TABLE OF CONTENTS

And in "Complete Edition" and "Library Edition"

INDEX

Pages 693–1204 *are omitted from the* Shorter Edition

Pages 693–1204 *are omitted from the* Shorter Edition

Pages 693–1204 are omitted from the Shorter Edition

Pages 693–1204 are omitted from the Shorter Edition

Pages 693–1204 *are omitted from the* Shorter Edition

Pages 693–1204 *are omitted from the* Shorter Edition

Pages 693–1204 *are omitted from the* Shorter Edition

Pages 693–1204 *are omitted from the* Shorter Edition

Pages 693–1204 *are omitted from the* Shorter Edition

Pages 693–1204 *are omitted from the* Shorter Edition

Pages 693–1204 *are omitted from the* Shorter Edition

Pages 693–1204 *are omitted from the* Shorter Edition

Pages 693–1204 *are omitted from the* Shorter Edition

Pages 693–1204 *are omitted from the* Shorter Edition

Pages 693–1204 *are omitted from the* Shorter Edition

Pages 693–1204 *are omitted from the* Shorter Edition

Pages 693–1204 *are omitted from the* Shorter Edition

Pages 693–1204 *are omitted from the* Shorter Edition

Pages 693–1204 are omitted from the Shorter Edition

Pages 693–1204 *are omitted from the* Shorter Edition

Pages 693–1204 *are omitted from the* Shorter Edition

Pages 693–1204 *are omitted from the* Shorter Edition

Pages 693–1204 are omitted from the Shorter Edition

Pages 693–1204 are omitted from the Shorter Edition

Pages 693–1204 *are omitted from the* Shorter Edition

Pages 693–1204 *are omitted from the* Shorter Edition

Pages 693–1204 *are omitted from the* Shorter Edition

Pages 693–1204 *are omitted from the* Shorter Edition

Pages 693–1204 *are omitted from the* Shorter Edition

Pages 693–1204 are omitted from the Shorter Edition

Pages 693–1204 *are omitted from the* Shorter Edition

Pages 693–1204 *are omitted from the* Shorter Edition

Pages 693–1204 *are omitted from the* Shorter Edition

Pages 693–1204 *are omitted from the* Shorter Edition

Pages 693–1204 *are omitted from the* Shorter Edition

Pages 693–1204 are omitted from the Shorter Edition

Pages 693–1204 *are omitted from the* Shorter Edition

Pages 693–1204 *are omitted from the* Shorter Edition

Pages 693–1204 *are omitted from the* Shorter Edition

Pages 693–1204 *are omitted from the* Shorter Edition

Pages 693–1204 *are omitted from the* Shorter Edition

Pages 693–1204 *are omitted from the* Shorter Edition

Pages 693–1204 *are omitted from the* Shorter Edition

Pages 693–1204 *are omitted from the* Shorter Edition

Pages 693–1204 *are omitted from the* Shorter Edition

Pages 693–1204 *are omitted from the* Shorter Edition

Pages 693–1204 *are omitted from the* Shorter Edition

Pages 693–1204 are omitted from the Shorter Edition

Pages 693–1204 *are omitted from the* Shorter Edition

DIVORCE STATISTICS

England and Wales

	1938	1960	1961
Dissolution			
Petitions filed . . .	9,970	27 870	31 124
By husbands . . .	4,649	12 109	13 321
By wives . . .	5,321	15 761	17,803
On grounds of			
Adultery . . .	4,989	12,896	13,876
Desertion . . .	3,909	9.074	8,820
Cruelty . . .	699	5,622	5,144
Lunacy . . .	226	162	147
Presumed death .	47	89	100
Rape, etc. . . .	..	27	73
Decrees ab. granted	6,092	23,369	24,936
Nullity of Marriage			
Petitions filed . . .	263	672	781
Decrees ab. granted	158	499	458
Judicial Separations . . .	25	118	124

Scotland

	1938	1960	1961
Divorce			
Actions completed .	822	1,856	1,879
By husbands . . .	402	786	802
By wives . . .	420	1,070	1,077
On grounds of			
Adultery, etc. . . .	453	793	829
Desertion . . .	369	675	634
Insanity . . .	..	14	14
Cruelty, etc. . . .	..	373	402
Divorces granted . .	812	1 804	1,804
Separation			
Actions completed .	2	7	6
Separation granted	2	6	4

Northern Ireland.

	1938	1960	1961
Divorce . . .	..	152	123
Nullity of marriage	1	4	1
Judicial Separation .	..	1	2

PUBLIC HOLIDAYS

BANK HOLIDAYS IN ENGLAND, WALES, NORTHERN IRELAND AND THE CHANNEL ISLANDS ARE :—Easter Monday, Whit Monday, first Monday in August and first week-day after Christmas (Boxing Day).

Banks are also closed on Good Friday and Christmas Day.

The Stock Exchange is closed on Bank Holidays, Good Friday and Christmas Day; and on Saturdays throughout the Year.

Custom House and Docks, as *Banks;* with the Queen's Birthday (when decreed).

Excise and Stamp Offices, as *Banks;* with Whit Tuesday and Coronation Day, if and when decreed.

Law Offices.—Good Friday, Easter Monday and Tuesday, Whit Monday, Christmas Day, and first week-day after Christmas.

BANK HOLIDAYS IN SCOTLAND ARE: New Year's Day, first Monday in May and first Monday in August.

Banks in Scotland are also closed on Good Friday and Christmas Day. There are also Spring and Autumn holidays in most Scottish cities and towns.

Scotland has special *Term* (*Quarter*) *Days:*—Candlemas, Feb. 2; Whit Sunday, May 15 (Fixed date); Lammas, Aug. 1; and Martinmas, Nov. 11; the *Removal Terms* are May 28 and Nov. 28.

OCCURRENCES DURING PRINTING

Politics, Official and General

Oct. 1.—Mr. Wilson, at Labour Party Conference, advocated programme of technological reform. Conference passed resolutions in favour of integrating public schools with state system, removing all National Health Service charges and abolishing pay-beds in N.H.S. hospitals.

Commissioner F. Coutts was elected new General of Salvation Army.

Oct. 2.—Mr. Anthony Greenwood was elected Chairman of Labour Party for ensuing year.

Mr. Macmillan returned to 10 Downing Street, after its rebuilding, which had occupied more than three years.

Oct. 4.—Labour Party Conference supported proposal for wealth tax.

Oct. 7.—Mr. A. R. Stamp, Chairman of L.C.C., resigned.

Oct. 8.—Mr. Macmillan was admitted to hospital for operation for prostate obstruction.

Oct. 9.—Conservative Party Conference opened at Blackpool.

Oct. 10.—Operation was successfully performed on Mr. Macmillan. Later, a message from him was read to Conservative Party Conference. He said that he would be unable to lead Party at next election and hoped that it would soon be possible for customary processes of consultation to be carried on within Party about future leadership. Lord Hailsham said that he intended to disclaim his peerage.

Oct. 18.—It was announced from Buckingham Palace that Mr. Macmillan had tendered to the Queen his resignation as Prime Minister and First Lord of the Treasury and that Her Majesty had been graciously pleased to accept it. The Queen visited Mr. Macmillan in hospital, and a further announcement said that Her Majesty had received the Earl of Home in audience and invited him to form an Administration.

Oct. 19.—The Queen again received in audience the Earl of Home, who kissed hands upon his appointment as Prime Minister and First Lord of the Treasury.

Oct. 20.—Lord Home announced the names of his Cabinet, which had been enlarged from 21 members to 23. Mr. R. A. Butler succeeded the new Prime Minister as Foreign Secretary. Mr. Selwyn Lloyd returned to the Cabinet as Lord Privy Seal and Leader of the House of Commons. Mr. J. H. Hare, previously Minister of Labour, became Chancellor of the Duchy of Lancaster, with a viscountcy, and was appointed Chairman of the Conservative Party. He was succeeded as Minister of Labour by Mr. J. B. Godber, formerly Secretary of State for War. Mr. E. R. G. Heath was given the new title of Secretary of State for Industry, Trade and Regional Development, and President of the Board of Trade. The former President of the Board of Trade, Mr. F. J. Erroll, was appointed Minister of Power. Mr. Enoch Powell's place as Minister of Health was taken by Mr. A. P. L. Barber who became a Privy Councillor. Lord Carrington, previously First Lord of the Admiralty, was made an additional Minister without Portfolio and Leader of the House of Lords.

Labour

Oct. 1.—Six hundred clerks went on strike at Standard-Triumph factories at Coventry; 2,000 assembly workers were sent home.

Oct. 8.—Railway workers' unions decided to put in immediate new wage claim.

Overseas

Oct. 1.—Nigeria became a Republic.

It was reported that Anglo-Malaysian security forces had clashed with Indonesian terrorists 35 miles inside Sarawak, casualties being caused on both sides.

Oct. 2.—Wives and children of Shell Company employees at Balikpapan, Indonesian Borneo, were evacuated to Singapore.

Oct. 3.—Armed forces of Honduras overthrew Government and exiled President Morales.

Archbishop Beran of Prague, who had been imprisoned for 14 years, was released together with four other bishops.

Oct. 4.—Gambia achieved full internal self-government.

The Kabaka of Buganda was elected first President of Uganda.

Oct. 6.—Hurricane, which had already caused much damage in Tobago, was reported to have killed about 5,000 persons in Haiti. Later it inflicted considerable damage in Cuba, where more than 1,000 lives were lost.

Oct. 10.—Water from Vaiont Dam swept down the Piave Valley in Italy; five villages were destroyed and death roll was estimated at more than 3,000.

Nobel Peace Prize for 1963 was awarded jointly to International Red Cross Committee and International League of Red Cross Societies.

Oct. 15.—Dr. Adenauer retired from Federal German Chancellorship and was succeeded on following day by Prof. Ludwig Erhard.

Obituary

Oct. 4.—Sir Frederic Hooper, Bt., prominent industrialist, aged 71. *Admiral* Sir Patrick Brind, G.B.E., K.C.B., aged 71. *Admiral* Sir Douglas Fisher, K.C.B., K.B.E., aged 72. Oct. 8.—Oliver Sylvain Balliol Brett, G.B.E., 3rd Viscount Esher, aged 82. Oct. 10.—*Brig.* Sir Henry Houldsworth, K.B.E., D.S.O., M.C., Lord Lieutenant of Moray, aged 67. Oct. 11.—Jean Cocteau, French man of letters, aged 74.

NEW MINISTRY

For Mr. Macmillan's Administration at the time of his resignation, *see* p. 310; and for the new Ministry formed by the Earl of Home in October, 1963, *see* p. 309.

FOREIGN EXCHANGE RATES

A. London Market Rates

Country	Denomination	1939 Average Rate to £ (approx.)	September 30, 1963 Middle Rates
Austria	*Schilling*	—	72·21§
Belgium	*Franc*	26·49 belgas	139·65§
Canada	*Dollar*	4·545	3·01 5/8§
Denmark	*Krone*	22·26	19·30 3/4§
Finland	*Markka*	217 1/4	9·00 1/2§
France	*Franc*	176·10	13·71 3/8§
Germany (Federal Republic)	*D'Mark*	—	11·13 1/2§
Italy	*Lira*	85	1741 1/2§
Japan	*Yen*	1/2‖	1013§
Netherlands	*Florin*	8·34	10·08 3/4§
Neth. W. Indies	*Florin*	8·34	5·26
Norway	*Krone*	19·45	20·02 1/8§
Portugal	*Escudo*	110·07	80·25§
Spain	*Peseta*	42·45	167 1/2§
Sweden	*Krona*	18·59	14·51 1/2§
Switzerland	*Franc*	19·87	12·07 1/2§
U.S.A.	*Dollar*	4·485	2·79 3/4§

B. Scheduled Territories

Country	Denomination	1939 Average Rate to £ (approx.)	September 30, 1963 Middle Rates
Australia	*Australian £*	A. £1·2525	125 1/4*
Bahamas	*Bahama £*	—	par
Barbados	*West Indian $*	—	4·80
Bermuda	*Bermuda £*	—	par
British Honduras	*British Honduras $*	—	4·00
Burma	*Kyat (Rupee)*	13·38	1/6‖
Ceylon	*Rupee*	13·38	1/6 1/32‖
Cyprus	*Cyprus £*	—	par
East Africa Aden Uganda Kenya Tanganyika	*East African Shilling*	—	20
Ghana	*Ghana £*	—	par
Hong Kong	*H.K. $*	—	1/3‖
Iceland	*Krona*	—	120·64
India	*Rupee*	13·38	1/6‖
Jamaica	*Jamaica £*	—	par
Jordan	*Dinar*	par	par
Kuwait	*Dinar*	—	par
Libya	*Libyan £*	—	par
Malaysia	*Mal. $*	8·571	2/4 1/32‖
Malta	*Maltese £*	—	par
New Zealand	*N.Z. £*	£1·2425	100 11/16*
Nigeria	*Nigeria £*	—	par
Nyasaland	*Rhodesia £*	—	par
Pakistan	*Rupee*	—	1/6‖
Rhodesia	*Rhodesia £*	—	par
South Africa	*Rand*	S.A. £1	2
Trinidad	*West Indian $*	—	4·80

C. Other Rates

Country	Denomination	1939 Average Rate to £ (approx.)	September 30, 1963 Middle Rates
Algeria	*New Algeria Franc*	—	13·71 3/8
Argentina	*Peso*	19	414†
Bolivia	*Bolivian Peso*	141·50	33
Brazil	*Cruzeiro*	82	1709·55†
Bulgaria	*Lev*	375	3·29
Chile	*Escudo*	116 1/2	8·40†
China	*Peoples $*	4 1/8	6·893
Colombia	*Peso*	7·59	27·95†
Congo	*Congolese Franc*	—	182·04
Costa Rica	*Colon*	25·16	18·55†
Cuba	*Peso*	4·386	2·79 3/4
Czechoslovakia	*Koruno*	—	20·16†
Ecuador	*Sucre*	66	54 1/8†
Egypt	*Egyptian £*	97 1/2	122*†
Ethiopia	*Eth. $*	—	7
Germany (East)	*Ostmark*	—	6·22†
Greece	*Drachma*	545	84
Guatemala	*Quetzal*	4·386	2·79 3/4
Guinea	*Guinea Franc*	—	683
Haiti	*Gourde*	22·4	13·99 1/16

* Per £100 London. † Indicates that other rates are also obtainable, varying according to the nature of the transaction. § Limited exchange fluctuations permitted. ‖ To avoid confusion rates quoted for the *rupee* or *dollar* in shillings and pence are indicated thus ‖.

Country	Denomination	1939 Average Rate to £ (approx.)	September 30, 1963 Middle Rates
Honduras, Rep. of	*Lempira*	8⅜	5·59⅝
Hungary	*Forint*	20¾	32·87†
Indonesia	*Rupiah*	—	882†
Iraq	*Dinar*	par	£1
Israel	*Israel £*	par	8·40
Lebanon	*Lebanon £*	9·65	8·69½†
Madagascar	*C.F.A. Franc*	175 (F. Fr.)	685⅝
Mexico	*Peso*	—	34·95
Morocco	*Dirham*	176·10 (F. Fr.)	14·064
Nicaragua	*Cordoba*	24	19·58 11/16
Paraguay	*Guarani*	—	351·07
Persia	*Rial*	80·50	212·10
Peru	*Sol*	24½	74·95
Philippines	*Peso*	—	10·93†
Poland	*Zloty*	23½	11·20†
Rumania	*Leu (Lei)*	655	16·80†
Salvador	*Colon*	11·20	7·04
Saudi Arabia	*Riyal*	—	12·55
Sudan	*Sudan £*	97½	97½ nom.*
Syria	*Syrian £*	—	11
Thailand	*Baht*	10·91	57·87
Tunisia	*Tunisian Dinar*	—	1·1669
Turkey	*T £*	—	25·26
Uruguay	*Peso*	9	48·75†
U.S.S.R.	*Rouble*	23·75	2·52
Venezuela	*Bolivar*	14·15	12·67†
Vietnam	*Piastre*	—	98†
Yugoslavia	*Dinar*	197½	2100†

See Notes, p. 83.

THE UNITED KINGDOM

Area.—The land area of the United Kingdom (England, Wales, Scotland and N. Ireland) is 93,024 sq. miles or 59,535,000 acres. The area of inland water* in the United Kingdom is 1,186 sq. miles. Total 94,210 sq. miles.

	Land Area		Inland water*	Total
	Sq. miles	'000 acres	Sq. miles	Sq. miles
England	50,056	32,036	276	50,332
Wales	7,967	5,099	49	8,016
Scotland	29,795	19,069	616	30,411
Northern Ireland	5,206	3,332	246	5,452

* Excluding tidal water.

POPULATION: CENSUS RESULTS, 1801–1961 — Thousands

	United Kingdom			England and Wales			Scotland			Northern Ireland†		
	Total	Males	Females	Total	Males	Females	Total	Males	Females	Total	Males	Females
1801	11,944	5,692	6,252	8,893	4,255	4,638	1,608	739	869	1,443	698	745
1811	13,368	6,368	7,000	10,165	4,874	5,291	1,806	826	980	1,397	668	729
1821	15,472	7,498	7,974	12,000	5,850	6,150	2,092	983	1,109	1,380	665	715
1831	17,835	8,647	9,188	13,897	6,771	7,126	2,364	1,114	1,250	1,574	762	812
1841	20,183	9,819	10,364	15,914	7,778	8,137	2,620	1,242	1,378	1,649	800	849
1851	22,259	10,855	11,404	17,928	8,781	9,146	2,889	1,375	1,513	1,443	698	745
1861	24,525	11,894	12,631	20,066	9,776	10,290	3,062	1,450	1,612	1,396	668	728
1871	27,431	13,309	14,122	22,712	11,059	11,653	3,360	1,603	1,757	1,359	647	712
1881	31,015	15,060	15,955	25,974	12,640	13,335	3,736	1,799	1,936	1,305	621	684
1891	34,264	16,593	17,671	29,003	14,060	14,942	4,026	1,943	2,083	1,236	590	646
1901	38,237	18,492	19,745	32,528	15,729	16,799	4,472	2,174	2,298	1,237	590	647
1911	42,082	20,357	21,725	36,070	17,446	18,625	4,761	2,309	2,452	1,251	603	648
1921	44,027	21,033	22,994	37,887	18,075	19,811	4,882	2,348	2,535	*1,258*	*610*	*648*
1931	46,038	22,060	23,979	39,952	19,133	20,819	4,843	2,326	2,517	*1,243*	*601*	*642*
1951	50,225	24,118	26,107	43,758	21,016	22,742	5,096	2,434	2,662	1,371	668	703
1961	52,676	25,478	27,198	46,072	22,299	23,773	5,178	2,484	2,694	1,425	695	731

† All figures refer to the area which is now Northern Ireland. Figures for N. Ireland in 1921 and 1931 are estimates based on the Censuses held in 1926 and 1937.

NOTES.—1. Before 1801 there existed no official return of the population of either England or Scotland. Estimates of the population of England at various periods, calculated from the number of baptisms, burials and marriages, are: in 1570, 4,160,221; 1600, 4,811,718; 1630, 5,600,517; 1670, 5,773,646; 1700, 6,045,008; 1750, 6,517,035.

2. By June 30, 1962, the total population of the United Kingdom was estimated to have risen to 53,301,000 (England, 44,017,660; Wales, 2,651,340; Scotland, 5,196,600; Northern Ireland, 1,435,400).

ABBREVIATIONS IN COMMON USE

Ψ = Seaport.

A

A.A., Automobile Association.
A.A.A., Amateur Athletic Association.
A.A.I., *Associate* of Chartered Auctioneers' and Estate Agent's Institute.
A. and M., Hymns Ancient and Modern.
A.B., Able-bodied Seaman.
A.B.C., Alphabet (also Aerated Bread Company).
a.c., alternating current.
a/c., accounts.
A.C. (*Ante Christum*), B.C.
A.C.A., *Associate* of Inst. of Chartered Accountants (of England and Wales).
A.C.C.S.—of the Corporation of Secretaries.
A.C.I.S.—of the Chartered Institute of Secretaries.
A.C.W.A.—of the Institute of Cost and Works Accountants.
A.D. (*Anno Domini*), In the year of our Lord.
A.D.C., Aide-de-Camp.
Ad lib. (*ad libitum*), At pleasure.
A.F.C., Air Force Cross.
A.F.M., Air Force Medal.
A.G., Adjutant-General.
A.H. (*Anno Hegirae*), In the year of the Hejira.
A.I.A., *Associate* of the Institute of Actuaries.
A.I.B.—of Bankers.
A.I.C.S.—of Chartered Shipbrokers.
A.I.M.T.A.—of Munic. Treas. and Accountants.
A. Inst.P.—of Physics.
A.I.Q.S.—of Quantity Surveyors.
A.K.C.—of King's College.
A.L. (*Anno Lucis*), in the year of Light.
A.L.A., *Associate* of the Library Association.
A.L.C.D.—of London College of Divinity.
A.M. (*Ante meridiem*), Before noon.
A.M. (*Anno mundi*), In the year of the world.
A.M.D.G. (*Ad majorem Dei Gloriam*), To the greater glory of God.
A.M.I.C.E., *Associate Member* of Institution of Civil Engrs.
A.M.I.Chem.E.—Do. Chemical Engineers.
A.M.I.E.E.—Do. Electrical Engineers.
A.M.I.Mech.E.—*Associate Member Institute* of Mechanical Engineers.
A.N.Z.A.C., Australian and New Zealand Army Corps.
A.O.C., Air Officer Commanding.
A.P., Associated Press.
A.R.A., *Associate* of Royal Academy.
A.R.A.M.—of Royal Academy of Music.
A.R.B.S.—of the Royal Society of British Sculptors.
A.R.C.A.—of Royal Coll. of Arts.
A.R.C.M.—of Royal College of Music.
A.R.C.O.—Do. Organists.
A.R.I.B.A.—of Royal Institute of British Architects.
A.R.I.C.—of Royal Institute of Chemistry.
A.R.I.C.S.—of Royal Institution of Chartered Surveyors.
A.R.P.S. *Associate* of Royal Photographic Society.
A.R.R.C.—of Royal Red Cross.
A.R.W.S.—of Royal Society of Painters in Water Colours.
A.S.A., Amateur Swimming Association.
A.S.D.I.C., Anti-Submarine Detector Indicator Committee.
A.S.L.I.B., Association of Special Libraries and Information Bureaux.
A.T.A., Air Transport Auxiliary.
A.T.C., Air Training Corps.
A.T.V.—Associated Television Authority.
A.U.C. (*Ab urbe condita*). In the year from the foundation of Rome.
A.W.O.L., Absent Without Leave.

B

B.A., *Bachelor* of Arts.
B.Arch.—of Architecture.
B.Ch. (or Ch.B.)—of Surgery.
B.C.L.—of Civil Law.
B.Com.—of Commerce.
B.D.—of Divinity.
B.D.S. (or B.Ch.D.)—of Dental Surgery.
B.Ed.—of Education.
B.Eng.—of Engineering.
B.Litt.—of Literature *or* of Letters.
B.Phil.—of Philosophy.
B.Sc.—of Science.
B.V.M.S.—of Veterinary Medicine and Surgery.
B.A.O.R., British Army of the Rhine.
B.B., Boys' Brigade.
B.B.C., British Broadcasting Corporation.
B.C., Before Christ.
B.D.A., British Dental Assocn.
B.E.A., British European Airways Corporation.
B.E.M., British Empire Medal.
B.M.A., British Medical Assocn.
B.N.C., Brasenose College (Oxon.).
B.O.A.C., British Overseas Airways Corporation.
B.R.C.S., British Red Cross Society.
B.S.T., British Summer Time.
Bt., Baronet.
B.Th.U., British Thermal Unit.
B.V.M., Blessed Virgin Mary.

C

C.—Conservative.
ca. (*circa*), about.
C.A., Chartered Accountant (*Scottish Institute*).
Cantab., Cambridge.
Cantuar., Canterbury.
Cap. (Chapter), Number of Act of Parliament.
C.B., Companion of the Bath.
C.B.E., Commander of Order of British Empire.
c.c., cubic centimetres.
C.C., County Council.
C.C.F., Combined Cadet Force.
C.E., Civil Engineer.
C.E.N.T.O., Central Treaty Organisation.
C. of E., Church of England.
cf. (*confer*), Compare.
C.F., Chaplain to the Forces.
C.G.M., Conspicuous Gallantry Medal.
C.G.S., Centimetre - gramme - second (system).
C.H., Companion of Honour.
Ch. Ch., Christ Church.
C.I., Lady of Imperial Order of the Crown of India.
C.I., Channel Islands.
C.I.D., Criminal Investigation Department.
C.I.E., Companion, Order of Indian Empire.
C.I.F. (usually cif.), Cost, Insurance and Freight.
C.I.G.S., Chief of Imperial General Staff.
C.-in-C., Commander-in-Chief.
C.I.O., Congress of Industrial Organizations (U.S.A.).
C.L.B., Church Lads' Brigade.
C.M. (*Chirurgiae Magister*), Master of Surgery.
C.M.G., Companion, Order of St. Michael and St. George.
C.M.S., Church Missionary Society.
C.O., Commanding Officer.
C.O.D., Cash on delivery.
C.O.I.—Central Office of Information.
C.P.R.E.—Council for Preservation of Rural England.
C.S.I., Companion, Order of Star of India.
C.T.C., Cyclists' Touring Club.
C.V.O., Commander, Royal Victorian Order.
cwt., Hundredweight.

D

d. (*denarius*), penny.
D.B.E., Dame Commander of Order of British Empire.
d.c., direct current.
D.C., District of Columbia.
D.C.L., *Doctor* of Civil Law.
D.D.—of Divinity.
D.D.S.—of Dental Surgery.
D.Litt.—of Letters, *or* of Literature.
D.Phil.—of Philosophy.

D.Sc.—of Science.
D.C.M., Distinguished Conduct Medal.
D.C.V.O.—Dame Commander of the Royal Victorian Order.
D.D.T., dichlorodiphenyltrichloroethane (insecticide).
del. (*delineavit*), He (she) drew it.
D.F.C., Distinguished Flying Cross.
D.F.M., Distinguished Flying Medal.
D.G. (*Dei gratia*), By the Grace of God.
D.I.C., *Diploma* of the Imperial College.
D.P.H.—in Public Health.
D.P.M.—in Psychological Medicine.
D.T.M.—in Tropical Medicine.
D.L., Deputy-Lieutenant.
D.N.B., Dictionary of National Biography.
Do. (ditto), The same. (Italian, *detto*).
D.O.M., *Dominus Omnium Magister*.
D.P., Displaced Person(s).
D.S.C., Distinguished Service Cross.
D.S.M., Do. Medal.
D.S.O., Companion of Distinguished Service Order.
d.s.p. (*decessit sine prole*), died without issue.
D.V. (*Deo volente*), God willing.
dwt., Pennyweight.

E

E. and O.E., Errors and omissions excepted.
Ebor, York.
E.C., East Central District.
E.C.S.C., European Coal and Steel Community.
E.D., Efficiency Decoration.
E.E.C., European Economic Community.
E.F.T.A., European Free Trade Association ("The Seven"—Austria, Denmark, Norway, Portugal, Sweden, Switzerland, U.K.).
e.g. (*exempli gratia*), for the sake of example.
E.M.A., European Monetary Agreement.
E.R., Elizabetha Regina, or Edwardus Rex.
E.R.D., Emergency Reserve Decoration.
etc. (*etcetera*). And the other things.
et seq. (*et sequentia*). And the following.
ex lib. (*ex libris*), from the books of.

F

F.A., Football Association.
F.A.I. *Fellow* of Chartered Auctioneers' and Estate Agents Institute.
F.A.L.P.A.—of Incorporated Society of Auctioneers.
F.B.A.—of the British Academy.
F.C.A.—of Institute of Chartered Accountants (of England and Wales).
F.C.C.S.—of Corporation of Secretaries.
F.C.G.I.—of City and Guilds Institute.
F.C.I.A.—of Corporation of Insurance Agents.
F.C.I.B.—of Corporation of Insurance Brokers.
F.C.I.I.—of the Chartered Insurance Institute.
F.C.I.S.—of the Chartered Institute of Secretaries.
F.C.P.—of the College of Preceptors.
F.C.W.A.—of the Institute of Cost and Works Accountants.
F.G.S.—of the Geological Society.
F.I.A.—of the Institute of Actuaries.
F.I.A.A.—Architect Member of Inc. Assoc. of Architects.
F.I.Arb.—of Arbitrators.
F.I.B.—of Bankers.
F.I.C.S.—of Chartered Shipbrokers.
F.I.M.T.A.—of Munic. Treas. and Accountants.
F.Inst.P.—of Physics.
F.I.Q.S.—of Quantity Surveyors.
F.J.I.—of Journalists.
F.L.A., Fellow of Library Assocn.
F.L.A.S.—of Land Agents Society.
F.L.S.—of the Linnean Society.
F.P.S.—of the Pharmaceutical Society.
F.R.A.I.—of Royal Anthropological Institute.
F.R.A.M.—of Royal Academy of Music.
F.R.A.S.—of the Royal Astronomical Society.
F.R.Ae.S.—of Royal Aeronautical Society.
F.R.B.S.—of the Royal Society of British Sculptors.
F.R.C.M.—of the Royal College of Music.
F.R.C.O.—of Royal College of Organists.
F.R.C.O.G.—of Royal College of Obstetricians and Gynaecologists.
F.R.C.P., F.R.C.P.Ed., and F.R.C.P.I.—of the Royal College of Physicians of London, of Edinburgh, and in Ireland respectively.
F.R.C.S.—of Royal College of Surgeons.
F.R.C.S.Ed., ditto of Edinburgh; F.R.C.S.I., of Ireland.
F.R.C.V.S.—of Royal College of Veterinary Surgeons.
F.R.Econ.S.—of Roy. Economic Society.
F.R.F.P.S.G.—of the Royal Faculty of Physicians and Surgeons of Glasgow.
F.R.G.S.—of the Royal Geographical Society.
F.R.H.S.—of the Royal Horticultural Society.
F.R.Hist.Soc., ditto Historical.
F.R.I.B.A.—of the Royal Institute of British Architects.
F.R.I.C.—of the Royal Institute of Chemistry.
F.R.I.C.S.—of the Royal Institution of Chartered Surveyors.
F.R.M.S.—of Royal Microscopical Society.
F.R. Met. S.—of Royal Meteorological Society.
F.R.N.S.—of Royal Numismatic Society.
F.R.P.S.—of Royal Photographic Society.
F.R.S.—of the Royal Society.
F.R.S.E., ditto of Edinburgh.
F.R.S.A.—of the Royal Society of Arts.
F.R.S.L.—Do. Literature.
F.S.A.—of the Society of Antiquaries.
F.S.S.—Do. Statistical Society.
F.Z.S.—of the Zoological Society.
F.A.N.Y., First Aid Nursing Yeomanry.
F.A.O., Food and Agriculture Organization.
F.B.I., Federation of British Industries.
fcp., Foolscap.
F.D. (*Fidei Defensor*) Defender of the Faith.
Fec. (*fecit*), He did it (or made it).
F.H., Fire Hydrant.
F.I.D.O., Fog Investigation Dispersal Operations.
fl. (*floruit*), he, or she, flourished.
F.O., Foreign Office.
FOB (*usually* f.o.b.), Free on board.

G

G.A.T.T., General Agreement on Tariffs and Trade.
G.B.E., Knight or Dame Grand Cross of British Empire.
G.C., George Cross.
G.C.B., Knight Grand Cross of the Bath.
G.C.I.E., Knight Grand Commander of Indian Empire.
G.C.M.G., Knight Grand Cross of St. Michael and St. George.
G.C.S.I., Knight Grand Commander of Star of India.
G.C.V.O., Knight or Dame Grand Cross of Royal Victorian Order.
G.H.Q., General Headquarters.
G.M., George Medal
G.M.T., Greenwich Mean Time.
G.O.C., General Officer Commanding.
G.P.O., General Post Office.
G.R. (*Georgius Rex*), King George.
G.R.C.M., Graduate of the Royal College of Music.
G.R.S.M., Graduate of the Royal Schools of Music (Royal Academy and Royal College).
G.S.O., General Staff Officer.

H

H.A.C., Honble. Artillery Coy.
H.C.F., Highest Common Factor.
H.E., His Excellency.
H.E.H., His [Her] Exalted Highness.
H.H., His [Her] Highness.
H.I.H., His [Her] Imperial Highness.

H.I.M., His [Her] Imperial Majesty.
H.J.S. (*Hic jacet sepultus*), Here lies buried. *cf.* H.S.E.
H.M., His, or Her, Majesty.
H.M.A.S., Her Majesty's Australian Ship.
H.M.L., Her Majesty's Lieutenant.
H.M.S., Her Majesty's Ship.
H.M.S.O., Her Majesty's Stationery Office.
h.p., horse power.
H.Q., Headquarters.
H.R.H., His [Her] Royal Highness.
H.S.E. (*Hic sepultus est*), Here lies buried. *cf.* H.J.S.
H.S.H., His [Her] Serene Highness.

I

I.A., Indian Army.
Ibid. (*ibidem*), In the same place.
IBRD., Internat. Bank for Reconstruction and Development.
I.C.B.M., Inter-Continental ballistic missile.
I.C.S., Indian Civil Service.
Id. (*idem*), The same.
I.C.A.O., International Civil Aviation Organization.
i.d.c., Graduate of Imperial Defence College.
i.e. (*id est*), That is.
IFC, International Finance Corporation.
I.H.S. (*Iesus Hominum Salvator*), Jesus the Saviour of Mankind; originally, these were the Greek Capital letters, ΙΗΣ.
I.L.O., International Labour Organization.
I.L.P., Independent Labour Party.
IMCO., Inter - Governmental Maritime Consultative Organization.
IMF, International Monetary Fund.
I.M.S., Indian Medical Service.
Incog. (*incognito*), Unknown.
In loc (*in loco*), In its place.
I.N.R.I. (*Iesus Nazarenus Rex Judaeorum*), Jesus of Nazareth King of the Jews.
Inst. (instant), current month.
I.O.M., Isle of Man.
I.O.U., I owe you.
I.O.W., Isle of Wight.
I.Q., Intelligence Quotient.
IRBM., Intermediate - range ballistic missile.
I.S.O., Imperial Service Order.
I.T.A., Independent Television Authority.
I.T.O.—International Trade Organization.
I.T.U.—International Telecommunication Union.

J

J., Judge.
J.P., Justice of the Peace.

K

K.B.E., Knight Commander of British Empire.
K.C.B.—Do. the Bath.
K.C.I.E.—Do. Indian Empire.
K.C.M.G.—Do. of St. Michael and St. George.
K.C.S.I.—Do, the Star of India.
K.C.V.O.—Do. Royal Victorian Order.
K.G., Knight of the Garter.
k.o., knock out (boxing).
K.P., Knight of St. Patrick.
K.T., Knight of the Thistle.
Kt.. Knight Bachelor.

L

L., Liberal.
Lab., Labour.
L.A.C., London Athletic Club.
L.A.H., *Licentiate* of Apothecaries' Hall, Dublin.
L.C.P., Do. of College of Preceptors.
L.D.S., Do. in Dental Surgery.
L.M., Do. in Midwifery.
L.M.S.S.A. Do. in Medicine and Surgery, Soc. of Apothecaries.
L.R.A.M., Do. of Royal Acad. of Music.
L.R.C.P., Do. of the Roy. Coll. of Physicians.
L.R.C.P.Ed., ditto Edinburgh.
L.R.C.S.Ed.—of Roy. Coll. Surg., Edinburgh.
L.R.F.P.S.G., Do. of the Royal Faculty of Physicians and Surgeons of Glasgow.
L.S.A., Do. of Society of Apothecaries.
L.T.M., Do. of Tropical Medicine.
Lat., Latitude.
lb. (*libra*). Pound weight.
l.c., "Lower case," *i.e.* small letter.
L.C.C., London County Council.
L.C.J., Lord Chief Justice.
L.C.M., Least Common Multiple.
Lit., Literally.
Litt.D., Doctor of Letters.
L.J., Lord Justice.
LL.B., Bachelor of Laws.
LL.D., Doctor of Laws.
LL.M., Master of Laws.
loc. cit. (*loco citato*), In the place, cited.
L.S. (*loco sigilli*), Place of the Seal.
L s. d. (*Librae, solidi, denarii*). Pounds, shillings, pence.
L.T.A., Lawn Tennis Association.
Ltd., Limited Liability.
LXX., Septuagint.

M

M.A., *Master* of Arts.
M.Ch.—of Surgery.
M.Ch.D.—of Dental Surgery.
M.S.—of Surgery.
M.Sc.—of Science.
M.Th.—of Theology.
M.B., Bachelor of Medicine.
M.D., Doctor of ditto.
M.B.E., *Member* of British Empire Order.
M.E.C.—of Executive Council.
M.I.C.E.—of Institution of Civil Engineers.
M.I.Chem.E.—of Chemical Engineers.
M.I.E.E.—of Electrical Engineers.
M.I.Mar.E.—of Institute of Marine Engineers.
M.I.Mech.E.—of Institution of Mechanical Engineers.
M.Inst.Met.—of Institute of Metals.
M.Inst.T.—of Institute of Transport.
M.J.I.—of Journalists.
M.L.A.—*Member* of Legislative Assembly.
M.L.C., ditto Council.
M.N.—Merchant Navy.
M.P.—of Parliament (also Military Police).
M.P.S. — of Pharmaceutical Society.
M.R.C.P.—of Royal College of Physicians.
M.R.C.S.—of Royal College of Surgeons.
M.R.C.V.S.—of Royal College of Veterinary Surgeons.
M.V.O.—of Royal Victorian Order.
M.C., Military Cross.
M.C.C., Marylebone Cricket Club.
M.F.H., Master of Fox Hounds.
Mgr., Monsignor.
Min. Plenip., Minister Plenipotentiary.
Mlle., Mademoiselle.
M.M., Military Medal (also Messieurs).
Mme., Madame.
M.O.H., Medical Officer of Health.
m.p.h., Miles per hour.
MS., manuscript (pl. MSS.).
Mus. D. [B.J.] Doctor, [Bachelor], of Music.

N

N.A.A.F.I., Navy, Army and Air Force Institutes.
N.A.T.O., North Atlantic Treaty Organization.
N.B., North Britain.
N.B. (*Nota bene*), Note well.
N.C.B., National Coal Board.
N.C.O., Non - commissioned Officer.
n.d., no date (of books).
Nem. con. (*Nemine contradicente*), No one contradicting.
N.F.U. — National Farmers' Union.
No. (*Numero*), Number.
N.P., Notary Public.
Non seq. (*non sequitur*), It does not follow.
N.R.A., National Rifle Association.
N.S., Nova Scotia.
N.S.P.C.C., National Society for the Prevention of Cruelty to Children.
N.S.W., New South Wales.
N.T., New Testament.
N.U.J., *National Union* of Journalists.
N.U.R.—of Railwaymen.
N.U.S.—of Students.
N.W.P.[T.], North West Provinces [Territory].
N.Y., New York.
N.Z., New Zealand.

O

O.B.E., Officer of British Empire Order.
ob., or *obiit.* died.
O.C., Officer Commanding.
O.E.C.D., Organisation for Economic Co-operation and Development.
O.E.D., Oxford English Dictionary.
O.H.M.S., On Her Majesty's Service.
O.M., Order of Merit (and member of).
O.P., Opposite Prompt side (of Theatre), Out of Print (of books).
op. cit. (*opere citato*), in the work cited.
Orse (*legal*), Otherwise.
O.S., Old Style.
O.S.B., Order of St. Benedict.
O.T., Old Testament.
O.U.D.S., Oxford University Dramatic Society.
Oxon., Oxford.
Oz., Ounce.

P

P.A., Press Association.
P.C., Privy Councillor.
P.E.N. (*Club*), Poets, Essayists, Novelists.
p.f.c., Passed Flying College.
Ph.D., Doctor of Philosophy.
pinx(*it*), he (or she) painted it.
P.L.A., Port of London Authority.
P.M. (*post meridiem*), Afternoon (also *post mortem*).
P.M.G., Postmaster-General.
P.N.E.U., Parents' National Educational Union.
p.p., or per pro. (*per procurationem*)—by proxy.
Pro tem. (*pro tempore*), For the time being.
Prox. (*proximo*), Next month.
P.S. (*Post scriptum*), Postscript.
p.s.c., Passed Staff College.
P.T., Physical Training.
P.T.O., Please turn over.

Q

Q.C., Queen's Counsel.
Q.e.d. (*quod erat demonstrandum*), which was to be proved.
Q.H.C., Honorary Chaplain to the Queen; Q.H.P., ditto Physician; Q.H.S., ditto Surgeon; Q.H.D.S., ditto Dental Surgeon; Q.H.N.S., ditto Nursing Sister.
Q.M.G., Quartermaster-General.
Q.S., Quarter Sessions.
q.v. (*quod vide*), "which see".

R

R.A., *Royal* Artillery or Royal Academy.
R.A.C.—Armoured Corps (also Royal Automobile Club).
R.A.E.C.—Army Educational Corps.
R.Ae.S., Royal Aeronautical Society.
R.A.F.—Air Force.
R.A.M.—Academy of Music.
R.A.M.C. — Army Medical Corps.
R.A.N.—Australian Navy.
R.A.P.C.—Army Pay Corps.
R.A.O.C.—Army Ordnance Corps.
R.A.S.C.—Army Service Corps.
R.A.V.C.—Army Veterinary Corps.
R.B.A.—Society of British Artists.
R.B.S.—Society of British Sculptors.
R.C.N.—Canadian Navy.
R.C.N.C.—Corps of Naval Constructors.
R.D.—Naval Reserve Decoration, or Rural Dean.
R.E.—Engineers.
R.E.M.E.—Electrical and Mechanical do.
R.H.A.—Horse Artillery or—Hibernian Academy.
R.I.A.—Irish Academy.
R.M.—Marines.
R.M.A.—Military Academy.
R.M.S.—Mail Steamer.
R.N.—Navy; R.N.R. Naval Reserve; R.N.V.R., Naval Volunteer Reserve.
R.O.I.—Institute of Oil Painters.
R.P.—Society of Portrait Painters.
R.Sigs.—Signals.
R.S.A.—Scottish Academician.
R.S.P.C.A.—Society for the Prevention of Cruelty to Animals.
R.W.S.—Water Colour Society.
R.Y.S.—Yacht Squadron.
R.C., Roman Catholic.
R.D., Refer to drawer (banking).
R.D.C., Rural District Council.
R.D.I., Designer for Industry of the Royal Society of Arts.
R.I.P. (*Requiescat in pace*), May he rest in peace.
Ro. (*recto*), On the right-hand page. (*See* Vo.)
R.O.C., Royal Observer Corps.
r.p.m., revolutions per minute.
R.R.C., Lady of Royal Red Cross.
R.S.V.P. (*Répondez, s'il vous plait*), Answer, if you please.
R.V., Revised Version (of Bible).

S

Sc. (*scilicet*), Let it be understood.
Sc.D., Doctor of Science.
S.E.A.T.O.—South East Asia Treaty Organization.
S.H.A.P.E.—Supreme Headquarters, Allied Powers, Europe.
Sic., So written.
S.J., Society of Jesus.
S.O.S. ("Save Our Souls") Distress Signal.
s.p. (*sine prole*), Without issue.
S.P.C.K., Society for the Promotion of Christian Knowledge.
S.P.G., Society for the Propagation of the Gospel.
S.P.Q.R. (*Senatus Populusque Romanus*), The Senate and People of Rome.
S.R.N., State Registered Nurse.
S.S.A.F.A., Soldiers', Sailors', and Airmen's Families Assocn.
S.S.C., Solicitor in the Supreme Court (Scotland).
Stet, Let it stand.
S.T.P. (=D.D.), *Sacrae Theologiae Professor*.

T

T.A.N., Twilight all night.
t.b., Tuberculosis.
T.D., Territorial Decoration.
T.C.D., Trinity College, Dublin.
T.N.T., Trinitrotoluene (explosive).
Toc. H., Talbot House.
T.U.C., Trades Union Congress.
T.V.A., Tennessee Valley Authority.

U

Ult. (*ultimo*), in the preceding month.
U.D.C., Urban District Council.
U.K., United Kingdom.
U.N.A.C., United Nations Appeal for Children.
U.N.E.S.C.O., United Nations Educational, Scientific and Cultural Organization.
U.N.O., United Nations Organization.
U.P., United Press.
U.P.U., Universal Postal Union.
U.S.A. or U.S., United States of America.
U.S.C.L., United Society for Christian Literature.
U.S.S.R., Union of Soviet Socialist Republics.

V

v. (*versus*), Against.
V.A., Victoria and Albert Order or Vicar Apostolic.
V.A.D., Voluntary Aid Detachment.
V.C., Victoria Cross.
V.D., Vol. Officers' Decoration.
Ven., Venerable.
Verb. sap. (*Verbum sapienti satis est*), A word to the wise is enough.
V.I.P., Very Important Person.
Viz. (*videlicet*), Namely.
Vo. (*verso*), On the left-hand page. (*See* Ro.)
V.R., Victoria Regina.
V.R.D.—Volunteer Reserve Decoration.

W

W.A.A.F., now W.R.A.F., Women's Auxiliary Air Force.
W.H.O., World Health Organization.
W.M.O. World Meteorological Organization.
W.O., Warrant Officer.
W.R.A.C., Woman's Royal Army Corps.
W.R.A.F., Women's Royal Air Force.
W.R.N.S., Women's Royal Naval Service.
W.S., Writer to the Signet.
W.V.S., Women's Voluntary Services.

Y

Y.M.C.A., Young Men's Christian Association.
Y.W.C.A., Young Women's do.

BEING BISSEXTILE OR LEAP YEAR AND 12 AND 13 OF QUEEN ELIZABETH II

Golden Number	VIII
Epact	16
Dominical Letter	E, D
Solar Cycle	13
Roman Indiction	2
Julian Period	6677
Julian Day, Jan. 1. Begins at noon	2,438,396
New Year's Day (Wednesday)	Jan. 1
Septuagesima Sunday	„ 26
Foundation Day (Australia)	„ 26
Accession of Queen Elizabeth II	Feb. 6
New Zealand Day	„ 6
Ash Wednesday	„ 12
Prince Andrew's Birthday (1960)	„ 19
St. David's Day	Mar. 1
St. Patrick's Day	„ 17
Good Friday	„ 27
Easter Day	„ 29
The Queen's Birthday (1926)	Apr. 21
St. George's Day	„ 23
Ascension Day	May 7
Moslem New Year (1384)	„ 13
Whit Sunday	„ 17
Trinity Sunday	„ 24
Corpus Christi	„ 28
Duke of Edinburgh's Birthday (1921)	June 10
Queen's Official Birthday	„ 13
Canada Day (1867)	July 1
The Queen Mother's Birthday (1900)	Aug. 4
Princess Anne's Birthday (1950)	„ 15
Jewish New Year (5725)	Sept. 7
Remembrance Sunday	Nov. 8
Prince of Wales's Birthday (1948)	„ 14
1st Sunday in Advent	„ 29
St. Andrew's Day	„ 30
Christmas Day (Friday)	Dec. 25

Spring Equinox	Sun enters Sign Aries	March	20*d* 14*h*
Summer Solstice	„ „ „ Cancer	June	21*d* 09*h*
Autumn Equinox	„ „ „ Libra	Sept.	23*d* 00*h*
Winter Solstice	„ „ „ Capricornus	Dec.	21*d* 20*h*

Calendar for the Year 1964

January

Su.	—	5	12	19	26	
M.	—	6	13	20	27	
Tu.	—	7	14	21	28	
W.	1	8	15	22	29	
Th.	2	9	16	23	30	
F.	3	10	17	24	31	
S.	4	11	18	25	—	

February

Su.	—	2	9	16	23
M.	—	3	10	17	24
Tu.	—	4	11	18	25
W.	—	5	12	19	26
Th.	—	6	13	20	27
F.	—	7	14	21	28
S.	1	8	15	22	29

March

Su.	1	8	15	22	29
M.	2	9	16	23	30
Tu.	3	10	17	24	31
W.	4	11	18	25	—
Th.	5	12	19	26	—
F.	6	13	20	27	—
S.	7	14	21	28	—

April

Su.	—	5	12	19	26
M.	—	6	13	20	27
Tu.	—	7	14	21	28
W.	1	8	15	22	29
Th.	2	9	16	23	30
F.	3	10	17	24	—
S.	4	11	18	25	—

May

Su.		3	10	17	24	31
M.		4	11	18	25	—
Tu.		5	12	19	26	—
W.		6	13	20	27	—
Th.		7	14	21	28	—
F.	1	8	15	22	29	—
S.	2	9	16	23	30	—

June

Su.	—	7	14	21	28
M.	1	8	15	22	29
Tu.	2	9	16	23	30
W.	3	10	17	24	—
Th.	4	11	18	25	—
F.	5	12	19	26	—
S.	6	13	20	27	—

July

Su.	—	5	12	19	26
M.	—	6	13	20	27
Tu.	—	7	14	21	28
W.	1	8	15	22	29
Th.	2	9	16	23	30
F.	3	10	17	24	31
S.	4	11	18	25	—

August

Su.	—	2	9	16	23	30
M.	—	3	10	17	24	31
Tu.	—	4	11	18	25	—
W.	—	5	12	19	26	—
Th.	—	6	13	20	27	—
F.	—	7	14	21	28	—
S.	1	8	15	22	29	—

September

Su.	—	6	13	20	27
M.	—	7	14	21	28
Tu.	1	8	15	22	29
W.	2	9	16	23	30
Th.	3	10	17	24	—
F.	4	11	18	25	—
S.	5	12	19	26	—

October

Su.	—	4	11	18	25
M.	—	5	12	19	26
Tu.	—	6	13	20	27
W.	—	7	14	21	28
Th.	1	8	15	22	29
F.	2	9	16	23	30
S.	3	10	17	24	31

November

Su.	1	8	15	22	29
M.	2	9	16	23	30
Tu.	3	10	17	24	—
W.	4	11	18	25	—
Th.	5	12	19	26	—
F.	6	13	20	27	—
S.	7	14	21	28	—

December

Su.	—	6	13	20	27
M.	—	7	14	21	28
Tu.	1	8	15	22	29
W.	2	9	16	23	30
Th.	3	10	17	24	31
F.	4	11	18	25	—
S.	5	12	19	26	—

Calendar for the Year 1965

January

Su.	—	3	10	17	24	31
M.	—	4	11	18	25	—
Tu.	—	5	12	19	26	—
W.	—	6	13	20	27	—
Th.	—	7	14	21	28	—
F.	1	8	15	22	29	—
S.	2	9	16	23	30	—

February

Su.	—	7	14	21	28
M.	1	8	15	22	—
Tu.	2	9	16	23	—
W.	3	10	17	24	—
Th.	4	11	18	25	—
F.	5	12	19	26	—
S.	6	13	20	27	—

March

Su.	—	7	14	21	28
M.	1	8	15	22	29
Tu.	2	9	16	23	30
W.	3	10	17	24	31
Th.	4	11	18	25	—
F.	5	12	19	26	—
S.	6	13	20	27	—

April

Su.	—	4	11	18	25
M.	—	5	12	19	26
Tu.	—	6	13	20	27
W.	—	7	14	21	28
Th.	1	8	15	22	29
F.	2	9	16	23	30
S.	3	10	17	24	—

May

Su.	—	2	9	16	23	30
M.	—	3	10	17	24	31
Tu.	—	4	11	18	25	—
W.	—	5	12	19	26	—
Th.	—	6	13	20	27	—
F.	—	7	14	21	28	—
S.	1	8	15	22	29	—

June

Su.	—	6	13	20	27
M.	—	7	14	21	28
Tu.	1	8	15	22	29
W.	2	9	16	23	30
Th.	3	10	17	24	—
F.	4	11	18	25	—
S.	5	12	19	26	—

July

Su.	—	4	11	18	25	
M.	—	5	12	19	26	
Tu.	—	6	13	20	27	
W.	—	7	14	21	28	
Th.	1	8	15	22	29	
F.	2	9	16	23	30	
S.	3	10	17	24	31	

August

Su.	1	8	15	22	29
M.	2	9	16	23	30
Tu.	3	10	17	24	31
W.	4	11	18	25	—
Th.	5	12	19	26	—
F.	6	13	20	27	—
S.	7	14	21	28	—

September

Su.	—	5	12	19	26
M.	—	6	13	20	27
Tu.	—	7	14	21	28
W.	1	8	15	22	29
Th.	2	9	16	23	30
F.	3	10	17	24	—
S.	4	11	18	25	—

October

Su.	—	3	10	17	24	31
M.	—	4	11	18	25	—
Tu.	—	5	12	19	26	—
W.	—	6	13	20	27	—
Th.	—	7	14	21	28	—
F.	1	8	15	22	29	—
S.	2	9	16	23	30	—

November

Su.	—	7	14	21	28
M.	1	8	15	22	29
Tu.	2	9	16	23	30
W.	3	10	17	24	—
Th.	4	11	18	25	—
F.	5	12	19	26	—
S.	6	13	20	27	—

December

Su.	—	5	12	19	26
M.	—	6	13	20	27
Tu.	—	7	14	21	28
W.	1	8	15	22	29
Th.	2	9	16	23	30
F.	3	10	17	24	31
S.	4	11	18	25	—

Janus, god of the portal, facing two ways, past and future.

Sun's Longitude 300° ♒ 21d 01h

Day of Month	Day of Week	
1	W.	Circumcision. Sir E. Lutyens d. 1944
2	Th.	Gen. Wolfe b. 1727. A. W. Kinglake d. 1891
3	F.	Josiah Wedgwood d. 1795. Earl Attlee b. 1883
4	S.	Rachel d. 1858. Visct. Waverley d. 1958
5	S.	2nd Sunday after Christmas. Dr. Adenauer b. 1876
6	M.	Epiphany. Twelfth Day
7	Tu.	English Channel crossed in balloon, 1785
8	W.	Lord Baden-Powell d. 1941. Sir Bruce Ingram d. [1963
9	Th.	Napoleon III d. 1873. Tommy Handley d. 1949
10	F.	Miss Mitford d. 1855. Chester Wilmot d. 1954
11	S.	Neville Duke b. 1922. Visct. Simon d. 1954
12	S.	1st Sunday after Epiphany. Sir Charles Wyndham d.
13	M.	HILARY LAW SITTINGS BEGIN. Plow Monday [1919
14	Tu.	A. Schweitzer b. 1875. Cardinal Manning d. 1892
15	W.	Lady Hamilton d. 1815. Morgan Phillips d. 1963
16	Th.	Duke of Connaught d. 1942. R. H. Tawney d. 1962
17	F.	Sir C. Mackenzie b. 1883. Moira Shearer b. 1926
18	S.	Rudyard Kipling d. 1936. H. T. N. Gaitskell d. 1963
19	S.	2nd Sunday after Epiphany. Ciudad Rodrigo 1812
20	M.	George V d. 1936. Sir Roy Welensky b. 1907
21	Tu.	Paul Scofield b. 1922. Lenin d. 1924
22	W.	Queen Victoria d. 1901. Cardinal Godfrey d. 1963
23	Th.	Lord Denning b. 1899. Dame Clara Butt d. 1936
24	F.	Dogger Bank, 1915. John Burns d. 1943
25	S.	Conversion of St. Paul Lord Hankey d. 1963
26	S.	Septuagesima. FOUNDATION DAY, AUSTRALIA
27	M.	Mozart b. 1756. Verdi d. 1901 [(1788)
28	Tu.	Dostoievsky d. 1881. W. B. Yeats d. 1939
29	W.	George III. d. 1820. Fritz Kreisler d. 1962 [1963
30	Th.	Sir Pelham Warner d. 1963. Francis Poulenc d.
31	F.	Sir C. B. Cochran d. 1951. A. A. Milne d. 1956

PHENOMENA

January 2 Perihelion (91,400,000 miles).

4d 14h Mercury in inferior conjunction with the Sun.

9d 22h Venus in conjunction with Saturn. Venus 0°·6 S.

13d 08h Mercury in conjunction with the Moon. Mercury 3° N.

14d Partial eclipse of the Sun.

17d 01h Saturn in conjunction with the Moon. Saturn 2° N.

17d 17h Venus in conjunction with the Moon. Venus 3° N.

20d 19h Jupiter in conjunction with the Moon. Jupiter 4° N.

27d 00h Mercury at greatest western elongation. (25°)

CONSTELLATIONS

The following constellations are near the meridian at

	d	h		d	h
Dec.	1	24	Dec.	16	23
Jan.	1	22	Jan.	16	21
Feb.	1	20	Feb.	15	19

Draco (below the Pole), Ursa Minor (below the Pole), Camelopardus, Perseus, Auriga, Taurus, Orion, Eridanus and Lepus.

MINIMA OF ALGOL

d	h	d	h
1	07	18	12
4	03	21	08
7	00	24	05
9	21	27	02
12	18	29	23
15	15		

PHASES OF THE MOON

	d	h	m
☾ Last Quarter	6	15	58
● New Moon	14	20	43
☽ First Quarter	22	05	29
○ Full Moon	28	23	23

	d	h
Apogee (251,920 miles)	10	00
Perigee (227,190 „)	26	01

Mean Longitude of Ascending Node on January 1, 101°.

MONTHLY NOTES

January 1. New Year's Day. Bank Holiday in Scotland.

—. County Quarter Sessions, Eng. and W., to be held within the period of 21 days immediately preceding or following Dec. 25 last.

6. Dividends on Consols, etc., due.

7. Christmas Fire Insurances must be paid.

16. Ramadân begins.

Day	The Sun s.d. 16′·3 Right Ascension	Dec. −	Equation of time	Rise 52°	Rise 56°	Transit	Set 52°	Set 56°	Sidereal Time	Transit of First Point of Aries
	h m s	° ′	m s	h m	h m	h m	h m	h m	h m s	h m s
1	18 41 45	23 06	− 3 00	8 08	8 32	12 03	15 58	15 35	6 38 45	17 18 25
2	18 46 10	23 01	− 3 28	8 08	8 32	12 04	15 59	15 36	6 42 41	17 14 29
3	18 50 34	22 56	− 3 57	8 08	8 31	12 04	16 00	15 37	6 46 38	17 10 33
4	18 54 59	22 50	− 4 24	8 08	8 31	12 05	16 01	15 39	6 50 34	17 06 37
5	18 59 23	22 44	− 4 52	8 08	8 31	12 05	16 03	15 40	6 54 31	17 02 41
6	19 03 46	22 38	− 5 19	8 08	8 30	12 06	16 04	15 41	6 58 27	16 58 45
7	19 08 10	22 31	− 5 46	8 07	8 30	12 06	16 05	15 43	7 02 24	16 54 49
8	19 12 32	22 24	− 6 12	8 07	8 29	12 06	16 06	15 44	7 06 21	16 50 53
9	19 16 55	22 16	− 6 38	8 06	8 28	12 07	16 08	15 46	7 10 17	16 46 57
10	19 21 16	22 08	− 7 03	8 06	8 28	12 07	16 09	15 47	7 14 14	16 43 02
11	19 25 38	21 59	− 7 28	8 05	8 27	12 08	16 10	15 49	7 18 10	16 39 06
12	19 29 58	21 50	− 7 52	8 05	8 26	12 08	16 12	15 51	7 22 07	16 35 10
13	19 34 19	21 40	− 8 15	8 04	8 25	12 08	16 13	15 52	7 26 03	16 31 14
14	19 38 38	21 31	− 8 38	8 03	8 24	12 09	16 15	15 54	7 30 00	16 27 18
15	19 42 57	21 20	− 9 01	8 03	8 23	12 09	16 16	15 56	7 33 57	16 23 22
16	19 47 15	21 09	− 9 22	8 02	8 22	12 10	16 18	15 58	7 37 53	16 19 26
17	19 51 33	20 58	− 9 44	8 01	8 21	12 10	16 19	16 00	7 41 50	16 15 30
18	19 55 50	20 47	−10 04	8 00	8 20	12 10	16 21	16 02	7 45 46	16 11 34
19	20 00 06	20 35	−10 23	7 59	8 18	12 11	16 23	16 03	7 49 43	16 07 38
20	20 04 22	20 22	−10 42	7 58	8 17	12 11	16 24	16 05	7 53 39	16 03 42
21	20 08 36	20 10	−11 01	7 57	8 15	12 11	16 26	16 07	7 57 36	15 59 47
22	20 12 50	19 57	−11 18	7 56	8 14	12 11	16 28	16 09	8 01 32	15 55 51
23	20 17 03	19 43	−11 35	7 55	8 13	12 12	16 29	16 11	8 05 29	15 51 55
24	20 21 16	19 29	−11 50	7 53	8 11	12 12	16 31	16 14	8 09 25	15 47 59
25	20 25 27	19 15	−12 05	7 52	8 10	12 12	16 33	16 16	8 13 22	15 44 03
26	20 29 38	19 00	−12 20	7 51	8 08	12 12	16 35	16 18	8 17 19	15 40 07
27	20 33 48	18 45	−12 33	7 49	8 06	12 13	16 37	16 20	8 21 15	15 36 11
28	20 37 57	18 30	−12 46	7 48	8 05	12 13	16 38	16 22	8 25 12	15 32 15
29	20 42 06	18 15	−12 57	7 47	8 03	12 13	16 40	16 24	8 29 08	15 28 19
30	20 46 13	17 59	−13 08	7 45	8 01	12 13	16 42	16 26	8 33 05	15 24 23
31	20 50 20	17 42	−13 18	7 44	7 59	12 13	16 44	16 28	8 37 01	15 20 27

Duration of Civil (C), Nautical (N), and Astronomical (A), Twilight (in minutes)

Lat.	Jan. 1			Jan. 11			Jan. 21			Jan. 31		
°	C	N	A	C	N	A	C	N	A	C	N	A
52	41	84	125	40	82	123	38	80	120	37	78	117
56	47	96	141	45	93	138	43	90	134	41	87	130

ASTRONOMICAL NOTES

MERCURY is invisible during the first half of the month, inferior conjunction occurring on the 4th. From the middle until almost the end of the month it is visible as a morning star (magnitude +0·6 to 0·0), low in the E.S.E. sky, at about the time of the beginning of morning civil twilight. Despite the fact that it is at greatest western elongation on the 27th it is not very well placed for observation because of its declination (−22°).

VENUS is an evening star, magnitude −3·4, visible in the S.W. after sunset. On the evening of the 9th Venus and Saturn will be less than 1° apart while on the evening of the 17th observers will see the crescent Moon passing 3°S. of Venus, having passed Saturn 16 hours earlier.

MARS is too close to the Sun for observation.

JUPITER is a conspicuous evening star, magnitude −1·9, in the constellation of Pisces. As darkness falls Jupiter becomes a prominent object in the southern sky, outshone only by Venus, lower down in the S.W.

SATURN may only be seen with difficulty as an evening star, magnitude +1·0. It may be seen low in the W.S.W. for a very short time around the end of nautical twilight. By the middle of the month Saturn will be lost in the evening twilight.

ECLIPSE. A partial eclipse of the Sun occurs on the 14th but it is not visible from the British Isles.

THE MOON

Day	R.A.	Dec.	Hor. Par.	Semi-diam.	Sun's Co-long.	P.A. of Bright Limb	Phase	Age	Rise 52°	Rise 56°	Transit	Set 52°	Set 56°
	h m	°	′	′	°	°		d	h m	h m	h m	h m	h m
1	8 12	+21·8	59·6	16·2	106	98	97	15·9	18 27	18 07	1 38	9 53	10 14
2	9 12	+19·2	58·8	16·0	118	103	91	16·9	19 45	19 29	2 35	10 28	10 45
3	10 08	+15·7	57·9	15·8	130	107	84	17·9	21 01	20 50	3 28	10 56	11 08
4	11 00	+11·4	57·0	15·5	142	110	76	18·9	22 14	22 08	4 17	11 18	11 26
5	11 48	+ 6·8	56·1	15·3	154	112	66	19·9	23 25	23 23	5 03	11 37	11 40
6	12 35	+ 2·0	55·4	15·1	166	113	56	20·9	..	..	5 46	11 54	11 54
7	13 20	− 2·8	54·8	14·9	178	112	47	21·9	0 33	0 36	6 28	12 11	12 07
8	14 04	− 7·3	54·4	14·8	191	111	37	22·9	1 41	1 47	7 10	12 28	12 20
9	14 49	−11·6	54·2	14·8	203	109	28	23·9	2 47	2 59	7 52	12 48	12 36
10	15 35	−15·4	54·1	14·7	215	106	20	24·9	3 54	4 09	8 36	13 11	12 54
11	16 23	−18·5	54·2	14·8	227	103	13	25·9	5 00	5 19	9 22	13 38	13 18
12	17 12	−21·0	54·4	14·8	239	98	8	26·9	6 03	6 26	10 10	14 13	13 50
13	18 04	−22·5	54·7	14·9	252	92	3	27·9	7 03	7 27	11 00	14 56	14 31
14	18 57	−23·0	55·0	15·0	264	83	1	28·9	7 55	8 20	11 51	15 49	15 24
15	19 51	−22·3	55·5	15·1	276	299	0	0·1	8 39	9 02	12 43	16 52	16 29
16	20 44	−20·6	55·9	15·2	288	265	1	1·1	9 15	9 34	13 34	18 01	17 42
17	21 37	−17·8	56·4	15·4	300	258	5	2·1	9 44	9 59	14 24	19 14	19 00
18	22 29	−14·0	56·9	15·5	312	254	10	3·1	10 08	10 19	15 13	20 29	20 19
19	23 20	− 9·6	57·4	15·6	325	251	17	4·1	10 29	10 36	16 01	21 45	21 41
20	0 10	− 4·6	57·9	15·8	337	249	26	5·1	10 49	10 51	16 49	23 02	23 03
21	1 00	+ 0·7	58·3	15·9	349	249	36	6·1	11 09	11 06	17 37	..	..
22	1 51	+ 6·1	58·8	16·0	1	250	47	7·1	11 29	11 22	18 27	0 21	0 26
23	2 44	+11·2	59·3	16·1	13	252	59	8·1	11 53	11 41	19 20	1 42	1 52
24	3 40	+15·7	59·6	16·2	25	255	70	9·1	12 22	12 06	20 16	3 04	3 19
25	4 38	+19·4	59·9	16·3	38	260	80	10·1	13 00	12 38	21 16	4 25	4 45
26	5 40	+21·9	60·0	16·3	50	266	88	11·1	13 48	13 23	22 17	5 41	6 05
27	6 42	+23·0	59·9	16·3	62	274	95	12·1	14 48	14 23	23 18	6 48	7 13
28	7 45	+22·4	59·6	16·2	74	285	99	13·1	16 00	15 37	..	7 42	8 05
29	8 46	+20·5	59·1	16·1	86	23	100	14·1	17 17	16 59	0 18	8 23	8 42
30	9 44	+17·3	58·5	15·9	98	95	99	15·1	18 35	18 22	1 14	8 54	9 09
31	10 38	+13·2	57·7	15·7	110	103	95	16·1	19 52	19 43	2 05	9 19	9 29

MERCURY ☿

Day	R.A.	Dec. −	Diam.	Phase	Transit	
	h m	°	″		h m	
1	19 16	20·6	10	6	12 33	Mercury is too close to the Sun for observation
4	19 00	20·2	10	0	12 04	
7	18 43	20·0	10	3	11 36	
10	18 29	19·9	10	12	11 11	
13	18 21	20·1	9	25	10 53	
16	18 19	20·5	8	33	10 40	

Day	R.A.	Dec. −	Diam.	Phase	5° high E. 52°	5° high E. 56°	Transit
	h m	°	″		h m	h m	h m
16	18 19	20·5	8	33	7 17	7 45	10 40
19	18 23	20·9	8	43	7 12	7 41	10 32
22	18 30	21·3	7	52	7 11	7 42	10 28
25	18 41	21·7	7	59	7 13	7 44	10 27
28	18 54	21·9	7	65	7 16	7 48	10 29
31	19 08	22·1	6	70	7 20	7 53	10 32

VENUS ♀

Day	R.A.	Dec −	Diam.	Phase	Transit	5° high W. 52°	5° high W. 56°
	h m	°	″		h m	h m	h m
1	20 52	19·4	12	87	14 14	17 48	17 23
6	21 17	17·6	12	85	14 19	18 07	17 45
11	21 42	15·6	13	84	14 24	18 25	18 06
16	22 05	13·5	13	83	14 28	18 43	18 27
21	22 29	11·2	13	82	14 31	19 00	18 47
26	22 51	8·8	14	80	14 34	19 17	19 06
31	23 14	6·2	14	79	14 37	19 34	19 25

MARS ♂

Day	R.A.	Dec. −	Diam.	Phase	Transit	
	h m	°	″		h m	
1	19 29	22·9	4	—	12 50	Mars is too close to the Sun for observation
6	19 46	22·3	4	—	12 47	
11	20 02	21·6	4	—	12 44	
16	20 19	20·7	4	—	12 40	
21	20 35	19·8	4	—	12 37	
26	20 51	18·8	4	—	12 33	
31	21 07	17·7	4	—	12 30	

SUNRISE AND SUNSET (G.M.T.)

Day	London		Bristol		Birmingham		Manchester		Newcastle		Glasgow		Belfast	
	a.m.	p.m.	a.m.	p.m.	a.m.	p.m.	a.m.	p.m.	a.m.	p.m.	a.m.	p.m.	a.m.	p.m.
	h m	h m	h m	h m	h m	h m	h m	h m	h m	h m	h m	h m	h m	h m
1	8 06	4 01	8 16	4 11	8 18	4 02	8 26	3 59	8 32	3 47	8 48	3 53	8 48	4 07
2	8 06	4 02	8 16	4 12	8 18	4 03	8 25	4 00	8 31	3 48	8 48	3 54	8 47	4 08
3	8 06	4 03	8 16	4 13	8 18	4 04	8 25	4 01	8 31	3 49	8 47	3 55	8 47	4 09
4	8 06	4 04	8 16	4 14	8 18	4 06	8 25	4 03	8 31	3 51	8 47	3 57	8 47	4 11
5	8 06	4 05	8 15	4 16	8 18	4 07	8 25	4 04	8 31	3 52	8 47	3 58	8 47	4 12
6	8 06	4 06	8 15	4 17	8 17	4 08	8 24	4 05	8 30	3 53	8 46	3 59	8 46	4 13
7	8 05	4 07	8 15	4 18	8 17	4 10	8 24	4 07	8 30	3 55	8 46	4 01	8 46	4 15
8	8 05	4 09	8 15	4 19	8 16	4 11	8 23	4 08	8 29	3 56	8 45	4 02	8 45	4 16
9	8 04	4 10	8 14	4 21	8 16	4 12	8 23	4 09	8 28	3 58	8 44	4 04	8 44	4 18
10	8 04	4 11	8 14	4 22	8 15	4 14	8 22	4 11	8 28	3 59	8 44	4 05	8 44	4 19
11	8 03	4 12	8 13	4 23	8 14	4 15	8 21	4 12	8 27	4 01	8 43	4 07	8 43	4 21
12	8 03	4 14	8 13	4 25	8 14	4 17	8 21	4 14	8 26	4 03	8 42	4 09	8 42	4 23
13	8 02	4 15	8 12	4 26	8 13	4 18	8 20	4 15	8 25	4 04	8 41	4 10	8 41	4 24
14	8 01	4 17	8 11	4 28	8 13	4 20	8 19	4 17	8 24	4 06	8 40	4 12	8 40	4 26
15	8 01	4 18	8 11	4 29	8 12	4 21	8 19	4 18	8 23	4 08	8 39	4 14	8 39	4 28
16	8 00	4 20	8 10	4 30	8 11	4 23	8 18	4 20	8 22	4 09	8 38	4 16	8 38	4 29
17	7 59	4 21	8 09	4 32	8 10	4 24	8 17	4 21	8 21	4 11	8 37	4 18	8 37	4 31
18	7 58	4 23	8 08	4 33	8 09	4 26	8 16	4 23	8 20	4 13	8 36	4 20	8 36	4 33
19	7 57	4 25	8 07	4 35	8 08	4 28	8 15	4 25	8 19	4 15	8 34	4 21	8 35	4 35
20	7 56	4 26	8 06	4 37	8 07	4 29	8 14	4 27	8 18	4 17	8 33	4 23	8 34	4 37
21	7 55	4 28	8 05	4 38	8 06	4 31	8 13	4 28	8 16	4 18	8 31	4 25	8 33	4 38
22	7 54	4 30	8 04	4 40	8 05	4 33	8 11	4 30	8 15	4 20	8 30	4 27	8 31	4 40
23	7 53	4 31	8 03	4 41	8 04	4 34	8 10	4 32	8 14	4 22	8 29	4 29	8 30	4 42
24	7 51	4 33	8 01	4 43	8 02	4 36	8 09	4 34	8 12	4 25	8 27	4 32	8 29	4 44
25	7 50	4 35	8 00	4 45	8 01	4 38	8 07	4 36	8 11	4 27	8 26	4 34	8 27	4 46
26	7 49	4 37	7 59	4 47	8 00	4 40	8 06	4 38	8 09	4 29	8 24	4 36	8 26	4 48
27	7 47	4 39	7 57	4 49	7 58	4 42	8 04	4 40	8 07	4 31	8 22	4 38	8 24	4 50
28	7 46	4 40	7 56	4 50	7 57	4 43	8 03	4 42	8 06	4 33	8 21	4 40	8 23	4 52
29	7 45	4 42	7 55	4 52	7 56	4 45	8 01	4 44	8 04	4 35	8 19	4 42	8 21	4 54
30	7 43	4 44	7 53	4 54	7 54	4 47	8 00	4 46	8 03	4 37	8 17	4 44	8 19	4 56
31	7 42	4 46	7 52	4 56	7 53	4 49	7 58	4 48	8 01	4 39	8 15	4 46	8 17	4 58

JUPITER ♃ SATURN ♄

Day	Jupiter R.A.	Jupiter Dec. +	Jupiter Transit	Jupiter 5° high West 52°	Jupiter 5° high West 56°	Saturn R.A.	Saturn Dec. —	Saturn Transit	Saturn 5° high West 52°	Saturn 5° high West 56°
	h m	°	h m	h m	h m	h m	°	h m	h m	h m
1	0 42	3·0	18 00	23 42	23 42	21 33	15·8	14 52	18 49	18 29
11	0 45	3·5	17 25	23 09	23 09	21 37	15·5	14 17	18 16	17 57
21	0 50	4·0	16 50	22 38	22 38	21 41	15·1	13 42	17 43	17 25
31	0 56	4·7	16 16	22 07	22 08	21 46	14·7	13 07	17 11	16 53

Equatorial diameter of Jupiter 39″; of Saturn 16″. Diameters of Saturn's rings 35″ and 8″.

URANUS ♅ NEPTUNE ♆

Day	Uranus R.A.	Uranus Dec. +	Uranus 10° high in East 52°	Uranus 10° high in East 56°	Uranus Transit	Neptune R.A.	Neptune Dec. —	Neptune 10° high in East 52°	Neptune 10° high in East 56°	Neptune Transit
	h m	° ′	h m	h m	h m	h m	° ′	h m	h m	h m
1	10 47·2	8 34	22 26	22 25	4 08	15 00·9	15 18	5 01	5 28	8 21
11	10 46·5	8 39	21 45	21 45	3 28	15 01·9	15 22	4 23	4 50	7 42
21	10 45·5	8 45	21 05	21 04	2 47	15 02·6	15 24	3 45	4 12	7 04
31	10 44·2	8 53	20 23	20 23	2 07	15 03·1	15 26	3 07	3 34	6 25

Uranus: Diameter 4″. Neptune: Diameter 2″.

Februa, Roman festival of Purification.

Sun's Longitude 330° ♓ 19d 15h

Day of Month	Day of Week	
1	S.	Stanley Matthews b. 1915
2	S.	Sexagesima. Purification. Candlemas
3	M.	Sir Roger Makins b. 1904. Pres. Wilson d. 1924
4	Tu.	Dr. Ludwig Erhard b. 1897. Lord Shawcross b. 1902
5	W.	Press Assoc. inaug. 1870. Visct. Samuel d. 1963
6	Th.	ACCESSION OF QUEEN ELIZABETH II (1952)
7	F.	Charles Dickens b. 1812. Earl of Harewood b. 1923
8	S.	Sir Giles Gilbert Scott d. 1960
9	S.	Quinquagesima. Dean Rusk b. 1909
10	M.	Lord Birkett d. 1962. J. H. Taylor d. 1963
11	Tu.	Shrove Tuesday. Louis Paulhan d. 1963
12	W.	Ash Wednesday. Kant d. 1804
13	Th.	Massacre of Glencoe, 1692. Wagner d. 1883
14	F.	VALENTINE'S DAY. Capt. Cook d. 1779
15	S.	H. M. Bateman b. 1887. Relief of Kimberley, 1900
16	S.	1st Sunday in Lent. Lord Franks b. 1905
17	M.	Heine d. 1856. Bruno Walter d. 1962
18	Tu.	Sir Arthur Bryant b. 1899
19	W.	PRINCE ANDREW BORN 1960 [d. 1960
20	Th.	Laurence Housman d. 1959. Sir Leonard Woolley
21	F.	Cardinal Newman b. 1801
22	S.	Washington b. 1732. Corot d. 1875
23	S.	2nd Sunday in Lent. Sir Edward Elgar d. 1934
24	M.	St. Matthias. David Langdon b. 1914
25	Tu.	Thomas Moore d. 1852. Sir John Tenniel d. 1914
26	W.	Wren d. 1723. Dean Inge d. 1954
27	Th.	John Evelyn d. 1706. John Steinbeck b. 1902
28	F.	Sir Basil Embry b. 1902. Henry James d. 1916
29	S.	E. F. Benson d. 1940. Agadir earthquake 1960

PHENOMENA

February 11^{d} 19^{h} Mercury in conjunction with the Moon. Mercury 0°·7 N.

15^{d} 06^{h} Saturn in conjunction with the Sun.

16^{d} 13^{h} Venus in conjunction with the Moon. Venus 5° N.

17^{d} 03^{h} Mars in conjunction with the Sun.

17^{d} 09^{h} Jupiter in conjunction with the Moon. Jupiter 4° N.

27^{d} 14^{h} Uranus at opposition.

28^{d} 02^{h} Mercury in conjunction with Saturn. Mercury 1°·0 S.

28^{d} 08^{h} Venus in conjunction with Jupiter. Venus 1°·7 N.

CONSTELLATIONS

The following constellations are near the meridian at

	d	h		d	h
Jan.	1	24	Jan.	16	23
Feb.	1	22	Feb.	15	21
Mar.	1	20	Mar.	16	19

Draco (below the Pole), Camelopardus, Auriga, Taurus, Gemini, Orion, Canis Minor, Monoceros, Lepus, Canis Major and Puppis (Argo).

MINIMA OF ALGOL

d	h	d	h
1	20	16	04
4	16	19	00
7	13	21	21
10	10	24	18
13	07	27	15

PHASES OF THE MOON

	d	h	m
☾ Last Quarter......	5	12	42
● New Moon.......	13	13	01
☽ First Quarter......	20	13	24
○ Full Moon........	27	12	39

	d	h
Apogee (251,350 miles)...	6	20
Perigee (230,000 „)...	21	08

Mean Longitude of Ascending Node on February 1, 100°.

MONTHLY NOTES

February 1. Pheasant and partridge shooting ends.
2. Scottish Term Day.
5. 12 Elizabeth II ends.
6. 13 Elizabeth II begins. New Zealand Day.
8. Half-Quarter Day.
12. Lent begins (ends midnight March 28).

QUARTER DAYS

(England, Wales and Northern Ireland)

Lady Day.........March 25 *Michaelmas*.......September 29
Midsummer........June 24 *Christmas*........December 25

HALF-QUARTER DAYS are Feb. 8, May 9, Aug. 11 and Nov. 11.

SCOTTISH TERM DAYS

Candlemas........February 2 *Lammas*.........August 1
Whitsunday.......May 15 *Martinmas*.......November 11

Removal Terms are May 28 and November 28.

Day	The Sun — Right Ascension	Dec. —	Equation of Time	Rise 52°	Rise 56°	Transit	Set 52°	Set 56°	Sidereal Time	Transit of First Point of Aries
	h m s	° ′	m s	h m	h m	h m	h m	h m	h m s	h m s
1	20 54 26	17 26	−13 28	7 42	7 58	12 14	16 46	16 30	8 40 58	15 16 31
2	20 58 31	17 09	−13 36	7 41	7 56	12 14	16 48	16 33	8 44 55	15 12 36
3	21 02 35	16 52	−13 44	7 39	7 54	12 14	16 49	16 35	8 48 51	15 08 40
4	21 06 38	16 34	−13 51	7 38	7 52	12 14	16 51	16 37	8 52 48	15 04 44
5	21 10 41	16 17	−13 57	7 36	7 50	12 14	16 53	16 39	8 56 44	15 00 48
6	21 14 43	15 59	−14 02	7 34	7 48	12 14	16 55	16 41	9 00 41	14 56 52
7	21 18 44	15 40	−14 07	7 33	7 46	12 14	16 57	16 44	9 04 37	14 52 56
8	21 22 44	15 22	−14 11	7 31	7 44	12 14	16 59	16 46	9 08 34	14 49 00
9	21 26 44	15 03	−14 14	7 29	7 42	12 14	17 01	16 48	9 12 30	14 45 04
10	21 30 43	14 44	−14 16	7 27	7 40	12 14	17 02	16 50	9 16 27	14 41 08
11	21 34 41	14 24	−14 17	7 25	7 37	12 14	17 04	16 52	9 20 24	14 37 12
12	21 38 38	14 05	−14 18	7 24	7 35	12 14	17 06	16 55	9 24 20	14 33 16
13	21 42 34	13 45	−14 18	7 22	7 33	12 14	17 08	16 57	9 28 17	14 29 21
14	21 46 30	13 25	−14 17	7 20	7 31	12 14	17 10	16 59	9 32 13	14 25 25
15	21 50 25	13 05	−14 15	7 18	7 29	12 14	17 12	17 01	9 36 10	14 21 29
16	21 54 19	12 44	−14 13	7 16	7 26	12 14	17 14	17 03	9 40 06	14 17 33
17	21 58 13	12 24	−14 10	7 14	7 24	12 14	17 15	17 05	9 44 03	14 13 37
18	22 02 05	12 03	−14 06	7 12	7 22	12 14	17 17	17 08	9 47 59	14 09 41
19	22 05 57	11 42	−14 02	7 10	7 19	12 14	17 19	17 10	9 51 56	14 05 45
20	22 09 49	11 20	−13 56	7 08	7 17	12 14	17 21	17 12	9 55 52	14 01 49
21	22 13 39	10 59	−13 50	7 06	7 15	12 14	17 23	17 14	9 59 49	13 57 53
22	22 17 29	10 37	−13 44	7 04	7 12	12 14	17 25	17 16	10 03 46	13 53 57
23	22 21 18	10 16	−13 36	7 02	7 10	12 14	17 27	17 19	10 07 42	13 50 01
24	22 25 07	9 54	−13 28	7 00	7 07	12 13	17 28	17 21	10 11 39	13 46 06
25	22 28 55	9 32	−13 20	6 58	7 05	12 13	17 30	17 23	10 15 35	13 42 10
26	22 32 42	9 09	−13 11	6 55	7 03	12 13	17 32	17 25	10 19 32	13 38 14
27	22 36 29	8 47	−13 01	6 53	7 00	12 13	17 34	17 27	10 23 28	13 34 18
28	22 40 15	8 25	−12 51	6 51	6 58	12 13	17 36	17 29	10 27 25	13 30 22
29	22 44 01	8 02	−12 40	6 49	6 55	12 13	17 38	17 31	10 31 21	13 26 26

The Sun s.d. 16′·2

Duration of Civil (C), Nautical (N), and Astronomical (A), Twilight (in minutes)

Lat.	Feb. 1			Feb. 11			Feb. 21			Feb. 28		
°	C	N	A	C	N	A	C	N	A	C	N	A
52	37	77	117	35	75	114	34	74	113	34	73	112
56	41	86	130	39	83	126	38	81	125	38	81	124

ASTRONOMICAL NOTES

Mercury is not suitably placed for observation.

Venus is a brilliant evening star, magnitude −3·6. It is slowly increasing in brightness and also noticeably getting farther from the Sun so that it is visible in the south-western and western sky for several hours after sunset. At the end of the month Venus and Jupiter are only a few degrees apart.

Mars is unsuitably placed for observation, conjunction occurring on the 17th.

Jupiter, still in Pisces, remains an evening star, magnitude −1·8, being a conspicuous object in the south-western sky. It is gradually drawing nearer to Venus, conjunction occurring on the 28th. On the evening of the 16th the crescent Moon will be seen a few degrees S. of the line joining Venus and Jupiter; the two planets being about 10° apart, with Venus nearer to the Sun.

Saturn is unsuitably placed for observation, conjunction occurring on the 15th

Zodiacal Light. The evening cone may be observed in the west after the end of twilight between the beginning of the month and the 14th and again on the 29th. Unfortunately observation of this faint phenomenon will be partly spoilt by the brilliance of Venus, and to a lesser extent by Jupiter as well.

THE MOON

Day	R.A.	Dec.	Hor. Par.	Semi-diam.	Sun's Co-long.	P.A. of Bright Limb	Phase	Age	Rise 52°	Rise 56°	Transit	Set 52°	Set 56°
	h m	°	′	′	°	°		d	h m	h m	h m	h m	h m
1	11 29	+ 8·6	56·9	15·5	123	107	89	17·1	21 05	21 02	2 54	9 40	9 45
2	12 17	+ 3·8	56·1	15·3	135	109	82	18·1	22 16	22 17	3 39	9 58	9 59
3	13 03	− 1·1	55·5	15·1	147	110	73	19·1	23 25	23 30	4 22	10 15	10 13
4	13 49	− 5·9	54·9	15·0	159	109	64	20·1	..	..	5 05	10 33	10 26
5	14 34	−10·3	54·5	14·8	171	108	55	21·1	0 33	0 42	5 47	10 51	10 41
6	15 20	−14·3	54·3	14·8	183	105	46	22·1	1 40	1 54	6 31	11 13	10 58
7	16 07	−17·7	54·2	14·8	195	102	36	23·1	2 47	3 04	7 16	11 38	11 19
8	16 56	−20·3	54·3	14·8	208	98	28	24·1	3 51	4 13	8 03	12 10	11 47
9	17 47	−22·2	54·6	14·9	220	92	19	25·1	4 52	5 16	8 52	12 49	12 24
10	18 39	−23·0	55·0	15·0	232	86	12	26·1	5 47	6 12	9 43	13 38	13 13
11	19 33	−22·7	55·5	15·1	244	79	7	27·1	6 34	6 59	10 34	14 38	14 14
12	20 27	−21·3	56·1	15·3	256	70	3	28·1	7 13	7 35	11 26	15 45	15 25
13	21 21	−18·7	56·6	15·4	269	47	0	29·1	7 45	8 02	12 18	16 58	16 43
14	22 14	−15·2	57·2	15·6	281	284	0	0·5	8 12	8 24	13 08	18 15	18 04
15	23 06	−10·8	57·7	15·7	293	261	3	1·5	8 34	8 42	13 57	19 32	19 26
16	23 57	− 5·8	58·2	15·9	305	255	7	2·5	8 55	8 58	14 46	20 51	20 50
17	0 48	− 0·4	58·5	16·0	317	252	14	3·5	9 14	9 13	15 35	22 10	22 14
18	1 39	+ 5·0	58·8	16·0	330	252	23	4·5	9 35	9 29	16 25	23 31	23 40
19	2 32	+10·2	59·0	16·1	342	253	33	5·5	9 57	9 47	17 16	..	..
20	3 27	+14·9	59·2	16·1	354	256	44	6·5	10 24	10 09	18 11	0 52	1 06
21	4 23	+18·8	59·2	16·1	6	260	55	7·5	10 57	10 37	19 07	2 12	2 32
22	5 23	+21·5	59·2	16·1	18	266	66	8·5	11 40	11 16	20 06	3 29	3 52
23	6 23	+22·9	59·1	16·1	30	272	76	9·5	12 35	12 09	21 06	4 37	5 03
24	7 25	+22·9	58·9	16·1	43	279	85	10·5	13 40	13 16	22 05	5 34	5 58
25	8 25	+21·4	58·6	16·0	55	287	92	11·5	14 54	14 34	23 01	6 19	6 40
26	9 23	+18·6	58·2	15·9	67	297	97	12·5	16 11	15 56	23 54	6 53	7 09
27	10 17	+14·9	57·7	15·7	79	322	100	13·5	17 28	17 18	..	7 20	7 32
28	11 09	+10·4	57·1	15·6	91	75	100	14·5	18 44	18 38	0 43	7 42	7 49
29	11 58	+ 5·6	56·5	15·4	103	99	97	15·5	19 57	19 55	1 30	8 01	8 04

MERCURY ☿

Day	R.A.	Dec. −	Diam.	Phase	Transit		Day	R.A.	Dec. −	Diam.	Phase	Transit	
	h m	°	″		h m			h m	°	″		h m	
1	19 13	22·1	6	71	10 33	Mercury is too close to the Sun for observation	16	20 41	19·9	5	86	11 02	Mercury is too close to the Sun for observation
4	19 29	22·0	6	75	10 37		19	21 00	18·9	5	88	11 09	
7	19 47	21·7	6	78	10 43		22	21 19	17·7	5	90	11 17	
10	20 04	21·3	6	81	10 49		25	21 39	16·2	5	92	11 24	
13	20 22	20·7	5	84	10 55		28	21 59	14·6	5	94	11 32	
16	20 41	19·9	5	86	11 02		31	22 18	12·8	5	96	11 41	

VENUS ♀

Day	R.A.	Dec.	Diam.	Phase	Transit	5° high W. 52°	5° high W. 56°
	h m	°	″		h m	h m	h m
1	23 18	−5·7	14	79	14 37	19 37	19 29
6	23 40	−3·1	14	77	14 39	19 53	19 47
11	0 02	−0·5	15	76	14 41	20 08	20 05
16	0 23	+2·1	15	74	14 43	20 24	20 22
21	0 44	+4·7	16	72	14 45	20 39	20 39
26	1 05	+7·3	16	71	14 46	20 53	20 56
31	1 27	+9·8	17	69	14 48	21 08	21 13

MARS ♂

Day	R.A.	Dec. −	Diam.	Phase	Transit	
	h m	°	″		h m	
1	21 10	17·5	4	—	12 29	Mars is too close to the Sun for observation
6	21 26	16·3	4	—	12 25	
11	21 41	15·0	4	—	12 21	
16	21 57	13·7	4	—	12 16	
21	22 12	12·3	4	—	12 12	
26	22 27	10·8	4	—	12 07	
31	22 42	9·4	4	—	12 02	

SUNRISE AND SUNSET (G.M.T.)

Day	London		Bristol		Birmingham		Manchester		Newcastle		Glasgow		Belfast	
	a.m.	p.m.	a.m.	p.m.	a.m.	p.m.	a.m.	p.m.	a.m.	p.m.	a.m.	p.m.	a.m.	p.m.
	h m	h m	h m	h m	h m	h m	h m	h m	h m	h m	h m	h m	h m	h m
1	7 41	4 48	7 50	4 48	7 52	4 51	7 57	4 50	8 00	4 41	8 14	4 48	8 16	5 00
2	7 39	4 50	7 49	5 00	7 50	4 53	7 55	4 52	7 58	4 43	8 12	4 51	8 14	5 03
3	7 38	4 51	7 47	5 01	7 48	4 55	7 53	4 54	7 56	4 45	8 10	4 53	8 12	5 05
4	7 37	4 53	7 46	5 03	7 46	4 57	7 51	4 56	7 54	4 47	8 08	4 55	8 10	5 07
5	7 35	4 55	7 44	5 05	7 44	4 59	7 49	4 58	7 52	4 49	8 06	4 57	8 08	5 09
6	7 33	4 57	7 42	5 07	7 43	5 01	7 48	5 00	7 50	4 51	8 04	4 59	8 07	5 11
7	7 32	4 58	7 41	5 08	7 41	5 03	7 46	5 02	7 48	4 54	8 02	5 02	8 05	5 13
8	7 30	5 00	7 39	5 10	7 39	5 05	7 44	5 04	7 46	4 56	8 00	5 04	8 03	5 15
9	7 28	5 02	7 38	5 12	7 37	5 07	7 42	5 06	7 44	4 58	7 58	5 06	8 01	5 17
10	7 26	5 04	7 36	5 14	7 35	5 08	7 40	5 07	7 42	5 00	7 56	5 08	7 59	5 19
11	7 24	5 05	7 34	5 15	7 33	5 10	7 38	5 09	7 40	5 02	7 54	5 10	7 57	5 21
12	7 23	5 07	7 32	5 17	7 32	5 12	7 37	5 11	7 38	5 04	7 52	5 12	7 55	5 23
13	7 21	5 09	7 31	5 19	7 30	5 14	7 35	5 13	7 36	5 06	7 50	5 14	7 53	5 25
14	7 19	5 11	7 29	5 21	7 28	5 16	7 33	5 15	7 34	5 08	7 48	5 16	7 51	5 27
15	7 17	5 13	7 27	5 23	7 26	5 18	7 31	5 17	7 32	5 10	7 46	5 18	7 49	5 29
16	7 15	5 15	7 25	5 25	7 24	5 20	7 29	5 19	7 29	5 12	7 43	5 20	7 47	5 31
17	7 13	5 16	7 23	5 26	7 22	5 21	7 27	5 21	7 27	5 14	7 41	5 22	7 45	5 33
18	7 11	5 18	7 21	5 28	7 20	5 23	7 25	5 23	7 25	5 17	7 39	5 25	7 43	5 35
19	7 09	5 20	7 19	5 30	7 18	5 25	7 22	5 25	7 22	5 19	7 36	5 27	7 40	5 37
20	7 07	5 22	7 17	5 32	7 16	5 27	7 20	5 27	7 20	5 21	7 34	5 29	7 38	5 39
21	7 05	5 24	7 15	5 34	7 14	5 29	7 18	5 29	7 18	5 23	7 32	5 31	7 36	5 41
22	7 03	5 26	7 13	5 36	7 12	5 31	7 16	5 31	7 16	5 25	7 29	5 33	7 33	5 43
23	7 01	5 28	7 11	5 38	7 10	5 33	7 14	5 33	7 14	5 27	7 27	5 36	7 31	5 46
24	6 59	5 29	7 09	5 39	7 08	5 34	7 11	5 35	7 11	5 29	7 24	5 38	7 28	5 48
25	6 57	5 31	7 07	5 41	7 06	5 36	7 09	5 37	7 09	5 31	7 22	5 40	7 26	5 50
26	6 54	5 33	7 04	5 43	7 03	5 38	7 07	5 39	7 07	5 33	7 20	5 42	7 42	5 52
27	6 52	5 35	7 02	5 45	7 01	5 40	7 04	5 41	7 04	5 35	7 17	5 44	7 21	5 54
28	6 50	5 37	7 00	5 47	6 59	5 42	7 02	5 43	7 02	5 37	7 15	5 46	7 19	5 56
29	6 48	5 39	6 58	5 49	6 57	5 44	7 00	5 45	6 59	5 39	7 12	5 48	7 17	5 58

JUPITER ♃ / SATURN ♄

Day	Jupiter R.A.	Jupiter Dec. +	Jupiter Transit	5° high West 52°	5° high West 56°	Saturn R.A.	Saturn Dec. −	Saturn Transit	
	h m	°	h m	h m	h m	h m	°	h m	
1	0 56	4·7	16 13	22 04	22 05	21 46	14·7	13 04	Saturn is too close to the Sun for observation
11	1 03	5·4	15 40	21 35	21 36	21 51	14·3	12 29	
21	1 10	6·2	15 08	21 07	21 09	21 56	13·9	11 54	
31	1 17	7·0	14 36	20 39	20 42	22 00	13·5	11 20	

Equatorial diameter of Jupiter 36″; of Saturn 15″. Diameters of Saturn's rings 35″ and 7″.

URANUS ♅ / NEPTUNE ♆

Day	Uranus R.A.	Uranus Dec. +	10° high in East 52°	10° high in East 56°	Uranus Transit	Neptune R.A.	Neptune Dec. −	10° high in East 52°	10° high in East 56°	Neptune Transit
	h m	° ′	h m	h m	h m	h m	° ′	h m	h m	h m
1	10 44·1	8 54	20 19	20 18	2 03	15 03·2	15 26	3 03	3 30	6 21
11	10 42·6	9 03	19 38	19 37	1 22	15 03·5	15 27	2 24	2 51	5 42
21	10 41·0	9 12	18 56	18 55	0 41	15 03·6	15 26	1 44	2 12	5 03
31	10 39·4	9 22	18 14	18 13	0 00 / 23 56	15 03·4	15 25	1 05	1 32	4 23

Uranus: Diameter 4″ Neptune: Diameter 2″

Mars, Roman god of battle.

Sun's Longitude 0° ♈ 20^{d} 14^{h}

Day of Month	Day of Week	
1	S.	St. David's Day. 3rd Sunday in Lent.
2	M.	John Wesley d. 1791. Sir Miles Thomas b. 1897
3	Tu.	Treaty of San Stefano, 1878. Ronald Searle b. 1920
4	W.	Raeburn d. 1756. Sir Charles Sherrington d. 1952
5	Th.	James I d. 1625. Rex Harrison b. 1908
6	F.	John Redmond d. 1918. Cologne captured 1945
7	S.	J. R. Green d. 1883. Lord Tovey b. 1885
8	S.	4th Sunday in Lent. William III d. 1702. [1963
9	M.	Visct. Dawson of Penn b. 1864.** Sir J. Crocker d.
10	Tu.	Sir W. W. Wakefield b. 1898. Owen Brannigan b.
11	W.	Harold Wilson b. 1916. Earl Beatty d. 1936 [1908
12	Th.	Sun Yat Sen d. 1925. Sir W. H. Bragg d. 1942
13	F.	G. E. Buckle d. 1935. Sir Cyril Norwood d. 1956
14	S.	Admiral Byng d. 1757. Karl Marx d. 1883
15	S.	5th Sunday in Lent. Visct. Chandos b. 1893
16	M.	R. S. Surtees d. 1864.** Lord Beveridge d. 1963
17	Tu.	St Patrick's Day. Bobby Jones b. 1902
18	W.	Sir R. Walpole d. 1745. Sir Hubert Gough d. 1963
19	Th.	Earl of Balfour d. 1930 [1929
20	F.	Sir Michael Redgrave b. 1908. Marshal Foch d.
21	S.	Aboukir 1801. Robert Southey d. 1843
22	S.	6th Sunday in Lent. Palm Sunday
23	M.	Jimmy Edwards b. 1920. Clement Davies d. 1962
24	Tu.	Queen Mary d. 1953. Mrs. Humphry Ward d. 1920
25	W.	Hilary Law Sittings End. Annunciation
26	Th.	Maundy Thursday. Earl Lloyd George d. 1945
27	F.	Good Friday
28	S.	Dame Flora Robson b. 1902. Rachmaninoff d. 1943
29	S.	Easter Day
30	M.	Easter Monday. Visct. Radcliffe b. 1899
31	Tu.	Easter Tuesday. Duke of Gloucester b. 1900

PHENOMENA

March 3^{d} 12^{h} Pluto at opposition.

12^{d} 05^{h} Saturn in conjunction with the Moon. Saturn 3° N.

13^{d} 08^{h} Mercury in superior conjunction with the Sun.

16^{d} 02^{h} Jupiter in conjunction with the Moon. Jupiter 4° N.

17^{d} 06^{h} Venus in conjunction with the Moon. Venus 6° N.

20^{d} 14^{h} Vernal Equinox.

31^{d} 23^{h} Mercury in conjunction with Jupiter. Mercury 3° N.

CONSTELLATIONS

The following constellations are near the meridian at

	d	h		d	h
Feb.	1	24	Feb.	15	23
Mar.	1	22	Mar.	16	21
April	1	20	April	15	19

Cepheus (below the Pole), Camelopardus, Lynx, Gemini, Cancer, Leo, Canis Minor, Hydra, Monoceros, Canis Major and Puppis (Argo).

MINIMA OF ALGOL

d	h	d	h
1	12	18	17
4	09	21	13
7	05	24	10
10	02	27	07
12	23	30	04
15	20		

PHASES OF THE MOON

	d	h	m
☾ Last Quarter	6	10	00
● New Moon	14	02	14
☽ First Quarter	20	20	39
○ Full Moon	28	02	48

	d	h
Apogee (251,190 miles) ...	5	17
Perigee (228,190 „) ...	17	16

Mean Longitude of Ascending Node on March 1, 98°.

Summer Time in 1964.—Begins: March 22 at 2 a.m. G.M.T.
Ends: October 25 at 2 a.m. G.M.T.

MONTHLY NOTES

March 1. Auditors of Boroughs, Eng. and W., to be elected.

17. Bank Holiday in Northern Ireland.

25. Lady Day. Quarter Day. Accounts of Local Government Authorities, Eng. and W., to be made up to 31st. Quarter Sessions to be held 21 days before or after this date.

28. First day of Jewish Passover.

30. Bank and General Holiday, England, Wales and N. Ireland.

31. Financial Year 1963-64 ends.

** Centenary.

Day	The Sun s.d. 16′·1 Right Ascension	Dec.	Equation of Time	Rise 52°	Rise 56°	Transit	Set 52°	Set 56°	Sidereal Time	Transit of First Point of Aries
	h m s	° ′	m s	h m	h m	h m	h m	h m	h m s	h m s
1	22 47 46	−7 39	−12 28	6 47	6 53	12 12	17 39	17 34	10 35 18	13 22 30
2	22 51 31	−7 17	−12 16	6 45	6 50	12 12	17 41	17 36	10 39 15	13 18 34
3	22 55 15	−6 54	−12 04	6 42	6 48	12 12	17 43	17 38	10 43 11	13 14 38
4	22 58 59	−6 31	−11 51	6 40	6 45	12 12	17 45	17 40	10 47 08	13 10 42
5	23 02 42	−6 07	−11 38	6 38	6 42	12 12	17 46	17 42	10 51 04	13 06 47
6	23 06 25	−5 44	−11 24	6 36	6 40	12 11	17 48	17 44	10 55 01	13 02 51
7	23 10 07	−5 21	−11 10	6 33	6 37	12 11	17 50	17 46	10 58 57	12 58 55
8	23 13 49	−4 58	−10 56	6 31	6 35	12 11	17 52	17 48	11 02 54	12 54 59
9	23 17 31	−4 34	−10 41	6 29	6 32	12 11	17 53	17 50	11 06 50	12 51 03
10	23 21 12	−4 11	−10 26	6 27	6 30	12 10	17 55	17 52	11 10 47	12 47 07
11	23 24 53	−3 47	−10 10	6 24	6 27	12 10	17 57	17 55	11 14 44	12 43 11
12	23 28 34	−3 24	− 9 54	6 22	6 24	12 10	17 59	17 57	11 18 40	12 39 15
13	23 32 15	−3 00	− 9 38	6 20	6 22	12 09	18 00	17 59	11 22 37	12 35 19
14	23 35 55	−2 36	− 9 22	6 17	6 19	12 09	18 02	18 01	11 26 33	12 31 23
15	23 39 35	−2 13	− 9 05	6 15	6 16	12 09	18 04	18 03	11 30 30	12 27 27
16	23 43 14	−1 49	− 8 48	6 13	6 14	12 09	18 06	18 05	11 34 26	12 23 32
17	23 46 54	−1 25	− 8 31	6 11	6 11	12 08	18 07	18 07	11 38 23	12 19 36
18	23 50 33	−1 01	− 8 14	6 08	6 09	12 08	18 09	18 09	11 42 19	12 15 40
19	23 54 12	−0 38	− 7 56	6 06	6 06	12 08	18 11	18 11	11 46 16	12 11 44
20	23 57 51	−0 14	− 7 38	6 04	6 03	12 07	18 13	18 13	11 50 13	12 07 48
21	0 01 30	+0 10	− 7 21	6 01	6 01	12 07	18 14	18 15	11 54 09	12 03 52
22	0 05 08	+0 33	− 7 03	5 59	5 58	12 07	18 16	18 17	11 58 06	11 59 56
23	0 08 47	+0 57	− 6 44	5 57	5 55	12 07	18 18	18 19	12 02 02	11 56 00
24	0 12 25	+1 21	− 6 26	5 54	5 53	12 06	18 20	18 21	12 05 59	11 52 04
25	0 16 03	+1 44	− 6 08	5 52	5 50	12 06	18 21	18 23	12 09 55	11 48 08
26	0 19 41	+2 08	− 5 50	5 50	5 48	12 06	18 23	18 25	12 13 52	11 44 12
27	0 23 20	+2 31	− 5 31	5 47	5 45	12 05	18 25	18 27	12 17 48	11 40 17
28	0 26 58	+2 55	− 5 13	5 45	5 42	12 05	18 26	18 29	12 21 45	11 36 21
29	0 30 36	+3 18	− 4 55	5 43	5 39	12 05	18 28	18 31	12 25 42	11 32 25
30	0 34 14	+3 42	− 4 37	5 41	5 37	12 04	18 30	18 34	12 29 38	11 28 29
31	0 37 53	+4 05	− 4 18	5 38	5 34	12 04	18 31	18 36	12 33 35	11 24 33

Duration of Civil (C), Nautical (N), and Astronomical (A), Twilight (in minutes)

Lat.	Mar. 1			Mar. 11			Mar. 21			Mar. 31		
°	C	N	A	C	N	A	C	N	A	C	N	A
52	34	73	112	34	73	113	34	74	116	34	76	120
56	38	81	124	37	80	125	37	82	129	38	84	136

ASTRONOMICAL NOTES

MERCURY is not suitably placed for observation at first, as it is at superior conjunction on the 13th. However it becomes an evening star (magnitude −1) by the 25th as it is still at an altitude of 5° above the W. horizon at the end of civil twilight. This evening apparition, which extends well into April, is the most suitable one of the year for observers in the northern hemisphere. On the evening of the 31st Mercury will be seen to be only about 3° from Jupiter. Note that Jupiter will be a whole magnitude brighter than Mercury and farther to the left.

VENUS is a brilliant evening star, magnitude −3·8, visible in the south western sky after sunset. On the evening of the 16th the thin crescent Moon will be seen a few degrees south of the line joining Venus and Jupiter.

MARS is unsuitably placed for observation.

JUPITER remains a conspicuous evening star, magnitude −1·6, though now moving noticeably towards the Sun.

SATURN is unsuitably placed for observation.

ZODIACAL LIGHT. The evening cone may be observed stretching up from the western horizon after the end of twilight between the beginning of the month and the 15th, and again on the 30th and 31st. Observers will notice that Venus and Jupiter again interfere with their observations.

THE MOON

Day	R.A.	Dec.	Hor. Par.	Semi-diam.	Sun's Co-long.	P.A. of Bright Limb	Phase	Age	Rise 52°	Rise 56°	Transit	Set 52°	Set 56°
	h m	°	′	′	°	°		d	h m	h m	h m	h m	h m
1	12 46	+ 0·6	55·9	15·2	115	104	93	16·5	21 07	21 11	2 14	8 19	8 18
2	13 32	− 4·3	55·3	15·1	128	106	87	17·5	22 17	22 24	2 58	8 36	8 31
3	14 18	− 8·9	54·8	14·9	140	106	80	18·5	23 25	23 37	3 41	8 54	8 45
4	15 04	−13·2	54·5	14·8	152	104	72	19·5	..	..	4 24	9 14	9 01
5	15 51	−16·8	54·3	14·8	164	101	63	20·5	0 32	0 49	5 09	9 38	9 20
6	16 39	−19·7	54·3	14·8	176	98	54	21·5	1 38	1 59	5 55	10 06	9 45
7	17 29	−21·9	54·4	14·8	188	93	44	22·5	2 41	3 04	6 43	10 42	10 18
8	18 20	−23·0	54·7	14·9	201	88	35	23·5	3 38	4 03	7 33	11 27	11 01
9	19 13	−23·1	55·2	15·0	213	82	26	24·5	4 28	4 53	8 24	12 21	11 56
10	20 07	−22·1	55·8	15·2	225	76	18	25·5	5 10	5 33	9 15	13 25	13 03
11	21 01	−19·9	56·5	15·4	237	70	11	26·5	5 45	6 04	10 07	14 36	14 18
12	21 54	−16·7	57·2	15·6	249	63	5	27·5	6 13	6 27	10 58	15 53	15 39
13	22 47	−12·5	57·9	15·8	262	51	2	28·5	6 37	6 47	11 48	17 11	17 03
14	23 39	− 7·5	58·6	16·0	274	171	0	29·5	6 58	7 03	12 38	18 32	18 28
15	0 31	− 2·1	59·1	16·1	286	269	1	0·9	7 18	7 19	13 28	19 53	19 55
16	1 24	+ 3·5	59·5	16·2	298	258	5	1·9	7 39	7 34	14 19	21 16	21 23
17	2 17	+ 9·0	59·7	16·3	310	256	11	2·9	8 01	7 51	15 11	22 39	22 52
18	3 13	+14·0	59·7	16·3	323	258	19	3·9	8 26	8 12	16 06	..	..
19	4 10	+18·2	59·6	16·2	335	261	29	4·9	8 58	8 38	17 03	0 02	0 20
20	5 09	+21·3	59·3	16·2	347	265	40	5·9	9 37	9 14	18 01	1 21	1 44
21	6 10	+23·0	59·0	16·1	359	271	52	6·9	10 28	10 02	19 01	2 32	2 58
22	7 10	+23·2	58·6	16·0	11	277	63	7·9	11 30	11 05	19 59	3 32	3 57
23	8 10	+22·1	58·2	15·9	24	283	73	8·9	12 40	12 18	20 54	4 19	4 42
24	9 07	+19·6	57·8	15·7	36	289	82	9·9	13 55	13 38	21 47	4 55	5 14
25	10 02	+16·2	57·3	15·6	48	295	90	10·9	15 11	14 59	22 37	5 23	5 37
26	10 53	+11·9	56·8	15·5	60	302	95	11·9	16 26	16 18	23 24	5 46	5 56
27	11 42	+ 7·2	56·4	15·4	72	313	98	12·9	17 39	17 36	..	6 06	6 10
28	12 30	+ 2·2	55·9	15·2	84	188	100	13·9	18 51	18 52	0 08	6 23	6 24
29	13 16	− 2·8	55·4	15·1	96	87	99	14·9	20 01	20 07	0 52	6 40	6 37
30	14 02	− 7·6	55·0	15·0	109	99	96	15·9	21 10	21 20	1 35	6 57	6 50
31	14 48	−12·0	54·6	14·9	121	101	92	16·9	22 19	22 33	2 18	7 16	7 05

MERCURY ☿

Day	R.A.	Dec. −	Diam.	Phase	Transit	
	h m	°	″		h m	
1	22 12	13·5	5	95	11 38	Mercury is too close to the Sun for observation
4	22 32	11·5	5	97	11 46	
7	22 52	9·4	5	98	11 55	
10	23 13	7·1	5	100	12 03	
13	23 34	4·6	5	100	12 13	
16	23 55	1·9	5	100	12 22	

Day	R.A.	Dec.	Diam.	Phase	Transit	5° high W. 52°	5° high W. 56°
	h m	°	″		h m	h m	h m
16	23 55	− 1·9	5	100	12 22	17 44	17 39
19	0 16	+ 0·8	5	97	12 31	18 08	18 06
22	0 37	+ 3·7	5	94	12 41	18 32	18 32
25	0 58	+ 6·5	5	88	12 50	18 55	18 58
28	1 18	+ 9·2	6	80	12 58	19 17	19 22
31	1 37	+11·7	6	70	13 05	19 36	19 44

VENUS ♀

Day	R.A.	Dec. +	Diam.	Phase	Transit	5° high W. 52°	5° high W. 56°
	h m	°	″		h m	h m	h m
1	1 22	9·3	17	69	14 47	21 05	21 09
6	1 44	11·7	17	67	14 49	21 19	21 26
11	2 05	14·0	18	65	14 50	21 33	21 42
16	2 26	16·2	19	63	14 52	21 46	21 57
21	2 48	18·3	19	61	14 54	22 00	22 12
26	3 09	20·2	20	59	14 56	22 12	22 27
31	3 31	21·8	21	56	14 57	22 24	22 41

MARS ♂

Day	R.A.	Dec. −	Diam.	Phase	Transit	
	h m	°	″		h m	
1	22 39	9·7	4	—	12 03	Mars is too close to the Sun for observation
6	22 54	8·2	4	—	15 58	
11	23 08	6·6	4	—	11 53	
16	23 23	5·1	4	—	11 48	
21	23 37	3·5	4	—	11 43	
26	23 52	1·9	4	—	11 37	
31	0 06	0·3	4	—	11 32	

Day	London		Bristol		Birmingham		Manchester		Newcastle		Glasgow		Belfast	
	SUNRISE AND SUNSET (G.M.T.)													
	a.m.	p.m.	a.m.	p.m.	a.m.	p.m.	a.m.	p.m.	a.m.	p.m.	a.m.	p.m.	a.m.	p.m.
	h m	h m	h m	h m	h m	h m	h m	h m	h m	h m	h m	h m	h m	h m
1	6 46	5 40	6 56	5 50	6 55	5 46	6 58	5 47	6 57	5 42	7 10	5 51	7 15	6 00
2	6 44	5 42	6 54	5 52	6 52	5 47	6 55	5 48	6 54	5 43	7 07	5 53	7 12	6 01
3	6 42	5 44	6 51	5 54	6 50	5 49	6 53	5 50	6 52	5 45	7 05	5 55	7 10	6 03
4	6 40	5 46	6 49	5 56	6 47	5 51	6 50	5 52	6 49	5 47	7 02	5 57	7 07	6 05
5	6 38	5 47	6 47	5 57	6 45	5 53	6 48	5 54	6 47	5 49	6 59	5 59	7 05	6 07
6	6 36	5 49	6 45	5 59	6 43	5 55	6 46	5 56	6 45	5 51	6 57	6 01	7 03	6 09
7	6 33	5 50	6 43	6 00	6 40	5 57	6 43	5 58	6 42	5 53	6 54	6 03	7 00	6 11
8	6 31	5 52	6 41	6 02	6 38	5 59	6 41	6 00	6 40	5 55	6 52	6 05	6 58	6 13
9	6 29	5 54	6 39	6 04	6 36	6 00	6 39	6 01	6 37	5 57	6 49	6 07	6 55	6 15
10	6 27	5 55	6 36	6 05	6 34	6 02	6 37	6 03	6 35	5 59	6 47	6 09	6 53	6 17
11	6 24	5 57	6 34	6 07	6 31	6 04	6 34	6 05	6 32	6 02	6 44	6 12	6 50	6 20
12	6 22	5 59	6 32	6 09	6 29	6 06	6 32	6 07	6 29	6 04	6 41	6 14	6 47	6 22
13	6 20	6 00	6 30	6 10	6 27	6 07	6 30	6 09	6 27	6 06	6 39	6 16	6 45	6 24
14	6 17	6 02	6 27	6 12	6 24	6 09	6 27	6 11	6 24	6 08	6 36	6 18	6 42	6 26
15	6 15	6 04	6 25	6 14	6 22	6 11	6 25	6 12	6 22	6 09	6 33	6 20	6 40	6 27
16	6 13	6 06	6 23	6 16	6 20	6 13	6 22	6 14	6 19	6 11	6 31	6 22	6 37	6 29
17	6 11	6 07	6 21	6 17	6 18	6 14	6 20	6 16	6 17	6 13	6 28	6 24	6 35	6 31
18	6 08	6 09	6 18	6 19	6 15	6 16	6 17	6 18	6 14	6 15	6 26	6 26	6 32	6 33
19	6 06	6 11	6 16	6 21	6 13	6 18	6 15	6 20	6 12	6 17	6 23	6 28	6 30	6 35
20	6 04	6 13	6 14	6 23	6 11	6 20	6 12	6 22	6 09	6 19	6 20	6 30	6 27	6 37
21	6 01	6 14	6 11	6 24	6 08	6 21	6 10	6 24	6 07	6 21	6 18	6 32	6 25	6 39
22	5 59	6 16	6 09	6 26	6 06	6 23	6 07	6 26	6 04	6 23	6 15	6 34	6 22	6 41
23	5 57	6 18	6 07	6 28	6 04	6 25	6 05	6 27	6 02	6 24	6 12	6 36	6 20	6 42
24	5 54	6 20	6 04	6 30	6 01	6 27	6 03	6 29	6 00	6 26	6 10	6 38	6 18	6 44
25	5 52	6 21	6 02	6 31	5 59	6 28	6 00	6 31	5 57	6 28	6 07	6 40	6 15	6 46
26	5 50	6 23	6 00	6 33	5 57	6 30	5 58	6 33	5 55	6 30	6 05	6 42	6 13	6 48
27	5 47	6 25	5 57	6 34	5 54	6 32	5 55	6 35	5 52	6 32	6 02	6 44	6 10	6 50
28	5 45	6 26	5 55	6 36	5 52	6 33	5 53	6 36	5 49	6 34	5 59	6 46	6 07	6 52
29	5 43	6 28	5 53	6 38	5 50	6 35	5 51	6 38	5 46	6 36	5 56	6 48	6 04	6 54
30	5 41	6 30	5 51	6 39	5 48	6 37	5 49	6 40	5 44	6 38	5 54	6 51	6 02	6 57
31	5 39	6 31	5 49	6 41	5 45	6 38	5 46	6 41	5 41	6 40	5 51	6 53	5 59	6 58

Day	JUPITER ♃ R.A.	Dec. +	Transit	5° high West 52°	56°	SATURN ♄ R.A.	Dec. −	Transit	
	h m	°	h m	h m	h m	h m	°	h m	
1	1 17	6·9	14 39	20 42	20 44	22 00	13·5	11 23	Saturn is too close to the sun for observation
11	1 25	7·8	14 08	20 15	20 18	22 04	13·2	10 48	
21	1 33	8·6	13 37	19 49	19 52	22 09	12·8	10 13	
31	1 42	9·5	13 07	19 22	19 27	22 13	12·4	9 38	

Equatorial diameter of Jupiter 34″; of Saturn 16″. Diameter of Saturn's rings 35″ and 6″.

Day	URANUS ♅ R.A.	Dec. +	Transit	10° high in West 52°	56°	NEPTUNE ♆ R.A.	Dec. −	10° high in East 52°	56°	Transit
	h m	° ′	h m	h m	h m	h m	° ′	h m	h m	h m
1	10 39·6	9 21	0 04	5 46	5 47	15 03·4	15 25	1 09	1 36	4 27
11	10 37·9	9 31	23 19	5 06	5 07	15 03·1	15 23	0 29	0 56	3 48
21	10 36·4	9 40	22 38	4 26	4 27	15 02·5	15 21	23 45	0 16	3 08
31	10 35·0	9 48	21 58	3 46	3 47	15 01·8	15 17	23 04	23 31	2 28

Uranus: Diameter 4″ — Neptune: Diameter 2″

Aperire, to open. Earth opens to receive seed.

Sun's Longitude 30° ♉ 20^{d} 01^{h}

Day of Month	Day of Week	
1	W.	Donizetti d. 1848. R.A.F. formed 1918
2	Th.	Sir Alex Guinness b. 1914
3	F.	Murillo d. 1682. Jean de Reszke d. 1925
4	S.	Goldsmith d. 1774. Sir Cuthbert Whitaker d. 1950
5	S.	1st S. after Easter. John Wisden d. 1884
6	M.	Albrecht Dürer d. 1528. John Stow d. 1605
7	Tu.	EASTER LAW SITTINGS BEGIN. C. H. Dodd b. 1884
8	W.	Sir Adrian Boult b. 1889. Henry Ford d. 1947
9	Th.	Bacon d. 1626. Benno Moiseiwitsch d. 1963
10	F.	U.S. nuclear submarine *Thresher* lost 1963
11	S.	American Civil War began 1861
12	S.	2nd Sunday after Easter. F. D. Roosevelt d. 1945
13	M.	Vienna captured 1945. Eric Kennington d. 1960
14	Tu.	Handel d. 1759. Ernest Bevin d. 1951
15	W.	Matthew Arnold d. 1888. Loss of *Titanic* 1912
16	Th.	Culloden 1746. Peter Ustinov b. 1921
17	F.	Benjamin Franklin d. 1790. N. S. Khrushchev b. [1894
18	S.	H. A. L. Fisher d. 1940. Einstein d. 1955
19	S.	3rd Sunday after Easter. Pierre Curie d. 1956
20	M.	Manet d. 1883. Sir Donald Wolfit b. 1902
21	Tu.	QUEEN ELIZABETH II BORN 1926
22	W.	Phil May b. 1864**. George du Maurier d. 1896
23	Th.	ST. GEORGE'S DAY. Shakespeare b. 1564**; d. 1616
24	F.	Princess Alexandra's Wedding Day 1963
25	S.	St. Mark. ANZAC DAY. Princess Royal b. 1897
26	S.	4th Sunday after Easter. Daniel Defoe d. 1730
27	M.	W. C. Macready d. 1873. Emerson d. 1882
28	Tu.	Dr. Salazar b. 1889. Val Gielgud b. 1900
29	W.	Sir Malcolm Sargent b. 1895
30	Th.	Fontenoy 1745. Queen Juliana b. 1909

PHENOMENA

April 7^{d} 18^{h} Mercury at greatest eastern elongation (19°).

8^{d} 20^{h} Saturn in conjunction with the Moon. Saturn 3° N.

10^{d} 09^{h} Venus at greatest eastern elongation (46°)

13^{d} 14^{h} Mercury in conjunction with the Moon. Mercury 8° N.

15^{d} 18^{h} Venus in conjunction with the Moon. Venus 6° N.

22^{d} 14^{h} Jupiter in conjunction with the Sun.

27^{d} 10^{h} Mercury in inferior conjunction.

CONSTELLATIONS

The following constellations are near the meridian at

	d	h		d	h
Mar.	1	24	Mar.	16	23
April	1	22	April	15	21
May	1	20	May	16	19

Cepheus (below the Pole), Cassiopeia (below the Pole), Ursa Major, Leo Minor, Leo, Sextans, Hydra and Crater.

MINIMA OF ALGOL

d	h	d	h
2	01	19	06
4	22	22	02
7	18	24	23
10	15	27	20
13	12	30	17
16	09		

PHASES OF THE MOON

	d	h	m
☾ Last Quarter	5	05	45
● New Moon	12	12	37
☽ First Quarter	19	04	09
○ Full Moon	26	17	50

	d	h
Apogee (251,520 miles)	2	12
Perigee (224 940 „)	14	10
Apogee (252,060 „)	30	02

Mean Longitude of Ascending Node on April 1, 97°.

See note on *Summer Time*, p. 98.

MONTHLY NOTES

April 1. Refreshment House Licences to be renewed.

5. Income Tax Year (1963-64) ends.

8. Lady Day Fire Insurances must be paid.

** Centenary.

Day	The Sun s.d. 16′·0 Right Ascension	Dec. +	Equation of Time	Rise 52°	Rise 56°	Transit	Set 52°	Set 56°	Sidereal Time	Transit of First Point of Aries
	h m s	° ′	m s	h m	h m	h m	h m	h m	h m s	h m s
1	0 41 31	4 28	− 4 00	5 36	5 32	12 04	18 33	18 38	12 37 31	11 20 37
2	0 45 10	4 51	− 3 42	5 34	5 29	12 04	18 35	18 40	12 41 28	11 16 41
3	0 48 49	5 14	− 3 24	5 31	5 26	12 03	18 37	18 42	12 45 24	11 12 45
4	0 52 28	5 37	− 3 07	5 29	5 24	12 03	18 38	18 44	12 49 21	11 08 49
5	0 56 07	6 00	− 2 49	5 27	5 21	12 03	18 40	18 46	12 53 17	11 04 53
6	0 59 46	6 23	− 2 32	5 24	5 19	12 02	18 42	18 48	12 57 14	11 00 57
7	1 03 25	6 45	− 2 15	5 22	5 16	12 02	18 43	18 50	13 01 10	10 57 02
8	1 07 05	7 08	− 1 58	5 20	5 13	12 02	18 45	18 52	13 05 07	10 53 06
9	1 10 45	7 30	− 1 42	5 18	5 11	12 02	18 47	18 54	13 09 04	10 49 10
10	1 14 25	7 53	− 1 25	5 15	5 08	12 01	18 49	18 56	13 13 00	10 45 14
11	1 18 06	8 15	− 1 09	5 13	5 06	12 01	18 50	18 58	13 16 57	10 41 18
12	1 21 46	8 37	− 0 53	5 11	5 03	12 01	18 52	19 00	13 20 53	10 37 22
13	1 25 28	8 59	− 0 38	5 09	5 00	12 01	18 54	19 02	13 24 50	10 33 26
14	1 29 09	9 20	− 0 23	5 06	4 58	12 00	18 55	19 04	13 28 46	10 29 30
15	1 32 51	9 42	− 0 08	5 04	4 55	12 00	18 57	19 06	13 32 43	10 25 34
16	1 36 33	10 03	+ 0 07	5 02	4 53	12 00	18 59	19 08	13 36 39	10 21 38
17	1 40 15	10 25	+ 0 21	5 00	4 50	12 00	19 00	19 10	13 40 36	10 17 43
18	1 43 58	10 46	+ 0 35	4 58	4 48	11 59	19 02	19 12	13 44 33	10 13 47
19	1 47 41	11 06	+ 0 48	4 56	4 45	11 59	19 04	19 14	13 48 29	10 09 51
20	1 51 25	11 27	+ 1 01	4 53	4 43	11 59	19 06	19 16	13 52 26	10 05 55
21	1 55 09	11 48	+ 1 14	4 51	4 40	11 59	19 07	19 18	13 56 22	10 01 59
22	1 58 53	12 08	+ 1 26	4 49	4 38	11 58	19 09	19 20	14 00 19	9 58 03
23	2 02 38	12 28	+ 1 37	4 47	4 36	11 58	19 11	19 22	14 04 15	9 54 07
24	2 06 23	12 48	+ 1 49	4 45	4 33	11 58	19 12	19 24	14 08 12	9 50 11
25	2 10 09	13 08	+ 2 00	4 43	4 31	11 58	19 14	19 26	14 12 08	9 46 15
26	2 13 55	13 27	+ 2 10	4 41	4 28	11 58	19 16	19 28	14 16 05	9 42 19
27	2 17 42	13 46	+ 2 20	4 39	4 26	11 58	19 17	19 30	14 20 02	9 38 23
28	2 21 29	14 05	+ 2 29	4 37	4 24	11 57	19 19	19 32	14 23 58	9 34 28
29	2 25 16	14 24	+ 2 38	4 35	4 21	11 57	19 21	19 34	14 27 55	9 30 32
30	2 29 05	14 43	+ 2 46	4 33	4 19	11 57	19 22	19 36	14 31 51	9 26 36

Duration of Civil (C), Nautical (N), and Astronomical (A), Twilight (in minutes)

Lat.	Apr. 1 C	Apr. 1 N	Apr. 1 A	Apr. 11 C	Apr. 11 N	Apr. 11 A	Apr. 21 C	Apr. 21 N	Apr. 21 A	Apr. 30 C	Apr. 30 N	Apr. 30 A
°												
52	34	76	121	35	79	128	37	84	138	39	89	152
56	38	85	137	40	90	148	42	96	167	44	105	200

ASTRONOMICAL NOTES

MERCURY is an evening star for the first half of the month, its magnitude decreasing from −0·6 to +1·5. It may be seen low in the W.N.W. sky about the time of end of civil twilight. For observers in the northern hemisphere this is the best evening apparition of the year.

VENUS is a brilliant evening star, magnitude −4·0. It is at greatest eastern elongation on the 10th and dominates the western sky throughout the evenings. On the 2nd Venus is passing just S. of the Pleiades. By the end of the month Venus is still visible, low in the W.N.W., as late as 23^h.

MARS is unsuitably placed for observation.

JUPITER may only be glimpsed as an evening star, magnitude −1·6, low in the west after sunset for the first few days of the month. During these few days Jupiter may be distinguished from Mercury by the fact that it is nearer to the Sun and at least a magnitude brighter than Mercury. Thereafter it is unsuitably placed for observation, conjunction occurring on the 22nd.

SATURN is unsuitably placed for observation.

THE MOON

Day	R.A.	Dec.	Hor. Par.	Semi-diam.	Sun's Co-long.	P.A. of Bright Limb	Phase	Age	Rise 52°	Rise 56°	Transit	Set 52°	Set 56°
	h m	°	′	′	°	°		d	h m	h m	h m	h m	h m
1	15 35	−15·9	54·3	14·8	133	100	86	17·9	23 26	23 45	3 03	7 38	7 22
2	16 23	−19·1	54·2	14·8	145	98	79	18·9	..	..	3 48	8 04	7 44
3	17 12	−21·5	54·2	14·8	157	94	71	19·9	0 30	0 53	4 36	8 37	8 13
4	18 03	−23·0	54·4	14·8	169	90	62	20·9	1 29	1 55	5 24	9 17	8 52
5	18 55	−23·5	54·7	14·9	182	85	52	21·9	2 22	2 48	6 14	10 07	9 41
6	19 48	−22·8	55·2	15·0	194	79	43	22·9	3 07	3 31	7 05	11 07	10 42
7	20 41	−21·1	55·8	15·2	206	74	33	23·9	3 43	4 05	7 56	12 14	11 54
8	21 33	−18·2	56·6	15·4	218	69	24	24·9	4 14	4 30	8 46	13 27	13 11
9	22 26	−14·4	57·5	15·7	230	65	16	25·9	4 39	4 51	9 36	14 44	14 33
10	23 18	− 9·7	58·3	15·9	243	60	9	26·9	5 01	5 08	10 26	16 04	15 58
11	0 10	− 4·4	59·2	16·1	255	53	3	27·9	5 21	5 23	11 16	17 26	17 25
12	1 03	+ 1·3	59·8	16·3	267	33	1	28·9	5 41	5 39	12 07	18 50	18 55
13	1 57	+ 7·1	60·3	16·4	279	285	0	0·5	6 02	5 55	13 00	20 16	20 26
14	2 53	+12·5	60·6	16·5	292	263	3	1·5	6 26	6 14	13 55	21 42	21 59
15	3 51	+17·2	60·5	16·5	304	262	9	2·5	6 55	6 38	14 53	23 07	23 28
16	4 52	+20·7	60·3	16·4	316	265	17	3·5	7 33	7 10	15 53	..	..
17	5 54	+22·9	59·8	16·3	328	270	26	4·5	8 21	7 55	16 54	0 24	0 49
18	6 56	+23·6	59·2	16·1	340	275	37	5·5	9 20	8 54	17 54	1 29	1 56
19	7 57	+22·7	58·6	16·0	353	281	48	6·5	10 29	10 06	18 51	2 21	2 45
20	8 55	+20·5	58·0	15·8	5	287	59	7·5	11 44	11 25	19 45	3 00	3 20
21	9 50	+17·2	57·3	15·6	17	291	69	8·5	13 00	12 45	20 35	3 30	3 45
22	10 41	+13·2	56·7	15·5	29	295	79	9·5	14 14	14 05	21 21	3 53	4 04
23	11 30	+ 8·5	56·2	15·3	41	299	86	10·5	15 27	15 22	22 06	4 13	4 19
24	12 17	+ 3·6	55·7	15·2	54	302	93	11·5	16 38	16 38	22 49	4 30	4 32
25	13 03	− 1·4	55·2	15·1	66	306	97	12·5	17 48	17 52	23 32	4 47	4 45
26	13 49	− 6·2	54·9	14·9	78	320	99	13·5	18 57	19 06	..	5 03	4 57
27	14 34	−10·8	54·5	14·9	90	53	100	14·5	20 06	20 20	0 15	5 21	5 11
28	15 21	−14·9	54·3	14·8	102	91	98	15·5	21 14	21 32	0 58	5 41	5 27
29	16 08	−18·4	54·1	14·7	115	95	95	16·5	22 20	22 42	1 44	6 05	5 47
30	16 57	−21·1	54·1	14·7	127	94	91	17·5	23 22	23 47	2 30	6 35	6 12

MERCURY ☿

Day	R.A.	Dec. +	Diam.	Phase	Transit	5° high W. 52°	5° high W. 56°	Day	R.A.	Dec. +	Diam.	Phase	Transit	
	h m	°	″		h m	h m	h m		h m	°	″		h m	
1	1 43	12·4	6	66	13 07	19 42	19 49	16	2 32	18·1	10	15	12 54	Mercury is too close to the Sun for observation
4	1 59	14·5	7	54	13 10	19 55	20 04	19	2 32	17·8	10	8	12 41	
7	2 12	16·1	7	43	13 11	20 04	20 15	22	2 29	17·1	11	3	12 25	
10	2 23	17·3	8	32	13 09	20 08	20 19	25	2 23	16·0	12	1	12 08	
13	2 29	17·9	9	23	13 03	20 04	20 16	28	2 17	14·6	12	0	11 50	
16	2 32	18·1	10	15	12 54	19 55	20 07	31	2 10	13·1	12	1	11 32	

VENUS ♀ MARS ♂

Day	R.A.	Dec. +	Diam.	Phase	Transit	5° high W. 52°	5° high W. 56°	Day	R.A.	Dec.	Diam.	Phase	Transit	
	h m	°	″		h m	h m	h m		h m	°	″		h m	
1	3 35	22·2	21	56	14 58	22 26	22 43	1	0 09	0·0	4	—	11 31	Mars is too close to the Sun for observation
6	3 56	23·6	23	53	14 59	22 37	22 56	6	0 23	+1·5	4	—	11 25	
11	4 18	24·8	24	51	15 01	22 46	23 06	11	0 37	+3·1	4	—	11 20	
16	4 38	25·8	25	48	15 02	22 53	23 15	16	0 51	+4·6	4	—	11 14	
21	4 58	26·6	27	45	15 02	22 58	23 21	21	1 05	+6·2	4	—	11 08	
26	5 17	27·1	29	42	15 01	23 00	23 24	26	1 19	+7·6	4	—	11 03	
31	5 35	27·4	31	38	14 59	23 00	23 25	31	1 34	+9·1	4	—	10 57	

SUNRISE AND SUNSET (G.M.T.)

Day	London a.m.	London p.m.	Bristol a.m.	Bristol p.m.	Birmingham a.m.	Birmingham p.m.	Manchester a.m.	Manchester p.m.	Newcastle a.m.	Newcastle p.m.	Glasgow a.m.	Glasgow p.m.	Belfast a.m.	Belfast p.m.
	h m	h m	h m	h m	h m	h m	h m	h m	h m	h m	h m	h m	h m	h m
1	5 37	6 33	5 47	6 42	5 43	6 40	5 44	6 43	5 39	6 42	5 49	6 55	5 57	7 00
2	5 35	6 35	5 45	6 44	5 40	6 42	5 41	6 45	5 36	6 44	5 46	6 57	5 54	7 02
3	5 32	6 36	5 42	6 46	5 38	6 44	5 39	6 47	5 34	6 46	5 43	6 59	5 52	7 04
4	5 30	6 38	5 40	6 47	5 35	6 46	5 36	6 49	5 31	6 48	5 41	7 01	5 49	7 06
5	5 28	6 39	5 38	6 49	5 33	6 48	5 34	6 51	5 29	6 50	5 38	7 03	5 47	7 08
6	5 25	6 41	5 35	6 51	5 31	6 50	5 32	6 53	5 27	6 52	5 36	7 05	5 45	7 10
7	5 23	6 43	5 33	6 52	5 28	6 51	5 29	6 54	5 24	6 54	5 33	7 07	5 42	7 11
8	5 21	6 44	5 31	6 54	5 26	6 53	5 27	6 56	5 21	6 56	5 30	7 09	5 40	7 13
9	5 19	6 46	5 29	6 56	5 24	6 55	5 24	6 58	5 19	6 58	5 28	7 11	5 37	7 15
10	5 16	6 48	5 26	6 58	5 21	6 57	5 22	7 00	5 16	7 00	5 25	7 13	5 35	7 17
11	5 14	6 49	5 24	6 59	5 19	6 58	5 20	7 02	5 14	7 02	5 23	7 15	5 33	7 19
12	5 12	6 51	5 22	7 01	5 17	7 00	5 17	7 04	5 11	7 04	5 20	7 17	5 30	7 21
13	5 10	6 53	5 20	7 03	5 15	7 02	5 15	7 05	5 09	7 05	5 17	7 19	5 27	7 23
14	5 07	6 54	5 17	7 04	5 12	7 03	5 12	7 07	5 06	7 07	5 15	7 21	5 24	7 25
15	5 05	6 56	5 15	7 06	5 10	7 05	5 10	7 09	5 04	7 09	5 12	7 23	5 22	7 27
16	5 03	6 58	5 13	7 08	5 08	7 07	5 08	7 11	5 02	7 11	5 10	7 25	5 20	7 29
17	5 01	6 59	5 11	7 09	5 06	7 08	5 05	7 13	4 59	7 13	5 07	7 27	5 17	7 31
18	4 59	7 01	5 09	7 11	5 04	7 10	5 03	7 15	4 57	7 15	5 05	7 29	5 15	7 33
19	4 57	7 03	5 07	7 13	5 02	7 12	5 01	7 17	4 54	7 17	5 02	7 31	5 13	7 35
20	4 54	7 05	5 04	7 15	4 59	7 14	4 58	7 18	4 51	7 19	5 00	7 33	5 10	7 36
21	4 52	7 06	5 02	7 16	4 57	7 15	4 56	7 20	4 49	7 21	4 57	7 35	5 08	7 38
22	4 50	7 08	5 00	7 18	4 55	7 17	4 54	7 22	4 47	7 23	4 55	7 37	5 06	7 40
23	4 48	7 10	4 58	7 20	4 53	7 19	4 52	7 24	4 45	7 25	4 53	7 39	5 04	7 42
24	4 46	7 11	4 56	7 21	4 51	7 20	4 50	7 25	4 42	7 27	4 50	7 41	5 01	7 44
25	4 44	7 13	4 54	7 23	4 49	7 22	4 48	7 27	4 40	7 29	4 48	7 43	4 59	7 46
26	4 42	7 15	4 52	7 24	4 47	7 24	4 46	7 29	4 38	7 31	4 46	7 45	4 57	7 48
27	4 40	7 16	4 50	7 26	4 45	7 26	4 44	7 31	4 36	7 33	4 44	7 47	4 55	7 50
28	4 38	7 18	4 48	7 27	4 43	7 28	4 42	7 32	4 34	7 34	4 42	7 48	4 53	7 51
29	4 37	7 20	4 47	7 29	4 40	7 29	4 39	7 34	4 31	7 36	4 39	7 50	4 50	7 53
30	4 35	7 21	4 45	7 30	4 35	7 31	4 37	7 36	4 29	7 38	4 37	7 52	4 48	7 55

JUPITER ♃ / SATURN ♄

Day	Jupiter R.A.	Jupiter Dec. +	Jupiter Transit		Saturn R.A.	Saturn Dec. —	Saturn Transit	
	h m	°	h m		h m	°	h m	
1	1 43	9·6	13 04	Jupiter is too close to the Sun for observation	22 13	12·4	9 34	Saturn is too close to the Sun for observation
11	1 52	10·4	12 33		22 17	12·1	8 59	
21	2 01	11·3	12 03		22 20	11·8	8 23	
31	2 10	12·1	11 33		22 23	11·5	7 46	

Equatorial diameter of Jupiter 33″; of Saturn 16″. Diameters of Saturn's rings 36″ and 6″.

URANUS ♅ / NEPTUNE ♆

Day	Uranus R.A.	Uranus Dec. +	Uranus Transit	Uranus 10° high in West 52°	Uranus 10° high in West 56°	Neptune R.A.	Neptune Dec. —	Neptune 10° high in East 52°	Neptune 10° high in East 56°	Neptune Transit
	h m	° ′	h m	h m	h m	h m	° ′	h m	h m	h m
1	10 34·9	9 49	21 54	3 42	3 43	15 01·7	15 17	23 00	23 27	2 24
11	10 33·7	9 55	21 13	3 02	3 03	15 00·9	15 13	22 19	22 46	1 44
21	10 32·8	10 00	20 33	2 22	2 24	14 59·9	15 08	21 39	22 05	1 03
31	10 32·2	10 03	19 53	1 43	1 44	14 58·8	15 04	20 58	21 24	0 23

Uranus: Diameter 4″ — Neptune: Diameter 2″

MAY XXXI DAYS

Maia, goddess of growth and increase.

Sun's Longitude 60° ♊ 21d 01h

Day of Month	Day of Week	
1	F.	SS. Philip and James. Sir Sydney Cockerell d.
2	S.	German Surrender in Italy 1945 [1962
3	S.	5th Sunday after Easter. Rogation Sunday
4	M.	Joseph Whitaker b. 1820. Edward Shanks d. 1953
5	Tu.	Napoleon d. 1821. Sir Gordon Richards b. 1904
6	W.	Edward VII d. 1910. Sir Bernard Fergusson b.
7	Th.	Ascension Day. *Lusitania* sunk 1915 [1911
8	F.	J. S. Mill d. 1873. Harry S. Truman b. 1894
9	S.	OFFICIAL END OF WAR IN EUROPE (1945)
10	S.	1st Sunday after Ascension. Léon Gaumont b. 1864**
11	M.	Earl of Chatham d. 1778. G. L. Jessop d. 1955
12	Tu.	Sir Arthur Quiller-Couch d. 1944
13	W.	Fridtjof Nansen d. 1930. Gary Cooper d. 1961
14	Th.	Visct. Allenby d. 1936. Sir J. Martin-Harvey d. 1944
15	F.	EASTER LAW SITTINGS END. E. R. Dexter b. 1935
16	S.	Albuera 1811. Sir Edmund Gosse d. 1928
17	S.	Whit Sunday. Pentecost.
18	M.	Meredith d. 1909. Dame Margot Fonteyn b. 1919
19	Tu.	Nathaniel Hawthorne d. 1864** T. E. Lawrence d.
20	W.	John Clare d. 1864** [1935
21	Th.	Lord Rosebery d. 1929
22	F.	Victor Hugo d. 1885. Earl of Ypres d. 1925
23	S.	Visct. De L'Isle b. 1909. J. D. Rockefeller d. 1937
24	S.	Trinity Sunday. COMMONWEALTH DAY
25	M.	Lord Beaverbrook b. 1879. Richard Dimbleby b.
26	Tu.	TRINITY LAW SITTINGS BEGIN [1913
27	W.	Sir John Cockcroft b. 1897. *Bismarck* sunk 1941
28	Th.	Corpus Christi. Ibsen d. 1906
29	F.	Restoration Day 1660. Pres. Kennedy b. 1917
30	S.	Duke of Norfolk b. 1908. Wilbur Wright d. 1912
31	S.	1st Sunday after Trinity. Peter Fleming b. 1907

PHENOMENA

May 6^d 08^h Saturn in conjunction with the Moon. Saturn 3° N.

7^d 00^h Neptune at opposition.

10^d 12^h Mars in conjunction with the Moon. Mars 4° N.

10^d 12^h Mercury in conjunction with the Moon. Mercury 2° N.

10^d 13^h Mercury in conjunction with Mars. Mercury 1°·9 S.

10^d 20^h Jupiter in conjunction with the Moon. Jupiter 4° N.

13^d 19^h Venus at greatest brilliancy.

14^d 16^h Venus in conjunction with the Moon. Venus 4° N.

19^d 19^h Mars in conjunction with Jupiter. Mars 0°·6 N.

24^d 20^h Mercury at greatest western elongation (25°).

25^d 14^h Mercury in conjunction with Jupiter. Mercury 3° S.

CONSTELLATIONS

The following constellations are near the meridian at

	d	h		d	h
April	1	24	April	15	23
May	1	22	May	16	21
June	1	20	June	15	19

Cepheus (below the Pole), Cassiopeia (below the Pole), Ursa Minor, Ursa Major, Canes Venatici, Coma Berenices, Bootes, Leo, Virgo, Crater, Corvus and Hydra.

ALGOL is inconveniently situated for observation during May.

PHASES OF THE MOON

	d	h	m
☾ Last Quarter	4	22	20
● New Moon	11	21	02
☽ First Quarter	18	12	42
○ Full Moon	26	09	29

	d	h
Perigee (222,670 miles)	12	16
Apogee (252,410 „)	27	09

Mean Longitude of Ascending Node on May 1, 95°

See note on *Summer Time*, page 98.

MONTHLY NOTES

May 4. Bank Holiday, Scotland.
9. Half-Quarter Day.
13. Moslem New Year (A.H. 1384).
15. Whitsunday (Scotland). Scottish Term Day.
17. Norway's National Day.
—. Jewish Pentecost (Feast of Weeks) begins.
18. Bank and General Holiday, England, Wales and N. Ireland.
28. Removal Day, Scotland.

** Centenary.

Day	The Sun s.d. 15′·8 Right Ascension	Dec. +	Equation of Time	Rise 52°	Rise 56°	Transit	Set 52°	Set 56°	Sidereal Time	Transit of First Point of Aries
	h m s	° ′	m s	h m	h m	h m	h m	h m	h m s	h m s
1	2 32 53	15 01	+ 2 54	4 31	4 17	11 57	19 24	19 38	14 35 48	9 22 40
2	2 36 43	15 19	+ 3 01	4 29	4 14	11 57	19 26	19 40	14 39 44	9 18 44
3	2 40 33	15 37	+ 3 08	4 27	4 12	11 57	19 27	19 42	14 43 41	9 14 48
4	2 44 23	15 55	+ 3 14	4 25	4 10	11 57	19 29	19 44	14 47 37	9 10 52
5	2 48 14	16 12	+ 3 20	4 24	4 08	11 57	19 31	19 46	14 51 34	9 06 56
6	2 52 06	16 29	+ 3 25	4 22	4 06	11 57	19 32	19 48	14 55 31	9 03 00
7	2 55 58	16 46	+ 3 29	4 20	4 04	11 56	19 34	19 50	14 59 27	8 59 04
8	2 59 50	17 02	+ 3 33	4 18	4 01	11 56	19 36	19 52	15 03 24	8 55 08
9	3 03 44	17 18	+ 3 36	4 16	3 59	11 56	19 37	19 54	15 07 20	8 51 13
10	3 07 38	17 34	+ 3 39	4 15	3 57	11 56	19 39	19 56	15 11 17	8 47 17
11	3 11 32	17 50	+ 3 41	4 13	3 55	11 56	19 40	19 58	15 15 13	8 43 21
12	3 15 27	18 05	+ 3 43	4 11	3 53	11 56	19 42	20 00	15 19 10	8 39 25
13	3 19 23	18 20	+ 3 43	4 10	3 51	11 56	19 44	20 02	15 23 06	8 35 29
14	3 23 19	18 35	+ 3 44	4 08	3 50	11 56	19 45	20 04	15 27 03	8 31 33
15	3 27 16	18 49	+ 3 44	4 06	3 48	11 56	19 47	20 06	15 31 00	8 27 37
16	3 31 13	19 03	+ 3 43	4 05	3 46	11 56	19 48	20 08	15 34 56	8 23 41
17	3 35 11	19 17	+ 3 42	4 03	3 44	11 56	19 50	20 09	15 38 53	8 19 45
18	3 39 09	19 31	+ 3 40	4 02	3 42	11 56	19 51	20 11	15 42 49	8 15 49
19	3 43 08	19 44	+ 3 37	4 01	3 40	11 56	19 53	20 13	15 46 46	8 11 53
20	3 47 08	19 56	+ 3 34	3 59	3 39	11 56	19 54	20 15	15 50 42	8 07 57
21	3 51 08	20 09	+ 3 31	3 58	3 37	11 57	19 56	20 17	15 54 39	8 04 02
22	3 55 08	20 21	+ 3 27	3 57	3 36	11 57	19 57	20 18	15 58 35	8 00 06
23	3 59 09	20 33	+ 3 22	3 55	3 34	11 57	19 58	20 20	16 02 32	7 56 10
24	4 03 11	20 44	+ 3 18	3 54	3 32	11 57	20 00	20 22	16 06 29	7 52 14
25	4 07 13	20 55	+ 3 12	3 53	3 31	11 57	20 01	20 23	16 10 25	7 48 18
26	4 11 16	21 06	+ 3 06	3 52	3 30	11 57	20 02	20 25	16 14 22	7 44 22
27	4 15 19	21 16	+ 3 00	3 51	3 28	11 57	20 04	20 27	16 18 18	7 40 26
28	4 19 22	21 26	+ 2 53	3 50	3 27	11 57	20 05	20 28	16 22 15	7 36 30
29	4 23 26	21 35	+ 2 45	3 49	3 26	11 57	20 06	20 30	16 26 11	7 32 34
30	4 27 30	21 45	+ 2 37	3 48	3 24	11 57	20 07	20 31	16 30 08	7 28 38
31	4 31 35	21 53	+ 2 29	3 47	3 23	11 58	20 09	20 32	16 34 04	7 24 42

Duration of Civil (C), Nautical (N), and Astronomical (A), Twilight (in minutes)

Lat.	May 1 C	May 1 N	May 1 A	May 11 C	May 11 N	May 11 A	May 21 C	May 21 N	May 21 A	May 31 C	May 31 N	May 31 A
°												
52	39	90	154	41	97	179	44	106	T.A.N.	46	116	T.A.N.
56	45	106	209	49	121	T.A.N.	53	143	T.A.N.	57	T.A.N.	T.A.N.

ASTRONOMICAL NOTES

MERCURY is unsuitably placed for observation despite the fact that it is at greatest western elongation on the 24th.

VENUS remains the dominating feature of the evening sky. It attains its greatest brilliancy on the 13th (magnitude −4·2). With good eyesight Venus may be visible in daylight if the observer knows exactly where to look for it. In a telescope Venus is a beautiful sight, exhibiting a crescent shape which gets noticeably thinner during the month (the area illuminated decreasing from about one-third to one-tenth); at the same time the crescent is increasing in length (the diameter increasing from 31″ to 49″). At the beginning of the month Venus may still be seen as late as 23^h but by the end of the month it will not be visible after 22^h.

MARS is unsuitably placed for observation.

JUPITER is unsuitably placed for observation.

SATURN gradually becomes a morning star, magnitude +1·2, during the month. It may be glimpsed with difficulty low above the E.S.E. horizon about the time of beginning of nautical twilight.

THE MOON

Day	R.A.	Dec.	Hor. Par.	Semi-diam.	Sun's Co-long.	P.A. of Bright Limb	Phase	Age	Rise 52°	Rise 56°	Transit	Set 52°	Set 56°
	h m	°	′	′	°	°		d	h m	h m	h m	h m	h m
1	17 48	−22·9	54·1	14·7	139	91	84	18·5	..	..	3 19	7 12	6 47
2	18 39	−23·7	54·3	14·8	151	86	77	19·5	0 17	0 44	4 08	7 58	7 31
3	19 31	−23·4	54·6	14·9	163	82	68	20·5	1 05	1 30	4 58	8 53	8 28
4	20 24	−22·0	55·1	15·0	175	77	59	21·5	1 44	2 07	5 48	9 57	9 34
5	21 15	−19·6	55·7	15·2	188	73	49	22·5	2 15	2 34	6 37	11 06	10 48
6	22 07	−16·1	56·5	15·4	200	69	39	23·5	2 41	2 56	7 26	12 20	12 07
7	22 58	−11·8	57·4	15·6	212	65	29	24·5	3 04	3 13	8 14	13 37	13 28
8	23 48	− 6·8	58·4	15·9	224	63	20	25·5	3 24	3 29	9 03	14 56	14 53
9	0 40	− 1·3	59·3	16·2	237	61	12	26·5	3 43	3 43	9 53	16 18	16 20
10	1 33	+ 4·5	60·1	16·4	249	59	5	27·5	4 03	3 58	10 44	17 43	17 51
11	2 28	+10·2	60·8	16·6	261	53	1	28·5	4 25	4 15	11 39	19 11	19 24
12	3 26	+15·3	61·1	16·7	273	318	0	0·1	4 52	4 37	12 37	20 39	20 59
13	4 27	+19·6	61·2	16·7	286	268	2	1·1	5 25	5 05	13 38	22 04	22 28
14	5 31	+22·4	60·9	16·6	298	269	7	2·1	6 09	5 45	14 41	23 18	23 44
15	6 35	+23·7	60·4	16·5	310	273	14	3·1	7 06	6 40	15 44	..	..
16	7 39	+23·3	59·7	16·3	322	278	23	4·1	8 15	7 50	16 44	0 17	0 42
17	8 40	+21·4	58·9	16·0	334	284	33	5·1	9 30	9 09	17 40	1 02	1 23
18	9 37	+18·3	58·0	15·8	347	288	44	6·1	10 47	10 31	18 32	1 35	1 52
19	10 30	+14·4	57·2	15·6	359	292	55	7·1	12 03	11 53	19 20	2 00	2 13
20	11 20	+ 9·8	56·5	15·4	11	295	65	8·1	13 17	13 11	20 05	2 21	2 29
21	12 07	+ 4·9	55·8	15·2	23	297	75	9·1	14 28	14 27	20 49	2 39	2 42
22	12 53	− 0·1	55·3	15·1	36	297	83	10·1	15 38	15 41	21 31	2 55	2 54
23	13 38	− 5·0	54·8	14·9	48	298	90	11·1	16 47	16 55	22 13	3 11	3 06
24	14 23	− 9·6	54·5	14·8	60	298	95	12·1	17 56	18 08	22 56	3 28	3 19
25	15 09	−13·9	54·2	14·8	72	299	98	13·1	19 04	19 20	23 41	3 47	3 34
26	15 56	−17·6	54·1	14·7	84	314	100	14·1	20 11	20 32	..	4 09	3 52
27	16 44	−20·5	54·0	14·7	96	82	100	15·1	21 15	21 39	0 27	4 36	4 15
28	17 34	−22·6	54·0	14·7	109	90	98	16·1	22 13	22 39	1 15	5 11	4 46
29	18 26	−23·7	54·1	14·7	121	88	94	17·1	23 03	23 30	2 04	5 53	5 26
30	19 18	−23·7	54·3	14·8	133	84	89	18·1	23 45	..	2 53	6 45	6 19
31	20 10	−22·6	54·7	14·9	145	80	82	19·1	..	0 09	3 43	7 46	7 22

MERCURY ☿

Day	R.A.	Dec. +	Diam.	Phase	Transit
	h m	°	″		h m
1	2 10	13·1	12	2	11 32
4	2 05	11·8	12	4	11 15
7	2 02	10·7	11	8	11 00
10	2 01	9·9	11	13	10 48
13	2 02	9·5	10	18	10 38
16	2 06	9·4	10	23	10 30

Mercury is too close to the Sun for observation

Day	R.A.	Dec. +	Diam.	Phase	Transit
	h m	°	″		h m
16	2 06	9·4	10	23	10 30
19	2 12	9·7	9	29	10 25
22	2 20	10·3	9	34	10 21
25	2 30	11·2	8	39	10 20
28	2 42	12·2	8	45	10 20
31	2 56	13·5	7	50	10 23

Mercury is too close to the Sun for observation

VENUS ♀

Day	R.A.	Dec. +	Diam.	Phase	Transit	5° high W. 52°	5° high W. 56°
	h m	°	″		h m	h m	h m
1	5 35	27·4	31	38	14 59	23 00	23 25
6	5 51	27·5	33	34	14 55	22 57	23 21
11	6 05	27·5	35	30	14 49	22 50	23 14
16	6 16	27·2	38	26	14 40	22 39	23 03
21	6 25	26·8	42	21	14 29	22 24	22 47
26	6 30	26·3	45	16	14 13	22 05	22 27
31	6 30	25·6	49	12	13 54	21 40	22 02

MARS ♂

Day	R.A.	Dec. +	Diam.	Phase	Transit
	h m	°	″		h m
1	1 34	9·1	4	—	10 57
6	1 48	10·5	4	—	10 52
11	2 02	11·8	4	—	10 46
16	2 17	13·1	4	—	10 41
21	2 31	14·4	4	—	10 36
26	2 45	15·6	4	—	10 31
31	3 00	16·7	4	—	10 25

Mars is too close to the Sun for observation

SUNRISE AND SUNSET (G.M.T.)

Day	London		Bristol		Birmingham		Manchester		Newcastle		Glasgow		Belfast	
	a.m.	p.m.	a.m.	p.m.	a.m.	p.m.	a.m.	p.m.	a.m.	p.m.	a.m.	p.m.	a.m.	p.m.
	h m	h m	h m	h m	h m	h m	h m	h m	h m	h m	h m	h m	h m	h m
1	4 33	7 23	4 43	7 32	4 36	7 33	4 35	7 38	4 27	7 40	4 35	7 54	4 46	7 57
2	4 31	7 24	4 41	7 34	4 34	7 35	4 33	7 40	4 24	7 42	4 32	7 56	4 44	7 59
3	4 29	7 26	4 39	7 35	4 32	7 36	4 31	7 42	4 22	7 44	4 30	7 58	4 42	8 01
4	4 27	7 27	4 37	7 37	4 30	7 38	4 29	7 43	4 20	7 46	4 28	8 00	4 40	8 02
5	4 26	7 29	4 36	7 39	4 29	7 40	4 27	7 45	4 18	7 48	4 26	8 02	4 38	8 04
6	4 24	7 30	4 34	7 40	4 27	7 41	4 25	7 47	4 16	7 50	4 24	8 04	4 36	8 06
7	4 22	7 32	4 32	7 42	4 25	7 43	4 23	7 49	4 14	7 52	4 22	8 06	4 34	8 08
8	4 20	7 34	4 30	7 44	4 23	7 45	4 21	7 50	4 12	7 53	4 19	8 08	4 31	8 10
9	4 18	7 35	4 28	7 45	4 21	7 46	4 19	7 52	4 10	7 55	4 17	8 10	4 29	8 12
10	4 17	7 37	4 27	7 47	4 20	7 48	4 17	7 54	4 08	7 57	4 15	8 12	4 27	8 14
11	4 15	7 38	4 25	7 48	4 18	7 49	4 16	7 56	4 06	7 59	4 13	8 14	4 26	8 16
12	4 13	7 40	4 23	7 50	4 16	7 51	4 14	7 58	4 04	8 01	4 11	8 16	4 24	8 18
13	4 12	7 42	4 22	7 52	4 15	7 53	4 12	7 59	4 02	8 03	4 09	8 18	4 22	8 19
14	4 10	7 43	4 20	7 53	4 13	7 54	4 10	8 01	4 01	8 05	4 08	8 20	4 20	8 21
15	4 08	7 45	4 18	7 55	4 11	7 56	4 09	8 03	3 59	8 07	4 06	8 22	4 19	8 23
16	4 07	7 46	4 17	7 56	4 10	7 57	4 07	8 04	3 57	8 08	4 04	8 24	4 17	8 24
17	4 05	7 48	4 16	7 58	4 08	7 59	4 05	8 06	3 55	8 10	4 02	8 25	4 15	8 26
18	4 04	7 49	4 14	7 59	4 07	8 00	4 04	8 07	3 54	8 12	4 00	8 27	4 14	8 28
19	4 03	7 51	4 13	8 01	4 06	8 02	4 03	8 09	3 52	8 13	3 58	8 29	4 12	8 29
20	4 01	7 52	4 12	8 02	4 04	8 03	4 01	8 10	3 51	8 15	3 57	8 31	4 11	8 31
21	4 00	7 54	4 11	8 04	4 03	8 05	4 00	8 12	3 49	8 17	3 55	8 33	4 09	8 33
22	3 59	7 55	4 10	8 05	4 02	8 06	3 59	8 13	3 48	8 18	3 54	8 34	4 08	8 34
23	3 57	7 56	4 08	8 06	4 00	8 07	3 57	8 14	3 46	8 20	3 52	8 36	4 06	8 36
24	3 56	7 58	4 07	8 08	3 59	8 09	3 56	8 16	3 44	8 22	3 50	8 38	4 04	8 38
25	3 55	7 59	4 06	8 09	3 58	8 10	3 55	8 17	3 43	8 23	3 49	8 39	4 03	8 39
26	3 54	8 00	4 05	8 10	3 57	8 11	3 54	8 19	3 42	8 25	3 48	8 41	4 02	8 41
27	3 53	8 02	4 04	8 11	3 55	8 13	3 52	8 20	3 40	8 26	3 46	8 43	4 00	8 42
28	3 52	8 03	4 03	8 12	3 54	8 15	3 51	8 22	3 39	8 28	3 45	8 44	3 59	8 44
29	3 51	8 04	4 02	8 14	3 53	8 16	3 50	8 23	3 38	8 29	3 44	8 46	3 58	8 45
30	3 51	8 05	4 01	8 15	3 52	8 17	3 49	8 24	3 37	8 30	3 42	8 47	3 57	8 46
31	3 50	8 07	4 00	8 16	3 51	8 18	3 48	8 26	3 36	8 32	3 41	8 48	3 56	8 48

JUPITER ♃ — SATURN ♄

Day	Jupiter R.A.	Jupiter Dec. +	Jupiter Transit		Saturn R.A.	Saturn Dec. —	Saturn 5° high East 52°	Saturn 5° high East 56°	Saturn Transit
	h m	°	h m		h m	°	h m	h m	h m
1	2 10	12·1	11 33	Jupiter is too	22 23	11·5	3 23	3 37	7 46
11	2 19	12·9	11 03	close to the	22 26	11·3	2 45	2 59	7 09
21	2 29	13·6	10 33	Sun for	22 28	11·2	2 06	2 20	6 32
31	2 37	14·3	10 02	observation	22 29	11·1	1 28	1 42	5 54

Equatorial diameter of Jupiter 33″; of Saturn 17″. Diameters of Saturn's rings 38″ and 5″.

URANUS ♅ — NEPTUNE ♆

Day	Uranus R.A.	Uranus Dec. +	Uranus Transit	Uranus 10° high in West 52°	Uranus 10° high in West 56°	Neptune R.A.	Neptune Dec. —	Neptune Transit	Neptune 10° high in West 52°	Neptune 10° high in West 56°
	h m	° ′	h m	h m	h m	h m	° ′	h m	h m	h m
1	10 32·2	10 03	19 53	1 43	1 44	14 58·8	15 04	0 23	3 44	3 18
11	10 32·0	10 04	19 14	1 03	1 05	14 57·7	14 59	23 39	3 04	2 38
21	10 32·1	10 03	18 34	0 24	0 25	14 56·7	14 55	22 58	2 25	1 59
31	10 32·5	10 00	17 56	23 41	23 42	14 55·7	14 50	22 18	1 45	1 19

Uranus: Diameter 4″ — Neptune: Diameter 2″

Junius, Roman *gens* (family).

♊

Sun's Longitude 90° ♋ 21^{d} 09^{h}

Day of Month	Day of Week	
1	M.	Battle of Ushant 1794. Sir Hugh Walpole d. 1941
2	Tu.	CORONATION DAY (1953). Garibaldi d. 1882
3	W.	George V b. 1865. Pope John XXIII d. 1963
4	Th.	George III b. 1738. Allies entered Rome 1944
5	F.	Stravinsky b. 1882. Roy Thomson b. 1894
6	S.	"D" Day (1944). Cavour d. 1861
7	S.	2nd Sunday after Trinity. David Cox d. 1859
8	M.	Sarah Siddons d. 1831. Sir Godfrey Tearle d. 1953
9	Tu.	Dickens d. 1870. Visct. Brookeborough b. 1888
10	W.	DUKE OF EDINBURGH BORN (1921)
11	Th.	St. Barnabas. Richard Strauss b. 1864**
12	F.	Visct. Cunningham of Hyndhope d. 1963
13	S.	Fanny Burney b. 1752
14	S.	3rd Sunday after Trinity. J. K. Jerome d. 1927
15	M.	Alcock and Brown's Atlantic Flight (1919)
16	Tu.	Marlborough d. 1722. S. C. Griffith b. 1914
17	W.	Addison d. 1719. Visct. Alanbrooke d. 1963
18	Th.	WATERLOO DAY. William Cobbett d. 1835
19	F.	W. R. Hammond b. 1903. Sir James Barrie d. 1937
20	S.	William IV d. 1837. Black Hole of Calcutta 1756
21	S.	4th Sunday after Trinity. Sir C. Auchinleck b. 1884
22	M.	Sir John Hunt b. 1910. Walter de la Mare d. 1956
23	Tu.	Sir Leonard Hutton b. 1916. Sir Charles Oman d.
24	W.	St. John Baptist. Midsummer Day [1946
25	Th.	Korean War began 1950
26	F.	George IV d. 1830. Earl of St. Andrews b. 1962
27	S.	Helen Keller b. 1880. Cherbourg captured 1944
28	S.	5th S. after Trinity. Alfred Noyes d. 1958
29	M.	St. Peter. Paderewski d. 1941
30	Tu.	Elizabeth Barrett Browning d. 1861

PHENOMENA

June 1^{d} 17^{h} Mercury in conjunction with Mars. Mercury 3° S.

2^{d} 18^{h} Saturn in conjunction with the Moon. Saturn 3° N.

7^{d} 17^{h} Jupiter in conjunction with the Moon. Jupiter 3° N.

8^{d} 10^{h} Mars in conjunction with the Moon. Mars 3° N.

8^{d} 19^{h} Mercury in conjunction with the Moon. Mercury 1° N.

10^{d} Partial eclipse of the Sun. See p. 148.

19^{d} 23^{h} Venus in inferior conjunction with the Sun.

21^{d} 09^{h} Summer Solstice.

24–25^{d} Total eclipse of the Moon. See p. 148.

27^{d} 07^{h} Mercury in superior conjunction with the Sun.

30^{d} 00^{h} Saturn in conjunction with the Moon. Saturn 3° N.

CONSTELLATIONS

The following constellations are near the meridian at

	d	h		d	h
May	1	24	May	16	23
June	1	22	June	15	21
July	1	20	July	16	19

Cassiopeia (below the Pole), Ursa Minor, Draco, Ursa Major, Canes Venatici, Bootes, Corona, Serpens, Virgo and Libra.

ALGOL is inconveniently situated for observation during June.

PHASES OF THE MOON

	d	h	m
☾ Last Quarter	3	11	07
● New Moon	10	04	22
☽ First Quarter	16	23	02
○ Full Moon	25	01	08

	d	h
Perigee (222,040 miles) ...	10	02
Apogee (252,370 „) ...	23	12

Mean Longitude of Ascending Node on June 1, 93°.

See note on *Summer Time*, page 98.

MONTHLY NOTES

June 5. Constitution Day, Denmark.

21. Longest day.

24. Midsummer Day. Quarter Day. Sheriffs of London to be elected by the Liverymen.

—. County Quarter Sessions, Eng. and W., to be held within the period of 21 days immediately preceding or following June 24.

** Centenary.

Day	The Sun: Right Ascension	Dec. +	Equation of Time	Rise 52°	Rise 56°	Transit	Set 52°	Set 56°	Sidereal Time	Transit of First Point of Aries
	s.d. 15′·8									
	h m s	° ′	m s	h m	h m	h m	h m	h m	h m s	h m s
1	4 35 41	22 02	+ 2 20	3 46	3 22	11 58	20 10	20 34	16 38 01	7 20 47
2	4 39 46	22 10	+ 2 11	3 45	3 21	11 58	20 11	20 35	16 41 58	7 16 51
3	4 43 52	22 17	+ 2 02	3 44	3 20	11 58	20 12	20 36	16 45 54	7 12 55
4	4 47 59	22 25	+ 1 52	3 44	3 19	11 58	20 13	20 38	16 49 51	7 08 59
5	4 52 06	22 32	+ 1 41	3 43	3 18	11 58	20 14	20 39	16 53 47	7 05 03
6	4 56 13	22 38	+ 1 31	3 42	3 17	11 59	20 15	20 40	16 57 44	7 01 07
7	5 00 20	22 44	+ 1 20	3 42	3 17	11 59	20 16	20 41	17 01 40	6 57 11
8	5 04 28	22 50	+ 1 09	3 41	3 16	11 59	20 17	20 42	17 05 37	6 53 15
9	5 08 36	22 55	+ 0 57	3 41	3 15	11 59	20 17	20 43	17 09 33	6 49 19
10	5 12 45	23 00	+ 0 45	3 40	3 15	11 59	20 18	20 44	17 13 30	6 45 23
11	5 16 54	23 04	+ 0 33	3 40	3 14	12 00	20 19	20 45	17 17 27	6 41 27
12	5 21 02	23 08	+ 0 21	3 40	3 14	12 00	20 20	20 46	17 21 23	6 37 32
13	5 25 11	23 12	+ 0 08	3 40	3 13	12 00	20 20	20 46	17 25 20	6 33 36
14	5 29 21	23 15	− 0 04	3 39	3 13	12 00	20 21	20 47	17 29 16	6 29 40
15	5 33 30	23 18	− 0 17	3 39	3 13	12 00	20 21	20 48	17 33 13	6 25 44
16	5 37 39	23 21	− 0 30	3 39	3 13	12 01	20 22	20 48	17 37 09	6 21 48
17	5 41 49	23 23	− 0 43	3 39	3 12	12 01	20 22	20 49	17 41 06	6 17 52
18	5 45 58	23 24	− 0 56	3 39	3 12	12 01	20 23	20 49	17 45 03	6 13 56
19	5 50 08	23 25	− 1 09	3 39	3 12	12 01	20 23	20 50	17 48 59	6 10 00
20	5 54 17	23 26	− 1 22	3 39	3 13	12 01	20 23	20 50	17 52 56	6 06 04
21	5 58 27	23 27	− 1 35	3 39	3 13	12 02	20 24	20 50	17 56 52	6 02 08
22	6 02 36	23 27	− 1 48	3 40	3 13	12 02	20 24	20 51	18 00 49	5 58 12
23	6 06 46	23 26	− 2 01	3 40	3 13	12 02	20 24	20 51	18 04 45	5 54 17
24	6 10 55	23 25	− 2 14	3 40	3 14	12 02	20 24	20 51	18 08 42	5 50 21
25	6 15 05	23 24	− 2 26	3 41	3 14	12 03	20 24	20 51	18 12 38	5 46 25
26	6 19 14	23 22	− 2 39	3 41	3 14	12 03	20 24	20 51	18 16 35	5 42 29
27	6 23 23	23 20	− 2 51	3 41	3 15	12 03	20 24	20 50	18 20 32	5 38 33
28	6 27 32	23 18	− 3 04	3 42	3 16	12 03	20 24	20 50	18 24 28	5 34 37
29	6 31 40	23 15	− 3 16	3 43	3 16	12 03	20 24	20 50	18 28 25	5 30 41
30	6 35 49	23 11	− 3 28	3 43	3 17	12 04	20 23	20 49	18 32 21	5 26 45

Duration of Civil (C), Nautical (N), and Astronomical (A), Twilight (in minutes)

Lat.	June 1			June 11			June 21			June 30		
°	C	N	A	C	N	A	C	N	A	C	N	A
52	47	117	T.A.N.	48	125	T.A.N.	49	128	T.A.N.	49	125	T.A.N.
56	58	T.A.N.	T.A.N.	61	T.A.N.	T.A.N.	63	T.A.N.	T.A.N.	62	T.A.N.	T.A.N.

ASTRONOMICAL NOTES

MERCURY is unsuitably placed for observation, superior conjunction occurring on the 27th.

VENUS is now moving rapidly towards the Sun and decreasing in brightness. It is only visible as an evening star, low in the W.N.W. sky, during the first twelve days of the month as inferior conjunction occurs on the 19th.

MARS is unsuitably placed for observation.

JUPITER becomes a morning star magnitude −1·7, during the first part of the month. It may be seen low above the E.N.E. horizon by about 03^h at the beginning of the month and by about $01^h\ 30^m$ at the end of the month. Jupiter is in the constellation of Aries.

SATURN is a morning star, magnitude +1·0, though the long duration of twilight does not make it an easy object to locate. Note that Saturn is nearly three magnitudes fainter than Jupiter and is to be found farther round to the south than Jupiter.

ECLIPSE. A partial eclipse of the Sun occurs on the 10th but it is not visible from the British Isles.

ECLIPSE. A total eclipse of the Moon occurs on the 24th–25th, visible from the British Isles. See p. 148, for details.

THE MOON

Day	R.A.	Dec.	Hor. Par.	Semi-diam.	Sun's Co-long.	P.A. of Bright Limb	Phase	Age	Rise 52°	Rise 56°	Transit	Set 52°	Set 56°
	h m	°	′	′	°	°		d	h m	h m	h m	h m	h m
1	21 01	−20·5	55·1	15·0	157	75	74	20·1	0 18	0 39	4 32	8 52	8 32
2	21 52	−17·4	55·7	15·2	170	72	65	21·1	0 46	1 02	5 20	10 03	9 48
3	22 42	−13·4	56·4	15·4	182	68	55	22·1	1 09	1 20	6 07	11 17	11 07
4	23 31	− 8·7	57·2	15·6	194	66	44	23·1	1 28	1 36	6 54	12 33	12 28
5	0 21	− 3·5	58·1	15·8	206	65	34	24·1	1 47	1 50	7 42	13 51	13 51
6	1 11	+ 2·1	59·1	16·1	219	65	24	25·1	2 06	2 04	8 31	15 12	15 17
7	2 04	+ 7·7	59·9	16·3	231	65	15	26·1	2 26	2 19	9 22	16 37	16 48
8	3 00	+13·1	60·7	16·5	243	67	7	27·1	2 49	2 37	10 18	18 05	18 21
9	3 59	+17·8	61·2	16·7	255	70	2	28·1	3 18	3 01	11 17	19 32	19 54
10	5 02	+21·4	61·4	16·7	268	56	0	29·1	3 57	3 34	12 20	20 54	21 20
11	6 07	+23·4	61·2	16·7	280	271	1	0·8	4 48	4 21	13 25	22 03	22 29
12	7 13	+23·7	60·8	16·6	292	274	5	1·8	5 53	5 26	14 29	22 56	23 20
13	8 17	+22·4	60·1	16·4	304	280	11	2·8	7 08	6 45	15 29	23 35	23 54
14	9 18	+19·6	59·2	16·1	317	285	20	3·8	8 28	8 10	16 25	..	..
15	10 14	+15·8	58·3	15·9	329	289	30	4·8	9 47	9 34	17 16	0 04	0 19
16	11 06	+11·2	57·3	15·6	341	292	40	5·8	11 04	10 56	18 03	0 27	0 37
17	11 55	+ 6·3	56·5	15·4	353	294	50	6·8	12 17	12 14	18 47	0 46	0 51
18	12 41	+ 1·3	55·7	15·2	5	294	61	7·8	13 28	13 30	19 30	1 03	1 04
19	13 27	− 3·7	55·1	15·0	18	294	70	8·8	14 38	14 44	20 12	1 19	1 15
20	14 12	− 8·5	54·7	14·9	30	293	79	9·8	15 46	15 57	20 55	1 35	1 28
21	14 57	−12·8	54·3	14·8	42	291	86	10·8	16 55	17 09	21 39	1 53	1 42
22	15 44	−16·7	54·1	14·7	54	288	92	11·8	18 02	18 21	22 24	2 14	1 58
23	16 32	−19·8	54·0	14·7	66	284	96	12·8	19 07	19 30	23 11	2 39	2 19
24	17 22	−22·1	54·0	14·7	79	279	99	13·8	20 07	20 33	..	3 11	2 47
25	18 13	−23·5	54·1	14·7	91	260	100	14·8	21 01	21 27	0 00	3 51	3 24
26	19 05	−23·8	54·3	14·8	103	90	99	15·8	21 45	22 10	0 50	4 40	4 13
27	19 57	−23·0	54·5	14·9	115	84	97	16·8	22 21	22 43	1 40	5 38	5 13
28	20 49	−21·1	54·9	15·0	127	79	92	17·8	22 51	23 08	2 29	6 43	6 22
29	21 40	−18·2	55·3	15·1	140	75	86	18·8	23 14	23 27	3 18	7 53	7 36
30	22 29	−14·5	55·8	15·2	152	72	78	19·8	23 35	23 43	4 05	9 05	8 53

MERCURY ☿

Day	R.A.	Dec. +	Diam.	Phase	Transit	
	h m	°	″		h m	
1	3 01	14·0	7	52	10 24	Mercury is too close to the Sun for observation
4	3 17	15·4	7	58	10 28	
7	3 35	17·0	6	65	10 35	
10	3 55	18·5	6	72	10 43	
13	4 17	20·1	6	78	10 54	
16	4 41	21·5	5	85	11 06	

Day	R.A.	Dec. +	Diam.	Phase	Transit	
	h m	°	″		h m	
16	4 41	21·5	5	85	11 06	Mercury is too close to the Sun for observation
19	5 07	22·8	5	92	11 20	
22	5 34	23·7	5	96	11 36	
25	6 03	24·3	5	99	11 53	
28	6 32	24·5	5	100	12 10	
31	7 00	24·3	5	98	12 27	

VENUS ♀

Day	R.A.	Dec. +	Diam.	Phase	Transit	5° high W. 52°	5° high W. 56°
	h m	°	″		h m	h m	h m
1	6 30	25·5	49	11	13 49	21 35	21 56
6	6 25	24·6	53	6	13 25	21 04	21 24
11	6 17	23·7	56	3	12 56	20 29	20 47
16	6 05	22·5	58	1	12 24	19 50	20 07
21	5 51	21·4	58	0	11 51	19 10	19 25
26	5 39	20·2	57	2	11 19	18 31	18 45
31	5 28	19·3	55	5	10 50	17 56	18 10

MARS ♂

Day	R.A.	Dec. +	Diam.	Phase	Transit	
	h m	°	″		h m	
1	3 03	16·9	4	—	10 24	Mars is too close to the Sun for observation
6	3 18	17·9	4	—	10 19	
11	3 32	18·9	4	—	10 14	
16	3 47	19·8	4	—	10 09	
21	4 02	20·6	4	—	10 05	
26	4 17	21·3	4	—	10 00	
31	4 32	21·9	4	—	9 55	

SUNRISE AND SUNSET (G.M.T.)

Day	London		Bristol		Birmingham		Manchester		Newcastle		Glasgow		Belfast	
	a.m.	p.m.	a.m.	p.m.	a.m.	p.m.	a.m.	p.m.	a.m.	p.m.	a.m.	p.m	a.m.	p.m.
	h m	h m	h m	h m	h m	h m	h m	h m	h m	h m	h m	h m	h m	h m
1	3 49	8 08	3 59	8 17	3 50	8 20	3 47	8 27	3 35	8 33	3 40	8 50	3 55	8 49
2	3 48	8 09	3 58	8 18	3 49	8 21	3 46	8 28	3 34	8 34	3 39	8 51	3 54	8 50
3	3 47	8 10	3 57	8 19	3 48	8 22	3 45	8 29	3 33	8 35	3 38	8 52	3 53	8 51
4	3 47	8 11	3 57	8 20	3 48	8 23	3 44	8 30	3 32	8 37	3 37	8 54	3 52	8 52
5	3 46	8 12	3 56	8 21	3 47	8 24	3 44	8 31	3 31	8 38	3 36	8 55	3 52	8 53
6	3 45	8 12	3 55	8 22	3 46	8 25	3 43	8 32	3 30	8 39	3 35	8 56	3 51	8 54
7	3 45	8 13	3 55	8 23	3 46	8 26	3 42	8 33	3 30	8 40	3 35	8 57	3 50	8 55
8	3 44	8 14	3 54	8 24	3 45	8 27	3 42	8 34	3 29	8 41	3 34	8 58	3 50	8 56
9	3 44	8 15	3 54	8 24	3 45	8 27	3 41	8 35	3 28	8 42	3 33	8 59	3 49	8 57
10	3 43	8 16	3 53	8 25	3 44	8 28	3 41	8 36	3 28	8 43	3 33	9 00	3 49	8 58
11	3 43	8 16	3 53	8 26	3 44	8 29	3 40	8 37	3 27	8 44	3 32	9 01	3 48	8 59
12	3 43	8 17	3 53	8 27	3 44	8 30	3 40	8 38	3 27	8 45	3 32	9 02	3 48	9 00
13	3 43	8 17	3 53	8 27	3 44	8 30	3 39	8 38	3 26	8 45	3 31	9 02	3 47	9 00
14	3 42	8 18	3 52	8 28	3 43	8 31	3 39	8 39	3 26	8 46	3 31	9 03	3 47	9 01
15	3 42	8 19	3 52	8 28	3 43	8 31	3 39	8 40	3 26	8 47	3 31	9 04	3 47	9 02
16	3 42	8 19	3 52	8 29	3 43	8 32	3 39	8 40	3 26	8 47	3 31	9 04	3 47	9 02
17	3 42	8 19	3 52	8 29	3 43	8 32	3 39	8 41	3 26	8 48	3 30	9 05	3 47	9 03
18	3 42	8 20	3 52	8 30	3 43	8 33	3 39	8 41	3 26	8 48	3 30	9 05	3 47	9 03
19	3 42	8 20	3 52	8 30	3 43	8 33	3 39	8 41	3 26	8 48	3 30	9 06	3 47	9 03
20	3 42	8 20	3 52	8 30	3 43	8 33	3 39	8 42	3 26	8 49	3 31	9 06	3 47	9 04
21	3 42	8 21	3 52	8 31	3 43	8 34	3 39	8 42	3 26	8 49	3 31	9 06	3 47	9 04
22	3 43	8 21	3 53	8 31	3 44	8 34	3 39	8 42	3 26	8 49	3 31	9 07	3 47	9 04
23	3 43	8 21	3 53	8 31	3 44	8 34	3 39	8 42	3 26	8 49	3 31	9 07	3 47	9 04
24	3 43	8 21	3 53	8 31	3 44	8 34	3 40	8 42	3 27	8 49	3 32	9 07	3 48	9 04
25	3 44	8 21	3 54	8 31	3 45	8 34	3 40	8 42	3 27	8 49	3 32	9 07	3 48	9 04
26	3 44	8 21	3 54	8 31	3 45	8 34	3 41	8 42	3 28	8 49	3 32	9 07	3 49	9 04
27	3 44	8 21	3 54	8 31	3 45	8 34	3 41	8 42	3 28	8 49	3 33	9 06	3 49	9 04
28	3 45	8 21	3 55	8 31	3 46	8 34	3 42	8 42	3 29	8 49	3 34	9 06	3 50	9 04
29	3 46	8 21	3 56	8 31	3 47	8 34	3 42	8 42	3 29	8 49	3 34	9 06	3 50	9 04
30	3 46	8 21	3 56	8 30	3 47	8 33	3 43	8 41	3 30	8 48	3 35	9 05	3 51	9 03

	JUPITER ♃					SATURN ♄				
Day	R.A.	Dec. +	5° high East 52°	5° high East 56°	Transit	R.A.	Dec. —	5° high East 52°	5° high East 56°	Transit
	h m	°	h m	h m	h m	h m	°	h m	h m	h m
1	2 38	14·4	3 18	3 09	9 59	22 29	11·1	1 24	1 38	5 50
11	2 47	15·1	2 44	2 34	9 28	22 30	11·1	0 45	0 59	5 11
21	2 55	15·7	2 09	1 59	8 57	22 30	11·1	0 06	0 20	4 32
31	3 03	16·2	1 35	1 24	8 26	22 29	11·2	23 23	23 37	3 52

Equatorial diameter of Jupiter 34″; of Saturn 18″. Diameters of Saturn's rings 40″ and 5″.

	URANUS ♅					NEPTUNE ♆				
Day	R.A.	Dec. +	Transit	10° high in West 52°	10° high in West 56°	R.A.	Dec. —	Transit	10° high in West 52°	10° high in West 56°
	h m	h m	° ′	h m	h m	h m	° ′	h m	h m	h m
1	10 32·5	10 00	17 52	23 37	23 38	14 55·6	14 50	22 14	1 41	1 15
11	10 33·3	9 55	17 13	22 58	22 59	14 54·7	14 46	21 34	1 01	0 35
21	10 34·4	9 48	16 35	22 19	22 20	14 53·9	14 43	20 54	0 21	23 52
31	10 35·7	9 40	15 57	21 40	21 42	14 53·3	14 41	20 14	23 38	23 12

Diameter 4″ Diameter 2″

Julius Caesar, formerly *Quintilis*, 5th month (from March).

Sun's Longitude 120° ♌ 22d 20h

Day of Month	Day of Week	
1	W.	Canada Day (1867). G. F. Watts d. 1904
2	Th.	King Olav b. 1903. Earl of Home b. 1903
3	F.	Joel Chandler Harris d. 1908 [d. 1963
4	S.	Independence Day, U.S.A. (1776). Lord Freyberg
5	S.	6th S. after Trinity. Cecil Rhodes b. 1853
6	M.	Sedgemoor 1685. William Faulkner d. 1962
7	Tu.	Sheridan d. 1816. Sir A. Conan Doyle d. 1930
8	W.	Shelley d. 1822. Alec Waugh b. 1898
9	Th.	Caen captured 1944
10	F.	Lord Fisher d. 1920. Albert Chevalier d. 1923
11	S.	Sir J. Rothenstein b. 1901. Sir A. Evans d. 1941
12	S.	7th Sunday after Trinity. Col. Dreyfus d. 1935
13	M.	Battle of the Pyramids 1798. Treaty of Berlin 1878
14	Tu.	Fête Nationale, France. F. R. Leavis b. 1895
15	W.	St. Swithin's Day. Dame Marie Tempest b. 1864**
16	Th.	Lord Plumer d. 1932 Hilaire Belloc d. 1953 [1959
17	F.	*Punch* first issued, 1841. Sir Alfred Munnings d.
18	S.	Jane Austen d. 1817. Visct. Snowden b. 1864**
19	S.	8th S. after Trinity. John Bratby b. 1928
20	M.	Marconi d. 1937. G. M. Trevelyan d. 1962 [1764**
21	Tu.	Matthew Prior b. 1664**. Sir Sidney Smith b.
22	W.	St. Mary Magdalen. Mackenzie King d. 1950
23	Th.	Visct. Alanbrooke b. 1883. Cordell Hull d. 1955
24	F.	Sacha Guitry d. 1957
25	S.	St. James. Blériot's Channel Flight 1909
26	S.	9th Sunday after Trinity. Peter Thorneycroft b.
27	M.	Korean Truce signed 1953 [1909
28	Tu.	J. S. Bach d. 1750. Bismarck d. 1898
29	W.	Van Gogh d. 1890. Joseph Grimond b. 1913
30	Th.	Gray d. 1771. Henry Moore b. 1898
31	F.	Trinity Law Sittings End. Liszt d. 1886

PHENOMENA

July 5d Aphelion (94,600,000 miles).

5d 12h Jupiter in conjunction with the Moon. Jupiter 3° N.

7d 06h Mars in conjunction with the Moon. Mars 2° N.

7d 17h Venus in conjunction with the Moon. Venus 4° S.

9d Partial eclipse of the Sun. See p. 148.

10d 12h Mercury in conjunction with the Moon. Mercury 0°·9 S.

18d 07h Venus in conjunction with Mars. Venus 5° S.

26d 16h Venus at greatest brilliancy.

27d 03h Saturn in conjunction with the Moon. Saturn 3° N.

CONSTELLATIONS

The following constellations are near the meridian at

	d	h		d	h
June	1	24	June	15	23
July	1	22	July	16	21
Aug.	1	20	Aug.	16	19

Ursa Minor, Draco, Corona, Hercules, Lyra, Serpens, Ophiuchus, Libra, Scorpius and Sagittarius.

MINIMA OF ALGOL

d	h	d	h
2	19	20	00
5	16	22	21
8	12	25	17
11	09	28	14
14	06	31	11
17	03		

PHASES OF THE MOON

	d	h	m
☾ Last Quarter	2	20	31
● New Moon	9	11	31
☽ First Quarter	16	11	47
○ Full Moon	24	15	58

	d	h
Perigee (223,110 miles)	8	11
Apogee (251,940 „)	20	21

Mean Longitude of Ascending Node on July 1, 92°.

See note on *Summer Time*, page 98.

MONTHLY NOTES

July 1. Special Session for Licences to deal in Game to be held this month.

3. Dog Days begin (end Aug. 15).
5. Dividends due. Tynwald Day, Isle of Man.
8. Midsummer Fire Insurances to be paid.
13. Bank and General Holiday, Northern Ireland.
15. Latest date for receiving corrections for next year's "WHITAKER."
21. Belgian Independence Day (1831).
31. Gun and Game Licences expire.

** Centenary.

Day	The Sun s.d. 15′·8 Right Ascension	Dec. +	Equation of Time	Rise 52°	Rise 56°	Transit	Set 52°	Set 56°	Sidereal Time	Transit of First Point of Aries
	h m s	° ′	m s	h m	h m	h m	h m	h m	h m s	h m s
1	6 39 57	23 08	− 3 39	3 44	3 18	12 04	20 23	20 49	18 36 18	5 22 49
2	6 44 05	23 03	− 3 51	3 44	3 19	12 04	20 23	20 49	18 40 14	5 18 53
3	6 48 13	22 59	− 4 02	3 45	3 20	12 04	20 22	20 48	18 44 11	5 14 57
4	6 52 20	22 54	− 4 13	3 46	3 20	12 04	20 22	20 47	18 48 07	5 11 01
5	6 56 28	22 49	− 4 24	3 47	3 21	12 04	20 21	20 47	18 52 04	5 07 06
6	7 00 35	22 43	− 4 34	3 48	3 22	12 05	20 21	20 46	18 56 01	5 03 10
7	7 04 41	22 37	− 4 44	3 49	3 24	12 05	20 20	20 45	18 59 57	4 59 14
8	7 08 48	22 30	− 4 54	3 50	3 25	12 05	20 20	20 44	19 03 54	4 55 18
9	7 12 53	22 23	− 5 03	3 51	3 26	12 05	20 19	20 44	19 07 50	4 51 22
10	7 16 59	22 16	− 5 12	3 52	3 27	12 05	20 18	20 42	19 11 47	4 47 26
11	7 21 04	22 08	− 5 21	3 53	3 28	12 05	20 17	20 41	19 15 43	4 43 30
12	7 25 08	22 00	− 5 29	3 54	3 30	12 06	20 16	20 40	19 19 40	4 39 34
13	7 29 13	21 52	− 5 36	3 55	3 31	12 06	20 16	20 39	19 23 36	4 35 38
14	7 33 16	21 43	− 5 43	3 56	3 33	12 06	20 15	20 38	19 27 33	4 31 42
15	7 37 19	21 34	− 5 50	3 57	3 34	12 06	20 14	20 37	19 31 30	4 27 46
16	7 41 22	21 24	− 5 56	3 58	3 36	12 06	20 13	20 35	19 35 26	4 23 51
17	7 45 24	21 14	− 6 01	4 00	3 37	12 06	20 12	20 34	19 39 23	4 19 55
18	7 49 25	21 04	− 6 06	4 01	3 39	12 06	20 10	20 33	19 43 19	4 15 59
19	7 53 26	20 53	− 6 11	4 02	3 40	12 06	20 09	20 31	19 47 16	4 12 03
20	7 57 27	20 42	− 6 15	4 03	3 42	12 06	20 08	20 30	19 51 12	4 08 07
21	8 01 27	20 31	− 6 18	4 05	3 43	12 06	20 07	20 28	19 55 09	4 04 11
22	8 05 26	20 19	− 6 20	4 06	3 45	12 06	20 06	20 27	19 59 05	4 00 15
23	8 09 25	20 07	− 6 23	4 08	3 47	12 06	20 04	20 25	20 03 02	3 56 19
24	8 13 23	19 55	− 6 24	4 09	3 48	12 06	20 03	20 23	20 06 59	3 52 23
25	8 17 20	19 42	− 6 25	4 10	3 50	12 06	20 01	20 22	20 10 55	3 48 27
26	8 21 17	19 29	− 6 25	4 12	3 52	12 06	20 00	20 20	20 14 52	3 44 31
27	8 25 13	19 16	− 6 25	4 13	3 54	12 06	19 58	20 18	20 18 48	3 40 36
28	8 29 09	19 02	− 6 24	4 15	3 55	12 06	19 57	20 16	20 22 45	3 36 40
29	8 33 04	18 48	− 6 23	4 17	3 57	12 06	19 55	20 14	20 26 41	3 32 44
30	8 36 59	18 34	− 6 21	4 18	3 59	12 06	19 54	20 12	20 30 38	3 28 48
31	8 40 53	18 19	− 6 18	4 19	4 01	12 06	19 52	20 11	20 34 34	3 24 52

Duration of Civil (C), Nautical (N), and Astronomical (A), Twilight (in minutes)

Lat.	July 1 C	July 1 N	July 1 A	July 11 C	July 11 N	July 11 A	July 21 C	July 21 N	July 21 A	July 31 C	July 31 N	July 31 A
°												
52	48	124	T.A.N.	46	116	T.A.N.	44	107	T.A.N.	41	98	180
56	61	T.A.N.	T.A.N.	58	T.A.N.	T.A.N.	53	144	T.A.N.	49	122	T.A.N.

ASTRONOMICAL NOTES

MERCURY is unsuitably placed for observation.

VENUS becomes a morning star, just visible very low in the E.N.E. before sunrise, at the beginning of the month. It attains its greatest brilliancy on the 26th (magnitude −4·2). Venus and Mars remain fairly close to each other in the sky throughout the second part of the month.

MARS becomes a morning star during the second half of the month, magnitude +1·7. It may be located low above the E.N.E. horizon near the time of beginning of nautical twilight. Mars is gradually passing Venus, and on the 18th, when conjunction occurs, Mars is 5°N. of it.

JUPITER is a morning star, magnitude −1·8 and by the very end of the month may be seen low in the E.N.E. shortly before midnight.

SATURN is a morning star, magnitude +0·9, and gradually drawing away from the Sun. Saturn is in the constellation of Aquarius and by the end of the month is visible before 22^{h}.

ECLIPSE. A partial eclipse of the Sun occurs on the 9th but it is not visible from the British Isles.

THE MOON

Day	R.A.	Dec.	Hor. Par.	Semi-diam.	Sun's Co-long.	P.A. of Bright Limb	Phase	Age	Rise 52°	Rise 56°	Transit	Set 52°	Set 56°
	h m	°	′	′	°	°		d	h m	h m	h m	h m	h m
1	23 18	−10·0	56·5	15·4	164	69	69	20·8	23 53	23 57	4 51	10 19	10 12
2	0 07	− 5·0	57·2	15·6	176	67	59	21·8	..	..	5 37	11 34	11 32
3	0 56	+ 0·3	58·0	15·8	189	67	48	22·8	0 11	0 10	6 24	12 52	12 55
4	1 46	+ 5·8	58·8	16·0	201	68	37	23·8	0 29	0 24	7 12	14 12	14 20
5	2 39	+11·1	59·5	16·2	213	70	27	24·8	0 50	0 40	8 04	15 36	15 49
6	3 35	+16·0	60·2	16·4	225	74	17	25·8	1 15	1 00	8 59	17 01	17 20
7	4 35	+20·0	60·8	16·6	237	79	9	26·8	1 48	1 28	9 59	18 25	18 49
8	5 38	+22·7	61·0	16·6	250	86	3	27·8	2 31	2 07	11 03	19 40	20 07
9	6 44	+23·8	61·0	16·6	262	101	0	28·8	3 29	3 02	12 07	20 42	21 08
10	7 50	+23·2	60·7	16·5	274	265	0	0·5	4 40	4 15	13 11	21 29	21 50
11	8 53	+20·9	60·1	16·4	286	278	3	1·5	6 01	5 40	14 10	22 03	22 20
12	9 52	+17·4	59·3	16·2	299	284	9	2·5	7 23	7 08	15 05	22 29	22 41
13	10 47	+12·9	58·4	15·9	311	288	16	3·5	8 43	8 33	15 55	22 50	22 57
14	11 38	+ 8·0	57·5	15·7	323	291	25	4·5	10 01	9 56	16 42	23 08	23 11
15	12 27	+ 2·8	56·6	15·4	335	292	35	5·5	11 14	11 14	17 26	23 25	23 23
16	13 13	− 2·3	55·8	15·2	348	292	45	6·5	12 25	12 30	18 10	23 41	23 35
17	13 59	− 7·2	55·2	15·0	360	291	55	7·5	13 35	13 44	18 52	23 59	23 49
18	14 45	−11·7	54·7	14·9	12	289	65	8·5	14 44	14 57	19 36	..	..
19	15 31	−15·7	54·3	14·8	24	286	73	9·5	15 52	16 10	20 21	0 19	0 04
20	16 19	−19·1	54·1	14·7	37	282	81	10·5	16 58	17 20	21 07	0 42	0 24
21	17 08	−21·6	54·1	14·7	49	277	88	11·5	18 00	18 25	21 56	1 12	0 49
22	17 59	−23·2	54·2	14·8	61	271	94	12·5	18 56	19 23	22 46	1 49	1 23
23	18 51	−23·8	54·3	14·8	73	262	97	13·5	19 44	20 10	23 36	2 35	2 08
24	19 44	−23·3	54·6	14·9	85	246	100	14·5	20 23	20 46	..	3 30	3 05
25	20 36	−21·6	54·9	15·0	98	113	100	15·5	20 54	21 13	0 26	4 34	4 12
26	21 27	−19·0	55·3	15·1	110	85	98	16·5	21 19	21 34	1 15	5 43	5 25
27	22 18	−15·4	55·8	15·2	122	78	95	17·5	21 41	21 51	2 03	6 56	6 42
28	23 07	−11·0	56·3	15·3	134	73	89	18·5	22 00	22 05	2 49	8 09	8 01
29	23 55	− 6·1	56·8	15·5	146	71	82	19·5	22 17	22 18	3 35	9 24	9 20
30	0 44	− 0·9	57·4	15·6	159	70	73	20·5	22 35	22 31	4 21	10 40	10 41
31	1 33	+ 4·5	58·0	15·8	171	70	63	21·5	22 54	22 46	5 08	11 58	12 04

MERCURY ☿

Day	R.A.	Dec. +	Diam.	Phase	Transit	
	h m	°	″		h m	
1	7 00	24·3	5	98	12 27	Mercury is too close to the Sun for observation
4	7 28	23·7	5	95	12 42	
7	7 54	22·8	5	91	12 56	
10	8 18	21·5	5	87	13 09	
13	8 41	20·1	5	82	13 19	
16	9 02	18·5	6	78	13 28	

Day	R.A.	Dec. +	Diam.	Phase	Transit	
	h m	°	″		h m	
16	9 02	18·5	6	78	13 28	Mercury is too close to the Sun for observation
19	9 22	16·7	6	73	13 36	
22	9 40	14·9	6	69	13 41	
25	9 56	13·1	6	65	13 46	
28	10 11	11·2	7	61	13 49	
31	10 24	9·4	7	57	13 50	

VENUS ♀

Day	R.A.	Dec. +	Diam.	Phase	5° high E. 52°	5° high E. 56°	Transit
	h m	°	″		h m	h m	h m
1	5 28	19·3	55	5	3 42	3 29	10 50
6	5 22	18·5	51	8	3 20	3 08	10 24
11	5 20	18·1	48	13	3 01	2 49	10 02
16	5 21	17·9	44	18	2 44	2 32	9 44
21	5 26	17·9	41	22	2 29	2 17	9 30
26	5 35	18·1	38	27	2 17	2 05	9 19
31	5 46	18·4	35	31	2 07	1 54	9 11

MARS ♂

Day	R.A.	Dec. +	Diam.	Phase	5° high E. 52°	5° high E. 56°	Transit
	h m	°	″		h m	h m	h m
1	4 32	21·9	4	97	2 30	2 14	9 55
6	4 47	22·4	4	97	2 22	2 05	9 50
11	5 01	22·9	4	97	2 15	1 57	9 45
16	5 16	23·3	4	96	2 07	1 49	9 40
21	5 31	23·5	4	96	2 01	1 42	9 36
26	5 46	23·7	4	96	1 55	1 36	9 31
31	6 01	23·8	4	96	1 49	1 30	9 26

SUNRISE AND SUNSET (G.M.T.)

Day	London a.m.	London p.m.	Bristol a.m.	Bristol p.m.	Birmingham a.m.	Birmingham p.m.	Manchester a.m.	Manchester p.m.	Newcastle a.m.	Newcastle p.m.	Glasgow a.m.	Glasgow p.m.	Belfast a.m.	Belfast p.m.
	h m	h m	h m	h m	h m	h m	h m	h m	h m	h m	h m	h m	h m	h m
1	3 47	8 21	3 57	8 30	3 48	8 33	3 44	8 41	3 31	8 48	3 36	9 05	3 52	9 03
2	3 47	8 20	3 57	8 30	3 48	8 33	3 44	8 41	3 32	8 48	3 37	9 05	3 52	9 03
3	3 48	8 20	3 58	8 29	3 49	8 32	3 45	8 40	3 33	8 47	3 38	9 04	3 53	9 02
4	3 49	8 19	3 59	8 29	3 50	8 32	3 46	8 40	3 33	8 46	3 38	9 03	3 54	9 02
5	3 50	8 19	4 00	8 28	3 51	8 31	3 47	8 39	3 34	8 46	3 39	9 03	3 55	9 01
6	3 51	8 18	4 01	8 28	3 52	8 31	3 48	8 39	3 35	8 45	3 40	9 02	3 56	9 01
7	3 52	8 18	4 02	8 27	3 53	8 30	3 49	8 38	3 37	8 44	3 42	9 01	3 57	9 00
8	3 53	8 17	4 03	8 27	3 54	8 30	3 50	8 37	3 38	8 43	3 43	9 00	3 58	8 59
9	3 54	8 17	4 04	8 26	3 55	8 29	3 51	8 36	3 39	8 43	3 44	9 00	3 59	8 58
10	3 55	8 16	4 05	8 25	3 56	8 28	3 52	8 35	3 40	8 41	3 45	8 58	4 00	8 57
11	3 56	8 15	4 06	8 24	3 57	8 27	3 53	8 35	3 41	8 41	3 46	8 57	4 01	8 57
12	3 57	8 14	4 07	8 24	3 58	8 26	3 55	8 34	3 43	8 40	3 48	8 56	4 03	8 56
13	3 58	8 14	4 08	8 23	3 59	8 26	3 56	8 33	3 44	8 39	3 49	8 55	4 04	8 55
14	3 59	8 13	4 09	8 22	4 00	8 25	3 57	8 32	3 45	8 38	3 51	8 54	4 05	8 54
15	4 00	8 12	4 10	8 21	4 01	8 24	3 58	8 31	3 46	8 37	3 52	8 53	4 06	8 53
16	4 01	8 11	4 11	8 20	4 03	8 22	4 00	8 29	3 48	8 35	3 54	8 51	4 08	8 51
17	4 02	8 10	4 13	8 19	4 04	8 21	4 01	8 28	3 49	8 34	3 55	8 50	4 09	8 50
18	4 03	8 08	4 14	8 18	4 05	8 20	4 02	8 27	3 51	8 33	3 57	8 49	4 11	8 49
19	4 04	8 07	4 15	8 17	4 07	8 19	4 04	8 26	3 52	8 31	3 58	8 47	4 12	8 47
20	4 06	8 06	4 16	8 16	4 08	8 17	4 05	8 24	3 54	8 30	4 00	8 46	4 14	8 46
21	4 07	8 05	4 18	8 15	4 10	8 16	4 07	8 23	3 55	8 28	4 01	8 44	4 15	8 44
22	4 08	8 04	4 19	8 14	4 11	8 15	4 08	8 22	3 57	8 27	4 03	8 43	4 17	8 43
23	4 10	8 02	4 20	8 12	4 13	8 13	4 10	8 20	3 59	8 25	4 05	8 41	4 19	8 41
24	4 11	8 01	4 22	8 11	4 14	8 12	4 11	8 19	4 00	8 23	4 06	8 39	4 20	8 39
25	4 12	7 59	4 23	8 09	4 15	8 10	4 12	8 17	4 02	8 22	4 08	8 38	4 22	8 38
26	4 14	7 58	4 24	8 08	4 17	8 09	4 14	8 16	4 04	8 20	4 10	8 36	4 24	8 36
27	4 15	7 56	4 26	8 06	4 18	8 07	4 15	8 14	4 05	8 19	4 12	8 34	4 25	8 35
28	4 17	7 55	4 27	8 05	4 20	8 06	4 17	8 13	4 07	8 17	4 13	8 32	4 27	8 33
29	4 19	7 53	4 29	8 03	4 22	8 04	4 19	8 11	4 09	8 15	4 15	8 30	4 29	8 31
30	4 20	7 52	4 30	8 02	4 23	8 03	4 20	8 10	4 10	8 13	4 17	8 28	4 30	8 30
31	4 21	7 50	4 31	8 00	4 24	8 01	4 22	8 08	4 12	8 12	4 19	8 27	4 32	8 28

JUPITER ♃ / SATURN ♄

Day	Jupiter R.A.	Jupiter Dec. +	Jupiter 5° high East 52°	Jupiter 5° high East 56°	Jupiter Transit	Saturn R.A.	Saturn Dec. −	Saturn 5° high East 52°	Saturn 5° high East 56°	Saturn Transit
	h m	°	h m	h m	h m	h m	°	h m	h m	h m
1	3 03	16·2	1 35	1 24	8 26	22 29	11·2	23 23	23 37	3 52
11	3 11	16·7	1 00	0 49	7 54	22 28	11·4	22 43	22 57	3 12
21	3 17	17·1	0 25	0 14	7 21	22 26	11·6	22 03	22 18	2 31
31	3 23	17·5	23 46	23 34	6 48	22 24	11·8	21 23	21 38	1 49

Equatorial diameter of Jupiter 37″; of Saturn 18″. Diameters of Saturn's rings 42″ and 6″.

URANUS ♅ / NEPTUNE ♆

Day	Uranus R.A.	Uranus Dec. +	Uranus Transit		Neptune R.A.	Neptune Dec. −	Neptune Transit	Neptune 10° high in West 52°	Neptune 10° high in West 56°
	h m	° ′	h m		h m	° ′	h m	h m	h m
1	10 35·7	9 40	15 57	Uranus is too	14 53·3	14 41	20 14	23 38	23 12
11	10 37·4	9 30	15 19	close to the	14 52·8	14 40	19 34	22 58	22 33
21	10 39·2	9 19	14 42	Sun for	14 52·6	14 39	18 54	22 19	21 53
31	10 41·2	9 07	14 04	observation	14 52·5	14 40	18 15	21 39	21 14

Uranus: Diameter 4″ — Neptune: Diameter 2″

Julius Caesar *Augustus*, formerly *Sextilis*, 6th month (from March).

Sun's Longitude 150° ♍ 23^{d} 03^{h}

Day of Month	Day of Week	
1	S.	Lord Dilhorne b. 1905. F. M. Worrell b. 1924
2	S.	10th Sunday after Trinity. A. Graham Bell d. 1922
3	M.	Grinling Gibbons d. 1721. Joseph Conrad d. 1924
4	Tu.	QUEEN ELIZABETH THE QUEEN MOTHER BORN 1900
5	W.	First Atom Bomb dropped 1945
6	Th.	Transfiguration. Ben Jonson d. 1637
7	F.	Sir Rabindranath Tagore d. 1941
8	S.	Canning d. 1827. Lord Evershed b. 1899
9	S.	11th Sunday after Trinity. Sir B. Partridge d. 1945
10	M.	President Hoover b. 1874. Treaty of Trianon 1921
11	Tu.	Sir Denis Brogan b. 1900.
12	W.	William Blake d. 1827. J. R. Lowell d. 1891
13	Th.	Sir Basil Spence b. 1907. H. G. Wells d. 1946
14	F.	Richard Jeffries d. 1887. Sir Landon Ronald d. [1938
15	S.	PRINCESS ANNE BORN 1950
16	S.	12th Sunday after Trinity. Margaret Mitchell d. 1949
17	M.	Admiral Blake d. 1657. Frederick the Great d. 1786
18	Tu.	Basil Cameron b. 1884. W. H. Hudson d. 1922
19	W.	Pascal d. 1662. Visct. Haldane d. 1928
20	Th.	General Booth d. 1912. Trotsky assassinated 1940
21	F.	PRINCESS MARGARET BORN 1930
22	S.	Bosworth Field 1485. Sir Oliver Lodge d. 1940
23	S.	13th Sunday after Trinity.
24	M.	St. Bartholomew. Lord Woolton b. 1883
25	Tu.	Michael Faraday d. 1867. Paris liberated 1944
26	W.	Prince Richard b. 1944. Mark Hambourg d. 1960
27	Th.	Lyndon Johnson b. 1908. Sir D. Bradman b. 1908
28	F.	Leigh Hunt d. 1869. General Botha d. 1919
29	S.	Lord Casey b. 1890. Vicki Baum d. 1960
30	S.	14th Sunday after Trinity. John Gunther b. 1901
31	M.	Sir Bernard Lovell b. 1913. Sir Hall Caine d. 1931

PHENOMENA

August 2^{d} 03^{h} Jupiter in conjunction with the Moon. Jupiter 2° N.

4^{d} 16^{h} Venus in conjunction with the Moon. Venus 5° S.

4^{d} 23^{h} Mars in conjunction with the Moon. Mars 0°·2 N.

5^{d} 19^{h} Mercury at greatest eastern elongation (27°).

9^{d} 14^{h} Mercury in conjunction with the Moon. Mercury 8° S.

23^{d} 07^{h} Saturn in conjunction with the Moon. Saturn 3° N.

24^{d} 20^{h} Saturn at opposition.

28^{d} 11^{h} Venus in conjunction with Mars. Venus 4° S.

29^{d} 10^{h} Venus at greatest western elongation. (46°).

29^{d} 13^{h} Jupiter in conjunction with the Moon. Jupiter 2° N.

CONSTELLATIONS

The following constellations are near the meridian at

	d	h		d	h
July	1	24	July	16	23
Aug.	1	22	Aug.	16	21
Sept.	1	20	Sept.	15	19

Draco, Hercules, Lyra, Cygnus, Sagitta, Ophiuchus, Serpens, Aquila and Sagittarius.

MINIMA OF ALGOL

d	h	d	h
3	08	17	16
6	05	20	13
9	01	23	09
11	22	26	06
14	19	29	03

PHASES OF THE MOON

	d	h	m
☾ Last Quarter	1	03	29
● New Moon	7	19	17
☽ First Quarter	15	03	19
○ Full Moon	23	05	25
☾ Last Quarter	30	09	15

	d	h
Perigee (225,600 miles)	5	15
Apogee (251,380 „)	17	12

Mean Longitude of Ascending Node on August 1, 90°.

See note on *Summer Time*, page 98.

MONTHLY NOTES

August 1. Lammas. Scottish Term Day.

3. Bank and General Holiday, Gt. Britain and N. Ireland.

5. Oyster season opens.

11. Half-Quarter Day, Eng. and W.

12. Grouse shooting begins.

Day	THE SUN s.d. 15′·8								Sidereal Time	Transit of First Point of Aries
	Right Ascension	Dec. +	Equation of Time	Rise 52°	Rise 56°	Transit	Set 52°	Set 56°		
	h m s	° ′	m s	h m	h m	h m	h m	h m	h m s	h m s
1	8 44 46	18 04	− 6 15	4 21	4 03	12 06	19 51	20 09	20 38 31	3 20 56
2	8 48 39	17 49	− 6 12	4 22	4 05	12 06	19 49	20 07	20 42 28	3 17 00
3	8 52 31	17 34	− 6 07	4 24	4 07	12 06	19 47	20 04	20 46 24	3 13 04
4	8 56 23	17 18	− 6 02	4 25	4 08	12 06	19 45	20 02	20 50 21	3 09 08
5	9 00 14	17 02	− 5 57	4 27	4 10	12 06	19 44	20 00	20 54 17	3 05 12
6	9 04 04	16 46	− 5 51	4 29	4 12	12 06	19 42	19 58	20 58 14	3 01 16
7	9 07 54	16 29	− 5 44	4 30	4 14	12 06	19 40	19 56	21 02 10	2 57 21
8	9 11 44	16 12	− 5 37	4 32	4 16	12 06	19 38	19 54	21 06 07	2 53 25
9	9 15 32	15 55	− 5 29	4 33	4 18	12 05	19 36	19 52	21 10 03	2 49 29
10	9 19 20	15 38	− 5 20	4 35	4 20	12 05	19 34	19 49	21 14 00	2 45 33
11	9 23 08	15 20	− 5 11	4 37	4 22	12 05	19 32	19 47	21 17 57	2 41 37
12	9 26 55	15 02	− 5 02	4 38	4 24	12 05	19 30	19 45	21 21 53	2 37 41
13	9 30 41	14 44	− 4 52	4 40	4 26	12 05	19 29	19 42	21 25 50	2 33 45
14	9 34 27	14 26	− 4 41	4 42	4 28	12 05	19 27	19 40	21 29 46	2 29 49
15	9 38 12	14 07	− 4 29	4 43	4 30	12 04	19 25	19 38	21 33 43	2 25 53
16	9 41 57	13 48	− 4 18	4 45	4 32	12 04	19 23	19 35	21 37 39	2 21 57
17	9 45 41	13 29	− 4 05	4 46	4 34	12 04	19 21	19 33	21 41 36	2 18 01
18	9 49 25	13 10	− 3 52	4 48	4 36	12 04	19 18	19 31	21 45 32	2 14 06
19	9 53 08	12 51	− 3 39	4 50	4 38	12 04	19 16	19 28	21 49 29	2 10 10
20	9 56 50	12 31	− 3 25	4 51	4 40	12 03	19 14	19 26	21 53 26	2 06 14
21	10 00 32	12 11	− 3 10	4 53	4 42	12 03	19 12	19 23	21 57 22	2 02 18
22	10 04 14	11 51	− 2 56	4 55	4 44	12 03	19 10	19 21	22 01 19	1 58 22
23	10 07 55	11 31	− 2 40	4 56	4 46	12 03	19 08	19 18	22 05 15	1 54 26
24	10 11 36	11 10	− 2 24	4 58	4 47	12 02	19 06	19 16	22 09 12	1 50 30
25	10 15 16	10 50	− 2 08	4 59	4 49	12 02	19 04	19 13	22 13 08	1 46 34
26	10 18 56	10 29	− 1 52	5 01	4 51	12 02	19 01	19 11	22 17 05	1 42 38
27	10 22 36	10 08	− 1 35	5 03	4 53	12 01	18 59	19 08	22 21 01	1 38 42
28	10 26 15	9 47	− 1 17	5 04	4 55	12 01	18 57	19 06	22 24 58	1 34 46
29	10 29 54	9 26	− 0 59	5 06	4 57	12 01	18 55	19 03	22 28 55	1 30 51
30	10 33 32	9 05	− 0 41	5 08	4 59	12 01	18 53	19 01	22 32 51	1 26 55
31	10 37 10	8 43	− 0 23	5 09	5 01	12 00	18 50	18 58	22 36 48	1 22 59

Duration of Civil (C), Nautical (N), and Astronomical (A), Twilight (in minutes)

Lat.	Aug. 1			Aug. 11			Aug. 21			Aug. 31		
°	C	N	A	C	N	A	C	N	A	C	N	A
52	41	97	177	39	89	153	37	83	138	35	79	127
56	48	120	T.A.N.	45	106	205	42	96	166	40	89	147

ASTRONOMICAL NOTES

MERCURY is not suitably placed for observation despite the fact that it is at greatest eastern elongation on the 5th.

VENUS is a brilliant morning star, magnitude −4·1, visible in the eastern sky long before dawn. It is interesting to note that Mars had overtaken Venus in July while the latter was near a stationary point. However Venus is now accelerating (as seen from the Earth) and passes Mars shortly before the end of the month.

MARS is a morning star, magnitude +1·7, drawing very slowly away from the Sun. On the morning of the 5th Mars will be seen only a few degrees west of the thin crescent Moon. Mars is moving eastwards in the constellation of Gemini. Because the distance of Mars from the Sun is now increasing the planet is actually $0^{m}\cdot4$ fainter than in February (when conjunction occurred) whilst Mars was almost at perihelion.

JUPITER is a conspicuous morning star, magnitude −2·0, in the constellation of Taurus. The Moon passes 2° S. of Jupiter on 2^{d} 03^{h} and again on 29^{d} 13^{h}.

SATURN, magnitude +0·6, is at opposition on the 24th and is thus visible all night.

METEORS. The maximum of the Perseid meteor shower occurs on the evening of the 11th. Conditions are favourable for observation as the Moon, only 4 days old, sets at about 21^{h} 30^{m}.

THE MOON

Day	R.A.	Dec.	Hor. Par.	Semi-diam.	Sun's Co-long.	P.A. of Bright Limb	Phase	Age	Rise 52°	Rise 56°	Transit	Set 52°	Set 56°
	h m	°	′	′	°	°		d	h m	h m	h m	h m	h m
1	2 24	+ 9·8	58·6	16·0	183	71	52	22·5	23 17	23 04	5 57	13 18	13 29
2	3 17	+14·7	59·2	16·1	195	74	40	23·5	23 45	23 27	6 50	14 40	14 57
3	4 14	+18·9	59·7	16·3	207	79	29	24·5	..	23 59	7 46	16 02	16 24
4	5 15	+22·0	60·1	16·4	220	85	19	25·5	0 22	..	8 46	17 19	17 46
5	6 18	+23·6	60·4	16·4	232	92	11	26·5	1 12	0 45	9 49	18 26	18 53
6	7 23	+23·7	60·4	16·5	244	101	5	27·5	2 16	1 49	10 52	19 19	19 43
7	8 26	+22·0	60·2	16·4	256	118	1	28·5	3 32	3 08	11 53	19 59	20 18
8	9 27	+19·0	59·7	16·3	269	234	0	0·2	4 54	4 36	12 50	20 29	20 43
9	10 24	+14·8	59·1	16·1	281	276	2	1·2	6 17	6 04	13 43	20 52	21 01
10	11 18	+ 9·9	58·3	15·9	293	284	6	2·2	7 37	7 30	14 33	21 12	21 16
11	12 08	+ 4·7	57·5	15·7	305	288	13	3·2	8 54	8 52	15 19	21 29	21 29
12	12 57	− 0·6	56·6	15·4	318	289	21	4·2	10 08	10 10	16 04	21 46	21 41
13	13 43	− 5·7	55·9	15·2	330	289	30	5·2	11 20	11 27	16 47	22 03	21 54
14	14 30	−10·5	55·2	15·0	342	288	39	6·2	12 30	12 42	17 31	22 22	22 09
15	15 16	−14·7	54·7	14·9	354	285	49	7·2	13 39	13 56	18 16	22 44	22 27
16	16 04	−18·3	54·4	14·8	7	282	58	8·2	14 47	15 07	19 02	23 11	22 50
17	16 53	−21·1	54·2	14·8	19	277	67	9·2	15 51	16 15	19 50	23 45	23 20
18	17 44	−23·0	54·2	14·8	31	272	76	10·2	16 49	17 16	20 39	..	..
19	18 35	−23·8	54·4	14·8	43	266	83	11·2	17 40	18 07	21 29	0 28	0 01
20	19 28	−23·6	54·6	14·9	55	259	90	12·2	18 22	18 46	22 20	1 20	0 54
21	20 21	−22·3	55·0	15·0	68	251	95	13·2	18 56	19 17	23 10	2 22	1 58
22	21 13	−19·8	55·5	15·1	80	239	98	14·2	19 23	19 39	23 58	3 30	3 10
23	22 04	−16·4	56·0	15·2	92	192	100	15·2	19 46	19 58	..	4 43	4 28
24	22 54	−12·2	56·5	15·4	104	95	99	16·2	20 06	20 12	0 46	5 57	5 47
25	23 43	− 7·3	57·0	15·5	116	79	96	17·2	20 23	20 26	1 33	7 13	7 08
26	0 32	− 2·0	57·5	15·7	128	74	91	18·2	20 41	20 39	2 19	8 29	8 29
27	1 21	+ 3·4	57·9	15·8	141	73	84	19·2	21 00	20 53	3 06	9 47	9 52
28	2 12	+ 8·8	58·3	15·9	153	73	76	20·2	21 21	21 09	3 55	11 07	11 17
29	3 05	+13·8	58·7	16·0	165	75	65	21·2	21 46	21 29	4 46	12 28	12 44
30	4 00	+18·1	59·1	16·1	177	79	54	22·2	22 19	21 58	5 40	13 49	14 10
31	4 58	+21·5	59·3	16·2	189	84	43	23·2	23 03	22 37	6 37	15 07	15 32

MERCURY ☿

Day	R.A.	Dec. +	Diam.	Phase	Transit	
	h m	°	″		h m	
1	10 29	8·8	7	55	13 50	Mercury is too close to the Sun for observation
4	10 40	7·1	7	51	13 50	
7	10 50	5·5	8	46	13 47	
10	10 58	4·0	8	41	13 43	
13	11 04	2·8	9	36	13 37	
16	11 08	1·8	9	30	13 29	

Day	R.A.	Dec. +	Diam.	Phase	Transit	
	h m	°	″		h m	
16	11 08	1·8	9	30	13 29	Mercury is too close to the Sun for observation
19	11 10	1·1	9	24	13 18	
22	11 08	0·9	10	18	13 04	
25	11 03	1·1	10	12	12 47	
28	10 56	1·9	11	6	12 28	
31	10 47	3·1	11	2	12 07	

VENUS ♀

Day	R.A.	Dec. +	Diam.	Phase	5° high E. 52°	5° high E. 56°	Transit
	h m		″		h m	h m	h m
1	5 48	18·5	34	32	2 05	1 52	9 09
6	6 02	18·8	32	35	1 57	1 44	9 03
11	6 17	19·0	30	39	1 52	1 38	8 59
16	6 34	19·2	28	42	1 48	1 34	8 57
21	6 53	19·3	26	45	1 46	1 33	8 55
26	7 12	19·2	25	48	1 46	1 33	8 55
31	7 32	19·0	23	51	1 48	1 35	8 56

MARS ♂

Day	R.A.	Dec. +	Diam.	Phase	5° high E. 52°	5° high E. 56°	Transit
	h m	°	″		h m	h m	h m
1	6 04	23·8	4	96	1 48	1 29	9 25
6	6 18	23·8	4	95	1 43	1 24	9 20
11	6 33	23·7	4	95	1 38	1 19	9 14
16	6 47	23·6	4	95	1 34	1 15	9 09
21	7 01	23·3	4	94	1 30	1 12	9 03
26	7 15	23·0	5	94	1 26	1 08	8 58
31	7 29	22·6	5	94	1 23	1 05	8 52

SUNRISE AND SUNSET (G.M.T.)

Day	London		Bristol		Birmingham		Manchester		Newcastle		Glasgow		Belfast	
	a.m.	p.m.	a.m.	p.m.	a.m.	p.m.	a.m.	p.m.	a.m.	p.m.	a.m.	p.m.	a.m.	p.m.
	h m	h m	h m	h m	h m	h m	h m	h m	h m	h m	h m	h m	h m	h m
1	4 23	7 49	4 33	7 59	4 26	8 00	4 23	8 06	4 14	8 10	4 21	8 25	4 33	8 26
2	4 24	7 47	4 34	7 57	4 27	7 58	4 25	8 04	4 16	8 08	4 23	8 23	4 35	8 24
3	4 26	7 45	4 36	7 55	4 29	7 56	4 27	8 02	4 18	8 05	4 25	8 20	4 37	8 22
4	4 27	7 43	4 37	7 53	4 30	7 54	4 28	8 00	4 19	8 03	4 26	8 18	4 38	8 20
5	4 29	7 42	4 39	7 52	4 32	7 53	4 30	7 59	4 21	8 02	4 28	8 16	4 40	8 18
6	4 31	7 40	4 41	7 50	4 34	7 51	4 32	7 57	4 23	8 00	4 30	8 14	4 42	8 16
7	4 32	7 38	4 42	7 48	4 35	7 49	4 34	7 55	4 25	7 58	4 32	8 12	4 44	8 14
8	4 34	7 37	4 44	7 46	4 37	7 47	4 35	7 53	4 26	7 56	4 34	8 10	4 46	8 12
9	4 35	7 35	4 45	7 44	4 38	7 45	4 37	7 51	4 28	7 54	4 36	8 08	4 48	8 10
10	4 37	7 33	4 47	7 42	4 40	7 43	4 39	7 48	4 30	7 51	4 38	8 05	4 50	8 07
11	4 39	7 31	4 49	7 40	4 42	7 41	4 41	7 46	4 32	7 49	4 40	8 03	4 52	8 05
12	4 40	7 29	4 50	7 39	4 44	7 39	4 43	7 44	4 34	7 47	4 42	8 01	4 54	8 03
13	4 42	7 28	4 52	7 37	4 46	7 37	4 45	7 42	4 36	7 44	4 44	7 58	4 55	8 01
14	4 43	7 26	4 53	7 35	4 47	7 35	4 46	7 40	4 38	7 42	4 46	7 56	4 57	7 59
15	4 45	7 24	4 55	7 33	4 49	7 33	4 48	7 38	4 40	7 40	4 48	7 54	4 59	7 57
16	4 46	7 22	4 56	7 31	4 51	7 31	4 50	7 36	4 42	7 38	4 50	7 52	5 01	7 55
17	4 48	7 20	4 58	7 29	4 52	7 29	4 51	7 34	4 43	7 36	4 51	7 50	5 02	7 53
18	4 49	7 17	4 59	7 27	4 54	7 26	4 53	7 31	4 45	7 33	4 53	7 48	5 04	7 50
19	4 51	7 15	5 01	7 25	4 56	7 24	4 55	7 29	4 47	7 31	4 55	7 45	5 06	7 48
20	4 52	7 13	5 02	7 23	4 57	7 22	4 56	7 27	4 49	7 29	4 57	7 43	5 08	7 46
21	4 54	7 11	5 04	7 21	4 59	7 20	4 58	7 25	4 51	7 26	4 59	7 40	5 10	7 43
22	4 56	7 09	5 06	7 19	5 01	7 18	5 00	7 23	4 53	7 24	5 01	7 38	5 11	7 41
23	4 57	7 07	5 07	7 17	5 02	7 16	5 01	7 21	4 55	7 21	5 03	7 35	5 13	7 39
24	4 59	7 05	5 09	7 15	5 04	7 14	5 03	7 19	4 56	7 19	5 04	7 33	5 15	7 37
25	5 00	7 03	5 10	7 13	5 05	7 12	5 05	7 16	4 58	7 16	5 06	7 30	5 17	7 34
26	5 02	7 00	5 12	7 10	5 07	7 09	5 07	7 14	5 00	7 14	5 08	7 28	5 19	7 32
27	5 04	6 58	5 14	7 08	5 09	7 07	5 08	7 12	5 02	7 12	5 10	7 25	5 20	7 29
28	5 05	6 56	5 15	7 06	5 10	7 05	5 10	7 09	5 04	7 09	5 12	7 23	5 22	7 27
29	5 07	6 54	5 17	7 04	5 12	7 03	5 12	7 07	5 06	7 07	5 14	7 20	5 24	7 24
30	5 09	6 52	5 19	7 02	5 14	7 01	5 14	7 04	5 08	7 04	5 16	7 18	5 26	7 22
31	5 10	6 49	5 20	6 59	5 15	6 58	5 15	7 02	5 09	7 02	5 18	7 15	5 28	7 19

JUPITER ♃ — SATURN ♄

Day	Jupiter R.A.	Dec. +	5° high East 52°	5° high East 56°	Transit	Saturn R.A.	Dec. −	Transit	5° high West 52°	5° high West 56°
	h m	°	h m	h m	h m	h m	°	h m	h m	h m
1	3 24	17·5	23 42	23 31	6 44	22 24	11·8	1 45	6 07	5 52
11	3 28	17·8	23 06	22 54	6 10	22 21	12·1	1 03	5 23	5 08
21	3 32	18·0	22 30	22 18	5 34	22 18	12·4	0 21	4 39	4 24
31	3 35	18·1	21 52	21 40	4 57	22 15	12·7	23 34	3 55	3 40

Equatorial diameter of Jupiter 40″; of Saturn 19″. Diameters of Saturn's rings 43″ and 7″.

URANUS ♅ — NEPTUNE ♆

Day	Uranus R.A.	Dec. +	Transit		Neptune R.A.	Dec. −	Transit	10° high in West 52°	10° high in West 56°
	h m	° ′	h m		h m	° ′	h m	h m	h m
1	10 41·4	9 05	14 01	Uranus is too close to the Sun for observation	14 52·6	14 40	18 11	21 35	21 10
11	10 43·6	8 52	13 24		14 52·7	14 41	17 32	20 56	20 31
21	10 45·9	8 38	12 47		14 53·2	14 44	16 53	20 17	19 51
31	10 48·2	8 24	12 10		14 53·8	14 47	16 14	19 38	19 12

Diameter 4″ (Uranus)   Diameter 2″ (Neptune)

Septem (seven), 7th month of Roman (pre-Julian) Calendar.

Sun's Longitude 180° ♎ $23^d\ 00^h$

Day of Month	Day of Week	
1	Tu.	Louis XIV d. 1715. W. W. Jacobs d. 1943
2	W.	Fire of London 1666. Omdurman 1898
3	Th.	Britain at War 1939. Allies landed in Italy 1943
4	F.	French Republic proclaimed 1870
5	S.	John Wisden b. 1826
6	S.	15th Sunday after Trinity. Edmund Gwenn d. 1959
7	M.	King Baudouin b. 1930. C. B. Fry d. 1956
8	Tu.	King Feisal I d. 1933. Richard Strauss d. 1949
9	W.	Flodden 1513
10	Th.	Terence O'Neill b. 1914. W. S. Blunt d. 1922
11	F.	Malplaquet 1709. J. C. Smuts d. 1950
12	S.	Blücher d. 1819. Guizot d. 1874
13	S.	16th S. after Trinity. Quebec 1759
14	M.	Wellington d. 1852. Hon. Angus Ogilvy b. 1928
15	Tu.	Battle of Britain Day. I. K. Brunel d. 1859
16	W.	Fire of Moscow 1812. Sir Ronald Ross d. 1932
17	Th.	Smollett d. 1771. W. S. Landor d. 1864**
18	F.	Matthew Prior d. 1721. Greta Garbo b. 1905
19	S.	Poitiers 1356
20	S.	17th Sunday after Trinity. Upton Sinclair b. 1878
21	M.	St. Matthew. King Haakon VII. d. 1957
22	Tu.	Boulogne reoccupied 1944. Ian Hay d. 1952 [1962
23	W.	Walter Lippmann b. 1889. Louis de Soissons d.
24	Th.	Sir A. P. Herbert b. 1890. Sir Howard Florey b. 1898
25	F.	Johann Strauss d. 1849. W. M. Hughes b. 1864**
26	S.	Pope Paul VI. b. 1897. W. H. Davies d. 1940.
27	S.	18th Sunday after Trinity. Adelina Patti d. 1919
28	M.	Louis Pasteur d. 1895
29	Tu.	St. Michael and All Angels. Zola d. 1902
30	W.	Donald Swann b. 1923. Calais reoccupied 1944

PHENOMENA

September $2^d\ 07^h$ Mercury in inferior conjunction with the Sun.

$2^d\ 13^h$ Mars in conjunction with the Moon. Mars 1° S.

$2^d\ 16^h$ Venus in conjunction with the Moon. Venus 5° S.

$2^d\ 22^h$ Uranus in conjunction with the Sun.

$6^d\ 14^h$ Pluto in conjunction with the Sun.

$18^d\ 12^h$ Mercury at greatest western elongation (18°).

$19^d\ 11^h$ Saturn in conjunction with the Moon. Saturn 3° N.

$23^d\ 00^h$ Autumnal Equinox.

$25^d\ 19^h$ Jupiter in conjunction with the Moon. Jupiter 1° N.

CONSTELLATIONS

The following constellations are near the meridian at

	d	h		d	h
Aug.	1	24	Aug.	16	23
Sept.	1	22	Sept.	15	21
Oct.	1	20	Oct.	16	19

Draco, Cepheus, Lyra, Cygnus, Vulpecula, Sagitta, Delphinus, Equuleus, Aquila, Aquarius and Capricornus.

MINIMA OF ALGOL

d	h	d	h
1	00	18	05
3	21	21	02
6	18	23	22
9	14	26	19
12	11	29	16
15	08		

PHASES OF THE MOON

	d	h	m
● New Moon	6	04	34
☽ First Quarter	13	21	24
○ Full Moon	21	17	31
☾ Last Quarter	28	15	01

	d	h
Perigee (228,690 miles) ...	2	02
Apogee (251,090 „) ...	14	07
Perigee (229,660 „) ...	27	05

Mean Longitude of Ascending Node on September 1, 88°.

See note on *Summer Time*, page 98.

MONTHLY NOTES

September 1. Partridge shooting begins. Salmon close-time begins.

7. Jewish New Year (A.M. 5725).
8. Malta's National Day (1565).
16. Yom Kippur (Jewish Day of Atonement).
21. Harvest Moon.
28. Sheriffs of London to be sworn in.
29. Michaelmas. Quarter day. Lord Mayor of London elected.
—. County Quarter Sessions, Eng. and W., to be held within the period of 21 days immediately preceding or following Sept. 29.

** Centenary.

Day	The Sun s.d. 15′·9								Sidereal Time	Transit of First Point of Aries
	Right Ascension	Dec.	Equation of Time	Rise 52°	Rise 56°	Transit	Set 52°	Set 56°		
	h m s	° ′	m s	h m	h m	h m	h m	h m	h m s	h m s
1	10 40 48	+8 21	− 0 04	5 11	5 03	12 00	18 48	18 56	22 40 44	1 19 03
2	10 44 26	+8 00	+ 0 15	5 12	5 05	12 00	18 46	18 53	22 44 41	1 15 07
3	10 48 03	+7 38	+ 0 34	5 14	5 07	11 59	18 44	18 50	22 48 37	1 11 11
4	10 51 40	+7 16	+ 0 53	5 16	5 09	11 59	18 41	18 48	22 52 34	1 07 15
5	10 55 17	+6 53	+ 1 13	5 17	5 11	11 59	18 39	18 45	22 56 30	1 03 19
6	10 58 54	+6 31	+ 1 33	5 19	5 13	11 58	18 37	18 43	23 00 27	0 59 23
7	11 02 30	+6 09	+ 1 53	5 21	5 15	11 58	18 34	18 40	23 04 24	0 55 27
8	11 06 06	+5 46	+ 2 14	5 22	5 17	11 58	18 32	18 37	23 08 20	0 51 31
9	11 09 42	+5 24	+ 2 34	5 24	5 19	11 57	18 30	18 35	23 12 17	0 47 36
10	11 13 18	+5 01	+ 2 55	5 26	5 21	11 57	18 27	18 32	23 16 13	0 43 40
11	11 16 54	+4 38	+ 3 16	5 27	5 23	11 57	18 25	18 29	23 20 10	0 39 44
12	11 20 29	+4 15	+ 3 37	5 29	5 25	11 56	18 23	18 27	23 24 06	0 35 48
13	11 24 05	+3 52	+ 3 58	5 30	5 27	11 56	18 20	18 24	23 28 03	0 31 52
14	11 27 40	+3 29	+ 4 19	5 32	5 29	11 56	18 18	18 21	23 31 59	0 27 56
15	11 31 15	+3 06	+ 4 40	5 34	5 31	11 55	18 16	18 19	23 35 56	0 24 00
16	11 34 51	+2 43	+ 5 02	5 35	5 33	11 55	18 13	18 16	23 39 53	0 20 04
17	11 38 26	+2 20	+ 5 23	5 37	5 35	11 54	18 11	18 13	23 43 49	0 16 08
18	11 42 01	+1 57	+ 5 44	5 39	5 36	11 54	18 09	18 11	23 47 46	0 12 12
19	11 45 36	+1 34	+ 6 06	5 40	5 38	11 54	18 06	18 08	23 51 42	0 08 16
20	11 49 11	+1 10	+ 6 27	5 42	5 40	11 53	18 04	18 05	23 55 39	0 04 21
21	11 52 47	+0 47	+ 6 49	5 44	5 42	11 53	18 02	18 03	23 59 35	{00 00 25 {23 56 29
22	11 56 22	+0 24	+ 7 10	5 45	5 44	11 53	17 59	18 00	0 03 32	23 52 33
23	11 59 57	0 00	+ 7 31	5 47	5 46	11 52	17 57	17 57	0 07 28	23 48 37
24	12 03 33	−0 23	+ 7 52	5 48	5 48	11 52	17 55	17 55	0 11 25	23 44 41
25	12 07 09	−0 46	+ 8 13	5 50	5 50	11 52	17 52	17 52	0 15 21	23 40 45
26	12 10 45	−1 10	+ 8 33	5 52	5 52	11 51	17 50	17 49	0 19 18	23 36 49
27	12 14 21	−1 33	+ 8 54	5 54	5 54	11 51	17 48	17 47	0 23 15	23 32 53
28	12 17 57	−1 57	+ 9 14	5 55	5 56	11 51	17 46	17 44	0 27 11	23 28 57
29	12 21 33	−2 20	+ 9 34	5 57	5 58	11 50	17 44	17 42	0 31 08	23 25 01
30	12 25 10	−2 43	+ 9 54	5 58	6 00	11 50	17 41	17 39	0 35 04	23 21 06

Duration of Civil (C), Nautical (N), and Astronomical (A), Twilight (in minutes)

Lat.	Sept. 1			Sept. 11			Sept. 21			Sept. 30		
°	C	N	A	C	N	A	C	N	A	C	N	A
52	35	79	127	34	76	120	34	74	115	34	73	113
56	39	89	146	38	84	135	37	82	129	37	80	126

ASTRONOMICAL NOTES

MERCURY becomes a morning star (magnitude +1·5 to −1·0) after the first ten days of the month when it may be seen low above the E. horizon at the beginning of civil twilight. This is the most suitable morning apparition of the year for observers in the northern hemisphere.

VENUS is a brilliant morning star, magnitude −3·8, visible in the eastern skies for several hours before dawn. An interesting spectacle will be afforded to observers on the mornings of the 2nd and 3rd with the old crescent Moon passing south of the Twins and north of the planets Venus and Mars.

MARS is a morning star, magnitude +1·6, and visible low in the eastern sky before 02^h. During the month Mars moves from Gemini into Cancer.

JUPITER is a conspicuous morning star, magnitude −2·2, situated about 6° S.S.W. of the Pleiades. On the late evening of the 25th, at moonrise, Jupiter will be seen only a few degrees above the gibbous Moon.

SATURN is an evening star, magnitude +0·7, retrograding in Aquarius.

ZODIACAL LIGHT. The morning cone may be seen stretching up from the eastern horizon before the beginning of twilight, between the 5th and the 20th. However the presence of Venus will again interfere with observation.

THE MOON

Day	R.A.	Dec.	Hor. Par.	Semi-diam.	Sun's Co-long.	P.A. of Bright Limb	Phase	Age	Rise 52°	Rise 56°	Transit	Set 52°	Set 56°
	h m	°	′	′	°	°		d	h m	h m	h m	h m	h m
1	5 59	+23·5	59·5	16·2	202	90	32	24·2	..	23 33	7 37	16 16	16 43
2	7 02	+24·0	59·6	16·2	214	97	22	25·2	0 00	..	8 38	17 12	17 38
3	8 04	+22·9	59·5	16·2	226	105	13	26·2	1 10	0 45	9 39	17 55	18 17
4	9 05	+20·3	59·3	16·2	238	113	6	27·2	2 28	2 08	10 37	18 28	18 44
5	10 03	+16·5	58·9	16·1	251	125	2	28·2	3 50	3 35	11 31	18 53	19 05
6	10 57	+11·9	58·4	15·9	263	175	0	29·2	5 12	5 02	12 22	19 14	19 20
7	11 49	+ 6·7	57·8	15·8	275	268	1	0·8	6 31	6 26	13 09	19 32	19 34
8	12 38	+ 1·3	57·1	15·6	287	282	4	1·8	7 47	7 47	13 55	19 49	19 47
9	13 26	− 4·0	56·4	15·4	299	285	9	2·8	9 01	9 06	14 40	20 06	19 59
10	14 13	− 9·0	55·7	15·2	312	286	16	3·8	10 13	10 23	15 24	20 24	20 13
11	15 00	−13·5	55·2	15·0	324	284	24	4·8	11 24	11 39	16 09	20 45	20 29
12	15 48	−17·4	54·7	14·9	336	282	32	5·8	12 33	12 53	16 55	21 10	20 50
13	16 37	−20·5	54·4	14·8	348	278	42	6·8	13 39	14 03	17 43	21 41	21 17
14	17 27	−22·7	54·3	14·8	1	273	51	7·8	14 40	15 07	18 31	22 20	21 53
15	18 18	−23·9	54·3	14·8	13	268	60	8·8	15 34	16 02	19 21	23 09	22 41
16	19 10	−24·0	54·5	14·9	25	262	69	9·8	16 19	16 45	20 11	..	23 41
17	20 03	−23·0	54·9	15·0	37	257	78	10·8	16 56	17 18	21 01	0 07	..
18	20 55	−20·9	55·4	15·1	49	251	85	11·8	17 25	17 44	21 51	1 13	0 51
19	21 47	−17·8	55·9	15·2	62	244	92	12·8	17 50	18 03	22 39	2 24	2 07
20	22 37	−13·7	56·6	15·4	74	236	96	13·8	18 10	18 19	23 26	3 39	3 26
21	23 27	− 8·9	57·2	15·6	86	218	99	14·8	18 29	18 33	..	4 55	4 48
22	0 17	− 3·6	57·8	15·8	98	122	100	15·8	18 46	18 46	0 14	6 13	6 11
23	1 07	+ 2·0	58·4	15·9	110	83	98	16·8	19 04	18 59	1 01	7 32	7 36
24	1 58	+ 7·6	58·8	16·0	122	77	94	17·8	19 25	19 14	1 50	8 54	9 02
25	2 51	+12·8	59·1	16·1	135	77	87	18·8	19 49	19 33	2 41	10 16	10 30
26	3 47	+17·5	59·3	16·1	147	79	78	19·8	20 19	19 59	3 35	11 39	11 59
27	4 45	+21·1	59·3	16·2	159	83	68	20·8	20 59	20 34	4 32	12 59	13 23
28	5 45	+23·4	59·3	16·2	171	89	57	21·8	21 52	21 24	5 32	14 11	14 38
29	6 47	+24·2	59·2	16·1	183	95	46	22·8	22 57	22 30	6 32	15 10	15 37
30	7 49	+23·5	59·0	16·1	195	101	35	23·8	..	23 49	7 32	15 56	16 19

MERCURY ☿

Day	R.A.	Dec. +	Diam.	Phase	5° high E. 52°	5° high E. 56°	Transit	Day	R.A.	Dec. +	Diam.	Phase	5° high E. 52°	5° high E. 56°	Transit
	h m	°	″		h m	h m	h m		h m	°	″		h m	h m	h m
1	10 44	3·6	11	1	6 15	6 15	11 59	16	10 30	9·5	8	37	4 34	4 29	10 50
4	10 34	5·2	10	1	5 45	5 44	11 38	19	10 41	9·2	7	50	4 35	4 30	10 49
7	10 27	6·9	10	5	5 18	5 16	11 20	22	10 55	8·3	6	64	4 42	4 39	10 52
10	10 23	8·3	9	13	4 56	4 52	11 05	25	11 12	7·0	6	75	4 55	4 52	10 58
13	10 24	9·2	8	24	4 41	4 36	10 55	28	11 31	5·2	6	84	5 11	5 10	11 05
16	10 30	9·5	8	37	4 34	4 29	10 50	31	11 50	3·2	5	90	5 29	5 30	11 12

VENUS ♀

Day	R.A.	Dec. +	Diam.	Phase	5° high E. 52°	5° high E. 56°	Transit
	h m	°	″		h m	h m	h m
1	7 36	18·9	23	51	1 49	1 36	8 56
6	7 57	18·4	22	54	1 53	1 40	8 57
11	8 19	17·8	21	57	1 58	1 46	8 59
16	8 41	16·9	20	59	2 05	1 54	9 01
21	9 03	15·9	19	61	2 14	2 03	9 04
26	9 25	14·6	18	63	2 23	2 14	9 06
31	9 47	13·2	18	65	2 33	2 26	9 09

MARS ♂

Day	R.A.	Dec. +	Diam.	Phase	5° high E. 52°	5° high E. 56°	Transit
	h m	°	″		h m	h m	h m
1	7 32	22·6	5	94	1 22	1 05	8 50
6	7 45	22·1	5	94	1 19	1 02	8 44
11	7 59	21·6	5	93	1 15	0 59	8 38
16	8 12	21·0	5	93	1 12	0 57	8 31
21	8 24	20·4	5	93	1 09	0 54	8 24
26	8 37	19·7	5	93	1 06	0 52	8 17
31	8 49	19·0	5	92	1 03	0 50	8 10

SUNRISE AND SUNSET (G.M.T.)

Day	London		Bristol		Birmingham		Manchester		Newcastle		Glasgow		Belfast	
	a.m.	p.m.	a.m.	p.m.	a.m.	p.m.	a.m.	p.m.	a.m.	p.m.	a.m.	p.m.	a.m.	p.m.
	h m	h m	h m	h m	h m	h m	h m	h m	h m	h m	h m	h m	h m	h m
1	5 12	6 47	5 22	6 57	5 17	6 56	5 17	7 00	5 11	7 00	5 20	7 13	5 30	7 17
2	5 13	6 45	5 23	6 55	5 18	6 54	5 19	6 57	5 13	6 57	5 22	7 10	5 32	7 14
3	5 15	6 43	5 25	6 53	5 20	6 52	5 21	6 55	5 15	6 54	5 24	7 07	5 34	7 12
4	5 17	6 40	5 27	6 50	5 22	6 49	5 23	6 52	5 17	6 52	5 26	7 05	5 36	7 09
5	5 18	6 38	5 28	6 48	5 23	6 47	5 24	6 50	5 19	6 49	5 28	7 02	5 37	7 07
6	5 20	6 36	5 30	6 46	5 25	6 44	5 26	6 47	5 21	6 47	5 30	7 00	5 39	7 04
7	5 22	6 34	5 32	6 43	5 27	6 42	5 28	6 45	5 23	6 44	5 32	6 57	5 41	7 02
8	5 23	6 32	5 33	6 41	5 29	6 40	5 30	6 43	5 25	6 41	5 34	6 54	5 43	7 00
9	5 25	6 30	5 35	6 39	5 31	6 37	5 32	6 40	5 27	6 39	5 36	6 52	5 45	6 57
10	5 27	6 27	5 37	6 36	5 32	6 35	5 33	6 38	5 28	6 37	5 38	6 49	5 46	6 55
11	5 28	6 25	5 38	6 34	5 34	6 32	5 35	6 35	5 30	6 34	5 40	6 46	5 48	6 52
12	5 30	6 23	5 40	6 32	5 36	6 30	5 37	6 33	5 32	6 32	5 42	6 44	5 50	6 50
13	5 31	6 20	5 41	6 30	5 37	6 27	5 38	6 30	5 34	6 29	5 44	6 41	5 52	6 47
14	5 32	6 18	5 42	6 28	5 39	6 25	5 40	6 28	5 36	6 26	5 46	6 38	5 54	6 44
15	5 34	6 16	5 44	6 26	5 41	6 23	5 42	6 26	5 38	6 24	5 48	6 36	5 56	6 42
16	5 36	6 13	5 46	6 23	5 42	6 20	5 43	6 23	5 40	6 21	5 50	6 33	5 58	6 39
17	5 37	6 11	5 47	6 21	5 44	6 18	5 45	6 21	5 42	6 18	5 52	6 30	6 00	6 36
18	5 39	6 09	5 49	6 19	5 46	6 16	5 47	6 19	5 43	6 16	5 53	6 28	6 02	6 34
19	5 40	6 06	5 50	6 16	5 47	6 13	5 48	6 16	5 45	6 14	5 55	6 25	6 03	6 31
20	5 42	6 04	5 52	6 14	5 49	6 11	5 50	6 14	5 47	6 11	5 57	6 22	6 05	6 29
21	5 44	6 02	5 54	6 12	5 51	6 09	5 52	6 11	5 49	6 08	5 59	6 20	6 07	6 26
22	5 45	5 59	5 55	6 09	5 52	6 06	5 54	6 09	5 51	6 06	6 01	6 17	6 09	6 24
23	5 47	5 57	5 57	6 07	5 54	6 04	5 56	6 06	5 53	6 03	6 03	6 14	6 11	6 21
24	5 48	5 55	5 58	6 05	5 55	6 02	5 57	6 04	5 54	6 01	6 05	6 12	6 12	6 19
25	5 50	5 52	6 00	6 02	5 57	5 59	5 59	6 01	5 56	5 58	6 07	6 09	6 14	6 16
26	5 52	5 50	6 02	6 00	5 59	5 57	6 01	5 59	5 58	5 56	6 09	6 06	6 16	6 14
27	5 54	5 48	6 04	5 58	6 01	5 55	6 03	5 56	6 00	5 53	6 11	6 04	6 18	6 11
28	5 55	5 46	6 05	5 56	6 02	5 53	6 05	5 54	6 02	5 51	6 13	6 01	6 20	6 09
29	5 57	5 44	6 07	5 54	6 04	5 51	6 06	5 52	6 03	5 48	6 15	5 59	6 21	6 06
30	5 58	5 41	6 08	5 51	6 05	5 48	6 08	5 49	6 05	5 46	6 17	5 56	6 23	6 04

JUPITER ♃ / SATURN ♄

Day	Jupiter R.A.	Jupiter Dec. +	Jupiter 5° high East 52°	Jupiter 5° high East 56°	Jupiter Transit	Saturn R.A.	Saturn Dec. −	Saturn Transit	Saturn 5° high West 52°	Saturn 5° high West 56°
	h m	°	h m	h m	h m	h m	°	h m	h m	h m
1	3 35	18·1	21 48	21 36	4 54	22 15	12·7	23 30	3 51	3 35
11	3 36	18·1	21 10	20 58	4 15	22 12	13·0	22 48	3 07	2 51
21	3 36	18·1	20 31	20 18	3 36	22 10	13·2	22 06	2 24	2 08
31	3 35	18·0	19 50	19 38	2 55	22 08	13·4	21 25	1 41	1 25

Equatorial diameter of Jupiter 44″; of Saturn 19″. Diameters of Saturn's rings 42″ and 8″.

URANUS ♅ / NEPTUNE ♆

Day	Uranus R.A.	Uranus Dec. +	Uranus Transit		Neptune R.A.	Neptune Dec. −	Neptune Transit	Neptune 10° high in West 52°	Neptune 10° high in West 56°
	h m	° ′	h m		h m	° ′	h m	h m	h m
1	10 48·5	8 23	12 06	Uranus is too	14 53·8	14 47	16 11	19 34	19 08
11	10 50·8	8 08	11 29	close to the	14 54·7	14 51	15 32	18 55	18 29
21	10 53·1	7 54	10 52	Sun for	14 55·7	14 56	14 54	18 16	17 50
31	10 55·4	7 41	10 15	observation	14 56·8	15 02	14 16	17 37	17 11

Uranus: Diameter 4″ — Neptune: Diameter 2″

Octo (eight), 8th month of Roman (pre-Julian) Calendar.

Sun's Longitude 210° ♏ 23^{d} 09^{h}

Day of Month	Day of Week	
1	Th.	MICHAELMAS LAW SITTINGS BEGIN
2	F.	Graham Greene b. 1904. Sir Thomas Lipton d. 1931
3	S.	William Morris d. 1896. Sir Arnold Bax d. 1953
4	S.	19th S. after Trinity. E. Hendren d. 1962
5	M.	Richard Wood b. 1920. R 101 Disaster 1930
6	Tu.	Tennyson d. 1892. R. Benaud b. 1930
7	W.	Sir Hubert Parry d. 1918. Marie Lloyd d. 1922
8	Th.	Wendell Willkie d. 1944. Kathleen Ferrier d. 1953
9	F.	Duke of Kent b. 1935. Pope Pius XII d. 1958
10	S.	Visct. Nuffield b. 1877. Sir W. Grenfell d. 1940
11	S.	20th Sunday after Trinity. Camperdown 1797
12	M.	Robert Stephenson d. 1859. Robert E. Lee d. 1870
13	Tu.	Anatole France d. 1924. Lord Passfield d. 1947
14	W.	Pres. de Valera b. 1882. Dwight D. Eisenhower b.
15	Th.	Gregorian Calendar introduced 1582 [1890
16	F.	Gen. George Marshall d. 1959
17	S.	Sir Philip Sidney d. 1586. Chopin d. 1849
18	S.	21st Sunday after Trinity. St Luke
19	M.	Swift d. 1748. Lord Rutherford d. 1937
20	Tu.	J. A. Froude d. 1894. George Woodcock b. 1904
21	W.	TRAFALGAR DAY (1805). Sir Dudley Pound d. 1943
22	Th.	Sir John Fortescue d. 1933. Lord Carson d. 1935
23	F.	Cézanne d. 1906. W. G. Grace d. 1915
24	S.	F. T. Palgrave d. 1897. Franz Lehar d. 1948
25	S.	22nd Sunday after Trinity. Picasso b. 1881
26	M.	William Hogarth d. 1764**
27	Tu.	Lascelles Abercrombie d. 1938. W. M. Hughes d.
28	W.	St. Simon and St. Jude. John Locke d. 1704 [1952
29	Th.	John Leech d. 1864**. Wilfred Rhodes b. 1877
30	F.	R. H. Mottram b. 1883. Bonar Law d. 1923
31	S.	Hallowmas Eve. Augustus John d. 1961

PHENOMENA

October 1^{d} 00^{h} Mars in conjunction with the Moon. Mars 2° S.

2^{d} 03^{h} Venus in conjunction with the Moon. Venus 5° S.

15^{d} 19^{h} Mercury in superior conjunction with the Sun.

16^{d} 18^{h} Saturn in conjunction with the Moon. Saturn 3° N.

22^{d} 23^{h} Jupiter in conjunction with the Moon. Jupiter 1° N.

29^{d} 09^{h} Mars in conjunction with the Moon. Mars 3° S.

31^{d} 23^{h} Venus in conjunction with the Moon. Venus 4° S.

CONSTELLATIONS

The following constellations are near the meridian at

	d	h		d	h
Sept.	1	24	Sept.	15	23
Oct.	1	22	Oct.	16	21
Nov.	1	20	Nov.	15	19

Ursa Major (below the Pole), Cepheus, Cassiopeia, Cygnus, Lacerta, Andromeda, Pegasus, Capricornus, Aquarius and Piscis Austrinus.

MINIMA OF ALGOL

d	h	d	h
2	13	19	18
5	10	22	15
8	07	25	11
11	03	28	08
14	00	31	05
16	21		

PHASES OF THE MOON

	d	h	m
● New Moon	5	16	20
☽ First Quarter	13	16	56
○ Full Moon	21	04	45
☾ Last Quarter	27	21	59

	d	h
Apogee (251,330 miles)...	12	03
Perigee (226,730 „)...	23	22

Mean Longitude of Ascending Node on October 1, 87°.

MONTHLY NOTES

October 1. Pheasant shooting begins.

12. Columbus Day, U.S.A.

14. Michaelmas Fire Insurances must be paid.

21. Hunter's Moon.

25. *Summer Time* ends at 2 a.m. G.M.T.

** Centenary.

Day	The Sun s.d. 16′·1 Right Ascension	Dec. −	Equation of Time	Rise 52°	Rise 56°	Transit	Set 52°	Set 56°	Sidereal Time	Transit of First Point of Aries
	h m s	° ′	m s	h m	h m	h m	h m	h m	h m s	h m s
1	12 28 47	3 07	+10 13	6 00	6 02	11 50	17 38	17 36	0 39 01	23 17 10
2	12 32 25	3 30	+10 32	6 02	6 04	11 49	17 36	17 34	0 42 57	23 13 14
3	12 36 02	3 53	+10 51	6 03	6 06	11 49	17 34	17 31	0 46 54	23 09 18
4	12 39 40	4 16	+11 10	6 05	6 08	11 49	17 31	17 28	0 50 50	23 05 22
5	12 43 19	4 39	+11 28	6 07	6 10	11 48	17 29	17 26	0 54 47	23 01 26
6	12 46 58	5 03	+11 46	6 08	6 12	11 48	17 27	17 23	0 58 44	22 57 30
7	12 50 37	5 26	+12 03	6 10	6 14	11 48	17 25	17 21	1 02 40	22 53 34
8	12 54 16	5 49	+12 20	6 12	6 16	11 48	17 22	17 18	1 06 37	22 49 38
9	12 57 56	6 11	+12 37	6 14	6 18	11 47	17 20	17 16	1 10 33	22 45 42
10	13 01 37	6 34	+12 53	6 15	6 20	11 47	17 18	17 13	1 14 30	22 41 47
11	13 05 18	6 57	+13 09	6 17	6 22	11 47	17 16	17 10	1 18 26	22 37 51
12	13 08 59	7 20	+13 24	6 19	6 24	11 46	17 13	17 08	1 22 23	22 33 55
13	13 12 41	7 42	+13 39	6 21	6 26	11 46	17 11	17 05	1 26 19	22 29 59
14	13 16 23	8 04	+13 53	6 22	6 28	11 46	17 09	17 03	1 30 16	22 26 03
15	13 20 06	8 27	+14 07	6 24	6 30	11 46	17 07	17 00	1 34 13	22 22 07
16	13 23 49	8 49	+14 20	6 26	6 32	11 46	17 05	16 58	1 38 09	22 18 11
17	13 27 33	9 11	+14 33	6 28	6 35	11 45	17 02	16 55	1 42 06	22 14 15
18	13 31 18	9 33	+14 45	6 29	6 37	11 45	17 00	16 53	1 46 02	22 10 19
19	13 35 03	9 55	+14 56	6 31	6 39	11 45	16 58	16 50	1 49 59	22 06 23
20	13 38 48	10 16	+15 07	6 33	6 41	11 45	16 56	16 48	1 53 55	22 02 27
21	13 42 35	10 38	+15 17	6 35	6 43	11 45	16 54	16 46	1 57 52	21 58 32
22	13 46 22	10 59	+15 27	6 36	6 45	11 44	16 52	16 43	2 01 48	21 54 36
23	13 50 09	11 20	+15 36	6 38	6 47	11 44	16 50	16 41	2 05 45	21 50 40
24	13 53 58	11 41	+15 44	6 40	6 49	11 44	16 48	16 38	2 09 42	21 46 44
25	13 57 47	12 02	+15 51	6 42	6 51	11 44	16 46	16 36	2 13 38	21 42 48
26	14 01 37	12 23	+15 58	6 43	6 53	11 44	16 44	16 34	2 17 35	21 38 52
27	14 05 27	12 43	+16 04	6 45	6 56	11 44	16 42	16 31	2 21 31	21 34 56
28	14 09 19	13 03	+16 09	6 47	6 58	11 44	16 40	16 29	2 25 28	21 31 00
29	14 13 11	13 23	+16 14	6 49	7 00	11 44	16 38	16 27	2 29 24	21 27 04
30	14 17 04	13 43	+16 17	6 50	7 02	11 44	16 36	16 25	2 33 21	21 23 08
31	14 20 57	14 03	+16 20	6 52	7 04	11 44	16 34	16 22	2 37 17	21 19 12

Duration of Civil (C), Nautical (N), and Astronomical (A), Twilight (in minutes)

Lat.	Oct. 1			Oct. 11			Oct. 21			Oct. 31		
°	C	N	A	C	N	A	C	N	A	C	N	A
52	34	73	113	34	73	112	34	74	113	36	75	114
56	37	80	125	37	80	124	38	81	124	40	83	126

ASTRONOMICAL NOTES

MERCURY is unsuitably placed for observation, superior conjunction occurring on the 15th.

VENUS remains a brilliant morning star, magnitude −3·6, visible in the eastern sky long before dawn. On the morning of the 5th it passes only 0°·4 S. of Regulus and on 17^d 00^h passes 0°·1 N. of Uranus.

MARS remains a morning star, magnitude +1·5, now visible in the south-eastern sky for several hours before dawn. The Moon passes 2° N. of Mars on the 1st at 00^h and again on the 29th at 09^h it passes 3°N. of the planet. Mars moves from Cancer into Leo during the month.

JUPITER is a conspicuous morning star, magnitude −2·4, retrograding on the borders of Aries and Taurus. The Moon passes 1° S. of Jupiter on the late evening of the 22nd. By the end of the month Jupiter is visible above the E.N.E. horizon before twilight has ended in the western sky. A good pair of binoculars, steadily supported, will show the four Galilean satellites. Details of the eclipses and shadow transits of its satellites are given on p. 150 for the convenience of observers with telescopes.

SATURN is an evening star, magnitude +0·8. By the end of the month it is unobservable after midnight.

The Moon

Day	R.A.	Dec.	Hor. Par.	Semi-diam.	Sun's Co-long.	P.A. of Bright Limb	Phase	Age	Rise 52°	Rise 56°	Transit	Set 52°	Set 56°
	h m	°	′	′	°	°		d	h m	h m	h m	h m	h m
1	8 49	+21·3	58·8	16·0	208	108	24	24·8	0 11	..	8 29	16 31	16 49
2	9 46	+17·9	58·4	15·9	220	113	15	25·8	1 31	1 14	9 23	16 57	17 11
3	10 40	+13·5	58·0	15·8	232	119	8	26·8	2 51	2 39	10 14	17 19	17 27
4	11 31	+ 8·5	57·6	15·7	244	126	3	27·8	4 10	4 03	11 02	17 37	17 41
5	12 21	+ 3·2	57·1	15·5	257	144	1	28·8	5 26	5 25	11 48	17 54	17 53
6	13 08	− 2·2	56·5	15·4	269	242	0	0·3	6 41	6 45	12 32	18 10	18 05
7	13 56	− 7·4	55·9	15·2	281	276	2	1·3	7 55	8 03	13 17	18 27	18 18
8	14 43	−12·2	55·4	15·1	293	281	6	2·3	9 07	9 20	14 02	18 47	18 32
9	15 31	−16·3	54·9	15·0	305	281	11	3·3	10 18	10 36	14 48	19 10	18 51
10	16 20	−19·8	54·6	14·9	318	278	18	4·3	11 26	11 49	15 35	19 38	19 15
11	17 10	−22·3	54·3	14·8	330	275	26	5·3	12 30	12 56	16 24	20 13	19 47
12	18 01	−23·9	54·2	14·8	342	270	34	6·3	13 27	13 55	17 13	20 58	20 30
13	18 53	−24·4	54·3	14·8	354	265	43	7·3	14 16	14 43	18 03	21 52	21 24
14	19 45	−23·7	54·5	14·9	6	260	53	8·3	14 55	15 20	18 52	22 54	22 30
15	20 37	−22·0	54·9	15·0	19	255	62	9·3	15 27	15 48	19 41	..	23 43
16	21 28	−19·2	55·5	15·1	31	250	71	10·3	15 53	16 08	20 29	0 03	..
17	22 18	−15·5	56·2	15·3	43	245	80	11·3	16 14	16 25	21 17	1 15	1 01
18	23 08	−11·0	57·0	15·5	55	241	88	12·3	16 33	16 39	22 04	2 31	2 21
19	23 58	− 5·8	57·8	15·7	67	237	94	13·3	16 50	16 52	22 52	3 49	3 44
20	0 48	− 0·2	58·5	15·9	79	230	98	14·3	17 08	17 05	23 41	5 08	5 09
21	1 39	+ 5·6	59·2	16·1	92	190	100	15·3	17 27	17 19	..	6 30	6 36
22	2 33	+11·2	59·7	16·3	104	90	99	16·3	17 50	17 36	0 32	7 55	8 07
23	3 29	+16·2	60·0	16·4	116	82	96	17·3	18 18	17 59	1 26	9 21	9 39
24	4 28	+20·3	60·1	16·4	128	83	89	18·3	18 56	18 31	2 24	10 45	11 09
25	5 30	+23·1	60·0	16·3	140	87	81	19·3	19 45	19 17	3 24	12 03	12 30
26	6 33	+24·4	59·7	16·3	152	93	71	20·3	20 47	20 19	4 26	13 08	13 36
27	7 35	+24·0	59·3	16·2	164	99	60	21·3	22 00	21 35	5 27	13 58	14 23
28	8 36	+22·2	58·8	16·0	177	105	49	22·3	23 18	22 59	6 25	14 36	14 56
29	9 33	+19·0	58·3	15·9	189	110	38	23·3	..	..	7 20	15 04	15 19
30	10 27	+14·8	57·8	15·7	201	114	28	24·3	0 38	0 24	8 11	15 26	15 36
31	11 19	+10·0	57·3	15·6	213	117	19	25·3	1 56	1 47	8 58	15 44	15 50

MERCURY ☿

Day	R.A.	Dec.	Diam.	Phase	Transit	
	h m	°	″		h m	
1	11 50	+3·2	5	90	11 12	Mercury is too close to the Sun for observation
4	12 09	+1·0	5	95	11 20	
7	12 29	−1·3	5	97	11 27	
10	12 48	−3·6	5	99	11 35	
13	13 07	−5·9	5	100	11 42	
16	13 26	−8·1	5	100	11 49	

Day	R.A.	Dec. −	Diam.	Phase	Transit	
	h m	°	″		h m	
16	13 26	8·1	5	100	11 49	Mercury is too close to the Sun for observation
19	13 44	10·2	5	100	11 55	
22	14 03	12·2	5	99	12 02	
25	14 21	14·2	5	99	12 08	
28	14 39	16·0	5	98	12 15	
31	14 58	17·7	5	97	12 21	

VENUS ♀

Day	R.A.	Dec. +	Diam.	Phase	5° high E. 52°	5° high E. 56°	Transit
	h m	°	″		h m	h m	h m
1	9 47	13·2	18	65	2 33	2 26	9 09
6	10 10	11·6	17	67	2 44	2 38	9 11
11	10 32	9·8	16	69	2 56	2 51	9 14
16	10 54	7·9	16	71	3 08	3 05	9 16
21	11 16	5·9	15	73	3 21	3 20	9 19
26	11 39	3·7	15	75	3 35	3 35	9 21
31	12 01	1·5	15	76	3 48	3 51	9 24

MARS ♂

Day	R.A.	Dec. +	Diam.	Phase	5° high E. 52°	5° high E. 56°	Transit
	h m	°	″		h m	h m	h m
1	8 49	19·0	5	92	1 03	0 50	8 10
6	9 02	18·2	5	92	1 00	0 47	8 02
11	9 13	17·4	5	92	0 56	0 44	7 54
16	9 25	16·6	5	91	0 52	0 42	7 46
21	9 36	15·8	5	91	0 49	0 39	7 38
26	9 47	15·0	6	91	0 44	0 35	7 29
31	9 58	14·1	6	91	0 40	0 32	7 20

SUNRISE AND SUNSET (G.M.T.)

Day	London		Bristol		Birmingham		Manchester		Newcastle		Glasgow		Belfast	
	a.m.	p.m.	a.m.	p.m.	a.m.	p.m.	a.m.	p.m.	a.m.	p.m.	a.m.	p.m.	a.m.	p.m.
	h m	h m	h m	h m	h m	h m	h m	h m	h m	h m	h m	h m	h m	h m
1	6 00	5 38	6 10	5 48	6 07	5 45	6 10	5 46	6 07	5 43	6 19	5 53	6 25	6 01
2	6 02	5 36	6 12	5 46	6 09	5 43	6 12	5 44	6 09	5 41	6 21	5 51	6 27	5 59
3	6 03	5 34	6 13	5 44	6 10	5 41	6 13	5 42	6 11	5 38	6 23	5 48	6 29	5 56
4	6 05	5 32	6 15	5 42	6 12	5 38	6 15	5 39	6 13	5 35	6 25	5 45	6 31	5 53
5	6 07	5 30	6 17	5 40	6 14	5 36	6 17	5 37	6 15	5 33	6 27	5 43	6 33	5 51
6	6 08	5 27	6 18	5 37	6 15	5 34	6 18	5 35	6 17	5 30	6 29	5 40	6 35	5 48
7	6 10	5 25	6 20	5 35	6 17	5 32	6 20	5 33	6 19	5 28	6 31	5 38	6 37	5 46
8	6 12	5 23	6 21	5 33	6 19	5 29	6 22	5 30	6 21	5 25	6 33	5 35	6 39	5 43
9	6 14	5 21	6 23	5 31	6 21	5 27	6 24	5 28	6 23	5 23	6 35	5 33	6 41	5 41
10	6 15	5 19	6 24	5 29	6 23	5 24	6 26	5 25	6 25	5 20	6 37	5 30	6 43	5 38
11	6 17	5 17	6 26	5 27	6 25	5 22	6 28	5 23	6 27	5 18	6 39	5 27	6 45	5 36
12	6 19	5 14	6 28	5 24	6 26	5 20	6 29	5 21	6 28	5 16	6 41	5 25	6 46	5 34
13	6 20	5 12	6 30	5 22	6 28	5 17	6 31	5 18	6 30	5 13	6 43	5 22	6 48	5 31
14	6 22	5 10	6 31	5 20	6 30	5 15	6 33	5 16	6 32	5 11	6 45	5 20	6 50	5 29
15	6 23	5 08	6 33	5 18	6 32	5 13	6 35	5 14	6 34	5 08	6 47	5 17	6 52	5 27
16	6 25	5 06	6 35	5 16	6 34	5 11	6 37	5 11	6 36	5 06	6 49	5 15	6 54	5 24
17	6 27	5 03	6 37	5 13	6 36	5 08	6 39	5 09	6 39	5 03	6 52	5 12	6 56	5 22
18	6 28	5 01	6 38	5 11	6 37	5 06	6 41	5 07	6 41	5 01	6 54	5 10	6 58	5 20
19	6 30	4 59	6 40	5 09	6 39	5 04	6 43	5 04	6 43	4 58	6 56	5 07	7 00	5 17
20	6 32	4 57	6 42	5 07	6 41	5 02	6 45	5 02	6 45	4 56	6 58	5 05	7 02	5 15
21	6 34	4 55	6 44	5 05	6 43	5 00	6 47	5 00	6 47	4 54	7 00	5 03	7 04	5 13
22	6 35	4 53	6 45	5 03	6 44	4 58	6 48	4 58	6 48	4 52	7 02	5 00	7 06	5 10
23	6 37	4 51	6 47	5 01	6 46	4 56	6 50	4 55	6 50	4 49	7 04	4 58	7 08	5 08
24	6 39	4 49	6 49	4 59	6 48	4 54	6 52	4 53	6 52	4 47	7 06	4 55	7 10	5 05
25	6 41	4 47	6 51	4 57	6 50	4 52	6 54	4 51	6 54	4 45	7 08	4 53	7 12	5 03
26	6 42	4 45	6 52	4 55	6 51	4 50	6 56	4 49	6 56	4 43	7 10	4 51	7 14	5 01
27	6 44	4 43	6 54	4 53	6 53	4 48	6 58	4 47	6 59	4 40	7 13	4 48	7 16	4 59
28	6 46	4 41	6 56	4 51	6 55	4 46	7 00	4 45	7 01	4 38	7 15	4 46	7 18	4 57
29	6 48	4 39	6 58	4 49	6 57	4 44	7 02	4 43	7 03	4 36	7 17	4 44	7 20	4 55
30	6 49	4 37	6 59	4 47	6 58	4 42	7 03	4 41	7 05	4 34	7 19	4 42	7 22	4 53
31	6 51	4 35	7 01	4 45	7 00	4 40	7 05	4 39	7 07	4 32	7 21	4 40	7 24	4 51

JUPITER ♃ / SATURN ♄

Day	Jupiter R.A.	Jupiter Dec. +	Jupiter 5° high East 52°	Jupiter 5° high East 56°	Jupiter Transit	Saturn R.A.	Saturn Dec. −	Saturn Transit	Saturn 5° high West 52°	Saturn 5° high West 56°
	h m	°	h m	h m	h m	h m	°	h m	h m	h m
1	3 35	18·0	19 50	19 38	2 55	22 08	13·4	21 25	1 41	1 25
11	3 32	17·8	19 09	18 57	2 13	22 06	13·5	20 44	1 00	0 43
21	3 28	17·6	18 27	18 15	1 30	22 05	13·6	20 04	0 19	0 02
31	3 23	17·3	17 45	17 33	0 46	22 04	13·6	19 24	23 35	23 18

Equatorial diameter of Jupiter 48″; of Saturn 18″. Diameters of Saturn's rings, 41″ and 8″.

URANUS ♅ / NEPTUNE ♆

Day	Uranus R.A.	Uranus Dec. +	Uranus 10° high in East 52°	Uranus 10° high in East 56°	Uranus Transit	Neptune R.A.	Neptune Dec. −	Neptune Transit	
	h m	° ′	h m	h m	h m	h m	° ′	h m	
1	10 55·4	7 41	4 41	4 42	10 15	14 56·8	15 02	14 16	Neptune is too
11	10 57·5	7 28	4 05	4 06	9 38	14 58·1	15 07	13 37	close to the
21	10 59·4	7 16	3 29	3 29	9 00	14 59·5	15 14	13 00	Sun for
31	11 01·1	7 06	2 52	2 53	8 23	15 00·9	15 20	12 22	observation

Diameter 4″ (Uranus) Diameter 2″ (Neptune)

Novem (nine), 9th month of Roman (pre-Julian) Calendar.

Sun's Longitude 240° ♐ 22d 07h

Day of Month	Day of Week	
1	S.	23rd Sunday after Trinity. All Saints.
2	M.	All Souls' Day. James Thurber d. 1961
3	Tu.	J. G. Winant d. 1947. Ralph Hodgson d. 1962
4	W.	Sir Robert Lorimer b. 1864**. Sir John Dill d. 1944
5	Th.	Guy Fawkes Day (1605). Inkerman 1854
6	F.	Sir Johnston Forbes-Robertson d. 1937 [1962
7	S.	Sir Godfrey Kneller d. 1723. Eleanor Roosevelt d.
8	S.	24th Sunday after Trinity. Tolstoy d. 1910
9	M.	Edward VII b. 1841. Neville Chamberlain d. 1940
10	Tu.	Catherine the Great d. 1796. P. Marquand b. 1893
11	W.	ARMISTICE DAY (1918). King of Sweden b. 1882
12	Th.	Mrs. Gaskell d. 1865. *Tirpitz* sunk 1944
13	F.	William Etty d. 1849. Francis Thompson d. 1907
14	S.	PRINCE OF WALES BORN (1948)
15	S.	25th Sunday after Trinity. Averill Harriman b. 1891
16	M.	Gustavus Adolphus d. 1632. Clark Gable d. 1960
17	Tu.	Visct. Montgomery b. 1887. Rodin d. 1917
18	W.	Niels Bohr d. 1962. Clifford Bax d. 1962
19	Th.	Charles I b. 1600. G. H. Elliott d. 1962
20	F.	QUEEN'S WEDDING DAY (1947) [1886
21	S.	Visct. Leathers b. 1883. Sir Harold Nicolson b.
22	S.	26th Sunday after Trinity. Pres. de Gaulle b. 1890
23	M.	Sir Arthur Pinero d. 1934. James Bone d. 1962
24	Tu.	Sir Henry Havelock d. 1857. Lilian Baylis d. 1937
25	W.	Isaac Watts d. 1748. Lord Devlin b. 1905
26	Th.	Marshal Soult d. 1851. Coventry Patmore d. 1896
27	F.	Dumas *fils* d. 1895. Eugene O'Neill d. 1953
28	S.	Wolsey d. 1530. Queen Wilhelmina d. 1962
29	S.	1st Sunday in Advent. Sir George Robey d. 1954
30	M.	St. Andrew. Sir Winston Churchill b. 1874

PHENOMENA

November 5d 07h Mercury in conjunction with the Moon. Mercury 4° S.

9d 23h Neptune in conjunction with the Sun.

13d 02h Saturn in conjunction with the Moon. Saturn 3° N.

13d 10h Jupiter at opposition.

19d 04h Jupiter in conjunction with the Moon. Jupiter 2° N.

26d 16h Mars in conjunction with the Moon. Mars 3° S.

30d 10h Mercury at greatest eastern elongation (21°).

CONSTELLATIONS

The following constellations are near the meridian at

	d	h		d	h
Oct.	1	24	Oct.	16	23
Nov.	1	22	Nov.	15	21
Dec.	1	20	Dec.	16	19

Ursa Major (below the Pole), Cepheus, Cassiopeia, Andromeda, Pegasus, Pisces, Aquarius and Cetus.

MINIMA OF ALGOL

d	h	d	h
3	02	17	10
5	23	20	07
8	20	23	04
11	16	26	00
14	13	28	21

PHASES OF THE MOON

	d	h	m
● New Moon	4	07	16
☽ First Quarter	12	12	20
○ Full Moon	19	15	43
☾ Last Quarter	26	07	10

	d	h
Apogee (251,950 miles)	8	22
Perigee (223,540 „)	21	00

Mean Longitude of Ascending Node on November 1, 85°.

MONTHLY NOTES

November 1. Hallowmas.

2. Fox-hunting begins.

8. Remembrance Sunday.

11. Martinmas. Scottish Term Day.

—. Half-Quarter Day, Eng. and W.

13. County Sheriffs, Eng. and W., for next year, nominated.

14. Lord Mayor's Day.

15. Solicitors', notaries', proctors' and sworn clerks' certificates expire. See note, Dec. 15.

26. Thanksgiving Day, U.S.A.

28. Removal Day, Scotland.

** Centenary.

Day	The Sun Right Ascension	Dec. —	Equation of Time	Rise 52°	Rise 56°	Transit	Set 52°	Set 56°	Sidereal Time	Transit of First Point of Aries
	h m s	° ′	m s	h m	h m	h m	h m	h m	h m s	h m s
1	14 24 52	14 22	+16 22	6 54	7 06	11 44	16 32	16 20	2 41 14	21 15 17
2	14 28 47	14 41	+16 23	6 56	7 08	11 44	16 30	16 18	2 45 11	21 11 21
3	14 32 43	15 00	+16 24	6 58	7 10	11 44	16 29	16 16	2 49 07	21 07 25
4	14 36 40	15 19	+16 23	7 00	7 13	11 44	16 27	16 14	2 53 04	21 03 29
5	14 40 38	15 37	+16 22	7 01	7 15	11 44	16 25	16 12	2 57 00	20 59 33
6	14 44 36	15 56	+16 20	7 03	7 17	11 44	16 23	16 10	3 00 57	20 55 37
7	14 48 36	16 14	+16 17	7 05	7 19	11 44	16 22	16 08	3 04 53	20 51 41
8	14 52 36	16 31	+16 14	7 07	7 21	11 44	16 20	16 06	3 08 50	20 47 45
9	14 56 37	16 49	+16 09	7 09	7 23	11 44	16 18	16 04	3 12 46	20 43 49
10	15 00 39	17 06	+16 04	7 10	7 25	11 44	16 17	16 02	3 16 43	20 39 53
11	15 04 42	17 22	+15 58	7 12	7 27	11 44	16 15	16 00	3 20 40	20 35 57
12	15 08 45	17 39	+15 51	7 14	7 30	11 44	16 14	15 58	3 24 36	20 32 02
13	15 12 50	17 55	+15 43	7 16	7 32	11 44	16 12	15 56	3 28 33	20 28 06
14	15 16 55	18 11	+15 34	7 18	7 34	11 45	16 11	15 55	3 32 29	20 24 10
15	15 21 01	18 26	+15 25	7 19	7 36	11 45	16 09	15 53	3 36 26	20 20 14
16	15 25 08	18 42	+15 14	7 21	7 38	11 45	16 08	15 51	3 40 22	20 16 18
17	15 29 15	18 56	+15 03	7 23	7 40	11 45	16 07	15 49	3 44 19	20 12 22
18	15 33 24	19 11	+14 51	7 25	7 42	11 45	16 05	15 48	3 48 15	20 08 26
19	15 37 33	19 25	+14 39	7 26	7 44	11 45	16 04	15 46	3 52 12	20 04 30
20	15 41 43	19 39	+14 25	7 28	7 46	11 46	16 03	15 45	3 56 09	20 00 34
21	15 45 54	19 53	+14 11	7 30	7 48	11 46	16 02	15 43	4 00 05	19 56 38
22	15 50 06	20 06	+13 55	7 31	7 50	11 46	16 00	15 42	4 04 02	19 52 42
23	15 54 19	20 18	+13 39	7 33	7 52	11 46	15 59	15 40	4 07 58	19 48 47
24	15 58 32	20 31	+13 22	7 35	7 54	11 47	15 58	15 39	4 11 55	19 44 51
25	16 02 46	20 43	+13 05	7 36	7 56	11 47	15 57	15 38	4 15 51	19 40 55
26	16 07 01	20 54	+12 46	7 38	7 57	11 47	15 56	15 37	4 19 48	19 36 59
27	16 11 17	21 06	+12 27	7 39	7 59	11 48	15 56	15 35	4 23 44	19 33 03
28	16 15 34	21 17	+12 07	7 41	8 01	11 48	15 55	15 34	4 27 41	19 29 07
29	16 19 51	21 27	+11 47	7 42	8 03	11 48	15 54	15 33	4 31 38	19 25 11
30	16 24 09	21 37	+11 25	7 44	8 05	11 49	15 53	15 32	4 35 34	19 21 15

s.d. 16′·2

Duration of Civil (C), Nautical (N), and Astronomical (A), Twilight (in minutes)

Lat. °	Nov. 1 C	N	A	Nov. 11 C	N	A	Nov. 21 C	N	A	Nov. 30 C	N	A
52	36	75	115	37	78	117	38	80	120	39	82	123
56	40	84	127	41	87	130	43	90	134	45	93	137

ASTRONOMICAL NOTES

MERCURY is unsuitably placed for observation.

VENUS crosses the equator going southwards and as its elongation from the Sun is steadily decreasing it is becoming visible later and later each morning in the south-eastern sky. Venus is still a brilliant morning star, magnitude −3·5, but it is no longer observable at such high altitudes as it was a few months ago. Venus passes 4° N. of Spica on the morning of the 18th.

MARS is a morning star, magnitude +1·3, and by the end of the month is visible shortly after midnight. Mars is in Leo and passes 1°·3 N. of Regulus on the 4th.

JUPITER is at opposition on the 13th, magnitude −2·4, and is visible all night. Jupiter is a conspicuous object in the constellation of Aries, about 15°–20° to the west of Aldebaran.

SATURN is an evening star, magnitude +0·9 and well situated for observation in the early evening. Even a small telescope will show Saturn's Rings, and also its largest satellite, Titan. Observation of the Rings themselves is getting more difficult now the apparent width is narrowing. At the moment the apparent width of the rings in a N.–S. direction is only half the planet's apparent diameter.

THE MOON

Day	R.A.	Dec.	Hor. Par.	Semi-diam.	Sun's Co-long.	P.A. of Bright Limb	Phase	Age	Rise 52°	Rise 56°	Transit	Set 52°	Set 56°
	h m	°	′	′	°	°		d	h m	h m	h m	h m	h m
1	12 07	+ 4·8	56·8	15·5	225	120	11	26·3	3 12	3 08	9 44	16 01	16 01
2	12 55	− 0·6	56·3	15·3	238	122	6	27·3	4 26	4 27	10 28	16 16	16 13
3	13 41	− 5·8	55·8	15·2	250	127	2	28·3	5 39	5 45	11 12	16 33	16 25
4	14 28	−10·7	55·4	15·1	262	155	0	29·3	6 51	7 02	11 56	16 51	16 38
5	15 15	−15·2	54·9	15·0	274	266	1	0·7	8 03	8 19	12 42	17 12	16 55
6	16 04	−18·9	54·6	14·9	286	276	3	1·7	9 13	9 34	13 29	17 37	17 16
7	16 54	−21·8	54·3	14·8	299	275	7	2·7	10 19	10 44	14 17	18 10	17 44
8	17 45	−23·7	54·1	14·8	311	272	12	3·7	11 20	11 48	15 06	18 50	18 22
9	18 36	−24·5	54·1	14·7	323	267	19	4·7	12 12	12 40	15 56	19 40	19 12
10	19 28	−24·3	54·2	14·8	335	263	27	5·7	12 55	13 21	16 45	20 39	20 13
11	20 20	−22·9	54·4	14·8	347	258	36	6·7	13 28	13 51	17 33	21 44	21 22
12	21 10	−20·5	54·8	14·9	0	253	45	7·7	13 56	14 14	18 21	22 54	22 37
13	22 00	−17·2	55·4	15·1	12	249	55	8·7	14 18	14 31	19 07	. .	23 55
14	22 49	−13·0	56·1	15·3	24	246	65	9·7	14 37	14 46	19 53	0 07	. .
15	23 37	− 8·1	57·0	15·5	36	244	74	10·7	14 54	14 59	20 40	1 22	1 15
16	0 26	− 2·7	57·9	15·8	48	242	83	11·7	15 11	15 11	21 27	2 39	2 37
17	1 16	+ 3·0	58·8	16·0	60	241	90	12·7	15 29	15 24	22 17	3 59	4 03
18	2 09	+ 8·7	59·7	16·3	72	241	96	13·7	15 50	15 39	23 10	5 23	5 32
19	3 04	+14·2	60·4	16·4	85	236	99	14·7	16 15	15 59	. .	6 50	7 05
20	4 03	+19·0	60·8	16·6	97	100	100	15·7	16 48	16 26	0 07	8 18	8 39
21	5 06	+22·3	61·0	16·6	109	86	97	16·7	17 33	17 06	1 09	9 43	10 09
22	6 11	+24·3	60·8	16·6	121	90	92	17·7	18 32	18 04	2 12	10 57	11 25
23	7 16	+24·5	60·4	16·5	133	95	84	18·7	19 44	19 18	3 16	11 55	12 21
24	8 19	+23·0	59·8	16·3	145	101	75	19·7	21 04	20 43	4 18	12 38	13 00
25	9 19	+20·0	59·1	16·1	157	107	64	20·7	22 25	22 10	5 15	13 09	13 26
26	10 15	+16·0	58·3	15·9	170	111	53	21·7	23 45	23 34	6 08	13 33	13 45
27	11 07	+11·3	57·6	15·7	182	114	42	22·7	. .	. .	6 57	13 52	13 59
28	11 57	+ 6·1	56·9	15·5	194	116	32	23·7	1 01	0 56	7 43	14 09	14 11
29	12 44	+ 0·8	56·3	15·3	206	116	23	24·7	2 15	2 15	8 27	14 24	14 22
30	13 30	− 4·5	55·7	15·2	218	116	15	25·7	3 28	3 32	9 10	14 40	14 34

MERCURY ☿

Day	R.A.	Dec. −	Diam.	Phase	Transit		Day	R.A.	Dec. −	Diam.	Phase	Transit	
	h m	°	″		h m			h m	°	″		h m	
1	15 04	18·2	5	96	12 24	Mercury is too close to the Sun for observation	16	16 37	24·3	5	87	12 57	Mercury is too close to the Sun for observation
4	15 22	19·8	5	95	12 30		19	16 55	25·0	5	84	13 04	
7	15 41	21·1	5	94	12 37		22	17 13	25·5	6	80	13 10	
10	15 59	22·4	5	92	12 44		25	17 30	25·8	6	75	13 15	
13	16 18	23·4	5	90	12 51		28	17 47	25·8	6	69	13 19	
16	16 37	24·3	5	87	12 57		31	18 01	25·7	7	61	13 22	

VENUS ♀

Day	R.A.	Dec.	Diam.	Phase	5° high E. 52°	5° high E. 56°	Transit
	h m	°	″		h m	h m	h m
1	12 05	+ 1·1	14	76	3 51	3 54	9 24
6	12 27	− 1·2	14	78	4 06	4 10	9 27
11	12 50	− 3·4	14	80	4 20	4 27	9 30
16	13 13	− 5·7	13	81	4 35	4 44	9 32
21	13 35	− 8·0	13	82	4 51	5 02	9 36
26	13 59	−10·1	13	84	5 07	5 20	9 39
31	14 22	−12·2	13	85	5 24	5 39	9 43

MARS ♂

Day	R.A.	Dec. +	Diam.	Phase	5° high E. 52°	5° high E. 56°	Transit
	h m	°	″		h m	h m	h m
1	10 00	14·0	6	91	0 39	0 31	7 18
6	10 11	13·1	6	91	0 35	0 27	7 09
11	10 21	12·2	6	90	0 29	0 23	6 59
16	10 30	11·4	6	90	0 24	0 18	6 49
21	10 40	10·6	6	90	0 18	0 13	6 39
26	10 49	9·7	7	90	0 12	0 07	6 29
31	10 58	9·0	7	90	0 05	0 01	6 18

SUNRISE AND SUNSET (G.M.T.)

Day	London		Bristol		Birmingham		Manchester		Newcastle		Glasgow		Belfast	
	a.m.	p.m.	a.m.	p.m.	a.m.	p.m.	a.m.	p.m.	a.m.	p.m.	a.m.	p.m.	a.m.	p.m.
	h m	h m	h m	h m	h m	h m	h m	h m	h m	h m	h m	h m	h m	h m
1	6 53	4 34	7 03	4 44	7 02	4 38	7 07	4 37	7 09	4 30	7 23	4 38	7 26	4 49
2	6 55	4 32	7 05	4 42	7 04	4 36	7 09	4 35	7 11	4 28	7 25	4 36	7 28	4 47
3	6 57	4 30	7 06	4 40	7 06	4 35	7 11	4 34	7 13	4 26	7 27	4 34	7 30	4 45
4	6 59	4 29	7 08	4 39	7 08	4 33	7 13	4 32	7 15	4 24	7 29	4 32	7 32	4 43
5	7 00	4 27	7 10	4 37	7 10	4 31	7 15	4 30	7 17	4 22	7 31	4 30	7 34	4 41
6	7 02	4 25	7 11	4 35	7 12	4 29	7 17	4 28	7 19	4 20	7 33	4 28	7 36	4 39
7	7 04	4 24	7 13	4 34	7 14	4 27	7 19	4 26	7 21	4 18	7 35	4 26	7 38	4 37
8	7 06	4 22	7 15	4 32	7 16	4 25	7 21	4 24	7 23	4 16	7 37	4 24	7 40	4 35
9	7 07	4 20	7 17	4 30	7 17	4 24	7 22	4 23	7 25	4 14	7 39	4 22	7 41	4 34
10	7 09	4 19	7 18	4 29	7 19	4 22	7 24	4 21	7 27	4 12	7 41	4 20	7 43	4 32
11	7 11	4 17	7 20	4 27	7 21	4 20	7 26	4 19	7 29	4 10	7 43	4 18	7 45	4 30
12	7 12	4 16	7 22	4 26	7 23	4 19	7 28	4 17	7 31	4 08	7 46	4 16	7 48	4 28
13	7 14	4 14	7 24	4 24	7 25	4 17	7 30	4 16	7 33	4 07	7 48	4 14	7 50	4 26
14	7 16	4 13	7 26	4 23	7 27	4 16	7 32	4 14	7 35	4 05	7 50	4 13	7 52	4 25
15	7 17	4 11	7 27	4 21	7 28	4 14	7 34	4 13	7 37	4 04	7 52	4 11	7 54	4 23
16	7 19	4 10	7 29	4 20	7 30	4 13	7 36	4 11	7 39	4 02	7 54	4 09	7 56	4 21
17	7 21	4 09	7 31	4 19	7 32	4 12	7 38	4 09	7 41	4 00	7 56	4 07	7 58	4 19
18	7 23	4 07	7 33	4 17	7 34	4 10	7 40	4 08	7 43	3 59	7 58	4 06	8 00	4 18
19	7 24	4 06	7 34	4 16	7 35	4 09	7 42	4 07	7 45	3 57	8 00	4 04	8 02	4 17
20	7 26	4 05	7 36	4 15	7 37	4 08	7 43	4 05	7 47	3 56	8 02	4 03	8 03	4 15
21	7 28	4 04	7 38	4 14	7 39	4 07	7 45	4 04	7 49	3 54	8 04	4 01	8 05	4 14
22	7 29	4 02	7 39	4 13	7 40	4 05	7 47	4 03	7 51	3 53	8 06	4 00	8 07	4 13
23	7 31	4 01	7 41	4 12	7 42	4 04	7 49	4 01	7 53	3 51	8 08	3 58	8 09	4 11
24	7 33	4 00	7 43	4 11	7 44	4 03	7 51	4 00	7 55	3 50	8 10	3 57	8 11	4 10
25	7 34	3 59	7 44	4 10	7 45	4 02	7 52	3 59	7 56	3 49	8 12	3 56	8 12	4 09
26	7 36	3 58	7 46	4 09	7 47	4 01	7 54	3 58	7 58	3 48	8 13	3 55	8 14	4 08
27	7 37	3 58	7 47	4 08	7 48	4 01	7 55	3 58	8 00	3 47	8 15	3 53	8 16	4 07
28	7 39	3 57	7 49	4 07	7 50	4 00	7 57	3 57	8 01	3 46	8 17	3 52	8 17	4 06
29	7 40	3 56	7 50	4 07	7 51	3 59	7 58	3 56	8 03	3 45	8 19	3 51	8 19	4 05
30	7 42	3 55	7 52	4 06	7 53	3 58	8 00	3 55	8 05	3 44	8 21	3 50	8 21	4 04

JUPITER ♃ SATURN ♄

Day	Jupiter R.A.	Jupiter Dec. +	Jupiter Transit	Jupiter 5° high West 52°	Jupiter 5° high West 56°	Saturn R.A.	Saturn Dec. —	Saturn Transit	Saturn 5° high West 52°	Saturn 5° high West 56°
	h m	°	h m	h m	h m	h m	°	h m	h m	h m
1	3 23	17·2	0 41	7 38	7 50	22 04	13·6	19 20	23 31	23 14
11	3 17	16·9	23 52	6 51	7 02	22 05	13·6	18 41	22 52	22 35
21	3 12	16·6	23 07	6 04	6 15	22 06	13·5	18 03	22 14	21 58
31	3 07	16·3	22 23	5 18	5 29	22 07	13·3	17 25	21 38	21 21

Equatorial diameter of Jupiter 49″; of Saturn 17″. Diameters of Saturn's rings 39″ and 7″.

URANUS ♅ NEPTUNE ♆

Day	Uranus R.A.	Uranus Dec. +	Uranus 10° high in East 52°	Uranus 10° high in East 56°	Uranus Transit	Neptune R.A.	Neptune Dec. —	Neptune Transit	
	h m	° ′	h m	h m	h m	h m	° ′	h m	
1	11 01·3	7 05	2 48	2 49	8 19	15 01·1	15 21	12 18	Neptune is too close to the Sun for observation
11	11 02·7	6 56	2 11	2 12	7 41	15 02·5	15 27	11 40	
21	11 03·9	6 50	1 34	1 35	7 03	15 04·0	15 33	11 02	
31	11 04·7	6 45	0 56	0 57	6 24	15 05·5	15 39	10 24	

Diameter 4″ Diameter 2″

Decem (ten), 10th month of Roman (pre-Julian) Calendar.

Sun's Longitude 270° ♑ 21^{d} 20^{h}

Day of Month	Day of Week	
1	Tu.	Queen Alexandra b. 1844
2	W.	Austerlitz 1805. Queen Adelaide d. 1849
3	Th.	R. L. Stevenson d. 1894. Nigel Balchin b. 1908
4	F.	Richelieu d. 1642. John Gay d. 1732
5	S.	Mozart d. 1791. Walt Disney b. 1901
6	S.	2nd Sunday in Advent. Thistle Sunday
7	M.	Pearl Harbour 1941. Kirsten Flagstad d. 1962
8	Tu.	De Quincey d. 1859. Herbert Spencer d. 1903
9	W.	Van Dyck d. 1641. R. A. Butler b. 1902
10	Th.	Earl Alexander of Tunis b. 1891
11	F.	Accession of George VI 1936
12	S.	Douglas Fairbanks d. 1939
13	S.	3rd Sunday in Advent. Sir J. Cunningham d. 1962
14	M.	George VI b. 1895. Prince Consort d. 1861
15	Tu.	H. M. Abrahams b. 1899. Charles Laughton d. 1962
16	W.	Sir J. B. Hobbs b. 1882. Lily Elsie d. 1962
17	Th.	Lord Kelvin d. 1907. *Graf von Spee* scuttled 1939
18	F.	Prince William b. 1941. Dorothy L. Sayers d. 1957
19	S.	J. M. W. Turner d. 1851. Sir Stanley Unwin b. 1884
20	S.	4th Sunday in Advent. Sir Robert Menzies b. 1894
21	M.	St. Thomas. MICHAELMAS LAW SITTINGS END
22	Tu.	George Eliot d. 1880. Sir Ninian Comper d. 1960
23	W.	Lord Rank b. 1888. Earl of Halifax d. 1959
24	Th.	Christmas Eve. Jean Forbes-Robertson d. 1962
25	F.	Christmas Day.
26	S.	St. Stephen. Visct. Amory b. 1899
27	S.	1st S. after Christmas. St. John.
28	M.	Holy Innocents'. St. John Ervine b. 1883
29	Tu.	City of London incendiary bomb fires 1940
30	W.	Josephine Butler d. 1906. Ruth Draper d. 1956
31	Th.	P. B. H. May b. 1929. Dr. C. F. Garbett d. 1955

PHENOMENA

December 1^{d} 04^{h} Venus in conjunction with the Moon. Venus 2° S.

$3\text{–}4^{d}$ Partial eclipse of the Sun. (*See* p. 148).

5^{d} 22^{h} Mercury in conjunction with the Moon. Mercury 0°·6 S.

10^{d} 12^{h} Saturn in conjunction with the Moon. Saturn 3° N.

16^{d} 09^{h} Jupiter in conjunction with the Moon. Jupiter 2° N.

18^{d} 21^{h} Mercury in inferior conjunction with the Sun.

19^{d} Total eclipse of the Moon. (*See* p. 148).

21^{d} 20^{h} Winter Solstice.

24^{d} 19^{h} Mars in conjunction with the Moon. Mars 3° S.

31^{d} 14^{h} Venus in conjunction with the Moon. Venus 0°·3 N.

31^{d} 22^{h} Mercury in conjunction with the Moon. Mercury 2° N.

CONSTELLATIONS

The following constellations are near the meridian at

	d	h		d	h
Nov.	1	24	Nov.	15	23
Dec.	1	22	Dec.	16	21
Jan.	1	20	Jan.	16	19

Ursa Major (below the Pole), Ursa Minor (below the Pole), Cassiopeia, Andromeda, Perseus, Triangulum, Aries, Taurus, Cetus and Eridanus.

MINIMA OF ALGOL

d	h	d	h
1	18	18	23
4	15	21	20
7	12	24	17
10	08	27	13
13	05	30	10
16	02		

PHASES OF THE MOON

	d	h	m
● New Moon	4	01	18
☽ First Quarter	12	06	01
○ Full Moon	19	02	41
☾ Last Quarter	25	19	27

	d	h
Apogee (252,480 miles)	6	12
Perigee (221,720 „)	19	11

Mean Longitude of Ascending Node on December 1, 84°.

MONTHLY NOTES

December 10. Grouse and Black Game Shooting ends.

15. Last day for renewing solicitors' certificates. Notices to owners and occupiers affected by private Bills in Parliament must be delivered.

21. Common Council Elections, City of London.

25. Quarter Day.

—. County Quarter Sessions, Eng. and W., to be held within the period of 21 days immediately preceding or following Dec. 25.

26. Boxing Day. Bank and General Holiday, Eng. and W., N. Ireland.

31. Various licences expire.

Day	The Sun s.d. 16′·3 Right Ascension	Dec. −	Equation of Time	Rise 52°	Rise 56°	Transit	Set 52°	Set 56°	Sidereal Time	Transit of First Point of Aries
	h m s	° ′	m s	h m	h m	h m	h m	h m	h m s	h m s
1	16 28 27	21 47	+11 03	7 45	8 06	11 49	15 52	15 31	4 39 31	19 17 19
2	16 32 47	21 56	+10 41	7 47	8 08	11 50	15 52	15 30	4 43 27	19 13 23
3	16 37 06	22 05	+10 17	7 48	8 10	11 50	15 51	15 30	4 47 24	19 09 27
4	16 41 27	22 13	+ 9 53	7 49	8 11	11 50	15 51	15 29	4 51 20	19 05 32
5	16 45 48	22 21	+ 9 29	7 51	8 13	11 51	15 50	15 28	4 55 17	19 01 36
6	16 50 10	22 28	+ 9 04	7 52	8 14	11 51	15 50	15 28	4 59 13	18 57 40
7	16 54 32	22 35	+ 8 38	7 53	8 16	11 52	15 49	15 27	5 03 10	18 53 44
8	16 58 54	22 42	+ 8 12	7 54	8 17	11 52	15 49	15 26	5 07 07	18 49 48
9	17 03 18	22 48	+ 7 45	7 56	8 18	11 52	15 49	15 26	5 11 03	18 45 52
10	17 07 41	22 54	+ 7 19	7 57	8 20	11 53	15 49	15 26	5 15 00	18 41 56
11	17 12 05	22 59	+ 6 51	7 58	8 21	11 53	15 49	15 25	5 18 56	18 38 00
12	17 16 29	23 04	+ 6 23	7 59	8 22	11 54	15 49	15 25	5 22 53	18 34 04
13	17 20 54	23 08	+ 5 55	8 00	8 23	11 54	15 49	15 25	5 26 49	18 30 08
14	17 25 19	23 12	+ 5 27	8 01	8 24	11 55	15 49	15 25	5 30 46	18 26 12
15	17 29 44	23 16	+ 4 58	8 02	8 25	11 55	15 49	15 25	5 34 42	18 22 16
16	17 34 10	23 19	+ 4 29	8 03	8 26	11 56	15 49	15 25	5 38 39	18 18 21
17	17 38 35	23 21	+ 4 00	8 03	8 27	11 56	15 49	15 25	5 42 36	18 14 25
18	17 43 01	23 23	+ 3 31	8 04	8 28	11 57	15 49	15 25	5 46 32	18 10 29
19	17 47 27	23 25	+ 3 01	8 05	8 29	11 57	15 50	15 26	5 50 29	18 06 33
20	17 51 54	23 26	+ 2 32	8 05	8 29	11 58	15 50	15 26	5 54 25	18 02 37
21	17 56 20	23 26	+ 2 02	8 06	8 30	11 58	15 50	15 27	5 58 22	17 58 41
22	18 00 46	23 27	+ 1 32	8 06	8 30	11 59	15 51	15 27	6 02 18	17 54 45
23	18 05 13	23 26	+ 1 02	8 07	8 31	11 59	15 51	15 28	6 06 15	17 50 49
24	18 09 39	23 26	+ 0 32	8 07	8 31	12 00	15 52	15 28	6 10 12	17 46 53
25	18 14 05	23 24	+ 0 03	8 08	8 31	12 00	15 53	15 29	6 14 08	17 42 57
26	18 18 32	23 23	− 0 27	8 08	8 32	12 01	15 53	15 30	6 18 05	17 39 01
27	18 22 58	23 20	− 0 57	8 08	8 32	12 01	15 54	15 30	6 22 01	17 35 06
28	18 27 24	23 18	− 1 26	8 08	8 32	12 02	15 55	15 31	6 25 58	17 31 10
29	18 31 50	23 15	− 1 56	8 08	8 32	12 02	15 56	15 32	6 29 54	17 27 14
30	18 36 16	23 11	− 2 25	8 08	8 32	12 03	15 57	15 33	6 33 51	17 23 18
31	18 40 41	23 07	− 2 54	8 08	8 32	12 03	15 58	15 34	6 37 47	17 19 22

Duration of Civil (C), Nautical (N), and Astronomical (A), Twilight (in minutes)

Lat.	Dec. 1 C	Dec. 1 N	Dec. 1 A	Dec. 11 C	Dec. 11 N	Dec. 11 A	Dec. 21 C	Dec. 21 N	Dec. 21 A	Dec. 31 C	Dec. 31 N	Dec. 31 A
°												
52	40	82	123	41	84	125	41	85	126	41	84	125
56	45	93	138	47	96	141	47	97	142	47	96	141

ASTRONOMICAL NOTES

MERCURY may only be seen as a morning star during the last few days of the month.

VENUS is still a morning star, magnitude −3·4, though by the end of the month it is only visible above the S.E. horizon for an hour before sunrise. A close conjunction with the old crescent Moon occurs on the 1st while the Moon will again be seen approaching Venus on the morning of the 31st.

MARS is still a morning star though visible before midnight by the end of the month. It is becoming a more noticeable object in the south-eastern sky as it increases in brightness from magnitude +1·0 to +0·5. Mars moves from Leo into Virgo towards the end of the month.

JUPITER is a conspicuous evening star, magnitude −2·3, in the constellation of Aries. As evening twilight grows Jupiter is already a prominent object of the south-eastern sky.

SATURN is still an evening star, magnitude +1·1, and visible in the southern sky after sunset. By the end of the month it is not visible after 20^h.

ECLIPSE. A partial eclipse of the Sun occurs on the 3rd–4th but it is not visible from the British Isles.

ECLIPSE. A total eclipse of the Moon occurs on the 19th, visible from the British Isles. See p. 148 for details.

METEORS. The maximum of the Geminid meteor shower occurs on the evening of the 12th. The Moon is at First Quarter and will therefore hamper observations made before midnight.

THE MOON

Day	R.A.	Dec.	Hor. Par.	Semi-diam.	Sun's Co-long.	P.A. of Bright Limb	Phase	Age	Rise 52°	Rise 56°	Transit	Set 52°	Set 56°
	h m	°	′	′	°	°		d	h m	h m	h m	h m	h m
1	14 16	− 9·4	55·2	15·0	230	115	9	26·7	4 39	4 49	9 54	14 57	14 46
2	15 02	−14·0	54·8	14·9	243	114	4	27·7	5 50	6 05	10 38	15 16	15 01
3	15 50	−17·9	54·5	14·9	255	113	1	28·7	7 01	7 20	11 24	15 40	15 20
4	16 40	−21·1	54·3	14·8	267	159	0	29·7	8 09	8 32	12 12	16 09	15 45
5	17 30	−23·3	54·1	14·7	279	273	1	0·9	9 12	9 39	13 01	16 47	16 19
6	18 22	−24·5	54·0	14·7	291	271	3	1·9	10 07	10 36	13 50	17 33	17 05
7	19 14	−24·5	54·0	14·7	304	266	8	2·9	10 53	11 21	14 40	18 29	18 02
8	20 05	−23·5	54·1	14·7	316	261	13	3·9	11 30	11 55	15 28	19 32	19 08
9	20 56	−21·4	54·3	14·8	328	257	20	4·9	11 59	12 19	16 16	20 40	20 21
10	21 45	−18·4	54·7	14·9	340	253	28	5·9	12 23	12 38	17 02	21 50	21 36
11	22 33	−14·5	55·3	15·1	352	250	38	6·9	12 42	12 53	17 47	23 02	22 53
12	23 21	−10·0	55·9	15·2	4	247	47	7·9	13 00	13 06	18 31	..	..
13	0 08	− 4·9	56·8	15·5	17	246	58	8·9	13 16	13 17	19 16	0 16	0 12
14	0 56	+ 0·6	57·7	15·7	29	245	68	9·9	13 32	13 29	20 03	1 32	1 33
15	1 46	+ 6·2	58·7	16·0	41	246	78	10·9	13 51	13 43	20 53	2 51	2 57
16	2 38	+11·7	59·6	16·2	53	248	86	11·9	14 13	13 59	21 47	4 14	4 26
17	3 35	+16·7	60·5	16·5	65	252	93	12·9	14 41	14 22	22 46	5 41	5 59
18	4 36	+20·9	61·1	16·6	77	258	98	13·9	15 19	14 55	23 50	7 09	7 32
19	5 40	+23·6	61·4	16·7	89	276	100	14·9	16 11	15 43	..	8 31	8 59
20	6 47	+24·6	61·4	16·7	102	88	99	15·9	17 19	16 52	0 55	9 40	10 08
21	7 54	+23·8	61·1	16·6	114	95	95	16·9	18 39	18 16	2 01	10 32	10 56
22	8 58	+21·3	60·4	16·5	126	102	88	17·9	20 04	19 46	3 03	11 09	11 29
23	9 57	+17·5	59·6	16·2	138	107	79	18·9	21 28	21 15	4 00	11 37	11 51
24	10 52	+12·8	58·7	16·0	150	110	69	19·9	22 48	22 41	4 52	11 59	12 07
25	11 44	+ 7·5	57·8	15·7	162	113	59	20·9	..	..	5 40	12 16	12 20
26	12 32	+ 2·1	56·9	15·5	174	114	48	21·9	0 04	0 02	6 26	12 32	12 32
27	13 19	− 3·2	56·1	15·3	187	113	38	22·9	1 18	1 21	7 09	12 48	12 43
28	14 05	− 8·3	55·5	15·1	199	112	28	23·9	2 30	2 37	7 53	13 04	12 55
29	14 51	−12·9	54·9	15·0	211	110	20	24·9	3 41	3 53	8 37	13 22	13 09
30	15 38	−17·0	54·5	14·9	223	106	13	25·9	4 51	5 08	9 22	13 44	13 26
31	16 27	−20·4	54·2	14·8	235	101	7	26·9	5 59	6 21	10 09	14 11	13 48

MERCURY ☿

Day	R.A.	Dec. −	Diam.	Phase	Transit		Day	R.A.	Dec. −	Diam.	Phase	Transit	
	h m	°	″		h m			h m	°	″		h m	
1	18 01	25·7	7	61	13 22	Mercury is too close to the Sun for observation	16	18 03	22·3	10	4	12 20	Mercury is too close to the Sun for observation
4	18 12	25·4	7	51	13 20		19	17 46	21·4	10	0	11 51	
7	18 20	24·8	8	40	13 15		22	17 29	20·5	10	5	11 23	
10	18 21	24·1	8	27	13 04		25	17 17	20·0	9	15	11 00	
13	18 16	23·3	9	15	12 45		28	17 12	19·9	9	27	10 44	
16	18 03	22·3	10	4	12 20		31	17 12	20·2	8	39	10 34	

VENUS ♀ MARS ♂

Day	R.A.	Dec. −	Diam.	Phase	5° high E. 52°	5° high E. 56°	Transit	Day	R.A.	Dec. +	Diam.	Phase	5° high E. 52°	5° high E. 56°	Transit
	h m	°	″		h m	h m	h m		h m	°	″		h m	h m	h m
1	14 22	12·2	13	85	5 24	5 39	9 43	1	10 58	9·0	7	90	0 05	23 59	6 18
6	14 46	14·2	12	86	5 40	5 58	9 47	6	11 06	8·2	7	90	23 56	23 53	6 06
11	15 11	16·1	12	87	5 57	6 17	9 52	11	11 14	7·5	7	90	23 48	23 45	5 55
16	15 36	17·8	12	88	6 14	6 37	9 58	16	11 22	6·8	8	90	23 39	23 37	5 42
21	16 01	19·3	12	89	6 31	6 56	10 03	21	11 28	6·2	8	91	23 29	23 27	5 30
26	16 27	20·5	11	90	6 46	7 15	10 10	26	11 35	5·6	8	91	23 18	23 17	5 16
31	16 54	21·6	11	91	7 01	7 33	10 16	31	11 41	5·1	9	91	23 07	23 06	5 02

SUNRISE AND SUNSET (G.M.T.)

Day	London		Bristol		Birmingham		Manchester		Newcastle		Glasgow		Belfast	
	a.m.	p.m.	a.m.	p.m.	a.m.	p.m.	a.m.	p.m.	a.m.	p.m.	a.m.	p.m.	a.m.	p.m.
	h m	h m	h m	h m	h m	h m	h m	h m	h m	h m	h m	h m	h m	h m
1	7 43	3 54	7 53	4 05	7 54	3 57	8 01	3 54	8 06	3 43	8 22	3 49	8 22	4 03
2	7 45	3 54	7 55	4 05	7 56	3 57	8 03	3 54	8 08	3 42	8 24	3 48	8 24	4 02
3	7 46	3 53	7 56	4 04	7 57	3 56	8 04	3 53	8 10	3 42	8 26	3 48	8 26	4 02
4	7 47	3 53	7 57	4 04	7 59	3 55	8 06	3 52	8 11	3 41	8 27	3 47	8 28	4 01
5	7 49	3 52	7 58	4 03	8 00	3 55	8 07	3 52	8 13	3 40	8 29	3 46	8 29	4 00
6	7 50	3 52	8 00	4 03	8 01	3 54	8 08	3 51	8 14	3 40	8 30	3 46	8 30	4 00
7	7 51	3 52	8 01	4 02	8 03	3 54	8 10	3 51	8 16	3 39	8 32	3 45	8 32	3 59
8	7 52	3 52	8 02	4 02	8 04	3 53	8 11	3 50	8 17	3 38	8 33	3 44	8 33	3 58
9	7 54	3 51	8 03	4 02	8 05	3 53	8 12	3 50	8 18	3 38	8 34	3 44	8 34	3 58
10	7 55	3 51	8 04	4 02	8 06	3 53	8 13	3 50	8 19	3 38	8 36	3 44	8 35	3 58
11	7 56	3 51	8 05	4 02	8 08	3 53	8 15	3 50	8 21	3 38	8 37	3 43	8 37	3 58
12	7 57	3 51	8 06	4 02	8 09	3 53	8 16	3 50	8 22	3 38	8 38	3 43	8 38	3 58
13	7 58	3 51	8 07	4 02	8 10	3 53	8 17	3 50	8 23	3 38	8 39	3 43	8 39	3 58
14	7 59	3 51	8 08	4 02	8 11	3 53	8 18	3 50	8 24	3 38	8 40	3 43	8 40	3 58
15	8 00	3 52	8 09	4 02	8 12	3 53	8 19	3 50	8 25	3 38	8 41	3 43	8 41	3 58
16	8 01	3 52	8 10	4 02	8 12	3 53	8 19	3 50	8 25	3 38	8 42	3 43	8 41	3 58
17	8 01	3 52	8 10	4 02	8 13	3 53	8 20	3 50	8 26	3 38	8 43	3 43	8 42	3 58
18	8 02	3 52	8 11	4 02	8 14	3 53	8 21	3 50	8 27	3 38	8 44	3 43	8 43	3 58
19	8 03	3 53	8 12	4 03	8 15	3 54	8 22	3 50	8 28	3 38	8 45	3 44	8 44	3 58
20	8 03	3 53	8 12	4 03	8 15	3 54	8 22	3 51	8 28	3 39	8 45	3 44	8 44	3 59
21	8 04	3 53	8 13	4 03	8 16	3 54	8 23	3 51	8 29	3 39	8 46	3 45	8 45	3 59
22	8 04	3 54	8 13	4 04	8 16	3 55	8 24	3 52	8 30	3 40	8 46	3 45	8 46	4 00
23	8 05	3 54	8 14	4 04	8 17	3 55	8 24	3 52	8 30	3 40	8 47	3 46	8 46	4 00
24	8 05	3 55	8 14	4 05	8 17	3 56	8 24	3 53	8 30	3 41	8 47	3 46	8 46	4 01
25	8 06	3 56	8 15	4 06	8 18	3 57	8 25	3 54	8 31	3 42	8 47	3 47	8 47	4 02
26	8 06	3 56	8 15	4 06	8 18	3 57	8 25	3 54	8 31	3 42	8 48	3 48	8 47	4 02
27	8 06	3 57	8 15	4 07	8 18	3 58	8 25	3 55	8 31	3 43	8 48	3 48	8 47	4 03
28	8 06	3 58	8 15	4 08	8 18	3 59	8 25	3 56	8 31	3 44	8 48	3 49	8 47	4 04
29	8 06	3 59	8 16	4 09	8 18	4 00	8 25	3 57	8 31	3 45	8 48	3 50	8 47	4 05
30	8 06	4 00	8 16	4 10	8 18	4 01	8 26	3 58	8 32	3 46	8 48	3 51	8 48	4 06
31	8 06	4 01	8 16	4 11	8 18	4 02	8 25	3 59	8 31	3 47	8 48	3 52	8 47	4 07

Day	JUPITER ♃ R.A.	Dec. +	Transit	5° high West 52°	5° high West 56°	SATURN ♄ R.A.	Dec. −	Transit	5° high West 52°	5° high West 56°
	h m	°	h m	h m	h m	h m	°	h m	h m	h m
1	3 07	16·3	22 23	5 18	5 29	22 07	13·3	17 25	21 38	21 21
11	3 02	16·0	21 39	4 33	4 43	22 09	13·1	16 48	21 02	20 46
21	2 59	15·8	20 57	3 49	3 59	22 12	12·8	16 11	20 27	20 11
31	2 57	15·7	20 15	3 07	3 16	22 15	12·5	15 35	19 53	19 38

Equatorial diameter of Jupiter 47″; of Saturn 17″. Diameters of Saturn's rings 37″ and 7″.

Day	URANUS ♅ R.A.	Dec. +	10° high in East 52°	10° high in East 56°	Transit	NEPTUNE ♆ R.A.	Dec. −	10° high in East 52°	10° high in East 56°	Transit
	h m	° ′	h m	h m	h m	h m	° ′	h m	h m	h m
1	11 04·7	6 45	0 56	0 57	6 24	15 05·5	15 39	7 08	7 35	10 24
11	11 05·2	6 42	0 17	0 18	5 45	15 06·9	15 44	6 30	6 58	9 46
21	11 05·4	6 42	23 34	23 35	5 06	15 08·2	15 49	5 53	6 21	9 08
31	11 05·2	6 43	22 54	22 55	4 27	15 09·3	15 54	5 15	5 43	8 30

Uranus: Diameter 4″ — Neptune: Diameter 2″

INTRODUCTION TO ASTRONOMICAL SECTION

GENERAL

The astronomical data are given in a form suitable for those who practise naked-eye astronomy or use small telescopes. No attempt has been made to replace the *Astronomical Ephemeris* for professional astronomers. Positions of the heavenly bodies are given only to the degree of accuracy required by amateur astronomers for setting telescopes, or for plotting on celestial globes or star atlases. Where intermediate positions are required, linear interpolation may be employed.

All data are, unless otherwise stated, for 0^h G.M.T., or the midnight at the beginning of the day named. No allowance is made for Summer Time, the dates of which, although given by the Summer Time Act, 1925, may be altered by Order in Council.

Definitions of the terms used cannot be given in an ephemeris of this nature. They must be sought in astronomical literature and text-books. Probably the best source for the amateur is Norton's *Star Atlas* (Gall and Inglis, 14th edition, 1959; 17*s*. 6*d*.), which contains an excellent introduction to observational astronomy, and the finest series of star maps yet produced for showing stars visible to the naked eye. Certain more extended ephemerides are available in the British Astronomical Association Handbook, an annual very popular among amateur astronomers. (Secretary: 303 Bath Road, Hounslow West, Middlesex.)

A special feature has been made of the times when the various heavenly bodies are visible in the British Isles. Since two columns, calculated for latitudes 52° and 56°, are devoted to risings and settings, the range 50° to 58° is covered by interpolation and extrapolation. The times given in these columns are G.M.T.'s for the meridian of Greenwich. An observer west of this meridian must add his longitude (in time) and vice versa. Allowance must also be made for Summer Time if in force.

In accordance with the usual convention in astronomy, + and − indicate respectively north and south latitudes or declinations.

PAGE I OF EACH MONTH

The Zodiacal signs through which the Sun is passing during each month are illustrated. The date of transition from one sign to the next, to the nearest hour, is also given.

The FASTS AND FESTIVALS in black-letter type are those so given in the Prayer Book. The line immediately to the right of the Day of Week is shown heavy when the Law Courts are sitting in London.

Under the heading PHENOMENA will be found particulars of the more important conjunctions of the Sun, Moon and planets with each other, and also the dates of eclipses and other astronomical phenomena of special interest.

The CONSTELLATIONS listed each month are those that are near the meridian at the beginning of the month at 22^h local mean time. Allowance must be made for Summer Time if necessary. The fact that any star crosses the meridian 4^m earlier each night or 2^h earlier each month may be used, in conjunction with the lists given each month, to find what constellations are favourably placed at any moment. The table preceding the list of constellations may be extended indefinitely at the rate just quoted.

Times of MINIMA OF ALGOL are approximate times of the middle of the period of diminished light (*see* p. 153).

The principal PHASES OF THE MOON are the G.M.T.'s when the difference between the longitude of the Moon and that of the Sun is 0°, 90°, 180° or 270°. The times of perigee and apogee are those when the Moon is nearest to, and farthest from the Earth, respectively. The nodes or points of intersection of the Moon's orbit and the ecliptic make a complete retrograde circuit of the ecliptic in about 19 years. From a knowledge of the longitude of the ascending node and the inclination, whose value does not vary much from 5°, the path of the Moon among the stars may be plotted on a celestial globe or star atlas.

The MONTHLY NOTES are self-explanatory.

PAGE II OF EACH MONTH

The Sun's semi-diameter, in arc, is given once a month.

The right ascension given is that of the true Sun. The right ascension of the mean Sun is obtained by applying the equation of time, with the sign given, to the right ascension of the true Sun, or, more easily, by applying 12^h to the column Sidereal Time. The direction in which the equation of time has to be applied in different problems is a frequent source of confusion and error. Apparent Solar Time is equal to the Mean Solar Time plus the Equation of Time. For example at noon on Aug. 8 the Equation of Time is $-5^m\ 37^s$ and thus at 12^h Mean Time on that day the Apparent Time is $12^h - 5^m\ 37^s = 11^h\ 54^m\ 23^s$.

The Sidereal Time at 0^h and the Transit of the First Point of Aries (which is really the mean time when the sidereal time is 0^h) are used for converting mean time to sidereal time and vice versa.

The G.M.T. of transit of the Sun at Greenwich may also be taken as the L.M.T. of transit in any longitude. It is independent of latitude. The G.M.T. of transit in any longitude is obtained by adding the longitude to the time given if west, and vice versa.

The legal importance of SUNRISE and SUNSET is that the Road Traffic Act, 1956, defines Lighting-up Time for vehicles as being from half an hour after sunset to half an hour before sunrise throughout the year. In all laws and regulations "sunset" refers to the local sunset, i.e. the time at which the Sun sets at the place in question. This common-sense interpretation has been upheld by legal tribunals. Thus the necessity for providing for different latitudes and longitudes, as already described, is evident.

The times of SUNRISE and SUNSET are those when the Sun's upper limb, as affected by refraction, is on the true horizon of an observer at sea-level. Assuming the mean refraction to be 34′, and the Sun's semi-diameter to be 16′, the time given is that when the true zenith distance of the

Sun's centre is $90° + 34' + 16'$ or $90° 50'$, or, in other words, when the depression of the Sun's centre below the true horizon is 50′. The upper limb is then 34′ below the true horizon, but is brought there by refraction. It is true, of course, that an observer on a ship might see the Sun for a minute or so longer, because of the dip of the horizon, while another viewing the sunset over hills or mountains would record an earlier time. Nevertheless, the moment when the true zenith distance of the Sun's centre is 90° 50′ is a precise time dependent only on the latitude and longitude of the place, and independent of its altitude above sea-level, the contour of its horizon, the vagaries of refraction or the small seasonal change in the Sun's semi-diameter; this moment is suitable in every way as a definition of sunset (or sunrise) for all statutory purposes.

It is well known that light reaches us before sunrise and also continues to reach us for some time after sunset. The interval between darkness and sunrise or sunset and darkness is called twilight. Astronomically speaking, twilight is considered to begin or end when the Sun's centre is 18° below the horizon, as no light from the Sun can then reach the observer. As thus defined twilight may last several hours; in high latitudes at the solstices the depression of 18° is not reached, and twilight lasts from sunset to sunrise.

The need for some sub-division of twilight was met some years ago by dividing the gathering darkness into four steps.

(1) *Sunrise or Sunset*, defined as above.

(2) *Civil twilight*, which begins or ends when the Sun's centre is 6° below the horizon. This marks the time when operations requiring daylight may commence or must cease. In England it varies from about 30 to 60 minutes after sunset.

(3) *Nautical twilight*, which begins or ends when the Sun's centre is 12° below the horizon. This marks the time when it is, to all intents and purposes, completely dark.

(4) *Astronomical twilight*, which begins or ends when the Sun's centre is 18° below the horizon. This marks theoretical perfect darkness. It is not of practical importance, especially if nautical twilight is tabulated.

To assist observers the durations of civil, nautical and astronomical twilights are given at intervals of ten days. The beginning of a particular twilight is found by subtracting the duration from the time of sunrise, while the end is found by adding the duration to the time of sunset. Thus the beginning of astronomical twilight in latitude 52°, on the Greenwich meridian, on March 11 is found as $06^h\ 24^m - 113^m = 04^h\ 31^m$ and similarly the end of civil twilight as $17^h\ 57^m + 34^m = 18^h\ 31^m$.

The letters T.A.N. are printed when twilight lasts all night.

Lighting-up time is a crude attempt to approximate to civil twilight over the British Isles.

Under the heading ASTRONOMICAL NOTES will be found notes describing the position and visibility of the planets and also of other phenomena; these are intended to guide naked-eye observers, or those using small telescopes.

PAGE III OF EACH MONTH

The Moon moves so rapidly among the stars that its position is given only to the degree of accuracy that permits linear interpolation. The right ascension and declination are geocentric, i.e. for an imaginary observer at the centre of the Earth. To an observer on the surface of the Earth the position is always different, as the altitude is always less on account of parallax which may reach 1°.

The lunar terminator is the line separating the bright from the dark part of the Moon's disk. Apart from irregularities of the lunar surface, the terminator is elliptical, because it is a circle seen in projection. It becomes the full circle forming the limb, or edge, of the Moon at New and Full Moon. The selenographic longitude of the terminator is measured from the mean centre of the visible disk, which may differ from the visible centre by as much as 8°, because of libration.

Instead of the longitude of the terminator the Sun's selenographic colongitude is tabulated. It is numerically equal to the selenographic longitude of the morning terminator, measured eastward from the mean centre of the disk. Thus its value is approximately 270° at New Moon, 360° at First Quarter, 90° at Full Moon and 180° at Last Quarter.

The Position Angle of the Bright Limb is the position angle of the midpoint of the illuminated limb, measured eastwards from the north point on the disk. The column PHASE shows the percentage of the area of the Moon's disk illuminated; this is also the illuminated percentage of the diameter at right angles to the line of cusps. The terminator is a semi-ellipse whose major axis is the line of cusps, and whose semi-minor axis is determined by the tabulated percentage; from New Moon to Full Moon the east limb is dark, and vice versa.

The times given as moonrise and moonset are those when the upper limb of the Moon is on the horizon of an observer at sea-level. The Sun's horizontal parallax is about 9″, and is negligible when considering sunrise and sunset, but that of the Moon averages about 57′. Hence the computed time represents the moment when the true zenith distance of the Moon is 90° 50′ (as for the Sun) minus the horizontal parallax. The time required for the Sun or Moon to rise or set is about four minutes.

The tables have been constructed for the meridian of Greenwich, and for latitudes 52° and 56°. They give Greenwich Mean Time (G.M.T.) throughout the year; if Summer Time (B.S.T.) is in force, one hour must be added to get the time shown by civil clocks. To obtain the G.M.T. of the phenomenon as seen from any other latitude and longitude, first interpolate or extrapolate for latitude by the usual rules of proportion. To the time thus found the longitude (expressed in time) is to be *added* if west (as it usually is in Great Britain) or *subtracted* if east. If the longitude is expressed in degrees and minutes of arc, it must be converted to time at the rate of $1° = 4^m$ and $15' = 1^m$.

The G.M.T. of transit of the Moon over the meridian of Greenwich is given: these times are independent of latitude, but must be corrected for longitude. For places in the British Isles it suffices to add the longitude if west, and vice versa. For more remote places a further correction is necessary because of the rapid movement of the Moon relative to the stars. The entire correction is conveniently determined by first finding the west longitude λ of the place. If the place is in west longitude, λ is the ordinary west longitude; if the place is in east longitude λ is the complement to 24^h (or 360°) of the longitude, and will be greater than 12^h (or 180°). The correction then consists of two positive portions, namely λ and the fraction λ/24 (or λ°/360) multiplied by the difference between consecutive transits. Thus for Sydney, N.S.W., the longitude is $10^h\ 05^m$ east, so $\lambda = 13^h\ 55^m$ and the fraction λ/24 is 0·58. The transit on the local date 1964 Aug. 9 is found as follows:

	d	h	m
G.M.T. of transit at Greenwich.... Aug.	8	12	50
λ..............................		13	55
$0{\cdot}58 \times (13^h\ 43^m - 12^h\ 50^m)$			31
G.M.T. of transit at Sydney........	9	03	16
Corr. to N.S.W. Standard Time....		10	00
Local standard time of transit	9	13	16

It is evident, of course, that for any given place the quantities λ and the correction to local standard time may be combined permanently, being here $23^h\ 55^m$.

Positions of Mercury are given for every third day, and those of Venus and Mars for every fifth day; they may be interpolated linearly. The column PHASE shows the illuminated percentage of the disk. In the case of the inner planets this approaches 100 at superior conjunction and 0 at inferior conjunction. When the phase is less than 50 the planet is crescent-shaped or horned; for greater phases it is gibbous. In the case of the exterior planet Mars, the phase approaches 100 at conjunction and opposition, and is a minimum at the quadratures.

Since the planets cannot be seen when on the horizon, the actual times of rising and setting are not given; instead, the time when the planet has an apparent altitude of 5° has been tabulated. The phenomenon tabulated is the one that occurs between sunset and sunrise; unimportant exceptions to this rule may occur because changes are not made during a month, except in the case of Mercury. The times given may be interpolated for latitude and corrected for longitude as in the case of the Sun and Moon.

The G.M.T. at which the planet transits the Greenwich meridian is also given. The times of transit are to be corrected to local meridians in the usual way, as already described.

PAGE IV OF EACH MONTH

The G.M.T.'s of Sunrise and Sunset may be used not only for these phenomena, but also for Lighting-up Times, which, under the Road Traffic Act, 1956, are from half an hour after sunset to half an hour before sunrise throughout the year.

The particulars for the four outer planets resemble those for the planets on Page III of each month, except that, under Uranus and Neptune, times when the planet is 10° high instead of 5° high are given; this is because of the inferior brightness of these planets. The polar diameter of Jupiter is about 3″ less than the equatorial diameter, while that of Saturn is about 2″ less. The diameters given for the rings of Saturn are those of the major axis (in the plane of the planet's equator) and the minor axis respectively. The former has a small seasonal change due to the slightly varying distance of the Earth from Saturn, but the latter varies from zero when the Earth passes through the ring plane every 15 years to its maximum opening half-way between these periods. The rings were completely closed in September, 1950, and open at their widest extent in the middle of 1958.

TIME

From the earliest ages, the natural division of time into recurring periods of day and night has provided the practical time scale for the everyday activities of mankind. Indeed, if any alternative means of time measurement is adopted, it must be capable of adjustment so as to remain in general agreement with the natural time scale defined by the diurnal rotation of the Earth on its axis. Ideally the rotation should be measured against a fixed frame of reference; in practice it must be measured against the background provided by the celestial bodies. If the Sun is chosen as the reference point, we obtain Apparent Solar Time, which is the time indicated by a sundial. It is not a uniform time, but is subject to variations which amount to as much as a quarter of an hour in each direction. Such wide variations cannot be tolerated in a practical time scale, and this has led to the concept of Mean Solar Time in which all the days are of exactly the same length and equal to the average length of the Apparent Solar Day.

The positions of the stars in the sky are specified in relation to a fictitious reference point in the sky known as the First Point of Aries (or the Vernal Equinox). It is therefore convenient to adopt this same reference point when considering the rotation of the Earth against the background of the stars. The time scale so obtained is known as Apparent Sidereal Time.

Greenwich Mean Time

The diurnal rotation of the Earth on its axis causes the Sun and the other heavenly bodies to appear to cross the sky from East to West. It is convenient to represent this relative motion as if the Sun really performed a daily circuit around a fixed Earth. Noon in Apparent Solar Time may then be defined as the time at which the Sun transits across the observer's meridian. In Mean Solar Time, noon is similarly defined by the meridian transit of a fictitious Mean Sun moving uniformly in the sky with the same average speed as the true Sun. Mean Solar Time observed on the meridian of the transit circle telescope of the Royal Observatory at Greenwich is called Greenwich Mean Time (G.M.T.) The mean solar day is divided into 24 hours and, for astronomical and scientific purposes, these are numbered 0 to 23, commencing at midnight. Civil time is usually reckoned in two periods of 12 hours, designated a.m. (before noon) and p.m. (after noon): Civil time is also usually advanced by one hour during summer time (see later), whereas G.M.T. remains unchanged.

Universal Time

Before January 1, 1925 G.M.T. was reckoned in 24 hours commencing at noon: since that date it has been reckoned from midnight. In view of the risk of confusion in the use of the designation G.M.T. before and after 1925, the International Astronomical Union recommended in 1928 that astronomers should, for the present, employ the term Universal Time, U.T. (or Weltzeit, W.Z.) to denote G.M.T. measured from Greenwich Mean Midnight.

In precision work it has now become necessary to take account of small variations, hitherto negligible, in Universal Time. These arise from small irregularities in the rotation of the Earth. Observed astronomical time is designated U.T.0. Observed time corrected for the effects of the motion of the poles (giving rise to a "wandering" in longitude) is designated U.T.1. There is also a seasonal fluctuation in the rate of rotation of the Earth arising from meteorological causes, often called the annual fluctuation. U.T.1 corrected for this effect is designated U.T.2, and provides a time scale free from short-period fluctuations. It is still subject to small secular and irregular changes.

Apparent Solar Time

As has been mentioned, the time shown by a sundial is called Apparent Solar Time. It differs from Mean Solar Time by an amount known as the Equation of Time, which is the total effect of two causes which make the length of the apparent solar day non-uniform. One cause of variation is that the orbit of the Earth is not a circle, but an ellipse, having the Sun at one focus. As a consequence, the angular speed of the Earth in its orbit is not constant; it is greatest at the beginning of January when the Earth is nearest the Sun. The other cause is due to the obliquity of the ecliptic; the plane of the equator (which is at right-angles to the axis of rotation of the Earth) does not coincide with the ecliptic (the plane defined by the apparent annual motion of the Sun around the celestial sphere) but is inclined to it at an angle of 23° 27′. As a result, the apparent solar day is shorter than average at the equinoxes and longer at the solstices. From the combined effects of the components due to obliquity and eccentricity, the equation of time reaches its maximum values in February (−14 mins.) and early November (+16 mins.). It has a zero value on four dates during the year, and it is only on these dates (approx. April 15, June 14, Sept. 1, and Dec. 25) that a sundial shows Mean Solar Time.

Sidereal Time

A sidereal day is the duration of a complete rotation of the Earth with reference to the First Point of Aries. The term sidereal (or "star") time is perhaps a little misleading since the time scale so defined is not exactly the same as that which would be defined by successive transits of a selected star, as there is a small progressive motion between the stars and the First Point of Aries due to the precession of the Earth's axis. This makes the length of the sidereal day shorter than the true period of rotation by 0·008 seconds. Superimposed on this steady precessional motion are small oscillations called nutation, giving rise to fluctuations in apparent sidereal time amounting to as much as 1·2 seconds. It is therefore customary to employ Mean Sidereal Time, from which these fluctuations have been removed. The conversion of G.M.T. to Greenwich sidereal time (G.S.T.) may be performed by adding the value of the G.S.T. at 0^h on the day in question (page II of each month) to the G.M.T. converted to sidereal time using the table on p. 146.

Example. To find the G.S.T. at $2^h\ 41^m\ 11^s$ G.M.T. on Aug. 8

	h	m	s
G.S.T. at 0^h	21	06	07
G.M.T.	2	41	11
Acceleration for 2^h			20
" " $41^m\ 11^s$			7
Sum = G.S.T. = ...	23	47	45

If the observer is not on the Greenwich meridian then his longitude, measured positively westwards from Greenwich, must be subtracted from the G.S.T. to obtain Local Sidereal Time (L.S.T.). Thus, in the above example, an observer 5^h east of Greenwich, or 19^h west, would find his L.S.T. as $4^h\ 47^m\ 45^s$.

Ephemeris Time

In the study of the motions of the Sun, Moon and planets, observations taken over an extended period are used in the preparation of tables giving the apparent position of the body each day. A table of this sort is known as an ephemeris, and may be used in the comparison of current observations with tabulated positions. A detailed examination of the observations made over the past 300 years shows that the Sun, Moon and planets appear to depart from their predicted positions by amounts proportional to their mean motions. The only satisfactory explanation is that the time scale to which the observations were referred was not uniform as had been supposed. Since the time scale was based on the rotation of the Earth, it follows that this rotation is subject to irregularities. The fact that the discrepancies between the observed and ephemeris positions were proportional to the mean motions of the bodies made it possible to secure agreement by substituting a revised time scale and recomputing the ephemeris positions. The time scale which brings the ephemeris into agreement with the observations has been named Ephemeris Time (E.T.).

The new unit of time has been defined in terms of the apparent annual motion of the Sun. Thus the second is now defined in terms of the annual motion of the Earth in its orbit around the Sun (1/31556925·9747 of the Tropical Year for 1900 January 0 at 12 h. E.T.) instead of in terms of the diurnal rotation of the Earth on its axis (1/86 400 of the Mean Solar Day). In many branches of scientific work other than astronomy there has been a demand for a unit of time that is invariable, and the second of Ephemeris time was adopted by the Comité International des Poids et Mésures in 1956. The length of the unit has been chosen to provide general agreement with U.T. throughout the 19th and 20th centuries. During 1964 the estimated difference E.T. − U.T. is 35 seconds. The precise determination of E.T. from astronomical observations is a lengthy process, as the accuracy with which a single observation of the Sun can be made is far less than that obtainable in, for instance, a comparison between clocks. It is therefore necessary to average the observations over an extended period. Largely on account of its faster motion, the position of the Moon may be observed with greater accuracy, and a close approximation to Ephemeris Time may be obtained by comparing observations of the Moon with its ephemeris position. Even in this case, however, the requisite standard of accuracy can only be achieved by averaging over a number of years.

Atomic Time

The fundamental standards of time and frequency must be defined in terms of a periodic motion adequately uniform, enduring and susceptible of measurement. This has led in the past to the adoption of standards based on the observed motions in the Solar System. Recent progress has made it possible to consider the use of other natural standards, such as atomic or molecular oscillations. The oscillations so far employed are not in fact continuous periodic motions such as the revolution of the electrons in their orbits around the nuclei. The continuous oscillations are generated in an electrical circuit, the frequency of which is then compared or brought into coincidence with the frequency characteristic of the absorption or emission by the atoms or molecules when they change between two selected energy levels. At the National Physical Laboratory regular comparisons have been made since the middle of 1955 between quartz clocks of high stability and a frequency defined by atoms of caesium. The standard has proved of great value in the precise calibration of frequencies and time intervals: it has also been possible to build up a scale of "atomic time" by using continuously-running quartz clocks calibrated in terms of the caesium frequency standard. Because of the high precision attained in the comparisons, cumulative errors in the integrated time scale do not become serious in the course of a few years, and the atomic time scale may thus be compared with the astronomical time scale.

Radio Time Signals

The establishment of a uniform time system by the assessment of the performance of standard clocks in terms of astronomical observations is the work of a national observatory, and standard time is then made generally available by means of radio time signals. In the United Kingdom, the Royal Greenwich Observatory is responsible for the legal standard of time, and controls the "6-pips" radio signals emitted by the British Broadcasting Corporation. Signals by land line from the Observatory correct the Post Office Speaking Clock, TIM.

For survey and scientific purposes in which the highest accuracy is required, special signals are transmitted from the Post Office Radio Station at Rugby. The International Signals, consisting of a five-minute series of pips, one-tenth of a second long, with the pips at the minutes lengthened for identification, are radiated at 02.55–03.00, 08.55–09.00, 09.55–10.00 and 14.55–15.00, 17.55–18.00 and 20.55–21.00 from GBR (16 kc/s) and associated H.F. transmitters. The seconds pulses superposed on the MSF standard frequency transmissions, which consist of five cycles of a 1,000 c.p.s. tone, are derived from the same master control at the transmitting station, and are radiated for ten minutes in each quarter-hour on 2½, 5, and 10 Mc/s for 24-hours per day, and on 60 kc/s from 14.29–15.30. The carrier frequencies of all the MSF transmissions, and of GBR, are closely controlled, and measured regularly at the National Physical Laboratory in terms of the caesium atomic resonance. The time signals, derived from the same master oscillator, and thus rigidly locked to the carrier frequencies, are monitored regularly at the Royal Greenwich Observatory. A uniform rate is maintained throughout the year and, if corrections are required to keep the time signals in agreement with UT2, a step adjustment of 50 milliseconds is made on all transmissions on the first day of a month. Since April 1960 the Rugby service has been run in close co-operation with the time services of the United States. By mutual agreement, the rates are adjusted to correspond, and the signals are synchronised. Any necessary adjustments are made simultaneously in the U.K. and U.S.A. services. The American transmissions concerned are: WWV (Beltsville) 2½, 5, 10, 15, 20, 25 Mc/s; WWVH (Hawaii) 5, 10, 15 Mc/s; NBA (Canal Zone) 18 kc/s. Other national Observatories have agreed to some measure of co-ordination.

SUMMER TIME

In the United Kingdom, Summer Time, one hour ahead of G.M.T., was in force in 1963 between 02^h G.M.T. on March 31 and 02^h G.M.T. on October 27. The Home Secretary announced in Parliament on May 31, 1963, that Summer Time in 1964 would be extended to run from March 22 to October 25.

Variations of the Standard time may be used abroad and the dates of adoption are decided annually. In British Honduras the variation occurs in winter and is called Winter Time.

British Commonwealth.—	*Foreign Countries.—*	
British Honduras	Albania	Macao
Canada (except Yukon)	Azores	Madeira
Channel Islands	Parts of China	Norway
Hong Kong	Dominican Republic	Pescadores Is.
	Egypt	Poland
	Formosa	Portugal
	Iceland	Parts of U.S.A.
	Irish Republic	Syria
		Turkey
		Uruguay

STANDARD TIME

In the year 1880 it was enacted by statute that the word "time", when it occurred in any legal document relating to Great Britain, was to be interpreted, unless otherwise specifically stated, as the Mean Time of the Greenwich meridian.* Other nations similarly used the time of their own capital, but since the year 1883 the system of Standard Time by Zones has been gradually accepted, and now almost throughout the world a Standard Time which differs from that of Greenwich by an integral number of hours, either fast or slow, is used. In some countries (†) Standard Time is no longer used and the time given in the table below is that in normal use.

The large territories of the United States, Canada and U.S.S.R. are divided into zones approximately 7½° on either side of central meridians. The important ones are given below; there are in addition zones from 5 to 13 hours fast in the U.S.S.R. centred at 60° E. to 180° E.

Fast on Greenwich Time.

12 hrs. F...Fiji, Gilbert and Ellice Is., New Zealand, Marshall Is., Caroline Is. (east of 160° E.).

11½ „ F...Norfolk I., Nauru I.

11 „ F...New Caledonia, New Hebrides, Santa Cruz and Solomon Is., Truk, Ponape.

10 „ F...Sakhalin north of 50° N., Victoria, N.S.W. (except Broken Hill Area), Queensland, Tasmania, British New Guinea, Admiralty Is., Caroline Is. (west of 160° E.), Australian Capital Territory, Marianas Is.

9½ „ F...South Australia, Northern Territory of Australia, N.S.W. (Broken Hill Area), Dutch New Guinea.

9 „ F...Japan, Kei, Aru, Schouten Is., Sakhalin south of 50° N., Kurile Is., Manchuria, Korea.

8½ „ F...Molucca Is.

8 „ F...China (coast), Hong Kong, Philippine Is., Labuan, Macao, Timor, West Australia, Celebes, Sarawak, N. Borneo, Formosa, Pescadores Is., Vietnam.

7½ „ F...Federation of Malaya, Singapore, Indonesian Borneo and Java.

7 „ F...S. Sumatra, Christmas I. (Indian Ocean), Thailand, Cambodia, Laos.

6½ „ F...Burma, Cocos-Keeling Is., N. Sumatra.

6 „ F...Pakistan (East).

5½ „ F...India, Ceylon, Laccadive Is., Andaman and Nicobar Is.

5 „ F...Chagos Archipelago, Pakistan (West).

4 „ F...Mauritius, Seychelles, Reunion, Oman, U.S.S.R., 40° E. to 52°30′ E.

3½ „ F...Persia.

3 „ F...U.S.S.R. west of 40° E., Iraq, Ethiopia, Aden, Socotra I., Somaliland, Comoro Is., Madagascar, Uganda, Kenya, Tanganyika, Zanzibar.

2 „ F...Turkey, Greece, Bulgaria, Roumania, Finland, Israel, Jordan, U.A.R., Syria*, Cyprus, Rhodesia and
E. European. Nyasaland, South Africa and Protectorates Mozambique, Sudan, Congolese Republic, Cyrenaica †, Crete, Lebanon, Tripolitania.

1 hr. F....Sweden, Norway, Denmark, Netherlands, Belgium, Germany, France †, Luxemburg †, Spain †, Gibraltar †, Monaco †, Balearic Is. †, Poland, Austria, Hungary, Switzerland,
Mid-European. Italy, Czechoslovakia, Yugoslavia, Albania, Tunisia, Nigeria, Malta, Sicily, Central African Republic, Cameroon Republic, Republic of Congo, Angola, Spitzbergen, Algeria, Dahomey, Corsica †, Sardinia.

Greenwich Time..Great Britain, Ireland, Faroë, Channel Is., Portugal, Algeria, Morocco, Mauritania, Sierra Leone, West African republics, Ghana, Principe I., St. Helena, Gambia, Canary Is. †, Ascension I., Tangier, São Thomé, Rio de Oro†.

Slow on Greenwich Time.

1 hr. S...Iceland, Madeira, Portuguese Guinea.

2 hrs. S...Azores, Cape Verde Is., Fernando Noronha I., Scoresby Sound, South Georgia.

3 „ S...Greenland (excluding Scoresby Sound and Thule), Eastern Brazil, Uruguay, Argentina †.

3½ „ S...Newfoundland, Labrador, Dutch Guiana.

3¾ „ S...British Guiana.

4 „ S...Canada east of 68° W., Greenland (Thule Area), Puerto Rico, Lesser
Atlantic. Antilles, Central Brazil, Falkland Is., Paraguay, Bermuda, Bolivia, French Guiana, Chile.

4½ hrs. S...Venezuela, Curaçao I.

5 „ S...Canada from 68° W. to 85° W. (north) or 90° W. (south) Eastern States of
Eastern. U.S.A., Jamaica, Bahama Is., Cuba, Haiti, Peru, Panama, W. Brazil, Colombia, Cayman Is., Ecuador, Dominican Republic.

6 hrs. S...Central parts of U.S.A., Canada from 85° W. (north) or 90° W. (south)
Central. to 102° W., Costa Rica, Salvador, Honduras, part of Mexico, Guatemala, Nicaragua.

7 hrs. S...Canada from 102° W. to 120° W.,
Mountain. Mountain States of U.S.A., part of Mexico.

8 hrs. S...Canada west of 120° W., Alaska
Pacific. (south-east coast), Western States of U.S.A., part of Mexico.

9 hrs. S...Alaska N. of Cross Sound to 141° W. Yukon. Christmas Is. (Pacific Ocean).

10 „ S...Alaska from 141° W. to 162° W., Low Archipelago, Austral and Society Is., Hawaii, Fanning I.

11 „ S...Aleutian Is., Alaska (west coast), Samoa, Midway Is.

In the Tonga Islands the time 13^h fast and in Chatham Is.† $12h\ 45m$ fast on Greenwich is used, as the Date line is to the East of them.

THE DATE OR CALENDAR LINE

The line where the change of date occurs is a modification of the 180th meridian, and is drawn so as to include islands of any one group on the same side of the line, or for political reasons. It is indicated by joining up the following nine points:

Lat.	Long.	Lat.	Long.	Lat.	Long.
60° S.	180°	15° S.	172½° W.	53° N.	170° E.
51° S.	180°	5° S.	180°	65½° N.	169° W.
45° S.	172½° W.	48° N.	180°	75° N.	180°

---

* Summer Time is the "legal" time during the period in which its use is ordained.

SUNRISE AND SUNSET TABLE

Dec.	Latitude and Declination of Opposite Signs							Latitude and Declination of Same Signs					
	50°	45°	40°	30°	20°	10°	0°	10°	20°	30°	40°	45°	50°
°	h m	h m	h m	h m	h m	h m	h m	h m	h m	h m	h m	h m	h m
0	6 05	6 05	6 04	6 04	6 04	6 03	6 03	6 03	6 04	6 04	6 04	6 05	6 05
1	6 00	6 01	6 01	6 02	6 02	6 03	6 03	6 04	6 05	6 06	6 08	6 09	6 10
2	5 56	5 57	5 58	5 59	6 01	6 02	6 03	6 05	6 06	6 08	6 11	6 13	6 15
3	5 51	5 53	5 54	5 57	5 59	6 01	6 03	6 06	6 08	6 11	6 14	6 17	6 20
4	5 46	5 49	5 51	5 55	5 58	6 01	6 03	6 06	6 09	6 13	6 18	6 21	6 24
5	5 41	5 45	5 48	5 52	5 56	6 00	6 03	6 07	6 11	6 15	6 21	6 25	6 29
6	5 36	5 41	5 44	5 50	5 55	5 59	6 03	6 08	6 12	6 18	6 25	6 29	6 34
7	5 32	5 37	5 41	5 48	5 53	5 58	6 03	6 08	6 14	6 20	6 28	6 33	6 39
8	5 27	5 32	5 37	5 45	5 52	5 58	6 03	6 09	6 15	6 23	6 32	6 37	6 44
9	5 22	5 28	5 34	5 43	5 50	5 57	6 03	6 10	6 17	6 25	6 35	6 41	6 49
10	5 17	5 24	5 30	5 41	5 49	5 56	6 03	6 11	6 18	6 27	6 38	6 46	6 54
11	5 12	5 20	5 27	5 38	5 47	5 56	6 03	6 11	6 20	6 30	6 42	6 50	6 59
12	5 07	5 16	5 23	5 36	5 46	5 55	6 03	6 12	6 21	6 32	6 46	6 54	7 04
13	5 02	5 12	5 20	5 33	5 44	5 54	6 03	6 13	6 23	6 35	6 49	6 58	7 09
14	4 56	5 07	5 16	5 31	5 43	5 53	6 03	6 14	6 24	6 37	6 53	7 03	7 15
15	4 51	5 03	5 13	5 28	5 41	5 53	6 03	6 14	6 26	6 40	6 57	7 07	7 20
16	4 46	4 58	5 09	5 26	5 40	5 52	6 03	6 15	6 28	6 42	7 00	7 12	7 26
17	4 40	4 54	5 05	5 23	5 38	5 51	6 03	6 16	6 29	6 45	7 04	7 16	7 31
18	4 35	4 49	5 01	5 21	5 37	5 50	6 04	6 17	6 31	6 47	7 08	7 21	7 37
19	4 29	4 45	4 58	5 18	5 35	5 50	6 04	6 18	6 33	6 50	7 12	7 26	7 43
20	4 23	4 40	4 54	5 16	5 33	5 49	6 04	6 18	6 34	6 53	7 16	7 31	7 49
21	4 17	4 35	4 50	5 13	5 32	5 48	6 04	6 19	6 36	6 55	7 20	7 36	7 55
22	4 11	4 30	4 46	5 10	5 30	5 47	6 04	6 20	6 38	6 58	7 24	7 41	8 02
23	4 05	4 25	4 42	5 08	5 28	5 47	6 04	6 21	6 39	7 01	7 29	7 46	8 08
24	3 58	4 20	4 37	5 05	5 27	5 46	6 04	6 22	6 41	7 04	7 33	7 51	8 15
25	3 52	4 15	4 33	5 02	5 25	5 45	6 04	6 23	6 43	7 07	7 38	7 57	8 22
26	3 45	4 09	4 28	4 59	5 23	5 44	6 04	6 24	6 45	7 10	7 42	8 03	8 30
27	3 38	4 04	4 24	4 56	5 21	5 43	6 04	6 24	6 47	7 13	7 47	8 09	8 37
28	3 30	3 58	4 19	4 53	5 20	5 42	6 04	6 25	6 49	7 16	7 52	8 15	8 45
29	3 22	3 52	4 14	4 50	5 18	5 41	6 04	6 26	6 51	7 19	7 57	8 21	8 53

The local mean time of sunrise or sunset (as defined on page 138) may be found by determining the appropriate hour angle from the table above and subtracting it from or adding it to the time of transit given in the ephemeris for each month. The resulting local mean time may be converted into the standard time of the country by taking the difference between the longitude of the standard meridian of the country and that of the place, and adding it to the local mean time if the place is west of the standard meridian, and subtracting it if the place is east of the standard meridian.

Example.—Required the N.Z. Mean Time (12^h fast on G.M.T.) of sunset on May 24 at Auckland. The latitude is 36° 50′ south (or minus) and the longitude $11^h 39^m$ east. Taking the declination as +20°·7, we find

	h m
Tabular entry for 30° Lat. and Dec. 20°, opposite signs................	5 16
Proportional part for 6° 50′ of Lat......	− 15
Proportional part for 0°·7 of Dec.......	− 3
Hour angle........................	4 58
Sun transits........................	11 57
Longitudinal correction...............	+ 21
N.Z. Mean Time...............	17 16

MOONRISE AND MOONSET

It is also possible to calculate the times of moonrise and moonset using the above table though the method is more complicated, mainly because the apparent motion of the Moon is much more rapid than that of the Sun. A further minor difference is that the parallax of the Moon causes slightly later rising times and earlier setting times than would be the case if the Moon was as distant as the Sun.

Using the notation given below the auxiliary table the method may be conveniently divided into five steps as follows:

Auxiliary Table for Moonrise and Moonset

A \ X	40^m	45^m	50^m	55^m	60^m	65^m	70^m
h	m	m	m	m	m	m	m
1	2	2	2	2	3	3	3
2	3	4	4	5	5	5	6
3	5	6	6	7	8	8	9
4	7	8	8	9	10	11	12
5	8	9	10	11	13	14	15
6	10	11	13	14	15	16	18
7	12	13	15	16	18	19	20
8	13	15	17	18	20	22	23
9	15	17	19	21	23	24	26
10	17	19	21	23	25	27	29
11	18	21	23	25	28	30	32
12	20	23	25	28	30	33	35
13	22	24	27	30	33	35	38
14	23	26	29	32	35	38	41
15	25	28	31	34	38	41	44
16	27	30	33	37	40	43	47
17	28	32	35	39	43	46	50
18	30	34	38	41	45	49	53
19	32	36	40	44	48	51	55
20	33	38	42	46	50	54	58
21	35	39	44	48	53	57	61
22	37	41	46	50	55	60	64
23	38	43	48	53	58	62	67
24	40	45	50	55	60	65	70

Determination of times (G.M.T.) of moonrise and moonset.

Notation

φ = latitude of observer
λ = longitude of observer (measured positively towards the west).
T_{-1} = time of transit of Moon on previous day
T_0 = time of transit of Moon on day in question
T_1 = time of transit of Moon on following day
δ_0 = approximate declination of Moon
δ_R = declination of Moon at moonrise
δ_S = declination of Moon at moonset
h_0 = approximate hour angle of Moon
h_R = hour angle of Moon at moonrise
h_S = hour angle of Moon at moonset
t_R = time of moonrise
t_S = time of moonset

METHOD

1. With arguments φ, δ_0 enter table on p. 144 to determine h_0 where h_0 is negative for moonrise and positive for moonset.
2. Form approximate times from
   $t_R = T_0 + \lambda + h_0$
   $t_S = T_0 + \lambda + h_0$
3. Determine δ_R, δ_S for times t_R, t_S respectively.
4. Re-enter table on p. 144 with—
   (*a*) arguments φ, δ_R to determine h_R
   (*b*) arguments φ, δ_S to determine h_S
5. Form $t_R = T_0 + AX + \lambda + h_R + y$
   $t_S = T_0 + AX + \lambda + h_S - y$

where $A = (\lambda + h)/24^h$

$X = (T_0 - T_{-1})$ if $(\lambda + h)$ is negative

and $X = (T_1 - T_0)$ if $(\lambda + h)$ is positive

also y, which is an approximate correction due to the moon's parallax, is taken as 4^m in latitude 0°, 6^m in latitude 40°, and 8^m in latitude 50°. The term AX is obtained directly from the auxiliary table.

Example.—To find the times of moonrise and moonset at Vancouver ($\varphi = +49°$, $\lambda = +8^h\ 12^m$) on 1964 October 10. The starting data (from p. 128) are

	h	m
T_{-1} =	14	47
T_0 =	15	34
T_1 =	16	23
δ_0 =	$-21°{\cdot}5$	

1. $h_0 = \pm 4^h\ 18^m$
2. Approximate values
   $t_R = 10^d 15^h 34^m + 8^h 12^m + (-4^h 18^m)$
   $= 10^d\ 19^h\ 28^m$
   $t_S = 10^d\ 15^h 34^m + 8^h 12^m + (+4^h 18^m)$
   $= 11^d\ 04^h\ 04^m$
3. $\delta_R = -21°{\cdot}9$
   $\delta_S = -22°{\cdot}7$
4. $h_R = -4^h\ 16^m$
   $h_S = +4^h\ 11^m$
5. $t_R = 10^d\ 15^h\ 34^m + (+8^m) + 8^h\ 12^m - 4^h\ 16^m + 8^m = 10^d\ 19^h\ 46^m$ G.M.T.
   $t_S = 10^d\ 15^h\ 34^m + (+26^m) + 8^h\ 12^m + 4^h\ 11^m - 8^m = 11^d\ 04^h\ 15^m$ G.M.T.

To get the L.M.T. of the phenomenon the longitude is subtracted from the G.M.T. thus

Moonrise = $10^d\ 19^h\ 46^m - 8^h\ 12^m = 10^d\ 11^h\ 34^m$
Moonset = $11^d\ 04^h\ 15^m - 8^h\ 12^m = 10^d\ 20^h\ 03^m$

ASTRONOMICAL CONSTANTS

Solar Parallax .... 8″·80
Precession for the year 1964 .... 50″·27
,, in R.A. .... $3^s{\cdot}074$
,, in Declination .... 20″·04
Constant of Nutation .... 9″·21
Constant of Aberration .... 20″·47
Mean Obliquity of Ecliptic (1964) .. 23° 26′ 38″
Moon's Equatorial Hor. Parallax .... 57′ 02″·70
Velocity of Light in vacuo *per sec.* 186,324 miles
Solar motion *per sec.* ..... 19·5 km. = 12·1 miles
Equatorial radius of the Earth .... 3963·35 miles
Polar radius of the Earth .... 3950·01 miles

North Galactic Pole (I.A.U. *Standard*) .. R.A. $12^h\ 49^m$. Dec. 27°·4 N. (1950·0).
Solar Apex (*Boss*) .... R.A. 270° Dec. 34° N.
Length of Year ... Tropical ...... 365·24220
(*In Mean Solar Days*) Sidereal .... 365·25636
Anomalistic .... 365·25964
(*Perihelion to Perihelion*)
Eclipse .... 346·6200

		d	h	m	s
Length of Month (*Mean Values*)	New Moon to New	29	12	44	02·9
	Sidereal	27	07	43	11·5
	Anomalistic ...... (*Perigee to Perigee*)	27	13	18	33·2

MEAN AND SIDEREAL TIME

Acceleration

h	m s	h	m s
1	0 10	13	2 08
2	0 20	14	2 18
3	0 30	15	2 28
4	0 39	16	2 38
5	0 49	17	2 48
6	0 59	18	2 57
7	1 09	19	3 07
8	1 19	20	3 17
9	1 29	21	3 27
10	1 39	22	3 37
11	1 48	23	3 47
12	1 58	24	3 57

m s	s
0 00	
	0
3 02	
	1
9 07	
	2
15 13	
	3
21 18	
	4
27 23	
	5
33 28	
	6
39 34	
	7
45 39	
	8
51 44	
	9
57 49	
	10
60 00	

Retardation

h	m s	h	m s
1	0 10	13	2 08
2	0 20	14	2 18
3	0 29	15	2 27
4	0 39	16	2 37
5	0 49	17	2 47
6	0 59	18	2 57
7	1 09	19	3 07
8	1 19	20	3 17
9	1 28	21	3 26
10	1 38	22	3 36
11	1 48	23	3 46
12	1 58	24	3 56

m s	s
0 00	
	0
3 03	
	1
9 09	
	2
15 15	
	3
21 21	
	4
27 28	
	5
33 34	
	6
39 40	
	7
45 46	
	8
51 53	
	9
57 59	
	10
60 00	

MEAN REFRACTION

Alt. ° ′	Ref. ′	Alt. ° ′	Ref. ′
1 20		4 30	
	21		10
1 30		5 06	
	20		9
1 41		5 50	
	19		8
1 52		6 41	
	18		7
2 05		7 54	
	17		6
2 19		9 27	
	16		5
2 35		11 39	
	15		4
2 52		15 00	
	14		3
3 12		20 42	
	13		2
3 34		32 20	
	12		1
4 00		62 17	
	11		0
4 30		90 00	

The length of a sidereal day in mean time is $23^h\ 56^m\ 04^s.09$. Hence 1^h M.T.$=1^h+9^s.86$ S.T. and 1^h S.T.$=1^h-9^s.83$ M.T.

To convert an interval of mean time to the corresponding interval of sidereal time, enter the acceleration table with the given mean time (taking the hours and the minutes and seconds separately) and add the acceleration obtained to the given mean time. To convert an interval of sidereal time to the corresponding interval of mean time, take out the retardation for the given sidereal time and subtract.

The columns for the minutes and seconds of the argument are in the form known as Critical Tables. To use these tables, find in the appropriate left-hand column the two entries between which the given number of minutes and seconds lies; the quantity in the right-hand column between these two entries is the required acceleration or retardation. Thus the acceleration for $11^m\ 26^s$ (which lies between the entries $9^m\ 07^s$ and $15^m\ 13^s$) is 2^s. If the given number of minutes and seconds is a tabular entry, the required acceleration or retardation is the entry in the right-hand column *above* the given tabular entry; e.g. the retardation for $45^m\ 46^s$ is 7^s.

Example.—Convert $14^h\ 27^m\ 35^s$ from S.T. to M.T.

	h m s
Given S.T.	14 27 35
Retardation for 14^h.	2 18
Retardation for $27^m\ 35^s$	5
Corresponding M.T.	14 25 12

For further explanation, see p. 141.

The refraction table is also in the form of a critical table.

THE SUMMER TIME ACTS

In 1916 an Act ordained that during a defined period of that year the legal time for general purposes in Great Britain should be one hour in advance of Greenwich Mean Time. The practice was stabilized (until the war) by the *Summer Time Acts*, 1922 to 1925, which enacted that "For the purposes of this Act, the period of summer time shall be taken to be the period beginning at two o'clock, Greenwich Mean Time, in the morning of the day next following the third Saturday in April, or, if that day is Easter Day, the day next following the second Saturday in April and ending at two o'clock, Greenwich Mean Time, in the morning of the day next following the first Saturday in Otober."

During the Second World War the duration of Summer Time was extended and in the years 1941–45 and in 1947, Double Summer Time (2 hrs. in advance of Greenwich Mean Time) was in force. Summer Time was extended in each year from 1948 to 1952 and again in 1961–1963, by Order in Council.

The duration of Summer Time during the last few years is given in the following table.

1951 Apr. 15—Oct. 21	1958 Apr. 20—Oct. 5
1952 Apr. 20—Oct. 26	1959 Apr. 19—Oct. 4
1953 Apr. 19—Oct. 4	1960 Apr. 10—Oct. 2
1954 Apr. 11—Oct. 3	1961 Mar. 26—Oct. 29
1955 Apr. 17—Oct. 2	1962 Mar. 25—Oct. 28
1956 Apr. 22—Oct. 7	1963 Mar. 31—Oct. 27
1957 Apr. 14—Oct. 6	

ASTRONOMERS ROYAL

John Flamsteed, first Astronomer Royal	1675–1719
Edmund Halley	1720–1742
James Bradley	1742–1762
Nathaniel Bliss	1762–1764
Nevil Maskelyne	1765–1811
John Pond	1811–1835
Sir George Biddell Airy	1835–1881
Sir William Henry Mahoney Christie	1881–1910
Sir Frank Watson Dyson	1910–1933
Sir Harold Spencer Jones	1933–1955
Sir Richard Woolley	1955–

PHENOMENA OF JUPITER'S SATELLITES, 1964

January

G.M.T. d h m	Sat.	Phen.
3 18 00	III	Ec f.
3 21 55	II	Sh c.
4 22 16	I	Sh c.
5 18 47	II	Ec f.
5 21 44	I	Ec f.
6 18 55	I	Sh.f.
10 19 34	III	Ec.c.
10 22 02	III	Ec.f.
12 19 00	II	Ec.c.
12 21 26	II	Ec.f.
12 23 40	I	Ec.f.
13 18 41	I	Sh.c.
13 20 51	I	Sh.f.
14 18 09	I	Ec.f.
19 21 39	II	Ec.c.
20 20 37	I	Sh.c.
20 22 47	I	Sh.f.
21 18 49	II	Sh.f.
21 20 04	I	Ec.f.
27 22 33	I	Sh.c.
28 17 35	III	Sh.c.
28 19 02	II	Sh.c.
28 19 58	III	Sh.f.
28 21 25	II	Sh.f.
28 21 59	I	Ec.f.
29 19 12	I	Sh.f.

February

G.M.T. d h m	Sat.	Phen.
4 21 38	II	Sh.c.
4 21 38	III	Sh.c.
5 18 58	I	Sh.c.
5 21 09	I	Sh.f.
6 18 23	I	Ec.f.
6 18 43	II	Ec.f.
12 20 54	I	Sh.c.
13 20 19	I	Ec.f.
13 21 22	II	Ec.f.
15 18 10	III	Ec.f.
21 19 30	I	Sh.f.
22 18 31	II	Sh.f.
22 19 48	III	Ec.c.
28 19 15	I	Sh.c.
29 18 38	I	Ec.f.
29 18 44	II	Sh.c.
29 21 07	II	Sh.f.

March

G.M.T. d h m	Sat.	Phen.
7 20 33	I	Ec.f.
9 18 37	II	Ec.f.
11 20 11	III	Sh.f.
15 19 46	I	Sh.f.
22 19 31	I	Sh.c.

July

G.M.T. d h m	Sat.	Phen.
6 02 51	I	Ec.c.
7 02 20	I	Sh.f.
8 02 28	III	Ec.f.
12 01 56	II	Ec.c.
22 01 08	I	Ec.c.
28 01 27	II	Sh.c.
29 03 02	I	Ec.c.
30 00 21	I	Sh.c.

August

G.M.T. d h m	Sat.	Phen.
2 02 17	III	Sh.c.
6 01 20	II	Ec.f.
6 23 25	I	Ec.c.
13 01 31	II	Ec.c.
13 03 55	II	Ec.f.
14 01 19	I	Ec.c.
15 00 45	I	Sh.f.
20 00 20	III	Ec.c.
20 02 30	III	Ec.f.
20 04 05	II	Ec.c.
21 03 13	I	Ec.c.
22 00 31	I	Sh.c.
22 01 00	II	Sh.f.
27 04 20	III	Ec.c.
29 01 14	II	Sh.c.
29 02 24	I	Sh.c.
29 23 36	I	Ec.c.
30 22 20	II	Ec.f.
30 23 01	I	Sh.f.

September

G.M.T. d h m	Sat.	Phen.
5 03 51	II	Sh.c.
6 01 30	I	Ec.c.
6 22 17	III	Sh.c.
6 22 30	II	Ec.c.
6 22 46	I	Sh.c.
7 00 25	III	Sh.f.
7 00 54	II	Ec.f.
7 00 55	I	Sh.f.
13 03 24	I	Ec.c.
14 00 40	I	Sh.c.
14 01 04	II	Ec.c.
14 02 17	III	Sh.c.
14 02 48	I	Sh.f.
14 03 29	II	Ec.f.
14 21 53	I	Ec.c.
15 21 16	I	Sh.f.
15 22 10	II	Sh.f.
20 05 19	I	Ec.c.
21 02 33	I	Sh.c.
21 03 39	II	Ec.c.
21 23 47	I	Ec.c.
22 21 02	I	Sh.c.
22 22 23	II	Sh.c.
23 23 10	I	Sh.f.
23 00 47	II	Sh.f.
24 22 33	III	Ec.f.
29 01 42	I	Ec.c.
29 22 55	I	Sh.c.
30 01 00	II	Sh.c.
30 01 04	I	Sh.f.
30 20 10	I	Ec.c.

October

G.M.T. d h m	Sat.	Phen.
2 00 23	III	Ec.c.
2 02 34	III	Ec.f.
6 03 36	I	Ec.c.
7 00 49	I	Sh.c.
7 02 58	I	Sh.f.
7 03 37	II	Sh.c.
7 22 05	I	Ec.c.
8 21 26	I	Sh.f.
8 22 04	II	Ec.c.
9 04 24	III	Ec.c.
12 20 26	III	Sh.f.
13 05 31	I	Ec.c.
14 02 42	I	Sh.c.
14 04 52	I	Sh.f.
14 23 59	I	Ec.c.
15 21 11	I	Sh.c.
15 23 20	I	Sh.f.
16 00 39	II	Ec.c.
17 19 34	II	Sh.c.
17 21 59	II	Sh.f.
19 22 17	III	Sh.c.
20 00 26	III	Sh.f.
22 01 54	I	Ec.c.
22 23 05	I	Sh.c.
23 01 14	I	Sh.f.
23 03 14	II	Ec.c.
23 20 23	I	Ec.c.
24 19 43	I	Sh.f.
24 22 11	II	Sh.c.
25 00 36	II	Sh.f.
27 02 18	III	Sh.c.
29 03 49	I	Ec.c.
30 00 59	I	Sh.c.
30 05 48	II	Ec.c.
30 22 17	I	Ec.c.
31 19 27	I	Sh.c.
31 21 37	I	Sh.f.

November

G.M.T. d h m	Sat.	Phen.
1 00 48	II	Sh.c.
2 19 06	II	Ec.c.
5 05 43	I	Ec.c.
6 02 53	I	Sh.c.
6 05 03	I	Sh.f.
6 20 27	III	Ec.c.
7 00 12	I	Ec.c.
7 21 22	I	Sh.c.
7 23 31	I	Sh.f.
8 05 51	II	Sh.f.
8 18 41	I	Ec.c.
9 18 00	I	Sh.f.
9 21 41	II	Ec.c.
11 19 10	II	Sh.f.
14 00 28	III	Ec.c.
14 02 39	III	Ec.f.
14 04 17	I	Ec.f.
14 23 16	I	Sh.c.
15 01 26	I	Sh.f.
15 22 46	I	Ec.f.
16 17 45	I	Sh.c.
16 19 55	I	Sh.f.
17 02 42	II	Ec.f.
17 17 15	I	Ec.f.
18 19 21	II	Sh.c.
18 21 47	II	Sh.f.
21 06 12	I	Ec.f.
22 01 11	I	Sh.c.
23 00 41	I	Ec.f.
23 19 40	I	Sh.c.
23 21 49	I	Sh.f.
24 05 18	II	Ec.f.
24 18 20	III	Sh.c.
24 19 10	I	Ec.f.
24 20 31	III	Sh.f.
25 21 58	II	Sh.c.
26 00 24	II	Sh.f.
27 18 36	II	Ec.f.
30 02 36	I	Ec.f.
30 21 34	I	Sh.c.
30 23 44	I	Sh.f.

December

G.M.T. d h m	Sat.	Phen.
1 21 05	I	Ec.f.
1 22 21	III	Sh.c.
2 00 32	III	Sh.f.
2 18 13	I	Sh.f.
3 00 35	II	Sh.c.
4 21 13	II	Ec.f.
7 04 32	I	Ec.f.
7 23 29	I	Sh.c.
8 01 39	I	Sh.f.
8 23 00	I	Ec.f.
9 17 58	I	Sh.c.
9 20 08	I	Sh.f.
10 17 29	I	Ec.f.
11 23 50	II	Ec.f.
12 16 32	III	Ec.c.
12 18 44	III	Ec.f.
13 18 58	II	Sh.f.
15 01 25	I	Sh.c.
16 00 56	I	Ec.f.
16 19 53	I	Sh.c.
16 22 03	I	Sh.f.
17 19 25	I	Ec.f.
19 02 26	II	Ec.f.
19 20 33	III	Ec.c.
19 22 46	III	Ec.f.
20 19 09	II	Sh.c.
20 21 35	II	Sh.f.
23 02 51	I	Ec.f.
23 21 49	I	Sh.c.
23 23 58	I	Sh.f.
24 21 20	I	Ec.f.
25 18 27	I	Sh.f.
27 00 35	III	Ec.c.
27 02 49	III	Ec.f.
27 21 46	II	Sh.c.
28 00 12	II	Sh.f.
29 18 22	II	Ec.f.
30 23 44	I	Sh.c.
31 23 15	I	Ec.f.

Jupiter's satellites transit across the disk from east to west, and pass behind the disk from west to east. The shadows that they cast also transit across the disk. With the exception at times of Satellite IV, the satellites also pass through the shadow of the planet, i.e. they are eclipsed. Just before opposition the satellite disappears in the shadow to the west of the planet, and reappears from occultation on the east limb. Immediately after opposition the satellite is occulted at the west limb, and reappears from eclipse to the east of the planet. At times approximately two to four months before and after opposition, both phases of eclipses of Satellite III may be seen. When Satellite IV is eclipsed, both phases may be seen.

The list of phenomena gives most of the eclipses and shadow transits visible in the British Isles under favourable conditions.

Ec. = Eclipse　　c. = commences
Sh. = Shadow transit　　f. = finishes

CELESTIAL PHENOMENA FOR OBSERVATION IN 1964

ECLIPSES, 1964

During 1964 there will be six eclipses; this is only one short of the maximum possible number. Only the two lunar eclipses will be visible from the British Isles.

1. A partial eclipse of the Sun on January 14, not visible from the British Isles. The eclipse will be seen from the southern part of Tasmania, Antarctica, the Falkland Islands and the Southern tip of South America.

2. A partial eclipse of the Sun on June 10, not visible from the British Isles. The eclipse is visible from Antarctica, Australia, and New Zealand.

3. A total eclipse of the Moon on June 24–25, visible from the British Isles. The eclipse is visible from the Indian Ocean, south-west Asia, Africa, Europe, the Atlantic Ocean, Antarctica and the Americas. The partial eclipse begins at $24^d\ 23^h\ 09^m$ and ends at $25^d\ 03^h\ 03^m$ while totality lasts from $25^d\ 00^h\ 16^m$ to $25^d\ 01^h\ 57^m$.

4. A partial eclipse of the Sun on July 9, not visible from the British Isles. The eclipse is visible from northern Canada, the Arctic and northern Asia.

5. A partial eclipse of the Sun on December 3–4, not visible from the British Isles. The eclipse is visible from north-east Asia, the north Pacific Ocean and Alaska.

6. A total eclipse of the Moon on December 19, visible from the British Isles. The eclipse is visible from western Asia, the Indian Ocean, Africa, Europe, the Atlantic Ocean, the Arctic, North and South America and the Pacific Ocean. The partial eclipse begins at $00^h\ 59^m$ and ends at $04^h\ 15^m$. Totality lasts from $02^h\ 07^m$ to $03^h\ 07^m$.

OCCULTATIONS, 1964

This year is a very poor one for occultation observers in the British Isles as not a single bright star or planet undergoes occultation. The brightest star occulted is ζ Tauri ($3^m{\cdot}0$), during the late evening of January 25.

No first magnitude star will be occulted again before 1967.

Occultation Observations.—Observations of the times of these occultations are made by both amateurs and professionals. Such observations are later analysed to yield accurate positions of the Moon; this is one method of determining the difference between ephemeris time and universal time.

Many of the observations made by amateurs are obtained with the use of a stop-watch which is compared with a time-signal immediately after the observation. Thus an accuracy of about one-fifth of a second is obtainable, though the observer's personal equation may amount to one-third or one-half of a second.

OCCULTATIONS OF STARS

The list on the opposite page includes all the occultations visible under favourable conditons in the British Isles. Disappearances of stars down to magnitude 6·9 are normally included, and reappearances to 5·9 magnitude. No occultation is included unless the star is at least 10° above the horizon and the Sun sufficiently far below the horizon to permit the star to be seen with the naked eye or in a small telescope. The altitude limit is reduced from 10° to 2° for stars and planets brighter than magnitude 2·0 and such occultations are also predicted in daylight.

The column Phase shows whether a disappearance (D) or reappearance (R) is to be observed. Times and position angles (*P*), reckoned from the north point in the direction north, east, south, west, are given for Greenwich (Lat. 51° 29′, Long. 0°) and Edinburgh (Lat. 55° 56′, Long. 3° 11′ west). The coefficients *a* and *b* are the variations in the G.M.T. for each degree of longitude (positive to the west) and latitude (positive to the north) respectively: they enable approximate times (to within about 1^m generally) to be found for any point in the British Isles. If the point of observation is $\Delta\lambda$ degrees west and $\Delta\phi$ degrees north, the approximate time is found by adding $a.\Delta\lambda + b.\Delta\phi$ to the given G.M.T.

As an illustration the disappearance of 33 Piscium on December 12 at Liverpool will be found from both Greenwich and Edinburgh.

	Greenwich	Edinburgh
	°	°
Longitude	0·0	+3·2
Long. of Liverpool	+3·0	+3·0
$\Delta\lambda$	+3·0	−0·2
Latitude	+51·5	+55·9
Lat. of Liverpool	+53·4	+53·4
$\Delta\phi$	+1·9	−2·5
	h m	h m
G.M.T.	22 14·8	22 11·0
$a.\Delta\lambda$	−1·8	+0·1
$b.\Delta\phi$	−1·1	+0·8
	22 11·9	22 11·9

If the occultation is given for one station but not the other, the reason for the suppression is given by the following code.

No. occn. = star not occulted.
Low = star's altitude less than 10° (2° for bright stars and planets).
Sun = Sun not sufficiently below the horizon.
Graze = occultation is of very short duration.

It will be noticed that in some cases the coefficients *a* and *b* are not given: this is because the occultation is so short that prediction for other places by means of these coefficients would not be reliable.

OCCULTATIONS OF STARS BY THE MOON, 1964

Date	Star	Mag.	Phase	Age of Moon	Greenwich G.M.T.	Greenwich a	Greenwich b	Greenwich P	Edinburgh G.M.T.	Edinburgh a	Edinburgh b	Edinburgh P
				d	h m	m	m	°	h m	m	m	°
Jan. 19	30 Piscium	4·7	D	4·9	19 41·9	−0·8	−1·1	80	19 35·6	−0·7	−0·7	64
22	434 B. (Ceti)	6·7	D	8·1	22 44·5	−0·6	−0·2	49	22 43·1	−0·6	+0·4	32
22	85 Ceti	6·3	D	8·1	23 20·3	−0·6	+2·6	6	No occn.	..	..	..
24	68 Tauri	4·2	D	9·9	16 41·9	−0·7	+1·5	80	16 47·2	−0·5	+1·7	70
24	+17° 724	6·9	D	9·9	17 35·9	−0·7	+1·9	53	17 43·2	−0·5	+2·2	40
25	ζ Tauri	3·0	D	11·1	22 21·7	−1·5	−2·2	127	22 10·3	−1·3	−1·0	109
25	ζ Tauri	3·0	R	11·1	23 13·6	−1·4	+1·3	219	23 13·1	−1·2	+0·4	236
Feb. 20	193 B. Tauri	6·3	D	7·2	Graze	..	..	..	18 07·5	−1·7	−0·9	116
21	68 Tauri	4·2	D	7·5	No occn.	..	..	..	0 47·9	—	—	159
21	+17° 724	6·9	D	7·5	Low	..	..	..	1 08·7	+0·1	−1·4	91
22	η Geminorum *f*	3·5	D	9·3	19 22·4	−1·1	+3·1	32	No occn.	..	..	..
22	η Geminorum *f*	3·5	R	9·3	20 08·5	−1·7	−2·5	316	No occn.	..	..	..
22	μ Geminorum	3·2	D	9·4	23 24·4	−1·3	+0·2	50	23 22·9	−1·4	+1·2	34
22	μ Geminorum	3·2	R	9·4	24 12·6	−0·2	−2·7	315	23 58·3	−0·1	−3·6	328
24	+22° 1687	6·9	D	10·5	0 45·4	−0·7	−1·6	104	0 36·2	−0·8	−1·4	97
24	49 B. Cancri	5·9	D	11·3	No occn.	..	..	..	20 47·1	−1·2	−2·0	150
25	η Cancri	5·5	D	11·6	2 58·1	−0·6	−1·1	69	2 51·3	−0·7	−1·0	64
Mar. 2	80 Virginis	5·8	R	17·5	0 50·6	−1·4	+0·9	276	0 50·4	−1·1	+0·8	285
18	162 B. Tauri	6·3	D	4·7	20 02·7	−0·9	+1·4	23	No occn.	..	..	..
18	173 B. Tauri	6·8	D	4·8	21 54·9	−0·7	+1·3	18	No occn.	..	..	..
18	180 B. Tauri	6·2	D	4·8	Low	..	..	..	22 51·7	+0·1	−1·4	88
19	106 Tauri	5·3	D	5·8	23 14·7	+0·1	−1·8	110	23 06·9	0·0	−1·7	101
20	141 (Tauri)	6·3	D	6·7	20 06·5	−1·4	0·0	65	20 03·7	−1·3	+0·6	50
20	14 B. Geminorum	6·0	D	6·9	23 42·2	0·0	−1·8	109	23 34·1	−0·2	−1·7	102
21	44 Geminorum	5·9	D	7·8	21 15·5	−1·1	−1·5	108	21 06·1	−1·1	−1·1	97
22	μ Cancri	5·4	D	8·8	22 24·3	−1·2	−1·0	87	22 16·9	−1·2	−0·6	78
Apr. 19	+20° 2232	6·8	D	7·4	23 17·4	−1·0	−0·8	61	23 10·9	−1·1	−0·6	54
22	398 B. Leonis	6·7	D	10·4	23 09·6	0·0	−3·1	176	22 56·6	−0·3	−2·6	170
28	ν Scorpii *m*	4·3	D	16·5	23 54·2	−0·9	0·0	133	23 52·4	−0·8	+0·4	129
29	ν Scorpii *m*	4·3	R	16·5	1 09·6	−1·7	+0·3	273	1 06·1	−1·4	+0·4	275
May 14	+22° 1352	6·8	D	3·0	No occn.	..	..	..	22 08·2	—	—	166
15	+22° 1735	6·9	D	4·1	Low	..	..	..	23 13·4	+0·4	−1·5	114
22	80 Virginis	5·8	D	11·0	21 15·1	−1·8	0·0	96	Sun	..	..	..
June 3	τ Aquarii	4·2	R	22·2	2 27·1	−0·9	+1·6	263	Low	..	..	..
Aug 22	φ Capricorni	5·4	D	14·2	0 24·2	−2·3	−1·7	124	0 12·8	−1·7	−0·8	112
28	147 B. Arietis	5·8	R	21·2	23 18·2	−0·4	+1·3	287	23 23·0	−0·3	+1·3	295
Sept. 1	3 Geminorum *m*	5·8	R	24·3	2 28·8	−0·8	+0·4	310	2 25·7	—	—	332
18	κ Capricorni	4·8	D	12·7	20 25·5	−1·4	+1·1	57	20 26·5	−1·2	+1·1	52
29	87 B. Geminorum	5·8	R	22·9	0 20·8	−0·2	+0·9	296	0 23·8	−0·3	+0·8	309
Oct. 13	51 Sagittarii	5·7	D	8·1	18 34·0	−1·6	−0·1	77	Low	..	..	..
13	52 Sagittarii	4·7	D	8·1	19 06·3	−2·0	−1·1	124	Low	..	..	..
19	30 Piscium	4·7	D	13·4	1 41·2	−0·9	−1·5	91	1 33·0	−0·8	−1·0	75
24	ο Tauri	4·8	R	19·3	No occn.	..	..	..	21 35·0	+0·9	+3·0	188
28	γ Cancri	4·7	R	22·4	1 22·6	−1·0	−0·9	333	No occn.	..	..	..
Nov. 9	ψ Sagittarii *m*	4·9	D	5·4	16 46·9	−1·6	−0·4	88	Low	..	..	..
12	154 B. Capricorni	6·1	D	8·5	18 31·1	−1·5	+0·2	69	18 28·1	−1·3	+0·4	62
14	252 G. Aquarii	6·8	D	10·7	23 59·8	−0·6	−1·0	72	23 54·6	−0·5	−0·6	57
18	ξ¹ Ceti	4·5	D	13·7	1 41·2	−0·6	+1·1	23	1 48·3	—	—	357
20	ι Tauri	4·7	R	16·6	21 53·0	−1·0	+1·1	275	21 54·4	−1·0	+0·9	289
21	109 Tauri	5·1	R	16·9	5 21·5	−1·1	+1·0	209	5 20·3	−0·9	0·0	225
21	1 Geminorum	4·3	D	17·6	19 20·6	+0·2	+1·2	91	19 27·0	+0·2	+1·4	83
21	1 Geminorum	4·3	R	17·6	20 11·0	+0·1	+1·6	247	20 18·4	+0·1	+1·6	257
Dec. 9	37 Capricorni	5·8	D	5·7	No occn.	..	..	..	17 49·4	—	—	127
12	30 Piscium	4·7	D	8·8	20 23·5	−0·5	+1·1	21	20 29·5	+0·1	+2·1	0
12	33 Piscium	4·7	D	8·9	22 14·8	−0·6	−0·6	62	22 11·0	−0·5	−0·3	47
17	33 B. Tauri	6·3	D	13·0	1 24·6	−0·8	−1·0	79	1 18·6	−0·8	−0·5	65

FIXED STARS, 1964

Name	Mag.	R.A.	Dec.	Spectrum
		h m	° ′	
α Andromedæ *Alpheratz*	2·1	0 06·5	+28 53	A0p
β Cassiopeiæ *Caph*	2·4	0 07·2	+58 57	F5
γ Pegasi *Algenib*	2·9	0 11·4	+14 59	B2
α Phœnicis	2·4	0 24·5	−42 30	K0
α Cassiopeiæ *Schedar*	2·3	0 38·5	+56 20	K0
β Ceti *Diphda*	2·2	0 41·8	−18 11	K0
γ Cassiopeiæ*	Var.	0 54·5	+60 31	B0p
β Andromedæ *Mirach*	2·4	1 07·7	+35 26	M0
δ Cassiopeiæ	2·8	1 23·4	+60 03	A5
α Eridani *Achernar*	0·6	1 36·4	−57 25	B5
β Arietis *Sheratan*	2·7	1 52·6	+20 38	A5
α Ursæ Minoris *Polaris*	2·1	1 58·6	+89 06	F8
γ Andromedæ *Almak*	2·3	2 01·7	+42 09	K0
α Arietis *Hamal*	2·2	2 05·1	+23 18	K2
β Persei *Algol**	Var.	3 05·8	+40 49	B8
α Persei *Mirfak*	1·9	3 21·7	+49 44	F5
η Tauri *Alcyone*	3·0	3 45·3	+24 00	B5p
α Tauri *Aldebaran*	1·1	4 33·9	+16 26	K5
β Orionis *Rigel*	0·3	5 12·8	− 8 15	B8p
α Aurigæ *Capella*	0·2	5 14·0	+45 58	G0
γ Orionis *Bellatrix*	1·7	5 23·2	+ 6 19	B2
β Tauri *Elnath*	1·8	5 24·0	+28 35	B8
δ Orionis	2·5	5 30·2	− 0 19	B0
α Leporis	2·7	5 31·1	−17 51	F0
ε Orionis	1·7	5 34·4	− 1 13	B0
ζ Orionis	2·0	5 38·9	− 1 58	B0
κ Orionis	2·2	5 46·0	− 9 41	B0
α Orionis *Betelgeuse**	Var.	5 53·2	+ 7 24	M0
β Aurigæ *Menkalinan*	2·1	5 56·9	+44 57	A0p
β Canis Majoris *Mirzam*	2·0	6 21·1	−17 56	B1
α Carinæ *Canopus*	−0·9	6 23·2	−52 41	F0
γ Geminorum *Alhena*	1·9	6 35·6	+16 26	A0
α Canis Majoris *Sirius*	−1·6	6 43·6	−16 40	A0
ε Canis Majoris	1·6	6 57·2	−28 55	B1
δ Canis Majoris	2·0	7 06·9	−26 20	F8p
α Geminorum *Castor*	1·6	7 32·3	+31 58	A0
α Canis Minoris *Procyon*	0·5	7 37·4	+ 5 19	F5
β Geminorum *Pollux*	1·2	7 43·1	+28 07	K0
ζ Puppis	2·3	8 02·3	−39 54	Od
γ Velorum	1·9	8 08·4	−47 14	Oap
ε Carinæ	1·7	8 21·8	−59 24	K0
δ Velorum	2·0	8 43·7	−54 35	A0
λ Velorum *Suhail*	2·2	9 06·7	−43 17	K5
β Carinæ	1·8	9 12·8	−69 34	A0
ι Carinæ	2·2	9 16·1	−59 07	F0
α Hydræ *Alphard*	2·2	9 25·8	− 8 30	K2
α Leonis *Regulus*	1·3	10 06·5	+12 09	B8
γ Leonis *Algeiba*	2·6	10 18·0	+20 01	K0
β Ursæ Majoris *Merak*	2·4	10 59·7	+56 35	A0
α Ursæ Majoris *Dubhe*	1·9	11 01·5	+61 57	K0

* γ Cassiopeiæ, 1963 mag. 2·7. β Persei, mag. 2·2 to 3·5. α Orionis, mag. 0·1 to 1·2.

The positions of heavenly bodies on the celestial sphere are defined by two co-ordinates, right ascension and declination, which are analogous to longitude and latitude on the surface of the Earth. If we imagine the plane of the terrestrial equator extended indefinitely, it will cut the celestial sphere in a great circle known as the celestial equator. Similarly the plane of the Earth's orbit, when extended, cuts in the great circle called the ecliptic. The two intersections of these circles are known as the First Point of Aries and the First Point of Libra. If from any star a perpendicular be drawn to the celestial equator, the length of this perpendicular is the star's declination. The arc, measured eastwards along the equator from the First Point of Aries to the foot of this perpendicular, is the right ascension. An alternative definition of right ascension is that it is the angle at the celestial pole (where the Earth's axis, if prolonged, would meet the sphere) between the great circles to the First Point of Aries and to the star.

The plane of the Earth's equator has a slow movement, so that our reference system for right ascension and declination is not fixed. The consequent alteration in these quantities from year to year is called precession. In right ascension it is an increase of about 3^s a year for equatorial stars, and larger or smaller amounts for stars near the pole. In declination it varies between +20″ and −20″ according to the right ascension of the star.

A star or other body crosses the meridian when the sidereal time is equal to its right ascension. The altitude is then a maximum, and may be deduced by remembering that the altitude of the elevated pole is numerically equal to the latitude, while that of the equator at its intersection with the meridian is equal to the co-latitude, or complement of the latitude.

FIXED STARS, 1964

Name	Mag.	R.A.	Dec.	Spectrum
		h m	° ′	
δ Leonis	2·6	11 12·2	+20 43	A3
β Leonis *Denebola*	2·2	11 47·2	+14 46	A2
γ Ursæ Majoris *Phecda*	2·5	11 51·9	+53 54	Ao
γ Corvi	2·8	12 14·0	−17 21	B8
α Crucis	1·0	12 24·6	−62 54	B1
γ Crucis	1·6	12 29·2	−56 55	M3
γ Centauri	2·4	12 39·5	−48 46	Ao
γ Virginis	2·9	12 39·8	− 1 15	Fo
β Crucis	1·5	12 45·6	−59 30	B1
ε Ursæ Majoris *Alioth*	1·7	12 52·4	+56 09	Aop
α Canum Venaticorum	2·9	12 54·3	+38 31	Aop
ζ Ursæ Majoris *Mizar*	2·4	13 22·5	+55 07	A2p
α Virginis *Spica*	1·2	13 23·3	−10 58	B2
η Ursæ Majoris *Alkaid*	1·9	13 46·1	+49 30	B3
β Centauri *Hadar*	0·9	14 01·3	−60 12	B1
θ Centauri	2·3	14 04·6	−36 12	Ko
α Bootis *Arcturus*	0·2	14 14·0	+19 22	Ko
α Centauri *Rigil Kent*	0·1	14 37·1	−60 41	Go
ε Bootis	2·7	14 43·4	+27 14	Ko
β Ursæ Minoris *Kochab*	2·2	14 50·8	+74 18	K5
α Coronæ Borealis *Alphecca*	2·3	15 33·2	+26 50	Ao
δ Scorpii	2·5	15 58·2	−22 31	Bo
β Scorpii	2·9	16 03·3	−19 42	B1
α Scorpii *Antares*	1·2	16 27·2	−26 21	Mo
α Trianguli Australis	1·9	16 44·8	−68 58	K2
ε Scorpii	2·4	16 47·8	−34 14	Ko
α Herculis*	Var.	17 13·0	+14 26	M3
λ Scorpii	1·7	17 31·2	−37 05	B2
α Ophiuchi *Rasalhague*	2·1	17 33·3	+12 35	A5
θ Scorpii	2·0	17 34·7	−42 59	Fo
κ Scorpii	2·5	17 40·0	−39 01	B2
γ Draconis	2·4	17 55·8	+51 30	K5
ε Sagittarii *Kaus Australis*	1·9	18 21·8	−34 24	Ao
α Lyræ *Vega*	0·1	18 35·7	+38 45	Ao
σ Sagittarii	2·1	18 53·0	−26 21	B3
β Cygni *Albireo*	3·2	19 29·3	+27 53	Ko
α Aquilæ *Altair*	0·9	19 49·0	+ 8 46	A5
β Capricorni	3·2	20 19·0	−14 54	Go
γ Cygni	2·3	20 20·9	+40 08	F8p
α Pavonis	2·1	20 22·8	−56 51	B3
α Cygni *Deneb*	1·3	20 40·2	+45 09	A2p
α Cephei *Alderamin*	2·6	21 17·7	+62 26	A5
ε Pegasi	2·5	21 42·4	+ 9 43	Ko
δ Capricorni	3·0	21 45·1	−16 18	A5
α Gruis	2·2	22 06·0	−47 08	B5
δ Cephei*	Var.	22 27·8	+58 14	*
β Gruis	2·2	22 40·5	−47 04	M3
α Piscis Austrini *Fomalhaut*	1·3	22 55·7	−29 49	A3
β Pegasi *Scheat*	2·6	23 02·0	+27 53	Mo
α Pegasi *Markab*	2·6	23 03·0	+15 01	Ao

*α Herculis, mag. 3·1 to 3·9.
δ Cephei, mag. 3·7 to 4·4, Spectrum F5 to Go.

Thus in London (Lat. 51° 30′) the meridian altitude of *Sirius* is found thus:

	°	′
Altitude of equator	38	30
Declination south	16	40
Difference	21	50

The Altitude of *Capella* (Dec. +45° 58′) at lower transit is:

	°	′
Altitude of pole	51	30
Polar distance of Star	44	02
Difference	7	28

The brightness of a heavenly body is denoted by its magnitude. Omitting the exceptionally bright stars *Sirius* and *Canopus*, the twenty brightest stars are of the first magnitude, while the faintest stars visible to the naked eye are of the sixth magnitude. The magnitude scale is a precise one, as a difference of five magnitudes represents a ratio of 100 to 1 in brightness. Typical second magnitude stars are *Polaris* and the stars in the Belt of Orion. The scale is most easily fixed in memory by comparing the stars with Norton's *Star Atlas* (see page 138). The stars *Sirius* and *Canopus* and the planets Venus and Jupiter are so bright that their magnitudes are expressed by negative numbers. A small telescope will show stars down to the ninth or tenth magnitude, while stars as faint as the twentieth magnitude may be photographed by long exposures with the largest telescopes.

Some of the astronomical information in this ALMANACK has been taken from the *Astronomical Ephemeris*, and is published here by arrangement with, and with the permission of, the Controller of H.M. Stationery Office.

THE STRUCTURE OF THE UNIVERSE

The Solar System, although occupying a volume of space large by terrestrial standards, is only a very tiny fraction of the whole Universe. The Sun itself is just one of the millions of stars which make up our Galaxy, and our Galaxy is just one of the millions of galaxies which are distributed through the visible Universe. All these stars and galaxies are in motion, many of them with enormous velocities; yet they are so remote that to the naked eye they present almost the same configurations for a period of many thousands of years, and even with telescopic aid the measurement of their motions is a delicate matter. The nearest star is about 250,000 times as far away as the Sun, the Great Nebula in Andromeda, one of the few galaxies visible to the naked eye, is over 500,000 times as far away as the nearest star, and the largest telescopes can penetrate to a distance of at least 500 times that of the Andromeda Nebula. It is convenient to express astronomical distances in terms of the time that light takes to accomplish the journey. Light travels at the rate of 186,000 miles a second; it takes 1⅓ seconds to reach us from the Moon, our nearest neighbour in space; just over 8 minutes to reach us from the Sun; four years from the nearest star; two million years from the Andromeda Nebula, and about 1000 million years from the most distant bodies yet photographed. We therefore talk about a star as being so many light years distant. Astronomers also use another unit of distance, the parsec. 1 parsec equals 3·26 light years.

THE STARS

The stars are classed according to their apparent brightness in magnitudes. A few of the brightest stars are brighter than the first magnitude. Stars as faint as the sixth magnitude can be seen by the naked eye. Stars fainter than this are not visible to the naked eye; the 200-inch telescope, the world's largest, on Mount Palomar in California, can photograph stars of the 23rd magnitude, which is about 650 million times fainter than the first magnitude. This large range in the apparent brightness of the stars is due to a combination of two factors. The first of these is distance. According to a standard law of optics, the apparent brightness of any given luminous object is inversely proportional to the square of its distance away. Thus, if two similar stars are at distances one of which is 10 times the other, the more distant star will appear to be 100 times fainter than the nearer star. The second factor affecting the apparent brightness of a star is its real intrinsic brightness. There are many different kinds of stars; some are very large luminous objects, others are small and faint.

The distances of the stars can be determined in a variety of ways. The direct trigonometric method consists in measuring the minute difference of direction of the star as seen from opposite sides of the Earth's orbit; this is always done photographically. The distances of about 15,000 stars have been measured in this way, but the method has very little accuracy for distances greater than about 250 light years. For more distant stars, distances may be estimated from a study of their spectra. The distances of some double and variable stars can be found from their special characteristics. A star is said to be at a distance of one parsec if the radius of the Earth's orbit round the Sun subtends an angle of one second of arc at the star. As mentioned earlier, light takes 3·26 years to travel a distance of one parsec.

When the distance of any star has been determined, and its apparent magnitude measured, the real intrinsic brightness of the star may be determined. As a convenient convention, astronomers adopt as the "absolute magnitude" of a star (or other object) that apparent magnitude which the star would have if it were moved from its real position to a distance of ten parsecs. Conversely, if the absolute magnitude of a star is known by spectroscopic or other methods, and its apparent magnitude is observed, its distance may be calculated.

STELLAR SPECTRA

A large number of stars have been examined spectroscopically, and it is found that their spectra fall, with very few exceptions, into a sequence of types, denoted by the letters O, B, A, F, G, K, M; the types merge imperceptibly one into the next. O and B stars, exemplified by the three stars which form *Orion's* belt, have spectra showing helium and hydrogen lines. A stars, like *Vega* and *Sirius*, are characterized by very strong hydrogen lines. F, G and K stars, like *Procyon*, our *Sun*, and *Arcturus*, respectively, have spectra showing large numbers of metallic lines, and hydrogen lines much weaker than in A stars. Finally, the M stars, like *Betelgeuse* and *Antares*, show very complex molecular spectra, chiefly of titanium oxide. This sequence of spectral types O to M is essentially a temperature sequence, the O stars being the hottest and the M stars the coolest. Approximate values of the surface temperatures of the stars are, a value for the middle of each type being quoted in degrees Centigrade: O, 30,000°; B, 18,000°; A, 10,000°; F, 7000°; G, 5500°; K, 4500°; M, 3000°. The sequence O to M is also a sequence of colour, the O stars being the bluest and the M stars the reddest. The colour of a star is capable of precise definition and measurement; there is a very close correlation between colour and surface temperature, and between colour and spectral type. The latter correlation is so good that for many astrophysical purposes colour measurements are used instead of spectral types. There is the further advantage that colours can be measured for stars too faint for study by spectroscopic techniques.

When the spectral types (or colours) of a large number of stars are correlated with their absolute magnitudes, a surprising result emerges. The sequence O to M is one of decreasing absolute brightness. Approximate values of the absolute magnitudes of the stars are, a value for the middle of each type being quoted: O, −4; B, −2; A, +1; F, +3; G, +5; K, +7; M, +11. A graphical illustration of this relation between spectral type and absolute magnitude is known as the Hertzsprung-Russell Diagram (or, when colours are used instead of spectral types, as a colour-magnitude diagram). The relationship represented by this diagram is one of the corner stones of modern astrophysics. The above series of stars of types O to M and absolute magnitude decreasing from −4 to +11, or fainter, is known as the "main sequence", and a large proportion of all known stars are members of this sequence. A relatively small proportion of the stars of spectral types O to M do not belong to the main sequence. Closer examination of the spectra of these stars reveals slight differences between their spectra and ordinary stars of nominally the same type on the main sequence. These differences are sufficiently characteristic to enable the two types of stars to be segregated spectroscopically without independent knowledge of their absolute magnitudes. These stars are found to be brighter than the corresponding main sequence stars of the same types. Most of those of types G, K and M have absolute magnitudes about 0; many of those of types O to F and a few of types G to M are still brighter, with absolute magnitudes ranging from −4 to −7. The exceptional brightness of these stars is believed to be due to their sizes: those with absolute magnitudes about 0 are called giants, those of −4 to −7 are called supergiants.

The sizes of the stars have been determined mostly by calculation from known surface temperatures and absolute magnitudes. In very few cases direct determinations have been made by means of an interferometer, and sizes can also be inferred from observations of some eclipsing binary stars. The Sun is 864,000 miles in diameter. The main sequence is found to be a sequence of diminishing radii; an O star has a radius of about 20 times that of the Sun, while an average M star has a radius of one-third of the Sun. The giant stars of types G to M have radii between 10 and 100 times the Sun; supergiants have radii between 30 and 1000 times the Sun.

It is possible to determine the chemical composition of a star from a study of its spectrum. This has been done for main sequence stars and for giants and supergiants. All these stars appear to be of similar chemical composition, about 80 per cent by numbers of atoms being hydrogen, most of the remainder helium, heavier elements being less than one per cent of the total. All the differences between types O to M and main sequence, giant and supergiant stars can be accounted for by variations of surface temperature and of size (affecting the spectrum through the surface gravity).

A few stars cannot be classified according to the standard sequence O to M. Among these those classified as R and N stars show strong bands of carbon compounds instead of the titanium oxide of M stars, and the S stars show zirconium oxide instead of titanium oxide. A number of still less common types of stars show anomalous lines of strontium, barium, manganese, silicon, europium, lanthanum and other elements. The reasons for all these peculiarities are not known; it is probable that many of them are genuine differences from the standard chemical composition of the majority of the stars.

DOUBLE STARS

Many stars which appear single to the naked eye are found to be double in the telescope. These are frequently found to be in orbital motion round one another in periods varying from about one year to many thousands of years. Some binary stars are so close together that they cannot be seen separately even in large telescopes; their binary nature is revealed by the spectroscope. The varying motions of the stars in their orbits can be detected by the Doppler shifts of lines in their spectra. The periods of these stars, known as spectroscopic binaries, vary from a few hours to a few years. Some spectroscopic binaries are of special interest in that during their orbital motion the two components periodically eclipse each other, and the combined light of the two stars will vary. This happens when the Earth is nearly in the plane of the binary star orbits. Such binaries are called eclipsing variables, of which the best known is *Algol*, or β Persei, a star normally of the second magnitude (see p. I of each month).

VARIABLE STARS

We have already referred to the eclipsing variables, whose light variation is due to a geometrical cause. Some single stars vary in light. These include Cepheid variables, with periods of from a few hours up to about fifty days, long-period variables with periods of from a hundred to a thousand days, and numerous types of variable stars in which the periods and light fluctuations are entirely irregular. Many of these variations are attributed to pulsation of the stars by alternate expansion and contraction. The Cepheids are of particular interest because of the period-luminosity relation: the longer the period of a Cepheid the brighter is its mean absolute magnitude. An observation of the period of variation of the star immediately tells us its absolute magnitude and thence its distance.

Novæ are stars whose light increases by 10 to 15 magnitudes in a few days, and then fades gradually to normal brightness, reached a year or two later. The cause of the brightening is the sudden expansion of the star, but the reason for this is unknown. Supernovæ are stars whose brightness increases by up to 20 magnitudes; they are believed to be caused by the explosion of the whole star.

STAR CLUSTERS

Stars frequently occur in clusters; two types of clusters are known. The first, called open (or galactic) clusters, are groups of up to two or three hundred stars; the second, globular clusters, contain over one hundred thousand stars. The open clusters are found mainly in the neighbourhood of the Milky Way, the globular clusters avoid the Milky Way. Several open clusters are visible to the naked eye: the Pleiades, the Hyades and Praesepe are the best known of these. The colour-magnitude diagrams of open clusters are generally similar to those of nearby single stars; the most important difference is that when a cluster contains blue O and B stars it does not also contain red giant stars. The colour-magnitude diagrams of globular clusters are very similar among themselves, but differ greatly from the diagrams of galactic clusters and nearby stars. The main sequence does not exist in any globular cluster for stars of types O, B and A; red giants are present in all the clusters, and they range up to absolute magnitude −3. There is an additional sequence of stars with absolute magnitudes about 0 which is quite unlike any sequence in the diagrams for nearby stars.

INTERSTELLAR MATTER

The space between the stars is not empty; it contains a mixture of gas and dust which serves to dim the light of distant objects and tends to make them appear redder than normal. Very distant objects may be obscured completely if they lie in or near the plane of the Milky Way. The density of interstellar gas averages one atom in each cubic centimetre; this may be compared with a density 26 million million million times as great in ordinary air at normal pressure and temperature. As is the case for cosmic material in general, hydrogen predominates in interstellar gas. In addition to this widely distributed matter, there are denser clouds of gas and dust existing locally. These are frequently in evidence as dark clouds in front of a brighter stellar background. Some clouds have hot stars embedded, and the interstellar gas may then shine either by reflection of the starlight or it may be heated until it glows and emits its own characteristic light. Such dense glowing clouds are termed galactic nebulæ. Sometimes the cloud is more regular in shape and is excited by one star; such clouds are termed planetary nebulæ, and the Ring Nebula in Lyra is an excellent example of these objects. Planetary nebulæ are among the denser interstellar formations; their densities range up to 20,000 atoms per cubic centimetre. Hot stars can make ordinary interstellar gas glow even when the density is low; the spherical region of glowing gas surrounding a hot star is termed an ionized-hydrogen region. These regions are of particular interest for the study of the Galaxy and of extragalactic nebulæ because they are relatively bright and can be seen at large distances.

THE GALAXY

A cursory glance at the sky is sufficient to show that the fainter stars are concentrated towards the region of the Milky Way. This implies that the stars form a flattened system, which extends farther in the direction of the Milky Way than it does at right angles to it. It is now known that this system, called the Galaxy, is about 100,000 light years in diameter, and has a thickness of less than 5000 light years. The Milky Way is the centre plane of the system. We in the Solar System are situated at about 27,000 light years from the centre, and not far from the central plane. All the objects mentioned earlier, single and multiple stars, variable stars, novæ and supernovæ, galactic and globular clusters, interstellar gas, dust and galactic and planetary nebulæ, form part of the Galaxy. The distribution of these various objects in the Galaxy is not all alike. The hot O and B stars, galactic clusters and interstellar matter are closely concentrated towards the Milky Way plane, mostly lying within 300 light years on either side of the plane. The stars of types A to M tend to be less closely concentrated to the plane; globular clusters show hardly any concentration, forming a nearly spherical distribution stretching to over 30,000 light years from the plane. Most Cepheid variables with periods of more than a day are closely concentrated to the galactic plane; those with periods of less than a day have a distribution similar to that of globular clusters.

The Galaxy has a spiral structure similar to that of some extragalactic nebulæ. This structure was first shown by studying the positions of O and B stars; these stars trace out spiral arms. Radio astronomers subsequently found that interstellar hydrogen gas emits radio waves on 21 centimetres wavelength. Studies of this radio radiation has enabled the density and distribution of interstellar hydrogen to be determined. The hydrogen gas is found to be situated along the same spiral arms as the O and B stars. Indeed, there is a remarkably close correlation between O and B stars and interstellar matter.

Observations by both optical and radio methods have proved that the whole Galaxy is rotating about an axis through its centre perpendicular to the galactic plane. The period of rotation varies with distance from the centre, an average value being 200 million years. The total mass of the Galaxy is about 100 thousand million times the mass of the Sun.

STELLAR POPULATIONS

The two different types of colour-magnitude (or Hertzsprung-Russell) diagram mentioned above appear to apply not only to star clusters but to other objects in our Galaxy and in other galaxies. There seems little doubt that there are two fundamentally different types of stellar population: Population I has a colour-magnitude diagram similar to that of nearby stars and open clusters, Population II has a diagram similar to that for globular clusters. Population I includes both open clusters, longer-period Cepheid variables and supergiant stars, and is intimately associated with interstellar matter; it occurs prominently in the spiral structure of our Galaxy, and is generally concentrated towards the galactic plane. Population II includes the globular clusters, short-period Cepheids and other objects, tends to avoid the spiral structure of the Galaxy, has little or no interstellar dust associated with it, but may be associated with interstellar hydrogen gas, and is not concentrated towards the galactic plane. All the available evidence suggests that Population II stars are old objects, with ages averaging 5000 million years, while Population I stars are much younger, with ages in a few cases of only a few million years. Population II stars have lower content of metals relative to hydrogen than Population I stars.

EXTRAGALACTIC NEBULÆ

Outside our own Galaxy there are large numbers of objects having a more or less hazy appearance on photographs. These are the extragalactic nebulæ, also known as external galaxies. Some show a well-defined spiral structure, some are elliptical in form with no marked structural features, and some are irregular in form. The spiral nebulæ consist of a

NEBULAE, CLUSTERS AND GALAXIES

Designation	Name	Type	Mag.	R.A. (1950·0) h m	Dec. (1950·0) °	Angular Size ′ ′
N.G.C. 104	47 Tucanae	GC	4	0 22	−72·4	42×42
M.31	Andromeda (Nebula)	G	4	0 40	+41·0	160×40
Nubecula Minor		—	—	0 50	−73·9	(10 sq. deg.)
M.33		G	7	1 31	+30·4	60×40
H. VI. 33, 34	Double Cluster	OC	4	2 18	+56·9	2(36×36)
M.45	Pleiades	OC	—	3 45	+23·9	90×60
	Hyades	OC	—	4 26	+15·8	180×180
Nubecula Major		—	—	5 25	−69·3	(42 sq. deg.)
M.1	"Crab" nebula	PN	10	5 32	+22·0	6×4
M.42	"Great" nebula	N	6	5 33	− 5·4	66×60
N.G.C. 2070	30 Doradus	OC+N	—	5 39	−69·1	—
M.44	"Praesepe" or "Beehive"	OC	4	8 37	+20·2	90×90
N.G.C. 3372	η Carinae	N	—	10 43	−59·4	80×80
N.G.C. 4755	κ Crucis	OC	—	12 51	−60·1	10×10
	ω Centauri	GC	3	13 24	−47·1	45×45
M.3		GC	6	13 40	+28·6	19×19
M.13		GC	6	16 40	+36·6	23×23
M.7		OC	5	17 51	−34·8	50×50
M.20	"Trifid" nebula	N	8	17 59	−23·0	29×27
M.8	"Lagoon" nebula	N	5	18 01	−24·4	90×40
M.57	"Ring" nebula	PN	9	18 52	+33·0	1×1
M.55		GC	5	19 37	−31·0	15×15
M.27	"Dumb-bell" nebula	PN	8	19 57	+22·6	8×4

Types: N—Nebula. PN—Planetary Nebula. OC—Open Cluster.
GC—Globular Cluster. G—Galaxy.

central bulge surrounded by spiral arms embedded in a disk-shaped structure. The elliptical nebulæ and the central bulges of the spiral nebulæ are believed to be composed of stars of Population II. The spiral arms are composed of Population I and some Population II, together with large quantities of gas and dust. The presence of dust is evident because of the dark patches of absorption which are a feature of the photographs of spiral nebulæ; the presence of hydrogen gas has been proved by the observation of regions of glowing gas and by the reception of radio waves on 21 centimetres wavelength. In a few of the nearer galaxies individual stars have been observed, and comparison with stars in our own Galaxy provides estimates of the distances and sizes of the galaxies. Many of them are found to be comparable with our own Galaxy—with diameters of 100,000 light years and masses 100 thousand million times the Sun. The two Magellanic Clouds are the nearest galaxies to our own, their distances being about 140,000 light years. The best known external galaxy is the Great Nebula in Andromeda, at a distance of 2,000,000 light years; this spiral nebula is believed to be similar to our own Galaxy in size and stellar content. Extragalactic nebulæ frequently occur in large clusters, each containing hundreds of nebulæ. Many extragalactic nebulæ are in rotation in a manner similar to our own Galaxy and with comparable periods.

RADIO SOURCES

In addition to the 21 centimetre hydrogen radiation received from interstellar gas, radio noise is received on other wavelengths. Some of this originates in well-known objects; one important source of radio noise is the Crab Nebula, which is known to be the remains of the supernova of A.D. 1054. Some extragalactic nebulæ are also sources of radio noise, but many of the apparently isolated sources, "radio stars", do not seem to coincide with any visible stars or nebulæ. A few strong sources have been identified with peculiar extragalactic nebulæ, and in other cases the source appears to be two colliding galaxies. There is a growing feeling that many of the radio stars may be very distant objects, perhaps even beyond the range of optical telescopes. The process by which the radio waves are generated has not yet been explained.

COSMOLOGY

The large scale problems of the Universe are concerned with the motions and distribution of the extragalactic nebulæ through the observable region of space. It has been found that in spite of the tendency of galaxies to cluster together, on a still larger scale the galaxies are distributed remarkably uniformly. Observations have shown that distant galaxies have spectra showing "red-shifts", which have been interpreted as Doppler shifts due to velocities of recession; all the distant galaxies appear to be moving away from us with velocities proportional to their distance. This suggests that the whole Universe is in expansion. There are two rival theories of the cause of this expansion. One postulates a gigantic initial explosion some 5,000 million years ago. The other postulates a steady state, with continuous creation of matter producing new galaxies which eventually force the existing ones to continually increasing distances. Observations have not yet succeeded in distinguishing between these theories.

THE SOLAR SYSTEM

The Sun is one of the millions of stars that make up the Universe. The energy that it radiates in the form of light and heat is maintained by nuclear reactions among the atoms in its interior. It is surrounded by an immense number of comparatively cold planets and comets, together with smaller particles that give rise to meteors and the zodiacal light.

The planets are solid bodies revolving about the Sun in elliptical orbits with the Sun at one focus, and at distances related to the periodic times in accordance with Kepler's third law: the squares of the periodic times vary as the cubes of the semi-major axes. All revolve in the same direction, the orbits being only slightly inclined to the plane of the ecliptic in which the Earth moves round the Sun. As seen from the Earth, therefore, the planets are always near the ecliptic, moving in general from west to east round the sky. Once in every such revolution the planet appears to become stationary and then retrograde, forming a looped path which is a consequence of the Earth's own orbital movement.

The nine major planets, of which the earth is one, are of special interest, the five that are visible to the naked eye having been known from the earliest times. Six have satellites or moons revolving round them. These, like the planets themselves, are not self-luminous, but shine by the reflected light of the Sun. Notes on these bodies are given in the following pages. The thousands of minor planets that are also known, although of less interest to the observer, afford many problems to the mathematical astronomer. Comets are also members of the solar system; their orbits are inclined at all angles to the ecliptic, and are generally highly eccentric, reaching out to immense distances in space. The light of a comet is not due entirely to reflected sunlight, but partly to fluorescence caused by selective absorption of solar radiation. The return of a comet of short period may be predicted with some accuracy, but most comets appear quite unexpectedly. Meteoric dust appears to have a common origin with the comets, since some meteor showers have been shown to follow the orbits of certain comets.

THE SUN

The Sun is the ultimate source of most of the chemical energy available on the Earth. Hence the origin of that energy, which reaches the Earth in the form of light and heat from within the Sun, is of particular interest. The spectral distribution of the light from the Sun's surface indicates a temperature of about 5,700° C., but a relatively short distance inside the surface the temperature reaches 1,000,000° and deeper in the interior, near the centre, it is believed to be in the region of 14,000,000°. Now the constitution of the Sun is similar to that of the Earth, as is shown by similarities in the chemical spectra of solar and terrestrial sources; but at these high temperatures the atoms become stripped of their outer layers of electrons. In this highly "ionized" state the substance of the Sun acts in much the same way as a "perfect gas" does on the Earth, even though the density is high. Furthermore, the thermal velocities are sufficiently great for nuclear collisions to take place. Nuclear energy can be released in the Sun by a variety of collision-processes, in each of which the light atoms of hydrogen, by far the most abundant element, are ultimately combined into the heavier atoms of helium. This energy, released almost entirely in the central regions, is transmitted by radiation and convection to the cooler outer layers of the Sun and thence to outer space, a very small proportion of it falling on the Earth. It is possible to infer with some certainty, by considering the Sun as a typical star, that this process has been going on for about three thousand million years and that it may be expected to continue similarly for perhaps a further ten thousand million years.

As viewed in a low-power telescope provided with heavily absorbing filters, the Sun presents various features. Over most of its surface a fine mottling can be seen under good observing conditions. This "granulation" is visible evidence of a turbulent convective layer near the surface. Much more noticeable surface-markings called sunspots appear sporadically in the equatorial zones of the Sun and up to latitudes of 40°–50° north and south. These sunspots, which are sometimes visible to the naked eye, provide direct evidence of the rotation of the Sun on an axis which is inclined about 7° to the line joining the poles of the ecliptic. They also indicate that the Sun does not rotate as a solid body but somewhat faster in equatorial regions than at higher latitudes. Its mean sidereal rotation-period is about 25 days but the motion of the Earth in its orbit around the Sun results in an apparent rotation-period, as viewed from the Earth, of approximately 27 days. Associated with sunspots are bright regions called faculae but these can not be seen when the spot is near the centre of the disk.

Sunspots vary in size from small dark specks, barely visible in a telescope, but actually with an area of about a million square miles, to large dark markings several thousand times as great. The largest spot ever measured (April, 1947) covered 7,000 million square miles at its greatest, or approximately 0·7 per cent. of the Sun's visible surface. Correspondingly, sunspots have lifetimes ranging from a few hours in the case of some of the smallest, to many weeks in the case of the most persistent spots, which are often regular in shape but not as a rule particularly large. The frequency of spots varies in a definite eleven-year cycle, though the number of spots may vary considerably in a haphazard way from week to week in a particular year. One of the observed properties of spots during the 11-year cycle is that high latitudes, north and south, are predominant towards the beginning of a cycle, while later on there is a gradual drift of the most densely occupied zones towards the equator. In addition, a strong magnetic-field is found to be associated with sunspots, as well as certain systematic drifts in the solar layers there. These and other observed properties, such as concern the detailed structure and movements of spots

ELEMENTS OF THE SOLAR SYSTEM

Orb	Mean Distance from Sun		Sidereal Period	Synodic Period	Inclination of Orbit to Ecliptic	Diameter	Mass compared with Earth	Period of Rotation on Axis
	Radii of Earth's Orbit	Millions of Miles						
			y d	Days	° ′	Miles		d h m
Sun	...	...	...	...	...	864,000	333,434	25 09
Mercury	0·39	36	88	116	7 00	3000	0·04	88
Venus	0·72	67	225	584	3 24	7600	0·83	Unknown
Earth	1·00	93	1 0	...	...	7927 *eq.*	1·00	23 56
Mars	1·52	142	1 322	780	1 51	4200	0·11	24 37
Jupiter	5·20	483	11 315	399	1 18	{ 88,700 *eq.* 82,800 *p.*	318	{ 9 50 9 56
Saturn	9·54	886	29 167	378	2 29	{ 75,100 *eq.* 67,200 *p.*	95	{ 10 14 10 38
Uranus	19·19	1783	84 6	370	0 46	30,900	15	10 49
Neptune	30·07	2793	164 288	367	1 46	33,000	17	15 40
Pluto	39·46	3666	247 255	367	17 09	Unknown	Unknown	Unknown

must be explained by any comprehensive physical theory of sunspots. At present no generally accepted theory exists, though it seems clear that the magnetic field of the spot inhibits convection in the turbulent layers near the Sun's surface and so produces local cooling.

The Table below gives dates of recent maxima and minima of the sunspot cycles. It will be seen that the intervals between successive maxima (or minima) vary considerably from the average value of 11·1 years.

Maxima		Minima	
1837·2	1907·0	1833·9	1901·7
1848·1	1917·6	1843·5	1913·6
1860·1	1928·4	1856·0	1923·6
1870·6	1937·4	1867·2	1933·8
1883·9	1947·5	1878·9	1944·2
1894·1	1957·9	1889·6	1954·3

The last sunspot maximum was unusual in its absence of giant spots, the intense activity being due to a very large number of smaller spots; the previous maxima in 1937–38 and 1947–49 were also notable for great activity.

Other features of the Sun may be detected in light of wavelengths other than those of normal integrated visual light. With the light from the centre of strong spectral absorption lines such as Hα, the C-line of hydrogen, or the H and K lines of calcium, bright regions can almost always be seen around sunspots and these regions occasionally become exceptionally bright for periods of an hour, or thereabouts. This is the phenomenon of the "solar flare", and its occurrence may be otherwise detected upon the Earth by immediate changes in propagation-conditions for long-distance radio-communication (changes in the ionosphere caused by a sudden increase in ionizing radiation) or, in the case of large flares, by the subsequent occurrence, a day or two later, of a magnetic storm. A very few large flares have had associated with them increases, occurring a few minutes later, of the high-energy cosmic-ray flux detected at the earth's surface.

Also visible in monochromatic wavelengths are the prominences, which extend outwards from the Sun's surface into its tenuous outer regions, called the corona. At the limb prominences appear as bright forms, often arched or branching, while against the Sun's disk they appear as dark filaments. The corona itself can normally only be observed in its brightest regions by using light from certain bright spectral lines in special instruments at a high altitude on the Earth. At lower altitudes, and in the outer corona at high altitudes, scattered sky-light is too great. However, when the Sun is obscured by the Moon at a total solar eclipse, the whole corona becomes easily seen. As well as the bright lines, it shows a weak continuous spectrum. It is also found that the corona has characteristically different appearances at sunspot maximum and sunspot minimum and that it frequently shows streamers extending outwards several million miles. When observed with radio wavelengths in the range 10 cm. to 5 m. the corona is normally detected, as well as short-lived emissions from disturbed regions around sunspots.

MERCURY

Mercury is the smallest planet and the nearest to the Sun. Because it moves in an orbit between the Sun and the Earth, it is never far west or east of the Sun. If east, it appears as an evening star; if west, as a morning star. The extremes of these apparent excursions are known as Greatest Elongations; their times and extent, measured by the angular distance from the Sun, are given on the first page of each month under the heading PHENOMENA. The great ellipticity of the orbit of Mercury causes the amount of these elongations to vary from 18° to 28°. The planet is best placed for naked-eye observation some days before eastern elongation on spring evenings, or after western elongation on autumn mornings, though in England at these times its actual distance from the Sun is near its minimum. In the southern hemisphere the conditions are, of course, reversed.

In a telescope, Mercury shows phases to the Earth like the Moon, resembling her at first quarter when at eastern elongation, and at last quarter when at western elongation. The planet is exceedingly difficult to observe telescopically and is best scrutin-

THE SATELLITES

Name	Star mag.	Mean distance from Primary	Sidereal Period of Revolution
The Earth		Miles	d h m
Moon	—	238,840	27 07 43
Mars			
Phobos	11	5,800	7 39
Deimos	12	14,600	1 06 18
Jupiter			
V. Unnamed	13	112,000	11 57
I. Io	5½	262,000	1 18 28
II. Europa	5½	417,000	3 13 14
III. Ganymede	5	665,000	7 03 43
IV. Callisto	6	1,169,000	16 16 32
VI. Unnamed	15	7,120,000	251
X. "	19	7,180,000	254
VII. "	18	7,290,000	260
XII. "	18	13,000,000	620
XI. "	19	14,000,000	692
VIII. "	17	14,600,000	739
IX. "	18½	14,700,000	745

Name	Star Mag.	Mean distance from Primary	Sidereal Period of Revolution
Saturn		Miles	d h m
Mimas	12	115,000	22 37
Enceladus	12	148,000	1 08 53
Tethys	11	183,000	1 21 18
Dione	11	234,000	2 17 41
Rhea	10	327,000	4 12 25
Titan	8½	759,000	15 22 42
Hyperion	15	919,000	21 06 38
Iapetus	11	2,211,000	79 07 56
Phoebe	14	8,000,000	550
Uranus			
Miranda	17	80,000	1 10 0[illegible]
Ariel	14	119,000	2 12 29
Umbriel	14½	166,000	4 03 28
Titania	14	272,000	8 16 56
Oberon	14	364,000	13 11 07
Neptune			
Triton	13½	220,000	5 21 03
Nereid	19½	3,500,000	359 10 00

ized with large apertures in full daylight. A recent map of the surface, made by Antoniadi, confirms in its essential features one made last century by Schiaparelli; these observers agree that Mercury always turns the same face to the Sun. The question of whether Mercury has an atmosphere cannot be regarded as settled.

VENUS

Venus, next from the Sun, has a diameter only two or three hundred miles less than that of the Earth. Its apparent movement with regard to the Sun is similar to that of Mercury, but, owing to the greater size of its orbit, its elongations extend as far as 47°. Venus is the brightest planet and is several times brighter than any star; it can often be seen in full daylight with the naked eye.

Apart from the beauty of its phases, Venus is a disappointing object in the telescope, its extensive atmosphere being so highly reflective, probably owing to cloud, that its true surface can never be observed. Vague dusky shadings may be seen or imagined, but conspicuous markings are both rare and evanescent.

Photographs of Venus in violet light were taken by Kuiper in 1950 and 1954 with the 82-inch reflector of the McDonald Observatory in Texas, and show that the surface of the planet is banded, three or more dark and bright bands being noted lying in a direction perpendicular to the terminator. These bands have been attributed to zones of ascending and descending currents in the atmosphere of Venus. Assuming that the bands are parallel to the equator, Kuiper deduced the position of the pole of Venus at $3^h\ 32^m$, +81°, which is in Cepheus. The equator of Venus is therefore tilted at an angle of about 32° to its orbit. Further observations will be required to deduce the period of rotation of the planet, but it is considered that this cannot exceed a few weeks.

The spectrum of the atmosphere above the reflecting layer reveals a considerable amount of carbon dioxide, but no oxygen; such might also be the conditions on the Earth, were it not for the constant absorption of carbon dioxide by vegetation and its replacement by oxygen. A remarkable feature of the upper atmosphere is the absence of all trace of water vapour.

MARS

Mars, the first planet whose orbit is exterior to that of the Earth, is a little larger than Mercury. Oppositions occur at intervals of about 2 years 2 months, but owing to the eccentricity of the orbit the opposition distance varies between 35 and 63 million miles. The most favourable approaches unfortunately take place when the planet is low in the sky for northern observers; but when, as in 1956, one occurs in the early autumn, the distance may be less than 40 million miles and the planet just north of the equator. It is only within two or three months of opposition that Mars is near enough for its surface to be successfully studied with a telescope; even at these times only the coarser details are likely to be recognized with instruments of less than 6 inches aperture.

Except for Mercury, Mars is the only planet whose true surface we are able to see This exhibits many well-defined markings, most of which are permanent, and from these the rotation period has been well determined; it is about 41½ minutes longer than that of the Earth. The axis of rotation is inclined at about 24° to the plane of the orbit. There are white spots at the poles which are deposited during the winter of each hemisphere and melt or evaporate during the summer. It is most probable that these consist of thick deposits of hoar frost, and the infra-red absorption spectra of the polar caps support this view. The major portion of the surface is of a featureless orange hue, which gives rise to the ruddy appearance of Mars. But there abound large areas, often with sharp boundaries, of a blue-grey colour. The latter were once thought to be seas; but it is now known that there are no large sheets of open water, and some regard areas of vegetation as their most likely interpretation, especially as they undergo change of tint. It has been claimed that these changes follow the Martian seasons; but as 15 or 17 years must elapse between the times when we can study Mars under similar conditions, it cannot yet be confirmed that there are any changes of a truly seasonal character apart from the waxing and waning of the polar caps.

The question of the so-called Martian "canals" is very controversial. Most skilled observers would probably deny the very existence of these excessively thin linear markings, attributing them to optical or physiological effects. To speculate on their being the work of intelligent beings is therefore, to say the least, premature.

Mars has an atmosphere believed to be considerably less dense than our own. The spectroscope has been unable to establish that it contains either oxygen or water vapour, which can therefore be present only in minute proportions. Recently, however, about the same amount of carbon dioxide has been detected as is found in our own atmosphere.

Mars has two faint satellites, Phobos and Deimos, which were discovered by Asaph Hall in 1877.

THE MINOR PLANETS

Moving in orbits which in general lie between those of Mars and Jupiter, are a large number of small bodies called minor planets or asteroids. It is estimated that at least 50,000 come within reach of present instruments. Scores of them are now found every year by photographing the sky. Their orbits are calculated as observations accrue, and when the results are reliable enough the new planets are given permanent numbers, and usually also names, by a central authority—now at the Cincinnati Observatory, U.S.A. At present there are over 1600 on the permanent list, and several dozen are likely to be added each year; and always there are many still under investigation. All are faint—none have ever been seen by an unaided eye except, just possibly, Vesta.

These celestial bodies are probably little more than masses of rock revolving round the Sun. The first four, found early in the 19th century, are also the largest: Ceres, 420 miles in diameter, Pallas 280, Juno 150, and Vesta 240 miles.

The periodic times of the revolutions about the Sun vary considerably around an average of 4½ years, but interesting groups and gaps occur among the values for these times owing to disturbances of the orbits caused by the attraction on these bodies of the massive planet Jupiter. Although some of the orbits are nearly circular, others are very elongated ovals (ellipses); and though the inclinations of their planes to the ecliptic are mostly less than 20°, several exceed 30°, including Pallas 35°. The highest known, 43°, is that of Hidalgo. This planet has also the longest period, 14 years, and travels out as far as Saturn's orbit. On the other hand Icarus, discovered in 1949, comes within the orbit of Mercury, and three others Apollo, Adonis and Hermes, within that of Venus. Another, Eros, is of importance because in some circumstances it can be within 13 or 14 million miles of the Earth. This happened in 1931 when carefully planned photographic recording of the planet and the surrounding stars enabled measures of its distance to be made, and hence a new value of the distance of the Sun from the Earth (the solar parallax) to be deduced.

Similarly, certain other minor planets with suitable orbits can be used for special purposes, as in the precise measurement of the equinox and equator, or in finding the masses of Mercury or Venus.

JUPITER

Jupiter, the largest planet, has a volume over 1000 times that of the Earth, but a density only one-quarter of ours. Its oblate shape is so marked, owing to its great size and rapid rotation, as to be obvious in quite small telescopes.

The characteristic surface features of Jupiter are bright zones separated by dusky belts, running practically parallel to the planet's equator. With telescopes of moderate size some of these may be resolved into finer detail, consisting of spots, wisp, streaks, etc., but the general banded appearance still remains. When the period of rotation is determined by timing objects such as these as they cross the planet's central meridian, it is found that spots within about 10° of the equator indicate a period of approximately $9^h\ 50\frac{1}{2}^m$, while most of those in higher latitudes give periods between $9^h\ 55^m$ and $9^h\ 56^m$, the transition from the shorter to the longer being usually quite abrupt. When the rotation periods are examined in greater detail, it is found that the surface may be divided into many zones, each having a particular period characteristic of its latitude, but that the distribution in latitude of the various periods is quite haphazard. This differs from the Sun, whose rotation is also fastest at the equator, for whereas a definite formula connects the periods of solar spots with their latitude, no such law can be found for Jupiter. Actually the fastest moving spots are confined to a narrow strip in latitude about +25°; the last outbreak of such spots occurred in 1939.

Few Jovian markings have any degree of permanence, having generally lost their individuality after a few months. Two objects, however, form notable exceptions. The well-known "Bay" or "Hollow" in the South Equatorial Belt, which is so closely associated with the Great Red Spot, made famous in 1878–80 by its darkness and colour, is known to have existed from 1831 and the Red Spot itself may be identical with a similar object first depicted in the 17th century and followed for many years. The physical nature of the Red Spot is a mystery; its long duration suggests some connection with the solid surface, but the non-uniformity of its period of rotation seems to rule out this explanation. The other feature displaying considerable permanence is known as the South Tropical Disturbance, which has the same latitude as the Red Spot. Its rotation period is somewhat shorter than that of the latter; since its first detection in 1901 it has overtaken and passed the Red Spot eight times.

The spectroscope shows that Jupiter's atmosphere contains ammonia and considerable quantities of methane (marsh gas). The main constituents are unknown, but it is probable that hydrogen and helium abound and that the light clouds of the surface are due to minute droplets or crystals of ammonia, the surface temperature having been found by measurement to be of the order $-120°$ C., which is not far from the calculated value. It has been suggested that this atmosphere is very deep; but if so, the pressure at depths below 50 miles or so must be such as to give it the properties of a liquid rather than a gas. A recent theory is that it may be dense enough to support in flotation a light solid body at some depth below the surface, and that what we see as the Red Spot may be a manifestation in the atmosphere above it of thermal changes in such a solid.

Jupiter has four principal satellites—the first celestial objects discovered by telescope by Galileo. The two inner major satellites are about the size of our Moon, while the two outer are about as large as Mercury. A fifth, very much smaller and fainter and nearer to Jupiter, was discovered visually by Barnard in 1892; this satellite has the most rapid motion of any in the solar system. Seven other satellites have been discovered photographically but all are minute objects; the four outermost of these have retrograde motion and are so greatly disturbed by the solar attractions that their orbits are not even approximately elliptical.

Intense but irregular bursts of radio noise were detected at the Carnegie Institute at Washington in January 1955, on wavelengths of 13·5 and 10 metres; these signals were received only during the few minutes while Jupiter was crossing the aerial beam. Similar evidence has been obtained from other quarters, and an investigation is now being made to discover possible correlations between these radio outbursts and the times at which visible markings on the belts of Jupiter transit across the centre of the disk.

SATURN

This planet is unique because of its encircling ring system, which makes it a very beautiful object in even a small telescope. There are two bright rings and an inner dusky one, which is transparent enough for the body of the planet to be seen through it. The dark line separating the two outer rings is known as Cassini's division in honour of its discoverer. The rings lie almost exactly in one plane, which is inclined at 27° to the planet's orbit and is sensibly that of its equator. It has been proved theoretically that the rings consist of a vast swarm of small individual particles, each pursuing its own orbit like a satellite around Saturn; this has been confirmed observationally by the spectroscope. This makes even more remarkable the extreme thinness of the rings, which is illustrated every 15 years, when the plane of the rings passes through the Earth; they then become invisible even in the greatest telescopes. Thus they cannot present when edgewise a width of more than a very few miles.

From the few spots that have been observed on Saturn's surface, the rotation period at the equator is about $10^h\ 15^m$, in higher latitudes $10^h\ 38^m$ has been found in the northern hemisphere and $10^h\ 37^m$ in the southern. There is thus some analogy with Jupiter, but we are ignorant of the behaviour of intermediate zones.

The density of Saturn is less than three-quarters that of water; the oblateness is even more marked than is Jupiter's, the equatorial diameter exceeding the polar by about one part in nine. The general appearance of the disk is banded, but the dusky belts are fewer and wider than those on Jupiter and present less contrast with the brighter zones. The atmosphere is known to contain methane and ammonia.

Among the more interesting results obtained from measurements of infra-red absorption spectra with the 82-inch reflector of the McDonald Observatory in Texas are those of the constitution of Saturn's rings and the five inner satellites. The only substance which gives similar absorption bands to those observed would appear to be frost deposited on a material at very low temperatures. The absorption curve is quite characteristic, and seems to be governed by the size of the frost crystals. Similar curves are given by the polar caps of Mars, but not by snow or ice. Estimates of the masses of Saturn's rings and of the five inner satellites show that their densities cannot be far from unity, and it is provisionally suggested that they are all composed of ice. Evaporation will be negligible at the low temperatures prevailing, and the small particles of which the ring is composed will suffer little or no loss.

Saturn has nine satellites, of which the largest, Titan, is easily seen with a small telescope. Titan is the largest satellite in the solar system, and the only one which shows definite evidence of possessing an atmosphere. The seven innermost satellites revolve nearly in the plane of the rings. When the rings are seen edgewise, these inner satellites may transit the planet or be eclipsed in the same manner as those of Jupiter. The faint outermost satellite, Phœbe, has a retrograde motion.

URANUS

This planet was discovered by William Herschel at Bath in 1781, and so has completed only two revolutions since its discovery. It is only just visible to the naked eye, but in a telescope is distinguishable by its disk, which is quite obvious, though less than 4″ in diameter, and by the different quality of its light. The two outer and brighter of its four main satellites were found by Herschel in 1787; the two inner by Lassell in 1851. Their movement is retrograde in a plane inclined 82° to the plane of the ecliptic. A fifth satellite was discovered by Kuiper in 1948. The period of rotation of Uranus has been determined spectroscopically to be $10\frac{3}{4}$ hours; the direction is the same as that of the satellites.

NEPTUNE

This planet is a telescopic object of about the 8th magnitude, presenting a disk of well over 2″ in diameter. A rotation period of $15\frac{1}{2}$ hours, inferred spectroscopically, is now generally adopted for the planet.

The planet was found in 1846 as a result of calculations, made independently by J. C. Adams and Le Verrier, which gave the position of an unknown planet which was responsible for perturbations of the motion of Uranus. The planet was found near the indicated place by Galle of the Berlin Observatory. Neptune has two satellites, of which the inner, Triton, was discovered by Lassell soon after the discovery of the planet. Triton revolves about Neptune in a retrograde direction at a distance a little less than that of the Moon from the Earth.

The other satellite, found by Kuiper in 1949, revolves in the normal direction in a period of about a year. Its orbit is remarkably eccentric, and the satellite's distance from Neptune varies from 800,000 to over 6 million miles.

PLUTO

The outermost planet of the solar system was discovered photographically at the Lowell Observatory in March 1930, as a result of a systematic search for a trans-Neptunian planet. The existence of such a planet had been suggested many years before, and although the predicted elements of the orbit differ in some respects from the true facts, yet these predictions were undoubtedly responsible for the ultimate discovery. The planet was called Pluto, and would appear to be small, with a mass possibly much less than that of the Earth. It would also appear to be a poor reflector of the Sun's light, since it shines only as a star of the 14th–15th magnitude.

THE MOON

The Moon is the Earth's satellite, and although its motion is highly complicated, it may be considered to revolve about the Earth in an elliptical orbit inclined about 5° to the plane of the ecliptic. Owing to perturbations, the ellipse is continually varying in shape, and the whole orbit twists round in space so that the nodes, or points where the orbit intersects the ecliptic, move in a retrograde direction, making one complete revolution in 18·6 years.

The Moon, whose diameter is 2160 miles, rotates in the same time that it revolves ($27^d\ 7^h\ 43^m$) so that the same face is always presented to the Earth. The tilt of its axis, and the variable speed in the orbit, cause it to undergo an apparent swaying motion called libration, which enables us, in the long run, to see rather more than an exact half of the lunar surface. In a telescope this surface shows many objects of great beauty and interest, the rugged ranges of mountains, the craters and plains forming an impressive picture of jet-black shadows and bright highlights.

The revolution of the Moon about the Earth with reference to the Sun takes rather longer than a sidereal revolution, so that the phases of the Moon repeat themselves in a period that varies slightly about a mean of 29½ days. Each month the Moon passes in front of all stars in its path. Such an *occultation* causes the light of the star to be extinguished instantly. This, together with the sharpness and intensity of the shadows on the Moon, indicates a complete lack of atmosphere. Eclipses occur at two "seasons" of the year, when the Moon is near one of its nodes and in line with the Earth and the Sun. A lunar eclipse takes place when the Full Moon passes through the Earth's shadow, and is visible over half the Earth at any one time. A solar eclipse takes place when the New Moon passes in front of the Sun, and is visible only from a rather small area of the Earth.

As a result of its eastward movement among the stars, the Moon rises later each day by a variable amount that depends on the inclination of its apparent path to the observer's horizon. When this angle is small, the Moon rises at much the same time for several days in succession. Although this occurs each month, it is most noticeable in high latitudes at the Full Moon nearest to the Autumnal Equinox. This is the Harvest Moon, although in this Almanack the name is always given to the Full Moon of September. The next Full Moon is called the Hunters' Moon.

THE AURORA BOREALIS (AND AUSTRALIS)

An aurora is the visible counterpart of a marked disturbance of the Earth's magnetic field (a "magnetic storm") apparently due to the action of a stream of electrified particles shot earthwards from localized regions of the Sun, such as that of a big sunspot. The glow of auroral patches, arches or streamers results from the action of this solar stream upon the constituent gases of the Earth's upper atmosphere. The usual height of the lower limit of the auroral luminescence is about 60 miles; upwards, it may extend to 300 miles or higher. Aurorae are very frequent in the so-called auroral zones (magnetic latitude about 67°); they are most frequent for the Earth as a whole near sunspot maximum. Although the solar origin of great displays (e.g. January 25, 1938 and January 24–26, 1949) can be traced to particular sunspots with solar flares, many lesser auroral displays cannot be thus associated. However, their solar origin is evidenced by their tendency to recur at intervals of 27 days, the time required for the Sun to turn once on its axis with respect to the Earth.

THE ZODIACAL LIGHT

This faint phenomenon of the late evening or early morning sky can be seen only when the air is sufficiently clear, the sky quite dark, and the ecliptic making a fairly steep angle with the horizon. It then appears as a cone of faint light stretching up from the position of the Sun (below the horizon) in the direction of the ecliptic, with its apex anything from 60° to 110° from the Sun. In our latitudes it is best seen after sunset in spring and before sunrise in the autumn, when it may appear brighter than the Galaxy in its brightest area.

Occasionally, under very good conditions, an extension of the Cone may be traced right round the ecliptic. This is known as the Zodiacal Band. The Gegenschein or "Counter-glow" may also be detected as a widening of the band at the anti-solar point.

Recent work shows that the zodiacal cloud is a continuation of the Sun's corona, and that much of this fine dust must fall on the earth every day. The particles are much too small, however, to become visible (by incandescence) as they fall through the atmosphere, and there is evidence to show that they settle in the form of micro-meteorites. These probably act as centres of condensation in the formation of rain.

METEORS

The scattered particles which move in streams about the Sun give rise to occasional showers of meteors ("shooting-stars") or fireballs—bodies that differ only in size. They are visible in varying numbers every night, being sometimes so abundant as to be quite spectacular. Often on a particular date or dates, meteors radiate from the same part of the heavens every year. This is because a stream of particles more or less dense, is moving in an orbit that intersects that of the Earth. The orbits of some of these streams, Lyrids, Pons-Winneckeids, Perseids, Giacobinids, Leonids, are known to be closely similar to those of certain comets, but modern work on the measurement of meteor velocities by photographic and radar methods has given very different results for the other streams. Thus the Geminids and the November Taurids have been shown by Whipple (from photographic results) to have small but eccentric orbits, more like those of minor planets. The radar methods of studying meteors have the advantage of being equally useful in daylight, and unaffected by cloud. Besides making measurements of the major showers noted above, the radar technique has shown the presence of a number of extensive showers in daylight hours, particularly in the summer months. These also show the same type of small eccentric orbit as those determined by Whipple.

METEOR SHOWERS

Date	Radiant		Name
	R.A.	Dec.	
	°	°	
January 3........	230	+52	Quadrantids
April 20–22.......	271	+33	Lyrids*
May 2–6..........	337	− 1	η Aquarids*
June 27–30........	213	+53	Pons-Winneckeids*
August 10–13.....	47	+58	Perseids
October 9........	264	+55	Giacobinids*
October 18–23....	96	+15	Orionids*
November 16–17..	152	+22	Leonids*
December 10–13..	113	+32	Geminids
December 22	205	+75	Bečvář's Stream*

* Not plentiful each year.

The real paths of a great number of meteors have been computed, and the average heights found to be about 70 miles at the beginning and about 48 miles at the end. The speeds vary from 10 to 45 miles per second. Fireballs, or very bright meteors, appear at all times of the year unexpectedly so that they are often imperfectly noted and computation of their flight is not practicable.

Fireballs would seem to have a different origin from the ordinary shooting star, and probably arise from the belt of minor planets. The largest fireballs, when not completely consumed, land on the earth as meteorites. The largest meteorite found weighs 30 tons, and considerable collections are to be seen in our museums. Very large falls were recorded in Siberia in 1908 and 1947, while craters (formed presumably by large meteorites) are found in Arizona, Ungava and elsewhere. At the other end of the scale are the micro-meteorites which are too small to become incandescent in the atmosphere and which drift slowly down to the earth's surface.

Above is a list of the nights when meteor showers may be expected, with the radiant points from which the meteors diverge. The dates given are those when the meteors are likely to be most abundant. In some cases, e.g. the Perseids, the apparition lasts beyond these limiting dates, and the position of the radiant, which changes from night to night, is given for the date of maximum.

COMETS

A comet is distinguished from other bodies in the solar system by its appearance: a hazy luminous patch moving in the sky, more or less round and usually brighter in the centre, sometimes with a star-like nucleus there; and from it not infrequently extends a tail which may, in bright comets, reach a length of as much as 100 million miles—a fine spectacle. Most comets are found accidentally and few observers search for these objects. One of the few is G. E. D. Alcock of Peterborough, Northants, who, after searching unsuccessfully for six years, found two new comets in August, 1959, within the space of 5 days. There have been unusually few bright ones for nearly half a century, and the two naked-eye comets which appeared in 1957 (Comet Arend–Roland in April, and Comet Mrkos in August) therefore aroused considerable interest.

Although generally large in volume, a comet is small in mass, probably less than one-millionth that of the Earth even in the largest comets—the centre being composed mainly of an aggregation of pieces of matter mostly of sizes between that of pebbles and fine dust, but probably containing also a solid core a few miles in diameter. According to a recent theory, the earthy material is held together by various "ices"—masses of frozen gases such as ammonia, carbon dioxide and methane—which, on approaching the Sun, begin to evaporate. The pressure of the Sun's radiation is great enough to repel these gases, together with fine dust, and thus form a tail. As the comet approaches the Sun, it grows brighter and as it recedes it grows fainter again, the tail now preceding it in its journey away from the Sun.

Most comets follow paths which are very elongated ovals (ellipses) and return to the Sun, if at all, only after hundreds or thousands of years. The arrival of such comets cannot therefore be predicted. A few dozen comets, however, mostly too faint ever to be seen with the unaided eye, move in smaller ellipses which are sufficiently accurately known to enable predictions to be made of their returns. The most famous and brightest of these periodic comets is Halley's comet, whose spectacular appearances about every 75 years have been traced back over more than 2000 years—it is next due early in 1986. Two very faint comets are known which travel in nearly circular orbits and, on this account, come within reach for photographic observation every year: Schwassmann-Wachmann (1), designated 1925 II, and Oterma. The former is of special interest, not only because its orbit is the only known one lying wholly between Jupiter and Saturn, but on account of the unexpected outbursts in brightness it occasionally manifests.

THE EARTH

The shape of the Earth is that of an oblate spheroid or solid of revolution whose meridian sections are ellipses not differing much from circles, whilst the sections at right angles are circles. The length of the equatorial axis is about 7927 miles, and that of the polar axis 7900 miles. The mean density of the Earth is 5·5 times that of water, although that of the surface layer is less. The Earth and Moon revolve about their common centre of gravity in a lunar month; this centre in turn revolves round the Sun in a plane known as the ecliptic, that passes through the Sun's centre. The Earth's equator is inclined to this plane at an angle of $23\frac{1}{2}°$. This tilt is the cause of the seasons. In mid-latitudes, and when the Sun is high above the Equator, not only does the high noon altitude make the days longer, but the Sun's rays fall more directly on the Earth's surface; these effects combine to produce summer. In equatorial regions the noon altitude is large throughout the year, and there is little variation in the length of the day. In higher latitudes the noon altitude is lower, and the days in summer are appreciably longer than those in winter.

The average velocity of the Earth in its orbit is $18\frac{1}{2}$ miles a second. It makes a complete rotation on its axis in about $23^h\ 56^m$ of mean time, which is the sidereal day. Because of its annual revolution round the Sun, the rotation with respect to the Sun, or the solar day, is more than this by about four minutes (*see* p. 140). The extremity of the axis of rotation, or the North Pole of the Earth, is not rigidly fixed, but wanders over an area roughly 60 feet in diameter.

THE TIDES

The tides are caused by the attraction of the Moon for the waters of the Earth, while a similar but smaller effect is due to the Sun. Normally there are two high tides every day, about $12\frac{1}{2}$ hours apart. They thus occur about 50 minutes later than those of the previous day, corresponding to the $24^h\ 50^m$ interval between consecutive meridian passages of the Moon. Briefly, a high tide occurs when the Moon is near the meridian because the attraction on the water is greater than on the solid earth. On the other side of the Earth the land is nearer to the Moon than the water hence the land is more strongly attracted to the Moon and a second high tide occurs at this point. The height of the tide varies considerably. The highest, called Spring Tides, always occur about the time of New or Full Moon, when the lunar and solar attractions act together. At Neap Tides, which occur about First and Last Quarter, the rise and fall is only about half as much as at Spring Tide.

The tidal flow of water across the Earth is greatly modified by the shape of the coastlines and other geographical conditions. The complicated motion of the Moon, its changing position north or south of the equator, and its varying distance from the Earth, all add small variations; it is thus impossible to predict tides theoretically. Tide-tables for any place are always constructed from an analysis of past observations of times and heights. It is found that the height can be expressed as the sum of a series of periodic terms, which can be carried forward.

High water does not necessarily occur at the same time as the meridian passage of the Moon, nor do springs and neaps necessarily occur on the same day as the phases stated. Thus at London Bridge the tide is high when the Moon is somewhat west of the meridian, while Spring Tides occur about $2\frac{1}{2}$ days after New or Full Moon.

The shape and depth of a channel or estuary very greatly modify the nature of the tides. At some places one of the daily tides becomes so small as to be negligible, while in other channels (e.g. Southampton Water) the high tides are doubled. The difference between high and low water, or range of the tide, may vary from a small amount, as in the land-locked Mediterranean, up to 40 feet in the Severn Estuary and 50 feet in the Bay of Fundy.

As the energy involved in this tidal flow is considerable, various schemes for harnessing tidal energy have been evolved. As a consequence of the friction caused by tidal flow, the Earth's period of rotation is increasing by about a thousandth of a second per day every century. Although very small at present, this effect was greater in the past, and has played a considerable part in the history of the Earth-Moon system.

High Water in the Thames, 1964

Occasions when predicted height at London Bridge is 23 feet or more

March	16–18	September	24–25
April	13–16	October	22–24
May	12–15	November	21–22
June	11–12	December	20–21

TERRESTRIAL MAGNETISM

In the earliest years of experimental science it was known that a light bar of iron rubbed with a piece of the commonly occurring iron ore, magnetite or lodestone, was subject to a directing force impelling it to take up a constant direction when freed from other restraint. Before the 12th century, voyagers were using this mysterious property to guide themselves, their method being to place a light magnetized needle on a reed floated on water. From this primitive device the Mariner's compass subsequently developed. The direction, though roughly north to south, was by no means accurately so. It was found by Columbus on his voyage across the Atlantic that whereas the needle pointed east of north at the outset, it pointed north-north-west at the end.

William Gilbert gave the first approximately correct explanation of the then known facts. Magnetized needles behave as if in proximity to a large magnetized sphere, which he conceived to be the Earth itself. It was soon found that the direction of the force in a particular locality slowly changed. Henry Gellibrand, observing near Greenwich in 1634, found the direction to be about 4° east of north, whereas there was undoubted evidence that in 1580 it had been about 11° east in the same neighbourhood. In 1722, Graham, the clockmaker, found that the direction oscillates slowly through a small angle every day. The movement is eastwards till about 8 a.m., then rather quickly westwards till about 2 p.m., after which there is a gradual return eastwards. The amplitude may be as much as 15′ in the summer.

The compass needle points along a magnetic line of force passing through the "magnetic poles." At these poles a freely suspended magnetized needle would be directed into the vertical. Recent investigations by Canadian surveying parties indicate a position for the North magnetic pole of approximately 75° N. 101° W., but the lines of force do not converge radially upon this point tending rather, on the north side, to concentrate into a channel. From observations by members of Mawson's Australian Antarctic Expedition in 1912 the inferred position of the South magnetic pole was approximately 71° S. 151° E. Results obtained during a French Antarctic Expedition in 1951–2 suggest a position for the South magnetic pole of 67° S. 142° E. The two magnetic poles are thus not antipodal, the line joining them passing the centre of the Earth at a distance of about 700 miles. The distances of the magnetic poles from the north and south geographical poles appear now to be about 1,000 and 1,600 miles respectively.

There is also a "magnetic equator", at all points of which the vertical force is nil and a magnetized needle remains horizontal on its axis. This line runs between 5° and 10° north of the geographical equator in the eastern hemisphere, turns sharply south off the West African coast, and crosses South America through Brazil, Bolivia and Peru; it recrosses the geographical equator in mid-Pacific.

Reference has already been made to secular changes in the Earth's field. The following table indicates the changes in magnetic declination (or variation of the compass). Similar, though much smaller, changes have occurred in "dip" or magnetic inclination. Combination of the two phenomena suggests that a whole cycle may perhaps occupy several hundred years; it is uncertain whether an exact repetition would then follow.

London		Greenwich	
1580	11° 15′ E.	1773	21° 09′ W.
1622	6 00 E.	1805	24 08 W.
1657	0 00	1820	24 21 W.
1692	6 00 W.	1860	21 14 W.
1723	14 17 W.	1900	16 29 W.

In order that up-to-date information on the variation of the compass may be available, many governments publish magnetic charts on which there are lines (called isogonals) passing through all places at which specified values of declination will be found at the date of the chart.

In the British Isles, isogonal lines now run from north-east to south-west, making an angle of about 20° with the meridians. Though there are considerable local deviations due to mineralogical causes, a rough value of magnetic declination may be obtained by assuming that at 50° N. on the meridian of Greenwich, the value in 1964 is 7° 16′ west and allowing an increase of 13′ for each degree of latitude northwards and one of 30′ for each degree of longitude westwards. For example, at 53° N., 5° W., declination will be about 7° 16′ +39′+150′, i.e. 10° 25′ west. The average annual change at the present time is about 6′ decrease.

The number of magnetic observatories now approaches 200—widely scattered over the globe. In Great Britain three are maintained by the Government, namely at Hartland, North Devon, at Eskdalemuir in Dumfriesshire, Scotland, and at Lerwick, Shetland Islands, while a fourth is maintained by Stonyhurst College, Lancashire. The new Hartland Observatory (a department of the Royal Greenwich Observatory) came into operation in 1957 to take the place of the magnetic observatory at Abinger, Surrey, which ceased to operate later in the year. The mean values of the magnetic elements at Abinger are given below.

The phenomena of terrestrial magnetism are due primarily to a field of magnetic force emanating from within the Earth, the origin and behaviour of which is still not satisfactorily explained, and secondarily to magnetic fields imposed from without by the flow of streams of ions or electric currents in the higher regions of the atmosphere. It is undoubted that the latter effects are closely associated with the position of the Sun and with the state of activity of that body, for the diurnal oscillation of the needle everywhere follows *local* time, and is also more than twice as great in summer as in winter in temperate latitudes. Again, it is considerably larger during years of increased solar activity (as indicated by the occurrence of many sunspots) than in the quiet years.

Year	Declination West	Dip or Inclination	Horizontal Force‡	Vertical Force‡
	° ′	° ′		
1935	11 30	66 41	0·1853	0·4298
1940	10 43	66 44	0·1853	0·4310
1945	10 00	66 44	0·1857	0·4321
1950	9 20	66 43	0·1863	0·4329
1955	8 44	66 37	0·1874	0·4335
1960†	8 12	66 33	0·1885	0·4345

† Deduced from Hartland values. ‡ In gauss.

Magnetic Storms. Occasionally—sometimes with great suddenness—the Earth's field is subject for several hours to marked disturbance, indicated by continuous irregular movements of the recording magnets and accompanied in many instances by a widespread display of auroræ. In severe magnetic storms, induced earth-currents also develop which seriously interfere with telegraphic communication. The disturbances are generally ascribed to the passage of the Earth through vast streams of ions or electrified particles that have been expelled from the Sun during an explosive outburst at the solar surface. Such eruptions can be seen and photographed. Often a conspicuous spot has been apparent near the centre of the Sun's disk a day or two before; but the appearance of a spot is by no means always followed by the occurrence of a magnetic storm. There is a tendency for disturbances to recur after intervals of 27 or 28 days, corresponding closely to the apparent period of rotation of the Sun on its axis; this would be explained if the source of the disturbance were located on a particular area of the Sun's surface.

ARTIFICIAL SATELLITES AND SPACE PROBES

The progress of rocket research during the last war led to the development by the Germans in 1944 of the V.2 rocket which, if fired vertically, attained a height of 110 miles. Before the end of the decade the U.S. rocket engineers had increased this maximum height to 250 miles by using a two-stage rocket, the first stage being a V.2 and the second a WAC Corporal. Plans for using multi-stage rockets to put artificial satellites into orbit around the earth during the International Geophysical Year (July 1957–December 1958) were announced by both the U.S. and the U.S.S.R. Such projects also called for an immense effort in establishing optical, radio, and radar tracking facilities around the world.

The historic event which heralded the Space Age occurred on October 4, 1957, when the U.S.S.R. successfully injected a "sputnik" into an orbit inclined at 65° to the earth's equator. One month later "Sputnik 2" was also put into orbit, carrying a dog that survived the ascent trajectory and lived for several days orbiting the earth. The rate of satellite launching has increased since 1957 and by the end of 1960 the number of artificial satellites in orbit around the Earth exceeded the number of natural satellites known to be in the Solar System. All the satellites launched up to the end of 1960 have been sent up in the same direction as the rotation of the Earth, *i.e.*, eastwards. Thus they are able to start with the benefit of the Earth's rotational velocity at the particular launching site. This is why these satellites always appear to move in an easterly direction. However, the first satellite launching of 1961 (*Samos 2*) achieved a retrograde orbit.

Satellite Orbits

To consider the orbit of an artificial satellite it is best to imagine that one is looking at the Earth from a distant point in space. The Earth would then be seen to be rotating about its axis inside the orbit described by the rapidly revolving satellite. The inclination of a satellite orbit to the Earth's equator (which generally remains almost constant throughout the satellite's lifetime) gives at once the maximum range of latitudes over which the satellite passes. Thus a satellite whose orbit has an inclination of 53° will pass overhead all latitudes between 53° S. and 53° N., but would never be seen in the zenith of any place nearer the poles than these latitudes. If we consider a particular place on the earth, whose latitude is less than the inclination of the satellite's orbit then the Earth's rotation carries this place under first the northbound part of the orbit and then, later on, under the southbound portion of the orbit, these two occurrences being always less than 12 hours apart for satellites moving in direct orbits (*i.e.* to the east). For satellites in retrograde orbits the words "northbound" and "southbound" should be interchanged in the preceding statement. As the value of the latitude of the observer increases and approaches the value of the inclination of the orbit, so this interval gets shorter until (when the latitude is equal to the inclination) only one overhead passage occurs each day.

Orbital Variations

The relatively simple picture described above is unfortunately complicated by the considerable variations in the shape, orientation and size of the orbit during a satellite's lifetime. The major variations are due to the Earth's oblateness and to air-drag. A third cause, radiation pressure from the Sun, is noticeable only on large satellites of extremely low density.

The oblate shape of the Earth—the equatorial diameter is 27 miles longer than the polar diameter—has two marked effects on a satellite orbit. It causes a regression of the nodes, amounting to several degrees a day for close satellites. Thus from a point in space, the whole orbit is seen to twist around the Earth, making a complete turn of 360° within a few months. This regression, which may also be described as the rotation of the orbital plane around the Earth's axis, is in the opposite direction to the satellite's motion, *i.e.* the orbit of a satellite with a direct motion regresses to the west. The actual amount of the regression depends, first, on the inclination of the orbit to the equator, being greatest at low inclinations and zero for a true polar orbit (inclination 90°). It is also dependent on the distance of the satellite from the Earth, being greatest for small orbits. At the distance of the Moon the regression is only 19° *a year.*

The orbit of *Samos 2* is extremely interesting from this point of view as its regression is to the east at almost an identical rate with the movement of the Sun. Thus there is hardly any change in the area of visibility over a long period of time.

The other effect the Earth's oblateness has on a satellite orbit is to cause a rotation of the line of apsides (*i.e.* the line joining the perigee and apogee points of the orbit). The rate of the rotation is dependent on the inclination of the orbit, and also on the distance of the satellite, again being greater for close satellites than for more distant ones. The value of this rotation has its greatest positive value (*i.e.* it moves forward along the orbit in the same direction as the satellite) at the equator and becomes zero at an inclination of 63°·4. As the inclination moves from 63°·4 to 90° the value increases again numerically, but with the opposite sign, the motion of the line of apsides being backwards along the orbit.

Even at heights of several hundred miles there is still sufficient atmosphere to cause a retarding effect on satellites. Although air-drag will have most effect around the perigee point the actual result is to reduce the height of the apogee point with hardly any change in perigee height and thus to decrease the eccentricity of the orbit until, in the final stage of a satellite's life-time, the orbit is almost circular. Unfortunately the air density at perigee height is not constant. It alters as the perigee moves from daylight into darkness and from darkness into daylight, and also as the latitude of perigee changes

SATELLITE HEIGHTS AND VELOCITIES

Period	Height, miles	Velocity, miles per hour
h m		
1 28	113	17,446
1 32	236	17,189
1 36	357	16,947
1 40	476	16,718
1 44	593	16,501
1 48	709	16,295
1 52	824	16,098
1 56	937	15,911
2 00	1,049	15,732
2 04	1,160	15,561
2 08	1,269	15,397
2 12	1,377	15,240
2 16	1,485	15,089
2 20	1,591	14,944
2 24	1,696	14,805
2 28	1,800	14,670
2 32	1,904	14,540
2 36	2,006	14,415
2 40	2,108	14,294
2 50	2,358	14,008
3 00	2,603	13,743
3 10	2,844	13,498
3 20	3,081	13,269
3 30	3,313	13,055
3 40	3,542	12,854
3 50	3,768	12,665
4 00	3,994	12,487
5 00	5,265	11,592
6 00	6,458	10,908
7 00	7,585	10,362
8 00	8,660	9,911
9 00	9,691	9,529
10 00	10,684	9,200
11 00	11,644	8,913
12 00	12,576	8,658
13 00	13,483	8,430
14 00	14,366	8,224
15 00	15,229	8,037
16 00	16,072	7,866
17 00	16,898	7,709
18 00	17,708	7,563
19 00	18,504	7,428
20 00	19,285	7,302
21 00	20,053	7,184
22 00	20,810	7,074
23 00	21,555	6,970
24 00	22,289	6,872

due to the rotation of the line of apsides. There is already some evidence that the atmospheric density varies with the sunspot cycle. In addition unpredictable short-period variations in the output of solar radiation may also occur and these have the effect of increasing the air density at any given height. Thus the air-drag on a satellite is by no means a constant factor and this is the reason why it is not possible to forecast accurately the position of a satellite for any considerable period of time. There is also some retardation due to electrified particles but this effect may be included with the air-drag.

Radiation pressure from the Sun only has any appreciable effect on large satellites of extremely low density such as the 100-ft. diameter balloon, *Echo* 1. For such satellites, however, this effect can be severe, and for heights greater than a few hundred miles, it can equal or even surpass that due to air drag. The effect on the orbit is very much more complicated than that due to air-drag, and even the signs of the variations can change periodically with time. Thus it is possible for the eccentricity to increase rather than decrease, with an increase in apogee height and a decrease in perigee height.

For close artificial satellites the gravitational attractions of the Sun and Moon are many thousand times weaker than that of the Earth's equatorial bulge and need only be considered in an extremely precise analysis of observational material.

Height and Velocity

The mean height of a satellite above the Earth's surface, which is determined by its orbital velocity, is related to its period of revolution around the Earth as is shown by the table above. This table is only strictly valid for circular orbits.

As the orbit shrinks due to air drag, both the mean height and the period decrease so that the retarding effect of air drag actually causes the satellite to move faster, though in a smaller orbit.

Satellite Launchings, 1957-63

Many different types of orbit have been achieved though the vast majority have had a direct motion. The majority of the Russian satellite orbits have had inclinations of 65° and orbits entirely below 1200 miles height. An important exception was Lunik 3 whose original inclination was 75° and initial apogee height 293,000 miles. This satellite orbited the Moon on its first revolution, returning with the first photographs of the other side of the Moon, which were transmitted back to the Earth when near perigee.

The American satellites have been injected into orbits of various inclinations. The early Explorers and Vanguards are in orbits of inclination about 28–35° while near-polar orbits were achieved with the Discoverers. Other series of launchings such as the Transit, Tiros and Echo put satellites in orbits of intermediate inclinations. In contrast to the heavy, but short-lived, Russian satellites, a number of those launched by the U.S. have been very small and have been put in larger orbits which have given them considerably longer life-times.

One launching project has caused great controversy amongst astronomers. This is the so-called "West Ford" project, involving the launching of a Midas satellite into a polar orbit, carrying a dispenser. The dispenser contains several hundred million small needles and these are released after the Midas has been successfully injected into a selected orbit. The needles form a belt around the Earth which is used as a reflector for radio signals. The first attempt (1961 α δ) failed but the second (1963–14) has been successful.

[*continued on p. 168*]

ARTIFICIAL SATELLITES LAUNCHED IN 1962-3

Designation	Name	Launch Date	i	P	e	Perigee Height, miles	Apogee Height, miles
		1962	°	m			
1962 ψ	?	June 17	?	?	?	?	?
1962 ω 1	?	June 18	82·1	92·4	0·003	230	255
1962 αα 1	Tiros 5	June 19	58·0	100·4	0·027	365	605
1962 αα 2	Tiros 5 Rocket		58·0	100·4	0·027	364	604
1962 αβ	?	June 23	75·0	90·0	0·006	132	182
1962 αγ	?	June 28	76·0	93·6	0·035	131	428
1962 αδ 1	*Cosmos 6*	June 30	49·0	90·5	0·006	164	214
1962 αδ 2	*Cosmos 6 Rocket*		49·0	90·5	0·006	163	213
1962 αε 1	Telstar 1	July 10	44·8	157·7	0·242	592	3,500
1962 αε 2	Telstar 1 Rocket		44·8	157·5	0·242	588	3,495
1962 αζ 1	?	July 18	96·1	88·7	0·004	114	147
1962 αη	?	July 21	70·3	90·4	0·013	129	237
1962 αθ	?	July 28	71·1	90·6	0·012	140	240
1962 αι 1	*Cosmos 7*	July 28	65·0	90·1	0·012	122	221
1962 αι 2	*Cosmos 7 Rocket*		65·0	90·0	0·010	129	212
1962 ακ 1	?	August 2	82·3	90·8	0·016	127	260
1962 αλ	?	August 5	96·3	88·6	0	127	127
1962 αμ 1	*Vostok 3**	August 11	65·0	88·3	0·004	103	135
1962 αμ 2	*Vostok 3 Rocket*		64·8	88·0	0·004	94	94
1962 αν 1	*Vostok 4**	August 12	65·0	88·4	0·004	105	138
1962 αν 2	*Vostok 4 Rocket*		64·8	88·4	0·004	105	137
1962 αξ 1	Cosmos 8	August 18	49·0	92·9	0·026	152	372
1962 αξ 2	*Cosmos 8 Rocket*		49·0	92·9	0·025	156	367
1962 αο 1	?	August 23	98·6	99·6	0·017	385	533
1962 αο 4	? Rocket			(similar to 1962 αο 1)			
1962 απ 1	*Sputnik 19*	August 25	64·9	88·7	0·006	107	157
1962 απ 2	*Sputnik 19 Rocket*		64·9	89·4	0·010	111	193
1962 αρ 1	Mariner 2			(artificial planet)			
1962 αρ 2	Mariner 2 Rocket			(artificial planet)			
1962 ασ	?	August 29	65·2	90·4	0·016	116	249
1962 ατ	*Sputnik 20*	September 1		(Orbit not known)			
1962 αυ	?	September 1	82·8	94·4	0·027	186	416
1962 αφ 1	*Sputnik 21*	September 12	64·8	88	0	109	109
1962 αχ 1	?	September 17	81·8	93·3	0·034	127	415
1962 αχ 2	*T.R.S. 1*	September 17		(similar to 1962 αχ 1)			
1962 αψ 1	Tiros 6	September 18	58·3	98·7	0·002	425	442
1962 αψ 2	Tiros 6 Rocket		58·3	98·7	0·002	425	442
1962 αω 1	*Cosmos 9*	September 27	65·0	90·9	0·004	181	215
1962 αω 2	*Cosmos 9 Rocket*		65·0	90·9	0·004	181	215
1962 βα 1	Alouette	September 29	80·5	105·5	0·002	619	641
1962 βα 2	Alouette Rocket		80·5	105·5	0·001	626	636
1962 ββ	?	September 29	65·4	90·3	0·013	126	234
1962 βγ 1	Explorer 14	October 2	33·0	2185	0·881	175	61,224
1962 βγ 2	Explorer 14 Rocket	October 2		(similar to 1962 βγ 1)			
1962 βδ 1	*Mercury 8**	October 3	32·6	88·8	0·010	95	177
1962 βδ 2	*Mercury 8 Rocket*		32·6	88·7	0·009	97	171
1962 βε	?	October 9	82·0	91·0	0·016	132	265
1962 βζ 1	*Cosmos 10*	October 17	65·0	90·2	0·013	122	228
1962 βζ 2	*Cosmos 10 Rocket*		64·9	89·1	0·005	122	162
1962 βθ 1	Cosmos 11	October 20	49·0	96·0	0·048	145	705
1962 βθ 2	*Cosmos 11 Rocket*		49·0	95·8	0·047	145	695
1962 βι	Sputnik 22	October 25	65	90	?	?	?
1962 βκ	Midas 6	October 26	71·4	147·9	0·290	123	3,461
1962 βλ 1	Explorer 15	October 27	18·0	315·2	0·564	194	10,961
1962 βλ 2	Explorer 15 Rocket			(similar to 1962 βλ 1)			
1962 βμ 1	Anna 1B	October 31	50·1	107·8	0·007	669	734
1962 βμ 2	Anna 1B Rocket		50·1	107·5	0·006	664	720
1962 βν 1	Mars 1	November 1		(artificial planet)			
1962 βν 3	*Sputnik 23*		65	90	?	?	?
1962 βξ 1	*Sputnik 24*	November 4	(similar to 1962 βξ 3)			122	367
1962 βξ 3	*Sputnik 24 Rocket*		64·7	92·4	0·029	122	367
1962 βο	?	November 5	75·0	90·7	0·015	129	254
1962 βπ	?	November 11	96·0	88·7	0	128	128
1962 βρ	?	November 24	65·1	89·9	0·010	127	209
1962 βσ	?	December 4	65·1	89·2	0·006	121	170
1962 βτ 1	?	December 13	70·4	116·3	0·162	144	1,731
1962 βτ 2	Injun 3		70·4	116·3	0·162	146	1,731
1962 βτ 6	Injun 3 Rocket		70·4	116·3	0·160	154	1,724
1962 βυ 1	Relay 1	December 13	47·5	185·0	0·284	821	4,622
1962 βυ 2	Relay 1 Rocket		47·5	184·7	0·282	836	4,597
1962 βφ	?	December 14	71·0	90·5	0·014	124	244

Designation	Name	Launch Date	*i*	*P*	*e*	Perigee Height, miles	Apogee Height, miles
		1962	°	m			
1962 $\beta\chi$	Explorer 16	December 16	52·0	104·3	0·029	466	734
1962 $\beta\psi$ 1	Transit 5A	December 19	90·6	99·1	0·002	434	450
1962 $\beta\psi$ 2	Transit 5A Rocket		90·7	97·9	0·011	357	455
1962 $\beta\omega$ 1	*Cosmos 12*	December 22	65·0	90·5	0·015	123	244
1962 $\beta\omega$ 2	*Cosmos 12 rocket*		65	90·2	0·013	122	230
		1963					
1963—01 A	*Sputnik 25*	January 1–3	?	?	?	?	?
1963—01 B	*Sputnik 25 Rocket*		?	?	?	?	?
1963—02 A	?	January 7	82·2	90·5	0·015	127	248
1963—02 B	?		82·2	90·3	0·012	130	234
1963—03 A	?	January 16	81·9	94·6	0·005	285	331
1963—04 A	Syncom 1	February 14	33·3	1425·5	0·028	21,370	22,829
1963—04 B	Syncom 1 Rocket		33·1	606·0	0·721	157	21,436
1963—05 A	Blue Scout 2	February 19	100·5	97·8	0·020	314	492
1963—05 B	Blue Scout 2 Rocket		100·5	97·8	0·020	317	490
1963—06 A	*Cosmos 13*	March 21	65·0	89·8	0·010	119	201
1963—06 B	*Cosmos 13 Rocket*		Initial orbit similar to 1963—06 A				
1963—07 A	?	April 1	75·4	90·7	0·015	125	254
1963—08 A	Luna 4	April 2	Initial earth-satellite orbit similar to 1963—08 C				
1963—08 C	*Sputnik 26?*		65?	90?			
1963—09 A	Explorer 17	April 3	57·6	96·4	0·048	158	570
1963—09 B	*Explorer 17 Rocket*		57·6	96·3	0·048	153	572
1963—10 A	Cosmos 14	April 13	49·0	92·1	0·018	157	310
1963—10 B	*Cosmos 14 Rocket*		(similar to 1963—10 A)				
1963—11 A	*Cosmos 15*	April 22	65·0	89·8	0·015	107	230
1963—11 B	*Cosmos 15 Rocket*		(similar to 1963—11 A)				
1963—12 A	*Cosmos 16*	April 28	65·0	90·4	0·014	121	240
1963—12 B	*Cosmos 16 Rocket*		65·0	90·5	0·014	122	246
1963—13 A	Telstar 2	May 7	42·7	225·1	0·401	604	6,712
1963—13 B	Telstar 2 Rocket		42·8	224·8	0·399	612	6,695
1963—14 A	Midas 6	May 9	87·4	166·5	0·004	2,239	2,287
1963—14 B	T.R.S. 2		87·4	166·5	0·004	2,239	2,288
1963—14 C	T.R.S. 3		87·4	166·5	0·004	2,239	2,287
1963—15 A	*Mercury 9**	May 15	32·5	88·7	0·008	101	167
1963—15 B	*Mercury 9 Rocket*		32·5	88·3	0·005	101	139
1963—16 A	?	May 18	?	?	?	?	?
1963—17 A	Cosmos 17	May 22	49·0	94·8	0·038	156	482
1963—17 G	Cosmos 17 Rocket		49·0	94·8	0·037	162	476
1963—18 A	*Cosmos 18*	May 24	65·0	89·4	0·006	127	173
1963—18 B	*Cosmos 18 Rocket*		65·0	89·3	0·004	125	168

A Thor-Delta vehicle, launched from Cape Canaveral, successfully injected an Anglo-American satellite into orbit on April 26, 1962. This satellite, named "Ariel 1", weighs 132 lbs. and has a diameter of 23 inches, with extending booms and aerials. Ariel 1 is transmitting on 136·408 Mc/s. The inclination of its orbit is 54° so that it is readily observable from the British Isles. The third stage Altair rocket is in a similar orbit. Both objects are likely to remain in orbit for a number of years.

Apart from their names, *e.g.* Cosmos 6 Rocket or Injun 3, the satellites are also classified according to their date of launch. Thus 1961 α refers to the launching of Samos 2. The next satellite launching was 1961 β and so on. A number following the Greek letter is intended to indicate the relative brightness of the satellites put in orbit. From the beginning of 1963 the Greek letters are replaced by numbers and the numbers by roman letters e.g. 1963—01A. In this table are given the designation and name of the satellite, the launch date and some initial orbital data. This data consists of the inclination to the equator (*i*), the nodal period of revolution (*P*), the perigee and apogee heights, and the eccentricity (*e*). The names of those satellites which have already disintegrated in the Earth's atmosphere or returned to the Earth's surface are printed in italics. A satellite which carried a human being is indicated by an asterisk.

Since the last edition of *Whitaker's Almanack* the following satellites launched in the years 1961 and 1962 have disintegrated in the Earth's atmosphere:—

1961 $\alpha\epsilon 1$, Discoverer 34; 1962 $\eta 1$, ?; 1962 $\eta 3$, Agena Rocket; 1962 $\upsilon 1$, Sputnik 15; 1962 $\upsilon 2$, Sputnik 15 Rocket.

Some American satellites are of military significance and details of their orbits are not disclosed. This is the reason for the gaps in the table.

It is interesting to note that the rate of successful satellite launchings reached a maximum in 1962 with an average of 6·0 per month but that during the first five months of 1963 the rate has fallen to 3·6 per month.

Observation of Satellites

The regression of the orbit around the Earth causes alternate periods of visibility and invisibility, though this is of little concern to the radio or radar observer. To the visual observer the following cycle of events normally occurs (though the cycle may start in any position): invisibility, morning observations before dawn, invisibility, evening observations after dusk, invisibility, morning observations before dawn, and so on. With reasonably high satellites and for observers in high latitudes around the summer solstice the evening observations follow the morning observations without interruption as sunlight passing over the polar regions can still illuminate satellites which are passing over temperate latitudes at local midnight. At the moment all satellites rely on sunlight to make them visible though a satellite with a flashing light has been suggested for a future launching. The observer must be in darkness or twilight in order to make any useful observations and the durations of twilight and the sunrise, sunset times given on page II of each month will be a useful guide.

Some of the satellites are visible to the naked eye and much interest has been aroused by the spectacle of a bright satellite disappearing into the Earth's shadow. The event is even more fascinating telescopically as the disappearance occurs gradually as the satellite traverses the Earth's penumbral shadow, and during the last few seconds before the eclipse is complete the satellite may change colour (under suitable atmospheric conditions) from yellow to red. This is because the last rays of sunlight are refracted through the denser layers of our atmosphere before striking the satellite.

Some satellites rotate about one or more axes so that a periodic variation in brightness is observed. This was particularly noticeable in several of the U.S.S.R. satellites. In some cases the brightness range was 4 or 5 magnitudes and at minimum brightness the satellite was invisible to the naked eye.

Although it is still possible to make useful observations with the naked eye many observers now use some form of optical aid to enhance the positional accuracy of their observations. A popular instrument is the "elbow" telescope with a wide field of view. However, for locating very faint satellites the more conventional astronomical telescope may be employed, though this involves the potential observer in some detailed calculations beforehand in order to set his telescope correctly.

The observer is normally supplied with details of the orbit of the satellite and the position of the satellite in this orbit for certain times. Using graphical methods or tables, the apparent altitude and azimuth of the satellite at a convenient time are derived and this information is then converted to right ascension and declination. A telescope may then be set on this point. Alternatively several such positions may be calculated, the apparent track across the sky plotted on a star map, and then binoculars or an elbow telescope may be used to scan this track at the predicted time.

The observer will start a stop-watch as the satellite crosses the line joining two identifiable stars, noting the relative distances involved. He will then compare his watch with a time signal as soon as possible—a short wave radio set to pick up such signals is a valuable asset. One of the most useful stations is DIZ (4·525 Mc/s) which gives a "pip" every second (the minute pip is noticeably lengthened). A big advantage of this station is that it is continuously transmitting. Regular observers send their observations to the Satellites Section of the D.S.I.R. Radio Research Station at Slough, from which they receive predictions.

As this subject is so new hardly any literature in book form about satellites has been published in this country. The only notable exceptions are (1) the *Artificial Satellite Memoir* produced by the British Astronomical Association and (2) *Satellites and Scientific Research* by D. King-Hele.

Satellite research has already provided some interesting results. Among them may be mentioned a revised value of the Earth's oblateness, 1/298·2, and the discovery of the Van Allen radiation belts. Apart from space travel itself great possibilities will be opened up in other fields in the years to come, *e.g.* communications, navigation and meteorology.

Space Probes

Several lunar probes have been launched. The only direct hits were scored by Lunik 2 and Lunik 2 Rocket in September, 1959, and by Ranger 4 in April, 1962.

There are a number of artificial planets in orbit including several resulting from the three Venus probes and the Mars probe.

THE ZODIAC

The Zodiac is an imaginary belt in the heavens within which lie the apparent paths of the Sun, Moon and major planets. It is bounded by two parallels generally taken as lying 8° on either side of the ecliptic or path of the Sun in its annual course. The Zodiac is divided into twelve equal parts of 30° called Signs, which are not used by astronomers, but have some import in astrology, for which the division of the Zodiac was probably made originally. The Signs of the Zodiac take their names from certain of the constellations with which they once coincided. They are assumed to begin at the vernal equinox or intersection of the plane of the ecliptic with that of the equator. This point is still called the First Point of Aries, although the Sign of Aries now lies in the constellation of Pisces, some 30° to the west. This retrograding of the equinox by about 50″ a year is due to precession; the signs no longer coincide with the constellations whose names they bear.

A catalogue has been made (Grimaldi, 1905) of all, so far as is known, sculptured or incised representations on ancient monuments or tablets of the traditional constellation figures, either Zodiacal or otherwise, together with many modern pictures of the Zodiac. The first in the list is a roughly shaped upright, black stone about 2½ feet high and 1½ feet broad in the Babylonian room of the British Museum on the front of which are lightly incised ten out of the twelve Signs and other constellation figures. This was found near Baghdad and its date is estimated to be about 1187–1175 B.C.

The hour when the Sun enters each Sign of the Zodiac, which varies year by year in accordance with the leap-year cycle, and slightly for other reasons, is given in the heading of page I of each month.

Tidal Constants

THE TIME OF HIGH WATER *at the undermentioned Ports and Places may be* approximately *found by taking the appropriate Time of High Water at the* Standard Port (*as shown on pp.* 172, 173, *etc.) and* adding thereto *the quantities annexed. The time thus found will be* G.M.T. *for British, Irish, French and Belgian ports, and for Netherlands Ports* G.M.T.+1 hour. *The columns headed "Springs" and "Neaps" show the height of the tide above datum for Mean High Water Springs and Mean High Water Neaps respectively.* During the period of SUMMER TIME one hour must be added to the times shown on pp. 172–183, before the system is applied.

Tidal data is no longer available for a number of places which formerly appeared in the list below. These places (with the name of the substitute now recorded) are: *Air Point* (Mostyn Quay); *Ardrishaig* (East Loch Tarbert); *Arisaig* (Loch Moidart); *Ayr Pt., I.o.M.* (Peel); *Beachy Head* (Eastbourne); *Beaumaris* (Menai Bridge); *Brielle* (Scheveningen); *Broughty Ferry* (Newburgh); *Burryport* (Whiteford Lighthouse); *Caen* (Cayeux); *Caernarvon* (Llanddwyn Isld.); *Chesilton* (Worthing); *Dumbarton* (Bowling); *Dumfries* (Port Carlisle); *Fareham* (Itchenor); *Fifeness* (Anstruther Easter); *Glasson Dock* (Tarn Pt.); *Gravesend* (Tilbury Dock); *Greenwich* (R. Albert Dock); *Hythe* (Totland Bay); *Lancaster* (Dudden Bar); *Lynmouth* (Porlock Bay); *Nash Pt.* (Chepstow); *Needles Pt.* (Freshwater Bay); *Neath* (Porthcawl); *Nore Lt.* (Chatham); *Port Harrington* (Hestan Islet); *Portishead* (Avonmouth); *St. Agnes* (Coverack); *St. Mary's* (Sennen Cove); *Start Pt.* (Lulworth Cove); *Stockton* (Seaham); *Sutton Bridge* (Blacktoft); *Torbay* (Torquay); *Woolwich* (Hammersmith Br.); *Worms Head* (Ferryside); *Honfleur Harbour* (Duclair).

Port	Diff.	Springs	Neaps	Port	Diff.	Springs	Neaps
	h. m.	ft.	ft.		h. m.	ft.	ft.
Aberdeen.......... *Leith*	−1 16	12·1	9·4	Coverack.......... *Btol*	−2 0	18·2	14·8
Aberdovey........ *L'pool*	−3 16	14·9	11·2	*Cowes (West)...... *Lon*	−2 30	11·8	9·3
Aberystwyth...... *L'pool*	−3 34	14·6	11·0	Cromarty.......... *Leith*	−2 51	13·7	11·1
Aldeburgh.......... *Lon*	−3 6	9·1	8·5	Cromer............ *Hull*	+0 36	15·9	12·2
Alderney............ *Lon*	+5 15	21·0	16·4	Dartmouth.......... *Lon*	+4 28	15·4	11·6
Alloa.............. *Leith*	+0 46	18·1	13·8	Deal.............. *Lon*	−2 32	17·8	14·2
Amlwch.......... *L'pool*	−0 40	21·4	16·1	Devonport Dock..... *Lon*	+4 0	16·1	12·5
Anstruther Easter... *Leith*	−0 22	17·8	14·1	Dieppe.............. *Lon*	−3 8	30·0	24·0
Antwerp............ *Lon*	+1 20	17·8	14·7	Dingle Harbour.... *L'pool*	−6 55	11·5	8·4
Appledore.......... *Btol*	−1 24	24·8	16·6	Donegal Harbour.. *L'pool*	+6 55	11·8	9·2
Arbroath.......... *Leith*	−0 30	14·6	11·6	Douglas.......... *L'pool*	−0 4	22·5	17·8
Ardrossan.......... *Grnk*	−0 20	9·2	7·6	Dover.............. *Lon*	−2 42	19·1	15·1
*Arundel............ *Lon*	−1 8	10·3	7·1	Duclair.............. *Lon*	−0 53	25·6	21·3
Avonmouth......... *Btol*	0	42·2	31·4	Dudden Bar....... *L'pool*	+0 3	26·5	20·5
Ayr.............. *Grnk*	−0 20	9·5	8·2	Dunbar........... *Leith*	−0 7	16·2	13·2
Ballycottin.......... *Btol*	−1 41	12·5	9·8	Dundalk (Pile Lt.). *L'pool*	−0 13	15·7	14·0
Banff.............. *Leith*	−2 41	10·4	8·2	Dundee............ *Leith*	+0 14	15·3	12·0
Bantry Harbour.... *L'pool*	+5 56	11·6	8·9	Dungeness.......... *Lon*	−2 56	23·6	18·6
Bardsey Island..... *L'pool*	−3 23	14·5	11·2	Dunkirk............ *Lon*	−1 57	19·0	15·7
Barmouth......... *L'pool*	−3 9	15·7	12·0	Eastbourne.......... *Lon*	−2 44	21·8	16·7
Barnstaple Bridge.... *Btol*	−1 7	13·4	4·6	East Loch Tarbert... *Grnk*	−0 5	14·6	10·7
Barrow........... *L'pool*	−0 9	28·4	22·9	Exmouth............ *Lon*	+4 50	12·4	8·7
Barry Island......... *Btol*	−0 25	35·8	26·7	Eyemouth.......... *Leith*	−0 20	15·0	11·9
Berwick........... *Leith*	−0 1	15·1	12·3	Falmouth............ *Lon*	+3 36	17·2	13·8
Bideford........... *Btol*	−1 24	19·5	11·9	Ferryside............ *Btol*	−1 0	25·7	19·3
Blacktoft........... *Hull*	+0 38	18·1	11·5	Filey Bay.......... *Leith*	+1 51	15·6	12·4
Blakeney........... *Hull*	+0 30	10·0	6·7	Fishguard......... *L'pool*	−4 9	13·7	9·0
Blyth.............. *Leith*	+0 51	14·5	10·9	Flushing............ *Lon*	+0 23	15·6	12·9
Bolt Head........... *Lon*	+4 5	15·9	12·4	Folkestone.......... *Lon*	−2 54	20·6	16·4
Boscastle........... *Btol*	−1 39	22·8	17·5	Formby Pt......... *L'pool*	−0 21	27·8	22·3
Boulogne............ *Lon*	−2 48	29·2	24·0	Fowey.............. *Lon*	+3 47	16·7	13·3
Bowling........... *Grnk*	+0 24	12·3	10·2	Fraserburgh......... *Leith*	−2 16	11·6	9·1
Brest............... *Lon*	−2 25	24·5	19·3	Freshwater Bay...... *Lon*	−3 23	6·9	5·9
Bridgwater Bar...... *Btol*	0	16·0	6·0	Galway Bay....... *L'pool*	+6 15	15·3	11·7
Bridlington......... *Leith*	+2 4	17·6	13·2	Glasgow........... *Grnk*	+0 41	13·4	10·7
Bridport............ *Lon*	+4 50	12·0	8·4	Goole.............. *Hull*	−1 12	17·8	11·7
Brighton............ *Lon*	−2 50	19·2	14·6	Granton Pier....... *Leith*	+0 1	17·8	14·4
Buckie............ *Leith*	−2 54	11·5	9·6	Granville............ *Lon*	+4 32	43·0	33·0
Bude Haven......... *Btol*	−1 34	22·8	17·5	Grimsby............ *Hull*	−0 27	20·4	15·8
Burntisland......... *Leith*	0	17·8	14·4	Hammersmith Bdge.. *Lon*	+0 35	18·0	14·3
Calais.............. *Lon*	−2 25	22·6	18·6	Hartlepool......... *Leith*	+0 59	15·9	12·3
Campbeltown...... *Grnk*	−0 32	8·9	7·5	Harwich............ *Lon*	−2 18	12·6	10·5
Cape Cornwall....... *Btol*	−2 04	17·4	14·0	Hastings............ *Lon*	−2 47	22·8	18·0
Cardiff............. *Btol*	−0 7	37·4	27·8	Haverfordwest .... *L'pool*	−4 36	6·9	1·5
Cardigan.......... *L'pool*	−4 7	14·2	10·7	Havre.............. *Lon*	−4 0	25·6	20·9
Carmarthen Bar..... *Btol*	−0 39	8·9	3·0	Hestan Islet....... *L'pool*	+0 25	26·7	20·5
Cayeux.............. *Lon*	−2 59	33·1	26·2	Hilbre Is.......... *L'pool*	−0 25	28·2	21·5
Chatham (N. Lock).. *Lon*	−1 4	18·6	15·2	Holyhead......... *L'pool*	−0 54	16·8	12·7
Chepstow........... *Btol*	+0 20	38·4	28·7	Hook of Holland..... *Lon*	+1 18	6·7	5·6
Cherbourg.......... *Lon*	−6 4	20·7	16·1	Hurst Camber....... *Lon*	−3 0	7·5	6·3
Chester........... *L'pool*	+1 5	13·4	5·5	Ilfracombe.......... *Btol*	−1 9	28·3	21·4
Chichester Harbour.. *Lon*	−2 30	14·2	11·0	Inverary........... *Grnk*	+0 11	11·0	10·1
*Christchurch Harb... *Lon*	−3 08	4·9	4·1	Invergordon........ *Leith*	−2 41	13·9	10·8

* Approximate figures only, owing to abnormality of tides in the area.

Port	Diff.	Springs	Neaps	Port	Diff.	Springs	Neaps
	h. m.	ft.	ft.		h. m.	ft.	ft.
Ipswich............*Lon*	−1 43	13.3	10.6	Ramsey (I.O.M.)...*L'pool*	+0 4	22.5	18.0
Itchenor............*Lon*	−2 21	14.6	11.1	Ramsgate Harbour...*Lon*	−2 22	16.2	13.0
Kinsale Harbour...*L'pool*	+6 14	12.5	9.7	Ribble Lt. House..*L'pool*	−0 4	26.7	19.7
Kirkcudbright.....*L'pool*	no data	22.8	18.0	Rosslare Harbour..*L'pool*	−5 29	5.8	4.3
Kirkwall..........*Leith*	−4 11	8.3	6.1	Rosyth............*Leith*	+0 6	17.5	13.9
Lamlash...........*Grnk*	−0 26	9.1	7.6	R.A. Dock..........*Lon*	−0 31	21.9	18.3
Lerwick Harbour...*Leith*	−3 46	5.7	4.2	Ryde...............*Lon*	−2 30	12.4	9.7
Limerick..........*L'pool*	−4 50	18.2	14.4	St. Helier..........*Lon*	+4 47	35.4	25.6
Littlehampton Bar....*Lon*	−2 38	16.6	12.9	St. Ives.............*Btol*	−2 9	22.8	17.8
Lizard.............*Btol*	−2 4	17.4	14.0	St. Malo............*Lon*	+4 26	39.7	30.6
Llanddwyn Island..*L'pool*	−1 47	14.2	10.9	St. Peter Port........*Lon*	+4 53	26.5	19.0
Llanelly Bar.........*Btol*	−0 52	25.5	19.2	Salcombe............*Lon*	+4 5	15.9	12.4
Loch Long.........*Grnk*	0	12.6	10.5	Saltash..............*Lon*	+4 9	16.2	12.6
Loch Moidart......*Grnk*	+5 48	14.2	10.1	Scarborough........*Leith*	+1 49	16.7	12.9
Looe (East)..........*Lon*	+3 58	17.0	13.6	Scheveningen........*Lon*	+1 28	6.8	5.6
Lossiemouth........*Leith*	−2 58	11.8	9.5	Seaham............*Leith*	+0 54	15.0	11.5
Lowestoft...........*Lon*	−4 26	6.9	5.7	Selsea Bill...........*Lon*	−2 33	15.8	12.4
Lulworth Cove......*Lon*	+5 7	6.5	4.2	Sennen Cove........*Btol*	−2 26	20.0	15.7
Lundy Island.........*Btol*	−1 19	22.8	17.3	Sharpness............*Btol*	+0 46	30.2	18.2
Lyme Regis..........*Lon*	+4 50	12.3	8.6	Sheerness............*Lon*	−1 19	17.9	14.8
Lymington..........*Lon*	−2 53	8.5	6.9	Shoreham Harbour...*Lon*	−2 43	18.1	13.9
Lynn Road.........*Hull*	+0 6	21.9	16.7	Silloth............*L'pool*	+0 37	27.4	21.5
Margate Pier.........*Lon*	−2 1	14.1	11.7	Southampton........*Lon*	−2 55	13.5	10.8
Maryport.........*L'pool*	+0 24	26.7	20.7	Southend............*Lon*	−1 29	18.4	15.2
Menai Bridge......*L'pool*	−0 25	24.0	19.1	Southwold...........*Lon*	−3 51	7.9	6.8
Mevagissey..........*Lon*	+3 36	18.3	14.9	Spurn Head.........*Hull*	−0 35	18.9	14.3
Middlesbrough......*Leith*	+1 10	17.3	13.4	Stirling............*Leith*	+1 12	8.4	4.6
Milford Haven.....*L'pool*	+7 13	23.0	17.2	Stonehaven.........*Leith*	−1 6	13.5	10.7
Minehead Pier.......*Btol*	no data	34.8	25.8	Stornoway........*L'pool*	+7 57	14.1	10.5
Montrose...........*Leith*	−0 26	14.1	11.2	Stranraer...........*Grnk*	−0 20	9.2	7.5
Morecambe.......*L'pool*	+0 1	28.2	22.3	Stromness..........*Leith*	−5 32	10.4	7.4
Mostyn Quay......*L'pool*	−0 10	28.4	22.7	Sunderland.........*Leith*	+0 52	15.6	12.0
Mull of Galloway...*Grnk*	−1 1	15.5	12.6	Swanage............*Lon*	−3 23	5.4	4.3
Naze...............*Lon*	−2 15	12.9	10.3	Swansea Bay........*Btol*	−0 51	28.7	21.7
Newburgh.........*Leith*	+0 51	13.4	9.7	Tarn Point........*L'pool*	+0 5	26.2	20.3
Newcastle on Tyne..*Leith*	+0 55	15.4	11.9	Tay River Bar......*Leith*	−0 18	15.1	11.8
Newhaven..........*Lon*	−2 55	20.7	15.9	Tees River Bar.... *Leith*	+1 9	16.8	12.8
Newport (Mon.).....*Btol*	−0 10	39.2	29.3	Teignmouth.........*Lon*	+4 32	13.1	9.5
Newquay (Town)....*Btol*	−1 59	22.4	17.3	Tenby..............*Btol*	−1 3	25.4	19.0
New Quay (Card.).*L'pool*	−3 41	14.3	10.8	Thurso.............*Leith*	−5 56	14.1	10.5
North Shields.......*Leith*	+0 52	14.5	11.2	Tilbury Docks.......*Lon*	−0 59	20.6	17.1
North Sunderland...*Leith*	+0 5	14.9	11.5	Tobermory.........*L'pool*	+7 1	13.5	9.4
Oban..............*Grnk*	+5 45	11.5	7.9	Torquay............*Lon*	+4 35	13.6	9.8
Orfordness..........*Lon*	−2 51	9.1	8.6	Totland Bay.........*Lon*	−3 20	6.9	6.1
Ostend..............*Lon*	−1 35	16.3	13.7	Troon..............*Grnk*	−0 20	9.1	7.3
Padstow.............*Btol*	−1 49	22.3	16.8	Truro...............*Lon*	+3 41	18.2	14.2
Peel (I.O.M.)......*L'pool*	−0 4	17.7	14.2	Tynemouth Bar.....*Leith*	+0 57	14.7	11.1
Pembroke Dock ...*L'pool*	+7 13	23.0	17.2	Ushant..............*Lon*	+2 28	24.9	19.5
Penzance............*Btol*	−2 16	17.7	13.9	Valentia Harbour..*L'pool*	+5 28	11.7	8.6
Peterhead..........*Leith*	−1 56	11.5	9.2	Waterford Hbr.....*L'pool*	+6 39	13.9	11.2
Plymouth B'water...*Lon*	+3 54	16.0	12.4	Weston S. Mare......*Btol*	−0 25	38.9	29.1
Poole...............*Lon*	−3 18	5.6	4.3	Wexford..........*L'pool*	−5 6	5.8	4.5
Porlock Bay.........*Btol*	−0 52	31.6	23.9	Whitby.............*Leith*	+1 23	16.1	12.1
Port Carlisle....... *L'pool*	+0 52	20.9	17.0	Whiteford Lt. House..*Btol*	−0 55	27.1	20.3
Portmadoc........*L'pool*	−3 8	15.4	11.7	Whitehaven.......*L'pool*	+0 2	25.9	20.0
Port Patrick.......*L'pool*	0	12.5	10.0	Wick...............*Leith*	−3 26	10.2	7.5
Port Talbot.........*Btol*	−0 54	29.1	21.9	Wisbech............*Hull*	+0 9	22.4	16.2
Porthcawl...........*Btol*	−0 49	29.9	21.8	Workington.......*L'pool*	+0 9	26.5	20.4
Portland Bill.........*Lon*	+4 50	9.3	6.8	Worthing...........*Lon*	−2 38	18.2	14.2
Portland B'water.....*Lon*	+5 5	7.0	4.5	Yarmouth Roads....*Lon*	−5 1	6.9	5.6
Portsmouth..........*Lon*	−2 28	13.4	10.5	Yarmouth (I.O.W)...*Lon*	−3 11	8.4	6.6
Preston............*L'pool*	0	27.0	21.0	Ymuiden............*Lon*	+2 13	6.9	5.5
Pwllheli...........*L'pool*	−3 18	15.5	11.4	Youghal..........*L'pool*	+6 32	13.0	10.3
Queenstown.......*L'pool*	+6 26	12.1	9.1				

The Standard Ports referred to in the heading are given in italic.

EXAMPLE.—Required times of high water at Stranraer on *April* 6, 1964:—

(*a*) *Morning Tide.*

Appropriate time of high water at *Greenock*	0604 hrs. (*April* 6)
Tidal difference.........	−0020 hrs.
H.W. at *Stranraer*...	0544 hrs.

(*b*) *Afternoon Tide.*

Appropriate time of high water at *Greenock*	1845 hrs. (*April* 6)
Tidal difference.........	−0020 hrs.
H.W. at *Stranraer*...	1825 hrs.

JANUARY

Time of High Water at the undermentioned Places—

Day of Month	Day of Week	London Bridge				Liverpool				Bristol (*Avonmouth*)				Hull				Greenock				Leith†				Dun Laoghaire			
		January 1964				January 1964				January 1964				January 1964				January 1964				January 1964				January 1964			
		Mn.	Ht.	Aft.	Ht.	Mn.	Ht.	Aft.	Ht.	Mn.	Ht.	Aft.	Ht.	Mn.	Ht.	Aft.	Ht.	Mn.	Ht.	Aft.	Ht.	Mn.	Ht.	Aft.	Ht.	Mn.	Ht.	Aft.	Ht.
		h.m.	ft.	h.m.	ft.	h.m.	ft.	h.m.	ft.	h.m.	ft.	h.m.	ft.	h.m.	ft.	h.m.	ft.	h.m.	ft.	h.m.	ft.	h.m.	ft.	h.m.	ft.	h.m.	ft.	h.m.	ft.
1	W	247	22·8	1511	22·9	0 3	29·5	1223	29·9	824	43·4	2051	43·2	725	22·5	1938	22·0	125	11·2	1322	12·4	328	18·5	1556	18·2	010	12·6	1231	13·3
2	Th	331	22·5	1558	22·6	050	29·0	13 8	29·5	910	43·1	2137	42·0	811	21·9	2021	21·6	216	10·9	14 7	12·5	417	18·2	1643	17·8	1 0	12·3	1320	13·1
3	F	414	21·9	1645	22·1	136	28·1	1353	28·6	953	41·9	2221	40·2	856	21·1	21 2	20·9	3 4	10·8	1452	12·4	5 5	17·5	1732	17·2	153	11·9	1412	12·8
4	S	457	21·2	1730	21·3	223	26·7	1438	27·2	1035	40·1	23 3	38·0	940	20·1	2143	20·1	349	10·5	1535	12·1	555	16·7	1822	16·4	245	11·3	15 5	12·4
5	**S**	540	20·3	1816	20·5	310	25·2	1524	25·6	1116	37·9	2344	35·6	1024	19·0	2226	19·2	433	10·1	1618	11·5	646	15·7	1913	15·6	341	10·8	16 1	11·8
6	M	622	19·5	19 3	19·6	359	23·8	1616	24·3	1158	35·4	—	—	1110	18·0	2317	18·3	518	9·7	17 5	10·8	740	14·9	20 6	15·0	443	10·2	17 4	11·2
7	Tu	710	18·8	1955	18·9	455	22·7	1714	23·1	028	33·3	1247	33·3	—	—	12 6	17·1	612	9·2	1759	10·0	837	14·3	21 3	14·5	550	9·9	1811	10·7
8	W	8 6	18·2	2057	18·6	558	22·5	1822	22·5	124	31·5	1347	31·7	019	17·6	1312	16·8	719	9·0	19 5	9·6	938	14·2	22 4	14·4	657	9·8	1919	10·5
9	Th	920	18·1	22 5	18·6	7 4	22·4	1933	22·6	229	31·0	1456	31·5	134	17·4	1421	17·1	833	9·1	2017	9·5	1041	14·3	23 6	14·4	756	10·0	2017	10·4
10	F	1033	18·5	23 5	19·2	8 9	23·1	2037	23·3	337	31·8	16 4	32·6	245	17·7	1522	18·0	931	9·5	2120	9·7	1137	14·6	—	—	846	10·3	21 6	10·6
11	S	1132	19·3	2359	19·9	9 2	24·3	2126	24·2	439	33·6	17 4	34·4	346	18·4	1614	18·9	1019	9·8	2212	10·0	0 2	14·7	1226	15·0	927	10·8	2149	10·8
12	**S**	—	—	1224	20·0	945	25·4	22 7	25·1	534	35·7	1755	36·3	438	19·1	1659	19·8	11 2	10·1	23 0	10·1	052	15·1	1313	15·6	10 4	11·2	2227	10·9
13	M	046	20·5	1310	20·6	1025	26·4	2244	25·9	621	37·7	1840	37·9	524	19·8	1737	20·5	1139	10·4	2344	10·1	137	15·5	1354	16·1	1038	11·6	23 3	11·1
14	Tu	128	21·0	1350	21·1	11 0	27·1	2320	26·3	7 2	39·2	1919	39·2	6 5	20·2	1813	21·0	—	—	1212	10·6	217	16·0	1433	16·6	1113	11·9	2338	11·2
15	W	2 5	21·3	1427	21·5	1135	27·9	2356	26·9	740	40·3	1956	40·0	641	20·5	1846	21·2	025	10·1	1247	10·7	255	16·4	15 8	16·9	1146	12·1	—	—
16	Th	239	21·5	15 4	21·6	—	—	1212	28·3	816	41·0	2033	40·5	718	20·7	1918	21·4	1 5	9·9	1321	10·8	330	16·8	1542	17·2	013	11·3	1222	12·3
17	F	314	21·6	1540	21·6	033	27·1	1247	28·6	851	41·0	2110	40·4	753	20·7	1952	21·5	145	9·9	1356	11·0	4 7	16·9	1618	17·2	050	11·3	1259	12·4
18	S	351	21·6	1618	21·6	1 8	27·1	1325	28·5	929	40·7	2148	39·9	828	20·7	2027	21·5	226	10·0	1434	11·2	444	16·7	1657	17·0	1 30	11·3	1339	12·4
19	**S**	427	21·4	1657	21·3	147	26·8	14 4	28·2	10 6	40·1	2226	38·9	9 6	20·4	21 5	21·4	3 5	10·2	1512	11·3	526	16·4	1740	16·7	211	11·2	1421	12·4
20	M	5 4	21·2	1737	21·1	227	26·2	1445	27·6	1043	38·9	23 5	37·6	947	20·0	2149	21·1	347	10·4	1555	11·5	613	15·9	1825	16·4	257	11·0	15 8	12·2
21	Tu	540	20·9	1819	20·6	315	25·6	1533	26·8	1123	37·4	2349	35·9	1034	19·3	2239	20·5	428	10·5	1641	11·3	7 2	15·5	1916	16·1	349	10·8	16 0	11·9
22	W	622	20·6	19 9	20·1	4 9	24·8	1633	25·8	—	—	1213	35·6	1128	18·5	2340	19·9	512	10·4	1734	10·9	758	15·1	2010	15·7	450	10·5	17 2	11·5
23	Th	715	20·1	2014	19·6	511	24·1	1739	25·0	045	34·5	1319	34·4	—	—	1233	18·0	6 4	10·2	1842	10·4	859	15·0	2115	15·5	559	10·4	1815	11·2
24	F	827	19·7	2133	19·6	623	23·9	1856	24·9	159	34·0	1441	34·5	051	19·4	1349	17·9	711	9·9	20 3	10·2	1010	15·1	2227	15·6	711	10·5	1929	11·2
25	S	954	19·8	2252	20·1	741	24·7	2012	25·5	321	34·9	16 5	36·2	213	19·3	15 4	18·5	831	10·1	2125	10·3	1117	15·5	2341	16·0	815	11·0	2037	11·4
26	**S**	1116	20·6	—	—	850	25·9	2120	26·7	438	37·0	1717	38·5	332	19·8	16 8	19·4	942	10·4	2232	10·5	—	—	1222	16·1	913	11·5	2136	11·7
27	M	0 1	20·8	1226	21·3	949	27·4	2215	27·7	544	39·4	1817	40·6	439	20·7	17 6	20·4	1040	10·9	2331	10·6	044	16·7	1320	16·8	10 4	12·0	2229	11·9
28	Tu	1 0	21·5	1326	22·0	1039	28·6	23 5	28·5	641	41·3	1910	42·0	538	21·4	1758	21·2	1134	11·4	—	—	143	17·4	1413	17·4	1051	12·5	2318	12·1
29	W	151	22·0	1418	22·4	1127	29·4	2352	28·8	730	42·6	1956	42·8	630	21·9	1844	21·7	028	10·6	1224	11·7	233	17·9	1459	17·9	1136	12·9	—	—
30	Th	236	22·2	15 4	22·5	—	—	1210	29·9	814	43·3	2040	42·9	717	22·0	1926	21·8	120	10·6	1312	12·1	320	18·1	1542	18·1	0 3	12·0	1221	13·0
31	F	318	22·3	1546	22·5	036	28·6	1253	29·5	856	43·3	2120	42·4	759	21·6	20 4	21·6	2 8	10·6	1356	12·3	4 4	18·0	1624	18·0	048	12·0	13 6	13·0

† See note, p. 173.

FEBRUARY

Time of High Water at the undermentioned Places—

Day of Month	Day of Week	London Bridge Mn.	Ht.	Aft.	Ht.	Liverpool Mn.	Ht.	Aft.	Ht.	Bristol (*Avonmouth*) Mn.	Ht.	Aft.	Ht.	Hull Mn.	Ht.	Aft.	Ht.
		February 1964				February 1964				February 1964				February 1964			
		h.m.	ft.	h.m.	ft.	h.m.	ft.	h.m.	ft.	h.m.	ft.	h.m.	ft.	h.m.	ft.	h.m.	ft.
1	S	357	22·1	1626	22·2	118	28·2	1333	29·1	934	42·6	2158	41·3	837	21·0	2041	21·2
2	**S**	436	21·7	17 4	21·7	159	27·4	1411	28·0	1011	41·4	2233	39·4	912	20·2	2115	20·6
3	M	512	21·2	1740	21·0	237	26·3	1449	26·6	1044	39·3	23 5	37·1	947	19·3	2151	19·9
4	Tu	547	20·5	1815	20·1	317	24·8	1529	24·9	1114	36·9	2336	34·6	1024	18·4	2231	18·9
5	W	622	19·7	1854	19·2	4 0	23·3	1616	23·3	1148	34·1	—	—	11 7	17·5	2321	17·8
6	Th	7 5	18·8	1943	18·4	453	22·0	1715	22·0	014	32·2	1233	31·6	—	—	12 2	16·7
7	F	8 4	18·1	2050	17·9	558	21·6	1828	21·3	1 8	30·2	1336	29·8	027	16·8	1315	16·3
8	S	927	17·8	2211	18·1	714	21·8	1950	21·5	221	29·7	1457	29·7	155	16·3	1435	16·6
9	**S**	1051	18·4	2324	18·7	823	22·8	2056	22·6	344	30·9	1618	31·5	316	16·7	1541	17·5
10	M	1156	19·4	—	—	919	24·2	2145	24·0	456	33·4	1724	34·2	418	17·6	1632	18·5
11	Tu	021	19·6	1248	20·2	10 3	25·7	2226	25·4	555	36·1	1817	36·8	5 6	18·6	1714	19·5
12	W	1 7	20·3	1332	20·9	1041	27·0	23 2	26·6	642	38·5	19 1	39·0	547	19·5	1751	20·4
13	Th	144	20·9	1410	21·4	1117	28·2	2339	27·6	722	40·4	1940	40·8	625	20·4	1826	21·2
14	F	220	21·4	1446	21·9	1153	29·1	—	—	8 0	41·9	2019	42·0	7 1	21·0	19 1	21·8
15	S	255	21·8	1523	22·3	015	28·2	1230	29·6	838	42·8	2057	42·7	736	21·4	1936	22·2
16	**S**	332	22·2	16 1	22·3	052	28·6	13 6	29·9	916	43·2	2136	42·7	813	21·5	2013	22·4
17	M	410	22·4	1639	22·2	130	28·4	1345	29·6	953	42·7	2212	41·7	851	21·2	2052	22·3
18	Tu	446	22·4	1717	22·0	2 8	27·8	1424	28·8	1028	41·3	2248	40·0	930	20·6	2134	21·8
19	W	522	22·0	1756	21·3	249	26·8	15 8	27·6	11 4	39·2	2325	37·5	1012	19·7	2221	21·0
20	Th	6 2	21·4	1842	20·4	339	25·5	16 3	26·0	1147	36·6	—	—	11 0	18·6	2316	19·8
21	F	653	20·5	1944	19·4	440	24·2	1713	24·5	012	34·9	1245	34·1	—	—	12 1	17·6
22	S	8 6	19·7	21 8	19·0	556	23·4	1837	23·8	121	33·1	1411	32·9	027	18·6	1319	17·0
23	**S**	942	19·5	2238	19·1	724	23·6	20 4	24·3	254	33·1	1549	34·2	2 0	18·0	1447	17·3
24	M	1111	20·1	2353	20·1	841	24·9	2115	25·6	425	35·1	17 8	36·8	330	18·6	16 1	18·4
25	Tu	—	—	1223	21·0	942	26·6	2210	27·0	537	38·1	1810	39·5	439	19·8	17 0	19·8
26	W	052	20·9	1322	21·7	1031	28·1	2257	28·0	632	40·6	19 2	41·3	535	20·9	1749	20·8
27	Th	141	21·5	1410	22·1	1114	29·0	2337	28·6	719	42·2	1942	42·4	622	21·5	1832	21·5
28	F	222	21·9	1451	22·3	1153	29·6	—	—	759	42·9	2021	42·8	7 4	21·7	1911	21·8
29	S	3 0	22·1	1527	22·5	016	28·8	1231	29·6	836	43·3	2056	42·5	739	21·4	1945	21·8

Day of Month	Day of Week	Greenock Mn.	Ht.	Aft.	Ht.	Leith† Mn.	Ht.	Aft.	Ht.	Dun Laoghaire Mn.	Ht.	Aft.	Ht.
		February 1964				February 1964				February 1964			
		h.m.	ft.	h.m.	ft.	h.m.	ft.	h.m.	ft.	h.m.	ft.	h.m.	ft.
1	S	250	10·5	1437	12·4	446	17·4	17 8	17·4	133	11·6	1351	12·8
2	**S**	330	10·5	1515	12·1	529	16·6	1751	16·7	217	11·3	1437	12·4
3	M	4 5	10·3	1552	11·7	613	15·7	1835	15·9	3 2	10·8	1523	11·7
4	Tu	439	10·0	1632	11·0	657	14·8	1918	15·0	351	10·2	1614	11·0
5	W	518	9·5	1717	10·3	744	14·1	20 5	14·3	447	9·6	1712	10·2
6	Th	6 3	9·2	1811	9·6	835	13·7	21 0	13·8	550	9·3	1822	9·7
7	F	7 6	8·9	1916	9·3	936	13·5	22 7	13·6	659	9·3	1932	9·5
8	S	829	8·9	2028	9·2	1046	13·6	2321	13·7	759	9·6	2032	9·7
9	**S**	942	9·3	2140	9·3	1151	14·1	—	—	851	10·1	2122	10·1
10	M	1035	9·7	2237	9·6	023	14·2	1247	14·8	935	10·7	22 4	10·5
11	Tu	1115	10·1	2326	9·8	116	14·9	1333	15·5	1014	11·3	2242	11·0
12	W	1152	10·4	—	—	2 1	15·7	1414	16·3	1051	11·8	2319	11·3
13	Th	010	9·7	1229	10·7	239	16·5	1449	16·9	1126	12·2	2353	11·5
14	F	051	9·7	13 5	10·9	314	17·0	1523	17·5	—	—	12 1	12·5
15	S	131	9·9	1342	11·2	348	17·4	1558	17·8	029	11·7	1238	12·8
16	**S**	211	10·1	1420	11·5	424	17·4	1636	17·8	1 7	11·8	1317	12·9
17	M	249	10·5	1459	11·8	5 5	17·1	1718	17·6	148	11·7	1359	12·8
18	Tu	327	10·9	1539	11·7	549	16·6	18 3	17·2	231	11·5	1445	12·5
19	W	4 5	11·0	1623	11·4	637	16·0	1850	16·6	319	11·2	1537	12·1
20	Th	446	10·9	1714	10·9	729	15·3	1944	15·9	416	10·7	1639	11·4
21	F	534	10·4	1816	10·2	829	14·8	2050	15·2	524	10·3	1754	10·9
22	S	633	9·9	1939	9·6	943	14·5	2213	15·1	642	10·3	1916	10·6
23	**S**	757	9·6	2121	9·5	11 4	14·8	2333	15·4	756	10·5	2031	10·8
24	M	930	9·8	2236	9·7	—	—	1215	15·5	9 1	11·1	2134	11·2
25	Tu	1035	10·4	2334	10·0	041	16·2	1314	16·4	956	11·7	2226	11·5
26	W	1126	10·9	—	—	138	17·0	14 4	17·1	1044	12·3	2313	11·8
27	Th	024	10·2	1214	11·4	226	17·5	1446	17·7	1127	12·6	2352	11·8
28	F	1 9	10·3	1259	11·7	3 7	17·7	1525	17·9	—	—	12 7	12·9
29	S	150	10·3	1341	12·0	344	17·7	16 2	17·8	030	11·8	1247	12·8

† To obtain depth of water over the sill at the entrance to the Imperial Dock, Leith, the constant of 12·60 ft. should be added to the above predictions.

MARCH

Time of High Water at the undermentioned Places—

Day of Month	Day of Week	London Bridge March 1964				Liverpool March 1964				Bristol (Avonmouth) March 1964				Hull March 1964			
		Mn.	Ht.	Aft.	Ht.	Mn.	Ht.	Aft.	Ht.	Mn.	Ht.	Aft.	Ht.	Mn.	Ht.	Aft.	Ht.
		h.m.	ft.	h.m.	ft.	h.m.	ft.	h.m.	ft.	h.m.	ft.	h.m.	ft.	h.m.	ft.	h.m.	ft.
1	**S**	336	22·3	16 1	22·4	054	28·5	13 8	29·1	910	42·9	2130	41·7	813	20·9	2017	21·5
2	M	410	22·2	1633	22·1	128	27·9	1340	28·1	941	41·8	2159	40·3	842	20·4	2047	21·0
3	Tu	442	21·9	17 2	21·5	2 1	27·0	1411	26·9	10 8	40·0	2225	38·2	912	19·7	2119	20·3
4	W	512	21·2	1732	20·6	234	25·7	1445	25·4	1032	37·5	2249	35·8	944	19·0	2156	19·2
5	Th	543	20·3	18 4	19·7	310	24·2	1525	23·7	1059	34·8	2319	33·2	1022	18·0	2239	17·9
6	F	620	19·2	1847	18·6	354	22·8	1616	21·9	1136	32·0	—	—	11 7	17·0	2335	16·4
7	S	712	18·3	1945	17·7	456	21·6	1725	20·8	0 2	30·8	1228	29·7	—	—	12 9	16·0
8	**S**	827	17·6	21 7	17·4	611	21·0	1855	20·6	1 8	29·2	1351	28·7	057	15·3	1335	15·6
9	M	10 3	17·9	2240	17·8	737	21·6	2019	21·7	244	29·3	1531	29·8	242	15·4	15 1	16·3
10	Tu	1123	18·9	2349	18·8	845	23·3	2116	23·5	416	31·7	1652	33·0	353	16·5	1558	17·5
11	W	—	—	1222	19·9	934	25·1	22 0	25·3	525	35·1	1750	36·3	442	17·9	1643	18·8
12	Th	039	19·8	13 7	20·9	1013	27·0	2238	27·0	616	38·3	1836	39·2	523	19·4	1724	20·2
13	F	119	20·9	1346	21·6	1051	28·5	2314	28·3	658	40·7	1917	41·6	6 1	20·7	18 2	21·4
14	S	154	21·6	1423	22·3	1128	29·8	2352	29·3	738	42·8	1958	43·3	639	21·7	1840	22·4
15	**S**	231	22·3	15 0	22·8	—	—	12 7	30·6	817	44·3	2037	44·5	717	22·2	1919	23·0
16	M	3 9	23·0	1538	23·1	030	29·7	1245	30·9	857	44·9	2115	44·6	755	22·2	1959	23·1
17	Tu	348	23·3	1618	23·0	1 9	29·5	1324	30·4	935	44·4	2153	43·4	833	21·8	2038	22·8
18	W	427	23·2	1657	22·6	148	28·9	14 6	29·4	1012	42·8	2229	41·3	911	21·0	2120	22·1
19	Th	5 6	22·7	1737	21·6	229	27·6	1451	27·7	1047	40·1	23 5	38·4	951	19·9	22 7	20·8
20	F	549	21·7	1824	20·4	317	26·0	1547	25·7	1129	36·7	2351	35·1	1038	18·7	23 2	19·3
21	S	643	20·5	1925	19·2	419	24·3	1659	23·9	—	—	1226	33·6	1135	17·4	—	—
22	**S**	759	19·5	2052	18·5	538	23·0	1827	23·0	059	32·7	1355	31·9	018	17·8	13 0	16·6
23	M	938	19·4	2226	18·7	712	23·1	1959	23·6	238	32·2	1539	33·1	2 0	17·3	1437	16·9
24	Tu	11 7	19·9	2342	19·5	831	24·5	21 8	25·1	414	34·4	1658	36·1	329	18·2	1551	18·2
25	W	—	—	1216	20·9	931	26·2	2159	26·6	524	37·6	1756	39·0	432	19·6	1648	19·6
26	Th	039	20·4	1310	21·6	1016	27·6	2240	27·7	617	40·1	1843	40·8	523	20·7	1733	20·7
27	F	125	21·0	1352	21·8	1056	28·5	2317	28·3	7 0	41·7	1922	41·8	6 5	21·3	1813	21·4
28	S	2 4	21·6	1429	22·1	1132	28·9	2352	28·5	737	42·3	1956	42·2	641	21·4	1849	21·7
29	**S**	238	22·0	15 1	22·3	—	—	12 7	29·0	810	42·5	2029	42·2	714	21·3	1921	21·8
30	M	311	22·3	1532	22·4	026	28·3	1240	28·6	842	42·3	2059	41·6	745	21·0	1952	21·6
31	Tu	344	22·4	16 1	22·3	057	27·9	1310	27·8	9 9	41·2	2126	40·4	813	20·6	2023	21·1

Day of Month	Day of Week	Greenock March 1964				Leith† March 1964				Dun Laoghaire March 1964			
		Mn.	Ht.	Aft.	Ht.	Mn.	Ht.	Aft.	Ht.	Mn.	Ht.	Aft.	Ht.
		h.m.	ft.	h.m.	ft.	h.m.	ft.	h.m.	ft.	h.m.	ft.	h.m.	ft.
1	**S**	228	10·4	1418	12·0	421	17·2	1640	17·4	1 7	11·6	1327	12·6
2	M	3 1	10·5	1451	11·9	459	16·6	1718	16·8	145	11·3	14 6	12·1
3	Tu	330	10·4	1523	11·4	536	15·7	1755	16·0	222	10·9	1446	11·5
4	W	358	10·2	1559	11·0	614	15·0	1833	15·2	3 3	10·4	1528	10·7
5	Th	430	9·9	1638	10·3	653	14·2	1915	14·3	349	9·8	1616	10·0
6	F	5 9	9·5	1726	9·6	737	13·7	20 4	13·5	442	9·4	1719	9·3
7	S	558	9·1	1823	9·1	835	13·2	2112	13·1	550	9·1	1838	9·0
8	**S**	659	8·8	1932	8·9	947	13·1	2239	13·1	7 4	9·2	1951	9·2
9	M	838	8·8	21 1	8·9	1110	13·4	2350	13·7	810	9·7	2051	9·8
10	Tu	10 0	9·2	2214	9·2	—	—	1216	14·2	9 1	10·4	2138	10·4
11	W	1047	9·7	23 4	9·4	049	14·6	13 7	15·1	945	11·1	2219	11·1
12	Th	1126	10·1	2347	9·6	134	15·6	1347	16·2	1025	11·8	2254	11·6
13	F	—	—	12 5	10·7	213	16·5	1423	17·1	11 2	12·4	2329	12·0
14	S	028	9·8	1244	11·0	249	17·3	1458	17·9	1137	12·8	—	—
15	**S**	1 9	10·1	1324	11·4	323	17·8	1533	18·4	0 5	12·2	1214	13·1
16	M	148	10·6	14 3	11·7	4 0	17·9	1613	18·5	043	12·3	1254	13·3
17	Tu	226	10·9	1442	11·9	440	17·7	1656	18·4	022	12·3	1338	13·1
18	W	3 2	11·3	1524	11·8	526	17·1	1742	17·7	2 6	12·0	1424	12·7
19	Th	340	11·4	16 9	11·4	615	16·4	1831	16·9	254	11·6	1517	12·1
20	F	421	11·2	1659	10·6	7 8	15·5	1928	15·8	350	11·1	1621	11·3
21	S	5 8	10·6	1759	9·8	8 9	14·7	2039	15·0	5 0	10·5	1740	10·5
22	**S**	6 4	9·9	1925	9·0	927	14·3	22 7	14·8	620	10·3	19 9	10·3
23	M	725	9·4	2128	8·8	1051	14·5	2328	15·2	740	10·5	2026	10·5
24	Tu	919	9·4	2237	9·2	—	—	12 5	15·3	849	11·0	2128	11·0
25	W	1025	9·9	2324	9·6	033	16·1	13 1	16·2	944	11·6	2218	11·4
26	Th	1113	10·4	—	—	126	16·7	1348	16·9	1031	12·2	2258	11·7
27	F	0 7	9·9	1157	10·8	210	17·1	1428	17·4	1113	12·5	2333	11·8
28	S	046	10·1	1239	11·2	247	17·4	15 3	17·6	1149	12·6	—	—
29	**S**	123	10·2	1317	11·4	321	17·3	1537	17·6	0 6	11·8	1225	12·5
30	M	157	10·3	1351	11·5	354	16·9	1611	17·2	040	11·6	13 0	12·2
31	Tu	227	10·4	1422	11·4	426	16·5	1645	16·7	112	11·4	1336	11·7

† See note, p. 173.

APRIL

Time of High Water at the undermentioned Places—

Day of Month	Day of Week	London Bridge				Liverpool				Bristol (Avonmouth)				Hull			
		April 1964				April 1964				April 1964				April 1964			
		Mn.	Ht.	Aft.	Ht.	Mn.	Ht.	Aft.	Ht.	Mn.	Ht.	Aft.	Ht.	Mn.	Ht.	Aft.	Ht.
		h.m.	ft.	h.m.	ft.	h.m.	ft.	h.m.	ft.	h.m.	ft.	h.m.	ft.	h.m.	ft.	h.m.	ft.
1	W	413	22·2	1629	21·9	127	27·3	1338	26·9	933	39·8	2147	38·6	841	20·2	2054	20·4
2	Th	441	21·5	1656	21·0	157	26·2	14 9	25·5	956	37·7	2210	36·5	912	19·5	2129	19·2
3	F	512	20·7	1727	20·0	230	24·8	1445	23·9	1020	35·2	2238	34·1	946	18·6	22 8	17·8
4	S	549	19·5	18 7	18·8	312	23·3	1534	22·3	1054	32·6	2315	31·8	1025	17·5	2256	16·4
5	**S**	638	18·5	19 0	17·9	4 7	22·1	1639	21·0	1142	30·3	—	—	1113	16·4	—	—
6	M	746	17·8	2012	17·3	520	21·2	18 5	20·5	016	29·9	1257	28·9	0 4	15·2	1222	15·6
7	Tu	915	17·8	2139	17·4	643	21·5	1932	21·4	147	29·3	1442	29·7	145	15·0	1355	15·7
8	W	1042	18·7	23 2	18·4	8 0	23·0	2039	23·3	332	31·2	1612	32·6	3 9	16·1	15 9	16·9
9	Th	1145	19·9	2359	19·6	855	24·9	2126	25·3	448	34·6	1715	36·2	4 4	17·8	16 4	18·6
10	F	—	—	1235	20·9	939	26·9	22 6	27·1	542	38·1	18 5	39·5	449	19·5	1651	20·3
11	S	044	20·7	1316	21·8	1020	28·7	2245	28·7	626	40·9	1848	41·9	530	21·1	1734	21·8
12	**S**	123	21·7	1355	22·6	11 0	30·1	2326	29·7	7 9	43·1	1931	43·8	611	22·1	1816	22·8
13	M	2 2	22·6	1435	23·1	1143	30·9	—	—	751	44·6	2012	44·9	652	22·6	1859	23·4
14	Tu	244	23·2	1516	23·4	0 6	30·2	1225	31·0	834	45·3	2053	45·0	731	22·6	1941	23·4
15	W	326	23·5	1558	23·2	048	30·1	13 7	30·4	915	44·7	2134	43·8	810	22·1	2023	22·8
16	Th	410	23·3	1640	22·5	130	29·2	1351	29·0	955	42·9	2212	41·6	851	21·2	21 8	21·8
17	F	455	22·6	1723	21·5	214	27·9	1440	27·2	1036	40·0	2253	38·5	932	20·1	2157	20·4
18	S	544	21·6	1813	20·2	3 5	26·1	1540	25·2	1121	36·5	2340	35·3	1020	18·9	2256	18·8
19	**S**	643	20·4	1914	18·9	4 8	24·4	1653	23·5	—	—	1221	33·4	1120	17·6	—	—
20	M	8 1	19·5	2036	18·2	527	23·1	1821	22·7	049	32·8	1346	31·8	016	17·5	1246	16·7
21	Tu	934	19·4	2211	18·5	657	23·2	1946	23·5	223	32·4	1521	33·1	155	17·3	1420	17·0
22	W	1057	20·0	2324	19·2	815	24·5	2051	24·9	354	34·3	1636	35·7	314	18·2	1530	18·2
23	Th	1159	20·7	—	—	912	25·9	2138	26·2	5 1	37·2	1730	38·3	413	19·4	1624	19·5
24	F	020	20·2	1248	21·3	956	27·1	2217	27·2	551	39·5	1816	40·1	459	20·3	17 7	20·5
25	S	1 3	20·8	1327	21·7	1033	27·8	2252	27·8	633	40·8	1853	41·0	537	20·9	1745	21·2
26	**S**	140	21·3	14 2	22·0	11 8	28·1	2326	28·0	7 9	41·4	1928	41·3	612	21·1	1821	21·6
27	M	215	21·7	1433	22·1	1141	28·1	2358	28·1	742	41·4	1959	41·3	645	21·1	1854	21·6
28	Tu	246	22·0	15 4	22·2	—	—	1213	27·8	811	41·1	2029	41·0	715	21·1	1927	21·4
29	W	318	22·2	1533	22·2	029	27·8	1242	27·2	839	40·3	2054	40·0	745	20·9	20 0	20·9
30	Th	349	22·1	16 2	21·7	058	27·3	1312	26·3	9 4	38·9	2118	38·5	815	20·6	2034	20·1

Day of Month	Day of Week	Greenock				Leith†				Dun Laoghaire			
		April 1964				April 1964				April 1964			
		Mn.	Ht.	Aft.	Ht.	Mn.	Ht.	Aft.	Ht.	Mn.	Ht.	Aft.	Ht.
		h.m.	ft.	h.m.	ft.	h.m.	ft.	h.m.	ft.	h.m.	ft.	h.m.	ft.
1	W	254	10·5	1454	11·0	459	15·9	1719	16·1	147	11·1	1411	11·1
2	Th	320	10·4	1527	10·6	533	15·3	1755	15·3	222	10·6	1450	10·5
3	F	351	10·2	16 7	10·0	6 9	14·6	1834	14·4	3 2	10·1	1535	9·8
4	S	427	9·9	1652	9·5	651	13·9	1923	13·5	350	9·7	1630	9·2
5	**S**	510	9·4	1744	9·0	745	13·3	2032	13·0	452	9·4	1743	9·0
6	M	6 4	8·9	1845	8·7	857	13·0	2153	13·0	6 3	9·3	19 9	9·1
7	Tu	716	8·6	2011	8·5	1020	13·2	2312	13·6	719	9·7	2013	9·7
8	W	910	8·8	2143	8·8	1132	14·0	—	—	822	10·4	21 5	10·5
9	Th	10 8	9·4	2234	9·3	011	14·6	1228	15·0	9 8	11·2	2146	11·3
10	F	1052	10·0	2315	9·6	1 0	15·6	1311	16·2	950	11·9	2225	11·9
11	S	1134	10·6	2356	9·9	141	16·7	1350	17·3	1030	12·6	23 0	12·3
12	**S**	—	—	1217	11·0	217	17·5	1428	18·1	11 9	13·0	2337	12·6
13	M	038	10·4	13 0	11·5	255	18·1	15 6	18·7	1147	13·3	—	—
14	Tu	119	10·8	1343	11·7	335	18·2	1548	18·9	015	12·7	1230	13·3
15	W	157	11·3	1425	11·8	418	18·0	1634	18·6	056	12·6	1317	13·1
16	Th	236	11·6	15 8	11·5	5 5	17·3	1723	17·9	143	12·4	14 8	12·5
17	F	317	11·7	1556	11·0	555	16·5	1817	16·8	234	12·0	15 4	11·8
18	S	4 0	11·3	1647	10·2	651	15·6	1919	15·8	332	11·4	1611	11·0
19	**S**	447	10·7	1749	9·2	755	14·7	2032	14·9	441	10·8	1730	10·3
20	M	543	9·8	1926	8·5	913	14·3	2155	14·9	6 1	10·4	1858	10·1
21	Tu	7 1	9·0	2124	8·6	1034	14·5	2311	15·3	724	10·5	2014	10·5
22	W	859	9·0	2221	9·1	1145	15·2	—	—	830	11·0	2114	10·9
23	Th	10 3	9·5	23 3	9·5	013	16·0	1240	16·0	927	11·6	22 0	11·3
24	F	1048	10·0	2340	9·8	1 3	16·5	1324	16·7	1012	12·0	2237	11·5
25	S	1130	10·4	—	—	144	16·9	14 3	17·0	1052	12·1	2311	11·6
26	**S**	016	9·9	1210	10·7	219	17·0	1437	17·3	1127	12·1	2341	11·4
27	M	051	10·1	1248	10·8	252	16·9	1510	17·2	—	—	12 1	11·9
28	Tu	123	10·4	1322	10·9	323	16·8	1543	17·0	011	11·5	1235	11·6
29	W	152	10·4	1354	10·7	354	16·5	1618	16·6	041	11·4	13 8	11·2
30	Th	218	10·5	1425	10·4	425	16·1	1650	16·0	114	11·2	1344	10·8

† See note, p. 173.

MAY

Time of High Water at the undermentioned Places—

Day of Month	Day of Week	London Bridge Mn.	Ht.	Aft.	Ht.	Liverpool Mn.	Ht.	Aft.	Ht.	Bristol (*Avonmouth*) Mn.	Ht.	Aft.	Ht.	Hull Mn.	Ht.	Aft.	Ht.
		May 1964				May 1964				May 1964				May 1964			
		h.m.	ft.	h.m.	ft.	h.m.	ft.	h.m.	ft.	h.m.	ft.	h.m.	ft.	h.m.	ft.	h.m.	ft.
1	F	420	21·6	1631	21·1	129	26·5	1314	25·2	928	37·1	2143	36·6	845	20·0	21 9	19·1
2	S	452	20·7	17 3	20·1	2 3	25·4	1420	24·0	955	35·1	2212	34·6	916	19·2	2146	17·9
3	**S**	531	19·7	1743	19·0	243	24·1	15 7	22·7	1032	33·1	2252	32·7	952	18·3	2230	16·8
4	M	618	18·7	1831	18·2	336	23·0	16 9	21·6	1120	31·4	2349	31·1	1035	17·4	2326	16·0
5	Tu	719	18·1	1932	17·6	441	22·3	1723	21·2	—	—	1229	30·3	1133	16·7	—	—
6	W	833	18·2	2047	17·8	556	22·3	1843	22·0	1 9	30·6	14 2	30·6	045	15·8	1250	16·5
7	Th	954	18·8	22 8	18·5	7 9	23·4	1952	23·5	245	32·0	1528	33·2	210	16·6	1413	17·4
8	F	11 1	19·8	2313	19·7	810	25·1	2046	25·4	4 3	34·9	1634	36·6	316	18·1	1519	18·9
9	S	1156	20·9	—	—	9 1	26·9	2131	27·3	5 1	38·2	1728	39·6	4 8	19·7	1614	20·6
10	**S**	0 6	20·8	1243	21·9	948	28·6	2215	28·7	552	40·9	1814	41·9	456	21·2	17 3	22·0
11	M	053	21·9	1328	22·6	1033	29·9	23 0	29·8	639	42·8	19 1	43·5	541	22·2	1751	23·0
12	Tu	139	22·8	1412	23·2	1119	30·5	2345	30·3	725	44·1	1947	44·5	625	22·6	1837	23·3
13	W	224	23·3	1458	23·3	—	—	12 5	30·6	812	44·7	2032	44·6	7 7	22·6	1924	23·2
14	Th	312	23·5	1542	23·1	030	30·1	1253	29·9	857	44·1	2117	43·6	749	22·2	2010	22·5
15	F	4 0	23·1	1627	22·4	116	29·4	1342	28·6	942	42·5	22 1	41·6	833	21·5	21 0	21·5
16	S	450	22·5	1714	21·4	2 4	28·1	1435	26·9	1029	40·0	2247	39·0	918	20·6	2152	20·3
17	**S**	543	21·5	18 5	20·2	258	26·6	1534	25·2	1119	37·1	2338	36·4	10 7	19·5	2252	18·9
18	M	644	20·5	19 3	19·2	358	25·0	1643	23·7	—	—	1218	34·4	11 6	18·3	—	—
19	Tu	755	19·7	2016	18·5	510	24·0	18 0	23·1	041	34·2	1329	32·9	0 4	17·9	1221	17·5
20	W	915	19·5	2141	18·4	628	23·9	1916	23·6	158	33·4	1448	33·3	124	17·5	1342	17·5
21	Th	1030	19·8	2253	18·9	742	24·5	2018	24·5	317	34·4	1558	34·9	237	18·0	1451	18·1
22	F	1128	20·4	2349	19·8	840	25·3	21 6	25·7	421	36·2	1653	36·9	335	18·7	1546	19·0
23	S	—	—	1215	20·9	926	26·2	2147	26·5	514	37·8	1739	38·4	422	19·5	1632	19·9
24	**S**	033	20·4	1255	21·1	10 5	26·7	2225	27·1	558	38·9	1820	39·3	5 2	20·1	1713	20·6
25	M	113	20·9	1332	21·4	1042	26·9	2258	27·3	637	39·4	1857	39·9	540	20·6	1752	21·0
26	Tu	150	21·3	14 6	21·7	1116	27·0	2332	27·5	714	39·6	1931	40·1	614	20·9	1830	21·1
27	W	225	21·6	1440	21·9	1149	26·9	—	—	746	39·6	20·3	40·0	647	21·1	19 7	20·9
28	Th	259	21·8	1511	21·8	0 4	27·5	1220	26·4	816	39·1	2033	39·4	720	21·1	1942	20·4
29	F	332	21·7	1542	21·7	036	27·2	1253	25·9	845	38·1	21 0	38·2	751	20·8	2017	19·8
30	S	4 6	21·3	1614	21·0	1 9	26·6	1327	25·2	913	36·8	2129	36·8	822	20·4	2052	19·1
31	**S**	441	20·6	1649	20·2	144	25·8	14 5	24·3	945	35·4	22 2	35·4	851	19·9	2128	18·4

Day of Month	Day of Week	Greenock Mn.	Ht.	Aft.	Ht.	Leith† Mn.	Ht.	Aft.	Ht.	Dun Laoghaire Mn.	Ht.	Aft.	Ht.
		May 1964				May 1964				May 1964			
		h.m.	ft.	h.m.	ft.	h.m.	ft.	h.m.	ft.	h.m.	ft.	h.m.	ft.
1	F	245	10·4	15 0	10·1	459	15·6	1726	15·4	151	10·9	1422	10·3
2	S	315	10·3	1539	9·8	536	14·9	18 6	14·5	231	10·5	15 4	9·8
3	**S**	351	10·0	1623	9·4	621	14·2	1858	13·8	317	10·2	1557	9·4
4	M	434	9·7	1712	9·1	712	13·8	20 0	13·4	411	10·0	17 3	9·1
5	Tu	523	9·2	18 9	8·7	817	13·4	2112	13·3	517	9·8	1818	9·3
6	W	625	8·9	1919	8·6	931	13·6	2225	13·8	627	10·0	1929	9·9
7	Th	8 1	8·9	2056	8·9	1040	14·2	2326	14·7	732	10·6	2025	10·6
8	F	921	9·5	2152	9·4	1140	15·2	—	—	828	11·3	2111	11·3
9	S	1012	10·1	2236	9 7	018	15·8	1229	16·3	916	12·0	2152	12·0
10	**S**	1059	10·6	2321	10·2	1 2	16·7	1313	17·3	10 0	12·5	2232	12·4
11	M	1146	11·0	—	—	144	17·4	1358	18·1	1042	12·9	2311	12·7
12	Tu	0 4	10·7	1233	11·3	226	18·0	1442	18·7	1125	13·1	2352	12·9
13	W	048	11·1	1321	11·4	310	18·2	1528	18·9	—	—	1212	13·0
14	Th	132	11·6	14 8	11·4	357	18·0	1618	18·6	036	12·8	13 1	12·7
15	F	214	11·8	1457	11·1	446	17·5	1711	17·8	124	12·6	1356	12·2
16	S	258	11·9	1547	10·5	539	16·8	18 7	16·9	217	12·2	1455	11·5
17	**S**	342	11·6	1640	9·8	636	15·9	19 8	15·9	317	11·7	16 0	10·9
18	M	430	10·9	1742	9·0	740	15·1	2016	15·2	424	11·2	1717	10·3
19	Tu	525	10·0	1910	8·4	850	14·6	2131	15·0	541	10·9	1837	10·1
20	W	636	9·2	2050	8·4	10 4	14·7	2242	15·3	656	10·9	1948	10·4
21	Th	814	8·9	2147	8·8	11 9	15·2	2340	15·6	8 3	11·1	2047	10·7
22	F	923	9·2	2229	9·2	—	—	12 7	15·7	9 0	11·3	2133	11·0
23	S	1012	9·6	23 6	9·6	030	16·0	1252	16·2	947	11·5	2211	11·2
24	**S**	1056	10·0	2342	9·9	112	16·2	1333	16·4	1027	11·6	2244	11·4
25	M	1138	10·2	—	—	150	16·4	1410	16·6	11 3	11·5	2317	11·5
26	Tu	018	10·1	1216	10·2	224	16·5	1445	16·7	1137	11·3	2345	11·5
27	W	051	10·2	1253	10·2	255	16·5	1519	16·6	—	—	1210	11·1
28	Th	121	10·3	1329	10·0	326	16·4	1554	16·4	017	11·5	1245	10·8
29	F	149	10·3	14 2	9·7	4 0	16·2	1630	16·0	051	11·3	1320	10·5
30	S	218	10·3	1439	9·5	435	15·8	17 6	15·5	128	11·2	14 0	10·2
31	**S**	249	10·2	1518	9·3	515	15·3	1748	14·9	2 7	11·0	1443	10·0

† *See note*, p. 173.

JUNE

Time of High Water at the undermentioned Places—

Day of Month	Day of Week	London Bridge Mn.	Ht.	Aft.	Ht.	Liverpool Mn.	Ht.	Aft.	Ht.	Bristol (Avonmouth) Mn.	Ht.	Aft.	Ht.
		June 1964				June 1964				June 1964			
		h.m.	ft.	h.m.	ft.	h.m.	ft.	h.m.	ft.	h.m.	ft.	h.m.	ft.
1	M	520	20·0	1727	19·4	224	25·1	1450	23·4	1023	34·1	2242	34·1
2	Tu	6 5	19·3	1810	18·9	312	24·3	1544	22·8	1110	32·9	2333	33·1
3	W	655	18·8	19 1	18·6	4 9	23·7	1648	22·4	—	—	12 9	32·2
4	Th	756	18·6	20 2	18·5	513	23·6	1756	22·9	040	32·5	1323	32·4
5	F	9 4	19·0	2113	19·0	620	24·3	19 2	23·9	159	33·2	1441	34·1
6	S	1014	19·7	2225	19·7	724	25·4	20 4	25·4	315	35·3	1550	36·5
7	**S**	1117	20·7	2329	20·8	824	26·8	2058	27·0	420	37·8	1649	39·1
8	M	—	—	1212	21·7	918	28·1	2149	28·3	517	40·0	1744	41·1
9	Tu	027	21·7	13 6	22·3	1010	29·2	2238	29·4	611	41·9	1835	42·5
10	W	121	22·5	1355	22·7	11 2	29·8	2326	29·9	7 4	43·1	1926	43·4
11	Th	213	23·0	1443	23·0	1152	19·8	—	—	755	43·5	2016	43·7
12	F	3 4	23·0	1529	22·7	015	29·9	1242	29·4	845	43·3	21 5	43·1
13	S	356	22·9	1616	22·2	1 4	29·4	1333	28·3	935	42·2	2153	41·9
14	**S**	447	22·4	17 3	21·4	153	28·4	1426	27·1	1024	40·4	2241	40·1
15	M	539	21·6	1753	20·5	246	27·3	1521	25·7	1113	38·2	2328	37·9
16	Tu	635	20·7	1845	19·6	341	25·9	1620	24·5	—	—	12 4	36·1
17	W	734	20·0	1944	19·0	442	24·9	1724	23·7	020	35·9	13 0	34·2
18	Th	838	19·5	2053	18·6	547	21·1	1830	23·5	119	34·5	14 1	33·4
19	F	945	19·3	22 5	18·7	655	23·9	1934	23·8	224	33·9	15 5	33·6
20	S	1044	19·6	23 7	19·2	758	24·2	2029	24·5	330	34·4	16 4	34·6
21	**S**	1136	19·9	2358	19·7	852	24·7	2114	25·2	427	35·5	1657	36·0
22	M	—	—	1222	20·4	937	25·2	2156	25·9	519	36·5	1745	37·2
23	Tu	044	20·3	13 3	20·8	1016	25·6	2234	26·6	6 5	37·3	1828	38·2
24	W	127	20·8	1343	21·2	1054	26·0	2310	27·0	646	37·9	19 7	38·9
25	Th	2 7	21·2	1420	21·4	1129	26·1	2344	27·3	724	38·2	1944	39·2
26	F	243	21·4	1453	21·6	—	—	12 4	26·1	759	38·3	2017	39·1
27	S	320	21·4	1527	21·4	019	27·3	1238	25·9	833	38·0	2050	38·7
28	**S**	355	21·3	16 0	21·1	054	27·0	1314	25·5	9 6	37·5	2124	37·9
29	M	431	20·9	1635	20·7	129	26·7	1351	25·1	941	36·8	2158	37·0
30	Tu	5 9	20·5	1712	20·2	2 7	26·3	1433	24·8	1019	36·0	2236	36·1

Day of Month	Day of Week	Hull Mn.	Ht.	Aft.	Ht.	Greenock Mn.	Ht.	Aft.	Ht.	Leith† Mn.	Ht.	Aft.	Ht.	Dun Laoghaire Mn.	Ht.	Aft.	Ht.
		June 1964				June 1964				June 1964				June 1964			
		h.m.	ft.	h.m.	ft.	h.m.	ft.	h.m.	ft.	h.m.	ft.	h.m.	ft.	h.m.	ft.	h.m.	ft.
1	M	926	19·3	22 8	17·8	325	10·1	16 2	9·2	557	14·8	1838	14·3	252	10·8	1533	9·7
2	Tu	10 7	18·7	2258	17·3	4 7	9·9	1648	9·1	648	14·5	1933	14·0	341	10·6	1629	9·6
3	W	11 0	18·2	—	—	453	9·6	1739	9·0	745	14·2	2034	13·9	437	10·5	1735	9·7
4	Th	0 1	17·1	12 7	18·1	548	9·4	1839	8·8	848	14·4	2139	14·3	541	10·5	1843	10·1
5	F	114	17·4	1321	18·5	7 4	9·3	1958	9·0	951	14·7	2240	14·8	648	10·9	1943	10·6
6	S	226	18·3	1433	19·5	830	9·6	21 6	9·4	1052	15·4	2335	15·7	748	11·3	2035	11·3
7	**S**	326	19·6	1536	20·7	933	10·1	2159	9·9	1149	16·2	—	—	842	11·8	2122	11·8
8	M	421	20·7	1634	21·8	1026	10·5	2248	10·3	028	16·5	1242	17·0	932	12·3	22 5	12·3
9	Tu	510	21·6	1727	22·5	1119	10·8	2337	10·8	116	17·1	1334	17·8	1021	12·5	2248	12·6
10	W	558	22·1	1819	22·7	—	—	1213	10·8	2 3	17·7	1425	18·4	11 9	12·6	2331	12·8
11	Th	646	22·3	1911	22·6	024	11·2	13 5	10·8	251	17·9	1517	18·6	1157	12·5	—	—
12	F	732	22·2	20 2	22·1	111	11·6	1358	10·7	340	18·0	16 7	18·4	020	12·9	1250	12·4
13	S	817	21·7	2052	21·4	158	11·9	1451	10·4	431	17·7	17 0	17·9	110	12·8	1346	12·0
14	**S**	9 4	21·1	2143	20·4	244	12·0	1541	10·1	524	17·1	1754	17·0	2 5	12·5	1444	11·5
15	M	952	20·2	2237	19·3	329	11·6	1633	9·6	619	16·3	1852	16·2	3 2	12·2	1545	10·9
16	Tu	1044	19·2	2334	18·3	416	11·1	1726	9·0	718	15·6	1952	15·5	4 4	11·7	1651	10·5
17	W	1141	18·4	—	—	5 6	10·3	1830	8·5	819	15·1	2055	15·0	512	11·3	18 4	10·2
18	Th	037	17·6	1249	17·9	6 5	9·5	1951	8·4	924	14·9	22 0	14·9	624	11·0	1912	10·2
19	F	144	17·4	1358	17·9	720	9·0	2059	8·6	1027	14·9	2259	15·1	729	10·9	2012	10·4
20	S	245	17·8	15 0	18·3	834	8·9	2149	8·9	1126	15·2	2352	15·3	828	10·9	21 1	10·6
21	**S**	339	18·4	1554	19·0	932	9·1	2233	9·3	—	—	1217	15·4	918	10·9	2142	10·9
22	M	425	19·2	1644	19·6	1021	9·4	2313	9·6	038	15·5	13 4	15·6	10 1	11·0	2218	11·1
23	Tu	5 7	20·0	1729	20·1	11 6	9·6	2350	9·9	120	15·7	1347	15·8	1040	10·9	2250	11·3
24	W	547	20·6	1811	20·3	1148	9·6	—	—	159	16·0	1426	16·0	1116	10·9	2323	11·5
25	Th	623	20·9	1850	20·3	025	10·0	1229	9·4	234	16·2	15 4	16·2	1151	10·8	2356	11·5
26	F	657	21·0	1928	20·1	058	10·1	13 9	9·2	3 9	16·3	1540	16·3	—	—	1224	10·6
27	S	730	20·9	20 2	19·8	128	10·1	1346	9·1	343	16·3	1615	16·1	031	11·6	13 1	10·6
28	**S**	759	20·8	2036	19·5	159	10·1	1425	9·0	418	16·2	1652	15·9	1 7	11·6	1341	10·5
29	M	831	20·6	2111	19·2	231	10·2	15 4	9·1	457	15·9	1733	15·5	147	11·5	1421	10·4
30	Tu	9 5	20·4	2149	18·9	3 8	10·2	1544	9·2	538	15·6	1817	15·0	228	11·5	15 6	10·3

† See note, p. 173.

JULY

Time of High Water at the undermentioned Places—

Day of Month	Day of Week	London Bridge July 1964 Mn.	Ht.	Aft.	Ht.	Liverpool July 1964 Mn.	Ht.	Aft.	Ht.	Bristol (Avonmouth) July 1964 Mn.	Ht.	Aft.	Ht.	Hull July 1964 Mn.	Ht.	Aft.	Ht.
		h.m.	ft.	h.m.	ft.	h.m.	ft.	h.m.	ft.	h.m.	ft.	h.m.	ft.	h.m.	ft.	h.m.	ft.
1	W	549	20·0	1749	19·9	249	25·8	1519	24·2	11 0	35·1	2319	35·3	946	20·1	2234	18·5
2	Th	630	19·6	1832	19·6	339	25·4	1612	23·8	1149	34·4	—	—	1034	19·8	2326	18·2
3	F	719	19·4	1922	19·5	434	24·9	1713	23·8	011	34·5	1247	33·9	1131	19·5	—	—
4	S	819	19·3	2025	19·5	537	24·9	1818	24·2	116	34·2	1354	34·3	029	18·0	1239	19·4
5	**S**	929	19·6	2142	19·9	645	25·4	1927	25·0	230	35·0	15 7	35·7	139	18·3	1352	19·6
6	M	1042	20·3	23 0	20·6	753	26·1	2031	26·3	344	36·7	1617	37·7	248	18·9	15 5	20·2
7	Tu	1149	21·0	—	—	857	27·2	2130	27·5	452	38·7	1721	39·6	350	19·8	1611	20·9
8	W	0 9	21·3	1248	21·7	956	28·1	2223	28·6	553	40·5	1819	41·2	446	20·7	1713	21·5
9	Th	112	22·0	1342	22·3	1050	28·8	2314	29·4	651	41·8	1913	42·3	540	21·4	1811	21·9
10	F	2 8	22·5	1432	22·5	1141	29·2	—	—	744	42·5	20 5	43·0	630	21·9	19 4	22·1
11	S	3 0	22·8	1518	22·4	0 3	29·6	1232	29·0	834	42·8	2054	43·1	720	22·1	1955	21·9
12	**S**	350	22·7	16 3	22·2	051	29·5	1321	28·5	923	42·4	2141	42·5	8 5	21·9	2041	21·4
13	M	438	22·3	1648	21·7	138	29·1	14 9	27·6	1010	41·4	2225	41·4	848	21·5	2126	20·6
14	Tu	525	21·7	1733	21·0	226	28·1	1457	26·4	1054	39·7	23 7	39·6	930	20·9	2210	19·6
15	W	611	21·0	1817	20·3	313	26·9	1546	25·2	1136	37·5	2347	37·3	1013	20·0	2255	18·6
16	Th	657	20·2	19 3	19·4	4 2	25·4	1637	24·0	—	—	1217	35·2	1059	19·1	2344	17·7
17	F	746	19·4	1954	18·9	457	24·2	1735	23·2	032	35·1	13 5	33·3	1151	18·3	—	—
18	S	842	18·8	21 0	18·5	559	23·2	1840	22·8	124	33·1	14 2	32·2	042	17·1	1257	17·6
19	**S**	946	18·6	2214	18·5	7 8	22·9	1943	23·2	226	32·3	15 6	32·3	148	17·0	1412	17·4
20	M	1050	18·9	2319	19·1	814	23·1	2041	23·9	334	32·5	1610	33·2	254	17·5	1521	17·8
21	Tu	1147	19·5	—	—	9 9	23·8	2131	24·9	438	33·6	17 9	35·0	353	18·3	1621	18·4
22	W	016	19·8	1238	20·2	956	24·6	2213	25·9	534	35·1	18 2	36·7	442	19·2	1712	19·1
23	Th	1 5	20·4	1322	20·7	1036	25·3	2251	26·7	623	36·5	1847	38·0	524	20·0	1755	19·6
24	F	150	20·9	14 0	21·0	1112	25·8	2326	27·3	7 6	37·7	1926	39·1	6 2	20·5	1835	19·9
25	S	228	21·2	1435	21·3	1148	26·3	—	—	744	38·5	20 3	39·7	636	20·9	1911	20·1
26	**S**	3 4	21·3	15 9	21·4	0 1	27·7	1222	26·6	820	39·0	2038	39·9	7 8	21·1	1945	20·3
27	M	339	21·4	1543	21·4	035	27·9	1258	26·7	856	39·3	2114	39·9	739	21·3	2019	20·3
28	Tu	414	21·4	1618	21·4	110	28·0	1333	26·6	933	39·1	2149	39·4	813	21·4	2052	20·2
29	W	448	21·3	1653	21·3	147	27·8	1410	26·2	10 8	38·6	2224	38·7	848	21·4	2129	19·9
30	Th	525	21·0	1727	21·1	225	27·4	1451	25·7	1045	37·6	23 1	37·4	926	21·3	2210	19·4
31	F	6 3	20·6	18 3	20·8	3 8	26·7	1539	25·0	1124	36·3	2343	35·9	1011	20·9	2256	18·8

Day of Month	Day of Week	Greenock July 1964 Mn.	Ht.	Aft.	Ht.	Leith† July 1964 Mn.	Ht.	Aft.	Ht.	Dun Laoghaire July 1964 Mn.	Ht.	Aft.	Ht.
		h.m.	ft.	h.m.	ft.	h.m.	ft.	h.m.	ft.	h.m.	ft.	h.m.	ft.
1	W	347	10·2	1626	9·3	625	15·3	19 6	14·8	313	11·4	1556	10·2
2	Th	431	10·1	1712	9·4	715	15·2	20 0	14·7	4 3	11·3	1655	10·2
3	F	521	9·9	18 4	9·3	8 9	15·1	2058	14·6	5 1	11·1	1759	10·3
4	S	625	9·7	19 7	9·3	9 8	15·2	2159	14·9	6 7	11·1	19 5	10·6
5	**S**	743	9·7	2019	9·4	1011	15·5	23 1	15·4	714	11·3	20 3	11·1
6	M	859	9·9	2125	9·8	1118	16·0	—	—	817	11·5	2056	11·6
7	Tu	10 2	10·1	2222	10·3	0 0	16·0	1221	16·5	914	11·9	2145	12·1
8	W	11 2	10·2	2316	10·7	057	16·6	1322	17·2	10 7	12·1	2231	12·5
9	Th	1159	10·2	—	—	150	17·3	1417	17·9	1058	12·2	2319	12·8
10	F	0 7	11·1	1258	10·1	241	17·7	15 9	18·2	1148	12·3	—	—
11	S	059	11·5	1353	10·1	329	18·0	1559	18·2	0 8	13·0	1240	12·1
12	**S**	148	11·8	1445	10·0	418	17·9	1649	17·9	057	13·0	1332	11·9
13	M	233	11·9	1531	9·8	5 7	17·4	1738	17·2	149	12·9	1424	11·5
14	Tu	317	11·8	1616	9·6	558	16·9	1829	16·3	242	12·6	1517	11·1
15	W	359	11·3	1659	9·3	650	16·1	1922	15·5	337	12·1	1616	10·6
16	Th	443	10·6	1746	8·9	742	15·5	2016	14·8	437	11·5	1719	10·2
17	F	532	9·8	1841	8·5	838	14·9	2112	14·4	542	10·9	1826	10·0
18	S	631	9·2	1951	8·4	937	14·5	2213	14·3	650	10·5	1929	10·0
19	**S**	740	8·9	21 2	8·6	1041	14·4	2312	14·4	753	10·3	2024	10·2
20	M	847	8·8	2159	9·0	1143	14·5	—	—	849	10·3	2111	10·5
21	Tu	949	9·0	2246	9·3	0 7	14·7	1239	14·7	937	10·5	2151	10·9
22	W	1042	9·1	2327	9·7	056	15·1	1328	15·1	1019	10·6	2227	11·3
23	Th	1129	9·1	—	—	139	15·4	1412	15·6	1055	10·8	23 2	11·6
24	F	0 3	9·8	1213	9·0	218	16·0	1450	16·1	1129	10·9	2335	11·8
25	S	038	9·9	1255	8·9	254	16·4	1527	16·4	—	—	12 4	11·0
26	**S**	113	10·0	1335	8·8	327	16·7	16 0	16·6	0 9	12·0	1240	11·1
27	M	145	10·2	1412	8·9	4 0	16·8	1635	16·6	045	12·2	1316	11·1
28	Tu	217	10·3	1448	9·1	436	16·7	1712	16·3	123	12·2	1355	11·1
29	W	253	10·5	1527	9·4	517	16·5	1754	15·9	2 2	12·3	1438	11·0
30	Th	330	10·6	16 5	9·8	6 1	16·3	1839	15·5	246	12·2	1523	10·9
31	F	413	10·7	1646	9·9	646	16·0	1924	15·1	333	12·0	1617	10·8

† *See note*, p. 173.

AUGUST

Time of High Water at the undermentioned Places—

London Bridge — August 1964

Day of Month	Day of Week	Mn. h.m.	Ht. ft.	Aft. h.m.	Ht. ft.
1	S	646	20·0	1847	20·4
2	**S**	739	19·5	1949	19·9
3	M	852	19·3	2111	19·7
4	Tu	1015	19·5	2242	20·2
5	W	1131	20·3	—	—
6	Th	0 0	21·1	1236	21·2
7	F	1 6	21·8	1332	21·8
8	S	2 3	22·4	1419	22·2
9	**S**	252	22·6	15 3	22·3
10	M	336	22·6	1544	22·3
11	Tu	418	22·5	1625	22·1
12	W	458	22·0	17 4	21·6
13	Th	536	21·3	1741	20·9
14	F	612	20·5	1816	20·1
15	S	648	19·5	1857	19·3
16	**S**	734	18·7	1951	18·5
17	M	834	18·0	2110	18·1
18	Tu	955	18·0	2237	18·4
19	W	11 9	18·6	2346	19·3
20	Th	—	—	1210	19·4
21	F	042	20·2	1258	20·2
22	S	128	20·9	1340	20·8
23	**S**	2 5	21·3	1410	21·3
24	M	240	21·6	1444	21·7
25	Tu	313	21·9	1518	22·1
26	W	348	22·1	1552	22·3
27	Th	424	22·1	1627	22·3
28	F	5 0	21·8	17 1	22·0
29	S	535	21·2	1738	21·5
30	**S**	616	20·4	1823	20·8
31	M	7 9	19·5	1927	19·9

Liverpool — August 1964

Day of Month	Day of Week	Mn. h.m.	Ht. ft.	Aft. h.m.	Ht. ft.
1	S	4 0	25·9	1635	24·4
2	**S**	5 2	25·1	1742	24·1
3	M	615	24·7	1859	24·3
4	Tu	735	25·0	2014	25·3
5	W	848	26·0	2118	26·8
6	Th	950	27·3	2214	28·2
7	F	1043	28·2	23 3	29·1
8	S	1131	28·9	2350	29·8
9	**S**	—	—	1217	29·1
10	M	035	29·9	13 2	28·8
11	Tu	117	29·4	1344	28·1
12	W	158	28·5	1425	27·1
13	Th	237	27·2	15 4	25·7
14	F	319	25·6	1547	24·3
15	S	4 5	23·9	1638	23·0
16	**S**	5 2	22·5	1740	22·0
17	M	612	21·5	1853	21·9
18	Tu	735	21·6	20 6	22·6
19	W	843	22·4	21 5	24·0
20	Th	935	23·7	2151	25·3
21	F	1016	25·1	2229	26·6
22	S	1052	26·1	23 4	27·7
23	**S**	1126	27·1	2338	28·5
24	M	—	—	12 0	27·7
25	Tu	013	29·0	1235	28·1
26	W	048	29·3	1310	28·0
27	Th	124	29·2	1346	27·7
28	F	2 0	28·6	1425	27·0
29	S	242	27·6	15 9	25·8
30	**S**	333	26·2	16 5	24·7
31	M	438	24·8	1717	23·8

Bristol (*Avonmouth*) — August 1964

Day of Month	Day of Week	Mn. h.m.	Ht. ft.	Aft. h.m.	Ht. ft.
1	S	—	—	1211	34·9
2	**S**	038	34·6	1315	34·0
3	M	153	34·0	1434	34·3
4	Tu	318	35·0	1556	36·0
5	W	437	37·1	17 9	38·3
6	Th	545	39·4	1811	40·5
7	F	644	41·2	19 5	42·0
8	S	734	42·3	1952	43·0
9	**S**	820	42·8	2038	43·4
10	M	9 4	42·8	2121	43·2
11	Tu	946	42·1	2159	42·3
12	W	1024	40·6	2235	40·6
13	Th	1058	38·6	23 7	38·1
14	F	1130	36·0	2340	35·2
15	S	—	—	12 5	33·4
16	**S**	020	32·6	1253	31·2
17	M	118	30·4	14 0	30·1
18	Tu	234	29·9	1521	30·8
19	W	357	31·1	1635	32·9
20	Th	5 5	33·4	1736	35·4
21	F	6 0	35·9	1825	37·7
22	S	645	37·9	19 6	39·5
23	**S**	724	39·5	1944	40·8
24	M	8 1	40·8	2019	41·7
25	Tu	838	41·5	2056	42·2
26	W	914	41·7	2132	42·0
27	Th	949	41·1	22 6	41·0
28	F	1024	39·8	2239	39·1
29	S	11 0	37·7	2319	36·6
30	**S**	1143	35·3	—	—
31	M	010	34·3	1243	33·2

Hull — August 1964

Day of Month	Day of Week	Mn. h.m.	Ht. ft.	Aft. h.m.	Ht. ft.
1	S	11 3	20·3	2352	18·2
2	**S**	—	—	12 5	19·6
3	M	1 0	17·9	1322	19·1
4	Tu	216	18·1	1447	19·1
5	W	329	18·9	16 4	19·8
6	Th	434	19·9	1710	20·8
7	F	531	21·0	18 8	21·6
8	S	622	21·8	1857	22·0
9	**S**	7 7	22·2	1942	21·9
10	M	749	22·2	2023	21·5
11	Tu	827	21·9	21 1	20·7
12	W	9 4	21·3	2136	19·8
13	Th	939	20·5	2213	18·9
14	F	1017	19·6	2252	18·0
15	S	11 3	18·5	2343	17·2
16	**S**	—	—	12 2	17·3
17	M	049	16·6	1325	16·5
18	Tu	210	16·7	1455	16·6
19	W	323	17·4	16 4	17·4
20	Th	418	18·5	1656	18·4
21	F	5 2	19·5	1738	19·3
22	S	540	20·3	1815	20·1
23	**S**	614	21·0	1849	20·7
24	M	646	21·6	1922	21·2
25	Tu	720	22·1	1956	21·3
26	W	755	22·3	2031	21·2
27	Th	830	22·3	21 8	20·8
28	F	9 8	22·0	2146	20·1
29	S	952	21·3	2230	19·2
30	**S**	1041	20·3	2322	18·2
31	M	1143	19·0	—	—

Greenock — August 1964

Day of Month	Day of Week	Mn. h.m.	Ht. ft.	Aft. h.m.	Ht. ft.
1	S	5 0	10·4	1732	9·8
2	**S**	558	10·0	1829	9·5
3	M	710	9·7	1941	9·4
4	Tu	834	9·5	21 0	9·6
5	W	953	9·6	22 7	10·0
6	Th	1059	9·6	23 5	10·5
7	F	1158	9·7	—	—
8	S	0 0	10·8	1254	9·7
9	**S**	050	11·3	1345	9·8
10	M	137	11·6	1431	9·8
11	Tu	220	11·8	1513	9·8
12	W	3 0	11·7	1549	9·8
13	Th	336	11·4	1624	9·6
14	F	415	10·8	17 1	9·3
15	S	457	10·0	1744	9·0
16	**S**	547	9·4	1838	8·5
17	M	649	8·8	1956	8·4
18	Tu	8 3	8·6	2119	8·6
19	W	919	8·6	2220	9·0
20	Th	1022	8·8	23 5	9·4
21	F	1121	8·8	2344	9·7
22	S	1156	8·8	—	—
23	**S**	019	9·9	1236	8·8
24	M	053	10·1	1313	8·9
25	Tu	127	10·3	1351	9·1
26	W	2 2	10·6	1428	9·5
27	Th	236	10·9	15 2	9·9
28	F	315	11·1	1541	10·3
29	S	355	11·0	1621	10·3
30	**S**	443	10·7	17 6	10·1
31	M	538	10·0	18 0	9·6

Leith† — August 1964

Day of Month	Day of Week	Mn. h.m.	Ht. ft.	Aft. h.m.	Ht. ft.
1	S	737	15·8	2023	14·9
2	**S**	834	15·5	2125	14·8
3	M	944	15·3	2236	15·0
4	Tu	11 1	15·5	2347	15·5
5	W	—	—	1214	16·1
6	Th	049	16·2	1318	16·8
7	F	144	16·9	1413	17·5
8	S	233	17·7	15 3	18·0
9	**S**	317	18·0	1548	18·1
10	M	4 2	18·1	1631	17·9
11	Tu	444	17·8	1713	17·2
12	W	530	17·2	1758	16·3
13	Th	617	16·4	1845	15·4
14	F	7 3	15·6	1933	14·7
15	S	751	14·7	2020	14·0
16	**S**	843	14·1	2118	13·8
17	M	951	13·6	2225	13·7
18	Tu	11 7	13·7	2334	13·9
19	W	—	—	1213	14·0
20	Th	031	14·5	13 6	14·7
21	F	119	15·2	1352	15·4
22	S	2 0	15·9	1431	16·1
23	**S**	233	16·6	15 6	16·8
24	M	3 6	17·1	1538	17·1
25	Tu	338	17·5	1611	17·3
26	W	414	17·5	1649	17·0
27	Th	454	17·5	1730	16·7
28	F	536	17·2	1814	16·1
29	S	622	16·7	19 2	15·5
30	**S**	712	16·0	1957	14·9
31	M	814	15·3	21 3	14·6

Dun Laoghaire — August 1964

Day of Month	Day of Week	Mn. h.m.	Ht. ft.	Aft. h.m.	Ht. ft.
1	S	4 30	11·6	1720	10·6
2	**S**	536	11·3	1829	10·6
3	M	650	11·1	1937	10·9
4	Tu	8 1	11·3	2038	11·4
5	W	9 5	11·5	2133	11·9
6	Th	10 2	11·8	2223	12·4
7	F	1053	12·0	2310	12·9
8	S	1140	12·2	2356	13·2
9	**S**	—	—	1226	12·2
10	M	043	13·3	1311	12·1
11	Tu	130	13·2	1358	11·8
12	W	216	12·8	1445	11·4
13	Th	3 5	12·3	1534	10·9
14	F	357	11·5	1627	10·3
15	S	455	10·8	1731	9·9
16	**S**	6 3	10·1	1838	9·8
17	M	716	9·8	1942	9·9
18	Tu	820	9·9	2037	10·3
19	W	913	10·2	2123	10·8
20	Th	955	10·6	22 2	11·4
21	F	1032	11·0	2237	11·9
22	S	11 7	11·4	2312	12·3
23	**S**	1141	11·7	2346	12·6
24	M	—	—	1214	11·9
25	Tu	020	12·8	1249	12·0
26	W	056	13·0	1328	12·0
27	Th	137	13·0	14 7	11·9
28	F	219	12·8	1453	11·7
29	S	3 7	12·4	1545	11·3
30	**S**	4 4	11·9	1648	10·9
31	M	513	11·3	18 2	10·8

† *See note*, p. 173.

SEPTEMBER

Time of High Water at the undermentioned Places—

Day of Month	Day of Week	London Bridge Mn.	Ht.	Aft.	Ht.	Liverpool Mn.	Ht.	Aft.	Ht.	Bristol (*Avonmouth*) Mn.	Ht.	Aft.	Ht.	Hull Mn.	Ht.	Aft.	Ht.
		September 1964				September 1964				September 1964				September 1964			
		h.m.	ft.	h.m.	ft.	h.m.	ft.	h.m.	ft.	h.m.	ft.	h.m.	ft.	h.m.	ft.	h.m.	ft.
1	Tu	824	18·7	2057	19·5	558	23·8	1841	23·7	129	32·7	1411	32·9	029	17·5	13 8	18·1
2	W	957	18·9	2235	19·9	728	24·0	20 6	24·7	3 7	33·4	1547	34·6	159	17·4	1448	18·3
3	Th	1120	19·7	2355	20·9	846	25·3	2113	26·3	435	36·1	17 5	37·7	323	18·3	16 8	19·5
4	F	—	—	1226	20·7	945	26·9	22 6	28·0	542	39·1	18 5	40·5	430	19·7	17 9	20·8
5	S	059	21·8	1318	21·6	1034	28·2	2251	29·2	634	41·3	1854	42·4	523	21·1	18 0	21·8
6	**S**	151	22·2	14 3	22·0	1116	29·0	2333	29·8	719	42·5	1937	43·3	6 9	22·0	1845	22·2
7	M	235	22·6	1442	22·3	1157	29·3	—	—	8 0	43·1	2016	43·7	652	22·4	1922	22·0
8	Tu	313	22·7	1519	22·5	013	29·9	1237	29·2	839	43·1	2054	43·5	728	22·4	1958	21·6
9	W	349	22·6	1556	22·4	051	29·5	1313	28·6	915	42·5	2128	42·5	8 2	22·1	2030	20·9
10	Th	422	22·3	1630	22·2	127	28·6	1349	27·6	947	41·2	2158	40·8	834	21·6	21 1	20·3
11	F	454	21·7	17 2	21·5	2 1	27·3	1423	26·2	1015	39·1	2225	38·3	9 7	20·8	2132	19·5
12	S	525	20·8	1734	20·6	236	25·7	15 0	24·8	1042	36·5	2251	35·3	943	19·8	22 8	18·7
13	**S**	556	19·8	1810	19·5	316	23·9	1544	23·3	1111	33·6	2325	32·3	1025	18·4	2252	17·7
14	M	635	18·7	19 0	18·5	4 6	22·1	1642	21·9	1152	31·0	—	—	1119	16·9	2351	16·7
15	Tu	730	17·8	2012	17·8	517	20·8	1758	21·2	015	29·7	1254	29·2	—	—	1240	15·7
16	W	849	17·3	2149	18·0	648	20·6	1925	21·7	134	28·3	1426	29·1	117	16·2	1430	15·6
17	Th	1023	17·7	2311	18·9	813	21·7	2034	23·2	313	29·3	16 0	31·3	247	16·6	1543	16·7
18	F	1136	18·5	—	—	9 8	23·4	2124	25·0	435	32·4	17 8	34·6	347	17·8	1632	18·1
19	S	011	20·0	1226	19·7	950	25·1	22 2	26·7	534	35·7	1759	37·8	432	19·0	1712	19·4
20	**S**	057	20·9	13 5	20·7	1025	26·8	2236	28·2	619	38·5	1840	40·1	510	20·3	1747	20·6
21	M	134	21·6	1338	21·5	1059	28·0	2311	29·4	658	40·7	1916	42·1	545	21·5	1822	21·6
22	Tu	2 8	22·1	1412	22·1	1133	28·9	2347	30·2	735	42·4	1954	43·4	620	22·4	1857	22·2
23	W	243	22·6	1448	22·7	—	—	1210	29·5	813	43·5	2032	44·0	657	22·9	1932	22·4
24	Th	319	22·8	1524	23·0	024	30·5	1246	29·5	851	43·8	2110	43·8	735	23·2	20 9	22·1
25	F	355	22·8	16 0	23·0	1 1	30·2	1323	28·9	928	43·1	2146	42·5	812	23·0	2045	21·5
26	S	433	22·4	1639	22·7	140	29·3	14 2	27·9	10 3	41·2	2222	40·1	852	22·3	2123	20·6
27	**S**	512	21·6	1720	21·9	223	27·8	1448	26·4	1040	38·6	23 1	37·0	936	21·3	22 6	19·5
28	M	554	20·6	1810	20·8	317	25·9	1545	24·8	1123	35·5	2354	33·9	1028	19·9	2258	18·3
29	Tu	649	19·4	1919	19·9	423	24·1	17 0	23·4	—	—	1226	32·9	1136	18·4	—	—
30	W	8 6	18·5	2053	19·4	551	23·0	1832	23·3	118	31·8	14 0	32·0	012	17·3	1314	17·5

Day of Month	Day of Week	Greenock Mn.	Ht.	Aft.	Ht.	Leith† Mn.	Ht.	Aft.	Ht.	Dun Laoghaire Mn.	Ht.	Aft.	Ht.
		September 1964				September 1964				September 1964			
		h.m.	ft.	h.m.	ft.	h.m.	ft.	h.m.	ft.	h.m.	ft.	h.m.	ft.
1	Tu	650	9·3	19 8	9·4	932	15·0	2224	14·7	635	10·9	1918	10·9
2	W	830	9·0	2044	9·3	1059	15·2	2341	15·1	755	11·0	2026	11·4
3	Th	10 1	9·1	22 4	9·7	—	—	1213	15·9	9 3	11·4	2125	12·0
4	F	11 3	9·4	23 2	10·3	044	15·9	1315	16·8	959	11·8	2216	12·6
5	S	1155	9·5	2351	10·8	137	16·9	14 6	17·5	1047	12·2	23 0	13·1
6	**S**	—	—	1242	9·6	221	17·7	1450	18·0	1128	12·3	2342	13·4
7	M	037	11·2	1327	9·8	3 2	18·1	1530	18·1	—	—	12 8	12·4
8	Tu	123	11·5	14 8	9·9	340	18·2	16 8	17·8	024	13·5	1247	12·3
9	W	2 2	11·6	1444	10·0	420	17·9	1648	17·2	1 5	13·3	1327	12·1
10	Th	237	11·6	1516	10·1	5 1	17·3	1727	16·4	148	12·8	14 7	11·7
11	F	310	11·3	1547	10·0	542	16·4	18 6	15·5	231	12·2	1450	11·2
12	S	345	10·8	1619	9·8	624	15·5	1847	14·7	315	11·4	1536	10·6
13	**S**	425	10·2	1657	9·4	7 6	14·6	1930	14·0	4 7	10·5	1632	10·1
14	M	512	9·5	1746	8·9	757	13·8	2025	13·4	510	9·8	1739	9·8
15	Tu	6 7	8·8	1844	8·5	9 5	13·3	2136	13·3	631	9·5	1853	9·8
16	W	716	8·4	2017	8·4	1029	13·2	2256	13·6	745	9·6	1958	10·3
17	Th	849	8·4	2146	8·8	1143	13·7	—	—	843	10·1	2049	10·9
18	F	10 6	8·7	2237	9·2	0 1	14·2	1238	14·5	927	10·8	2130	11·6
19	S	1052	9·0	2316	9·6	051	15·1	1324	15·5	10 6	11·4	22 8	12·2
20	**S**	1129	9·1	2352	10·1	132	16·0	14 3	16·5	1040	12·0	2243	12·8
21	M	—	—	12 8	9·2	2 6	16·9	1438	17·1	1114	12·4	2317	13·2
22	Tu	027	10·4	1245	9·4	239	17·6	1511	17·7	1146	12·6	2352	13·4
23	W	1 5	10·8	1324	9·7	312	18·1	1545	18·0	—	—	1221	12·8
24	Th	141	11·1	14 1	10·2	349	18·4	1624	17·7	030	13·6	1258	12·8
25	F	218	11·3	1436	10·7	430	18·3	17 5	17·4	111	13·5	1340	12·6
26	S	259	11·4	1515	10·9	513	17·8	1751	16·6	156	13·1	1425	12·3
27	**S**	341	11·2	1557	11·0	6 1	17·0	1842	15·8	247	12·6	1518	11·8
28	M	431	10·7	1643	10·6	657	16·1	1939	15·0	347	11·9	1622	11·3
29	Tu	527	9·9	1737	10·0	8 6	15·2	2051	14·5	5 1	11·2	1741	11·0
30	W	640	9·0	1845	9·4	930	14·9	2215	14·6	629	10·8	19 3	11·1

† *See note*, p. 173.

OCTOBER

Time of High Water at the undermentioned Places—

Day of Month	Day of Week	London Bridge Mn.	Ht.	Aft.	Ht.	Liverpool Mn.	Ht.	Aft.	Ht.	Bristol (Avonmouth) Mn.	Ht.	Aft.	Ht.
		October 1964				October 1964				October 1964			
		h.m.	ft.	h.m.	ft.	h.m.	ft.	h.m.	ft.	h.m.	ft.	h.m.	ft.
1	Th	946	18·5	2231	20·0	728	23·3	20 1	24·4	3 7	32·6	1545	34·3
2	F	11 9	19·5	2346	21·0	843	25·2	21 6	26·3	431	35·9	1659	37·8
3	S	—	—	1212	20·5	937	26·9	2154	28·0	531	39·2	1753	40·9
4	**S**	045	21·8	13 1	21·3	1019	28·2	2235	29·1	619	41·6	1837	42·7
5	M	130	22·3	1341	21·9	1058	29·0	2312	29·7	7 0	42·7	1916	43·6
6	Tu	210	22·6	1417	22·3	1135	29·3	2348	29·6	735	43·2	1951	43·6
7	W	244	22·6	1452	22·5	—	—	12 8	29·1	8 9	43·0	2024	43·2
8	Th	317	22·6	1525	22·6	023	29·2	1242	28·7	841	42·4	2054	42·2
9	F	347	22·5	1557	22·4	056	28·3	1313	27·8	910	41·2	2120	40·4
10	S	416	21·9	1626	21·8	125	27·0	1345	26·7	932	39·3	2144	38·1
11	**S**	443	21·2	1657	20·9	157	25·5	1418	25·3	957	36·9	22 8	35·4
12	M	514	20·1	1734	19·8	234	23·8	1459	23·8	1025	34·3	2240	32·7
13	Tu	552	18·9	1822	18·7	321	22·1	1553	22·3	112	31·7	2326	30·0
14	W	642	18·0	1928	17·9	428	20·7	17 6	21·3	1158	29·6	—	—
15	Th	751	17·2	2054	17·8	554	20·1	1830	21·4	038	28·2	1328	28·7
16	F	919	17·3	2223	18·5	725	21·1	1948	22·7	223	28·5	1515	30·3
17	S	1044	18·1	2328	19·6	830	23·0	2044	24·7	356	31·6	1631	33·9
18	**S**	1142	19·3	—	—	915	25·0	2124	26·6	459	35·4	1724	37·5
19	M	016	20·8	1225	20·5	952	26·9	22 2	28·3	546	38·8	18 7	40·4
20	Tu	056	21·6	13 1	21·5	1027	28·4	2240	29·7	628	41·4	1848	42·6
21	W	133	22·3	1339	22·3	11 5	29·6	2319	30·6	7 7	43·3	1928	44·1
22	Th	211	22·9	1417	23·0	1143	30·2	2359	30·8	747	44·5	20 8	44·9
23	F	250	23·1	1457	23·3	—	—	1222	30·2	828	44·7	2049	44·5
24	S	331	23·1	1540	23·2	041	30·4	13 3	29·5	9 7	43·9	2129	42·9
25	**S**	412	22·5	1623	22·8	124	29·2	1347	28·4	947	41·9	22 9	40·4
26	M	455	21·6	1712	21·8	212	27·5	1436	26·7	1028	39·0	2256	37·2
27	Tu	541	20·4	18 9	20·7	3 9	25·5	1535	25·0	1115	36·0	2352	34·1
28	W	638	19·3	1920	19·7	420	23·6	1651	23·6	—	—	1220	33·4
29	Th	754	18·4	2049	19·5	545	22·8	1819	23·4	114	32·1	1352	32·5
30	F	927	18·4	2218	20·1	715	23·5	1943	24·7	252	32·9	1527	34·5
31	S	1047	19·2	2326	21·0	824	25·0	2046	26·1	411	35·7	1637	37·6

Day of Month	Day of Week	Hull Mn.	Ht.	Aft.	Ht.	Greenock Mn.	Ht.	Aft.	Ht.
		October 1964				October 1964			
		h.m.	ft.	h.m.	ft.	h.m.	ft.	h.m.	ft.
1	Th	155	17·2	1456	18·2	850	8·6	2037	9·1
2	F	319	18·4	16 7	19·7	10 9	9·1	22 0	9·6
3	S	419	20·1	1659	21·1	1059	9·4	2250	10·2
4	**S**	5 9	21·4	1742	22·0	1141	9·8	2336	10·7
5	M	551	22·3	1822	22·2	—	—	1221	9·9
6	Tu	629	22·7	1856	22·0	018	11·1	13 0	10·1
7	W	7 3	22·6	1928	21·7	059	11·3	1336	10·2
8	Th	735	22·3	1957	21·3	136	11·4	14 9	10·4
9	F	8 6	21·8	2026	20·8	2 9	11·3	1439	10·5
10	S	838	20·9	2056	20·2	242	11·1	1510	10·5
11	**S**	915	19·8	2130	19·4	315	10·7	1541	10·3
12	M	956	18·3	2210	18·3	353	10·2	1616	9·9
13	Tu	1043	16·8	2257	17·1	436	9·5	1658	9·5
14	W	1 52	15·5	—	—	527	9·0	1750	8·9
15	Th	0 6	16·2	1338	15·3	632	8·5	1859	8·6
16	F	142	16·2	1459	16·3	756	8·4	2057	8·7
17	S	258	17·2	1551	17·9	932	8·8	2153	9·3
18	**S**	349	18·7	1634	19·6	1017	9·2	2236	9·9
19	M	432	20·4	1711	21·1	1055	9·5	2317	10·5
20	Tu	513	21·8	1749	22·2	1133	9·9	2357	10·9
21	W	552	22·9	1827	22·8	—	—	1212	10·1
22	Th	633	23·5	19 5	22·9	038	11·2	1252	10·5
23	F	714	23·6	1943	22·6	118	11·5	1333	11·0
24	S	755	23·1	2023	21·9	2 0	11·5	1412	11·4
25	**S**	838	22·3	21 2	21·0	243	11·4	1452	11·7
26	M	927	21·0	2149	19·8	329	11·1	1536	11·6
27	Tu	1024	19·5	2245	18·6	423	10·5	1625	11·1
28	W	1138	18·1	—	—	522	9·6	1721	10·3
29	Th	0 2	17·6	1315	17·7	645	8·9	1826	9·5
30	F	141	17·7	1442	18·5	854	8·8	2020	9·3
31	S	258	18·8	1544	19·8	956	9·2	2135	9·6

Day of Month	Day of Week	Leith† Mn.	Ht.	Aft.	Ht.	Dun Laoghaire Mn.	Ht.	Aft.	Ht.
		October 1964				October 1964			
		h.m.	ft.	h.m.	ft.	h.m.	ft.	h.m.	ft.
1	Th	1058	15·3	2334	15·2	755	10·9	2017	11·5
2	F	—	—	12 7	16·1	9 1	11·5	2116	12·2
3	S	034	16·2	13 4	17·0	953	12·0	22 5	12·8
4	**S**	123	17·1	1349	17·6	1035	12·3	2247	13·3
5	M	2 4	17·7	1429	17·9	1113	12·5	2326	13·4
6	Tu	241	18·1	15 6	17·9	1147	12·6	—	—
7	W	316	18·1	1540	17·6	0 3	13·3	1221	12·5
8	Th	352	17·8	1616	17·1	041	13·1	1255	12·3
9	F	429	17·3	1651	16·5	118	12·6	1332	12·0
10	S	5 5	16·5	1726	15·8	157	11·9	1410	11·5
11	**S**	544	15·6	18 3	14·9	240	11·1	1452	11·0
12	M	624	14·6	1844	14·2	326	10·4	1540	10·5
13	Tu	717	13·7	1937	13·5	422	9·8	1639	10·1
14	W	823	13·1	2045	13·2	538	9·4	1753	10·0
15	Th	943	13·1	22 6	13·3	7 0	9·5	19 6	10·3
16	F	1059	13·6	2316	14·0	8 4	10·1	20 5	11·0
17	S	1159	14·6	—	—	852	10·9	2052	11·7
18	**S**	0 9	15·0	1247	15·6	931	11·6	2132	12·4
19	M	053	16·1	1327	16·6	10 8	12·3	2210	13·0
20	Tu	131	17·1	14 4	17·4	1042	12·8	2246	13·4
21	W	2 7	17·9	1441	18·0	1116	13·1	2324	13·6
22	Th	244	18·6	1517	18·3	1151	13·2	—	—
23	F	323	18·8	1557	18·2	0 3	13·7	1230	13·2
24	S	4 7	18·7	1643	17·8	048	13·5	1313	13·0
25	**S**	454	18·1	1730	17·0	137	13·0	14 2	12·7
26	M	547	17·1	1825	16·1	232	12·4	1459	12·2
27	Tu	649	16·2	1928	15·2	336	11·6	16 5	11·6
28	W	759	15·3	2041	14·7	453	10·9	1723	11·3
29	Th	922	15·1	22 1	14·8	622	10·7	1847	11·3
30	F	1041	15·5	2314	15·5	743	11·0	1959	11·8
31	S	1147	16·3	—	—	846	11·5	2057	12·3

† *See note, p. 173.*

NOVEMBER

Time of High Water at the undermentioned Places—

Day of Month	Day of Week	London Bridge Mn.	Ht.	Aft.	Ht.	Liverpool Mn.	Ht.	Aft.	Ht.	Bristol (Avonmouth) Mn.	Ht.	Aft.	Ht.	Hull Mn.	Ht.	Aft.	Ht.
		November 1964				November 1964				November 1964				November 1964			
		h.m.	ft.	h.m.	ft.	h.m.	ft.	h.m.	ft.	h.m.	ft.	h.m.	ft.	h.m.	ft.	h.m.	ft.
1	**S**	1147	20·3	—	—	916	26·6	2133	27·6	5 9	38·7	1730	40·3	356	20·2	1634	20·8
2	M	018	21·6	1234	21·1	957	27·8	2214	28·4	555	40·8	1812	42·0	443	21·3	1716	21·5
3	Tu	1 1	22·0	1314	21·6	1034	28·5	2249	28·7	634	41·9	1850	42·6	524	22·1	1752	21·8
4	W	139	22·2	1350	21·9	11 8	28·7	2324	28·6	710	42·3	1924	42·5	6 1	22·4	1826	21·8
5	Th	213	22·3	1424	22·1	1142	28·7	2356	28·3	743	42·2	1957	42·1	636	22·4	1857	21·7
6	F	245	22·3	1458	22·3	—	—	1214	28·4	813	41·8	2025	41·1	710	22·1	1926	21·5
7	S	315	22·3	1530	22·3	027	27·6	1245	27·8	841	40·8	2051	39·7	743	21·6	1957	21·2
8	**S**	344	22·0	16 1	21·7	058	26·6	1315	26·8	9 6	39·1	2116	37·7	819	20·8	2027	20·7
9	M	414	21·3	1634	20·9	131	25·3	1349	25·8	931	37·2	2143	35·5	855	19·7	2059	19·9
10	Tu	446	20·2	1713	20·0	2 8	24·0	1427	24·5	10 0	35·0	2216	33·2	933	18·4	2134	19·0
11	W	523	19·2	1759	19·0	251	22·6	1517	23·2	1036	32·8	23 0	31·2	1017	17·2	2218	18·0
12	Th	610	18·3	1855	18·3	351	21·3	1621	22·3	1128	30·9	—	—	1110	16·3	2314	17·1
13	F	7 7	17·6	20 5	18·0	5 4	20·7	1733	22·1	0 4	29·6	1242	29·9	—	—	1226	15·9
14	S	817	17·5	2124	18·3	624	21·3	1848	22·9	134	29·5	1421	30·7	029	16·8	1350	16·4
15	**S**	936	18·0	2233	19·2	735	22·8	1951	24·4	3 5	31·7	1542	33·6	152	17·4	1456	17·8
16	M	1045	19·0	2328	20·4	829	24·8	2042	26·3	413	35·2	1643	37·1	258	18·8	1547	19·5
17	Tu	1138	20·2	—	—	913	26·8	2126	28·0	5 7	38·6	1731	40·2	351	20·5	1634	21·0
18	W	015	21·4	1224	21·4	955	28·4	2211	29·3	555	41·0	1817	42·3	439	22·0	1716	22·2
19	Th	1 0	22·3	13 8	22·3	1037	29·6	2255	30·2	639	43·2	19 2	43·8	524	23·0	1758	22·8
20	F	143	22·8	1353	22·9	1120	30·2	2341	30·5	723	44·3	1947	44·7	6 9	23·6	1840	23·0
21	S	228	23·1	1439	23·2	—	—	12 5	30·4	8 7	44·6	2033	44·4	656	23·6	1921	22·8
22	**S**	312	23·1	1526	23·2	027	30·1	1249	29·8	852	44·1	2119	43·3	742	23·1	20 4	22·3
23	M	357	22·6	1617	22·7	115	29·0	1336	28·8	938	42·5	22 6	41·0	831	22·2	2048	21·4
24	Tu	442	21·8	17 9	21·9	2 7	27·5	1428	27·4	1025	40·1	2256	38·3	923	21·1	2137	20·4
25	W	532	20·7	18 7	21·0	3 4	25·8	1526	25·8	1114	37·5	2351	35·5	1022	19·8	2234	19·3
26	Th	627	19·6	1914	20·1	4 9	24·2	1634	24·6	—	—	1213	35·2	1130	18·6	2344	18·4
27	F	734	18·8	2030	19·8	525	23·4	1751	24·1	1 1	33·7	1328	33·9	—	—	1249	18·0
28	S	854	18·5	2148	19·9	642	23·5	19 9	24·5	220	33·3	1449	34·4	1 7	18·1	14 6	18·2
29	**S**	1013	19·0	2253	20·4	751	24·5	2014	25·4	332	34·9	1559	36·2	221	18·7	15 9	18·9
30	M	1115	19·8	2344	20·9	845	25·7	21 4	26·4	432	37·0	1654	38·3	320	19·6	1558	19·7

Day of Month	Day of Week	Greenock Mn.	Ht.	Aft.	Ht.	Leith† Mn.	Ht.	Aft.	Ht.	Dun Laoghaire Mn.	Ht.	Aft.	Ht.
		November 1964				November 1964				November 1964			
		h.m.	ft.	h.m.	ft.	h.m.	ft.	h.m.	ft.	h.m.	ft.	h.m.	ft.
1	**S**	1036	9·6	2227	10·2	011	16·3	1240	16·9	935	12·0	2147	12·8
2	M	1115	10·0	2310	10·6	058	17·1	1325	17·4	1017	12·3	2229	13·0
3	Tu	1153	10·2	2351	11·0	139	17·5	14 3	17·5	1052	12·5	23 7	13·0
4	W	—	—	1230	10·3	216	17·7	1439	17·4	1124	12·5	2342	12·8
5	Th	031	11·2	13 5	10·5	251	17·7	1512	17·3	1154	12·4	—	—
6	F	1 9	11·2	1336	10·7	326	17·5	1546	17·0	016	12·4	1226	12·3
7	S	142	11·0	14 5	10·9	4 1	17·0	1617	16·6	052	12·0	13 0	12·1
8	**S**	217	10·7	1434	10·8	435	16·4	1651	16·0	129	11·5	1337	11·7
9	M	249	10·3	15 7	10·6	514	15·6	1729	15·4	2 8	10·8	1417	11·3
10	Tu	327	10·0	1542	10·3	556	14·8	1811	14·6	253	10·3	15 2	10·9
11	W	411	9·6	1623	9·9	647	13·9	19 2	14·0	344	9·8	1555	10·6
12	Th	457	9·2	1714	9·5	746	13·4	20 4	13·7	447	9·5	1658	10·4
13	F	554	8·9	1814	9·1	856	13·5	2112	13·8	6 3	9·6	18 7	10·5
14	S	7 5	8·7	1937	9·2	10 8	13·8	2220	14·3	713	10·0	1914	11·0
15	**S**	834	9·0	2059	9·6	11 9	14·7	2318	15·1	8 9	10·8	20 8	11·6
16	M	928	9·5	2154	10·3	—	—	12 0	15·7	854	11·5	2055	12·3
17	Tu	1013	9·9	2240	10·9	0 9	16·1	1246	16·5	934	12·2	2138	12·8
18	W	1056	10·5	2325	11·2	053	17·0	1328	17·4	1012	12·8	2220	13·3
19	Th	1140	10·8	—	—	135	17·9	14 9	18·0	1049	13·1	23 0	13·4
20	F	011	11·5	1223	11·2	218	18·6	1452	18·3	1127	13·3	2343	13·4
21	S	057	11·5	13 5	11·7	3 2	18·8	1536	18·3	—	—	12 9	13·3
22	**S**	145	11·6	1351	12·0	350	18·8	1623	18·1	032	13·2	1255	13·2
23	M	234	11·3	1436	12·2	442	18·2	1715	17·4	124	12·8	1348	13·0
24	Tu	326	10·9	1523	12·1	538	17·3	1812	16·6	221	12·2	1445	12·6
25	W	418	10·4	1611	11·6	639	16·4	1912	15·8	324	11·5	1549	12·1
26	Th	514	9·7	17 5	10·9	745	15·7	2020	15·2	439	10·9	17 3	11·7
27	F	633	9·0	1810	10·1	857	15·3	2132	15·2	6 1	10·7	1821	11·6
28	S	815	8·9	1937	9·5	1010	15·6	2241	15·6	717	10·8	1932	11·8
29	**S**	921	9·2	21 0	9·7	1115	16·0	2341	16·2	820	11·2	2033	12·0
30	M	10 6	9·7	2153	10·1	—	—	12 9	16·4	911	11·6	2125	12·3

† *See note*, p. 173.

DECEMBER

Time of High Water at the undermentioned Places—

Day of Month	Day of Week	London Bridge December 1964				Liverpool December 1964				Bristol (Avonmouth) December 1964				Hull December 1964			
		Mn.	Ht.	Aft.	Ht.	Mn.	Ht.	Aft.	Ht.	Mn.	Ht.	Aft.	Ht.	Mn.	Ht.	Aft.	Ht.
		h.m.	ft.	h.m.	ft.	h.m.	ft.	h.m.	ft.	h.m.	ft.	h.m.	ft.	h.m.	ft.	h.m.	ft.
1	Tu	—	—	12 4	20·4	929	26·6	2147	26·9	520	38·7	1741	39·6	410	20·5	1642	20·4
2	W	029	21·2	1247	20·9	10 8	27·3	2226	27·3	6 4	39·8	1821	40·4	453	21·2	1720	20·9
3	Th	1 9	21·4	1325	21·3	1044	27·7	23 2	27·3	643	40·5	1859	40·7	534	21·6	1756	21·3
4	F	145	21·7	14 2	21·6	1119	28·0	2336	27·1	719	40·8	1933	40·2	623	21·8	1830	21·5
5	S	220	22·0	1438	21·8	1151	27·9	—	—	750	40·6	20 4	39·8	650	21·6	19 3	21·5
6	**S**	252	22·0	1511	21·8	0 8	26·7	1224	27·7	821	40·0	2034	39·0	728	21·1	1934	21·3
7	M	324	21·9	1544	21 6	041	26·1	1256	27·1	949	39·0	21 2	37·6	8 3	20·5	20 4	20·9
8	Tu	355	21·4	1620	21·1	113	25·4	1330	26·3	916	37·5	2131	35·9	838	19·7	2035	20·4
9	W	428	20·5	1658	20·3	149	24·5	14 7	25·5	948	35·9	22 5	34·4	913	18·9	21 9	19·7
10	Th	5 5	19·7	1739	19·5	230	23·5	1451	24·6	1024	34·5	2246	33·1	951	18·1	2147	19·0
11	F	545	19·0	1824	18·9	319	22·7	1542	23·9	11 8	33·3	2339	32·0	1035	17·5	2236	18·4
12	S	630	18·5	1919	18·5	417	22·1	1641	23·4	—	—	12 6	32·3	1133	17·1	2337	18·0
13	**S**	726	18·3	2022	18·6	524	22·0	1747	23·5	045	31·4	1321	32·0	—	—	1241	17·1
14	M	830	18·4	2133	19·0	633	22·8	1853	24·3	2 5	32·2	1443	33·4	050	18·2	1356	17·8
15	Tu	943	19·0	2239	19·9	738	24·2	1957	25·6	321	34·3	1554	35·9	2 3	19·0	1459	19·0
16	W	1051	20·0	2339	20·8	835	25·9	2054	27·1	425	37·2	1655	38·7	3 8	20·2	1554	20·3
17	Th	1151	21·2	—	—	926	27·5	2146	28·4	521	39·9	1749	41·1	4 7	21·4	1643	21·4
18	F	033	21·8	1247	22·0	1015	28·8	2237	29·4	614	42·0	1842	42·8	5 0	22·4	1731	22·1
19	S	123	22·4	1340	22·7	11 3	29·8	2328	29·7	7 4	43·2	1932	43·8	552	22·9	1819	22·5
20	**S**	213	22·8	1431	23·1	1151	30·2	—	—	753	44·0	2022	43·9	644	23·1	19 5	22·6
21	M	259	22·9	1521	23·0	017	29·6	1240	30·1	842	44·0	2111	43·4	736	22·8	1952	22·4
22	Tu	345	22·5	1612	22·8	1 7	29·1	1328	29·5	931	43·2	22 0	42·0	827	22·2	2038	21·8
23	W	432	21·9	17 5	22·2	159	27·9	1418	28·4	1018	41·8	2249	40·1	918	21·3	2126	21·0
24	Th	522	21·1	1758	21·4	252	26·6	1510	27·1	11 5	39·8	2338	37·7	1010	20·2	2217	20·0
25	F	612	20·3	1854	20·6	348	25·2	16 6	25·7	1155	37·5	—	—	11 4	19·0	2313	19·1
26	S	7 6	19·5	1955	19·8	449	24·1	1710	24·6	030	35·6	1250	35·5	—	—	12 6	18·0
27	**S**	810	18·9	21 1	19·4	555	23·4	1820	24·0	130	33·7	1353	34·2	810	18·4	1312	17·5
28	M	923	18·7	22 7	19·4	7 3	23·4	1929	24·0	235	33·4	15 2	34·1	128	18·1	1420	17·6
29	Tu	1032	19·0	23 4	19·7	8 5	24·1	2030	24·4	340	34·1	16 6	34·8	235	18·4	1518	18·2
30	W	1129	19·6	2355	20·1	857	24·9	2122	25·0	439	35·2	17 3	36·1	334	19·1	16 8	19·0
31	Th	—	—	1219	20·2	943	25·8	22 4	25·5	531	36·9	1753	37·4	426	19·8	1652	19·8

Day of Month	Day of Week	Greenock December 1964				Leith† December 1964				Dun Laoghaire December 1964			
		Mn.	Ht.	Aft.	Ht.	Mn.	Ht.	Aft.	Ht.	Mn.	Ht.	Aft.	Ht.
		h.m.	ft.	h.m.	ft.	h.m.	ft.	h.m.	ft.	h.m.	ft.	h.m.	ft.
1	Tu	1045	10·1	2239	10·5	029	16·6	1254	16·7	953	11·9	22 8	12·3
2	W	1121	10·4	2324	10·7	113	16·9	1336	16·8	1029	12·0	2247	12·2
3	Th	1159	10·6	—	—	152	17·0	1413	16·9	11 2	12·1	2323	12·0
4	F	0 5	10·8	1236	10·8	229	17·0	1448	16·9	1132	12·2	2357	11·8
5	S	042	10·8	1310	11·0	3 6	16·9	1521	16·8	—	—	12 4	12·1
6	**S**	121	10·6	1339	10·9	341	16·7	1554	16·6	031	11·4	1237	12·0
7	M	156	10·4	1410	10·9	416	16·3	1628	16·2	1 6	11·0	1313	11·8
8	Tu	231	10·0	1443	10·8	453	15·7	17 4	15·8	145	10·6	1352	11·6
9	W	3 9	9·8	1519	10·6	533	15·1	1746	15·2	226	10·3	1434	11·4
10	Th	350	9·7	1557	10·3	619	14·5	1832	14·7	310	10·0	1519	11·1
11	F	432	9·5	1643	10·2	712	14·1	1925	14·5	4 5	9·8	1612	11·0
12	S	519	9·4	1734	9·9	810	14·0	2023	14·5	5 7	9·8	1712	10·9
13	**S**	613	9·4	1838	9·8	913	14·2	2123	14·7	616	10·0	1819	11·0
14	M	725	9·4	20 0	10·0	1015	14·7	2225	15·2	720	10·5	1923	11·4
15	Tu	840	9·8	21 8	10·5	1113	15·4	2323	15·9	814	11·2	2019	11·9
16	W	932	10·3	22 5	11·0	—	—	12 8	16·1	9 1	11·8	2110	12·3
17	Th	1022	10·8	2259	11·3	017	16·6	1258	16·9	945	12·3	2157	12·7
18	F	1111	11·2	2351	11·4	110	17·5	1345	17·6	1027	12·8	2244	12·8
19	S	1158	11·6	—	—	2 0	18·1	1434	18·1	11 9	13·1	2331	12·9
20	**S**	043	11·3	1247	12·0	250	18·5	1521	18·3	1154	13·3	—	—
21	M	138	11·2	1336	12·3	341	18·6	1610	19·2	022	12·7	1243	13·3
22	Tu	231	11·0	1425	12·5	434	18·3	17 0	17·8	115	12·4	1336	13·1
23	W	322	10·8	1512	12·4	527	17·6	1754	17·1	210	12·0	1432	12·9
24	Th	412	10·4	16 0	12·0	622	16·8	1852	16·5	3 9	11·5	1531	12·5
25	F	5 3	9·9	1649	11·3	721	16·0	1951	15·8	414	10·9	1636	12·0
26	S	6 2	9·4	1746	10·5	824	15·4	2054	15·5	526	10·6	1748	11·6
27	**S**	712	9·0	1853	9·9	930	15·2	2159	15·3	639	10·4	1859	11·4
28	M	827	9·1	20 9	9·6	1035	15·2	23 1	15·4	744	10·6	20 4	11·3
29	Tu	926	9·4	2115	9·7	1133	15·5	2358	15·6	840	10·8	2059	11·4
30	W	1013	9·9	22 7	10·0	—	—	1225	15·7	927	11·1	2148	11·4
31	Th	1056	10·3	2257	10·3	044	15·9	1310	15·9	10 7	11·4	2229	11·3

† *See note*, p. 173.

Chronological Notes

TIME MEASURES

Kelvin (1883) estimated the age of the earth's crust at 20–400 million years. Study of radio-activity has since shown cooling to have been slower. Holmes and others gave 1,500–2,000 million years as the age of the oldest known rocks. Jeffreys suggests an age not exceeding 8,000 million years for the separate existence of the earth, which, probably with other related planets, separated from the sun after a star-collision. Very early rocks, almost without traces of fossils, are variously named in North America and Europe and account for a period down to about 500 million years ago.

PALÆOZOIC (Old Animal Life) PERIODS include:—

Cambrian, Ordovician and Silurian rocks, all named from Wales (Cambria, Ordovices, Silures, the two latter ancient Celtic peoples). These rocks account for about 200 million years and there then followed a major phase of mountain-building, called *Caledonian* because studied early in Scotland, characterized by N.E.–S.W. lines of hills and valleys in several areas.

Devonian, including the Old Red Sandstone.

Carboniferous, including Mountain Limestone, Millstone Grit and Coal Measures.

These rocks account for about 100 million years and then there followed a major phase of mountain-building called *Hercynian* because widespread in W. Germany and adjacent areas. In Britain there are E.–W. lines of hills and valleys, and some N.–S.

MESOZOIC (Middle Forms of Life) PERIODS include:—

Permian rocks, widespread in Perm district, U.S.S.R. *Triassic*, including New Red Sandstone. *Jurassic*, important in the Jura Mts. *Cretaceous*, including the Greensands and the Chalk of England. In the Mesozoic, modern large land groups of animals, reptiles, birds and mammals first appear, but almost no modern genera or species of animals are known.

CAINOZOIC or CENOZOIC (Recent forms of Life) PERIODS include:—

Eocene. A few existing genera or species. *Oligocene*. A minority of existing forms. *Miocene*. Approach to a balance of existing and extinct forms. *Pliocene*. A majority of existing forms. *Pleistocene*. A very large majority of existing forms. *Holocene*. Existing forms only, save for a few exterminated by man. In the last 50 million years, from the Miocene through the Pliocene, the Alpine-Himalayan and the circum-Pacific phases of mountain building reached their climax.

During the Pleistocene period icesheets repeatedly locked up masses of water as land ice, its weight depressed the land, but the locking up of water lowered sea-level by 100–200 metres. Milankovitch has worked out variations of radiation theoretically receivable from the sun and has reached conclusions not very markedly different as to dates from those of Penck who studied sediments, and both can fit into Deperet's scheme based on study of river terraces. Milankovitch gives 600,000 years for the Pleistocene.

Phases of the Pleistocene:—

(*a*) Early Glaciations (probably 2), Gunz glaciations of Penck's Alpine series. About 600 to 500 thousand years ago.

(*b*) An interglacial phase with high sea level, Milazzian terraces (of Deperet's series) around the Mediterranean. About 500,000 years ago.

(*c*) A second pair of Glaciations, the Mindel of Penck's series. About 500 to rather before 400 thousand years ago.

(*d*) A long interglacial phase with high sea level, but less high than during (*b*). Tyrrhenian terraces around the Mediterranean. From about 400 to about 200 thousand years ago.

(*e*) The penultimate series of glaciations (probably 3), the Riss of Penck's series. About 200 to 150 thousand years ago.

(*f*) An interglacial phase with fairly high sea level, less high than during (*d*). Monastirian terraces around the Mediterranean. From about 150 to about 120 thousand years ago.

(*g*) The ultimate series of glaciations (probably 3, preceded perhaps by a cool phase), the Wurm of Penck's series. From about 115 to rather more than 20 thousand years ago.

(*h*) The last glacial retreat merging into the Holocene period about 10,000 or 8,000 years ago.

MAN IN THE PLEISTOCENE

In the East African Miocene have been found by Hopwood and Leakey fragmentary remains of apes with possible human links in thigh bone characters.

In S. Africa at Taungs, Sterkfontein and Kroomdraai have been found remains of *Australopithecus*, *Plesianthropus* and *Paranthropus*, possibly linked with early man in limb characters and some features of skull and teeth though the brains are small and rather ape-like. The cave deposits in which they occur are supposed to be late Pliocene or early Pleistocene. The late Dr. Broom inferred that *Australopithecus prometheus* made use of fire, *i.e.*, was, at any rate, near-human.

Java and Peking finds began with Dubois' discovery (1892) of an imperfect skull cap, some teeth and a possibly related femur indicating the erect posture. Later finds by von Koenigswald and by Weidenreich (1937–41) have emphasized the human relationship of the Java specimens, and also give evidence of gigantism (the name *Meganthropus* has been used). The specimens are usually given a Middle Pleistocene age. Oppenoorth (1932) discovered robust skulls and human Pleistocene bones on a terrace of the Solo river, Java. Twelve specimens from Chou Kou Tien near Peking studied by Black and Weidenreich and called *Sinanthropus* are broadly like the Java finds; the name *Pithecanthropus* had better be used for all.

A jaw from Mauer, Heidelberg, found 1902, and dated to the mid Pleistocene is very large but human in form. A skull cap from Neandertal near Düsseldorf, Germany, has been under discussion for 100 years. It and later found congeners belong to the onset of the 4th series of Glaciations (Penck's Wurm). The best preserved of these skulls is that of La Chapelle aux Saints (France) with very strong brow-ridges. Related skulls of rather earlier date from Steinheim, Ehringsdorf, Krapina and elsewhere are less specialized and more akin to modern man. Skulls from Sacco Pastore and Circeo in Italy are related to the Neandertal group.

Mt. Carmel, Palestine, has yielded to Professor Dorothy Garrod and Dr. McCown several mid- or late Pleistocene specimens apparently related both to modern types and to the Neandertal group.

A skull from Galilee, and a skull from Broken Hill, Rhodesia, are related to the Neandertal group.

Recently Oakley has estimated the age of Pleistocene fossil bones from their fluorine content. The back part of a skull from Swanscombe, N. Kent, has in this way been dated to the mid Pleistocene. Its discoverer, Marston, has won widespread support for his view linking it with modern types.

Controversy over the Piltdown skull and jaw is ended. The skull is dated by Oakley's method as late Pleistocene, or later, so the old name *Eoanthropus* is inappropriate. The ape-like jaw is found to be modern and to have nothing to do with the skull.

With the last retreat of the ice sheets it seems that the Neandertal group, and probably the Pithecanthropus group, became extinct. Well-known specimens of man of modern type with diversity of form have been found at Combe Capelle, Cro-Magnon, Chancelade and elsewhere in the later Pleistocene in France and others in Czechoslovakia.

HUMAN CULTURAL STAGES

Until about 8 or 7 thousand years ago men lived by hunting and collecting. In the middle of the Pleistocene they already made finely shaped hand axes (Abbevillean and Acheulian) from stone cores by chipping off flakes, using flint, chert, obsidian, rhyolite, quartzite, etc. in many regions, and these cultures spread from Africa to Spain, France and Britain during some interglacial periods. Apparently the men hunted and made pitfalls for animals as Leakey has shown at Olorgesailie in Kenya, while women and children collected. Fire was used very early. In the continental interior of Eurasia rough stone flakes were long used rather than shaped stone cores and apparently in cold periods at any rate this culture spread west to Britain. In the later part of the Riss-Wurm interglacial, stone flakes became finer especially in regions where contact was made with makers of core-tools, and in some groups both cores and flakes were used.

With the last retreat of the ice-sheets stone flakes became the dominant tools, with diverse types suited to scraping, boring, sawing, etc.—Aurignacian, followed in France by Solutrian, in which long leaf-like flakes were treated as cores and shaped very skilfully by pressing off flakes. The Magdalenian stage next following used flakes but specialized in implements of bone, horn and ivory. In some areas the Aurignacian grades into the Magdalenian and this seems to be largely the case in parts of Britain. All the above cultures are often grouped as Palæolithic.

About 8 or 7 thousand years ago people in S.W. Asia began to cultivate cereals on river mud laid down by annual floods, thus keeping the soil fertile and allowing durable settlement with concomitant advances in mud brick construction, pot-making, stone grinding, which had begun earlier and gave an improved control of shape, carpentering, weaving and other inventions. In all this development the Nile valley was early concerned and its regular floods from summer rains in Abyssinia could be managed to give such an advantage that Egypt gained a unique primacy in early history. Domestication of animals was added very early to cultivation of crops, most probably as a source of milk, flesh, leather, sinews, etc. Neolithic Culture was thus characterized by stone axes shaped by grinding or rubbing, by cultivation, usually by domestic animals, often by durable settlements and a variety of arts and crafts.

Especially after the practice of castration of surplus male animals was introduced, domestic beasts were used for work, notably for pulling a modified hoe to scratch the drying surface of river-mud and so keep it from caking too hard. This is the early plough, valuable in lands where plant food in the soil is drawn up nearly to the surface as moisture rises and evaporates. Animals were also used as porters and tractors.

Heating stones in fires, probably for water-heating, led to the discovery of impure copper and the invention of bronze (standardized at about 10 per cent. tin and 90 per cent. copper) at the beginning of the Bronze Age in S.W. Asia and/or Egypt. By that time, about 5,000 years ago, cities and trade were developing and the basic arts were spreading to the Indus basin, the Mediterranean and the loess areas of Central Europe. Western Europe on the one hand and N. China on the other were affected somewhat later but more than 4,000 years ago; and China rapidly advanced to a high skill in pottery and bronze. Over 3,000 years ago in Anatolia the smelting of iron was developed, and it spread thence in the next centuries, beginning the Iron Age. Iron nails and tools made possible larger boats, houses, furniture and especially larger ploughs, working deeper into the earth and so suited to cooler lands, where plant food was often deep in the soil because evaporation was not very strong and rain might occur at every season. So the farmer needed to bring up the deeper layers to the surface in northwest Europe. With the spread of iron, especially about 2,000 to 1,000 years ago, northwest Europe emerged from its former low status and went ahead, still more after houses were improved with more privacy, chimneys and beds.

The evolution of culture in the Americas is much discussed. Early drifts of hunters via Alaska may have occurred in the late Pleistocene. Probably a good deal of Neolithic culture (stone implements, pottery, etc.) spread by the same route to America about or after 5,000 years ago but did not take Asiatic cereals or domestic animals. America also received contributions to its life by maritime routes especially following the North Pacific currents.

TIME MEASUREMENT AND CALENDARS

MEASUREMENTS OF TIME

Measurements of Time.—These are based on the time taken by the earth to rotate on its axis (*Day*); by the moon to revolve round the earth (*Month*); and by the earth to revolve round the sun (*Year*). From these, which are not commensurable, certain average or mean intervals have been adopted for ordinary use. Of these the first is the *Day*, which begins at midnight and is divided into 24 hours of 60 minutes, each of 60 seconds. The hours are counted from midnight up to 12 at noon (when the sun crosses the meridian), and these hours are designated A.M. (*ante meridiem*); and again from noon up to 12 at midnight, which hours are designated P.M. (*post meridiem*), except when the *Twenty-four Hour* reckoning is employed. The 24-hour reckoning ignores A.M. and P.M., and the hours are numbered 0 to 23 from midnight to midnight.

Colloquially the 24 hours are divided into *day* and *night*, day being the time while the sun is above the horizon (including the four stages of twilight defined on p. 139). Day is subdivided further into *morning*, the early part of daytime, ending at noon; *afternoon* from noon to 6 p.m. and *evening*, which may be said to extend from 6 p.m. until midnight. *Night*, the dark period between day and day, begins at the close of Astronomical Twilight (*see* p. 139) and extends beyond midnight to sunrise the next day.

The names of the *Days*—Sunday, Monday, Tuesday (Tiw=God of War), Wednesday (Woden or Odin), Thursday (Thor), Friday (Frig=wife of Odin), and Saturday are derived from Old English translations or adaptations of the Roman titles (Sol, Luna, Mars, Mercurius, Jupiter, Venus and Saturnus).

The *Week* is a period of 7 days.

The *Month* in the ordinary calendar is approximately the twelfth part of a year, but the lengths of the different months vary from 28 (or 29) days to 31.

The Year.—The *Equinoctial or Tropical Year* is the time that the earth takes to revolve round the sun from equinox to equinox, or 365·2422 mean solar days. The *Calendar Year* consists of 365 days, but a year the date of which is divisible by 4, without remainder, is called *bissextile* (see Roman Calendar) or *Leap Year* and consists of 366 days, one day being added to the month February, so that a date "leaps over" a day of the week. The last year of a century is not a leap year unless its number is divisible by 400 (*e.g.* the years 1800 and 1900 had only 365 days).

The Historical Year.—Before the year 1752, two Calendar systems were in use in England. The Civil or Legal Year began on March 25, while the Historical Year began on January 1. Thus the Civil or Legal date 1658 March 24, was the same day as 1659 March 24 Historical; and a date in that portion of the year is written as: March 24 $165\frac{8}{9}$, the lower figure showing the Historical year.

The Masonic Year.—Two dates are quoted in warrants, dispensations, etc., issued by the United Grand Lodge of England, those for the current year being expressed as *Anno Domini* 1964—*Anno Lucis* 5964. This *Year of Light* is based on the Book of Genesis I: 3, the 4000 year difference being derived from *Ussher's Notation*, published in 1654, which placed the Creation of the World in 4,000 B.C.

Regnal Years.—These are the years of a sovereign's reign, and each begins on the anniversary of his or her accession: *e.g.* Regnal year 12 of the present Queen began on Feb. 6, 1963. The system was used for dating Acts of Parliament until 1962. The *Summer Time Act* of 1925, for example, is quoted as 15 and 16 Geo. V. c. 64, because it became law in the session which extended over part of both of these regnal years. The regnal years of Edward VII began on January 22, which was the day of Queen Victoria's death in 1901, so that Acts passed in that reign are, in general, quoted with only one year number, but year 10 of the series ended on May 6, 1910, being the day on which King Edward died, and Acts of the Parliamentary Session 1910 are headed 10 Edw. VII. and 1 Geo. V.; Acts passed in 1936 were dated 1 Edw. VIII. and 1 Geo. VI.; Acts passed in 1952 were dated 16 Geo. VI. and 1 Elizabeth II. An Act to effect the dating of Acts of Parliament by the calendar year, from Jan. 1, 1963, received the Royal Assent on July 19, 1962.

New Year's Day.—In England in the seventh century, and as late as the thirteenth, the year was reckoned from Christmas Day, but in the twelfth century the Anglican Church began the year with the Feast of The Annunciation of the Blessed Virgin (Lady Day) on March 25 and this practice was adopted generally in the fourteenth century. The Civil or Legal year in the British Dominions (exclusive of Scotland), as opposed to the Historical, which already began on Jan. 1, began with "Lady Day" until 1751. But in and since 1752 the civil year has begun with Jan. 1. Certain dividends are still paid by the Bank of England on dates based on Old Style. The Income Tax year begins on April 6 (the New Style equivalent of March 25, Old Style) in accordance with Act of Parliament (39 Geo. III. 1798). New Year's Day in *Scotland* was changed from March 25 to Jan. 1 in 1600. On the Continent of Europe, Jan. 1 was adopted as the first day of the year by Venice in 1522, Germany in 1544, Spain, Portugal, and the Roman Catholic Netherlands in 1556, Prussia, Denmark and Sweden in 1559, France 1564, Lorraine 1579, Protestant Netherlands 1583, Russia 1725, Tuscany 1751.

The Longest Day.—The longest day measured from sunrise to sunset at any place is the day on which the Sun attains its greatest distance from the Equator, north or south, accordingly as the place is in the northern or southern hemisphere; in other words, it is the day of the Calendar on which a Solstice falls. If a Solstice falls on June 21 late in the day, by Greenwich Time, that day will be the longest of the year at Greenwich, though it may be by only a second of time or a fraction thereof, but it will be on June 22 (local date) in Japan, and therefore June 22 will be the longest day there and at places in Eastern longitudes.

But leaving this question of locality and confining consideration to Greenwich, the Solstices are events in the Tropical Year whose length is $365\frac{1}{4}$ days less about 11 minutes, and therefore, if a Solstice happens late on June 21 in one year, it will be nearly six hours later in the next, or early on June 22, and that will be the longest day. This delay of the Solstice is not permitted to continue because the extra day in Leap Year brings it back a day in the Calendar, and at the present time three of the four years in the Leap Year cycle have the longest day on June 21, one on June 22. By the end of the century the longest day will fall each year on June 21.

Because of the 11 minutes above mentioned the additional day in Leap Year brings the Solstice back too far by 44 minutes, and the time of the Solstice in the calendar is earlier as the century progresses, being about 18 hours too soon at the end of the hundred years.

To remedy this the last year of a century is in most cases not a Leap Year, and the omission of the extra day puts the date of the Solstice later by about six hours too much, compensation for which is made by making the fourth centennial year a Leap Year.

The Shortest Day.—Similar considerations apply to the shortest day of the year, or the day of the Winter Solstice. At the present time one year of the Leap Year cycle has the shortest day on Dec. 21 and the rest on Dec. 22, but in roughly the last quarter of the century the shortest day will fall on Dec. 21 in two years of each four and on Dec. 22 in the remaining two years. The difference due to locality also prevails in the same sense as for the longest day.

At Greenwich the Sun sets at its earliest by the clock about ten days before the shortest day, which is a circumstance that may require explanation. The daily change in the time of sunset is due in the first place to the Sun's movement southwards at this time of year, which diminishes the interval between the Sun's southing or Apparent noon, and its setting, and, secondly, because of the daily decrease of the Equation of Time subtractive from Apparent time, which causes the time of Apparent noon to be continuously later, day by day, and so in a measure counteracts the first effect. The rates of the resulting daily acceleration and retardation are not equal, nor are they uniform, but are such that their combination causes the date of earliest sunset to be Dec. 13 or 14 at Greenwich. In more southerly latitudes the effect of the movement of the Sun is less, and the change in the time of sunset depends on that of the Equation of Time to a greater degree, and the date of earliest sunset is earlier than it is at Greenwich.

Lord Mayor's Day.—The Lord Mayor was previously elected on the day of the Feast of St. Simon and St. Jude (Oct. 28), and from the time of

Edward I, at least, was presented to the King or to the Barons of the Exchequer on the following day, except that day be a Sunday.

The day of election was altered to Oct. 16 in 1346, and after some further changes was fixed for Michaelmas Day in 1546, but the ceremonies of admittance and swearing-in of the Lord Mayor continued to take place on Oct. 28 and 29 respectively until 1751. In 1752, when Sept. 3 was reckoned as Sept. 14 at the reform of the Calendar, the Lord Mayor was continued in office until Nov. 8, the "New Style" equivalent of Oct. 28. The Lord Mayor is now presented to the Lord Chief Justice at the Royal Courts of Justice, on the second Saturday in November to make the final declaration of office, having been sworn in at Guildhall on the preceding day.

Dog Days.—The days about the heliacal rising of the Dog Star, noted from ancient times as the hottest and most unwholesome period of the year in the Northern Hemisphere. Their incidence has been variously calculated as depending on the Greater or Lesser Dog Star (Sirius or Procyon) and their duration has been reckoned as from 30 to 54 days. A generally accepted period is from July 3 to August 15.

Metonic (Lunar, or Minor) *Cycle.*—In the year 432 B.C. Meton, an Athenian astronomer, found that 235 Lunations are very nearly, though not exactly, equal in duration to 19 Solar Years, and, hence, after 19 years the Phases of the Moon recur on the same days of the month (nearly). The dates of Full Moon in a cycle of nineteen years were inscribed in *figures of gold* on public monuments in Athens, and the number showing the position of a year in the Cycle is called the *Golden Number* of that year.

Solar (or Major) *Cycle.*—A period of twenty-eight years, in any corresponding year of which the days of the week recur on the same days of the month.

Julian Period.—Proposed by Joseph Scaliger in 1582. The period is 7980 Julian years, and its first year coincides with the year 4713 B.C. 7980 is the product of the number of years in the Solar Cycle, the Metonic Cycle and the cycle of the Roman Indiction (28 × 19 × 15).

Roman Indiction.—A period of fifteen years, instituted for fiscal purposes about A.D. 300.

Epact.—The age of the calendar Moon on Jan. 1 in each year, formerly used in determining the date of Easter.

THE FOUR SEASONS

SPRING, the first season of the year, is defined astronomically to begin in the *Northern Hemisphere* at the Vernal Equinox when the Sun enters the sign Aries (*i.e.* about March 21) and crosses the Equator, thus causing day and night to be of equal length all over the world; and to terminate at the Summer Solstice. In *Great Britain*, Spring in popular parlance comprises the months of February, March and April; in *North America* the months of March, April and May. In the *Southern Hemisphere* Spring corresponds with Autumn in the Northern Hemisphere.

SUMMER, the second and warmest season, begins astronomically at the Summer Solstice when the Sun enters the sign Cancer (about June 21). The Sun then attains its greatest northern declination and appears to stand still, the times of sunrise and sunset and the consequent length of the day showing no variation for several days together, before and after the Longest Day (June 21 or 22). Summer terminates at the Autumnal Equinox. In popular parlance Summer in *Great Britain* includes the months of May, June, July and August, Midsummer Day being June 24. In *North America* the season includes the months of June, July and August.

AUTUMN, the third season, begins astronomically at the Autumnal Equinox (*i.e.*, about September 21) when the Sun enters the sign Libra, the beginning of which sign is at the intersection of the Equator and the Ecliptic, the point in the sky where the Sun crosses from N. to S. of the Equator and causes the length of day and night to be equal all over the world. In *Great Britain* it is popularly held to include the months of September and October. A warm period sometimes occurs round about St. Luke's Day (Oct. 18) and is known as "St. Luke's Summer." In *North America*, Autumn, or "The Fall," comprises September, October and November. Autumn ends at the Winter Solstice. In the *Southern Hemisphere* it corresponds with Spring of the Northern Hemisphere.

WINTER, the fourth and coldest season, begins astronomically at the Winter Solstice (*i.e.* about Dec. 21) when the Sun enters the sign Capricornus, and ends at the Vernal Equinox. In *Great Britain* the season is popularly held to comprise the months of November, December and January, midwinter being marked by the Shortest Day. A warm period sometimes occurs round about Martinmas (Nov. 11) and is known as "St. Martin's Summer." In *North America* the season includes the months of December, January and February. In the *Southern Hemisphere* it corresponds with Summer of the Northern Hemisphere.

THE ROMAN CALENDAR

Roman.—Roman historians adopted as an epoch the Foundation of Rome, which is believed to have happened in the year 753 B.C., and the ordinal number of the years in Roman reckoning is followed by the letters A.U.C. (*Ab Urbe Condita*), so that the year A.D. 1964 is MMDCCXVII (2717), A.U.C. The Calendar that we know has developed from one established by Romulus, who is said to have used a year of 304 days divided into ten months, beginning with March, to which Numa added January and February, making the year consist of 12 months of 30 and 29 days alternately, with an additional day so that the total was 355. It is also said that Numa ordered an intercalary month of 22 or 23 days in alternate years, making 90 days in eight years, to be inserted after Feb. 23, but there is some doubt as to the origination and the details of the intercalation in the Roman Calendar, though it is certain that some scheme of this kind was inaugurated and not fully carried out, for in the year 46 B.C. Julius Cæsar, who was then Pontifex Maximus, found that the Calendar had been allowed to fall into some confusion. He therefore sought the help of the Egyptian astronomer Sosigenes, which led to the construction and adoption (45 B.C.) of the Julian Calendar, and, by a slight alteration, to the Gregorian now in use. The year 46 B.C. was made to consist of 445 days, and is called the *Year of Confusion*. In the Roman (Julian) Calendar the days of the month were counted backwards from three fixed points, or days, and an intervening day was said to be so many days *before* the next coming point, the first *and* last being counted. These three points were (1) the Kalends; (2) the Nones; and (3) the Ides. Their positions in the months and the method of counting from them will be seen in the Table on p. 188. The year containing 366 days was called *bissextilis annus*, as it had a doubled sixth day (*bissextus dies*) before the March Kalends on Feb. 24—*ante diem sextum Kalendas Martias*, or VI Kal. Mart.

Present Days of the Month	March, May, July, October have thirty-one days	January, August, December have thirty-one days	April, June, September, November have thirty days	February has twenty-eight days, and in Leap Year twenty-nine
1	Kalendis.	Kalendis.	Kalendis.	Kalendis.
2	VI. } Ante Nonas.	IV. } Ante Nonas.	IV. } Ante Nonas.	IV. } Ante Nonas.
3	V.	III.	III.	III.
4	IV.	Pridie Nonas.	Pridie Nonas.	Pridie Nonas.
5	III.	Nonis.	Nonis.	Nonis.
6	Pridie Nonas.	VIII. } Ante Idus.	VIII. } Ante Idus.	VIII. } Ante Idus.
7	Nonis.	VII.	VII.	VII.
8	VIII. } Ante Idus.	VI.	VI.	VI.
9	VII.	V.	V.	V.
10	VI.	IV.	IV.	IV.
11	V.	III.	III.	III.
12	IV.	Pridie Idus.	Pridie Idus.	Pridie Idus.
13	III.	Idibus.	Idibus.	Idibus.
14	Pridie Idus.	XIX. } Ante Kalendas (of the month following).	XVIII. } Ante Kalendas (of the month following).	XVI. } Ante Kalendas Martias.
15	Idibus.	XVIII.	XVII.	XV.
16	XVII. } Ante Kalendas (of the month following).	XVII.	XVI.	XIV.
17	XVI.	XVI.	XV.	XIII.
18	XV.	XV.	XIV.	XII.
19	XIV.	XIV.	XIII.	XI.
20	XIII.	XIII.	XII.	X.
21	XII.	XII.	XI.	IX.
22	XI.	XI.	X.	VIII.
23	X.	X.	IX.	VII.
24	IX.	IX.	VIII.	VI.
25	VIII.	VIII.	VII.	V.
26	VII.	VII.	VI.	IV.
27	VI.	VI.	V.	III.
28	V.	V.	IV.	Pridie Kalendas Martias.
29	IV.	IV.	III.	
30	III.	III.	Pridie Kalendas (of the month following).	
31	Pridie Kalendas (of the month following).	Pridie Kalendas (of the month following).		

THE CHRISTIAN CALENDAR

In the Christian chronological system the years are distinguished by cardinal numbers before or after the Incarnation, the period being denoted by the letters B.C. (Before Christ) or, more rarely, A.C. (*Ante Christum*), and A.D. (*Annus Domini*). The correlative dates of the epoch are the 4th year of the 194th Olympiad, the 753rd year from the Foundation of Rome, A.M. 3761 (Jewish Chronology), and the 4714th year of the Julian Period. This was introduced into Italy in the sixth century, and though first used in France in the seventh it was not universally established there until about the eighth century. It has been said that the system was introduced into England by St. Augustine (A.D. 596), but was probably not generally used until some centuries later. It was ordered to be used by the Bishops at the Council of Chelsea, A.D. 816. The actual date of the birth of Christ is somewhat uncertain. Dec. 25, 4 B.C., is supported by several lines of argument.

Old and New Style.—In the Julian Calendar all the centennial years were Leap Years, and for this reason towards the close of the sixteenth century there was a difference of 10 days between the tropical and calendar years; or, in other words, the equinox fell on March 11 of the Calendar, whereas at the time of the Council of Nicaea, A.D. 325, it had fallen on March 21. In 1582 Pope Gregory ordained that Oct. 5th should be called Oct. 15th, and that of the end-century years only the fourth should be a Leap Year (*see* p. 186). This change was adopted by Italy, France, Spain, and Portugal in 1582; by Prussia, the German Roman Catholic States, Switzerland, Holland, and Flanders on Jan. 1, 1583, Poland 1586, Hungary 1587, the German and Netherland Protestant States and Denmark 1700, Sweden (gradually) by the omission of eleven leap days, 1700–1740; Great Britain and her Dominions (including the North American Colonies) in 1752, by the omission of eleven days (Sept. 3 being reckoned as Sept. 14). This *Gregorian Calendar* was adopted by Japan in 1872, China in 1912, Bulgaria in 1915, Turkey and Soviet Russia in 1917, by Yugoslavia and Roumania in 1919, and by Greece in February, 1923. The Russian, Greek, Serbian and Roumanian Churches did not abandon the Julian Calendar until May, 1923, when the Gregorian, slightly modified, was adopted. The *difference* between the Old and New Styles was 11 days after 1752, 12 days after 1800, and has been 13 days since 1900. It happened that a change of the beginning of the year from March 25 to January 1 was made in England in 1752, the year in which the change from Julian to Gregorian Calendar was made, and for that reason the words Old and New Style have been used in a sense which is not strictly correct, but is nevertheless expressive.

The Dominical Letter is one of the letters A–G which are used to denote the Sundays (Lord's Days) in successive years. If the first day of the year is a Sunday the letter is A; if the second, B; the third, C; and so on. Leap year requires two letters, the first for Jan. 1—Feb. 29, the second for March 1—Dec. 31.

Epiphany.—The Feast of the Epiphany, commemorating the manifestation of the infant Jesus to the Gentiles, later became associated with the offering of gifts by the Magi. The day was of

Continued on page 191

A TABLE OF EASTER DAYS AND SUNDAY LETTERS
FROM THE YEAR 1500 TO 2000

	1500—1599	1600—1699	1700—1799	1800—1899	1900—2000	
d Mar. 22	1573	1668	1761	1818		d Mar. 22
e „ 23	1505-16	1600	1788	1845-56	1913	e „ 23
f „ 24		1611-95	1706-99		1940	f „ 24
g „ 25	1543-54	1627-38-49	1722-33-44	1883-94	1951	g „ 25
A „ 26	1559-70-81-92	1654-65-76	1749-58-69-80	1815-26-37	1967-78-89	A „ 26
b Mar. 27	1502-13-24-97	1608-87-92	1785-96	1842-53-64	1910-21-32	b Mar. 27
c „ 28	1529-35-40	1619-24-30	1703-14-25	1869-75-80	1937-48	c „ 28
d „ 29	1551-62	1635-46-57	1719-30-41-52	1807-12-91	1959-64-70	d „ 29
e „ 30	1567-78-89	1651-62-73-84	1746-55-66-77	1823-34	1902-75-86-97	e „ 30
f „ 31	1510-21-32-83-94	1605-16-78-89	1700-71-82-93	1839-50-61-72	1907-18-29-91	f „ 31
g April 1	1526-37-48	1621-32	1711-16	1804-66-77-88	1923-34-45-56	g April 1
A „ 2	1553-64	1643-48	1727-38-52(NS)	1809-20-93-99	1961-72	A „ 2
b „ 3	1575-80-86	1659-70-81	1743-63-68-74	1825-31-36	1904-83-88-94	b „ 3
c „ 4	1507-18-91	1602-13-75-86-97	1708-79-90	1847-58	1915-20-26-99	c „ 4
d „ 5	1523-34-45-56	1607-18-29-40	1702-13-24-95	1801-63-74-85-96	1931-42-53	d „ 5
e April 6	1539-50-61-72	1634-45-56	1729-35-40-60	1806-17-28-90	1947-58-69-80	e April 6
f „ 7	1504-77-88	1667-72	1751-65-76	1822-33-44	1901-12-85-96	f „ 7
g „ 8	1509-15-20-99	1604-10-83-94	1705-87-92-98	1849-55-60	1917-28	g „ 8
A „ 9	1531-42	1615-26-37-99	1710-21-32	1871-82	1939-44-50	A „ 9
b „ 10	1547-58-69	1631-42-53-64	1726-37-48-57	1803-14-87-98	1955-66-77	b „ 10
c April 11	1501-12-63-74-85-96	1658-69-80	1762-73-84	1819-30-41-52	1909-71-82-93	c April 11
d „ 12	1506-17-28	1601-12-91-96	1789	1846-57-68	1903-14-25-36-98	d „ 12
e „ 13	1533-44	1623-28	1707-18	1800-73-79-84	1941-52	e „ 13
f „ 14	1555-60-66	1639-50-61	1723-34-45-54	1805-11-16-95	1963-68-74	f „ 14
g „ 15	1571-82-93	1655-66-77-88	1750-59-70-81	1827-38	1900-06-79-90	g „ 15
A April 16	1503-14-25-36-87-98	1609-20-82-93	1704-75-86-97	1843-54-65-76	1911-22-33-95	A April 16
b „ 17	1530-41-52	1625-36	1715-20	1808-70-81-92	1927-38-49-60	b „ 17
c „ 18	1557-68	1647-52	1731-42-56	1802-13-24-97	1954-65-76	c „ 18
d „ 19	1500-79-84-90	1663-74-85	1747-67-72-78	1829-35-40	1908-81-87-92	d „ 19
e „ 20	1511-22-95	1606-17-79-90	1701-12-83-94	1851-62	1919-24-30	e „ 20
f April 21	1527-38-49	1622-33-44	1717-28	1867-78-89	1935-46-57	f April 21
g „ 22	1565-76	1660	1739-53-64	1810-21-32	1962-73-84	g „ 22
A „ 23	1508	1671		1848	1905-16-2000	A „ 23
b „ 24	1519	1603-14-98	1709-91	1859		b „ 24
c „ 25	1546	1641	1736	1886	1943	c „ 25

A TABLE OF THE MOVABLE FEASTS FOR 10 YEARS—1960–1969

Year	Ash Wednesday	Easter	Ascension	Whit Sunday	Suns. after Trin.	Advent
1960	March 2	April 17	May 26	June 5	xxiii	Nov. 27
1961	Feb. 15	April 2	May 11	May 21	xxvi	Dec. 3
1962	March 7	April 22	May 31	June 10	xxiii	Dec. 2
1963	Feb. 27	April 14	May 23	June 2	xxiv	Dec. 1
1964	Feb. 12	March 29	May 7	May 17	xxvi	Nov. 29
1965	March 3	April 18	May 27	June 6	xxiii	Nov. 28
1966	Feb. 23	April 10	May 19	May 29	xxiv	Nov. 27
1967	Feb. 8	March 26	May 4	May 14	xxvii	Dec. 3
1968	Feb. 28	April 14	May 23	June 2	xxiv	Dec. 1
1969	Feb. 19	April 6	May 15	May 25	xxv	Nov. 30

NOTES CONCERNING TABLE OF MOVABLE FEASTS

Ash Wednesday (first Day in *Lent*) can fall at earliest on February 4 and at latest on March 10.
Easter Day can fall at earliest on March 22 and at latest on April 25.
Ascension Day can fall at earliest on April 30 and at latest on June 3.
Whit Sunday can fall at earliest on May 10 and at latest on June 13.
Rogation Sunday is the Sunday next before *Holy Thursday* (Ascension Day).
Trinity Sunday is the Sunday next after *Whit Sunday*.
Corpus Christi falls on the Thursday next after *Trinity Sunday*.
There are not less than xxii and not more than xxvii *Sundays after Trinity*.
Advent Sunday is the Sunday nearest to November 30.

PERPETUAL CALENDAR

OR TABLES FOR FINDING THE DAY OF THE WEEK FOR ANY DATE A.D.

(Copyright by A. F. L. Wilkinson)

TO USE THE CALENDAR:—Look up the Index Numbers corresponding to the Century, the Year (last two figures) and the Month, respectively, in the first three tables; add these three numbers together and add also the Day of the Month; in the fourth table, *opposite the sum obtained*, read the day of the Week.

(1)

Century					Index No.
001–099	700 - 799	1400–1499	1752‡–1799	2100–2199, &c.	5
100–199	800 - 899	1500–1599	...	...	4
200–299	900 - 999	1600–1699	1800 –1899	2200–2299, &c.	3
300–399	1000–1099	1700–1752†	...	...	2
400–499	1100–1199	...	1900 –1999	2300–2399, &c.	1
500–599	1200–1299	...	2000 –2099	2400–2499, &c.	0
600–699	1300–1399	...	...	...	6

† Up to September 2nd inclusive. ‡ From September 14th inclusive. (*See* footnote)

(2)

Year (last two figures)				Index No.§ A	Index No.§ B
00*				6	0
00**				0	0
01	29	57	85	1	1
02	30	58	86	2	2
03	31	59	87	3	3
04	32	60	88	4	5
05	33	61	89	6	6
06	34	62	90	0	0
07	35	63	91	1	1
08	36	64	92	2	3
09	37	65	93	4	4
10	38	66	94	5	5
11	39	67	95	6	6
12	40	68	96	0	1
13	41	69	97	2	2
14	42	70	98	3	3
15	43	71	99	4	4
16	44	72	—	5	6
17	45	73	—	0	0
18	46	74	—	1	1
19	47	75	—	2	2
20	48	76	—	3	4
21	49	77	—	5	5
22	50	78	—	6	6
23	51	79	—	0	0
24	52	80	—	1	2
25	53	81	—	3	3
26	54	82	—	4	4
27	55	83	—	5	5
28	56	84	—	6	0

§ Use column A for January and February and column B for March to December.
* For years up to 1700 inclusive, and also for 2000, 2400, etc.
** For the years 1800, 1900, 2100, 2200, 2300, 2500, etc.

(3)

Month	Index No.	Month	Index No.
January ...	0	July	6
February	3	August ...	2
March......	3	September	5
April	6	October ...	0
May	1	November	3
June	4	December	5

(4)

Sum of Index Numbers							Day
1	8	15	22	29	36	43	Sunday
2	9	16	23	30	37	44	Monday
3	10	17	24	31	38	45	Tuesday
4	11	18	25	32	39	46	Wednesday
5	12	19	26	33	40	47	Thursday
6	13	20	27	34	41	48	Friday
7	14	21	28	35	42	49	Saturday

Examples

1914, *August 4th*	*Index No.*	1215, *June 19th*	*Index No.*
Table 1 1900–1999	1	Table 1 ...1200 1299	0
Table 2 ......14 (B)	3	Table 2 ... 15 (B)	4
Table 3 ......August	2	Table 3 ...June	4
4th	4	19th	19
Sum	10	Sum	27
Table 4 ... 10=Tuesday		Table 4 ... 27=Friday	

NOTE.—In England the change from the Julian System or Old Style to the Gregorian System or New Style, was made in September, 1752, when the 11 days 3rd to 13th inclusive were omitted, and Wednesday Sept. 2 was immediately followed by Thursday Sept. 14. Other countries made the change at dates varying from 1582 to 1940. (*See* p. 188.)

If it is desired to look up a date after 1752 in Old Style, or before 1752 in New Style, it can be done by taking a date 700 years earlier in the first case or 400 years later in the second case; *e.g.* 1923 in Old Style is the same as 1223, and 1582 in New Style is the same as 1982.

exceptional importance from the time of the Council of Nicaea (A.D. 325) as the primate of Alexandria was charged at every Epiphany Feast with the announcement in a letter to the Churches of the date of the forthcoming Easter. The day was of considerable importance in Britain as it influenced dates, ecclesiastical and lay, *e.g. Plow Monday*, when work was resumed in the fields, falls upon the Monday in the first full week after the Epiphany.

Lent.—The Teutonic word *Lent*, which denotes the Fast preceding Easter, originally meant no more than the Spring season; but from Anglo-Saxon times, at least, it has been used as the equivalent of the more significant Latin term *Quadragesima*, meaning the "Forty Days" or, more literally, the fortieth day. As early as the fifth century some of the Fathers of the Church put forward the view that the forty days Fast is of Apostolic origin, but this is not supported or believed by modern scholars; and it appears to some that it dates from the early years of the fourth century. There is some suggestion that the Fast was kept originally for only forty hours. *Ash Wednesday* is the first day of Lent, which ends at midnight before Easter Day.

Sexagesima and Septuagesima.—It has been suggested that the unmeaning application of the names *Sexagesima* and *Septuagesima* to the second and third Sundays before Lent was made by analogy with the names *Quadragesima* and *Quinquagesima*. Another less likely conjecture is that *Septuagesima* means the seventieth day before the Octave of Easter. It is not certain whether the name *Quinquagesima* is due to the fact that the Sunday in question is the fiftieth day before Easter (reckoned inclusive) or was simply formed on the analogy of *Quadragesima* (*New English Dictionary*).

Palm Sunday commemorates the triumphal entry of Our Lord into Jerusalem and is celebrated in Britain (where palm is not available) by branches of willow gathered for use in the decoration of churches on that day.

Maundy Thursday, the day before Good Friday, the name itself being a corruption of *dies mandati* (day of the mandate) when Christ washed the feet of the disciples and gave them the mandate to love one another.

Easter-Day is the first Sunday after the full moon which happens upon, or next after, the 21st day of March; and if the full moon happens upon a Sunday, Easter-Day is the Sunday after. This definition is contained in an Act of Parliament (24 Geo. II., cap. 23), and explanation is given in the preamble to the Act that the day of Full Moon depends on certain tables that have been prepared. These are the tables whose essential points are given in the early pages of the Book of Common Prayer. The Moon referred to is not the real moon of the heavens, but a hypothetical Moon on whose "Full" the date of Easter depends, and the lunations of this "Calendar" Moon consist of twenty-nine and thirty days alternately with certain necessary modifications to make the date of its Full agree as nearly as possible with that of the real Moon, which is known as the *Paschal Full Moon*.

A Fixed Easter.—As at present ordained, Easter falls on one of 35 days (March 22—April 25). On June 15, 1928, the House of Commons agreed to a motion for the third reading of the Bill that Easter Day shall, in the Calendar year next but one after the commencement of the Act and in all subsequent years, be *the first Sunday after the second Saturday* in April. Easter would thus fall between April 9 and 15, both inclusive—that is, on the second or third Sunday in April. A clause in the Bill provided that before it shall come into operation regard shall be had to any opinion expressed officially by the various Christian Churches. Although there has been some support, there is no present prospect of the adoption of a Fixed Easter.

Holy Days and Saints Days were the normal factors in early times for settling the dates of future and recurrent appointments, *e.g.* the *Quarter Days* in England and Wales are the Feast of the Nativity, the Feast of the Annunciation, the Feast of St. John the Baptist and the Feast of St. Michael and All the Holy Angels, while *Term Days* in Scotland are Candlemas (Feast of the Purification), Whitsunday (a fixed date), Lammas (Loaf Mass) and Martinmas (St. Martin's Day). *Law Sittings* in England and Wales commence on the Feast of St. Hilary and the term which begins on Old Michaelmas Day ends on the Feast of St. Thomas the Apostle.

The number of Saints commemorated in the Calendar of the Book of Common Prayer is 73, but (with the exception of All Saints' Day) "days" are appointed only for those whose names are mentioned in Scripture. *Red Letter Days* (*see also* p. 222) were Holy Days and Saints Days indicated in early ecclesiastical calendars by letters printed in red ink. The days to be distinguished in this way were finally approved at the Council of Nicaea, A.D. 325, and special services are set apart for them in the Book of Common Prayer.

Rogation Days.—These are the Monday, Tuesday and Wednesday preceding Ascension Day, "Holy Thursday", and in the fifth century were ordered by the Church to be observed as public Fasts with solemn processions and supplications. The processions were discontinued as religious observances at the Reformation, but survive in the ceremony known as "Beating the Parish Bounds."

Ember Days.—The Ember Days at the Four Seasons are the Wednesday, Friday and Saturday after (1) the First Sunday in Lent, (2) the Feast of Pentecost, (3) September 14, (4) December 13.

Whit Sunday.—It is generally said that this name is a variant of White Sunday, and was so called from the albs or white robes of the newly baptised. But other derivations have been suggested. An early writer says: "This day is called Wyte Sonday because the Holy Ghost brought Wyte and Wisdom unto Christ's disciples, and filled them full of ghostly wit."

Trinity Sunday.—The Festival in honour of the Trinity is observed on the Sunday following Whit Sunday, and subsequent Sundays are reckoned in the Church of England as "after Trinity"; in the Roman Catholic Church Sundays are reckoned "after Pentecost."

Thomas Becket, called by his contemporaries Thomas of London (*born* 1118; *murdered* Dec. 29, 1170), was consecrated Archbishop of Canterbury on the Sunday after Whit Sunday and his first act was to ordain that the day of his consecration should be held as a new festival in honour of the Holy Trinity. The observance thus originated spread from Canterbury throughout the whole of Christendom.

Advent Sunday is the Sunday nearest to St. Andrew's Day, Nov. 30, which allows three Sundays between Advent and Christmas Day in all cases. The Sunday preceding Advent is the 27th after Trinity if Easter falls on one of the days, March 22–26 inclusive. It is the 22nd after Trinity when Easter Day is on April 24 or 25. If the date of Easter were determined as proposed (*see Fixed Easter*), there would generally be 24 Sundays after Trinity, the number being 25 only in the years when Easter fell on April 9. As the rubric ordains that the Epistle and Gospel for the

25th Sunday after Trinity shall always be read upon the Sunday next before Advent, it follows that those offices appointed for the 24th Sunday would be little used. With a Fixed Easter there would never be a sixth Sunday after Epiphany. There would be a fifth Sunday when Easter Day fell on April 15 or on April 14, the year being a leap year.

Thistle Sunday (Scotland) is the first Sunday after St. Andrew's Day.

THE JEWISH CALENDAR

Origin.—The story in the Book of Genesis that the Flood began on the seventeenth day of the second month; that after the end of 150 days the waters were abated; and that on the seventeenth day of the seventh month the Ark rested on Mount Ararat, indicates a calendar of some kind and that the writers recognized 30 days as the length of a lunation. There is other mention of months by their ordinal numbers in the Book of Genesis and in establishing the rite of the Passover Moses spoke of *Abib* as the month when the Israelites came out from Egypt and Abib was to be the first month of the year. In the First Book of Kings three months are mentioned by name, Zif the second month, Ethanim the seventh and Bul the eighth, but these are not names now in use. After the Dispersion, Jewish communities were left in considerable doubt as to the times of Fasts and Festivals, and this led to the formation of the Jewish Calendar as used to-day, which, it is said by some, was done in A.D. 358 by Rabbi Hillel II., a descendant of Gamaliel—though some assert that it did not happen until much later. This calendar is luni-solar, and is based on the lengths of the lunation and of the tropical year as found by Hipparchus (*Circ.* 120 B.C.) which differ little from those adopted at the present day. The year 5724 (1963–64 A.D.) is the 5th year of the 302nd *Metonic* (Minor or Lunar) *Cycle* of 19 years and the 12th year of the 205th *Solar* (or Major) *Cycle* of 28 years since the Era of the Creation, which the Jews hold to have occurred at the time of the Autumnal Equinox in the year known in the Christian Calendar as 3760 B.C. (954 of the Julian Period) and the epoch or starting point of Jewish Chronology corresponds to Oct. 7, 3761 B.C. At the beginning of each Solar Cycle the *Tekufah* of Nisan (the vernal equinox) returns to the same day and to the same hour.

The hour is divided into 1080 *minims* and the month between one new Moon and the next is reckoned as 29 days, 12 hours, 793 minims. The normal calendar year, called a Common Regular year, consists of 12 months of 30 days and 29 days alternately. Since 12 months such as these comprise only 354 days, in order that each of them shall not diverge greatly from an average place in the solar year, a thirteenth month is occasionally added after the fifth month of the Civil year (which commences on the first day of month Tishri), or as the penultimate month of the Ecclesiastical (which commences on the first day of month Nisan), the years when this happens being called Embolismic. Of the 19 years that form a Metonic cycle, 7 are embolismic; they occur at places in the cycle indicated by the numbers 3, 6, 8, 11, 14, 17, 19 these places being chosen so that the accumulated excesses of the solar years should be as small as possible. The first of each month is called the day of New Moon, though it is not necessarily the day of astronomical New Moon, that being the day on which conjunction of Sun and Moon occurs, but there is generally a difference of a day or two. In practice, in a month which follows one of 30 days, the day preceding its first day is also observed as a day of New Moon. The dates in the Christian calendar of the first days of the months depend on that of the first of Tishri, which

JEWISH CALENDARS 5724–5726

Jewish Month		A.M. 5724			A.M. 5725			A.M. 5726		
Tishri	1 ..	1963	September	19 ..	1964	September	7 ..	1965	September	27
Marcheshvan	1 ..		October	19 ..		October	7 ..		October	27
Kislev	1 ..		November	17 ..		November	6 ..		November	25
Tebet	1 ..		December	17 ..		December	6 ..		December	24
Shebat	1 ..	1964	January	15 ..	1965	January	4 ..	1966	January	22
Adar	1 ..		February	14 ..		February	3 ..		February	21
Ve-Adar	1 ..		..	..		March	5 ..		..	
Nisan	1 ..		March	14 ..		April	3 ..		March	22
Iyar	1 ..		April	13 ..		May	3 ..		April	21
Sivan	1 ..		May	12 ..		June	1 ..		May	20
Tammuz	1 ..		June	11 ..		July	1 ..		June	19
Ab	1 ..		July	10 ..		July	30 ..		July	18
Ellul	1 ..		August	9 ..		August	29 ..		August	17

JEWISH FASTS AND FESTIVALS

Tishri	1	Rosh Hoshanah (New Year).
,,	2	,, ,, (2nd day).
,,	3	*Fast of Gedaliah.
,,	10	Yom Kippur (Day of Atonement).
,,	15–22	Succoth (Feast of Tabernacles).
,,	21	Hoshana Rabba.
,,	22	Solemn Assembly
,,	23	Rejoicing of the Law.
Kislev	25	Dedication of the Temple.
Tebet	10	Fast of Tebet.
Adar	13	§Fast of Esther.
,,	14	Purim.
,,	15	Shushan Purim.
Nisan	15–21	Passover
Sivan	6 and 7	Shavuot (Pentecost or Feast of Weeks).
Tammuz	17	*Fast of Tammuz.
Ab	9	*Fast of Ab.

A Common abundant year of 12 months, 51 Sabbaths and 355 days.

A.M. 5724 (known as 724 in the short system) is a Common Regular year of 12 months, 51 Sabbaths and 354 days.

A.M. 5725 (725) is an Embolismic Abundant year of 13 months, 55 Sabbaths and 385 days.

A.M. 5726 (726) is a Common Deficient year of 12 months, 50 Sabbaths and 353 days.

NOTES.—* If these dates fall on the Sabbath the Fast is kept on the following day.
This fast is observed on Adar 11 (or Ve-Adar 11 in Embolismic years) if Adar 13 falls on a Sabbath.

therefore controls the dates of fasts and festivals in the Jewish year. For certain ceremonial reasons connected with these, the first of Tishri must not fall on a Sunday, Wednesday or Friday, and if this should happen as the result of the computation it is postponed to the next day in the Christian calendar. Also, if the New Moon of Tishri falls on any day of the week at noon or later than noon, then the following day is to be taken for the celebration of that New Moon and is Tishri 1, provided that it is not one of the forbidden days, in which case there is a further postponement of a day. These rules and others have been considered in detail, and finally a calendar scheme has been drawn up in which a Jewish year is of one of the following six types: Common Deficient (353 days), Common Regular (354 days), Common Abundant (355 days), Embolismic Deficient (383 days), Embolismic Regular (384 days), or Embolismic Abundant (385 days).

The Regular year has an alternation of 30 and 29 days. In an Abundant year, whether Common or Embolismic, Marcheshvan, the second month of the Civil year, has 30 days instead of 29; in Deficient years Kislev, the third month, has 29 instead of 30. The additional month in Embolismic years which is called Adar I., and precedes the month called Adar in Common years and Adar II., or Ve-Adar, in Embolismic, always has 30 days, but neither this, nor the other variations mentioned, is allowed to change the number of days in the other months which still follow the alternation of the normal twelve. In Embolismic years the month intercalated precedes Adar and usurps its name, but the usual Adar festivals are kept in Ve-Adar.

These are the main features of the Jewish Calendar which must be considered permanent, because as a Jewish law it cannot be altered except by a great Synhedrion.

The Jewish day begins between sunset and nightfall. The time used is that of the meridian of Jerusalem, which is *2h. 21m.* in advance of Greenwich Mean Time. Rules for the beginning of Sabbaths and Festivals were laid down for the latitude of London in the eighteenth century and hours for nightfall are now fixed annually by the Chief Rabbi.

THE MOSLEM CALENDAR

The basic date of the Moslem Calendar is the *Hejira*, or Flight of Muhammad from Mecca to Medina, the corresponding date of which is A.D. 622, July 16, in the Julian Calendar. Hejira years are used principally in Persia, Turkey, Arabia, Egypt, in certain parts of India and in Malaya. The system was adopted about A.D. 632, commencing from the first day of the month preceding the Hejira. The years are purely lunar and consist of 12 months containing in alternate sequence 30 or 29 days, with the intercalation of one day at the end of the 12th month at stated intervals in each cycle of 30 years, the object of the intercalation being to reconcile the date of the first of the month with the date of the actual New Moon. Some adherents still take the date of the evening of the first visibility of the crescent as that of the first of the month. In each cycle of 30 years 19 are common and contain 354 days and 11 are intercalary (355 days), the latter being called *kabishah*.

The mean length of the Hejira year is 354 days, 8 hours, 48 minutes and the period of mean lunation is 29 days, 12 hours, 44 minutes.

To ascertain if a Hejira year is common or *kabishah* divide it by 30; the quotient gives the number of completed cycles and the remainder shows the place of the year in the current cycle. If the remainder is 2, 5, 7, 10, 13, 16, 18, 21, 24, 26 or 29 the year is *kabishah* and consists of 355 days.

Hejira year 1383 gives a quotient of 46 with a remainder of 3 and is a common year. A.H. 1384, with remainder 4, is a common year and A.H. 1385 is *kabishah*.

Hejira Years 1383 and 1384

Name and Length of Month	A.H. 1383		A.H. 1384	
Muharram (30)..	1963	May 25	1964	May 13
Saphar (29).....		June 24		June 12
Rabia I (30)		July 23		July 11
Rabia II (29)....		Aug. 22		Aug. 10
Jomada I (30)...		Sept. 20		Sept. 8
Jomada II (29)...		Oct. 20		Oct. 8
Rajab (30)......		Nov. 18		Nov. 6
Shaaban (29)....		Dec. 18		Dec. 6
Ramadân (30)...	1964	Jan. 16	1965	Jan. 4
Shawwâl (29)...		Feb. 15		Feb. 3
Dulkaada (30)...		Mar. 15		Mar. 4
Dulheggia (29 or 30)..........		April 14		April 3

NOTE.—A.H. 1385 (*kabishah* year of 355 days) begins on 1965, May 2.

OTHER EPOCHS AND CALENDARS

China.—Until the year A.D. 1911 a Lunar Calendar was in force in China, but with the establishment of the Republic the Government adopted the Gregorian Calendar, and the new and old systems were used simultaneously by the people for several years. Since 1930 the publication and use of the old Calendar have been banned by the Government, and an official Chinese Calendar, corresponding with the European or Western system, is compiled, but the old Lunar Calendar is still in use to some extent in China. The old Chinese Calendar, with a cycle of 60 years, is still in use in Tibet, Hong Kong, Singapore, Malaya and elsewhere in South-East Asia.

Ethiopia.—In the Coptic Calendar, which is used by part of the population of Egypt and Abyssinia, the year is made up of 12 months of 30 days each, followed, in general, by 5 complementary days. Every fourth year is an Intercalary or Leap year and in these years there are 6 complementary days. The Intercalary year of the Coptic Calendar immediately precedes the Leap year of the Julian Calendar. The Era is that of Diocletian or the Martyrs, the origin of which is fixed at A.D. 284, Aug. 29 (Julian date).

Greece.—Ancient Greek chronology was reckoned in *Olympiads*, cycles of 4 years corresponding with the periodic Olympic Games held on the plain of Olympia in Elis once in 4 years, the intervening years being the first, second, etc., of the Olympiad which received the name of the victor at the Games, The first recorded Olympiad is that of Choroebus, 776 B.C.

India.—In addition to the Moslem reckoning there are six eras used in India. The principal astronomical system was the *Kaliyuga Era*, which appears to have been adopted in the fourth century A.D. It began on Feb. 18, 3102 B.C. The chronological system of Northern India, known as the *Vikrama Samvat Era*, prevalent in Western India, began on Feb. 23, 57 B.C. The year A.D. 1964 is, therefore, the year 2021 of the Vikrama Era.

The *Saka Era* of Southern India dating from March 3, A.D. 78, was declared the uniform national calendar of the Republic of India with effect from March 22, 1957, to be used concurrently with the Gregorian Calendar. As revised, the year of the new *Saka Era* begins at the spring equinox, with five successive months of 31 days and seven of 30 days in ordinary years; six months of each length in leap years. The year A.D. 1964 is 1886 of the revised *Saka Era*.

In the Hills, the *Saptarshi Era* dates from the

moment when the Saptarshi, or saints, were translated and became the stars of the Great Bear in 3076 B.C.

The *Buddhists* reckoned from the death of Buddha in 543 B.C. (the actual date being 487 B.C.); and the epoch of the *Jains* was the death of Vardhamana, the founder of their faith, in 527 B.C.

Iran.—The chronology of Iran (Persia) is the Era of Hejira, which began on A.D. 622, July 16. The *Zoroastrian Calendar* was used in pre-Moslem days and is still employed by Zoroastrians in Iran and India (Parsees) with era beginning A.D. 632, June 16.

Japan.—The Japanese Calendar is the Gregorian, and is essentially the same as that in use by Western nations, the years, months and weeks being of the same length and beginning on the same days as those of the Western Calendar. The numeration of the years is different, for Japanese chronology is based on a system of epochs or periods, each of which begins at the accession of an Emperor or other important occurrence, the method being not unlike the former British system of Regnal years, but differing from it in the particular that each year of a period closes on Dec. 31. The Japanese scheme begins about A.D. 650 and the three latest epochs are defined by the reigns of Emperors, whose actual names are not necessarily used:—

Epoch Meiji from 1868 Oct. 13 to 1912 July 31
„ Taishō „ 1912 Aug. 1 to 1926 Dec. 25
„ Shōwa „ 1926 Dec. 26

Hence the year Shōwa 39 begins 1964 Jan. 1. The months are not named. They are known as First Month, Second Month, etc., first month being the equivalent to January. The days of the week are Nichiyōbi (Sun-day), Getsuyōbi (Moon-day), Kayōbi (Fire-day), Suiyōbi (Water-day), Mokuyōbi (Wood-day), Kinyōbi (Metal-day), Doyōbi (Earth-day).

EARTHQUAKES SINCE 1531

(Approximate numbers of persons killed appear in brackets.)

1531	Jan. 26	Portugal, Lisbon (30,000).
1556	Jan. 24	China, Shensi (830,000).
1693	Jan. 11	Catania (60,000).
1703	Dec. 30	Japan (200,000).
1731	Oct.–Nov.	China.
1737	Oct. 11	India, Calcutta (300,000).
1746		Peru.
1754	Sept. 2	Egypt, Cairo.
1755	Nov. 1	Portugal, Lisbon (60,000). Fire and tidal wave.
1783	Feb. 5–Mar. 28	Calabria (60,000). Followed until 1786 by further series of shocks (38 severe).
1811		Madrid.
1819		Kutch.
1822		Syria, Aleppo (20,000). Chile.
1835		Chile.
1857	Dec. 16	Naples, Salerno (12,000).
1859	Mar. 22	Ecuador, Quito.
1868	Aug. 13–15	Peru (25,000).
1883	July–Aug.	Italy, Ischia.
1886	Aug. 31	U.S.A., Charleston.
1891	Oct. 28	Japan, Mino Awari.
1895		Ljubljana (Laibach).
1895–1905		Japan. 257 earthquakes.
1896		Japan, Sanikro. Krakatoa, with volcanic disturbance.
1897	June 12	India, Assam.
1899		Alaska, Yakutat Bay.
1902		West Indies, Mont Pelée (20,000).
1905		India, Kangra (20,000).
1906	April 18	U.S.A., California. Large part of San Francisco destroyed.
	Aug. 17	Chile, Valparaiso (2,500).
1907	Jan. 17	Jamaica, Kingston.
1908	Dec. 28	Italy, Messina (77,000).
1909		Persia, Luristan.
1911		Mexico.
1923	Sept. 1–1924 Jan. 15	Japan, Tokyo and Yokohama destroyed. Deaths 180,000; houses destroyed by fire, 447,128; by collapse, 128,266.
1926		Azores, Horta.
1927		Herzegovina and Dalmatia.
1927	Feb. 16	North Japan and Kamchatka.
	Mar. 7	Japan, Tadjima.
	July 11	Palestine.
1928	Dec.	Chile, Talca.
1930	July 23	Italy, Naples (2,142; injured 4,551).
1931	Mar. 31	Nicaragua, Manaquao (Managua) destroyed.
	Feb. 3	New Zealand.
1932	June 3	Mexico.
1933	Sept. 19	China.
1935	May 31	Baluchistan, Quetta (Town destroyed) (60,000).
1936		West Indies, Montserrat.
1937	June 2.	New Britain, Rabaul.
1938	April 19–20	Turkey, Anatolia.
1939	Jan. 26	Chile (20,000). Dec.–Feb. 1940. Turkey, Anatolia (30,000).
1950	May 21	Peru, Cuzco (100).
	July 8–9	Colombia (270).
	Aug. 15	India, Assam (1,500).
1951	May 6	Salvador (1,000).
1953	Mar. 18	Turkey (266).
	Aug. 10	Greece, Ionian Islands (476).
	Sept. 10	Cyprus, Paphos (40).
1954	April 30 and May 12	Greece, Thessaly (21).
	Sept. 9	Algeria, Orleansville (1,409).
1956	June 10–17	Afghanistan (2,000).
	Nov. 4	Persia, Luristan (350).
1957	April 24	Turkey, Fethiye (10).
	May 26	Anatolia (26).
	July 2–11	Persia, Sangchal (180).
	July 28	Mexico (56).
	Dec. 4	Mongolia (30).
	Dec. 13	Persia, Kermanshah, Hamadan and Sanandraj (1,306). 29 villages destroyed, including Farsinaj (950).
1958	Aug. 16–21	Persia (191).
1960	Feb. 29	Morocco, Agadir. 12,000 killed in the total destruction of the town. Accompanied by a tidal wave.
	April 25	Persia, Lar and Herash (3,000).
1960	May 21–25	Chile (5,000). Heavy destruction in Concepcion, Puerto Montt and on Chiloe Island. Accompanied by tidal waves and the eruption of 3 new volcanoes.
1963	July 26	Yugoslavia (1,029). Much of the town of Skopje destroyed and 100,000 persons made homeless.

The World

THE *Superficial Area* of the Earth is estimated to be 196,836,000 square miles, of which 55,786,000 square miles are Land and 141,050,000 square miles Water. The *Diameter* of the Earth at the Equator is 7,926¼ English miles, and at the Poles 7,900 English miles. The Equatorial *Circumference* is 24,901·8 English miles, divided into 360 Degrees of Longitude, each of 69·17 English (or 60 Geographical) miles; these Degrees are measured from the Meridian of Greenwich, and numbered East and West of that point to meet in the Antipodes at the 180th Degree. Distance North and South of the Equator is marked by Parallels of Latitude, which proceed from zero (at the Equator) to 90° at the Poles.

The velocity of a given point of the Earth's surface at the Equator exceeds 1,000 miles an hour (24,901·8 miles in 24 hours); the Earth's velocity in its orbit round the Sun is about 66,600 miles an hour (584,000,000 miles in 365¼ days). The Earth is distant from the Sun 93,000,000 miles, on the average.

AREA AND POPULATION

The total population of the world in June, 1961, was estimated by the *United Nations Statistical Yearbook* at 3,069,000,000 compared with 2,509,000,000 in 1950 and 1,811,000,000 in 1920. Figures of areas in the following table are of land area and inland water, but exclude uninhabited polar regions and some uninhabited islands. Figures for Europe and Asia exclude U.S.S.R. which is shown separately. Figures for Oceania include Hawaii.

Continent, etc.	Area		Estimated Population, 1961
	Sq. miles '000	Sq. km. '000	
Europe	1,913	4,955	430,000,000
Asia*	10,401	26,940	1,721,000,000
U.S.S.R.	8,649	22,402	218,000,000
Africa	11,684	30,366	261,000,000
America	16,379	42,041	422,000,000
Oceania	3,304	8,558	17,000,000
Total	52,225	135,262	3,069,000,000

* Includes Asiatic Turkey.

A United Nations report (*The Future Growth of World Population*) in 1958, pointed out that the population of the world had increased since the beginning of the 20th Century at an unprecedented rate: in 1850 it was estimated at 1,094,000,000 and in 1900 at 1,550,000,000, an increase of 42 per cent. in 50 years. By 1925 it had risen to 1,907,000,000—23 per cent. in 25 years—and by 1950 it had reached 2,500,000,000, an increase of 31 per cent. in 25 years. Levels of population and the trend in distribution of the population by continents as forecast for the years 1975 and 2000 were:— [millions]

Continent	1975		2000	
	Estimated Population	Per cent.	Estimated Population	Per cent.
Europe‡	751	19·6	947	15·1
Asia*	2,210	57·7	3,870	61·8
Africa	303	7·9	517	8·2
N. America	240	6·3	312	5·0
Latin America†	303	7·9	592	9·4
Oceania	21	0·5	29	0·5
World	3,828	100	6,267	100

* Excluding U.S.S.R. † Mexico and the remainder of America south of U.S.A. ‡ Including U.S.S.R.

THE CONTINENTS.

Europe (including European Russia) forms about one-fourteenth of the land surface of the globe. Its length from the North Cape, 71° 12′ N., to Cape Matapan, in the south of Greece, 36° 23′ N., is about 2,400 miles, and its breadth from Cape St. Vincent to the Urals is about 3,300 miles. The political boundary between Europe and Asia extends some distance beyond the Urals, to include the mining regions; in the south-east it follows the valley of the Manych, north of the Caucasus.

Asia (including Asiatic Russia) extends over nearly one-third of the land surface of the globe. The distance between its extreme longitudes, the west coast of Asia Minor (26° E.) and the East Cape (170° W.), is 6,000 miles. The extreme latitudes, Cape Chelyuskin (78° 30″ N.) and Cape Bulus (76 miles north of the Equator), are 5,350 miles apart. Asia is bounded by the ocean on all sides except the west. The Isthmus of Suez connects it with Africa. The land boundary between Europe and Asia is formed on the west mainly by the Ural Mountains and the Ural River. In the south-west the valley of the Manych, which stretches from the Caspian Sea to the mouth of the Don, is now taken as the line between the two continents, although the Caucasus was formerly considered as belonging to Europe. The islands of the archipelago which lie in the south-east between the continents of Asia and Australia may be divided into two groups by a line passing east of Timor, Timor Laut, the Kei Islands and the Moluccas.

Africa is about three times the area of Europe. its extreme longitudes are 17° W. at Cape Verde and 51° 27′ 52″ E. at Ras Hafun. The extreme latitudes are Cape Blanco in 37° N. and Cape Agulhas in 35° S., at a distance of about 5,000 miles. It is surrounded by seas on all sides, except in the narrow isthmus through which is cut the Suez Canal, and may be considered as a great peninsula of the Eurasian continent.

North America, including Mexico, is a little less than twice the size of Europe. Its extreme longtitudes extend from a little west of 170° W. to 52½° W. in the east of Newfoundland, and its extreme latitudes from about 80° N. lat. to 15° N. lat. in the south of Mexico. It is surrounded by seas on all sides except in the south, where it joins the Isthmian States of *Central America*, which have an area of about 200,000 square miles. The area of the *West Indies* is about 65,000 square miles, a little more than half that of the United Kingdom. They extend from about 27° N. latitude to 10° N. latitude.

South America is a little more than 1¾ times the size of Europe. The extreme longitudes are Cape Branco 35° W. and Punta Parina 81° W., and the extreme latitudes, Punta Gallinas, 12½° N. and Cape Horn 56° S. South America is surrounded by the ocean, except where it is joined to Central America by the narrow isthmus through which is cut the Panama Canal.

Oceania extends over an area 1½ times the size of Europe, from Australia (in the West) to the most easterly islands of Polynesia, and from New Zealand (in the south) to the Sandwich Islands (Hawaii) in the north.

Area and Population of the World by Continents

The appended tables of area and population are based on such information as is immediately available.

With regard to areas it will be realized that no complete survey of many countries has yet been either achieved or even undertaken and that consequently accurate area figures are not available. In addition, among the results of the war of 1939–1945 is a readjustment of boundaries which have not yet been definitely settled. For the constituent parts of the United Kingdom and for the area and population of separate departments, overseas provinces, etc., of foreign countries, see main articles.

The populations given hereunder are derived from various sources; some have as their basis an authenticated census; some are official and some are unofficial estimates. In certain cases later information is given in the Dominions, Colonies or Foreign Countries Sections of the ALMANACK. What has been said about the survey of many of the world's countries applies equally to the question of census.

EUROPE AND THE MEDITERRANEAN

COUNTRY	Form of Government	Area Sq. Miles	Population	Per Sq. Mile	Capital	Population of Capital
Albania	Republic	10,700	1,394,000	130	Tirana	50,000
Andorra	Republic	180	6,000	33	Andorra La Vella	2,200
Austria	Republic	32,000	7,128,000	223	Vienna	1,627,566
Belgium	Kingdom	11,800	9,251,000	784	Brussels	1,029,693
Bulgaria	Republic	43,000	7,798,000	181	Sofia	725,756
Cyprus	Republic	3,500	563,000	161	Nicosia	87,000
Czechoslovakia	Republic	53,000	13,742,000	259	Prague	1,003,341
Denmark	Kingdom	16,600	4,585,000	276	Ψ Copenhagen	923,974
Finland	Republic	130,000	4,490,000	35	Ψ Helsinki	467,500
France	Republic	213,000	46,200,000	217	Paris	3,075,678
Germany:—						
Federal Republic of Germany	Republic	95,700	53,975,000	565	Bonn	145,000
Eastern Germany	Republic	41,400	17,300,000	418	East Berlin	1,200,000
Gibraltar	British	2	24,502	12,251	Ψ Gibraltar	20,000
Greece	Kingdom	51,000	8,389,000	164	Athens	1,852,709
Hungary	Republic	36,000	9,998,000	278	Budapest	1,807,030
Iceland	Republic	40,500	183,000	4	Ψ Reykjavik	74,664
Irish Republic	Republic	26,600	2,818,000	106	Ψ Dublin	537,448
Italy	Republic	131,000	50,003,000	382	Rome	2,160,773
Liechtenstein	Principality	60	17,800	297	Vaduz	3,620
Luxemburg	Grand Duchy	1,000	314,800	315	Luxemburg	71,653
Malta and Gozo	British	122	329,000	2,697	Ψ Valletta	18,287
Monaco	Principality	½	20,000	..	Monaco	2,422
Netherlands	Kingdom	13,500	11,938,000	884	The Hague Ψ Amsterdam	604,112 866,830
Norway	Kingdom	125,183	3,604,000	29	Ψ Oslo	461,591
Poland	Republic	121,000	30,133,000	249	Warsaw	1,171,000
Portugal	Republic	34,500	8,981,000	260	Ψ Lisbon	1,397,213
Roumania	Republic	91,600	18,567,000	203	Bucharest	1,225,507
San Marino	Republic	23	17,000	739	San Marino	2,000
Spain	Kingdom	197,000	30,947,000	157	Madrid	2,000,000
Sweden	Kingdom	173,000	7,542,000	44	Ψ Stockholm	807,127
Switzerland	Republic	15,950	5,608,000	351	Berne	168,900
Turkey in Europe	Republic	9,250	2,262,000	244	*See* Asia	..
United Kingdom of Great Britain and Northern Ireland†	Kingdom	93,000	53,301,000	573	Ψ London	8,176,810
U.S.S.R. (Europe):						
*R.S.F.S.R.**	Republic	1,970,000	*117,494,000*	60	Moscow	5,032,000
Ukraine	Republic	232,000	41,893,000	181	Kiev	1,102,000
Belorussia	Republic	80,000	8,060,000	101	Minsk	509,000
Moldavia	Republic	13,000	2,880,000	222	Kishinev	214,000
Estonia	Republic	17,400	1,196,000	69	Ψ Tallinn	280,000
Latvia	Republic	25,000	2,094,000	84	Ψ Riga	605,000
Lithuania	Republic	26,000	2,713,000	104	Vilnius	235,000
Vatican City State	State	109 *acres*	940	..	Vatican City	940
Yugoslavia	Republic	99,000	18,841,000	190	Belgrade	594,000

*Total population, Europe and Asia. †Estimated, June 30, 1962. Ψ Seaport.

ASIA

The expressions "The Near East," "The Middle East" and "The Far East" often appear in the Press of English-speaking countries, but have no definite boundaries. The following limits have been suggested:—*Near East* (Turkey to Persia) 25°–60° E. long., *Middle East* (Baluchistan to Burma) 60°–100° E. long., *Far East* (Siam to Japan) 100°–160° long.

COUNTRY	Form of Government	Area Sq. miles	Population	Per Sq. Mile	Capital	Population of Capital
Aden	British	75	200,000	2,666	Ψ Aden	32,500
Aden Protectorate	..	112,000	1,000,000	9	..	..
Afghanistan	Kingdom	250,000	11,000,000	44	Kabul	300,000
Bahrain	Shaikhdom	213	143,000	671	Ψ Manama	61,726
Bhutan	Kingdom	18,000	700,000	39	Punakha	..
Brunei	British	2,226	84,000	38	Ψ Brunei	37,000
Burma	Republic	262,000	21,527,000	82	Ψ Rangoon	740,000
Cambodia	Kingdom	70,000	5,000,000	71	Ψ Phnom Penh	550,000
Ceylon	Dominion	25,000	8,098,000	323	Ψ Colombo	48,800
China	Republic	4,300,000	656,630,000	153	Peking	4,010,000
Formosa (Taiwan)	Republic	13,800	10,050,000	728	Taipeh	927,400
Macau	Portuguese	5	188,000	37,600	Ψ Macau	157,175
Hong Kong	British	398	3,527,000	8,862	Ψ Victoria	767,000
India	Republic	1,260,000	433,619,000	344	Delhi	2,344,051
Indonesia	Republic	735,000	97,000,000	132	Ψ Djakarta	3,000,000
Iraq	Republic	172,000	6,538,000	38	Baghdad	552,047
Israel	Republic	8,000	2,332,000	291	Jerusalem	166,301
Japan	Kingdom	183,000	95,180,000	520	Tokyo	10,003,055
Jordan	Kingdom	30,000	1,752,000	58	Amman	244,599
Korea:—						
North Korea	Republic	48,000	6,500,000	136	Pyongyang	286,000
South Korea	Republic	37,000	26,278,000	710	Seoul	2,444,883
Kuwait	Amirate	5,800	322,000	56	Ψ Kuwait	210,000
Laos	Kingdom	90,000	2,500,000	28	Vientiane	80,000
Lebanon	Republic	4,300	1,750,000	407	Ψ Beirut	500,000
Malaysia	Federation	130,000	10,215,000	79	Kuala Lumpur	316,230
Malaya	Federation	51,000	7,250,533	142	Kuala Lumpur	316,230
*Sabah**		30,000	454,000	15	Ψ Jesselton	21,497
Sarawak		48,000	777,000	16	Kuching	50,576
Singapore		224	1,733,000	7,737	..	..
Maldive Islands	Sultanate	115	90,000	783	Ψ Malé	10,000
Muscat and Oman	Sultanate	82,000	550,000	7	Ψ Muscat	6,208
Nepal	Kingdom	54,000	9,388,000	174	Katmandu	122,507
Pakistan	Republic	365,000	93,812,000	257	Rawalpindi	240,000
Persia (Iran)	Kingdom	628,000	21,000,000	33	Tehran	1,500,000
Philippine Islds.	Republic	115,000	27,455,000	239	Ψ Manila	3,006,627
Qatar	Shaikhdom	4,000	45,000	11	Doha	40,000
Saudi Arabia	Kingdom	927,000	6,000,000	6	Riyadh	100,000
Syria	Republic	71,000	4,500,000	63	Damascus	450,000
Thailand (Siam)	Kingdom	198,000	30,000,000	152	Ψ Bangkok	2,318,000
Timor, Eastern	Portuguese	7,329	442,000	60	Ψ Dili	7,000
Trucial States	Shaikhdoms	32,000	110,000	3	..	..
Turkey in Asia	Republic	285,000	21,850,000	77	Ankara	500,000
U.S.S.R. (Asia):—						
R.S.F.S.R. (Asia)	Republic	6,640,000	*See* Europe			
Armenia (Hyastan)	Republic	11,000	1,768,000	161	Erevan	509,000
Azerbaidjan	Republic	33,000	3,700,000	112	Baku	968,000
Georgia	Republic	27,000	4,049,000	150	Tbilisi	664,000
Turkmenistan	Republic	188,000	1,520,000	8	Ashkhabad	170,000
Uzbekistan	Republic	158,000	8,113,000	51	Tashkent	911,000
Tadjikistan	Republic	54,000	1,982,000	37	Dushanbe	224,000
Kazakhstan	Republic	1,064,000	9,301,000	9	Alma Ata	455,000
Kirghizia	Republic	77,000	2,063,000	27	Frunze	217,000
Vietnam:—						
Northern Zone	Republic	63,000	16,500,000	262	Hanoi	750,000
Southern Zone	Republic	66,000	14,072,000	213	Saigon	1,400,000
Yemen	Kingdom	74,000	4,000,000	54	Taiz	20,000

Ψ Seaport. * *Formerly* British North Borneo and Labuan.

AFRICA

Country	Form of Government	Area Sq. Miles	Population	Per Sq. Mile	Capital	Population of Capital
Algeria	Republic	856,000	7,500,000	9	Ψ Algiers	850,000
Angola	Portuguese	488,000	4,145,000	8	Ψ St. Paul de Luanda	40,000
Basutoland	British Protect.	11,700	642,000	55	Maseru	5,739
Bechuanaland	British Protect.	222,000	294,000	1	Mafeking	..
Burundi	Kingdom	10,700	2,213,000	207	Kitega	..
Cameroon	Republic	432,000	4,907,000	11	Yaoundé	60,000
Cape Verde Islands	Portuguese	1,516	148,000	98	Ψ Praia	6,000
Central African Republic	Republic	234,000	1,227,000	5	Bangui	82,300
Chad	Republic	488,000	2,675,000	5	Fort Lamy	45,600
Congo	Republic	130,000	864,000	7	Brazzaville	136,000
Congolese Republic†	Republic	906,000	14,150,000	16	Leopoldville	900,000
Dahomey	Republic	47,000	1,934,000	41	Ψ Porto Novo	58,500
Egypt, *see* U.A.R.						
Ethiopia (Abyssinia)	Kingdom	400,000	21,800,000	54	Addis Ababa	449,021
Gaboon	Republic	101,400	440,000	4	Ψ Libreville	16,700
Gambia	British	4,000	264,000	66	Ψ Bathurst	23,600
Ghana	Republic	92,000	6,691,000	53	Ψ Accra	491,060
Guinea	Republic	97,000	3,000,000	31	Ψ Conakry	100,000
Ivory Coast	Republic	189,000	3,300,000	17	Ψ Abidjan	212,000
Kenya	British	220,000	7,287,000	33	Nairobi	297,000
Liberia	Republic	43,000	1,250,000	29	Ψ Monrovia	70,000
Libya	Kingdom	810,000	1,195,000	1	Ψ Tripoli	170,000
Madagascar	Republic	228,000	5,658,000	25	Antananarivo	254,271
Mali	Republic	582,000	4,100,000	7	Bamako	110,000
Mauritania	Republic	322,000	727,000	2	Nouakchott	..
Mauritius, etc.	British	805	680,000	844	Ψ Port Louis	92,400
Morocco	Kingdom	180,000	11,626,000	65	Ψ Rabat	227,445
Mozambique	Portuguese	298,000	5,732,000	19	Ψ Lourenço Marques	48,000
Niger	Republic	484,000	2,870,000	6	Niamey	24,300
Nigeria	Federation	357,000	40,000,000	112	Ψ Lagos	400,000
Nyasaland	British	37,000	2,921,000	79	Zomba	7,500
Portuguese Guinea	Portuguese	14,000	511,000	36	Ψ Bissau	6,000
Réunion	French Dept.	1,000	330,400	330	St. Denis	41,863
Rhodesia, North	British	288,000	2,515,000	9	Lusaka	*9,440
Rhodesia, South	British	150,300	3,839,000	25	Salisbury	299,900
Ruanda	Republic	10,000	2,634,000	263	Kigali	..
St. Helena	British	47	4,624	98	Ψ Jamestown	1,568
Ascension	British	38	336	9	Ψ Georgetown	..
Tristan da Cunha	British	45	..	..	Ψ Edinburgh	..
St. Tomé & Principé	Portuguese	372	60,159	162	Ψ São Tomé	3,187
Senegal	Republic	78,000	2,973,000	38	Ψ Dakar	383,000
Seychelles	British	156	44,000	282	Ψ Victoria	10,500
Sierra Leone	Dominion	28,000	2,400,000	86	Ψ Freetown	85,000
Somalia	Republic	246,000	1,990,000	8	Ψ Mogadishu	150,000
Somaliland, French	French	9,000	67,000	7	Ψ Jibuti	17,000
South Africa	Republic	473,000	15,983,000	34	Pretoria Ψ Cape Town	422,590 807,211
S.W. Africa	Mandate	318,000	525,000	1	Windhoek	13,000
Spanish Guinea	Spanish	10,000	204,000	20	Ψ Santa Isabel	9,000
Spanish Presidios:—						
Ceuta	Spanish	5	64,000	..	..	..
Melilla	Spanish	72	87,000	..	..	..
Sahara	Spanish	125,000	36,000	..	Villa Cisneros	250
Sudan	Republic	977,000	12,109,000	12	Khartoum	124,000
Swaziland	British	6,700	269,500	40	Mbabane	1,092
Tanganyika	Republic	363,000	9,404,000	26	Ψ Dar es Salaam	128,742
Togo	Republic	20,000	1,440,000	72	Lomé	70,000
Tunisia	Republic	45,000	4,198,000	93	Ψ Tunis	680,000
Uganda	Dominion	80,000	6,538,000	82	Kampala	12,000
United Arab Republic	Republic	386,000	26,059,000	68	Cairo	3,346,000
Voltaic Republic	Republic	100,000	3,635,000	36	Ouagadougou	63,000
Zanzibar	British	1,020	299,000	293	Ψ Zanzibar	45,284

† *Formerly* Belgian Congo. * European population. Ψ Seaport.

NORTH AMERICA

COUNTRY	Form of Government	Area Sq. Miles	Population	Per Sq. Mile	Capital	Population of Capital
Canada	Dominion	3,560,000	18,238,000	5	Ottawa	268,206
Mexico	Republic	758,000	34,626,000	46	Mexico City	4,829,402
St. Pierre and Miquelon	French	93	4,900	53	Ψ St. Pierre	3,500
United States*	Republic	3,554,000	183,285,000	52	Washington, D.C.	763,956

* The 50 states and Federal *District of Columbia*; for area and population of individual States, *see* main article.

CENTRAL AMERICA AND WEST INDIES

COUNTRY	Form of Government	Area Sq. Miles	Population	Per Sq. Mile	Capital	Population of Capital
Bahamas	British	4,400	107,000	24	Ψ Nassau	54,557
Bermuda	British	21	46,342	2,207	Ψ Hamilton	2,814
British Honduras	British	8,900	90,000	10	Ψ Belize	32,000
Costa Rica	Republic	19,600	1,302,000	66	San José	167,573
Cuba	Republic	44,000	6,499,000	148	Ψ Havana	783,162
Dominican Republic	Republic	19,300	3,014,000	156	Santa Domingo	462,192
Guadeloupe	French Dept.	688	266,400	387	Ψ Pointe à Pitre	26,200
Guatemala	Republic	42,000	4 017,000	96	Guatemala	417,218
Haiti	Republic	10,000	4,000 000	400	Ψ Port au Prince	250,000
Honduras	Republic	43,000	1,887,000	44	Tegucigalpa	133 877
Jamaica	Dominion	4,400	1,613,000	367	Ψ Kingston	445,797
Martinique	French Dept.	400	274,400	686	Ψ Fort de France	60,600
Netherlands Antilles	Netherlands	394	187,041	480	Ψ Willemstad	45,000
Nicaragua	Republic	57,000	1,605,000	28	Managua	241,409
Panama	Republic	31,900	1,068,000	33	Ψ Panama City	271,425
Panama Canal Zone	U.S.A.	362	42,000	116	Ψ Balboa Heights	..
Puerto Rico	U.S.A.	3,400	2,350,000	691	Ψ San Juan	588,805
Salvador	Republic	7,700	2,501,000	325	San Salvador	248,100
Trinidad and Tobago	Dominion	1,980	828,000	418	Ψ Port of Spain	93,954
Virgin Islands:—						
British	British	59	7,350	125	Ψ Road Town	900
U.S.	U.S.A.	133	32,000	241	Ψ Charlotte Amalie	11,000
West Indies, Brit.:—						
Antigua and Barbuda	British	171	57,000	333	Ψ St. John	21,000
Barbados	British	166	235,000	1,416	Ψ Bridgetown	11,452
Cayman Islds.	British	100	7,616	76	Ψ George Town	2 558
Dominica	British	290	59,000	203	Ψ Roseau	12,577
Grenada	British	133	89,000	669	Ψ St. George's	7,305
Montserrat	British	32	12,000	375	Ψ Plymouth	3,500
St. Kitts-Nevis	British	153	57,000	373	Ψ Basseterre	15,897
St. Lucia	British	238	86,000	361	Ψ Castries	32,215
St. Vincent	British	150	80,000	533	Ψ Kingstown	16,141
Turks and Caicos	British	166	5,700	34	Ψ Grand Turk	2,339

Ψ Seaport.

ROMAN EMPERORS

[The *First Triumvirate* (Julius Cæsar, Pompey and Crassus) 60-53 B.C.]

THE TWELVE CÆSARS

I. Caius **JULIUS CÆSAR**, *born* A.U.C. 651 (102 B.C.); *Dictator* A.U.C. 705 (48 B.C.); *Assassinated* A.U.C. 709. (44 B.C.).

[The *Second Triumvirate* (Octavian, Antony and Lepidus) 44-31 B.C.]

II. Caius Julius Cæsar Octavianus **AUGUSTUS**, *born* 63 B.C.; *Emperor* 27 B.C.; *Died* A.D. 14.
III. Claudius Nero Cæsar **TIBERIUS**, *born* 24 B.C.; *Emperor* A.D. 14; *Died* A.D. 37.
IV. Caius Cæsar **CALIGULA**, *born* A.D. 12; *Emperor* A.D. 37; *Assassinated* A.D. 41.
V. Tiberius Drusus **CLAUDIUS**, *born* 10 B.C.; *Emperor* A.D. 41; *Assassinated* A.D. 54.
VI. Claudius **NERO**, *born* A.D. 37; *Emperor* A.D. 54; *Suicide* A.D. 68.
VII. Servius Sulpicius **GALBA**, *born* 3 B.C.; *Emperor* A.D. 68; *Assassinated* A.D. 69.
VIII. Marcus Salvius **OTHO**, *born* A.D. 32; *Emperor* A.D. 69; *Suicide* A.D. 69.
IX. Aulus **VITELLIUS**, *born* A.D. 15; *Emperor* A.D. 69; *Assassinated* A.D. 69.
X. Titus Flavius **VESPASIAN**, *born* A.D. 9; *Emperor* A.D. 69; *Died* A.D. 79.
XI. Flavius Sabinus Vespasianus **TITUS**, *born* A.D. 48; *Emperor* A.D. 79; *Died* A.D. 81.
XII. Titus Flavius **DOMITIAN**, *born* A.D. 52; *Emperor* A.D. 81; *Assassinated* A.D. 96.

SOUTH AMERICA

Country	Form of Government	Area Sq. Miles	Population	Per Sq. Mile	Capital	Population of Capital
Argentina	Republic	1,080,000	20,959,000	19	Ψ Buenos Aires	4,500,000
Bolivia	Republic	415,000	3,462,000	8	La Paz	347,394
Brazil	Republic	3,289,000	66,302,000	20	Brasilia	142,000
Chile	Republic	290,000	7,440,000	25	Santiago	1,627,962
Colombia	Republic	462,000	13,500,000	29	Bogotá	1,064,740
Ecuador	Republic	226,000	4,169,000	18	Quito	267,798
Falkland Islands	British	4,700	2,172	..	Ψ Stanley	1,074
Guiana, *British*	British	83,000	603,000	7	Ψ Georgetown	72,991
French	French Dept.	35,000	30,900	1	Ψ Cayenne	13,300
Netherlands' (Surinam)	Netherlands	54,000	302,000	6	Paramaribo	86,400
Paraguay	Republic	157,000	1,800,000	12	Ψ Asunción	300,000
Peru	Republic	531,000	10,365,000	20	Lima	1,715,971
Uruguay	Republic	72,000	3,000,000	42	Ψ Monte Video	900,000
Venezuela	Republic	352,000	7,524,000	22	Caracas	1,257,515

OCEANIA

Country	Form of Government	Area Sq. Miles	Population	Per Sq. Mile	Capital	Population of Capital
Australia	Commonwealth	2,971,000	10,508,000	3	Canberra	63,313
Norfolk Island	Australian	15	877	58	Ψ Kingston	..
Antarctica	Australian	2,472,000	..	..	..	..
British Solomon Is.	Brit. Protectorate.	11,500	130,000	11	Ψ Honiara	..
Fiji	British	7,100	427 851	60	Ψ Suva	37,371
French Polynesia	French	2,500	77,000	31	Ψ Papeete	15,220
Gilbert and Ellice Is.	British	360	47,500	132	Tarawa	..
Guam	U.S.A.	209	67,000	321	Agaña	..
Mariana, Caroline and Marshall Islands†	United Nations	687	81,000	119	Saipan	..
Nauru	Brit. Mandate	8	4,599	575	Ψ Nauru	..
New Caledonia	French	7,200	68,000	9	Ψ Noumea	..
New Hebrides	Condominium	5,700	60,000	11	Ψ Vila	4,000
New Zealand	Dominion	104,000	2,440,000	23	Ψ Wellington	153,300
Cook Islands and Niue	N.Z.	200	23,000	115	Avarua	..
Ross Dependency	N.Z.	175,000	198	..	..	..
Papua and New Guinea	Australian Mandate	184,000	1,972,000	11	Ψ Port Moresby	3,000
Samoa:—						
Eastern	U.S.A.	76	20,000	260	Ψ Pago Pago	1,251
Western	Republic	1,130	114,000	100	Ψ Apia	25,000
Tonga, etc.	Brit. Protectorate.	270	65,600	230	Ψ Nukualofa	..

† Trust Territory of the Pacific Islands. Ψ Seaport.

OCEAN AREAS AND DEPTHS

The greatest known Ocean Depth (in the Pacific, off the Philippines, 36,198 feet) is not much greater than the greatest land height (in the Himalayas); but the mean depth of the Ocean floor exceeds 12,000 feet, while the mean height of the surface of the land area of the Earth above sea level is only 2,300 feet. The following table gives the areas of the principal oceans and seas, with the greatest known depth of each:—

Oceans

Name	Area of Basin (sq. miles)	Greatest Depth (feet)
Pacific	63,986,000	Mariana Trench 36,198
Atlantic	31,530,000	Porto Rico Trench, 27,498
Indian	28,350,000	Diamantina, 26,400
Arctic	5,541,600	17,850

Seas

Name	Area of Basin (sq. miles)	Greatest Depth (feet)
Malay	3,137,000	Kei Trench, 21,342
Central American	1,770,170	Cayman, 23,000
Mediterranean	1,145,000	Matapan, 14,435
Behring	878,000	Buldir Trough, 13,422
Okhotsk	582,000	Kurile Trough, 11,154
East China	480,000	*about* 10,500
Hudson Bay	472,000	*about* 1,500
Japan	405,000	*about* 10,200
Andaman	305,000	*about* 11,000
North Sea	221,000	Skaggerak, 1,998
Red Sea	178,000	20° N., 7,254
Baltic	158,000	*about* 1,300

THE LARGEST CITIES OF THE WORLD

Ψ = Seaport.	Pop.
TOKYO, Japan (1962)	10,003,055
Ψ LONDON, England (1962)	8,176,810
Ψ New York, U.S.A. (1960)	7,781,984
Ψ Shanghai, China (1957)	6,900,000
MOSCOW, U.S.S.R. (1959)	5,032,000
MEXICO CITY, Mexico (1960)	4,829,402
Ψ BUENOS AIRES, Argentina (1958)	4,500,000
Ψ Bombay, India (1961)	4,152,056
PEKING, China (1957)	4,010,000
Sao Paulo, Brazil (1960)	3,850,000
Chicago, U.S.A. (1960)	3,550,404
Ψ Calcutta, India (1962)	3,439,887
BERLIN, Germany (1960)	3,402,200
CAIRO, U.A.R. (1960)	3,346,000
Ψ Leningrad, U.S.S.R. (1959)	3,300,000
Ψ Rio de Janeiro, Brazil (1960)	3,288,000
Tientsin, China (1957)	3,220,000
Ψ Osaka, Japan (1962)	3,140,000
PARIS, France (1962)	3,075,678
Ψ MANILA, Philippines (1960)	3,006,627
Ψ Djakarta, Indonesia (196[illegible])	3,000,000
Ψ Los Angeles, U.S.A. (1960)	2,479,015
SEOUL, Korea (1960)	2,444,883
Shenyang (Mukden), China (1957)	2,411,000
DELHI, India (1961)	2,344,051
Ψ BANGKOK, Thailand (1960)	2,318,000
Ψ Sydney, New South Wales (1962)	2,215,970
ROME, Italy (1962)	2,160,773
Wuhan, China (1957)	2,146,000
Chunking, China (1957)	2,121,000
Hyderabad, India (1962)	2,062,995
Ψ Philadelphia, U.S.A. (1960)	2,002,512
MADRID, Spain (1958)	2,000,000
Ψ Melbourne, Victoria (1962)	1,946,500
Ψ Karachi, Pakistan (1961)	1,916,000
ATHENS, Greece (1961)	1,852,709
Ψ Hamburg, Germany (1961)	1,845,107
Ψ Canton, China (1957)	1,840,000
BUDAPEST, Hungary (1960)	1,807,030
Ψ Barcelona, Spain (1960)	1,800,000
Ψ Singapore, Malaysia (1962)	1,733,000
Ψ Madras, India (1951)	1,725,216
LIMA, Peru (1963)	1,715,971
Detroit, U.S.A. (1960)	1,670,144
Ψ Nagoya, Japan (1962)	1,655,000
SANTIAGO, Chile (1956)	1,627,962
VIENNA, Austria (1961)	1,627,566
Ψ Toronto, Canada (1961)	1,618,787
Milan, Italy (1961)	1,580,978
Harbin, China (1957)	1,552,000
Ψ Alexandria, Egypt (1960)	1,513,000
Lushun-Dairen, China (1957)	1,508,000
TEHRAN, Persia (1956)	1,500,000
Ψ Yokohama, Japan (1962)	1,459,000
Nanking, China (1957)	1,409,000
SAIGON, S. Vietnam (1957)	1,400,000
Ψ LISBON, Portugal (1960)	1,397,213
Sian, China (1957)	1,310,000
Kyoto, Japan (1962)	1,299,000
Lahore, Pakistan (1961)	1,297,000
CARACAS, Venezuela (1961)	1,257,515
BUCHAREST, Roumania (1960)	1,225,507
Ψ Istanbul, Turkey (1960)	1,214,616
Ψ Montreal, Canada (1961)	1,191,062
Ψ Naples, Italy (1961)	1,179,608
WARSAW, Poland (1961)	1,171,000
Ψ Pusan, Korea (1960)	1,163,614
Kobé, Japan (1962)	1,149,000
Ψ Tsingtao, China (1957)	1,121,000
Birmingham, England (1962)	1,115,080
Johannesburg, S. Africa (1961)	1,110,905
Chengtu, China (1957)	1,107,000
Kiev, U.S.S.R. (1959)	1,102,000
Munich, Germany (1961)	1,080,000
BOGOTA, Colombia (1958)	1,064,740
Ψ Glasgow, Scotland (1962)	1,049,115
BRUSSELS, Belgium (1963)	1,029,693
Taiyuan, China (1957)	1,020,000
Turin, Italy (1961)	1,019,230
PRAGUE, Czechoslovakia (1959)	1,003,341
Baku, U.S.S.R. (1959)	968,000
Gorky, U.S.S.R. (1959)	942,000
Ψ Baltimore, U.S.A. (1960)	939,024
Ψ Houston, U.S.A. (1960)	938,219
Kharkov, U.S.S.R. (1959)	930,000
TAIPEH, Formosa (1961)	927,400
Ψ COPENHAGEN, Denmark (1960)	923,974
Tashkent, U.S.S.R. (1959)	911,000
LEOPOLDVILLE, Congolese Rep. (1963)	900,000
Ψ MONTE VIDEO, Uruguay (1959)	900,000
Novosibirsk, U.S.S.R. (1959)	887,000
Kanpur, India (1961)	881,177
Cleveland, U.S.A. (1960)	876,050
AMSTERDAM, Netherlands (1963)	866,830
ALGIERS, Algeria (1963)	850,000
Ψ CAPE TOWN, S. Africa (1961)	807,211
Ψ STOCKHOLM, Sweden (1962)	807,127
Kuibyshev, U.S.S.R. (1959)	806,000
HANOI, N. Vietnam (1963)	800,000
Cologne, Germany (1961)	795,183
Ψ Vancouver, Canada (1961)	790,165
Ahmedabad, India (1958)	788,333
Recife, Brazil (1960)	784,000
Ψ HAVANA, Cuba (1953)	783,162
Sverdlovsk, U.S.S.R. (1959)	777,000
Ψ Genoa, Italy (1961)	775,107
Ψ VICTORIA, Hong-Kong (1951)	767,000
WASHINGTON, U.S.A. (1960)	763,956
St. Louis, U.S.A. (1960)	750,026
Ψ Liverpool, England (1962)	745,230
Milwaukee, U.S.A. (1960)	741,324
Ψ San Francisco, U.S.A. (1960)	740,316
Ψ RANGOON, Burma (1953)	740,000
Ψ Rotterdam, Netherlands (1963)	730,963
Essen, Germany (1961)	726,000
SOFIA, Bulgaria (1956)	725,756
Lodz, Poland (1961)	723,000
Ψ Donetsk, U.S.S.R. (1959)	701,000

THE SEVEN WONDERS OF THE WORLD

I. THE PYRAMIDS OF EGYPT.—From Gizeh (near Cairo) to a southern limit 60 miles distant. The oldest is that of Zoser, at Saggara, built about 2,700 B.C. The Great Pyramid of Cheops covers more than 12 acres and was originally 481 ft. in height and 756 × 756 ft. at the base.

II. THE HANGING GARDENS OF BABYLON.—Adjoining Nebuchadnezzar's palace, 60 miles south of Baghdad. Terraced gardens, ranging from 75 to 300 ft. above ground level, watered from storage tanks on the highest terrace.

III. THE TOMB OF MAUSOLUS.—At Halicarnassus, in Asia Minor. Built by the widowed Queen Artemisia about 350 B.C. The memorial originated the term mausoleum.

IV. THE TEMPLE OF DIANA AT EPHESUS.—A marble temple designed by Ctesiphon and erected by cities of Ionia in honour of the goddess about 480 B.C.

V. THE COLOSSUS OF RHODES.—A bronze statue of Apollo, set up about 280 B.C. with legs astride the harbour entrance at the seaport of Rhodes.

VI. THE STATUE OF JUPITER OLYMPUS.—At Olympia in the plain of Elis, constructed of marble inlaid with ivory and gold by the sculptor Phidias, about 430 B.C.

VII. THE PHAROS OF ALEXANDRIA.—A marble watch tower and lighthouse on the island of Pharos in the harbour of Alexandria.

THE WORLD'S LAKES

Name	Country	Length (Miles)	Area. (Sq. Miles)
Caspian Sea	Asia	680	170,000
Superior	North America	383	31,820
Victoria Nyanza	Africa	200	26,200
Aral	U.S.S.R.	265	24,400
Huron	North America	247	23,010
Michigan	North America	321	22,400
Nyasa	Africa	350	14,200
Tanganyika	Africa	420	12,700
Great Bear	Canada	175	11,660
Baikal	U.S.S.R.	330	11,580
Great Slave	Canada	325	11,170
Erie	North America	241	9,940
Winnipeg	Canada	260	9,398
Maracaibo	South America	..	8,296
Ontario	North America	193	7,540
Balkhash	U.S.S.R.	323	7,050
Ladoga	U.S.S.R.	125	7,000
Chad	Africa	..	6.000
Nettiling	Baffin Land	120	5,000

Name	Country	Length (Miles)	Area (Sq. Miles)
Amadjuak	Baffin Land	75	4,000
Onega	U.S.S.R.	145	3,800
Eyre	Australia	..	3,700
Rudolf	Africa	185	3,500
Titicaca	South America	120	3,200
Athabasca	Canada	100	3,058
Nicaragua	Central America	195	3,000
Gairdner	Australia	..	3,000
Van	Asia Minor	80	2,500
Reindeer	Canada	160	2,444
Torrens	Australia	130	2,400
Koko-Nor	Tibet	68	2,300
Issyk-Kul	U.S.S.R.	115	2,250
Vänern	Sweden	93	2,150
Winnipegosis	Canada	122	2,086
Bangweolo	Africa	150	2,000
Nipigon	Canada	70	1,870
Manitoba	Canada	191	1,817

VOLCANOES OF THE WORLD

ACTIVE

Volcano	Locality	Height in Feet
Cotopaxi	Ecuador	19,612
Kluchevskaya	U.S.S.R.	16,130
Mount Wrangel	U.S.A.	14,000
Mauna Loa	Hawaii	13,675
Erebus	Antarctic Continent	13,000
Nyiragongo	Congo	11,560
Iliamna	Aleutian Islands, U.S.A.	11,000
Etna	Sicily	10,800
Chillan	Chile	10,500
Nyamuragira	Congo	10,150
Ruapehu	New Zealand	9,175
Paricutin	Mexico	9,000
Asama	Japan	8,200
Ngauruhoe	New Zealand	7,515
Hecla	Iceland	5,100
Kilauea	Hawaii	4,090
Vesuvius	Italy	3,700
Stromboli	Lipari Islands, Italy	3,000
Volcanello	Lipari Islands, Italy	2,500

QUIESCENT

Volcano	Locality	Height in Feet
Llullaillaco	Chile	20,244
Demavend	Persia	18,600
Semerou	Indonesia	12,050
Haleakala	Hawaii	10,032
Guntur	Indonesia	7,300
Tongariro	New Zealand	6,458
Pelée	Martinique, W. Indies	4,430
Tarawera	New Zealand	3,646
Soufrière	St. Vincent Is., W.I.	3,000
Krakatoa	Sunda Strait	2,600
Two-Shima	Japan	2,480

BELIEVED EXTINCT

Volcano	Locality	Height in Feet
Aconcagua	Chile and Argentina	22,834
Chimborazo	Ecuador	20,500
Kilimanjaro	Tanganyika	19,340
Antisana	Ecuador	18,850
Elbruz	Caucasus	18,526
Popocatapetl	Mexico	17,540
Orizaba	Mexico	17,400
Karisimbi	Congo	15,020
Mikeno	Congo	14,780
Fujiyama	Japan	12,395

THE HIGHEST MOUNTAINS

The following list contains the principal peaks of such ranges as the Himalayas and the Andes, and the highest mountains in other ranges.

Name	Range	Height in Feet
Everest	Himalayas	29,002
K 2	Karakoram	28,250
Kinchinjanga	Himalayas	28,146
Nanga Parbat	"	26,629
Nanda Devi	"	25,645
Kamet	"	25,447
Minyaa Konka	China	24,900
Pik Communizmu	Pamirs	24,590
Pik Pobedy	Tian Shan	24,410
Aconcagua	Andes	22,834
Huascaran	"	22,211
Nandakhat	Himalayas	21,690
Sorata (Illampu)	Andes	21,500
Sahama	"	21,480
Illimani	"	21,221
Huandoy	"	20,855
Chimborazo	"	20,500
McKinley	Alaska	20,320
Llullaillaco	Andes	20,244
Mount Logan	Yukon	19,850
Cotopaxi	Andes	19,612
North Peak	Alaska	19,370
Kilimanjaro	Tanganyika	19,340
Antisana	Andes	18,850
Demavend	Elbruz	18,600
Elbruz	Caucasus	18,526
Tolima	Andes	18,320
Mount St. Elias	Alaska	18,008
Popocatapetl	S. Madre	17,540
Orizaba	S. Madre	17,400
Foraker	Alaska	17,395
Ararat	Armenia	17 160
Mount Lucania	Yukon	17,150
King's Peak	"	17,130
Sangay	Andes	17,124
Koshtan Tau	Caucasus	17,096
Kenya	Kenya	17,058
Ruwenzori	Uganda	16,800
Carstenz	New Guinea	16,500
Kluchevskaya	Miakovski	16,130
Mont Blanc	Alps	15,782

THE LONGEST RIVERS

River	Outflow	Length in Miles
Nile	Mediterranean	4,160
Amazon	Atlantic	4,050
Missouri-Mississippi-Red Rock	Gulf of Mexico	3,710
Yangtse	North Pacific	3,400
Yenisei	Arctic Sea	3,300
Congo	Atlantic	3,000
Lena	Arctic Sea	2,800
Mekong	China Sea	2,800
Obi	Arctic Sea	2,700
Niger	Gulf of Guinea	2,600
Hoangho	North Pacific	2,600
Amur	,, ,,	2,500
Paranâ	Atlantic	2,450
Volga	Caspian Sea	2,400
Mackenzie	Beaufort Sea	2,300
Yukon	Behring Sea	2,000
Arkansas	Mississippi	2,000
Madeira	Amazon	2,000
Colorado	Gulf of California	2,000
St. Lawrence	Gulf of St. Lawrence	1,800
Rio Grande del Norte	Gulf of Mexico	1,800
Sao Francisco	Atlantic	1,800
Salween	Gulf of Martaban	1,800
Danube	Black Sea	1,725
Euphrates	Persian Gulf	1,700
Indus	Arabian Sea	1,700
Brahmaputra	Bay of Bengal	1,680
Zambesi	Indian Ocean	1,633
Murray	Indian Ocean	1,609
Severn	Bristol Channel	220
Thames	North Sea	210

THE LONGEST BRIDGES

(With length, in feet, of *waterway*.)

Lower Zambesi, Africa	11,322
Storsstromsbroen, Denmark	10,499
Tay Bridge, Scotland	10,289
Upper Sone, India	9,839
Godavari, India	8,881
Forth Railway Bridge, Scotland	8,291
Rio Salado, Argentina	6,703
Golden Gate, San Francisco, U.S.A.	6,260
Rio Dulce, Argentina	5,866
Hardinge, India	5,384
Victoria Jubilee, Montreal	5,325
Moerdijk, Netherlands	4,698
Harbour, Sydney, N.S.W.	4,124
Jacques Cartier, Montreal	3,888
Queensborough, U.S.A.	3,720
Brooklyn, U.S.A.	3,451
Torun, Poland	3,291
Quebec Bridge, Quebec	3,205

PRINCIPAL HEIGHTS ABOVE SEA LEVEL

	Feet
Europe: Alps—Mont Blanc*	15,782
England: Scafell Pike	3,210
Wales: Snowdon	3,560
Scotland: Ben Nevis	4,406
Ireland: Carrantuohill	3,414
Asia: Everest	29,002
Africa: Kilimanjaro	19,340
North America: McKinley	20,320
South America: Aconcagua	22,976
Australia: Kosciusko	7,328
New Zealand: Cook	12,349
Oceania: Charles Louis	18,000

* The Caucasus being taken physically, if not politically, as in Asia.

THE LARGEST ISLANDS

Name of Island	Ocean	Area in Sq. miles
Greenland (Danish)	Arctic	827,300
New Guinea (Brit.-Neth.)	Pacific	347,450
Borneo (Brit.-Indonesian)	,,	307,000
Baffin Land (Canadian)	Arctic	231,000
Madagascar	Indian	228,000
Sumatra (Indonesian)	Indian	163,000
Great Britain	Atlantic	88,745
Honshiu (Japanese)	Pacific	87,500
Celébes (Indonesian)	Indian	73,000
Prince Albert (Canadian)	Arctic	60,000
South Island, N.Z.	Pacific	58,500
Java (Indonesian)	Indian	48,400
North Island, N.Z.	Pacific	44,500
Cuba (Independent)	Atlantic	44,000
Newfoundland (Canadian)	,,	42,750
Luzon (Philippines)	Pacific	41,000
Ellesmere (Canadian)	Arctic	41,000
Iceland (Independent)	Atlantic	40,000
Mindanao (Philippines)	Pacific	37,000
Ireland	Atlantic	32,600
Hokkaido (Japanese)	Pacific	30,000
Novaya Zemlya (Russian)	Arctic	30,000
Sakhalin (Russian)	Pacific	29,100
Haiti (Independent)	Atlantic	29,000
Tasmania (Australian)	Pacific	26,215
Ceylon	India	25,400
Banks (Canadian)	Arctic	25,000
North Devon (Canadian)	,,	24,000
Melville Land (Canadian)	,,	20,000

GREAT SHIP CANALS OF THE WORLD

Canal	Opened year	Length, miles	Depth, feet	Width,§ feet
Amsterdam (Netherlands)	1876	16½	23	88
Corinth (Greece)	1893	4	26·25	72
Elbe and Trave (Germany)	1900	41	10	72
Gota (Sweden)*	1832	115	10	47
Kiel (Germany)†	1895	61	45	150
Manchester (England)	1894	35·5	28–30	120
Panama (U.S.A.)	1914	50·5	45	300
Princess Juliana (Netherlands)	1935	20	16	52
Saulte Ste. Marie (U.S.A.)	1855	1·6	22	100
Saulte Ste. Marie (Canada)	1895	1·11	20·25	142
Suez (Egypt)	1869	100	34	197
Welland (Canada) ‡	1887	26·75	25	200

* Reconstructed 1916. † Reconstructed 1914. ‡ Reconstructed 1929–30. § At the bottom.

WATERFALLS OF THE WORLD

In order of height

Fall	Locality		Height in Feet
Angel Falls	Venezuela		3,212
Ribbon Fall	Yosemite, U.S.A.		1,612
Upper Yosemite	Yosemite, U.S.A.	(a)	1,430
Gavarnie	Pyrenees		1,385
Wollomombie	New South Wales	(b)	1,100
Staubbach	Switzerland		980
Vettisfoss	Norway		856
King Edward VIII.	British Guiana		840
Gersoppa	Mysore, India	(c)	830
Sutherland	New Zealand	(d)	815
Kaietur (Köituök)	British Guiana		741
Kalambo	Tanganyika	(e)	704
Maletsunyane	Basutoland		630
Bridalveil	Yosemite, U.S.A.		620
Nevada	Yosemite, U.S.A.		594
Skjeggedalsfoss	Norway		525
Sterling	New Zealand		505

In order of volume

Fall	Locality	Width in Yards
Khon Cataracts (1)	Indo-China	15,840
Guayra (2)	Brazil	5,300
Victoria (3)	Rhodesia	1,760
Niagara (4)	Canada—U.S.A.	1,200

On the basis of annual flow the Guayra Falls in Brazil are the most spectacular, with a flow of 470,000 cubic feet per second (annual average).

NOTES.—(a) Out of a total fall of 2,565 ft.; (b) 1,700 ft.; (c) 960 ft.; (d) 1,904 ft.; (e) 3,000 ft.

(1) Height, 50–70 ft.; (2) 90–130 ft.; (3) 236–354 ft.; (4) 158–175 ft.

LONGEST RAILWAY TUNNELS

E.R. = Eastern Region; L.M.R. = London Midland Region; N.E.R. = North Eastern Region; S.R. = Southern Region; W.R. = Western Region

United Kingdom

Tunnel	Region	Miles	Yards
Severn	W.R.	4	628
Totley	L.M.R.	3	950
Standedge	N.E.R.	3	66
Woodhead	L.M.R.	3	66
Sodbury	W.R.	2	924
Disley	L.M.R.	2	346
Bramhope	N.E.R.	2	241
Festiniog	L.M.R.	2	338
Cowburn	L.M.R.	2	182
Sevenoaks	S.R.	1	1693
Rhondda	W.R.	1	1683
Morley	N.E.R.	1	1609
Box	W.R.	1	1452
Catesby	L.M.R.	1	1240
Dove Holes	L.M.R.	1	1224
Littleborough (Summit)	L.M.R.	1	1125
Vict. Waterloo (Liverpool)	L.M.R.	1	946
Ponsbourne	E.R.	1	924
Polhill	S.R.	1	851
Queensbury	N.E.R.	1	741
Merthyr	W.R.	1	737
Kilsby	L.M.R.	1	666
Bleamoor	L.M.R.	1	869
Shepherd's Well	S.R.	1	609
Gildersome	N.E.R.	1	571
Strood	S.R.	1	569
Clayton	S.R.	1	499
Oxted	S.R.	1	501
Sydenham	S.R.	1	381
Drewton	N.E.R.	1	354
Merstham New (Quarry)	S.R.	1	353
Wapping	L.M.R.	1	351
Mersey	Mersey	1	350
Greenock	Scottish Region	1	351
Bradway	E.R.	1	267
Sough	L.M.R.	1	255
Watford, New	L.M.R.	1	230
Caerphilly	W.R.	1	173
Llangyfelach	W.R.	1	192
Abbot's Cliff	Southern R.	1	182
Corby	L.M.R.	1	166
Halton	L.M.R.	1	176
Wenvoe	W.R.	1	107
Sapperton	W.R.	1	100
Sharnbrook	L.M.R.	1	100

(The London Underground *Northern Line* between Morden and East Finchley by the City Branch serves 25 stations and uses tunnels totalling 17½ miles in length).

The World

Tunnel	Country	Miles	Yards
Simplon	Switzerland–Italy	12	560
Apennine	Italy	11	880
St. Gothard	Switzerland	9	550
Lötschberg	Switzerland	9	130
Mont Cenis	Italy	8	870
Cascade	United States	7	1410
Arlberg	Austria	6	650
Moffat	United States	6	200
Shimizu	Japan	6	70

DISTANCE OF THE HORIZON

THE limit of distance to which one can see varies with the height of the spectator. The greatest distance at which an object on the surface of the sea, or of a level plain, can be seen by a person whose eyes are at a height of 5 feet from the same level is nearly 3 miles. At a height of 20 feet the range is increased to nearly 6 miles, and an approximate rule for finding the range of vision for small heights is to increase the square root of the number of feet that the eye is above the level surface by a third of itself, the result being the distance of the horizon in miles, but is slightly in excess of that in the table below, which is computed by a more precise formula. The table may be used conversely to show the distance of an object of given height that is just visible from a point in the surface of the earth or sea. Refraction is taken into account both in the approximate rule and in the Table.

At a height of	the range is	At a height of	the range is	At a height of	the range is
5 ft.	2·9 miles	500 ft.	29·5 miles	4,000 ft.	83·3 miles
20 ,,	5·9 ,,	1,000 ,,	41·6 ,,	5,000 ,,	93·1 ,,
50 ,,	9·3 ,,	2,000 ,,	58·9 ,,	20,000 ,,	186·2 ,,
100 ,,	13·2 ,,	3,000 ,,	72·1 ,,		

RULERS OF FOREIGN COUNTRIES

Country	Ruler	Born	Acceded
Afghanistan	Mohamed Zahir Shah, *King*	Oct. 15, 1914	Nov. 8, 1933
Algeria	Ahmed Ben Bella, *President*	..	Sept. 26, 1962
Argentine Republic	Dr. Arturo Illia, *President*	..	Oct. 12, 1963
Austria	Adolf Schaerf, *President*	1890	May 5, 1957
Bahrain	Isa bin Sulman, *Shaik*	1932	Nov. 2, 1961
Belgium	Baudouin, *King*	Sept. 7, 1930	July 17, 1951
Bolivia	Victor Paz Estenssoro, *President*	..	Aug. 6, 1960
Brazil	Joao Belchior Marques Goulart, *President*	..	Sept. 1961
Bulgaria	Dimiter Ganev, *President*	..	Nov. 30, 1958
Burma	Gen. Ne Win, *Chairman, Revolutionary Govt*	..	Mar. 2, 1962
Burundi	Mwambutsa IV, *Ruler*	..	July 1, 1962
Cambodia	Kossamak Nearirat, *Queen Dowager*	..	June 20, 1960
Cameroon	Ahmadou Ahidjo, *President*	..	May 5, 1960
Cent. African Rep.	David Dacko, *President*	..	Aug. 17, 1960
Chad	Francois Tombalbaye, *President*	..	Aug. 11, 1960
Chile	Jorge Alessandri Rodriguez, *President*	..	Nov. 4, 1958
China	Liu Shao-ch'i, *President*	..	April 27, 1959
Colombia	Guillermo-Leon Valencia, *President*	..	May 4, 1962
Congo*	Abbé Fulbert Youlou, *President*	..	Aug. 17, 1960
Congolese Republic	Joseph Kasavubu, *President*	..	June 30, 1960
Costa Rica	Francisco J. Orlich, *President*	..	Feb. 1962
Cuba	Dr. Osvaldo Dorticos Torrado, *President*	..	July 18, 1959
Czechoslovakia	Antonin Novotny, *President*	Dec. 10, 1904	Nov. 19, 1957
Dahomey	Hubert Maga, *President*	..	Dec. 11, 1960
Denmark	Frederik IX, *King*	Mar. 11, 1899	April 20, 1947
Dominican Republic	Juan Bosch, *President*	1910	Feb. 27, 1963
Ecuador	(vacant) (*Military Junta*)	..	July 11, 1963
Ethiopia	Haile Selassie, *Emperor*	July 23, 1892	April 2, 1930
Finland	Dr. U. K. Kekkonen, *President*	1900	Feb. 15, 1956
Formosa	Gen. Chiang Kai-Shek, *President*	1886	1949
France	Gen. Charles de Gaulle, *President*	Nov. 22, 1890	Dec. 21, 1958
Gaboon	Leon M'ba, *President*	..	Aug. 17, 1960
Germany (Fed.Rep.)	Heinrich Lübke, *President*	Oct. 14, 1894	Sept. 15, 1959
Germany (Eastern)	W. Ulbricht, *Chairman, Council of State*	..	Sept. 12, 1960
Greece	Paul I, *King of the Hellenes*	Dec. 14, 1901	April 1, 1947
Guatemala	Col. Enrique Peralta Azurdia, *Head of Govt.*	..	March 31, 1963
Guinea	Sékou Touré, *President*	..	Oct. 2, 1958
Haiti	Dr. François Duvalier, *President*	..	Oct. 22, 1957
Honduras	Dr. J. R. V. Morales, *President*	..	Dec. 21, 1957
Hungary	István Dobi, *President*	..	July 1953
Iceland	Asgeir Asgeirsson, *President*	..	Aug. 1, 1952
Indonesia	Dr. Sukarno, *President*	June 6, 1901	Dec. 17, 1949
Iraq	Marshal Abdul Salam Mohammed Arif, *President*	1921	Feb. 1963
Irish Republic	Eamon de Valéra, *President*	Oct. 14, 1882	June 18, 1959
Israel	Zalman Shazar, *President*	1889	May 22, 1963
Italy	Antonio Segni, *President*	1895	May 6, 1962
Ivory Coast	Felix Houphouët-Boigny, *President*	..	Nov. 27, 1960
Japan	Hirohito, *Emperor*	April 29, 1901	Dec. 25, 1926
Jordan	Hussein, *King*	Nov. 14, 1935	Aug. 11, 1952
Korea, South	Gen. Pak Chung Hi, *Acting President*	..	Mar. 22, 1962
Kuwait	Abdulla as-Salim al-Subah, *Amir*	1895	Feb. 25, 1950
Laos	Setha Khatya (..Savang Vatthana), *King*	1908	Nov. 4, 1959
Lebanon	Gen. Fuad Chehab, *President*	..	Sept. 23, 1958
Liberia	William V. S. Tubman, *President*	..	May 6, 1943
Libya	Idriss I., *King*	1890	Dec. 24, 1951
Liechtenstein	Franz Joseph II., *Prince*	Aug. 16, 1906	Aug. 25, 1938
Luxemburg	Charlotte, *Grand Duchess*	Jan. 23, 1896	Jan. 9, 1919
Madagascar	Philibert Tsiranana, *President*	..	June 26, 1960
Mali	Modibo Keita, *President*	..	April 4, 1959
Mauritania	Moktar Ould Dadda, *President*	..	Nov. 28, 1958
Mexico	Adolfo Lopez Mateos, *President*	1910	Dec. 1, 1958
Monaco	Rainier, *Prince*	May 31, 1923	May 9, 1949
Morocco	Hassan II, *King*	July 9, 1929	Feb. 26, 1961
Muscat and Oman	Said bin Taimur, *Sultan*	Aug. 13, 1910	Feb. 10, 1932
Nepal	Mahendra Bir Bikram Shah, *King*	1920	Mar. 13, 1955
Netherlands	Juliana, *Queen*	April 30, 1909	Sept. 6, 1948
Nicaragua	Dr. René Schick Guttierez, *President*	..	May 1, 1963
Niger	Hamani Diori, *President*	..	July 11, 1960
Norway	Olav V., *King*	July 2, 1903	Sept. 21, 1957
Panama	Roberto Chiara, *President*	..	Oct. 1, 1960
Paraguay	Gen. Alfredo Stroessner, *President*	..	Aug. 15, 1954
Persia	Shahpoor Mohammed Reza Pahlevi, *Shah*	Oct. 26, 1919	Sept. 16, 1941
Peru	Fernando Belaunde Terry, *President*	..	July 28, 1963

*Formerly French Congo.

RULERS OF FOREIGN COUNTRIES—*continued*

Country	Ruler	Born	Acceded
Philippine Islands	Diosdado Macapagal, *President* [*Ministers*	1910	Dec. 30, 1961
Poland	Aleksander Zawadski, *Chairman of Council of*	..	Dec. 1952
Portugal	Americo D. Rodrigues, *President*	..	Aug. 9, 1958
Qatar	Ahmad al Thani, *Shaikh*	..	Oct. 24, 1960
Roumania	Gheorghe Gheorghiu-Dej, *President*	..	March 21, 1961
Ruanda	Grégoire Kayibanda, *President*	1925	July 1, 1962
Salvador	Col. Julio A. Rivera, *President*	..	July 1, 1962
Saudi Arabia	Saud ibn Abdul Aziz, *King*	1902	Nov. 9, 1953
Senegal	Leopold Senghor, *President*	..	Sept. 5, 1960
Somalia	Aden Abdulie Osman, *President*	..	May 31, 1961
South Africa	Charles Robberts Swart, *President*	1894	May 31, 1961
Spain	General Francisco Franco Bahamonde, *Regent*	Dec. 4, 1892	Aug. 9, 1939
Sudan	Ferik Ibrahim Abboud, *President*	..	Nov. 17, 1958
Sweden	Gustaf VI Adolf, *King*	Nov. 11, 1882	Oct. 29, 1950
Switzerland	Willy Spühler, *President*	1902	Jan. 1, 1963
Syria	*National Council of the Revolution Command*	..	May 14, 1963
Thailand	Bhumibol Adulyadej, *King*	Dec. 5, 1927	June 9, 1946
Togo	Nicholas Grunitsky, *President*	..	May 10, 1963
Tunisia	Habib Bourguiba, *President*	..	July 25, 1957
Turkey	Cemal Gürsel, *President*	1884	Oct. 26, 1961
United Arab Rep.	Lt. Col. Gamal Abdel Nasser, *President*	Jan. 15, 1918	Feb. 21, 1958
United States	John F. Kennedy, *President*	May 29, 1917	Jan. 20, 1961
Uruguay	Faustino Harrison, *President*	..	Mar. 1, 1962
U.S.S.R.	Leonid I. Brezhnev, *President*	1907	May 7, 1960
Vatican City State	Paul VI, *Pope*	Sept. 26, 1897	June 21, 1963
Venezuela	Romulo Betancourt, *President*	Feb. 22, 1908	Feb. 13, 1959
Vietnam, North	Ho Chin Minh, *President*	..	1945
Vietnam, South	Ngo Dinh Diem, *President*	..	Oct. 26, 1955
Voltaic Republic	Maurice Yaméogo, *President*	..	July 11, 1960
Yemen	Saif al Islam Muhammad al Badr, *King*	1920	Sept. 19, 1962
Yugoslavia	Josip Broz Tito, *President*	May 25, 1892	Jan. 14, 1953

PRESIDENTS OF THE FRENCH REPUBLIC

	Acceded
Committee of Public Defence	4 Sept. 1870
Louis Adolphe Thiers	31 Aug. 1871
Marshal MacMahon	24 May, 1873
Jules Grévy	30 Jan. 1879
Sadi Carnot (assass.: 14 June, 1894)	3 Dec. 1887
Jean Casimir Périer	27 June, 1894
François Félix Faure	17 Jan. 1895
Emile Loubet	18 Feb. 1899
Armand Fallières	18 Jan. 1906
Raymond Poincaré	17 Jan. 1913
Paul Deschanel	18 Feb. 1920
Alexandre Millerand	20 Sept. 1920
Gaston Doumergue	13 June, 1924
Paul Doumer (assass.: 7 May, 1932)	13 June, 1931
Albert Lebrun (deposed 1940)	10 May, 1932
Maréchal Pétain, "Vichy" nominee	11 July, 1940

[After the liberation of Paris, General Charles de Gaulle entered the capital and formed a provisional government on Sept. 10, 1944. This was regarded as a continuation of the *Third Republic*. De Gaulle was named provisional President. He resigned and was succeeded by Fèlix Gouin on Jan. 23, 1946. A new National Assembly was elected and on June 2, 1946, Gouin resigned and was succeeded by Georges Bidault.

A new Constitution (*Fourth Republic*), adopted on Oct. 13, 1946, and amended in 1954, was in force until 1958.]

	Acceded
Vincent Auriol, *born* 1884	Jan. 16, 1947
René Coty, *born* 1882	Jan. 17, 1954

[The *Fifth French Republic* came into being on October 5, 1958, following the approval of its constitution by a national referendum in September, 1958.]

Charles de Gaulle, *born* 1890	Jan. 8, 1959

POPES FROM 1621

Sovereign Pontiff.	*Family Name.*	*Elected.*
Gregory XV	Ludovisi	1621
Urban VIII	Barberini	1623
Innocent X	Pamphili	1644
Alexander VII	Chigi	1655
Clement IX	Rospigliosi	1667
Clement X	Altieri	1676
Innocent XI	Odescalchi	1670
Alexander VIII	Ottoboni	1689
Innocent XII	Pignatelli	1691
Clement XI	Albani	1700
Innocent XIII	Conti	1721
Benedict XIII	Orsini	1724
Clement XII	Corsini	1730
Benedict XIV	Lambertini	1740
Clement XIII	Rezzonico	1758
Clement XIV	Ganganelli	1769
Pius VI	Braschi	1775
Pius VII	Chiaramonti	1800
Leo XII	della Genga	1823
Pius VIII	Castiglion	1829
Gregory XVI	Cappellari	1831
Pius IX	Mastai-Ferretti	1846
Leo XIII	Pecci	1878
Pius X	Sarto	1903
Benedict XV	della Chiesa	1914
Pius XI	Ratti	1922
Pius XII	Pacelli	1939
John XXIII	Roncalli	1958
Paul VI	Montini	1963

Adrian IV (Nicholas Breakspear, the only Englishman elected Pope) was born at Langley, near St. Albans; elected Pope, on the death of Anastasius IV, 1154; died 1159.

ENGLISH KINGS AND QUEENS A.D. 827 TO 1603

Name	DYNASTY	MARRIED	Access.	Died	Age	Rgnd.
	Saxons and Danes					
EGBERT	King of Wessex and all England		827	839	—	12
ETHELWULF	Son of Egbert		839	858	—	19
{ETHELBALD	Son of Ethelwulf		858}	860	—	2
{ETHELBERT	Second son of Ethelwulf		858}	866	—	8
ETHELRED	Third son of Ethelwulf		866	871	—	5
ALFRED THE GREAT	Fourth son of Ethelwulf	Ealhswith of Gaini	871	901	52	30
EDWARD THE ELDER	Son of Alfred the Great	1, Egwyn; 2, Elfled; 3, Eadgifu	901	925	55	24
ATHELSTAN	Eldest son of Edward the Elder (by 1)		925	940	45	15
EDMUND	Third son of Edward the Elder (by 3)	1, Elgifu; 2, Ethelfled	940	946	25	6
EDRED	Fourth son of Edward the Elder (by 3)		946	955	32	9
EDWY	Son of Edmund (by 1)		955	959	18	3
EDGAR	Second son of Edmund (by 1)	1, Ethelfled; 2, Elfthryth	959	975	32	17
EDWARD THE MARTYR	Son of Edgar (by 1)		975	978	17	4
ETHELRED II	Younger son of Edgar (by 2)	1, Elfgifu; 2, Emma, dau. of Richard, Duke of Normandy	978	1016	48	37
EDMUND IRONSIDE	Eldest son of Ethelred II (by 1)	[II	1016	1016	27	0
CANUTE THE DANE	By conquest and election	1, Elfgifu of Deiar; 2, Emma, widow of Ethelred	1017	1035	40	18
HAROLD I	Son of Canute (by 1)		1035	1040	—	5
HARDICANUTE	Son of Canute (by 2)		1040	1042	24	2
EDWARD THE CONFESSOR	Son of Ethelred II (by 2)	Edith, dau. of Earl Godwin	1042	1066	62	24
HAROLD II	Son of Earl Godwin		1066	1066	44	0
	The House of Normandy					
WILLIAM I	Obtained the Crown by Conquest	Matilda, dau. of Baldwin, Count of Flanders.	1066	1087	60	21
WILLIAM II	Third son of William I	(Died unmarried)	1087	1100	43	13
HENRY I	Youngest son of William I	*1st* Matilda, dau. of Malcolm Canmore, K. of Scotland; *2nd* Adelicia, dau. of Godfrey, D. of Louvaine.	1100	1135	67	35
STEPHEN	Third son of Stephen, Count of Blois, by Adela, fourth dau. of William I.	Matilda, dau. of Eustace, Count of Boulogne.	1135	1154	50	19
	The House of Plantagenet					
HENRY II	Son of Geoffrey Plantagenet by Matilda, only dau. of Henry I; his grandmother, Matilda of Scotland, was a lineal descendant of Alfred and of Egbert.	Eleanor, dau. of D. of Guienne and divorced Queen of Louis VII of France.	1154	1189	56	35
RICHARD I	Eldest surviving son of Henry II	Berengaria, dau. of Sancho VI, K. of Navarre.	1189	1199	42	10
JOHN	Sixth and youngest son of Henry II	*1st* Avisa, dau. of E. of Gloucester, divorced upon grounds of consanguinity; *2nd* Isabella dau. of Aymer, Count of Angoulême.	1199	1216	50	17
HENRY III	Eldest son of John	Eleanor, dau. of Raymond, Count of Provence.	1216	1272	65	56
EDWARD I	Eldest son of Henry III	*1st* Eleanor, dau. of Ferdinand III, K. of Castile; *2nd* Margaret, dau. of Philip III, the Hardy, K. of France.	1272	1307	68	35
EDWARD II	Eldest surviving son of Edward I	Isabella, dau. of Philip IV, the Fair, K. of France	1307	1327	43	20

Name	DYNASTY	MARRIED	Access.	Died	Age	Rgnd.
EDWARD III	Eldest son of Edward II.	Philippa, dau. of William, Count of Holland and Hainault.	1327	1377	65	50
RICHARD II.	Son of the Black Prince, eldest son of Edward III, (died 1400)	*1st* Anne, dau. of Emp. Charles IV; *2nd* Isabel, dau. of Charles VI of France.	1377	dep. 1399	34	22
	The House of Lancaster					
HENRY IV	Son of John of Gaunt, 4th son of Edward III.	*1st* Mary de Bohun, dau. of the E. of Hereford; *2nd* Joanna of Navarre, widow of John de Montford, D. of Bretagne.	1399	1413	47	13
HENRY V.	Eldest son of Henry IV	Katherine, dau. of Charles VI, K. of France.	1413	1422	34	9
HENRY VI	Only son of Henry V, (died 1471)	Margaret of Anjou, dau. of René, D. of Anjou.	1422	dep. 1461	49	39
	The House of York					
EDWARD IV	Son of Richard, grandson of Edmund, fifth son of Edward III; and of Anne, great-grand-daughter of Lionel, third son of Edward III.	Elizabeth Widvile (or Woodville), dau. of Sir Richard Widvile and widow of Sir John Grey of Groby.	1461	1483	41	22
EDWARD V	Eldest son of Edward IV	(Died unmarried)	1483	1483	13	0
RICHARD III	Younger brother of Edward IV	Anne, dau. of the E. of Warwick, and widow of Edward, Prince of Wales.	1483	1485	35	2
	The House of Tudor					
HENRY VII	Son of Edmund, eldest son of Owen Tudor, by Katherine, widow of Henry V; his mother, Margaret Beaufort, was great-grand-daughter of John of Gaunt.	Elizabeth, dau. of Edward IV	1485	1509	53	24
HENRY VIII	Only surviving son of Henry VII.	*1st* Katharine of Arragon, widow of his elder brother Arthur, (divorced); *2nd* Anne, dau. of Sir Thomas Boleyn, (beheaded); *3rd* Jane, dau. of Sir John Seymour, (died in childbirth of a son, aft. Edward VI); *4th* Anne, sister of William, D. of Cleves, (divorced); *5th* Katharine Howard, niece of the Duke of Norfolk, (beheaded); *6th* Katharine, dau. of Sir Thomas Parr and widow of Edward Nevill, Lord Latimer.	1509	1547	56	38
EDWARD VI	Son of Henry VIII by Jane Seymour	(Died unmarried)	1547	1553	16	6
JANE	Grand-daughter of Mary, younger sister of Henry VIII, (beheaded Feb. 12, 1554).	Lord Guilford Dudley	1553	1554	17	14 days
MARY I	Daughter of Henry VIII by Katharine of Arragon.	Philip II of Spain	1553	1558	43	5
ELIZABETH I	Daughter of Henry VIII by Anne Boleyn.	(Died unmarried)	1558	1603	69	44

Name	DYNASTY	MARRIED	Access.	Died	Age	Rgnd.
	The House of Stuart					
JAMES I (VI OF SCOT.) . . .	Son of Mary, Queen of Scots, granddaughter of James IV and Margaret, daughter of Henry VII.	Anne, dau. of Frederick II of Denmark.	1603	1625	59	22
CHARLES I	Only surviving son of James I.	Henrietta-Maria, dau. of Henry IV of France.	1625	Beh. 1649	48	24
	Commonwealth	*declared May 19, 1649*				
	Oliver Cromwell, Lord Protector, 1653–8.	*Richard Cromwell, Lord Protector, 1658–9*				
CHARLES II	Eldest son of Charles I, (restored 1660) . . .	The Infanta Catharine of Portugal, dau. of John IV and sister of Alphonso VI.	1649	1685	55	36
JAMES II (VII OF SCOT.) . .	Second son of Charles I, (died Sept. 16, 1701) (Interregnum, Dec. 11, 1688—Feb. 13, 1689)	*1st* Lady Anne Hyde, dau. of Edward, E. of Clarendon, who died before James ascended the throne; *and* Mary Beatrice Eleanor d'Este, dau. of Alphonso, D. of Modena.	1685	Dep. 1688 Dec. 1701	68	3
WILLIAM III and	Son of William Prince of Orange and grandson of Charles I.	. . . .	1689	1702	51	13
MARY II.	Eldest daughter of James II.		1689	1694	33	6
ANNE.	Second daughter of James II	Prince George of Denmark.	1702	1714	49	12
	The House of Hanover					
GEORGE I	Son of Elector of Hanover, by Sophia, daughter of Elizabeth, daughter of James I	Sophia Dorothea, dau. of George William, D. of Zell.	1714	1727	76	13
GEORGE II	Only son of George I.	Wilhelmina Caroline, dau. of John Frederick, Margrave of Brandenburg-Anspach.	1727	1760	77	33
GEORGE III	Grandson of George II.	Charlotte Sophia, dau. of Charles Lewis Frederick, D. of Mecklenburg-Strelitz.	1760	1820	81	59
GEORGE IV	Eldest son of George III, (Regent from February 5, 1811)	Caroline Amelia Elizabeth, dau. of Charles William Ferdinand, D. of Brunswick-Wolfenbuttel, by Augusta, eldest sister of George III.	1820	1830	67	10
WILLIAM IV.	Third son of George III	Amelia Adelaide Louisa Theresa Caroline, dau. of George Frederick Charles, D. of Saxe-Meiningen.	1830	1837	71	7
VICTORIA.	Daughter of Edward, 4th son of George III.	Francis Albert Augustus Charles Emmanuel, D. of Saxe, pr. of Saxe-Coburg and Gotha.	1837	1901	81	63
	The House of Saxe-Coburg					
EDWARD VII	Eldest son of Victoria	Princess Alexandra of Denmark.	1901	1910	68	9
	The House of Windsor					
GEORGE V.	Surviving son of Edward VII.	H.S.H. Princess Victoria Mary of Teck	1910	1936	70	25
EDWARD VIII.	Eldest son of George V, (abdicated 1936). .	(Mrs. Wallis Warfield, June 3, 1937.)	1936	—	—	325 days
GEORGE VI.	Second son of George V	The Lady Elizabeth Angela Marguerite, dau. of 14th Earl of Strathmore and Kinghorne (HER MAJESTY QUEEN ELIZABETH THE QUEEN MOTHER).	1936	1952	56	15
ELIZABETH II.	Elder daughter of George VI.	Philip, son of Prince Andrew of Greece (H.R.H. THE DUKE OF EDINBURGH).	1952	WHOM GOD PRESERVE.		

The House of Windsor is in direct descent from (*inter alios*) Egbert, King of Wessex, Alfred the Great and William the Conqueror; also from the Emperor Charlemagne (*b.* 742, *d.* 814), Rodrigo the Cid (*b.* 1030, *d.* 1099), the Emperor Barbarossa (*b.* 1123, *d.* 1190) and St. Louis, King of France (*b.* 1215, *d.* 1270).

SCOTTISH KINGS AND QUEENS A.D. 1057 TO 1603

Sovereign		Married	Access.	Died
MALCOLM III (CANMORE)	Son of Duncan I	*1st* Ingibiorg, widow of Thorfinn, Earl of Orkney; *2nd* Margaret, sister of Edgar the Atheling.	1057	1093
DONALD BÀN	Brother of Malcolm Canmore		1093	—
DUNCAN II	Son of Malcolm Canmore, by first marriage.		1094	1094
DONALD BÀN	(Restored)		1094	1097
EDGAR	Son of Malcolm Canmore, by second marriage	Died unmarried.	1097	1107
ALEXANDER I	Son of Malcolm Canmore	Sybilla, natural daughter of Henry I of England.	1107	1124
DAVID I	Son of Malcolm Canmore	Matilda, daughter of Waltheof, Earl of Northumbria, widow of Simon, Earl of Northampton.	1124	1153
MALCOLM IV (THE MAIDEN)	Son of Henry, eldest son of David I	Died unmarried	1153	1165
WILLIAM I (THE LION)	Brother of Malcolm the Maiden	Ermengarde, daughter of Richard, Viscount of Beaumont,	1165	1214
ALEXANDER II	Son of William the Lion	*1st* Joanna, daughter of King John; *2nd* Mary, daughter of Ingelram de Coucy (*Picardy*).	1214	1249
ALEXANDER III	Son of Alexander II, by second marriage	*1st* Margaret, daughter of Henry III of England; *2nd* Joleta, daughter of the Count de Dreux.	1249	1286
MARGARET, MAID OF NORWAY	Daughter of Eric II of Norway, grand-daughter of Alexander III.	Died unmarried	1286	1290
JOHN BALIOL	Grandson of eldest daughter of David, Earl of Huntingdon, brother of William the Lion.		1292	1296
ROBERT I (BRUCE)	Great-grandson of 2nd daughter of David, Earl of Huntingdon, brother of William the Lion.	*1st* Isabella, daughter of Donald, Earl of Mar; *2nd* Elizabeth de Burgh, sister of Earl of Ulster.	1306	1329
DAVID II	Son of Robert I, by second marriage	*1st* Joanna, daughter of Edward II of England; *2nd* Margaret, widow of Sir John Logie (divorced, 1369).	1329	1371
ROBERT II (STEWART)	Son of Marjorie, daughter of Robert I by first marriage, and Walter the Steward.	*1st* Elizabeth, dau., of Sir Robert Mure (or More) of Rowallan; *2nd* Euphemia, dau., of Hugh, Earl of Ross, widow of John, Earl of Moray.	1371	1390
ROBERT III	(John, Earl of Carrick) son of Robert II.	Annabella, daughter of Sir John Drummond of Stobhall, niece of Margaret Logie.	1390	1406
JAMES I	Son of Robert III	Jane Beaufort, daughter of John, Earl of Somerset, 4th son of John of Gaunt and grandson of Edward III of England.	1406	1437
JAMES II	Son of James I	Mary, daughter of Arnold, Duke of Gueldres	1437	1460
JAMES III	Eldest son of James II	Margaret, daughter of Christian I of Denmark, Norway and Sweden.	1460	1488
JAMES IV	Eldest son of James III	Margaret Tudor, daughter of Henry VII	1488	1513
JAMES V	Son of James IV	*1st* Madeleine, daughter of Francis I of France; *2nd* Mary of Lorraine, daughter of Duc de Guise, widow of Duc de Longueville.	1513	1542
MARY	Daughter of James V, by second marriage	*1st* Francis, Dauphin of France; *2nd* Henry, Lord Darnley; *3rd* James, Earl of Bothwell.	1542	1587
JAMES VI (Ascended the Throne of England 1603)	Son of Mary, by second marriage	Anne, daughter of Frederick II of Denmark	1567	1625

WELSH SOVEREIGNS AND PRINCES

WALES was ruled by Sovereign Princes from the "earliest times" until the death of Llywelyn in 1282. The first English Prince of Wales was the son of Edward I, and was born in Caernarvon town on April 25, 1284. According to a discredited legend, he was presented to the Welsh chieftains as their Prince, in fulfilment of a promise that they should have a Prince who "could not speak a word of English" and should be native born. This son, who afterwards became Edward II, was created "Prince of Wales and Earl of Chester" at the famous Lincoln Parliament on February 7, 1301. The title Prince of Wales is borne after individual conferment and is not inherited at birth; it was conferred on Prince Charles by Her Majesty the Queen on July 26, 1958.

INDEPENDENT PRINCES, A.D. 844 to 1282

Rhodri the Great	844–878
Anarawd, son of Rhodri	878–916
Hywel Dda, the Good	916–950
Iago ab Idwal (or Ieuaf)	950–979
Hywel ab Ieuaf, the Bad	979–985
Cadwallon, his brother	985–986
Maredudd ab Owain ap Hywel Dda	986–999
Cynan ap Hywel ab Ieuaf	999–1008
Llewelyn ap Sitsyhlt	1018–1023
Iago ab Idwal ap Meurig	1023–1039
Gruffydd ap Llywelyn ap Seisyll	1039–1063
Bleddyn ap Cynfyn	1063–1075
Trahaern ap Caradog	1075–1081
Gruffydd ap Cynan ab Iago	1081–1137
Owain Gwynedd	1137–1170
Dafydd ab Owain Gwynedd	1170–1194
Llywelyn Fawr, the Great	1194–1240
Dafydd ap Llywelyn	1240–1246
Llywelyn ap Gruffydd ap Llywelyn	1246–1282

ENGLISH PRINCES, SINCE A.D. 1301

Edward, b. 1284 (Edwd. II), cr. Pr. of Wales	1301
Edward the Black Prince, s. of Edward III	1343
Richard (Richard II), s. of the Black Prince	1377
Henry of Monmouth (Henry V)	1399
Edward of Westminster, son of Henry VI	1454
Edward of Westminster (Edward V)	1472
Edward, son of Richard III, (d. 1484)	1483
Arthur Tudor, son of Henry VII	1489
Henry Tudor (Hen. VIII), s. of Henry VII	1503
Henry Stuart, son of James I, (d. 1612)	1610
Charles Stuart (Charles I), s. of James I	1616
Charles (Charles II), son of Charles I	1630
James Francis Edward, "The Old Pretender" (d. 1766)	1688
George Augustus (Geo. II), s. of George I	1714
Frederick Lewis, s. of George II, (d. 1751)	1727
George William Frederick (George III)	1751
George Augustus Frederick (George IV)	1762
Albert Edward (Edward VII)	1841
George (George V)	1901
Edward (Edward VIII)	1911
Charles Philip Arthur George	1958

THE FAMILY OF QUEEN VICTORIA

QUEEN VICTORIA was *born* May 24, 1819; *succeeded* to the Throne June 20, 1837; *married* Feb. 10, 1840, Albert, PRINCE CONSORT (*born* Aug. 26, 1819, *died* Dec. 14, 1861); *died* Jan. 22, 1901. Her Majesty had issue:—

1. H.R.H. Princess Victoria (*Princess Royal*), born Nov. 21, 1840, married, 1858, Frederick, German Emperor; died Aug. 5, 1901, leaving issue:—

(1) H.I.M. William II., *German Emperor* 1888–1918, born Jan. 27, 1859, died June 4, 1941, having married Princess Augusta Victoria of Schleswig-Holstein-Sonderburg-Augustenburg (born 1858, died 1921), and secondly, Princess Hermine of Reuss (born 1887, died 1947). The late German Emperor's family:—

(*a*) The late Prince William (*Crown Prince* 1888–1918), born May 6, 1882, married Duchess Cecilia of Mecklenburg-Schwerin (who died May 6, 1954); died July 20, 1951. (The Crown Prince's children:—Prince Wilhelm, born July 4, 1906, died 1940; Prince Ludwig, born Nov. 9, 1907, married (1938) Grand Duchess Kira, daughter of Grand Duke Cyril of Russia (and has issue two sons); Prince Hubertus, born Sept. 30, 1909, died April 8, 1950; Prince Frederick George, born Dec. 19, 1911; Princess Alexandrine Irene, born April 7, 1915; Princess Cecilia, born Sept. 5, 1917).

(*b*) The late Prince Eitel Frederick, born July 7, 1883, married Duchess Sophie of Oldenburg (marriage dissolved 1926); died Dec. 7, 1942.

(*c*) The late Prince Adalbert (born July 14, 1884, died Sept. 22, 1948), married Duchess Adelaide of Saxe-Meiningen. (Prince Adalbert's children:—Princess Victoria Marina, born Sept. 11, 1917; Prince William Victor, born Feb. 15, 1919.)

(*d*) The late Prince Augustus William, born Jan. 29, 1887, married Princess Alexandra of Schleswig-Glucksburg (marriage dissolved 1920); died March, 1949. (Prince Augustus's son is Prince Alexander, born Dec. 26, 1912.)

(*e*) The late Prince Oscar, born July 27, 1888, married Countess von Ruppin, died Jan. 27, 1958. (Prince Oscar's children:—Prince Oscar, born July 12, 1915, died 1939; Prince Burchard, born Jan. 8, 1917; Princess Herzeleida, born Dec. 25, 1918; Prince William, born Jan. 30, 1922).

(*f*) The late Prince Joachim, born Dec. 17, 1890, married Princess Marie of Anhalt, died July 17, 1920 (leaving issue, Prince Karl, born Dec. 15, 1916, married 1940 Princess Henrietta of Schoenaich-Carolath).

(*g*) Princess Victoria, born Sept. 13, 1892, married (1913) the then reigning Duke of Brunswick. (Princess Victoria's children:—Prince Ernest, born March 18, 1914, married Princess Ortrud von Glucksburg, 1951; Prince George, born March 25, 1915; Princess Frederica, born April 18, 1917, married Paul I., King of the Hellenes (*see* p. 212); Prince Christian Oskar, born Sept 1, 1919; Prince Weif Heinrich, born March 11, 1923, married Princess Alexandra of Ysemburg, 1960).

(2) The late Princess Charlotte, born July 24, 1860, married (1878) the late Duke of Saxe-Meiningen, died Oct. 1, 1919. (Princess Charlotte's daughter, Princess Feodora, born May 12, 1879, married (1898) the late Prince Henry XXX. of Reuss, died Aug. 26, 1945).

(3) The late Prince Henry, born Aug. 14, 1862, married (1888) the late Princess Irene of Hesse, died April 20, 1929 (issue, Prince Waldemar, born March 20, 1889, died May 2, 1945; Prince Sigismund, born Nov. 27, 1896).

(4) The late Princess Victoria, born April 12, 1866, married firstly (1890) Prince Adolphus of Schaumburg-Lippe, secondly (1927) Alexander Zubkov, died Nov. 13, 1929.

(5) The late Princess Sophia, born June 14, 1870, married (1889) the late Constantine, *King of the Hellenes*, died Jan. 13, 1932, leaving issue:—

(*a*) The late George II., *King of the Hellenes* 1922-24 and 1935-47, born July 7, 1890, married Princess Elisabeth of Roumania (marriage dissolved 1935); died April 1947.

(*b*) The late Alexander, *King of the Hellenes* 1917-1920, born Aug. 1, 1893, married (1919) Aspasia Manos; died Oct. 25, 1920, leaving issue Princess Alexandra (born 1921) who married, March 20, 1944, King Petar II. of Yugoslavia.

(*c*) Princess Helena, born May 2, 1896, married (1921) late King Carol of Roumania, (marriage dissolved 1928), having issue, King Michael, G.C.V.O., born Oct. 25, 1921, married (1948) Princess Anne of Bourbon Parma, and has issue, Princess Marguerite, born March 26, 1949, Princess Helene, born Nov. 15, 1950, and Princess Irina, born Feb. 28, 1953.

(*d*) Paul (*Paul I., King of the Hellenes*), born Dec. 4, 1901, *acceded* April 1, 1947, married Jan. 9, 1938, Princess Frederica of Brunswick (*see* p. 211), having issue Constantine (*Diadoch*), born June 2, 1940; Sophia, born Nov. 2. 1938, married (1962), Don Juan Carlos of Spain; and Irene, born May 11, 1942.

(*e*) Princess Eirene, born Feb. 13, 1904, married (1939) the Duke of Aosta, and has issue.

(*f*) Princess Catherine, born May 4, 1913, married (1947) Major R. C. A. Brandram and has issue.

(6) The late Princess Margarete, born April 22, 1872, married (1893) the late Prince Frederick Charles of Hesse, died Jan. 21, 1954 (issue the late Prince Frederick William, born 1893, died 1916; the late Prince Maximilian, born 1894, died 1914; Prince Philipp, born 1896, married (1925) Princess Mafalda, daughter of King Victor Emmanuel III. of Italy (and has issue, Prince Maurice, born 1926, and Prince Henry, born 1927); Prince Wolfgang, born 1896, married (1924) Princess Marie of Baden; Prince Richard, born May 14, 1901).

2. H.M. KING EDWARD VII. (*see* p. 213).

3. H.R.H. Princess Alice, born April 25, 1843, married Prince Louis (afterwards reigning Grand Duke) of Hesse; died Dec. 14, 1878. Issue:—

(i) Victoria Alberta, born April 5, 1863, married Admiral of the Fleet the late Marquess of Milford Haven, died Sept. 24, 1950, leaving issue:—

(*a*) Alice (*H.R.H. Princess Andrew of Greece*), born Feb. 25, 1885, married Prince Andrew of Greece having issue (*see* p. 214).

(*b*) Lady Louise Mountbatten (*Queen of Sweden*), born July 13, 1889; married Nov. 3, 1923, H.R.H. The Crown Prince of Sweden, now King Gustaf VI. Adolf.

(*c*) George, Marquess of Milford Haven, G.C.V.O., born Nov. 6, 1892, Capt. R.N., married (1916) Countess Nadejda (died Jan. 22, 1963), daughter of late Grand Duke Michael of Russia; died April 8, 1938, leaving issue:—Lady Elizabeth, born 1917; David Michael, *Marquess of Milford Haven*, O.B.E., D.S.C., Lieutenant, R.N. (ret.), born 1919, married, and has issue, Earl of Medina, *b.* 1961.

(*d*) Louis, Admiral of the Fleet Earl Mountbatten of Burma, K.G., P.C., G.C.B., G.C.S.I., G.C.I.E., G.C.V.O., D.S.O., born June 25, 1900, Governor-General of the Dominion of India 1947-48, Viceroy of India 1947, Personal A.D.C. to the Queen; married July 18, 1922, Edwina Cynthia Annette (died Feb. 20, 1960), daughter of Lord Mount Temple, and has issue two daughters, the Lady Patricia (Lady Brabourne), born 1924 and the Lady Pamela Hicks, born 1929.

(ii) Elizabeth Fedorovna (*Grand Duchess Sergius of Russia*), born Nov. 1, 1864; died July 1918.

(iii) Irene (*Princess Henry of Prussia*), born July 11, 1866, married the late Prince Henry of Prussia, and died Nov. 11, 1953 (*see* p. 211).

(iv) Ernest Ludwig, Grand Duke of Hesse, born Nov. 25, 1868, died Oct. 9, 1937, having married (1905) Princess Eleonore of Solms-Hohensolmslich, with issue (*a*) George, Grand Duke of Hesse, born Nov. 8, 1906, married Princess Cecilie of Greece and Denmark (*see* p. 214); *accidentally killed* (with mother, wife and two sons) Nov. 16, 1937; (*b*) Ludwig, Grand Duke of Hesse, born Nov. 20, 1908, married (Nov. 17, 1937) Margaret, daughter of 1st Lord Geddes.

(v) Alix (*Tsaritsa of Russia*), born June 6, 1872, married (Nov. 25, 1894) the late Nicholas II. (*Tsar of All the Russias*), assassinated July 16, 1918, with the Tsar and their issue (Grand Duchess Olga; Grand Duchess Tatiana; Grand Duchess Marie; Grand Duchess Anastasia, and the Tsarevitch).

(vi) Mary, born May 24, 1874, died Nov. 15, 1878.

4. Admiral of the Fleet H.R.H. Prince Alfred, *Duke of Edinburgh*, born Aug. 6, 1844, married Jan. 23, 1874, Marie Alexandrovna (died Oct. 25, 1920), only daughter of Alexander II., Emperor of Russia; succeeded as *Duke of Saxe-Coburg and Gotha*, Aug. 22, 1893; died July 30, 1900, leaving issue:—

(1) Alfred (*Prince of Saxe-Coburg*), born Oct. 15, 1874, died Feb. 6, 1899.

(2) Marie (*Queen of Roumania*), born Oct. 29, 1875, married (1893) the late King Ferdinand of Roumania; died July 18, 1938, having issue:—

(*a*) King Carol II. of Roumania, K.G., born Oct. 15, 1893, married (1921) Princess Helena of Greece (*see* col. 1), died April 4, 1953.

(*b*) Elisabeth (*Queen of the Hellenes*), born Oct. 11, 1894, married (1921) the late King George II of the Hellenes, died Nov. 15, 1956.

(*c*) Marie, born Jan. 8, 1900, married (1922) the late King Alexander of Yugoslavia, died June 22, 1961 (having issue:—Petar, King of Yugoslavia, born Sept. 6, 1923, married (1944) Princess Alexandra of Greece, and has issue, Prince Alexander, born July 17, 1945; Prince Tomislav, born Jan. 19, 1928, married (1957) Princess Margarita of Baden (see p. 214) and has issue, Prince Nicholas, born 1958; Prince Andrej, born 1929, married 1956, Princess Christina of Hesse).

(*d*) H.R.H. Prince Nicolas, born Aug. 7, 1903, married, Nov. 7, 1931, Jeanne Lucie Doletti.

(*e*) H.R.H. Princess Ileana, born Jan. 5, 1909; married 1st, Archduke Anton of Austria (having issue:—Stephan, born Aug. 15, 1932); 2nd, Dr. Stefan Issarescu.

(*f*) Prince Mircea, born Jan. 3, 1913, died Nov. 1916.

(3) Victoria, born Nov. 25, 1876, married (1894) Grand Duke of Hesse and (1905) the late Grand Duke Cyril of Russia; died March 2, 1936, having issue:—

(*a*) Marie, born Feb. 2, 1907, married (1925) Prince Friedrich Carl of Leiningen, died Oct. 27, 1951.

(*b*) Kira Cyrillovna, born May 22, 1909, married (1938) Prince Ludwig of Germany.

(*c*) Vladimir Cyrillovitch, born Aug. 17, 1917, married (1948) Princess Leonide Bagration-Moukhransky, and has issue, a daughter.

(4) Alexandra, born Sept. 1, 1878, married (1896) the late Prince of Hohenlohe Langenburg; died April 16, 1942, leaving issue:—

(*a*) Gottfried, born March, 24, 1897; died May 11, 1960.

(*b*) Maria (*Princess Friedrich of Holstein-*

Glucksburg), born Jan. 18, 1899.

(*c*) Princess Alexandra, born April 2, 1901.

(*d*) Princess Irma, born July 4, 1902.

(5) Princess Beatrice, V.A., born April 20, 1884, married (1909) Infante Alfonso Maria of Orleans, having issue.

5. H.R.H. Princess Helena Augusta Victoria, born May 25, 1846, married July 5, 1866, General H.R.H. *Prince Christian of Schleswig-Holstein* (died Oct. 28, 1917); died June 9, 1923. Issue:—

(i) H.H. Prince Christian Victor, born April 14, 1867, died Oct. 29, 1900.

(ii) H.H. Prince Albert, born Feb. 26, 1869, died April 27, 1931.

(iii) H.H. Princess Helena Victoria, born May 3, 1870; died March 13, 1948.

(iv) H.H. Princess Marie Louise, born Aug. 12, 1872; died Dec. 8, 1956.

(v) H.H. Prince Harold, born May 12, died May 20, 1876.

6. H.R.H. Princess Louise, born March 18, 1848, married March 21, 1871, the Marquess of Lorne, afterwards the 9th Duke of Argyll K.G.; died Dec. 3, 1939, without issue.

7. Field Marshal H.R.H. Prince Arthur, *Duke of Connaught*, born May 1, 1850, married March 13, 1879, H.R.H. Princess Louisa of Prussia (died March 14, 1917); died Jan. 16, 1942. Issue:—

(i) H.R.H. Princess Margaret, born Jan. 15, 1882, married H.R.H. the Crown Prince of Sweden, now *King Gustaf VI. Adolf*, G.C.B., G.C.V.O., died May 1, 1920, leaving issue:—

(*a*) Duke of Westerbotten, born April 22, 1906, married (1932) Princess Sybil of Saxe-Coburg-Gotha, died Jan. 26, 1947, leaving issue one son, now the Crown Prince of Sweden, and 4 daughters.

(*b*) Duke of Upland (Count Sigvard Bernadotte), born June 7, 1907.

(*c*) Princess Ingrid (*Queen of Denmark*), born March 28, 1910, married (1935) the Crown Prince (now King Frederick IX.) of Denmark, and has issue 3 daughters.

(*d*) Duke of Halland, born Feb. 28, 1912.

(*e*) Duke of Dalecarlia, born Oct. 31, 1916.

(ii) Major-Gen. H.R.H. Prince Arthur, born Jan. 13, 1883; married Oct. 15, 1913, H.H. the Duchess of Fife; died Sept. 12, 1938, leaving issue (see below).

(iii) H.R.H. Princess Patricia (*Lady Patricia Ramsay*) V.A., C.I., born March 17, 1886, married Feb. 27, 1919, Adm. Hon. Sir Alexander Ramsay, G.C.V.O., K.C.B., D.S.O., having issue Alexander Arthur Alfonso David, born Dec. 21, 1919.

8. H.R.H. Prince Leopold, *Duke of Albany*, born April 7, 1853, married Princess Helena of Waldeck (died Sept. 1, 1922); died March 28, 1884. Issue:—

(i) H.R.H. Princess Alice (*Countess of Athlone*), V.A., G.C.V.O., G.B.E., Commandant in Chief Women's Transport Service, Chancellor of the University College of the West Indies, born Feb. 25, 1883, married Feb. 10, 1904, Maj.-Gen. the Earl of Athlone (who died Jan. 16, 1957), having issue—

(*a*) Lady May Helen Emma, born Jan. 23, 1906, married (1931) Sir Henry Abel-Smith, K.C.V.O., D.S.O., and has issue a son and 2 daughters.

(*b*) The late *Viscount Trematon*, born 1907, died April 15, 1928.

(ii) Charles Edward, *Duke of Saxe-Coburg-Gotha* (1900–1918), born July 19, 1884, married (1905) Princess Victoria of Schleswig-Holstein, died March 6, 1954, leaving surviving issue 2 sons and 2 daughters.

9. H.R.H. Princess Beatrice, born April 14, 1857, married July 23, 1885, H.R.H. Prince Henry of Battenberg (born Oct. 5, 1858, died Jan. 20, 1896); died Oct. 26, 1944, leaving issue:—

(i) Alexander, *Marquess of Carisbrooke*, born Nov. 23, 1886, married Lady Irene Denison (died July 15, 1956); died Feb. 23, 1960, leaving issue a daughter, Lady Iris Mountbatten, born Jan. 13, 1920, married (1941) Capt. H. J. O'Malley (marriage dissolved, 1946).

(ii) Victoria Eugénie, born Oct. 24, 1887, married May 31, 1906, His late Majesty Alfonso XIII. (*King of Spain* 1886–1931; born 1886, died 1941), having issue.

(iii) Major Lord Leopold Mountbatten, G.C.V.O., born May 21, 1889; died April 23, 1922.

(iv) Maurice, born Oct. 3, 1891; died of wounds received in action, Oct. 27, 1914.

THE FAMILY OF KING EDWARD VII

KING EDWARD VII., eldest son of Queen Victoria, *born* Nov. 9, 1841; *married* March 10, 1863, Her Royal Highness Princess Alexandra, eldest daughter of King Christian IX. of Denmark; *succeeded* to the Throne Jan. 22, 1901; *died* May 6, 1910. Issue:—

1. H.R.H. Prince ALBERT VICTOR, *Duke of Clarence and Avondale and Earl of Athlone*, born Jan. 8, 1864, died Jan. 14, 1892.

2. H.M. KING GEORGE V. (*see* p. 214). Assumed by Royal Proclamation (June 17, 1917) for his House and Family as well as for all descendants in the male line of Queen Victoria who are subjects of these Realms, the name of WINDSOR; died Jan. 20, 1936, having had issue (*see* p. 214).

3. H.R.H. LOUISE, *Princess Royal*, born Feb. 20, 1867; married July 27, 1889, 1*st Duke of Fife* (who died Jan. 29, 1912); died Jan. 4, 1931. Issue:—

(i) H.H. Princess Alexandra, Duchess of Fife (*H.R.H. Princess Arthur of Connaught*), born May 17, 1891; married Oct. 15, 1913, to H.R.H. the late Prince Arthur. died Feb. 26, 1959. Issue:—

Alastair Arthur, Duke of Connaught, born Aug. 9, 1914; died April 26, 1943.

(ii) H.H. Princess Maud, born April 3, 1893; married Nov. 12, 1923, 11th Earl of Southesk; died Dec. 14, 1945, leaving issue:—

The Duke of Fife, born Sept. 23, 1929; married (1956) Hon. Caroline Dewar and has issue, The Earl of Macduff, born 1961.

4. H.R.H. Princess VICTORIA, born July 6, 1868; died Dec. 3, 1935.

5. H.R.H. Princess MAUD, born Nov. 26, 1869; married July 22, 1896, to Haakon VII., King of Norway, who died Sept. 21, 1957; died Nov. 20, 1938. Issue:—

H.M. Olav V., K.G., K.T., G.C.B., KING OF NORWAY, born July 2, 1903, *married* March 21, 1929, H.R.H. Princess Marthe of Sweden (who died April 5, 1954). Issue:—

(*a*) H.R.H. Princess Ragnhild, born June 9, 1930.

(*b*) H.R.H. Princess Astrid, born Feb. 12, 1932.

(*c*) H.R.H. Harald, Crown Prince of Norway, G.C.V.O., born Feb. 21, 1937.

THE FAMILY OF PRINCE ANDREW OF GREECE

Prince Andrew of Greece, *born* Feb. 2, 1882; *married* Princess Alice of Battenberg (*H.R.H. Princess Andrew of Greece*) (*see* p. 212); *died* Dec. 2, 1944, having had issue:—

(1) Princess Margarita, *born* April 17, 1905, *married* Prince Gottfried of Hohenlohe-Langenburg (*see* p. 212), and has issue, Prince Kraft, *born* 1935, Princess Beatrix, *born* 1936, Prince George, *born* 1938.

(2) Princess Theodora, *born* May 30, 1906, *married* Prince Berthold of Baden, and has issue, Princess Margarita, *born* 1932 (married, 1957, Prince Tomislav of Yugoslavia (see p. 212)), Prince Max, *born* 1933, Prince Louis, *born* 1937.

(3) Princess Cecilie, *born* June 22, 1911, *married* George, Grand Duke of Hesse, accidentally killed with husband and two sons, Nov. 16, 1937 (*see* p. 212).

(4) Princess Sophie, *born* June 26, 1914, *married* (i) Prince Christopher of Hesse (who died, 1944, leaving issue, Princess Christina, born 1933 (married Aug. 1956, Prince Andrej of Yugoslavia), Princess Dorothea, *born* 1934 (married 1959 Prince Friedrich Karl Windisch-Grätz), Prince Charles, *born* 1937, Prince Rainer, *born* 1939, Princess Clarissa, *born* 1944), *married* (ii) Prince George of Hanover, and has further issue, Prince Guelf, *born* 1947, Prince George, *born* 1950, Princess Friederike-Elizabeth, *born* 1954.

(5) Prince Philip (*H.R.H. the Prince Philip, Duke of Edinburgh*), *born* June 10, 1921 (*see* p. 215).

THE FAMILY OF KING GEORGE V

KING GEORGE V, second son of King Edward VII, *born* June 3, 1865; *married* July 6, 1893, Her Serene Highness Princess Victoria Mary Augusta Louise Olga Pauline Claudine Agnes (Queen Mary), *succeeded* to the throne May 6, 1910; *died* Jan. 20, 1936. Queen Mary died March 24, 1953. Issue:—

H.R.H. THE DUKE OF WINDSOR (EDWARD Albert Christian George Andrew Patrick David) K.G., K.T., K.P., G.C.B., G.C.S.I., G.C.M.G., G.C.I.E., G.C.V.O., G.B.E., I.S.O., M.C., F.R.S., Royal Victorian Chain, Admiral of the Fleet, Field Marshal, Marshal of the Royal Air Force, *born* June 23, 1894, *succeeded* to the Throne as KING EDWARD VIII., Jan. 20, 1936; *abdicated* Dec. 11, 1936; *married* June 3, 1937, Mrs. Wallis Warfield (The Duchess of Windsor). *Resident abroad.*

H.M. KING GEORGE VI (Albert Frederick Arthur George), *born* at York Cottage, Sandringham, Dec. 14, 1895; *married* April 26, 1923, to Lady Elizabeth Angela Marguerite (HER MAJESTY QUEEN ELIZABETH THE QUEEN MOTHER), daughter of the 14th Earl of Strathmore and Kinghorne, *succeeded* to the throne Dec. 11, 1936; *crowned* in Westminster Abbey, May 12, 1937; *died* Feb. 6, 1952, having had issue (*see* p. 215).

H.R.H. THE PRINCESS ROYAL (Victoria Alexandra Alice MARY), *Dowager Countess of Harewood*, C.I., G.C.V.O., G.B.E., E.D., R.R.C., D.C.L., Hon. General, Col.-in-Chief Royal Corps of Signals, Royal Scots, Prince of Wales' Own (Regiment of Yorkshire), Royal Canadian Signals, Canadian Scottish Regiment (Highlanders), Royal Australian Corps of Signals, Royal New Zealand Corps of Signals, Hon. Col. Barbados Regt., Leeds University Officers' Training Corps, Controller Commandant W.R.A.C., Air Chief Commandant, Princess Mary's Royal Air Force Nursing Service, Chancellor of Leeds University, *born* April 25, 1897, *married* Feb. 28, 1922, the 6th Earl of Harewood, K.G., G.C.V.O., D.S.O., T.D. (*born* Sept. 9, 1882; *died* May 24, 1947). *Residences*—Friary Court, St. James's Palace, S.W.1; Harewood House, Leeds.

Children of the Princess Royal—

(1) George Henry Hubert, 7th Earl of Harewood, *born* Feb. 7, 1923; *married* Sept. 29, 1949, Maria Donata (Marion), daughter of the late Erwin Stein, and has issue, David Henry George, Viscount Lascelles, *born* Oct. 21, 1950; Hon. James Edward Lascelles, *born* Oct. 5, 1953; Hon. Robert Jeremy Hugh Lascelles, *born* Feb. 14, 1955; (2) Hon. Gerald David Lascelles, *born* Aug. 21, 1924, *married* July 15, 1952, Miss Angela Dowding, and has issue, Henry Ulick, *born* May 19, 1953.

H.R.H. THE DUKE OF GLOUCESTER (HENRY William Frederick Albert), Duke of Gloucester, Earl of Ulster and Baron Culloden, High Steward of Windsor, K.G., P.C., K.T., K.P., Great Master of the Most Honourable Order of the Bath, G.C.M.G. G.C.V.O., LL.D., F.R.S., Royal Victorian Chain; Personal A.D.C. to the Queen; Grand Prior of the Order of St. John of Jerusalem; Field Marshal, Marshal of the Royal Air Force, Colonel Scots Guards, Col.-in-Chief 10th Hrs., R. Innis. Fus., Gloster Regt., Gordons, Rifle Bde., R.A.S.C., Royal Winnipeg Rifles, Royal Canadian Army Service Corps, Royal Australian Army Service Corps, Royal New Zealand Army Service Corps; Hon. Col. Camb. U.O.T.C. and 245th (Ulster) L.A.A. Regt., R.A. (T.A.) and Ceylon Light Infantry, Hon. Commodore, R.N.R., Master of the Corporation of Trinity House; *born* March 31, 1900, *married* Nov. 6, 1935, Lady Alice Montagu-Douglas-Scott, daughter of the 7th Duke of Buccleuch (H.R.H. the Duchess of Gloucester, C.I., G.C.V.O., G.B.E., Grand Cordon of Al Kamal, Colonel-in-Chief the King's Own Scottish Borderers and 2nd East Anglian Regt. (Duchess of Gloucester's Own Royal Lincolnshire and Northamptonshire), Air Chief Commandant W.R.A.F., *born* Dec. 25, 1901). *Children of the Duke of Gloucester*—

H.R.H. Prince WILLIAM Henry Andrew Frederick, *born* Dec. 18, 1941; H.R.H. Prince RICHARD Alexander Walter George, *born* Aug. 26, 1944. *Residences*—York House, St. James's Palace, S.W.1; Barnwell Castle, Northamptonshire.

H.R.H. THE DUKE OF KENT (GEORGE Edward Alexander Edmund), Duke of Kent, Earl of St. Andrews and Baron Downpatrick, K.G., P.C., K.T., G.C.M.G., G.C.V.O., Royal Victorian Chain, Personal A.D.C. to the King, *born* Dec. 20, 1902, *married* Nov. 29, 1934, H.R.H. Princess Marina of Greece and Denmark (H.R.H. Princess Marina, Duchess of Kent, C.I., G.C.V.O., G.B.E., Colonel-in-Chief The Devonshire and Dorset Regiment, Colonel, The Queen's Own Buffs, The Royal Kent Regiment; Chief Commandant, Women's Royal Naval Service, Honorary Colonel, 431st L.A.A. Regt., R.A. (T.A.), Honorary Colonel, 299 Field Regiment, R.A. (T.A.), *born* Nov. 30, O.S., 1906). *Killed on Active Service*, Aug. 25, 1942, leaving issue:—

(1) H.R.H. Prince EDWARD George Nicholas Paul Patrick, *Duke of Kent*, G.C.V.O., *born* Oct. 9, 1935, Capt. The Royal Scots Greys, *married* June 8, 1961, Katharine Lucy Mary, daughter of Sir William Worsley, Bt., and has issue, George Philip Nicholas, Earl of St. Andrews, *born* June 26, 1962. (2) H.R.H. Princess ALEXANDRA Helen Elizabeth Olga Christabel, G.C.V.O., *born* Dec. 25, 1936, Colonel-in-Chief, Durham Light Infantry, Hon. Colonel, North Irish Horse, *married*, April 24, 1963, Hon. Angus Ogilvy, son of the Earl of Airlie, *born* Sept. 14, 1928; (3) H.R.H. Prince MICHAEL George Charles Franklin, *born* July 4, 1942. *Residence of the Duke of Kent.*—Coppins, Iver, Bucks.

Residence of Princess Marina, Duchess of Kent.—Kensington Palace, W.8.

H.R.H. PRINCE JOHN, *born* July 12, 1905; *died* Jan. 18, 1919.

The House of Windsor

Her Most Excellent Majesty ELIZABETH THE SECOND (Elizabeth Alexandra Mary of Windsor), by the Grace of God, of the United Kingdom of Great Britain and Northern Ireland and of Her other Realms and Territories Queen, Head of the Commonwealth, Defender of the Faith, Sovereign of the British Orders of Knighthood, Captain General of the Royal Regiment of Artillery, and the Honourable Artillery Company, Colonel-in-Chief of the Life Guards, the Royal Horse Guards, the Royal Scots Greys (2nd Dragoons), the 16th/5th The Queen's Royal Lancers, the Royal Tank Regiment, the Corps of Royal Engineers, the Grenadier Guards, the Coldstream Guards, the Scots Guards, the Irish Guards, the Welsh Guards, the Royal Welch Fusiliers, the Loyal Regiment (North Lancashire), 2nd Green Jackets, K.R.R.C., the Argyll and Sutherland Highlanders, Royal Malta Artillery, R.A.O.C., Duke of Lancaster's Own Yeomanry, Hon. Colonel Queen's Own Warwickshire and Worcestershire Yeomanry, Captain-General, Combined Cadet Force, Captain-General, Royal Canadian Artillery, Colonel-in-Chief, the Regiment of Canadian Guards, Royal Canadian Engineers, King's Own Calgary Regiment, Royal 22e Régiment, Governor-General's Footguards, Canadian Grenadier Guards, the Royal New Brunswick Regt. (Carleton and York), Le Régiment de la Chaudière, the 48th Highlanders of Canada, Argyll and Sutherland Highlanders of Canada, Royal Canadian Ordnance Corps, Royal Australian Artillery, Royal Australian Engineers, Royal Australian Infantry Corps, Royal Australian Army Ordnance Corps, Royal Australian Army Nursing Corps, Captain-General, Royal New Zealand Artillery, Royal New Zealand Armoured Corps, Colonel-in-Chief, Royal New Zealand Engineers, Auckland Regiment (Countess of Ranfurly's Own), Wellington Regiment (City of Wellington's Own), Colonel-in-Chief, Royal Rhodesia Regiment, King's African Rifles, Northern Rhodesia Regiment, Royal Nigerian Military Forces, Royal Sierra Leone Military Forces, Air-Commodore-in-Chief, R.A.A.F., R.A.F. Regiment, Royal Observer Corps, Royal Canadian Air Force Auxiliary, Australian Citizen Air Force, Commandant-in-Chief, Royal Air Force College, Cranwell, Hon. Commissioner, Royal Canadian Mounted Police, Master of the Merchant Navy and Fishing Fleets, Head of the Civil Defence Corps, Head of the National Hospital Service Reserve.

Elder daughter of His late Majesty King George VI and of Her Majesty Queen Elizabeth the Queen Mother; *born* at 17 Bruton Street, London, W.1, April 21, 1926, *succeeded* to the throne February 6, 1952, *crowned* June 2, 1953; having *married*, November 20, 1947, in Westminster Abbey, Philip, Duke of Edinburgh, Earl of Merioneth and Baron Greenwich (H.R.H. the Prince Philip, Duke of Edinburgh), K.G., P.C., K.T., G.M.B.E., F.R.S., Admiral of the Fleet, Field Marshal, Marshal of the Royal Air Force, Admiral of the Fleet, Royal Australian Navy, Field Marshal, Australian Military Forces, Marshal of the Royal Australian Air Force, Captain-General of the Royal Marines, Colonel-in-Chief, The Queen's Royal Irish Hussars, The Duke of Edinburgh's Royal Regiment (Berkshire and Wiltshire), Queen's Own Highlanders (Seaforths and Camerons), Royal Canadian Regiment, Hawkes Bay Regiment, New Zealand, Colonel of the Welsh Guards, Commandant-in-Chief, R.A.F. Technical College, Hon. Colonel, Leicestershire and Derbyshire Yeomanry, Edinburgh University Officers Training Corps, Admiral, Sea Cadet Corps, Royal Canadian Sea Cadets, Colonel-in-Chief, Army Cadet Force, Royal Canadian Army Cadets, Air Commodore-in-Chief Air Training Corps, Royal Canadian Air Cadets, Ranger of Windsor Park. *See* p. 214.

CHILDREN OF HER MAJESTY

H.R.H. THE PRINCE OF WALES (CHARLES Philip Arthur George), Prince of Wales and Earl of Chester, Duke of Cornwall and Duke of Rothesay, Earl of Carrick and Baron Renfrew, Lord of the Isles and Great Steward of Scotland, K.G., *born* at Buckingham Palace, November 14, 1948.

H.R.H. PRINCESS ANNE ELIZABETH ALICE LOUISE, *born* at Clarence House, August 15, 1950.

H.R.H. PRINCE ANDREW ALBERT CHRISTIAN EDWARD, *born* at Buckingham Palace, Feb. 19, 1960.

MOTHER OF HER MAJESTY

H.M. QUEEN ELIZABETH THE QUEEN MOTHER (Elizabeth Angela Marguerite) (daughter of the 14th Earl of Strathmore and Kinghorne), Lady of the Garter, Lady of the Thistle, Order of the Crown of India, Grand Master of the Royal Victorian Order, Dame Grand Cross of the Order of the British Empire, Royal Victorian Chain, Doctor of Civil Law, Doctor of Literature, Colonel-in-Chief 1st the Queen's Dragoon Guards, Queen's Own Hussars, 9th/12th Royal Lancers (Prince of Wales's), 3rd East Anglian Regiment (16th/44th Foot), Black Watch, K.O.Y.L.I., the King's Regiment (Manchester and Liverpool), R.A.M.C., and the Royal Australian Army Medical Corps, Commandant-in-Chief W.R.A.C., Hon. Colonel London Scottish, City of London Yeomanry, Colonel-in-Chief Toronto Scottish and Black Watch (Royal Highland Regiment) of Canada, Commandant-in-Chief R.A.F. Central Flying School. *Born* Aug. 4, 1900, *married* April 26, 1923, Prince Albert Frederick Arthur George of Windsor, Duke of York, who *succeeded* to the throne as KING GEORGE VI, Dec. 11, 1936, and *died* February 6, 1952.

Residences.—Clarence House, St. James's, S.W.1.; Castle of Mey, Caithness, Scotland.

SISTER OF HER MAJESTY

H.R.H. PRINCESS MARGARET ROSE (The Princess Margaret, Countess of Snowdon), C.I., G.C.V.O., Colonel-in-Chief, 15th–19th The King's Royal Hussars, 1st East Anglian Regiment (Royal Norfolk and Suffolk), The Royal Highland Fusiliers (Princess Margaret's Own Glasgow and Ayrshire Regiment), Queen Alexandra's Royal Army Nursing Corps, Women's Royal Australian Army Corps, Commandant-in-Chief, St. John Ambulance Brigade Cadets, Dame Grand Cross of the Order of St. John of Jerusalem, Commodore Sea Ranger Section of the Girl Guides Association; *born* at Glamis Castle, Angus, Scotland, Aug. 21, 1930; *married* May 6, 1960, Antony Charles Robert Armstrong-Jones (*born* March 7, 1930), son of Ronald Armstrong-Jones, Q.C. and the Countess of Rosse, *created* Earl of Snowdon, 1961, Constable of Caernarvon Castle, and has issue, David Albert Charles, Viscount Linley, *born* Nov. 3, 1961.

Residence.—Kensington Palace, W.8.

ORDER OF SUCCESSION TO THE THRONE

The Queen's sons and daughter are in the order of succession to the throne, and after the Princess Margaret and her son, the Duke of Gloucester and his sons; then the Duke of Kent, his son, his brother and his sister; then the Princess Royal, her elder son and his sons and her younger son and his son; then the Duke of Fife, son of the late Countess of Southesk, and his son; then King Olav of Norway and his children, then the children of the second daughter of the late Duke of Saxe-Coburg (his eldest daughter, the late Queen Marie of Roumania, having formally renounced on her marriage all possibility of claim to the British Throne); then the children of the third daughter (the late Princess Alexandra of Hohenlohe-Langenburg); then the children of the eldest son of the late Princess Margaret of Connaught (Crown Princess of Sweden), her other sons and her daughter (Queen Ingrid of Denmark) and her children; then the younger daughter of the first Duke of Connaught and Strathearn (Lady Patricia Ramsay) and her son; then the Princess Alice (Countess of Athlone) and her daughter and grandchildren. Having thus exhausted the families of all Queen Victoria's sons we turn to her daughters, beginning with the house of the late Empress Frederick, but as this line is wholly out of practical bounds it would be profitless to pursue the investigation any further.

Precedence in England

The Sovereign.

The Prince Philip, Duke of Edinburgh.

The Prince of Wales.

The Prince Andrew.

The Duke of Gloucester.

The Duke of Windsor.

Archbishop of Canterbury.

Lord High Chancellor.

Archbishop of York.

The Prime Minister.

Lord President of the Council.

Speaker of the House of Commons.

Lord Privy Seal.

High Commissioners of Commonwealth Countries and Ambassadors of Foreign States.

Dukes, according to their Patents of Creation:

(1) Of England; (2) of Scotland; (3) of Great Britain; (4) of Ireland; (5) those created since the Union.

Ministers and Envoys.

Eldest sons of Dukes of Blood Royal.

Marquesses, in same order as Dukes.

Dukes' eldest Sons.

Earls, in same order as Dukes.

Younger sons of Dukes of Blood Royal.

Marquesses' eldest Sons.

Dukes' younger Sons.

Viscounts, in same order as Dukes.

Earls' eldest Sons.

Marquesses' younger Sons.

Bishops of London, Durham and Winchester.

All other English Bishops, according to their seniority of Consecration.

Secretaries of State, if of the degree of a Baron.

Barons, in same order as Dukes.

Treasurer of H.M.'s Household.

Comptroller of H.M.'s Household.

Vice-Chamberlain of H.M.'s Household.

Secretaries of State under the degree of Baron.

Viscounts' eldest Sons.

Earls' younger Sons.

Barons' eldest Sons.

Knights of the Garter if Commoners.

Privy Councillors if of no higher rank.

Chancellor of the Exchequer.

Chancellor of the Duchy of Lancaster.

Lord Chief Justice of England.

Master of the Rolls.

President of the Probate Court.

The Lords Justices of Appeal.

Judges of the High Court.

Vice-Chancellor of County Palatine of Lancaster.

Viscounts' younger Sons.

Barons' younger Sons.

Sons of Life Peers.

Baronets of either Kingdom, according to date of Patents.

Knights of the Thistle if Commoners.

Knights Grand Cross of the Bath.

Members of the Order of Merit.

Knights Grand Commanders of the Star of India.

Knights Grand Cross of St. Michael and St. George.

Knights Grand Commanders of the Indian Empire.

Knights Grand Cross of the Royal Victorian Order.

Knights Grand Cross of Order of the British Empire.

Companions of Honour.

Knights Commanders of the above Orders.

Knights Bachelor.

Official Referees of The Supreme Court.

Judges of County Courts and Judges of the Mayor's and City of London Court.

Companions and Commanders *e.g.* C.B.; C.S.I.; C.M.G.; C.I.E.; C.V.O.; C.B.E.; D.S.O.; M.V.O. (4th); O.B.E.; I.S.O.

Eldest Sons of younger Sons of Peers.

Baronets' eldest Sons.

Eldest Sons of Knights in the same order as their Fathers.

M.V.O. (5th); M.B.E.

Younger Sons of the younger Sons of Peers.

Baronets' younger Sons.

Younger Sons of Knights in the same order as their Fathers.

Naval, Military, Air, and other Esquires by Office.

WOMEN

Women take the same rank as their husbands or as their eldest brothers; but the daughter of a Peer marrying a Commoner retains her title as Lady or Honourable. Daughters of Peers rank next immediately after the wives of their elder brothers, and before their younger brother's wives. Daughters of Peers marrying Peers of lower degree take the same order of precedency as that of their husbands; thus the daughter of a Duke marrying a Baron becomes of the rank of Baroness only, while her sisters married to commoners retain their rank and take precedence of the Baroness. Merely official rank on the husband's part does not give any similar precedence to the wife.

For Dames Grand Cross, *see* pp. 297–8.

LOCAL PRECEDENCE

ENGLAND AND WALES.—No written code of county or city order of precedence has been promulgated, but in Counties the Lord Lieutenant stands first, and secondly the Sheriff, and therefore in Cities and Boroughs the Lord Lieutenant has social precedence over the mayor; but at City or Borough functions the Lord Mayor or Mayor will preside. At Oxford and Cambridge the High Sheriff takes precedence of the Vice-Chancellor.

SCOTLAND.—*See* Index.

The Queen's Household

Lord Chamberlain, The Lord Cobbold, P.C., G.C.V.O.
Lord Steward, The Duke of Hamilton and Brandon, P.C., K.T., G.C.V.O., A.F.C.
Master of the Horse, The Duke of Beaufort, K.G., P.C., G.C.V.O.
Treasurer of the Household, M. H. C. Hughes-Young, M.C., M.P.
Comptroller of the Household, R. Chichester-Clark, M.P.
Vice-Chamberlain, G. B. Finlay, E.R.D., M.P.

Gold Sticks, Field-Marshal the Lord Harding of Petherton, G.C.B., C.B.E., D.S.O., M.C.; Field-Marshal Sir Gerald Templer, G.C.B., G.C.M.G., K.B.E., D.S.O.
Vice-Admiral of the United Kingdom, Admiral Sir John Edelsten, G.C.B., G.C.V.O., C.B.E.
Rear-Admiral of the United Kingdom, Admiral Sir Peter Reid, G.C.B., C.V.O.
First and Principal Naval Aide-de-Camp, Admiral Sir Wilfrid Woods, G.B.E., K.C.B., D.S.O.
Aides-de-Camp General, General Henry Crerar, C.H., C.B., D.S.O., C.D.; General Sir Richard Hull, G.C.B., D.S.O.; General Sir Gerald Lathbury, G.C.B., D.S.O., M.B.E.; General Sir Roderick McLeod, K.C.B., C.B.E.; General Sir Michael West, K.C.B., D.S.O.
Principal Air Aides-de-Camp, Air Chief Marshal Sir Edmund Hudleston, G.C.B., C.B.E.; Air Chief Marshal Sir Walter Merton, G.B.E., K.C.B.

Mistress of the Robes, The Dowager Duchess of Devonshire, G.C.V.O., C.B.E.
Ladies of the Bedchamber, The Countess of Leicester; The Countess of Euston.
Extra Lady of the Bedchamber, The Marchioness of Abergavenny.
Women of the Bedchamber, Lady Margaret Hay, C.V.O.; Lady Rose Baring; Miss Mary Morrison; Lady Susan Hussey (*temp.*).
Extra Women of the Bedchamber, Hon. Mrs. Andrew Elphinstone, C.V.O.; Mrs. Alexander Abel Smith; Mrs. John Dugdale.

THE PRIVATE SECRETARY'S OFFICE

Buckingham Palace, S.W.1.

Private Secretary to the Queen, Lt.-Col. Rt. Hon. Sir Michael Adeane, G.C.V.O., K.C.B.
Assistant Private Secretaries to the Queen, Sir Edward Ford, K.C.V.O., C.B.; Lt.-Col. Hon. Sir Martin Charteris, K.C.V.O., C.B., O.B.E.
Press Secretary, Commander Richard Colville, C.B., C.V.O., D.S.C., R.N.
Assistant Press Secretary, Miss Anne Hawkins.
Assistant Information Officer, H. Freeman-Greene (*temp.*).
Chief Clerk, Miss Jean Taylor.
Secretary to the Private Secretary, A. C. Neal, M.V.O., B.E.M.
Clerks, Miss O. M. Short, M.V.O.; Miss J. M. Munro; Miss W. M. Balcomb; Miss S. F. Phillips; Miss M. D. H. Smith; Miss S. A. Douglas Smith; Miss C. W. Austin; Miss A. M. Downes (*Press*); Miss F. M. Simpson (*Press*).

The Queen's Archives,

Norman Tower, Windsor Castle.

Keeper of the Queen's Archives, Lt.-Col. Rt. Hon. Sir Michael Adeane, G.C.V.O., K.C.B.
Assistant Keeper, R. C. Mackworth-Young, M.V.O.
Registrar, Miss Enid Price Hill, M.V.O.
Historical Adviser, Sir John Wheeler-Bennett, K.C.V.O., C.M.G., O.B.E.

DEPARTMENT OF THE KEEPER OF THE PRIVY PURSE AND TREASURER TO THE QUEEN

Buckingham Palace, S.W.1.

Keeper of the Privy Purse and Treasurer to the Queen, Brigadier the Lord Tryon, K.C.B., K.C.V.O., D.S.O.
Deputy Treasurer to the Queen, Commander P. J. Row, M.V.O., O.B.E., R.N.
Assistant Keeper of the Privy Purse, Major J. R. Maudslay, M.V.O., M.B.E.

Privy Purse Office

Chief Accountant, Edmund F. Grove, M.V.O.
Clerk to the Keeper of the Privy Purse, D. Waters, M.V.O.
Accountant, Peter Wright, M.V.O.
Clerk, E. Smith.

Land Agent, Sandringham, Capt. William A. Fellowes, C.V.O.
Resident Factor, Balmoral, Brigadier the Earl of Caithness, C.V.O., C.B.E., D.S.O.
Land Steward, Windsor, Adrian Pelly, M.V.O.
Consulting Engineers, James A. Banks, C.V.O., O.B.E. (*Balmoral*); Ralph Freeman, C.B.E. (*Sandringham*).

Treasurer's Office.

Chief Accountant and Paymaster, Henry G. Pinnock, M.V.O.
Establishment Officer, Miss R. McLennan, M.V.O.
Accountant, Charles Warner, M.V.O.
Clerk to the Deputy Treasurer, Miss E. S. Colquhoun, M.V.O., M.B.E.
Comptroller of Supply, Philip Venning.
Deputy Comptroller of Supply, M. D. Tims, M.V.O.
Chief Clerk, Comptroller of Supply's Office, S. S. Haimes.

Royal Almonry

High Almoner, The Rt. Rev. the Lord Bishop of St. Albans.
Hereditary Grand Almoner, The Marquess of Exeter, K.C.M.G.
Sub-Almoner, Rev. M. F. Foxell, C.V.O.
Secretary, Lawrence E. Tanner, C.V.O., F.S.A.
Assistant Secretary, Peter Wright, M.V.O.

THE LORD CHAMBERLAIN'S OFFICE

St. James's Palace, S.W.1.

Comptroller, Brigadier Sir Norman Gwatkin, G.C.V.O., D.S.O.
Assistant Comptroller, Lt.-Col. E. C. W. Penn, O.B.E., M.C.
Secretary, A. J. Galpin, C.B.E., M.V.O.
Assistant Secretary R. J. Hill, M.V.O., M.B.E.
Clerks, D. V. G. Buchanan, M.V.O.; J. E. P. Titman, M.V.O. (*State Invitation Assistant*); W. E. O. Munro; Miss M. Fisher, B.E.M.; Miss J. Kirby; Miss M. Greiner; Mrs. T. J. H. Downing.
Examiners of Plays, C. D. Heriot, M.V.O.; Lt.-Col. Sir St. Vincent Troubridge, Bt., M.B.E.; M. Coles.
Examiner of Plays (Welsh), Rev. A. E. Jones, C.B.E. (Cynan).

Permanent Lords in Waiting, Lt.-Col. The Lord Nugent, G.C.V.O., M.C.; The Earl of Scarbrough, K.G., P.C., G.C.S.I., G.C.I.E., G.C.V.O., T.D.
Lords in Waiting, The Earl of Eldon, G.C.V.O.; The Earl of Westmorland; The Lord Denham; The Marquess of Lothian; The Earl Ferrers.

Gentlemen Ushers, Capt. Sir Humphrey C. LLoyd, K.C.V.O., M.C.; Lt.-Col. Sir Henry Bache de Satgé, K.C.V.O., C.M.G., D.S.O.; Col. Sir Geoffrey Ronald Codrington, K.C.V.O., C.B., C.M.G., D.S.O., O.B.E., T.D.; Capt. William Duncan Phipps, C.V.O., R.N.; Capt. Philip Lloyd Neville, C.V.O., R.N.; Lt.-Col. John Mandeville Hugo, C.V.O., O.B.E.; Col. John Sidney North Fitzgerald, C.V.O., M.B.E., M.C.; Maj.-Gen. Frederick George Beaumont-Nesbitt, C.V.O., C.B.E., M.C.; Air Vice-Marshal Arthur Percy Ledger, C.B., C.B.E.; H. L. Carron Greig.

Extra Gentlemen Ushers, Capt. Charles Alexander Lindsay Irvine, C.V.O., O.B.E.; Sir John C. Hanbury-Williams, C.V.O.; Sir John Monck, G.C.V.O., C.M.G.; Sir Algar Howard, K.C.B., K.C.V.O., M.C., T.D.; Capt. Andrew Yates, M.V.O., R.N.; Major Thomas Harvey, C.V.O., D.S.O.; Ernest Frederick Orby Gascoigne, T.D.; Brig. Charles Richard Britten, M.C.; Frederic Hudd, C.B.E.; Brig. I. Ahmad Khan; Capt. Sir John Dashwood, Bt., C.V.O.; Air Vice-Marshal Sir Ranald Reid, K.C.B., D.S.O., M.C.; Esmond Butler; Brig. Sir Ivan De la Bere, K.C.V.O., C.B., C.B.E.; Sir Austin Strutt, K.C.V.O., C.B.; William Richard Cumming, C.V.O.; Brigadier Richard Frank Sherlock Gooch, D.S.O., M.C.

Gentleman Usher to the Sword of State, Air Chief Marshal Sir Arthur Sheridan Barratt, K.C.B., C.M.G., M.C.

Gentleman Usher of the Black Rod, Air Chief Marshal Sir George Mills, G.C.B., D.F.C.

Serjeants at Arms, H. G. Pinnock, M.V.O.; A. J. Galpin, C.B.E., M.V.O.; R. J. Hill, M.V.O., M.B.E.

Constable & Governor of Windsor Castle (vacant).

Deputy Constable and Lieutenant Governor (vacant).

Keeper of the Jewel House, Tower of London, Maj.-Gen. H. D. W. Sitwell, C.B., M.C., F.S.A.

Surveyor of the Queen's Pictures, Professor Sir Anthony Frederick Blunt, K.C.V.O.

Deputy Surveyor of the Queen's Pictures, Oliver Nicholas Millar, C.V.O., F.S.A.

Librarian, R. C. Mackworth-Young, M.V.O.

Keeper of the Prints and Drawings, Miss A. Scott-Elliot, M.V.O., F.S.A.

Library Assistant, Miss O. Hedley.

Surveyor of the Queen's Works of Art, Francis Watson, M.V.O., F.S.A.

Deputy Surveyor, Geoffrey de Bellaigue.

Master of the Music, Sir Arthur Bliss, Mus.D. Ll.D.

Poet Laureate, John Edward Masefield, O.M., Litt.D., Ll.D., F.S.A.

Bargemaster, H. A. Barry.

Keeper of the Swans, F. J. Turk.

Caretaker of St. James's Palace, L. Wyatt, M.B.E.,

Housekeeper (Hampton Court Palace), Miss G. Pooley.

ASCOT OFFICE

St. James's Palace, S.W.1.

Her Majesty's Representative at Ascot, The Duke of Norfolk, K.G., P.C., G.C.V.O.

Secretary, Miss D. M. L. Collins.

ECCLESIASTICAL HOUSEHOLD

The College of Chaplains.

Clerk of the Closet, The Bishop of Chichester.

Deputy Clerk of the Closet, Rev. M. F. Foxell, C.V.O., M.A.

Chaplains to the Queen, Canon T. G. Rogers, M.C., B.D.; Canon C. E. Raven, D.D., D.Sc.; Canon W. J. T. Phythian-Adams, D.S.O., M.C., D.D.; Rev. P. T. B. Clayton, C.H., M.C., D.D., M.A.; Canon S. E. Swann, M.A.; Ven. F. Boreham, M.A.; Canon L. Martin Andrews, C.V.O., M.B.E., M.C., M.A.; Rev. R. R. Churchill, C.B.E., M.A.; Canon R. C. Meredith, M.A.; Preb. W. G. Arrowsmith, M.A.; Preb. H. H. Treacher; Rev. P. L. Gillingham, M.V.O., M.A.; Canon L. G. Mannering, M.C., M.A.; Ven. A. S. Bean, M.B.E., M.A., B.D.; Ven. J. F. Richardson, M.A.; Rev. W. G. Fallows, M.A.; Canon H. D. Anderson, M.V.O., B.D.; Rev. E. J. G. Ward, M.A.; Preb. C. J. Brown, O.B.E., M.A.; Ven. D. H. Booth, M.B.E., M.A.; Canon D. P. Low, T.D., M.A.; Canon C. B. Sampson, M.A.; Rev. J. R. W. Stott, M.A.; Ven. E. H. Stenning, M.B.E., T.D., M.A.; Rev. A. C. Don, K.C.V.O., D.D.; Rev. S. A. Williams, M.A.; Ven. W. S. Hayman, M.A.; Canon T. J. Pugh, T.D., M.A.; Ven. K. G. Thompson, M.A.; Rev. H. C. Blackburne, M.A.; Rev. C. E. M. Roderick, M.A.; Ven. I. D. Neill, C.B., O.B.E., M.A.; Canon W. E. Norris, M.A.

Chapels Royal.

Dean of the Chapels Royal, The Bishop of London.

Sub-Dean of the Chapels Royal, Rev. M. F. Foxell, C.V.O., M.A.

Priests in Ordinary, Rev. E. F. Donne, M.A.; Rev. G. E. Sage, M.A.; Rev. F. J. Glendenning, M.A.

Deputy Priests, Rev. C. T. H. Dams, M.A.; Rev. R. Simpson; Rev. G. R. Dunstan, M.A., F.S.A.

Organist, Choirmaster and Composer, W. H. Gabb, M.V.O., F.R.C.O., A.R.C.M.

Domestic Chaplain—Windsor Castle, The Dean of Windsor.

Domestic Chaplain—Sandringham, Rev. P. T. Ashton, M.V.O., M.A.

Chaplain—Royal Chapel, Windsor Great Park, Rev. E. J. G. Ward, M.V.O., M.A.

Chaplain—Hampton Court Palace, Preb. W. G. Cameron, M.A.

Organist and Choirmaster—Hampton Court Palace, Norman Askew, F.R.A.M., F.R.C.O., A.R.C.M.

MEDICAL HOUSEHOLD

Physicians, Sir John Weir, G.C.V.O., M.B., Ch.B.; The Lord Evans, G.C.V.O., D.Sc., M.D., F.R.C.P.; R. Bodley Scott, D.M., F.R.C.P.

Physician-Paediatrician, Sir Wilfrid Sheldon, K.C.V.O. M.D., F.R.C.P.

Extra Physician, Sir Daniel Thomas Davies, K.C.V.O., M.D., B.Sc., F.R.C.P.

Serjeant Surgeon, Sir Arthur Espie Porritt, Bt., K.C.M.G., K.C.V.O., C.B.E., M.B., M.Ch., F.R.C.S.

Surgeons, Professor Sir James Ross, Bt., K.C.V.O., M.S., F.R.C.S.; Sir Ralph Marnham, K.C.V.O., M.Chir., F.R.C.S., L.R.C.P.

Surgeon Oculist, Sir Stewart Duke-Elder, G.C.V.O., D.Sc., Ph.D., M.D., F.R.S., F.R.C.S., F.A.C.S.

Extra Orthopædic Surgeon, Sir Reginald Watson-Jones, F.R.C.S., M.Ch.Orth., B.Sc., M.B., Ch.B., L.R.C.P.

Surgeon Gynaecologist, Sir John Peel, K.C.V.O., F.R.C.S., F.R.C.O.G.

Surgeon Dentist, Alan McLeod, C.V.O., F.D.S., R.C.S. (ENG.), D.D.S.

Aurist, J.C. Hogg, C.V.O., F.R.C.S.

Physician to the Household, William Neville Mann, M.D., F.R.C.P.

Surgeon to the Household, Edward Grainger Muir M.S., F.R.C.S.

Surgeon Oculist to the Household, Allen Goldsmith, C.V.O., M.B., B.S., F.R.C.S., L.R.C.P.

Apothecary to the Household, J. Nigel Loring, C.V.O., M.R.C.S., L.R.C.P.

Surgeon Apothecary to the Household at Windsor, Richard May, C.V.O., M.B., B.Ch., M.R.C.S., L.R.C.P.

Surgeon Apothecary to the Household at Sandringham, J. L. B. Ansell, M.V.O., M.R.C.S., L.R.C.P.

Coroner of the Queen's Household, A. G. Davies, M.B., B.S., M.R.C.S., L.R.C.P.

Marshal of the Diplomatic Corps, Rear-Adm. The Earl Cairns, C.B.
Vice-Marshal, Dugald Malcolm, T.D.

CENTRAL CHANCERY OF THE ORDERS OF KNIGHTHOOD

8 Buckingham Gate, S.W.1.

Secretary, Maj.-Gen. C. H. Colquhoun, C.B., O.B.E.
Chief Clerk, G. A. Harris, M.V.O., M.B.E.
Clerks, D. Morrison, M.V.O.; Mrs. L. C. A. Bell, M.V.O.; Miss A. A. Hamersley, M.V.O.; Miss M. P. Horsfield, M.V.O.; Miss S. Wells; Mrs. E. Rogers; Miss D. M. Mason; Mrs. A. M. Hughes.

The Honorable Corps of Gentlemen at Arms

St. James's Palace, S.W.1.

Captain, The Earl St. Aldwyn, P.C., T.D.; *Lieutenant,* Maj.-Gen. W. A. F. L. Fox-Pitt, D.S.O., M.V.O., M.C.; *Standard Bearer,* Brig. Sir Henry Floyd, Bt., C.B., C.B.E.; *Clerk of the Cheque & Adjutant,* Col. Sir Robert Gooch, Bt., D.S.O.; *Harbinger,* Maj.-Gen. A. R. Chater, C.B., D.S.O., O.B.E.

Gentlemen of the Corps.

Brigadiers, Sir Henry Houldsworth, K.B.E., D.S.O., M.C., T.D.; J. N. Cheney, O.B.E.; R. B. T. Daniell, D.S.O.; A. H. Pepys, D.S.O.; J. O. E. Vandeleur, D.S.O.; Hon. R. G. Hamilton-Russell, D.S.O.; J. E. Swetenham, D.S.O.
Colonels, Sir John Carew Pole, Bt., D.S.O., T.D.; C. Mitford-Slade; S. Enderby, D.S.O., M.C.; K. E. Savill, D.S.O.; F. F. B. St. George, C.V.O.; H. N. Clowes, D.S.O., O.B.E.; P. F. I. Reid, O.B.E.
Lieutenant-Colonels, John F. Colvin, O.B.E., M.C.; J. F. C. K. E. Previté, O.B.E.; F. E. A. Fulford; W. Heathcoat-Amory, D.S.O.; Sir William Makins, Bt.; G. J. Kidston-Montgomerie, D.S.O., M.C.; J. Chandos-Pole, O.B.E.; R. S. G. Perry, D.S.O.; Hon. M. G. Edwardes, M.B.E.; P. T. Clifton, D.S.O.; Sir William Lowther, Bt., O.B.E.; J. Granville; H. A. Hope, O.B.E., M.C.

The Queen's Bodyguard of the Yeomen of the Guard

St. James's Palace, S.W.1.

Captain, Col. the Viscount Goschen, O.B.E.; *Lieutenant,* Maj.-Gen. Sir Allan Adair, Bt., C.B., C.V.O., D.S.O., M.C.; *Clerk of the Cheque & Adjutant,* Lt.-Col. V. B. Turner, V.C.; *Ensign,* Brig. W. G. Carr, D.S.O.; *Exons,* Col. the Duke of Westminster, D.S.O.; Lt.-Col. J. D. Hornung, O.B.E., M.C.

MASTER OF THE HOUSEHOLD'S DEPARTMENT

Board of Green Cloth.

Buckingham Palace, S.W.1.

Master of the Household, Major Sir Mark Milbank, K.C.V.O., M.C.
Deputy Master of the Household, Major the Lord Plunket, M.V.O.
Chief Clerk, T. J. Barnham, M.V.O.
Clerk, G. H. Franklin.

Superintendent, Buckingham Palace, S. A. Williams, M.V.O.

Superintendent, Windsor Castle, S. Lucking, M.V.O.

Palace Steward, C. Oulton.

Housekeeper, Buckingham Palace, Mrs. J. E. Findlater.

Housekeeper, Windsor Castle, Mrs. Edith Holmes.

ROYAL MEWS DEPARTMENT

Buckingham Palace, S.W.1.

Crown Equerry, Lt.-Col. John Mansel Miller, D.S.O., M.C.

Equerries, Major the Lord Plunket, C.V.O.; Captain P. C. Harvey (*temp.*); Lieut. J. Garnier, R.N. (*temp.*).

Senior Air Equerry, Air Vice-Marshal Sir Edward Fielden, K.C.V.O., C.B., D.F.C., A.F.C.

Extra Equerries, Vice-Admiral Sir Conolly Abel-Smith, G.C.V.O., C.B.; Lt.-Col. Rt. Hon. Sir Michael Adeane, G.C.V.O., K.C.B.; Col. Sir John Renton Aird, Bt., M.V.O., M.C.; Rt. Hon. Sir James Ulick Francis Canning Alexander, G.C.B., G.C.V.O., C.M.G., O.B.E.; Capt. P. W. B. Ashmore, M.V.O., D.S.C., R.N.; Lt.-Gen. Sir Frederick A. M. Browning, G.C.V.O., K.B.E., C.B., D.S.O.; Cdr. Colin Buist, C.V.O., R.N.; Capt. Sir Harold Campbell, G.C.V.O., D.S.O., R.N.; Lt.-Col. Hon. Sir Martin Michael Charles Charteris, K.C.V.O., C.B., O.B.E.; Cdr. Sir Dudley Colles, K.C.B., K.C.V.O., O.B.E., R.N.; Vice-Admiral Sir Peter Dawnay, K.C.V.O., C.B., D.S.C.; Sir Edward William Spencer Ford, K.C.V.O., C.B.; Brigadier Walter Douglas Campbell Greenacre, C.B., D.S.O., M.V.O.; Brig. Sir Norman Gwatkin, G.C.V.O., D.S.O.; Capt. Lord Claud Hamilton, G.C.V.O., C.M.G., D.S.O.; Rear-Adm. Sir Joseph Charles Cameron Henley, K.C.V.O., C.B.; Rt. Hon. Sir Alan Lascelles, G.C.B., G.C.V.O., C.M.G., M.C.; Lt.-Col. the Earl of Leicester, M.V.O.; Adm. Hon. Sir Herbert Meade-Featherstonhaugh, G.C.V.O., C.B., D.S.O.; Major Sir Mark Vane Milbank, K.C.V.O., M.C.; Air Commodore Dennis Mitchell, C.V.O., D.F.C., A.F.C. (*Captain of the Queen's Flight*); Capt. Charles Joseph Henry O'Hara Moore, C.V.O., M.C.; Lt.-Col. Ryrid Myddleton, M.V.O.; Lt.-Col. the Lord Nugent, G.C.V.O., M.C.; Lt.-Col. Eric Charles William Mackenzie Penn, O.B.E., M.C.; Sir George Arthur Ponsonby, K.C.V.O.; Brig. Walter Morley Sale, C.V.O., O.B.E.; Maj.-Gen. Sir Arthur Guy Salisbury-Jones, G.C.V.O., C.M.G., C.B.E., M.C.; Group Capt. Peter Wooldridge Townsend, C.V.O., D.S.O., D.F.C.

Hon. Veterinary Surgeon, A. C. Fraser, Ph.D., B.V.Sc., M.R.C.V.S.

Supt. Royal Mews, Buckingham Palace, Capt. N. H. Morgan, M.V.O., M.M.

Comptroller of Stores, J. W. McNelly, M.V.O.

Chief Clerk, Miss Winifred M. Bateson, M.V.O.

HER MAJESTY'S HOUSEHOLD IN SCOTLAND

Hereditary Lord High Constable, The Countess of Erroll.

Hereditary Master of the Household, The Duke of Argyll.

Lyon King of Arms, Sir Thomas Innes of Learney, K.C.V.O.

Hereditary Standard-Bearer, The Earl of Dundee, P.C.

Hereditary Keepers:—
Holyrood, The Duke of Hamilton and Brandon, P.C., K.T., G.C.V.O., A.F.C.

Falkland, Maj. Michael Duncan David Crichton-Stuart, M.C.
Dunstaffnage, The Duke of Argyll.
Stirling, The Earl of Mar and Kellie.
Keeper of Dumbarton Castle, Admiral Sir Angus E. M. B. Cunninghame Graham of Gartmore, K.B.E., C.B.
Keeper of Rothesay Castle, The Marquess of Bute.
Governor of Edinburgh Castle, Lieut.-Gen. Sir William Turner, K.B.E., C.B., D.S.O.
Dean of the Chapel Royal and of the Order of the Thistle, Very Rev. Charles Laing Warr, K.C.V.O., D.D., LL.D., F.R.S.E.
Chaplains in Ordinary, Very Rev. C. L. Warr, K.C.V.O., D.D., LL.D., F.R.S.E.; Very Rev. A. N. Davidson, D.D.; Rev. Prof. J. S. Stewart, D.D.; Very Rev. J. A. Fraser, M.B.E., T.D., D.D.; Rev. Prof. E. P. Dickie, M.C., D.D.; Very Rev. Sir George McLeod, Bt., M.C., D.D.; Rev. J. B. Longmuir, T.D., M.A., B.I.; Rev. H. O. Douglas, C.B.E., M.A., D.D.; Rev. R. W. V. Selby Wright, T.D., D.D., F.S.A. (Scot.); Rev. H. C. Whitley, M.A., Ph.D.
Extra Chaplains, Very Rev. J. Hutchinson Cockburn, D.D.; Rev. T. B. Stewart Thomson, M.C., T.D., D.D.; Rev. A. Nicol, M.A.
Domestic Chaplain, Balmoral, Rev. John Lamb, C.V.O., D.D.
Historiographer Emeritus, Prof. John Duncan Mackie, C.B.E., M.C., LL.D.
Botanist (vacant).
Painter and Limner, Stanley Cursiter, C.B.E., R.S.A., R.S.W., F.R.S.E.
Sculptor, Benno Schotz, R.S.A.
Physicians in Scotland, Prof. E. J. Wayne, M.D., F.R.C.P.; Prof. I. G. W. Hill, C.B.E., T.D., M.B., Ch.B., F.R.C.P.; Prof. Sir Derrick Dunlop, B.A., M.D., F.R.C.P., F.R.C.P.E., F.R.S.E.
Extra Physician in Scotland, Prof. Sir Stanley Davidson, M.D., F.R.C.P., F.R.S.E.
Surgeons in Scotland, Prof. John Bruce, C.B.E., T.D., F.R.C.S.E.; George G. Bruce, M.B., Ch.B., M.D., F.R.C.S.E., L.R.C.P.
Extra Surgeon in Scotland, Prof. Sir James Learmonth, K.C.V.O., C.B.E., M.B., Ch.M., F.R.C.S.E.
Surgeon Oculist in Scotland, John Marshall, M.C., T.D., M.B., Ch.B., F.R.F.P.S.
Surgeon Dentist in Scotland, John Crawford Shiach, F.D.S., L.R.C.P., L.R.C.S.
Surgeon Apothecary to the Household at Balmoral, Sir George Proctor Middleton, K.C.V.O., M.B., Ch.B.
Surgeon Apothecary to the Household at Holyroodhouse, George Brewster, M.D., D.P.H.

THE QUEEN'S BODY GUARD FOR SCOTLAND

The Royal Company of Archers,
Archers' Hall, Edinburgh.

Captain General and Gold Stick for Scotland, Col. the Duke of Buccleuch and Queensberry, P.C., K.T., G.C.V.O., T.D.
Captains, The Earl of Rosebery, P.C., K.T., D.S.O., M.C.; Wing-Comdr. the Earl of Haddington, K.T., M.C., T.D.; Col. the Earl of Elgin and Kincardine, K.T., C.M.G., T.D.; Lt.-Col. the Earl of Airlie, K.T., G.C.V.O., M.C.
Lieutenants, Brigadier Thomas Grainger Stewart, C.B., M.C., T.D.; Col. the Earl of Stair, M.B.E. (*Adjutant*); The Lord Elphinstone; Major the Marquess of Tweeddale.
Ensigns, Major Sir Hugh Rose, Bt., T.D.; Admiral Sir Frederick H. G. Dalyrymple-Hamilton, K.C.B.; Air Commodore the Duke of Hamilton and Brandon, P.C., K.T., G.C.V.O., A.F.C; Major the Earl of Home, P.C., K.T.
Brigadiers, Brigadier the Lord Stratheden and Campbell; Major Sir R. Ian A. Forbes-Leith, Bt., M.B.E.; The Earl of Dalkeith; Admiral Sir Angus E. M. B. Cunninghame Graham, K.B.E., C.B.; Major J. M. Askew; Lt.-Col. Sir John E. Gilmour, Bt., D.S.O., T.D., M.P.; The Earl of Mansfield; Major A. C. Blair, C.V.O., T.D.; Col. The Lord Clydesmuir, M.B.E., T.D.; Col. the Lord Polwarth, T.D.; Major Sir Charles H. F. Maclean, Bt.; Major Sir Hew Hamilton-Dalrymple, Bt.
Adjutant, Col. the Earl of Stair, M.B.E.
Surgeon, Lt.-Col. D. N. Nicholson, T.D., M.B., F.R.C.P.E.
Chaplain, Very Rev. C. L. Warr, K.C.V.O., D.D.
President of the Council and Silver Stick for Scotland, Wing-Comdr. the Earl of Haddington, K.T., M.C., T.D.
Vice-President, Lt.-Col. the Earl of Airlie, K.T., G.C.V.O., M.C.
Secretary, Major C. K. Murray, T.D.
Treasurer, Col. G. R. Simpson, D.S.O., T.D.

HOUSEHOLD OF THE PRINCE PHILIP, DUKE OF EDINBURGH

Treasurer, Rear-Admiral C. D. Bonham-Carter C.B., C.V.O.
Private Secretary, J. B. V. Orr, M.V.O.
Equerry, Sqn. Ldr. D. J. Checketts.
Extra Equerries, Lieut-Gen. Sir Frederick Browning, G.C.V.O., K.B.E., C.B., D.S.O.; Capt. P. M. L. Mann, R.M.; Capt. D. R. P. Lewis.
Chief Clerk and Accountant, L. A. J. Treby, M.V.O., M.B.E., B.E.M.

HOUSEHOLD OF QUEEN ELIZABETH THE QUEEN MOTHER

Lord Chamberlain, Lt.-Col. the Earl of Airlie, K.T., G.C.V.O., M.C.
Comptroller, The Lord Adam Gordon, C.V.O., M.B.E.
Private Secretary and Equerry, Lt.-Col. Sir Martin Gilliat, K.C.V.O., M.B.E.
Treasurer, Asst. Private Secretary and Equerry, Major Sir Ralph Anstruther, Bt., M.C.
Equerry, Major the Hon. Francis Legh.
Press Secretary and Extra Equerry, Major Arthur J. S. Griffin,
Extra Equerries, The Lord Sinclair, M.V.O.; Maj. Raymond Seymour.
Equerry (Tempy.), Capt. David McMicking.
Apothecary to the Household, J. Nigel Loring, C.V.O., M.R.C.S., L.R.C.P.
Surgeon-Apothecary (Royal Lodge, Windsor), Richard May, C.V.O., M.A., M.B., B.Ch., M.R.C.S., L.R.C.P.
Mistress of the Robes, The Dowager Duchess of Northumberland, G.C.V.O., C.B.E.
Ladies of the Bedchamber, The Countess Spencer, D.C.V.O., O.B.E.; The Dowager Viscountess Hambleden, D.C.V.O.
Extra Ladies of the Bedchamber, The Dowager Countess of Halifax, C.I., D.C.V.O.; The Lady Harlech, D.C.V.O.; The Countess of Scarbrough, D.C.V.O.
Women of the Bedchamber, The Lady Jean Rankin, C.V.O.; The Hon. Mrs. John Mulholland, C.V.O.; The Lady Fermoy, O.B.E.; The Lady Caroline Douglas-Home (*temp.*).
Extra Women of the Bedchamber, The Lady Victoria Wemyss, C.V.O.; The Hon. Mrs. Geoffrey Bowlby, C.V.O.; Alexandra, Lady Worsley, C.B.E., The Lady Delia Peel, D.C.V.O.; The Lady Katharine Seymour, D.C.V.O.; The Lady Elizabeth Basset; The Lady Hyde, D.C.V.O.
Clerk Comptroller, Lieut. (S) R. E. Lambert, M.V.O., R.N.
Clerk Accountant, M. Blanch.
Clerks, J. P. Kyle; Miss M. V. Dunlop; Mrs. J. J. Mays-Smith; Miss C. Clark; Miss Z. Morris.

HOUSEHOLD OF THE PRINCESS MARGARET, COUNTESS OF SNOWDON

Treasurer and Private Secretary, Major The Hon. Francis Legh.
Equerry, Maj. M. P. A. Mitchell (*temp.*).
Lady in Waiting, Miss Jane Allday.
Extra Ladies in Waiting, Mrs. John Lowther; The Lady Elizabeth Cavendish; Mrs. Alastair Aird.

HOUSEHOLD OF THE PRINCESS ROYAL

Comptroller, Major Geoffrey H. Eastwood, C.V.O., C.B.E.
Ladies in Waiting, Miss Gwynedd LLoyd, C.V.O.; The Hon. Mrs. Francis Balfour; Dame Mary Colvin, D.B.E., T.D.; The Hon. Mrs. Thorold, O.B.E. (*temp.*).
Extra Ladies in Waiting, Joan, Countess of Cavan, D.B.E.; Lady Paynter, M.B.E.

THE DUKE AND DUCHESS OF GLOUCESTER'S HOUSEHOLD

Private Secretary and Equerry, Maj. Michael Hawkins, C.V.O.,. M.B.E.
Assistant Private Secretary and Equerry, Maj. S. C. M. Bland.
Equerry, Maj. Philip Erskine.
Extra Equerries, Rt. Hon. Sir Godfrey Thomas, Bt., G.C.V.O., K.C.B., C.S.I.; Lt.-Col. Sir Howard Kerr, K.C.V.O., C.M.G., O.B.E.; Lt.-Col. R. T. Stanyforth, C.V.O., M.C.
Ladies in Waiting, Mrs. Cedric Holland; Miss Jean Maxwell Scott.
Extra Ladies in Waiting, The Lady Cecily Vesey; Miss Dorothy Meynell, C.V.O.

THE DUKE AND DUCHESS OF KENT'S HOUSEHOLD

Treasurer, Sir Philip Hay, K.C.V.O., T.D.
Private Secretary, Lieut.-Cdr. Richard Buckley, R.N.
Comptroller, Bernard Parkes, M.V.O., O.B.E.

HOUSEHOLD OF PRINCESS MARINA, DUCHESS OF KENT

Treasurer and Private Secretary, Sir Philip Hay, K.C.V.O., T.D.
Assistant Private Secretary, Major P. C. Clarke.
Comptroller, Bernard Parkes, M.V.O., O.B.E.
Ladies in Waiting, The Lady Rachel Pepys, C.V.O.; Lady Balfour.

Extra Ladies in Waiting, The Countess of Pembroke and Montgomery, C.V.O.; The Lady Constance Milnes-Gaskell, D.C.V.O.

HOUSEHOLD OF THE PRINCESS ALEXANDRA

Lady in Waiting, The Lady Moyra Hamilton, C.V.O.

HONORARY PHYSICIANS TO THE QUEEN (CIVIL)

(Appointed until September 30, 1965)

Dr. D. Thomson, *Deputy Chief Medical Officer, Ministry of Health*; Dr. P. Henderson, *Principal Medical Officer, Ministry of Education*; Dr. A. R. Culley, C.B.E., *Medical Member, Welsh Board of Health*; Dr. A. B. Semple, *Medical Officer of Health, Liverpool and Professor of Public Health, University of Liverpool*; Dr. J. B. Ewen, *Senior Administrative Medical Officer, East Anglian Regional Hospital Board*; Dr. E. N. Reid, *Medical Officer of Health, Stirlingshire*.

THE QUEEN'S BIRTHDAY, 1964

The date for the observance of the Queen's Birthday in 1964, both at home and abroad, will be Saturday, June 13. For the Customs and Excise Department, and the officers and servants of the dock companies in England and Northern Ireland, the day appointed for the observance will be Saturday, June 27.

ROYAL SALUTES

On the Anniversaries of the Birth, Accession and Coronation of the Sovereign a salute of 62 guns is fired on the wharf at the Tower of London.

On extraordinary and triumphal occasions, such as on the occasion of the Sovereign opening, proroguing or dissolving Parliament in Person, or when passing through London in procession, except when otherwise ordered, 41 guns only are fired.

On the occasion of the birth of a Royal infant, a salute of 41 guns is fired from the two Saluting Stations in London, *i.e.* Hyde Park and the Tower of London.

Constable of the Royal Palace and Fortress of London, Field-Marshal the Earl Alexander of Tunis, K.G., P.C., G.C.B., O.M., G.C.M.G., C.S.I., D.S.O., M.C. (1960).
Lieutenant of the Tower of London, Lieut.-Gen. Sir William Pike, K.C.B., C.B.E., D.S.O.
Major and Resident Governor, Col. Sir Thomas Butler, Bt., D.S.O., O.B.E.
Master Gunner of St. James's Park, General Sir Robert Mansergh, G.C.B., K.B.E., M.C. (1960).

THE ROYAL ARMS

QUARTERLY.—1st and 4th *gules*, three lions passant guardant in pale *or* (*England*); 2nd *or*, a lion rampant within a double tressure flory counterflory *gules* (*Scotland*); 3rd *azure*, a harp *or*, stringed *argent* (*Ireland*); the whole encircled with the Garter.

SUPPORTERS.—*Dexter*: A lion rampant guardant *or*, imperially crowned. *Sinister*: a unicorn *argent*, armed crined and unguled *or*, gorged with a coronet composed of crosses patées and fleurs de lis, a chain affixed passing between the forelegs and reflexed over the back.

BADGES.—The red and white rose united (*England*), a thistle (*Scotland*); a harp *or*, the strings *argent*, with a shamrock leaf *vert* (*Ireland*); upon a mount *vert*, a dragon passant wings elevated *gules* (*Wales*).

ANNUITIES TO THE ROYAL FAMILY

The annuities payable to Her Majesty are known as the *Civil List*, which is granted by Parliament upon the recommendation of a Select Committee. The Civil List of King George VI amounted to £410,000. A Select Committee appointed to consider the Civil List in May, 1952, made the following recommendations, which were embodied in the Civil List Consolidated Fund (Appropriation) Act, which received the Royal Assent on Aug. 1. The annual provision made for Her Majesty the Queen and other members of the Royal Family under the Acts of 1937 and 1952 is as follows:—

Her Majesty's Privy Purse	£60,000
Salaries of Household	185,000
Expenses of Household	121,800
Royal Bounty, alms and special services	13,200
Supplementary Provision	95,000
	£475,000

Queen Elizabeth the Queen Mother	£70,000
The Duke of Edinburgh	40,000
The Duke of Gloucester	35,000
The Princess Margaret	15,000
The Princess Royal	6,000

These payments are separately charged on the Consolidated Fund, and do not form part of the Civil List.

THE UNION JACK

Days for hoisting the Union Flag on Government and Public Buildings (from 8 A.M. to sunset).

February 6 (1952).—Her Majesty's Accession.
February 19 (1960).—Birthday of Prince Andrew.
March 1.—St. David's Day (in Wales only).
March 31 (1900).—Birthday of Duke of Gloucester.
April 21 (1926).—Birthday of Her Majesty the Queen.
April 23.—St. George's Day (in England only). Where a building has two or more flagstaffs the Cross of St. George may be flown in addition to the Union Jack but not in a superior position.
April 25 (1897).—Birthday of the Princess Royal.
May 24.—Commonwealth Day.
June 2 (1953).—Coronation Day.
June 10 (1921) Birthday of the Duke of Edinburgh.
June 13.—Queen's Official Birthday, 1964.
Aug. 4 (1900).—Birthday of Her Majesty Queen Elizabeth the Queen Mother.
Aug. 15 (1950).—Birthday of the Princess Anne.
Aug. 21 (1930).—Birthday of the Princess Margaret.
Nov. 8.—Remembrance Sunday, 1964.
Nov. 14 (1948).—Birthday of the Prince of Wales.
Nov. 20 (1947).—Her Majesty's Wedding Day.
Nov. 30.—St. Andrew's Day (in Scotland only).

And on the occasion of the opening and closing of Parliament by the Queen, flags should be flown on public buildings in the Greater London area, whether or not Her Majesty performs the ceremony in person.

The only additions to the above list will be those notified to the Ministry of Public Building and Works by Her Majesty's command and communicated by the Ministry to the other Departments. The list applies equally to Government and Public Buildings in London and elsewhere in the United Kingdom. In cases where it has been the practice to fly the Union Jack daily, *e.g.* on some Custom Houses, that practice may continue.

Flags will be flown at half-mast on the following occasions:—

(*a*) From the announcement of the death up to the funeral of the Sovereign, except on Proclamation Day, when they are hoisted right up from 11 a.m. to sunset.

(*b*) The funerals of members of the Royal Family, subject to special commands from Her Majesty in each case.

(*c*) The funerals of Foreign Rulers, subject to special commands from Her Majesty in each case.

(*d*) The funerals of Prime Ministers and ex-Prime Ministers of the United Kingdom.

(*e*) Other occasions by special command of Her Majesty.

On occasions when days for flying flags coincide with days for flying flags at half mast the following rules will be observed. Flags will be flown: (*a*) although a member of the Royal Family, or a near relative of the Royal Family, may be lying dead, unless special commands be received from Her Majesty to the contrary, and (*b*) although it may be the day of the funeral of a Foreign Ruler. If the body of a very distinguished subject is lying at a Government Office the flag may fly at half mast on that office until the body has left (provided it is a day on which the flag would fly) and then the flag is to be hoisted right up. On all other Public Buildings the flag will fly as usual.

The *Royal Standard* is only to be hoisted when the Queen is actually present in the building, and never when Her Majesty is passing in procession.

RED-LETTER DAYS

Scarlet Robes are worn by the Judges of the Queen's Bench Division on *Red-Letter Days* at the sittings of a Criminal Court or of the Court of Criminal Appeal and on all State Occasions.

RED-LETTER DAYS AND STATE OCCASIONS, 1964.

Jan.	25.	Conversion of St. Paul.
Feb.	2.	Purification.
"	6.	Queen's Accession.
"	12.	Ash Wednesday.
"	24.	St. Matthias.
Mar.	25.	Annunciation.
Apr.	21.	Queen's Birthday.
"	25.	St. Mark.
May	1.	St. Philip and St. James.
"	7.	Ascension Day.
June	2.	Coronation Day.
"	10.	Birthday of the Duke of Edinburgh.
"	11.	St. Barnabas.
"	13.	Queen's Official Birthday.
"	24.	St. John the Baptist.
"	29.	St. Peter.
July	25.	St. James.
Aug.	4.	Birthday of Queen Elizabeth the Queen Mother.
Oct.	18.	St. Luke.
"	28.	St. Simon and St. Jude.
Nov.	1.	All Saints.
"	9.	Lord Mayor's Day.
"	14.	Birthday of the Prince of Wales.
"	30.	St. Andrew.
Dec.	21.	St. Thomas.

THE MILITARY KNIGHTS OF WINDSOR

Founded in 1348 after the Wars in France to assist English Knights, who, having been prisoners in the hands of the French, had become impoverished by the payments of heavy ransoms. They received a pension and quarters in Windsor Castle. Edward III founded the Order of the Garter later in the same year, incorporating the Knights of Windsor and the College of St. George into its foundation and raising the number of Knights to 26 to correspond with the number of the Knights of the Garter. Known later as the Alms Knights or Poor Knights of Windsor, their establishment was reduced under the will of King Henry VIII to 13 and Statutes were drawn up by Queen Elizabeth I.

In 1833 King William IV changed their designation to The Military Knights and granted them their present uniform which consists of a scarlet coatee with white cross sword-belt, crimson sash and cocked hat with plume. The badges are the Shield of St. George and the Star of the Order of the Garter. The Knights receive a small stipend in addition to their Army pensions and quarters in Windsor Castle. They take part in all ceremonies of the Noble Order of the Garter and attend Sunday morning service in St. George's Chapel as representatives of the Knights of the Garter.

Applications for appointment should be made to The Military Secretary, The War Office.

Governor, Maj.-Gen. Edmund Hakewill Smith, C.B., C.B.E., M.C.

Military Knights, Lt.-Colonel C. L. Hodgson; Major H. K. Clough, O.B.E.; Colonel A. H. W. Haywood, C.M.G., C.B.E., D.S.O.; Lt.-Colonel J. M. Mackenzie, D.S.O.; Lt.-Colonel L. Holbech, C.V.O., D.S.O., O.B.E., M.C.; Lt.-Colonel R. F. Squibb, M.C.; Brigadier E. K. B. Furze, D.S.O., O.B.E., M.C.; Lt.-Colonel E. P. O. Boyle, M.V.O.; Brigadier W. P. A. Robinson, M.C.; Major T. W. Garnett, M.B.E.; Lt.-Colonel G. F. G. Turner, O.B.E., D.C.M.

The Peerage §

THE PEERAGE AND ITS DEGREES

The rules which govern the arrangements of the Peerage are marked by so many complications that even an expert may occasionally be perplexed. All Peers of England are Peers of Parliament. In Scotland and Ireland there are Peerages of equally long standing and upon the successive Unions of those two Kingdoms with the Kingdom of England a certain number of Scottish and Irish Peers received titles in the Peerage of Great Britain, or of the United Kingdom, carrying the right of summons to the House of Lords.

All Peers of Parliament up to June 20, 1707, are classed as Peers of England and rank before all others of like degree; from that date to December 31, 1800, all fresh creations either in England or in Scotland were called Peers of Great Britain, and creations from January 1, 1801, onwards, either in Great Britain or Ireland, are known as Peers of the United Kingdom, save only that the Sovereign retains the power to create one new Peer of Ireland for every three Irish Peerages of older date than the Union which have become extinct. In 1868 the Barony of Rathdonnell was so created and in 1898 that of Curzon of Kedleston, the latter being designed to permit the holder (who was Viceroy of India from 1898 to 1905) to return to the House of Commons instead of entering the House of Lords.

From the date of the Union with Scotland 16 Scottish Peers, not entitled to sit in the House of Lords by virtue of a British or United Kingdom Peerage, are elected as Representative Peers for the duration of each Parliament. By the Peerage Act, 1963, all hereditary Scottish Peers, and all Peeresses in their own Right, became entitled to seats.

No Fees for Dignities have been payable since 1937.

PEERAGES CREATED SINCE THE LAST ISSUE

EARL—Alexander of Hillsborough.
BARONS (2)—Normanbrook; Silsoe.
For Life Peers created under the Life Peerages Act, 1958, see p. 247.

PEERAGES EXTINCT SINCE THE LAST ISSUE

VISCOUNTCIES (3)—Cunningham of Hyndhope (cr. 1946); Elibank (cr. 1911); Hyndley (cr. 1948).
BARONIES (4)—Beveridge (cr. 1946); Dorchester (cr. 1899); Normand (Life Peerage) (cr. 1947); Tredegar (cr. 1859).

RENUNCIATION OF PEERAGES

The following former peers have renounced their peerages under the Peerage Act, 1963: Viscount Stansgate; Lord Altrincham.

PEERS WHO ARE MINORS

(As at Jan. 1, 1964)

THE PRINCE OF WALES (Duke of Cornwall) (*b.* 1948).
EARLS (2): Belmore (*b.* 1951); Chichester (*b.* 1944).
BARONS (3): Hesketh (*b.* 1950); O'Hagan (*b.* 1945); Sysonby (*b.* 1945).

The following Peers will come of age during 1964:—
EARL (1): Kingston (Sept. 23).
VISCOUNT (1): Torrington (July 13).

	Hereditary	Peeresses	Minors	No Seat	Life or Term	In House of Lords
Royal Dukes	5	..	1	..	..	4
Archbishops	..	..	..	..	2	2
Dukes	27	..	..	..	1	27
Marquesses	38	..	..	..	..	38
Earls	206	6	3	18	8	191
Viscounts	134	..	1	16	..	117
Bishops	..	..	..	17	24	24
Barons	536	14	3	37	23	510
Life Peers (under the 1958 Act)	..	7	..	..	37	44
Totals	946	27	8	88	95	957

Note.—This table will not cross-check because, e.g., the 16 Scottish Representative Peers elected to Parliament in Oct. 1959 are included both as Hereditary Peers and Peers for a Term; Irish Peers have no seats, but some are also Minors; one Peeress in her own Right also holds a Life Peerage.

ROYAL DUKES

Style, His Royal Highness the Duke of ——

Addressed as, Sir, or more formally, May it please your Royal Highness.

1947 *Edinburgh*. The Prince Philip, Duke of Edinburgh, K.G., P.C., K.T., G.B.E., *b.* 1921, *m.* (*see* pp. 214 and 215).
1337 *Cornwall*, Charles, Prince of Wales, Duke of Cornwall, (*Scottish Duke, Rothesay*, 1398), K.G., *b.* 1948, *M.* (*see* p. 215).
1928 *Gloucester*. Henry, Duke of Gloucester. K.G., P.C., K.T., K.P., etc., *b.* 1900, *m.* (*see* p. 214).
1934 *Kent* (2nd), Edward, Duke of Kent, G.C.V.O., *b.* 1935, *s.* 1942, *m.* (*see* p. 214).
1936 *Windsor*, Edward, Duke of Windsor, K.G., K.T., K.P., etc., *b.* 1894, *m.* (*see* p. 214).

§ *For list of Contractions used, see p.* 251.

ARCHBISHOPS

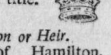

Style, The Most Rev. His Grace the Lord Archbishop of ——.
Addressed as, My Lord Archbishop; or, Your Grace.

Trans.

1961 *Canterbury* (100th), Arthur Michael Ramsey, P.C., D.D., *b.* 1904. *Consecrated Bishop of Durham*, 1952, *translated to York*, 1956.

1961 *York* (93rd), Frederick Donald Coggan, P.C., D.D., *b.* 1909. *Consecrated Bishop of Bradford*, 1956

DUKES

Style, His Grace the Duke of ——. *Addressed as*, My Lord Duke; or, Your Grace. The eldest sons of Dukes and Marquesses take, by courtesy, their father's second title. The other sons and the daughters are styled Lord Edward, Lady Caroline, etc.

Created.	*Title, Order of Succession, Name, etc.*	*Eldest Son or Heir.*
1868 I.*	*Abercorn* (4th), James Edward Hamilton (5th *Brit. Marq.*. 1790, and 13th *Scott. Earl*, 1606, both *Abercorn*), *b.* 1904, *s.* 1953, *m.*	Marquess of Hamilton, *b.* 1934.
1701 S. } 1892 * }	*Argyll*, Ian Douglas Campbell (11th *Scottish* and 4th *U.K. Duke*, *Argyll*), *b.* 1903, *s.* 1949, *m.*	Marquess of Lorne, *b.* 1937.
1703 S.	*Atholl* (10th), George Iain Murray, *b.* 1931, *s.* 1957.	Arthur S. P. M. *b.* 1899.
1682	*Beaufort* (10th), Henry Hugh Arthur FitzRoy Somerset, K.G., P.C., G.C.V.O., Royal Victorian Chain, *b.* 1900, *s.* 1924, *m.* (*Master of the Horse*).	Henry R. S. F. de V. *S.*, D.S.O., *b.* 1898.
1694	*Bedford* (13th), John Robert Russell, *b.* 1917, *s.* 1953, *m.*	Marquess of Tavistock, *b.* 1940.
1663 S.*	*Buccleuch* (8th) & (10th) *Queensberry* (1706), Walter John Montagu-Douglas-Scott, P.C., K.T., G.C.V.O., T.D. (7th *Engl. Earl, Doncaster* 1662), *b.* 1894, *s.* 1935, *m.*	Earl of Dalkeith, M.P. *b.* 1923.
1694	*Devonshire* (11th), Andrew Robert Buxton Cavendish, M.C., *b.* 1920, *s.* 1950, *m.*	Marquess of Hartington, *b.* 1944.
1900	*Fife* (3rd), James George Alexander Bannerman Carnegie, *b.* 1929, *s.* 1959, *m.* (*see* p. 212).	Earl of Macduff, *b.* 1961.
1675	*Grafton* (10th), Charles Alfred Euston FitzRoy, *b.* 1892, *s.* 1936, *m.*	Earl of Euston, *b.* 1919.
1643 S.*	*Hamilton* (14th), Douglas Douglas-Hamilton, P.C., K.T., G.C.V.O., A.F.C. (*Premier Peer of Scotland*; 11th *Brit. Duke, Brandon*, 1711) (*Lord Steward*), *b.* 1903, *s.* 1940, *m.*	Marquess of Douglas and Clydesdale, *b.* 1938.
1694	*Leeds* (12th), Francis D'Arcy Godolphin Osborne, K.C.M.G. (11th *Scott. Visct., Dunblane*), *b.* 1884, *s.* 1963.	(None.)
1766 I.*	*Leinster* (7th), Edward FitzGerald (*Premier Duke, Marquess and Earl of Ireland*; 7th *Brit. Visct., Leinster*, 1747), *b.* 1892, *s.* 1922, *w.*	Marquess of Kildare, *b.* 1914.
1719	*Manchester* (10th), Alexander George Francis Drogo Montagu, O.B.E., *b.* 1902, *s.* 1947, *m.*	Visct. Mandeville, *b.* 1929.
1702	*Marlborough* (10th), John Albert Edward William Spencer-Churchill, *b.* 1897, *s.* 1934, *w.*	Marquess of Blandford, *b.* 1926.
1707 S.*	*Montrose* (7th), James Angus Graham (5th *Brit. Earl, Graham*, 1722), *b.* 1907, *s.* 1954, *m.*	Marquess of Graham, *b.* 1935.
1756	*Newcastle* (*under Lyme*) (9th), Henry Edward Hugh Pelham-Clinton-Hope O.B.E., *b.* 1907, *s.* 1941, *m.*	Capt. Henry C. F. *Pelham-Clinton*, *b.* 1892.
1483	*Norfolk* (16th), Bernard Marmaduke Fitzalan-Howard, K.G., P.C., G.C.V.O., Royal Victorian Chain (*Premier Duke and Earl*, 13th *Scott. Baron, Herries*, 1489), *b.* 1908, *s.* 1917, *m.* (*Earl Marshal*).	Lord Howard of Glossop, b. 1885 (*see* p. 240) (to Dukedom); to Herries Barony, Lady Anne *F.-H.*, *b.* 1938.
1766	*Northumberland* (10th), Hugh Algernon Percy, K.G., T.D., *b.* 1914, *s.* 1940, *m.*	Earl Percy, *b.* 1953.
1716	*Portland* (7th), William Arthur Henry Cavendish-Bentinck, K.G., T.D., *b.* 1893, *s.* 1943, *m.*	Major Sir Ferdinand W. *C.-B.*, K.B.E., C.M.G., *b.* 1888.
1675	*Richmond* (9th) & *Gordon* (4th, 1876), Frederick Charles Gordon-Lennox (9th *Scott. Duke, Lennox*, 1675), *b.* 1904, *s.* 1935, *m.*	Earl of March, *b.* 1929.
1707 S.*	*Roxburghe* (9th), George Victor Robert John Innes-Ker (4th *U.K. Earl, Innes*, 1837), *b.* 1913, *s.* 1932, *m.* (*Premier Baronet of Scotland*).	Marquess of Bowmont, *b.* 1954.
1703	*Rutland* (10th), Charles John Robert Manners, C.B.E., *b.* 1919, *s.* 1940, m.	Marquess of Granby, *b.* 1959.
1684	*St. Albans* (12th), Osborne de Vere Beauclerk, T.D., *b.* 1874, *s.* 1934, *w.*	Charles A. F. de V. *B.*, O.B.E., *b.* 1915.
1547	*Somerset* (18th), Percy Hamilton Seymour, *b.* 1910, *s.* 1954, *m.*	Lord Seymour, *b.* 1952.
1833	*Sutherland* (6th), John Sutherland Egerton, *b.* 1915, *s.* 1963, *m.*	Cyril R. *E.*, *b.* 1905.
1814	*Wellington* (7th), Gerald Wellesley, K.G. (8th *Irish Earl, Mornington*, 1746), *b.* 1885, *s.* 1943. *w*	Col. Marquess Douro, M.V.O., O.B.E., M.C., *b.* 1915.
1874	*Westminster* (4th), Gerald Hugh Grosvenor, D.S.O., *b.* 1907, *s.* 1963, *m.*	Lt.-Col. Lord Robert G., T.D. M.P., *b.* 1910.

MARQUESSES

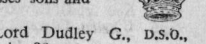

Style, The Most Hon. the Marquess of ——. *Addressed as*, My Lord Marquess. In titles marked ° the "of" is *not* used. For the style of Marquesses' sons and daughters, *see* under "DUKES," above.

1915	*Aberdeen and Temair* (2nd), George Gordon, O.B.E. (8th *Scott. Earl, Aberdeen*, 1682), *b.* 1879, *s.* 1934, *w.*	Lord Dudley G., D.S.O., *b.* 1883.

Created.	*Title, Order of Succession, Name, etc.*	*Eldest Son or Heir.*
1876	*Abergavenny* (5th), John Henry Guy Larnach-Nevill, O.B.E., *b.* 1914, *s.* 1954, *m.*	Earl of Lewes, *b.* 1948.
1821	*Ailesbury* (7th), Chandos Sidney Cedric Brudenell-Bruce, *b.* 1904, *s.* 1961, *m.*	Viscount Savernake, *b.* 1926.
1831	*Ailsa* (7th), Archibald David Kennedy (19th *Scott. Earl, Cassillis,* 1509), *b.* 1925, *s.* 1957, *m.*	Earl of Cassillis, *b.* 1956.
1815	*Anglesey* (7th), George Charles Henry Victor Paget, *b.* 1922, *s.* 1947, *m.*	Earl of Uxbridge, *b.* 1950.
1789	*Bath* (6th), Henry Frederick Thynne, E.D., *b.* 1905, *s.* 1946, *m.*	Viscount Weymouth, *b.* 1932.
1826	*Bristol* (6th), Victor Frederick Cochrane Hervey, *b.* 1915, *s.* 1960, *m.*	Earl Jermyn, *b.* 1954.
1796	*Bute* (6th), John Crichton-Stuart (11th *Scott. Earl, Dumfries,* 1633), *b.* 1933, *s.* 1956, *m.*	Earl of Dumfries, *b.* 1958.
1917	*Cambridge* (2nd), George Francis Hugh Cambridge, G.C.V.O., *b.* 1895, *s.* 1927, *m.*	(None).
1812	°*Camden* (5th), John Charles Henry Pratt, *b.* 1899, *s.* 1943, *m.*	Earl of Brecknock, *b.* 1930.
1815	*Cholmondeley* (5th), George Horatio Charles Cholmondeley, G.C.V.O. (9th *Irish Viscount, Cholmondeley,* 1628), *b.* 1883, *s.* 1923, *m.* (*Lord Great Chamberlain*).	Earl of Rocksavage, M.C., *b.* 1919.
1816 I.*	°*Conyngham* (6th), Frederick William Burton Conyngham (6th *U.K. Baron, Minster,* 1821), *b.* 1890, *s.* 1918, *m.*	Earl of Mount Charles, *b.* 1924.
1791 I.*	*Donegall* (6th), Edward Arthur Donald St. George Hamilton Chichester (6th *Brit. Baron, Fisherwick,* 1790), *b.* 1903, *s.* 1904, *m.*	Lord Templemore, *b.* 1916 (*see* p. 245).
1789 I.*	*Downshire* (7th), Arthur Wills Percy Wellington Blundell Trumbull Sandys Hill (7th *Brit. Earl, Hillsborough,* 1772), *b.* 1894, *s.* 1918, *m.*	A. Robin I. *H.*, *b.* 1929.
1888	*Dufferin & Ava* (5th), Sheridan Frederick Terence Hamilton-Temple-Blackwood (11th *Irish Baron, Dufferin & Clandeboye,* 1800), *b.* 1938, *s.* 1945.	(None to Marquessate), to Irish Barony, Sir Francis E. T. *Blackwood,* Bt., *b.* 1901.
1801 I.*	*Ely* (7th), George Henry Wellington Loftus (7th *U.K. Baron, Loftus,* 1801), *b.* 1903, *s.* 1935, *m.*	Guy A. G. *L.*, *b.* 1899.
1801	*Exeter* (6th), David George Brownlow Cecil, K.C.M.G., *b.* 1905, *s.* 1956, *m.*	Lord Martin *C.*, *b.* 1909.
1800 I.*	*Headfort* (6th), Thomas Geoffrey Charles Michael Taylour (4th *U.K. Baron, Kenlis,* 1831), *b.* 1932, *s.* 1960, *m.*	Earl of Bective, *b.* 1959.
1793	*Hertford* (8th), Hugh Edward Conway Seymour (9th *Irish Baron, Conway,* 1712), *b.* 1930, *s.* 1940, *m.*	Earl of Yarmouth, *b.* 1958.
1599 S.*	*Huntly* (12th), Douglas Charles Lindsay Gordon (*Premier Marquess of Scotland*) (4th *U.K. Baron, Meldrum,* 1815), *b.* 1908, *s.* 1937, *m.*	Earl of Aboyne *b.* 1944.
1784	*Lansdowne* (8th), George John Charles Mercer Nairne Petty-Fitzmaurice (8th *Irish Earl, Kerry,* 1722), *b.* 1912, *s.* 1944, *m.*	Earl of Shelburne, *b.* 1941.
1902	*Linlithgow* (3rd), Charles William Frederick Hope, M.C. (10th *Scott. Earl, Hopetoun* 1703), *b.* 1912, *s.* 1952, *m.*	Earl of Hopetoun, *b.* 1946.
1816 I.*	*Londonderry* (9th), Alexander Charles Robert Vane-Tempest-Stewart (6th *U.K. Earl, Vane,* 1823), *b.* 1937, *s.* 1955, *m.*	Francis C. J. *Vane-Tempest*, *b.* 1911.
1701 S.*	*Lothian* (12th), Peter Francis Walter Kerr (6th *U.K. Baron, Ker* 1821), *b.* 1922, *s.* 1940, *m.*	Earl of Ancram, *b.* 1945.
1917	*Milford Haven* (3rd), David Michael Mountbatten, O.B.E., D.S.C., *b.* 1919, *s.* 1938, *m.* (*see also* p. 212).	Earl of Medina, *b.* 1961.
1838	*Normanby* (4th), Oswald Constantine John Phipps, M.B.E. (8th *Irish Baron, Mulgrave,* 1767), *b.* 1912, *s.* 1932, *m.*	Earl of Mulgrave, *b.* 1954.
1812	*Northampton* (6th), William Bingham Compton, D.S.O., *b.* 1885, *s.* 1913, *m.*	Earl Compton, *b.* 1946.
1825 I.*	*Ormonde* (6th), James Arthur Norman Butler, C.V.O., M.C. (6th *U.K. Baron, Ormonde,* 1821), *b.* 1893, *s.* 1949, *m.*	James H. T. C. *B.*, M.B.E., 1899.
1682 S.	*Queensberry* (12th), David Harrington Angus Douglas, *b.* 1929, *s.* 1954.	Lord Gawain *D.*, *b.* 1948.
1926	*Reading* (3rd), Michael Alfred Rufus Isaacs, M.B.E., M.C., T.D., *b.* 1916, *s.* 1960, *m.*	Viscount Erleigh, *b.* 1942.
1789	*Salisbury* (5th), Robert Arthur James Gascoyne-Cecil, K.G., P.C., *b.* 1893, *s.* 1947, *m.*	Viscount Cranborne, *b.* 1916.
1800 I.*	*Sligo* (10th), Denis Edward Browne (10th *U.K. Baron, Monteagle,* 1806), *b.* 1908, *s.* 1952, *m.*	Earl of Altamont, *b.* 1939.
1787	°*Townshend* (7th), George John Patrick Dominic Townshend, *b.* 1916, *s.* 1921, *m.*	Viscount Raynham, *b.* 1945.
1694 S.*	*Tweeddale* (11th), William George Montagu Hay (2nd *U.K. Baron, Tweeddale,* 1881), *b.* 1884, *s.* 1911, *m.*	David G. M. *H.*, *b.* 1921.
1789 I.*	*Waterford* (8th), John Hubert de la Poer Beresford (8th *Brit. Baron, Tyrone,* 1786), *b.* 1933, *s.* 1934, *m.*	Earl of Tyrone, *b.* 1958.
1936	*Willingdon* (2nd), Inigo Brassey Freeman-Thomas, *b.* 1899, *s.* 1941, *m.*	(None.)
1551	*Winchester* (17th), Richard Charles Paulet (*Premier Marquess of England*), *b.* 1905, *s.* 1962.	George C. *P.*, *b.* 1905.
1892	*Zetland* (3rd), Lawrence Aldred Mervyn Dundas, (5th *U.K. Earl of Zetland,* 1838, 6th *Brit. Baron Dundas,* 1794), *b.* 1908, *s.* 1961, *m.*	Earl of Ronaldshay, *b.* 1937.

EARLS

Style (*see also* note, p. 253). The Right Hon. the Earl of ——. *Addressed as*, My Lord. The eldest sons of Earls take, by courtesy, their father's second title, the younger sons being styled the Hon., *e.g.* the Hon. John ——, but the daughters Lady Elizabeth ——, etc. Where marked ° the " of " is not used.

Created.	*Title, Order of Succession, Name, etc.*	*Eldest Son or Heir.*
1639 S.	*Airlie* (12th), David Lyulph Gore Wolseley Ogilvy, K.T., G.C.V.O., M.C., *b.* 1893, *s.* 1900, *m.*	Lord Ogilvy, *b.* 1926.
1696	*Albemarle* (9th), Walter Egerton George Lucian Keppel, M.C., *b.* 1882, *s.* 1942, *m.*	Viscount Bury, *b.* 1911.
1963	°*Alexander of Hillsborough* (1st), Albert Victor Alexander, P.C., C.H., *b.* 1885, *m.*	(None.)
1952	°*Alexander of Tunis* (1st), Harold Rupert Leofric George Alexander, K.G., P.C., G.C.B., O.M., G.C.M.G., C.S.I., D.S.O., M.C., *Field Marshal, Constable of the Royal Palace and Fortress of London*, *b.* 1891, *m.*	Lord Rideau, *b.* 1935.
1826	°*Amherst* (5th), Jeffery John Archer Amherst, M.C., *b.* 1896, *s.* 1927.	Hon. Humphrey W. *A.*, *b.* 1903.
1892	*Ancaster* (3rd), Gilbert James Heathcote-Drummond-Willoughby, T.D., *b.* 1907, *s.* 1951, *m.*	Lord Willoughby de Eresby, *b.* 1936.
1789 I.	°*Annesley* (9th), Robert Annesley, *b.* 1900, *s.* 1957, *m.*	Viscount Glerawly, *b.* 1924.
1785 I.	*Antrim* (8th), Randal John Somerled McDonnell, *b.* 1911, *s.* 1932, *m.*	Viscount Dunluce, *b.* 1935.
1762 I.*	*Arran* (8th), Arthur Strange Kattendyke David Archibald Gore (4th U.K. *Baron Sudley*, 1884), *b.* 1910, *s.* 1958, *m.*	Viscount Sudley, *b.* 1938.
1955	°*Attlee* (1st), Clement Richard Attlee, K.G., P.C., O.M., C.H., *b.* 1883, *m.*	Viscount Prestwood, *b.* 1927.
1961	*Avon* (1st), (Robert) Anthony Eden, K.G., P.C., M.C., *b.* 1897, *m.*	Viscount Eden, *b.* 1930.
1714	*Aylesford* (11th), Charles Ian Finch-Knightley *b.* 1918, *s.* 1958, *m.*	Lord Guernsey, *b.* 1947.
1937	°*Baldwin of Bewdley* (3rd), Arthur Windham Baldwin, *b.* 1904, *s.* 1958, *m.*	Viscount Corvedale, *b.* 1938.
1922	*Balfour* (3rd) Robert Arthur Lytton Balfour, *b.* 1902, *s.* 1945, *m.*	Viscount Traprain, *b.* 1925.
1800 I.	*Bandon* (5th), Percy Ronald Gardner Bernard, G.B.E., C.B., C.V.O., D.S.O., *b.* 1904, *s.* 1924, *m.*	Maj. Hon. Charles B. A. *B.*, C.B.E., *b.* 1904 (Twin).
1772	°*Bathurst* (8th), Henry Allen John Bathurst, *b.* 1927, *s.* 1943, *m.*	Lord Apsley, *b.* 1961.
1919	°*Beatty* (2nd), David Field Beatty, D.S.C., *b.* 1905, *s.* 1936, *m.*	Viscount Borodale, *b.* 1946.
1815	°*Beauchamp* (8th), William Lygon, *b.* 1903, *s.* 1938, *m.*	Hon. Richard E. *L.*, *b.* 1916.
1797 I.	*Belmore* (8th), John Armar Lowry-Corry, *b.* 1951, *s.* 1960, *M.*	Sir Henry C. *L.-C.*, M.C., *b.* 1887.
1739 I. } 1937* }	*Bessborough* (2nd), Frederick Edward Neuflize Ponsonby, (10th *Irish Earl Bessborough*), *b.* 1913, *s.* 1956, *m.*	Arthur M.L. *P.*, *b* 1912 (to Irish Earldom only).
1922	*Birkenhead* (2nd), Frederick Winston Furneaux Smith, T.D., *b.* 1907, *s.* 1930, *m.*	Viscount Furneaux, *b.* 1936.
1815	*Bradford* (6th), Gerald Michael Orlando Bridgeman, T.D., *b.* 1911, *s.* 1957, *m.*	Viscount Newport, *b.* 1947.
1677 S.	*Breadalbane and Holland* (10th), John Romer Boreland Campbell, *b.* 1919, *s.* 1959. *m.*	(None.)
1469 S.*	*Buchan* (16th), Donald Cardross Flower Erskine, (7th U.K. *Baron Erskine*), *b.* 1899 *s.* (to Barony), 1957, (to Earldom) 1960, *m.*	Lord Cardross, *b.* 1930.
1746	*Buckinghamshire* (9th), Vere Frederick Cecil Hobart-Hampden, *b.* 1901, *s.* 1963.	Cyril L. *H.-H.* *b.* 1902.
1800	°*Cadogan* (7th), William Gerald Charles Cadogan, M.C., *b.* 1914, *s.* 1933, *m.*	Viscount Chelsea, *b.* 1937.
1878	°*Cairns* (5th). David Charles Cairns, C.B., *b.* 1909, *s.* 1946, *m.*	Viscount Garmoyle, *b.* 1939.
1543 S.	*Caithness* (19th), James Roderick Sinclair, C.V.O., C.B.E., D.S.O., *b.* 1906, *s.* 1947, *m.*	Lord Berriedale, *b.* 1948.
1800 I.	*Caledon* (5th), Erik James Desmond Alexander, *b.* 1885, *s.* 1898.	Lt.-Col. Hon. Herbrand *A.*, D.S.O., *b.* 1888.
1661	*Carlisle* (12th), Charles James Ruthven Howard, M.C., *b.* 1923, *s.* 1963, *m.*	Viscount Morpeth, *b.* 1949.
1793	*Carnarvon* (6th), Henry George Alfred Marius Victor Francis Herbert, *b.* 1898, *s.* 1923.	Lord Porchester, *b.* 1924.
1748 I.*	*Carrick* (9th), Brian Stuart Theobald Somerset Caher Butler (3rd U.K. *Baron, Butler*, 1912), *b.* 1931, *s.* 1957, *m.*	Viscount Ikerrin, *b.* 1953.
1800 I.	°*Castle Stewart* (8th), Arthur Patrick Avondale Stuart, *b.* 1928, *s.* 1961, *m.*	Viscount Stuart, *b.* 1953.
1814	°*Cathcart* (6th), Alan Cathcart, D.S.O., M.C. (15th *Scott. Baron, Cathcart*), *b.* 1919, *s.* 1927, *m.*	Lord Greenock, *b.* 1952.
1647 I.	*Cavan* (12th), Michael Edward Oliver Lambart, T.D., *b.* 1911, *s.* 1950, *m.*	Oliver F. W. *L.*, *b.* 1895.
1827	°*Cawdor* (5th), John Duncan Vaughan Campbell, T.D., *b.* 1900, *s.* 1914.	Viscount Emlyn, *b.* 1932.
1801	*Chichester* (9th), John Nicholas Pelham, *b.* 1944, *s.* 1944, *M.*	Anthony G. *P.*, *b.* 1911.
1803 I.*	*Clancarty* (6th), Richard Frederick John Donough Le Poer Trench (5th *U.K. Visct. Clancarty*, 1823), *b.* 1891, *s.* 1929, *m.*	Hon. Greville S. R. *Le P. T.*, *b.* 1902.
1776 I.*	*Clanwilliam* (6th), John Charles Edmund Carson Meade (4th *U.K. Baron Clanwilliam*, 1828), *b.* 1914, *s.* 1953, *m*	Adm. Hon. Sir Herbert *Meade - Fetherstonhaugh*, G.C.V.O., C.B., D.S.O., *b.* 1875.

Created.	Title, Order of Succession, Name, etc.	Eldest Son or Heir.
1776	*Clarendon* (7th), George Frederick Laurence Villiers, *b.* 1933, *s.* 1955.	Hon. Nicholas *V.*, *b.* 1916.
1620 I.*	*Cork & Orrery* (1660), William Henry Dudley Boyle,, G.C.B., G.C.V.O. (12th *Irish Earl* and 8th. *Brit. Baron, Boyle of Marston*, 1711), *Admiral of the Fleet*, *b.* 1873, *s.* 1934, *w.*	Maj. Patrick R. *B.*, *b.* 1910.
1850	*Cottenham* (7th), John Digby Thomas Pepys, *b.* 1907, *s.* 1943, *m.*	Viscount Crowhurst, *b.* 1943.
1762 I.*	*Courtown* (8th), James Montagu Burgoyne Stopford, O.B.E., T.D. (7th *Brit. Baron, Saltersford*, 1796), *b.* 1908, *s.* 1957, *m.*	Viscount Stopford, *b.* 1954.
1697	*Coventry* (11th), George William Coventry, *b.* 1934, *s.* 1940.	Viscount Deerhurst, *b.* 1957.
1857	*Cowley* (5th), Denis Arthur Wellesley, B.E.M., *b.* 1921, *s.* 1962, *m.*	Viscount Dangan, *b.* 1946.
1892	*Cranbrook* (4th), John David Gathorne-Hardy, C.B.E., *b.* 1900, *s.* 1915, *m.*	Lord Medway, *b.* 1933.
1801	*Craven* (6th), William Robert Bradley Craven, *b.* 1917, *s.* 1932, *m.*	Viscount Uffington, *b.* 1957.
1398 S.*	*Crawford* (28th) *and Balcarres* (11th), David Alexander Robert Lindsay, K.T., G.B.E. (*Premier Earl on Union Roll and* 4th *U.K. Baron, Wigan*, 1826), *b.* 1900, *s.* 1940, *m.*	Lord Balniel, M.P., *b.* 1927.
1861	*Cromartie* (4th), Roderick Grant Francis Mackenzie, M.C., *b.* 1904, *s.* 1962, *m.*	Viscount Tarbat, *b.* 1948.
1901	*Cromer* (3rd), George Rowland Stanley Baring, M.B.E., *b.* 1918, *s.* 1953.	Viscount Errington, *b.* 1946.
1633 S.*	*Dalhousie* (16th) Simon Ramsay, G.B.E., M.C. (4th *U.K. Baron, Ramsay* 1875), *b.* 1914, *s.* 1950, *m.*	Lord Ramsay, *b.* 1948.
1725 I.*	*Darnley* (10th), Peter Stuart Bligh (19th *English Baron, Clifton of Leighton Bromswold*, 1608), *b.* 1915, *s.* 1955.	Hon. Adam I. S. *B.*, *b.* 1941.
1711	*Dartmouth* (9th), Gerald Humphry Legge, *b.* 1924, *s.* 1962, *m.*	Viscount Lewisham, *b.* 1949
1761	°*De La Warr* (9th), Herbrand Edward Dundonald Brassey Sackville, P.C., G.B.E., *b.* 1900, *s.* 1915, *m.*	Lord Buckhurst, *b.* 1921.
1622	*Denbigh* (10th) *and Desmond* (9th), William Rudolph Stephen Feilding (9th *Irish Earl, Desmond*, 1622), *b.* 1912, *s.* 1939, *m.*	Viscount Feilding, *b.* 1943.
1485	*Derby* (18th) Edward John Stanley, M.C., *b.*, 1918, *s.* 1948, *m.*	Hon. Richard *S.*, M.P., *b.* 1920.
1553	*Devon* (17th), Charles Christopher Courtenay, *b.* 1916, *s.* 1935, *m.*	Lord Courtenay, *b.* 1942.
1800 I.*	*Donoughmore* (7th), John Michael Henry Hely-Hutchinson, (7th *U.K. Visct. Hutchinson*, 1821), *b.* 1902, *s.* 1948, *m.*	Viscount Suirdale, *b.* 1927.
1661 I.*	*Drogheda* (11th), Charles Garrett Moore, O.B.E. (2nd *U.K. Baron, Moore* 1954) *b.* 1910, *s.* 1957, *m.*	Viscount Moore, *b.* 1937.
1837	*Ducie* (6th), Basil Howard Moreton, *b.* 1917, *s.* 1952, *m.*	Lord Moreton, *b.* 1951.
1860	*Dudley* (3rd), William Humble Eric Ward, M.C., T.D., *b.* 1894, *s.* 1932, *m.*	Viscount Ednam, *b.* 1920.
1660 S.*	*Dundee* (11th), Henry James Scrymgeour-Wedderburn, P.C. (1st *U.K. Baron, Glassary*, 1954) *b.* 1902, *s.* 1924 (*claim admitted*, 1953), *m* (*Hereditary Standard Bearer, Scotland*).	Lord Scrymgeour, *b.* 1949.
1669 S.	*Dundonald* (14th), Ian Douglas Leonard Cochrane, *b.* 1918, *s.* 1958, *m.*	Lord Cochrane, *b.* 1961.
1686 S.*	*Dunmore* (9th), John Alexander Murray (4th *U.K. Baron, Dunmore*, 1831), *b.* 1939, *s.* 1962.	Arthur C. *M.*, *b.* 1882.
1822 I.	*Dunraven and Mount Earl* (6th), Richard Southwell Windham Robert Wyndham-Quin, C.B., C.B.E., M.C., *b.* 1887, *s.* 1952, *m.*	Viscount Adare, *b.* 1939.
1833	*Durham* (5th), John Frederick Lambton, *b.* 1884, *s.* 1929, *m.*	Viscount Lambton, M.P., *b.* 1922.
1837	*Effingham* (6th), Mowbray Henry Gordon Howard, *b.* 1905, *s.* 1946. *m.*	Hon. John A. F. C. *H.*, *b.* 1907.
1507 S. } 1859* }	*Eglinton* (17th) & (8th) *Winton* (1600), Archibald William Alexander Montgomerie (5th *U.K. Earl Winton*, 1859), *b.* 1914, *s.* 1945, *m.*	Lord Montgomerie, *b.* 1939.
1733 I.*	*Egmont* (11th), Frederick George Moore Perceval (9th *Brit. Baron, Lovel & Holland*, 1762), *b.* 1914, *s.* 1932, *m.*	Viscount Perceval, *b.* 1934.
1821	*Eldon* (4th), John Scott, G.C.V.O., *b.* 1899, *s.* 1926, *m.*	Viscount Encombe, *b.* 1937.
1633 S.*	*Elgin* (10th) & *Kincardine* (14th) (1647), Edward James Bruce, K.T., C.M.G., T.D. (3rd *U.K. Baron, Elgin*, 1849), *b.* 1881, *s.* 1917, *m.*	Lord Bruce, *b.* 1924.
1789 I.*	*Enniskillen* (6th), David Lowry Cole, M.B.E., (4th *U.K. Baron, Grinstead*, 1815), *b.* 1918, *s.* 1963, *m.*	Viscount Cole, *b.* 1942.
1781 I.*	*Erne* (6th), Henry George Victor John Crichton (3rd *U.K. Baron, Fermanagh*, 1876), *b.* 1937, *s.* 1940, *m*,	David G. C., *b.* 1914.
1661	*Essex* (8th), Algernon George de Vere Capell, *b.* 1884, *s.* 1916, *m.*	Viscount Malden, T.D., *b.* 1906.
1711	ᶜ*Ferrers* (13th), Robert Washington Shirley, *b.* 1929, *s.* 1954, *m.*	Viscount Tamworth, *b.* 1952.
1868	*Feversham* (3rd), Charles William Slingsby Duncombe, D.S.O., T.D. (6th *U.K. Baron Feversham*, 1826), *b.* 1906, *s.* 1916, *m.*	(None to Earldom), to Barony, Charles A. P. *Duncombe-Anderson*, *b.* 1945.
1628 I.*	*Fingall* (12th), Oliver James Horace Plunkett, M.C. (5th *U.K. Baron, Fingall*, 1831), *b.* 1896, *s.* 1929, *m.*	(None to Earldom), to Barony of Killeen Lord Dunsany (*see* p. 238).

Created.	Title, Order of Succession, Name, etc.	Eldest Son or Heir.
1746*	°*Fitzwilliam* (10th) William Thomas George Wentworth-Fitzwilliam (10th *Irish Earl, Fitzwilliam*, 1716), *b.* 1904, *s.* 1952, *m.*	(None.)
1789	°*Fortescue* (6th), Denzil George Fortescue, M.C., T.D., *b.* 1893, *s.* 1958, *m.*	Viscount Ebrington, *b.* 1922.
1841	*Gainsborough* (5th), Anthony Gerard Edward Noel, *b.* 1923, *s.* 1927, *m.*	Viscount Campden, *b.* 1950.
1623 S.*	*Galloway* (12th), Randolph Algernon Ronald Stewart (5th *Brit. Baron, Stewart of Garlies*, 1796), *b.* 1892, *s.* 1920, *m.*	Lord Garlies, *b.* 1928.
1703 S.*	*Glasgow* (8th), Patrick James Boyle, D.S.O. (2nd *U.K. Baron, Fairlie*, 1897), *b.* 1874, *s.* 1915, *m.*	Rear-Adm. Viscount Kelburn, C.B., D.S.C., *b.* 1910.
1806 I.*	*Gosford* (6th), Archibald Alexander John Stanley Acheson, O.B.E., (4th *U.K. Baron, Worlingham*, 1835), *b.* 1911, *s.* 1954, *m.*	Viscount Acheson, *b.* 1942.
1945	*Gowrie* (2nd), Alexander Patrick Greysteel Hore-Ruthven (3rd *U.K. Baron Ruthven of Gowrie*, 1919), *b.* 1939, *s.* 1955, *m.*	Hon. Malise W. M. K. *H-R*, *b.* 1942.
1684 I.*	*Granard* (9th) Arthur Patrick Hastings Forbes, A.F.C. (4th *U. K. Baron, Granard*. 1806), *b.* 1915, *s.* 1948, *m.*	Hon. John *F.*, *b.* 1920.
1833	°*Granville* (5th), Granville James Leveson-Gower, M.C., *b.* 1918, *s.* 1953. [*m.*	Lord Leveson, *b.* 1959.
1806	°*Grey* (6th), Richard Fleming George Charles Grey, *b.* 1939, *s.* 1963.	Philip K. *G.*, *b.* 1940.
1752	*Guilford* (9th), Edward Francis North, *b.* 1933, *s.* 1949, *m.*	Hon. John M. W. *N.*, *b.* 1905.
1619 S.	*Haddington* (12th), George Baillie-Hamilton, K.T., M.C., T.D., *b.* 1894, *s.* 1917, *m.*	Lord Binning, *b.* 1941.
1919	°*Haig* (2nd), George Alexander Eugene Douglas Haig *b.* 1918, *s.* 1928, *m.*	Viscount Dawick, *b.* 1961.
1944	*Halifax* (2nd), Charles Ingram Courtenay Wood (4th *U.K. Viscount, Halifax*, 1866), *b.* 1912. *s.* 1959, *m.*	Lord Irwin, *b.* 1944.
1898	*Halsbury* (3rd), John Anthony Hardinge Giffard, *b.* 1908, *s.* 1943, *m.*	Viscount Tiverton, *b.* 1934.
1754	*Hardwicke* (9th), Philip Grantham Yorke, *b.* 1906, *s.* 1936, *m.*	Viscount Royston, *b.* 1938.
1812	*Harewood* (7th), George Henry Hubert Lascelles, *b.* 1923, *s.* 1947, *m.* (*See also* p. 214).	Viscount Lascelles, *b.* 1950.
1742	*Harrington* (11th), William Henry Leicester Stanhope, *b.* 1922, *s.* 1929.	Viscount Petersham, *b.* 1945.
1809	*Harrowby* (6th), Dudley Ryder, *b.* 1892, *s.* 1956. *m.*	Viscount Sandon, *b.* 1922.
1604 S.*	*Home* (14th), Alexander Frederick Douglas-Home, P.C., K.T. (4th *U.K. Baron, Douglas*, 1875), *b.* 1903, *s.* 1951, *m.*	Lord Dunglass, *b.* 1943.
1821	°*Howe* (5th), Francis Richard Henry Penn Curzon, P.C., C.B.E., V.D., *b.* 1884, *s.* 1929, *m.*	Viscount Curzon, C.B.E., *b.* 1908.
1529	*Huntingdon* (15th), Francis John Clarence Westenra Plantagenet Hastings, *b.* 1901, *s.* 1939, *m.*	David F. G. *H.*, *b.* 1909.
1885	*Iddesleigh* (3rd), Henry Stafford Northcote, *b.* 1901, *s.* 1927, *m.*	Viscount St. Cyres, *b.* 1932.
1756	*Ilchester* (7th), Edward Henry Charles James Fox-Strangways, *b.* 1905, *s.* 1959, *m.*	Walter A. *F.-S.*, *b.* 1887.
1929	*Inchcape* (3rd), Kenneth James William Mackay, *b.* 1917, *s.* 1939.	Viscount Glenapp, *b.* 1943.
1919	*Iveagh* (2nd), Rupert Edward Cecil Lee Guinness, K.G., C.B., C.M.G., *b.* 1874, *s.* 1927, *m.*	Viscount Elveden, *b.* 1937.
1925	°*Jellicoe* (2nd), George Patrick John Rushworth Jellicoe, D.S.O., M.C., *b.* 1918, *s.* 1935, *m.*	Viscount Brocas, *b.* 1950.
1697	*Jersey* (9th), George Francis Child-Villiers (12th *Irish Visct., Grandison*, 1620), *b.* 1910, *s.* 1923, *m.*	Viscount Villiers, *b.* 1948.
1822 I.	*Kilmorey* (5th), Francis Jack Richard Patrick Needham, *b.* 1915, *s.* 1961, *m.*	Viscount Newry and Mourne, *b.* 1942.
1962	*Kilmuir* (1st), David Patrick Maxwell Fyfe, P.C., G.C.V.O., *b.* 1900, *m.*	(None.)
1866	*Kimberley* (4th), John Wodehouse, *b.* 1924, *s.* 1941, *m.*	Lord Wodehouse, *b.* 1951.
1768 I.	*Kingston* (11th), Barclay Robert Edwin King-Tenison, *b.* 1943, *s.* 1948, *M.*	Capt. R. D. *King-Harman*, D.S.O., D.S.C., R.N., *b.* 1891.
1633 S.*	*Kinnoull* (15th), Arthur William George Patrick Hay (9th *Brit. Baron, Hay of Pedwardine*, 1711), *b.* 1935, *s.* 1938, *m.*	Viscount Dupplin, *b.* 1962.
1677 S.*	*Kintore* (10th), Arthur George Keith (4th *U.K. Baron, Kintore*, 1838, 12th *Scott. Baron Falconer of Halkerton*, 1646), *b.* 1879, *s.* 1930, *m.*	To Earldom, Sydney, Viscountess Stonehaven, *b.* 1874; to U.K. Barony, None; to Scott. Barony, The Master of Halkerton, *b.* 1916.
1914	°*Kitchener of Khartoum* (3rd), Henry Herbert Kitchener, *b.* 1919, *s.* 1937.	Hon. Charles E. *K.*, *b.* 1920.
1756 I.	*Lanesborough* (9th), Denis Anthony Brian Butler, *b.* 1918, *s.* 1959.	*Lt. Comdr.* Terence B. J. D. *B.*, *b.* 1913.
1624 S.	*Lauderdale* (16th), Rev. Alfred Sydney Frederick Maitland, *b.* 1904, *s.* 1953, *m.*	The Master of Lauderdale, *b.* 1911.
1837	*Leicester* (5th), Thomas William Edward Coke, M.V.O., *b.* 1908, *s.* 1949, *m.*	Anthony L. *C.*, *b.* 1909.
1641 S.	*Leven* (14th) & (13th) *Melville* (1690), Alexander Robert Leslie-Melville, *b.* 1924, *s.* 1947, *m.*	Lord Balgonie, *b.* 1954.
1831	*Lichfield* (5th), Thomas Patrick John Anson, *b.* 1939, *s.* 1960.	Hon. Rupert A., *b.* 1889.
1803 I.*	*Limerick* (5th), Edmund Colquhoun Pery, G.B.E., C.H., K.C.B., D.S.O., T.D. (4th *U.K. Baron, Foxford*, 1815), *b.* 1888, *s.* 1929, *m.*	Viscount Glentworth, *b.* 1930.
1633 S.	*Lindsay* (14th), William Tucker Lindesay-Bethune, *b.* 1901, *s.* 1943, *m.*	Viscount Garnock, *b.* 1926.

Created.	Title, Order of Succession, Name, etc.	Eldest Son or Heir.
1626	*Lindsey* (13th) *and Abingdon* (8th) (1682), Montagu Henry Edmund Cecil Bertie, *b.* 1887, *s.* 1928, *m.*	Richard H. R. *B.*, *b.* 1931.
1776 I.	*Lisburne* (7th), Ernest Edmund Henry Malet Vaughan, *b.* 1892, *s.* 1899, *w.*	Viscount Vaughan, *b.* 1918.
1822 I.*	*Listowel* (5th), William Francis Hare, P.C., G.C.M.G. (3rd *U.K. Baron, Hare* 1869), *b.* 1906, *s.* 1931.	Hon. Richard G. *H.*, *b.* 1907.
1905	*Liverpool* (4th), Robert Anthony Edward St. Andrew Savile Foljambe, *b.* 1887, *s.* 1962.	Hon. Victor A. C. S. *F.*, *b.* 1895.
1945	°*Lloyd George of Dwyfor* (2nd), Richard Lloyd George, *b.* 1889, *s.* 1945, *m.*	Viscount Gwynnedd, *b.* 1924.
1785 I.*	*Longford* (7th), Francis Aungier Pakenham, P.C. (9th *U.K. Baron, Silchester*, 1821; 1st U.K. *Baron Pakenham*, 1945), *b.* 1905, *s.* 1961, *m.*	Lord Silchester, *b.* 1933.
1807	*Lonsdale* (7th), James Hugh William Lowther, *b.* 1922, *s.* 1953, *m.*	Viscount Lowther, *b.* 1949.
1838	*Lovelace* (4th), Peter Malcolm King (11th *British Baron King*, 1725), *b.* 1905, *s.* 1929, *m.*	Viscount Ockham, *b.* 1951.
1795 I.*	*Lucan* (6th), George Charles Patrick Bingham, M.C. (2nd *U.K. Baron, Bingham*, 1934), *b.* 1898, *s.* 1949, *m.*	Lord Bingham, *b.* 1934.
1880	*Lytton* (4th), Noel Anthony Scawen Lytton (17th *English Baron, Wentworth*, 1529), *b.* 1900, *s.* 1951, *m.*	Viscount Knebworth, *b.* 1950.
1721	*Macclesfield* (7th), George Loveden William Henry Parker, *b.* 1888, *s.* 1896, *m.*	Viscount Parker, *b.* 1914.
1800	*Malmesbury* (6th), William James Harris, T.D., *b.* 1907, *s.* 1950, *m.*	Viscount FitzHarris, *b.* 1946.
1776 & 1792	*Mansfield and Mansfield* (7th), Mungo David Malcolm Murray (13th *Scott, Visct., Stormont*, 1621), *b.* 1900, *s.* 1935, *m.*	Viscount Stormont, *b.* 1930.
1404 S.	*Mar* (33rd), Lionel Walter Young Erskine (*Premier Earl of Scotland*), *b.* 1891, *s.* 1932.	Master of Mar, *b.* 1914.
1565 S.	*Mar* (13th) & (14th) *Kellie* (1616), John Francis Hervey Erskine, *b.* 1921, *s.* 1955, *m.*	Lord Erskine, *b.* 1949.
1785 I.	*Mayo* (10th), Terence Patrick Bourke, *b.* 1929, *s.* 1962, *m.*	Lord Naas, *b.* 1953.
1627 I.*	*Meath* (14th), Anthony Windham Normand Brabazon (5th *U.K. Baron, Chaworth*, 1831), *b.* 1910, *s.* 1949, *m.*	Lord Ardee, *b.* 1941.
1766 I.	*Mexborough* (7th), John Raphael Wentworth Savile, *b.* 1906, *s.* 1945, *m.*	Viscount Pollington, *b.* 1931.
1920	*Midleton* (2nd), George St. John Brodrick, M.C. (10th *Irish Viscount, Midleton*, 1717), *b.* 1888, *s.* 1942, *m.*	(None to Earldom), to Irish Viscountcy, W. J. H. *B.*, O.B.E., *b.* 1874.
1813	*Minto* (5th), Victor Gilbert Lariston Garnet Elliot-Murray-Kynynmound, *b.* 1891, *s.* 1914, *m.*	Viscount Melgund, M.B.E., *b.* 1928.
1562 S.*	*Moray* (19th) (Archibald) John Morton Stuart (11th *Brit. Baron, Stuart of Castle Stuart*, 1796), *b.* 1894, *s.* 1943, *m.*	Lord Doune, *b.* 1928.
1815	*Morley* (6th), John St. Aubyn Parker, *b.* 1923, *s.* 1962, *m.*	Visct. Boringdon, *b.* 1956.
1458 S.	*Morton* (21st), Sholto Charles John Hay Douglas, *b.* 1907, *s.* 1935.	Hon. Charles *D.*, *b.* 1881.
1947	°*Mountbatten of Burma* (1st), Louis Francis Albert Victor Nicholas Mountbatten, K.G., P.C., G.C.B., G.C.S.I., G.C.I.E., G.C.V.O., D.S.O., *b.* 1900, *w.* (*Personal A.D.C. to the Queen*), *Admiral of the Fleet.* (*See also p.* 212.)	Baroness Brabourne, *b.* 1934 (*see* pp. 212 and 236).
1789	*Mount Edgcumbe* (6th), Kenelm William Edward Edgcumbe, T.D., *b.* 1873, *s.* 1944, *m.*	Edward P. *E.*, *b.* 1903.
1831	*Munster* (5th), Geoffrey William Richard Hugh FitzClarence, P.C., K.B.E., *b.* 1906, *s.* 1928, *m.*	Edward C. *FitzC.*, *b.* 1899.
1805	°*Nelson* (7th), Henry Edward Joseph Horatio Nelson, *b.* 1894, *s.* 1957.	Hon. Charles S. J. H. *N.*, *b.* 1896.
1827 I.	*Norbury* (6th), Noel Terence Graham-Toler, *b.* 1939, *s.* 1955.	
1806 I.*	*Normanton* (5th), Edward John Sidney Christian Welbore Ellis Agar (3rd *U.K. Baron, Somerton*, 1873), *b.* 1910, *s.* 1933, *m.*	Viscount Somerton, *b.* 1945.
1647 S.	*Northesk* (11th), David Ludovic George Hopetoun Carnegie, *b.* 1901 *s.* 1921, *m.*	John Douglas *C.*, *b.* 1895.
1801	*Onslow* (6th), William Arthur Bampfylde Onslow, K.B.E., M.C., T.D., *b.* 1913, *s.* 1945, *m.*	Viscount Cranley, *b.* 1938.
1925	*Oxford & Asquith* (2nd), Julian Edward George Asquith, C.M.G., *b.* 1916, *s.* 1928, *m.*	Viscount Asquith of Morley, *b.* 1952.
1929	°*Peel* (2nd), Arthur William Ashton Peel (3rd *U.K. Viscount Peel*, 1895), *b.* 1901, *s.* 1937, *m.*	Viscount Clanfield, *b.* 1947.
1551	*Pembroke* (16th) & (13th) *Montgomery* (1605), Sidney Charles Herbert, C.V.O., *b.* 1906, *s.* 1960, *m.*	Lord Herbert, *b.* 1939.
1605 S.	*Perth* (17th), John David Drummond, P.C., *b.* 1907, *s.* 1951, *m.*	Viscount Strathallan, *b.* 1935.
1905	*Plymouth* (3rd), Other Robert Ivor Windsor-Clive (*English Baron, Windsor*, 1529), *b.* 1923, *s.* 1943, *m.*	Viscount Windsor, *b.* 1951.
1785 I.	*Portarlington* (7th), George Lionel Yuill Seymour Dawson-Damer, *b.* 1938, *s.* 1959, *m.*	Hon. Lionel J. C. S. *D.-D*, *b.* 1940.
1743	*Portsmouth* (9th), Gerard Vernon Wallop, *b.* 1898, *s.* 1943, *m.*	Viscount Lymington, *b.* 1923.
1706	°*Poulett* (8th), George Amias Fitzwarrine Poulett, *b.* 1909, *s.* 1918, *w.*	(None.)
1804	*Powis* (5th), Edward Robert Henry Herbert, C.B.E., T.D. (6th *Irish Baron, Clive*, 1762), *b.* 1889, *s.* 1952, *m.*	Hon. Christian V. C. *H.*, *b.* 1904.

Created.	*Title, Order of Succession, Name, etc.*	*Eldest Son or Heir.*
1765	*Radnor* (7th) William Pleydell-Bouverie, K.G., K.C.V.O., *b.* 1895, *s.* 1930, *m.*	Viscount Folkestone, *b.* 1927.
1831 I.★	*Ranfurly* (6th), Thomas Daniel Knox, K.C.M.G. (7th *U.K. Baron, Ranfurly*, 1826), *b.* 1913, *s.* 1933, *m.*	Capt. John N. *K.*, R.N., *b.* 1890.
1771 I.	*Roden* (9th), Robert William Jocelyn, *b.* 1909, *s.* 1956, *m.*	Viscount Jocelyn, *b.* 1938.
1801	*Romney* (6th), Charles Marsham, *b.* 1892, *s.* 1933, *m.*	Michael H. *M.*, *b.* 1910.
1703 S.★	*Rosebery* (6th), Albert Edward Harry Mayer Archibald Primrose, P.C., K.T., D.S.O., M.C. (2nd *U.K. Earl of Midlothian*, 1911), *b.* 1882, *s.* 1929, *m.*	Lord Primrose, *b.* 1929.
1806 I.	*Rosse* (6th), Laurence Michael Harvey Parsons, M.B.E., *b.* 1906, *s.* 1918, *m.*	Lord Oxmantown, *b.* 1935.
1801	*Rosslyn* (6th), Anthony Hugh Francis Harry St. Clair-Erskine, *b.* 1917, *s.* 1939.	Lord Loughborough, *b.* 1958.
1457 S.	*Rothes* (20th), Malcolm George Dyer Edwardes Leslie, *b.* 1902, *s.* 1927, *m.*	Lord Leslie, *b.* 1932.
1861	‘*Russell* (3rd), Bertrand Arthur William Russell, O.M., F.R.S., *b.* 1872, *s.* 1931, *m.*	Viscount Amberley, *b.* 1921.
1915	°*St. Aldwyn* (2nd), Michael John Hicks-Beach, P.C., T.D., *b.* 1912, *s.* 1916, *m.*	Viscount Quenington, *b.* 1950.
1815	*St. Germans* (9th), Nicholas Richard Michael Eliot, *b.* 1914, *s.* 1960, *m.*	Lord Eliot, *b.* 1941.
1660	*Sandwich* (10th), Alexander Victor Edward Paulet Montagu, *b.* 1906, *s.* 1962, *m.*	Viscount Hinchingbrooke, *b.* 1943.
1690	*Scarbrough* (11th), (Lawrence) Roger Lumley, K.G. P.C., G.C.S.I., G.C.I.E., G.C.V.O., T.D., Royal Victorian Chain (12th *Irish Visct., Lumley*, 1628), *b.* 1896, *s.* 1945, *m.*	Viscount Lumley, *b.* 1932.
1771 I. ★	*Sefton* (7th), Hugh William Osbert Molyneux (6th *U.K. Baron, Sefton*, 1831), *b.* 1898, *s.* 1930, *w.*	(None.)
1882	*Selborne* (3rd), Roundell Cecil Palmer, P.C., C.H., *b.* 1887, *s.* 1942, *w.*	Viscount Wolmer, *b.* 1940.
1646 S.	*Selkirk* (7th) (George) Nigel Douglas-Hamilton, P.C., G.C.M.G., O.B.E., A.F.C., *b.* 1906, *s.* 1940, *m.*	Lord Malcolm *D.-H.*, O.B.E., D.F.C., *b.* 1909.
1672	*Shaftesbury* (10th), Anthony Ashley-Cooper, *b.* 1938, *s.* 1961.	Hon. John P. H. M. *A.-C.*, *b.* 1915.
1756 I.★	*Shannon* (8th), Robert Henry Boyle (7th *Brit. Bn. Carleton*, 1786), *b.* 1900, *s.* 1917, *m.*	Viscount Boyle, *b.* 1924.
1442	*Shrewsbury* (21st) & *Waterford* (I. 1446), John George Charles Henry Alton Alexander Chetwynd Chetwynd-Talbot (*Premier Earl of England and Ireland, Earl Talbot*, 1784), *b.* 1914, *s.* 1921.	Viscount Ingestre, *b.* 1952.
1961	*Snowdon* (1st), Antony Charles Robert Armstrong-Jones, *b.* 1930, *m.* (*See also* p. 215.)	Viscount Linley, *b.* 1961 (*see* p. 215).
1880	‘*Sondes* (4th), George Henry Milles-Lade, *b.* 1914, *s.* 1941, *m.*	Viscount Throwley, *b.* 1940.
1633 S.★	*Southesk* (11th), Charles Alexander Carnegie, K.C.V.O. (3rd *U.K. Baron, Balinhard*, 1869), *b.* 1893, *s.* 1941, *m.*	The Duke of Fife, *b.* 1929 (*see* pp. 213 and 224).
1765	°*Spencer* (7th), Albert Edward John Spencer, T.D., *b.* 1892, *s.* 1922, *m.*	Viscount Althorp, M.V.O., *b.* 1924.
1703 S.★	*Stair* (13th), John Aymer Dalrymple, M.B.E. (6th *U.K. Baron, Oxenfoord*, 1841), *b.* 1906, *s.* 1961, *m.*	Viscount Dalrymple, *b.* 1961.
1628	*Stamford* (10th), Roger Grey, *b.* 1896, *s.* 1910.	(None.)
1718	‘*Stanhope* (7th) James Richard Stanhope, K.G., P.C., D.S.O., M.C. (13th *Earl of Chesterfield*, 1628) (7th *U.K. Viscount Stanhope of Mahon*, 1717), *b.* 1880, *s.* (*to Earldom of Stanhope*), 1905 (*to Earldom of Chesterfield*), 1952, *w.*	None to Earldoms, to Viscountcy, Earl of Harrington, *b.* 1922, (*see* p. 228).
1821	*Stradbroke* (4th), John Anthony Alexander Rous, *b.* 1903, *s.* 1947, *m.*	Hon. Keith *R.* *b.* 1907.
1847	*Strafford* (7th), Robert Cecil Byng, *b.* 1904, *s.* 1951, *m.*	Viscount Enfield, *b.* 1936.
1937	*Strathmore* (3rd), Timothy Patrick Bowes-Lyon (16th *Scottish Earl, Strathmore & Kinghorne* 1606), *b.* 1918, *s.* 1949, *m.*	Fergus M. C. *B.-L.*, *b.* 1928.
1603	*Suffolk* (21st) & (14th) *Berkshire* (1626), Michael John James George Robert Howard, *b.* 1935, *s.* 1941, *m.*	Hon. Maurice *H.*, *b.* 1936.
1955	*Swinton* (1st), Philip Cunliffe-Lister, P.C., G.B.E., C.H., M.C., *b.* 1884, *m.*	Lord Masham, *b.* 1937.
1714	*Tankerville* (8th), Charles Augustus Ker Bennet, *b.* 1897, *s.* 1931, *m.*	Lord Ossulston, *b.* 1921.
1822	°*Temple of Stowe* (6th), Chandos Grenville Temple-Gore-Langton, *b.* 1909, *s.* 1940, *m.*	Hon. Ronald *T.-G.-L.*, *b.* 1910.
1815	*Verulam* (6th), John Grimston (10th *Irish Visct., Grimston*, 1719; 15th *Scott. Baron, Forrester*, 1633), *b.* 1912, *s.* 1960, *m.*	Lord Forrester of Corstorphine, *b.* 1951.
1729	°*Waldegrave* (12th), Geoffrey Noel Waldegrave, T.D., *b.* 1905, *s.* 1930, *m.*	Viscount Chewton, *b.* 1940.
1759	*Warwick* & °*Brooke* (1746), Charles Guy Fulke Greville (7th *Earl Brooke* and 7th *Earl of Warwick*), *b.* 1911, *s.* 1928.	Lord Brooke, *b.* 1934.
1633 S.★	*Wemyss* (12th) & (8th) *March* (1697), Francis David Charteris (5th *U.K. Baron, Wemyss*, 1821), *b.* 1912, *s.* 1937, *m.*	Lord Neidpath, *b.* 1943.
1621 I.	*Westmeath* (12th), Gilbert Charles Nugent, *b.* 1880, *s.* 1933, *m.*	Lord Delvin, *b.* 1923.
1624	*Westmorland* (15th), David Anthony Thomas Fane, *b.* 1924, *s.* 1948, *m.*	Lord Burghersh, *b.* 1951.
1876	*Wharncliffe* (4th) Alan James Montagu-Stuart-Wortley-Mackenzie, *b.* 1935, *s.* 1953, *m.*	Ralph *Montagu - Stuart Wortley*, *b.* 1897.

Created.	Title, Order of Succession, Name, etc.	Eldest Son or Heir.
1793 I.	*Wicklow* (8th) William Cecil James Philip John Paul Forward-Howard, *b.* 1902, *s.* 1946, *m.*	Cecil A. *F.-H.*, *b.* 1909.
1801	*Wilton* (7th), Seymour William Arthur John Egerton, *b.* 1921, *s.* 1927, *m.*	Lord Ebury, *b.* 1934 (*see* p. 238).
1628	*Winchilsea* (16th) & (11th) *Nottingham* (1681), Christopher Denys Stormont Finch-Hatton, *b.* 1936, *s.* 1950.	Hon. Robin H. *F.-H.*, *b.* 1939.
1766 I.	°*Winterton* (7th), Robert Chad Turnour, *b.* 1915, *s.* 1962, *m.*	Cecil N. *T.*, *b.* 1919.
1956	*Woolton* (1st), Frederick James Marquis, P.C., C.H., *b.* 1883, *m.*	Viscount Walberton, *b.* 1922.
1837	*Yarborough* (6th), Marcus Herbert Pelham, *b.* 1893, *s.* 1948, *m.*	Lord Worsley, *b.* 1920.
1922	*Ypres* (3rd), John Richard Charles Lambart French, *b.* 1921, *s.* 1958, *m.*	Maj. Hon. E. Gerald F. *F.*, D.S.O., *b.* 1883.

VISCOUNTS

Style (*see* note, p. 253), The Right Hon. the Viscount ——. *Addressed as*, My Lord. The eldest sons of Viscounts and Barons have no distinctive title; they, as well as their brothers and sisters, are styled the Hon. Robert, Hon. Mary, &c.

1945	*Addison* (2nd), Christopher Addison, *b.* 1904, *s.* 1951, *m.*	Hon. Michael *A.* *b.* 1914.
1946	*Alanbrooke* (2nd), Thomas Brooke, *b.* 1920, *s.* 1963.	Hon. Alan V. H. *B.*, *b.* 1932.
1919	*Allenby* (2nd), Dudley Jaffray Hynman Allenby, *b.* 1903, *s.* 1936, *m.*	Hon. Michael *A.*, *b.* 1931.
1911	*Allendale* (3rd), Wentworth Hubert Charles Beaumont, *b.* 1922, *s.* 1956, *m.*	Hon. Wentworth P. I. *B.*, *b.* 1948.
1960	*Amory* (1st), Derick Heathcoat Amory, P.C., G.C.M.G., *b.* 1899.	(None.)
1641 S.	*Arbuthnott* (15th), Robert Keith Arbuthnott, C.B., C.B.E., D.S.O., M.C., *b.* 1897, *s.* 1960, *m.*	Master of Arbuthnott, D.S.C., *b.* 1924.
1751 I.	*Ashbrook* (10th), Desmond Llowarch Edward Flower, M.B.E., *b.* 1905, *s.* 1936, *m.*	Hon. Michael *F.*, *b.* 1935.
1917	*Astor* (3rd), William Waldorf Astor, *b.* 1907, *s.* 1952, *m.*	Hon. William W. *A.*, *b.* 1951.
1781 I.	*Bangor* (7th), Edward Henry Harold Ward, *b.* 1905, *s.* 1950.	Hon. William M. D. *W.*, *b.* 1948.
1720 I.*	*Barrington* (11th), Patrick William Daines Barrington (5th *U.K. Baron Shute*, 1880), *b.* 1908, *s.* 1960.	Hon. Rupert E. S. *B.*, D.S.O., *b.* 1877
1925	*Bearsted* (3rd), Marcus Richard Samuel, T.D., *b.* 1909, *s.* 1948, *m.*	Hon. Peter *S.*, M.C., T.D., *b.* 1911.
1935	*Bledisloe* (2nd), Benjamin Ludlow Bathurst, Q.C., *b.* 1899, *s.* 1958, *m.*	Hon. Christopher H. L. *B.*, *b.* 1934.
1712	*Bolingbroke & St. John* (6th), Vernon Henry St. John, *b.* 1896, *s.* 1899.	Capt. Geoffrey R. *St. J.*, M.C., *b.* 1889.
1960	*Boyd of Merton* (1st), Alan Tindal Lennox-Boyd, P.C., C.H., *b.* 1904, *m.*	Hon. Simon D. R. N. *L.-B.*, *b.* 1939.
1717 I.*	*Boyne* (10th), Gustavus Michael George Hamilton-Russell (4th *U.K. Baron, Brancepeth*, 1866), *b.* 1931, *s.* 1942, *m.*	Hon. Richard *H.-R.*, D.S.O., *b.* 1909.
1929	*Brentford* (3rd), Lancelot William Joynson-Hicks, *b.* 1902, *s.* 1958, *m.*	Hon. Crispin W. *J.-H.*, *b.* 1933.
1929	*Bridgeman* (2nd), Robert Clive Bridgeman, K.B.E., C.B., D.S.O., M.C., *b.* 1896, *s.* 1935, *m.*	Hon. Geoffrey *B.*, M.C., *b.* 1898.
1868	*Bridport* (3rd), Rowland Arthur Herbert Nelson Hood (6th *Duke of Brontë in Sicily and* 5th *Irish Baron, Bridport* 1794), *b.* 1911, *s.* 1924, *m.*	Hon. Alexander N. *H.*, *b.* 1948.
1952	*Brookeborough* (1st), Basil Stanlake Brooke, P.C. (N.I.), C.B.E., M.C., *b.* 1888, *m.*	Hon. John W. *B.*, *b.* 1922.
1947	*Bruce of Melbourne* (1st), Stanley Melbourne Bruce, P.C., C.H., M.C., F.R.S., *b.* 1883, *m.*	(None.)
1932	*Buckmaster* (2nd), Owen Stanley Buckmaster, *b.* 1890, *s.* 1934, *m.*	Hon. Martin S. *B.*, *b.* 1921.
1939	*Caldecote* (2nd), Robert Andrew Inskip, D.S.C., *b.* 1917, *s.* 1947, *m.*	Hon. Piers J. H. *I.*, *b.* 1947.
1941	*Camrose* (2nd), (John) Seymour Berry, T.D., *b.* 1909, *s.* 1954.	Hon. Michael *B.*, M.B.E., T.D., *b.* 1911.
1954	*Chandos* (1st), Oliver Lyttelton, P.C., D.S.O., M.C., *b.* 1893, *m.*	Hon. Antony A. *L.*, *b.* 1920.
1916	*Chaplin* (3rd), Anthony Freskyn Charles Hamby Chaplin, *b.* 1906, *s.* 1949 *m.*	
1665 I.	*Charlemont* (9th) Charles Edward St. George Caulfeild (13th *Irish Baron, Caulfeild of Charlemont*, 1620), *b.* 1887, *s.* 1949, *m.*	Harry F. St. G. *C.*, *b.* 1881.
1921	*Chelmsford* (2nd), Andrew Charles Gerald Thesiger, *b.* 1903, *s.* 1933, *m.*	Hon. Frederic *T.*, *b.* 1931.
1717 I.	*Chetwynd* (9th), Adam Duncan Chetwynd, T.D., *b.* 1904, *s.* 1936, *m.*	Hon. Adam *C.*, *b.* 1935.
1911	*Chilston* (3rd), Eric Alexander Akers-Douglas, *b.* 1910, *s.* 1947.	Alastair G. *A.-D.*, *b.* 1946.
1902	*Churchill* (2nd), Victor Alexander Spencer, *b.* 1890, *s.* 1934, *w.*	Hon. Victor G. *S.*, *b.* 1934.
1781 I.*	*Clifden* (7th), Francis Gerald Agar-Robartes, K.C.V.O. (7th *Brit. Baron, Mendip* 1794), *b.* 1883, *s.* 1930.	Major Hon. Victor *A.-R.*, M.C., *b.* 1887.
1718	*Cobham* (10th), Charles John Lyttelton, G.C.M.G. (7th *Irish Baron, Westcote* 1618), *b.* 1909, *s.* 1949, *m.*	Hon John W. L. *L.*, *b.* 1943.

Created.	Title, Order of Succession, Name, etc.	Eldest Son or Heir.
1902	*Colville of Culross* (4th), John Mark Alexander Colville (13th *Scott. Baron, Colville of Culross*, 1604), *b.* 1933, *s.* 1945., *m.*	Master of Colville, *b.* 1959.
1827	*Combermere* (4th), Francis Lynch Wellington Stapleton-Cotton, *b.* 1887, *s.* 1898, *m.*	Hon. Michael *S.-C.*, *b.* 1929.
1917	*Cowdray* (3rd), Weetman John Churchill Pearson (3rd *U.K. Baron, Cowdray*, 1910), *b.* 1910, *s.* 1933, *m.*	Hon. Michael *P.*, *b.* 1944.
1927	*Craigavon* (2nd), James Craig, *b.* 1906 *s.* 1940, *m.*	Hon. Janric *C.*, *b.* 1944.
1886	*Cross* (3rd), Assheton Henry Cross, *b.* 1920, *s.* 1932, *m.*	(None.)
1943	*Daventry* (2nd), Robert Oliver FitzRoy, *b.* 1893, *s.* 1962, *m.*	Cdr. Hon. John M. *FitzRoy-Newdegate*, *b.* 1897.
1937	*Davidson* (1st), John Colin Campbell Davidson, P.C., G.C.V.O., C.H., C.B., *b.* 1889, *m.*	Hon. John A. *D.*, *b.* 1928.
1956	*De L'Isle* (1st), William Philip Sidney, V.C., P.C., G.C.M.G., G.C.V.O., (6th *Baron De L'Isle and Dudley*, 1835), *b.* 1909, *w.* (*Governor-General of Australia*).	Hon. Philip *S.*, *b.* 1945.
1776 I.	*De Vesci* (6th), John Eustace Vesey (7th *Irish Baron, Knapton*, 1750), *b.* 1919, *s.* 1958, *m.*	Hon. Thomas E. *V.*, *b.* 1955.
1917	*Devonport* (2nd), Gerald Chester Kearley, *b.* 1890, *s.* 1934, *m.*	Hon. Terence *K.*, *b.* 1944.
1622 I.	*Dillon* (20th), Michael Eric Dillon, *b.* 1911, *s.* 1946, *m.*	Hon. Charles *D.*, *b.* 1945.
1785 I.	*Doneraile* (9th), Richard St. John St. Leger, *b.* 1923, *s.* 1957, *m.*	Hon. Richard A. *St. L.*, *b.* 1946.
1680 I.*	*Downe* (10th), Richard Dawnay, O.B.E. (3rd *U.K. Baron, Dawnay*, 1897), *b.* 1903, *s.* 1931, *m.*	Hon. John C. G. *D.*, *b.* 1935.
1959	*Dunrossil* (2nd), John William Morrison, *b.* 1926, *s.* 1961, *m.*	Hon. Andrew W. R. *M.*, *b.* 1953.
1897	*Esher* (3rd), Oliver Sylvain Baliol Brett, G.B.E., *b.* 1881, *s.* 1930, *m.*	Hon. Lionel *B.*, *b.* 1913.
1816	*Exmouth* (9th), Pownoll Irving Edward Pellew, *b.* 1908, *s.* 1951, *m.*	Hon. Paul *P.*, *b.* 1940.
1620 S.	*Falkland* (14th), Lucius Henry Charles Plantagenet Cary, *b.* 1905, *s.* 1961. *m.*	Master of Falkland, *b.* 1935.
1720	*Falmouth* (9th), George Hugh Boscawen (26th *Eng. Baron, Le Despencer*, 1264), *b.* 1919, *s.* 1962, *m.*	Hon. Evelyn A. H. *B.*, *b.* 1955.
1918	*Furness* (2nd), William Anthony Furness, *b.* 1929, *s.* 1940.	(None.)
1720 I.*	*Gage* (6th), Henry Rainald Gage, K.C.V.O (5th *Brit. Baron, Gage*, 1790), *b.* 1895, *s.* 1912, *m.*	Hon. George J. St. C. *G.*, *b.* 1932.
1727 I.*	*Galway* (9th), Simon George Robert Monckton-Arundell (3rd *U.K. Baron, Monckton*, 1887), *b.* 1929, *s.* 1943, *m.*	William A. *Monckton*, *b.* 1894.
1478 I.*	*Gormanston* (17th), Jenico Nicholas Dudley Preston (*Premier Viscount of Ireland*; 5th *U.K. Baron, Gormanston*, 1868), *b.* 1939, *s.* 1940.	Hon. Robert *Shaw-Preston*, *b.* 1915.
1816 I.	*Gort* (7th), Standish Robert Gage Prendergast Vereker, M.C., *b.* 1888, *s* 1946, *m.*	Colin L. P. *V.*, *b.* 1916.
1900	*Goschen* (3rd), John Alexander Goschen, O.B.E., *b.* 1906, *s.* 1952. *m.*	(None.)
1849	*Gough* (5th), Shane Hugh Maryon Gough, *b.* 1941, *s.* 1951.	(None.)
1937	*Greenwood* (2nd), David Henry Hamar Greenwood, *b.* 1914, *s.* 1948.	Hon. Michael G. H. *G.*, *b.* 1923.
1929	*Hailsham* (2nd), Quintin McGarel Hogg, P.C., Q.C., *b.* 1907, *s.* 1950, *m.*	Hon. Douglas M. *H.*, *b.* 1945
1946	*Hall* (1st), George Henry Hall, P.C., *b.* 1881, *w.*	Hon. W. G. Leonard *H.*, *b.* 1913.
1891	*Hambleden* (4th), William Herbert Smith, *b.* 1930, *s.* 1948, *m.*	Hon. William H. *S.*, *b.* 1955.
1884	*Hampden* (4th), Thomas Henry Brand, C.M.G. (26th *Eng. Baron, Dacre*, 1307), *b.* 1900, *s.* 1958, *m.*	Hon. David F. *B.*, *b.* 1902.
1936	*Hanworth* (2nd), David Bertram Pollock, *b.* 1916, *s.* 1936, *m.*	Hon. David *P.*, *b.* 1946.
1791 I.	*Harberton* (9th), Henry Ralph Martyn Pomeroy, *b.* 1908, *s.* 1956.	Hon. Thomas De V. *P.*, *b.* 1910.
1917	*Harcourt* (2nd), William Edward Harcourt, K.C.M.G., O.B.E., *b.* 1908, *s.* 1922, *w.*	(None.)
1846	*Hardinge* (4th), Caryl Nicholas Charles Hardinge, M.B.E., *b.* 1905, *s.* 1924, *m.*	Hon. Henry N. *H.*, *b.* 1929.
1791 I.	*Hawarden* (8th), Robert Leslie Eustace Maude, *b.* 1926, *s.* 1958, *m.*	Hon. Robert C. W. L., *M.*, *b.* 1961.
1960	*Head* (1st), Antony Henry Head, P.C., G.C.M.G., C.B.E., M.C., *b.* 1906, *m.*	Hon. Richard A. *H.*, *b.* 1937.
1550	*Hereford* (18th), Robert Milo Leicester Devereux (*Premier Viscount of England*), *b.* 1932, *s.* 1952.	Rodney de B. *D.*, *b.* 1903.
1940	*Hewart* (2nd), Hugh Vaughan Hewart, *b.* 1896, *s* 1943.	(None.)
1842	*Hill* (7th), Gerald Rowland Clegg-Hill, *b.* 1904, *s.* 1957, *m.*	Hon. Antony R. *C-H.*, *b.* 1931.
1796	*Hood* (6th), Samuel Hood, K.C.M.G. (6th *Irish Baron, Hood*, 1782), *b.* 1910, *s.* 1933.	Hon. Alexander L. *H.*, *b.* 1914.
1952	*Hudson* (2nd), Robert William Hudson, *b.* 1924, *s.* 1957.	(None.)
1956	*Ingleby* (1st), Osbert Peake, P.C., *b.* 1897, *m.*	Hon. Martin *P.*, *b.* 1926.
1945	*Kemsley* (1st), (James) Gomer Berry, G.B.E., *b.* 1883, *m.*	Hon. Lionel *B.*, *b.* 1909.

Created.	Title, Order of Succession, Name, etc.	Eldest Son or Heir.
1911	*Knollys* (2nd), Edward George William Tyrwhitt Knollys, G.C.M.G., M.B.E., D.F.C., *b.* 1895, *s.* 1924, *m.*	Hon. David F. D. *K.*, *b.* 1931.
1895	*Knutsford* (4th), Thurstan Holland-Hibbert, *b.* 1888, *s.* 1935, *m.*	Hon. Julian *H.-H.*, *b.* 1920.
1945	*Lambert* (2nd), George Lambert, T.D., *b.* 1909, *s.* 1958, *m.*	Hon. George *L.*, *b.* 1941.
1954	*Leathers* (1st), Frederick James Leathers, P.C., C.H., *b.* 1883, *m.*	Hon. Fredk. A. *L.*, *b.* 1908.
1922	*Leverhulme* (3rd), Philip William Bryce Lever, T.D., *b.* 1915, *s.* 1949, *m.*	(None.)
1781 I.	*Lifford* (8th), Alan William Wingfield Hewitt, *b.* 1900, *s.* 1954, *m.*	Hon. Edward J. W. *H.*, *b.* [1949.
1921	*Long* (3rd) (Richard) Eric (Onslow) Long, T.D., *b.* 1892, *s.* 1944, *w.*	Hon. Richard *L.*, *b.* 1929.
1957	*Mackintosh of Halifax* (1st), Harold Vincent Mackintosh, *b.* 1891, *m.*	Hon. John *M.*, *b.* 1921.
1955	*Malvern* (1st), Godfrey Martin Huggins, P.C., C.H., K.C.M.G., *b.* 1883, *m.*	Hon. John G. *H.*, *b.* 1922.
1945	*Marchwood* (2nd) Peter George Penny, M.B.E., *b.* 1912, *s.* 1955, *m.*	Hon. David G. S. *P.*, *b.* 1936.
1942	*Margesson* (1st), Henry David Reginald Margesson, P.C., M.C., *b.* 1890.	Hon. Francis V. H. *M.*, *b.* 1922.
1660 I.*	*Massereene* (13th) & (6th) *Ferrard* (1797), John Clotworthy Talbot Foster Whyte-Melville Skeffington (6th *U.K. Baron*, *Oriel*, 1821), *b.* 1914, *s.* 1956, *m.*	Hon. John D.C.W.M. *S.*, *b.* 1940.
1939	*Maugham* (2nd), Robert Cecil Romer Maugham, *b.* 1916, *s.* 1958.	(None.)
1802	*Melville* (8th), Henry Charles Patric Brouncker Dundas, *b.* 1909, *s.* 1935.	Robert *D.*, *b.* 1937.
1916	*Mersey* (3rd), Edward Clive Bigham, *b.* 1906, *s.* 1956, *m.*	Master of Nairne, *b.* 1934.
1962	*Mills* (1st), Percy Herbert Mills, P.C., K.B.E., *b.* 1890, *m.*	Hon. Roger C. *M*, *b.* 1919.
1716 I.	*Molesworth* (11th), Richard Gosset Molesworth, *b.* 1907, *s.* 1961, *m.*	Hon. Robert B. K., *M.*, *b.* 1959.
1801 I.*	*Monck* (6th), Henry Wyndham Stanley Monck, O.B.E., (3rd *U.K. Baron*, *Monck*, 1866), *b.* 1905, *s.* 1927, *m.*	Hon. Charles S. *M.*, *b.* 1953.
1957	*Monckton of Brenchley* (1st), Walter Turner Monckton, P.C., K.C.M.G. K.C.V.O., M.C., Q.C., *b.* 1891, *m.*	Maj. Gen. Hon. Gilbert W. R. *M.*, O.B.E., M.C., *b.* 1915.
1935	*Monsell* (1st), Bolton Meredith Eyres-Monsell, P.C., G.B.E., *b.* 1881, *m.*	Hon. Graham *E-M.*, *b.* 1905.
1946	*Montgomery of Alamein* (1st), Bernard Law Montgomery, K.G., G.C.B., D.S.O., *Field Marshal*, *b.* 1887, *w.*	Hon. David *M.*, *b.* 1928.
1550 I.*	*Mountgarret* (16th), Piers Henry Augustine Butler (3rd *U.K. Baron*, *Mountgarret*, 1911), *b.* 1903, *s.* 1918, *m.*	Hon. Richard H. *B.*, *b.* 1936.
1952	*Norwich* (2nd), John Julius Cooper, *b.* 1929, *s.* 1954, *m.*	(None.)
1938	*Nuffield* (1st), William Richard Morris, G.B.E., C.H., F.R.S., *b.* 1877, *w.*	(None.)
1946	*Portal of Hungerford* (1st), Charles Frederick Algernon Portal, K.G., G.C.B., O.M., D.S.O., M.C. (1st *U.K. Baron Portal of Hungerford*, 1945), *Marshal of the Royal Air Force*, *b.* 1893, *m.*	Hon. Rosemary Ann *P.*, *b.* 1923 (to Barony only).
1873	*Portman* (8th) Gerald William Berkeley Portman, *b.* 1903, *s.* 1948, *m.*	Edward H. B. *P.*, *b.* 1934.
1743 I.*	*Powerscourt* (9th) Mervyn Patrick Wingfield, (3rd *U.K. Baron*, *Powerscourt*, 1885), *b.* 1905, *s.* 1947, *m.*	Hon. Mervyn *W.*, *b.* 1935.
1962	*Radcliffe* (1st), Cyril John Radcliffe, P.C., G.B.E., *b.* 1899, *m.* (*Lord of Appeal*).	(None).
1900	*Ridley* (3rd), Matthew White Ridley, C.B.E., *b.* 1902, *s.* 1916, *m.*	Hon. Matthew W. *R.*, *b.* 1925.
1960	*Rochdale* (1st), John Durival Kemp, O.B.E., T.D. (2nd U.K. *Baron*, *Rochdale*, 1913), *b.* 1906, *s.* 1945, *m.*	Hon. St. John *K.*, *b.* 1938.
1919	*Rothermere* (2nd), Esmond Cecil Harmsworth *b.* 1898, *s.* 1940.	Hon. Vere *H.*, *b.* 1925.
1937	*Runciman of Doxford* (2nd), Walter Leslie Runciman, O.B.E., A.F.C. (3rd. *U.K. Baron*, *Runciman*, 1933), *b.* 1900, *s.* 1949, *m.*	Hon. Walter G. *R.*, *b.* 1934.
1918	*St. Davids* (2nd), Jestyn Reginald Austen Plantagenet Philipps, *b.* 1917, *s.* 1938, *m.*	Hon. Colwyn *P.*, *b.* 1939.
1801	*St. Vincent* (7th), Ronald George James Jervis, *b.* 1905, *s.* 1940, *m.*	Hon. Edward R. J. *J.*, *b.* 1951.
1937	*Samuel* (2nd), Edwin Herbert Samuel, C.M.G., *b.* 1898, *s.* 1963, *m.*	Hon. David H. *S.*, *b.* 1922.
1911	*Scarsdale* (2nd), Richard Nathaniel Curzon, T.D. (6th *Brit. Baron*, *Scarsdale*, 1761), *b.* 1898, *s.* 1925, *m.*	Francis J. N *C.*, *b.* 1924.
1905	*Selby* (4th), Michael Guy John Gully, *b.* 1942, *s.* 1959.	Hon. James E. H. G. *G.*, *b.* 1945.
1805	*Sidmouth* (6th), Raymond Anthony Addington, *b.* 1887, *s.* 1953, *m.*	Hon. John T. *A.*, *b.* 1914.
1940	*Simon* (2nd), John Gilbert Simon, C.M.G., *b.* 1902, *s.* 1954, *m.*	Hon. Jan D. *S.*, *b.* 1940.
1954	*Simonds* (1st), Gavin Turnbull Simonds, P.C. *b.* 1881, *m.*	(None.)
1960	*Slim* (1st), William Joseph Slim, K.G., G.C.B., G.C.M.G., G.C.V.O., G.B.E., D.S.O., M.C., *Field Marshal*, *b.* 1891, *m.*	Maj. Hon. John *S.*, *b.* 1929.
1954	*Soulbury* (1st) Herwald Ramsbotham, P.C., G.C.M.G., G.C.V.O., O.B.E., M.C., *b.* 1887, *m.*	Hon. J. Herwald *R.*, *b.* 1915.
1776 I.	*Southwell* (7th), Pyers Anthony Joseph Southwell, *b.* 1930, . 1960, *m.*	Hon. Richard A. P. *S.*, *b.* 1956
1938	*Stonehaven* (2nd), (James) Ian Baird, *b.* 1908, *s.* 1941, *m.*	Hon. Michael *B.*, *b.* 1939.
1959	*Stuart of Findhorn* (1st), James Gray Stuart, P.C., C.H., M.V.O., M.C., *b.* 1897, *m.*	Hon. David R. M. *S.*, *b.* 1924.

Created.	Title, Order of Succession, Name, etc.	Eldest Son or Heir.
1806 I.	*Templetown* (5th), Henry Augustus George Mountjoy Heneage Upton, *b.* 1894, *s.* 1939, *m.*	Hon. Henry U. *b.* 1917.
1957	*Tenby* (1st), Gwilym Lloyd George, P.C., T.D., *b.* 1894, *m.*	Hon. David L. G., *b.* 1922.
1952	*Thurso* (1st), Archibald Henry Macdonald Sinclair, P.C., K.T., C.M.G., *b.* 1890, *m.*	Hon. Robin M. *S.*, *b.* 1922. [1943.
1721	*Torrington* (11th), Timothy Howard St. George Byng, *b.* 1943, *s.* 1961.	John L. *B.*, M.C., *b.* 1919.
1936	*Trenchard* (2nd), Thomas Trenchard, M.C., *b.* 1923, *s.* 1956, *m.*	Hon. Hugh *T.*, *b.* 1951.
1921	*Ullswater* (2nd), Nicholas James Christopher Lowther, *b.* 1942, *s.* 1949.	Hon. Arthur J. B. *L.*, *b.* 1888.
1621 I.	*Valentia* (14th), Francis Dighton Annesley, M.C., *b.* 1888, *s.* 1951 (*claim established*, 1959), *m.*	Hon. Richard J. D. *A.*, *b.* 1929.
1960	*Ward of Witley* (1st), George Reginald Ward, P.C., *b.* 1907, *m.*	Hon. Anthony G. H. *W.*, *b.* 1943.
1952	*Waverley* (2nd), David Alastair Pearson Anderson, *b.* 1911, *s.* 1958, *m.*	Hon. John D. F. *A.*, *b.* 1949.
1938	*Weir* (2nd), (James) Kenneth Weir, C.B.E., *b.* 1905, *s.* 1959, *m.*	Hon. William K. J. *W.*, *b.* 1933.
1918	*Wimborne* (2nd), Ivor Grosvenor Guest, O.B.E. (3rd U.K. *Baron, Wimborne*, 1880), *b.* 1903, *s.* 1939, *m.*	Hon. Ivor *G.*, *b.* 1939.
1923	*Younger of Leckie* (3rd), Edward George Younger, O.B.E., T.D. *b.* 1906, *s.* 1946, *m.*	Hon. George *Y.*, *b.* 1931.

BISHOPS

Style, The Right Rev. the Lord Bishop of ——. *Addressed as*, My Lord. [Those marked * always sit; of the others, except †Sodor and Man, 21 sit by date, those awaiting admission in order shown (in parentheses)].

Apptd.		Entd. Lords
1961	**London* (114th), Robert Wright Stopford, P.C., C.B.E., D.D., *b.* 1901, *cons.* 1955, *trans.* 1956 and 1961	1961
1956	**Durham* (89th), Maurice Henry Harland, D.D., *b.* 1896, *cons.* 1942, *trans.* 1947 and 1956	1954
1961	**Winchester* (93rd), Sherard Falkner Allison, D.D., *b.* 1907, *cons.* 1951, *trans.* 1961	1958
1960	*Bath & Wells* (73rd), Edward Barry Henderson, D.S.C., D.D, *b.* 1910, *cons.* 1955, *trans.* 1960	(5)
1953	*Birmingham* (4th), John Leonard Wilson, C.M.G., D.D., *b.* 1897, *cons.* 1941, *trans.* 1953	1958
1960	*Blackburn* (4th), Charles Robert Claxton, D.D., *b.* 1903, *cons.* 1946, *trans.* 1960	(6)
1961	*Bradford* (4th), Clement George St. Michael Parker, D.D., *b.* 1900, *cons.* 1954, *trans.* 1961	(9)
1958	*Bristol* (52nd), Oliver Stratford Tomkins, D.D., *b.* 1908, *cons.* 1959	1963
1946	*Carlisle* (62nd), Thomas Bloomer, D.D., *b.* 1895, *cons.* 1946	1953
1962	*Chelmsford* (5th), John Gerhard Tiarks, M.A., *b.* 1903, *cons.* 1962	(12)
1955	*Chester* (37th), Gerald Alexander Ellison, D.D., *b.* 1910, *cons.* 1950, *trans.* 1955	1960
1958	*Chichester* (98th) Roger Plumpton Wilson, D.D., *b.* 1905, *cons.* 1949, *trans.* 1958	1955
1956	*Coventry* (5th), Cuthbert Killick Norman Bardsley, C.B.E., D.D., *b.* 1907, *cons.* 1947, *trans.* 1956	1962
1959	*Derby* (3rd), Geoffrey Francis Allen, D.D., *b.* 1902, *cons.* 1947, *trans.* 1959	(2)
1956	*Ely* (64th), Noel Baring Hudson, D.S.O., M.C., D.D., *b.* 1893, *cons.* 1931, *trans.* 1941 and 1956	1949
1949	*Exeter* (67th), Robert Cecil Mortimer, D.D., *b.* 1902, *cons.* 1949	1955
1962	*Gloucester* (36th), Basil Tudor Guy, M.A., *b.* 1910, *cons.* 1957, *trans.* 1962	(14)
1961	*Guildford* (5th), George Edmund Reindorp, D.D., *b.* 1911, *cons.* 1961	(8)
1961	*Hereford* (102nd), Mark Allin Hodson, D.D., *b.* 1907, *cons.* 1956, *trans.* 1961	(10)
1953	*Leicester* (3rd), Ronald Ralph Williams, D.D., *b.* 1906, *cons.* 1953	1959
1953	*Lichfield* (95th), Arthur Stretton Reeve, D.D., *b.* 1907, *cons.* 1953	1959
1956	*Lincoln* (68th), Kenneth Riches, D.D., *b.* 1908, *cons.* 1952, *trans.* 1956	1961
1944	*Liverpool* (4th), Clifford Arthur Martin, D.D., *b.* 1895, *cons.* 1944	1953
1947	*Manchester* (7th), William Derrick Lindsay Greer, D.D., *b.* 1902, *cons.* 1947	1955
1957	*Newcastle* (8th), Hugh Ernest Ashdown, D.D., *b.* 1904, *cons.* 1957	1962
1959	*Norwich* (68th), William Launcelot Scott Fleming, D.D., *b.* 1906, *cons.* 1949, *trans.* 1959	1956
1955	*Oxford* (38th), Harry James Carpenter, D.D., *b.* 1901, *cons.* 1955	1960
1961	*Peterborough* (34th), Cyril Eastaugh, M.C., M.A., *b.* 1897, *cons.* 1950, *trans.* 1961	(11)
1960	*Portsmouth* (5th), John Henry Lawrence Phillips, D.D., *b.* 1910, *cons.* 1960	(4)
1959	*Ripon* (9th), John Richard Humpidge Moorman, D.D., *b.* 1905, *cons.* 1959	(1)
1961	*Rochester* (104th), Richard David Say, D.D., *b.* 1914, *cons.* 1961	(7)
1950	*St. Albans* (6th), Edward Michael Gresford Jones, D.D., *b.* 1901, *cons.* 1942, *trans.* 1950	1956
1954	*St. Edmundsbury & Ipswich* (5th), Arthur Harold Morris, D.D., *b.* 1898, *cons.* 1949, *trans.* 1954	1959
1963	*Salisbury* (74th), Joseph Edward Fison, D.D., *b.* 1906, *cons.* 1963	(15)
1962	*Sheffield* (3rd), Francis John Taylor, M.A., *b.* 1912, *cons.* 1962	(13)
1954	†*Sodor & Man* (75th), Benjamin Pollard, T.D., D.D, *b.* 1890, *cons.* 1936, *trans.* 1954.	
1959	*Southwark* (6th), Arthur Mervyn Stockwood, D.D., *b.* 1913, *cons.* 1959	1963
	Southwell (vacant)	
1959	*Truro* (10th), John Maurice Key, D.D., *b.* 1905, *cons.* 1947, *trans.* 1959	(3)
1958	*Wakefield* (7th), John Alexander Ramsbotham, D.D., *b.* 1906, *cons.* 1949, *trans.* 1958	1962
1955	*Worcester* (109th), Lewis Mervyn Charles-Edwards, D.D., *b.* 1902, *cons.* 1955	1960

BARONS

Style (see note, p. 253). The Right Hon. the Lord ——.
Addressed as, My Lord.

Created.	Title, Order of Succession, Name, etc.	Eldest Son or Heir.
1911	*Aberconway* (3rd), Charles Melville McLaren, *b.* 1913, *s.* 1953, *m.*	Hon. Henry C. *McL.*, *b.* 1948.
1873	*Aberdare* (4th), Morys George Lyndhurst Bruce, *b.* 1919, *s.* 1957, *m.*	Hon. Alastair J. L. *B.*, *b.* 1947.
1835	*Abinger* (8th), James Richard Scarlett, *b.* 1914, *s.* 1943, *m.*	Hon. James H. *S.*, *b.* 1959.
1869	*Acton* (3rd), John Emerich Henry Lyon-Dalberg-Acton, M.B.E., *b.* 1907, *s.* 1924, *m.*	Hon. Richard *L.-D.-A.*, *b.* 1941.
1887	*Addington* (3rd), John Gellibrand Hubbard, O.B.E., *b.* 1883, *s.* 1915.	Hon. Raymond *H.*, *b.* 1884.
1955	*Adrian* (1st), Edgar Douglas Adrian, O.M., M.D., F.R.S., *b.* 1889, *m.*	Hon. Richard H. *A.*, *b.* 1927.
1921	*Ailwyn* (3rd), Eric William Edward Fellowes, C.B.E., *b.* 1887, *s.* 1936, *m.*	Hon. Carol A. *F.*, T.D., *b.* 1895.
1907	*Airedale* (4th) Oliver James Vandeleur Kitson, *b.* 1915, *s.* 1958.	(None.)
1896	*Aldenham* (4th) *and* (2nd) *Hunsdon of Hunsdon* (1923), Walter Durant Gibbs, *b.* 1888, *s.* 1935 and 1939, *m.*	Hon. Antony *G.*, *b.* 1922.
1962	*Aldington* (1st), Toby Austin Richard William Low, P.C., K.C.M.G., C.B.E., D.S.O., T.D., *b.* 1914, *m.*	Hon. Charles H. S. *L.*, *b.* 1948.
1902	*Allerton* (3rd), George William Lawies Jackson, *b.* 1903, *s.* 1925, *m.*	Hon. Edward L. *J.*, *b.* 1928.
1929	*Alvingham* (2nd), Robert Guy Eardley Yerburgh, *b.* 1926, *s.* 1955, *m.*	Hon. Robert R. G. *Y.*, *b.* 1956.
1892	*Amherst of Hackney* (3rd), William Alexander Evering Cecil, C.B.E., *b.* 1912, *s.* 1919, *m.*	Hon. William *C.*, *b.* 1940.
1881	*Ampthill* (3rd), John Hugo Russell, C.B.E., *b.* 1896, *s.* 1935, *m*	Hon. Geoffrey *R.*, *b.* 1921.
1929	*Amulree* (2nd), Basil William Sholto Mackenzie, M.D., *b.* 1900, *s.* 1942.	(None.)
1947	*Amwell* (1st), Frederick Montague, C.B.E., *b.* 1876, *m.*	Hon. Frederick *M.*, *b.* 1912.
1863	*Annaly* (4th), Luke Henry White, M.C., *b.* 1885, *s.* 1922, *m.*	Hon. Luke R. *W.*, *b.* 1927.
1949	*Archibald* (1st), George Archibald, *b.* 1898, *m.*	Hon. George Christopher *A.*, *b.* 1926.
1903	*Armstrong* (2nd), William John Montagu Watson-Armstrong, *b.* 1892, *s.* 1941, *m.*	Hon. William H. C. J. R. *W.-A.*, *b.* 1919.
1885	*Ashbourne* (3rd), Edward Russell Gibson, C.B., D.S.O., *b.* 1901, *s.* 1942, *m.*	Hon. Edward B. G. *G.*, *b.* 1933.
1835	*Ashburton* (6th), Alexander Francis St. Vincent Baring, K.C.V.O., *b.* 1898, *s.* 1938, *m.*	Hon. John F. H. *B.*, *b.* 1928.
1892	*Ashcombe* (4th), Henry Edward Cubitt, *b.* 1924, *s.* 1962, *m.*	Maj. Hon. Archibald E. *C.*, *b.* 1901.
1911	*Ashton of Hyde* (2nd), Thomas Henry Raymond Ashton, *b.* 1901, *s.* 1933, *m.*	Hon. Thomas J. *A.*, *b.* 1925.
1800 I.	*Ashtown* (4th), Robert Power Trench, *b.* 1897, *s.* 1946, *m.*	Hon. Dudley *T.*, *b.* 1901.
1956	*Astor of Hever* (1st), John Jacob Astor, *b.* 1886, *m.*	Hon. Gavin *A.*, *b.* 1918.
1789 I. } 1793* }	*Auckland* (9th), Ian George Eden (9th *Brit. Baron, Auckland*), *b.* 1926, *s.* 1957, *m.*	Hon. Robert I. B. *E.*, *b.* 1962.
1900	*Avebury* (3rd), John Lubbock, *b.* 1915, *s.* 1929, *m.*	Eric R. *L.*, M.P., *b.* 1928.
1718 I.	*Aylmer* (9th), John Frederick Whitworth Aylmer, *b.* 1880, *s.* 1923, *m.*	Hon. Kenneth A. *A.*, *b.* 1883.
1929	*Baden-Powell* (3rd), Robert Crause Baden-Powell, *b.* 1936, *s.* 1962, *m.*	Hon. David M. *B.-P.*, *b.* 1940.
1780	*Bagot* (7th), Harvey Eric Bagot, *b.* 1894, *s.* 1961, *w.*	Reginald W. B., *b.* 1897.
1953	*Baillieu* (1st), Clive Latham Baillieu, K.B.E., C.M.G. *b.* 1889, *w.*	Hon. William L. *B.*, *b.* 1915.
1607 S.	*Balfour of Burleigh* (7th), George John Gordon Bruce, *b.* 1883, *s.* 1921, *m.*	Master of Burleigh, *b.* 1927.
1945	*Balfour of Inchrye* (1st), Harold Harington Balfour, P.C., M.C., *b.* 1897, *m.*	Hon. Ian *B.*, *b.* 1924.
1924	*Banbury of Southam* (2nd), Charles William Banbury, *b.* 1915, *s.* 1936.	Hon. Charles W. *B.*, *b.* 1953.
1698	*Barnard* (10th), Christopher William Vane, C.M.G., O.B.E., M.C., T.D., *b.* 1888, *s.* 1918, *m.*	Hon. Harry J. N. *V.*, *b.* 1923.
1922	*Barnby* (2nd), Francis Vernon Willey, C.M.G., C.B.E., M.V.O., T.D., *b.* 1884, *s.* 1929, *m.*	(None.)
1887	*Basing* (3rd), John Limbrey Robert Sclater-Booth, T.D., *b.* 1890, *s.* 1919, *m.*	George L. *S.-B.*, *b.* 1903.
1917	*Beaverbrook* (1st), (William) Maxwell Aitken, P.C., *b.* 1879, *m.*	Group Capt. Hon. Maxwell *A.*, D.S.O., D.F.C., *b.* 1910.
1647 S.	*Belhaven & Stenton* (13th), Robert Anthony Carmichael Hamilton, *b.* 1927, *s.* 1961, *m.*	Master of Belhaven, *b.* 1953.
1848 I.	*Bellew* (5th), Edward Henry Bellew, M.B.E., *b.* 1889, *s.* 1935, *m.*	Hon. Bryan *B.*, M.C., *b.* 1890.
1856	*Belper* (4th), (Alexander) Ronald George Strutt, *b.* 1912, *s.* 1956.	Hon. Richard H. *S.*, *b.* 1941.
1938	*Belstead* (2nd), John Julian Ganzoni, *b.* 1932, *s.* 1958.	(None.)
1922	*Bethell* (2nd), John Raymond Bethell, *b.* 1902, *s.* 1945, *m.*	Hon. Guy *B.*, *b.* 1928.

Created.	*Title, Order of Succession, Name, etc.*	*Eldest Son or Heir.*
1938	*Bicester* (2nd), Randal Hugh Vivian Smith, *b.* 1898, *s.* 1956, *m.*	Angus E. V. *S.*, *b.* 1932.
1903	*Biddulph* (3rd), Michael William John Biddulph, *b.* 1898, *s.* 1949, *m.*	Hon. Robert M. C. *B.*, *b.* 1931.
1950	*Bilsland* (1st), (Alexander) Steven Bilsland, K.T., M.C., *b.* 1892, *m.*	(None.)
1938	*Birdwood* (3rd), Mark William Ogilvie Birdwood, *b.* 1938, *s.* 1962, *m.*	
1958	*Birkett* (2nd), Michael Birkett, *b.* 1929, *s.* 1962, *m.*	
1935	*Blackford* (2nd), Glyn Keith Murray Mason, C.B.E., D.S.O., *b.* 1887, *s.* 1947, *m.*	Hon. Keith *M.*, D.F.C., *b.* 1923.
1907	*Blyth* (3rd), Ian Audley James Blyth, *b.* 1905, *s.* 1943, *m.*	Hon. Anthony *B.*, *b.* 1931.
1797	*Bolton* (7th), Richard William Algar Orde-Powlett, *b.* 1929, *s.* 1963, *m.*	Hon. Harry A. N. *O.-P.* *b.* 1954.
1922	*Borwick* (4th), James Hugh Myles Borwick, M.C., *b.* 1917, *s.* 1961, *m.*	Hon. George S. *B.*, *b.* 1922.
1761	*Boston* (8th), Cecil Eustace Irby, M.C., *b.* 1897, *s.* 1958.	Gerald H. B. *I.*, M.B.E., *b.* 1897.
1949	*Boyd-Orr* (1st), John Boyd Orr, D.S.O., M.C., M.D., F.R.S., *b.* 1880, *m.*	(None.)
1942	*Brabazon of Tara* (1st), John Theodore Cuthbert Moore-Brabazon, P.C., G.B.E., M.C., *b.* 1884, *m.*	Hon. Derek C. *M.-B.*, C.B.E., *b* 1910.
1880	*Brabourne* (7th), John Ulick Knatchbull, *b.* 1924, *s.* 1943, *m.*	Hon. Norton *K.*, *b.* 1947.
1925	*Bradbury* (2nd), John Bradbury, *b.* 1914, *s.* 1950, *m.*	Hon. John *B.*, *b.* 1940.
1962	*Brain* (1st), (Walter) Russell Brain, D.M., F.R.C.P., *b.* 1895, *m.*	Hon. Christopher L. *B.*, *b.* 1926.
1946	*Brand* (1st), Robert Henry Brand, C.M.G., *b.* 1878, *w.*	(None.)
1938	*Brassey of Apethorpe* (2nd), Bernard Thomas Brassey, M.C., T.D., *b.* 1905, *s.* 1958, *m.*	Hon. David H. *B.*, *b.* 1932.
1788	*Braybrooke* (9th), Henry Seymour Neville, *b.* 1897, *s.* 1943, *m.*	Hon. Robin *N.*, *b.* 1932.
1529	*Braye* (7th), Thomas Adrian Verney-Cave, *b.* 1902, *s.* 1952, *m.*	Hon. Penelope M. *V.-C.*, *b.* 1941.
1958	*Brecon* (1st), David Vivian Penrose Lewis, P.C., *b.* 1905, *m.*	(None.)
1957	*Bridges* (1st), Edward Ettingdene Bridges, P.C., G.C.B., G.C.V.O., M.C., F.R.S., *b.* 1892, *m.*	Hon. Thomas E. *B.* *b.* 1927.
1945	*Broadbridge* (2nd), Eric Wilberforce Broadbridge, *b.* 1895, *s.* 1952, *m.*	Hon. Peter H. *B.*, *b.* 1938.
1933	*Brocket* (2nd), Arthur Ronald Nall Nall-Cain, *b.* 1904, *s.* 1934. *m.*	Charles R. G. *N.-C.*, b. 1952.
1860	*Brougham and Vaux* (4th), Victor Henry Peter Brougham, *b.* 1909, *s.* 1927, *m.*	Hon. Michael J. *B.*, *b.* 1938.
1945	*Broughshane* (2nd), Patrick Owen Alexander Davison, *b.* 1903, *s.* 1953, *m.*	Hon. Alexander *D.*, *b.* 1936.
1776	*Brownlow* (6th), Peregrine Francis Adelbert Cust, *b.* 1899, *s.* 1927, *m.*	Hon. Edward *C.*, *b.* 1936.
1942	*Bruntisfield* (1st), Victor Alexander George Anthony Warrender, M.C., *b.* 1899, *m.*	Hon. John R. *W.*, M.C., *b.* 1921.
1950	*Burden* (1st), Thomas William Burden, C.B.E., *b.* 1885, *m.*	Hon. Philip *B.*, *b.* 1916.
1529	*Burgh* (7th), Alexander Peter Willoughby Leith, *b.* 1935, *s.* 1959, *m.*	Hon. Alexander G. D. *L.*, *b.* 1958.
1903	*Burnham* (5th), William Edward Harry Lawson, *b.* 1920, *s.* 1963, *m.*	Hon. Hugh J. F. *L.*, *b.* 1931.
1897	*Burton* (3rd), Michael Evan Victor Baillie, *b.* 1924, *s.* 1962, *m.*	Hon. Evan *B.*, *b.* 1949.
1643	*Byron* (11th), Rupert Frederick George Byron, *b.* 1903, *s.* 1949, *m.*	Richard G. G. *B.*, D.S.O., *b.* 1899.
1937	*Cadman* (2nd), John Basil Cope Cadman, *b.* 1909, *s.* 1941, *m.*	Hon. John A. *C.*, *b.* 1938.
1796	*Calthorpe* (10th), Peter Waldo Somerset Gough-Calthorpe, *b.* 1927, *s.* 1945, *m.*	(None.)
1945	*Calverley* (2nd), George Raymond Orford Muff, *b.* 1914, *s.* 1955, *m.*	Hon. Charles R. *M.*, *b.* 1946.
1383	*Camoys* (5th), Ralph Francis Julian Stonor, *b.* 1884, *s.* 1897, *w.*	Hon. Sherman *S.*, *b.* 1913.
1715 I.	*Carbery* (10th), John Evans Carberry, *b.* 1892, *s.* 1898, *m.*	Hon. Ralfe *Evans-Freke*, M.B.E., *b.* 1897.
1834 I. 1838 *	*Carew* (6th), William Francis Conolly-Carew (6th *U.K. Baron, Carew*, 1838), *b.* 1905, *s.* 1927, *m.*	Hon. Patrick Thomas *C.-C.*, *b.* 1938.
1916	*Carnock* (3rd), Erskine Arthur Nicolson, D.S.O., *b.* 1884, *s.* 1952, *m.*	Hon. David H. A. *N.*, *b.* 1920.
1796 I. 1797*	*Carrington* (6th), Peter Alexander Rupert Carington, P.C., K.C.M.G., M.C. (6th *Brit. Baron, Carrington*, 1797), *b.* 1919, *s.* 1938, *m.*	Hon. Rupert F. J. *C.*, *b.* 1948.
1812 I.	*Castlemaine* (7th), John Michael Schomberg Staveley Handcock, *b.* 1904, *s.* 1954, *m.*	Hon. Roland T. J. *H.*, *b.* 1943.
1936	*Catto* (2nd), Stephen Gordon Catto, *b.* 1923, *s.* 1959, *m.*	Hon. Innes G. *C.*, *b.* 1950.
1918	*Cawley* (3rd), Frederick Lee Cawley, *b.* 1913 *s.* 1954, *m.*	Hon. John F. *C.*, *b.* 1946.
1937	*Chatfield* (1st), (Alfred) Ernle Montacute Chatfield, P.C., G.C.B., O.M., K.C.M.G., C.V.O., *Admiral of the Fleet*, *b* 1873, *m.*	Hon. Ernle D. L. *C.*, *b.* 1917.
1858	*Chesham* (5th), John Charles Compton Cavendish, *b.* 1916, *s.* 1952, *m.*	Hon. Nicholas *C.*, *b.* 1941.
1945	*Chetwode* (2nd), Philip Chetwode, *b.* 1937, *s.* 1950.	Hon. Christopher R. *C.*, *b.* 1940.
1887	*Cheylesmore* (4th), Francis Ormond Henry Eaton, D.S.O., *b.* 1893, *s.* 1925, *m.*	Hon. Herbert *E.*, *b.* 1895.
1945	*Chorley* (1st), Robert Samuel Theodore Chorley, Q.C., *b.* 1895, *m.*	Hon. Roger *C.*, *b.* 1930.
1858	*Churston* (4th), Richard Francis Roger Yarde-Buller, V.R.D., *b.* 1910, *s.* 1930, *m.*	Hon. John *Y.-B.*, *b.* 1934.
1946	*Citrine* (1st), Walter McLennan Citrine, P.C., G.B.E., *b.* 1887, *m.*	Hon. Norman *C.*, *b.* 1914.

Created.	Title, Order of Succession, Name, etc.	Eldest Son or Heir
1800 I.	*Clanmorris* (7th), John Michael Ward Bingham, *b.* 1908, *s.* 1960. *m.*	Hon. Simon J. W. *B.*, *b.* 1937.
1672	*Clifford of Chudleigh* (12th), Lewis Joseph Hugh Clifford, *b.* 1889, *s.* 1962, *m.*	Hon. Lewis H. *C.*, *b.* 1916.
1955	*Clitheroe* (1st), Ralph Assheton, P.C., *b.* 1901, *m.*	Hon. Ralph J. *A.*, *b.* 1929.
1919	*Clwyd* (2nd), (John) Trevor Roberts, *b.* 1900, *s.* 1955, *m.*	Hon. John A. *R.*, *b.* 1935.
1947	*Clydesmuir* (2nd) Ronald John Bilsland Colville, M.B.E., T.D., *b.* 1917, *s.* 1954, *m.*	Hon. David R. *C.*, *b.* 1949.
1960	*Cobbold* (1st), Cameron Fromanteel Cobbold, P.C., G.C.V.O., *b.* 1904, *m.* (*Lord Chamberlain*)	Hon. David A. F. *C.*, *b.* 1937.
1919	*Cochrane of Cults* (2nd), Thomas George Frederick Cochrane, D.S.O., *b.* 1883, *s.* 1951, *m.*	Hon. Thomas C. A. *C.*, *b.* 1922.
1951	*Cohen*, Lionel Leonard Cohen, P.C., *b.* 1888, *w.* (*Lord of Appeal, retired*).	(Life Peerage.)
1956	*Cohen of Birkenhead* (1st), Henry Cohen, M.D., D.SC., LL.D., F.R.C.P., F.S.A., *b.* 1900.	(None.)
1954	*Coleraine* (1st), Richard Kidston Law, P.C. *b.* 1901, *m.*	Hon. James M.B. *L.*, *b.* 1931.
1873	*Coleridge* (4th), Richard Duke Coleridge, C.B.E., *b.* 1905, *s.* 1955, *m.*	Hon. William D. *C.*, *b.* 1937.
1946	*Colgrain* (2nd), Donald Swinton Campbell, M.C., *b.* 1891, *s.* 1954, *m.*	Hon. David C. *C.*, *b.* 1920.
1917	*Colwyn* (2nd), Frederick John Vivian Smith, *b.* 1914, *s.* 1946, *m.*	Hon. Ian A. H. *S.*, *b.* 1942.
1956	*Colyton* (1st), Henry Lennox D'Aubigné Hopkinson, P.C., C.M.G., *b.* 1902, *m.*	Hon. Nicholas H. E. *H.*, *b.* 1932.
1955	*Conesford* (1st), Henry George Strauss, Q.C., *b.* 1892, *m.*	(None.)
1841	*Congleton* (7th), William Jared Parnell, *b.* 1925, *s.* 1932.	Hon. Christopher *P.*, *b.* 1930.
1927	*Cornwallis* (2nd), Wykeham Stanley Cornwallis, K.B.E., M.C., *b.* 1892, *s.* 1935, *m.*	Hon. Fiennes *C.*, *b.* 1921.
1874	*Cottesloe* (4th), John Walgrave Halford Fremantle, G.B.E., T.D., *b.* 1900, *s.* 1956, *m.*	Hon. John T. *F.*, *b.* 1927.
1914	*Cozens-Hardy* (4th), Herbert Arthur Cozens-Hardy, *b.* 1907, *s.* 1956.	(None.)
1929	*Craigmyle* (3rd), Thomas Donald Mackay Shaw, *b.* 1923, *s.* 1944, *m.*	Hon. Thomas C. *S.*, *b.* 1960.
1899	*Cranworth* (2nd), Bertram Francis Gurdon, K.G., M.C., *b.* 1877, *s.* 1902, *m.*	Philip B. *G.*, *b.* 1940.
1959	*Crathorne* (1st), Thomas Lionel Dugdale, P.C., T.D., *b.* 1897, *m.*	Hon. Charles J. *D.*, *b.* 1939.
1892	*Crawshaw* (4th), William Michael Clifton Brooks, *b.* 1933, *s.* 1946.	Hon. David *B.* *b.* 1934.
1940	*Croft* (2nd), Michael Henry Glendower Page Croft, *b.* 1916, *s.* 1947, *m.*	Hon. Bernard W. H. P. *C.*, *b.* 1949.
1797 I.	*Crofton* (5th), Edward Blaise Crofton, *b.* 1926, *s.* 1942.	Hon. Charles E.P. *C.*, *b.* 1949.
1375	*Cromwell* (5th), Robert Godfrey Wolseley Bewicke-Copley, D.S.O., M.C., *b.* 1893, *called out of abeyance* 1923, *m.*	Hon. David *B.-C.*, *b.* 1929.
1947	*Crook* (1st), Reginald Douglas Crook, *b.* 1901, *m.*	Hon. Douglas *C.*, *b.* 1925.
1920	*Cullen of Ashbourne* (2nd), Charles Borlase Marsham Cokayne, M.B.E., *b.* 1912, *s.* 1932, *m.*	Hon. Edmund *C.* *b.* 1916.
1914	*Cunliffe* (2nd), Rolf Cunliffe, *b.* 1899, *s.* 1920, *m.*	Hon. Roger *C.*, *b.* 1932.
1927	*Daresbury* (2nd), Edward Greenall, *b.* 1902, *s.* 1938, *w.*	Hon. Edward G. *G.*, *b.* 1928.
1924	*Darling* (2nd), Robert Charles Henry Darling, *b.* 1919, *s.* 1936, *m.*	Hon. Robert *D.*, *b.* 1944.
1946	*Darwen* (2nd), Cedric Percival Davies, *b.* 1915, *s.* 1950, *m.*	Hon. Roger M. *D.*, *b.* 1938.
1923	*Daryngton* (2nd), Jocelyn Arthur Pike Pease, *b.* 1908, *s.* 1949.	(None.)
1932	*Davies* (3rd), David Davies, *b.* 1940, *s.* 1944.	Hon. Jonathan H. *D.*, *b.* 1944.
1812 I.	*Decies* (6th), Arthur George Marcus Douglas de la Poer Beresford, *b.* 1915, *s.* 1944, *m.*	Hon. Marcus *de la P.B.*, *b.* 1948.
1299	*De Clifford* (26th), Edward Southwell Russell, O.B.E., E.D., *b.* 1907, *s.* 1909.	Hon. John *R.*, *b.* 1928.
1851	*De Freyne* (7th), Francis Arthur John French, *b.* 1927, *s.* 1935, *m.*	Hon. Fulke C. J. A. *F.*, *b.* 1957.
1821	*Delamere* (4th), Thomas Pitt Hamilton Cholmondeley, *b.* 1900, *s.* 1931, *m.*	Hon. Hugh G. *C.*, *b.* 1934.
1700	*De Longueuil* (10th) (*Peerage of Canada*), Ronald Charles Grant, *b.* 1888, *s.* 1938, *m.*	Hon. Raoul *G.*, *b.* 1919.
1838	*De Mauley* (6th), Gerald John Ponsonby, *b.* 1921, *s.* 1962, *m.*	Hon. Thomas M. *P.*, *b.* 1930.
1937	*Denham* (2nd), Bertram Stanley Mitford Bowyer, *b.* 1927, *s.* 1948, *m.*	Hon. Richard G. *B.*, *b.* 1959.
1834	*Denman* (4th), Thomas Denman, *b.* 1905, *s.* 1954.	Sir Charles S. *D.*, Bt., M.C., *b.* 1916.
1957	*Denning*, Alfred Thompson Denning, P.C., *b.* 1899, *m.* (*Master of the Rolls*).	(Life Peerage.)
1885	*Deramore* (5th), Stephen Nicholas de Yarburgh-Bateson, *b.* 1903, *s.* 1943, *m.*	Hon. Richard A. *de Y.-B.*, *b.* 1911.
1887	*De Ramsey* (3rd), Ailwyn Edward Fellowes, *b.* 1910, *s.* 1925, *m.*	Hon. John A. *F.*, *b.* 1942.
1881	*Derwent* (4th), Patrick Robin Gilbert Vanden-Bempde-Johnstone, *b.* 1901, *s.* 1949, *m.*	Hon. Robin *V.-B.-J.*, *b.* 1930.
1831	*De Saumarez* (5th), James St. Vincent Broke Saumarez, *b.* 1889, *s.* 1937, *m.*	Hon. James V. B. *S.*, *b.* 1924.
1910	*De Villiers* (3rd), Arthur Percy De Villiers, *b.* 1911, *s.* 1934, *m.*	Hon. Alexander C. *de V.*, *b.* 1940.

Created.	*Title, Order of Succession, Name, etc.*	*Eldest Son or Heir.*
1961	*Devlin*, Patrick Arthur Devlin, P.C., F.B.A., *b.* 1905, *m.* (*Lord of Appeal*).	(Life Peerage.)
1930	*Dickinson* (2nd), Richard Clavering Hyett Dickinson, *b.* 1926, *s.* 1943, *m.*	Hon. Martin H. *D.*, *b.* 1961.
1620 I. 1765*	*Digby* (11th), Edward Kenelm Digby, K.G., D.S.O., M.C., T.D. (5th *Brit. Baron, Digby*), *b.* 1894, *s.* 1920, *m.*	Hon. Edward H. K. *D.*, *b.* 1924.
1962	*Dilhorne* (1st), Reginald Edward Manningham-Buller, P.C., *b.* 1905, *m.* (*Lord Chancellor*).	Hon. John M. *M.-B.*, *b.* 1932.
1615	*Dormer* (15th), Charles Walter James Dormer, *b.* 1903, *s.* 1922, *m.*	Hon. Joseph *D.*, *b.* 1914.
1950	*Douglas of Barloch* (1st), Francis Campbell Ross Douglas, K.C.M.G., *b.* 1889, *m.*	(None.)
1948	*Douglas of Kirtleside* (1st), (William) Sholto Douglas, G.C.B., M.C., D.F.C., *Marshal of the Royal Air Force*, *b.* 1893, *m.*	(None.)
1943	*Dowding* (1st), Hugh Caswall Tremenheere Dowding, G.C.B., G.C.V.O., C.M.G., *b.* 1882, *m.*	Hon. Derek *D.*, *b.* 1919.
1439	*Dudley* (13th), Ferdinando Dudley Henry Lea Smith, *b.* 1910, *s.* 1936, *m.*	Hon. Mrs. Guy *Wallace*, *b.* 1907.
1929	*Dulverton* (2nd), (Frederick) Anthony Hamilton Wills, T.D., *b.* 1915, *s.* 1956, *m.*	Hon. Gilbert M. H. *W.*, *b.* 1944.
1800 I.	*Dunalley* (6th), Henry Desmond Graham Prittie, *b.* 1912, *s.* 1948, *m.*	Hon. Henry *P.*, *b.* 1948.
1324 I.	*Dunboyne* (28th), Patrick Theobald Tower Butler, *b.* 1917, *s.* 1945, *m.*	Hon. John F. *B.*, *b.* 1951.
1802	*Dunleath* (4th), Charles Edward Henry John Mulholland, *b.* 1933, *s.* 1956, *m.*	Rt. Hon. Sir Henry G. H. *M.*, Bt., *b.* 1888.
1439 I.	*Dunsany* (19th), Randal Arthur Henry Plunkett, *b.* 1906, *s.* 1957, *m.*	Hon. Edward *P.*, *b.* 1939.
1780	*Dynevor* (9th), Richard Charles Uryan Rhys, *b.* 1935, *s.* 1962, *m.*	
1928	*Ebbisham* (2nd) Rowland Roberts Blades, T.D., *b.* 1912, *s.* 1953, *m.*	(None.)
1857	*Ebury* (6th), Francis Egerton Grosvenor, *b.* 1934, *s.* 1957.	Hon Julian F. M. *G.*, *b.* 1959.
1962	*Eccles* (1st), David McAdam Eccles, P.C., K.C.V.O., *b.* 1904, *m.*	Hon. John D. *E.*, *b.* 1931.
1643 S.	*Elibank* (13th), James Alastair Frederick Campbell Erskine-Murray, *b.* 1902, *s.* 1962.	Alan D'A. *E.-M.*, *b.* 1923.
1802	*Ellenborough* (8th), Richard Edward Cecil Law, *b.* 1926, *s.* 1945, *m.*	Hon. Rupert E. H. *L.*, *b.* 1955.
1509 S.*	*Elphinstone* (17th), John Alexander Buller-Fullerton-Elphinstone, (3rd *U.K. Baron Elphinstone*, 1885), *b.* 1914, *s.* 1955.	Rev. the Hon. A. C. V. *B.-F.-E.*, *b.* 1918.
1934	*Elton* (1st), Godfrey Elton, *b.* 1892, *m.*	Hon. Rodney *E.*, *b.* 1930.
1939	*Ennisdale* (1st), Henry Edward Lyons, O.B.E., *b.* 1878, *m.*	(None.)
1932	*Essendon* (2nd), Brian Edmund Lewis, *b.* 1903, *s.* 1944, *m.*	(None.)
1957	*Evans* (1st), Horace Evans, G.C.V.O., M.D., *b.* 1903, *m.*	(None.)
1956	*Evershed* (1st), (Francis) Raymond Evershed, P.C., *b.* 1899, *m.* (*Lord of Appeal*).	(None.)
1627 S.	*Fairfax of Cameron* (13th), Thomas Brian McKelvie Fairfax, *b.* 1923, *s.* 1939, *m.*	Hon. Nicholas J. A. *F.*, *b.* 1956.
1929 & 1961	*Fairhaven* (1st), Urban Huttleston Rogers Broughton, *b.* 1896.	Hon. Henry R. *B.*, (to 1961 Barony only) *b.* 1900.
1910	*Faringdon* (2nd), Alexander Gavin Henderson, *b.* 1902, *s.* 1934.	Charles M. *H.*, *b.* 1937.
1756 I.	*Farnham* (12th), Barry Owen Somerset Maxwell, *b.* 1931, *s.* 1957, *m.*	Vice-Adm. Hon. Sir Denis C. *M.*, K.C.B., C.B.E., *b.* 1892.
1893	*Farrer* (5th), Anthony Thomas Farrer, *b.* 1910, *s.* 1954, *m.*	(None.)
1856 I.	*Fermoy* (5th), Edmund James Burke Roche, *b.* 1939, *s.* 1955.	Alexis M. B. *R.*, *b.* 1922.
1798 I.	*ffrench* (7th), Peter Martin Joseph Charles John ffrench, *b.* 1926, *s.* 1955, *m.*	Hon. Robuck J. P. C. M. *ff.*, *b.* 1956.
1909	*Fisher* (3rd), John Vavasseur Fisher, D.S.C. *b.* 1921, *s.* 1955, *m.*	Hon. Patrick V. *F.*, *b.* 1953.
1295	*Fitzwalter* (21st), Fitzwalter Brook Plumptre, *b.* 1914, *called out of abeyance*, 1953, *m.*	Hon. Julian B. *P.*, *b.* 1952.
1961	*Fleck* (1st), Alexander Fleck, K.B.E., F.R.S., *b.* 1889, *w.*	(None.)
1776	*Foley* (8th), Adrian Gerald Foley, *b.* 1923, *s.* 1927, *m.*	Hon. Thomas H. F., *b.* 1961.
1445 S.	*Forbes* (23rd), Nigel Ivan Forbes, K.B.E. (*Premier Baron of Scotland*), *b.* 1918, *s.* 1953, *m.*	Master of Forbes, *b.* 1946.
1821	*Forester* (7th), Cecil George Wilfrid Weld-Forester, *b.* 1899, *s.* 1932, *m.*	Hon. George C. B. *W.-F.*, *b.* 1938.
1922	*Forres* (3rd), John Archibald Harford Williamson, *b.* 1922, *s.* 1954, *m.*	Hon. Alastair S. G. *W.*, *b.* 1946.
1959	*Forster of Harraby* (1st), John Forster, K.B.E., Q.C., *b.* 1888, *m.*	(None.)
1917	*Forteviot* (3rd), Henry Evelyn Alexander Dewar, M.B.E., *b.* 1906, *s.* 1947, *m.*	Hon. J. J. Evelyn *D.*, *b.* 1938.
1946	*Fraser of North Cape* (1st), Bruce Austin Fraser, G.C.B., K.B.E., *Admiral of the Fleet*, *b.* 1888.	(None.)
1951	*Freyberg* (2nd), Paul Richard Freyberg, M.C., *b.* 1923, *s.* 1963, *m.*	
1917	*Gainford* (2nd), Joseph Pease, T.D., *b.* 1889, *s.* 1943, *m.*	Hon. Joseph *P.*, *b.* 1921.
1818 I.	*Garvagh* (5th), (Alexander Leopold Ivor) George Canning, *b.* 1920, *s.* 1956, *m.*	Hon. Spencer G. S. de R. *C.*, *b.* 1953.
1942	*Geddes* (2nd), Ross Campbell Geddes, C.B.E., *b.* 1907, *s.* 1954, *m.*	Hon. Euan M. R. *G.*, *b.* 1937.

Created.	*Title, Order of Succession, Name, etc.*	*Eldest Son or Heir.*
1876	*Gerard* (4th), Robert William Frederick Alwyn Gerard, *b.* 1918, *s.* 1953.	Lt.-Col. Charles R. T. M. G., D.S.O., O.B.E., *b.* 1894.
1824	*Gifford* (6th), Anthony Maurice Gifford, *b.* 1940, *s.* 1961.	
1917	*Gisborough* (3rd), Thomas Richard John Long Chaloner, *b.* 1927, *s.* 1951, *m.*	Hon. Thomas P. L. *C.*, *b.* 1961.
1960	*Gladwyn* (1st), (Hubert Miles) Gladwyn Jebb, G.C.M.G., G.C.V.O., C.B., *b.* 1900, *m.*	Hon. Miles A. *J.*, *b.*, 1931.
1899	*Glanusk* (4th), David Russell Bailey, *b.* 1917, *s.* 1948, *m.*	Hon. Christopher *B.*, *b.* 1942.
1918	*Glenarthur* (3rd), Matthew Arthur, O.B.E., *b.* 1909, *s.* 1942, *m.*	Hon. Simon M. *A.*, *b.* 1944.
1921	*Glenavy* (3rd), Patrick Gordon Campbell, *b.* 1913, *s.* 1963, *m.*	Hon. Michael *C.*, *b.* 1924.
1911	*Glenconner* (2nd), Christopher Grey Tennant, *b.* 1899, *s.* 1920, *m.*	Hon. Colin *T.*, *b.* 1926.
1922	*Glendyne* (2nd), John Nivison, *b.* 1878, *s.* 1930, *m.*	Hon. Robert *N.*, *b.* 1926.
1916	*Glentanar* (2nd), Thomas Coats, K.B.E., *b.* 1894, *s.* 1918, *w.*	(None.)
1939	*Glentoran* (2nd), Daniel Stewart Thomas Bingham Dixon, P.C., (N.I.), *b.* 1912, *s.* 1950, *m.*	Hon. Thomas R. V. *D.*, *b.* 1935.
1956	*Godber* (1st), Frederick Godber, *b.* 1888, *m.*	(None.)
1944	*Goddard*, Rayner Goddard, P.C., G.C.B., *b.* 1877, *w.* (*Lord Chief Justice, retired*).	(Life Peerage.)
1909	*Gorell* (4th), Timothy John Radcliffe Barnes, *b.* 1927, *s.* 1963, *m.*	Hon. Ronald A. H. *B.*, *b.* 1931.
1953	*Grantchester* (1st), Alfred Jesse Suenson-Taylor, O.B.E., *b.* 1893, *m.*	Hon. Kenneth *S.-T.*, *b.* 1921.
1782	*Grantley* (7th), John Richard Brinsley Norton, M.C., *b.* 1923, *s.* 1954, *m.*	Hon. Richard W. B. *N.*, *b.* 1956.
1794 I.	*Graves* (7th), Henry Algernon Claud Graves, *b.* 1877, *s.* 1937.	Hon. Peter G. W. *G.*, *b.* 1911.
1445 S.	*Gray* (22nd), Angus Diarmid Ian Campbell-Gray, *b.* 1931, *s.* 1946, *m.*	Master of Gray, *b.* 1934.
1950	*Greenhill* (1st), Ernest Greenhill, O.B.E., *b.* 1887, *m.*	Hon. Stanley E. *G.*, M.D., *b.* 1917.
1927	*Greenway* (3rd), Charles Paul Greenway, *b.* 1917, *s.* 1963, *m.*	Hon. Ambrose C. D. *G.*, *b.* 1941.
1902	*Grenfell* (2nd), Pascoe Christian Victor Francis Grenfell, *b.* 1905, *s.* 1925, *m.*	Hon. Julian *G.*, *b.* 1935.
1944	*Gretton* (2nd), John Frederic Gretton, O.B.E., *b.* 1902, *s.* 1947, *m.*	Hon. John H. *G.*, *b.* 1941.
1869	*Greville* (4th), Ronald Charles Fulke Greville, *b.* 1912, *s.* 1952.	(None.)
1324	*Grey de Ruthyn* (25th), John Lancelot Wykeham Butler-Bowdon, *b.* 1883, *called out of abeyance*, 1939.	
1955	*Gridley* (1st), Arnold Babb Gridley, K.B.E., *b.* 1878, *w.*	Hon. Arnold H. *G.*, *b.* 1905.
1880	*Grimthorpe* (4th), Christopher John Beckett, O.B.E., *b.* 1915, *s.* 1963, *m.*	Hon. Edward J. *B.*, *b.* 1954.
1961	*Guest*, Christopher William Graham Guest, P.C., *b.* 1901, *m.* (*Lord of Appeal*).	(Life Peerage.)
1945	*Hacking* (2nd), Douglas Eric Hacking, *b.* 1910, *s.* 1950, *m.*	Hon. Douglas D. *H.*, *b.* 1938.
1950	*Haden-Guest* (2nd), Stephen Haden-Guest, *b.* 1902, *s.* 1960, *m.*	Hon. Richard *H.-G.*, *b.* 1904.
1957	*Hailes* (1st), Patrick George Thomas Buchan-Hepburn, P.C., G.B.E., C.H., *b.* 1901, *m.*	(None.)
1936	*Hailey* (1st), (William) Malcolm Hailey, P.C., O.M., G.C.S.I., G.C.M.G., G.C.I.E., *b.* 1872, *w.*	(None.)
1886	*Hamilton of Dalzell* (3rd), John D'Henin Hamilton, M.C., *b.* 1911, *s.* 1952, *m.*	Hon. James L. *H.*, *b.* 1938.
1874	*Hampton* (5th), Humphrey Arthur Pakington, O.B.E., *b.* 1888, *s.* 1962, *w.*	Hon. Richard H. R. *P.*, *b.* 1925.
1939	*Hankey* (2nd), Robert Maurice Alers Hankey, K.C.M.G., K.C.V.O., *b.* 1905, *s.* 1963, *m.*	Hon. Donald R. A. *H.*, *b.* 1938.
1958	*Harding of Petherton* (1st), John Harding, G.C.B., C.B.E., D.S.O., M.C., *Field Marshal*, *b.* 1896, *m.*	Capt. Hon. John C. *H.*, *b.* 1928.
1910	*Hardinge of Penshurst* (3rd), George Edward Charles Hardinge, *b.* 1921, *s.* 1960, *m.*	Hon. Julian A. *H.*, *b.* 1945.
1877	*Harlech* (4th), William George Arthur Ormsby-Gore, K.G., P.C., G.C.M.G., *b.* 1885, *s.* 1938, *m.*	Rt. Hon. Sir David *O.-G.*, K.C.M.G., *b.* 1918.
1939	*Harmsworth* (2nd), Cecil Desmond Bernard Harmsworth, *b.* 1903, *s.* 1948, *m.*	Hon. Eric *H.*, *b.* 1905.
1815	*Harris* (5th), George St. Vincent Harris, M.C., *b.* 1889, *s.* 1932, *m.*	Hon. George R. *H.*, *b.* 1920.
1954	*Harvey of Tasburgh* (1st), Oliver Charles Harvey, G.C.M.G., G.C.V.O., C.B., *b.* 1893, *m.*	Hon. Peter C. O. *H.*, *b.* 1921.
1295	*Hastings* (22nd), Edward Delaval Henry Astley, *b.* 1912, *s.* 1956, *m.*	Hon. Delaval T. H. *A.*, *b.* 1960.
1835	*Hatherton* (5th), Edward Thomas Walhouse Littleton, *b.* 1900, *s.* 1944, *m.*	Hon. John W. S. *L.*, *b.* 1906.
1776	*Hawke* (9th), Bladen Wilmer Hawke, *b.* 1901, *s.* 1939, *m.*	Hon. Julian *H.*, *b.* 1904.
1927	*Hayter* (2nd), Charles Archibald Chubb, *b.* 1871, *s.* 1946, *m.*	Hon. George C. H. *C.*, *b.* 1911.
1945	*Hazlerigg* (2nd), Arthur Grey Hazlerigg, M.C., *b.* 1910, *s.* 1949, *m.*	Hon. Arthur G. *H.*, *b.* 1951.
1797 I.	*Headley* (6th), Rowland Patrick John George Allanson-Winn, *b.* 1901, *s.* 1935, *m.*	Hon. Charles *A.-W.*, *b.* 1902.
1943	*Hemingford* (2nd), Dennis George Ruddock Herbert, *b.* 1904, *s.* 1947, *m.*	Hon. Dennis *H.*, *b.* 1934.

Created.	*Title, Order of Succession, Name, etc.*	*Eldest Son or Heir.*
1906	*Hemphill* (5th), Peter Patrick Fitzroy Martyn Hemphill-Martyn, *b.* 1928, *s.* 1957, *m.*	Hon. Charles A. M. *H-M.*, *b.* 1954.
1945	*Henderson* (1st), William Watson Henderson, P.C., *b.* 1891.	(None.)
1896	*Heneage* (3rd), Rev. Thomas Robert Heneage, *b.* 1877, *s.* 1954.	(None.)
1799 I.*	*Henley* (7th), Michael Francis Eden (5th *U.K. Baron, Northington,* 1885), *b.* 1914, *s.* 1962, *m.*	Hon. Oliver M. R. *E.*, *b.* 1953.
1800 I.*	*Henniker* (7th), John Ernest de Grey Henniker-Major (3rd *U.K. Baron, Hartismere,* 1866), *b.* 1883, *s.* 1956, *w.*	Hon. John P. E. C. *H.-M.*, C.M.G., C.V.O., M.C., *b.* 1916.
1886	*Herschell* (3rd), Rognvald Richard Farrer Herschell, *b.* 1923, *s.* 1929, *m.*	(None.)
1935	*Hesketh* (3rd) Thomas Alexander Fermor-Hesketh, *b.* 1950, *s.* 1955, *M.*	Hon. Robert *F.-H.*, *b.* 1951.
1828	*Heytesbury* (5th), William Leonard Frank Holmes à Court, *b.* 1906, *s.* 1949, *m.*	Hon. Francis *H. à C.*, *b.* 1931.
1955	*Heyworth* (1st), Geoffrey Heyworth, *b.* 1894, *m.*	(None.)
1886	*Hillingdon* (4th), Charles Hedworth Mills, *b.* 1922, *s.* 1952, *m.*	Hon. Charles J. *M.*, *b.* 1951.
1886	*Hindlip* (4th), Charles Samuel Victor Allsopp, *b.* 1906, *s.* 1931, *m.*	Hon. Henry R. *A.*, *b.* 1912.
1950	*Hives* (1st), Ernest Walter Hives, C.H., M.B.E., *b.* 1886, *w.*	Hon. John W. *H.*, *b.* 1913.
1960	*Hodson*, Francis Lord Charlton Hodson, P.C., M.C., *b.* 1895, *m.* (*Lord of Appeal*).	(Life Peerage.)
1912	*Hollenden* (2nd), Geoffrey Hope Hope-Morley, *b.* 1885, *s.* 1929, *m.*	Hon. Claude H. *H.-M.*, *b.* 1887.
1897	*Holm Patrick* (3rd), James Hans Hamilton, *b.* 1928, *s.* 1942, *m.*	Hon. H. J. D. *H.*, *b.* 1955.
1933	*Horder* (2nd), Thomas Mervyn Horder, *b.* 1911, *s.* 1955.	(None.)
1797 I.	*Hotham* (7th), Henry Frederick Hotham, C.B.E., *b.* 1899, *s.* 1923, *m.*	Hon. Henry D. *H.*, *b.* 1940.
1881	*Hothfield* (4th), Thomas Sackville Tufton, *b.* 1916, *s.* 1961	Lt.-Col. George W. A. *T.*, T.D., *b.* 1904.
1597	*Howard de Walden* (9th), John Osmael Scott-Ellis (5th *U.K. Baron, Seaford,* 1826), *b.* 1912, *s.* 1946, *m.*	Coheiresses. To U.K. Barony, W. F. *Ellis*, *b.* 1912.
1869	*Howard of Glossop* (3rd), Bernard Edward Fitzalan-Howard, M.B.E., *b.* 1885, *s.* 1924, *m.*	Brig. Hon. Miles *F.-H.*, C.B.E., M.C., *b.* 1915.
1930	*Howard of Penrith* (2nd), Francis Philip Howard, *b.* 1905, *s.* 1939, *m.*	Hon. Philip *H.*, *b.* 1945.
1960	*Howick of Glendale* (1st), Evelyn Baring, G.C.M.G., K.C.V.O., *b.* 1903, *m.*	Hon. Charles E., *B.*, *b.* 1937.
1951	*Hungarton* (1st), Archibald Crawford, *b.* 1890, *m.*	(None.)
1796 I.	*Huntingfield* (5th), William Charles Arcedeckne Vanneck, K.C.M.G., *b.* 1883, *s.* 1915, *w.*	Hon. G. C. Arcedeckne *V.*, *b.* 1935.
1950	*Hurcomb* (1st), Cyril William Hurcomb, G.C.B., K.B.E., *b.* 1883, *w.*	(None.)
1866	*Hylton* (4th) William George Hervey Jolliffe, *b.* 1898, *s.* 1945, *m.*	Hon. Raymond *J.*, *b.* 1932.
1933	*Iliffe* (2nd), Edward Langton Iliffe, *b.* 1908, *s.* 1960, *m.*	Robert P. R. *I*, *b.* 1944.
1543 I.	*Inchiquin* (16th), Donough Edward Foster O'Brien (*O'Brien of Thomond*), *b.* 1897, *s.* 1929, *m.*	Hon. Phadrig *O'B.*, *b.* 1900.
1962	*Inchyra* (1st), Frederick Robert Hoyer Millar, G.C.M.G., C.V.O., *b.* 1900, *m.*	Hon. Robert *H. M.*, *b.* 1953.
1946	*Inman* (1st), Philip Albert Inman, P.C., *b.* 1892, *m.*	Hon. Philip J. *I.*, *b.* 1929.
1919	*Inverforth* (2nd), Andrew Alexander Morton Weir, *b.* 1897, *s.* 1955, *m.*	Hon. Andrew C. R. *W.*, *b.* 1932.
1941	*Ironside* (2nd), Edmund Oslac Ironside, *b.* 1924, *s.* 1959, *m.*	Hon. Charles E.G. *I.*, *b.* 1956.
1947	*Ismay* (1st), Hastings Lionel Ismay, K.G., P.C., G.C.B., C.H., D.S.O., *b.* 1887, *m.*	(None.)
1952	*Jeffreys* (2nd), Mark George Christopher Jeffreys, *b.* 1932, *s.* 1960, *m.*	Hon. Christopher H. M. *J.*, *b.* 1957.
1959	*Jenkins*, David Llewelyn Jenkins, P.C., *b.* 1899 (*Lord of Appeal.*)	(Life Peerage.)
1924	*Jessel* (2nd), Edward Herbert Jessel, C.B.E. *b.* 1904, *s.* 1950, *m.*	Hon. Timothy E. *J.*, *b.* 1935.
1906	*Joicey* (3rd), Hugh Edward Joicey, D.S.O., *b.* 1881, *s.* 1940, *m.*	Hon. Michael *J.*, *b.* 1925.
1953	*Keith of Avonholm*, James Keith, P.C., *b.* 1886, *m.* (*Lord of Appeal, retired*).	(Life Peerage.)
1937	*Kenilworth* (2nd), Cyril Davenport Siddeley, C.B.E., T.D., *b.* 1894, *s.* 1953, *m.*	Hon. John D. *S.*, *b.* 1924.
1935	*Kennet* (2nd), Wayland Hilton Young, *b.* 1923, *s.* 1960, *m.*	Hon. William A. *Y.*, *b.* 1957.
1776 I. } 1886* }	*Kensington* (7th), William Edwardes (4th *U.K. Baron, Kensington*), *b.* 1904, *s.* 1938.	Hugh I. *E.*, *b.* 1933.
1951	*Kenswood* (2nd), John Michael Howard Whitfield, *b.* 1930, *s.* 1963, *m.*	Hon. Michael C. *W.*, *b.* 1955.
1788	*Kenyon* (5th), Lloyd Tyrell-Kenyon, *b.* 1917, *s.* 1927, *m.*	Hon. Lloyd *T.-K.*, *b.* 1947.
1947	*Kershaw* (4th), Edward John Kershaw, *b.* 1936, *s.* 1962, *m.*	Hon. Donald A. *K.*, *b.* 1915.
1943	*Keyes* (2nd), Roger George Bowlby Keyes, *b.* 1919, *s.* 1945, *m.*	Hon. Charles W. P. *K.*, *b.* 1951.
1909	*Kilbracken* (3rd), John Raymond Godley, D.S.C., *b.* 1920, *s.* 1950.	Hon. Christopher J. *G.*, *b.* 1945.
1900	*Killanin* (3rd), Michael Morris, M.B.E., T.D., *b.* 1914, *s.* 1927, *m.*	Hon. George R. F. *M.*, *b.* 1947.
1943	*Killearn* (1st), Miles Wedderburn Lampson, P.C., G.C.M.G., C.B., M.V.O., *b.* 1880, *m.*	Maj. Hon. Graham *L.*, *b.* 1919.

Created.	Title, Order of Succession, Name, etc.	Eldest Son or Heir.
1789 I.	*Kilmaine* (6th), John Francis Archibald Browne, C.B.E., *b.* 1902, *s.* 1946, *m.*	Hon. John D. H. *B.*, *b.* 1948.
1831	*Kilmarnock* (6th), Gilbert Allan Rowland Boyd, M.B.E., *b.* 1903, *s.* 1941, *m.*	Hon. Alastair *B.*, *b.* 1927.
1941	*Kindersley* (2nd), Hugh Kenyon Molesworth Kindersley, C.B.E., M.C., *b.* 1899, *s.* 1954, *m.*	Hon. Robert H. M., *K.*, *b.* 1929.
1223 I.	*Kingsale* (34th), Michael William Robert de Courcy, D.S.O. (*Premier Baron of Ireland*), *b.* 1882, *s.* 1931.	John *de C.*, *b.* 1941.
1682 S. } 1860* }	*Kinnaird* (12th), Kenneth FitzGerald Kinnaird, K.T., K.B.E. (4th *U.K. Baron, Kinnaird*), *b.* 1880, *s.* 1923, *w.*	Master of Kinnaird, *b.* 1912.
1902	*Kinross* (3rd), John Patrick Douglas Balfour, *b.* 1904, *s.* 1939.	Hon. David A. *B.*, T.D., *b.* 1906.
1951	*Kirkwood* (2nd), David Kirkwood, *b.* 1903, *s.* 1955, *m.*	Hon. David H. *K.*, *b.* 1931.
1962	*Lambury* (1st), Leonard Percy Lord, K.B.E., *b.* 1896, *m.*	(None.)
1800 I.	*Langford* (9th), Geoffrey Alexander Rowley-Conway, C.B.E., *b.* 1912, *s.* 1953, *m.*	Hon. Owen G. *R-C.*, *b.* 1958.
1942	*Latham* (1st), Charles Latham, *b.* 1888, *m.*	Hon. Francis *L.*, *b.* 1917.
1431	*Latymer* (7th), Thomas Burdett Money-Coutts, *b.* 1901, *s.* 1949, *m.*	Hon. Hugo N. *M.-C.*, *b.* 1926.
1869	*Lawrence* (4th), John Anthony Edward Lawrence, *b.* 1908, *s.* 1947, *m.*	Hon. David *L.*, *b.* 1937.
1950	*Lawson* (1st), John James Lawson, P.C., *b.* 1881, *m.*	(None.)
1947	*Layton* (1st), Walter Thomas Layton, C.H., C.B.E., *b.* 1884, *w.*	Hon. Michael J. *L.*, *b.* 1912.
1859	*Leconfield* (5th), Edward Scawen Wyndham, D.S.O., *b.* 1883, *s.* 1963, *m.*	Hon. John E. R. *W.*, M.B.E. *b.* 1920.
1839	*Leigh* (4th), Rupert William Dudley Leigh, *b.* 1908, *s.* 1938, *m.*	Hon. John P. *L.*, *b.* 1935.
1962	*Leighton of St. Mellons* (1st), (George) Leighton Seager, C.B.E., *b.* 1896, *m.*	Hon. John L. *S.*, *b.* 1922.
1797	*Lilford* (7th), George Vernon Powys, *b.* 1931, *s.* 1949.	Frank L. *P.*, *b.* 1902.
1945	*Lindsay of Birker* (2nd), Michael Francis Morris Lindsay, *b.* 1909, *s.* 1952, *m.*	Hon. James F. *L.*, *b.* 1945.
1758 I.	*Lisle* (7th), John Nicholas Horace Lysaght, *b.* 1903, *s.* 1919, *m.*	Hon. Horace *L.*, *b.* 1908.
1925	*Lloyd* (2nd), Alexander David Frederick Lloyd, M.B.E., *b.* 1912, *s.* 1941, *m.*	Hon. Charles G. D. *L.*, *b.* 1949.
1895	*Loch* (3rd), George Henry Compton Loch, *b.* 1916, *s.* 1942, *m.*	Hon. Spencer *L.*, M.C., *b.* 1920.
1850	*Londesborough* (6th), Ernest William Denison, M.B.E., *b.* 1876, *s.* 1937, *m.*	Capt. Edward C. *D.*, M.V.O., R.N., *b.* 1888.
1541 I.	*Louth* (16th), Otway Michael James Oliver Plunkett, *b.* 1929, *s.* 1950, *m.*	Hon. Jonathan O.*P.* *b.* 1952.
1458 S. } 1837* }	*Lovat* (15th), Simon Christopher Joseph Fraser, D.S.O., M.C. (4th *U.K. Baron, Lovat*), *b.* 1911, *s.* 1933, *m.*	Master of Lovat, *b.* 1939.
1946	*Lucas of Chilworth* (1st), George William Lucas, *b.* 1896, *m.*	Hon. Michael *L.*, *b.* 1925.
1929	*Luke* (2nd), Ian St. John Lawson-Johnston, *b.* 1905, *s.* 1943, *m.*	Hon. Arthur *L.-J.*, *b.* 1933.
1839	*Lurgan* (4th), William George Edward Brownlow, *b.* 1902, *s.* 1937.	John D. C. *B.*, O.B.E., *b.* 1911.
1914	*Lyell* (3rd), Charles Lyell, *b.* 1939, *s.* 1943.	(None.)
1945	*Lyle of Westbourne* (2nd), Charles John Leonard Lyle, *b.* 1905, *s.* 1954, *m.*	(None.)
1859	*Lyveden* (4th), Robert FitzPatrick Courtenay Vernon, *b.* 1892, *s.* 1926, *m.*	Sydney M. *V.*, *b.* 1888.
1962	*Mabane* (1st), William Mabane, P.C., K.B.E., *b.* 1895, *m.*	(None.)
1959	*MacAndrew* (1st), Charles Glen MacAndrew, P.C., T.D., *b.* 1888, *m.*	Hon. Colin N. G. *Mac A.* *b.* 1919.
1955	*McCorquodale of Newton* (1st), Malcolm Stewart McCorquodale, P.C., *b.* 1901, *w.*	(None.)
1947	*MacDermott*, John Clarke MacDermott, P.C., M.C., *b.* 1896, *m.* (*Lord Chief Justice of Northern Ireland*).	(Life Peerage.)
1776 I.	*Macdonald* (7th), Alexander Godfrey Macdonald, M.B.E., T.D., *b.* 1909, *s.* 1947, *m.*	Hon. Godfrey *M.*, *b.* 1947.
1949	*Macdonald of Gwaenysgor* (1st), Gordon Macdonald, P.C., K.C.M.G., *b.* 1888, *m.*	Hon. Gordon R. *M.*, *b.* 1915.
1937	*McGowan* (2nd), Harry Wilson McGowan, *b.* 1906, *s.* 1961, *m.*	Hon. Harry *McG.*, *b.* 1938.
1955	*McNair* (1st), Arnold Duncan McNair, C.B.E., Q.C., LL.D., F.B.A., *b.* 1885, *m.*	Hon. John *McN.*, *b.* 1915.
1922	*Maclay* (2nd), Joseph Paton Maclay, K.B.E., *b.* 1899, *s.* 1951, *m.*	Hon. Joseph P. *M.*, *b.* 1942.
1951	*Macpherson of Drumochter* (1st), Thomas Macpherson, *b.* 1888, *m.*	Hon. J. Gordon *M.*, *b.* 1924.
1937	*Mancroft* (2nd), Stormont Mancroft Samuel Mancroft, K.B.E., *b.* 1914, *s.* 1942, *m.*	Hon. Benjamin L. S. *M.*, *b.* 1957.
1807	*Manners* (4th), Francis Henry Manners, M.C., *b.* 1897, *s.* 1927, *m.*	Hon. John R. C. *M.*, *b.* 1923.
1922	*Manton* (2nd), George Miles Watson, *b.* 1899, *s.* 1922, *m.*	Hon. Joseph *W.*, *b.* 1924.
1908	*Marchamley* (3rd), John William Tattersall Whiteley, *b.* 1922, *s.* 1949.	(None.)
1961	*Marks of Broughton* (1st), Simon Marks, *b.* 1888, *m.*	Hon. Michael *M.*, *b.* 1920.
1930	*Marley* (2nd), Godfrey Pelham Leigh Aman, *b.* 1913, *s.* 1952, *m.*	(None.)

Created.	*Title, Order of Succession, Name, etc.*	*Eldest Son or Heir.*
1776 I.	*Massy* (9th), Hugh Hamon John Somerset Massy, *b.* 1921, *s.* 1958, *m.*	Hon. David H. S. *M.*, *b.* 1947.
1951	*Mathers* (1st), George Mathers, P.C., K.T., *b.* 1886, *m.*	(None.)
1935	*May* (3rd), Michael St. John May, *b.* 1931, *s.* 1950, *m.*	
1928	*Melchett* (3rd), Julian Edward Alfred Mond, *b.* 1925, *s.* 1949, *m.*	Hon. Peter R. H. *M.*, *b.* 1948.
1925	*Merrivale* (3rd), Jack Henry Edmond Duke, *b.* 1917, *s.* 1951, *m.*	Hon. Derek J. P. *D.*, *b.* 1935.
1911	*Merthyr* (3rd), William Brereton Couchman Lewis, T.D., *b.* 1901, *s.* 1932, *m.*	Hon. Trevor O. *L.*, *b.* 1948.
1919	*Meston* (2nd), Dougall Meston, *b.* 1894, *s.* 1943, *m.*	Hon. James *M.*, *b.* 1950.
1838	*Methuen* (4th), Paul Ayshford Methuen, R.A., *b.* 1886, *s.* 1932, *w.*	Hon. Anthony P. *M.*, *b.* 1891.
1905	*Michelham* (2nd), Herman Alfred Stern, *b.* 1900, *s.* 1919, *w.*	Hon. Jack *Michelham*, *b.* 1903.
1711	*Middleton* (11th), Michael Guy Percival Willoughby, K.G., M.C., T.D., *b.* 1887, *s.* 1924, *m.*	Hon. Michael G. J. *W.*, M.C., *b.* 1921.
1939	*Milford* (2nd), Wogan Philipps, *b.* 1902, *s.* 1962, *m.*	Hon. Hugo J. L. *P.*, *b.* 1929.
1933	*Milne* (2nd), George Douglass Milne, *b.* 1909, *s.* 1948, *m.*	Hon. George *M.*, *b.* 1941.
1951	*Milner of Leeds* (1st), James Milner, P.C., M.C., T.D., *b.* 1889, *m.*	Hon. Michael *M.*, *b.* 1923.
1947	*Milverton* (1st), Arthur Frederick Richards, G.C.M.G., *b.* 1885, *m.*	Hon. Fraser *R.*, *b.* 1930
1873	*Moncreiff* (5th), Harry Robert Wellwood Moncreiff, *b.* 1915, *s.* 1942, *m.*	Hon. Rhoderick H. W. *M.*, *b.* 1954.
1884	*Monk Bretton* (3rd), John Charles Dodson, *b.* 1924, *s.* 1933, *m.*	(None.)
1885	*Monkswell* (3rd), Robert Alfred Hardcastle Collier, *b.* 1875, *s.* 1909, *m.*	William A. L. *C.*, *b.* 1913.
1728	*Monson* (11th), John Monson, *b.* 1932, *s.* 1958, *m.*	Hon. Nicholas J. *M.*, *b.* 1955.
1885	*Montagu of Beaulieu* (3rd), Edward John Barrington Douglas-Scott-Montagu, *b.* 1926, *s.* 1959, *m.*	Hon. Ralph *D-S-M.*, *b.* 1961.
1839	*Monteagle of Brandon* (6th), Gerald Spring Rice, *b.* 1926, *s.* 1946, *m.*	Hon. Charles J. S. *R.*, *b.* 1953.
1943	*Moran* (1st), Charles McMoran Wilson, M.C., M.D., *b.* 1882, *m.*	Hon. Richard *W.*, *b.* 1924.
1918	*Morris* (2nd), Michael William Morris, *b.* 1903, *s.* 1935.	Hon. Michael *M.*, *b.* 1937.
1960	*Morris of Borth-y-Gest*, John William Morris, P.C., C.B.E., M.C., *b.* 1896. (*Lord of Appeal*).	(Life Peerage.)
1950	*Morris of Kenwood* (2nd), Philip Geoffry Morris, *b.* 1928, *s.* 1954, *m.*	
1945	*Morrison* (2nd), Dennis Morrison, *b.* 1914, *s.* 1953, *m.*	(None.)
1947	*Morton of Henryton*, Fergus Dunlop Morton, P.C., M.C., *b.* 1887, *m.* (*Lord of Appeal, retired*).	(Life Peerage.)
1831	*Mostyn* (4th), Edward Llewelyn Roger Lloyd-Mostyn, *b.* 1885, *s.* 1929, *m.*	Hon. Roger *L.-M.*, M.C., *b.* 1920.
1933	*Mottistone* (3rd), (Arthur) Patrick William Seely, T.D., *b.* 1905, *s.* 1963.	Capt. Hon. David P. *S.* R.N., *b.* 1920.
1945	*Mountevans* (2nd), Richard Andvord Evans, *b.* 1918, *s.* 1957, *m.*	Hon. Edward P. B. *E.*, *b.* 1943.
1283	*Mowbray* (25th), *Segrave* (26th) (1283), *&* *Stourton* (22nd) (1448), William Marmaduke Stourton, M.C. (*Premier Baron of England*), *b.* 1895, *s.* 1936, *m.*	Hon. Charles *S.*, *b.* 1923.
1932	*Moyne* (2nd), Bryan Walter Guinness, *b.* 1905, *s.* 1944, *m.*	Hon. Jonathan *G.*, *b.* 1930.
1929	*Moynihan* (2nd), Patrick Berkeley Moynihan, O.B.E., T.D., *b.* 1906, *s.* 1930, *m.*	Hon. Antony *M.*, *b.* 1936.
1781 I.	*Muskerry* (7th), Mathew Fitzmaurice Tilson Deane, *b.* 1874, *s.* 1954, *w.*	Hon. Hastings F. T. *D.*, *b.* 1907.
1627 S.*	*Napier and Ettrick* (14th), Francis Nigel Napier (5th *U.K. Baron, Ettrick*, 1872), *b.* 1930, *s.* 1954, *m.*	Master of Napier, *b.* 1962.
1868	*Napier of Magdala* (5th), (Robert) John Napier, O.B.E., *b.* 1904, *s.* 1948, *m.*	Hon. Robert *N.*, *b.* 1940.
1940	*Nathan* (1st), Harry Louis Nathan, P.C., T.D., *b.* 1889, *m.*	Hon. Roger *N.*, *b.* 1922.
1960	*Nelson of Stafford* (2nd), Henry George Nelson, *b.* 1917, *s.* 1962, *m.*	Hon. Henry R. G. *N.*, *b.* 1943.
1959	*Netherthorpe* (1st), James Turner, *b.* 1908, *m.*	Hon. Andrew *T.*, *b.* 1936.
1940	*Newall* (1st), Cyril Louis Norton Newall, G.C.B., O.M., G.C.M.G., C.B.E., *Marshal of the Royal Air Force*, *b.* 1886, *m.*	Hon. Francis *N.*, *b.* 1930.
1776 I.	*Newborough* (6th), Robert Vaughan Wynn, O.B.E., *b.* 1877, *s.* 1957, *w.*	Hon. Robert C. M. V. *W.*, D.S.C., *b.* 1917.
1892	*Newton* (4th), Peter Richard Legh, *b.* 1915, *s.* 1960, *m.*	Hon. Richard T. *L.*, *b.* 1950.
1930	*Noel Buxton* (2nd), Rufus Alexander Buxton, *b.* 1917, *s.* 1948, *m.*	Hon. Martin C. *B.*, *b.* 1940.
1963	*Normanbrook* (1st), Norman Craven Brook, P.C., G.C.B., *b.* 1902, *m.*	(None.)
1957	*Norrie* (1st), (Charles) Willoughby (Moke) Norrie, G.C.M.G., G.C.V.O., C.B., D.S.O., M.C., *b.* 1893, *m.*	Hon. George W. M. *N.*, *b.* 1936.
1884	*Northbourne* (4th), Walter Ernest Christopher James, *b.* 1896, *s.* 1932, *m.*	Hon. Christopher G. W. *J.*, *b.* 1926.
1866	*Northbrook* (5th), Francis John Baring, *b.* 1915, *s.* 1947, *m.*	Hon. Francis T. *B.*, *b.* 1954.
1878	*Norton* (7th), John Arden Adderley, *b.* 1915, *s.* 1961, *m.*	Hon. James N. A. *A.*, *b.* 1947.
1960	*Nugent* (1st), Terence Edward Gascoigne Nugent, G.C.V.O., M.C., *b.* 1895, *m.*	(None.)
1906	*Nunburnholme* (3rd), Charles John Wilson, *b.* 1904, *s.* 1924, *m.*	Hon. Ben Charles *W.*, *b.* 1928.
1950	*Ogmore* (1st), David Rees Rees-Williams, P.C., T.D., *b.* 1903, *m.*	Hon. Gwilym *R.-W.*, *b.* 1931.

Created.	*Title, Order of Succession, Name, etc.*	*Eldest Son or Heir.*
1870	*O'Hagan* (4th), Charles Towneley Strachey, *b.* 1945, *s.* 1961, *M.*	Hon. Richard T. *S.*, *b.* 1950.
1868	*O'Neill* (4th), Raymond Arthur Clanaboy O'Neill, *b.* 1933, *s.* 1944, *m.*	Hon. Terence *O'N.*, *b.* 1914.
1836 I.*	*Oranmore and Browne* (4th), Dominick Geoffrey Edward Browne (2nd *U.K. Baron Mereworth*, 1926), *b.* 1901, *s.* 1927, *m.*	Hon. Dominick G. T. *B.*, *b.* 1929.
1868	*Ormathwaite* (6th), John Arthur Charles Walsh, *b.* 1912, *s.* 1944.	(None.)
1933	*Palmer* (3rd), Raymond Cecil Palmer, *b.* 1916, *s.* 1950, *m.*	Hon. Gordon W. N. *P.*, O.B.E., *b.* 1918.
1958	*Parker of Waddington*, Hubert Lister Parker, P.C., *b.* 1900, *m.* (*Lord Chief Justice of England*).	(Life Peerage.)
1914	*Parmoor* (2nd), Alfred Henry Seddon Cripps, *b.* 1882, *s.* 1941.	Hon. Frederick H. *C.*, D.S.O., T.D., *b.* 1885.
1962	*Pearce*, Edward Holroyd Pearce, P.C., *b.* 1901, *m.* (*Lord of Appeal*).	(Life Peerage.)
1937	*Pender* (2nd), John Jocelyn Denison-Pender, C.B.E., *b.* 1907, *s.* 1949, *m.*	Hon. John W. *D.-P.*, *b.* 1933.
1866	*Penrhyn* (5th), Frank Douglas-Pennant, *b.* 1865, *s.* 1949, *m.*	Col. Hon. Malcolm F. *D.-P.*, D.S.O., M.B.E., *b.* 1908.
1909	*Pentland* (2nd), Henry John Sinclair, *b.* 1907, *s.* 1925, *m.*	(None.)
1603	*Petre* (17th), Joseph William Lionel Petre, *b.* 1914, *s.* 1915, *m.*	Hon. John *P.*, *b.* 1942.
1918	*Phillimore* (3rd), Robert Godfrey Phillimore, *b.* 1939, *s.* 1947.	Hon. Claud *P.*, *b.*, 1911.
1945	*Piercy* (1st), William Piercy, C.B.E., *b.* 1886, *w.*	Hon. Nicholas P. *P.*, *b.* 1918.
1827	*Plunket* (7th), Patrick Terence William Span Plunket, C.V.O., *b.* 1923, *s.* 1938.	Hon. Robin *P.*, *b.* 1925.
1831	*Poltimore* (4th), George Wentworth Warwick Bampfylde, *b.* 1882, *s.* 1918, *w.*	Hon. Arthur B. W. *B.*, *b.* 1883.
1690 S.	*Polwarth* (10th), Henry Alexander Hepburne-Scott, T.D., *b.* 1916, *s.* 1944, *m.*	Master of Polwarth, *b.* 1947.
1930	*Ponsonby of Shulbrede* (2nd), Matthew Henry Hubert Ponsonby, *b.* 1904, *s.* 1946, *m.*	Hon. Thomas A. *P.*, *b.* 1930.
1958	*Poole* (1st), Oliver Brian Sanderson Poole, P.C., C.B.E., T.D., *b.* 1911, *m.*	Hon. David C. *P.*, *b.* 1945.
1852	*Raglan* (4th), FitzRoy Richard Somerset, *b.* 1885, *s.* 1921, *m.*	Hon. FitzRoy *S.*, *b.* 1927.
1957	*Rank* (1st), Joseph Arthur Rank, *b.* 1888, *m.*	(None.)
1932	*Rankeillour* (3rd), Henry John Hope, *b.* 1899, *s.* 1958, *m.*	Hon. Peter T. M. *H.*, *b.* 1935.
1953	*Rathcavan* (1st), (Robert William) Hugh O'Neill, P.C., *b.* 1883, *m.*	Hon. Phelim R. H. *O'N.*, M.P., *b.* 1909.
1916	*Rathcreedan* (2nd), Charles Patrick Norton, T.D., *b.* 1905, *s.* 1930, *m.*	Hon. Christopher J. *N.*, *b.* 1949.
1868 I.	*Rathdonnell* (5th), Thomas Benjamin McClintock-Bunbury, *b.* 1938, *s.* 1959.	(None.)
1821	*Ravensworth* (8th), Arthur Waller Liddell, *b.* 1924, *s.* 1950, *m.*	Hon. Thomas A. H. *L.*, *b.* 1954.
1821	*Rayleigh* (5th), John Arthur Strutt, *b.* 1908, *s.* 1947, *m.*	Hon. Charles *S.*, *b.* 1910.
1937	*Rea* (2nd) Philip Russell Rea, P.C., O.B.E., *b.* 1900, *s.* 1948, *m.*	John N. *R.*, *b.* 1928.
1628 S.	*Reay* (14th), Hugh William Mackay, *b.* 1937, *s.* 1963.	Hon. Alexander W. R. *R.* *b.* 1907.
1902	*Redesdale* (4th), John Power Bertram Ogilvy Freeman-Mirford, *b.* 1885, *s.* 1962.	Clement N. B. *F.-M.*, *b.* 1932.
1948	*Reid*, James Scott Cumberland Reid, P.C., *b.* 1890, *m.* (*Lord of Appeal*)	(Life Peerage.)
1940	*Reith* (1st), John Charles Walsham Reith, P.C., G.C.V.O., G.B.E., C.B., T.D., *b.* 1889, *m.*	Hon. Christopher J. *R.*, *b.* 1928.
1923	*Remnant* (2nd), Robert John Farquharson Remnant, M.B.E., *b.* 1895, *s.* 1933, *m.*	Hon. James W. *R.*, *b.* 1930.
1806 I.	*Rendlesham* (8th), Charles Anthony Hugh Thellusson, *b.* 1915, *s.* 1943, *m.*	Hon. Charles W. B. *T.*, *b.* 1954.
1933	*Rennell* (2nd), Francis James Rennell Rodd, K.B.E., C.B., *b.* 1895, *s.* 1941, *m.*	Hon. Peter *R.*, *b.* 1904.
1885	*Revelstoke* (4th), Rupert Baring, *b.* 1911, *s.* 1934.	Hon. John *B.*, *b.* 1934.
1905	*Ritchie of Dundee* (3rd), John Kenneth Ritchie, *b.* 1902, *s.* 1948, *w.*	Hon. Colin *R.*, *b.* 1908.
1935	*Riverdale* (2nd), Robert Arthur Balfour, *b.* 1901, *s.* 1957, *m.*	Hon. Mark R. *B.*, *b.* 1927.
1961	*Robertson of Oakridge* (1st), Brian Hubert Robertson, G.C.B., G.B.E., K.C.M.G., K.C.V.O., D.S.O., M.C., b. 1896, *m.*	Hon. William R. *R.*, *b.* 1930.
1938	*Roborough* (2nd), Massey Henry Edgcumbe Lopes, *b.* 1903, *s.* 1938, *m.*	Hon. Henry *L.*, *b.* 1940.
1931	*Rochester* (2nd), Foster Charles Lowry Lamb, *b.* 1916, *s.* 1955, *m.*	Hon. David C. *L.*, *b.* 1944.
1934	*Rockley* (2nd), Robert William Evelyn Cecil, *b.* 1901, *s.* 1941, *m.*	Hon. James H. *C.*, *b.* 1934.
1782	*Rodney* (8th), George Bridges Harley Guest Rodney, *b.* 1891, *s.* 1909, *m.*	Hon. John F. *R.*, *b.* 1920.
1651 S.	*Rollo* (13th), Eric John Stapylton Rollo (4th *U.K. Baron, Dunning*, 1869), *b.* 1915, *s.* 1947, *m.*	Master of Rollo, *b.* 1943.
1866	*Romilly* (4th), William Gaspard Guy Romilly, *b.* 1899, *s.* 1905, *w.*	(None.)
1959	*Rootes* (1st), William Edward Rootes, G.B.E., *b.* 1894, *m.*	Hon. Geoffrey *R.*, *b.* 1917.

Created.	Title, Order of Succession, Name, etc.	Eldest Son or Heir.
1796 I. 1838*	*Rossmore* (7th), William Warner Westenra (6th *U.K. Baron, Rossmore*), *b.* 1931, *s.* 1958.	(None.)
1939	*Rotherwick* (2nd), (Herbert) Robin Cayzer, *b.* 1912, *s.* 1958, *m.*	Hon. H. Robin *C.*, *b.* 1954.
1885	*Rothschild* (3rd), Nathaniel Mayer Victor Rothschild, G.M., F.R.S., *b.* 1910, *s.* 1937, *m.*	Hon. Nathaniel *R.*, *b.* 1936.
1911	*Rowallan* (2nd), Thomas Godfrey Polson Corbett, K.T., K.B.E., M.C., T.D., *b.* 1895, *s.* 1933, *m.*	Hon. Arthur *C.*, *b.* 1919.
1947	*Rugby* (1st), John Loader Maffey, G.C.M.G., K.C.B., K.C.V.O., C.S.I., C.I.E., *b.* 1877, *m.*	Hon. Alan L. *M.*, *b.* 1913.
1945	*Rusholme* (1st), Robert Alexander Palmer, *b.* 1890.	(None.)
1919	*Russell of Liverpool* (2nd), Edward Frederick Langley Russell, C.B.E., M.C., T.D., *b.* 1895, *s.* 1920. *m.*	Hon. Langley G. H. *R.*, M.C., *b.* 1922.
1876	*Sackville* (5th), Edward Charles Sackville-West, *b.* 1901, *s.* 1962.	Lionel B. *S.-W.*, *b.* 1913.
1911	*St. Audries* (2nd), Alexander Peregrine Fuller-Acland-Hood, *b.* 1893, *s.* 1917.	Hon. A. John *F.-A.-H.*, *b.* 1906.
1559	*St. John of Bletso* (19th), John Moubray Russell St. John, *b.* 1917, *s.* 1934.	Comdr. Oliver *St. J.*, D.S.C., R.N., *b.* 1914.
1935	*St. Just* (2nd), Peter George Grenfell, *b.* 1922, *s.* 1941, *m.*	(None.)
1852	*St. Leonards* (3rd), Frank Edward Sugden, *b.* 1890, *s.* 1908.	Arthur H. *S.*, *b.* 1889.
1887	*St. Levan* (3rd), Francis Cecil St. Aubyn, *b.* 1895, *s.* 1940, *m.*	Hon. John F. A. *St. A.*, D.S.C., *b.* 1919.
1885	*St. Oswald* (4th), Rowland Denys Guy Winn, M.C., *b.* 1916, *s.* 1957, *m.*	Hon. Derek E. A. *W.*, *b.* 1919.
1953	*Salter* (1st), (James) Arthur Salter, P.C., G.B.E., K.C.B., *b.* 1881, *m.*	(None.)
1445 S.	*Saltoun* (19th), Alexander Arthur Fraser, M.C., *b.* 1886, *s.* 1933, *m.*	Hon. Flora M. *Ramsay*, *b.* 1930.
1960	*Sanderson of Ayot* (1st), Basil Sanderson, M.C., *b.* 1894, *w.*	Hon. Alan L. *S.*, *b.* 1931.
1945	*Sandford* (2nd), Rev. John Cyril Edmondson, *b.* 1920, *s.* 1959, *m.*	Hon. James J. M. *E.*, *b.* 1949.
1871	*Sandhurst* (4th), Ralph Sheldon Mansfield, O.B.E., *b.* 1892, *s.* 1933, *w.*	Hon. J. E. Terence *M.*, D.F.C., *b.* 1920.
1802	*Sandys* (7th), Richard Michael Oliver Hill, *b.* 1931, *s.* 1961.	Lt.-Col. Hon. George *C. H.*, *b.* 1887.
1888	*Savile* (3rd), George Halifax Lumley-Savile, *b.* 1919, *s.* 1931.	Hon. Henry L. T. *L.-S.*, *b.* 1923.
1447	*Saye and Sele* (20th), Ivo Murray Twisleton-Wykeham-Fiennes, O.B.E., M.C., *b.* 1885, *s.* 1949, *m.*	Hon. Nathaniel *T.-W.-F.*, *b.* 1920.
1932	*Selsdon* (3rd), Malcolm McEacharn Mitchell-Thomson, *b.* 1937, *s.* 1963.	
1489 S.	*Sempill* (19th), William Francis Forbes-Sempill, A.F.C., *b.* 1893, *s.* 1934, *m.*	Hon. Ann Moira *Chant*, *b.* 1920.
1916	*Shaughnessy* (3rd), William Graham Shaughnessy, *b.* 1922, *s.* 1938, *m.*	Hon. Patrick J. *S.*, *b.* 1944.
1783 I. 1839*	*Sheffield* (6th), Edward John Stanley (6th *U.K. Baron, Stanley of Alderley and* 5th *U.K. Baron Eddisbury*, 1848), *b.* 1907, *s.* 1931, *m.*	Hon. Lyulph H. V. O. *S.*, *b.* 1915.
1946	*Shepherd* (2nd), Malcolm Newton Shepherd, *b.* 1918, *s.* 1954, *m.*	Hon. Grahame G. *S.*, *b.* 1949.
1784	*Sherborne* (7th), Charles Dutton, *b.* 1911, *s.* 1949, *m.*	Hon. George E. *D*, *b.* 1912.
1941	*Sherwood* (1st), Hugh Michael Seely, *b.* 1898.	(None.)
1902	*Shuttleworth* (4th), Charles Ughtred John Kay-Shuttleworth, M.C., *b.* 1917, *s.* 1942, *m.*	Hon. Charles G. N. *S.*, *b.* 1948.
1950	*Silkin* (1st), Lewis Silkin, P.C., *b.* 1889, *w.*	Hon. Arthur *S.*, *b.* 1916.
1963	*Silsoe* (1st), (Arthur) Malcolm Trustram Eve, G.B.E., M.C., T.D., Q.C., *b.* 1894, *m.*	Hon. David M. T. *E.*, *b.* 1930.
1947	*Simon of Wythenshawe* (2nd), Roger Simon, *b.* 1913, *s.* 1960, *m.*	Hon. Matthew *S*, *b.* 1955.
1449 S.	*Sinclair* (17th), Charles Murray Kennedy St. Clair, M.V.O., *b.* 1914, *s.* 1957.	Malcolm A. J. *St. C.*, *b.* 1927.
1957	*Sinclair of Cleeve* (1st), Robert John Sinclair, K.C.B., K.B.E., *b.* 1893, *m.*	Maj. Hon. John R. K. *S.*, M.B.E., *b.* 1919.
1919	*Sinha* (2nd), Aroon Kumar Sinha, *b.* 1887, *s.* 1928, *m.*	Hon. Sudhindro *S.*, *b.* 1920.
1828	*Skelmersdale* (5th), Arthur George Bootle-Wilbraham, M.C., *b.* 1876, *s.* 1930.	Claude *B.-W.*, *b.* 1877.
1916	*Somerleyton* (3rd), Savile William Francis Crossley, *b.* 1928, *s.* 1959, *m.*	Hon. Richard *N. C.*, *b.* 1932.
1784	*Somers* (8th), John Patrick Somers Cocks, *b.* 1907, *s.* 1953, *m.*	John S. S. *C.*, *b.* 1907.
1780	*Southampton* (5th), Charles FitzRoy, *b.* 1904, *s.* 1958, *m.*	Hon. Charles J. *F.*, *b.* 1928.
1917	*Southborough* (3rd), Francis John Hopwood, *b.* 1897, *s.* 1960, *m.*	Hon. Francis M. *H.*, *b.* 1922.
1959	*Spens* (1st), William Patrick Spens, P.C., K.B.E., Q.C., *b.* 1885, *m.*	Hon. William G. M. *S.*, M.B.E., *b.* 1914.
1640	*Stafford* (14th), Basil Francis Nicholas Fitzherbert, *b.* 1926, *s.* 1941, *m.*	Hon. Francis M. W. *F.*, *b.* 1954.
1938	*Stamp* (3rd), Trevor Charles Stamp, *b.* 1907, *s.* 1941, *m.*	Hon. Trevor *S.*, *b.* 1935.
1318	*Strabolgi* (11th), David Montague de Burgh Kenworthy, *b.* 1914, *s.* 1953.	Rev. the Hon. Jonathan M. A. *K.*, *b.* 1916.
1911	*Strachie* (2nd), Edward Strachey, *b.* 1882, *s.* 1936, *w.*	(None.)
1954	*Strang* (1st), William Strang, G.C.B., G.C.M.G., M.B.E., *b.* 1893, *m.*	Hon. Colin *S.*, *b.* 1922.
1955	*Strathalmond* (1st), William Fraser, C.B.E., *b.* 1888, *m.*	Hon. William *F.*, *b.* 1915.
1936	*Strathcarron* (2nd), David William Anthony Blyth Macpherson, *b.* 1924, *s.* 1937, *m.*	Hon. Ian D. P. *M.*, *b.* 1949.

Created	*Title, Order of Succession, Name, etc.*	*Eldest Son or Heir.*
1955	*Strathclyde* (1st), Thomas Dunlop Galbraith, P.C., *b.* 1891, *m.*	Hon. Thomas G. D. *G.*, M.P., *b.* 1917.
1900	*Strathcona and Mount Royal* (4th), Donald Euan Palmer Howard, *b.* 1923, *s.* 1959, *m.*	Hon. Donald A. *H.*, *b.* 1961.
1836	*Stratheden & Campbell* (1841) (4th), Alastair Campbell, *b.* 1899, *s.* 1918, *w.*	Maj. Hon. Gavin *C.*, *b.* 1901.
1884	*Strathspey* (5th), Donald Patrick Trevor Grant, *b.* 1912, *s.* 1948, *m.*	Hon. James P. *G.*, *b.* 1943.
1838	*Sudeley* (7th), Merlyn Charles Sainthill Hanbury-Tracy, *b.* 1939, *s.* 1941.	Ninian J. *H.-T.*, *b.* 1910.
1786	*Suffield* (11th), Anthony Philip Harbord-Hamond, M.C., *b.* 1922, *s.* 1951, *m.*	Hon. Charles A. A. *H.-H.* *b.* 1953.
1893	*Swansea* (4th), John Hussey Hamilton Vivian, *b.* 1925, *s.* 1934. *m.*	Hon. Richard A. H. *V.*, *b.* 1957.
1907	*Swaythling* (3rd), Stuart Albert Samuel Montagu, O.B.E., *b.* 1898, *s.* 1927, *m.*	Hon. David C. *M.*, *b.* 1928.
1919	*Swinfen* (2nd), Charles Swinfen Eady, *b.* 1904, *s.* 1919, *m.*	Hon. Roger M. *E.*, *b.* 1938.
1935	*Sysonby* (3rd), John Frederick Ponsonby, *b.* 1945, *s.* 1956, *M.*	(None.)
1831 I. } 1856* }	*Talbot of Malahide* (7th), Milo John Reginald Talbot, C.M.G. (4th *U.K. Baron, Talbot de Malahide*), *b.* 1912, *s.* 1948.	Francis J. R. *T.*, *b.* 1889 (to Irish Barony).
1946	*Tedder* (1st), Arthur William Tedder, G.C.B., *Marshal of the Royal Air Force*, *b.* 1890, *m.*	Hon. John M. *T.*, *b.* 1926.
1797 I.	*Teignmouth* (6th), Hugh Aglionby Shore, *b.* 1881, *s.* 1926, *m.*	Hon. Frederick *S.*, D.S.C., *b.* 1920.
1831	*Templemore* (5th), Dermot Richard Claud Chichester, *b.* 1916, *s.* 1953, *m.*	Hon. Arthur P. *C.*, *b.* 1952.
1884	*Tennyson* (4th), Harold Christopher Tennyson, *b.* 1919, *s.* 1951.	Lieut.-Com. Hon. Mark A. *T.*, D.S.C., R.N., *b.* 1920.
1918	*Terrington* (4th), (James Allen) David Woodhouse, *b.* 1915, *s.* 1961, *m.*	Hon. C. Montague *W.*, D.S.O., O.B.E., M.P., *b.* 1917.
1940	*Teviot* (1st), Charles Iain Kerr, D.S.O., M.C., *b.* 1874, *m.*	Hon. Charles J. *K.*, *b.* 1934.
1616	*Teynham* (19th), Christopher John Henry Roper-Curzon, D.S.O., D.S.C., *b.* 1896, *s.* 1936, *m.*	Hon. John *R.-C.*, *b.* 1928.
1792	*Thurlow* (7th), Henry Charles Hovell-Thurlow-Cumming-Bruce, C.B., C.B.E., D.S.O., *b.* 1910, *s.* 1952.	Hon. Sir Francis E. *H.-T.-C.-B.*, K.C.M.G., *b.* 1912.
1876	*Tollemache* (4th), John Edward Hamilton Tollemache, M.C., *b.* 1910, *s.* 1955, *m.*	Hon. Timothy J. E. *T.*, *b.* 1939.
1564 S.	*Torphichen* (13th), John Gordon Sandilands, *b.* 1886, *s.* 1915, *m.*	Master of Torphichen, *b.* 1917.
1946	*Tovey* (1st), John Cronyn Tovey, G.C.B., K.B.E., D.S.O., *Admiral of the Fleet*, *b.* 1885, *m.*	(None.)
1947	*Trefgarne* (2nd), David Garro Trefgarne, *b.* 1941, *s.* 1960.	Hon. Trevor G. *T.*, *b.* 1944.
1921	*Trevethin* (3rd) *and Oaksey* (1st), Geoffrey Lawrence, P.C., D.S.O., T.D. (1st *U.K. Baron, Oaksey*, 1947), *b.* 1880, *s.* 1959, *m.*	Hon. John G. T. *L.*, *b.* 1929.
1880	*Trevor* (4th), Charles Edwin Hill-Trevor, *b.* 1928, *s.* 1950.	Hon. Nevill E. *H.-T.*, *b.* 1931.
1461 I.	*Trimlestown* (19th), Charles Aloysius Barnewall, *b.* 1899, *s.* 1937, *w.*	Hon. Anthony *B.*, *b.* 1923.
1940	*Tryon* (2nd), Charles George Vivian Tryon, K.C.B., K.C.V.O., D.S.O., *b.* 1906, *s.* 1940, *m.*	Hon. Anthony *T.*, *b.* 1940.
1950	*Tucker* (Frederick) James Tucker, P.C., *b.* 1888 (*Lord of Appeal, retired*), *m.*	(Life Peerage.)
1935	*Tweedsmuir* (2nd), John Norman Stuart Buchan, O.B.E., *b.* 1911, *s.* 1940, *m.*	Hon. William *B.*, *b.* 1916.
1946	*Uvedale of North End* (1st), Ambrose Edgar Woodall, M.D., F.R.C.S., *b.* 1885, *m.*	(None).
1523	*Vaux of Harrowden* (9th), Rev. Peter Hugh Gordon Gilbey, *b.* 1914, *s.* 1958.	Hon. John H. P. *G.*, *b.* 1915.
1800 I.	*Ventry* (7th), Arthur Frederick Daubeney Eveleigh-de-Moleyns, *b.* 1898, *s.* 1936.	Hon. Francis *E.-de-M.*, *b.* 1901.
1762	*Vernon* (10th), John Lawrance Venables-Vernon, *b.* 1923, *s.* 1963, *m.*	
1922	*Vestey* (3rd), Samuel George Armstrong Vestey, *b.* 1941, *s.* 1954.	Mark W. *V.*, *b.* 1943.
1841	*Vivian* (5th), Anthony Crespigny Claude Vivian, *b.* 1906, *s.* 1940, *m.*	Hon. Nicholas *V.*, *b.* 1935.
1934	*Wakehurst* (2nd), John de Vere Loder, K.G., K.C.M.G., *b.* 1895, *s.* 1936, *m.* (*Governor of Northern Ireland*).	Hon. John C. *L.*, *b.* 1925.
1905	*Waleran* (2nd), William George Hood Walrond, *b.* 1905, *s.* 1925.	(None.)
1723	*Walpole* (9th), Robert Henry Montgomerie Walpole, *b.* 1913, *s.* 1931, *m.*	Hon. Robert H. *W.*, *b.* 1938.
1780	*Walsingham* (8th), George de Grey, D.S.O., O.B.E., *b.* 1884, *s.* 1929, *m.*	Hon. John *de G.*, M.C., *b.* 1925.
1936	*Wardington* (2nd), Christopher Henry Beaumont Pease, *b.* 1924, *s.* 1950	Hon. William S. *P.*, *b.* 1925.
1792 I.	*Waterpark* (7th), Frederick Caryll Phillip Cavendish, *b.* 1926, *s.* 1948, *m.*	Hon. Roderick A. *C.*, *b.* 1959.
1942	*Wedgwood* (3rd), Hugh Everard Wedgwood, *b.* 1921, *s.* 1959, *m.*	Hon. Piers A. W. *W.*, *b.* 1954.

Created.	*Title, Order of Succession, Name, etc.*	*Eldest Son or Heir.*
1861	*Westbury* (5th), David Alan Bethell, M.C., *b.* 1922, *s.* 1961, *m.*	Hon. Richard N. *B.*, *b.* 1950.
1944	*Westwood* (2nd), William Westwood, *b.* 1907, *s.* 1953, *m.*	Hon. William G. *W.*, *b.* 1944.
1544	*Wharton* (9th), Charles John Halswell Kemeys-Tynte, *b.* 1908, *s.* 1934.	Hon. Elizabeth D. *Vincent*, *b.* 1906.
1912	*Whitburgh* (1st), Thomas Banks Borthwick, *b.* 1874.	(None.)
1935	*Wigram* (2nd), (George) Neville (Clive) Wigram, M.C., *b.* 1915, *s.* 1960, *m.*	Hon. Andrew F. C. *W.*, *b.* 1949.
1948	*Williams* (1st), Thomas Edward Williams, *b.* 1892, *m.*	(None.)
1491	*Willoughby de Broke* (20th), John Henry Peyto Verney, M.C., A.F.C., *b.* 1896, *s.* 1923, *m.*	Hon. Leopold D. *V.*, *b.* 1938.
1950	*Wilmot of Selmeston* (1st), John Wilmot, P.C., *b.* 1895.	(None.)
1946	*Wilson* (1st), Henry Maitland Wilson, G.C.B., G.B.E., D.S.O., *Field Marshal*, *b* 1881, *m.*	Hon. Patrick M. *W.*, *b.* 1915.
1937	*Windlesham* (3rd), David James George Hennessy, *b.* 1932, *s.* 1962.	Hon. Frederick F. G. *H.*, M.B.E., *b.* 1906.
1951	*Wise* (1st), Frederick John Wise, *b.* 1887, *m.*	Hon. John C. *W.*, *b.* 1923.
1869	*Wolverton* (5th), Nigel Reginald Victor Glyn, *b.* 1904, *s.* 1932.	Sir Francis M. G. *G.*, K.C.M.G., *b.* 1901.
1928	*Wraxall* (2nd), George Richard Lawley Gibbs, *b.* 1928, *s.* 1931.	Hon. Eustace H. B. *G.*, *b.* 1929.
1915	*Wrenbury* (3rd), John Burton Buckley, *b.* 1927, *s.* 1940, *m.*	Hon. Colin *B.*, *b.* 1899.
1932	*Wright*, Robert Alderson Wright, P.C., G.C.M.G., F.B.A., *b.* 1869, *m.* (*Lord of Appeal, retired*)	(Life Peerage.)
1838	*Wrottesley* (5th), Richard John Wrottesley, M.C., *b.* 1918, *s.* 1962, *m.*	Hon. Richard F. G. *W.*, *b.* 1942.
1919	*Wyfold* (3rd), Hermon Robert Fleming Hermon-Hodge, *b.* 1915, *s.* 1942.	(None.)
1829	*Wynford* (8th), Robert Samuel Best, M.B.E., *b.* 1917, *s.* 1943, *m.*	Hon. John P. R. *B.*, *b.* 1950.

Peeresses in Their Own Right

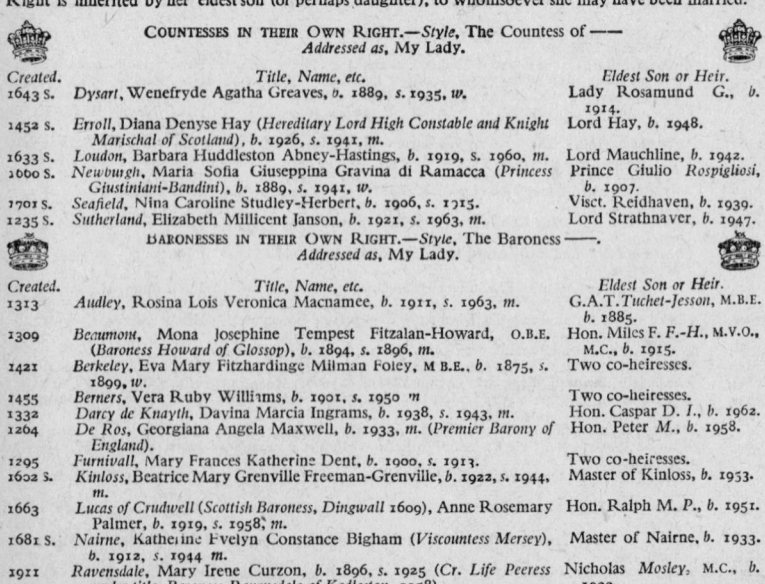

Peerages are occasionally granted immediately to ladies of distinction or the widows of distinguished men; but frequently the instances falling under this heading are the result of regular inheritance in lines which are open to females in default of males. A Peeress in her Own Right retains her title after marriage, and if her husband's rank is the superior she is designated by the two titles jointly, the inferior one last: her hereditary claim still holds good in spite of any marriage whether higher or lower. No rank held by a woman can confer any title or even precedence upon her husband but the rank of a Peeress in her Own Right is inherited by her eldest son (or perhaps daughter), to whomsoever she may have been married.

COUNTESSES IN THEIR OWN RIGHT.—*Style*, The Countess of ——
Addressed as, My Lady.

Created.	*Title, Name, etc.*	*Eldest Son or Heir.*
1643 S.	*Dysart*, Wenefryde Agatha Greaves, *b.* 1889, *s.* 1935, *w.*	Lady Rosamund *G.*, *b.* 1914.
1452 S.	*Erroll*, Diana Denyse Hay (*Hereditary Lord High Constable and Knight Marischal of Scotland*), *b.* 1926, *s.* 1941, *m.*	Lord Hay, *b.* 1948.
1633 S.	*Loudon*, Barbara Huddleston Abney-Hastings, *b.* 1919, *s.* 1960, *m.*	Lord Mauchline, *b.* 1942.
1660 S.	*Newburgh*, Maria Sofia Giuseppina Gravina di Ramacca (*Princess Giustiniani-Bandini*), *b.* 1889, *s.* 1941, *w.*	Prince Giulio *Rospigliosi*, *b.* 1907.
1701 S.	*Seafield*, Nina Caroline Studley-Herbert, *b.* 1906, *s.* 1915.	Visct. Reidhaven, *b.* 1939.
1235 S.	*Sutherland*, Elizabeth Millicent Janson, *b.* 1921, *s.* 1963, *m.*	Lord Strathnaver, *b.* 1947.

BARONESSES IN THEIR OWN RIGHT.—*Style*, The Baroness ——.
Addressed as, My Lady.

Created.	*Title, Name, etc.*	*Eldest Son or Heir.*
1313	*Audley*, Rosina Lois Veronica Macnamee, *b.* 1911, *s.* 1963, *m.*	G.A.T.*Tuchet-Jesson*, M.B.E. *b.* 1885.
1309	*Beaumont*, Mona Josephine Tempest Fitzalan-Howard, O.B.E. (*Baroness Howard of Glossop*), *b.* 1894, *s.* 1896, *m.*	Hon. Miles F. *F.-H.*, M.V.O., M.C., *b.* 1915.
1421	*Berkeley*, Eva Mary Fitzhardinge Milman Foley, M.B.E., *b.* 1875, *s.* 1899, *w.*	Two co-heiresses.
1455	*Berners*, Vera Ruby Williams, *b.* 1901, *s.* 1950 *m*	Two co-heiresses.
1332	*Darcy de Knayth*, Davina Marcia Ingrams, *b.* 1938, *s.* 1943, *m.*	Hon. Caspar D. *I.*, *b.* 1962.
1264	*De Ros*, Georgiana Angela Maxwell, *b.* 1933, *m.* (*Premier Barony of England*).	Hon. Peter *M.*, *b.* 1958.
1295	*Furnivall*, Mary Frances Katherine Dent, *b.* 1900, *s.* 1913.	Two co-heiresses.
1602 S.	*Kinloss*, Beatrice Mary Grenville Freeman-Grenville, *b.* 1922, *s.* 1944, *m.*	Master of Kinloss, *b.* 1953.
1663	*Lucas of Crudwell* (*Scottish Baroness, Dingwall* 1609), Anne Rosemary Palmer, *b.* 1919, *s.* 1958, *m.*	Hon. Ralph M. *P.*, *b.* 1951.
1681 S.	*Nairne*, Katherine Evelyn Constance Bigham (*Viscountess Mersey*), *b.* 1912, *s.* 1944 *m.*	Master of Nairne, *b.* 1933.
1911	*Ravensdale*, Mary Irene Curzon, *b.* 1896, *s.* 1925 (*Cr. Life Peeress under title, Baroness Ravensdale of Kedleston*, 1958).	Nicholas *Mosley*, M.C., *b.* 1923.

Created.	Title, Name, etc.	Eldest Son or Heir.
1651 S.	*Ruthven*, Bridget Helen Monckton, C.B.E. (*Viscountess Monckton of Brenchley*) *b.* 1896, *s.* 1956, *m.*	Earl of Carlise, M.C., *b.* 1923 (*see* p. 226).
1299	*Strange of Knokin*, 1426 *Hungerford and* 1445 *De Moleyns*. Elizabeth Philipps (*Dowager Viscountess St. Davids*), *b.* 1884, *s.* 1921, *w.*	Viscount St. Davids, *b.* 1917. (*see* p. 233).
1308	*Zouche*, Mary Cecil Frankland, *b.* 1875, *s.* 1917, *w.*	Sir James F., Bt., *b.* 1943.

LIFE PEERS

Created under Life Peerages Act, 1958

BARONS

1961 *Alport*, Cuthbert James McCall Alport, P.C., T.D., *b.* 1912, *m.*
1963 *Balerno*, Alick Drummond Buchanan-Smith, C.B.E., T.D., D.SC., F.R.S.E., *b.* 1898, *w.*
1958 *Boothby*, Robert John Graham Boothby, K.B.E., *b.* 1900.
1960 *Bossom*, Alfred Charles Bossom, *b.* 1881, *w.*
1960 *Casey*, Richard Gardiner Casey, P.C., C.H., D.S.O., M.C., *b.* 1890, *m.*
1962 *Champion*, Arthur Joseph Champion, *b.* 1897, *m.*
1963 *Chelmer*, Eric Cyril Boyd Edwards, M.C., T.D., *b.* 1914, *m.*
1961 *Coutanche*, Alexander Moncrieff Coutanche, *b.* 1892, *m.*
1959 *Craigton*, Jack Nixon Browne, P.C., C.B.E., *b.* 1904.
1958 *Ferrier*, Victor Ferrier Noel-Paton, *b.* 1900, *m.*
1961 *Fisher of Lambeth*, Most Rev. Geoffrey Francis Fisher, P.C., G.C.V.O., D.D., Royal Victorian Chain, *b.* 1887, *m.*
1962 *Francis-Williams*, (Edward) Francis Williams, C.B.E., *b.* 1903, *m.*
1962 *Franks*, Oliver Shewell Franks, P.C., G.C.M.G., K.C.B., C.B.E., F.B.A., *b.* 1905, *m.*
1958 *Fraser of Lonsdale* (William Jocelyn) Ian Fraser, C.H., C.B.E., *b.* 1897, *m.*
1958 *Geddes of Epsom*, Charles John Geddes, C.B.E., *b.* 1897, *m.*
1958 *Granville-West*, Daniel Granville West, *b.* 1904, *m.*
1963 *Hill of Luton*, Charles Hill, P.C., M.D., *b.* 1904, *m.*
1961 *Hughes*, William Hughes, C.B.E., *b.* 1911, *m.*
1962 *Ilford*, Geoffrey Clegg Hutchinson, M.C., T.D., Q.C., *b.* 1893, *m.*
1959 *James of Rusholme*, Eric John Francis James, *b*, 1909, *m.*
1961 *Lindgren*, George Samuel Lindgren, *b.* 1900, *m.*
1961 *Molson*, (Arthur) Hugh (Elsdale) Molson, P.C., *b.* 1903, *m.*
1959 *Morrison of Lambeth*, Herbert Stanley Morrison, P.C., C.H., *b.* 1888, *m.*
1961 *Peddie*, James Mortimer Peddie, M.B.E., *b.* 1906, *m.*
1959 *Plowden*, Edwin Noel Plowden, K.C.B., K.B.E., *b.* 1907, *m.*
1959 *Robbins*, Lionel Charles Robbins, C.B., F.B.A., *b.* 1898, *m.*
1961 *Robens of Woldingham*, Alfred Robens, P.C., *b.* 1910, *m.*
1962 *Sainsbury*, Alan John Sainsbury, *b.* 1902, *m.*
1958 *Shackleton*, Edward Arthur Alexander Shackleton, O.B.E., *b.* 1911, *m.*
1959 *Shawcross*, Hartley William Shawcross, P.C., Q.C., *b.* 1902, *m.*
1958 *Stonham*, Victor John Collins, O.B.E., *b.* 1903, *m.*
1958 *Taylor*, Stephen James Lake Taylor, M.D., *b.* 1910, *m.*
1962 *Todd*, Alexander Robertus Todd, D.SC., D.Phil., F.R.S., *b.* 1907, *m.*
1958 *Twining*, Edward Francis Twining, G.C.M.G., M.B.E., *b.* 1899, *m.*
1961 *Walston*, Henry David Leonard George Walston, *b.* 1912, *m.*
1961 *Williams of Barnburgh*, Tom Williams, P.C., *b.* 1888, *m.*
1962 *Williamson*, Thomas Williamson, C.B.E., *b.* 1897, *m.*

BARONESSES

1962 *Burton of Coventry*, Elaine Frances Burton, *b.* 1904.
1958 *Elliot of Harwood*, Katharine Elliot, D.B.E., *b.* 1903, *w.*
1959 *Horsbrugh*, Florence Gertrude Horsbrugh, P.C., G.B.E., *b.* 1889.
1958 *Ravensdale of Kedleston*, see Baronesses in their own Right, "Ravensdale", above.
1958 *Swanborough*, Stella, Dowager Marchioness of Reading, G.B.E., *w.*
1961 *Summerskill*, Edith Summerskill, P.C., *b.* 1901, *m.*
1958 *Wootton of Abinger*, Barbara Frances Wright, *b.* 1897, *m.*

Surnames of Peers and Peeresses differing from their Titles

Abney Hastings — *Loudoun*
Acheson—*Gosford*
Adderley—*Norton*
Addington—*Sidmouth*
Agar—*Normanton*
Agar Robartes—*Clifden*
Aitken—*Beaverbrook*
Akers Douglas—*Chilston*
Alexander—*Alexander of Tunis*
Alexander—*Alexander of Hillsborough*
Alexander—*Caledon*
Allanson Winn—*Headley*
Allsopp—*Hindlip*
Aman—*Marley*
Anderson—*Waverley*
Annesley—*Valentia*
Anson—*Lichfield*
Armstrong Jones—*Snowdon*
Arthur—*Glenarthur*
Ashley Cooper—*Shaftesbury*
Ashton—*Ashton of Hyde*
Assheton—*Clitheroe*
Asquith—*Oxford & A.*
Astley—*Hastings*
Astor—*Astor of Hever*
Bailey—*Glanusk*
Baillie—*Burton*
Baillie Hamilton—*Haddington*
Baird—*Stonehaven*
Baldwin — *Baldwin of Bewdley*
Balfour—*Kinross*
Balfour—*Riverdale*
Balfour — *Balfour of Inchrye*
Bampfylde—*Poltimore*
Banbury — *Banbury of Southam*
Baring—*Ashburton*
Baring—*Cromer*
Baring — *Howick of Glendale*
Baring—*Northbrook*
Baring—*Revelstoke*
Barnes—*Gorell*
Barnewall—*Trimlestown*
Bathurst—*Bledisloe*
Beauclerk—*St. Albans*
Beaumont—*Allendale*
Beckett—*Grimthorpe*
Bennet—*Tankerville*
Beresford—*Decies*
Beresford—*Waterford*
Bernard—*Bandon*
Berry—*Camrose*
Berry—*Kemsley*
Bertie—*Lindsey*
Best—*Wynford*
Bethell—*Westbury*
Bewicke Copley—*Cromwell*
Bigham—*Mersey*
Bigham—*Nairne*
Bingham—*Clanmorris*

Bingham—*Lucan*
Blades—*Ebbisham*
Bligh—*Darnley*
Blunt Mackenzie—*Cromartie*
Bootle Wilbraham — *Skelmersdale*
Borthwick—*Whitburgh*
Boscawen—*Falmouth*
Bourke—*Mayo*
Bowes Lyon—*Strathmore*
Bowyer—*Denham*
Boyd—*Kilmarnock*
Boyle—*Cork and Orrery*
Boyle—*Glasgow*
Boyle—*Shannon*
Brabazon—*Meath*
Brand—*Hampden*
Brassey — *Brassey of Apethorpe*
Brett—*Esher*
Bridgeman—*Bradford*
Brodrick—*Midleton*
Brook—*Normanbrook*
Brooke—*Alanbrooke*
Brooke—*Brookeborough*
Brooks—*Crawshaw*
Brougham — *Brougham and Vaux*
Broughton—*Fairhaven*
Browne—*Craigton*★
Browne—*Kilmaine*
Browne — *Oranmore and Browne*
Browne—*Sligo*
Brownlow—*Lurgan*
Bruce—*Aberdare*
Bruce—*Balfour of Burleigh*
Bruce—*Bruce of Melbourne*
Bruce — *Elgin and Kincardine*
Brudenell Bruce — *Ailesbury*
Buchan—*Tweedsmuir*
Buchan-Hepburn—*Hailes*
Buchanan-Smith — *Balerno*★
Buckley—*Wrenbury*
Burton—*Burton of Coventry*★
Butler—*Carrick*
Butler—*Dunboyne*
Butler—*Lanesborough*
Butler—*Mountgarret*
Butler—*Ormonde*
Butler-Bowdon—*Grey de Ruthyn*
Buxton—*Noel-Buxton*
Byng—*Strafford*
Byng—*Torrington*
Campbell—*Argyll*
Campbell — *Breadalbane and Holland*
Campbell—*Cawdor*
Campbell—*Colgrain*
Campbell—*Glenavy*
Campbell—*Stratheden and Campbell*
Campbell Gray—*Gray*
Canning—*Garvagh*
Capell—*Essex*
Carberry—*Carbery*
Carington—*Carrington*
Carnegie—*Fife*
Carnegie—*Northesk*
Carnegie—*Southesk*
Cary—*Falkland*
Caulfeild—*Charlemont*
Cavendish—*Chesham*
Cavendish—*Devonshire*
Cavendish—*Waterpark*
Cavendish Bentinck — *Portland*
Cayzer—*Rotherwick*
Cecil—*Amherst of Hackney*
Cecil—*Exeter*
Cecil—*Rockley*
Chaloner—*Gisborough*
Charteris—*Wemyss and March*
Chetwynd Talbot — *Shrewsbury*
Chichester—*Donegall*
Chichester — *Templemore*
Child Villiers—*Jersey*
Cholmondeley — *Delamere*
Chubb—*Hayter*
Clegg Hill—*Hill*
Clifford — *Clifford of Chudleigh*
Coats—*Glentanar*
Cochrane — *Cochrane of Cults*
Cochrane—*Dundonald*
Cocks—*Somers*
Cohen—*Cohen of Birkenhead*
Cokayne — *Cullen of Ashbourne*
Coke—*Leicester*
Cole—*Enniskillen*
Collier—*Monkswell*
Collins—*Stonham*★
Colville—*Clydesmuir*
Colville—*Colville of Culross*
Compton—*Northampton*
Conolly Carew—*Carew*
Cooper—*Norwich*
Corbett—*Rowallan*
Courtenay—*Devon*
Craig—*Craigavon*
Crawford—*Hungarton*
Crichton—*Erne*
Crichton Stuart—*Bute*
Cripps—*Parmoor*
Crossley—*Somerleyton*
Cubitt—*Ashcombe*
Cunliffe Lister—*Swinton*
Curzon—*Howe*
Curzon—*Ravensdale*
Curzon—*Scarsdale*
Cust—*Brownlow*
Dalrymple—*Stair*
Davies—*Darwen*
Davison—*Broughshane*
Dawnay—*Downe*
Dawson Damer — *Portarlington*
De Courcy—*Kingsale*
De Grey—*Walsingham*
De Yarburgh Bateson—*Deramore*
Deane—*Muskerry*
Denison—*Londesborough*
Denison Pender—*Pender*
Dent—*Furnivall*
Devereux—*Hereford*
Dewar—*Forteviot*
Dixon—*Glentoran*
Dodson—*Monk Bretton*
Douglas—*Douglas of Barloch*
Douglas — *Douglas of Kirtleside*
Douglas—*Morton*
Douglas—*Queensberry*
Douglas Hamilton — *Hamilton*
Douglas Hamilton — *Selkirk*
Douglas Home—*Home*
Douglas Pennant—*Penrhyn*
Douglas Scott Montagu —*Montagu of Beaulieu*
Drummond—*Perth*
Duff—*Fife*
Dugdale—*Crathorne*
Duke—*Merrivale*
Duncombe—*Feversham*
Dundas—*Melville*
Dundas—*Zetland*
Dutton—*Sherborne*
Eady—*Swinfen*
Eaton—*Cheylesmore*
Eden—*Auckland*
Eden—*Avon*
Eden—*Henley*
Edgcumbe—*Mount Edgcumbe*
Edmondson—*Sandford*
Edwardes—*Kensington*
Edwards—*Chelmer*★
Egerton—*Sutherland*
Egerton—*Wilton*
Eliot—*St. Germans*
Elliot—*Elliot of Harwood*★
Elliot—*Minto*
Erskine—*Buchan*
Erskine—*Mar & Kellie*
Erskine Murray—*Elibank*
Evans—*Mountevans*
Eve—*Silsoe*
Eveleigh de Moleyns—*Ventry*
Eyres Monsell—*Monsell*
Fane—*Westmorland*
Feilding—*Denbigh*
Fellowes—*Ailwyn*
Fellowes—*De Ramsey*
Fermor Hesketh—*Hesketh*
Finch Hatton—*Winchilsea*
Finch Knightley—*Aylesford*
Fisher—*Fisher of Lambeth*★
Fitzalan Howard—*Beaumont*
Fitzalan Howard — *Howard of Glassop*
Fitzalan Howard—*Norfolk*
FitzClarence—*Munster*
FitzGerald—*Leinster*
Fitzherbert—*Stafford*
FitzRoy—*Daventry*
FitzRoy—*Grafton*
FitzRoy—*Southampton*
Flower—*Ashbrook*
Foley—*Berkeley*
Foljambe—*Liverpool*
Forbes—*Granard*
Forbes Sempill—*Sempill*
Forster—*Forster of Harraby*
Forward Howard — *Wicklow*
Fox Strangways — *Ilchester*
Frankland—*Zouche*
Fraser—*Fraser of Lonsdale*★
Fraser—*Lovat*
Fraser—*Saltoun*
Fraser—*Strathalmond*
Freeman Grenville—*Kinloss*
Freeman Mitford — *Redesdale*
Freeman Thomas—*Willingdon*
Fremantle—*Cottesloe*
French—*De Freyne*
French—*Ypres*
Fuller Acland Hood—*St. Audries*
Fyfe—*Kilmuir*
Galbraith—*Strathclyde*
Ganzoni—*Belstead*
Gascoyne Cecil—*Salisbury*
Gathorne Hardy—*Cranbrook*
Geddes—*Geddes of Epsom*★
Gibbs—*Aldenham*
Gibbs—*Wraxall*
Gibson—*Ashbourne*
Giffard—*Halsbury*
Gilbey—*Vaux of Harrowden*
Glyn—*Wolverton*
Godley—*Kilbracken*
Gordon—*Aberdeen*
Gordon—*Huntly*
Gordon Lennox—*Richmond*
Gore—*Arran*
Gough Calthorpe—*Calthorpe*
Graham—*Montrose*
Graham Toler—*Norbury*
Grant—*De Longueuil*
Grant—*Strathspey*
Greaves—*Dysart*
Greenall—*Daresbury*
Grenfell—*St. Just*
Greville—*Warwick*
Grey—*Stamford*
Grimston—*Verulam*
Grosvenor—*Ebury*
Grosvenor—*Westminster*
Guest—*Wimborne*
Guinness—*Iveagh*
Guinness—*Moyne*
Gully—*Selby*
Gurdon—*Cranworth*
Hamilton—*Abercorn*
Hamilton—*Belhaven and Stenton*
Hamilton — *Hamilton of Dalzell*
Hamilton — *Holm Patrick*
Hamilton Russell—*Boyne*
Hamilton Temple Blackwood—*Dufferin*
Hanbury Tracy—*Sudeley*
Handcock—*Castlemaine*

★ Life Peer created under Life Peerages Act, 1958.

Harbord Hamond — *Suffield*
Harding—*Harding of Petherton*
Hardinge — *Hardinge of Penshurst*
Hare—*Listowel*
Harmsworth — *Rothermere*
Harris—*Malmesbury*
Harvey—*Harvey of Tasburgh*
Hastings—*Huntingdon*
Hay—*Erroll*
Hay—*Kinnoull*
Hay—*Tweeddale*
Heathcote Drummond Willoughby—*Ancaster*
Hely Hutchinson—*Donoughmore*
Hemphill Martyn—*Hemphill*
Henderson—*Faringdon*
Hennessy—*Windlesham*
Henniker Major — *Henniker*
Hepburne Scott — *Polwarth*
Herbert—*Carnarvon*
Herbert—*Hemingford*
Herbert—*Pembroke*
Herbert—*Powis*
Hermon Hodge—*Wyfold*
Hervey—*Bristol*
Hewitt—*Lifford*
Hicks Beach—*St. Aldwyn*
Hill—*Downshire*
Hill—*Hill of Luton*★
Hill—*Sandys*
Hill Trevor—*Trevor*
Hobart Hampden—*Buckinghamshire*
Hogg—*Hailsham*
Holland Hibbert—*Knutsford*
Holmes à Court—*Heytesbury*
Hood—*Bridport*
Hope—*Linlithgow*
Hope—*Rankeillour*
Hope Morley—*Hollenden*
Hopkinson—*Colyton*
Hopwood — *Southborough*
Hore Ruthven—*Gowrie*
Hovell Thurlow Cumming Bruce—*Thurlow*
Howard—*Carlisle*
Howard—*Effingham*
Howard—*Howard of Penrith*
Howard—*Strathcona*
Howard—*Suffolk*
Hoyer Millar—*Inchyra*
Hubbard—*Addington*
Huggins—*Malvern*
Hutchinson—*Ilford*★
Ingrams—*Darcy de Knayth*
Innes Ker—*Roxburghe*
Inskip—*Caldecote*
Irby—*Boston*
Isaacs—*Reading*
Isaacs—*Swanborough*★
Jackson—*Allerton*
James—*James of Rusholme*★
James—*Northbourne*
Janson—*Sutherland*
Jebb—*Gladwyn*
Jervis—*St. Vincent*
Jocelyn—*Roden*
Jolliffe—*Hylton*
Joynson Hicks—*Brentford*
Kaye Shuttleworth — *Shuttleworth*
Kearley—*Devonport*
Keith—*Keith of Avonholm*
Keith—*Kintore*
Kemeys Tynte—*Wharton*
Kemp—*Rochdale*
Kennedy—*Ailsa*
Kenworthy—*Strabolgi*
Keppel—*Albemarle*
Kerr—*Lothian*
Kerr—*Teviot*
King—*Lovelace*
King Tenison—*Kingston*
Kitchener — *Kitchener of Khartoum*
Kitson—*Airedale*
Knatchbull—*Brabourne*
Knox—*Ranfurly*
Lamb—*Rochester*
Lambart—*Cavan*
Lambton—*Durham*
Lampson—*Killearn*
Larnach Nevill — *Abergavenny*
Lascelles—*Harewood*
Law—*Coleraine*
Law—*Ellenborough*
Lawrence—*Trevethin and Oaksey*
Lawson—*Burnham*
Lawson Johnston—*Luke*
Le Poer Trench—*Clancarty*
Legge—*Dartmouth*
Legh—*Newton*
Leith—*Burgh*
Lennox Boyd—*Boyd of Merton*
Leslie—*Rothes*
Leslie Melville—*Leven*
Lever—*Leverhulme*
Leveson Gower—*Granville*
Lewis—*Brecon*
Lewis—*Essendon*
Lewis—*Merthyr*
Liddell—*Ravensworth*
Lindesay Bethune — *Lindsay*
Lindsay—*Crawford*
Lindsay — *Lindsay of Birker*
Littleton—*Hatherton*
Lloyd George — *Lloyd George of Dwyfor*
Lloyd George—*Tenby*
Lloyd Mostyn—*Mostyn*
Loder—*Wakehurst*
Loftus—*Ely*
Lopes—*Roborough*
Lord—*Lambury*
Low—*Aldington*
Lowry Corry—*Belmore*
Lowther—*Lonsdale*
Lowther—*Ullswater*
Lubbock—*Avebury*
Lumley—*Scarbrough*
Lumley Savile—*Savile*
Lygon—*Beauchamp*
Lyle—*Lyle of Westbourne*
Lyon Dalberg Acton—*Acton*
Lyons—*Ennisdale*
Lysaght—*Lisle*
Lyttelton—*Chandos*
Lyttelton — *Cobham* (*Viscountcy*)
McClintock Bunbury—*Rathdonnell*
McCorquodale—*McCorquodale of Newton*
Macdonald — *Macdonald of Gwaenysgor*
McDonnell—*Antrim*
Mackay—*Inchcape*
Mackay—*Reay*
Mackenzie—*Amulree*
Mackintosh—*Mackintosh of Halifax*
McLaren—*Aberconway*
Macnamee—*Audley*
Macpherson — *Macpherson of Drumochter*
Macpherson—*Strathcarron*
Maffey—*Rugby*
Maitland—*Lauderdale*
Manners—*Rutland*
Manningham Buller—*Dilhorne*
Mansfield—*Sandhurst*
Marks—*Marks of Broughton*
Marquis—*Woolton*
Marsham—*Romney*
Mason—*Blackford*
Maude—*Hawarden*
Maxwell—*De Ros*
Maxwell—*Farnham*
Meade—*Clanwilliam*
Milles Lade—*Sondes*
Mills—*Hillingdon*
Milner—*Milner of Leeds*
Mitchell Thomson — *Selsdon*
Molyneux—*Sefton*
Monckton—*Monckton of Brenchley*
Monckton—*Ruthven*
Monckton Arundell — *Galway*
Mond—*Melchett*
Money-Coutts—*Latymer*
Montagu—*Manchester*
Montagu—*Sandwich*
Montagu—*Swaythling*
Montagu Douglas Scott —*Buccleuch*
Montagu Stuart Wortley Mackenzie — *Wharncliffe*
Montague—*Amwell*
Montgomerie—*Eglinton*
Montgomery — *Montgomery of Alamein*
Moore—*Drogheda*
Moore Brabazon—*Brabazon of Tara*
Moreton—*Ducie*
Morris—*Killanin*
Morris — *Morris of Borth-y-Gest*
Morris—*Morris of Kenwood*
Morrison—*Dunrossil*
Morrison — *Morrison of Lambeth*★
Morris—*Nuffield*
Morton—*Morton of Henryton*
Mountbatten — *Carisbrooke*
Mountbatten—*Edinburgh*
Mountbatten — *Milford Haven*
Mountbatten — *Mountbatten of Burma*
Muff—*Calverley*
Mulholland—*Dunleath*
Murray—*Atholl.*
Murray—*Dunmore*
Murray—*Mansfield and Mansfield*
Nall Cain—*Brocket*
Napier — *Napier and Ettrick*
Napier — *Napier of Magdala*
Needham—*Kilmorey*
Nelson—*Nelson of Stafford*
Neville—*Braybrooke*
Nicolson—*Carnock*
Nivison—*Glendyne*
Noel—*Gainsborough*
Noel Paton—*Ferrier*★
North—*Guilford*
Northcote—*Iddesleigh*
Norton—*Grantley*
Norton—*Rathcreedan*
Nugent—*Westmeath*
O'Brien—*Inchiquin*
Ogilvy—*Airlie*
O'Neill—*Rathcavan*
Orde Powlett—*Bolton*
Ormsby Gore—*Harlech*
Osborne—*Leeds*
Paget—*Anglesey*
Pakenham—*Longford*
Pakington—*Hampton*
Palmer—*Lucas of Crudwell*
Palmer—*Rusholme*
Palmer—*Selborne*
Parker—*Macclesfield*
Parker—*Morley*
Parker—*P. of Waddington*
Parnell—*Congleton*
Parsons—*Rosse*
Paulet—*Winchester*
Peake—*Ingleby*
Pearson—*Cowdray*
Pease—*Daryngton*
Pease—*Gainford*
Pease—*Wardington*
Pelham—*Chichester*
Pelham—*Yarborough*
Pelham Clinton Hope—*Newcastle*
Pellew—*Exmouth*
Penny—*Marchwood*
Pepys—*Cottenham*
Perceval—*Egmont*
Percy—*Northumberland*
Pery—*Limerick*
Petty Fitzmaurice—*Lansdowne*
Philipps—*Milford*
Philipps—*St. Davids*
Philipps—*Strange of Knokin*
Phipps—*Normanby*
Pleydell Bouverie—*Radnor*
Plumptre—*Fitzwalter*

★ Life Peer created under Life Peerages Act, 1958.

Plunkett—Dunsany
Plunkett—Fingall
Plunkett—Louth
Pollock—Hanworth
Pomeroy—Harberton
Ponsonby—Bessborough
Ponsonby—De Mauley
Ponsonby—P. of Shulbrede
Ponsonby—Sysonby
Portal—Portal of Hungerford
Powys—Lilford
Pratt—Camden
Preston—Gormanston
Primrose—Rosebery
Prittie—Dunalley
Ramacca—Newburgh
Ramsay—Dalhousie
Ramsbotham—Soulbury
Rees Williams—Ogmore
Rhys—Dynevor
Richards—Milverton
Ritchie—Ritchie of Dundee
Robens—Robens of Woldingham★
Roberts—Clwyd
Robertson—Robertson of Oakridge
Roche—Fermoy
Rodd—Rennell
Roper Curzon—Teynham
Rous—Stradbroke
Rowley Conwy—Langford
Runciman — Runciman of Doxford
Russell—Ampthill
Russell—Bedford
Russell—De Clifford
Russell—R. of Liverpool
Ryder—Harrowby
Sackville—De La Warr
Sackville West—Sackville
St. Aubyn—St. Levan
St. Clair—Sinclair
St. Clair Erskine—Rosslyn
St. John—St. J. of Bletso
St. John—Bolingbroke and St. John
St. Leger—Doneraile
Samuel—Bearsted
Sanderson — Sanderson of Ayot
Sandilands—Torphichen
Saumarez—De Saumarez
Savile—Mexborough
Scarlett—Abinger
Sclater Booth—Basing
Scott—Eldon
Scott Ellis—Howard de Walden
Scrymgeour Wedderburn—Dundee
Seager—Leighton of St. Mellons
Seely—Mottistone
Seely—Sherwood
Seymour—Hertford
Seymour—Somerset
Shaw—Craigmyle
Shirley—Ferrers
Shore—Teignmouth
Siddeley—Kenilworth
Sidney—De L'Isle
Simon—Simon of Wythenshawe
Sinclair—Caithness
Sinclair—Pentland
Sinclair—Sinclair of Cleeve
Sinclair—Thurso
Skeffington—Massereene
Smith—Bicester
Smith—Birkenhead
Smith—Colwyn
Smith—Dudley (Barony)
Smith—Hambleden
Somerset—Beaufort
Somerset—Raglan
Spencer—Churchill
Spencer Churchill — Marlborough
Spring Rice—Monteagle of Brandon
Stanhope—Harrington
Stanley—Derby
Stanley—Sheffield
Stapleton Cotton—Combermere
Stern—Michelham
Stewart—Galloway
Stonor—Camoys
Stopford—Courtown
Stourton—Mowbray
Strachey—O'Hagan
Strachey—Strachie
Strauss—Conesford
Strutt—Belper
Strutt—Rayleigh
Stuart—Castle Stewart
Stuart—Moray
Stuart—Stuart of Findhorn
Studley Herbert — Seafield
Suenson Taylor—Grantchester
Sugden—St. Leonards
Talbot—T. de Malahide
Taylour—Headfort
Temple Gore Langton—Temple of Stowe
Tennant—Glenconner
Thellusson—Rendlesham
Thesiger—Chelmsford
Thynne—Bath
Trench—Ashtown
Tufton—Hothfield
Turner—Netherthorpe
Turnour—Winterton
Twisleton Wykeham Fiennes—Saye and Sele
Tyrrell Kenyon—Kenyon
Upton—Templetown
Vanden Bempde Johnstone—Derwent
Vane—Barnard
Vane Tempest Stewart—Londonderry
Vanneck—Huntingfield
Vaughan—Lisburne
Vavasseur Fisher—Fisher
Venables Vernon—Vernon
Vereker—Gort
Verney—Willoughby de Broke
Verney Cave—Braye
Vernon—Lyveden
Vesey—De Vesci
Villiers—Clarendon
Vivian—Swansea
Wallop—Portsmouth
Walrond—Waleran
Walsh—Ormathwaite
Ward—Bangor
Ward—Dudley (Earldom)
Ward—Ward of Witley
Warrender — Bruntisfield
Watson—Manton
Watson Armstrong — Armstrong
Weir—Inverforth
Weld Forester—Forester
Wellesley—Cowley
Wellesley—Wellington
Wentworth Fitzwilliam—Fitzwilliam
West—Granville-West★
Westenra—Rossmore
White—Annaly
Whiteley—Marchamley
Whitfield—Kenswood
Willey—Barnby
Williams—Berners
Williams—Francis-Williams★
Williams—Williams of Barnburgh★
Williamson—Forres
Willoughby—Middleton
Wills—Dulverton
Wilmot—Wilmot of Selmeston
Wilson—Moran
Wilson—Nunburnholme
Windsor—Cornwall
Windsor—Gloucester
Windsor—Kent
Windsor Clive — Plymouth
Wingfield—Powerscourt
Winn—St. Oswald
Winn—Headley
Wodehouse—Kimberley
Wood—Halifax
Woodall — Uvedale of North End
Woodhouse—Terrington
Wright—Wootton of Abinger★
Wyndham—Leconfield
Wyndham Quin—Dunraven
Wynn—Newborough
Yarde Buller—Churston
Yerburgh—Alvingham
Yorke—Hardwicke
Young—Kennet
Young Erskine—Mar
Younger—Y. of Leckie

★ Life Peer created under Life Peerages Act, 1958.

Courtesy Titles (*in actual use in 1964*)

Holders of Courtesy Titles are addressed in the manner shown for holders of substantive titles

From this list it will be seen that the "Marquess of Blandford" *is the heir to the* Dukedom of Marlborough *and the* "Earl of Aboyne" *to the* Marquessate of Huntly, *and* "Viscount Acheson" *heir to the* Earldom of Gosford: ★*the titles of second heirs are also given*; *e.g.* Earl of Offaly, *son of the* "Marquess of Kildare" *heir to the* Dukedom of Leinster.

∴ *In addition to these Titles of Courtesy the eldest son of some Scottish peers is usually styled* "The Master of —— " *e.g.* "The Master of Falkland," *eldest son of* Viscount Falkland.

Marquesses.

★Blandford—Marlborough
Bowmont—Roxburghe
Douglas & Clydesdale—Hamilton
★°Douro—Wellington
Graham—Montrose
Granby—Rutland
Hamilton—Abercorn
Hartington —Devonshire
★Kildare—Leinster
Lorne—Argyll
Tavistock—Bedford

Earls.

Aboyne—Huntly
Altamont—Sligo
Ancram—Lothian
Bective—Headfort
Brecknock—Camden
Cassillis—Ailsa
°Compton — Northampton
★Dalkeith—Buccleuch
Dumfries—Bute
★Euston—Grafton
Hopetoun—Linlithgow
°Jermyn—Bristol
Lewes—Abergavenny
Macduff—Fife
March—Richmond
Medina—Milford Haven
Mornington—★Douro
★Mount Charles — Conyngham
Mulgrave—Normanby
Offaly—★Kildare
°Percy—Northumberland
Rocksavage — Cholmondeley
Ronaldshay—Zetland
St. Andrews—Kent
Shelburne—Lansdowne
Sunderland—★Blandford
Tyrone—Waterford
Uxbridge—Anglesey
Yarmouth—Hertford

Viscounts.

Acheson—Gosford
Adare—Dunraven
Althorp—Spencer
Amberley—Russell
Asquith of Morley—Oxford and Asquith
Boringdon—Morley
Borodale—Beatty
Boyle—Shannon
Brocas—Jellicoe
Bury—Albemarle
Campden—Gainsborough
Chelsea—Cadogan
Chewton—Waldegrave
Clanfield—Peel
Cole—Enniskillen

Corvedale — *Baldwin of Bewdley*
Cranborne—*Salisbury*
Cranley—*Onslow*
Crowhurst—*Cottenham*
Curzon—*Howe*
Dalrymple—*Stair*
Dangan—*Cowley*
Dawick—*Haig*
Deerhurst—*Coventry*
Dunluce—*Antrim*
Dupplin—*Kinnoull*
Ebrington—*Fortescue*
Eden—*Avon*
Ednam—*Dudley*
Elveden—*Iveagh*
Emlyn—*Cawdor*
Encombe—*Eldon*
Enfield—*Strafford*
Erleigh—*Reading*
Errington—*Cromer*
Feilding—*Denbigh*
FitzHarris—*Malmesbury*
Folkestone—*Radnor*
Furneaux—*Birkenhead*
Garmoyle—*Cairns*
Garnock—*Lindsay*
Glenapp—*Inchcape*
Glentworth—*Limerick*
Glerawly—*Annesley*
Gwynnedd—*Lloyd George of Dwyfor* [*wich*
Hinchingbrooke—*Sand-*
Ikerrin—*Carrick*
Ingestre—*Shrewsbury*
Ipswich—**Euston*
Jocelyn—*Roden*
Kelburn—*Glasgow*
Knebworth—*Lytton*
Lambton—*Durham*
Lascelles—*Harewood*
Lewisham—*Dartmouth*
Linley—*Snowdon*
Lowther—*Lonsdale*
Lumley—*Scarbrough*
Lymington—*Portsmouth*
Malden—*Essex*
Mandeville—*Manchester*
Melgund—*Minto*
Moore—*Drogheda*
Morpeth—*Carlisle*
Newport—*Bradford*
Newry and Mourne—*Kilmorey*
Ockham—*Lovelace*
Parker—*Macclesfield*
Perceval—*Egmont*
Petersham—*Harrington*
Pollington—*Mexborough*
Prestwood—*Attlee*
Quenington—*St. Aldwyn*
Raynham—*Townshend*
Reidhaven—*Seafield*
Royston—*Hardwicke*
St. Cyres—*Iddesleigh*
Sandon—*Harrowby*
Savernake—*Ailesbury*
Slane—**Mount Charles*
Somerton—*Normanton*
Stopford—*Courtown*
Stormont—*Mansfield*
Strathallan—*Perth*
Stuart—*Castle Stewart*
Sudley—*Arran*
Suirdale—*Donoughmore*
Tamworth—*Ferrers*
Tarbat—*Cromartie*
Throwley—*Sondes*
Tiverton—*Halsbury*
Traprain—*Balfour*
Uffington—*Craven*
Vaughan—*Lisburne*
Villiers—*Jersey*
Walberton—*Woolton*
Weymouth—*Bath*
Windsor—*Plymouth*
Wolmer—*Selborne*

Barons (Lord —)

Apsley—*Bathurst*
Ardee—*Meath* [*Melville*
Balgonie — *Leven and*
Balniel—*Crawford*
Berriedale—*Caithness*
Bingham—*Lucan*
Binning—*Haddington*
Brooke—*Warwick*
Bruce—*Elgin*
Buckhurst—*De La Warr*
Burghersh—*Westmorland*
Cardross—*Buchan*
Cochrane—*Dundonald*
Courtenay—*Devon*
Delvin—*Westmeath*
Doune—*Moray*
Dunglass—*Home*
Eliot—*St. Germans*
Erskine—*Mar & Kellie*
Eskdaill—**Dalkeith*
Forrester of Corstorphine —*Verulam*
Garlies—*Galloway*
Greenock—*Cathcart*
Guernsey—*Aylesford*
Hay—*Erroll*
Herbert—*Pembroke*
Howland—**Tavistock*
Irwin—*Halifax*
Leslie—*Rothes*
Leveson—*Granville*
Loughborough—*Rosslyn*
Masham—*Swinton*
Mauchline—*Loudoun*
Medway—*Cranbrook*
Montgomerie—*Eglinton*
Moreton—*Ducie*
Naas—*Mayo* [*March*
Neidpath—*Wemyss &*
Ogilvy—*Airlie*
Ossulston—*Tankerville*
Oxmantown—*Rosse*
Porchester—*Carnarvon*
Primrose—*Rosebery*
Ramsay—*Dalhousie* [*Tunis*
Rideau — *Alexander of*
Scrymgeour—*Dundee*
Seymour—*Somerset*
Silchester—*Longford*
Strathnaver—*Sutherland*
Willoughby de Eresby —*Ancaster*
Wodehouse—*Kimberley*
Worsley—*Yarborough*

CONTRACTIONS AND SYMBOLS

Contractions and Symbols.—S. or I. appended to the date of creation denotes a *Scottish* or *Irish* title, the furthur addition of a * implies that the Peer in question holds also an *Imperial* title, which is specified (after the name) by its more definite description as *Engl.*, *Brit.*, or *U.K.* When both titles are alike, as in the case of Argyll, this star is appended to the conjoined date below, and it then denotes that such date is that of the imperial creation. The mark ° signifies that there is no " of " in the Marquessate or Earldom so designated; *b.* signifies born; *s.*, succeeded; *m.*, married: *w.*, widower or widow: *M.*, minor.

Her Majesty's Most Honourable Privy Council

The Privy Council is of very ancient origin. A Council, the number of which was about twelve, was instituted by Alfred, 895, and it discharged the functions of State now confined to members of the Cabinet. In the Middle Ages the chief advisers of the King who were permanently about him formed the Privy Council. Having become unwieldy, it was reconstituted in 1679. At present it consists of certain eminent persons whose names are given below. Members of the Cabinet must be Privy Councillors, and they principally form the acting Privy Council. The Council is summoned as such to act " with others " upon the demise of the Crown, and many matters are referred by the Sovereign to Committees of the Council, some of which are standing Committees, and others constituted to deal with particular cases, *e.g.*, the Judicial Committee, the Board of Trade, *q.v.* The Lord President of the Council is one of the Great Officers of State, and as such is always a prominent member of the Cabinet.

H.R.H. the Prince Philip, Duke of Edinburgh.....	1951
H.R.H. the Duke of Gloucester............	1925
Adeane, Sir Michael......	1953
Ademola, Sir Adetokunbo	1962
Aldington, Lord..........	1954
Alexander of Hillsborough, Earl..................	1929
Alexander of Tunis, Earl..	1952
Alexander, Sir Ulick....,	1952
Alport, Lord............	1934
Amery, Julian...........	1960
Amory, Viscount........	1953
Attlee, Earl.............	1935
Avon, Earl of............	1934
Azikiwe, Nnamdi........	1960
Baker, Philip J. Noel-....	1945
Balewa, Sir Abubakar Tafawa	1961
Balfour of Inchrye, Lord..	1941
Barnes, Alfred...........	1945
Barrowclough, Sir Harold	1954
Beaufort, Duke of.......	1936
Beaumont, Sir John......	1944
Beaverbrook, Lord.......	1918
Bellenger, Frederick John .	1946
Bevins, John Reginald....	1959
Birch, Nigel............	1955
Bottomley, Arthur George	1952
Bowden, Herbert William	1962
Boyd of Merton, Viscount	1951
Boyle, Sir Edward, Bt.....	1962
Brabazon of Tara, Lord...	1940
Brecon, Lord............	1960
Bridges, Lord............	1953
Brooke, Henry...........	1955
Brown, George Alfred....	1951
Bruce of Melbourne, Viscount.................	1923
Buccleuch and Queensberry, Duke of........	1937
Bucknill, Sir Alfred	1945
Butler, Richard Austen...	1939
Cadogan, Sir Alexander ..	1946
Campbell, Rt. Rev. Henry Colville Montgomery-.	1956
Campbell, Sir Ronald Ian.	1950
Canterbury, The Archbishop of	1956
Carpenter, John Archibald Boyd-..................	1954
Carr, Robert............	1963
Carrington, Lord	1959
Casey, Lord.............	1939
Chandos, Viscount.......	1940
Chatfield, Lord..........	1939

Churchill, Sir Winston Spencer	1907
Citrine, Lord	1940
Clayden, Sir John	1962
Clitheroe, Lord	1944
Clyde, Lord	1951
Cobbold, Lord	1959
Cohen, Lord	1946
Coleraine, Lord	1943
Colyton, Lord	1952
Craigton, Lord	1961
Crathorne, Lord	1951
Cross, Sir Ronald, Bt.	1940
Danckwerts, Sir Harold	1961
Davidson, Viscount	1928
Davies, Sir William Arthian	1961
Deedes, William Francis	1962
De La Warr, Earl	1936
De L'Isle, Viscount	1951
Denning, Lord	1948
Devlin, Lord	1960
Diefenbaker, John	1957
Dilhorne, Lord	1954
Diplock, Sir Kenneth	1961
Dixon, Sir Owen	1951
Donovan, Sir Terence	1960
Dundee, Earl of	1959
Eccles, Lord	1951
Ede, James Chuter	1944
Edwards, Ness	1947
Erroll, Frederick James	1960
Evatt, Herbert Vere	1942
Evershed, Lord	1947
Fadden, Sir Arthur	1942
Fisher of Lambeth, Lord	1939
Forde, Francis Michael	1944
Foster, Sir Harry Hylton-	1957
Franks, Lord	1949
Fraser, Hugh	1962
Godber, Joseph Bradshaw	1963
Goddard, Lord	1938
Gore, Sir David Ormsby-	1957
Grant, Lord	1958
Gray, Sir William Anstruther-	1962
Grenfell, David Rhys	1951
Gresson, Sir Kenneth	1962
Griffiths, James	1945
Grigg, Sir James	1942
Grimond, Joseph	1961
Guest, Lord	1960
Hailes, Lord	1951
Hailey, Lord	1949
Hailsham, Viscount (*Lord President*)	1956
Hall, Viscount	1942
Hamilton and Brandon, Duke of	1940
Hare, John Hugh	1955
Harlech, Lord	1927
Harman, Sir Charles	1959
Harrison, Sir Eric John	1952
Head, Viscount	1951
Headlam, Sir Cuthbert, Bt.	1945
Heald, Sir Lionel	1954
Heath, Edward Richard George	1955
Henderson, Lord	1950
Henderson, Arthur	1947
Hilbery, Sir Malcolm	1959
Hill of Luton, Lord	1963
Hobson, Sir John	1963
Hodson, Lord	1951
Holloway, Edward James	1950
Holt, Harold Edward	1953
Holyoake, Keith Jacka	1954
Home, Earl of	1951
Hope, Lord John	1959
Horsbrugh, Lady	1945
Howe, Earl	1929
Ilsley, James Lorimer	1946
Ingleby, Viscount	1943
Inman, Lord	1947
Isaacs, George Alfred	1945
Ismay, Lord	1951
Jay, Douglas	1952
Jenkins, Lord	1949
Johnston, Thomas	1931
Jones, Arthur Creech	1946
Jones, Aubrey	1955
Joseph, Sir Keith, Bt.	1962
Keith of Avonholm, Lord	1953
Key, Charles William	1947
Killearn, Lord	1941
Kilmuir, Earl of	1945
Kitto, Sir Frank	1962
Kotelawala, Sir John	1954
Lascelles, Sir Alan	1943
Latham, Sir John	1933
Lawson, Lord	1945
Leathers, Viscount	1941
Lee, Sir Frank	1962
Listowel, Earl of	1946
Lloyd, Geoffrey William	1943
Lloyd, John Selwyn Brooke	1951
London, The Bishop of	1961
Longford, Earl of	1948
Mabane, Lord	1944
MacAndrew, Lord	1952
McBride, Sir Philip	1959
McCorquodale of Newton, Lord	1945
MacDermott, Lord	1947
Macdonald of Gwaenysgor, Lord	1951
MacDonald, Malcolm	1935
McEwen, John	1953
McKell, Sir William	1948
Maclay, John Scott	1952
Macleod, Iain	1952
Macmillan, Harold	1942
Macpherson, Niall Malcolm Stewart	1962
McTiernan, Sir Edward	1962
Malvern, Viscount	1947
Margai, Sir Milton	1961
Margesson, Viscount	1933
Marples, Alfred Ernest	1957
Marquand, Hilary Adair	1949
Massey, Vincent	1941
Mathers, Lord	1947
Maudling, Reginald	1955
Menzies, Sir Douglas	1962
Menzies, Sir Robert	1937
Milligan, Lord	1955
Mills, Viscount	1957
Milner of Leeds, Lord	1945
Molson, Lord	1956
Monckton of Brenchley, Viscount	1951
Monsell, Viscount	1923
Morgan, Sir John Vaughan-	1961
Morris of Borth-y-Gest, Lord	1951
Morrison of Lambeth, Lord	1931
Morton of Henryton, Lord	1944
Mountbatten of Burma, Earl	1947
Munster, Earl of	1954
Nair, Sir Madhavan	1941
Nash, Walter	1946
Nathan, Lord	1946
Nkrumah, Kwame	1959
Noble, *Cdr.* Sir Allan Herbert Percy	1956
Noble, Michael Antony Cristobal	1962
Norfolk, Duke of	1936
Normanbrook, Lord	1953
Nugent, Sir Richard, Bt.	1962
Nutting, Harold Anthony	1954
Ogmore, Lord	1951
Ormerod, Sir Benjamin	1957
Owen, Sir William	1962
Paling, Wilfred	1944
Parker of Waddington, Lord	1954
Patrick, Lord	1949
Pearce, Lord	1957
Pearson, Sir Colin	1961
Pearson, Lester	1963
Perth, Earl of	1957
Poole, Lord	1963
Powell, Enoch	1960
Radcliffe, Viscount	1949
Rathcavan, Lord	1937
Rea, Lord	1962
Redmayne, Martin	1959
Reid, Lord	1941
Reith, Lord	1940
Renton, David	1962
Rippon, Aubrey Geoffrey Frederick	1962
Robens of Woldingham, Lord	1951
Robinson, Sir Roland	1962
Romer, Sir Charles	1951
Rosebery, Earl of	1945
Russell, Sir Charles	1962
St. Aldwyn, Earl	1959
St. Laurent, Louis Stephen	1940
Salisbury, Marquess of	1940
Salter, Lord	1941
Sandys, Duncan	1944
Scarbrough, Earl of	1952
Selborne, Earl of	1929
Selkirk, Earl of	1955
Sellers, Sir Frederic	1957
Shakespeare, Sir Geoffrey, Bt.	1945
Shawcross, Lord	1946
Shearer, Ian Hamilton	1962
Shinwell, Emanuel	1945
Silkin, Lord	1945
Simon, Sir Jocelyn	1961
Simonds, Viscount	1944
Slesser, Sir Henry	1929
Smith, Sir Ben	1943
Smith, Sir Derek Colclough Walker-, Bt.	1957
Smith, Dame Patricia Hornsby-	1959
Smith, Sir Reginald Dorman-	1939
Smyth, Sir John, Bt.	1962
Soames, Arthur Christopher John	1958
Soskice, Sir Frank	1948
Soulbury, Viscount	1939
Spens, Lord	1953
Stanhope, Earl	1929
Strathclyde, Lord	1953
Strauss, George Russell	1947
Stuart of Findhorn, Visct.	1939
Summerskill, Lady	1949
Swinton, Earl of	1922
Taylor, Sir Alan Russell	1962
Tenby, Viscount	1941
Thomas, Sir Godfrey, Bt.	1958
Thorneycroft, Peter	1951
Thurso, Viscount	1931
Touche, Sir Gordon	1959
Tredgold, Sir Robert	1957

Trevethin and Oaksey, Lord.......... 1944
Tucker, Lord.......... 1945
Turton Robert Hugh.... 1955
Upjohn, Sir Gerald....... 1960
Vanier, *Maj.-Gen.* Georges Philias.......... 1963
Vosper, Dennis Forwood.. 1957
Walker, Patrick Chrestien Gordon-.......... 1950
Wand, *Rt. Rev.* John William Charles....... 1945
Ward of Witley, Viscount 1957
Waterhouse, *Capt.* Charles 1945
Watkinson, Harold Arthur 1954
Welensky, Sir Roy...... 1960
Wheatley, Lord.. 1947
White, Henry Graham.... 1945
Williams of Barnburgh, Lord.......... 1941
Willink, Sir Henry Urmston, Bt.......... 1943
Willmer, Sir Henry Gordon 1958
Wilmot of Selmeston, Lord 1945
Wilson, James Harold 1947
Windeyer, Sir Victor..... 1962
Wood, Richard Frederick. 1959
Woodburn, Arthur...... 1947
Woolton, Earl of........ 1940
Wright, Lord.......... 1932
York, The Archbishop of. 1961
Younger, Kenneth....... 1951

Clerk of the Council, W. G. Agnew. *Deputy Clerk of the Council*, E. N. Landale.

THE PREFIX RIGHT HONOURABLE

"Right Honourable."—By long established custom, or courtesy, members of Her Majesty's Most Honourable Privy Council are entitled to be designated "The Right Honourable," but, in practice, this prefix is sometimes absorbed in other designations; for example, a Prince of the Blood admitted a Privy Councillor remains "His Royal Highness"; a Duke remains "His Grace"; a Marquess is still styled "Most Honourable". The style of all other Peers, whether Privy Councillors or not, is "Right Honourable", although it is more usual to describe them with the prefix "The", omitting the more elaborate styles. A Privy Councillor who is not a Peer should be addressed as The Right (or Rt.) Hon. ——. A Peer below the rank of Marquess who is a Privy Councillor should be addressed as The Right (or Rt.) Hon. the Lord (or Earl or Viscount) ——, P.C., or, less elaborately, The Lord (or Earl or Viscount) —— P.C.

THE DISTINGUISHED SERVICE ORDER (1886)—D.S.O.

Ribbon, Red, with Blue Edges.

Bestowed in recognition of especial services in action of commissioned officers in the Navy, Army and Royal Air Force and (1942) Mercantile Marine. The members are Companions only and rank immediately before the 4th Class of the Royal Victorian Order. A Bar may be awarded for any additional act of service.

THE IMPERIAL SERVICE ORDER (1902, enlarged 1912)—I.S.O.

Ribbon, Crimson, with Blue Centre.

Restricted to members of the administrative or clerical (clerk) branches of the Civil Service and consists of the SOVEREIGN and Companions (not exclusively male) to a number not exceeding 740, of whom 360 may belong to the Home Services, 180 to the services of Dominions and 200 to the services of the Colonies and Protectorates.

OTHER PRINCIPAL DECORATIONS AND MEDALS (in order of Precedence)

Victoria Cross.—1856.—V.C. *See* pp. 299-302.

George Cross.—1940.—G.C. *See* p. 302.

British Orders of Knighthood.

Royal Red Cross.—R.R.C. (Class I.).—For ladies, founded 1883.

Distinguished Service Cross.—1914.—D.S.C.—In substitution for the Conspicuous Service Cross, 1901; is for officers of the R.N. below the rank of Captain, and for Warrant Officers.

Military Cross.—Dec. 1914.—M.C.—Awarded to Captains, Lieutenants, and Warrant Officers (Cl. I.) in the Army and Indian and Colonial Forces.

Distinguished Flying Cross.—1918.—D.F.C.—For bestowal upon Officers and Warrant Officers in the Royal Air Force (and Fleet Air Arm from April 9, 1941) for acts of gallantry when flying in active operations against the enemy.

Air Force Cross.—1918.—A.F.C.—Instituted as preceding but for acts of courage or devotion to duty when flying, although not in active operations against the enemy (extended to Fleet Air Arm since April 9, 1941).

Royal Red Cross (Class II).

Order of British India.

Kaisar-i-Hind Medal.

Order of St. John.

Albert Medal.—A.M.—Dates from 1866, with extensions in 1867 and 1877, "For Gallantry in Saving Life at Sea" or "on Land."

Union of South Africa Queen's Medal for Bravery, in Gold.

Medal for Distinguished Conduct in the Field.—D.C.M.—Awarded to warrant officers, non-commissioned officers and men of the Army and R.A.F.

Conspicuous Gallantry Medal.—C.G.M.—Is bestowed upon warrant officers and men of the R.N., and since 1942 of Mercantile Marine and R.A.F.

The George Medal.—G.M.—Established by King George VI in 1940 is a recognition of acts of gallantry.

Queen's Police and Fire Services Medal for Gallantry.

The Edward Medal.—Established by King Edward VII in 1907, is a recognition of heroic acts performed by miners and quarrymen, or of others who have endangered their lives in rescuing those so employed.

Royal West African Frontier Force Distinguished Conduct Medal.

King's African Rifles Distinguished Conduct Medal.

Union of South Africa Queen's Medal for Bravery, in Silver.

Distinguished Service Medal.—1914.—D.S.M.—For chief petty officers, petty officers, men, and boys of all branches of the Royal Navy, and since 1942 of Mercantile Marine, to non-commissioned officers and men of the Royal Marines, and to all other persons holding corresponding positions in Her Majesty's Service afloat.

Military Medal.—M.M.—For warrant and non-commissioned officers and men of the Army, and since June 21, 1916, for serving women.

Distinguished Flying Medal.—1918.—D.F.M.—and the **Air Force Medal.**—A.F.M.—for warrant and non-commissioned officers and men for equivalent services as for D.F.C. and A.F.C. (extended to Fleet Air Arm, April 9, 1941).

Constabulary Medal (Ireland).

Medal for Saving Life at Sea.

Colonial Police Medal for Gallantry.

British Empire Medal.—B.E.M.—(formerly the Medal of the Order of the British Empire, for Meritorious Service; also includes the Medal of the Order awarded before Dec. 29, 1922).

Canada Medal.

Queen's Police, and Fire Services Medal, for Distinguished Service.

Queen's Medal for Chiefs.

War Medals and Stars (in order of date).

Polar Medals (in order of date).

Royal Victorian Medal (Gold, Silver and Bronze).

Imperial Service Medal.

Police Medals for Valuable Service.

Badge of Honour.

Jubilee, Coronation and Durbar Medals.

King George V, King George VI and Queen Elizabeth II, Long and Faithful Service Medals.

Long Service and Good Conduct Medal.

Naval Long Service and Good Conduct Medal.

Medal for Meritorious Service.

Royal Marine Meritorious Service Medal.

Royal Air Force Meritorious Service Medal.

Royal Air Force Long Service and Good Conduct Medal.

Royal West African Frontier Force Long Service and Good Conduct Medal.

King's African Rifles Long Service and Good Conduct Medal.

Police and Fire Brigade Long Service and Good Conduct Medal.

African Police Medal for Meritorious Services.

Colonial Police and Fire Brigades Long Service Medal.

Colonial Prison Service Medal.

Army Emergency Reserve Decoration.

Volunteer Officers' Decoration.—V.D.
Volunteer Long Service Medal.
Volunteer Officers' Decoration (for India and the Colonies).
Volunteer Long Service Medal (for India and the Colonies).
Colonial Auxiliary Forces Officers' Decoration.
Colonial Auxiliary Forces Long Service Medal.
Medal for Good Shooting (Naval).
Militia Long Service Medal.
Imperial Yeomanry Long Service Medal.
Territorial Decoration.—1908.—T.D.
Efficiency Decoration.—E.D.
Territorial Efficiency Medal.
Efficiency Medal.
Special Reserve Long Service and Good Conduct Medal.
Decoration for Officers, Royal Naval Reserve.—1910.—R.D.
Decoration for Officers, R.N.V.R.—V.R.D.
Royal Naval Reserve Long Service and Good Conduct Medal.
R.N.V.R. Long Service and Good Conduct Medal.
Royal Naval Auxiliary Sick Berth Reserve Long Service and Good Conduct Medal.
Royal Fleet Reserve Long Service and Good Conduct Medal.
Royal Naval Wireless Auxiliary Reserve Long Service and Good Conduct Medal.
Air Efficiency Award.—1942.
The Queen's Medal.—(For Champion Shots in the Army, Territorial Army and R.A.F.)
Cadet Forces Medal.
Coast Life Saving Corps Long Service Medal.
Special Constabulary Long Service Medal.
Royal Observer Corps Medal.
Civil Defence Long Service Medal.
Service Medal of the Order of St. John.
Badge of the Order of the League of Mercy.
Voluntary Medical Service Medal.—1932.
Woman's Voluntary Service Medal.
Colonial Special Constabulary Medal.
Foreign Orders, Decorations and Medals (in order of date).

Orders of Chivalry

THE MOST NOBLE ORDER OF THE GARTER (1348)—K.G.

Ribbon, Garter Blue. *Motto*, Honi soit qui mal y pense (*Shame on him who thinks evil of it*).
The number of Knights Companions is limited to 26.

SOVEREIGN OF THE ORDER—THE QUEEN

Ladies of the Garter—H.M. QUEEN ELIZABETH THE QUEEN MOTHER, 1936.
H.M. THE QUEEN OF THE NETHERLANDS, 1958.

ROYAL KNIGHTS
H.R.H. the Prince Philip, Duke of Edinburgh, 1947.
H.R.H. the Prince of Wales, 1958.
H.R.H. the Duke of Gloucester, 1921.
H.R.H. the Duke of Windsor, 1910.

EXTRA KNIGHTS
H.M. King Leopold III, 1935.
H.M. the King of Denmark, 1951.
H.M. the King of Sweden, 1954.
H.I.M. the Emperor of Ethiopia, 1954.
H.M. the King of Norway, 1959.
H.M. the King of the Belgians, 1963.
H.M. the King of the Hellenes, 1963.
H.R.H. Prince Paul of Yugoslavia, 1939.

KNIGHTS COMPANIONS
The Earl Stanhope, 1934.
The Duke of Norfolk, 1937.
The Duke of Beaufort, 1937.
The Marquess of Salisbury, 1946.
The Earl Mountbatten of Burma, 1946.
The Viscount Portal of Hungerford, 1946.
The Earl Alexander of Tunis, 1946.
The Viscount Montgomery of Alamein, 1946.
The Duke of Portland, 1948.
The Lord Harlech, 1948.
The Earl of Scarbrough, 1948.
The Lord Cranworth, 1948.
The Duke of Wellington, 1951.
Sir Winston Churchill, 1953.
The Earl of Avon, 1954.
The Earl of Iveagh, 1955.
The Earl Attlee, 1956.
The Lord Ismay, 1957.
The Lord Middleton, 1957.
The Viscount Slim, 1959.
The Duke of Northumberland, 1959.
The Earl of Radnor, 1960.
The Lord Digby, 1960.
The Lord Wakehurst, 1962.

Prelate, The Bishop of Winchester.
Chancellor, The Marquess of Salisbury, K.G., P.C.
Register, The Dean of Windsor.
Garter King of Arms, Sir Anthony Richard Wagner, K.C.V.O., F.S.A.
Usher of the Black Rod, Air Chief Marshal Sir George Mills, G.C.B., D.F.C.
Secretary, Hon. Sir George Rothe Bellew, K.C.B., K.C.V.O., F.S.A.

THE MOST ANCIENT AND MOST NOBLE ORDER OF THE THISTLE (1687)—K.T.

Ribbon, Green. *Motto*, Nemo me impune lacessit (*No one provokes me with impunity*).
The number of Knights (other than Royal Knights) is limited to 16.

SOVEREIGN OF THE ORDER—THE QUEEN

Lady of the Thistle—H.M. QUEEN ELIZABETH THE QUEEN MOTHER, 1937.

ROYAL KNIGHTS
H.R.H. the Prince Philip, Duke of Edinburgh, 1952.
H.R.H. the Duke of Gloucester, 1933.
H.R.H. the Duke of Windsor, 1922.

EXTRA KNIGHT
H.M. the King of Norway, 1962.

KNIGHTS COMPANIONS
The Earl of Elgin and Kincardine, 1933.
The Viscount Thurso, 1941.
The Earl of Airlie, 1942.
The Earl of Rosebery, 1947.
The Duke of Buccleuch and Queensberry, 1949.
The Duke of Hamilton and Brandon, 1951.
The Earl of Haddington, 1951.
The Earl of Crawford and Balcarres, 1955.
The Lord Bilsland, 1955.
Sir John Stirling of Fairburn, 1956.
The Lord Mathers, 1956.
The Lord Kinnaird, 1957.
The Lord Rowallan, 1957.
The Earl of Home, 1962
Sir Robert Menzies, 1963

Chancellor, The Earl of Airlie, K.T., G.C.V.O., M.C.
Dean, Very Rev. Charles Laing Warr, K.C.V.O., D.D., LL.D.
Lord Lyon King of Arms and Secretary, Sir Thomas Innes of Learney, K.C.V.O.
Usher of the Green Rod, Sir Reginald Graham of Larbert, Bt., V.C., O.B.E.

THE MOST ILLUSTRIOUS ORDER OF SAINT PATRICK (1783)—K.P.

Ribbon, Sky Blue. *Motto*, Quis separabit? (*Who shall separate?*) (No conferments since 1934).

SOVEREIGN OF THE ORDER—THE QUEEN

ROYAL KNIGHTS
H.R.H. the Duke of Gloucester, 1934.
H.R.H. the Duke of Windsor, 1927.

Norroy and Ulster King of Arms Registrar and Knight Attendant, Aubrey John Toppin, C.V.O., F.S.A.

THE MOST HONOURABLE ORDER OF THE BATH (1725)

Ribbon, Crimson, *Motto*, Tria juncta in uno (*Three joined in one*). (Remodelled 1815, and enlarged thirteen times since. The Order is divided into civil and military divisions.)

G.C.B. Mil.

G.C.B. Civ.

K.C.B. Mil.

K.C.B. Civ.

C.B. Mil.

THE SOVEREIGN; *Great Master and Principal Knight Grand Cross*, Field Marshal H.R.H. the Duke of Gloucester, K.G., P.C., K.T., K.P., G.C.B., G.C.M.G., G.C.V.O.; *Dean of the Order*, The Dean of Westminster; *Bath King of Arms*, Air Chief Marshal Sir James Robb, G.C.B., K.B.E. D.S.O., D.F.C. A.F.C.; *Registrar and Secretary*, Maj.-Gen. D. N. Wimberley, C.B., D.S.O., M.C.; *Genealogist*, Sir Anthony Wagner, K.C.V.O., *Gentleman Usher of the Scarlet Rod*, Rear-Adm. R. St. V. Sherbrooke, V.C., C.B., D.S.O.; *Deputy Secretary*, The Secretary, Central Chancery of the Orders of Knighthood; *Chancery*, Central Chancery of the Orders of Knighthood, 8 Buckingham Gate, S.W.1.—G.C.B., Knight Grand Cross; K.C.B., Knight Commander; C.B. Companion.

THE ORDER OF MERIT (1902)—O.M. *Ribbon*, Blue and Crimson.

O.M. Mil.

O.M.Civ.

This Order is designed as a special distinction for eminent men and women—without conferring a knighthood upon them. The Order is limited in numbers to 24, with the addition of foreign honorary members. Membership is of two kinds, Military and Civil, the badge of the former having crossed swords, and the latter oak leaves. Membership is denoted by the suffix O.M., which follows the first class of the Order of the Bath and precedes the letters designating membership of the inferior classes of the Bath and all classes of the lesser Orders of Knighthood.

John Masefield, 1935.
Admiral of the Fleet the Lord Chatfield, 1939.
Marshal of the Royal Air Force the Lord Newall, 1940.
The Lord Adrian, 1942.
Sir Henry Hallett Dale, 1944.
Sir Winston Leonard Spencer Churchill, 1946.
Marshal of the Royal Air Force the Visct. Portal of Hungerford, 1946
Thomas Stearns Eliot, 1948.
Sir Robert Robinson, 1949.
The Earl Russell, 1949.
Sir Alexander George Montagu Cadogan, 1951.
The Earl Attlee, 1951.
Wilder Graves Penfield, 1953.
The Lord Hailey, 1956.
Sir John Douglas Cockcroft, 1957.
Sir (Frank) Macfarlane Burnet, 1958.
Field Marshal the Earl Alexander of Tunis, 1959.
Sir Cyril Hinshelwood, 1960.
Graham Vivian Sutherland, 1960.
Sir Basil Urwin Spence, 1962
Sir Geoffrey de Havilland, 1962.
Sir Owen Dixon, 1963.

Honorary Members, Dwight David Eisenhower, 1945. Dr. Albert Schweitzer, 1955. Dr. Sarvepalli Radhakrishnan, 1963.
Secretary and Registrar, (vacant).

THE MOST EXALTED ORDER OF THE STAR OF INDIA (1861).

G.C.S.I.

Ribbon, Light Blue, with White Edges. *Motto*, Heaven's Light our Guide.

THE SOVEREIGN; *Registrar*, The Secretary of the Central Chancery of the Orders of Knighthood; G.C.S.I., Knight Grand Commander; K.C.S.I., Knight Commander; C.S.I., Companion. No conferments made since 1947.

THE MOST DISTINGUISHED ORDER OF ST. MICHAEL AND ST. GEORGE (1818).

G.C.M.G.

Ribbon, Saxon Blue, with Scarlet Centre. *Motto*, Auspicium melioris ævi (*Token of a better age*).

THE SOVEREIGN; *Grand Master*, The Earl Alexander of Tunis, K.G., P.C., G.C.B., O.M., G.C.M.G., C.S.I., D.S.O., M.C.; *Prelate*, The Bishop of Birmingham; *Chancellor*, The Lord Norrie, G.C.M.G., G.C.V.O., C.B., D.S.O., M.C.; *Secretary*, Sir Hilton Poynton, K.C.M.G.; *Registrar*, Sir Saville Garner, K.C.M.G.; *King of Arms*, The Lord Inchyra, G.C.M.G., C.V.O.; *Gentleman Usher of the Blue Rod*, Sir George Beresford Stooke, K.C.M.G.; *Chancery*, Colonial Office, S.W.1.—G.C.M.G., Knight Grand Cross; K.C.M.G., Knight Commander; C.M.G., Companion.

THE MOST EMINENT ORDER OF THE INDIAN EMPIRE (1877).

G.C.I.E.

Ribbon, Imperial Purple. *Motto*, Imperatricis auspiciis (*Under the auspices of the Empress*).

THE SOVEREIGN; *Registrar*, The Secretary of the Central Chancery of the Orders of Knighthood; G.C.I.E., Knight Grand Commander; K.C.I.E., Knight Commander; C.I.E., Companion. No conferments made since 1947.

THE ROYAL VICTORIAN ORDER (1896).

Ribbon, Blue, with Red and White Edges. *Motto*, Victoria.

THE SOVEREIGN; *Grand Master*, H.M. Queen Elizabeth the Queen Mother; *Chancellor*, The Lord Chamberlain; *Secretary*, The Keeper of the Privy Purse; *Registrar*, The Secretary of the Central Chancery of the Orders of Knighthood; *Chaplain*, The Rev. R. L. Roberts; G.C.V.O., Knight or Dame Grand Cross; K.C.V.O., Knight Commander; D.C.V.O., Dame Commander; C.V.O., Commander; M.V.O., Member, marked 4th or 5th Class.

THE ROYAL VICTORIAN CHAIN (1902).

Founded by King Edward VII, in 1902. It confers no precedence on its holders.

H.M. THE QUEEN

H.M. QUEEN ELIZABETH THE QUEEN MOTHER (1937).

H.R.H. the Duke of Windsor (1921).
H.R.H. the Duke of Gloucester (1932).
H.E.H. The Nizam of Hyderabad and Berar (1946).
Lord Fisher of Lambeth (1949).
Sir John Weir (1949).
The Duke of Norfolk (1953).
The Duke of Beaufort (1953).
The Rt. Hon. Vincent Massey (1960).
The Earl of Scarbrough (1963).
H.M. The King of Sweden (1923).
H.I.M. The Emperor of Ethiopia (1930).
H.R.H. Prince Paul of Yugoslavia (1934).
H.M. King Leopold III (1937).
H.I.M. The Shahinshah of Persia (1948).
H.M. Queen Juliana of the Netherlands (1950).
H.M. The King of Norway (1955).
President Craveiro Lopes (1957).
H.M. the King of Denmark (1957). [(1960).
President Charles de Gaulle
H.M. the King of Thailand (1960).
H.M. The King of Nepal (1961).

G.B.E.

THE MOST EXCELLENT ORDER OF THE BRITISH EMPIRE (1917).

K.B.E.

Ribbon, Rose pink edged with pearl grey with vertical pearl stripe in centre (Military Division); without vertical pearl stripe (Civil Division). *Motto*, For God and the Empire. THE SOVEREIGN: *Grand Master*, H.R.H. the Prince Philip, Duke of Edinburgh K.G., P.C., K.T., G.B.E.; *Prelate*, The Bishop of London; *King of Arms*, Air Marshal Sir Roderick Carr, K.B.E., C.B., D.F.C., A.F.C. *Registrar*, The Secretary of the Central Chancery of the Orders of Knighthood; *Secretary*, The Permanent Secretary to the Treasury; *Dean*, The Dean of St. Paul's; *Gentleman Usher of the Purple Rod*, The Viscount Silsoe, G.B.E., M.C., T.D., Q.C. *Sub-Dean*, The Rev. Canon A. F. Hood, M.A. *Chancery*, Central Chancery of the Orders of Knighthood, 8 Buckingham Gate, S.W.1. G.B.E., Knight Grand Cross or Dame Grand Cross; K.B.E., Knight Commander; D.B.E., Dame Commander; C.B.E., Commander; O.B.E., Officer; M.B.E., Member. The Order was divided into *Military* and *Civil* divisions in Dec. 1918.

ORDER OF THE COMPANIONS OF HONOUR (June 4, 1917)—C.H.

Ribbon, Carmine, with Gold Edges.

This Order consists of one Class only and carries with it no title. It ranks after the 1st Class of the Order of the British Empire, *i.e.*, Knights and Dames Grand Cross (Mil. and Civ. Div.). The number of awards is limited to 65 and the Order is open to both sexes. *Secretary and Registrar*, The Secretary of the Central Chancery of the Orders of Knighthood.

Adams, William George Stewart, 1936.
Alexander of Hillsborough, The Earl, 1941.
Astor, Nancy, Viscountess, 1937.
Attlee, The Earl, 1945.
Beazley, Sir John, 1959.
Boyd of Merton, The Viscount, 1960.
Britten, Edward Benjamin, 1953.
Bruce of Melbourne, The Viscount, 1927.
Butler, Rt. Hon. Richard Austen, 1954.
Casey, The Lord, 1944.
Cecil, Lord David Gascoyne, 1949.
Churchill, Rt. Hon. Sir Winston S., 1922.
Clark, Sir Kenneth, 1959.
Clayton, Rev. Philip T. B., 1933.
Craig, Edward Henry Gordon, 1956.
Crerar, *General* Henry Duncan Graham, 1945.
Davidson, The Viscount, 1923.
Dodd, Rev. Charles Harold, 1961.
Ede, Rt. Hon. James Chuter, 1953.
Forster, Edward Morgan, 1953.
Fraser of Lonsdale, The Lord, 1953.
Gooch, George Peabody, 1939.
Hailes, The Lord, 1962.
Hill, *Prof.* Archibald Vivian, 1946.
Hives, The Lord, 1943.
Holyoake, Rt. Hon. Keith Jacka, 1963.
Ismay, *General* The Lord, 1945.
Johnston, Rt. Hon. Thomas, 1953.
Kotelawala, Rt. Hon. Sir John, 1956.
Layton, The Lord, 1919.
Leathers, The Viscount, 1943.
Limerick, The Earl of, 1961.
Lloyd, Rt. Hon. Selwyn, 1962.
Maclay, Rt. Hon. John, 1962.
McNaughton, *General* Andrew George Latta, 1946.
Malvern, The Viscount, 1944.
Mann, Arthur Henry, 1941.
Martin, Rev. Hugh, 1955.
Massey, Rt. Hon. Vincent, 1946.
Matthews, Very Rev. Walter Robert, 1962.
Maugham, William Somerset, 1954.
Menzies, Rt. Hon. Sir Robert, 1951.
Moore, Henry Spencer, 1955.
Morrison of Lambeth, The Lord, 1951.
Nash, Rt. Hon. Walter, 1959.
Nuffield, The Viscount, 1958.
Raliman, Tunku Abdul, 1961.
Selborne, The Earl of, 1945.
Sitwell, Sir Osbert, Bt., 1958.
Stuart of Findhorn, The Viscount, 1957.
Swinton, The Earl of, 1943.
Toynbee, *Prof.* Arnold Joseph, 1956.
Waley, Arthur David, 1956.
Watkinson, Rt. Hon. Harold, 1962.
Wilson, *Prof.* John Dover, 1936.
Woolton, The Earl of, 1942.
Honarary Members, M. René Massigli, 1954; M. Paul-Henri Spaak, 1963.

THE ROYAL ORDER OF VICTORIA AND ALBERT (for Ladies)—V.A.

Instituted in 1862, and enlarged in 1864, 1865, and 1880, but no conferments have been made since 1902. Badge, in the first three Classes a medallion of Queen Victoria and the Prince Consort, differing in the width and jewelling of the border as the Classes descend, whilst the fourth substitutes a jewelled cipher. All four are surmounted by a crown, which is attached to a bow of white moiré ribbon. The honour does not confer any rank or title upon the recipient.

FIRST CLASS.

H.R.H. the Princess Alice, Countess of Athlone.

SECOND CLASS.

H.R.H. the Princess Alfonso d'Orleans-Bourbon (the Infanta Beatrix of Spain).
Lady Victoria Patricia Helena Ramsay.

THE IMPERIAL ORDER OF THE CROWN OF INDIA (for Ladies)—C.I.

Instituted January 1, 1878. Badge, the royal cipher in jewels within an oval, surmounted by an Heraldic Crown and attached to a bow of light blue watered ribbon, edged white. The honour does not confer any rank or title upon the recipient. No conferments have been made since 1948.

H.M. THE QUEEN, 1947.
H.M. Queen Elizabeth the Queen Mother, 1931.
H.R.H. the Princess Margaret, Countess of Snowdon, 1947.
H.R.H. the Princess Royal, 1919.
H.R.H. the Duchess of Gloucester, 1937.
H.R.H. Princess Marina, Duchess of Kent, 1937.
H.H. Maharani Sahab Chimna Bai Gaekwar of Baroda, 1892.
Lady Victoria Patricia Helena Ramsay, 1911.
Margaret Etrenne Hannah, Marchioness of Crewe, 1911.
Dorothy Evelyn Augusta, Countess of Halifax, 1926.
Pamela, Countess of Lytton, 1927.
H.H. Maharani Regent of Travancore, 1929.
Doreen Maud, Marchioness of Linlithgow, 1936.
Doreen Geraldine, Dowager Baroness Brabourne, 1937.
Eugenie Marie, Countess Wavell, 1943.
Florence Amery, 1945.
H.H. Maharani Tara Devi of Jammu and Kashmir, 1946.
Agnes Anne, Baroness Clydesmuir, 1948.

Baronets, Knights Grand Cross, Knights Grand Commanders, Knights Commanders and Knights Bachelor

Badge of Baronets of England, Great Britain, U.K., (and Ireland marked I.).

Badge of Baronets of Scotland or Nova Scotia (marked S.).

NOTES CONCERNING BARONETS

Clause II. of the Royal Warrant of February 8, 1910, ordains as follows:—"That no person whose name is not entered upon the Official Roll shall be received as a Baronet, or shall be addressed or mentioned by that title in any Civil or Military Commission, Letters Patent or other official document." When an obelisk (†) precedes a name it indicates that, *at the time of going to press*, the Baronet concerned has not been registered on the Official Roll of the Baronetage. The date of creation of the Baronetcy is given in parenthesis ( ).

Baronets are addressed as "Sir" (with Christian name) and in writing as "Sir Robert *A*—, Bt." Baronets' wives are addressed (formally) as "Your Ladyship" or "Lady *A*—," without any Christian name unless a daughter of a Duke, Marquess or Earl, in which case "The Lady Mary *A*—"; if daughter of a Viscount or Baron "The Hon. Lady *A*—."

NOTES CONCERNING KNIGHTS GRAND CROSS, ETC.

Knights Grand Cross, Knights Grand Commanders and Knights Commanders are addressed in the same manner as Baronets (*q.v.*), but in writing the appropriate initials (G.C.B., K.C.B., &c.) are appended to surname in place of "Bt." Knights Bachelor are addressed as "Sir —— (first or Christian name)" and in writing as "Sir A—— B——." The wife of a Knight Grand Cross, Knight Grand Commander, Knight Commander or Knight Bachelor is addressed as stated for the wife of a Baronet.

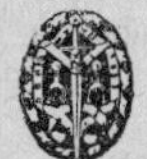

NOTES CONCERNING KNIGHTS BACHELOR

The Knights Bachelor do not constitute a Royal Order, but comprise the surviving representation of the ancient State Orders of Knighthood. The Register of Knights Bachelor, instituted by James I. in the 17th century, lapsed. and in 1908 a voluntary Association under the title of "The Society of Knights" (now "The Imperial Society of Knights Bachelor" by Royal command) was formed with the primary objects of continuing the various registers dating from 1257 and obtaining the uniform registration of every created Knight. In 1926 a design for a badge to be worn by Knights Bachelor was approved and adopted, a miniature reproduction being shown above. The Officers of the Society are:—*Knight Principal*, Sir Anthony Wagner, K.C.V.O., *Deputy Knight Principal*, Hon. Sir George Bellew, K.C.B., K.C.V.O.; *Hon. Registrar*, Sir John Weir Russell; *Clerk*, Mrs. Rodney; *Registry and Library*, 21 Old Buildings, Lincoln's Inn, W.C.1.

BARONETAGE AND KNIGHTAGE

(Revised to Aug. 9, 1963)

Peers are not included in this list

A full entry in italic type indicates that the recipient of a Knighthood died during the year in which the honour was conferred. The name is included for purposes of record.

Abayomi, Sir Kofo Adekunle, Kt.
Abbiss, Sir George, Kt., O.B.E.
Abdy, Sir Robert Henry Edward, Bt. (1850).
Abell, Sir Anthony Foster, K.C.M.G.
Abell, Sir George Edmond Brackenbury, K.C.I.E., O.B.E.
Abercromby, *Col.* Sir George William, Bt., D.S.O. (S. 1636).
Abrahall, Sir Theo Chandos Hoskyns-, Kt., C.M.G.
Abrahams, Sir Adolphe, Kt., O.B.E., M.D.
Acheson, Sir James Glasgow, Kt., C.I.E.
Ackroyd, Sir Cuthbert Lowell, Bt. (1956).
Acland, Sir Richard Thomas Dyke, Bt. (1644).
Acland, Sir William Henry Dyke, Bt., M.C., A.F.C., T.D. (1890).
Acutt, Sir Keith Courtney K.B.E.
Adair, *Maj.-Gen.* Sir Allan Henry Shafto, Bt., C.B., C.V.O., D.S.O., M.C. (1838).
Adam, *General* Sir Ronald Forbes, Bt., G.C.B., D.S.O., O.B.E. (1917).
Adams, Sir Ernest Charles, Kt., C.B.E.
Adams, *Hon.* Sir Francis Boyd, Kt.
Adams, Sir Grantley Herbert, Kt., C.M.G., Q.C.
Adams, Sir Maurice Edward, K.B.E.
Adcock, Sir Frank Ezra, Kt., O.B.E., F.B.A.
Adcock, Sir Robert Henry, Kt., C.B.E.

Addis, Sir William, K.B.E., C.M.G.
Adeane, *Lt.-Col. Rt. Hon.* Sir Michael Edward, G.C.V.O., K.C.B.
Adeane, *Col.* Sir Robert Philip Wyndham, Kt., O.B.E.
Ademola, *Rt. Hon.* Sir Adetokunbo Adegboyega, Kt.
Adjaye, Sir Edward Otchere Asafu-, Kt.
Agarwala, *Hon.* Sir Clifford Manmohan, Kt.
Agnew, Sir Fulque Melville Gerald Noel, Bt. (S 1629).
Agnew, Sir (John) Anthony Stuart, Bt. (1895).
Agnew, *Cdr.* Sir Peter Garnett, Bt., M.P. (1957).
Aikman, Sir Alexander, Kt., C.I.E.
Ainley, Sir (Alfred) John, Kt., M.C.
Ainscough, Sir Thomas Martland, Kt., C.B.E.
Ainsworth, Sir Thomas, Bt. (1917).
Aird, *Col.* Sir John Renton, Bt., M.V.O., M.C. (1901).
Airey, *Lt.-Gen.* Sir Terence Sydney, K.C.M.G., C.B., C.B.E.
Aitchison, Sir Charles Walter de Lancey, Bt. (1938).
Aitchison, *Capt.* Sir David, K.C.V.O.
Aitken, Sir Robert Stevenson, Kt., M.D., D.Phil.
Aitken, Sir William Traven, K.B.E., M.P.
Alban, Sir Frederick John, Kt., C.B.E.
Albery, Sir Bronson (James), Kt.
Albery, Sir Irving James, Kt., M.C.
Albu, Sir George, Bt. (1912).
Alderson, Sir Harold George, Kt., M.B.E.
Aldridge, Sir Frederick, Kt.
Alexander, Sir Charles Gundry, Bt. (1945).
Alexander, Sir Claud Hagart-, Bt. (1886).
Alexander, Sir Desmond William Lionel Cable, Bt. (1809).
Alexander, Sir Douglas Hamilton, Bt. (1921).
Alexander, *Maj. Rt.Hon.* Sir Ulick, G.C.B., G.C.V.O., C.M.G., O.B.E.
Alexander, Sir William Picken, Kt., Ph.D.
Alford, Sir Robert Edmund, K.B.E., C.M.G.
Alison, *Cdr.* Sir Archibald, Bt., O.B.E., R.N. (1852).
Allan, Sir Henry Ralph Moreton Havelock-, Bt. (1858).
Allan, Sir Robert George, Kt., C.I.E.
Allchin, Sir Geoffrey Cuthbert, K.B.E., C.M.G., M.C.
Allen, Sir Carleton Kemp, Kt., M.C., Q.C.
Allen, Sir Donald Richard, Kt., O.B.E., M.C.
Allen, Sir George Vance, Kt., C.B.E.
Allen, Sir Richard Hugh Sedley, K.C.M.G.
Allen, Sir Roger, K.C.M.G.
Allen, *Col.* Sir Stephen Shepherd, K.B.E., C.M.G., D.S.O., V.D.
Allen, Sir (William) Denis, K.C.M.G., C.B.
Allen, Sir William Kenneth Gwynne, Kt.
Alleyne, *Capt.* Sir John Meynell, Bt., D.S.O., D.S.C., R.N. (1769).
Allfrey, *Lt.-Gen.* Sir Charles Walter, K.B.E., C.B., D.S.O., M.C.
Allison, Sir (William) John, K.B.E.
Allsop, *Hon.* Sir James Joseph Whittlesea, Kt.
Allum, Sir John Andrew Charles, Kt., C.B.E.
Almond, Sir James, Kt.
Aluwihare, Sir Richard, K.C.M.G., C.B.E.
Amcotts, *Lt.-Col.* Sir Weston Cracroft-, Kt., M.C.
Ameer Ali, Sir Torick, Kt.
Amies, *Prof.* Sir Arthur Barton Pilgrim, Kt., C.M.G.
Amory, Sir John Heathcoat-, Bt. (1874).
Anderson, Sir Alexander James, Kt., C.S.I., V.D.
Anderson, Sir Austin Innes, Kt.
Anderson, Sir Colin Skelton, Kt.
Anderson, Sir David Stirling, Kt., Ph.D.
Anderson, *Lt.-Gen.* Sir Desmond Francis, K.B.E., C.B., C.M.G., D.S.O.
Anderson, Sir Donald Forsyth, Kt.
Anderson, Sir Duncan Law, K.B.E., T.D.
Anderson, Sir Edward Arthur, Kt.
Anderson, Sir Gilmour Menzies, Kt., C.B.E.
Anderson, Sir James Drummond, K.C.I.E.
Anderson, Sir John, K.B.E., C.B.
Anderson, *Lt.-Gen*, Sir John D'Arcy, K.C.B., C.B.E., D.S.O.
Anderson, Sir Kenneth, K.B.E., C.B.
Anderson, *Lt.-Gen.* Sir Richard Neville, K.C.B., C.B.E., D.S.O.
Andrew, Sir (George) Herbert, K.C.M.G., C.B.
Andrew, Sir John, K.B.E.
Andrewes, Sir Christopher Howard, Kt., M.D., F.R.S.
Andrewes, *Admiral* Sir William Gerrard, K.B.E., C.B., D.S.O.
Andrews, Sir Edwin Arthur Chapman-, K.C.M.G., O.B.E.
Andrews, Sir Ernest Herbert, Kt., C.B.E.
Andrews, Sir (William) Linton, Kt.
Angas, Sir John Keith, Kt.
Angell, Sir Norman, Kt.
Ankole, The Omugabe of, Kt.
Anson, Sir (George) Wilfrid, Kt.
Anson, *Cdr.* Sir Peter, Bt., R.N. (1831).
Ansorge, Sir Eric Cecil, Kt., C.S.I., C.I.E.
Anstice, *Vice-Adm.* Sir Edmund Walter, K.C.B.
Anstruther, Sir Ralph Hugo, Bt., M.C. (S 1694).
Anstruther, Sir Windham Eric Francis Carmichael-, Bt. (S. 1700; G.B. 1798).
Anthony, Sir Michael Mobolaji Bank-, K.B.E.
Antrobus, Sir Philip Humphrey, Bt., M.C. (1815).
Appleby, Sir Robert Rowland, K.B.E.
Appleton, Sir Edward Victor, G.B.E., K.C.B., D.Sc., F.R.S.
Arbuckle, Sir William Forbes, K.B.E., C.B.
Arbuthnot, Sir Hugh Fitzgerald, Bt. (1823).
Archdale, *Comdr.* Sir Edward Folmer, Bt. D.S.C., R.N. (1928).
Archer, Sir Clyde Vernon Harcourt, Kt.
Archer, Sir Geoffrey Francis, K.C.M.G.
Archey, Sir Gilbert Edward, Kt., C.B.E.
Arkell, *Capt.* Sir (Thomas) Noel, Kt.
Armer, Sir (Isaac) Frederick, K.B.E., C.B., M.C.
Armitage, *General* Sir (Charles) Clement, K.C.B., C.M.G., D.S.O.
Armitage, Sir Robert Perceval, K.C.M.G., M.B.E.
Armstrong, Sir Andrew St. Clare, Bt. (1841).
Armstrong, Sir Godfrey George, Kt., O.B.E., M.C., V.D.
Armstrong, Sir John Dunamace Heaton-, Kt., M.V.O.
Armstrong, Sir Thomas Henry Wait, Kt., D.MUS.
Armstrong, Sir William, K.C.B., M.V.O.
Armytage, *Capt.* Sir (John) Lionel, Bt. (1738).
Arnold, Sir William Henry, Kt., C.B.E.
Arnott, Sir Robert John, Bt. (1896).
Arrowsmith, Sir Edwin Porter, K.C.M.G.
Arthur, Sir Basil Malcolm, Bt. (1841).
Arthur, Sir (Oswald) Raynor, K.C.M.G., C.V.O.
Arundell, *Brig.* Sir Robert Duncan Harris, K.C.M.G., O.B.E.
Ashbridge, Sir Noel, Kt.
Ashburnham, Sir Denny Reginald, Bt. (1661).
Ashby, Sir Eric, Kt., D.Sc., F.R.S.
Ashenheim, Sir Neville Noel, Kt., C.B.E.
Ashton, Sir (Arthur) Leigh (Bolland), Kt.
Ashton, Sir Frederick William Mallandaine, Kt., C.B.E.
Ashton, Sir Hubert, K.B.E., M.C., M.P.
Ashton, Sir John William, Kt., O.B.E.
Ashwin, Sir Bernard Carl, K.B.E., C.M.G.
Ashworth, *Hon.* Sir John Percy, Kt., M.B.E.
Aske, Sir Conan, Bt., (1922).
Astley, Sir Francis Jacob Dugdale, Bt. (1821).
Atcherley, *Air Marshal* Sir Richard Llewellyn Roger, K.B.E., C.B., A.F.C.
Atkinson, Sir Cyril, Kt.
Atkinson, *Hon.* Sir Fenton, Kt.
Atkinson, Sir (John) Kenneth, Kt.

Attygalle, *Hon.* Sir Nicholas, Kt.
Auchinleck, *Field Marshal* Sir Claude John Eyre, G.C.B., G.C.I.E., C.S.I., D.S.O., O.B.E.
Austin, Sir John (Byron Fraser), Bt. (1894).
Austin, Sir Thomas, K.C.I.E.
Axon, Sir Albert Edwin, K.B.E.
Aykroyd, Sir Alfred Hammond, Bt. (1920).
Aykroyd, Sir Cecil William, Bt. (1929).
Aylmer, Sir Fenton Gerald, Bt. (I 1622).
Aylwen, Sir George, Bt. (1949).
Aynsley, Sir Charles Murray Murray-, Kt.
Ayre, Sir Wilfrid, Kt.
Ayres, Sir Reginald John, K.B.E., C.B.
Babington, *Rt. Hon.* Sir Anthony Brutus, Kt., Q.C.
Babington, *Air Marshal* Sir Philip, K.C.B., M.C., A.F.C.
Backhouse, Sir Jonathan Roger, Bt. (1901).
Bacon, Sir Edmund Castell, Bt., O.B.E., T.D. *Premier Baronet of England* (1611 and 1627).
Baddeley, Sir Frank Morrish, K.B.E., C.M.G.
Baddeley, Sir John Beresford, Bt. (1922).
Badenoch, Sir (Alexander) Cameron, K.C.I.E., C.S.I.
Bagge, Sir (John) Picton, Bt., C.M.G. (1867).
Bagrit, Sir Leon, Kt.
Baguley, Sir John Minty, Kt.
Bahawalpur, *Lt.-Gen.* H.H. the Amir of, G.C.S.I., G.C.I.E., K.C.V.O.
Bahr, Sir Philip Manson-, Kt. C.M.G., D.S.O., M.D.
Bailey, Sir Derrick Thomas Louis, Bt., D.F.C. (1919).
Bailey, Sir Donald Coleman, Kt., O.B.E.
Bailey, Sir Edward Battersby, Kt., M.C., D.SC., F.R.S.
Bailey, Sir George Edwin, Kt., C.B.E.
Bailey, *Prof.* Sir Harold Walter, Kt., D.Phil., F.B.A.
Bailey, Sir Kenneth Hamilton, Kt., C.B.E.
Baillie, Sir Gawaine George Hope, Bt. (1823).
Bairamian, *Hon.* Sir Vahe Robert, Kt.
Baird, Sir David Charles, Bt. (1809).
Baird, *Prof.* Sir Dugald, Kt., M.D.
Baird, Sir James Hozier Gardiner, Bt., M.C. (S. 1695).
Bairstow, *Prof.* Sir Leonard, Kt., C.B.E., F.R.S.
Baker, *Air Marshal* Sir Brian Edmund, K.B.E., C.B., D.S.O., M.C., A.F.C.
Baker, Sir Frederick Spencer Arnold, Kt.
Baker, *Hon.* Sir George Gillespie, Kt., O.B.E.
Baker, *Hon.* Sir Henry Seymour, K.C.M.G., D.S.O.
Baker, Sir Humphrey Dodington Benedict Sherston-, Bt. (1796).
Baker, *Prof.* Sir John Fleetwood, Kt., O.B.E., SC.D., F.R.S.
Baker, *Air Chief Marshal* Sir John Wakeling, G.B.E., K.C.B., M.C., D.F.C.
Baker, Sir (Stanislaus) Joseph, Kt, C.B.
Baker, *Lt.-Gen.* Sir William Henry Goldney, K.C.I.E., C.B., D.S.O., O.B.E.
Balcon, Sir Michael, Kt.
Baldwin, Sir Archer Ernest, Kt., M.C.
Baldwin, *Air Marshal* Sir John Eustace Arthur, K.B.E., C.B., D.S.O.
Balewa, *Rt. Hon.* Sir Abubakar Tafawa, K.B.E.
Balfour, Sir John G.C.M.G., G.B.E.
Balfour, *Lt.-Gen.* Sir Philip Maxwell, K.B.E., C.B., M.C.
Ball, Sir Edmund Lancaster, Kt.
Ball, Sir Nigel Gresley, Bt. (1911).
Bancroft, Sir Oswald Lawrence, Kt., Q.C.
Bankart, *Vice-Adm.* (S.), Sir (George) Harold, K.C.B., C.B.E.
Banks, *Maj.-Gen.* Sir Donald, K.C.B., D.S.O., M.C., T.D.
Banks, Sir John Garnett, Kt., C.B.E.
Banner, Sir George Knowles Harmood-, Bt. (1924).
Bannerman, *Lt.-Col.* Sir Donald Arthur Gordon, Bt. (S 1682).
Banwell, Sir (George) Harold, Kt.
Barber, *Lt.-Gen.* Sir Colin Muir, K.B.E., C.B., D.S.O.
Barber, Sir Herbert William, Kt.
Barber, *Lt.-Col.* Sir William Francis, Bt., T.D. (1960).
Barbirolli, Sir Giovanni Battista, Kt.
Barclay, Sir Colville Herbert Sanford, Bt. (S 1668).
Barclay, Sir Roderick Edward, K.C.M.G., K.C.V.O.
Baring, Sir Charles Christian, Bt. (1911).
Barker, *General* Sir Evelyn Hugh, K.C.B., K.B.E., D.S.O., M.C.
Barlow, Sir Christopher Hilaro, Bt. (1803).
Barlow, Sir (James) Alan (Noel), Bt., G.C.B., K.B.E. (1902).
Barlow, Sir John Denman, Bt., M.P. (1907).
Barlow, Sir Robert, Kt.
Barlow, Sir Thomas Dalmahoy, G.B.E.
Barnard, Sir (Arthur) Thomas, Kt., C.B., O.B.E.
Barnard, *Vice-Adm.* Sir Geoffrey, K.C.B., C.B.E., D.S.O.
Barnard, Sir Henry William, Kt.
Barnes, Sir James Horace, K.C.B., K.B.E.
Barnes, Sir Thomas James, G.C.B., C.B.E.
Barnes, Sir William Lethbridge Gorell-, K.C.M.G., C.B.
Barnett, Sir Ben Lewis, K.B.E., C.B., M.C.
Barnett, *Air Chief Marshal* Sir Denis Hensley Fulton, K.C.B., C.B.E., D.F.C.
Barnett, Sir Geoffrey Morris, Kt.
Barnett, Sir George Percy, Kt.
Barnewall, Sir Reginald Robert, Bt. (I 1623).
Baroda, *Col.* H.H. The Maharaja Gaekwar of, G.C.I.E.
Barotseland, The Paramount Chief of (Mwanawina III), K.B.E.
Barraclough, *Brig.* Sir John Ashworth, Kt., C.M.G., D.S.O., O.B.E., M.C.
Barran, Sir John Leighton, Bt. (1895).
Barratt, *Air Chief Marshal* Sir Arthur Sheridan, K.C.B., C.M.G., M.C.
Barratt, *Capt.* Sir Francis Henry Godolphin Layland-, Bt., M.C. (1908).
Barratt, Sir Sydney, Kt.
Barrett, Sir Arthur George, Kt.
Barrie, Sir Walter, Kt.
Barrington, Sir Charles Bacon, Bt. (1831).
Barrow, Sir Malcolm Palliser, Kt.
Barrow, Sir Richard John Uniacke, Bt. (1835).
Barrowclough, *Rt. Hon.* Sir Harold Eric, K.C.M.G., C.B., D.S.O., M.C., E.D.
Barry, Sir (Claude) Francis, Bt. (1809).
Barry, Sir Gerald Reid, Kt.
Barry, *Hon.* Sir John Vincent William, Kt.
Barry, *Hon.* Sir Patrick Redmond Joseph, Kt., M.C.
Barstow, Sir George Lewis, K.C.B.
Barter, Sir Percy, Kt., C.B.
Bartlett, *Lt.-Col.* Sir Basil Hardington, Bt. (1913).
Bartlett, Sir Frederic Charles, Kt., C.B.E., F.R.S.
Bartley, Sir Charles, Kt.
Barttelot, Sir Brian Walter de Stopham, Bt. (1875).
Barwick, Sir Garfield Edward John, Kt., Q.C.
Barwick, Sir Richard Llewellyn, Bt. (1912).
Basser, Sir Adolph, Kt., C.B.E.
Bassett, Sir Walter Eric, K.B.E., M.C.
Bastyan, *Lt.-Gen.* Sir Edric Montague, K.C.M.G., K.C.V.O., K.B.E., C.B.
Bateman, Sir Charles Harold, K.C.M.G., M.C.
Bates, Sir Alfred, Kt., M.C.
Bates, Sir Geoffrey Voltelin, Bt., M.C. (1880).
Bates, Sir (John) Dawson, Bt., (1937).
Bates, *Air Vice-Marshal* Sir Leslie John Vernon, K.B.E., C.B.
Bateson, Sir Dingwall Latham, Kt., C.B.E., M.C.

Batho, Sir Maurice Benjamin, Bt., (1928).
Bathurst, Sir Frederick Peter Methuen Hervey-, Bt. (1818).
Batterbee, Sir Harry Fagg, G.C.M.G., K.C.V.O.
Baulkwill, Sir (Reginald) Pridham, Kt., C.B.E.
Baxter, Sir (Arthur) Beverley, Kt., M.P.
Bayer, Sir Horace, Kt.
Baynes, Sir William Edward Colston, Bt., M.C. (1801).
Bazley, Sir Thomas Stafford, Bt. (1869).
Bazl-ul-lah, *Sahib Bahadur* K. B., Sir Muhammad, Kt., C.I.E., O.B.E.
Beadle, Sir Gerald Clayton, Kt., C.B.E.
Beadle, *Hon.* Sir Thomas Hugh William, Kt., C.M.G., O.B.E.
Beale, Sir Louis, K.C.M.G., C.B.E.
Beale, *Hon.* Sir (Oliver) Howard, K.B.E., Q.C.
Beale, Sir Samuel Richard, K.B.E.
Beale, Sir William Francis, Kt., O.B.E.
Beamish, *Air Marshal* Sir George Robert, K.C.B., C.B.E.
Beamish, *Col.* Sir Tufton Victor Hamilton, Kt., M.C., M.P.
Bean, Sir Edgar Layton, Kt., C.M.G.
Beatty, Sir (Alfred) Chester, Kt., F.S.A.
Beatty, Sir Kenneth James, Kt.
Beauchamp, Sir Brograve Campbell, Bt. (1911).
Beauchamp, Sir Douglas Clifford, Bt. (1918).
Beauchamp, Sir Ivor Cuthbert Proctor-, Bt. (1745).
Beaumont, Sir George (Howland Francis), Bt. (1661).
Beaumont, *Rt. Hon.* Sir John William Fisher, Kt., Q.C.
Beaver, Sir Hugh Eyre Campbell, K.B.E.
Beazley, *His Hon.* Sir Hugh Loveday, Kt.
Beazley, *Prof.* Sir John Davidson, Kt., C.H.
Becher, Sir William Fane Wrixon, Bt., M.C. (1831).
Becker, Sir Jack Ellerton, Kt.
Beckett, *Capt.* Sir (Martyn) Gervase, Bt., M.C., (1921).
Beckett, Sir (William) Eric, K.C.M.G., Q.C.
Bedale, *Rear-Adm.* (E.) Sir John Leigh K.B.E., C.B.
Beddington, *Brig.* Sir Edward Henry Lionel, Kt., C.M.G., D.S.O., M.C.
Bedingfeld, *Capt.* Sir Edmund George Felix Paston-, Bt. (1661).
Bednall, *Maj.-Gen.* Sir Peter, K.B.E., C.B., M.C.
Bedson, Sir Samuel Phillips, Kt., M.D., F.R.S.
Beecham, Sir Adrian Welles, Bt. (1914).
Beeley, Sir Harold, K.C.M.G., C.B.E.
Beeman, *Eng.-Rear-Adm.* Sir Robert, K.B.E., C.B., C.M.G.
Beetham, Sir Edward Betham, K.C.M.G., C.V.O., O.B.E.
Beevor, Sir Thomas Agnew, Bt. (1784).
Begg, *Admiral* Sir Varyl Cargill, K.C.B., D.S.O., D.S.C.
Beharrell, Sir (George) Edward, Kt.
Behrens, *Maj.* Sir Edward Beddington-, Kt., C.M.G., M.C., Ph.D.
Beit, Sir Alfred Lane, Bt. (1924).
Belcher, Sir Charles Frederic, Kt., O.B.E.
Belgrave, Sir (Charles) Dalrymple, K.B.E.
Bell, Sir Arthur Capel Herbert, Kt.
Bell, Sir Charles Reginald Francis Morrison-, Bt. (1905).
Bell, Sir (Francis) Gordon, K.B.E.
Bell, Sir Frederick (Archibald), Kt., O.B.E., M.C.
Bell, Sir Gawain Westray, K.C.M.G., C.B.E.
Bell, Sir Harold Idris, Kt., C.B., O.B.E.
Bell, Sir Hugh Francis, Bt. (1885).
Bell, Sir Stanley, Kt., O.B.E.
Bellew, Sir Arthur John Grattan-, Kt., C.M.G., Q.C.
Bellew, Hon. Sir George Rothe, K.C.B., K.C.V.O., F.S.A.
Bellew, Sir Henry Charles Grattan-, Bt. (1838).
Bellingham, Sir Roger Carroll Patrick Stephen, Bt. (1796).
Bemrose, Sir (John) Maxwell, Kt.
Benn, *Capt.* Sir (Patrick Ion) Hamilton, Bt. (1920).
Benn, Sir John Andrews, Bt. (1914).
Bennett, Sir John (Cecil) Sterndale, K.C.M.G.
Bennett, Sir John Wheeler Wheeler-, K.C.V.O., C.M.G., O.B.E.
Bennett, Sir Ronald Wilfrid Murdoch, Bt. (1929).
Bennett, Sir Thomas Penberthy, K.B.E.
Bennett, Sir William Gordon, Kt.
Benson, Sir Arthur Edward Trevor, G.C.M.G.
Benson, *Rev.* Sir Clarence Irving, Kt., C.B.E.
Benson, Sir George, Kt., M.P.
Benson, *Lt.-Col.* Sir Reginald Lindsay, Kt., D.S.O., M.V.O., M.C.
Benstead, Sir John, Kt., C.B.E.
Benthall, Sir (Arthur) Paul, K.B.E.
Bentinck, *Maj.* Sir Ferdinand William Cavendish-, K.B.E., C.M.G.
Berar, H.H. the Prince of, G.C.I.E., G.B.E.
Berendsen, Sir Carl August, K.C.M.G.
Berlin, Sir Isaiah, Kt., C.B.E.
Bernard, Sir Dallas Gerald Mercer, Bt. (1954).
Berney, *Capt.* Sir Thomas Reedham, Bt., M.C. (1620).
Berry, Sir (Henry) Vaughan, Kt.
Berryman, *General* Sir Frank Horton, K.C.V.O., C.B., C.B.E., D.S.O.
Berthoud, Sir Eric Alfred, K.C.M.G.
Best, Sir John Victor Hall, Kt.
Beste, *Capt.* Sir Henry Aloysius Bruno Digby-, Kt., C.I.E., O.B.E., R.N.
Betham, *Lt.-Col.* Sir Geoffrey Lawrence, K.B.E., C.I.E., M.C.
Bethune, Sir Alexander Maitland Sharp, Bt. (S 1683).
Bevan, Sir David Martyn Evans, Bt. (1958).
Bevan, *Rear-Adm.* Sir Richard Hugh Loraine, K.B.E., C.B., D.S.O., M.V.O.
Beverley, *Vice-Adm.* Sir (William) York (La Roche), K.B.E., C.B.
Bevir, Sir Anthony, K.C.V.O., C.B.E.
Bhagchand Soni, *Rai Bahadur* Sir Seth, Kt., O.B.E.
Bibby, *Maj.* Sir (Arthur) Harold, Bt., D.S.O. (1959).
Biddle, Sir Reginald Poulton, Kt., C.B.E., T.D.
Biddulph, Sir Francis Henry, Bt. (1664).
Bigge, Sir John Amherst Selby-, Bt., O.B.E., (1919).
Biggs, *Vice-Adm.* Sir Hilary Worthington, K.B.E., C.B., D.S.O.
Bignold, Sir Charles Robert, Kt.
Binder, Sir Bernhard Heymann, Kt.
Bingley, *Admiral* Sir Alexander Noel Campbell, G.C.B., O.B.E.
Binney, Sir George, Kt., D.S.O.
Binns, Sir Arthur Lennon, Kt., C.B.E., M.C.
Birchall, Sir (Walter) Raymond, K.C.B., K.B.E.
Bird, *Lt.-Gen.* Sir Clarence August, K.C.I.E., C.B., D.S.O.
Bird, Sir Cyril Handley, Kt., C.B.E.
Bird, Sir Donald Geoffrey, Bt. (1922).
Bird, Sir Hugh Stonehewer-, K.C.M.G., O.B.E.
Birkin, Sir Charles Lloyd, Bt. (1905).
Birkmyre, Sir Henry, Bt. (1921).
Birtchnell, Sir Cyril Augustine, K.C.M.G., C.B.
Bishop, Sir Harold, Kt., C.B.E.
Bishop, *Instructor Rear-Adm.*, Sir William Alfred, K.B.E., C.B.
Bishop, Sir William Poole, Kt., C.M.G.
Bisset, *Commodore* Sir James Gordon Partridge, Kt., R.N.R.
Black, Sir Cyril Wilson, Kt., M.P.
Black, *Capt.* Sir John Paul, Kt.
Black, Sir Robert Andrew Stransham, Bt. (1922).
Black, Sir Robert Brown, G.C.M.G. O.B.E.
Black, Sir William Rushton, Kt.
Blackall, Sir Henry William Butler, Kt., Q.C.
Blackburn, Sir Arthur Dickinson, K.C.M.G., C.B.E.
Blackburn, *Lt.-Col.* Sir Charles Bickerton, K.C.M.G., O.B.E., M.D.

Blackburne, Sir Kenneth William, G.C.M.G., G.B.E.
Blackett, *Maj.* Sir Charles Douglas, Bt. (1673).
Blackmore, Sir Charles Henry, Kt., C.B.E.
Blackwell, Sir Basil Henry, Kt.
Blackwood, Sir Francis Elliot Temple, Bt. (1819).
Blackwood, Sir Robert Rutherford, Kt.
Blair, Sir James Hunter-, Bt. (1786).
Blair, *Col.* Sir Patrick James, K.B.E., D.S.O., T.D.
Blake, *Cdr.* Sir Cuthbert Patrick, Bt., D.S.O., R.N. (1772).
Blake, Sir (Francis) Michael, Bt. (1907).
Blake, *Vice-Adm.* Sir Geoffrey, K.C.B., D.S.O.
Blake, Sir Ulick Temple, Bt. (I 1622).
Blaker, Sir Reginald, Bt., T.D. (1919).
Blakiston, Sir Arthur Frederick, Bt., M.C. (1763).
Bland, Sir (George) Nevile (Maltby), K.C.M.G., K.C.V.O.
Bland, Sir Thomas Maltby, Kt., T.D.
Blatch, Sir (William) Bernard, Kt., M.B.E.
Blennerhassett, Sir Marmaduke Adrian Francis William, Bt. (1809).
Bligh, Sir Edward Clare, Kt.
Bliss, Sir Arthur, Kt., MUS.D., Ll.D.
Bloch, Sir Maurice, Kt.
Blois, *Capt.* Sir Gervase Ralph Edmund, Bt., M.C. (1686).
Blomefield, Sir Thomas Edward Peregrine, Bt. (1807).
Blood, Sir Hilary Rudolph Robert, G.B.E., K.C.M.G.
Blosse, Sir Robert (Geoffrey) Lynch-, Bt., R.N. (1622).
Blount, Sir Edward Robert, Bt. (1642).
Blundell, Sir Michael, K.B.E.
Blundell, Sir Robert Henderson, Kt.
Blunden, Sir William, Bt. (I 1766).
Blunt, *Prof.* Sir Anthony Frederick, K.C.V.O., F.B.A.
Blunt, Sir John Lionel Reginald, Bt., (1720).
Boag, Sir George Townsend, K.C.I.E., C.S.I.
Board, Sir (Archibald) Vyvyan, Kt., D.S.O., M.C.
Bodkin, *Hon.* Sir William Alexander, K.C.V.O.
Boevey, Sir Launcelot Valentine Hyde Crawley-, Bt. (1784).
Boileau, Sir Gilbert George Benson, Bt. (1838).
Boles, Sir Jeremy John Fortescue, Bt. (1922).
Bolitho, *Lt.-Col.* Sir Edward Hoblyn Warren, K.B.E., C.B., D.S.O.
Bolton, Sir George Lewis French, K.C.M.G.
Bolton, Sir (Horatio) Norman, K.C.I.E., C.S.I.
Bolton, Sir Ian Frederick Cheney, Bt., K.B.E. (1927).
Bonallack, Sir Richard Frank, Kt., C.B.E.
Bond, Sir Ralph Stuart, Kt., C.B.E.
Bonham, *Maj.* Sir Antony Lionel Thomas, Bt. (1852).
Bonsor, Sir Bryan Cosmo, Bt., M.C., T.D. (1925).
Boord, Sir Richard William, Bt. (1896).
Booth, Sir Douglas Allen, Bt. (1916).
Booth, Sir G. Arthur W., K.B.E.
Booth, Sir Michael Savile Gore-, Bt. (I 1760).
Booth, Sir Paul Henry Gore-, K.C.M.G., K.C.V.O.
Boothby, Sir Hugo Robert Brooke, Bt. (1660).
Boreel, Sir Alfred, Bt. (1645).
Bornu, The Shehu of, K.B.E.
Bornu, The Waziri of, K.C.M.G., C.B.E.
Borwick, *Lt.-Col.* Sir Thomas Faulkner, Kt., C.I.E., D.S.O.
Boston, Sir Henry Josiah Lightfoot, G.C.M.G.
Boswall, Sir Thomas Houstoun-, Bt. (1836).
Bottomley, *Air Chief Marshal* Sir Norman Howard, K.C.B., C.I.E., D.S.O., A.F.C.
Bouchier, *Air Vice-Marshal* Sir Cecil Arthur, K.B.E., C.B., D.F.C.
Boughey, Sir Richard James, Bt. (1798).
Boult, Sir Adrian Cedric, Kt., D.MUS.
Boulton, Sir (Denis Duncan) Harold (Owen), Bt. (1905).
Boulton, Sir Edward John, Bt. (1944).
Bourke, *Maj.* Sir (Edward Alexander) Henry Legge-, K.B.E., M.P.
Bourke, *Hon.* Sir Paget John, Kt.
Bourne, *General* Sir Alan George Barwys, K.C.B., D.S.O., M.V.O., R.M.
Bourne, Sir Frederick Chalmers, K.C.S.I., C.I.E.
Bourne, *General* Sir Geoffrey Kemp, G.C.B., K.B.E., C.M.G.
Bovell, Sir (Conrad Swire) Kerr, Kt., C.M.G.
Bovenschen, Sir Frederick Carl, K.C.B., K.B.E.
Bowater, Sir Noel Vansittart, Bt., G.B.E., M.C. (1939).
Bowater, Sir (Thomas) Dudley (Blennerhassett), Bt. (1944).
Bowden, Sir Frank, Bt. (1915).
Bowen, Sir (John) William, Kt., C.B.E.
Bowen, Sir Thomas Frederic Charles, Bt. (1921).
Bower, Sir Frank, Kt., C.B.E.
Bower, Sir John Reginald Hornby Nott-, K.C.V.O.
Bower, *Air Marshal* Sir Leslie William Clement, K.C.B., D.S.O., D.F.C.
Bower, *Lt.-Gen.* Sir Roger Herbert, K.C.B., K.B.E.
Bower, Sir (William) Guy Nott-, K.B.E., C.B.
Bowker, Sir Leslie Cecil Blackmore, K.C.V.O., O.B.E., M.C.
Bowker, Sir (Reginald) James, G.B.E., K.C.M.G.
Bowlby, Sir Anthony Hugh Mostyn, Bt. (1923).
Bowman, Sir James, Bt., K.B.E. (1961).
Bowman, Sir John Paget, Bt. (1884)
Bowra, Sir (Cecil) Maurice, Kt., F.B.A.
Bowyer, Sir Eric Blacklock, K.C.B., K.B.E.
Boyce, Sir Richard Leslie, Bt. (1952).
Boyd, Sir Alexander Walter, Bt. (1916).
Boyd, *Admiral* Sir Denis William, K.C.B., C.B.E., D.S.C.
Boyd, *Prof.* Sir John, Kt.
Boyd, *Brig.* Sir John Smith Knox, Kt., O.B.E., M.D., F.R.S.
Boyle, *Marshal of the Royal Air Force* Sir Dermot Alexander, G.C.B., K.C.V.O., K.B.E., A.F.C.
Boyle, *Rt. Hon.* Sir Edward Charles Gurney, Bt., M.P. (1904).
Boynton, *Cdr.* Sir Griffith Wilfrid Norman, Bt., R.N. (1618).
Brabin, *Hon.* Sir Daniel James, Kt., M.C.
Bracegirdle, *Rear-Adm.* Sir Leighton Seymour, K.C.V.O., C.M.G., D.S.O.
Brackenridge, Sir Alexander, K.B.E., M.C.
Bradbeer, Sir Albert Frederick, Kt.
Braddell, Sir Roland St. John, Kt.
Bradfield, *Lt.-Gen.* Sir Ernest William Charles, K.C.I.E., O.B.E.
Bradford, Sir Edward Alexander Slade, Bt. (1902).
Bradford, Sir Thomas Andrews, Kt., D.S.O.
Bradley, *Air Marshal* Sir John Stanley Travers, K.C.B., C.B.E.
Bradley, Sir Kenneth Granville, Kt., C.M.G.
Bradman, Sir Donald George, Kt.
Bragg, *Prof.* Sir (William) Lawrence, Kt., O.B.E., M.C., F.R.S.
Brain, Sir Henry Norman, K.B.E., C.M.G.
Braithwaite, Sir John Bevan, Kt.
Brand, *Air Chief Marshal* Sir (Christopher Joseph) Quintin, K.B.E., D.S.O., M.C., D.F.C.
Branigan, Sir Patrick Francis, Kt., Q.C.
Branson, *Col.* Sir Douglas Stephenson, K.B.E., C.B., D.S.O., M.C., T.D.
Braund, *His Hon.* Sir Henry Benedict Linthwaite, Kt.
Bray, *Capt.* Sir Jocelyn, Kt.
Bray, *Lt.-Gen.* Sir Robert Napier Hubert Campbell, K.C.B., C.B.E., D.S.O.
Brebner, Sir Alexander, Kt., C.I.E.
Brett, *Hon.* Sir Lionel, Kt.
Brickwood, Sir Rupert Redvers, Bt. (1927).
Bridge, *Admiral* Sir Arthur Robin Moore, K.B.E., C.B.

Bridgeford, *Lt.-Gen.* Sir William, K.B.E., C.B., M.C.
Bridgland, Sir Aynsley Vernon, Kt., C.B.E.
Briercliffe, Sir Rupert, Kt., C.M.G., O.B.E., M.D.
Briggs, Sir (Alfred) George (Ernest), Kt.
Briggs, *Hon.* Sir Francis Arthur, Kt.
Brinckman, *Col.* Sir Roderick Napoleon, Bt. D.S.O., M.C. (1831).
Brind, *Admiral* Sir (Eric James) Patrick, G.B.E., K.C.B.
Brisbane, Sir Hugh Lancelot, Kt., M.B.E.
Brisco, Sir Hylton Musgrave Campbell, Bt. (1782).
Briscoe, Sir John Leigh Charlton, Bt., D.F.C. (1910).
Brise, Sir John Archibald Ruggles-, Bt., C.B., O.B.E., T.D. (1935).
Bristow, Sir Charles Holditch, Kt., C.I.E.
Bristow, Sir Robert Charles, Kt., C.I.E.
Brittain, Sir Harry, K.B.E., C.M.G.
Broad, *Lt.-Gen.* Sir Charles Noel Frank, K.C.B., D.S.O.
Broadbent, Sir William Francis, Bt. (1893).
Broadfoot, *Hon.* Sir Walter James, K.B.E.
Broadhurst, *Air Chief Marshal* Sir Harry, G.C.B., K.B.E., D.S.O., D.F.C., A.F.C.
Broadley, Sir Herbert, K.B.E.
Broadmead, Sir Philip Mainwaring, K.C.M.G., M.C.
Brock, Sir Russell Claude, Kt., F.R.C.S.
Brocklebank, Sir John Montague, Bt. (1885).
Brockehurst, Sir Philip Lee, Bt., T.D. (1903).
Brodie, *Capt.* Sir Benjamin Collins, Bt., M.C. (1834).
Brogan, *Prof.* Sir Denis William, Kt.
Bromet, *Air Vice-Marshal* Sir Geoffrey Rhodes, K.B.E., C.B., D.S.O.
Bromhead, *Lt.-Col.* Sir Benjamin Denis Gonville, Bt., O.B.E. (1806).
Bromley, Sir Rupert Howe, Bt. (1757).
Brooke, *Lt.-Gen.* Sir Bertram Norman Sergison-, K.C.B., K.C.V.O., C.M.G., D.S.O.
Brooke, Sir Edward Geoffrey de Capell, Bt., C.B.E. (1803).
Brooke, *Maj.* Sir George Cecil Francis, Bt. (1903).
Brooke, *Maj.* Sir John Weston, Bt. (1919).
Brooke, Sir Richard Christopher, Bt. (1662).
Brookes, *Capt.* Sir Ernest Geoffrey, Kt.
Brookes, Sir Norman Everard, Kt.
Brooks, *General* Sir (Reginald Alexander) Dallas, G.C.M.G., K.C.B., K.C.V.O., D.S.O., R.M.
Brooksbank, Sir (Edward) William, Bt. (1919).
Broughton, Sir Evelyn Delves, Bt. (1661).
Broun, Sir (James) Lionel, Bt. (S 1686).
Brown, Sir Allen Stanley, Kt., C.B.E.
Brown, *Lt.-Col.* Sir (Charles Frederick) Richmond, Bt. (1863).
Brown, Sir Edward Joseph, Kt., M.B.E.
Brown, Sir (George) Lindor, Kt., C.B.E., F.R.S.
Brown, *Eng. - Vice - Adm.* Sir Harold Arthur, G.B.E., K.C.B.
Brown, Sir Harry Percy, Kt., C.M.G., M.B.E.
Brown, Sir James Birch, K.C.I.E., C.S.I.
Brown, Sir James Raitt, Kt.
Brown, Sir John Douglas Keith, Kt.
Brown, Sir Kenneth Alfred Leader, Kt.
Brown, *Air Vice-Marshal* Sir Leslie Oswald, K.C.B., C.B.E., D.S.C., A.F.C.
Brown, *Lt.-Col.* Sir Norman Seddon Seddon-, Kt., T.D.
Brown, Sir Samuel Harold, Kt.
Brown, *Air Commodore* Sir Vernon Sydney, Kt., C.B., O.B.E.
Brown, Sir William Brian Pigott-, Bt. (1903).
Brown, Sir William Robson-, Kt., M.P.
Brown, Sir William Scott, K.C.I.E., C.S.I.
Browne, Sir Denis John, K.C.V.O.
Browne, *Col.* Sir Eric Gore-, Kt., D.S.O., O.B.E., T.D.
Browne, *Lt.-Col.* Sir Stewart Gore-, Kt., D.S.O.
Browning, *Lt.-Gen.* Sir Frederick Arthur Montague, G.C.V.O., K.B.E., C.B., D.S.O.
Brownjohn, *General* Sir Nevil Charles Dowell, G.B.E., K.C.B., C.M.G., M.C.
Brownrigg, Sir Nicholas (Gawen), Bt. (1816).
Bruce, Sir Arthur Atkinson, K.B.E., M.C.
Bruce, Hon. Sir Francis Edward Hovell - Thurlow - Cumming-, K.C.M.G.
Bruce, Sir (Francis) Michael Ian, Bt. (S 1628).
Bruce, Sir Hervey John William, Bt. (1804).
Bruce, *Prof.* Sir John, Kt., C.B.E., T.D.
Brundrett, Sir Frederick, K.C.B., K.B.E.
Brune, Sir Humphrey Ingelram Prideaux, K.B.E., C.M.G.
Brunner, Sir Felix John Morgan, Bt. (1895).
Brunt, *Prof.* Sir David, K.B.E., F.R.S.
Brunton, Sir (Edward Francis) Lauder, Bt. (1908).
Bruxner, *Lt.-Col. Hon.* Sir Michael Frederick, K.B.E., D.S.O.
Bryan, Sir Andrew Meikle, Kt.
Bryant, Sir Arthur Wynne Morgan, Kt., C.B.E.
Buchanan, Sir Charles James, Bt. (1878).
Buchanan, Sir George Hector Macdonald Leith-, Bt. (1775).
Buchanan, Sir John Cecil Rankin, K.C.M.G., M.D.
Buchanan, Sir John Scoular, Kt., C.B.E.
Buchanan, *Maj.-Gen.* Sir Kenneth Gray, Kt., C.B., C.M.G., D.S.O.
Bucher, *General* Sir Roy, K.B.E., C.B., M.C.
Buckley, Hon. Sir Denys Burton, Kt., M.B.E.
Buckley, *Rear-Adm.* Sir Kenneth Robertson, K.B.E.
Bucknill, *Rt. Hon.* Sir Alfred Townsend, Kt., O.B.E.
Buganda, H.H. The Kabaka of, K.B.E.
Bulkeley, Sir Richard Harry David Williams-, Bt. (1661).
Bull, Sir George, Bt. (1922).
Bullard, Sir Edward Crisp, Kt., Ph.D., SC.D., F.R.S.
Bullard, Sir Reader William, K.C.B., K.C.M.G., C.I.E.
Bullin, *Maj.* Sir Reginald, Kt., O.B.E., T.D.
Bullock, Sir Christopher Llewellyn, K.C.B., C.B.E.
Bullock, Sir Ernest, Kt., C.V.O., Mus.D.
Bullock, *Capt.* Sir Malcolm, Bt., M.B.E. (1954).
Bunbury, Sir Henry Noel, K.C.B.
Bunbury, Sir John William Napier, Bt. (1681).
Bunbury, Sir (Richard David) Michael Richardson-, Bt. (I 1787).
Bunyoro-Kitara, The Omukama of, Kt., C.B.E.
Burbidge, Sir Richard (Grant Woodman), Bt., C.B.E. (1916).
Burbury, *Hon.* Sir Stanley Charles, K.B.E.
Burder, Sir John Henry, Kt.
Burdett, Sir Savile Aylmer, Bt. (1665).
Burgess, *Maj.-Gen.* Sir William Livingstone Hatchwell Sinclair-, K.B.E., C.B., C.M.G., D.S.O.
Burgis, *His Hon.* Sir Edwin Cooper, Kt.
Burgoyne, Sir John, Kt., O.B.E.
Burke, Sir Aubrey Francis, Kt., O.B.E.
Burke, Sir Thomas Stanley, Bt. (I 1797)
Burman, Sir (John) Charles, Kt.
Burnand, Sir (Richard) Frank, Kt., C.B.E.
Burne, Sir Lewis Charles, Kt., C.B.E., A.F.C.
Burnet, Sir (Frank) Macfarlane, Kt., O.M., M.D., F.R.S.
Burnett, *Maj.* Sir David Humphery, Bt., M.B.E., T.D. (1913).

Burney, *Cmdr.* Sir (Charles) Dennistoune, Bt., C.M.G., R.N. (1921).
Burns, Sir Alan Cuthbert, G.C.M.G.
Burns, Sir Charles Ritchie, K.B.E., M.D.
Burns, Sir John Crawford, Kt.
Burns, *Maj.-Gen.* Sir (Walter Arthur) George, K.C.V.O., C.B., D.S.O., O.B.E., M.C.
Burrard, *Maj.* Sir Gerald, Bt., D.S.O. (1769).
Burrell, *Vice-Adm.* Sir Henry Mackay, K.B.E., C.B.
Burrell, Sir Walter Raymond, Bt., C.B.E., T.D. (1774).
Burrough, *Admiral* Sir Harold Martin, G.C.B., K.B.E., D.S.O.
Burrows, Sir Bernard Alexander Brocas, K.C.M.G.
Burrows, Sir Frederick John, G.C.S.I., G.C.I.E.
Burrows, Sir Robert Abraham, K.B.E.
Burt, Sir Cyril Lodowic, Kt., D.SC., LL.D.
Burt, Sir George Mowlem, K.B.E.
Burton, Sir Geoffrey Pownall, K.C.S.I., K.C.I.E.
Buscarlet, *Air Vice-Marshal* Sir Willett Amalric Bower Bowen-, K.B.E., C.B., D.F.C.
Busk, Sir Douglas Laird, K.C.M.G.
Busoga, The Kyabazinga of, Kt.
Bustamante, Sir (William) Alexander, Kt.
Butcher, Sir Herbert Walter, Bt., M.P. (1960).
Butler, Sir (Charles) Owen, K.B.E., C.M.G., E.D.
Butler, Sir Gerald Snowden, Kt., C.I.E.
Butler, Sir James Ramsay Montagu, Kt., M.V.O., O.B.E.
Butler, Sir Nevile Montagu, K.C.M.G., C.V.O.
Butler, Sir (Reginald) Michael (Thomas), Bt. (1922).
Butler, *Hon.* Sir Richard Layton, K.C.M.G.
Butler, *Lt.-Col.* Sir Thomas Pierce, Bt., D.S.O., O.B.E. (1628).
Butt, Sir (Alfred) Kenneth Dudley, Bt. (1929).
Butterfield, Sir Harry Durham, Kt., C.B.E.
Butters, Sir John Henry, Kt., C.M.G., M.B.E., V.D.
Buxton, Sir Thomas Fowell Victor, Bt. (1840).
Buzzard, *Rear-Adm.* Sir Anthony Wass, Bt., C.B., D.S.O., O.B.E. (1929).
Byass, *Col.* Sir Geoffrey Robert Sidney, Bt., T.D. (1926).
Byrne, Sir Laurence Austin, Kt.
Cabot, Sir Daniel Alfred Edmund, Kt.
Caccia, Sir Harold Anthony, G.C.M.G., G.C.V.O.
Cadbury, *Maj.* Sir Egbert, Kt., D.S.C., D.F.C.
Cade, *Air Vice-Marshal* Sir Stanford, K.B.E., C.B.
Cader, Sir Hussein Hassanaly Abdool, Kt., C.B.E.
Cadogan, *Rt. Hon.* Sir Alexander George Montagu, O.M., G.C.M.G., K.C.B.
Cadzow, Sir Norman James Kerr, Kt., V.R.D.
Caffyn, *Brig.* Sir Edward Roy, K.B.E., C.B., T.D.
Cahn, Sir Albert Jonas, Bt. (1934).
Cain, Sir Ernest, Bt. (1920).
Caine, Sir Derwent Hall, Bt. (1937).
Caine, Sir Sydney, K.C.M.G.
Cairns, *Hon.* Sir David Arnold Scott, Kt.
Calder, Sir John Alexander, K.C.M.G.
Callander, *Lt.-Gen.* Sir Colin Bishop, K.C.B., K.B.E., M.C.
Calthorpe, *Brig.* Sir Richard Hamilton Anstruther-Gough-, Bt., C.B.E., (1929).
Cameron, *Lt.-Gen.* Sir Alexander Maurice, K.B.E., C.B., M.C.
Cameron, *Lt.-Col.* Sir Donald Charles, K.C.M.G., D.S.O., V.D.
Cameron, Sir Donald Charles, Kt.
Cameron, *Hon.* Sir Ewen Paul, Kt.
Cameron, *Prof.* Sir Gordon Roy, Kt., F.R.S.
Cameron, Sir John, Bt. (1893).
Cameron, *Hon.* Sir John, Kt., D.S.C., Q.C. (Lord Cameron).
Camilleri, *His Hon.* Sir Luigi Antonio, Kt, LL.D.
Camm, Sir Sydney, Kt., C.B.E.
Campbell, *Maj.-Gen.* Sir (Alexander) Douglas, K.B.E., C.B., D.S.O., M.C.
†Campbell, Sir Bruce Colin Patrick, Bt. (S 1804).
Campbell, Sir Charles Rudolph, Kt., C.B.E.
Campbell, Sir Clifford Clarence, G.C.M.G.
Campbell, Sir Colin, Kt., O.B.E.
Campbell, Sir Colin Moffat, Bt., M.C. (S 1668).
Campbell, *Prof.* Sir David, Kt., M.C., M.D., LL.D., F.R.S.E.
Campbell, Sir George Ilay, Bt. (1808).
Campbell, Sir George Riddoch, K.C.I.E.
Campbell, Sir Gerald, G.C.M.G.
Campbell, *Col.* Sir Guy Theophilus Halswell, Bt., O.B.E., M.C. (1815).
Campbell, *Maj.-Gen.* Sir Hamish Manus, K.B.E., C.B.
Campbell, *Capt.* Sir Harold George, G.C.V.O., D.S.O., R.N.
Campbell, *Rt. Rev.* Henry Colville Montgomery, K.C.V.O., M.C., D.D.
Campbell, *Vice-Adm.* Sir Ian Murray Robertson, K.B.E., C.B., D.S.O.
Campbell, Sir Ian Vincent Hamilton, Bt., C.B. (1831).
Campbell, Sir James Clark, Kt., T.D.
Campbell, Sir John Johnston, Kt.,
Campbell, Sir John Middleton, Kt.
Campbell, Sir Matthew, K.B.E., C.B., F.R.S.E.
Campbell, Sir Norman Dugald Ferrier, Bt. (S 1628).
Campbell, Sir Ralph Abercromby, Kt.
Campbell, *Rt. Hon.* Sir Ronald Ian, G.C.M.G., C.B.
Campbell, Sir Thomas Cockburn-, Bt. (1821).
Campbell, *Lt.-Col.* Sir Walter Fendall, K.C.I.E.
Campion, Sir Harry, Kt., C.B., C.B.E.
Canning, Sir Ernest R., Kt.
Cantlie, *Admiral* Sir Colin, K.B.E., C.B., D.S.C.
Cantlie, Sir Keith, Kt., C.I.E.
Cantlie, *Lt.-Gen.* Sir Neil, K.C.B., K.B.E., M.C.
Carberry, Sir John Edward Doston, Kt.
Carden, *Maj.* Sir Frederick Henry Walter, Bt. (1887).
Carden, Sir John Craven, Bt. (I 1787).
Carew, Sir Thomas Palk, Bt. (1661).
Carlill, *Vice-Adm.* Sir Stephen Hope, K.B.E., C.B., D.S.O.
Carmichael, Sir Archibald Henry William Gibson-Craig-, Bt. (S 1702 and 1831).
Carmichael, Sir John, K.B.E.
Carnac, Sir Henry George Crabbe Rivett-, Bt. (1836).
Caroe, Sir Olaf Kirkpatrick, K.C.S.I., K.C.I.E.
Carpendale, *Vice-Adm.* Sir Charles Douglas, Kt., C.B.
Carpenter, Sir Eric Ashton, Kt., O.B.E.
Carr, Sir Arthur Strettell Comyns, Kt., Q.C.
Carr, Sir Cecil Thomas, K.C.B., Q.C., LL.D.
Carr, *Air Marshal* Sir (Charles) Roderick, K.B.E., C.B., D.F.C., A.F.C.
Carr, Sir (Frederick) Bernard, Kt., C.M.G.
Carr, *Air Marshal* Sir John Darcy Baker-, K.B.E., C.B., A.F.C.
Carr, Sir William Emsley, Kt.
Carrington, *Lt.-Gen.* Sir Robert Harold, K.C.B., D.S.O.
Carrington, Sir William Speight, Kt.
Carroll, Sir Alfred Thomas, K.B.E.
Carroll, Sir John Anthony, K.B.E., Ph.D., F.R.S.E.
Carron, Sir William John, Kt.
Carson, Sir Norman John, Kt., C.M.G.
Carter, *Admiral* Sir Stuart Sumner Bonham-, K.C.B., C.V.O., D.S.O.
Cartland, Sir George Barrington, Kt., C.M.G.
Carver, Sir Stanley Roy, Kt., O.B.E.
Cary, Sir Robert Archibald, Bt., M.P. (1955).
Cash, Sir Thomas James, K.B.E., C.B.

Cash, Sir William, Kt.
Cassel, Sir Francis Edward, Bt. (1920).
Cassels, *General* Sir (Archibald) James Halkett, G.C.B., K.B.E., D.S.O.
Cassels, Sir James Dale, Kt.
Casson, Sir Hugh Maxwell, Kt., A.R.A., F.R.I.B.A.
Casson, Sir Lewis, Kt., M.C.
Cator, Sir Geoffrey Edmund, Kt., C.M.G.
Cave, Sir Charles Edward Coleridge, Bt. (1896).
Cave, Sir Robert Cave-Browne-, Bt. (1641).
Cawthorn, *Maj.-Gen.* Sir Walter Joseph, Kt., C.B., C.I.E., C.B.E.
Cayley, Sir Kenelm Henry Ernest, Bt. (1661).
Cayzer, Sir James Arthur, Bt. (1904).
Cayzer, Sir (William) Nicholas, Bt. (1921).
Cazalet, *Vice-Adm.* Sir Peter Grenville Lyon, K.B.E., C.B., D.S.O., D.S.C.
Chadwick, Sir James, Kt., M.D., F.R.S.
Chadwick, Sir Robert Burton Burton-, Bt. (1935).
Chadwick, Sir Thomas, K.C.V.O., C.B.E.
Chamberlain, Sir Henry Wilmot, Bt. (1828).
Chamier, *Air Commodore* Sir (John) Adrian, Kt., C.B., C.M.G., D.S.O., O.B.E.
Champion, *Prof.* Sir Harry George, Kt., C.I.E., D.SC.
Champion, *Rev.* Sir Reginald Stuart, K.C.M.G., O.B.E.
Champneys, *Capt.* Sir Weldon Dalrymple-, Bt., C.B. (1910).
Chance, Sir Roger James Ferguson, Bt., M.C. (1900).
Chance, Sir (William) Hugh (Stobart), Kt., C.B.E.
Chancellor, Sir Christopher John, Kt., C.M.G.
Chandler, Sir John De Lisle, Kt.
Chaplin, Sir George Frederick, Kt., C.B.E.
Chapman, Sir Robert Macgowan, Bt., C.B.E., T.D. (1958).
Chapman, *Air Chief Marshal* Sir Ronald Ivelaw-, G.C.B., K.B.E., D.F.C., A.F.C.
Charles, Sir John Alexander, K.C.B., M.D.
Charles, Sir Noel Hughes Havelock, Bt., K.C.M.G., M.C. (1928).
Charlton, *Commodore* Sir William Arthur, Kt., D.S.C.
Charrington, Sir John, Kt.
Charteris, *Lt.-Col.* Hon. Sir Martin Michael Charles, K.C.V.O., C.B., O.B.E.
Chau, Sik-nin, Sir, Kt., C.B.E.
Chau Tsun-nin, Sir, Kt., C.B.E.
Chaytor, Sir William Henry Clervaux, Bt. (1831).
Chegwidden, Sir Thomas Sidney, Kt., C.B., C.V.O.
Cheshire, *Air Chief Marshal* Sir Walter Graemes, K.C.B., C.B.E.
Chetwynd, Sir (Arthur Henry) Talbot, Bt., O.B.E., M.C. (1795).
Cheyne, Sir Joseph Lister Watson, Bt. (1908).
Chichester, Sir (Edward) John, Bt. (1641).
Chick, Sir (Alfred) Louis, K.B.E.
Chiesman, Sir Walter Eric, Kt., C.B., M.D.
Child, Sir (Coles) John, Bt. (1919).
Chilton, *Air Marshal* Sir (Charles) Edward, K.B.E., C.B.
Chinoy, Sir Sultan Meherally, Kt.
Chippindall, Sir Giles Tatlock, Kt., C.B.E.
Chisholm, Sir (Albert) Roderick, Kt.
Chitham, Sir Charles Carter, Kt., C.I.E.
Chitty, Sir Thomas Willes, Bt. (1924).
Cholmeley, *Col.* Sir Hugh John Francis Sibthorp, Bt., C.B., D.S.O. (1896).
Chrimes, Sir (William) Bertram, Kt., C.B.E.
Christie, Sir William, K.C.I.E., C.S.I., M.C.
Christison, *Gen.* Sir (Alexander Frank) Philip, Bt., G.B.E., C.B., D.S.O., M.C. (1871).
Christopher, Sir George Perrin, Kt.
Christophers, *Col.* Sir Samuel Rickard, Kt., C.I.E., O.B.E., F.R.S.
Church, *Brig.* Sir Geoffrey Selby, Bt., C.B.E., M.C., T.D. (1901).
Churchill, *Rt. Hon.* Sir Winston (Leonard Spencer), K.G., O.M., C.H., M.P.
Cilento, Sir Raphael West, Kt., M.D.
Clark, Sir Andrew Edmund James, Bt., M.B.E., M.C., Q.C. (1883).
Clark, *Capt.* Sir George Anthony, Bt. (1917).
Clark, Sir George Norman, Kt., D.Litt.
Clark, Sir Henry Laurence Urling, Kt.
Clark, Sir (John) Beresford, K.C.M.G., C.B.E.
Clark, Sir Kenneth MacKenzie, C.H., K.C.B.
Clark, Sir Stewart Stewart-, Bt. (1918).
Clark, Sir Thomas, Bt. (1886).
Clark, *Prof.* Sir Wilfrid Edward Le Gros, Kt., F.R.S., D.SC.
Clark, Sir (William) Arthur (Weir), K.C.M.G., C.B.E.
Clarke, *Rear-Adm.* (L.) Sir (Charles) Philip, K.B.E., C.B., D.S.O.
Clarke, Sir Douglas, Kt.
Clarke, *Maj.-Gen.* Sir Edward, M.C., K.B.E., C.B.
Clarke, Sir Ellis Emmanuel Innocent, Kt., C.M.G.
Clarke, Sir (Henry) Ashley, G.C.M.G., G.C.V.O.
Clarke, Sir Humphrey Orme, Bt., (1831).
Clarke, Sir Percy Selwyn Selwyn-, K.B.E., C.M.G., M.C., M.D.
Clarke, *Col.* Sir Ralph Stephenson, K.B.E., T.D.
Clarke, Sir Rupert William John, Bt., M.B.E. (1882).
Claughton, Sir Harold, Kt., C.B.E.
Clauson, Sir Gerard Leslie Makins, K.C.M.G., O.B.E.
Clavering, Sir Albert, Kt., O.B.E.
Clay, Sir Charles Travis, Kt., C.B.
Clay, Sir Geoffrey Fletcher, K.C.M.G., O.B.E., M.C.
Clay, Sir Henry Felix, Bt. (1841).
Clayden, *Rt. Hon.* Sir (Henry) John, Kt.
Claye, *Prof.* Sir Andrew Moynihan, Kt., M.D.
Clayton, Sir Arthur Harold, Bt., D.S.C. (1732).
Cleary, Sir William Castle, K.B.E., C.B.
Clee, Sir (Charles) Beaupré Bell, Kt., C.S.I., C.I.E.
Clegg, Sir Cuthbert Barwick, Kt.
Cleland, *Brig.* Sir Donald Mackinnon, Kt., C.B.E.
Clerk, Sir John Dutton, Bt. (S 1679).
Clerke, Sir John Edward Longueville, Bt. (1660).
Cleverly, Sir Osmund Somers, Kt., C.B., C.V.O.
Clifford, *Capt.* Hon. Sir Bede Edmund Hugh, G.C.M.G., C.B., M.V.O.
Clifford, *Vice-Adm.* Sir Eric George Anderson, K.C.B., C.B.E.
Clifford, Sir (Geoffrey) Miles, K.B.E., C.M.G., E.D.
Clifford, *Rev.* Sir Lewis Arthur Joseph, Bt. (1887).
Clough, Sir Robert, Kt.
Cloutman, *His Hon.* Sir Brett Mackay, Kt., V.C., M.C., Q.C.
Clowes, Sir Harold, Kt., O.B.E.
Clutterbuck, Sir (Peter) Alexander, G.C.M.G., M.C.
Clutton, Sir George Lisle, K.C.M.G.
Clyde, *Col.* Sir David, Kt., C.I.E., M.D.
Clyne, *Hon.* Sir Thomas Stuart, Kt.
Coates, Sir Albert Ernest, Kt., O.B.E., M.D.
Coates, *Maj.* Sir Clive Milnes-, Bt., O.B.E. (1911).
Coates, Sir Eric Thomas, Kt., C.S.I., C.I.E.
Coates, Sir Frederick Gregory Lindsay, Bt. (1921).
Coats, *Lt.-Col.* Sir James Stuart, Bt., M.C. (1905).
Cobham, Sir Alan John, K.B.E., A.F.C.
Coburn, Sir (Marmaduke) Robert, Kt., C.S.I., C.I.E., O.B.E.
Cochrane, Sir Desmond Oriel Alastair George Weston, Bt. (1903).
Cochrane, *Rear-Adm.* Sir Edward Owen, K.B.E.

Cochrane, *Air Chief Marshal* Hon. Sir Ralph Alexander, G.B.E., K.C.B., A.F.C.
Cockburn, Sir John Elliot, Bt. (S 1671).
Cockburn, Sir Robert, K.B.E., C.B., Ph.D.
Cockcroft, Sir John Douglas, O.M., K.C.B., C.B.E., F.R.S.
Cocker, Sir William Wiggins, Kt., O.B.E.
Cocks, Sir (Thomas George) Barnett, K.C.B., O.B.E.
Codrington, Sir Christopher William Gerald Henry, Bt. (1876).
Codrington, *Col.* Sir Geoffrey Ronald, K.C.V.O., C.B., C.M.G., D.S.O., O.B.E., T.D.
Codrington, Sir William Alexander, Bt. (1721).
Coen, Sir Terence Bernard Creagh, K.B.E., C.I.E.
Coghill, *Capt.* Sir (Marmaduke Nevill) Patrick (Somerville), Bt. (1778).
Cohen, Sir Andrew Benjamin, K.C.M.G., K.C.V.O., O.B.E.
Cohen, Sir Bernard Nathaniel Waley-, Bt. (1961).
Cohen, Sir Edgar Abraham, K.C.M.G.
Cohen, Sir Herbert (Benjamin), Bt., O.B.E., T.D. (1905).
Cohen, *Maj.* Sir (Jack Benn) Brunel, K.B.E.
Coker, Sir Salako Ambrosius Benka-, Kt., O.B.E.
Coldstream, Sir George Phillips, K.C.B., Q.C.
Coldstream, *Prof.* Sir William Menzies, Kt., C.B.E.
Coleman, *Lieut.-Gen.* Sir (Cyril Frederick) Charles, K.C.B., C.M.G., D.S.O., O.B.E.
Coles, Sir Arthur William, Kt.
Coles, Sir Edgar Barton, Kt.
Coles, Sir George James, Kt., C.B.E.
Coles, Sir Kenneth Frank, Kt.
Colfox, *Lt.-Col.* Sir (William) Philip, Bt., M.C. (1939).
Colles, *Cmdr.* (S.) Sir (Ernest) Dudley, K.C.B., K.C.V.O., O.B.E., R.N.
Collett, Sir Henry Seymour, Bt. (1934).
Collier, *Air Vice-Marshal* Sir (Alfred) Conrad, K.C.B., C.B.E.
Collier, Sir Laurence, K.C.M.G.
Collingwood, Sir Charles Arthur, Kt.
Collingwood, Sir Edward Foyle, Kt., C.B.E., Ph.D., Sc.D.
Collingwood, *Lt.-Gen.* Sir (Richard) George, K.B.E., C.B., D.S.O.
Collins, Sir Charles Henry, Kt., C.M.G.
Collins, Sir Geoffrey Abdy, Kt.
Collins, Sir James Patrick, Kt.
Collins, *Vice-Adm.* Sir John Augustine, K.B.E., C.B., R.A.N.
Colman, Sir Michael Jeremiah, Bt. (1907).
Colman, Sir Nigel Claudian Dalziel, Bt. (1952).
Colquhoun of Luss, Sir Ivar Iain, Bt. (1786).
Colson, *Surgeon Vice-Adm.* Sir Henry St. Clair, K.C.B., C.B.E.
Colston, Sir Charles Blampied, Kt., C.B.E., M.C., D.C.M.
Colt, Sir Edward William Dutton, Bt. (1694).
Colthurst, Sir Richard La Touche, Bt. (1744).
Colville, Sir (Henry) Cecil, Kt.
Compton, Sir Edmund Gerald, K.B.E., C.B.
Conant, Sir Roger John Edward, Bt., C.V.O. (1954).
Connell, Sir Charles, Kt.
Connell, Sir Charles Gibson, Kt.
Conroy, Sir Diarmaid William, Kt., C.M.G., O.B.E., T.D.
Constable, Sir Henry Marmaduke Strickland-, Bt. (1641).
Constantine, Sir George Baxandall, Kt.
Constantine, *Air Chief Marshal* Sir Hugh Alex, K.B.E., C.B., D.S.O.
Constantine, *Hon.* Sir Learie Nicholas, Kt., M.B.E.
Conybeare, *Air Vice-Marshal* Sir John Josias, K.B.E., M.C., M.D.
Cooch Behar, *Maj.* H.H. the Maharaja of, K.C.I.E.
Cook, Sir Francis Ferdinand Maurice, Bt. (1886).
Cook, Sir James Wilfred, Kt., D.Sc., Ph.D., F.R.S.
Cook, *Lt.-Col.* Sir Thomas Russell Albert Mason, Kt.
Cook, Sir William Richard Joseph, Kt., C.B., F.R.S.
Cooke, *Air Marshal* Sir Cyril Bertram, K.C.B., C.B.E.
Cooke, Sir John Fletcher-, Kt., C.M.G.
Cooke, Sir William Henry Charles Wemyss, Bt. (1661).
Coomaraswamy, Sir Velupillai, Kt., C.M.G.
Cooper, *Maj.* Sir Charles Eric Daniel, Bt. (1863).
Cooper, Sir (Harold) Stanford, Kt.
Cooper, Sir (Henry) Guy, Kt., M.C., D.C.M.
Cooper, Sir Patrick Graham Astley, Bt. (1821).
Cooper, *Hon.* Sir Walter Jackson, Kt., M.B.E.
Cooper, Sir William Herbert, Bt. (1905).
Cooper, *Prof.* Sir (William) Mansfield, Kt.
Coote, *Capt.* Sir Colin Reith, Kt., D.S.O.
Coote, *Rear-Adm.* (E.) Sir John Ralph, Bt., C.B., C.B.E., D.S.C., *Premier Baronet of Ireland* (I 1621).
Cope, Sir Anthony Mohun Leckonby, Bt. (1611).
Cope, *Brig.-Gen.* Sir Thomas George, Bt., C.M.G., D.S.O. (1918).
Cope, Sir (Vincent) Zachary, Kt., M.D.
Copeman, *Vice-Adm.* Sir Nicholas Alfred, K.B.E., C.B., D.S.C.
Copland, Sir Douglas Berry, K.B.E., C.M.G., D.Sc.
Coppock, Sir Richard, Kt., C.B.E.
Corah, Sir John Harold, Kt.
Corbet, Sir John Vincent, Bt., M.B.E. (1808).
Cordingley, *Air Vice-Marshal* Sir John Walter, K.C.B., K.C.V.O., C.B.E.
Corfield, Sir Conrad Laurence, K.C.I.E., C.S.I., M.C.
Cornwall, *General* Sir James Handyside Marshall-, K.C.B., C.B.E., D.S.O., M.C.
Corrie, Sir Owen Cecil Kirkpatrick, Kt., M.C.
Corry, *Lt.-Col.* Sir Henry Charles Lowry-, Kt., M.C.
Corry, Sir James Perowne Ivo Myles, Bt. (1885).
Cory, Sir Clinton James Donald, Bt. (1919).
Cory, *Lt.-Gen.* Sir George Norton, K.C.B., K.B.E., D.S.O.
Coryton, *Air Chief Marshal* Sir (William) Alec, K.C.B., K.B.E., M.V.O., D.F.C.
Cosgrove, *Hon.* Sir Robert, K.C.M.G.
Coslett, *Air Marshal* Sir (Thomas) Norman, K.C.B., O.B.E.
Costain, Sir Richard Rylandes, Kt., C.B.E.
Costar, Sir Norman Edgar, K.C.M.G.
Costello, Sir Leonard Wilfred James, Kt., C.B.E.
Cotter, *Lt.-Col.* Sir Delaval James Alfred, Bt., D.S.O. (I. 1763).
Cotterell, Sir Richard Charles Geers, Bt. (1805).
Cotton, Sir Charles Andrew, K.B.E.
Cotton, Sir James Temple, Kt., C.B., O.B.E.
Cottrell, Sir Edward Baglietto, Kt., C.B.E.
Cotts, Sir (William) Campbell Mitchell-, Bt. (1921).
Couchman, *Admiral* Sir Walter Thomas, K.C.B., C.V.O., D.S.O., O.B.E.
Coulson, Sir John Eltringham, K.C.M.G.
Couper, Sir Guy, Bt. (1841).
Courtauld, Sir Stephen Lewis, Kt., M.C.
Courtney, *Air Chief Marshal* Sir Christopher Lloyd, G.B.E., K.C.B., D.S.O.
Coutts, Sir Walter Fleming, G.C.M.G., M.B.E.
Covell, *Maj.-Gen.* Sir Gordon, C.I.E., M.D.
Cowan, Sir Christopher George Armstrong, Kt.
Cowan, Sir (Henry) Kenneth, Kt., M.D., F.R.S.E.
Cowell, *Maj.-Gen.* Sir Ernest Marshall, K.B.E., C.B., D.S.O., T.D., M.D.
Cowley, *Lt.-Gen.* Sir John Guise, K.B.E., C.B.
Cox, Sir Christopher William Machell, K.C.M.G.
Cox, Sir (George) Trenchard, Kt., C.B.E., F.S.A.
Cox, Sir Harold Roxbee, Kt., D.Sc., Ph.D.
Cox, Sir Herbert Charles Fahie, Kt.

Cox, Sir Ivor Richard, Kt., D.S.O.
Cox, Sir John William, Kt., C.B.E.
Cox, *Brig.* Sir Matthew Henry, Kt., C.I.E., O.B.E. M.C.
Cox, Sir Reginald Kennedy-Kt., C.B.E.
Crabbe, Sir Cecil Brooksby, Kt.
Crace, *Admiral* Sir John Gregory, K.B.E., C.B.
Craddock, Sir (George) Beresford, Kt., M.P.
Craddock, *Lt.-Gen.* Sir Richard Walter, K.B.E., C.B., D.S.O.
Craddock, Sir Walter Merry, Kt., D.S.O., M.C.
Craig, Sir Arthur John Edward, Kt.
Craig, Sir (Ernest) Gordon, Kt.
Craig, Sir John Herbert Mc-Cutcheon, K.C.V.O., C.B., LL.D.
Crankshaw, *Col.* Sir Eric Norman Spencer, K.C.M.G., M.B.E.
Craster, Sir John Montagu, Kt.
Craufurd, Sir Alexander John Fortescue, Bt. (1781).
Craw, Sir Henry Hewat, K.B.E., C.I.E.
Crawford, Sir (Archibald James) Dirom, Kt.
Crawford, Sir Frederick, G.C.M.G., O.B.E.
Crawford, Sir John Grenfell, Kt., C.B.E.
Crawford, Sir (Walter) Ferguson, K.B.E., C.M.G.
Crawford, *Vice-Adm.* Sir William Godfrey, K.B.E., C.B., D.S.C.
Creagh, *Maj.-Gen.* Sir (Kilner) Rupert Brazier-, K.B.E., C.B., D.S.O.
Creagh, *Maj.-Gen.* Sir Michael O'Moore, K.B.E., M.C.
Creasy, *Admiral of the Fleet* Sir George Elvey, G.C.B., C.B.E., D.S.O., M.V.O.
Creasy, Sir Gerald Hallen, K.C.M.G., K.C.V.O., O.B.E.
Creed, Sir Thomas Percival, K.B.E., M.C., Q.C.
Creedy, Sir Herbert James, G.C.B., K.C.V.O.
Cresswell, *Rev.* Cyril Leonard, K.C.V.O.
Creswell, Sir Michael Justin, K.C.M.G.
Cribbett, Sir (Wilfrid Charles) George, K.B.E., C.M.G.
Crichton, Sir Andrew James Maitland-Makgill-, Kt.
Crichton, Sir Robert, C.B.E.
Crisp, Sir (John) Peter, Bt. (1913).
Critchett, Sir Ian (George Lorraine), Bt. (1908).
Crocker, Sir William Charles, Kt., M.C.
Croft, Sir Bernard Hugh Denman, Bt. (1671).
Croft, Sir John William Graham, Bt. (1818).
Croft, Sir William Dawson, K.C.B., K.B.E., C.I.E., C.V.O.
Crofton, Sir (Hugh) Patrick Simon, Bt. (1801).
Crofton, Sir Malby Sturges, Bt. (1828).
Crombie, Sir James Ian Cormack, K.C.B., K.B.E., C.M.G.
Cross, *Hon.* Sir (Arthur) Geoffrey (Neale), Kt.
Cross, *Air Marshal* Sir Kenneth Brian Boyd, K.C.B., C.B.E., D.S.O., D.F.C.
Cross, *Rt. Hon.* Sir Ronald Hibbert, Bt., K.C.M.G., K.C.V.O. (1941).
Crossley, Sir Christopher John, Bt. (1909).
Crosthwaite, Sir Bertram Maitland, Kt., V.D.
Crosthwaite, Sir (Ponsonby) Moore, K.C.M.G.
Crosthwaite, Sir William Henry, Kt.
Crow, Sir Alwyn Douglas, Kt., C.B.E.
Crowe, Sir Colin Tradescant, K.C.M.G.
Crowther, Sir Geoffrey, Kt.
Croysdale, Sir James, Kt.
Crutchley, *Admiral* Sir Victor Alexander Charles, V.C., K.C.B., D.S.C.
Cudmore, *Hon.* Sir Collier Robert, Kt.
Cuke, Sir (Hampden) Archibald, Kt., C.B.E.
Cumings, Sir Charles Cecil George, K.B.E.
Cumming, Sir Duncan Cameron, K.B.E., C.B.
Cumming, Sir William Gordon Gordon-, Bt. (1804).
Cunard, Sir Henry Palmes, Bt. (1859).
Cuninghame, Sir John Christopher Foggo Montgomery-, Bt. (N.S. 1672).
Cuninghame, Sir William Alan Fairlie-, Bt., M.C. (S 1630).
Cunliffe, Sir Cyril Henley, Bt. (1759).
Cunliffe, Sir John Robert Ellis, Kt.
Cunningham, *General* Sir Alan Gordon, G.C.M.G., K.C.B., D.S.O., M.C.
Cunningham, Sir Charles Banks, Kt., C.S.I.
Cunningham, Sir Charles Craik, K.C.B., K.B.E., C.V.O.
Cunningham, Sir George, G.C.I.E., K.C.S.I., O.B.E.
Cunningham, Sir Graham, K.B.E.
Cunynghame, Sir (Henry) David St. Leger Brooke Selwyn, Bt. (S 1702).
Curgenven, Sir Arthur Joseph, Kt.
Currie, Sir George Alexander, Kt.
Currie, Sir Walter Mordaunt Cyril, Bt. (1847).
Cursetjee, *Maj.-Gen.* Sir Heerajee Jehangir Manockjee, K.C.I.E., C.S.I., D.S.O.
Curteis, *Capt.* Sir Gerald, K.C.V.O., R.N.
Curtis, *Sq.-Ldr.* Sir Arthur Randolph Wormeley, K.C.V.O., C.M.G., M.C.
Curtis, Sir George Harold, Kt., C.B.
Curtis, Sir Peter, Bt. (1802).
Cushion, *Air Vice-Marshal* Sir William Boston, K.B.E., C.B.
Cutforth, *Maj.-Gen.* Sir Lancelot Eric, K.B.E., C.B.
Cuthbert, *Vice-Adm.* Sir John Wilson, K.B.E., C.B.
Dain, Sir Harry Guy, Kt.
D'Albiac, *Air Marshal* Sir John Henry, K.C.V.O., K.B.E., C.B., D.S.O.
Dale, *His Hon.* Sir Edgar Thorniley, Kt.
Dale, Sir Henry Hallett, O.M., G.B.E., M.D., D.SC., F.R.S.
Daley, Sir Dennis Leo, Kt.
Daley, Sir (William) Allen, Kt., M.D.
Dalling, Sir Thomas, Kt.
Dalrymple, Sir (Charles) Mark, Bt. (1887).
Dalrymple, Sir Hew Fleetwood Hamilton-, Bt. (S 1697).
Dalton, Sir Henry, Kt., C.B.E.
Dalton, *Vice-Adm.* Sir Norman Eric, K.C.B, O.B.E.
Daly, *Lt.-Col.* Sir Clive Kirkpatrick, Kt., C.S.I., C.I.E.
D'Ambrumenil, Sir Philip, Kt.
Danckwerts, *Rt. Hon.* Sir Harold Otto, Kt.
Daniel, *Admiral* Sir Charles Saumarez, K.C.B., C.B.E., D.S.O.
Dannatt, Sir Cecil, Kt., O.B.E., M.C.
Dannreuther, Sir Sigmund, Kt., C.B.
Darell, Sir Jeffrey Lionel, Bt., M.C. (1795).
Darling, *Lt.-Gen.* Sir Kenneth Thomas, K.C.B., C.B.E., D.S.O.
Darling, Sir Malcolm Lyall, K.C.I.E.
Darvall, *Air Vice Marshal* Sir Lawrence, K.C.B., M.C.
Dash, Sir Arthur Jules, Kt., C.I.E.
Dash, Sir Roydon Englefield Ashford, Kt., D.F.C.
Dashwood, Sir Henry George Massy, Bt. (1684).
Dashwood, Sir John Lindsay, Bt., C.V.O., *Premier Baronet of Great Britain* (1707).
Datar Singh, *Sardar Bahadur* Sir, Kt.
Davenport, Hon. Sir George Arthur, K.B.E., C.M.G.
Davenport, *Lt.-Col.* Sir Walter Henry Bromley-, Kt., T.D., M.P.
David, Sir Edgeworth Beresford K.B.E., C.M.G.
David, Sir Percival Victor, Bt. (1911).
Davidson, *Air Vice-Marshal* Sir Alexander Paul, K.B.E., C.B.
Davidson, *Prof.* Sir (Leybourne) Stanley (Patrick), Kt., M.D., F.R.S.E.
Davie, *Rev.* Sir Arthur Patrick Ferguson-, Bt. (1847).
Davies, Sir Daniel Thomas, K.C.V.O., M.D.

Davies, *His Hon.* Sir David, Kt., Q.C.
Davies, *Hon.* Sir Edward John, Kt.
Davies, *Hon.* Sir (Herbert) Edmund, Kt.
Davies, Sir Robert John, Kt., O.B.E.
Davies, *Rt. Hon.* Sir (William) Arthian, Kt.
Davis, Sir Gilbert, Bt. (1946).
Davis, Sir Godfrey, Kt.
Davis, Sir Herbert, Kt., C.B.E.
Davis, Sir Robert Henry, Kt.
Davis, *Admiral* Sir William Wellclose, G.C.B., D.S.O.
Dawnay, *Vice-Adm.* Sir Peter, K.C.V.O., C.B., D.S.C.
Dawson, Sir Benjamin, Bt. (1929).
Dawson, *Cdr.* Sir Hugh Trevor, Bt., C.B.E., R.N. (1920).
Dawson, Sir (Joseph) Bernard, K.B.E., M.D.
Dawson, *Air Chief Marshal* Sir Walter Lloyd, K.C.B., C.B.E., D.S.O.
Day, Sir Albert James Taylor, Kt., C.B.E.
Day, *Vice-Adm.* Sir Archibald, K.B.E., C.B., D.S.O.
D'Costa, Sir Alfred Horace, Bt.
Dean, Sir Arthur William Henry, Kt., C.I.E., M.C., E.D.
Dean, *Hon.* Sir Arthur, Kt.
Dean, Sir John Norman, Kt.
Dean, Sir Maurice Joseph, K.C.B., K.C.M.G.
Dean, Sir Patrick Henry, G.C.M.G.
de Beer, Sir Gavin Rylands, Kt., D.SC., F.R.S.
Debenham, Sir Piers Kenrick, Bt. (1931).
De Bunsen, Sir Bernard, Kt., C.M.G.
De Burgh, *General* Sir Eric, K.C.B., D.S.O., O.B.E.
Deedes, *General* Sir Charles Parker, K.C.B., C.M.G., D.S.O.
Deeley, Sir Anthony Meyrick Mallaby-, Bt. (1922).
D'Egville, Sir Howard, K.B.E.
de Freitas, Sir Geoffrey Stanley, K.C.M.G.
De Guingand, *Maj.-Gen.* Sir Francis W., K.B.E., C.B., D.S.O.
de Havilland, *Capt.* Sir Geoffrey, Kt., O.M., C.B.E.
De Hoghton, Sir Henry Philip Anthony Mary, Bt. (1611).
De La Bere, *Brig.* Sir Ivan, K.C.V.O., C.B., C.B.E.
De la Bère, Sir Rupert, Bt., K.C.V.O. (1953).
Delacombe, *Maj.-Gen.* Sir Rohan, K.B.E., C.B., D.S.O.
De la Poer Beresford, *Maj.-Gen.* Sir George, Kt., C.B., M.C.
De la Rue, Sir Eric Vincent, Bt. (1898).
De Lestang, Sir Marie Charles Emmanuel Clement Nageon, Kt.
Delve, Sir Frederick William, Kt., C.B.E.
de Montmorency, Sir Miles Fletcher, Bt., (I 1631).
Dempsey, *General* Sir Miles Christopher, G.B.E., K.C.B., D.S.O., M.C.,
Denholm, Sir John Carmichael, Kt., C.B.E.
Dening, Sir (Maberly) Esler, G.C.M.G., O.B.E.
Denman, Sir Charles Spencer Douglas, Bt., M.C. (1945).
Denning, *Vice-Adm.* Sir Norman Egbert, K.B.E., C.B.
Denning, *Lt.-Gen.* Sir Reginald Francis Stewart, K.B.E., C.B.
Denny, Sir Alistair Maurice Archibald, Bt., (1913).
Denny, Sir Anthony Coningham de Waltham, Bt.(I 1782).
Denny, Sir (Jonathan) Lionel (Percy), Kt., M.C.
Denny, *Admiral* Sir Michael Maynard, G.C.B., C.B.E., D.S.O.
de Normann, Sir Eric, K.B.E., C.B.
Dent, Sir Robert Annesley Wilkinson, Kt., C.B.
Derbyshire, Sir Harold, Kt., M.C., Q.C.
Dering, *Lt.-Col.* Sir Rupert Anthony Yea, Bt. (1627).
De Satgé, *Lt.-Col.* Sir Henry Valentine Bache, K.C.V.O., C.M.G., D.S.O.
Des Forges, Sir Charles Lee, Kt., C.B.E.
De Silva, Sir (Albert) Ernest, Kt.
De Soysa, Sir (Lambert) Wilfrid (Alexander), Kt.
De Stein, Sir Edward, Kt.
De Trafford, *Capt.* Sir Humphrey Edmund, Bt., M.C. (1841).
Deverell, Sir Colville Montgomery, G.B.E., K.C.M.G., C.V.O.
Devitt, Sir Thomas Gordon, Bt. (1916).
Dewey, Sir Anthony Hugh, Bt., (1917).
D'Eyncourt, Sir (Eustace) Gervais Tennyson-, Bt. (1930).
De Zoysa, *Hon.* Sir Cyril, Kt.
Dhrangadhra, H.H. the Maharaja Raj Saheb of, K.C.I.E.
Dickson, *Marshal of the Royal Air Force* Sir William Forster, G.C.B., K.B.E., D.S.O., A.F.C.
Dilke, Sir John Fisher Wentworth, Bt. (1862).
Dill, Sir Nicholas Bayard, Kt., C.B.E.
Dillon, Sir Robert William Charlier, Bt. (1801).
Dimsdale, Sir John Holdsworth, Bt. (1902).
Diplock, *Rt. Hon.* Sir (William John) Kenneth, Kt.
Dixie, Sir (Alexander Archibald Douglas) Wolstan, Bt. (1660).
Dixon, Sir Arthur Lewis, Kt., C.B., C.B.E.
Dixon, Sir Charles William, K.C.M.G., K.C.V.O., O.B.E.
Dixon, Sir Francis Netherwood, Kt., C.B.
Dixon, *Air Vice-Marshal* Sir (Francis Wilfred) Peter, K.B.E.
Dixon, Sir John, Bt. (1919).
Dixon, *Rt. Hon.* Sir Owen, O.M., G.C.M.G.
Dixon, Sir Pierson John, G.C.M.G., C.B.
Dixon, Sir Samuel Gurney-, Kt.
Doak, Sir James, Kt.
Dobbie, *Lt.-Gen.* Sir William George Shedden, G.C.M.G., K.C.B., D.S.O.
Dobson, Sir Roy Hardy, Kt., C.B.E.
Docker, Sir Bernard Dudley Frank, K.B.E.
Dodd, Sir John Samuel, Kt.
Dodds, Sir (Edward) Charles, Kt., M.V.O., D.SC., Ph.D., M.D., F.R.S.
Dodds, Sir James Leishman, K.C.M.G.
Dods, *Prof.* Sir Lorimer Fenton, Kt., M.V.O.
Dodson, Sir Gerald, Kt.
Dodsworth, Sir John Christopher Smith-, Bt. (1784).
Dodsworth, Sir (Leonard) Lumley (Savage), Kt.
Domvile, *Admiral* Sir Barry Edward, K.B.E., C.B., C.M.G.
Domville, Sir (Gerald) Guy, Bt. (1814).
Don, *Very Rev.* Alan Campbell, K.C.V.O., D.D.
Donald, *Air Marshal* Sir Grahame, K.C.B., D.F.C., A.F.C.
Donner, Sir Patrick William, Kt.
Donovan, *Rt. Hon.* Sir Terence Norbert, Kt.
Dorman, *Maj.* Sir Charles Geoffrey, Bt., M.C. (1923).
Dorman, Sir Maurice Henry, G.C.M.G., G.C.V.O.
Dormer, Sir Cecil Francis Joseph, K.C.M.G., M.V.O.
Dos Santos, Sir Errol Lionel, Kt., C.B.E.
Doubleday, Sir Leslie, Kt.
Douglas, Sir James Boyd, Kt., C.B.E.
Douglas, Sir James Louis Fitzroy Scott, Bt. (1786).
Douglas, Sir Sholto Courtenay Mackenzie, Bt., M.C. (1831).
Dow, Sir Hugh, G.C.I.E., K.C.S.I.
Dowbiggin, Sir Herbert Layard, Kt., C.M.G.
Dowding, *Vice-Adm.* Sir Arthur Ninian, K.C.V.O., K.B.E., C.B.
Dowler, *Lt.-Gen.* Sir Arthur Arnold Bullick, K.C.B., K.B.E.
Dowling, *Vice-Adm.* Sir Roy Russell, K.C.V.O., K.B.E., C.B., D.S.O.
Down, *Lt.-Gen.* Sir Ernest Edward, K.B.E., C.B.
Downie, Sir Harold Frederick, K.B.E., C.M.G.
Dowse, *Maj.-Gen.* Sir Maurice Brian, K.C.V.O., C.B., C.B.E.

Dowty, Sir George Herbert, Kt.
Doyle, *Capt.* Sir John Francis Reginald William Hastings, Bt. (1828).
D'Oyly, *Cdr.* Sir John Rochfort. Bt., R.N. (1663).
Drake, Sir Eugen (John Henry Vanderstegen) Millington-, K.C.M.G.
Drake, Sir (Hugh) Garrard Tyrwhitt-, Kt.
Drax, *Admiral* Hon. Sir Reginald Aylmer Ranfurly Plunkett-Ernle-Erle-, K.C.B., D.S.O.
Drew, Sir Ferdinand Caire, Kt., C.M.G.
Drewe, Sir Cedric, K.C.V.O.
Dreyer, *Vice-Adm.* Sir Desmond Parry, K.C.B., C.B.E., D.S.C.
Dring, *Lt.-Col.* Sir Arthur John, K.B.E., C.I.E.
Driver, Sir Arthur John, Kt.
Drummond, Sir James Hamlyn Williams Williams-, Bt. (1828).
Drummond, Sir Walter James, Kt.
Drummond, *Lieut.-Gen.* Sir (William) Alexander (Duncan), K.B.E., C.B.
Drury, Sir Alan Nigel, Kt., C.B.E., M.D., F.R.S.
Dryden, Sir Noel Percy Hugh, Bt. (1733 and 1795).
Duckworth, *Maj.* Sir Richard Dyce, Bt. (1909).
Du Cros, Sir Philip Harvey, Bt. (1916).
Dudley, Sir Alan Alves, K.B.E., C.M.G.
Duff, Sir (Charles) Michael (Robert Vivian), Bt. (1911).
Duff, Sir (Charles) Patrick, K.C.B., K.C.V.O.
Duff, Sir James Fitzjames, Kt.
Dugdale, Sir William (Francis Stratford), Bt., F.S.A. (1930).
du Heaume, Sir Francis Herbert, Kt., C.I.E., O.B.E.
Duhig, *Most Rev.* James, K.C.M.G.
Duke, Sir Charles Beresford, K.C.M.G., C.I.E., O.B.E.
Duke, Sir (Robert) Norman, K.B.E., C.B., D.S.O., M.C.
Dukes, Sir Paul, K.B.E.
Dumas, Sir Lloyd, Kt.
Dumas, Sir Russell John, Kt. C.M.G.
Dunbar, Sir Adrian Ivor, Bt., (S 1694).
Dunbar, Sir (Archibald) Edward, Bt., M.C. (S 1700).
Dunbar, Sir David Hope-, Bt. (S 1664).
Dunbar, Sir Drummond Cospatrick Ninian, Bt., M.C. (S 1698).
Dunbar, Sir John Greig, Kt.
Duncan, *Col.* Sir Alan Gomme Gomme-, Kt., M.C.
Duncan, Sir Arthur Bryce, Kt.
Duncan, Sir (Charles Edgar) Oliver, Bt. (1905).
Duncan, *Capt.* Sir James Alexander Lawson, Bt., M.P. (1957).
Duncan, *Hon.* Sir Walter Gordon, Kt.
Duncombe, Sir Everard Philip Digby Pauncefort-, Bt., D.S.O. (1859).
Dundas, Sir Ambrose Dundas Flux, K.C.I.E., C.S.I.
Dundas, Sir James Durham, Bt., O.B.E. (1898).
Dundas, Sir Robert Whyte Melville, Bt. (1821).
Dunfield, Sir Brian (Edward Spencer), Kt., Q.C.
Dungarpur, H.H. the Maharawal of, G.C.I.E., K.C.S.I.
Dunk, Sir William Ernest, Kt., C.B.E.
Dunkley, Sir Herbert Francis, Kt.
Dunlop, *Prof.* Sir Derrick Melville, Kt., M.D.
Dunlop, *Brig.* Sir John Kinninmont, K.B.E., M.C., T.D.
Dunlop, Sir Thomas, Bt. (1916).
Dunn, Sir John Henry, Bt. (1917).
Dunn, *Maj.* Sir Philip Gordon, Bt. (1921).
Dunne, Sir Laurence Rivers, Kt., M.C.
Dunnett, Sir George Sangster, K.B.E., C.B.
Dunnett, Sir (Ludovic) James, K.C.B., C.M.G.
Dunning, Sir Simon William Patrick, Bt. (1930).
Dunphie, *Maj.-Gen.* Sir Charles Anderson Lane, Kt., C.B., C.B.E., D.S.O.
Duntze, Sir George Edwin Douglas, Bt., C.M.G. (1774).
Dupree, Sir Vernon, Bt. (1921).
Durand, *Col.* Sir Alan Algernon Marion, Bt., M.C. (1892).
Durlacher, *Admiral* Sir Laurence George, K.C.B., O.B.E., D.S.C.
Durrant, Sir William Henry Estridge, Bt. (1784).
Duthie, Sir William Smith, Kt., O.B.E., M.P.
Dutton, Sir Ernest Rowe-, K.C.M.G., C.B.
Duveen, Sir Geoffrey, Kt., R.D.
Dwyer, Sir John Patrick, K.C.M.G.
Dyer, Sir Leonard Schroeder Swinnerton, Bt. (1678).
Dyett, Sir Gilbert (Joseph Cullen), Kt., C.M.G.
Dyke, Sir Oliver Hamilton Augustus Hart, Bt. (1677).
Dyson, Sir Cyril Douglas, Kt.
Dyson, Sir George, K.C.V.O., Mus.D.
Eades, Sir Thomas, Kt.
Eager, Sir Clifden Henry Andrews, K.B.E., Q.C.
Earle, *Air Marshal* Sir Alfred, K.B.E., C.B.
Earle, Sir George Foster, Kt., C.B.E.
Earle, Sir Hardman Alexander Mort, Bt. (1869).
Eastham, *His Hon.* Sir Tom, Kt., Q.C.
Easton, *Air Commodore* Sir James Alfred, K.C.M.G., C.B., C.B.E.
Eaton, *Vice-Adm.* Sir John Willson Musgrave, K.B.E., C.B., D.S.O., D.S.C.
Eborall, Sir (Ernest) Arthur, Kt., C.B.E.
Ebrahim, Sir (Mahomed) Currimbhoy, Bt. (1910).
Eccles, *Admiral* Sir John Arthur Symons, G.C.B., K.C.V.O., C.B.E.
Eccles, *Prof.* Sir John Carew, Kt., D.Phil., F.R.S.
Eccles, Sir Josiah, Kt., C.B.E., M.M.
Echlin, Sir Norman David Fenton, Bt. (I 1721).
Edden, *Vice-Adm.* Sir (William) Kaye, K.B.E., C.B.
Eddis, Sir Basil Eden Garth, Kt.
Eddy, Sir (Edward) George, Kt., O.B.E.
Edelsten, *Admiral* Sir John Hereward, G.C.B., G.C.V.O., C.B.E.
Eden, Sir John Benedict, Bt., M.P. (1672 and 1776).
Edge, Sir Knowles, Bt. (1937).
Edmenson, Sir Walter Alexander, Kt., C.B.E.
Edmonstone, Sir Archibald Bruce Charles, Bt. (1774).
Edwards, *Lt.-Col.* Sir Bartle Mordaunt Marsham, Kt., C.V.O., M.C.
Edwards, Sir Christopher John Churchill, Bt. (1866).
Edwards, Sir David, Kt.
Edwards, Sir George Robert, Kt., C.B.E.
Edwards, Sir Ifan ab Owen, Kt.
Edwards, Sir John Clive Leighton, Bt. (1921).
Edwards, *Prof.* Sir (John) Goronwy, Kt., D.Litt., F.B.A.
Edwards, Sir Lawrence, K.B.E.
Edwards, Sir Ronald Stanley, K.B.E.
Edye, Sir Benjamin Thomas, Kt., C.B.E.
Egerton, Sir (Philip) John (Caledon) Grey-, Bt. (1617).
Elder, Sir Stewart Duke-, G.C.V.O., M.D., F.R.S.
Elderton, Sir Thomas Howard, K.C.I.E.
Eldridge, *Lt.-Gen.* Sir (William) John, K.B.E., C.B., D.S.O., M.C.
Eliott, Sir Arthur Francis Augustus Boswell, Bt. (S 1666).
Elkins, Sir Anthony Joseph, Kt., C.B.E.
Elkins, *Vice-Adm.* Sir Robert Francis, K.C.B., C.V.O., O.B.E.
Ellerman, Sir John Reeves, Bt. (1905).

Ellington, *Marshal of the Royal Air Force* Sir Edward Leonard, G.C.B., C.M.G., C.B.E.
Elliot, Sir John Blumenfeld, Kt.
Elliot, *Air Chief Marshal* Sir William, G.C.V.O., K.C.B., K.B.E., D.F.C.
Elliott, Sir Claude Aurelius, Kt., O.B.E.
Elliott, Sir Hugh Francis Ivo, Bt., O.B.E. (1917).
Elliott, *Vice-Adm.* Sir Maurice Herbert, K.C.B., C.B.E.
Ellis, Sir Arthur William Mickle, Kt., O.B.E., M.D.
Ellis, Sir Charles Drummond, Kt., Ph.D., F.R.S.
Ellis, Sir Thomas Hobart, Kt.
Ellwood, *Air Marshal* Sir Aubrey Beauclerk, K.C.B., D.S.C.
Elmhirst, *Air Marshal* Sir Thomas Walker, K.B.E., C.B., A.F.C.
Elphinstone, Sir Alexander Logie, Bt. (S 1701).
Elphinstone, Sir Howard (Graham), Bt. (1816).
Elphinstone, Sir Lancelot Henry, Kt.
Elton, Sir Arthur Hallam Rice, Bt. (1717).
Elwes, *Hon.* Sir Richard Everard Augustine, Kt. O.B.E., T.D.
Elworthy, *Air Chief Marshal* Sir (Samuel) Charles, G.C.B., C.B.E., D.S.O., M.V.O., D.F.C., A.F.C.
Emberton, Sir (John) Wesley, Kt.
Embry, *Air Chief Marshal* Sir Basil Edward, G.C.B., K.B.E., D.S.O., D.F.C., A.F.C.
Emerson, *Col.* Sir Ralf Billing, Kt., C.I.E., O.B.E.
Emery, Sir (James) Frederick, Kt.
Emmerson, Sir Harold Corti, G.C.B., K.C.V.O.
Empson, Sir Charles, K.C.M.G.
Enever, Sir Francis Alfred, Kt., C.B., M.C.
Enfield, Sir Ralph Roscoe, Kt., C.B.
Engineer, Sir Noshirwan Phirozshah, Kt.
Engledow, *Prof.* Sir Frank Leonard, Kt., C.M.G., F.R.S.
Entwistle, *Maj.* Sir Cyril Fullard. Kt., M.C., Q.C.
Entwistle, Sir John Nuttall Maxwell, Kt.
Errington, Sir Eric, Bt., M.P. (1963).
Erskine, *General* Sir George Watkin Eben James, G.C.B., K.B.E., D.S.O.
Erskine, Sir John Maxwell, Bt., G.B.E. (1961).
Erskine, Sir (Robert) George, Kt., C.B.E.
Erskine, Sir (Thomas) David, Bt. (1821).
Esmonde, Sir Anthony Charles, Bt. (I 1629).
Esplen, Sir William Graham, Bt., (1921)
Evans, Sir Anthony Adney, Bt. (1920).

I*

Evans, Sir Arthur Trevor, Kt.
Evans, Sir Athol Donald, K.B.E.
Evans, Sir (Benjamin) Ifor, Kt., D.Lit.
Evans, Sir Bernard, Kt., D.S.O., E.D.
Evans, Sir Charles (Arthur) Lovatt, Kt., F.R.S.
Evans, *Vice-Adm.* Sir Charles Leo Glandore, K.C.B., C.B.E., D.S.O., D.S.C.
Evans, Sir (David) Emrys, Kt.
Evans, Sir David Lewis, Kt., O.B.E., D.Litt.
Evans, Sir Evelyn Ward, Bt. (1902).
Evans, Sir Francis Edward, G.B.E., K.C.M.G.
Evans, Sir Geoffrey, Kt., C.I.E.
Evans, *Lt.-Gen.* Sir Geoffrey Charles, K.B.E., C.B., D.S.O.
Evans, Sir Guildhaume Myrddin-, K.C.M.G., C.B.
Evans, Sir Ian William Gwynne-, Bt. (1913).
Evans, Sir John Harold, K.B.E., C.B.
Evans, Sir Lincoln, Kt., C.B.E.
Evans, *His Hon.* Sir (William) Shirley (Worthington) Worthington-, Bt. (1916).
Everard, Sir Nugent Henry, Bt. (1911).
Every, Sir John Simon, Bt. (1641).
Evetts, *Lt.-Gen.* Sir John Fullerton, Kt., C.B., C.B.E., M.C.
Evill, *Air Chief Marshal* Sir Douglas Claude Strathern, G.B.E., K.C.B., D.S.O., A.F.C.
Ewart, Sir (William) Ivan (Cecil), Bt., D.S.C. (1887).
Ewbank, Sir Robert Benson, Kt., C.S.I., C.I.E.
Ewing, *Prof.* Sir Alexander William Gordon, Kt., Ph.D.
Ewing, Sir Charles Ian Orr-, Bt., O.B.E., M.P. (1963).
Ewing, *Vice-Adm.* Sir (Robert) Alastair, K.B.E., C.B., D.S.C.
Ewing, Sir Ronald Archibald Orr-. Bt. (1886).
Eyre, *Lt.-Col.* Sir Oliver Eyre Crosthwaite-, Kt., M.P.
Ezra, Sir Alwyn, Kt.
Fadahunsi, Sir Joseph Odeleye, K.C.M.G.
Fadden, *Rt. Hon.* Sir Arthur William, G.C.M.G.
Fagge, Sir John William Frederick, Bt. (1660).
Fair, *Hon.* Sir Arthur, Kt., M.C.
Fairbairn, Sir William Albert, Bt. (1869).
Fairley, Sir Andrew Walker, K.B.E., C.M.G.
Fairley, Sir Neil Hamilton, K.B.E., F.R.S.
Fairweather, Sir Charles Edward Stuart, Kt., C.I.E.
Falconer, *Lt.-Col.* Sir George Arthur, K.B.E., C.I.E.
Falkiner, *Lt.-Col.* Sir Terence Edmond Patrick, Bt. (I. 1778).
Fanshawe, *Maj.-Gen.* Sir Evelyn Dalrymple, Kt., C.B., C.B.E.

Faridkot, *Col.* H.H. the Raja of, K.C.S.I.
Farquhar, *Lt.-Col.* Sir Peter (Walter), Bt., D.S.O. (1796).
Farquharson, Sir James Robbie, K.B.E.
Farrant, Sir Geoffrey Upcott, Kt., C.B.E.
Farren, Sir William Scott, Kt., C.B., M.B.E., F.R.S.
Farrer, Sir (Walter) Leslie, K.C.V.O.
Farrington, *Maj.* Sir Henry Francis Colden, Bt. (1818).
Fass, Sir (Herbert) Ernest, K.C.M.G., C.B., O.B.E.
Faulks, *Hon.* Sir Neville Major Ginner, Kt., M.B.E., T.D.
Fayrer, Sir Joseph Herbert Spens, Bt., D.S.C. (1896).
Fedden, Sir Roy, Kt., M.B.E., D.Sc.
Feilden, *Maj.-Gen.* Sir Randle Guy, K.C.V.O., C.B., C.B.E.
Feilden, Sir William Morton Buller, Bt., M.C. (1846).
Feiling, Sir Keith Grahame, Kt., O.B.E., D.Litt.
Fellowes, Sir Edward Abdy, K.C.B., C.M.G., M.C.
Fennelly, Sir (Reginald) Daniel, Kt., C.B.
Fenton, *Col.* Sir William Charles, Kt., M.C.
Ferens, Sir Thomas Robinson, Kt., C.B.E.
Ferguson, Sir Edward Brown, Kt.
Ferguson, Sir Gordon, Kt., M.C.
Ferguson, *Hon.* Sir John Alexander, Kt., O.B.E.
Ferguson, *Maj.* Sir John Frederick, Kt., C.B.E.
Ferguson, *Lt.-Col.* Sir Neil Edward Johnson-, Bt., T.D. (1906).
Fergusson, *Brig.* Sir Bernard Edward, G.C.M.G., G.C.V.O., D.S.O., O.B.E.
Fergusson, Sir Ewen MacGregor Field, Kt.
Fergusson of Kilkerran, Sir James, Bt. (S. 1703).
Fergusson, Sir James Herbert Hamilton Colyer-, Bt. (1866).
Ferranti, Sir Vincent Ziani de, Kt., M.C.
Festing, *Field Marshal* Sir Francis Wogan, G.C.B., K.B.E., D.S.O.
Fetherstonhaugh, *Admiral* Hon. Sir Herbert Meade-, G.C.V.O., C.B., D.S.O.
Fetherstonhaugh, *Lt.-Col.* Sir Timothy, Kt., O.B.E., T.D.
ffolkes, Sir Robert Francis Alexander, Bt. (1774).
fforde, Sir Arthur Frederic Brownlow, Kt.
Field, Sir Ernest Wensley Lapthorn, Kt., C.B.E.
Field, Sir John Osbaldiston, Kt., C.M.G.
Fielden, *Air Vice-Marshal* Sir Edward Hedley, K.C.V.O., C.B., D.F.C., A.F.C.
Fieldhouse, Sir Harold, K.B.E., C.B.
Fiennes, Sir Ranulph Twisleton-Wykeham-, Bt. (1916).

Fildes, Sir Paul, Kt., O.B.E., SC.D., F.R.S.
Findlay, *Lt.-Col.* Sir Roland Lewis, Bt. (1925).
Finlay, *Hon.* Sir George Panton, Kt.
Finnemore, *Hon.* Sir Donald Leslie, Kt.
Firebrace, *Cdr.* Sir Aylmer Newton George, Kt., C.B.E., R.N.
Fish, Sir (Eric) Wilfred, Kt., C.B.E., M.D., D.SC.
Fisher, *Lt.-Gen.* Sir Bertie Drew, K.C.B., C.M.G., D.S.O.
Fisher, *Admiral* Sir Douglas Blake, K.C.B., K.B.E.
Fisher, *Brig.* Sir Gerald Thomas, K.B.E., C.S.I., C.I.E.
Fisher, Sir Godfrey Arthur, K.C.M.G.
Fisher, Sir John, Kt.
Fisk, Sir Ernest Thomas, Kt.
Fison, Sir (Frank Guy) Clavering, Kt.
Fison, Sir (William) Guy, Bt., M.C. (1905).
Fitton, *Col.* Sir Charles Vernon, Kt., O.B.E., M.C.
Fitts, Sir Clive Hamilton, Kt., M.D.
Fitzgerald, Sir (Adolf) Alexander, Kt., O.B.E.
FitzGerald, Sir Arthur Henry Brinsley, Bt., *The Knight of Kerry* (1880).
FitzGerald, Sir John Joseph, Bt. (1903).
Fitz-Gerald, Sir Patrick Herbert, Kt., O.B.E.
Fitzgerald, Sir William James, Kt., M.C., Q.C.
Fitzgerald, Sir (William) Raymond, Kt.
FitzHerbert, Sir William, Bt. (1784).
Fitzmaurice, *Lt.-Col.* Sir Desmond FitzJohn, Kt., C.I.E.
Fitzmaurice, Sir Gerald Gray, G.C.M.G., Q.C.
Flavelle, Sir (Joseph) Ellsworth, Bt. (1917).
Flaxman, *Hon.* Sir Hubert James Marlowe, Kt., C.M.G.
Fleming, *Instr. Rear-Adm.* Sir John, K.B.E., D.S.C.
Flemming, Sir Gilbert Nicolson, K.C.B.
Fletcher, *Lt.-Col.* Sir (Edward) Lionel, Kt., C.B.E., R.M.
Fletcher, *Maj.* Sir Henry Lancelot Aubrey-, Bt., C.V.O., D.S.O. (1782).
Fletcher, Sir James, Kt.
Fletcher, *Hon.* Sir Patrick Bisset, K.B.E., C.M.G.
Flint, Sir William Russell, Kt., R.A.
Florey, *Prof.* Sir Howard Walter, Kt., P.R.S.
Floud, Sir Francis Lewis Castle, K.C.B., K.C.S.I., K.C.M.G.
Flower, *Lt.-Col.* Sir Fordham, Kt., O.B.E.
Flower, Sir (Walter) Newman, Kt.
Floyd, *Brig.* Sir Henry Robert Kincaid, Bt., C.B., C.B.E. (1816).
Fogarty, *Air Chief-Marshal* Sir Francis Joseph, G.B.E., K.C.B., D.F.C., A.F.C.
Foley, Sir (Ernest) Julian, Kt., C.B.
Follows, Sir (Charles) Geoffry (Shield), Kt., C.M.G.
Fooks, Sir Raymond Hatherell, Kt., C.B.E.
Foot, Sir Hugh Mackintosh, G.C.M.G., K.C.V.O., O.B.E.
Forbes, *Hon.* Sir Alastair Granville, Kt.
Forbes, Sir Archibald Finlayson, G.B.E.
Forbes of Pitsligo, Sir Charles Edward Stuart-, Bt., (S 1626).
Forbes, *Col.* Sir John Stewart, Bt., D.S.O. (1823).
Ford, *Capt.* Sir Aubrey St. Clair-, Bt., D.S.O., R.N. (1793).
Ford, *Vice-Adm.* (E.) Sir Denys Chester, K.C.B., C.B.E.
Ford, *Prof.* Sir Edward, Kt., O.B.E., M.D.
Ford, *Maj.* Sir Edward William Spencer, K.C.V.O., C.B.
Ford, Sir Henry Russell, Bt. (1929).
Ford, Sir Leslie Ewart, Kt., O.B.E.
Ford, *Maj.-Gen.* Sir Peter St. Clair-, K.B.E., C.B., D.S.O.
Ford, *Admiral* Sir Wilbraham Tennyson Randle, K.C.B., K.B.E.
Forsdyke, Sir (Edgar) John, K.C.B.
Forwood, Sir Dudley Richard, Bt. (1895).
Foster, Sir Frank Savin, Kt., C.B.E.
Foster, *Rt. Hon.* Sir Harry Braustyn Hylton Hylton-, Kt., Q.C., M.P.
Foster, Sir John Gregory, Bt. (1930).
Foster, *Gen.* Sir Richard Foster Carter, K.C.B., C.M.G., D.S.O.
Foster, *Air Chief Marshal* Sir Robert Mordaunt, K.C.B., C.B.E., D.F.C.
Foulis, Sir Ian Primrose Liston-, Bt. (S 1634).
Fowke, Sir Frederick (Woollaston Rawdon), Bt. (1814).
Fox, Sir Cyril Fred, Kt., Ph.D., F.S.A.
Fox, Sir John, Kt., O.B.E.
Fox, *Maj.* Sir John St. Vigor, Kt.
Fox, Sir Robert David John Scott, K.C.M.G.
Fox, Sir Theodore Fortescue, Kt., M.D., LL.D.
Foy, Sir Thomas Arthur Wyness, Kt., C.S.I., C.I.E.
Francis, Sir (Cyril Gerard) Brooke, Kt., Q.C.
Francis, Sir Frank Chalton, K.C.B., F.S.A.
Francis, *Hon.* Sir Josiah, Kt.
Frank, Sir Robert John, Bt. (1920).
Frankau, Sir Claude (Howard Stanley), Kt., C.B.E., D.S.O.
Frankland, Sir James Assheton, Bt. (1660).
Franklin, Sir Eric Alexander, Kt., C.B.E.
Fraser, Sir Arthur Ronald, K.B.E., C.M.G.
Fraser, Sir Basil Malcolm, Bt. (1921).
Fraser, Sir Bruce Donald, K.C.B.
Fraser, Sir Francis Richard, Kt., M.D.
Fraser, *Air Marshal* Sir (Henry) Paterson, K.B.E., C.B., A.F.C.
Fraser, Sir Hugh, Bt. (1961).
Fraser, Sir Ian, Kt., D.S.O., O.B.E.
Fraser, Sir James David, Bt. (1943).
Fraser, Sir Keith Charles Adolphus, Bt. (1806).
Fraser, *Brig.* Sir Kenneth Barron, Kt., C.B.E., E.D.
Fraser, Sir (Richard) Michael, Kt., C.B.E.
Fraser, Sir Robert Brown, Kt., O.B.E.
Fraser, Sir Stuart (Mitford), K.C.S.I., C.I.E.
Fraser, Sir (William) Robert, K.C.B., K.B.E.
Frazer, Sir Thomas, Kt., O.B.E.
Frederick, *Maj.* Sir Charles Boscawen, Bt. (1723).
Freeman, Sir John Keith Noel, Bt. (1945).
French, Sir Henry Leon, G.B.E., K.C.B.
Fressanges, *Air Marshal* Sir Francis Joseph, K.B.E., C.B.
Fretwell, Sir George Herbert, K.B.E., C.B.
Frew, *Air Vice-Marshal* Sir Matthew Brown, K.B.E., C.B., D.S.O., M.C., A.F.C.
Frew, *Eng. Rear-Adm.* Sir Sydney Oswell, K.B.E., C.B.
Frome, Sir Norman Frederick, Kt., C.I.E., D.F.C.
Froom, Sir Arthur Henry, Kt.
Fry, Sir Leslie Alfred Charles, K.C.M.G., O.B.E.
Fry, Sir (Theodore) Penrose, Bt. (1894).
Fry, Sir William Kelsey, Kt., C.B.E., M.C.
Fryars, Sir Robert Furness, Kt.
Fuchs, Sir Vivian Ernest, Kt., Ph.D.
Fuller, *Maj.* Sir (John) Gerard (Henry Fleetwood), Bt. (1910).
Furlonge, Sir Geoffrey Warren, K.B.E., C.M.G.
Furness, Sir Christopher, Bt. (1913).
Furse, *Maj.* Sir Ralph Dolignon, K.C.M.G., D.S.O.
Fyfe, Sir William Hamilton, Kt.
Fysh, Sir (Wilmot) Hudson, K.B.E., D.F.C.
Gadsdon, Sir Lawrence Percival, Kt.
Gage, Sir Berkeley Everard Foley, K.C.M.G.
Gaggero, Sir George, Kt., O.B.E.
Gainer, Sir Donald St. Clair, G.B.E., K.C.M.G.
Gairdner, *General* Sir Charles Henry, K.C.M.G., K.C.V.O., K.B.E., C.B.

Gaisford, *Lt.-Col.* Sir Philip, Kt., C.I.E.
Gale, *Lt.-Gen.* Sir Humfrey Myddelton, K.B.E., C.B., C.V.O., M.C.
Gale, *General* Sir Richard Nelson, G.C.B., K.B.E., D.S.O., M.C.
Galer, Sir (Frederic) Bertram, Kt.
Galloway, *Lt.-Gen.* Sir Alexander, K.B.E., C.B., D.S.O., M.C.
Gallwey, Sir Reginald Frankland Payne-, Bt. (1812).
Galpern, Sir Myer, Kt., M.P.
Gamage, Sir Leslie Carr, Kt., M.C.
Gamble, Sir David Arthur Josias, Bt. (1897).
Gammell, *Lt.-Gen.* Sir James Andrew Harcourt, K.C.B., D.S.O., M.C.
Gane, Sir Irving Blanchard, K.C.V.O.
Garbett, Sir Colin Campbell, K.C.I.E., C.S.I., C.M.G.
Gardener, Sir Alfred John, K.C.M.G., C.B.E.
Gardiner, Sir Alan Henderson, Kt., D.Litt.
Gardiner, Sir Thomas Robert, G.C.B., G.B.E.
Gardner, Sir Douglas Bruce Bruce-, Bt. (1945).
Gardner, Sir George William Hoggan, K.B.E., C.B.
Garner, Sir Harry Mason, K.B.E., C.B.
Garner, Sir (Joseph John) Saville, K.C.M.G.
Garran, Sir Isham Peter, K.C.M.G.
Garrett, *Lt.-Gen.* Sir (Alwyn) Ragnar, K.B.E., C.B.
Garrett, Sir (Arthur) Wilfrid, K.B.E.
Garrett, Sir (Joseph) Hugh, K.C.I.E., C.S.I.
Garrett, Sir Ronald Thornbury, Kt.
Garrett, Sir William Herbert, Kt., M.B.E.
Garrod, *Air Chief Marshal* Sir (Alfred) Guy (Roland), G.B.E., K.C.B., M.C., D.F.C.
Garthwaite, Sir William Francis Cuthbert, Bt., D.S.C. (1910).
Garvey, Sir Ronald Herbert, K.C.M.G., K.C.V.O., M.B.E.
Gascoigne, Sir Alvary Douglas Frederick, G.B.E., K.C.M.G.
Gascoigne, *Maj.-Gen.* Sir Julian Alvery, K.C.M.G., K.C.V.O., C.B., D.S.O.
Gass, Sir Neville Archibald, K.B.E., M.C.
Gasson, Sir Lionel Bell, Kt.
Gault, *Brig.* Sir James Frederick, K.C.M.G., M.V.O., O.B.E.
Gauntlett, Sir (Mager) Frederic, K.C.I.E., K.B.E.
Gavin, Sir William, Kt., C.B.E.
Gentle, Sir Frederick (William), Kt., Q.C.
Gentry, *Maj.-Gen.* Sir William George, K.B.E., C.B., D.S.O.
George, Sir John Clarke, K.B.E., M.P.
George, *Air Vice-Marshal* Sir Robert Allingham, K.C.M.G., K.C.V.O., K.B.E., C.B., M.C.
Gepp, *Maj.-Gen.* Sir (Ernest) Cyril, K.B.E., C.B., D.S.O.
Gerahty, Sir Charles Cyril, Kt., Q.C.
German, Sir Ronald Ernest, Kt., C.M.G.
Gerrard, Sir Albert Denis, Kt.,
Gethin, *Lt.-Col.* Sir Richard Patrick St. Lawrence, Bt. (I 1665).
Gibb, *Prof.* Sir Hamilton Alexander Roskeen, Kt., F.B.A.
Gibbons, Sir John Edward, Bt. (1752).
Gibbs, Sir Frank Stannard, K.B.E., C.M.G.
Gibbs, *Hon.* Sir Geoffery Cokayne, K.C.M.G.
Gibbs, *Air Marshal* Sir Gerald Ernest, K.B.E., C.I.E., M.C.
Gibbs, Hon. Sir Humphrey Vicary, K.C.M.G., O.B.E.
Gibson, Sir Christopher Herbert, Bt. (1931).
Gibson, Sir Donald Edward Evelyn, Kt., C.B.E.
Gibson, Sir Edmund Currey, K.C.I.E.
Gibson, *Hon.* Sir Frank Ernest, Kt.
Gibson, Sir (Horace) Stephen, Kt., C.B.E.
Gibson, Sir Kenneth Lloyd, Bt. (1926).
Gibson, Sir William, Waymouth, Kt.
Gidney, Sir Claude Henry, K.C.I.E., C.S.I.
Gielgud, Sir (Arthur) John, Kt.
Giffard, *General* Sir George James, G.C.B., D.S.O.
Gilbert, Sir Ian Anderson Johnson-, Kt., C.B.E.
Gilbert, *Hon.* Sir (Joseph) Trounsell, Kt., C.B.E., Q.C.
Gilbey, Sir (Walter) Derek, Bt. (1893).
Gilchrist, Sir James Albert, Kt., Q.C.
Giles, *Lt.-Col.* Sir Oswald Bissill, Kt.
Gill, Sir Archibald Joseph, Kt.
Gill, *Commodore* Sir Roy, K.B.E., R.D.
Gillan, *Lt.-Col.* Sir George van Baerle, K.C.I.E.
Gillan, Sir (James) Angus, K.B.E., C.M.G.
Gillett, Sir Edward Bailey, Kt.
Gillett, Sir Michael Cavenagh, K.B.E., C.M.G.
Gillett, Sir Stuart, Kt., C.M.G.
Gillett, Sir (Sydney) Harold, Bt., M.C. (1959).
Gilliat, *Lt.-Col.* Sir Martin John, K.C.V.O., M.B.E.
Gillies, Sir Alexander, Kt.
Gilmour, Sir John Edward, Bt., D.S.O., T.D., M.P. (1897).
Gilmour, Sir John Little, Bt. (1926).
Gimson, Sir Franklin Charles, K.C.M.G.
Gladstone, Sir Albert Charles, Bt., M.B.E. (1846).
Gladstone, *Admiral* Sir Gerald Vaughan, G.B.E., K.C.B.
Glanville, Sir William Henry, Kt., C.B., C.B.E., D.Sc., Ph.D., F.R.S.
Glen, Sir Alexander, K.B.E., C.B., M.C.
Glenday, Sir Vincent Gonçalves, K.C.M.G., O.B.E.
Glennie, *Admiral* Sir Irvine Gordon, K.C.B.
Glover, *Col.* Sir Douglas, Kt., T.D., M.P.
Glover, *Maj.-Gen.* Sir Guy de Courcy, K.B.E., C.B., D.S.O., M.C.
Glubb, *Lt.-Gen.* Sir John Bagot, K.C.B., C.M.G., D.S.O., O.B.E., M.C.
Gluckstein, Sir Louis Halle, Kt., T.D., Q.C.
Glyn, Sir Anthony Geoffrey Leo Simon, Bt. (1927).
Glyn, Sir Francis Maurice Grosvenor, K.C.M.G.
Glyn, *Col.* Sir Richard Hamilton, Bt., O.B.E., T.D., M.P. (1759 and 1800).
Godber, Sir George Edward, K.C.B., D.M.
Goddard, *Air Marshal* Sir (Robert) Victor, K.C.B., C.B.E.
Godfrey, Sir John Albert, Kt.
Godfrey, Sir William Maurice, Bt. (I 1785).
Godley, *Brig.* Sir Francis William Crewe Fetherston-, Kt., O.B.E.
Goenka, *Rai Bahadur* Sir Badridas, Kt., C.I.E.
Goff, Sir Ernest (William) Davis-, Bt. (1905).
Goldie, Sir Noel Barré, Kt., Q.C.
Goldney, Sir Henry Hastings, Bt., M.C. (1880).
Goldsmid, Sir Henry Joseph D'Avigdor-, Bt., D.S.O., M.C., M.P. (1934).
Gomes, Sir Stanley Eugene, Kt.
Gonzi, *Most Rev. Monsignor* Michael, K.B.E., D.D. (*Archbishop of Malta*).
Gooch, Sir Robert Douglas, Bt. (1866).
Gooch, *Col.* Sir Robert Eric Sherlock, Bt., D.S.O. (1746).
Goodale, Sir Ernest William, Kt., C.B.E., M.C.
Goodall, Sir Stanley Vernon, K.C.B., O.B.E.
Goodbody, *General* Sir Richard Wakefield, G.C.B., K.B.E., D.S.O.
Goode, Sir William Allmond Codrington, G.C.M.G.
Goodenough, Sir Richard Edmund, Bt. (1943).
Goodeve, Sir Charles Frederick, Kt., O.B.E., V.D., F.R.S.
Goodfellow, Sir William, Kt.
Goodhart, Sir John Gordon, Bt. (1911).
Goodman, Sir Victor Martin Reeves, K.C.B., O.B.E., M.C.
Goodson, *Lt.-Col.* Sir Alfred Lassam, Bt. (1922).
Goodwin, *Maj.-Gen.* Sir Richard Elton, K.C.B., C.B.E., D.S.O.
Goodwin, Sir Stuart Coldwell, Kt.
Goold, Sir George Ignatius, Bt., (1801).
Goonetilleke, Sir Oliver Ernest, G.C.M.G., K.C.V.O., K.B.E.

Gordon, Sir (Archibald) Douglas, Kt., C.I.E.
Gordon, Sir Archibald McDonald, Kt., C.M.G.
Gordon, Sir Douglas Frederick Duff-, Bt. (1813).
Gordon, Sir Eyre, Kt., C.S.I., C.I.E.
Gordon, Sir Garnet Hamilton, Kt., C.B.E., Q.C.
Gordon, *Capt.* Sir Henry Robert, Kt., D.S.C.
Gordon, Sir John Charles, Bt. (S 1706).
Gordon, Sir Lionel Eldred Pottinger Smith-, Bt. (1838).
Gore, *Lt.-Col.* Sir Ralph St. George Brian, Bt. (I 1622).
Gore, *Rt. Hon.* Sir (William) David Ormsby-, K.C.M.G.
Goring, Sir William Burton Nigel, Bt. (1627).
Gorman, *Hon.* Sir William, Kt.
Goschen, Sir Edward Christian, Bt., D.S.O. (1916).
Gosling, Sir Arthur Hulin, K.B.E., C.B., F.R.S.E.
Gothard, Sir Clifford Frederic, Kt., O.B.E.
Gott, Sir Charles Henry, Kt.
Gotz, Sir Frank Leon Aroho, K.C.V.O.
Gould, Sir Robert Macdonald, K.B.E., C.B.
Gould, Sir Ronald, Kt.
Gould, *Hon.* Sir Trevor Jack, Kt.
Goulding, Sir William Basil, Bt. (1904).
Gower, Sir (Robert) Patrick (Malcolm), K.B.E., C.B., C.V.O.
Gowers, Sir Ernest Arthur, G.C.B., G.B.E.
Graaff, Sir de Villiers, Bt., M.B.E. (1911).
Grace, Sir (Oliver) Gilbert, Kt., C.I.E., O.B.E.
Grace, Sir Raymond Eustace, Bt. (1795).
Gracey, *General* Sir Douglas David, K.C.B., K.C.I.E., C.B.E., M.C.
Graeme, Sir Egerton Hood Murray Hamond-, Bt., T.D. (1783).
Graham, *Admiral* Sir Angus Edward Malise Bontine Cunninghame, K.B.E., C.B.
Graham, Sir Clarence Johnston, Kt.
Graham, Sir (Frederick) Fergus, Bt., K.B.E., T.D. (1783).
Graham, Sir George Goldie, Kt.
Graham, Sir John Gibson, Kt., M.C.
Graham, Sir John Reginald Noble, Bt., V.C., O.B.E. (1906).
Graham, *Maj.-Gen.* Sir Miles William Arthur Peel, K.B.E., C.B., M.C.
Graham, Sir Montrose Stuart, Bt. (1629).
Graham, Sir Richard Bellingham, Bt., O.B.E. (1662).
Grandy, *Air Marshal* Sir John, K.B.E., C.B., D.S.O.
Gransden, Sir Robert, Kt., C.B.E.
Grant, Sir (Albert) William, Kt., C.B.E.
Grant, *Air Marshal* Sir Andrew, K.B.E., C.B.
Grant, *Maj.* Sir Ewan George Macpherson-, Bt. (1838).
Grant, Sir Francis Cullen, Bt. (S 1705).
Grant, Sir Kenneth Lindsay, Kt., O.B.E.
Grant, Sir Kerr, Kt.
Grant, Sir Patrick Alexander Benedict, Bt. (S 1688).
Grantham, Sir Alexander William George Herder, G.C.M.G.
Grantham, *Admiral* Sir Guy, G.C.B., C.B.E., D.S.O.
Grasett, *Lt.-Gen.* Sir (Arthur) Edward, K.B.E., C.B., D.S.O., M.C.
Gravely, Sir Walter Booth-, K.C.M.G., C.S.I., C.I.E.
Graves, Sir Hubert Ashton, K.C.M.G., M.C.
Gray, Sir Alexander, Kt., C.B.E.
Gray, Sir Alexander George, Kt.
Gray, Sir Archibald (Montague Henry), K.C.V.O., C.B.E., M.D.
Gray, *Prof.* Sir James, Kt., C.B.E., M.C., SC.D., D.SC., LL.D., F.R.S.
Gray, Sir John Milner, Kt.
Gray, Sir William, Bt. (1917).
Gray, *Maj. Rt. Hon.* Sir William John Anstruther-, Bt., M.C., M.P. (1956).
Grayson, Sir Ronald Henry Rudyard, Bt. (1922).
Greaves, Sir John Bewley, Kt., C.M.G., O.B.E.
Greaves, Sir John Brownson, Kt., C.B.E.
Green, Sir (Edward) Stephen (Lycett), Bt. (1886).
Green, Sir George Edward, Kt.
Green, Sir John, Kt.
Green, *Lt.-Gen.* Sir (William) Wyndham, K.B.E., C.B., D.S.O., M.C.
Greenaway, Sir Derek Burdick, Bt. (1933).
Greene, Sir Edward Allan, Bt., M.C., T.D. (1900).
Greenfield, Sir Harry, Kt., C.S.I., C.I.E.
Greenfield, Sir Henry Challen, Kt., C.S.I., C.I.E.
Greenwell, Sir Peter McClinbock, Bt. (1906).
Greenwood, Sir James Mantle, Kt., C.B.E.
Greeson, *Surgeon Vice-Adm.* Sir Clarence Edward, K.B.E., C.B., Q.H.P.
Greeves, *Maj.-Gen.* Sir Stuart, K.B.E., C.B., D.S.O., M.C.
Gregg, Sir Norman McAlister, Kt., M.C.
Gregory, Sir Theodore, Kt., D.SC.
Gresley, Sir Nigel, Bt. (1612).
Gresson, *Rt. Hon.* Sir Kenneth Macfarlane, K.B.E.
Gretton, *Vice-Adm.* Sir Peter William, K.C.B., D.S.O., O.B.E., D.S.C.
Grey, Sir Paul Francis, K.C.M.G.
Grey, Sir Ralph Francis Alnwick, K.C.M.G., K.C.V.O., O.B.E.
Grey, Sir Robin Edward Dysart, Bt. (1814).
Grierson, Sir Richard Douglas, Bt. (S 1685).
Grieve, Sir (Herbert) Ronald (Robinson), Kt.
Griffin, Sir Arthur Cecil, K.C.I.E., K.B.E.
Griffin, Sir Herbert John Gordon, Kt., C.B.E.
Griffin, Sir John Bowes, Kt., Q.C.
Griffin, Sir (Lancelot) Cecil (Lepel), Kt., C.S.I., C.I.E.
Griffith, *Lt.-Col.* Sir Ralph Edwin Hotchkin, K.C.S.I., C.I.E.
Griffiths, Sir Percival Joseph, K.B.E., C.I.E.
Griffiths, Sir Peter Norton-, Bt. (1922).
Grigg, *Rt. Hon.* Sir (Percy) James, K.C.B., K.C.S.I.
Grime, Sir Harold Riley, Kt.
Grimston, Sir Robert Villiers, Bt., M.P. (1952).
Groom, Sir Thomas Reginald, Kt.
Groom, *Air Marshal* Sir Victor Emmanuel, K.C.V.O., K.B.E., C.B., D.F.C.
Grotrian, Sir John (Appelbe) Brent, Bt. (1934).
Grove, Sir Walter Philip, Bt. (1874).
Grubb, Sir Kenneth George, Kt., C.M.G.
Grundy, *Air Marshal* Sir John, K.B.E., C.B.
Gubbins, *Maj.-Gen.* Sir Colin McVean, K.C.M.G., D.S.O., M.C.
Guest, *Air Marshal* Sir Charles Edward Neville, K.B.E., C.B.
Guest, *Col. Hon.* Sir Ernest Lucas, K.B.E., C.M.G., C.V.O.
Guinness, Sir Alec, Kt., C.B.E.
Guinness, Sir Kenelm Ernest Lee, Bt. (1867).
Guise, Sir Anselm William Edward, Bt. (1783).
Gull, Sir Michael Swinnerton Cameron, Bt. (1872).
Gunn, Sir (Herbert) James, Kt. R.A.
Gunn, Sir William Archer, K.B.E., C.M.G.
Gunning, Sir (Orlando) Peter, Kt., C.M.G.
Gunning, Sir Robert Charles, Bt. (1778).
Gunson, Sir James Henry, Kt., C.M.G., C.B.E.
Gunston, *Maj.* Sir Derrick Wellesley, Bt., M.C. (1938).
Gunter, Sir Ronald Vernon, Bt. (1901).
Gurney, Sir Hugh, K.C.M.G., M.V.O.
Gutch, Sir John, K.C.M.G., O.B.E.
Guthrie, Sir Giles Connop McEacharn, Bt., O.B.E., D.S.C. (1936).
Guthrie, Sir (William) Tyrone, Kt.
Gwatkin, *Maj.-Gen.* Sir Frederick, Kt., C.B., D.S.O., M.C.
Gwatkin, *Brig* Sir Norman Wilmshurst, G.C.V.O., D.S.O.
Gwynne, *Lieut.-Col.* Sir Roland Vaughan, Kt., D.S.O.

Hackett, *Lt.-Gen.* Sir John Winthrop, K.C.B., C.B.E., D.S.O., M.C.
Hacking, Sir John, Kt.
Haddon, Sir Richard Walker, Kt., C.B.E.
Hadow, Sir Gordon, Kt., C.M.G., O.B.E.
Haggard, Sir Godfrey, K.C.M.G., C.V.O., O.B.E.
Haggerston, Sir (Hugh) Carnaby de Marie, Bt. (1642).
Hague, Sir (Charles) Kenneth (Felix), Kt.
Haines, Sir Cyril Henry, K.B.E.
Hale, Sir Edward, K.B.E., C.B.
Hale, Sir William Edward, Kt., C.B.E.
Haley, Sir William John, K.C.M.G.
Halid Bey, Sir Mehmed, Kt.
Hall, Sir Arnold Alexander, Kt., F.R.S.
Hall, Sir Douglas Basil, K.C.M.G.
Hall, Sir (Frederick) John (Frank), Bt. (1923).
Hall, Sir Herbert Hall, K.C.M.G.
Hall, Sir John Bernard, Bt. (1919).
Hall, Sir John Hathorn, G.C.M.G., D.S.O., O.B.E., M.C.
Hall, Sir Julian Henry, Bt. (S 1687).
Hall, Sir Noel Frederick, Kt.
Hall, Sir Robert de Zouche, K.C.M.G.
Hall, *Air Marshal* Sir Robert Hamilton Clark-, K.B.E., C.M.G., D.S.O.
Hall, Sir Robert Lowe, K.C.M.G., C.B.
Hall, Sir Roger Evans, Kt., C.B.E.
Hall, *Cdr.* Sir (William) Stephen (Richard) King-, Kt.
Hallam, Sir Clement Thornton, Kt.
Hallett, *Vice-Adm.* Sir Cecil Charles Hughes-, K.C.B., C.B.E.
Hallett, Sir Hugh Imbert Periam, Kt., M.C.
Hallett, Sir Maurice Garnier, G.C.I.E., K.C.S.I.
Halliday, *General* Sir Lewis Stratford Tollemache, V.C., K.C.B., R.M.
Halliday, Sir William Reginald, Kt., LL.D.
Hallinan, Sir Charles Stuart, Kt., C.B.E.
Hallinan, Sir Eric, Kt.
Hallstrom, Sir Edward John Lees, Kt.
Hallsworth, Sir Joseph, Kt.
Halsey, *Capt.* Sir Thomas Edgar, Bt., D.S.O., R.N. (1920).
Hambling, Sir (Herbert) Guy (Musgrave), Bt. (1924).
Hambro, Sir Charles Jocelyn, K.B.E., M.C.
Hamer, Sir George Frederick, Kt., C.B.E.
Hames, Sir George Colvile Hayter, Kt., C.B.E.
Hamilton, *Capt.* Lord Claud Nigel, G.C.V.O., C.M.G., D.S.O.
Hamilton, *Admiral* Sir Frederick Hew George Dalrymple-, K.C.B.
Hamilton, Sir George Rostrevor, Kt.
Hamilton, Sir Horace Perkins, G.C.B.
Hamilton, *Vice-Adm.* Sir John Graham, K.B.E., C.B.
Hamilton, Sir Patrick George, Bt. (1937).
Hamilton, Sir (Robert Charles) Richard Caradoc, Bt. (S 1646).
Hamilton, *Capt.* Sir Robert William Stirling-, Bt., R.N. (S 1673).
Hamilton, Sir (Thomas) Sydney (Perceval), Bt. (1776 and 1819).
Hammick, Sir George Frederick, Bt. (1834).
Hammond, Sir John, Kt., C.B.E., F.R.S.
Hampson, Sir Cyril Aubrey Charles, Bt. (1642).
Hancock, *Lt.-Col.* Sir Cyril Percy, K.C.I.E., O.B.E., M.C.
Hancock, Sir Henry Drummond, G.C.B., K.B.E., C.M.G.
Hancock, *Air Marshal* Sir Valston Eldridge, K.B.E., C.B., D.F.C.
Hancock, *Prof.* Sir (William) Keith, Kt., F.B.A.
Hanham, Sir Henry Phelips, Bt. (1667).
Hankinson, Sir Walter Crossfield, K.C.M.G., O.B.E., M.C.
Hanmer, Sir (Griffin Wyndham) Edward, Bt. (1774).
Hannays, Sir Leonard Courtney, Kt., Q.C.
Hanson, Sir Anthony Leslie Oswald, Bt. (1887).
Hanson, Sir (Charles) John, Bt. (1918).
Happell, Sir Alexander John, Kt., O.B.E.
Happell, Sir Arthur Comyn, Kt.
Harcourt, Sir (Robert) John (Rolston), Kt.
Hardinge, Sir Charles Edmund, Bt. (1801).
Hardman, Sir Henry, K.C.B.
Hardman, *Air Chief Marshal* Sir (James) Donald (Innes), G.B.E., K.C.B., D.F.C.
Hardwicke, Sir Cedric Webster, Kt.
Hardy, *Prof.* Sir Alister Clavering, Kt., D.Sc., F.R.S.
Hardy, *General* Sir Campbell Richard, K.C.B., C.B.E., D.S.O., R.M.
Hardy, Sir Edward, Kt.
Hardy, Sir Harry, Kt.
Hardy, Sir James Douglas, Kt., C.B.E.
Hardy, Sir Rupert John, Bt., (1876).
Hare, Sir Ralph Leigh, Bt. (1818).
Harford, Sir (George) Arthur, Bt. (1934).
Harford, Sir James Dundas, K.B.E., C.M.G.
Har Govind Misra, Sir, Kt., O.B.E.
Hargreaves, *His Hon.* Sir Gerald De La Pryme, Kt.
Hargreaves, Sir Thomas, Kt.
Harington Sir Charles Robert, K.B.E., Ph.D., F.R.S.
Harington, Sir Richard Dundas, Bt. (1611).
Harkness, Sir Douglas Alexander Earsman, K.B.E.
Harley, Sir Stanley Jaffa, Kt.
Harley, Sir Thomas Winlack, Kt., M.B.E., M.C.
Harman, Sir Cecil William Francis Stafford-King-, Bt. (1914).
Harman, *Rt. Hon.* Sir Charles Eustace, Kt.
Harmsworth, Sir (Arthur) Geoffrey (Annesley,) Bt. (1918).
Harmsworth, Sir Hildebrand Alfred Beresford, Bt. (1922).
Harper, Sir Arthur Grant, K.C.V.O., C.B.E.
Harper, Sir Richard Stephenson, Kt.
Harragin, Sir Walter, Kt., C.M.G., Q.C.
Harries, *Air Vice-Marshal* Sir Douglas, K.C.B., A.F.C.
Harrington, *Vice-Adm.* Sir Wilfred Hastings, K.B.E., C.B., D.S.O.
Harris, Sir Archibald, Kt.
Harris, *Marshal of the Royal Air Force* Sir Arthur Travers, Bt., G.C.B., O.B.E., A.F.C. (1953).
Harris, Sir Charles Joseph William, K.B.E.
Harris, Sir Douglas Gordon, K.B.E., C.S.I., C.I.E.
Harris, *Lt.-Gen.* Sir Frederick, K.B.E., C.B., M.C., Q.H.S.
Harris, Sir Jack Wolfred Ashford, Bt. (1932).
Harris, Sir Lionel Herbert, K.B.E., T.D.
Harris, Sir Percy Wyn, K.C.M.G., M.B.E.
Harris, Sir Ronald Montague Joseph, K.C.V.O., C.B.
Harris, Sir William Henry, K.C.V.O., D.Mus.
Harrison, Sir Archibald Frederick, Kt., C.B.E.
Harrison, Sir (Bernard) Guy, Kt.
Harrison, Sir Cyril Ernest, Kt.
Harrison, *Rt. Hon.* Sir Eric John, K.C.M.G., K.C.V.O.
Harrison, Sir Geoffrey Wedgwood, K.C.M.G., K.C.V.O.
Harrison, *Col.* Sir (James) Harwood, Bt., T.D., M.P. (1961).
Harrison, Sir Robert Colin, Bt. (1922).
Harrod, Sir (Henry) Roy Forbes, Kt., F.B.A.
Harston, *Maj.* Sir Ernest Sirdefield, Kt., C.B.E.
Hart, *Brig.-Gen.* Sir Herbert Ernest, K.B.E., C.B., C.M.G., D.S.O., V.D.
Hart, Sir Robert, Bt. (1893).
Hart, Sir William Ogden, Kt., C.M.G.
Hartley, *Air Marshal* Sir Christopher Harold, K.C.B., C.B.E., D.F.C., A.F.C.
Hartley, *Brig.-Gen.* Sir Harold, G.C.V.O., C.B.E., M.C., F.R.S.
Hartopp, Sir John Edmund Cradock-, Bt. (1796).

Hartwell, Sir Brodrick William Charles Elwin, Bt. (1805).
Hartwell, Sir Charles Herbert, Kt., C.M.G.
Harvey, *Air Commodore* Sir Arthur Vere, Kt., C.B.E., M.P.
Harvey, *Col.* Sir (Charles) Malcolm Barclay-, K.C.M.G.
Harvey, *Maj.-Gen.* Sir Charles Offley, Kt., C.B., C.V.O., C.B.E., M.C.
Harvey, *Air Vice-Marshal* Sir George David, K.B.E., C.B., D.F.C.
Harvey, *Air Vice-Marshal* Sir Leslie Gordon, K.B.E., C.B.
Harvey, Sir Richard Musgrave, Bt. (1933).
Harvey, Sir Robert James Paterson, K.B.E., C.B.
Harwood, Sir Edmund George, K.B.E., C.B.
Hassan, Sir Joshua Abraham, Kt., C.B.E., M.V.O., Q.C.
Hatton, Sir Ronald George, Kt., C.B.E., F.R.S.
Hatty, Sir Cyril James, Kt.
Havelock, Sir Thomas Henry, Kt., D.SC., F.R.S.
Havelock, Sir Wilfrid Bowen, Kt.
Havers, *Hon.* Sir Cecil Robert, Kt.
Havers, *Air Vice-Marshal* Sir (Ephraim) William, K.B.E., C.B.
Hawes, Sir Richard Brunel, Kt., C.M.G.
Hawes, Sir Ronald Nesbitt-, Kt., C.B.E., E.D.
Hawke, Sir (Edward) Anthony, Kt.
Hawker, Sir (Frank) Cyril, Kt.
Hawkey, Sir Roger Pryce, Bt. (1945).
Hawkins, *Admiral* Sir Geoffrey Alan Brooke, K.B.E., C.B., M.V.O., D.S.C.
Hawkins, Sir Humphry Villiers Caesar, Bt. (1778).
Hawley, *Maj.* Sir David Henry, Bt. (1795).
Haworth, Sir (Arthur) Geoffrey, Bt. (1911).
Hawton, Sir John Malcolm Kenneth, K.C.B.
Hawtrey, Sir Ralph George, Kt., C.B., F.B.A.
Hay, Sir (Alan) Philip, K.C.V.O., T.D.
Hay, Sir Arthur Thomas Erroll, Bt. (S 1663).
Hay, Sir Duncan Edwyn, Bt. (S 1635).
Hay, Sir Frederick Baden-Powell, Bt. (S 1793).
Hay, Sir James Brian Dalrymple-, Bt., (1798).
Hay, Sir James Lawrence, Kt., O.B.E.
Hay, Sir John George, Kt.
Hay, *Lt.-Gen.* Sir Robert, K.C.I.E.
Haygarth, *Col.* Sir Joseph Henry, Kt., C.B.E.
Hayman, Sir (Cecil George) Graham, Kt.
Haynes, Sir George Ernest, Kt., C.B.E.
Hayter, Sir William Goodenough, K.C.M.G.
Hayward, Sir Alfred, K.B.E.
Hayward, Sir Edward Waterfield, Kt.
Hayward, Sir Isaac James, Kt.
Hayward, Sir Maurice Henry Weston, K.C.S.I.
Head, Sir Francis David Somerville, Bt. (1838).
Heading, *Hon.* Sir James Alfred, Kt., C.M.G., D.C.M., M.M.
Headlam, *Lt.-Col. Rt. Hon.* Sir Cuthbert Morley, Bt., D.S.O., O.B.E., T.D. (1935).
Heald, *Rt. Hon.* Sir Lionel Frederick, Kt., Q.C., M.P.
Healey, *Maj.* Sir Edward Randal Chadwyck-, Bt., M.C. (1919).
Heath, *Air Marshal* Sir Maurice Lionel, K.B.E., C.B.
Heathcote, Sir Michael Perryman, Bt. (1833).
Heaton, Sir John Victor Peregrine, Bt. (1912).
Hedges, Sir John Francis, Kt., C.B.E.
Heinze, *Prof.* Sir Bernard Thomas, Kt., LL.D.
Helm, Sir (Alexander) Knox, G.B.E., K.C.M.G.
Helmore, Sir James (Reginald Carroll), K.C.B., K.C.M.G.
Helsby, Sir Laurence Norman, G.C.B., K.B.E.
Henderson, Sir Charles James, K.B.E.
Henderson, Sir David Kennedy, Kt., M.D.
Henderson, Sir Guy Wilmot McLintock, Kt., Q.C.
Henderson, Sir Ian Leslie, K.B.E., C.M.G.
Henderson, Sir James, K.B.E.
Henderson, Sir James Thyne, K.B.E., C.M.G.
Henderson, Sir (John James) Craik, Kt.
Henderson, Sir Malcolm Siborne, K.C.M.G.
Henderson, *Vice-Adm.* Sir Nigel Stuart, K.C.B., O.B.E.
Henderson, *Lt.-Col.* Sir Vivian Leonard, Kt., M.C.
Hendy, Sir Philip, Kt.
Heneage, *Lt.-Col.* Sir Arthur Pelham, Kt., D.S.O.
Henley, *Rear-Adm.* Sir Joseph Charles Cameron, K.C.V.O., C.B.
Hennessy, *Hon.* Sir Alfred Theodore, K.B.E.
Hennessy, Sir Patrick, Kt.
Henniker, *Brig.* Sir Mark Chandos Auberon, Bt., C.B.E., D.S.O., M.C. (1813).
Henriques, Sir Cyril George Xavier, Kt.
Henry, Sir David, Kt.
Henry, Sir James Holmes, Bt., C.M.G., M.C., T.D., Q.C. (1923).
Hepburn, Sir Ninian Buchan Archibald John Buchan-, Bt. (1815).
Herbert, Sir Alan Patrick, Kt.
Herbert, Sir Charles Gordon, K.C.I.E., C.S.I.
Herbert, *Lt.-Gen.* Sir (Edwin) Otway, K.B.E., C.B., D.S.O.
Herbert, Sir Edwin Savory, K.B.E.
Herbert, *Rt. Rev.* Percy Mark, K.C.V.O., D.D.
Herchenroder, Sir (Marie Joseph Barnabe) Francis, Kt., Q.C.
Hercus, Sir Charles Ernest, Kt., D.S.O., O.B.E., V.D., M.D.
Herring, *Lt.-Gen. Hon.* Sir Edmund Francis, K.C.M.G., K.B.E., D.S.O., M.C., E.D., Q.C.
Hetherington, Sir Hector James Wright, G.B.E., LL.D.
Hewetson, *Lt.-Gen.* Sir Reginald Hackett, K.C.B., C.B.E., D.S.O.
Hewett, Sir John George, Bt., M.C. (1813).
Hewitt, *Air Chief Marshal* Sir Edgar Rainey Ludlow-, G.C.B., G.B.E., C.M.G., D.S.O., M.C.
Hewitt, Sir Joseph, Bt. (1921).
Hewson, *Hon.* Sir Joseph Bushby, Kt.
Heyes, Sir Tasman Hudson Eastwood, Kt., C.B.E.
Heygate, Sir John Edward Nourse, Bt. (1831).
Heysen, Sir Hans, Kt., O.B.E.
Heywood, Sir Oliver Kerr, Bt. (1838).
Hickinbotham, Sir Tom, K.C.M.G., K.C.V.O., C.I.E., O.B.E.
Hickman, Sir (Alfred) Howard (Whitby), Bt. (1903).
Hicks, Sir (Cedric) Stanton, Kt., M.D., Ph.D.
Hicks, *Col.* Sir Denys Theodore, Kt., O.B.E., T.D.
Hilbery, *Rt. Hon.* Sir Malcolm, Kt.
Hildred, Sir William Percival, Kt., C.B., O.B.E.
Hildyard, *Gen.* Sir Reginald John Thoroton, K.C.B., C.M.G., D.S.O.
Hiles, Sir Herbert, Kt., M.B.E.
Hill, *Prof.* Sir Austin Bradford, Kt., C.B.E., Ph.D., D.SC., F.R.S.
Hill, Sir (George) Cyril Rowley, Bt. (I 1779).
Hill, Sir James, Bt. (1917).
Hill, Sir (James William) Francis, Kt., C.B.E.
Hill, Sir Reginald Herbert, K.B.E., C.B.
Hill, Sir Robert Erskine-, Bt. (1945).
Hillary, Sir Edmund, K.B.E.
Hills, Sir Reginald Playfair, Kt., O.B.E., M.C.
Himsworth, Sir Harold Percival, K.C.B., M.D., F.R.S.
Hinchcliffe, *Hon.* Sir George Raymond, Kt.
Hinchliffe, Sir (Albert) Henry (Stanley), Kt.
Hinde, *Maj.-Gen.* Sir (William) Robert (Norris), K.B.E., C.B., D.S.O.
Hinshelwood, Sir Cyril Norman, Kt., O.M., D.SC., F.R.S.
Hinton, Sir Christopher, K.B.E., F.R.S.
Hirst, Sir (Frank) Wyndham, K.B.E.
Hitchman, Sir (Edwin) Alan, K.C.B.
Hoare, Sir Archer, Kt., C.B.E.

Hoare, Sir Edward O'Bryen, Bt. (I 1784).
Hoare, Sir Frederick Alfred, Bt. (1962).
Hoare, Sir Peter William, Bt. (1786).
Hoare, Sir Samuel, Kt., C.B.
Hobart, *Lt.-Cdr.* Sir Robert Hampden, Bt., R.N. (1914).
Hobbs, Sir John Berry, Kt.
Hobhouse, Sir Arthur Lawrence, Kt.
Hobhouse, Sir Charles Chisholm, Bt., T.D. (1812).
Hobson, Sir Henry Arthur, K.B.E.
Hobson, *Rt. Hon.* Sir John Gardiner Sumner, Kt., O.B.E., T.D., Q.C., M.P.
Hobson, Sir Patrick, Kt.
Hochoy, Sir Solomon, G.C.M.G., O.B.E.
Hodge, Sir John Rowland, Bt., M.B.E. (1921).
Hodge, *Prof.* Sir William Vallance Douglas, Kt., SC.D., F.R.S., F.R.S.E.
Hodges, Sir Reginald John, Kt.
Hodgson, Sir Gerald Hassall, Kt.
Hodgson, Sir Mark, Kt., O.B.E.
Hodsoll, *Wing-Cdr.* Sir John, Kt., C.B.
Hodson, *Maj.* Sir Edmond Adair, Bt., D.S.O. (I 1789).
Hogan, Sir Michael Joseph Patrick, Kt., C.M.G.
Hogg, Sir Anthony Henry Lindsay-, Bt. (1905).
Hogg, Sir John Nicholson, Kt., T.D.
Hogg, *Lieut.-Col.* Sir Kenneth Weir, Bt., O.B.E. (1846).
Holbrook, *Col.* Sir Claude Vivian, Kt., C.B.E.
Holcroft, Sir Reginald Culcheth, Bt. (1921).
Holden, Sir Edward, Bt. (1893).
Holden, Sir George, Bt. (1919).
Holden, Sir Harry Cassie, Bt. (1909).
Holden, Sir James Robert, Kt.
Holder, Sir Frank Wilfred, Kt., C.M.G.
Holder, Sir John Eric Duncan, Bt. (1898).
Holderness, Sir Ernest William Elsmie, Bt., C.B.E. (1920).
Holford, *Prof.* Sir William Graham, Kt.
Holland, Sir Alfred Herbert, Kt.
Holland, Sir Eardley Lancelot, Kt., M.D.
Holland, Sir Edward Milner, Kt., C.B.E., Q.C.
Holland, Sir Henry Tristram, Kt., C.I.E.
Holland, Sir Jim Sothern, Bt. (1917).
Holland, Sir Robert Erskine, K.C.I.E., C.S.I., C.V.O., V.D.
Hollinghurst, *Air Chief Marshal* Sir Leslie Norman, G.B.E., K.C.B., D.F.C.
Hollis, *General* Sir Leslie Chasemore, K.C.B., K.B.E., R.M.
Hollis, Sir Roger Henry, Kt., C.B., O.B.E.
Holman, Sir Adrian, K.B.E., C.M.G., M.C.
Holmes, Sir Gordon Morgan, Kt. C.M.G., C.B.E., M.D., D.SC., F.R.S.
Holmes, Sir Maurice Gerald, G.B.E., K.C.B.
Holmes, *Maj.-Gen.* Sir Noel Galway, K.B.E., C.B., M.C.
Holmes, Sir Stephen Lewis, K.C.M.G., M.C.
Holmes, *Lt.-Gen.* Sir William George, K.B.E., C.B., D.S.O.
Holroyd, Sir Ronald, Kt., Ph.D., F.R.S.
Holt, Sir Edward, Bt. (1916).
Holt, Sir James Arthur, Kt.
Holt, Sir John Anthony Langford-, Kt., M.P.
Home, Sir David George, Bt. (S 1671).
Hone, Sir Evelyn Denison, K.C.M.G., C.V.O., O.B.E.
Hone, *Maj.-Gen.* Sir (Herbert) Ralph, K.C.M.G., K.B.E., M.C., T.D., Q.C.
Honeyman, Sir George Gordon, Kt., C.B.E., Q.C.
Honywood, *Col.* Sir William Wynne, Bt., M.C. (1660).
Hood, *Lt.-Gen.* Sir Alexander, G.B.E., K.C.B., K.C.V.O., M.D.
Hood, Sir Harold Joseph, Bt., T.D. (1922).
Hooke, Sir Lionel Alfred George, Kt.
Hooper, Sir Frederic Collins, Bt. (1962).
Hope, Sir Archibald Philip, Bt., O.B.E., D.F.C. (S 1628).
Hope, Sir James, Bt., M.M. (1932).
Hope, *Lt.-Col.* Sir Percy Mirehouse, Kt., O.B.E.
Horlick, *Lt.-Col.* Sir James Nockells, Bt., O.B.E., M.C. (1914).
Hornby, Sir (Henry) Russell, Bt. (1899).
Hornby, Sir Roger Antony, Kt.
Horne, Sir Alan Edgar, Bt. M.C. (1929).
Hornibrook, Sir Manuel Richard, Kt., O.B.E.
Horobin, Sir Ian Macdonald, Kt.
Horrocks, *Lt.-Gen.* Sir Brian Gwynne, K.C.B., K.B.E., D.S.O., M.C.
Horsfall, Sir (John) Donald, Bt. (1909).
Horsman, Sir Henry Kt., M.C.
Hort, Sir James Fenton, Bt. (1767).
Horwill, Sir Lionel Clifford, Kt.
Hoskins, Sir Cecil Harold, Kt.
Hoskyns, Sir Benedict Leigh, Bt. (1676).
Hotham, *Admiral* Sir Alan Geoffrey, K.C.M.G., C.B.
Houldsworth, *Brig.* Sir Henry Walter, K.B.E., D.S.O., M.C., T.D.
Houldsworth, Sir (Harold) Basil, Bt. (1956).
Houldsworth, Sir Reginald Douglas Henry, Bt., O.B.E., T.D. (1887).
Houlton, Sir John Wardle, Kt., C.S.I., C.I.E.
How, Sir Friston Charles, Kt., C.B.
Howard, Sir Algar Henry Stafford, K.C.B., K.C.V.O., M.C., T.D.
Howard, Hon. Sir Arthur Jared Palmer, K.B.E., C.V.O.
Howard, Sir Douglas Frederick, K.C.M.G., M.C.
Howard, *Lt.-Gen.* Sir Geoffrey Weston, K.C.B., C.M.G., D.S.O.
Howard, Sir Harold Walter Seymour, Bt. (1955).
Howard, *Maj.* Sir Henry (George), Kt., C.I.E., M.C.
Howard, Sir Henry Rudolph, K.B.E.
Howard, Sir John Alfred Golding, Kt.
Howard, Sir John Curtois, Kt.
Howard, Sir (Stanley) Herbert, Kt.
Howard, *Hon.* Sir (Stephen) Gerald, Kt.
Howard, Sir Walter Stewart, Kt., M.B.E.
Howe, Sir Robert George, G.B.E., K.C.M.G.
Howe, Sir Ronald Martin, Kt., C.V.O., M.C.
Howell, Sir Evelyn Berkeley, K.C.I.E., C.S.I.
Howitt, Sir Harold Gibson, G.B.E., D.S.O., M.C.
Howorth, Sir Rupert Beswicke, K.C.M.G., K.C.V.O., C.B., F.S.A.
Htoon Aung Gyaw, Sir, Kt.
Hubback, *Vice-Adm.* Sir (Arthur) Gordon (Voules), K.B.E., C.B.
Hubback, Sir John Austen, K.C.S.I.
Hudleston, *Air Chief Marshal* Sir Edmund Cuthbert, G.C.B., C.B.E.
Hudson, Sir Edmund Peder, Kt., F.R.S.E.
Hudson, Sir William, K.B.E.
Hugessen, Sir Hughe Montgomery Knatchbull-, K.C.M.G.
Huggins, Sir John, G.C.M.G., M.C.
Hughes, Sir Richard Edgar, Bt. (1773).
Hughes, *Hon.* Sir Wilfred Selwyn Kent, K.B.E., M.V.O., M.C., E.D.
Huish, Sir Raymond Douglas, Kt., C.B.E.
Hulbert, *Wing-Cdr.* Sir Norman John, Kt., M.P.
Hull, Sir Hubert, Kt., C.B.E.
Hull, Sir Percy Clarke, Kt., MUS.DOC.
Hull, *General* Sir Richard Amyatt, G.C.B., D.S.O.
Hulse, Sir (Hamilton) Westrow, Bt. (1739).
Hulton, Sir Edward George Warris, Kt.
Hulton, Sir Geoffrey Alan, Bt. (1905).
Hume, Sir (Hubert) Nutcombe, K.B.E., M.C.
Humphrys, *Lt.-Col.* Sir Francis Henry, G.C.M.G., G.C.V.O., K.B.E., C.I.E.
Hungerford, Sir (Alexander) Wilson, Kt.
Hunt, Sir David Wathen Stather, K.C.M.G., O.B.E.
Hunt, *Brig.* Sir (Henry Cecil) John, Kt., C.B.E., D.S.O.

Hunt, Sir Reuben James, Kt.
Hunt, Sir William Edgar, Kt., C.M.G., C.B.E.
Hunter, *Col.* Sir Herbert Patrick, Kt., C.B., C.B.E.
Hunting, Sir Percy Llewellyn, Kt.
Hunton, *General* Sir Thomas Lionel, K.C.B., M.V.O., O.B.E., R.M.
Hurd, Sir Anthony Richard, Kt., M.P.
Hurley, Sir Wilfred Hugh, Kt.
Hurst, Sir Alfred (William), K.B.E., C.B.
Hurst, Sir (James Henry) Donald, Kt.
Hutchings, Sir Robert Howell, K.C.I.E., C.M.G.
Hutchinson, Sir Arthur Sydney, K.B.E., C.B., C.V.O.
Hutchinson, Sir Herbert John, K.B.E., C.B.
Hutchinson, Sir Joseph Burtt, Kt., C.M.G., SC.D., F.R.S.
Hutchinson, Sir Lewis Bede, K.B.E., C.B.
Hutchison, *Lt.-Gen.* Sir Balfour Oliphant, K.B.E., C.B.
Hutchison, *Brig.* Sir Eric Alexander Ogilvy, Bt. (1923).
Hutchison, *Lt.-Cdr.* Sir (George) Ian Clark, Kt., R.N.
Hutchison, *Hon.* Sir James Douglas, Kt.
Hutchison, Sir James Riley Holt, Bt., D.S.O., T.D. (1956).
Hutchison, Sir John Colville, K.B.E.
Hutchison, Sir Peter, Bt. (1939).
Hutchison, Sir (William) Kenneth, Kt., C.B.E.
Hutchison, Sir William Oliphant, Kt., P.R.S.A.
Hutson, Sir Francis Challenor, Kt., C.B.E.
Hutt, Sir (Alexander McDonald) Bruce, K.B.E., C.M.G.
Hutton, Sir Leonard, Kt.
Hutton, Sir Maurice Inglis, Kt., C.M.G.
Hutton, Sir Noel Kilpatrick, K.C.B., Q.C.
Hutton, *Lt.-Gen.* Sir Thomas, K.C.I.E., C.B., M.C.
Huxley, Sir Julian Sorell, Kt., D.SC., F.R.S.
Hyde, Sir Robert Robertson, K.B.E., M.V.O.
Hyderabad and Berar, *Lt.-Gen.* H.E.H. the Nizam of, G.C.S.I., G.B.E., Royal Victorian Chain.
Hyland, *Hon.* Sir Herbert John Thornhill, Kt.
Hyne, *Hon.* Sir Ragnar, Kt.
Ibadan, The Olubadan of, Kt., O.B.E.
Ibiam, Sir Francis Akanu, K.C.M.G., K.B.E.
Idun, Sir Samuel Okie Quashie-, Kt.
Ife, The Oni of, K.C.M.G., K.B.E.
Iliff, Sir William Angus Boyd, Kt., C.M.G., M.B.E.
Illingworth, *Prof.* Sir Charles Frederick William, Kt., C.B.E.
Ilott, Sir John Moody Albert, Kt.
Imrie, Sir John Dunlop, Kt., C.B.E.
Indore, H.H. *ex*-Maharaja Holkar of, G.C.I.E.
Ingilby, Sir Joslan William Vivian, Bt. (1866).
Inglefield, *Col.* Sir John Frederick Crompton-, Kt., T.D.
Inglis, Sir Claude Cavendish, Kt., C.I.E., F.R.S.
Inglis, *Maj.-Gen.* Sir Drummond, K.B.E., C.B., M.C.
Inglis, *Vice-Adm.* Sir John Gilchrist Thesiger, K.B.E., C.B.
Inglis of Glencorse, Sir Maxwell Ian Hector, Bt. (S 1703).
Ingold, *Prof.* Sir Christopher Kelk, Kt., D.SC., F.R.S.
Ingram, Sir Herbert, Bt. (1893).
Innes, Sir Charles Alexander, K.B.E.
Innes of Learney, Sir Thomas, K.C.V.O.
Innes, Sir Walter James, Bt. (S 1628).
Inniss, *Hon.* Sir Clifford de Lisle, Kt.
Iqbal Ahmad, Sir, Kt.
Iredell, *Air Vice-Marshal* Sir Alfred William, K.B.E., C.B.
Irving, Sir Stanley Gordon, K.B.E., C.M.G.
Isaachsen, Sir Oscar Lionel, Kt.
Isham, Sir Gyles, Bt. (1627).
Isitt, *Air Vice-Marshal* Sir Leonard Monk, K.B.E.
Ismay, Sir George, K.B.E., C.B.
Jackman, *Air Marshal* Sir (Harold) Douglas, K.B.E., C.B.
Jackson, Sir Donald Edward, Kt.
Jackson, *Col.* Sir Francis James Gidlow, Kt., M.C., T.D.
Jackson, Sir George Christopher Mather-, Bt. (1869).
Jackson, Sir Harold Warters, Kt.
Jackson, *General* Sir Henry Cholmondeley, K.C.B., C.M.G., D.S.O.
Jackson, Sir Hugh Nicolas, Bt. (1913).
Jackson, Sir John Montrésor, Bt. (1815).
Jackson, Sir Michael Roland, Bt. (1902).
Jackson, Sir Richard Leofric, Kt., C.B.E.
Jackson, Sir Robert Gillman Allen, K.C.V.O., C.M.G., O.B.E.
Jackson, Sir Wilfrid Edward Francis, G.C.M.G.
Jackson, Sir Willis, Kt., D.SC., D.Phil., F.R.S.
Jacob, *Lt.-Gen.* Sir (Edward) Ian (Claud), G.B.E., C.B.
Jacob, *Hon.* Sir George Harold Lloyd-, Kt.
Jacobs, Sir Roland Ellis, Kt.
Jaffray, Sir William Otho, Bt. (1892).
Jaipur, *Lt.-Gen.* H.H. the Maharaja of, G.C.S.I., G.C.I.E.
James, *Wing-Cdr.* Sir Archibald William Henry, K.B.E., M.C.
James, Sir David John, Kt.
James, Sir Frederick Ernest, Kt., O.B.E.
James, Sir Gerard Bowes Kingston, Bt. (1823).
James, Sir (John) Morrice (Cairns), K.C.M.G., C.V.O., M.B.E.
James, *Admiral* Sir William Milbourne, G.C.B.
Jameson, *Rear-Adm* (E.) Sir William Scarlett, K.B.E., C.B.
Jamkhandi, Raja of, K.B.E.
Janes, Sir Herbert Charles, Kt.
Janner, Sir Barnett, Kt., M.P.
Jansz, Sir Herbert Eric, Kt., C.M.G.
Jardine, *Maj.* Sir Ian Liddell, Bt., M.C. (1916).
Jardine, Sir John, Bt., O.B.E., T.D. (1919).
Jardine, *Capt.* Sir John William Buchanan-, Bt. (1885).
Jardine, Sir William Edward, Bt. (S 1672).
Jarratt, Sir William Smith, Kt.
Jarrett, Sir Clifford George, K.B.E., C.B.
Jarvis, Sir (Arnold) Adrian, Bt. (1922).
Jayetileke, *Hon.* Sir Edward George Perera, Kt., Q.C.
Jefferis, *Maj.-Gen.* Sir Millis Rowland, K.B.E., M.C.
Jefferson, *Lt.-Col.* Sir John Alexander Dunnington-, Bt., D.S.O. (1958).
Jeffreys, *Prof.* Sir Harold, Kt., D.SC., F.R.S.
Jeffries, Sir Charles Joseph, K.C.M.G., O.B.E.
Jeffries, *Hon.* Sir Shirley Williams, Kt.
Jehanghir, Sir Hirjee Cowasjee, Bt. (1908).
Jejeebhoy, Sir Jamsetjee, Bt. (1857).
Jenkin, Sir William Norman Prentice, Kt., C.S.I., C.I.E.
Jenkins, Sir Evan Meredith, G.C.I.E., K.C.S.I.
Jenkins, Sir Owain Trevor, Kt.
Jenkins, Sir (Thomas) Gilmour, K.C.B., K.B.E. M.C.
Jenkins, Sir William Albert, Kt.
Jenkinson, Sir Anthony Banks, Bt. (1661).
Jenks, Sir Richard Atherley, Bt. (1932).
Jennings, Sir Roland, Kt.
Jennings, Sir (William) Ivor, K.B.E., Q.C., Litt.D.
Jenour, Sir (Arthur) Maynard (Chesterfield), Kt., T.D.
Jensen, Sir John Klunder, Kt., O.B.E.
Jephcott, Sir Harry, Bt. (1962).
Jerram, Sir (Cecil) Bertrand, K.C.M.G.
Jerram, *Rear-Adm.* (S.) Sir Rowland Christopher, K.B.E., D.S.O.
Jessel, Sir George, Bt., M.C. (1883).
Jessel, Sir Richard Hugh, Kt.
Jivanjee, Sir Yusufali Alibhai Karimjee, Kt.
John, *Admiral of the Fleet* Sir Caspar, G.C.B.
Johnson, Sir Frederic Charles, Kt., C.B.
Johnson, *Maj.-Gen.* Sir George Frederick, K.C.V.O., C.B., C.B.E., D.S.O.

Johnson, Sir Henry Allen Beaumont, Bt. (1818).
Johnson, Sir John Paley, Bt., M.B.E. (1755).
Johnson, Sir Philip Bulmer, Kt.
Johnson, Sir William Clarence, Kt., C.M.G., C.B.E.
Johnston, Sir Alexander, G.C.B., K.B.E.
Johnston, Sir Charles Hepburn, K.C.M.G.
Johnston, Sir Gaston, Kt., Q.C.
Johnston, Sir Thomas Alexander, Bt. (S 1626).
Johnstone, Sir Frederic Allan George, Bt. (S. 1700).
Joint, Sir (Edgar) James, K.C.M.G., O.B.E.
Jones, *Maj.-Gen.* Sir (Arthur) Guy Salisbury-, G.C.V.O., C.M.G., C.B.E., M.C.
Jones, Sir Austin Ellis Lloyd, Kt., M.C.
Jones, *Prof.* Sir (Bennett) Melvill, Kt., C.B.E., A.F.C., F.R.S.
Jones, *Lt.-Gen.* Sir Charles Phibbs, K.C.B., C.B.E., M.C.
Jones, Sir Clement Wakefield, Kt., C.B.
Jones, Sir Cyril Edgar, K.C.I.E., C.S.I.
Jones, Sir Edward Redmayne-, Kt.
Jones, Sir Eric Malcolm, K.C.M.G., C.B., C.B.E.
Jones, Sir Eric Newton Griffith-, K.B.E., C.M.G., Q.C.
Jones, *Prof.* Sir Ewart Ray Herbert, Kt., D.Sc., Ph.D., F.R.S.
Jones, *Air Marshal* Sir George, K.B.E., C.B., D.F.C.
Jones, Sir (George) Basil Todd-, Kt.
Jones, Sir Glyn Smallwood, K.C.M.G., M.B.E.
Jones, *Hon.* Sir Harry Vincent Lloyd-, Kt.
Jones, Sir Henry Frank Harding, Kt., M.B.E.
Jones, *Hon.* Sir Hildreth Glyn-, Kt., T.D.
Jones, Sir (John) Henry Morris-, Kt., M.C.
Jones, *Air Marshal* Sir (John) Humphrey Edwardes, K.C.B., C.B.E., D.F.C., A.F.C.
Jones, Sir John Prichard-, Bt. (1910).
Jones, *Air Chief Marshal* Sir John Whitworth, G.B.E., K.C.B.
Jones, Sir Lawrence Evelyn, Bt., M.C., T.D., (1831).
Jones, Sir Lewis, Kt.
Jones, Sir Owen Haddon Wansbrough-, K.B.E., C.B., Ph.D.
Jones, Sir Reginald Watson-, Kt.
Jones, *Air Marshal* Sir (Robert) Owen, K.B.E., C.B., A.F.C.
Jones, Sir Vincent Strickland, K.B.E.
Jones, Sir Walter Benton, Bt. (1910).
Jones, Sir (William John) Andrew, Kt., C.M.G.
Jones, Sir Wynne Cemlyn-, Kt.
Jordan, *Air Marshal* Sir Richard Bowen, K.C.B., D.F.C.
Jose, Sir Ivan Bede, Kt., C.B.E.
Joseph, *Maj.* Sir (Herbert) Leslie, Kt.
Joseph, *Rt. Hon.* Sir Keith Sinjohn, Bt., M.P. (1943).
Joseph, Sir Norman Samuel, Kt., C.B.E.
Joubert de la Ferté, *Air Chief Marshal* Sir Philip Bennet, K.C.B., C.M.G., D.S.O.
Joy, Sir George Andrew, K.B.E., C.M.G.
Julian, Sir (Kenneth) Ivor, Kt., C.B.E.
Jungwirth, Sir William John, Kt., C.M.G.
Kaberry, Sir Donald, Bt., T.D., M.P. (1960).
Kalat, *Maj.* H.H. the Khan of, G.C.I.E.
Karimjee, Sir Tayabali Hassanali Alibhoy, Kt.
Karminski, *Hon.* Sir Seymour Edward, Kt.
Kater, *Hon.* Sir Norman William, Kt.
Katsina, The Emir of, K.B.E., C.M.G.
Kaula, Sir Ganga, Kt., C.I.E.
Kay, Sir James Reid, Kt.
Kaye, Sir John Christopher Lister Lister-, Bt., (1812).
Kaye, Sir Stephen Henry Gordon, Bt. (1923).
Keane, Sir Richard Michael, Bt., (1801).
Keatinge, Sir Edgar Mayne, Kt., C.B.E.
Keay, Sir John, Kt.
Keay, Sir Lancelot Herman, K.B.E.
Keefe, Sir Ronald Barry, Kt.
Keeling, Sir John Henry, Kt.
Keen, Sir Bernard Augustus, Kt., D.Sc., F.R.S.
Keevil, *Col.* Sir Ambrose, K.B.E., M.C.
Keightley, *General* Sir Charles Frederick, G.C.B., G.B.E., D.S.O.
Keir, Sir David Lindsay, Kt.
Kellett, Sir Henry de Castres, Bt. (1801).
Kelliher, Sir Henry Joseph, Kt.
Kelly, Sir Arthur John, Kt., C.B.E.
Kelly, Sir Gerald Festus, K.C.V.O., R.A.
Kelly, Sir Patrick Aloysius, Kt., C.I.E.
Kemp, Sir Leslie Charles, K.B.E.
Kemsley, *Col.* Sir Colin Norman Thornton-, Kt., O.B.E., T.D., M.P.
Kendal, Sir Norman, Kt., C.B.E.
Kendrew, *Maj.-Gen.* Sir Douglas Anthony, K.C.M.G., C.B., C.B.E., D.S.O.
Kendrick, Sir Thomas Downing, K.C.B., F.B.A., F.S.A.
Kennard, Sir Lawrence Ury Charles, Bt. (1891).
Kennaway, Sir John Lawrence, Bt. (1791).
Kennedy, Sir (Henry Charles) Donald (Cleveland) Mackenzie-, K.C.M.G.
Kennedy, *Maj.-Gen.* Sir John Noble, G.C.M.G., K.C.V.O., K.B.E., C.B., M.C.
Kennedy, Sir John Ralph Bayly Bt. (1836).
Kennedy, *Hon.* Sir Robert, Kt.
Kent, Sir Harold Simcox, G.C.B.
Kenyon, Sir Bernard, Kt.
Kerr, Sir Hamilton William, Bt., M.P. (1957).
Kerr, *Maj.-Gen.* Sir (Harold) Reginald, K.B.E., C.B., M.C.
Kerr, *Lt.-Col.* Sir Howard, K.C.V.O., C.M.G., O.B.E.
Kerridge, Sir Robert James, Kt.
Kettle, Sir Russell, Kt.
Keville, Sir (William) Errington, Kt., C.B.E.
Key, Sir Charles Edward, K.B.E., C.B.
Key, Sir Neill Cooper-, Kt., M.P.
Keynes, Sir Geoffrey Langdon, Kt., M.D.
Killick, *Brig.* Sir Alexander Herbert, Kt., C.B.E., D.S.O., M.C.
Killick, Sir Anthony Bernard, K.B.E., C.M.G.
Kimber, Sir Charles Dixon, Bt. (1904).
Kimmins, *Lt.-Gen.* Sir Brian Charles Hannam, K.B.E., C.B.
Kinahan, *Admiral* Sir Harold Richard George, K.B.E., C.B.
Kinahan, Sir Robert George Caldwell, Kt., E.R.D.
King, Sir Alexander Boyne, Kt., C.B.E.
King, Sir Alexander William, Bt. (1815).
King, Sir Anthony Highmore, Kt., C.B.E.
King, Sir Arthur Henry William, K.B.E.
King, *Lt.-Gen.* Sir Charles John Stuart, K.B.E., C.B.
King, Sir (Clifford) Robertson, K.B.E.
King, Sir Geoffrey Stuart, K.C.B., K.B.E., M.C.
King, Sir James Granville Le Neve, Bt., T.D. (1888).
King, Sir John Richard Duckworth-, Bt. (1792).
Kingham, Sir Robert Dixon, Kt., C.B.E.
Kingsley, Sir Patrick Graham Toler, K.C.V.O.
Kinloch, Sir Alexander Davenport, Bt. (S 1686).
Kinloch, Sir John, Bt. (1873).
Kipping, Sir Norman Victor, K.B.E.
Kirby, Sir Arthur Frank, K.B.E., C.M.G.
Kirby, Sir James Norman, Kt., C.B.E.
Kirby, *Hon.* Sir Richard Clarence, Kt.
Kirkbride, Sir Alec Seath, K.C.M.G., O.B.E., M.C.
Kirkman, *General* Sir Sidney Chevalier, G.C.B., K.B.E., M.C.
Kirkpatrick, Sir Ivone Augustine, G.C.B., G.C.M.G.
Kirkpatrick, Sir Ivone Elliott, Bt. (S. 1685).
Kirkwood, Sir Robert Lucien Morrison, Kt.
Kitchen, Sir Geoffrey, Kt., T.D.

Kitson, Sir George Vernon, K.B.E.
Kitto, *Rt. Hon.* Sir Frank Walters, K.B.E.
Kleinwort, Sir Alexander Santiago, Bt. (1909).
†Knill, Sir Stuart, Bt. (1893).
Knott, *Lt.-Gen.* Sir Harold Edwin, K.C.B., O.B.E., M.D.
Knowles, Sir Francis Gerald William, Bt. (1765).
Knox, *Maj.-Gen.* Sir Alfred William Fortescue, K.C.B., C.M.G.
Knox, Sir Edward Ritchie, Kt., M.C.
Knox, *General* Sir Harry Hugh Sidney, K.C.B., D.S.O.
Knox, Sir Robert Uchtred Eyre, K.C.B., K.C.V.O., D.S.O.
Knox, Sir Robert Wilson, Kt.
Knox, Sir (Thomas) Malcolm, Kt.
Koelle, *Vice-Adm.* Sir Harry Philpot, K.C.B.
Kolhapur, *Maj.* H.H. Maharaja of, G.C.S.I.
Kotalawala, Sir Don Henry, Kt.
Kotalawala, *Col. Rt. Hon.* Sir John Lionel, C.H., K.B.E.
Krebs, *Prof.* Sir Hans Adolf, Kt., M.D., F.R.S.
Krishnamachariar, *Rao Bahadur* Sir Vangal Thiruvenkatachari, K.C.S.I., K.C.I.E.
Kyle, *Air Marshal* Sir Wallace Hart, K.C.B., C.B.E., D.S.O., D.F.C.
Labouchere, Sir George Peter, K.C.M.G.
Lacey, Sir Ralph Wilfred, K.B.E.
Lacon, Sir George Vere Francis, Bt. (1818).
Lacy, Sir Maurice John Pierce, Bt. (1921).
Lagos, The Oba of, K.B.E.
Laidlaw, Sir George Palmer, Kt., O.B.E.
Laing, Sir John William, Kt., C.B.E.
Laird, Sir Patrick Ramsay, K.B.E., C.B., F.R.S.E.
Laithwaite, Sir (John) Gilbert, G.C.M.G., K.C.B., K.C.I.E., C.S.I.
Lake, *Capt.* Sir Atwell Henry, Bt., C.B., O.B.E., R.N. (1711).
Lakin, Sir Henry, Bt. (1909).
Lakshmanaswami Mudaliar, *Diwan Bahadur* Sir Arcot, Kt.
Lala Gujjar Mal, *Rai Bahadur* Sir, Kt.
Lamb, Sir Lionel Henry, K.C.M.G., O.B.E.
Lambart, Sir Oliver Francis, Bt. (1911).
Lambert, *Rear-Adm.* (S.) Sir David Sidney, K.C.B., O.B.E.
Lambert, Sir Edward Thomas, K.B.E., C.V.O.
†Lambert, Sir Greville Foley, Bt. (1711).
Lamond, Sir William, Kt.
Lampson, Sir Curtis George, Bt., (1866).
Lancaster, *Vice-Adm.* Sir John Strike, K.B.E., C.B.
Lane, Sir Allen Lane Williams, Kt.
Lane, *Maj.-Gen.* Sir Charles Reginald Cambridge, K.C.I.E., C.B., C.B.E., M.C.
Lane, Sir William Arbuthnot, Bt., C.B.E. (1913).
Lang, Sir John Gerald, G.C.B.
Langham, Sir John Charles Patrick, Bt. (1660).
Langley, Sir Carleton George, Kt.
Langman, Sir John Lyell, Bt. (1906).
Langrishe, Sir Terence Hume, Bt. (I 1777).
Larcom, Sir Philip, Bt. (1868).
Larmor, Sir (John) Graham, Kt.
Lascelles, *Rt. Hon.* Sir Alan Frederick, G.C.B., G.C.V.O., C.M.G., M.C.
Lascelles, Sir Daniel William, K.C.M.G.
Lascelles, Sir Francis William, K.C.B., M.C.
Latham, *Hon.* Sir Charles George, Kt.
Latham, *Rt. Hon.* Sir John Greig, G.C.M.G., Q.C.
Latham, Sir Joseph, Kt., C.B.E.
Latham, Sir Richard Thomas Paul, Bt. (1919).
Lathbury, *General* Sir Gerald William, G.C.B., D.S.O., M.B.E.
Lauder, *Maj.* Sir George Andrew Dick-, Bt. (S. 1690).
Laurence, *Admiral* Sir Noel Frank, K.C.B., D.S.O.
Laurent, Sir Edgar, Kt., C.M.G., M.D.
Laurie, *Maj.-Gen.* Sir John Emilius, Bt., C.B.E., D.S.O. (1834).
Law, Sir Charles Ewan, Kt.
Lawes, Sir John Claud Bennet, Bt. (1882).
Lawrance, *Maj.* Sir Arthur Salisbury, K.C.M.G., K.B.E., D.S.O.
Lawrence, Sir David Roland Walter, Bt. (1906).
Lawrence, Sir Frederick, Kt., O.B.E.
Lawrence, Sir (Frederick) Geoffrey, Kt., Q.C.
Lawrence, Sir Henry Eustace Waldemar, Bt. (1858).
Lawrence, Sir William, Bt. (1867)
Lawson, Sir Henry Brailsford, Kt., M.C.
Lawson, *Lt.-Col.* Sir John Charles Arthur Digby, Bt., D.S.O., M.C. (1900).
Lawson, *Lt.-Col.* Sir Peter Grant, Bt. (1905).
Lawson, Sir Ralph Henry, Bt. (1841).
Lawson, Sir William Halford, Kt., C.B.E.
Lawther, Sir William, Kt.
Lawton, *Hon.* Sir Frederick Horace, Kt.
Laycock, *Maj.-Gen.* Sir Robert Edward, K.C.M.G., C.B., D.S.O.
Layton, *Admiral* Sir Geoffrey, G.B.E., K.C.B., K.C.M.G., D.S.O.
Lea, Sir Thomas Claude Harris, Bt. (1892).
Leadbitter, Sir Eric Cyril Egerton, K.C.V.O.
Leale, *Rev.* Sir John, Kt.
Learmonth, *Prof.* Sir James Rögnvald, K.C.V.O., C.B.E.
Leather, Sir Edwin Hartley Cameron, Kt., M.P.
Lechmere, Sir Ronald Berwick Hungerford, Bt. (1818).
Ledger, Sir Joseph Francis, Kt.
Lee, *Lt.-Col.* Sir (Albert) George, Kt., O.B.E., M.C.
Lee, *Rt. Hon.* Sir Frank Godbould, G.C.M.G., K.C.B.
Lee Hau Shik, *Col.* Sir, K.B.E.
Lee, Sir (Henry) Desmond (Pritchard), Kt.
Lee, Sir Kenneth, Bt., LL.D. (1941).
Lee, *Hon.* Sir Walter Henry, K.C.M.G.
Leeds, *Cdr.* Sir Reginald Arthur St. John, Bt., R.N. (1812).
Leeper, Sir Reginald Wildig Allen, G.B.E., K.C.M.G.
Lees, *Air Marshal* Sir Alan, K.C.B., C.B.E., D.S.O., A.F.C.
Lees, Sir Charles Archibald Edward Ivor, Bt. (1804).
Lees, *Air Marshal* Sir (Ronald) Beresford, K.C.B., C.B.E., D.F.C.
Lees, Sir Thomas Edward, Bt., (1897).
Lees, Sir (William) Hereward Clare, Bt. (1937).
Leese, *Lt.-Gen.* Sir Oliver William Hargreaves, Bt., K.C.B., C.B.E., D.S.O. (1908).
Le Fanu, *Vice-Adm.* Sir Michael, K.C.B., D.S.C.
Le Fleming, Sir Frank Thomas, Bt. (1705).
Lefroy, Sir Edward Henry Bruce, Kt.
Legard, Sir Thomas Digby, Bt. (1660).
Leggatt, *Col. Hon.* Sir William Watt, Kt., D.S.O., M.C., E.D.
Leggett, Sir Frederick William, K.B.E., C.B.
Leicester, *Lt.-Col.* Sir Charles Byrne Warren, Bt. (I 1671).
Leigh, Sir John, Bt. (1918).
Leighton, Sir Michael John Bryan, Bt. (1693).
Leitch, Sir William, K.B.E., C.B.
Leith, Sir (Robert) Ian (Algernon) Forbes-, Bt., M.B.E. (1923).
Le Marchant, Sir Denis, Bt. (1841).
Lennard, *Lt.-Col.* Sir Stephen Arthur Hallam Farnaby, Bt. (1880).
Lennard, Sir Thomas Richard Fiennes Barrett-, Bt. (1801).
Leon, Sir Ronald George, Bt. (1911).
Le Rougetel, Sir John Helier, K.C.M.G., M.C.
Leslie, Sir (Henry John) Lindores, Bt. (S 1625).
Leslie, Sir (John Randolph) Shane, Bt. (1876).
Lethbridge, *Capt.* Sir Hector Wroth, Bt. (1804).
Lett, Sir Hugh, Bt., K.C.V.O., C.B.E. (1941).
Lever, Sir Ernest Harry, Kt.
Lever, Sir Tresham (Joseph Philip), Bt. (1911).
Levinge, *Maj.* Sir Richard Vere Henry, Bt., M.B.E. (I 1704).
Levy, Sir (Enoch) Bruce, Kt., O.B.E.

Levy, Sir Ewart Maurice, Bt. (1913).
Lewey, Sir Arthur Werner, Kt.
Lewis, *Prof.* Sir Aubrey Julian, Kt., M.D.
Lewis, *Brig.* Sir Clinton Gresham, Kt., O.B.E.
Lewis, Sir Edward Roberts, Kt.
Lewis, Sir (John) Duncan Orr-, Bt. (1920).
Lewis, *Maj.-Gen.* Sir Richard George, K.C.M.G., C.B., C.B.E.
Lewis, Sir William Arthur, Kt.
Lewis, Sir (William) Hawthorne, K.C.S.I., K.C.I.E.
Lewthwaite, Sir William Anthony, Bt. (1927).
Ley, Sir Gerald Gordon, Bt., T.D. (1905).
Leyland, Sir Vivyan Edward Naylor-, Bt. (1805).
Liardet, *Maj.-Gen.* Sir Claude Francis, K.B.E., C.B., D.S.O., T.D.
Lidbury, Sir Charles, Kt.
Lidbury, Sir David John, K.C.M.G., C.B., D.S.O.
Lienhop, *Hon.* Sir John Henry, Kt.
Liesching, Sir Percivale, G.C.M.G. K.C.B., K.C.V.O.
Ligertwood, *Hon.* Sir George Coutts, Kt.
Light, Sir Edgar William, K.C.V.O., C.M.G., O.B.E.
Lighton, Sir Christopher Robert, Bt., M.B.E. (I 1791).
Lillico, *Hon.* Sir Alexander, Kt.
Lillicrap, Sir Charles Swift, K.C.B., M.B.E.
Lim, Sir Han Hoe, Kt., C.B.E.
Lind, *Hon.* Sir Albert Eli, Kt.
Lindsay, Sir Ernest Daryl, Kt.
Lindsay, *Maj.* Sir (George) Humphry (Maurice) Broun-, Kt., D.S.O.
Lindsay, Sir Martin Alexander, Bt., C.B.E., D.S.O. M.P., (1962).
Lindsay, Sir William, Kt., C.B.E.
Lindsay, Sir William O'Brien, K.B.E.
Lindsell, *Lt.-Gen.* Sir Wilfrid Gordon, G.B.E., K.C.B., D.S.O., M.C.
Linstead, Sir Hugh Nicholas, Kt., O.B.E., M.P.
Linstead, Sir (Reginald) Patrick, Kt., C.B.E., D.SC., F.R.S.
Lintott, Sir Henry John Bevis, K.C.M.G.
Lister, Sir (Charles) Percy, Kt.
Lister, Sir (Thomas) Frederick, Kt., C.B.E.
Lithgow, Sir William James, Bt., (1925).
Little, *Admiral* Sir Charles James Colebrooke, G.C.B., G.B.E.
Little, Sir (Rudolf) Alexander, K.C.B.
Littlewood, Sir Sydney Charles Thomas, Kt.
Livingston, *Air Marshal* Sir Philip Clermont, K.B.E., C.B., A.F.C.
Llewellyn, Sir David Treharne, Kt.
Llewellyn, *Lt.-Col.* Sir Rhys, Bt. (1922).
Llewellyn, *Col.* Sir (Robert) Godfrey, Bt., C.B., C.B.E., M.C., T.D. (1959).
Llewelyn, Sir Charles Michael Dillwyn-Venables-, Bt., M.V.O., (1890).
Lloyd, *Maj.* Sir (Ernest) Guy (Richard), Bt., D.S.O. (1960).
Lloyd, *Air Chief Marshal* Sir Hugh Pughe, G.B.E., K.C.B., M.C., D.F.C.
LLoyd, *Capt.* Sir Humphrey Clifford, K.C.V.O., M.C.
Lloyd, Sir Robert Owen, Kt., O.B.E.
Lloyd, Sir Thomas Ingram Kynaston, G.C.M.G., K.C.B.
Lockhart, Sir Allan Robert Eliot, Kt., C.I.E.
Lockhart, Sir John Beresford Sinclair-, Bt., E.D. (S 1636).
Lockhart, *General* Sir Rob (McGregor Macdonald), K.C.B., C.I.E., M.C.
Lockhart, Sir Robert (Hamilton) Bruce, K.C.M.G.
Lockspeiser, Sir Ben, K.C.B., F.R.S.
Lockwood, Sir John Francis, Kt.
Lockwood, Sir Joseph Flawith, Kt.
Locock, Sir Charles Bird, Bt. (1857).
Loder, Sir Giles Rolls, Bt. (1887).
Loder, Sir Louis Francis, Kt., C.B.E.
Loehnis, Sir Clive, K.C.M.G.
Loewen, *General* Sir Charles Falkland, G.C.B., K.B.E., D.S.O.
Logan, Sir Douglas William, Kt., D.Phil.
Logan, Sir William Marston, K.B.E., C.M.G.
Lomax, Sir John Garnett, K.B.E., C.M.G., M.C.
Lombe, *Vice-Adm.* Sir Edward Malcolm Evans-, K.C.B.
Long, Sir Bertram, Kt., M.C., T.D.
Longmore, *Air Chief Marshal* Sir Arthur Murray, G.C.B., D.S.O.
Lord, Sir Frank, K.B.E.
Lovell, *Prof.* Sir (Alfred Charles) Bernard, Kt., O.B.E., F.R.S.
Low, Sir David Alexander Cecil, Kt.
Low, Sir Francis, Kt.
Low, Sir Henry Telfer, Kt., C.B.E.
Low, Sir James Richard Morrison-, Bt. (1908).
Lowe, Sir (Albert) George, Kt.
Lowe, *Hon.* Sir Charles John, K.C.M.G.
Lowe, Sir David, Kt., C.B.E.
Lowe, *Air Vice-Marshal* Sir Edgar Noel, K.B.E., C.B.
Lowe, Sir Francis Gordon, Bt. (1918).
Lowson, Sir Denys Colquhoun Flowerdew, Bt. (1951).
Lowther, *Lt.-Col.* Sir (William) Guy, Bt., O.B.E. (1824).
Loyd, *General* Sir Henry Charles, K.C.B., K.C.V.O., D.S.O., M.C.
Lubbock, Sir Alan, Kt., F.S.A.
Lucas, *Maj.* Sir Jocelyn Morton, Bt., K.B.E., M.C., M.P. (1887).
Luce, *Admiral* Sir (John) David, G.C.B., D.S.O., O.B.E.
Luce, Sir William Henry Tucker, G.B.E., K.C.M.G.
Luckhoo, *Hon.* Sir Joseph Alexander, Kt.
Lucy, *Capt.* Sir (Henry) Montgomerie (Ramsay) Fairfax-, Bt., M.C. (1836).
Luke, Sir Harry Charles, K.C.M.G.
Luke, Sir Kenneth George, Kt., C.M.G.
Luke, Sir Stephen Elliot Vyvyan, K.C.M.G.
Lumley, Sir Dudley Owen, K.B.E., C.B.
Lumsden, Sir James Robert, Kt., C.B.E.
Lund, Sir Thomas George, Kt., C.B.E.
Lunn, Sir Arnold Henry Moore, Kt.
Lushington, Sir Herbert Castleman, Bt. (1791).
Lydford, *Air Marshal* Sir Harold Thomas, K.B.E., C.B., A.F.C.
Lyell, *Hon.* Sir Maurice Legat, Kt.
Lyle, Sir Gavin Archibald, Bt. (1929).
Lyle, Sir Ian Duff, Kt., D.S.C.
Lyons, Sir William, Kt.
Lythgoe, Sir James, Kt., C.B.E.
Maby, Sir Charles George, Kt., C.B.E.
Macadam, Sir Ivison Stevenson, Kt. C.V.O., C.B.E F.R.S.E.
McAdden, Sir Stephen James, Kt., C.B.E., M.P.
Macalister, Sir Robert Lachlan, Kt.
McAlpine, Sir (Alfred) Robert, Bt. (1918).
McAlpine, Sir Robert Edwin, Kt.
McAlpine, Sir (Thomas) Malcolm, K.B.E.
Macara, Sir (Charles) Douglas, Bt. (1911).
McArthur, Sir Gordon Stewart, Kt.
MacArthur, *Lt.-Gen.* Sir William Porter, K.C.B., D.S.O., O.B.E.
†Macartney, Sir John Barrington, Bt. (I 1799).
Macaulay, Sir Hamilton, Kt., C.B.E.
McBride, *Rt. Hon.* Sir Philip Albert Martin, K.C.M.G.
McCall, Sir Alexander, Kt., M.D.
McCall, *Admiral* Sir Henry William Urquhart, K.C.V.O., K.B.E., C.B., D.S.O.
MacCallum, Sir Peter, Kt., M.C.
McCance, Sir Andrew, Kt., D.SC., F.R.S.
McCarthy, *Admiral* Sir (Edward) Desmond (Bewley), K.C.B., D.S.O.
McCarthy, Sir Edwin, Kt., C.B.E.
M'Carthy, Sir Leslie Ernest Vivian, Kt.
McCarthy, Sir Mortimer Eugene, Kt., C.B.E.
McCaughey, Sir (David) Roy, Kt., C.M.G.
McCauley, *Air Marshal* Sir John Patrick Joseph, K.B.E., C.B.
McCay, *Lt.-Gen.* Sir Ross Cairns, K.B.E., C.B., D.S.O.

McConnell, *Cdr.* Sir Robert Melville Terence, Bt., V.R.D. (1900).
McCowan, Sir David James Cargill, Bt. (1934).
McCreery, *General* Sir Richard Loudon, G.C.B., K.B.E., D.S.O., M.C.
McCullagh, Sir (Joseph) Crawford, Bt. (1935).
McCulloch, Sir Malcolm McLeod, Kt., C.B.E.
McDavid, Sir Edwin Frank, Kt., C.M.G., C.B.E.
McDavid, Sir Herbert Gladstone, Kt., C.B.E.
MacDermot, Sir Dermot Francis, K.C.M.G., C.B.E.
McDonald, *Air Marshal* Sir Arthur William Baynes, K.C.B., A.F.C.
McDonald, Sir Charles George, Kt., C.B.E.
Macdonald of Sleat, Sir Ian Godfrey Bosville, Bt. (S 1625).
Macdonald, Sir John, Kt.
McDonald, *Hon.* Sir John Gladstone Black, Kt.
Macdonald, Sir John Ronald Maxwell-, Bt. (S 1682 and S 1707).
Macdonald, Sir Peter George, Kt.
McDonald, Sir (Robert) Ross, Kt., Q.C.
Macdonald, *Hon.* Sir Thomas Lachlan, K.C.M.G.
McDonald, *Hon.* Sir William John Farquhar, Kt.
MacDonald, *Air Marshal* Sir William Laurence Mary, K.C.B., C.B.E., D.F.C.
Macdougall, Sir (George) Donald (Alastair), Kt., C.B.E.
McDougall, Sir Malcolm, Kt.
McElwaine, Sir Percy Alexander, Kt.
McEvoy, *Air Chief Marshal* Sir Theodore Newman, K.C.B., C.B.E.
McEwen, Sir James Napier Finnie, Bt. (1953).
McEwin, *Hon.* Sir (Alexander) Lyell, K.B.E.
McFadyean, Sir Andrew, Kt.
Macfadyen, *Air Vice-Marshal* Sir Douglas, K.C.B., C.B.E.
Macfadyen, Sir Eric, Kt.
McFadzean, Sir William Hunter, Kt.
McFarland, Sir Basil (Alexander Talbot), Bt., C.B.E. (1914).
MacFarquhar, Sir Alexander, K.B.E., C.I.E.
MacGillivray, Sir Donald Charles, G.C.M.G., M.B.E.
McGlashan, *Rear-Adm.* (E) Sir Alexander Davidson, K.B.E., C.B., D.S.O.
McGlashan, Sir George Tait, Kt., C.B.E.
McGovern, Sir Patrick Silvesta, Kt., C.B.E.
MacGregor, Sir Alexander Stuart Murray, K.B.E., M.D.
MacGregor, Sir Colin Malcolm, Kt.
MacGregor of MacGregor, Sir Gregor, Bt. (1795).
McGregor, *Air Marshal* Sir Hector Douglas, K.C.B., C.B.E., D.S.O.
McGregor, Sir James Robert, K.B.E.
Macgregor, Sir Robert James McConnell, Bt., M.M. (1828).
McGrigor, *Capt.* Sir Charles Edward, Bt. (1831).
Machtig, Sir Eric Gustav, G.C.M.G., K.C.B., O.B.E.
McIlrath, Sir Martin, Kt.
Macintosh, *Prof.* Sir Robert Reynolds, Kt., M.D.
Macintyre, Sir Donald, Kt., C.B.E.
McIntyre, Sir Laurence Rupert, Kt., C.B.E.
Mack, Sir (William) Henry (Bradshaw), G.B.E., K.C.M.G.
McKay, Sir Charles Holly, Kt., C.B.E.
Mackay, *Lt.-Gen.* Sir Iven Giffard, K.B.E., C.M.G., D.S.O., V.D.
McKean, *Air Vice-Marshal* Sir Lionel Douglas Dalzell, K.B.E., C.B.
McKee, *Air Marshal* Sir Andrew, K.C.B., C.B.E., D.S.O., D.F.C., A.F.C.
McKee, *Maj.* Sir William Cecil, Kt., E.R.D.
McKell, *Rt. Hon.* Sir William John, G.C.M.G., Q.C.
MacKenna, *Hon.* Sir Bernard Joseph Maxwell, Kt.
McKenzie, Sir Alexander, K.B.E.
Mackenzie, Sir (Alexander George Anthony) Allan, Bt. (1890).
Mackenzie, Sir Clutha Nantes, Kt.
Mackenzie, Sir Duncan George, K.C.I.E.
Mackenzie, Sir (Edward Montague) Compton, Kt., O.B.E.
Mackenzie, Sir (Lewis) Roderick Kenneth, Bt (S. 1703).
Mackenzie, Sir Robert Evelyn, Bt. (S 1673).
Mackenzie, *Capt.* Sir Robert Henry Muir, Bt. (1805).
McKerron, Sir Patrick Alexander Bruce, K.B.E., C.M.G.
Mackeson, *Brig.* Sir Harry Ripley, Bt. (1954).
McKie, Sir William Neil, Kt., M.V.O., D.Mus.
Mackinlay, Sir George Mason, Kt.
McKinnon, Sir James, Kt.
McKisack, Sir Audley, Kt.
Macklin, Sir Albert Sortain Romer, Kt.
Mackworth, *Cdr.* Sir David Arthur Geoffrey, Bt. (1776).
McLaggan, Sir (John) Douglas, K.C.V.O.
Maclaren, Sir Hamish Duncan, K.B.E., C.B., D.F.C.
Maclean, *Maj.* Sir Charles Hector Fitzroy, Bt. (S 1631).
Maclean, Sir Fitzroy Hew, Bt., C.B.E., M.P. (1957).
MacLean, *Vice-Adm.* Sir Hector Charles Donald, K.B.E., C.B., D.S.C.
McLean, *Lt.-Gen.* Sir Kenneth Graeme, K.C.B., K.B.E.
McLean, Sir Robert, Kt.
Maclean, Sir Robert Alexander, Kt.
McLean, Sir William Hannah, K.B.E.
McLeay, *Hon.* Sir John, K.C.M.G., M.M.
Maclennan, Sir Ian Morrison Ross, K.C.M.G.
McLennan, Sir Ian Munro, K.B.E.
MacLennan, Sir Robert Laing, Kt., C.I.E.
McLeod, Sir Charles Henry, Bt. (1925).
McLeod, *Rev.* Sir George Fielden, Bt., M.C., D.D. (1924).
MacLeod, Sir John, Kt., T.D., M.P.
McLeod, *General* Sir Roderick William, K.C.B., C.B.E.
McLintock, Sir William Traven, Bt. (1934).
Maclure, *Lt.-Col.* Sir John William Spencer, Bt., O.B.E. (1898).
McMahon, Sir (William) Patrick, Bt. (1817).
MacMichael, Sir Harold (Alfred), G.C.M.G., D.S.O.
Macmillan, Sir Ernest Campbell, Kt., Mus. Doc.
MacMillan, *General* Sir Gordon Holmes Alexander, K.C.B., K.C.V.O., C.B.E., D.S.O., M.C.
McMullen, *Maj.-Gen.* Sir Donald Jay, K.B.E., C.B., D.S.O.
McMullin, *Hon.* Sir Alister Maxwell, K.C.M.G.
Macnab, *Brig.* Sir Geoffrey Alex Colin, K.C.M.G., C.B.
Macnaghten, Sir Antony, Bt. (1836).
McNair, Sir (George) Douglas, Kt., M.B.E.
McNair, *Hon.* Sir William Lennox, Kt.
MacNalty, Sir Arthur Salusbury, K.C.B., M.D.
McNaughton, Sir George Matthew, Kt., C.B.
Macneal, Sir Hector Murray, K.B.E.
McNee, Sir John William, Kt., D.S.O., M.D., D.Sc.
McNeice, Sir (Thomas) Percy (Fergus), Kt., C.M.G., O.B.E.
McNeill, Sir James McFadyen, K.C.V.O., C.B.E., M.C., F.R.S.
Macpherson, Sir John Stuart, G.C.M.G.
Macready, Sir Nevil John Wilfrid, Bt. (1923).
McRobert, *Col.* Sir George Reid, Kt., C.I.E.
MacTaggart, Sir Andrew McCormick, Kt.
Mactaggart, Sir Ian Auld, Bt. (1938).
MacTaggart, Sir William, Kt., P.R.S.A.
MacTier, Sir (Reginald) Stewart, Kt., C.B.E.
McTiernan, *Rt. Hon.* Sir Edward Aloysius, K.B.E.
McVey, Sir Daniel, Kt., C.M.G.
McWatters, Sir Arthur Cecil, Kt., C.I.E.
Madden, *Admiral* Sir Alexander Cumming Gordon, K.C.B., C.B.E.

Madden, *Admiral* Sir Charles Edward, Bt., K.C.B. (1919).
Maddex, Sir George Henry, K.B.E.
Maddocks, Sir Kenneth Phipson, K.C.M.G., K.C.V.O.
Madhorao Genesh Deshpande *Rao Bahadur* Sir, K.B.E.
Madsen, *Prof.* Sir John Percival Vissing, Kt., D.SC.
Magee, Sir Cuthbert Gaulter, Kt., C.B.E.
Magill, Sir Ivan Whiteside, K.C.V.O.
Magnus, Sir Philip, Bt. (1917).
Mahadeva, Sir Arunachalam, K.C.M.G.
Mahon, Sir George Edward John, Bt. (1819).
Mahon, *Hon.* Sir Gerald Mac Mahon, Kt.
Mahoney, Sir John Andrew, Kt., O.B.E.
Maihar, The Maharaja of, K.C.I.E.
Maini, Sir Amar Nath, Kt., C.B.E.
Maitland, Sir Alexander, Kt., Q.C.
Maitland, *Cdr.* Sir John Francis Whitaker, Kt., M.P.
Maitland, Sir Keith Richard Felix Ramsay-Steel-, Bt. (1917).
Maitland, Richard John, Bt. (1818).
Makhdum Murid Hussain Quraishi, *Khau Bahadur Nawab* Sir, Kt.
Makgill, *Maj.* Sir (John) Donald (Alexander Arthur), Bt. (S 1627).
Makins, Sir (Alfred) John (Ware) Kt.
Makins, Sir Roger Mellor, G.C.B., G.C.M.G.
Makins, *Lt.-Col.* Sir William Vivian, Bt. (1903).
Malcolm, Sir Michael Albert James, Bt. (S 1665).
Malet, *Col.* Sir Edward William St. Lo, Bt., O.B.E. (1791).
Malik Khizar Hayat Khan Tiwana, *Lt.-Col. Nawab* Sir, K.C.S.I., O.B.E.
Mallaby, Sir (Howard) George (Charles), K.C.M.G., O.B.E.
Mallet, Sir Victor Alexander Louis, G.C.M.G., C.V.O.
Mallet, Sir (William) Ivo, G.B.E., K.C.M.G.
Mallinson, *Col.* Sir Stuart Sidney, Kt., C.B.E., D.S.O., M.C.
Mallinson, Sir William Paul, Bt. (1935).
Malone, Sir Clement, Kt., O.B.E., Q.C.
Maltby, *Air Vice-Marshal* Sir Paul Copeland, K.C.V.O., K.B.E., C.B., D.S.O., A.F.C.
Maltby, Sir Thomas Karran, Kt.
Mamo, Sir Anthony Joseph, Kt., O.B.E.
Mance, *Brig.-Gen.* Sir H. Osborne, K.B.E., C.B., C.M.G., D.S.O.
Mander, Sir Charles Marcus, Bt. (1911).
Mander, Sir Frederick, Kt.
Mandi, *Col.* H.H. the Raja of, K.C.S.I.
Manifold, *Hon.* Sir (Thomas) Chester, Kt.
Manilal Balabhai Nanavati, Sir, Kt.
Manktelow, Sir (Arthur) Richard, K.B.E., C.B.
Mann, Sir (Edward) John, Bt. (1905).
Mansel, Sir Philip, Bt. (1622).
Mansergh, *Vice-Adm.* Sir (Cecil) Aubrey (Lawson), K.B.E., C.B., D.S.C.
Mansergh, *General* Sir (Eric Carden) Robert, G.C.B., K.B.E., M.C.
Mansergh, *Admiral* Sir Maurice James, K.C.B., C.B.E.
Mansfield, *Hon.* Sir Alan James, K.C.M.G.
Manuwa, Sir Samuel Layinka Ayodeji, Kt., C.M.G. O.B.E.
Manzoni, Sir Herbert John Baptista, Kt., C.B.E.
Mappin, Sir Frank Crossley, Bt. (1886).
Marchant, Sir Herbert Stanley, K.C.M.G., O.B.E.
Margai, *Rt. Hon.* Sir Milton Augustus Strieby, Kt., M.B.E.
Margetson, *Maj.* Sir Philip Reginald, K.C.V.O., M.C.
Markar, Haji Sir Mohammed Macan-, Kt.
Markham, Sir Charles John, Bt. (1911).
Markham, Sir (Sydney) Frank, Kt., M.P.
Marling, *Lt.-Col.* Sir John Stanley Vincent, Bt., O.B.E. (1882).
Marnham, Sir Ralph, K.C.V.O.
Marr, Sir Leslie Lynn, Bt. (1919).
Marriott, *Maj.-Gen.* Sir John Charles Oakes, K.C.V.O., C.B., D.S.O., M.C.
Marriott, Sir Ralph George Cavendish Smith-, Bt. (1774).
Marriott, Sir Robert Ecklin, Kt., V.D.
Marsden, Sir Ernest, Kt., C.M.G., C.B.E., M.C., F.R.S.
Marsden, Sir John Denton, Kt. (1924).
Marsh, Sir Percy William, Kt., C.S.I., C.I.E.
Marshall, *Hon.* Sir Archie Pellow, Kt.
Marshall, Sir Douglas, Kt., M.P.
Marshall, Sir Geoffrey, K.C.V.O., C.B.E., M.D.
Marshall, Sir Hugo Frank, K.B.E., C.M.G.
Marshall, Sir James, Kt.
Marshall, Sir Sidney Horatio, Kt.
Marshall, Sir William Marchbank, Kt.
Martin, Sir Alec, K.B.E.
Martin, Sir Charles Carnegie, Kt., C.B.E.
Martin, *Admiral* Sir Deric Holland-, K.C.B., D.S.O., D.S.C.
Martin, Sir George William, K.B.E.
Martin, *Prof.* Sir (John) Leslie, Kt., Ph.D.
Martin, Sir John Miller, K.C.M.G., C.B., C.V.O.
Martin, *Prof.* Sir Leslie Harold, Kt., C.B.E.
Martin, *Hon.* Sir Norman (Angus), Kt.
Martineau, Sir Wilfrid, Kt., M.C., T.D.
Marwick, Sir Brian Allan, K.B.E., C.M.G.
Masani, Sir Rustom Pestonji, Kt.
Mason, Sir Dan Hurdis, Kt., O.B.E., E.R.D.
Mason, *Vice-Adm.* (E.) Sir Frank Trowbridge, K.C.B.
Mason, Sir Laurence, Kt., C.I.E., O.B.E., M.C.
Mason, Sir Paul, K.C.M.G., K.C.V.O.
Massey, Sir Arthur, Kt., C.B.E.
Massey, *Prof.* Sir Harrie Stewart Wilson, Kt., Ph.D., F.R.S.
Massiah, Sir (Hallam) Grey, Kt., C.B.E.
Masson, Sir John Robertson, Kt.
Masterman, Sir Christopher Hughes, Kt., C.S.I., C.I.E.
Masterman, Sir John Cecil, Kt., O.B.E.
Matheson, *General* Sir Torquhil George, Bt., K.C.B., C.M.G. (1882).
Mathew, Sir Charles, Kt., C.M.G., Q.C.
Mathew, Sir Theobald, K.B.E., M.C.
Mathias, Sir Richard Hughes, Bt. (1917).
Matters, Sir (Reginald) Francis, Kt., V.R.D., M.D.
Matthew, *Prof.* Sir Robert Hogg, Kt., C.B.E., A.R.S.A.
Matthews, Sir Arthur, Kt., O.B.E.
Matthews, Sir Bryan Harold Cabot, Kt., C.B.E., SC.D., F.R.S.
Matthews, *Very Rev.* Walter Robert, C.H., K.C.V.O., D.D.
Matthews, Sir William Thomas, K.C.M.G., C.B., O.B.E.
Maud, Sir John Primatt Redcliffe, G.C.B., C.B.E.
Maufe, Sir Edward Brantwood, Kt., R.A.
Mawby, Sir Maurice Alan Edgar, Kt., C.B.E.
Maxwell, Sir Alexander Hyslop, K.C.M.G.
Maxwell, Sir Aymer, Bt. (S. 1681).
Maxwell, *Maj.-Gen.* Sir Aymer, Kt., C.B.E., M.C.
Maxwell, *Vice-Adm.* (E.) Hon. Sir Denis Crichton, K.C.B., C.B.E.
Maxwell, Sir John, Kt., C.B.E.
Maxwell, Sir Patrick Ivor Heron-, Bt. (S 1683).
Maxwell, Sir Reginald Maitland, G.C.I.E., K.C.S.I.
Maxwell, Sir Robert Hugh, K.B.E.
Maxwell, *Rear-Adm.* Sir Wellwood George Courtenay, K.B.E., C.M.G., D.C.L.
May, *Surg. Vice-Adm.* Sir (Robert) Cyril, K.B.E., C.B., M.C.
Mayer, Sir Robert, Kt.
Mayhew, Sir Basil Edgar, K.B.E.
Mayo, *Hon.* Sir Herbert, Kt.
Mayurbhanj, *Flight-Lt.* The Maharaja of, G.C.I.E.

Mbanefo, Sir Louis Nwachukwu, Kt.
Meade, Sir Richard Geoffrey Austin, K.B.E., C.M.G., C.V.O.
Meagher, Sir Thomas, Kt.
Mealing, Sir Kenneth William, Kt.
Medlicott, *Brig.* Sir Frank, Kt., C.B.E.
Medlycott, Sir Hubert Mervyn, Bt. (1808).
Meek, Sir David Burnett, Kt., C.I.E., O.B.E.
Meere, Sir Francis Anthony, Kt., C.B.E.
Megaw, *Hon.* Sir John, Kt., C.B.E., T.D.
Mehta, Sir Chunilal Baichand, Kt.
Meiklereid, Sir (Ernest) William, K.B.E., C.M.G.
Mellor, Sir John Serocold Paget, Bt. (1924).
Melville, Sir Harry Work, K.C.B., Ph.D., D.Sc., F.R.S.
Melville, Sir Leslie Galfreid, K.B.E.
Mensforth, Sir Eric, Kt., C.B.E.
Menteth, Sir James Wallace Stuart-, Bt. (1838).
Menzies, *Rt. Hon.* Sir Douglas Ian, K.B.E.
Menzies, Sir Laurence James, Kt.
Menzies, Sir Robert, Kt., O.B.E., V.D.
Menzies, *Rt. Hon.* Sir Robert Gordon, K.T., C.H., Q.C.
Menzies, *Maj.-Gen.* Sir Stewart Graham, K.C.B., K.C.M.G., D.S.O., M.C.
Mercer, *Prof.* Sir Walter, Kt.
Mercieca, *Hon.* Sir Arturo, Kt., LL.D.
Meredith, *Air Vice-Marshal* Sir Charles Warburton, K.B.E., C.B., A.F.C.
Meredith, Sir Vincent Robert Sissons, Kt.
Merriam, Sir Laurence Pierce Brooke, Kt., M.C.
Merrick, Sir John Edward Siegfried, Kt., C.M.G., O.B.E.
Merriman, Sir Walter Thomas, Kt.
Merton, Sir Thomas Ralph, K.B.E., F.R.S.
Merton, *Air Chief Marshal* Sir Walter Hugh, G.B.E., K.C.B.
Messent, Sir Philip Santo, Kt.
Messer, Sir Frederick, Kt., C.B.E.
Messervy, *General* Sir Frank Walter, K.C.S.I., K.B.E., C.B., D.S.O.
Metcalfe, Sir Frederic William, K.C.B.
Metcalfe, Sir Ralph Ismay, Kt.
Metcalfe, Sir Theophilus John, Bt. (1802).
Methven, Sir Harry Finlayson, Kt.
Meyer, Sir Anthony John Charles, Bt. (1910).
Meynell, Sir Francis, Kt.
Meyrick, *Lt.-Col.* Sir George David Elliott Tapps-Gervis-, Bt., M.C. (1791).
Meyrick, *Admiral* Sir Sidney Julius, K.C.B.
Meyrick, *Maj.* Sir Thomas Frederick, Bt. (1880).
Michaelis, *Brig. Hon.* Sir Archie, Kt.
Michelmore, Sir Walter Harold Strachan, Kt., M.B.E.
Michelmore, *Maj.-Gen.* Sir (William) Godwin, K.B.E., C.B., D.S.O., M.C., T.D.
Middlebrook, Sir Harold, Bt. (1930).
Middlemore, Sir William Hawkslow, Bt. (1919).
Middleton, Sir George Humphrey, K.C.M.G.
Middleton, Sir George Proctor, K.C.V.O.
Middleton, Sir Stephen Hugh, Bt. (1662).
Miers, *Rear-Adm.* Sir Anthony Cecil Capel, V.C., C.B.E., C.B., D.S.O.
Miéville, Sir Eric Charles, G.C.I.E., K.C.V.O., C.S.I., C.M.G.
Milbank, Sir Frederick Richard Powlett, Bt. (1882).
Milbank, *Maj.* Sir Mark Vane, K.C.V.O., M.C.
Milburn, Sir John Nigel, Bt. (1905).
Mildmay, Sir Verus Arundell Maunder St. John-, Bt. (1772).
Miles, Sir Charles Watt, Kt., O.B.E.
Miles, Sir Charles William, Bt., O.B.E. (1859).
Miles, *Admiral* Sir Geoffrey John Audley, K.C.B., K.C.S.I.
Millais, Sir Ralph Regnault, Bt. (1885).
Millbourn, Sir (Philip) Eric, Kt., C.M.G.
Miller, Sir Alastair George Lionel Joseph, Bt. (1788).
Miller, *Lt.-Gen.* Sir Euan Alfred Bews, K.C.B., K.B.E., D.S.O., M.C.
Miller, *Col.* Sir Geoffrey Christie-, K.C.B., D.S.O., M.C.
Miller, Sir (Ian) Douglas, Kt.
Miller, Sir James, Kt.
Miller, *Col.* Sir James MacBride, Kt., M.C., T.D.
Miller, Sir John Holmes, Bt. (1705).
Miller, Sir Richard Hope, Kt.
Miller, Sir Stanley Norie-, Bt., M.C. (1936).
Mills, *Maj.-Gen.* Sir Arthur Mordaunt, Kt., C.B., D.S.O.
Mills, *Air Chief Marshal* Sir George Holroyd, G.C.B., D.F.C.
Mills, *Col.* Sir John Digby, Kt., T.D.
Mills, Sir Peter Frederick Leighton, Bt. (1921).
Milman, Sir Dermot Lionel Kennedy, Bt. (1800).
Milne, Sir David, G.C.B.
Milne, Sir James Allan, Kt., C.B.E.
Milne, Sir John (Sydney) Wardlaw-, K.B.E.
Milner, Sir (George Edward) Mordaunt, Bt. (1717).
Minter, Sir Frederick Albert, G.C.V.O.
Misra, Sir Lakshmipati, Kt.
Missenden, Sir Eustace James, Kt., O.B.E.
Mitchell, Sir Godfrey Way, Kt.
Mitchell, *Col.* Sir Harold Paton, Bt. (1945).
Mitchell, Sir James, Kt., C.B.E.
Mitchell, Sir Kenneth Grant, K.C.I.E.
Mitchell, *Prof.* Sir Mark Ledingham, Kt.
Mitchell, *Maj.-Gen.* Sir Philip Euen, G.C.M.G., M.C.
Mitchell, Sir (Seton) Steuart Crichton, K.B.E., C.B.
Mitra, Sir Dhirendra Nath, Kt., C.B.E.
Moberly, Sir Walter (Hamilton), G.B.E., K.C.B., D.S.O., D.Litt.
Mocatta, *Hon.* Sir Alan Abraham, Kt., O.B.E.
Mockett, Sir Vere, Kt., M.B.E.
Mody, Sir Hormasji Peroshaw, K.B.E.
Moffat, Sir John Smith, Kt., O.B.E.
Moir, Sir Ernest Ian Royds, Bt. (1916).
Molony, Sir Hugh Francis, Bt. (1925).
Monck, Sir John Berkeley, G.C.V.O., C.M.G.
Moncreiffe, Sir (Rupert) Iain (Kay), Bt. (S 1685).
Moncrieff, *Admiral* Sir Alan Kenneth Scott-, K.C.B., C.B.E., D.S.O.
Monson, Sir Edmund St. John Debonnaire John, Bt., K.C.M.G. (1905).
Montgomery, Sir Basil Purvis-Russell-Hamilton-, Bt. (1801).
Montgomery, Sir Frank Percival, Kt., M.C.
Mookerjee, Sir Birendra Nath, Kt.
Moon, Sir Edward Penderel, Kt., O.B.E.
Moon, Sir John Arthur, Bt. (1887).
Moon, Sir (Peter) Wilfred Giles, Bt. (1855).
Moore, Sir Edward Stanton, Bt. (1923).
Moore, Sir Harold (John de Courcy), Kt.
Moore, Sir Henry Monck-Mason, G.C.M.G.
Moore, *Admiral* Sir Henry Ruthven, G.C.B., C.V.O., D.S.O.
Moore, *Lt.-Gen.* Sir (James Newton) Rodney, K.C.B., K.C.V.O., C.B.E., D.S.O.
Moore, Sir Norman Winfrid, Bt. (1919).
Moore, Sir Richard Greenslade, Kt., O.B.E.
Moore, *Lt.-Col.* Sir Thomas Cecil Russell, Bt., C.B.E., M.P. (1956).
Moore, *Hon.* Sir Walter K., Kt., C.B.E.
Moore, Sir William Samson, Bt. (1932).
Mooring, Sir (Arthur) George (Rixson), K.C.M.G.
Mootham, Sir Orby Howell, Kt.
Mordaunt, Sir Nigel John, Bt., M.B.E. (1611).
Mordecai, Sir John Stanley, Kt., C.M.G.

Morgan, Sir Edward James Ranembe, Kt.
Morgan, Sir Frank William, Kt., M.C.
Morgan, *Lt.-Gen.* Sir Frederick Edgworth, K.C.B.
Morgan, *Rt. Hon.* Sir John Kenyon Vaughan-, Bt., M.P. (1960).
Morgan, Sir John Vernon Hughes-, Bt. (1925).
Morgan, *Admiral* Sir Vaughan, K.B.E., C.B., M.V.O., D.S.C.
Morgan, *General* Sir William Duthie, G.C.B., D.S.O., M.C.
Morison, Sir Ronald Peter, Kt., Q.C.
Morland, Sir Oscar Charles, G.B.E., K.C.M.G.
Morley, Sir Alexander Francis, K.C.M.G., C.B.E.
Morrell, *Capt.* Sir Arthur Routley Hutson, K.B.E.
Morren, Sir William Booth Rennie, Kt., C.B.E., M.V.O.
Morris, *Air Vice-Marshal* Sir (Alfred) Samuel, K.B.E., C.B.
Morris, Sir Charles Richard, K.C.M.G.
Morris, Sir Cedric Lockwood, Bt. (1806).
Morris, *Air Marshal* Sir Douglas Griffith, K.C.B., C.B.E., D.S.O., D.F.C.
Morris, *General* Sir Edwin Logie, K.C.B., O.B.E., M.C.
Morris, Sir Harold, Kt., M.B.E., Q.C.
Morris, *Air Marshal* Sir Leslie Dalton-, K.B.E., C.B.
Morris, Sir Parker, Kt.
Morris, Sir Philip Robert, K.C.M.G. C.B.E.
Morrow, Sir Arthur William, Kt., D.S.O., E.D.
Morse, Sir Arthur, K.B.E.
Morshead, Sir Owen Frederick, G.C.V.O., K.C.B., D.S.O., M.C.
Mortimer, *Rev.* Sir Charles Edward, Kt., C.B.E.
Morton, *Maj.* Sir Desmond John Falkiner, K.C.B., C.M.G., M.C.
Morton, Sir Ralph John, Kt., C.M.G., O.B.E., M.C.
Moses, Sir Charles Joseph Alfred, Kt., C.B.E.
Mosley, Sir Oswald Ernald, Bt. (1781).
Moss, Sir Eric de Vere, Kt., C.I.E.
Moss, Sir John Herbert Theodore Edwards-, Bt. (1868).
Mossop, Sir Allan George, Kt.
Mostyn, Sir Jeremy John Antony, Bt. (1670).
Mott, Sir Adrian Spear, Bt. (1930).
Mott, *Prof.* Sir Nevill Francis, Kt., F.R.S.
Mounsey, Sir George Augustus, K.C.M.G., C.B., O.B.E.
Mount, Sir William Malcolm, Bt. (1921).
Mountain, Sir Brian Edward Stanley, Bt. (1922).
Mountford, Sir James Frederick, Kt., D.Litt.
Mowat, *Col.* Sir Alfred Law, Bt., D.S.O., O.B.E., M.C. (1932).
Mowbray, Sir George Robert, Bt., K.B.E. (1880).
Moxham, Sir Harry Cuthbertson, Kt.
Moylan, Sir John FitzGerald, Kt., C.B., C.B.E.
Mudaliar, *Diwan Bahadur* Sir Arcot Ramaswami, K.C.S.I.
Mudie, Sir (Robert) Francis, K.C.S.I., K.C.I.E., O.B.E.
Muhamad Noor, *Khan Bahadur* Sir Khaja, Kt., C.B.E.
Muhammad Ahmad Sa'id Khan *Nawab* Sir, G.B.E., K.C.S.I., K.C.I.E.
Muhammad Nawaz, *Col.* Sir, K.C.I.E.
Muir, Sir David John, Kt., C.M.G.
Muir, Sir Edward Francis, K.C.B.
Muir, Sir John Harling, Bt. (1892).
Muirhead, Sir John Spencer, Kt. D.S.O., M.C., T.D.
Mulholland, *Rt. Hon.* Sir Henry George Hill, Bt. (1945).
Mulholland, Sir William Walter, Kt., O.B.E.
Mullens, Sir Harold Hill, Kt.
Mullens, Sir William John Herbert deWette, Kt., D.S.O., T.D.
Mumford, Sir Albert Henry, K.B.E.
Munro, Sir Arthur Herman, Bt. (S. 1634).
Munro, *Hon.* Sir Leslie Knox, K.C.M.G., K.C.V.O.
Munro, Sir (Richard) Gordon, K.C.M.G., M.C.
Munro, Sir Torquill (Thomas Alfonso), Bt. (1825).
Murphy, Sir Alexander Paterson, Kt.
Murphy, Sir Oswald Ellis Joseph, Kt.
Murphy, Sir William Lindsay, K.C.M.G.
Murrant, Sir Ernest Henry, K.C.M.G., M.B.E.
Murray, Sir Alan John Digby, Bt. (S 1628).
Murray, Sir Andrew Hunter Arbuthnot, Kt., O.B.E.
Murray, Sir (Francis) Ralph (Hay), K.C.M.G., C.B.
Murray, *Brig.* Sir (George David) Keith, Kt., O.B.E., M.C., T.D.
Murray, *General* Sir Horatius, G.C.B., K.B.E., D.S.O.
Murray, Sir John, K.C.V.O., D.S.O., T.D., F.S.A.
Murray, *Hon.* Sir John Murray, Kt.
Murray, Sir (John) Stanley, Kt.
Murray, Sir Keith Anderson Hope, K.C.B., Ph.D.
Murray, Sir Kenneth, Kt.
Murray, Sir Robert Alistair, Kt., O.B.E.
Murray, Sir Rowland William Patrick, Bt. (S 1630).
Murray, Sir William Patrick Keith, Bt. (S 1673).
Murrie, Sir William Stuart, K.B.E., C.B.
Musgrave, Sir Charles, Bt. (1611).
Musgrave, Sir (Frank) Cyril, K.C.B.
Musgrave, Sir Richard James, Bt. (I 1782).
Musker, Sir John, Kt.
Muspratt, *General* Sir Sydney Frederick, K.C.B., C.S.I., C.I.E., D.S.O.
Musto, Sir Arnold Albert, Kt., C.I.E.
Mutta Venkatasubba Rao, Sir, Kt.
Mya Bu, Sir, Kt.
Mynors, *Prof.* Sir Roger Aubrey Baskerville, Kt., F.B.A.
Mysore, H.H. the Maharaja of, G.C.B., G.C.S.I.
Nabarro, Sir Gerald David Nunes, Kt., M.P.
Nair, *Rt. Hon.* Sir Chettur Madhavan, Kt.
Nairac, *Hon.* Sir André Laurence, Kt., C.B.E., Q.C.
Nairn, Sir Douglas Leslie Spencer-Bt., T.D. (1933).
Nairn, Sir (Michael) George, Bt. (1904).
Nall, *Lt.-Cdr.* Sir Michael Joseph, Bt., R.N. (1954).
Napier, Hon. Sir Albert Edward Alexander, K.C.B., K.C.V.O., Q.C.
Napier, *Hon.* Sir John Mellis, K.C.M.G.
Napier, Sir Joseph William Lennox, Bt., O.B.E. (1867).
Napier, Sir Robert Archibald, Bt. (S 1627).
Narang, Sir Gokul Chand, Kt., Ph.D.
Nasmith, *Admiral* Sir Martin Eric Dunbar-, V.C., K.C.B., K.C.M.G.
Nathan, Sir Maurice Arnold, K.B.E.
Nawanagar, *Lt.-Gen.* H.H. Maharaja Jam Sahib of, G.C.S.I., G.C.I.E.
Nayudu, *Sri Diwan Bahadur* Sir Madura Balasundram, Kt., C.I.E.
Neale, *Prof.* Sir John Ernest, Kt., F.B.A.
Neale, *Lt.-Col.* Sir (Walter) Gordon, K.C.V.O., C.I.E.
Neame, *Lt.-Gen.* Sir Philip, V.C., K.B.E., C.B., D.S.O.
Neame, Sir Thomas, Kt., F.S.B.
Neave, Sir Arundell Thomas Clifton, Bt. (1795).
Neden, Sir Wilfred John, Kt., C.B., C.B.E.
Needham, Sir Raymond Walter, Kt., Q.C.
Neerunjun, Sir Rampersad, Kt., O.B.E.
Negus, Sir Victor Ewings, Kt.
Neill, *Col.* Sir Frederick Austin, Kt., C.B.E., D.S.O., T.D.
Nelson, Sir Frank, K.C.M.G.
Nelson, *Air Marshal* Sir (Sidney) Richard (Carlyle), K.C.B., O.B.E.
Nelson, *Maj.* Sir William Vernon Hope, Bt., O.B.E. (1912).
Nepean, *Lt.-Col.* Sir Evan Yorke, Bt. (1802).
Nethersole, Sir Michael (Henry Braddon), K.B.E., C.S.I., C.I.E., D.S.O.
Nevile, Sir Sydney Oswald, Kt.
Nevill, *Air Vice-Marshal* Sir Arthur de Terrotte, K.B.E., C.B.

Neville, *Lt.-Col.* Sir (James) Edmund (Henderson), Bt., M.C. (1927).
Neville, *Maj.-Gen.* Sir Robert Arthur Ross, K.C.M.G., C.B.E., R.M.
Newboult, Sir Alexander Theodore, K.B.E., C.M.G., M.C., E.D.
Newland, Sir Henry Simpson, Kt., C.B.E., D.S.O.
Newman, Sir Gerard Robert Henry Sigismund, Bt. (1912).
Newman, Sir Ralph Alured, Bt. (1836).
Newns, Sir Alfred Foley Francis Polden, K.C.M.G., C.V.O.
Newsam, Sir Frank Aubrey, G.C.B., K.B.E., C.V.O., M.C.
Newton, Sir Basil Cochrane, K.C.M.G.
Newton, Sir Charles Henry, Kt.
Newton, Sir Edgar Henry, Bt. (1924).
Newton, Sir (Harry) Michael (Rex), Bt. (1900).
Nicholetts, *Air Marshal* Sir Gilbert Edward, K.B.E., C.B., A.F.C.
Nicholls, Sir Harmar, Bt., M.P. (1960).
Nicholls, Sir John Walter, K.C.M.G., O.B.E.
Nicholls, *Maj.-Gen.* Sir Leslie Burtonshaw, K.C.M.G., C.B., C.B.E.
Nicholls, *Hon.* Sir Robert Dove, Kt.
Nicholson, *General* Sir Cameron Gordon Graham, G.C.B., K.B.E., D.S.O., M.C.
Nicholson, Sir Godfrey, Bt., M.P. (1958).
Nicholson, Sir John Charles, Bt. (1859).
Nicholson, Sir John Norris, Bt., C.I.E. (1912).
Nicholson, Sir John William, Kt., M.M.
Nicholson, *Admiral* Sir Randolph Stewart Gresham, K.B.E., C.B., D.S.O., D.S.C.
Nicoll, Sir John Fearns, K.C.M.G.
Nicolls, Sir Basil Edward, Kt., C.V.O., C.B.E.
Nicolson, Hon. Sir Harold George, K.C.V.O., C.M.G.
Nicolson, Sir Kenneth, Kt., M.C.
Nield, *Hon.* Sir Basil Edward, Kt., C.B.E., Q.C.
Niemeyer, Sir Otto (Ernst), G.B.E., K.C.B.
Nightingale, Sir Geoffrey Slingsby, Bt. (1628).
Nihill, *Hon.* Sir (John Harry) Barclay, K.B.E., M.C., Q.C.
Nimmo, Sir Robert, Kt.
Niven, Sir (Cecil) Rex, Kt., C.M.G., M.C.
Nixon, Sir (Charles) Norman, Kt.
Nixon, *Maj.* Sir Christopher John Louis Joseph, Bt., M.C. (1906).
Nixon, Sir Frank Horsfall, K.C.M.G., C.B.
Noble, *Cmdr. Rt. Hon.* Sir Allan Herbert Percy, K.C.M.G., D.S.O., D.S.C., R.N.
Noble, Sir Andrew Napier, Bt., K.C.M.G. (1923).
Noble, Sir Humphrey Brunel, Bt., M.B.E., M.C. (1902).
Nock, Sir Norman Lindfield, Kt.
Norman, Sir Edward James, Kt.
Norman, *Vice-Adm.* Sir (Horace) Geoffrey, K.C.V.O., C.B., C.B.E.
Norman, Sir Mark Annesley, Bt. (1915).
Normand, Sir Charles William Blyth, Kt., C.I.E., D.Sc.
Norris, Sir Alfred Henry, K.B.E.
Norris, *Vice-Adm.* Sir Charles Fred Wivell, K.B.E., C.B., D.S.O.
Norris, *Maj.-Gen.* Sir Frank Kingsley, K.B.E., C.B., D.S.O., E.D
North, *Hon.* Sir Alfred Kingsley, Kt.
North, Sir George, Kt., C.B., M.C.
North, Sir (William) Jonathan (Frederick), Bt. (1920)
Northam, Sir Reginald, Kt., C.B.E.
Northcott, *General* Sir John, K.C.M.G., K.C.V.O., C.B.
Northey, Sir Armand Hunter Kennedy Wilbraham, Kt.
Norton, Sir Clifford John, K.C.M.G., C.V.O.
Norton, Sir (Walter) Charles, Kt., M.B.E., M.C.
Norwood, Sir Charles John Boyd, Kt.
Nosworthy, *Lt.-Gen.* Sir Francis Poitiers, K.C.B., D.S.O., M.C.
Nosworthy, Sir Richard Lysle, K.C.M.G.
Nott, *Cmdr.* Sir James Grenville Pyke-, Kt., C.M.G., R.N.
Nottidge, Sir William Rolfe, Kt.
Nugent, Sir (George) Guy (Bulwer), Bt. (1806).
Nugent, *Rt. Hon.* Sir (George) Richard (Hodges), Bt., M.P. (1960).
Nugent, Sir Hugh Charles, Bt. (I 1795).
Nugent, *Maj.* Sir Peter Walter James, Bt. (1831).
Nussey, Sir Thomas Moore, Bt. (1909).
Nuttall, Sir Nicholas Keith Lillington, Bt. (1922).
Nutting, Sir Harold Stansmore, Bt. (1903).
Nye, *Lt.-Gen.* Sir Archibald Edward, G.C.S.I., G.C.M.G., G.C.I.E., K.C.B., K.B.E., M.C.
Nye, Sir Geoffrey Walter, K.C.M.G., O.B.E.
Oakeley, Sir (Edward) Atholl, Bt. (1790).
Oakes, Sir Sydney, Bt. (1939).
Oakshott, Sir Hendrie Dudley, Bt., M.B.E., M.P. (1959).
Obeyesekere, Sir James Peter, Kt.
O'Brien, Sir (Frederick) Lucius, Kt.
O'Brien, Sir John Edmond Noel, Bt., M.C. (1849).
O'Brien, Sir Tom, Kt.
O'Bryan, *Hon.* Sir Norman, Kt.
Ochterlony, Sir Charles Francis, Bt. (1823).
O'Connell, Sir Morgan Donal Conail, Bt. (1869).
O'Connor, *Lt.-Gen.* Sir Denis Stuart Scott, K.B.E., C.B.
O'Connor, Sir Kenneth Kennedy, K.B.E., M.C., Q.C.
O'Connor, *General* Sir Richard Nugent, G.C.B., D.S.O., M.C.
Odgers, Sir Charles Edwin, Kt.
Oehlers, Sir George Edward Noel, Kt., O.B.E.
Officer, Sir (Frank) Keith, Kt., O.B.E., M.C.
Ogden, Sir Alwyne George Neville, K.B.E., C.M.G.
Ogg, Sir William Gammie, Kt.
Ogilvie, Sir Charles (MacIvor Grant) Kt., C.S.I., C.B.E.
Ogilvie, *Lt.-Col.* Sir George Drummond, K.C.I.E., C.S.I.
Ogilvie, *Maj.-Gen.* Sir (William) Heneage, K.B.E.
Ogilvy, Sir David John Wilfrid, Bt. (S 1626)
Ohlson, Sir Eric James, Bt. (1920).
Ojukwu, Sir Odumegwu, Kt., O.B.E.
Okeover, *Lieut.-Col.* Sir Ian Peter Andrew Monro Walker-, Bt., D.S.O., T.D. (1886).
Oliphant, Sir Lancelot, K.C.M.G., C.B.
Oliphant, Sir Marcus Laurence Elwin, K.B.E., F.R.S.
Oliver, Sir (Frederick) Ernest, Kt., C.B.E., T.D.
Oliver, *Admiral* Sir Geoffrey Nigel, G.B.E., K.C.B., D.S.O.
Oliver, *Admiral of the Fleet* Sir Henry Francis, G.C.B., K.C.M.G., M.V.O.
Oliver, Sir Roland Giffard, Kt., M.C.
Oliver, *Lt.-Gen.* Sir William Pasfield, K.C.B., K.C.M.G., O.B.E.
Olivier, Sir Laurence Kerr, Kt.
O'Loghlen, Sir Coleman Michael, Bt. (1838).
O'Malley, Sir Owen St. Clair, K.C.M.G.
O'Neill, Hon. Sir Con Douglas Walter, K.C.M.G.
Onslow, Sir Geoffrey Henry Hughes-, K.B.E., D.S.C.
Onslow, Sir John Roger Wilmot, Bt. (1797).
Onslow, *Admiral* Sir Richard George, K.C.B., D.S.O.
Oppenheim, Sir Alexander, Kt., O.B.E., D.Sc., F.R.S.E.
Oppenheim, Sir Duncan Morris, Kt.
Oppenheimer, Sir Michael Bernard Grenville, Bt. (1921).
Oram, Sir Matthew Henry, Kt., M.B.E.
Orde, Sir Charles William, K.C.M.G.
Orde, Sir Percy Lancelot, Kt., C.I.E.
Orde, *Maj.* Sir Simon Arthur Campbell-, Bt. (1790).
Ormerod, *Rt. Hon.* Sir Benjamin, Kt.
Ormerod, *Maj.* Sir Cyril Berkeley, K.B.E.

Ormrod, *Hon.* Sir Roger Fray Greenwood, Kt.
Orr, Sir Samuel, Kt.
Osborn, Sir Danvers Lionel Rouse, Bt. (1662).
Osborn, Sir Frederic James, Kt.
Osborne, Sir Cyril, Kt., M.P.
Osborne, Sir Peter George, Bt. (I 1629).
Osbourne, *Air Commodore* Sir Henry Percy Smyth-, Kt., C.M.G., C.B.E.
O'Sullivan, *Hon.* Sir Neil, K.B.E.
Oulsnam, Sir (Samuel) Harrison (Yardley), Kt., C.S.I., C.I.E.
Outerbridge, *Col. Hon.* Sir Leonard Cecil, Kt., C.B.E., D.S.O.
Outram, Sir Alan James, Bt. (1859).
Overton, Sir Arnold Edersheim, K.C.B., K.C.M.G., M.C.
Overy, Sir Thomas Stuart, Kt.
Owen, Sir Alfred George Beech, Kt., C.B.E.
Owen, Sir (Arthur) Douglas, K.B.E., C.B.
Owen, Sir Dudley Herbert Cunliffe-, Bt. (1920).
Owen, *Lt.-Col.* Sir Goronwy, Kt., D.S.O.
Owen, Sir John Arthur, Bt. (1813).
Owen, *Rt. Hon.* Sir William Francis Langer, K.B.E.
Owen, Sir (William) Leonard, Kt., C.B.E.
Owens, *Capt.* Sir Arthur Lewis, Kt., R.D., R.N.R.
Owo, The Olowo of, Kt.
Packard, *Lieut.-Gen.* Sir (Charles) Douglas, K.B.E., C.B., D.S.O.
Packer, Sir (Douglas) Frank (Hewson), Kt., C.B.E.
Paddon, *Lt.-Col.* Sir Stanley Somerset Wreford, Kt., C.I.E.
Padmore, Sir Thomas, K.C.B.
Paget, *Capt.* Sir James Francis, Bt., R.N. (1871).
Paget, Sir John Starr, Bt. (1886).
Paine, Sir (Herbert) Kingsley, Kt., C.M.G.
Paley, *Maj.-Gen.* Sir (Alexander George) Victor, K.B.E., C.B., D.S.O.
Palitana, Thakore Saheb of, K.C.S.I., K.C.I.E.
Palmer, Sir Charles Mark, Bt. (1886).
Palmer, Sir Geoffrey Christopher John, Bt. (1660).
Palmer, Sir John Edward Somerset, Bt. (1791).
Palmer, *Brig.* Sir Otho Leslie Prior-, Kt., D.S.O., M.P.
Palmer, Sir William, G.B.E., C.B.
Panabokke, Sir Tikiri Banda, Kt.
Panckridge, *Surgeon Vice-Adm.* Sir (William) Robert (Silvester), K.B.E., C.B.
Panna, *Maj.* H.H. Maharaja of, K.C.S.I., K.C.I.E.
Papworth, *Rev.* Sir Harold Charles, K.B.E.
Pararajasingam, Sir Sangarapillai, Kt.
Parham, *Admiral* Sir Frederick Robertson, G.B.E., K.C.B., D.S.O.
Paris, Sir Edward Talbot, Kt., C.B., D.SC.
Park, *Air Chief Marshal* Sir Keith Rodney, G.C.B., K.B.E., M.C., D.F.C.
Parker, Sir Harold, K.C.B., K.B.E., M.C.
Parker, Sir Karl Theodore, Kt., C.B.E., Ph.D., F.B.A.
Parker, Sir Richard (William) Hyde, Bt. (1681).
Parker, *Capt.* Sir William Lorenzo, Bt., O.B.E. (1844).
Parkes, Sir Roderick Wallis, K.C.M.G., O.B.E.
Parkin, Sir Ian, Kt., C.B.E.
Parkinson, Sir (Arthur Charles) Cosmo, G.C.M.G., K.C.B., O.B.E.
Parkinson, Sir Harold, K.B.E.
Parkinson, Sir John, Kt., M.D.
Parkinson, Sir Kenneth Wade, Kt.
Parlakimedi, *Capt.* Raja of, K.C.I.E.
Parr, Sir Robert, K.B.E., C.M.G.
Parry, *Prof.* Sir David Hughes, Kt., Q.C.
Parry, Sir Henry Wynn, Kt.
Parry, *Brig.* Sir Richard Gambier-, K.C.M.G.
Parry, *Admiral* Sir (William) Edward, K.C.B.
Parsons, Sir (Alfred) Alan Lethbridge, K.C.I.E.
Parsons, *Maj-Gen.* Sir Arthur Edward Broadbent, K.C.I.E., C.B.E., D.S.O.
Partabgarh, H.H. the Maharawab of, K.C.S.I.
Paskin, Sir (Jesse) John, K.C.M.G., M.C.
Pasley, Sir Rodney Marshall Sabine, Bt. (1794).
Patch, Sir Edmund Leo Hall-, G.C.M.G.
Patch, *Air Chief Marshal* Sir Hubert Leonard, K.C.B., C.B.E.
Paterson, Sir (Alexander) Swinton, K.B.E., C.M.G.
Paterson, Sir George Mutlow, Kt., O.B.E., Q.C.
Patiala, *Lt.-Gen.* H.H. the Maharaja of, G.C.I.E., G.B.E.
Patna, Maharaja of, K.C.I.E.
Paton, *Prof.* Sir George Whitecross, Kt.
Paton, Sir Leonard Cecil, Kt., C.B.E., M.C.
Patrick, Sir Paul Joseph, K.C.I.E., C.S.I.
Patron, Sir Joseph, Kt., O.B.E., M.C.
Patterson, Sir John Robert, K.B.E., C.M.G.
Pattinson, *Hon.* Sir Baden, K.B.E.
Paul, Sir John Warburton, K.C.M.G., O.B.E., M.C.
Paul, Sir Brian Kenneth Dean, Bt. (1821).
Paull, *Hon.* Sir Gilbert James, Kt.
Pavlides, Sir Paul George, Kt., C.B.E.
Pawsey, Sir Charles Ridley, Kt., C.S.I., C.I.E., M.C.
Payne, *Hon.* Sir Reginald Withers, Kt.
Payne, Sir William Labatt, Kt., C.M.G., O.B.E.
Peacock, Sir Kenneth Swift, Kt.
Peake, Sir Francis Harold, Kt.
Pearce, Sir (Charles) Frederick (Byrde), Kt., C.B.E.
Pearce, Sir George Alfred, Kt., O.B.E.
Peard, *Rear-Adm.* Sir Kenyon Harry Terrell, K.B.E.
Pearson, *Rt. Hon.* Sir Colin Hargreaves, Kt., C.B.E.
Pearson, Sir James Denning, Kt.
Pearson, Sir James Reginald, Kt., O.B.E.
Pearson, Sir Neville, Bt. (1916).
Pease, Sir Alfred Vincent, Bt. (1882).
Pease, Sir Richard Arthur, Bt. (1920).
Pechell, *Lt.-Col.* Sir Paul, Bt., M.C. (1797).
Peck, Sir James Wallace, Kt., C.B.
Pedder, *Vice-Adm.* Sir Arthur Reid, K.B.E., C.B.
Peek, Sir Francis Henry Grenville, Bt. (1874).
Peel, *Capt.* Sir (Francis Richard) Jonathan, Kt., C.B.E., M.C.
Peel, Sir John Harold, K.C.V.O.
Peile, *Vice-Adm.* Sir Lancelot Arthur Babington, K.B.E., C.B., D.S.O., M.V.O.
Peirse, Sir Henry Campbell de la Poer Beresford-, Bt., C.B. (1814).
Peirse, *Air Chief Marshal* Sir Richard Edmund Charles, K.C.B., D.S.O., A.F.C.
Pelham, Sir (George) Clinton, K.B.E., C.M.G.
Pelly, *Air Chief Marshal* Sir Claude Bernard Raymond, G.B.E., K.C.B., M.C.
Pelly, Sir Harold Alwyne, Bt., M.C. (1840).
Pelly, Sir Kenneth Raymond, Kt., M.C.
Pendred, *Air Marshal* Sir Lawrence Fleming, K.B.E., C.B., D.F.C.
Pengilly, Sir Alexander, Kt.
Penney, Sir William George, K.B.E., D.SC., Ph.D., F.R.S.
Penney, *Maj.-Gen.* Sir (William) Ronald Campbell, K.B.E., C.B., D.S.O., M.C.
Penny, Sir James Downing, K.C.I.E., C.S.I.
Pennycuick, *Hon* Sir John, Kt.
Penton, Sir Edward, K.B.E.
Peppiatt, Sir Kenneth Oswald, K.B.E., M.C.
Peppiatt, Sir Leslie Ernest, Kt., M.C.
Pereira, Sir Horace Alvarez de Courcy, Kt.
Peren, *Prof.* Sir Geoffrey Sylvester, K.B.E.
Perez, Sir Joseph Leon Mathieu-, Kt.
Peries, Sir (Pattiya Pathirannahalage) Albert Frederick, K.B.E.
Perkins, Sir (Walter) Robert Dempster, Kt.
Perks, Sir (Robert) Malcolm Mewburn, Bt. (1908).
Perring, Sir Ralph Edgar, Kt.

Perrott, Sir Donald Cyril Vincent, K.B.E.
Perry, *Hon.* Sir Frank Tennyson, Kt., M.B.E.
Perry, *Hon.* Sir William, Kt.
Peters, *Admiral* Sir Arthur Malcolm, K.C.B., D.S.C.
Peters, *Prof.* Sir Rudolph Albert, Kt., M.C., F.R.S.
Peters, Sir William, Kt., C.M.G.
Petit, Sir Dinshaw Manockjee, Bt. (1890).
Peto, *Cdr.* Sir (Henry) Francis (Morton), Bt., R.N. (1855).
Peto, *Lt.-Col.* Sir (James) Michael, Bt. (1927).
Petrie, Sir Charles Alexander, Bt., C.B.E. (1918).
Phaltan, *Maj.* the Raja of, K.C.I.E.
Phibbs, Sir Charles, Kt.
Phillimore, *Hon.* Sir Henry Josceline, Kt., O.B.E.
Philipps, *Lt.-Col.* Sir Grismond Picton, Kt., C.V.O.
Phillips, *Maj.-Gen.* Sir Edward, K.B.E., C.B., D.S.O., M.C.
Phillips, Sir (Edward) Charles, Kt., C.B.E.
Phillips, *Vice-Adm.* Sir Henry Clarmont, K.B.E., C.B.
Phillips, *Maj.-Gen.* Sir Leslie Gordon, K.B.E., C.B., M.C.
Phillips, Sir Leslie Walter, Kt., C.B.E.
Phillips, Sir Robin Francis, Bt. (1912).
Phillips, Sir Thomas Williams, G.B.E., K.C.B.,
Phillipson, Sir Sidney, K.B.E., C.M.G.
Philp, *Hon.* Sir Roslyn Foster Bowie, K.B.E.
Pickering, Sir George Hunter, Kt.
Pickering, *Prof.* Sir George White, Kt., F.R.S.
Pickford, Sir Anthony Frederick Ingham, Kt.
Pickles, Sir John Sydney, Kt.
Pickthorn, Sir Kenneth William Murray, Bt., Litt.D., M.P. (1959).
Pierre, Sir Joseph Henry, Kt.
Piers, Sir Charles Robert Fitzmaurice, Bt. (I 1661).
Pierssené, Sir Stephen Herbert, Kt., T.D.
Pigot, *Brig.-Gen.* Sir Robert, Bt., D.S.O., M.C. (1764).
Pigott, *Maj.* Sir Berkeley, Bt. (1808).
Pike, Sir Theodore Ouseley, K.C.M.G.
Pike, *Marshal of the Royal Air Force*, Sir Thomas Geoffrey, G.C.B., C.B.E., D.F.C.
Pike, *Lt.-Gen.* Sir William Gregory Huddleston, K.C.B., C.B.E., D.S.O.
Pilcher, Sir Gonne St. Clair, Kt., M.C.
Pilditch, Sir Denys, Kt., C.I.E.
Pilditch, Sir Richard Edward, Bt. (1929).
Pile, *General* Sir Frederick Alfred, Bt., G.C.B., D.S.O., M.C. (1900).
Pilkington, *Capt.* Sir Richard Antony, K.B.E., M.C., M.P.
Pilkington, Sir Thomas Henry Milborne - Swinnerton-, Bt. (S 1635).
Pilkington, Sir (William) Henry, Kt.
Pim, *Capt.* Sir Richard Pike, K.B.E., V.R.D., R.N.V.R.
Pink, Sir Ivor Thomas Montague, K.C.M.G.
Pinsent, Sir Roy, Bt. (1938).
Pipon, *Vice-Adm.* Sir James Murray, K.B.E., C.B., C.M.G., M.V.O.
Pirbhai, Sir Eboo, Kt., O.B.E.
Pirie, *Air Chief Marshal* Sir George Clark, K.C.B., K.B.E., M.C., D.F.C.
Pitman, Sir Hubert Percival Lancaster, Kt., O.B.E.
Pitman, Sir (Isaac) James, K.B.E., M.P.
Pizey, *Admiral* Sir (Charles Thomas) Mark, G.B.E., C.B., D.S.O.
Plant, *Prof.* Sir Arnold, Kt.
Platt, Sir Harry, Bt., M.D. (1958).
Platt, *Prof.* Sir Robert, Bt., M.D. (1959).
Platt, *General* Sir William, G.B.E., K.C.B., D.S.O.
Playfair, Sir Edward Wilder, K.C.B.
Playfair, *Air Marshal* Sir Patrick Henry Lyon, K.B.E., C.B., C.V.O., M.C.
Playford, *Hon.* Sir Thomas, G.C.M.G.
Pleass, Sir Clement John, K.C.M.G., K.C.V.O., K.B.E.
Plimsoll, Sir James, Kt., C.B.E.
Plowman, *Hon.* Sir (John) Anthony, Kt.
Pode, Sir Edward Julian, Kt.
Poett, *General* Sir (Joseph Howard) Nigel, K.C.B., D.S.O.
Poland, *Vice-Adm.* Sir Albert Lawrence, K.B.E., C.B., D.S.O., D.S.C.
Pole, *Col.* Sir John Gawen Carew, Bt., D.S.O., T.D. (1628).
Pole, Sir Peter Van Notten-, Bt. (1791).
Pollard, Sir Charles Herbert, Kt., C.B.E.
Pollard, *Lt.-Gen.* Sir Reginald George, K.B.E., C.B., D.S.O.
Pollen, Sir John Michael Hungerford, Bt. (1795).
Pollen, *Capt.* Sir Walter Michael Hungerford, Kt., M.C.
Pollock, Sir George, Kt., Q.C.
Pollock, Sir George Frederick, Bt. (1866).
Pollock, Sir George Seymour Montagu-, Bt. (1872).
Pollock, Sir Ronald Evelyn, Kt.
Pollock, Sir William Horace Montagu-, K.C.M.G.
Ponsonby, *Col.* Sir Charles Edward, Bt., T.D. (1956).
Ponsonby, Sir George Arthur, K.C.V.O.
Poole, *Vice-Adm.* Sir Richard Hayden Owen Lane-, K.B.E., C.B.
Pooley, Sir Ernest Henry, Bt., G.C.V.O. (1953).
Poore, Sir Herbert Edward, Bt. (1795).
Pope, Sir Sidney Barton, Kt.
Porbandar, *Lt.-Col.* H.H. Maharaja of, K.C.S.I.
Porritt, Sir Arthur Espie, Bt., K.C.M.G., K.C.V.O., C.B.E. (1963).
Portal, Sir Francis Spencer, Bt. (1901).
Portal, *Admiral* Sir Reginald Henry, K.C.B., D.S.C.
Porter, Sir Andrew Marshall Horsbrugh-, Bt., D.S.O. (1902).
Porter, Sir George Swinburne, Bt. (1880).
Pott, Sir Leslie, K.B.E.
Potter, Sir Alan Graeme, Kt.
Potter, Sir Henry Steven, K.C.M.G.
Potter, *Air Marshal* Sir Patrick Brunton Lee, K.B.E., M.D.
Potter, Sir (William) Ian, Kt.
Pound, Sir Derek Allen, Bt. (1905).
Powell, *Maj.* Sir Richard George Douglas, Bt., M.C. (1897).
Powell, Sir Richard Royle, K.C.B., K.B.E., C.M.G.
Power, Sir John Patrick McLannahan, Bt. (1924).
Power, *Admiral* Sir Manley Laurence, K.C.B., C.B.E., D.S.O.
Powles, Sir Guy Richardson, K.B.E., C.M.G., E.D.
Powlett, *Vice-Adm.* Sir Peveril Barton Reibey Wallop William-, K.C.B., K.C.M.G., C.B.E., D.S.O.
Poynter, Sir Hugh Edward, Bt. (1902).
Poynton, Sir (Arthur) Hilton, K.C.M.G.
Prain, Sir Ronald Lindsay, Kt., O.B.E.
Pratt, Sir (Edward) Bernard, Kt.
Pratt, Sir John Thomas, K.B.E., C.M.G.
Prempeh II., Otumfuo Sir Osei Agyeman, K.B.E.
Prescott, Sir Richard Stanley, Bt. (1938).
Preston, *Lt.-Col.* Sir Edward Hulton, Bt., D.S.O., M.C. (1815).
Preston, Sir Kenneth Huson, Kt.
Preston, *Admiral* Sir Lionel George, K.C.B.
Pretty, *Air Vice-Marshal* Sir Walter Philip George, K.B.E., C.B.
Prevost, *Capt.* Sir George James Augustine, Bt. (1805).
Preziosi, Sir Luigi, Kt., M.D.
Price, Sir (Archibald) Grenfell, Kt., C.M.G.
Price, *Lt.-Col.* Sir Charles James Napier Rugge-, Bt. (1804).
Price, Sir (Charles) Roy, K.C.M.G.
Price, Sir Henry Philip, Bt. (1953).
Price, *Capt.* Sir John Green-, Bt. (1874).
Price, Sir Rose Francis, Bt. (1815).
Prichard, Sir John, Kt., C.B.E.
Pridham, *Vice-Adm.* Sir (Arthur) Francis, K.B.E., C.B.
Pridie, Sir Eric Denholm, K.C.M.G., D.S.O., O.B.E.
Priestley, Sir Gerald William, K.C.I.E.
Priestley, Sir Raymond Edward, Kt., M.C.
Primrose, Sir John Ure, Bt. (1903).
Primrose, Sir John Ure, Kt.
Pringle, Sir Stuart Robert, Bt. (S 1683).

Prior, Sir Charles Geoffrey, K.C.I.E.
Prior, Sir Henry Carlos, K.C.I.E., C.S.I.
Pritchard, Sir Fred Eills, Kt., M.B.E.
Pritchard, Sir Neil, K.C.M.G.
Pritchett, Sir Theodore Beal, Kt., M.C.
Proby, *Maj.* Sir Richard George, Bt., M.C. (1952).
Proctor, Sir (Philip) Dennis, K.C.B.
Pryke, Sir David Dudley, Bt. (1926).
Puckey, Sir Walter Charles, Kt.
Puckle, Sir Frederick Hale, K.C.I.E., C.S.I.
Pugh, *His. Hon.* Sir (John) Alun, Kt.
Pugh, *Prof.* Sir William John, Kt., O.B.E., D.SC., F.R.S.
Pugsley, *Prof.* Sir Alfred Grenvile, Kt., O.B.E., D.SC., F.R.S.
Pugsley, Sir Reuben James, Kt., O.B.E.
Puttick, *Lt.-Gen.* Sir Edward, K.C.B., D.S.O.
Pym, *Maj.* Sir Charles Evelyn, Kt., C.B.E.
Pyman, *General* Sir Harold English, G.B.E., K.C.B., D.S.O.
Quartermaine, Sir Allan Stephen, Kt., C.B.E., M.C.
Quénet, *Hon.* Sir Vincent Ernest, Kt.
Quilter, Sir Anthony Raymond Leopold Cuthbert, Bt. (1897).
Raby, Sir Victor Harry, K.B.E., C.B., M.C.
Radcliffe, Sir Clifford Walter, Kt., C.B.E.
Radcliffe, Sir Everard Joseph, Bt. (1813).
Radcliffe, Sir Ralph Hubert John Delmé-, Kt.
Radclyffe, Sir Charles Edward Mott-, Kt., M.P.
Radley, Sir (William) Gordon, K.C.B., C.B.E., Ph.D.
Rae, Sir Alexander Montgomery Wilson, K.C.M.G., M.D.
Rae, Sir Robert, Kt., C.B.
Raeburn, Sir Colin, Kt., C.B.E.
Raeburn, Sir Edward Alfred, Bt. (1923).
Raffray, Sir Philippe, Kt., C.B.E., Q.C.
Raggatt, Sir Harold George, Kt., C.B.E.
Raghunath Purushottam Paranjpye, Sir, Kt.
Rahimtoola, Sir Fazil Ibrahim, Kt., C.I.E.
Raikes, *Maj.-Gen.* Sir Geoffrey Taunton, Kt., C.B., D.S.O.
Raikes, Sir (Henry) Victor (Alpin MacKinnon), K.B.E.
Railing, Sir Harry, Kt.
Raisman, Sir (Abraham) Jeremy, G.C.M.G., G.C.I.E., K.C.S.I.
Rajagopalachari, Sir Shrinivas Prasonna, Kt.
Rajapakse, Sir Lalita Abhaya, Kt., Q.C.
Ralli, Sir Strati, Bt., M.C. (1912).
Ram, Sir Shri, Kt.
Ram Chandra Mardarai Deo, *Raja Bahadur*, Sir, Kt.
Ramage, Sir Richard Ogilvy, Kt., C.M.G.
Raman, Sir (Chandrasekhara) Venkata. Kt., F.R.S.
Ramaswami Aiyar, Sir Chetpat P. A., K.C.S.I., K.C.I.E.
Rampur, *Maj.-Gen.* H.H. the Nawab of, G.C.I.E., K.C.S.I.
Ramsay, *Maj.-Gen.* Sir Alan Hollick, Kt., C.B., C.B.E., D.S.O.
Ramsay, Sir Alexander, Kt., O.B.E.
Ramsay, Sir Alexander Burnett, Bt. (1806).
Ramsay, *Admiral* Hon. Sir Alexander Robert Maule, G.C.V.O., K.C.B., D.S.O.
Ramsay, Sir Neis Alexander, Bt. (S 1666).
Ramsden, Sir Geoffrey Charles Frescheville, Kt., C.I.E.
Ramsden, Sir (Geoffrey) William Pennington-, Bt. (1689).
Ramsey, *Admiral* Sir Charles Gordon, K.C.B.
Ranasinha, Sir Arthur Godwin, Kt., C.M.G., C.B.E.
Rance, *Maj.-Gen.* Sir Hubert Elvin, G.C.M.G., G.B.E., C.B.
Randall, Sir Alec Walter George, K.C.M.G., O.B.E.
Randall, *Prof.* Sir John Turton, Kt., D.SC., F.R.S.
Rankin, Sir Hugh (Charles Rhys), Bt. (1898).
Rankine, Sir John Dalziel, K.C.M.G., K.C.V.O.
Ransford, *Col.* Sir Alister John, Kt., C.I.E.
Rapp, Sir Thomas Cecil, K.B.E., C.M.G., M.C.
Rasch, *Maj.* Sir Richard Guy Carne, Bt. (1903).
Rashleigh, Sir Harry Evelyn Battie, Bt. (1831).
Rattray, *Rear-Adm.* Sir Arthur Rullion, K.B.E., C.B., C.I.E.
Rau, Sir Benegal Rama, Kt., C.I.E.
Raw, *Vice-Adm.* Sir Sydney Moffat, K.B.E., C.B.
Rawlinson, Sir (Alfred) Frederick, Bt. (1891).
Rawlinson, Sir Joseph, Kt., C.B.E.
Rawlinson, Sir Peter Anthony Grayson, Q.C., M.P.
Rawson, Sir Stanley Walter, Kt.
Rayner, *Brig.* Sir Ralph Herbert, Kt.
Read, Sir Herbert, Kt., D.S.O., M.C.
Reade, Sir Clyde Nixon, Bt. (1661).
Readhead, Sir James Templeman, Bt. (1922).
Rebbeck, Sir Frederick Ernest, K.B.E.
Rebbeck, *Rear-Adm.* Sir (Leopold) Edward, K.B.E., C.B.
Reddish, Sir Halford Walter Lupton, Kt.
Redfern, Sir (Arthur) Shuldham, K.C.V.O., C.M.G.
Redgrave, Sir Michael Scudamore, Kt., C.B.E.
Redman, *Lt.-Gen.* Sir Harold, K.C.B., C.B.E.
Redman, Sir (Herbert) Vere, Kt., C.M.G., O.B.E.
Redwood, Sir Thomas Boverton, Bt. (1911).
Reece, Sir Gerald, K.C.M.G., C.B.E.
Reed, Sir Carol, Kt.
Reed, *Hon.* Sir Geoffrey Sandford, Kt.
Reed, Sir John Seymour Blake-, Kt., O.B.E.
Reed, Sir Stanley, K.B.E., LL.D.
Rees, *Hon.* Sir (Charles William) Stanley, Kt., T.D.
Rees, Sir Frederic Tavinor, Kt., C.B.E., M.C., T.D.
Rees, Sir Hugh Ellis-, K.C.M.G., C.B.
Rees, Sir (James) Frederick, Kt.
Rees, Sir Richard Lodowick Edward Montagu, Bt. (1919).
Reid, Sir Alexander James, Kt., C.M.G., I.S.O.
Reid, Sir Douglas Neilson, Bt. (1922).
Reid, Sir Edward James, Bt., O.B.E. (1897).
Reid, *Air Vice-Marshal* Sir (George) Ranald Macfarlane, K.C.B., D.S.O. M.C.
Reid, Sir George Thomas, K.B.E., C.B.
Reid, *Admiral* Sir (John) Peter (Lorne), G.C.B., C.V.O.
Reid, Sir Robert Niel, K.C.S.I., K.C.I.E.
Reilly, *Lt.-Col.* Sir Bernard Rawdon, K.C.M.G., C.I.E., O.B.E.
Reilly, Sir (D'Arcy) Patrick, K.C.M.G., O.B.E.
Renals, Sir, Stanley Bt. (1895).
Rendel, Sir George William, K.C.M.G.
Renison, Sir Patrick Muir, G.C.M.G.
Rennie, *Hon.* Sir Alfred Baillie, Kt.
Rennie, Sir Gilbert (McCall), G.B.E., K.C.M.G., M.C.
Rennie, Sir John Shaw, K.C.M.G., O.B.E.
Renold, Sir Charles Garonne, Kt.
Renshaw, Sir (Charles) Stephen (Bine), Bt. (1903).
Renwick, Sir Eustace Deuchar, Bt. (1921).
Renwick, Sir Robert Burnham, Bt., K.B.E. (1927).
Rey, *Lt.-Col.* Sir Charles Fernand, Kt., C.M.G.
Reynolds, *Air Marshal* Sir Bryan Vernon, K.C.B., C.B.E.
Reynolds, Sir David James, Bt. (1923).
Reynolds, Sir Jeffery Fellowes Crofts, Kt., C.I.E., M.C.
Reynolds, *Maj.* Sir Percival Reuben, K.B.E.
Rhodes, Sir Christopher George, Bt. (1919).
Rhodes, *Brig.-Gen.* Sir Godfrey Dean, Kt., C.B., C.B.E., D.S.O.
Ricardo, Sir Harry Ralph, Kt., LL.D., F.R.S.
Rich, Sir Almeric Frederic Conness, Bt. (1791).
Richards, Sir Gordon, Kt.
Richardson, *Prof.* Sir Albert Edward, K.C.V.O., R.A., F.S.A.

Richardson, *Lt.-Gen.* Sir Charles Leslie, K.C.B., C.B.E., D.S.O.
Richardson, Sir (Horace) Frank, Kt.
Richardson, Sir Ian Rory Hay Stewart-, Bt. (S 1630).
Richardson, Sir (John) Henry (Swain), Kt.
Richardson, Sir John Samuel, Kt., M.V.O., M.D.
Richardson, Sir Leslie Lewis, Bt. (1924).
Richardson, Sir Ralph David, Kt.
Richardson, Sir William Wigham, Bt., M.B.E. (1929).
Riches, Sir Derek Martin Hurry, K.C.M.G.
Riches, Sir Eric William, Kt., M.C.
Riches, *General* Sir Ian Hurry, K.C.B., D.S.O.
Richmond, Sir Arthur Cyril, Kt., C.B.E.
Richmond, Sir Bruce Lyttelton, Kt.
Richmond, Sir John Christopher Blake, K.C.M.G.
Richmond, Sir John Frederick, Bt. (1929).
Richmond, *Vice-Adm.* Sir Maxwell, K.B.E., C.B., D.S.O.
Rickett, Sir Denis Hubert Fletcher, K.C.M.G., C.B.
Ricketts, Sir Robert Cornwallis Gerald St. Leger, Bt. (1828).
Riddell, Sir John Charles Buchanan-, Bt. (S 1628).
Ride, Sir Lindsay Tasman, Kt., C.B.E., E.D.
Rideal, Sir Eric Keightley, Kt., M.B.E., F.R.S., D.SC.
Ridley, Sir Sidney, Kt.
Rieu, Sir (Jean) Louis, K.C.S.I.
Rigby, *Lt.-Col.* Sir (Hugh) John (Macbeth), Bt. (1920).
Rigg, Sir Theodore, K.B.E.
Riley, *Maj.-Gen.* Sir (Henry) Guy, K.B.E., C.B.
Ripley, Sir Hugh, Bt. (1880).
Ritchie, Sir James Edward Thomson, Bt. (1918).
Ritchie, Sir (John) Douglas, Kt., M.C.
Ritchie, Sir John Neish, Kt., C.B.
Ritchie, *Capt.* (S) Sir Lewis Anselm, K.C.V.O., C.B.E., R.N.
Ritchie, *General* Sir Neil Methuen, G.B.E., K.C.B., D.S.O., M.C.
Ritchie, Sir Thomas Malcolm, Kt.
Ritson, Sir Edward Herbert, K.B.E., C.B.
Road, Sir Alfred, Kt., C.B.E.
Robb, Sir (George) Douglas, Kt., C.M.G., M.D.
Robb, *Air Chief Marshal* Sir James Milne, G.C.B., K.B.E. D.S.O., D.F.C., A.F.C.
Roberts, Sir Alfred, Kt., C.B.E.
Roberts, Sir Ernest Handforth Goodman, Kt., Q.C.
Roberts, Sir Frank Kenyon, G.C.M.G.
Roberts, Sir George William Kelly, Kt., C.B.E.
Roberts, Sir Harold Charles West, Kt., C.B.E., M.C.
Roberts, Sir James Denby, Bt. (1909).
Roberts, Sir (James Reginald) Howard, Kt., C.B.E.
Roberts, Sir John, Kt.
Roberts, Sir Leslie, Kt., C.B.E.
Roberts, Sir Norman Stanley, K.B.E., C.M.G.
Roberts, *General* Sir Ouvry Lindfield, G.C.B., K.B.E., D.S.O.
Roberts, Sir Peter Geoffrey, Bt., M.P. (1919).
Roberts, Sir Sydney Castle, Kt.
Roberts, *Col.* Sir Thomas Langdon Howland, Bt. (1809).
Roberts, Sir Walter St. Clair Howland, K.C.M.G., M.C.
Roberts, Sir William, Kt., C.I.E.
Robertshaw, *Vice-Adm.* Sir Ballin Illingworth, K.B.E., C.B.
Robertson, Sir Alexander, Kt., D.C.M.
Robertson, Sir Carrick Hey, Kt.
Robertson, Sir David, Kt., M.P.
Robertson, Sir Frederick Wynne, Kt., C.S.I., C.I.E.
Robertson, Sir George Stuart, Kt., Q.C., F.S.A.
Robertson, Sir James (Jackson), Kt., O.B.E., LL.D.
Robertson, Sir James Wilson, G.C.M.G., G.C.V.O., K.B.E.
Robieson, Sir William Dunkeld, Kt., LL.D.
Robins, Sir Reginald Edwin, Kt., C.M.G., O.B.E.
Robinson, Sir Albert Edward Phineas, Kt.
Robinson, Sir Foster Gotch, Kt.
Robinson, *Maj.* Sir Frederick Villiers Laud, Bt., M.C. (1660).
Robinson, Sir George Gilmour, Kt.
Robinson, Sir Harold Ernest, Kt.
Robinson, Sir John Beverley, Bt. (1854).
Robinson, Sir John Edgar, Kt.
Robinson, *Rt. Hon.* Sir (John) Roland, Kt., M.P.
Robinson, Sir Leslie Harold, K.B.E., C.B.
Robinson, Sir (Montague) Arnet, Kt.
Robinson, Sir Niall Bryan Lynch-, Bt., D.S.C. (1920).
Robinson, Sir Norman de Winton, Kt.
Robinson, Sir Robert, Kt., O.M., D.SC., F.R.S.
Robinson, Sir Victor Lloyd, Kt., C.B.E., Q.C.
Robinson, Sir (Wilfred Henry) Frederick Bt. (1908).
Robinson, Sir William Henry, K.C.M.G., C.B.E.
Robson, Sir Thomas Buston, Kt., M.B.E.
Robson, *Vice-Adm.* Sir (William) Geoffrey (Arthur), K.B.E., C.B., D.S.O., D.S.C.
Roche, Sir Standish O'Grady, Bt., D.S.O. (1938).
Rodrigo, Sir (Senapathige Theobald) Philip, Kt., O.B.E.
Roe, *Maj.-Gen.* Sir William Gordon, K.B.E., C.B.
Rogers, Sir Philip James, Kt., C.B.E.
Roll, Sir Eric, K.C.M.G., C.B.
Roll, *Rev.* Sir James William Cecil, Bt. (1921).
Rolland, *Very Rev.* Sir Francis William, Kt., C.M.G., O.B.E., M.C.
Romer, *Rt. Hon.* Sir Charles Robert Ritchie, O.B.E.
Ronald, Sir Nigel Bruce, K.C.M.G., C.V.O.
Roome, *Maj.-Gen.* Sir Horace Eckford, K.C.I.E., C.B., C.B.E., M.C.
Rooney, *Maj.-Gen.* Sir Owen Patrick James, K.B.E., C.B.
Rootes, Sir Reginald Claud, Kt.
Roper, Sir Harold, Kt., C.B.E., M.C.
Ropner, *Col.* Sir Leonard, Bt., M.C., T.D. (1952).
Ropner, Sir Robert Desmond, Kt.
Ropner, Sir Robert Douglas, Bt. (1904).
Ropner, Sir (William) Guy, Kt.
Rose, Sir Alan Edward Percival, K.C.M.G., Q.C.
Rose, Sir Charles Henry, Bt. (1909).
Rose, Sir Francis Cyril, Bt. (1872).
Rose, Sir Hugh, Bt., T.D. (1935).
Rose, Sir Philip (Humphrey Vivian), Bt. (1874).
Roseveare, Sir Martin Pearson, Kt.
Roseway, Sir (George) David, K.B.E., C.B.
Roskill, *Hon.* Sir Eustace Wentworth, Kt.
Ross, Sir Archibald David Manisty, K.C.M.G.
Ross, *Hon.* Sir Dudley Bruce, Kt.
Ross, Sir Frederick William Leith-, G.C.M.G., K.C.B.
Ross, Sir Henry James, Kt.
Ross, *Prof.* Sir James Paterson, Bt., K.C.V.O. (1960).
Ross, Sir (William) David, K.B.E., D.Litt.
Rothenstein, Sir John Knewstub Maurice, Kt., C.B.E., Ph.D.
Rous, Sir Stanley Ford, Kt., C.B.E.
Rouse, Sir Alexander Macdonald, Kt., C.I.E.
Rowan, Sir (Thomas) Leslie, K.C.B., C.V.O.
Rowcroft, *Maj.-Gen.* Sir (Eric) Bertram, K.B.E., C.B.
Rowe, Sir Michael Edward, Kt., C.B.E., Q.C.
Rowell, Sir Andrew Herrick, Kt.
Rowell, Sir (Herbert Babington) Robin, Kt., C.B.E., A.F.C.
Rowell, Sir Reginald Kaye, Kt.
Rowell, *Lt.-Gen.* Sir Sydney Fairbairn, K.B.E., C.B.
Rowland, Sir John Edward Maurice, Kt.
Rowland, Sir Wentworth Lowe, Bt. (1950).
Rowlands, *Surg.-Rear-Adm.* Sir (Richard) Alun, K.B.E., M.D.
Rowlandson, Sir (Stanley) Graham, Kt., M.B.E.
Rowley, Sir Joshua Francis, Bt. (1786).

Rowley, *Lt.-Col.* Sir William Joshua, Bt. (1836).
Roxburgh, Sir Ronald Francis, Kt.
Roxburgh, Sir (Thomas) James (Young), Kt., C.I.E.
Roy, Sir Asoka Kumar, Kt.
Royden, Sir John Ledward, Bt. (1905).
Royle, Sir Lancelot Carrington, K.B.E.
Rucker, Sir Arthur Nevil, K.C.M.G., C.B., C.B.E.
Ruddle, *Lt.-Col.* Sir (George) Kenneth (Fordham), Kt., T.D.
Rugg, Sir (Edward) Percy, Kt.
Rumball, *Air Vice-Marshal* Sir (Campion) Aubrey, K.B.E.
Rumbold, Sir (Horace) Algernon (Fraser), K.C.M.G., C.I.E.
Rumbold, Sir (Horace) Anthony (Claude), Bt., K.C.M.G., C.B. (1779).
Runciman, *Hon.* Sir James Cochran Stevenson, Kt.
Rundall, Sir Francis Brian Anthony, K.C.M.G., O.B.E.
Russell, Sir Arthur Edward Ian Montagu, Bt. (1812).
Russell, Sir Charles Ian, Bt. (1916).
Russell, *Rt. Hon.* Sir Charles Ritchie, Kt.
Russell, *Lt.-Gen.* Sir Dudley, K.B.E., C.B., D.S.O., M.C.
Russell, Sir (Edward) John, Kt., O.B.E., F.R.S.
Russell, Sir (Edward) Lionel, Kt. C.B.E.
Russell, *Admiral* Hon. Sir Guy Herbrand Edward, G.B.E., K.C.B., D.S.O.
Russell, Sir John Weir, Kt.
Russell, Sir Robert Edwin, Kt., C.S.I., C.I.E.
Russell, Sir (Sydney) Gordon, Kt., C.B.E., M.C.
Russon, Sir (William) Clayton, Kt., O.B.E.
Rutherford, Sir John George, Kt.
Ryan, Sir Derek Gerald, Bt., (1919).
Rycroft, Sir Benjamin William, Kt., O.B.E., M.D.
Rycroft, Sir (Richard) Newton, Bt. (1784).
Rye, Sir Eudo John, Bt. (S 1706).
Rymill, Sir Arthur Campbell, Kt.
Sachs, *Hon.* Sir Eric, Kt., M.B.E., T.D.
Saint, Sir (Sidney) John, Kt., C.M.G., O.B.E.
St. Aubyn, Sir John Molesworth-, Bt. (1689).
St. George, Sir Robert Alan, Bt. (I 1766).
Salisbury, Sir Edward James, Kt., C.B.E., D.SC., F.R.S.
Salmon, *Hon.* Sir Cyril Barnet, Kt.
Salmon, Sir Samuel Isidore, Kt.
Salmond, *Marshal of the Royal Air Force* Sir John Maitland, G.C.B., C.M.G., C.V.O., D.S.O.
Salt, Sir David Shirley, Bt. (1869).
Salt, Sir Edward William, Kt.
Salt, *Lt.-Col.* Sir Thomas Henry, Bt. (1899).
Samson, Sir William Frederick, Kt.
Samuel, Sir Harold, Kt.
Samuel, Sir Jon Michael Glen, Bt. (1898).
Samuels, Sir Alexander, Kt., C.B.E.
Samuelson, Sir Francis Henry Bernard, Bt. (1884).
Sanders, Sir Harold George, Kt., Ph.D.
Sandars, *Vice-Adm.* Sir (Reginald) Thomas, K.B.E., C.B.
Sanders, *Air Chief Marshal* Sir Arthur Penrose Martyn, G.C.B., K.B.E.
Sanderson, *Air Marshal* Sir (Alfred) Clifford, K.B.E., C.B., D.F.C.
Sanderson, Sir Frank Bernard, Bt. (1920).
Sanderson, Sir Harold Leslie, Kt., D.C.M.
Sandford, Sir Folliott Herbert, K.B.E., C.M.G.
Sansom, Sir George Bailey, G.B.E., K.C.M.G.
Sargent, Sir John Philip, Kt., C.I.E.
Sargent, Sir Malcolm, Kt., Mus.D.
Sargent, Sir (Sidney) Donald, K.B.E., C.B.
Satow, Sir Harold Eustace, K.C.M.G., O.B.E.
Saundby, *Air Marshal* Sir Robert Henry Magnus Spencer, K.C.B., K.B.E., M.C., D.F.C., A.F.C.
Saunders, Sir Alexander Morris Carr-, K.B.E.
Saunders, Sir Harold Leonard, Kt.
Saunders, *Air Chief Marshal* Sir Hugh William Lumsden, G.C.B., K.B.E., M.C., D.F.C., M.M.
Savage, Sir Alfred William Lungley, K.C.M.G.
Savage, Sir (Edward) Graham, Kt., C.B.
Savill, Sir Eric Humphrey, K.C.V.O., C.B.E., M.C.
Savory, Sir Douglas Lloyd, Kt.
Savory, *Lt.-Gen.* Sir Reginald Arthur, K.C.I.E., C.B., D.S.O., M.C.
Sayad Muhammad, *Nawab* Sir, Kt.
Sayer, *Vice-Adm.* Sir Guy Bourchier, K.B.E., C.B., D.S.C.
Sayers, Sir Frederick, Kt., C.I.E.
Scarlett, Sir Peter William Shelley Yorke, K.C.M.G., K.C.V.O.
Scarman, *Hon.* Sir Leslie George, Kt., O.B.E.
Scherger, *Air Marshal* Sir Frederick Rudolph William, K.B.E., C.B., D.S.O., A.F.C.
Schonell, *Prof.* Sir Fred Joyce, Kt. Ph.D., D.Litt.
Schonland, Sir Basil Ferdinand Jamieson, Kt., C.B.E., Ph.D., F.R.S.
Schreiber, *Lt.-Gen.* Sir Edmond Charles Acton, K.C.B., D.S.O.
Schuster, Sir (Felix) James Moncrieff, Bt., O.B.E. (1906).
Schuster, Sir George Ernest, K.C.S.I., K.C.M.G., C.B.E., M.C.
Scicluna, Sir Hannibal Publius, Kt., M.B.E.
Scobie, *Lt.-Gen.* Sir Ronald Mackenzie, K.B.E., C.B., M.C.
Scoones, *General* Sir Geoffry Allen Percival, K.C.B., K.B.E., C.S.I., D.S.O., M.C.
Scoones, *Maj.-Gen.* Sir Reginald Laurence, K.B.E., C.B., D.S.O.
Scopes, Sir Frederick, Kt.
Scopes, Sir Leonard Arthur, K.C.V.O., C.M.G., O.B.E.
Scott, Sir David John Montagu-Douglas-, K.C.M.G., O.B.E.
Scott, *Lt.-Col.* Sir Douglas Winchester, Bt. (1913).
Scott, Sir Edward Arthur Dolman, Bt. (1806).
Scott, Sir Harold Richard, G.C.V.O., K.C.B., K.B.E.
Scott, *Brig.* Sir Henry (Lawrence), Kt., C.B., D.S.O., M.C.
Scott, Sir Ian Dixon, K.C.M.G., C.I.E.
Scott, *Col.* Sir Jervoise Bolitho, Bt. (1962).
Scott, *Col.* Sir Malcolm Stoddart-, Kt., O.B.E., T.D., M.P.
Scott, Sir Oliver Christopher Anderson, Bt. (1909).
Scott, Sir Robert, K.C.M.G.
Scott, Sir (Robert) Donald, Kt.
Scott, Sir Robert Heatlie, G.C.M.G., C.B.E.
Scott, Sir Walter, Bt. (1907).
Scott, Sir William, Kt., O.B.E.
Scott, *Maj.-Gen.* Sir William Arthur, K.C.M.G., C.B., C.B.E.
Scott, Sir William Dalgliesh, Kt., C.B.E.
Scragg, *Air Vice-Marshal* Sir Colin, K.B.E., C.B., A.F.C.
Scrivener, Sir Patrick Stratford, K.C.M.G.
Scrivenor, Sir Thomas Vaisey, Kt., C.M.G.
Seaford, Sir Frederick Jacob, Kt., C.M.G., C.B.E.
Seal, Sir Eric Arthur, K.B.E., C.B.
Seale, Sir John Carteret Hyde, Bt. (1838).
Sebright, Sir Hugo Giles Edmund, Bt. (1626).
Seeds, Sir William, K.C.M.G.
Seel, Sir George Frederick, K.C.M.G.
Selby, Sir Walford Harmood Montague, K.C.M.G., C.B., C.V.O.
Self, Sir (Albert) Henry, K.C.B., K.C.M.G., K.B.E.
Selleck, Sir Francis Palmer, K.B.E., M.C.
Sellers, *Rt. Hon.* Sir Frederic Aked, Kt., M.C.
Sellors, Sir Thomas Holmes, Kt., D.M.
Selway, *Air Marshal* Sir Anthony Dunkerton, K.C.B., D.F.C.
Senter, Sir John Watt, Kt., Q.C.
Seton, Sir Bruce Lovat, Bt. (S 1663).
Seton, Sir Claud Ramsay Wilmot, Kt., M.C.
Seton, Sir Robert James, Bt. (S 1683).
Seward, Sir Eric John, K.B.E.
Seymour, Sir George Seymour, Kt., O.B.E.
Seymour, Sir Horace James, G.C.M.G., C.V.O.
Seymour, *Cdr.* Sir Michael Culme-, Bt., R.N. (1809).

Shakerley, *Maj.* Sir Cyril Holland, Bt. (1838).
Shakespeare, *Rt. Hon.* Sir Geoffrey Hithersay, Bt. (1942).
Shankland, Sir Thomas Murray, Kt., C.M.G.
Shapcott, *Brig.* Sir Henry, K.B.E., C.B., M.C.
Sharp, Sir Edward Harold Wilfred, Bt. (1022).
Sharp, Sir Milton Reginald, Bt. (1920).
Sharpe, Sir Reginald Taaffe, Kt., Q.C.
Sharpe, Sir William Rutton Searle, Kt.
Shaw, Sir Bernard Vidal, Kt.
Shaw, Sir Evelyn Campbell, K.C.V.O., LL.D.
Shaw, *Cdr.* Sir John James Kenward Best-, Bt., R.N. (1665).
Shaw, Sir John Valentine Wistar, K.C.M.G.
Shaw, Sir Robert de Vere, Bt., M.C. (1821).
Shea, *General* Sir John Stuart Mackenzie, G.C.B., K.C.M.G., D.S.O.
Shearer, Sir James Greig, Kt.
Shedden, Sir Frederick Geoffrey, K.C.M.G., O.B.E.
Sheepshanks, Sir Thomas Herbert, K.C.B., K.B.E.
Sheffield, Sir Robert Arthur, Bt. (1755).
Sheldon, Sir Wilfrid Percy Henry, K.C.V.O.
Shelley, *Brig.* Sir John Frederick, Bt. (1611).
Shelley, Sir Sydney Patrick, Bt. (1806).
Shenton, Sir William Edward Leonard, Kt.
Shepheard, Sir Victor George, K.C.B.
Shepherd, Sir (Edward) Henry Gerald, K.C.M.G.
Sheppard, Sir John Tresidder, Kt., M.B.E.
Sheridan, Sir Joseph, Kt.
Sherwill, Sir Ambrose James, K.B.E., M.C.
Shiffner, Sir Henry David, Bt. (1818).
Shipway, Sir Francis Edward Shipway, K.C.V.O., M.D.
Shires, Sir Frank, Kt.
Sholl, *Hon.* Sir Reginald Richard, Kt.
Shone, Sir Robert Minshull, Kt., C.B.E.
Shone, Sir Terence Allen, K.C.M.G.
Shoobert, Sir (Wilfred) Harold, Kt., C.I.E., E.D.
Shoobridge, *Hon.* Sir Rupert Oakley, Kt.
Shuckburgh, Sir (Charles Arthur) Evelyn, K.C.M.G., C.B.
Shuckburgh, Sir Charles Gerald Stewkley, Bt. (1660).
Sikkim, H.H. the Maharaja of, K.C.S.I., K.C.I.E.
Sim, Sir (George) Alexander (Strachan), Kt.
Sim, Sir Wilfrid Joseph, K.B.E., Q.C.
Simeon, Sir John Edmund Barrington, Bt. (1815).
Simmonds, Sir Oliver Edwin, Kt.
Simon, *Rt. Hon.* Sir Jocelyn Edward Salis, Kt.
Simon, Sir Leon, Kt., C.B.
Simpson, Sir Basil Robert James, Bt., O.B.E. (1935).
Simpson, *General* Sir Frank Ernest Wallace, G.B.E., K.C.B., D.S.O.
Simpson, Sir George Clarke, K.C.B., C.B.E., F.R.S.
Simpson, Sir James Dyer, Kt.
Simpson, Sir James Fletcher, Kt.
Simpson, Sir John Roughton, Kt., C.B.
Simpson, Sir Joseph, K.B.E.
Sims, Sir Alfred John, K.C.B., O.B.E.
Sims, Sir Arthur, Kt.
Sinclair, Sir George Evelyn, Kt., C.M.G., O.B.E.
Sinclair, *Maj.-Gen.* Sir John Alexander, K.C.M.G., C.B., O.B.E.
Sinclair, Sir John Rollo Norman Blair, Bt. (S. 1704).
Sinclair, Sir Kenneth Duncan Leckey, Kt.
Sinclair, *Air Vice-Marshal* Sir Laurence Frank, K.C.B., G.C., C.B.E., D.S.O.
Sinclair, Sir Leonard, Kt.
Sinclair, Sir Ronald Ormiston, K.B.E.
Sinclair, Sir William, Kt., C.B.E.
Sinderson, Sir Harry Chapman, K.B.E., C.M.G., M.V.O., M.D.
Singhania, Sir Padampat, Kt.
Sinker, Sir (Algernon) Paul, K.C.M.G., C.B.
Sita Ram, *Rai Bahadur* Sir, Kt.
Sitwell, *Capt.* Sir (Francis) Osbert (Sacheverell), Bt., C.H., C.B.E. (1808).
Skiffington, Sir Donald MacLean, Kt., C.B.E.
Skinner, Sir (Thomas) Hewitt, Bt. (1912).
Skipwith, Sir Patrick Alexander D'Estoteville, Bt. (1622).
Skrine, Sir Clarmont Percival, Kt., O.B.E.
Slade, Sir Benjamin Julian Alfred, Bt. (1831).
Slater, *Admiral* Sir Robin (Leonard Francis) Durnford-, K.C.B.
Slater, Sir William Kershaw, K.B.E., D.SC., F.R.S.
Slattery, *Rear-Adm.* Sir Matthew Sausse, K.B.E., C.B.
Slayter, *Admiral* Sir William Rudolph, K.C.B., D.S.O., D.S.C.
Sleeman, *Col.* Sir James Lewis, Kt., C.B., C.M.G., C.B.E., M.V.O., T.D.
Sleight, Sir John Frederick, Bt. (1920).
Slesser, *Rt. Hon.* Sir Henry, Kt.
Slessor, *Marshal of the Royal Air Force* Sir John Cotesworth, G.C.B., D.S.O., M.C.
Sloan, Sir Tennant, K.C.I.E., C.S.I.
Smallpeice, Sir Basil, K.C.V.O.
Smiley, Sir Hugh Houston, Bt. (1903).
Smirk, *Prof.* Sir Frederick Horace, K.B.E., M.D.
Smith, Sir Allan Chalmers, Kt., M.C.
Smith, Sir (Alexander) Rowland, Kt.
Smith, Sir Andrew, Kt., C.B.E.
Smith, *Lieut-Gen.* Sir Arthur Francis, K.C.B., K.B.E., D.S.O., M.C.
Smith, *Rt. Hon.* Sir Ben, K.B.E.
Smith, Sir Bracewell, Bt., K.C.V.O. (1947).
Smith, Sir Bryan Evers Sharwood-, K.C.M.G., K.C.V.O., K.B.E.
Smith, Sir Cecil Furness-, Kt., Q.C.
Smith, *Maj.-Gen.* Sir Cecil Miller, K.B.E., C.B., M.C.
Smith, Sir Christopher Sydney Winwood, Bt. (1809).
Smith, *Rt. Hon.* Sir Derek Colclough Walker-, Bt., T.D., Q.C. (1960).
Smith, *Vice-Adm.* Sir (Edward Michael) Conolly Abel, G.C.V.O., C.B.
Smith, Sir Frank Edward, G.C.B., G.B.E., F.R.S.
Smith, Sir Frank Edwin Newson-, Bt. (1944).
Smith, Sir (Frank) Ewart, Kt.
Smith, *Vice-Adm.* Sir Geoffrey Thistleton-, K.B.E., C.B., G.M.
Smith, *Col.* Sir Harold Charles, K.B.E.
Smith, Sir (Harold) Gengoult, Kt., V.D.
Smith, *Col.* Sir Henry Abel, K.C.M.G., K.C.V.O., D.S.O.
Smith, Sir Henry Thompson, K.B.E., C.B.
Smith, Sir Henry Wilson, K.C.B., K.B.E.
Smith, Sir John Alfred Lucie-, Kt., O.B.E., V.D.
Smith, Sir John Hamilton-Spencer-, Bt. (1804).
Smith, Sir Jonah Walker-, Kt.
Smith, Sir Laurence Barton Grafftey-, K.C.M.G., K.B.E.
Smith, Sir Norman Percival Arthur, Kt., C.I.E., O.B.E.
Smith, *Col. Rt. Hon.* Sir Reginald Hugh Dorman-, G.B.E.
Smith, Sir Richard Rathborne Vassar-, Bt. (1917).
Smith, *Prof.* Sir Sydney Alfred, Kt., C.B.E., M.D.
Smith, Sir Thomas, Kt., V.D.
Smith, Sir Thomas Dalrymple Straker-, Kt.
Smith, *Lt.-Col.* Sir (Thomas) Eustace, Kt., C.B.E., T.D.
Smith, Sir Thomas Gilbert, Bt. (1897).
Smith, Sir Tom Elder Barr, Kt.
Smith, Sir (William) Gordon, Bt., V.R.D. (1945).
Smith, Sir William Prince-, Bt., O.B.E., M.C. (1911).
Smith, Sir William Proctor, Kt.
Smith, Sir William Reardon Reardon-, Bt. (1920).
Smith, Sir (William) Reginald Verdon, Kt.
Smith, *Capt.* Sir (William Robert) Dermot (Joshua) Cusack-, Bt. (I 1799).

Smithers, Sir Arthur Tennyson, Kt., C.B.E.
Smyth, *Brig. Rt. Hon.* Sir John George, Bt., V.C., M.C., M.P. (1955).
Smyth, *Capt.* Sir Philip Weyland Bowyer-. Bt., R.N. (1661).
Snedden, Sir Richard, Kt., C.B.E.
Snelling, Sir Arthur Wendell, K.C.M.G., K.C.V.O.
Snelson, Sir Edward Alec Abbott, K.B.E.
Snow, Sir Charles Percy, Kt., C.B.E.
Snow, Sir Harold Ernest, Kt., C.B.E.
Soame, Sir Charles Burnett Buckworth-Herne-, Bt. (1697).
Sobha Singh, *Hon. Sardar Bahadur* Sir Sardar, Kt., O.B.E.
Sokhey, *Maj.-Gen.* Sir Sahibsingh, Kt., M.D.
Sokoto, *Hon.* The Sardauna of, K.B.E.
Somerville, Sir John Livingston, Kt., F.R.S.E.
Somerville, Sir Robert, K.C.V.O.
Sopwith, Sir Thomas Octave Murdoch, Kt., C.B.E.
Sorley, *Air Marshal* Sir Ralph Squire, K.C.B., O.B.E., D.S.C., D.F.C.
Soskice, *Rt. Hon.* Sir Frank, Kt., Q.C., M.P.
Soulsby, Sir Llewellyn T. G., Kt.
Souter, Sir William Alfred, Kt.
Southby, *Cdr.* Sir Archibald Richard James, Bt., R.N. (1937).
Southwell, Sir (Charles Archibald) Philip, Kt., C.B.E., M.C.
Southwell, Sir Richard Vynne, Kt., F.R.S.
Souttar, Sir Henry Sessions, Kt., C.B.E.
Soysa, Sir Warusahennedige Abraham Bastian, Kt., C.B.E.
Sparks, Sir Ashley, K.C.M.G., K.B.E.
Spearman, Sir Alexander Bowyer, Bt. (1840).
Spearman, Sir Alexander (Cadwallader) Mainwaring, Kt., M.P.
Spears, *Maj.-Gen.* Sir Edward (Louis), Bt., K.B.E., C.B., M.C. (1953).
Speed, Sir Eric Bourne Bentinck, K.C.B., K.B.E., M.C.
Speed, Sir Robert William Arney, Kt., C.B., Q.C.
Speelman, *Jonkheer* Sir Cornelis Jacob, Bt. (1686).
Spence, *Maj.* Sir Basil Hamilton Hebden Neven-, Kt.
Spence, Sir Basil Urwin, Kt., O.M., O.B.E., T.D., R.A.
Spencer, Sir Henry Francis, Kt.
Spencer, Sir Kelvin Tallent, Kt., C.B.E., M.C.
Spencer, Sir Thomas George, Kt.
Spender, *Hon.* Sir Percy Claude, K.C.V.O., K.B.E., Q.C.
Sperling, Sir Rowland Arthur Charles, K.C.M.G., C.B.
Spicer, Sir (Albert) Dykes, Bt. (1906).
Spicer, *Hon.* Sir John Armstrong, Kt.
Spooner, *Hon.* Sir William Henry, K.C.M.G., M.M.
Spreckley, *Air Marshal* Sir Herbert Dorman, K.B.E., C.B.
Spriggs, Sir Frank Spencer, K.B.E.
Spurrier, Sir Henry, Kt.
Srinivasa Varadachariar, Sir, Kt.
Stable, *Hon.* Sir Wintringham Norton, Kt., M.C.
Stacey, Sir Ernest, Kt.
Stallard, Sir Peter Hyla Gawne, K.C.M.G., C.V.O., M.B.E.
Stamer, Sir (Lovelace) Anthony, Bt. (1809).
Stanier, *Brig.* Sir Alexander Beville Gibbons, Bt., D.S.O., M.C. (1917).
Stanier, Sir William Arthur, Kt., F.R.S.
Stanley, Sir Robert Christopher Stafford, K.B.E., C.M.G.
Stanton, *Hon.* Sir Joseph, Kt.
Stapledon, Sir Robert de Stapeldon, K.C.M.G., C.B.E.
Staples, Sir Robert George Alexander, Bt. (I 1628).
Stapleton, Sir Miles Talbot, Bt. (1679).
Starkey, *Lt.-Col.* Sir William Randle, Bt. (1935).
Stedeford, Sir Ivan Arthur Rice, G.B.E.
Stedman, Sir George Foster, K.B.E., C.B., M.C.
Steel, Sir Christopher Eden, G.C.M.G., M.V.O.
Steel, *Maj.* Sir (Fiennes) William Strang, Bt., (1938).
Steel, *Air Chief Marshal* Sir John Miles, G.C.B., K.B.E., C.M.G.
Steele, *Air-Marshal* Sir Charles Ronald, K.C.B., D.F.C.
Steele, Sir Henry, Kt.
Steele, *General* Sir James Stuart, G.C.B., K.B.E., D.S.O., M.C.
Stenhouse, Sir Nicol, Kt.
Stenton, Sir Frank Merry, Kt., LL.D., D.Litt., F.B.A.
Stephen, Sir Alexander Murray, Kt., M.C.
Stephen, Sir James Alexander, Bt. (1891).
Stephens, Sir (Leon) Edgar, Kt., C.B.E.
Stephenson, Sir Arthur George, Kt., C.M.G., M.C.
Stephenson, *Vice-Adm.* Sir Gilbert Owen, K.B.E., C.B., C.M.G.
Stephenson, *Lt.-Col.* Sir (Henry) Francis (Blake), Bt., O.B.E., T.D. (1936).
Stephenson, Sir Hugh Southern, K.C.M.G., C.I.E., C.V.O., O.B.E.
Stephenson, *Hon.* Sir John Frederick Eustace, Kt.
Stephenson, Sir William Samuel, Kt., M.C., D.F.C.
Stern, *Lt.-Col.* Sir Albert, K.B.E., C.M.G.
Stern, *Col.* Sir Frederick Claude, Kt., O.B.E., M.C.
Stevens, *Air Marshal* Sir Alick Charles, K.B.E., C.B.
Stevens, *Hon.* Sir Bertram Sydney Barnsdale, K.C.M.G.
Stevens, Sir Harold Samuel Eaton, K.C.I.E., C.S.I., M.C.
Stevens, *Maj.-Gen.* Sir Jack Edwin Stawell, K.B.E., C.B., D.S.O., E.D.
Stevens, *Vice-Adm.* Sir John Felgate, K.B.E., C.B.
Stevens, Sir Roger Bentham, K.C.M.G.
Stevenson, *Hon.* Sir (Aubrey) Melford (Steed), Kt.
Stevenson, Sir Hubert Craddock, K.C.M.G., O.B.E., M.C.
Stevenson, Sir Ralph (Clarmont) Skrine, G.C.M.G.
Stevenson, Sir Roy Hunter, Kt., M.B.E.
Steward, Sir William Arthur, Kt.
Stewart, Sir Bruce Fraser, Bt. (1920).
Stewart, Sir David James Henderson-, Bt. (1957).
Stewart, Sir Herbert Kay, Kt., C.I.E.
Stewart, Sir Hugh Charlie Godfray, Bt. (1803).
Stewart, Sir James Watson, Bt. (1920).
Stewart, Sir Jocelyn Harry, Bt. (I 1623).
Stewart, *Maj.-Gen.* Sir Keith Lindsay, K.B.E., C.B., D.S.O.
Stewart, Sir Kenneth Dugald, Bt., G.B.E. (1960).
Stewart, Sir Robert Sproul, Kt., C.B.E.
Stewart, Sir Ronald Compton, Bt. (1937).
Stewart, Sir Thomas Alexander, K.C.S.I., K.C.I.E.
Stewart, *Lt.-Col.* Sir (Walter) Guy Shaw-, Bt., M.C. (S 1667).
Stirling, Sir Charles Norman, K.C.M.G., K.C.V.O.
Stirling, Sir John, K.T., M.B.E., T.D.
Stirling, *General* Sir William Gordon, K.C.B., C.B.E., D.S.O.
Stoby, Sir Kenneth Sievewright, Kt.
Stockdale, Sir Edward Villiers Minshull, Bt. (1960).
Stockwell, *General* Sir Hugh Charles, G.C.B., K.B.E., D.S.O.
Stone, Sir Gilbert, Kt.
Stone, Sir (John) Leonard, Kt., O.B.E., Q.C.
Stoneham, Sir Ralph Thompson, K.B.E.
†Stonhouse, Sir Arthur Allan, Bt. (1628).
Stooke, Sir George Beresford-, K.C.M.G.
Stopford, *General* Sir Montagu George North, G.C.B., K.B.E., D.S.O., M.C.
Storey, Sir Samuel, Bt., M.P. (1960).
Storrar, Sir John, Kt., C.B.E., M.C.
Stott, Sir Philip Sidney, Bt., (1920).
Stourton, Sir Ivo Herbert Evelyn Joseph, Kt., C.M.G., O.B.E.
Stout, Sir Thomas Duncan Macgregor, Kt., C.B.E., D.S.O., E.D.
Stow, Sir Frederic Lawrence Philipson-, Bt. (1907).
Stow, Sir John Montague, K.C.M.G.
Stracey, Sir Michael George Motley, Bt. (1818).

Strachan, Sir Andrew Henry, Kt., C.B.E.
Strangman, Sir Thomas Joseph, Kt., Q.C.
Strath, Sir William, K.C.B.
Stratton, *Lt.-Gen.* Sir William Henry, K.C.B., C.V.O., C.B.E., D.S.O.
Streat, Sir (Edward) Raymond, K.B.E.
Streatfield, *Hon.* Sir Geoffrey Hugh Benbow, Kt., M.C.
Street, *Hon.* Sir Kenneth Whistler, K.C.M.G.
Strohmenger, Sir Ernest John, G.B.E., C.B.
Strong, *Maj.-Gen.* Sir Kenneth William Dobson, Kt., C.B., O.B.E.
Stronge, *Capt. Rt. Hon.* Sir (Charles) Norman (Lockhart), Bt., M.C. (1803).
Stronge, Sir Herbert Cecil, Kt., Q.C.
Strutt, Sir (Henry) Austin, K.C.V.O., C.B.
Stuart, Sir Alexander Moody, Kt., O.B.E., M.C.
Stuart, Sir Campbell, G.C.M.G., K.B.E.
†Stuart, Sir Phillip Luttrell, Bt. (1660).
Stucley, Sir Dennis Frederic Bankes, Bt. (1859).
Studd, Sir Eric, Bt., O.B.E. (1929).
Studdy, Sir Henry, Kt., C.B.E.
Studholme, Sir Henry Gray, Bt., C.V.O., M.P. (1956).
Sturdee, *Rear-Adm.* Sir Lionel Arthur Doveton, Bt., C.B.E. (1916).
Sturdee, *Lt.-Gen.* Sir Vernon Ashton Hobart, K.B.E., C.B., D.S.O.
Sturges, *Lt.-Gen.* Sir Robert Grice, K.B.E., C.B., D.S.O., R.M.
Style, Sir William Montague, Bt. (1627).
Sugden, *Maj.-Gen.* Sir Henry Haskins Clapham, K.B.E., C.B., D.S.O.
Suleman Cassum Mitha, *Hon. Sardar Sahib* Sir, Kt., C.I.E.
Sullivan, Sir Richard Benjamin Magniac, Bt. (1804).
Sullivan, Sir William, K.C.M.G.
Sullivan, Sir William John, K.B.E., C.M.G.
Summerhayes, Sir Christopher Henry, K.B.E., C.M.G.
Summers, Sir Geoffrey, Bt., C.B.E. (1952).
Summers, Sir (Gerard) Spencer, Kt., M.P.
Summers, Sir Richard Felix, Kt.
Summerscale, Sir John Percival, K.B.E.
Summerson, Sir John Newenham, Kt., C.B.E., F.B.A., F.S.A,
Surridge, Sir (Ernest) Rex (Edward), Kt., C.M.G.
Sutherland, Sir Benjamin Ivan, Bt. (1921).
Sutherland, Sir Gordon Brims Black McIvor, Kt., F.R.S.
Suttie, Sir George Philip Grant-, Bt. (S 1702).
Sutton, Sir (Oliver) Graham, Kt., C.B.E., D.SC., F.R.S.
Sutton, Sir Robert Lexington, Bt. (1772).
Sutton, Sir Stafford William Powell Foster-, K.B.E., C.M.G., Q.C.
Swan, Sir Kenneth Raydon, Kt., O.B.E., Q.C.
Swann, Sir Anthony Charles Christopher, Bt., C.M.G., O.B.E., (1906).
Swayne, *Lt.-Gen.* Sir John George Des Réaux, K.C.B., C.B.E.
Swift, Sir Brian Herbert, Kt., M.C., M.D.
Swinburne, Sir Spearman Charles, Bt. (1660).
Swiney, *Maj.-Gen.* Sir George Alexander Neville, K.B.E., C.B., M.C.
Syers, Sir Cecil George Lewis, K.C.M.G., C.V.O.
Syfret, *Admiral* Sir (Edward) Neville, G.C.B., K.B.E.
Sykes, Sir (Benjamin) Hugh, Bt. (1921).
Sykes, Sir Francis Godfrey, Bt. (1781).
Sykes, Sir (Mark Tatton) Richard, Bt. (1783).
Sylvester, Sir (Arthur) Edgar, K.B.E.
Syme, Sir Colin York, Kt.
Syme, *Prof.* Sir Ronald, Kt., F.B.A.
Symon, Sir Alexander Colin Burlington, K.C.M.G., K.C.V.O. O.B.E.
Symonds, *Air Vice-Marshal* Sir Charles Putnam, K.B.E., C.B.
Symonette, Sir Roland Theodore, Kt.
Synge, Sir Robert Carson, Bt. (1801).
Tait, Sir Frank Samuel, Kt.
Tait, Sir James Blair, Kt., Q.C.
Tait, Sir John, Kt.
Tait, *Air Vice-Marshal* Sir Victor Hubert, K.B.E., C.B.
Talbot, *Vice-Adm.* Sir Cecil Ponsonby, K.C.B., K.B.E., D.S.O.
Tallack, Sir Hugh Mackay, Kt.
Tancred, Sir Henry Lawson-, Bt. (1662).
Tandy, Sir Arthur Harry, K.B.E.
Tange, Sir Arthur Harold, Kt., C.B.E.
Tangye, *Capt.* Sir Basil Richard Gilzean, Bt. (1912).
Tansley, Sir Eric Crawford, Kt., C.M.G.
Tapp, *Maj.-Gen.* Sir Nigel Prior Hanson, K.B.E., C.B., D.S.O.
Tarbat, Sir John Allan, Kt.
Targett, Sir Robert William, Kt., C.I.E.
Tasker, Sir Theodore James, Kt., C.I.E., O.B.E.
Tate, *Lt.-Col.* Sir Henry, Bt. (1898).
Tayler, *Admiral* Sir Richard Victor Symonds-, K.B.E., C.B., D.S.C.
Taylor, *Rt. Hon.* Sir Alan Russell, K.B.E.
Taylor, Sir Charles Stuart, Kt., M.P.
Taylor, Sir (Eric) Stuart, Bt., O.B.E., M.D. (1917).
Taylor, *Vice-Adm.* Sir Ernest Augustus, Kt., C.M.G., C.V.O.
Taylor, *Prof.* Sir Geoffrey Ingram, Kt., F.R.S.
Taylor, Sir George, Kt., D.SC., F.R.S.E.
Taylor, *Maj.-Gen.* Sir (George) Brian (Ogilvie), K.B.E., C.B.
Taylor, *Prof.* Sir Hugh Stott, K.B.E., D.SC., F.R.S.
Taylor, Sir John, Kt.
Taylor, Sir John William, K.B.E., C.M.G.
Taylor, *Lt.-Gen.* Sir Malcolm Cartwright Cartwright-, K.C.B., R.M.
Taylor, *Capt.* Sir Patrick Gordon, Kt., G.C., M.C.
Taylor, Sir Reginald William, Kt., C.M.G.
Taylor, Sir Robert Mackinlay, Kt., C.B.E.
Taylor, Sir William Johnson, Bt., C.B.E., M.P. (1963).
Taylor, Sir William Ling, Kt., C.B.E.
Teale, Sir Edmund Oswald, Kt., D.SC.
Teeling, Sir (Luke) William Burke, Kt., M.P.
Tek Chand, Sir, Kt.
Temple, *Maj.* Sir Richard Anthony Purbeck, Bt., M.C. (1876).
Templer, *Field Marshal* Sir Gerald Walter Robert, G.C.B., G.C.M.G., K.B.E., D.S.O.
Tennant, Sir William Robert, Kt., C.I.E.
Tennyson, Sir Charles Bruce Locker, Kt., C.M.G.
Terrell, *Capt.* Sir Thomas Antonio Reginald, Kt.
Terry, *Maj.* Sir Edward Henry Bouhier Imbert-, Bt., M.C. (1917).
Tew, Sir Mervyn Lawrence, Kt.
Tewson, Sir (Harold) Vincent, Kt., C.B.E., M.C.
Thelwell, Sir Arthur Frederick, Kt., C.B.E.
Thesiger, *Admiral* Sir Bertram Sackville, K.B.E., C.B., C.M.G.
Thesiger, *Hon.* Sir Gerald Alfred, Kt., M.B.E.
Thirkill, Sir Henry, Kt., C.B.E., M.C.
Thomas, *Hon.* Sir (Arwyn) Lynn Ungoed-, Kt.
Thomas, Sir Ben Bowen, Kt.
Thomas, Sir Clement Price-, K.C.V.O.
Thomas, Sir Frederick William, Kt.
Thomas, Sir George Alan, Bt. (1766).
Thomas, Sir George Hector, Kt.
Thomas, *Rt. Hon.* Sir Godfrey John Vignoles, Bt., G.C.V.O., K.C.B., C.S.I. (1694).
Thomas, *General* Sir (Gwilym) Ivor, G.C.B., K.B.E., D.S.O., M.C.
Thomas, Sir (James William) Tudor, Kt., D.SC., M.D.

Thomas, Sir Leslie Montagu, Kt., M.B.E., T.D., M.P.
Thomas, Sir Percy Edward, Kt., O.B.E., LL.D.
Thomas, *Lt.-Col.* Sir Reginald Aneurin, Kt., C.B.E.
Thomas, Sir William James Cooper, Bt. (1929).
Thomas, Sir (William) Michael (Marsh), Bt. (1918).
Thomas, Sir (William) Miles (Webster), Kt., D.F.C.
Thompson, *Capt.* Sir Algar de Clifford Charles Meysey-, Bt. (1874).
Thompson, *Capt.* Sir (Cyril) Ivan, Kt.
Thompson, Sir Edward Walter, Kt.
Thompson, Sir Geoffrey Harington, G.B.E., K.C.M.G.
Thompson, *Lt.-Gen.* Sir Geoffrey Stuart, K.B.E., C.B., D.S.O.
Thompson, *Hon.* Sir John, Kt.
Thompson, Sir (Joseph) Herbert, Kt., C.I.E.
Thompson, Sir Kenneth Pugh, Bt., M.P. (1963).
Thompson, Sir (Louis) Lionel (Harry), Kt., C.B.E.
Thompson, Sir Peile Beaumont, Bt. (1890).
Thompson, Sir Richard Hilton Marler, Bt., M.P. (1963).
Thompson, *Lt.-Col.* Sir Thomas Raikes Lovett, Bt., M.C. (1806).
Thompson, *Lt.-Gen.* Sir Treffry Owen, K.C.S.I., C.B., C.B.E.
Thompstone, Sir Eric Westbury, K.B.E., C.M.G., M.C.
Thomson, Sir (Arthur) Landsborough, Kt., C.B., O.B.E., D.SC.
Thomson, *Prof.* Sir Arthur Peregrine, Kt., M.C., M.D.
Thomson, Sir George Paget, Kt., F.R.S.
Thomson, *Rear-Adm.* Sir George Pirie, Kt., C.B., C.B.E.
Thomson, Sir Ivo Wilfrid Home, Bt. (1925).
Thomson, *Hon.* Sir James Beveridge, Kt.
Thomson, Sir (James) Douglas (Wishart), Bt. (1929).
Thomson, Sir John Mackay, Kt., C.B.
Thomson, Sir Ronald (Jordan), Kt.
Thorne, *General* Sir (Augustus Francis) Andrew (Nicol), K.C.B., C.M.G., D.S.O.
Thorne, Sir John Anderson, K.C.I.E., C.S.I.
Thornley, Sir Colin Hardwick, K.C.M.G., C.V.O.
Thornton, Sir (Henry) Gerard, Kt., D.SC., F.R.S.
Thorold, Sir Guy Frederick, K.C.M.G.
Thorold, Sir James (Ernest), Bt., (1642).
Thorpe, Sir Fred Garner, Kt.
Throckmorton, Sir Robert George Maxwell, Bt. (1642).
Thumboo Chetty, Sir Bernard, Kt., O.B.E.
Thuraisingham, Sir Ernest Emmanuel Clough, Kt., C.B.E.
Thwin, Sir U, Kt.
Tibbits, Sir Cliff, Kt.
Tichborne, Sir Anthony Joseph Henry Doughty-, Bt., (1621).
Tickell, *Maj.-Gen.* Sir Eustace Francis, K.B.E., C.B., M.C.
Tirikatene, *Hon.* Sir Eruera Tihema, K.C.M.G.
Titman, Sir George Alfred, Kt., C.B.E., M.V.O.
Tivey, Sir John Proctor, Kt.
Tod, Sir Alan Cecil, Kt., T.D.
Todd, Sir Geoffrey Sydney, K.C.V.O., O.B.E.
Todd, Sir Herbert John, Kt., C.I.E.
Tollemache, Sir (Cecil) Lyonel (Newcomen), Bt. (1793).
Tomlinson, Sir Thomas Symonds, Kt.
Tong, Sir Walter Wharton, Kt.
Tooth, Sir Hugh Veer Huntly Duff Lucas-, Bt., M.P. (1920).
Toro, The Omukama of, Kt.
Tory, Sir Geofroy William, K.C.M.G.
Tottenham, *Admiral* Sir Francis Loftus, K.C.B., C.B.E.
Tottenham, Sir (George) Richard (Frederick), Kt., K.C.I.E., C.S.I.
Touche, *Rt. Hon.* Sir Gordon Cosmo, Bt., M.P. (1962)
Touche, Sir Norman George, Bt. (1920).
Tower, *Vice-Adm.* Sir Francis Thomas Butler, K.B.E., C.B.
Town, Sir (Hugh) Stuart, Kt.
Townley, Sir John Barton, Kt.
Townend, Sir Harry Douglas, Kt.
Tozer, *Maj.* Sir James Clifford, Kt.
Train, Sir (John Cumberland) Landale, Kt., C.B.E., M.C.
Travancore, *Maj.-Gen.* H.H. the Maharajah of, G.C.S.I., G.C.I.E.
Tredgold, *Rt. Hon.* Sir Robert Clarkson, K.C.M.G., Q.C.
Trelawny, Sir John Barry Salusbury-, Bt. (1628).
Tremayne, *Air Marshal* Sir John Tremayne, K.C.B., C.B.E., D.S.O.
Trench, Sir David Clive Crosbie, K.C.M.G., M.C.
Trend, Sir Burke St. John, K.C.B., C.V.O.
Trevaskis, Sir Gerald Kennedy Nicholas, K.C.M.G.
Trevelyan, Sir George Lowthian, Bt. (1874).
Trevelyan, Sir Humphrey, K.C.M.G., C.I.E., O.B.E.
Trevelyan, Sir Willoughby John, Bt. (1662).
Trevor, Sir Cecil Russell, Kt., C.I.E.
Trimmer, Sir George (William Arthur), Kt.
Tritton, *Maj.* Sir Geoffrey Ernest, Bt., C.B.E. (1905).
Trivedi, Sir Chandulal Madhavlal, K.C.S.I., C.I.E., O.B.E.
Trollope, Sir Anthony Owen Clavering, Bt. (1642).
Trott, *Hon.* Sir William James Howard, Kt., C.B.E.
Troubridge, *Lt.-Col.* Sir (Thomas) St. Vincent (Wallace), Bt., M.B.E. (1799).
Troup, *Vice-Adm.* Sir James Andrew Gardiner, K.B.E., C.B.
Trout, Sir Herbert Leon, Kt.
Troutbeck, Sir John Monro, G.B.E., K.C.M.G.
Trower, Sir William Gosselin, Kt.
Troyte, *Lt.-Col.* Sir Gilbert John Acland-, Kt., C.M.G., D.S.O.
Truscott, Sir Denis Henry, G.B.E., T.D.
Truscott, Sir Eric Homewood Stanham, Bt. (1909).
Trustam, Sir Charles Frederick, Kt.
Trusted, Sir Harry Herbert, Kt., Q.C.
Tuck, Sir Bruce Adolph Reginald, Bt. (1910).
Tucker, Sir Henry James, Kt., C.B.E.
Tucker, Sir James Millard, Kt., Q.C.
Tucker, Sir Norman Sanger, Kt., O.B.E.
Tudor, *Maj.-Gen.* Sir (Henry) Hugh, K.C.B., C.M.G.
Tudsbery, Sir Francis Cannon Tudsbery, Kt., C.B.E.
Tuite, Sir Brian Hugh Morgan, Bt. (I 1622).
Tuker, *Lt.-Gen.* Sir Francis Ivan Simms, K.C.I.E., C.B., D.S.O., O.B.E.
Tupper, Sir James Macdonald, Bt. (1888).
Turing, Sir Robert Andrew Henry, Bt. (S 1638).
Turnbull, *Lt.-Col.* Sir Hugh Stephenson, K.C.V.O., K.B.E.
Turnbull, Sir Richard Gordon, G.C.M.G.
Turner, *Hon.* Sir Alexander Kingcome, Kt.
Turner, *Eng. Vice-Adm.* Sir Frederick Richard Gordon, K.C.B., O.B.E.
Turner, Sir George Wilfred, K.C.B., K.B.E.
Turner, Sir Henry Samuel Edwin, Kt.
Turner, Sir Michael William, Kt., C.B.E.
Turner, *Prof.* Sir Ralph Lilley, Kt., M.C., F.B.A.
Turner, *Vice-Adm.* Sir Robert Ross, K.B.E., C.B., D.S.O.
Turner, Sir (Ronald) Mark (Cunliffe), Kt.
Turner, Sir Sidney, Kt., C.B.E.
Turner, Sir Victor (Alfred Charles), Kt., C.S.I., C.I.E., M.B.E.
Turner, *Lt.-Gen.* Sir William Francis Robert, K.B.E., C.B., D.S.O.
Tuttle, *Air Marshal* Sir Geoffrey William, K.B.E., C.B., D.F.C.
Twyford, Sir Harry Edward Augustus, K.B.E.
Twynam, Sir Henry Joseph, K.C.S.I., C.I.E.
Twysden, *Lt.-Cdr.* Sir William Adam Duncan, Bt., R.N. (1611).
Tyler, *Maj.-Gen.* Sir Leslie Norman, K.B.E., C.B.

Tymms, Sir Frederick, K.C.I.E., M.C.
Tyndall, *Hon.* Sir Arthur, Kt., C.M.G.
Tyrrell, Sir Francis Graeme, K.B.E., C.M.G.
Tyrrell, *Air Vice-Marshal* Sir William, K.B.E., D.S.O., M.C.
Tyrwhitt, Sir Reginald Thomas Newman, Bt. (1919).
Tyson, Sir John (Dawson), K.C.I.E., C.S.I., C.B.E.
Tytler, *Lt.-Col.* Sir William Kerr Fraser-, K.B.E., C.M.G., M.C.
Unsworth, Sir Edgar Ignatius Godfrey, Kt., C.M.G., Q.C.
Unwin, Sir Stanley, Kt., LL.D.
Upcott, Sir Gilbert Charles, K.C.B.
Upjohn, *Rt. Hon.* Sir Gerald Ritchie, Kt., C.B.E.
Upjohn, Sir William George Dismore, Kt., O.B.E., M.D.
Urquhart, Sir Andrew, K.C.M.G., M.B.E.
Urquhart, Sir Robert William, K.B.E., C.M.G.
Urton, Sir William Holmes Lister, Kt., M.B.E., T.D.
Usher, Sir George Clemens, Kt.
Usher, Sir Peter Lionel, Bt. (1899).
Uvarov, Sir Boris Petrovitch, K.C.M.G., D.SC., F.R.S.
Vaisey, Sir Harry Bevir, Kt.
Vallat, Sir Francis Aimé, K.C.M.G., Q.C.
Vandepeer, Sir Donald (Edward), K.C.B., K.B.E.
Van Ryneveld, *General* Sir Pierre, K.B.E., C.B., D.S.O., M.C.
Vasey, Sir Ernest Albert, K.B.E., C.M.G.
Vaughan, Sir George Edgar, K.B.E.
Vavasour, *Cdr.* Sir Geoffrey William, Bt., D.S.C., R.N. (1828).
Veale, Sir Douglas, Kt., C.B.E.
Veale, *Hon.* Sir Geoffrey de Paiva, Kt.
Venables, Sir Percy Frederick Ronald, Kt., Ph.D.
Venning, *General* Sir Walter King, G.C.B., C.M.G., C.B.E., M.C.
Verdin, *Lt.-Col.* Sir Richard Bertram, Kt., O.B.E., T.D.
Vereker, Sir (George) Gordon (Medlicott), K.C.M.G., M.C.
Verity, Sir Edgar William, K.B.E., C.B.
Verity, Sir John, Kt.
Verner, Sir Edward Derrick Wingfield, Bt. (1846).
Verney, Sir Harry (Calvert Williams), Bt., D.S.O. (1818).
Verney, Sir John, Bt., M.C. (1946).
Vernon, Sir Sydney, Kt.
Vernon, Sir Wilfred Douglas, Kt.
Vernon, Sir (William) Norman, Bt. (1914).
Vesey, *General* Sir Ivo Lucius Beresford, K.C.B., K.B.E., C.M.G., D.S.O.
Vestey, Sir (John) Derek, Bt. (1921).
Vian, *Admiral of the Fleet* Sir Philip, G.C.B., K.B.E., D.S.O.
Vickers, Sir (Charles) Geoffrey, Kt., V.C.
Vickery, Sir Philip Crawford, Kt., C.I.E., O.B.E.
Victoria, Sir (Joseph Aloysius) Donatus, Kt., C.B.E.
Villiers, Sir (Francis) Edward (Earle), Kt.
Villiers, *Vice-Adm.* Sir (John) Michael, K.C.B., O.B.E.
Vincent, Sir Alfred, Kt.
Vincent, Sir (Harold) Graham, K.C.M.G., C.B., C.V.O.
Vincent, Sir Lacey Eric, Bt. (1936).
Vizianagram, Rajkumar of, Kt.
Vyse, *Lt.-Gen.* Sir Edward Dacre Howard-, K.B.E., C.B., M.C.
Vyvyan, Sir Richard Philip, Bt. (1645).
Wace, Sir (Ferdinand) Blyth, K.C.I.E., C.S.I.
Wackett, Sir Lawrence James, Kt., D.F.C., A.F.C.
Waddell, Sir Alexander Nicol Anton, K.C.M.G., D.S.C.
Wade, Sir Armigel de Vins, Kt., C.M.G., O.B.E.
Wade, *Col.* Sir George Albert, Kt., M.C.
Wadham, *Prof.* Sir Samuel McMahon, Kt.
Wadsworth, Sir Sidney, Kt.
Waechter, Sir Harry Leonard D'Arcy, Bt. (1911).
Wagner, Sir Anthony Richard, K.C.V.O.
Wake, Sir Hereward, Bt., M.C. (1621).
Wakefield, Sir Edward Birkbeck, Bt., C.I.E. (1962).
Wakefield, Sir (William) Wavell, Kt., M.P.
Wakeley, Sir Cecil Pembrey Grey, Bt., K.B.E., C.B., D.SC. (1952).
Wakely, Sir Clifford Holland, K.B.E.
Wakeman, *Capt.* Sir Offley, Bt., C.B.E. (1828).
Walch, Sir Geoffrey Archer, K.B.E., C.V.O.
Waldock, *Prof.* Sir (Claud) Humphrey (Meredith), Kt., C.M.G., O.B.E., Q.C., D.C.L.
Walker, Sir Baldwin Patrick, Bt. (1856).
Walker, *Maj.* Sir Cecil Edward, Bt., D.S.O., M.C. (1906).
Walker, Sir (Charles) Michael, K.C.M.G.
Walker, Sir Edward Ronald, Kt., C.B.E.
Walker, Sir Francis William, Kt., C.B.E.
Walker, *Air Marshal* Sir (George) Augustus, K.C.B., C.B.E., D.S.O., D.F.C., A.F.C.
Walker, *Maj.* Sir George Ferdinand Forestier-, Bt. (1835).
Walker, *Admiral* Sir Harold Thomas Coulthard, K.C.B.
Walker, Sir Hubert Edmund, Kt., C.B.E.
Walker, Sir James Heron, Bt. (1868).
Walker, Sir John, K.C.M.G., O.B.E.
Walker, Sir Ronald FitzJohn, Kt.
Walker, Sir William Giles Newsom, Kt., T.D.
Wall, Sir (George) Rolande (Percival), Kt., M.C.
Wallace, Sir Martin Kelso, Kt.
Waller, Sir John Stanier, Bt. (1815).
Waller, Sir Robert William, Bt. (I 1780).
Wallinger, Sir Geoffrey Arnold, G.B.E., K.C.M.G.
Walmsley, *Air Marshal* Sir Hugh Sydney Porter, K.C.B., K.C.I.E., C.B.E., M.C., D.F.C.
Walsh, Sir David Philip, K.B.E., C.B.
Walsh, *Prof.* Sir John Patrick, K.B.E.
Walsham, *Rear-Adm.* Sir John Scarlett Warren, Bt., C.B., O.B.E. (1831).
Walshe, Sir Francis Martin Rouse, Kt., O.B.E., M.D., D.SC., F.R.S.
Walton, *Col.* Sir Cusack, Kt., D.S.O.
Walton, *Brig.* Sir George Hands, K.B.E., C.B., T.D.
Walton, Sir Richmond, K.B.E., C.B.
Walton, Sir William Turner, Kt., Mus., Doc.
Wand, *Rt. Rev.* John William Charles, P.C., K.C.V.O., D.D.
Ward, *General* Sir (Alfred) Dudley, G.C.B., K.B.E., D.S.O.
Ward, Sir John Guthrie, K.C.M.G.
Ward, Sir Joseph George Davidson, Bt. (1911).
Ward, *Cdr.* Sir Melvill Willis, Bt., D.S.C., R.N. (1914).
Ward, Sir (Victor) Michael Barrington-, K.C.V.O., C.B.E., D.S.O.
Wardlaw, Sir Henry, Bt. (S 1631).
Ware, Sir Frank, Kt., C.I.E.
Waring, Sir Alfred Harold, Bt. (1935).
Waring, Sir (Arthur) Bertram, Kt.
Waring, Sir Douglas Tremayne, Kt., C.B.E.
Warmington, *Lt.-Cdr.* Sir Marshall George Clitheroe, Bt., R.N. (1908).
Warner, *Hon.* Sir Arthur George, K.B.E.
Warner, Sir Edward Courtenay Henry, Bt. (1910).
Warner, Sir George Redston, K.C.V.O., C.M.G.
Warr, *Very Rev.* Charles Laing, K.C.V.O., D.D.
Warren, Sir Brian Charles Pennefather, Bt. (1784).
Warren, *Hon.* Sir Edward Emerton, K.B.E., C.M.G.
Warren, Sir Mortimer Langton, Kt.
Warter, Sir Philip, Kt.
Waterer, Sir (Robert) Bernard, Kt., C.B.
Waterfield, Sir (Alexander) Percival, K.B.E., C.B.
Waterhouse, Sir Nicholas Edwin, K.B.E.
Waterlow, Sir Philip Alexander, Bt. (1873).
Waterlow, *Col.* Sir (William) James, Bt., M.B.E., T.D. (1930).

Waterman, Sir Ewen McIntyre, Kt.
Waters, *Maj.* Sir Arnold Horace Santo, Kt., V.C., C.B.E., D.S.O., M.C.
Waters, Sir George Alexander, Kt., LL.D.
Watherston, Sir David Charles, K.B.E., C.M.G.
Watkinson, Sir (George) Laurence, K.B.E., C.B., M.C.
Watney, *Col.* Sir Frank Dormay, K.C.V.O., C.B.E., T.D.
Watson, Sir Alfred Henry, Kt.
Watson, Sir Arthur Egerton, Kt., C.B., C.B.E.
Watson, *General* Sir Daril Gerrard, G.C.B., C.B.E., M.C.
Watson, Sir (David) Ronald Milne-, Bt. (1937).
Watson, *Capt.* Sir Derrick William Inglefield Inglefield-, Bt., T.D. (1895).
Watson, Sir Hugh, Kt.
Watson, Sir James Anderson Scott, Kt., C.B.E., M.C.
Watson, Sir James Andrew, Bt. (1866).
Watson, Sir Norman James, Bt. (1912).
Watson, *Vice-Adm.* Sir (Robert) Dymock, K.C.B., C.B.E.
Watson, Sir William, Kt.
Watt, Sir Alan Stewart, Kt., C.B.E.
Watt, *Brig.* Sir George Steven Harvie-, Bt., T.D., Q.C. (1945).
Watt, Sir Robert Alexander Watson-, Kt., C.B.
Watt, *Prof.* Sir Robert Dickie, Kt.
Wauchope, Sir Patrick George Don-, Bt. (S 1667).
Waugh, Sir Arthur Allen, K.C.I.E., C.S.I.
Way, Sir Richard George Kitchener, K.C.B., C.B.E.
Weatherby, Sir Francis, Kt., M.C.
Weatherhead, Sir Arthur Trenham, Kt., C.M.G.
Webb, Sir (Ambrose) Henry, Kt.
Webb, Sir Charles Morgan, Kt., C.I.E.
Webb, *Hon.* Sir William Flood, K.B.E.
Webbe, Sir Harold, Kt., C.B.E.
Webster, Sir David Lumsden, Kt.
Webster, Sir Robert Joseph, Kt., C.M.G., C.B.E., M.C.
Webster, *General* Sir Thomas Sheridan Riddell-, G.C.B., D.S.O.
Wedderburn, *Cdr.* Sir John Peter Ogilvy-, Bt., R.N. (1803).
Wedderspoon, Sir Thomas Adam, Kt.
Wedgwood, Sir John Hamilton, Bt., T.D. (1942).
Weedon, *Air Vice-Marshal* Sir Colin Winterbotham, K.B.E., C.B.
Weir, Sir John, G.C.V.O., Royal Victorian Chain.
Weir, *Maj.-Gen.* Sir Stephen Cyril Ettrick, K.B.E., C.B., D.S.O.
Welby, Sir Oliver Charles Earle, Bt. (1801).
Welch, *Lt.-Col.* Sir (George James) Cullum, Bt., O.B.E., M.C. (1957).
Weldon, Sir Anthony Edward Wolseley, Bt. (I 1723).
Welensky, *Rt. Hon.* Sir Roy (Roland), K.C.M.G.
Wellington, Sir (Reginald Everard) Lindsay, Kt., C.B.E.
Wells, Sir Charles Maltby, Bt. (1944).
Wells, Sir Frederick Michael, Bt. (1948).
Wells, *Lt.-Gen.* Sir Henry, K.B.E., C.B., D.S.O.
Wells, *Admiral* Sir Lionel Victor, K.C.B., D.S.O.
Wenham, Sir John Henry, Kt.
Wernher, *Maj.-Gen.* Sir Harold Augustus, Bt., G.C.V.O., T.D. (1905).
West, Sir Frederick John, Kt., O.B.E.
West, Sir Harold Ernest Georges, Kt.
West, *General* Sir Michael Montgomerie Alston Roberts, K.C.B., D.S.O.
Westall, *General* Sir John Chaddesley, K.C.B., C.B.E., R.M.
Westerman, Sir Wilfred Alan, Kt., C.B.E.
Westlake, Sir Charles Redvers, Kt.
Weston, Sir Arthur Reginald Astley, Kt., C.B.E.
Weston, Sir Eric, Kt.
Westrup, *Prof.* Sir Jack Allan, Kt.
Wetherall, *Lt.-Gen.* Sir (Harry) Edward de Robillard, K.B.E., C.B., D.S.O. M.C.
Wheatley, *Lt.-Col.* Sir Mervyn James, K.B.E.
Wheeler, Sir Arthur (Frederick Pullman Derek), Bt. (1920).
Wheeler, Sir Charles Thomas, K.C.V.O., C.B.E., P.R.A.
Wheeler, Sir (Robert Eric) Mortimer, Kt., C.I.E., M.C., F.B.A., F.S.A.
Wheler, *Capt.* Sir Trevor Wood, Bt. (1660).
Whishaw, Sir Ralph, Kt., C.B.E.
Whitaker, Sir (Frederick) Arthur, K.C.B.
Whitaker, *Maj.* Sir James Herbert Ingham, Bt. (1936).
Whitby, Sir Bernard James, Kt.
White, Sir (Alfred Edward) Rowden, Kt., C.M.G., M.D.
White, Sir Bernard Kerr, K.B.E.
White, *Brig.* Sir Bruce Gordon, K.B.E.
White, Sir Dennis Charles, K.B.E., C.M.G.
White, Sir Dick Goldsmith, K.C.M.G., K.B.E.
White, Sir (Eric) Richard Meadows, Bt. (1937).
White, Sir Frederick William George, K.B.E., Ph.D.
White, Sir (George) Stanley, Bt. (1904).
White, *Wing-Cdr.* Sir Henry Arthur Dalrymple-, Bt., D.F.C. (1926).
White, *Surgeon Rear-Adm.* Sir Henry Ellis Yeo, K.C.V.O., O.B.E., M.D.
White, *Lt.-Gen.* Sir Maurice Fitzgibbon Grove-, K.B.E., C.B., D.S.O.
White, *Maj.* Sir (Rudolph) Dymoke, Bt. (1922).
White, Sir Thomas Astley Woollaston, Bt. (1802).
Whitehead, *Hon.* Sir Edgar Cuthbert Fremantle, K.C.M.G., O.B.E.
Whitehead, Sir Rowland John Rathbone, Bt. (1889).
Whiteley, *Capt.* Sir (Herbert) Maurice Huntington-, Bt., R.N. (1918).
Whiteley, *General* Sir John Francis Martin, G.B.E., K.C.B., M.C.
Whiteside, Sir Cuthbert William, Kt.
Whitford, *Air Vice-Marshal* Sir John, K.B.E., C.B.
Whitley, *Brig.-Gen.* Sir Edward Nathan, K.C.B., C.M.G., D.S.O., T.D.
Whitley, *Air Marshal* Sir John René, K.B.E., C.B., D.S.O., A.F.C.
Whitmore, Sir John Henry Douglas, Bt. (1954).
Whittingham, *Air Marshal* Sir Harold Edward, K.C.B., K.B.E.
Whittington, Sir Richard, K.C.M.G., C.B.E.
Whittle, *Air Commodore* Sir Frank, K.B.E., C.B.
Whittome, Sir Maurice Gordon, Kt., C.B.
Whitworth, *Admiral* Sir William Jock, K.C.B., D.S.O.
Whyatt, Sir John, Kt., Q.C.
Whyte, Sir (Alexander) Frederick, K.C.S.I.
Wickham, *Lt.-Col.* Sir Charles George, K.C.M.G., K.B.E., D.S.O.
Widgery, *Hon.* Sir John Passmore, Kt., O.B.E., T.D.
Wigan, Sir Frederick Adair, Bt. (1898).
Wiggin, Sir Charles Richard Henry, Bt., T.D. (1892).
Wigglesworth, *Air Marshal* Sir (Horace Ernest) Philip, K.B.E., C.B., D.S.C.
Wigram, *Rev.* Sir Clifford Woolmore, Bt. (1805).
Wijeyeratne, Sir Edwin Aloysius Perera, K.B.E.
Wijeyewardene, *Hon.* Sir (Edwin) Arthur (Lewis), Kt.
Wilberforce, *Hon.* Sir Richard Orme, Kt., C.M.G., O.B.E.
Wilbraham, Sir Randle John Baker, Bt. (1776).
Wildish, *Eng.-Rear-Adm.* Sir Henry William, K.B.E., C.B.
Wiles, Sir Harold Herbert, K.B.E., C.B.
Wilkinson, Sir George Henry, Bt., K.C.V.O. (1941).
Wilkinson, Sir Russell Facey, K.C.V.O.
Wilkinson, Sir Thomas Crowe Spenser-, Kt.
Willan, Sir Harold Curwen, Kt., C.M.G., M.C.
Willcox, *Lt.-Gen.* Sir Henry Beresford Dennitts, K.C.I.E., C.B., D.S.O., M.C.

Willert, Sir Arthur, K.B.E.
Williams, Sir Alan Meredith, K.C.M.G.
Williams, Sir Alexander Thomas, K.C.M.G., M.B.E.
Williams, Sir Brandon Meredith Rhys-, Bt. (1918).
Williams, Sir (Daniel) Thomas, Kt., O.B.E.
Williams, Sir David Philip, Bt. (1915).
Williams, Sir Ernest Hillas, Kt.
Williams, Sir (Evan) Owen, K.B.E.
Williams, Sir Griffith Goodland, K.B.E., C.B.
Williams, Sir Gwilym Ffrangcon, Kt., C.B.E.
Williams, *Lt.-Gen.* Sir Harold, K.B.E., C.B.
Williams, Sir Harold Herbert, Kt., F.B.A.
Williams, Sir Henry Morton Leech, Kt., M.B.E.
Williams, Sir Ifor, Kt., D.Litt.
Williams, Sir John Coldbrook Hanbury-, Kt., C.V.O.
Williams, Sir John Francis, Kt.
Williams, Sir John Lias Cecil Cecil-, Kt.
Williams, Sir John Rolleston Lort-, Kt., Q.C.
Williams, *Maj.-Gen.* Sir Leslie Hamlyn, K.B.E., C.B., M.C.
Williams, Sir Osmond, Bt., M.C. (1909).
Williams, Sir Peter Watkin, Kt.
Williams, Sir Reginald Lawrence William, M.B.E. (1798).
Williams, *Air Marshal* Sir Richard, K.B.E., C.B., D.S.O.
†Williams, Sir Robert Ernest, Bt. (1866).
Williams, Sir Robin Philip, Bt. (1953).
Williams, Sir Roy Ellis Hume-, Bt. (1922).
Williams, Sir Thomas Herbert Parry-, Kt., D.Litt.
Williams, Sir William Emrys, Kt., C.B.E.
Williamson, Sir Alexander, Kt., C.B.E.
Williamson, Sir George Alexander, Kt.
Williamson, Sir Horace, Kt., C.I.E., M.B.E.
Williamson, Sir (Nicholas Frederick) Hedworth, Bt. (1642).
Willink, *Rt. Hon.* Sir Henry Urmston, Bt., M.C., Q.C., D.C.L. (1957).
Willis, *Admiral of the Fleet* Sir Algernon Usborne, G.C.B., K.B.E., D.S.O.
Willis, Sir (Zwinglius) Frank, Kt., C.B.E.
Willmer, *Rt. Hon.* Sir (Henry) Gordon, Kt., O.B.E., T.D.
Willmott, Sir Maurice Gordon, Kt., M.C.
Wills, *Lt.-Col.* Sir (Ernest) Edward de Winton, Bt. (1904).
Wills, Sir Gerald, Kt., M.B.E., M.P.
Wills, Sir John Vernon, Bt. (1923).
Wills, *Brig.* Sir Kenneth Agnew, K.B.E., M.C. E.D.
Wilmot, *Capt.* Sir John Eardley-, Bt. (1821).
Wilmot, Sir Robert Arthur, Bt. (1759).
Wilshaw, Sir Edward, K.C.M.G.
Wilson, Sir Alan Herries, Kt., F.R.S.
Wilson, Sir Arton, K.B.E., C.B.
Wilson, Sir Bertram, Kt.
Wilson, Sir Garnet Douglas, Kt.
Wilson, Sir George, K.B.E.
Wilson, *Rev.* Sir (George) Percy (Maryon) Maryon-, Bt. (1661).
Wilson, *Lt.-Gen.* Sir Gordon, K.C.S.I., C.B., C.B.E., M.C.
Wilson, *Prof.* Sir Graham Selby, Kt., M.D.
Wilson, Sir Horace John, G.C.B., G.C.M.G., C.B.E.
Wilson. Sir James Robertson, Bt. (1906).
Wilson, Sir (James) Steuart, Kt.
Wilson, Sir John Mitchell Harvey, Bt., K.C.V.O. (1920).
Wilson, Sir Leonard, K.C.I.E.
Wilson, Sir Mathew Martin, Bt. (1874).
Wilson, Sir Reginald Holmes, Kt.
Wilson, *General* Sir Roger Cochrane, K.C.B., D.S.O., M.C.
Wilson, Sir Roland, Kt., C.B.E.
Wilson, Sir Roy Mickel, Kt., Q.C.
Windeyer, *Prof.* Sir Brian Wellingham, Kt.
Windeyer, *Rt. Hon.* Sir (William John) Victor, K.B.E., C.B., D.S.O., E.D.
Windham, *Hon.* Sir Ralph, Kt.
Windley, Sir Edward Henry, K.C.M.G., K.C.V.O.
Wingate, *Col.* Sir Ronald Evelyn Leslie, Bt., C.B., C.M.G., C.I.E., O.B.E. (1920).
Winn, *Hon.* Sir (Charles) Rodger (Noel), Kt., C.B., O.B.E.
Winneke, Sir Henry Arthur, Kt., O.B.E.
Winnifrith, Sir (Alfred) John (Digby), K.C.B.
Winnington, Sir Francis Salwey William, Bt. (1755).
Winstedt, Sir Richard (Olaf), K.B.E., C.M.G., F.B.A.
Winterbotham, Sir Geoffrey Leonard, Kt.
Winterton, *Maj.-Gen.* Sir (Thomas) John (Willoughby), K.C.B., K.C.M.G., C.B.E.
Wise, Sir John Humphrey, K.C.M.G., C.B.E.
Wiseman, Sir John William, Bt. (1628).
Wolfenden, Sir John Frederick, Kt., C.B.E.
Wolff, *Hon.* Sir Albert Asher, K.C.M.G.
Wolffsohn, Sir Arthur Norman, Kt.
Wolfit, Sir Donald, Kt., C.B.E.
Wolfson, Sir Isaac, Bt., F.R.S. (1962).
Wolseley, Sir Charles Garnet Mark Richard, Bt. (1628).
Wolseley, Sir Garnet, Bt. (I 1745).
Wombwell, Sir (Frederick) Philip (Alfred William), Bt., M.B.E. (1778).
Womersley, Sir Peter John Walter, Bt. (1945).
Wood, Sir Anthony John Page, Bt. (1837).
Wood, Sir David Basil Hill-, Bt. (1921).
Wood, *Lt.-Gen.* Sir Ernest, K.B.E., C.B., C.I.E., M.C.
Wood Sir John Arthur Haigh, Bt., M.C., D.S.C. (1918).
Wood, Sir William Wilkinson, Kt.
Woodall, *Lt.-Gen.* Sir John Dane, K.C.M.G., K.B.E., C.B., M.C.
Woodhead, Sir John Ackroyd, G.C.I.E., K.C.S.I.
Woodhouse, *Admiral* Sir Charles Henry Lawrence, K.C.B.
Wooding, Sir Hugh Olliviere Beresford, Kt., C.B.E.
Woodley, Sir (Frederick George) Richard, Kt.
Woods, *Admiral* Sir Wilfrid John Wentworth, G.B.E., K.C.B., D.S.O.
Woodward, *Lt.-Gen.* Sir Eric Winslow, K.C.M.G., K.C.V.O., C.B., C.B.E., D.S.O.
Woodward, Sir (Ernest) Llewellyn, Kt.
Woolford, Sir Eustace Gordon, Kt., O.B.E., Q.C.
Woolley, Sir Charles Campbell, G.B.E., K.C.M.G., M.C.
Woolley, Sir Richard van der Riet, Kt., O.B.E., F.R.S.
Wootten, *Maj.-Gen.* Sir George Frederick, K.B.E., C.B., D.S.O., E.D.
Worboys, Sir Walter John, Kt.
Worley, Sir Newnham Arthur, K.B.E., Q.C.
Worlledge, Sir John Leonard, K.B.E., C.M.G.
Worsley, *Col.* Sir William Arthington, Bt. (1938).
Wort, Sir Alfred William Ewart, Kt.
Worthington, *Air Vice-Marshal* Sir Geoffrey Luis, K.B.E., C.B.
Wrangham, *Hon.* Sir Geoffrey Walter, Kt.
Wraxall, Sir Morville William Lascelles, Bt. (1813).
Wray, Sir Kenneth Owen Roberts-, G.C.M.G., Q.C.
Wrench, Sir (John) Evelyn (Leslie), K.C.M.G.
Wrey, Sir (Castel) Richard Bourchier, Bt. (1628).
Wright, Sir Andrew Barkworth, K.C.M.G., C.B.E., M.C.
Wright, Sir Denis Arthur Hepworth, K.C.M.G.
Wright, Sir Geoffrey Cory-, Bt. (1903).
Wright, Sir Charles Seymour, K.C.B., O.B.E., M.C.
Wright, Sir Leonard Morton, Kt.
Wright, Sir Michael Robert, G.C.M.G.
Wright, Sir Norman Charles, Kt., C.B., D.Sc., Ph.D., F.R.S.E.
Wright, *Admiral* Sir Royston Hollis, K.C.B., D.S.O.

Wrightson, Sir John Garmondsway, Bt. (1900).
Wrigley, Sir John Crompton, K.B.E., C.B.
Wrisberg, *Lt.-Gen.* Sir Frederick George, K.B.E., C.B.
Wunderly, Sir Harry Wyatt, Kt., M.D.
Wyatt, *Vice-Adm.* Sir (Arthur) Guy (Norris), K.B.E., C.B.
Wyatt, Sir Myles Dermot Norris, Kt., C.B.E.
Wyatt, Sir Stanley, Kt.
Wycherley, Sir (Robert) Bruce, Kt., M.C.
Wylie, Sir Campbell, Kt., Q.C., E.D.
Wylie, Sir Francis Verner, G.C.I.E., K.C.S.I.
Wynn, *Lt.-Col.* Sir Owen Watkin Williams-, Bt. (1688).
Yamin Khan, Sir Muhammad, Kt., C.I.E.
Yarrow, Sir Eric Grant, Bt., M.B.E. (1916).
Yates, Sir Thomas, Kt., C.B.E.
Yeabsley, Sir Richard Ernest, Kt., C.B.E.
Yeaman, Sir Ian David, Kt.
Young, Sir Alastair Spencer Templeton, Bt. (1945).
Young, Sir George Samuel Knatchbull, Bt. (1813).
Young, Sir James Reid, Kt.
Young, Sir (John) Douglas, Kt.
Young, Sir John William Roe, Bt. (1821).
Young, Sir Mark Aitchison, G.C.M.G.
Young, Sir (Thomas) Eric (Boswell), Kt.
Young, Sir William Neil, Bt. (1769).
Younger, *Capt.* Sir James Paton, Kt. C.B.E.
Younger, Sir William Robert, Bt. (1911).
Yusuf, Sir Mohamad, Kt.
Zealley, Sir Alec Thomas Sharland, Kt.
Zuckerman, *Prof.* Sir Solly, Kt., C.B., M.D., D.SC., F.R.S.

Baronetcies Extinct (Since last issue)—

Anderson (U.K. 1920); Blair of Harrow Weald (U.K. 1945); Cross of Marchbankwood (U.K. 1912); Cornwall (U.K. 1918); Foley-Philipps (U.K. 1887); Hollins (U.K. 1907); Murphy (U.K. 1913); Nugent of Porthferry (U.K. 1961); Pryce-Jones (U.K. 1918); Rouse-Boughton (U.K. 1641 and 1791).

Baronetcies Created—

Errington; Orr-Ewing of Hendon; Hoare of Fleet Street; Porritt; Taylor of Cawthorne; Thompson of Reculver; Thompson of Walton-on-the-Hill.

Dames Grand Cross and Dames Commanders of the Royal Victorian Order and of the Order of the British Empire

NOTE.—Dames Grand Cross (G.C.V.O. or G.B.E.) and Dames Commanders (D.C.V.O. or D.B.E.) are addressed in a manner similar to that of Knights Grand Cross or Knights Commanders, *e.g.* "Miss Florence Smith," after receiving the honour would be addressed as "Dame Florence," and in writing, as "Dame Florence Smith, G. (or D.) C.V.O., or G. (or D.) B.E." Where such award is made to a lady already in enjoyment of a higher title the appropriate letters are appended to her name, *e.g.* "The Countess of ——, G.C.V.O." Dames Grand Cross rank after wives of Baronets and before wives of Knights Grand Cross. Dames Commanders rank after the wives of Knights Grand Cross and before the wives of Knights Commanders.

DAMES GRAND CROSS AND DAMES COMMANDERS

H.M. Queen Elizabeth The Queen Mother, K.G., K.T., C.I. G.M.V.O.
H.R.H. The Princess Margaret, Countess of Snowdon, C.I., G.C.V.O.
H.R.H. The Princess Royal, C.I., G.C.V.O., G.B.E.
H.R.H. The Duchess of Gloucester, C.I., G.C.V.O. G.B.E.
H.R.H. Princess Marina, Duchess of Kent, C.I., G.C.V.O., G.B.E.
H.R.H. The Princess Alice, Countess of Athlone, V.A., G.C.V.O., G.B.E.
H.R.H. The Princess Alexandra of Kent, G.C.V.O.
Acton, Dame (Ellen) Marian, D.B.E.
Albemarle, The Countess of, D.B.E.
Alexander of Tunis, The Countess, G.B.E.
Anderson, Dame Judith, D.B.E.
Anderson, Dame Kitty, D.B.E., Ph.D.
Ashcroft, Dame Peggy (Mrs. Hutchinson), D.B.E.
Baden-Powell, Olave St. Clair, Baroness, G.B.E.
Barnett, *Air Commandant* Dame (Mary) Henrietta, D.B.E.
Beale, Dame Doris Winifred, D.B.E., R.R.C.
Berry, Dame Alice Miriam, D.B.E.
Bevin, Dame Florence Anne, D.B.E.
Bishop, Dame Margaret Joyce, D.B.E.
Blair, *Matron in Chief* Dame Emily Mathieson, D.B.E., R.R.C.
Brock, Dame (Madeline) Dorothy, D.B.E., Litt.D.
Brooke, Dame Barbara Muriel, D.B.E.
Brookeborough, The Viscountess, D.B.E.
Brookes, Mabel Balcombe, Lady, D.B.E.
Bryans, Dame Anne Margaret, D.B.E.
Buckley, *Hon.* Dame Ruth Burton, D.B.E.
Cargill, *Air Commandant* Dame Helen Wilson, D.B.E.
Carter, Lady (Helen) Violet Bonham, D.B.E.
Cavan, Joan, Countess of, D.B.E.
Chick, Dame Harriette, D.B.E., D.Sc.
Churchill, Clementine, Lady, G.B.E.
Cockayne, Dame Elizabeth, D.B.E.
Colville, Lady (Helen) Cynthia, D.C.V.O., D.B.E.
Colvin, *Brig.* Dame Mary Katherine Rosamund, D.B.E., T.D.
Connor, Dame (Annie) Jean, D.B.E., M.D.
Cook, Mary, Lady, D.B.E.
Cosgrove, Dame Gertrude Ann, D.B.E.
Couchman, Dame Elizabeth May Ramsay, D.B.E.
Coulshed, *Brig.* Dame (Mary) Frances, D.B.E., T.D.
Courtney, Dame Kathleen D'Olier, D.B.E.
Cox, Dame Marjorie Sophie, D.B.E.
Cozens, *Brig.*, Dame (Florence) Barbara, D.B.E., R.R.C.
Cripps, Hon. Isobel, Lady, G.B.E.
Crowdy, Dame Rachael Eleanor (Mrs. Thornhill), D.B.E.
Curtis, Dame Myra, D.B.E.
Curwen, Dame (Anne) May, D.B.E.
Daly, Dame Mary Dora, D.B.E.
Davenport, Dame Lilian Emily Isabel Jane Bromley-, D.B.E.
Davidson, The Viscountess, D.B.E.
Davidson, Margaret Agnes, Lady, D.B.E.
Davies, *Commandant* Dame Jean, D.B.E.
de Valois, Dame Ninette, D.B.E.
Devonshire, Mary Alice, Duchess of, G.C.V.O., C.B.E.
Dixon, Edith, Lady, D.B.E.
Doyle, *Air Commandant* Dame Jean Lena Annette Conan, D.B.E.
Elgin & Kincardine, The Countess of, D.B.E.
Evans, Dame Edith Mary (Mrs. Booth), D.B.E.
Evans, Dame Regina Margaret, D.B.E.
Farrer, Hon. Dame Frances Margaret, D.B.E.

Fell, Dame Honor Bridget, D.B.E.
Fonteyn, Dame Margot, D.B.E.
Forbes, *Air Chie Commandant* Dame Katherine Trefusis, D.B.E.
Freyberg, The Dowager Baroness, G.B.E.
Gardiner, Dame Helen Louise, D.B.E., M.V.O.
Gaskell, Lady Constance Milnes-, D.C.V.O.
Genée, Dame Adeline (Mrs. Genée-Isitt), D.B.E., Mus. Doc.
Gillespie, *Brig.* Dame Helen Shiels, D.B.E., R.R.C.
Godwin, Dame (Beatrice) Anne, D.B.E.
Goodrich, Dame Matilda, D.B.E., R.R.C.
Granville, Rose, Countess, G.C.V.O.
Greenwood, The Viscountess, D.B.E.
Halifax, Dorothy, Countess of, D.C.V.O.
Hambleden, Patricia, Viscountess, D.C.V.O.
Hanbury, *Air Commandant* Dame Felicity Hyde, D.B.E.
Hancock, Dame Florence May, D.B.E.
Hardy, Lady Isobel Constance Mary Gathorne-, D.C.V.O.
Harlech, The Baroness, D.C.V.O.
Haydon, *Brigadier* Dame Anne, D.B.E.
Herring, Mary, Lady, D.B.E.
Hess, Dame Myra, D.B.E., Mus.D.
Hillingdon, Edith Mary, Lady, D.B.E.
Humphrys, Gertrude Mary, Lady, D.B.E.
Hyde, The Lady, D.C.V.O.
Johnson, *Brig.* Dame (Cecilie) Monica, D.B.E., R.R.C.
Jones, Dame Katharine Henrietta, D.B.E., R.R.C.
Jones, Dame Mary Latchford Kingsmill, D.B.E.
Kilroy, Dame Alix Hester Marie (Lady Meynell), D.B.E.
Kilmuir, The Countess of, D.B.E.
Knight, Dame Laura, D.B.E., R.A.
Limerick, The Countess of, G.B.E.
Livingstone, Dame Adelaide Lord, D.B.E
Lloyd, Dame Hilda Nora, D.B.E.
Lloyd, *Commandant* Dame Mary Kathleen, D.B.E.
Lonsdale, *Prof.* Dame Kathleen, D.B.E., D.SC., F.R.S.
Loughlin, Dame Anne, D.B.E.
Lowrey, *Air Commandant* Dame Alice, D.B.E., R.R.C.
Lyons, Dame Enid Muriel, G.B.E.
McIlroy, Dame Louise, D.B.E., M.D.
Macleod of Macleod, Dame Flora, D.B.E.
Markova, Dame Alicia, D.B.E.
Marsham, Dame Joan (Hon. Mrs. Sydney Marsham), D.B.E.
Maxse, Dame Marjorie, D.B.E.
Menzies, Dame Pattie Maie, G.B.E.
Millar, *Commandant* Dame (Evelyn Louisa) Elizabeth Hoyer-, D.B.E.
Monro, Hon. Mary Caroline, Lady, D.B.E.
Murdoch, Elizabeth Joy, Lady, D.B.E.
Myer, Dame (Margery) Merlyn Baillieu, D.B.E.
Northumberland, Helen, Duchess of, G.C.V.O., C.B.E.
Oliver, Beryl, Lady, G.B.E., R.R.C.
Oliver, *Hon.* Dame Annie Florence Gillies Cardell-, D.B.E.
Oudendyk, Dame Margaret, D.B.E.
Parker, *Rt. Hon.* Dame Dehra, G.B.E.
Peel, Lady Adelaide Margaret, D.C.V.O.
Pentland, Marjorie Adeline, Baroness, D.B.E.
Pitt, Dame Edith Maud, D.B.E., M.P.
Portland, The Duchess of, D.B.E.
Railton, *Brig.* Dame Mary, D.B.E.
Rambert, Dame Marie (Mrs. Ashley Dukes), D.B.E.
Rankin, Dame Annabelle Jane Mary, D.B.E.
Richmond and Gordon, Hilda Madeleine, Duchess of, D.B.E.
Roberts, Dame Jean, D.B.E.
Robertson, *Commandant* Dame Nancy Margaret, D.B.E.
Robson, Dame Flora McKenzie, D.B.E.
Rosebery, The Countess of, D.B.E.
Salt, Dame Barbara, D.B.E.
Scarbrough, The Countess of, D.C.V.O.
Seymour, Lady Katharine, D.C.V.O.
Sharp, Dame Evelyn Adelaide, G.B.E.
Sitwell, Dame Edith Louisa, D.B.E.
Smieton, Dame Mary Guillan, D.B.E.
Smith, Dame Enid Mary Russell Russell-, D.B.E.
Smith, *Rt. Hon.* Dame (Margaret) Patricia Hornsby-, D.B.E., M.P.
Snagge, *Air Commandant* Dame Nancy Marion, D.B.E.
Spencer, The Countess, D.C.V.O.
Stephens, *Air Commandant* Dame Anne, D.B.E.
Strickland, Barbara, Lady, D.B.E.
Teyte, Dame Maggie (Mrs. Cottingham), D.B.E.
Thorndike, Dame Sybil, D.B.E. (Lady Casson).
Tonga, *Queen* Salote Tubou of, G.C.V.O., G.B.E.
Turner, Dame Eva, D.B.E.
Tyrwhitt, *Brigadier* Dame Mary Joan Caroline, D.B.E.
Vaisey, Dame Dorothy May, D.C.V.O.
Vaughan, Dame Helen Charlotte Isabella Gwynne-, G.B.E., D.Sc.
Vaughan, Dame Janet Maria, (Mrs. Gourlay), D.B.E.
Walwyn, Eileen Mary, Lady, D.B.E.
Ward, Dame Irene Mary Bewick, D.B.E., M.P.
Watt, Dame Katherine Christie, D.B.E., R.R.C.
Welsh, *Air Chief Commandant* Ruth Mary, Lady, D.B.E.
West, Dame Rebecca (Mrs. Andrews), D.B.E.
Whateley, *Chief Controller* Dame Leslie Violet, D.B.E.
Wheeler, Dame Olive Annie, D.B.E.
Whyte, *Air Commandant* Dame Roberta Mary, D.B.E., R.R.C.
Wilkinson, *Matron-in-Chief* Dame Louisa Jane, D.B.E., R.R.C.
Williams, Juliet Evangeline, Lady Rhys-, D.B.E.
Williamson, *Air Commandant* Dame Alice Mary, D.B.E., R.R.C., Q.H.N.S.
Wills, Dame Violet Edith, D.B.E.
Woollcombe, Dame Jocelyn May, D.B.E.

NOTABLE HONOURS OF THE YEAR

Among the honours notified in the New Year and Birthday Honours Lists, 1963, and at other times during the year, were the following: (For Peerages created *see* pp. 223 and 247; for Baronetcies created, *see* p. 297).

KNIGHT OF THE THISTLE

Rt. Hon. R. G. Menzies.

COMPANION OF HONOUR

Rt. Hon. K. J. Holyoake.

G.C.B. (Military)

General Sir Richard Goodbody.
Air Chief Marshal Sir Edmund Hudleston.
Admiral Sir John Luce.

G.C.B. (Civil)

Sir Laurence Helsby.
Sir Harold Kent.

G.C.M.G.

Sir Patrick Dean.
Sir William Goode.
Viscount Head.
Sir Frank Roberts.

G.C.V.O.

Lord Cobbold.
Visct. De L'Isle.
The Earl of Eldon.
Brig. Sir Bernard Fergusson.
Brig. Sir Norman Gwatkin.

G.B.E. (Military)

Air Chief Marshal Sir Walter Merton.
General Sir Harold Pyman.
Admiral Sir Wilfrid Woods.

G.B.E. (Civil)

Sir Colville Deverell.
Sir Geoffrey Wallinger.

K.C.B. (Military)

Lt.-Gen. M. C. Cartwright-Taylor, R.M.
Air Marshal T. N. Coslett.

Lt.-Gen. K. T. Darling.
Vice-Adm. D. P. Dreyer.
Maj.-Gen. R. E. Goodwin.
Vice-Adm. P. W. Gretton.
Air Marshal C. H. Hartley.
Lt.-Gen. H. E. Knott.
Vice-Adm. M. Le Fanu.
Air Marshal S. R. C. Nelson.

K.C.B. (Civil)

William Armstrong.
T. G. B. Cocks.
Sir Keith Murray.

K.C.M.G.

G. H. Andrew.
N. E. Costar.
C. T. Crowe.
P. F. Grey.
D. W. S. Hunt.
Maj.-Gen. D. A. Kendrew.
H. S. Marchant.
Sir Charles Morris.
I. T. M. Pink.
D. M. H. Riches.
J. C. B. Richmond.
R. D. J. Scott Fox.
G. K. N. Trevaskis.
C. M. Walker.
A. M. Williams.

K.C.V.O.

Vice-Adm. J. C. C. Henley.
Vice-Adm. H. G. Norman.

K.B.E. (Military)

Maj.-Gen. H. M. Campbell.
Lt.-Gen. R. W. Craddock.
Vice-Adm. N. E. Denning.
Air Marshal E. M. F. Grundy.
Vice-Adm. J. G. Hamilton.
Lt.-Gen. D. S. S. O'Connor.
Air Vice-Marshal C. Scragg.

D.B.E. (Military)

Air Commandant Jean Conan Doyle.
Brigadier Barbara Cozens.
Commandant Jean Davies.

K.B.E. (Civil)

W. T. Aitken, M.P.
H. N. Brain.
Brigadier E. R. Caffyn.
Matthew Campbell.
R. S. Edwards.
J. C. George, M.P.
Sir Percival Griffiths.
Sir Harry Howard.
B. A. Marwick.
R. G. A. Meade.
A. H. Mumford.
Sir Ronald Sinclair.
G. E. Vaughan.

D.B.E. (Civil)

Miss M. J. Bishop.
Miss H. B. Fell.
Mme. Alicia Markova.
Miss Barbara Salt.

KNIGHTS BACHELOR

W. H. Arnold.
A. C. H. Bell.
R. F. Bonallack.
K. G. Bradley.
Prof. D. W. Brogan.
K. A. L. Brown.
Prof. John Bruce.
W. J. Carron.
J. W. Cook.
Prof. W. M. Cooper.
Col. J. F. Crompton-Inglefield.
J. L. P. Denny.
J. N. M. Entwistle.
Ian Fraser.
James Gunn, R.A.
C. E. Harrison.
J. N. Hogg.
Ronald Holroyd.
W. S. Howard.
E. P. Hudson.
R. L. Jackson.
Prof. E. R. H. Jones.
N. S. Joseph.
Geoffrey Kitchen.
Frederick Lawrence
Geoffrey Lawrence, Q.C.
H. B. Lawson.
William Lindsay.
Alan Lubbock.
R. E. McAlpine.
P. G. Macdonald.
Capt. John MacLeod, M.P.
A. J. Maitland-Makgill-Crichton.
Douglas Marshall, M.P.
H. H. Mullens.
W. J. H. Mullens.
Prof. R. A. B. Mynors.
G. D. N. Nabarro, M.P.
K. S. Peacock.
J. D. Pearson.
M. A. Robinson.
M. E. Rowe, Q.C.
Harold Samuel.
Alexander Samuels.
H. G. Sanders.
T. H. Sellors.
H. F. Spencer.
L. M. Thomas, M.P.
Rear Adm. G. P. Thomson.
N. S. Tucker.
P. F. R. Venables.
M. K. Wallace.
R. E. L. Wellington.
R. van der R. Woolley.
N. C. Wright.
M. D. N. Wyatt.

THE VICTORIA CROSS. V.C.

The ribbon is *Crimson* for all Services (until 1918 it was *Blue* for Royal Navy).

FOR CONSPICUOUS BRAVERY. INSTITUTED *January 29th, 1856.*

The V.C. is worn before all other decorations, on the left breast, and consists of a cross-pattee of bronze, 1½ inches in diameter, with the Royal Crown surmounted by a lion in the centre, and beneath there is the inscription "For Valour." Holders of the V.C. receive a tax-free annuity of £100, irrespective of need or other conditions. In 1911, the right to receive the Cross was extended to Indian soldiers, and in 1920 a Royal Warrant extended the right to Matrons, Sisters and Nurses, and the Staff of the Nursing Services and other services pertaining to Hospitals and Nursing, and to Civilians of either sex regularly or temporarily under the orders, direction or supervision of the Naval, Military or Air Forces of the Crown.

Surviving Recipients of the Victoria Cross

Adlam, *Lt.-Col.* T. E. (Bedf. R.), *Gt. War*.. 1918
Agansing Raj, *Havildar* (Gurkha Rifles), *World War*.............................. 1944
Agar, *Commodore* Augustine W. S., D.S.O. (R.N.), *Gt. War*.. 1919
Ali Haidar, *Sepoy* (Frontier Force Rifles), *World War*.......................... 1945
Anderson, *Lt.-Col.* C. G. W. (Australian M.F.), *World War* 1942
Andrew, *Brig.* Leslie W., D.S.O. (N. Z. Inf.), *Gt. War*........... 1917
Annand, *Capt.* R. W. (Durham L.I.), *World War*.............................. 1940
Auten, *Capt.* H., D.S.C. (R.N.R.), *Gt. War*. 1918
Axford, *Corpl.* T. L., M.M. (A.I.F.), *Gt. War* 1918
Barrett, *Col.* John C. (R. Leic. R.), *Gt. War* .. 1918
Bassett, *Col.* Cyril R. G. (N.Z.), *Gt. War*... 1915
Beak, *Maj.-Gen.* Daniel M. William, D.S.O., M.C. (R. Scots. Fus.), *Gt. War*........... 1918
Beattie, *Capt.* S. H. (R.N.), *World War*..... 1942
Beesley, *Corpl.* W. (Rif. Bgde.), *Gt. War*... 1918
Bennett, *Capt.* E. P., M.C. (Wor. R.), *Gt. War* 1917
Bent, *R.-S.-M.* S. J. (East Lancs. R.), *Gt. War* 1914
Bhanbhagta Gurung, *Lance-Naik* (2nd Gurkha Rifles), *World War*.................. 1945
Bhandari Ram, *Lance-Naik* (Baluch R.), *World War*.............................. 1944
Bissett, *Maj.* W. D. (A. & S. H.), *Gt. War*... 1918
Borella, *Capt.* A. C., M.M. (Australia), *Gt. War* 1918
Boyle, *Rear-Adm.* E. C. (R.N.), *Gt. War*.... 1915
Brereton, *C.-S.-M.* A. (Manitoba R.), *Gt. War*.............................. 1918
Burman, *Sergt.* W. F. (Rif. Bgde.), *Gt. War*.. 1917
Burton, *Corpl.* R. H. (Duke of Wellington's R.), *World War*........................ 1944
Butler, *Pte.* Wm. B. (W. Yorks. R.), *Gt. War* 1917
Bye, *Sergt.* Robert (Welsh Gds.), *Gt. War* . 1917
Cain, *Maj.* R. H. (R. Northumberland Fus.), *World War*........................... 1944

Caldwell, *C.-S.-M.* Thomas (Lanark Yeo. & R. Scots. Fus.), *Gt. War* ... 1918
Calvert, *Sergt.* L., M.M. (K.O.Y.L.I.), *Gt. War* 1918
Campbell, *Brigadier* L. M., D.S.O., T.D. (A. & S. Highrs.), *World War* ... 1943
Carmichael, *Sergt.* J. (N. Staff. R.), *Gt. War.* 1917
Carne, *Col.* J. P., D.S.O. (Glos. R.), *Korea*... 1951
Carroll, *Pte.* John (Aus. Inf.), *Gt. War*... 1917
Cartwright, *Pte.* George (Aust.), *Gt. War*... 1918
Cator, *Capt.* Harry, M.M. (E. Surr. R.) *Gt. War* ... 1917
Chafer, *Pte.* G. W. (E. York. R.), *Gt. War* . 1916
Chapman, *Sergt.* E. T. (Monmouthshire R.), *World War* ... 1945
Chatta Singh, *Havildar* (Bhopal Inf.), *Gt. War* 1916
Cheshire, *Group Capt.* G. L., D.S.O., D.F.C. (R.A.F.), *World War* ... 1944
Christian, *Pte.* H. (K. O. Royal R.), *Gt. War.* 1916
Christie, *L.-Cpl.* J. A. (Lond. R.), *Gt. War*.. 1918
Cloutman, His Honour Sir Brett M., M.C., Q.C. (R.E.), *Gt. War* ... 1918
Coltman, *Capt.* William H., D.C.M., M.M. (N. Staff. R.), *Gt. War* ... 1918
Cooper, *Lt.* E. (K.R.R.C.), *Gt. War*... 1917
Coppins, *L/Sgt.* F. G. (Manitoba R.), *Gt. War* 1918
Counter, *Corpl.* Jack T. (King's R.), *Gt. War.* 1918
Craig, *Wing Cdr.* J. M. (R.A.F.), *Gt. War*.. 1917
Cross, *Corpl.* Arthur H. (M.G.C.), *Gt. War*.. 1918
Crowe, *Capt.* John (Worc. R.), *Gt. War*.... 1918
Cruickshank, *Fl. Lt.* J. A. (R.A.F.V.R.), *World War* ... 1944
Cruickshank, *Pte.* R. E. (Lond. R.), *Gt. War* 1918
Crutchley, *Admiral* Sir Victor Alexander, K.C.B., D.S.C. (R.N.), *Gt. War* ... 1918
Cumming, *Brig.* A. E., O.B.E., M.C. (Indian Army), *World War* ... 1942
Currie, *Maj.* D. V., C.B.E. (S. Alberta R., Canada), *World War* ... 1944
Curtis, *Sergt.* H. A. (R. Dub. Fus.), *Gt. War.* 1918
Cutler, *Lt.* A. R. (Australia), *World War*.... 1941
Dalziel, *Sergt.* Henry (Aust. I.F.), *Gt. War*... 1918
Davies, *Corp.* J. T. (S. Lancs. R.), *Gt. War*.. 1918
Davies, *Sergt.* J. (R. Welch Fus.), *Gt. War*.. 1916
Davies, *Maj.-Gen.* L. A. E. Price-, C.B., C.M.G., D.S.O. (K.R.R.C.), *S. Africa* ... 1901
Davies, *Vice-Adm.* Richard B., C.B., D.S.O., A.F.C., *Gt. War* ... 1915
Dawson, *Col.* James Lennox (R.E.), *Gt. War.* 1915
Dean, *Col.* D. J., O.B.E. (R. W. Kent R.), *Gt. War* ... 1918
De L'Isle, *Maj.* Viscount, P.C., G.C.M.G., G.C.V.O. (*Hon.* W. P. Sidney) (Gren. Gds.), *World War* ... 1944
Dinesen, *Lt.* T. (Roy. Highlanders of Canada), *Gt. War* ... 1918
Dorrell, *Lt.-Col.* G. T., M.B.E. (R.H.A.), *Gt. War* ... 1914
Downie, *Sergt.* R. (R. Dub. F.), *Gt. War*... 1916
Drain, *Sergt.* J. H. C. (R.H.A.), *Gt. War*.... 1914
Dresser, *Pte.* T. (Green Howards), *Gt. War.* 1914
Duffy, *Pte.* James (R. Innis. Fus.), *Gt. War*.. 1918
Eardley, *Sergt.* G. H., M.M. (K.S.L.I.), *World War* ... 1944
Edwards, *Corpl.* F. J. (Middx. R.), *Gt. War*.. 1916
Edwards, *Air Commodore* H. I., C.B., D.S.O., O.B.E., D.F.C. (R.A.F.), *World War*... 1941
Edwards, *Capt.* W. (K.O.Y.L.I.), *Gt. War*.. 1917
Egerton, *Sergt.* E. A. (Sherwood F.), *Gt. War* 1917
Elliott, *Lt.* the Rev. K. (N.Z.M.F.), *World War* 1942
Ervine-Andrews, *Lt.-Col.* H. M. (E. Lancs. R.), *World War* ... 1940
Finch, *Lt.* (*Q.M.*) N. A. (R.M.A.), *Gt. War.* 1918
Findlay, *Col.* George de C. E., M.C. (R.E.), *Gt. War* ... 1918
Foote, *Maj.Gen.* H. R. B., C.B., D.S.O. (R. Tank R.), *World War* ... 1942
Foote, Rev. J. W. (Canada), *World War*... 1942
Fraser, *Cdr.* I. E., D.S.C. (R.N.R.), *World War* 1945
Frickleton, *Capt.* Samuel (N.Z.), *Gt. War*... 1917
Fuller, *Sgt.* W. (Welch Regt.), *Gt. War*... 1914
Ganju Lama, M.M., *Jemadar* (Gurkha Rifles), *World War* ... 1944
Gardner, *Capt.* P. J., M.C. (R.T.R.), *World War* ... 1941
Garforth, *Sergt.* C. E. (15th Hrs.), *Gt. War*.. 1914
Geary, Rev. B. H., C.F. (E. Surr. R.), *Gt. War* 1915
Ghale, *Subedar*, Gaje (Gurkha Rif.). *Wld. War* 1943
Gian Singh, *Jemadar* (Punjab R.), *World War.* 1945
Good, *Corpl.* H. J. (Quebec R.), *Gt. War*.... 1918
Gordon, *L.-Cpl.* B. S., M.M. (Aust.), *Gt. War* 1917
Gordon, *W.O. II* J. H. (Australia), *World War* 1917
Gould, *Lt.* T. W. (R.N.), *World War* ... 1942
Gourley, *2nd Lt.* C. E., M.M. (R.F.A.), *Gt. War* ... 1918
Graham, *Lt.-Col.* Sir Reginald, Bt., O.B.E. (M.G.C.), *Gt. War* ... 1917
Grant, *Col.* John D., C.B., D.S.O. (I.A.), *Thibet* 1904
Grant, *Lt.* J. G. (Well. R., N.Z.), *Gt. War*.. 1918
Greaves, *Sergt.* Fred. (Sherwood F.), *Gt. War* 1917
Gregg, *Brig.* Hon. Milton F., C.B.E., M.C. (Nova Scotia R.), *Gt. War* ... 1918
Gregg, *Sergt.* W., D.C.M., M.M. (R.B.), *Gt. War* ... 1918
Grimshaw, *Lt.-Col.* John (Lanc. Fus.), *Gt. War* 1917
Haine, *Lt.-Col.* R. L. M.C. (H.A.C.), *Gt. War.* 1917
Hall, *Sergt.* Arthur (Australia), *Gt. War*.... 1918
Halliday, *Gen.* Sir Lewis S. T., K.C.B. (R.M.L.I.), *China* ... 1900
Halton, *Pte.* A. (K. O. Royal R.), *Gt. War.* 1917
Hamilton, *Lt.* J. B. (H.L.I.), *Gt. War*... 1917
Hanna, *Lt.* Robert (Can. Inf.), *Gt. War*.... 1914
Harvey, *Brig.* F. M. W. (Can. Inf.), *Gt. War* 1917
Hayward, *Lt.-Col.* Reginald F. Johnson, M.C. (Wilts. R.), *Gt. War* ... 1918
Herring, *Maj.* A. C. (N'thants R.), *Gt. War*.. 1918
Hewitt, *2nd Lieut.* William Henry (S. Afr. Inf.), *Gt. War* ... 1917
Hill, *Pte.* Albert (R. Welch Fus.), *Gt. War*.. 1916
Hinton, *Sergt.* J. D. (N.Z.M.F.), *World War*.. 1941
Holbrook, *Com.* N. D. (R.N.), *Gt. War*.... 1914
Holland, *Capt.* John V. (Leinster R.), *Gt. War* 1916
Hollis, *C.S.M.* S. E. (Green Howards), *World War* ... 1944
Holmes, *Capt.* F. W. (K.O.Y.L.I.), *Gt. War*.. 1914
Howell, *Corpl.* G. J., M.M. (Aust. Inf.), *Gt. War* 1917
Huffam, *Maj.* J. P. (Duke of Wellington's R.), *Gt. War* ... 1918
Hulme, *Sergt.* A. C. (N.Z.M.F.), *World War.* 1941
Hunter, *Sergt.* D. F. (H.L.I.), *Gt. War*... 1918
Hutchinson, *Corpl.* J. (Lanc. Fus.), *Gt. War*... 1916
Insall, *Group Capt.* Gilbert S. M., M.C. (R.A.F.), *Gt. War* ... 1915
Inwood, *Corpl.* R. R. (Aust. Imp. Fce.), *Gt. War* ... 1917
Ishar Singh, *Lt.* (Punjabis), *Waziristan*... 1921
Jackson, *W.O.* N. C. (R.A.F.V.R.), *Wld. War* 1945
James, *Brig.* Manley Angell, D.S.O., M.C. (Glouc. R.), *Gt. War* ... 1918
Jamieson, *Maj.* D. A. (R. Norfolk R.), *World War* ... 1944
Jefferson, *L.-Corpl.* F. A. (Lancs. Fus.), *Wld. War* ... 1944
Jerrard, *F/Lt.* Alan (R.A.F.), *Gt. War*... 1918
Johnson, *Maj.-Gen.* Dudley G., C.B., D.S.O., M.C. (S. Wales B.), *Gt. War* ... 1918
Joynt, *Lt.-Col.* W. D. (Aust. I. F.), *Gt. War*.. 1918
Judson, *Capt.* Reginald Stanley, D.C.M., M.M. (Auckland R., N.Z.), *Gt. War* ... 1918
Kamal Ram, *Havildar* (Punjab R.), *Wld. War* 1944
Karanbahadur Rana, *Naik* (Gurkha Rifles), *Gt. War* ... 1918

Kenna, *Pte.* E. (Australian M.F.), *Wld. War*. 1945
Kenneally, *C.-Q.-M.-S.* J. P. (Irish Gds.), *Wld. War* 1943
Kenny, *Pte.* H. E. (Loyal R.), *Gt. War* 1916
Khudadad Khan, *Subedar* (129th Bal.), *Gt. War* 1914
Knight, *2nd Lt.* A. J., M.B.E. (Sher. F.), *Gt. War*. 1917
Lachiman Gurung, *Rifleman* (Gurkha Rifles), *World War* 1945
Lalbahadur, Thapa, *Subedar-Major* (Gurkah Rifles), *World War* 1943
Lauder, *Pte.* D. R. (R. Scots Fus.), *Gt. War*. 1916
Laurent, *Lt.* H. J. (N.Z. Rif. Bgde.), *Gt. War*. 1918
Leak, *Pte.* John (Australia), *Gt. War* 1916
Learoyd, *Wing-Cmdr.* R. A. B. (R.A.F.), *World War* 1940
Le Patourel, *Col.* H. W. (R. Hampshire R.), *World War* 1942
Lewis, *Pte.* H. W. (Welch R.), *Gt. War* 1916
Luke, *Sergt.* F. (R.H.A.), *Gt. War* 1914
McCarthy, *Lt.* L. D. (Aust.), *Gt. War* 1913
McDougall, *Sergt.* S. R. (A.I.F.), *Gt. War* 1916
MacIntyre, *Lt.* David Lowe, C.B. (Arg. & Suth. High.), *Gt. War* 1918
McNally, *Sergt.* William, M.M. (Green Howards), *Gt. War* 1918
McNamara, *Corpl.* John (E. Surrey R.), *Gt. War* 1918
Magennis, *L/S* J. J. (R.N.), *World War* 1945
Mahony, *Lt.-Col.* J. K. (Westminster R., Canada), *World War* 1944
Malleson, *Com.* W. St. A. (R.N.), *Gt. War* 1915
Martin, *Brig.* C. G., C.B.E., D.S.O. (R.E.), *Gt. War* 1915
Maxwell, *Lt.* J., M.C., D.C.M. (Aust.), *Gt. War* 1918
Merritt, *Lt.-Col.* C. C. I. (S. Saskatchewan R.), *World War* 1942
Metcalf, *L.-Sergt.* William Henry, M.M. (Manitoba R.), *Gt. War* 1918
Miers, *Rear-Adm.* Sir A. C. C., K.B.E., C.B., D.S.O. (R.N.), *World War* 1942
Miles, *Pte.* Francis G. (Glouc. R.), *Gt. War*. 1918
Mitchell, *Lt.-Col.* Coulson N., M.C. (Canad. Engrs.), *Gt. War* 1918
Molyneux, *Sergt.* John (R. Fus.), *Gt. War* 1917
Moon, *Lt.* Rupert V. (Aust. Inf.), *Gt. War* 1917
Moore, *Capt.* M. S. S. (R. Hants. R.), *Gt. War* 1917
Mott, *Sergt.* E. J., D.C.M. (Border R.), *Gt. War* 1917
Mountain, *Sergt.* A. (W. Yorks. R.), *Gt. War* 1918
Moyney, *Sergt.* John (Irish Gds.), *Gt. War* 1917
Murray, *Lt.-Col.* Henry Wm., C.M.G., D.S.O., D.C.M. (Aust. Inf.), *Gt. War* 1917
Myles, *Capt.* E. K., D.S.O. (Worc. R.), *Gt. War* 1916
Namdeo Jadhao, *Havildar* (Mahratta L. I.), *World War* 1945
Nasmith, *Adm.* Sir M. E. Dunbar-, K.C.B., K.C.M.G., (R.N.), *Gt. War* 1915
Neame, *Lt.-Gen.* Sir Philip, K.B.E., C.B., D.S.O. (R.E.), *Gt. War* 1915
Newman, *Lt.-Col.* A. C., O.B.E., T.D. (Essex R.), *World War* 1942
Nicholls, *L.-Cpl.* H. (G. Gds.), *World War* 1940
Norton, *Capt.* G. R., M.M. (S.A.M.F.), *World War* 1944
Ockenden, *Sergt.* J. (R. Dub. Fus.), *Gt. War*. 1917
Parkash Singh, *Capt.* (Punjab R.), *World War* 1943
Partridge, *Pte.* F. J. (Australia), *World War* 1945
Pearkes, *Maj.-Gen.* George Randolph, C.B., D.S.O., M.C. (Can. Ind.), *Gt. War* 1918
Peeler, *W.O.* Walter (Aust. I. F.), *Gt. War* 1917
Phillips, *Capt.* R. E. (R. War. R.), *Gt. War*. 1917
Pitcher, *Petty Off.* E., D.S.M. (R.M.), *Gt. War* 1917
Place, *Capt.* B. C. G., D.S.C. (R.N.), *Wld. War* 1943
Pooll, *Capt.* A. H. Batton-, M.C. (R. Muns. F.), *Gt. War* 1916
Porteous, *Brig.* P. A. (R.A.), *World War* 1942
Premindra Singh Bhagat, *Capt.* (Corps. of Ind. Engineers), *World War* 1941
Procter, Rev. A. H. (King's R.) *Gt. War* 1916
Ratcliffe, *Pte.* W., M.M. (S. Lanc. R.), *Gt. War* 1917
Rattey, *Sergt.* R. R. (Australia), *World War*. 1945
Readitt, *Sergt.* John (S. Lanc. R.), *Gt. War* 1917
Rees, *Sergt.* Ivor (S. Wales Bord.), *Gt. War*. 1917
Reid, *Fl.-Lt.* W. (R.A.F.V.R.), *World War*. 1943
Ricketts, *Sgt.* T. (R. Newf'land R.), *Gt. War* 1918
Ritchie, *Corpl.* W. (Seaforth H.), *Gt. War* 1916
Roberts, *Maj.-Gen.* F. C., C.B.E., D.S.O., M.C. (Worc. R.), *Gt. War* 1918
Roberts, *Lt.-Com.* P. S. W., D.S.C. (R.N.), *World War* 1942
Robinson, *Rear-Adm.* E. G., O.B.E. (R.N.), *Gt. War* 1915
Robson, *Pte.* H. H. (Royal Scots), *Gt. War* 1914
Roupell, *Brig.* G. R. P., C.B. (E. Surrey R.), *Gt. War* 1915
Rutherford, *Capt.* C. B., M.C., M.M. (Quebec R.), *Gt. War* 1918
Ruthven, *Maj.* William (Aust. I. F.), *Gt. War* 1918
Ryder, *Sergt.* Robert (Middx. R.), *Gt. War* 1916
Ryder, *Capt.* R. E. D. (R.N.), *World War* 1942
Sadlier, *Lt.* C. W. K. (Aust. I. F.), *Gt. War* 1918
Shankland, *Lt.-Col.* Robert, D.C.M. (Can. Inf.), *Gt. War* 1917
Shepherd, *Rflm.* A. E. (K.R.R.C.), *Gt. War*. 1918
Sherbrooke, *Rear-Adm.* R. St. V., C.B., D.S.O. (R.N.), *World War* 1942
Smith, *Sergt.* E. A. (Seaforth Highrs. of Canada), *World War* 1944
Smith, *Pte.* James (Border R.), *Gt. War* 1914
Smyth, *Brig.* Rt. Hon. Sir J. G., Bt., M.C., M.P. (Ludhiana Sikhs), *Gt. War* 1915
Smythe, *Lt.* G. Q. M. (S.A.M.F.), *Wld. War* 1942
Spackman, *Sergt.* Charles Edward (Border R.), *Gt. War* 1918
Speakman, *Sergt.* W. (Black Watch), *Korea* 1951
Stannard, *Capt.* R. B., D.S.O., R.D. (R.N.R.), *World War* 1940
Starcevich, *Pte.* L. T. (Australia), *World War*. 1945
Steele, *Com.* G. C. (R.N.), *Gt. War* 1918
Steele, *Sergt.* T. (Seaforth H.), *Gt. War* 1917
Storkey, His Honour P. V. (Aust. I. F.), *Gt. War* 1918
Strachan, *Maj.* H., M.C. (Can. Cav.), *Gt. War* 1917
Stringer, *Pte.* G. (Manch. R.), *Gt. War* 1916
Tandey, *L/Corpl.* H., D.C.M., M.M. (W. Riding R.), *Gt. War* 1918
Tilston, *Maj.* F. A. (Essex Scottish, Canada), *World War* 1945
Tombs, *Corpl.* J. (King's R.), *Gt. War* 1915
Topham, *Corpl.* F. G. (1st Canadian Parachute Bn.). *World War* 1945
Towers, *Pte.* James (Cameronians), *Gt. War*. 1918
Towner, *Maj.* Edgar Thomas, M.C. (Aust. M.G.C.), *Gt. War* 1918
Train, *Corpl.* C. W. (Lond. R.), *Gt. War* 1918
Trent, *Group Capt.* L. H., D.F.C. (R.N.Z.A.F.), *World War* 1943
Triquet, *Brig.* P. (R. 22R. of Canada), *World War* 1943
Tulbahadur Pun, *W.O.I.* (Gurkha Rifles), *World War* 1944
Turner, *Lt.-Col.* V. B. (R.B.), *World War* 1942
Turrall, *Pte.* Thos. G. (Worc. R.), *Gt. War*. 1916
Umrao Singh, *Havildar* (I.A.), *World War* 1917
Upham, *Capt.* C. H. (and Bar, 1942), (N.Z.M.F.) *World War* 1941
Veale, Corpl. T. W. H. (Devon R.), *Gt. War* 1919

Vickers, *Capt.* Sir C. Geoffrey (Sherwood For.), *Gt. War* 1915
Wakeford, *Maj.* R. (R. Hampshire R.), *World War* 1944
Wallace, *Capt.* S. T. D. (R.F.A.), *Gt. War* .. 1917
Waters, *Maj.* Sir Arnold, C.B.E., D.S.O., M.C. (R.E.), *Gt. War* 1918
Watkins, *Maj.* T. (Welch R.), *World War* . 1944
Welch, *Sgt.* J. (R. Berk. R.), *Gt. War* 1917
West, *Air Commodore* Ferdinand M. F., C.B.E., M.C. (R.A.F.), *Gt. War* 1918
White, *Col.* Archie Cecil T., M.C. (Green Howards), *Gt. War* 1916
White, *Lt.* Wm. A. (M. G. Corps), *Gt. War* .. 1918
Whitfield, *Sergt.* H. (K. Shrop. L. I.), *Gt. War* 1918
Williams, *Seaman* W. (R.N.R.), *Gt. War* ... 1917
Wilson, *Lt.-Col.* E. C. T. (E. Surrey R.), *World War* 1940
Wood, *Pte.* W. (R. Northd. Fus.), *Gt. War*. 1918
Woolley, Rev. Geoffrey H., O.B.E., M.C., Q.H.C. (Qn. Vic. Rif.), *Gt. War* 1915
Wright, *C.S.M.* P. H. (Coldstream Gds.), *World War* 1944
Wyatt, *L.-Sergt.* G. H. (Cold. Gds.), *Gt. War* 1915
Young, *Pte.* T. (Durh. L.I.), *Gt. War* 1918
Zengel, *Sergt.* Raphael L., M.M. (Saskatchewan R.), *Gt. War* 1918

THE GEORGE CROSS, G.C.

The ribbon is *dark blue* threaded through a bar adorned with laurel leaves

FOR GALLANTRY

INSTITUTED *September 24th*, 1940 (with amendments, *November 3rd*, 1942)

The George Cross is worn before all other decorations (except the V.C.) on the left breast § and consists of a plain silver cross with four equal limbs, the cross having in the centre a circular medallion bearing a design showing St. George and the Dragon. The inscription "For Gallantry" appears round the medallion and in the angle of each limb of the cross is the Royal cypher "G VI" forming a circle concentric with the medallion. The reverse is plain and bears the name of the recipient and the date of the award. The cross is suspended by a ring from a bar adorned with laurel leaves on dark blue ribbon $1\frac{1}{2}$ inches wide.

The cross is intended primarily for civilians and awards to the fighting services are confined to actions for which purely military honours are not normally granted. It is awarded only for acts of the greatest heroism or of the most conspicuous courage in circumstances of extreme danger.

§ When worn by a woman it may be worn on the left shoulder from a ribbon of the same width and colour fashioned into a bow.

Empire Gallantry Medal.—The Royal Warrant which ordained that the grant of the Empire Gallantry Medal should cease authorized holders of that medal to return it to the Central Chancery of the Order of Knighthood and to receive in exchange the George Cross. A similar provision applied to posthumous awards of the Empire Gallantry Medal made after the outbreak of war in 1939.

THE GRAND PRIORY IN THE BRITISH REALM OF THE MOST VENERABLE ORDER OF THE HOSPITAL OF ST. JOHN OF JERUSALEM

(INCORPORATED MAY 14, 1888, WITH ADDENDA 1888, 1890, 1907, 1926, 1955 and 1958), St. John's Gate, Clerkenwell, E.C.1.

Sovereign Head .... H.M. the Queen.
Grand Prior .... H.R.H. The Duke of Gloucester, K.G., P.C., K.T., K.P., G.M.B., G.C.M.G., G.C.V.O.
Lord Prior .... The Lord Wakehurst, K.G., K.C.M.G.

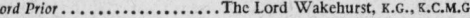

The Order had its origin in Jerusalem where a hospice for the relief of Christian pilgrims was founded in the eleventh century. Initially a monastic order, it later became militarized and its Knights fought alongside the Crusaders against the spread of Islam. After the loss of the Holy Land, the Order became sovereign in Rhodes and then in Malta. Like other ancient Orders of Chivalry, the Order of St. John was represented in most European countries, though its Priories in England and Scotland were dissolved at the same time as the monasteries. The Order was expelled from Malta by Napoleon in 1798 and the Grand Magistracy eventually settled in Rome.

In 1827 the Knights of France, with the authority of the Grand Magistracy, assisted in the revival of what is now the Grand Priory in the British Realm of the Most Venerable Order of the Hospital of St. John of Jerusalem, whose Chancery is at St. John's Gate, the surviving gatehouse of the former Priory of England in Clerkenwell. A Royal Charter was granted to the Order in 1888 by Queen Victoria, and the first Grand Prior was King Edward VII, while Prince of Wales. The Badge is a white eight-pointed cross, embellished in alternate angles with a lion and an unicorn; the riband is of black watered silk. By a Royal Charter of March 15, 1955, members are divided into six grades:—(1) Bailiffs and Dames Grand Cross; (2) Knights and Dames of Justice and of Grace; (3) Commanders; (4) Officers; (5) Serving Brothers and Sisters; and (6) Esquires. The Chaplains of the Order form a special class, taking precedence between the Knights and Commanders. A notification of these distinctions having been conferred appears in the London Gazette, but they do not confer any rank, title or precedence.

The work of the Order consists of the maintenance of its three Foundations—The Ophthalmic Hospital in Jerusalem (founded 1882); The St. John Ambulance Association, which is concerned with education in First Aid and kindred subjects; and the St. John Ambulance Brigade, the main object of which is to provide trained personnel for attendance on the public where the rendering of First Aid may be required.

THE EXECUTIVE

The Crown (the Queen in Council) "makes peace and war, issues charters, increases the peerage, is the fountain of honour, of office, and of justice." The Sovereign entrusts the executive power to Ministers of the Crown, appointed on the advice of the accredited leader of the party in Parliament which enjoys, or can secure, a majority of votes in the House of Commons.

The Cabinet

The Cabinet has no corporate existence, but under the *Ministers of the Crown Act* (1937), provision is made for 17 Ministers of the first rank (Cabinet Ministers) of whom not more than 15 may be members of the House of Commons. The *Ministers of the Crown (Parliamentary Secretaries) Act* (1960) laid down aggregate limit of 33 Parliamentary Secretaries.

The Prime Minister

The Prime Minister is appointed by the Sovereign. When a party is in opposition and its leadership becomes vacant it makes its free choice among the various personalities available; but if the party is in office, the Sovereign's choice may anticipate, and in a certain sense forestall, the decision of the party. In 1905 the office of Prime Minister, which had been in existence for nearly 200 years, was officially recognized and its holder was granted a place in the Table of Precedence.

The Leader of the Opposition

In 1937 the office of Leader of the Opposition was similarly recognized and a salary of £2,000 per annum was assigned to the post, thus following a practice which had prevailed in the Dominion of Canada since 1906. In 1957 the salary was increased to £3,000.

THE PRINCIPAL PARTIES IN PARLIAMENT

(1900–1959)

General Election	Conservative and Unionist	Liberal	Labour
1900..........	402	185	11
1906..........	158	387	41
1910 (Jan.).....	273	275	40
1910 (Dec.)....	272	272	42
1918..........	382 (*a*)	161 (*b*)	74 (*c*)
1922..........	347	118 (*d*)	142
1923..........	258	151	191
1924..........	41[illegible]	39	150
1929..........	260	59	287
1931..........	471	72 (*e*)	65 (*f*)
1935..........	387	54 (*g*)	166 (*h*)
1945..........	189	25 (*i*)	396 (*j*)
1950..........	298 (*k*)	9	315 (*l*)
1951..........	320 (*m*)	6	296 (*l*)
1955..........	344 (*m*)	6	277 (*n*)
1959..........	365 (*m*)	6	258 (*o*)

NOTES.—(*a*) Including 48 Non-Coalition Unionists. (*b*) Including 28 Non-Coalition Liberals. (*c*) Including 63 Non-Coalition Labour. (*d*) Liberal National 59; Liberal 59. (*e*) Liberal National 35 (Simon); Liberal 33 (Samuel); 4 (Lloyd George). (*f*) National Labour 13 (MacDonald); Labour 52 (Henderson). (*g*) Liberal National 33; Liberal 21. (*h*) National Labour 8; Labour 154; I.L.P. 4. (*i*) Liberal National 13. Liberal 12. (*j*) Labour 393; I.L.P. 3. (*k*) Incl. Nat. Liberal. (*l*) Irish Nationalists (2) and Speaker make total of 625. (*m*) Including associates. (*n*) Sinn Fein (2) and Speaker make total of 630. (*o*) Independent (1) makes total of 630.

Conservatives and associates have subsequently gained one seat from Labour and lost three seats to Labour at by-elections and the Conservative candidate in S.E. Bristol by-election was declared to have been elected. Liberals have gained one seat from Conservatives.

LEGISLATION

Legislation is initiated in the Houses of Parliament in the form of Bills. Public Bills are of two kinds, those introduced by the Government of the day, and those introduced by a private member. A Bill (except a Money Bill, which must originate in the House of Commons) can be introduced in either House and when presented receives its *First Reading*, after which it is printed and circulated to members. The next stage is the *Second Reading*, in the debate on which the broad issues raised are discussed. If passed it reaches the *Committee Stage* and is referred to a Committee (of the whole House, Select, or Standing—*see* "Committees," pp. 314–15). Bills of major importance are usually, and Money Bills are always, sent to a Committee of the whole House. In committee, a Bill is discussed clause by clause, and is returned to the House with or without amendment. A Private Bill, which is introduced to enable an individual or a body corporate to acquire or vary certain powers, is referred to a *Select Committee*, and if opposed, witnesses may be called and counsel heard by the Committee. The next step is the *Report Stage*, when the Bill is accepted by the House, or sent back to the same, or sent back to another, Committee for further consideration. Finally the Bill receives its *Third Reading* (during which, in the House of Commons, only verbal amendments are permissible) and is sent to the other House. When a Bill has been passed by both Houses it becomes an *Act of Parliament*, on receiving the *Royal Assent*, which is signified by the Sovereign on the Throne, or by Commissioners (normally three Peers), in the Chamber of the House of Lords. The power to withhold assent (colloquially known as the *Royal Veto*) resides in the Sovereign, but has not been exercised in the United Kingdom since 1707, in the reign of Queen Anne.

COUNCILLORS OF STATE

On every occasion that the Sovereign leaves the realm for distant parts of the Commonwealth or a foreign country, it is necessary to appoint Councillors of State under Letters Patent to carry out the chief functions of the monarch, including the holding of Privy Councils and the signature of Acts passed by Parliament. The normal procedure is to appoint as Councillors three or four members of the Royal Family who are next in succession to the Throne among those remaining in the United Kingdom. For instance, during the Queen's African tour in 1961, the Councillors of State were Queen Elizabeth the Queen Mother, Princess Margaret, the Duke of Gloucester and the Duke of Kent.

In the event of the Sovereign on accession being under the age of eighteen years or at any time unavailable or incapacitated by infirmity of mind or body for the performance of the royal functions provision is made for a Regency. The Regency Act, 1953, has designated the Duke of Edinburgh as Regent, should a Regency become necessary during the minority of the children of her present Majesty.

GOVERNMENT BY PARTY

Towards the close of Charles II's reign the Exclusion Bill debates in Parliament (1679–80) were marked by the rise of two parties in the political life of the nation and they became known as *Whigs* and *Tories*, names given by the opponents to each other but afterwards mutually accepted, to continue as political labels until Whig was changed to *Liberal* and Tory to *Conservative*.

The Oxford English Dictionary explains the terms as follows:—

Whig [origin obscure; probably shortening of *Whiggamore*].—An adherent of the Presbyterian cause in Scotland in the seventeenth century. Applied to the Exclusioners who opposed the succession of James, Duke of York, to the crown, on the ground of his being a Roman Catholic.

Tory [Anglicized spelling of Irish *toraidhe* "pursuer"] . . . applied to any Irish Papist or Royalist in arms. A nickname given 1679–80 by the Exclusionists to those who opposed the exclusion of James, Duke of York (a Roman Catholic), from the succession to the crown.

Before the reign of William and Mary (1688–1702) the principal Officers of State were chosen by and were responsible to the Sovereign alone and not to Parliament or the nation at large. Such officers acted sometimes in concert with one another, but more often independently, and the fall of one did not, of necessity, involve that of others, although all were liable to be dismissed at any moment.

In 1693 the Earl of Sunderland recommended to William III the advisability of selecting a Ministry from the political party which enjoyed a majority in the House of Commons and the first united Ministry was drawn in 1696 from the Whigs, to which party the King owed his throne, the principal members being Russell (the Admiral), Somers (the Advocate), Lord Wharton and Charles Montague (afterwards Chancellor of the Exchequer). This group became known as the *Junto* and was regarded with suspicion as a novelty in the political life of the nation, being a small section meeting in secret apart from the main body of Ministers. It may be regarded as the forerunner of the *Cabinet* and in course of time it led to the establishment of the principle of joint responsibility of Ministers, so that internal disagreement caused a change of *personnel* or resignation of the whole body of Ministers.

The *Act of Settlement* (1701) secured the Protestant succession to the throne and with the accession of George I (1714) the main cause of the political division was removed, leaving the Whigs as the dominant party for many years, the Tories being regarded as Jacobites in permanent opposition to the Hanoverians; but before the close of George II's reign (1760) they had become reconciled to the dynasty and during the French wars they secured an ascendency in Parliament.

The accession of a King unfamiliar with the English language led to a disinclination on the part of the Sovereign to preside at meetings of his Ministers and caused the appearance of a *Prime Minister*, a position first acquired by Robert Walpole in 1721 and retained without interruption for 20 years and 326 days.

In 1828 the old party of the Whigs became known as *Liberals*, a name originally given to it by its opponents to imply laxity of principles, but gradually accepted by the party to indicate its claim to be pioneers and champions of political reform and progressive legislation. In 1861 a Liberal Registration Association was founded and Liberal Associations became widespread. As the outcome of a conference at Birmingham in 1877 a National Liberal Federation was formed, with headquarters in London. The Liberal Party was in power for long periods during the second half of the nineteenth century in spite of the set-back during the Home Rule crisis of 1886, which resulted in the secession of the Liberal Unionists, and for several years during the first quarter of the twentieth century, but after a further split into National and Independent Liberals it numbered only 59 in all after the General Election of 1929, with a further fall to 12 (excluding National Liberals) after the 1945 Election, 9 after the 1950 Election and 6 after the 1951, 1955 and 1959 Elections.

Soon after the change from Whig to Liberal the Tory Party became known as *Conservative*, a name traditionally believed to have been invented by John Wilson Croker in 1830 and to have been generally adopted about the time of the passing of the Reform Act of 1832 to indicate that the preservation of national institutions was the leading principle of the party. After the Home Rule crisis of 1886 the dissentient Liberals entered into a compact with the Conservatives, under which the latter undertook not to contest their seats, but a separate *Liberal Unionist* organization was maintained until 1912, when it was united with the Conservatives under the title of National Unionist Association of Conservative and Liberal Unionist Organizations, the members of which became known as *Unionists*.

The Labour Party.—Labour candidates for Parliament made their first appearance at the General Election of 1892, when there were 27 standing as "Labour" or "Liberal-Labour." Of this number John Burns (Battersea) and J. Keir Hardie (West Ham) were elected "Labour" Members of Parliament and 13 others as "Liberal-Labour" members. At the General Election of 1895 the number of successful candidates fell to 12, with a further fall to 11 at the election of 1900.

On Feb. 27, 1900, as a result of a resolution passed by the Trades Union Congress in the previous September, a Conference of Trade Union and Socialist bodies was held in the Memorial Hall, Farringdon Street, London, and an organization called the *Labour Representative Committee* was set up in order to establish a distinct Labour Group in Parliament, with its own whips, its own policy, and a readiness to co-operate with any party which may be engaged in promoting legislation in the direct interest of labour. In 1906 the L.R.C. became known as *The Labour Party*.

Parliamentary Whips

In order to secure the attendance of Members of a particular party in Parliament on all occasions, and particularly on the occasion of an important division, *Whips* (originally known as "Whippers-in") are appointed for the purpose. The written appeal or circular letter issued by them is also known as a "whip," its urgency being denoted by the number of times it is underlined. Neglect to respond to a three-lined whip, headed "Most Important," is tantamount to secession (at any rate temporarily) from the party.

Whips are officially recognized by Parliament and are provided with office accommodation in both Houses. Government Whips receive salaries from public funds, the Parliamentary (Patronage) Secretary to the Treasury (*Chief Whip in the Commons*) receiving £3,750; the Captain of the Gentlemen-at-Arms (*Chief Whip in the Lords*), the Captain of the Yeomen of the Guard (*Assistant do.*) and the first of the Junior Lords of the Treasury (*Deputy Chief Whip in the Commons*), each £2,200; the (Political) Lords in Waiting and the remaining Junior Lords of the Treasury, each £2,000.

The House of Lords

The *Government Whips* are: The Captain of the Honourable Corps of the Gentlemen at Arms (The Earl St. Aldwyn), the Captain of the Queen's Bodyguard of the Yeomen of the Guard (Viscount Goschen) and the (Political) Lords in Waiting (The Marquess of Lothian, Earl Ferrers and Lord Denham).

The *Labour Whips* are: The Earl of Lucan (*Chief Whip*); The Lords Burden and Shepherd.

The *Liberal Whip* is The Lord Amulree.

The House of Commons

The *Government Whips* are: The Parliamentary (Patronage) Secretary to the Treasury (*Chief Whip*) and the Junior Lords of the Treasury. *Assistant Whips* (who are unpaid) are also usually appointed.

The *Labour Whips* are Rt. Hon. H. W. Bowden (*Chief Whip*); G. H. R. Rogers; C. A. Howell; G. M. Lawson; S. Irving; E. C. Redhead; I. Davies; J. McCann; A. D. Broughton; C. F. Grey.

The *Liberal National Whip* is Sir Herbert Walter Butcher, Bt.

The Liberal Whip is E. R. Lubbock.

SCOTTISH REPRESENTATIVE PEERS

(Elected at the Palace of Holyroodhouse, Oct, 1959).

Sixteen Representative Peers are elected for each Parliament by the entire adult Peerage of Scotland specially convened for that purpose.

Duke of Atholl.	Lord Forbes.
Earl of Caithness.	Lord Saltoun.
Earl of Perth.	Lord Sempill.
Earl of Haddington.	Lord Balfour of Burleigh.
Earl of Airlie.	
Earl of Selkirk.	Lord Fairfax of Cameron.
Earl of Mar and Kellie.	
Earl of Northesk.	Lord Polwarth.
Earl of Dundonald.	Lord Sinclair.

The *Peerage Act*, 1963, abolished Scottish Representative Peers.

IRISH REPRESENTATIVE PEERS

No elections were held after the passing of the Government of Ireland Act in 1920, and the last Irish Representative Peer (the 4th Earl of Kilmorey) died in 1961.

PARLIAMENTS SINCE 1802

Assembled	Dissolved	Duration yrs.	m.	d.
	George III			
1802 Oct. 29	1806 Oct. 25	3	11	26
1806 Dec. 15	1807 April 29	0	4	14
1807 June 22	1812 Sept. 29	5	3	7
1812 Nov. 24	1818 June 10	5	6	16
1819 Jan. 14	1820 Feb. 29	1	1	15
	George IV			
1820 April 23	1826 June 2	6	1	10
1826 Nov. 14	1830 July 24	3	8	10
	William IV			
1830 Oct. 26	1831 April 22	0	5	27
1831 June 14	1832 Dec. 3	1	5	19
1833 Jan. 29	1834 Dec. 30	1	11	1
1835 Feb. 19	1837 July 17	2	4	28
	Victoria			
1837 Nov. 15	1841 June 23	3	7	8
1841 Aug. 19	1847 July 23	5	11	4
1847 Nov. 18	1852 July 1	4	7	13
1852 Nov. 4	1857 March 21	4	4	17
1857 April 30	1859 April 23	1	11	23
1859 May 31	1865 July 6	6	1	6
1866 Feb. 1	1868 Nov. 11	2	9	10
1868 Dec. 10	1874 Jan. 26	5	1	16
1874 March 5	1880 March 25	6	0	20
1880 April 29	1885 Nov. 18	5	6	20
1886 Jan. 12	1886 June 26	0	5	14
1886 Aug. 5	1892 June 28	5	10	24
1892 Aug. 4	1895 July 9	2	11	5
1895 Aug. 12	1900 Sept. 25	5	1	14
	Victoria and Edward VII			
1900 Dec. 3	1906 Jan. 8	5	1	6
	Edward VII			
1906 Feb. 13	1910 Jan. 15	3	11	2
	Edward VII and George V			
1910 Feb. 15	1910 Nov. 28	0	9	13
	George V			
1911 Jan. 31	1918 Nov. 25	7	9	25
1919 Feb. 4	1922 Oct. 26	3	8	22
1922 Nov. 20	1923 Nov. 16	0	11	27
1924 Jan. 8	1924 Oct. 9	0	9	1
1924 Dec. 2	1929 May 10	4	5	7
1929 June 25	1931 Oct. 6	2	3	11
1931 Nov. 3	1935 Oct. 25	3	11	22
	George V, Edward VIII and *George VI*			
1935 Nov. 16	1945 June 15	9	6	25
	George VI			
1945 Aug. 1	1950 Feb. 3	4	6	3
1950 March 1	1951 Oct. 5	1	7	4
	George VI and Elizabeth II			
1951 Oct. 31	1955 May 6	3	6	6
	Elizabeth II			
1955 June 9	1959 Sept. 18	4	3	9
1959 Oct. 27	..			

MAJORITIES IN THE HOUSE OF COMMONS

(*Since the Reform Bill*, 1832)

Year	Party	Majority
1833	*Whig*	307
1835	*Whig*	107
1837	*Whig*	51
1841	*Conservative*	81
1847	*Whig*	1
1852	*Liberal*	13
1857	*Liberal*	79
1859	*Liberal*	43
1865	*Liberal*	67
1868	*Liberal*	128
1874	*Conservative*	46
1880	*Liberal*	62
1885	*Liberal* (84) and *Irish Nationalist* (82)	166
1886	*Unionist*	114
1892	*Liberal*	40
1895	*Unionist*	152
1900	*Unionist*	134
1906	*Liberal*	356
1910 (Jan.)	*Liberal*	124
1910 (Dec.)	*Liberal*	126
1918	*Coalition*	263
1922	*Conservative*	79
1923	No Majority.	
1924	*Conservative*	225
1929	No Majority.	
1931	*National Government*	425
1935	*National Government*	247
1945	*Labour*	186
1950	*Labour*	8
1951	*Conservative*	16
1955	*Conservative*	59
1959	*Conservative*	100

SPEAKERS OF THE COMMONS SINCE 1660

PARLIAMENT OF ENGLAND.

1660. Sir H. Grimston.	1685. Sir John Trevor.
1661. Sir E. Turner.	1688. H. Powle.
1673. Sir J. Charlton.	1694. Paul Foley.
1673. Edwd. Seymour.	1698. Sir T. Lyttleton.
1678. Sir Robt. Sawyer.	1700. Robert Harley (*Earl of Oxford and Mortimer*).
1679. Serjeant William Gregory.	1702. John Smith.
1680. W. Williams.	

PARLIAMENT OF GREAT BRITAIN.

1708 Sir Richard Onslow (*Lord Onslow*).	1761. Sir John Cust.
1710. Wm. Bromley.	1770. Sir F. Norton.
1713. Sir Th. Hanmer.	1780. C. W. Cornwall.
1715. Spencer Compton (*Earl of Wilmington*).	1788. Hon. W. Grenville (*Lord Grenville*).
1727. Arthur Onslow.	1789. Henry Addington (*Viscount Sidmouth*).

PARLIAMENT OF UNITED KINGDOM.

1801. Sir John Mitford (*Lord Redesdale*).
1802. Charles Abbot (*Lord Colchester*).
1817. Charles M. Sutton (*Viscount Canterbury*)
1835. James Abercromby (*Lord Dunfermline*).
1839. Charles Shaw-Lefevre (*Viscount Eversley*).
1857. J. Evelyn Denison (*Viscount Ossington*).
1872. Sir H. W. B. Brand (*Viscount Hampden*).
1884. Arthur Wellesley Peel (*Viscount Peel*).
1895. William Court Gully (*Viscount Selby*).
1905. James W. Lowther (*Viscount Ullswater*).
1921. John Henry Whitley.
1928. Hon. Edward Algernon FitzRoy.
1943. Col. D. Clifton Brown (*Viscount Ruffside*).
1951. William Shepherd Morrison (*Viscount Dunrossil*).
1959. Sir Harry Hylton-Foster.

WOMEN MEMBERS OF PARLIAMENT

A movement to grant parliamentary franchise to women was supported in the mid-nineteenth century by Richard Cobden, Benjamin Disraeli and John Stuart Mill, but the vote was not accorded to women until 1918, although they had been included in the County Councils electorate by the Local Government Act of 1888. After a *Speaker's Conference* of all parties, which reported in favour of a limited form of women's suffrage, a clause enfranchising women was carried in both Houses and the *Parliament (Qualification of Women) Act* containing the clause which removed the sex disqualification for membership of the House of Commons, and conferred the franchise on women at the age of 30, received the Royal Assent in 1918. A further Act of 1928 granted them the vote on the same terms as men at the age of 21. Twenty-five women were elected at the 1959 Election (13 Labour, 11 Conservative and 1 Ulster Unionist), 2 fewer than at the Dissolution. One more woman Conservative member has since been returned at a by-election, but there is now one Labour woman member fewer.

FORFEITED DEPOSITS

Candidates at parliamentary elections who fail to obtain more than one-eighth of the total votes cast in their constituencies forfeit the deposit of £150 which all candidates must lodge. This law has been in force since the 1918 election.

Deposits forfeited at the 1959 Election totalled 116, 16 more than in 1951. Deposits were lost by 55 Liberal candidates, 17 Communists, 14 Welsh Nationalists, 7 Sinn Fein, 3 Scottish Nationalists, 2 Conservatives, 1 Labour and 17 others. Seventeen out of 18 Communist candidates forfeited their deposits. In 1950 the record number of 443 deposits was lost.

THE INTER-PARLIAMENTARY UNION

6 Rue Constantin, Geneva, Switzerland.

The Inter-Parliamentary Union has been in existence since 1889; originally started to popularize the idea of International Arbitration, it achieved its object very substantially in helping to create the Permanent Court of Arbitration by the First Hague Conference and to bring about the convocation of the Second Conference of The Hague. In 1945, the Union resumed work on all questions connected with peace and reconstruction, which have been studied under various aspects. Some of them are as follows:—

The development of international law; economic development; national sovereignty; principles of international morality; social problems; immigration and emigration; intellectual relations.

In addition to member groups in national Parliaments, the Union works largely through standing study committees, which meet each Spring, and annual plenary conferences, which meet in the late summer.

BRITISH GROUP.

Hon. Presidents, The Lord Chancellor; Mr. Speaker.
President, The Rt. Hon. Harold Macmillan, M.P.
Vice-Presidents, The Marquess of Salisbury, K.G.; The Earl of Scarbrough, K.G.; The Rt. Hon. J. S. B. Lloyd, C.H., C.B.E., T.D., Q.C., M.P.; The Earl of Home, P.C., K.T.; The Rt. Hon. J. H. Wilson, M.P.
Chairman, Sir Herbert Butcher, Bt., M.P.
Secretary, Maj-Gen. W. A. Dimoline, C.B., C.M.G., C.B.E., D.S.O., M.C.

COMMONWEALTH PARLIAMENTARY ASSOCIATION

The Commonwealth Parliamentary Association was formed under the title "Empire Parliamentary Association" in 1911, Its object was, then as now, to facilitate the exchange of information, closer understanding and more frequent intercourse between those engaged in the parliamentary government of the Commonwealth. In 1949, the Association was reorganized as the Commonwealth Parliamentary Association, and a General Council was instituted as the governing body.

The Association now consists of fifteen main branches in the Parliaments of the self-governing countries of the Commonwealth—the United Kingdom, Canada, Australia, New Zealand, India, Pakistan, Ceylon, Ghana, the Federation of Malaya, the Federation of Nigeria, Sierra Leone, Tanganyika, Jamaica, Trinidad and Tobago and Uganda—and three auxiliary branches, in the Parliaments of the Federation of Rhodesia and Nyasaland, Malta and Singapore. There are also branches in State, Provincial and Territorial Legislatures, as well as in the Parliaments of Northern Ireland, the Isle of Man, and the States of Jersey. In addition, there are 22 affiliated branches in Legislatures of those Commonwealth countries which are not completely self-governing, and 14 subsidiary branches in colonial territories making a total of 90 branches. Commonwealth Parliamentary Conferences and General Meetings are held every year in different countries of the Commonwealth.

Chairman of the General Council, Dr. Hon. Lim Swee Aun (Federation of Malaya).
Secretary-General, R. V. Vanderfelt, O.B.E., Houses of Parliament, S.W.1.
Secretary, United Kingdom Branch, P. G. Molloy, M.C., Westminster Hall, Houses of Parliament, S.W.1.

Date	Prime Minister	Exchequer	Lord President	Foreign	Home	Commonwealth*	Board of Trade
1929 June 8.......	J. R. MacDonald	P. Snowden	Parmoor	A. Henderson	J. R. Clynes	J. H. Thomas, *D* Passfield, *C*	W. Graham
1931 Aug. 25.....	J. R. MacDonald	P. Snowden N. Chamberlain	S. Baldwin	Reading Sir J. Simon	Sir H. Samuel Sir J. Gilmour	J. H. Thomas, *D* Sir P. C.-Lister, *C*	Sir P. C.- Lister W. Runciman
1935 June 7.......	S. Baldwin	N. Chamberlain	J. R. MacDonald	Sir S. Hoare	Sir J. Simon	J. H. Thomas, *D* M. MacDonald, *C*	W. Runciman
1935 Nov. 22.....	S. Baldwin	N. Chamberlain	J. R. MacDonald	Sir S. Hoare A. Eden	Sir J. Simon	M. MacDonald, *D* J. H. Thomas, *C* W. Ormsby- Gore, *C*	W. Runciman
1937 May 28......	N. Chamberlain	Sir J. Simon	Halifax Hailsham Runciman	A. Eden Halifax	Sir S. Hoare	W. O.-Gore, *C* Stanley, *D* M. MacDonald, *C* Sir T. Inskip, *D*	O. Stanley
1939 Sept. 3......	N. Chamberlain	Sir J. Simon	Stanhope	Halifax	Sir J. Anderson	A. Eden, *D* M. MacDonald, *C*	O. Stanley Sir A. Duncan
1940 May 11......	W. S. Churchill	Sir K. Wood Sir J. Anderson	N. Chamberlain Sir J. Anderson C. R. Attlee	Halifax A. Eden	Sir J. Anderson H. Morrison	Caldecote, *D* Cranborne, *D* Lloyd, *C* Moyne, *C* C. R. Attlee, *D* Cranborne, *D* O. Stanley, *C*	Sir A. Duncan O. Lyttelton Sir A. Duncan H. Dalton J. J. Llewellin
1945 May 23......	W. S. Churchill	Sir J. Anderson	Woolton	A. Eden	Sir D. Somervell	Cranborne, *D* O. Stanley, *C*	O. Lyttelton
1945 July 26......	C. R. Attlee	H. Dalton Sir S. Cripps H. T. N. Gaitskell	H. Morrison Addison	E. Bevin H. Morrison	J. Chuter Ede	Addison, *D* G. H. Hall, *C* A. C. Jones, *C* P. Noel Baker, *C-R* P. C. Gordon- Walker, *C-R*	Sir S. Cripps J. H. Wilson Sir H. Shawcross
1951 Oct. 26......	W. S. Churchill	R. A. Butler	Woolton Salisbury	Sir A. Eden	Sir D. Maxwell Fyfe G. Lloyd-George	O. Lyttelton, *C* A.T.Lennox-Boyd Ismay, *C-R* [*C* Salisbury, *C-R* Swinton, *C-R*	G. E. P. Thorney- croft
1955 April 7......	Sir A. Eden	R. A. Butler H. Macmillan	Salisbury	H. Macmillan J. S. B. Lloyd	G. Lloyd-George	Home, *C-R* [*C* A.T.Lennox-Boyd	G. E. P. Thorney- croft.
1957 Jan. 13......	H. Macmillan	G. E. P. Thorney- croft D. H-Amory J. S. B. Lloyd R. Maudling	Salisbury Home Hailsham Home Hailsham	J. S. B. Lloyd Home	R. A. Butler H. Brooke	Home, *C-R* [*C* A.T.Lennox-Boyd I. N. Macleod, *C* D. Sandys, *C-R* R. Maudling, *C* D.Sandys, *C-R* &*C*	Sir D. Eccles R. Maudling F. J. Errol

* *C* = Secretary of State for the Colonies (1854); *D* = for the Dominions (1925–1947); *C-R* = for Commonwealth Relations (1947)

Date	Ld. Chancellor	Admiralty (1673)	War (1794)	Air (1922)	Health (1854)	Agriculture (1890)	Education (1857)
1929 June 8	Sankey	A. V. Alexander	T. Shaw	Thomson Amulree	A. Greenwood	N. Buxton C. Addison	Sir C. P. Trevelyan H. B. Lees-Smith
1931 Aug. 25	Sankey	Sir A. Chamber-lain Sir B. E.-Monsell	Crewe Hailsham	Amulree Londonderry	N. Chamberlain Sir E. Hilton-Young	Sir J. Gilmour W. E. Elliot	Sir D. Maclean Irwin
1935 June 7	Hailsham	Sir B. E.-Monsell	Halifax	Sir P. C.-Lister	Sir K. Wood	W. E. Elliot	O. Stanley
1935 Nov. 22	Hailsham	Monsell Sir S. Hoare	A. Duff-Cooper	Swinton	Sir K. Wood	W. S. Morrison	O. Stanley
1937 May 28	Hailsham Maugham	A. Duff-Cooper Stanhope	L. Hore-Belisha	Swinton Sir K. Wood	Sir K. Wood W. E. Elliot	W. S. Morrison Sir R. Dorman-Smith	Stanhope De la Warr
1939 Sept. 3	Caldecote	W. S. Churchill	L. Hore-Belisha O. Stanley	Sir K. Wood Sir S. Hoare	W. E. Elliot	Sir R. Dorman-Smith	De La Warr
1940 May 11	Simon	A. V. Alexander	A. Eden D. Margesson Sir J. Grigg	Sir A. Sinclair	M. MacDonald E. Brown H. U. Willink	R. S. Hudson	H. Ramsbotham R. A. Butler
1945 May 23	Simon	B. Bracken	Sir J. Grigg	H. Macmillan	H. U. Willink	R. S. Hudson	R. K. Law
1945 July 26	Jowitt	A. V. Alexander Hall Pakenham	J. J. Lawson F. J. Bellenger E. Shinwell E. J. St. L. Strachey	Stansgate P. J. Noel Baker A. Henderson	A. Bevan H. A. Marquand	T. Williams	Ellen Wilkinson G. Tomlinson
1951 October 26	Simonds Kilmuir	J. P. L. Thomas	A. H. Head	De L'Isle and Dudley	H. F. C. Crook-shank I. N. Macleod	Sir T. L. Dugdale D. Heathcoat-Amory	Florence Hors-brugh Sir D. Eccles
1955 April 7	Kilmuir	J. P. L. Thomas (Cilcennin) Hailsham	A. H. Head J. H. Hare	De L'Isle and Dudley E. N. C. Birch	I. N. Macleod R. H. Turton	D. Heathcoat-Amory	Sir D. Eccles
1957 Jan. 13	Kilmuir Dilhorne	Selkirk Carrington	J. H. Hare A. C. J. Soames J. D. Profumo J. B. Godber	G. R. Ward J. Amery H. C. P. J. Fraser	D. F. Vosper D. C. Walker-Smith J. E. Powell	D. Heathcoat-Amory J. H. Hare A. C. J. Soames	Hailsham G. W. Lloyd Sir D. Eccles Sir E. Boyle

PRIME MINISTERS.—Sir Robert Walpole, First Lord of the Treasury and Chancellor of the Exchequer from 1721 to 1742, rose to a power no Minister had ever before attained and was the subject of a protest entered in the journal of the House of Lords, the grievance being that the Sovereign should repose confidence in any one Minister to the exclusion od the remainder. He is usually regarded as the first Prime Minister and the eminence he achieved was repeated in the reign of George III, when the illness of the Sovereign necessitated the appearance of a leading and presiding minister, the Prince Regent not taking the Sovereign's place in this respect. After the Regency the Sovereign ceased to preside at Cabinet Meetings and the leading Minister became, in fact, Prime Minister.

(October 24, 1963)

THE CABINET

Prime Minister and First Lord of the Treasury, THE RT. HON. SIR ALEXANDER FREDERICK DOUGLAS-HOME, K.T., *born* July 2, 1903.
Secretary of State for Foreign Affairs, The Rt. Hon. Richard Austen Butler, C.H., M.P., *born* Dec. 9, 1902.
Chancellor of the Exchequer, The Rt. Hon. Reginald Maudling, M.P., *born* March 7, 1917.
Lord President of the Council and Minister for Science, The Rt. Hon. Visct. Hailsham, Q.C., *born* Oct. 9, 1907.
Lord High Chancellor, The Rt. Hon. Lord Dilhorne, *born* Aug. 1, 1905.
Lord Privy Seal and Leader of the House of Commons, The Rt. Hon. (John) Selwyn (Brooke) Lloyd, C.H., C.B.E., T.D., Q.C., M.P., *born* July 28, 1904.
Secretary of State for the Home Department, The Rt. Hon. Henry Brooke, M.P., *born* April 9, 1903.
Chancellor of the Duchy of Lancaster, The Rt. Hon. John Hugh Hare, O.B.E., *born* Jan. 22, 1911.
Chief Secretary to the Treasury and Paymaster-General, The Rt. Hon. J. A. Boyd-Carpenter, M.P., *b.* June 2, 1908.
Secretary of State for Commonwealth Relations and for the Colonies, The Rt. Hon. Duncan Sandys, M.P., *born* Jan. 24, 1908.
Secretary of State for Scotland, The Rt. Hon. Michael Antony Cristobal Noble, M.P., *born* March 19, 1913.
Secretary of State for Industry, Trade and Regional Development and President of the Board of Trade, The Rt. Hon. Edward Richard George Heath, M.B.E., M.P., *born* July 9, 1916.
Minister of Labour, The Rt. Hon. Joseph Bradshaw Godber, M.P., *born* March 17, 1914.
Minister of Housing and Local Government and Minister for Welsh Affairs, The Rt. Hon. Sir Keith Sinjohn Joseph, Bt., M.P., *born* Jan. 17, 1918.
Minister of Agriculture, Fisheries and Food, The Rt. Hon. Christopher Soames, C.B.E., M.P., *b.* Oct. 12, 1920.
Minister of Education, The Rt. Hon. Sir Edward Charles Gurney Boyle, Bt., M.P., *born* Aug. 31, 1923.
Minister of Transport, The Rt. Hon. Ernest Marples, M.P., *born* Dec. 9, 1907.
Minister of Defence, The Rt. Hon. (George Edward) Peter Thorneycroft, M.P., *born* July 26, 1909.
Minister of Health, The Rt. Hon. Anthony Perrinott Lysberg Barber, T.D., M.P., *born* July 4, 1920.
Minister of Power, The Rt. Hon. Frederick James Erroll, M.P., *born* May 27, 1914.
Minister of Public Building and Works, The Rt. Hon. Geoffrey Rippon, M.P., *born* May 28, 1924.
Minister without Portfolio and Leader of the House of Lords, The Rt. Hon. Lord Carrington, K.C.M.G., M.C., *born* June 6, 1919.
Minister without Portfolio, The Rt. Hon. William Francis Deedes, M.C., M.P., *born* June 1, 1918.

MINISTERS OF CABINET RANK

First Lord of the Admiralty, The Rt. Hon. Earl Jellicoe, D.S.O., M.C., *born* April 4, 1918.
Secretary of State for War, The Rt. Hon. James Edward Ramsden, M.P., *born* Nov. 1, 1923.
Secretary of State for Air, The Rt. Hon. Hugh Charles Patrick Joseph Fraser, M.B.E., M.P., *born* Jan. 23, 1918.
Ministers of State (Foreign Affairs), The Rt. Hon. the Earl of Dundee, *born* May 3, 1902; Peter John Mitchell Thomas, M.P., *born* July 31, 1920.
Minister of State (Colonial Affairs), The Marquess of Lansdowne, *born* Nov. 27, 1912.
Minister of State (Scottish Office), The Rt. Hon. Lord Craigton, C.B.E., *born* Sept. 3, 1904.
Ministers of State (Board of Trade), Rt. Hon. Niall Malcolm Stewart Macpherson, *born* Aug. 3, 1908; Edward Dillon Lott du Cann, M.P., *born* May 28, 1924.
Minister of State (Welsh Affairs), The Rt. Hon. Lord Brecon, *born* August 14, 1905.
Minister of State (Technical Co-operation), The Rt. Hon. Robert Carr, M.P., *born* Nov. 11, 1916.
Minister of State (Home Affairs), The Lord Derwent, *born* Oct. 26, 1901.
Minister of State (Commonwealth Relations), The Duke of Devonshire, M.C., *born* Jan. 2, 1920.
Minister of Pensions and National Insurance, The Rt. Hon. Richard Frederick Wood, M.P., *born* Oct. 5, 1920.
Postmaster General, The Rt. Hon. John Reginald Bevins, M.P., *born* August 20, 1908.
Minister of Aviation, The Rt. Hon. Julian Amery, M.P., *born* March 27, 1919.

PARLIAMENTARY UNDER SECRETARIES AND OTHER MINISTERS

Attorney-General, Rt. Hon. Sir John Hobson, O.B.E., T.D., Q.C., M.P.
Solicitor-General, Sir Peter Rawlinson, Q.C., M.P.
Lord Advocate, Rt. Hon. I. H. Shearer, Q.C.
Solicitor-General for Scotland, D. C. Anderson, V.R.D., Q.C.
Admiralty (Civil Lord), J. A. Hay, M.P.
Agriculture and Fisheries (Joint), The Lord St. Oswald, M.C.; J. S. R. Scott-Hopkins, M.P.
Air, J. E. Ridsdale, M.P.
Aviation, H. N. Marten, M.P.
Colonies, N. T. L. Fisher, M.C., M.P.
Commonwealth Relations (Joint), J. D. R. T. Tilney, T.D., M.P.; R. P. Hornby, M.P.
Education, C. J. Chataway, M.P.
Foreign, P. H. B. O. Smithers, V.R.D., D.Phil., M.P.
Health (Joint), B. R. Braine, M.P.; The Lord Newton.
Home (Joint), Hon. C. M. Woodhouse, D.S.O., O.B.E., M.P.; Miss I. M. P. Pike, M.P.
Housing and Local Govt. (Joint), Capt. F. V. Corfield, M.P.; The Lord Hastings.
Labour, W. S. I. Whitelaw, M.C., M.P.
Pensions and National Insurance (Joint), Mrs. M. H. Thatcher, M.P.; Lt.-Cdr. S. L. C. Maydon, D.S.O., D.S.C., M.P.
Post Office (Asst. P.M.G.), R. L. Mawby, M.P.
Power, J. W. W. Peyton, M.P.
Public Building and Works, R. C. Sharples, O.B.E., M.C., M.P.
Science, The Earl of Bessborough.
Scottish Office (Joint), R. C. Brooman-White, M.P.; The Lady Tweedsmuir, M.P.
Trade, D. E. C. Price, M.P.
Transport (Joint), The Lord Chesham; Vice-Adm. J. Hughes-Hallett, C.B., D.S.O., M.P.; Hon. T. G. D. Galbraith, M.P.
Treasury, Rt. Hon. M. Redmayne, D.S.O., M.P.; (*do.*) *Financial Secretary*, A. Green, M.P.; (*do.*) *Economic Secretary*, M. V. Macmillan, M.P.
Junior Lords, J. E. B. Hill, M.P.; W. J. Peel, M.P.; F. F. Pearson, M.B.E., M.P.; G. T. C. Campbell, M.C., M.P.; M. C. Hamilton, M.P.
War Office, P. M. Kirk, M.P.

Leader of the Opposition, The Rt. Hon. James Harold Wilson, O.B.E., M.P., *born* March 11, 1916.

NOTE.—The page giving the names of holders of certain Ministerial offices since 1940 has been temporarily displaced from the Almanack to afford space for the above information. Several index entries are therefore superseded.

MR. MACMILLAN'S ADMINISTRATION
(As reconstructed in July 1962, with subsequent minor changes)

THE CABINET

Prime Minister and First Lord of the Treasury, THE RT. HON. HAROLD MACMILLAN, M.P., *born* Feb. 10, 1894.
First Secretary of State, The Rt. Hon. Richard Austen Butler, C.H., M.P., *born* Dec. 9, 1902.
Secretary of State for Foreign Affairs, The Rt. Hon. The Earl of Home, K.T. *born* July 2, 1903.
Chancellor of the Exchequer, The Rt. Hon. Reginald Maudling, M.P., *born* March 7, 1917.
Lord President of the Council, Minister for Science and Leader of the House of Lords, The Rt. Hon. Viscount Hailsham, Q.C., *born* Oct. 9, 1907.
Lord High Chancellor, The Rt. Hon. Lord Dilhorne, *born* Aug. 1, 1905.
Lord Privy Seal, The Rt. Hon. Edward Richard George Heath, M.B.E., M.P., *born* July 9, 1916.
Secretary of State for the Home Department, The Rt. Hon. Henry Brooke, M.P., *born* April 9, 1903.
Chancellor of the Duchy of Lancaster and Leader of the House of Commons, The Rt. Hon. Iain Norman Macleod, M.P., *born* Nov. 11, 1913.
Chief Secretary to the Treasury and Paymaster-General, The Rt. Hon. John Archibald Boyd-Carpenter, M.P., *born* June 2, 1908.
Secretary of State for Commonwealth Relations and for the Colonies, The Rt. Hon. Duncan Sandys, M.P., *born* Jan. 24, 1908.
Secretary of State for Scotland, The Rt. Hon. Michael Antony Cristobal Noble, M.P., *born* March 19, 1913.
Minister of Labour, The Rt. Hon. John Hugh Hare, O.B.E., M.P., *born* Jan. 22, 1911.
President of the Board of Trade, The Rt. Hon. Frederick James Erroll, M.P., *born* May 27, 1914.
Minister of Housing and Local Government and Minister for Welsh Affairs, The Rt. Hon. Sir Keith Sinjohn Joseph, Bt., M.P., *born* Jan. 17, 1918.
Minister of Agriculture, Fisheries and Food, The Rt. Hon. (Arthur) Christopher (John) Soames, C.B.E., M.P., *born* Oct. 12, 1920.
Minister of Education, The Rt. Hon. Sir Edward Charles Gurney Boyle, Bt., M.P., *born* Aug. 31, 1923.
Minister of Transport, The Rt. Hon. Ernest Marples, M.P., *born* Dec. 9, 1907.
Minister of Defence, The Rt. Hon. (George Edward) Peter Thorneycroft, M.P., *born* July 26, 1909.
Minister of Health, The Rt. Hon. (John) Enoch Powell, M.B.E., M.P., *born* June 16, 1912.
Minister without Portfolio, The Rt. Hon. William Francis Deedes, M.C., M.P., *born* June 1, 1918.

MINISTERS OF CABINET RANK

First Lord of the Admiralty, The Rt. Hon. Lord Carrington, K.C.M.G., M.C., *born* June 6, 1919.
Secretary of State for War, The Rt. Hon. Joseph Bradshaw Godber, M.P., *born* March 17, 1914.
Secretary of State for Air, The Rt. Hon. Hugh Charles Patrick Joseph Fraser, M.B.E., M.P., *born* Jan. 23, 1918.
Ministers of State (Foreign Affairs), The Rt. Hon. the Earl of Dundee, *born* May 3, 1902; Peter John Mitchell Thomas, M.P., *born* July 31, 1920.
Minister of State (Colonial Affairs), The Marquess of Lansdowne, *born* Nov. 27, 1912.
Minister of State (Scottish Office), The Rt. Hon. Lord Craigton, C.B.E., *born* Sept. 3, 1904.
Ministers of State (Board of Trade), Alan Green, M.P., *born* Sept. 29, 1911; The Lord Derwent, *born* Oct. 26, 1901.
Minister of State (Welsh Affairs), The Rt. Hon. Lord Brecon, *born* August 14, 1905.
Minister of State (Technical Co-operation). The Rt. Hon. Robert Carr, M.P., *born* Nov. 11, 1916.
Minister of State (Home Affairs), The Earl Jellicoe, D.S.O., M.C., *born* April 4, 1918.
Minister of State (Commonwealth Relations), The Duke of Devonshire, M.C., *born* Jan. 2, 1920.
Minister of Pensions and National Insurance, The Rt. Hon. N. M. S. Macpherson, M.P., *born* Aug. 3, 1908.
Postmaster-General, The Rt. Hon. John Reginald Bevins, M.P., *born* August 20, 1908.
Minister of Public Building and Works, The Rt. Hon. Geoffrey Rippon, M.P., *b.* May 28, 1924.
Minister of Power, The Rt. Hon. Richard Frederick Wood, M.P., *born* Oct. 5, 1920.
Minister of Aviation, The Rt. Hon. Julian Amery, M.P., *born* March 27, 1919.

PARLIAMENTARY UNDER SECRETARIES AND OTHER MINISTERS

Attorney-General, Rt. Hon. Sir John Hobson, O.B.E., T.D., Q.C., M.P.
Solicitor-General, Sir Peter Rawlinson, Q.C., M.P.
Lord Advocate, Rt. Hon. I. H. Shearer, Q.C.
Solicitor-General for Scotland, D. C. Anderson, V.R.D., Q.C.
Admiralty (Civil Lord), J. A. Hay, M.P.
Agriculture and Fisheries (Joint), The Lord St. Oswald, M.C.; J. S. R. Scott-Hopkins, M.P.
Air, J. E. Ridsdale, M.P.
Aviation, H. N. Marten, M.P.
Colonies, N. T. L. Fisher, M.C., M.P.
Commonwealth Relations, J. D. R. T. Tilney, T.D., M.P.
Education, C. J. Chataway, M.P.
Foreign, P. H. B. O. Smithers, V.R.D., D.Phil., M.P.
Health (Joint), B. R. Braine, M.P.; The Lord Newton.
Home (Joint), Hon. C. M. Woodhouse, D.S.O., O.B.E., M.P.; Miss I. M. P. Pike, M.P.
Housing and Local Govt. (Joint), Capt. F. V. Corfield, M.P.; The Lord Hastings.
Labour, W. S. I. Whitelaw, M.C., M.P.
Pensions and National Insurance (Joint), Mrs. M. H. Thatcher, M.P.; Lt.-Cdr. S. L. C. Maydon, D.S.O., D.S.C., M.P.
Post Office (Asst. P.M.G.), R. L. Mawby, M.P.
Power, J. W. W. Peyton, M.P.
Public Building and Works, R. C. Sharples, O.B.E., M.C., M.P.
Science, D. K. Freeth, M.P.
Scottish Office (Joint), R. C. Brooman-White, M.P.; The Lady Tweedsmuir, M.P; J. A. Stodart, M.P.
Trade, D. E. C. Price, M.P.
Transport (Joint), The Lord Chesham; Vice-Adm. J. Hughes-Hallett, C.B., D.S.O., M.P.; Hon. T. G. D. Galbraith, M.P.
Treasury, Rt. Hon. M. Redmayne, D.S.O., M.P.; (do.) *Financial Secretary*, A. P. L. Barber, T.D., M.P.; (do.) *Economic Secretary*, E. D. L. du Cann, M.P.
Junior Lords, J. E. B. Hill, M.P.; W. J. Peel, M.P.; F. F. Pearson, M.B.E., M.P.; G. T. C. Campbell, M.C., M.P.; M. C. Hamilton, M.P.
War Office, J. E. Ramsden, M.P.

For the October, 1963 Ministry, see previous page.

THE HOUSES OF PARLIAMENT

Parliament originated in the demand of the King's Great Council, consisting of prelates, earls and barons, that there should be discussion about the affairs of state and in 1242 the word "parliament" was first used in an official document to describe such an assembly. In 1265 Simon de Montfort in the king's name summoned to a parliament not only the great men but also for the first time two representatives elected by each county, city and town, and by the end of the reign of Edward I it had become usual to summon the Commons.

The House of Lords is the ultimate Court of Appeal for all Courts in Great Britain and Northern Ireland, except for criminal cases in Scotland. The Lords surrendered the ancient right of peers to be tried for treason or felony by their peers in 1948. Each House has the right to control its own internal proceedings and to commit for contempt.

The Commons claim exclusive control in respect of national taxation and expenditure and in respect of local rates and charges upon them. Bills such as the Finance Bill, which imposes taxation, and the Consolidated Fund Bills, which authorise expenditure, and are commonly known as Supply Bills, must begin in the Commons and have not been amended by the Lords in any respect in modern times. A bill of which the financial provisions are subsidiary may begin in the Lords; and the Commons may waive their rights in regards to Lords amendments affecting finance.

Normally a bill must be agreed to by both Houses before it receives the Royal Assent, but under the Parliament Acts, 1911 and 1948—(*a*) a bill which the Speaker has certified as a Money Bill, i.e. as concerned solely with national taxation, expenditure or borrowing, if not agreed to by the Lords within one month of its being sent to them, receives the Royal Assent and becomes law without their concurrence; (*b*) any other public bill (except one to extend the life of a Parliament) which has been passed by the Commons in two successive sessions and twice rejected by the Lords, receives the Royal Assent and becomes law, provided that one year has elapsed between its Second Reading in the first session and its Third Reading in the second session in the Commons.

The Parliament Act of 1911 also limited the duration of Parliament, if not previously dissolved, to 5 years. The term is reckoned from the date given on the writs for the new Parliament. During the War of 1914–18 the duration of Parliament was extended by successive Acts from 5 to 8 years, but a General Election was held before the end of the term finally prescribed and the Parliament which first met on Jan. 31, 1911, was dissolved on Nov. 25, 1918, fourteen days after the Armistice. At the outbreak of war in 1939 a similar course was followed and Parliament which first met on Nov. 26, 1935, was not dissolved until June 15, 1945.

Parliament is dissolved (as it is summoned) by the Sovereign, and until the passing of the Representation of the People Act (1867), Parliament was dissolved by the Demise of the Crown, but in that Act provision was made for its continuance to the normal duration, unless previously dissolved.

The longest recorded sitting of the House of Commons is 41 hours 30 minutes (from 4 p.m., Jan. 31 to 9.30 a.m. Feb. 2, 1881), that of the House of Lords is 11 hrs. 57 minutes (from 4.15 p.m. to 4.12 a.m. Nov. 1934).

Since 1803 reports of the proceedings of Parliament in open session have been published. From 1803–1888 these were known as *Hansard's Parliamentary Debates*, and in 1943 the word "Hansard" was restored to the title page. Copies are obtainable from H.M. Stationery Office and periodical issues are on sale throughout the country.

Payment of Members.—Members of the House of Lords are unpaid. They are entitled to re-imbursement of travelling expenses from their residence to the House in respct of regular attendance and repayment of expenses within a maximum of £3 3*s*. for each day of such attendance.

Since 1911 members of the House of Commons have received payments and travelling facilities, the payment of £400 being increased in 1937 to £600, and in 1946 to £1,000 per annum. Since 1957, members have received payment of £1,750 per annum; they are entitled to claim income tax relief on expenses incurred in the course of parliamentary duties. Members of Parliament contribute towards a Fund to provide pensions or grants to ex-members, their widows and orphans whose incomes are below certain limits; the income of the Fund in 1961–62 was £41,157 and expenditure grants £32,473. The Capital Account (1962) stood at £117,312. An Act was passed in 1957 enabling the Treasury to make an annual contribution to the fund. £22,000 was so contributed in 1962–63.

THE HOUSE OF LORDS

The House of Lords consists of some 900 Lords Spiritual and Temporal. The Lords Spiritual are the two Archbishops, the Bishops of London, Durham and Winchester, and the 21 senior Bishops from the remaining English sees. The Lords Temporal are: Peers by descent of England, Scotland, Great Britain or the United Kingdom, peers of new creation, Lords of Appeal in Ordinary (who are life peers), Peeresses in their own right, and Life Peers and Life Peeresses created under the Life Peerages Act, 1958. An Irish Peer not in the House of Lords is eligible for election as a member of the House of Commons for an English, Welsh or Scottish constituency.

THE HOUSE OF COMMONS

By the *Representation of the People Act* (1885) membership was increased from 658 (at which it had stood since 1801 through the *Act of Union with Ireland*) to 670, and by a similar Act (1918) it was increased to 707. By the *Government of Ireland Act* (1920) and the *Irish Free State Agreement Act* (1922) membership was decreased to 615, Irish representation being reduced from 105 to 13 members. By the *Representation of the People Act* of 1945 25 new constituencies were created, making the total 640; and by a similar Act of 1948 the total membership was reduced to 625. As the result of Orders in Council made in 1955 under the *House of Commons (Redistribution of Seats) Act*, 1949, the total membership has now been increased to 630.

Elected by	General Elections 1950 and 1951	General Elections 1955 and 1959
London Boroughs	43	42
English Boroughs	248	247
English Counties	215	222
Welsh Boroughs	10	10
Welsh Counties	26	26
Scottish Burghs	32	32
Scottish Counties	39	39
N. Irish Boroughs	4	4
N. Irish Counties	8	8
Total	625	630

THE PALACE OF WESTMINSTER

An ordinance issued in the reign of Richard II stated that "Parliament shall be holden or kepid wheresoever it pleaseth the King" and at the present day the Sovereign summons parliament to meet and prescribes the time and place of meeting. The royal palace at Westminster, built according to legend by Edward the Confessor, and enlarged by William the Conqueror (Westminster Hall being added by William Rufus) was the normal place of Parliament from about 1340. St. Stephen's Chapel (originally built for King Stephen) was used from 1547 for the meetings of the House of Commons, which had previously been held in the Chapter House or Refectory of Westminster Abbey. The House of Lords met in an apartment of the royal palace.

The disastrous fire of 1834 destroyed the whole palace, except Westminster Hall, and the present Houses of Parliament were erected on the site from the designs of Sir Charles Barry and Augustus Pugin, between the years 1840 and 1867, at a cost of £2,198,000.

The Victoria Tower of the House of Lords is 330 feet high and when Parliament is sitting the Union Jack flies from sunrise to sunset from its flag-staff. The clock tower of the House of Commons is 320 feet high and contains "Big Ben," the 13½-ton Hour Bell named after Sir Benjamin Hall, First Commissioner of Works when the original bell was cast in 1856. The dials of the clock are 22½ feet in diameter, the hands being 11 feet (hour) and 14 feet (minute) in length. The chimes and strike of "Big Ben" have achieved world-wide fame from broadcasting.

A light is displayed in the clock tower from sundown to sunrise during the hours the House is in session.

The Chamber of the House of Commons was destroyed by enemy action in 1941 and the foundation stone of a new building, from the designs of Sir Giles Gilbert Scott, was laid by the Speaker on May 26, 1948. The new Chamber was used for the first time on Oct. 26, 1950.

THE LORD CHANCELLOR

The Lord High Chancellor of England is (although not addressed as such) the Speaker of the House of Lords. Unlike the Speaker of the House of Commons, he takes part in debates and votes in divisions. He sits on one of the *Woolsacks*, couches covered with red cloth and stuffed with wool. If the Lord Chancellor wishes to address the House in any way except formally as Speaker, he leaves the Woolsack and steps towards his proper place as a peer, below the Royal Dukes.

PRIME MINISTER'S RESIDENCE

Number 10, Downing Street, S.W.1, is the official town residence of the Prime Minister, No. 11 of the Chancellor of the Exchequer and No. 12 is the office of the Government Whips. The street was named after Sir George Downing, Bt., soldier and diplomatist, who was M.P. for Morpeth from 1660 to 1684.

Chequers, a Tudor mansion in the Chilterns, about 3 miles from Princes Risborough, was presented together with a maintenance endowment by Lord and Lady Lee of Fareham in 1917 to serve, from Jan. 1, 1921, as a country residence for the Prime Minister of the day, the Chequers estate of 700 acres being added to the gift by Lord Lee in 1921. The mansion contains a famous collection of Cromwellian portraits and relics.

PRIME MINISTERS

Sir Robert Walpole, *Whig*, April 3, 1721.
Earl of Wilmington, *Whig*, Feb. 16, 1742.
Henry Pelham, *Whig*, Aug. 25, 1743.
Duke of Newcastle, *Whig*, May 18, 1754.
Duke of Devonshire, *Whig*, Nov. 16, 1756.
Duke of Newcastle, *Whig*, July 2, 1757.
Earl of Bute, *Tory*, May 28, 1762.
George Grenville, *Whig*, April 15, 1763.
Marquess of Rockingham, *Whig*, July 10, 1765.
Earl of Chatham, *Whig*, Aug. 2, 1766.
Duke of Grafton, *Whig*, Dec. 1767.
Lord North, *Tory*, Feb. 6, 1770.
Marquess of Rockingham, *Whig*, March 27, 1782.
Earl of Shelburne, *Whig*, July 13, 1782.
Duke of Portland, *Coalition*, April 4, 1783.
William Pitt, *Tory*, Dec. 7, 1783.
Henry Addington, *Tory*, March 21, 1801.
William Pitt, *Tory*, May 16, 1804.
Lord Grenville, *Whig*, Feb. 10, 1806.
Duke of Portland, *Tory*, March 31, 1807.
Spencer Perceval, *Tory*, Dec. 6, 1809.
Earl of Liverpool, *Tory*, June 16, 1812.
George Canning, *Tory*, April 30, 1827.
Viscount Goderich, *Tory*, Sept. 8, 1827.
Duke of Wellington, *Tory*, Jan. 26, 1828.
Earl Grey, *Whig*, Nov. 24, 1830.
Viscount Melbourne, *Whig*, July 13, 1834.
Sir Robert Peel, *Tory*, Dec. 26, 1834.
Viscount Melbourne, *Whig*, March 14, 1835.
Sir Robert Peel, *Tory*, Sept. 6, 1841.
Lord John Russell, *Whig*, July 6, 1846.
Earl of Derby, *Tory*, Feb. 28, 1852.
Earl of Aberdeen, *Peelite*, Dec. 28, 1852.
Viscount Palmerston, *Liberal*, Feb. 10, 1855.
Earl of Derby, *Conservative*, Feb. 25, 1858.
Viscount Palmerston, *Liberal*, June 13, 1858.
Earl Russell, *Liberal*, Nov. 6, 1865.
Earl of Derby, *Conservative*, July 6, 1866.
Benjamin Disraeli, *Conservative*, Feb. 27, 1868.
W. E. Gladstone, *Liberal*, Dec. 9, 1868.
Benjamin Disraeli, *Conservative*, Feb. 21, 1874.
W. E. Gladstone, *Liberal*, April 28, 1880.
Marquess of Salisbury, *Conservative*, June 24, 1885.
W. E. Gladstone, *Liberal*, Feb. 6, 1886.
Marquess of Salisbury, *Conservative*, Aug. 3, 1886.
W. E. Gladstone, *Liberal*, Aug. 18, 1892.
Earl of Rosebery, *Liberal*, March 3, 1894.
Marquess of Salisbury, *Conservative*, July 2, 1895.
A. J. Balfour, *Conservative*, July 12, 1902.
Sir H. Campbell-Bannerman, *Liberal*, Dec. 5, 1905.
H. H. Asquith, *Liberal*, April 8, 1908.
H. H. Asquith, *Coalition*, May 26, 1915.
D. Lloyd George, *Coalition*, Dec. 7, 1916.
A. Bonar Law, *Conservative*, Oct. 23, 1922.
S. Baldwin, *Conservative*, May 22, 1923.
J. R. MacDonald, *Labour*, Jan. 22, 1924.
S. Baldwin, *Conservative*, Nov. 4, 1924.
J. R. MacDonald, *Labour*, June 8, 1929.
J. R. MacDonald, *Coalition*, Aug. 25, 1931.
S. Baldwin, *Coalition*, June 7, 1935.
N. Chamberlain, *Coalition*, May 28, 1937.
W. S. Churchill, *Coalition*, May 11, 1940.
W. S. Churchill, *Conservative*, May, 23, 1945.
C. R. Attlee, *Labour*, July 26, 1945.
Sir W. S. Churchill, *Conservative*, Oct. 26, 1951.
Sir A. Eden, *Conservative*, April 6, 1955.
H. Macmillan, *Conservative*, Jan. 13, 1957.

Of the 43 Prime Ministers 18 sat in the House of Lords and 24 in the House of Commons during their term of office. One, Lord John Russell (afterwards Earl Russell) sat in his first Ministry in the House of Commons, and in his second in the House of Lords. Benjamin Disraeli was raised to the peerage as Earl of Beaconsfield during his second term of office.

Lord Palmerston, as an Irish peer, and Lord North, as the holder of a courtesy title, both sat in the House of Commons.

OFFICERS OF THE HOUSE OF LORDS

Speaker, The Rt. Hon. Reginald Edward Manningham-Buller, Lord Dilhorne (+£8,000 *as Lord Chancellor*) £4,000
Private Secretary to the Lord Chancellor, A. D. M. Oulton.
Lord Chairman of Committees, The Lord Merthyr, T.D. £3,250

Clerk of the Parliaments, D. Stephens, C.V.O.. £7,015
Clerk Assistant, H. M. Burrows, C.B.E..... £4,715
Reading Clerk and Clerk of the Journals, R. W. Perceval.......£4,115
Counsel to Lord Chairman of Committees, T. G. Talbot, C.B., Q.C.......£4,115
Principal Clerks, R. P. Cave (*Judicial Office*); E. D. Graham (*Private Bills in Committees*); P. G. Henderson (*Public Bills*).......£3,815
Senior Clerk, J. C. Sainty (*seconded as Secretary to the Leader of the House and the Chief Whip*).
Senior Clerks, J. V. D. Webb; J. E. Grey £1,959 to £2,711
Clerks, M. A. J. Wheeler-Booth; J. A. Valance White; D. Dewar.
Clerk of the Records, M. F. Bond, O.B.E. £2,493 to £2,865
Assistant Clerks of the Records, Miss E. R. Poyser; H. S. Cobb.......£1,498 to £2,544
Accountant, R. W. Hill, O.B.E... £1,680 to £2,349
Assistant Accountant, E. W. Field. £1,369 to £1,747
Examiner of Private Acts, etc., Miss R. J. Griffith, M.B.E.
Librarian, C. S. A. Dobson.....£2,865 to £3,215
Asst. Librarian, R. M. Price.....£1,498 to £2,544
Examiners of Petitions for Private Bills, T. G. Odling; F. D. Graham.
Gentleman-Usher of the Black Rod, Air Chief Marshal Sir George Mills, G.C.B., D.F.C.......£2,865
Yeoman Usher of the Black Rod, Serjeant-at-Arms, and Secretary to the Lord Great Chamberlain, Capt. K. L. Mackintosh, R.N.......£3,008
Staff Superintendent, Lt.-Cdr. S. E. Glover, M.B.E., D.S.C.
Shorthand Writer, A. R. Kennedy.......*fees*
Editor, Official Report (Hansard), S. C. Ireland M.B.E.......£2,126
Asst. do., W. M. Stuart......£1,574 to £1,785

OFFICERS OF THE HOUSE OF COMMONS

Speaker (First elected Oct. 20, 1959), Rt. Hon. Sir Harry (Braustyn Hylton) Hylton-Foster, Q.C., M.P. for Cities of London and Westminster.......£5,000
Chairman of Ways and Means, Rt. Hon. Sir William Anstruther-Gray, Bt., M.C., M.P. for Berwick and East Lothian.......£3,250
Deputy Chairman of Ways and Means, Sir Robert Grimston, Bt., M.P. for Westbury.......£2,500

DEPT. OF THE CLERK OF THE HOUSE

Clerk of the House of Commons, Sir Barnett Cocks, K.C.B., O.B.E.......£7,015
Clerk Asst., D. W. S. Lidderdale, C.B...... £5,015
Second do., R. D. Barlas, O.B.E.......£4,115
Principal Clerks—
Public Bills, K. R. Mackenzie.......£4,115
Journals, S. C. Hawtrey.......£4,115
Committees, H. R. M. Farmer.......£4,115
Fourth Clerk at the Table, C. A. S. S. Gordon £3,815
Private Bills, T. G. Odling.......£3,665
Standing Committees, A. C. Marples..... £3,665
Deputy Principal Clerks, D. Scott; E. S. Taylor, Ph.D.; M. H. Lawrence; F. G. Allen; A. A. Birley.......£2,865 to £3,565
Senior Clerks, R. S. Lankester; K. A. Bradshaw; D. A. M. Pring, M.C.; J. H. Willcox; J. P. S. Taylor; C. A. James; H. M. Barclay; M. T. Ryle; D. McW. Millar; C. J. Boulton; J. F. Sweetman; A. A. Barrett; D. W. Limon; R. V. R. James; J. R. Rose each £1,959 to £2,711
Assistant Clerks, G. S. Ecclestone; C. B. Winnifrith; A. J. Hastings; W. R. McKay; R. J. Willoughby.
Examiners of Private Bills, T. G. Odling; F. D. Graham.
Taxing Officer, T. G. Odling.

DEPT. OF THE SPEAKER

Speaker's Secretary, Brig. F. S. Reid, C.B.E. £2,371 to £2,813
Counsel to the Speaker, Sir Robert Speed, C.B., Q.C.......£4,115
Chaplain to the Speaker, Rev. Canon M. S. Stancliffe, M.A.......£668
Librarian, Strathearn Gordon, O.B.E. £2,865 to £3,565
Assistant Librarians, A. B. Pepin; D. C. L. Holland.......£2,566 to £2,865
Deputy Assistant Librarian, D. Menhennet, D.Phil.......£1,653 to £2,699
Senior Library Clerks, R. F. C. Butcher, V.R.D.; E. C. Thompson; R. H. V. C. Morgan; D. J. T. Englefield; H. J. Palmer; G. F. Lock.......£1,498 to £2,544
Accountant, F. J. Wilkin, D.F.M... £1,874 to £2,572
Deputy Accountant, H. Mc. E. Allen £1,358 to £1,842
Editor, Official Report (Hansard), L. W. Bear £2,438 to £2,848
Shorthand Writer, A. R. Kennedy.......*fees*
Vote Office, Principal Clerk, P. K. Marsden £1,874 to £2,505

DEPT. OF THE SERJEANT AT ARMS

Serjeant at Arms, Rear-Admiral A. H. C. Gordon Lennox, C.B., D.S.O.......£3,565
Deputy do., Lt.-Col. P. F. Thorne.......£2,711
Assistant do., Cdr. D. Swanston, D.S.O., D.S.C., R.N. (*ret.*).......£2,164 to £2,499
Deputy Assistant do., Major G. V. S. Le Fanu £2,043 to £2,293

NOTES ON PARLIAMENTARY PROCEDURE

WRITS FOR A NEW PARLIAMENT, ETC.—Writs for a new Parliament are issued, on the Sovereign's warrant, by the Lord Chancellor to Peers individually, but in the case of the Commons to the returning officers of the various constituencies. A Writ of Summons to the House of Lords, before the time when baronies were created by Letters Patent, is held (should the writ be good and the Parliament legally summoned) to create a barony for the recipient and his heirs. The oldest English peerages, the baronies of De Ros and Mowbray, are founded on writs of summons issued in 1264 and 1283 respectively. The right to sit in the House of Lords is determined by the House. A newly-created Peer may not sit or speak in the House of Lords until he has been introduced by two sponsors of his own degree in the Peerage.

VACANT SEATS.—When a vacancy occurs in the House of Commons the Writ for a New Election is generally moved, during a session of Parliament, by the Chief Whip of the party to whom the member whose seat has been vacated belonged. If the House is in recess, the Speaker can issue a writ, should two members certify to him that a seat is vacant. He cannot, however, issue such a writ if the seat has been vacated through the former member's lunacy or his acceptance of the office of Bailiff of the *Chiltern Hundreds*, or Steward of the *Manor of Northstead*, a legal fiction which enables a member to retire from the House, for it has long been established that a member cannot, by his own volition, relieve himself of the responsibilities to his constituents which his membership involves. Until 1926, however, it was necessary for a member to retire from the House on accepting an office of profit under the Crown, which, it may be noted, subjected a private member who accepted ministerial office to the trouble and expense of seeking re-election in his constituency. The Act of 1926, which removed this necessity, retained the Chiltern Hundreds and the Manor of Northstead as offices of profit and thus perpetuated the fiction.

HOURS OF MEETING, ETC.—The House of Lords normally meets during the Session at 2.30 p.m. on Tuesday and Wednesday, and at 3 p.m. on Thursday. The House of Commons meets on Monday, Tuesday, Wednesday and Thursday at 2.30, and on Friday at 11. *Strangers* are present during the debates of both Houses on sufferance, and may be excluded at any time; this applies equally to the *Press Gallery*. Time has modified what was once a rigid exclusion and strangers have in recent years generally been admitted except during the secret sessions of war time. The proceedings are opened by Prayers in both Houses. The *Quorum* of the House of Commons is forty members, including the Speaker, and should a member point out to the Speaker at any time that fewer than forty members are present, the division bells are rung, and if forty members have not appeared within four minutes, the House is said to be *Counted Out*, and the sitting is adjourned. The *Quorum* of the Lords is three.

PROROGATION AND DISSOLUTION.—A session of Parliament is brought to an end by its Prorogation to a certain date, while Parliament itself comes to an end either by Dissolution by the Sovereign or the expiration of the term of 5 years for which it was elected (*see* p. 311).

ELECTION PETITIONS.—The right of a member of the House of Commons to sit in Parliament can be challenged by petition on several grounds, *e.g.* ineligibility to sit owing to his bribery or corruption of the electors. Such petitions were originally decided by the House itself, but as party feeling was too much inclined to dictate the decision, their trial was in 1868 referred to the High Court of Justice.

STANDING ORDERS.—These are rules, which have from time to time been established by both Houses of Parliament, to regulate the conduct of business. These orders are not irrevocable, and like the Statutory Laws of England they can be easily revised, amended or repealed. The custom and precedents of Parliament, which dictate the bulk of Parliamentary procedure, have acquired, in seven centuries, prescriptive rights of obedience as firmly seated as the Common Law. *Sessional Orders* are applicable only to the session in which they are passed.

GENERAL PROCEDURE.—There are differences in the rules which govern the conduct of debates in the House of Lords and in the House of Commons. The Speaker in the Commons is responsible for the preservation of order and discipline in the House, but the only duty of the Lord Chancellor or the presiding Peer is to put the question. A Peer prefaces his remarks with "My Lords," whereas a member of the House of Commons addresses himself to Mr. Speaker.

A member of the House of Commons wishing to speak "rises in his place uncovered." When several members rise together the one whom the Speaker calls to continue the debate is described as *having caught the Speaker's eye*. In the House of Lords in similar circumstances, the House itself decides who shall speak.

Broadly speaking, a member may not, except in Committee, speak more than once to a question except in explanation or reply, and this privilege is granted only to the mover of a motion, or to the Minister or Member in charge of a bill.

A member may address the House from notes but must not read his speech, a distinction sometimes without a difference. In the Commons members must not be mentioned by name; the proceedings of the other House and matters *sub judice* must not be discussed; offensive words or epithets must not be used; a member may not speak after a question has been put, except on a point of order, and then he must address the Speaker "*seated and covered*." He must bow to the Speaker on entering and leaving the House.

QUESTION TIME.—After Prayers the first business of importance in the House of Commons is Question Time, which lasts from 2.45 until 3.30. Two days' notice of questions must be given to the *Clerk of the House of Commons*, the senior official of the House, who presides over it in the brief interval between the first assembly of a new Parliament and the election of a Speaker, and whose counterpart in the House of Lords is the *Clerk of the Parliaments*. Members of the House may put an unlimited number of questions to Ministers, but forty-eight hours' notice must be given, and not more than two demanding an oral answer may be made in any one day. Supplementary questions may be put either by the member asking the original question, or by other members, to obtain clarification of a Minister's answer.

COMMITTEES.—On the Assembly of a new Parliament, after the election of the Speaker, the

House of Commons deals with the subject of Committees, which are of three kinds:—*Committees of the Whole House, Select Committees* (appointed for a specific purpose) and the *Standing Committees* which consider public bills and whose composition, though laid down by Standing Orders, is frequently modified by Sessional Orders. When a bill dealing *exclusively* with Scotland or with Wales and Monmouthshire is referred to a Standing Committee, in the first place all Scottish, and in the second, all Welsh, members are automatically members thereof. Two of the most important Committees of the whole House of Commons are the *Committee of Supply* and that of *Ways and Means*. The former votes the money to provide for the service of the State, the amount being based on the estimates presented by the Government for the Services. Twenty days are allotted for debates on Supply before August 5, and there may be three other days before or after that date. The other Committee decides the methods to be adopted to raise the money voted by the Committee of Supply. These methods are foreshadowed by the *Budget* and put into effect by the *Finance Act*, while the *Appropriation Act* ensures that money voted for a certain purpose is applied to that purpose only.

CLOSURE AND THE GUILLOTINE.—To prevent deliberate waste of Parliamentary time, a procedure known as the *Closure* (colloquially known as "The Gag") was brought into effect on Nov. 10, 1882. A motion may be made *that the question be now put*. If the Speaker decides that the rights of a minority are not being prejudiced and 100 members support the motion, it is put to the vote, and, if carried, the original motion is put to the House, without further debate. The *Guillotine* represents a more rigorous and systematic application of the Closure. Under this system, a bill proceeds in accordance with a rigid time table and discussion is limited to the time allotted to each group of clauses. If the number of amendments put down appears likely to require more time than has been allotted for their discussion, the Speaker selects those which he considers are most important. The guillotine was first put into use on June 17, 1887, after prolonged debates on the Crimes Bill.

THE PREVIOUS QUESTION.—When the House is disinclined to give a decision on a particular question it is possible to avoid the issue by moving the Previous Question, which is done by one of several motions, *e.g.* "That the Question be not now put" or "That the House do now proceed to the Orders of the Day."

MOTION FOR ADJOURNMENT.—Adjournment ends the sitting of either House and takes place either under the provisions of a Standing Order or through an *ad hoc* resolution. In the Commons a method of obtaining immediate discussion of a matter of urgency is by moving *The adjournment on a matter of urgent public importance*. A member may ask leave to make this motion by giving written notice to the Speaker after Question Time and if it obtains the support of 40 members and the Speaker considers the matter of sufficient importance, it is discussed at 7 p.m. on that day. A Committee of the Whole House cannot adjourn but its proceedings may be interrupted by a motion *That the Chairman report Progress*. This brings the Speaker back to the House and the Committee seeks permission to sit on a future date.

PRIVILEGES OF PARLIAMENT.—There are certain rights and jurisdictions peculiar to each House of Parliament, but privileges in their accepted meaning are common to both Houses. The right of imprisoning persons who commit what are in the opinion of the House breaches of privilege is beyond question, and such persons cannot be admitted to bail nor is any Court competent to investigate the causes of commitment. Each House is the sole and absolute judge of its own privileges and where law and privilege have seemed to clash a conflict of jurisdiction has arisen between Parliament and the Courts. Breaches of privilege may be described briefly as disobedience to the orders of either House; assaults or insults to Members or libels on them; and interference with the officers of the House in the carrying out of their duties. The House of Lords may imprison for a period, or may inflict a fine, but the House of Commons only commits generally and the commitment ceases on the prorogation of Parliament. The Bill of Rights established the principle that "freedom of speech and debates and proceedings in Parliament should not be impeached or questioned in any court or place out of parliament." Consequently the House itself is the only authority which can punish a member for intemperance in debate. Freedom from arrest was a much prized privilege, but it applied only to civil arrest for debt (now abolished) and arbitrary arrest by the Government; members are amenable to all other processes of the Law. Freedom from arrest, in the case of members of the House of Commons, applies to the forty days after the prorogation and the forty days before the next meeting of Parliament.

THE SPEAKER.—The *Speaker of the House of Commons* is the spokesman and president of the Chamber. He is elected by the House at the beginning of each Parliament. He was originally a partisan but throughout a century of development between Speaker Onslow (1728) and Speaker Shaw-Lefevre (1839), the theory of the non-partisan Speaker was perfected, and he now neither speaks in debates, nor votes in divisions, except when the voting is equal. His order in the precedence of the Kingdom is high, only the Prime Minister and the Lord President of the Council going before him. He takes precedence of all Peers, except the two Archbishops, and Speakers are almost invariably raised to the Peerage on vacating their office, though Speaker Whitley is believed to have declined the offer of a Viscountcy. The Speaker's most severe disciplinary measure against a member is to *Name* him. When a member has been named, i.e. contrary to the practice of the House called by surname and not addressed as the "Hon. Member for . . ." (his constituency), the Leader of the House moves that he "be suspended from the service of the House" for (in the case of a first offence) a period of a week. The period of suspension is increased, should the member offend again. Speaker Denison has left it on record that "The House is always kind and indulgent, but it expects its Speakers to be right. If he should be found tripping, his authority must soon be at an end." The Speaker's Deputy is the *Chairman of Committees*, officially the *Chairman of Ways and Means*, who presides in the absence of the Speaker and when the House has resolved itself into Committee by the passage of the motion *that the Speaker do now leave the Chair*. He, like the Speaker, is elected at the beginning of each Parliament, and when he is presiding as chairman of a committee neither speaks in debate nor votes. A *Deputy Chairman* of *Ways and Means* is also appointed, and several temporary chairmen, who frequently preside either over a Committee of the Whole House or over Standing Committees.

VOTES CAST AT THE GENERAL ELECTIONS, 1945, 1950, 1951, 1955 AND 1959 AND AT BY-ELECTIONS SINCE 1945

General Election, 1945

Labour	11,985,733
Conservative	8,693,858
Liberal	2,253,197
Liberal National	759,884
Ulster Unionist	441,109
Independent	287,345
Irish Nationalist	148,078
National	125,299
Communist	102,780
Common Wealth	96,247
Independent Conservative	40,948
Independent Labour Party	36,153
Scottish Nationalist	30,594
Welsh Nationalist	14,887
Democratic	1,809
Independent Socialist	472
Total	25,018,393

By-elections, 1945–50

At 50 by-elections between the General Elections of 1945 and 1950, the following votes were cast:—

Labour	740,914
Conservative and National Liberal	641,540
Ulster Unionist	87,435
Liberal	49,730
Independent	35,647
Irish Nationalist	24,422
Scottish Nationalist	13,040
Welsh Nationalist	12,775
Independent Labour Party	8,367
Communist	5,087

General Election, 1950

Labour	13,265,610
Conservative	11,166,026
National Liberal and Conservative	983,623
Ulster Unionist	352,334
Liberal	2,621,489
Independent	112,318
Communist	91,815
Irish Nationalist	65,211
Irish Labour	52,715
Labour Independent	26,014
Welsh Nationalist	17,680
Scottish Nationalist	10,630
Independent Labour Party	4,112
Total	28,769,577

By-elections, 1950–51

At 15 by-elections between the General Elections of 1950 and 1951 the following votes were cast:—

Conservative and Associate	265,535
Labour	264,977
Irish Labour	30,883
Liberal	2,752
Independent Labour Party	1,366
Communist	729
Independent	453

General Election, 1951

Labour	13,949,105
Conservative and Associate	*13,718,069
Liberal	730,552
Irish Nationalist	94,587
Communist	19,640
Welsh Nationalist	10,920
Scottish Nationalist	7,299
Independent Labour Party	4,388
Others	62,135
Total	28,596,695

* Four Ulster Unionists were returned unopposed.

By-elections 1951–55

At 45 contested by-elections between the General Elections of 1951 and 1955, the following votes were cast:—

Conservative and Associate	751,421
Labour	705,176
Liberal	28,216
Welsh Nationalist	10,243
Independent	3,405
Scottish Nationalist	2,931
Communist	1,457

General Election, 1955

Conservative and Associate	13,311,938
Labour	12,405,246
Liberal	722,395
Sinn Fein	152,310
Welsh Nationalist	45,119
Communist	33,144
Scottish Nationalist	12,112
Others	78,490
Total	26,760,754

By-elections, 1955–59

At 52 contested by-elections between the General Elections of 1955 and 1959, the following votes were cast:—

Labour	784,656
Conservative and Associate	779,577
Liberal	174,904
Sinn Fein	54,516
Independent	40,986
Welsh Nationalist	7,719
Anti-Partition	6,421

General Election, 1959

Conservative and Associate	13,750,965
Labour	12,195,765
Liberal	1,661,262
Welsh Nationalist	77,571
Sinn Fein	63,915
Communist	30,897
Scottish Nationalist	21,738
Others	61,225
Total	27,863,338

By-elections, 1959–63

At 47 by-elections since the General Election of 1959, the following votes have been cast:

Labour	646,972
Conservative and Associate	518,103
Liberal	347,509
Independent	24,338
Scottish Nationalist	15,861
Welsh Nationalist	3,711
Communist	2,954

The Conservatives have gained one seat (Brighouse and Spenborough) from Labout, lost three (Middlesbrough, West; Glasgow, Woodside, and S. Dorset) to Labout and lost one (Orpington) to Liberals.

ALPHABETICAL LIST OF MEMBERS OF THE HOUSE OF COMMONS

(Elected October 8, 1959)

For abbreviations, see page 324. The number before the name of each constituency is for easy reference and corresponds to the number of that constituency given on pp. 324–345.

	Maj.
*Abse, L. (*b.* 1917), *Lab.*, 465*Pontypool*	17,852
*Agnew, Cmdr. Sir P. G., Bt. (*b.* 1900), *C.*, 622*Worcs. S.*	14,940
*Ainsley, J. W. (*b.* 1889). *Lab.*, 198*Durham, N.W.*	14,892
*Aitken, Sir W. T. (*b.* 1905), C., 117 *Bury St. Edmunds*	7,962
*Albu, A. H. (*b.* 1903), *Lab.*, 216*Edmonton*	461
*Allan, R. A. (*b.* 1914), *C.*, 453*Paddington S.*	7,287
*Allason, J. H. (*b.* 1912), C., 287*Hemel Hempstead*	8,235
*Allaun, F. (*b.* 1913), *Lab.*, 505*Salford, E.*	3,468
*Allen, S. S. (*b.* 1898), *Lab.*, 161*Crewe*	3,781
*Amery, Rt. Hon. J. (*b.* 1919), *C.*, 472 *Preston, N.*	4,461
Anderson, Miss M. B. H. (*b.* 1915), *C.*, 477 *Renfrew, E.*	15,093
*Arbuthnot, J. S. W. (*b.* 1912), *C.*, 187 *Dover*	3,241
Arton, Maj. A. T. Bourne- (*b.* 1913), *C.*, 167*Darlington*	4,417
*Ashton, Sir H. (*b.* 1898), *C.*, 136*Chelmsford*	9,868
*Atkins, H.E. (*b.* 1922), *C.*, 401*Merton and Morden*	8,159
*Awbery, S. S. (*b.* 1888), *Lab.*, 104*Bristol, Central*	2,696
Awdry, D. E. (*b.* 1924), C., 145*Wilts., Chippenham*	1,588
*Bacon, Miss A. M., *Lab.*, 352*Leeds, S.E.*	9,649
*Baird, J. (*b.* 1906), *Lab.*, 615*Wolverhampton, N.E.*	3,797
*Baker, F. E. Noel- (*b.* 1920), *Lab.*, 561 *Swindon*	3,909
*Baker, Rt. Hon. P. J. Noel- (*b.* 1889), *Lab.*, 174*Derby, S.*	3,431
*Balniel, Lord (*b.* 1927), *C.*, 294*Hertford*	8,821
*Barber, A. P. L. (*b.* 1920), *C.*, 181*Doncaster*	3,586
*Barlow, Sir J. D., Bt. (*b.* 1898), *C.*, 404 *Middleton and Prestwich*	10,168
Barnett, N. G. (*b.* 1928), *Lab.*, 185 *Dorset, S.*	704
*Barter, J. W. (*b.* 1917), *C.*, 199*Ealing, N.*	4,276
*Batsford, B. C. C. (*b.* 1910), *C.*, 200*Ealing, S.*	12,722
*Baxter, Sir A. B. (*b.* 1891), *C.*, 530*Southgate*	16,736
Baxter, W. (*b.* 1911), *Lab.*, 540*Stirling, W.*	5,511
*Beach, Maj. W. W. Hicks (*b.* 1907), *C.*, 138 *Cheltenham*	9,272
*Beamish, Col. Sir T. V. H. (*b.* 1917), *C.*, 361*Lewes*	16,577
Beaney, A. (*b.* 1905), *Lab.*, 288*Hemsworth*	35,365
*Bell, R. M. (*b.* 1914), *C.*, 113*Bucks, S.*	21,104
*Bellenger, Rt. Hon. F. J. (*b.* 1894), *Lab.*, 39*Bassetlaw*	7,713
*Bence, C. R. (*b.* 1902), *Lab.*, 192*Dunbarton, E.*	3,349
*Bennett, F. M. (*b.* 1918), *C.*, 568*Torquay.*	17,743
Bennett, J. *Lab.*, 245 *Bridgeton*	6,995
*Bennett, R. F. B. (*b.* 1911), *C.*, 264*Gosport and Fareham*	16,154
*Benson, Sir G. (*b.* 1889), *Lab.*, 142*Chesterfield*	13,450
Berkeley, H. J. (*b.* 1926), *C.* 347*Lancaster*	5,528
*Bevins, Rt. Hon. J. R. (*b.* 1908), *C.*, 373 *Toxteth*	3,915
*Bidgood, J. C. (*b.* 1914), *C.*, 116*Bury and Radcliffe*	3,908
Biffen, W. J. (*b.* 1930), *C.*, 450*Oswestry*	3,781
*Bingham, R. M. (*b.* 1915), *C.*, 370*Liverpool, Garston*	14,157
*Birch, Rt. Hon. E. N. C. (*b.* 1906), *C.*, 237*Flint, W.*	7,521
*Bishop, F. P. (*b.* 1900), *C.*, 280*Harrow, Central*	9,764
*Black, Sir C. W. (*b.* 1902), *C.*, 609*Wimbledon*	10,860
*Blackburn, F. (*b.* 1902), *Lab.*, 537*Stalybridge and Hyde*	1,423
*Blyton, W. R. (*b.* 1899), *Lab.*, 308 *Houghton-le-Spring*	24,562
*Boardman, H. (*b.* 1907), *Lab.*, 359*Leigh*	14,775
Bossom, Hon. C. (*b.* 1918), *C.*, 360 *Leominster*	9,737
†Bottomley, Rt. Hon. A. G. (*b.* 1907), *Lab.*, 402*Middlesbrough, E.*	11,783
*Bourke, Maj. Sir E. A. H. Legge-(*b.* 1914), *C.*, 325*Isle of Ely*	6,468
*Bowden, Rt. Hon. H. W. (*b.* 1905), *Lab.*, 358*Leicester, S.W.*	2,743
*Bowen, E. R. (*b.* 1913), *L.*, 130*Cardigan.*	9,309
*Bowles, F. G. (*b.* 1902), *Lab.*, 442*Nuneaton*	9,540
Box, D. S. (*b.* 1917), *C.*, 127*Cardiff, N.*	10,683
Boyden, H. J. (*b.* 1910), *Lab.*, 76*Bishop Auckland*	8,329
*Boyle, Rt. Hon. Sir E. C. G., Bt. (*b.* 1923) *C.*, 67*Handsworth*	10,127
*Braddock, Mrs. E. M. (*b.* 1899), *Lab.*, 369 *Liverpool, Exchange*	6,971
Bradley, T. G. (*b.* 1926), *Lab.*, 355*Leicester, N.E.*	1,948
*Braine, B. R. (*b.* 1914), *C.*, 223*Essex, S.E.*	10,133
Bray, Dr. J. W. (*b.* 1930), *Lab.*, 403 *Middlesbrough, W.*	2,270
*Brewis, H. J. (*b.* 1920), *C.*, 241*Galloway.*	9,042
*Brockway, A. F. (*b.* 1888), *Lab.*, 224*Eton and Slough*	88
*Brooke, Rt. Hon. H. (*b.* 1903), *C.*, 277 *Hampstead*	12,006
*Broughton, A. D. D. (*b.* 1902), *Lab.*, 41 *Batley and Morley*	7,666
Brown, A. G. (*b.* 1913), *Ind.*, 571*Tottenham*	6,637
*Brown, Rt. Hon. G. A. (*b.* 1914), *Lab.*, 54 *Belper*	4,337
*Brown, T. J. (*b.* 1886), *Lab.*, 321*Ince*	18,957
*Brown, Sir W. Robson- (*b.* 1900), *C.*, 222 *Esher*	24,221
Browne, P. B. (*b.* 1923), *C.*, 569*Torrington*	2,265
*Bryan, P. E. O. (*b.* 1913), *C.*, 310*Howden*	12,872
Buck, P. A. F. (*b.* 1928), *C.*, 153*Colchester*	5,344
Bullard, D. G. (*b.* 1912), *C.*, 338*King's Lynn*	1,765
*Bullus, Wing-Cdr. E. E. (*b.* 1906), *C.*, 593*Wembley, N.*	11,080
*Burden, F. F. A. (*b.* 1905), *C.*, 244 *Gillingham*	7,279
*Butcher, Sir H. W., Bt. (*b.* 1901), *Nat. L. and C.*, 302*Holland with Boston*	11,174
*Butler, H. W. (*b.* 1897), *Lab.*, 272*Hackney, Central*	9,502
*Butler, Mrs. J. S. (*b.* 1910), *Lab.*, 618*Wood Green*	1,134
*Butler, Rt. Hon. R. A. (*b.* 1902), *C.*, 499 *Saffron Walden*	6,782
*Callaghan, L. J. (*b.* 1912), *Lab.*, 128*Cardiff, S.E.*	868
*Campbell, G. T. C. (*b.* 1921), *C.*, 410 *Moray and Nairn*	7,203
Carmichael, N. G. (*b.* 1921) *Lab.*, 259 *Glasgow, Woodside*	1,368
*Carpenter, Rt. Hon. J. A. Boyd- (*b.* 1908), *C.*, 339*Kingston-on-Thames*	16,241

	Maj.
*Carr, Rt. Hon. L. R. (*b.* 1916), *C.*, 407 *Mitcham*	9,816
Carr, W. C. (*b.* 1918), *C.*, 35 *Barons Court*	913
*Cary, Sir R. A., Bt. (*b.* 1898), *C.*, 394 *Withington*	9,694
*Castle, Mrs. B. A. (*b.* 1911), *Lab.*, 77 *Blackburn*	2,866
*Channon, H. P. G. (*b.* 1935), *C.*, 528 *Southend, W.*	17,035
*Chapman, W. D. (*b.* 1923), *Lab.*, 69 *Birmingham, Northfield*	940
Chataway, C. J. (*b.* 1931), *C.*, 362 *Lewisham, N.*	4,613
*Churchill, Rt. Hon. Sir W. S. (*b.* 1874), *C.*, 617 *Woodford*	14,797
Clark, H. (*b.* 1929), *U.U.*, 16 *Antrim, N.*	40,527
*Clark, R. Chichester- (*b.* 1928), *U.U.*, 378 *Londonderry*	23,657
Clark, W. G. A. (*b.* 1917), *C.*, 440 *Nottingham, S.*	7,372
*Clarke, Brig. T. H. (*b.* 1904), *C.*, 471 *Portsmouth, W.*	6,266
Cleaver, L. H. (*b.* 1909), *C.*, 75 *Yardley*	1,385
*Cliffe, M. (*b.* 1904), *Lab.*, 518 *Shoreditch and Finsbury*	11,566
*Cole, N. J. (*b.* 1909), *L. and C.*, 48 *Beds., S.*	4,759
*Collick, P. H. (*b.* 1897), *Lab.*, 62 *Birkenhead*	3,629
*Cooke, C. Fletcher- (*b.* 1914), *C.*, 169 *Darwen*	8,342
*Cooke, R. G. (*b.* 1907), *C.*, 573 *Twickenham*	17,039
*Cooke, R. G. (*b.* 1930), *C.*, 109 *Bristol, W.*	20,117
*Cooper, A. E. (*b.* 1910), *C.*, 319 *Ilford, S.*	7,307
*Corbet, Mrs. F. K. (*b.* 1900), *Lab.*, 122 *Peckham*	11,382
*Cordeaux, Lt.-Col. J. K. (*b.* 1902), *C.*, 438 *Nottingham, Central*	2,135
Cordle, J. H. (*b.* 1912), *C.*, 89 *Bournemouth, E. and Christchurch*	19,792
*Corfield, Capt. F. V. (*b.* 1915), *C.*, 261 *Glos., S.*	4,601
Costain, A. P. (*b.* 1910), *C.*, 238 *Folkestone and Hythe*	12,380
Coulson, J. M. (*b.* 1927), *C.*, 314 *Hull, N.*	702
*Courtney, Cmdr. A. T. (*b.* 1908), *C.*, 281 *Harrow, E.*	5,947
*Craddock, G. (*b.* 1897), *Lab.*, 93 *Bradford, S.*	3,014
*Craddock, Sir G. B. (*b.* 1898), *C.*, 535 *Spelthorne*	8,093
Crawley, A. M. (*b.* 1908), *C.*, 177 *Derbyshire W.*	1,220
Critchley, J. M. G. (*b.* 1930), *C.*, 485 *Rochester and Chatham*	1,023
*Cronin, J. D. (*b.* 1916), *Lab.*, 379 *Loughborough*	3,747
Crosland, C. A. R. (*b.* 1918), *Lab.*, 270 *Grimsby*	101
*Crossman, R. H. S. (*b.* 1907), *Lab.*, 158 *Coventry, E.*	7,762
*Crowder, F. P. (*b.* 1919), *C.*, 493 *Ruislip-Northwood*	13,056
*Cullen, Mrs. A. (*b.* 1892), *Lab.*, 249 *Gorbals*	10,659
*Cunningham, S. K. (*b.* 1909), *U.U.*, 17 *Antrim, S.*	50,041
Curran, C. (*b.* 1903), *C.*, 575 *Uxbridge*	1,390
*Currie, G. B. H. (*b.* 1905), *U.U.*, 188 *Down, N.*	50,734
Dalkeith, Earl of (*b.* 1923), *C.*, 212 *Edinburgh, N.*	5,334
Dalyell, T. (*b.* 1932), *Lab.* 601 *West Lothian*	11,516
*Dance, J. C. G. (*b.* 1907), *C.*, 111 *Bromsgrove*	9,040
*Darling, G. (*b.* 1905), *Lab.*, 515 *Hillsborough*	5,043
*Davenport, Lt.-Col. Sir W. H. Bromley- (*b.* 1903), *C.*, 341 *Knutsford*	19,153
Davies, G. E. (*b.* 1913), *Lab.*, 479 *Rhondda, E.*	15,985
*Davies, H. (*b.* 1904), *Lab.*, 354 *Leek*	1,149
Davies, I. (*b.* 1910), *Lab.*, 265 *Gower*	17,604
*Davies, S. O. (*b.* 1886), *Lab.*, 400 *Merthyr Tydfil*	18,723
*Davies, W. R. Rees- (*b.* 1916), *C.*, 326 *Isle of Thanet*	11,898
*Davison, J. A. Biggs- (*b.* 1918), *C.*, 144 *Chigwell*	5,562
*Deedes, Rt. Hon. W. F. (*b.* 1913), *C.*, 22 *Ashford*	10,400
*Deer, G. (*b.* 1890), *Lab.*, 417 *Newark*	1,772
*de Ferranti, B. R. Z. (*b.* 1930), *C.*, 411 *Morecambe and Lonsdale*	15,975
*Delargy, H. J. (*b.* 1908), *Lab.*, 565 *Thurrock*	12,082
Dempsey, J. (*b.* 1917), *Lab.*, 152 *Coatbridge and Airdrie*	794
*Diamond, J. (*b.* 1907), *Lab.*, 260 *Gloucester*	2,771
*Digby, K. S. D. W. (*b.* 1910), *C.*, 186 *Dorset, W.*	8,211
*Dodds, N. N. (*b.* 1903), *Lab.*, 221 *Erith and Crayford*	5,760
*Donaldson, Cmdr. C. E. M. (*b.* 1903), *C.*, 491 *Roxburgh, Selkirk and Peebles*	9,513
*Donnelly, D. L. (*b.* 1920), *Lab.*, 455 *Pembroke*	5,322
*Doughty, C. J. A. (*b.* 1902), *C.*, 556 *Surrey, E.*	25,934
*Drayson, G. B. (*b.* 1913), *C.*, 520 *Skipton*	9,100
Driberg, T. E. N. (*b.* 1905), *Lab.*, 31 *Barking*	12,000
*du Cann, E. D. L. (*b.* 1924), *C.*, 562 *Taunton*	6,498
Duffy, A. E. P. (*b.* 1920), *Lab.* 154 *Colne Valley*	2,039
*Duncan, Capt. Sir J. A. L., Bt. (*b.* 1899), *L. and C.*, 15 *S. Angus*	11,296
*Duthie, Sir W. S. (*b.* 1892), *C.*, 30 *Banff*	8,367
*Ede, Rt. Hon. J. C. (*b.* 1882), *Lab.*, 532 *South Shields*	8,939
*Edelman, M. (*b.* 1911), *Lab.*, 159 *Coventry, N.*	1,241
*Eden, Sir J. B., Bt. (*b.* 1925), *C.*, 90 *Bournemouth, W.*	17,618
*Edwards, Rt. Hon. N. (*b.* 1897), *Lab.*, 119 *Caerphilly*	20,973
*Edwards, R. J. (*b.* 1906), *Lab.*, 61 *Bilston*	3,545
*Edwards, W. J. (*b.* 1900), *Lab.*, 538 *Stepney*	18,309
Elliot, Capt. W. (*b.* 1910), *C.*, 134 *Carshalton*	8.925
*Elliott, R. W. (*b.* 1920), *C.*, 422 *Newcastle, N.*	11,272
Emery, P. F. H. (*b.* 1926), *C.*, 475 *Reading*	3,942
*Emmet, Mrs. E. V. E. (*b.* 1899), *C.*, 203 *East Grinstead*	21,655
*Errington, Sir E., Bt. (*b.* 1900), *C.*, 11 *Aldershot*	12,891
*Erroll, Rt. Hon. F. J. (*b.* 1914), *C.*, 12 *Altrincham and Sale*	15,851
*Evans, A. (*b.* 1903), *Lab.*, 330 *Islington, S.W.*	10,388
*Ewing, Sir C. I. Orr-, Bt. (*b.* 1912), *C.*, 289 *Hendon, N.*	5,332
*Eyre, Lt.-Col. Sir O. E. Crosthwaite- (*b.* 1913), *C.*, 424 *New Forest*	16,282
Farr, J. A. (*b.* 1922), *C.*, 278 *Harborough*	12,514
*Fell, A. (*b.* 1914), *C.*, 628 *Yarmouth*	3,579
*Fernyhough, E. (*b.* 1908), *Lab.*, 331 *Jarrow*	10,352
*Ferris, Wing-Cdr. R. G. Grant- (*b.* 1907), *C.*, 414 *Nantwich*	6,737
*Finch, H. J. (*b.* 1898), *Lab.*, 49 *Bedwellty*	23,880
*Finlay, G. B. (*b.* 1917), *C.*, 219 *Epping*	4,393

	Maj.
*Fisher, N. T. L. (*b.* 1913), *C.*, 555 *Surbiton*	12,425
*Fitch, E. A. (*b.* 1915), *Lab.*, 606 *Wigan*	16,049
*Fletcher, E. G. M. (*b.* 1903), *Lab.*, 328 *Islington, E.*	4,669
Foley, M. A. (*b.* 1925), *Lab.*, 595 *West Bromwich*	12,264
*Foot, D. M. (*b.* 1905). *Lab.*, 324 *Ipswich*	3,235
Foot, M. M. (*b.* 1913), *Lab.*, 207 *Ebbw Vale*	16,729
*Forman, J. C. (*b.* 1884), *Lab.*, 258 *Springburn*	6,130
*Forrest, G. (*b.* 1922), *Ind. U.U.*, 406 *Mid Ulster*	18,923
†Foster, Rt. Hon. Sir H. B. H. Hylton- (*b.* 1905), *The Speaker*, 149 *Cities of London and Westminster*	17,188
*Foster, J. G. (*b.* 1904), *C.*, 435 *Northwich*	7,970
*Fraser, Rt. Hon. H. C. P. J. (*b.* 1918), *C.*, 536 *Stafford and Stone*	10,073
Fraser, I. M. (*b.* 1916), *C.*, 463 *Plymouth, Sutton*	6,761
*Fraser, T. (*b.* 1911), *Lab.*, 275 *Hamilton*	15,913
*Freeth, D. K. (*b.* 1924), *C.*, 38 *Basingstoke*	11,244
*Galbraith, Hon. T. G. D. (*b.* 1917), *C.*, 251 *Hillhead*	10,777
Galpern, Sir M. (*b.* 1903), *Lab.*, 257 *Shettleston*	8,173
*Gammans, Lady (*b.* 1898), *C.*, 306 *Hornsey*	12,338
Gardner, E. L. (*b.* 1912), *C.*, 60 *Billericay*	4,822
*George, Sir J. C. (*b.* 1902), *C.*, 254 *Pollok*	7,266
*George, Lady M. Lloyd (*b.* 1902), *Lab.*, 133 *Carmarthen*	6,633
Gilmour, I. H. J. (*b.* 1926), *C.*, 427 *Norfolk, Cent.*	220
Gilmour, Sir J. E., Bt, (*b.* 1912), *C.*, 233 *Fife, E.*	7,066
Ginsburg, D. (*b.* 1923), *Lab.*, 180 *Dewsbury*	3,669
*Glover, Col. Sir D. (*b.* 1908), *C.*, 448 *Ormskirk*	18,251
Glyn, Dr. A. J. (*b.* 1918), *C.*, 584 *Clapham*	1,876
*Glyn, Col. Sir R. H., Bt. (*b.* 1907), *C.*, 184 *Dorset, N.*	8,651
*Godber, Rt. Hon. J. B. (*b.* 1914), *C.*, 266 *Grantham*	6,615
*Goldsmid, Sir H. J. d'Avigdor-, Bt. (*b.* 1909), *C.*, 580 *Walsall, S.*	8,782
*Gooch, E. G. (*b.* 1889), *Lab.*, 428 *Norfolk, N.*	658
*Goodhart, P. C. (*b.* 1925), *C.*, 45 *Beckenham*	23,133
Goodhew, V. H. (*b.* 1919), *C.*, 500 *St. Albans*	8,507
*Gordon, P. W. Wolrige- (*b.* 1935), *C.*, 5 *Aberdeenshire, E.*	8,002
*Gough, C. F. H. (*b.* 1901), *C.*, 307 *Horsham*	13,263
Gourlay, H. P. H. (*b.* 1916), *Lab.*, 340 *Kirkcaldy*	11,242
*Gower, H. R. (*b.* 1916), *C.*, 37 *Barry*	9,523
*Gray, Maj. Rt. Hon. Sir W. J. Anstruther-, Bt. (*b.* 1905), *C.*, 56 *Berwick and E. Lothian*	2,850
*Green, A. (*b.* 1911), *C.*, 473 *Preston, S.*	3,019
*Greenwood, A. W. J. (*b.* 1911), *Lab.*, 487 *Rossendale*	2,591
*Grey, C. F. (*b.* 1903), *Lab.*, 197 *Durham*	16,689
*Griffiths, D. (*b.* 1896), *Lab.*, 489 *Rother Valley*	28,593
*Griffiths, Rt. Hon. J. (*b.* 1890), *Lab.*, 377 *Llanelly*	24,497
*Griffiths, W. D. (*b.* 1912), *Lab.*, 390 *Manchester, Exchange*	8,724
*Grimond, Rt. Hon. J. (*b.* 1913) *L.*, 447 *Orkney and Zetland*	8,612
*Grimston, Sir. R. V., Bt. (*b.* 1897), *C.*, 596 *Westbury*	5,826
*Grosvenor, Lt.-Col. Lord Robert (*b.* 1919), *U.U.*, 232 *Fermanagh and S. Tyrone*	24,732
Gunter, R. J. (*b.* 1909), *Lab.*, 533 *Southwark*	12,340
*Gurden, H. E. (*b.* 1903), *C.*, 71 *Selly Oak*	8,356
*Hale, C. L. (*b.* 1902), *Lab.*, 446 *Oldham, W.*	4,119
*Hall, J. (*b.* 1911), *C.*, 627 *Wycombe*	10,870
*Hallett, Vice-Adm. J. Hughes- (*b.* 1901), *C.*, 163 *Croydon, N.E.*	8,905
Hamilton, M. C. (*b.* 1918), *C.*, 591 *Wellingborough*	606
*Hamilton, W. W. (*b.* 1917), *Lab.*, 234 *Fife, W.*	14,297
*Hann n, W. (*b.* 1906), *Lab.*, 253 *Maryhill*	9,582
*Hare, Rt. Hon. J. H. (*b.* 1911), *C.*, 552 *Sudbury and Woodbridge*	9,882
Harper, J. (*b.* 1915), *Lab.*, 464 *Pontefract*	19,828
*Harris, F. W. (*b.* 1915), *C.*, 164 *Croydon, N.W.*	10,453
*Harris, R. R. (*b.* 1913), *C.*, 296 *Heston and Isleworth*	8,850
*Harrison, A. B. C. (*b.* 1921), *C.*, 386 *Maldon*	2,240
*Harrison, Col. Sir J. H., Bt. (*b.* 1907), *C.*, 266 *Eye*	2,484
Hart, Mrs. J. C. M. (*b.* 1924), *Lab.*, 345 *Lanark*	540
*Harvey, Air Cdre. Sir A. V. (*b.* 1906), *C.*, 384 *Macclesfield*	9,326
*Harvey, J. E. (*b.* 1920), *C.*, 581 *Walthamstow, E.*	2,901
Hastings, S. L. E. (*b.* 1921), *C.* 47 *Mid-Beds.*	6,222
*Hay, J. A. (*b.* 1919), *C.*, 291 *Henley*	9,403
*Hayman, F. H. (*b.* 1894), *Lab.*, 227 *Falmouth and Camborne*	4,197
*Heald, Rt. Hon. Sir L. F. (*b.* 1897), *C.*, 139 *Chertsey*	10,686
*Healey, D. W. (*b.* 1917), *Lab.*, 348 *Leeds, E.*	4,785
*Heath, Rt. Hon. E. R. G. (*b.* 1916), *C.*, 59 *Bexley*	8,633
*Henderson, Rt. Hon. A. (*b.* 1893), *Lab.*, 490 *Rowley Regis and Tipton*	9,977
*Henderson, J. (*b.* 1888), *C.*, 246 *Cathcart*	9,574
Hendry, A. F. (*b.* 1908), *C.*, 6 *Aberdeenshire, W.*	12,395
*Herbison, Miss M. (*b.* 1907), *Lab.*, 346 *Lanark, N.*	6,269
*Hewitson, M. (*b.* 1897), *Lab.*, 315 *Hull, W.*	2,435
Hiley, J. (*b.* 1902), *C.*, 474 *Pudsey*	6,511
*Hill, Mrs. E. (*b.* 1897), *C.*, 395 *Wythenshawe*	1,309
*Hill, J. E. B. (*b.* 1912), *C.*, 429 *Norfolk, S.*	2,733
Hill, J. M. (*b.* 1899), *Lab.*, 405 *Midlothian*	9,660
*Hilton, A. V. (*b.* 1908), *Lab.*, 430 *Norfolk, S.W.*	78
*Hirst, G. A. N. (*b.* 1905), *C.*, 517 *Shipley*	5,511
*Hobson, Rt. Hon. Sir J. G. S. (*b.* 1912), *C.*, 588 *Warwick and Leamington*	13,079
Hocking, P. N. (*b.* 1925), *C.*, 160 *Coventry, S.*	1,830
Holland, P. W. (*b.* 1917), *C.*, 10 *Acton*	923
Hollingworth, J. H. (*b.* 1930), *C.*, 63 *Birmingham, All Saints*	20
*Holman, P. (*b.* 1891), *Lab.*, 58 *Bethnal Green*	16,815
*Holt, A. F. (*b.* 1914), *L.*, 85 *Bolton, W.*	3,988
*Holt, Sir J. A. Langford- (*b.* 1916), *C.*, 519 *Shrewsbury*	8,632
Hooson, H. E. (*b.* 1925), *L.*, 409 *Montgomeryshire*	7,549
*Hope, Rt. Hon. Lord John (*b.* 1912), *C.*, 213 *Pentlands*	8,792
Hopkins, A. C. N. (*b.* 1926), *C. and Nat. L.*, 105 *Bristol, N.E.*	2,684
Hopkins, J. S. R. Scott- (*b.* 1921), *C.*, 157 *Cornwall, N.*	989
*Hornby, R. P. (*b.* 1922), *C.*, 567 *Tonbridge*	10,506

Member	Maj.
*Houghton, A. L. N. D. (*b.* 1898), *Lab.*, 534*Sowerby*	1,956
*Howard, G. R. (*b.* 1909), *Nat. L. and C.*, 502*St. Ives*	6,898
*Howard, J. M. (*b.* 1913), *C.*, 526*Southampton, Test*	6,766
*Howell, C. A. (*b.* 1905), *Lab.*, 70*Perry Bar*	183
†Howell, D. H. (*b.* 1923), *Lab.*, 72*Small Heath*	6,259
*Hoy, J. H. (*b.* 1909), *Lab.*, 211*Leith*	3,074
*Hughes, C. (*b.* 1916), *Lab.*, 13*Anglesey*	6,244
*Hughes, E. (*b.* 1894), *Lab.*, 28*Ayrshire, S.*	10,669
*Hughes, H. S. J. (*b.* 1887), *Lab.*, 3*Aberdeen, N.*	17,656
*Hulbert, Wing-Cdr. Sir N. J. (*b.* 1903), *C.*, 542*Stockport, N.*	3,222
*Hunter, A. E. (*b.* 1900), *Lab.*, 231*Feltham*	2,250
*Hurd, Sir A. R. (*b.* 1901), *C.*, 418 *Newbury*	9,916
*Hutchison, A. M. C. (*b.* 1914), *C.*, 214 *Edinburgh, S.*	11,514
*Hynd, H. (*b.* 1900), *Lab.*, 9*Accrington*	600
*Hynd, J. B. (*b.* 1902), *Lab.*, 511*Attercliffe*	18,372
Hyslop, R. J. Maxwell- (*b.* 1931), *C.*, 566 *Tiverton*	3,040
*Iremonger, T. L. (*b.* 1916), *C.*, 318*Ilford, N.*	13,647
*Irvine, A. J. (*b.* 1909), *Lab.*, 368*Edge Hill*	699
*Irvine, B. G. (*b.* 1909), *C.*, 498*Rye*	19,916
*Irving, S. (*b.* 1918), *Lab.*, 168*Dartford*	1,276
Jackson, F. L. J. (*b.* 1919), *C.*, 176*Derbyshire, S.E.*	12
James, D. P. (*b.* 1919), *C.*, 102*Brighton, Kemptown*	5,746
*Janner, Sir B. (*b.* 1892), *Lab.*, 356*Leicester, N.W.*	1,773
*Jay, Rt. Hon. D. P. T. (*b.* 1907), *Lab.*, 42 *Battersea, N.*	10,306
*Jeger, G. (*b.* 1903), *Lab.*, 263*Goole*	9,771
*Jenkins, R. C. D. (*b.* 1900), *C.*, 121 *Dulwich*	2,251
*Jenkins, R. H. (*b.* 1920), *Lab.*, 74*Stechford*	2,923
*Jennings, J. C. (*b.* 1903), *C.*, 115*Burton*	5,894
Johnson, C. A. (*b.* 1903), *Lab.*, 363 *Lewisham, S.*	3,081
*Johnson, Dr. D. M. (*b.* 1903), *C.*, 131 *Carlisle*	1,998
*Johnson, E. S. T. (*b.* 1897), *C.*, 388 *Blackley*	4,373
*Jones, Rt. Hon. A. (*b.* 1911), *C.*, 66*Hall Green*	13,717
Jones, A. A. (*b.* 1915), *C.*, 433*Northants. S.*	917
*Jones, Rt. Hon. A. Creech- (*b.* 1891), *Lab.*, 576*Wakefield*	9,591
Jones, D. (*b.* 1908), *Lab.*, 114*Burnley*	6,773
*Jones, F. E. (*b.* 1909), *Lab.*, 599*West Ham, S.*	22,829
*Jones, F. W. Farey- (*b.* 1904), *C.*, 589 *Watford*	2,901
*Jones, J. I. J. (*b.* 1900), *Lab.*, 626*Wrexham*	12,957
*Jones, T. W. (*b.* 1898), *Lab.*, 399*Merioneth*	976
*Joseph, Sir K. S., Bt. (*b.* 1918), *C.*, 349 *Leeds, N.E.*	11,531
*Kaberry, Sir D., Bt. (*b.* 1907), *C.*, 350 *Leeds, N.W.*	16,702
Kelley, R. (*b.* 1904), *Lab.*, 182*Don Valley*	24,148
*Kemsley, Sir C. N. Thornton- (*b.* 1903), *L. and C.*, 14*North Angus and Mearns*	9,050
*Kenyon, C. (*b.* 1896), *Lab.*, 147*Chorley*	676
Kerans, Cmdr. J. S. (*b.* 1915), *C.*, 283*The Hartlepools*	182
*Kerby, Capt. H. B. (*b.* 1914), *C.*, 20 *Arundel and Shoreham*	24,289
*Kerr, Sir H. W., Bt. (*b.* 1903), *C.*, 123 *Cambridge*	6,807
*Kershaw, J. A. (*b.* 1915), *C.*, 551*Stroud*	5,112
*Key, Rt. Hon. C. W. (*b.* 1883), *Lab.*, 468 *Poplar*	15,871
*Key, Sir N. Cooper- (*b.* 1907), *C.*, 285 *Hastings*	8,882
*Kimball, M. R. (*b.* 1928), *C.*, 240 *Gainsborough*	6,809
*King, H. M. (*b.* 1901), *Lab.*, 525*Southampton, Itchen*	3,733
*Kirk, P. M. (*b.* 1928), *C.*, 267*Gravesend*	2,162
Kitson, T. P. G. (*b.* 1931), *C.*, 482*Richmond, Yorks*	19,067
*Lagden, G. W. (*b.* 1906), *C.*, 305*Hornchurch*	7,322
*Lambton, Visct. (*b.* 1922), *C.*, 57*Berwick-on-Tweed*	8,267
*Lancaster, Col. C. G. (*b.* 1899), *C.*, 529 *South Fylde*	24,467
*Lawson, G. M. (*b.* 1906), *Lab.*, 413*Motherwell*	4,396
*Leather, Sir E. H. C. (*b.* 1919), *C.*, 523 *Somerset, N.*	6,783
*Leavey, J. A. (*b.* 1915), *C.*, 298*Heywood and Royton*	2,154
*Ledger, R. J. (*b.* 1920), *Lab.*, 486*Romford*	607
*Lee, F. (*b.* 1906), *Lab.*, 426*Newton*	7,976
*Lee, Miss J. (*b.* 1904), *Lab.*, 125*Cannock*	7,139
*Lever, L. M. (*b.* 1905), *Lab.*, 387*Ardwick*	6,742
*Lever, N. H. (*b.* 1914), *Lab.*, 389*Cheetham*	9,336
*Lewis, A. W. J. (*b.* 1917), *Lab.*, 598*West Ham, N.*	14,778
Lewis, K. (*b.* 1916), *C.*, 497*Rutland and Stamford*	4,941
Lilley, F. J. P. (*b.* 1907), *C.*, 252*Kelvingrove*	1,101
*Lindsay, Sir M. A., Bt. (*b.* 1905), *C.*, 522 *Solihull*	23,180
*Linstead, Sir H. N. (*b.* 1901), *C.*, 588*Putney*	5,121
*Lipton, Lt.-Col. M. (*b.* 1900), *Lab.*, 342 *Brixton*	2,112
Litchfield, Capt. J. S. S. (*b.* 1903) *C.*, 137 *Chelsea*	14,677
*Lloyd, Rt. Hon. G. W. (*b.* 1902), *C.*, 558*Sutton Coldfield*	21,754
*Lloyd, Rt. Hon. J. S. B. (*b.* 1904), *C.*, 612*Wirral*	21,002
*Logan, D. G. (*b.* 1871). *Lab.*, 372*Liverpool, Scotland*	7,667
Longbottom, C. B. (*b.* 1930), *C.*, 630*York.*	4,074
*Longden, G. J. M. (*b.* 1902), *C.*, 295 *Herts, S.W.*	10,237
Loughlin, C. W. (*b.* 1914), *Lab.*, 262 *Glos., W.*	5,411
*Loveys, W. H. (*b.* 1920), *C.*, 143*Chichester*	21,209
Lubbock, E. R. (*b.* 1928), *L.*, 449*Orpington*	7,855
*Lucas, Sir J. M., Bt. (*b.* 1889), *C.*, 470 *Portsmouth, S.*	15,913
*Mabon, Dr. J. D. (*b.* 1925), *Lab.*, 268 *Greenock*	9,082
*McAdden, Sir S. J. (*b.* 1907), *C.*, 527 *Southend, E.*	7,725
MacArthur, I. (*b.* 1925), *C.*, 459*Perth and E. Perthshire*	14,580
McBride, N., *Lab.*, 559*Swansea, E.*	14,014
*McCann, J. (*b.* 1910), *Lab.*, 484*Rochdale*	2,740
*MacColl, J. E. (*b.* 1908), *Lab.*, 605*Widnes*	1,598
†MacDermot, N. (*b.* 1916), *Lab.*, 173 *Derby, N.*	8,018
*McInnes, J. (*b.* 1901), *Lab.*, 247*Glasgow, Central*	7,206
*McKay, J. (*b.* 1885), *Lab.*, 578*Wallsend*	8,766
Mackie, J. (*b.* 1906), *Lab.*, 217*Enfield, E.*	3,624
McLaren, M. (*b.* 1914), *C.*, 106*Bristol, N.W.*	1,919
*McLaughlin, Mrs. F. P. A. (*b.* 1916), *U.U.*, 53*Belfast, W.*	8,836
*Maclay, Rt. Hon. J. S. (*b.* 1905), *L. and C.*, 478*Renfrew, W.*	2,753

	Maj.
†Maclean, Sir F. H. R., Bt. (*b.* 1911), *C.*, 26*Bute and N. Ayrshire*	8,052
*McLean, N. L. D. (*b.* 1918), *C.*, 322 *Inverness*	4,075
*McLeavy, F. (*b.* 1899), *Lab.*, 91*Bradford, E.*	5,527
*Macleod, Rt. Hon. I. N. (*b.* 1913), *C.*, 218*Enfield, W.*	13,830
*Macleod, Sir J. (*b.* 1913), *Nat. L.*, 323*Ross and Cromarty*	2,998
*McMaster, S. R. (*b.* 1927), *U.U.*, 50 *Belfast, E.*	10,098
*Macmillan, Rt. Hon. H. (*b.* 1894), *C.*, 110*Bromley*	15,452
*Macmillan, M. K. (*b.* 1913), *Lab.*, 597 *Western Isles*	1,167
*Macmillan, M. V. (*b.* 1921), *C.*, 273 *Halifax*	2,515
*MacPherson, M. (*b.* 1904), *Lab.*, 541 *Stirling and Falkirk*	2,626
*Macpherson, Rt. Hon. N. M. S. (*b.* 1908), *Nat. L. and C.*, 191*Dumfries*	7,430
*Maddan, M. F. M. (*b.* 1920), *C.*, 300 *Hitchin*	4,375
Maginnis, J. E. (*b.* 1919), *U.U.*, 19 *Armagh*	33,502
*Mahon, S. (*b.* 1914), *Lab.*, 86*Bootle*	2,915
*Maitland, Comdr. Sir J. F. W. (*b.* 1903), *C.*, 304*Horncastle*	9,871
*Mallalieu, E. L. (*b.* 1905), *Lab.*, 100*Brigg*	2,104
*Mallalieu, J. P. W. (*b.* 1908), *Lab.*, 311 *Huddersfield, E.*	3,085
Manuel, A. C. (*b.* 1901), *Lab.*, 27*Ayshire, Central*	1,676
Mapp, C. (*b.* 1903), *Lab.*, 445*Oldham, E.*	1,830
*Markham, Sir S. F. (*b.* 1897), *C.*, 112 *Buckingham*	1,746
*Marlowe, A. A. H. (*b.* 1904), *C.*, 309*Hove*	23,944
*Marples, Rt. Hon. A. E. (*b.* 1907), *C.*, 577*Wallasey*	15,066
Marsh, R. W. (*b.* 1928), *Lab.*, 269*Greenwich*	5,525
*Marshall Sir D. (*b.* 1906), *C.*, 82*Bodmin*	2,801
Marten, H. N. (*b.* 1916), *C.*, 29*Banbury*	6,714
*Mason, R. (*b.* 1924), *Lab.*, 34*Barnsley*	27,376
*Mathew, R. (*b.* 1911), *C.*, 303*Honiton*	13,053
Matthews, G. R. (*b.* 1908), *C.*, 398 *Meriden*	263
Maude, A. E. U. (*b.* 1912), *C.*, 549*Stratford*	3,470
*Maudling, Rt. Hon. R. (*b.* 1917), *C.*, 33 *Barnet*	13,399
*Mawby, R. L. (*b.* 1922), *C.*, 570*Totnes*	13,809
*Maydon, Lt.-Cmdr. S. L. C. (*b.* 1913), *C.*, 592*Wells*	6,905
*Mayhew, C. P. (*b.* 1915), *Lab.*, 619 *Woolwich, E.*	9,715
*Mellish, R. J. (*b.* 1913), *Lab.*, 55*Bermondsey*	14,341
*Mendelson, J. J. (*b.* 1917), *Lab.*, 456 *Penistone*	11,308
Millan, B. (*b.* 1927), *Lab.*, 248*Craigton*	602
Mills, W. S. (*b.* 1932), *U.U.*, 51*Belfast, N.*	13,533
Milne, E. J. (*b.* 1915), *Lab.*, 81*Blyth*	16,072
Miscampbell, N. A. (*b.* 1925), *C.*, 78 *Blackpool, N.*	973
*Mitchison, G. R. (*b.* 1890), *Lab.*, 335 *Kettering*	3,485
*Monslow, W. (*b.* 1895), *Lab.*, 36*Barrow-in-Furness*	3,974
Montgomery, W. F. (*b.* 1927), *C.*, 421 *Newcastle, E.*	98
*Moody, A. S. (*b.* 1891), *Lab.*, 242*Gateshead, E.*	7,665
*Moore, Sir T. C. R., Bt. (*b.* 1886), *C.*, 25*Ayr*	3,356
More, J. (*b.* 1907), *C.*, 382*Ludlow*	5,650
*Morgan, Rt. Hon. Sir J. K. Vaughan-, Bt. (*b.* 1905), *C.*, 476*Reigate*	12,501
Morgan, W. G. O. (*b.* 1920), *C.*, 171 *Denbigh*	4,625
Morris, J. (*b.* 1929), *Lab.*, 1*Aberavon*	17,638
*Morrison, J. G. (*b.* 1906), *C.*, 507*Salisbury.*	7,709
*Moyle, A. (*b.* 1894), *Lab.*, 444*Oldbury and Halesowen*	2,383
*Mulley, F. W. (*b.* 1918), *Lab.*, 516*Sheffield, Park*	15,480
*Nabarro, Sir G. D. N. (*b.* 1914), *C.*, 336 *Kidderminster*	9,343
*Neal, H. (*b.* 1897), *Lab.*, 83*Bolsover*	23,460
*Neave, A. M. S. (*b.* 1916), *C.*, 8*Abingdon.*	10,972
*Nicholls, Sir H., Bt. (*b.* 1912), *C.*, 460 *Peterborough*	4,584
*Nicholson, Sir G., Bt. (*b.* 1910), *C.*, 228 *Farnham*	13,738
*Noble, Rt. Hon. M. A. C. (*b.* 1913), *C.*, 18*Argyll*	9,243
*Nugent, Rt. Hon. Sir G. R. H., Bt. (*b.* 1907), *C.*, 271*Guildford*	13,442
*Oakshott, Sir H. D., Bt. (*b.* 1904), *C.*, 44 *Bebington*	9,861
*Oliver, G. H. (*b.* 1888), *Lab.*, 320*Ilkeston*	21,644
O'Malley, B. K. (*b.* 1930), *Lab.*, 488 *Rotherham*	13,232
*Oram, A. E. (*b.* 1913), *Lab.*, 205*East Ham, S.*	6,808
*Orr, Capt. L. P. S. (*b.* 1918), *U.U.*, 189 *Down, S.*	29,947
Osborn, J. H. (*b.* 1922), *C. and L.*, 513 *Hallam*	16,809
*Osborne, Sir C. (*b.* 1898), *C.*, 380*Louth*	8,803
*Oswald, T. (*b.* 1904), *Lab.*, 209*Edinburgh, Central*	617
*Owen, W. J. (*b.* 1901), *Lab.*, 412*Morpeth*	16,719
*Padley, W. E. (*b.* 1916), *Lab.*, 443*Ogmore*	23,265
Page, A. J. (*b.* 1919), *C.*, 282*Harrow, W.*	11,426
*Page, R. G. (*b.* 1911), *C.*, 162*Crosby*	15,056
*Paget, R. T. (*b.* 1908), *Lab.*, 432*Northampton*	2,717
*Palmer, Brig. Sir O. L. Prior- (*b.* 1897), *C.*, 624*Worthing*	23,778
*Pannell, N. A. (*b.* 1901), *C.*, 371*Kirkdale.*	2,747
*Pannell, T. C. (*b.* 1902), *Lab.*, 353*Leeds, W.*	4,593
*Pargiter, G. A. (*b.* 1897), *Lab.*, 524*Southall*	2,319
*Parker, J. (*b.* 1906), *Lab.*, 166*Dagenham*	20,383
*Parkin, B. T. (*b.* 1906), *Lab.*, 452*Paddington, N.*	768
*Partridge, E. (*b.* 1895), *C.*, 43*Battersea, S.*	1,752
*Paton, J. (*b.* 1886), *Lab.*, 436*Norwich, N.*	6,483
Pavitt, L. A. (*b.* 1914), *Lab.*, 608*Willesden, W.*	7,734
*Pearson, A. (*b.* 1897), *Lab.*, 466*Pontypridd*	15,957
Pearson, F. F. (*b.* 1911), *C.*, 151*Clitheroe*	6,211
*Peart, T. F. (*b.* 1914), *Lab.*, 623*Workington*	8,643
*Peel, W. J. (*b.* 1912), *C.*, 387*Leicester, S.E.*	14,630
*Pentland, N. (*b.* 1912), *Lab.*, 141*Chester-le-Street*	23,063
Percival, W. I. (*b.* 1921), *C.*, 531*Southport*	15,613
*Peyton, J. W. W. (*b.* 1919), *C.*, 629*Yeovil*	6,133
*Pickthorn, Sir K. W. M., Bt. (*b.* 1892), *C.*, 132*Carlton*	8,077
*Pike, Miss I. M. P. (*b.* 1918), *C.*, 397*Melton*	12,821
*Pilkington, Capt. Sir R. A. (*b.* 1908), *C.*, 467*Poole*	11,631
*Pitman, Sir I. J. (*b.* 1901), *C.*, 40*Bath*	6,533
*Pitt, Dame Edith (*b.* 1906), *C.*, 65*Edgbaston*	14,928
*Popplewell, E. (*b.* 1899), *Lab.*, 423*Newcastle, W.*	5,023
*Pott, H. P. (*b.* 1908), *C.*, 178*Devizes*	3,838
*Powell, Rt. Hon. J. E. (*b.* 1912), *C.*, 616 *Wolverhampton, S.W.*	11,167
*Prentice, R. E. (*b.* 1923), *Lab.*, 204*E. Ham, N.*	3,826

	Maj.
*Price, D. E. C. (*b.* 1924), C., 206 *Eastleigh*	3,256
*Price, H. A. (*b.* 1911), C., 364 *Lewisham, W.*	6,233
*Price, J. T. (*b.* 1902), Lab., 600 *Westhoughton*	10,725
Prior, J. M. L. (*b.* 1927), C., 381 *Lowestoft*	1,489
*Probert, A. R. (*b.* 1909), Lab., 2 *Aberdare*	24,305
*Proctor, W. T. (*b.* 1896), Lab., 208 *Eccles*	1,986
Proudfoot, G. W. (*b.* 1921), C., 150 *Cleveland*	1,655
*Pursey, Cmdr. H. (*b.* 1891), Lab., 313 *Hull, E.*	13,019
Pym, F. L. (*b.* 1922), C., 124 *Cambridgeshire*	6,077
Quennell, Miss J. M., C., 461 *Petersfield*	7,303
*Radclyffe, Sir C. E. Mott- (*b.* 1911), C., 611 *Windsor*	14,078
*Ramsden, J. E. (*b.* 1923), C., 279 *Harrogate*	19,270
*Randall, H. E. (*b.* 1899), Lab., 243 *Gateshead, W.*	9,768
*Rankin, J. (*b.* 1890), Lab., 250 *Govan*	9,820
*Rawlinson, Sir P. A. G. (*b.* 1919), C., 220 *Epsom*	24,445
*Redhead, E. C. (*b.* 1902), Lab., 582 *Walthamstow, W.*	8,108
*Redmayne, Rt. Hon. M. (*b.* 1910), C., 495 *Rushcliffe*	4,440
Rees, J. E. H. (*b.* 1928), C., 560 *Swansea, W.*	403
Rees, M. (*b.* 1920), Lab., 351 *Leeds, S.*	12,789
*Reid, W. (*b.* 1889), Lab., 255 *Provan*	4,367
*Renton, Rt. Hon. D. L. M. (*b.* 1908), *Nat. L. & C.*, 316 *Hunts*	8,271
*Reynolds, G. W. (*b.* 1927), Lab., 329 *Islington, N.*	3,898
*Rhodes, H. (*b.* 1895), Lab., 23 *Ashton-under-Lyne*	2,752
Ridley, Hon. N. (*b.* 1929), C., 148 *Cirencester and Tewkesbury*	11,855
*Ridsdale, J. E. (*b.* 1915), C. and Nat. L., 284 *Harwich*	12,065
*Rippon, Rt. Hon. A. G. F. (*b.* 1924), C., 437 *Norwich, S.*	2,244
*Roberts, A. (*b.* 1908), Lab., 431 *Normanton*	18,503
*Roberts, G. O. (*b.* 1913), Lab., 118 *Caernarvon*	7,942
*Roberts, Sir P. G., Bt. (*b.* 1912), C. and L., 514 *Heeley*	10,127
*Robertson, Sir D. (*b.* 1890), Ind., 120 *Caithness and Sutherland*	5,725
Robertson, J. (*b.* 1913), Lab., 454 *Paisley*	1,658
*Robinson, Rt. Hon. Sir J. R. (*b.* 1907), C., 79 *Blackpool, S.*	12,430
*Robinson, K. (*b.* 1911), Lab., 504 *St. Pancras, N.*	6,307
*Rodgers, J. C. (*b.* 1906), C., 510 *Sevenoaks*	13,921
Rodgers, W. T., Lab. 544 *Stockton-on-Tees*	7,582
*Rogers, G. H. R. (*b.* 1906), Lab., 333 *Kensington, N.*	877
Roots, W. L. (*b.* 1911), C., 334 *Kensington, S.*	21,940
*Ropner, Sir L., Bt. (*b.* 1895), C., 32 *Barkston Ash*	7,553
*Ross, W. (*b.* 1911), Lab., 337 *Kilmarnock*	10,292
Royle, A. H. F. (*b.* 1927), C., 481 *Richmond, Surrey*	14,186
*Royle, C. (*b.* 1896), Lab., 506 *Salford, W.*	2,861
*Russell, R. S. (*b.* 1904), C., 594 *Wembley, S.*	7,567
*Sandys, Rt. Hon. D. (*b.* 1908), C., 586 *Streatham*	12,705
*Scott, Col. Sir M. Stoddart- (*b.* 1901), C., 483 *Ripon*	12,966
Seymour, L. G. (*b.* 1900), C., 73 *Sparkbrook*	885
*Sharples, R. C. (*b.* 1916), C., 557 *Sutton and Cheam*	15,398
Shaw, M. N. (*b.* 1920), L. & C., 101 *Brighouse and Spenborough*	666
*Shepherd, W. S. (*b.* 1912), C., 135 *Cheadle*	17,318
*Shinwell, Rt. Hon. E. (*b.* 1884), Lab., 201 *Easington*	27,293
*Short, E. W. (*b.* 1912), Lab., 420 *Newcastle, Central*	11,566
Silkin, Hon. J. E. (*b.* 1923), Lab. 172 *Deptford*	7,483
*Silverman, J. (*b.* 1905), Lab., 64 *Aston*	2,531
*Silverman, S. S. (*b.* 1895), Lab., 416 *Nelson and Colne*	1,264
Skeet, T. H. H. (*b.* 1918), C., 607 *Willesden, E.*	2,210
*Skeffington, A. M. (*b.* 1909), Lab., 286 *Hayes and Harlington*	4,152
*Slater, Mrs. H. (*b.* 1903), Lab., 547 *Stoke, N.*	12,814
*Slater, J. (*b.* 1904), Lab., 509 *Sedgefield*	8,871
Small, W. W. (*b.* 1909), Lab., 256 *Scotstoun*	3,370
*Smith, Rt. Hon. Sir D. C. Walker-, Bt. (*b.* 1910), C., 293 *Herts, E.*	10,181
Smith, D. G. (*b.* 1926), C., 96 *Brentford and Chiswick*	2,919
*Smith, E. (*b.* 1896), Lab., 548 *Stoke, S.*	9,260
Smith, G. Johnson (*b.* 1924), C., 301 *Holborn and St. Pancras, S.*	656
*Smith Rt. Hon. Dame Patricia Hornsby- (*b.* 1914), C., 146 *Chislehurst*	6,679
*Smithers, P. H. B. O. (*b.* 1913), C., 610 *Winchester*	12,792
*Smyth, Brig. Rt. Hon Sir J. G., Bt. (*b.* 1893), C., 343 *Norwood*	6,983
*Snow, J. W. (*b.* 1910), Lab., 366 *Lichfield and Tamworth*	1,550
*Soames, Rt. Hon. A. C. J. (*b.* 1920), C., 46 *Bedford*	6,767
*Sorensen, R. W. (*b.* 1891), Lab., 365 *Leyton*	3,919
*Soskice, Rt. Hon. Sir F. (*b.* 1902), Lab., 425 *Newport*	3,648
*Spearman, Sir A. C. M. (*b.* 1901), C., 508 *Scarborough and Whitby*	14,467
*Speir, R. M. (*b.* 1910), C., 297 *Hexham*	10,520
*Spriggs, L. (*b.* 1910), Lab., 501 *St. Helens*	14,005
*Stanley, Hon. R. O. (*b.* 1920), C., 434 *North Fylde*	15,738
*Steele, T. (*b.* 1905), Lab., 193 *Dunbartonshire, W.*	2,141
*Stevens, G. P. (*b.* 1902), C., 469 *Langstone*	18,281
*Steward, H. M. (*b.* 1904), C., 543 *Stockport, S.*	2,540
*Stewart, R. M. M. (*b.* 1906), Lab., 239 *Fulham*	2,944
Stodart, J. A. (*b.* 1916), C., 215 *Edinburgh, W.*	11,932
*Stonehouse, J. T. (*b.* 1925), Lab. 590 *Wednesbury*	6,683
*Stones, W. (*b.* 1904), Lab., 155 *Consett*	16,270
*Storey, Sir S., Bt. (*b.* 1896), C., 550 *Stretford*	9,350
*Strauss, Rt. Hon. G. R. (*b.* 1901), Lab., 344 *Vauxhall*	7,125
*Stross, Dr. B. (*b.* 1899), Lab., 546 *Stoke, Central*	10,425
*Studholme, Sir H. G., Bt. (*b.* 1899), C., 563 *Tavistock*	10,770
*Summers, Sir G. S. (*b.* 1902), C., 24 *Aylesbury*	8,955
Swain, T. (*b.* 1912), Lab., 175 *Derbyshire, N.E.*	15,332
*Swingler, S. T. (*b.* 1915), Lab., 419 *Newcastle-under-Lyme*	6,002

	Maj.
*Symonds, J. B. (_b._ 1901), _Lab._, 604 _Whitehaven_	6,130
Talbot, J. E. (_b._ 1906), _C._, 99 _Brierley Hill_	4,133
Tapsell, P. H, B. (_b._ 1930), _C._, 441 _Nottingham, W._	164
Taverne, D. (_b._ 1928), _Lab._, 367 _Lincoln_	7,652
*Taylor, Sir C. S. (_b._ 1910), _C._, 202 _Eastbourne_	16,037
Taylor, E. (_b._ 1905), _C._, 84 _Bolton, E._	641
Taylor, F. H. (_b._ 1907), _C._, 392 _Moss Side_	3,086
*Taylor, H. B. (_b._ 1895), _Lab._, 396 _Mansfield_	16,366
*Taylor, Sir W. J., Bt. (_b._ 1902), _C. and Nat. L._, 92 _Bradford, N._	2,671
*Teeling, Sir L. W. B. (_b._ 1903), _C._, 103 _Brighton, Pavilion_	15,974
*Temple, J. M. (_b._ 1910), _C._, 140 _Chester_	10,355
Thatcher, Mrs. M. H. (_b._ 1925), _C._, 235 _Finchley_	16,260
*Thomas, I. R. (_b._ 1896), _Lab._, 480 _Rhondda, W._	16,152
*Thomas, Sir L. M. (_b._ 1906), _C._, 126 _Canterbury_	15,100
*Thomas, P. J. M. (_b._ 1920), _C._, 156 _Conway_	4,535
*Thomas, T. G. (_b._ 1909), _Lab._, 129 _Cardiff, W._	3,132
Thompson, Dr. A. E. (_b._ 1924), _Lab._, 196 _Dunfermline_	8,734
*Thompson, Sir K. P., Bt. (_b._ 1909), _C._, _Walton_	4,034
*Thompson, Sir R. H. M., Bt. (_b._ 1912), _C._, 165 _Croydon, S._	8,215
*Thomson, G. M. (_b._ 1921), _Lab._, 194 _Dundee, E._	4,181
*Thorneycroft, Rt. Hon. G. E. P. (_b._ 1909), _C._, 408 _Monmouth_	6,257
*Thornton, E. (_b._ 1905), _Lab._, 229 _Farnworth_	8,037
Thorpe, J. J. (_b._ 1929), _L._, 179 _Devon, N._	362
*Tiley, A. (_b._ 1910), _C. and Nat. L._, 94 _Bradford, W._	5,105
*Tilney, J. D. (_b._ 1907), _C._, 375 _Wavertree_	16,232
*Timmons, J. (_b._ 1891), _Lab._, 88 _Bothwell_	4,352
*Tomney, F. (_b._ 1908), _Lab._, 276 _Hammersmith, N._	6,747
*Tooth, Sir H. Lucas-, Bt. (_b._ 1903), _C._, 290 _Hendon, S._	11,955
*Touche, Rt. Hon. Sir G. C., Bt. (_b._ 1895), _C._, 183 _Dorking_	14,959
Turner, C. W. C. (_b._ 1922), _C._, 620 _Woolwich, W._	3,695
*Turton, Rt. Hon. R. H. (_b._ 1903), _C._, 564 _Thirsk and Malton_	15,095
*Tweedsmuir, Lady (_b._ 1915), _C._, 4 _Aberdeen, S._	8,122
van Straubenzee, W. R. (_b._ 1924), _C._, 614 _Wokingham_	15,991
*Vane, W. M. F. (_b._ 1909), _C._, 602 _Westmorland_	11,692
*Vickers, Miss J. H. (_b._ 1907), _C. and Nat. L._, 462 _Devonport_	6,454
*Vosper, Rt. Hon. D. F. (_b._ 1916), _C._, 494 _Runcorn_	12,778
*Wade, D. W. (_b._ 1904), _L._, 312 _Huddersfield, W._	9,652
Wainwright, E. (_b._ 1908), _Lab._, 170 _Dearne Valley_	27,883
*Wakefield, Sir W. W. (_b._ 1898), _C._, 503 _St. Marylebone_	14,771
*Walder, A. D. (_b._ 1928), _C._, 299 _High Peak_	1,868
*Walker, Rt. Hon. P. C. Gordon- (_b._ 1907), _Lab._, 521 _Smethwick_	3,544
Walker, P. E. (_b._ 1931), _C._, 621 _Worcester_	3,597
*Wall, P. H. B. (_b._ 1916), _C._, 274 _Haltemprice_	16,352
*Warbey, W. N. (_b._ 1903), _Lab._, 21 _Ashfield_	20,742
*Ward, Dame Irene, _C._, 574 _Tynemouth_	13,944
*Watkins, T. E. (_b._ 1903), _Lab._, 95 _Brecon and Radnor_	6,472
*Watkinson, Rt. Hon. H. A. (_b._ 1910), _C._, 613 _Woking_	17,311
*Watt, J. D. Gibson- (_b._ 1918), _C._, 292 _Hereford_	7,578
*Webster, D. W. E. (_b._ 1923), _C._, 603 _Weston-super-Mare_	16,904
*Weitzman, D. (_b._ 1898), _Lab._, 545 _Stoke Newington and Hackney, W._	8,435
Wells, J. J. (_b._ 1925), _C._, 385 _Maidstone_	10,463
*Wells, P. L. (_b._ 1891), _Lab._, 230 _Faversham_	253
*Wells, W. T. (_b._ 1908), _Lab._, 579 _Walsall, N._	9,952
*White, Mrs. E. L. (_b._ 1909), _Lab._, 236 _Flint, E._	75
*White, R. C. Brooman- (_b._ 1912), _C._, 496 _Rutherglen_	1,522
*Whitelaw, W. S. I. (_b._ 1918), _C._, 457 _Penrith and the Border_	14,209
Whitlock, W. C. (_b._ 1918), _Lab._, 439 _Nottingham, N._	5,053
*Wigg, G. E. C. (_b._ 1900), _Lab._, 190 _Dudley_	5,725
*Wilkins, W. A. (_b._ 1899), _Lab._, 107 _Bristol, S._	9,582
*Willey, F. T. (_b._ 1910), _Lab._, 553 _Sunderland, N._	2,208
*Williams, D. J. (_b._ 1897), _Lab._, 415 _Neath_	20,206
*Williams, Rev. L. (_b._ 1911), _Lab._, 7 _Abertillery_	22,191
*Williams, P. G. (_b._ 1922), _C._, 554 _Sunderland, S._	990
*Williams, R. D. (_b._ 1908), _C._, 225 _Exeter_	5,661
*Williams, W. R. (_b._ 1895), _Lab._, 393 _Openshaw_	8,438
†Williams, W. T. (_b._ 1915), _Lab._, 587 _Warrington_	7,000
*Willis, E. G. (_b._ 1903), _Lab._, 210 _Edinburgh, E._	312
*Wills, Sir G. (_b._ 1905), _C._, 97 _Bridgwater_	8,296
*Wilson, H. G. B. (_b._ 1903), _C._, 572 _Truro_	4,487
*Wilson, Rt. Hon. J. H. (_b._ 1916), _Lab._, 317 _Huyton_	5,927
*Winterbotton, R. E. (_b._ 1899), _Lab._, 512 _Brightside_	16,033
Wise, Lt.-Col. A. R. (_b._ 1901), _C._, 492 _Rugby_	470
*Wood, Rt. Hon. R. F. (_b._ 1920), _C._, 98 _Bridlington_	17,391
*Woodburn, Rt. Hon. A. (_b._ 1890), _Lab._, 539 _Clackmannan and E. Stirling_	7,872
Woodhouse, Hon. C. M. (_b._ 1917), _C._, 451 _Oxford_	8,488
Woodnutt, H. F. M. (_b._ 1918), _C._, 327 _Isle of Wight_	12,832
*Woof, R. E. (_b._ 1911), _Lab._, 80 _Blaydon_	12,250
*Woollam, J. V. (_b._ 1927), _C._, 376 _Liverpool, West Derby_	3,333
Worsley, W. M. J. (_b._ 1925), _C._, 332 _Keighley_	170
Wyatt, W. L. (_b._ 1918), _Lab._, 87 _Bosworth_	1,394
*Yates, V. F. (_b._ 1900), _Lab._, 68 _Ladywood_	6,323
*Yates, W. (_b._ 1921), _C._, 625 _The Wrekin_	2,978
*Young, M. H. C. Hughes- (_b._ 1912), _C._, 583 _Wandsworth, Central_	1,972
*Zilliacus, K. (_b._ 1894), _Ind. Lab._, 391 _Gorton_	857

THE HOUSE OF COMMONS BY CONSTITUENCIES

The figures following the name of the Constituency denote the total number of *Electors* in the Parliamentary Division at the General Election of 1959.

ABBREVIATIONS.—*C.* = Conservative; *Comm.* = Communist; *I.L.P.* = Independent Labour Party; *Ind.* = Independent; *L.* = Liberal; *Lab.* = Labour; *Nat. L.* = National Liberal; *Scot. Nat.* = Scottish Nationalist; *S.F.* = Sinn Fein; *U.U.* = Ulster Unionist; *Welsh Nat.* = Welsh Nationalist. An asterisk * denotes membership of the last House for the same division; an obelisk †, for a different division.

Aberavon (Glamorgan)
E. 56,316
1 *J. Morris, Lab.* 30,397
R. E. G. Howe, *C.* 12,759
I. M. Lewis, *Welsh Nat.* .. 3,066
Lab. maj. *17,638*
(1955 Lab. maj. 16,297)

Aberdare (Welsh Borough)
E. 49,124
2***A. R. Probert, Lab.* 30,889
B. McGlynn, *C.* 6,584
K. P. Thomas, *Welsh Nat.* 3,367
Lab. maj. *24,305*
(1955 Lab. maj. 23,366)

Aberdeen (2)
NORTH E. 66,351
3**H. S. J. Hughes*, Q.C., *Lab.* 32,793
J. Stewart-Clark, *C.* 15,137
W. A. Milne, *Scot. Nat.* .. 2,964
Lab. maj. *17,656*
(1955 Lab. maj. 16,796)
SOUTH E. 58,086
4**Lady Tweedsmuir, C.* 25,471
P. M. Doig, *Lab.* 17,349
Mrs. E. T. Dangerfield, *L.* 4,558
C. maj. *8,122*
(1955 C. maj. 7,190)

Aberdeenshire (2)
EAST E. 44,628
5**P. W. Wolrige-Gordon, C.* 18,982
J. B. Urquhart, *Lab.* 10,980
C. maj. *8,002*
(Nov. 1958, by-election, C. maj. 6,328) (1955 C. maj. 10,057)
WEST E. 46,429
6 *A. F. Hendry, C.* 22,937
W. Kemp, *Lab.* 10,542
C. maj. *12,395*
(1955 C. maj. 10,928)

Abertillery (Monmouthshire)
E. 38,674
7**Rev. L. Williams, Lab.* .. 26,931
R. J. Maddocks, *C.* 4,740
Lab. maj. *22,191*
(1955 Lab. maj. 21,518)

Abingdon (Berkshire)
E. 63,844
8**A. M. S. Neave*, D.S.O., O.B.E., M.C., T.D., *C.* .. 27,943
P. Picard, *Lab.* 16,971
Mrs. V. I. Perl, *L.* 6,651
C. maj. *10,972*
(1955 C. maj. 8,634)

Accrington (English Borough)
E. 49,933
9**H. Hynd, Lab.* 22,242
M. Henry, *C.* 21,642
Lab. maj. *600*
1955 Lab. maj. 1,345)

Acton (English Borough)
E. 46,835
10 *P. W. Holland, C.* 19,358
*J. A. Sparks, *Lab.* 18,438
C. maj. *920*
(1955 Lab. maj. 525)

Aldershot (Hampshire)
E. 56,820
11**Sir E. Errington, Bt. C.* .. 25,161
R. E. Brooks, *Lab.* 12,270
Miss E. Lakeman, *L.* 5,679
C. maj. *12,891*
(1955 C. maj. 9,572)

ALL SAINTS—*See* Birmingham

Altrincham and Sale (English Borough)
E. 64,860
12**Rt. Hon. F. J. Erroll*, T.D., *C.* 29,992
N. Atkinson, *Lab.* 14,141
D. F. Burden, *L.* 9,415
C. maj. *15,851*
(1955 C. maj. 18,412)

Anglesey
E. 36,281
13**C. Hughes, Lab.* 13,249
O. M. Roberts, *C.* 7,005
Dr. R. T. Jones, *Welsh Nat.* 4,121
R. G. Lloyd, *L.* 3,796
Lab. maj. *6,244*
(1955 Lab. maj. 4,573)

Angus and Kincardine (2)
NORTH ANGUS AND MEARNS
E. 36,513
14**Sir C. N. Thornton-Kemsley*, O.B.E., T.D., *L. & C.* 17,536
R. Hughes, *Lab.* 8,486
L. & C. maj. 9,050
(1955 L. & C. maj. 10,193)
SOUTH E. 44,840
15**Capt. Sir J. A. L. Duncan, Bt., L. & C.* 19,435
G. Y. Mackie, *L.* 8,139
J. L. Stewart, *Lab.* 6,477
L. & C. maj. *11,296*
(1955 L. & C. maj. 14,971)

Antrim (2)
NORTH E. 69,880
16 *H. Clark, U.U.* 42,807
J. Dougan, *S.F.* 2,280
U.U. maj. *40,527*
(1955 U.U. maj. 34,954)
SOUTH E. 93,634
17**S. K. Cunningham*, Q.C., *U.U.* 52,786
M. Traynor, *S.F.* 2,745
U.U. maj. *50,041*
(1955 U.U. maj. 45,192)

ARDWICK—*See* Manchester

Argyll
E. 40,015
18**Rt. Hon. M. A. C. Noble, C.* 16,599
D. Nisbet, *Lab.* 7,356
Hon. G. E. W. Noel, *L.* 4,469
C. maj. *9,243*
(June 1958, by-election, C. maj. 5,166) (1955 C. maj. 10,028)

Armagh
E. 73,416
19 *J. E. Maginnis, U.U.* ... 40,325
J. Lynch, *S F.* 6,823
U.U. maj. *33,502*
(1955 U.U. maj. 17,254)

Arundel and Shoreham (West Sussex) E. 75,601
20**Capt. H. B. Kerby, C.* .. 37,034
A. L. Bell, *Lab.* 12,745
A. L. Ford, *L.* 8,081
C. maj. *24,289*
(1955 C. maj. 19,992)

Ashfield (Nottinghamshire)
E. 61,139
21**W. N. Warbey, Lab.* ... 35,432
J. G. W. Sandys, *C.* ... 14,690
Lab. maj. *20,742*
(1955 Lab. maj. 20,069)

Ashford (Kent)
E. 52,097
22**Rt. Hon. W. F. Deedes*, M.C., *C.* 25,383
R. G. Ward, *Lab.* 14,983
C. maj. *10,400*
(1955 C. maj. 8,307)

Ashton under Lyne (English Borough)
E. 60,706
23* *H. Rhodes*, D.F.C., *Lab.* 25,991
R. Horrocks, *C.* 23,239
Lab. maj *2,752*
(1955 Lab. maj. 1,965)

ASTON—*See* Birmingham
ATTERCLIFFE—*See* Sheffield

Aylesbury (Buckinghamshire)
E. 54,089
24**Sir G. S. Summers, C.* . 22,504
H. Gray, *Lab.* 13,549
H. L. Fry, L. 7,897
C. maj. *8,955*
(1955 C. maj. 5,761)

Ayrshire and Bute (5)
AYR E. 45,444
25**Sir T. C. R. Moore, Bt.*, C.B.E., *C.* 19,659
A. Eadie, *Lab.* 16,303
C. maj. *3,356*
(1955 C. maj. 6,140)
BUTE AND NORTH AYRSHIRE
E. 44,291
26†*Sir F. H. R. Maclean, Bt.*, C.B.E., M.C., *C.* ... 20,270
D. Lambie, *Lab.* 12,218
C. maj. *8,052*
(1955 C. maj. 9,155)
CENTRAL E. 48,596
27 *A. C. Manuel, Lab.* 21,901
*D. L. Spencer-Nairn, *C.* 20,225
Lab. maj. *1,676*
(1955 C. maj. 167)
SOUTH E. 48,063
28**E. Hughes, Lab.* 24,774
W. H. Hunter, *C.* 14,105
Lab. maj. *10,669*
(1955 Lab. maj. 8,209)

See also Kilmarnock

Banbury (Oxfordshire)
E. 64,414
29 *H. N. Marten, C.* 26,413
D. J. Buckle, *Lab.* 19,699
K. Colman, *L.* 6,074
C. maj. *6,714*
(1955 C. maj. 4,125)

Banff
E. 32,129
30**Sir W. S. Duthie*, O.B.E., C. 14,359
R. W. Irvine, *Lab.* 5,992
C. maj. *8,367*
(1955 C. maj. 8,306)

Barking (English Borough)
E. 51,654
31 *T. E. N. Driberg, Lab.* 23,454
K. F. Dibben, *C.* 11,454
D. E. Evans, *L.* 5,648
Lab. maj. *12,000*
(1955 Lab. maj. 15,047)

Barkston Ash (Yorks, W.R.)
E. 54,448
32**Sir L. Ropner, Bt.*, M.C., T.D., *C.* 26,200
R. W. Bowes, *Lab.* 18,647
C. maj. *7,553*
(1955 C. maj. 6,167)
E. 64,739

Barnet (Hertfordshire)
33**Rt. Hon. R. Maudling, C.* 33,136
R. M. Prideaux, *Lab.* 19,737
C. maj. *13,399*
(1955 C. maj. 10,729)

Barnsley (English Borough)
E. 69,833
34**R. Mason, Lab.* 42,565
J. P. H. Bent, *C.* 15,189
Lab. maj. *27,376*
(1955 Lab. maj. 24,709)

Barons Court (London Borough)
E. 50,032
35 *W. C. Carr, C.* 18,658
*W. T. Williams, *Lab.* 17,745
S. H. J. A. Knott, *Ind. L.* 1,766
C. maj. *913*
(1955 Lab. maj. 125)

Barrow in Furness
(English Borough) *E.* 51,904
36**W. Monslow, Lab.* 23,194
M. Metcalf, *C.* 19,220
Lab. maj. *3,974*
(1955 Lab. maj. 2,759)

Barry (Glamorgan)
E. 60,206
37**H. R. Gower, C.* 30,313
D. R. Evans, *Lab.* 20,790
C. maj. *9,523*
(1955 C. maj. 7,363)

Basingstoke (Hampshire)
E. 60,979
38**D. K. Freeth, C.* 25,314
S. G. Conbeer, *Lab.* 14,070
Dr. L. G. Housden, *L.* .. 9,126
C. maj. *11,244*
(1955 C. maj. 6,290)

Bassetlaw (Nottinghamshire)
E. 59,907
39**Rt. Hon. F. J. Bellenger, Lab.* 27,875
M. J. Cowling, *C.* 20,162
Lab. maj. *7,713*
(1955 Lab. maj. 7,498)

Bath (English Borough)
E. 57,150
40**Sir I. J. Pitman*, K.B.E., *C.* 24,048
G. E. Mayer, *Lab.* 17,515
G. R. Allen, *L.* 6,214
C. maj. *6,533*
(1955 C. maj. 6,843)

L+

Batley and Morley
(English Borough) *E.* 56,031
41**A. D. D. Broughton, Lab.* 26,781
Mrs. B. M. Garden, *C.* .. 19,115
Lab. maj. *7,666*
(1955 Lab. maj. 9,208)

Battersea (2)
NORTH *E.* 40,937
42**Rt. Hon. D. P. T. Jay, Lab.* 19,595
R. G. Taylor, *C.* 9,289
Lab. maj. *10,306*
(1955 Lab. maj. 12,922)

SOUTH *E.* 37,320
43**E. Partridge, C.* 14,208
G. W. Rhodes, *Lab.* 12,451
W. B. Mattinson, *L.* 2,774
C. maj. *1,752*
(1955 C. maj. 679)

Bebington (English Borough)
E. 70,374
44**Sir H. D. Oakshott, Bt.*, M.B.E., *C.* 33,705
G. J. Oakes, *Lab.* 23,844
C. maj. *9,861*
(1955 C. maj. 9,423)

Beckenham (English Borough)
E. 73,421
45**P. C. Goodhart, C.* 36,528
H. Ferguson, *Lab.* 13,395
H. H. Monroe, *L.* 9,365
C. maj. *23,133*
(March, 1957, by-election, C. maj. 12,176)
(1955 C. maj. 21,237)

Bedfordshire (3)
BEDFORD *E.* 55,278
46**Rt. Hon. A. C. J. Soames*, C.B.E., *C.* 23,495
M. A. Foley, *Lab.* 16,728
M. L. Rowlandson, L. 5,966
C. maj. *6,767*
(1955 C. maj. 4,941)

MID *E.* 53,889
47**Rt. Hon. A. T. Lennox-Boyd*, C.H., *C.* 21,301
B. E. Magee, *Lab.* 16,127
W. G. Matthews, *L.* 8,099
C. maj. *5,174*
(By-election, Nov. 16, 1960)
S. L. E. Hastings, C. 17,503
B. E. Magee, *Lab.* 11,281
W. G. Matthews, *L.* 9,550
C. F. H. Gilliard, *Ind.* .. 235
C. maj. *6,222*
(1955 C. maj. 3,964)

SOUTH *E.* 65,416
48**N. J. Cole*, V.R.D., *L. & C.* 25,861
W. H. Johnson, *Lab.* .. 21,102
Mrs. R. R. Soskin, *L.* .. 7,912
L. & C. maj. *4,759*
(1955 L. & C. maj. 2,468)

Bedwellty (Monmouthshire)
E. 44,890
49**H. J. Finch, Lab.* 30,697
C. J. Cox, *C.* 6,817
Lab. maj. *23,880*
(1955 Lab. maj. 23,692)

Belfast (4)
EAST *E.* 58,663
50**S. R. McMaster, U.U.* .. 26,510
J. S. Gardner, *N.I.Lab.* .. 16,412
B. Boswell, *S.F.* 1,204
U.U. maj. *10,098*
(March 1959, by election, U.U. maj. 5,260)
(1955 U.U. maj. 13,897)

NORTH *E.* 74,494
51 *W. S. Mills, U.U.* 32,173
J. W. McDowell, *N.I. Lab.* 18,640
F. McGlade, *S.F.* 2,156
U.U. maj. *13,533*
(1955 U.U. maj. 18,680)

SOUTH *E.* 50,861
52**Rt. Hon. Sir D. C. Campbell*, K.B.E., C.M.G., *U.U.* 30,164
N. Searight, *N.I. Lab.* .. 9,318
Miss S. M. Murnaghan, *L.* 3,253
B. O'Reilly, *S.F.* 434
U.U. maj. *20,846*
(1955 U.U. maj. 25,884)
(By-election pending)

WEST *E.* 73,405
53**Mrs. F. P. A. McLaughlin, U.U.* 28,898
J. Brennan, *Ind. Lab.* .. 20,062
T. A. Heenan, *S.F.* 4,416
U.U. maj. *8,836*
(1955 U.U. maj. 18,141)

Belper (Derbyshire)
E. 69,336
54**Rt. Hon. G. A. Brown, Lab.* 31,344
Mrs. J. Ratcliffe, *C.* 27,007
Lab. maj. *4,337*
(1955 Lab. maj. 6,099)

Berkshire (4). *See* **Abingdon, Newbury, Windsor and Wokingham**

Bermondsey (London Borough)
E. 37,921
55**R. J. Mellish, Lab.* 20,528
K. P. Payne, *C.* 6,187
Lab. maj. *14,341*
(1955 Lab. maj. 17,400)

Berwick and East Lothian
E. 50,569
56**Maj. Rt. Hon. Sir W. J. Anstruther-Gray, Bt.*, M.C., *C.* 22,472
P. Jones, *Lab.* 19,622
C. maj. *2,850*
(1955 C. maj. 2,710)

Berwick upon Tweed
(Northumberland)
E. 40,951
57**Viscount Lambton, C.* .. 19,904
R. C. Jelley, *Lab.* 11,637
C. maj. *8,267*
(1955 C. maj. 6,277)

Bethnal Green
(London Borough)
E. 57,617
58**P. Holman, Lab.* 24,228
P. R. Roney, *C.* 7,412
J. Hart, *L.* 5,508
J. L. Read, *Soc. Party of G.B.* 899
Lab. maj. *16,816*
(1955 Lab. maj. 20,701)

Bexley (English Borough)
E. 64,906
59**Rt. Hon. E. R. G. Heath*, M.B.E., *C.*.... 32,025
E. A. Bramall, *Lab.*.... 23,392
C. maj..... *8,633*
(1955 C. maj. 4,499)

Billericay (Essex)
E. 78,328
60 *E. L. Gardner*, Q.C., *C.*.. 29,224
Mrs. R. A. Smythe, *Lab.* 24,402
P. M. T. Sheldon-Williams, *L.*.... 9,347
C. maj..... *4,822*
(1955 C. maj. 4,206)

Bilston (English Borough)
E. 65,861
61**R. J. Edwards, Lab.*.... 27,068
F. J. Oxford, *C.*.... 23,523
Lab. maj..... *3,545*
(1955 Lab. maj. 7,008)

Birkenhead (English Borough)
E. 59,960
62**P. H. Collick, Lab.*.... 22,990
K. G. Routledge, *C.*.... 19,361
G. F. Bilson, *L.*.... 4,658
Lab. maj..... *3,629*
(1955 Lab. maj. 3,174)

Birmingham (13)

All Saints *E.* 48,611
63 *J. H. Hollingworth, C.*.. 17,235
*D. H. Howell, *Lab.*.... 17,215
C. maj..... *20*
(1955 Lab. maj. 1,307)

Aston *E.* 57,593
64**J. Silverman, Lab.*.... 21,518
A. M. Beaumont-Dark, *C.*.... 18,984
Lab. maj..... *2,534*
(1955 Lab. maj. 8,262)

Edgbaston *E.* 55,719
65**Dame Edith Pitt*, D.B.E., *C.*.... 26,401
Mrs. N. F. Hinks, *Lab.*. 11,473
C. maj..... *14,928*
(1955 C. maj. 14,094)

Hall Green *E.* 61,066
66**Rt. Hon. A. Jones, C.*.... 29,148
D. H. V. Fereday, *Lab.*. 15,431
H. W. Maynard, *Ind. C.* 1,955
C. maj..... *13,717*
(1955 C. maj. 10,697)

Handsworth *E.* 55,596
67**Rt. Hon. Sir E. C. G. Boyle, Bt., C.*.... 23,243
A. Murie, *Lab.*.... 13,116
S. W. Keatley, *Ind.*.... 1,867
C. maj..... *10,127*
(1955 C. maj. 10,285)

Ladywood *E.* 39,131
68**V. F. Yates, Lab.*.... 14,717
T. G. John, *C.*.... 8,393
Lab. maj..... *6,324*
(1955 Lab. maj. 8,811)

Northfield *E.* 74,269
69**W. D. Chapman, Lab.*.. 29,587
R. E. Eyre, *C.*.... 28,647
Lab. maj..... *940*
(1955 Lab. maj. 2,884)

Perry Barr *E.* 50,306
70**C. A. Howell, Lab.*.... 16,811
S. C. Greatrix, *C.*.... 16,628
W. L. Lawler, *L.*.... 5,611
H. Pearce, *Comm.*.... 424
Lab. maj..... *183*
(1955 Lab. maj. 1,680)

Selly Oak *E.* 58,017
71**H. E. Gurden, C.*.... 24,950
J. O. Rhydderch, *Lab.*. 16,594
C. maj..... *8,356*
(1955 C. maj. 6,720)

Small Heath *E.* 51,004
72**W. E. Wheeldon, Lab.*.. 19,213
B. C. Owens, *C.*.... 14,282
Lab. maj..... *4,931*
(By-election, March 23, 1961)
†*D. H. Howell, Lab.*.... 12,182
B. C. Owens, *C.*.... 5,923
W. Kirk, *L.*.... 2,476
Lab. maj..... *6,259*
(1955 Lab. maj. 7,960)

Sparkbrook *E.* 47,731
73 *L. G. Seymour, C.*.... 17,751
J. T. Webster, *Lab.*.... 16,865
C. maj..... *886*
(1955 Lab. maj. 3,211)

Stechford *E.* 55,674
74**R. H. Jenkins, Lab.*.... 21,919
J. M. Bailey, *C.*.... 18,996
Lab. maj..... *2,923*
(1955 Lab. maj. 6,740)

Yardley *E.* 59,135
75 *L. H. Cleaver, C.*.... 23,482
*H. C. Usborne, *Lab.* .. 22,097
C. maj..... *1,385*
(1955 Lab. maj. 3,124)

Bishop Auckland (Durham)
E. 48,865
76 *H. J. Boyden, Lab.*.... 21,706
N. W. Murray, *C.*.... 13,377
J. G. Pease, *L.*.... 4,377
Lab. maj..... *8,329*
(1955 Lab. maj. 5,845)

Blackburn (English Borough)
E. 60,362
77**Mrs. B. A. Castle, Lab.*.. 27,356
J. M. A. Yerburgh, *C.*. 24,490
Lab. maj..... *2,866*
(1955 Lab. maj. 489)

Blackley—*See* **Manchester**

Blackpool (2)

North *E.* 57,078
78**Rt. Hon. Sir T. Low*, K.C.M.G., C.B.E., D.S.O., T.D., *C.*.... 25,297
W. H. Dugdale, *Lab.*.. 9,440
H. Hague, *L.*.... 8,990
C. maj..... *15,857*
(By-election, March 13, 1962)
N. A. Miscampbell, C... 12,711
H. Hague, *L.*.... 11,738
Miss S. Summerskill, *Lab.* 8,776
C. maj..... *973*
(1955 C. maj. 16,030)

South *E.* 52,927
79**Rt. Hon. Sir J. R. Robinson, C.*.... 25,767
P. P. Hall, *Lab.*.... 13,337
C. maj..... *12,430*
(1955 C. maj. 12,225)

Blaydon (Durham)
E. 47,854
80**R. E. Woof, Lab.*.... 25,969
G. W. Iredell, *C.*.... 13,719
Lab. maj..... *12,250*
(Feb. 1956, by-election, Lab. maj. 10,714) (1955 Lab. maj. 12,523)

Blyth (English Borough)
E. 62,599
81**Rt. Hon. A. Robens, Lab.* 38,615
D. M. Walters, *C.*.... 13,122
Lab. maj..... *25,494*
(By-election, Nov. 24, 1960)
E. J. Milne, Lab..... 23,438
D. M. Walters, *C.*.... 7,366
C. Pym, *Ind.*.... 3,223
Lab. maj..... *16,072*
(1955 Lab. maj. 23,093)

Bodmin (Cornwall)
E. 45,000
82**Sir D. Marshall, C.*.... 16,853
P. J. Bessell, *L.*.... 14,052
T. F. Mitchell, *Lab.*.... 5,769
C. maj..... *2,801*
(1955 C. maj. 7,659)

Bolsover (Derbyshire)
E. 50,455
83**H. Neal, Lab.*.... 32,536
R. G. Marlar, *C.*.... 9,076
Lab. maj..... *23,460*
(1955 Lab. maj. 22,019)

Bolton (2)

East *E.* 60,580
84**P. I. Bell*, T.D., Q.C., *C.*. 25,885
R. Haines, *Lab.*.... 23,153
C. maj..... *2,732*
(By-election, Nov. 16, 1960)
E. Taylor, C..... 15,499
R. L. Howarth, *Lab.*.... 14,858
C. F. Byers, O.B.E., *L.*. 10,173
J. E. Dayton, *Ind.*.... 493
C. maj..... *641*
(1955 C. maj. 3,511)

West *E.* 54,035
85**A. F. Holt, L.*.... 23,533
P. Cameron, *Lab.*.... 19,545
L. maj..... *3,988*
(1955 L. maj. 4,813)

Bootle (English Borough)
E. 50,647
86**S. Mahon, Lab.*.... 21,294
H. O. Cullen, *C.*.... 18,379
Lab. maj..... *2,915*
(1955 Lab. maj. 1,438)

Bosworth (Leicestershire)
E. 65,115
87 *W. L. Wyatt, Lab.*.... 27,734
P. L. Braithwaite, *C.*.. 26,341
Lab. maj..... *1,393*
(1955 Lab. maj. 4,100)

Bothwell (Lanarkshire)
E. 55,845
88**J. Timmons, Lab.*.... 25,119
W. G. Greig, *C.*.... 20,767
Lab. maj..... *4,352*
(1955 Lab. maj. 3,610)

Bournemouth (2)

East and Christchurch
E. 60,657
89 *J. H. Cordle, C.*.... 29,014
J. D. Rutland, *Lab.*.... 9,222
W. J. Wareham, *L.*.... 8,308
C. maj..... *19,792*
(1955 C. maj. 18,498)

West *E.* 68,209
90**Sir J. B. Eden, Bt., C.*.. 33,575
G. W. Spicer, *Lab.*.... 15,957
C. maj..... *17,618*
(1955 C. maj. 16,784)

Bradford (4)

EAST *E.* 47,514
91**F. McLeavy, Lab.* 20,056
D. A. Dalgleish, *C. & Nat. L.* 14,529
Lab. maj. *5,527*
(1955 Lab. maj. 8,875)

NORTH *E.* 51,957
92**Sir W. J. Taylor, Bt.*, C.B.E., *C. & Nat. L.* ... 22,850
J. Marshall, M.B.E., *Lab.* 20,179
C. & Nat. L. maj. *2,671*
(1955 C. & Nat. L. maj. 69)

SOUTH *E.* 57,018
93**G. Craddock, Lab.* 21,172
R. Winston Jones, *C. & Nat. L.* 18,158
H. Womersley, *L.* 6,850
Lab. maj. *3,014*
(1955 Lab. maj. 3,710)

WEST *E.* 50,044
94**A. Tiley, C. & Nat. L.* .. 23,012
S. Hyam, *Lab.* 17,906
C. & Nat. L. maj. *5,106*
1955 C. & Nat. L. maj. 3,159)

Brecon and Radnor
E. 51,357
95**T. E. Watkins, Lab.* 25,411
J. H. Davies, *C.* 18,939
Lab. maj. *6,472*
(1955 Lab. maj. 7,541)

Brentford and Chiswick
(English Borough) *E.* 39,881
96 *D. G. Smith, C.* 17,869
Dr. H. B. O. Cardew, *Lab.* 14,950
C. maj. *2,919*
(1955 C. maj. 2,105)

Bridgwater (Somerset)
E. 55,770
97**Sir G. Wills*, M.B.E., *C.* 23,002
J. Finnigan, *Lab.* 14,706
P. G. Watkins, *L.* 7,893
C. maj. *8,296*
(1955 C. maj. 7,717)

Bridlington (Yorkshire E.R.)
E. 55,006
98**Rt. Hon. R. F. Wood, C.* 27,438
H. Moor, *Lab.* 10,047
C. maj. *17,391*
(1955 C. maj. 15,266)

Brierley Hill (Staffordshire)
E. 71,161
99 *J. E. Talbot, C.* 31,202
*C. J. Simmons, *Lab.* ... 27,069
C. maj. *4,133*
(1955 Lab. maj. 949)

Brigg (Lincolnshire)
E. 71,138
100**E. L. Mallalieu*, Q.C., *Lab.* 28,997
R. C. Baker, *C.* 26,893
Lab. maj. *2,104*
(1955 Lab. maj. 5,021)

Brighouse and Spenborough
(English Borough) *E.* 54,422
101**Rt. Hon. L. J. Edwards*, O.B.E., *Lab.* 23,290
M. N. Shaw, *L. & C.* 23,243
Lab. maj. *47*
(By-election, March 17, 1960)
M. N. Shaw, L. & C. 22,472
G. C. Jackson, *Lab.* ... 21,806
L. & C. maj. *666*
(1955 Lab. maj. 1,626)

Brighton (2)

KEMPTOWN *E.* 61,119
102 *D. P. James, C.* 25,411
L. C. Cohen, *Lab.* 19,665
C. maj. *5,746*
(1955 C. maj. 5,257)

PAVILION *E.* 57,238
103**Sir L. W. B. Teeling, C.* 27,972
R. G. White, *Lab.* 11,998
C. maj. *15,974*
(1955 C. maj. 14,386)

Bristol (6)

CENTRAL *E.* 49,476
104**S. S. Awbery, Lab.* 19,905
L. G. Pine, *C.* 17,209
Lab. maj. *2,696*
(1955 Lab. maj. 8,752)

NORTH EAST *E.* 64,319
105 *A. C. N. Hopkins, C. & Nat. L.* 24,258
*W. Coldrick, *Lab.* 21,574
Mrs. A. M. Pearce, *L.* 5,030
C. & Nat. L. maj. .. *2,684*
(1955 Lab. maj. 876)

NORTH WEST *E.* 57,831
106 *M. McLaren, C.* 24,938
*T. C. Boyd, *Lab.* 23,019
C. maj. *1,919*
(1955 Lab. maj. 1,655)

SOUTH *E.* 58,671
107**W. A. Wilkins, Lab.* .. 27,010
G. E. McWatters, *C.* .. 17,428
Lab. maj. *9,582*
(1955 Lab. maj. 10,976)

SOUTH EAST *E.* 57,416
108**Hon. A. N. W. Benn, Lab.* 26,273
M. A. J. St. Clair, *C.* .. 20,446
Lab. maj. *5,827*
(By-election, May 4, 1961)
**Visct. Stansgate (A. N. W. Benn), Lab.* 23,275
M. A. J. St. Clair, *C.* .. 10,231
Lab. maj. *13,044*
(On July 28, 1961, *M. A. J. St. Clair, C.* was declared to have been elected).
(1955 Lab. maj. 8,047)
(By-election pending)

WEST *E.* 56,080
109**R. G. Cooke, C.* 27,768
M. Cocks, *Lab.* 7,651
C. A. Hart-Leverton, *L.* 5,835
C. maj. *20,117*
(March 1957, by-election, C. maj. 14,162) (1955 C. maj. 22,001)

BRIXTON—*See* **Lambeth**

Bromley (English Borough)
E. 48,937
110**Rt. Hon. H. Macmillan, C.* 27,055
A. J. Murray, *Lab.* 11,603
C. maj. *15,452*
(1955 C. maj. 13,139)

Bromsgrove (Worcestershire)
E. 66,924
111**J. C. G. Dance*, E.R.D., *C.* 32,473
C. B. B. Norwood, *Lab.* 23,433
C. maj. *9,040*
(1955 C. maj. 5,174)

Buckinghamshire (4)

BUCKINGHAM *E.* 54,905
112**Sir S. F. Markham, C.* .. 22,304
Capt. I. R. Maxwell, *Lab.* 20,558
E. L. F. Richards, *L.* .. 4,577
C. maj. *1,746*
(1955 C. maj. 1,140)

SOUTH *E.* 72,466
113**R. M. Bell, C.* 34,154
Dr. R. J. Sankey, *Lab.* 13,050
R. K. Brown, O.B.E., T.D., Q.C., *L.* 10,589
C. maj. *21,104*
(1955 C. maj. 17,981)

See also **Aylesbury and Wycombe**

Burnley (English Borough)
E. 57,990
114 *D. Jones, Lab.* 27,675
E. Brooks, *C.* 20,902
Lab. maj. *6,773*
(1955 Lab. maj. 5,636)

Burton (Staffordshire)
E. 58,220
115**J. C. Jennings, C.* 26,926
E. McGarry, *Lab.* 21,032
C. maj. *5,894*
(1955 C. maj. 2,973)

Bury and Radcliffe
(English Borough) *E.* 64,897
116**J. C. Bidgood, C.* 28,623
R. P. Walsh, *Lab.* 24,715
C. maj. *3,908*
(1955 C. maj. 3,749)

Bury St. Edmunds (Suffolk)
E. 57,908
117**Sir W. T. Aitken*, K.B.E., *C.* 26,730
Mrs. A. M. A. Walter, *Lab.* 18,768
C. maj. *7,962*
(1955 C. maj. 4,570)

Bute and North Ayrshire—*See* **Ayrshire and Bute**

Caernarvonshire (2)

CAERNARVON *E.* 41,202
118**G. O. Roberts, Lab.* ... 17,506
T. E. Hooson, *C.* 9,564
D. O. Jones, *Welsh Nat.* 7,293
Lab. maj. *7,942*
(1955 Lab. maj. 9,221)

See also **Conway**

Caerphilly (Glamorgan)
E. 46,671
119**Rt. Hon. N. Edwards, Lab.* 28,154
W. R. Lewis, *C.* 7,181
J. D. A. Howell, *Welsh Nat.* 3,420
Lab. maj. *20,973*
(1955 Lab. maj. 18,672)

Caithness and Sutherland
E. 26,716
120**Sir D. Robertson, Ind.* .. 12,163
R. K. Murray, *Lab.* .. 6,438
Ind. maj. *5,725*
(1955 C. maj. 5,089)

Camberwell (2)

DULWICH *E.* 66,988
121**R. C. D. Jenkins, C.* .. 24,991
A. L. Hill, *Lab.* 22,740
W. J. Searle, *L.* 5,324
C. maj. *2,251*
(1955 C. maj. 1,851)

PECKHAM *E.* 57,850
122★*Mrs. F. K. Corbet, Lab.* 24,389
A. F. Lockwood, *C.*.. 13,007
Lab. maj.......... *11,382*
(1955 Lab. maj. 13,768)

Cambridge (English Borough)
E. 59,745
123★*Sir H. W. Kerr, Bt., C.* 24,350
R. M. D. Davies, *Lab*.............. 17,543
A. G. de Montmorency, *L*........ 5,792
C. maj........... *6,807*
(1955 C. maj. 7,127)

Cambridgeshire
E. 60,698
124★*S. G. Howard,* Q.C., *C.* 27,407
W. Royle, *Lab*....... 19,928
C. maj........... *7,479*
(By-election, March 16, 1961)
F. L. Pym, C......... 17,643
R. M. D. Davies, *Lab*.. 11,566
R. Moore, *L*........ 9,219
C. maj........... *6,077*
(1955 C. maj. 3,974)

Cannock (Staffordshire)
E. 65,472
125★*Miss J. Lee, Lab*....... 29,624
P. H. Lugg, *C. & L*... 22,485
Lab. maj.......... *7,139*
(1955 Lab. maj. 8,298)

Canterbury (Kent)
E. 62,011
126★*Sir L. M. Thomas,* M.B.E., T.D., *C*...... 30,846
G. E. Peters, *Lab*...... 15,746
C. maj........... *15,100*
(1955 C. maj. 14,295)

Cardiff (3)

NORTH *E.* 59,986
127 *D. S. Box, C.*....... 28,737
G. S. Viner, *Lab*...... 18,054
E. P. Roberts, *Welsh Nat*.............. 2,553
S. G. Worth, *Ind*..... 408
C. maj........... *10,683*
(1955 C. maj. 9,185)

SOUTH EAST *E.* 64,574
128★*L. J. Callaghan, Lab*.... 26,915
M. H. A. Roberts, *C*.. 26,047
Lab. maj.......... *868*
(1955 Lab. maj. 3,240)

WEST *E.* 59,524
129★*T. G. Thomas, Lab*.... 25,390
A. L. Hallinan, *C*..... 22,258
Lab. maj.......... *3,132*
(1955 Lab. maj. 4,962)

Cardiganshire
E. 38,878
130★*E. R. Bowen,* Q.C., *L*.. 17,868
Mrs. L. Rees Hughes, *Lab*.............. 8,559
G. W. Evans, *Welsh Nat*.............. 3,880
L. maj........... *9,309*
(1955 L. maj. 8,817)

Carlisle (English Borough)
E. 49,519
131★*Dr. D. M. Johnson, C*.. 21,948
A. Hargreaves, *Lab*... 19,950
C. maj........... *1,998*
(1955 C. maj. 370)

Carlton (Nottinghamshire)
E. 64,554
132★*Sir K. W. M. Pickthorn, Bt., C*....... 30,722
P. Myers, *Lab*........ 22,645
C. maj........... *8,077*
(1955 C. maj. 6,857)

Carmarthenshire (2)

CARMARTHEN *E.* 57,195
133★*Lady Megan Lloyd-George, Lab*....... 23,399
A. T. Davies, *L*...... 16,766
J. B. Evans, *C*....... 6,147
H. H. Roberts, *Welsh Nat*.............. 2,545
Lab. maj.......... *6,633*
(Feb. 1957, by-election, Lab. maj. 3,069) (1955 L. maj. 3,333)
See also **Llanelly**

Carshalton (Surrey)
E. 68,391
134★*Rt. Hon. A. H. Head,* C.B.E., M.C., *C*...... 30,454
J. H. Powell, *Lab*..... 17,210
J. H. G. Browne, *L*.... 8,744
C. maj........... *13,244*
(By-election, Nov. 16, 1960)
Capt. W. Elliot, D.S.C., R.N., *C*........... 19,175
J. H. G. Browne, *L*... 10,250
B. Thomas, *Lab*...... 7,696
C. maj........... *8,925*
(1955 C. maj. 11,505)

CATHCART—*See* **Glasgow**

Cheadle (Cheshire)
E. 71,205
135★*W. S. Shepherd, C*.... 32,787
R. N. Cuss, *L*........ 15,469
C. R. Morris, *Lab*.... 11,373
C. maj........... *17,318*
(1955 C. maj. 19,974)

CHEETHAM—*See* **Manchester**

Chelmsford (Essex)
E. 61,630
136★*Sir H. Ashton,* K.B.E., M.C., *C*........... 29,992
B. R. Clapham, *Lab*.. 20,124
C. maj........... *9,868*
(1955 C. maj. 5,149)

Chelsea (London Borough)
E. 47,085
137 *Capt. J. S. S. Litchfield,* R.N., *C*........... 20,985
L. Goldstone, *Lab*..... 6,308
K. G. Wellings, *L*.... 3,662
C. maj........... *14,677*
(1955 C. maj. 15,052)

Cheltenham (English Borough)
E. 52,946
138★*Maj. W. W. Hicks Beach,* T.D., *C*...... 21,997
Dr. K. G. Pendse, *Lab.* 12,725
G. G. Watson, *L*..... 8,428
C. maj........... *9,272*
(1955 C. maj. 7,621)

Chertsey (Surrey)
E. 55,609
139★*Rt. Hon. Sir L. F. Heald,* Q.C., *C*...... 24,836
J. S. Barr, *Lab*........ 14,150
A. R. Mayne, *L*....... 5,146
C. maj........... *10,686*
(1955 C. maj. 8,365)

Cheshire (10). *See* **Cheadle, Chester (City of), Crewe, Knutsford, Macclesfield, Nantwich, Northwich, Runcorn, Stalybridge and Hyde** and **Wirral**

Chester (City of) (Cheshire)
E. 57,617
140★*J. M. Temple, C*...... 27,847
L. Carter-Jones, *Lab*... 17,492
C. maj........... *10,355*
(Nov. 1956, by-election, C. maj. 6,348) (1955 C. maj. 11,002)

Chester-le-Street (Durham)
E. 53,884
141★*N. Pentland, Lab*...... 33,901
W. R. Rees-Mogg, *C.* 10,838
Lab. maj.......... *23,063*
(Sept. 1956, by-election, Lab. maj. 21,287) (1955 Lab. maj. 22,276)

Chesterfield (English Borough)
E. 65,270
142★*Sir G. Benson, Lab*..... 30,534
J. A. Lemkin, *C. & Nat. L*........... 17,084
G. R. Smedley-Stevenson, *L*....... 6,360
Lab. maj.......... *13,450*
(1955 Lab. maj. 7,854)

Chichester (West Sussex)
E. 63,958
143★*W. H. Loveys, C*..... 30,755
J. S. Spooner, *Lab*..... 9,546
J. Newman, *L*........ 6,913
C. maj........... *21,209*
(Nov. 1958, by-election, C. maj. 13,654) (1955 C. maj. 18,122)

Chigwell (Essex)
E. 50,213
144★*J. A. Biggs-Davison, C.* 23,422
A. S. Harman, *Lab*.... 17,860
C. maj........... *5,562*
(1955 C. maj. 1,875)

Chippenham (Wiltshire)
E. 51,923
145★*Rt. Hon. Sir D. M. Eccles,* K.C.V.O., *C*... 21,696
R. W. Portus, *Lab*.... 12,911
J. C. Hall, *L*........ 7,059
C. maj........... *8,785*
(By-election, Nov. 22, 1962)
D. E. Awdry, C...... 13,439
Hon. C. W. Layton, *L*. 11,851
R. W. Portus, *Lab*... 10,633
K. Jerrome, *Ind*...... 260
J. P. Naylor, *Ind*...... 237
M. J. A. Smith, *Ind*... 88
C. maj........... *1,588*
(1955 C. maj. 6,695)

Chislehurst (Kent)
E. 59,646
146★*Rt. Hon. Dame Patricia Hornsby-Smith,* D.B.E., *C*.................25,748
Mrs. M. Reid, *Lab*... 19,069
D. C. Blackburn, *L*... 6,366
C. maj........... *6,679*
(1955 C. maj. 3,870)

Chorley (Lancashire)
E. 59,086
147★*C. Kenyon, Lab*....... 25,641
F. H. Taylor, *C*...... 24,965
Lab. maj.......... *676*
(1955 Lab. maj. 1,338)

Cirencester and Tewkesbury
(Gloucestershire)
E. 58,099
148 *Hon. N. Ridley, C.*... 28,169
J. M. Bowyer, *Lab.*... 16,314
C. maj............ *11,855*
(1955 The Speaker's maj. 12,978)

Cities of London and Westminster
E. 68,896
149†*Rt. Hon. Sir H. B. H. Hylton-Foster*, Q.C., *C.* (now *The Speaker*).. 27,489
W. Howie, *Lab.*..... 10,301
D. Monsey, *L.*....... 4,409
C. maj............ *17,188*
(1955 C. maj. 18,044)

Clackmannan and East Stirling—*See* **Stirling and Clackmannan**
CLAPHAM—*See* **Wandsworth**

Cleveland (Yorkshire, N.R.)
E. 71,281
150 *G. W. Proudfoot, C.*... 30,445
*A. M. F. Palmer, *Lab.*. 28,790
C. maj............ *1,655*
(1955 Lab. maj. 181)

Clitheroe (Lancashire)
E. 44,350
151 *F. F. Pearson, C.*..... 22,314
W. Rutter, *Lab.*..... 16,103
C. maj............ *6,211*
(1955 C. maj. 4,944)

Coatbridge and Airdrie
(Scottish Burgh)
E. 53,223
152 *J. Dempsey, Lab.*...... 22,747
Mrs. C. S. Morton, *C.* 21,953
Lab. maj........... *794*
(1955 Lab. maj. 4,664)

Colchester (Essex)
E. 57,776
153*Rt. *Hon. C. J. M. Alport*, T.D., *C.*..... 24,592
Mrs. J. I. Edmondson, *Lab.*............. 17,096
P. M. Linfoot, *L.*..... 5,942
C. maj............ *7,496*
(By-election, March 16, 1961)
P. A. F. Buck, C...... 17,891
J. W. Fear, *Lab.*...... 12,547
Capt. H. Fry, *L.*...... 7,487
C. maj............ *5,344*
(1955 C. maj. 4,898)

Colne Valley (Yorks, W.R.)
E. 51,777
154**Rt. Hon. W. G. Hall, Lab.*............. 19,284
C. J. Barr, *C.*........ 13,030
R. S. Wainwright, *L.* 11,254
Lab. maj........... *6,254*
(By-election, March 21, 1963)
A. E. P. Duffy, Lab... 18,033
R. S. Wainwright, *L.* 15,994
A. Alexander, *C.*..... 6,238
A. Fox, *Ind.*......... 266
Lab. maj........... *2,039*
(1955 Lab. maj. 3,596)

Consett (Durham)
E. 59,206
155**W. Stones, Lab.*...... 32,307
D. A. Orde, *C.*....... 16,037
Lab. maj........... *16,270*
(1955 Lab. maj. 15,755)

Conway (Caernarvonshire)
E. 45,660
156**P. J. M. Thomas, C.*.. 17,795
S. Jones, *Lab.*........ 13,260
J. H. Bellis, *L.*....... 3,845
I. B. Rees, *Welsh Nat.* 2,852
C. maj............ *4,535*
(1955 C. maj. 4,824)

Cornwall (5)
NORTH *E.* 42,764
157 *J. S. R. Scott-Hopkins, C.*............... 16,701
E. T. Malindine, *L.*... 15,712
W. C. Ferman, *Lab.*.. 3,389
C. maj............ *989*
(1955 C. maj. 1,604)
See also **Bodmin, Falmouth and Camborne, St. Ives and Truro**

Coventry (3)
EAST *E.* 70,689
158**R. H. S. Crossman*, O.B.E., *Lab.*........ 32,744
W. J. Biffen, *C.*...... 24,982
Lab. maj........... *7,762*
(1955 Lab. maj. 6,104)
NORTH *E.* 53,598
159**M. Edelman, Lab.*..... 23,035
F. C. Maynard, *C.*.... 21,794
Lab. maj........... *1,241*
(1955 Lab. maj. 3,173)
SOUTH *E.* 67,394
160 *P. N. Hocking, C.*.... 28,584
*Miss E. F. Burton, *Lab.* 26,754
C. maj............ *1,830*
(1955 Lab. maj. 1,688)
CRAIGTON—*See* **Glasgow**

Crewe (Cheshire)
E. 50,971
161**S. S. Allen*, Q.C., *Lab.*. 22,811
G. L. Beaman, *C.*.... 19,030
Lab. maj........... *3,781*
(1955 Lab. maj. 6,356)

Crosby (English Borough)
E. 57,495
162**R. G. Page*, M.B.E., *C.* 29,801
D. E. Brown, *Lab.*... 14,745
C. maj............ *15,056*
(1955 C. maj. 15,436)

Croydon (3)
NORTH EAST *E.* 57,174
163**Vice-Adm. J. Hughes-Hallett*, C.B., D.S.O., *C.*............... 24,345
W. J. Wolfgang, *Lab.*. 15,440
Dr. A. E. Bender, *L.*.. 6,109
C. maj............ *8,905*
(1955 C. maj. 8,481)
NORTH WEST *E.* 58,177
164**F. W. Harris, C.*...... 25,111
D. W. Chalkley, *Lab.*. 14,658
Miss I. E. Thurston, *L.* 6,061
C. maj............ *10,453*
(1955 C. maj. 10,537)
SOUTH *E.* 63,636
165**Sir R. H. M. Thompson, Bt., C.*........ 29,284
F. A. Messer, *Lab.*.... 21,069
C. maj............ *8,215*
(1955 C. maj. 6,700)

Cumberland (3). *See* **Penrith and the Border, Whitehaven and Workington**

Dagenham (English Borough)
E. 73,968
166**J. Parker, Lab.*........ 37,009
A. F. Waley, *C.*...... 16,626
Lab. maj........... *20,383*
(1955 Lab. maj. 25,093)

Darlington (English Borough)
E. 59,342
167 *A. T. Bourne-Arton, C.* 24,318
R. H. Lewis, *Lab.*.... 19,901
J. P. McQuade, *L.*.... 5,863
C. maj............ *4,417*
(1955 C. maj. 2,581)

Dartford (Kent)
E. 66,599
168**S. Irving, Lab.*........ 25,323
P. E. Walker, *C.*...... 24,047
B. C. Davis, *L.*...... 5,881
Lab. maj........... *1,276*
(1955 Lab. maj. 4,198)

Darwen (Lancashire)
E. 55,461
169**C. Fletcher-Cooke*, Q.C., *C.*........... 27,483
T. Park, *Lab.*........ 19,141
C. maj............ *8,342*
(1955 C. maj. 7,916)

Dearne Valley (Yorks, W.R.)
E. 59,444
170 *E. Wainwright*, B.E.M., *Lab.*............. 39,088
D. S. W. Blacker, *C.*. 11,205
Lab. maj........... *27,883*
(1955 Lab. maj. 26,316)

Denbighshire (2)
DENBIGH *E.* 53,000
171 *W. G. O. Morgan, C.*. 17,893
Dr. G. T. Hughes, *L.*. 13,268
S. Williams, *Lab.*..... 8,620
Dr. D. A. Jones, *Welsh Nat.*............. 3,077
C. maj............ *4,625*
(1955 Nat. L. maj. 4,641)
See also **Wrexham**

Deptford (London Borough)
E. 49,412
172**Sir L. A. Plummer, Lab.*............. 21,226
J. D. Brimacombe, *C.*. 13,038
Lab. maj........... *8,188*
(By-election, July 4, 1963)
Hon. J. E. Silkin, Lab.. 12,209
D. J. Penwarden, *L.*.. 4,726
J. D. Brimacombe, *C.* 4,023
Lab. maj........... *7,483*
(1955 Lab. maj. 11,453)

Derby (2)
NORTH *E.* 55,976
173**Group-Capt. C. A. B. Wilcock*, O.B.E., A.F.C., *Lab.*........ 22,673
R. J. Maxwell-Hyslop, *C.*............... 20,266
Lab. maj........... *2,407*
(By-election, April 17, 1962)
†*N MacDermot*, Q.C., *Lab.* 16,497
L. Irving, *L.*......... 8,479
T. M. Wray, *C.*...... 7,502
T. Lynch, *Ind.*....... 886
Lab. maj........... *8,018*
(1955 Lab. maj. 5,006)
SOUTH *E.* 54,131
174**Rt. Hon. P. J. Noel-Baker, Lab.*........ 20,776
T. M. Wray, *C.*..... 17,345
A. L. Smart, *L.*...... 4,746
Lab. maj........... *3,431*
(1955 Lab. maj. 6,509)

Derbyshire (7)
NORTH EAST *E.* 73,678
175 *T. Swain, Lab.*....... 37,444
R. A. Ward, *C.*..... 22,112
Lab. maj........... *15,332*
(1955 Lab. maj. 17,344)

SOUTH EAST E. 65,457
176 *F. L. J. Jackson, C.* ... 25,374
★A. J. Champion, *Lab*.. 25,362
T. Lynch, *L*. ... 4,980
C. maj. ... *12*
(1955 Lab. maj. 1,581)
WEST E. 43,881
177★*E. B. Wakefield*, C.I.E., *C*. ... 22,034
A. E. Kitts, *Lab*. ... 13,925
C. maj. ... *8,109*
(By-election, June 6, 1962)
A. M. Crawley, M.B.E. *C*. 12,455
Lt.-Col. R. Gardner-Thorpe, *L*. ... 11,235
J. Dilks, *Lab*. ... 9,431
R. E. Gregory, *Ind*. ... 1,433
C. maj. ... *1,220*
(1955 C. maj. 6,756)
See also **Belper, Bolsover, High Peak and Ilkeston**

Devizes (Wiltshire)
E. 50,779
178★*H. P. Pott, C*. ... 20,682
W. E. Cave, *Lab*. ... 16,844
J. Norton, *Ind*. ... 2,707
C. maj. ... *3,838*
(1955 C. maj. 2,075)
DEVONPORT—*See* **Plymouth**

Devonshire (6)
NORTH E. 43,486
179 *J. J. Thorpe, L*. ... 15,831
★Hon. J. L. Lindsay, *C*. 15,469
G. W. Pitt, *Lab*. ... 5,567
L. maj. ... *362*
(1955 C. maj. 5,226)
See also **Honiton, Tavistock, Tiverton, Torrington and Totnes**

Dewsbury (English Borough)
E. 54,894
180 *D. Ginsburg, Lab*. ... 20,870
J. M. Fox, *C*. ... 17,201
J. M. McLusky, *L*. ... 7,321
Lab. maj. ... *3,669*
(1955 Lab. maj. 7,417)

Doncaster (English Borough)
E. 58,505
181★*A. P. L. Barber*, T.D., *C*. 26,521
W. E. Garrett, *Lab*. ... 22,935
C. maj. ... *3,586*
(1955 C. maj. 1,660)

Don Valley (Yorks, W.R.)
E. 68,876
182 *R. Kelley, Lab*. ... 40,935
G. H. Dodsworth, *C*.. 16,787
Lab. maj. ... *24,148*
(1955 Lab. maj. 24,732)

Dorking (Surrey)
E. 51,092
183★*Rt. Hon. Sir G. C. Touche, Bt. C*. ... 24,564
S. R. Mills, *Lab*. ... 9,605
W. S. Watson, *L*. ... 6,582
C. maj. ... *14,959*
(1955 C. maj. 12,509)

Dorset (3)
NORTH E. 46,844
184★*Col. Sir R. H. Glyn, Bt.*, O.B.E., T.D., *C*. .. 20,255
J. A. Emlyn-Jones, *L*.. 11,604
H. J. Dutfield, *Lab*. ... 6,548
C. maj. ... *8,651*
(June 1957, by-election, C. maj. 3,102) (1955 C. maj. 7,159)
SOUTH E. 56,196
185★*Viscount Hinchingbrooke, C*. ... 22,050
C. F. Ascher, *Lab*. ... 15,357
L. I. Norbury-Williams, *L*. ... 6,887
C. maj. ... *6,693*
(By-election, Nov. 22, 1962)
N. G. Barnett, Lab. ... 13,783
A. E. U. Maude, T.D. *C*. 13,079
L. I. Norbury-Williams, *L*. ... 8,910
Sir P. K. Debenham, Bt., *Ind*. ... 5,057
P. Burn, *Ind*. ... 181
M. Fudge, *Ind*. ... 82
J. C. O'Connor, *Ind*. . 45
Lab. maj. ... *704*
(1955 C. maj. 5,417)
WEST E. 44,109
186★*K. S. D. W. Digby*, T.D., *C*. ... 19,747
L. W. King, *Lab*. ... 11,536
J. H. Goodden, *L*. ... 4,850
C. maj. ... *8,211*
(1955 C. maj. 6,763)

Dover (Kent)
E. 63,512
187★*J. S. W. Arbuthnot*, M.B.E., T.D., *C*. ... 27,939
H. W. Lee, *Lab*. ... 24,698
C. maj. ... *3,241*
(1955 C. maj. 3,018)

Down (2)
NORTH E. 89,686
188★*G. B. H. Currie*, M.B.E., *U.U*. ... 51,773
J. Campbell, *S.F*. ... 1,039
U.U. maj. ... *50,734*
(1955 U.U. maj. 48,678)
SOUTH E. 77,628
189★*Capt. L. P. S. Orr, U.U*. ... 36,875
K. O'Rourke, *S.F*. ... 6,928
U.U. maj. ... *29,947*
(1955 U.U. maj. 18,297)

Dudley (English Borough)
E. 72,829
190★*G. E. C. Wigg, Lab*. .. 31,826
F. E. Spiller, *C*. ... 26,101
Lab. maj. ... *5,725*
(1955 Lab. maj. 11,051)
DULWICH—*See* **Camberwell**

Dumfries
E. 57,212
191★*Rt. Hon. N. M. S. Macpherson, Nat. L. & C*. 25,867
G. C. Moodie, *Lab*. ... 18,437
Nat. L. & C. maj. .. *7,430*
(1955 Nat. L. & C. maj. 9,078)

Dunbartonshire (2)
EAST E. 64,961
192★*C. R. Bence, Lab*. ... 27,942
D. C. Anderson, V.R.D., Q.C., *C*. ... 24,593
A. E. Henderson, *Comm*. ... 2,200
Lab. maj. ... *3,349*
(1955 Lab. maj. 1,130)
WEST E. 50,277
193★*T. Steele, Lab*. ... 22,105
N. M. Glen, *C*. ... 19,964
Lab. maj. ... *2,141*
(1955 Lab. maj. 1,952)

Dundee (2)
EAST E. 58,537
194★*G. M. Thomson, Lab*.. 26,263
R. A. McCrindle, *C. & Nat. L*. ... 22,082
Lab. maj. ... *4,181*
(1955 Lab. maj. 4,040)
WEST E. 62,804
195★*Rt. Hon. E. J. St. L. Strachey, Lab*. ... 25,857
Dr. R. R. Taylor, *C*.. 25,143
D. P. Bowman, *Comm*. 1,087
Lab. maj. ... *714*
(1955 Lab. maj. 1,874)
(By-election pending)

Dunfermline (Scottish Burgh)
E. 47,737
196 *Dr. A. E. Thompson, Lab*. ... 23,478
W. A. Elliott, *Nat. L. & C*. ... 14,744
Lab. maj. ... *8,734*
(1955 Lab. maj. 7,976)

Durham (9)
DURHAM E. 62,192
197★*C. F. Grey, Lab*. ... 33,795
C. P. MacCarthy, *C*.. 17,106
Lab. maj. ... *16,689*
(1955 Lab. maj. 15,772)
NORTH WEST E. 50,629
198★*J. W. Ainsley, Lab*. ... 28,064
Mrs. O. Sinclair, *C*. .. 13,172
Lab. maj. ... *14,892*
(1955 Lab. maj. 14,006)
See also **Bishop Auckland, Blaydon, Chester-le-Street, Consett, Easington, Houghton-le-Spring and Sedgefield**

Ealing (2)
NORTH E. 59,768
199★*J. W. Barter, C*. ... 27,312
W. S. Hilton, *Lab*. ... 23,036
C. maj. ... *4,276*
(1955 C. maj. 246)
SOUTH E. 53,296
200★*B. C. C. Batsford, C*. ... 24,761
H. G. Garside, *Lab*. ... 12,039
Sir J. J. A. Mostyn, Bt., *L*. ... 4,842
C. maj. ... *12,722*
(June, 1958, by-election, C. maj., 6,159)
(1955 C. maj. 12,530)

Easington (Durham)
E. 56,690
201★*Rt. Hon. E. Shinwell, Lab*. ... 36,552
G. W. Rossiter, *C*. ... 9,259
Lab. maj. ... *27,293*
(1955 Lab. maj. 25,257)

Eastbourne (East Sussex)
E. 62,971
202★*Sir C. S. Taylor, C*. ... 27,874
A. A. Dumont, *Lab*. .. 11,837
Lt.-Col. R. L. Gardner-Thorpe, *L*. ... 8,955
C. maj. ... *16,037*
(1955 C. maj. 14,218)

East Grinstead (East Sussex)
E. 65,437
203★*Mrs. E. V. E. Emmet, C*. ... 31,759
R. W. G. Humphreys, *Lab*. ... 10,104
P. A. T. Furnell, *L*. ... 9,100
C. maj. ... *21,655*
(1955 C. maj. 16,700)

East Ham (2)
NORTH E. 38,014
204★*R. E. Prentice, Lab*. ... 16,001
J. H. S. Bangay, *C*. ... 12,175
Lab. maj. ... *3,826*
(May, 1957, by-election, Lab. maj. 5,979)
(1955 Lab. maj. 5,545)

SOUTH E. 39,764
205★*A. E. Oram, Lab.* 18,230
R. J. Watts, *C.* 11,422
Lab. maj. *6,808*
(1955 Lab. maj. 8,699)

Eastleigh (Hampshire)
E. 55,215
206★*D. E. C. Price, C.* 24,949
C. J. S. Rowland, *Lab.* 21,693
C. maj. *3,256*
(1955 C. maj. 545)

Ebbw Vale (Monmouthshire)
E. 39,299
207★*Rt. Hon. A. Bevan, Lab.* 27,326
A. G. Davies, *C.* 6,404
Lab. maj. *20,922*
(By-election, Nov. 17, 1960)
M. M. Foot, Lab. 20,528
Sir B. M. Rhys-Williams, Bt., *C.* 3,799
Lt.-Col. P. H. Lort-Phillips, *L.* 3,449
E. Roberts, *Welsh Nat.* 2,091
Lab. maj. *16,729*
(1955 Lab. maj. 19,236)

Eccles (English Borough)
E. 59,315
208★*W. T. Proctor, Lab.* 25,566
B. R. O. Bell, *C.* 23,580
Lab. maj. *1,986*
(1955 Lab. maj. 2,326)

EDGBASTON—*See* **Birmingham**
EDGE HILL—*See* **Liverpool**

Edinburgh (7)
CENTRAL E. 42,781
209★*T. Oswald, Lab.* 15,849
N. R. Wylie, *C.* 15,232
Lab. maj. *617*
(1955 Lab. maj. 939)
EAST E. 54,756
210★*E. G. Willis, Lab.* 22,244
Earl of Dalkeith, *C.* 21,932
Lab. maj. *312*
(1955 Lab. maj. 2,042)
LEITH E. 39,750
211★*J. H. Hoy, Lab.* 15,092
G. Stewart, *Nat. L. & C.* 12,018
Sir A. H. A. Murray, O.B.E., *L.* 4,475
Lab. maj. *3,074*
(1955 Lat. maj. 5,644)
NORTH E. 42,270
212★*Rt. Hon. W. R. Milligan,* Q.C., *C.* 19,991
G. G. Stott, Q.C., *Lab.* 11,235
C. maj. *8,756*
(By-election, May 19, 1960)
Earl of Dalkeith, C. 12,109
R. King Murray, *Lab.* 6,775
R. McPake, *L.* 3,458
C. maj. *5,334*
(1955 C. maj. 7,761)
PENTLANDS E. 53,178
213★*Rt. Hon. Lord John Hope, C.* 25,742
J. P. Mackintosh, *Lab.* 16,950
C. maj. *8,792*
(1955 C. maj. 7,485)
SOUTH E. 48,767
214★*A. M. C. Hutchison, C.* 22,799
A. D. Reid, *Lab.* 11,285
Hon. W. Douglas-Home, *L.* 5,505
C. maj. *11,514*
(May, 1957, by-election, C. maj. 4,640)
(1955 C. maj. 12,887)
WEST E. 57,293
215 *J. A. Stodart, C.* 25,976
J. K. Stocks, *Lab.* 14,041
D. F. Leach, *L.* 5,962
C. maj. *11,932*
(1955 C. maj. 13,216)

Edmonton (English Borough)
E. 67,837
216★*A. H. Albu, Lab.* 25,958
W. H. Bishop, *C.* 25,497
Lab. maj. *461*
(1955 Lab. maj. 7,038)

Enfield (2)
EAST E. 47,183
217 *J. Mackie, Lab.* 20,101
F. J. V. Brown, *C.* 16,477
Lab. maj. *3,624*
(1955 Lab. maj. 7,701)
WEST E. 44,983
218★*Rt. Hon. I. N. Macleod, C.* 24,861
G. Hickman, *Lab.* 11,058
C. maj. *13,803*
(1955 C. maj. 11,518)

Epping (Essex)
E. 83,647
219★*G. B. Finlay, C.* 31,507
D. F. W. Ford, *Lab.* 27,114
L. T. J. Arlott, *L.* 11,913
C. maj. *4,393*
(1955 C. maj. 3,523)

Epsom (Surrey)
E. 69,592
220★*Sir P. A. G. Rawlinson,* Q.C., *C.* 35,484
D. E. Heather, *Lab.* 11,039
R. W. M. Walsh, *L.* 9,910
C. maj. *24,445*
(1955 C. maj. 22,073)

Erith and Crayford (English Borough)
E. 53,057
221★*N. N. Dodds, Lab.* 24,523
J. J. Davis, *C.* 18,763
Lab. maj. *5,760*
(1955 Lab. maj. 8,618)

Esher (Surrey)
E. 72,183
222★*Sir W. Robson-Brown, C.* 37,155
P. E. Vanson, *Lab.* 12,934
G. E. Owen, *L.* 8,730
C. maj. *24,221*
(1955 C. maj. 20,642)

Essex (10)
SOUTH EAST E. 60,316
223★*B. R. Braine, C.* 28,124
R. M. Fryer, *Lab.* 17,991
C. maj. *10,133*
(1955 C. maj. 6,690)
See also **Billericay, Chelmsford, Chigwell, Colchester, Epping, Harwich, Maldon, Saffron Walden** and **Thurrock**

Eton and Slough (English Borough)
E 52,114
224★*A. F. Brockway, Lab.* 20,851
A. J. Page, *C.* 20,763
Lab. maj. *88*
(1955 Lab. maj. 2,443)

EXCHANGE—*See* **Liverpool** and **Manchester**

Exeter (English Borough)
E. 54,084
225★*R. D. Williams, C.* 21,579
A. J. Rogers, *Lab.* 15,918
G. C. Taylor, *L.* 6,852
C. maj. *5,661*
(1955 C. maj. 5,388)

Eye (Suffolk)
E. 56,395
226★*Col. Sir J. H. Harrison, Bt.,* T.D., *C.* 22,333
E. L. Granville, *Lab.* 19,849
Mrs. S. Robson, *L.* 5,215
C. maj. *2,484*
(1955 C. maj. 889)

Falmouth and Camborne (Cornwall)
E. 53,763
227★*F. H. Hayman, Lab.* 20,083
Miss A. M. Tennant, *C.* 15,886
N. A. S. Gibson, *L.* 7,890
Lab. maj. *4,197*
(1955 Lab. maj. 1,047)

Farnham (Surrey)
E. 50,249
228★*Sir G. Nicholson, Bt., C.* 23,538
Dr. J. G. Turner, *Lab.* 9,800
D. W. Saunders, *L.* 6,538
C. maj. *13,738*
(1955 C. maj. 10,906)

Farnworth (Lancashire)
E. 56,094
229★*E. Thornton,* M.B.E., *Lab.* 27,393
A. S. Royse, *C.* 19,356
Lab. maj. *8,037*
(1955 Lab. maj. 6,598)

Faversham (Kent)
E. 57,760
230★*P. L. Wells, Lab.* 24,327
Mrs. E. M. S. Olsen, *C.* 24,074
Lab. maj. *253*
(1955 Lab. maj. 59)

Feltham (English Borough)
E. 53,417
231★*A. E. Hunter, Lab.* 20,320
J. B. W. Turner, *C.* 18,070
L. A. de Pinna, *L.* 4,533
Lab. maj. *2,250*
(1955 Lab. maj. 3,350)

Fermanagh and South Tyrone
E. 64,022
232★*Lt.-Col. Lord Robert Grosvenor,* T.D., *U.U.* 32,080
J. H. Martin, *S.F.* 7,348
U.U. maj. *24,732*
(Sept. 1955, U.U. declared elected)
(1955 S.F. maj. 261)

Fife (2)
EAST E. 50,537
233★*Sir J. Henderson-Stewart, Bt., L. & C.* 26,585
J. Nicol, *Lab.* 11,421
L. & C. maj. *15,164*
(By-election, Nov. 8, 1961)
Sir J. E. Gilmour, Bt., D.S.O., T.D., *C.* 15,948
J. Smith, *Lab.* 8,882
D. Leach, *L.* 8,786
C. maj. *7,066*
(1955 L. & C. maj. 15,232)

WEST *E.* 55,992
234***W. W. Hamilton, Lab.*. 25,554
A. L. Buchanan-Smith, *C.* 11,257
L. Daly, *Ind.* 4,886
W. Lauchlan, *Comm.* 3,828
Lab. maj. 14,297
(1955 Lab. maj. 16,211)

Finchley (English Borough) *E.* 69,123
235 *Mrs. M. H. Thatcher, C.* 29,697
E. P. Deakins, *Lab.* 13,437
H. I. Spence, *L.* 12,701
C. maj. 16,260
(1955 C. maj. 12,825)

Flintshire (2)
EAST *E.* 52,635
236***Mrs. E. L. White, Lab.*. 22,776
F. Hardman, *C.* 22,701
Lab. maj. 75
(1955 Lab. maj. 2,274)

WEST *E.* 47,490
237***Rt. Hon. E. N. C. Birch,* O.B.E., *C.* 20,446
R. G. Waterhouse, *Lab.* 12,925
L. E. Roberts, *L.* 4,319
E. N. C. Williams, *Welsh Nat.* 1,594
C. maj. 7,521
(1955 C. maj. 8,352)

Folkestone and Hythe (Kent) *E.* 50,825
238 *A. P. Costain, C.* 21,726
W. E. Simpkins, *Lab.* 9,346
R. D. Emerson, *L.* 7,351
C. maj. 12,380
(1955 C. maj. 11,002)

Fulham (London Borough) *E.* 52,088
239***R. M. M. Stewart, Lab.* 21,525
Mrs. M. L. de la Motte, *C.* 18,581
Lab. maj. 2,944
(1955 Lab. maj. 4,394)

Gainsborough (Lincolnshire) *E.* 50,051
240***M. R. Kimball, C.* 20,056
H. D. L. G. Walston, *Lab.* 13,247
Dr. R. I. Douglas, *L.* 7,147
C. maj. 6,809
(Feb. 1956, by-election, C. maj. 1,006)
(1955 C. maj. 4,469)

Galloway *E.* 36,296
241***H. J. Brewis, C.* 15,454
S. B. Mackay, *L.* 6,412
J. Pickett, *Lab.* 5,590
C. maj. 9,042
(April, 1959, by-election, C. maj. 6,483)
(1955 C. mai. 8,014)

GARSTON—*See* Liverpool

Gateshead (2)
EAST *E.* 52,662
242***A. S. Moody, Lab.* 25,319
G. Glover, *C.* 17,654
Lab. maj. 7,665
(1955 Lab. maj. 4,947)

WEST *E.* 42,643
243***H. E. Randall, Lab.* 21,277
D. A. Wright, *C.* 11,509
Lab. maj. 9,768
(Dec. 1955, by-election, Lab. maj. 6,535)
(1955 Lab. maj. 10,331)

Gillingham (English Borough) *E.* 48,390
244***F. F. A. Burden, C.* 23,142
G. B. Kaufman, *Lab.* 15,863
C. maj. 7,279
(1955 C. maj. 4,145)

Glamorganshire (7). *See* **Aberavon, Barry, Caerphilly, Gower, Neath, Ogmore and Pontypridd**

Glasgow (15)
BRIDGETON *E.* 48,473
245***J. Carmichael, Lab.* 21,048
R. J. Docherty, *C.* 12,139
Lab. maj. 8,909
(By-election, Nov. 16, 1961)
J. Bennett, Lab. 10,930
M. McNeill, *C.* 3,935
I. Macdonald, *Scottish Nat.* 3,549
G. W. Stone, *I.L.P.* 586
Lab. maj. 6,995
(1955 Lab. maj. 8,101)

CATHCART *E.* 64,703
246***J. Henderson, C.* 30,743
J. Jarvie, *Lab.* 21,169
C. maj. 9,574
(1955 C. maj. 15,751)

CENTRAL *E.* 36,540
247***J. McInnes,* M.B.E., *Lab.* 15,918
I. D. Barber-Fleming, *C.* 8,712
Lab. maj. 7,206
(1955 Lab. maj. 6,367)

CRAIGTON *E.* 46,768
248 *B. Millan, Lab.* 19,649
*J. N. Browne, *C.* 19,047
Lab. maj. 602
(1955 C. maj. 210)

GORBALS *E.* 48,004
249***Mrs. A. Cullen, Lab.* 20,732
W. C. Hunter, *C.* 10,073
P. Kerrigan, *Comm.* 1,931
Lab. maj. 10,659
(1955 Lab. maj. 10,728)

GOVAN *E.* 51,084
250***J. Rankin, Lab.* 23,139
A. G. Hutton, *C.* 13,319
G. McLennan, *Comm.* 1,869
Lab. maj. 9,820
(1955 Lab. maj. 9,602)

HILLHEAD *E.* 38,154
251***Hon. T. G. D. Galbraith, C.* 20,094
T. B. Duncan, *Lab.* 9,317
C. maj. 10,777
(1955 C. maj. 10,458)

KELVINGROVE *E.* 34,319
252 *F. J. P. Lilley, C.* 12,355
*Mrs. M. A. McAlister, *Lab.* 11,254
W. C. Park, *I.L.P.* 740
C. maj. 1,101
(March, 1958, by-election, Lab. maj. 1,360)
(1955 C. maj. 2,888)

MARYHILL *E.* 46,422
253***W. Hannan, Lab.* 21,893
N. J. Adamson, *C.* 12,311
Lab. maj. 9,582
(1955 Lab. maj. 8,638)

POLLOK *E.* 52,472
254***Sir J. C. George,* K.B.E., *C.* 24,338
J. M. Smith, *Lab.* 17,072
C. maj. 7,266
(1955 C. maj. 8,845)

PROVAN *E.* 49,284
255***W. Reid, Lab.* 21,608
R. D. Kernohan, *C.* 17,241
Lab. maj. 4,367
(1955 Lab. maj. 180)

SCOTSTOUN *E.* 56,278
256 *W. W. Small, Lab.* 24,690
J. Bias, *C.* 21,320
Lab. maj. 3,370
(1955 C. maj. 428)

SHETTLESTON *E.* 49,987
257 *Sir M. Galpern, Lab.* 22,916
D. E. Donaldson, *C.* 14,743
Lab. maj. 8,173
(1955 Lab. maj. 5,819)

SPRINGBURN *E.* 38,147
258*J. C. Forman, *Lab.* 16,297
E. M. Taylor, *C.* 10,167
F. Hart, *Comm.* 1,235
Lab. maj. 6,130
(1955 Lab. maj. 5,773)

WOODSIDE *E.* 44,746
259***Rt. Hon. W. Grant,* T.D., Q.C., *C.* 16,567
J. McGinley, *Lab.* 14,483
G. V. McLaughlin, *L.* 2,583
C. maj. 2,084
(By-election, Nov. 22, 1962)
N. G. Carmichael, Lab. 8,303
N. M. Glen, *C.* 6,935
J. House, *L.* 5,000
A. Niven, *Scott. Nat.* 2,562
G. A. A. Aldred, *Ind. Soc.* 134
R. Vallar, *Soc. Party of G.B.* 83
Lab. maj. 1,368
(1955 C. maj. 4,303)

Gloucester (English Borough) *E.* 52,836
260***J. Diamond, Lab.* 19,450
H. D. K. Scott, *C.* 16,679
Lt.-Col. P. H. Lort-Phillips, *L.* 7,336
Lab. maj. 2,771
(Sept. 1957, by-election, Lab. maj. 8,374)
(1955 Lab. maj. 748)

Gloucestershire (4)
SOUTH *E.* 57,026
261***Capt. F. V. Corfield, C.* 26,168
J. Holland, *Lab.* 21,567
C. maj. 4,601
(1955 C. maj. 1,726)

WEST *E.* 54,202
262 *C. W. Loughlin, Lab.* 21,634
Miss O. K. L. Lloyd-Baker, C.B.E., *C.* 16,223
E. J. Radley, *L.* 5,921
Lab. maj. 5,411
(1955 Lab. maj. 4,020)
See also **Cirencester and Tewkesbury and Stroud**

Goole (Yorks W. R.) *E.* 53,191
263***G. Jeger, Lab.* 26,352
D. Sisson, *C. and L.* 16,581
Lab. maj. 9,771
(1955 Lab. maj. 9,964)

GORBALS—*See* **Glasgow**
GORTON—*See* **Manchester**

Gosport and Fareham
(English Borough) *E.* 73,284
264* *R. F. B. Bennett*, V.R.D., *C.* 35,808
A. S. Pratley, *Lab.* 19,654
C. maj. *16,154*
(1955 C. maj. 12,486)

GOVAN—*See* Glasgow

Gower (Glamorgan)
E. 49,480
265 *I. Davies, Lab.* 27,441
M. R. D. Heseltine, *Nat. L. & C.* 9,837
Dr. J. G. Griffiths, *Welsh Nat.* 3,744
Lab. maj. *17,604*
(1955 Lab. maj. 18,169)

Grantham (Lincolnshire)
E. 59,026
266* *Rt. Hon. J. B. Godber, C.* 27,482
T. C. Skeffington-Lodge, *Lab.* 20,867
C. maj. *6,615*
(1955 C. maj. 2,375)

Gravesend (Kent)
E. 63,299
267* *P. M. Kirk, C.* 27,124
C. J. V. Mishcon, *Lab.* 24,962
C. maj. *2,162*
(1955 C. maj. 2,909)

Greenock (Scottish Burgh)
E. 48,366
268* *Dr. J. D. Mabon, Lab.* . 19,320
W. T. C. Riddell, *L.* . 10,238
L. M. Turpie, *C.* 8,616
Lab. maj. *9,082*
(Dec. 1955, by-election, Lab. maj. 2,694)
(1955 Lab. maj. 1,033)

Greenwich (London Borough)
E. 60,561
269 *R. W. Marsh, Lab.* 25,204
J. R. Holmes, *C.* 19,679
Lab. maj. *5,525*
(1955 Lab. maj. 7,939)

Grimsby (English Borough)
E. 64,350
270 *C. A. R. Crosland, Lab.* 24,729
W. Pearson, *C.* 24,628
Lab. maj. *101*
(1955 Lab. maj. 3,522)

Guildford (Surrey)
E. 58,963
271* *Rt. Hon. Sir G. R. H. Nugent, Bt., C.* 27,198
G. R. Beilerby, *Lab.* .. 13,756
Maj. A. R. Braybrooke, *L.* 6,318
C. maj. *13,442*
(1955 C. maj. 11,328)

Hackney, Central
(London Borough)
E. 62,561
272* *H. W. Butler, Lab.* 25,407
J. C. T. Waring, *C.* .. 15,905
Lab. maj. *9,502*
(1955 Lab. maj. 11,800)

Halifax (English Borough)
E. 67,149
273* *M. V. Macmillan, C.* .. 29,212
P. Shore, *Lab.* 26,697
C. maj. *2,515*
(1955 C. maj. 1,535)

HALL GREEN—*See* Birmingham

HALLAM—*See* Sheffield

Haltemprice (Yorkshire, E.R.)
E. 53,906
274* *P. H. B. Wall*, M.C., V.R.D., *C.* 26,102
D. N. Bancroft, *Lab.* . 9,750
W. I. Cooper, *L.* 7,562
C. maj. *16,352*
(1955 C. maj. 14,342)

Hamilton (Lanarkshire)
E. 51,995
275* *T. Fraser, Lab.* 27,423
J. A. Davidson, *C.* 11,510
D. R. Rollo, *Scot. Nat.* 2,586
Lab. maj. *15,913*
(1955 Lab. maj. 13,526)

Hammersmith, North
(London Borough) *E.* 51,680
276* *F. Tomney, Lab.* 21,409
W. D. A. Bagnell, *C.* . 14,662
Lab. maj. *6,747*
(1955 Lab. maj. 8,863)

Hampshire (6). *See* **Aldershot, Basingstoke, Eastleigh, New Forest, Petersfield and Winchester**

Hampstead (London Borough)
E. 69,438
277* *Rt. Hon. H. Brooke, C.* 25,506
Dr. D. T. Pitt, *Lab.* ... 13,500
H. C. Seigal, *L.* 8,759
C. maj. *12,006*
(1955 C. maj. 12,186)

HANDSWORTH—*See* **Birmingham**

Harborough (Leicestershire)
E. 67,790
278 *J. A. Farr, C.* 29,281
J. R. Mably, *Lab.* 16,767
E. G. Rushworth, *L.* . 11,333
C. maj. *12,514*
(1955 C. maj. 10,184)

Harrogate (Yorks, W.R.)
E. 53,248
279* *J. E. Ramsden, C.* 29,466
F. B. Singleton, *Lab.* .. 10,196
C. maj. *19,270*
(1955 C. maj. 16,541)

Harrow (3)

CENTRAL *E.* 47,615
280* *F. P. Bishop*, M.B.E., *C.* 23,813
F. W. Powe, *Lab.* 14,049
C. maj. *9,764*
(1955 C. maj. 8,041)

EAST *E.* 49,273
281* *Cmdr. A. T. Courtney*, O.B.E., *C.* 23,554
M. Rees, *Lab.* 17,607
C. maj. *5,947*
(March 1959, by-election. C. maj. 2,220)
(1955 C. maj. 3,622)

WEST *E.* 54,295
282* *Sir A. N. Braithwaite*, D.S.O., M.C., *C.* 30,512
P. J. Jenkins, *Lab.* 12,512
C. maj. *18,000*
(By-election, March 17, 1960.)
A. J. Page, C. 18,526
J. Wallbridge, *L.* 7,100
P. J. Jenkins, *Lab.* 6,030
J. E. Dayton, *Ind.* 1,560
C. maj. *11,426*
(1955 C. maj. 17,297)

The Hartlepools
(English Borough)
E. 60,888
283 *Cdr. J. S. Kerans, C.* .. 25,463
*D. T. Jones, *Lab.* 25,281
C. maj. *182*
(1955 Lab. maj. 1,585)

Harwich (Essex)
E. 58,194
284* *J. E. Ridsdale, C. & Nat. L.* 23,653
W. O. J. Robinson, *Lab.* 11,588
T. E. Dale, *L.* 5,507
L. F. Rose, *Ind.* 3,744
C. & Nat. L. maj. ... *12,065*
(1955 C. & L. maj. 9,464)

Hastings (English Borough)
E. 48,569
285* *Sir N. Cooper-Key, C.* 22,458
J. P. Bryant, *Lab.* 13,576
C. maj. *8,882*
(1955 C. maj. 8,536)

Hayes and Harlington
(English Borough)
E. 46,244
286* *A. M. Skeffington, Lab.* 18,301
J. A. Grant, *C.* 14,149
S. Gay, *L.* 4,235
F. Foster, *Comm.* 527
Lab. maj. *4,152*
(1955 Lab. maj. 6,148)

HEELEY—*See* **Sheffield**

Hemel Hempstead
(Hertfordshire)
E. 70,962
287 *J. H. Allason*, O.B.E., *C.* 30,189
B. F. C. Floud, *Lab.* .. 21,954
Miss M. Neilson, *L.* .. 8,358
C. maj. *8,235*
(1955 C. maj. 6,136)

Hemsworth (Yorks. W.R.)
E. 65,705
288 *A. Beaney, Lab.* 45,153
W. H. Leay, *C.* 9,788
Lab. maj. *35,365*
(1955 Lab. maj. 34,042)

Hendon (2)

NORTH *E.* 52,729
289* *Sir C. I. Orr-Ewing*, *Bt.*, O.B.E., *C.* 21,898
C. H. Genese, *Lab.* ... 16,566
Lady Hills, *L.* 4,598
C. maj. *5,332*
(1955 C. maj. 4,060)

SOUTH *E.* 53,545
290* *Sir H. Lucas-Tooth, Bt., C.* 22,971
P. K. Archer, *Lab.* 11,016
P. H. Billenness, *L.* ... 7,134
C. maj. *11,955*
(1955 C. maj. 10,436)

Henley (Oxon.) *E.* 58,319
291* *J. A. Hay, C.* 24,417
A. Ledger, *Lab.* 15,014
C. Truman, *L.* 6,261
C. maj. *9,403*
(1955 C. maj. 7,081)

Herefordshire (2)

HEREFORD *E.* 45,340
292* *J. D. Gibson-Watt*, M.C., *C.* 17,763
R. Day, *L.* 10,185
J. W. Wardle, *Lab.* ... 8,097
C. maj. *7,578*
(Feb. 1956, by-election, C. maj. 2,150)
(1955 C. maj. 9,400)

See also Leominster

Hertfordshire (7)

EAST *E.* 66,913
293**Rt. Hon. Sir D. C. Walker-Smith, Bt.*, T.D., Q.C., *C.* 28,201
S. J. Bidwell, *Lab.* 18,020
K. J. W. Spargo, *L.* ... 8,656
C. maj. *10,181*
(1955 C. maj. 6,518)

HERTFORD *E.* 64,106
294**Lord Balniel, C.* 31,418
G. D. Southgate, *Lab.* . 22,597
C. maj. *8,821*
(1955 C. maj. 5,984)

SOUTH WEST *E.* 69,291
295**G. J. M. Longden*, M.B.E. *C.* 29,724
A. J. Whiteside, *Lab.* .. 19,487
D. A. H. Banks, *L.* ... 9,278
C. maj. *10,237*
(1955 C. maj. 6,969)

See also **Barnet, Hemel Hempstead and St. Albans**

Heston and Isleworth
(English Borough)
E. 55,121
296**R. R. Harris, C.* 24,486
T. Ponsonby, *Lab.* 15,636
W. P. Letch, *L.* 4,867
C. maj. *8,850*
(1955 C. maj. 6,512)

Hexham (Northumberland)
E. 49,906
297**R. M. Speir, C.* 25,500
W. H. W. Roberts, *Lab.* 14,980
C. maj. *10,520*
(1955 C. maj. 10,264)

Heywood and Royton
(Lancashire)
E. 57,868
298**J. A. Leavey, C.* 19,742
H. Nevin, *Lab.* 17,588
G. E. MacPherson, *L.* 11,713
C. maj. *2,154*
(1955 C. maj. 3,210)

High Peak (Derbyshire)
E. 49,196
299**Rt. Hon. A. H. E. Molson, C.* 18,738
B. Conlan, *Lab.* 13,827
Hon. S. R. Cawley, *L.* 8,138
C. maj. *4,911*
(By-election, March 16, 1961)
A. D. Walder, C. 13,069
W. M. Halsall, *Lab.* .. 11,201
D. Wrigley, *L.* 10,674
C. maj. *1,868*
(1955 C. maj. 5,442)

HILLHEAD—*See* **Glasgow**
HILLSBOROUGH—*See* **Sheffield**

Hitchin (Hertfordshire)
E. 75,493
300**M. F. M. Maddan, C.* . 30,193
P. J. H. Benenson, *Lab.* 25,818
R. Glenton, *L.* 8,481
C. maj. *4,375*
(1955 C. maj. 965)

Holborn and St. Pancras, South (London Borough)
E. 48,504
301 *G. Johnson Smith, C.* .. 17,065
*Mrs. L. M. Jeger, *Lab.* 16,409
C. maj. *656*
(1955 Lab. maj. 931)

Holland with Boston
(Lincolnshire)
E. 70,588
302**Sir H. W. Butcher, Bt., Nat. L. & C.* 29,013
J. D. T. Williamson, *Lab.* 17,839
C. Valentine, *L.* 7,334
Nat. L. & C. maj. ... *11,174*
(1955 Nat. L. & C. maj. 9,083)

Honiton (Devonshire)
E. 57,172
303**R. Mathew*, T.D., *C.* .. 25,959
J. B. Halse, *L.* 12,906
F. W. Morgan, *Lab.* .. 6,928
C. maj. *13,053*
(1955 C. maj. 14,741)

Horncastle (Lincolnshire)
E. 42,262
304**Comdr. Sir J. F. W. Maitland, C.* 19,799
H. W. Peck, *Lab.* 9,928
C. maj. *9,871*
(1955 C. maj. 10,270)

Hornchurch (English Borough)
E. 87,544
305**G. W. Lagden, C.* 34,852
Miss J. Richardson, *Lab.* 27,530
L. H. Jones, *L.* 11,056
C. maj. *7,322*
(1955 C. maj. 1,372)

Hornsey (English Borough)
E. 71,151
306**Lady Gammans, C.* 30,048
F. E. Mostyn, *Lab.* 17,710
S. Solomon, *L.* 5,706
G. J. Jones, *Comm.* 1,107
C. maj. *12,338*
(May 1957, by-election, C. maj. 3,131)
(1955 C. maj. 12,726)

Horsham (West Sussex)
E. 76,618
307**C. F. H. Gough*, M.C., T.D., *C.* 37,275
A. E. Pegler, *Lab.* 24,012
C. maj. *13,263*
(1955 C. maj. 11,510)

Houghton-le-Spring (Durham)
E. 56,780
308**W. R. Blyton, Lab.* 35,960
A. R. C. Arbuthnot, *C.* 11,398
Lab. maj. *24,562*
(1955 Lab. maj. 22,899)

Hove (English Borough)
E. 67,018
309**A. A. H. Marlowe*, Q.C., *C.* 36,150
T. J. Marsh, *Lab.* 12,206
C. maj. *23,941*
(1955 C. maj. 22,353)

Howden (Yorkshire, E.R.)
E. 47,310
310**P. E. O. Bryan*, D.S.O., M.C., *C.* 20,681
J. Rhodes, *Lab.* 7,809
R. H. Hargreaves, *L.* . 7,384
C. maj. *12,872*
(1955 C. maj. 11,398)

Huddersfield (2)

EAST *E.* 52,729
311**J. P. W. Mallalieu, Lab.* 22,474
P. M. Beard, *C.* 19,389
Lab. maj. *3,085*
(1955 Lab. maj. 4,224)

WEST *E.* 51,284
312**D. W. Wade, L.* 25,273
J. Marsden, *Lab.* 15,621
L. maj. *9,652*
(1955 L. maj. 7,927)

Hull (3)

EAST *E.* 72,441
313**Cmdr. H. Pursey, Lab.* . 30,667
Mrs. F. C. M. Heath, M.B.E., *C.* 17,648
J. J. McCallum, *L.* 10,043
Lab. maj. *13,019*
(1955 Lab. maj. 12,706)

NORTH *E.* 63,918
314 *J. M. Coulson, C.* 23,612
J. H. Foord, *Lab.* 22,910
A. Butcher, *L.* 5,604
C. maj. *702*
(1955 C. maj. 590)

WEST *E.* 64,100
315**M. Hewitson, Lab.* 25,446
T. H. F. Farrell, *C.* ... 23,011
Lab. maj. *2,435*
(1955 Lab. maj. 5,523)

Huntingdonshire
E. 46,794
316**Rt. Hon. D. L. M. Renton*, T.D., Q.C., *Nat. L. & C.* 20,254
J. W. Fear, *Lab.* 11,983
R. E. W. Vanderplank, *L.* 5,389
Nat. L. & C. maj. .. *8,271*
(1955 Nat. L. & C. maj. 5,939)

Huyton (Lancashire)
E. 77,371
317**Rt. Hon. J. H. Wilson*, O.B.E., *Lab.* 33,111
G. B. Woolfenden, *C.* 27,184
Lab. maj. *5,927*
(1955 Lab. maj. 2,558)

Ilford (2)

NORTH *E.* 67,208
318**T. L. Iremonger, C.* 29,609
C. F. H. Green, *Lab.* .. 15,962
D. K. Mills, *L.* 7,915
C. maj. *13,647*
(1955 C. maj. 10,501)

SOUTH *E.* 60,678
319**A. E. Cooper*, M.B.E., *C.* 23,876
G. J. Borrie, *Lab.* 16,569
R. V. Netherclift, *L.* .. 6,832
C. maj. *7,307*
(1955 C. maj. 6,478)

Ilkeston (Derbyshire)
E. 69,719
320**G. H. Oliver*, Q.C., *Lab.* 39,930
G. I. Walters, *C.* 18,286
Lab. maj. *21,644*
(1955 Lab. maj. 21,693)

Ince (Lancashire)
E. 51,273
321**T. J. Brown, Lab.* 30,752
W. Clegg, *C.* 11,795
Lab. maj. *18,957*
(1955 Lab. maj. 18,647)

Inverness-shire and Ross and Cromarty (3)

INVERNESS *E.* 49,546
322**N. L. D. McLean*, D.S.O., *C.* 15,728
J. M. Bannerman, *L.* .. 11,653
J. F. Coulter, *Lab.* 8,073
C. maj. *4,075*
1955 C. maj. 966)

ROSS AND CROMARTY E. 25,350
323★*Sir J. Macleod*, T.D., *Nat. L.* 7,813
Mrs. J. B. Saggar, *Lab.* 4,815
C. Murchison, *L.* 3,918
Nat. L. maj. *2,998*
(1955 Nat. L. maj. 3,926)
See also **Western Isles**

Ipswich (English Borough)
E. 77,633
324★*D. M. Foot*, Q.C., *Lab.*. 25,858
J. C. Cobbold, *C.* 22,623
Miss A. M. P. H. Sykes, *L.* 14,359
Lab. maj. *3,235*
(Oct. 1957, by-election, Lab. maj 7,737)
(1955 Lab. maj. 3,582)

Isle of Ely
E. 61,387
325★*Maj. Sir E. A. H. Legge-Bourke*, K.B.E., *C.* 26,173
J. D. Page, *Lab.* 19,705
C. maj. *6,468*
(1955 C. maj. 6,446)

Isle of Thanet (Kent)
E. 71,952
326★*W. R. Rees-Davies, C.* 29,453
H. A. Fountain, *Lab.*.. 17,555
G. E. MacDonald-Jones, *L.* 6,998
C. maj. *11,898*
(1955 C. maj. 12,289)

Isle of Wight
E. 66,939
327 *H. F. M. Woodnutt, C.* 31,228
E. C. Amey, *Lab.* 18,396
C. maj. *12,832*
(1955 C. maj. 12,637)

Islington (3)
EAST E. 48,613
328★*E. G. M. Fletcher, Lab.*. 17,766
K. C. Burden, *C.* 13,097
Lab. maj. *4,669*
(1955 Lab. maj. 6,702)

NORTH E. 54,120
329★*G. W. Reynolds, Lab.*.. 18,718
R. D. Bartle, *C.* 14,820
Lab. maj. *3,898*
(May, 1958, by-election, Lab. maj. 7,461)
(1955 Lab. maj. 7,578)

SOUTH WEST E. 56,620
330★*A. Evans, Lab.* 22,362
N. P. Scott, *C.* 11,974
Lab. maj. *10,388*
(1955 Lab. maj. 13,268)

ITCHEN—*See* **Southampton**

Jarrow (English Borough)
E. 50,958
331★*E. Fernyhough, Lab.*... 25,638
T. T. Hubble, *C.* 15,286
Lab. maj. *10,352*
(1955 Lab. maj. 10,402)

Keighley (English Borough)
E. 47,981
332 *W. M. J. Worsley, C.*. 20,626
★C. R. Hobson, *Lab.*.. 20,456
C. maj. *170*
(1955 Lab. maj. 3,403)

KELVINGROVE—*See* **Glasgow**
KEMPTOWN—*See* **Brighton**

Kensington (2)
NORTH E. 51,492
333★*G. H. R. Rogers, Lab.*. 14,925
R. W. Bulbrook, *C.*.. 14.048
M. Hydleman, *L.* 3,118
Sir O. E. Mosley, Bt., *Union Movement*.... 2,821
Lab. maj. *877*
(1955 Lab. maj. 2,943)

SOUTH E. 58,023
334 *W. L. Roots*, Q.C., *C.*. 26,606
G. C. H. Millar, *L.* ... 4,666
I. S. Richard, *Lab.* 4,525
C. maj. *21,940*
(1955 C. maj. 25,247)

Kent (13). *See* **Ashford, Canterbury, Chislehurst, Dartford, Dover, Faversham, Folkestone and Hythe, Gravesend, Isle of Thanet, Maidstone, Orpington, Sevenoaks and Tonbridge**

Kettering (Northants)
E. 74,696
335★*G. R. Mitchison*, C.B.E., Q.C., *Lab.* 32,933
J. H. Lewis, *C.* 29,448
Lab. maj. *3,485*
(1955 Lab. maj. 5,903)

Kidderminster (Worcestershire)
E. 58,223
336★*Sir G. D. N. Nabarro*, *C.* 27,699
Mrs. J. Tomlinson, *Lab.* 18,356
C. maj. *9,343*
(1955 C. maj. 8,224)

Kilmarnock (Ayrshire)
E. 49,090
337★*W. Ross*, M.B.E., *Lab.* . 25,379
R. I. McNaught, *C.*.. 15,087
Lab. maj. *10,292*
(1955 Lab. maj. 8,341)

King's Lynn (Norfolk)
E. 52,125
338 *D. G. Bullard, C.* 21,671
G. C. Jackson, *Lab.*... 19,906
C. maj. *1,765*
(1955 C. maj. 1,338)

Kingston upon Thames (English Borough)
E. 60,403
339★*Rt. Hon. J. A. Boyd-Carpenter, C.* 31,649
T. Braddock, *Lab.* 15,408
C. maj. *16,241*
(1955 C. maj. 14,965)

Kinross and West Perthshire—*See* **Perthshire and Kinross**

Kirkcaldy (Scottish Burgh)
E. 54,232
340 *H. P. H. Gourlay, Lab.*. 25,428
J. Law, *C.* 14,186
D. Blyth, *L.* 4,020
Lab. maj. *11,242*
(1955 Lab. maj. 7,469)

KIRKDALE—*See* **Liverpool**

Knutsford (Cheshire)
E. 52,999
341★*Lt.-Col. Sir W. H. Bromley - Davenport*, T.D., *C.* 27,270
F. R. Tetlow, *L.* 8,117
N. Selwyn, *Lab.* 7,945
C. maj. *19,153*
(1955 C. maj. 19,486)

LADYWOOD—*See* **Birmingham**

Lambeth (3)
BRIXTON E. 52,261
342★*Lt.-Col. M. Lipton*, O.B.E., *Lab.* 18,117
Dr. B. Warren, *C.* 16,005
Lab. maj. *2,112*
(1955 Lab. maj. 5,035)

NORWOOD E. 57,807
343★*Brig. Rt. Hon. Sir J. G. Smyth, Bt.*, V.C., M.C., *C.* 22,958
L. L. Reeves, *Lab.* 15,975
D. Chapman, *L.* 4,744
C. maj. *6,983*
(1955 C. maj. 5,032)

VAUXHALL E. 45,802
344★*Rt. Hon. G. R. Strauss*, *Lab.* 18,437
Miss A. E. O. Havers, *C.* 11,312
Lab. maj. *7,125*
(1955 Lab. maj. 8,728)

Lanark (Lanarkshire)
E. 57,094
345 *Mrs. J. C. M. Hart*, *Lab.* 25,171
★Hon. P. F. Maitland, *C.* 24,631
Lab. maj. *540*
(1955 C. maj. 958)

Lanarkshire (6)
NORTH E. 43,505
346★*Miss M. Herbison, Lab.* 21,152
G. K. H. Younger, *C.* 14,883
Lab. maj. *6,269*
(1955 Lab. maj. 5,523)
See also **Bothwell, Hamilton, Lanark, Motherwell and Rutherglen**

Lancashire (16). *See* **Chorley, Clitheroe, Darwen, Farnworth, Heywood and Royton, Huyton, Ince, Lancaster, Middleton and Prestwich, Morecambe and Lonsdale, Newton, North Fylde, Ormskirk, South Fylde, Westhoughton and Widnes**

Lancaster (Lancashire)
E. 43,714
347 *H. J. Berkeley, C.* 20,783
E. Gardner, *Lab.* 15,255
C. maj. *5,528*
(1955 C. maj. 4,549)

LANGSTONE—*See* **Portsmouth**

Leeds (6)
EAST E. 66,074
348★*D. W. Healey*, M.B.E., *Lab.* 28,707
J. A. Fawcett, *C.* 23,922
Lab. maj. *4,785*
(1955 Lab. maj. 4,939)

NORTH EAST E. 54,594
349★*Rt. Hon. Sir K. S. Joseph, Bt., C.* 26,240
H. M. Waterman, *Lab.* 14,709
C. maj. *11,531*
(Feb. 1956, by-election, C. maj. 5,869)
(1955 C. maj. 9,279)

NORTH WEST E. 69,243
350★*Sir D. Kaberry, Bt.*, T.D., *C.* 35,210
D. B. Matthews, *Lab.*. 18,508
C. maj. *16,702*
(1955 C. maj. 15,329)

SOUTH *E.* 52,822
351★*Rt. Hon. H. T. N. Gaitskell*, C.B.E., *Lab.* 24,442
J. F. W. Addey, *C.* ... 12,956
J. B. Meeks, *L.* ... 4,340
Lab. maj. ... 11,486
(By-election, June 20, 1963)
M. Rees, Lab. ... 18,785
J. Udal, *C.* ... 5,996
B. Walsh, *L.* ... 4,399
B. Ramelson, *Comm.*. 670
Lab. maj. ... 12,789
(1955 Lab. maj. 12,016)

SOUTH EAST *E.* 48,457
352★*Miss A. M. Bacon*, C.B.E., *Lab.* ... 21,795
J. B. Womersley, *C.* .. 12,146
Lab. maj. ... 9,649
(1955 Lab. maj. 12,572)

WEST *E.* 60,269
353★*T. C. Pannell, Lab.* ... 25,878
D. L. Crouch, *C.* ... 21,285
Lab. maj. ... 4,593
(1955 Lab. maj. 6,264)

Leek (Staffordshire) *E.* 72,777
354★*H. Davies, Lab.* ... 31,096
Sir J. H. Wedgwood, Bt., T.D., *C.* ... 29,947
Lab. maj. ... 1,149
(1955 Lab. maj. 1,059)

Leicester (4)
NORTH EAST *E.* 47,733
355★*Sir A. L. Ungoed-Thomas*, Q.C., *Lab.* .. 19,421
Miss A. H. Spokes, *C.* 17,990
Lab. maj. ... 1,431
(By-election, July 12, 1962)
T. G. Bradley, Lab. ... 11,274
D. Bond, *L.* ... 9,326
R. G. Marlar, *C.* ... 6,578
Lab. maj. ... 1,948
(1955 Lab. maj. 5,170)

NORTH WEST *E.* 51,922
356★*Sir B. Janner, Lab.* ... 21,515
F. A. Tomlinson, *C.* .. 19,742
Lab. maj. ... 1,773
(1955 Lab. maj. 3,510)

SOUTH EAST *E.* 53,810
357★*W. J. Peel, C.* ... 28,390
D. J. Williams, *Lab.* ... 13,760
C. maj. ... 14,630
(Nov. 1957, by-election, C. maj. 6,482)
(1955 C. maj. 11,541)

SOUTH WEST *E.* 47,762
358★*Rt. Hon. H. W. Bowden*, C.B.E., *Lab.* ... 17,395
A. D. Walder, *C.* ... 14,652
J. W. Ward, *L.* ... 5,438
Lab. maj. ... 2,743
(1955 Lab. maj. 4,489)

Leicestershire (4). *See* **Bosworth, Harborough, Loughborough and Melton**

Leigh (English Borough) *E.* 58,911
359★*H. Boardman, Lab.* ... 31,672
W. Cameron, *C.* ... 16,897
Lab. maj. ... 14,775
(1955 Lab. maj. 11,956)

Leominster (Herefordshire) *E.* 39,306
360 *Hon. C. Bossom, C.* ... 16,642
T. G. Jones, *L.* ... 6,905
F. W. Bowerman, *Lab.* 6,475
C. maj. ... 9,737
(1955 C. maj. 8,747)

Lewes (East Sussex) *E.* 56,338
361★*Col. Sir T. V. H. Beamish*, M.C., *C.* ... 29,642
W. Reay, *Lab.* ... 13,065
C. maj. ... 16,577
(1955 C. maj. 12,546)

Lewisham (3)
NORTH *E.* 52,415
362 *C. J. Chataway, C.* ... 22,125
★N. MacDermot, *Lab.*. 17,512
K. J. Brookes, *L.* ... 2,921
C. maj. ... 4,613
(Feb. 1957, by-election, Lab. maj. 1,110)
(1955 C. maj. 3,236)

SOUTH *E.* 53,962
363 *C. A. Johnson*, C.B.E., *Lab.* ... 22,354
J. L. Hunt, *C.* ... 19,273
G. Forrester, *Alert Party* ... 788
Lab. maj. ... 3,081
(1955 Lab. maj. 6,343)

WEST *E.* 54,069
364★*H. A. Price*, C.B.E., *C.* .. 22,466
R. C. Edmonds, *Lab.*. 16,233
T. A. Smith, *L.* ... 4,721
C. maj. ... 6,233
(1955 C. maj. 4,325)

Leyton (English Borough) *E.* 70,996
365★*R. W. Sorensen, Lab.* .. 28,367
R. C. Buxton, *C.* ... 24,448
Lab. maj. ... 3,919
(1955 Lab. maj. 8,204)

Lichfield and Tamworth (Staffordshire) *E.* 50,240
366★*J. W. Snow, Lab.* ... 21,341
Dr. F. R. Roberts, *C.* 19,791
Lab. maj. ... 1,550
(1955 Lab. maj. 3,105)

Lincoln (English Borough) *E.* 50,973
367★*G. S. de Freitas, Lab.* .. 23,629
L. H. Priestley, *C.* ... 19,240
Lab. maj. ... 4,389
(By-election, March 8, 1962)
D. Taverne, Lab. ... 19,038
W. P. Grieve, *C.* ... 11,386
P. Furnell, *L.* ... 6,856
Capt. A. Taylor, *Ind.*.. 412
Lab. maj. ... 7,652
(1955 Lab. maj. 5,222)

Lincolnshire and Rutland (7). *See* **Brigg, Gainsborough, Grantham, Holland with Boston, Horncastle, Louth and Rutland and Stamford**

Liverpool (9)
EDGE HILL *E.* 54,824
368★*A. J. Irvine*, Q.C. *Lab.* .. 19,725
J. Norton, *C.* ... 19,026
Lab. maj. ... 699
(1955 Lab. maj. 1,120)

EXCHANGE *E.* 51,052
369★*Mrs. E. M. Braddock, Lab.* ... 18,916
T. Beattie-Edwards, *C.* 11,945
Lab. maj. ... 6,971
(1955 Lab. maj. 7,186)

GARSTON *E.* 65,506
370★*R. M. Bingham*, T.D., Q.C., *C.* ... 31,441
B. Crookes, *Lab.* ... 17,284
C. maj. ... 14,157
(Dec. 1957, by-election, C. maj. 4,304)
(1955 C. maj. 11,969)

KIRKDALE *E.* 57,102
371★*N. A. Pannell, C.* ... 22,416
T. H. Hockton, *Lab.* .. 19,669
C. maj. ... 2,747
(1955 C. maj. 1,814)

SCOTLAND *E.* 51,914
372★*D. G. Logan*, C.B.E., *Lab.* 20,051
J. F. Bradley, *C.* ... 12,384
Lab. maj. ... 7,667
(1955 Lab. maj. 10,107)

TOXTETH *E.* 49,686
373★*Rt. Hon. J. R. Bevins, C.* 19,575
W. H. Sefton, *Lab.* ... 15,660
C. maj. ... 3,915
(1955 C. maj. 4,539)

WALTON *E.* 57,312
374★*Sir K. P. Thompson, Bt., C.* ... 24,288
G. McCartney, *Lab.* .. 20,254
C. maj. ... 4,034
(1955 C. maj. 2,862)

WAVERTREE *E.* 55,679
375★*J. D. Tilney*, T.D., *C.* . 26,624
Mrs. M. Aspin, *Lab.* .. 10,392
T. S. Rothwell, *L.* ... 5,161
C. maj. ... 16,232
(1955 C. maj. 15,620)

WEST DERBY *E.* 54,804
376★*J. V. Woollam, C.* ... 22,719
A. D. G. Paxton, *Lab.*. 19,386
C. maj. ... 3,333
(1955 C. maj. 2,584)

Llanelly (Carmarthenshire) *E.* 64,048
377★*Rt. Hon. J. Griffiths, Lab.* ... 34,625
H. Gardner, *C.* ... 10,128
Rev. D. E. Morgan, *Welsh Nat.* ... 7,176
Lab. maj. ... 24,497
(1955 Lab. maj. 23,381)

Londonderry *E.* 73,262
378★*R. Chichester-Clark, U.U.* ... 37,529
M. Canning, *S.F.* ... 13,872
U.U. maj. ... 23,657
(1955 U.U. maj. 16,033)

Loughborough (Leicestershire) *E.* 54,225
379★*J. D. Cronin, Lab.* ... 21,496
C. G. Waite, *C.* ... 17,749
R. E. Hancock, *L.* ... 6,303
Lab. maj. ... 3,747
(1955 Lab. maj. 4,263)

Louth (Lincolnshire) *E.* 51,773
380★*Sir C. Osborne, C.* ... 24,211
F. R. Macdonald, *Lab.* 15,408
C. maj. ... 8,803
(1955 C. maj. 6,520)

Lowestoft (Suffolk) *E.* 57,814
381 *J. M. L. Prior, C.* ... 24,324
★E. Evans, C.B.E., *Lab.* .. 22,835
C. maj. ... 1,489
(1955 Lab. maj. 1,915)

Ludlow (Shropshire) *E.* 46,735
382★*C. J. Holland-Martin, C.* 21,464
J. Garwell, *Lab.* ... 14,138
C. maj. ... 7,326
(By-election, Nov. 16, 1960)
J. More, C. ... 13,777
D. Rees, *L.* ... 8,127
J. Garwell, *Lab.* ... 7,812
C. maj. ... 5,650
(1955 C. maj. 7,879)

Luton (English Borough)
E. 59,769
383★*Rt. Hon. C. Hill,* M.D., *L. & C.*.......... 27,153
C. R. Fenton, *Lab*.... 22,134
L. & C. maj........ *5,019*
(1955 L. & C. maj. 4,418)
(By-election pending)

Macclesfield (Cheshire)
E. 58,892
384★*Air Cdre. Sir A. V. Harvey,* C.B.E., *C*.... 28,978
J. F. Bex, *Lab*........ 19,652
C. maj............ *9,326*
(1955 C. maj. 9,189)

Maidstone (Kent)
E. 63,304
385 *J. J. Wells, C*......... 30,115
A. B. S. Soper, *Lab*.... 19,652
C. maj............ *10,463*
(1955 C. maj. 7,406)

Maldon (Essex)
E. 54,401
386★*A. B. C. Harrison, C*... 21,772
S. G. Richards, *Lab*... 19,532
L. C. M. Walsh, *L*.... 3,860
C. maj............ *2,240*
(1955 C. maj. 550)

Manchester (9)
ARDWICK *E.* 57,166
387★*L. M. Lever, Lab*...... 24,134
H. Sharp, *C*.......... 17,392
Lab. maj.......... *6,742*
(1955 Lab. maj. 2,082)

BLACKLEY *E.* 57,851
388★*E. S. T. Johnson,* M.C., *C*................ 22,163
R. B. Chrimes, *Lab*... 17,790
R. M. Hammond, *L*.. 7,223
C. maj............ *4,373*
(1955 C. maj. 5,436)

CHEETHAM *E.* 47,156
389★*N. H. Lever, Lab*...... 20,941
Miss M. P. O'Gara, *C*. 11,605
Lab. maj.......... *9,336*
(1955 Lab. maj. 8,531)

EXCHANGE *E.* 47,067
390★*W. D. Griffiths, Lab*... 19,328
L. Smith, *C*.......... 10,604
Lab. maj.......... *8,724*
(1955 Lab. maj. 7,281)

GORTON *E.* 55,846
391★*K. Zilliacus, Lab. (now Ind. Lab.)*......... 23,337
D. H. Moore, *C*...... 22,480
Lab. maj.......... *857*
(1955 Lab. maj. 269)

MOSS SIDE *E.* 51,271
392 *J. Watts, C*.......... 22,090
N. Morris, *Lab*....... 13,371
C. maj............ *8,719*
(By-election, Nov. 7, 1961)
F. H. Taylor, C....... 9,533
R. H. Hargreaves, *L*.. 6,447
G. J. Oakes, *Lab*...... 5,980
W. Hesketh, *Union Movement*......... 1,212
C. maj............ *3,086*
(1955 C. maj. 10,528)

OPENSHAW *E.* 54,610
393★*W. R. Williams, Lab*... 24,975
M. B. Scholfield, *C*... 16,537
Lab. maj.......... *8,438*
(1955 Lab. maj. 8,042)

WITHINGTON *E.* 59,457
394★*Sir R. A. Cary, Bt., C*.. 23,170
R. E. Sheldon, *Lab*.... 13,476
G. V. Davies, *L*....... 7,675
C. maj............ *9,694*
(1955 C. maj. 12,653)

WYTHENSHAWE *E.* 69,925
395★*Mrs. E. Hill, C*....... 28,934
A. Morris, *Lab*....... 27,625
C. maj............ *1,309*
(1955 C. maj. 2,822)

Mansfield (Nottinghamshire)
E. 56,674
396★*H. B. Taylor, Lab*..... 31,066
M. R. V. Eliot, *C*..... 14,700
Lab. maj.......... *16,366*
(1955 Lab. maj. 16,033)

MARYHILL—*See* **Glasgow**

Melton (Leicestershire)
E. 70,233
397★*Miss I. M. P. Pike, C*.. 34,997
C. W. Shepherd, *Lab*. 22,176
C. maj............ *12,821*
(Dec. 1956, by-election, C. maj. 2,362)
(1955 C. maj. 10,780)

Meriden (Warwickshire)
E. 62,449
398 *G. R. Matthews, C*.... 26,498
★R. Moss, *Lab*........ 26,235
C. maj............ *263*
(1955 Lab. maj. 1,105)

Merionethshire
E. 26,435
399★*T. W. Jones, Lab*...... 9,095
B. G. Jones, *L*........ 8,119
G. Evans, *Welsh Nat*.. 5,127
Lab. maj.......... *976*
(1955 Lab. maj. 2,682)

Merthyr Tydfil
(Welsh Borough)
E. 42,153
400★*S. O. Davies, Lab*..... 26,608
Mrs. M. M. M. Greenaway, *C*.......... 7,885
Lab. maj.......... *18,723*
(1955 Lab. maj. 18,082)

Merton and Morden
(English Borough)
E. 52,178
401★*H. E. Atkins, C*....... 25,603
R. W. Kerr, *Lab*...... 17,444
C. maj............ *8,159*
(1955 C. maj. 6,390)

Middlesbrough (2)
EAST *E.* 62,666
402★*Rt. Hon. H. A. Marquand, Lab*......... 29,391
D. R. Chapman, *C*... 18,365
Lab. maj.......... *11,026*
(By-election, March 14, 1962)
†*Rt. Hon. A. G. Bottomley,* O.B.E., *Lab*...... 18,928
G. Scott, *L*.......... 7,145
F. A. S. Wood, *C*..... 4,613
J. Hamm, *Union Movement*............ 550
Lab. maj.......... *11,783*
(1955 Lab. maj. 10,758)

WEST *E.* 53,059
403★*Rt. Hon. Sir J. E. S. Simon,* Q.C., *C*..... 24,603
E. J. Fletcher, *Lab*..... 15,892
G. W. I. Hodgson, *L*.. 4,336
C. maj............ *8,710*
(By-election, June 6, 1962)
Dr. J. W. Bray, Lab.... 15,095
B. Connelly, *C*....... 12,825
G. Scott, *L*.......... 9,829
R. E. Eckley, *Ind*..... 189
M. Thompson, *Ind*....... 117
Lab. maj.......... *2,270*
(1955 C. maj. 7,361)

Middlesex (2). *See* **Spelthorne and Uxbridge**

Middleton and Prestwich
(Lancashire)
E. 65,855
404★*Sir J. D. Barlow, Bt., C*................ 31,416
F. G. Barton, *Lab*..... 21,248
C. maj............ *10,168*
(1955 C. maj. 10,107)

Midlothian
E. 58,092
405 *J. M. Hill, Lab*........ 28,457
W. S. How, *C*....... 18,797
Lab. maj.......... *9,660*
(1955 Lab. maj. 8,786)

Mid-Ulster
E. 66,585
406★*G. Forrest, Ind. U.U*... 33,093
T. J. Mitchell, *S.F*.... 14,170
Ind. U.U. maj...... *18,923*
(May, 1956, by-election, Ind. U.U. maj. 4,481)
(1955 S.F. maj. 260)

Mitcham (English Borough)
E. 70,463
407★*Rt. Hon. L. R. Carr, C*. 33,661
E. J. C. Smythe, *Lab*. . 23,845
C. maj............ *9,816*
(1955 C. maj. 7,590)

Monmouth (Monmouthshire)
E. 53,628
408★*Rt. Hon. G. E. P. Thorneycroft, C*..... 25,422
G. S. D. Parry, *Lab*.... 19,165
C. maj............ *6,257*
(1955 C. maj. 5,797)

Monmouthshire (5). *See* **Abertillery, Bedwellty, Ebbw Vale, Monmouth and Pontypool**

Montgomeryshire
E. 31,152
409★*Rt. Hon. E. Clement Davies,* Q.C., *L*...... 10,970
F. L. Morgan, *C*...... 8,176
D. C. Jones, *Lab*...... 6,950
L. maj............ *2,794*
(By-election, May 15, 1962)
H. E. Hooson, Q.C., *L*. . 13,181
R. H. Dawson, *C*..... 5,632
T. Davies, *Lab*........ 5,299
I. F. Elis, *Welsh Nat*.. 1,594
L. maj............ *7,549*
(1955 L. maj. 8,500)

Moray and Nairn
E. 35,487
410 *G. T. C. Campbell,* M.C., *C*.......... 13,742
M. Mackay, *Lab*...... 6,539
D. C. MacDonald, *L*.. 5,831
C. maj............ *7,203*
(1955 C. maj. 5,129)

Morecambe and Lonsdale (Lancashire) *E.* 57,654
411★*B. R. Z. de Ferranti, C.* 30,228
F. R. McManus, *Lab.*. 14,253
C. maj. 15,975
(Nov. 1958, by-election, C. maj. 11,231)
(1955 C. maj. 17,701)

Morpeth (Northumberland) *E.* 45,361
412★*W. J. Owen, Lab.* 27,435
D. Bloom, *C.* 10,716
Lab. maj. 16,719
(1955 Lab. maj. 14,833)

MOSS SIDE—*See* **Manchester**

Motherwell (Lanarkshire) *E.* 50,503
413★*G. M. Lawson, Lab.* 22,009
B. Brogan, *C.* 17,613
D. Murray, *Ind.* 1,331
Lab. maj. 4,396
(1955 Lab. maj. 2,885)

Nantwich (Cheshire) *E.* 43,655
414★*Wing-Cdr. R. G. Grant-Ferris, C.* 17,613
L. Knight, *Lab.* 10,876
G. M. Harvey, *L.* 7,983
C. maj. 6,737
(1955 C. maj. 7,366)

Neath (Glamorgan) *E.* 51,711
415★*D. J. Williams, Lab.* 30,469
D. N. I. Pearce, *C.* 10,263
J. J. David, *Comm.* 1,962
Lab. maj. 20,206
(1955 Lab. maj. 21,114)

Nelson and Colne *E.* 48,472
416★*S. S. Silverman, Lab.* 20,407
J. Crabtree, *C.* 19,143
T. C. Emmott, *Ind.* 1,889
Lab. maj. 1,264
(1955 Lab. maj. 2,291)

Newark (Nottinghamshire) *E.* 54,597
417★*G. Deer*, O.B.E., *Lab.* 24,072
P. Jenkin-Jones, *C.* 22,300
Lab. maj. 1,772
(1955 Lab. maj. 2,141)

Newbury (Berkshire) *E.* 62,854
418★*Sir A. R. Hurd, C.* 29,703
D. L. Stoddart, *Lab.* 19,787
C. maj. 9,916
(1955 C. maj. 7,237)

Newcastle under Lyme (English Borough) *E.* 63,623
419★*S. T. Swingler, Lab.* 29,840
T. Prendergast, *C.* 23,838
Lab. maj. 6,002
(1955 Lab. maj. 6,745)

Newcastle upon Tyne (4)

CENTRAL *E.* 49,929
420★*E. W. Short, Lab.* 24,051
W. D. Rutter, *C.* 12,485
Lab. maj. 11,566
(1955 Lab. maj. 13,003)

EAST *E.* 50,616
421 *W. F. Montgomery, C.* 21,457
★A. Blenkinsop, *Lab.* 21,359
C. maj. 98
(1955 Lab. maj. 1,822)

NORTH *E.* 47,930
422★*R. W. Elliott, C.* 24,588
Mrs. M. F. L. Prichard, *Lab.* 13,316
C. maj. 11,272
(March, 1957, by-election, C. maj. 6,462)
(1955 L. & C. maj. 10,933)

WEST *E.* 64,509
423★*E. Popplewell*, C.B.E., *Lab.* 28,956
C. D. Larrow, *C.* 23,933
Lab. maj. 5,023
(1955 Lab. maj. 5,184)

New Forest (Hampshire) *E.* 58,958
424★*Lt.-Col. Sir O. E. Crosthwaite-Eyre, C.* 29,949
R. C. Mitchell, *Lab.* 13,667
C. maj. 16,282
(1955 C. maj. 14,742)

Newport (Welsh Borough) *E.* 71,342
425★*Rt. Hon. Sir F. Soskice*, Q.C., *Lab.* 31,125
A. D. Arnold, *C.* 27,477
Lab. maj. 3,648
(July, 1956, by-election, Lab. maj. 8,485)
(1955 Lab. maj. 4,360)

Newton (Lancashire) *E.* 65,124
426★*F. Lee, Lab.* 31,041
N. A. Miscampbell, *C.* 23,065
Lab. maj. 7,976
(1955 Lab. maj. 7,955)

Norfolk (6)

CENTRAL *E.* 54,436
427 *R. C. M. Collard*, D.S.O., D.F.C., *C. & Nat. L.* 21,918
F. H. Stone, *Lab.* 15,131
G. M. Goode, *L.* 6,465
C. & Nat. L. maj. 6,787
(By-election, Nov. 22, 1962)
I. H. J. Gilmour, C. & Nat. L. 13,268
G. Bennett, *Lab.* 13,048
G. M. Goode, *L.* 7,915
K. Coleman, *Ind. L.* 909
J. Andrews, *Ind.* 79
C. maj. 220
(1955 Nat. L. & C. maj. 5,563)

NORTH *E.* 48,756
428★*E. G. Gooch*, C.B.E., *Lab.* 19,784
F. H. Easton, *C. & Nat. L.* 19,126
Lab. maj. 658
(1955 Lab. maj. 1,242)

SOUTH *E.* 43,458
429★*J. E. B. Hill, C.* 19,275
J. M. Stewart, *Lab.* 16,542
C. maj. 2,733
(1955 C. maj. 1,475)

SOUTH WEST *E.* 40,283
430★*A. V. Hilton, Lab.* 16,858
Mrs. M. E. Kellett, *C.* 16,780
Lab. maj. 78
(March, 1959, by-election, Lab. maj. 1,354)
(1955 Lab. maj. 193)

See also **King's Lynn** and **Yarmouth**

Normanton (Yorks, W.R.) *E.* 49,139
431★*A. Roberts, Lab.* 29,672
J. A. C. Briggs, *C.* 11,169
Lab. maj. 18,503
(1955 Lab. maj. 17,806)

Northampton (English Borough) *E.* 72,521
432★*R. T. Paget*, Q.C., *Lab.* 27,823
Mrs. J. C. J. Knight, *C.* 25,106
A. T. Smith, *L.* 7,170
Lab. maj. 2,717
(1955 Lab. maj. 3,348)

Northamptonshire (4)

SOUTH *E.* 51,403
433★*Rt. Hon. Sir R. E. Manningham-Buller, Bt.*, Q.C., *C.* 24,226
A. Richardson, *Lab.* 18,292
C. maj. 5,934
(By-election, Nov. 22, 1962)
A. A. Jones, C. 14,921
I. Wilde, *Lab.* 14,004
N. Picarda, *L.* 7,002
P. Buchan, *Ind.* 332
C. maj. 917
(1955 C. maj. 4,158)

See also **Kettering, Peterborough** and **Wellingborough**

NORTHFIELD—*See* **Birmingham**

North Fylde (Lancashire) *E.* 53,864
434★*Hon. R. O. Stanley, C.* 27,045
J. Myerscough, *Lab.* 11,307
C. maj. 15,738
(1955 C. maj. 14,660)

Northumberland (3). *See* **Berwick upon Tweed, Hexham** and **Morpeth**

Northwich (Cheshire) *E.* 44,305
435★*J. G. Foster*, Q.C., *C.* 20,396
J. Crawford, *Lab.* 12,426
R. E. Lewis, *L.* 4,602
C. maj. 7,970
(1955 C. maj. 6,555)

Norwich (2)

NORTH *E.* 41,221
436★*J. Paton, Lab.* 19,092
D. R. Chance, *C.* 12,609
Lab. maj. 6,483
(1955 Lab. maj. 6,595)

SOUTH *E.* 43,789
437★*Rt. Hon. A. G. F. Rippon, C.* 19,128
G. D. Wallace, *Lab.* 16,884
C. maj. 2,244
(1955 C maj. 1,758)

Nottingham (4)

CENTRAL *E.* 52,491
438★*Lt.-Col. J. K. Cordeaux*, C.B.E., *C.* 24,004
I. Winterbottom, *Lab.* 21,869
C. maj. 2,135
(1955 C. maj. 758)

NORTH *E.* 59,638
439 *W. C. Whitlock, Lab.* 24,005
A. G. Blake, *C.* 18,952
S. Thomas, *L.* 6,581
J. Peck, *Comm.* 1,331
Lab. maj. 5,053
(1955 Lab. maj. 6,090)

SOUTH *E.* 71,520
440 *W. G. A. Clark, C.* 29,607
Hon. J. E. Silkin, *Lab.* 22,235
C. maj. 7,372
(1955 C. maj. 7,053)

WEST *E.* 62,030
441 *P. H. B. Tapsell, C.* 22,052
★Sir T. O'Brien, *Lab.* 21,888
C. maj. 164
(1955 Lab. maj. 3,908)

Nottinghamshire (6). *See* Ashfield, Bassetlaw, Carlton, Mansfield, Newark and Rushcliffe

Nuneaton (Warwickshire)
E. 58,038
442**F. G. Bowles, Lab.* 24,894
C. G. Miller, *C.* 15,354
J. Campbell, *L.* 7,227
Lab. maj. 9,540
(1955 Lab. maj. 10,284)

Ogmore (Glamorgan)
E. 57,192
443**W. E. Padley, Lab.* 35,170
T. O. Ewart-James, *C.* .. 11,905
Lab. maj. 23,265
(1955 Lab. maj. 22,524)

Oldbury and Halesowen
E. 68,892
444**A. Moyle,* C.B.E., *Lab.* .. 23,861
J. F. Vernon, *C.* 21,478
D. Mirfin, *L.* 10,343
Lab. maj. 2,383
(1955 Lab. maj. 5,055)

Oldham (2)
EAST *E.* 54,520
445 *C. Mapp, Lab.* 19,329
*Sir I. M. Horobin, *C.* .. 17,499
D. Wrigley, *L.* 6,660
Lab. maj. 1,830
(1955 C. maj. 380)
WEST *E.* 51,845
446**C. L. Hale, Lab.* 22,624
J. H. V. Sutcliffe, *C.* .. 18,505
Lab. maj. 4,119
(1955 Lab. maj. 3,899)

OPENSHAW—*See* Manchester

Orkney and Zetland
E. 26,435
447**Rt. Hon. J. Grimond,* T.D., *L.* 12,099
R. H. W. Bruce, *C.* .. 3,487
R. S. McGowan, *Lab.* 3,275
L. maj. 8,612
(1955 L. maj. 7,993)

Ormskirk (Lancashire)
E. 61,420
448**Col. Sir D. Glover, C.* 32,952
G. E. Roberts, *Lab.* ... 14,701
C. maj. 18,251
(1955 C. maj. 14,539)

Orpington (Kent)
E. 51,872
449**W. D. M. Sumner,* O.B.E., Q.C., *C.* 24,303
N. J. Hart, *Lab.* 9,543
J. O. Galloway, *L.* 9,092
C. maj. 14,760
(By-election, March 14, 1962)
E. R. Lubbock, L. 22,846
P. Goldman, *C.* 14,991
A. Jinkinson, *Lab.* 5,350
L. maj. 7,855
(1955 C. maj. 11,936)

Oswestry (Shropshire)
E. 50,772
450**Rt. Hon. W. D. Ormsby-Gore, C.* 21,055
G. Thomas, *Lab.* 10,531
D. G. Rees, *L.* 6,068
C. maj. 10,524
(By-election, Nov. 8, 1961)
W. J. Biffen, C. 12,428
J. Buchanan, *L.* 8,647
A. B. Walden, *Lab.* 8,519
J. A. Dayton, *Ind.* 839
C. maj. 3,781
(1955 C. maj. 10,425)

Oxford (English Borough)
E. 66,655
451 *Hon. C. M. Woodhouse,* D.S.O., O.B.E., *C.* 26,798
L. N. Anderton, *Lab.* . 18,310
I. R. M. Davies, *L.* ... 7,491
C. maj. 8,488
(1955 C. maj. 7,778)

Oxfordshire (2). *See* Banbury and Henley

Paddington (2)
NORTH *E.* 40,952
452**B. T. Parkin, Lab.* 14,397
H. H. S. Montefiore, *C.* 13,629
Lab. maj. 768
(1955 Lab. maj. 2,092)
SOUTH *E.* 40,951
453**R. A. Allan,* D.S.O., O.B.E., *C.* 16,006
D. J. Nisbet, *Lab.* 8,719
C. maj. 7,287
(1955 C. maj. 7,047)

Paisley (Scottish Burgh)
E. 63,097
454**D. H. Johnston,* Q.C., *Lab.* 28,519
G. R. Rickman, *C.* .. 21,250
Lab. maj. 7,269
(By-election, April 20, 1961)
J. Robertson, Lab. 19,200
J. M. Bannerman, *L.* . 17,542
G. R. Rickman, *C.* ... 5,597
Lab. maj. 1,658
(1955 Lab. maj. 6,098)

PARK—*See* Sheffield

PAVILION—*See* Brighton

PECKHAM—*See* Camberwell

Pembrokeshire
E. 62,372
455**D. L. Donnelly, Lab.* .. 27,623
H. G. Partridge, *C.* ... 22,301
W. Williams, *Welsh Nat.* 2,253
Lab. maj. 5,322
(1955 Lab. maj. 1,592)

Penistone (Yorks, W.R.)
E 61,397
456**J. J. Mendelson, Lab.* .. 31,117
J. B. Deby, *C.* 19,809
Lab. maj. 11,308
(June, 1959, by-election, Lab. maj. 11,119)
(1955 Lab. maj. 11,636)

Penrith and the Border (Cumberland)
E. 51,190
457**W. S. I. Whitelaw,* M.C., *C.* 23,551
B. P. Atha, *Lab.* 9,342
B. G. Ashmore, *L.* ... 7,602
C. maj. 14,209
(1955 C. maj. 13,672)

PENTLANDS—*See* Edinburgh

PERRY BARR—*See* Birmingham

Perthshire and Kinross (2)
KINROSS AND WEST *E.* 33,582
458**W. G. Leburn,* T.D., *C.* 16,256
J. G. Mackenzie, *Lab.* . 4,008
A. Donaldson, *Scott. Nat.* 3,568
C. maj. 12,248
(By-election pending)
(1955 C. maj. 12,158)

PERTH AND EAST *E.* 55,064
459 *I. MacArthur, C.* 24,217
Dr. R. D. McIntyre, *Scot. Nat.* 9,637
T. W. Moore, *Lab.* ... 7,781
C. maj. 14,580
(1955 C. maj. 13,721)

Peterborough (Northamptonshire)
E. 60,545
460**Sir H. Nicholls, Bt., C.* 27,414
Miss B. Boothroyd, *Lab.* 22,830
C. maj. 4,584
(1955 C. maj. 3,238)

Petersfield (Hampshire) *E* 52,796
461**Hon. P. R. Legh, C.* .. 23,687
J. S. P. Davey, *Lab.* ... 8,278
Lt.-Col. R. M. Digby, *L.* 6,912
C. maj. 15,409
(By-election, Nov. 16, 1960)
Miss J. M. Quennell, C. 15,613
Lt.-Col. R. M. Digby, *L.* 8,310
W. Royle, *Lab.* 4,777
C. maj. 7,303
(1955 C. maj. 14,090)

Plymouth (2)
DEVONPORT *E.* 64,236
462**Miss J. H. Vickers,* M.B.E., *C. & Nat. L.* 28,481
M. M. Foot, *Lab.* 22,027
C. & Nat. L. maj. .. 6,454
(1955 C. & Nat. L. maj. 100)
SUTTON *E.* 74,078
463 *I. M. Fraser,* M.C., *C.* .. 32,752
J. D. Richards, *Lab.* .. 25,991
C. maj. 6,761
(1955 C. maj. 3,810)

POLLOK—*See* Glasgow

Pontefract (English Borough)
E. 54,677
464**G. O. Sylvester, Lab.* .. 35,194
E. T. Bowman, *C.* ... 10,884
Lab. maj. 24,310
(By-election, March 22, 1962)
J. Harper, Lab. 26,461
P. Dean, *C.* 6,633
R. E. Eckley, *Ind.* 1,146
Lab. maj. 19,828
(1955 Lab. maj. 22,463)

Pontypool (Monmouthshire)
E. 47,452
465**L. Abse, Lab.* 26,755
P. S. Thomas, *C.* 8,903
B. C. L. Morgan, *Welsh Nat.* 2,519
Lab. maj. 17,852
(Nov. 1958, by-election, Lab. maj. 13,727)
(1955 Lab. maj. 16,572)

Pontypridd (Glamorgan)
E. 53,903
466**A. Pearson,* C.B.E., *Lab.* 29,853
Sir B. M. Rhys-Williams, Bt., *C.* 13,896
Lab. maj. 15,957
(1955 Lab. maj. 17,163)

Poole (English Borough)
E. 63,554
467**Capt. Sir R. A. Pilkington,* K.B.E., M.C., *C.* . 26,956
A. J. Williams, *Lab.* .. 15,325
J. C. Holland, *L.* 8,735
C. maj. 11,631
(1955 C. maj. 9,562)

Poplar (London Borough)
E. 44,412
468★*Rt. Hon. C. W. Key, Lab.* 22,506
P. B. Black, *C.* 6,635
Lab. maj. *15,871*
(1955 Lab. maj. 19,828)

Portsmouth (3)
LANGSTONE *E.* 79,885
469★*G. P. Stevens, C.* 38,834
D. G. Reynolds, *Lab.*. 20,553
C. maj. *18,281*
(1955 C. maj. 14,155)
SOUTH *E.* 55,121
470★*Sir J. M. Lucas, Bt., K.B.E., M.C., C.* 27,892
F. Towell, *Lab.* 11,979
C. maj. *15,913*
(1955 C. maj. 14,287)
WEST *E.* 53,206
471★*Brig. T. H. Clarke, C.B.E., C.* 23,600
Dr. M. Bresler, *Lab.*.. 17,334
C. maj. *6,266*
(1955 C. maj. 3,669)

Preston (2)
NORTH *E.* 52,212
472★*Rt. Hon. J. Amery, C.*. 23,990
A. Davidson, *Lab.* 19,529
C. maj. *4,461*
(1955 C. maj. 2,903)
SOUTH *E.* 49,809
473★*A. Green, C.* 21,954
T. G. Bradley, *Lab.* ... 18,935
C. maj. *3,019*
(1955 C. maj. 474)

PROVAN—*See* Glasgow

Pudsey (English Borough)
E. 52,285
474 *J. Hiley, C.* 22,752
V. P. Richardson, *Lab.* 16,241
J. S. Snowden, *L.* 6,429
C. maj. *6,511*
(1955 C. maj. 4,564)

PUTNEY—*See* Wandsworth

Reading (English Borough)
E. 58,772
475 *P. F. H. Emery, C.* ... 26,314
★I. Mikardo, *Lab.* 22,372
C. maj. *3,942*
(1955 Lab. maj. 238)

Reigate (Surrey)
E. 60,266
476★*Rt. Hon. Sir J. K. Vaughan-Morgan, Bt., C.* 26,966
C. J. Garnsworthy, *Lab.* 14,465
Mrs. A. H. Scott, *L.*.. 8,205
C. maj. *12,501*
(1955 C. maj. 10,307)

Renfrewshire (2)
EAST *E.* 61,060
477 *Miss M. B. H. Anderson, O.B.E., C.* 29,672
A. J. Houston, *Lab.* ... 14,579
D. M. H. Starforth, *L.* 6,339
C. maj. *15,093*
(1955 C. maj. 16,588)
WEST *E.* 47,395
478★*Rt. Hon. J. S. Maclay, C.H., C.M.G., L. & C.* 20,959
C. Minihan, *Lab.* 18,206
L. & C. maj. *2,753*
(1955 L. & C. maj. 4,040)

Rhondda (2)
EAST *E.* 37,908
479 *G. E. Davies, Lab.* 20,565
Mrs. A. Powell, *Comm.* 4,580
D. H. Peace, *C.* 3,629
N. Williams, *Welsh Nat.* 2,776
Lab. maj. *15,985*
(1955 Lab. maj. 17,315)
WEST *E.* 34,450
480★*I. R. Thomas, Lab.* 21,130
G. P. James, *Welsh Nat.* 4,978
F. L. Pym, *C.* 3,242
Lab. maj. *16,152*
(1955 Lab. maj. 16,864)

Richmond, Surrey (English Borough)
E. 59,852
481 *A. H. F. Royle, C.* ... 27,161
C. H. Archibald, *Lab.* 12,975
J. A. Baker, *L.* 7,359
C. maj. *14,186*
(1955 C. maj. 12,955)

Richmond (Yorkshire, N.R.)
E. 52,416
482 *T. P. G. Kitson, C.* ... 28,270
Mrs. M. McMillan, *Lab.* 9,203
C. maj. *19,067*
(1955 C. maj. 16,005)

Ripon (Yorkshire, W.R.)
E. 41,184
483★*Col. Sir M. Stoddart-Scott, O.B.E., T.D., M.D., C.* 22,757
J. H. Swann, *Lab.* 9,791
C. maj. *12,966*
(1955 C. maj. 12,065)

Rochdale (English Borough)
E. 61,191
484★*J. McCann, Lab.* 21,689
L. H. C. Kennedy, *L.*. 18,949
T. Normanton, *C.* ... 11,665
Lab. maj. *2,740*
(Feb. 1958, by-election, Lab. maj. 4,530)
(1955 C. maj. 1,590)

Rochester and Chatham (English Borough)
E. 64,386
485 *J. M. G. Critchley, C.*. 26,510
★Rt. Hon. A. G. Bottomley, O.B.E., *Lab.*. 25,487
C. maj. *1,023*
(1955 Lab. maj. 2,447)

Romford (English Borough)
E. 73,082
486★*R. J. Ledger, Lab.* 25,558
R. J. S. Harvey, *C.* ... 24,951
D. Geary, *L.* 8,228
Lab. maj. *607*
(1955 Lab. maj. 2,625)

Ross and Cromarty—*See* Inverness-shire and Ross and Cromarty

Rossendale (English Borough)
E. 50,577
487★*A. W. J. Greenwood, Lab.* 20,743
J. R. T. Holt, *C.* 18,152
A. Cooper, *L.* 4,752
Lab. maj. *2,591*
(1955 Lab. maj. 2,911)

Rotherham (English Borough)
E. 57,080
488★*J. H. Jones, Lab.* 28,298
R. Hall, *C.* 16,759
Lab. maj. *11,539*
(By-election, March 28, 1963)
B. K. O'Malley, Lab.. 22,441
M. Barras, *C.* 9,209
R. E. Eckley, *Ind.* 742
Lab. maj. *13,232*
(1955 Lab. maj. 11,541)

Rother Valley (Yorks, W.R.)
E. 71,652
489★*D. Griffiths, Lab.* 43,962
W. A. V. Hoskins, *C.*. 15,369
Lab. maj. *28,593*
(1955 Lab. maj. 27,052)

Rowley Regis and Tipton
E. 59,895
490★*Rt. Hon. A. Henderson, Q.C., Lab.* 27,151
A. Taylor, *C.* 17,174
Lab. maj. *9,977*
(1955 Lab. maj. 13,168)

Roxburgh, Selkirk and Peebles
E. 55,459
491★*Cmdr. C. E M. Donaldson, V.R.D., C.* 22,275
Dr. J. M. MacCormick, *L.* 12,762
T. Dalyell, *Lab.* 9,336
C. maj. *9,513*
(1955 C. maj. 7,170)

Rugby (Warwickshire)
E. 47,809
492 *Lt.-Col. A. R. Wise, M.B.E., T.D., C.* 17,429
★J. Johnson, *Lab.* 16,959
S. Goldblatt, *L.* 6,413
A. S. Frost, *Ind.* 142
C. maj. *470*
(1955 Lab. maj. 1,378)

Ruislip-Northwood (English Borough)
E. 49,198
493★*F. P. Crowder, C.* 23,480
J. L. King, *Lab.* 10,424
R. A. Walker, *L.* 7,295
C. maj. *13,056*
(1955 C. maj. 11,555)

Runcorn (Cheshire)
E. 49,584
494★*Rt. Hon. D. F. Vosper, T.D., C.* 26,615
J. Barnett, *Lab.* 13,837
C. maj. *12,778*
(1955 C. maj. 10,830)

Rushcliffe (Nottinghamshire)
E. 58,971
495★*Rt. Hon. M. Redmayne, D.S.O., C.* 27,392
N. D. Sandelson, *Lab.* 22,952
C. maj. *4,440*
(1955 C. maj. 1,643)

Rutherglen (Lanarkshire)
E. 42,833
496★*R. C. Brooman-White, C.* 19,146
E. J. Milne, *Lab.* 17,624
C. maj. *1,522*
(1955 C. maj. 2,101)

Rutland and Stamford (Lincolnshire and Rutland)
E. 41,061
497 *K. Lewis, C.* 19,078
C. S. B. Attlee, *Lab.*.. 14,137
C. maj. *4,941*
(1955 C. maj. 2,819)

Rye (East Sussex)
E. 54,599
498**B. G. Irvine, C.*......... 27,465
J. R. Murray, *L.*...... 7,549
D. S. Tilbé, *Lab.*...... 7,359
C. maj............. *19,916*
(1955 C. maj. 17,940)

Saffron Walden (Essex)
E. 48,454
499**Rt. Hon. R. A. Butler,* C.H., *C.*........... 20,955
Rev. H. N. Horne, *Lab.*............... 14,173
D. J. Ridley, *L.*...... 4,245
C. maj............. *6,782*
(1955 C. maj. 6,418)

St. Albans (Hertfordshire)
E. 52,823
500 *V. H. Goodhew, C.*.... 23,157
L. W. Carroll, *Lab.*.... 14,650
W. A. N. Jones, *L.*.... 5,948
C. maj............. *8,507*
1955 C. maj. 5,721)

St. Helens (English Borough)
E. 75,280
501**L. Spriggs, Lab.*....... 35,961
M. Carlisle, *C.*....... 21,956
Lab. maj........... *14,005*
(June, 1958, by-election, Lab. maj. 11,994)
(1955 Lab. maj. 15,883)

St. Ives (Cornwall)
E. 44,010
502**G. R. Howard, C. & Nat. L.*............ 15,700
D. Longden, *Lab.*..... 8,802
G. E. L. Whitmarsh, *L.*................ 8,258
C. & Nat. L. maj... *6,898*
(1955 C. & Nat. L. maj. 7,335)

St. Marylebone (London Borough)
E. 55,080
503**Sir W. W. Wakefield, C.*............... 23,278
B. Hooberman, *Lab.*.. 8,507
E. M. Wheeler, *L.*.... 4,304
C. maj............. *14,771*
(1955 C. maj. 15,399)

St. Pancras, North (London Borough)
E. 59,194
504**K. Robinson, Lab.*..... 22,256
D. B. Mitchell, *C.*.... 15,949
W. Webster, *Ind.*..... 1,685
J. Nicolson, *Comm.*... 1,230
Lab. maj........... *6,307*
(1955 Lab. maj. 7,082)

Salford (2)
EAST *E.* 51,231
505**F. Allaun, Lab.*....... 20,639
J. H. Franks, *C.*...... 17,171
Lab. maj........... *3,468*
(1955 Lab. maj. 1,728)
WEST *E.* 56,490
506**C. Royle, Lab.*....... 23,167
H. H. Davies, *C.*..... 20,306
Lab. maj........... *2,861*
(1955 Lab. maj. 859)

Salisbury (Wiltshire)
E. 49,997
507**J. G. Morrison,* T.D., *C.* 20,641
Dr. J. A. Cannon, *Lab.* 12,932
J. M. Booker, *L.*...... 5,516
C. maj............. *7,709*
(1955 C. maj. 7,639)

Scarborough and Whitby (Yorkshire, N.R.)
E. 63,938
508**Sir A. C. M. Spearman, C.*................ 25,226
G. Gray, *L.*......... 10,759
N. G. Barnett, *Lab.*... 10,468
C. maj............. *14,467*
(1955 C. maj. 16,645)

SCOTLAND—*See* Liverpool

SCOTSTOUN—*See* Glasgow

Sedgefield (Durham)
E. 63,535
509**J. Slater,* B.E.M., *Lab.*.. 30,642
D. F. M. Appleby, *C.*. 21,771
Lab. maj........... *8,871*
(1955 Lab. maj. 8,853)

SELLY OAK—*See* Birmingham

Sevenoaks (Kent)
E. 62,701
510**J. C. Rodgers, C.*...... 28,186
R. C. Ogley, *Lab.* 14,265
Mrs. N. Penman, *L.*.. 7,819
C. maj............. *13,921*
(1955 C. maj. 11,078)

Sheffield (6)
ATTERCLIFFE *E.* 65,024
511**J. B. Hynd, Lab.*...... 33,676
Lt.-Col. H. L. Lambert, *C. & L.*...... 15,304
Lab. maj........... *18,372*
(1955 Lab. maj. 19,568)
BRIGHTSIDE *E.* 57,090
512**R. E. Winterbottom, Lab.*............... 28,302
H. C. Holmes, *C. & L.* 12,269
H. Hill, *Comm.*...... 1,373
Lab. maj........... *16,033*
(1955 Lab. maj. 15,404)
HALLAM *E.* 60,225
513 *J. H. Osborn, C. & L.*. 28,747
E. S. Sachs, *Lab.*..... 11,938
B. Roseby, *L.*....... 5,119
C. & L. maj....... *16,809*
(1955 C. & L. maj. 14,739)
HEELEY *E.* 72,648
514**Sir P. G. Roberts, Bt., C. & L.*.......... 33,236
Miss J. Mellors, *Lab.*.. 23,109
C. & L. maj....... *10,127*
(1955 C. & L. maj. 11,051)
HILLSBOROUGH *E.* 51,023
515**G. Darling, Lab.*...... 21,888
S. K. Arnold, *C.*..... 16,845
Lab. maj........... *5,043*
(1955 Lab. maj. 7,010)
PARK *E.* 51,533
516**F. W. Mulley, Lab.*... 26,078
J. Neill, *C. & L.*..... 10,598
Lab. maj........... *15,480*
(1955 Lab. maj. 18,339)

SHETTLESTON—*See* Glasgow

Shipley (Yorkshire, W.R.)
E. 45,460
517**G. A. N. Hirst,* T.D., *C.* 22,536
M. R. English, *Lab.*.. 17,025
C. maj............. *5,511*
(1955 C. maj. 5,331)

Shoreditch and Finsbury (London Borough)
E. 53,210
518**M. Cliffe, Lab.*........ 22,744
T. H. M. Whipham, *C.*................ 11,178
Lab. maj........... *11,566*
(Nov. 1958, by-election, Lab. maj. 6,995)
(1955 Lab. maj. 16,284)

Shrewsbury (Shropshire)
E. 46,846
519**Sir J. A. Langford-Holt, C.*................ 19,970
K. V. Russell, *Lab.*... 11,338
H. Shaw, *L.*......... 6,387
C. maj............. *8,632*
(1959 C. maj. 7,593)

Shropshire (4) *See* **Ludlow, Oswestry, Shrewsbury and Wrekin**

Skipton (Yorkshire, W.R.)
E. 49,037
520**G. B. Drayson,* T.D., *C.* 20,278
F. O. Hooley, *Lab.*... 11,178
Miss K. C. Graham, *L.* 10,543
C. maj............. *9,100*
(1955 C. maj. 9,182)

SMALL HEATH—*See* Birmingham

Smethwick (English Borough)
E. 49,794
521**Rt. Hon. P. C. Gordon-Walker, Lab.*....... 20,670
P. H. S. Griffiths, *C.*.. 17,126
Lab. maj........... *3,544*
(1955 Lab. maj. 6,495)

Solihull (Warwickshire)
E. 60,227
522**Sir M. A. Lindsay, Bt.,* C.B.E., D.S.O., *C.*.... 35,862
E. J. Bowen, *Lab.*.... 12,682
C. maj............. *23,180*
(1955 C. maj. 18,023)

Somerset (6)
NORTH *E.* 63,231
523**Sir E. H. C. Leather, C.* 30,432
E. F. Wilde, *Lab.*..... 23,649
C. maj............. *6,783*
(1955 C. maj. 4,183)
See also **Bridgwater, Taunton, Wells, Weston-super-Mare and Yeovil**

Southall (English Borough)
E. 55,290
524**G. A. Pargiter, Lab.*... 22,285
M. T. B. Underhill, *C.* 19,966
Lab. maj........... *2,319*
(1955 Lab. maj. 6,335)

Southampton (2)
ITCHEN *E.* 69,886
525**H. M. King,* D.Phil., *Lab.*............... 29,123
E. M. King, *C.* 25,390
Lab. maj........... *3,733*
(1955 Lab. maj. 5,771)
TEST *E.* 67,087
526**J. M. Howard, C.*..... 30,176
Mrs. S. V. T. B. Williams, *Lab.*........ 23,410
C. maj............. *6,766*
(1955 C. maj. 3,842)

Southend (2)
EAST *E.* 55,265
527**Sir S. J. McAdden,* C.B.E., *C.*................ 24,712
E. J. Trevett, *Lab.*.... 16,987
C. maj............. *7,725*
(1955 C. maj. 6,758)

WEST *E.* 60,999
528★*H. P. G. Channon, C.*. 27,612
Miss H. J. Harvey, *L.*. 10,577
A. Pearson-Clarke, *Lab*. 9,219
C. maj. 17,035
(Jan. 1959, by-election, C. maj. 8,179)
(1955 C. maj. 18,460)

South Fylde (Lancashire)
E. 65,310
529★*Col. C. G. Lancaster, C.* 36,988
N. Holding, *Lab*. 12,521
C. maj. 24,467
(1955 C. maj. 22,395)

Southgate (English Borough)
E. 54,869
530★*Sir A. Beverley Baxter, C.* 25,704
G. J. Bridge, *L.* 8,968
S. J. Chapman, *Lab*. 7,613
C. maj. 16,736
(1955 C. maj. 18,210)

Southport (English Borough)
E. 62,466
531 *W. I. Percival*, Q.C., *C.* 26,905
S. Goldberg, *L.* 11,292
C. W. Hadfield, *Lab*. 9,805
C. maj. 15,613
(1955 C. maj. 17,441)

South Shields (English Borough)
E. 75,538
532★*Rt. Hon. J. C. Ede*, C.H., *Lab*. 32,577
J. Chalmers, *C.* 23,638
Lab. maj. 8,939
(1955 Lab. maj. 10,252)

Southwark (London Borough)
E. 61,747
533 *R. J. Gunter, Lab*. 25,036
J. M. Greenwood, *C.* 12,696
S. P. Bent, *Comm*. 1,395
Lab. maj. 12,340
(1955 Lab. maj. 17,230)

Sowerby (Yorkshire, W.R.)
E. 52,560
534★*A. L. N. D. Houghton, Lab*. 18,949
R. K. McKim, *C.* 16,993
J. G. Walker, *L.* 7,654
Lab. maj. 1,956
(1955 Lab. maj. 2,783)

SPARKBROOK—*See* **Birmingham**

Spelthorne (Middlesex)
E. 52,115
535★*Sir G. B. Craddock, C.* 25,221
J. P. Carruthers, *Lab*. 17,128
C. maj. 8,093
(1955 C. maj. 5,982)

SPRINGBURN—*See* **Glasgow**

Stafford and Stone (Staffordshire)
E. 57,078
536★*Rt. Hon. H. C. P. J. Fraser*, M.B.E., *C.* 28,107
A. Gregory, *Lab*. 18,034
C. maj. 10,073
(1955 C. maj. 8,656)

Staffordshire (6). *See* **Brierley Hill, Burton, Cannock, Leek, Lichfield and Tamworth** and **Stafford and Stone**

Stalybridge and Hyde (Cheshire)
E. 55,183
537★*F. Blackburn, Lab*. 23,732
E. J. Brown, *C.* 22,309
Lab. maj. 1,423
(1955 Lab. maj. 155)

STECHFORD—*See* **Birmingham**

Stepney (London Borough)
E. 63,932
538★*W. J. Edwards, Lab*. 26,875
P. B. Calwell, *C.* 8,566
S. Kaye, *Comm*. 2,548
Lab. maj. 18,309
(1955 Lab. maj. 21,944)

Stirling and Clackmannan (2)
CLACKMANNAN AND EAST
E. 52,200
539★*Rt. Hon. A. Woodburn, Lab*. 25,004
R. C. Aitchison, *C.* 17,132
Lab. maj. 7,872
(1955 Lab. maj. 7,009)

WEST *E.* 43,686
540 *W. Baxter, Lab*. 21,008
W. A. Gay, *C.* 15,497
Lab. maj. 5,511
(1955 Lab. maj. 3,167)

Stirling and Falkirk (Scottish Burgh) *E.* 55,759
541★*M. MacPherson*, M.B.E., *Lab*. 22,423
R. S. Johnston, *C.* 19,797
J. Halliday, *Scot. Nat*. 2,983
Lab. maj. 2,626
(1955 Lab. maj. 1,306)

Stockport (2)
NORTH *E.* 53,287
542★*Wing-Cdr. Sir N. J. Hulbert, C.* 23,487
M. E. J. Swain, *Lab*. 20,265
C. maj. 3,222
(1955 C. maj. 4,567)

SOUTH *E.* 47,265
543★*H. M. Steward, C.* 20,522
S. Orme, *Lab*. 17,982
C. maj. 2,540
(1955 C. maj. 4,086)

Stockton on Tees (English Borough)
E. 53,224
544★*G. R. Chetwynd, Lab*. 23,961
G. J. K. Coles, *C.* 20,684
Lab. maj. 3,277
(By-election, April 5, 1962)
W. T. Rodgers, Lab. 19,694
G. J. K. Coles, *C.* 12,112
J. H. Mulholland, *L.* 11,722
Lab. maj. 7,582
(1955 Lab. maj. 3,815)

Stoke Newington and Hackney, North (London Borough)
E. 64,723
545★*D. Weitzman*, Q.C., *Lab*. 22,950
R. L. White, *C.* 14,515
P. Phillips, *L.* 6,076
Lab. maj. 8,435
(1955 Lab. maj. 10,088)

Stoke on Trent (3)
CENTRAL *E.* 62,220
546★*Dr. B. Stross, Lab*. 28,630
J. P. H. Harrison, *C.* 18,205
Lab. maj. 10,425
(1955 Lab. maj. 12,355)

NORTH *E.* 58,336
547★*Mrs. H. Slater, Lab*. 29,336
S. F. Middup, M.B.E., *C.* 16,522
Lab. maj. 12,814
(1955 Lab. maj. 14,874)

SOUTH *E.* 63,777
548★*E. Smith, Lab*. 29,578
G. S. Tucker, *C.* 20,318
Lab. maj. 9,260
(1955 Lab. maj. 13,264)

Stratford (Warwickshire)
E. 49,660
549★*J. D. Profumo*, O.B.E., *C.* 26,146
J. Stretton, *Lab*. 12,017
C. maj. 14,129
(By-election, August 15, 1963)
A. E. U. Maude, T.D., *C.* 15,846
A. Faulds, *Lab*. 12,376
D. Mirfin, *L.* 7,622
M. S. Blair, *Ind*. 281
D. F. Sutch, *Ind*. 209
C. maj. 3,470
(1955 C. maj. 13,312)

STREATHAM—*See* **Wandsworth**

Stretford (English Borough)
E. 71,304
550★*Sir S. Storey, Bt., C.* 32,888
E. Reid, *Lab*. 23,538
C. maj. 9,350
(1955 C. maj. 11,834)

Stroud (Gloucestershire)
E. 57,222
551★*J. A. Kershaw*, M.C., *C.* 23,448
A. T. Evans, *Lab*. 18,336
C. J. McNair, *L.* 6,988
C. maj. 5,112
(1955 C. maj. 3,943)

Sudbury and Woodbridge (Suffolk)
E. 60,756
552★*Rt. Hon. J. H. Hare*, O.B.E., *C.* 26,130
R. B. Stirling, *Lab*. 16,248
A. Herbert, *L.* 6,914
C. maj. 9,882
(1955 C. maj. 7,190)

Suffolk (4). *See* **Bury St. Edmunds, Eye, Lowestoft** and **Sudbury and Woodbridge**

Sunderland (2)
NORTH *E.* 57,763
553★*F. T. Willey, Lab*. 24,341
P. E. Heselton, *C.* 22,133
Lab. maj. 2,208
(1955 Lab. maj. 2,836)

SOUTH *E.* 68,014
554★*P. G. Williams, C.* 27,825
E. Armstrong, *Lab*. 26,835
C. maj. 990
(1955 C. maj. 1,774)

Surbiton (English Borough)
E. 45,165
555★*N. T. L. Fisher*, M.C., *C.* 24,058
A. Imisson, *Lab*. 11,633
C. maj. 12,425
(1955 C. maj. 10,483)

Surrey (10)
EAST *E.* 69,996
556★*C. J. A. Doughty*, Q.C., *C.* 36,310
K. S. Vaus, *L.* 10,376
J. C. Hunt, *Lab*. 10,102
C. maj. 25,934
(1955 C. maj. 24,709)

See also **Carshalton, Chertsey, Dorking, Epsom, Esher, Farnham, Guildford, Reigate and Woking**
East Sussex (4). *See* Eastbourne, East Grinstead, Lewes and Rye
West Sussex (3). *See* **Arundel and Shoreham, Chichester and Horsham**
SUTTON—*See* **Plymouth**

Sutton and Cheam (English Borough)
E. 58,898
557* *R. C. Sharples*, O.B.E., M.C., *C.*........... 27,344
F. A. Judd, *Lab.*....... 11,946
J. Montgomerie, *L.*.... 7,600
C. maj........... *15,398*
(1955 C. maj. 14,333)

Sutton Coldfield (English Borough)
E. 65,347
558* *Rt. Hon. G. W. Lloyd, C.*.............. 33,064
R. S. G. Hattersley, *Lab.*............. 11,310
K. J. Hovers, *L.*...... 7,543
C. maj........... *21,754*
(1955 C. maj. 17,987)

Swansea (2)
EAST *E.* 55,301
559* *D. L. Mort, Lab.*...... 29,884
H. J. F. Crum Ewing, *C.*............. 9,754
E. C. Rees, *Welsh Nat.* 4,651
Lab. maj........... *20,130*
(By-election, March 28, 1963)
N. McBride, Lab....... 18,909
R. Owens, *L.*........ 4,895
Rev. L. Atkin, *Ind.* .. 2,462
Miss A. P. Thomas, *C.* 2,272
E. C. Rees, *Welsh Nat.* 1,620
B. Pearce, *Comm.*.... 773
Lab. maj........... *14,014*
(1955 Lab. maj. 17,472)
WEST *E.* 58,045
560 *J. E. H. Rees, C.*...... 24,043
*P. Morris, *Lab.*....... 23,640
C. maj........... *403*
(1955 Lab. maj. 1,021)

Swindon (English Borough)
E. 53,339
561* *F. E. Noel-Baker, Lab.*. 24,087
G. L. Pears, *C.*....... 20,178
Lab. maj........... *3,909*
(1955 Lab. maj. 3,939)

Taunton (Somerset)
E. 52,675
562* *E. D. L. du Cann, C.*.. 22,680
L. V. Pike, *Lab.*....... 16,182
C. M. K. Bruton, *L.*.. 7,031
C. maj........... *6,498*
(Feb. 1956, by-election, C. maj. 657)
(1955 C. maj. 5,542)

Tavistock (Devonshire)
E. 46,908
563* *Sir H. G. Studholme, Bt.*, C.V.O., *C.*...... 19,778
R. G. Moore, *L.*..... 9,008
B. R. Weston, *Lab.*.. 8,022
C. maj........... *10,770*
(1955 C. maj. 10,236)
TEST—*See* **Southampton**

Thirsk and Malton (Yorkshire, N.R.)
E. 52,517
564* *Rt. Hon. R. H. Turton*, M.C., *C.*........... 27,413
Dr. J. W. Bray, *Lab.*.. 12,318
C. maj........... *15,095*
(1955 C. maj. 14,085)

Thurrock (Essex)
E. 67,054
565* *H. J. Delargy, Lab.*... 32,270
W. E. McNamara, *C.* 20,188
Lab. maj........... *12,082*
(1955 Lab. maj. 15,329)

Tiverton (Devonshire)
E. 48,416
566* *Rt. Hon. D. Heathcoat Amory*, T.D., *C.*.... 21,714
Dr. J. E. O. Dunwoody, *Lab.*....... 9,836
J. J. Collier, *L.*....... 7,504
C. maj........... *11,878*
(By-election, Nov. 16, 1960)
R. J. Maxwell-Hyslop, C............... 15,308
J. J. Collier, *L.*....... 12,268
R. F. H. Dobson, *Lab.*. 5,895
C. maj........... *3,040*
(1955 C. maj. 10,424)

Tonbridge (Kent)
E. 67,320
567* *R. P. Hornby, C.*..... 31,687
K. W. May, *Lab.*.... 21,181
C. maj........... *10,506*
(June, 1956, by-election, C. maj. 1,602)
(1955 C. maj. 10,196)

Torquay (English Borough)
E. 67,608
568* *F. M. Bennett, C.*..... 29,527
W. V. Cooper, *Lab.*.. 11,784
T. O. Kellock, *L.*.... 10,685
C. maj........... *17,743*
(Dec. 1955, by-election, C. maj. 10,581)
(1955 C. maj. 17,230)

Torrington (Devonshire)
E. 44,029
569 *P. B. Browne, C.*..... 17,283
*M. R. Bonham-Carter, *L.*.............. 15,018
R. F. H. Dobson, *Lab.* 5,633
C. maj........... *2,265*
(March, 1958, by-election, L. maj. 219)
(1955 Nat. L. & C. maj. 9,312)

Totnes (Devonshire)
E. 63,071
570* *R. L. Mawby, C.* 26,925
T. J. B. Heelas, *Lab.*.. 13,116
T. C. Jones, *L.*.......10,719
C. maj........... *13,809*
(1955 C. maj. 11,594)

Tottenham (English Borough)
E. 59,794
571 *A. G. Brown, Lab.* (*now Ind.*)............ 22,325
D. J. G. Hennessy, *C.*. 15,688
L. G. Lepley, *L.*...... 5,030
Lab. maj........... *6,637*
(1955 Lab. maj. 8,883)
TOXTETH—*See* **Liverpool**

Truro (Cornwall)
E. 55,185
572* *H. G. B. Wilson, C.*.. 19,544
R. J. R. Blindell, *Lab.* 15,057
Miss B. N. Seear, *L.*.. 9,637
C. maj........... *4,487*
(1955 C. maj. 4,717)

Twickenham (English Borough)
E. 73,852
573* *R. G. Cooke*, C.B.E., *C.* 33,677
Mrs. A. P. Clark, *Lab.* 16,638
K. A. Powell, *L.*..... 8,589
C. maj........... *17,039*
(1955 C. maj. 16,276)

Tynemouth (English Borough)
E. 72,273
574* *Dame I. M. B. Ward*, D.B.E., *C.*......... 32,810
W. H. Hutchison, *Lab.* 18,866
D. N. Thompson, *L.*. 6,525
C. maj........... *13,944*
(1955 C. maj. 10,836)

Uxbridge (Middlesex)
E. 56,997
575 *C. Curran, C.*........ 22,360
*F. Beswick, *Lab.*..... 20,970
G. R. Goodall, *L.*.... 4,746
C. maj........... *1,390*
(1955 Lab. maj. 876)
VAUXHALL—*See* **Lambeth**

Wakefield (English Borough)
E. 60,790
576* *Rt. Hon. A. Creech Jones, Lab.*......... 29,705
T. M. Jopling, *C.*.... 20,114
Lab. maj........... *9,591*
(1955 Lab. maj. 9,745)

Wallasey (English Borough)
E. 72,660
577* *Rt. Hon. A. E. Marples, C.*.............. 35,567
G. Woodburn, *Lab.*.. 20,501
C. maj........... *15,066*
(1955 C. maj. 14,218)

Wallsend (English Borough)
E. 80,235
578* *J. McKay, Lab.*....... 37,862
R. B. Baird, *C.*...... 29,096
Lab. maj........... *8,766*
(1955 Lab. maj. 9,350)

Walsall (2)
NORTH *E.* 59,257
579* *W. T. Wells*, Q.C., *Lab.*.............. 27,693
J. G. Ackers, *C.*...... 17,741
Lab. maj........... *9,952*
(1955 Lab. maj. 10,695)
SOUTH *E.* 62,804
580* *Sir H. J. d'Avigdor-Goldsmid, Bt.*, D.S.O., M.C., *C.*........... 30,471
J. A. F. Ennals, *Lab.*.. 21,689
C. maj........... *8,782*
(1955 C. maj. 2,426)

Walthamstow (2)
EAST *E.* 43,892
581* *J. E. Harvey, C.*...... 16,622
Mrs. M. McKay, *Lab.* 13,721
N. H. Cork, *L.*...... 4,974
W. H. Christopher, *I.L.P.*........... 183
C. maj........... *2,901*
(1955 C. maj. 1,129)

WEST E. 38,226
582**E. C. Redhead, Lab.*...15,980
H. C. Midgley, C.... 7,872
W. O. Smedley, L.... 5,229
Lab. maj........... *8,108*
(March, 1956, by-election, Lab. maj. 9,204)
(1955 Lab. maj. 9,250)

WALTON—*See* Liverpool

Wandsworth (4)

CENTRAL E. 61,831
583**M. H. C. Hughes-Young, M.C., C.*.... 23,655
Mrs. A. P. Llewelyn Davies, *Lab.*....... 21,683
R. A. Locke, *L.*...... 4,287
C. maj........... *1,972*
(1955 C. maj. 1,093)

CLAPHAM E. 55,894
584 *Dr. A. J. Glyn, C.*.... 22,266
*C. W. Gibson, *Lab.*.. 20,390
C. maj........... *1,876*
(1955 Lab. maj. 225)

PUTNEY E. 71,772
585**Sir H. N. Linstead, O.B.E., C.*........ 28,236
D. Taverne, *Lab.*.... 23,115
M. F. Burns, *L.*..... 6,166
C. maj........... *5,121*
(1955 C. maj. 7,195)

STREATHAM E. 50,916
586**Rt. Hon. D. Sandys, C.* 23,479
Dr. D. L. Kerr, *Lab.*.. 10,773
R. S. Rubin, *L.*...... 5,039
C. maj........... *12,706*
(1955 C. maj. 12,268)

Warrington (English Borough)
E. 52,884
587**Rt. Hon. Edith Summerskill, Lab.*........ 22,890
F. O. Stansfield, C... 17,791
Lab. maj........... *5,099*

(By-election, April 20, 1961)
†*W. T. Williams, Lab.*. 16,149
Mrs. B. A. Arnold, *C.* 9,149
F. R. Tetlow, *L.*..... 3,623
Lab. maj........... *7,000*
(1955 Lab. maj. 5,646)

Warwick and Leamington (Warwickshire)
E. 62,849
588**Rt. Hon. Sir J. G. S. Hobson, O.B.E., T.D., Q.C., C.*.......... 32,513
W. Wilson, *Lab.*..... 19,434
C. maj........... *13,079*
(March, 1957, by-election, C. maj. 2,157).
(1955 C. maj. 13,466)

Warwickshire (6). *See* Meriden, Nuneaton, Rugby, Solihull, Stratford and Warwick and Leamington

Watford (English Borough)
E. 53,388
589**F. W. Farey-Jones, C.*. 21,216
Mrs. R. Short, *Lab.*.. 18,315
I. S. Steers, *L.*........ 5,753
C. maj........... *2,901*
(1955 C. maj. 1,717)

WAVERTREE—*See* Liverpool

Wednesbury (English Borough)
E. 60,297
590**J. T. Stonehouse, Lab.*. 24,147
E. Knight, *C.*........ 17,464
F. B. Willmott, *L.*.... 4,780
Lab. maj........... *6,683*
(Feb. 1957, by-election, Lab. maj. 12,236)
(1955 Lab. maj. 8,944)

Wellingborough (Northamptonshire)
E. 52,261
591 *M. C. Hamilton, C.*...22,964
*G. S. Lindgren, *Lab.*.. 22,358
C. maj........... *606*
(1955 Lab. maj. 926)

Wells (Somerset)
E. 57,455
592**Lt.-Cmdr. S. L. C. Maydon, D.S.O., D.S.C., C.* 23,357
J. A. A. Evans, *Lab.*.. 16,452
P. R. Hobhouse, *L.*... 8,220
C. maj........... *6,905*
(1955 C. maj. 5,879)

Wembley (2)

NORTH E. 47,554
593**Wing-Cdr. E. E. Bullus, C.*............. 22,211
R. M. Lewis, *Lab.*.... 11,131
Dr. D. G. Valentine, *L.*.............. 6,171
C. maj........... *11,080*
(1955 C. maj. 10,109)

SOUTH E. 45,150
594**R. S. Russell, C.*..... 19,733
E. Mackenzie, *Lab.*... 12,166
J. E. C. Perry, *L.*..... 5,403
C. maj........... *7,567*
(1955 C. maj. 6,456)

West Bromwich (English Borough)
E. 64,111
595**Rt. Hon. J. Dugdale, Lab.*............. 26,702
A. H. Windrum, *C.*.. 19,809
Lab. maj........... *6,893*
(By-election July 4, 1963)
M. A. Foley, Lab..... 20,510
G. Hawkins, *C.*...... 8,246
N. R. W. Mawle, *L.* 6,161
Lab. maj........... *12,264*
(1955 Lab. maj. 10,020)

Westbury (Wiltshire)
E. 53,238
596**Sir R. V. Grimston, Bt., C.*............. 20,396
J. G. Ridley, *Lab.*.... 14,570
B. T. Wigoder, *L.*... 9,816
C. maj........... *5,826*
(1955 C. maj. 3,389)

WEST DERBY—*See* Liverpool

Western Isles (Inverness-shire and Ross and Cromarty)
E. 25,178
597**M. K. Macmillan, Lab.*. 8,663
D. Macleod, *L. & C.* 7,496
Lab. maj........... *1,167*
(1955 Lab. maj. 2,172)

West Ham (2)

NORTH E. 57,828
598**A. W. J. Lewis, Lab.*.. 24,096
J. G. Jones, *C.*....... 9,318
D. A. S. Brooke, *L.*.. 7,271
Lab. maj........... *14,778*
(1955 Lab. maj. 16,537)

SOUTH E. 52,341
599**F. E. Jones, Q.C., Lab.*. 28,017
P. Goldman, *C.*...... 5,188
O. French, *L.*........ 4,020
Lab. maj........... *22,829*
(1955 Lab. maj. 23,454)

Westhoughton (Lancashire)
E. 56,948
600**J. T. Price, Lab.*..... 29,359
Lt.-Col. J. E. Gouldbourn, *C.*.........18,634
Lab. maj........... *10,725*
(1955 Lab. maj. 10,052)

West Lothian
E. 58,457
601**J. Taylor, Lab.*....... 27,454
W. I. Stewart, *C.*.... 18,083
Lab. maj........... *9,371*
(By-election, June 14, 1962)
T. Dalyell, Lab....... 21,266
W. C. Wolfe, *Scot. Nat.*............. 9,750
W. I. Stewart, *C.*.... 4,784
D. Bryce, *L.*......... 4,537
G. McLennan, *Comm.* 1,511
Lab. maj........... *11,516*
(1955 Lab. maj. 8,307)

Westmorland
E. 46,991
602**W. M. F. Vane, T.D., C.*.............. 20,676
A. G. D. Acland, *L.*.. 8,984
C. Hughes-Stanton, *Lab.*............. 7,359
C. maj........... *11,692*
(1955 C. maj. 13,147)

Weston-super-Mare (Somerset)
E. 60,795
603**D. W. E. Webster, C.*.. 27,881
S. E. Hampton, *Lab.*.. 10,977
E. B. Taylor, *L.*...... 9,609
C. maj........... *16,904*
(June, 1958, by-election, C. maj. 9,976)
(1955 C. maj. 11,082)

Whitehaven (Cumberland)
E. 46,650
604**J. B. Symonds, Lab.*... 22,783
H. J. Pedraza, *C.*..... 16,653
Lab. maj........... *6,130*
(June, 1959, by-election, Lab. maj. 6,324)
(1955 Lab. maj. 6,194)

Widnes (Lancashire)
E. 48,966
605**J. E. MacColl, Lab.*.... 21,218
Lt.-Cdr. B. L. Butcher, *C.*.............. 19,620
Lab. maj........... *1,598*
(1955 Lab. maj. 1,449)

Wigan (English Borough)
E. 55,155
606**E. A. Fitch, Lab.*...... 30,664
J. J. Hodgson, *C.*..... 14,615
M. Weaver, *Comm.*.. 945
Lab. maj........... *16,049*
(June, 1958, by-election, Lab. maj. 17,167)
(1955 Lab. maj. 14,872)

Willesden (2)

EAST E. 58,865
607 *T. H. H. Skeet, C.*.... 22,709
*M. Orbach, *Lab.*..... 20,499
C. maj........... *2,210*
(1955 Lab. maj. 659)

WEST *E.* 61,534
608 *L. A. Pavitt, Lab.* 25,680
Mrs. P. S. Brookes, *C.* 17,946
L. Burt, *Comm.* 1,324
Lab. maj. *7,734*
(1955 Lab. maj. 11,111)

Wiltshire (4). *See* **Chippenham, Devizes, Salisbury and Westbury**

Wimbledon (English Borough)
E. 42,151
609**Sir C. W. Black, C.* ... 21,538
L. M. Kershaw, *Lab.* .. 10,678
C. maj. *10,860*
(1955 C. maj. 10,490)

Winchester (Hampshire)
E. 48,321
610**P. H. B. O. Smithers,* V.R.D., D.Phil., *C.* .. 24,924
Mrs. M. J. Manning, *Lab.* 12,132
C. maj. *12,792*
(1955 C. maj. 11,236)

Windsor (Berkshire)
E. 60,673
611**Sir C. E. Mott-Radclyffe, C.* 29,942
W. E. Robinson, *Lab.* . 15,864
C. maj. *14,078*
(1955 C. maj. 10,724)

Wirral (Cheshire)
E. 71,025
612**Rt. Hon. J. S. B. Lloyd,* C.H., C.B.E., T.D., Q.C., *C.* 39,807
F. W. Venables, *Lab.* . 18,805
C. maj. *21,002*
(1955 C. maj. 17,051)

WITHINGTON—*See* **Manchester**

Woking (Surrey)
E. 64,295
613**Rt. Hon. H. A. Watkinson,* C.H., *C.* 33,521
R. D. V. Williams, *Lab.* 16,210
C. maj. *17,311*
(1955 C. maj. 12,467)

Wokingham (Berkshire)
E. 67,144
614 *W. R. van Straubenzee,* M.B.E., *C.* 30,896
T. G. Boston, *Lab.* ... 14,905
C. W. J. Rout, *L.* 7,899
C. maj. *15,991*
(1955 C. maj. 12,948)

Wolverhampton (2)
NORTH EAST *E.* 51,217
615**J. Baird, Lab.* 20,436
O. A. Pomeroy, *C.* ... 16,639
Lab. maj. *3,797*
(1955 Lab. maj. 9,209)

SOUTH WEST *E.* 51,293
616**Rt. Hon. J. E. Powell,* M.B.E., *C.* 25,696
E. L. J. Thorne, *Lab.* .. 14,529
C. maj. *11,167*
(1955 C. maj. 8,420)

Woodford (English Borough)
E. 45,070
617**Rt. Hon. Sir W. S. Churchill,* K.G., O.M., C.H., *C.* 24,815
A. C. Latham, *Lab.* 10,018
C. maj. *14,797*
(1955 C. maj. 15,808)

Wood Green (English Borough)
E. 59,380
618**Mrs. J. S. Butler, Lab.* . 22,869
R. G. Shillingford, *C.* 21,735
Lab. maj. *1,134*
(1955 Lab. maj. 3,712)

WOODSIDE—*See* **Glasgow**

Woolwich (2)
EAST *E.* 46,349
619**C. P. Mayhew, Lab.* ... 22,353
E. J. Porter, *C.* 12,638
Lab. maj. *9,715*
(1955 Lab. maj. 10,346)

WEST *E.* 54,563
620 *C. W. C. Turner, C.* .. 24,373
W. Hamling, *Lab.* 20,678
R. S. Mallone, *Fellowship Party* 1,189
C. maj. *3,695*
(1955 C. maj. 1,880)

Worcester (English Borough)
E. 59,117
621**Rt. Hon. G. R. Ward, C.* 27,024
B. C. Stanley, *Lab.* ... 19,832
C. maj. *7,192*
(By-election, March 16, 1961)
P. E. Walker, C. 15,087
B. C. Stanley, *Lab.* 11,490
R. Glenton, *L.* 11,435
C. maj. *3,597*
(1955 C. maj. 6,102)

Worcestershire (3)
SOUTH *E.* 57,657
622**Comdr. Sir P. G. Agnew, Bt., C.* 25,824
D. W. Young, *Lab.* .. 10,884
Dr. E. H. L. Harries, *L.* 6,890
C. maj. *14,940*
(1955 C. maj. 12,980)

See also **Bromsgrove and Kidderminster**

Workington (Cumberland)
E. 49,401
623**T. F. Peart, Lab.* 25,537
T. M. Brannan, *C.* ... 16,894
Lab. maj. *8,643*
(1955 Lab. maj. 7,928)

Worthing (English Borough)
E. 60,505
624**Brig. Sir O. L. Prior-Palmer,* D.S.O., *C.* ... 31,396
F. R. Mason, *Lab.* 7,618
D. R. E. Abel, *L.* 7,045
C. maj. *23,778*
(1955 C. maj. 21,875)

The Wrekin (Shropshire)
E. 48,789
625**W. Yates, C.* 22,030
D. W. T. Bruce, *Lab.* 19,052
C. maj. *2,978*
(1955 C. maj. 478)

Wrexham (Denbighshire)
E. 66,150
626**J. I. J. Jones, Lab.* 30,101
G. H. Pierce, *C. & Nat. L.* 17,144
D. E. Morgan, *Welsh Nat.* 6,579
Lab. maj. *12,957*
(1955 Lab. maj. 11,659)

Wycombe (Buckinghamshire)
E. 68,199
627**J. Hall,* O.B.E., T.D., *C.* 30,774
W. G. Fordham, *Lab.* 19,904
A. D. Dennis, *L.* 7,068
C. maj. *10,870*
(1955 C. maj. 7,940)

WYTHENSHAWE—*See* **Manchester**

YARDLEY—*See* **Birmingham**

Yarmouth (Norfolk)
E. 52,847
628**A. Fell, C.* 22,827
S. C. Davis, *Lab.* 19,248
C. maj. *3,579*
(1955 C. maj. 917)

Yeovil (Somerset)
E. 59,739
629**J. W. W. Peyton, C.* .. 23,771
W. A. Baker, *Lab.* ... 17,638
Col. G. F. Taylor, *L.* .. 9,484
C. maj. *6,133*
(1955 C. maj. 4,266)

York (English Borough)
E. 73,717
630 *C. B. Longbottom, C.* .. 33,099
Dr. D. R. L. M. Poirier, *Lab.* 29,025
C. maj. *4,074*
(1955 C. maj. 1,104)

Yorkshire, East Riding (3). *See* **Bridlington, Haltemprice and Howden**

Yorkshire, North Riding (4). *See* **Cleveland, Richmond, Scarborough and Whitby and Thirsk and Malton**

Yorkshire, West Riding (14). *See* **Barkston Ash, Colne Valley, Dearne Valley, Don Valley, Goole, Harrogate, Hemsworth, Normanton, Penistone, Ripon, Rother Valley, Shipley, Skipton and Sowerby**

PARLIAMENTARY SUMMARY, LORDS AND COMMONS, 1962–63

THE QUEEN OPENS BUSY SESSION.—When Parliament reassembled after the summer recess on *Oct.* 25, 1962, the third session was quickly ended, and on *Oct.* 30 the Queen opened in State the new session, which, in addition to a heavy legislative programme, was destined to deal with many problems and which saw a number of changes affecting the membership of both Houses. The Opposition lost its leader in the Commons, Mr. Hugh Gaitskell, early in the session, and he was succeeded by Mr. Harold Wilson. The collapse of the negotiations for Britain's entry into the Common Market, a reform in the nation's defence system, with a unified Ministry of Defence over the heads of the three Services, and a measure enabling Peers to disclaim their titles during their lifetime and permit them to sit in the Commons were among the main fruits of the session. Finally the signing of the partial ban on nuclear tests by the Soviet, Great Britain and the United States brought congratulations from all sides of each Chamber to Mr. Macmillan. The Commons adjourned on *Aug.* 2 until *Oct.* 24, when it was intended to prorogue Parliament and to open the fifth session on *Oct.* 29.

In the Speech from the Throne the Queen said that the Government had been shocked by the invasion of Indian territory by Chinese armies and fully supported India's decision to defend her rightful territory. They would continue to work for international agreement on general and complete disarmament and would persevere in their efforts to secure a treaty banning nuclear tests. Gravely concerned at the dangers of the recent introduction of offensive missiles into Cuba, the Government were glad to learn that those missiles were to be dismantled. They would continue, in conjunction with our allies, to seek to negotiate a settlement of the Berlin question which would preserve the security and freedom of the people of west Berlin. Turning to home problems, the Speech promised that Ministers would continue to promote efficient and sound expansion of the national economy with a high and stable level of employment, and were resolved to maintain an efficient and prosperous agricultural industry. Plans would be laid before Parliament for the development in England and Wales over the next decade of the health and welfare services of the local authorities, in parallel with the development of the hospitals.

Among the other legislation foreshadowed were Bills to reorganize local government in Greater London, to extend the powers of local authorities in connection with the care of children, to provide for the health, safety and welfare of persons employed in shops and offices, to bring up-to-date and extend the Weights and Measures Acts and establish a Consumers' Council to promote the interests of consumers, to require employers to give their employees written statements about terms of employment and prescribe minimum periods of notice and to extend and continue the operation of the Television Act.

The Address in reply was moved in the House of Commons by Mr. W. T. Aitken (Bury St. Edmunds) and seconded by Mr. Hocking (Coventry, South), and that in the Upper Chamber by Lady Elliot of Harwood (the first lady to introduce the traditional motion) and Lord Dynevor respectively. Mr. Hugh Gaitskell, referring to the Cuban crisis, said they had drawn back from the brink, and perhaps they could get some advantage out of having been so near to it. "We must make every possible effort to grasp for a real break-through towards peace", he said. The Prime Minister emphasized Britain's sympathy with India as a result of China's "ruthless application of policies based upon the most naked and realistic concepts of power" and assured India that what India had asked the British Government to do to help them they would do. On the following day, Mr. Harold Wilson welcomed this assurance and suggested that Britain should offer to India to institute a massive programme of lend-lease. Mr. Heath, Lord Privy Seal, said this suggestion would certainly be considered.

Sir Keith Joseph, the Minister of Housing and Local Government, promised on *Nov.* 1 that the Government would increase the pace with which the work of improving the housing of the people was tackled. The final Ministerial speaker in the debate was the Chancellor of the Exchequer, Mr. Maudling, who on *Nov.* 5, outlined a number of stimulants to economic expansion, including an immediate reduction in purchase tax on cars from 45 to 25 per cent., and increased allowances from 20 to 30 per cent. for capital expenditure on new plant and machinery. An Opposition amendment was defeated by 320 to 227 and the Address was agreed to. The Lords adopted their Address on *Nov.* 7 after rejecting by 79 to 32 a Labour amendment on the economic situation.

THE TEST BAN TREATY.—Shortly before Parliament adjourned for the summer recess, the agreement reached at Moscow by the U.S.S.R., the United Kingdom, and the United States to ban all nuclear tests except those underground received the necessary ratification, the customary delay of 21 days after a treaty had been laid before Parliament being modified with the agreement of the Labour Party. When Mr. Macmillan entered the House on *July* 25, to announce the initialling of the treaty, he was greeted with warm cheers, and these were renewed when, after reading the text of the treaty, the Prime Minister said he was sure the House would understand his own feelings at seeing at last "the result of efforts made over many years and of hopes long deferred". He went on: "I am deeply grateful that it has fallen to me to report this agreement to the House, not only because of the value which it has in itself but also because of the hope which it offers of further progress in the future." Mr. Harold Wilson said people all over the world would be thankful at the conclusion of the agreement and offered his congratulations to all concerned, and the Liberal spokesman expressed the wish that the agreement would be a step towards general disarmament, other congratulations following from all parts of the Chamber.

SECURITY IN WHITEHALL.—As a sequel to the conviction of an Admiralty clerk on a charge of espionage, the Prime Minister announced that an inquiry by three senior civil servants had been set up to consider the question of security. An interim report containing copies of letters sent to the clerk by Mr. T. G. D. Galbraith, at the period in question Civil Lord of the Admiralty, refuted completely any insinuation against the Minister, but he offered his resignation, which Mr. Macmillan accepted. Opposition speakers declared that instead of the civil servants' inquiry, an independent person should be appointed, and on *Nov.* 13 the Prime Minister told the House that there had been "a number of developments" which had led him to decide to set up a tribunal of inquiry under the Act of 1921. On the following day, Mr. Macmillan, moving the necessary resolution, stated that Lord Radcliffe would preside over the tribunal and that the other members would be Mr. Justice Barry and Sir Milner Holland, Q.C. He said that stories had been set about reflecting upon the loyalty of the First Lord of the Admiralty, Lord Carrington, and the Board of Admiralty, alleging that they had been negligent to a degree which amounted to a betrayal of the Service, and therefore he had decided, with the approval of his colleagues, to bring forward the motion for setting up the tribunal of eminent men. The time had come, declared the Prime Minister, for men of propriety and decency not to tolerate "the growth of the spirit of Titus Oates and Senator McCarthy", and the tribunal would be a "trial of the truth". Mr. Gaitskell said that the Opposition welcomed the establishment of the tribunal, and after a debate marked by a good deal of acrimony, the motion was agreed to without a division. Both Houses subsequently discussed the report of the tribunal, which completely vindicated both Lord Carrington and Mr. Galbraith, the latter of whom was reappointed to a post in the administration. In the Commons on *May* 7, the Prime Minister said the Government had decided that subordinate staff to the Service attachés should in future be subject to Service discipline and recruited from the Services. The procedure for reporting from the Embassies abroad had been reviewed so that all Embassy staffs would be on the alert for any development affecting security. Mr. Macmillan warned the House that he thought future cases would arise and that more spies would be caught. As to methods of investigation he thought the present position was rather unsatisfactory. He suggested that it might well be advantageous to set up a small standing body, consisting of a judicial chairman assisted and supported by two other members, as a permanent body to act as a security commission. In addition they might have a small standing committee of Privy Councillors of both sides, to enable the Government to decide whether an inquiry by the security commission was called for. Mr. Harold Wilson contended that confidence had not been restored by the report of the tribunal, and that there was ground for deep concern about the state of our security. He hoped the announcement of new machinery would be taken as indicating the gravity of the situation that they faced, and suggested that the Government should consider appointing a select committee to consider the working of the Act of 1921 under which the tribunal had been set up. Mr. Iain Macleod said that the Government would consider this suggestion. During the Lords debate on *May* 8, Lord Morrison of Lambeth said he did not agree with the proposal for a standing committee. Speakers in both Chambers expressed pleasure at the complete vindication of Lord Carrington and Mr. Galbraith.

The Profumo Case.—Mr. Macmillan told the House of Commons on *June* 17 that early in the year he was informed by his principal private secretary that he had been told of certain rumours linking the name of a woman witness in an Old Bailey case with Mr. John Profumo, the Secretary of State for War, and Captain Ivanov, a former member of the Soviet Embassy in London. Mr. Profumo emphatically denied that there was anything more than an innocent social friendship. He was warned of the security risk of his connection with an artist named Stephen Ward because of the latter's friendship with Ivanov. The Prime Minister recounted the negotiations which led to the personal statement of his innocence by Mr. Profumo on *March* 22, and after the Lord Chancellor had begun an inquiry into the security aspects, Mr. Profumo's confession that his protestations of innocence had been untrue and his consequent resignation of office. The debate had been opened by Mr. Wilson who said that they had done everything in their power to prevent this becoming a matter of public discussion or of party controversy. He declared: "To have a Secretary of State, a member of the Defence Committee of the Cabinet, with full access to all military secrets and to the military secrets of our Allies, part of this dingy quadrilateral reveals a degree of security risk that no Prime Minister could tolerate for one moment after the facts were conveyed to him." Though he personally acquitted the Prime Minister of foreknowledge or complicity in the matter of misleading the House, he could not be acquitted of grave dereliction of duty in failing to find out. Mr. Macmillan said that as head of the administration what had happened had inflicted a deep, bitter and lasting wound. "I know I have acted honourably", he declared later, "I believe I have acted justly." At no time until the confession had he any indications, either from the security services or from the police, that there was any reason to doubt Mr. Profumo's statement as to his connection with Mr. Ward or the girl in question. He claimed that he was entitled to the sympathetic understanding and confidence of the House and of the country. Mr. George Brown, on behalf of the Opposition, asked the Government to establish a select committee of the House to go further into the matter but Mr. Iain Macleod thought an independent judicial inquiry would be a better method. On a technical motion, the Government had a majority of 69, the voting being 321 against 252. The House, on *June* 20, agreed without a division to a motion declaring Mr. Profumo guilty of grave contempt in stating untruths in his personal statement, and on the following day Mr. Macmillan announced that Lord Denning, the Master of the Rolls, would conduct the inquiry into the security aspects of the affair. Mr. Wilson said this was inadequate and thought it could be better conducted by a select committee or by a tribunal of inquiry. Lord Denning's report on his investigation had not been completed when Parliament adjourned. Another security affair was brought to the notice of both Houses on *July* 1, when Mr. Heath told the Commons that Mr. Harold Philby, a former Foreign Office official who became a journalist in 1951, and who had disappeared from Beirut in the spring, was the "third man" in the Burgess and Maclean case in 1951, had warned them in time to permit their escape and was now presumed to be behind the "iron curtain" himself, a presumption which was subsequently confirmed in Moscow.

An Expansion Budget.—When Mr. Reginald Maudling unveiled his first Budget in the Commons on *April* 3 he broke an old tradition by which a Chancellor of the Exchequer revealed his main proposals only in the final stages of his speech. After describing the theme of his Budget as "expansion without inflation", Mr. Maudling announced almost in his opening sentences that the income tax on owner-occupiers' residential premises would be abolished in the current financial year, and this change was followed later by a number of income tax reliefs designed primarily to help both old persons and younger ones with low incomes. Equally important were his measures to aid areas of serious unemployment, including grants for new buildings and plant. The Chancellor said the purpose of the Budget was to do the Government's part in achieving the rate of growth, briefly described as the 4 per cent. target, and he was confident that this could be attained. Total revenue last year was £6,794,000,000, and expenditure above the line £6,441,000,000, a surplus of £353,000,000, but with payments below the line at £419,000,000, there was an overall deficit of £66,000,000. Remarking that he had never regarded Schedule A as justifiable, Mr. Maudling aroused loud Ministerial cheers by his announcement that in the case of owner-occupiers of residential property, the tax should be brought to an end in one operation this year. In the case of properties owned and let for profit a system of direct taxation of rents and other income arising from property would be substituted later for Schedule A, and Schedule B on amenity lands would be abolished. The cost of these changes would be about £35,000,000 in 1963–64 and of the order of £48,000,000 in a full year. The Land Tax, which now yielded only £200,000 a year, would be abolished from the end of the last Land Tax year. Next, Mr. Maudling briefly referred to "one other agreeable consequence": the abolition of the Schedule A valuation system provided a convenient opportunity for getting rid of the excise licences on beer brewed by farmers and others for their own consumption, or for that of their workpeople. He also proposed to abolish the system of excise licences for the sale of tobacco. The £1 television licence excise duty would be dropped but without affecting the cost to the viewer as the licence fee would be raised from £3 to £4. The Chancellor said that he proposed to extend for a further year the power enabling the Treasury to operate the "Customs regulator"—the power to raise or lower certain indirect taxes—and would seek the agreement of the House in the Finance Bill for making reductions, and only reductions, subject to affirmative resolution. Coming to income tax, he increased the income limit for purposes of the dependent relative allowance from £155 to £180, and announced that from 1964–65 the child allowance would not be wholly lost when a child's income exceeded the income limit but reduced, pound for pound, by the excess of the child's income over the income limit. The limitation of tax allowance for expensive business cars would be changed to a system restricting the allowance in the early years of the car and diminishing the restriction subsequently. Next, Mr. Maudling raised from £4,000 to £5,000 the exemption limit on estate duty, with appropriate adjustments in the rates for estates just over that amount. The cost of the minor tax changes, he estimated, would be £10,000,000 in 1963–64, and £26,000,000 in a full year. As to the taxation of gambling, the Chancellor said that he needed to make much wider studies of the practical and social issues involved before he could recommend a new tax which would be fair, effective, and socially desirable. He proposed that the Customs and Excise should compile a register of all gaming institutions, including those often very profitable machines known as "one-arm bandits". After stating that an investigation was to be made into the practical effects of instituting a turnover tax, either in addition to existing taxation or in substitution for purchase tax or profits tax, or both, Mr. Maudling said he had reached the conclusion that tax concessions in the current year of the order of some £250,000,000 were required to stimulate the economy if we were to realize the target of vigorous expansion without a return to inflation. On the basis of existing taxation he estimated the total revenue for the current year at £7,108,000,000, or £314,000,000 more than last year's revenue, and expenditure above the line at £6,929,000,000 giving a surplus of £179,000,000, compared with last year's estimate of £433,000,000 and a realized surplus of £353,000,000. Net payments below the line were expected to be £597,000,000 so that the over-all deficit, or net borrowing requirements of the Budget, would be £418,000,000. The measures which he was proposing were designed to achieve a growth target of 4 per cent. a year without inflation, and, emphasizing that expansion and incomes policy were entirely inter-dependent, he accepted the view that the appropriate rate of increase in money incomes was about 3 to 3½ per cent. on the average. Dealing with the availability of skilled manpower, Mr. Maudling said he had provisionally allocated up to £10,000,000 as a start in establishing industrial training boards, and to assist regional employment he would increase the grants to local authorities for expenditure on the clearance and rehabilitation of derelict sites in development districts. In Scotland the Government would make a loan to finance the construction of an important pulp and paper mill at Fort William, and in the north-east they would make a loan to the Tees Conservancy Commissioners for dock development. They had decided also to introduce standard grants of 25 per cent. of the cost of buildings and 10 per cent. of the cost of plant and machinery for firms setting up or expanding in development districts. As a further help industrialists in development districts in Great Britain and the whole of Northern Ireland would be allowed to write off their capital equipment at any rate they chose. This system of "free depreciation", he said, would cost about £25,000,000 next year and might rise to a maximum of £45,000,000 in 1966–67. He proposed to raise from 2 to 4 per cent. the annual allowance on new industrial buildings and announced a number of changes in the stamp duty. The Chancellor said that the cost of all the tax changes so far announced amounted to £83,000,000 this year, leaving room for further relief which he had decided should be concentrated in the field of direct taxation. The changes, which, he said, would involve remissions of £186,000,000 this year and £240,000,000 in a full year, would be greatest in the lower ranges of income. The limits of exemption from income tax would in future be £325 for single persons of 65 and £520 for married couples, of whom one was 65, and the earned income relief for investment income would become £900 where the taxpayer or his wife was 65, while the small income relief which would apply to a taxpayer under 65 was raised to incomes of £450. He abolished the lowest rate of income tax (1/9*d.* on the first £60), raised allowances for single persons by £60 and for married couples by £80, and replaced the next two categories (each of £150 with tax at 4/3*d.* and 6/3*d.*) by categories of £100 at 4/– and £200 at 6/–. In addition all the child allowances would be raised by £15. The effect of all these proposals was to exempt from tax some three and three quarter million people, said Mr. Maudling. In total the changes would reduce revenue receipts by £269,000,000 by next year and would convert the surplus above the line of £179,000,000 into a deficit of £90,000,000. He ended by stressing once again that the Government alone could not ensure success. There was a need for a national effort led by the Government, management and unions. He thought he could claim that they were doing the Government's share. Mr. Harold Wilson said that the Opposition welcomed the income tax concessions, but declared that the Government's expansion policy was not a continuing philosophy but a quadrennial inspiration animated by factors other than purely economic ones. On the following day, Mr. Erroll, the President of the Board of Trade, said that his department would at once discuss with the chairmen of leading companies with growth prospects in the development districts the many advantages to be gained from taking work to those areas. The Minister of Labour, Mr. John Hare, told the House on *April* 8 that the Board of Trade would build 13 small advance factories in the areas of high unemployment—6 in the north of England, 5 in Scotland and 2 in Wales. He also proposed to provide 15 more training centres and enlarge some of the existing 16 centres. In his first Commons speech since he left the Treasury, Mr. Selwyn Lloyd, the former Chancellor, said he was glad that Mr. Maudling had continued the "regulator", hoped he would think again about the idea of a Commonwealth Economic Development Council, and congratulated his successor on "a most able Budget". Winding up the general debate on *April* 9, Mr. Maudling claimed that he had avoided going so far in developing the economy and the purchasing power as to bring the country once again to a situation in which incomes, costs and prices were rising too fast. "This is the circle from which we must break out", he said. "We can break out if we all do it together." The resolution to amend the law relating to the national debt was agreed to, and on *April* 10 the Budget resolutions were agreed to on report and the Finance Bill was presented and read a first time. The Bill received its second reading without a division on *May* 6 when Mr. Barber, Financial Secretary to the Treasury, said that the clause enabling the Customs and Excise to compile a register of gambling institutions was a fact-finding operation to enable the Treasury to build up a detailed picture of the variety of forms of gambling throughout Britain to help the review being made of the possibility of introducing duties. Mr. Maudling said he had not given up the hunt for a gambling Bill, but he wanted to be sure that they knew what they were doing before a tax on gambling was introduced. The committee stage opened on *May* 14, and two days later the clause abolishing Schedule A tax was agreed to after the rejection by 222 to 154 of a Labour amendment which proposed that the relief afforded should not apply to an owner-occupier in respect of more than one house in the year of assessment. The stage was completed on *May* 30, and on *June* 28 the Bill was read a third time without a division. The Chancellor said we were now seeing an expansion in the economy, and our central task must be to ensure that that expansion was as rapid as was consistent with the avoidance of a return to inflation and maintaining a rate of growth in whose steadiness businessmen could have confidence. The House of Lords gave the Bill a second reading and passed the remaining stages on *July* 23, and it received the Royal Assent on *July* 31.

PEERS AS M.P.s.—Undertakings were given in both Chambers on *March* 28 that before the next general election the Government would introduce legislation to enable Peers to surrender their peerages during their own lifetime, thus permitting them to stand as candidates for election as M.P.s. Both Houses agreed to a motion "taking note" of the report of the joint committee which had considered the question, raised by the wish of Viscount Stansgate to continue to sit in the Commons after his succession to his father's title. Mr. Iain Macleod, Leader of the House of Commons, said that, subject to one or two points of detail, the Government view was that the recommendations of the committee could be implemented and the machinery set up without much difficulty. The Lord Chancellor said in the Upper Chamber that the necessary Bill might be exceedingly controversial. Although Peers and M.P.s agreed to the motion without a division some Opposition members reiterated their wish for a wider reform of the House of Lords. Mr. Harold Wilson said that a Labour Government would reserve the right to propose legislation on reform, adding that their criticisms related to the delaying powers of "another place" and the right to reject statutory instruments, although the latter power was not used. Moving the second reading of the Bill to give effect to the report on *June* 19, Mr. Macleod said that it would come into force on the dissolution of the present Parliament. Mr. Gordon Walker, for the Labour Party, suggested that it might become operative on receiving the Royal Assent, but the second reading was given without a division. In committee on *June* 27 an amendment to provide that a disclaimer of a peerage should be valid for all time was rejected by 185 to 134, and another to bring the Bill into operation on receiving the Royal Assent was defeated by 174 to 113. The committee stage was concluded with the Bill unaltered, and it was read a third time. The Lords gave it an unopposed second reading on *July* 4, although Labour Peers reiterated their opposition to the hereditary principle. Lord Salisbury supported the Bill but suggested that some of them would have liked a much more drastic reform which would cut out the dead wood of those who never attended. For the first time their lordships heard a speech from a Communist peer, Lord Milford, who declared "The Bill is of no great value to me or to my party". In committee on *July* 11, an amendment moved by Lord Boothby providing that if a peerage were disclaimed it would be extinguished was rejected by 106 to 25, and another to permit Irish peers to attend the Lords by 90 to 5. The Peers clashed with a decision of the Commons on *July* 16, when, by 105 to 25 they carried by a majority of 80 against the Government an amendment moved by Lord Silkin deleting the words bringing the proposals into force on the dissolution of the present Parliament, which had the effect of putting them into operation immediately the Bill received the Royal Assent. Another alteration was made on *July* 18 when, on the proposal of the Earl of Swinton, it was agreed to give sitting peers twelve months in which to decide whether they should disclaim their titles. The Bill was read a third time and passed on *July* 22. On Mr. Macleod's advice the Commons on *July* 30 agreed to the amendment bringing the operation of the Bill into immediate force and to the other Lords amendments. Mr. Malcolm St. Clair, who became M.P. for Bristol, South-East, when Lord Stansgate was disqualified, announced during the debate that he would shortly resign, and immediately the Royal Assent was given on *July* 31, Lord Stansgate forwarded his Instrument of Disclaimer, and again became Mr. Anthony Wedgwood Benn and eligible for election to the Commons. He was quickly followed by Lord Altrincham, who became Mr. John Grigg.

COUNCIL FOR GREATER LONDON.—A considerable proportion of the time occupied for Parliamentary discussion of new legislation was devoted to the London Government Bill, which Sir Keith Joseph, Minister of Housing and Local Government, explained in moving the second reading in the Commons on *Dec.* 10, was intended to deal with the structure of London's local government, unchanged in any major way since 1889. Its main feature, he said, was the creation of an overall authority to meet needs which by their nature were needs of Greater London as a whole by setting up a substantially unified system of borough administration. Under the new measure there would be a body directly elected by the people of London charged with the responsibility of watching over the whole physical environment and having powers and resources to match their responsibilities. This body, the Greater London Council, would be a planning authority and a traffic authority for the Greater London area and would be the highway authority for metropolitan roads, but the Government was satisfied that the borough councils would be competent to carry the full responsibilities of local education authorities except for the central area. The L.C.C. service would be taken over by a special education committee of the Greater London Council. There would be 32 boroughs formed by the existing boroughs and district councils inside the continuously built-up area within the Green Belt. Sir Keith said that the Government believed that London government was at the cross roads and they would welcome all constructive criticism to improve the Bill. For the Opposition, Mr. Michael Stewart suggested that members of the Greater London Council should be paid, and Sir Cyril Black, a London Conservative M.P., said that the Government had no vestige of mandate for the Bill. On the following day, Mr. Enoch Powell, Minister of Health, said that in the Government's view the London boroughs would be entirely adequate authorities for the health and welfare services and would be able to develop those services more rapidly. The second reading was carried by 314 to 236, a majority of 78. A long struggle opened in the committee stage on *Jan.* 23, and the Government had later to allocate time for some of the discussion. An amendment to delay by three years the date for the first election was rejected by 215 to 166 on *Jan.* 24, and on *Feb.* 5 another urging that aldermen should not serve on the Greater London Council was defeated by 23 to 1 by the standing committee after the Minister had promised to consider the proposal, the clause setting up the Greater London Council being then agreed to by 25 to 18. On *Feb.* 2 a Government amendment, making it possible for the Minister of Transport to intervene in traffic affairs in the Greater London area when it was necessary, was carried by 24 to 19. The Bill was returned to the whole House on *Feb.* 13, when it was decided that the City of London should remain a local authority, an amendment being rejected that it should be combined with other boroughs. The standing committee on *Feb.* 14 dealt with and agreed to a Government amendment which ensured that the Greater London Council should have full powers for re-housing people displaced as a result of major development or traffic schemes carried out by the Greater London Council as part of their overall planning decisions. Another Government amendment to safeguard the conditions of the transferred staff was agreed to on *April* 1, and on the following day the third reading was carried by 285 to 226 after an Opposition spokesman declared that they did not accept the pattern imposed on London by the Bill. The House of Lords on *April* 24 passed the second reading by 55 to 27, and began the committee stage on *May* 9. On *May* 14 they rejected an amendment moved by Lord Morrison of Lambeth to absorb the boroughs of Finsbury, Shoreditch, Stepney and Southwark with the City of London. The committee stage was concluded on *May* 30, and the Bill was read a third time and passed on *July* 8, after the defeat by 72 to 41 of a Labour amendment declining to pass a Bill which failed to set up a system of local government which would assure adequate services to the people. The Commons agreed to the Lords amendments and the Royal Assent was given on *July* 31.

Railway Reorganization Approved.—Under the shadow of a threatened three-day strike by the National Union of Railwaymen as a protest against the proposals of Dr. Beeching for re-shaping Britain's railway system, both Houses discussed the plan. The Commons on *April* 30 agreed to a Government motion approving the report "as a major contribution to the development of a sound and well-balanced transport system for the country", after rejecting by 323 to 248 an Opposition amendment calling for a transport policy for road and rail. The Upper Chamber on *May* 2 accepted a motion urging the need for the utilization of each form of transport for the purposes for which it was most suitable. Moving the Commons resolution, Mr. Marples, the Minister of Transport, said that a strike would be a tragedy; it would harm everybody and benefit nobody. He said that the Government were determined that transport policy must be related to national planning, to the growth and movement of industry and population. They intended to appoint an independent committee of inquiry to examine the whole question of licensing road haulage, and its report would enable them to get the right size, shape and function of the railway system. Mr. George Strauss, introducing the amendment, claimed that transport must be the servant and not the master of our social planning, and Mr. Harold Wilson, on the second day of the debate, said he regarded the battle of the future of the British Transport system as a political one, which should take place in the House and ultimately at the polling booths. His Party certainly did not want a strike, nor did the unions, but if there was a strike the responsibility would be on a Government which for ten years had virtually destroyed the integrated transport system. Mr. Wilson contended that the only way to solve the rail crisis was by an integrated transport policy which ensured that profits creamed off from rail to road were brought into the transport pool, and he challenged the Government to refer the whole plan to the National Economic Development Council before a decision was taken. Before the Peers agreed to their resolution, Viscount Hailsham said that Dr. Beeching's plan was not one that could be implemented all at once, and his guess was that the process would take about seven years and that only after the most elaborate series of arguments on each set of proposals.

Protection For The Consumer.—When the Commons gave an unopposed second reading to the Weights and Measures Bill on *Nov.* 12, Mr. Erroll, as President of the Board of Trade, said the measure sought to bring together and modernize a great amount of out-of-date legislation, and to give the consumer better protection. The Government had endeavoured to create order from the chaotic mass of national and local legislation, and to ensure that the Bill would give adequate powers to meet future developments in trading methods. They would go ahead with the establishment of a Consumers' Council as soon as possible, and the Bill gave them the powers they were likely to need to give effect to any recommendations on weights and measures which the Council might make. The yard and pound were defined by relationship to the metre and kilogram, and a commission of units and standards of measurements would be set up to advise the Government of any changes in the definition of the law. The Bill did away with the rod, pole or perch and after five years the bushel, peck and pennyweight would also disappear, and the Board was empowered to ban the apothecaries system which covered such things as the drachm. It regulated all the devices of weighing and measuring to be used and the checking of equipment by local inspectors. One of the aims was to provide shoppers with accurate information about the quantity of goods they were buying, and to enable them to exercise judgment more effectively. There would also for the first time be protection for the consumer against short weight or measure of all kinds, including pre-packed goods after an interval. For the Opposition, Mr. Darling welcomed the Bill, but he said there were confusing, and, in some cases, contradictory rules. Other members urged the adoption of the metiic system, but the Parliamentary Secretary said that half the world's trade was conducted on the Imperial system, notably in the United States and the Commonwealth. He added that the situation was being kept under review. In standing committee on *Nov.* 27, Mr. Freeth, for the Government, said that for some parts of the world exporters had to pack goods in the units used by the country to which they were selling, and he instanced the picul in Hong Kong, the oki in Sudan and the kati in Burma. The Bill was read a third time on *March* 26, and after being discussed by the Lords received the Royal Assent on *July* 31.

BETTER CONDITIONS FOR OFFICE WORKERS.—The Royal Assent was given on *July* 31 to a Bill described by Mr. Hare, Minister of Labour, when he obtained a second reading on *Nov.* 15, as intended to raise the standard of working conditions in shops, offices and certain railway premises so as to protect the health, welfare and safety of workers. It laid down conditions for temperatures, overcrowding, lighting and cleanliness, and Mr. Hare told the Commons that a great variety of premises would be covered, from the corner shop to the huge departmental store and from a signal box to Waterloo Station. He said that the measure was part of wider plans to improve the conditions of employment for all workers. It would benefit a massive body of people who worked in offices and shops and would give them protection of a kind which workers in industry already enjoyed. Mr. Ray Gunter, for the Labour Party, said the Bill was not quite the lusty thing they hoped it would be, but they would do everything they could to help the Minister improve it. In standing committee on *Nov.* 29, a Labour proposal that theatres should be brought within the Bill was rejected by 18 to 13, and on *March* 6 the Commons agreed to a new Government clause which made provision for the appointment of a small central inspectorate to supervise the work of local authorities in the enforcement of the Bill. The Lords agreed to the second reading without a division, Lord Carrington explaining that it was expected that the Bill would cover more than 8,000,000 workers in over a million premises, and the Bill was read a third time and passed on *May* 13.

CONTRACTS FOR WORKERS.—Fixed periods of notice with pay for workers and the creation of machinery by which unofficial strikers might in some circumstances forfeit this right were the main features of the Contracts of Employment Bill, which received an unopposed second reading in the Commons on *Feb.* 14. The measure provided that when it came into operation employers would have to give two weeks' notice to workers who had been in continuous employment by them for two years, and four weeks to those who had been employed for five years. The Minister of Labour, Mr. John Hare, said the Bill was a part of the Government's plans to provide greater security for the workers. At present the great majority of manual workers had a right to only one week's notice, no matter how long their service might have been, and in some industries they had a right to even less. After a reasonable time a minimum period of notice would be laid down, and every worker would know precisely what the conditions of his contract would be. Speaking of unofficial strikes, Mr. Hare said there was a strong body of public opinion, by no means based on party political lines, which was demanding that the Government should introduce legislation to protect the public interest, and it would be quite wrong to underestimate how strong that feeling was. For the Opposition, Mr. Ray Gunter said he could not believe that the Bill would do anything to eliminate the causes of industrial unrest or bring greater discipline into industry. He agreed that there were cases where a tiny handful of evil men were given some authority over their workmates and were incapable of bearing that authority. In standing committee, Government amendments were adopted providing that a man who went on strike without breach of contract would not lose his continuity of employment but that one who did so in breach of contract would lose that continuity. The Bill was passed by the Lords on *July* 22 and received the Royal Assent on *July* 31.

PUBLIC ORDER, TELEVISION AND CHILD WELFARE.—Among the other measures which were placed on the Statute Book on *July* 31 was the Public Order Bill, intended by the Government to ensure that public order was maintained and to arm the courts adequately so that those who disturbed it did not get off lightly. The Bill increased the penalties for stirring up racial prejudice in public places, the maximum being raised to three months' imprisonment and/or a £100 fine on summary conviction and to twelve months' imprisonment and/or a £500 fine on indictment. Another measure laid down the procedure to be followed by the Independent Television Authority and the Postmaster-General to secure economic rents from the programme companies for payment into the Exchequer. Mr. Bevins, the Postmaster-General, told the Commons on *Feb.* 25 that he estimated that the revenue to the Exchequer under the proposals would amount to £18,000,000 in a full year, and that the television advertising duty, which produced about £8,000,000 would be abolished in 1964 and the new scheme would begin to operate at the same time when new contracts were awarded to the programme companies. During the second reading debate in the Upper Chamber on *July* 9 Lord Morrison of Lambeth protested against the appointment of Lord Hill of Luton as chairman of the I.T.A. on the ground of his party associations. The Children and Young Persons Bill was described by Earl Jellicoe in the House of Lords on *Nov.* 20 as aimed mainly at increasing the power of local authorities to promote the welfare of children, including those living in their own homes. It also enlarged the present scheme of licensing children to take part in theatrical and similar entertainments to cover film-making and broadcasting. The Lords on *Jan.* 24 reduced the age of criminal responsibility from 12 to 10, after an amendment had been carried earlier fixing the higher age. In the Commons it was stated that the changes proposed would affect in particular child care in approved schools and probation services, and later Mr. Brooke announced that a comprehensive review of the approved school rules was being undertaken by the Home Office. Another Bill passed before the adjournment gave the Minister of Education power to enforce his determination of the salary increase to teachers which differed from that of the Burnham Committee.

CHANGES IN THE COMMONWEALTH.—After many conferences between opposing sections in some overseas territories, Parliament quickly passed Bills based on and accepting agreements reached at those negotiations. The first measure of the kind established the Tanganyika Republic. Another empowered the Queen to make provisions for the dissolution of the Federation of Rhodesia and Nyasaland or the secession from the Federation of any of its constituent territories, although it did not itself dissolve the Federation. A third created the Federation of Malaysia out of four territories of Malaya. Both the latter received the Royal Assent on *July* 31, and on the following day it was announced that Malta would become independent in May, 1964.

PUBLIC ACTS OF PARLIAMENT, 1962–63

The list below commences with notes on ten Public Acts of Parliament which received the Royal Assent before September, 1962, and some of which were only mentioned briefly in the last summary. Those Public Acts which follow received the Royal Assent after September, 1962. The date stated after each Act is the date on which it came into operation.

BUILDING SOCIETIES ACT, 1962 (October 1, 1962) consolidates with corrections and improvements the Building Societies Acts, 1874 to 1960.

TOWN AND COUNTRY PLANNING ACT, 1962 (April 1, 1963) consolidates certain enactments relating to town and country planning in England and Wales.

FINANCE ACT, 1962 (August 1, 1962): Part I of this Act deals with Customs, Excise and Purchase Tax, whilst Part II deals with Income Tax and Profits Tax, increasing the tax reliefs for small incomes and for certain registered blind persons. An innovation is provided by the introduction of capital gains tax; capital gains made by the disposition of land within three years and of other property within six months become chargeable to income tax and profits tax. Part III of the Act, dealing with Estate Duty, grants relief in the case of small estates, and Part IV, dealing with Stamp Duties, abolishes settlement duty but introduces a unit trust duty.

APPROPRIATION ACT, 1962 (August 1, 1962) applies a sum out of the Consolidated Fund to the service of the year ending March 31, 1963, and appropriates the supplies granted in the then current Sessions of Parliament.

TRANSPORT ACT, 1962 (days to be appointed) provides for the re-organization of the nationalized transport undertakings carried on under the Transport Act, 1947, and provides for the establishment of public authorities (the British Railways Board, the London Transport Board, the British Transport Docks Board and the British Waterways Board) as successors to the British Transport Commission among whom the functions and property of the British Transport Commission are to be divided. The Act further provides that the British Railways Board is to set up Regional Railways Boards (the Eastern Railway Board, the London Midland Railway Board, the North Eastern Railway Board, the Scottish Railway Board, the Southern Railway Board and the Western Railway Board) which will share between them responsibility for all parts of the national railway system.

EDUCATION (SCOTLAND) ACT, 1962 (October 1, 1962 and other dates) consolidates the enactments relating to education in Scotland.

LANDLORD AND TENANT ACT, 1962 (November 1, 1962) provides that where a person is granted by contract or by statute a right to occupy any premises as a residence in consideration of a rent which is payable weekly, then it is the duty of the landlord to provide a rent book, or other similar document for use in respect of the premises, unless the rent includes a payment in respect of board and the value of that board to the tenant forms a substantial proportion of the whole rent. The Act also deals with the information which has to be contained in rent books.

LICENSING (SCOTLAND) ACT, 1962 (dates to be appointed) makes provision in Scotland for the grant by licensing courts of new forms of certificate for the sale by retail of exciseable liquor, amends the law in Scotland regarding the sale and supply of exciseable liquor and regarding licensed premises and clubs, prescribes the hours during which premises in Scotland licensed for the sale and supply of exciseable liquor for consumption off the premises may remain open for the serving of customers with such liquor, and restricts the carriage of exciseable liquor in public service vehicles used as contract carriages (public service vehicles not carrying passengers at separate fares).

PIPE-LINES ACT, 1962 (dates to be appointed) regulates and facilitates the construction of, and secures the safe operation of, pipe-lines.

ROAD TRAFFIC ACT, 1962 (dates to be appointed) makes important changes in the law relating to road traffic and road safety. The Act first imposes a more severe test in relation to unfitness to drive through drink or drugs, and deals with evidence to be regarded on a charge of unfitness to drive. The Act then contains detailed provisions in regard to disqualification, endorsement and penalties. Thus, when a person is convicted of certain offences, such as manslaughter, driving under the influence of drink or drugs, and driving while disqualified, the court must order him to be disqualified for such period not less than twelve months as the court thinks fit unless the court for special reasons thinks fit to order him to be disqualified for a shorter period or not to order him to be disqualified. Again, when a person is convicted of certain other offences, *e.g.*, speeding, being in charge of a motor vehicle while under the influence of drink or drugs, the court may order him to be disqualified for such period as it thinks fit. Other provisions of the Act deal with endorsement of licence, speed limits, construction, use and equipment of vehicles, driving instruction, minimum age and test fees, and highway powers and parking places.

TANGANYIKA REPUBLIC ACT, 1962 (December 6, 1962) makes provision as to the operation of the law upon Tanganyika becoming a Republic within the Commonwealth.

PENSIONS INCREASE ACT, 1962 (December 20, 1962) provides for increases or supplements in respect of certain pensions.

EXPIRING LAWS CONTINUANCE ACT, 1962 (December 20, 1962) continues in force certain Acts of Parliament, *e.g.*, the Furnished Houses (Rent Control) Act, 1946, which would otherwise expire.

FOREIGN COMPENSATION ACT, 1962 (December 20, 1962) provides for the payment out of moneys provided by Parliament of additional compensation in respect of claims arising in connection with certain events in Egypt. The Act requires the Foreign Compensation Commission to pay sums into the Exchequer in respect of deductions made in meeting such claims, and makes provision in relation to pensions and other payments to or in respect of members, officers and servants of the Commission.

AIR CORPORATIONS ACT, 1962 (December 20, 1962) increases the borrowing powers of B.O.A.C. and of B.E.A.C., makes further provision for the payment of pension benefits in the case of employees of the Corporations, and provides in certain cases for compensating members of the Corporations for loss of office.

COAL INDUSTRY ACT, 1962 (December 20, 1962) makes further provision regarding temporary advances to the National Coal Board, and alters the financial year of the Board by providing that the financial year of the Board which begins at midnight on December 29, 1962 is to continue until midnight on March 28, 1964; thereafter the financial year of the Board is the period beginning at midnight of the last Saturday in March in one calendar year and ending at midnight of the last Saturday in March in the next following calendar year.

ELECTRICITY (BORROWING POWERS) (SCOTLAND) ACT, 1962 (December 20, 1962) extends the borrowing powers of the South of Scotland Electricity Board.

CONSOLIDATED FUND ACT, 1963 (February 28, 1963) applies a sum out of the Consolidated Fund to the service of the year ending March 31, 1963.

THE BETTING, GAMING AND LOTTERIES ACT, 1963 (February 28, 1963) consolidates certain of the enactments relating to betting, gaming, lotteries and connected matters.

BETTING DUTIES ACT, 1963 (February 28, 1963) consolidates certain enactments relating to the pool betting and bookmakers' licence duties.

TOWYN TREWAN COMMON ACT, 1963 (February 28, 1963) extinguishes certain rights of common and private rights of way in respect of lands forming part of Towyn Trewan Common in the county of Anglesey, and enables new drain and accessory works to be carried out on other parts of the Common. The Act also provides for compensation in respect of the extinguishment of the above rights, and provides for the use by the public of a track across part of the Common.

COUNTY COURTS (JURISDICTION) ACT, 1963 (April 1, 1963) extends the jurisdiction of county courts in consequence of the coming into force, on April 1, 1963, of the new valuation list for rating whereby the net annual value for rating of property throughout the country has been considerably increased.

COMMONWEALTH SCHOLARSHIPS (AMENDMENT) ACT, 1963, (February 28, 1963) amends the Commonwealth Scholarships Act, 1959, to give power to select persons from the Channel Islands and the Isle of Man as candidates for Commonwealth Scholarships.

NATIONAL INSURANCE ACT, 1963 (February 28, 1963) increases ungraduated contributions and benefits under the National Insurance Acts, and contributions and benefits under the National Insurance (Industrial Injuries) Acts, and, in connection with the increase of benefits, modifies the method of computing national assistance grants for any period before all the increases have taken effect. The Act also modifies the widowed mother's allowance under the 1946 Act, amends section 24 of that Act as respects conditions for payment of benefit under that section, and alters graduated contributions and benefits under the 1959 Act by enlarging the amount of pay taken into account in fixing contributions. It also amends the 1959 Act as respects non-participating employments, and improves the allowances payable out of the Industrial Injuries Fund in respect of incapacities arising from pre-1948 employment.

CONSOLIDATED FUND (NO. 2) ACT, 1963 (March 28, 1963) applies certain sums out of the Consolidated Fund to the service of the years ending March 31, 1962, 1963 and 1964.

PURCHASE TAX ACT, 1963 (April 1, 1963) consolidates the enactments relating to purchase tax.

DRAINAGE RATES ACT, 1963 (March 28, 1963) provides for the assessment of drainage rates by reference to values determined under section 8 of the Agricultural (Miscellaneous Provisions) Act, 1943, notwithstanding the repeal of that section.

AGRICULTURE (MISCELLANEOUS PROVISIONS) ACT, 1963 (May 15, 1963) makes further provisions as to grants and contributions for agricultural and certain horticultural purposes and otherwise amends the law relating to agriculture, agricultural produce and agricultural land, and provides for the purchase by the Sugar Board of sugar from the Republic of Ireland. The Act also contains provisions in relation to notices to quit agricultural holdings, and provides in effect that where a landlord is seeking to obtain possession of the land on the ground that the tenant has failed to comply with a notice requiring him to remedy a breach of the terms and conditions of the tenancy, that the notice must be in a prescribed form and must specify the period within which the breach is to be remedied, and that where such a notice requires the doing of any repair or maintenance work, any further notice requiring the doing of such work which is served on the tenant within twelve months of the earlier notice is to be disregarded, unless the earlier notice is withdrawn with the tenant's written consent. A period of less than six months is not to be treated as a reasonable period within which to do the work.

LOCAL GOVERNMENT (FINANCIAL PROVISIONS) (SCOTLAND) ACT, 1963 (May 15, 1963) continues, with amendments, the provisions relating to the payment of Exchequer Equalisation and Transitional Grants to local authorities in Scotland, increases the limit of contributions payable to such authorities under the Rural Water Supplies and Sewerage Act, 1944, alters the basis of apportionment among such authorities of certain sums, and amends the law of Scotland with respect to the valuation for rating of industrial and freight transport lands and heritages and to other matters relating to valuation, rating, and local authorities' financial administration.

NURSING HOMES ACT, 1963 (May 15, 1963) authorizes the Minister of Health to make regulations as to the conduct of nursing homes, including the provision of facilities and services in such homes.

CORN RENTS ACT, 1963 (May 15, 1963) makes further provision for the apportionment and redemption of corn rents and other payments wholly or partly payable in lieu of tithes and for the extinguishment thereof in certain cases. The Act also transfers to the Treasury certain functions of the Minister of Agriculture, Fisheries and Food in relation to the extinguishment of corn rents.

FORT WILLIAM PULP AND PAPER MILLS ACT, 1963 (May 15, 1963) authorises the Board of Trade to make advances to Wiggins, Teape & Co., Ltd., not exceeding £10 million in all, for the purpose of the construction and equipment of pulp and paper mills in the neighbourhood of Fort William in Inverness.

PROTECTION OF DEPOSITORS ACT, 1963 (October 10, 1963) penalises fraudulent inducements to invest in deposit, restricts and regulates the issue of advertisements for deposits, and makes special provision with respect to the accounts to be delivered by and the supervision of companies which issue such advertisements.

TOWN AND COUNTRY PLANNING ACT, 1963 (February 25, 1963) makes further provision with respect to development comprised in Schedule 3 to the Town and Country Planning Act, 1962, and Schedule 3 to the Town and Country Planning (Scotland) Act, 1947.

STOCK TRANSFER ACT, 1963 (various dates) amends the law with respect to the transfer of securities by providing for a simplified form of transfer of securities.

LOCAL EMPLOYMENT ACT, 1963 (July 10, 1963) makes further provision for the payment of grants under the Local Employment Act, 1960, towards the cost of machinery, plant and buildings required by undertakings in development districts, and enables the Board of Trade to fulfil certain agreements in localities which have ceased to be development districts.

REMUNERATION OF TEACHERS ACT, 1963 (July 10, 1963) empowers the Minister of Education to make provision by order for securing that the remuneration of teachers shall be determined, and remuneration paid to them by local education authorities, in accordance with the scales and other provisions contained in reports of the Burnham Committee and of the Committee on Scales and Salaries for the Teaching Staff of Farm Institutes and for Teachers of Agricultural (including Horticultural) Subjects.

EDUCATION (SCOTLAND) ACT, 1963 (July 10, 1963) provides for the establishment of a board in Scotland for the purpose of discharging certain functions relating to examinations for pupils receiving secondary education and others, and deals with certain other matters relating to education in Scotland.

SHERIFF COURTS (CIVIL JURISDICTION AND PROCEDURE) (SCOTLAND) ACT, 1963 (October 1, 1963) increases the amount by reference to which actions are classified as summary causes in the sheriff court in Scotland, increases the amount by reference to which the small debt jurisdiction of the sheriff is limited and amends the law with regard to the bringing of actions between spouses for interim aliment of small amounts in the sheriff's small debt court and with regard to the jurisdiction of the sheriff in such actions.

FORESTRY (SALE OF LAND) (SCOTLAND) ACT, 1963 (July 10, 1963) extends the power of the Secretary of State to sell forestry land.

BRITISH MUSEUM ACT, 1963 (day to be appointed) alters the composition of the Committee of Trustees of the British Museum, provides for the separation from the British Museum of the Natural History Museum and makes new provision with respect to the regulations of the two Museums and their collections in place of that made by the British Museum Act, 1753.

OATHS AND EVIDENCE (OVERSEAS AUTHORITIES AND COUNTRIES) ACT 1963 (July 31, 1963) authorizes the administration of oaths and the performance of notarial acts by representatives of, and other persons empowered by the authorities of, countries overseas, and by representatives of Her Majesty in posts overseas.

OIL IN NAVIGABLE WATERS ACT, 1963 (days to be appointed) enables effect to be given to certain amendments of the International Convention for the Prevention of Pollution of the Sea by Oil 1954, and otherwise to extend the Oil in Navigable Waters Act, 1955.

LOCAL AUTHORITIES (LAND) ACT, 1963 (July 31, 1963) makes amendments of the law relating to the functions of local authorities in relation to land to the like effect as those commonly made in local Acts. It enables local authorities to make advances for the erection of buildings and to provide accommodation for keeping motor vehicles, amends the provisions of the National Parks and Access to the Countryside Act, 1949, relating to the treatment of derelict land, and amends the law with respect to the powers of municipal boroughs to use the general rate fund and borrow for non-statutory purposes.

STATUTE LAW REVISION ACT, 1963 (July 31, 1963) revises the statute law by repealing obsolete, spent, unnecessary or superseded enactments.

PUBLIC LAVATORIES (TURNSTILES) ACT, 1963 (July 31, 1963) makes it the duty of local authorities to abolish turnstiles in public lavatories and sanitary conveniences.

RHODESIA AND NYASALAND ACT, 1963 (July 31, 1963) confers on Her Majesty in Council powers requisite to provide for the dissolution of the Federation of Rhodesia and Nyasaland on the secession therefrom of any of the Territories comprised in the Federation.

DEER ACT, 1963 (August 31, 1963 and other dates) provides close seasons for deer, prohibits the killing and taking of deer by certain devices and at certain times, and restricts the use of vehicles in connection with the killing and taking of deer.

DOG RACING (BETTING DAYS) ACT, 1963 (July, 31 1963) provides for the fixing of days when betting facilities may be provided on licensed tracks being dog racecourses in place of betting days lost due to weather conditions or other circumstances.

ANIMAL BOARDING ESTABLISHMENTS ACT, 1963 (January 1, 1964) regulates the keeping of boarding establishments for animals.

WILLS ACT, 1963 (January 1, 1964) repeals the Wills Act, 1861, and makes new provisions in lieu thereof. It also provides that certain testamentary instruments shall be probative for the purpose of the conveyance of heritable property in Scotland.

MATRIMONIAL CAUSES ACT, 1963 (July 31, 1963) amends the law relating to matrimonial causes, and facilitates reconciliation in such causes.

PEERAGE ACT, 1963 (July 31, 1963) authorizes the disclaimer for life of certain hereditary peerages. It also includes among the peers qualified to sit in the House of Lords all peers in the peerages of Scotland and peeresses in their own right in the peerages of England, Scotland, Great Britain, and the United Kingdom. It removes certain disqualifications of peers in the peerage of Ireland in relation to the House of Commons and elections thereto.

PUBLIC ORDER ACT, 1963 (July 31, 1963) increases the penalties for offences under section 5 of the Public Order Act, 1936, and section 1 of the Public Meeting Act, 1908.

PERFORMERS' PROTECTION ACT, 1963 (August 31, 1963) amends the law relating to the protection of performers so as to enable effect to be given to a Convention entered into at Rome on October 26, 1961.

FINANCE ACT, 1963.
CONSOLIDATED FUND (APPROPRIATION) ACT, 1963.
LONDON GOVERNMENT ACT, 1963.
TELEVISION ACT, 1963.
WEIGHTS AND MEASURES ACT, 1963.
MALAYSIA ACT, 1963.
CHILDREN AND YOUNG PERSONS ACT, 1963.
WATER RESOURCES ACT, 1963.
CRIMINAL JUSTICE (SCOTLAND) ACT, 1963.
COMMONWEALTH DEVELOPMENT ACT, 1963.
OFFICES, SHOPS AND RAILWAY PREMISES ACT, 1963.
LOCAL GOVERNMENT (FINANCIAL PROVISIONS) ACT, 1963.
LIMITATION ACT, 1963.
CONTRACTS OF EMPLOYMENT ACT, 1963.
LAND COMPENSATION (SCOTLAND) ACT, 1963.

Government and Public Offices

The Civil Service in the United Kingdom is divided into classes, each with a series of grades. The *Administrative Class*, which consists largely of university graduates, advises Ministers on policy, deals with any difficulties arising from current policy and forecasts the probable effects of new measures and regulations. The *Executive Class* is responsible for the day to day conduct of Government business within the framework of established policy. The *Clerical Class* undertakes all the clerical work of departmental business, *e.g.* the preparation of accounts and keeping of records and the handling of particular claims in accordance with known rules. The *Professional, Scientific and Technical Classes* include doctors, lawyers, engineers, etc. *Departmental Classes*, confined to one or two departments, include the Tax Inspectorate, Factory Inspectorate and Customs Waterguard.

NOTE.—The salaries shown are in most cases those actually received. In certain instances, however, the National Scale without corresponding London weighting is given.

ADMIRALTY

(*see* Royal Navy)

MINISTRY OF AGRICULTURE, FISHERIES AND FOOD

Whitehall Place, S.W.1. †
[Trafalgar: 7711]

The Ministry of Agriculture, Fisheries and Food was established in April 1955 and assumed the responsibilities previously discharged by the Ministry of Agriculture and Fisheries and the Ministry of Food.

The Ministry has a general responsibility for food supplies, both home produced and imported, and for food manufacture, distribution and storage.

The Ministry provides financial assistance and free technical advice to the agricultural, horticultural and fishing industries in England and Wales. Financial assistance under the Agriculture Acts of 1947 and 1957 takes the form of deficiency payments in respect of the main agricultural products to ensure a fair return to the producer. There are also a number of production grants and subsidies designed generally to improve the efficiency of farming. Free advice is available on farm management, and the technical aspects of agricultural production, including farm buildings and fixed equipment, land drainage, and crop and animal husbandry.

The Ministry is also responsible for schemes designed to improve the quality of livestock and of other agricultural products through the dissemination of the results of research carried out by the Agricultural Research Council and other institutions and through the control and eradication of animal and plant disease and of pests. It is also concerned with the safety, health, welfare and wages of agricultural workers.

The Ministry is concerned with the interests and development of the fishing industry in England and Wales, including the processing and distributive trades, whaling and research.

The Ministry has primary responsibility for administering part of the food and drugs legislation, in particular the composition, labelling and advertising of food; for slaughterhouses and meat inspection, and for the quality and cleanliness of milk; the Ministry maintains relations with Commonwealth and other countries and participates in the work of a number of international bodies, concerned with agriculture and food.

The Ministry is also responsible for the Royal Botanic Gardens, Kew, and the Ordnance Survey Department.

Minister of Agriculture, Fisheries and Food, THE RT. HON. (ARTHUR) CHRISTOPHER (JOHN) SOAMES, C.B.E., M.P. £5,000
Private Sec., M. D. M. Franklin.
Assistant Private Secs., Miss J. E. Arthur; P. Pooley.
Parliamentary do., R. D. Williams, M.P. ... *unpaid*
Parliamentary Clerk, M. F. Grant. £1,615 to £2,061
Parliamentary Secretaries, The Lord St. Oswald, M.C.; J. S. R. Scott-Hopkins, M.P. £2,500
Permanent Secretary, Sir John Winnifrith, K.C.B. £7,015

† Unless otherwise stated, Divisions of the Ministry are at this address.

Chief Scientific Advisers, (*Agriculture*) Sir Harold Sanders, £5,015; (*Food*) Dr. H. R. Barnell £3,865
Liaison Officers, The Lord Amherst of Hackney, C.B.E.; E. M. Howard; The Lord de Ramsey, T.D.; The Lord Hamilton of Dalzell, M.C.; Lt.-Col. F. G. W. Lane-Fox; The Earl of Malmesbury, T.D.; E. G. Parsons, C.B.E.; H. G. Partridge; Col. N. V. Stopford Sackville, C.B.E., T.D.; Sir Donald Scott; R. W. Trumper, C.B.E.; Lt.-Col. Sir Richard Verdin, O.B.E., T.D.; Capt. N. G. Garnons Williams, M.B.E., R.N. (*ret.*); Lt.-Col. Sir Watkin Williams-Wynn, Bt. . *unpaid*

Administrative Departments

GROUP A

Deputy Secretary, G. P. Humphreys-Davies, C.B. £5,015

SUB-GROUP (1)

Under Secretary, H. G. Button £4,115

LAND IMPROVEMENT DIVISION

Great Westminster House, Horseferry Road, S.W.1
[Victoria: 8511]

Assistant Secretary, Miss I. O. H. Lepper £2,800 to £3,500
Principals, H. J. Brice; A. Jeffrey Smith; R. A. Thorne, M.B.E. .... £1,894 to £2,646
Senior Executive Officer, G. E. Howell £1,615 to £2,061

AGRICULTURAL LAND SERVICE

Director, Maj. E. S. Dobb, C.B. £4,115
Deputy Director, D. A. Hole, C.B.E. £3,565
Regional Land Commissioners, R. E. Dowse; F. G. Eaton-Evans; J. Phillips Jones; A. J. Langdon; R. G. A. Lofthouse; C. Robinson; J. R. Rundle; D. M. Sims; H. Walton ..... £2,800 to £3,150
Chief Architect and Buildings Officer, F. W. Holder £3,215
Land Commissioners, W. T. Baker, T.D.; J. R. Booth, M.C.; R. G. Brighten; T. D. Cameron; H. Cartwright, T.D.; J. H. Dernie; D. H. Draper; J. H. L. Dunster; H. S. Dyer; F. C. Elliott; N. F. Finn, M.B.E.; J. D. Foster; C. M. Green; N. K. Green; A. Halhead, O.B.E.; J. P. Harrison; J. F. Hoare; E. Hodgson; H. Hollinrake, O.B.E.; T. Jones; J. Keir; K. S. Lycett; J. L. McGrath; W. Magson; A. C. Middleton; B. H. Moore; H. G. Penfold; H. D. Pennington; A. K. J. Quinney; P. G. M. Riding; O. W. Rowntree, O.B.E.; G. T. Roy; R. B. Sayce; R. F. Smith; J. F. Smithies; R. W. Soden, T.D.; R. H. Twinch; E. Vaughan; W. S. Waters; T. H. F. Whitton, T.D.; L. J. Williams; F. J. W. Winship; N. B. Wood .... £2,228 to £2,563
Senior Research Officer, D. J. Griffiths £1,894 to £2,563

LAND USE AND SMALLHOLDINGS DIVISION

Great Westminster House, Horseferry Road, S.W.1
[Victoria: 8511]

Assistant Secretary, G. L. Wilde .. £2,800 to £3,500
Principals, Miss M. E. Vince; R. A. E. Williams, C.I.E. .... £1,894 to £2,646
Chief Executive Officers, H. W. Durrant; R. A. Hughes, O.B.E. .... £2,172 to £2,507
Senior Executive Officers, K. W. Evans; L. W. Tolladay; J. A. Walker ...... £1,615 to £2,061

LAND DRAINAGE, WATER SUPPLY, AND MACHINERY DIVISION

Great Westminster House, Horseferry Road, S.W.1.
[Victoria: 8511]

Assistant Secretary, J. Crooks.... £2,800 to £3,500
Principals, W. R. Small; D. White £1,894 to £2,646
Senior Executive Officers, R. J. Crowe; Miss D. Hastings; S. T. K. Hester.... £1,615 to £2,061
Chief Drainage Engineer, E. A. G. Johnson, C.B.E. £3,815
Deputy Chief Drainage Engineer, J. V. Spalding £2,800 to £3,150
Senior Drainage Engineers, Major F. D. Ashton; C. L. Clayton; G. Cole; K. T. H. Langton; R. H. Miers, M.B.E.......... £2,228 to £2,563
Principal Scientific Officer, A. N. Ede £1,894 to £2,646

SUB-GROUP (2)

Under Secretary, C. H. M. Wilcox........ £4,115

ADVISORY SERVICE AND INFESTATION CONTROL DIVISION

Great Westminster House, Horseferry Road S.W.1
[Victoria: 8511]
Hook Rise South, Tolworth, Surbiton, Surrey
[Derwent: 6611]

Assistant Secretary, A. B. Bartlett £2,800 to £3,500
Principals, W. J. B. Hopkinson, O.B.E.; D. F. Williamson................ £1,894 to £2,646
Chief Executive Officer, H. W. Foot £2,172 to £2,507
Senior Executive Officers, Miss C. M. Marston, M.B.E.; H. S. Newman............. £1,615 to £2,061
Architect, A. G. Jenson......... £1,559 to £2,089

NATIONAL AGRICULTURAL ADVISORY SERVICE

Director, W. E. Jones.................... £4,115
Senior Advisory Officers, P. H. Brown; N. H. Pizer; J. W. Reid, O.B.E.................... £3,565
Chief Farm Management Advisory Officer, A. Jones (+*allce.*) £2,975 to £3,275
Director of Experiments, P. J. Macfarlan £2,975 to £3,275
Chief Livestock Husbandry Advisory Officer, W. P. Dodgson.................. £2,975 to £3,275
Deputy Chief Livestock Husbandry Advisory Officer, T. Allsop..........(+*allce.*) £2,100 to £2,600
Chief Poultry Advisory Officer, R. Coles £2,975 to £3,275
Chief Farm Machinery Advisory Officer, C. Culpin O.B.E..............(+*allce.*) £2,100 to £2,600
Regional Directors, R. Bruce, O.B.E.; H. Burr; H. E. Evans; R. B. Ferro; E. Ll. Harry, C.B.E.; N. F. McCann; E. Rea; D. H. Robinson £2,975 to £3,275
Deputy Regional Directors, A. J. Davies; O. G. Dorey; R. Gardner; H. C. Gough; E. G. Griffiths; S. L. Huthnance; W. S. Rayfield; W. R. Smith; F. W. Shepherd; J. R. Stubbs; M. W. Taylor, M.B.E.; O. G. Williams (+*allce.*) £2,100 to £2,600
County Advisory Officers, Grade I, D. C. Barber; E. A. Bartlett; J. C. M. Bearder; W. J. Brimacombe; D. M. Bryant; J. Butt-Evans; E. S. Carter; G. J. Clarke; V. Cory; P. E. Cross, O.B.E.; E. Davies; Emlyn Davies; D. S. Downey; R. Duncan; H. Edmunds; R. A. Engledow; E. J. Evans; J. V. Evans; A. H. Fitton; B. J. Fricker; J. Gibbons; H. J. Gill; A. T. Haesler; W. H. Helme; P. Holmes; R. Hope; J. S. Hopkins; G. H. Hughes; J. H. Humphreys; P. M. T. Jones; W. H. Jones, O.B.E.; J. R. Judson; J. B. Kerr; J. R. Keyworth; A. L. Lewis; L. J. McHardy; A. W. Mardon; K. M. Pearman; G. Precious; A. W. Prowel; H. E. Roberts; E. Shaw; K. W. Silverthorne, M.B.E.; J. A. M. Sutherland; W. E. H. Telford; W. Bowen-Thomas; P. J. O. Trist, O.B.E.; S. E. Turner; L. M. Waud; J. Wilkie; H. M. Williams; T. Williamson £2,100 to £2,600
County Advisory Officers, Grade II, J. Hardy; J. D. Laurence; P. D. Lees; J. J. S. Webster £1,821 to £2,250
Grade I Advisory Officers:
Special Duties, K. Dexter; R. Ede (+*allce.*); J. A. Rudderham; R. E. Taylor... £2,100 to £2,600
Bacteriologists, J. W. Edgell; J. Harrison; Miss A. A. Nichols; C. A. Scarlett; S. B. Thomas; C. H. Westwater................ £2,100 to £2,600
Crop Husbandry, D. W. Beesley; W. Q. Connold; H. Jackson; C. Kinsey; T. E. Miller; E. I. Prytherch; J. N. Sharrock.... £2,100 to £2,600
Entomologists, C. A. Collingwood; B. A. Cooper; J. H. Fidler; H. C. F. Newton; L. N. Staniland; J. D. Thomas; J. H. White... £2,100 to £2,600
Farm Machinery, H. J. Hine; H. T. Horsman, M.B.E.; H. B. Huntley; F. C. Richards £2,100 to £2,600
Grassland Husbandry, S. Campbell; H. G. Chippendale; J. Davies; T. W. Evans; G. P. Hughes; D. J. C. Jones, O.B.E.; J. Jones; C. D. Price £2,100 to £2,600
Horticulture, L. F. Clift; K. V. Cramp; J. B. Duggan; W. S. English; J. W. Ewan; A. D. Harrison; E. C. Herwin; W. G. Hume; P. S. Milne; R. Peake; J. Rhodes; F. A. Roach; E. E. Skillman; B. D. A. Tucker; G. C. Williams £2,100 to £2,600
Livestock Husbandry, J. E. Campion; F. J. Fullbrook; R. J. Gayton; E. L. Jones; W. Longrigg; G. H. Proffit, M.M.; G. E. G. Robinson; A. T. G. Trew; G. W. Whitehouse... £2,100 to £2,600
Milk Production, Miss J. Bide; W. E. Buck; Miss D. M. Evans; J. Hutchison; Miss M. Jones; Miss K. D. Maddever, O.B.E.; Miss D. M. Phillips; Miss B. Thornborrow....... £2,100 to £2,600
Nutrition Chemists, S. M. Boden; A. Eden; J. Featherstone; J. R. Griffiths; D. J. C. Jones; W. Lewis; J. R. Lloyd; N. Trinder £2,100 to £2,600
Plant Pathologists, G. H. Brenchley; W. Campbell; H. E. Croxall; D. L. G. Davies; H. H. Glasscock; L. Ogilvie; I. F. Storey...... £2,100 to £2,600
Poultry, W. M. O. Allcroft; G. E. Burkitt; W. Evans; R. F. Hall; Miss B. Lang; W. J. Lintin; Capt. M. C. Morgan; J. B. Morrison; I. W. Rhys; C. T. Riley; W. F. Wood £2,100 to £2,600
Soil Chemists, J. W. Blood; W. Dermott; J. B. E. Patterson; E. Roberts; T. H. Rose; J. E. Watkin; J. Webber; R. Williams, O.B.E. £2,100 to £2,600

EXPERIMENTAL HUSBANDRY FARMS

Directors, E. R. Bullen; G. P. Chater; S. Culpin; W. M. R. Evans; P. N. Harvey; P. J. Jones; C. H. Mudd; M. Roberts; R. W. Shepherd; F. E. Shotton; J. M. Willcock. £2,100 to £2,600

EXPERIMENTAL HORTICULTURE STATIONS

Directors, A. J. Bedding; S. P. Craze; H. J. Eaton; T. Laflin; J. M. S. Potter, O.B.E.; F. G. Smith £2,100 to £2,600

PLANT PATHOLOGY LABORATORY

Hatching Green, Harpenden
[Harpenden: 5241]

Deputy Chief Scientific Officer (Director), M. Cohen, Ph.D. .... £3,275 to £3,600
Senior Principal Scientific Officers, I. W. Prentice (*Deputy Director*); R. de B. Ashworth; F. H. Jacob £2,800 to £3,150
Principal Scientific Officers, E. C. Large, O.B.E.; E. J. Miller; Miss F. J. H. Moore; J. F. Southey; A. H. Strickland; H. L. G. Stroyan £1,894 to £2,646

INFESTATION CONTROL LABORATORY

Hook Rise South, Tolworth, Surbiton, Surrey
[Derwent: 6611]

Deputy Chief Scientific Officer, I. Thomas £3,275 to £3,600
Senior Principal Scientific Officers, J. A. Freeman, O.B.E.; E. E. Turtle, M.B.E.... £2,800 to £3,150
Principal Scientific Officers, E. W. Bentley; G. A.

Brett; R. A. Davies; D. S. Papworth; R. H. Thompson.................£1,894 to £2,646

FIELD RESEARCH STATION

Tangley Place, Worplesdon, Surrey
[Worplesdon: 2581]

Principal Scientific Officer, H. V. Thompson £1,894 to £2,646

LABOUR, SAFETY AND SEEDS DIVISION

Great Westminster House, Horseferry Road, S.W.1
[Victoria: 8511]

Assistant Secretary, L. J. Smith...£2,800 to £3,500
Principals, Miss M. L. Dhonau, O.B.E.; R. C. Hinton; D. N. M. Moore, D.S.O., M.C. £1,894 to £2,646
Chief Executive Officer, S. R. Males £2,172 to £2,507
Senior Executive Officer, Mrs. P. E. Holloway £1,615 to £2,061
Safety Inspectorate:
Chief Inspector, G. S. Wilson.............£2,711
Deputy Chief Inspector, J. C. Weeks £2,172 to £2,507

INFORMATION AND INVESTIGATION DIVISION

Assistant Secretary, J. A. Barrah..£2,800 to £3,500
Principal, C. H. Shillito........£1,894 to £2,646
Chief Executive Officers, A. W. Bunn; G. Carmichael, O.B.E.; T. A. McDowell, M.B.E. (*Press Officer*)...................£2,172 to £2,507
Senior Executive Officers, S. R. O'Hanlon, M.B.E.; Miss G. E. Pegler, M.B.E......£1,615 to £2,061
Librarian (Grade I), F. C. Hirst..£2,172 to £2,507

GRASSLAND AND CROP IMPROVEMENT DIVISION

Assistant Secretary, B. I. Felton..£2,800 to £3,500
Principals, W. T. Barker; J. B. Foxlee £1,894 to £2,646
Chief Executive Officer, F. A. Baker £2,172 to £2,507
Senior Executive Officers, P. G. Horscroft; C. L. Huntingford, M.B.E..........£1,615 to £2,061
Chief Technical Officer, G. L. Gray £2,190 to £2,380

SUB-GROUP (3)

Under Secretary, J. Hensley..............£4,115

ANIMAL HEALTH DIVISION

Hook Rise South, Tolworth, Surbiton, Surrey
[Derwent: 6611]

Assistant Secretary, J. G. Carnochan £2,800 to £3,500
Principal, L. Hurst...........£1,894 to £2,646
Chief Executive Officers, W. E. Crump; I. P. M. Macdonald..............£2,172 to £2,507
Chief Veterinary Officer, Sir John Ritchie, C.B. £4,110
Director of Field Services, John Reid.......£3,800
Deputy Directors of Field Services, A. G. Beynon; W. D. Macrae; James Reid............£3,350
Regional Veterinary Officers, H. B. Allan; J. C. Bennison, T.D.; A. C. L. Brown; J. Cameron; E. Clark; B. A. Claxton; E. R. Corrigall; H. M. M. Duff; J. K. S. Elmslie; F. J. Hill; A. Kelly; J. R. Kerr; J. W. R. Pearce; J. W. Simpson; G. Tullis; A. M. Urquhart £2,825 to £3,125
Deputy Regional Veterinary Officers, A. D. Campbell; J. A. Graham; W. Grant; E. F. Hardwick; E. Lowes; A. M. K. McLeod; H. G. Silcock; T. W. Stobo; E. P. Thorne; A. J. Wilsdon; W. W. Wilson..........................£2,775
Divisional Veterinary Officers, F. H. Addison; J. R. Anderson; J. C. Baird; P. Baird; N. M. Barrie; R. A. A. Beament; G. S. Beattie; J. G. S. Boyle; I. Brennan; J. M. Brown; D. K. Bryson; D. E. Callender; S. R. Campbell; E. T. Camps; T. D. Carrigan; G. S. R. Chalmers; D. Christie; D. M. Cochrane; H. Cremlyn-Hughes; J. G. Crowhurst; D. B. Davies; H. S. Davies; J. A. de Garis; J. C. Dring; D. J. Drummond; R. Dudlyke; T. P. Duffy; F. Dunlop; A. J. Dwyer; W. H. Dymock; H. Edwards; J. H. Findlay; J. M. Fraser; A. C. Gillespie; C. J. N. Godfrey; F. A. Gordon; A. M. Grant; H. C. Gregory; L. H. Green; E. G. Griffith; Lt.-Col. J. B. Griffiths, M.B.E.; A. Hamilton; P. Harvey; M. Herlihy; R. Hunnan; T. T. Hunter; H. M. John; D. Johnston; T. Johnston; D. K. Jones; H. N. Kennedy; R. S. Kyle; G. V. Langier; H. P. Lightfoot; R. C. Locke; J. G. Loxam; A. McAinsh; D. J. Macaulay; D. H. Macdonald; W. J. McIlroy; W. S. Mackay; J. M. McKellar; J. J. McLaren; J. D. McLaughlan; R. McNeil; R. I. Macrae; P. M. Marshall; R. T. H. Massey; R. C. Matheson; M. H. W. Miller; G. A. Moore; A. L. F. Mullen; R. B. T. Munro; G. Ord; L. E. Perkins; G. F. Pickering; R. A. Richards; R. W. Ross; S. Sharp; A. Shaw; J. L. Shaw; W. Simpson; A. J. Skea; A. W. Smith; J. Smith; R. J. Smith; J. G. Souter; A. Steele; J. Steele; R. L. Steele; John Stewart (*Cambridge*); John Stewart (*Ayr*); A. Sutherland; A. M. Taylor; G. B. Taylor; J. E. Taylor; J. G. Taylor; D. L. Thomson; Capt. W. Tweed; T. J. Tyrrell; J. M. Ware; J. Watson; G. Wight; A. Wilson; W. R. Wilson...£2,090 to £2,700

VETERINARY LABORATORIES

New Haw, Weybridge
[Byfleet: 41111]
Eskgrove, Lasswade, Midlothian
[Lasswade: 2025-6-7]

Director Veterinary Laboratories and Veterinary Investigation Service, H. I. Field.........£3,800
Deputy Director, Veterinary Laboratory, J. L. McGirr £3,350
Senior Research Officers, Grade I, Mrs. R. Allcroft, O.B.E.; F. D. Asplin; N. H. Hole; E. C. Hulse; S. B. Kendall; J. R. Lawson; A. B. Paterson; G. Slavin; J. E. Wilson.........£2,650 to £3,000
Senior Research Officers, Grade II, G. H. Bennett; I. Davidson; S. F. M. Davies; J. T. Done; R. H. Duff; T. E. Gibson; B. S. Hanson; R. A. Huck; L. P. Joyner; I. W. Lesslie; A. F. Machin; D. J. Mackinnon; L. M. Markson; J. F. Michel; P. G. Millar; W. J. B. Morgan; N. S. Saba; G. B. Simmins, O.B.E.; W. J. Sojka; H. N. Spears; D. L. Stewart; P. Stuart; C. D. Wilson £2,090 to £2,700
Principal Scientific Officer, M. K. Lloyd £1,894 to £2,646
Deputy Director Veterinary Investigation Service, D. W. Menzies.......................£3,350
Superintending Veterinary Investigation Officer, L. E. Hughes...................£2,650 to £3,000
Veterinary Investigation Officers, D. R. Allen; N. H. Brooksbank; D. Buntain; J. C. Buxton; I. H. Fincham; E. A. Gibson; M. Gitter; G. B. S. Heath; G. F. Kershaw; R. M. Loosmore; W. H. Parker; J. D. Paterson; H. E. Roberts; W. T. Rowlands, O.B.E.; I. G. Shaw; W. B. V. Sinclair; A. J. Stevens; D. M. Thomson; J. A. J. Venn; J. G. Wilson...............£2,090 to £2,700
Senior Executive Officer (*Laboratory Secretary*), G. C. Hampson..................£1,615 to £2,061

FOOD SCIENCE AND PLANT HEALTH DIVISION

Great Westminster House, Horseferry Road, S.W.1
[Victoria: 8511]

Assistant Secretary, Miss E. Walker, O.B.E. £2,800 to £3,500
Principal, Mrs. E. A. Attridge...£1,894 to £2,646
Senior Executive Officers, E. A. Airriess; J. N. Jackson £1,615 to £2,061
Senior Principal Scientific Officer, W. T. L. Neal £2,800 to £3,150
Senior Grade, Works Group, J. A. Carr £2,228 to £2,563
Principal Scientific Officers, H. S. Burton; R. E. J. Goodman; J. F. Hearne; Miss D. F. Hollingsworth, O.B.E.; A. C. Hughes; K. B. W. Jones £1,894 to £2,646

PLANT HEALTH INSPECTORATE

Chief Inspector, C. E. Pearson, O.B.E. £2,100 to £2,600

Senior Plant Health Inspectors, J. P. Cleary; D. Page; G. Rough; R. Varley.......£1,615 to £2,061

EMERGENCY SERVICES DIVISION
Great Westminster House, Horseferry Road, S.W.1
[Victoria: 8511]

Assistant Secretary, R. J. E. Taylor £2,800 to £3,500
Principals, W. R. Harper, O.B.E.; Brig. J. R. Reynolds, C.I.E., O.B.E.......£1,894 to £2,646
Chief Executive Officers, L. G. Hanson; R. Martin £2,172 to £2,507
Assistant Director (Technical), E. Whalley £2,228 to £2,563
Services Supplies Officer, Brig. J. A. Mullington, O.B.E.......................£2,172 to £2,507
Senior Executive Officers, M. E. Blackman; F. H. Hall; J. R. Stirling, M.B.E.; K. P. Stones £1,615 to £2,061

FOOD STANDARDS, HYGIENE AND SLAUGHTERHOUSE POLICY DIVISION
Great Westminster House, Horseferry Road, S.W.1
[Victoria: 8511]

Assistant Secretary, G. O. Lace, D.F.C. £2,800 to £3,500
Principal, G. O. Kermode......£1,894 to £2,646
Chief Executive Officer, K. A. Bird £2,172 to £2,507
Senior Executive Officers, L. C. Gaskell; Miss H. J. Morey...................£1,615 to £2,061
Chief Technical Adviser on Meat Inspection, L. B. A. Grace....................£2,825 to £3,125
Deputy Chief Technical Adviser on Meat Inspection, R. V. Blamire........................£2,775
Principal Scientific Officer, W. M. Shortt, O.B.E. £1,894 to £2,646

GROUP B

Deputy Secretary, F. A. Bishop, C.B., C.V.O.. £5,015

SUB-GROUP (4)

Under Secretary, B. C. Engholm...........£4,115

INTERNATIONAL CEREALS DIVISION

Assistant Secretary, R. P. Askew. £2,800 to £3,500
Principal, M. M. A. Gray.......£1,894 to £2,646
Senior Executive Officer, W. A. Files £1,615 to £2,061
Senior Trade Officer, A. V. Bryant, M.B.E. £1,615 to £2,061

HOME-GROWN CEREALS DIVISION
Government Buildings, (Block C), Tolcarne Drive, Pinner
[Field End: 7161]

Assistant Secretary, H. G. Lambert £2,800 to £3,500
Principals, F. H. Goodwin; J. S. W. Henshaw £1,894 to £2,646
Chief Executive Officer, S. W. Woods £2,172 to £2,507
Senior Executive Officers, G. A. Millington; A. G. Simpson; H. E. Smith.......£1,615 to £2,061
Marketing Officer (Grade II), A. Lawrance £1,821 to £2,250

SUB-GROUP (5)

Under Secretary, J. A. Payne, O.B.E.........£4,115

HORTICULTURE DIVISION I
Great Westminster House, Horseferry Road, S.W.1
[Victoria: 8511]

Assistant Secretary, G. R. Woodward £2,800 to £3,500
Principals, N. E. D. Burton; B. D. Hayes £1,894 to £2,646
Senior Executive Officer, E. H. High £1,615 to £2,061
Trade Adviser on Fruit and Vegetables, R. I. Payne, C.B.E....................£2,172 to £2,507
Marketing Officer (Grade I), F. J. Goldsmith £2,100 to £2,600

HORTICULTURE DIVISION II

Assistant Secretary, A. Savage...£2,000 to £3,500
Head of Branch, G. Wiglesworth...£2,800 (*personal*)
Principal, R. V. Allen..........£1,894 to £2,646
Senior Executive Officer, H. Pease £1,615 to £2,061

SUB-GROUP (6)

Under Secretary, W. A. Nield.............£4,115

EXTERNAL RELATIONS DIVISION I

Assistant Secretary, F. M. Kearns, M.C. £2,800 to £3,500
Principals, J. H. V. Davies; P. Parkhouse £1,894 to £2,646
Senior Executive Officer, Miss E. J. Marston, M.B.E. £1,615 to £2,061

EXTERNAL RELATIONS DIVISION II

Assistant Secretary, (vacant)
Principals, J. E. Dixon; A. C. McCarthy £1,894 to £2,646
Senior Executive Officer, Miss G. D. McElnea £1,615 to £2,061

EXTERNAL RELATIONS DIVISION III

Assistant Secretary, J. G. Kelsey.. £2,800 to £3,500
Principals, D. H. Andrews; M. L. David £1,894 to £2,646

GROUP C

Deputy Secretary, R. G. R. Wall, C.B......£5,015

SUB-GROUP (7)

Under Secretary, J. H. Kirk, C.B.E..........£4,115

ECONOMIC ADVICE, MARKETING AND EGGS DIVISION

Assistant Secretary, D. H. McPhail £2,800 to £3,500
Head of Branch, G. W. Day.....£2,800 (*personal*)
Principals, A. L. Irving, O.B.E.; G. P. Jupe; S. H. Moore....................£1,894 to £2,646
Chief Executive Officer, P. G. Ellis £2,172 to £2,507
Senior Executive Officers, P. M. Reason; A. D. Thomas..................£1,615 to £2,061

STATISTICS DIVISION

Chief Statistician, C. J. Brown.. £2,800 to £3,500
Statisticians, A. H. J. Baines; S. Clayton £1,894 to £2,646
Chief Executive Officer, A. N. Croxford, O.B.E., £2,172 to £2,507
Senior Executive Officers, A. J. Carrington; W. N. T. Roberts; D. Salton..........£1,615 to £2,061

SUB-GROUP (8)

Under Secretary, A. C. Sparks £4,115

AGRICULTURAL ECONOMICS DIVISION

Chief Agricultural Economist, L. Napolitan £3,340 to £3,665
Senior Principal Agricultural Economists, J. Ashton; E. A. G. Shrimpton.........£2,865 to £3,215
Principal Agricultural Economists, B. E. Cracknell; J. A. Evans; G. Sharp.......£1,839 to £2,590
Statisticians, E. L. Snowdon; Miss A. O. G. Tanner £1,894 to £2,646
Chief Executive Officer, K. T. Wasley £2,172 to £2,507
Senior Executive Officers, K. W. Battrick; F. Bradbury..................£1,615 to £2,061

AGRICULTURAL GUARANTEES DIVISION

Assistant Secretary, J. M. Grant.. £2,800 to £3,500
Principal, Miss S. Campbell.....£1,894 to £2,646

SUB-GROUP (9)

Under Secretary, W. C. Tame, C.B.........£4,115

MEAT AND LIVESTOCK DIVISION

Assistant Secretary, N. J. P. Hutchison £2,800 to £3,500
Principals, W. E. Mason; G. E. Myers; E. S. Virgo £1,894 to £2,646
Senior Executive Officers, H. C. Carter, M.B.E.; A. R. Parselle, M.B.E.; D. Rundle £1,615 to £2,061

FATSTOCK MARKETING DIVISION
Government Buildings, Epsom Road, Guildford, Surrey
[Guildford: 68121]
Whitehall Place, S.W.1
[Trafalgar: 7711]

Assistant Secretary, J. R. Moss... £2,800 to £3,500
Head of Branch, R. H. P. Meen, M.B.E. £2,700 (*personal*)
Principal, Miss M. J. Crighton... £1,894 to £2,646
Chief Executive Officers, C. D. Spencer; R. O. Williams.................. £2,172 to £2,507
Senior Executive Officer, E. W. Warren £1,568 to £1,947
Chief Fatstock Officers, W. M. Gillespie; A. M. Taylor.................. £2,618 to £2,800
Deputy Chief Fatstock Officers, R. Kyles; J. T. Robinson.................. £2,172 to £2,507
Marketing Officer (Grade II), A. A. N. Beveridge £1,821 to £2,250

SUB-GROUP (10)

Under Secretary, E. Jones-Parry.......... £4,115

MILK AND MILK PRODUCTS DIVISION
Great Westminster House, Horseferry Road, S.W.1
[Victoria: 8511]

Assistant Secretary, C. E. Coffin.. £2,800 to £3,500
Head of Branch, R. C. Simpkin, O.B.E. £2,810 (*personal*)
Principals, Mrs. H. I. Pinkerton; O. A. Robertson; Mrs. J. J. Tait.............. £1,894 to £2,646
Senior Executive Officers, D. K. Gilbert; W. E. Rushforth.................. £1,615 to £2,061
Chief Milk Officer, G. T. Morgan, O.B.E. £2,975 to £3,275
Regional Milk Officers, J. Beever; J. Boag; H. J. Brooks; Miss E. L. Coleman; T. I. Jones; A. H. Moseley; C. C. Orwin; S. Swift, M.B.E. £2,100 to £2,600

SUGAR, TROPICAL AND MANUFACTURED FOODSTUFFS DIVISION
Great Westminster House, Horseferry Road, S.W.1.
[Victoria: 8511]

Assistant Secretary, I. H Locke.. £2,800 to £3,500
Head of Division, R. Wentworth, O.B.E.(+*allce.*) £1,894 to £2,646
Principals, R. A. Isaacson; E. J. G. Smith £1,894 to £2,646
Senior Executive Officers, J. A. Bamford; J. Stopforth; C. J. Young.............. £1,615 to £2,061

FISHERIES DEPARTMENT

Fisheries Secretary, H. Gardner, C.B.E....... £4,115
Assistant Secretaries, E. H. Bott; J. Graham £2,800 to £3,500
Principals, A. K. H. Atkinson; H. F. Greenfield; E. D. Hardy; L. W. N. Homan £1,894 to £2,646
Senior Executive Officers, G. T. Adams; E. R. Fiske £1,615 to £2,061
Chief Inspector, H. T. Blaney............ £2,800
Deputy Chief Inspector, P. G. Jeffrey £2,172 to £2,473
Chief Salmon and Freshwater Fisheries Officer, F. T. K. Pentelow.................. £2,800 to £3,150
Deputy do., I. R. H. Allan...... £1,894 to £2,646

FISHERIES LABORATORY
Pakefield, Lowestoft
[Lowestoft: 4251]

Director of Fishery Research (Chief Scientific Officer), H. A. Cole.......................... £3,863
Deputy Director (Deputy Chief Scientific Officer), R. J. H. Beverton.......... £3,275 to £3,600
Senior Principal Scientific Officers, D. H. Cushing; A. J. Lee, D.S.C.; A. C. Simpson £2,800 to £3,150
Principal Scientific Officers, J. S. Alabaster; A. C. Burd; J. G. Cattley; J. Corlett; J. A. Gulland; D. A. Hancock; W. G. Hartley; F. R. Harden Jones; M. N. Mistakidis; F. Morgan; N. Reynolds; J. E. Shelbourne; A. Swain; G. C. Trout; P. R. Walne; G. D. Waugh.. £1,894 to £2,646

ESTABLISHMENTS AND ORGANISATION DEPARTMENT
Great Westminster House, Horseferry Road, S.W.1.
[Victoria: 8511]

Under Secretary (Director of Establishments and Organisation), H. Pitchforth £4,115

Division I

Assistant Secretary, J. A. K. Christie £2,800 to £3,500
Principals, E. H. Doling; Miss M. Hooley £1,894 to £2,646
Chief Executive Officers, B. Dennis; A. Tibbitts £2,172 to £2,507
Senior Executive Officers, S. Brookes; Miss I. E. M. Carpenter, M.B.E.; C. W. Chapman; J. A. Christianson; V. G. Codd; V. T. Humphreys; D. F. Mogg; D. W. Peddie; R. Townsend, D.F.C. £1,615 to £2,061

Division II

Assistant Secretary, C. H. A. Duke £2,800 to £3,500
Principal, W. Savage.......... £1,894 to £2,646
Chief Executive Officers, R. Dickeson; A. J. Hoare £2,172 to £2,507
Senior Executive Officers, J. A. Covell; A. R. Heath; J. N. Jotcham; F. C. Parker; G. Seymour; H. Smeethe.................. £1,615 to £2,061

Division III

Office Controller, G. H. B. King (*Principal Executive Officer*).......................... £3,150
Chief Executive Officers, H. M. Allix; G. E. Marriott; R. Nightingale............ £2,172 to £2,507
Senior Executive Officers, J. H. S. Baker; S. A. Botelle; W. E. N. Charnley; A. S. J. Cox; H. W. Emery; D. Kimber; G. W. Raymond M.B.E. (*Chief Welfare Officer*); C. S. Taylor, M.C.; B. Vernon.............. £1,615 to £2,061

FINANCE DEPARTMENT

Principal Finance Officer, M. Compton..... £4,115
Accountant General, W. Russell........... £3,815
Assistant Secretary, J. W. Pugsley £2,800 to £3,500
Directors (Professional), H. Fitzgerald, O.B.E.; R. H. Higginbotham, C.B.E......... £2,800 to £3,325
Head of Branch, W. F. C. Clark, O.B.E. £3,225 (*personal*)
Assistant Directors (Professional), E. P. Bennetts; K. V. Stephens; L. E. Wintersgill £2,418 to £2,750
Principal Executive Officer, A. Fillmore, O.B.E. £3,150
Principals, Mrs. J. M. Archer; W. G. Boss, O.B.E.; E. Pendlebury; Miss B. M. Shedden £1,894 to £2,646
Chief Accountants (Professional), L. C. Bentley; (£2,800) (*personal*); R. W. Meikle; D. P. Scott; R. Yuill.................. £1,851 to £2,293
Chief Executive Officers, J. L. Cope; J. W. Hewitt; R. W. Newman.......... £2,172 to £2,507
Senior Executive Officers, F. S. Anderson; A. W. Bridges; F. L. Charlton; N. Critchley; B. I. Hagel; D. Hall; J. Hallam; J. Lindsay; A. F Longworth; H. McCrae; W. McLaren; W. G. Madge, M.B.E.; H. Mayor; A. J. J. Mullan; A. G. Robinson; G. B. Ross; R. I. Sellers; R. G. Taylor; R. W. Turner; L. W. Wayne £1,615 to £2,061

LEGAL DEPARTMENT

Legal Adviser and Solicitor, C. S. Davis, C.B.. £5,015
Principal Assistant Solicitor, H. H. Rutter... £4,115
Assistant Solicitors, G. F. Aronson; E. C. Harris; A. J. Harriss; F. P. R. Mallows, O.B.E.; W. M. Wadham-Smith; J. D. Westlake £2,900 to £3,500
Senior Legal Assistants, A. J. Bligh; R. W. Brown; J. Collier; W. D. Curnock; T. B. Foster; H. P.

Hall; A. Hall-Brown; F. R. Hamp; K. P. Hickman Miss E. H. Kirkby-Gomes; R. D. Mainwaring; N. Monro; H. R. Reade; F. A. Richards; H. G. Roberts; F. H. C. Taylor £2,239 to £2,800

Senior Litigation Clerk, H. Davies, M.B.E. £1,615 to £2,061

REGIONAL OFFICES

Regional Controllers, G. H. C. Amos (*West Midland*); W. F. Darke (*East Midlands*); G. W. Ford (*South Western*); R. F. Giles (*Northern*); K. Harrison-Jones (*Yorks/Lancs.*); T. P. Marten (*South Eastern*); J. H. Perrin (*Eastern*). £2,800 to £3,500

DIVISIONAL OFFICES

Divisional Executive Officers, G. H. Barlow, M.B.E. (*Maidstone*); P. B. Barraud (*Truro*); G. Bishop (*Gloucester*); S. Booth (*Shrewsbury*); A. E. Bray (*Preston*); A. E. Brewer (*Alnwick*); R. J. Bricknell, M.B.E. (*Exeter*); A. F. Brocklebank (*Carlisle*); S. W. Charlton (*Beverley*); H. A. S. Doughty (*Harrogate*); D. R. Dow (*Bury St. Edmunds*); P. Ebbage (*Norwich*); R. Elphick (*Nottingham*); J. Farrell, T.D. (*Lincoln*); W. J. Hazeldine (*Oxford*); F. L. Hobson (*March*); A. R. Hughes (*Huntingdon*); G. H. D. Hunt (*Chelmsford*); T. Johnston (*Guildford*); J. Kerr (*Durham*); E. A. Leslie (*Crewe*); J. T. Muncaster (*Northampton*); W. H. Pedley (*Northallerton*); C. J. Sampson, O.B.E. (*Taunton*); N. F. V. Williams (*Winchester*); T. B. Wood (*Worcester*) .... £2,172 to £2,507

WALES

Welsh Department

Caerleon, 8, Victoria Terrace, Aberystwyth [Aberystwyth: 7561]

Under Secretary [*Welsh Secretary*], J. Morgan Jones, C.B.E. £4,050

Senior Chief Executive Officer, R. F. Kyle £2,618 to £2,800

Chief Executive Officers, D. B. L. Davies; T. L. Jones .... £2,172 to £2,507

Senior Executive Officers, W. J. Duckham; J. Medway .... £1,615 to £2,061

DIVISIONAL OFFICES

Divisional Executive Officers (*Chief Executive Officers*), W. E. Evans (*Caernarvon*); F. Haddon (*Ruthin*); W. G. Jones (*Cardiff*); T. A. Ivey (*Llandrindod Wells*); L. G. Keeley (*Carmarthen*) £2,172 to £2,507

ROYAL BOTANIC GARDENS, KEW

Open daily, 10 a.m. to Sunset or 8 p.m. House: 1 p.m. to dusk or 5 p.m. (weekdays), 1 p.m. to dusk or 6 p.m. (Sundays). Admission, 3*d*. Closed on Christmas Day. In 1962 there were 1,080,076 visitors to Kew Gardens Dogs not admitted.

Director of Royal Botanic Gardens, Sir George Taylor, D.SC., F.R.S.E., F.L.S., V.M.H. £4,110

Deputy Director, C. E. Hubbard, O.B.E. £3,275 to £3,600

Senior Principal Scientific Officer, E. W. B. H. Milne-Redhead, T.D. .... £2,800 to £3,150

Principal Scientific Officers, J. P. M. Brenan; A. A. Bullock; R. W. G. Dennis; F. N. Howes (*Keeper of Museums*); K. Jones; C. R. Metcalfe (*Keeper, Jodrell Laboratory*); R. D. Meikle; R. Melville; T. A. Russell; N. Y. Sandwith; J. R. Sealy; V. S. Summerhayes, O.B.E. £1,894 to £2,646

Librarian, Grade II, R. G. C. Desmond £1,615 to £2,061

Curator, L. Stenning, M.B.E. .... £1,615 to £2,155

Secretary (*Senior Executive Officer*), R. W. King, D.F.C. .... £1,615 to £2,061

ORDNANCE SURVEY DEPARTMENT

Leatherhead Road, Chessington, Surrey [Epsom: 2660]

Director-General, Major-Gen. A. H. Dowson, C.B.E.

Directors:

Map Publication and Production, Brig. R. A. Gardiner, M.B.E.

Field Survey, Brig. R. C. A. Edge, M.B.E.

Establishment and Finance, G. D. Lundie. £2,800 to £3,500

Deputy Directors:

Field Survey, Col. W. A. Seymour.

Large Scale Drawing and Reproduction, Col. M. H. Cobb.

Small and Medium Scale Drawing and Reproduction, Col. D. L. Griffith, O.B.E.

Establishment, R. W. Gough .. £2,172 to £2,507

Finance, T. Birtwistle .... £2,172 to £2,507

Assistant Directors, Lt.-Col. C. R. Bourne; Lt.-Col. C. W. Farrow; Lt.-Col. D. V. Hutchinson, M.B.E.; Lt.-Col. A. W. Pritchard.

CHAIRMEN OF COUNTY AGRICULTURAL EXECUTIVE COMMITTEES (ENGLAND AND WALES)

J. M. Angell, C.B.E. (*Glos.*); H. B. Atkinson (*Lincs.* (*Holland*)); H. Barker (*Yorks.* (*West Riding*)); T. R. Bayston (*Yorks* (*East Riding*)); Lt.-Col. The Hon. R. E. B. Beaumont, T.D. (*Montgomery*); T. R. C. Blofeld, C.B.E. (*Norfolk*); Sir Richard Boughey, Bt. (*Sussex* (*East*)); S. J. Buxton (*Notts.*); D. A. Carter (*Herts.*); W. J. Colfox (*Dorset*); J. H. Cooke (*Staffs.*); A. C. Cropper, T.D. (*Westmorland*); J. O. Cullimore, C.B.E. (*Monmouth*); R. Lloyd Davies (*Anglesey*); J. Gwyn Evans (*Cardigan*); H. R. Finn (*Kent*); W. T. Godber (*Beds.*); J. Goring (*Sussex* (*West*)); T. Greenshields (*Durham*); Sir Peter Greenwell, Bt., T.D. (*Suffolk*); F. Griffiths, M.B.E. (*Caernarvon*); The Lord Hamilton of Dalzell, M.C. (*Surrey*); J. R. Hardern, O.B.E. (*Isles of Scilly*); J. G. Henson, C.B.E. (*Lincs.* (*Kesteven*)); J. Heyes, O.B.E. (*Lancs.*); Lt.-Col. J. H. V. Higgon, O.B.E. (*Pembroke*); J. B. Holliday (*Cumberland*); C. H. Hollis (*Rutland*); L. G. F. Horrell (*Devon*); A. B. Howie, C.B.E. (*Northumberland*); P. Hughes (*Worcs.*); E. R. Jackson, C.B.E. (*Yorks.* (*North Riding*)); E. O. Jones, O.B.E. (*Brecon*); J. G. Jones (*Merioneth*); I. H. Lamb (*Cambs.*); W. J. Layton, O.B.E. (*Hereford*); H. Lewis, C.B.E. (*Radnor*); The Earl of Malmesbury, T.D. (*Hants.*); J. R. D. Morten (*Derbyshire*); R. J. Padfield (*Essex*); Col. The Hon. R. G. H. Phillimore, O.B.E. (*Oxon.*); The Lord De Ramsey, T.D, (*Hunts and Soke of Peterborough*); H. J. Rathbone, O.B.E. (*Denbigh*); G. B. Read (*Lincs.* (*Lindsey*)); G. Richards (*Glamorgan*); W. J. S. Richards (*Carmarthen*); A. S. Rickwood, C.B.E. (*Isle of Ely*); E. K. Robarts (*Middlesex*); J. W. Shirley (*Bucks.*); W. J. Simmons, O.B.E. (*Berks.*); Col. N. V. Stopford Sackville, C.B.E. (*Northants.*); H. W. Standring (*Warwicks.*); W. F. Stanley (*Leics.*); R. A. Stark (*Isle of Wight*); Lt.-Col. Sir Richard Verdin, O.B.E., T.D. (*Cheshire*); F. W. Ward (*Salop*); G. Comer White, C.B.E. (*Somerset*); H. Williams (*Flint*); P. M. Williams, O.B.E. (*Cornwall*); C. P. Wookey (*Wilts.*).

AGRICULTURAL RESEARCH COUNCIL

Cunard Building, 15 Regent Street, S.W.1

The Agricultural Research Council was incorporated by Royal Charter on July 23, 1931. In accordance with the provisions of the *Agricultural Research Act*, 1956, the Council is charged, under a Committee of the Privy Council, with the organization and development of agricultural and food research and may, in particular, establish or develop institutions or departments of institutions and make grants for investigation and research relating to the advance of agriculture. The Council's finance is, under the 1956 Act, derived from the Agricultural Research Fund into which monies provided by Parliament for the purpose of the Act, and other sums received by the Council, are paid.

Council, The Duke of Northumberland, K.G., T.D. (*Chairman*); Sir David Lowe, C.B.E., F.R.S.E. (*Deputy Chairman*); J. D. Alston; Prof. T. A. Bennet-Clark, Ph.D., F.R.S.; Prof. F. W. R. Brambell, D.SC., Ph.D., F.R.S.; Major J. E. M. Dugdale, T.D.; Prof. A. C. Frazer, C.B.E., M.D., D.SC., Ph.D.; R. E. Glover, D.SC.; Prof. J. E. Harris, C.B.E., Ph.D., F.R.S.; Prof. J. W. Howie,

M.D.; Prof. Sir Hans Krebs, M.D., D.SC., F.R.S.; The Lord Netherthorpe; Sir John Ritchie, C.B., F.R.S.E.; Prof. A. Robertson, Ph.D., Ll.D., F.R.S.; Sir Harold Sanders, Ph.D.; W. H. Senior, F.R.S.E.; C. H. M. Wilcox; Prof. W. T. Williams, D.SC., Ph.D.

Secretary, E. G. Cox, T.D., D.SC., F.R.S.
Deputy Secretary, W. G. Alexander, C.B.E.
Assistant Secretaries, W. E. Berry, Ph.D.; E. D. T. Jourdain; A. Oates.
Scientific Advisers to the Secretary, E. E. Cheesman, C.B.E., D.SC.; R. Scarisbrick, Ph.D.; J. Lamb, O.B.E.; D. L. Gunn, C.B.E., D.SC.; F. H. Moult; D. Rudd Jones, Ph.D.
Principals, F. J. S. Culley; D. J. Parkinson, O.B.E.; L. S. Porter.
Chief Executive Officers. F. V. Bird; J. H. Shimwell.
Senior Executive Officers, M. R. Beauchamp; K. H. J. Clarke.

For the Research Institutes under the control of the council, *see Index*.

EXECUTIVE COUNCIL OF THE COMMONWEALTH AGRICULTURAL BUREAUX

Farnham House, Farnham Royal, Bucks.

This Commonwealth organization, governed by an Executive Council composed of nominees of the various Commonwealth Governments, and of the Colonial Office, was set up in 1929 to administer bureaux organized to act as clearing houses of information on research in eight specialized fields of agricultural science, and financed from a common fund provided by the Governments of the Commonwealth. The Governments of the Commonwealth and Empire instructed it in 1933 to supervise the administration and finances of the Commonwealth (formerly Imperial) Institute of Entomology, the Commonwealth (formerly Imperial) Mycological Institute and the Commonwealth Institute of Biological Control (formerly the Imperial Parasite Service), and in 1937 to organize bureaux for Forestry and Dairy Science. The Annual Reports of the Council are submitted to each of the Governments through their several members on the Council. The bureaux are attached to appropriate research institutions, but are distinct from them.

Chairman, W. A. C. Mathieson, C.M.G., M.B.E.
Vice-Chairman, H. E. Seneviratne.
Secretary, Sir Thomas Scrivenor, C.M.G.

Institutes

Commonwealth Institute of Entomology, Natural History Museum, S.W.7. *Director*, E. O. Pearson.
Commonwealth Mycological Institute, Ferry Lane, Kew, Surrey. *Director*, J. C. Hopkins, C.M.G., D.SC.
Commonwealth Institute of Biological Control, Gordon Street, Curepe, Trinidad. *Director*, F. J. Simmonds, Ph.D., D.SC.

Bureaux

Animal Breeding and Genetics, Institute of Animal Genetics, King's Buildings, West Mains Road, Edinburgh 9, Scotland.—*Director*, J. P. Maule.
Animal Health, Central Veterinary Laboratory, New Haw, Weybridge, Surrey.—*Director*, M. Crawford.
Animal Nutrition, Rowett Research Institute Bucksburn, Aberdeen, Scotland.—*Director*, D. Harvey, Ph.D.
Dairy Science and Technology, National Institute for Research in Dairying, Shinfield, nr. Reading. —*Director*, E. J. Mann.
Forestry, Commonwealth Forestry Institute. South Parks Road, Oxford.—*Director*, F. C. Ford Robertson, O.B.E.
Helminthology, The White House, 103 St. Peter's Street, St. Albans, Herts.—*Director*, Miss S. M. Willmott, Ph.D.
Horticulture and Plantation Crops, East Malling Research Station, East Malling, nr. Maidstone, Kent.—*Director*, G. K. Argles.
Commonwealth Bureau of Pastures and Field Crops, Hurley, nr. Maidenhead, Berks.—*Director*, A. G. G. Hill.
Plant Breeding and Genetics, School of Agriculture, Downing Street, Cambridge—*Director*, P. S. Hudson, O.B.E., Ph.D.
Soils, Rothamsted Experimental Station, Harpenden, Herts.—*Director* G. V. Jacks.

AIR MINISTRY

(*see* Royal Air Force)

AIR REGISTRATION BOARD

Chancery House, Chancery Lane, W.C.2
[Chancery: 2811]

Set up on Feb. 26, 1937, under the *Companies Act*, the Board is an autonomous non-profit making limited company. Delegated to the Board are certain powers relating to the design, construction and maintenance of civil aircraft; investigation by surveyors of aircraft and associated equipment for the purpose of recommending to the Minister concerning issues and renewals of certificates of airworthiness. The Board also conducts technical examinations for licences of aircraft maintenance engineers, flight engineers and commercial pilots.

Chairman, Lord Brabazon of Tara, P.C., G.B.E., M.C.
Secretary, R. E. Hardingham, C.M.G., O.B.E.

AIR TRANSPORT LICENSING BOARD

Therese House, 29–30 Glasshouse Yard, Aldersgate Street, E.C.1.
[Clerkenwell: 8841]

Established by the *Civil Aviation (Licensing) Act*, 1960, to license air services (with certain exceptions). The Board considers representations in relation to air transport services by U.K. registered aircraft, or to facilities, tariffs or charges in connection therewith, reporting their conclusions and recommendations to the Minister of Aviation.

Chairman, D. T. Jack, C.B.E. £5,000
Deputy Chairman, J. J. Taylor, O.B.E. £3,500
Members, Prof. R. G. D. Allen, C.B.E.; F. C. Bagnall, C.B.E.; E. Baldry, O.B.E.; C. P. Harvey, Q.C.; Sir Friston How, C.B.; W. P. James, O.B.E.; A. H. Wilson, C.B., C.B.E.
each 15 gns. per session
Secretary, J. E. Barnes. . . . . £2,865 to £3,565

COLLEGE OF ARMS OR HERALDS COLLEGE

Queen Victoria Street, E.C.4
[City: 2762]

The College of Arms is open daily from 10–4 when an Officer of Arms is in attendance to deal with enquiries by the public, though such enquiries may also be directed to any of the Officers of Arms, either personally or by letter.

There are 13 officers of the College, 3 Kings of Arms, 6 Heralds and 4 Pursuivants, who specialise in genealogical and heraldic work for their respective clients. The College possesses the finest records on these subjects in the world. It is the official repository of the Arms and pedigrees of English, Northern Irish, and Commonwealth families and their descendants, and its records include official copies of the records of Ulster King of Arms, the originals of which remain in Dublin.

Arms have been and still are granted by Letters Patent from the Kings of Arms under Authority delegated to them by the Sovereign, such authority having been expressly conferred on them since at least the fifteenth century. A right to Arms can only be established by the registration in the official records of the College of Arms of a pedigree showing direct male line descent from an ancestor already appearing therein as being entitled to Arms, or by making application to the College of Arms for a Grant of Arms.

Earl Marshal, His Grace the Duke of Norfolk, K.G., P.C., G.C.V.O., Royal Victorian Chain.

Kings of Arms

Garter, Sir Anthony Richard Wagner, K.C.V.O., D.Litt., F.S.A.
Clarenceux, Sir John Dunamace Heaton-Armstrong, M.V.O.
Norroy and Ulster, Aubrey John Toppin, C.V.O., F.S.A.

Heralds

Windsor, Richard Preston Graham-Vivian, M.V.O., M.C.
Somerset, Michael Roger Trappes-Lomax, F.S.A.
Lancaster (and Registrar), John Riddell Bromhead Walker, M.V.O., M.C.
York, The Lord Sinclair, M.V.O.
Chester, Walter John George Verco, M.V.O. (*Earl Marshal's Secretary*).
Richmond, Robin de la Lanne Mirrlees.

Pursuivants

Bluemantle, John Philip Brooke Brooke-Little.
Portcullis, Alexander Colin Cole.
Rouge Croix, Lt.-Col. Rodney Onslow Dennys, O.B.E.
Rouge Dragon, Conrad Marshall John Fisher Swan, Ph.D.

Wales (Herald Extraordinary), Maj. Francis Jones.

COURT OF THE LORD LYON

H.M. Register House, Edinburgh
[Edinburgh: 30137]

The Scottish Court of Chivalry, including the genealogical jurisdiction of the *Ri-Sennachie* of Scotland's Celtic Kings, adjudicates rights to arms and administration of *The Scottish Public Register of All Arms and Bearings* (under 1672 cap. 47) and *Public Register of All Genealogies*. The Lord Lyon presides and judicially establishes rights to existing arms or succession to Chiefship, or for cadets with scientific "differences" showing position in clan or family. Pedigrees are also established by decrees of Lyon Court, and by Letters Patent. As *Royal Commissioner in Armory*, he grants Patents of Arms (which constitute the grantee and heirs noble in the Noblesse of Scotland) to "virtuous and well-deserving" Scotsmen, and petitioners (personal or corporate) in Her Majesty's overseas realms of Scottish connection, and issues birth-brieves. In Scots Law, Arms are protected by Statute; their usurpation is punishable, and the Registration Fees of Honour on patents (£80) and matriculations (£20) are payable to H.M. Exchequer.

Lord Lyon King of Arms, Sir Thomas Innes of Learney, K.C.V.O., LL.D., F.S.A.*Scot.*, Advocate £1,200

Three Heralds (£25 each)

Rothesay, Lt.-Col. H. A. B. Lawson, M.V.O., F.S.A. *Scot.*
Marchmont, James Monteith Grant, W.S.
Albany, Sir Iain Moncreiffe of that Ilk, Bt., Ph.D., Advocate.

Three Pursuivants (£16 13*s.* 4*d.* each)

Kintyre, Charles Eliot Jauncey of Tullichettle, Q.C.
Carrick Malcolm Rognvald Innes of Edingight, F.S.A., *Scot.*
Unicorn, John Inglis Drever Pottinger.

Lyon Clerk and Keeper of Records, Harold Andrew Balvaird Lawson, M.V.O., F.S.A. *Scot*....... £900
Procurator-Fiscal, Ivor Reginald Guild, W.S.
Herald Painter, Mrs. Katherine Chart.
Macer, Thomas C. Gray.

ART GALLERIES, ETC.

ROYAL FINE ART COMMISSION

5 Old Palace Yard, S.W.1
[Whitehall: 3935]

Appointed in May, 1924, "to enquire into such questions of public amenity or of artistic importance as may be referred to them from time to time by any of our Departments of State, and to report thereon to such Department; and, furthermore, to give advice on similar questions when so requested by public or quasi-public bodies, where it appears to the said Commission that their assistance would be advantageous." In August, 1933, a Royal Warrant extended the Terms of Reference of the Commission—"so that it shall also be open to the said Commission, if they so desire, to call the attention of any of Our Departments of State, or of the appropriate public or quasi-public bodies, to any project or development which in the opinion of the said Commission may appear to affect amenities of a national or public character"; in May, 1946, a Royal Warrant further extended the Terms of Reference of the Commission as follows:—

We Do give and grant unto you, or any three or more of you, full power to call before you such persons as you shall judge likely to afford you any information upon the subject of this Our Commission; and also to call for, have access to and examine all such books, documents, registers and records as may afford you the fullest information on the subject, and to inquire of and concerning the premises by all other lawful ways and means whatsoever: We Do authorize and empower you, or any three or more of you, to visit and personally inspect such places as you may deem it expedient so to inspect for the more effectual carrying out of the purposes aforesaid:

Chairman, The Lord Bridges, P.C., G.C.B., G.C.V.O., M.C., F.R.S.
Commissioners, Sir Colin Anderson; John Betjeman, C.B.E.; Hon. Lionel Brett; Sir Hugh Casson, A.R.A., F.R.I.B.A.; Howard Colvin; Prof. R. Llewelyn Davies, F.R.I.B.A.; Raymond Erith, A.R.A.; Arthur Floyd, C.B.E.; Frederick Gibberd, C.B.E., A.R.A.; Sir William Holford, A.R.A.; G. A. Jellicoe, C.B.E.; Sir Leslie Martin, C.B.E.; Henry Moore, O.M., C.H.; John Piper; Sir Edward Playfair, K.C.B.; J. M. Richards, C.B.E.; Sir Basil Spence, O.M., O.B.E., T.D., R.A.
Secretary, Hon. Godfrey Samuel.

ROYAL FINE ART COMMISSION FOR SCOTLAND

22 Melville Street,
Edinburgh 3
[Edinburgh Caledonian: 5434]

Appointed in 1927 "to enquire into such questions of public amenity or of artistic importance relating to Scotland as may be referred to them by any of our Departments of State, and to report thereon to such Departments; and, furthermore, to give advice on similar questions when so requested by public or quasi-public bodies when it appears to the said Commission that their assistance would be advantageous." Under Royal Warrant of May 8, 1953, the terms of reference of the Commission were extended so that it is now open to the Commission, if it so desires, to call the attention of any Department of State or of the appropriate public or quasi-public bodies, to any project or development which in the opinion of the Commission may appear to affect amenities of a national or public character; and to call before it any persons, examine any documents or visit any places it might deem expedient for the more effectual carrying out of its duties.

Commissioners, Sir Hector Hetherington, G.B.E. (*Chairman*); T. Coughtrie, C.B.E., LL.D.; J. L. Gleave, R.S.A.; C. d'O. Pilkington Jackson, A.R.S.A., F.R.S.A.; W. H. Kininmonth, R.S.A., F.R.I.B.A.; I. G. Lindsay, O.B.E., R.S.A., F.R.I.B.A.; The Hon. Lady MacGregor of MacGregor, O.B.E.; Sir Robert Matthew, C.B.E., A.R.S.A., P.R.I.B.A.; J. Cameron Smail, O.B.E., LL.D., F.R.S.E.
Secretary, Lt.-Col. J. T. Bannatyne, M.B.E.

NATIONAL GALLERY

Trafalgar Square, W.C.2
[Whitehall: 7618–9]

Hours of opening.—Weekdays 10 to 6 (June–Sept., Tuesdays and Thursdays 10 to 9), Sundays 2 to 6.

Admission free. Closed on Good Friday, Christmas Eve, and Christmas Day.

The National Gallery is the result of a Parliamentary grant of £60,000 in 1824 for the purchase and Exhibition of the Angerstein collection of pictures, the present building being opened in 1838 and enlarged in 1876, 1887, 1911, 1928, 1930, 1937 and 1961. Expenses for 1963–64 were estimated at £291,000.

TRUSTEES

The Lord Robbins, C.B., F.B.A. (*Chairman*); Henry Moore, O.M., C.H.; Denis Mahon; Sir William Coldstream, C.B.E.; The Viscount Chandos, P.C., D.S.O., M.C.; The Marquess of Salisbury, K.G., P.C., F.R.S.; The Earl of Plymouth; The Duke of Devonshire, M.C.;, Miss C. V. Wedgwood, C.B.E. Sir Patrick Linstead, C.B.E. F.R.S., D.Sc.; Sir Karl Parker, C.B.E. Ph.D.

OFFICERS

Director, Sir Philip Hendy £4,115
Keeper, M. Davies .... £2,865 to £3,215
Deputy Keeper, C. H. M. Gould . £2,493 to £2,865
Scientific Adviser to the Trustees, R. G. H. Thomson £2,493 to £2,865
Assistant Keeper, (*I*) M.V. Levey . £1,498 to £2,554
Chief Restorer, A. W. Lucas ..... £2,510 to £2,813

NATIONAL PORTRAIT GALLERY

St. Martin's Place, Charing Cross Road, W.C.2
[Whitehall: 8511]

Open Monday to Friday 10 to 5. Saturday 10 to 6. Sunday 2 to 6.

The first grant was made in 1856 to form a gallery of the portraits of the most eminent persons in British history, the collections being successively housed in Great George Street, Westminster, in South Kensington, and in Bethnal Green. The present building was opened in 1896, £80,000 being contributed to its cost by Mr. W. H. Alexander; an extension erected at the expense of Lord Duveen was opened in 1933. The amount for salaries and expenses, including a grant of £4,100 for purchase of portraits, was estimated at £47,000 for 1963–64.

Director, Keeper and Secretary, C. K. Adams, C.B.E. £3,240
Assistant Keepers (I), D. T. Piper; J. F. Kerslake; R. C. Strong .... £1,498 to £2,554

TATE GALLERY

Millbank, S.W.1
[Tate Gallery: 4444]

Hours of opening.—Weekdays 10 to 6. Sundays 2 to 6. Admission free, except to certain temporary exhibitions. Closed on Good Friday, Christmas Eve, and Christmas Day.

The Tate Gallery, which constitutes the National Collection of British painting, of modern foreign painting and of modern sculpture, was opened in 1897, the cost of erection (£80,000), being defrayed by the late Sir Henry Tate, who also contributed the nucleus of the present collection. The *Turner Wing*, built at the expense of Sir Joseph Duveen and his son, Lord Duveen, was opened in 1910. There are also special collections by Blake, Watts and Alfred Stevens. Lord Duveen also defrayed the cost of galleries to contain the collection of modern foreign painting, completed in 1926, and a new sculpture hall, completed in 1937. Expenses for 1963–64 were estimated at £118,000.

Director, Sir John Rothenstein, C.B.E., Ph.D.. £3,815
Keeper, N. R. Reid .... £2,865 to £3,215
Deputy Keeper, R. E. Alley ...... £2,566 to £2,865
Assistant Keepers (*Grade I*), Mary Chamot; Judith Cloake; D. L. A. Farr; M. R. F. Butlin. £1,508 to £2,544
Chief Restorer, S. Slabczynski ... £2,510 to £2,813

WALLACE COLLECTION

Hertford House Manchester Square, W.1
[Welbeck: 0687-8]

Admission free. Open on weekdays 10 a.m. to 5 p.m.; Sundays 2 p.m. to 5 p.m. Closed on Good Friday, Christmas Eve and Christmas Day.

The Wallace Collection was bequeathed to the nation by the widow of Sir Richard Wallace, Bt., K.C.B., M.P., on her death in 1897, and Hertford House was subsequently acquired by the Government. The collection includes pictures, drawings and miniatures, French furniture, sculpture, bronzes, porcelain, armour and miscellaneous *objets d'art*. The total net expenses were estimated at £67,000 in 1963–64.

Dirctor, F. J. B. Watson, M.V.O., F.S.A. £3,215
Assistant Director, R. A. Cecil ... £1,498 to £2,544

NATIONAL GALLERIES OF SCOTLAND

Mound, Edinburgh
[Edinburgh Caledonian: 6824]

Comprising:—
National Gallery of Scotland, Mound, Edinburgh, 1.
Scottish National Portrait Gallery, Queen Street, Edinburgh 2.
Scottish National Gallery of Modern Art, Inverleith House, Royal Botanic Gardens, Edinburgh, 4.

Director of the National Galleries of Scotland, David K. Baxandall, C.B.E. £3,500
Chief Restorer, H. R. H. Woolford £2,390 to £2,739
Keeper of Paintings, C. E. Thompson £1,438 to £2,479
Keeper of Prints and Drawings, K. K. Andrews £1,438 to £2,479
Keeper, Scottish National Portrait Gallery, Robert E. Hutchison..(+*allce*. £181) £1,438 to £2,479
Assistant Keeper, Scottish National Portrait Gallery, B. C. Skinner .... £1,438 to £2,479
Keeper, Scottish National Gallery of Modern Art, W. D. Hall .... £1,438 to £2,479
Secretary, Accountant and Establishment Officer, R. J. Inglis .... £1,615 to £2,061

(For other British Art Galleries, *see* Index.)

UNITED KINGDOM ATOMIC ENERGY AUTHORITY

11 Charles II Street, S.W.1
[Whitehall: 6262]

Established by the *Atomic Energy Authority Act*, 1954, the Authority took over, on August 1, 1954, the control of atomic energy research and development. The Minister for Science is responsible to Parliament for general atomic energy policy and for money provided for the Authority.

The Authority is organized in five groups, as shown below:—

(*a*) the *Research Group*. The Research Establishment at Harwell, Berks., conducts fundamental research into nuclear physics and atomic energy and provides information to the other establishments. It includes the Isotope School (1951) and Reactor School (1954). The Radiochemical Centre at Amersham, Bucks., prepares radio-active substances such as radium, radon and isotopes produced in the atomic reactors, for medical, scientific and industrial purposes.

(*b*) the *Weapons Group*. Research work on atomic weapons is carried on at the Research Establishment, Aldermaston, Berks.

(*c*) the *Reactor Group*. Responsible for the design, construction and development of nuclear power reactors, including the Dounreay Experimental Reactor in Caithness, the Advanced Gas-cooled Reactor experiment at Windscale, Cumberland, and the Atomic Energy Establishment at Winfrith, Dorset. It also acts as engineering consultant for the Electricity Boards, overseas organisations and the British Consortia formed for the building of nuclear power stations. Headquarters are at Risley, Lancs.

(*d*) the *Production Group*. Responsible for the operation of the nuclear reactors at Calder Hall and Chapelcross and for management of the uranium and plutonium production factories at Springfields in Lancashire, Windscale, and Capenhurst in Cheshire. Consults with industry on the sale of nuclear fuel exploitation patents and other commercial activities. Headquarters of the Group are at Risley.

(*e*) the *Engineering Group*. Responsible for the design and construction of Authority plants, works and buildings and for the design and inspection of fuel elements for production purposes. Headquarters are at Risley.

Chairman, Sir Roger Makins, G.C.B., G.C.M.G. £10,000

Vice-Chairman, Sir William Penney, K.B.E., F.R.S. £8,000

Members (Full-time), Sir William Cook, C.B., F.R.S. (*Reactors*); Sir Alan Hitchman, K.C.B. (*Finance and Administration*); J. C. C. Stewart (*Production*) each £7,500

Air Chief Marshal Sir Claude Pelly, G.B.E., K.C.B., M.C. (*Weapons Research and Development*). £6,500

(*Part-time*) Sir John Cockcroft, O.M., K.C.B., C.B.E., F.R.S. £3,000

Prof. A. H. Cottrell, F.R.S.; C. F. Kearton, O.B.E., F.R.S.; S. J. Pears; R. M. Geddes, O.B.E.; Sir Leonard Owen, C.B.E.; The Lord Geddes of Epsom, C.B.E. .... each £1,000

Secretary, D. E. H. Peirson.

MINISTRY OF AVIATION

Shell Mex House, Strand, W.C.2
[Temple Bar: 1207]

The Ministry of Aviation is responsible for the supply of aircraft to the Services and undertakes research on and development of aircraft, electronic equipment, etc., for the Services, and of certain classes of equipment for civil use, *e.g.*, civil aircraft and industrial gas turbines. The Ministry undertakes the organization, implementation and encouragement of measures for the development of civil aviation; the promotion of safety and efficiency in the use of aircraft; research concerning navigation and operation of civil aircraft; general oversight of the activities of the Air Corporations; the investigation of aircraft accidents; the licensing and supervision of training arrangements for aircrews; the operation of over thirty civil aerodromes, air traffic control and telecommunications services.

Minister of Aviation, THE RT. HON. JULIAN AMERY, M.P. £5,000

Private Secretary, C. B. Benjamin.

Assistant Private Secretary, N. D. Paren.

Parliamentary Private Secretary, A. Royle, M.P. unpaid

Parliamentary Secretary, H. N. Marten, M.P. .. £2,500

Permanent Secretary, Sir Richard Way, K.C.B., C.B.E. £7,015

Private Secretary, A. G. Manzie.

Deputy Secretary (*A*)., J. M. Wilson, C.B. ... £5,015

Deputy Secretary (*B*.), R. Burns, C.B., C.M.G. £5,015

Deputy Secretary (C.), D. W. G. L. Haviland, C.B. £5,015

Controller of Aircraft, M. B. Morgan, C.B. .. £5,015

Deputy Controller of Aircraft (*Royal Navy*), Rear Admiral J. A. Ievers, C.B., O.B.E.

Deputy Controller of Aircraft (*Royal Air Force*), Air Vice-Marshal Sir Colin Scragg, K.B.E., C.B., A.F.C.

Deputy Controller of Aircraft (*Research and Development*) (vacant)

Director-General of Flying (*Research and Development*), Air Vice-Marshal C. D. C. Boyce, C.B., C.B.E. (*ret*.) £2,800

Controller of Guided Weapons and Electronics, Air Marshal Sir Edouard Grundy, K.B.E., C.B.

Deputy Controller of Electronics, Air Vice-Marshal T. U. C. Shirley, C.B., C.B.E.

Director-General Atomic Weapons, L. T. D. Williams, C.M.G. £4,115

Directors, S. Chard, O.B.E.; S. A. Hunwicks, O.B.E. £3,703

Controller of National Air Traffic Control Services, Air Vice-Marshal Sir Laurence Sinclair, G.C., K.C.B., C.B.E., D.S.O. (*ret*.) £4,415

Chief Scientist, Sir Robert Cockburn, K.B.E., C.B. £5,815

Administration and Finance

Under-Secretaries, D. F. Allen; L. H. Curzon, C.B.;. F. J. Doggett; W. G. Downey; R. R. Goodison; V. P. Harries, C.B.; G. V. Hole; E. S. Jackson, C.B.; N. V. Meeres, C.B.; G. I. Morris, C.B.; J. H. Riddoch, C.M.G.; T. M. Wilson £4,115

Director of Contracts (*A*.), S. G. McKay £3,715

Director of Contracts (*B*.), L. J. T. Clifton ... £3,715

Accountant General, W. Gairns, C.B.E. £3,715

Assistant Secretaries, W. W. Abson; B. D. Airey; R. Anderson; J. E. Barnes; J. K. Batey; R. H. W. Bullock; C. M. Colbeck; N. Craig; A. V. Davies, M.B.E.; R. S. S. Dickinson; E. S. Foster; D. F. A. R. Freeman; R. W. N. B. Gilling; A. Goodson; G. A. Haig, O.B.E.; N. Hartley; E. W. G. Haynes; G. S. Hill; P. G. Hudson; J. A. Jaggers; G. P. Jefferies; C. R. F. Lark; R. E. M. LeGoy; D. A. Lovelock; G. C. Lowe; C. F. McFarlane, C.B.E.; E. I. R. MacGregor; R. B. Marshall, M.B.E.; L. C. J. Orchard; R. F. Prosser, M.C.; G. T. Rogers; Miss M. L. Senior; W. P. Shovelton; Mrs. L. Silverston, O.B.E.; W. W. Simpson; R. S. Swann; C. E. H. Tuck; P. F. G. Twinn; S. R. Walton; L. Williams; K. J. Willoughby; G. McD. Wilson £2,715 to £3,415

Chief Information Officer, D. D. Grant £2,715 to £3,415

Inspection

Director-General of Inspection, F. E. McGinnety, C.B.E. £4,115

Directors, R. E. Swift, C.B.E. (£4,110); E. D. Whitehead, M.B.E. (£3,560).

Representatives of Ministry of Aviation Overseas

Director-General, Defence Research Staff (*Washington*), Dr. H. M. Wilson, M.B.E. £4,115

Directors, Air Commodore D. N. Kingston-Blair-Oliphant, O.B.E.; Brig. J. A. Fitzpatrick

Head of United Kingdom Defence Research and Supply Staff, Australia, T. M. Wilson £4,115

Counsellor (*Defence Research and Supply*), *Canada*, C. J. Francis £3,565

Aircraft

Director-General of Aircraft Equipment Research and Development, N. Coles £3,928

Director-General of Aircraft General Services, A. E. Woodward-Nutt £4,115

Director-General of Engine Research and Development, P. Lloyd, C.B.E. £3,928

Director-General of Aircraft Research and Development (*R.A.F.*), D. E. Morris £3,928

Director-General, Scientific Research (*Air*), L. F. Nicholson, C.B. £4,115

Directors, Captain J. E. Dyer-Smith, R.N.; W. O. Broughton; Dr. N. J. L. Megson, C.B.E.; Air Commodore E. M. T. Howell, C.B.E.; Air Commodore H. M. Russell, O.B.E.; F. G. R. Cook; E. B. Carter; E. A. Poulton; C. Moore *Varying rates to* £3,665

Director, Royal Aircraft Establishment, M. J. Lighthill, F.R.S. £5,000

Director, National Gas Turbine Establishment, R. H. Weir, C.B. £4,050

Director-General, Aircraft Production, L. R. Beesly £4,365

Directors, H. J. Curnow, O.B.E.; B. D. Davies; H. E. Hancocke, O.B.E.; H. P. Baker £3,565

Chief Superintendent, Aeroplane and Armament Experimental Establishment, Dr. D. Cameron £3,275 to £3,600

Director, Air Technical Publications, E. R. Stables £3,560

Guided Weapons and Electronics

Deputy Controller of Guided Weapons, J. E. Serby, C.B., C.B.E. £4,415

Director-General, Guided Weapons, Dr. B. G. Dickins, C.B.E. £4,115

Directors, Captain A. F. Caswell, R.N.; Air Commodore F. W. Thompson, C.B.E., D.S.O., D.F.C., A.F.C.; Air Commodore J. H. Hunter-Tod; Brig. F. Grant, T.D.; C. P. Fogg; C. J. Stephens; Brig. W. M. Greenway .... £3,275 to £3,600

Director, Royal Radar Establishment, Dr. G. G. MacFarlane £4,150

Director-General of Electronics Research and Development, Dr. W. H. Penley, C.B.E. £4,115

Directors, J. H. Briggs; R. G. Friend; R. W. Willmer; E. V. Truefitt ..... £3,275 to £3,600
Director-General, Guided Weapons and Electronics Production, R. E. Sainsbury £4,115
Directors, H. E. Drew; J. G. Brown; H. R. Reid £3,565
Director, Explosives Research and Development Establishment, Dr. C. H. Johnson, C.B.E... £3,923
Director, Rocket Propulsion Establishment, J. E. P. Dunning .... £3,275 to £3,600
Director, Signals Research and Development Establishment, R. J. Lees £3,800

CIVIL AVIATION

Aviation Economics and Aircraft

Chief Statistician, A. H. Watson. £2,715 to £3,415

Aviation Safety

Director, W. E. B. Griffiths, C.B.E. £2,925 to £3,350
Deputy Directors, W. F. Rimmer; J. R. Neill £2,397 to £2,875
Flight Safety Director, G. W. Stallibrass, O.B.E. £2,925 to £3,350
Deputy Directors, J. A. Karran; M. H. Vivian £2,397 to £2,875

Accidents Investigation (Civil Aviation)

Chief Inspector, Group Capt. J. B. Veal, C.B.E., A.F.C. £3,715

AVIATION GROUND SERVICES

Aerodromes Technical

Director, Sir John Briscoe, Bt., D.F.C. £2,925 to £3,350

Directorate of Control

Director (Plans), V. A. M. Hunt, C.B.E. £2,925 to £3,350
Director (Operations), Air Cdre, H. J. Hickey, C.B.E. £2,925 to £3,350

Telecommunications Engineering Staff

Chief Telecommunications Engineer, C. G. Phillips O.B.E. £3,715
Deputy Chief Telecommunications Engineer, E. L. T. Barton, O.B.E. £3,415
Assistant Chief Telecommunications Engineers, G. E. Graham M.B.E.; W. H. Garnett, O.B.E.; J. F. Montgomerie; W. A. J. Thorn, O.B.E. £2,650 to £3,000

Aviation Operational Research

Senior Principal Scientific Officer, F. L. Sawyer £2,650 to £3,000

Aviation Works Directorate

Director, C. E. Foster, C.B.E., E.R.D.

Civil Aviation Ground Services

London Airports

General Manager, F. L. Passmore £3,860
Aerodrome Commandants, Special Grade, G. J. Warcup (*London Airport*) (£2,925 to £3,350); B. A. Oakley (*Gatwick*) ..... £2,305 to £2,875

Southern Division

Heston Aerodrome, Hounslow, Middlesex
[Hayes: 6171]

Divisional Controller, C. M. Colbeck £2,710 to £3,410
Assistant Chief Telecommunications Engineer, J. C. Farmer .... £2,650 to £3,000
Deputy Director (Operations), G. F. K. Donaldson, D.F.C., A.F.C. .... £2,397 to £2,875
Divisional Air Traffic Control Officer, G. W. Monk, O.B.E., D.F.C. .... £2,750 to £3,000

Scottish Division

Divisional Offices, Broomhouse Drive, Saughton, Edinburgh, 11.
[Craiglockhart: 4040]

Divisional Controller, G. M. Macintosh, O.B.E. £2,925 to £3,350
Assistant Chief Telecommunications Engineer, D. E. Horne .... £2,650 to £3,000
Deputy Director (Operations), S. G. Hall £2,397 to £2,875
Aerodrome Commandant Special Grade (Prestwick), C. D. Waldron .... £2,397 to £2,875
Aerodrome Commandant Grade I (Renfrew), W. F. Murray, O.B.E. .... £2,236 to £2,525
Divisional Air Traffic Control Officer, M. A. Young £2,319 to £2,497

Northern Division

24–26, Grove Park, Liverpool 8
[Sefton Park: 1421]

Divisional Controller, W. M. Hargreaves, C.B.E. £2,925 to £3,350
Assistant Chief Telecommunications Engineer, G. A. Glossop .... £2,650 to £3,000
Aerodrome Commandant Grade I (Belfast), J. B. Selway, D.F.C. .... £2,236 to £2,525
Deputy Director (Operations) (vacant)
Divisional Air Traffic Control Officer, J. Middlemas, O.B.E. .... £2,319 to £2,497

BRITISH BROADCASTING CORPORATION

Broadcasting House, Portland Place, W.1
[Langham: 4468]

The BBC was incorporated under Royal Charter as successor to the British Broadcasting Company, Ltd., whose licence expired Dec. 31, 1926. Its present Charter came into force July 1, 1952, and expires July 29, 1964. The Chairman, Vice-Chairman and other Governors are appointed by the Crown. The BBC is financed by means of revenue from receiving licences for the Home services and by a Grant in Aid from Parliament for the External services. The total number of licences in force in March 1963 was 15,698,991, of which 12,442,806 were for television as well as sound broadcasting.

Chairman, Sir Arthur fforde £4,000
Vice-Chairman, Sir James Duff £1,500
Governors, Sir David Milne, G.C.B. (*Scotland*), £1,500; Mrs. R. M. Jones (*Wales*), £1,500; Sir Richard Pim, K.B.E., V.R.D. (*N. Ireland*); G. E. Coke; R. F. Lusty; Dame Anne Godwin, D.B.E.; Sir Ashley Clarke, G.C.M.G., G.C.V.O. (*each* £1,000)
Director-General, H. Carleton Greene, O.B.E.
Directors, Sir Beresford Clark, K.C.M.G., C.B.E. (*External Broadcasting*); H. J. G. Grisewood, C.B.E. (*Chief Assistant to the Director-General*); Sir Harold Bishop, C.B.E. (*Engineering*); J. H. Arkell, C.B.E. (*Administration*); K. Adam, C.B.E. (*Television*); F. C. McLean, C.B.E. (*Engineering*); F. G. Gillard, C.B.E. (*Sound Broadcasting*).
Deputy Director of Engineering, M. J. L. Pulling.
Assistant Director of External Broadcasting, E. Tangye Lean, C.B.E.
Assistant Director of Sound Broadcasting, R. D'A. Marriott, D.F.C.
Controller, Programmes, Television, S. C. Hood, M.B.E.
Controller, Finance, J. G. L. Francis.
General Manager, Publications, R. S. C. Hall.
Legal Adviser, E. C. Robbins, C.B.E.
Secretary, C. J. Curran.

Controllers of Regional Offices

Scotland, A. Stewart, C.B.E., Broadcasting House, Queen Margaret Drive, Glasgow, W.2.
Northern Ireland, R. McCall, C.M.G., Broadcasting House, Ormeau Avenue, Belfast, 2.
Wales, A. B. Oldfield-Davies, C.B.E., Broadcasting House, Park Place, Cardiff.
Midland, H. J. Dunkerley, C.B.E., Broadcasting House, 52 Carpenter Road, Edgbaston, Birmingham, 15.
North, R. Stead, Broadcasting House, Piccadilly, Manchester.
West, S. J. de Lotbinière, C.V.O., O.B.E., Broadcasting House, Whiteladies Road, Clifton, Bristol.

BRITISH EUROPEAN AIRWAYS CORPORATION

Bealine House, Ruislip, Middlesex
[Viking: 1234]

Chairman, Marshal of the Royal Air Force Lord Douglas of Kirtleside, G.C.B., M.C., D.F.C. (*and expenses* £1,000) £8,500

Deputy Chairman, Sir John Keeling*
Other Members, A. H. Milward, C.B.E. (*and expenses* £750) (£7,500) (*Chief Executive*); The Lord Balfour of Inchrye, P.C., M.C., £1,000; S. K. Davies, C.B.E.*; Sir Walter Edmenson, C.B.E.*; A. C. Ping, £2,000; R. L. Weir, O.B.E. (*and expenses* £400) (£6,000); Sir Giles Guthrie, Bt., O.B.E., D.S.C.*; B. S. Shenstone (*and expenses* £400) (£6,000).
Chief Executive, A. H. Milward, C.B.E.
Flight Operations and Communications Director, J. W. G. James, O.B.E.
Commercial and Sales Director, P. C. F. Lawton, D.F.C.
Chief Engineer, B. S. Shenstone.
Traffic Director, E. P. Whitfield, O.B.E.
Financial Controller, R. L. Weir, O.B.E.
Secretary, H. E. Marking, M.C.
Personnel Director, C. A. Herring.
Director of Medical Services, Dr. A. Buchanan Barbour, O.B.E.
Chief Public Relations Officer, W. Simpson, O.B.E., D.F.C.

* Fees not drawn.

BRITISH OVERSEAS AIRWAYS CORPORATION

B.O.A.C. Headquarters, London Airport, Hounslow, Middlesex
[Skyport: 5511]

Established in 1939, British Overseas Airways Corporation acquired, on April 1, 1940, the air transport undertakings of Imperial Airways and British Airways, which had been at the disposal of the Secretary of State for Air since the outbreak of war.

B.O.A.C. is the larger of the two Government Corporations which are charged with the task of developing and operating British scheduled air transport services under the provisions of the Air Corporations Act, 1949. It operates a round-the-world service and services to Africa, the Middle, Near and Far East, Australia and New Zealand, and North and South America. In June 1963, the Corporation was operating about 70 routes, with a total gross service mileage of just over 400,000. On these routes there were more than 120 services weekly in each direction.

The members of the Corporation are appointed by the Minister of Aviation.

Chairman, Rear-Admiral Sir Matthew Slattery, K.B.E., C.B. (*allowances* £1,000) £8,500
Deputy Chairman (part-time), Sir Wilfred Neden, C.B., C.B.E. (*allowances* £250) £4,500
Managing Director, Sir Basil Smallpeice, K.C.V.O.

BRITISH RAILWAYS BOARD

222 Marylebone Road, N.W.1.
[Ambassador 3232]

The British Railways Board was established by the *Transport Act*, 1962 and assumed the railway and certain other associated assets of the former British Transport Commission on January 1, 1963. The Board's duty is to provide railway services in Great Britain and such other ancilliary services and facilities as appear expedient. These include hotel and catering and cross-channel shipping services.

Its Members are appointed by the Minister of Transport and, with the approval of the Minister, the Board has set up six Regional Railway Boards to whom it delegates certain management and operational functions. The Board reserves to itself general financial control, industrial relations of a national character, determination of the future size and shape of the system, design and manufacture of equipment, and approval of major engineering projects.

Chairman, Dr. R. Beeching £24,000
Vice-Chairman, Sir Steuart Mitchell, K.B.E., C.B. £7,500
Full time Members, A. R. Dunbar, O.B.E. (£7,500); F. C. Margetts, M.B.E. (£7,500); J. Ratter, C.B.E. (£7,500); Maj.-Gen. G. N. Russell, C.B., C.B.E. (£7,500); P. H. Shirley (£12,000); L. H. Williams (£7,500).
Part time Members, H. P. Barker; D. H. Cameron of Lochiel, T.D.; F. Donachy, O.B.E.; F. Hayday; J. MacN. Sidey, D.S.O.; T. H. Summerson (£1,000 *each*)
Secretary, Maj.-Gen. Ll. Wansbrough-Jones, C.B., C.B.E.
Solicitor and Legal Adviser, M. H. B. Gilmour.
Financial Controller, P. G. James.
Technical Adviser, R. C. Bond.
Chief Commercial Officer, R. A. Long.
Chief Operating Officer, G. F. Fiennes, O.B.E.
Chief Industrial Relations Officer, C. S. McLeod, O.B.E.
Chief Management Staff Officer, J. E. M. Roberts.
Public Relations Adviser, S. K. Garratt.

Eastern Railway Board

Liverpool Street Station, E.C.2

Chairman, J. MacN. Sidey, D.S.O.
Members, J. R. Hammond, M.B.E.; A. MacLeod; A. F. Pegler; J. B. Peile; W. J. Evans.
Secretary, L. S. Plastow.

London Midland Railway Board

Euston Station, N.W.1

Chairman, H. C. Johnson, C.B.E.
Members, L. Cooke, O.B.E.; J. Haworth; J. Bonham-Carter, D.S.O.; F. H. Culpin; R. L. E. Lawrence, O.B.E., E.R.D.; Sir Richard Summers; W. G. Thorpe.
Secretary, M. T. Howard-Williams, M.B.E.

North Eastern Railway Board

Railway Headquarters Offices, York

Chairman, T. H. Summerson.
Members, A. Dean, C.B.E.; G. H. Kitson, O.B.E., T.D.; L. H. McRobert, C.B.E., T.D.; D. S. M. Barrie, M.B.E.; J. W. Fraser; Sir George Walton, K.B.E., C.B., T.D.
Secretary, N. C. R. Barker.

Scottish Railway Board

302 Buchanan Street, Glasgow, C.2.

Chairman, D. H. Cameron of Lochiel, T.D.
Members, J. W. Armit, Ph.D.; F. Donachy, O.B.E.; J. Ness; Sir Hugh Rose, Bt., T.D.; Sir William Walker, T.D.; R. B. W. Bolland, E.R.D.; J. O. Blair Cunynghame, O.B.E.; G. W. Stewart.
Secretary, C. A. Scott.

Southern Railway Board

Waterloo Station, S.E.1

Chairman, D. McKenna, O.B.E.
Members, C. P. Hopkins; D. L. T. Oppé; Sir Kenneth Preston; A. V. Barker, O.B.E.; P. A. White.
Secretary, D. A. Verdon-Smith.

Western Railway Board

Paddington Station, W.2

Chairman, S. E. Raymond.
Members, J. R. G. Flynn; L. W. Ibbotson, M.B.E.; J. Ryan, C.B.E., M.C.; J. B. Drongeson, M.B.E.; R. F. Hanks.
Secretary, A. H. Curtis Welch.

BRITISH TRANSPORT DOCKS BOARD

Melbury House, Melbury Terrace, N.W.1
[Hunter: 6621]

Constituted under the *Transport Act*, 1962, to operate the harbours owned or managed by the Board. Harbours at 32 ports in Great Britain were taken over from the British Transport Commission.

Chairman, Sir Arthur Kirby, K.B.E., C.M.G.
Vice Chairman, Sir Andrew Crichton.
Members, G. H. Lowthain, M.B.E.; A. G. McCrae; The Lord Melchett; E. D. Nicholson; R. B. Southall, C.B.E.; R. L. J. Wills, C.B.E., M.C.
Secretary and Solicitor, H. A. Chapman.

BRITISH TRAVEL AND HOLIDAYS ASSOCIATION

Headquarters and Tourist Information Centre
Queen's House, 64/65 St. James's Street, S.W.1
[Mayfair: 9191]

Overseas Offices

British Travel Association: 680 Fifth Avenue, New York 19; 39 South La Salle Street, Chicago 3;

612 South Flower Street, Los Angeles 17; 50 Young Street, Sydney; 151 Bloor Street West, Toronto; 661 Howe Street, Vancouver; 6 Place Vendôme, Paris; 22 Neue Mainzerstrasse, Frankfurt/Main; Leidseplein 29, Amsterdam; Norrmalmstorg 1, Stockholm C; Avda. Santa Fé 854, Buenos Aires; Rua Aurora 960, Sala 2, Sao Paulo; Union Castle Building, 36 Loveday Street, Johannesburg; 41 Boulevard Adophe Max, Brussels; 21B Via Torino, Rome; Pearl Assurance House, Jamieson Avenue, Salisbury, Southern Rhodesia.

The functions of the Association can be summarized as follows: (*a*) to increase the number of visitors from overseas and (*b*) to ensure that overseas visitors and home holiday makers are well received and accommodated and have the best facilities that can be provided. The Association is a Company limited by guarantee and registered under the Companies Act and draws its membership from all sections of the tourist and holiday industry. The Association is supported by H.M. Government and receives a Grant-in-Aid from the Board of Trade. The Board consists of a Chairman who is appointed by the President of the Board of Trade, and 19 members, 8 of whom are nominated by the President of the Board of Trade: 7 are elected by the members of the Association and the remainder nominated by the Scottish Tourist Board (2), the Welsh Tourist and Holidays Board (1) and the Northern Ireland Tourist Board (1). Four additional members representing the various interests concerned with travel and holidays in the United Kingdom may be appointed.

Chairman, The Lord Mabane, P.C., K.B.E.
General Manager, L. J. Lickorish.

BRITISH WATERWAYS BOARD

Melbury House, Melbury Terrace, N.W.1
[Ambassador: 6711]

Chairman, Sir John Hawton, K.C.B. (*full-time*).

Vice-Chairman, Adm. Sir Frederick Parham, G.B.E., K.C.B., D.S.O. (*part-time*).

Members, Mrs. J. Dower, O.B.E.; E. C. R. Hadfield, C.M.G.; Hon. Alexander Hood; J. Matthews, O.B.E. (*all part-time*).

Secretary, H. E. Candy (*acting*).

CABINET OFFICE

Great George Street, S.W.1
[Whitehall: 5422]

Secretary of the Cabinet, Sir Burke Trend, K.C.B., C.V.O. £7,515
Private Secretary, J. H. Robertson.
Deputy Secretary of the Cabinet, A. L. M. Cary £5,015
Under Secretaries, Miss J. J. Nunn; P. A. Wilkinson, C.M.G., D.S.O., O.B.E. £4,115
Asst. Secs., P. R. Baldwin; J. T. A. Howard-Drake; J. McKenzie, M.B.E.; K. M. McLeod (*Establishment Officer*); J. C. A. Roper, M.C.; Maj.-Gen. L. de M. Thuillier, C.B., O.B.E. .... £2,865 to £3,565
Central Statistical Office:
Director, Sir Harry Campion, C.B., C.B.E. .. £5,015
Deputy Director, R. E. Beales, C.B.E. £4,115
Chief Statisticians, H. E. Bishop, D.F.C.; G. Penrice; T. S. Pilling; W. D. Stedman Jones £2,865 to £3,565
Historical Section:
Chief Historians, Prof. Sir James Butler, M.V.O., O.B.E. (*Military*); Sir Keith Hancock (*Civil*).
Administrative Officer in Charge and Departmental Records Officer, A. J. D. Woods, C.B.E. £2,865 to £3,565
Chief Clerk, H. L. Theobald.... £1,680 to £2,126

CABLE AND WIRELESS LIMITED

Head Office—Mercury House, Theobald's Road, W.C.1
[Chancery: 4433]

The Company was formed in 1929 (as Imperial and International Communications, Ltd., the name being changed in 1934) to unify the oversea communications of the Empire, consequent upon the Imperial Wireless and Cable Conference of 1928. Cable and Wireless, Ltd., was acquired (under the *Cable and Wireless Act*, 1946) by the U.K. Government as from January 1, 1947.

Cable and Wireless Ltd., with its associated companies, operates oversea telecommunications services by means of a system comprising 12,000 nautical miles of telephone cable, 131,000 nautical miles of telegraph cable, and 320,000 miles of radio circuits. The Company has 88 branches overseas, a cable station and an engineering college in Britain, and a fleet of seven cable ships—one cable layer and six cable repair ships. It is responsible for financing, laying and maintaining the British share of the Commonwealth comprehensive telephone cable system. Its operations include public service telegraphy and telephony by both cable and radio; telex; leased circuits for telegraphy, telephony, and data transmission; phototelegraphy; ship-shore services; aeronautical services; inland telephone systems, etc.

Chairman, Sir John Macpherson, G.C.M.G. £3,500 (and expenses up to £350)
Managing Directors, N. C. Chapling, C.B.E.; H. H. Eggers, C.M.G., O.B.E. £4,700 each (and expenses up to £200 and £150 respectively)
Other Directors, H. E. Matthews, O.B.E. (£1,000); E. J. L. Howitt, O.B.E. (£4,000); Col. D. McMillan, C.B., O.B.E.; R. J. Halsey, C.M.G... (*unpaid*)
Secretary, R. H. Hensman, O.B.E.
Chief Accountant, R. A. Rice.
Staff Manager, W. H. Davies.

CHARITY COMMISSION

Ryder Street, St. James's, S.W.1.
[Whitehall: 7621]
Official Custodian's Division, Wellington House, Buckingham Gate, S.W.1
[Sullivan: 6693]

The Charity Commission was constituted under Act of Parliament in 1853 and reconstituted under the Charities Act, 1960, with the general function of promoting the effective use of charitable monies and a duty to keep a register of charities. The powers of the Commissioners over endowments held for educational purposes are exercised by the Minister of Education. The Official Custodian for Charities holds investments for charities and remits for income, free of income tax, to trustees.

Chief Commissioner, C. P. Hill, C.B.E. £4,115
Commissioners, S. P. Grounds; W. E. A. Lewis, O.B.E. (*also Secretary and Establishment Officer*) £3,140 to £3,565
Assistant Solicitors, O. H. Toyne; E. L. Hayes £2,965 to £3,565
Asst. Commissioners, W. J. Wolfe; J. MacC. Armstrong; J. P. L. Redfern; F. H. Pratt; C. W. E. Shelley; W. C. Over; D. B. Hodgkinson; T. Keith; C. A. Weston, D.F.C., G.M. £2,239 to £2,865
Principal, P. J. Mantle, C.M.G.... £1,959 to £2,711
Official Custodian for Charities, H. A. Anderton, I.S.O. £2,607 to £2,865
Accountant, Securities Division, H. O'Neill, M.B.E. £2,237 to £2,572
Senior Executive Officers, L. A. Jimenez; H. M. Taylor; Miss M. L. O. Williams, M.B.E.; R. Booth; Miss C. M. Clark; R. S. Morgan; D. W. Peel; E. G. Saunders.. £1,680 to £2,126

CHURCH COMMISSIONERS

1 Millbank, Westminster, S.W.1
[Whitehall: 5444]

The Church Commissioners were established on April 1, 1948, by the amalgamation of *Queen Anne's Bounty* (established 1704) and the *Ecclesiastical*

Commissioners (established 1836). The Commissioners have three main tasks:—

(1) the management of their capital assets so that they may earn income;

(2) the proper distribution of that income; and

(3) the discharge of a large number of administrative duties conferred on them by Acts of Parliament and Measures of the Church Assembly.

In the financial year 1962/3 the Commissioners' income was:—

Stock Exchange Securities	£9,215,294
Agricultural and Urban Estates	4,653,415
Mortgages	1,691,556
Miscellaneous	1,602,333
	£17,162,598

This income was spent as follows:—

Payment of clergy stipends and pensions	£12,601,405
Provision of better houses for the clergy	600,000
Provision of Church buildings in housing areas	255,932
Additions to capital mainly to add to gifts by the laity	370,630
Reserves, sinking funds, administration and other miscellaneous purposes	3,334,631
	£17,162,598

Constitution

The 2 Archbishops, the 41 diocesan Bishops, 5 deans, 10 other clerks and 10 laymen appointed by the Church Assembly; 4 laymen nominated by the Queen; 4 persons nominated by the Archbishop of Canterbury; The Lord Chancellor; The Lord President of the Council; the First Lord of the Treasury; The Chancellor of the Exchequer; The Secretary of State for the Home Dept.; The Speaker of the House of Commons; The Lord Chief Justice; The Master of the Rolls; The Attorney-General; The Solicitor-General; The Lord Mayor and two Aldermen of the City of London; The Lord Mayor of York and one representative from each of the Universities of Oxford and Cambridge.

Church Estates Commissioners and Joint Treasurers:—

First, The Lord Silsoe, G.B.E., M.C., T.D., Q.C.
Second, J. S. W. Arbuthnot, M.B.E., T.D., M.P.
Third, Sir Hubert Ashton, K.B.E., M.C., M.P.
Secretary, Sir Mortimer Warren.
Financial and Administrative Secretary, K. S. Ryle, M.C.
Estates Secretary, D. A. Collenette, O.B.E.
Assistant Secretaries, R. C. Edwards (*Investments*); A. W. J. Savidge (*Legislative and Special Matters*); L. N. King (*General*); L. A. Speller (*Estates*).
Accountant, H. M. G. Pryor.
Establishment Officer, R. G. Williams.
Trust Officer, D. G. Ward.
Principals, J. D. M. Barnes; E. C. Buckley; E. Denselow; L. J. Dent; W. T. Leech; E. W. Lyons; A. I. McDonald; R. K. Pears, D.F.C.; C. C. W. Rodd; L. D. Walker.
Senior Executive Officers, K. A. L. Argent; D. R. Baird; J. Facer; A. Godbold; A. Holley; H. H. T. Munden; L. E. Nelson; G. H. Penn; N. H. Rawlings; R. McN. Roxburgh; S. E. Smith.

Legal Department

Official Solicitor, O. H. Woodforde, M.B.E.
Deputy Solicitor, R. H. Rogers.
Assistant Solicitor, J. W. Cook.
Senior Legal Assistants, H. K. Benham; A. J. L. Campbell; R. A. G. Lees; P. Leslie; S. J. Palmer.
Legal Assistant, P. Lambert.
Special Duties, M. P. Simpson.

Architectural Department

Official Architect, R. G. Wood.
Deputy Architect. B. H. Dowland.
Senior Asst. Architect, H. A. Scarth.
Asst. Architects, L. T. Channing; J. A. Whittaker; P. F. Roach.

Surveyor's Department

Official Surveyor, W. R. Paice.
Deputy Surveyor, H. M. Rigby, M.B.E., T.D.

Agents

Messrs. Clutton, 5 Great College Street, Westminster, S.W.1; Messrs. Smith, Gore & Co., 4 Cowley Street, Westminster, S.W.1; Messrs. Chesterton & Sons, 116 Kensington High Street, W.8; Messrs, Hunt & Steward, 45 Parliament Street, Westminster, S.W.1.

CIVIL SERVICE COMMISSION

23 Savile Row, W.1

The Civil Service Commission was first constituted by Order in Council in 1855. The Commissioners' primary function is to test the qualifications of persons proposed to be appointed to situations in Her Majesty's Civil Establishments: in addition they have from time to time undertaken certain examinations of candidates for other public services.

First Commissioner, Sir George Mallaby, K.C.M.G., O.B.E. £5,015
Commissioner, Secretary and Establishment Officer, J. C. Seddon .... £2,865 to £3,565
Deputy Establishment Officer, C. J. Floyd £2,237 to £2,572
Assistant Secretaries, P. J. M. Fry; G. M. Smeaton £2,237 to £2,572
Advisory Officer, Miss E. M. Young £2,237 to £2,572

Examinations Directorate

Commissioner and Director of Examinations, Dr. H. A. Needham, C.B.E. .... £2,865 to £3,565
Senior Assistant Directors of Examinations, F. J. R. Bartlett; F. Bateman; K. M. Reader £2,527 to £2,813
Assistant Directors of Examinations, R. N. Burton; J. R. Foster; R. H. Howorth; Miss B. M. J. Hurden; A. S. Pratley; Miss E. M. Pumfrey; Miss A. C. Wanstall; Dr. W. E. Wightman £1,336 to £2,522
Chief Superintendent of Examinations, H. Kroll, O.B.E. .... £2,237 to £2,572

Scientific and Engineering Directorate

Commissioner, Scientific and Engineering Adviser, Sir Frederick Brundrett, K.C.B., K.B.E. (*part-time*) £2,950
Deputy Commissioners, T. A. Oxley; J. D. S. Rawlinson, O.B.E. .... £3,340 to £3,665
Assistant Commissioners, J. W. A. Chorley, O.B.E. (£2,865 to £3,215), C. F. Blanks (£1,954 to £2,760), D. A. R. Hall (£2,293 to £2,628).

Civil Service Selection Board

Commissioner and Chairman, J. H. T. Goldsmith, C.B.E. (*part-time*) £2,852
Assistant Commissioner and Deputy to the Chairman, K. A. G. Murray .... £2,865 to £3,215
Principal, M. J. Moriarty .... £1,959 to £2,711

Research Unit

Principal Psychologist, Miss M. S. Stevenson £1,959 to £2,628

Accountant, H. Ingram .... £1,680 to £2,126
Senior Executive Officers, Miss L. M. Alessi; R. A. McKenzie; W. H. L. Mayer; G. A. Rochester; G. S. Wishart .... £1,680 to £2,126

COLONIAL OFFICE

The Church House, Great Smith Street, S.W.1
[Abbey: 1266]

The business of the Colonies was, until 1801, included in the functions of the Home Secretary, to be transferred in that year to the newly-created "Secretary for War." In 1854 the outbreak of the Russian War led to the appointment of a Secretary of State for the Colonies (to relieve the War Secretary of Colonial business).

Secretary of State for the Colonies, THE RT. HON. DUNCAN SANDYS, M.P. £5,000
Principal Private Secretary, N. B. J. Huijsman.
Assistant Private Secretary, D. F. Milton.

Parliamentary Private Secretary, J. H. Osborn M.P. . . . . unpaid
Minister of State for Colonial Affairs, THE MARQUESS OF LANSDOWNE £3,750
Parliamentary Under-Secretary of State, N. T. L. Fisher, M.C., M.P. £2,500
Permanent Under-Secretary of State, Sir Hilton Poynton, K.C.M.G. £6,950
Private Secretary, Miss M. Fairlie.
Deputy Under-Secretary, Sir John Martin, K.C.M.G. C.B., C.V.O. £4,950
Assistant Under-Secretaries, C. G. Eastwood, C.M.G.; W. B. L. Monson, C.M.G.; A. R. Thomas, C.M.G.; §C. Y. Carstairs, C.M.G.; A.N. Galsworthy, C.M.G.; T. Smith, C.M.G.; W. I. J. Wallace, C.M.G., O.B.E. £4,050
Assistant Secretaries, § W. A. Morris, C.M.G.; J. E. Marnham, C.M.G., M.C., T.D.; J. D. Higham, C.M.G.; F. D. Webber, C.M.G., M.C., T.D.; §N. D. Watson, C.M.G.; B. O. B. Gidden, C.M.G. (*Establishment and Organization Officer*); A. M. MacKintosh, C.M.G.; J. W. Vernon; *H. P. Hall, C.M.G., M.B.E.; J. M. Kisch; *I. B. Watt; A. Campbell; T. C. Jerrom; J. N. A. Armitage-Smith; D. Williams; R. W. Piper; §J. T. A. Howard-Drake; N. B. J. Huijsman; D. J. Kirkness; *C. S. Roberts; §S. P. Whitley. £2,800 to £3,500

Advisory and Specialist Staff

Senior Economic Adviser, †P. Selwyn £2,800 to £3,500
Chief Information Officer, P. R. Noakes, O.B.E. £2,800 to £3,500
Press Officer, R.W. Francis . . . . . £2,172 to £2,807
Principal Information Officer, R. H. Young £2,172 to £2,507
Senior Information Officers, L.W. Forsdick; †Mrs. N. Good; †E. M. Glover . . . . £1,615 to £2,061
Legal Adviser, J. C. McPetrie, C.M.G., O.B.E. £4,950
Assistant Legal Advisers, J. A. Peck; A. R. Rushford, C.M.G. . . . . £2,900 to £3,500
Senior Legal Assistants, D. G. Gordon-Smith; I. C. Saul; H. Steel; M. G. De Winton, C.B.E., M.C. £2,239 to £2,800
Temporary Senior Legal Assistants, T. H. H. Perrott; I. H. Cruchley, O.C.; Sir Arthur Grattan-Bellew, C.M.G., Q.C. . . . . £2,239 to £2,800
Librarian, B. Cheeseman, O.B.E. . £2,172 to £2,507
Deputy Librarian, C.D. Overton. £1,615 to £2,001
Inspector General of Colonial Police, †Sir Ivo Stourton, C.M.G., O.B.E. . . . . £2,800 to £3,150
Deputy Inspector General of Colonial Police, J. W. Deegan, C.M.G., C.V.O. . . . . . . £1,894 to £2,646
Principals, R. Terrell; A. McN. Webster; J. R. Downie; H.W. Atterbury, O.B.E. (*Deputy Establishment Officer*); *J. D. Hennings; I. H. Harris; A. J. Fairclough; C. G. Gibbs; E. C. Burr; §G. W. Jamieson; P. J. Kitcatt; *R. H. Hobden, D.F.C.; §K. J. Neal, O.B.E.; W. H. Formoy; J. W. Stacpoole; D. J. Derx; *W. A. Ward; §J. H. Robertson; D. J. C. Jones; E. R. Hammer; §J. A. Sankey; J. E. Whitelegg; §W. S. Ryrie; I. S. Wheatley; E. G. Donohoe; W. S. Carter, C.V.O.; D. A. Shepherd; R. G. Pettitt; P. V. Dixon; B. L. Barder; Miss M. Z. Terry; Hon. A. P. H. T. Cumming-Bruce O.B.E.; M. L. Woods; J. W.Widdell, O.B.E.; T. M. Jenkins £1,894 to £2,646
Temporary Principals, H. C. Baker; Maj.-Gen. D. Dunlop, C.B., C.B.E. (*Chief Security Officer*); D.W. Russell; Lt.-Col. W. M. L. Adler, O.B.E. (*Military Staff Officer*); J. Watson, O.B.E.; R. F. A. Shegog; N. L. Mayle; I. M. Glennie; M. F. Page, C.B.E.; L. G. Maurice; K. W. S. Mackenzie, C.M.G. £1,894 to £2,646
Chief Executive Officers, D. K. Malone, M.B.E.; S. A. Gibbins, M.B.E.; K. O. H. Osborne £2,172 to £2,507
Senior Executive Officers, L. Abbott; C. E. R. Darby, E.D.; J. P. Mullarky; J. H. H. Vaughan; B. H. J. Lane; D. F. Smith; W. G. Gathercole; D. R. Lockhart . . . . £1,615 to £2,061
Research Officers (Economic), †Mrs. M. E. Maccoll; †J. Inman . . . . £1,894 to £2,646
Controller of Overseas Communications, S. H. Field. £2,172 to £2,507
Controller of Office Services, F. C. Lamacq, I.S.O., M.B.E. . . . . £2,061 to £2,507
Accountant, L. H. Day . . . . £1,615 to £2,061
§On loan to other Government Departments.
*Serving Overseas.
†Temporary.

COMMONWEALTH DEVELOPMENT CORPORATION

33 Hill Street, W.1
[Mayfair: 8484]

The Corporation was formerly known as the Colonial Development Corporation. The change of name was effected by the Commonwealth Development Act, 1963, which also restored the Corporation's full powers of operation in all those countries which had achieved independence within the Commonwealth since 1948.

Under the original Overseas Resources Development Act of 1948 the Corporation was charged with securing development in dependent Commonwealth territories at that date with a view to increasing their general productive capacity and trade. It is authorised to borrow up to £160,000,000.

Chairman (part-time), The Lord Howick of Glendale, G.C.M.G., K.C.V.O. £5,250
Deputy Chairman (part-time), J. F. Prideaux, O.B.E. £1,500
Members (part-time), A. P. H. Aitken; Sir John Elliot; A. Gaitskell, C.M.G.; The Lord Ogmore, P.C., T.D.; Sir Clem Pleass, K.C.M.G., K.C.V.O., K.B.E.; Sir Eric Tansley, C.M.G. . . . . . *each* £1,000

COMMONWEALTH RELATIONS OFFICE

Downing Street, S.W.1
[Whitehall: 2323]

Secretary of State for Commonwealth Relations, THE RIGHT HON. DUNCAN SANDYS, M.P. . . . £5,000
Private Sec., W. I. McIndoe.
Ceremonial and Protocol Sec., Lt.-Col. J M. Hugo, C.V.O., O.B.E. £2,040
Minister of State, THE DUKE OF DEVONSHIRE, M.C. £3,750
Parliamentary Under-Secretary of State, J. D. R. T. Tilney, T.D., M.P. £2,500
Permanent Under-Secretary of State, Sir Saville Garner, K.C.M.G. £7,015
Private Secretary, A. J. Hunter.
Deputy Under-Secretaries of State, Sir Algernon Rumbold, K.C.M.G., C.I.E.; Sir Arthur Snelling, K.C.M.G., K.C.V.O. £5,015
Assistant Under-Secretaries of State, W. A. B. Hamilton, C.M.G.; Sir Neil Pritchard, K.C.M.G.; G. E. B. Shannon, C.M.G.; M. R. Metcalf, C.M.G., O.B.E.; G. P. Hampshire, C.M.G.; G. W. St. J. Chadwick, C.M.G.; L. B. Walsh Atkins, C.M.G., C.V.O.; C. S. Pickard; R. W. D. Fowler, C.M.G.; R. H. Belcher, C.M.G.; E. G. Norris, C.M.G.; G. Kimber, C.M.G.; L. J. D. Wakely, O.B.E.; R. C. C. Hunt; N. Aspin £4,115
Director of Information Services, Maj.-Gen. W. H. A. Bishop, C.B., C.M.G., C.V.O., O.B.E. £3,865
Principal Staff Officer to the Secretary of State, Maj.-Gen. C. R. Price, C.B., C.B.E. £3,715
Assistant Secretaries, G. E. Crombie, C.M.G.; D. M. Cleary; C. G. Costley-White, C.M.G.; E. L. Sykes; H. E. Davies; B. R. Curson; R. L. D. Jasper, C.M.G.; J. C. Morgan; H. G. M. Bass; H. A. Twist, O.B.E.; F. A. K. Harrison; M. J. Moynihan, M.C.; M. E. Allen, C.V.O.; E. N. Larmour; W. G. Lamarque, M.B.E.; T. L. Crosthwait, M.B.E.; B. J. Greenhill; T. W. Keeble; J. R. A. Bottomley; J. O. Moreton, M.C.; G. S. Whitehead, M.V.O.; J. D. Fraser, C.V.O., M.B.E.; D. A. Scott; S. J. G. Fingland; H. Smedley, M.B.E.; R.W. Newsam, C.V.O.; W. J. Smith; D. L. Cole, M.C.; V. C. Martin; R. C. Ormerod; G. D. Anderson; A. R. Adair, C.V.O., M.B.E.; P. Gautrey, C.V.O.; J. S. Gandee, O.B.E.; H. S. H. Stanley; E. G. Le Tocq; K. A. East; Miss E. J. Emery; W. J. Coe; W. S. Bates; A. A. Golds, M.V.O.; C. E. Diggines; R. G. Britten; A. H. Reed; Miss L. E. T. Storar;

J. D. B. Shaw, M.V.O.; J. R. Williams; M. Scott, M.V.O.; F. S. Miles.......... £2,865 to £3,565
Adviser, Sir Charles Dixon, K.C.M.G., K.C.V.O., O.B.E.
Principals, G. J. Price-Jones; J. Gordon, O.B.E.; R. G. Chisholm; P. A. Carter; W. R. Bickford, M.B.E.; J. Bourn; L. G. Heptinstall; T. J. O'Brien, M.C.; D. J. King; J. A. Molyneux; J. E. A. Miles, O.B.E.; A. J. Brown; K. R. Crook; B. G. Smallman; R. Walker; G. L. Simmons, M.V.O.; M. H. G. Rogers; F. Mills; W. L. Allinson, M.V.O.; T. W. Aston; J. W. Nicholas; J. K. Hickman; R. B. Dorman; D. G. R. Bentliff; M. McMullen; O. G. Forster, M.V.O.; The Viscount Dunrossil; M. P. Preston; M. K. Ewans; E. V. Vines; S. Fryer; J. F. Barrow; P. J. S. Moon; T. D. O'Leary; W. I. McIndoe; W. Peters, M.V.O., M.B.E.; R. H. Oakeley; R. A. R. Barltrop; K. F. X. Burns; G. G. Collins; J. A. Davidson; E. O. Laird, M.B.E.; Miss M. Archer, M.B.E.; D. E. Richards; Brig. G. F. Lushington, C.B.E.; O. R. Blair; Cdr. J. E. Smallwood, R.N.(*ret.*); G. V. Britten, C.B.E.; J. N. Allan; J. A. Scott, M.V.O.; A. H. Brind; S. F. St. C. Duncan; M. A. McConville, M.B.E.; W. J. Watts; A. S. Fair; Mrs. M. B. Chitty; Air Commodore F. F. Rainsford, C.B.E., D.F.C.; C. H. Imray; J. A. G. Banks; R. C. Cox, M.B.E.; S. W. F. Martin; F. A. Reynolds; P G. P. D. Fullerton; D. H. Christie; P. A. Grier; A. B. Moore; N. A. I. French; I. A. C. Kinnear; A. C. Watson; D. Connelly........ £1,959 to £2,711
Temporary Principals, H. A. Arthington-Davy, M.B.E.; A. W. Redpath, C.B.E.; H. G. Hammett; H. R. E. Browne, C.M.G., O.B.E.; W. D. Drysdale, M.B.E.; V. E. Davies, O.B.E.; W. F. G. Le Bailly; T. J. Lennard, M.B.E.; C. E. Wool-Lewis, O.B.E.; C. W. F. Footman, C.M.G.; H. R. M. Beattie; H. G. Turner, C.M.G.; J. W. H. O'Regan, O.B.E.; E. H. M. Counsell, C.B.E.; E. G. Lewis, O.B.E.; Sir Charles Duke, K.C.M.G., C.I.E., O.B.E.; D. F. B. Le Breton; P. C. Petrie; P. W. Heap £1,959 to £2,711
Principal Executive Officer, F. H. Davey, O.B.E. (*Accountant-General and Controller of Pension Funds*)............................ £3,065
Senior Chief Executive Officers, R. G. Tracy, O.B.E. (*Deputy Accountant-General*); W. Clarkson, O.B.E., I.S.O................. £2,683 to £2,865
Chief Executive Officers, W. R. Lythgo; Miss M. L. Dalgleish, M.B.E.; N. A. Sales, M.B.E.; H. J. Turner; K. M. Critchley; R. H. Davies, M.B.E., D.F.C.; P. F. Walker; W. D. J. Morgan; D. W. H. Wickson, M.B.E.; L. Collett, M.V.O.; J. A. Pugh £2,237 to £2,572
Senior Executive Officers, R. J. Hicks; R. J. Jenkins, M.B.E.; D. R. Avery; A. E. Huttly; C. A. Lovitt, M.B.E.; J. A. Stockwell, M.B.E.; J. E. S. Clayden; R. R. G. Watts; D. H. C. Phillips; K. D. Forster; D. H. Fowler, M.B.E.; G. R. Lee; D. W. Goodman; F. R. Evans; J. H. D. Gambold; D. M. R. Skinner; L. G. Smith; C. G. R. Sewell, M.B.E.; S. Wellington; C. J. Hanbury; T. Bambury, M.V.O.; R. W. S. Carr; A. T. Smith; J. Plant; B. Rose; H. Thompson £1,670 to £2,126
Legal Adviser, W. L. Dale, C.M.G.
Assistant Legal Adviser, H. L. M. Oxley, O.B.E. £2,965 to £3,565
Senior Legal Assistants, C. H. Butterfield; Sir Orby Mootham................ £2,304 to £2,865
Chief Information Officers (*A*), J. T. Hughes, O.B.E.; J. S. Ellis, O.B.E............... £2,865 to £3,565
Chief Information Officers, (*B*) D. F. Kerr, C.V.O., O.B.E.; R. McC. Samples, D.S.O., O.B.E.; A. C. Hall; W. S. G. Smele; D. D. Condon; T. A. H. Scott; Col. I. C. Edwards, C.V.O., O.B.E., T.D......................... £2,683 to £2,865
Principal Information Officers, R. Hickling; J. Borthwick, M.B.E.; E. Bailey; F. R. Morgan; A. J. Gilmour; B. D. Brown; Cdr. R. D. Wall, R.N.; D. R. F. Brower; Mrs. M. E. Barraclough, O.B.E.; H. E. Rigney; R. I. Hall; D. A. Wehl; J. C. E. Hyde; A. D. Trounson; W. D. Nightingale; G. J. A. Slater; Miss E. M. Booker, M.B.E.; J. R. E. Carr-Gregg; W. S. Ashford; C. G. Mortlock; P. J. F. Storrs; J. H. Reiss; G. d'Arnaud Taylor; J. McQuiggan, M.B.E.; R. W. Baxter; F. O. Darvall, C.B.E.,; R. P. Ross Williamson; A. R. D'Astugues; F. W. Bustin (*temp.*) £2,237 to £2,572
Senior Information Officers, J. L. Hayden, O.B.E.; T. J. Sigsworth; E. M. Manvell; Miss O. M. Barton, M.B.E.; E. Young; K. J. Maconochie; G. E. Bell; L. R. H. Rowdon; Miss R. A. Vining; D. B. L. Chudleigh; J. A. Potter; W. D. Symington; C. E. Greatorex, M.B.E.; D. K. Middleton; J. A. Clewley, M.B.E.; W. E. Hall; G. Needham; J. A. Chaplin, D.S.O., D.F.C.; P. B. Porter; S. G. Chandler; J. S. Jasper; N. A. Leadbitter. £1,670 to £2,126
Temporary Senior Information Officers, C. Le G. Eaton; J. D. G. Walker-Brash; Col. T. L. Laister, O.B.E.; R. Hayward; G. W. Baker; H. Kay £1,670 to £2,126
Senior Research Officer, A. A. Halliley, M.B.E. £1,959 to £2,628
Liaison Officer with the Ministry of Defence, Capt. J. A. W. Tothill, D.S.C., R.N. (*ret*)........ £1,402

Commonwealth Relations Office Library

Librarian, *B. Cheeseman, O.B.E........... £2,747
Deputy Librarian, C. D. Overton......... £2,126

India Office Library

King Charles Street, S.W.1

Founded by the Honourable East India Company in 1801. Oriental Library containing 250,000 printed books and 15,000 MSS. in both European and Oriental (mostly Indian) languages.

Librarian, S. C. Sutton, C.B.E.............. £3,065

*Also for Colonial Office.

COMMONWEALTH TELECOMMUNICATIONS BOARD

28 Pall Mall, S.W.1
[Whitehall: 5511]

On May 31, 1949, the Commonwealth Telecommunications Board was incorporated by Act of Parliament, and superseded the former Commonwealth Communications Council.

Chairman, D. Donaldson.
Members, Col. D. McMillan, C.B., O.B.E. (*United Kingdom*); H. A. L. Pattison, C.B.E. (*Canada*); H. A. de Dassel, O.B.E. (*Australia*); T. N. Morrison (*New Zealand*); M. V. Pai (*India*); C. K. Reheem (*Pakistan (Observer)*); H. E. Seneviratne (*Ceylon*); J. H. Wagstaff (*Federation of Malaya*); G. T. Anstey, C.B. (*Rhodesia & Nyasaland*); A. H. Sheffield, C.B.E. (*Other Commonwealth Territories*).
Secretary-General, W. Stubbs, C.B.E., M.C.

CONSERVANCY BOARDS

THAMES CONSERVANCY

2–3 Norfolk Street, Strand, W.C.2
[Temple Bar: 4982]

The conservation of the River Thames was originally granted to twelve Conservators in 1857. In 1909 the Port of London Authority took over all rights, powers and duties of the Conservators in respect of the river below Teddington. The Conservators of the River Thames under the Thames Conservancy Acts, 1932 to 1959, now have jurisdiction over the River Thames from Cricklade in Wiltshire to a point about 265 yards below Teddington Lock; and under the Land Drainage Act, 1930, the Conservators are constituted the Drainage Board of the Thames Catchment Area. The principal duties of the Conservators as a Navigation Authority are the maintenance and improvement of the navigation, and the registration and regulation of craft; the Conservators also exercise jurisdiction for the prevention of pollution over the Thames Catchment Area, and over the fisheries in the River Thames from Cricklade to Teddington. Their income for these purposes is derived from various tolls, fees, rents, licences, payments from the Metropolitan Water Board and certain water undertakers, and contributions by the councils of various riparian counties and county boroughs in the Thames Valley; while the funds for carrying out the powers and duties of a Drainage Board are obtained by precept from the county councils and county borough councils as prescribed by the Land Drainage Act. The Board consists of 41 Conservators and their term of office is three years.

Chairman, Rt. Hon. Sir Richard Nugent, Bt., M.P.
Vice-Chairman, Col. F. A. Sudbury, O.B.E., E.R.D.
Secretary, Solicitor and Parliamentary Officer, G. E. Walker, O.B.E.
Chief Engineer, H. C. Bowen, O.B.E., T.D.
Treasurer and Accountant, E. A. James.

FORTH CONSERVANCY BOARD

Instituted by the Forth Conservancy Order Confirmation Act, 1921, for the preservation, maintenance and improvement of the River and Firth of Forth within the limits prescribed in the Order.

Chairman, The Earl of Mar and Kellie.
Clerk and Treasurer, M. D. Kennedy, W.S., Benview, Wellside Place, Falkirk.
Engineers, Messrs. Leslie & Reid, C.E., 53 Manor Place, Edinburgh.
Marine Superintendent, Lt.-Cdr. R. M. Roberts, D.S.C., R.N. (*ret.*).

COTTON BOARD

Royal Exchange 6th Floor, Manchester 2

Established under the Cotton Industry Development Council Order, 1948.

Chairman, F. Rostron, M.B.E.
Other Independent Members, J. Broatch, C.B.E.; J. C. Robinson.
Members representing the Employers, W. T. Winterbottom, C.B.E.; J. M. H. Grey; G. D. Hughes; R. T. Alcock.
Members representing Employees, L. T. Wright; L. Sharp, M.B.E.; J.W.Whitworth; J. King.
Director-General, T. D. F. Powell.

CROWN AGENTS FOR OVERSEA GOVERNMENTS AND ADMINISTRATIONS

4 Millbank, Westminster, S.W.1
[Abbey: 7730]

(*Stock Transfer Office*, Lloyd's Bank Buildings, Moorgate, E.C.2) [Central 8575]
(*Shipping Department* (*City Branch*), 77 and 78 Gracechurch Street, E.C.3. [Mansion House 2016]

The Crown Agents are the officially appointed business and financial agents of a large number of Governments and public authorities. These include independent Governments such as Bahrain, Ceylon, Cyprus, Ghana, Jamaica, Jordan, Libya, the Federation of Malaya, the Federal and Regional Governments of Nigeria, Sierra Leone, the Somali Republic, Tanganyika, Trinidad and Uganda, as well as all the territories overseas under British administration or trusteeship. Other authorities for whom they act include the United Nations, municipalities, universities, and public utilities such as railway, electricity, broadcasting and water undertakings. The office is not a Department of the United Kingdom Government, and no vote for it comes before the United Kingdom Parliament. It is self-supporting, its funds being derived from fees charged to principals from whom instructions are received direct.

The work of the Crown Agents' office includes the purchase, inspection, shipment and insurance of engineering plant and equipment and of stores of all kinds; the design of engineering structures; the issue and management of loans and the investment of funds; the payment of salaries to officers on leave; the engagement of staff for certain oversea Government appointments; the booking of passages for Government officers and their families; and many other functions.

Senior Crown Agent, Sir Stephen Luke, K.C.M.G.
Assistant Crown Agent and Engineer in Chief, Sir James Farquharson, K.B.E.
Assistant Crown Agent, W. G. Bawden, C.B.E.

CROWN ESTATE COMMISSIONERS

Whitehall, S.W.1
[Trafalgar: 2211]

THE CROWN ESTATE (formerly The Crown Lands).—The Land Revenues of the Crown in *England and Wales* have been collected on the public account since 1760, when George III. surrendered them and received a fixed annual payment or *Civil List*. At the time of the surrender the gross revenues amounted to about £89,000 and the net return to about £11,000.

In the year ended March 31, 1963, the total Receipts by the Commissioners were £4,169,234. The Expenditure (including property tax allowed) was £673,950. The sum of £2,380,000 was paid to the Exchequer in 1962–63 as *Surplus Revenue*, being a net sum from which no deductions have to be made for administration.

The Land Revenues in *Ireland* have been carried to the Consolidated Fund since 1820; from April 1, 1923, as regards Southern Ireland, they have been collected and administered by the Irish Free State (Republic of Ireland).

The Land Revenues in *Scotland* were transferred to the Commissioners in 1833.

First Commissioner and Chairman (*part-time*), The Earl of Perth, P.C.
Second Commissioner (*and Secretary*) J. A. Sutherland-Harris, C.B. £5,000
Commissioners (*part-time*), M. F. Berry; The Earl of Bradford, T.D.; D. H. Cameron of Lochiel, T.D.; W. C. Farnsworth, C.B.E.; Sir Edward Gillett; The Lord Williams.
Deputy Commissioner, H. A. C. Gill £2,800 to £3,500
Assistant Commissioner, P. S. Bolshaw £1,894 to £2,646
Crown Estate Surveyor, L. E. C. Osborne, C.B.E. £3,215
Deputy Crown Estate Surveyor, E. J. Shaw £2,228 to £2,563
Clerk to the Board and Establishment Officer, J. Griffiths .... £2,172 to £2,507
Accountant and Receiver-General, F. V. Mills £1,615 to £2,061
Senior Executive Officers, D. W. Broughton; A. R. Brown; W. H. Cosslett; C. J. Heather; E. F. Richards; C. R. Smith; D. T. Hunt (*Edinburgh*) £1,615 to £2,061
Legal Adviser and Solicitor, J. G. Allan £2,900 to £3,500
Senior Legal Assistant, A. W. Robinson £2,239 to £2,800
Solicitor, Scotland, N. C. Grant.
Director of Forestry, R. Lindsay, M.V.O., B.E.M.

Windsor Estate

Surveyor and Deputy Ranger, Maj. A. W. Haig, M.V.O.
Director of Gardens, Sir Eric Savill, K.C.V.O., C.B.E., M.C.

BOARD OF CUSTOMS AND EXCISE

King's Beam House, Mark Lane, E.C.3
[Mansion House: 1515]

Commissioners of Customs were first appointed in 1671 and housed by the King in London, the present "Long Room" in the Custom House, Lower Thames Street, E.C.3, replacing that built by Charles II and rebuilt after destruction by fire in 1718 and 1814. The Excise Department was formerly under the Inland Revenue Department, and was amalgamated with the Customs Department on April 1, 1909.

The Board

Chairman, Sir John Anderson, K.B.E., C.B. .. £6,950
Private Sec., P. G. Wallis.
Deputy Chairman, Sir Douglas Owen, K.B.E., C.B. £4,950
Director of Establishment and Organization and Commissioner, J. E. B. Finlay, C.B., O.B.E., T.D. £4,050
Commissioners, C. H. Blake; G. Imms; K. B. Pepper (*Joint Secretaries*) £4,050

Secretaries' Office

Assistant Secretaries, A. R. Ashford, C.M.G.; H. F. Christopherson; C. T. Cross; G. C. English; H. F. Hewett; J. K. Hulme, O.B.E.; Mrs. D. C. L. Johnstone, C.B.E.; E. A. Knight; F. Lee; G. G. Leighton-Boyce; J. Mair; T. H. Pratt; R. W. Radford, M.B.E.; C. H. Veale; L. J. White; J. M. Woolf................£2,800 to £3,500
Principals, A. Aldous; R. Bamfield; A. H. Barrett; N. E. Campion; H. D. Davis, D.S.O., M.B.E.; G. B. Diamond; E. L. Fletcher; J. C. Fletcher; F. J. French, O.B.E., D.F.C., A.F.C.; P. N. Gerosa; A. R. H. Glover; N. E. Godfrey; E. N. Griffiths; L. S. Gross; F. T. Hallett; D. J. Harbour; L. D. Hawken; R. J. Hayman; S. H. P. Holt; J. C. Leeming; A. J. Lippitt; K. C. Messere; J. Midgley; A. C. Ralph; B. Rose; M. H. Smith; M.W. Townley; D. Turnell; W. L. Vonderahe; J. E.White................£1,897 to £2,646
Controller of Valuation Branch, R. H. Watson £3,150
Deputy Controllers of Valuation Branch, F. J. Kumpf; E. J. Piper................£2,618 to £2,800
Chief Executive Officers, L. A. Barber; S. Bellew; S. A. Cheetham; A. O. Davies; I. E. de Groot; B. T. Dobson; F. G. Evans; H. F. Johnson; C. H. Gill; H. A. King; L. L. Kirby; T. H. Morley; C.W. Mothersill; A. Radcliffe; W. A. J. Taft; G. Tiplin; H. J. White; L. A. Widden; G. E. Wright................£2,172 to £2,507
Senior Executive Officers, J. G. Acton; Miss E. Armstrong; Miss E. M. Baker; J. Barber; F. E. Bartlett; W. A. Bassett; H. T. Bigg; Mrs. D. Biggam; P. Calvert; J. Clary; L. W. Cousins; Miss M. I. Crane; D. K. Dawson; J. K. Dornom; F. D. Garnett; W. J. Glover; H.W. Goodfellow; R. W. Grimer; A. H. Hart; H. F. Hercock; Miss B. T. Huggett; Miss S. A. Jacobs; R. L. Jeffery; S. F. Jordan; H. S. R. Lindsey; D. G. Lovibond; D. E. Maidwell; F. G. Marshall; S. G. Mier; Miss G. E. Moger; W. Newman; B. Nicholls; S. N. Owen; G. Payne; K. W. V. Payne; K. C. Piper; R. J. Powell; D. C. Priddon; E. F. Reader; L. J. Rose; Miss B. E. Smith; A. Strachan; Miss J. M. Tobias; A. C. Vince; W. T.C. Wakefield; E. G.Webster; G. S.Welch; Miss E. K.White; Miss M.Wood; R. H. Yates £1,615 to £2,061
Superintendent of Registry, A. J. Ellis, M.B.E. £1,615 to £2,061

Intelligence Branch and Library

Chief of Branch and Library (Asst. Secretary), R. J. S. Cory................£2,800 to £3,500
Principals, C. Bamfield; C. Freedman £1,894 to £2,646
Chief Executive Officer, R. Coleman £2,172 to £2,507
Press and Information Officer, M. Nockies £2,172 to £2,507
Intelligence Officer and Librarian, R. C. Jarvis, I.S.O. £1,615 to £2,061

Solicitor's Office

Solicitor, D. J. Willson, C.B.E., T.D.........£4,950
Assistant Solicitors, R. K. F. Hutchings; J. N. B. Lainé; E. G. Mosely; J.W. Reid; C. A. Ryves; J. L. Willis, T.D.............£2,900 to £3,500
Senior Legal Assistants, J. L. Bowen, M.C.; V. E. Eaton; W. L. Fearnehough, T.D.; G. F. Gloak; V. E. Jenvey; G. Krikorian; F. J. de T. Mandley; P. C. R. Noble, O.B.E.; W. Rawlinson; J. L. Stewart; P. J. Sutton; F. Townley; F. N.Walker £2,239 to £2,800

Chief Inspector's Office

Chief Inspector, B. Mitchell, C.B...........£3,863
Dep. Ch. Insp., L. F. W.Lawrence; W. D.Leckonby £3,325
Principal Inspectors, E. P. Brown; H. Davey; W. F. Joyce; G. N. Madgen; E. L. Martin; W. D. Milne; E. D. Roberts; B. F. Sander; S. Sparke; W. C. V. Tait.............................£3,150
Senior Inspectors, R. H. Abbott; S. R. J. Abraham; S. G. Allchin; D. C. Armstrong; W. A. R. Armstrong; T. R. Barber; H. D. Beak; N. Brazil; A. J. Brown; F. Clegg; N. E. Ellis; D. Ewings; B. M. Field; F. R. Frost; A. O. Gibson, I.S.O.; T. C. Gosling; L. A. Hardham, T.D.; R. Hopwood; J. G. Howells; J. T. Hughes; R. T. Jenkinson; P. C. Kerridge, M.C.; J. K. Kidson; K. E. Lefever; W. W. Loudon; W. McKeown; R. P. Outhwaite; B. S. R. Penney; F. Pilkington; J. D. Price; C. Rice; G. E. A. Rice; E. R. J. Scarrett; R. E. Skilbeck; W. Slatter; J. P. Smith; R. B. Spence; D. B. Stanley; F. Turner; W. E. Tyzzer; G. A.Wagstaffe; W. L.Wells; K. P.Wharton; G. W. Winsor £2,681 to £2,900
Inspectors, G. N. Austin; M. K. Barford; A. R. Beach; H. C. Chapman; W. R. Chave; G. W. Cox; N. Dixon; R. A. Ewin; G. J. Gale; R. E. Giles; J. Henderson; S. J. House; F. W. Jones; H. C. Kenway; G. G. Lawrance; J. K. Lawson; W.H.Leach; M. H. Macfarlane; P. P. McNamara; D. C. McNeil; T. R. Moore, M.M.; R. F. Mountjoy; R. N. Reeve; D. C. Restorick; D. R. R. Robinson; L. J. Shew; J. D. Spence; W. Surtees; C. E. Wilson ...£2,172 to £2,507

Accountant and Comptroller-General's Office

Accountant and Comptroller-General, L. E. Dove £3,750
Deputy Accountant-General, G. Wilson.....£3,150
Assistant Accountants-General, K. J. Macrae; S. R. Richards, O.B.E.............£2,618 to £2,800
Chief Accountants, S. J. T. Beck; C. Birkin; W. M. Cowper; R. S. Graddon; E. B. W. Johnston; H. A. O'Neill; W. G.Wright. £2,172 to £2,507
Accountants, Miss D. L. Banwell; S. Best; R. F. Boyce; F. E. Butler; W. J. Cannon, M.B.E.; D. L. Carpenter; R. E. Collett; D.W. P. Crooks; R. Dutton; T. E. Ellerington; Miss O. L. Fuller; H.W. Gales, M.B.E.; L. Gregory; G. S. Harriss; A. C. Holdstock; J. H. Oliver; C. A. Pilgrim; Miss E. M. Scotchmer; R. D. Shearer; R. F. Snowdon; D. Vandenbergh; R.Williamson £1,615 to £2,061

Statistical Office

Controller, E. B. Thomson, O.B.E. £2,618 to £2,800
Deputy Controllers, J. M. Boreham; D. R. King £2,172 to £2,507
Senior Executive Officers, W. H. Gorton; J. C. Lewis, D.S.C.; C. A. Plumb; S. C. Slade; C. G. Smith; J. R.Williamson; S. C.Wood; W. L. Woodliffe £1,615 to £2,061

Office of Inspector-General of Waterguard

Insp.-Gen. of Waterguard, C. M. Douglas ..£3,325
Dep. Insp.-Gen., R. Beswick; T. R. Snellgrove, O.B.E...............................£2,900
Inspectors, L. Battersby; F. Coaker; J.W. Edmonson; H. L. Ford; F. Hanson; E. J. Hulbert; C. M. Porter; N. A. Ramsay; W. J. Tasker; S.Webster £2,172 to £2,507
Asst. Inspectors, D. Barnard; J. W. H. Berry; A. E. Burnham; R. Colling; J. G. Davies; E. H. Elliott; W. E. Hopkins; T. L. McCarthy; R. Mould; R. F. Stephenson; J. N. White. £1,539 to £1,903

Stores Branch

Superintendent, C. F. Burrell, M.B.E. £1,615 to £2,061

Collectors of Customs and Excise and Waterguard Superintendents

England and Wales

Birmingham: Higher Collector, H. F. J. Clapson (*c*); *Senior Assistant Collector*, K. C. Newnham (*e*); *Assistant*, E. T. C. Joyce (*f*).
Brighton: E. P. Furby (*e*).
Bristol: Higher Collector, J. Amos (*c*); *Senior Assistant*, P. J. Muir (*e*); *Assistant Collector*, H. C. Reid (*f*); *Asst. Waterguard Supt.*, J. M. Cutler (*g*).
Cardiff and Newport: B. W. Eames (*e*); *Assistant*, C. B. E. Williams (*f*); *Waterguard Supt.*, G. R. Elliott (*f*).

Chester: A. A. Brack (*e*); *Assistant Collector*, H. J. Webb (*f*).
Douglas: (*Collector-Surveyor*): D. R. Cashin (*h*).
Dover: T. D. Crellin (*e*); *Assistant*, E. F. Elfick (*f*); *Waterguard Supt.* F. Jackson (*f*); *Asst. Waterguard Supt.*, J. R. Cooper (*g*).
Harwich: W. A. Stubbles (*e*); *Assistant*, S. Cooper (*f*); *Waterguard Supt.*, A. F. Mathews (*f*); *Asst. Waterguard Supt.*, J. K. Kennedy (*g*).
Hull: Higher Collector, S. F. Howard (*c*); *Senior Assistant*, G. D. Laws, M.B.E., D.S.C. (*e*); *Assistant Collector*, R.W. H. Baxter (*f*); *Waterguard Supt.*, C.W. Harrison (*f*); *Asst. Waterguard Supt.*, P. H. J. Ryan (*g*).
Leeds: Higher Collector, S. L. Smith (*c*); *Senior Assistant*, J. Lavery (*e*); *Assistant*, W. D. Doyle (*f*).
Liverpool: P. Fallon (*b*); *Deputy Collector*, E. W. Thompson (*c*); *Senior Assistant Collectors*, R. Davies; J. D. Reed; R. F. A. Webber (*e*); *Assistant Collectors*, F. J. Blunt; W. F. Egerton; G. A. Hughes (*f*); *Higher Waterguard Supt.*, N. E. McKinna, O.B.E. (*d*); *Deputy Waterguard Supt.*, R. Linford (*f*); *Asst. Waterguard Supts.*, O. Ford; H. P. Langley; W. E. Smith (*g*).
London Airports: Higher Collector, A. F. Davis (*c*); *Senior Assistant Collector*, W. Threlfall (*e*); *Assistant Collector*, C. W. Watson (*f*); *Higher Waterguard Supt.*, G. E. B. Morrison (*d*); *Deputy Waterguard Sutp.*, A. E. Fry (*f*).
London Port: F. G. J. Sherwin (*a*); *Deputy Collector*, G. W. Cossum (*c*); *Senior Assistant Collectors*, A. M. Brebner; R. Chapman; S. E. Macdonald; H. A. Shenton (*e*); *Assistant Collectors*, J. R. M. McCormack; J. E. Ruberry; H. F. Strevens; H. Tennant (*f*).
London Central: Higher Collector, R. B. Button (*c*); *Senior Assistant Collector*, W. R. Pickett (*e*); *Assistant Collector*, J. Hall (*f*).
London North: Higher Collector, L. R. N. David (*c*); *Senior Assistant Collector*, F.W. Perry (*b*); *Assistant Collector*, J. Hoile (*f*).
London South: Higher Collector, D. J. Jones (*c*); *Senior Assistant Collector*, L. J. Boulter (*e*); *Assistant Collector*, N. H. Harrild (*f*).
London West: Higher Collector, H. C. Lewis (*c*); *Senior Assistant Collector*, A. N. Lowe (*e*); *Assistant Collector*, C. S. Killingley (*f*).
Manchester: Higher Collector, O. C. Clark, O.B.E. (*c*); *Senior Assistant Collectors*, J. M. Carter; W. S. Stead (*e*); *Assistant Collector*, D. A. Jordan (*f*); *Waterguard Supt.*, W. C. Henderson (*f*).
Newcastle: Higher Collector, G. E. T. Harmer (*c*); *Senior Assistant*, R. V. J. Neeves (*e*); *Assistant Collector*, W. J. Campbell, M.B.E. (*f*); *Waterguard Supt.*, J. I. S. Downie (*f*); *Asst. Waterguard Supts.*, M. M. MacLaren (*North Shields*); B. Mitchell (*Middlesbrough*) (*g*).
Northampton: G.W. F. Short (*e*); *Assistant*, J. R. Allsopp (*f*).
Norwich: T. L. Christmas (*e*); *Assistant*, D. C. Rose (*f*).
Nottingham: Higher Collector, L. Payne (*c*); *Senior Assistant Collector*, J. C. Clemett (*e*); *Assistant Collector*, V. M. Brown (*f*).
Plymouth: S. C. Lawrence (*e*); *Assistant*, J. D. Adams (*f*); *Waterguard Supt.*, D. C. Morrison (*f*); *Asst. Waterguard Supt.*, L. Bulford (*g*).
Preston: A. B. Day (*e*); *Assistant*, E. F. W. Willis (*f*).
Reading: G. A. Jones (*e*); *Assistant*, C. J. Wilcox (*f*).
Sheffield: A. Borlace (*e*).
Southampton: Higher Collector, H. L. Burden (*c*); *Senior Assistant Collector*, J. S. H. Plummer (*e*); *Assistant Collector*, H. Peart (*f*); *Higher Waterguard Supt.*, G. T. Clarke (*d*); *Deputy Waterguard Supt.*, J. P. Williams (*f*); *Asst. Waterguard Supt.*, T. Hill (*g*).
Swansea: A. W. Rolte (*e*); *Asst. Waterguard Supt.*, W. G. Sutton (*g*).

Scotland

Aberdeen: W. Taylor (*e*); *Assistant*, G. H. Tyson (*f*); *Waterguard Supt.*, W. G. Shannon (*f*).
Dundee: H. T. Walker (*e*); *Assistant*, K.W. Thayer (*f*).
Edinburgh: Higher Collector, C. E. Jackson (*c*); *Senior Assistant Collector*, G. H. Moore (*e*); *Assistant Collector*, W. Welch (*f*); *Waterguard Supt.* (*Leith*), F. Gotts (*f*).
Glasgow: Higher Collector, A. S. Knight (*c*); *Senior Assistant Collectors*, T. J. Gilchrist; W. W. McHowat (*e*); *Assistant Collector*, L. Beaty (*f*); *Waterguard Supt.* J. Mc L. Crombie (*g*).
Greenock: W. N. Heasley (*e*); *Assistant*, R. L. Mitchell (*f*).
Inverness: J. R. Campbell (*e*); *Assistant Collector*, H. D. Thorne, M.B.E., T.D. (*f*).

Northern Ireland

Belfast: Higher Collector, J. Bell (*c*); *Senior Assistant Collector*, H. J. Dunhill (*e*); *Assistant Collector*, A. S. Lochhead (*f*); *Waterguard Supt.*, J. Howard (*f*); *Asst. Waterguard Supt.*, G. E. M. White (*g*).

London Waterguard

Superintendent of Waterguard, L. E. Kieran... £2,900
Deputy Waterguard Supts., J. Spence (*f*); D. Donald (*Gravesend*) (*f*).
Asst. Waterguard Supts., J. Grice; E. G. Richards (*g*).
Salaries:
(*a*) £3,600; (*b*) £3,375 (*c*) £3,150; (*d*) £2,800; (*e*) £2,681 to £2,900; (*f*) £2,172 to £2,507; (*g*) £1,539 to £1,903; (*h*) £1,615 to £2,055.

MINISTRY OF DEFENCE

Storey's Gate, S.W.1
[Whitehall: 7000]

The Ministry of Defence was formally constituted on January 1, 1947, under the *Ministry of Defence Act*, 1946. The Minister of Defence is responsible for the formulation and general application of a unified policy relating to the Armed Forces of the Crown as a whole and their requirements, as defined in White Papers under the heading *Central Organization for Defence* (Cmd. 6923/1946 and Cmd. 476/1958). He has authority to decide (subject to the responsibilities of the Cabinet and the Defence Committee), all major matters of defence policy affecting the size, shape, organization and disposition of the Armed Forces and their weapons and war-like equipment and supply (including defence research and development). He has further responsibilities arising from United Kingdom participation in international defence organizations.

The Minister of Defence is the Deputy Chairman of the Defence Committee of the Cabinet, of which the Prime Minister is Chairman.

Minister of Defence, THE RT. HON (GEORGE EDWARD) PETER THORNEYCROFT, M.P. £5,000
Private Secretary, A. P. Hockaday.
Assistant Private Secretaries, H. Godfrey, M.B.E., Miss B. R. Gwilliam.
Parliamentary Private Secretary, Wing-Cdr. E. E. Bullus, M.P.
Permanent Secretary, Sir Henry Hardman, K.C.B. £7,015
Chief of the Defence Staff, Admiral of the Fleet the Earl Mountbatten of Burma, K.G., P.C., G.C.B., G.C.S.I., G.C.I.E., G.C.V.O., D.S.O...... *Service pay*
Chief Scientific Adviser, Sir Solly Zuckerman, C.B., F.R.S. £7,015
Deputy Secretaries, F. W. Mottershead, C.B.; F. Wood, C.B.; A. D. Peck, M.B.E. £5,015
Deputy Chief of Defence Staff, Lt.-Gen. Sir Denis O'Connor, K.B.E., C.B. .... *Service pay*
Under-Secretaries, J. A. Drew, C.B.; Capt. M. Hodges, O.B.E., R.N. (*ret.*); I. Montgomery, C.B.; G. Wheeler, C.B.; H. L. Lawrence-Wilson; C. W. Wright £4,115
Chief Scientific Officers, E. C. Cornford; B. T. Price; Dr. R. Press, O.B.E. £4,115
Assistant Secretaries, F.W. Armstrong; C. Benwell; H. L. Emmett; F. A. Kendrick; P. D. Martyn, C.I.E., C.B.E.; J. A. Millson; G. Moses (*Establishment Officer*); E. H. St. G. Moss; L. J. Savatini £2,865 to £3,565
Principals, R. J. Andrews; J. G. Ashcroft; D. M. Dell; A. P. Hockaday; M. Holton; C. J. Hooker, C.B.E.; G. F. Kear; C. T. McDonnell; N. K.

Reeve; C. L. Silver; F. J. Stephens, M.B.E. £1,959 to £2,711
Director of Public Relations, Brig. G. P. Hobbs, C.B.E. (ret.) £3,325
Deputy Establishment Officers, E. A. Eagles (*Finance*) J. H. Maslen (*Personnel*) ..... £2,237 to £2,572
Chief Clerk, A. C. Beer........ £1,680 to £2,127
Accountant, N. H. West......... £1,680 to £2,127

Military Staff

Secretary, Chiefs of Staff Committee, Commodore J. K. Watkins, O.B.E., R.N. .... *Service pay*

British Defence Staffs, Washington

Chairman, Gen. Sir Michael West, K.C.B., D.S.O. *Service pay*
Chief of Staff to Chairman, Rear-Adm. M. C. Greig, C.B., D.S.C. .... *Service pay*
Secretary, Commander T. B. Homan, R.N. *Service pay*

Joint Intelligence Bureau

Metropole Buildings, Northumberland Avenue, W.C.2
[Whitehall: 8474]

Director, Major-General Sir Kenneth Strong, C.B., O.B.E. (*ret.*)........ £4,750
Deputy Directors, M. Y. Watson, C.B.E.; Maj.-Gen. R. E. Lloyd, C.B., C.B.E., D.S.O. (*ret.*).... £3,863
A. Potts.................. £3,340 to £3,665

Imperial Defence College

Seaford House, 37 Belgrave Square, S.W.1
[Belgravia: 1091]

Commandant, Air Chief Marshal Sir Hugh Constantine, K.B.E., C.B., D.S.O.
Directing Staff, Rear-Adm. G. T. S. Gray, D.S.C.; Maj.-Gen. F. H. Brooke, C.B., C.B.E., D.S.O.; Air Vice-Marshal E. G. Jones, C.B., C.B.E., D.S.O., D.F.C. (*Service pay*); M. N. F. Stewart, C.M.G., O.B.E. (*Under Secretary*)............. £4,115

Joint Warfare Staff

10–14 Spring Gardens, S.W.1
[Whitehall: 8122]

Director, Air Vice-Marshal P. G. Wykeham, C.B., D.S.O., O.B.E., D.F.C., A.F.C. .... *Service pay*
Deputy Director, Brigadier P. W. C. Hellings, D.S.O., M.C. .... *Service pay*
Secretariat, Lt.-Col. J. M. Petit, M.B.E.; Lt.-Cdr. E. N. Gregory, R.N. .... *Service pay*

Joint Services Staff College

Latimer, Chesham, Bucks.
[Little Chalfont: 2761/3]

Commandant, Maj.-Gen. C. M. F. Deakin, C.B., C.B.E.
Senior Directing Staff, Captain E. S. Carver, D.S.C., R.N.; Colonel C. Blair, O.B.E., M.C.; Group Capt. K. P. Smales, D.S.O., D.F.C. .... *Service pay*
Administrative Commandant, *Latimer*, Lt.-Col. P. Kemmis-Betty, M.C. .... *Service Pay*

DEVELOPMENT COMMISSION

3 Dean's Yard, Westminster, S.W.1
[Abbey: 1177]

The Development Commission was established and constituted under the *Development and Road Improvement Funds Act*, 1909, and the amending Act of 1910. The Act of 1909 as affected by the *Forestry Act*, 1919, the *Ministry of Transport Act*, 1919 and the *Fisheries Act*, 1955, empowers the Treasury, on the recommendation of the Development Commission, to make advances by way of grant or loan to Government departments, public authorities, universities, colleges, schools, institutions, or associations not trading for profit. At the present time the Fund may be used to promote the economic advancement of the rural community through schemes designed to help and expand directly or indirectly agriculture and rural industries, and widen the opportunities of rural life; and secondly to promote the development and improvement of fisheries by a variety of means, including the promotion of research, both marine and freshwater.

Chairman, The Countess of Albemarle, D.B.E.
Other Commissioners, Lt.-Col. Hon. R. E. B. Beaumont, T.D.; C. I. C. Bosanquet; L. K. Elmhirst; J. L. Longland; W. Scholes; Prof. R. C. Tress; W. J. Wright, C.B.E.
Secretary, F. S. O. Broughton... £2,865 to £3,565

THE DUCHY OF CORNWALL

Buckingham Gate, S.W.1
[Victoria: 7346-8]

The Duchy of Cornwall was instituted by Edward III. in 1337 for the support of his eldest son, Edward, the Black Prince, and since that date the eldest son of the Sovereign has succeeded to the Dukedom by inheritance.

The Council

H.R.H. The Prince Philip, Duke of Edinburgh, K.G., K.T., G.M.B.E.; The Earl of Radnor, K.G., K.C.V.O. (*Lord Warden of the Stannaries*); The Lord Ashburton, K.C.V.O. (*Receiver General*); The Lord Roborough: Brig. The Lord Tryon, K.C.B., K.C.V.O., D.S.O.; J. T. Molony, Q.C. (*Attorney-General of the Duchy*); Sir John Carew Pole, Bt., D.S.O., T.D.; Sir Patrick Kingsley, K.C.V.O. (*Secretary*).

Other Officers of the Duchy of Cornwall

Auditor, W. E. Parker, C.B.E.
Solicitor, B. B. D. Stopford.
Asst. Secretary, M. R. E. Ruffer, T.D.
Deputy Receiver, R. F. H. Adams.
Sheriff (1963–64), Cmdr. R. M. Favell, D.S.C.

THE DUCHY OF LANCASTER

Lancaster Place, Strand, W.C.2
[Temple Bar: 8277]

The estates and jurisdiction known as the Duchy and County Palatine of Lancaster have been attached to the Crown since 1399, when John of Gaunt's son came to the throne as Henry IV. As the Lancaster inheritance it goes back to 1265. Edward III. erected Lancashire into a County Palatine for his son John of Gaunt, Duke of Lancaster, in 1377.

Chancellor of the Duchy of Lancaster, The RIGHT HON. IAIN NORMAN MACLEOD, M.P. £5,000
Private Secretary, N. S. Forward.
Parliamentary Private Secretaries, R. F. B. Bennett, V.R.D., M.P.; C. B. Longbottom, M.P.
Attorney-General and Attorney and Serjeant within the County Palatine of Lancaster, Sir Milner Holland, C.B.E., Q.C.
Receiver-General, Brig. The Lord Tryon, K.C.B., K.C.V.O., D.S.O.
Vice-Chancellor, T. A. C. Burgess.
Clerk of Council and Keeper of Records, Sir Robert Somerville, K.C.V.O.
Solicitor, K. R. E. Taylor, C.V.O.
Chief Clerk, E. R. Wheeler, M.B.E.
Registrar, *Manchester District*, R. A. Forrester.
Do. *Liverpool District*, W. E. Helsby.
Do. *Preston District*, W. E. Helsby.

COURT OF CHANCERY OF THE COUNTY PALATINE OF DURHAM

Registrar's Chambers, Old Elvet, Durham

It is uncertain when the existing "Palatine" privileges were first exercised, but these rights were recognized by Parliament in 1289 during the Episcopate of Bishop Bek and as having then existed "time out of mind" and long prior to the Norman Conquest. William I., in reorganizing his Kingdom was, so far as Durham was concerned, content to confirm the Laws of St. Cuthbert which previously Guthred, King of Northumbria and Alfred the Great appear in turn to have confirmed. Palatine Counties were formed for the protection and defence of the Border, in this case against the Scots, and the Lands of the See were far more extensive than the present County of Durham as is shown by the Jurisdiction of the present Palatine Court extending over Norham and Islandshire (roughly the northern quarter of Northumberland) and Bedlingtonshire. Palatinate rights were exercised by succeeding Prince Bishops till resumed

by the Crown in 1836; but this Court of co-ordinate Jurisdiction with the Chancery Division of the High Court still exists and continues in large measure to exercise its ancient powers on behalf of the Crown.
Chancellor, H. E. Salt, Q.C.
Attorney-General, G. S. Waller, O.B.E., Q.C.
Solicitor-General, R. Lyons, Q.C.
Registrar of Chancery Court, H. Curry, D.F.C.

MINISTRY OF EDUCATION

Curzon Street, W.1
[Hyde Park: 7070]

The Government Department of Education was, until the establishment of a separate office, a Committee of the Privy Council appointed in 1839 to supervise the distribution of certain grants which had been made by Parliament since 1834. The Act of 1899 established the Board of Education, with a President and Parliamentary Secretary, and created a Consultative Committee. The Education Act of 1944 established the Ministry of Education. The cost of administration for the financial year 1962 was estimated at £3,592,000.
Minister of Education, THE RT. HON. SIR EDWARD CHARLES GURNEY BOYLE, Bt., M.P. £5,750
Private Sec., G. F. Cockerill .. £1,894 to £2,646
Asst. Private Sec., C. Priestley.
Parliamentary Private Secretary, Hon Nicholas Ridley, M.P. .... *Unpaid*
Parliamentary Secretary, C. J. Chataway, M.P. £3,250
Permanent Secretary, Sir Herbert Andrew, K.C.M.G., C.B. £7,015
Private Sec., M. J. E. Rabarts,
Deputy Secretaries, H. F. Rossetti, C.B.; T. R. Weaver, C.B. £4,950
Permanent Secretary of Welsh Department, E. Davies, Ph.D.
Under-Secretary and Director of Establishments and Organization, R. Howlett, C.B. £4,050
Under-Secretary for Finance and Accountant-General, J. F. Embling £4,050
Under-Secretaries, H. T. Bourdillon, C.M.G.; L. R. Fletcher; D. H. Leadbetter, C.B.; P. R. Odgers, M.B.E.; W. D. Pile, M.B.E.; J. A. R. Pimlott, C.B. £4,050
Legal Adviser, W. L. Dale, C.M.G. £4,950
Senior Chief Inspector, P. Wilson, C.B. £4,700
Chief Architect (vacant)
Chief Medical Officer (at Ministry of Health), Sir George Godber, K.C.B., D.M.
Principal Medical Officer, P. Henderson, M.D., Q.H.P. £4,050

Schools Branch

Assistant Secretaries, Miss W. P. Harte; Miss K. A. Kennedy; A. R. M. Maxwell-Hyslop; D. H. Morrell .... £2,800 to £3,600
Principals, D. L. Corder; A. S. Gann; M. L. Herzig; M. Kogan; L. W. Norwood; Miss M. E. Small; V. H. Stevens; I. R. M. Thom £1,894 to £2,646
Chief Executive Officers, L. G. Cook; L. G. Gibbs, E.R.D. .... £2,172 to £2,507

Further Education Branch I

Assistant Secretaries, J. S. Arthur; Miss S. M. E. Goodfellow; D. A. Routh ... £2,800 to £3,500
Principals, R. J. Baker, O.B.E.; H. Jordan; H. G. M. Peters; J. A. Swindale .... £1,894 to £2,646
Chief Executive Officers, G. H. Radmore; D. F. Robinson .... £2,172 to £2,507
Senior Executive Officers, J. G. Bagley; Miss N. E. Jones .... £1,615 to £2,061

Further Education Branch II

Assistant Secretaries, E. B. H. Baker, O.B.E.; D. Evan Morgan; A. Thompson ..... £2,800 to £3,500
Principals, H. Barkley; Miss M. S. Hardwick; J. I. Jones; F. N. Withers ..... £1,894 to £2,646
Library Adviser, P. H. Sewell £2,250
Senior Executive Officers, J. Blatcher; V. C. Clark; P. R. Green .... £1,615 to £2,061

External Relations Branch

Assistant Secretaries, L. C. J. Martin; M. A. Walker £2,800 to £3,500
Principals, H. O. Dovey; Miss S. K. L. Guiton; P. S. Litton; J. O. Roach, O.B.E. £1,894 to £2,646
Senior Executive Officers, G. J. Sheppard; A. W. Thompson .... £1,615 to £2,061

Teachers Branch I (Supply)

Assistant Secretaries, J. D. Brierley; E. H. Simpson £2,800 to £3,500
Principals, R. Dellar; A. G. Hurrell; J. A. Richards £1,894 to £2,646
Senior Executive Officers, H. G. Jenkins; Mrs. I. F. T. Martin, M.B.E. .... £1,615 to £2,061

Teachers Branch II (Training)

Assistant Secretaries, H. C. Rackham; G. L. Thornton £2,800 to £3,500
Principals, R. E. Duff; C. Graham; W. K. Reid £1,894 to £2,646
Chief Executive Officer, S. B. Hallett £2,172 to £2,507
Senior Executive Officers, P. H. Bidgood; W. G. Easeman, T.D.; R. Klein; H. C. Riddett £1,615 to £2,061

Salaries Branch

Honeypot Lane, Stanmore, Middlesex
[Edgware: 2366]

Principal Executive Officer, S. J. Barker, D.S.C. £3,150
Chief Executive Officers, M. A. Barry, E.R.D.; D. J. Brazier, D.S.M. .... £2,172 to £2,507
Senior Executive Officers, F. G. Clayton; E. R. Gibbs; M. Moss .... £1,615 to £2,061

Pensions Branch

Honeypot Lane, Stanmore, Middlesex
[Edgware: 2366]

Principal Executive Officer, L. P. Angell £3,150
Chief Executive Officers, G. L. Macey; K. H. R. Maynard .... £2,172 to £2,507
Senior Executive Officers, W. J. Archibald; Miss V. D. M. Chapman; Miss M. E. E. Mills; J. T. Say; D. F. H. Taylor .... £1,615 to £2,061

Special Services Branch

Assistant Secretaries, G. W. W. Browne; J. A. Hudson .... £2,800 to £3,500
Principals, W. F. Dawson, M.B.E.; Miss J. M. Grinham; L. J. Melhuish; Miss J. M. Scrimshaw £1,894 to £2,646
Senior Executive Officers, R. Carpenter, D.S.C.; G. L. Emmett; Miss A. M. Sheehan, M.B.E.; S. M. Smith .... £1,615 to £2,061
Senior Medical Officers, C. B. Huss; Miss D. M. Llewellin, M.D. £3,500
Medical Officers, J. N. Horne, M.D.; Miss E. E. Simpson, M.D.; Miss M. Scott Stevenson; T. K. Whitmore; Mrs. M. M. Wilson, O.B.E. (*Leeds*); A. T. Wynne .... £2,412 to £3,075
Cost Accountant, A. G. Smith ... £2,618 to £2,800
Assistant Cost Accountant, A. T. Forbes £1,615 to £2,061

Establishments and Organization Branch

Assistant Secretaries, J. A. Hudson; D. Neylan, O.B.E. £2,800 to £3,500
Chief Executive Officers, J. H. Comper; H. A. Hewitt, I.S.O.; K. R. Rowberry £2,172 to £2,507
Senior Executive Officers, R. Burgess; M. Cohen; Miss V. G. Ford; V. A. C. Willis £1,615 to £2,061

Accountant General's Department and Awards Branch

Assistant Secretary (Deputy Accountant General), D. E. Lloyd Jones, M.C. ...... £2,800 to £3,500
Director of Cost Investigation Unit, T. A. J. Warlow £2,800 to £3,325
Deputy Director, T. H. Hopkins .. £1,851 to £2,293
Chief Executive Officers, W. H. G. Harvey; D. F. E. King; Miss M. Nicholls ..... £2,172 to £2,507
Senior Executive Officers, Miss K. T. Hosegood, M.B.E.; R. F. Smith .... £1,615 to £2,061

Awards
13 Cornwall Terrace, N.W.1
[Hunter: 1455]
Assistant Secretary, D. E. Lloyd Jones M.C. £2,800 to £3,500
Principal, A. E. Marrington, C.B.E. £1,894 to £2,646
Chief Executive Officer, J. W. B. Ireson, I.S.O. £2,172 to £2,507
Senior Executive Officer, R. K. Usher £1,615 to £2,061

Statistics Branch
Chief Statistician, P. Redfern.... £2,800 to £3,500
Statisticians, D. B. Halpern; W. B. Wakefield; M. V. Wilde.................... £1,894 to £2,646
Senior Executive Officer, Miss E. Maher £1,615 to £2,061

Research and Intelligence Branch
Assistant Secretary, P. Sloman... £2,800 to £3,500
Principal, P. G. B. Giles....... £1,894 to £2,646
Information Department
Chief Information Officer, N. F. Cowen £2,800 to £3,500
Principal Information Officer, H. L. James £2,172 to £2,507
Senior Information Officer, Mrs. B. Hoddinott £1,615 to £2,061
Senior Executive Officer, D. M. Basey £1,615 to £2,061
Library
Librarian, Miss P. M. Downie... £1,615 to £2,061

Architects and Building Branch
Assistant Secretary, J. N. Archer. £2,800 to £3,500
Principals, N. T. Hardyman; J. A. Humphreys; D.W. MacDowall; K.W. Morris; R. H. Stone £1,894 to £2,646
Principal Architects, J. C. Loyd; D. L. Medd, O.B.E.; G. H. Wigglesworth........ £2,800 to £3,150
Principal Quantity Surveyor, R. C. King £2,800 to £3,150
Senior Architects, W. R. C. Cleary; J. S. B. Coatman; B. H. Cox; Miss M. B. Crowley, O.B.E.; S. C. Halbritter; J. D. Kay; J. L. H. Kitchen; J. M. P. Price; J. B. Smith; J. E. Toomer £2,228 to £2,563
Senior Quantity Surveyor, P. F. Bottle £2,228 to £2,563
Senior Heating and Ventilating Engineer, L. E. J. Piper £2,228 to £2,563
Architects, G. W. Ballard; Miss O. Emmerson-Price; R. L. Fitzwilliam; W. A. Fletcher; K. E. Foster; F. P. R. Gibbs; J. L. Grove; L. J. P. Halstead; L. S. Holland; F. Jackson; D. S. Pearce; A. P. Roach; O. M. Stepan; Mrs. A. G. J. Swain; R. L. Thompson; G. A. Webber... £1,559 to £2,089
Quantity Surveyors, C. L. Payne; B. A. Staples; B. G. Whitehouse............... £1,559 to £2,089
Senior Executive Officer, K. S. Roelich £1,615 to £2,061

Legal Branch
Assistant Legal Advisers, H. B. C. Horrell; M. L. Longhurst, C.B.E............ £2,900 to £3,500
Senior Legal Assistants, G. R. Hughes; E. K. Kitson; G. J. Morgan; A. B. Rabagliati; Mrs. E. M. E. Sims; J. L. B. Todhunter, O.B.E. £2,239 to £2,800
Senior Executive Officer, B. Lowe £1,615 to £2,061

Central Advisory Council for Education (England)
Secretary, M. Kogan........... £1,894 to £2,646

H.M. Inspectorate (England)
Chief Inspectors, J. G. M. Allcock; J. E. H. Blackie, C.B.; W. R. Elliott; C. R. English; C. J. Gill; R. D. Salter Davies................ £3,750
Divisional Inspectors, J. A. Barclay; C. H. Barry; L. J. Burrows; M. J. G. Hearley; Miss P. Nanney; G. S. V. Petter; Miss M. R. Power, C.B.E.; E. S. Snelling, C.B.E.; H. L. Willoughby; J. S. Wingate-Saul.. £3,380
Staff Inspectors, R. H. Adams, T.D.; G. C. Allen, C.B.E.; A. D. Atkinson; D. G. O. Ayerst; E. I. Baker; M. F. Bird; F. Caunce; F. E. Charlton; A. D. Collop; L. C. Comber; J. A. Edgar; Miss R. Foster; H. W. French; L. F. Gibbon, C.B.E.; J. H. Goldsmith; A. G. Gooch; Miss V. L. Gray; E. E. Y. Hales; Miss W. S. Hargreaves; C. W. Harvey; J. W. Horton; Miss M. E. Johnston; Miss E. M. Langley; J. A. Lefroy, M.B.E.; V. J. Long; L. E. Lowe; J. Lumsden; R. C. Lyness; Miss E. McDougall; J. Maitland-Edwards; E. C. Marchant, C.I.E.; J. C. G. Mellars; R.W. Morris; Miss M. E. Nicholls; E. Parkinson; G. F. Peaker, C.B.E.; A. Pollard; D. I. R. Porter; M. W. Pritchard; O. J. E. Pullen; D. C. Riddy, C.B.E.; H. Sagar; J. A. Simpson; H. Spibey, C.B.E.; R. J. W. Stubbings; G. Sutton; K. G. Todd; J. R. Tolson; W. B. Tudhope, C.B.E.; J.W. Withrington £3,085 to £3,380

H. M. Inspectors, Miss K. Addison; Mrs. J. N. C. Alington; J. P. Allen; Mrs. H. G. Alston; Miss D. V. Armstrong; F. A. Arrowsmith; Miss P. M. Ash; K. L. Ashurst; Lady H. Asquith; M. F. Atkins; Miss N. M. Ayre; A. B. Baddeley; Miss M. A. Badland; R. C. Baker; W. T. Barber; J. W. Barks; E. E. Barnard; Miss H. M. Barratt; Miss N. B. Batley; W. K. Beal; Miss D. M. Beatley; M. J. Beaver; Miss M. R. Beckwith; R. H. Beevers; L. F. Bennett; Miss A. F. H. Berwick; Miss E. E. Biggs; M. Birchenough; F. H. Birks; R.W. Blake; H. H. Blissett; R. W. Boon; N. Booth; Miss J. M. Bosdêt; G. J. Boyden; H. A. Boyer; A. Bray; R. S. Breckon; J. K. Brierley; Miss B. S. Briggs; Mrs. B. M. Brook; R. F. J. Brown; Miss S. J. Browne; Miss C. M. Brunt; K. R. Bull; E. Bullock; P. M. Burns; Miss K. M. P. Burton; R. J. Butchers; A. A. Campbell; W. F. Campbell; N. S. Capper; Mrs. K. M. Catlin; C. W. E. Cave; Miss F. M. Chamberlain; J. T. G. Chugg; Miss D. Clark; Miss G. D. Clark; L. Clark; A. L. Clay; G. D. Clay; Mrs. V. A. Clifford; Miss E. M. Collin; Miss C. Collingwood; Miss A. D. Collins; J. A. Cook; E. D. Cooke; Mrs. U. A. Cooling; R. M. Cooper; T. J. Corbin; Miss N. K. Cornforth; N. G. Cottrell; Miss K. B. Cowan; T. C. Cradock; R. C. H. Crawford; Miss E. H. Crowther; C. J. Crumpler; G. Crwys Williams; Mrs. I. L. Cutforth; Miss D. Dain; J. Dalglish; P. C. Davey; D. M. Davies; Miss E. Davies; F. R. Davies; H. E. Davies; I. Davies; Mrs. O. H. Davis; Miss M. B. Davison; Miss I. M. M. Dean, O.B.E.; Miss J. H. Deas; Miss W. E. Deavin; F. A. Dellar; Miss K. M. Dencer; J. Denham; Mrs. A. C. Dennis; Miss K. V. Dewar; Miss R. M. Dewey, O.B.E.; Miss G. J. Diment; Miss E. Dodds; Mrs. H.W. Doubleday; R. C. Dove; F. J. Downs; A. W. Doyle; W. Drabble; Miss E. J. DuCane; P. D. Dudley; Miss S. M. C. Duncan; W. M. Dutton; W. J. H. Earl; A. E. Ecclestone; F. Edwards; H. J. Edwards; Miss O. E. J. Ellicott; K. T. Elsdon; G.W. Elsmore; D. W. Emery; L. F. Ennever; Miss M. D. Erskine; Miss G. L. O. Evans; L. M. Evans; W. J. Evans; E. Fanthorpe; E. J. Fedarb; R. B. Feilden; H. L. Fenn; H. Firth; J. R. Fish; T. J. Fletcher; W. S. Fowler; Miss J. M. Francis; Miss M. G. Fraser; W. W. French; A. W. Fuller; R. Gardner; J. L. Gayler; Miss V. Ghaleb; Miss D. S. Gilbert; Miss P. M. Giles; O. O.W. Ginn; D. R. T. Goodwin; C. B. Gordon; L. F. Gordon; Miss M. I. Gordon; F. C. Gould; J. F. Graber; J. Graham; Miss S. E. Grant; E. A. Greatwood; W. Green; R. E. Greenway; R. P. Greenwood; W. A. Grier; Miss D. M. Griffin; L. S. Grimsdale; R. D. Guest; S. E. Gunn, T.D.; Miss D. Haigh; A. A. Haimes; Miss E. M. Hale; Miss Y. M. Hale; P. N. Hallifax; W. G. Hamflett; J. R. Hampton; Mrs. E. W. Hancock; G. Hankin; A. N. Harris; J. R. G. Harris; G. B. Harrison; Miss K. Harrison; M. F. Harrold; D. F. Harrop; B. W. V. Hawes; Miss C. M. Hawkes; C. G. Hayter; R. Heworth; Miss A. A. Hill; Miss B. E. Hill; W. G. D. Hill; D. Hilton; J. E. A. Hinton; Miss M. K. Hircock;

Miss N. Hitchman; Miss M. E. Hodkinson; Miss D'A. V. Hogg; L. Holdsworth; R. Holmes; R. O. Hopkins; D. M. Hopkinson; E. Houghton; F. Howe; A. H. Howlett; P. H. Hoy; Miss A. M. Hughes; L. J. Hughes; W. E. Husband; L. C. Hyde; K. Jary; W. J. F. Jeff, T.D.; R. A. Jeffery; T. R. Jenkyn; H. Johns; Miss E. M. Johnson; Miss M. Knox Johnston; D. T. Jones, O.B.E.; H. Jones; J. S. Jones; T. C. Keay; G. S. Keeney; F. Keggins; H. R. Keys; A. G. King; M. Kingston; L. S. Laid; Miss C. M. Lambert; J. G. Lavender; S. G. Lawrence; Miss V. M. Lawson; A. J. Legge; Miss M. D. Lewis; T. McG. Leyden; I. B. Licence; Miss M. K. Lightowler; Miss M. Lockyer; E. Lord; B.W. Lucke; A. G. J. Luffman, O.B.E.; D. Luffman; Miss M. T. McBride; Miss M. McCullough; F. O. Machin; Miss W. B. McIntosh; Miss H. MacA. McIntyre; Miss B. H. Mackay; Miss D. F. McKenna; Miss E. M. Mackenzie; Miss M. S. Macmorran; F. Makin; H. J. J. Malcolm; Miss K. L. Malcolm; Miss J. L. Maltby; H. E. S. Marks; Miss Z. A. Marsh; Miss M. J. Marshall; T. L. Marsters; T. S. Matthewson; Miss P. Maurice; W. H. Mawson; C. H. Melanefy; G. W. Milburn; P. C. K. Millins; Miss M. Mitchell; R. Money; A. Monkman; G. G. Moore, M.B.E.; Miss S. I. J. Moore; Miss P. M. W. Morecombe; A. G. Morris; C. W. Morris; J. W. Morris; R. C. Morton; E. A. Mount Haes; Miss N. R. Mulcahy; A. M. Munday; J. H. Mundy; R. Munro; T. M. Murray-Rust, T.D.; A. W. Newton; Miss N. M. Newton-Smith; D. B. Nield; Mrs. V. M. F. M. A. de R. O'Byrne; Miss K. M. O'Leary; F. E. Olney; J. A. Page; Miss S. E. Parfitt; A. T. Parnham; A. J. Parr; Mrs. B. Parr; W. H. Parry; H. Pashley; Miss J. Paterson; Miss K. Payne; W. Peach; E. Pearson; Miss M. J. Pedley; L. F. Pendlebury; P. Phillips; C. L. Pickering; Miss L. M. Pickering; J. R. Pocock; Miss E. G. Pollard; Miss E. M. Potts; Miss M. M. Potts; J.W. Powell, T.D.; S. Price; G. B. Priest; J. M. Pullan; Miss F. M. Pursglove; T. M. Pyke, O.B.E., T.D.; Miss B. E. Rabley; J. C. D. Rainbow; Miss A. V. Rambaut; Miss R. C. Ramirez; Miss B. E. Rawlins; Miss M. Rayment; J. H. P. Rae; C. J. Read; C. P. Read; Mrs. M. H. Reay, M.B.E.; R. I. Redfern; D. L. Rees; Miss M. T. Rhys; R. A. Richardson; V. C. E. Rickwood; Miss M. R. Rishworth; R. R. Roberts; Miss E. M. Robinson; J. Robinson; C. P. Rochester; G. R. Romans; A. A. Rossi; R. Roundhill; C. W. Rowland; F. C. Ruffett; D. Sadler; I. P. Salisbury; P. Samuel; K. J. Sargent; I. Secker; C. H. Selby; Mrs. M. Sessions; J. H. Shackley; D. R. Shannon; Miss E. M. Sharman; B. E. Shaw; I. V. Shelby, M.B.E. T.D.; L. J. V. Shepherd; W. W. Sheppard; R. Sibson; E. J. Sidebottom; Miss M. Sidwell; E. Sims; Miss C. M. Smale; P. F. Smart; J. L. Smedley; J. E. Smith; Miss L. Smith; L. G. Smith; Miss N. M. Smith; E. W. Snook; G. Snowball; W. H. Snowdon; Mrs. M. H. Somers; J. F. Spencer; M. E. Sprakes; M. E. Sprinks; A. P. J. Staton; Miss A. E. Stephen; B. C. G. Stevens; T. L. Stewart; L. A. Stockdale; Mrs. D. K. Stone; H. C. Story; C. E. Strafford; G. C. Streeton; T. Stultiens; E. W. Sudale; J. J. Sullivan; F. Sutcliffe; E. F. A. Suttle; J. L. Swain; Miss M. F. H. Sweny; Miss J. M. Sykes; D. F. Symes; F. E. Tandy; R. F. A. Tanner; G. L. I. Tarrant; B. Taylor; H. Taylor; Miss S. A. Taylor; T. Taylor; W. W. Taylor; Miss E. W. Temple; N. Thomas; R. V. Thomas; W. B. Thompson; Miss A. Thubrun; Miss K. M. M. Tobin; R. J. Todd; D. G. Toose; G. E. Trodd; F. A. Tucker; Miss M. Turner; B. G. G. Uden; A. Urie; R. A. Wake; R. L. Wakeford; Miss N. M. Walley; Miss J. R. Warner; Miss R. Watson; Miss P. M. Webb; Miss M. F. Weedon; Miss M. M. Weemys; Miss R. E. A. Wertheimer; Miss H. Westbrook; W. M. White; E. Whiteley; A. Wigglesworth; M. R. Wigram; E. Wilkinson; C. L. Williams; Miss G. M. B. Williams; G. L. O. Williamson; Miss F. M. Willis; P. G. Willmore; Miss B. Wooldridge; Miss N. W. Wooldridge; J. T. Woodend; E. H. Wright; J. L. Wright; J. R. Yorke-Radleigh; T. R. Young .... £2,023 to £2,905

Welsh Department
8 Cathedral Road, Cardiff
[Cardiff: 21547]

Assistant Secretary, J. H. Brook, C.M.G. (*a*) £2,800 to £3,500
Principal, Miss O. R. Arnold.... £1,894 to £2,646
Chief Executive Officer, D. H. Grattidge (*a*) £2,172 to £2,507
Senior Executive Officer, G. C. Kitts £1,615 to £2,061
Senior Architect, S. C. Halbritter . £2,228 to £2,563
Central Advisory Council for Education (Wales), Secretaries, Miss O. R. Arnold; E. O. Davies

(*a*) In London.

H.M. Inspectorate (Wales)

Chief Inspector, W. Ll. Lloyd C.B. £3,750
Staff Inspectors, T. I. Davies; E. G. Lewis; M. D. Owen; I. G. Richards; B. E. Thomas; A. H. Williams; T. E. Williams ..... £3,085 to £3,380
H.M. Inspectors, G. Bowen; W. J. Bowyer; F. H. Cleaver; E. Ll. Davies; Miss E. M. Davis; E. O. Davies; H. R. Davies; Miss E. C. Edwards; T. R. Edwards; Miss E. O. Evans; Miss G. Evans; Miss J. Evans; R. W. Evans; G. Gratton; Miss W. M. Hopkins-Jones; I. E. Hughes; E. H. Hutton; W. J. Jenkins; C. H. B. Jones; Miss G. Jones; R. H. Jones; Miss M. M. L. Lewis; W. G. Lewis; G. A. V. Morgan; Miss H. E. Morgan; P. E. Owen; W. Pickles; Miss D. Rees; C. Reid; D. E. A. Roberts; Miss M. K. Roderick; D. A. Thomas; G. Thomas; Miss G. M. Thomas; W. J. Thomas; I. R. Walters, O.B.E.; P. C. Webb £1,876 to £2,755

ELECTRICITY AUTHORITIES

THE ELECTRICITY COUNCIL

30 Millbank, S.W.1
[Victoria: 2333]

The Electricity Act, 1957, provided for the dissolution of the Central Electricity Authority, as from Jan. 1, 1958, and for the allocation of its duties and powers to an Electricity Council and a Central Electricity Generating Board. These bodies were set up on Sept. 1, 1957, and as from Jan. 1, 1958, all liabilities and obligations of the Central Authority in respect of British Electricity Stock issued before that date were tranferred to the Electricity Council, and all property, rights, liabilities and obligations which before that date pertained to the Central Authority, with certain exceptions which by agreement under the Act vested in the Council, were transferred to the Generating Board.

Electricity Council

Chairman Sir Ronald Edwards K.B.E. £10,000
Deputy Chairmen C. T. Melling C.B.E.; N. F. Marsh £7,500
Members, P. Briggs, £7,000; The Lord Geddes of Epsom, C.B.E. (*part-time*) £1,000
Members from Central Electricity Generating Board, Sir Christopher Hinton, K.B.E., F.R.S.; F. H. S. Brown, C.B.E.; O. Francis, C.B. and the Chairmen of the 12 Area Electricity Boards.

Secretary and Solicitor, R. A. Finn.

CENTRAL ELECTRICITY GENERATING BOARD

Bankside House, Sumner Street, S.E.1
[Waterloo: 2011]

The Board owns and operates the power stations and main transmission lines in England and Wales, and is responsible for the bulk supply of electricity to the Area Electricity Boards.

Chairman, Sir Christopher Hinton, K.B.E., F.R.S. £10,000
Deputy Chairman, F. H. S. Brown, C.B.E. £7,500
Members, O. Francis, C.B.; A. R. Cooper; L. Rotherham; E. S. Booth, each £7,000; (*part-time*) Sir William Holford; P. T. Menzies; Sir Leslie Nicholls, K.C.M.G., C.B., C.B.E.; S. Watson, C.B.E. each £1,000
Secretary, E. J. Turner.

ELECTRICITY BOARDS

The 12 Area Electricity Boards

(The Chairmen of Area Boards receive a salary of £6,500).

London, 46–47 New Broad Street, E.C.2. *Chairman*, D. B. Irving. *Sec.*, S. M. Gore.
South Eastern, 10 Queen's Gardens, Hove 3, Sussex. *Chairman*, H. V. Pugh. *Sec.*, G. Wray, O.B.E.
Southern, Southern Electricity House, Littlewick Green, Maidenhead, Berks. *Chairman*, R. R. B. Brown. *Sec.*, F. W. Kempton.
South Western, Electricity House, Colston Avenue, Bristol 1. *Chairman*, A. N. Irens. *Sec.*, D. S. Bentham.
Eastern, Wherstead, nr. Ipswich, Suffolk. *Chairman*, H. D. B. Wood, O.B.E. *Sec.*, J. S. Mills.
East Midlands, Mapperley Hall, Lucknow Avenue, Nottingham. *Chairman*, A. N. Todd, *Sec.*, J. A. MacKerrell.
Midlands, Mucklow Hill, Halesowen, nr. Birmingham. *Chairman*, G. F. Peirson, *Sec.*, F. W. Cater.
South Wales, St. Mellons, Cardiff, *Chairman*, W. D. D. Fenton, C.B.E. *Sec.* R. G. Williams.
Merseyside and North Wales, Electricity House, Love Lane, Pall Mall, Liverpool 3. *Chairman*, D. G. Dodds. *Sec.*, M. M. Parker.
Yorkshire, Wetherby Road, Scarcroft, Leeds. *Chairman*, A. Bond. *Sec.* E. K. Richmond, T.D.
North Eastern, Carliol House, Newcastle upon Tyne, 1. *Chairman*, G. N. Green. *Sec.*, J. E. Hayes.
North Western, Cheetwood Road, Manchester 8. *Chairman*, R. F. Richardson. *Sec.*, J. W. K. Evans.

NORTH OF SCOTLAND HYDRO-ELECTRIC BOARD

16 Rothesay Terrace, Edinburgh 3
[Edinburgh Caledonian: 1361]

Chairman, The Lord Strathclyde, P.C. £3,750
Deputy Chairman, A. I. Mackenzie.
Members (part-time), The Lord Macdonald, M.B.E., T.D. (*Chairman of Consultative Council*) (£1,500); A. Macrae, C.B.E.; I. A. D. Millar, M.C.; The Lord Hughes, C.B.E.; Maj. P. H. Gordon, M.C.; N. Hogg, *each* £1,000.
General Manager and Member of Board, A. A. Fulton, C.B.E.
Secretary, H.W. Simpson.

SOUTH OF SCOTLAND ELECTRICITY BOARD

Inverlair Avenue, Glasgow, S.4
[Merrylee: 7177]

Chairman, N. R. Elliott, C.B.E. £7,500
Deputy-Chairman, W. Hutton, C.B.E. £6,000
Part-time Members, Sir David Anderson; J. Ballantyne; W. Macfarlane Gray; Sir Maxwell Inglis (*Chairman of Consultative Council*) £1,500); J. McBoyle; P. L. Meldrum; A. Sutherland *each* £1,000
Chief Engineer, E. H. Jones.
Secretary, A. A. Wallace.

EXCHEQUER AND AUDIT DEPARTMENT

Audit House, Victoria Embankment, E.C.4
[Fleet Street: 8901]

This is the Department of the Comptroller and Auditor General, an office created by the Act 29 & 30 Vict. c. 39 (1866) to replace, with extended powers, the separate offices of Comptroller General of the Receipt and Issue of the Exchequer and of the Commissioners for Auditing the Public Accounts. This officer is appointed by Letters Patent under the Great Seal, and is irremovable except upon an address from the two Houses of Parliament. In his capacity of Comptroller General of the Receipt and Issue of the Exchequer, he authorizes all issues from the Exchequer after satisfying himself that Parliament has given authority for them. He examines the Exchequer accounts and makes an annual report on them to Parliament. In his capacity of Auditor General of Public Accounts, he is charged with the duty of examining on behalf of the House of Commons the accounts of expenditure out of funds provided by Parliament, the accounts of the receipt of revenue, and generally all other public accounts, including the accounts of Government stores and of trading services conducted by Government Departments. The results of his examination of those accounts are reported to the House of Commons.

Comptroller and Auditor General, Sir Edmund Compton, K.B.E., C.B. £7,000
Private Secretary, P. J. C. Keemer.
Secretary, P. J. Curtis, C.B., C.B.E. £4,115
Deputy Secretary, A. R. Slyth, O.B.E. £3,815
Director of Establishments and Accounts, R. C. Hooper £3,215
Directors of Audit, W. S. J. Thornington, O.B.E.; H. C. Hepburn; D. V. Boyd; F. Brown; W. E. Coles, O.B.E.; R. A. Cheeseman; H. A. Long; C. H. Davies; G. P. Morrell £3,215
Deputy Directors of Audit, E. J. Lowe; R. W. Tizard; W. H. Nichols; R. H. Plaister; T. N. Finch; R. A. Best; Miss W. M. Cragg, M.B.E.; P. G. Spary; H. R. Francis; J. French; J. H. D. Sant; S. L. Teasdale; J. F. T. Cheetham; D. F. Smith; P. H. Elsley; P. R. Billett; J. C. McDowell £2,683 to £2,865

EXPORT CREDITS GUARANTEE DEPARTMENT

59–67 Gresham Street, E.C.2
[Monarch: 6699]

REGIONAL OFFICES: *City of London and South Eastern*—Marlon House, Mark Lane, E.C.3 (Royal 3491). *West London*—Cunard Building, 15 Regent Street, S.W.1 (Whitehall 9061). *South London*—Clements House, Gresham Street, E.C.2 (Monarch 4581). *South Western*—The Gaunts House, Denmark Street, Bristol 1 (22011). *Midland*—Chamber of Commerce House, Harborne Road, Birmingham 15 (Edgbaston 4375). *East Midland*—Equitable House, Market Square, Nottingham (46585). *North-Western*—Britannic Building, Fountain Street, Manchester 2 (Blackfriars 6236). *North-Eastern*—Britannia House, Bridge Street, Bradford 1 (25147). *Northern*—36/38 Moseley Street, Newcastle 1 (29838). *Scotland*—7 West George Street, Glasgow, C.2 (Central 3056). *Northern Ireland*—7 Donegall Square West, Belfast (29428).
AREA OFFICES: *Sheffield*—Fargate House, Fargate (29151). *Liverpool*—India Buildings, Water Street, 2 (Central 5756). *Leeds*—Headrow House, 42 The Headrow, 1 (30082). *Edinburgh*—108 George Street (Caledonian 3004). *Cardiff*—St. David's House, Wood Street (26657).

The Export Guarantees Acts, 1949 to 1961, empower the Board of Trade to give guarantees to United Kingdom exporters for the purpose of encouraging export trade. This power is administered by the Export Credits Guarantee Department. Commercial guarantees, under Section 1 of the 1949 Act, are given after consultation with an Advisory Council set up for the purpose.

Minister, The President of the Board of Trade.

Export Guarantees Advisory Council

Chairman, Sir John Hogg.
Deputy Chairman, The Lord Catto.
Other Members, A. D. Chesterfield, C.B.E.; L. Cooke, O.B.E.; L. G. T. Farmer; J. M. Laing; R. M. Lee; J. McLean, C.B.E.; The Lord Melchett;

Sir Frank Nixon, K.C.M.G., C.B.; Sir Kenneth Preston; J. M. Reynolds; H. H. Thackstone; G. E. Thomson.

Officers

Headquarters

Secretary, A. E. Percival, C.B. £5,015
Under Secretaries, A. T. K. Grant, C.M.G.; J. B. L. Munro, C.B., C.M.G. £4,115
Establishment and Finance Officer, J. T. G. Smith £2,865 to £3,565
Assistant Secretaries, C. K. Baylis; R. A. Dickinson; P. H. Garrity, D.F.C.; C. P. Rawlings; A. F. Toms; F. H. Whitaker, O.B.E. . . . . £2,865 to £3,565
Principals, G. F. B. Corti; K. Cotterill; R. A. Freeman; J. Gill; D. C. W. Hill; E. J. Jackson; R. T. Kemp; H. G. B. Lynch; D. C. Smith; E. T. Walton; I. Whaley. . . . £1,959 to £2,711
Senior Chief Executive Officers, C. F. Catt, O.B.E.; E. Edwards, O.B.E.; F. Greenwood, O.B.E.,; F. J. Waller, O.B.E.; A. Watson . . . . £2,607 to £2,865
Chief Executive Officers, A. E. J. Berry; T. F. B. Crossfield; L. Elmes; M. W. Gentle; K. C. Harrison; E. G. Lowton; R. F. L. Martin; W. H. Neuff, O.B.E.; C. L. Palmer; Mrs. D. M. Phillips, M.B.E.; W. J. Sharland; Miss M. E. Shiach; Miss K. M. Sleven; H. L. H. Stevens, M.B.E. £2,237 to £2,572
Principal Information Officer, P. A. D. Jones, O.B.E. £2,751
Senior Executive Officers, F. C. Argent; Miss L. D. Bolwell; L. M. Broad; J. E. M. Bury; J. Caldwell; J. W. Coggins; T. H. Collinson; J. A. Crossen; J. Cunningham; A. R. Currie; Mrs. E. Davidson; W. B. Davies; A. Dawson; P. C. B. Duncan; A. J. Dunstan; G. W. Ethall; F. H. Fishpool; D. H. J. Furbank; A. J. Gentry; Miss E. D. Gush; J. H. Hall; L. Halligan; G. W. Hopcroft; K. F. Jackson; W. H. Johnson, D.F.C., D.F.M.; H. K. Jones; N. F. Lowe; F. C. Mann; P. W. Mayer; R. A. Napier-Andrews; E. Panton; R. M. Payne; N. S. Pollard; G. P. Reeve; P. W. Shaw; W. E. Smith; J. G. Sorbie; E. Thornton; A. H. Vine; J. F. Vose; P. J. Wells; V. E. Young. £1,680 to £2,126

Regional Organization

Regional Managers, C. C. Birch, M.B.E.; J. A. Bookless; J. A. Dyer; W. Ford; A. A. L. MacManus, M.B.E.; R. K. Pearson; W. C. Pettigrew; J. N. Smales . . . . £1,680 to £2,126
Representative in U.S.A., R. S. Kinsey £1,959 to £2,711

FOREIGN OFFICE

Downing Street, S.W.1
[Whitehall: 8440]

The Office of Secretary of State for Foreign Affairs was created in 1782, superseding that of the former Secretary for the Northern Department and assuming the foreign affairs functions of the former Secretary for the Southern Department. The Secretary of State is assisted by the Lord Privy Seal, two Ministers of State, a Parliamentary Under-Secretary and a staff of permanent officials headed by one Permanent Under-Secretary, six Deputy Under-Secretaries, and eight Assistant Under-Secretaries. The chief function is the conduct of relations with foreign Powers and other functions include certain formal duties, the general administration of Her Majesty's Foreign Service and receiving and answering communications from individuals, other Government Departments and diplomatic and consular representatives in this country and abroad.

Salaries and expenses of the Foreign Office, including missions and consulates abroad, were estimated at £27,283,000 in 1963-4.

Secretary of State for Foreign Affairs, THE EARL OF HOME, P.C., K.T. £5,000
Private Secretary, J. O. Wright, D.F.C. £2,865 to £3,565
Assistant Private Secretaries, Hon. T. E. Bridges; J. C. Thomas; N. H. Young.
Lord Privy Seal, The Rt. Hon. EDWARD RICHARD GEORGE HEATH, M.B.E., M.P. £5,000
Private Secretary, C. D. Wiggin, D.F.C., A.F.C.
Parliamentary Private Secretary, J. M. Howard, M.P.
Ministers of State, THE EARL OF DUNDEE, P.C.; PETER JOHN MITCHELL THOMAS, M.P. £3,750
Parliamentary Under- Secretary of State, P. H. B. O. Smithers, V.R.D., D.Phil., M.P. £2,500
Permanent Under-Secretary of State, Sir Harold Caccia, G.C.M.G., G.C.V.O. £7,015
Private Secretary, Lord Nicholas Gordon-Lennox, M.V.O.
Deputy Under-Secretaries of State, Sir Patrick Reilly, K.C.M.G., O.B.E.; Sir John Nicholls, K.C.M.G., O.B.E.; Sir Geoffrey Harrison, K.C.M.G., K.C.V.O.; Sir Bernard Burrows, K.C.M.G.,; The Viscount Hood, K.C.M.G. £5,015
Assistant Under-Secretaries of State, N. J. A. Cheetham, C.M.G.; M. S. Williams, C.M.G.; A. D. Wilson, C.M.G.; J. A. Pilcher, C.M.G.; R. S. Crawford, C.M.G., C.V.O.; J. A. M. Marjoribanks, C.M.G.; L. C. Glass, C.M.G.; E. H. Peck, C.M.G. . . . £4,115
Legal Adviser, Sir Francis Vallat, K.C.M.G., Q.C. £5,015
Deputy Legal Adviser, W. V. J. Evans, C.M.G., M.B.E, £4,115
Legal Counsellors, J. L. Simpson, C.M.G., T.D.; P. L. Bushe-Fox, C.M.G. . . . . £2,865 to £3,565
Assistant Legal Advisers, I. M. Sinclair; H. G. Darwin; F. Burrows; A. D. Watts . . . . £2,304 to £2,865
Director of Communications, E. F. Maltby, C.B.E. £3,500
Director of Research, Librarian and Keeper of the Papers, R. W. Mason, C.M.G. £3,565
Historical Adviser (part-time), R. d' O. Butler £1,720
Her Majesty's Vice-Marshal of the Diplomatic Corps, D. Malcolm, T.D. . . . . £2,865 to £3,565
Corps of Inspectors:
Inspectors, B. J. Garnett, C.M.G., O.B.E. (£4,115); J. V. Rob, C.M.G.; J. F. Brewis, C.M.G., C.V.O.; P. L. Carter; J. O. McCormick, M.C.; W. I. Combs, C.M.G.; H. A. N. Brown, C.M.G., C.V.O. £2,805 to £3,565
Judge of the Chief Court of the Persian Gulf, Sir John Whyatt, Q.C. £4,100
Foreign Service Counsellors, G. G. Arthur, C.M.G.; C. F. R. Barclay; E. J. W. Barnes, M.B.E.; T. F. Brenchley; R. Cecil, C.M.G.; D. S. L. Dodson, C.M.G., M.C.; P. S. Falla; S. Falle, D.S.C.; R. M. Hadow, C.M.G.; J. N. Henderson; E. S. Jones, C.B.E.; H. B. C. Keeble; W. B. J. Ledwidge; D. A. Logan; C. M. MacLehose, M.B.E.; D. Malcolm, T.D.; F. C. Mason, C.M.G.; R. H. Mason, C.M.G., O.B.E.; G. E. Millard, C.M.G., C.V.O.; A. R. Moore; W. Morris; D. F. Muirhead, C.V.O.; A. D. F. Pemberton-Pigott; R. F. G. Sarell, C.M.G.; H. R. Sawbridge, C.B.E.; R. S. Scrivener; R. M. K. Slater, C.M.G.; A. A. S. Stark; J. E. D. Street; D. C. Tebbit; I. F. S. Vincent, M.B.E.; J. W. Wall, C.M.G.; F. A. Warner, C.M.G.; R. G. H. Watts, C.B.E.; P. A. G. Westlake, M.C.; J. O. Wright, D.S.C. £2,865 £3,565
Head of Archives Department, Miss D. A. Denny, O.B.E. . . . . £2,683 to £2,865
Head of Claims Department, E. A. S. Brooks £2,865 to £3,565
Head of Conference and Supply Department, Brig. C. D. Steel, C.M.G., O.B.E. . . . . £2,865 to £3,565
Head of Treaty and Nationality Department, Miss C. J. Polak, M.B.E. . . . . £2,683 to £2,865
Assistants in Departments—First Secretaries, R. McC. Andrew; A. C. Buxton; J. E. Cable; D. C. Carden; P. Cradock; S. Y. Dawbarn; H. J. Downing; J. K. Drinkall; T. A. K. Elliott; J. A. Ford, M.C.; P. M. Foster; J. A. Grant; W. W. Hillier-Fry; R. C. Hope-Jones; D. K. Jamieson; H. B. McK. Johnston; P. H. Lawrence, M.C.; J. H. Lewen; A. F. Maddocks; H. T. A. Overton; Miss J. C. Petrie; J. E. Powell-Jones; C. M. Rose; T. R. M. Sewell; H. B. Shepherd, T.D.; E. Sniders, M.B.E.; D. J. Speares; R. J. Stratton; D. M. Summerhayes; C. A. Thompson; J. P. Waterfield; J. F. Wearing; D. T. West; A. J. Williams; E. Youde, M.B.E. . . . £1,959 to £2,711

Foreign Service Branch B (Grade II), F. B. G. Bevan; D. G. Crichton; W. F. M. Davies, O.B.E.; L. E. Hanham; E. G. Harman; R. T. Landale; J. L. N. O'Loughlin; H. V. Richardson; W. Sharpe; A. Shepherd; D. W. T. Smithies; Miss M. L. C. Woodham, O.B.E.; E. E. Young; Miss F. M. Young .... £2,237 to £2,572
Foreign Service Branch B (Grade III), D. R. M. Acland; I. C. L. Alexander, O.B.E.; Miss E. M. Baker; A. G. Banks; Miss D. E. Betts; D. F. Burden; R. Clark; J. W. S. Corbett; L. Cox; E. C. C. Crapp; Miss E. E. Crotty, M.B.E.; R. N. Dawson; J. S. Dixon; A. Dockerill; R. E. Gamble; Miss B. M. Gill, M.B.E.; F. W. Hall; A. Harrington; A. F. R. Harvey; H. Holmes; J. D. Lambert, M.B.E.; J. Lee, D.F.C.; Miss W. M. Lloyd; W. R. Loveridge; Miss M. B. McBride; J. A. MacLeod; Hon. Mrs. B. E. Miller; Miss D. E. Puleston; Miss E. A. Redhouse; G. L. Scullard; B. Spencer; E. Sullivan; D. Tonkin; Mrs. N. E. Wallace, M.B.E.; L. E. Webb; J. B. Wright .... £1,680 to £2,126
Signals Department (Government Communications Headquarters), Priors Road, Cheltenham.
Director, Sir Clive Loehnis, K.C.M.G. £4,950
Deputy Director, L. J. Hooper, C.M.G., C.B.E. £4,150
Principal Establishment Officer, W. Millward, C.B.E. £4,050
London Communications—Electronic Security Agency, 8 Palmer Street, S.W.1.
Director, R. F. T. Stannard, O.B.E., D.S.C. ... £4,050
Deputy Director and Establishment Officer, Brig. C. D. Gardiner, C.B.E. (*ret.*) .... £2,800 to £3,500

Passport Office

Clive House, Petty France, S.W.1
[Abbey: 8010]

Branch Passport Office, India Buildings, Water Street, Liverpool 2.
Branch Passport Office, 14 Princes Square, 48 Buchanan Street, Glasgow, C.2.
Passport Agency, 1 May Street, Belfast.
Chief Passport Officer, P. L. Rex, C.B.E. £3,215
Deputy Chief Passport Officer, M. G. Dixon. £2,174 to £2,499
Assistant Passport Officers, Mrs. D. Mumford, M.B.E.; Miss M. A. Ashley; Miss J. K. Gilliam; R. W. Dennis .... £1,633 to £2,061
Establishment Officer and Accountant, R. P. B. Cave £2,174 to £2,499
Officer-in-Charge, Branch Passport Office, Liverpool, Miss C. F. Withers .... £2,109 to £2,434
Officer-in-Charge, Branch Passport Office, Glasgow, Miss S. C. Small .... £1,568 to £2,001

Queen's Foreign Service Messengers

Superintending Queen's Foreign Service Messenger, Lt.-Col. G. P. Murray, D.S.O.
Queen's Foreign Service Messengers, R. A. Perryman; Maj. J. C. G. Dunolly, M.C.; W. Kirkwood, M.B.E.; Lt.-Comdr. S. J. R. G. Woodhouse; Wing-Comdr. T. A. Jefferson, A.F.C.; T. D. Nettleton; Maj. E. J. Wallis; Wing-Comdr. S. C. Norris, D.F.C.; Capt. J. G. Canning; Col. G. W. C. Montgomery, O.B.E.; Maj. M. Godley; Col. J. H. Wakefield; Lt.-Col. F. A. H. Wilson; Lt.-Col. L. A. Villiers; Group Capt. J. P. Scorgie, O.B.E., B.E.M.; Col. A. W. Malcolm, C.V.O.; Col. C. R. Buchanan; Lt.-Col. F. D. Richardson; A. E. C. Moore; Brig. J. P. C. MacKinlay; Capt. H. C. Browne, C.B.E., D.S.O., R.N. (*ret.*); Air Commodore H. F. G. Southey, C.B.; Lt.-Col. P. F. Metcalfe; Col. B. L. Standley; Lt.-Col. A. F. Rowe; Lt.-Col. H. S. Stansfeld; Lt.-Col. D. C. G. Seymour-Evans, M.C.; Lt.-Col. P. de Robeck; Lt.-Col. R. K. Constantine; Lt.-Col. C. F. V. Bagot, O.B.E.; Lt.-Col. J. M. B. Poyntz, O.B.E.; Maj. M. P. D. Cruickshank; Sq.-Ldr. A. P. Hollick; J. D. Blake; A. W. J. Eyers; Maj. H. S. Lyons, M.B.E.; A. P. H. Lousada; Lt.-Col. P. H. Huth; Lt.-Col. A. I. G. Ramsay, O.B.E.; Wing-Comdr. T. Stevenson, A.F.C.; Maj. E. C. Hargreaves; Lt.-Col. A. J. M. Parry; Sq.-Ldr. S. O. R. White.

FORESTRY COMMISSION

25 Savile Row, W.1
[Regent: 0221]

The Forestry Commission, a Body Corporate, is appointed under the *Forestry Acts*, 1919 to 1951. The Commissioners are charged with the general duty of promoting the interests of forestry, the development of afforestation, the production and supply of timber and the maintenance of reserves of growing trees in Great Britain. Including the former Crown Woods, transferred to it in 1924, the Commission has acquired about 2,585,000 acres of land (66 per cent. being plantable), of which 1,399,000 acres are under plantations. Under various grant schemes, financial assistance is given to private owners and local authorities in respect of approved works of afforestation.

Chairman, The Earl Waldegrave, T.D. (*part-time*) £3,000
Forestry Commissioners (Unpaid), Maj. D. C. Bowser, O.B.E.; Lt.-Col. Sir Richard Cotterell, Bt.; E. G. Davies; E. B. Latham, M.M.; Capt. J. Maxwell Macdonald; Maj. Sir William Strang Steel, Bt.; T. Taylor.
Director-General, Sir Henry Beresford-Peirse, Bt., C.B. £5,015
Deputy Director-General, G. B. Ryle £4,115
Secretary, H. A. Turner £4,115
Directors (England) J. R. Thom (25 Savile Row, W.1.); (*Scotland*), J. A. Dickson (25 Drumsheugh Gardens, Edinburgh); (*Wales*), J. Q. Williamson, M.B.E. (Victoria House, Aberystwyth); (*Research*), A. Watt, C.B.E. (Alice Holt Lodge, Farnham, Surrey) .... £3,000 to £3,565

REGISTRY OF FRIENDLY SOCIETIES (CENTRAL OFFICE) AND OFFICE OF THE INDUSTRIAL ASSURANCE COMMISSIONER

17 North Audley Street, W 1
[Mayfair: 7001]

A Barrister was appointed in 1828 to certify the Rules of Savings Banks, and in 1829 to certify those of Friendly Societies. In 1846 he was constituted Registrar of Friendly Societies. By the Friendly Societies Act, 1875, the Central Office of the Registry of Friendly Societies was created, consisting of the Chief Registrar and the Assistant Registrars for England. It exercises numerous and important functions under the Friendly Societies Acts, the Industrial and Provident Societies Acts, the Building Societies Acts, the Trade Union Acts, the Scientific Societies Act, the Trustee Saving Banks and Post Office Savings Bank Acts, the Loan Societies Act, the Shop Clubs Act, the Superannuation and other Trust Funds (Validation) Act and the Prevention of Fraud (Investments) Act. Under the Industrial Assurance Acts, the Chief Registrar is charged with various powers and duties in relation to Industrial Assurance Companies and Collecting Societies, and in that capacity is styled the Industrial Assurance Commissioner.

Chief Registrar and Industrial Assurance Commissioner, S. D. Musson, C.B., M.B.E. £5,015
Private Sec., Miss M. E. Blake.
Assistant Registrar and Deputy Industrial Assurance Commissioner, R. E. Grindle £3,815
Asst. Registrar, A. Vollmar ...... £2,965 to £3,565
Executive Registrar, A. A. C. Soper (*also Establishment Officer*) .... £2,683 to £2,865
Senior Legal Assistant, J. E. Gower, M.C. £2,239 to £2,865
Registration Branch (Head), A. J. Gilliver, £2,237 to £2,572; (*Assist. Head*), H. F. Denyer £1,680 to £2,126
Returns and Statistics Branch (Head) J. A. Walter, £2,237 to £2,572; (*Assist. Head*), A. Theaker £1,680 to £2,126
Establishment and Records Branch (Head), J. W. D. Goss .... £1,680 to £2,126

Investigations Branch (Head), E. S. Burgess £1,680 to £2,126
Disputes Branch (Head), E. C. Jones £1,680 to £2,126

Registry of Friendly Societies, Scotland
19 Heriot Row, Edinburgh, 3
[Edinburgh Waverley: 4371]
Assistant Registrar, J. Craig, W.S.

THE GAS COUNCIL
1 Grosvenor Place, S.W.1
[Belgravia: 4321]

The Gas Council was set up by the Gas Act, 1948, to advise the Minister of Power on the affairs of the gas industry and to assist the Area Boards in the discharge of their functions. It is responsible for the creation and issue of British Gas Stock.
Chairman, Sir Henry Jones, M.B.E. (*plus allowances* £1,000) £8,500
Deputy Chairman, Sir William Hutchison, C.B.E. (*plus allowances* £500) £7,500
The Members are the Chairmen of the 12 Area Gas Boards.
Secretary, R. G. Huxtable, M.B.E.

Chairmen of Area Gas Boards

Scottish, S. Smith, C.B.E.
Northern, Dr. J. Burns, G.M.
North Western, D. P. Welman.
North Eastern, Dr. R. S. Edwards.
East Midlands, R. S. Johnson, M.B.E., T.D.
West Midlands, C. H. Leach, C.B.E.
Wales, T. Mervyn Jones, C.B.E.
Eastern, J. H. Dyde, O.B.E.
North Thames, M. Milne-Watson, C.B.E.
South Eastern, R. N. B. D. Bruce, O.B.E., T.D.
Southern, A. F. Hetherington, D.S.C.
South Western, C. H. Chester, C.B.E.
each £6,500 (*plus allowances* £500)

GENERAL REGISTER OFFICE
(England and Wales)
Somerset House, W.C.2
[Temple Bar: 2407]

All departments close at noon on Saturdays.
Registrar General, M. Reed, C.B. £4,215
Assistant Secretaries, R. M. Blaikley (*Establishment Officer*); F. A. Rooke-Matthews £2,800 to £3,500
Chief Statisticians, C. C. Spicer (*Medical*), £3,750; A. J. Boreham (*Population*)... £2,800 to £3,500
Statisticians (Medical), L. Lipworth; W. A. Wilson £1,904 to £3,075
Statisticians (Population), S. Day; J. A. Rowntree; J. R. L. Schneider.......... £1,894 to £2,646
Principals, L. M. Feery; Miss A. B. Graham; J. Murray.................. £1,894 to £2,646
Chief Executive Officers, V. M. Harris; I. Hutchinson; J. R. Jeffery; D. J. Smale; R. P. Thorby £2,172 to £2,507

Scotland
See under SCOTTISH OFFICE

THE GOVERNMENT ACTUARY
Caxton House East, Tothill Street, S.W.1
[Abbey: 4234]

Government Actuary, H. Tetley, C.B. £5,815
Deputy Government Actuary, P. R. Cox.... £4,115
Principal Actuaries, C. E. Clarke, C.B.E.; L. V. Martin; F. Gordon Smith; C. M. Stewart £2,865 to £3,565
Actuaries, J. R. Ford; R. C. Gilder; G. T. Humphrey; E. A. Johnston; Miss I. A. Laurence; W. M. Low; G. G. Newton; W. V. Webb £2,237 to £2,711

THE GOVERNMENT CHEMIST
(*See under* DEPARTMENT OF SCIENTIFIC AND INDUSTRIAL RESEARCH).

GOVERNMENT HOSPITALITY FUND
The Treasury, Whitehall, S.W.1
[Whitehall: 1481]

Instituted in 1908 for the purpose of organizing official hospitality on a regular basis, with a view to the promotion of international goodwill.
Minister in Charge, RT. HON. GEOFFREY RIPPON, M.P.
Secretary, Brigadier Sir Geoffrey Macnab, K.C.M.G., C.B. £3,300

MINISTRY OF HEALTH
Alexander Fleming House, Elephant and Castle, S.E.1.
[Hop: 5522]

The Ministry of Health was established by the *Ministry of Health Act*, 1919, to exercise in England and Wales functions with respect to health and local government which, in the main, were previously exercised by the Local Government Board and the National Health Insurance Commission. Responsibility for the National Health Insurance and the Widows', Orphans' and Old Age Contributory Pensions Schemes was transferred to the Ministry of National Insurance on April 1, 1945. The functions of the Ministry relating to local government, rating and valuation, public health, housing, rent control, burials and coast protection were transferred to the Ministry of Housing and Local Government on January 30, 1951. The responsibility for hospitals, limb-fitting, the supply of surgical appliances and certain treatment services formerly undertaken by the Ministry of Pensions was assumed on August 31, 1953. Since 1955 the Ministry has assumed responsibilities for food hygiene and welfare foods which were previously carried out by the Ministry of Food. On May 1, 1957, responsibility for certain aspects of the recruitment of nurses and midwives was transferred from the Ministry of Labour and National Service to the Ministry of Health. The main administrative divisions in the Ministry of Health deal with general practitioner services; nursing; general relations with various health professions; Local Authority health and welfare services; hospitals and specialist services; mental health services; nutrition, and international health. The Department is also responsible for the National Hospital Service Reserve and, in conjunction with the Home Office, for the Ambulance and First Aid Section of the Civil Defence Corps under the Civil Defence Act, 1948.

Minister, THE RT. HON. (JOHN) ENOCH POWELL, M.B.E., M.P. £5,000
Private Secretary, L. H. Brandes.
Assistant Private Sec., B. A. Harrison.
Parliamentary Private Secretary, M. Maddan, M.P.
Parliamentary Secretaries, B. R. Braine, M.P.; The Lord Newton £2,500
Permanent Secretary, Sir Bruce Fraser, K.C.B.. £7,015
Private Secretary, P. J. Wormald.
Deputy Secretary, A. W. France, C.B. £5,015
Chief Medical Officer, Sir George Godber, K.C.B. £5,815
Solicitor and Legal Adviser, J. C. Blake, C.B... £5,015
Under-Secretary for Finance and Accountant-General, F. A. Adams £4,115
Under-Secretary and Director of Establishments and Organization, J. E. Pater, C.B. £4,115
Under Secretaries, A. R. W. Bavin; J. P. Dodds, C.B.; D. Emery; R. Gedling; T. E. H. Hodgson, C.B.; D. Somerville £4,115
Assistant Secretaries, E. B. S. Alton, M.B.E., M.C.; P. Benner; L. H. Brandes; R. L. Briggs; Mrs. E. G. Croft; A. Emanuel, C.M.G.; M. R. P. Gregson; E. Halliday; Mrs. J. A. Hauff; Miss H. M. Hedley; M. J. Hewitt; J. F. Hunt; W. J. Littlewood; L. G. S. Mason, O.B.E.; P. V. Muston; Mrs. D. M. O'Brien; E. T. Prideaux, O.B.E.; R. T. P. Pronger; H. N. Roffey; M. H. Rossington; H. C. Salter, D.F.C.; S. I. Smith; R. F. Tyas;

T. B. Williamson; W. G. Wilson, O.B.E.; J. T. Woodlock .... £2,865 to £3,565
Principal Regional Officers, C. E. Asher (£2,925); T. H. Carruthers; Miss A. E. Earlam; C. P. Goodale; V. F. Jones (£2,411 to £2,746); L. R. Macbeth, O.B.E.; J. McCree, I.S.O.; A. J. Merritt (£2,411 to £2,746); J. G. Paterson; C. N. Rhodes (£2,411 to £2,746) . £2,133 to £2,885
Principals, Miss M. F. B. Boys; J. R. Brough; J. P. Cashman; R. E. Clark; G. S. Downey; T. E. Dutton; R. Ellerington; W. F. Farrant; S. H. Findlay; J. M. Foster; W. A. Fuller, D.S.C.; H. Herzmark; Miss P. Hirst; Miss P. A. Hooper; G. G. Hulme; W. Hutchison; N. Illingworth; D. U. Jackson; C. R. O. Jones; W. N. Judd, D.F.C.; E. W. L. Keymer, M.C.; J. E. King; W. F. Lake; S. G. Mackenzie; Miss S. M. Masel; R. S. Matthews; R. B. Mayoh; E. L. Mayston; E. B. Midgley; K. J. Moyes, M.B.E.; J. Murray; T. E. Nodder; W. D. Paget; Mrs. V. J. M. Poole; Mrs. K. M. Potter; Mrs. A. M. Reisner; W. O. Roberts; Miss M. A. J. Robinson; C. L. Sargent; H. W. Seabourn; H. W. Silver; A. L. Thompson; W. Turner; E. L. Wallis; F. D. K. Williams; Mrs. P. M. Williamson ...... £1,959 to £2,711
Public Relations and Principal Press Officer, S. A. Heald, O.B.E. .... £2,715 to £3,415
Press Officer, H. S. Harding, O.B.E. £2,237 to £2,572
Assistant Press Officers, A. M. Paton; Mrs. J. E. Samson .... £1,680 to £2,126
Senior Publicity Assistants, Miss B. J. Crawter; Mrs. H. M. Robins .... £1,680 to £2,126
Librarian, A. E. Fountain ...... £1,680 to £2,126
Chief Statistician, B. Benjamin .. £2,865 to £3,565
Medical Statistician, M. A. Heasman £3,500
Statisticians, R. Ash; E. R. Bransby (*Social Economist*); Miss E. M. Brooks; Mrs. C. M. Firth; K. M. Francis .... £1,959 to £2,711
Principal Executive Officers, J. B. Cornish,; S M. Davies; R. C. Millward £3,215
Senior Chief Executive Officers, N. Hollens; G. E. John; W. Perkins, O.B.E.; C. G. Taylor
£2,607 to £2,865
Chief Executive Officers, L. G. Barter; B. H. Betts; C. S. Brady; R. Cattran; Miss E. C. Corry-Smith; B. J. Crisp; Miss J. Davison; P. W. Day; P. C. Denny; F. W. Harris; A. W. Hornsby; F. R. Howes; Mrs. M. M. Perry; R. P. Pole; A. B. Rees; C. H. Robinet; A. M. Storrie; J. Thompson; R. C. Trant; T. F. Trevail; P. J. Ward; C. K. Whitaker; E. G. White, M.B.E.; H. V. White; J. E. Worth, D.F.C.; R. Wright; L. Yates
£2,237 to £2,572
Senior Executive Officers, C. G. R. Alderman; B. R. Aldridge; D. R. Armitage; L. Beren; J. Beveridge; K. W. Blakey; J. S. F. Blanchard; K. B. Bocking; R. Bolton; W. Brewer; B. A. R. Cheeseman; M. H. Clark; G. F. C. Clarke; R. R. Coleman; E. F. Cooper; H. R. Dowling; S. C. Edwards; F. J. Farrell, M.B.E.; A. Forbes; Miss K. V. Green; Miss J. Harrington; Miss D. F. Hawthorn; E. C. Haxton; L. Hitchen; G. L. Hughes; A. N. Jackson; P. W. Jenden; H. G. Jones; D. E. McCarthy; J. G. Martin; P. C. R. Masters; E. J. Mattison; Miss N. I. Maynard; W. G. Molyneux; J. Muir; Miss M. P. Newton; T. P. O'Mara; L. R. Payne; Miss L. R. Prescott, M.B.E.; J. E. T. Rankin; Miss E. M. Reeve; A. F. Richards, M.B.E.; E. Robinson; G. L. Scales; J. Seaward; F. E. Smith; B. H. Street; P. H. Sullivan; R. E. Taylor; J. O. Thorn; G. R. Totman; F. E. Webb; R. H. Westlake; M. Wilson; R. V. Woodroof.... £1,680 to £2,126
Chief Inspector, C. W. G. Barton £2,715
Chief Technical Inspector, J. Walker
£1,516 to £2,015
Senior Technical Officers, R. L. Bellis; R. W. H. Cook; E. H. Fagg; E. Fawcitt; R. Higson; R. Walker .... £1,599 to £1,921

Accountant-General's Department

Under-Secretary for Finance and Accountant-General, F. A. Adams £4,115
Principal Executive Officers, F. J. Aldridge; C. L. Bourton; C. W. Hales-Hunt £3,065
Senior Chief Executive Officers, J. Hegarty; L. B. Jacques; R. A. Owen; G. W. H. Woodman
£2,607 to £2,865
Chief Executive Officers, E. A. Arnold; S. Bayfield; Mrs. J. Coyne; R. A. French; H. W. Goodfellow; R. L. Gordon; Miss E. F. Musto; K. Shuttleworth; T. A. Sidford; E. R. Stuart; B. G. Tozer .... £2,237 to £2,572
Senior Executive Officers, V. J. Alcock; J. Allan; L. Best; H. E. T. Booth; T. I. Butler; J. Chadwick; N. S. Collins; L. Devine; J. B. Filburn; H. J. Foster; I. G. Gardiner; J. H. Gawley; Miss M. E. Hammond; J. W. Joy; G. T. King; W. J. Lester; J. F. Mann; A. J. Martinsen; R. Melvin; A. Miller; W. A. O'Connor; M. W. Perry; K. Shackleton; F. W. Shaw; Miss R. W. Taylor; T. R. Thain; T. C. Threlfall; Miss D. C. Trew; W. Trueblood; J. A. Warwick; N. Waters; B. Wilcox; D. Williamson ..... £1,680 to £2,126

Health Services Superannuation Division

Principal Executive Officer, Mrs. J. G. Pillar . £3,060
Senior Chief Executive Officer, D. L. Ibbott
£2,607 to £2,865
Chief Executive Officers, T. K. Alcock; Mrs. E. A. Hutchinson .... £2,237 to £2,572
Senior Executive Officers, J. R. Briggs; P. H. Brown; B. K. Chambers; K. R. Creedy; A. B. Great-Rex; D. R. Knight; D. H. S. Ward
£1,680 to £2,126

Medical Staff

Chief Medical Officer, Sir George Godber, K.C.B.
£5,815
Deputy Chief Medical Officers, D. Thomson, C.B., Q.H.P.; Miss A. L. Winner, O.B.E. £4,415
Principal Medical Officers, R. H. L. Cohen; I. G. Davies; R. K. Freudenberg, £4,115; E. T. Conybeare, O.B.E.; D. W. Jolly, O.B.E.; W. H. P. Minto; L. H. Murray, O.B.E.; A. T. Roden; J. M. Ross; R. M. Shaw; D. S. Todd-White; G. C. Tooth; H. Yellowlees £3,815
Senior Medical Officers, R. H. Barrett; W. T. C. Berry; C. A. Boucher, O.B.E.; D. H. Burbridge, O.B.E.; T. E. A. Carr; Miss R. N. Chamberlain; Mrs. C. N. Dennis; P. F. Early; A. J. Eley; R. Goulding; T. J. B. Green; A. B. Harrington; J. H. T. Harrington; W. Lees; D. S. McKenzie; J. L. McLetchie, C.M.G., O.B.E.; A. E. Martin; C. Muir; E. C. Murphy, T.D.; Brig. R. V. Phillipson, O.B.E.; F. Riley; E. D. Robb; C. Seeley; P. Seelig; G. S. Thompson; J. G. Thomson; J. N. Twohig; Col. E. E. S. Wheatley, C.B.E., D.F.C., T.D.; G. W. Whittall; R. Wilkins; J. M. G. Wilson
£3,415
Medical Officers, G. L. Alcock; H. M. Archibald, M.B.E.; R. B. Bell; J. F. E. Bloss; J. C. Brass; R. G. Bryce; R. G. Buxton; M. H. Cosbie; A. Cruickshank, O.B.E.; R. D. L. Davies; H. J. B. Day; Brig. A. B. Dempsey; D. Dooley; W. N. Dunnet; H. M. Elliott; J. A. Fitzgerald; Mrs. P. W. Fleming; J. Fletcher; Miss M. G. Gorrie; C. E. Halliday; D. L. Harbinson, O.B.E.; E. E. Harris; E. E. Henderson; R. Hudson-Evans; J. L. Hunt; Miss M. A. C. Kuck; W. C. Lawrence; E. D. T. Lewis; K. W. Lovel; L. P. McCullagh; A. McGregor; Sir Arthur MacNalty, K.C.B.; Mrs. M. M. Manson; Brig. G. M. Marsden, C.B.E.; C. C. D. Martin; P. A. Maughan; Surg. Rear-Adm. R. W. Mussen, C.B., C.B.E.; C. G. M. Nicol; G. R. Parry; R. H. Purnell; J. H. Ramage; R. G. Redhead; V. Roman; Miss M. D. H. Sheridan; Mrs. E. C. Shore; Lt.-Col. E. A. Smyth; D. S. Toole; M. Vitali; T. G. Williams; R. Williamson .... £2,477 to £3,140

Regional General Medical Staff

Principal Medical Officer in Charge of Regional Medical Services, C. E. Gallagher, O.B.E. £4,115
Principal Medical Officer, K. A. Boughton-Thomas
£3,750

Senior Medical Officers, R. W. Bone; A. W. Lilley; W. Meikle; E. Mence; I. E. Phelps; J. E. Struthers £3,500
Medical Officers, J. Adam, O.B.E.; W. D. Anderson; A. T. Ashcroft; J. Barr; J. C. H. Bird; P. F. Bishop; J. D. Black; J. C. B. Bone; C. M. Boucher; A. Brebner; G. Bridge; D. W. E. Burridge; S. Campbell; J. M. Canning; G. Cornah; E. J. S. Evans; G. I. G. Findlay; H. J. Gibson; P. B. Hanbury; T. S. Hanlin; R. C. Hill; P. N. Holmes; M. Hutchinson; P. W. Jack; A. G. Jackson; A. T. L. Kingdon; H. J. Lee; C. J. Livingstone; C. E. B. Lynch; A. F. Macbean; J. R. McBoyle; J. Mackellar; A. Maclaine; E. G. L. Mark; A. Markson; C. R. Morison; M. A. Nicholson; D. B. Robb; E. D. Robb; J. D. Robertson; A. W. M. Rooke; S. Ruttle; G. R. M. Sichel; A. B. Stewart; H. A. Tuck; B. C. Welshman; J. A. Whyte; W. Wilson £2,412 to £3,075

Dental Staff

Chief Dental Officer, Surgeon Rear-Adm. (*D.*) W. Holgate, C.B., O.B.E., R.N.(*ret.*) £3,865
Deputy Chief Dental Officer, F. S. S. Whiter, O.B.E. £3,515
Senior Dental Officers, R. A. Campbell; H. A. Dixey; Miss J. R. Forrest, O.B.E.; L. G. Hitching, T.D.; Miss E. M. Knowles, O.B.E.; G. A. Rowse; A. G. Smith £3,240
Dental Officers, R. D. Buchan; E. S. Cross; P. A. Crow; A. Ferrari; I. C. S. Fraser; M. A. Freeman, M.C.; F. D. R. Geldard; A. R. Gillies; A. W. Holman; V. Howarth; E. E. Jackson; I. H. Jones; N. I. MacMillan; A. McPherson; R. W. Mather; R. Middleton; W. N. M. Niven; J. A. O'Connor, M.B.E.; Miss J. D. Oswald; D. S. Prichard; G. B. Roberts; P. D. M. Rowland; A. J. Vaughton; H. Walker; R. B. Whalley; J. H. Whittle; G. V. L. Williams, T.D.,; J. C. Williams £2,153 to £2,800

Pharmaceutical, Nursing and Welfare Staff, etc.

Chief Pharmacist, H. Davis, C.B.E. £3,190
Senior Technical Officer, R. Higson £1,599 to £1,921
Ambulance Adviser, T. G. Mullen £2,353
Adviser on Radio-active Substances, W. Binks (*part time*) £1,700
Chief Nursing Officer, Miss K. A. Raven £2,990
Deputy Chief Nursing Officers, Miss E. Jackson, O.B.E.; Miss D. M. White £2,041
Mental Nursing Officers, F. J. Ely; Miss O. F. Griffith .... £1,422 to £1,693
Public Health Nursing Officers, Misses M. M. Bathgate, M.B.E.; M. H. Cook, M.B.E.; K. Drage; A. E. Girling; F. L. Gray; F. A. Heaney; R. E. Maguire; M. W. Slight; E. M. Trehearn; A. Webster £1,362 to £1,628
Hospital Nursing Officers, Miss C. Biddulph; Mrs. J. Heywood; Misses M. le Q. Mitchell; P. I. M. Robson; M. Simpson; E. West; J. G. Whitehead; M. Williams ... £1,362 to £1,628
Artificial Limb Research Officer, N. A. M. Swettenham, O.B.E. £2,528
Chief Welfare Officer, Miss A. M. Sheridan . £2,129
Deputy Chief Welfare Officers, Miss E. L. Hope-Murray; Mrs. D. Ottley ..... £1,817 to £1,947
Welfare Officers, J. Castelow; Mrs. W. M. Curzon; Mrs. D. Leaf; Misses H. Brown; K. Buchanan; K. E. G. Davidge; C. M. Gavin; M. G. M. Gordon; F. E. Handasyde; A. D. Kelly; L. M. Mason; J. R. Mijouain; M. E. Openshaw; B. H. Roberts; D. Sharp; M. B. Wann; H. Wheatcroft, M.B.E. .... £1,362 to £1,628
Inspector of Welfare of the Blind, Miss W. L. Adams, M.B.E. £1,693
Senior Adviser on Catering and Dietetics, Miss E. Washington (+*allce.* £120) £1,688
Advisers on Catering and Dietetics, Misses J. B. F. Beveridge; H. G. Cairney, M.B.E.; A. K. Chalmers; E. C. B. Ross .... £1,412 to £1,688
Advisers on Hospital Domestic Management, Miss J. M. Howat; Mrs. M. J. Brash-Smith; Mrs. E. E. M. Stew .... £1,412 to £1,688
Food Hygiene Advisory Officer, M. T. Parry .. £2,197

Architects

Chief Architect, W. E. Tatton Brown £4,115
Superintending Architect, M. C. Tebbitt, C.B.E. £3,715
Principal Architects, R. H. Goodman; R. F. Radford; A. Roberts; A. V. Robertson, O.B.E.; W. E. Sidnell .... £2,715 to £3,065
Architects (Senior Grade), M. J. Bench; W. J. H. Dungey; G. L. Martin; W. L. Nicholson; D. J. Petty, M.B.E. .... £2,145 to £2,457
Architects (Main Grade), L. J. Connor; C. Davies; J. E. Deleuse; A. Diprose; J. R. B. Green; R. Grunberg; L. E. Knight; V. A. Liff; D. R. J. Martin; A. J. Noakes; Mrs. A. M. Nutting; Z. P. Słaski; Miss E. B. J. Thomas; J. D. Twells-Grosse; J. Ward .... £1,516 to £2,015
Chief Quantity Surveyor, L. McL. Watson £2,715 to £3,065
Quantity Surveyors (Senior Grade), R. T. V. Amery; E. G. Lasseter .... £2,145 to £2,457
Quantity Surveyors (Main Grade), G. R. Barber; N. G. M. Barton; B. R. Broadway; W. V. Buckle; S. G. Cooke; P. Coy; D. E. Hook £1,516 to £2,015

Engineering Staff

Chief Engineer, D. A. Hughes £3,715
Superintending Engineers, L. T. Davis; M. Drury; G. S. Gillard; C. A. Powell .. £2,715 to £3,065
Engineering Inspectors, J. S. Alton; J. H. H. Marshall £1,905 to £2,465
Engineers, Senior Grade, D. Clayton; A. K. Dobbie; S. Fidler; P. M. Harms; B. Joseph; T. A. Nicholls £2,145 to £2,457
Laundry Engineers, C. Haggas; S. J. Whitaker £1,516 to £2,015
Engineers, Main Grade, B. E. Jannaway; P. Y. M. Duncan; D. L. Mumford; A. Smith; R. F. Stephens; J. A. Sutherland; H. Weatherley £1,516 to £2,015

Legal Branch

Solicitor and Legal Adviser, J. C. Blake, C.B. .. £5,015
Principal Assistant Solicitor, E. H. Watson ... £4,115
Asst. Solicitors, J. Austin; S. H. Brookfield, C.B.E.; J. B. Davidson; H. R. Green; J. C. Hales; V. J Lewis; J. S. Ryan; P. N. Townsend. £2,815 to £3,415
Senior Legal Assistants, N. G. Bird; Mrs. M. D. Charles; K. A. T. Davey; R. G. C. Davison; R. P. A. Douglas; Miss E. H. Forbes; G. E. Gammie; I. C. M. Hamilton; Miss L. M. Hammond; J. M. Keidan; F. D. Kennedy; Miss P. B. Morris; W. H. J. Parish; Miss F. Potter, M.B.E.; G. D. Wheway £2,103 to £2,715

NATIONAL HEALTH SERVICE

(For main article, *see* Index)

Regional Hospital Boards

England and Wales are divided into 15 hospital regions, each with its own Regional Hospital Board which administers the hospital and specialist services in the area. The Regional Hospital Boards do not, however, administer Teaching Hospitals, which have their own Boards of Governors.

The Chairmen and members of Regional Hospital Boards and Boards of Governors are appointed by the Minister of Health in accordance with the third schedule to the National Health Service Act, 1946.

Areas

Newcastle, Benfield Road, Newcastle upon Tyne 6. *Chairman*, Sir Edward Collingwood, C.B.E. *Secretary*, R. Dobbin.
Leeds, Park Parade, Harrogate, Yorks. *Chairman*, L. F. Laycock, O.B.E. *Secretary*, W. A. Shee.

Sheffield, Fulwood House, Old Fulwood Road, Sheffield, 10. *Chairman*, A. V. Martin, C.B.E. *Secretary*, L. W. Faulkner.
East Anglian (*Cambridge*), 117 Chesterton Road, Cambridge. *Chairman*, Sir Stephen Green, Bt. *Secretary*, K. V. F. Morton, C.I.E.
North West Metropolitan, 40 Eastbourne Terrace, W.2. *Chairman*, The Lord Moynihan, O.B.E. *Secretary*, A. J. Bennett.
North East Metropolitan, 40 Eastbourne Terrace, W.2. *Chairman*, Sir Graham Rowlandson, M.B.E. *Secretary*, C. E. Nicol, O.B.E.
South East Metropolitan, 40 Eastbourne Terrace, W.2. *Chairman*, Sir Ivor Julian, C.B.E. *Secretary*, C. M. Ker, O.B.E.
South West Metropolitan, 40 Eastbourne Terrace, W.2. *Chairman*, A. G. Linfield, C.B.E. *Secretary*, E. G. Braithwaite.
Oxford, 43 Banbury Road, Oxford. *Chairman*, Mrs. I. Graham-Bryce. *Secretary*, G. Watts, O.B.E.
South Western, 27 Tyndalls Park Road, Bristol 8. *Chairman*, Col. H. A. Guy, O.B.E., T.D. *Secretary* H. W. White.
Wales, Temple of Peace and Health, Cathays Park, Cardiff. *Chairman*, Sir Godfrey Llewellyn, Bt., C.B., C.B.E., M.C., T.D. *Secretary*, A. E. Newell.
Birmingham, 10 Augustus Road, Edgbaston, Birmingham 15. *Chairman*, J. T. Lewis. *Secretary*, W. F. Newstead.
Manchester, Cheetwood Road, Manchester 8. *Chairman*, Sir James Lythgoe, C.B.E. *Secretary*, J. Gibbon.
Liverpool, Pearl Assurance House, 55 Castle Street, Liverpool 2. *Chairman*, Sir Thomas Harley, M.B.E., M.C. *Secretary*, V. Collinge.
Wessex, Highcroft, Romsey Road, Winchester, Hants. *Chairman*, P. G. Templeman. *Secretary*, G. Bowden.

(SCOTLAND)
See under Scottish Office

WELSH BOARD OF HEALTH

Cathays Park, Cardiff
[Cardiff: 28066]

Chairman, A. F. Williams, C.M.G. £4,050
Members of Board, A. R. Culley, C.B.E., M.D., Q.H.P. (*Medical*), £4,050; A. Owen, M.C. £2,800 to £3,500.
Principals, F. D. Riddett; J. G. Stephens (*Chief Accountant and Establishment Officer*); H. E. Leonard .... £1,894 to £2,646
Chief Executive Officer, M. G. Evans £2,172 to £2,507
Senior Executive Officers, Mrs. E. O. James; G. H. Nowell; G. Roberts; T. Williams £1,615 to £2,061
Senior Medical Officer, R. T. Bevan, M.D. .. £3,500
Senior Medical Officer (*Regional Medical Service*), T. J. M. Gregg, O.B.E. £3,500
Medical Officers, Mrs. M. W. Jenkins; G. J. Roberts, M.D.; T. D. L. Thomas ...... £2,412 to £3,075
Medical Officers (*Regional Medical Service*), E. A. Wilson; J. O. Williams; G. M. Evans; H. A. Mullen, T.D., Q.H.P.; A. J. R. Hudson £2,412 to £3,075
Medical Officers (*Artificial Limb and Appliance Service*), G. A. L. Jones; A. A. G. Dean, M.D. £2,412 to £3,075
Dental Officers, G. E. Morgan; G. Morris; T. W. Beer .... £2,306 to £2,950
Legal Adviser, D. E. Davies ...... £2,239 to £2,800
Senior Legal Assistant, G. Davies . £2,239 to £2,800
Legal Assistant, A. Howe .... £1,232 to £2,061
Architect (*Senior Grade*), J. T. Darch £2,228 to £2,563
Architect (*Main Grade*), J. K. Harding £1,559 to £2,089

DEPARTMENT OF HEALTH FOR SCOTLAND

See Scottish Office

HERRING INDUSTRY BOARD

1 Glenfinlas Street, Edinburgh 3
[Caledonian: 4241]

Chairman, Sir John Carmichael, K.B.E. (*part-time*) £2,500
Members, W. J. L. Dean, O.B.E. (*part-time*) £2,500 *in respect of this and other appointments in White Fish Authority*; The Lord Lloyd, M.B.E.; E. H. M. Cluttenbuck, O.B.E. (*part-time*) £1,000
Gen. Manager, H. H. Goodwin, C.B.E.
Secretary, A. Fairley.

HISTORIC BUILDINGS COUNCILS

Established under the *Historic Buildings and Ancient Monuments Act*, 1953, to advise the Minister of Public Building and Works on the exercise of his powers under the Act to make grants towards the repair or maintenance of buildings of outstanding historic or architectural interest, their contents and adjoining land, and, where necessary, to acquire such buildings or to assist the National Trusts or local authorities to acquire them. In 1963–64, £500,000 is available for allocation as repair and maintenance grants.

England

Abell House, John Islip Street, S.W.1

Chairman, The Lord Hailes, P.C., G.B.E., C.H.
Members, R. S. Dutton, F.S.A.; Rt. Hon. J. Chuter Ede, C.H., M.P.; Miss D. M. Elliott, C.B.E.; The Earl of Euston, F.S.A.; Sir William Holford; C. E. C. Hussey, C.B.E., F.S.A.; Sir Charles Mott-Radclyffe, M.P.; The Countess of Radnor, O.B.E.; Sir John Summerson, C.B.E., F.S.A., F.B.A.
Secretary T. L. Jones.

Wales

St. Agnes Road, Gabalfa, Cardiff

Chairman, Col. Sir Grismond Philipps, C.V.O.
Members, The Marquess of Anglesey, F.S.A.; S. Colwyn Foulkes, O.B.E.; J. D. K. Lloyd, O.B.E., F.S.A.; Maj H. J. Lloyd-Johnes, T.D., F.S.A.; G. O. Robers, M.P.; Prof. Glanmor Williams.
Secretary (vacant).

Scotland

122 George Street, Edinburgh

Chairman, The Earl Cawdor, T.D.
Members, Sir Arthur Duncan; J. L. Gleave, R.S.A.; The Countess of Haddington; I. G. Lindsay, O.B.E., R.S.A., F.R.I.B.A., F.S.A.Scot.; The Lord Polwarth, T.D.; D. C. Scott-Moncrieff, C.V.O., W.S.; A. A. Templeton, C.B.E.; Rt. Hon. A. Woodburn, M.P.
Secretary, G. D. Crane.

HISTORICAL MANUSCRIPTS COMMISSION

See Record Office

ROYAL COMMISSION ON HISTORICAL MONUMENTS (ENGLAND)

Fielden House, Great College Street, S.W.1
[Abbey: 7041]

The Royal Commission on Historical Monuments (England) was appointed in 1908 to survey and publish in inventory form an account of every building, earthwork or stone construction up to the year 1714. The terminal date was extended after the late war to 1850. The Commission has published up to present date inventories covering seven counties, three cities and Roman York. It is a purely recording body and while the Commissioners may recommend that certain structures should be preserved, they have no power to implement their recommendations.

Chairman, The Marquess of Salisbury, K.G., P.C., F.S.A.
Commissioners, Sir Albert Richardson, K.C.V.O., R.A., Litt.D., F.S.A., F.R.I.B.A.,; Professor I. A. Richmond, C.B.E., D.Litt., Ll.D., F.B.A., F.S.A.; Professor V. H. Galbraith, D.Lit., Litt.D., F.B.A.; Professor S.

Piggott, F.B.A., F.S.A.; Sir John Summerson, C.B.E., F.B.A., F.S.A., A.R.I.B.A.; Professor H. C. Darby, O.B.E., Ph.D.; Christopher Hussey, C.B.E., F.S.A.; C. A. Ralegh Radford, F.B.A., F.S.A.; Prof. J. G. D. Clark, Ph.D., F.B.A., F.S.A.; Prof. F. Wormald, Litt.D., F.B.A., F.S.A.; and the Lords Lieutenant of the counties at the time of survey.
Secretary, A. R. Dufty £3,000

ROYAL COMMISSION ON ANCIENT MONUMENTS IN WALES AND MONMOUTHSHIRE

17 Queens Road, Aberystwyth
[Aberystwyth: 256]

The Commission was appointed in 1908 to make an inventory of the Ancient and Historical Monuments in Wales and Monmouthshire.
Chairman, Prof. Sir Goronwy Edwards, D.Litt., F.B.A.
Commissioners, R. J. C. Atkinson, F.S.A.; Prof. A. H. Dodd; Prof. I. Ll. Foster, F.S.A.; Prof. W. F. Grimes, C.B.E., F.S.A.; Prof. E. M. Jope, F.S.A.; A. J. Taylor, F.S.A.; Prof. Glanmor Williams; R. B. Wood-Jones, Ph.D., F.S.A.
Secretary, A. H. A. Hogg, F.S.A.

ROYAL COMMISSION ON ANCIENT AND HISTORICAL MONUMENTS OF SCOTLAND

7 Coates Gardens, Edinburgh 12
[Edinburgh: Don. 7680]

The Commission was appointed in 1908 to make an inventory of the Ancient and Historical Monuments of Scotland from the earliest times to 1707, and to specify those that seem most worthy of preservation. The terms of reference were extended by Royal Warrant dated Jan. 1, 1948, to cover the period since 1707 at the Commissioners' discretion.
Chairman, The Earl of Wemyss and March Ll.D.
Commissioners, Prof. I. A. Richmond, C.B.E., Ll.D., Litt.D., D.Lit., F.B.A., F.S.A.; Prof. S. Piggott, D.Litt., F.B.A., F.S.A.; W. Douglas Simpson, C.B.E., D.Litt., Ll.D., F.S.A.; I. G. Lindsay, O.B.E., R.S.A., F.R.I.B.A.; Mrs. A. I. Dunlop, O.B.E., Ph.D., D.Litt., L.D.; A. Graham, F.S.A.
Secretary, K. A. Steer, Ph.D., F.S.A. £2,497

ANCIENT MONUMENTS BOARDS

England

Lambeth Bridge House, S.E.1

Chairman, Sir Eric de Normann, K.B.E., C.B., F.S.A.
Members, M. S. Briggs, F.R.I.B.A.; R. L. S. Bruce-Mitford, F.S.A.; Prof. J. G. D. Clark, Sc.D., F.B.A., V.-P.S.A.; Sir Trenchard Cox, C.B.E., F.S.A., F.B.A.; A. R. Dufty, Sec. S.A.; Prof. W. F. Grimes, C.B.E.; D.Litt., F.S.A.; D. B. Harden, O.B.E., Ph.D., F.S.A.; Prof. C. F. C. Hawkes, F.S.A., F.B.A.; J. N. L. Myres, Ll.D., V.-P.S.A.; Nigel Nicolson, M.B.E., F.S.A.; C. A. Ralegh Radford, F.S.A., F.B.A.; Prof. I. A. Richmond, C.B.E., D.Litt., Dir.S.A., F.B.A.; Marshall Sisson, C.B.E., A.R.A, F.S.A., F.R.I.B.A.; Sir Mortimer Wheeler, C.I.E., M.C., T.D., D.Litt., F.S.A., F.B.A.
Secretary, K. F. Huggons, V.R.D.

Wales

Gabalfa, Cardiff

Chairman, J. D. K. Lloyd, O.B.E., F.S.A.
Members, Prof. R. J. C. Atkinson, F.S.A.; Prof. E. G. Bowen, F.S.A.; Prof. A. H. Dodd; Prof. Sir Goronwy Edwards, D.Litt., F.B.A.; Prof. W. F. Grimes, C.B.E., D.Litt., F.S.A.; A. H. A. Hogg, F.S.A.; C. A. Ralegh Radford, F.B.A., F.S.A.; Dr. H. N. Savory, F.S.A.; Sir Ben Bowen Thomas; Prof. David Williams, D.Litt.
Secretary, C. A. Gresham, F.S.A.

Scotland

122 George Street, Edinburgh 2

Chairman, W. D. Simpson, C.B.E., D.Litt., Ll.D., F.S.A., F.S.A.Scot.
Members, The Earl of Haddington, K.T., M.C., Ll.D., F.S.A.Scot.; A. R. Cross, M.C., T.D., F.S.A.Scot.; I. G. Lindsay, O.B.E., R.S.A., F.R.I.B.A., F.S.A.Scot.; Prof. J. D. Mackie, C.B.E., M.C., Ll.D., F.S.A.Scot.; Prof. Stuart Piggott, D.Litt., F.B.A., F.R.S.E., F.S.A., F.S.A.Scot.; Miss A. S. Robinson, F.S.A., F.S.A.Scot.; Prof. W. J. Smith, M.C., F.R.I.B.A., F.S.A.; R. B. K. Stevenson, F.S.A.
Secretary, G. D. Crane.

HOME OFFICE

Whitehall, S.W.1
[Whitehall: 8100]

The Home Office deals with such internal affairs of England and Wales as are not assigned to other Departments. The Home Secretary is the channel of communication between Her Majesty the Queen and Her subjects, and between the U.K. Government and the Government of Northern Ireland, the Channel Islands and the Isle of Man. The chief matters with which the Home Office is concerned are—The maintenance of law and order; the efficiency of the police service; the control and administration of prisons and borstal institutions; the treatment of offenders, including juvenile offenders; the efficiency of the probation service; the organization of magistrates' courts; legislation on criminal justice; the supervision of the fire service; the preparations for civil defence services; the care of children by local authorities and voluntary societies; the regulation of the employment of children and young persons; the control of Commonwealth immigrants and aliens and the naturalization of aliens; the law relating to parliamentary and local government elections. In addition, many miscellaneous subjects are dealt with, including explosives, dangerous drugs, poisons, intoxicating liquor and State Management Districts (England and Wales), shops, public safety, entertainments, bye-laws on good rule and government and other subjects, cremations and burials, betting and gambling; addresses and petitions to the Queen, ceremonials and formal business connected with honours.

Secretary of State for Home Affairs, THE RT. HON. HENRY BROOKE, M.P. £5,000
Private Secretary, G. J. Otton.
Assistant Private Secretary, A. H. Turney.
Parliamentary Private Secretary, A. T. Bourne-Arton, M.P. .... *unpaid*
Minister of State, THE EARL JELLICOE, D.S.O., M.C. £3,750
Parliamentary Under-Secretaries of State, Miss I. M. P. Pike, M.P.; Hon. Christopher Woodhouse, D.S.O., O.B.E., M.P. £2,500
Permanent Under-Secretary of State, Sir Charles Cunningham, K.C.B., K.B.E., C.V.O. £7,015
Private Secretary, Miss M. M. Peck.
Deputy Under-Secretaries of State, E. H. Gwynn, C.B.; F. L. T. Graham-Harrison, C.B. £5,015
Chief Medical Officer (at Ministry of Health), Sir George Godber, K.C.B., D.M.
Honorary Catering Adviser, Sir Norman Joseph, C.B.E.

General Department

Assistant Under-Secretary of State, R. J. Guppy £4,115
Assistant Secretaries, S. H. E. Burley; T. C. Green; R. J. P. Hewison; H. W. Stotesbury £2,865 to £3,565
Principals, P. Beedle; J. F. D. Buttery; J. M. Clift; G. I. De Deney; K. Eddy; A. H. Hewins; Miss M. Hornsby; A. J. Langdon; Miss G. P. Wise £1,959 to £2,711
Senior Executive Officers, Miss M. I. F. Green; F.W. Stacey; J. Stephens; Miss F. G. F. Wakeman £1,680 to £2,126

Dangerous Drugs Branch

Chief Inspector, A. L. Dyke.... £2,607 to £2,865
Deputy Chief Inspector, C. G. Jeffery £2,192 to £2,533

Explosives Branch

Chief Inspector, H. K. Black.............£3,340
Second Inspector, D. Simmons...£2,628 to £2,915
Inspectors, F. W. Ireland; G. J. Jeacocke; C. Johnstone; A. Reed..................£1,781 to £2,549

Inspectors under Cruelty to Animals Act, 1876

Chief Inspector, R. S. Vine..............£3,715
Inspectors, Group Capt. J. R. Cellars, A.F.C.; R. L. Macpherson, M.B.E.; Group Capt. I. Mackay; R. Mitchell; H. G. B. Slack, M.D. £2,265 to £2,990

State Management Scheme
(Carlisle District)
19 Castle Street, Carlisle
[Carlisle: 25213]

General Manager, J. N. Adams............£3,150
Assistant General Manager, L. F. Ambler £2,272 to £2,607
Head Brewer, J. W. Monk......£2,256 to £2,677
Manager of Wholesale Spirits Stores, L. Bell £1,615 to £2,061
Superintendent of Managed Houses, F. M. Stewart £2,172 to £2,507
Superintendent of Hotels and Restaurants, M. R. Jones £2,172 to £2,507

Immigration and Nationality Department
Princeton House, 271/277 High Holborn, W.C.1
[Chancery: 8811]

Assistant Under-Secretary of State, K. B. Paice £4,115
Assistant Secretaries, I. B. Macdonald Ross; J. M. Ross; J. H. Walker; R. F. Wood £2,865 to £3,565
Principals, N. F. Carrington, D.S.C.; Miss K. N. Coates, O.B.E.; W. N. Hyde; A. S. Oakley, M.B.E.; G. W. Penn; J. B. Sharp £1,959 to £2,711
Chief Executive Officer, S. G. Baker £2,237 to £2,572
Senior Executive Officers, A. J. Bellett; S. J. Gregory; J. Hamilton; K. E. Hughes; J. P. Jarvis; L. Snowden, M.B.E.; E. C. Walduck; R. M. Whitfield £1,680 to £2,126
Chief Inspector, F. G. Chinchen...........£3,215
Assistant Chief Inspectors, H. V. Bowles; A. J. Clarke; A. E. Nicholls, M.B.E. £2,237 to £2,572
Inspectors, C. J. Allen; R. I. Collison; I. L. Davis; H. S. Humphrey; L. J. Perry; C. D. Rawbone; H. J. G. Richards; T. W. E. Roche; J. H. B. Sanders; E. L. Ward........£1,734 to £2,126

Children's Department
Thames House South, Millbank, S.W.1
[Victoria: 1288]

Assistant Under-Secretary of State, J. B. Howard £4,115
Assistant Secretaries, E. R. Cowlyn; E. N. Kent; R. J. Whittick.............£2,865 to £3,565
Principals, J. H. J. Beck; W. J. Bohan; K. H. Dawson; B. A. E. Harrold; H. C. P. McGregor; G. H. Roberts..............£1,959 to £2,711
Chief Executive Officer, E. A. Sedgley £2,237 to £2,572
Senior Executive Officers, Miss E. M. Chadwell; J. E. Johnson; G. T. Newton; B. D. H. Phillips £1,680 to £2,126

Children's Department Inspectorate

Chief Inspector, Miss A. M. Scorrer, C.B.E...£3,565
Deputy Chief Inspectors, J. Kilgour; G. Revell £3,215
Senior Medical Inspector, G. M. Fleming....£3,415
Medical Inspectors, Mrs. M. Bates; Miss M. A. Hay; Miss M. E. McLaughlin.....£2,265 to £2,990
Superintending Inspectors, B. Evans; S. A. Gwynn, O.B.E.; C. P. Huggard; C. E. Shipley; P. F. Tipping; L. J. Wardle........£2,623 to £3,025
Inspectors (Grade I), J. M. Arlidge; Miss S. C. Brown, O.B.E.; Miss O. Chandler; Miss G. E. Chesters; Mrs. K. E. Cuffe; R. S. Davies; N. Desbrow; A. N. Dyson; Miss M. L. Edwards; Miss J. P. Francis; Miss R. M. Ganderton; A. B. Hadley; Miss A. Haigh-Loney; C. Hamlin; N. Higson; L. S. Jenkins; V. E. Jenkins, M.B.E.; W. W. Jones; M. C. Joseph; J. E. Knight; D. S. Lyle; H. B. Mackay; E. C. Morris; Miss M. C. Rose; Miss L. M. E. Smart; G. E. Whittaker; Miss K. A. Wood..............£2,190 to £2,602
Inspectors (Grade II), Miss D. M. Armstrong; Miss J. W. Barnes; W. F. Brien; Miss G. Browne-Wilkinson; Mrs. A. W. Chisholm; Miss Y. Cowell; I. J. Croft; V. Davies; Mrs. M. W. Delgado; D. F. Earley; W. H. Fletcher; F. Flower; J. K. Ford; Miss M. Freeman; W. A. Hollingbery; D. P. Hughes; Miss C. F. Jayne; D. L. Jones; R. L. Jones; Miss A. C. Kennedy; T. H. Lewis; J. McCarthy; L. Pugh; S. Reed; G. W. Smith; A. J. L. Southwell; Miss P. P. Thayer; R. J. N. Tod; B. W. Vincent; Miss J. M. Wakeham; Miss E. C. Woodall; J. B. Woods; S. Woollock £1,521 to £2,005
Inspectors (Old Style), Miss E. M. Hall; Miss A. Murray; Miss M. S. Stainforth, M.B.E. £2,023 to £2,602

Civil Defence and Fire Service Department
Horseferry House, Dean Ryle Street, S.W.1
[Victoria: 6655]

Assistant Under-Secretary of State, G. H. McConnell £4,115
Inspector-General of Civil Defence, Air Chief Marshal Sir Walter Merton, G.B.E., K.C.B.
Assistant Secretaries, R. H. F. Firth; R. A. James, M.C.; R. L. Jones; R. M. North; N. S. Ross; K. P. Witney..............£2,865 to £3,565
Principals, P. V. Collyer; Mrs. H. E. Forbes; H. V. Marks; R. W. Mott; W. A. Newsome; Miss K. A. O'Neill; G. P. Renton; G. T. Rudd; G. M. Tucker; D. E. H. Wynter, M.V.O. £1,959 to £2,711
Regional Directors of Civil Defence, Maj.-Gen. C. L. Firbank, C.B., C.B.E., D.S.O.; Lieut.-Gen. E. N. Goddard, C.B., C.I.E., C.B.E., M.V.O., M.C.; Maj.-Gen. G. P. Gregson, C.B., C.B.E., D.S.O., M.C.; Capt. K. L. Harkness, C.B.E., D.S.C., R.N.; Maj.-Gen. F. C. Horton, C.B., O.B.E.; Maj.-Gen. R. W. Jelf, C.B.E.; Maj.-Gen. S. Lamplugh, C.B., C.B.E.; Maj.-Gen. F. R. G. Matthews, C.B., D.S.O.; Air Marshal Sir Lawrence Pendred, K.B.E., C.B., D.F.C.; Rear-Adm. A. D. Torlesse, C.B., D.S.O.; J. R. S. Watson....................£3,200
Assistant Regional Directors of Civil Defence, V. G. Barry, D.F.C.; H. A. Bingley; J. F. Boxell; S. W. Briggs; P. W. H. Chapman; W. E. Farrant; J. P. Gelly; G. Hutchinson, O.B.E.; C. C. Hutton; E. S. Moran; H. Wallwork, O.B.E. £2,172 to £2,507
Chief Executive Officer, L. C. Sones £2,237 to £2,572
Senior Executive Officers, R. Atwell; S. R. Cameron; W. F. Delamare; E. Hutchings; N. F. Law; P. Leyshon; F. C. Millward; J. Richards; J. D. F. Turnham; G. C. Woods....£1,680 to £2,126
Chief Training Officer, Brig. G. H. C. Pennycook, C.B.E.....................£1,959 to £2,711
Assistant Chief Training Officers, Lt.-Col. G. W. Laverick; T. N. Storer; V. H. Wallis £1,785 to £2,136
Principal Warning Officers, Wing-Cmdr. W. J. Marshall, O.B.E.; Brig. W. H. G. Rogers, C.B.E. £2,237 to £2,572

Civil Defence Staff College
Sunningdale Park, Ascot, Berks

Commandant, Maj.-Gen. R. B. B. B. Cooke, C.B., C.B.E., D.S.O.......................£3,200

Civil Defence Schools
Eastwood Park, Falfield, Gloucester

Commandant, Lt.-Col. A. J. Batchelor £2,017 to £2,334

The Hawkhills, Easingwold, Yorkshire

Commandant, Lt.-Col. A. A. H. Ewin £2,017 to £2,334

Taymouth Castle, Kenmore, nr. Aberfeldy, Perthshire
Commandant, Brig. D. C. Mullen, C.B.E. £2,017 to £2,334

Fire Service Inspectorate

Horseferry House, Dean Ryle Street, S.W.1
Chief Inspector, H. M. Smith, C.B.E. £3,565
Inspectors, S. H. Charters, O.B.E.; F. Dann, O.B.E.; D. G. M. Middleton; W. E. Norwood, M.B.E.; D. V. M. Staples, M.B.E.; A. V. Thomas, G.M.; P. S. Wilson-Dickson, M.B.E.. £2,605 to £2,965
Engineering Inspector, F. C. A. Shirling £2,293 to £2,628
Engineering Inspector (Water), R. Killey, M.B.E. (+ *allce.*) £1,624 to £2,144

Fire Service College

Wotton House. Abinger Common, Dorking, Surrey
Commandant, W. W. Paramor, C.B.E. £2,540 to £2,900

Fire Service Training Centre
Moreton-in-Marsh, Glos.
Commandant, E. Anderson...... £2,195 to £2,390

Criminal and Probation Department

Assistant Under-Secretary of State, H. B. Wilson £4,115
Assistant Secretaries, A. J. E. Brennan; N. F. Cairncross; Miss W. M. Goode, C.B.E.; C. T. H. Morris £2,865 to £3,565
Principals, B. J. Burrows; D. E. J. Dowler; R. S. King; W. M. Lee; C. H. Prior; M. L. Priss; R. F. D. Shuffrey .... £1,959 to £2,711
Senior Executive Officers, A. E. Corbin; A. K. Guymer; G. T. L. Hubert; S. C. Jackson; T. G. Mead; Miss J. M. Northover; D. G. Turner; W. J. Wright.............. £1,630 to £2,126
Principal Probation Inspector, F. J. MacRae, O.B.E. D.F.C............................. £3,090
Inspectors (Grade I), Miss M. Irvine; H. M. Morton; E. Rocksborough Smith; Miss W. R. Vandy £2,255 to £2,622
Inspectors (Grade II), S. A. Barrett; Miss J. T. Dodds, M.B.E.; R. J. W. Foren; M. H. Hogan; H. A. Prins; Miss M. D. Samuels; Miss J. Shepherd; R. W. Spiers; F. N. Stephens; C. T. Swann; P. Westland................ £1,586 to £2,070
Inspector (Old Style), Miss M. J. R. Hutchinson £2,088 to £2,667

Establishment and Organization Department

Assistant Under-Secretary of State (Principal Establishment Officer), A. R. Bunker......... £4,115
Assistant Secretaries, C. Parkinson; R. R. Pittam; T. G. Weiler .... £2,865 to £3,565
Principals, F. W. Durndell; J. McIntyre; D. A. Peach; R. W. G. Smith; F. J. Woodward £1,959 to £2,711
Chief Executive Officers, E. Goodbody, I.S.O.; A. J. Kennedy, M.B.E............ £2,237 to £2,572
Senior Executive Officers, C. Archer; D. V. Bailey; N. E. Clark; H. W. Gillies; R. J. P. Hayes; T. J. Kempton; I. D. King; D. E. Luke; R. G. Oram; H. G. Pearson; H. R. Pendlebury; E. A. Slater; J. A. Wallace; F. B. Warner; D. J. Wilkes; D. A. R. Wood............ £1,680 to £2,126

Communications Branch

Director, N. H. Elgood......... £2,715 to £3,065

Public Relations Branch

Chief Information Officer, A. Richardson, O.B.E. £2,865 to £3,565
Principal Information Officer, T. D. McCaffrey £2,237 to £2,572

Statistics and Research

Statistical Adviser and Director of Research, T. S. Lodge.................... £2,865 to £3,565
Statisticians, Mrs. E. H. Gibson; C. A. F. Russell; L. T. Wilkins............... £1,959 to £2,711

Kingston By-Pass Road, Surbiton, Surrey
[Emberbrook: 5541]
Senior Executive Officer, R. T. Tudor £1,675 to £2,121

Finance Department

Horseferry House, Dean Ryle Street, S.W.1
[Victoria: 6655]
Assistant Under-Secretary of State, (Principal Finance Officer), I. Roy...................... £4,115
Assistant Secretary (Finance Officer) R. L. Thomas £2,865 to £3,565
Senior Chief Executive Officers, E. J. W. Durrant; M. T. Leddy.............. £2,683 to £2,865
Chief Executive Officers, L. H. Foss; L. W. Goringe; L. T. Norman, I.S.O.; J. F. Quirk £2,237 to £2,572
Senior Executive Officers, A. E. Coleshill; T. S. Fookes; A. H. Stringer; M. G. Thompson; P. H. L. Trodden; J. R. Troop.... £1,680 to £2,126

Legal Advisers

Legal Adviser, J. K. T. Jones, C.B.E......... £5,015
Assistant Legal Advisers, G. B. T. Barr, C.B.E.; G. V. Hart; H. W. Wollaston...... £2,965 to £3,565
Senior Legal Assistants, P. N. S. Farrell; P. Harvey; J. D. Semken, M.C........... £2,304 to £2,865

Police Department

Assistant Under-Secretary of State, K. A. L. Parker, C.B.................................... £4,115
Assistant Secretaries, T. A. Critchley; A. W. Glanville; D. A. C. Morrison; P. L. Taylor £2,865 to £3,565
Principals, G. H. Baker, D.S.C.; D. H. J. Hilary; J. C. H. Holden; W. Middlemass; Miss G. M. B. Owen; D. J. Trevelyan ..... £1,959 to £2,711
Forensic Science Adviser, F. G. Tryhorn, C.B.E. £3,340 to £3,665
Chief Executive Officers, T. A. Moy; Miss M. Turner, M.B.E..................... £2,237 to £2,572
Senior Executive Officers, R. F. Elliott; B. C. Holmes; R. K. Prescott; C. F. Whitfield £1,680 to £2,126

H.M. Inspectors of Constabulary

Chief Inspector, Sir William Johnson, C.M.G., C.B.E. £5,353
Inspectors, B. N. Bebbington, O.B.E.; J. S. H. Gaskain, M.B.E.; Sir Charles Martin, C.B.E.; J. T. Manuel; A. U. R. Scroggie, O.B.E.; Cdr. W. J. A. Willis, C.B.E., M.V.O., R.N. (*ret.*) £4,675
Assistant Inspectors of Constabulary, Miss K. M. Hill, M.B.E.; Miss J. S. S. Law..... £2,121 to £2,742

Police College

Bramshill House, Hartley Wintney, Basingstoke, Hants.
Commandant, S. Lawrence, C.B.E.......... £2,890
Deputy Commandant, T. Lockley, O.B.E. £1,765 to £1,960

Prison Department

Horseferry House, Dean Ryle Street, Westminster, S.W.1
[Victoria: 6655]
Assistant Under-Secretary of State, A. W. Peterson, C.B., M.V.O. (*Chairman of Prisons Board*... £4,115
Assistant Secretaries, *M. G. Russell; *N. Storr, O.B.E..................... £2,865 to £3,565
Chief Director, *R. D. Fairn............. £3,415
Director of Prison Administration, *J. Holt, O.B.E. £3,315
Director of Borstal Administration, *H. J. Taylor £3,315

*The above, with T. G. Weiler, constitute the Prisons Board.

Assistant Directors, J. E. Henderson; H. Kenyon; R. E. Owen; Lt.-Col. J. S. Haywood; D. G. Waddilove; Lady Taylor; C. T. Cape; G. Hair; G. B. Smith. £3,015

Principals, N. W. R. Baker; G. Emerson; D. E. R. Faulkner; T. J. H. Hetherington £1,959 to £2,711
Chief Executive Officers, H. Lynn; D. R. Sands; H. Winson........£2,237 to £2,572
Senior Executive Officers, W. R. Dallingwater; G. F. Gartan; R. Gooderham; L. I. Lerego; P. R. Wall; R. J. H. West........£1,680 to £2,126
Director of Works, Lt.-Col. S. P. Sartain ...£3,565
Deputy Director of Works, E. Cruddas £2,865 to £3,215
Senior Architects, A. Ball; N. E. Hill £2,293 to £2,628
Senior Quantity Surveyor, R. G. Read £2,293 to £2,628
Senior Engineers, G. McLean; S. B. Nash £2,410 to £2,745
Senior Surveyor, L. O. L. Lee...£2,293 to £2,628
Director of Prison Medical Services, I. G. W. Pickering, V.R.D., M.D........£4,050
Assistant to the Director of Prison Medical Services, C. E. Caudwell........£3,565
Director of Industries and Stores, R. J. Davis. £3,215
Chaplain General, Rev. L. L. Rees........£2,164
Chief Psychologist, A. Straker...£2,865 to £3,215
Catering Adviser, F. G. T. Belcham £1,574 to £2,012
Organiser of Physical Education, A. Healey £1,720 to £1,945

PRISONS

Governors

Appleton Thorn, M. D. McLeod. £1,784 to £2,106
Ashwell, Rutland, L. C. Oxford. £1,784 to £2,106
Askham Grange, Yorks., Miss M. E. G. Stocker £1,784 to £2,106
Aylesbury, J. H. Waylen, M.B.E... £2,284 to £2,618
Bedford, R. S. Llewelyn........£1,784 to £2,016
Bela River, Westmorland, R. A. B. A. Howden £1,784 to £2,061
Birmingham, R. Harris........£2.776
Blundeston, Suffolk, E. A. Towndrow £2,284 to £2,618
Bristol, J. L. Scott........£2,284 to £2,618
Brixton, S.W.2, C. H. Shoemake £2,776
Camp Hill, I.O.W., L. J. Simpson £2,284 to £2,618
Canterbury, A. R. Moreton....£1,784 to £2,106
Cardiff, Lt.-Col. C. C. Markes..£2,284 to £2,618
Chelmsford, N. H. Golding.....£2,284 to £2,618
Dartmoor, D. G. W. Malone........£2,776
Dorchester, T. Ryan........£1,784 to £2,016
Drake Hall, Staffs., G. E. Griffiths £1,784 to £2,016
Durham, L. Newcombe........£2,776
Eastchurch, Kent, G. F. Bride....£2,284 to £2,618
Exeter, P. C. Jones........£2,284 to £2,618
Ford, Sussex, J. A. Dennett.....£2,284 to £2,618
Gloucester, L. W. F. Steinhausen. £1,784 to £2,106
Grendon, Bucks., W. J. Gray (*Medical Superintendent*) £3,750
Hill Hall, Essex, Miss M. Patterson £1,784 to £2,106
Holloway, N.7, Mrs. J. E. Kelley........£2,836
Hull, E. A. Esquilant........£1,784 to £2,106
Kirkham, Lancs, N. Clay.......£1,784 to £2,106
Lancaster, L. R. Ogier ....£1,784 to £2,106
Leeds, H. G. Reeve........£2,776
Leicester, R. F. Owens........£1,784 to £2,106
Lewes, J. R. Watson........£2,284 to £2,618
Leyhill, Glos., D. G. Hewlings, D.F.C., A.F.C. £2,284 to £2,618
Lincoln, Cdr. C. S. Cooke, R.N.. £2,284 to £2,618
Liverpool, S. G. Clarke........£2,776
Maidstone, R. M. Ffinch........£2,776
Manchester, A. A. Coomes........£2,776
Moor Court, Staffs., Miss L. S. White £1,784 to £2,106
Northallerton, B. Fletcher.......£1,784 to £2,106
Norwich, R. W. Downton.....£1,784 to £2,106
Nottingham, G. Footer........£1,784 to £2,106
Oxford, J. Brophy........£1,784 to £2,106
Parkhurst, I.O.W., A. C. Packham........£2,776
Pentonville, N., P. M. Burnett £2,841
Preston, Maj. G. Nash........£2,284 to £2,618
Shrewsbury, Lt.-Col. R. A. Shebbeare £1,784 to £2,106
Spring Hill, Bucks., R. K. Leslie. £1,784 to £2,106
Stafford, G. G. S. Chambers.....£2,284 to £2,618
Styal, Cheshire, Miss I. M. McWilliam £2,284 to £2,618
Sudbury, Derby, P. A. M. Heald £2,284 to £2,618
Swansea, Capt. W. I. Davies....£1,784 to £2,016
Thorp Arch, Yorks., K. F. Watson £1,784 to £2,106
The Verne, Dorset, R. C. Townsend £2,284 to £2,618
Wakefield, A. Bainton........£2,776
Wandsworth, S.W.18, M. S. Gale, M.C.....£2,836
Winchester, J. J. Beisty........£2,284 to £2,618
Wormwood Scrubs, W.12, T. W. H. Hayes..£2,836

BORSTALS

Governors

Bullwood Hall, Essex, Miss J. Martyn, O.B.E. £2,284 to £2,618
Dover, A. Gould........£2,284 to £2,618
East Sutton Park, Kent, Miss E. Hooker, M.B.E. £1,784 to £2,106
Everthorpe, Yorks., E. E. Gregory £2,284 to £2,618
Feltham, Middx., G. Macfarlane. £2,223 to £2,548
Gaynes Hall, Hunts., R. K. Lawson £1,784 to £2,106
Guys Marsh, Dorset, B. J. Chilvers £1,784 to £2,106
Hatfield, Yorks., M. H. P. Coombs £1,784 to £2,106
Hewell Grange, Worcs., A. B. Roberton £1,784 to £2,106
Hindley, Lancs., A. C. Miller, M.B.E., T.D. £2,284 to £2,618
Hollesley Bay Colony, Suffolk, J. L. Gilder £2,284 to £2,618
Huntercombe, Oxon., L. J. F. Wheeler £1,784 to £2,106
Latchmere House, Surrey, D. W. Fisher £1,844 to £2,166
Lowdham Grange, Notts., W. R. B. Noall, D.S.O. £2,284 to £2,618
Morton Hall, Lincs., W. A. Brister £1,784 to £2,106
North Sea Camp, Lincs., H. H. Harrison £1,784 to £2,106
Pollington, Yorks, G. Lister.....£1,784 to £2,106
Portland, Dorset, F. V. Elvy.....£2,284 to £2,618
Portsmouth, S. A. Bester........£1,784 to £2,106
Reading, N. C. Honey........£1,784 to £2,106
Rochester, G.W. Fowler........£2,284 to £2,618
Swinfen Hall, Staffs., D. T. Cross £1,784 to £2,106
Usk, Mon., W. Taylor ....£1,784 to £2,106
Wetherby, Yorks., C. M. Miles..£1,784 to £2,106

REMAND CENTRE

Governor

Ashford, Middx., A. D. W. Sanderson, M.C. £2,284 to £2,618

DETENTION CENTRES

Wardens

Aldington, Kent, W. S. Smith, D.S.C.
Aylesbury, D. St. L. Simon.
Blantyre House, Kent, D. R. N. Maxwell.
Buckley Hall, Lancs., W. H. T. Carmichael.
Campsfield House, Oxford, D. W. Higman.
Erlestoke House, Wilts., D. F. Dennis.
Foston Hall, Derby, J. P. Cox.
Haslar, Hants., Capt. P. E. Marshall, V.R.D.
Kirklevington, Yorks,. D. E. Preston, M.B.E.
Medomsley, Co. Durham, R. E. Adams.
New Hall, Yorks, J. B. B. Plummer.
Send, Surrey, S. Mitchell.
Werrington House, Staffs., Capt. L. V. D. Dewar.
(*All* £1,784 to £2,106)

Scientific Advisers' Branch

Horseferry House, Dean Ryle Street, S.W.1
[Victoria: 6655]

Chief Scientific Adviser, H. A. Sargeaunt, C.B., O.B.E. £4,115

Senior Principal Scientific Officers, E. Leader-Williams; G. R. Stanbury...£2,865 to £3,215
Principal Scientific Officers, N. E. Hand; D. T. Jones; J. McAulay; T. Martin; J. A. Miles; F. H. Pavry; A. M. Western.............£1,904 to £2,655

Supply and Transport Branch
Kingston By-Pass Road, Surbiton, Surrey
[Emberbrook: 5541]

Director of Supply, F. S. T. Cleave.........£3,210
Deputy Director, W. H. Stephens £2,678 to £2,860
Senior Executive Officers, W. Heggie; A. H. Mc-Creadie-Smith.............£1,675 to £2,121
Senior Engineer, J. W. Arnot... £2,348 to £2,265

Women's Voluntary Service
41 Tothill Street, Westminster, S.W.1

Chairman, The Dowager Marchioness of Reading, G.B.E.................................*unpaid*
Vice-Chairman, The Dowager Lady Hillingdon, D.B.E.................................*unpaid*
Social Services Administrator, Miss A. C. Johnston, C.B.E.................................*unpaid*
Chief Administrator (Regions), Miss K. M. Halpin, C.B.E.................................£1,140

HORSERACE TOTALISATOR BOARD

163 Euston Road, N.W.1
[Euston: 5871]

Established by the Betting Levy Act, 1961, as successor in title to the Racecourse Betting Control Board established by the Racecourse Betting Act, 1928.

Its function is to operate totalisators on approved horse racecourses in Great Britain, and thus to provide moneys for the improvement of breeds of horses, the sport of horse racing and the advancement and encouragement of veterinary science and education, by means of an annual levy paid to the Horserace Betting Levy Board established under the same Act in 1961.

Members

Apptd. by the Home Secretary: Sir Alexander Sim (*Chairman*); Hon. J. J. Astor, M.B.E.; Sir Dingwall Bateson, C.B.E., M.C.; Col. G. E. C. Wigg, M.P.
Secretary, Captain E. T. Graham, R.N. (*ret.*).

MINISTRY OF HOUSING AND LOCAL GOVERNMENT

Whitehall, S.W.1
[Whitehall: 4300]

The Ministry of Housing and Local Government was set up in 1951 under the title of Ministry of Local Government and Planning and took over the housing and local government functions of the Ministry of Health and the functions of the Ministry of Town and Country Planning. It is responsible for the administration of Government housing policy, housing standards and the general supervision of local authority housing programmes; the administration of the planning acts concerning the use and development of land in England and Wales; and it is the department principally concerned in the supervision of the work of local authorities.

Minister (and Minister for Welsh Affairs), THE RT. HON. SIR KEITH SINJOHN JOSEPH, BT... £5,000
Private Secretary, G. W. Moseley.
Assistant Private Secretary, B. H. Chapman.
Parliamentary Private Secretary, G. W. Proudfoot, M.P.
Minister of State for Welsh Affairs, THE LORD BRECON, P.C.*.....................£3,750
Private Secretary, V. C. Davies.*
Joint Parliamentary Secretaries, F. V. Corfield, M.P.; The Lord Hastings.................£2,500
Permanent Secretary, Dame Evelyn Sharp, G.B.E. £7,015
Private Secretary, R. E. Head.
Deputy Secretaries, J. D. Jones; J. H. Waddell, C.B. £5,015
Under-Secretaries, J. E. Beddoe; R. Brain; J. Crocker (*Principal Finance Officer and Accountant-General*); Miss W. M. Fox; S. W. C. Phillips, C.B. (*Principal Establishment Officer*); I. V. Pugh; J. Rogerson; J. W. M. Sibery (*Welsh Secretary*)*; J. H. Street.......................£4,115
Solicitor and Legal Adviser, J. C. Blake, C.B. (*also Solicitor and Legal Adviser to Ministry of Health*) £5,015
Chief Architect, A. W. Cleeve Barr........£4,415
Chief Engineer, C. H. Spens, C.B...........£4,415
Chief Housing and Planning Inspector, L. P. Ellicott, C.B.E.....................£4,215 (*personal*).
Chief Planner, J. R. James, O.B.E...........£4,415
Chief Inspector of Audit, J. B. B. Kendrick... £4,115
Chief Alkali Inspector, Dr. J. S. Carter, C.B.E.. £3,703
Chief Estate Officer, G. S. Wheldon, C.B.E.. £3,565
Assistant Secretaries, G. L. Barber; H. H. Browne; E. W. Bryant; J. Catlow; P. D. Coates; G. R. Coles; W. R. Corrie; W. R. Cox; L. Goodman; A. E. Hickinbotham; P. L. Hughes; A. R. Isserlis; J. D. W. Janes; L. Mann; J. R. Niven; C. J. Pearce; A. G. Rayner; H. J. Ryan; H. R. Savage, M.C.; F. Schaffer; A. Sylvester-Evans; A. L. Vincent; F. J. Ward; Miss M. M. Wilkins; S. G. G. Wilkinson; W. A. Wood £2,865 to £3,565
Ironstone Adviser, Sir Henry Prior, K.C.I.E., C.S.I. (*part-time*)
Deputy Accountants-General, W. Lloyd-Davies; R. D. Widdas.......................£3,215
Assistant Accountants-General, Miss K. C. Close; B. Dobson................£2,683 to £2,865
Principals, R. G. Adams; Miss C. E. Barson, O.B.E.; Miss P. J. Cairns; N. H. Calvert; G. H. Chipperfield; Miss A. M. Constantine; P. Critchley; H. A. M. Cruickshank; V. G. Curtis; W. Dawson; J. Delafons; R. Ditchfield; C. W. Dodge; J. M. Douglas; S. W. Gilbert; F. W. Girling; E. R. Gordon; P. F. Grant; L. B. Grimshaw; J. A. Hall; J. E. Hannigan; P. J. Harrop; T. M. Heiser; M. Hoffman; K. Lightfoot; J. G. Littler; P. C. McQuail; H. W. Marshall; R. Metcalfe; D. C. Milefanti; J. E. Morton; G. W. Moseley; K. F. Munn; L. R. Mustill, M.B.E.; Miss M. E. Petzche; H. R. Pollitzer; B. S. Quilter; F. G. Rickard; J. P. G. Rowcliffe; L. F. Saw; Mrs. M. I. Schofield; W. M. Schwab; H. G. C. Sutcliffe; B. Taylor; J. S. M. Vinter; Mrs. M. M. Ward; G. M. Wedd; T. D. Wickenden; Miss W. Williams; E. H. T. Wiltshire, C.B.E.; P. I. Wolf; Hon. Mrs. R. J. Youard £1,959 to £2,711
Chief Executive Officers, C. W. Baldwin; C. F. Curtis; E. S. Foster; Miss B. M. George; S. H. Godsell; N. Hamilton; S. J. B. Hurden; T. A. James; Miss M. Knights; R. C. Lawrence; C. H. Leedham; G. H. W. Lewis, M.B.E.; T. Mackenzie; C. Nettleton; S. H. Norris; G. M. Orpwood; P. P. B. Rickard; R. T. Scowen; J. Stobart; A. H. Thom..............£2,237 to £2,572
Senior Executive Officers, Miss E. M. Barber; Miss I. Bartlett; A. G. W. C. Birs; W. E. Bradbury; W. L. Brimmer; E. D. Burr; K. F. A. Cain; H. Chapman; J. W. E. Cheal; E. Cheesbrough; Miss J. E. Collins; E. J. Dovey; Miss J. Farrar; K. Fowkes; J. A. Fowler; Miss H. M. Gooding; F. W. Goodfellow; Miss M. B. Green; A. T. Gregory; A. F. Hayes; H. J. Hobbs; C. T. Jones; D. W. Jones; G. P. Jupp; J. C. H. Marlow; R. W. J. Mitchell; D. A. S. O'Driscoll; D. W. Plamping; Miss D. G. Pomeroy; A. W. Ponsford, M.B.E.; R. W. Porteous; Miss D. J. Price; D. Richardson; Miss M. M. Ruskin; Mrs. M. H. H. Segal; J. Shepperson; Miss W. A. Stansfeld; J. W. Storr; C. P. Taylor; G. D. Vaughan; J. Wallis; K. Weedon ....£1,689 to £2,216

* Office at Cathays Park, Cardiff.

Librarian, W. Pearson.........£1,680 to £2,216
Chief Press and Information Officer, A. P. G. Brown £2,865 to £3,565
Deputy Chief Engineers, R. A. Elliott; A. A. L. Lane £3,815

Senior Engineering Inspectors, A. G. Boulton; A. A. Cowie; I. H. Hainsworth; J. W. M. Hawksworth; A. K. Pollock; M. W. Summers; H. S. Tricker; A. R. Vail; B. C. W. Wood £3,165 to £3,565
Engineering Inspectors, J H. Abbott; R. Best; R. F. Caple; S. G. Cotton; G. E. Forward; A. J. Gerrard; Col. S. K. Gilbert; E. Hockley; T. P. Hughes; W. H. Norris; R. E. Smith; J. Sumner, O.B.E.; S. F.White; R. S.Wood £2,349 to £2,915
Senior Engineers (Hydrology), R. B. W. Bannerman; C. L. Berg; W. A. R. Robertson £2,293 to £2,628
Public Cleansing Inspector, E. R. Green £1,876 to £2,505
Engineer, G. Henderson........£1,920 to £2,422
Senior Chemical Inspector, Dr. A. Key, C.B.E. £3,165 to £3,565
Chemical Inspectors, D. Mercer; D. H. A. Price £2,349 to £2,915
Senior Radio Chemical Inspector, A. W. Kenny £3,165 to £3,565
Radio Chemical Inspectors, N. D. Baines; R. N. Crooks; G. E. Hesketh; B. R. Hookway; R. G. D. Osmond................£2,293 to £2,628
Deputy Chief Alkali Inspectors, F. E. Ireland; Dr. E. A. J. Mahler.............£2,865 to £3,215
District Alkali Inspectors, J. Beighton; H. Brigg; J. E. Colehan; Dr. E. T. J. Fuge; Dr. W. E. Grant; H. Heron; Dr. L. E. Hockin; L. W. Mullinger; R. L. Pawson; J. C. Peabody; R. H. Smith; J. Swaine...........£2,293 to £2,628
Alkali Inspectors, G. H. Bott; A. H. Brown; J. P. Fletcher; F. Gardner; S. J. Hart; G. W. Orchard; S. D. Phillips; A. Ridley; E. S. Tomlinson £1,624 to £2,154
Deputy Chief Architect, M. B. Blackshaw, C.B.E. £3,815
Assistant Chief Architects, O. J. Cox; A. D. H. Embling...........................£3,565
Chief Quantity Surveyor, D. W. Nunn, O.B.E. £3,565
Principal Architects, A. A. Bellamy; J. S. Conway; A. D. R. Cowley; O.B.E., J. R. Hunter; K. R. Lack; E. T. Salter, O.B.E.....£2,865 to £3,215
Senior Architects, B. Annable; G. A. S. Atkinson; C. M. Bond; F. V. S. Chard; J. Clay; A. C. Couch; J. S. Cunningham; K. Exell; Sir Arthur Hay, Bt.; E. H. H. Higham; G. J. Kelly; Miss G. M. McKenzie; F. A. Morrison; P. G. Negus; T. O'Toole; C. J. Smith; J. P. Stott; R. C. Symonds; F. N. E. Thompson; Miss P. R. Tindale; J. M. Welbank; L. Whitaker £2,293 to £2,628
Architects (Main Grade), A. J. Adkins; A. G. Armstrong; J. Bartlett; K. Beale; J. M. Bridges; L. M. Cordwell-Smith; J. Cunningham; I. Fraser; A. G. Gosling; M. W. Howard; K. F. J. Humphreys; R. D. Lawson; I. C. Macpherson; J. L. Merry; J. D. Noble; P. Randall; B. Seddon; W. J. Simmonds; A. L. Vasbenter; J. P. Vevers; A. Watson; Mrs. R. J. Wilson £1,624 to £2,154
Senior Quantity Surveyors, W. S. Adam, M.C.; G. E. Bromley; R. W. Churchill; B. H. Critchlow; G. H. Mallett; H. L. Millward; D. Schofield £2,293 to £2,628
Quantity Surveyors (Main Grade), B. S. Griffiths; A. G. Rayner; R. M. Sharp . £1,624 to £2,154
Deputy Chief Planners, J. F. P. Kacirek; J. L. Parkinson...........................£3,815
Principal Planners, H. Armistead; T. C. Coote, M.B.E.; P. L. Joseph; F. H. Littler; W. F. B. Lovett; W. M. Ogden; R. H. Shaw; R. S. Taylor; E. R. Voyce; W. M. White; Dr. E. C. Willetts, O.B.E.......................£2,865 to £3,215
Senior Planning Officers, G. C. Booth; T. F. W. Clarke; G. B. Dearden; C. E. D. Gibson; J. H. Hopper; D. E. Johnson; B. C. Maynard; J. R. Oxenham, T.D.; H. J. Smith-Boyes; E. Thompson; P. S. Waddington; D. Walpole; F. A. G. White; J. T. Wilkinson.....£2,293 to £2,628
Planning Officers, N. P. Allen; P. N. Atlee; J. C. Ball; J. R. Burgess; J. R. Coward; G. A. Deans; W. D. Gash; C. H. Glover; R. A. Hooker; W. A. Hutchinson; Miss K. R. Jervis; A. Mapletoft; Miss M. Marston; J. W. Mason; R. G. Maw; H. L. Nicholson; Miss K. B. Pailing; J. Peake; P. W. Peck; P. R. Phillips; D. T. B. Pope; Miss M. E. Raffloer; C. E. Scanlon; P. S. Vafidis; E. C. Wearing; L. F. I. Wolters; G. P. Woodford; C. B. Wringley............£1,624 to £2,154
Senior Research Officers (Geologists), L. M. Dunstan; R. O. Warburg...........£1,904 to £2,655
Senior Research Officers, H. C. Andrews; F. T. Burnett, M.C.; D. T. M. Davies; A. Fawcett; J. R. Jarmain; R. Kiff; W. D. McPherson; P. H Massey; J. Stephenson; R. S. Walshaw £1,959 to £2,682
Statistician, Dr. E. H. Rutland..£1,959 to £2,711
Deputy Chief Housing and Planning Inspector, F. H. Carr, C.B.E.........................£3,565
Principal Housing and Planning Inspectors, C. F. Allan; J. G. Birkett; F. J. K. Brindley; R. G. M. Chase; E. L. Crawford; S. J. Docking, O.B.E.; R. H. Evans; E. Farricker; V. H. Loney; H. W. Lovell; D. F. Offord; G. E. Pike; C. E. Pinel; E. W. Riley; A. E. Rochard-Thomas; M. B. Tetlow; R. F. F. Williams; H. F. Yeomans £2,865 to £3,215
Senior Housing and Planning Inspectors, M. Adamson; F. Appleton; C. J. D. Benton; E. W. Berridge; C. T. Blackall; J. Botterill; G. Marfleet Brown; A. R. Chown; S. R. Clarke; T. H. Clayton; A. Coates; L. J. Collman; F. R. Day; W. A. Devereux; K. Dodds; G. J. Easterbrook; W. H. Fennell; V. R. Fothergill; A. G. Harcourt; H. C. Harris; K. M. Hart; R. H. Heath; C. Hilton; J. A. B. Holborn; A. J. Hunt; C. Johnson; J. A. Kent; D. H. Komlosy; D. R. McKinlay; G. N. Maynard; J. L. M. Metcalfe; V. L. Nash; W. Orbell; W. H. Owen; L. G. H. Pannell; A. K. Park, M.B.E.; S. J. Parnell; J. R. M. Poole; D. I. Pryde; A. M. Roberts; S. T. Roberts; F. C. Sabin; A. B. Salmon; D. Senior; G. A. Simpson; E. A. Sykes; A. C. Todd; H. R. Wardill, O.B.E.; J. K Weston; J. L. Wetton; R. St. G. Whelan; G. P. G. Whitaker; P. J. Williams, O.B.E.; W. G. Wookey; F. H. M. Young . . £2,293 to £2,628
Housing and Planning Inspectors, Miss J. M. Albery; R. L. Armstrong; N. Ashworth; A. S. Barnes; R. E. Barry; C. J. Bartlett; F. Birkbeck; J. D. Blacklock; G. Borough-Copley, O.B.E.; L. P. Bradshaw; S. T. Bramble; L. S. I. Buck; F. M. Burgess; A. Burton-Stibbon; J. P. Chalke; K. Cleaver; B. J. Cornelius, T.D.; F. T. Cornhill; G. J. D. Cowley; J. B. S. Dahl; W. T. Davies; H. D. Dawson; R. W. Deans, G.M.; S. Dicks, M.B.E.; J. Eyre; B. J. Fleming; J. Gates; L. F. Goodwin; J. R. Hale; L. C. Hall; H. A. Hamilton; F. A. Haris; R. J. Harris; N. L. Harrop; A. D. Hawkins; A. R. Head; L. Howell, M.C.; C. A. K. Innes-Wilson, C.B.E.; J. P. Jackson; B. P. Janes; G. M. Jefferis; D. Jones; D. J. Kealey; L. T. B. Kealey; A. G. Kelly; P. H. King; S. R. H. King; B. W. Knott; Miss D. R. Lane; J. F. A. Lees; A. L. MacIver; J. S. Mappin; B. R. Matthew; G. W. Maycock, V.R.D.; P. S. Maynard; S. W. Midwinter; G. Mill; A. Millar; N. S. Miller; S. R. Mollison; R. H. Moody; E. Oakley; A. D. Owen; H. R. Parkin; H. N. F. Patterson; B. Pearson; A. W. Pyonor; V. C. Radmore; S. Roberton; E. M. Roberts; S. H. A. Rollison; D. K. Rubie; K. M. Sargeant; R. le B. Shelton; R. J. Sissons; A. A. Sloma; A. F. M. Smith, C.B.E.; H. M. A. Stedham; G. Swayne-Thomas; W. E. Tait, T.D.; J. K. Watson, C.B.E.; P. C. Williams; P. H. Winter; R. Woodford; T. S. Wright £1,791 to £2,154
Deputy Chief Estate Officer, W. J. N. Oswald £2,865 to £3,215
Senior Estate Officers, J. M. Berncastle; T. W. R. Bridson; D. L. Brocklesby, A.F.C.; K. J. W. Brown; R. M. Buckley, E.R.D.; P. G. Burnett; B. E. Cresswell; J. A. Fox; J. R. Hodgson, T.D.; A. L. Horton; J. A. Speak; E. Thomas £2,293 to £2,628

Estate Officers, J. H. Baker, M.C.; T. A. L. Banks; H. J. Bedford; H. E. Bellas; R. W. Castle; E. A. Hall; R. A. M. Jordan; P. W. Jupp, C.B.E.; K. Keasley; E. H. M. Knight; R. F. Martin; W. S. Munday; S. Rose; A. R. Sanders £1,624 to £2,154
Deputy Chief Inspector of Audit, W. D. Munrow, C.B.E. £3,815
District Auditors, O. Barraclough; P. A. Chater; E. M. Clarke; S. V. Collins; G. Davies; T. Eagle; E. Fieth; S. A. Hills; R. Jones; E. E. Keys; A. Long; A. R. Parr, O.B.E.; F. R. Smith; M. C. C. Sullivan; L. Tovell; A. W. Vale £3,215
Deputy District Auditors, R. C. Bannermann; J. Carmichael; C. H. Chidgey; R. K. Edwards; R. F. B. Elliston; S. T. Evans; H. Harrison; F. Holdsworth; C. D. Lacey; L. J. May; N. S. Middleton; B. Northey; E. S. Sant; C. E. Seward; J. Speirs; J. G. Teesdale; R. W. Thirwell .... £2,683 to £2,865

Welsh Office

Cathays Park, Cardiff
[Cardiff: 28066]

Welsh Secretary, J. W. M. Siberry £4,050
Assistant Secretaries, I. Davey; H. N. Jerman £2,800 to £3,500
Principals, J. H. Clement; B. H. Evans; D. Morgan; J. L. Palmer; J. L. Pinder .... £1,894 to £2,646
Chief Executive Officer, W. B. Jones (*Establishment Officer*) .... £2,172 to £2,507
Senior Executive Officers, J. E. H. Booker; J. G. W. Butcher; M. A. Crabbe; G. M. Jenkins; J. E. L. Rees; H. I. W. Sparkes; A. D. Williams £1,615 to £1,061

Architectural Staff

Principal Architect, J. Hughes .... £2,800 to £3,150
Senior Architect, I. J. Lewis ..... £2,228 to £2,563
Senior Quantity Surveyor, A. D. Hill £2,228 to £2,563

Engineering Staff †

Senior Engineering Inspector, A. F. Brennand £3,100 to £3,500
Engineering Inspectors, T. J. Crews; H. Cronshaw; G. Davies; W. F. George; R. S. Offord; C. S. Trapp .... £2,284 to £2,850

Planning Staff

Principal Planner, G. H. C. Cooper £2,800 to £3,150
Senior Planning Officer, W. L. Hulley £2,228 to £2,563
Planning Officers, I. N. Jones; P. A. Sydney; J. W. Tester .... £1,559 to £2,089
Senior Research Officer, D. S. Prosser £1,894 to £2,563
Senior Estate Officer, B. J. Robe .. £2,228 to £2,563
Estate Officer, W. Bradley ...... £1,559 to £2,089

†Also serve the Welsh Board of Health.

CENTRAL OFFICE OF INFORMATION

Hercules Road, Westminster Bridge Road, S.E.1
[Waterloo: 2345]

The Central Office of Information is a common service department which produces information and publicity material, and supplies publicity services, required by all other Government departments. In the United Kingdom it conducts Government display press, television and poster advertising (except for the National Savings Committee), produces and distributes booklets, leaflets, films, television material, exhibitions, photographs and other visual material; carries out social surveys, and distributes departmental press notices. For the overseas departments it supplies British Information posts overseas with press, radio and television material, booklets, magazines, reference services, films, exhibitions, photographs, display and reading room material; manages schemes for promoting the overseas sale of British books, periodicals and newspapers; arranges tours in the United Kingdom for official visitors from overseas; and provides exhibition stands at trade fairs (for the Board of Trade). Administratively, the Central Office of Information is responsible to Treasury ministers, while the ministers whose departments it serves are responsible for the policy expressed in its work.

Director-General, T. Fife Clark, C.B.E. £5,015
Private Secretary, Miss E. M. Butler, M.B.E.

Group 1—Overseas

Controller, D. F. Kerr, C.V.O. £3,928
Assistant Controller, C. Barns, O.B.E. £2,683 to £2,865
Senior Information Officer, Miss G. R. Hembry £1,676 to £2,126

Films, Television and Newsreels Divisions

Director, C. F. A. de V. Beauclerk, O.B.E. £2,865 to £3,565
Chief Information Officer, R. A. Fleming £2,683 to £2,865
Principal Information Officers, J. Baird; Miss D. V. G. Cockburn; L. Croft; H. C. Wheeler £2,237 to £2,572
Senior Information Officers, A. J. L. Bourne; A. S. Brettell; P. G. Broderick; Mrs. R. Brownrigg; C. G. Cave; P. W. Coldham; P. D. Dann; J. Fares; R. J. Hall; Miss A. B. I. James; J. Maddison, M.B.E.; D. B. Mayne; K. H. Sanders; A. A. Vessello .... £1,676 to £2,126
Senior Executive Officer, D. J. Etheridge £1,676 to £2,126

Radio Division

Director, J. P. Langston, O.B.E. .. £2,865 to £3,565
Principal Information Officer, A. M. Kittermaster £2,237 to £2,572
Senior Information Officers, C. W. W. Ryan; H. J. Swift .... £1,676 to £2,126

Photographs Division

Director, A. H. M. Harrison, O.B.E. £2,683 to £2,865
Principal Information Officer, A. H. Midgley, O.B.E. £2,237 to £2,572
Senior Information Officers, Miss H. R. Dunt; R. E. Hicks; R. N. Stone, M.B.E. ... £1,676 to £2,126
Senior Executive Officer, G. W. M. Pearson £1,676 to £2,126

Publications Division

Director, J. H. McMillan, C.B.E. .. £2,865 to £3,565
Chief Information Officer, N. Bicknell, D.S.O., D.F.C. £2,683 to £2,865
Principal Information Officers, J. C. Bayliss; J. D. Gilbert, M.B.E.; R. F. Hoddinott; W. J. Masters, O.B.E.; J. S. Tetley, M.B.E. .... £2,237 to £2,572
Senior Information Officers, B. H. Atkinson; H. C. Baillie; S. C. Bignell; R. D. Binfield, M.B.E.; J. L. Bishop; C. H. Bourchier; V. G. Cockersell; H. J. S. Collett; H. Dunn, M.B.E.; A. E. Gatland; D. F. Grant; A. R. Harris; H. P. Jolowicz; J. G. King; H. D. Liversidge; D. A. Loxley; W. W. Miller; K. Roden; A. E. Rodwell; R. T. Ronan; L. C. K. Vaughan-Jones ..... £1,676 to £2,126

Overseas Press Services Division

Director, M. H. Lovell, C.B.E. ... £2,865 to £3,565
Chief Information Officer, J. M. Spey, M.B.E. £2,683 to £2,865
Prcinipal Information Officers, J. C. B. Hannah; E. R. Kelly; Dr. E. C. Roberson; K. W. Sutton; H. J. Watters .... £2,237 to £2,572
Senior Information Officers, Mrs. A. A. Beattie; P. T. Brazier; Miss R. Clifford; W. D. Clifford; R. E. Collins; Mrs. C. Comber; T. Cooban; F. S. Cox; J. W. Dunscombe; Miss M. M. Foster; B. C. Freestone; G. P. H. Garton; S. F. J. Godfrey; J. A. K. Goldthorpe; L. Haffner; D. W. Harvey; L. A. J. Hawkings; J. K. Holroyd; G. Holt; T. J. Hughes; L. Ledesma; Miss D. J. Littlefield; T. H. Mapp; S. W. Mason, O.B.E.; Miss E. C. C. Mayson; H. Miller; D. J. Payton-Smith; F. R.

Pickering, M.B.E.; G. A. Repath; J. Smallwood; C. F. G. Wills . . . . £1,676 to £2,126

Reference Division

Director, Miss N. M. Chown . . . £2,683 to £2,865
Principal Information Officers, A. E. Bevens; E. G. Farmer . . . . £2,237 to £2,572
Senior Information Officers, Mrs. J. Bonnor; F. Lees; Mrs. D. L. Long (*part-time*); J. H. C. Mannock; K. Mather; W. H. Turnbull, M.B.E.; N. L. Webster; H. Witheford . . . . . £1,676 to £2,126
Senior Executive Officer, A. J. Courtney £1,676 to £2,126

Group 2—Administration

Controller, B. C. Thomas, C.B.E. £3,928

Advertising Division

Director, O. G. Thetford . . . . £2,683 to £2,865
Principal Information Officers, J. Bessant; D. G. Marsh £2,237 to £2,572
Senior Information Officers, P. G. Hutchings; A. F. Lamb; Miss V. E. Thorne . . . £1,676 to £2,126
Senior Executive Officer, I. U. McLauchlan £1,676 to £2,126

Exhibitions Division

Director, E. T. W. Swaine, M.B.E. £2,865 to £3,565
Chief Information Officer, H. J. Bewg £2,683 to £2,865
Principal Information Officers, E. R. I. Allan; S. Hart-Still; N. J. Holland; H. H. Rossney £2,237 to £2,572
Senior Information Officers, G. W. Bennett; H. O. Bryant; C. P. Carter; P. R. Daniell; A. D. Estill; G. E. C. Farndell; W. H. Farrow; A. E. Humphries; A. W. Jones; F. Lightfoot; L. A. Miller; R. J. Reeves; A. V. Whitehead; D. Wilkes £1,676 to £2,126
Senior Executive Officer, H. Cook £1,676 to £2,126

Social Survey Division

Director, L. Moss . . . . £2,865 to £3,565
Principal Information Officers, P. G. Gray; Miss A. I. Harris; W. F. F. Kemsley; C. G. Thomas; H. D. Willcock, O.B.E. . . . . £2,237 to £2,572
Senior Information Officers, Miss J. Atkinson; R. M. Blunden; Dr. A. C. McKennell; Miss R. Morton-Williams; Dr. D. Sheppard; D. F. O. Stuart . . . . £1,676 to £2,126
Senior Executive Officer, S. Witzenfeld £1,676 to £2,126

Finance and Accounts Division

Director, N. S. O'Connell . . . . . . £2,865 to £3,565
Chief Executive Officers, S. Griffin; G. E. Iles £2,237 to £2,572
Senior Executive Officers, R. K. Evans; D. Hall, D.F.M.; D. F. Parsons . . . . £1,676 to £2,126

Establishment and Organization Division

Director, G. Meara, C.B.E. . . . . . . £2,865 to £3,565
Chief Executive Officers, R. W. Kingsbury; C. T. Sawyer . . . . £2,237 to £2,572
Senior Executive Officers, M. Collins; G. A. Dixon; W. F. Garnett; A. E. Youngs £1,676 to £2,126

Tours and Production Services Division

Director, R. G. Biggs, O.B.E. . . . . £2,865 to £3,565
Chief Information Officer, M. F. Hackett, O.B.E. £2,638 to £2,865
Principal Information Officers, R. Blundell, D.F.C.; F. C. Cooke; A. A. Garnett, M.B.E.; A. W. Jenkins, M.B.E.; W. H. J. Thornton £2,237 to £2,572
Senior Information Officers, A. E. Bates; C. P. Jeaffreson; E. J. Kirtland; A. W. Patten; E. H. Putnam; D. N. Steward; E. W. Taylor; F. G. E. Terry; J. Wilson, M.B.E. . . . . . £1,676 to £2,126
Senior Executive Officers, J. B. F. Foster, M.B.E.; A. H. Kemp . . . . £1,676 to £2,126

Regional Unit

Principal Information Officer, K. C. F. Davies £2,237 to £2,572

News Distribution Service

Duty Officers, T. P. Blakiston; Miss W. F. Reeves.

Regional Offices

Northern—Prudhoe House, Prudhoe Street, Newcastle-upon-Tyne, 1

Chief Regional Officer, J. W. Shand, O.B.E. £2,172 to £2,507
Senior Information Officer, L. W. Mandy. £1,615 to £2,061

East and West Ridings—42 Eastgate, Leeds, 2

Chief Regional Officer, T. J. Hunt, O.B.E. £2,172 to £2,507
Senior Information Officer, S. Gannon £1,615 to £2,061

North Midland—Walton House, Granby Street, Nottingham

Chief Regional Officer, D. de M. Guilfoyle £2,172 to £2,507
Senior Information Officer, D. C. Boyd £1,615 to £2,061

Eastern—Block D, Government Buildings, Brooklands Avenue, Cambridge

Chief Regional Officer, P. L. K. Schwabé, M.V.O. £2,172 to £2,507

London and South Eastern—Hercules Road, Westminster Bridge Road, S.E.1

Chief Regional Officer, E. A. Hunt £2,237 to £2,572
Senior Information Officer (vacant)

Southern—Government Buildings No. 3, Whiteknights, Reading

Chief Regional Officer, P. T. Ede. £2,172 to £2,507

South Western—61–63 Queen's Road, Bristol, 8

Chief Regional Officer, W. J. D. Irving £2,172 to £2,507
Senior Information Officer, F. Barrett £1,615 to £2,061

Midland—Windsor House, Temple Row, Birmingham, 2

Chief Regional Officer, R. Dean, M.B.E. £2,172 to £2,507
Senior Information Officer, R. R. Boyce £1,615 to £2,061

North Western—Coronation House, 1 New Brown Street, Manchester, 4

Chief Regional Officer, H. V. Tillotsun £2,172 to £2,507
Senior Information Officer, H. Cope £1,615 to £2,061

Welsh Office—42 Park Place, Cardiff

Chief Officer, Idris Evans, M.V.O. £2,618 to £2,800
Senior Information Officer, P. L. Marshall £1,615 to £2,061

BOARD OF INLAND REVENUE

Somerset House, W.C.2

[Temple Bar: 2407]

The Board of Inland Revenue was constituted under the Inland Revenue Board Act, 1849, by the consolidation of the Board of Excise and the Board of Stamps and Taxes. In 1909 the administration of excise duties was transferred to the Board of Customs. The Board of Inland Revenue is responsible for the management and collection of income tax, surtax, profits tax, estate duty, stamp duties and other direct taxes, and also for the valuation of freehold and leasehold property for Inland Revenue taxation, for certain purposes on behalf of other Government Departments and public authorities and, in England and Wales, for local authority rating. Since April 1, 1960, the Board has also been responsible for the management and collection of tithe redemption annuities. Salaries and expenses of the Board for 1963/64 were estimated at £62,885,000.

The Board

Chairman, Sir Alexander Johnston, G.C.B. K.B.E. £7,015
Private Secretary, J. M. Crawley.

Deputy Chairmen, Sir John Evans, K.B.E., C.B.; J. R. McK. Willis, C.B., C.M.G. £5,015
Other Members, E. R. Brookes, C.B.; E. S. McNairn, C.B.; A. J. N. Miller, C.B.; R. O. M. Nicholas, C.B.

Secretaries' Office

Secretaries, E. R. Brookes, C.B.; E. S. McNairn, C.B.; A. J. N. Miller, C.B.; R. O. M. Nicholas, C.B. £4,115

Establishments Division

Director of Establishments, E. S. McNairn, C.B.
Assistant Secretaries, R. F. Bailey; D. G. Daymond; J. M. Green; D. A. Smith.... £2,865 to £3,565
Principals, W. R. Atkinson; J. M. Stevenson, I.S.O.; A. F. Taggart .... £1,959 to £2,711
Principal Clerks, S. G. Ash, M.B.E.; R. V. Binding; J. B. Sweeting .... £2,237 to £2,572
Assistant Principal Clerks, J. D. Benson; Miss N. Curtis; L. J. E. Hatchett; G. T. Street £1,680 to £2,126
Accommodation Officer, C. H. W. Hall £2,237 to £2,572
Deputy Accommodation Officers, A. L. Cowden; F. C. Harris, M.B.E. .... £1,680 to £2,126
Senior Organization and Methods Officer, L. S. Jowsey £2,237 to £2,572
Principal Clerks, H. R. Brockwell; S. G. Day £2,237 to £2,572
Organization and Methods Officers, J. W. E. Clutterbuck; D. M. McL. Loudon; R. A. Newbery; A. J. Rawlins .... £1,680 to £2,126

Stamps and Taxes Division

Assistant Secretaries, D. E. Barrett; W. E. Bruce; A. H. Dalton; J. H. Gracey; G. B. N. Hartog; W. H. B. Johnson; J. A. Johnstone; J. G. Lewis; §A. Lord; Miss A. H. McNicol; §D. G. McPherson; N. C. Price; J. P. Strudwick; J. Webb; Miss G. E. M. Wolters........... £2,865 to £3,565
Principals, L. J. H. Beighton; M. H. Collins; C. E. K. Fear; F. B. Harrison; B. T. Houghton; G. M. Kirby; H. V. Lewis; T. J. Painter; §W. D. Pattinson; F. I. Robertson; J. C. Rowley; G. Smith; §J. D. Taylor Thompson; D. B. Vernon £1,959 to £2,711
Principal Clerk, E. A. Rapsey... £2,237 to £2,572
Assistant Principal Clerks, Miss W. J. Blanchard; C. L. Deller; Miss M. I. Fetherston; S. G. Hawkins; S. F. Marlow; A. F. Royle; R. A. White.................... £1,680 to £2,126
Principal Accountant, D. Graneek. £2,478 to £2,810
Chief Accountants, A. E. Allchurch; G. B. Baron; J. M. Fulton; R. Halsall; W. A. Heslop; E. Lawson; C. U. Mack; S. R. F. Porter; W. H. Simon; A. Wilson; N. J. Wykes..... £1,851 to £2,358

Statistics and Intelligence Division

Somerset House, W.C.2

Director, G. Paine............. £2,865 to £3,565
Statisticians, R. F. Burch; S. F. James £1,959 to £2,711
Principal Clerks, E. F. J. Eustace; T. I. Williams £2,237 to £2,572
Assistant Principal Clerks, J. B. Berry; A. J. Green, M.B.E.; D. H. Pooley........ £1,680 to £2,126

Assessments Division

Barrington Road, Worthing, Sussex

Controller, H. Leigh........... £2,618 to £2,800
Principal Clerks, Mrs. M. E. Hughes; N. E. Nolan £2,172 to £2,507
Assistant Principal Clerks, B. E. Greville; J. R. Griffin; R. Heeley; D. R. Laver; R. W. Marsh; P. E. Nielsen; F. G. Thompson; §S. E. S. Whitby; J. R. Wilson....... £1,615 to £2,061

Office of Special Commissioners of Income Tax

Hinchley Wood, Surrey

Presiding Special Commissioner, R. A. Furtado £4,215
Special Commrs., W. E. Bradley; G. R. East, C.M.G.; F. Gilbert; B. James; R. W. Quayle, O.B.E.; N. F. Rowe; H. G. Watson; each £3,815; F. H. Brooman; H. H. Leedale; J. N. Wright, O.B.E. *unpaid*
Clerk to Special Commissioners of Income Tax and Inspector of Foreign Dividends, F. H. Brooman £3,560
Assistant Clerk to Special Commissioners of Income Tax and Assistant Inspector of Foreign Dividends, H. H. Leedale..................... £3,085
Senior Principal Clerks, G. Briddon; D. S. Kirtley; R. C. Tebboth; E. E. Wheeler; J. N. Wright, O.B.E. .... £2,678 to £2,860
Principal Clerks, Miss D. B. Bickmore; F. W. J. Boggiss; R. O. Burnett; J. A. Cargill; W. H. Day; J. N. Gosling; S. G. Hammond; W. H. S. Howell; W. J. Hunt; W. M. Imlay; §E. J. King; G. S. Lancaster; A. McKenzie; W. J. Maddren; W. J. Moore; F. A. Oelman; J. Richardson; N. W. Sydee; C. A. Thorpe; W. E. Webb; C. H. Windeatt.................. £2,232 to £2,567
Assistant Principal Clerks, G. M. Abrams; W. P. Ashton; S. W. Banyard; P. Beever; R. J. Bitton; R. D. Blair; H. Booth; §C. S. Brady; R. Burns; A. Campbell; E. L. Cannon; R. Carrington; A. H. Carter; A. W. Coates; Miss M. A. Connell; A. R. Cooper; A. D. Crombie; G. Edmiston; H. Elsworth; H. B. Every; R. K. Ewan; C. G. Field; J. T. Forsythe; R. A. Forth; W. F. Francis; H. R. Game; Miss M. V. Gifford; C. S. Goodwin; A. R. Grove; R. W. S. Haines; L. W. Harris; R. P. Hawkins; Miss M. L. Hayward; T. G. Hodgson; §C. E. Howick; T. Hudson; R. G. Hughes; A. C. Johns; R. E. M. Kirkman; B. Lyons; Miss J. Madgwick; D. W. Mason; G. E. P. Matthews; F. W. Newcombe; A. F. Newson; G. H. Pentelow; M. W. Potter; C. W. Price; D. V. Roberts; W. Roberts; Miss D. E. Robertson; O. F. Sellers; A. J. Simmons; J. Sinfield; F. C. Smith; Mrs. M. Steane; W. J. Stewart; Miss E. Stone; B. S. Taylor; J. D. Thomas; §A. Thompson; W. E. Thorpe; A. E. Wadey; N. Wainwright; H. L. Warburton; E. V. Wigglesworth; J. R. Wilding; D. B. Willis; P. L. Wolsey; T. D. Youl, M.B.E. £1,675 to £2,121

Estate Duty Office

Minford House, Rockley Road, West Kensington, W.14

Controller of Death Duties, H. T. Veall, C.B. £3,923
Deputy Controllers of Death Duties, E. W. C. Lewis; H. W. Hewitt £3,285
Asst. Controllers of Death Duties, E. J. Ashman, O.B.E.; R. D. J. Dean; C. D. Harding; R. K. Johns; I. D. Lorde; D. H. McCartie; C. A. Robertson; E. J. Salter; J. B. Wells..... £2,910
Chief Examiners, W. J. G. Allen; J. D. Armour; W. J. Atkinson; E. H. Baker; J. A. Banks; J. W. Bogle; W. G. Cannon; C. G. Carter; W. G. Carter; K. W. Chetwood; Miss M. Clark; W. R. G. Coleman; M. F. B. Couzens, O.B.E.; E. N. Crowther; W. E. Dallas; G. F. Dawe; J. F. Daykin; Miss M. Dexter; P. Dunphy; B. E. Glaze; C. P. Grant; G. E. Hayman; R. Horrex; F. G. Hoyle; C. D. Hughes; F. Irwin; H. H. Jago; Miss M. M. Jones; K. S. Lake; K. J. Lees; §E. G. Marriott; D. W. Meacock; A. D. Mitchner; P. H. Moss; S. Noden; E. W. J. Panting; G. F. Parrott; G. Patrick; J. Pearce; N. L. Pearce; C. M. Phillips; W. K. Sisman; P. B. Smallwood; E. Sykes; H. E. Thomas; R. W. Thomas; G. Thompson; F. H. Thornton; R. F. J. Thornton; P. Vernon; Miss M. S. Whitley, O.B.E.; W. Wright £2,232 to £2,706
Sen. Examiners, G. Allcock; A. C. Allen; D. J. Allen; E. M. Andrew; R. J. H. Anton; Miss H. M. Atherden; T. E. Austen; R. M. Balsillie; R. Barber; M. W. Barnett; J. P. Barter; A. L. Barton; R. A. Beare; G. A. Beasley; J. H. Bell; R. G. Bigmore; G. E. Bird; D. J. F. Boiling; H. Booth, M.B.E.; J. T. Bow; J. E. Brereton; J. Bugden; J. H. Bunn; E. C. Burden; A. J. Burley; A. Cherns; D. D. Chittey; J. G. Colebrook; S.

Collingwood; W. W. Cornforth; P. C. B. Cox; F. Cuerden; J. F. Cunningham; T. C. Dale; E. E. Davies; L. Drew; J. E. Dyer; §T. F. Evans; B. W. Eyre; R. D. Finner; T. D. Flavin; R. D. Fleming; P. H. Fletcher; S. H. Forshaw; H. J. A. Fox; A. B. Gardner; A. W. George; P. K. Gerhold; H. Gilhespy; W. Gonzalez; R. Grant; R. R. Greenfield; Miss C. P. Grudgings; N. B. Gudgin; I. P. Gunn; H. J. Hall; W. Hall; D. C. Hamilton; L. S. Harris; F. A. Hastings; Miss B. R. Hewens; J. Hillas; A. F. Hiscock; R. W. Holliday; S. Holmden; K. H. Holmes; E. J. Holt; C. P. Hudson; H. J. D. Hunkin; D. J. Hyland; A. F. Jaques; A. S. Johnson; J. F. Johnson; W. G. Johnston; B. T. Jones; Miss F. M. Jones; C. W. Jordan; R. T. Kablean; G. J. Kennard; J. G. Kingsley; D. J. Lawday; F. W. Leigh; J. P. O. Lewis; P. B. Lugg; Miss M. Macaulay; L. A. Mackay; W. A. McLaren; E. J. Mann; V. R. Marfell; P. Marshall; R. C. Mason; R. K. Miller; C. E. Milner; E. A. Owen; A. R. Payne; R. T. Peak; R. J. Pearson; E. G. Peel; D. J. Perks; N. C. Phillips; R. F. Pittman; C. R. Ponter; L. F. Poole; A. P. Primett; D. F. Reading; E. Readhead; J. E. Redman; O. E. Rice; E. H. R. Router; W. H. Rundle; D. H. Salloway; H. S. Smith; L. Smith; Miss V. C. Smith; G. A. Spencer; F. E. Spurrell; R. A. Suckling; §E. J. Sutton; M. Swann; Miss M. C. Taylor; J. Thorndycraft; B. W. Wainwright; Miss J. E. Wakeford; D. H. Weddell; G. A. Wignall; A. W. Wilcox; F. Wood; L. Worth; W. F. Worth; G. W. Youngman.......... £1,675 to £2,121

Assistant Principal Clerk, W. R. Howard, M.B.E. £1,675 to £2,121

Accountant and Comptroller-General's Office

Bush House, South-West Wing, Strand, W.C.2

Accountant and Comptroller-Gen., W. F. B. Smith £3,565

Deputy do., G. F. Manfield £3,090

Assistant Accountants and Comptrollers-General, E. J. Parker; F. F. Swalwell; R. A. J. Webber; G. D. Wroe............... £2,618 to £2,865

General Accounting and Collection of Taxes Divisions

Principal Collectors, H. Edwards; E. E. Hill; J. F. Hill; A. F. Jackson; J. W. Sidford, O.B.E.; J. J. Stokes; G. B. Walker....... £2,172 to £2,572

Regional Collectors, E. R. Bailey; D. J. Barcham; O. H. Boord; H. V. Campbell-White; F. G. Coppage; L. A. E. Crick; J. L. Cridge; G. M. Culpan; H. Daker; K. L. Fickling; D. C. Geddes; L. C. Gilbertson; E. J. Goslin, M.B.E.; H. G. Grimshaw; L. W. Guyatt; W. B. Hindle; W. Holmes; W. A. Impey; N. D. Jones; E. G. Lewin; G. R. Lister; L. A. Martin; A. J. Morrison; R. A. Newbery; W. Pickersgill; J. V. Pickles; G. M. Poole; H. W. Reynolds; A. G. H. Richards, M.B.E.; W. H. J. Sharp; A. L. Smith; J. T. Terry; A. R. Titley £1,615 to £2,126

Audit Division

Principal Clerks, A. E. Bleksley; F. W. Etherington £2,237 to £2,572

Assistant Principal Clerks, R. A. Baldwin; P. D. Connell; G. O. Hughes; D. J. S. Seaman; Miss E. A. Sharples; T. N. Simpson; Miss M. J. Wingfield.................. £1,680 to £2,126

Office of the Controller of Stamps

Bush House, South-West Wing, Strand, W.C.2

Controller, A. A. E. E. Ettinghausen....... £2,965

Principal Clerks, Miss M. C. Bird, O.B.E.; S. J. C. Boucher.................. £2,237 to £2,572

Assistant Principal Clerks, A. Blaney; A. W. G. Boughton; R. A. Chattaway; J. S. Ewing; G. H. Glanville; J. G. Hull; R. H. Molineux; C. L. Spence; H. E. Stammus; G. F. Wise £1,680 to £2,126

Director of Stamping

Somerset House, W.C.2

Director, J. Green............. £2,237 to £2,572

Office of the Chief Inspector of Taxes

Somerset House, W.C.2

Chief Inspector, Sir Edward Norman........ £5,015

Deputy Chief Inspectors, L. Barford; S. H. H. Hildersley, C.B.E....................... £3,928

Senior Principal Inspectors, G. L. Ayres; G. T. Baney; E. Bramley; J. T. Cannon; J. E. Caro; D. H. Diack; J. E. Firth; C. H. Godden; V. H. T. Grout; R. A. Hogg; W. J. Lofthouse; A. W. Mason; C. H. Morrell; W. A. T. Morton; W. H. Nelson; F. H. Ostime, O.B.E.; R. M. Owen, C.B.E.; W. A. Purdie; R. W. Rae; F. Seale; A. Stocks; D. A. Swift; E. V. Symons; H. G. Thomas; J. H. Walker, C.B.E........... £3,515

Principal Inspectors (attached to Head Office), E. V. Adams; J. N. Allen; W. G. Ayerst; L. R. Barker; R. O. Bearne; N. E. Beck; H. J. R. Bennett; B. J. Bentley; T. Bingham; A. D. M. Brown; F. Carr; J. E. Comben; C. E. Cox; E. Croppin; A. D. Ellis; A. W. Fifield; C. G. V. Fleming; H. D. Grinham; E. G. Heath, O.B.E.; J. Hutton, O.B.E.; E. Jacques; K. A. Job; R. F. McKie; L. L. Milner; C. W. Moir; D. H. Moorcraft; C. G. Newman; W. A. Perry; A. J. Philbin; F. H. Phillips; J. A. Quinney; T. Scott; I. R. E. Symons; I. D. Thomson; P. Tillson; P. E. Woodcock............. £3,215

Senior Inspectors (attached to Head Office), J. F. S. Banks; Miss D. M. Bates; W. J. Blanch; C. W. Bland; R. A. Blythe; J. F. Bowman; J. F. Boyd; R. O. Brennand; G. I. Brown; B. S. Caley; J. A. Cattermole; J. M. Chadburn; V. C. Chapman; L. O. Clarke; A. M. Clelland; R. C. Cook; F. S. Creed; P. C. H. Crozier; H. Cunliffe; T. B. Curry; L. R. Davies; W. M. Dermit; D. W. R. Doggett; E. D. Evans; L. J. Fillmore; D. A. W. Furbank; Miss E. M. Fyvie; G. Galey; A. B. Hadden; D. A. Hamill; J. W. Harman; R. V. Harrison; D. P. Harwood; D. Herdman; G. M. Howell; P. Hudson; Miss A. Hume; S. R. Hunt; C. M. Jeanes; J. L. Jeffries; E. Jones; K. J. D. Keighley; W. G. Knight; Miss E. M. Lacey; J. E. Lawrance; W. T. Legon; J. Livesey; W. I. McJannet; F. T. J. Magee; H. C. Mansfield, M.B.E.; D. Meredith; R. C. Mitchell; J. S. Moore; R. S. Morrow, M.B.E.; T. Nichol; K. E. Norman; L. H. Northam; H. O'Donnell; R. W. Parker; J. S. Phillips; G. R. Pickard; C. G. Porritt; A. Prothero; L. R. Restorick; R. T. Rogers; W. J. Scarpello; F. H. Shea; C. P. Sherlock; Miss D. M. Sirett; P. C. Slaney; G. E. Smith; S. G. H. Spelman; Miss S. T. Stephen; E. M. R. Thompstone; T. W. M. Tuite; D. K. Turner; Miss K. B. Walker; J. K. Ward; R. F. Ward; W. Watson; A. F. Weightman; A. W. Whalley; R. H. Wilson; S. G. C. Wilson, O.B.E.; C. A. Winterton; S. J. Wood... .. £2,404 to £2,865

Inspectors Higher Grade (attached to Head Office), J. B. Anderson; W. Anderson; J. S. Ashton; H. Bailey; L. C. Baldwyn; Miss M. W. Barham; Miss J. A. Bartlett; H. S. Bendell; R. W. Burgess; E. J. Burnett; W. B. Burrows; A. J. Bye; I. Civval, M.B.E.; K. Clark; Miss M. A. Collyer; E. R. Courtney; P. W. Deal; J. S. Doherty, M.B.E.; W. R. Dunsford; H. D. Evans, S. A. Evans; Miss S. J. Frazer; E. G. Goddard; J. Gould, M.B.E.; D. G. E. Grocott; G. Guest; G. F. Hamilton; R. S. Hanchett, T.D.; J. W. Hart; W. G. Hawes; H. Heap; Miss D. E. Hill; C. A. Hollands, M.B.E.; J. J. H. Hopkins; I. N. Hunter; P. J. Hytch; Miss A. W. Jones; H. L. Jones; I. Jones; Mrs. W. M. Kidd; E. C. Kirton; A. E. Leak; K. A. Letch; A. E. Lloyd; D. M. M. Loudon; M. McDonald; A. T. McKechnie; J. McNulty; J. Mangan; D. F. Martin; Miss W. M. Melbourne; R. Metcalfe; J. H. Morphet; H. Morrell; J. R. Morris; W. A. Page; E. B. Paterson; B. Pollard; L. Pritchard; T. Pullen; M. J. Quirk; W. Ralph; Miss C. L. Read; E. A. Roe; P. G. Rolfe; Miss B. L. Sheminant; K. A. Skinner; H. L. Smeardon; A. Smith; S. H.

Smith; Miss V. M. Spilling; Miss A. M. Taylor; Miss L. B. Taylor; R. Taylor; J. E. Thompson; Miss A. M. Thomson; H. J. Tombs; K. V. Tucker; F. F. Wadsworth; J. F. Warren, M.B.E.; B. G. Webb; H. F. G. Wellington; A. D. Wilkins; W. B. Williamson; Miss J. H. Wilson; T. McD. Wray.................... £1,615 to £2,321

Solicitor's Office
Somerset House, W.C.2

Solicitor, C. R. Sopwith................. £5,015
Principal Assistant Solicitor, H. G. Rowland. £4,115
Assistant Solicitors, K. G. Blake; K. Brading, M.B.E.; J. C. Doggett; D. M. Hatton; J. B. Hodgson; J. F. Josling; H. G. Kingston; F. P. Laws; R. J. Lloyd; E. G. R. Moses; J. W. Weston £2,965 to £3,565
Senior Legal Assistants, D. S. Blair; R. S. Boden; R. T. Brand; P. Carter; J. S. Clarke, M.C.; F. R. Davies; J. F. Easton; M. C. Furey; P. D. Hall; Miss A. Hopkin; E. O. Jackson; D. G. Passmore, O.B.E.; B. J. Reynolds; A. K. Tavaré; P. Towle; A. Wheaten; R. H. Widdows £2,304 to £2,865
Assistant Principal Clerks, L. E. Armstrong; I. P. Dunkley.................. £1,680 to £2,126

Valuation Office
Somerset House, W.C.2

Chief Valuer, Sir Kenneth Atkinson....... £5,015
Deputy Chief Valuers, J. A. Edwards, C.B.E.; D. P. Iggulden, C.B.E., D.S.O., T.D............. £3,928
Assistant Chief Valuers, T. Broad; W. R. T. Eveling, C.B.E.; W. A. Hobbs; D. F. Mills; E. M. Neville; L. N. Roddis, C.B.E.; J. J. Scott........ £3,665
Superintending Valuers, S. V. Abel; G. Alexander; H. E. Bailey; F. G. Burge; J. R. Burton; H. Coley; R. J. Cowling; R. J. Crown; R. F. Davey; C. V. Edis; G. Edwards; C. S. Farnes; H. S. Ford; R. L. Fraquet; H. B. Freeman; W. H. Gibson; H. C. Grenyer; A. F. Guy; G. A. Higgens; G. M. Hughes; G. L. Kirk; J. H. Lucas, O.B.E.; A. F. Meire; A. Molony; K. J. Morgan; E. Passingham; C. J. Pither, O.B.E.; W. P. Rees, M.C.; F. P. G. Rudge; F. G. Scrase; N. Simmonds; E. J. Smith; G. Thomas; M. C. Thorne; C. H. Tinsley; E. L. Woodruff..... £2,975 to £3,340
First Class Valuers (attached to Head Office), J. V. C. Anthony; C. J. Bailey; R. M. Barraball; R. G. Edwards; H. R. Elford; M. C. Fuller-Hall; R. D. E. Gilbard; J. K. Harris; S. G. Hope; J. B. Hyne; W. A. Stewart Jones; V. E. A. Morris; G. W. Robinson; D. E. J. Rottenbury; G. S. Teviotdale; K. C. Walter £2,410 to £2,915
Chief Executive Officer, R. G. West £2,237 to £2,572
Senior Executive Officer, D. W. G. Bragg £1,680 to £2,126

Tithe Redemption Office
Finsbury Square House, 33/37, Finsbury Square, E.C.2.

Controller, G. F. K. Grant...... £2,683 to £2,865
Deputy Controller, H. A. Cox, M.B.E. £2,237 to £2,572
Assistant Principal Clerks, E. A. Bourchier, M.B.E.; P. W. Davenport; C. W. Hill; A. D. Seymour £1,680 to £2,126

Inland Revenue (Scotland)
10 Waterloo Place, Edinburgh 1
Stamps and Taxes

Comptroller, R. W. Stanton, C.B.E £2,800 to £3,500
Deputy Comptroller, D. Glass ... £1,894 to £2,646
Principal Clerks, W. M. Stewart; D. M. Watson £2,172 to £2,507
Asst. Principal Clerks, S. Brown; W. T. Lyons; M. L. Reardon............. £1,615 to £2,061

Solicitor's Office

Solicitor, J. K. W. Dunn................. £3,600
Senior Legal Assistants, G. H. Brown; A. H. S. Neave; G. K. Petrie-Hay........... £2,239 to £2,800

Estate Duty Office
6 Waterloo Place, Edinburgh 1

Registrar of Death Duties, W. H. Cartwright £3,225
Deputy Registrar of Death Duties, R. L. Balfour £2,850
Chief Examiners, J. W. B. Crombie; I. W. Grant; R. A. Grieve; A. J. Kilpatrick; E. G. Lucas; J. A. Taylor; Miss A. C. Tennant. £2,172 to £2,646
Senior Examiners, G. P. H. Aitken; P. C. Anderson; Miss M. M. Armstrong; I. S. Beveridge; J. Carlin, D.F.C.; J. B. Donald; M. Finnigan; G. T. Graham, D.S.C.; J. W. Grant; G. G. McGregor; J. B. M. McKean; G. Mackie; A. M. McPake; D. J. Ritchie; R. Robertson; J. Stewart; V. D. E. Webb; D. A. White........ £1,615 to £2,061

Valuation Office, Scotland
43 Rose Street, Edinburgh 2

Chief Valuer for Scotland, C. Short, C.B.E... £3,675
Asst. Chief Valuers, D. S. Glen, I.S.O.; N. E. MacKay, I.S.O..................... £2,975 to £3,275

‡ Temporary.
§ Seconded to other Government Departments.

IRON AND STEEL BOARD

Norfolk House, St. James's Square, S.W.1
[Trafalgar: 8833]

Established by the *Iron and Steel Act*, 1953, for the supervision of the iron and steel industry.

Chairman, Sir Cyril Musgrave, K.C.B....... £6,000
Deputy Chairman, Sir Lincoln Evans, C.B.E... £1,500
Executive Member, R. W. Foad (*full-time*).. £7,000
Members, H. Douglass; Sir Kenneth Hague; G. Wilton Lee; N. C. Macdiarmid; Sir Richard Summers; A. H. White, C.B.E.; The Lord Williamson, C.B.E.; Sir Alan Wilson, F.R.S. (*each* £1,000).
Secretary, J. P. Keane.

MINISTRY OF LABOUR

8 St. James's Square, S.W.1.
[Whitehall 6200]

The Ministry of Labour was set up in 1916 to take over certain duties of the Board of Trade, including the administration throughout Great Britain of employment exchanges established under the *Labour Exchanges Act*, 1909. The first 62 had opened on February 1, 1910, and there are now over 1,000 local offices. The Ministry provides a free service for employers seeking labour and for workers who are unemployed or wish to change their jobs. The arrangements cover all categories of labour, including men and women with technical and scientific qualifications, professional and executive workers, those released from H. M. Forces, discharged prisoners and foreign workers. The exchanges also act as agencies for other Government Departments in such matters as the payment of unemployment benefit and the issue of passports.

Through its 17 Industrial Rehabilitation Units the Ministry helps disabled and handicapped men and women to regain working fitness, and in 16 Government Training Centres provides courses to help individuals in need of training and to reduce the shortages of skilled labour. It is also responsible for the central, and some local, administration of the Youth Employment Service; the promotion of safety, health and welfare amongst workpeople in factories and certain other premises; the enforcement of statutory minimum wages, holidays and hours of work laid down by Wages Councils; and the collection and publication of statistics about manpower, wages, hours of work, and the index of retail prices.

The Department, through its advisory and conciliation services, assists in the prevention or settlement of industrial disputes, and its activities overseas include the maintenance of labour attachés in certain foreign countries and liaison with the International Labour Organisation.

Minister of Labour, THE RT. HON. JOHN HUGH HARE, O.B.E., M.P. £5,000
Private Secretary, J. H. Galbraith.
Assistant Private Secretary, M. Wake.
Parliamentary Private Secretary, M. N. Shaw, M.P. *unpaid*
Parliamentary Secretary, W. S. I. Whitelaw, M.C., M.P. £2,500
Permanent Secretary, Sir James Dunnett, K.C.B., C.M.G. £7,015
Private Secretary, R. S. Allison.
Deputy Secretaries, D. C. Barnes; P. H. St. John Wilson, C.B., C.B.E. £5,015
Solicitor, H. W. W. Huxham., C.B.E. £5,015

Employment Department

Under-Secretary, C. J. Maston, C.B.E. £4,115
Assistant Secretaries, J. R. Davies; J. L. Edwards; A. M. Morgan, C.M.G. ...... £2,800 to £3,500
Chief Technical Nursing Officer, Miss H. M. Cousens £1,416 to £1,693

Establishments Department

Director of Establishments, C. H. Sisson £4,115
Assistant Secretaries, I. F. Hudson; R. F. Keith £2,800 to £3,500
Controller of Services, I. C. Webley, O.B.E. £3,215
Chief Inspector, Miss J. M. Campbell, O.B.E. £2,618 to £2,800

Finance Department

Accountant-General, G. J. Nash C.B. £4,115
Director of Accounts and Audit, E. Betterton .. £3,215
Assistant Accountants-General, A. R. Cooke; A. A. D'Encer; C. P. Field; D. W. J. Orchard £2,618 to £2,800
Regional Finance Officers, J. Bayliss (*Wales and South Western*); V. P. Clark (*London and South Eastern*); A. R. Jenkins (*Midlands*); J. C. Potts (*North Western*); L. Reason (*Eastern and Southern*); W. H. Simons (*Yorkshire and Lincolnshire and Northern*); J. S. Rew (*Scotland*) £2,172 to £2,507

Industrial Relations Department

Under-Secretaries, C. F. Heron, O.B.E.; A. S. Marre, C.B. £4,115
Assistant-Secretaries, K. Barnes; Z. T. Claro, M.V.O., O.B.E. (*Chief Conciliation Officer*); Miss B. Green; C. A. Larsen; R. M. Walker. £2,800 to £3,500
Chief Wages Inspector, D. G. Cox £2,618 to £2,800

Office of Wages Councils

Secretary of Wages Councils, J. J. Watson £2,172 to £2,507

Information Branch

Chief Information Officer, C. W. Birdsall, O.B.E. £2,865 to £3,565
Chief Press Officer, J. McIntosh .. £2,172 to £2,507

Overseas Department

Under-Secretary, G. C. H. Slater, C.B.E. £4,115
Assistant Secretaries, E. A. Ferguson; J. M. Vincent Smith .... £2,800 to £3,500

Safety, Health and Welfare Department

Under-Secretary, N. Singleton £4,115
Assistant Secretaries, J. R. Lloyd Davies, C.M.G.; A. J. S. James; A. F. A. Sutherland; D. R. F. Turner .... £2,800 to £3,500

H.M. Factory Inspectorate

Chief Inspector of Factories, R. K. Christy ... £4,040
Deputy Chief Inspectors of Factories, Miss A. S. Bettenson, O.B.E.; C. Mainwaring; W. J. C. Plumbe; H. Woods, C.B.E. £3,515
Senior Medical Inspector, T. A. Lloyd Davies. £3,815
Deputy Senior Medical Inspectors, A. H. Baynes; W. D. Buchanan; A. T. Doig (*Glasgow*) .. £3,500
Medical Inspectors, S. G. Rainsford, C.B. (*Headquarters*); G. O. Williams (*Headquarters*); A. H. Baynes (*Sheffield*); Mrs. J. E. Cottrell (*London*); H. J. Davies (*Cardiff*); L. E. Euinton (*Nottingham*); M. D. Kipling (*Birmingham*); R. Morley (*Newcastle*); R. Owen (*London*); G. L. Ritchie, O.B.E. (*Wolverhampton*); G. F. Smith (*Bristol*); J. B. L. Tombleson (*Manchester*); D. G. Trott (*London*); A. Watt (*Liverpool*); G. J. S. West (*Sheffield*); R. Whitelaw (*Glasgow*) .... £2,412 to £3,075
Senior Electrical Inspector, S. J. Emerson, O.B.E. († *allce.*) £2,865 to £3,215
Senior Chemical Inspector, D. Matheson £2,865 to £3,215
Senior Engineering Inspector, W. A. Attwood £2,865 to £3,215
Senior Inspector (Building and Civil Engineering) W. D. Short .... († *allce.*) £2,228 to £2,563
Superintending Inspectors, Miss M. Brand (*Midlands (Birmingham)*); Miss N. L. Forster (*Eastern and Southern*); Miss K. M. Haddock, M.B.E. (*Headquarters*); B. H. Harvey (*Yorks. and Lincs. (Leeds)*); R. Hillier (*Yorks and Lincs. (Sheffield)*); J. L. Hobson (*North Western (Manchester)*); F. J. Kirk (*London (North)*); A. B. E. Lovett (*Wales*); W. S. Moore (*London (South)*); W. G. Symons (*North Western (Liverpool)*); F. W. Thompson (*Scotland*); R. H. Thompson (*Northern*); E. Waller (*Midlands (Nottingham)*); E. I. Wilson (*South Western*) £2,675 to £3,035

Industrial Health and Safety Centre, 97 Horseferry Road, Westminster, S.W.1.—A permanent exhibition of methods, arrangements and appliances for promoting safety, health and welfare of industrial workers.
Director, E. W. Hodgson († *allce.*) £2,228 to £2,563

Government Wool Disinfecting Station

Manager, H. Neal ..... († *allce.*) £1,688 to £2,005

Solicitor's Department

Solicitor, H. W. W. Huxham, C.B.E. £5,015
Assistant Solicitors, D. E. Belham; F. D. Lawton; T. N. Lockyer .... £2,965 to £3,565
Senior Legal Assistants, J. B. H. Billam, D.F.C.; D. Bowdon-Dan; D. M. D. D. Grazebrook; Miss M. Howells; G. E. McClelland; H. T. Morgan, T.D. .... £2,239 to £2,800

Statistics Department

Director of Statistics, R. F. Fowler, C.B.E. ... £4,115
Deputy Director, P. D. Ward, O.B.E. £2,618 to £2,800

Training Department

Under Secretary, J. G. Stewart, C.B., C.B.E. . £4,115
Assistant Secretaries, K. H. Clucas; J. G. Robertson, C.M.G. .... £2,500 to £3,500
Chief Inspector of Training, A. A. G. McNaughton £2,618 to £2,800

Youth Employment and Disabled Persons Department

Under-Secretary, J. G. Stewart, C.B., C.B.E. .. £4,115
Assistant Secretaries, H. W. Evans; D. Pointon £2,800 to £3,500
H.M. Inspector of Schools (on loan), H. E. Edwards £2,023 to £2,905

Regional Organization

Northern Region

Controller, W. R. Iley, O.B.E. ... £2,800 to £3,500
Deputy Controller, M. Abbott, O.B.E. £2,618 to £2,800

Yorkshire and Lincolnshire Region

Controller, G. F. Blumer .... £2,800 to £3,500
Deputy Controller, Miss M. A. Mackie, O.B.E. £2,618 to £2,800

Eastern and Southern Region

Controller, W. A. Treganowan . £2,800 to £3,500
Deputy Controller, E. V. Eves, O.B.E. £2,618 to £2,800

London and South Eastern Region

Controller K. D. Jones, O.B.E. ... £2,800 to £3,500
Deputy Controller, J. C. Healey . £2,618 to £2,800

South Western Region
Controller, E. Robbie.......... £2,800 to £3,500
Deputy Controller, E. Barber, O.B.E.
£2,618 to £2,800

Wales
Controller, B. M. Evans, O.B.E.... £2,800 to £3,500
Deputy Controller, W. R. Joslin . £2,618 to £2,800

Midlands Region
Controller, C. J. German........ £2,800 to £3,500
Deputy Controller, T. C. Southworth, O.B.E.
£2,618 to £2,800

North Western Region
Controller, G. C. Wilson, C.B.E.., £2,800 to £3,500
Deputy Controller, Miss F. M. Sower, O.B.E.
£2,618 to £2,800

Scotland
Controller, J. A. Diack, C.B.E..... £2,800 to £3,500
Deputy Controller, Miss I. Robertson, O.B.E.
£2,618 to £2,800

INDEPENDENT OFFICES

The Industrial Court
1 Abbey Garden, Great College Street, Westminster, S.W.1
[Whitehall: 4571]

The Industrial Court is a standing arbitration tribunal set up by the Industrial Courts Act, 1919, for the settlement of trade disputes.

President, Sir Roy Wilson, Q.C............ £5,800
Independent Members, A. Ll. Armitage; W. I. R. Fraser, Q.C.; Prof. H. G. Hanbury, Q.C., D.C.L.; Sir George Honeyman, C.B.E., Q.C.; D. T. Jack, C.B.E.; D. Karmel, Q.C.; Miss B. L. Napier.
Representative Members, S. M. Caffyn, C.B.E.; W. L Clarke, C.B.E.; H. Douglass; Dame Anne Godwin, D.B.E.; A. J. Hubbard; N. Longley, C.B.E.; A. H. Mathias, C.B.E.; A. T. Ormrod; J. M. Prain, D.S.O., O.B.E., T.D.; Sir Alfred Roberts, C.B.E.; S. A. Robinson; A. G. Tomkins, C.B.E.; A. L. Trundle, O.B.E.
Secretary, L. F. Kemp, M.B.E..... £1,643 to £2,122

Office of the Umpire
6 Grosvenor Gardens, S.W.1
[Sloane: 9236]

Independent statutory authority—appointed by the Crown to decide appeals under Reinstatement in Civil Employment Act and National Service Acts.

Umpire, D. W. E. Neligan, O.B.E............ *fees*
Deputy Umpire, S. J. W. Price............... *fees*
Secretary, W. H. James........ £1,643 to £2,122

H.M. LAND REGISTRY
Lincoln's Inn Fields, W.C.2
[Holborn: 3488]

H.M. Land Registry was established in pursuance of a recommendation of a Royal Commission by the Land Registry Act, 1862. The aim of the Act was to render dealings with land more simple and economical by establishing a State register of landowners who voluntarily submitted the titles to their land for examination and approval by the Registrar on behalf of the State. The Registry was reformed by the Land Transfer Act, 1875, which, while making many changes in the system, continued its voluntary basis. In 1897 the Land Transfer Act introduced the principle of compulsory registration, and four Orders in Council under that Act between 1898 and 1902 made the system compulsory on sale in the administrative county of London. By further Orders registration was made compulsory on sale in 1925 in Eastbourne; in 1928 in Hastings, in 1936 in the administrative county of Middlesex, in 1938 in the County Borough of Croydon, in 1952 in the administrative County of Surrey, in 1954 in the City of Oxford, in 1956 in the County Borough of Oldham, in 1957 in the Medway area of Kent and in the County Borough of Leicester, in 1958 in eastern areas of Kent and the City of Canterbury, in 1961 in the remainder of Kent, and the Cities of Manchester and Salford, in 1962 in the County Boroughs of Blackburn, Huddersfield and Reading, and in 1963 in the County Borough of Rochdale and the administrative County of Berkshire. The Land Registration Act, 1925, consolidated the previous Acts, and made such changes in the system as the experience of a generation had shown to be necessary. The keynote of the system is that the machinery for the purchase and sale of land is assimilated to that for stocks and shares. Absolute titles granted by the Land Registry are guaranteed by the State. Simple forms, analogous to those used on transfers of stocks and shares, are provided. The cost of buying, selling or mortgaging registered land is much less than the cost in the case of unregistered land. It is open to any County Council or Council of a County Borough to apply to the Privy Council for an order making registration of title compulsory in its area. The Land Registry is administered under the Lord Chancellor by the Chief Land Registrar, who also controls the Land Charges Department under the Land Charges Act, 1925, and the Agricultural Credits Act, 1928 (Sec. 9).

Registration of Title
Chief Land Registrar, T. B. F. Ruoff, C.B.E. £4,700
Senior Registrar, T. I. Casswell............ £3,900
Registrars, E. D. Wetton, C.B.E.; W. E. B. Pryer; R. S. Hood; S. L. Whiteley; C. C. Scarth; C. N. T. Waterer; S. Jacey; C. W. K. Donaldson; A. G. W. James; D. P. Chivers; U. Davidson
£2,900 to £3,500
Asst. Registrars, G. E. O. Nutt; Miss M. M. F. G. Walker; A. O. Viney; C. W. Furneaux; R. B. Roper; P. Kendall; N. U. A. Hogg; W. D. Hosking; Miss J. E. Bagshaw; R. E. Shorrocks; A. D. Dewar; A. P. Roberts; Miss N. Gray; G. A. Weddell; J. S. R. Bevington; Miss C. M. Bannister; B. E. Berry; Miss A. M. Phillips; J. S. Hunt; R. Tate............. £2,239 to £2,800
Organization Officer, A. J. Jenkins, O.B.E.
£2,618 to £2,800
Chief Executive Officers, P. Gittings; H. R. Goose; E. W. Hannam............. £2,172 to £2,507
Senior Executive Officers, C. D. Garrett; R. T. Adams; K. C. Walpole; J. L. Memory; B. J. Moulden; F. E. J. Allen; P. J. Dix; J. C. Eames, M.B.E.; V. P. Sterlini; G. H. Fisher; R. Palmer; G. H. Scuffle; A. G. Caudle; A. W. Pardey; J. R. Boulter; W. Gledhill; R. G. W. Brazier; G. A. Whyman; E. F. A. Jones; W. H. Norris; H. Walter; J. H. Sex; R. C. Martin; A. L. Moore; A. J. Sexton; H. G. D. Wright; J. Q. Pembroke; T. A. Davies; C. T. Vince; L. J. Cutler; R. J. Moss; E. D. B. Head; T. Chipperfield; R. S. Walter; A. C. Forrester; A. W. Watson
£1,615 to £2,061
Chief Superintendent (Plans Branch), C. J. Sweeney, M.B.E..................... £2,618 to £2,800
Deputy Chief Superintendent, B. M. White
£2,172 to £2,507
Senior Superintendents, G. E. Rice; P. A. Orsich; D. C. King; H. J. Wiles; A. J. Davies; J. F. A. Rowland; J. D. Henderson; H. J. Houseman; L. A. Jenks; F. H. Braithwaite; F. W. Barber; J. Mairs................ £1,615 to £2,061
Chief Assistant (Establishment and Accounts), C. C. Woods, M.B.E......................... £3,150
Deputy Chief Assistant, K. E. Aris
£2,172 to £2,507

Land Charges and Agricultural Credits Departments
Station Approach Buildings, Kidbrooke, S.E.3
[Lee Green: 9191]
Superintendent, S. A. Durrant, M.B.E.
£1,615 to £2,061

LAW OFFICERS' DEPARTMENT

Royal Courts of Justice, W.C.2

[Holborn: 7641]

The Law Officers of the Crown for England and Wales (the Attorney-General and the Solicitor-General) represent the Crown in courts of justice, advise Government departments and represent them in court. The Attorney-General has also certain administrative functions, including supervision of the Director of Public Prosecutions.

Attorney-General, The Rt. Hon. Sir John Hobson, O.B.E., T.D., Q.C., M.P. £10,000

Parliamentary Private Secretary, E. L. Gardner, Q.C., M.P.

Solicitor-General, Sir Peter Rawlinson, Q.C., M.P. £7,000

Parliamentary Private Secretary, J. M. Coulson, M.P.

Legal Secretary, G. E. Dudman £2,500 to £3,000

Asst. Legal Sec., H. J. Davies.. £1,720 to £2,400

LIBRARIES

BRITISH MUSEUM

See under MUSEUMS

NATIONAL LIBRARY OF SCOTLAND

George IV Bridge, Edinburgh 1

[Caledonian: 4104]

Open free. Reading Room, weekdays, 9.30 a.m. to 8.30 p.m. (During July, August and September closes at 5 p.m. on Mondays, Tuesdays and Fridays); Saturdays, 9.30 to 1. Map Room, weekdays, 9.30 a.m. to 5 p.m.; Saturdays, 9.30 to 1. Exhibition, weekdays, 9.30 a.m. to 6 p.m., Saturdays, 9.30 to 1; Sundays, 2 to 5. During Edinburgh International Festival open till 8.30 p.m. on weekdays.

The Library, which had been founded as the Advocates' Library in 1682, became the National Library of Scotland by Act of Parliament in 1925. It continues to share the rights conferred by successive Copyright Acts since 1709. Its collections of printed books and MSS., augmented by purchase and gift, are very large and it has an unrivalled Scottish collection. The present building was opened by H.M. the Queen in 1956.

The Reading Room is for reference and research which cannot conveniently be pursued elsewhere. Admission is by ticket issued to an approved applicant.

Chairman of the Trustees, The Earl of Crawford and Balcarres, K.T., G.B.E.

Librarian and Secretary to the Trustees, William Beattie, C.B.E., LL.D. £3,500

Secretary of the Library, J. R. Seaton £1,438 to £2,479

Keeper of Printed Books, D. M. Lloyd £2,428 to £2,800

Deputy Keepers, J. H. Loudon; Margaret I. Johnston (+allce. £181) .... £1,438 to £2,479

Assistant Keepers, First Class, R. Donaldson; Alexandra M. Graham; L. J. G. Heywood; Marion P. Linton; M. A. Pegg £1,438 to £2,479

Senior Research Assistant, Margaret E. Gramb £1,615 to £2,005

Keeper of Manuscripts, William Park £2,428 to £2,800

Assistant Keepers, First Class, T. I. Rae; J. S. Ritchie; E. F. D. Roberts.... £1,438 to £2,479

THE NATIONAL LIBRARY OF WALES

LLYFRGELL GENEDLAETHOL CYMRU

Aberystwyth

Readers' room open on weekdays, 9.30 a.m. to 6 p.m. (Saturdays, 5 p.m.); closed on Sundays. Admission by Reader's Ticket.

Founded by Royal Charter, 1907, and maintained by annual grant from the Treasury. One of the six libraries entitled to certain privileges under Copyright Act. Contains nearly 2,000,000 printed books, 30,000 manuscripts, 3,500,000 deeds and documents, and numerous maps, prints and drawings. Specializes in manuscripts and books relating to Wales and the Celtic peoples. Repository for pre-1858 Welsh probate records. Approved by the Master of the Rolls as a repository for manorial records and tithe documents, and by the Lord Chancellor for certain legal records. Bureau of the Regional Libraries Scheme for Wales and Monmouthshire.

Librarian, E. D. Jones.

Deputy Librarian, G. Tibbott.

NATIONAL CENTRAL LIBRARY

Malet Place, W.C.1

[Euston: 6262]

Incorporated by Royal Charter and maintained by annual grants from the Treasury, Municipal and County Authorities, University and special libraries, adult education bodies, and public Trusts.

The Library is the national centre for the loan of books (other than fiction and students' text-books) and periodicals to readers in all parts of the British Isles, through their public, university, or other library; and also to and from foreign libraries through their national centres. It is able to draw on over 21,000,000 books in nearly all the principal British libraries. Other work undertaken by the Library includes loans to organized classes of adult students; and the recording of duplicates and discarded books and periodicals and their distribution to appropriate libraries at home and abroad; also the establishment of a catalogue of Russian books and periodicals in British libraries. The Library's own stock for loan comprises about 260,000 volumes.

Applications to borrow books must be made through the reader's library and not directly to the National Central Library.

Librarian and Secretary to the Trustees, S. P. L. Filon.

Deputy Librarian, I. P. Gibb.

NATIONAL LENDING LIBRARY FOR SCIENCE AND TECHNOLOGY

Boston Spa, Yorkshire.

Officially opened on November 5, 1962, the library provides a postal loan service to organizations, including industrial companies, learned societies and educational establishments. Individuals can borrow through the public library system. It has a stock of about 450,000 volumes and nearly 20,000 current periodicals. Part of the initial stock was drawn from the library of the Science Museum, London. Gross total annual expenditure £370,000.

Director, D. J. Urquhart, Ph.D.

SCOTTISH CENTRAL LIBRARY

Lawnmarket, Edinburgh, 1

Carries out in Scotland functions similar to those of the National Central Library, i.e. acts as a clearing-house for inter-library lending, and maintains a Union Catalogue and other records of books held by Scottish libraries. Its own stock of 35,000 books is freely available to all. *Applications to borrow books must be made through the reader's library.*

Librarian and Secretary to the Trustees, M. C. Pottinger, D.S.C.

Deputy Librarian, Miss E. M. Swinton.

LOCAL GOVERNMENT. *See* HOUSING AND LOCAL GOVERNMENT

LONDON TRANSPORT BOARD

55 Broadway, Westminster, S.W.1
[Abbey: 5600]

Constituted under the *Transport Act*, 1962, "to provide or secure the provision of an adequate and properly co-ordinated system of passenger transport for the London Passenger Transport Area and to have due regard to efficiency, economy and safety of operation as respects the services and facilities provided by them".

Chairman, A. B. B. Valentine............£8,500
Deputy Chairman and Managing Director, A. H. Grainger..........................£7,000
Members, A. Bull, O.B.E.; E. C. Ottaway (*each* £6,000); *and* (*part-time*) The Lord Geddes of Epsom, C.B.E.; J. Bedford, O.B.E.; The Lord Catto..........................(*each* £1,000)
Secretary, W. E. G. Hewings.

LORD ADVOCATE'S DEPARTMENT

3 Dean's Yard, Westminster, S.W.1.

The Law Officers for Scotland are the Lord Advocate and the Solicitor-General for Scotland. The Lord Advocate's Department is responsible for drafting Scottish legislation, for providing legal advice to other departments on Scottish questions and for assistance to the Law Officers for Scotland in certain of their legal duties.

Lord Advocate, The Rt. Hon. Ian Hamilton Shearer, Q.C.................................£5,000
Solicitor-General for Scotland, D. C. Anderson, V.R.D., Q.C..........................£3,750
Legal Secretary and First Parliamentary Draftsman, J. H. Gibson, C.B. Q.C.................£5,000
Deputy Legal Secretary and Parliamentary Draftsman, G. I. Mitchell......................£4,100
Asst. Legal Secs. and Parlty. Draftsmen, J. M. Moran; A. C. B. Reid.....£3,280 to £3,880
Junior Legal Secs. and Parlty. Draftsmen, J. F. Wallace; G. S. Douglas....£2,304 to £2,865

LORD GREAT CHAMBERLAIN'S OFFICE

House of Lords, S.W.1.
[Whitehall: 6240]

The Lord Great Chamberlain is the Sixth Great Officer of State, the office being hereditary since the grant of Henry I to the family of De Vere, Earls of Oxford.

Lord Great Chamberlain, The Marquess of Cholmondeley, G.C.V.O.
Secretary to the Lord Great Chamberlain, Capt. K. L. Mackintosh, R.N.
Clerks to the Lord Great Chamberlain, Miss M. Firth; Miss A. R. Cook.

OFFICE OF THE LORD PRESIDENT OF THE COUNCIL AND MINISTER FOR SCIENCE

2, Richmond Terrace, Whitehall, S.W.1
[Trafalgar: 6371]

On October 28, 1959, a new post of Minister for Science was created. By an Order in Council the functions previously exercised by the Prime Minister under the Atomic Energy Acts were transferred to the Minister for Science, together with those functions relating to scientific research which were previously performed by the Lord President of the Council.

Lord President of the Council, Minister for Science and Leader of the House of Lords, THE RT. HON. THE VISCOUNT HAILSHAM, P.C., Q.C...£5,000
Private Secretary, C. Herzig.
Assistant Private Secretaries, A. S. Gordon; K. R. Mears.
Parliamentary Secretary for Science, D. K. Freeth, M.P. £2,500
Secretary, Office of the Minister for Science, F. F. Turnbull, C.B., C.I.E.
Under-Secretaries, M. I. Michaels, C.B. (*Atomic Energy Division*); R. N. Quirk, C.B. (*General Science Division*)....................£4,050
Deputy Chief Scientific Officer, M. D. Robins £3,275 to £3,600
Assistant Secretaries, G. I. Crawford; J. F. Hosie, O.B.E.; D. le B. Jones; J. G. Liverman; R. A. Thompson..............£2,800 to £3,500
Chief Information Officer, L. J. Cheney £2,542 to £2,800

Privy Council Office

Old County Hall, Spring Gardens S.W.1

Clerk of the Council, W. G. Agnew, C.V.O....£3,788
Deputy Clerk of the Council, E. N. Landale £2,374 to £3,015
Senior Clerk, N. E. Leigh......£1,798 to £2,255

LORD PRIVY SEAL

(*see* Foreign Office)

MEDICAL RESEARCH COUNCIL

20 Park Crescent, W.1
[Museum: 5422]

The Council, formerly the Medical Research Committee established in 1913 under the National Health Insurance Act, was incorporated under its present title by Royal Charter on April 1, 1920. It is under the administrative direction of a Committee of the Privy Council, consisting of the Minister for Science, the Secretaries of State for Scotland, for Commonwealth Relations, for the Colonies, and for Home Affairs, the Minister of Health and the Minister of Labour; the Secretary of the Medical Research Council is *ex officio* Secretary to this Committee.

The Council applies moneys voted by Parliament or received from private sources for the furtherance of medical research. Its reports, published by H.M. Stationery Office, are obtainable through any bookseller.

Members, The Lord Shawcross, P.C., Q.C. (*Chairman*); Sir Edward Collingwood, C.B.E., SC.D. (*Treasurer*); Prof. T. Crawford, M.D.; Sir Hugh Linstead, O.B.E., M.P.; Prof. W. M. Millar, M.D.; Prof. M. L. Rosenheim, C.B.E., M.D.; Prof. Wilson Smith, M.D., F.R.S.; Prof. G. M. Bull, M.D.; Prof. A. Neuberger, Ph.D., M.D., F.R.S.; Prof. M. M. Swann, Ph.D., F.R.S.; Prof. W. D. M. Paton, F.R.S.; Prof. H. J. B. Atkins, D.M.
Secretary, Sir Harold Himsworth, K.C.B., M.D., F.R.S.
Deputy Secretary, C. Y. Carstairs, C.M.G.
Principal Medical Officers, F. J. C. Herrald; B. S. Lush, M.D.
Principal Administrative Officer, J. G. Duncan.
Senior Medical Officers, Mrs. J. M. Faulkner; R. C. Norton.
Assistant Secretaries, J. D. Whittaker, M.B.E.; C. A. Kirkman.
Medical Officers, E. M. B. Clements; Mrs. M. Gorrill; P. J. Chapman; H. W. Bunjé, M.D.; M. P. W. Godfrey; M. J. T. Adams.
Administrative Officers, D. J. Cawthron; J. C. R. Hudson; R. F. Smart; F. R. Rushton; A. E. Turner.
Consultant Adviser to the Secretary, Sir Charles Harington, K.B.E., SC.D., F.R.S.

National Institute for Medical Research

Mill Hill, N.W.7
[Mill Hill: 3666]

Director, P. B. Medawar, C.B.E., D.SC., F.R.S.

Research Units

Unit for Research on Occupational Aspects of Ageing, Department of Psychology, University of Liverpool, Liverpool 7. *Hon. Director*, Prof. L. S. Hearnshaw.
Air Pollution Research Unit, St. Bartholomew's Hospital, Medical College, Charterhouse Square, E.C.1. *Director*, P. J. Lawther.

Atheroma Research Unit, Western Infirmary, Glasgow, W.1. *Director*, B. Bronte-Stewart, M.D.
Unit for the Experimental Investigation of Behaviour, Department of Psychology, University College, Gower Street, W.C.1. *Hon. Director*, Prof. G. C. Drew.
Biophysics Research Unit, King's College, Strand, W.C.2. *Director*, Prof. Sir John Randall, D.SC., F.R.S. (*part-time*).
Blood Coagulation Research Unit, Churchill Hospital, Headington, Oxford. *Director*, R. G. Macfarlane, M.D., F.R.S. (*part-time*).
Blood Group Reference Laboratory (administered for Ministry of Health), Gatliff Road, S.W.1. *Director*, A. E. Mourant, D.M., D.Phil.
Blood Group Research Unit, Lister Institute, Chelsea Bridge Road, S.W.1. *Director*, R. R. Race, Ph.D., F.R.S.
Body Temperature Research Unit, Dept. of the Regius Professor of Medicine, The Radcliffe Infirmary, Oxford. *Hon. Director*, Prof. Sir George Pickering, M.D., F.R.S.
Bone-seeking Isotopes Research Unit, Churchill Hospital, Headington, Oxford. *Hon. Director*, Dame Janet Vaughan, D.B.E., D.M.
Carcinogenic Substances Research Unit, Washington Singer Laboratories, The University, Exeter. *Hon. Director*, Sir James Cook, D.SC., F.R.S.
Cell Metabolism Research Unit, Department of Biochemistry, South Parks Road, Oxford. *Hon. Director*, Prof. Sir Hans Krebs, M.D., D.SC., F.R.S.
Chemotherapy Research Unit, Molteno Institute, Cambridge. *Director*, Miss A. Bishop, SC.D., F.R.S.
Department of Clinical Research, University College Hospital Medical School, W.C.1. *Director*, E. E. Pochin, C.B.E., M.D.
Common Cold Research Unit (*National Institute for Medical Research*), Harvard Hospital, Salisbury. *Medical Superintendent*, M. L. Bynoe.
Cyclotron Unit, Hammersmith Hospital, Ducane Road, W.12. *Director*, D. D. Vonberg.
Wernher Research Unit on Deafness, King's College Hospital Medical School, Denmark Hill, S.E.5. *Director*, T. S. Littler, Ph.D.
Dental Research Unit, Dental School, Lower Maudlin Street, Bristol 1. *Hon. Director*, Prof. A. I. Darling, D.SC.
Clinical Endocrinology Research Unit 2 Forrest Road, Edinburgh. *Director*, J. A. Loraine, D.SC.
Unit for the Study of Environmental Factors in Mental and Physical Illness, London School of Economics and Political Science, Houghton Street, W.C.2. *Director*, J. W. B. Douglas.
Epidemiological Research Unit (*Jamaica*), University College of the West Indies, Kingston, Jamaica. *Director*, W. E. Miall.
Epidemiological Research Unit (*South Wales*), 4 Richmond Road, Cardiff. *Hon. Director*, Prof. A. L. Cochrane, M.B.E.
Department of Experimental Medicine, Tennis Court Road, Cambridge. *Director*, Prof. R. A. McCance, C.B.E., M.D., Ph.D., F.R.S.
Medical Research Council Laboratories, Gambia, Fajara, Gambia, W. Africa. *Director*, I. A. McGregor, O.B.E.
Gastroenterology Research Unit, Central Middlesex Hospital, Park Royal, N.W.10. *Director*, E. N. Rowlands, M.D.
Clinical Genetics Research Unit, Institute of Child Health, The Hospital for Sick Children, Great Ormond Street, W.C.1. *Director*, J. A. Fraser Roberts, M.D., D.SC., F.R.S.
Experimental Genetics Research Unit, Dept. of Genetics, University College, W.C.1. *Hon. Director*, Prof. H. Grüneberg, M.D., D.SC., F.R.S.
Human Biochemical Genetics Research Unit, Dept. of Biochemistry, King's College, Strand, W.C.2. *Hon. Director*, Prof. H. Harris, M.D.
Microbial Genetics Research Unit, Hammersmith Hospital, Ducane Road, W.12. *Director*, W. Hayes, D.SC.
Population Genetics Research Unit, Old Road, Headington, Oxford. *Director*, A. C. Stevenson, M.D.
Psychiatric Genetics Research Unit, Institute of Psychiatry, Maudsley Hospital, Denmark Hill, S.E.5. *Director*, E. T. O. Slater, M.D. (*part-time*).
Experimental Haematology Research Unit, St. Mary's Hospital Medical School, W.2. *Director*, Prof. P. L. Mollison, M.D.
Abnormal Haemoglobin Research Unit, Department of Chemical Pathology, St. Bartholomew's Hospital, E.C.1. *Director*, H. Lehmann, M.D., SC.D.
Industrial Injuries and Burns Research Unit, Birmingham Accident Hospital, Bath Row, Birmingham 15. *Director*, J. P. Bull, M.D.
Laboratory Animals Centre, M.R.C. Laboratories, Woodmansterne Road, Carshalton, Surrey. *Director*, W. Lane-Petter.
Infantile Malnutrition Research Unit, Mulago Hospital, Kampala, Uganda. *Director*, Prof. R. F. A. Dean, Ph.D.
Unit for Research on the Chemical Pathology of Mental Disorders, Dept. of Physiology, The Medical School, Birmingham 15. *Hon. Director*, Prof. I. E. Bush, Ph.D.
Metabolic Disturbances in Surgery Research Unit, The General Infirmary, Leeds 1. *Hon. Director*, Prof. L. N. Pyrah, C.B.E.
Laboratory of Molecular Biology, University Postgraduate Medical School, Hills Road, Cambridge. *Chairman of Board*, M. F. Perutz, C.B.E., Ph.D., F.R.S.
Mutagenesis Research Unit, Institute of Animal Genetics, West Mains Road, Edinburgh 9. *Hon. Director*, Miss C. Auerbach, D.SC., F.R.S.
Neuroendocrinology Research Unit, Dept. of Human Anatomy, South Parks Road, Oxford. *Hon. Director*, Prof. G. W. Harris, M.D., D.SC., F.R.S.
Neuropharmacology Research Unit, Dept. of Experimental Neuropharmacology, The Medical School, Birmingham 15. *Hon. Director*, P. B. Bradley, D.SC.
Neuropsychiatric Research Unit, M.R.C. Laboratories, Woodmansterne Road, Carshalton, Surrey. *Director*, D. Richter, Ph.D.
Human Nutrition Research Unit, Nutrition Building, National Institute for Medical Research, Mill Hill, N.W.7. *Director*, Prof. B. S. Platt, C.M.G., Ph.D.
Dunn Nutritional Laboratory, Milton Road, Cambridge. *Director*, E. H. Kodicek, M.D., Ph.D.
Obstetric Medicine Research Unit, Aberdeen University Medical School, Foresterhill, Aberdeen. *Hon. Director*, Prof. Sir Dugald Baird, M.D.
Wernher Research Unit on Ophthalmological Genetics, Royal College of Surgeons, Lincoln's Inn Fields, W.C.2. *Hon. Director*, Prof. A. Sorsby, M.D.
Otological Research Unit, National Hosp. for Nervous Diseases, Queen Square, W.C.1. *Director*, C. S. Hallpike, C.B.E., F.R.S.
Environmental Physiology Research Unit, London School of Hygiene and Tropical Medicine, Keppel Street, W.C.1. *Director*, J. S. Weiner, Ph.D.
Pneumoconiosis Research Unit, Llandough Hospital, Penarth, Glam. *Director*, J. C. Gilson, O.B.E.
Unit for Research on the Epidemiology of Psychiatric Illness, Dept. of Psychological Medicine, University of Edinburgh, 2 George Square, Edinburgh, 8. *Hon. Director*, Prof. G. M. Carstairs, M.D.
Clinical Psychiatry Research Unit, Graylingwell Hospital, Chichester. *Director*, P. Sainsbury, M.D.
Social Psychiatry Research Unit, Maudsley Hospital, Denmark Hill, S.E.5. *Hon. Director*, Prof. Sir Aubrey Lewis, M.D.
Applied Psychology Research Unit, 15 Chaucer Road, Cambridge. *Director*, D. E. Broadbent.
Industrial Psychology Research Unit, Dept. of Psychology, University College, Gower Street, W.C.1. *Hon. Director*, Prof. G. C. Drew.

Clinical Effects of Radiation Research Unit, Dept. of Radiotherapy, Western General Hospital, Crewe Road, Edinburgh 4. *Director*, W. M. Court Brown. O.B.E.

Environmental Radiation Research Unit, Dept. of Medical Physics, The General Infirmary, Leeds 1. *Hon. Director*, Prof. F. W. Spiers, C.B.E., D.Sc.

Radiobiological Research Unit, Harwell, Berks. *Director*, J. F. Loutit, C.B.E., D.M., F.R.S.

Radiological Protection Service (jointly with the Ministry of Health), Clifton Avenue, Belmont, Sutton, Surrey. *Director*, W. Binks.

Experimental Radiopathology Research Unit, Hammersmith Hospital, Ducane Road, W.12. *Director*, Miss T. Alper.

Rheumatism Research Unit, Canadian Red Cross Memorial Hospital, Taplow, Maidenhead, Berks. *Hon. Director*, Prof. E. G. L. Bywaters.

Unit for Research on Experimental Pathology of the Skin, The Medical School, Birmingham 15. *Director*, C. N. D. Cruickshank, M.D.

Social Medicine Research Unit, The London Hospital, E.1. *Director*, Prof. J. N. Morris, D.Sc.

Statistical Research Unit, University College Hospital Medical School, Gower Street, W.C.1. *Director*, W. R. S. Doll, O.B.E., M.D., D.Sc.

Toxicology Research Unit, M.R.C. Laboratories, Woodmansterne Road, Carshalton. *Director*, J. M. Barnes, C.B.E.

Trachoma Research Unit, Lister Institute, Chelsea Bridge Road, S.W.1 and M.R.C. Laboratories, Gambia. *Hon. Director*. L. H. Collier, M.D.

Tropical Metabolism Research Unit, University of the West Indies, Mona, St. Andrew, Jamaica. *Director*, Prof. J. C. Waterlow, M.D.

Tuberculosis Research Unit, M.R.C. Laboratories, Holly Hill, Hampstead, N.W.3. *Director*, P. M. D'Arcy Hart, C.B.E., M.D.

Unit for Research on Drug Sensitivity in Tuberculosis, Postgraduate Medical School, Ducane Road, W.12. *Hon. Director*, D. A. Mitchison.

Virus Research Unit, M.R.C. Laboratories, Woodmansterne Road, Carshalton, Surrey. *Director*, F. K. Sanders, D. Phil.

Experimental Virus Research Unit, Institute of Virology, Church Street, Glasgow, W.1. *Hon. Director*, Prof. M. G. P. Stoker, M.D.

Vision Research Unit, Institute of Ophthalmology, Judd Street, W.C.1. *Director*, H. J. A. Dartnall, D.Sc.

External Staff

J. D. Blainey, M.D., R. G. H. B. Boddy, Ph.D., G. H. Davis, Ph.D., C. Osorio, Dr.Med., S. L. Rowles, Ph.D., *Birmingham*; Miss J. M. Allen, C. R. Austin, D.Sc., G. Clarke, Ph.D., R. Davies, Ph.D., Miss R. Deanesley, D.Sc., (*part-time*); J. T. Dingle, Miss A. W. Heim, Ph.D.; W. E. Hick, M.D., Miss S. F. Jackson, Ph.D., Mrs. O. Kennard, H. W. Laser, M.D., Sc.D., J. A. Lucy, Ph.D., D. A. T. New, Ph.D., B. A. Newton, Ph.D., Miss M. A. Vince, Mrs. A. J. Watson (*part-time*), Miss K. P. Watts, M. Webb, Ph.D., L. Weiss, M.D., *Cambridge*; R. E. Hope Simpson, O.B.E., *Cirencester*; J. P. Laidlaw (*part-time*), W. Sircus, M.D., Ph.D. (*part-time*), *Edinburgh*; J. Newsome, M.D., *Hertford*; J. B. Dawson, Ph.D., M. Hamilton, M.D., *Leeds*; N. Ambache, A. Antonis, Ph.D., J. A. V. Bates (*part-time*), E. J. M. Bowlby, Ph.D., D. S. Brown, Ph.D., F. B. Byrom, M.D., J. Colover, M.D. (*part-time*), C. N. Davies, D.Sc., H. Davson, D.Sc., E. J. Delorme, M.D., Mrs. J. M. Dolby, Ph.D., J. L. de C. Downer, Ph.D., A. Elithorn, M.D. (*part-time*), W. A. Gaunt, Mrs. I. Gore, Ph.D., D. W. Green, Ph.D., A. M. Halliday, P. Hugh-Jones, M.D. (*part-time*), L. Juhasz, Ph.D., Mrs. M. Kerr (*part-time*), D. Kingston, A. B. Kinnier Wilson, Mrs. V. J. Lankester, B. Lewis, M.D., Ph.D., D. J. Lewis, Sc.D., O. M. Lidwell, Ph.D., B. McArdle, M.D., Mrs. M. W. McGrath, Ph.D., Miss M. E. Mackay, Ph.D., J. S. McKinley-McKee, Ph.D., A. McPherson, R. P. J. G. McWilliam, N. B. Myant, D.M., P. W. Nathan, M.D., A. C. T. North, Ph.D., Miss J. R. Parriss; V. Parsons; D. C. Phillips, Ph.D., J. W. I. Redfearn, M.D. (*part-time*), Mrs. M. C. Sherwood, M.D., N. Veall, Mrs. J. M. C. Whiting, P. Wolf, M.D., A. W. Zbrozyna, *London*; A. S. Hallsworth, Ph.D., H. Jackson, Ph.D., S. A. Leach, Ph.D., *Manchester*; R. W. Parnell, D.M., J. C. F. Poole, D.M., D. S. Robinson, Ph.D., F. D. Stott, D.Phil., Miss A. A. Wieneka, A. M. Woodin, Ph.D., L. I. Woolf, Ph.D., *Oxford*, R. N. P. Sutton, H. F. West, M.D. (*part-time*), *Sheffield*; M. C. S. Kennedy (*part-time*), *Stoke-on-Trent*; J. Dawson, *Wickford, Essex*; J. H. S. Petitt, M.D., *Malaya*; A. Davis, *Tanganyika*; A. D. Berrie, *Uganda*.

Tropical Medicine Research Board

(*Appointment in consultation with the Department of Technical Co-operation.*)

Chairman, Sir Harold Himsworth, K.C.B., M.D., F.R.S.

Secretary, B. S. Lush, M.D.

Clinical Research Board

(*Appointed in consultation with the Ministry of Health and the Scottish Home and Health Department.*)

Chairman, Prof. E. J. Wayne, M.D., Ph.D.

Secretary, F. J. C. Herrald.

MERSEY DOCKS AND HARBOUR BOARD

Dock Office, Liverpool 3

The Mersey Docks and Harbour Board was constituted by Act of Parliament in 1857 to take over the entire control of the port accommodation at Liverpool and Birkenhead. It is also responsible for the conservancy of the River Mersey and for approach channels, buoyage and lighting. It is also the pilotage authority. The Board consists of 28 members. Twenty-four are elected by the dock ratepayers and 4 appointed by the Minister of Transport, in whom is vested the powers originally granted to the Mersey Conservancy Commissioners. The borrowing powers of the Board authorised to July 1, 1962, were £96,141,103 and the capital expenditure at this date was £86,643,380.

Elective Members, A. C. Morrell, C.B.E., M.C. (*Chairman*); M. D. Oliphant, M.B.E., T.D. (*Deputy Chairman*); J. E. Alexander; V. A. Arnold, M.C.; N. M. Bacon; D. A. Barber; A. J. Kentish Barnes; Maj. Sir Harold Bibby, Bt., D.S.O.; N. M. Bibby; W. B. Briscoe; Sir John Brocklebank, Bt.; P. G. Clarke; R. N. Cornelius; C. H. T. Gilchrist; M. B. Glasier, C.B.E.; G. P. Holt, M.B.E.; K. R. Monroe; B. Nelson, C.B.E.; C. J. Palk; James Paton; Sir Arnet Robinson; J. C. Taylor; M. S. Webster; J. D. Wilson.

Nominee Members (*appointed by the Minister of Transport*), J. K Batty; J. J. Cleary; Robert W. Johnson, C.B.E.; J. H. Wall.

General Manager, C. A. Dove, C.B.E., E.R.D.

METROPOLITAN WATER BOARD

New River Head, Rosebery Avenue, E.C.1

[Terminus: 3300]

The Board serves an area of 540 sq. miles. The charges are levied on net annual value at such rate not exceeding 10 per cent., as the Board may fix, the charge for 1963–64 being 2¾ per cent. on net annual value. The Capital Debt on March 31, 1963, amounted to £66,366,983. The supply for the year 1962–63 was 134,833,000,000 gallons (representing 602,000,000 tons), a daily average of 369.4 million gallons.

Chairman of the Metropolitan Water Board, T. W. Smith.

Clerk of the Board, S. D. Askew.

THE ROYAL MINT

Tower Hill, E.C. 3

[Royal: 8261]

Admission is by order only, application for which should be made to the Deputy Master of the Mint at least 6 weeks in advance of intended visit. Hours of admission Monday to Friday 9.20 a.m. to 2.50 p.m. (Public holidays excepted.)

Master Worker and Warden, The Chancellor of the Exchequer (*ex officio*).

Deputy Master and Comptroller, and ex officio Engraver of H.M. Seals, J. H. James, C.B. £4,400

Assistant Secretary, P. J. Moss (*temp.*) £3,565

Chief Clerk, C. Hewertson ..... £2,683 to £2,865

Establishment Officer, F. L. McHenry, O.B.E. £2,711

Senior Executive Officers, A. J. Dowling, D.F.C.; H. A. Wright; G. F. Howell; C. L. Powell; J. D. Goddard; A. T. Layzell ..... £1,680 to £2,126

Superintendent, Operative Department, D. R. Cooper, T.D. £3,215

Deputy do., E. M. Phillips .... £2,293 to £2,628

Mechanical Engineers, J. F. Harrington; S. J. Wellington; M. R. Tidmarsh £1,624 to £2,154

Chemist and Assayer, E. G. V. Newman, O.B.E. £2,865 to £3,215

Deputy Chemist and Assayer, A. Dunning £1,959 to £2,711

Senior Experimental Officer, D. J. Harvey £1,680 to £2,126

Branches of the Royal Mint

Melbourne, Victoria

Deputy Master, L. A. Webb.

Perth, Western Australia

Deputy Master, C. A. M. Cook.

MONOPOLIES COMMISSION

8 Cornwall Terrace, Regent's Park, N.W.1

[Museum: 8801]

The Monopolies and Restrictive Practices Commission, which was set up under the Monopolies and Restrictive Practices (Inquiry and Control) Act, 1948, was reconstituted on Oct. 31, 1956, as the Monopolies Commission in accordance with a provision of the Restrictive Trade Practices Act, 1956. The Commission has the duty of investigating and reporting on the existence, in industries referred to it by the Board of Trade, of monopoly, restrictive practices affecting exports and other arrangements not registrable under Part I of the Restrictive Trade Practices Act, 1956, and, where so required by the Board, to report on the effect of such arrangements on the public interest.

Chairman, R. F. Levy, Q.C. £4,700

Members, Prof. T. Barna; B. Davidson; Dr. L. T. M. Gray; I. C. Hill, C.B.E.; W. E. Jones, C.B.E.; O. B. Miller; A. W. Roskill, Q.C.; J. M. A. Smith; Sir Laurence Watkinson, K.B.E., C.B., M.C.

Secretary, A. S. Gilbert, C.B.E.

Assistant Secretary, E. T. Harvey.

Assistant Director of Accountants, J. H. Drayson, O.B.E.

Principals, Miss I. M. Asbury; Mrs. E. R. Brinton, O.B.E.; J. L. Prescott; J. P. L. Scott.

Chief Accountant, T. A. Wells.

Establishment Officer, F. A. Bear, O.B.E.

MUSEUMS

STANDING COMMISSION ON MUSEUMS AND GALLERIES

6 Carlton House Terrace, S.W.1

[Whitehall: 4341]

First appointed Feb. 11, 1931. The functions of the Commission are:—(1) To advise generally on questions relevant to the most effective development of the National Institutions as a whole and on any specific questions which may be referred to them from time to time; (2) to promote co-operation between the National Institutions themselves and between the National and Provincial Institutions; (3) to stimulate the generosity and direct the efforts of those who aspire to become public benefactors.

Chairman, The Earl of Rosse, LL.D., F.S.A.

Members, The Countess of Albemarle, D.B.E.; The Earl of Crawford and Balcarres, K.T., G.B.E.; Dr. E. Davies; B. L. Hallward; The Earl of Halsbury; Sir William Hayter, K.C.M.G.; Sir Cyril Hinshelwood, O.M., F.R.S., D.SC.; Sir Gilbert Laithwaite, G.C.M.G., K.C.B., K.C.I.E., C.S.I.; J. L. E. Smith; The Earl Spencer, T.D., F.S.A.; J. C. Witt, F.S.A.

Secretary, Miss A. L. T. Oppé.

THE BRITISH MUSEUM

Bloomsbury, W.C.1

[Museum: 1555]

Exhibitions.—Manuscripts, Printed Books, Egyptian, Assyrian, Greek and Roman Sculptures, Romano-British, Prehistoric and Oriental Antiquities and Ethnography (Main Entrance, Great Russell Street, W.C.1). Select Exhibition of works of art and antiquities in the King Edward VII Gallery. Prints and Drawings, Oriental Paintings, Egyptian and Babylonian antiquities (North Entrance, Montague Place, W.C.1). Open weekdays (including Bank Holidays) 10 to 5 and Sundays 2.30 to 6. Closed on Good Friday and Christmas Day. Admission free.

Reading-room open daily to readers, from 9 to 5, (Tues.—Thurs., 9 p.m.), and Newspaper Room, (at Colindale), from 10 to 5 throughout the year, except Good Friday, Christmas and Boxing Day and Sundays. Closed for cleaning the week beginning with first Monday in May. Long-period tickets of admission for purposes of research and reference which cannot be carried on elsewhere, are granted on written application beforehand to the Director. The applicant should state abode, business or profession and full particulars of purpose, and should send a recommendation from a person of recognized position.

The British Museum may be said to date from 1753, when Parliament granted funds to purchase the collections of Sir Hans Sloane and the Harleian manuscripts, and for their proper housing and maintenance. The building (Montague House) was opened in 1759. The present buildings were erected between 1823 and the present day, and the original collection has increased to its present dimensions by gifts and purchases, and by the operation of the Copyright Acts. The administrative expenses were estimated at £1,122,000 in 1963–64, and were met by a vote under "Museums, Galleries and the Arts," Class VIII of the Civil Estimates.

STANDING COMMITTEE

The Three Principal Trustees, The Archbishop of Canterbury; The Lord High Chancellor; The Speaker of the House of Commons—*ex officio*; *Appointed by the Sovereign*, The Marquess of Cambridge, G.C.V.O.; *Other Trustees*, Earl of Crawford and Balcarres, K.T., G.B.E.; Visct. De L'Isle, V.C., P.C., G.C.M.G.; Visct Boyd of Merton, P.C., C.H.; Lord Hurcomb, G.C.B., K.B.E.; Visct. Radcliffe, P.C., G.B.E.; Rt. Hon. J. Chuter Ede, C.H., M.P.; Hon. Sir Steven Runciman, F.B.A.; Sir Henry Dale, O.M., G.B.E., F.R.S.; Professor A. V. Hill, C.H., O.B.E., D.SC., F.R.S.; Sir Victor Goodman, K.C.B., O.B.E., M.C.; Sir William Hayter, K.C.M.G.; Professor D. M. S. Watson, F.R.S.; Rev. Canon C. E. Raven, D.D., D.SC., F.B.A.; T. S. R. Boase, M.C., LL.D.; Prof. C. F. A. Pantin, SC.D., F.R.S.

OFFICERS

Director and Principal Librarian, Sir Frank Francis, K.C.B. £4,215

Secretary, B. P. C. Bridgewater £2,865 to £3,215
Assistant Secretary, D. L. Paisey . . £1,498 to £2,544
Publications Officer, H. Jacob . . . . £1,498 to £2,544
Senior Executive Officers, Elsie G. Ding; J. F. W. Ryde . . . . £1,680 to £2,126
Guide Lecturers, O. E. Holloway; F. S. Leigh-Browne £1,680 to £2,126
Principal Keeper of Printed Books, R. A. Wilson, C.B. £3,340 to £3,565
Keepers, N. F. Sharp; A. H. Chaplin £2,865 to £3,215
Deputy Keepers, R. A. Skelton; P. Brown; A. H. King; G. H. Spinney; H. M. Nixon; J. L. Wood; R. F. L. Bancroft . . . . £2,566 to £2,865
Superintendent of Reading Room, R. F. L. Bancroft.
Assistant Keepers, R. G. Lyde; G. A. F. Scheele; Annie O'Donovan; Margaret S. Scheele; Audrey C. Brodhurst; G. D. Painter; E. J. Miller; A. F. Allison; H. G. Whitehead; *F. J. Hill; *R. S. Pine-Coffin; *R. J. Fulford; Anna E. C. Simoni; L. J. Thomas; G. J. R. Arnold; T. T. Tuckey-Smith; D. F. Foxon; D. F. Rhodes; O. W. Neighbour; Helen M. Wallis; P. A. H. Brown; I. R. Willison; P. R. Harris; P. J. Fairs; Lorna M. Arnold (*part-time*); A. M. Cain; C. E. N. Childs; P. C. Meade; J. W. Jolliffe; R. J. Roberts; M. G. Atkins; Hanna M. Swiderska; D. B. Chrastek; Cynthia M. Howard; G. B. Morris; Barbara J. Youngman; S. P. Cooper; Eiluned Rees; D. T. Thorratt.
Superintendent, Newspaper Library (Colindale), P. E. Allen.
Keeper of Manuscripts and Egerton Librarian, T. C. Skeat . . . . £2,865 to £3,215
Deputy Keepers, C. E. Wright; G. R. C. Davis; L. J. Gorton . . . . £2,566 to £2,865
Assistant Keepers, Margery L. Hoyle; *G. I. Bonner; Pamela J. Willetts; J. P. Hudson; D. H. Turner; P. D. A. Harvey; M. A. F. Borrie; J. L. M. Gulley; T. A. J. Burnett; Janet H. Backhouse; L. R. H. Smith; T. S. Pattie; Anita J. Lewis.
Keeper of Oriental Printed Books and Manuscripts, K. B. Gardner . . . . £2,865 to £3,215
Assistant Keepers, *G. M. Meredith-Owens; M. Lings; E. D. Grinstead; J. Rosenwasser; M. R. C. I. Suprapto; W. Zwalf; R. F. Hosking.
Keeper of Prints and Drawings, E. F. Croft-Murray £2,865 to £3,215
Deputy Keeper, P. M. R. Pouncey £2,566 to £2,865
Assistant Keepers, J. A. G. Gere; P. H. Hulton; C. J. White.
Keeper of Coins and Medals, J. Walker, C.B.E. £2,865 to £3,215
Deputy Keeper, G. K. Jenkins . . . £2,566 to £2,865
Assistant Keepers, R. A. G. Carson; J. P. C. Kent; N. M. Lowick.
Keeper of Egyptian Antiquities, I. E. S. Edwards £2,865 to £3,215
Assistant Keepers, *T. G. H. James; A. F. Shore.
Keeper of Western Asiatic Antiquities, R. D. Barnett £2,865 to £3,215
Assistant Keepers, E. Sollberger; A. R. Hillard.
Keeper of Greek and Roman Antiquities, D. E. L. Haynes . . . . £2,865 to £3,215
Assistant Keepers, *R. A. Higgins; D. E. Strong; Ann Birchall.
Keeper of British and Medieval Antiquities, R. L. S. Bruce-Mitford . . . . £2,865 to £3,215
Deputy Keeper, J. W. Brailsford . £2,566 to £2,865
Assistant Keepers, P. E. Lasko; G. H. Tait; G. de G. Sieveking; D. M. Wilson; K. S. Painter; I. H. Longworth.
Keeper of Oriental Antiquities, B. Gray, C.B.E. £2,865 to £3,215
Deputy Keepers, R. S. Jenyns; D. E. Barrett £2,566 to £2,865
Assistant Keepers, W. Watson; R. H. Pinder-Wilson; D. B. Waterhouse.
Keeper of Ethnography, A. Digby . £2,865 to £3,215
Deputy Keeper, W. B. Fagg . . . . . . £2,566 to £2,865
Assistant Keepers, B. A. L. Cranstone; D. B. Tayler; D. M. Boston.
Keeper of Laboratory, A. E. A. Werner £2,865 to £3,215
Principal Scientific Officer, A. D. Baynes-Cope £1,904 to £2,655
Chief Experimental Officers, H. Barker; R. M. Organ £2,182 to £2,516

* Receives an allowance.

THE BRITISH MUSEUM (NATURAL HISTORY)

Cromwell Road S.W.7
[Kensington: 6323]

Open free on week-days (except Good Friday and Christmas Day) 10 to 6, and on Sundays from 2.30 to 6.

The Natural History Collections were removed from the British Museum (Bloomsbury) to South Kensington in 1881–85, the new Museum being opened to the public in 1881. The collections comprise all branches of natural history. The Zoological Museum, Tring [Tring: 2255], bequeathed by the second Lord Rothschild, has formed part of the British Museum (Natural History) since 1938.

Official Guide-lectures conduct visitors round some of the exhibition galleries at 3 p.m. daily on weekdays free of charge, and their services are available at other times for special parties (also free of charge) by arrangement with the Director. Students are admitted daily for the special study of the collections, and to make drawings and take photographs of specimens, under special regulations to be obtained from the Director. The Museum issues a large variety of publications, comprising scientific monographs and catalogues, popular guide-books and manuals, instructions for collectors, economic pamphlets, and picture post-cards, both monochrome and in colour.

The administrative expenses were estimated at £657,000 in 1963–64.

Director, T. C. S. Morrison-Scott, D.S.C., D.SC. £4,115
Secretary, W. A. Ferguson . . . . . £1,959 to £2,711
Assistant Secretary, W. L. Rombach £1,680 to £2,126
Librarian, A. C. Townsend . . . . . £2,865 to £3,215
Chief Exhibition Officer, Miss M. R. J. Edwards, M.B.E. . . . . £2,237 to £2,572
Senior Experimental Officers, S. L. Stammwitz; A. G. Leutscher . . . . £1,680 to £2,126
Keeper of Zoology, F. C. Fraser, C.B.E. £3,340 to £3,665
Deputy Keepers, J. D. Macdonald; J. P. Harding £2,865 to £3,215
Senior Principal Scientific Officer, N. B. Marshall £2,865 to £3,215
Principal Scientific Officers, Miss I. Gordon, O.B.E.; W. I. Rees; G. O. Evans; Miss A. M. Clark; N. Tebble; R. H. Hedley; Miss A. G. C. Grandison; I. C. J. Galbraith; C. G. Adams; C. A. Wright; P. H. Greenwood . . . . £1,959 to £2,711
Chief Experimental Officers, R. W. Hayman; S. Prudhoe . . . . £2,237 to £2,572
Senior Experimental Officers, F. C. Sawyer; E. White; P. E. Purves; W. A. Smith; G. Palmer; R. P. D. Goodwin . . . . £1,680 to £2,126
Keeper of Entomology, J. P. Doncaster £2,865 to £3,215
Deputy Keeper, J. F. Perkins . . . . . £2,865 to £3,215
Senior Principal Scientific Officer, R. B. Benson £2,865 to £3,215
Principal Scientific Officers, E. B. Britton; H. Oldroyd; P. F. Mattingly; P. Freeman; J. W. A. F. Balfour-Browne; Miss T. R. Clay; I. H. H. Yarrow; D. E. Kimmins; V. F. Eastop £1,959 to £2,711
Senior Experimental Officers, R. J. Izzard; R. L. Coe; S. J. Turpin; N. H. Bennett . . £1,680 to £2,126
Keeper of Palaeontology, E. I. White, C.B.E., F.R.S. £3,240 to £3,665
Deputy Keepers, K. P. Oakley; H. D. Thomas £2,865 to £3,215

Principal Scientific Officers, L. Bairstow; H. W. Ball; W. T. Dean ....£1,959 to £2,711
Chief Experimental Officers, H. A. Toombs; F. M. Wonnacott................£2,237 to £2,572
Senior Experimental Officers, C. P. Castell; A. E. Rixon....................£1,680 to £2,126
Keeper of Mineralogy, G. F. Claringbull
£2,865 to £3,215
Deputy Keeper, A. A. Moss.....£2,865 to £3,215
Senior Principal Scientific Officer, M. H. Hey
£2,865 to £3,215
Principal Scientific Officers, J. D. H. Wiseman; S. E. Ellis......................£1,959 to £2,711
Keeper of Botany, J. E. Dandy...£3,340 to £3,665
Deputy Keeper, R. Ross.......£2,865 to £3,215
Principal Scientific Officers, W. T. Stearn; A. Melderis; Mrs. F. L. Balfour-Browne; J. Lewis
£1,959 to £2,711
Senior Experimental Officers, E. B. Bangerter; L. H. J. Williams; J. B. Evans
£1,680 to £2,126

THE LONDON MUSEUM

Kensington Palace, W.8

[Western: 9816]

The Museum illustrates the history of London from the earliest times to the present. It has good collections of archaeological remains, topographical pictures and models, costumes and royal relics. Originally at Kensington Palace, the collections were transferred to Lancaster House in 1914. After the second world war, when most of Lancaster House was converted for use solely as a centre for government hospitality, the Museum was granted temporary accommodation for its offices, and for such of its exhibition as space permitted, at Kensington Palace by King George VI. In 1956 the State Apartments at Kensington Palace were re-opened to the public under the administrative control of the London Museum. The Apartments contain pictures from the royal collections, royal costumes and furniture formerly belonging to Queen Mary.

Director and Accounting Officer, D. B. Harden, O.B.E., F.S.A...............................£3,215
Asst. Keepers, M. R. Holmes, F.S.A.; B. W. Spencer, F.S.A.; J. T. Hayes.

THE SCIENCE MUSEUM

South Kensington, S.W.7

[Kensington: 6371]

Open free on weekdays 10 to 6; Sundays 2.30 to 6. Closed on Good Friday and Christmas Day.

For Science Museum Library, see below.

The Science Museum, which is the National Museum of Science and Industry, was instituted in 1853 under the Science and Art Department as a part of the South Kensington Museum, and opened in 1857; to it was added in 1883 the Collections of the Patent Museum. In 1909 the administration of the Science Collections was separated from that of the Art Collections, which were transferred to the Victoria and Albert Museum. The Collections in the Science Museum illustrate the development of science and engineering and related industries.

The seven departments into which the exhibits are grouped are shown below.

The administrative expenses of the Museum and Library were estimated at £358,000 in 1963-64 to be met by a vote under Education.

Director and Secretary, D. H. Follett........£4,115
Museum Superintendent, J. A. Reeve
£2,237 to £2,572

Department of Physics

Keeper, F. A. B. Ward.........£2,865 to £3,215
Assistant Keepers (First Class), V. K. Chew; A. B. Sahiar....................£1,498 to £2,544

Department of Chemistry

Keeper, S. E. Janson...........£2,865 to £3,215
Deputy Keepers, F. Greenaway; W. Winton
£1,679 to £2,725

Assistant Keeper (First Class), D. B. Thomas
£1,498 to £2,544

Department of Transport and Mining

Keeper, F. Lebeter.............£2,865 to £3,215
Deputy Keeper, H. P. Spratt.... £1,679 to £2,725
Assistant Keepers (First Class), P. L. Sumner; T. M. Simmons.................£1,498 to £2,544

Department of Electrical Engineering and Communications

Keeper, D. Chilton............£2,865 to £3,215
Deputy Keepers, G. R. M. Garratt; Miss M. K. Weston...................£1,679 to £2,725

Department of Aeronautics and Sailing Ships

Keeper, W. T. O'Dea.........£2,865 to £3,215
Deputy Keeper, G. W. B. Lacey.. £1,679 to £2,725
Assistant Keeper (First Class), W. J. Tuck
£1,498 to £2,544

Department of Mechanical and Civil Engineering

Keeper, K. R. Gilbert.........£2,865 to £3,215
Assistant Keepers (First Class), C. St. C. B. Davison; R. J. Law; G. B. L. Wilson.. £1,498 to £2,544

Department of Astronomy and Geophysics

Keeper, H. R. Calvert.........£2,865 to £3,215
Deputy Keeper, J. Wartnaby ... £1,679 to £2,725
Assistant Keeper (First Class), A. G. Thoday
£1,498 to £2,544

Library

SCIENCE MUSEUM LIBRARY, Imperial Institute Road, S.W.7.—A national library especially devoted to pure and applied science, 372,000 volumes, 18,300 periodicals and transactions of learned societies, about 4,700 current. Bibliographies supplied.—Open on weekdays 10 to 5.30. Closed on Sundays and Bank Holiday weekends. Admission free. Photo-copying service.

Keeper, J. A. Chaldecott........£2,865 to £3,215
Deputy Keeper, Miss H. J. Parker £1,679 to £2,725
Assistant Keeper (First Class), R. C. Kenedy
£1,498 to £2,544

THE VICTORIA AND ALBERT MUSEUM

South Kensington, S.W.7

[Kensington: 6371]

Hours 10 to 6 (weekdays and Bank Holidays); Sundays, 2.30 to 6. Admission Free. Art Library (10 to 6) and Print Room (10 to 5) open free (closed Sunday). Is a museum of all branches of fine and applied art, under the Ministry of Education.

The Museum descends direct from the Museum of Manufactures (later called Museum of Ornamental Art) opened in Marlborough House in 1852. The nucleus was a selection of objects bought for £5,000 from the Great Exhibition of 1851 which, with objects illustrating historic styles, was to be devoted to the "application of fine art to the ob ects of utility" and "the improvement of the public taste in design." The Museum was moved in 1857 to become part of the collective South Kensington Museum. Most of the older buildings date from 1860-82; the new parts from 1899-1909. The South Kensington Museum was re-named the Victoria and Albert Museum in 1899, and only became an exclusively art museum in 1909. Besides comprising the departments named below, the Museum contains the national collections of post-classical sculpture (excluding modern), of British miniatures and of water-colours, the National Art Library, and of art lantern slides. The branch museum at Bethnal Green (composed of a building formerly at South Kensington) was opened in 1872. The Victoria and Albert Museum also administers the Wellington Museum (Apsley House); Ham House, Richmond and Osterley Park, Middlesex.

Director and Secretary, Sir Trenchard Cox, C.B.E., F.S.A.......................................£4,115

Department of Architecture and Sculpture

Keeper, J. W. Pope-Hennessy, C.B.E. £2,865 to £3,215
Keeper, T. W. I. Hodgkinson, C.B.E. (*also Sec. to Advisory Council*). £2,325 to £2,865
Deputy Keeper, J. G. Beckwith. . £1,498 to £2,544†
Assistant Keeper, H. D. K. Baxandall £1,498 to £2,544

Department of Ceramics

Keeper, R. J. Charleston. . . . . . . £2,865 to £3,215
Assistant Keeper, J. G. Ayers. . . . £1,498 to £2,544

Department of Circulation

Keeper, H. G. Wakefield. . . . . . . £2,865 to £3,215
Assistant Keepers, C. Hogben; Mrs B. J. Morris £1,498 to £2,544

Library

Keeper, J. P. Harthan. . . . . £2,865 to £3,215
Assistant Keepers, T. M. MacRobert; R. W. Lightbown; Mrs. S. J. Bury . . . . . . £1,498 to £2,544

Department of Metalwork

Keeper, C. C. Oman. . . . . £2,865 to £3,215
Deputy Keeper, B. W. Robinson. £1,498 to £2,544†
Assistant Keeper, C. Blair. . . . . . . £1,498 to £2,544

Department of Museum Extension Services

Keeper, C. H. Gibbs-Smith. . . . . £2,865 to £3,215

Department of Prints and Drawings

Keeper, A. G. Reynolds. . . . . £2,865 to £3,215
Deputy Keepers, J. H. Mayne; B. E. Reade £1,498 to £2,544†
Assistant Keepers, P. W. Ward-Jackson; C. M. Kauffmann. . . . . £1,498 to £2,544

Department of Textiles

Keeper, G. F. Wingfield Digby. £2.865 to £3,215
Deputy Keeper, D. King. . . . . . . £1,498 to £2,544†
Assistant Keeper, Miss N. K. A. Rothstein £1,498 to £2,544

Department of Woodwork

Keeper, H. D. Molesworth. . . . . £2,865 to £3,215
Deputy Keeper, J. F. Hayward. . £1,498 to £2,544†
Assistant Keeper, P. K. Thornton £1,498 to £2,544

Indian Section

Keeper, J. C. Irwin. . . . . £2,865 to £3,215
Keeper Emeritus, W. G. Archer. . £1,498 to £2,544
Assistant Keeper, R. W. Skelton. £1,498 to £2,544

Conservation Department

Keeper, N. S. Brommelle. . . . . . £2,325 to £2,865

Secretariat

Assistant to the Director, J. E. Lowe £1,498 to £2,544
Museum Superintendent, P. Winter £2,237 to £2,572

† Plus *Allce.* £181.

BETHNAL GREEN MUSEUM

Cambridge Heath Road, Bethnal Green, E.2

A branch of the Victoria and Albert Museum, opened in 1872 (admission free). (1) British paintings. (2) British ceramics. (3) British domestic silver and furniture. (4) Costumes, etc. (5) Children's Section.

Officer-in-Charge, C. M. Weekley (*Deputy Keeper*) (plus *allce.* £181) £1,438 to £2,479

THE COMMONWEALTH INSTITUTE

Kensington High Street, W.8

[Western: 8252]

The management of the Institute is vested in a Board of Governors of which Sir James Robertson, G.C.M.G., G.C.V.O., K.B.E. is the Chairman and Sir Gilbert Laithwaife, G.C.M.G., K.C.B., K.C.I.E., C.S.I., Vice-Chairman. Membership of the Board consists of the High Commissioners in London of the Commonwealth Governments and of representatives of Colonial, educational, cultural and commercial interests as appointed by the Minister. United Kingdom Government Departments are represented by Assessors.

Exhibition Galleries open weekdays, 10 a.m. to 5.30 p.m.; Sundays, 2.30 p.m. to 6 p.m. Admission free. Cinema. Closed Good Fridays, Christmas Eve and Christmas Day.

Director, Sir Kenneth Bradley, C.M.G. £3,565
Deputy Director, Mrs. M. Burke. £2,237 to £2,572
Accountant and Establishment Officer, B. Daly £2,232 to £2,567
Curator, Exhibition Galleries, R. V. Hatt £1,680 to £2,126
Senior Information Officer, D. A. Ashley £1,680 to £2,126
Education Officer, Miss J. Foster. . £1,680 to £2,126
Conference Organizer, Sir James Harford, K.B.E., C.M.G. £1,886

IMPERIAL WAR MUSEUM

Lambeth Road, S.E.1

[Reliance: 2636]

Open free daily (except Good Friday and Christmas Day), 10 a.m.; Sundays, 2 p.m. Closes at 6 p.m. Reference Section open Monday–Friday (except on public holidays), 10 a.m.–5 p.m.

The Museum was founded in 1917, and established by Act of Parliament in 1920 to record all aspects of the First World War. In 1939 its scope was enlarged to cover the Second World War and in 1953 it was enlarged again to include all war-like operations in which Britain or the Commonwealth have been involved since August, 1914. The Museum was opened in its present home, formerly the Royal Bethlem Hospital, by the Duke of York in 1936. The Exhibition Galleries contain a wide range of the vessels, vehicles, weapons and accoutrements of war at sea, on land and in the air as well as many models and dioramas to explain their construction or the manner of their employment. The Museum is also an art gallery and possesses some 9,000 paintings, drawings and sculptures which show artists' impressions of the landscape, machinery and personalities of war. The Reference Library contains some 90,000 printed and manuscript items dealing with the origins, conduct and consequences of war since 1914. These embrace the political, military, economic, social and literary aspects of the subject. The Photographic Library consists of more than 3,000,000 prints, copies of which may be purchased and reproduction of which may be authorised. The Film Library contains thousands of miles of material taken in both wars on the military fronts, at sea and from the air and from both sides.

Director, A. N. Frankland, D.F.C., D.Phil. . . . £3,150
Keeper of Art Department, W. P. Mayes, F.S.A.(Scot.) £1,438 to £2,479
Keeper of Department of Exhibits, W. Y. Carman, F.S.A. . . . . £1,438 to £2,479
Keeper of Department of Records, C. H. Roads, Ph.D. £1,438 to £2,479

NATIONAL MARITIME MUSEUM

Greenwich, S.E.10

[Greenwich: 4422]

Open weekdays 10 till 6; Sundays 2.30 to 6. Closed on Good Friday, Christmas Eve and Christmas Day. Admission free. The old Royal Observatory now forms part of the Museum, and a part of it, now called Flamsteed House, was opened by H.M. The Queen in July, 1960.

Reading Room and Students' Section of the Print Room open on weekdays 10 to 5 (Saturdays, 12.30); tickets of admission on written application to the Director.

The National Maritime Museum was established by Act of Parliament on July 24, 1934, for the illustration of the maritime history, archaeology and art of Great Britain. The Museum, which has absorbed the Royal Naval Museum and the Painted Hall Collections, is accommodated in the Queen's House (built by Inigo Jones, 1617–35) and the Caird Galleries (converted at the expense of Sir James Caird, Bt.). The collections include paintings; ship-models; ships' lines; prints and drawings; maps, atlases and charts; navigational instruments; relics; books and MSS. The amount for salaries and expenses, including a Grant-in-Aid, was estimated at £99,000 in 1962–63.

Director and Accounting Officer, Frank G. G. Carr, C.B.E. £3,560
Deputy Director, Cmdr. W. E. May, R.N. £2,561 to £2,860
Assistant Keepers (First Class), J. Munday; Lt.-Cdr. G. P. B. Naish, R.N.R.; A. W. H. Pearsall; M. S. Robinson, M.B.E.; Lt.-Cdr. D. W. Waters, R.N. £1,488 to £2,539
Establishment Officer, E. A. Philp.

(For other Museums in England—*see* Index).

THE NATIONAL MUSEUM OF WALES

AMGUEDDFA GENEDLAETHOL CYMRU

Cardiff

Open free on weekdays, 10 a.m. to 5 p.m. (on Thursdays in Summer to 8 p.m.). Sundays (admission 6*d*.) 2.30 to 5 p.m.

Founded by Royal Charter, 1907, and maintained by Annual Grant from the Government and Museum rate from the Cardiff City Council. The collections consist of:—(Geology), Collections of geological specimens (rocks, minerals, and fossils) from all parts of Wales, with comparative material from other regions. Relief maps, models and photographs illustrating the structure and scenery of Wales. (Botany), the Welsh National Herbarium, illustrating especially the flora of Wales and comprising the Griffith, D. A. Jones, Vachell, Salter, Shoolbred, Wheldon and other herbaria, and display collections illustrating general and forest botany and the ecology of Welsh plants. (Zoology), Collections of skins, British mammals and birds, eggs of British birds, extensive entomological collections, Melvill-Tomlin collection of molluscs, spirit collections, chiefly of Welsh interest. (Archæology), Welsh prehistoric, Roman and medieval antiquities, casts of pre-Norman monuments of Wales, important numismatic collection. (Industry), Models and specimens illustrating the history and present status of the industries of Wales. (Art), The works of Richard Wilson, Augustus John, O.M., and Sir Frank Brangwyn, are well represented; the Gwendoline and Margaret Davies Bequests of works of the 19th-century French School, the British School and Old Masters, Pyke Thompson collection of water-colour drawings, and a general collection of paintings in oil; sculpture, including many works by Sir W. Goscombe John, R.A., Swansea and Nantgarw porcelain, the De Winton collection of Continental porcelain and the Jackson collection of silver, etc.

President, The Marquess of Anglesey, F.S.A.
Vice-President, The Earl of Plymouth.
Director, Dr. D. Dilwyn John, C.B.E., T.D.
Secretary, R. J. H. Lloyd, T.D.
Keepers (Geology), Dr. D. A. Bassett; (*Botany*), S. G. Harrison; (*Zoology*), Colin Matheson; (*Archæology*), H. N. Savory, D.Phil., F.S.A.; (*Industry*), D. Morgan Rees; (*Art*), R. L. Charles, M.C.

Welsh Folk Museum

Amgueddfa Werin Cymru

St. Fagans

The museum is situated 4 miles west of Cardiff. Open weekdays (except Monday) 11 a.m. to 7 p.m. April to September, and 11 a.m. to 5 p.m. October to March (admission 1*s*.). Open Sundays from 2.30 p.m. The museum was made possible by the gift of St. Fagans Castle and its grounds by the Earl of Plymouth in 1947. The rooms of the Castle contain period furniture; the gardens are maintained. A woollen factory from Brecknockshire, a 16th-century barn from Flintshire, four farmhouses, a cottage and an 18th-century chapel have been re-erected and other typical Welsh buildings are being re-erected in an area adjoining the Castle to picture the old Welsh way of life and to show the rural crafts of the past. Part of the Welsh Folk Collection is exhibited in a museum gallery.

Curator, Dr. Iorwerth C. Peate, F.S.A.

Legionary Museum of Caerleon

Caerleon, Mon.

Open on weekdays (April–September) 11 a.m. to 1 p.m.; 2.30 p.m. to 5 p.m., and at other times on application to the Caretaker.

Contains material found on the site of the Roman fortress of Isca and its suburbs.

Turner House Art Gallery

Penarth, Nr. Cardiff

Open daily (except Mondays), 2 p.m. to 6 p.m. in summer; 2 p.m. to 5 p.m. in winter.

ROYAL SCOTTISH MUSEUM

Chambers Street, Edinburgh, 1

[Edinburgh Caledonian: 7534–5]

Open free on weekdays, 10 a.m. to 5 p.m.; and on Sundays 2 to 5 p.m.

Director, W. I. R. Finlay £3,500
Keeper of Art and Archæology Department, C. Aldred .... £2,524 to £2,820
Keeper, Technological Department, R. W. Plenderleith .... £2,524 to £2,820
Keeper, Natural History Department, A. R. Waterston, O.B.E. .... £2,524 to £2,820
Keeper, Geology Department, C. D. Waterston, Ph.D. £2,524 to £2,820
Assistant Keepers (First Class), A. S. Clarke; R. Oddy; H. G. Macpherson; A. G. Thomson; E. C. Pelham-Clinton .... £1,438 to £2,479

NATIONAL MUSEUM OF ANTIQUITIES OF SCOTLAND

Queen Street, Edinburgh, 2

[Edinburgh Waverley: 5984]

Founded in 1781 by the Society of Antiquaries of Scotland, and transferred to the Nation in 1858. Open free. Weekdays, 10 a.m. to 5 p.m.; Sundays, 2–5 p.m. Annexe at 18 Shandwick Place (closed on Sundays).

Keeper, R. B. K. Stevenson £3,000
Assistant Keepers, S. Maxwell; Miss A. S. Henshall; A. Fenton.

NATIONAL ASSISTANCE BOARD

6 St. Andrew Street, E.C.4

[Central: 2090]

Chairman, The Lord Ilford, M.C., T.D., Q.C. .. £5,000
Private Secretary and Clerk to the Board, T. S. Heppell.
Deputy Chairman, Miss A. C. Johnston, C.B.E.
Other Members, E. Bayliss, O.B.E.; Mrs. M. A. McAlister; P. Morris, C.B.E.; Dr. H. Pigott.
Secretary, Sir Donald Sargent, K.B.E., C.B. ... £5,015
Private Secretary, Mrs. A. A. Lowe.
Under-Secretaries, Miss J. Hope-Wallace, C.B.E.; T. D. Kingdom, C.B. (*Director of Establishments and Organization*) £4,115
Assistant Secretaries, A. G. Beard; G. W. Cole, C.B.E.; T. M. Logan, C.B.E.; E. T. Randall; R. Windsor £2,800 to £3,500
Solicitor to the Board, A. E. W. Ward, C.B.E.
Principals, Miss J. I. Barnes; G. G. Beltram; N. E. Clarke; H. W. Harvey; K. R. Stowe; D. C. Ward; R. D. F. Whitelaw ... £1,894 to £2,646
Principal Excutive Officer, F. Jackson, O.B.E., £3,150
Deputy Finance Officer, J. H. Dobson, £2,684 to £3,035

Chief Executive Officers, A. Bisset; B. R. Brewer; E. A. Connell; R. J. Forrest; W. T. Hartland; F. R. Kisby; D. B. Powell; I. G. Scanlan; W. D. Shipton; J. M. Watts........ £2,172 to £2,507
Senior Executive Officers, J. F. G. Bishop; E. V. A. Brown; F. J. Burls; R. V. Court; R. C. Curd; J. A. Denton; E. E. C. Frew; D. F. M. Greaves; N. Hanson; V. G. Hilbourne; G. G. Hilton; D. D. Jameson; E. J. Knight; A. N. B. Malyn; G. H. Marsh; T. L. Midwood; Miss V. E. Preddle; A. F. Raven; L. Roper; A. J. Selman-Smith; Miss G. F. White; S. E. Wilkins £1,615 to £2,061

Regional Organization

Northern Region

Regional Controller, R. Fish..... £2,684 to £3,035
Deputy Regional Controller, J. M. Makin £2,172 to £2,507
Assistant Regional Controllers, O. H. Holme; O. Hughes; G. D. W. Middleton; F. Roberts; T. D. Walton; L. Ward .... £1,615 to £2,061

East and West Ridings Region

Regional Controller, W. Norris, O.B.E £2,684 to £3,035
Deputy Regional Controller, M. Duncan £2,172 to £2,507
Assistant Regional Controllers, F. G. Dyson; G. Fowler; J. C. Lancaster; B. V. Magee; A. R. Pirie; T. Y. B. Shaw........ £1,615 to £2,061

North-Midland Region

Regional Controller, L. G. Ballard, I.S.O. £2,684 to £3,035
Deputy Regional Controller, G. K. Mann £2,172 to £2,507
Assistant Regional Controllers, R. A. Banks; H. E. C. Brookman; J. E. Glynn; C. A. Jennings; B. C. Phillips .... £1,615 to £2,061

London (North) Region

Regional Controller, F. W. Goodchild, O.B.E. £2,684 to £3,035
Deputy Regional Controllers, J. Begbie; Miss E. M. Scott................ £2,172 to £2,507
Assistant Regional Controllers, M. Alderton; Miss E. Cocker; S. A. Evans; M. Fagan; H. C. Godfrey; W. McL. Gray; R. C. Harris; H. J. Kimble; E. R. D. Lunn; J. Rae; A. F. Thacker; Miss K. N. R. Whyte; Miss E. E. Wilkinson, M.B.E. £1,615 to £2,061

London (South) Region

Regional Controller, D. F. Rae .. £2,684 to £3,035
Deputy Regional Controllers, W. S. Duthie; H. A. C. Ferraro................ £2,172 to £2,507
Assistant Regional Controllers, Miss V. M. Baker; F. Blunden; D. Clegg; Miss H. M. Cobb; J. P. Harrisson; G. S. Johnstone; J. E. Micklewright; G. B. Pegge; R. B. Pullan; W. G. F. West £1,615 to £2,061

South-Western Region

Regional Controller, W. S. Smethurst £2,684 to £3,035
Deputy Regional Controller, R. E. Ball £2,172 to £2,507
Assistant Regional Controllers, W. T. Appleby; F. G. Bullen; W. C. Burgoyne; H. Hall; I. R. J. Inglefield; W. J. Lee........ £1,615 to £2,061

Wales

Controller, Miss A. Evans...... £2,684 to £3,035
Deputy Controller, V. W. P. Bellamy £2,172 to £2,507
Assistant Controllers, A. O. B. Bevan; T. J. Collins; D. G. H. Davies; M. J. Griffiths; I. Jones; L. G. Williams; P. B. Wiltshire.... £1,615 to £2,061

Midland Region

Regional Controller, F. Hill..... £2,684 to £3,035
Deputy Regional Controller, R. G. Trent £2,172 to £2,507
Assistant Regional Controllers, H. Green; J. B. Harris; G. F. Maltby, M.C.; A. Smith; H. S. Stringer; H. T. A. Tregear............. £1,615 to £2,061

North-Western Region

Regional Controller, R. E. Higginson £2,684 to £3,035
Deputy Regional Controllers, R. L. Cornes, I.S.O.; Miss C. M. Liptrot.......... £2,172 to £2,507
Assistant Regional Controllers, L. B. Bloore; R. A. W. Cork; G. Garrick; E. A. C. Hall; J. B. Jeffrey; S. J. Kelly; W. Riste; W. C. Selly; E. Smith £1,615 to £2,061

Scotland

Controller, J. M. Anderson...... £2,783 to £3,185
Deputy Controllers, W. R. D. Greenan; J. K. Nicol £2,172 to £2,507
Assistant Controllers, L. Boyd; J. W. Britain; W F. Campbell; G. F. Cobban; M. Glen; T. Jeff; J. R. Lambie; J. S. MacDougall; E. D. Potter; Miss M. Pringle; A. Provan; M. Sutherland £1,615 to £2,061

NATIONAL COAL BOARD

Hobart House, Grosvenor Place, S.W.1

[Belgravia: 2020]

The *Coal Industry Nationalization Act* received the Royal Assent on July 12, 1946, and the National Coal Board was constituted on July 15, 1946. It took over the mines on January 1, 1947. The Board was reconstituted on August 1, 1951, and in February, 1955.

Chairman, The Lord Robens of Woldingham, P.C. (*plus allowances* £1,000) £10,000
Deputy Chairman, E. H. Browne, C.B.E. (*plus allowances* £500) £8,000
Members, H. E. Collins, C.B.E.; A. W. John, O.B.E.; C. A. Roberts, C.B.E.; W. J. P. Webber, C.B.E.; F. Wilkinson; A. H. A. Wynn (*plus allowances* £500) *each* £7,500
Part-time Members, Sir Regionald Ayres, K.B.E., C.B.; S. Watson, C.B.E.; L. G. Whyte....*each* £1,000
Secretary, R. G. C. Cowe.
Deputy Secretary, P. W. E. Currie.
Legal Adviser, D. H. Haslam.
Director-General of Finance, D. M. Clement.
Director-General of Industrial Relations (vacant)
Director-General of Marketing, D. J. Ezra, M.B.E.
Director-General of Staff, C. G. Simpson, O.B.E.
Director-General of Purchasing and Stores, W. M. Crooks.
Director-General of Production, W. V. Sheppard, C.B.E.
Director of Statistics, E. H. Sealy, Ph.D.
Chief Public Relations Officer, J. G. Kirk.
Chief Medical Officer, Dr. J. M. Rogan.
Chairmen of Divisional Boards, A. W. John, O.B.E. (*Coal Products*); R. W. Parker, C.B.E. (*Scottish Division*); W. Reid, C.B.E., Ph.D. (*Northumberland and Durham*); W. H. Sales (*Yorkshire*); J. Anderton, O.B.E. (*North Western*); W. L. Miron, O.B.E., T.D. (*East Midlands*); J. Brass (*West Midlands*); A. H. Kellett (*South Western*); J. H. Plumptre (*Divisional General Manager*) (*South Eastern*).

NATIONAL DEBT OFFICE

and Office for Payment of Government Life Annuities

Bank Buildings, 19 Old Jewry, E.C.2

Secretary to the National Debt Commissioners and Comptroller-General, A. H. M. Hillis, C.M.G. £4,115
Asst. Comptroller, H. S. Mileman, O.B.E. £2,683 to £2,863

Chief Clerk, S. J. Payne.........£1,680 to £2,126
Principal Clerks, F. T. Roberts; F. D. Ashby £1,680 to £2,126
Brokers, Messrs. Mullens & Co............ £2,000

NATIONAL DOCK LABOUR BOARD

22–26 Albert Embankment, S.E.1

The National Dock Labour Board administers the scheme for giving permanent employment to dock workers under the *Dock Workers (Regulation of Employment) Act*, 1946.

Chairman, The Lord Crook.
General Manager and Secretary, M. R. Haddock, C.B.E.

NATIONAL GALLERIES

See ART GALLERIES

NATIONAL HEALTH SERVICE

See HEALTH SERVICE

NATIONAL PARKS COMMISSION

1 Cambridge Gate, Regent's Park, N.W.1
[Welbeck: 0366]

The National Parks Commission, a body corporate, was established under the National Parks and Access to the Countryside Act, 1949. Members are appointed by the Minister of Housing and Local Government, to whom the Commission reports annually. This report is laid before each House of Parliament.

The Commission is entrusted with the task of designating National Parks and areas of outstanding natural beauty in England and Wales. The former are extensive tracts of country affording facilities for open-air recreation. The Parks, when approved by the Minister of Housing and Local Government, are administered by Local Planning Authorities, subject to a general supervision by the Parks Commission. Ten National Parks, covering in all some 5,246 square miles, and twelve areas of outstanding natural beauty have been established. For main article, *see* Index.

The Commission is also required to report to the Minister of Housing and Local Government on long-distance routes, along which there will be continuous right of way for walkers and riders, e.g. the Pennine Way; to make representations to Ministers or Local Planning Authorities on any proposed development likely to be prejudicial to the natural beauty of any area; and to provide information services for the public.

Chairman, The Lord Strang, G.C.B., G.C.M.G., M.B.E. £2,000
Deputy Chairman, Mrs. J. Dower, O.B.E.....£1,000
Members, Prof. H. C. Darby, O.B.E., D.Litt; Mrs. Elwyn Davies, Ph.D.; J. C. P. de Winton; Sir Herbert Griffin, C.B.E.; G. Huxley, C.M.G., M.C.; Sir William Lindsay, C.B.E.; Lt.-Col. G. W. F. Luttrell, M.C.; F. Ritchie, O.B.E.; Prof. J. A. Steers; H. Wardale; Col. J. F. Williams-Wynne, D.S.O.; W. B. Yapp.................. *unpaid*
Secretary, M. F. B. Bell.................£3,500
Principals, J. R. B. Ferguson; Miss G. V. Chesterman £1,894 to £2,646
Field Officer, L. J. Watson...............£2,061
Senior Executive Officer, E. J. S. Burbidge..£2,061

NATIONAL RESEARCH DEVELOPMENT CORPORATION

1 Tilney Street, W.1
[Grosvenor: 5431]

The National Research Development Corporation is a Public Corporation set up by the Board of Trade under the provisions of the Development of Inventions Act, 1948, to develop or exploit in the public interest inventions resulting from research carried out by Government Departments or other public bodies, or any other research in respect of which financial assistance has been provided out of public funds; and also worthwhile inventions from other sources which are not already being developed or exploited.

Chairman, Sir William Black..............*unpaid*
Managing Director, J. C. Duckworth........£7,000

THE NATURE CONSERVANCY

19, Belgrave Square, S.W.1
[Belgravia: 3241]

The Nature Conservancy was set up by Royal Charter in March, 1949, and is directly responsible to the Lord President of the Council and Minister for Science as Chairman of the Privy Council Committee for Nature Conservation. The National Parks and Access to the Countryside Act, 1949, provided the necessary powers for the proper discharge of the responsibilities laid on the Conservancy.

In Great Britain 101 Nature Reserves, covering 211,233 acres, had been declared up to June 30, 1963. The Conservancy has powers under Part III of the National Parks and Access to the Countryside Act, 1949, to make byelaws for the protection of National Nature Reserves.

Research stations have been set up at Grange-over-Sands, Lancashire; Wareham, Dorset; Bangor, Caernarvonshire and Aviemore, Inverness-shire. An experimental station is being set up at Monks' Wood, Huntingdon. Field stations have been set up at Moor House, Westmorland and Kinlochewe, Ross-shire.

Chairman, The Lord Howick of Glendale, G.C.M.G., K.C.V.O.

Members, Prof. A. R. Clapham, Ph.D., F.R.S.; Sir Charles Connell, W.S.; F. Fraser Darling, D.Sc., LL.D., F.R.S.E.; Lt.-Col. C. M. Floyd, O.B.E.; Lt.-Col. J. P. Grant, M.B.E.; Prof. Sir Joseph Hutchinson, C.M.G., Sc.D., F.R.S.; G. V. Jacks; J. A. Kitching, O.B.E., Sc.D., F.R.S.; Major J. G. Morrison, T.D., M.P.; Prof. C. F. A. Pantin, Sc.D., F.R.S.; Prof. W. H. Pearsall, D.Sc., F.R.S.; T. F. Peart, M.P.; The Lord Porchester; Prof. P. W. Richards, Sc.D.; Prof. L. D. Stamp, C.B.E., D.Sc., LL.D., D.Litt.; Prof. J. A. Steers; The Lord Strang, G.C.B., G.C.M.G., M.B.E.

Scottish Committee

Chairman, Sir Charles Connell, W.S.
Members, Prof. J. H. Burnett, F.R.S.E.; The Lord Forbes, K.B.E.; Prof. T. N. George, D.Sc., F.R.S.E.; Lt.-Col. J. P. Grant, M.B.E.; Commander Sir Geoffrey Hughes-Onslow, K.B.E., D.S.C.; E. J. Ivory; Major S. F. Macdonald Lockhart of the Lee; Sir James Roberts, Bt.; A. R. Wannop, O.B.E., F.R.S.E.; Prof. V. C. Wynne-Edwards; Prof. C. M. Yonge, C.B.E., D.Sc., F.R.S., F.R.S.E.

Director-General, E. M. Nicholson, C.B.

Deputy Director-General (Scientific), E. B. Worthington, Ph.D.

Administrative Secretary, P. H. Cooper.

Director, Scotland, J. Berry, Ph.D., F.R.S.E., 12. Hope Terrace, Edinburgh, 9.

Director, Wales, R. E. Hughes, Ph.D., Penrhos Road, Bangor.

Director, Merlewood, J. B. Cragg, Merlewood Research Station, Grange-over-Sands, Lancashire.

Director, Monks' Wood, K. Mellanby, C.B.E., Sc.D., Abbots Ripton, Huntingdon.

Regional Offices

Wales, The Nature Conservancy Headquarters for Wales and Bangor Research Station, Penrhos Road, Bangor.

South Wales Region, Department of Zoology, University College of Swansea, Singleton Park, Swansea.

North Region, Merlewood Research Station, Grange-over-Sands, Lancashire.
East Anglia Region, Government Offices, Bishopgate, Norwich.
South Region; South-West Region, Furzebrook Research Station, Wareham, Dorset.
South-East Region, 19 Belgrave Square, S.W.1.
Midland Region, The Nature Conservancy, Attingham Park, Shrewsbury, Salop.

ROYAL OBSERVATORIES

Royal Greenwich Observatory

[Herstmonceux: 3171]

The Royal Observatory was established at Greenwich in 1675 by Charles II for improving methods of navigation. Latterly the growth of London, with its smoke and bright lights, seriously hampered astronomical observations there, and it was decided in 1946 to move the telescopes to Herstmonceux Castle in Sussex. The removal was completed by 1958. The meridian of zero longitude still passes through the old site, which now houses the astronomical section of the National Maritime Museum.

At the Observatory astronomical measurements are made of the positions, motions and distances of the heavenly bodies, and of such physical characteristics as their luminosities, masses and temperatures. Two meridian instruments and six equatorially-mounted telescopes are devoted to this work. The Observatory is responsible for the time service of the United Kingdom, for the maintenance of chronometers and watches used by H.M. armed forces, and for the periodical issue of world magnetic charts. At an outstation at Hartland, Devon, continuous observations are made of the strength and direction of the earth's magnetic field.

Astronomer Royal, Sir Richard van der Riet Woolley, O.B.E., SC.D., F.R.S. £4,050
Deputy Chief Scientific Officer, R. d'E. Atkinson, Ph.D. .... £3,275 to £3,600
Senior Principal Scientific Officers, A. Hunter, Ph.D.; B. E. J. Pagel, Ph.D. .... £2,800 to £3,150
Principl Scientific Officers, H. F. Finch; C. A. Murray; H. M. Smith; P. A. Wayman, Ph.D. £1,839 to £2,950

H.M. Nautical Almanac Office

c/o The Royal Greenwich Observatory

The *Nautical Almanac* was first published for 1767 by the Board of Longitude. The Office is now a branch of the Royal Greenwich Observatory. Annual publications—Astronomical Ephemeris, Nautical Almanac, Air Almanac, Star Almanac.

Superintendent, D. H. Sadler, O.B.E. £3,275 to £3,600
Principal Scientific Officers, Mrs. F. McBain Sadler (*part-time*); G. A. Wilkins, Ph.D. £1,839 to £2,950

SCOTLAND

Royal Observatory

Blackford Hill, Edinburgh 9

[Newington: 3321]

The Observatory was founded by the Astronomical Institution in 1818. Originally situated on Calton Hill, near the centre of the city, it was moved southwards to its present site in 1896. It is primarily a research institution concerned with work in astrophysics and stellar astronomy, and undertakes spectroscopic and photometric observations. The Observatory also houses a major centre of seismology. The Observatory operates an outstation at Earlyburn in Peeblesshire. The Library contains the valuable collection of Lord Crawford.

Astronomer Royal for Scotland and Regius Professor of Astronomy in the University of Edinburgh, H. A. Brück, Ph.D., D.Phil. .... £3,275 to £3,600
Principal Scientific Officers, H. E. Butler, Ph.D.; P. B. Fellgett, Ph.D.; V. C. Reddish, Ph.D. £1,894 to £2,646
Senior Seismologist, P. L. Willmore, Ph.D. £2,300 to £2,675

Royal Observatory, Cape of Good Hope

The Cape Observatory was founded by order in Council in 1820 to continue in the Southern Hemisphere the work being undertaken by Greenwich in the North. Extensive programmes are carried out to ascertain the positions, distances, magnitudes and radial velocities of stars.

Astronomer, R. H. Stoy, C.B.E., Ph.D. £3,600
Chief Asst. D. S. Evans, Ph.D. ... £2,800 to £3,150

OVERSEAS AUDIT DEPARTMENT

Queen Anne's Chambers, Dean Farrar Street, S.W.1

[Whitehall: 8307]

The Accounts of most of the dependent territories overseas are audited on behalf of the Secretary of State for the Colonies by Audit Officers acting under the supervision of the Director General of the Overseas Audit Service. The cost of this audit is borne by the territories affected.

Director General of the Overseas Audit Service, P. H. Jennings, C.B.E. £4,215
Deputy Director General, F. E. L. Carter, C.B.E. £3,815
Assistant Directors, R. J. S. Orwin, O.B.E.; G. C. Jarvis £2,865

OVERSEAS TERRITORIES INCOME TAX OFFICE

26 Grosvenor Gardens, S.W.1

The Official Representative is appointed by the Secretary for Technical Co-operation and acts in respect of those territories, Protectorates, etc., which have decided to avail themselves of his services in connection with territorial Income Tax.

Official Representative, W. M. Wedderspoon, C.B.E. £3,550
Deputy, F. C. Yandell £3,250

PATENT OFFICE

(and Industrial Property Department, Board of Trade).

25 Southampton Buildings, W.C.2

[Holborn: 8721]

The duties of the Department, which deals mainly with the granting of patents, the registration of designs and trade marks, and with questions relating to literary and artistic copyright, are performed by a Comptroller-General with a staff of officials. In 1962 the Patent Office sealed 27,721 patents and registered 7,431 designs and 9,754 trade marks.

Comptroller-General, G. Grant, C.B. £4,415
Assistant Comptrollers, A. E. Tollerfield, C.B.; £3,928
W. Wallace, C.M.G.; R. G. Atkinson, C.B.E. £3,815
Superintending Examiners, R. D. Satchell, C.B.E.; J. V. Hudson, C.B.E.; S. H. Biles; E. T. Vincent; T. C. Taylor; L. F. W. Knight; J. Field; J. E. Mirams; E. Armitage £3,665

Patent Office Library

The Library (383,450 volumes) is open to the public daily from 10 a.m. to 9 p.m. Mondays to Fridays; Saturdays 10 a.m. to 1 p.m.

Librarian, Miss M. Webb ...... £2,566 to £2,865

Manchester Office
51 Regent House, Cannon Street, Manchester, 4. [Blackfriars: 3759]
Keeper of Manchester Branch, W. E. Edwards £1,615 to £2,061

PAYMASTER GENERAL'S OFFICE
Russell Square House, Russell Square, W.C.1
[Museum; 8646]

The Paymaster General's Office was formed by the consolidation in 1835 of various separate pay departments then existing, some of which dated back at least to the Restoration of 1660. Other offices were incorporated in 1884. Its function is that of paying agent for Government Departments, other than the Revenue Departments. Most of its payments are made through banks, to whose accounts the necessary transfers are made at the Bank of England. The payment of many types of public service pensions is an important feature of its work. The Establishment expenses were estimated at £700,000 in 1963–64.

Paymaster-General (and Chief Secretary to the Treasury), RT. HON. JOHN ARCHIBALD BOYD-CARPENTER, M.P. £5,000
Assistant Paymaster General, J. H. Vetch £2,865 to £3,565
Dep. Asst. Paymaster Gen., F. J. Clay £2,683 to £2,865
Chief Executive Officers, F. T. Simmons; N. C. Norfolk; S. A. H. Guille, M.B.E. £2,237 to £2,572
Senior Executive Officers, K. G. L. Harrold; D. M. Wheble; A. A. C. Jackson; Miss H. M. Bottrill; P. J. Sheppard; R. C. Ward; A. J. Kennett; R. S. Harris; Miss E. M. Hart; A. Lawrence; I. J. Pells; H. C. Leng .... £1,680 to £2,126

MINISTRY OF PENSIONS AND NATIONAL INSURANCE
10 John Adam Street, W.C.2
[Whitehall: 9066]

The Ministry of Pensions and National Insurance is responsible for the administration of war pensions, family allowances and national insurance, including industrial injuries insurance. The schemes administered by the Ministry are explained in detail in the main article (*see* Index).

Minister, RT. HON. NIALL MALCOLM STEWART MACPHERSON, M.P. £5,000
Principal Private Secretary, C. M. Regan.
Assistant Private Secretary, B. G. James.
Parliamentary Private Secretary, G. Johnson Smith, M.P. .... *unpaid*
Joint Parliamentary Secretaries, Mrs. M. H. Thatcher, M.P.; Lt.-Cdr. S. L. C. Maydon, D.S.O., D.S.C., M.P. £2,500
Secretary, Sir Eric Bowyer, K.C.B., K.B.E. £7,015
Private Secretary, M. J. A. Partridge.
Deputy Secretary, J. Walley, C.B. £5,015

War Pensions
(War Pensions and Overseas Matters)
Under Secretary, D. C. H. Abbot, C.B. £4,115
Assistant Secretaries, A. Patterson, C.M.G.; A. J. G. Crocker; E. W. Whittemore, M.M. £2,865 to £3,565
Principals, D. J. Carter; R. B. Hodgetts; Mrs. M. M. Davison .... £1,959 to £2,711
Chief Executive Officers, G. T. Flock; J. M. Tones; G. B. Holding; T. S. Ferguson £2,237 to £2,572

Insurance Department A
(Industrial Injuries and Family Allowances)
Under Secretary, G. Edwards, C.B.E. £4,115
Assistant Secretaries, J. C. Hobbs; G. D. Caldwell £2,865 to £3,565
Principals, J. E. Ashford; Miss J. A. Bates; J. Cartmell, C.B.E.; T. A. Howell £1,959 to £2,711
Chief Executive Officers, G. W. Horn; L. G. Reffell; C. J. Russell .... £2,237 to £2,572

Insurance Department B
(National Insurance Scheme Benefits)
Under Secretary, R. S. Swift £4,115
Assistant Secretaries, Miss N. Hellon, C.B.E.; D. H. Fulcher, D.S.C.; S. B. Kibbey. £2,865 to £3,565
Principals, R. Dronfield; H. S. McPherson; N. M. Hale; R. E. Tringham; P. R. Oglesby £1,959 to £2,711
Chief Executive Officers, J. S. Campbell-Dick; T. C. Naylor .... £2,237 to £2,572

Insurance Department C
(Insurability, Contributions, Statistics, etc.)
Under Secretary, S. S. Menneer £4,115
Assistant Secretaries, Miss G. M. Jones; F. K. Forrester, M.B.E.; T. C. Stephens; W. F. Morris £2,865 to £3,565
Principals, J. Vaughan; Mrs. M. Parsons; B. J. Ellis .... £1,959 to £2,711
Statistician, D. Newman .... £1,959 to £2,711
Chief Executive Officers, L. C. H. Stadames; B. C. James; A. L. Parrott; W. T. Cotton £2,237 to £2,572

Establishments and Organization Department
Under Secretary, L. Errington, C.B. *(Director of Establishments and Organization)* £4,115
Assistant Secretaries, D. F. Herring, C.B.E., J. E. McDonnell, O.B.E.; H. B. Lewin, M.B.E.; H. Archer, D.F.C. .... £2,865 to £3,565
Chief Information Officer, R. G. S. Hoare, M.V.O., M.B.E. .... £2,865 to £3,565
Principals, G. T. Williams; M. Nelson £1,959 to £2,711
Heads of Branch, M. Innes *(Controller of Office Services)*; D. Pilkington *(Chief Instructions Officer)*; P. J. Haddy .... £2,683 to £2,865
Chief Executive Officers, M. Eastaugh, I.S.O.; J. F. C. Parsons; F. J. Goodridge; J. H. C. Nightingall; J. C. C. Smith; T. J. Salmon; D. W. Polley; K. Shuttleworth; J. F. C. Cheater; G. W. Watters £2,237 to £2,572
Principal Information Officer, J. Pilkington £2,237 to £2,572

Finance Department
Under Secretary for Finance and Accountant General, D. Overand £4,115
Assistant Secretary for Finance, J. A. Atkinson, D.F.C. £2,865 to £3,565
Principal, G. C. F. Sladden .... £1,959 to £2,711
Directors of Accounts, H. E. Morgan, C.B.E.; W. L. Williams £3,215
Assistant Accountants General, R. Taylor, O.B.E.; L. C. Donohoe; J. A. Worrall; D. W. Scarth £2,618 to £2,800
Chief Executive Officers, J. T. Perkins; G. Cox; R. G. Cope; J. Grieve; L. J. Hayward; C. Pagdin; N. S. Sunderland .... £2,172 to £2,507
Regional Finance Officers, J. B. Boyes *(Northern)*; R. Orchard *(North Midlands)*; W. Rowlinson *(London North)*; W. M. Baker, O.B.E. *(London South)*; W. P. Sheppard *(South Western)*; W. A. Gregory *(Wales)*; J. Burns *(Midland)*; T. J. Crosbie *(North Western)*; J. E. Smail *(Scotland)* £2,172 to £2,507

Legal Department
Solicitor, A. E. W. Ward, C.B.E. £5,015
Principal Assistant Solicitor, R. L. Garbutt, C.B.E. £4,115
Assistant Solicitors, G. H. Brinkworth, C.B.E.; J. R. B. Hodgetts, C.B.E.; W. H. M. Clifford; H. W. Hornsby; M. W. M. Osmond; R. F. N. Thoyts £2,965 to £3,565
Senior Legal Assistants, R. H. Prendergast; Miss C. K. Bridgewater; D. O. Robinson; T. C. A. Butcher; W. H. C. Hodges; W. H. D. Winder; R. N. Williams; M. O'Connor; A. J. A. Compton; H. L. Palmer; E. W. Howard; T. A. Parsons; A. S. Dinnis; S. E. Ingram; H. Knorpel; N. F. MacCabe; C. A. Emanuel; H. M. Jones; R. J. Butcher; D. R. Mendham; E. O. F.

Stocker; Mrs. G. M. Y. Williams; Dr. H. F. Davis; Mrs. A. B. Farthing . . £2,304 to £2,865

Medical Department

Chief Medical Officer, E. G. Dryburgh £4,415
Deputy Chief Medical Officer, J. Watkins-Pitchford, £4,115
Principal Medical Officers, T. H. Sims, O.B.E.; G. D. Gordon, O.B.E.; M. Newman; J. W. James; J. C. McVittie, O.B.E. £3,750
Senior Medical Officers, S. Vatcher, O.B.E.; D. E. V. Jones; G. A. Miller; G. S. Moran; W. D. T. Brunyate; E. D. Robson; C. Huddlestone; A. J. Lea; N. C. Simpson; B. Yuill; J. M. Cribb; J. Black; W. W. Jones; R. W. Thomas; M. S. Patrick; R. T. Fletcher, M.B.E.; H. W. Farrell, O.B.E.; J. R. Connelly; J. K. Steel, T.D.; J. N. Heales, M.B.E.; P. B. Atkinson; W. Sagar; A. M. Campbell, D.S.O., O.B.E., T.D.; C. C. Harvey; S. Conlan; A. Caplan £3,500
Medical Officers (H.Q. Regions and Central Office, Blackpool), C. W. A. Emery, C.B.E.; G. P. Thorold; S. J. V. Mouat; J. H. Williams; D. T. Lewis; D. R. P. Wilkie; J. N. U. Russell, M.B.E.; F. M. Collins; G. N. Hunt; Sir David Clyde, K.C.I.E.; D. C. Farquharson, O.B.E.; E. L. Brittain, T.D.; M. R. Hayes; Mrs. A. D. Maclaine; A. R. Woodforde; G. Shearer; W. Hosie; Miss B. T. M. Douglas; H. A. D. Doyle; S. B. Davis; A. M. Roberts; H. S. Hamlin; N. G. Clements; G. T. Cribb; E. G. Houghton; R. S. Parkin; R. St. J. R. Johnston; W. Lawie; G. O. Airey; N. Macleod; Miss B. Winterton; J. B. McCallum; J. L. Cox, V.R.D.; L. H. Buckland; R. P. Liston; J. Weir; W. Smith; A. D. Bourne; W. H. Stephen, T.D.; F. W. Whiteman, C.B.E.; G. L. Pett; J. F. H. Gaussen; J. B. Evans; E. Livingstone; H. G. G. Bernstein, M.B.E.; M. D. Edwards; R. J. C. Hamilton, T.D.; W. S. Shaw; J. E. M. Barnes; J. W. Laird; R. Dudley-Paget; W. S. Brown, T.D.; W. M. Quin; T. G. S. James; E. C. Vardy; R. Medlicott; J. H. F. Pankhurst; E. Haigh; R. D. Menzies; P. S. Hawkins; Miss A. C. N. Swanston; E. A. L. Murphy, T.D.; W. R. C. Spicer; A. M. Langwill; D. S. Gideon; R. S. Flynn; G. O. Mayne; J. A. G. Carmichael; W. G. Greene; G. Longworth-Krafft; E. G. Wright, O.B.E.; G. S. Caithness; J. G. S. Holman, M.C.; J. H. Morrison; E. Bradbury; J. E. L. Morris; B. Lee; R. S. F. Adam; R. S. Ellis-Brown; G. E. Stoker, M.C.; G. M. M. Menzies; H. B. C. Wallace, O.B.E.; J. A. Barclay; T. B. Purdy; M. C. Anderson; A. M. Muir; R. D. Simpson; T. R. Wilkie Millar; H. P. Clark . . £1,904 to £3,075
Medical Officers (Pneumoconiosis), J. M. Tyrrell; R. M. McGowan; G. B. Murray, D.C.M.; P. K. Walker; Mrs. M. L. Williams; W. B. Lister; W. C. Sharp; T. J. Reid; A. H. Pritchard; J. E. M. Hutchinson; H. D. McGorry; S. F. Seelig; M. K. Coles; D. R. Mackintosh; J. P. Lyons; W. N. Pringle; Miss A. F. Roberts; D. L. Cran; A. C. Byles; A. N. Dempsey; M. G. Ellis; F. H. Morrell; B. Roberts; R. L. Sadler, E.R.D.; R. G. B. Williamson; C. Y. Bland; G. J. Ryder; W. R. Parkes; G. Ashe; W. R. Brown; E. R. Cole; R. Paul, O.B.E.; T. J. G. Phillips; C. Michie . . . . £1,904 to £3,075

Blackpool Central Office

(War Pensions Awards and Appeals, War Pensions Issue Office)

Controller, E. L. Trew £3,150
Heads of Branch, H. Wilson; V. W. B. Slater; J. Johnston . . . . £2,618 to £2,800
Chief Executive Officers, L. J. Birtles; S. Watson, D.F.C.; D. J. Robertson; D. Jenner; V. M. Thomson; C. Byrne; A. Richardson £2,172 to £2,507

Newcastle upon Tyne Central Office

(Records Branch, Family Allowances, etc.)

Controller, J. H. McCarthy, C.B. £4,050
Heads of Division, W. H. Watling; W. B. Cowie £3,150
Heads of Branch, R. J. Eayrs; G. H. A. Othen; L. M. Maclean; J. A. Corry . . . . £2,618 to £2,800
Chief Executive Officers, W. T. Elsworth; Miss H. Marshall; G. Cryer; E. Turner; J. M. Nicholson; W. H. Wiseman; J. Crawford; J. Drummond; H. F. Thomas; D. N. Clark; W. Hampson; Miss A. Smith . . . . £2,172 to £2,507

Scotland

39 Drumsheugh Gardens, Edinburgh 3

Controller, I. Mc. G. Roberton, C.B.E. £2,800 to £3,500
Deputy do., G. T. Davidson . . . . . £2,618 to £2,800
Assistant do., Miss C. F. Murray; J. S. Mill; T. D. Brown; J. R. Henry . . . . £2,172 to £2,507
Chief Executive Officer, A. J. M. Petrie £2,172 to £2,507

Wales

Government Buildings, Gabalfa, Cardiff

Controller, E. Evans, C.B.E. . . . . . £2,800 to £3,500
Deputy do., D. E. Thomas . . . . . . £2,618 to £2,800
Assistant do., G. T. Huws; D. M. Watt, M.M.; C. Randalls . . . . £2,172 to £2,507

Regional Organization (England)

Northern—Newcastle

Regional Controller, C. Kenwright £3,150
Deputy do., F. B. Hindmarsh . . . . £2,618 to £2,800
Assistant do., J. Kennedy; G. Ward £2,172 to £2,507

East and West Riding—Leeds

Regional Controller, M. H. Mackellar, O.B.E. £3,150
Deputy do., Miss D. A. Wade . . £2,618 to £2,800
Assistant do., W. G. Kuhnel; G. R. Kemp; G. Collins . . . . £2,172 to £2,507

North Midland—Nottingham

Regional Controller, J. W. Farnsworth £3,150
Deputy do., R. Mather . . . . £2,618 to £2,800
Assistant do., J. C. Moy; A. L. Heath; W. H. Arthur £2,172 to £2,507
Chief Executive Officers, T. C. Pitkin, O.B.E.; J. Coates . . . . £2,172 to £2,507

London North

Regional Controller, R. H. G. Garside, C.B.E. £3,150
Deputy do., S. H. Bate . . . . £2,618 to £2,800
Assistant do., H. E. Knott, O.B.E.; F. W. Jones; S. Reeves; A. E. Goddard; R. Graham £2,172 to £2,507

London South

Regional Controller, F. D. S. Waterton £3,150
Deputy do., W. R. Denaro . . . . . . £2,618 to £2,800
Assistant do., T. C. Sutton, O.B.E.; H. F. Marshall; J. Bizley; L. C. Baxer . . . . £2,172 to £2,507
Principal, E. Franks . . . . £1,894 to £2,646

South Western—Bristol

Regional Controller, R. Hobbins £3,150
Deputy do., J. K. Studley . . . . £2,618 to £2,800
Assistant do., R. K. Meatyard; E. H. Cordwell; G. F. Kilshaw . . . . £2,172 to £2,507

Midland—Birmingham

Regional Controller, H. V. O'Toole £3,150
Deputy do., E. M. Fillmore, O.B.E. £2,618 to £2,800
Assistant do., A. E. Howells, O.B.E.; R. W. Turner; E. F. Thomas . . . . £2,172 to £2,507
Chief Executive Officer, S. F. J. Pilgrim £2,172 to £2,507

North Western—Manchester

Regional Controller, G. H. Childs £3,150
Deputy do., J. C. Lewis . . . . £2,618 to £2,800
Assistant do., F. Turnbull, O.B.E.; J. F. Crampton; R. M. Kelly; A. J. Farmer; J. H. Ward £2,172 to £2,507

Canada

Ministry Representative, R. A. E. Tow £2,618 to £2,800

NATIONAL INSURANCE ADVISORY COMMITTEE

10 John Adam Street, W.C.2

[Whitehall: 9066]

The National Insurance Advisory Committee was appointed on Oct. 28, 1947, under the National Insurance Act, 1946, to give advice and assistance to the Minister of Pensions and National Insurance in connection with the discharge of his functions under the Act, and to perform any other duties allotted to it under the Act. These other duties include the consideration of preliminary drafts of regulations to be made under the National Insurance Acts, and of representations received thereon. When the regulations are laid before Parliament, the Committee's Report on the preliminary draft is laid with them, together with a statement by the Minister showing what amendments to the preliminary draft have been made, what effect has been given to the Committee's recommendations, and, if effect has not been given to any recommendation, the reasons for not adopting it. The Minister may also refer to the Committee for consideration and advice any questions relating to the operation of the Acts (including questions as to the advisability of amending the Acts).

Chairman, Sir Ifor Evans.

Members, H. Collison, C.B.E.; J. A. Faris; Mrs. I. M. Howell, C.B.E.; J. C. Lennox, O.B.E.; H. M. D. Parker, C.B., C.B.E.; Sir Richard Sneddon, C.B.E.; Prof. R. M. Titmuss; N. C. Turner.

Secretary, R. Dronfield.

INDUSTRIAL INJURIES ADVISORY COUNCIL

10 John Adam Street, W.C.2

[Whitehall: 9066]

The Industrial Injuries Advisory Council, established under the National Insurance (Industrial Injuries) Act, 1946, considers and advises the Minister of Pensions and National Insurance on the Regulations proposed under the Act, and on other questions which the Minister refers to it.

Chairman, Prof. Sir Arnold Plant.

Members, A. Bridges; S. Chapman, C.B.E.; W. L. Clarke, C.B.E.; C. R. Dale; E. C. Happold; T. A. E. Layborn, C.B.E.; Prof. R. E. Lane, C.B.E.; G. H. Lowthian, C.B.E.; J. L. McQuitty, Q.C.; S. A. S. Malkin, C.B.E.; A. Martin; J. G. C. Milligan; Dr. D. G. Morgan, O.B.E.; Dr. L. G. Norman, C.B.E.; L. Sharp, M.B.E.; Dr. Alice M. Stewart; W. Taylor, C.B.

Secretary, T. A. Howell.

NATIONAL INSURANCE JOINT AUTHORITY

1 Adam Street, W.C.2

[Whitehall: 9066]

Members, The Minister of Pensions and National Insurance; the Minister of Labour and National Insurance for Northern Ireland.

Deputies, Sir Eric Bowyer, K.C.B., K.B.E.; D. C. H. Abbot, C.B.; J. E. Greeves; H. A. Lowry.

Joint Financial Advisers, H. Tetley, C.B.; D. Overend; J. E. Aiken.

Secretary, D. J. Carter.

WORKMEN'S COMPENSATION SUPPLEMENTATION BOARD and PNEUMOCONIOSIS AND BYSSINOSIS BENEFIT BOARD

Thames House South, Millbank, S.W.1

[Abbey: 1200]

Chairman, D. M. Campbell, Q.C.

Deputy Chairman, Sir George Honeyman, C.B.E., Q.C.

Members, P. E. Coxhead; H. Hewitt, O.B.E.; J. C. Hobbs; A. Martin; R. Pilkington; L. G. Reffell.

Secretary, C. W. F. Gower.

OFFICE OF THE CHIEF INSURANCE OFFICER FOR NATIONAL INSURANCE

287 High Holborn, W.C.1

[Chancery: 9020]

Chief Insurance Officer, Mrs. E. M. Kemp-Jones £3,815

Principal, J. H. Ward.......... £1,959 to £2,711

Chief Executive Officers, J. L. Oxlade; S. H. Duckering...................... £2,237 to £2,572

OFFICE OF THE REGISTRAR OF NON-PARTICIPATING EMPLOYMENTS

287 High Holborn, W.C.1

[Chancery: 9020]

Registrar, K. R. Malcolm....... £2,865 to £3,565

Deputy Registrar, A. J. Ashman.. £2,237 to £2,572

OFFICE OF THE NATIONAL INSURANCE COMMISSIONER

6 Grosvenor Gardens, S.W.1

[Sloane: 9236]

23 Melville Street, Edinburgh 3

[Edinburgh Caledonian: 2201]

7 Park Place, Cardiff

[Cardiff: 32623]

The Commissioner is the final Statutory Authority to decide claims under the Family Allowances Acts, the National Insurance Acts and the National Insurance (Industrial Injuries) Acts.

Commissioner, R. G. Micklethwait, Q.C.

Deputy Commissioners, N. P. d'Albuquerque; G. Owen George; H. A. Shewan, O.B.E., Q.C.; H. I. Nelson, Q.C.; D. W. E. Neligan, O.B.E.; R. G. Clover, T.D., Q.C.; D. Reith, Q.C.

Legal Assistants, J. R. C. Walford, M.B.E.; The Lord Swinfen; Mrs. C. R. Corbett.

Secretary, A. G. Atkinson.

POLITICAL HONOURS SCRUTINY COMMITTEE

H.M. Treasury, Great George Street, S.W.1

[Whitehall: 1234]

Chairman, The Lord Crathorne, P.C. T.D.

Members, The Lord Williams of Barnburgh, P.C.; The Lord Rea, P.C., O.B.E.

Secretary, Sir Robert Knox, K.C.B., K.C.V.O., D.S.O.

PORT OF LONDON AUTHORITY

Head Office, Trinity Square, E.C. 3

[Royal: 2000]

The Port of London Authority, established under the Port of London Act, 1908 (8 Edw. VII. c. 68), on the 31st March, 1909, for the purpose of administering, preserving, and improving the Port of London, consists of 28 members—10 appointed and 18 elected, with a Chairman and Vice-Chairman appointed by the Authority; these offices may (but need not be) filled by an elected or appointed member.

The following undertakings were transferred to the Port Authority as from the 31st March, 1909:—Thames Conservancy (all rights, powers and duties of the Conservators of the Thames in respect of the river below Teddington); London and India Docks Company; Surrey Commercial Dock Company; Millwall Dock Company; and Watermen's Company, except certain property and funds. The working of the Port for the year ended March 31, 1963 showed a surplus of £326,909, leaving a surplus balance of £803,098 carried forward.

Chairman, The Viscount Simon, C.M.G.

Vice-Chairman, The Lord Cottesloe, G.B.E., T.D.

Appointed Members

By the Admiralty, Vice-Admiral Sir Archibald Day, K.B.E., C.B., D.S.O.; *By the Ministry of Transport*; B. Fry; The Lord Cottesloe, G.B.E., T.D.; *By the Corporation of London*, S. G. Gates, C.B.E.; T. K. Collett, C.B.E.; *By the London County Council*, The Lord Macpherson of Drumochter; T. O'Leary, O.B.E.; N. W. Farmer, C.B.E.; E. E. Woods, O.B.E.; *By Trinity House*, Capt. G. C. H. Noakes, R.D., R.N.(*ret.*).

Elected Members

(Eighteen members are elected by payers of rates, wharfingers and owners of rivercraft.)

C. F. B. Arthur; J. S. Bevan; Sir David Burnett, Bt., M.B.E., T.D.; H. M. Gordon Clark; W. Frame; G. D. Hodge; W. C. Longstaff; Sir Herbert McDavid, C.B.E.; J. McLean, C.B.E.; D. F. Martin-Jenkins, T.D.; Sir Ralph Metcalfe; J. M. M. Meyer; G. Milling; C. D. Scriven; H. G. Sorrell, O.B.E;. Sir John Tait; M. T. Turnbull; A. Lawrence Williams.

Officers

General Manager, Sir Leslie Ford, O.B.E.
Joint Deputy General Managers, P. W. J. Martin, M.B.E.; G. D. G. Perkins.
Chief Engineer, G. A. Wilson.
Chief Accountant, E. P. J. Lunch.
Solicitor and Secretary, A. G. Robinson.
River Superintendent and Harbour Master, Cmdr. G. V. Parmiter, R.N. (*ret.*).
Establishment Officer, A. L. Leach.
Chief Information Officer, E. W. King.
Chief Police Officer, T. J. Oliver, O.B.E.
Supplies Officer, E. T. F. Hubbard.
Estate Officer, H. W. Ellis.
Medical Officer, A. M. Lawrence-Smith.
Commercial Superintendent, H. A. Lingwood.
Traffic Superintendent, G. W. Smith.
Research Officer, R. J. Sadler.
Staff Relations Officer, E. J. Enderby.

Docks and Warehouses, etc.

London and St. Katharine Docks, Superintendent, C. Gosling; *Dockmaster*, Capt. F. A. C. Bishop.
Surrey Commercial Docks, Superintendent. G. A. G. Ansell; *Dockmaster*, Capt. E. V. Henday.
India and Millwall Docks, Superintendent, E. S. Tooth; *Dockmaster*, Capt. W. G. Lloyd.
Royal Victoria, Albert and King George V. Docks, Superintendent, K. R. Oakley; *Dockmaster*, Capt. H. E. Morison, D.S.C.
Tilbury Docks, Superintendent, G. W. Watkins; *Dockmaster*, E. Ashworth.
Railway Dept., Superintendent, G. E. D. Toomey.

Australia and New Zealand

42 Bridge Street, Sydney, N.S.W.
Representative, W. C. Perkins.

South Africa and Southern Rhodesia

P.O. Box 3034, Cape Town
Representative, W. H. A. Webster, C.I.E.

THE POST OFFICE

St. Martin's-le-Grand, E.C.1
[Headquarters: 1234]

Postmaster General, RT. HON. (JOHN) REGINALD BEVINS, M.P. £5,000
Principal Private Secretary, T. C. Carpenter.
Assistant Private Secretaries, Miss R. O. Corke; N. M. Johnson.
Parliamentary Private Secretary, G. R. Matthews, M.P.
Assistant Postmaster General, R. L. Mawby, M.P. £2,500
Director General, Sir Ronald German, C.M.G. £6,950
Private Secretary, M. Morris.
Deputy Directors General, Sir Robert Harvey, K.B.E., C.B.; W. A. Wolverson, C.B. £4,950
Deputy Director General and Comptroller and Accountant General, Sir Kenneth Anderson, K.B.E., C.B. £4,950
Engineer-in-Chief, Sir Albert Mumford, K.B.E. £5,750
Director of Postal Services, Brig. K. S. Holmes, C.B., C.B.E. £4,050
Director of Inland Telecommunications, A. W. C. Ryland £4,050
Director of External Telecommunications Executive, Col. D. McMillan, C.B., O.B.E. £4,050
Director of Radio Services, A. Wolstencroft, C.B. £4,050
Director of Establishments and Organization, H. A. Daniels £4,050
Director of Personnel, J. M. Newton......... £4,050
Director of Finance and Accounts, E. W. Shepherd £4,050
Director of Clerical Mechanization and Buildings, A. H. Ridge £4,050

Administrative Departments

Assistant Secretaries, A. Hibbs; S. Horrox, E.R.D.; R. J. S. Baker; J. T. Baldry; Miss P. Bridger, M.B.E.; H. N. Pickering, O.B.E.; G. H. Coates, M.B.E.; D. C. Balaam; R. Martin, M.B.E.; H. G. Lillicrap; M. O. Tinniswood; C. R. Smith, O.B.E.; K. Hind, E.R.D.; Mrs. M. Swaffield; D. G. C. Lawrence, O.B.E.; C. E. Lovell; H. A. Longley; L. Hill; R. J. Broadbent; E. F. H. Gould; J. O. Thompson; D. Wesil; W. A. Kirkpatrick £2,800 to £3,500
Principals, N. A. Perkins; E. E. Wilkins, E.R.D.; J. F. Parry; B. L. Savage; P. W. F. Fryer; A. V. Leaver; E. Sharpe, M.B.E.; T. C. Carpenter; G. H. G. Tilling; Miss D. J. Fothergill; T. U. Meyer; L. T. Andrew; J. L. Judd; D. E. Baptiste; A. H. Mowatt; T. P. Hornsey; J. V. R. Birchall; F. H. Goldsmith; J. M. Morris, M.B.E.; *J. Hodgson; J. E. Golothan, T.D., E.R.D.; A. G. Smith; Miss C. Kennedy; Mrs. D. E. Mitchell; Miss P. A. Peverett; D. P. Wratten; Miss E. A. Knight; E. H. Truslove; H. G. Corpe; G. McMorran; N. E. A. Moore; R. W. Story, D.F.C.; T. Scott; Miss S. P. M. Fisher; J. R. Baxter; H. Beastall; J. M. Harper; J. M. Norman; R. A. Giles; R. A. Neate; K. C. Lawrance; G. J. Pocock; D. Pearman; A. P. Hawkins; R. A. Browne; Miss C. L. Crump; J. F. Hanson; Miss J. M. Emery; B. Traynor; B. T. Wright; F. Lawson; H. D. Bickley; N. A. Hawkins; A. G. Brown; K. F. Leeson; D. J. Kinder; C. H. Briscoe .... £1,894 to £2,646
Senior Chief Executive Officers, N. O. Johnson; R. Davies .... £2,618 to £2,800
Chief Executive Officers, J. E. Sayers; R. H. Jebb; G. W. Shepheard; C. H. Selby; H. A. Fricker; L. W. Addis; J. Evans; G. J. N. Bolster; D. H. Sutcliffe; A. O. Martin; R. C. Catterson; F. G. Phillips; Miss D. E. A. Furbank; R. W. Groves; W. W. Norris; A. A. Mead; L. C. Brunning; A. E. Endecott; I. H. Slee; A. M. James; H. G. Robson; R. J. Johnson; J. W. Judd; K. H. Maunder; Miss J. M. Milne.. £2,172 to £2,507
Senior Executive Officers, R. J. Boone; D. G. Clarke; H. W. Bray; R. V. Hatton; J. W. Morris; W. S. Ryan; S. T. B. Johns; A. J. Walmsley; H. A. J. Logan; R. O. Bradbury; E. H. Garner, M.B.E.; Miss W. A. Purnell; M. D. L. Bevis; A. O. Carter; R. J. Boggis; P. E. A. Faulkner; R. J. Johnson; A. L. Evans; G. H. Aldridge; R. V. T. Pryor; L. G. Hart; G. A. L. Everitt; Miss M. G. E. Newman; Miss E. A. Scillitoe; A. R. Marsh; Miss P. M. James; E. V. Hills; Miss H. Whaley; J. E. Link; Miss M. M. McLauchlan; F. R. Massy; C. B. Davis; Miss H. I. Robinson; Miss M. M. Randall; S. G. Munday; G. R. Brandon .... £1,615 to £2,061
Headquarters Inspector of Clerical Establishments, N. H. Harper......(+*allce.*) £1,615 to £2,061

Postal Inspectorate

Chief Inspector, W. C. Harvey............£3,150
Deputy Chief Inspectors, C. H. Rose; B. G. Genn; D. J. McDougall............£2,618 to £2,950
Postal Controller, R. O. Bonnett £2,618 to £2,950
Assistant Postal Controllers, Class I, V. C. Lucas; A. G. Gomm; H. S. Hughes; W. J. Rowe; A. Heaton; V. A. Huckerby; S. V. F. Hurrell; J. H. B. Cantley; D. M. Elliott; A. McRobert; A. G. Scott; M. W. Colgan; K. A. Fowler; L. H. Kingsbury; J. J. Wheatley; I. Barr; R. V. Watkins; B. D. Chainey; P. B. Milne £1,853 to £2,423

Telecommunications Sales Establishment

Controller of Sales, A. Ashforth..£2,172 to £2,507
Assistant Controllers of Sales, C. A. Richardson; R. M. Watson; P. A. Long; R. W. Clarke £1,615 to £2,061

Wireless Telegraph Establishment

Inspector, R. M. Billington, T.D. £2,800 to £3,150
Deputy Inspectors, W. Swanson; G. H. M. Gleadle £2,184 to £2,472
Assistant Inspectors, A. Whalley; G. F. Wilson; R. Wilson; R. M. Gibson....£1,720 to £2,180

Public Relations Department

Public Relations Officer, T. A. O'Brien, C.B.E. £3,750 (*personal*)
Deputy to Public Relations Officer, F. B. Savage £2,618 to £2,800
Controller of Publicity, A. H. Endecott £2,172 to £2,507
Principal Information Officers, E. J. Grove; K. J. Ley £2,172 to £2,507
Senior Information Officers, W. H. Armitage; B. Hogben..................£1,615 to £2,061
Assistant Controllers of Publicity, H. G. Petherick; W. J. Rawles............ £1,615 to £2,061

External Telecommunications Executive

Director, Col. D. McMillan, C.B., O.B.E.....£4,050
Deputy Directors, J. T. Baldry; E. F. H. Gould; J. O. Thompson...............£2,800 to £3,500
Deputy Director (Operations), H. Leigh.....£3,150
Staff Controller, C. H. G. Eburne, M.B.E. £2,618 to £2,950
Asst. Controllers, Lt.-Col. D. T. Gibbs, M.V.O., O.B.E., T.D.; R. W. Chandler, M.B.E.; A. T. Gray £2,172 to £2,507
Telegraph Manager, R. A. Harrison........£2,681
Deputy Telegraph Manager, E. Bowden.....£2,451

Investigation Branch

Controller, C. G. Osmond, O.B.E.........£3,150
Deputy Controller, A. C. Hawksworth £2,542 to £2,800
Asst. Controllers, R. J. Mitchell; W. G. Sharp; R. F. Yates....................£2,109 to £2,434
Senior Investigation Officers, W. H. C. Thomas, M.B.E., T.D.; W. J. Edwards; C. J. Saunders; B. A. E. Evans; J. Johnston; E. J. Passmore; W. Bowles; P. E. Whetter; F. A. Carr; A. J. Foster; J. B. Taylor; F. S. Upton; J. M. Murray; G. Woodin; J. Culbert; K. J. Thomas; F. A. Harper; W. I. Shaw; E. C. Comerford; W. S. Marsh; A. A. Darke; J. G. Jacquest; W. Tulip; F. L. Cook; D. L. Jeffery; K. Havard £1,568 to £2,001

Joint Post Office—Ministry of Works Research Development Group

Lambeth Bridge House, Albert Embankment, S.E.1

Deputy Regional Director in Charge, C. McCarthy £3,150
Assistant Staff Engineers, A. W. Hall; D. J. Harris £2,339 to £2,660
Assistant Postal Controllers, Class I, H. S. Hughes; D. G. J. Wilkey, D.S.C.......£1,853 to £2,423
Senior Executive Officer (Finance), Accountant General's Department, C. E. Steele.....£1,615 to £2,061

Accountant General's Department

Deputy Director General and Comptroller and Accountant General, Sir Kenneth Anderson, K.B.E., C.B. £4,950
Director of Finance and Accounts, E. W. Shepherd £4,050
Chief Statistician, S. Wood.....£2,800 to £3,500
Deputy Director of Finance (Policy), H. G. Lillicrap £2,800 to £3,500
Deputy Directors of Finance and Accounts, H. W. Barnes; N. F. Tolman; J. W. Grady....£3,150
Senior Chief Executive Officers, E. C. Shanks; A. J. Levell; C. E. Haynes, D.F.C.; R. C. Westlake; K. S. Nash; D. S. Nagle....£2,618 to £2,800
Principals, P. W. F. Fryer; B. Traynor £1,894 to £2,646
Statisticians, P. J. Lane; M. L. M. Neifield; J. H. Hayter; R. A. Hastie; N. A. Perkins £1,894 to £2,646
Chief Executive Officers, H. V. Holden; W. J. F. Wells; D. Slater; R. Murray; W. H. Durant; C. E. Beauchamp; T. S. Cocker; R. J. Stormer £2,172 to £2,507
Senior Executive Officers, Miss C. E. Skelton; E. S. Pritchard; R. Brumby; J. H. Outhwaite; W. F. Smith; C. A. E. Chandler (+ *allce.*); L. A. Marsh; Miss G. J. Gobby; W. D. Boyling; J. Roberts; J. V. Bond; Miss R. L. Spencer; J. Hall; E. J. Walton; G. P. Olver; R. J. J. Hunt; P. Wade; T. W. Woolmore; Miss S. R. Muir; C. E. Steele; Miss I. R. Fenning; P. D. Badrock; W. A. S. Verbi; I. S. Davies, A.F.C.; Miss E. A. Lovelock; A. W. Jones; E. R. H. Perry; E. C. Wood; C. C. W. White; G. Cramp; S. A. Owen; J. D. Norton; S. D. Selway; E. L. Graves £1,615 to £2,061

Engineering Department

Engineer-in-Chief, Sir Albert Mumford, K.B.E. £5,750
Deputy Engineer-in-Chief, D. A. Barron, C.B.E. £4,050
Director of Research, R. J. Halsey, C.M.G....£4,050
Asst. Engineers-in-Chief, R. E. Jones, M.B.E.; H. Williams; C. E. Calveley, O.B.E., E.R.D.; J. H. H. Merriman, O.B.E....................£3,750
Deputy Directors of Research, G. H. Metson, M.C., D.SC.; H. Stanesby.....................£3,750
Staff Controller (Engineer-in-Chief's Office), W. J. Manning..................£2,618 to £2,950
Chief Engineer (Scotland), (Edinburgh), R. J. Hines £2,800 to £3,150
Chief Engineer (Wales and Border Counties), (Cardiff), D. C. Blair...............£2,800 to £3,150
Chief Regional Engineers, G. S. Berkeley; Lt.-Col. J. Baines, O.B.E.; Lt.-Col. F. N. Lucas, E.R.D.; G. M. Mew; S. J. Edwards; A. H. C. Knox; W. L. A. Coleman; C. A. L. Nicholls, O.B.E. £2,800 to £3,150
Regional Engineer and Telecommunications Controller (Northern Ireland), (Belfast), J. Knox £2,339 to £2,660
Staff Engineers, L. F. Scantlebury; T. H. Flowers, M.B.E.; R. S. Phillips; R. H. Franklin, E.R.D.; R. O. Carter; J. J. Edwards; R. A. Brockbank, O.B.E., Ph.D.; F. J. D. Taylor, O.B.E.; W. J. E. Tobin; L. F. Salter; A. Cook; J. W. H. Freebody; E. W. Anderson; H. T. Mitchell; W. J. Bray; G. N. Davison; J. Balcombe; H. E. Francis; J. Rhodes, M.B.E.; N. C. C. de Jong; C. W. Sowton, O.B.E.; J. A. Lawrence; R. O. Boocock; H. B. Law; T. Kilvington; H. Barker; W. H. Maddison, T.D.............£2,800 to £3,150
Chief Executive Officers (Engineers-in-Chief's Office), H. K. Kirby; S. A. Norris...£2,172 to £2,507
Senior Executive Officers (Engineer-in-Chief's Office), H. T. B. Bourn; Miss J. M. Root; A. F. R. Sturges; Miss D. M. Roope; J. Smith; N. L. Faulkner; R. A. Attrill; T. R. Parry; A. E. Merrony; W. B. Diamond..£1,615 to £2,061
Chief Motor Transport Officer, Lt.-Col. F. A. Hough, O.B.E.....................£2,800 to £3,150

Motor Transport Officers, Class I, E. L. Collman; P. E. Brownlow............£2,339 to £2,660
Submarine Supt., I. R. Finlayson. £2,800 to £3,150
Deputy Submarine Supt., J. P. F. Betson, O.B.E. £2,339 to £2,660
Commanders, O. R. Bates (+*allce.*) (*H.M.T.S. Monarch*); J. P. Ruddock, O.B.E. (+*allce*). (*H.M.T.S. Alert*); C. M. G. Evans, M.B.E. (*H.M.T.S. Ariel*); J. B. Smith (*H.M.T.S. Iris*) £1,871 to £2,363
Regional Engineers, H. F. Epps; A. J. Jackman; J. G. Straw; S. I. Brett; A. J. Leckenby, M.B.E.; P. R. Couch; F. Summers; R. MacWhirter; S. M. E. Rousell; P. R. W. Brock; S. D. Mellor; E. Blackburn; E. S. Rusbridge; H. S. Thomsett; F. Warren; W. Hawking; T. H. A. Mascall; J. Duff; A. J. Cawsey; F. C. Haliburton; C. G. Grant; A. M. Hunt; R. C. Devereux; E. Hoare; C. D. S. G. Robertson; L. A. Triffitt; W. E. Adams; T. J. Rees; G. A. Probert; G. C. Greenwood; H. C. Stevenson, M.B.E.; R. N. Palmer; W. L. Surman; R. P. Glover; T. Moxon; G. Jackson; Lt.-Col. J. E. Z. Bryden £2,339 to £2,660
Assistant Staff Engineers, R. W. Palmer; F. Hollinghurst; *W. G. N. Chew, O.B.E.; A. W. C. Pearson; D. A. Thorn; L. L. Hall; F. C. Mead; J. L. Creighton; R. H. Chapman; H. C. S. Hayes; R. S. Salt; A. E. Wood; G. Spears; W. C. Ward; E. C. H. Seaman; F. C. G. Greening; F. E. Williams; H. E. Wilcockson; C. F. Floyd; N. V. Knight; C. J. Cameron, I.S.O.; H. R. Brown; E. F. S. Clarke; S. Welch; G. E. Styles; J. Piggott; L. K. Wheeler; F. Scowen; D. E. Watt-Carter; A. C. Hales; F. W. J. Webber; R. W. Hopwood; M. H. James; E. C. Swain; R. W. White; W. D. Cooper; T. F. A. Urben; T. C. Harding; A. J. Forty; D. L. Richards; W. A. Humphries; A. J. Thompson; W. T. Duerdoth; W. B. Jago; R. N. Renton, E.R.D.; J. Smith; G. P. Copping; J. K. S. Jowett; R. L. Corke; J. C. Billen; D. G. Jones; W. H. Lee; J. P. Harding; H. Knee, E.R.D.; R. K. Hayward; J. F. Bampton; M. B. Williams; S. C. Gordon; R. O. Bennett; M. Mitchell, M.B.E., E.R.D.; N. Walker; W. J. Smith; A. C. Eley; T. Pilling; A. E. Jemmeson; B. R. Horsfield; C. F. Davidson; Dr. P. R. Bray; A. W. Hall; S. G. Young; D. Wray; L. R. F. Harris; G. J. Alston; J. S. Whyte; N. B. Rymer, M.B.E.; F. G. Balcombe; J. E. Haworth, M.B.E.; D. B. Balchin; C. E. E. Clinch; A. C. Frost; D. J. Harris; C. A. M. May; T. Nicholson..................£2,339 to £2,660
Senior Principal Scientific Officers (*Engineer-in-Chief's Office*), R. J. F. Jarvis, Ph.D.; N. W. J. Lewis, Ph.D.; J. R. Tillman, D.Sc., A. C. Lynch; E. A. Speight, Ph.D.; M. F. Holmes £2,800 to £3,150
Principal Scientific Officers (*Engineer-in-Chief's Office*), A. W. M. Coombs, Ph.D.; A. Fairweather, Ph.D.; R. Taylor, Ph.D.; H. D. Bickley; E. V. Walker; R. L. Bull; E. W. Ayers; F. F. Roberts; W. E. Thomson; E. F. Rickard; J. M. Linke, Ph.D.; H. G. Bassett; J. I. Carasso; W. W. Chandler; A. A. New; E. S. Parkes; D. C. Shotton; J. H. Ellis; F. H. Reynolds; I. F. Macdiarmid; J. C. Harrison, Ph.D.; R. W. Lawson; H. N. Daglish, Ph.D.; M. M. Faktor, Ph.D......................£1,839 to £2,590
Chief Experimental Officers (*Engineer-in-Chief's Office*), H. J. Bowcott; P. E. Taylor, Ph.D. £2,117 to £2,451
Inspector of Drawing Offices, R. J. Jury £1,955 to £2,196
Chief Draughtsmen (*Engineer-in-Chief's Office*), E. C. Benstead; R. G. White; L. M. Pusey £1,615 to £1,950

* On loan to another Government Department.

London Postal Region

Director, G. R. Downes..................£4,050
Deputy Regional Director, F. G. Fielder.....£3,150
Controllers, W. Pounder; E. G. White; P. Dunn, M.B.E., E.R.D.; G. S. Pitman; D. E. Roberts, M.B.E........................£2,618 to £2,950
Staff Controller, L. P. Palmer...£2,618 to £2,950
Chief Regional Engineer, G. M. Mew £2,800 to £3,150
Regional Finance Officer, A. F. Andrews £2,618 to £2,800
Chief Executive Officer (*Deputy Staff Controller*), L. F. Weatherhead..........£2,172 to £2,507
Assistant Controllers, A. E. Chappell; J. L. T. Buckley; R. B. Trowbridge; W. R. Ward; J. M. Mudd; R. Brown; H. S. Boddy; S. T. Hodges; J. M. Richards; F. W. B. Gaunt; R. K. Francis; E. A. Lovegrove; S. J. Bowskill; D. Shaw; S. G. Dawkins; A. R. E. Bowles...£2,172 to £2,507
Chief Supts., G. M. Pollock; W. Shires; G. H. A. Newell; R. Askew; F. J. S. Crabb; B. H. Stroud £2,172 to £2,507
Senior Executive Officers, L. F. Burr; S. H. Gilbert; S. R. Weston; A. G. Chandler; R. E. Hails; A. Smith; C. V. Bell; F. H. Collingbourne; G. T. Woods; G. J. Norton; C. J. Blowers; J. Orr; A. D. Price................£1,615 to £2,061
Regional Inspector of Clerical Establishments, L. W. Hinton....................£1,615 to £2,061
Chief Welfare Officer, J. L. Henderson £1,615 to £2,061
Regional Engineer, T. H. A. Mascall £2,339 to £2,660
Court Postmaster, W. A. King

North and South Postal Engineering Sections

Senior Executive Engineers, S. E. Pugh; D. W. Roy £1,671 to £2,200

Metropolitan District Offices

West Central, 181 High Holborn, W.C.1
District Postmaster, B. Charlton..£2,172 to £2,507
Western, 1a Wimpole Street, W.1
District Postmaster, R. L. Jeffery £2,172 to £2,507
Paddington, London Street, W.2
District Postmaster, G. C. Flagg..£2,172 to £2,507
Eastern, 206 Whitechapel Road, E1.
District Postmaster, G. G. Bremner £2,172 to £2,507
South-Western, 9 Howick Place, Victoria Street, S.W.1
District Postmaster (vacant)......£2,172 to £2,507
Battersea, 202 Lavender Hill, S.W.11
District Postmaster, L. C. E. Bennett £2,172 to £2,507
South-Eastern, 239 Borough High Street, S.E.1
District Postmaster, R. B. Salmon £2,172 to £2,507
Northern, 116 Upper Street, N.1
District Postmaster, W. E. Stygle. £2,172 to £2,507
North-Western, 220 Eversholt Street, N.W.1
District Postmaster, G. W. Robson £2,172 to £2,507

Post Office Savings Department

Director of Savings, H. W. Smart...........£4,050
Deputy Directors, J. Wiltshire; F. J. L. Clark, £3,150; R. F. Armstrong £2,900
Senior Chief Executive Officers, P. E. Plummer; J. P. Wilde; J. Higson; Miss B. K. Billot; H. R. West.....................£2,618 to £2,800
Chief Executive Officers, G. E. Peters; Miss R. Saint; Miss P. M. Dothie, M.B.E.; A. F. Johns; A. E. Webber; C. W. Hand; F. L. Picton; R. Bailey; M. Marshall; R. H. Dryden; G. W. Mantle; Miss J. A. Tapsfield; E. F. King; Mrs. M. Werrell £2,172 to £2,507
Senior Executive Officers, S. C. Blazdell (+*allce.*); Miss B. J. Wyvill; B. C. Smith, M.B.E.; Miss E. A. French; Miss C. S. Archer; S. J. Allison; K. G. Taylor; Miss B. A. Clair; R. G. Lock; R. Mills; T. A. Martin; M. Morris; S. A. Ingham; A. Green; Miss P. J. Bennett; R. McIlven; W. Buckley; Miss K. D. Caffyn; D. M.

Jones; Miss E. F. Smith; C. F. Robertson; Miss C. N. Lall; C. M. Roberts; F. Shaw; F. H. Hill; R. F. Reville; Miss E. D. Boxhall; Miss M. A. Surguy; K. H. Denchfield; Miss L. M. Sykes; I. H. Smith; Miss M. R. Dawson; Miss E. A. Jackson; L. W. Sturt; R. S. Robinson; Miss V. G. Pollard; T. Wilson; Miss E. G. Kirk; C. F. H. Taylor; A. Watson; A. T. Perkins; J. Hilton; W. S. H. Wicks; Mrs. E. Milligan; R. J. F. Linsay; C. L. Dann; Miss F. A. Hayward; J. Saynor; F. W. Austin; Mrs. M. E. Broadbent; A. Hirst; G. E. Long; J. G. Booth £1,615 to £2,061

Inspectors of Clerical Establishments, Miss D. L. Cox; R. J. Bongard; J. M. Anderson; S. Green £1,615 to £2,061

Chief Welfare Officer, J. McChesney £1,615 to £2,061

Supplies Department

Controller, C. J. Gill ... £3,500

Deputy Controller (vacant) ... £2,950

Asst. Controllers, G. M. Punnett; L. L. Ellis; G. Luxton ... £2,618 to £2,800

Chief Executive Officers, R. E. T. Saunderson; C. A. Powis; J. H. Howard-Smith; H. A. Jenkinson; R. E. Carter ... £2,172 to £2,507

Senior Executive Officers, D. R. Busst; L. Carnie; W. W. W. H. Brown; J. Borlace; Miss E. I. Fallon; M. D. Cluse; W. L. Cooper; W. Williamson; K. R. Foskett; E. D. Cooper; D. H. Pratt; W. J. Tanner; R. Coles; E. A. Walling; V. H. Spurrier; G. E. Rugless; P. N. Tiffany; S. G. Hutton; R. H. Clarke ... £1,615 to £2,061

Solicitor's Department

Solicitor, J. P. Ricks ... £4,950

Principal Assistant Solicitor, P. Turner ... £4,050

Assistant Solicitors, A. T. Roberts; W. Vaughan Williams; A. R. C. Griffiths; C. B. Maxted; J. H. Weston; S. Rothstein .. £2,900 to £3,500

Senior Legal Assistants, A. G. E. Price; J. C. Fetherston; L. J. N. Stainton; D. Howells; B. A. Ritchie; E. L. Orkin; D. B. Broad; R. L. Johnstone; A. S. Alcock; R. H. Snell; C. L. Morrow; J. B. Collins; B. C. Gould; D. E. Follett; I. L. L. Jones; R. J. Harris; P. A. Sanderson; A. J. Harris; J. E. Levetus; W. B. Sneade ... £2,239 to £2,800

Senior Executive Officer, W. T. Adams £1,615 to £2,061

Factories Department

Controller, W. A. Hibberd ... £3,350

Deputy Controller, T. H. Southerton ... £2,800

Chief Factories Engineer, A. C. Croisdale £2,339 to £2,660

Factories Senior Executive Engineers, E. D. Forbes; F. A. L. Goddard (*London*); D. C. Smith (*Birmingham*) ... £1,671 to £2,200

Chief Executive Officer, J. V. Young £2,172 to £2,507

Senior Executive Officers, R. Harry; R. J. Tunnicliff (*London*); N. A. Hogarth (*Birmingham*) £1,615 to £2,061

Factory Managers, D. J. Woods (*London*) £2,507; R. A. Cooper (*Birmingham*), £2,507; T. Bradley (*Cwmcarn*), £2,233.

Contracts Department

Director, P. J. Mapplebeck ... £3,750

Deputy Director, R. Oliver ... £3,150

Assistant Directors, G. H. Arnold; E. Williams; T. J. Taylor; G. P. S. Coy ... £2,618 to £2,800

Principal Accountant, P. J. Bolton £2,418 to £2,750

Principal Technical Costs Officer, B. S. Burns, M.B.E. £2,228 to £2,563

Deputy Principal Accountant, E. Harmer (+*allce.*) £1,851 to £2,293

Chief Accountants, J. W. Breckenridge; S. H. G. Clarke; J. C. Gray; A. W. Webb £1,851 to £2,293

Senior Executive Officers, G. W. Hancock; L. Folds; L. Hudson; N. G. Carty; F. J. Giddins; J. R. Gregory; Miss D. M. Watson; Miss D. M. Williams; R. J. East; S. W. Saddington; Miss M. E. Cook ... £1,615 to £2,061

Senior Technical Cost Officers, W. A. H. Venus (+*allce.*); J. W. Horwood; M. S. Nodder; G. H. Roberts ... £1,559 to £2,089

Post Office Headquarters, Scotland

Director, W. H. Penny ... £3,750

Deputy Regional Director, E. T. Vallance ... £3,150

Postal Controller, J. S. Blake ... £2,542 to £2,950

Chief Regional Engineer, R. J. Hines £2,800 to £3,150

Telecommunications Controller, C. F. Perryman £2,542 to £2,950

Staff Controller, T. Frankland ... £2,542 to £2,950

Finance Officer (*and Chief Accountant for Scotland*), B. E. Hearn (+*allc.*) £2,542 to £2,800

Deputy Finance Officer, J. Anderson ... £2,284

Accountant (*Edinburgh*), W. Carr ... £2,284

Senior Executive Officers. E. Harrison; T. P. Taylor; Miss V. Smithies; E. W. Dixon £1,615 to £2,061

Solicitor, K. M. Croft-Gray.

Head Postmaster (*Glasgow*), K. E. F. Gowen, M.B.E. £3,025

Head Postmaster (*Edinburgh*), D. Stewart £2,629 to £2,800

Assistant Postal Controllers (*Class I*), W. W. Service; H. A. Greening; A. J. S. Wightman; K. S. Noble £1,853 to £2,423

Senior Assistant Controller of Telecommunications, H. Scarborough ... £1,853 to £2,423

Chief Telecommunications Superintendents, E. G. Crisp; E. R. P. Chant ... £1,615 to £2,061

Regional Inspector of Clerical Establishments, R. R. Golding ... £1,615 to £2,061

Regional Public Relations Officer, J. D. Drummond £1,615 to £2,061

Chief Welfare Officer, W. H. Procter £1,615 to £2,061

Regional Training Officer, J. Ferguson £1,615 to £2,061

Telephone Managers, *Aberdeen*, R. C. Birnie, M.B.E.; *Dundee*, R. B. Munro (£2,434 to £2,507); *Edinburgh*, I. Matheson (£2,622); *Glasgow*, M. W. Ramsay (£2,950); *Scotland West*, H. J. Revell £2,622

Post Office Headquarters, Northern Ireland

Director, Col. M. G. Holmes ... £3,500

Regional Engineer and Telecommunications Controller J. Knox ... £2,339 to £2,660

Staff Controller, D. Johnson ... £2,172 to £2,641

Finance Officer, G. H. Clemitson. £2,172 to £2,507

Senior Assistant Telecommunications Controller, W. D. Kay ... £1,853 to £2,423

Postal Controller, F. M. Ash ... £2,172 to £2,641

Assistant Postal Controller (*Class I*), J. R. Hall £1,853 to £2,423

Regional Public Relations Officer, S. G. Coulson £1,504 to £1,883

Regional Training Officer, H. Lawson £1,504 to £1,883

Chief Welfare Officer, L. W. H. Stevens £1,504 to £1,883

Head Postmaster, *Belfast*, J. C. Williams £2,686 to £2,800

Telephone Manager, *Belfast*, J. L. Howard ... £2,681

North-Eastern Region

Director, D. E. Knapman ... £3,750

Deputy Regional Director, F. W. Lister ... £3,150

Postal Controller, A. H. Woodland, E.R.D. £2,618 to £2,950

Chief Regional Engineer, Lt.-Col. J. Baines, O.B.E. £2,800 to £3,150

Telecommunications Controller, N. F. Sephton, O.B.E. £2,618 to £2,950

Staff Controller, P. S. Bell ... £2,618 to £2,950

Regional Finance Officer, P. D. H. King
£2,618 to £2,800
Assistant Postal Controllers (Class I), E. E. Mason; R. P. Hassell; J. R. Kibble; F. C. Buckley
£1,853 to £2,423
Senior Executive Officers, C. Fletcher; W. W. McKechnie.................£1,615 to £2,061
Senior Assistant Telecommunications Controller, H. S. Holmes.............£1,853 to £2,423
Chief Telecommunications Superintendent, W. W. Seed......................£1,615 to £2,061
Regional Inspector of Clerical Establishments, J. Murdoch..................£1,615 to £2,061
Regional Public Relations Officer, P. Frost
£1,615 to £2,061
Regional Training Officer, L. Wilson
£1,615 to £2,061
Chief Welfare Officer, W. C. Taylor
£1,615 to £2,061
Telephone Managers.—Bradford, J. Dixon; *Leeds*, J. P. Bell (*each* £2,681); *Lincoln*, F. O. Watson; *Middlesbrough*, Col. J. R. Sutcliffe, O.B.E., T.D. (*each* £2,507); *Newcastle*, H. A. Harman (£2,681); *Sheffield*, J. D. H. Martin; *York*, H. A. Clibbon
each £2,507

North-Western Region

Director, J. V. Greenlaw..................£3,750
Deputy Regional Director, E. E. Neal........£3,150
Postal Controller, L. E. Nice.....£2,618 to £2,950
Telecommunications Controller, R. R. Walker
£2,618 to £2,950
Chief Regional Engineer, Lt.-Col. F. N. Lucas
£2,800 to £3,150
Staff Controller, E. K. May......£2,618 to £2,950
Head Postmaster, Manchester, W. Scott, O.B.E.
£3,025
Head Postmaster, Liverpool, J. Johnstone.....£3,025
Regional Finance Officer, J. E. Morris
£2,618 to £2,800
Assistant Postal Controllers (Class I), R. Allen; A. G. Kruger; A. E. F. Lane; G. E. Duckett; E. W. Pearcey.............£1,853 to £2,423
Senior Assistant Telecommunications Controller, E. A. Petche...................£1,853 to £2,423
Chief Telecommunications Superintendents, J. H. W. Tatum; W. Palk; J. Ellison; A. Savage
£1,615 to £2,061
Senior Executive Officers, R. Arthur; C. R. Watts; O. J. Luker................£1,615 to £2,061
Regional Inspector of Clerical Establishments, S. F. Kelly....................£1,615 to £2,061
Regional Public Relations Officer, J. B. Crockatt
£1,615 to £2,061
Regional Training Officer, A. D. Burgoyne
£1,615 to £2,061
Chief Welfare Officer, F. Cowper £1,615 to £2,061
Telephone Managers.—Liverpool, H. C. Jones, O.B.E.; *Manchester*, H. W. Peddie, *each* £2,950; *Blackburn*, W. R. Beach; *Lancaster*, C. A. Atkinson; *Preston*, B. Lloyd................*each* £2,507

Home Counties Region

Director, A. Kemp, C.B.E.................£3,750
Deputy Directors, A. F. James (£2,800 to £3,500); L. J. Glanfield £3,150
Postal Controller, L. W. Higgins. £2,618 to £2,950
Telecommunications Controller, S. L. Holcombe
£2,618 to £2,950
Chief Regional Engineer, A. H. C. Knox
£2,800 to £3,150
Staff Controller, J. T. Beddoe... £2,618 to £2,950
Regional Finance Officer, T. E. Stappard
£2,618 to £2,800
Chief Executive Officers, L. Wilson; E. W. Smale
£2,172 to £2,507
Assistant Postal Controllers (Class I), W. E. Phillips; A. W. B. Strachan; H. R. H. White; P. J. Manson, M.C., E.R.D.; R. F. Haynes; W. F. Stacey....................£1,853 to £2,423
Senior Assistant Telecommunications Controllers, L. G. Hawker; V. F. B. Medland..£1,853 to £2,423
Chief Telecommunications Superintendents, R. S. Clippingdale; G. D. Curr; S. Wright; J. A. Hills
£1,615 to £2,061
Senior Executive Officers, W. J. Johnson; F. E. Bailey; Miss N. K. Simes; J. Tattersall; E. B. T. Williams ....£1,615 to £2,061
School Principal and Chief Regional Training Officer, A. F. J. Lee................£2,122 to £2,306
Regional Public Relations Officer, E. J. Lally
£1,615 to £2,061
Regional Training Officer, G. Davis
£1,615 to £2,061
Chief Welfare Officer, Miss M. E. Evans
£1,615 to £2,061
Regional Inspectors of Clerical Establishments, W. A. Lewington; R. E. Lack......£1,615 to £2,061
Telephone Managers.—Brighton, R. J. Cook £2,681; *Bedford*, H. Jeffs; *Cambridge*, S. J. Marsh; *Canterbury*, C. W. A. Kent; *Colchester*, R. N. Hamilton; *Guildford*, E. A. Mayne; *Norwich*, W. T. Warnock; *Oxford*, A. D. V. Knowers; *Portsmouth*, A. D. Neate; *Reading*, G. A. Bennet; *Southend*, G. Dawson; *Tunbridge Wells*, J. S. Meikleham.....................*each* £2,507

Midland Region

Director, H. T. W. Millar................£3,750
Deputy Regional Director, E. G. Hucker....£3,150
Postal Controller, P. J. W. de Grouchy
£2,618 to £2,950
Telecommunications Controller, R. E. Jordan
£2,618 to £2,950
Chief Regional Engineer, W. L. A. Coleman
£2,800 to £3,150
Staff Controller, T. H. Davies...£2,618 to £2,950
Head Postmaster, Birmingham, W. H. Blunt
£3,025
Regional Finance Officer, R. Lock £2,618 to £2,800
Assistant Postal Controllers (Class I), R. M. Clemence; W. G. Jones; D. J. Bartlett; A. B. Barlow; J. S. Newcomb.....£1,853 to £2,423
Senior Assistant Telecommunications Controller (vacant)..................£1,853 to £2,423
Chief Telecommunications Superintendents, R. Clinnick; R. Thompson.....£1,615 to £2,061
Senior Executive Officers, M. G. Sims; Miss B. E. Coggins; H. W. Izzard......£1,615 to £2,061
Regional Inspector of Clerical Establishments, J. A. Wilkinson................£1,615 to £2,061
Regional Public Relations Officer, W. J. Lewis
£1,615 to £2,061
Regional Training Officer, A. Roney
£1,615 to £2,061
Chief Welfare Officer, C. Hartless
£1,615 to £2,061
Telephone Managers.—Birmingham, E. W. Weaver, £2,950; *West Midland*, C. W. Lemmey; *Nottingham*, Lt.-Col. A. T. J. Beard, M.B.E. (*each* £2,681); *Coventry*, N. Gandon; *Stoke-on-Trent*, H. Todkill; *Leicester*, P. H. Paul; *Peterborough*, Lt.-Col. W. E. Gill, T.D..........*each* £2,507

Post Office Headquarters, Wales and Border Counties

Director, K. H. Cadbury, M.C............£3,750
Deputy Regional Director, F. R. B. Bucknall, E.R.D.
£3,150
Telecommunications Controller, H. C. Andrews
£2,618 to £2,950
Postal Controller, F. W. Guenier, M.B.E.
£2,618 to £2,950
Chief Regional Engineer, D. C. Blair
£2,800 to £3,150
Staff Controller, D. S. Pullin....£2,618 to £2,950
Finance Officer, D. J. Richman..£2,618 to £2,800
Assistant Postal Controllers (Class I), Lt.-Col. R. G. Treagus; K. Thomas; A. Fish £1,853 to £2,423
Senior Assistant Telecommunications Controller, R. F. Bradburn.................£1,853 to £2,423

Chief Telecommunications Superintendents, J. W. Moore; G. L. Wright........£1,615 to £2,061
Senior Executive Officers, C. E. Clifton; H. W. Lewis; J. M. G. Lynch, M.B.E..£1,615 to £2,061
Chief Welfare Officer, Col. H. R. Humphries, T.D. £1,615 to £2,061
Regional Public Relations Officer, J. T. Smith £1,615 to £2,061
Regional Training Officer, H. J. C. White £1,615 to £2,061
Inspector of Clerical Establishments, L. Davenport £1,615 to £2,061
Telephone Managers:—Cardiff, E L. Perkins, £2,681; *Swansea*, J. F. Hetzel; *Chester*, W. G. Luxton; *Shrewsbury*, F. Bate........*each* £2,507

South-Western Region

Director, S. Scott, O.B.E., M.C.............£3,750
Deputy Regional Director, G. H. Farnes......£3,150
Postal Controller, W. Park......£2,618 to £2,950
Telecommunications Controller, E. A. Bracken £2,618 to £2,950
Chief Regional Engineer, C. A. L. Nicholls, O.B.E. £2,800 to £3,150
Staff Controllers, D. C. Jones....£2,618 to £2,950
Finance Officer, D. W. Knott...£2,618 to £2,800
Assistant Postal Controllers (Class I), J. A. V. Teesdale; K. W. Mills; C. C. Warren..£1,853 to £2,423
Senior Assistant Telecommunications Controller, V. Roberts..................£1,853 to £2,423
Chief Telecommunications Superintendents, W. F. Westaway; B. E. Raker.....£1,615 to £2,061
Senior Executive Officers, G. E. Trusler; E. Jones; C. Beardsmore................£1,615 to £2,061
Regional Inspector of Clerical Establishments (vacant)
Regional Public Relations Officer, F. J. Hart £1,615 to £2,061
Regional Training Officer (vacant)
Chief Welfare Officer, R. D. Hope £1,615 to £2,061
Telephone Managers.—Bristol, M. E. Tufnail, £2,681; *Bournemouth*, W. R. Tyson, O.B.E.; *Southampton*, (vacant); *Taunton*, W. F. Hickox, E.R.D.; *Exeter*, H. G. Dean, O.B.E.; *Gloucester*, S. A. F. Adam; *Plymouth*, H. C. O. Stanbury (*each*) £2,507

London Telecommunications Region

Director, A. B. Harnden................£4,050
Deputy Regional Directors, H. M. Turner, O.B.E.; F. E. Jones..........................£3,150
Telecommunications Controllers, G. J. Millen; D. Smith....................£2618, to £2,950
Chief Regional Engineers, S. J. Edwards; G. S. Berkeley.................£2,800 to £3,150
Deputy Chief Regional Engineers, J. G. Straw; H. F. Epps..............(+*allce.*) £2,339 to £2,660
Staff Controller, E. W. Cross....£2,618 to £2,950
Deputy Staff Controllers, J. Bellew; D. C. Thompson £2,172 to £2,507
Regional Finance Officer, J. Baillie £2,618 to £2,800
Principal Telecommunications Superintendents, R. F. Bloxham; A. D. Rollings; S. R. Valentine; Lt.-Col. W. A. Stripp..........£2,172 to £2,507
Assistant Controller (Telegraphs), S. W. Dabbs £2,172 to £2,507
Senior Executive Officers, Miss L. A. Ralph; Miss K. N. Hunt; G. S. C. Page; Miss M. M. Wittich; Miss N. H. Howard; D. R. G. Kelly; H. G. McQ. Pullen; L. A. G. Clifford; E. C. Lloyd; J. A. Clarke; W. G. H. Russell; Miss D. R. Hill; A. J. W. Moss; D. M. McFarland; H. J. M. Huxley.....................£1,615 to £2,061
Telephone Manager, (Centre Area), C. W. Davies £2,950
Telephone Managers (other Areas), C. Turner; H. S. M. Hall; C. G. Brooks; H. M. de Borde; G. C. Goodman; C. R. Dancey; E. J. Markby; E. S. Loosemore.....................£2,681
Deputy Telephone Manager (Centre Area), S. A. T. Payne..............................£2,507
Deputy Telephone Managers (other Areas), C. H. Howard; J. Boyd, E.R.D.; W. H. Owens; D. F. Hamilton; G. E. Brett; T. Gibson; A. E. Bavin £2,451
Chief Telecommunications Superintendents, A. P. W. McCarthy; W. G. Aylett; W. H. Cleaves; E. W. Sansom; *J. L. Brooker; W. E. Tyzack; H. H. W. Merrick; L. W. Craft; J. D. Rollings, M.B.E.; E. A. Thorogood; L. B. Kerwin; R. C. Friend; R. N. Milton; R. J. G. Blackett, E.R.D.; E. W. M. Mann; C. Bell; H. S. Cooper; G. R. Clayton; E. W. G. Knight; S. H. P. Croft; R. F. Gurney; A. H. Donnell; W. L. Starling £1,615 to £2,061
Chief Sales Superintendents, A. E. Jones; H. A. Morris; F. Barber; M. G. Bonar; A. J. Weston; A. E. L. Roylance; *W. A. Lloyd; K. J. Bullingham; P. H. Toy; R. F. Chesher; L. W. Dixon £1,615 to £2,061
Chief Clerks (Senior Executive Officers), Miss O. M. Kinnard (£1,568 to £1,947); F. W. Bucknell; L. J. Ray; W. R. Parry; H. E. Bromley; G. E. Price; W. W. Armstrong; F. A. Ascott; Miss N. D. L. Hollman..(+*allce.*) £1,615 to £2,061
Regional Training Officer, J. R. Brunton £1,615 to £2,061
Chief Welfare Officer, E. M. McEvoy £1,615 to £2,061
Regional Public Relations Officer, C. E. Conway-Gordon...............£1,615 to £2,061
Regional Engineers, S. I. Brett; H. M. W. Ackerman; S. M. E. Rousell; C. G. Grant; R. C. Devereux; A. J. Jackman; Lt.-Col. J. E. Z. Bryden £2,271 to £2,590
Senior Executive Engineers, W. S. Mabe; H. J. S. I. Mason; R. H. Crooks; W. H. Lamb; R. C. W. Walker; E. M. Gleadle-Richards; J. A. Sheppard; L. W. Medcalf; D. M. Rogers; G. E. Alexander; R. J. A. Eagle; J. D. Rae; T. J. Morgan £1,671 to £2,200
Area Engineers, G. E. Smith; E. B. M. Beaumont; J. Prescott; H. T. A. Sharpe; A. B. Cooper; C. N. Smith; A. Blight; L. R. Watson; L. G. Wootten; W. T. Wooding; E. Palk; S. J. Mayo; C. A. Pride; R. W. G. Carden; F. C. Gould-Bacon; L. P. Johnson; C. A. Morgan; R. J. Griffiths; C. E. C. Watling; L. W. Rapkin; A. E. J. Sims; D. E. Wadeson; F. J. Smith; B. H. Moore; J. G. Donovan; D. G. Pocock; E. McDowell; S. Davis; J. R. G. Smith; A. M. Stonebanks, M.B.E.; D. J. Marks; W. E. Chisnall......£1,671 to £2,200

* On loan to another Government Department.

MINISTRY OF POWER

Thames House South, Millbank, S.W.1

[Abbey: 7000]

The Ministry of Power has a general responsibility for the fuel and power industries and for iron and steel. The Minister appoints the boards in the nationalised coal, electricity and gas industries and their capital investment plans and programmes of research are subject to his approval. The Ministry is responsible for Government relations with the petroleum industry. The Minister appoints the Iron and Steel Board which has the oversight of the development of that industry and which has also certain powers to control prices. The Minister has a statutory responsibility for safety and health in mines and quarries, a function which he discharges largely through the Inspectorate of Mines and Quarries. Under the Chief Scientist to the Ministry, the work of the Safety in Mines Research Establishment reflects the Minister's special responsibility in this field. The Minister is also responsible for the licensing and inspection of nuclear installations (other than those of the Atomic Energy Authority or of other Governments Departments) in England and Wales with particular reference to safety. Since 1962 the construction and operation of pipe-lines has also been subject to his control.

Minister of Power, RT. HON. RICHARD WOOD, M.P. £5,000
Private Sec., D. Eagers.
Parliamentary Private Secretary, F. J. P. Lilley, M.P. (*unpaid*)
Parliamentary Secretary, J. W. W. Peyton, M.P. £2,500
Secretary, Sir Dennis Proctor, K.C.B. £7,015
Private Sec., R. Mountfield.
Deputy Secretaries, M. P. Murray, C.B.; M. Stevenson, C.B., C.M.G. £5,015
Chief Scientist, C. M. Cawley, C.B.E., D.SC. Ph.D. £5,015
Deputy Chief Scientific Officers, L. H. Leighton; R. G. Voysey ....£3,340 to £3,665
Under Secretaries, J. A. Beckett, C.M.G.; P. Chantler, C.M.G.; D. H. Crofton, O.B.E.; G. H. Daniel, C.B.; B. Gottlieb; A. A. Jarratt; E. J. Meadon, C.B.; A. M. Rake, C.B.E.; K. L. Stock, C.B. ... £4,115
Assistant Secretaries, J. R. Baker, C.B.E.; W. R. G. Bell; A. C. Campbell; R. E. L. Cleaver; E. J. C. Dixon, I.S.O.; J. W. Farrell; C. I. K. Forster; M. R. Garner; L. J. Goss; H. J. Gummer; J. R. Jenkins; N. E. Martin, D.F.C.; A. H. Norris; A. B. Powell; W. C. C. Rose, C.B.E.; H. Scholes; Mrs. J. M. Spencer, C.B.E.; C. G. Thorley; D. J. Turner, C.B.E.; R. Wakefield; J. R. Wilson £2,865 to £3,565
Chief Engineering Inspector, A. H. F. Linton. £3,565
Chief Fuel Inspector, F. C. Lant, O.B.E. £3,465
Chief Information Officer, H. P. Haddow, O.B.E., M.C. £2,683 to £2,865
Pipe-lines Inspector, W. M. C. Jones £2,293 to £2,628

Mines Inspectorate

Chief Inspector of Mines and Quarries, H. S. Stephenson £4,415
Deputy Chief Inspectors of Mines and Quarries, W. Brown; R. H. Clough, O.B.E.; G. Hoyle, C.M.G. £3,928
Principal Inspector for Special Development Duties, W. H. N. Carter £3,703
Principal Inspector of Mechanical Engineering, S. J. Ayres £3,703
Principal Medical Inspector, J. M. Davidson, M.D. £3,815
Principal Electrical Inspector, D. E. Fox £3,703
Divisional Inspectors, W. Widdas (*Durham*); G. Miller (*West Midlands and Southern*); H. Hyde, Ph.D. (*Scotland*); J. W. Calder, O.B.E. (*East Midland*); H. F. Wilson, O.B.E. (*Northumberland and Cumberland*); C. Leigh (*South Western*); J. A. Peasegood, T.D. (*North Eastern*), G. D. Nursey, T.D. (*North Western*) £3,638

Inspectorate of Nuclear Installations

Chief Inspector of Nuclear Installation, Maj.-Gen. S. W. Joslin, C.B., C.B.E. £4,115
Assistant Chief Inspector, T. Griffiths £3,565

Safety in Mines Research Establishment

Central Laboratories, Red Hill, Off Broad Lane, Sheffield, 3.
and Field Laboratories, Harpur Hill, Buxton, Derbyshire

Director, H. T. Ramsay, C.B.E. £4,050
Deputy Chief Scientific Officers, E. M. Guenault, Ph.D., J. G. Nagelschmidt, D.Phil., C. A. A. Wass, Ph.D. ....£3,275 to £3,600

Regional Organization

Senior Scottish Officer, J. L. Warrander, C.B.E. £2,800 to £3,500
Senior Officer for Wales, H. Deadman £2,800 to £3,500

LORD PRIVY SEAL

(*see* Foreign Office)

MINISTRY OF PUBLIC BUILDING AND WORKS

Head Office, Lambeth Bridge House, Albert Embankment, S.E.1
[Reliance: 7611]

The Ministry of Works was constituted in 1940. It took over the functions of the Commissioners of H.M. Works and Public Buildings who had been incorporated by the Commissioners of Works Act, 1852. The principal functions of the Commissioners were to provide, furnish and maintain buildings required for the public service, including buildings overseas, manage the Royal Parks, maintain the Royal Palaces and certain historic buildings and to administer the Ancient Monuments Acts.

The Ministry is now also responsible for coordinating the work of the building and civil engineering industries and of the building materials industries. It encourages efficiency and increased production by supplying technical information and making known the results of research.

In July 1962 the Ministry was renamed the Ministry of Public Building and Works. Responsibility has recently been added for design, construction and maintenance of the building and civil engineering works at home and abroad for the Admiralty, War Office and Air Ministry.

Minister of Public Building and Works, Rt. Hon. (AUBREY) GEOFFREY (FREDERICK) RIPPON, M.P. £5,000
Private Secretary, W. O. Ulrich.
Parliamentary Private Secretary, A. P. Costain, M.P.
Parliamentary Secretary, R. C. Sharples, O.B.E., M.C., M.P. £2,500
Private Secretary, G. Lord.
Secretary, Sir Edward Muir, K.C.B. £6 950
Deputy Secretaries, A. A. Part, C.B., M.B.E.; F. J. Root, C.B. £4,950

Secretariat

Under-Secretaries, H. H. Hobbs, C.B.; K. Newis, M.V.O.; E. H. A. Stretton £4,050
Assistant Secretaries, R. W. Barrow; M. W. Bennitt; J. H. S. Burgess; H. A. Cridland; A. W. Cunliffe, M.B.E.; H. Leadbeater; G. May; P. H. Ogle-Skan, T.D.; T. H. Shearer; E. Vickers; G. H. M. Williams ....£2,800 to £3,500

Directorate of Establishments

Under-Secretary, W. P. D. Skillington (*Director of Establishments*) £4,050
Assistant Secretaries, R. P. Cooke, T.D.; A. A. Creamer, D.F.C.; A. H. Elwell; A. W. J. Scoble £2,800 to £3,500
Chief Information Officer, R. W. B. Howarth, O.B.E. £2,618 to £2,800

Directorate General of Research and Development

Director General, Sir Donald Gibson, C.B.E.. £6,000
Under Secretary, A. B. Hume, C.B. £4,050
Deputy Director General, R. T. Walters.... £4,350
Director of Development, J. T. Redpath, M.B.E. £3,750
Assistant Secretary, A. B. Saunders £2,800 to £3,500
Director of Building Management, C. E. D. Wooster £3,750
Assistant Secretary, O. H. Lawn . £2,800 to £3,500
Director of Research and Information, W. J. Reiners £3,250
Director of Economic Intelligence, N. Digney £2,800 to £3,500
Chief Statistician, Mrs. F. E. Lea, O.B.E. £2,800 to £3,500

Finance

Under-Secretary, L. T. Foster.............£4,050

Finance Division

Assistant Secretary, Mrs. J. Tookey £2,800 to £3,500

Accounts Division

Comptroller of Accounts, B. Roberts........£3,500

Directorate of Contracts

Director, A. Chadwick £3,500

Directorate General of Works

C. G. Mant, C.B.E. (*Controller-General*) £5,750; W. G. Harris, C.B. (*Director-General*), £4,950; E. Bedford, C.B., C.V.O. (*Chief Architect*), £4,350; W. L. Wilson, O.B.E. (*Chief Mechanical and Electrical Engineer*), £4,350; K. C. Mann, C.B.E. *Asst. Civil Engineer*), £4,350.

Directors of Works, C. F. Marshall, O.B.E. (£4,250); C. A. Richards, O.B.E. (£4,000); G. L. Wraige, C.B.E.; W. T. Jackson, M.B.E.; J. M. Curry, C.B.E.; R. Turner, C.M.G.; E. H. Thomson; R. Struthers; W. J. Glenn; F. B. Allcock; M. T. Shaw; C. L. Champion; J. Brierley; J. Nisbet; E. P. Stewart, C.B.E. (£3,750); P. McKearney, O.B.E. (£3,650); G. L. Hargreaves; B. E. Willett £3,500

Director of Lands, L. F. Savournin, C.B.E. £3,750

Chief Quantity Surveyor, R. Menzies, O.B.E. £3,750

Assistant Directors of Works, W. J. Wight; A. E. Chatterton; G. L. Wilson; J. Martin, O.B.E.; J. S. Crichton; T. A. Burnside; A. F. J. Grant; A. J. Dow, O.B.E.; J. C. R. Woodside, C.B.E.; C. E. Loveridge, C.B.E.; A. Goode; A. R. Macrae; L. G. Hiddleston; L. P. Rees, C.B.E.; J. W. Gardner (*Lands*); A. C. B. Evans (*Lands*). £3,500

Assistant Chief Architects, G. Ford, O.B.E.; G. H. Shepherd; S. R. Driver, O.B.E.; W. S. Bryant, M.B.E. £3,500

Assistant Chief Civil Engineers, R. Johnson; R. P. Haines, O.B.E.; L. R. Creasy, O.B.E.; G. L. Ackers, O.B.E. £3,500

Assistant Chief Mechanical and Electrical Engineers, C. E. Bedford; A. L. Parker; A. B. Watson; W. J. F. Wellard, O.B.E.; J. E. Carpenter £3,500

Assistant Chief Quantity Surveyors, C. A. Wales; R. C. Miller; N. E. Higgitt; T. Rishworth; K. C. H. Martin, O.B.E.; S. P. Simcocks, O.B.E. £3,500

Supplies Division

Controller of Supplies, H. Glover £3,500

Inspectorate of Ancient Monuments and Historic Buildings

Chief Inspector, A. J. Taylor £2,950

Royal Parks Division

Bailiff of the Royal Parks, Maj. I. K. C. Hobkirk, M.C. £2,618 to £2,800

Regional Organization

North Eastern (Leeds)

Director, A. W. T. Ellis .... £2,800 to £3,500

Home Counties (Reading)

Director, A. J. Isaac .... £2,800 to £3,500

South Western (Bristol)

Director, D. F. Mann .... £2,800 to £3,500

Midland (Birmingham)

Director, A. B. Moore .... £2,800 to £3,500

North Western (Manchester)

Director, S. Ashburner .... £2,800 to £3,500

Wales (Cardiff)

Director, G. G. Walters, C.B.E. ... £2,800 to £3,500

SCOTTISH HEADQUARTERS

122 George Street, Edinburgh 2
[Edinburgh Caledonian: 2533]

Administration

Under-Secretary, T. Brockie £4,050

Assistant Secretary, G. M. Patrick, D.S.C. £2,800 to £3,500

Directorate General

Director of Works and Services, H. A. Snow. £3,500

Superintending Architect, G. A. H. Pearce £2,800 to £3,150

Senior Architects, D. C. Ireland; R. Saddler; H. G. White, M.V.O. .... £2,228 to £2,563

Senior Structural Engineer, E. A. Mackay £2,228 to £2,563

Public Health Engineer, R. H. Shepherd £1,559 to £2,089

Superintending Estate Surveyor, F. S. Borley £2,800 to £3,150

Senior Estate Surveyor, P. E. Rayner £2,228 to £2,563

Superintending Quantity Surveyor, R. A. S. Jamieson .... £2,800 to £3,150

Senior Quantity Surveyors, I. Morrison; A. M. Murdoch .... £2,228 to £2,563

Senior Surveyor, G. I. Hunter ... £2,228 to £2,563

Senior Engineer, A. Mitchell .... £2,228 to £2,563

Royal Botanic Garden, Edinburgh

Regius Keeper, Dr. H. R. Fletcher £3,275 to £3,600

PUBLIC HEALTH LABORATORY SERVICE

24 Park Crescent, W.1
[Museum: 2223]

The Service was originally set up in 1939 as an emergency service to augment the existing public health resources of England and Wales in combating outbreaks of infectious diseases such as might arise from enemy action or abnormal conditions in time of war. In 1945 the Government decided to retain the Service on a permanent footing, and statutory authority for doing so was included in the National Health Service Act, 1946, the Minister of Health being empowered to provide a Bacteriological Service in England and Wales for the control of the spread of infectious diseases. The Service was administered by the Medical Research Council, as agents of the Ministry of Health until August 1, 1961, when, under the provision of the Public Health Laboratory Service Act, 1960, a new Public Health Laboratory Service Board was established as a statutory body capable of acting in its own right as agent for the Ministry.

Members of the Board

E. T. C. Spooner, M.D. (*Chairman*); P. Alwyn-Smith; A. H. Clough, C.M.G., O.B.E.; Prof. A. W. Downie, D.SC., M.D., F.R.S.; E. Hughes, M.D.; J. Stevenson Logan; J. R. McGregor, C.B., C.B.E., M.C.; Prof. A. A. Miles, C.B.E., M.D., F.R.S.; C. C. Stevens; Prof. C. H. Stuart-Harris, C.B.E., M.D.; D. Thomson, C.B., M.D.; G. I. Watson, M.D.

Director, J. W. Howie, M.D.

Secretary, D. V. T. Fairrie.

CENTRAL PUBLIC HEALTH LABORATORY, LONDON, N.W.9

Administrative Director, S. T. Cowan, M.D.

REFERENCE LABORATORIES
(*With names of Directors*)

Enteric Reference Laboratory, E. S. Anderson, M.D.

Salmonella Reference, Mrs. J. Taylor.

Streptococcus and Staphylococcus Reference and Cross-Infection Reference, M. T. Parker, M.D.

Virus Reference, A. D. Macrae, M.D.

Disinfection Reference, J. C. Kelsey, M.D.

Dysentery Reference, Mrs. K. P. Carpenter.

Mycological Reference (London School of Hygiene and Tropical Medicine), I. G. Murray.

Venereal Diseases Reference, London Hospital, E.1. A. E. Wilkinson, O.B.E. (*part-time*).

Tuberculosis Reference Laboratory, The Parade, Cardiff. J. Marks, M.D.

SPECIAL LABORATORIES
(*With names of Directors*)

Epidemiology Research Laboratory, J. C. McDonald, M.D.

Epidemiology Research Unit, Cirencester, R. E. Hope-Simpson, O.B.E. (*part-time*).

Food Hygiene, Miss B. C. Hobbs, PH.D.

National Collection of Type Cultures, S. T. Cowan. M.D.
Standards Laboratory for Serological Reagents, Mrs. C. M. P. Bradstreet.

CONSTITUENT PUBLIC HEALTH LABORATORIES
(*With names of Directors*)

Bath, P. G. Mann, M.D.; *Bedford*, W. F. Lane; *Birmingham*, B. R. Sandiford, M.D.; *Bournemouth*, G. J. G. King; *Bradford*, H. G. M. Smith, Ph.D.; *Brighton*, J. E. Jameson; *Bristol*, H. R. Cayton; *Cambridge*, G. R. E. Naylor, M.D.; *Cardiff*, Prof. Scott Thomson, M.D.; *Carlisle*, D. G. Davies, M.D.; *Carmarthen*, H. D. S. Morgan; *Chelmsford*, R. Pilsworth, M.D.; *Chester*, Miss P. M. Poole, M.D.; *Conway*, A. J. Kingsley Smith; *County Hall, London*, A. J. H. Tomlinson, M.D.; *Coventry*, J. E. M. Whitehead; *Derby*, J. L. G. Iredale; *Dorchester*, G. H. Tee, Ph.D.; *Epsom*, D. R. Gamble; *Exeter*, B. Moore, M.D.; *Guildford*, G. T. Cook, M.D., *Hereford*, D. R. Christie; *Hull*, J. H. McCoy; *Ipswich*, J. M. S. Dixon, M.D.; *Leeds*, G. B. Ludlam, M.D.; *Leicester*, N. S. Mair; *Lincoln*: J. M. Croll; *Liverpool*, Prof. D. T. Robinson; *Luton*, H. D. Holt; *Maidstone*, A. L. Furniss, M.D.; *Manchester*, J. O'H. Tobin; *Middlesbrough*, A. R. Blowers, M.D.; *Newcastle*, J. H. Hale, O.B.E., M.D.; *Newport (Mon.)*, R. D. Gray, M.D.; *Northallerton*, D. J. H. Payne; *Northampton*, L. Hoyle; *Norwich*, Miss L. M. Dowsett, M.D.; *Nottingham*, E. R. Mitchell; *Oxford*, R. Vollum, D.Phil (*part-time*); *Peterborough*, E. J. G. Glencross; *Plymouth*, C. H. Jellard; *Portsmouth*, K. E. A. Hughes, M.B.E.; *Preston*, L. Robertson; *Reading*, N. Wood, M.D.; *Salisbury*, P. J. Wormald, M.D.; *Sheffield*, E. H. Gillespie; *Shrewsbury*, A. C. Jones; *Southampton*, Miss R. I. Hutchinson, M.D. (*part-time*); *Southend*, J. A. Rycroft; *Stafford*, E. M. Mackay-Scollay; *Sunderland*, P. B. Crone, M.D.; *Swansea*, W. Kwantes; *Taunton*, J. A. Boycott, D.M.; *Truro*, F. D. M. Hocking (*acting*); *Wakefield*, L. A. Little; *Watford*, Mrs. B. H. E. Cadness Graves (*part-time*); *Winchester*, M. H. Hughes, D.M.; *Worcester*, R. J. Henderson, M.D.

PUBLIC RECORD OFFICE
See RECORD OFFICES

PUBLIC TRUSTEE OFFICE
Sardinia Street, Kingsway, W.C.2
[Holborn: 4300]

This is a Government Office (opened in 1908) by means of which the State acts as executor and trustee under a will, or as trustee under a settlement, and in other capacities of a like nature. The value of the trusts accepted up to March 31, 1963, was £659,000,000.

The facts of any trust, new or old, in which it is desired that the Public Trustee should act may be brought to his notice by letter or by personal interview. The appointment is effected in the same way as a private trustee, or by an Order of the Court. He can act solely or jointly with others.

In the case of a will, all that the testator need say is, "I appoint the Public Trustee executor and trustee of this my Will"; or the appointment may be a joint one with others. Executors who have obtained probate can transfer their duties to him under an Order of the Court. He can also act as administrator with, or without, the will annexed.

Strict secrecy is observed in all matters dealt with in the Department. Accounts in simple form are furnished to the beneficiaries as required. An interview with the Public Trustee or with any of his senior officers can be arranged at any time. A pamphlet giving particulars and details of the fees can be obtained free of cost from the Office of the Public Trustee, Kingsway, W.C.2.

Public Trustee, E. W. Eldridge, O.B.E. £4,715
Assistant Public Trustee, C. F. Jackson £4,115
Chief Administrative Officers, H. L. Pettitt, O.B.E., C. A. J. N. O'Sullivan. . . . . . . £2,965 to £3,565
Acceptance Officer, S. A. Williams £2,304 to £2,865
Officer in Charge of Legality of Investments, W. Ross Taylor. £2,304 to £2,865
Trust Officers, G. M. O. Briegel; V. J. Burt; B. L. M. Davies; J. M. B. Dove; H. H. W. Duffy; F. Haynes; J. H. Horne; H. K. Mackinder; N. D. Ouvry; J. Radford; J. C. Rowe; D. A. Wakeford; R. O. A. Wertheim; F. Wheatley £2,304 to £2,865
Establishment Officer (and Secretary, National Disasters Relief Fund) J. C. McCathie, I.S.O. £2,237 to £2,572
Deputy Establishment Officer, H. P. Callow, M.B.E. £1,680 to £2,126
Chief Accountant, H. T. Bowden . £2,683 to £2,865
Asst. Chief Accountant, G. J. Harrup £2,237 to £2,572
Accountants, F. A. Boocock; P. Habgood; E. N. T. Platt; Miss J. E. Randles. . . . . £1,680 to £2,126
Income Tax Officer, M. J. Blyth . £1,680 to £2,126
Chief Investment Managers, F. R. Lee; A. C. B. Urwin . . . . £2,683 to £2,865
Investment Managers, F. A. Beecham; M. F. Dawes; J. J. Olliffe; K. Stilliard; R. Wilson £1,680 to £2,126
Securities Officer, F. A. W. Fry . . . £1,680 to £2,126
Chief Property Adviser, S. Vidler . £2,293 to £2,628
Senior Property Advisers, G. L. Jennings; H. N. Venner, M.B.E. . . . . £1,624 to £2,154

PUBLIC WORKS LOAN BOARD
19 Old Jewry, E.C.2
[Monarch: 6234]

The Board is an independent statutory body, consisting of 12 unpaid Commissioners appointed by the Crown to hold office for 4 years; 3 Commissioners retire each year and may be re-appointed.

The functions of the Commissioners, derived chiefly from the Public Works Loans Act, 1875, and the Local Authorities Loans Act, 1945, are to consider applications for loans by Local Authorities and other prescribed bodies, and, when loans are approved, to collect the repayments.

Funds for loans are provided from time to time by Acts of Parliament and are drawn from the Local Loans Fund through the National Debt Commissioners. Rates of interest on the Board's loans and fees to cover management expenses are fixed by the Treasury.

During the year ended March 31, 1963, 3,066 applications for loans totalling £38,907,630 were approved and advances totalling £39,390,747 were made.

Chairman, Sir Jeremy Raisman, G.C.M.G., G.C.I.E., K.C.S.I. . . . . *unpaid*
Deputy Chairman, J. Binns, C.B.E. . . . . *unpaid*
Other Commissioners, J. Boydell; C. J. J. Clay; J. E. A. R. Guinness; F. Haywood; J. W. Hough, O.B.E.; Sir John Imrie, C.B.E.; Sir James Lythgoe, C.B.E.; A. Mackinnon, D.S.O., M.C., T.D.; J. S. E. Todd, C.B.E.; F. W. Warwick . . . . *unpaid*
Secretary, A. H. M. Hillis, C.M.G. (*Secretary to National Debt Commissioners—q.v.*).
Asst. Secretary and Establishment Officer, H. W. Darvill. £2,172 to £2,507
Accountant, T. Carrick . . . . £1,615 to £2,061

RECORD OFFICES, ETC.

THE PUBLIC RECORD OFFICE
Chancery Lane, W.C.2
[Holborn: 0741-4]

National Records since the Norman Conquest brought together from Courts of Law and Government Departments. Search rooms open daily from 9.30 to 5; Saturdays, 9.30 to 1. The Museum (open

Monday to Friday, 1 to 4 p.m., and to organized parties at other times by arrangement) contains *Domesday Book* (2 vols.), made by order of William the Conqueror in 1085, and *Domesday Chest*; *the Gunpowder Plot* papers (1605); bull of Pope Clement VIII, confirming Henry VIII as *Fidei Defensor* (1524); the Log Book of H.M.S. *Victory* at Trafalgar (1805); and many other documents of national interest.

Keeper of Public Records, S. S. Wilson, C.B.... £4,515

Deputy Keeper and Secretary, H. C. Johnson, C.B.E. £2,865 to £3,565

Records Administration Officer, J. H. Collingridge, C.B.E. .... £2,865 to £3,565

Establishment Officer, W. L. White, M.B.E. £2,237 to £2,572

Principal Assistant Keepers, H. N. Blakiston, O.B.E. (*Modern Records*); J. R. Ede (*Records Administration*); L. C. Hector, O.B.E. (*Publications and Editorial*); R. E. Latham (*Public Search Rooms*); D. B. Wardle, O.B.E. (*Repository and Technical, including Repairs and Photography*) £2,566 to £2,865

Assistant Keepers, First Class, Miss P. M. Barnes; L. Bell; E. W. Denham; N. E. Evans; Miss D. H. Gifford; R. F. Hunnisett; A. A. H. Knightbridge; A. W. Mabbs; Miss M. R. McGuinness; C. A. F. Meekings; P. A. Penfold; M. Roper; E. K. Timings; N. J. Williams. £1,498 to £2,544

Inspecting Officers, J. A. Gavin; H. A. Johnston; R. F. Monger, M.B.E.; F. T. Williams, D.F.M. £1,680 to £2,126

HOUSE OF LORDS RECORD OFFICE

House of Lords, S.W.1

[Whitehall: 6240]

Until 1497 the records of Parliament were normally transmitted at the end of a session to Chancery, and are now therefore preserved in the Public Record Office. Since 1497 the records of Parliament as a whole, and also of the House of Lords, have been kept within the Palace of Westminster. They are in the custody of the Clerk of the Parliaments, who in 1946 established a record department to supervise their preservation and production to students. The Search Room of this office is open to the public throughout the year, Mondays to Fridays inclusive, from 10 to 5. The records preserved number some 1,500,000 documents, and include Acts of Parliament from 1497, Journals of the House from 1510, Minutes and Committee proceedings from 1621, and Papers laid before Parliament, from 1531. Amongst the records are the Petition of Right, the Death Warrant of Charles I, the Declaration of Breda and the Bill of Rights. The House of Lords Record Office can also arrange access for students to the Journals of the House of Commons (from 1547), and to the other surviving records of the Commons (from 1572). The records of both Houses are preserved in the Victoria Tower at the Houses of Parliament.

Clerk of the Records, M. F. Bond, O.B.E., F.S.A. £2,493 to £2,865

Assistant Clerks of the Records, Miss E. R. Poyser; H. S. Cobb .... £1,498 to £2,544

ROYAL COMMISSION ON HISTORICAL MANUSCRIPTS

Quality House, Quality Court, Chancery Lane W.C.2

[Chancery: 2981]

National Register of Archives, [Chancery: 3205]

The Historical Manuscripts Commission was first appointed by Royal Warrant in 1869, and was empowered to make enquiry into the place of deposit of collections of manuscripts and papers of historical interest and with the consent of the owners to publish their contents. The Commission was reconstituted by Royal Warrant in 1959, with wider terms of reference, including the preservation of records and assistance to other bodies working in the same field. The Master of the Rolls, who is the Chairman of the Commission, now exercises through the Commission his responsibility under the Law of Property Act, 1922, and the Tithe Act, 1936, for manorial and tithe documents. The Commission has published over 200 volumes of printed reports upon manuscripts of historical import, and under its authority is compiled the *National Register of Archives*, which now contains over 9,000 typed reports upon privately-owned records, with extensive indexes, and may be consulted by historical scholars. At present a grant-in-aid is made through the Commission to the *Records Preservation Section* of the British Records Association. The Commission undertakes to advise owners upon the preservation and use of their manuscripts and records.

Chairman, The Master of the Rolls.

Commissioners, The Lord Evershed, P.C.; The Marquess of Salisbury, K.G., P.C.; The Earl of Harrowby; Sir Kenneth Pickthorn, Bt., Litt.D., M.P.; Prof. E. F. Jacob, D.Phil., F.B.A., F.S.A.; Prof. Sir J. G. Edwards, D.Litt., F.B.A.; Prof. G. R. Potter, Ph.D., F.S.A.; Miss C. V. Wedgwood, C.B.E., Ll.D.; Sir David L. Evans, O.B.E., D.Litt.; Sir James Fergusson of Kilkerran, Bt. Ll.D.; The Very Rev. S. J. A. Evans, F.S.A.; Sir John Summerson, C.B.E., F.B.A., F.S.A.; Sir Edgar Stephens, C.B.E., F.S.A.; R. N. Quirk, C.B., F.S.A.; Prof. J. C. Beckett.

Secretary, R. H. Ellis, F.S.A.

Registrar, National Register of Archives, Miss W. D. Coates.

SCOTTISH RECORD OFFICE

Register House, Edinburgh

[Edinburgh Waverley: 6585]

The Scottish Record Office has a continuous history from the 13th century. Its present home, the General Register House, was founded in 1774 and built to designs by Robert Adam, later modified by Robert Reid. Here are preserved, in accordance with the Treaty of Union, the public records of Scotland and many collections of private muniments lodged with the national records. Search Rooms open daily from 9.30 to 4.30; Saturdays, 9.30 to 12.30. Museum section open daily, 10 to 4.30 (Saturdays 10-12) in the summer months for exhibitions, and at other times by arrangement. Permanent exhibits include Bull of Pope Honorius III (1218), Declaration of Arbroath (1320), Treaty of Northampton (1328), National Covenant (1638) and Treaty of Union (1707).

Keeper of the Records of Scotland, Sir James Fergusson of Kilkerran, Bt...................... £3,150

Curator of Historical Records, J. Imrie £2,501 to £2,800

Senior Executive Officer, R. G. Bonnington £1,615 to £2,061

Assistant Keepers (*1st Class*), A. Anderson; G. R. Barbour; J. K. Bates; A. M. Broom; P. Gouldesbrough; A. L. Murray; G. G. Simpson; C. J. H. Sinclair; Miss M. D. Young... £1,438 to £2,479

DEPARTMENT OF THE REGISTERS OF SCOTLAND

Register House, Edinburgh

[Waverley: 2561]

The Registers of Scotland consist of:—

(1) General Register of Sasines; (2) Register of Deeds in the Books of Council and Session; (3) Register of Protests; (4) Register of English and Irish Judgments; (5) Register of Service of

Heirs; (6) Register of the Great Seal; (7) Register of the Quarter Seal; (8) Register of the Prince's Seal; (9) Register of Crown Grants; (10) Register of Sheriffs' Commissions; (11) Register of the Cachet Seal; (12) Register of Inhibitions and Adjudications; (13) Register of Entails; (14) Register of Hornings.

The largest of these is the General Register of Sasines, which forms the chief security in Scotland of the rights of land and other heritable (or real) property.

Keeper of the Registers of Scotland, G. Black. £2,950
Deputy Keeper, W. P. Armit....£2,265 to £2,600
Assistant Keepers, J. Maccabe; D. R. Peatie £2,172 to £2,507
Accountant, J. S. C. Gill........£1,790 to £2,236
Senior Examiners, W. A. J. Cunningham; J. Galloway; G. M. MacGregor; A. M. Manson; T. R. Wilson....................£1,615 to £2,061

CORPORATION OF LONDON RECORDS OFFICE

Guildhall, E.C.2
[Monarch: 3030]

Contains the municipal archives of the City of London which are regarded as the most complete collection of ancient municipal records in existence. Includes charters of William the Conqueror, Henry II, and later Kings and Queens to 1957; ancient custumals: Liber Horn, Dunthorne, Custumarum, Ordinacionum, Memorandum and Albus, Liber de Antiquis Legibus, and collections of Statutes; continuous series of judicial rolls and books from 1252 and Council minutes from 1275; records of the Old Bailey and Guildhall Sessions from 1603, and financial records from the 16th century, together with the records of London Bridge from the 12th century and numerous subsidiary series and miscellanea of historical interest. A Guide was published in 1951. Readers' Room open Monday to Friday, 9.30 A.M. to 5 P.M.; Saturday, 9.30 A.M. to 12.30 P.M.

Keeper of the City Records, The Town Clerk.
Deputy Keeper, P. E. Jones.
Assistant Keeper, M. J. Chandler.

THE CONVENTION OF THE ROYAL BURGHS OF SCOTLAND

Agents' Chambers, 51 Castle Street, Edinburgh 2

Instituted about 1150, and extended in 1405 and 1487: Annual General Convention meets in Edinburgh; Committees meet in Edinburgh City Chambers.—*Preses*, The Lord Provost of Edinburgh; *Chaplain*, The Very Rev Charles Laing Warr, K.C.V.O., D.D., LL.D.; *Standing Counsel*, H. R. Leslie, Q.C.; *Engineer*, W. P. Haldane, M.B.E.; *Convention Officer*, William H. Young (City Chambers, Edinburgh); *Party Agents*, Beveridge & Co.; *Agent, Clerk, and Treasurer*, J. Gibson Kerr, W.S., F.R.S.E., 51 Castle Street, Edinburgh 2.

ROYAL COMMISSION FOR THE EXHIBITION OF 1851

1 Lowther Gardens, Exhibition Road, S.W.7
[Kensington: 3665]

Incorporated by Supplemental Charter as a permanent Commission after winding up the affairs of the Great Exhibition of 1851. It has for its object the promotion of scientific and artistic education by means of funds derived from its Kensington Estate, purchased with the surplus left over from the Great Exhibition.

President of the Royal Commission, H.R.H. the Princess Royal.
Chairman, Board of Management, Sir Keith Murray, K.C.B.
Chairman, Science Scholarships Committee, Sir Eric Rideal, M.B.E., F.R.S.
Secretary to Commissioners, W. D. Sturch.

THE NATIONAL SAVINGS COMMITTEE

1 Princes Gate, S.W.7
[Kensington: 5166]

President and Chairman, The Viscount Mackintosh of Halifax.
Vice-Presidents, Sir Harold Parkinson, K.B.E.; Sir Kenneth Stewart, Bt., G.B.E.
Vice-Chairmen, Sir Gwilym Ffrangcon Williams, C.B.E.; G. Woodcock, C.B.E.; Air Chief Marshal Sir Hugh Saunders, G.C.B., K.B.E., M.C., D.F.C., M.M.; Sir Alfred Owen, C.B.E.
Members, J. Archbold (*National Union of Teachers*); R. C. Ashman, O.B.E.; M. Barnett, O.B.E.; R. Bennettt, O.B.E.; P. J. C. Bovill; W. Brown, C.B.E.; E. A. G. Caröe, C.B.E. (*Trustee Savings Banks Association*); A. D. Chesterfield, C.B.E. (*Joint Stock Banks*); Sir William Cocker, O.B.E.; Sir George Eddy, O.B.E.; W. R. Elliott (*Ministry of Education*); Mrs. O. Farquharson (*National Federation of Women's Institutes*); W. Fisk, C.B.E.; G. Freeman, O.B.E.; J. Gayler, O.B.E.; C. A. Harrison, C.B.E.; Sir George Haynes, C.B.E. (*National Council of Social Service*); P. R. Hicks, O.B.E. (*Stock Exchange*); The Dowager Lady Hillingdon, D.B.E. (*Women's Voluntary Services*); A. H. M. Hillis, C.M.G. (*National Debt Office*); R. B. Hopkins, O.B.E.; G. C. Jones (*Institute of Municipal Treasurers and Accountants*); W. E. Jones, C.B.E. (*Trades Union Congress*); J. Killey, O.B.E.; C. L. Lawton, O.B.E., LL.D. (*Trustee Savings Bank Association*); D. D. Livesey, C.B.E.; J. Macpherson (*Treasury*); Sir Andrew McC. MacTaggart (*British Employers' Confederation*); L. F. Milner, C.B.E.; A. V. Mussett (*Association of Education Committees*); Sir Tom O'Brien (*Trades Union Congress*); D. H. Peacock, O.B.E.; Mrs. E. Perkins, C.B.E. (*National Street and Village Groups Advisory Committee*); H. G. Reynolds, C.B.E.; R. G. Robinson, C.B.E.; A. L. Ruscoe (*Post Office*); H. W. Smart (*Post Office*); A. G. Stickland, O.B.E.; J. H. Trower, C.B.E.; E. J. N. Warburton.

OFFICERS

Secretary, D. R. Davidson, O.B.E..........£3,550
Director of Establishment and Finance, J. Hurst £2,618 to £2,800
Director of Publicity, J. W. King..£2,618 to £2,800
Chief Commissioner, R. H. Dowler, O.B.E. £2,618 to £2,800
Chief Executive Officer, A. G. Craner £2,172 to £2,507
Commissioners, S. Burke; F. J. Cooper; D. J. Cresswell, M.B.E.; J. Dean, I.S.O.; J. R. Dutton, I.S.O.; H. G. D. Gabriel, M.B.E.; K. J. Griffin; H. Houston, M.B.E.; J. S. Jephcott, I.S.O.; K. T. Pinch; R. Rees, M.B.E.; J. C. Timms £2,172 to £2,507

SCOTTISH SAVINGS COMMITTEE

68 George Street, Edinburgh 2
[Edinburgh Caledonian: 5486]

President, Sir John Maxwell Erskine, G.B.E.
Chairman, J. M. Archer, C.B.E..
Members, A. R. Abercromby; A. Bonthrone; D. S. Carmichael; J. Craig; Mrs. E. M. B. Forrest, O.B.E.; J. S. Govan; The Lord Greenhill, O.B.E.; R. J. Hastings, O.B.E.; H. Humble, M.B.E. A. L. Imrie, C.B.E.; Sir John D. Imrie, C.B.E.; J. Innes; Col. J. Jamieson; J. Keir, M.B.E.; The Countess of Mar and Kellie; M. Neil; The Very Rev. Canon O'Hanlon; E. G. Paton, M.B.E.; W. H. Penny; Mrs. R. E. Purvis, O.B.E.; Sir James F. Simpson; W. Steel; The Rev. Canon A. W. Stevenson; Mrs. J. Stewart; J. B. Thomson, O.B.E.; A. Tweeddale; A. Yeaman, O.B.E.
Secretary, A. M. Swanson......£2,542 to £2,800
Deputy Secretary, R. F. Johnson. £1,864 to £2,306

DEPARTMENT OF SCIENTIFIC AND INDUSTRIAL RESEARCH

State House, High Holborn, W.C.1. (Chancery: 1262); Africa House, Kingsway, W.C.2 (Holborn: 3422) (*Overseas Liaison Group*). North East Branch Office: Clarendon House, Clayton Street Court, Newcastle-upon-Tyne 1 (Newcastle: 27550). Scottish Branch Office: 20 Walker Street, Edinburgh 3 (Caledonian: 2383). Welsh Branch Office: 69 Park Place, Cardiff (Cardiff: 36671).

A Committee of the Privy Council was appointed by Order in Council dated July 28, 1915 (amended February 6, 1928), to direct the application of any sums of money provided by Parliament for the organization and development of Scientific and Industrial Research. On December 15, 1916, a separate Department was created for the service of the Committee. The Department of Scientific and Industrial Research Act, 1956, placed the Department under the charge of the Council for Scientific and Industrial Research, and redefined the Department's functions and the purposes for which it may make grants.

The aggregate net estimate for the Department in 1963–64 amounts to £20,609,000, a net increase of £2,509,000 on the same estimate for 1962–63. The gross estimate amounts to £23,053,000.

Chairman of the Committee of the Privy Council for Scientific and Industrial Research, The Lord President of the Council.

Research Council, Sir Harold Roxbee Cox, D.SC., Ph.D. (*Chairman*); L. H. Bedford, C.B.E.; Sir William Carron; C. F. Carter; Sir James Cook, D.SC., Ph.D., F.R.S.; F. Cousins; S. C. Curran, D.SC. Ph.D., F.R.S.; G. B. R. Feilden, F.R.S.; Prof. Sir Ewart Jones, D.SC., Ph.D., F.R.S.; Vice-Admiral Sir Frank Mason, K.C.B.; Sir Harry Melville, K.C.B., D.SC., F.R.S. (*Secretary*); Prof. O. A. Saunders, D.SC., F.R.S.; C. Sykes, C.B.E., D.SC., F.R.S.; H. C. Tett.

Headquarters Office

Secretary, Sir Harry Melville, K.C.B., D.SC., F.R.S. £6,950

Private Secretary, G. Hopkinson.

Deputy Secretary, B. K. Blount, C.B., D.Phil. £4,950

GROUP A

Director of Establishment and Finance, R. G. Elkington, C.B. £4,050

Establishment Division

Deputy Director, S. H. Smith, O.B.E. £2,800 to £3,500

Senior Principal Scientific Officers, S. H. Clarke, C.B.E.; Mrs. J. O. Paton....... £2,800 to £3,150

Principal, T. Lacey, I.S.O. .... £1,894 to £2,646

Principal Scientific Officers, *H. W. Nightingale; R. A. A. Taylor; D. G. Tobin, M.B.E. £1,894 to £2,646

Chief Executive Officer, F. A. Foott £2,172 to £2,507

Senior Executive Officers, C. W. Andrews; C. L. Clark; A. E. R. Dobbins; S. B. Watson £1,615 to £2,061

Finance Division

Deputy Director, R. St. J. Walker £2,800 to £3,500

Principals, F. Bath, Ph.D.; G. Hubbard £1,894 to £2,646

Chief Executive Officer, C. F. Fryer £2,172 to £2,507

Senior Executive Officers, R. L. Knott; W. A. Rickard, D.F.C.; R. L. Taylor. £1,615 to £2,061

GROUP B

Director, E. Lee, Ph.D. £4,050

Stations Division

Deputy Director, H. Wooldridge, O.B.E. £3,275 to £3,600

Senior Principal Scientific Officers, Miss P. K. Piercy; S. E. B. Solomons; J. Wallace. £2,800 to £3,150

Principal Scientific Officers, *D. Broyd; *G. H. O. Dines; R. Edmonds; L. L. Fox; E. B. Wright; Miss A. G. Allen .... £1,894 to £2,646

Senior Executive Officer, L. White £1,615 to £2,061

Senior Experimental Officer, H. A. Howe £1,615 to £2,061

Industry Division

Deputy Director, J. Knox....... £3,275 to £3,600

Senior Principal Scientific Officers, T. E. Easterfield, Ph.D.; P. D. Greenall; A. B. Hammond, Ph.D., W. M. Rodgers .... £2,800 to £3,150

Principal Scientific Officers, G. L. Milward; Miss N. Sullivan, M.B.E. .... £1,894 to £2,646

Development Section

Senior Principal Scientific Officer, D. Neville-Jones £2,800 to £3,150

Principal Scientific Officers, *F. R. Carling; C. Clarke; *R. A. Fereday, O.B.E., Ph.D., J. S. Linton £1,894 to £2,646

GROUP C

Director, W. L. Francis, C.B.E., Ph.D. £4,050

Grants Division

Deputy Director, C. Jolliffe..... £3,275 to £3,600

Senior Principal Officers, R. O. Jones, Ph.D.; L. S. Smith.......... £2,800 to £3,150

Principal Scientific Officers, F. E. Brown; A. B. Cherns; I. A. Learmouth; Miss M. O. Morris; E. Rudd, Ph.D. .... £1,894 to £2,646

Senior Executive Officer, J. F. Hayes, M.M. £1,615 to £2,061

Information Division

Deputy Director, H. E. Beckett.. £3,275 to £3,600

Senior Principal Scientific Officers, M. A. Vernon, Ph.D. (*Overseas Liaison Group*); *J. C. Gray; E. Martindale.......... £2,800 to £3,150

Principal Scientific Officers, K. V. Aubrey; *W. C. Brown; Miss H. M. T. Clay; A. P. J. Edwards; E. G. Hill; A. C. Low (*Scotland*); A. R. M. Murray, Ph.D.; R. E. Overbury; H. Powell (*Newcastle*); J. B. Reed; F. R. J. Spearman (*Overseas Liaison Group*); E. E. Williams (*Wales*) £1,894 to £2,646

Chief Information Officer, H. S. Winterbourne £2,542 to £2,800

Principal Information Officers, L. E. E. Jeanes; A. A. Morris .... £2,172 to £2,507

Senior Executive Officer, A. C. Locke (*Overseas Liaison Group*) .... £1,615 to £2,061

Senior Experimental Officers, G. E. Denyer; D. Hastings; H. H. V. Owen ... £1,615 to £2,061

Building Research Station

Bucknalls Lane, Garston, near Watford

[Garston: 4040]

Chairman of Board, R. M. Wynne-Edwards, C.B.E., D.S.O., M.C.

Director, F. M. Lea, C.B., C.B.E., D.SC. £4,150

Deputy Director, T. W. Parker, Ph.D. £3,863

Deputy Chief Scientific Officers, R. C. Bevan; L. F. Cooling, D.SC.; F. G. Thomas, Ph.D.; J. C. Weston, Ph.D. .... £3,275 to £3,600

Senior Principal Scientific Officers, K. Alsop; S. C. C. Bate, Ph.D.; J. B. Dick; J. W. Harding, Ph.D.; F. C. Harper, Ph.D.; R. G. Hopkinson, Ph.D.; R. W. B. Nurse, D.SC.; P. H. Parkin; A. T. Pickles, O.B.E.; J. W. Rice; A. Short; W. H. Ward, D.SC.; R. H. Wood, D.SC. £2,800 to £3,150

Principal Scientific Officers, Miss F. W. Black; B. Butterworth; N. W. B. Clarke; J. B. Collins; R. W. Cooke; E. Danter; L. F. Daws; T. J. Griffiths; *Miss W. V. Hole; D. B. Honeyborne; R. E. Jeanes; W. Kinniburgh; F. J. Langdon, D.Phil.; C. R. Lee; H. M. Llewellyn; A. G. Loudon; G. W. Mack; R. J. Mainstone; A. Marsland; H. G. Midgley, Ph.D.; G. R. Mitchell; C. W. Newberry; A. D. M. Penman; A. W. Pratt; H. J. Purkis; M. H. Roberts, Ph.D.; R. J. Schaffer; E. C. Sewell; K. J. Seymour Walker; A. Sobolev; P. A. Stone, Ph.D.; L. S. Vallance; *C. G. Webb; T. Whitaker; *P. Whiteley; *A. F. E. Wise .... £1,894 to £2,646

Superintending Architects, G. A. Atkinson, O.B.E.; W. M. Woodhouse.......... £2,800 to £3,150

Senior Architects, H. L. Gloag; A. Miller; G. D. Nash.......... £2,228 to £2,563

Superintending Engineer, J. F. Eden £2,800 to £3,150

Senior Engineers, D. Bishop, M.C.; J. Comrie; W. S. Forbes .... £2,228 to £2,563
Chief Experimental Officers, C. N. Craig; H. J. Eldridge; H. H. Neville, Ph.D.; A. J. Newman; L. G. Simms .... £2,172 to £2,507
Senior Executive Officer, J. D. Willcock £1,615 to £2,061

Scottish Laboratory
Thorntonhall, Glasgow
[Busby: 1171]

Officer-in-Charge, D. K. Baron (+*allce.*) £2,228 to £2,563

Fire Research Organization
(A joint organization in conjunction with the Fire Offices' Committee)
Fire Research Station, Boreham Wood, Herts.
[Elstree: 1341 and 1797]

Chairman of the Board, Prof. F. H. Garner, O.B.E., Ph.D.
Director, D. I. Lawson .... £3,275 to £3,600
Senior Principal Scientific Officers, R. G. Silversides; (*Assistant Director*); F. E. T. Kingman, Ph.D.; P. H. Thomas, Ph.D. .... £2,800 to £3,150
Principal Scientific Officers, J. F. Fry; P. Nash; K. N. Palmer; D. J. Rasbash, Ph.D.; D. L. Simms £1,894 to £2,646
Chief Experimental Officer, L. A. Ashton £2,172 to £2,507

Forest Products Research Laboratory
Princes Risborough, Bucks.
[Princes Risborough: 101]

Director, J. Bryan .... £3,275 to £3,600
Senior Principal Scientific Officers, F. H. Armstrong; E. J. Gibson, Ph.D.; D. A. Senior, O.B.E., Ph.D. £2,800 to £3,150
Principal Scientific Officers, J. D. Bletchly; J. D. Brazier; J. F. S. Carruthers; W. T. Curry; R. H. Farmer, D.Sc.; R. F. S. Hearmon; R. A. G. Knight; R. A. Laidlaw, Ph.D.; F. G. O. Pearson; E. W. J. Phillips, Ph.D.; B. J. Rendle; J. G. Savory; D. N. R. Smith; W. C. Stevens; J. G. Sunley .... £1,894 to £2,646

Geological Survey of Great Britain and Museum of Practical Geology
Head Office: Exhibition Road, South Kensington, S.W.7 [Kensington: 9441–5] with 15 and 17 Young Street, Kensington, W.8 [Western: 9651–4]. Scottish Office: South Park, 19 Grange Terrace, Edinburgh 9 [Newington: 5203]; North of England Office, Ring Road, Halton, Leeds 15 [Leeds: 64–9161/3]; Northern Ireland Office: 20 College Gardens, Belfast [Belfast: 28041].

Chairman of Geological Survey Board, Prof. J. C. Mitcheson, C.B.E.
Director of Survey and Museum, C. J. Stubblefield, D.Sc., F.R.S. £4,050
Assistant Directors, S. Buchan, Ph.D.; A. W. Woodland, Ph.D. (*Northern England*); G. H. Mitchell, D.Sc., F.R.S. (*Scotland*); V. Wilson, Ph.D. £3,275 to £3,600
District Geologists, F. W. Anderson, D.Sc., F.R.S.E. (*Chief Palæontologist*); G. Bisson; S. H. U. Bowie; W. Bullerwell, Ph.D. (*Chief Geophysicist*); A. J. Butler, O.B.E.; J. R. Earp, Ph.D.; R. A. Eden; E. H. Francis; S. C. A. Holmes; J. Ineson, Ph.D.; G. S. Johnstone; G. A. Kellaway; T. R. M. Lawrie; D. R. A. Ponsford; J. A. Robbie (*Belfast*); P. A. Sabine, Ph.D. (*Chief Petrographer*); B. J. Taylor; H. E. Wilson ...... £2,800 to £3,150
Principal Geologists, P. J. Adams, Ph.D.; A. A. Archer; K. E. Beer; M. A. Calver; R. Casey, Ph.D.; A. G. Darnley, Ph.D.; J. B. W. Day; F. W. Dunning; E. A. Edmonds; W. N. Edwards; R. W. Elliot; W. B. Evans; I. H. Forsyth; E. A. Francis; D. A. Gray; G. W. Green; D. C. Greig; R. K. Harrison; J. E. T. Horne; E. A. Jobbins; D. H. Land; G. I. Lumsden; J. M. Miller; W. Mykura; D. Ostle; J. D. Peacock, Ph.D.; E. G. Poole; W. H. C. Ramsbottom, Ph.D.; W. A. Read; G. H. Rhys; J. G. O. Smart; D. B. Smith; E. G. Smith; I. P. Stevenson; W. Tulloch; R. B. Wilson; B. C. G Worssam; J. E. Wright £1,894 to £2,646

Museum of Practical Geology
Exhibition Road, South Kensington, S.W.7

Open *free* on weekdays, 10 to 6; Sundays, 2.30 to 6. Closed on Good Friday and Christmas Day.
Curator, A. J. Butler, O.B.E.

Laboratory of the Government Chemist
Cornwall House, Stamford Street, S.E.1
[Waterloo: 7900]

Government Chemist, D. T. Lewis, C.B., D.Sc., Ph.D. £4,050
Deputy Government Chemist, J. Longwell, D.Sc. £3,275 to £3,600
Senior Principal Scientific Officers, H. L. Bolton; J. L. Buchan; D. I. Coomber, Ph.D.; H. Egan, Ph.D.; J. F. Hirst, O.B.E.; E. I. Johnson £2,800 to £3,150
Principal Scientific Officers, D. C. Abbott, Ph.D.; A. A. Christie; G. B. Collins; P. J. Cooper; C. G. Daubney; J. R. Fraser; C. F. M. Fryd; J. G. N. Gaskin; P. I. Hardwick, Ph.D.; C. R. Hoskins, Ph.D.; R. A. Jones; E. G. Kellett, D.Phil.; E. Q. Laws; G. W. G. Maclennan, Ph.D.; J. A. C. McClelland, Ph.D.; W. D. Maniece; Miss S. J. Patterson; B. A. Rose, Ph.D.; A. A. W. Russell; R. I. Savage; G. A. Sergeant; G. E. W. Sexton; H. G. Smith, Ph.D.; J. O'G. Tatton; W. F. Waters; R. E. Weston; R. Wood, Ph.D.; J. W. A. Woodley. .... £1,894 to £2,646
Chief Experimental Officers, D. A. Crighton (*Liverpool*); R. G. Stone .... £2,172 to £2,507
Senior Executive Officer, F. W. Wyatt £1,615 to £2,061

Hydraulics Research Station
Wallingford, Berks.
[Wallingford: 2381]

Chairman of Board, Prof. C. E. H. Bawn, C.B.E., Ph.D., F.R.S.
Director, F. H. Allen.................... £3,863
Senior Principal Scientific Officers, A. E. Seddon (*Assistant Director*); R. C. H. Russell; *P. Ackers £2,800 to £3,150
Principal Scientific Officers, H. R. A. Dedow; D. R. P. Farleigh; J. Grindley, Ph.D.; L. J. Jaffrey; F. J. T. Kestner; G. H. Lean; W. A. Price; N. P. Radley; *J. V. Sutcliffe, Ph.D.; M. J. Wilkie................ £1,894 to £2,646

National Chemical Laboratory
Teddington, Middlesex
[Teddington Lock: 3222]

Chairman of Steering Committee, Prof. C. E. H. Bawn, C.B.E., Ph.D., F.R.S.
Director, J. W. Mitchell, D.Sc., F.R.S. £4,050
Assistant Director, E. A. Coulson, D.Sc. £2,800 to £3,150
Deputy Chief Scientific Officers, R. A. Wells; E. F. G. Herington, D.Sc. .... £3,275 to £3,600
Senior Principal Scientific Officers, R. K. Barnes; G. R. Davies, Ph.D.; J. I. Jones, D.Sc.; H. S. Turner, Ph.D.; F. Wormwell, D.Sc. £2,800 to £3,150
Principal Scientific Officers, D. Ambrose, Ph.D.; A. Audsley, Ph.D.; G. H. Booth, Ph.D.; G. Butler, Ph.D.; J. D. Cox, Ph.D.; S. C. Ellis, Ph.D.; D. A. Everest, Ph.D.; J. H. S. Green, Ph.D.; D. K. Hale; J. L. Hales, Ph.D.; A. J. Head, Ph.D.; A. S. Lindsey, Ph.D.; J. F. Martin, Ph.D.; R. P. Miller; A. A. North; D. Reichenberg; F. M. Reynolds, Ph.D.; W. Slough, Ph.D.; J. G. N. Thomas, Ph.D.; S. L. S. Thomas, Ph.D.; N. E. Topp, Ph.D.; M. F. Vaughan; A. A. Woolf, Ph.D.; C. R. Veale, Ph.D.; Miss D. M. Brasher; Miss E. Napier £1,894 to £2,646
Chief Experimental Officer, R. Handley £2,172 to £2,507

National Engineering Laboratory
East Kilbride, Glasgow
[East Kilbride: 20222]

Chairman of Steering Committee, Vice-Admiral Sir Frank Mason, K.C.B.
Director, D. G. Sopwith, C.B.E., D.Sc. £4,050
Deputy Director, F. D. Penny £3,863
Deputy Chief Scientific Officers, L. Grunberg, D.Sc.; C. E. Phillips; C. Timms, D.Eng. £3,275 to £3,600
Senior Principal Scientific Officers, A. J. Ede; D. Firth; N. E. Frost; A. E. Johnson, D.Sc.; W. H. P. Leslie; A. A. Milne; H. Ll. D. Pugh; A. L. Smith; E. A. Spencer, Ph.D.; C. F. Watkinson £2,800 to £3,150
Principal Scientific Officers, R. W. Bain; J. S. Bateman; R. B. Campbell, Ph.D.; D. Chisholm, Ph.D.; M. G. Cockcroft, Ph.D.; *J. R. Dixon; *W. H. Emerson, Ph.D.; A. J. Fenner; H. A. G. Fletcher; R. J. Franklin; L. J. Griffin, Ph.D., A. T. J. Hayward; J. Holden, Ph.D.; M. J. Hughes; O. R. Hunter; A. A. King; D. Murray; *D. J. Myles, Ph.D.; B. D. J. Osment; I. S. Pearsall, Ph.D.; L. A. Sayce, C.B.E., Ph.D.; D. Scott; R. Sharp; D. W. Slimming; M. T. Watkins; G. G. Watson; R. G. Woolacott, Ph.D.; K. H. R. Wright, Ph.D.; H. L. Wunsch £1,894 to £2,646
Chief Experimental Officers, T. W. Aitchison; A. Bailey; C. S. Colgan; S. E. Mitchell £2,172 to £2,507
Senior Executive Officer, E. J. Gatrell £1,615 to £2,061

National Lending Library for Science and Technology
Walton, Boston Spa, Yorks
[Boston Spa: 2031]

Chairman of Consultative Committee, Sir Lindor Brown, C.B.E., F.R.S.
Director, D. J. Urquhart, Ph.D.. . £3,275 to £3,600
Principal Scientific Officer, B. C. Vickery £1,894 to £2,646

National Physical Laboratory
Teddington, Middlesex
[Teddington Lock: 3222]

Chairman of the General Board, The President of the Royal Society.
Vice-Chairman of General Board and Chairman of the Executive Committee, Sir Basil Schonland, C.B.E., F.R.S.
Director, Sir Gordon Sutherland, Sc.D., LL.D., F.R.S. £4,950
Deputy Director, J. V. Dunworth, C.B.E., Ph.D. £4,050
Secretary, H. J. Hadow......... £3,275 to £3,600
Assistant to the Secretary, W. J. Clenshaw £2,800 to £3,150
Principal Scientific Officers, T. C. Crawhall, O.B.E.; J. R. Illingworth; L. H. McDermott £1,894 to £2,646
Chief Experimental Officer, G. I. Robinson £2,172 to £2,507
Chief Executive Officer, G. W. Shott, M.B.E. £2,172 to £2,507
Senior Executive Officer, E. F. C. Nunn £1,615 to £2,061

Aerodynamics Division

Superintendent, W. P. Jones, D.Sc. £3,275 to £3,600
Senior Principal Scientific Officers, R. W. G. Gandy; R. C. Pankhurst, Ph.D.; H. H. Pearcey; E. W. E. Rogers; C. Scruton; J. T. Stuart, Ph.D. £2,800 to £3,150
Principal Scientific Officers, A. Chinneck; H. C. Garner; R. W. F. Gould; N. Gregory; N. C. Lambourne; K. C. Lapworth, Ph.D.; R. C. Lock, Ph.D.; L. Pennelegion, Ph.D.; C. Salter £1,894 to £2,646
Chief Experimental Officers, D. W. Bryer; D. Giles; R. J. North .... £2,172 to £2,507

Applied Physics Division

Superintendent, B. W. Robinson, Ph.D. £3,275 to £3,600
Senior Principal Scientific Officers, P. J. Campion, D.Phil.; E. A. Newman; D. W. Robinson £2,800 to £3,150
Principal Scientific Officers, G. H. Aston, Ph.D.; E. J. Axton; G. P. Barnard, D.Sc.; W. J. Callow; A. Felton; F. J. Wilkins ..... £1,894 to £2,646
Chief Experimental Officers, J. J. Hill; W. O. Jennings; W. Wilson, M.B.E. £2,172 to £2,507

Autonomics Division

Superintendent, A. M. Uttley, Ph.D. £3,275 to £3,600
Senior Principal Scientific Officers, D. W. Davies; P. H. Hammond............ £2,800 to £3,150
Principal Scientific Officers, D. L. A. Barber; D. O. Clayden; J. McDaniel; A. R. Meetham, D.Sc.; L. J. Page; P. R. Stuart, Ph.D.. £1,894 to £2,646
Chief Experimental Officer, C. F. Osborne £2,172 to £2,507

Basic Physics Division

Superintendent, J. A. Pople, Ph.D., F.R.S. £3,275 to £3,600
Deputy Chief Scientific Officer, D. H. Whiffen, D.Sc....................... £3,275 to £3,600
Senior Principal Scientific Officers, G. Bradfield; H. L. Cox; *H. A. Gebbie, Ph.D.; R. W. Powell, D.Sc. .... £2,800 to £3,150
Principal Scientific Officers, A. F. C. Brown; E. G. Butcher; M. F. Markham; M. J. P. Musgrave; H. Pursey; P. L. Smith, D.Phil. £1,894 to £2,646
Chief Experimental Officer, M. J. Hickman £2,172 to £2,507

Light Division

Superintendent, J. Dyson, Sc.D. . . £3,275 to £3,600
Senior Principal Scientific Officers, J. M. Burch, Ph.D; B. H. Crawford, D.Sc.; K. J. Habell; J. S. Preston £2,800 to £3,150
Principal Scientific Officers, J. W. C. Gates; E. J. Gillham; A. Jackson; *A. H. McIlraith, Ph.D. £1,894 to £2,646

Mathematics Division

Superintendent, E. T. Goodwin, Ph.D. £3,275 to £3,600
Deputy Chief Scientific Officer, J. H. Wilkinson £3,275 to £3,600
Senior Principal Scientific Officers, C. W. Clenshaw; J. G. L. Michel............. £2,800 to £3,150
Principal Scientific Officers, G. G. Alway; T. B. Boss; A. R. Curtis; P. Dean, Ph.D. J. G. Hayes; D. W. Martin, D.Phil.; J. L. Martin, Ph.D.; G. F. Miller; M. Woodger............... £1,894 to £2,646
Chief Experimental Officer, T. Vickers £2,172 to £2,507

Metallurgy Division

Superintendent, N. P. Allen, D.Sc., F.R.S.. . . . £4,050
Senior Principal Scientific Officers, B. E. Hopkins; *F. P. O. Kubaschewski, D.Sc.; D. McLean, D.Sc.; H. G. Short; H. A. Sloman £2,800 to £3,150
Principal Scientific Officers, J. A. Catterall, Ph.D.; J. F. Duke; P. G. Forrest, Ph.D.; A. Franks, Ph.D.; B. Gale, Ph.D.; K. F. Hale, Ph.D.; L. M. T. Hopkin, Ph.D.; J. H. Rendall; T. H. Schofield £1,894 to £2,646

Ship Division

Superintendent, A. Silverleaf. . . . £3,275 to £3,600
Senior Principal Scientific Officers, J. Dawson; G. Hughes, D.Sc.. .... £2,800 to £3,150
Principal Scientific Officers, W. E. A. Acum; D. V. Blake; R. E. Clements; D. J. Doust; G. E. Gadd, Ph.D.; G. J. Goodrich; N. Hogben, Ph.D.; J. R Shearer................... £1,894 to £2,646
Chief Experimental Officer, W. J. Marwood £2,172 to £2,507

Standards Division

Superintendent, H. Barrell, C.B.E., D.SC. £3,275 to £3,600

Deputy Chief Scientific Officer, L. Essen, O.B.E., D.SC., F.R.S. .... £3,275 to £3,600

Senior Principal Scientific Officers, P. H. Bigg; A. H. Cook, Ph.D.; K. D. Froome, D.SC.; L. W. Nickols; J. E. P. L. Vigoureux, D.SC. £2,800 to £3,150

Principal Scientific Officers, C. R. Barber; R. S. Dadson; E. J. Evans; P. W. Harrison; G. H. Rayner; J. McA. Steele; B. Swindells £1,894 to £2,606

Chief Experimental Officers, R. S. Marriner; T. R. J. Oakley; V. W. Stanley...... £2,172 to £2,507

Radio Research Station
Ditton Park, Slough, Bucks.
(Slough: 24411)

Chairman of Board, E. Eastwood, C.B.E., Ph.D.

Director, J. A. Ratcliffe, C.B.E., F.R.S. £3,863

Deputy Director, J. A. Saxton, D.SC. £3,275 to £3,600

Senior Principal Scientific Officers, R. Dalziel; H. G. Hopkins, O.B.E., Ph.D.; F. Horner; W. R. Piggott, O.B.E.; A. F. Wilkins, O.B.E. £2,800 to £3,150

Principal Scientific Officers, W. C. Bain, Ph.D.; E. N. Bramley, Ph.D.; C. Clarke; B. N. Harden; F. Kift; J. W. King, Ph.D.; J. A. Lane; G. W. Luscombe; R. W. Meadows; ‡F. H. C. M. Minnis, D.SC.; ‡B. G. Pressey, Ph.D. £1,894 to £2,646

Road Research Laboratory
Harmondsworth, West Drayton, Middlesex
[Skyport: 1421]

Chairman of Board, R. M. Wynne-Edwards, C.B.E., D.S.O., M.C.

Director, Sir William Glanville, C.B., C.B.E., D.SC., F.R.S. £4,150

Head Office and Materials and Construction Division and Tropical Section

Harmondsworth, West Drayton, Middlesex
[Skyport: 1421]

Deputy Director (Materials and Construction), A. R. Lee, Ph.D. .... £3,275 to £3,600

Deputy Chief Scientific Officers (Tropical Section), R. S. Millard, Ph.D.; *(Administration)* G. Charlesworth, Ph.D. .... £3,275 to £3,600

Senior Principal Scientific Officers, D. Croney; R. Jones, Ph.D.; R. H. H. Kirkham, Ph.D.; D. J. Maclean; J. H. Nicholas; W. I. J. Price; A. C. Whiffin, Ph.D. .... £2,800 to £3,150

Principal Scientific Officers, A. R. Atherton; H. G. Barnes; W. P. M. Black; *A. E. Burks; K. E. Clare; J. D. Coleman; M. J. Dumbleton, Ph.D.; G. D. Grainger; W. A. Lewis; N. W. Lister; J. A. Loe; *G. A. B. McIvor; D. H. Mathews; A. Please; G. F. Salt; W. J. O. Scott; F. N. Sparkes, O.B.E.; J. P. Stott, Ph.D.; J. C. Tanner; E. D. Tingle, Ph.D.; J. O. Tresidder; J. J. Trott; L. H. Watkins; F. H. P. Williams; P. J. F. Wright £1,894 to £2,646

Chief Experimental Officers, Mrs. R. G. Knight; F. A. Shergold; F. G. Taylor.. £2,172 to £2,507

Senior Executive Officer, W. H. Adams £1,615 to £2,061

Traffic and Safety Division

Langley Hall, Langley, Bucks.
[Slough: 43144]

Deputy Director (Traffic and Safety), R. J. Smeed, Ph.D. .... £3,275 to £3,600

Senior Principal Scientific Officers F. Garwood. Ph.D.; C. G. Giles; G. Grime, O.B.E.; R. L Moore .... £2,800 to £3,150

Principal Scientific Officers, K. N. Chandler, Ph.D.; A. W. Christie; T. M. Coburn; A. J. Harris; J. A. Hillier; V. J. Jehu; R. D. Lister; *J. A. Martin; Miss B. E. Sabey; H. J. H. Starks, Ph.D.; S. J. Thurlow; J. G. Wardrop; F. V. Webster, Ph.D.; P. D. Whiting........ £1,894 to £2,646

Chief Experimental Officer, Miss G. O. Jeffcoate £2,172 to £2,507

Scottish Laboratory

Thorntonhall, Glasgow
[Busby: 1171]

Principal Scientific Officer, J. R. Lake £1,894 to £2,646

Torry Research Station
Aberdeen
[Aberdeen: 24258]

Director, G. A. Reay, C.B.E., Ph.D., F.R.S.E. £3,275 to £3,600

Senior Principal Scientific Officers, A. Banks, Ph.D. *(Assistant Director)*; J. A. Lovern, O.B.E., D.SC., F.R.S.E.; J. M. Shewan, Ph.D., F.R.S.E. £2,800 to £3,150

Principal Scientific Officers, C. R. Baines; J. J. Connell, Ph.D.; ‡G. C. Eddie; S. W. F. Hanson; A. C. Jason, Ph.D.; N. R. Jones, Ph.D.; R. M. Love, Ph.D.; Miss J. N. Olley, Ph.D.; T. H. Simpson, Ph.D. .... £1,894 to £2,646

Humber Laboratory

Wassand Street, Kingston-upon-Hull
[Hull Central: 38283]

Officer in Charge, G. H. O. Burgess, Ph.D. £2,800 to £3,150

Principal Scientific Officer, D. L. Nicol, Ph.D. £1,894 to £2,646

Tropical Products Institute
56–62 Gray's Inn Road, W.C.1
[Chancery: 5412]

Chairman of Committee, Prof. Sir Ewart Jones, D.SC., Ph.D., F.R.S.

Director, E. S. Hiscocks, C.B.E... £3,275 to £3,600

Deputy Director, *P. C. Spensley, D.Phil. £2,800 to £3,150

Assistant Directors, R. H. Kirby, Ph.D.; W. D. Raymond, O.B.E., Ph.D. ..... £2,800 to £3,150

Principal Scientific Officers, H. J. Dothie; A. J. Feuell, Ph.D.; L. H. Greenwood-Barton; *Miss E. Orr; G. B. Pickering, D.Phil; *E. M. Thain, Ph.D. £1,894 to £2,646

Chief Experimental Officers, A. E. Chittenden; E. H. G. Smith............ £2,117 to £2,451

Warren Spring Laboratory
Gunnels Wood Road, Stevenage, Herts.
[Stevenage: 2080]

Chairman of Steering Committee, Sir Harry Melville, K.C.B., D.SC., F.R.S.

Director, C. C. Hall, Ph.D. £4,050

Senior Principal Scientific Officers, S. R. Craxford, D.Phil.; A. J. Robinson, Ph.D.; W F. B. Shaw; J. W. Smith; F. H. H. Valentin, Ph.D. £2,800 to £3,150

Principal Scientific Officers, P. R. P Claridge; Miss M. Clifton, M.D.; E. Douglas; A. W. Fletcher; D. Gall, Ph.D.; P. G. Jeffrey, Ph.D.; A. S. Joy; R. L. Moss, Ph.D.; P. L. Palmer; A. Poll; L. E. Reed, Ph.D.; J. Sandor; W. Smith, Ph.D.; F. A. Sweett; D. W. Tanner, Ph.D. £1,894 to £2,646

Chief Experimental Officer, L. D. Muller £2,172 to £2,507

Senior Executive Officer, R. Pizzey £1,615 to £2,061

Scottish Laboratory

Thorntonhall, Glasgow
[Busby: 1171]

Officer-in-Charge, H. L. Nicholson £1,615 to £2,061

Water Pollution Research Laboratory
Elder Way, Stevenage, Herts.
[Stevenage: 820]

Chairman of Board, C. J. Jackson, O.B.E., Ph.D.

Director, B. A. Southgate, C.B.E., D.SC...... £3,863

Senior Principal Scientific Officers, A. E. J. Petett (*Assistant Director*); A. L. Downing; G. E. Eden £2,800 to £3,150
Principal Scientific Officers, R. W. Edwards; A. L. H. Gameson; D. W. M. Herbert; G. Knowles; E. V. Mills, Ph.D.; H. A. Painter, Ph.D.; *J. D. Swanwick, Ph.D.; T. G. Tomlinson; A. B. Wheatland; R. Wilkinson, Ph.D. £1,894 to £2,646

*Temporary
‡ Seconded to another department.

SCOTTISH OFFICE

Dover House, Whitehall, S.W.1
[Whitehall: 6151]

Secretary of State for Scotland, THE RT. HON. MICHAEL ANTONY CRISTOBAL NOBLE, M.P. £5,000
Private Secretary, A. L. Rennie.
Assistant Private Secretary, J. Glendinning, M.B.E.
Parliamentary Private Secretary, The Earl of Dalkeith, M.P. .... *unpaid*
Minister of State, THE LORD CRAIGTON, P.C., C.B.E. £3,750
Private Secretary, W. Baird.
Joint Parliamentary Under-Secretaries of State, R. C. Brooman-White, M.P.; The Lady Tweedsmuir, M.P. £2,500
Permanent Under-Secretary of State, Sir William Murrie, K.B.E., C.B. £7,000
Private Secretary, W. A. P. Weatherston.
Assistant Under-Secretary of State, I. M. Robertson, M.V.O. £4,050

Administrative Departments of the Secretary of State for Scotland

I. *Department of Agriculture and Fisheries for Scotland.*
II. *Scottish Education Department.*
III. *Scottish Home and Health Department.*
IV. *Scottish Development Department.*

DEPARTMENT OF AGRICULTURE AND FISHERIES FOR SCOTLAND

St. Andrew's House, Edinburgh, 1
[Edinburgh Waverley: 8404]

Dover House, Whitehall, London, S.W.1
[Whitehall: 6151]

Secretary, Sir Matthew Campbell, K.B.E., C.B., F.R.S.E. £4,950
Fisheries Secretary, A. J. Aglen, C.B., F.R.S.E. .. £4,050
Deputy Secretary (Agriculture), W. H. Senior, F.R.S.E. £4,050
Under-Secretary, H. Whitby £4,050
Assistant Secretaries, A. T. Brooke; J. A. Ford, M.C.; W. W. Gauld; J. S. Gibson; Miss I. F. Haddow; T. F. S. Hetherington; J. Lawless; W. Russell; J. I. Smith; N. J. Steele; R. C. Tucker £2,800 to £3,500
Assistant Secretary (Finance Officer and Accountant), D. Henderson .... £2,800 to £3,500
Principals, R. Barrie; A. H. Bishop; J. Cormack; †W. J. L. Dobson; R. A. Fasken; J. R. Gordon; D. A. Leitch; Miss I. S. Montgomery; G. S. Murray; J. G. C. Richardson; H. G. Robertson; A. G. Ross; Miss J. L. Ross; A. T. Rush; I. L. Sharp; J. Smith; S. M. Ward; A. Woodburn; S. H. Wright .... £1,894 to £2,646
Deputy Finance Officer and Accountant, J. C. Walker £2,172 to £2,507
Assistant Finance Officer and Accountant, G. B. Robinson .... £2,172 to £2,507
Chief Executive Officers, J. C. Bannatyne, M.B.E.; J. Borland; J. W. Dougal; J. A. Downie; D. A. Flett; B. Gordon; Miss A. Murdison; T. G. Strong; R. M. Williamson ... £2,172 to £2,507
Senior Executive Officers, O. Beattie; D. A. Brown; D. F. Campbell; J. Cruickshank; J. N. Dick; J. A. C. Fairbairn; J. A. M. McLeod; H. McNamara; A. S. Neilson; J. S. Robertson; W. A. Strain; D. C. Thompson ..... £1,615 to £2,061

Inspectorate

Chief Inspector (Agriculture), W. Craib £3,500
Chief Inspector (Sea Fisheries), C. Sim £2,650
Deputy Chief Inspectors (General Duties), S. Isbister; J. P. Struthers; (*Livestock*), G. C. Smith, £2,800 to £3,150; (*Sea Fisheries*), J. M. Steven £2,172 to £2,473
Senior Inspectors (General Duties), A. H. Boggon; A. M. Calder; H. M. David; J. M. Esslemont; G. S. Lawrie; D. F. Mackenzie; I. L. Mackenzie; H. Robertson; R. J. Scott; J. W. Smith; G. S. Whimster, £2,228 to £2,563; (*Livestock*), D. C. Collie; J. Dean; (*Horticulture*), T. Robertson; (*Poultry*), F. H. Jones .... £2,100 to £2,600
Inspector (Salmon Fisheries), S. D. Sedgwick £2,005 to £2,590

Scientific Services (Seed Testing, Plant Registration, Plant Pathology, Entomology)

East Craigs, Corstorphine, Edinburgh 12
[Corstorphine: 3361]

Director, C. E. Foister, F.R.S.E. ... £3,275 to £3,600
Deputy Director, D. W. Williams £2,800 to £3,150
Principal Scientific Officers, J. L. Hardie; N. C. Morgan; Miss M. J. M. Noble; J. R. Thomson; J. M. Todd .... £1,839 to £2,590

Lands Staff

Chief Lands Officer, J. S. Weddell £3,500
Divisional Lands Officers, G. D. Davidson; J. S. Gibson, O.B.E. .... £2,800 to £3,150
Senior Lands Officers, J. Bett; A. N. Black; S. L. Hamilton, M.B.E.; P. C. Jack; T. B. Macdonald; A. Manson; D. Miller; A. W. Renfrew; J. White .... £2,228 to £2,563

† At Dover House.

Engineering and Surveying Staff

Chief Surveyor, D. Grant £3,500
Chief Engineer, F. W. Waddell, O.B.E. £3,150
Deputy Chief Surveyor, G. D. Mowat £2,800 to £3,150
Senior Surveyors, J. Alexander; F. G. G. Angus; Q. Bone, M.B.E.; A. P. Borrie; C. R. N. Duncan; J. P. Hastie; F. C. McLachlan; A. Malcolm; J. D. Young .... £2,228 to £2,563
Senior Civil Engineers, A. L. Archibald; T. P. Bulloch; W. G. Parker, M.B.E., G.M., E.R.D.; C. R. Wallace; J. K. C. Wilson £2,228 to £2,563

Miscellaneous Appointments

Technical Development Officer, W. O. Kinghorn £3,275
Advisory Officer in Agricultural Economics, O. J. Beilby .... £2,800 to £3,150
Chief Marketing Officer, A. M. N. Steward £2,172 to £2,507
Chief Fatstock Officer, A. Scott .. £2,172 to £2,507
Marine Superintendent, Capt. D. T. MacCallum, D.S.C., R.N.(ret.) .... £1,955 to £2,175
Engineer Superintendent, S. G. Blyth £1,760 to £1,930
Librarian, Miss E. V. Handlen, M.B.E. £1,615 to £2,061

Crofters Commission

9 Ardross Terrace, Inverness
[Inverness: 32711]

Chairman, J. S. Grant, O.B.E. £4,100
Members (part-time), R. H. W. Bruce; Air Vice-Marshal D. M. T. Macdonald, C.B.; J. MacDonald; A. J. Mackay; D. J. MacKenzie; J. N. McNaughton, C.B.E.; J. C. Robertson £850
Secretary and Solicitor, D. J. MacCuish £2,800 to £3,500
Chief Executive Officer, A. E. Mitchell £2,172 to £2,507
Chief Technical Officer, A. McArthur. £2,800 to £3,150

Red Deer Commission
Elm Park, Island Bank Road, Inverness

Chairman (part-time), Maj. M. D. D. Crichton-Stuart.....£1,000
Senior Executive Officer, T. M. Brown £1,615 to £2,061

Fisheries
Marine Laboratory
Victoria Road, Torry, Aberdeen
[Aberdeen: 25218]

Director, C. E. Lucas, C.M.G.....£3,863
Deputy Chief Scientific Officer, J. B. Tait £3,275 to £3,600
Assistant Director, B. B. Rae.....£2,800 to £3,150
Senior Principal Scientific Officers, J. H. Fraser; B. B. Parish.....£2,800 to £3,150
Principal Scientific Officers, R. E. Craig; W. Dickson; R. Johnston; R. Jones; A. D. McIntyre; J. A. Pope; A. Saville; J. H. Steele; H. J. Thomas £1,839 to £2,590

Freshwater Fisheries Laboratory
Faskally House, Pitlochry
[Pitlochry: 329]

Senior Principal Scientific Officer, K. A. Pyefinch £2,800 to £3,150
Principal Scientific Officers, A. V. Holden; T. A. Stuart.....£1,839 to £2,590

SCOTTISH EDUCATION DEPARTMENT
St. Andrew's House, Edinburgh 1
[Edinburgh Waverley: 6591]
Dover House, Whitehall,
London, S.W.1
[Whitehall: 6151]

The Scottish Education Department is responsible for the administration of the *Education (Scotland) Acts* and in general for the development of public education in Scotland.

Secretary, Sir William Arbuckle, K.B.E., C.B..£4,950
Deputy Secretary, H. H. Donnelly, C.B.E.....£4,050
Under-Secretary, A. G. Rodger, O.B.E.....£4,050
Assistant Secretaries, R. P. Fraser; R. A. Dingwall-Smith; F. M. M. Gray (*Establishment Officer*); S. C. Aldridge; J. A. M. Mitchell, C.V.O., M.C. J. B. Beaumont; I. M. Wilson; P. C. Rendle £3,500
Principals, J. J. Farrell; D. R. McFarlane; J. O. Johnston; W. A. M. Good; J. F. McClellan; B. J. Bennett; D. G. McCulloch; A. W. Brodie; Miss J. H. Renwick (*Asst. Estab. Officer*); R. Scott; Miss E. C. G. Wilson..£1,894 to £2,646
Chief Executive Officers, W. R. Adam, M.B.E.; D. G. Blyth; A. J. C. Mitchell; G. A. T. Hanks, M.B.E.; T. Drummond (*Accountant*) £2,172 to £2,507
Senior Executive Officers, W. A. Bruce; Miss W. J. Strongman; Miss I. W. Inglis; L. C. Watterson; Miss M. F. Irvine, M.B.E.; A C. Easson; R. Scott; Miss C. M. Steele; R. J. Edie, D.F.C.; G. H. J. Bell.....£1,615 to £2,001

H.M. Inspectors of Schools

Senior Chief Inspector, J. S. Brunton, C.B.....£3,863
Chief Inspectors, Miss E. I. Young; J. G. Strachan, Ph.D.; D. Dickson, Ph.D.; P. M. Gillan; J. P. Forsyth; J. Shanks.....£3,380
Inspectors, J. J. Davidson; A. S. Kelly, O.B.E.; A. Law, O.B.E., Ph.D.; J. Stevenson; R. Macleod, O.B.E.; W. S. Gray; C. A. Forbes; A. J. Mee; J. C. Holmes; L. Pendleton; Miss M. S. Thomson, O.B.E.; J. Dryburgh; A. T. Emond; N. Fullwood; J. Gilbert, Ph.D.; J. A. McPherson; K. E. Miller, O.B.E.; A. G. Skinner; J. H. Smith; T. L. Taylor; C. Murray; W. Gillies; J. J. Reid; J. Bennett, M.B.E.; Miss L. Boyd, D.Sc.....£3,085
E. W. Thomas, Ph.D.; W. Macdonald; Miss J. T. Duncanson; W. Christie; W. A. Milne; B. S. Fraser; J. B. Caird; Miss M. G. Watt; J. Deans; J. Robertson, Ph.D.; Miss E. B. Taylor; R. Morrison; W. F. Kerr, M.B.E.; I. A. MacDonald; D. Young; J. R. M. M. Brown; A. Garden; J. F. MacDonald; J. Cumming; T. Crippin; W. Cunningham; E. F. Thompkins; R. Allan; W. K. Ferguson; D. S. Petrie; W. Anderson; Miss M. K. G. Fraser; Miss M. I. Brown; Miss A. M. C. Mathewson; Miss M. G. Sibbald; Miss B. McQueen; Miss C. S. Cameron; J. Anderson; J. Rankin; J. Mackinnon; D. B. Kane; G. J. Brown; Miss M. M. Lawson; W. C. Brown; W. Mitchell; A. A. Macpherson; Miss E. M. W. Thomson; G. C. Morrison; J. F. McGarrity; A. D. Chirnside; G. S. Mutch; D. G. Marwick; A. Nisbet; J. C. Leitch; P. D. B. Walker; G. M. McGavin; A. K. Forbes; Miss A. H. M. Prain; J. H. Thomson; W. A. Gatherer, Ph.D.; J. Kiely; J. G. Morris; J. S. Murphy; G. M. Sinclair, Ph.D.; J. A. Ferguson; J. Stark, Ph.D.; M. G. Scott; A. G. Robertson; H. Smith; A. R. Gallon; H. L. Philip; S. T. S. Skillen; Miss H. J. S. Sandison; J. A. Sloggie; S. Thornton, Ph.D.; Mrs. J. G. Pillans; R. S. Johnston; G. Wallis.....£2,023 to £2,905

SCOTTISH HOME AND HEALTH DEPARTMENT
St. Andrew's House, Edinburgh 1
[Edinburgh Waverley: 8501]
Dover House, Whitehall, London, S.W.1
[Whitehall: 6151]

The Scottish Home and Health Department was constituted in June 1962 following a redistribution of the functions of the former Scottish Home Department and the former Department of Health for Scotland, and is responsible for the central administration in Scotland of functions relating to law and order and of the National Health Service and associated welfare services. It is the Department concerned with the Scottish police and probation services, criminal justice, legal aid and the services needed by the courts; and it is directly responsible for the administration of Scottish prisons and Borstal institutions. The Department is the central authority in Scotland for the fire service and civil defence and for legislation concerning shops, theatres, cinemas and licensed premises.

The Department is responsible for the central administration in Scotland of the National Health Service comprising the hospital service, the general medical, dental and ophthalmic services and the local authority health services. The associated welfare services include the supervision of local arrangements for the care of the aged and handicapped, and medical and surgical treatment of war pensioners.

Secretary, R. E. C. Johnson, C.B.....£4,950
Under-Secretaries, N. W. Graham, C.B.; J. Hogarth; R. H. Law (*Establishment Officer*).....£4,050
Assistant Secretaries, D. J. Cowperthwaite; E. U. E. Elliott-Binns; J. M. Fearn; R. G. Forrest; A. A. Hughes; J. B. Hume; †J. Kidd; Miss M. K. Macdonald; A. MacLehose; N. K. McCallum; T. M. Martin (*Director of Scottish Prisons and Borstal Services*); I. A. H. More; T. B. Skinner; P. Stevenson; Miss L. C. Watson, O.B.E. £2,800 to £3,500
Principals, G. F. Belfourd; R. G. S. Brown; Brig. A. I. Buchanan-Dunlop, C.B.E., D.S.O.; Miss H. M. Connor; F. H. Cowley; *Miss P. A. Cox; J. E. Fraser; W. K. Fraser; G. Gilbraith; J. J. Haughney; J. Inglis; J. Keeley; W. P. Lawrie; G. A. M. McIntosh; D. G. Mackay; T. H. McLean; A. M. Macpherson; A. T. F. Oglivie; †A. F. Reid; F. H. Roberts; J. Scrimgeour; A. M. Stephen; V. C. Stewart; A. W. Tait; J. E. Tinkler; J. Utterson; J. Walker £1,894 to £2,646
Chief Executive Officers, G. Aithie; D. H. Bayes; W. R. Butcher; C. S. Donaldson; W. H.

Fraser; A. Mackenzie; D. S. MacKenzie; A. D. Robertson; G. Robertson; I. S. Scott; W. T. A. Scott; J. Topping........... £2,172 to £2,507
Senior Executive Officers, I. M. L. Batts; Miss M. W. Baxter; R. D. M. Calder; D. Clark; C. S. W. Forbes; J. P. Fraser; T. B. Hamilton; J. J. Hunter, D.F.C.; *R. J. Inglis; J. S. C. Little; W. H. McCulloch; A. B. McLanachan; W. R. Miller; G. Paterson; E. Redmond; Mrs. M. A. S. Robertson, M.B.E.; W. Robertson; W. J. Shiels; J. E. Smith; G. G. Stewart; W. H. A. Thrower; A. Walker; J. Will; R. W. Williamson £1,615 to £2,061

Solicitor's Office

(For the Scottish Department and certain U.K. services, including H.M. Treasury, in Scotland).

Solicitor, J. M. Dick, C.B., C.B.E., V.R.D.....£4,350
Assistant Solicitors, J. S. Dalgetty; K. J. A. Greig; J. A. Beaton; R. W. Deans; A. G. Brand, M.B.E. £2,900 to £3,500
Senior Legal Assistants, E. S. Robertson; W. Thomson; R. A. Lawrie; W. Moffat; D. Cunningham; C. J. Workman; A. A. McMillan; A. J. F. Tannock, M.C.............. £2,239 to £2,800
Counsel to the Secretary of State for Scotland, under Private Legislation Procedure (Scotland) Act, 1936 (3 Parliament Square, Edinburgh), *Counsel*, C. N. Fraser, Q.C.; D. M. K. Grant, Advocate.

Scottish Information Office

St. Andrew's House, Edinburgh, 1
[Edinburgh Waverley: 8501]

Director, W. M. Ballantine, C.B.E., M.V.O. £2,650 to £3,350
Principal Information Officers, J. W. P. Dundas, M.V.O.; †D. A. S. Anderson... £2,172 to £2,507
Senior Information Officers, T. L. Speirs; D. F. Mackenzie; E. Reoch....... £1,615 to £2,061

† At Dover House.
* Seconded to another department.

Medical Staff

Chief Medical Officer, Sir Kenneth Cowan, M.D., F.R.S.E., Q.H.P.......................... £4,350
Deputy Chief Medical Officer, J. Smith, O.B.E. £4,050
Principal Medical Officers, H. B. Craigie; J. M. Johnston, C.B.E., F.R.S.E.; I. N. Sutherland; A. B. Walker............................ £3,750
Senior Medical Officers, A. L. Wilson; I. M. Macgregor; W. K. Henderson; J. K. Hunter.. £3,500
Medical Officers, R. M. Gordon; R. P. J. McBroom; R. D. Martin; Catherine H. S. Begg; Mabel E. Mitchell; A. Menzies; Patricia O'Kane; A. Lawrie; E. A. Smith; W. W. Sinclair; Elspeth M. Warwick; R. Steele..... £2,412 to £3,075
Regional Medical Officers, J. B. Barr; T. W. Buchan; A. A. Gordon; I. B. K. MacGregor; D. E. Walker; Jean W. Symington; G. H. Clement; R. I. T. Dunnachie; J. Watson; J. H. Leckie; J. W. Gibb.............. £2,412 to £3,075
Chief Dental Officer, J. W. Galloway....... £3,600
Senior Dental Officer, A. J. Ritchie......... £3,325
Dental Officers, R. A. Morrison; A. Pacitti; A. B. Potts..................... £2,306 to £2,950

Miscellaneous Appointments

Chief Inspector, Child Care and Probation, 23 Ainslie Place, Edinburgh 3, C. R. Corner £2,623 to £3,025
Chairman, After Care Council, Rev. Sir George F. MacLeod, Bt., M.C., D.D.
H.M. Inspector of Constabulary for Scotland, St. Andrew's House, Edinburgh, 1, T. Renfrew, C.B.E.................................. £3,400
Commandant, Scottish Police College, S. A. Kinnear, C.B.E.................................. £3,400
H.M. Inspector of Fire Services, A. D. Wilson £2,540 to £2,900
Chief Food and Dairy Officer, C. H. Chalmers, O.B.E. £2,100 to £2,600

State Managements Districts. Scotland

30 George Square, Glasgow
[Central: 4191]

General Manager, G. Thwaytes.. £2,618 to £2,800

Prisons Divisions

Broomhouse Drive, Edinburgh 11
[Craiglockhart: 4040]

Director of Scottish Prison and Borstal Services, T. M. Martin................... £2,800 to £3,500
Visiting Physician and Medical Adviser, T. D. Inch, C.B.E., M.C. (*part-time*).
Psychiatrist, W. Boyd, M.D. (*part-time*).

Prison Governors

Aberdeen, A. Angus........... £1,784 to £2,106
Edinburgh, J. McIntyre......... £2,284 to £2,618
Glasgow (Barlinnie), A. H. Anderson, O.B.E.. £2,776
Greenock, Miss E. L. W. Hobkirk, C.B.E., T.D. £1,784 to £2,106
Perth, G. S. W. Laidlaw....... £2,284 to £2,618
Peterhead, J. H. A. Frisby...... £2,284 to £2,618
Polmont Borstal Institution, D. Mackenzie £2,284 to £2,618

Mental Welfare Commission for Scotland

St. Andrew's House, Edinburgh, 1

Commissioners, Sir Hugh Rose Bt., T.D. (*Chairman*) £750; F. W. F. O'Brien, Q.C.; Mrs. Joan Wolrige-Gordon; Prof. W. M. Millar; Lt. Col. R. C. M. Monteith, M.C., T.D.; R. W. Patterson.... £210
Medical Commissioners, Dr. E. J. C. Hewitt; Dr. Anne N. M. Brittain................. £3,500
Medical Officers, Dr. R. P. J. McBroom; Dr. Catherine H. S. Begg; Dr. Patricia O'Kane £2,412 to £3,075
Secretary, J. Will.............. £1,615 to £2,061

Regional Hospital Boards

Northern, Reay House, Old Edinburgh Road, Inverness. *Chairman*, E. H. Macintosh. *Secretary*, W. A. Stevens.
North-Eastern, 1 Albyn Place, Aberdeen. *Chairman*, Lady Baird, C.B.E. *Secretary*, A. R. Batchelor.
Eastern, Vernonholme, Riverside Drive, Dundee. *Chairman*, L. F. Robertson. *Secretary*, J. K. Johnston.
South-Eastern, 11 Drumsheugh Gardens, Edinburgh. *Chairman*, C. S. Gumley, W.S. *Secretary*, W. L. Douglass.
Western, 351 Sauchiehall Street, Glasgow, C.2. *Chairman*, J. Dunlop. *Secretary*, P. S. Watt.

General Registry Office

New Register House, Edinburgh 2
[Edinburgh Waverley: 3952]

Registrar General of Births, Deaths and Marriages for Scotland, A. B. Taylor, C.B.E., D.Litt. £2,800 to £3,500
Secretary, R. MacLeod........ £2,172 to £2,507
Senior Executive Officer, C. F. Robertson £1,615 to £2,061

SCOTTISH DEVELOPMENT DEPARTMENT

St. Andrew's House, Edinburgh, 1
[Waverley: 8545]
Dover House, Whitehall, London, S.W.1
[Whitehall: 6151]

Secretary, T. D. Haddow, C.B............ £4,950
Under Secretaries, R. D. M. Bell; D. Caplan; J. H. McGuinness; W. G. Pottinger, C.V.O. ... £4,950
Assistant Secretaries, A. C. Cowan; F. Dawson; J. B. Fleming; E. L. Gillett; T. V. Hughson; H. F. G. Kelly; J. M. Ross; A. C. Sheldrake; C. D. Smith; J. E. Stark; H. H. A. Whitworth, M.B.E.; J. S. Scott Whyte..... £2,800 to £3,500
Principals, R. F. Butler; J. A. Cowell; R. D. Cramond; I. R. Duncan; G. M. Fair; B. J. Fiddes; T. R. H. Godden; I. D. Hamilton; P. K.

Harrison; R. I. Hulley; J. Kerr; J. B. Kirkwood, O.B.E.; T. L. Lister; J. G. S. Macphail; A. Milne, O.B.E.; J. B. More; G. J. Murray; G. Philipson; T. Rarity; N. E. Sharp; Miss S. D. Riddell; Miss B. S. Thomson........£1,894 to £2,646
Economic Adviser, P. M. Smith...£1,894 to £2,646
Statistician, J. Grant...........£1,894 to £2,646
Senior Chief Executive Officer, F. E. Bland £2,618 to £2,800
Chief Executive Officers, D. H. Collier; F. B. Drysdale; H. Forrest; H. Neville; L. A. Wells £2,172 to £2,507
Senior Executive Officers, A. J. Crawford; A. Gow; J. Henderson; C. T. Hole; G. P. McConnell; K. Mackay; R. Mowat; T. Moyes; S. G. Patterson; J. Pettigrew; J. Ramsay; J. Rodger; J. M. Thomson; J. Torrance; B. A. F. Vincent; Miss M. E. Hay; Miss M. A. McPherson £1,615 to £2,061

Professional Staff

Chief Engineer, J. B. Dempster............£3,750
Deputy Chief Engineer, J. W. Shiell £3,100 to £3,600
Chief Architect, T. A. Jeffryes.............£3,750
Chief Planning Officer, R. Grieve £3,750
Deputy Chief Architects, G. H. Lawrence; R. S. Morton; R. Woodcock.....£2,800 to £3,150
Regional Planning Officers, F. J. Connell; F. J. Evans, O.B.E.; G. Lyall.............£2,800 to £3,150
Chief Quantity Surveyor, J. C. Tait £2,800 to £3,150
Chief Road Engineer, J. S. McNeil £3,750
Deputy Chief Road Engineers, R. A. H. Allen; G. C. W. Hurry ....£2,800 to £3,150
Senior Civil Engineers, J. Crichton-Brown; W. Henderson, M.B.E. (*Bridge Engineer*); A. N. Sutherland.................£2,228 to £2,563
Chief Chemical Inspector, Dr. E. A. B. Birse..£3,150

HER MAJESTY'S STATIONERY OFFICE

Atlantic House, Holborn Viaduct, E.C.1
[City: 9876]

Bookshops in London:—

Retail.—York House, Kingsway, W.C.2., and 423 Oxford St., W.1.
Wholesale.—Cornwall House, Stamford Street, S.E.1.

H.M. Stationery Office was established in 1786 and is the British Government's central organization for the supply of printing, binding, office supplies and office machinery of all kinds, and published books and periodicals, for the Public Service at home and abroad; it also undertakes duplicating and distributing services for government departments. The Stationery Office is the publisher for the government, and has bookshops for the sale of government publications in London, Edinburgh, Cardiff, Manchester, Bristol, Birmingham and Belfast; leading booksellers in the larger towns act as agents; and there are wholesale departments in London, Edinburgh and Belfast from which booksellers may obtain supplies. It is also the agent for the sale of publications of the United Nations and its specialized agencies and for certain other international organizations. The Controller of the Stationery Office is under Letters Patent the *Queen's Printer of Acts of Parliament* and in him is vested the *Copyright in all British Government documents*.

Government publications are of a wide and varied range and over 6,000 publications are produced each year. They include the *London Gazette*, which has been issued twice weekly since 1665, and *Hansard*, the verbatim report of the proceedings in both Houses of Parliament, available on the morning following the debate. The Stationery Office has in stock some 40,000 current titles and its subscriptions and standing order lists contain 153,000 names. The annual sales total about 17,000,000 copies.

The aggregate net estimate for the department in 1963–64 was £20,378,000 (an increase of £1,679,000 on the same estimate for 1962–63).

Generally the department obtains its supplies from commercial sources by competitive tender. For printing and binding, however, the Stationery Office has its own printing works and binderies which produce about one-third of the total requirement, including telephone directories, pension allowance books, national savings certificates and stamps, postal orders, premium bonds, National Insurance stamps, road fund licences, television and wireless licences.

The staff employed on April 4, 1963, was 6,881, including 1,766 in warehouses and 2,482 at printing works; the total space occupied was two million square feet, including 1,250,000 sq. ft. for warehouse space and 475,000 sq. ft. for the printing works.

Controller, P. Faulkner, C.B...............£4,950
Private Secretary, W. S. Porter
Deputy Controller, R. H. Owen, C.M.G.....£4,050
Assistant Controllers, W. Donaldson (Group 1) (£3,500); H. Pickford, O.B.E. (Group 2); J. J. Cherns (Group 3) £3,150
Adviser on Typography, Sir Francis Meynell..*unpaid*

Group 1

Accounts Division

Director, C. W. Blundell.......£2,618 to £2,800
Deputy Director, R. H. Chisholm £1,615 to £2,061
Assistant Directors, E. J. Woods; Miss M. Beech; P. W. Buckerfield; P. Jefford. £1,615 to £2,061
Chief Examiner of Printers' and Binders' Accounts, A. J. C. Canham............£1,615 to £2,061

Establishments and Organization Division

Director, A. J. Long, I.S.O., M.B.E. £2,618 to £2,800
Deputy Director, R. F. Norris...£2,172 to £2,507
Assistant Directors, W. D. Forrester; G. L. Birch; T. S. Harris...............£1,615 to £2,061
Head of Survey Unit, D. C. Dashfield £2,172 to £2,507

Contracts Division

Director, J. W. E. Bates, O.B.E...£2,618 to £2,800
Deputy Director, R. H. Sloane..£1,615 to £2,061
Assistant Directors, A. W. Symons; J. Carpenter £1,615 to £2,061

Group 2

Printing Works Division

Director, J. P. Turner, O.B.E.....£2,618 to £2,800
Assistant Directors, D. A. Jamieson; A. H. Phillips £1,615 to £2,061
Senior Works Managers, J. Brookes; J. V. Westlake £2,172 to £2,507
Works Managers, J. W. H. Elvin; C. J. Errington; E. Warburton.............£1,615 to £2,061
Senior Deputy Works Managers, J. H. Hynes; J. McCausland; W. J. Scott.....£1,615 to £2,061

Printing and Binding Division

Director, D. E. Masson, M.B.E. £2,618 to £2,800
Deputy Director, A. S. Powis ...£1,615 to £2,061
Assistant Directors, J. E. Chapman; G. J. Hillier £1,615 to £2,061

Duplicating Division

Director, V. H. Morley........£2,172 to £2,507
Deputy Director, R. J. Crang....£1,615 to £2,061
Assistant Director, E. G. N. Calver £1,615 to £2,061

Co-ordination of Reproduction Services Section

Co-ordinator, J. W. Eyres........£2,172 to £2,507
Deputy Co-ordinator, H. M. Dodge, M.B.E. £1,615 to £2,061

Group 3

Publications Division

Director, N. G. Thompson.....£2,618 to £2,800
Deputy Director, F. E. Davey...£2,172 to £2,507
Assistant Directors, G. P. Brown; A. H. MacDonald; Miss A. R. Head; H. W. Leader; A. M. Foote £1,615 to £2,061

Typographic Design and Layout Section
Head of Section, W. J. Westwood £1,682 to £2,144

Supplies Division
Director, H. V. Roe.......... £2,618 to £2,800
Deputy Director, C. P. Bradshaw £1,615 to £2,061
Assistant Directors, C. White; P. J. George £1,615 to £2,061

Inspection, Transport and Warehouses Division
Director, C. Pengelly, M.B.E..... £2,618 to £2,800
Deputy Director, J. L. Wilkinson. £1,615 to £2,061
Deputy Director (Warehouses), A. R. Heritage £1,615 to £2,061
Chief Examiner of Paper and Office Requisites, J. Shore.................... £1,806 to £2,147

REGIONAL OFFICES

Scotland

Government Buildings, Bankhead Avenue, Edinburgh 11.
Bookshop: 13a Castle Street, Edinburgh 2.
Director, J. P. Morgan......... £2,172 to £2,507
Deputy Director, S. L. Palmer... £1,615 to £2,061

Wales

Bookshop: 109 St. Mary Street, Cardiff.
Officer in Charge, J. Holden.

Northern Ireland

Chichester House, Chichester Street, Belfast 1
Retail Bookshop: 80 Chichester Street, Belfast.
Wholesale Bookshop: Custom House, Belfast.
Director, J. L. Jones, O.B.E....... £2,172 to £2,507

Manchester

Broadway, Chadderton, Lancs.
Bookshop: 39–41 King Street, Manchester 2.
Director, R. E. Pysden.......... £2,172 to £2,507
Deputy Director, B. A. Smith... £1,615 to £2,061

Bristol

Ashton Vale Road, Bristol 3
Bookshop: 50 Fairfax Street, Bristol 1.
Superintendent (vacant).

Birmingham

Bookshop: 35 Smallbrook, Ringway, Birmingham 5.

STATUTE LAW COMMITTEE

House of Lords, S.W.1

President, The Lord Chancellor.
Members, Sir Cecil Carr, K.C.B., Q.C., LL.D.; Sir George Coldstream, K.C.B., Q.C.; Sir Charles Cunningham, K.C.B., K.B.E., C.V.O.; P. Faulkner, C.B.; E. G. M. Fletcher, M.P.; J. H. Gibson, C.B., Q.C.; Sir Laurence Helsby, G.C.B., K.B.E.; The Rt. Hon. Sir John Hobson, O.B.E., T.D., Q.C., M.P.; Sir Noel Hutton, K.C.B., Q.C.; Sir Harold Kent, G.C.B.; Sir Hugh Lucas-Tooth, Bt., M.P.; The Lord Morris of Borth-y-Gest, P.C., C.B.E., M.C.; Sir William Murrie, K.B.E., C.B.; H. W. Pritchard; The Lord Reid, P.C.; The Rt. Hon. I. H. Shearer, Q.C.; The Viscount Simonds, P.C.; Sir Robert Speed, C.B., Q.C.; T. G. Talbot, C.B., Q.C.; Sir Burke Trend, K.C.B., C.V.O.
Secretary, R. W. Perceval.

Statutory Publications Office

Queen Anne's Chambers, 41 Tothill Street, S.W.1
[Whitehall: 7363]
Editors, S. G. G. Edgar; A. B. Lyons £2,650 to £3,000

SUGAR BOARD

52, Mark Lane, E.C.3
[Royal : 6221]

The Sugar Board was constituted under the Sugar Act, 1956, on October 15, 1956. The Board buys the sugar which the United Kingdom has contracted to buy under the Commonwealth Sugar Agreement at prices negotiated annually by the Government and resells the sugar commercially at world prices. The Board also provides temporary finance for the British Sugar Corporation and receives from or pays to the Corporation any surplus or deficit arising on the production and refining of home grown beet sugar. The Board, in turn, balances its accounts, taking one year with another, by receiving a surcharge or making a distribution payment, on all imported and home produced sugar and molasses.

Chairman, Sir George Dunnett, K.B.E., C.B.. £5,000
Vice-Chairman, J. A. Dyson, C.B.E........ £3,500
Members (part-time), F. E. Harmer, C.M.G. (*salary not drawn*); G. F. A. Burgess; Sir Leslie Phillips, C.B.E.................................. £750
Secretary, A. V. Parsons, M.B.E.
Chief Marketing Officer, R. C. W. Gunner, M.B.E.
Chief Accountant, G. Keddie, M.B.E.

DEPARTMENT OF TECHNICAL CO-OPERATION

Eland House, Stag Place, Victoria, S.W.1
[Victoria: 2377]

The Department of Technical Co-operation was established in July, 1961. Its functions include the coordination of technical assistance to countries outside the United Kingdom, previously undertaken by the three Overseas Departments.

Secretary for Technical Co-operation, THE RT. HON. (L.) ROBERT CARR, M.P.............. £3,750
Private Secretary, J. D. Anderson, M.C.
Parliamentary Private Secretary, D. G. Smith, M.P.
Director-General, Sir Andrew Cohen, K.C.M.G., K.C.V.O., O.B.E.......................... £4,950
Private Secretary, Miss M. Norman.
Under-Secretaries, Sir Alan Dudley, K.B.E., C.M.G.; N. Leach; W. A. C. Mathieson, C.M.G., M.B.E.; P. Rogers, C.M.G. £4,050
Controller for Special Projects, A. H. P. Humphrey, C.M.G., O.B.E........................ £3,800
Assistant Secretaries, C. L. S. Cope; R. B. M. King, M.C.; A. A. W. Landymore; O. H. Morris; R. W. Newsam, C.V.O.; D. L. Pearson (*Establishment Officer*); D. M. Smith; M. G. Smith; W. J. Smith; W. D. Sweaney; J. K. Thompson, C.M.G. £2,800 to £3,500

Advisory and Specialist Staff

Head of Overseas Information Co-ordination Office, J. A. Bergin............. £2,800 to £3,500
**Head of Administrative Services Branch*, R. S. Hudson, C.M.G. .... (+ £239 allce.) £2,646
**Land Tenure Adviser*, S. R. Simpson, C.B.E. £1,894 to £2,646
**Local Government Adviser*, C. A. G. Wallis, O.B.E. £1,894 to £2,646
**Agricultural Adviser*, Sir Geoffrey Nye, K.C.M.G., O.B.E.................. £3,275 to £3,600
**Deputy Agricultural Adviser*, G. M. Roddan, C.M.G. £2,800 to £3,150
**Adviser on Agricultural Research*, D. Rhind, C.M.G., O.B.E.................. £3,275 to £3,600
**Adviser on Animal Health*, K. D. S. MacOwen, C.B.E.................. £3,275 to £3,600
**Adviser on Co-operatives*, B. J. Surridge, C.M.G., O.B.E.................. £2,800 to £3,150
Educational Adviser, Sir Christopher Cox, K.C.M.G. £3,275 to £3,600
Deputy Educational Adviser, H. Houghton, C.B.E. £2,800 to £3,150
Woman Educational Adviser, Miss F. H. Gwilliam, O.B.E.................. £2,800 to £3,150
**Adviser on Technical Education*, J. C. Jones, C.B.E. £2,800 to £3,150

**Assistant Educational Adviser*, D. J. S. Crozier, C.M.G. .... £1,839 to £2,590
**Adviser on Engineering Appointments*, F. H. Woodrow, C.B.E. .... £1,894 to £2,646
**Films Adviser (part-time)*, W. Sellers, O.B.E. .. £682
**Forestry Adviser*, C. Swabey, C.M.G. £3,275 to £3,600
Head of Information Department, C. G. Moyle £2,618 to £2,800
**Secretary, Inter-University Council and University Grants Advisory Committee*, I. C. M. Maxwell £2,800
**Secretary, Council for Technical Education and Training for Overseas Countries*, H. M. Collins (+£350 *allce.*) £2,418
Labour Adviser, G. Foggon, C.M.G., C.B.E. £3,275 to £3,600
Assistant Labour Adviser, Miss S. A. Ogilvie, O.B.E. £1,839 to £2,590
Adviser on Land Drainage and Irrigation (part-time), D. S. Ferguson £500
**Medical Adviser*, J. M. Liston, C.M.G. £4,150
**Deputy Medical Adviser*, P. W. Dill-Russell, C.B.E. £3,275 to £3,600
**Adviser on Medical Research*, R. Lewthwaite, C.M.G. O.B.E. .... £3,275 to £3,600
**Nursing Adviser*, Miss F. N. Udell, C.B.E. £1,888 to £2,028
Adviser on Social Development, W. H. Chinn, C.M.G. £2,800 to £3,150
Scientific Advisers, *D. C. Mandeville; W. Railston, Ph.D. .... £2,800 to £3,150
Director of Overseas (Geodetic and Topographic) Surveys and Surveys Adviser, G. J. Humphries, O.B.E. .... £3,125 to £3,450
Director of Overseas Geological Surveys and Geological Surveys Adviser, S. H. Shaw, C.M.G., O.B.E., Ph.D. .... £3,275 to £3,600
**Head of Middle East Development Division (Beiru)*, P. P. Howell, O.B.E. £3,625
Director of Anti-Locust Research Centre, P. T. Haskell, Ph.D. .... £3,275 to £3,600
**Special Adviser (Delhi Engineering College)*, W. G. Wormal.
Principals, J. D. Anderson, M.C.; K. G. Ashton; R. L. Baxter; R. A. Browning; J. L. F. Buist; S. A. Bunce; M. L. Cahill; G. K. Caston; W. T. A. Cox; F. P. Dunnill; Hon. C. A. Hankey, O.B.E.; Miss E. O. Mercer, M.B.E., Ph.D.; H. Nield; A. J. Peckham; C. R. A. Rae; J. E. Rednall; A. K. Robertson; B. E. Rolfe; A. K. Russell, D.Phil.; D. I. Scanlan, M.V.O., O.B.E.; B. G. Stone, O.B.E.; G. W. Thom, O.B.E.; A. M. Turner £1,894 to £2,641
Temporary Principals, B. A. Astley, O.B.E.; B. Abbott, O.B.E.; J. R. V. H. Bromage, C.B.E.; J. A. Burgess, O.B.E.; A. B. Cozens, O.B.E.; G. E. Fane-Smith, C.M.G.; E. J. Gibbons, C.M.G., C.B.E.; D. E. Glason; F. L. Greenland; R. C. H. Greig; C. M. H. Harrison; L. M. Heaney, C.M.G.; F. D. Hibbert, C.M.G.; R. J. J. Hill, C.I.E.; A. B. Hodgson, C.M.G.; H. E. O. Hughes, C.B.E.; S. J. Moore; C. N. F. Odgers, C.M.G.; A. E. Ridley, M.V.O.; R. K. M. Saker, C.B.E. £1,894 to £2,646
Chief Executive Officers, F. K. Boyle; G. G. Kesby, M.B.E. .... £2,172 to £2,507
Senior Executive Officers, F. W. Attwell; B. D. Barber; E. A. C. Bents; R. F. R. Deare; D. C. Fincham; K. G. Fry; D. Hinshelwood; Miss H. N. Lane; K. D. Law; B. G. Meara; Miss E. M. Murphy; V. R. B. Shalson; F. E. Sitch; A. H. Tansley; A. M. Trick (*Accountant*); T. J. Wilshire .... £1,615 to £2,061
Statistician, W. L. Kendall ...... £1,894 to £2,646

Overseas Service Resettlement Bureau

**Director and Head of Bureau*, H. A. S. Johnston, C.M.G., O.B.E., D.F.C.

*Temporary.

THAMES CONSERVANCY

See CONSERVANCY BOARDS

BOARD OF TRADE

Horse Guards Avenue, S.W.1
[Trafalgar: 8855]

The Board of Trade has general responsibility for the United Kingdom's commerce, industry and overseas trade, and particular responsibility in relation to all industries, except those which are the direct concern of other Departments, e.g. food, agriculture and fisheries, building and quarrying, electronics, ship building, fuel and power, and transport.

The Divisions of the Board form four main groups, the Overseas group, the Home group, the Regulative group, and the Common Service Divisions such as the Accountant's, Statistics, Finance, and Establishment Divisions, and the Solicitor's Department. The Board of Trade is represented in the Commonwealth by Trade Commissioners, and in foreign countries is assisted by Commerical Departments of H.M. missions and consulates.

President of the Board of Trade, THE RT. HON. FREDERICK JAMES ERROLL, T.D., M.P. £5,000
Private Secretaries, P. W. Carey; Hon. W. J. L. Plowden; I. Cumming; Miss C. H. Welch.
Parliamentary Private Secretary, J. M. L. Prior. M.P. .... *unpaid.*
Ministers of State, ALAN GREEN, M.P.; THE LORD DERWENT £3,750
Parliamentary Secretary, D. E. C. Price, M.P. .. £2,500
Parliamentary Clerk, B. M. Bird . £2,237 to £2,572
Permanent Secretary, Sir Richard Powell, K.C.B., K.B.E., C.M.G. £7,015
Private Secretary, D. O'Connell.
Second Secretaries, J. Leckie C.B.; W. Hughes, C.B., D. R. Serpell, C.B., C.M.G., O.B.E. £5,015
Solicitor, G. Ryder £5,015
Accountant Adviser, Sir Richard Yeabsley, C.B.E. *unpaid*

Commercial Relations and Exports Department

Under-Secretaries, A. E. Welch, C.B., C.M.G.; S. Golt; C. M. P. Brown, C.M.G.; D. Carter. £4,115
Adviser on Commercial Policy, C. W. Jardine £4,115
Assistant Secretaries, A. G. White; T. H. Sinclair; Miss M. W. Dennehy, C.B.E.; K. E. Mackenzie; E. L. Phillips, C.M.G.; S. L. Edwards; A. N. Halls, M.B.E., T.D.; R. L. Davies; W. P. W. Barnes; J. R. D. Gildea; Miss Y. Lovat-Williams; P. W. Ridley .... £2,865 to £3,565

General Departments

Under-Secretaries, G. Bowen, C.B., C.M.G.; S. Golt £4,115
Assistant Secretaries, V. I. Chapman; Mrs. P. B. M. James; J. M. Reynolds; K. Taylor £2,865 to £3,565

Export Licensing Branch

Hillgate House, 35 Old Bailey, E.C.4
[City: 5757]

Controller, E. J. Cornell .... £2,683 to £2,865

Export Services Branch

Hillgate House, 35 Old Bailey, E.C.4
[City: 5757]

Director, H. Birtles, C.B.E. £3,215

Export Publicity and Fairs Branch

Export Publicity and Fairs Officer, M. L. G. Balfour, C.B.E. .... £2,865 to £3,565
Principal Information Officer, A. B. Savage £2,237 to £2,572
Chief Executive Officers, R. H. Edmondson; D. Hacker .... £2,237 to £2,572
Senior Information Officer, D. M. Edwards £1,680 to £2,126

News Branch

Chief Information Officer, N. Shepherd £2,865 to £3,565
Editor, Board of Trade Journal, J. E. Holroyd £2,237 to £2,572
Chief Press Officer, Miss M. I. Lee £2,237 to £2,572

Deputy Chief Press Officer, R. J. J. Tuite, M.B.E. £1,680 to £2,126
Senior Information Officers, C. D. Wright; M. R. F. Young .... £1,680 to £2,126

Industries and Manufactures Department

Under-Secretaries, C. W. Sanders, C.B.; M. M. Ord-Johnstone; G. Parker £4,115
Assistant Secretaries, R. B. Tippetts; W. G. Onslow; J. L. May, C.B.E.; A. L. Burgess; P. Harris; D. Caplan; H. F. Heinemann; J. A. Turpin; Miss K. E. Boyes; Mrs. E. L. K. Sinclair £2,865 to £3,565

Standard Weights and Measures Department
26 Chapter Street, S.W.1
[Victoria: 7032]

Controller, T. G. Poppy, O.B.E. .. £2,293 to £2,628

Jute Control

Controller, A. B. Ferguson, O.B.E. £2,900 to £3,150

Distribution of Industry and Regional Division

Under-Secretary, Miss N. K. Fisher £4,115
Assistant Secretaries, S. H. Levine, C.B.E.; F. W. Glaves-Smith; E. V. Marchant £2,865 to £3,565

Regional Organization

Northern (Newcastle-upon-Tyne)
Controller, R. Wood £3,150

Yorkshire and Lincolnshire (Leeds)
Controller, E. Atherton .... £2,800 to £3,500

London and South Eastern
(Cromwell House, Dean Stanley Street, S.W.1)
Controller, B. W. T. Kay, C.B.E. .. £2,865 to £3,565

Eastern
(Cromwell House, Dean Stanley Street, S.W.1)
Controller, D. A. Wilson, C.B.E. .. £2,865 to £3,565

South Western (Bristol)
Controller, M. Weber £3,150

Office for Wales (Cardiff)
Controller, R. W. Daniel, C.B.E. .. £2,800 to £3,500

Midland (Birmingham)
Controller, P. J. L. Homan ...... £2,800 to £3,500

North Western (Manchester)
Controller, R. J. Forbes, C.B.E. £3,150

Office for Scotland (Glasgow)
Controller, C. J. A. Whitehouse, O.B.E. £2,800 to £3,500

Tariff and Import Policy Division

Under-Secretary, A. D. Neale, M.B.E. £4,115
Assistant Secretaries, Miss H. Barkley; P. B. Hypher; G. R. Denman .... £2,865 to £3,565

Import Licensing Branch
Hillgate House, 35 Old Bailey, E.C.4
[City: 5757]

Controller, E. J. Cornell .... £1,959 to £2,711

Insurance and Companies Department* and Bankruptcy Department

Under-Secretary, R. J. W. Stacy, C.B. £4,115
Assistant Secretaries, J. B. Smith; C. J. Homewood £2,865 to £3,565
Inspector General of Companies, Companies Liquidation and Bankruptcy, G. F. Morris £3,565

* Annual Returns and other documents filed with the Registrar of Companies are available for inspection at the Public Search Room, Companies House, 55–71 City Road, E.C.1.

Accountants Division
Hillgate House, 35 Old Bailey, E.C.4
[City: 5757]

Director, H. A. Parfitt, O.B.E. £3,565

Finance Division

Principal Finance Officer, A. C. Hill, C.B. £4,115
Assistant Secretary, S. W. T. Mitchelmore £2,865 to £3,565

Enemy Property Branch
Gavrelle House, Bunhill Row, E.C.1
[Monarch: 4071]

Controller, R. H. M. Clayton ... £1,959 to £2,711

Solicitor's Department

Solicitor, G. Ryder £5,015
Principal Assistant Solicitor, E. W. Dean, C.B.E. £4,115
Assistant Solicitors, J. F. Brown; R. W. Rainsford-Hannay; W. T. Beynon; H. C. Cotman, M.C.; F. A. Bayly; J. A. E. Davies .. £2,965 to £3,565

Establishment Division

Principal Establishment and Organization Officer, R. C. Bryant, C.B. £4,115
Assistant Secretaries, Dr. F. E. Budd; S. R. Raffan; P. E. Thornton; S. D. Wilks . £2,865 to £3,565

Statistics Division

Director of Statistics, J. Stafford, C.B. £4,115
Deputy Director of Statistics, Miss J. M. Maton, C.B.E. £3,815
Chief Statisticians, H. C. Stanton; W. Rudoe; T. Paterson; H. E. Browning; A. G. Carruthers £2,865 to £3,565

Board of Trade Advisory Committee
(Local Employment Act, 1960)
Neville House, Page Street, S.W.1
[Victoria: 9040]

Chairman, W. K. M. Slimmings, C.B.E.
Members, H. Ballantyne; Brig. L. H. McRobert, C.B.E., T.D.; L. Poole; S. A. H. Whetmore, C.B.E.; P. O. Williams, C.B.E.
Secretary, J. Darragh.

MINISTRY OF TRANSPORT

St. Christopher House, S.E.1
[Waterloo: 7999]

Minister, RT. HON. ERNEST MARPLES, M.P. .. £5,000
Private Secretary, C. N. Tebay.
Assistant Private Secretaries, B. Strong; Miss C. O. Blake.
Parliamentary Private Secretary, Miss J. M. Quennell, M.P.
Joint Parliamentary Secretaries, The Lord Chesham; The Hon. Thomas Galbraith, M.P.; Vice-Admiral J. Hughes-Hallett, C.B., D.S.O., M.P. £2,500
Permanent Secretary, Sir Thomas Padmore, K.C.B. £7,015
Private Secretary, E. J. D. Pearson.
Deputy Secretaries, R. C. Chilver, C.B. (*Shipping*); R. N. Heaton, C.B. (*Highways*); M. M. V. Custance, C.B. (*Inland Transport*) £5,015

Advisers to the Minister

Hon. Advisers on Marine Insurance Matters, Sir Philip D'Ambrumenil; H. Dumas.
Hon. Adviser on Shipping in Port, Sir Eric Millbourn, C.M.G.
Hon. Adviser on London Traffic Management, Sir Alexander Samuels, C.B.E.
Economic Adviser, Sir Robert Hall, K.C.M.G., C.B.

Marine

Under-Secretary, B. E. Bellamy £4,115

Crews
Assistant Secretary, A. W. Wood £2,865 to £3 565

Navigational Aids
Assistant Secretary, O. Cochran, O.B.E. £2,865 to £3,565

H.M. Coastguard
Chief Inspector, Cdr. D. F. White, R.D., R.N.R. (*ret.*) £2,445
Deputy do., Cdr. S. H. Pinchin, O.B.E., D.S.C., R.N., (*ret.*) £2,120

Safety
Assistant Secretary, H. E. Robson £2,865 to £3,565

Professional and Consultative Staff
Professional Officer (Chief Nautical Surveyor), Capt. J. H. Quick, C.B.E. £3,565
Engineer Surveyor in Chief, A. T. Willens .. £3,565
Chief Ship Surveyor, G. R. Weir £3,565
Professional Officer (Navigational Aids), Capt. H. Menzies, R.N. £2,865

General Register and Record Office of Shipping and Seamen
Llantrisant Road, Llandaff, Cardiff
(Cardiff: 71221)
Registrar General, G. T. Plant ... £2,172 to £2,507

Ports and Shipping Operations
Under-Secretary, D. E. O'Neill, C.B. £4,115

Ports
Assistant Secretary, D. G. Fagan .. £2,865 to £3,565

Sea Transport
Assistant Secretary and Director, R. W. Bullmore, M.B.E. .... £2,865 to £3,565

Shipping Planning
Assistant Secretary, A. R. Hiscock £2,865 to £3,565

Shipping Policy and Shipbuiding
Under-Secretary, T. F. Bird, C.B. £4,115

Foreign Shipping Relations A
Assistant Secretary (vacant) .... £2,865 to £3,565

Foreign Shipping Relations B
Assistant Secretary, S. M. A. Banister £2,865 to £3,565

General Shipping Policy
Assistant Secretary, R. D. Poland £2,865 to £3,565

Shipbuilding and Ship Repairs
Assistant Secretary, J. H. P. Draper £2,865 to £3,565
Director of Merchant Shipbuilding and Repairs, A. Sutcliffs £3,065

General, Statistics and International Transport
Under-Secretary, L. S. Mills £4,115

Statistics
Chief Statistician, Mrs. M. Venning £2,865 to £3,565

General
Assistant Secretary, J. R. Madge . £2,865 to £3,565

International Transport
Assistant Secretary, W. J. Sharp .. £2,865 to £3,565

Lands and Contracts
Under-Secretary, R. B. Lang, O.B.E. £4,115

Highways Lands and Development
Assistant Secretary, C. H. Wykes. £2,865 to £3,565

Highways Management and Services
Assistant Secretary, G. G. D. Hill . £2,865 to £3,565

Contracts
Deputy Director, S. Emm, M.B.E. £3,215

Highways and Traffic, Southern
Under-Secretary, J. N. Wood £4,115

London Traffic
Assistant Secretary, E. S. Ainley ... £2,865 to £3,565

Highways A
Assistant Secretary, G. Cockerham £2,865 to £3,565

Highways B
Assistant Secretary, J. E. Sanderson £2,865 to £3,565

Highways and Traffic, Northern
Under-Secretary, B. P. H. Dickinson £4,115

Highways N
Assistant Secretary, R. H. Lawrence £2,865 to £3,565

Highways R
Assistant Secretary, L. E. Dale ... £2,865 to £3,565

Highways Special Roads
Assistant Secretary, T. R. Newman £2,865 to £3,565

General Traffic
Assistant Secretary, T. G. Usborne £2,865 to £3,565

Highways Engineering
Chief Engineer, J. F. A. Baker, C.B. £4,415
Deputy Chief Engineers, C. E. Hollinghurst; J. E. Jones; J. G. Smith £3,815
Assistant Chief Engineers, H. C. Adams, M.C.; H. N. Ginns; P. J. Lyth; A. M. Ker; H. S. Keep, C.B.E., M.C.; W. H. Spencer .. £3,040 to £3,565

London Traffic Management Unit
Head of Unit, J. T. Duff .... £2,865 to £3,215

Road Safety, Road Transport and Vehicle Regulation
Under-Secretary, D. C. Haselgrove, C.B. £4,115

Road Transport
Assistant Secretary, J. M. Moore, D.S.C. £2,865 to £3,565

Road Safety
Assistant Secretary, A. M. Houghton £2,865 to £3,565

Vehicle Regulation
Assistant Secretary, J. W. L. Ivimy £2,865 to £3,565

Driving and Motor Licences
Head of Branch, P. A. Waller .... £2,683 to £2,865

Area Road Safety Units
Hampshire Unit (63/65 Above Bar, Southampton).
Head of Unit, Maj.-Gen. G. D. G. Heyman, C.B., C.B.E. £2,500
Warwickshire Unit (King Edward Building, 205 Corporation Street, Birmingham 4).
Head of Unit, G. E. Ridley £2,500

Mechanical Engineering
Chief Mechanical Engineer, H. Perring £3,815

Railways
Under-Secretary, C. P. Scott-Malden £4,115

Railways A
Assistant Secretary, H. Gillender .. £2,865 to £3,565

Railways B
Assistant Secretary, E. C. V. Goad. £2,865 to £3,565

Nationalised Transport
Under-Secretary, O. F. Gingell £4,115

Nationalised Transport A
Assistant Secretary, K. T. Harrison £2,865 to £3,565

Nationalised Transport B
Assistant Secretary, A. H. M. Irwin £2,865 to £3,565

Railway Inspectorate
Chief Inspecting Officer, Col. D. McMullen, R.E. (*ret.*) £3,715

COMMON SERVICES

Establishment, General and Organization

Under-Secretary, J. E. Hampson, C.B. (*Principal Establishment and Organization Officer*)..... £4,115

Establishment Staffing

Assistant Secretary, G. C. Wardale £2,865 to £3,565

Office Services

Controller, H. F. S. Rickerby, O.B.E. £2,683 to £2,865

Establishment Organization

Assistant Secretary, P. E. Lazarus £2,865 to £3,565

Information

Chief Information Officer, F. D. Bickerton £2,865 to £3,565

Welfare

Chief Welfare Officer, Miss C. H. Henry, M.B.E. £1,680 to £2,126

Finance

Under-Secretary (Finance), H. W. Cauthery.. £4,115

Finance Highways and Accounts

Head of Division, C. F. Rigby, O.B.E....... £3,215

Finance Transport and Shipping

Assistant Secretary, A. S. Robertson £2,865 to £3,565

REGIONAL OFFICES

Marine Survey Offices

Bristol Channel—Cardiff: *Principal Officer*, Capt. H. W. D. Story............ £2,800 to £3,000

East England—Hull: *Principal Officer* A. M. Daniels, O.B.E.............. £2,800 to £3,000

East of Scotland—Leith, Edinburgh 6; *Principal Officer*, F. J. Girling...... ....£2,800 to £3,000

Liverpool—Liverpool 3: *Principal Officer*, Capt. E. W. Lewis.............. £2,800 to £3,000

London—Walsingham House, Seething Lane, E.C.3: *Principal Officer*, Capt. W. A. Hann £2,865 to £3,065

North East England—Newcastle 1: *Principal Officer*, J. Graham, O.B.E............ £2,800 to £3,000

Northern Ireland—Belfast: *Principal Officer*, I. M. Lorimer .... £2,800 to £3,000

South and South West England—Southampton: *Principal Officer*, Capt. D. W. Jones £2,800 to £3,000

West of Scotland—Glasgow, C.2: *Principal Officer*, J. W. Bull .... £2,800 to £3,000

Mercantile Marine Offices

St. Christopher House, S.E.1: *Inspector of Mercantile Marine Offices*, C. A. Ashley.. £2,237 to £2,572

Bristol Channel—Cardiff: *District Superintendent*, F. S. Hammond............ £1,615 to £2,061

Liverpool—Liverpool 1: *District Superintendent*, A. H. Lynam.............. £1,615 to £2,061

London—Dock Street, E.1: *District Superintendent*, T. A. Patterson............ £1,680 to £2,126

North East England—Newcastle 1: *District Superintendent*, R. W. Forster....... £1,615 to £2,061

Scotland and Northern Ireland—Glasgow, C.2: *District Superintendent*, R. A. Parkin £1,615 to £2,061

South England—Southampton: *District Superintendent*, H. W. C. Wernham, M.B.E. £1,615 to £2,061

Divisional Road Engineers

Eastern—Bedford: A. K. Richards £2,975 to £3,500

Metropolitan—St. Christopher House, S.E.1: J. A. S. Dakers .... £3,040 to £3,565

Midland—Birmingham 3: J. S. Berry £2,975 to £3,500

North Eastern—Leeds 1: R. B. S. Chettoe £2,975 to £3,500

North Midland—Nottingham: A. D. Holland, T.D. £2,975 to £3,500

North Western—Manchester 3: J. L. Paisley, M.B.E. £2,975 to £3,500

South Eastern—Guildford: T. E. Hutton £2,975 to £3,500

South Western—Exeter: L. P. F. Hubbard £2,975 to £3,500

Wales and Monmouth—Cardiff: J. J. Liptrott £2,975 to £3,500

Transport Commissioner for Wales and Monmouthshire—Cardiff: A. G. Curtis, O.B.E....... £3,788

Traffic Commissioners and Licensing Authorities

Traffic Areas and Chairmen

East Midland—Nottingham: C. R. Hodgson, O.B.E. £3,550

Eastern—Cambridge: W. P. S. Ormond... £3,550

Metropolitan—Stuart House, Soho Square, W.1. D. I. R. Muir, O.B.E. (*Traffic Commissioner*) £3,638

Northern—Newcastle 1: J. A. T. Hanlon.... £3,550

North Western—Manchester 3; Maj.-Gen. A. F. J. Elmslie, C.B....................... £3,550

Scottish—Edinburgh 1: W. F. Quin........ £3,550

South Eastern—Southbridge House, Southwark Bridge Road, S.E.1: H. J. Thom, C.I.E., C.B.E., M.C............................. £3,550

South Wales—Cardiff: R. R. Jackson..... £3,550

West Midland—Birmingham 15: J. Else, M.B.E., T.D. £3,550

Western—Bristol: S. W. Nelson, C.B.E..... £3,550

Yorkshire—Leeds 2: F. S. Eastwood, C.B.E... £3,550

THE TRANSPORT HOLDING COMPANY

Melbury House, Melbury Terrace, N.W.1
[Paddington: 1281]

The Transport Holding Company is a statutory company established under the Transport Act, 1962, to own and manage all the transport investments of the former British Transport Commission except those transferred to the Railways, London, Docks and British Waterways Boards, and any other such investments which may be acquired from time to time.

The transferred investments are in the form of shares in companies, including bus companies, road haulage activities, travel agencies and shipping services. These vested in the Holding Company on January 1, 1963.

The road passenger interests transferred comprise the Tilling Group companies in England and Wales and the Scottish Omnibuses Group. There is also a number of companies in which shares are owned in equal parts with the British Electric Traction Group. The road haulage interests transferred are those of the former British Road Services Division of the Transport Commission. Travel agencies are represented by the Thos. Cook group of companies, and shipping by Atlantic Steam Navigation Co. Ltd., and Associated Humber Lines Ltd.

Chairman, Sir Philip Warter.

Deputy Chairman and Managing Director, Sir Reginald Wilson.

Directors, D. H. Cameron of Lochiel, T.D.; R. C. Clifford-Turner; B. H. Harbour; W. E. Jones, C.B.E.; H. L. Roy Matthews, C.B.E.; Sir Mark Turner.

Chief Secretary, G. W. Quick Smith, C.B.E.

Comptroller, H. E. Osborn, C.B.E.

Secretary, L. H. Mapleston.

THE TREASURY

Great George Street, S.W.1
[Whitehall: 1234]

The office of the Lord High Treasurer has been continuously in commission for well over 200 years. The Lords Commissioners of H.M. Treasury consist of the First Lord of the Treasury (who is also the Prime Minister), the Chancellor of the Exchequer and five Junior Lords. This Board of Commissioners is assisted at present by a Chief Secretary, a Parliamentary Secretary, a Financial Secretary and an Economic Secretary who are also

Ministers, and joint Permanent Secretaries. The Prime Minister and First Lord is not primarily concerned in the day-to-day aspects of Treasury business, and the Junior Lords and the Parliamentary Secretary are Government Whips in the House of Commons. The management of the Treasury therefore devolves on the Chancellor of the Exchequer and the Chief Secretary to the Treasury, who are both members of the Cabinet. The Chancellor is responsible for the general direction of economic and financial policy, at home and overseas. The Chief Secretary is responsible, under the general direction of the Chancellor, for the control of public expenditure and the management of the Civil Service. The Chancellor and the Chief Secretary are assisted at ministerial level by the Financial and Economic Secretaries, the Financial Secretary discharging in particular the traditional responsibility of the Treasury for the procedures for securing the voting of funds by Parliament.

Prime Minister and First Lord of the Treasury, THE RT. HON. HAROLD MACMILLAN, M.P.....£10,000 (*£4,000 free of tax*)

Principal Private Secretary, T. J. Bligh, D.S.O., O.B.E., D.S.C.

Private Secretaries, P. F. de Zulueta (*Overseas Affairs*); P. J. Woodfield (*Parliamentary and Home Affairs*); J. E. R. Wyndham, M.B.E. (*Home Affairs and General*).

Secretary for Appointments, J. F. Hewitt.

Adviser on Public Relations, S. H. Evans, C.M.G., O.B.E.............................£3,863

Assistant Private Secretaries, Miss J. Summers; Miss S. A. Minto, O.B.E.

Parliamentary Private Secretary, S. K. Cunningham, Q.C., M.P.

Lords Commissioners of the Treasury

The Prime Minister (*First Lord*); The Chancellor of the Exchequer.

Junior Lords of the Treasury

J. E. B. Hill, M.P.; W. J. Peel, M.P.; F. F. Pearson, M.B.E., M.P.; G. T. C. Campbell, M.C., M.P.; M. C. Hamilton, M.P..............*each* £2,000

Chancellor of the Exchequer, THE RT. HON. REGINALD MAUDLING, M.P........................£5,000

Principal Private Secretary, D. J. Mitchell.

Private Secretaries, T. H. Caulcott; Mrs. R. E. J. Gilmore.

Assistant Private Secretary and Parliamentary Clerk, R. A. Bell-Berry.

Parliamentary Private Secretary, J. D. Gibson-Watt, M.C., M.P.......................*unpaid.*

Chief Secretary to the Treasury (and Paymaster-General), THE RT. HON. JOHN ARCHIBALD BOYD-CARPENTER, M.P.................£5,000

Private Secretaries, K. E. Couzens; F. G. Burrett; J. W. Whitaker.

Assistant Private Secretary, E. A. Whitear.

Parliamentary Private Secretary, P. W. Holland, M.P.

Parliamentary Secretary of the Treasury, Rt. Hon. M. Redmayne, D.S.O., M.P.............£3,750

Private Secretaries, A. H. Warren, M.B.E.; Miss D. A. Truman; A. T. R. Fletcher.

Financial Secretary, A. P. L. Barber, T.D., M.P. £3,750

Private Secretary, A. M. H. Battishill,

Economic Secretary, E. D. L. Du Cann, M.P. £3,750

Private Secretary, C. W. France.

Joint Permanent Secretaries, Sir William Armstrong, K.C.B., M.V.O.; Sir Laurence Helsby, G.C.B., K.B.E. £7,515

Ceremonial Officer, Sir Robert Knox, K.C.B., K.C.V.O., D.S.O.

Second Secretaries, P. Allen, C.B.; R. W. B. Clarke, C.B., O.B.E.; Sir Denis Rickett, K.C.M.G., C.B. £7,015

Economic Adviser to the Government, A. K. Cairncross, C.M.G...................................£5,265

Third Secretaries, Mrs. E. M. Abbot, C.B.E.; D. A. V. Allen, C.B.; S. Goldman; Sir Ronald Harris, K.C.V.O., C.B.; W. W. Morton, C.B.; L. Petch; D. B. Pitblado, C.B., C.V.O.............£5,015

Under-Secretaries, G. R. Bell; G. B. Blaker, C.M.G.; T. J. Bligh, D.S.O., O.B.E., D.S.C.; R. F. Bretherton, C.B.; H. A. Harding, C.M.G.; D. F. Hubback; M. E. Johnston; S. L. Lees, M.V.O.; D. McKean; E. W. Maude; P. S. Milner-Barry, C.B., O.B.E.; S. P. Osmond; J. G. Owen; I. de L. Radice; J. J. S. Shaw; A. W. Taylor, C.B.; F. R. P. Vinter £4,115

Assistant Secretaries, I. P. Bancroft; F. R. Barratt; D. K. Burdett (*Chief Statistician*); J. P. Carswell; A. J. Collier; H. A. Copeman; K. E. Couzens; P. H. F. Dodd; T. Fitzgerald; C. W. Fogarty; C. J. Hayes; D. O. Henley; J. F. Hewitt; C. H. W. Hodges; J. J. B. Hunt; H. L. Jenkyns; C. D. E. Keeling (*Director, Centre for Administrative Studies*); G. S. Knight; H. S. Lee; J. Littlewood; C. C. Lucas; J. Mark, M.B.E.; D. J. Mitchell; P. Nicholls; D. O. Donovan; Miss J. F. H. Orr; A. J. Platt, O.B.E.; A. J. Phelps; I. Pliatzky; J. L. Rampton; A. K. Rawlinson; J. I. McK. Rhodes; P. S. Ross; Mrs. P. M. Rossiter (*Director of Training and Education*); R. L. Sharp; D. W. G. Wass; M. Widdup; O. L. Williams; A. L. Workman...........£2,865 to £3,565

Treasury Medical Adviser, Sir Walter Chiesman, C.B., M.D.

Deputy Treasury Medical Adviser (*also Chief Medical Adviser to G.P.O.*), M. C. W. Long, T.D.

Senior Medical Officers, Miss E. C. Evans, O.B.E.; P. R. Gilbert; V. C. Medvei, M.D.; J. W. Parks, M.B.E., M.D.; D. P. H. Schafer.

Principals, L. Airey; W. G. Angle; J. A. Annand; J. Anson; R. T. Armstrong; G. R. Ashford; A. M. Bailey; M. P. Beazley; C. S. Bennett; Mrs. E. H. Boothroyd; J. B. Bourn; J. M. Bridgeman; Miss L. Bristow; Miss M. R. Bruce; F. G. Burrett; C. J. Carey; T. H. Caulcott; S. T. Charles; P. F. Clifton; Miss D. R. A. Cooper; K. R. Cooper; Miss P. A. Cox; P. Cousins; Miss R. Culhane, M.V.O., O.B.E. (*Treasury Welfare Adviser*); R. E. Dearing; Miss D. J. Fothergill; A. McK. Fraser; I. G. Gilbert; J. S. Goldsmith; M. G. F. Hall; Mrs. D. J. Halley, M.B.E.; D. J. S. Hancock; J. E. Hansford; Mrs. M. Hedley-Miller; R. D. M. Hegarty; J. E. Herbecq; A. J. G. Isaac; G. H. S. Jordan; Miss J. Kelley; B. H. Knox; J. G. Littler; Mrs. S. Littler; Miss F. M. Loughnane; J. E. Lucas; M. P. J. Lynch; J. T. McAulay; K. C. Macdonald; J. A. Marshall; Miss G. E. Miles; A. H. M. Mitchell; P. Mountfield; Miss A. E. Mueller; T. E. Nodder; A. K. Ogilvy-Webb; Miss J. A. M. Oliver; R. J. Painter; L. Parnwell, O.B.E.; W. D. Pattinson; C. V. Peterson; R. W. Phelps; D. W. Royle; M. Rudd; W. S. Ryrie; D. L. Skidmore; J. F. Slater; Mrs. M. B. Sloman; Mrs. A. K. Stubbs; B. M. Thimont; J. G. Thompson; P. L. Towers; Miss K. Whalley; C. Wigfull; R. W. L. Wilding; P. J. Woodfield; S. H. Wright; A. W. Wyatt...................£1,959 to £2,711

Treasury Officer of Accounts, A. J. Platt.

Assistant to Treasury Officer of Accounts, L. J. Taylor £2,683 to £2,865

Accountant, R. F. Lloyd, M.V.O...........£3,215

Assistant Accountants, N. C. Harvey; R. C. Robin £2,237 to £2,572

Chief Catering Adviser, Miss M. V. Scott Carmichael.

Secretary to Civil Service Council for Further Education, T. F. Evans.

Senior Chief Executive Officers, D. C. Lee (*Chief Clerk*); N. S. Kiernan......£2,683 to £2,865

Chief Executive Officers, S. Barraclough; L. H. Bunker; W. Clowser; R. Cockram; W. J. Derbyshire; A. J. Gautrey; E. L. Hampson; C. J. Hancock; G. D. Jones; S. D. Light; K. H. McNeil; Miss M. E Moody, M.B.E.; J. D. Skinner; L. H. Stevenson; W. Winnard; W. A. R. Wolfe £2,237 to £2,572

Senior Organization Officers, W. J. Appleton; R. O.

Bradbury; B. Crichton; H. E. N. Cullingford; P. L. Davies; T. W. Ellison; E. H. Hollis; J. T. Whittaker, O.B.E. .... £2,237 to £2,572
Senior Executive Officers, W. A. Allman; A. D. Buchanan; B. G. Buckley (*Secretary, Civil Service Sports Council*); A. D. Bull; R. G. K. Burgess; P. Chapman; W. W. Clague; J. L. Clark; A. P. Coleman; A. Duke; P. L. Dyer; T. F. Evans; Miss M. Fountain; D. J. Francis; R. Gapp; E. R. Gauntlett; Miss M. C. Gibson; A. R. Gubbay; W. F. Hartman; J. G. Head; G. S. Herlihy, M.V.O.; R. F. Hickish; Miss E. A. Hogg, M.B.E.; S. C. Hutton; Mrs. L. R. E. Jarvis, M.B.E.; C. H. A. Judd; B. J. McCarthy; D. F. Mackay; B. V. Mills; P. R. Money; Miss M. M. Pedder; Miss M. E. Pickering; J. C. Poynter; G. W. Pullinger; M. C. L. Simms; P. A. Smith; G. H. Sparks (*Chief Registrar*); K. L. Spiers; E. J. Sutton; F. N. Swales; W. L. Tjaden; D. R. J. Tratner; C. Walsingham; J. R. Whitbread £1,680 to £2,126
Organization Officers, E. C. Biddie; A. J. Bidgood; A. E. Bishop; R. D. M. Calder; D. Campbell; E. W. Close; J. A. Dean; W. B. Diamond; W. Dinnie; A. S. Donkin; A. F. Dowling; R. F. Gillett; H. K. Good; L. C. Harmer; J. Hay; N. P. Howard; D. E. Jackson; S. F. King; G. A. Lavers; G. O. Naftel; R. B. O'Kane; H. R. Pope; D. F. Reed; G. H. Smith; C. B. Taylor; J. Thomson; J. A. Tiffen; E. H. Tooley; C. B. Taylor; S. D. Walker; J. W. West; S. E. Wigmore .... £1,680 to £2,126

Economic Section

Deputy Director, W. A. B. Hopkin, C.B.E. .. £4,115
Senior Economic Advisers, J. C. R. Dow; Hon. W. A. H. Godley .... £2,865 to £3,565
Economic Advisers, Miss M. P. Brown; J. L. Carr; M. C. Kennedy; T. A. Kennedy £1,959 to £2,711

Treasury Representatives Abroad

U.S.A.:—
Economic Minister, Financial Adviser and Head of U.K. Treasury and Supply Delegation, Sir Eric Roll, K.C.M.G., C.B.
Assistant Secretary, N. M. P. Reilly, C.M.G.
Principal, Miss J. M. Forsyth.
Senior Executive Officers, G. W. Baldock; E. H. Merry.
Economic Adviser, H. Christie.
South Asia, A. Mackay.
Assistant, A. H. Lovell.
U.K. Executive Director, International Monetary Fund and International Bank for Reconstruction and Development, Washington, Sir Eric Roll, K.C.M.G., C.B.

Information Division

Head of Division, C. Raphael, O.B.E. £3,863
Deputy Head of Division and Chief Press Officer, R. T. G. Miles .... £2,392 to £2,650
Principal Information Officers, H. R. Hayles; F. C. Crosfield .... £2,109 to £2,434

Capital Issues Committee

Chairman, Sir Thomas Frazer, O.B.E.
Members, Sir Otto Niemeyer, G.B.E., K.C.B.; Sir Percy Lister; H. B. Turle, C.B.E.
Secretary, A. T. Ripley.

Parliamentary Counsel
Parliament Square House, 34–36 Parliament Street, S.W.1

First Counsel, Sir Noel Hutton, K.C.B., Q.C.. £7,015
Private Sec., J. U. Reid.
Second Counsel, J. S. Fiennes. C.B. £5,815
Counsel, C. H. Chorley, C.B.; S. M. Krusin, C.B.; J. C. P. Elliston; A. N. Stainton; H. P. Rowe £4,265 to £5,015
Deputy Counsel, Mrs. E. A. Eadie £4,115
Senior Assistant Counsel, T. R. F. Skemp; F. A. R. Bennion; A. P. Irby .... £2,965 to £3,565

Rating of Government Property
Palace Chambers, Bridge Street, W.1

Treasury Valuer, J. G. Cook, C.B.E., M.V.O. . £3,600
Deputy Valuer, J. L. Powell ..... £2,975 to £3,275
Inspector of Rates, J. E. Long .... £2,237 to £2,572

Queen's and Lord Treasurer's Remembrancer
See Scottish Law Courts and Offices, p. 458.

NATIONAL ECONOMIC DEVELOPMENT COUNCIL

21–41 Millbank, S.W.1
[Victoria: 3811]

The creation of a National Economic Development Council was proposed by the Chancellor of the Exchequer on September 23, 1961. The tasks of the Council, as defined at the inaugural meeting on March 7, 1962, are "to examine the economic performance of the nation with particular concern for plans for the future in both the private and the public sectors of industry; to consider together what are the obstacles to quicker growth, what can be done to improve efficiency, and whether the best use is being made of our resources; and to seek agreement upon ways of improving economic performance, competitive power, and efficiency, and . . . to increase the rate of sound growth."

The Council has a full-time staff, drawn partly from the Civil Service and partly from industry, the commercial world and elsewhere.

Chairman, The Chancellor of the Exchequer.
Members, The President of the Board of Trade; The Minister of Labour; Dr. R. Beeching; Sir William Carron; F. A. Cockfield; F. Cousins; H. Douglass; The Lord Franks, P.C., G.C.M.G., K.C.B., C.B.E.; R. M. Geddes, O.B.E.; S. F. Greene; Sir Cyril Harrison; E. J. Hunter, O.B.E.; J. M. Laing; Prof. E. H. Phelps Brown, M.B.E., F.B.A.; The Lord Robens of Woldingham, P.C.; Sir Robert Shone, C.B.E.; R. Smith; J. N. Toothill, C.B.E.; G. Woodcock, C.B.E.
Director-General, Sir Robert Shone, C.B.E.
Economic Director, Sir Donald MacDougall, C.B.E.
Industrial Director, T. C. Fraser, M.B.E., T.D.
Administrative Secretary, F. Pickford.

THE TREASURY SOLICITOR

Department of H.M. Procurator-General and of the Solicitor to the Treasury
35 Old Queen Street, S.W.1
[Whitehall: 7363 and 1124]

Procurator-General and Treasury Solicitor, Sir Harold Kent, G.C.B. £7,015
Deputy Treasury Solicitor, W. A. H. Druitt, C.B. £4,715
Principal Assistant Solicitor, F. N. Charlton, C.B., C.B.E. £4,115
Assistant Solicitors, R. J. B. Anderson, C.B.E.; C. F. Brooke; E. M. Cockburn, M.B.E.; B. B. Hall, M.C., T.D.; J. H. Humphreys; D. Neill, M.C.; R. K. Price; H. G. Ware; L. A. Wolfe £2,965 to £3,565
Senior Legal Assistants, B. Arnold; J. Bailey; A. W. Baker; N. L. Braund; A. Bridge; L. M. Burridge; A. J. M. Chitty; W. H. Godwin; D. H. Harrison; M. E. Mead; K. G. Morris; J. L. Parker; G. S. Payne; G. A. Peacock; G. A. Preston; D. Rippengal; F. C. Scorah; D. A. Watson £2,304 to £2,865
Senior Executive Officers, S. F. D. Black; E. J. King; F. L. Parker .... £1,680 to £2,126

Accounts Branch

Chief Accountant, C. A. Briggs .. £2,237 to £2,572
Accountant, G. J. Judge .... £1,680 to £2,126

Establishments Branch

Establishment Officer, A. J. M. Chitty.

Deputy Establishment Officer, R. J. Muskette, M.B.E. £1,680 to £2,126

Queen's Proctor's Office

Queen's Proctor, Sir Harold Kent, G.C.B.
Assistant Queen's Proctor, C. Worsfold £2,965 to £3,565
Senior Legal Assistant, L. M. Burridge £2,304 to £2,865

Conveyancing Division

Principal Assistant Solicitor, E. A. K. Ridley, C.B. £4,115
Assistant Solicitors, R. R. Cole; A. A. R. Martin; G. A. Sifton; S. D. Stubbs; G. H. Wigglesworth £2,965 to £3,565
Senior Legal Assistants, B. G. Bradley; E. K. Bridges; R. W. Corbett; J. P. de Rees; E. J. D. Eastham; S. M. Fox; G. V. Freeman; R. B. Gardner; D. H. Godkin; J. Holdron; K. A. M. Johnson; J. E. H. Jones; W. S. Karran; *W. T. Kermode; N. J. Orchard; P. M. Sprott; C. F. S. Spurrell; J. B. Sweetman; J. A. Thompson; J. M. Venables £2,304 to £2,865
Senior Executive Officers, H. G. Kay; M. R. Tollow, M.B.E. .... £1,680 to £2,126

Bona Vacantia Division

28 The Broadway, S.W.1
[Whitehall: 7363 and 1124]

Assistant Solicitor, P. C. Carter.. £2,965 to £3,565
Senior Legal Assistants, J. C. Leck; R. N. Ogle £2,304 to £2,865
Senior Executive Officer, G. B. Gibson £1,680 to £2,126

Ministry of Aviation Branch

Shell Mex House, Strand, W.C.2.
[Temple Bar: 1207]

Assistant Solicitor, A. W. G. Kean £2,965 to £3,565
Senior Legal Assistants, W. C. Beckett; T. D. Salmon .... £2,304 to £2,865

Claims Commission Branch, War Office

York House, Kingsway, W.C.2
[Temple Bar: 3511]

Senior Legal Assistant, H. Parke.. £2,304 to £2,865

Ministry of Power Branch

Thames House South, Millbank, S.W.1
[Abbey: 7000]

Principal Assistant Solicitor, G. E. Johnstone, C.B. £4,115
Assistant Solicitors, R. M. Mainwaring; J. P. H. Trevor .... £2,965 to £3,565
Senior Legal Assistants, P. G. Ashcroft; †I. M. P. Evans; P. A. Featherstone-Witty; K. J. S. Ritchie .... £2,304 to £2,865

Office of Registrar of Restrictive Trading Agreements Branch

Chancery House, Chancery Lane, W.C.2
[Chancery: 2858]

Principal Assistant Solicitor, R. L. Allen..... £4,115
Assistant Solicitor, L. J. Brett.... £2,965 to £3,565
Senior Legal Assistants, †M. N. Ben-Levi, M.C.; A. J. C. Hay; C. H. A. Lewes; C. J. Macmahon; R Vincent .... £2,304 to £2,865

Ministry of Transport Branch

St. Christopher House, Southwark Street, S.E.1
[Waterloo: 7999]

Principal Assistant Solicitor, R. L. A. Hankey, C.B. £4,115
Assistant Solicitors, A. H. Kent; G. D. Seagrim; H. Woodhouse .... £2,965 to £3,565
Senior Legal Assistants, M. Abrahams; G. L. Close; R. B. A. Cushman; L. S. Falk; J. D. Harries-Jones; *M. A. Lush; D. L. Smithers, M.B.E. £2,304 to £2,865

* Temporary.
† Seconded to another Department.

COUNCIL ON TRIBUNALS

6 Spring Gardens, Cockspur Street, S.W.1
[Whitehall: 8691]

The Council on Tribunals, with its Scottish Committee, was constituted in 1958 under the provisions of the *Tribunals and Inquiries Act* of that year to act as an advisory body in the field of administrative tribunals and statutory inquiries.

Its principal functions under the *Tribunals and Inquiries Act* are (*a*) to keep under review the constitution and working of the various tribunals which have been placed under its general supervision by the Act; (*b*) to report on particular matters relating to any tribunal which may be referred to it by the Lord Chancellor and the Secretary of State for Scotland; and (*c*) to report on matters relating to statutory inquiries which may be similarly referred to it or which the Council may determine to be of special importance. In addition, the Council must be consulted both about rules of procedure for statutory inquiries and before rules are made for any of the tribunals under its general supervision, and it may make general recommendations about appointments to membership of such tribunals. The numerous tribunals which have been placed under the Council's supervision are concerned with a wide variety of matters varying from agriculture and road traffic to independent schools and pensions. They include the National Assistance appeal tribunals, and the main National Health Service and National Insurance Tribunals, together with such tribunals as the Air Transport Licensing Board, the Lands Tribunal, the Mental Health Review Tribunals, the Performing Right Tribunal and the Transport Tribunal.

The Scottish Committee of the Council considers Scottish tribunals and matters relating only to Scotland.

The Members of the Council are appointed by the Lord Chancellor and the Secretary of State for Scotland. The Scottish Committee is composed partly of members of the Council designated by the Secretary of State for Scotland and partly of other persons appointed by him.

The Council submits an annual report on its proceedings and those of the Scottish Committee to the Lord Chancellor and the Secretary of State for Scotland, which must be laid before Parliament.

Chairman, The Viscount Tenby, P.C., T.D.
Members, D. B. Bogle, W.S.; The Hon. R. E. B. Beaumont, T.D.; Mrs. K. M. Bell; H. Collison, C.B.E.; The Earl of Cranbrook, C.B.E.; Sir Harold Emmerson, G.C.B., K.C.V.O.; The Hon. H. A. P. Fisher, Q.C.; The Hon. Sylvia Fletcher-Moulton, C.B.E.; Col. W. I. French, D.S.O., O.B.E., T.D.; Brig. Sir Henry Houldsworth, K.B.E., D.S.O., M.C., T.D.; H. W. Pritchard; N. J. B. Raymond; Prof. H. W. R. Wade, LL.D., D.C.L.; The Baroness Wootton of Abinger.
Secretary, A. Macdonald.

Scottish Committee

51 Melville Street, Edinburgh 3
[Caledonian: 3236]

Chairman, D. B. Boyle, W.S.
Members, G. C. Emslie, Q.C.; Col. W. I. French, D.S.O., O.B.E., T.D.; Brig. Sir Henry Houldsworth, K.B.E., D.S.O., M.C., T.D.; W. P. McGinniss, O.B.E.; J. P. Morrison, O.B.E.; T. H. Thorneycroft.
Secretary, C. Gilbraith.

TRINITY HOUSE

Tower Hill, E.C.3
[Royal: 6601]

Trinity House, the first General Lighthouse and Pilotage Authority in the Kingdom, was a body of importance when Henry VIII. granted the Institution its first charter in 1514, *inter alia* " for the relief, increase and augmentation of the Shipping of this

Realm of England." Since that period the duty of erecting and maintaining lighthouses and other marks and signs of the sea has by Royal Charter and Acts of Parliament been entrusted to the Corporation of Trinity House, and until 1874 Masters of the Navy were examined by the Elder Brethren of the Corporation. In the present day, the principal duty of the Corporation of Trinity House, as a Public Department, is the administration of the Lighthouse, &c., Service of England and Wales with certain statutory jurisdiction in regard to lighthouses and other seamarks in Scotland, Ireland, the Channel Islands and Gibraltar, while the Corporation is also the chief Pilotage Authority in the United Kingdom, and in its capacity as a private corporation or guild it administers certain Charitable Trusts specifically dedicated to the relief of aged and distressed master mariners, their widows and spinster daughters. The Corporation controls some 60 lighthouses and 40 lightships, and maintains a fleet of 9 steam and motor vessels. The Active Elder Brethren of the Corporation also sit with the Judges of the Admiralty Division of the High Court of Justice to act as Nautical Assessors in Marine Causes tried in that Court. The Lighthouse Service of Trinity House is maintained out of the General Lighthouse Fund, this fund being provided by means of special dues called Light Dues levied on shipping using the ports of the United Kingdom. The accounts are submitted annually to Parliament.

Elder Brethren

Master, H.R.H. the Duke of Gloucester, K.G. *Deputy Master*, Captain G. E. Barnard. *Elder Brethren*, H.R.H. The Prince Philip, Duke of Edinburgh, K.G.; Rt. Hon. Sir Winston Spencer Churchill, K.G., O.M., C.H., M.P.; H.R.H. The Duke of Windsor, K.G.; Capt. Sir Arthur Morrell, K.B.E.; Capt. W. R. Chaplin, C.B.E.; Capt. W. E. Crumplin; The Viscount Monsell, P.C., G.B.E.; Capt. Sir Gerald Curteis, K.C.V.O., R.N. (*ret.*); Commodore R. L. F. Hubbard, C.B.E., R.D., R.N.R. (*ret.*); The Earl Alexander of Hillsborough, P.C., C.H. Capt. G. C. H. Noakes, R.D., R.N.R. (*ret.*); Admiral of the Fleet the Earl Mountbatten of Burma, K.G., P.C., G.C.B., G.C.S.I., G.C.I.E., G.C.V.O., D.S.O.; Capt. D. Dunn; The Earl Attlee, K.G., P.C., O.M., C.H.; Capt. K. McM. Drake, R.D.; Field-Marshal the Earl Alexander of Tunis, K.G., P.C., G.C.B., O.M., G.M.M.G., C.S.I., D.S.O., M.C.; Capt. G. P. McCraith; Capt. R. J. Galpin, R.D., R.N.R. (*ret.*); The Earl of Avon, K.G., P.C., M.C.; Capt. R. N. Mayo; Capt. D. S. Tibbits, D.S.C., R.N. (*ret.*); Capt. D. A. G. Dickens; Capt. J. E. Bury.

Officers

Secretary, R. S. McLernon, O.B.E., T.D.
Deputy Secretary, G. D. D'Ombrain.
Heads of Departments, D. C. Henry (*Lights*); S. W. Heesom (*Chief Accountant*).
Chief Staff Officer, A. R. W. Ransley.
Establishment Officer, J. H. J. Rogers.
Higher Executive Officers, L. N. Potter; W. Torkington; R. S. Beckett; J. R. Snipper; G. S. Ingram; J. R. Backhouse; D. J. Clark; G. Warnes.
Engineer-in-Chief, P. W. Hunt.
Deputy Engineer-in-Chief, I. C. Clingan.
Assistant Engineer-in-Chief, R. J. Shergold.
Chief Research Officer, A. C. MacKellar.
Engineers, C. A. Woollard, M.B.E.; W. J. Campbell; E. G. Beshaw; R. M. Gordon.
Senior Experimental Officers, L. G. Reynolds; W. L. Rew.
Surveyor of Shipping and Marine Engineer, W. D. Seaman.
Deputy do., W. R. Foley.
Pilotage Dept., S. R. Smith, O.B.E. (*Asst. Secretary for Pilotage*); E. Babbs.
Corporate Dept., V. G. Stamp (*Principal*).
Estates Surveyors, Messrs. Drivers, Jonas & Co.

COMMISSIONERS OF NORTHERN LIGHTHOUSES

84 George St., Edinburgh 2
[Edinburgh Caledonian: 2868 and 2922]

The Commissioners of Northern Lighthouses are the General Lighthouse Authority for Scotland and the Isle of Man. The present Board owes its origin to an Act of Parliament passed in 1786 which authorized the erection of 4 lighthouses; 19 Commissioners were appointed to carry out the Act. At the present time the Commissioners operate under the Merchant Shipping Act, 1894.

The Commissioners control 77 Major Lighthouses, 1 Manned Lightvessel, 92 Minor Lights and many Lighted and Unlighted Buoys. They have a fleet of 4 Motor Vessels.

Commissioners

The Lord Advocate, the Solicitor General, the Lord Provost and Senior Bailie of Edinburgh, the Lord Provost and Senior Bailie of Glasgow, the Lord Provosts of Aberdeen and Dundee, and the Provosts of Inverness, Campbeltown, and Greenock, the Sheriffs of the Lothians and Peebles; Lanark; Renfrew and Argyll; Inverness, Moray, Nairn, and Ross and Cromarty; Aberdeen, Kincardine and Banff; Ayr and Bute; Fife and Kinross; Perth and Angus; Caithness, Sutherland, Orkney and Zetland; Dumfries and Galloway; Roxburgh, Berwick and Selkirk; and Stirling, Dunbarton and Clackmannan.

Officers:

General Manager and Secretary, W. Alastair Robertson, D.S.C.
Deputy Secretary, A. R. Stewart.
Senior Executive Officer, A. R. Malcolm.
Accountant, T. A. R. Tait.
Superintendent, J. F. Bremner.
Engineer, P. H. Hyslop, D.S.C.
Radio Engineer, G. E. Rowe.

CLYDE LIGHTHOUSES TRUST

3 Somerville Place, Sauchiehall Street, Glasgow, C.3

Chairman, Col. T. H. Lawrie, C.B.E., T.D.
Clerk, L. E. Dickson, M.C., T.D.
Engineer, Ritchie M. Campbell.

CLYDE NAVIGATION TRUST

16 Robertson Street, Glasgow C.2

Chairman, I. C. Macfarlane.
General Manager and Secretary, J. R. Proudfoot, C.B.E.
Engineer, R. B. Braithwaite.

TRUSTEE SAVINGS BANKS

INSPECTION COMMITTEE

3–4 Clement's Inn, W.C.2.

This Committee was established under the *Savings Bank Act*, 1891, and is responsible for the inspection of the books and accounts of Trustee Savings Banks and for other duties set out in this and subsequent Acts.

Chairman, A. R. B. Haldane, D.Litt., W.S.
Vice-Chairman, A. E. Barber.
Other Members, Sir Bernard Blatch, M.B.E.; W. G. Densem; Sir John Fox, O.B.E.; O. S. Francis, M.C.; J. Renwick.
Secretary, N. E. Sheldon.

UNIVERSITY GRANTS COMMITTEE

38 Belgrave Square, S.W.1
[Belgravia: 4801]

The Committee was appointed by the Chancellor of the Exchequer in July, 1919, and its present terms of reference are as follows:

" To inquire into the financial needs of university education in Great Britain; to advise the Government as to the application of any grants made by Parliament towards meeting them; to collect, examine, and make available information relating to university education throughout the United Kingdom; and to assist, in consultation with the universities and other bodies concerned, the preparation and execution of such plans for the development of the universities as may from time to time be required in order to ensure that they are fully adequate to national needs."

Chairman, Sir John Wolfenden, C.B.E....... £5,800
Other Members, Professor W. M. Arnott, T.D., M.D.; Sir Eric Ashby, D.Sc., Sc.D., Ll.D.; Sir John Baker, O.B.E., D.Sc., Sc.D., F.R.S.; Miss M. J. Bishop, C.B.E.; Professor F. W. R. Brambell, D.Sc., F.R.S.; Professor A. Briggs; Sir Ronald Edwards; J. C. Gridley, C.B.E.; The Lord Heyworth; Sir Willis Jackson, D.Sc., D.Phil., F.R.S.; Professor C. H. Philips, Ph.D.; Professor J. M. Robertson, Ph.D., D.Sc., F.R.S., F.R.S.E.; Sir Lionel Russell, C.B.E.; F. A. Vick, O.B.E., Ph.D.; K. C. Wheare, C.M.G., D.Litt., F.B.A.; Professor T. E. Wright.
Members (for salary questions only), The Countess of Albemarle, D.B.E.; The Lord Morris of Borth-y-Gest, P.C., C.B.E., M.C.
Secretary, E. R. Copleston, C.B. £5,000
Deputy Secretary, R. C. Griffiths............ £4,050
Asst. Secretaries, W. H. Fisher, M.V.O.; A. E. L. Parnis .... £2,650 to £3,350
Principal, Mrs. D. R. Williams .. £1,716 to £2,418
Superintending Architect, S. Meyrick £2,650 to £3,000
Senior Architect, G. B. Oddie .... £2,080 to £2,392
Architects, G. H. Dodd; M. V. S. Smith; P. Whitely £1,456 to £1,950
Senior Quantity Surveyor, P. E. Bathurst £2,080 to £2,392

WAR DAMAGE COMMISSION

Eagle House, 90–96 Cannon Street, E.C.4
[Mincing Lane: 2000]

The War Damage Commission was appointed on March 27, 1941, to administer Part I of the *War Damage Act*, 1941, 4 & 5 Geo. 6, ch. 12. The 1941 Act, and two subsequent amending Acts, were consolidated in the *War Damage Act*, 1943, 6 & 7 Geo. 6, ch. 21. Its operations are related only to war damage to *land and buildings*, those parts of the Act which are concerned with *goods and chattels* being administered through the Board of Trade. There are technical centres in Hull, Sheffield, Liverpool, Manchester, Birmingham, Bristol, Plymouth, Southampton, Norwich, and Glasgow.

Headquarters

Chairman (part-time), Sir Alexander Johnston, G.C.B., K.B.E.
Commissioner, R. O. M. Nicholas, C.B.
Commissioner and Secretary, D. G. McPherson £2,800 to £3,500
Deputy Commissioners, W. E. A. Bull; G. A. Coombe, M.C.; J. R. Edwards, M.B.E.; T. C. Howitt, D.S.O., O.B.E.; F. Scarlett.
Principal, Miss S. D. Clements, O.B.E. £1,894 to £2,646
Chief Executive Officer, B. H. Du Feu, M.B.E. £2,172 to £2,507
Senior Executive Officers, F. G. Alder; Mrs. C. J. Field; C. E. Howick .... £1,615 to £2,061
Senior Technical Adviser, W. H. Martin, O.B.E. £2,228 to £2,563
Technical Advisers, H. J. B. Tufton; J. P. Ward £2,228 to £2,563

COMMONWEALTH WAR GRAVES COMMISSION

32 Grosvenor Gardens, S.W.1
[Sloane: 0751]

The Commonwealth War Graves Commission was incorporated by Royal Charter in 1917 under its then title "Imperial War Graves Commission"; its title was changed on April 1, 1960, by a Supplemental Royal Charter. The Commission's duty is to commemorate individually and in perpetuity each one of those, from whatever part of the Commonwealth they came, who fell in the two world wars of 1914–18 and 1939–45. More than one million graves are maintained in War Cemeteries, large and small, which have been constructed in nearly one hundred and fifty different countries throughout the world, and about 750,000 names are commemorated on memorials to those with no known grave. The funds of the Commission are derived from the seven Governments participating in their work—The United Kingdom, Canada, Australia, New Zealand, South Africa, India and Pakistan.

President, H.R.H. The Duke of Gloucester, K.G.
Chairman, The Secretary of State for War.
Vice-Chairman, Admiral Sir Guy Grantham, G.C.B., C.B.E., D.S.O.
Members, The Secretary of State for the Colonies; The Minister of Public Building and Works; The High Commissioners for Canada, the Commonwealth of Australia, New Zealand, India and Pakistan; the Ambassador for the Republic of South Africa; The Lord Spens, P.C., K.B.E., Q.C.; Air Chief Marshal Sir Arthur Longmore, G.C.B., D.S.O.; Sir Arthur Rucker, K.C.M.G., C.B., C.B.E.; Air Marshal Sir Charles Guest, K.B.E., C.B.; Sir John Hogg, T.D.; D. Griffiths, M.P.; Lt.-Gen. Sir John Anderson, K.C.B., C.B.E., D.S.O.
Director-General, W. J. Chalmers, C.B.E.
Director of External Relations and Records, W. Wynne Mason, M.C.
Director of Finance and Establishments, A. K. Pallot.
Director of Works, Maj.-Gen. J. F. D. Steedman, C.M.G., C.B.E., M.C.
Legal Adviser and Solicitor, H. L. Simmons.
Chief Horticultural Officer, W. F. W. Harding, O.B.E.
Honorary Chief Architect and Artistic Adviser, Sir Edward Maufe, R.A.
Hon. Consulting Engineer, H. D. Morgan.
Hon. Botanical Adviser, Sir George Taylor, D.Sc., F.R.S.E.
Hon. Literary Adviser, Professor Edmund Blunden, C.B.E., M.C.

Imperial War Graves Endowment Fund

Trustees, Col. Sir Eric Gore-Browne, D.S.O., O.B.E., T.D.; A. H. Carnwath; Admiral Sir Guy Grantham, G.C.B., C.B.E., D.S.O.
Hon. Secretary to the Trustees, W. J. Chalmers, C.B.E.

WAR WORKS COMMISSION

Eagle House, 90–96 Cannon Street, E.C.4
[Mincing Lane: 2000]

Appointed Sept. 6, 1945. It is an independent body, charged with the adjudication of disputes which might have arisen in cases where the Government is desirous of acquiring land on which works for war purposes had been created at the public expense, or where it was sought to make permanent the stopping up of certain highways and footpaths which had been found necessary in connection with such works.

Chairman (part-time), Sir Thomas W. Phillips, G.B.E., K.C.B.
Commissioners (part-time), Sir Harold Emmerson, G.C.B., K.C.V.O.; A. Lubbock, F.S.A.; The Lord Williams; D. MacLeod Matheson, C.B.E.; Sir David Hughes Parry, Q.C., Ll.D., D.C.L.
Secretary (part-time), H. N. V. Clarke.

WHITE FISH AUTHORITY

Lincoln's Inn Chambers, 2/3 Cursitor Street, E.C.4
[Chancery: 9441]

Chairman, H. L. R. Matthews, C.B.E. *(part-time)* £3,500
Deputy-Chairman, Sir John Ure Primrose *(part-time)* £3,000
Members (part-time), The Lord Lloyd, M.B.E., W. J. L. Dean, O.B.E.; N. Wood £1,000

COMMISSIONS, ETC.

Foreign Compensation Commission

1 Princes Gate, S.W.7

The Commission was set up by the *Foreign Compensation Act*, 1950, to distribute funds paid by foreign governments as compensation for expropriated British property and other losses sustained by British nationals. The *Foreign Compensation Act*, 1962, provided, *inter alia*, for the payment out of moneys provided by Parliament of additional compensation in respect of claims arising in connection with certain events in Egypt. The Commission has completed the final distribution of the funds contributed by Yugoslavia, Czechoslovakia, Bulgaria and Poland. Agreements with Hungary and Roumania to create similar funds have been made, and the Commission is registering certain British claims in Czechoslovakia and the Baltic States and other States acquired by the Soviet Union. A limited distribution is being made on Hungarian claims. The £27,500,000 compensation paid by the Government of the United Arab Republic under the financial agreement of Feb. 28, 1959, is being distributed by the Commission. The Final Distribution Order enables the Commission to pay compensation in respect of claims registered up to Dec. 31, 1962, and thereafter on notification from the Foreign Office.

Chairman, C. Montgomery White, Q.C.

Deputy Chairman, R. A. J. Mullarkey.

Commissioners, C. Middleton; W. Temple; Sir James Henry, Bt., C.M.G., M.C., T.D., Q.C.; Sir George Lowe; Sir Harold Willan, C.M.G., M.C.; D. Eifion Evans, Q.C.

Secretary, H. H. Butcher.

Local Government Commission for England

State House, High Holborn, W.C.1

Set up on October 31, 1958, under the *Local Government Act*, 1958, with "the duty of reviewing the organization of local government (*a*) in the areas specified in the Third Schedule to the Act (the conurbations of Tyneside, West Yorkshire, South East Lancashire, Merseyside and West Midlands), and (*b*) in the remainder of England exclusive of the Metropolitan Area;" and of making such proposals as were authorized in the Act "for effecting changes appearing to the Commission desirable in the interests of effective and convenient local government". The Commission has submitted five final reports relating to the West and East Midlands, to the South West and to Tyneside, and has published draft proposals for the North Eastern for York and North Midlands and the Lincolnshire and East Anglia general review areas and for the West Yorkshire special review areas.

Chairman, Sir Henry Hancock, G.C.B., K.B.E., C.M.G.

Deputy Chairman, Sir Michael Rowe, C.B.E., Q.C.

Members, Hon. Dame Ruth Buckley, D.B.E.; B. D. Storey, C.B.E.; L. R. Missen, C.M.G., M.C.; Prof. E. Devons; R. H. Parry, M.D.

Secretary, H. F. Summers, C.B.

Local Government Commission for Wales

69 Park Place, Cardiff

Set up on December 18, 1958, under the *Local Government Act*, 1958, with the duty of reviewing the organization of local government in Wales and of making such proposals as are authorized in the Act for effecting changes appearing to them to be desirable in the interests of effective and convenient local government. The Commission has presented its final report to the Minister of Housing and Local Government.

Chairman, Sir Guildhaume Myrddin-Evans, K.C.M.G., C.B.

Deputy Chairman, Sir Emrys Evans, LL.D.

Members, Prof. C. E. Gittins; W. Jones, O.B.E.; Mrs. J. Morgan.

Secretary, I. Davey.

THE NATIONAL TRUST

40-42 Queen Anne's Gate, Westminster, S.W.1

The National Trust was founded in 1895 by Miss Octavia Hill, Sir Robert Hunter and Canon Rawnsley, their object being to preserve as much as possible of the history and beauty of their country for its people. It has since become an organization incorporated by Act of Parliament to ensure the preservation of lands and buildings of historic interest or natural beauty for public access and benefit. It is independent of the State and relies mainly on the voluntary support of private individuals for working funds. The State, however, allows it certain tax exemptions. A further, and only recently instituted, branch of the Trust's work is the acquisition and preservation, with the co-operation of the Royal Horticultural Society, of gardens of national importance. It also has under its care bird sanctuaries and nature reserves, together with several hundred farms.

The National Trust now administers more than 300,000 acres of land in England, Wales and Northern Ireland; and in this area are over 1,000 properties. These properties have come into its hands mainly by gift or bequest; but since 1946 certain land and buildings accepted by the Treasury in lieu of death duties have been handed over to the Trust, the Treasury recompensing itself from the National Land Fund. The properties acquired by the National Trust before last year include the Ashridge Estate (Bucks. and Herts.); Cliveden (Bucks.); West Wycombe Park and village (Bucks.); Wicken Fen (Cambs.); Lyme Park (Cheshire); Cotehele House (Cornwall); Pentire Head (Cornwall); St. Michael's Mount (Cornwall); Trerice (Cornwall); Dovedale (Derbys. & Staffs.); Arlington Court Estate (Devon); Hatfield Forest (Essex); Chedworth Roman Villa (Glos.); Hidcote Manor Gdn. (Glos.); Knole (Kent); over 30,000 acres in the Lake District including the Buttermere Valley, Monk Coniston Estate, Scafell Pike and Troutbeck Park Farm; Tattershall Castle (Lincs.); Osterley Park (Middx.); Blickling Hall Estate (Norfolk); Farne Islands (Northumberland); Clumber Park (Notts.); Holnicote Estate (Somerset); Montacute House (Somerset); Flatford Mill (Suffolk); Box Hill (Surrey); Ham House (Surrey); Bodiam Castle (Sussex); Petworth House (Sussex); Charlecote Park (Warwicks.); Lacock Abbey and village (Wilts.); Stourhead Estate (Wilts.); Derwent Estate (Yorks. and Derbys.); Hardwick Hall (Derbys.); Bodnant Gardens (N. Wales); Powis Castle (Mont.); Castlecoole (N. Ireland); Hanbury Hall (Warwicks.); Lanhydrock (Cornwall); Tintinhull House (Somerset); Nymans Gardens (Sussex); Sheffield Park Gardens (Sussex); Uppark (Sussex); Nostell Priory (Yorks.); Staunton Harold Church (Leics.); Penard Cliff (Glam); Blundell's Old School (Deon); Castleward (N. Ireland).

Acquisitions last year include: Ormsby Hall (Yorkshire); The Temple of the Winds, Mount Stewart Gardens (Northern Ireland); The Long and Short Lythes, Selborne (Hampshire); Glendurgan House and Garden (Cornwall); and land at Mawnan

Glebe, Godrevy, Zennor and Nare Head (Cornwall).

THE CIVIC TRUST

79 Buckingham Palace Road, S.W.1
[Tate Gallery: 0891]

Founded in 1957, to promote high standards of architecture and civic planning in Great Britain and to encourage a wider interest in the appearance of our towns and villages. The Trust's income is provided by leading industrial and commercial companies and its funds and general policy are controlled by a board of trustees. Among its activities, the Trust, in co-operation with local authorities and traders, initiates schemes to brighten and tidy up streets all over Britain. With the help of volunteers it removes "eyesores" which mar the countryside. It obtains gifts of grown trees and replants them on urban sites. By conferences and exhibitions, it focuses attention on current problems of planning and architecture. It provides a centre from which some 400 local amenity societies can obtain advice and support. Whenever possible, it seeks to co-operate with existing organizations which are already working effectively in these fields.

Director, L. Lane.

THE CIVIC TRUST FOR THE NORTH WEST

Century House, St. Peter's Square, Manchester 2.
[Central: 0333]

Inaugurated on October 11, 1961, the Civic Trust for the North West is an independent non-profitmaking body. Its declared object is to make the great industrial, commercial and residential area centred on Manchester and Salford into an attractive, healthy and stimulating place in which to live and work. While the area has purposely not been closely defined, the Trust envisages working mainly in the industrial belt lying roughly between Preston and Macclesfield (but excluding Merseyside) and occupied by about three million people. Industry is heavily concentrated here in two cities, more than 40 towns and many villages.

The Civic Trust hopes to bring home to the people the realization that the area is one of ugliness and dirt and that much can be done even by individuals to put this right. The Trust proposes to support clean air and anti-litter drives; to illustrate by films, lectures and pamphlets attractive ways of painting and decorating houses and streets on a "help yourself" basis; to enlist the support of press, radio, and television; and to promote architectural competitions and awards. The Trust will support municipal projects in the area, where they fall in with the objects of the Trust and assist if required with the co-ordination of private development in official schemes. It also hopes to investigate and encourage improvement schemes for streets, squares or groups of houses, including redecoration of all the properties at the same time to fit an attractive overall plan; to encourage improvement of street signs, design of street furniture, and the planting of trees and gardens.

The Trust hopes to support and strengthen existing amenity societies and to promote the growth of new ones and finally to sponsor research into planning problems in the North West industrial area with the hope of it becoming the world's most efficient industrial concentration while at the same time paying regard to amenities, the Arts and social aspects. The income of the Civic Trust is drawn from subscriptions by important industrial and commercial firms in the area.

Chairman, W. L. Mather, O.B.E., M.C., T.D.
Deputy Chairman, L. P. Scott.
Trustees, G. H. Kenyon; R. M. Bateman; S. L. Bernstein; S. B. J. Z. de Ferranti; Sir Cyril Harrison; The Lord Peddie, M.B.E.; A. Tillotson.
Director, Lt.-Col. J. M. Barton, M.C.

THE PILGRIM TRUST

Millbank House, 2 Great Peter Street, S.W.1

Trustees, The Lord Evershed, P.C. (*Chairman*); The Lord Franks, P.C., G.C.M.G., K.C.B., C.B.E.; Richard Fleming, M.C.; The Earl of Crawford and Balcarres, K.T., G.B.E.; W. F. Oakeshott; The Lord Bridges, P.C., G.C.B., G.C.V.O., M.C.
Secretary, The Lord Kilmaine, C.B.E.

The Pilgrim Trust was founded in 1930 by the late Edward S. Harkness of New York, who placed in the hands of British trustees £2,000,000 for the benefit of Great Britain. Since then the Trust has been able to make substantial grants for the repair of ancient buildings, the preservation of historical records, the support of learned societies, the purchase of works of art and the assistance of social welfare schemes.

Since its foundation the Trust has made grants amounting to over £4,000,000 and in 1962 the Trustees voted sums totalling £305,145. These grants were made under the following three heads:—

Preservation...... £140,945
Art and Learning.. £150,700
Social Welfare.... £13,500

A further £75,000 was voted to the Historic Churches Preservation Trust for the next 5 years, and an additional £45,000 was granted to the Oxford Historic Buildings Fund. The Trustees contributed £57,000 towards the purchase of Leonardo da Vinci's cartoon for the nation; £25,000 to assist the National Trust to acquire Brownsea Island in Poole Harbour, Dorset; £10,000 to the National Trust for Scotland towards the restoration of ancient buildings in the old coastal towns of Fife; and £7,400 to cover the cost of two of the great nave windows in the new Coventry Cathedral.

Other grants during the year included £6,000 for Research in the humanities and the arts, and £5,000 each towards the repair of the buildings of Lord Leycester's Hospital, Warwick, and the preservation of the coast of Ulster.

THE ARTS COUNCIL OF GREAT BRITAIN

4 St James's Square, S.W.1

The Arts Council of Great Britain was incorporated under Royal Charter on August 9, 1946, "for the purpose of developing greater knowledge, understanding and practice of the fine arts exclusively and in particular to increase the accessibility of the fine arts to the public . . . to improve the standard of execution of the fine arts and to advise and co-operate with . . . Government Departments, Local Authorities and other bodies on any matters concerned directly or indirectly with those objects. . . ."

The Members of the Council, who may not exceed 16 in number, are appointed by the Chancellor of the Exchequer after consultation with the Minister of Education and the Secretary of State for Scotland. With the consent of the Secretary of State for Scotland and the Minister of Education, the Council appoints separate committees for Scotland and Wales.

The Council receives a grant-in-aid from the Treasury. For the year 1963–64 the amount was £2,730,000.

Chairman, The Lord Cottesloe, G.B.E., T.D.
Secretary-General, N. J. Abercrombie.

COUNCIL OF INDUSTRIAL DESIGN

28 Haymarket, S.W.1

The Council of Industrial Design, with its Scottish Committee, was set up in December, 1944, by the President of the Board of Trade, "to promote . . . the improvement of design in the products of British Industry." For manufacturers, the Council provides advice on the application of design policy, and recommends designers from its Record of Designers. For retailers, it provides courses for buyers and salesmen on design appreciation, and organizes exhibitions in retail stores. For the public it provides selective exhibitions of well designed goods.

The Council has a Design Centre for British Industries at 28 Haymarket, S.W.1. and a Scottish Design Centre at 46 West George Street, Glasgow, C.2.

The Council maintains a selective, pictorial and sample record of well designed goods in current production known as *Design Index*, which is available for consultation at the Design Centre. The Council also maintains a photograph and slide library, press and information services and a lecture panel, and publishes a monthly journal *Design*.

Chairman, Sir Duncan Oppenheim.
Chairman of Scottish Committee, I. W. S Wilson.
Director, Paul Reilly.
Chief Executive, Scottish Committee, R. G. Clark, 46 West George Street, Glasgow, C.2.

LONDON COURT OF ARBITRATION

69 Cannon Street, E.C.4.

The London Court of Arbitration, formed in 1892, is an impartial body prepared to appoint arbitrators at the request of disputants to settle disputes which may, under the law of England, be submitted to arbitration. The Court is administered by members appointed by the Corporation of London and the London Chamber of Commerce.

The Court's Services are available to any person, firm, company or organization of any nationality. Parties in the British Commonwealth and in foreign countries often request the Court to appoint an arbitrator to settle their disputes.

Chairman, C. G. Hayes, C.C.
Deputy Chairman, A. L. Stock.
Registrar, J. G. Allanby.

THE BRITISH COUNCIL

65 Davies Street, W.1

The British Council was established in 1934 to promote abroad a wider knowledge of the United Kingdom and of the English language, and to develop closer cultural relations between the United Kingdom and other countries. Most of the Council's funds are derived from grants voted by Parliament. Grants for 1963–64 amounted to £8,634.000.

The Council's activities include the promotion of English language teaching and British studies in universities, training colleges and schools. It gives particular attention to the maintenance and expansion of British libraries and cultural centres, Anglophile societies and British schools abroad; the fostering of personal contacts between British and overseas people, especially in the educational, scientific and professional fields. Scholarships and bursaries for study in this country of British institutions, methods and achievements are granted to overseas graduates and others.

In June, 1963, the Council had staffs at work in most countries of the Commonwealth and of Europe, Latin-America, the Middle East, S.E. Asia and in Japan. It promotes educational and other exchanges with the Soviet Union and other Eastern European countries, primarily by sponsoring visits in both directions by professional groups.

The Council maintains centres in the United Kingdom, mainly in university cities, to provide services for students, professional visitors, holders of U.N. and Colombo Plan awards and others from overseas. It makes available welfare services and leisure-time facilities to all full-time overseas Students in the U.K., and also provides certain special services, including reception on arrival and help with accommodation, for students of nearly all Commonwealth countries and territories and certain foreign countries.

President, General Sir Ronald Adam, Bt., G.C.B., D.S.O., O.B.E.
Chairman, The Lord Bridges, P.C., G.C.B., G.C.V.O., M.C., F.R.S.
Director-General, Sir Paul Sinker, K.C.M.G., C.B.

THE PRESS COUNCIL

In April, 1947, a Royal Commission was appointed to enquire into the control, management and ownership, etc., of the Press and news agencies and to make recommendations thereon. The Commission, in its report of June, 1949, recommended *inter alia* that a voluntary Press Council be formed.

A constitution ultimately set up provided for the establishment of such a council on July 1, 1953. This constitution was materially amended in 1963 by the introduction of an independent chairman and up to 20 per cent. lay membership. The objects of the Council are (1) to preserve the established freedom of the British Press; (2) to maintain the character of the British Press in accordance with the highest professional and commercial standards; (3) to consider complaints about the conduct of the Press or the conduct of persons and organizations towards the Press; to deal with these complaints in whatever manner might seem practical and appropriate and record resultant action; (4) to keep under review developments likely to restrict the supply of information of public interest and importance; (5) to report publicly on developments that may tend towards greater concentration or monopoly in the Press (including changes in ownership, control and growth of Press undertakings) and to publish statistical information relating thereto; and (6) to publish periodical reports recording the Council's work and to review, from time to time, developments in the Press and the factors affecting them.

The membership of the Council consists of editorial and managerial nominees of The Newspaper Proprietors Association Ltd. (5), The Newspaper Society (3), The Periodical Proprietors Association Ltd. (2), The Scottish Daily Newspaper Society (1), Scottish Newspaper Proprietors' Association (1), The Guild of British Newspaper Editors (2), The National Union of Journalists (4) and The Institute of Journalists (2).

Chairman (vacant).
Vice-Chairman, H. Bate.
Professional Members, M. Chapman Walker, C.B.E., M.V.O.; E. M. Clayson; Mrs. G. Clemetson; C. Eade; J. S. Forrest; G. R. French; D. Greenslade; C. D. Hamilton, D.S.O.; C. Hamnett; S. Jacobson, M.C.; C. Jervis; F. M. Johnston; A. M. Lee; A. Lofts; R. J. Erskine Orr, O.B.E.; C. A. Ramsden; Col. Sir James Waterlow, Bt., M.B.E., T.D.; M. Williamson; (one vacancy).
Lay Members (five vacancies).
Secretary, Col. W. C. Clissitt, T.D., Ludgate House, 110–111, Fleet Street, E.C.4.

THE BANK OF ENGLAND

Threadneedle Street, E.C.2

The Bank of England was incorporated in 1694 under Royal Charter. It is the banker of the Government on whose behalf it manages the Note Issue, the profits on which are paid to H.M. Treasury. It also manages the National Debt and administers the Exchange Control regulations. As central reserve bank of the country, the Bank keeps the accounts of British banks, who maintain with it a proportion of their cash resources, and of most overseas central banks; but it has gradually withdrawn from new commercial business.

As from March 1, 1946, the capital stock, amounting to £14,553,000, was transferred to a nominee of the Treasury (the Treasury Solicitor), under the provisions of the Bank of England Act, 1946, holders receiving in exchange 3 per cent. Treasury Stock, to such an amount as provided them with annual interest equal to the annual gross dividend of the previous 20 years, namely, 12 per cent.

Governor, The Earl of Cromer, M.B.E. (*1966).
Deputy Governor, Humphrey Charles Baskerville Mynors (*1964).
Directors, Sir George Edmond Brackenbury Abell, K.C.I.E., O.B.E. (*1964); The Lord Bicester (*1966); Sir George Lewis French Bolton, K.C.M.G. (*1964); Geoffrey Cecil Ryves Eley, C.B.E. (*1966); William Johnston Keswick (*1967); The Lord Kindersley, C.B.E., M.C. (*1967); John Maurice Laing (*1964); The Lord Nelson of Stafford (*1967); Leslie Kenneth O'Brien (*1966); Maurice Henry Parsons (*1965); Sir Harry (William Henry) Pilkington (*1964); Sir Alfred Roberts, C.B.E. (*1966); The Lord Sanderson of Ayot, M.C. (*1965); Michael James Babington Smith, C.B.E. (*1965); John Melior Stevens, D.S.O., O.B.E. (*1965).

* Date of Retirement.

Chief Cashier, J. Q. Hollom.
Chief Accountant, J. V. Bailey.
Chief of the Central Banking Information Dept., G. M. Watson.
Secretary, H. M. Neatby.
Chief of Establishments, C. H. H. White.
Advisers to the Governors, W. M. Allen; R. A. O. Bridge; Sir Laurence Menzies; G. R. Raw; J. St. J. Rootham; L. P. Thompson-McCausland.

ACCOUNT FOR THE WEEK ENDED AUGUST 14, 1963

Issue Department

	£		£
Notes issued:		Govt. Debt	11,015,100
In Circulation...	2,471,788,186	Other Govt. Securities	2,488,019,273
In Banking Department	28,572,354	Other Securities.......	703,675
		Coin other than gold	261,592
		Amount of Fiduciary Issue	2,500,000,000
		Gold Coin and Bullion*..	360,540
	£2,500,360,540		£2,500,360,540

Banking Department

	£		£
Capital......	14,553,000	Govt. Securities.....	205,161,912
Rest........	3,821,587	Other Securities—	
Public Deposits	8,384,268	Discounts & Advances	74,215,526
Other Deposits—			
Bankers'...	229,169,203		
Other Accts.	73,809,180	Securities..	20,958,991
		Notes.....	28,572,354
		Coin......	828,455
	£329,737,238		£329,737,238

* 250*s.* 7*d.* per oz. fine.

BRITISH MONETARY UNITS

COIN

Gold Coins
†Five Pound £5
†Two Pound £2
†Sovereign £1
†Half-Sovereign 10*s.*
† Discontinued.

Bronze Coins
Penny 1*d.*
Halfpenny ½*d.*

Cupro-Nickel
Crown 5*s.*
Half-Crown 2*s.* 6*d.*
Florin 2*s.*
Shilling 1*s.*
Sixpence 6*d.*
*Threepence 3*d.*

Nickel-Brass
Threepence 3*d.*

Silver
Maundy Money
Fourpence 4*d.*
Threepence 3*d.*
Twopence 2*d.*
Penny 1*d.*

* Not yet struck in cupro-nickel.

Gold Coin.—Gold ceased to circulate during the First World War. Under Exchange Control laws it is now illegal for a resident in the U.K. to hold gold coin other than collectors' pieces. The English sovereign, however, is still used as currency in certain Middle East countries and to meet foreign demand the Royal Mint during the years 1957–59 struck 12,000,000 sovereigns.

Silver.—Prior to 1920 our silver coins were struck from standard silver—an alloy of silver 925 parts and alloy 75 parts. In 1920 the proportion of silver was reduced to 500 parts and that of alloy increased to 500 parts. From January 1, 1947 all 'silver' coins, except Maundy money, have been struck from cupro-nickel—an alloy of copper 75 parts and nickel 25 parts. Maundy coins since 1947 have been struck from standard silver, *i.e.* 92½ per cent. pure silver.

Nickel-brass is an alloy of copper 79 parts, zinc 20 parts and nickel 1 part.

Bronze, introduced in 1860 to replace copper, is an alloy of copper 97 parts, zinc 2½ parts and tin ½ part. These proportions are subject to slight variation.

The 'Remedy' is the amount of variation from standard permitted in weight and fineness of coins when first issued from the Mint.

The legal weight of a penny is one-third and of a halfpenny one-fifth of an ounce avoirdupois. The halfpenny is one inch in diameter.

Legal tender of coin.—Gold, dated 1838 onwards, if of or above least current weight, is legal tender to any amount. Silver, dated 1816 onwards, and cupro-nickel are legal tender for sums up to £2, nickel-brass 3*d.* up to two shillings and bronze up to one shilling.

Work of the Royal Mint in 1962.—The number of United Kingdom coins struck at the Royal Mint in 1962 was 492,344,020 with a face value of £14,347,100. This is the highest annual output on record, easily surpassing the previous highest figure of 429,737,597 in 1948.

There was, however, a fall in the number of coins struck for overseas governments—282,320,787 (82,402,391 Commonwealth and 199,918,396 Foreign) compared with 538,041,671 in 1961. The grand total for the year, therefore, was 774,664,807—a figure which has only once been exceeded, in 1961 with 836,337,756. The strikings of domestic coins in 1962 included 23,998,112 half-crowns and 35,129,903 florins. The florin continues to gain in popularity at the expense of the half-crown. Shillings at 52,673,689 and threepences at 47,241,600 were respectively 10,000,000 and 6,000,000 higher than in 1961. It is in the lower denominations that increases are most marked. Because of a glut in circulation the minting of pennies was suspended in 1949 and, apart from token quantities in 1950, 1951 and 1953, was not resumed until 1961, when 39 million were struck. In 1962, 137,640,000 were struck. Although no halfpennies were struck in 1961, minting was resumed in 1962 with an output of 37,300,800. The public appetite for sixpences is insatiable. In 1962 the record number of 158,355,270 was struck.

Coinages for overseas represented 36 per cent. of the year's output, comprising 87 different denominations for 24 Commonwealth and foreign governments. Nearly 10 million coins were struck in silver for the Republic of Panama. Other customers of the Royal Mint during the year were Burma, Ceylon, Jordan, Kuwait, Muscat, Nicaragua, Uruguay and Vietnam.

The Mint also produced 45,846 medals and decorations.

1963 Operations.—All United Kingdom denominations, except crown pieces, were struck during the first six months. There was a strong demand for sixpences and halfpennies. Issues of shillings were heavier than usual. In the first half of the year 50,000,000 were issued and it was planned to strike a further 30,000,000 in the second half. This compares with an annual average of 40,000,000. Sovereigns were again minted but only for sale against dollars or gold—not for home circulation. The most interesting order from an overseas government was that from Tonga for 1,500 coins of pure gold.

Coins in Circulation.—On January 1, 1963, a total of 6,450,000,000 coins of all denominations was estimated to be in circulation in the United Kingdom: Crown, 10,000,000; Halfcrown, 431,000,000; Florin, 469,000,000; Shilling, 975,000,000; Sixpence, 1,406,000,000; Silver 3*d*., 71,000,000; Nickel-brass 3*d*., 718,000,000; Penny, 1,650,000,000; Halfpenny, 720,000,000.

NOTES

Bank of England Notes.—Bank of England notes are issued for sums of 10*s*., £1 and £5. Notes of 10*s*. and £1 are legal tender in Great Britain and Northern Ireland for the payment of any amount: those of £5 are legal tender in England and Wales only. Change cannot be demanded for notes except from the Bank of England. Notes for £10, £20, £50, £100, £500 and £1,000 were issued until April 22, 1943. These ceased to be legal tender on May 1, 1945. But on February 28, 1963, notes of these values were outstanding to a total of £1,696,000—including 74 notes of £1,000.

The old series of £1 notes issued during the years 1928 to 1960 and the 10*s*. notes of the same type issued from 1928 to 1961—those without the portrait of the Queen—ceased to be legal tender on May 28 and October 29, 1962, respectively. In August, 1963, about £26,000,000 in old £1 notes and £9,000,000 in old 10*s*. notes remained outstanding. It is estimated that the effect of this withdrawal was to reduce the total of notes in the hands of the public by about £90,000,000. The last of the old white £5 notes, dated up to September 20, 1956, were legal tender until March 13, 1961, when they were called in. Bank notes which are no longer legal tender are payable when presented at the head office of the Bank of England in London.

The note circulation is highest at the two peak spending periods of the year—around Christmas and August Bank Holiday. The record figure of £2,504,000,000 was reached on July 31, 1963. This was £46,000,000 higher than the previous peak figure of £2,458,000,000 on December 27, 1961. The actual increase in active circulation is somewhat greater than these figures indicate if the effect of the withdrawal of the old £1 and 10*s*. notes is taken into account.

The £5 note is proving increasingly popular. The smaller blue one was introduced on February 21, 1957, and on February 21, 1963, a further £5 note of new design was issued. These series are circulating together for the time being. The newest £5 note is the third in the series that bears the portrait of the Queen. On February 28, 1957, the value of the £5 notes in circulation was 14.5 per cent. of the total. On February 28, 1963, the proportion was 48.7 per cent., compared with 42.6 per cent. for £1 notes and 4.1 per cent. for 10*s*. notes. On that date the approximate values of these notes in circulation were: £5, £1,124,132,000; £1, £982,963,000 and 10*s*., £95,481,000.

The £10 note—after an interval of 21 years—is to be restored early in 1964. This will be the fourth and the final one in the current series bearing the portrait of the Queen.

Currency Notes.—Under the provisions of the Currency and Bank Notes Act, 1928, Currency Notes (popularly known as Treasury Notes) of the value of 10*s*. and £1 were replaced by the issue of Bank of England notes of the same denominations as from November 22, 1928.

BANK PROFITS, 1960–1962

Bank	1960	1961	1962
Barclays	£5 452,000	£6 074,000	£6,014,000
District	1,082,000	1,192,000	1,181,277
Lloyds	4,606,000	4,935 000	4,817,000
Martins	1,420,000	1,449 000	1,435,000
Midland	4,501,000	5,013,000	4 984,000
National Provincial	3,566,000	4,250,000	4 631,800
Westminster	3,413 000	3 924,000	3,851,836
TOTAL	£24 040 000	£26 873,000	£26 914 913

In the middle of 1939 United Kingdom net external liabilities amounted to rather more than £500 million. During the war years overseas sterling holdings rose extremely fast, reaching nearly £3,600 million at the end of 1945. Of this total a large proportion represented obligations to other countries arising from the exigencies of war rather than their working balances or normal reserves voluntarily held in London. The trends in the sterling holdings of different regions since the war are shown in the following table.

£ million

31st December	1945	1948	1951	1954	1959	1962
United Kingdom Colonies	411	519	919	1,221	635	2,675
Other sterling area countries	1,986	1,636	1,717	1,703	2,069	
Total sterling area countries	2,397	2,155	2,636	2,924	2,704	
Up to December 31, 1957:						
Dollar area	34	19	38	97	..	..
Other western hemisphere	163	135	57	8	..	..
O.E.E.C. countries	351	309	328	244	..	..
Other non-sterling countries	622	534	518	430	..	..
From December 31, 1958:						
North America	..	..	..	..	60	80
Latin America	..	..	..	..	12	−27
Western Europe	..	..	..	..	387	521
Other non-sterling countries	..	..	..	..	341	252
Total non-sterling countries	1,170	997	941	779	803	8[illegible]6
Total—all countries	3,567	3,152	3,577	3,703	3,507	3,501
Non-Territorial Organizations	..	398	566	476	705	605
TOTAL	3,567	3,550	4,143	4,179	4,212	4,106

The statistical series from which the above table is derived has now been discontinued and has been replaced by a new series of U.K. External Liabilities and Claims in Sterling. On the new basis, net external liabilities, excluding £606 million held by international bodies such as the International Monetary Fund, stood at £2,937,000,000 at end-December, 1962. Some £2,203,000,000 represented sterling held by central monetary institutions and, of this, £1,759,000,000 was held by overseas sterling countries. The remaining £734,000,000 represented balances held in London by overseas banks, corporations and individuals—£535,000,000 being owned by sterling area residents. These balances represent, to a great extent, the day-to-day working balances of the overseas banking and business community, although some part is held as a short-term investment. They are therefore more volatile than the official balances; nevertheless, they have not fallen below £725,000,000 during the last decade even when sterling has been under pressure.

The existence of currency and many other funds in sterling is due to the fact that the colonies do not possess developed local capital markets and therefore hold in London the very large funds which governments require for many and diverse purposes. Colonial currencies are very largely backed by sterling securities. The steadily increasing circulations which have accompanied rising populations, the increased use of money and increasing external incomes have thus produced an almost automatic increase in the Currency Boards' investments in United Kingdom and other government securities. Special funds, particularly those of savings banks, have also risen steadily, as have general government funds for planned development expenditures and for current working balances. The other funds, which are held with United Kingdom banks, represent the general banking assets of commercial banks operating in the colonies and the known liquid funds of companies and individuals resident there, held in London.

The underlying reason for the growth of the total holdings was the expansion of colonial economies at a time of rising prices and, in particular, the unprecedentedly high level of export earnings in the years following the outbreak of the Korean War. More recently, the colonial territories have been in deficit on current account but as there has also been a large capital inflow there has been little change in the general level of sterling holdings.

Independent sterling area holdings.—It is the normal practice of central banks in independent sterling area countries to hold the bulk of their foreign exchange reserves in sterling. Moreover, they are often required by statute to hold certain minimum reserves in foreign exchange (which may include sterling) against local currency issues. A large proportion of these statutory reserves is in practice held in sterling.

Much of the fall in the holdings of independent sterling area countries took place in the first few years after the war and represented the reduction of surplus balances built up during the war years. During the last few years trends in individual countries have been diverse. India's holding has recently been run down further to finance their five-year development plans and the holdings of Australia and New Zealand have fluctuated widely, largely under the influence of changes in the prices of their exports of primary products and their import policies. On the other hand, the balances of the middle east sterling area countries have increased considerably.

Non-sterling countries.—The holdings of the O.E.C.D. countries now represent sterling held by residents of these countries for commercial and financial reasons. Their size varies with the scale of the holders' business in sterling and the attractions of London as a financial centre in which to hold funds. The same generalization applies to the small net balances of sterling held by the dollar area countries. The very large fall in the holdings of other non-sterling countries since the war was due to the fact that several of these countries had accumulated large surpluses of sterling well beyond their normal commercial requirements during the war period. Egypt was an outstanding example, and in this and some other cases the funds were transferred to special or " blocked " accounts and provisions made for regular annual releases. Apart from these special accumulations, which have now been mainly used up, most of the countries in this group (including countries in the far east, middle east, western hemispheres and Soviet bloc) only hold sterling funds for financing foreign trade, particularly with sterling area countries.

PRESENT VALUE OF A LEASE, FREEHOLD ESTATE, OR ANNUITY

Years	3%	4%	5%	6%	7%	Years	3%	4%	5%	6%	7%
½	49	48	48	48	47	44	24 25	20 55	17 66	15 38	13 56
1	97	96	95	94	93	45	24 52	20 72	17 77	15 46	13 61
2	1 91	1 89	1 86	1 83	1 81	46	24 77	20 88	17 88	15 52	13 65
3	2 83	2 78	2 72	2 67	2 62	47	25 02	21 04	17 98	15 59	13 69
4	3 72	3 63	3 55	3 47	3 39	48	25 26	21 20	18 08	15 65	13 73
5	4 58	4 45	4 33	4 21	4 10	49	25 50	21 34	18 17	15 71	13 77
6	5 42	5 24	5 08	4 92	4 77	50	25 73	21 48	18 26	15 76	13 80
7	6 23	6 00	5 79	5 58	5 39	51	25 95	21 62	18 34	15 81	13 83
8	7 02	6 73	6 46	6 21	5 97	52	26 16	21 75	18 42	15 86	13 86
9	7 78	7 44	7 11	6 80	6 51	53	26 37	21 87	18 49	15 90	13 89
10	8 53	8 11	7 72	7 36	7 02	54	26 58	21 99	18 56	15 95	13 91
11	9 25	8 76	8 31	7 89	7 50	55	26 77	22 11	18 63	15 99	13 94
12	9 95	9 39	8 86	8 38	7 94	56	26 96	22 22	18 70	16 03	13 96
13	10 63	9 99	9 39	8 85	8 36	57	27 15	22 32	18 76	16 06	13 98
14	11 29	10 56	9 90	9 29	8 75	58	27 33	22 43	18 82	16 10	14 00
15	11 94	11 12	10 38	9 71	9 11	59	27 50	22 53	18 87	16 13	14 02
16	12 56	11 65	10 84	10 11	9 45	60	27 67	22 62	18 93	16 16	14 04
17	13 16	12 17	11 27	10 48	9 76	61	27 84	22 71	18 98	16 19	14 05
18	13 75	12 66	11 69	10 83	10 06	62	28 00	22 80	19 03	16 22	14 07
19	14 32	13 13	12 08	11 16	10 34	63	28 15	22 89	19 07	16 24	14 08
20	14 88	13 59	12 46	11 47	10 59	64	28 30	22 97	19 12	16 26	14 10
21	15 41	14 03	12 82	11 76	10 84	65	28 45	23 04	19 16	16 29	14 11
22	15 94	14 45	13 16	12 04	11 06	66	28 59	23 12	19 20	16 31	14 12
23	16 44	14 86	13 49	12 30	11 27	67	28 73	23 19	19 24	16 33	14 13
24	16 93	15 25	13 80	12 55	11 47	68	28 87	23 26	19 27	16 35	14 14
25	17 41	15 62	14 09	12 78	11 65	69	29 00	23 33	19 31	16 37	14 15
26	17 87	15 98	14 38	13 00	11 83	70	29 12	23 39	19 34	16 38	14 16
27	18 33	16 33	14 64	13 21	11 99	71	29 24	23 45	19 37	16 40	14 17
28	18 76	16 66	14 90	13 41	12 14	72	29 36	23 51	19 40	16 41	14 17
29	19 19	16 98	15 14	13 59	12 28	73	29 48	23 57	19 43	16 43	14 18
30	19 60	17 29	15 37	13 76	12 41	74	29 59	23 63	19 46	16 44	14 19
31	20 00	17 59	15 59	13 93	12 53	75	29 70	23 68	19 48	16 45	14 19
32	20 39	17 87	15 80	14 08	12 65	76	29 81	23 73	19 51	16 47	14 20
33	20 76	18 15	16 00	14 23	12 75	77	29 91	23 78	19 53	16 48	14 21
34	21 13	18 41	16 19	14 37	12 85	78	30 01	23 82	19 55	16 49	14 21
35	21 49	18 66	16 37	14 50	12 95	79	30 10	23 87	19 57	16 50	14 22
36	21 83	18 91	16 55	14 62	13 03	80	30 20	23 91	19 59	16 51	14 22
37	22 17	19 14	16 71	14 74	13 12	85	30 63	24 11	19 68	16 55	14 24
38	22 49	19 37	16 87	14 85	13 19	90	31 00	24 27	19 75	16 58	14 25
39	22 81	19 58	17 02	14 95	13 26	95	31 32	24 40	19 80	16 60	14 26
40	23 11	19 79	17 16	15 05	13 33	100	31 60	24 50	19 85	16 62	14 27
41	23 41	19 99	17 29	15 14	13 39						
42	23 70	20 19	17 42	15 22	13 45	In Perpetuity.					
43	23 98	20 37	17 55	15 31	13 51		33 33	25 00	20 00	16 66	14 28

EXAMPLE 1.—What is the present value of a Lease having 37 years to run of the net annual value of £100, interest being reckoned at 4 per cent.? ANSWER:—19·14 years' purchase, or £1,914.

EXAMPLE 2.—A man, aged 55, in receipt of a pension or annuity of £100 a year net, wishes to commute that for a present payment, interest being reckoned at 5 per cent. How much will he receive? ANSWER:—Looking at the Table of Expectation of Life (*See* Index), it will be seen that the expectation for age 50 is about 23 years; and from the above table an annuity certain for 23 years interest at 5 per cent., is worth 13 49 years purchase. The present payment required would therefore be £1,349 *approximately*.

Note to Example 2.—This method is only approximate. The values of annuities which depend on lives of a given present age, when properly calculated according to a given mortality table and a given rate of interest, are always somewhat less than those given by the method used in this Example.

A TABLE OF THE NUMBER OF DAYS FROM ANY DAY IN ONE MONTH TO THE SAME IN ANY OTHER MONTH IN ORDINARY YEARS

	Jan.	Feb.	Mar.	April	May	June	July	Aug.	Sept.	Oct.	Nov.	Dec.
January........	365	31	59	90	120	151	181	212	243	273	304	334
February.......	334	365	28	59	89	120	150	181	212	242	273	303
March..........	306	337	365	31	61	92	122	153	184	214	245	275
April..........	275	306	334	365	30	61	91	122	153	183	214	244
May............	245	276	304	335	365	31	61	92	123	153	184	214
June...........	214	245	273	304	334	365	30	61	92	122	153	183
July...........	184	215	243	274	304	335	365	31	62	92	123	153
August.........	153	184	212	243	273	304	334	365	31	61	92	122
September......	122	153	181	212	242	273	303	334	365	30	61	91
October........	92	123	151	182	212	243	273	304	335	365	31	61
November.......	61	92	120	151	181	212	242	273	304	334	365	30
December.......	31	62	90	121	151	182	212	243	274	304	335	365

Law Courts and Offices

LAW SITTINGS (1964).—*Hilary*, Jan. 13 to March 25; *Easter*, April 7 to May 15; *Trinity*, May 26 to July 31; *Michaelmas*, Oct. 1 to Dec. 21.

THE JUDICIAL COMMITTEE

The Judicial Committee of the Privy Council consists of the Lord Chancellor, Lord President, ex-Lords President, the Lords of Appeal in Ordinary (*see* below) and such other members of the Privy Council as shall from time to time hold or have held "high judicial office." Among the last are included The Earl of Kilmuir, Viscount Simonds, Lord Goddard, Lord Trevethin and Oaksey, Lord Wright, Lord Morton of Henryton, Lord MacDermott, Lord Tucker, Lord Cohen, Lord Keith of Avonholm, Sir John Beaumont, and the following judges from the Commonwealth: Sir John Greig Latham, H. V. Evatt, Sir Owen Dixon, Sir Harold Barrowclough, Sir Kenneth Gresson and Sir Robert Clarkson Tredgold.

Office—Downing Street, S.W.1.

Registrar of the Privy Council and Registrar of Ecclesiastical Causes, L. W. S. Upton, M.B.E.

Chief Clerk (Judicial), E. R. Mills.

THE HOUSE OF LORDS

The Supreme Judicial Authority for Great Britain and Northern Ireland is the House of Lords, which is the ultimate Court of Appeal from all the Courts in Great Britain and Northern Ireland (except criminal courts in Scotland).

The Lord High Chancellor—

The Rt. Hon. Reginald Edward Manningham-Buller, LORD DILHORNE, *born* 1905 (*apptd.* 1962), (£8,000 as Judge and £4,000 as Speaker of the House of Lords) £12,000.

Lords of Appeal in Ordinary (each £9,000)

	Apptd.
Rt. Hon. Lord Reid, *born* 1890	1948
Rt. Hon. Viscount Radcliffe, G.B.E., *born* 1899	1949
Rt. Hon. Lord Evershed, *born* 1899	1962
Rt. Hon. Lord Jenkins, *born* 1899	1959
Rt. Hon. Lord Morris of Borth-y-Gest, C.B.E., M.C., *born* 1896	1960
Rt. Hon. Lord Hodson, M.C., *born* 1895	1960
Rt. Hon. Lord Guest, *born* 1901	1961
Rt. Hon. Lord Devlin, *born* 1905	1962
Rt. Hon. Lord Pearce, *born* 1901	1962

Registrar: The Clerk of the Parliaments, D. Stephens, C.V.O.

SUPREME COURT OF JUDICATURE

COURT OF APPEAL

Ex officio Judges.—The Lord High Chancellor, the Lord Chief Justice of England, the Master of the Rolls, and the President of the Probate, Divorce, and Admiralty Division.

The Master of the Rolls (£9,000)

The Rt. Hon. Alfred Thompson, Lord Denning (*born* 1899, *apptd.* 1962).

Sec., A. H. Ormerod; *Clerk*, C. L. King.

Lords Justices of Appeal (each £8000)—

	Apptd.
Rt. Hon. Sir Frederic Aked Sellers, M.C., *born* 1893	1957
Rt. Hon. Sir Benjamin Ormerod, *born* 1890	1957
Rt. Hon. Sir Henry Gordon Willmer, O.B.E., T.D., *born* 1899	1958
Rt. Hon. Sir Charles Eustace Harman, *born* 1894	1959
Rt. Hon. Sir Gerald Ritchie Upjohn, C.B.E., *born* 1903	1960
Rt. Hon. Sir Terence Norbert Donovan, *born* 1898	1960
Rt. Hon. Sir Harold Otto Danckwerts, *born* 1888	1961
Rt. Hon. Sir Colin Hargreaves Pearson, C.B.E., *born* 1899	1961
Rt. Hon. Sir William Arthian Davies, *born* 1901	1961
Rt. Hon. Sir (William John) Kenneth Diplock, *born* 1907	1961
Rt. Hon. Sir Charles Ritchie Russell, *born* 1908	1962

HIGH COURT OF JUSTICE

Chancery Division

President, The Lord High Chancellor

Judges (each £8,000)—

	Apptd.
Hon. Sir George Harold Lloyd-Jacob, *born* 1897	1950
Hon. Sir (Arthur) Geoffrey (Neale) Cross, *born* 1904	1960
Hon. Sir Denys Burton Buckley, M.B.E. *born* 1906	1960
Hon. Sir John Pennycuick, *born* 1899	1960
Hon. Sir Richard Orme Wilberforce, C.M.G., O.B.E., *born* 1907	1961
Hon. Sir (John) Anthony Plowman, *born* 1905	1961
Hon. Sir (Arwyn) Lynn Ungoed-Thomas, *born* 1904	1962

Queen's Bench Division

The Lord Chief Justice of England (£10,000)

The Rt. Hon. Hubert Lister, LORD PARKER OF WADDINGTON (*born* 1900, *apptd.* 1958)

Secretary, P. Stephenson; *Clerk*, A. E. Shelton.

Judges (each £8,000)—

	Apptd.
Hon. Sir Wintringham Norton Stable, M.C., *born* 1888	1938
Hon. Sir Donald Leslie Finnemore, *born* 1889	1947
Hon. Sir Geoffrey Hugh Benbow Streatfeild, M.C., *born* 1897	1947
Hon. Sir William Gorman, *born* 1890	1950
Hon. Sir Patrick Redmond Joseph Barry, M.C., *born* 1898	1950
Hon. Sir William Lennox McNair, *born* 1892	1950
Hon. Sir Cecil Robert Havers, *born* 1889	1951
Hon. Sir Hildreth Glyn-Jones, *born* 1895	1953
Hon. Sir Eric Sachs, M.B.E., T.D., *born* 1898	1954
Hon. Sir John Percy Ashworth, M.B.E., *born* 1906	1954
Hon. Sir George Raymond Hinchcliffe, *born* 1900	1957
Hon. Sir Gilbert James Paull, *born* 1896	1957
Hon. Sir Cyril Barnet Salmon, *born* 1903	1957
Hon. Sir (Aubrey) Melford (Steed) Stevenson *born* 1902	1957
Hon. Sir (Herbert) Edmund Davies, *born* 1906	1958
Hon. Sir Richard Everard Augustine Elwes, O.B.E., T.D., *born* 1901	1958
Hon. Sir Gerald Alfred Thesiger, M.B.E., *born* 1902	1958
Hon. Sir Archie Pellow Marshall, *born* 1899	1959
Hon. Sir Henry Josceline Phillimore, O.B.E., born 1910	1959
Hon. Sir (Charles) Rodger (Noel) Winn, C.B., O.B.E., *born* 1903	1959
Hon. Sir Fenton Atkinson, *born* 1906	1960
Hon. Sir Basil Edward Nield, C.B.E., *born* 1903	1960
Hon. Sir (Stephen) Gerald Howard, *born* 1896	1961
Hon. Sir Geoffrey de Paiva Veale, *born* 1906	1961
Hon. Sir John Megaw, C.B.E., T.D., *born* 1909	1961
Hon. Sir Frederick Horace Lawton, *born* 1911	1961

Hon. Sir John Passmore Widgery, C.B.E., T.D., *born* 1911 1961
Hon. Sir Bernard Joseph Maxwell MacKenna, *born* 1906 1961
Hon Sir Alan Abraham Mocatta, O.B.E., *born* 1907 1961
Hon. Sir John Thompson, *born* 1907 1961
Hon. Sir Daniel James Brabin, M.C., *born* 1913 1962
Hon. Sir Eustace Wentworth Roskill, *born* 1911 1962
Hon. Sir Maurice Legat Lyell, *born* 1901 1962
Hon. Sir John Frederick Eustace Stephenson, *born* 1910 1962
Clerk of The Lists, Q.B.D.—W. J. Fell.

Court of Criminal Appeal

Judges, The Lord Chief Justice of England and all the Judges of the Queen's Bench Division.

Probate, Divorce and Admiralty Division

President (£8,000)

Rt. Hon. Sir Jocelyn Edward Salis Simon (*born* 1911, *apptd.* 1962).
Sec., Miss M. E. Manisty, M.B.E.; *Clerk*, B. H. Erhard.

Judges (each £8,000)— Apptd.
Hon. Sir Seymour Edward Karminski, *born* 1902 1951
Hon Sir Geoffrey Walter Wrangham, *born* 1900 1958
Hon. Sir Joseph Bushby Hewson, *born* 1902 1958
Hon. Sir Harry Vincent Lloyd-Jones, *born* 1901 1960
Hon. Sir David Arnold Scott Cairns, *born* 1902 1960
Hon. Sir George Gillespie Baker, O.B.E., *born* 1910 1961
Hon. Sir Leslie George Scarman, O.B.E., *born* 1911 1961
Hon Sir Roger Fray Greenwood Ormrod, *born* 1911 1961
Hon Sir Charles William Stanley Rees, T.D., *born* 1907 1962
Hon. Sir Reginald Withers Payne, *born* 1904 1962
Hon. Sir Neville Major Ginner Faulks, M.B.E., T.D., *born* 1908 1963
Judge Advocate of the Fleet, Hon. E. E. S. Montagu, C.B.E., Q.C.
Queen's Proctor, Sir Harold S. Kent, G.C.B.

LORD CHANCELLOR'S OFFICE

House of Lords, S.W.1

Clerk of the Crown in Chancery and Permanent Secretary to the Lord Chancellor, Sir George Coldstream, K.C.B., Q.C. £7,015
Private Sec. to the Lord Chancellor and Deputy Sergeant-at-Arms, A. D. M. Oulton £2,454 to £3,015
Deputy Clerk of the Crown in Chancery, D. W. Dobson, C.B., O.B.E. £4,415
Principal Establishment Officer, R. E. K. Thesiger, O.B.E. .... £2,965 to £3,565
Deputy Establishment Officer, A. C. E. Cook £2,237 to £2,572
Assistant Establishment Officers, Miss A. Barry; E. J. Brittain.
Secretary for Ecclesiastical Patronage, Brigadier B. S. Watkins, C.B.E. .... £1,798 to £2,561
Secretary of Commissions of the Peace, W. T. C. Skyrme, C.B.E., T.D. £3,815
Deputy, J. M. Cartwright Sharp £2,304 to £2,865
Assistant Solicitors, H. Boggis-Rolfe, C.B.E., K. M. Newman .... £2,965 to £3,565
Senior Legal Assistants, R. C. L. Gregory; J. W. Bourne .... £2,304 to £2,865

Vote Office of the Supreme Court

(Room 192, Royal Courts of Justice, W.C.2)

Accounting Officer, Sir George Coldstream, K.C.B., Q.C.
Clerk of Accounts, T. C. Spicer ... £1,680 to £2,126
Deputy Clerk of Accounts, B. Burns

Royal Courts of Justice Attendant Staff

(Room 466, Royal Courts of Justice, W.C. 2)

Superintendent, Major J. A. Kennedy-Davis.

SUPREME COURT OFFICES, ETC.

Conveyancing Counsel of the Supreme Court

W. T. Elverston; B. G. Burnett-Hall; R. R. A. Walker.

Examiners of the Court

(Empowered to take Examination of Witnesses in all Divisions of the High Court.)

Miss L. H. MacGarvey; M. H. Lush; S. L. Langdon; F. J. Telling.

Official Referees of the Supreme Court

Courts—Royal Courts of Justice, W.C.2

His Hon. Sir Brett Cloutman, V.C., M.C., Q.C.; His Honour Walker Kelly Carter, Q.C.; His Honour Percy Charles Lamb, Q.C. . each £4,700

Official Solicitor's Department

Room 213B—Royal Courts of Justice, W.C.2.

Official Solicitor to the Supreme Court, J. M. L. Evans, C.B.E. .... £3,550 to £4,100
Asst. do., N. H. Turner .... £2,965 to £3,565
Senior Legal Assts., R. Andreae; R. W. D. Auld; R. S. Dhondy; T. W. Swift . £2,304 to £2,865
Legal Asst., H. D. S. Venables, D. C. Relf £1,292 to £2,126
Chief Clerk, C. W. Vickery ... £2,220 to £2,383
Principal Clerks, K. A. Scollay; H. R. Wilson; B. C. Harris; C. T. Davies; R. F. Dunn; S. J. Rist; F. R. Blott; I. D. Abbot .... £1,874 to £2,126

Supreme Court Pay Office

Royal Courts of Justice, W.C.2

Accountant-General, Sir George Coldstream, K.C.B., Q.C.
Chief Accountant, C. D. G. Cook. £2,237 to £2,572
Senior Executive Officers, H. E. Hewett; W. P. Coult; E. D. Fagg .... £1,680 to £2,126
Stockbrokers, Messrs. W. Mortimer & Son.

Central Office of the Supreme Court

Royal Courts of Justice, W.C.2.

Senior Master of the Supreme Court (Q.B.D.) and Queen's Remembrancer, C. H. Grundy. ... £4,400
Masters of the Supreme Court (Q.B.D.), B. A. Harwood; W. R. Lawrence; C. Clayton; A. S. Diamond; I. H. Jacob; J. Ritchie, M.B.E. H. A. Palmer, T.D. .... each £3,550 to £4,100

Action Department

Head Clerk, W. H. Redman, M.B.E. £1,715 to £1,943

*Writ, Appearance and Judgment Section**

Chief Clerk, W. E. Garrod ...... £1,442 to £1,686

Summons and Order Section‡

Chief Clerk, R. C. Newman ... £1,442 to £1,686

*Filing Department**

Chief Clerk, C. W. C. Kentish .. £1,442 to £1,686

*Masters' Secretary's Department and Queen's Remembrancer's Department**

Chief Clerk (*Secretary to the Masters*), W. N. Last .... £1,442 to £1,686

Crown Office and Associates' Dept.

Clerk of the Lists (Q.B.D.), W. J. Fell £2,088 to £2,149
Head Clerk (*Crown Office*), V. W. Judd £1,715 to £1,943
Chief Associate, F. W. Player ... £1,715 to £1,943

Criminal Appeal Office

(Royal Courts of Justice, W.C.2)

Registrar, H. A. Palmer, T.D.
Assistant Registrar, D. R. Thompson £2,850 to £3,325

Deputy Assistant Registrars, W. H. Greenwood; M. P. Palmer..............£2,304 to £2,865
Chief Clerk, H. B. Hinton.....£1,536 to £1,837

Courts-Martial Appeals Office
(Royal Courts of Justice, W.C.2)

Registrar, D. R. Thompson.
Assistant Registrar, W. H. Greenwood.
* Office hours, 10 to 4; Vacations, 10 to 2; Saturdays, closed.
‡ Office hours, 10.30 to 4.30 Vacations, 10.30 to 2.30; Saturdays, closed.

Supreme Court Taxing Office

Chief Master, Paul Adams, T.D............£4,400
Masters of the Supreme Court, William Francis Hood; Ernest Marshall Foster; Graham John Graham-Green, T.D.; Charles Edgar Cullis; Dennis Robert Clarke; Leonard Humphrey Razzall £3,550 to £4,100
Chief Clerk (vacant).
Principal Clerks, G. N. H. Harris; H. C. Aiton; E. W. Pinder; R. S. Stanton; J. H. Ayers; A. G. Warren; E. P. A. Jack, H. J. C. Rainbird £1,874 to £2,126

CHANCERY DIVISION

Chancery Judges' Chambers
Royal Courts of Justice, W.C.2

Chief Master (attached to all the Judges), William Francis Spencer Hawkins............£4 400
Chief Clerk and Secretary to Chief Master, W. D. Verrall.

GROUP A

At Chambers.—Masters of the Supreme Court, A to F, Thomas Lutwyche Dinwiddy; *G to N*, Robert Edward Ball, M.B.E.; *O to Z*, Edmund Rawlings Heward..................£3,550 to £4,100

GROUP B

At Chambers.—Masters of the Supreme Court, A to F, James Stephen Neave; *G to N*, Arthur Edmund Frost; *O to Z*, William Lister Pengelly £3,550 to £4,100

Chancery Registrars' Office
Royal Courts of Justice, W.C.2

Chief Registrar, D. C. Smith, £3,550; *Registrars*, C. M. Kidd; P. Halliday; H. J. Wilson; D. G. Leach....................£2,850 to £3,325
Senior Assistant Registrar, M. S. Edwards £2,091 to £2,598
Assistant Registrars, A. Williams, O.B.E., L. F. Manning, H. W. Nicholls, A. W. Hancock £1,258 to £1,987
Chief Clerk and Secretary to Chief Registrar, W. D. Verrall.....................£1,773 to 2,001
Petition and Entry Clerk, S. S. Holloway.

Companies Court
Victory Buildings, Kingsway, W.C.2

Judges, The Hon. Mr. Justice Buckley, M.B.E.; The Hon. Mr. Justice Pennycuick; Mr. Justice Plowman
Registrar, A. F. M. Berkeley....£3,550 to £4,100
Principal Clerks, E. L. Russell, O.B.E. (£1,873 to £2,101); J. G. Usher.......£1,715 to £1,943
Senior Official Receiver, Companies Department, A. T. Cheek......................£3,350

PROBATE, DIVORCE AND ADMIRALTY DIVISION

PRINCIPAL PROBATE REGISTRY
Somerset House, W.C.2

Senior Registrar, Sir Bertram Long, M.C., T.D..£4,400
Registrars, J. F. Compton Miller, M.B.E., T.D.; C. H. G. Forbes, O.B.E.; H. C. T. Millers; J. P. Kinsley; J. E. N. Russell; D. A. Newton £3,550 to £4,100
Secretary, W. D. S. Caird......£1,797 to £2,243
Establishment Officer, D. H. Colgate £1,680 to £2,126
Principal Clerks, C. Kenworthy; B. W. Campbell; D. R. L. Holloway; W. R. Hurst; W. J. Pickering; J. R. Turner; R. W. Elliott; Miss K. W. Simes; J. D. Drayson; Miss L. M Farmborough; Miss J. J. Learmonth £1,680 to £2,126
Clerk of Rules and Orders (Royal Courts of Justice), J. Turner..................£1,680 to £2,126

DISTRICT PROBATE REGISTRIES

Birmingham and *Northampton*, G. H. Hayden.
Bodmin, D. P. Lazzerini.
Bristol, *Gloucester* and *Hereford*, T. B. Williams.
Chester, *Bangor* and *St. Asaph*, H. W. Jackson.
Exeter, F. C. Ottway.
Lancaster and *Carlisle*, H. M. Hall.
Lewes, W. A. Worrell.
Liverpool, G. Wentworth.
Llandaff and *Carmarthen*, F. J. Taylor.
Manchester, H. A. Gurney.
Newcastle and *Durham*, F. B. Birdsall, O.B.E.
Norwich, *Peterborough* and *Ipswich*, R. C. Robinson.
Nottingham, *Leicester*, *Lincoln* and *Derby*, W. A. Swan.
Oxford, A. Crawshaw.
Wakefield, F. J. E. Bools.
Winchester and *Salisbury*, C. F. Walker.
York, H. Wilkinson.

Admiralty Registry and Marshal's Office
Royal Courts of Justice, W.C. 2

Registrar, K. C. McGuffie.....£3,550 to £4,100
Marshal and Chief Clerk, P. V. Gray £1,684 to £2,059

Bankruptcy (High Court) Department
Victory House, Kingsway W.C.2

Judges, The Hon. Mr. Justice Cross; The Hon. Mr. Justice Wilberforce, C.M.G., O.B.E.; The Hon. Mr. Justice Ungoed-Thomas.
Chief Registrar, John Francis Bowyer.......£4,400
Registrar, Thomas Cunliffe.....£3,550 to £4,100
Principal Clerk, F. W. A. Bates..£1,874 to £2,126

Official Receivers' Department

Senior Official Receiver, A. A. Walter £2,750 to £3,125
Official Receiver, W. Whitehead, O.B.E. £2,392 to £2,750
Assistant do., B. J. Longley; R. B. Howard; J. B. Clemetson; R. L. Lockhead; S.Dirs. £1,976 to £2,382

OFFICE OF THE MASTER OF THE COURT OF PROTECTION
25 Store Street, W.C.1

Master, R. W. Jennings, Q.C..............£4,400
Deputy Master, M. E. Reed, C.B.E. £2,850 to £3,325
Assistants to the Master, W. J. Tabner, O.B.E.; D. G. Hunt; R. H. Phillips........£2,326 to £2,832
Chief Clerk, L. A. Douglass....£2,220 to £2,383
Assistant Chief Clerk, G. F. Porter £1,874 to £2,126
Principal Clerks, R. A. G. Whiteman; H. Rowland; H. F. Compton; N. F. Chidley £1,874 to £2,126

OFFICE OF THE LORD CHANCELLOR'S VISITORS

Legal Visitor, R. O. L. Armstrong-Jones, M.B.E., Q.C. £3,638
Medical Visitors, Dr. G. Somerville; Dr. W. D. Nicol; Dr. J. S. Harris..................£3,638

RESTRICTIVE PRACTICES COURT
Royal Courts of Justice, W.C.2

Judges nominated to sit in the Restrictive Practices Court: Mr. Justice Megaw (*President*); Mr. Justice Buckley; Mr. Justice Mocatta; Lord Cameron; Mr. Justice McVeigh.
Lay Members, Maj.-Gen. W. E. V. Abraham, C.B.E. (*part time*); Sir Stanford Cooper; E. L. Denny (*part time*); Sir Gilbert Flemming, K.C.B. (*part time*); Brig. T. Grainger-Stewart, C.B., M.C., T.D. (*part time*); C. C. W. Havell, M.C. (*part time*); W. L. Heywood, O.B.E.; D. V. House.

Clerk of the Court, Mr. Registrar Bowyer.

NOTE ON CIVIL COURTS.—Smaller civil actions are heard locally in County Courts which, with some exceptions, deal with all common law cases where the sum involved is less than £400. Jurisdiction given by special statutes is of the widest range and cases under such statutes are dealt with irrespective of the amount involved. County Courts are presided over by a paid judge sitting alone. The county court for the City of London is the Mayor's and City of London Court, which deals with small cases and has also jurisdiction unlimited in amount. Bankruptcy cases arising in London are dealt with in the London Bankruptcy Court, Carey Street, W.C.2; those arising out of London are dealt with in the county courts.

Actions in the High Court are distributed among the several Divisions of the High Court according to their nature. Certain classes of actions, *e.g.*, those dealing with the administration of estates of deceased persons, partnerships, trusts and mortgages, specific performance of contracts between vendors and purchasers of real estates, including contracts for leases, partition or sale of real estates, wardship of infants and the care of infants, estates, and company and bankruptcy cases, are usually commenced in the Chancery Division. The Queen's Bench Division deals with most ordinary civil cases. Actions may be tried in London or the Assizes. The Probate, Divorce and Admiralty Division has jurisdiction in matters concerning wills, divorces, and Admiralty, prize and shipping cases.

COUNTY COURTS

In 1962 the total number of proceedings in County Courts of England and Wales (including the Mayor's and City of London Court) was 1,693,626 (as against 1,699,430 for the year 1961). The number of debtors imprisoned under the *Debtors Act*, 1869, was 6,323 (1961) and 7,913 (1962) and of the last number 5,752 served the full terms of imprisonment for "Contempt of Court" in failing to comply with the order for payment.

County Court Judges (each £4,400)

[*County Court Judges are addressed as* "*His Honour*" *and* "*Your Honour.*"]

The figures in parentheses indicate the number of the County Court Circuit in which the Judges sit.

Addleshaw, John Lawrence (10), Cheshire.
Andrew, William Monro, M.B.E. (43), Marylebone.
Armstrong, Arthur Henry (55), Dorset, Hants., etc.
Barrington, John Harcourt, T.D. (48), Lambeth.
Bassett, John Henry, Q.C. (58), Essex.
Baxter, Herbert James, O.B.E. (40), Bow.
Bell, Philip Ingress, T.D., Q.C. (4), Blackburn.
Beresford, Eric George Harold (25), Staffs.
Blagden, John Basil (44), Westminster.
Braund, Sir Henry (19), Derbyshire.
Brown, Harold John, M.C., Q.C. (50), Sussex.
Buckee, Henry Thomas, D.S.O. (62), Southend, etc.
Carr, Norman Alexander (22), Worcs.
Clark, Reginald, Q.C. (41), Clerkenwell.
Cohen, Clifford Theodore, M.C., T.D. (11), Stockton-on-Tees.
Cohen, Nathaniel Arthur Jim (56), Croydon.
Dewar, Thomas (59), Cornwall.
Dow, Ronald Graham (41), Clerkenwell.
Drabble, John Frederick, Q.C. (1), Newcastle, etc.
Duveen, Claude Henry, M.B.E., Q.C. (61), Reading.
Edgedale, Samuel Richards, Q.C. (47), Dartford. etc.
Evans, Carey (32), Norfolk.
Evans, David Meurig (29), Caernarvonshire.
Evans, Sir Shirley Worthington-, Bt. (34), Brentford and Uxbridge.
Flint, Abraham John (18), Nottingham, etc.
Gage, Conolly Hugh (35), Cambridge.
Glazebrook, Francis Kirkland (63), Kent.
Hamilton, Allister McNicoll (23), Warwickshire.
Harding, Rowe (30), Glamorgan.
Harington, John Charles Dundas, Q.C. (26), Staffs.
Harper, Norman (16), Hull.
Herbert, Jesse Basil, M.C., Q.C. (44), Westminster.
Hillard, Richard Arthur Loraine, M.B.E. (54), Bristol.
Jellinek, Lionel, M.C. (60), Surrey.
Jones, Hugh Emlyn- (7), Cheshire.
Jones, Thomas Elder- (52), Somerset and Wilts.
Lambert, Robert (5), Bolton, etc.
Lane, Mrs. Elizabeth Kathleen, Q.C. (38), Edmonton.
Lee, Arthur Michael, D.S.C., Q.C. (51), Hampshire.
Leigh, Christopher Thomas Bowes, O.B.E., T.D. (8), Manchester and Leigh.
Leon, Henry Cecil, M.C. (46), Willesden.
Leslie, Gilbert Frank (46), Willesden.
Lewis, Edward Daly (17), Lincolnshire.
Lloyd. Ifor Bowen, Q.C. (37), West London.
McIntyre, Frederick Donald Livingstone, Q.C. (40), Bow.
McKee, Dermot St. Oswald (14), Yorks.
MacMillan, James (39), Shoreditch.
Maddocks, George (3), Cumberland.
Mais, Robert Hugh (43), Marylebone.
Morgan, (Hopkin) Trevor, M.C., Q.C. (31), Carmarthenshire.
Morris, O. T. Temple-, Q.C. (24), Monmouthshire.
Morris, William Gerard (6), Liverpool.
Nicholas, Montagu Richmond (45), Wandsworth.
Nicklin, Robert Shenstone (21), Birmingham.
Ould, Ernest (13), Sheffield.
Paton, Harold William, D.S.C. (54), Glos. and Somerset.
Pennant, David Edward Thornton (28), Shropshire and Mid-Wales.
Potter, Douglas Charles Loftus (56), Croydon.
Pratt, Hugh Macdonald (57), Devon.
Pugh, Sir (John) Alun (42), Bloomsbury.
Rawlins, Percy Lionel Edwin (36), Oxford.
Reid, John Alexander, M.C. (45), Wandsworth, etc.
Robson, Denis Hicks, Q.C. (20), Leicester, etc.
Ruttle, Henry Samuel Jacob (48), Lambeth.
Saul, Bazil Sylvester Wingate- (47), Southwark.
Sharp, Alastair George, M.B.E., Q.C. (2), Durham.
Smith, Gerard Gustave Lind- (21), Birmingham.
Smith, Stuart Hayne Granville, O.B.E. (38), Edmonton, etc.
Southall, Thomas Frederick (33), Suffolk.
Steel, Edward (8), Manchester and Leigh.
Sumner, William Donald Massey, O.B.E., Q.C. (49), Kent.
Talbot. Hilary Gwynne (39), Shoreditch.
Trotter, Richard Stanley (6), Lancs.
Willis, Roger Blenkiron, T.D. (42), Bloomsbury.

County Courts Branch

3 Dean's Yard, Westminster, S.W.1
Registry of County Courts Judgments, etc.
(Hours for searching, Monday to Friday, 11 to 4.)

Head of Branch, J. D. Kewish, C.B., T.D. £3,325
Asst. Head of Branch and Finance Officer, J. W. Twiss .... £2,172 to £2,507
Establishment Officer, H. Slater . . £2,172 to £2,507
Establishment Inspectors, P. G. Jefferson; W. A. Evans, T.D.; B. Kelley; F. H. Sadler £1,615 to £2,061
Senior Excecutive Officer, Miss A. M. Hart £1,615 to £2,061
Auditors, E. H. R. Ezard; W. L. Wright; J. E. Woodhouse; W. E. Hoile; R. L. Baker; S. E.

Skidmore; S. L. Padmore; G. F. Allen; H. Rusbridge; R. J. Skeldon; R. L. Rees; C. F. Stratton; H. Mark; J. C. White; F. Poppleston; F. E. Mayers; G. McMullan; R. J. Steele; J. W. Jackson; D. J. Raddan; K. A. R. Laycock; D. W. Jackson .... £1,438 to £2,061

CENTRAL CRIMINAL COURT

Old Bailey, E.C.4.

Judges, The Lord Mayor, the Lord Chancellor, any person who has been Lord Chancellor or Judge of the High Court, and the present Judges of the High Court; the Aldermen, Recorder, Common Serjeant, and Judges of the Mayor's and City of London Court for time being.

Clerk of the Court, Leslie Balfour Boyd.

Deputies, William Hugh Corbett Lowe; Drummond Garnar Blackaller.

Under-Sheriffs.

Under Sheriffs, (1963-64), Col. Colin Fraser Tod, The Old Mill House, Westcott, Dorking, Surrey and Col. Reginald Joseph Cooke-Hurle, Flat 10, 23A Grove End Road, N.W.8.

CIRCUITS OF JUDGES

South Eastern Circuit.

Special Itinerary

Norfolk (Norwich)—W., S. and adjourned S. and A. (City of Norwich)—W., S. and adjourned S. and A.

Essex (Chelmsford)—W., S. and adjourned S. and A.

Surrey (Kingston)—W., S. and adjourned S. and A

Kent (Maidstone)—W., S. and adjourned S. and A.

Sussex (Lewes)—W., S. and adjourned S. and A.

Ordinary Itinerary

Huntingdonshire (Huntingdon)—W. and S.

Cambridge (Cambridge)—W., S. and A.

Suffolk (Ipswich)—W. (Bury St. Edmunds)—S. and alternatively A. (Ipswich 1964).

Hertfordshire (Hertford)—W., S. and A.

Clerk of Assize, R. C. Lancaster. £2,085 to £3,175

Assistant Clerk of Assize, R. E. Gorton.

Clerk of Indictments, W. A. J. Brooks.

Associates, F. H. Hearn; N. F. Phillips.

Office, Royal Courts of Justice, W.C.2.

Midland Circuit.

(Counties in order of visit.)

Bucks (Aylesbury)—W., S. and A.

Beds (Bedford)—W., S. and A.

Lincolnshire (Lincoln)—W., S. and A.

Derbyshire (Derby)—W., S. and A.

Leicestershire (Leicester)—W., S. and A.

Rutlandshire (Oakham)—W. and S.

Northants (Northampton)—W., S. and A.

Notts (Nottingham)—W., S. and A.

Warwickshire (Warwick Div.)—W., S. and A.

Do. (Birmingham Div.)— W., S. and A.

Clerk of Assize, H. C. Naldrett. £2,085 to £3,175

Assistant Clerk of Assize, B. H. Sayer.

Clerks of Indictments, S. Carlton; L. V. Gebbett.

Associates, M. H. Snowdon; A. Evans.

Circuit Office, King Edward Building, 205 Corporation Street, Birmingham.

Northern Circuit.

Cumberland (Carlisle)—W., S. and A. (for Winter Assize County No. 1).

Westmorland (Appleby)—W. and S.

Lancashire, Northern Div (Lancaster)—W., S. and A.

Salford Division (Manchester)—W., S. and A.

West Derby Division (Liverpool)—W., S. and A.

Clerk of Assize, I. A. Macaulay, C.B.E., Liverpool. £2,085 to £3,175

Assistant Clerk of Assize, W. H. McNeile.

Associates, R. O. Jones; C. A. White; J. Tebay.

P+

North Eastern Circuit.

Northumberland and City of Newcastle (Newcastle)—W. S. and A.

Durham (Durham)—W., S. and A.

Yorkshire, N. & E. Riding, and City of York (York)—W., S. and A.

Yorkshire, Sheffield Division—W. S. and A.

Yorkshire, Leeds Division—W., S. and A.

Clerk of Assize, P. D. Robinson, Castle of York, York..................... £2,085 to £3,175

Assistant Clerk of Assize, A. L. Edwards.

Circuit Officers, A. H. Page; D. G. Gardiner; G. B. Wood; J. Winter; E. Lord.

Oxford Circuit.

Assizes are held three times a year at *Reading, Oxford, Worcester* (for County and City), *Gloucester* (for County and City), *Newport (Mon.), Hereford, Shrewsbury, Stafford.* Divorce business is taken at Gloucester, Newport and Shrewsbury only. Civil business is taken at every town at every Assize.

Clerk of Assize, William Lewis, T.D. £2,085 to £3,175

Assistant Clerk of Assize, P. E. Underwood.

Circuit Officers, H. P. McDermott; H. S. Jones.

Circuit Office, Government Offices, Whittington Road, Worcestor.

Western Circuit.

Divorce is taken W., S. and A. at Bodmin Exeter, Bristol and Winchester.

Wilts (Devizes) W., (Salisbury) S., (Devizes and Salisbury alternately A., 1964 Salisbury; *Dorset* (Dorchester) W., S. and A.; *Somerset*, (Taunton) W., (Wells) S., (Taunton and Wells alternately) A.; 1964 Wells; *Cornwall*, (Bodmin) W., S. and A.; *Devon*, (Exeter) W., S. and A.; *City of Exeter* (The Guildhall), W., S. and A.; *Bristol* (The Guildhall), W., S. and A.; *Hants.*, (Winchester) W., S. and A.

Clerk of Assize, S. E. Lloyd, Alexandra House, New Street, Salisbury....... £2,085 to £3,175

Assistant Clerk of Assize, C. E. Blake.

Circuit Officers, C. W. Langford; D. S. Jacobs; R. Potter.

Wales and Chester Circuit.

Criminal and Civil business is taken at all towns, together with Matrimonial Causes at Caernarvon, Carmarthen, Chester and Cardiff or Swansea.

Itinerary No. 6 (1 Judge)

Montgomeryshire—(Welshpool) W. S. and A.

Merioneth—(Dolgellau) W. S. and A.

Caernarvonshire—(Caernarvon) W. S. and A.

Anglesey—(Beaumaris) W. S. and A.

Denbighshire—(Ruthin) W. S. and A.

Flintshire—(Mold) W. S. and A.

Radnorshire—(Presteigne) W. S. and A.

Brecknock—(Brecon) W. S. and A.

Cardiganshire—(Lampeter) W. S. and A.

Pembrokeshire and Town and County of Haverfordwest—(Haverfordwest) W. S. and A.

Carmarthenshire and County of the Borough of Carmarthen—(Carmarthen) W. S. and A.

Itinerary No. 7 (2 Judges)

Cheshire—(Chester Castle) W. 1st and 2nd (adjourned) S. and A.

Glamorgan—(Cardiff) W. and 2nd S.; (Swansea) 1st S. and A.

Clerk of the Crown and Clerk of Assize, E. H. Thomas.................. £2,085 to £3,175

Assistant Clerk of Assize, L. R. Beckett.

Associates, E. J. Trowbridge; H. B. Thomas; D. J. Williams.

Circuit Office, Law Courts, Cardiff.

CROWN COURTS

The Criminal Justice Administration Act, 1956, authorized the setting up of two new courts, known as the Crown Court of Liverpool and the Crown Court of Manchester. These Courts took over the jurisdiction of the former Courts of Quarter Session for Liverpool and Manchester and the criminal jurisdiction of the Assize Courts for the West Derby and Salford Divisions of Lancashire. The Courts are normally presided over by the Recorders of Liverpool and Manchester who have power to refer assize cases for trial by a judge of the High Court.

RECORDERS

(*The Recorder of London is addressed as "Right Worshipful" and, when sitting as a Commissioner in the Central Criminal Court, as "My Lord." Others as "The Worshipful" and "Your Worship."*)

Abingdon, Anthony Clare Bulger (1962).
Andover, Michael Richard Hoare (1962).
Banbury, Richard Michael Arthur Chetwynd Talbot (1955).
Barnstaple, Alan Stewart Trapnell (1962).
Barrow-in-Furness, Thomas Alfred Cunliffe (1962).
Bath, Jeremy Nicolas Hutchinson, Q.C. (1962).
Bedford, Charles Lamond Henderson, Q.C. (1948).
Birkenhead, William Lloyd Mars-Jones, M.B.E., Q.C. (1959).
Birmingham, Joseph Arthur Grieves, Q.C. (1960).
Blackburn, Sydney Scholefield Allen, Q.C., M.P. (1948).
Blackpool, Joseph Stanley Watson, M.B.E., Q.C. (1961).
Bolton, Alexander David Karmel, Q.C. (1962).
Bournemouth, Edgar Stewart Fay, Q.C. (1961).
Bradford, Bernard Benjamin Gillis, Q.C. (1958).
Bridgwater, Leslie Herrick Collins, O.B.E. (1962).
Brighton, Charles John Addison Doughty, Q.C. M.P. (1955).
Bristol, Norman Roy Fox-Andrews, Q.C. (1961).
Burnley, Miss Rose Heilbron, Q.C. (1956).
Burton-on-Trent, Edward Walter Eveleigh, Q.C. (1961).
Bury St. Edmunds, Robert Ives (1963).
Cambridge, (vacant).
Canterbury, Hon. Henry Arthur Pears Fisher, Q.C. (1962).
Cardiff, Frederick Elwyn Jones, Q.C., M.P. (1960).
Carlisle, (vacant).
Chester, Francis John Watkin Williams, Q.C. (1958).
Colchester, Andrew Aiken Watson, Q.C. (1949).
Coventry, John Mervyn Guthrie Griffith-Jones, M.C. (1959).
Croydon, Malcolm John Morris, Q.C. (1962).
Deal, Richard Marven Hale Everett, Q.C. (1959).
Derby, Theobald Richard Fitzwalter Butler, O.B.E. (1962).
Devizes, Stephen Alastair Morton, T.D. (1957).
Doncaster, John Francis Scott Cobb, Q.C. (1961).
Dover, Robert Michael Oldfield Havers (1962).
Dudley, Gilbert Griffiths (1944).
**Durham*, James Kenneth Hope, C.B.E.
Exeter, Hugh Eames Park, Q.C. (1960).
Folkestone. Neil Lawson, Q.C. (1962).
Gloucester, Ralph Vincent Cusack, Q.C. (1961).
Grantham, William Arnold Sime, M.B.E., Q.C. (1959).
Gravesend, Frederick Petre Crowder, M.P. (1960).
Great Grimsby, Arthur Evan James, Q.C. (1962).
Guildford, Travers Christmas Humphreys, Q.C. (1959).
Halifax, Alter Max Hurwitz (1957).
**Hartlepool*, Leslie Othen Williams (1949).
Hastings, The Lord Dunboyne (1961).
Hereford, Robert Boyd Cochrane Parnall (1956).
Huddersfield, John Brooke Willis (1959).
Hull, Peter Stanley Price, Q.C. (1958).
Ipswich, Sebag Shaw, Q.C. (1958).
King's Lynn, John Charles Llewellyn (1961).
**Kingston* (vacant).
Leeds, George Stanley Waller, O.B.E., Q.C. (1961).
Leicester, Graham Russell Swanwick, M.B.E., Q.C. (1959).
Lichfield, Max Ernest Holdsworth, O.B.E. (1939).
Lincoln, Col. Ralph Kilner Brown, O.B.E., T.D., Q.C. (1960).
Liverpool (Crown Court), Stephen Chapman, Q.C. (1961).
London, Sir (Edward) Anthony Hawke (1959).
Maidstone, Neil Nairn McKinnon, Q.C. (1961).
Manchester (Crown Court), John Robertson Dunn Crichton, Q.C. (1960).
Margate, William Hugh Griffiths, M.C. (1962).
Merthyr Tydfil, Norman Grantham Lewis Richards, O.B.E., Q.C. (1960).
Middlesbrough, Henry Gaunt Suddards (1961).
Newark, Niall MacDermot, O.B.E., Q.C., M.P. (1962).
Newbury, Edward Terrell, O.B.E., Q.C. (1935).
Newcastle under Lyme, William Field Hunt (1945).
Newcastle upon Tyne, Arthur Bryan Boyle, C.B.E., Q.C. (1961).
Northampton, Michael Victor Argyle, M.C., Q.C. (1962).
Norwich, Peter Colin Duncan, M.C., Q.C. (1963).
Nottingham, Matthew Anthony Leonard Cripps, D.S.O., T.D., Q.C. (1961).
Oldham, Richard Martin Bingham, O.B.E., T.D., Q.C. (1960).
Oxford, John Galway Foster, Q.C., M.P. (1956).
Penzance, Raymond Stock (1962).
Plymouth, Norman John Lee Brodrick, Q.C. (1962).
Pontefract, Herbert Bewick (1961).
Poole, Malcolm McGougan (1954).
Portsmouth, Norman John Skelhorn. Q.C. (1962).
**Preston*, William Harrison Openshaw (1958).
Reading, Robert Crompton Hutton (1951).
Rochester, Donald Charles Bain. M.C., Q.C. (1961).
Rotherham, Charles Raymond Dean, Q.C. (1962).
Salford, Richard Haddow Forrest, Q.C. (1956).
Salisbury, Derek Aldwin Grant, D.S.O., Q.C. (1962).
Scarborough, Joseph Stanley Snowden (1951).
Sheffield, Rudolph Lyons, Q.C. (1961).
Shrewsbury, John Francis Bourke (1945).
Smethwick, Paul Henry Layton (1952).
Southampton, Joseph Thomas Molony, Q.C. (1960).
Southend, Patrick McCarthy O'Conner, Q.C. (1961).
Stoke on Trent, George Kenneth Mynett, Q.C. (1961).
Sunderland, Rupert Rawden Rawden-Smith (1961).
Swansea, Evan Roderic Bowen, Q.C., M.P. (1960).
Swindon, Desmond James Conrad Ackner, Q.C. (1962).
Walsall, James Charles Beresford-Whyte Leonard (1951).
**Wells*, William Mack Huntley.
West Bromwich, Edward Brian Gibbens, Q.C. (1959).
West Ham, Walter Augustus Leopold Raeburn, Q.C. (1949).
Wigan, John Glyn Burrell, Q.C. (1962).
Winchester, David Powell Croom-Johnson, D.S.C., V.R.D., Q.C. (1962).
Windsor, New, Alan Stewart Orr, O.B.E., Q.C. (1958).
Wolverhampton, Myer Alan Barry King-Hamilton, Q.C. (1961).
Worcester, Hon. Thomas Gabriel Roche, Q.C. (1959).
Yarmouth, Great, John Huxley Buzzard (1958).
York, Henry Cooper Scott, Q.C. (1961).

*Boroughs having no Quarter Sessions.

METROPOLITAN MAGISTRATES

(Under the Metropolitan Police Courts Act, 1839).

Bow Street, Covent Garden, W.C.2.

Chief Metropolitan Magistrate, Sir Robert Henderson Blundell £4,400

Magistrates, Kenneth James Priestley Barraclough, O.B.E., T.D.; Richard Geraint Rees; William Henry Hughes..................*each* £4,100

Senior Chief Clerk and Establishments Officer, Edward Hughes, C.B.E.......................£3,670

Chief Clerks, C. J. Collinge; A. V. E. J. Mindham £2,865 to £3,255

Chief Clerk, Juvenile Court, J. R. Nicol £2,865 to £3,255

Clerkenwell, King's Cross Road, W.C.1.

Magistrates, Lancelot Elliot Barker; Charles Richard Beddington; John Denis Purcell...each £4,100

Chief Clerks, F. M. Worthen (£3,255); D. V. Wainwright...............£2,865 to £3,255

Great Marlborough Street, W.1.

Magistrates, Leo Joseph Anthony Gradwell, D.S.C.; Edward George Haydon Robey; John Henry Lancelot Aubrey-Fletcher .... each £4,100

Chief Clerks, A. E. Jones; J. T. Taylor, M.C. £2,865 to £3,255

Greenwich (Blackheath Road, S.E.10) and Woolwich (Market Street, S.E.18).

Magistrates, Alan Leslie Stevenson; St. John Bernard Vyvyan Harmsworth ....each £4,100

Chief Clerk, G. Crankshaw.....£2,865 to £3,255

Lambeth, Renfrew Road, S.E.11.

Magistrates, Clive Stuart Saxon Burt, Q.C.; Thomas Ker Edie...........................each £4,100

Chief Clerk, P. J. Calnan...............£3,255

Marylebone, 181 Marylebone Road, N.W.1.

Magistrates, Geoffrey G. Raphael; Walter Bennett Frampton, O.B.E.; John Constantine Phipps; Nigel Francis Maltby Robinson; David Mure Wacher........................each £4,100

Chief Clerks, L. S. Penfold; Dr. B. Geidt £2,865 to £3,255

North London, Stoke Newington Road, N.16.

Magistrates, Frank Milton; Evelyn Charles Sackville Russell..........................each £4,100

Chief Clerk, C. A. Reston.....£2,865 to £3,255

Old Street, E.C.1.

Magistrates, Harold Francis Ralph Sturge; Neil Martin McElligott..............each £4,100

Chief Clerk, Douglas Edward Hughes.....£3,255

Thames, Aylward Street, Stepney, E.1.

Magistrates, Cecil Campion; Donaldson Loudoun *each* £4,100

Chief Clerk, Stanley French..............£3,255

Tower Bridge, Tooley Street, S.E.1.

Magistrates, Henry Hollingdrake Maddocks; John Robert Thomas Hooper..........each £4,100

Chief Clerk, F. A. Green..................£3,255

Chief Clerk, Justices' Court, J. V. Hayward . £3,170

West London, Southcombe Street, W. Kensington, W.14.

Magistrates, Eric Ronald Guest; Seymour John Collins.........................each £4,100

Chief Clerk, K. Edwards.......£2,865 to £3,255

South Western, Lavender Hill, S.W.11

Magistrates, Arthur Hugh Glenn Craske; Sir John Cameron, Bt.; Herbert Christopher Beaumont; Edgar Dennis Smith.............each £4,100

Chief Clerks, E. F. Turrill; H. R. C. Trenchard £2,865 to £3,255

Balham, 217 Balham High Road, S.W.17.

Magistrate, Tobias Springer.

Chief Clerk, W. E. C. Robins..£2,865 to £3,255

JUVENILE COURTS.

Juvenile Courts, in separate buildings from Magistrates' Courts, are held at 58B Bow Road, E.3; Methodist Church Hall, Elm Park, Brixton Hill, S.W.2; Church Hall, Ashburnham Place, Greenwich, S.E.10; Chelsea Juvenile Court, Walton Street, S.W.3; Anchor Mission, 273 Garratt Lane, Wandsworth, S.W.18; 163A Seymour Place, W.1.

STIPENDIARY MAGISTRATES

Birmingham, John Frederic Milward (1951).
Cardiff, Philip Guy Dudley Sixsmith (1948).
Huddersfield, Leslie Mervyn Pugh (1956).
Kingston upon Hull, Dennis Neil O'Sullivan (1952).
Leeds, Ralph Cleworth, Q.C. (1950).
Liverpool, Arthur McFarland (1947).
Manchester, Frederick Bancroft Turner (1951).
Merthyr Tydfil, David Powys Rowland (1961).
Middlesbrough, Alfred Pearson Peaker, M.C. (1939).
Pontypridd, Wyndham Matabele Davies, Q.C. (1949).
Salford, Leslie Walsh (1951).
Stoke, Geoffrey Arthur John Smallwood (1960).
Wolverhampton, Howard William Maitland Coley (1961).

CITY OF LONDON JUSTICE ROOMS

MANSION HOUSE JUSTICE ROOM.

Magistrate, The Lord Mayor, or an Alderman.

Chief Clerk, J. H. Tratt..................£3,175

Assistant Clerk, H. P. Jacob...............£2,305

GUILDHALL

Magistrate, An Alderman (in rotation).

Senior Chief Clerk, Clerk to the Licensing Justices and Clerk of Special Sessions, A. G. J. Chandler £3,645

Assistant Clerk, F. A. Treeby.............£2,695

DIRECTOR OF PUBLIC PROSECUTIONS

12 Buckingham Gate, S.W.1.

Director, Sir Theobald Mathew, K.B.E., M.C.. £5,815

Deputy Director, W. M. E. Crump, C.B.E.... £4,115

Assistant Directors, F. D. Barry, C.B.E.; J. F. Claxton; E. C. J. Jones...............£2,965 to £3,565

Assistant Solicitor, R. L. D. Thomas £2,965 to £3,565

Senior Legal Assistants, K. S. Lewis, T.D.; I. H. L. Smith; D. Prys Jones; E. G. MacDermott; M. D. Hutchison; M. J. Jardine; O. Nugent; J. M. Evelyn; P. F. Y. Radcliffe; P. M. J. Palmes; D. A. Hopkin; A. G. Flavell; P. R. Barnes; J. E. Leck; T. J. Taylor......£2,304 to £2,865

Legal Assistants, C. J. I. Bourke; J. H. Robbins; J. Wood; F. H. R. Burr; J. M. Walker; K. M. Horn; D. G. Williams; C. H. Cossham; K. G. Lawrence; B. Cooke; A. H. Whitfield; K. Dowling; P. E. Abbott; T. D. Tetlow.......£1,292 to £2,126

Establishment Officer, J. M. Evelyn.

Senior Executive Officer, H. Smethurst £1,680 to £2,126

OFFICE OF THE JUDGE ADVOCATE GENERAL OF THE FORCES

(Lord Chancellor's Establishment; Joint Service for the Army and the Royal Air Force)

6 Spring Gardens, Cockspur Street, S.W.1.

Judge Advocate General, O. C. Barnett, C.B.E., Q.C...................................£4,750

Vice Judge Advocate General, C. M. Cahn, C.B.E. £4,100

Assistant Judge Advocates General, J. E. M. Gunning, C.B.E.; B. A. C. Duncan, C.B.E.; B. de H. Pereira, T.D.; F. H. Dean, £3,215 to £3,565; O. Bertram

T.D.; W. St. J. C. Tayleur; E. H. V. Harington; R. H. Browne; C. E. Depinna £2,865 to £3,215
Deputy Judge Advocates, A. E. McDonald; W. E. Stubbs, M.B.E.; J. G. Morgan-Owen, M.B.E.; I. D. Turner, T.D.; R. G. Greene, M.C.; N. B. Birrell; G. H. L. Rhodes, T.D.; J. Stuart-Smith; B. R. Allen; G. Ll. Chapman...... £2,304 to £2,865
Legal Assistant, G. D. Lindley.
Registrar, K. A. Arnold.

METROPOLITAN POLICE OFFICE

New Scotland Yard, S.W.1
(Whitehall: 1212)

Commissioner, Sir Joseph Simpson, K.B.E.... £7,000
Deputy Commissioner, D. E. Webb, C.V.O., O.B.E. £5,355

"A" Department
Administration and Operations

Assistant Commissioner, J. L. Waldron, C.V.O. £4,840
Commander, A. Townsend, M.B.E., B.E.M. £3,390 to £3,780
Assistant Secretary, R. A. Bearman £2,237 to £2,572
Deputy Commander, J. R. Wray, M.B.E. £2,820 to £3,050
Chief Superintendents, D. E. J. Lightwood; H. A. Griffin; C. P. Attwood...... £2,375 to £2,530
Chief Superintendent of Women Police, Miss W. T. Barker .... £2,140 to £2,275
Principal Executive Officer, C. J. Fairfull, M.B.E. £1,680 to £2,126

"B" Department
Traffic and Transport

Assistant Commissioner, A. G. P. Way, C.M.G. £4,840
Commander (vacant)
Assistant Secretaries, A. R. Pike; C. W. Hutchings £2,237 to £2,572
Deputy Commander, N. Radford. £2,820 to £3,050
Chief Superintendents, R. A. Fairbank; E. W. Challands; R. R. Reynolds.. £2,375 to £2,530
Principal Executive Officers, R. D. Orr-Ewing; W. J. Porter; R. A. Root; G. W. Barns; H. V. Hyde; G. H. T. Shrimpton, C.B.E., T.D.; E. C. Cox.................... £1,680 to £2,126

"C" Department
Criminal Investigation

Assistant Commissioner, R. R. M. Bacon... £4,840
Commanders, G. H. Hatherill, O.B.E.; E. W. Jones, M.V.O. ....£3,390 to £3,780
Deputy Commanders, R. W. L. Spooner; C. L. MacDougall; J. C. Bliss..... £2,820 to £3,050
Chief Superintendents, G. W. C. Davis, M.B.E.; A. V. Griffin, M.B.E.; D. C. Grant; J. V. R. du Rose; J. W. Godsell; E. G. W. Millen; G. E. Salter; J. M. Davies; F. R. Pollard, M.B.E. £2,375 to £2,530

"D" Department
Organization and Training

Assistant Commissioner, T. E. Mahir, G.M... £4,840
Commanders, G. F. Payne, O.B.E., B.E.M.; J. T. Manuel £3,390 to £3,780
Assistant Secretaries, A. E. Cattle; J. L. Carter, M.B.E.................... £2,237 to £2,572
Chief Superintendents, T. G. Wall; F. H. Banfield; E. J. E. Tickle; A. McLean £2,375 to £2,530
Principal Executive Officers, G. A. Perry; S. H. Scard £1,680 to £2,126
Welfare Officer, Capt. J. S. Dalglish, C.V.O., C.B.E. £1,680 to £2,126

Metropolitan Police Cadet Corps

Commandant, Col. N. A. C. Croft, D.S.O. £3,100 to £3,330
Director of Academic Training, K. H. Patterson, V.R.D. £1,680 to £2,126

"S" Department
Secretariat

Secretary, G. C. Richardson £3,815
Deputy Secretary and Establishment Officer, R. L. Wynn-Williams, M.B.E...... £2,683 to £2,965
Assistant Secretaries, R. A. Cousins; G. S. Downes £2,237 to £2,572
Public Information Officer, P. H. Fearnley £2,237 to £2,572
Senior Information Officer, J. C. D. Dodds £1,680 to £2,126
Principal Executive Officers, G. R. Peel; A. E. Mitchell; H. L. Stark; C. A. F. Gibbs, M.C.; F. C. B. Varney; W. E. Wright; D. Meyler, D.S.C.................... £1,680 to £2,126

"L" Department
Solicitors

Solicitor, J. S. Williams.................. £4,115
Assistant Solicitors, W. C. Sharpe; R. I. Graham; E. O. Lane, D.F.C., A.F.C.; R. E. T. Birch; G. E. Clark; C. N. Winston...... £2,965 to £3,565
Senior Legal Assistants, N. M. Weston; A. H. Simpson; R. G. Mays; D. W. Warran; D. M. O'Shea; W. H. S. Relton; A. C. Staples £2,304 to £2,865
Legal Assistants, R. L. Kiley; M. R. Holmes; R. Wait-Brown; E. Thistlethwaite; J. M. Tuff; J. B. Egan; R. E. Marsh; H. B. Hargrave; F. W. Bakewell; D. W. Ellis; W. S. Frost; R. P. Coupland; R. B. Vince; C. S. Porteous; J. O'Keeffe; Miss P. M. Long; I. G. F. Graham; M. H. Wilmot............. £1,292 to £2,126
Chief Managing Clerks, J. P. Worboys; W. McCrorie; E. Worboys; F. J. Treasure; W. E. Ball; C. W. White.............. £1,633 to £2,012

Research and Planning Branch

Deputy Commander, N. J. H. Darke £2,820 to £3,050
Chief Superintendents, A. H. Thomson; B. M. Acott, D.F.C. .... £2,375 to £2,530
Principal Executive Officer, J. E. Mitchell, D.F.C. £1,680 to £2,126

Medical and Dental Branch

Chief Surgeon, R. W. Nevin, T.D.
Consulting Physician and Deputy to Chief Surgeon, Sir John Richardson, M.V.O.
Medical Officer, R. C. A. Bott.
Chief Dental Surgeon, M. J. O'Donnell.

Metropolitan Police Laboratory

Director, L. C. Nickolls......... £3,340 to £3,665
Principal Scientific Officers, E. D. Sweet; I. G. Holden; T. H. Jones......... £1,904 to £2,655

Districts of the Metropolitan Police

No. 1 District

Commander, H. J. Evans, O.B.E... £3,390 to £3,780
Deputy Commander, R. E. Rogers, M.B.E. £2,820 to £3,050
Detective Chief Superintendent, T. M. J. Butler £2,375 to £2,530

No. 2 District

Commander, F. W. C. Pennington £3,390 to £3,780
Deputy Commander, A. Walker, M.B.E. £2,820 to £3,050
Detective Chief Superintendent, D. W. Hawkins £2,375 to £2,530

No. 3 District

Commander, J. M. Hill, D.F.C..... £3,390 to £3,780
Deputy Commander, W. C. Batson, O.B.E. £2,820 to £3,050
Detective Chief Superintendent, J. Mannings £2,375 to £2,530

No. 4 District

Commander, G. C. F. Duncan... £3,390 to £3,780

Deputy Commander, J. Lawlor... £2,820 to £3,050
Detective Chief Superintendent, R. C. Lewis £2,375 to £2,530

Metropolitan Special Constabulary

Chief Commandant, Capt. C. D. Jackman, C.B.E.

OFFICE OF THE RECEIVER
FOR THE METROPOLITAN POLICE DISTRICT

Tintagel House, Albert Embankment, S.E.1.

Receiver, W. H. Cornish, C.B. £4,215
Secretary and Deputy Receiver, W. D. Cooper, C.B.E. £3 390
Deputy Secretary, S. R. Walker.. £2,683 to £2,865
Accountant, P. J. G. Buckley.... £2,683 to £2,865
Establishment Officer, J. W. Syms. £2,683 to £2,865
Chief Executive Officers, F. T. Allaway; J. J. Dolan; J. Last; S. A. Mudd......... £2,237 to £2,572
Senior Executive Officers, R. W. Coysh; B. G. David; C. N. Hill; L. Joughin; F. A. W. Pilborough; E. H. Sadler.... £1,680 to £2,126
Superintendent Printer, W. J. Merrett, M.B.E. £1,680 to £2,126
Senior Accident Claims Officer, A. Morley £1,680 to £2,126
Chief Architect and Surveyor, J. I. Elliott...... £3,565
Deputy do., G. B. Townsend... £2 865 to £3,215
Deputy Chief Architect, D. T. Edwards £2,865 to £3,215
Senior Surveyors, D. N. Fogden; W. J. Triggs, O.B.E. £2 293 to £2,628
Senior Architects, R. H. Cowley; S. J. Hanchet; C. A. Legerton; C. G. Liardet; G. B. Vint £2,293 to £2,628
Senior Public Health Engineer, C. L. Langshaw £2,293 to £2,628
Chief Engineer, W. M. S. Cawley......... £3,390
Deputy Chief Engr. (vacant).
Senior Engineers, J. L. Breese; R. H. Campin; H. L. Perry.................... £2,293 to £2,628

CITY OF LONDON POLICE
26 Old Jewry, E.C.2

Commissioner, Col. A. E. Young, C.M.G., C.V.O. £5,355
Assistant Commissioner, J. W. Goyder £3,390 to £3,780

Administration

Chief Superintendent, B. R. Platt £2,435 to £2,595

Criminal Investigation Department

Chief Superintendent, I. Davies... £2,435 to £2,595
Superintendents, W. G. French (*C.I.D.*); F. Lea (*C.I.D.*); E. H. Webster ("*A*" *Dept.*); H. W. Staples ("*B*" *Dept.*); T. Howard ("*B*" *Divn.*); F. H. Leggett ("*C*" *Divn.*); A. Lucas, M.B.E. ("*D*" *Divn.*).............. £2,040 to £2,160

City of London Special Constabulary.

Commandant, Col. Alexander Woods, T.D.
Chief Staff Officer, F. E. Shannon.

INDUSTRIAL AND OTHER TRIBUNALS
Compensation (Defence) Act, 1939.

SHIPPING CLAIMS TRIBUNAL.

President, The Rt. Hon. Lord Justice Willmer.
Member, F. G. Hogg.
Registrar, K. C. McGuffie, The Admiralty Registrar, Admiralty Registry, Royal Courts of Justice, W.C.2.

Lands Tribunal.
(3 Hanover Square, W.1)

President, Sir William James Fitzgerald, M.C., Q.C.
Members, C. E. W. Simes, Q.C.; H. P. Hobbs; J. R. Laird; J. A. F. Watson; R. C. G. Fennell; R. C. Walmsley.
Registrar, A. W. Bird.

Patents and Registered Designs Appeal Tribunal.
(Room 160, Royal Courts of Justice, W.C.2.)

Judge, The Hon. Mr. Justice Lloyd-Jacob.
Registrar, C. L. R. Dalley.

Performing Right Tribunal.
24 Kingsway (6th floor), W.C.2.

Chairman, W. A. L. Raeburn, Q.C.
Members, C. C. W. Havell, M.C.; Dame Alix Meynell, D.B.E.; J. A. Walker, C.B.E.; W. K. M. Slimmings, C.B.E.
Secretary, B. J. D. Styles.

Transport Tribunal
Watergate House, 15 York Buildings, W.C.2 [Trafalgar: 7194]

President, G. D. Squibb, Q.C.
Permanent Members, J. C. Poole, C.B.E., M.C., H. H. Phillips, O.B.E.; Sir Thomas Robson, M.B.E.; R. C. Moore, O.B.E.

Board of Referees Income Tax Act, 1952
(Room 552 Royal Courts of Justice, W.C.2.)

Registrar, F. H. Cowper.

Parliamentary and Local Government Election Petitions Office.
(Room 120, Royal Courts of Justice, W.C.2.)

Prescribed Officer, C. H. Grundy (*Master of the Supreme Court*).
Clerk to do., W. H. Redman, M.B.E.

Pensions Appeals Tribunals.
(Staffordshire House, Store St., W.C.1.)

President, Sir Stafford Foster-Sutton, K.B.E., C.M.G., Q.C.................................. £3 000
Secretary, C. J. Smitten......... £1,633 to £2,012

Benefices Act, 1898.
(Room 120, Royal Courts of Justice, W.C.2.)

Registrar of the Court, B. A. Harwood (*Master of the Supreme Court*).

ECCLESIASTICAL COURTS

Judge, The Rt. Hon. and Rt. Worshipful Sir Henry Urmston Willink, Bt., M.C., Q.C., D.C.L. [Judge of the Provincial Courts of Canterbury and York under "The Public Worship Regulation Act, 1874."]

Court of Arches.

Registry, 1 The Sanctuary, Westminster, S.W.1
Dean, The Rt. Hon. and Rt. Worshipful Sir Henry Urmston Willink, Bt., M.C., Q.C., D.C.L.
Registrar, D. M. M. Carey.

Court of Faculties.

[Registry and Office for Marriage Licences (Special and Ordinary). Appointment of Notaries Public, &c., 1, The Sanctuary, Westminster, S.W.1. Office hours, 10 to 4; Saturdays, 10 to 12.]

Master, The Rt. Hon. and Rt. Worshipful Sir Henry Urmston Willink, Bt., M.C., Q.C., D.C.L.
Registrar, D. M. M. Carey.

Vicar General's Office,

for granting Marriage Licences for Churches in the Province of Canterbury, and COURT OF PECULIARS, 1 The Sanctuary, Westminster, S.W.1. Office hours, 10 to 4; Saturdays, 10 to 12. Closed on Sundays, Good Friday, Christmas Day, and Bank Holidays.

Vicar General & Chancellor, The Rt. Hon. and Rt. Worshipful Sir Henry Urmston Willink, Bt., M.C., Q.C., D.C.L.
Registrar, D. M. M. Carey.
Apparitor General, Lt.-Col. J. B. Barron, O.B.E., M.C.

OFFICE OF THE VICAR GENERAL OF THE PROVINCE OF YORK.

Vicar General & Chancellor, Walter Somerville Wigglesworth, D.C.L.
Registrar, I. N. Ware, O.B.E.

Chancery Court of York.

Official Principal, The Rt. Hon. and Rt. Worshipful Sir Henry Urmston Willink, Bt., M.C., Q.C., D.C.L.
Registrar, I. N. Ware, O.B.E., Minster Yard, York.

SCOTTISH LAW COURTS AND OFFICES

COURT OF SESSION (Established 1532).

Lord President, Lord Clyde (Rt. Hon. James Latham McDiarmid Clyde).

INNER HOUSE.—*First Division.*

The Lord President £8,000
Lord Carmont, John Francis Carmont £6,600
Lord Sorn, James Gordon McIntyre, M.C... £6,600
Lord Guthrie, Henry Wallace Guthrie..... £6,600

Second Division.

Lord Justice Clerk, Lord Grant, Rt. Hon. William Grant, T.D. £7,800
Lord Patrick, Rt. Hon. William Donald Patrick £6,600
Lord Mackintosh Charles Mackintosh, M.C. £6,600
Lord Strachan, James Frederick Strachan... £6,600

OUTER HOUSE.

Lord Migdale, J. F. Gordon Thomson..... £6,600
Lord Wheatley, Rt. Hon. John Wheatley . £6,600
Lord Walker, James Walker............ £6,600
Lord Cameron, Sir John Cameron, D.S.C... £6,600
Lord Kilbrandon, Charles James Dalrymple Shaw £6,600
Lord Milligan, Rt. Hon. William Rankine Milligan £6,600
Lord Johnston, Douglas Harold Johnston, T.D. £6,600
Lord Hunter, John Oswald Mair Hunter.. £6,600

NOTE.—The word "Lord" prefixed to the names of Judges of the Court of Session, or to titles different from their names, is strictly an official honour and may be compared with the terms "Hon. Mr. Justice" and "Lord Chief Justice" in England.

Principal Clerk of Session, George MacDonald, O.B.E. £2,800
Deputy Principal Clerk, George H. Robertson (+allce.) £2,109 to £2,434
Depute Clerks, Inner House H. G. Manson; T. I. McWhannell.............. £1,568 to £2,001
Depute Clerks, Outer House, N. D. Richardson; D. Scott; Walter Steele; J. Watson; A. S. D. Rodger; P. Whitten; H. C. Macpherson; E. Smith.................... £1,568 to £2,001

High Court of Justiciary (1672)

Lord Justice General, Rt. Hon. Lord Clyde.
Lord Justice Clerk, Lord Grant.
Lords Comm. of Justiciary. all the other Judges.
Circuit Clerks D. J. Stevenson and Robert Johnston.

Auditor of Court of Session.
3 Parliament Square, Edinburgh.

Auditor, A. A. Innes Wedderburn, W.S.

Extracts Department

Extractor of the Court of Session, D. M. Candlish.

Minute Book Office and Record of Edictal Citations, etc., Office.
Parliament House, Edinburgh.

Keeper, D. M. Candlish........ £1,568 to £2,001

Court of Lords Commissioners for Teinds.

The Judges of the Inner House, and Lord Milligan, *Lord Ordinary on Teinds.*
Clerk of Teinds & Extractor, James H. Watt £1,568 to £2,001

Accountant of Court (Judicial Factories and Bankruptcy).

Accountant, J. Allan.................... £2,950
Depute do., A. L. Borthwick, I.S.O. £2,172 to £2,507
Chief Clerk, D. M. Young...... £1,615 to £2,061

Lord Advocate's Department
See p. 399.

Crown Office,
9 Parliament Square, Edinburgh, 2.

Crown Agent, Lionel I. Gordon, C.B.E. £4,050
Principal Assistant, Stanley Bowen. £2,356 to £3,050
Clerks, Roland R. Wright; Miss A. C. McGibbon; Miss A. Pollock; Miss C. MacNeill.

Justiciary Office,
2 Parliament Square, Edinburgh, 1

Clerk of Justiciary, James G. Leechman, Q.C. (*part time*) £700
Depute & 1st Assistant, D. J. Stevenson £2,172 to £2,507
Depute & 2nd Asst., Robert Johnston £1,615 to £2,061

Exchequer,
102 George Street, Edinburgh, 2.

Lord Ordinary, Lord Walker.
Queen's and Lord Treasurer's Remembrancer, W. Steel................................ £2,800
Chief Clerk, J. B. I. McTavish.. £2,109 to £2,434
Senior Executive Officers, J. Hardie; A. T. M. Anderson.
Higher Executive Officers, D. E. D. Robertson; Miss S. Y. Bryson; R. Wilkie.

Companies Registration Office
102 George Street, Edinburgh 2.

Registrar (also of Limited Partnership and of Business Names), W. Steel.

Edinburgh Gazette Office,
102 George Street, Edinburgh, 2.

Keeper, W. Steel.

Sheriff Court of Chancery.
Sheriff Court, Edinburgh.
Office: 21 York Place, Edinburgh.

Sheriff of Chancery, W. Ross McLean, V.R.D., Q.C.
Sheriff Clerk of Chancery, William George Purves, W.S.
Sheriff Clerk Deputes, A. H. Crerar, W.S.; J. D. Crerar, W.S.

H.M. Commissary Office,
Sheriff Court, Edinburgh.

Commissary Clerk, R. D. Gould.
Depute do., Alexander E. McRae.

Lord Clerk Register's Department.
H.M. General Register House, Edinburgh.

Lord Clerk Register and Keeper of the Signet, The Duke of Buccleuch and Queensberry, P.C., K.T., G.C.V.O., T.D.
Keeper of the Records of Scotland, Sir James Fergusson of Kilkerran, Bt.

Crown Estate Commissioners
2 St. Andrew Square, Edinburgh 2.

Crown Estate Receiver, D. T. Hunt.
Bishopric of Orkney, Francis McGinn, Kirkwall.

SCOTTISH LAND COURT.
1 Grosvenor Crescent, Edinburgh.

Members, Lord Gibson (*Chairman*); M. Montgomery; C. M. S. Grant; A. McDiarmid; W. Bankier.
Principal Clerk, T. MacD. Wilson.
Depute Clerks of Court and Senior Legal Assessors, S. Forrest; D. H. Cameron; J. D. Shepherd.
Depute Clerk of Court and Legal Assessor, J. B. S. Lewis.
Clerk of Accounts and Establishment, R. Landels.

SHERIFFS, SHERIFFS SUBSTITUTE, SHERIFF CLERKS AND PROCURATORS FISCAL OF COUNTIES IN SCOTLAND

SHERIFFS	SHERIFFS SUBSTITUTE	SHERIFF CLERKS	PROCURATORS FISCAL
Caithness, Sutherland, Orkney and Zetland.— Harald Robert Leslie, C.B.E., T.D., Q.C., 27 Queensferry Road, Edinburgh, 4.	*Wick*, E. Stewart	W. Howard	C. J. H. Campbell.
	Kirkwall, D. B. Keith, M.C.	A. M. Campbell	F. McGinn.
	Lerwick, A. A. Macdonald	R. A. Johnson	L. H. Mathewson.
	Dornoch, D. V. Irvine-Jones	D. MacDonald	G. A. Mackenzie.
	Fort William, J. B. Patrick	G. Proctor	J. M. Hogg.
Inverness, Moray, Nairn and Ross & Cromarty.— Douglas Mason Campbell, Q.C., 10 Forres Street, Edinburgh 3.	*Inverness*, D. A. Donald	G. Proctor	W. M. Paterson.
	Elgin, C. C. Ross	R. J. Macdonald	M. T. Macneill.
	Nairn, C. C. Ross	W. J. Cruikshank	M. T. Macneill.
	Portree, J. B. Patrick	G. Proctor	D. Macmillan.
	Lochmaddy, J. Allan	G. Proctor	D. S. Shaw.
	Dingwall & Tain, D. V. Irvine-Jones.	J. B. Blair	T. F. Aitchison
	Stornoway, J. Allan	J. B. Blair	C. S. Mackenzie.
Aberdeen, Kincardine & Banff.— Thomas Pringle McDonald, Q.C., 68 Northumberland Street, Edinburgh, 3.	*Aberdeen*, A. Hamilton; J. A. Smith.	T. Muirhead, O.B.E.	A. S. McNicol.
	Stonehaven, A. Hamilton; J. A. Smith.	Miss L. E. Cameron	W. B. Agnew.
	Peterhead, R. R. Kerr	T. Muirhead, O.B.E.	
	Banff, R. R. Kerr	D. Moir	N. Milne.
Perth & Angus.— Hector McKechnie, Q.C., LL.D., 64 Great King Street, Edinburgh 3.	*Perth & Dunblane*, A. M. Prain.	J. D. Penny	W. R. Macmillan.
	Dundee, J. B. W. Christie (*and Perth*); R. A. Inglis (*and Perth*)	J. D. Cochrane	J. Clark.
	Forfar, H. F. Ford	J. D. Cochrane	J. W. Gibb.
	Arbroath, H. F. Ford	J. D. Cochrane	J. Clark.
Fife and Kinross.— John Adam Lillie, Q.C., 45 Great King Street, Edinburgh 3.	*Cupar*, R. R. Kydd	P. Manzie	C. G. Hogg.
	Kirkcaldy, G. P. S. Shaw	P. Manzie	J. Houston.
	Dunfermline, J. S. Mowat	P. Manzie	J. G. McLean.
	Kinross, R. R. Kydd	D. A. R. Cuthbert, M.C.	J. G. McLean.
Stirling, Dunbarton and Clackmannan.— Francis Clifford Watt, Q.C., 52 Inverleith Place, Edinburgh 3.	*Alloa*, C. L. D. Murray	D. G. MacGregor	W. Hawthorn.
	Stirling, C. D. L. Murray	J. A. Johnston	V. E. Cuthbert.
	Dumbarton, J. M. Mackay	T. R. Marshall	W. F. Irvine.
	Falkirk, V. D. B. Skae	J. A. Johnston	W. S. Heatlie.
Renfrew and Argyll.— Alexander Thomson, Q.C., 11 Moray Place, Edinburgh, 3.	*Paisley*, A. K. F. Hunter; A. C. Horsfall.	G. S. Stirling	H. Herron.
	Greenock, W. T. Hook	G. S. Stirling	A. W. Wishart.
	Campbeltown, R. B. Miller	J. McGhie	A. I. B. Stewart.
	Dunoon, G. M. Bryson	J. McGhie	D. S. Thaw.
	Oban, J. M. Peterson	J. McGhie	J. Stevenson.
The Lothians and Peebles.— William Ross McLean, T.R.D., Q.C., 39 Moray Place, Edinburgh 3.	*Edinburgh*, E. J. Keith; G. W. I. C. Cohen; A. J. Stevenson; K. W. B. Middleton; J. G. Wilson, Q.C.	R. D. Gould	A. Macleod.
	Haddington, K. W. B. Middleton	D. McMillan	W. Macnab.
	Linlithgow, V. D. B. Skae; D. I. McLeod	I. F. MacKenzie	P. F. Hamilton.
	Peebles, D.I.McLeod (*and Selkirk*).	R. D. Gould	E. Laverock.
Lanark.— (vacant)	*Glasgow*, A. G. Walker; W. J. Bryden; H. W. Pirie; F. Middleton; H. S. Wilson; M. G. Gillies, T.D., Q.C.; J. M. Cowan, Q.C.; J. Bayne; T. A. U. Wood; S. E. Bell; C. H. Johnston, Q.C.; L. H. Daiches; W. D. Pattullo.	W. R. Docherty.	R. MacDonald.
	Airdrie, T. Young, C.B.E., T.D.	W. R. Docherty.	J. Farrell.
	Lanark, M. G. Gillies, T.D., Q.C.	W. R. Docherty.	T. J. Cochrane.
	Hamilton, J. A. Forsyth; I. A. Dickson; P. Thompson.	T. S. Neilson	D. B. Copeland.
Roxburgh, Berwick and Selkirk.— George Gordon Stott, Q.C., 32 Dundas Street, Edinburgh.	*Duns*, J. V. Paterson	Miss J. S. Cunningham	G. S. Morrison.
	Jedburgh, J. V. Paterson	R. R. Dale	J. Skeen.
	Hawick, J. V. Paterson	R. R. Dale	J. Skeen.
	Selkirk, D. I. Macleod	R. R. Dale	F. Woodward.
Ayr and Bute.— Ian McDonald Robertson, T.D., Q.C., 49 Moray Place, Edinburgh 3.	*Ayr*, G. S. Reid; J. Frame.	H. M. Barron	R. J. Cruickshank.
	Kilmarnock, R. N. Levitt, M.B.E., T.D.; J. Frame.	A. McDougall	J. Brown.
	Rothesay, G. M. Bryson	H. McMartin	J. M. Cullen.
Dumfries & Galloway.— Miss Margaret Henderson Kidd, Q.C., 5 India Street, Edinburgh 3.	*Dumfries*, W. E. R. Hendry	W. S. Rae	C. F. M. Burrell.
	Kirkcudbright, S. A. Lockhart	J. Davidson	A. Henry.
	Wigtown, S. A. Lockhart	J. Davidson	J. H. Douglas.
	Stranraer, S. A. Lockhart	J. Davidson	J. H. Douglas.

The Royal Navy

THE QUEEN

The Board of Admiralty, Whitehall, S.W.1

[Whitehall: 9000]

First Lord of the Admiralty, THE LORD CARRINGTON, P.C., K.C.M.G., M.C. .... (*with house*) £5,000
Naval Secretary, Rear Admiral J. O. C. Hayes,, O.B.E.
Private Secretary, W. I. Tupman.
Asst. Private Secretary, W. Vause.
First Sea Lord and Chief of Naval Staff, Admiral Sir David Luce, G.C.B., D.S.O., O.B.E. .... *Service pay*
Second Sea Lord and Chief of Naval Personnel, Admiral Sir Royston Wright, K.C.B., D.S.C. .... *Service pay*
Third Sea Lord and Controller, Vice-Admiral Sir Michael Le Fanu, K.C.B., D.S.O. .... *Service pay*
Fourth Sea Lord (Chief of Supplies and Transport and Vice-Controller), Rear-Admiral R. S. Hawkins, C.B. .... *Service pay*
Deputy Chief of Naval Staff and Fifth Sea Lord, Vice-Admiral F. H. E. Hopkins, C.B., D.S.O., D.S.C. .... *Service pay*
Vice-Chief of Naval Staff, Vice-Admiral J. B. Frewen, C.B. .... *Service pay*
Civil Lord, J. A. Hay, M.P. £2,500
Permanent Secretary, Sir Clifford Jarrett, K.B.E., C.B. £6,950

Deputy Controller (Research and Development), Sir John Carroll, K.B.E., Ph.D., F.R.S.E. £4,950
Director, W.R.N.S., Commandant Dame Jean Davies, D.B.E. .... *Service pay*

The Secretary's Department

Deputy Secretary (Personnel), P. N. N. Synnott, C.B. £4,950
Deputy Secretary (General Policy and Finance), J. M. Mackay £4,950
Under Secretaries, C. E. F. Gough, C.M.G.; P. H. Jones; G. J. MacMahon, C.B., C.M.G.; P. S. Newell, C.B.; E. A. Shillito; J. H. Taylor. £4,050
Assistant Secretaries, J. V. Battersby; C. G. H. Cardo; W. R. Darracott, D.S.C.; G. C. B. Dodds; W. N. Hanna, M.V.O.; F. C. Herd; A. R. M. Jaffray; R. N. P. Lewin; J. E. Makin, C.B.E.; W. Marshall; P. D. Nairne, M.C.; K. T. Nash; I. K. Petre; E. S. Roberts; R. C. Shawyer; L. Solomon; E. A. Turner; C. Wallworth £2,800 to £3,500
Principals, R. J. E. Abraham; J. P. Buchanan, M.B.E.; T. Cullen; R. A. Devereux; A. G. Draper; M. M. Du Mertor; D. N. Forbes; J. M. Gibbon; W. J. Hanman; J. P. Kelly; P. Lawrence, I.S.O.; N. P. Lewis, M.B.E.; R. A. Lloyd-Jones; F. H. Mawer; P. Mehew; P. Nailor; D. A. Nichols; J. Peters; G. F. C. Plowden; A. A. Pritchard; K. J. Pritchard; T. F. Ronayne; W. I. Tupman £1,894 to £2,646
Archivist-Librarian and Head of Historical Section, Lieut.-Cdr. P. K. Kemp, O.B.E., R.N. (*ret*) (+*allce.* £150) £2,507
Principal Director of Accounts, L. R. Palmer.. £3,650
Directors of Accounts, M. W. Tebby (*Costs*); J. G. Ross (*Payments*) .... £2,800 to £3,500
Assistant Directors of Accounts, H. G. Blair; J. E. Kay; F. W. J. Lawrance; J. C. Jones; F. G. S. Whitehouse; J. B. Lewis .... £2,618 to £2,800

The Hydrographic Department

Hydrographer of the Navy, Rear-Admiral E. G. Irving, C.B., O.B.E.
Chief Civil Assistant, F. N. Marshall £2,237 to £2,572
Chief Civil Hydrographic Officer and Assistant Superintendent of Charts, L. N. Pascoe £2,756 to £3,210

Department of Naval Weather Service

Director of Naval Weather Service, Instr. Capt. G. P. Britton, R.N.
Deputy Director, Instr. Capt. J. R. Thorp, O.B.E., R.N.

Second Sea Lord's Department

Director General of Personal Services and Officer Appointments, Rear-Admiral R. A. J. Owen, C.B.
Directors of Officer Appointments:
Seaman Officers, Capt. D. L. Davenport, O.B.E., R.N.
Supply and Secretariat Officers, Capt. G. A. Henderson, R.N.
Engineer Officers, Capt. T. H. Maxwell, R.N.
Electrical Officers, Capt. P. P. M. Green, R.N.
Director of Service Conditions and Fleet Supply Duties Division, Capt. H. S. Spittle, R.N.
Director General of Manpower, Rear-Admiral P. N. Buckley, D.S.O.
Manning—Director, Capt. H. R. Hewlett, R.N.
Planning and Complementing—Director, A. S. Osley .... £2,800 to £3,500
Naval Manpower Statistics, E. Jones £2,800 to £3,500
Senior Psychologist, N. A. B. Wilson, O.B.E., Ph.D. £2,800 to £3,150

Medical Departments

Director-General, Surgeon Vice-Admiral D. D. Steele-Perkins, C.B., C.V.O., Q.H.S.
Deputy Do., Surgeon Commodore F. W. Baskerville, C.B.E.
Deputy Do. for Dental Services, Surgeon Rear-Admiral (D) P. S. Turner, C.B., Q.H.D.S.

The Chaplain of the Fleet

Chaplain of the Fleet, The Ven. Archdeacon R. W. Richardson, Q.H.C.

Reserves Office

Admiral Commanding Reserves and Inspector of Recruiting, Rear-Admiral H. C. Martell, C.B., C.B.E.

Director General of Training, Rear-Admiral J. M. D. Gray, O.B.E.
Seamen and General Training—Director, Capt. R. E. Lloyd, D.S.C., R.N.
Engineering and Electrical Training—Director, Rear-Admiral J. S. Raven.
Supply and Secretariat Training—Director, Capt. G. A. Henderson, R.N.

Naval Education Service

Director, Instructor Rear-Admiral C. R. Darlington.

Ship Department

Director General, Sir Alfred Sims, K.C.B., O.B.E. £5,750
Chief Scientific Adviser, S. Bolshaw........£3,863
Chief Personnel Officer, H. D. Spitteler £3,100 to £3,500
Directors:—
Naval Construction, A. N. Harrison, C.V.O., O.B.E. £4,650
Marine Engineering, Rear-Admiral H. G. H. Tracy, D.S.C.
Electrical Engineering, J. C. Thompson, C.B.E. £4,650
Naval Equipment, Capt. G. J. Kirkby, D.S.C.
Ship Production, Capt. W. A. Haynes, O.B.E. £4,150
Deputy Directors:—
Naval Construction, C. E. Sherwin; R. N. Newton; R. H. Richards..........£4,050
Marine Engineering, Capt. L. E. S. H. Le Bailly, O.B.E.; Capt. W. B. S. Milln.
Electrical Engineering, W. E. C. Lampert, C.B.E. £4,050
Naval Equipment, Capt. J. A. R. Troup, D.S.C.
Assistant Directors:—
Naval Construction, J. L. Bessant; F. G. Bogie; H. R. Mason; W. G. Perry; M. K. Purvis; H. J. Tabb; A. J. Vosper; H. J. Fulthorpe; N. Hancock; J. E. S. Vincent £3,275 to £3,600
Marine Engineering, Captains J. R. Llewellyn; L. D. Dymoke; D. J. I. Garstin; N. H. Malim, M.V.O.; A. C. W. Wilson.
Marine Engineering Production, T. B. Gray £3,275
Electrical Engineering, H. C. Fitzer, O.B.E.; T. G. Hewitson; P. Smith; Capt. J. G. Watson; W. Ford; G. P. Swift.....£2,500 to £3,100
Ship Production, A. J. T. Gibbons; F. J. Jenvey; Capt. F. T. Healy; E. C. Pound £3,275 to £3,600
Chief Constructors, W. R. Andrew, O.B.E.; A. A. Austin; L. G. Bell; E. A. Brokensha; L. J. Brooks; H. R. P. Chatten; H. W. J. Chislett; R. J. Daniel, O.B.E.; K. G. Evans; L. J. Evans; G. S. Ferris; N. E. Gundry; A. F. Honnor; W. R. Seward; J. W. Harrington; R. Hawkes; F. V. Jolliffe; J. C. Lawrence; C. H. Mace; A. Mitchell; M. McMurray; J. A. H. Paffett; A. E. Reeves; L. J. Rydill, O.B.E.; G. J. Stunden; T. Thorpe; E. F. Wood; F. H. J. Yearling................£2,800 to £3,150
Superintending Electrical Engineers, F. W. Butler; S. W. Bullen; R. E. Cocks; H. L. Denman; Capt. G. P. Fulcher; Capt. E. W. Goodman, O.B.E.; Capt. K. A. Goudge, O.B.E., D.S.C.; L. W. Groom; F. E. Hutchins; W. T. Johnson; F. R. W. K. Mansell; F. E. Marks; Capt. A. J. B. Naish, C.B.E.; R. F. Nicholas; H. Summers; B. E. Vieyra; Capt. T. V. R. Wilson.................£2,563 to £2,900
Commodore (Engineering), R. C. Watkin.
Captains (Engineering), G. W. Dibben, O.B.E.; J. Sidgwick; E. G. Griffin; J. K. Pearsall; P. T. Hoath, M.B.E.; H. D. Nixon, M.V.O.; A. G. Reid, O.B.E.

Weapons Department

Director General, Weapons, Rear-Admiral C. P. Mills, C.B.E., D.S.C.

Surface Division

Director (D.W.S.), Capt. G. H. Carew-Hunt, R.N.
Deputy Directors, Capt. R. C. C. Greenlees, R.N.; Capt. A. W. Allen, R.N.
Head of Guided Weapon Projects, H. W. Pout, O.B.E. £3,275 to £3,600
Assistant Directors, Capt. W. A. Humphrey, R.N.; Capt. J. R. Marigold, R.N.; Capt. J. H. Murray, R.N.; A. E. Brown, M.B.E.....£2,800 to £3,150
Superintending Electrical Engineer, W. T. Edwards £2,392 to £2,750

Inspection Division

Director and Chief Inspector of Naval Ordnance, Capt. W. R. J. Redman C.B.E., R.N....£3,400
Deputies to the Chief Inspector of Naval Ordnance, Capt. R. Burrell, O.B.E., R.N. (*ret.*) (£2,540 to £2,850); Capt. J. C. Rowe, R.N. (*ret*) £2,228 to £2,563
Assistants to the Chief Inspector of Naval Ordnance, Lt.-Col. L. S. C. Pickering, R.M. (*ret.*); Commanders T. G. Davison, R.N.; L. E. Elwell, R.N. (£2,130 to £2,440); W. J. F. Collings, D.S.C., R.N.; W. D. Moseley, D.S.O., R.N. £1,559 to £2,089

Underwater Weapons Division

Director, Capt. W. D. S. White, R.N.
Deputy Director, Capt. J. G. Cannon, R.N.
Assistant Directors, Capt. A. G. Smalley, D.S.C., R.N.; Capt. J. G. Stott, R.N.; A. W. Miller £2,800 to £3,150

Radio Division

Director, Capt. R. L. Clode, R.N.
Deputy Director, Capt. D. V. Morgan, M.B.E., R.N.
Assistant Directors, Commanders R. D. Johnston, R.N.; L. L. Grey, D.S.C., R.N.; J. A. Bedford, R.N.; S. L. Cox.................£2,228 to £2,563

Compass Division

Director, Capt. T. D. Ross, R.N. (*ret.*) £2,700 to £3,000
Deputy Director, Commander A. E. Fanning, M.B.E., D.S.C., R.N. (*ret.*)...........£1,508 to £1.914

Central Services

Capt. L. H. J. Masters, R.N.

Weapons Systems Tuning Group

Capt. H. R. Wykeham-Martin, R.N.

Production Pool

Superintendent of Production Personnel, G. W. A. Birkett, C.B.E........................£3,250

Armament Supply Department

Director, N. P. Luscombe, C.B............£4,050
Deputy Directors, R. G. Gatehouse; K. A. Haddacks, M.B.E.; W. F. Woods...............£3,150
Assistant Directors, R. R. Bailey; G. E. Ballyn, O.B.E.; S. R. Callis; G. H. Chandler, M.B.E.; A. F. McLeod; P. R. Ody; E. de C. Tillett; W. E. S. Trigg; W. B. Winsor.....£2,542 to £2,800

Royal Naval Scientific Service

Chief of Royal Naval Scientific Service, R. H. Purcell, C.B., Ph.D.........................£4,350
Chief Scientific Officers, S. Bolshaw; W. L. Borrows; G. E. R. Deacon, C.B.E., F.R.S.; A. W. Ross, O.B.E.; R. W. Sutton, C.B., O.B.E.; B. W. Lythall; D. S. Watson, O.B.E......................£3,863
Deputy Chief Scientific Officers, R. Benjamin; F. S. Burt; F. F. Butterworth, C.B.E.; H. C. Calpine, M.B.E.; I. J. Good; H. E. Hogben; W. W. Jackson; J. L. King; A. C. Law, C.B.E.; G. W. Morgan, C.B.E.; T. C. J. Ovenston; J. H. Phillips; H. W. Pout, O.B.E.; W. E. Pretty; O. L. Ratsey; O. Simpson; J. Tunstead; E. J. Vaughan, C.B.E. £3,275 to £3,600

Department of Dockyards and Maintenance

Director General, Rear-Admiral C. P. G. Walker, D.S.C.
Director of Dockyards, D. W. Smithers......£4,150
Director of Fleet Maintenance, Capt. D. B. H. Wildish, R.N.
Director of Marine Services. Capt, D. F. Chilton, D.S.C., R.N.
Deputy Director of Dockyards, L. A. Sansbury £3,863

Deputy Director of Fleet Maintenance and Capt i/c Ship Maintenance Authority, Capt. K. J. Douglas-Morris, R.N.
Deputy Director of Marine Services, Commander C. G. Forsberg, O.B.E., R.N.
Assistant Director (Special Duties), Capt. B. S. Blanchford, R.N.
Assistant Director (Ships). M. C. Dunstan £3,275 to £3,600
Assistant Director (Shore), S. M. Gardiner £3,100 to £3,500
Assistant Director (Engineering), Capt. A. J. Osborne, R.N.
Assistant Director (Electrical), Capt. F. J. Perks, R.N.
Assistant Director (Management Techniques), S. T. Flannery.................£3,100 to £3,500
Assistant Director (Personnel), A. H. Couzens, C.B.E. £2,246 to £2,750
Assistant Director (Mechanical Engineering), Rear-Admiral H. C. Hogger, C.B., D.S.C. (*ret.*) £3,100 to £3,500
Assistant Director (Telecommunications), J. H. S. Gillingham................£3,100 to £3,500
Chief Marine Engineer, Capt. R. L. McClement, R.N.
Chief Electrical Engineer, Capt. F. J. Perks, R.N.
Assistant Director (General), V. M. Hall £3,125 to £3,450
Superintendents of Dockyard Machinery Installations, S. H. Dimmick; W. E. Morecroft, B.E.M. £2,689 to £2,900
Superintendent of Dockyard Electrical Installations, L. R. Hompstead...........£2,689 to £2,900
Managers, Constructive, S. H. Watson; H. E. Skinner, O.B.E.; H. E. Newnham £3,275 to £3,600
Managers, Engineering, Capt. H. G. Southwood, D.S.C., R.N.; Capt. J. G. Little, O.B.E., R.N.; Capt. R. P. Pratt, O.B.E., R.N.
Managers, Electrical, L. E. Hogan, O.B.E.; C. F. Hollman.................£3,100 to £3,500
Chief Constructors, L. Kirkpatrick, O.B.E.; R. H. Howarth; E. S. Gibbons; W. G. Warren; I. McD. Black; J. R. F. Moss, O.B.E.; E. McCallin; J. H. Froud; R. E. Tozer; L. W. A. Rayner; A. H. Matthews; A. J. Cope; J. T. Revans; F. P. Skinner; J. C. Allen; C. P. Oldridge; R. P. Collas; N. W. Honey ......£2,800 to £3,150
Chief Engineers, Capt. P. Carter, R.N.; Capt. T. G. B. Pearce, R.N.
Superintending Electrical Engineers, H. J. Steggall; G. Evans; E. R. Evans; Capt. B. H. Champion, M.B.E., R.N.; K. S. B. Lindsey; B. C. Caddy, M.B.E.; E. W. J. Satchell; A. L. J. Miller; N. G. Watson; T. D. Donovan; R. N. J. Edmonds; H. E. S. Thomas...........£2,563 to £2,900
General Managers, F. S. Sutherby; H. R. Mann, O.B.E.; Capt. D. P. Sparham, O.B.E., R.N. (*ret.*) £3,863
Manager, Organisation Development, E. R. Evans £3,100 to £3,500
Production Manager, E. W. Tucker....... £3,600
Planning Manager, Capt. J. F. Lewin, R.N.
Personnel Manager, F. W. Matthews £3,275 to £3,600
Personnel Superintendent, T. G. Barber £2,563 to £2,900
Superintendents, Yard Services, Cdr. M. A. Wilson, M.B.E., D.S.C., R.N.; N. S. Hallett £2,563 to £2,900
Superintendent of Management Planning and Review, Capt. M. H. Griffin, R.N.

Director of Stores

Director, F. C. Wilkins, C.B...............£4,050
Deputy Directors, E. J. Braybrook; G. T. Glue; A. W. Holden; J. P. Lovett, M.B.E.; F. L. Marwood, O.B.E.; W. J. Robinson, O.B.E..........£3,150
Assistant Directors, H. M. Blewett; B. A. Britton; J. M. Marshall; J. A. W. Peter; T. G. Robb; G. Smalley; L. J. S. Spry; R. P. Stevens; G. Strother; L. S. Davis, O.B.E.; T. H. J. Dethridge; F. A. Frost................£2,618 to £2,800

Victualling Department

Director, J. M. Widdecombe, O.B.E. £3,500
Deputy Directors, R. H. Shipway, M.B.E.; K. A. Hayward..........................£3,150
Assistant Directors, W. R. Balkwill, O.B.E.; E. J. D. Bullock; A. Clingan; J. D. Cocker £2,542 to £2,800
Head of Technical Branch, F. Brookhouse, O.B.E. £3,150

Movements Department

Director, L. J. Osborne, C.B.E..............£3,150
Deputy Director, D. R. S. Pursey £2,618 to £2,800

Department of the Director General, Aircraft

Director General, Rear-Admiral D. A. Williams, D.S.C.
Director of Air Equipment and Naval Photography, Capt. G. W. D. Spriggs, M.B.E., R.N.
Director of Aircraft Maintenance and Repair, Capt. P. H. C. Illingworth, R.N.
Director of Aircraft Electrics and Armament, Capt. P. L. V. Slater, O.B.E., R.N.
Assistant Directors, Capt. A. G. B. Griffiths, R.N.; Capt. T. W. Lamb, R.N.; Capt. M. W. Sylvester, R.N.; Capt. R. H. Webber, R.N.

Department of the Chief of Naval Information

Chief of Naval Information, Capt. A. H. Wallis, C.B.E., R.N. (*ret.*).....................£3,150
Deputy Director, W. Hayes .....£2,172 to £2,507

Lands Department

Chief Surveyor of Lands, E. H. Palmer......£3,500
Deputy Chief Surveyor of Lands, R. S. Tizzard, O.B.E. £2,800 to £3,150
Senior Surveyors of Lands, A. R. J. Baldwin; F. Cull; A. B. Dain; A. Fairley; R. S. Hodge; E. S. Jubb; A. K. Stanley, O.B.E.; K. P. Tanner; J. H. M. Tapley.....................£2,228 to £2,563

Contract and Purchase Department

Director of Contracts (D. of C.), P. T. Williams £3,750
Deputy Directors (D.D. of C.), E. F. Hedger; J. S. Kay; B. E. Orren, C.B.E.; L. W. Smith...£3,150
Assistant Directors (A.D. of C.), T. J. Beynon; S. G. R. Champ; H. G. Clement; F. A. Entwistle; G. E. Jackson; E. H. R. Lubbock; R. W. Ludman; R. Manvell; L. W. Pedrick; G. E. Sandell; D. S. Sargent; S. A. Varney £2,618 to £2,800

Accountancy Division

Principal Accountant, W. J. Kimpton, C.B.E.. £3,500

Judge Advocate of the Fleet

Judge Advocate of the Fleet, Hon. E. E. S. Montagu, C.B.E., Q.C., 3 Pump Court, Temple, E.C.4.
Chief Naval Judge Advocate, Capt. E. N. Hickson, R.N., Royal Naval College, Greenwich, S.E.10.

Queen Alexandra's Royal Naval Nursing Service

Matron-in-Chief, Miss J. M. Woodgate, R.R.C., Q.H.N.S.

ADMIRALS OF THE FLEET

Sir Henry F. Oliver, G.C.B., K.C.M.G., M.V.O., *born* Jan. 22, 1865 .... Jan. 21, 1928
The Lord Chatfield, P.C., G.C.B., O.M., K.C.M.G. C.V.O., *born* Sept. 27, 1873 .... May 8, 1935
H.R.H. the Duke of Windsor, K.G., K.T., K.P., G.C.B., G.C.S.I., G.C.M.G., G.C.I.E., G.C.V.O., G.B.E., I.S.O., M.C., *born* June 23, 1894 .... Jan. 21, 1936
The Earl of Cork and Orrery, G.C.B., G.C.V.O., *born* Nov. 30, 1873 .... Jan. 21, 1938
The Lord Tovey, G.C.B., K.B.E., D.S.O., *born* Mar. 7, 1885 .... Oct. 22, 1943
The Lord Fraser of North Cape, G.C.B., K.B.E., *born* Feb. 5, 1888 .... Oct. 22, 1948
Sir Algernon U. Willis, G.C.B., K.B.E., D.S.O., *born* May 17, 1889 .... Mar. 20, 1949
Sir Philip L. Vian, G.C.B., K.B.E., D.S.O., *born* June 15, 1894 .... June 1, 1952
H.R.H. the Prince Philip, Duke of Edinburgh, K.G., P.C., K.T., G.M.B.E., *born* June 10, 1921 .. Jan. 15, 1953
Sir George E. Creasy, G.C.B., C.B.E., D.S.O., M.V.O., *born* Oct. 13, 1895 .... April 22, 1955
The Earl Mountbatten of Burma, K.G., P.C., G.C.B., G.C.S.I., G.C.I.E., G.C.V.O., D.S.O. (*Chief of Defence Staff*), *born* June 25, 1900 .... Oct. 21, 1956
Sir Caspar John, G.C.B., *born* March 22, 1903 .... May 22, 1962

ADMIRALS

Sir J. David Luce, G.C.B., D.S.O., O.B.E. (*First Sea Lord and Chief of Naval Staff*).
Sir Wilfrid J. W. Woods, G.B.E., K.C.B., D.S.O. (*Commander-in-Chief, Portsmouth*).
Sir Deric Holland-Martin, K.C.B., D.S.O., D.S.C. (*Commander-in-Chief, Mediterranean*).
Sir Charles E. Madden, Bt., K.C.B. (*Commander-in-Chief, Home Fleet and C.-in-C., Allied Forces, Eastern Atlantic*).
Sir Royston H. Wright, K.C.B., D.S.C. (*Second Sea Lord and Chief of Naval Personnel*).
Sir Varyl C. Begg, K.C.B., D.S.O., D.S.C. (*Commander-in-Chief, Far East*).
Sir Nigel S. Henderson, K.C.B., O.B.E. (*Commander-in-Chief, Plymouth*).

VICE-ADMIRALS

Sir Desmond P. Dreyer, K.C.B., C.B.E., D.S.C. (*F.O. Commanding-in-Chief, Far East Fleet*).
Sir John G. Hamilton, K.B.E., C.B., (*F.O. Air (Home)*).
Sir Michael Le Fanu, K.C.B., D.S.C. (*Third Sea Lord and Controller of the Navy*).
Sir Norman E. Denning, K.B.E., C.B. (*Director of Naval Intelligence*).
R. M. Smeeton, C.B., M.B.E. (*Deputy Supreme Allied Commander, Atlantic*).
A. R. Hezlet, C.B., D.S.O., D.S.C. (*F.O., Scotland and Northern Ireland*).
J. B. Frewen, C.B. (*Vice-Chief of Naval Staff*).
A. A. F. Talbot, C.B., D.S.O. (*C.-in-C., South Atlantic and South America*).
F. H. E. Hopkins, C.B., D.S.O., D.S.C. (*Deputy Chief of Naval Staff and Fifth Sea Lord*).
F. R. Twiss, C.B., D.S.C. (*F.O. (Flotillas) Home Fleet*).
G. D. A. Gregory, C.B., D.S.O. (*Admiral Superintendent, Devonport*).
A. B. Cole, C.B., D.S.C. (*Chief of Staff to C.-in-C., Allied Forces, Mediterranean*).
R. V. Brockman, C.S.I., C.I.E., C.B.E. (*Principal Staff Officer to Chief of Defence Staff*).
I. W. T. Beloe, C.B., D.S.C.
J. P. Scatchard, C.B., D.S.C. (*F.O., Second-in-Command, Far East Station*).

REAR-ADMIRALS

E. G. Irving, C.B., O.B.E. (*Hydrographer of the Navy*).
Sir Joseph C. C. Henley, K.C.V.O., C.B. (*F.O., Royal Yachts*).
J. A. Ievers, C.B., O.B.E. (*Deputy Controller of Aircraft (R.N.), Ministry of Aviation*).
J. Howson, C.B., D.S.C. (*Acting Commander, Allied Naval Forces, Northern Europe*).
J. F. D. Bush, C.B., D.S.C. (*Commander British Naval Staff, Washington*).
R. S. Hawkins, C.B. (*Fourth Sea Lord and Vice-Controller*).
H. S. Mackenzie, C.B., D.S.O., D.S.C. (*Chief Polaris Executive*).
H. R. Law, C.B., O.B.E., D.S.C. (*F.O., Submarines*).
P. D. Gick, C.B., O.B.E., D.S.C. (*F.O., Flying Training*).
R. A. J. Owen, C.B. (*Director-General of Personal Services and Officer Appointments*).
F. Dossor, C.B.E. (*Polaris Project Officer, Minister of Aviation*).
H. C. Martell, C.B., C.B.E. (*Admiral Commanding Reserves and Inspector of Recruiting*).
E. N. Sinclair, C.B., D.S.C. (*F.O. and Admiral Superintendent, Gibraltar*).
M. G. Greig, C.B., D.S.C. (*Chief of Staff to Chairman, British Defence Staff, Washington*).
P. J. Hill-Norton (*Assistant Chief of Naval Staff*).
M. A. McMullen, O.B.E. (*F.O., Admiralty Interview Board*).
C. P. G. Walker, D.S.C. (*Director-General, Dockyards and Maintenance*).
P. N. Buckley, D.S.O. (*Director-General of Manpower*).
R. L. Alexander, D.S.O., D.S.C. (*Vice Naval Deputy to Supreme Allied Commander, Europe*).
J. M. D. Gray, O.B.E. (*Director-General of Training*).
J. E. Scotland, D.S.C. (*F.O., Middle East*).
J. H. Walwyn, O.B.E. (*F.O. (Flotillas), Mediterranean*).
J. O. C. Hayes, O.B.E. (*Naval Secretary to First Lord*).
J. S. Raven (*Director, Engineering and Electrical Training and Deputy Chief Naval Engineering Officer*).
R. H. Tribe, M.B.E. (*Chief Staff Officer (Technical) to C.-in-C., Home Fleet and Inspector-General, Fleet Maintenance*).
H. C. Lyddon, O.B.E. (*Rear-Admiral (Personnel) Home Air Command*).
G. T. S. Gray, D.S.C. (*Senior Naval Member, Directing Staff, Imperial Defence College*).
A. Davies (*Head of British Defence Liaison Staff, Australia*).
I. L. T. Hogg, D.S.C., (*F.O. Medway and Admiral Superintendent, Chatham*).
M. C. Giles, D.S.O., O.B.E., G.M. (*President, Royal Naval College, Greenwich*).
C. P. Mills, C.B.E., D.S.C. (*Director-General, Weapons*).
D. P. Mansfield (*Chief Staff Officer (Technical) to F.O. Air (Home)*).
D. A. Williams, D.S.C. (*Director-General, Aircraft*).
D. G. Clutterbuck (*Chief of Staff to C.-in-C., Home Fleet*).
P. U. Bayly, D.S.C. (*F.O., Sea Training*).
F. B. P. Brayne-Nicholls, D.S.C. (*Chief of Staff to F.O. Commanding-in-Chief, Far East Fleet*).

D. C. E. F. Gibson, D.S.C. (*F.O. Aircraft Carriers*).
J. G. B. Cooke, D.S.C. (*Assistant Chief of Naval Staff (Warfare)*).
J. G. Watson (*Admiral Superintendent, Rosyth*).
H. G. H. Tracy, D.S.C. (*Director of Marine Engineering*).
J. L. Blackham (*Admiral Superintendent, Portsmouth*).
A. Woodifield, C.B.E., M.V.O.

ROYAL MARINES

The Corps of Royal Marines (instituted 1664) is trained for service on sea and land. The primary duty of the Royal Marines is the provision of five commando units, three of which are at present serving abroad. They also serve at sea in H.M. Ships and provide landing-craft crews, special boat sections (frogmen) and other detachments for amphibious operations. The Corps also provides bands for H.M. ships and R.N. and R.M. shore establishments. Estimated strength of the Royal Marines in 1963–1964, 9,200 all ranks.

Commandant-General, Royal Marines, Lt.-Gen. Sir Malcolm C. Cartwright-Taylor, K.C.B.

Major-Generals, R. D. Houghton, C.B., O.B.E., M.C.; R. A. Pigot, O.B.E.; N. H. Tailyour, D.S.O.

PRINCIPAL SHIPS OF HER MAJESTY'S FLEET, 1963-64

Ship (with date of completion)	Standard Displacement (tons)	Speed (knots)
Aircraft Carriers:—		
Ark Royal (1955)	43,060	30
Hermes (1959)	23,150	28
Victorious (1941)	30,530	31
Centaur (1953)	23,500	25
Commando Ships:—		
Bulwark (1954)	23,310	27
Albion (1954)	23,170	27
Cruisers:—		
Tiger Class		
Tiger (1959)	9,550	31
Blake (1961)	9,550	31
Lion (1960)	9,550	31
Submarine Depot Ships:—		
Adamant (1942)	12,700	16
Maidstone (1938)	9,100	19
Repair Ship:—		
Ausonia (1944)	19,020	15
Escort Maintenance Ship:—		
Hartland Point (1945)	9,300	11
Minesweeper Support Ships:—		
Woodbridge Haven (1945)	1,652	19
Manxman (1943)	3,000	—
Mull of Kintyre (1945)	8,500	11
Mine Countermeasures Support and Diving Trials Ship:—		
Reclaim (1948)	1,360	—

Destroyers:—

Guided Missile Destroyers 5,225 tons

Devonshire (*l.* 1962) Hampshire (*l.* 1961)
Kent (*l.* 1961) London (1961)

Daring Class:—
3,061 tons 31–34 knots
Diamond (1952) Decoy (1953)
Duchess (1952) Diana (1954)

Battle Class
2,460 tons 30 knots
Agincourt (1947) Barrosa (1947)
Aisne (1947) Corunna (1947)

CA Class (1944)*:—*
2,106 tons 30 knots
Cavendish Cambrian
Cassandra Carron
Caesar

THE UNION JACK SERVICES CLUBS

Patron-in-Chief: H.R.H. the Duke of Gloucester.
Patroness-in-Chief: H.R.H. The Princess Royal.
President: Admiral Sir William James, G.C.B.
Vice-President: Major-Gen. Sir Julian Gascoigne, K.C.M.G., K.C.V.O., C.B., D.S.O.
Hon. Treasurer: Capt. S. J. L. Egerton.
Comptroller and Secretary: Major R. S. Walker, M.B.E.

THE UNION JACK CLUB

Waterloo Road, S.E.1. Tel.: Waterloo 6401.

This is one of our great National Institutions where Sailors, Soldiers and Airmen can go when on leave or passing through London; a place where they may obtain at moderate charges good meals and comfortable bedrooms and where they find the usual amenities of a club, including Library and Writing Room, Billiards Room, Television, Baths, Barber's Shop, and also a Club Shop in which articles of everyday use and almost everything that Service men require may be purchased. It is open throughout the day and night and has a total accommodation of 962 beds.

The Union Jack Club was erected by public subscription as a National Memorial to those who had fallen in the South African War, and other campaigns, and was opened in 1907. Membership is open to those below Commissioned ranks who are serving on the Active List of the Regular Forces, honorary membership being extended to the Colonial Permanent Forces and to the Navies, Armies and Air Forces of Foreign Powers visiting England. A limited number of ex-Service personnel below commissioned rank may also be elected members.

THE UNION JACK FAMILIES CLUB

Exton Street, Waterloo Road, S.E.1.
[Waterloo: 4087]

Warden: Miss L. V. Byers.

This Club was established in 1913, largely as a result of grants made by the South African Garrison Institutes, and provides board and temporary accommodation at moderate rates for the wives and children (with or without their husbands and fathers) of members and ex-members of the Royal Navy, Army and Royal Air Force, below commissioned rank.

THE UNION JACK WOMEN'S SERVICES CLUB

Exton Street, Waterloo Rd., S.E.1. (Opened October, 1952. Adjoins the Families Club.)

All serving W.R.N.S., Q.A.R.A.N.C., W.R.A.C., and W.R.A.F. below commissioned rank are members of this Club which has 44 beds and all facilities of a residential club.

SERVICE PAY AND PENSIONS

Pay and Pensions of the Armed Forces are reviewed regularly at intervals of not more than two years, taking into account movements in civilian earnings in a range of occupations. Increases of pay effective in two stages from April 1, 1962, and April 1, 1963, were announced in March, 1962. The following tables show the rates of pay with effect from April 1, 1963, and of retirement benefits effective from April 1, 1962. In general the rates shown below are for United Kingdom-based regulars of the three Services; where Army ranks only are shown, rates apply equally to equivalent ranks in the other Services. Full details appear in *Service Pay and Pensions* (Cmnd. 1666, 1962).

Increases 1962–63

On each of the dates above, annual increases for male officers on normal rates applied to the following Army ranks (and equivalent ranks in the other Services): Second-Lieutenant/Lieut., £27 7*s*. 6*d*.; Captain, £36 10*s*.; Major, £45 12*s*. 6*d*.; Lieutenant-Colonel, £54, 15*s*.; Colonel, £91 5*s*.; Brigadier and Major-General, £127 15*s*.,

and increases for the majority of regular ratings, soldiers and airmen in the following ranges of weekly amounts: Private, 5*s*. 3*d*. to 12*s*. 3*d*.; Lance-Corporal, 7*s*. to 14*s*.; Corporal, 10*s*. 6*d*. to 17*s*. 6*d*.; Sergeant, 12*s*. 3*d*. to 21*s*.; Staff Sergeant/Warrant Officer Class II, 14*s*. to 22*s*. 9*d*.; and Warrant Officer Class I, 15*s*. 9*d*. to 24*s*. 6*d*.

Women's rates of pay were also increased to maintain the ratio of approximately 85 per cent. of the equivalent men's rates.

ROYAL NAVY AND ROYAL MARINES
Officers

Rank (and equivalent rank, R.M.)	Basic Pay Daily		Basic Pay Annual
	s.	*d.*	£
Cadet	14	0	255
Midshipman at Dartmouth	17	6	319
Midshipman in Ship of Fleet	26	0	474
Acting Sub-Lieutenant	31	0	566
Sub-Lieutenant	35	0	639
Lieutenant R.N.	42	0	766
After 2 years*	54	0	985
After 4 years*	56	0	1,022
After 6 years*	58	0	1,058
Lieutenant-Commander	70	0	1,277
After 2 years*	73	0	1,332
After 4 years*	76	0	1,387
After 6 years*	79	0	1,442
After 8 years*	82	0	1,496
After 10 years*	85	0	1,551
After 12 years*	89	0	1,642
Commander	99	0	1,807
After 2 years*	102	0	1,861
After 4 years*	105	0	1,916
After 6 years*	108	0	1,971
After 8 years*	111	0	2,026
Captain	126	0	2,299
After 2 years*	130	0	2,372
After 4 years*	134	0	2,445
After 6 years*	138	0	2,518
After 8 years*	152	0	2,774
Rear-Admiral	194	0	3,540
Vice-Admiral§	226	0	4,124
Admiral§	276	0	5,037
Admiral of the Fleet§	326	0	5,949

* In this rank. § Unchanged from rates in 1960-62

ARMY
Officers

Rank	Basic Pay Daily		Basic Pay Annual
	s.	*d.*	£
Second-Lieutenant	32	0	584
Lieutenant	37	0	675
After 1 year*	39	0	712
After 2 years*	41	0	748
After 3 years*	43	0	785
Captain	50	0	912
After 1 year*	52	0	949
After 2 years*	54	0	985
After 3 years*	56	0	1,022
After 4 years*	58	0	1,058
After 5 years*	60	0	1,095
After 6 years*	62	0	1,131
Major	73	0	1,332
After 1 year*	75	0	1,369
After 2 years*	77	0	1,405
After 3 years*	79	0	1,442
After 4 years*	81	0	1,478
After 6 years*	83	0	1,515
After 8 years*	85	0	1,551
After 10 years*	87	0	1,588
After 12 years*	89	0	1,624
Lieutenant-Colonel with less than 19 years' service	98	0	1,788
After 2 years* or with 19 years' service	101	0	1,843
After 4 years* or with 21 years' service	104	0	1,898
After 6 years* or with 23 years' service	107	0	1,953
After 8 years* or with 25 years' service	110	0	2,007
Colonel	126	0	2,299
After 2 years*	130	0	2,372
After 4 years*	134	0	2,445
After 6 years*	138	0	2,518
After 8 years*	142	0	2,591
Brigadier	152	0	2,774
Major-General	194	0	3,540
Lieutenant-General†	226	0	4,124
General†	276	0	5,037
Field-Marshal†	326	0	5,949

*In this rank †Unchanged from rates in 1960–62.

NOTE:—A subaltern holding the temporary rank of Captain draws a rate of 46*s*. 0*d*. a day (£839 a year) in the first year in that rank.

Quarter-master Rates

On appointment, as for Captain (above), with annual increase of 1*s*. per day after each of first five years' service in the rank; after 6, 8 and 10 years' service, increases of 2*s*. per day. After 12 years' service, 77*s*. per day (£1,405); after 14, 16 and 18 years' service, increases of 2*s*. per day. Lieutenant-Colonel, 94*s*. per day (£1,715); after 3 years' in the rank, 96*s*. per day (£1,752).

Officer Cadets.—Cadet at R.M.A., Sandhurst, R.A.F. College or R.A.F. Technical College, basic pay weekly, 98*s*.; after 1 year's service, 122*s*. 6*d*.; Cadet at Officer Cadet Schools and Arms Schools, basic pay weekly, 98*s*.

ROYAL AIR FORCE

Officers. Basic Pay

Rank * In this rank	Daily	Annual
	s. d.	£
Acting Pilot Officer	26 0	474
After 6 months* (aircrew officers only)	28 0	511
After 1 year* (other officers)	28 0	511
Pilot Officer	32 0	584
Flying Officer	35 0	639
After 1 year* or 2 years' service	37 0	675
After 2 years* or 3 years' service	39 0	712
After 3 years* or 4 years' service	41 0	748
After 4 years* or 5 years' service	43 0	785
Flight Lieutenant	48 0	876
After 1 year* or 6 years' service	50 0	912
After 2 years* or 7 years' service	52 0	949
After 3 years* or 8 years' service	54 0	985
After 4 years* or 9 years' service	56 0	1,022
After 5 years* or 10 years' service	58 0	1,058
After 6 years* or 11 years' service	60 0	1,095
After 7 years* or 12 years' service	62 0	1,131

Rank * In this rank	Daily	Annual
	s. d.	£
Squadron Leader	73 0	1,332
After 1 year*	75 0	1,369
After 2 years*	77 0	1,405
After 3 years*	79 0	1,442
After 4 years*	81 0	1,478
After 6 years*	83 0	1,515
After 8 years*	85 0	1,551
After 10 years*	87 0	1,588
After 12 years*	89 0	1,624
Wing Commander	98 0	1,788
After 2 years* or 19 years' service	101 0	1,843
After 4 years* or 21 years' service	104 0	1,898
After 6 years* or 23 years' service	107 0	1,953
After 8 years* or 25 years' service	110 0	2,007
Group Captain	126 0	2,299
After 2 years*	130 0	2,372
After 4 years*	134 0	2,445
After 6 years*	138 0	2,518
After 8 years*	142 0	2,591
Air Commodore	152 0	2,774
Air Vice-Marshal	194 0	3,540
Air Marshal	226 0	4,124
Air Chief Marshal	276 0	5,037
Marshal of the Royal Air Force	326 0	5,949

ROYAL NAVY

Seamen Branch and R.M.* (General duties, tradesmen and musicians) Weekly rates	C		B		A	
	7-year Rate	9-year Rate	7-year Rate	9-year Rate	7-year Rate	9-year Rate
	s. d.	s. d.	s. d.	s. d.	s. d.	s. d.
Ordinary Rating or Marine 2nd Class	—	—	—	—	119 0	147 0
Able Rating or Marine 1st Class	—	—	136 6	164 6	147 0	175 0
Leading Rating or Corporal R.M.	182 0	210 0	187 3	215 3	192 0	220 6
Petty Officer or Sergeant R.M.	227 6	255 6	234 6	262 6	241 6	269 6
Chief Petty Officer or Colour Sergeant R.M.	259 0	287 0	266 0	294 0	273 0	301 0
Quarter-Master Sergeant R.M.	—	—	—	—	—	322 0
Regimental Sergeant Major R.M.	—	—	—	—	—	339 6

Artificers*	7-year Rate	9-year Rate
	s. d.	s. d.
Artificer 3rd Class (Leading Rating)	182 0	210 0
Artificer Acting 2nd Class (Petty Officer)	241 6	269 6
Artificer 2nd Class (Petty Officer)	259 0	287 0
Artificer 1st Class (Chief Petty Officer)	276 6	304 6
After 2 years	294 0	322 0
After 4 years	301 0	329 0
After 6 years	308 0	336 0
Chief Artificer (Chief Petty Officer)	332 6	360 6

Mechanicians* (9-year Rate)	s. d.
Mechanician 5th Class (Able Rating)	175 0
Mechanician Acting 4th Class (Leading Rating)	217 0
*Mechanicians (contd.)**	
Mechanician 4th Class (Leading Rating)	227 6
Mechanician 3rd Class (Petty Officer)	266 0
Mechanician 2nd Class (Petty Officer)	283 6
Mechanician 1st Class (Chief Petty Officer)	304 6
After 2 years	322 0
After 4 years	329 0
After 6 years	336 0
Chief Mechanician (Chief Petty Officer)	360 6

Artisans* (9-year Rate)	s. d.
Artisan 5th Class (Able Rating)	175 0
Artisan Acting 4th Class (Leading Rating)	210 0
Artisan 4th Class (Leading Rating)	220 6
Artisan 3rd Class / Artisan 2nd Class / Artisan 1st Class (Petty Officer)	259 6
Chief Artisan (Chief Petty Officer)	301 0

* Trade and Charge Pay are included where applicable. Additional pay for service after 9, 14 and 18 years ranges from 7*s.* to 21*s.* weekly.

ARMY

Other Ranks. Basic Pay

Rank	Weekly Rates of Pay for those committed to serve for:									
	Scale A★		Scale B★		Scale C★		Scale D★		Scale E★	
Technicians	*s.*	*d.*	*s.*	*d.*	*s.*	*d.*	*s.*	*d.*	*s.*	*d.*
Private	154	0	175	0	203	0	213	6	213	6
Lance-Corporal	171	6	192	6	220	6	231	0	231	0
Corporal	196	0	217	0	245	0	259	0	273	0
Sergeant	252	0	273	0	301	0	322	0	339	6
Staff-Sergeant	290	6	311	6	339	6	364	0	381	6
Warrant Officer Class I	301	0	322	0	350	0	374	6	392	0
Warrant Officer Class II	318	6	339	6	367	6	392	0	409	6
Group A Tradesmen	*s.*	*d.*	*s.*	*d.*	*s.*	*d.*	*s.*	*d.*	*s.*	*d.*
Private—										
Class III	122	6	143	6	171	6	182	0	182	0
Class II	129	6	150	6	178	6	189	0	189	0
Class I	140	0	161	0	189	0	199	6	199	6
Lance-Corporal—										
Class III	140	0	161	0	189	0	199	6	199	6
Class II	147	0	168	0	196	0	206	6	206	6
Class I	157	6	178	6	206	6	217	0	217	0
Corporal—										
Class II	168	0	189	0	217	0	231	0	245	0
Class I	175	0	196	0	224	0	238	0	252	0
Sergeant	220	6	241	6	269	6	290	6	308	0
Staff-Sergeant	248	6	269	6	297	6	322	0	339	6
Warrant Officer Class II	259	0	280	0	308	0	332	6	350	0
Warrant Officer Class I	276	6	297	6	325	6	350	0	367	6
Group B Tradesmen	*s.*	*d.*	*s.*	*d.*	*s.*	*d.*	*s.*	*d.*	*s.*	*d.*
Private—										
Class III	115	6	136	6	164	6	175	0	175	0
Class II	122	6	143	6	171	6	182	0	182	0
Class I	133	0	154	0	182	0	192	6	192	6
Lance-Corporal—										
Class III	133	0	154	0	182	0	192	6	192	6
Class II	140	0	161	0	189	0	199	6	199	6
Class I	150	6	171	6	199	6	210	0	210	0
Corporal—										
Class II	161	0	182	0	210	0	224	0	238	0
Class I	168	0	189	0	217	0	231	0	245	0
Sergeant	206	6	227	6	255	6	276	6	294	0
Staff-Sergeant	234	6	255	6	283	6	308	0	325	6
Warrant Officer Class II	245	0	266	0	294	0	318	6	336	0
Warrant Officer Class I	262	6	283	6	311	6	336	0	353	6
Non-Tradesmen	*s.*	*d.*	*s.*	*d.*	*s.*	*d.*	*s.*	*d.*	*s.*	*d.*
Private—										
Grade IV	98	0	119	0	147	0	—		—	
Grade III	115	6	136	6	164	6	175	0	175	0
Grade II	122	6	143	6	171	6	182	0	182	0
Grade I	133	0	154	0	182	0	192	6	192	6
Lance-Corporal—										
Grade III	133	0	154	0	182	0	192	6	192	6
Grade II	140	0	161	0	189	0	199	6	199	6
Grade I	150	6	171	6	199	6	210	0	210	0
Corporal—										
Grade II	161	0	182	0	210	0	224	0	238	0
Grade I	168	0	189	0	217	0	231	0	245	0
Sergeant	206	6	227	6	255	6	276	6	294	0
Staff-Sergeant	234	6	255	6	283	6	308	0	325	6
Warrant Officer Class II†	245	0	266	0	294	0	318	6	336	0
Warrant Officer Class I	262	6	283	6	311	6	336	0	353	6

★ SCALES.—A = Less than 6 years; B = 6 years but less than 9 years; C = 9 years or more; D = 15 years, having completed 9 years' service; E = 21 years or more, having completed 15 years' service.

NOTES:—† A Warrant Officer Class II, holding the appointment of R.Q.M.S. receives additional pay of 7*s*. 0*d*. a week. INCREMENTS.—In addition to the rates shown above, increments of 10*s*. 6*d*. a week are granted to sergeants and above on completion of eighteen years' service. FLYING PAY.—Weekly rates of additional pay for flying duties range from 42*s*. while under training as a pilot to 98*s*. for a Warrant Officer on the permanent cadre.

ROYAL AIR FORCE

Basic Pay

Rank	A	B	C
Aircrew	*s. d.*	*s. d.*	*s. d.*
(i) *Pilots and Navigators:*			
Sergeant	220 6	241 6	269 6
Flight Sergeant	252 0	273 0	301 0
Master Aircrew	276 6	297 6	325 6
(ii) *Air Signallers (A), Air Engineers (A), Radio Observers (A) and Air Meteorological Observers:*			
Sergeant	220 6	241 6	269 6
Flight Sergeant	252 0	273 0	301 0
Master Aircrew	276 6	297 6	325 6
(iii) *Air Signallers, Engineers and Radio Observers:*			
Sergeant	206 6	227 6	255 6
Flight Sergeant	234 6	255 6	283 6
Master Aircrew	262 6	283 6	311 6
Ground Tradesmen			
(i) *Skilled Trades and Trade Assistants:*			
Aircraftman 2	98 0	119 0	147 0
Aircraftman 1	108 6	129 6	157 6
Leading Aircraftman	115 6	136 6	164 6
Senior Aircraftman	133 0	154 0	182 0
Corporal	161 0	182 0	210 0
Sergeant	206 6	227 6	255 6
Flight Sergeant	234 6	255 6	283 6
Warrant Officer	262 6	283 6	311 6
(ii) *Advanced Trades (Aircraft Engineering, Radio Engineering, Armament Engineering and Electrical and Instrument Engineering Trade Groups) attracting Trade Pay at Scale A rates†:*			
Junior Technician	175 0	196 0	224 0
Corporal	199 6	220 6	248 6
Corporal Technician	210 0	231 0	259 0
Sergeant (i)	245 0	266 0	294 0
Sergeant (ii)	255 6	276 6	304 6
Senior Technician	255 6	276 6	304 6
Flight Sergeant (iii)	287 0	308 0	336 0
Ground Tradesmen	*s. d.*	*s. d.*	*s. d.*
(ii) (*contd.*)			
Flight Sergeant (iv)	301 0	322 0	350 0
Chief Technician	294 0	315 0	343 0
Warrant Officer (iii)	311 6	332 6	360 6
Warrant Officer (iv)	325 6	346 6	374 6
Master Technician	325 6	346 6	374 6
(iii) *Advanced Trades (Aircraft Engineering, Radio Engineering, Armament Engineering, Electrical and Instrument Engineering, General Engineering, Airfield Construction and Medical Trade Groups) attracting Trade Pay at Scale B rates†:*			
Junior Technician	164 6	185 6	213 6
Corporal	189 0	210 0	238 0
Corporal Technician	199 6	220 6	248 6
Sergeant (i)	234 6	255 6	283 6
Sergeant (ii)	245 0	266 0	294 0
Senior Technician	245 0	266 0	294 0
Flight Sergeant (iii)	276 6	297 6	325 6
Flight Sergeant (iv)	287 0	308 0	336 0
Chief Technician	280 0	301 0	329 0
Warrant Officer (iii)	301 0	322 0	350 0
Warrant Officer (iv)	311 6	332 6	360 6
Master Technician	311 6	332 6	360 6
(iv) *Other Advanced Trades:*			
Junior Technician	150 6	171 6	199 6
Corporal	175 0	196 0	224 0
Corporal Technician	175 0	196 0	224 0
Sergeant	220 6	241 6	269 6
Senior Technician	220 0	241 6	269 6
Flight Sergeant	252 0	273 0	301 0
Chief Technician	245 0	266 0	294 0
Warrant Officer	276 6	297 6	325 6
Master Technician	276 6	297 6	325 6

* BASIC PAY.—Weekly rates for those committed to serve for: A, less than 5 years; B, less than 9 years but not less than 5 years; C, not less than 9 years.

† TRADE PAY, ETC.—Includes trade pay at rates varying from 14*s.* 0*d.* to 49*s.* a week depending on trade, rank and technical qualification. (i) Not qualified Corporal Technician standard. (ii) Qualified Corporal Technician standard. (iii) Not qualified Senior Technician standard. (iv) Qualified Senior Technician standard.

INCREMENTAL PAY

Increments on the following scale will be payable after completion of 12 years' service to airmen aircrew and ground tradesmen:—

Corporal/Corporal Technician	21*s.* a week
Sergeant/Senior Technician; Flight Sergeant/Chief Technician	31*s.* 6*d.* a week
Warrant Officer/Master Aircrew; Master Technician	38*s.* 6*d.* a week

In addition increments for service in particular ranks will be payable as follows:—

Sergeant/Senior Technician	3*s.* 6*d.* a week for each 4 years in the rank
Flight Sergeant/Chief Technician	7*s.* 0*d.* a week for each 4 years in the rank
Warrant Officer/Master Aircrew; Master Technician	10*s.* 6*d.* a week for each 4 years in the rank

WOMEN'S SERVICES

Officers of W.R.N.S., W.R.A.C., W.R.A.F. Basic Pay

Rank	W.R.N.S.			W.R.A.C. and W.R.A.F.		
	Daily		Annual	Daily		Annual
	s.	*d.*	£	*s.*	*d.*	£
Acting Pilot Officer	—		—	21	6	392
After 1 year in the rank	—		—	23	6	429
Probationary Third Officer/Second Lieutenant/Pilot Officer	26	6	484	27	6	502
Third Officer on confirmation	29	6	538	—		—
Third Officer after 3 years/Lieutenant/Flying Officer	31	6	575	31	6	575
*Lieutenant/Flying Officer after 1 year	—		—	33	0	602
*Lieutenant/Flying Officer after 2 years	—		—	34	6	630
*Lieutenant/Flying Officer after 3 years	—		—	36	6	666
Second Officer/Captain/Flight Officer	37	6	684	42	6	776
After 1 year*	—		—	44	0	803
After 2 years*	40	6	739	46	0	839
After 3 years*	—		—	47	6	867
After 4 years*	43	6	794	49	0	894
After 5 years*	—		—	50	6	922
After 6 years*	46	6	849	52	6	958
After 8 years*	49	6	903	—		—
After 10 years*	52	6	958	—		—
After 12 years*	55	6	1,013	—		—
First Officer/Major/Squadron Officer	60	0	1,095	62	0	1,131
After 1 year*	—		—	63	6	1,159
After 2 years*	63	0	1,150	65	6	1,195
After 3 years*	—		—	67	0	1,223
After 4 years*	66	0	1,204	68	6	1,250
After 6 years*	69	0	1,259	70	6	1,287
After 8 years*	72	6	1,323	72	6	1,323
After 10 years*	74	0	1,350	74	0	1,350
After 12 years*	75	6	1,378	75	6	1,378
Chief Officer/Lieutenant-Colonel/Wing Officer	83	6	1,524	83	6	1,524
After 2 years or 19 years' service*	86	6	1,579	86	6	1,579
After 4 years or 21 years' service*	88	6	1,615	88	6	1,615
After 6 years or 23 years' service*	90	6	1,652	90	6	1,652
After 8 years or 25 years' service*	92	6	1,688	92	6	1,688
Superintendent/Colonel/Group Officer	106	6	1,944	106	6	1,944
After 2 years*	110	6	2,017	110	6	2,017
After 4 years*	113	6	2,071	113	6	2,071
After 6 years*	117	6	2,144	117	6	2,144
After 8 years*	—		—	120	6	2,199
Commandant/Brigadier/Air Commandant	129	0	2,354	129	0	2,354

*In the rank.

Q.A.R.N.N.S., Q.A.R.A.N.C., AND P.M.R.A.F.N.S.

Basic Pay

Rank	Daily	Annual
Nursing Sister/Lieutenant/Flying Officer	34*s.* 6*d.*–39*s.*	£630–£712
Senior Nursing Sister/Captain/Flight Officer	42*s.* 6*d.*–52*s.* 6*d.*	£776–£958
Superintendent Sister/Matron/Major/Squadron Officer	62*s.*–75*s.* 6*d.*	£1,131–£1,378
Principal Matron/Lieut.-Colonel/Wing Officer	83*s.* 6*d.*–92*s.* 6*d.*	£1,524–£1,688
Colonel/Group Officer	106*s.* 6*d.*–120*s.* 6*d.*	£1,944–£2,199
Matron-in-Chief/Brigadier/Air Commandant	129*s.*	£2,354

WOMEN'S SERVICES

(Weekly Rates)

W.R.N.S.

	B		A	
	s.	*d.*	*s.*	*d.*
Wren (Ordinary)	—		84	0
Wren (Able)	98	0	112	0
Leading Wren	136	6	150	6
Petty Officer Wren	175	0	189	0
Chief Wren	203	0	213	6

Q.A.R.A.N.C. AND W.R.A.C.

Sergeants and Higher Ranks

Rank	Technicians	Tradeswomen		Non-Tradeswomen
		Group A	Group B	
	s. d.	s. d.	s. d.	s. d.
Sergeant	213 6	189 0	175 0	175 0
Staff-Sergeant	245 0	210 0	196 0	196 0
Warrant Officer Class II*	255 6	220 6	206 6	206 6
Warrant Officer Class I	269 6	234 6	220 6	220 6

* A Warrant Officer Class II holding the appointment of R.Q.M.S. receives additional pay of 7*s.* per week.

Mechanicians and Tradeswomen

Rank	Mechanicians	Tradeswomen, Group A			Tradeswomen, Group B		
		Class III	Class II	Class I	Class III	Class II	Class I
	s. d.	s. d.	s. d.	s. d.	s. d.	s. d.	s. d.
Private	129 6	105 0	112 0	119 0	98 0	105 0	112 0
Lance-Corporal	143 6	119 0	126 0	133 0	112 0	119 0	126 0
Corporal	168 0	—	143 6	150 6	—	136 6	143 6

Non-Tradeswomen	Grade IV	Grade III	Grade II	Grade I
	s. d.	s. d.	s. d.	s. d.
Private	84 0	98 0	105 0	112 0
Lance-Corporal	—	112 0	119 0	126 0
Corporal	—	—	136 6	143 6

W.R.A.F.

Skilled Trades and Trade Assistants

Rank	Basic Pay	Rank	Basic Pay
	s. d.		s. d.
Aircraftwoman 2	84 0	Corporal	136 6
Aircraftwoman 1	94 6	Sergeant	175 0
Leading Aircraftwoman	98 0	Flight Sergeant	196 0
Senior Aircraftwoman	112 0	Warrant Officer	220 6

Advanced Tradeswomen

Rank	Trade Groups attracting rates in		Other Trade Groups
	Scale A*	Scale B†	
	s. d.	s. d.	s. d.
Junior Technician	147 0	140 0	126 0
Corporal	171 6	164 6	150 6
Corporal Technician	182 0	171 6	150 6
Sergeant (i)	210 0	203 0	} 189 0
Sergeant (ii)	220 6	210 0	
Senior Technician	220 6	210 0	189 0
Flight Sergeant (iii)	245 0	234 6	} 213 6
Flight Sergeant (iv)	255 6	245 0	
Chief Technician	248 6	238 0	206 6
Warrant Officer (iii)	266 0	255 6	} 234 6
Warrant Officer (iv)	276 6	265 0	
Master Technician	276 6	266 0	

* Aircraft, Radio, Armament and Electrical and Instrument Engineering Groups.

† The foregoing, together with General Engineering and Airfield Construction Trade Groups. Both Scales include trade pay at rates varying from 14*s.* to 42*s.* per week, (i)–(iv).—*See* notes for R.A.F. Ground Tradesmen.

RETIREMENT BENEFITS

Officers and Men—All Services

£ per annum

Years of reckonable service over age 21	Capt.	Major	Lt.-Col.	Col.	Brigadier	Maj.-Gen.	Lt.-Gen.§	General §	Field Marshal §
16*	485	545	660	—	—	—	—	—	—
17	510	575	695	—	—	—	—	—	—
18	530	605	730	930	—	—	—	—	—
19	550	630	760	965	—	—	—	—	—
20	570	655	790	1,000	—	—	—	—	—
21	585	680	820	1,035	—	—	—	—	—
22	600	705	850	2,070	1,100	—	—	—	—
23	615	730	880	1,105	1,225	—	—	—	—
24	625	750	905	1,140	1,260	1,450	—	—	—
25	635	770	930	1,175	1,295	1,505	—	—	—
26	645	790	955	1,210	1,330	1,560	—	—	—
27	655	810	980	1,240	1,365	1,615	1,810	—	—
28	665	830	1,005	1,270	1,400	1,670	1,880	—	—
29	675	850	1,030	1,300	1,435	1,725	1,950	—	—
30	685	870	1,055	1,330	1,470	1,780	2,020	2,440	—
31	695	885	1,080	1,360	1,505	1,835	2,090	2,530	—
32	705	900	1,100	1,390	1,535	1,890	2,160	2,620	—
33	715	915	1,120	1,420	1,565	1,945	2,230	2,710	—
34†	725	930	1,140	1,450	1,595	2,000	2,300	2,800	3,300

* Minimum rates. † Maximum rates. § Unchanged from 1960–62 rates.

NOTES:—The above rates apply to all officers serving on permanent regular commissions except in the case of certain R.N. Special Duties List Officers and of Lieutenant-Colonels (Quartermaster) and equivalent ranks in the other services who receive a lead of £75 over the Major's scale above. Rates shown are for compulsory retirement; there will be a reduction in certain circumstances for voluntary retirement. Terminal grants continue to be three times the rate of retired pay.

OFFICERS' GRATUITIES (All Services).—Rate of gratuity for an officer retiring compulsorily for age or non-employment, or voluntarily, before becoming eligible for retired pay and who has at least 10 years' qualifying service:

For the first 10 years' qualifying service, £1,150
For each further year's qualifying service, £230
Standard rate of Short Service gratuity for each year of service, £155

Ratings, Soldiers and Airmen—Basic Weekly Rates of Pension

Rank (and equivalents R.N. and R.A.F.)	For each of first 22 years	For each additional year	Rank (and equivalents R.N. and R.A.F.)	For each of first 22 years	For each additional year
	s. d.	s. d.		s. d.	s. d.
Below Corporal	2 4	4 8	Staff Sergeant	4 4	8 8
Corporal	3 0	6 0	Warrant Officer Class II	4 9	9 6
Sergeant	3 10	7 8	Warrant Officer Class I	5 0	10 0

EXAMPLES OF PENSIONS AND APPROXIMATE TERMINAL GRANTS.—PRIVATE, with 22 years' service: Pension 51*s*. 4*d*.; Grant, £400; with 37 years' service; Pension, 121*s*. 4*d*.; Grant, £946. SERGEANT, with 22 years' service; Pension, 84*s*. 4*d*.; Grant, £658; with 37 years' service: Pension, 199*s*. 4*d*.; Grant, £1,555. WARRANT OFFICER CLASS I, with 22 years' service: Pension, 110*s*.; Grant, £858; with 37 years' service; Pension, 260*s*.; Grant, £2,028. GRATUITIES.—Rate of gratuity payable to ratings, soldiers and airmen who leave the service with at least 12 years' qualifying service, £130; 13 years, £170; 14 yrs., £210; 15 yrs., £250; 16 yrs., £300; 17 yrs., £350; 18 yrs., £400; 19 yrs., £450; 20 yrs., £510; 21 yrs., £570.

WOMEN'S RETIREMENT BENEFITS

OFFICERS' GRATUITIES.—For the first 10 years' qualifying service, £977 10*s*.; for each further year's qualifying service an addition of £195 10*s*.

OFFICERS' RETIRED PAY.—*Minimum after 16 years' reckonable service:* Captain and below, £412 5*s*. per annum; Major, £463 5*s*.; Lt.-Colonel, £561 *Maximum after 34 years' reckonable service:* Captain and below, £616 5*s*. per annum; Major, £790 10*s*.; Lt.-Colonel, £969. These rates are subject to a deduction for voluntary retirement in certain circumstances. Terminal grants are three times the annual rate of pension.

OTHER RANKS' PENSIONS

Rank (and equivalents, W.R.N.S. and W.R.A.F.)	For each of first 22 years	For each additional year
	s. d.	s. d.
Below Corporal	2 0	4 0
Corporal	2 6	5 0
Sergeant	3 3	6 6
Staff Sergeant	3 8	7 4
Warrant Officer Class II	4 0	8 0
Warrant Officer Class I	4 3	8 6

Terminal grants are three times the annual rate of pension.

OTHER RANKS' GRATUITIES.—Rate of gratuity to women who leave the Service with at least 12 years' reckonable service, £110 10*s*.; 13 years, £144 10*s*.; 14 yrs., £178 10*s*.; 15 yrs., £212 10*s*.; 16 yrs., £225 0*s*.; 17 yrs., £297 10*s*.; 18 yrs., £340 0*s*.; 19 yrs., £382 10*s*.; 20 yrs., £433 10*s*.; 21 yrs., £484 10*s*.

The Army

THE QUEEN

The Army Council, The War Office, Whitehall, S.W.1

[Whitehall: 9400]

Secretary of State for War (President of the Army Council), The Rt. Hon. JOSEPH BRADSHAW GODBER, M.P.
Parliamentary Under-Secretary of State for War and Financial Secretary of the War Office (Vice-President of the Army Council), J. E. Ramsden, M.P.
Chief of the Imperial General Staff, General Sir Richard Hull, G.C.B., D.S.O., A.D.C. (*Gen.*)
Adjutant-General to the Forces, General Sir James Cassels, G.C.B., K.B.E., D.S.O.
Quarter-Master-General to the Forces, General Sir Gerald Lathbury, G.C.B., D.S.O., M.B.E., A.D.C. (*Gen.*)
Vice-Chief of the Imperial General Staff, Lt.-Gen. G. H. Baker, C.B., C.M.G., C.B.E., M.C.
Deputy Chief of Imperial General Staff, Lt.-Gen. Sir John Hackett, K.C.B., C.B.E., D.S.O., M.C.
Master-General of the Ordnance, Lt.-Gen. Sir Charles Jones, K.C.B., C.B.E., M.C.
Permanent Under-Secretary of State for War (Secretary of the Army Council), A. C. W. Drew, C.B.

The Secretary of State for War

Secretary of State, The Rt. Hon. JOSEPH BRADSHAW GODBER, M.P. £5,000
Principal Private Secretary, G. W. Wilson.
Assistant Private Secretary C. A. Whitmore.
Parliamentary Private Secretary, P. F. H. Emery, M.P. .... *unpaid*

Department of the Military Secretary

Military Secretary to the Secretary of State for War (Secretary of the Selection Board), Lt.-Gen. Sir John Anderson, K.C.B., C.B.E., D.S.O.

The Parliamentary Under-Secretary of State for War and Financial Secretary of the War Office

Parliamentary Under-Secretary, J. E. Ramsden, M.P. £2,500
Private Secretary, B. M. Norbury.

Department of the Chief of the Imperial General Staff

Chief of the Imperial General Staff, General Sir Richard Hull, G.C.B., D.S.O., A.D.C. (*Gen.*)
Aide-de-Camp, Capt. P. J. A. Mallaby.
Military Assistant, Lt.-Col. M. J. P. O'Cock, M.C.
Vice-Chief of the Imperial General Staff, Lt.-Gen. G. H. Baker, C.B., C.M.G., C.B.E., M.C.
Military Assistant, Maj. J. R. West.
Directors, Major-Generals M. St. J. Oswald, C.B.E., D.S.O., M.C.; G. R. D. Fitzpatrick, C.B., D.S.O., M.B.E., M.C.; Brigadier J. H. Gibbon, O.B.E.
Deputy Chief of the Imperial General Staff, Lt.-Gen. Sir John Hackett, K.C.B., C.B.E., D.S.O., M.C.
Director-General of Military Training, Lt.-Gen. G. C. Gordon-Lennox, C.B., C.V.O., D.S.O.
Engineer-in-Chief, Maj.-Gen. G. W. Duke, C.B., C.B.E., D.S.O.
Directors, Major-Generals G. P. L. Weston, C.B., C.B.E., D.S.O.; W. D. M. Raeburn, D.S.O., M.B.E.; E. J. H. Bates, O.B.E., M.C.; A. P. W. Hope, C.B., C.B.E.; G. S. Cole, C.B., C.B.E.; J. A. d'Avigdor-Goldsmid, O.B.E., M.C.; F. J. Swainson, O.B.E.; P. Gleadell, C.B., C.B.E., D.S.O.; T. H. Birkbeck, C.B., C.B.E., D.S.O.
Brigadiers G. W. H. Peters, C.B.E., D.S.O., M.C.; J. B. Ashworth, C.B.E., D.S.O., A.D.C.; E. I. E. Mozley; A. E. C. Bredin, D.S.O., M.C.

Department of the Adjutant-General to the Forces

Adjutant-General to the Forces, General Sir James Cassels, G.C.B., K.B.E., D.S.O.
Military Assistant, Maj. J. R. L. Howard.
Private Secretary, Maj. T. G. Laidler.
Vice-Adjutant-General, Maj.-Gen. G. R. D. Musson, C.B., C.B.E., D.S.O.
Director-General of Army Medical Services, Lt.-Gen. Sir Harold Knott, K.C.B., O.B.E., Q.H.P.
Directors, Major-Generals A. R. Fyler, O.B.E.; D. A. B. Clarke, C.B.E.; J. E. L. Morris, C.B., C.B.E., D.S.O.; A. L. Gadd, C.B.E.; P. J. L. Capon, C.B., Q.H.P.; A. N. Moon, C.B.E.
Brigadiers G. A. Rimbault, C.B.E., D.S.O., M.C. (*ret.*); G. Barratt, O.B.E.
Matron-in-Chief and Director of Army Nursing Services, Brig. Dame Barbara Cozens, D.B.E., R.R.C., Q.H.N.S.
Director, Women's Royal Army Corps, Brig. J. E. R. Rivett-Drake, M.B.E., A.D.C. (*Hon.*).

Department of the Quarter-Master-General to the Forces

Quarter-Master-General to the Forces, General Sir Gerald Lathbury, G.C.B., D.S.O., M.B.E., A.D.C. (*Gen.*)
Military Assistant, Maj. P. Hudson.
Vice-Quarter-Master-General, Maj.-Gen. A. Jolly, C.B., C.B.E., D.S.O.
Directors, Major-Generals W. J. Potter, C.B.E.; L. H. Atkinson, O.B.E.; P. G. Turpin, C.B., O.B.E.; H. J. C. Hildreth, C.B.E.; G. W. Duke, C.B., C.B.E., D.S.O. (*Engineer-in-Chief*).
Directors, Brigadiers D. N. H. Tyacke, O.B.E.; R. A. J. Eggar, O.B.E.; J. N. Drew, O.B.E.; R. M. N. Patrick; A. D. Seton; C. R. Nicholls, M.B.E.; M. W. Biggs, C.B.E.; W. T. Campbell, C.B.E.; L. E. Hayward.
Assistant Secretary, F. J. Burlace.

Department of the Master-General of the Ordnance

Master-General of the Ordnance, Lt.-Gen. Sir Charles Jones, K.C.B., C.B.E., M.C.
Deputy Master-General of the Ordnance, Maj.-Gen. H. M. Liardet, C.B., C.B.E., D.S.O.
Assistant Masters-General of the Ordnance, (*A*) Maj.-Gen. Sir William Roe, K.B.E., C.B. (*ret.*); (*B*) Maj.-Gen. E. S. Lindsay, C.B., C.B.E., D.S.O., (*ret.*); (*I*) J. E. Jackson, C.B.E.
Assistant Under-Secretaries of State (*A*) G. Leitch, C.B., O.B.E.; (*B*) H. O. Hooper, C.M.G.
Assistant Secretaries, G. A. C. Witheridge; L. V. Sumner; E. S. Wilson; J. M. Parkin; J. G. Stott.
Deputy Chief Scientist, (*A*) W. B. Littler, C.B., Ph.D.
Directors General, Maj.-Gen. W. M. Hutton, C.B.E., D.S.O., M.C.; L. G. Gale, C.B., O.B.E.; Maj.-Gen. C. T. D. Lindsay; F. H. Harrison, C.B.E.
Directors, Maj.-Gen. R. J. Moberly, C.B., O.B.E. (*ret.*); D. H. Chaddock, C.B.E.; E. E. Haddon; Brig. W. J. C. Hayward, O.B.E.; T. D. Jacobs; W. E. Denny, G.M.; Brig. W. P. St. J. Becher, C.B.E.; C. J. Tafft; H. Ison-Porter; E. L. Hill; Brig. J. R. G. Finch, O.B.E.; E. W. Chivers, C.B.; Brig. R. H. Bright, O.B.E.; C. Dunbar; R. A. Foulkes; Brig. H. A. T. Jarrett-Kerr; Comdr. F. W. Hornsby, R.N. (*ret.*); R. Cox; E. D. Jenkins; D. A. Hutton-Williams, M.B.E.; Dr. D. W. Henderson, C.B., F.R.S.; E. K. G. James.

Secretary, R.A.R.D.E. Fort Halstead, A. H. Broadbent.
Chief Superintendent of Ranges, Capt. W. F. C. Wreford, R.N. (*ret.*).

Department of the Permanent Under-Secretary of State for War

Permanent Under-Secretary of State, A. C. W. Drew, C.B.

Army Council Secretariat, J. H. Thomas.

Deputy Under-Secretaries of State, (*A*), W. Geraghty, C.B. (*B*); R. H. Melville, C.B.

Assistant Under-Secretaries of State, C. M. Fife, C.B.; E. K. Stopford, C.B. (*Director of Finance (B)*); G. S. Whittuck, C.B. (*Director of Finance (A)*); S. Redman, C.B. (*Royal Ordnance Factories and Labour*); N. G. Morrison (*Director of Establishments*); V. G. F. Bovenizer, C.M.G. (*Comptroller of Lands and Claims*).

Assistant Secretaries, G. H. Williams, C.B.E.; E. M. Bowen; G. M. Ratcliffe, O.B.E.; H. C. Budden; D. Hammond; A. J. Hall; C. H. W. Murphy, C.B.E.; F. S. Brown; P. F. R. Beards; D. M. Evans; R. W. Barrow; R. G. Alexander, O.B.E.; P. C. Thomson; E. D. Wright; C. E. Starling; H. B. Brenan, O.B.E.; J. E. Gale; W. C. Day, O.B.E.; W. T. Horsley; G. R. R. East; G. F. Carpenter, E.R.D.; D. B. Frudd; D. R. J. Stephen; F. J. Burlace; P. T. E. England.

Librarian, D. W. King, O.B.E.

Chaplain-General to the Forces, Ven. I. D. Neill, C.B., O.B.E., Q.H.C.

Chief Scientist, W. Cawood, C.B., C.B.E., Ph.D.

Electronics Adviser, D. H. Black, C.M.G., Ph.D.

Directors, Dr. E. R. R. Holmberg; G. N. Gadsby.

Director of Public Relations, Maj.-Gen. the Hon. G. W. R. Monckton, O.B.E., M.C.

Director of Army Contracts, H. Robbins.

Controller of Audit and Accounts, F. M. W. Smith, M.B.E.

Director of Ordnance Factories (Accounts), G. Smith.

Paymaster-in-Chief and Inspector of Pay Services, Maj.-Gen. R. D. Coate.

FIELD MARSHALS

H.R.H. the Duke of Windsor, K.G., K.T., K.P., G.C.B., G.C.S.I., G.C.M.G., G.C.I.E., G.C.V.O., G.B.E., I.S.O., M.C., *born* June 23, 1894 .... Jan. 21, 1936

The Earl Alexander of Tunis, K.G., P.C., G.C.B., O.M., G.C.M.G., C.S.I., D.S.O., M.C., Col. I. G. and 3/2 Punjab R., Hon. Col. London Irish Rif. (T.A.) (*Constable of the Royal Palace and Fortress of London*), *born* Dec. 10, 1891 .... June 4, 1944

The Viscount Montgomery of Alamein, K.G., G.C.B., D.S.O., Col. R. Warwick R., Col. Comdt. A.P.T.C., *born* Nov. 17, 1887 .... Sept. 1, 1944

The Lord Wilson, G.C.B., G.B.E., D.S.O., *born* Sept. 5, 1881 .... Dec. 29, 1944

Sir Claude J. E. Auchinleck, G.C.B., G.C.I.E., C.S.I., D.S.O. O.B.E., Col. 1 Punjab R. and Indian Grenadiers, *born* June 21, 1884 .... June 1, 1946

The Viscount Slim, K.G., G.C.B., G.C.M.G., G.C.V.O., G.B.E., D.S.O., M.C., *born* Aug. 6, 1891 .. Jan. 4, 1949

H.R.H. the Prince Philip, Duke of Edinburgh, K.G., P.C., K.T., G.M.B.E., Field-Marshal, Australian Military Forces, Col.-in-Chief, Q.R.I.H., D.E.R.R., Camerons, A.C.F., The Royal Canadian Regt., The Hawkes Bay Regt. and the Otago and Southland Regt., New Zealand, Royal Canadian Army Cadets and Australian Cadet Corps, Col. W. G. Hon. Col. L. D. Y. (T.A.) and Edin. O.T.C., *born* June 10, 1921 Jan. 15, 1953

The Lord Harding of Petherton, G.C.B., C.B.E., D.S.O., M.C., Col. L. G. and 6 G.R., *born* Feb. 10, 1896 July 21, 1953

H.R.H. the Duke of Gloucester, K.G., P.C., K.T., K.P., G.M.B., G.C.M.G., G.C.V.O., Col.-in-Chief 10 H., R. Innisks., Glosters, Gordons, P. B., R.A.S.C., Royal Winnipeg Rifles, Royal Canadian Army Service Corps, Royal Australian Army Service Corps, Royal Australian Armoured Corps, Royal New Zealand Army Service Corps and Ceylon Light Infantry, Col. S. G. (*Hon. Col., R.A. (T.A.) and O.T.C.*) (*Personal A.D.C. to the Queen*) *born* March 31, 1900 .... March 31, 1955

Sir Gerald W. R. Templer, G.C.B., G.C.M.G., K.B.E., D.S.O., Col. R. H. G. and 7 G. R., *born* Sept. 11, 1898 Nov. 27, 1956

Sir Francis W. Festing, G.C.B., K.B.E., D.S.O., Col. R.N.F., Col. Comdt. R.B., *born* Aug. 28, 1902 Sept. 1, 1960

GENERALS

Sir Dudley Ward, G.C.B., K.B.E., D.S.O. (*Governor and Commander-in-Chief of Gibraltar*).

Sir Hugh C. Stockwell G.C.B., K.B.E., D.S.O., Col. R.W.F., Col. Comdt., A.A.C. and R.A.E.C.

Sir A. James H. Cassels, G.C.B., K.B.E., D.S.O., Col. Q. O. Hldrs., Col. Comdt., R.M.P. and A.P.T.C. (*Adjutant-General*).

Sir Richard A. Hull, G.C.B., D.S.O., A.D.C. (*Gen.*), Hon. Col., O.T.C. (*Chief of the Imperial General Staff*).

Sir Gerald W. Lathbury, G.C.B., D.S.O., M.B.E., A.D.C. (*Gen.*), Col. Commdt., 1 Green Jackets and Para., Col. Jamaica Regt. (*Quarter-Master-General*).

Sir Harold E. Pyman, G.B.E., K.C.B., D.S.O., Col. Comdt., R. Tks and R.A.C., Hon. Col. R.A.C. (T.A.).

Sir Roderick W. McLeod, K.C.B., C.B.E., A.D.C. (*Gen.*), Col. Comdt., R.A.

Sir Michael M. A. R. West, K.C.B., D.S.O., A.D.C. (*Gen.*).

Sir Nigel Poett, K.C.B., D.S.O., Col. D.L.I.

Sir William G. Stirling, K.C.B., C.B.E., D.S.O., Col. Comdt., R.A.

LIEUTENANT-GENERALS

Sir Charles P. Jones, K.C.B., C.B.E., M.C., Col. Comdt., R.E. (Hon. Col. R.E. (A.E.R.)) (*Master-General of the Ordnance*).

Sir Rodney Moore, K.C.B., K.C.V.O., C.B.E., D.S.O.

Sir John Anderson, K.C.B., C.B.E., D.S.O., Col. 5 Innis. D.G., Hon. Col. O.T.C. (*Military Secretary*).

Sir Richard N. Anderson, K.C.B., C.B.E., D.S.O., Col. King's Own Border and 10 G. R.

Sir William G. H. Pike, K.C.B., C.B.E., D.S.O., Col. Comdt., R.A., Hon. Col. R.A. (T.A.)

Sir Robert N. H. C. Bray, K.C.B., C.B.E., D.S.O.

Sir Charles L. Richardson, K.C.B., C.B.E., D.S.O., Col. Comdt., R.E.

Sir Edward D. Howard-Vyse, K.B.E., C.B., M.C., Col. Comdt., R.A.

Sir Reginald H. Hewetson, K.C.B., C.B.E., D.S.O., Col. Comdt., R.A.

Sir John W. Hackett, K.C.B., C.B.E., D.S.O., M.C. Col. Comdt., R.E.M.E. (*Deputy C.I.G.S.*).

Sir William F. R. Turner, K.B.E., C.B., D.S.O., Col. K.O.S.B., (*Governor of Edinburgh Castle*).

Sir Harold E. Knott, K.C.B., O.B.E., Q.H.P. (*Director-General of Army Medical Services*).
Sir Denis S. S. O'Connor, K.B.E., C.B., Col. Comdt., R.A.
Sir Kenneth T. Darling, K.C.B., C.B.E., D.S.O.
G. H. Baker, C.B., C.M.G., C.B.E., D.S.O. (*Vice-C.I.G.S.*).
Sir Richard Craddock, K.B.E., C.B., D.S.O.
G. C. Gordon Lennox, C.B., C.V.O., D.S.O. (*Director-General of Military Training*).
C. H. P. Harington, C.B., C.B.E., D.S.O., M.C., Col. Cheshire.

MAJOR-GENERALS

R. W. Ewbank, C.B., C.B.E., D.S.O. (*Commandant, Royal Military College of Science*).
Sir Richard E. Goodwin, K.C.B., C.B.E., D.S.O., Col. I. E. Anglian.
G. R. D. Musson, C.B., C.B.E., D.S.O. (*Vice-Adjutant-General*).
J. A. R. Robertson, C.B., C.B.E., D.S.O., Col. 6 G.R.
C. H. Tarver, C.B., C.B.E., D.S.O.
D. E. B. Talbot, C.B., C.B.E., D.S.O., M.C.
H. M. Liardet, C.B., C.B.E., D.S.O., Col. Comdt., R.Tks.
J. F. Metcalfe, C.B., C.B.E., Col. Queen's Surreys.
D. G. Moore, C.B., Col. R.Innisks.
R. H. Batten, C.B., C.B.E., D.S.O.
C. M. F. Deakin, C.B., C.B.E. (*Commandant Joint Services Staff College*).
The Lord Thurlow, C.B., C.B.E., D.S.O.
A. P. W. Hope, C.B., C.B.E.
N. L. Foster, C.B., D.S.O.
D. S. Gordon, C.B., C.B.E., D.S.O.
G. R. D. Fitzpatrick, C.B., D.S.O., M.B.E., M.C.
P. Gleadell, C.B., C.B.E., D.S.O.
A. Jolly, C.B., C.B.E., D.S.O. (*Vice-Quartermaster-General*).
G. W. Duke, C.B., C.B.E., D.S.O., Col. Comdt., M.P.S.C. (*Engineer-in-Chief*).
G. S. Cole, C.B., C.B.E.
W. R. M. Drew, C.B., C.B.E., Q.H.P.
H. T. Alexander, C.B., C.B.E., D.S.O.
E. A.W. Williams, C.B., C.B.E., M.C.
I. C. Harris, C.B., C.B.E., D.S.O., Col. R.V.R.
J. H. Cubbon, C.B., C.B.E.
W. J. Officer, C.B., C.B.E., Q.H.S.
C. H. McVittie, C.B., C.B.E., Hon. Col. R.A.O.C. (A.E.R.)
J. K. Shepheard, C.B., D.S.O., O.B.E.
G. P. L. Weston, C.B., C.B.E., D.S.O.
P. G. Turpin, C.B., O.B.E., Col.. Gurkha A.S.C.
J. W. Channing-Williams, C.B., D.S.O., O.B.E.
D. A. K. Redman, C.B., O.B.E.
A. N. T. Meneces, C.B., C.B.E., D.S.O., Q.H.P.
T. H. Birkbeck, C.B., C.B.E., D.S.O.
J. E. L. Morris, C.B., C.B.E., D.S.O.
A. M. W. Whistler, C.B., C.B.E., Hon. Col. R. Sigs. (T.A.).
D. Peel-Yates, C.B., D.S.O., O.B.E., Col. S.W.B.
C. T. D. Lindsay, C.B.
R. G. F. Frisby, C.B., C.B.E., D.S.O., M.C.
J. F. Worsley, C.B., O.B.E., M.C. (*Commandant, Staff College, Camberley*).
W. C. Walker, C.B.E., D.S.O.
F. J. C. Piggott, C.B., C.B.E., D.S.O.
T. C. H. Pearson, C.B.E., D.S.O.
M. A. H. Butler, C.B.E., D.S.O., M.C.
I. H. Freeland, D.S.O.
J. D. Frost, D.S.O., M.C.
G. F. de Gex, O.B.E.
W. M. Hutton, C.B.E., D.S.O., M.C.
R. H. Farrant.
A. H. Dowson, C.B.E., Hon. Col. R.E. (T.A.).
A. R. Fyler, O.B.E.
H. J. Mogg, C.B.E., D.S.O., (*Commandant, R.M.A. Sandhurst*).
R. A. Fyffe, D.S.O., O.B.E., M.C.
D. B. Lang, D.S.O., M.C.
G. H. Lea, D.S.O., M.B.E.
J. A. J. Read, C.B.E., D.S.O., M.C.
W. Odling, C.B., O.B.E., M.C.
W. A. Robinson, O.B.E., M.D., Q.H.S.
E. J. H. Bates, O.B.E., M.C.
H. J. C. Hildreth, C.B.E.
L. T. Furnival, D.S.O., Q.H.S.
W. H. Hargreaves, O.B.E.
R. A. Stephen, C.B.E., M.D., Q.H.S.
J. C. Barnetson, O.B.E., Q.H.P.
E. J. B. Nelson, D.S.O., M.V.O., O.B.E., M.C.
E. H. W. Grimshaw, C.B.E., D.S.O.
M. St. J. Oswald, C.B.E., D.S.O., M.C.
R. E. T. St. John, M.C.
D. A. B. Clarke, C.B.E.
J. A. d'Avigdor-Goldsmid, O.B.E., M.C., Col. 4/7 D.G.
R. C. MacDonald, D.S.O., O.B.E.
J. R. Holden, C.B.E., D.S.O.
R. G. V. FitzGeorge-Balfour, C.B.E., D.S.O., M.C.
J. L. Gordon, O.B.E.
A. L. Gadd, C.B.E.
P. J. Glover, O.B.E.
R. M. P. Carver, C.B., C.B.E., D.S.O.
G. F. Upjohn, C.B.E.
F. J. Swainson, O.B.E.
F. B. Wyldbore-Smith, D.S.O., O.B.E.
P. G. F. Young, C.B.E.
W. D. M. Raeburn, D.S.O., M.B.E.
J. E. F. Willoughby, C.B.E., Col. Mx.
P. B. Gillett, O.B.E.
Hon. G. W. R. Monckton, O.B.E., M.C. (*Director of Public Relations, War Office*).
W. J. Potter, C.B.E.
R. D. Coate (*Paymaster-in-Chief*).
A. N. Moon, C.B.E.

CONSTITUTION OF THE BRITISH ARMY

The Regular Forces include the following Arms, Branches and Corps. Soldiers' Records Offices are shown at the end of each group; the records of officers are maintained at the War Office.

Details of the re-organization of the Army, published in July, 1957 showed a reduction in the number of units, effected in the case of regiments of the Royal Armoured Corps and Infantry of the Line by permanent amalgamation of units. Composition of the re-organized infantry brigades appears below, units amalgamated are shown under their new title.

Household Cavalry.—The Life Guards and Royal Horse Guards. *Records*, Horse Guards, London, S.W.1.

Royal Armoured Corps.—Cavalry Regiments and the Royal Tank Regiment. *Records*, Friern Barnet Lane, Whetstone, N.20.

Artillery.—The Royal Regiment of Artillery and the Royal Malta Artillery, *Records*, Foots Cray, Sidcup, Kent; Record Office, Malta.

Engineers.—The Corps of Royal Engineers. *Records*, Ditchling Road, Brighton.

Signals.—The Royal Corps of Signals. *Records*, Balmore House, Caversham, Reading.

Infantry.—The Brigade of Guards: Grenadier, Coldstream, Scots, Irish and Welsh Guards. *Records*, Birdcage Walk, London, S.W.1.

The Lowland Brigade: The Royal Scots (The Royal Regiment); The Royal Highland Fusiliers (Princess Margaret's Own Glasgow and Ayrshire Regiment); The King's Own Scottish Borderers; The Cameronians (Scottish Rifles). *Depôt*, Dreghorn Camp, Colinton, Edinburgh 13. *Records*, Cavalry Barracks, Fulford Road, York.

The Home Counties Brigade: The Queen's Royal Surrey Regiment; The Queen's Own Buffs, the Royal Kent Regiment; The Royal Sussex Regiment; The Middlesex Regiment (Duke of Cambridge's Own). *Depôt*, Wemyss Barracks, Canterbury, Kent. *Records*, Higher Barracks, Exeter.

The Lancastrian Brigade: The King's Own Royal Border Regiment; The King's Regiment (Manchester and Liverpool); The Lancashire Regiment (Prince of Wales's Volunteers); The Loyal Regiment (North Lancashire). *Depôt*, Fulwood Barracks, Preston, Lancs. *Records*, Cavalry Barracks, Fulford Road, York.

The Fusilier Brigade: The Royal Northumberland Fusiliers; The Royal Fusiliers (City of London Regiment); The Lancashire Fusiliers; The Royal Warwickshire Fusiliers. *Depôt*, Tower of London, E.C.3. *Records*, Higher Barracks, Exeter.

The East Anglian Brigade: 1st East Anglian Regiment (Royal Norfolk and Suffolk); 2nd East Anglian Regiment (Duchess of Gloucester's Own Royal Lincolnshire and Northamptonshire); 3rd East Anglian Regiment (16th/44th Foot); The Royal Leicestershire Regiment. *Depôt*, Blenheim Camp, Bury St. Edmunds. *Records*, Higher Barracks, Exeter.

The Wessex Brigade: The Devonshire and Dorset Regiment; The Gloucestershire Regiment; The Royal Hampshire Regiment; The Duke of Edinburgh's Royal Regiment (Berkshire and Wiltshire), *Depôt*, Topsham Barracks, Exeter. *Records*, Higher Barracks, Exeter.

The Light Infantry Brigade: The Somerset and Cornwall Light Infantry; The King's Own Yorkshire Light Infantry; The King's Shropshire Light Infantry; The Durham Light Infantry. *Depôt*, Copthorn Barracks, Shrewsbury, Shropshire. *Records*, Higher Barracks, Exeter.

The Yorkshire Brigade: The Prince of Wales's Own Regiment of Yorkshire; The Green Howards (Alexandra, Princess of Wales's Own Yorkshire Regiment); The Duke of Wellington's Regiment (West Riding); The York and Lancaster Regiment. *Depôt*, Queen Elizabeth Barracks, Strensall, Yorks. *Records*, Cavalry Barracks, Fulford Road, York.

The Mercian Brigade: The Cheshire Regiment; The Worcestershire Regiment; The Staffordshire Regiment (The Prince of Wales's); The Sherwood Foresters (Nottinghamshire and Derbyshire Regiment). *Depôt*, Whittington Barracks, Lichfield. *Records*, Cavalry Barracks, Fulford Road, York.

The Welsh Brigade: The Royal Welch Fusiliers; The South Wales Borderers; The Welch Regiment. *Depôt*, Cwrt y Gollen, Crickhowell, Breconshire. *Records*, Cavalry Barracks, Fulford Road, York.

The North Irish Brigade: The Royal Inniskilling Fusiliers; The Royal Ulster Rifles; The Royal Irish Fusiliers (Princess Victoria's). *Depôt*, Eglinton, Nr. Londonderry, Co. Londonderry. *Records*, Cavalry Barracks, Fulford Road, York.

The Highland Brigade: The Black Watch (Royal Highland Regiment); The Queen's Own Highlanders(Seaforth and Cameron); The Gordon Highlanders; The Argyll and Sutherland Highlanders (Princess Louise's). *Depôt*, Highland House, St. Catherine's Road, Perth. *Records*, Cavalry Barracks, Fulford Road, York.

The Green Jackets Brigade: 1st Green Jackets, 43rd and 52nd; 2nd Green Jackets, The King's Royal Rifle Corps; 3rd Green Jackets, The Rifle Brigade. *Depôt*, Upper Barracks, Winchester. *Records*, Higher Barracks, Exeter.

The Brigade of Gurkhas. *G.H.Q.* Records, Singapore.

Royal Army Service Corps, Army Catering Corps. *Records*, Ore Place, Hastings.

Royal Army Medical Corps, Royal Army Dental Corps, Queen Alexandra's Royal Army Nursing Corps, and Women's Royal Army Corps. *Records*, Lower Barracks, Winchester.

Royal Army Ordnance Corps, Royal Electrical and Mechanical Engineers. *Records*, Glen Parva Barracks, South Wigston, Leicester.

Small Arms School Corps. *Records*, Higher Barracks, Exeter.

General Service Corps. *Records*, Cavalry Barracks, Fulford Road, York.

Special Air Service Regiment, Army Air Corps, Royal Military Police, Royal Army Pay Corps, Royal Army Veterinary Corps, Royal Army Educational Corps, Royal Pioneer Corps, Intelligence Corps, and other ancillary corps not listed above. *Records*, Compton House, Fir Vale Road, Bournemouth.

THE TERRITORIAL ARMY

The Territorial Army has now reverted to its traditional all volunteer status and consists of both men and women. National Service men on completion of their two years with the Regular Army continue to have their 3½ years' reserve liability with the Territorial Army, but compulsory part-time training for them has been suspended.

The *rôle* of the Territorial Army is to form a reserve of trained and disciplined manpower in the country, trained to fight in any emergency.

The Territorial Army is organised on a divisional/district basis. It has centres in towns and villages all over the country. Each unit carries out 15 days training in camp annually. During the remainder of the year units train in the evenings and at weekends.

The Territorial Army Emergency Reserve (the "Ever Readies") is a special force of volunteers, raised from within the Territorial Army, who will accept a pre-proclamation liability and may in times of tension be called upon, for a period not exceeding 6 months in any one year, to serve anywhere in the world and bring Regular Army units temporarily up to war strength.

THE ARMY EMERGENCY RESERVE

Like the Territorial Army the Army Emergency Reserve consists of volunteers (men and women) and also National Service men who are allotted to units but do no part-time training. Its *role* is to provide units and individuals required overseas in peace-time emergencies, and to provide units and individuals to complete the mobilization order of battle of the Army on the outbreak of war. The majority of units are of a specialist nature. A.E.R. training is 15 days annually. One category of the A.E.R., which has a pre-proclamation liability for service overseas when warlike operations are in preparation or in progress, carries out some training in the evenings or at weekends.

NAVY, ARMY AND AIR FORCE RESERVES ACT, 1959

From June 30, 1959, men who served between September 1939 and December 31, 1948, and were generally known as "Z" Reservists (from 1954, R.N. and R.M. Emergency Reservists or Army General Reservists Group "P") and R.A.F. "G" Reservists, ceased to have any further liability for service. The number of men affected by the Act is nearly 3,000,000 and the Minister of Defence hoped that many of them would volunteer for the Civil Defence Service or for the Royal Naval Reserve, the Royal Marine Forces Volunteer Reserve, R.N. Minewatching Service, The Territorial Army, Army Emergency Reserve, Royal Auxiliary Air Force or the Royal Observer Corps, where they would be welcomed.

National Servicemen and volunteers joining the Forces after 1948, on completion of the normal period of whole or part-time service become Royal Naval Special Reservists, Army General Reservists Group "N" or R.A.F. Reservists Class "G", with liability to recall in a grave national emergency until June 30, 1964. The Act does not affect the position of men in the other reserves.

Officers whose service is similar in date to the groups above are similarly affected.

The Royal Air Force

THE QUEEN

THE AIR COUNCIL

Secretary of State for Air and President of the Air Council, The Rt. Hon. HUGH CHARLES PATRICK JOSEPH FRASER, M.B.E., M.P.
Parliamentary Under-Secretary of State for Air and Vice-President of the Air Council, J. E. Ridsdale, M.P.
Chief of the Air Staff, Air Chief Marshal Sir Charles Elworthy, G.C.B., C.B.E., D.S.O., M.V.O., D.F.C., A.F.C.
Air Member for Personnel, Air Chief Marshal Sir Walter Cheshire, K.C.B., C.B.E.
Air Member for Supply and Oganization, Air Marshal J. G. Davis, C.B., O.B.E.
Additional Members, Air Marshal Sir Wallace Kyle, K.C.B., C.B.E., D.S.O., D.F.C. (*Vice-Chief of the Air Staff*); Air Marshal Sir Christopher Hartley, K.C.B., C.B.E., D.F.C., A.F.C. (*Deputy Chief of Air Staff*).
Permanent Under-Secretary of State for Air, Sir Maurice Dean, K.C.B., K.C.M.G.

THE AIR MINISTRY

Whitehall, S.W.1.
[Trafalgar: 8811]
Adastral House, Theobalds Road, W.C.1.
[Holborn: 3434]

Secretary of State

Secretary of State, The Rt. Hon. HUGH CHARLES PATRICK JOSEPH FRASER, M.B.E., M.P. £5,000
Private Secretary, J. D. Bryars.
Assistant Private Secretary, G. J. Gammon.
Personal Air Secretary, Squadron Leader D. C. A. Lloyd.
Parliamentary Private Secretary, Hon. Clive Bossom, M.P.
Parliamentary Under-Secretary of State, J. E. Ridsdale, M.P. £2,500
Private Secretary, M. J. Culham.

Department of the Permanent Under-Secretary of State for Air.

Permanent Under-Secretary of State, Sir Maurice Dean, K.C.B., K.C.M.G.
Private Secretary, J. F. Mayne.
Deputy Under-Secretaries of State, M. T. Flett, C.B.; Sir Henry Smith, K.B.E., C.B.
Assistant Under-Secretaries of State, J. S. Orme, C.B., O.B.E.; B. Humphreys-Davies; T. A. G. Charlton; R. Haynes; F. Cooper, C.M.G.; E. G. Cass, O.B.E.
Assistant Secretaries, K. H. S. Edwards; S. W. Warran, C.B.E.; H. A. Shaw; R. H. Prince; J. H. Francis; W. J. B. Crotch; T. C. G. James; L. T. G. Sully, C.B.E.; R. F. Havell; R. J. Penney; E. F. C. Stanford; M. McF. Davis; P. J. Hudson; W. E. Dowling; E. Broadbent; F. L. F. Devey; G. H. Green; D. C. Humphreys; W. C. Curtis; R. N. Noyes; J. T. Williams; Miss E. P. Kruse; J. H. Nelson; W. E. Fitzsimmons; J. Roberts.
Director-General, Sir Graham Sutton, C.B.E., D.S.C., F.R.S.
Chief Information Officer, Air Commodore J. Barraclough, C.B.E., D.F.C., A.F.C.

Department of the Chief of the Air Staff

Chief of the Air Staff, Air Chief Marshal Sir Charles Elworthy, G.C.B., C.B.E., D.S.O., M.V.O., D.F.C., A.F.C.
Vice-Chief of the Air Staff, Air Marshal Sir Wallace Kyle, K.C.B., C.B.E., D.S.O., D.F.C.
Deputy Chief of the Air Staff, Air Marshal Sir Christopher Hartley, K.C.B., C.B.E., D.F.C., A.F.C.
Assistant Chiefs of the Air Staff, Air Vice-Marshal D. G. Smallwood, C.B.E., D.S.O., D.F.C.; Air Vice-Marshal R. H. E. Emson, C.B., C.B.E., A.F.C.; Air Vice-Marshal T. O. Prickett, C.B., D.S.O., D.F.C.; Air Vice-Marshal A. Foord-Kelcey, C.B.E., A.F.C.
Commandant-General, Air Vice-Marshal B. A. Chacksfield, C.B., O.B.E.
Directors, Air Commodores R. H. C. Burwell, C.B.E., D.F.C.; F. O. S. Dobell, C.B.E.; A. G. Dudgeon, C.B.E., D.F.C.; I. G. Esplin, O.B.E., D.F.C.; P. C. Fletcher, O.B.E., D.F.C., A.F.C.; A. D. Frank, C.B.E., D.S.O., D.F.C.; A. W. Howard, O.B.E., D.F.C., A.F.C.; F. D. Hughes, C.B.E., D.S.O., D.F.C., A.F.C.; A. H. Humphrey, C.B., O.B.E., D.F.C., A.F.C.; E. James, D.F.C., A.F.C.; R. I. Jones, C.B., A.F.C.; B. R. Macnamara, C.B.E., D.S.O.; L. D. Mavor, A.F.C.; E. J. Morris, C.B.E., D.S.O., D.F.C.; A. B. Riall, C.B.E.; J. R. Whelan, D.S.O., D.F.C.
Scientific Adviser, H. Constant, C.B., C.B.E., F.R.S.
Assistant Scientific Advisers, J. B. Parry, O.B.E.; J. E. Henderson; D. M. Clemmow.
Senior Principal Scientific Officers, R. W. Bevan, O.B.E.; T. H. Kerr, O.B.E.

Department of the Air Member for Personnel.

Air Member for Personnel, Air Chief Marshal Sir Walter Cheshire, K.C.B., C.B.E.
Air Secretary, Air Chief Marshal Sir William MacDonald, K.C.B., C.B.E., D.F.C.
Deputy Air Secretary, Air Vice-Marshal T. A. B. Parselle, C.B., C.B.E.
Directors-General, Air Marshal Sir Richard Nelson, K.C.B., O.B.E., Q.H.P.; Air Vice-Marshals W. E. Coles, C.B.E., D.S.O., D.F.C., A.F.C.; M. K. D. Porter, C.B., C.B.E.; J. G. W. Weston, C.B., O.B.E.
Deputy Director-General, Air Vice-Marshal J. B. Wallace, C.B., O.B.E., Q.H.S.
Directors, Air Vice-Marshal E. Knowles, C.B.E.; Air Vice-Marshal R. Scoggins, C.B.E., Q.H.D.S.; Air Commodores J. E. Allen-Jones, O.B.E.; R. E. Craven, O.B.E., D.F.C.; A. Gollan, O.B.E.; G. R. Gunn, O.B.E.; A. V. R. Johnstone, D.F.C.; F. J. Manning, C.B., C.B.E.; J. C. Millar, D.S.O.; P. E. Warcup, C.B.E.; Air Commandant Dame Jean Conan Doyle, D.B.E., A.D.C. (*Director, W.R.A.F.*); Air Commandant V. M. Ashworth, *R.R.C.* (*Matron-in-Chief*); Group Captains J. L. Crosbie, O.B.E.; J. S. Mason; C. V. G. Usher.
G. A. Roberts, C.B.E.
Chaplain-in-Chief, Ven. F. W. Cocks, C.B., Q.H.C.

Department of the Air Member for Supply and Organization.

Air Member for Supply and Organization, Air Marshal J. G. Davis, C.B., O.B.E.
Controller of Engineering and Equipment, Air Marshal Sir John Baker-Carr, K.B.E., C.B., A.F.C.
Directors-General, Air Vice-Marshals C. Broughton, C.B., C.B.E.; Sir Edgar Lowe, K.B.E., C.B.; M. E. M. Perkins, C.B., C.B.E.; C. M. Stewart, C.B., C.B.E.

Deputy Director-General, K. C. Mann, C.B.E.
Directors, Air Commodores A. G. P. Brightmore; L. C. Dennis, C.B.E.; H. I. Edwards, V.C., C.B., D.S.O., O.B.E., D.F.C., A.D.C.; T. E. J. Fitton, C.B.E.; A. Foden, C.B.E.; I. G. S. Hemming, C.B.E.; F. Hume, C.B.E.; L. A. Jackson, C.B.E., A.D.C.; N. W. Kearon, O.B.E.; W. MacI. King, C.B., C.B.E.; S. W. Lane, C.B.E.; A. R. D. MacDonald, D.F.C.; W. J. Maggs, O.B.E.; A. G. Powell; J. A. Robinson, O.B.E.; S. G. Walker, O.B.E.; Group Capt. N. H. Bennett.
C. F. Burden, O.B.E.

THE METEOROLOGICAL OFFICE

London Road, Bracknell, Berks.
[Bracknell: 2420]

The Meteorological Office is the State Meteorological Service. It forms part of the Air Ministry, the Director-General being responsible to the Secretary of State for Air through the Permanent Under-Secretary of State.

Except for the common services provided by other Government Departments as part of their normal function, the cost of the Meteorological Office is borne by Air Votes.

The gross annual expenditure by the Exchequer, including that on the common services, is of the order of £5,800,000. Of the expenditure chargeable to Air Votes, about £4,200,000 represents expenditure associated with staff and £1,400,000 expenditure on stores, communications and miscellaneous services. Of the total expenditure, over £1,200,000 is recovered from other Government Departments and outside bodies in respect of special services rendered, sales of meteorological equipment, etc.

Director-General of Meteorological Office, Sir Graham Sutton, C.B.E., D.SC., F.R.S.
Chief Scientific Officers, R. C. Sutcliffe, C.B., O.B.E.; A. C. Best, C.B.E.
Deputy Chief Scientific Officers, G. D. Robinson; J. S. Sawyer, F.R.S.; B. C. V. Oddie; P. J. Meade, O.B.E.
Senior Principal Scientific Officers, T. W. V. Jones, I.S.O.; H. L. Wright; C. J. Boyden; F. Pasquill, D.SC.; A. G. Forsdyke; J. C. Cumming, O.B.E.; C. W. G. Daking; A. L. Maidens; V. R. Coles; L. Jacobs; R. J. Murgatroyd, O.B.E.; L. H. Starr, M.B.E.; R. H. Clements; E. Knighting; J. M. Craddock; R. Frith, O.B.E.; S. E. Virgo; L. P. Smith; G. A. Bull; J. Harding; J. K. Bannon; R. F. Jones; G. A. Corby; R. F. Zobel, O.B.E.

ROYAL OBSERVER CORPS

Bentley Priory, Stanmore, Middlesex.

Raised during the First World War and officially established in 1925, the Royal Observer Corps is a voluntary civilian organization. A part of Fighter Command, it has the task in war of identifying and plotting the movements of aircraft, and since 1955 has had the additional *role* of reporting and tracking radioactive "fall-out" for the Services and for the National Warning System.

Air Commodore-in-Chief, H.M. THE QUEEN.
Commandant, Air Commodore C. M. Wight-Boycott, C.B.E., D.S.O.

ROYAL AIR FORCE RESERVE

The Royal Air Force Reserve (including W.R.A.F. Reserve of Officers) consists of officers and men who have served in the regular air force; officers employed on air force duties under special conditions of service; and officers commissioned in ground branches during National Service and transferred to the R.A.F. Reserve of Officers (N.S. List); airmen liable to recall under the Navy, Army and Air Force Reserves Act, 1959 (Class G.); airmen transferred to Class H. of the Reserve for part-time service under the National Service Acts. The Royal Air Force Reserve also includes the Royal Air Force Volunteer Reserve, a pool of officers, airmen and airwomen who train voluntarily on a part-time basis.

MARSHALS OF THE ROYAL AIR FORCE

Sir John M. Salmond, G.C.B., C.M.G., C.V.O., D.S.O., D.C.L., LL.D., *born* July 17, 1881 .... Jan. 1, 1933
H.R.H. the Duke of Windsor, K.G., K.T., K.P., G.C.B., G.C.S.I., G.C.M.G., G.C.I.E., G.C.V.O., G.B.E., I.S.O., M.C., *born* June 23, 1894 .... Jan. 21, 1936
Sir Edward L. Ellington, G.C.B., C.M.G., C.B.E., *born* Dec. 30, 1877 .... Jan. 1, 1937
The Lord Newall, G.C.B., O.M., G.C.M.G., C.B.E., *born* Feb. 15, 1886 .... Oct. 4, 1940
The Viscount Portal of Hungerford, K.G., G.C.B., O.M., D.S.O., M.C., D.C.L., LL.D., *born* May 21, 1893 .... Jan. 1, 1944
The Lord Tedder, G.C.B., D.C.L., LL.D., *born* July 11, 1890 .... Sept. 12, 1945
The Lord Douglas of Kirtleside, G.C.B., M.C., D.F.C., *born* Dec. 23, 1893 .... Jan. 1, 1946
Sir Arthur T. Harris, Bt., G.C.B., O.B.E., A.F.C., LL.D., *born* April 13, 1892 .... Jan. 1, 1946
Sir John C. Slessor, G.C.B., D.S.O., M.C., *born* June 3, 1897 .... June 8, 1950
H.R.H. the Prince Philip, Duke of Edinburgh, K.G., P.C., K.T., G.M.B.E. (*Air Commodore-in-Chief, Air Training Corps, Marshal of the R.A.A.F.*), *born* June 10, 1921 .... Jan. 15, 1953
Sir William F. Dickson, G.C.B., K.B.E., D.S.O., A.F.C., *born* Sept. 24, 1898 .... June 1, 1954
Sir Dermot A. Boyle, G.C.B., K.C.V.O., K.B.E., A.F.C., *born* Oct. 2, 1904 .... Jan. 1, 1958
H.R.H. the Duke of Gloucester, K.G., P.C., K.T., K.P., G.M.B., G.C.M.G., G.C.V.O. (*Personal Aide-de-Camp to the Queen*), *born* March 31, 1900 .... June 12, 1958
Sir Thomas G. Pike, G.C.B., C.B.E., D.F.C. (*Deputy to Supreme Allied Commander, Europe*), *born* June 29, 1906 .... April 6, 1962

AIR CHIEF MARSHALS

Sir Edmund Hudleston, G.C.B., C.B.E., A.D.C. (*Commander Allied Air Forces, Central Europe*).

Sir Hugh A. Constantine, K.B.E., C.B., D.S.O. (*Commandant, Imperial Defence College*).

Sir Denis H. F. Barnett, K.C.B., C.B.E., D.F.C. (*A.O.C.-in-C., Near East Air Force and Commander, British Forces in Cyprus*).

Sir Charles Elworthy, G.C.B., C.B.E., D.S.O., M.V.O., D.F.C. A.F.C. (*Chief of Air Staff*).

Sir Walter G. Cheshire, K.C.B., C.B.E. (*Air Member for Personnel*)

Sir William L. M. MacDonald, K.C.B., C.B.E., D.F.C. (*Air Secretary*).

AIR MARSHALS

Sir Richard Nelson, K.C.B., O.B.E., Q.H.P. (*Director-General of Medical Services*).

Sir Paterson Fraser, K.B.E., C.B., A.F.C. (*Inspector-General*).

Sir Hector McGregor, K.C.B., C.B.E., D.S.O. (*A.O.C.-in-C., Far East Air Force*).

Sir Alfred Earle, K.B.E., C.B. (*A.O.C.-in-C., Technical Training Command*).

Sir Anthony Selway, K.C.B., D.F.C. (*A.O.C.-in-C., Coastal Command*).

Sir Wallace Kyle, K.C.B., C.B.E., D.S.O., D.F.C. (*Vice-Chief of Air Staff*).

Sir Beresford Lees, K.C.B., C.B.E., D.F.C. (*C.-in-C., R.A.F., Germany*).

Sir Kenneth Cross, K.C.B., C.B.E., D.S.O., D.F.C. (*A.O.C.-in-C., Transport Command*).

Sir Douglas Morris, K.C.B., C.B.E., D.S.O., D.F.C. (*A.O.C.-in-C., Fighter Command*).

Sir John Grandy, K.B.E., C.B., D.S.O., (*A.O.C.-in-C., Bomber Command*).

Sir John Baker-Carr, K.B.E., C.B., A.F.C. (*Controller of Engineering and Equipment*).

Sir Leslie Bower, K.C.B., D.S.O., D.F.C.

Sir Maurice Heath, K.B.E., C.B. (*Chief of Staff, Allied Air Force, Central Europe*).

Sir John Grundy, K.B.E., C.B.

Sir Augustus Walker, K.C.B., C.B.E., D.S.O., D.F.C., A.F.C. (*A.O.C.-in-C., Flying Training Command*).

Sir Norman Coslett, K.C.B., O.B.E. (*A.O.C.-in-C., Maintenance Command*).

Sir Christopher Hartley, K.C.B., C.B.E., D.F.C., A.F.C. (*Deputy Chief for the Air Staff*).

J. G. Davis, C.B., O.B.E. (*Air Member for Supply and Organization*).

AIR VICE-MARSHALS

J. G. W. Weston, C.B., O.B.E. (*Director-General of Manning*).

Sir Walter P. G. Pretty, K.B.E., C.B. (*A.O.C.-in-C., Signals Command*).

J. F. Hobler, C.B., C.B.E. (*A.O.A., Far East Force*).

H. J. Kirkpatrick, C.B., C.B.E., D.F.C.

Sir Peter Dixon, K.B.E., Q.H.S.

D. R. Evans, C.B., C.B.E., D.F.C. (*Assistant Chief of the Defence Staff*).

J. Worrall, C.B., D.F.C.

M. H. Dwyer, C.B., C.B.E. (*A.O.A., Bomber Command*).

T. A. B. Parselle, C.B., C.B.E. (*Deputy Air Secretary*).

Sir Edgar Lowe, K.B.E., C.B. (*Director-General of Equipment*).

R. Scoggins, C.B.E., Q.H.D.S. (*Dir., R.A.F. Dental Services*).

D. J. P. Lee, C.B., C.B.E., (*Commandant, R.A.F. Staff College, Bracknell*).

B. K. Burnett, C.B., D.F.C., A.F.C. (*A.O.C., No. 3 Group*).

C. T. Weir, C.B., C.B.E., D.F.C. (*Commandant, School of Land-Air Warfare*).

P. H. Dunn, C.B., C.B.E., D.F.C. (*A.O.C., No. 1 Group*).

F. S. Stapleton, C.B., D.S.O., D.F.C. (*S.A.S.O., Transport Command*).

Sir Aubrey Rumball, K.B.E., Q.H.P. (*Senior Consultant, Central Medical Establishment*).

The Ven. F. W. Cocks, C.B., Q.H.C. (*Chaplain-in-Chief*).

P. D. Holder, D.S.O., D.F.C. (*A.O.C., No. 25 Group*).

A. Foord-Kelcey, C.B.E., A.F.C. (*Assistant Chief of the Air Staff (Intelligence)*).

Sir Colin Scragg, K.B.E., C.B., A.F.C. (*Deputy Controller, R.A.F., Ministry of Aviation*).

H. J. Maguire, C.B., D.S.O., O.B.E. (*S.A.S.O., Far East Air Force*).

R. N. Bateson, D.S.O., D.F.C. (*S.A.S.O., Fighter Command*).

P. G. Wykeham, C.B., D.S.O., O.B.E., D.F.C., A.F.C. (*Director, Joint Warfare Staff*).

H. Ford, C.B., C.B.E., A.F.C.

T. U. C. Shirley, C.B., C.B.E. (*Deputy Controller of Electronics, Ministry of Aviation*).

C. Broughton, C.B., C.B.E. (*Director-General of Organization*).

T. O. Prickett, C.B., D.S.O., D.F.C. (*Assistant Chief of the Air Staff (Policy and Planning)*).

T. W. Piper, C.B.E., A.F.C. (*A.O.C., No. 38 Group*).

H. B. Wrigley, C.B., C.B.E. (*S.T.S.O., Fighter Command*).

G. C. Eveleigh, O.B.E. (*A.O.A., Fighter Command*).

J. R. Gordon-Finlayson, D.S.O., D.F.C.

W. E. Coles, C.B., C.B.E., D.S.O., D.F.C., A.F.C. (*Director-General of Personal Services*).

E. L. Colbeck-Welch, C.B., O.B.E., D.F.C.

M. E. M. Perkins, C.B., C.B.E. (*Director-General of Engineering*).

E. Knowles, C.B.E., (*Director of Educational Services*).

P. T. Philpott, C.B.E. (*A.O.C., No. 23 Group*).

F. E. Rosier, C.B., C.B.E., D.S.O.

E. G. Jones, C.B., C.B.E., D.S.O., D.F.C. (*Senior Directing Staff, Imperial Defence College*).

D. F. Spotswood, C.B., C.B.E., D.S.O., D.F.C. (*A.C.O.S., Air Defence, S.H.A.P.E.*)

J. S. Wilson, C.B.E., Q.H.P. (*P.M.O., Bomber Command*).

G. H. White, C.B., C.B.E.

K. V. Garside, C.B., D.F.C., (*A.O.C., No. 18 Group*).

R. B. Thomson, C.B., D.S.O., D.F.C. (*A.O.A., Flying Training Command*).

A. A. Case, C.B.E. (*A.O.C., No. 22 Group*).

G. T. B. Clayton, C.B., D.F.C. (*A.O.C., R.A.F., Germany*).

R. H. E. Emson, C.B., C.B.E. (*Assistant Chief of the Air Staff (Operational Requirements)*).

T. C. Macdonald, C.B., A.F.C., Q.H.P. (*P.M.O., Technical Training Command*).

G. H. Morley, C.B.E., Q.H.S.

B. A. Chacksfield, C.B., O.B.E. (*Commandant-General, R.A.F. Regiment and Inspector of Ground Defences*).

S. W. R. Hughes, C.B.E., A.F.C. (*A.O.C., No. 19 Group*).

M. K. D. Porter, C.B., C.B.E. (*Director-General of Ground Training*).

J. B. Wallace, C.B., O.B.E., Q.H.S. (*Deputy Director-General of Medical Services*).

C. M. Stewart, C.B., C.B.E. (*Director-General of Signals*).

S. W. B. Menaul, C.B., C.B.E., D.F.C., A.F.C. (*S.A.S.O., Bomber Command*).

D. C. McKinley, C.B.E., D.F.C., A.F.C. (*Deputy C.-in-C. (Air), Allied Forces, Mediterranean and A.O.C., Malta*).

J. E. Johnson, C.B.E., D.S.O., D.F.C. (*A.O.C., Air Forces, Middle East*).

I. G. Esplin, C.B., O.B.E., D.F.C. (*Commander, R.A.F. British Defence Staffs (U.S.A.) and Air Attaché, Washington*).

C. J. R. Salmon, C.B., O.B.E. (*S.A.S.O., Maintenance Command*).

J. L. Barker, C.B., C.B.E., D.F.C.

J. B. Russell, C.B.E., D.S.O. (*S.A.S.O., Coastal Command*).

B. Ball, C.B., C.B.E. (*S.A.S.O., Technical Training Command*).

W. V. Crawford-Compton, C.B.E., D.S.O., D.F.C. (*S.A.S.O., Near East Air Force*).

D. C. Stapleton, C.B., C.B.E., D.F.C., A.F.C.

P. H. Holmes, O.B.E. (*A.O.A., Maintenance Command*).

J. K. Rotherham, C.B., C.B.E. (*A.O.C., No. 24 Group*).

AIR COMMODORES (ACTING AIR VICE-MARSHALS)

N. C. S. Rutter, C.B.E. (*S.T.S.O., Bomber Command*).

R. C. Ayling, C.B.E. (*S.A.S.O., Flying Training Command*).

F. J. Manning, C.B., C.B.E. (*A.O.A., Near East Air Force*).

D. G. Smallwood, C.B.E., D.S.O., D.F.C. (*Assistant Chief of the Air Staff (Operations)*).

D. N. Kingston-Blair-Oliphant, O.B.E. (*Vice-President, Ordnance Board*).

H. G. Leonard-Williams, C.B.E., (*A.O.A., Far East Air Force*).

H. N. G. Wheeler, C.B.E., D.S.O., D.F.C., A.F.C. (*S.A.S.O., R.A.F., Germany*).

G. L. Seabrook (*A.O.A., Technical Training Command*).

The Church of England

Province of Canterbury

CANTERBURY. £7,500.

100th *Archbishop and Primate of All England*, Rt. Hon. and Most Rev. Arthur Michael Ramsey, D.D. (Lambeth Palace, S.E.1.), *cons.* 1952, *trs.* 1956 and 1961. [Signs Michael Cantuar:]... 1961
Assistant Bishops, Rt. Rev. Alfred Carey Wollaston Rose, M.A.; (*cons.* 1935)................1956
Rt. Rev. Kenneth Charles Harman Warner, D.D. (*cons.* 1947)..........................1962
Rt. Rev. Norman Harry Clarke, M.A. (*cons.* 1950)..................................1962

Bishops Suffragan.

Dover, Rt. Rev. Lewis Evans Meredith, M.A. (Upway, St. Martin's Hill, Canterbury).....1957
Croydon, Rt. Rev. John Taylor Hughes, M.A. (44 Birdhurst Rise, South Croydon)...........1956
Maidstone, Rt. Rev. Stanley Woodley Betts, M.A. (21 Streatham Common South, S.W.16)....1956

Dean (£2,000 nominal).

Very Rev. Ian Hugh White-Thomson, M.A...1963

Canons Residentiary (each £1,000 nominal).

F. J. J. Shirley, Ph.D. 1935 | Archdn. Strutt.....1959
Archdn. Sargent..1939 | H. M. Waddams, M.A. 1961

Organist, Allan Wicks, M.A................1961

Archdeacons.

Canterbury, Ven. Alexander Sargent, M.A.....1942
Croydon, Ven. J. A. M. Clayson, A.K.C.......1957
Maidstone, Ven. R. G. Strutt, B.D............1959

Beneficed Clergy, 274; *Licensed under Seal, etc.* 57; *Curates*, 65.

Vicar-General of Province and Diocese, Rt. Hon. Sir Henry Willink, Bt., M.C., Q.C., D.C.L.
Commissary of Diocese, Lord Dunboyne.......1959
Registrar of the Province and Archbishop's Legal Sec., D. M. M. Carey, M.A., 1 The Sanctuary, S.W.1.
Registrar of the Diocese of Canterbury, D. M. M. Carey, M.A., Diocesan House, Lady Wootton's Green, Canterbury.

LONDON. £5,000.

114th *Bishop*, Rt. Hon. and Rt. Rev. Robert Wright Stopford, C.B.E., D.D., D.C.L., *cons.* 1955, *trs.* 1956 and 1961 (Fulham Palace, S.W.6) [Signs Robert Londin:]..........................1961

Bishops Suffragan.

Willesden, Rt. Rev. George Ernest Ingle, M.A. (20 West Heath Avenue, N.W.11) (*cons.* 1949). 1955
Kensington, Rt. Rev. Edward James Keymer Roberts, M.A. (19 Campden Hill Square, W.8) (*cons.* 1956)..............................1962
Stepney, Rt. Rev. Francis Evered Lunt, M.A. (25 Compton Terrace, N.1)..................1957
Fulham (*for North and Central Europe*), Rt. Rev. Roderic Norman Coote, D.D. (Woodham Parkway, nr. Byfleet, Surrey) (*cons.* 1951)......1957
Assistant Bishops, Rt. Rev. Frederick William Thomas Craske, B.A. (*cons.* 1953) 1961; Rt. Rev. Nathaniel William Newnham-Davis, M.A. (*cons.* 1944) 1961; Rt. Rev. Richard Ambrose Reeves, S.T.D. (*cons.* 1949)...........................1962

Dean of St. Pauls (£2,000).

Very Rev. Walter Robert Matthews, K.C.V.O., C.H., D.Lit., D.D., The Deanery, Dean's Court, E.C.4 1934

Canons Residentiary (each £1,000).

L. J. Collins, M.A...1948 | A. F. Hood, M.A...1960
Rt. Hon. and Rt. Rev. J. W. C. Wand, K.C.V.O., D.D.....1955 | Archd. Sullivan...1963

Organist, J. Dykes Bower, C.V.O., M.A., Mus. Doc., F.R.C.O...................................1936

Receiver of St. Paul's, E. T. Floyd Ewin, M.V.O.

Archdeacons.

London, Ven. M. G. Sullivan, M.A............1963
Middlesex, Ven. A. J. Morcom, M.A..........1953
Hampstead, Ven. G. D. Leonard, M.A.........1962
Hackney, Ven. M. M. Hodgins...............1951

Beneficed Clergy, 553; *Curates, &c.*, 597.

Chancellor and Commissary of the Dean and Chapter (1961), W. S. Wigglesworth, M.A., Ll.B. D.C.L. 1954
Registrar, Graham D. Heath, 1 The Sanctuary, S.W.1..................................1939
Chapter Clerk, Graham D. Heath, 1 The Sanctuary, S.W.1.

Westminster. £3,000.

(*The Collegiate Church of St. Peter—A Royal Peculiar*)

Dean, Very Rev. Eric Symes Abbott, M.A...1959

Canons Residentiary (£1,200 to £1,400)

Archd. Carpenter. 1951 | M. A. C. Warren, M.A.,
M.S. Stancliffe, M.A.1957 | D.D...........1963

Archdeacon, Ven. E. F. Carpenter, Ph.D., M.A., D.D.......................................1963
Chapter Clerk and Receiver General, W. R. J. Pullen, Ll.B.................................1963
Registrar, T. Hebron, C.B.E., M.V.O., M.A......1938
Precentor, Rev. R. Simpson..................1963
Organist, D. Guest, M.A., Mus.B., A.R.C.O......1963
Legal Secretary, J. S. Widdows, M.B.E.........1963

WINCHESTER. £3,000.

93rd *Bishop*, Rt. Rev. Sherard Falkner Allison, D.D., Ll.D., (*cons.* 1951). (Wolvesey, Winchester) [Signs Falkner Winton:]..................1961

Bishop Suffragan.

Southampton, Rt. Rev. Kenneth Edward Norman Lamplugh, M.A. (The Close, Winchester)...1951
Assistant Bishop, Rt. Rev. Nigel Edmund Cornwall, C.B.E., M.A. (*cons.* 1949)...................1963

Dean (£2,000).

Very Rev. Oswin Harvard Gibbs-Smith, C.B.E., M.A..1961

Dean of Jersey, Very Rev. Alan Stanley Giles, C.B.E., M.A......................1959
Dean of Guernsey, Very Rev. Edward Louis Frossard, M.A.............................1947

Canons Residentiary (£1,000).

R. B. Lloyd, M.A 1937 | E. A. de Mendieta, Ph.D............ 1962
W. D. Maundrell, M.A. 1961 | Bp. Cornwall 1963

Precentor, Rev. Canon J. P. Boden..........1939
Organist, Alwyn Surplice, F.R.C.O.............1949

Archdeacons

Winchester, Ven. J. R. Beynon..............1962
Basingstoke, Ven. R. C. Rudgard, O.B.E.. T.D...1958

Beneficed Clergy, 289; *Curates, &c.*, 70.

Chancellor, D. C. Bain, M.C., Q.C............1962
Registrar, G. H. Gardner, O.B.E., Winchester ..1939
Legal Secretary, Graham D. Heath, 1 The Sanctuary, S.W.1.

BATH AND WELLS. £2,700.

73rd *Bishop*, Rt. Rev. Edward Barry Henderson, D.S.C., D.D., *cons.* 1955. (The Palace, Wells.) [Signs Edward Bath: et Well:]...........1960

Bishop Suffragan.

Taunton, Rt. Rev. Francis Horner West, M.A..1962
Assistant Bishops, Rt. Rev. Douglas John Wilson, M.A. (*cons.* 1938).......................1956
Rt. Rev. Fabian Menteath Elliot Jackson, M.A. (*cons.* 1946)..........................1950

Dean (£1,200)
Very Rev. Irven David Edwards, M.A. 1963
Canons Residentiary of Wells (each £600).
J. S. L. Jones, B.A., 1947 D. S. Bailey, D.D... 1962
Bp. Wilson........1956 Archd. Lance......1963
Organist, D. D. R. Pouncey, Mus.Bac., F.R.C.O.. 1936
Archdeacons
Bath, Ven. A. Hopley 1962
Taunton, Ven. G. F. Hilder, M.A. 1951
Wells, Ven. J. du B. Lance, M.C., M.A. 1963
Beneficed Clergy, 490; *Curates, &c.*, 70.
Chancellor, W. S. Wigglesworth, M.A., LL.B...1942
Registrar, Sec. & Chapt. Clerk, C. W. Harris, Wells.

BIRMINGHAM. £2,200

4th Bishop, Rt. Rev. John Leonard Wilson, C.M.G., D.D., *cons.* 1941. (Bishop's Croft, Harborne, Birmingham 17.) [Signs Leonard Birmingham] 1953
Bishop Suffragan.
Aston, Rt. Rev. David Brownfield Porter, M.A. (139 Salisbury Road, Moseley, Birmingham 13) 1962
Provost, Rt. Rev. George Sinker, M.A. 1962
Archdeacons.
Aston, Ven. M. T. Dunlop, M.A. 1955
Birmingham, Ven S. Harvie Clark, M.A. 1947
Beneficed Clergy, 167. *Curates, &c.*, 72.
Organist, T. N. Tunnard, M.A., B.Mus., A.R.C.O.. 1958
Chancellor, H. E. Salt, Q.C. 1957
Registrar and Legal Secretary, R. L. Ekin, B.A. (85 Cornwall Street, Birmingham 3).

BRISTOL. £2,200.

52nd Bishop, Rt. Rev. Oliver Stratford Tomkins, D.D. (Bishop's House, Clifton Hill, Bristol 8) [Signs Oliver Bristol] 1959
Bishop Suffragan.
Malmesbury, Rt. Rev. Clifford Leofric Purdy Bishop, B.A. (73 Pembroke Road, Clifton, Bristol 8) 1962
Dean.
Very Rev. Douglas Ernest William Harrison, M.A. 1957
Canons Residentiary.
J. R. Peacey M.C., M.A. ....1945 | C. S. Milford, M.C., M.A. 1962
B. S. Moss, M.A. ... 1960 | Bishop of Malmesbury 1962
Organist, Clifford Harker, B.Mus., F.R.C.O., A.R.C.M. 1949
Archdeacons.
Bristol, Ven. P. G. Reddick, M.A. 1950
Swindon, Ven. C. W. J. Bowles, M.A. 1963
Beneficed Clergy, 144; *Curates, &c.*, 54.
Chancellor, J. Clifford Perks, M.C., M.A. 1950
Registrar and Sec., J. L. Press, M.A. 1949

CHELMSFORD. £3,000.

5th Bishop, Rt. Rev. John Gerhard Tiarks, M.A. (Bishopscourt, Chelmsford) [Signs John Chelmsford] 1962
Bishops Suffragan.
Colchester, Rt. Rev. Frederick Dudley Vaughan Narborough, B.D. (Derby House, Colchester) 1946
Barking, Rt. Rev. William Frank Percival Chadwick, M.A. (West Dene, Whitehall Lane, Buckhurst Hill) 1959
Provost, Very Rev. George Eric Gordon, M.A.. 1951
Organist, P. S. Ledger, B.A., B. Mus., F.R.C.O..... 1962
Archdeacons
Southend, Ven. W. N. Welch, M.A. 1953
West Ham, Ven J. E. Elvin 1957
Colchester, Ven. A. V. G. Cleall, M.A. 1959
Beneficed Clergy, 448; *Curates, &c.*, 192.
Chancellor, Sir Ernest Goodman Roberts, Q.C.. 1950
Diocesan Registrar, D. W. Faull, 1 The Sanctuary, S.W.1 1963

CHICHESTER. £2,200.

98th Bishop Rt Rev. Roger Plumpton Wilson D.D. (*cons.* 1949, *trans.* 1958) (The Palace, Chichester) [Signs Roger Cicestr.] 1958
Bishop Suffragan.
Lewes, Rt. Rev. James Herbert Lloyd Morrell, M.A. (83 Davigdor Road, Hove) 1959
Dean
Very Rev. John Walter Atherton Hussey, M.A. 1955
Canons Residentiary.
W. K. L. Clarke D.D. 1945 | D. R. Hutchinson, M.A. 1961
Archd. Mason......1949 |
Organist J. A. Birch, F.R.C.O. 1958
Archdeacons.
Chichester, Ven. L. Mason, M.A. 1946
Hastings, Ven. G. Mayfield, M.A. 1959
Lewes, Ven. D. H. Booth, M.B.E., M.A. 1956
Beneficed Clergy, 360; *Curates, &c.*. 133.
Chancellor, B. T. Buckle, M.A. 1960
Legal Secretary to the Bishop, and Diocesan Registrar, J. S. Widdows, M.B.E.

COVENTRY. £2,200.

5th Bishop, Rt. Rev. Cuthbert Killick Norman Bardsley, C.B.E., D.D. (The Bishop's House, 23 Davenport Road, Coventry.) [Signs Cuthbert Coventry.] 1956
Assistant Bishop, Rt. Rev. John David McKie, M.A. (*cons.* 1946) 1960
Provost, Very Rev. Harold Claude Noel Williams, B.A. 1958
Organist, D. F. Lepine 1961
Canons Residentiary.
E. H. Patey, M.A. ....1958 J. W. Poole, M.A.. 1963
Archdeacons.
Coventry, Ven. L. J. Stanford, M.A. 1946
Warwick, Ven. J. H. Proctor, M.A. 1958
Beneficed Clergy, 164, *Curates, &c.*, 42.
Chancellor, His Hon. Conolly Hugh Gage, M.A. 1948
Registrar, S. L. Penn, Coventry 1957

DERBY. £2,500.

3rd Bishop, Rt. Rev. Geoffrey Francis Allen, D.D., (*cons.* 1947) (Bishop's House, Breadsall, Derby.) [Signs Geoffrey Derby] 1959
Assistant Bishop, Rt. Rev. Thomas Richards Parfitt, M.A. (*cons.* 1952) 1962
Provost, Very Rev. Ronald Alfred Beddoes, M.A. 1953
Canons Residentiary.
Archd. Richardson. 1955 | W. James 1955
Archdeacons.
Derby, Ven. J. F. Richardson, M.A. 1952
Chesterfield Ven. T. W. I. Cleasby, M.A. 1963
Organist, W. M. Ross, Mus. Bac., F.R.C.O. 1958
Beneficed Clergy, 252; *Curates, &c.*, 45.
Chancellor, W. S. Wigglesworth, M.A., LL.B. .. 1944
Registrar, J. R. S. Grimwood-Taylor, Derby.

ELY. £2,500.

64th Bishop, Rt. Rev. Noel Baring Hudson, D.S.O., M.C., D.D. (*cons.* 1931, *trans.* 1941 *and* 1956) (The Bishop's House, Ely) [Signs Noel Ely].... 1956
Assistant Bishop, Rt. Rev. Gordon John Walsh, D.D. (*cons.* 1927) 1942
Dean (£1,700).
Very Rev. Cyril Patrick Hankey, M.A. 1950
Canons Residentiary (each £850).
Bp. Walsh.........1942 | D. G. Hill, M.A.... 1960
B. C. Pawley, M.A...1959 | G. W. Lampe, M.C., D.D. 1960
Organist, A. W. Wills, Mus. Doc., F.R.C.O. 1959
Archdeacons.
Ely, Ven. M. S. Carey, M.A. 1961

Huntingdon, Ven. A. Royle, M.A. 1954
Wisbech, Ven. J. P. Pelloe, M.A. 1953
Beneficed Clergy, 250; *Curates, &c.*, 85.
Chancellor, Kenneth M. Macmorran, Q.C., LL.B. 1924
Deputy Registrar, B. D. Boyd, Cintra House, 16 Hills Road, Cambridge
Secretary, D. M. Moir Carey, M.A., 1 The Sanctuary, S.W.1.

EXETER. £2,200.

67th Bishop, Rt. Rev. Robert Cecil Mortimer, D.D. (The Palace, Exeter). [Signs Robert Exon:]. 1949

Bishops Suffragan.

Crediton, Rt. Rev. Wilfrid Arthur Edmund Westall, B.A. (The Close, Exeter) 1954
Plymouth, Rt. Rev. Wilfrid Guy Sanderson, M.A. (Lynn, Bainbridge Avenue, Hartley, Plymouth) 1962

Dean (£2,000).

Very Rev. Marcus Knight, B.D. 1960

Canons Residentiary (each £1,000).

H. Balmforth, M.A. 1956 | Archd. Hawkins ...1962
Archd. Babington 1958

Organist, L. Dakers 1957
Chapter Clerk, D. Lyon-Smith, B.A. 1960

Archdeacons.

Barnstaple, Ven. A. F. Ward, B.A. 1962
Totnes, Ven. J. S. Hawkins, M.A. 1962
Plymouth, Ven. F. A. J. Matthews, M.A. 1962
Exeter, Ven. R. H. Babington, M.A. 1958
Beneficed Clergy, 400; *Curates, &c.*, 69
Chancellor, W. S. Wigglesworth, M.A., LL.B. ...1941
Registrar and Secretary, J. F. G. Michelmore, 18 Cathedral Yard, Exeter.

GLOUCESTER. £2,500

36th Bishop, Rt. Rev. Basil Tudor Guy, M.A. (*cons.* 1957) (Palace House, Gloucester) [Signs Basil Gloucestr:] 1962

Bishop Suffragan.

Tewkesbury, Rt. Rev. Forbes Trevor Horan, M.A. 1960

Dean (about £1,500).

Very Rev. Seiriol John Arthur Evans, M.A., F.S.A 1953

Canons Residentiary (each about £750).

J. McIntyre, D.D. 1940 | C. F. Pare, M.A. ...1963

Organist, Herbert Sumsion, C.B.E., D.Mus., F.R.C.O. 1923

Archdeacons.

Gloucester, Ven. W. T. Wardle, M.A. 1948
Cheltenham, Ven. R. H. Sutch, M.A. 1951
Beneficed Clergy, 260; *Curates, &c.*, 29.
Chancellor & Vicar-Gen., Rev. E. Garth Moore, M.A. 1957
Registrar & Sec., H. A. Gibson, 34 Brunswick Road, Gloucester 1957
Legal Sec., D. M. M. Carey, 1 The Sanctuary, Westminster, S.W.1.

GUILDFORD. £3,000.

5th Bishop, Rt. Rev. George Edmund Reindorp, D.D. (Willow Grange, Stringer's Common, Guildford) [Signs George Guildford] 1961
Assistant Bishops, Rt. Rev. Basil Montague Dale, M.A. (*cons.* 1950) 1957
Rt. Rev. Francis Featherstonhaugh Johnston, C.B.E., M.A. (*cons.* 1952) 1961
Rt. Rev. St. John Surridge Pike, D.D. (*cons.* 1958) 1963
Dean, Rt. Rev. George William Clarkson, M.A. 1961

Canons Residentiary

C. T. Chapman, Ph.D. 1961 | A. C. G. Oldham, A.K.C. 1961
Archd. Evans ...1963

Organist, B. Rose 1906

Archdeacons.

Surrey, Ven. A. J. de C. Studdert, M.A. 1957
Dorking, Ven. K. D. Evans, M.A. 1963
Beneficed Clergy, 152; *Curates, &c.*, 77.
Chancellor, K. M. Macmorran, Q.C., LL.B.
Legal Sec., Graham D. Heath, M.A.
Registrar of Diocese, Graham D. Heath, M.A.
Registrar of the Archdeaconries, D. M. Moir Carey, M.A.

HEREFORD. £3,000.

102nd Bishop, Rt. Rev. Mark Allin Hodson, B.A. (The Palace, Hereford), *cons.* 1956 [Signs Mark Hereford] 1961
Assistant Bishop, Right Rev. William Arthur Partridge, B.A. (*cons.* 1953) 1963

Dean (£2,000).

Very Rev. Robert Peel Price, M.A. 1961

Canons Residentiary (£933).

H. A. V. Moreton, D.Litt. 1935 | E. F. H. Dunnicliff, M.A. 1960
Archd. Randolph ...1961

Organist, Melville Cook, D.Mus., F.R.C.O. 1956

Archdeacons.

Hereford, Ven. T. B. Randolph, M.A. 1959
Ludlow, Ven J. W. Lewis, M.A. 1960
Beneficed Clergy, 226; *Curates, &c.*, 18.
Chancellor, K. J. T. Elphinstone 1952
Registrar, Philip Gwynne James, 5 St. Peter Street, Hereford.

LEICESTER. £2,500.

3rd Bishop, Rt. Rev. Ronald Ralph Williams, D.D. (Bishop's Lodge, Leicester.) [Signs Ronald Leicester] 1953
Assistant Bishops, Rt. Rev. Harold Alexander Maxwell, M.A. (*cons.* 1943) 1950
Rt. Rev. James Lawrence Cecil Horstead, C.M.G., C.B.E., D.D. (*cons.* 1936) 1961
Provost, Very Rev. John Chester Hughes, M.A. 1963

Canons Residentiary.

*F. M. Cray, B.A. 1951 | F. W. Pratt, B.A. ...1958
*R. Chalmers, T.D., M.A. 1954 | D. W. Gundry, B.D., M.Th. 1963

*Without residence or stipend.

Organist, George C. Gray, Mus.Bac., F.R.C.O. ..1930

Archdeacons.

Leicester, Ven. R. B. Cole 1963
Loughborough, Ven. H. Lockley, Ph.D. 1963
Beneficed Clergy, 220; *Curates, &c.*, 45.
Chancellor, R. A. Forrester, M.A. 1953

LICHFIELD. £3,000.

95th Bishop, Right Rev. Arthur Stretton Reeve, D.D. (22 The Close, Lichfield.) [Signs Stretton Lichfield] 1953

Bishops Suffragan.

Shrewsbury, Rt. Rev. William Alonzo Parker, M.A. (10 St. Mary's Place, Shrewsbury) 1959
Stafford, Rt. Rev. Richard George Clitherow, M.A. (Eversley, Bramshall Road, Uttoxeter) 1958

Dean (£1,500).

Very Rev. William Stuart Macpherson, M.A. . 1953

Canons Residentiary (each £900).

A. B. Lavelle, M.A., B.D., Ph.D. ......1959 | Archd. Stratton ...1960
D. K. Robertson, B.A. 1960

Organist, R. G. Greening, M.A., B.Mus., F.R.C.O. 1959

Archdeacons.

Stafford, Ven. B. Stratton, M.A. 1959
Salop, Ven. S. D. Austerberry 1959
Stoke on Trent, Ven. G. Youell 1956
Beneficed Clergy, 406; *Curates, &c.*, 141.
Chancellor, His Hon. C. H. Gage 1954
Diocesan Registrar and Bishop's Sec., M. B. S. Exham.

LINCOLN. £3,000.

68th Bishop, Rt. Rev. Kenneth Riches, D.D. (*cons.* 1952, *trans.* 1956 (Bishop's House, Eastgate, Lincoln). [Signs Kenneth Lincoln:] 1956

Bishops Suffragan.
Grimsby, Rt. Rev. Kenneth Healey, M.A. (48 Lee Road, Lincoln) 1958
Grantham, Rt. Rev. Anthony Otter, M.A. (Stoke Rectory, Grantham) 1949

Dean (£2,000).
Rt. Rev. David Colin Dunlop, M.A. 1949

Canons Residentiary (each £1,000).
M. H. R. Synge, M.A. 1959 | Archd. Jarvis 1960
N. S. Rathbone, M.A. 1956 | P. B. G. Binnall, M.A., F.S.A. 1962

Organist, Gordon Slater, Mus.Doc. 1930

Archdeacons.
Stow, Ven. M. R. Sinker, M.A. 1963
Lindsey, Ven. A. C. Jarvis, M.A. 1960
Lincoln, Ven. A. C. Smith, V.R.D., M.A. 1960
Beneficed Clergy, 370; *Curates, &c.*, 110.
Chancellor, K. M. Macmorran, Q.C., LL.B. 1937
Registrar, H. J. J. Griffith, 2 Bank Street, Lincoln.

NORWICH. £2,500.

68th Bishop (109th of *East Anglia*), Rt. Rev. William Launcelot Scott Fleming, D.D. (*cons.* 1949, *trans.* 1959) (Bishop's House, Norwich) [Signs Launcelot Norvic] 1959

Bishops Suffragan.
Lynn, Rt. Rev. William Somers Llewellyn, M.A. 1963
Thetford, Rt. Rev. Eric William Bradley Cordingly, M.B.E. 1963
Dean (£1,500), Very Rev. Norman Hook, M.A. 1952

Canons Residentiary.
R. A. Edwards, M.A. 1948 Bp. of Thetford 1962
J. Waring, M.A. 1951
Organist, Heathcote Statham, Mus.Doc. 1928

Archdeacons.
Norfolk, The Bishop of Thetford 1962
Norwich, Ven. W. A. Aitken, M.A. 1961
Lynn, The Bishop of Lynn 1961
Beneficed Clergy, 388; *Curates, &c.*, 30.
Chancellor, J. H. Ellison, M.A. 1955
Registrar & Sec., B. O. L. Prior.
London Sec., D. M. Moir Carey, M.A.

OXFORD. £2,500.

38th Bishop, Rt. Rev. Harry James Carpenter, D.D. (Cuddesdon, Oxford) [Signs Harry Oxon] . 1955

Bishops Suffragan.
Reading, Rt. Rev. Eric Henry Knell, M.A. (Christ Church Vicarage, Reading) 1955
Dorchester, Rt. Rev. David Goodwin Loveday, M.A. (Wardington, Banbury) 1957
Buckingham, Rt. Rev. Gordon David Savage, M.A. 1960
Assistant Bishop, Rt. Rev. Robert Milton Hay, M.A., B.D. (*cons.* 1944) 1960

Dean of Christ Church (£3,000)
Very Rev. Cuthbert Aikman Simpson, D.D. .. 1959

Canons Residentiary (£1,500).
The Canons of Christ Church (with the exception of the Archdeacon of Oxford) are Professors in the University of Oxford.
F. L. Cross, D.Phil. . 1944 | H. Chadwick, D.D. 1958
V. A. Demant, D.D. 1949 | S. L. Greenslade, D.D. 1959
Archd. Witton-Davies 1956

Organist, Sydney Watson, M.A., D.Mus. ... 1955

Archdeacons.
Oxford, Ven. C. Witton-Davies, M.A. 1956
Berks, Bishop of Reading 1954
Bucks, Ven. J. F. I. Pratt, M.A. 1961
Beneficed Clergy, 542; *Curates, &c.*, 310.
Chancellor, P. T. S. Boydell 1958
Registrar and Legal Sec., Peter Winckworth 1948

Windsor. £2,600.

(*The Queen's Free Chapel of St. George within Her Castle of Windsor—A Royal Peculiar*)
Dean, Very Rev. Robert Wylmer Woods, M.A. 1962

Canons Residentiary (each £1,500).
G. B. Bentley, M.A. 1957 | J. A. Fisher, M.A. .. 1958
R. H. Hawkins, M.A. 1958

Organist, S. S. Campbell, D.Mus., F.R.C.O. 1961
Chapter Clerk, D. Alexander.

PETERBOROUGH £3,000.

34th Bishop, Rt. Rev Cyril Eastaugh, M.C., M.A. (The Palace, Peterborough) [Signs Cyril Petriburg] (*cons.* 1949) 1961
Assistant Bishops, Rt. Rev. Weston Henry Stewart, C.B.E., D.D. (*cons.* 1943) 1957
Rt. Rev. Hugh Van Lynden Otter-Barry, C.B.E., M.A. (*cons.* 1931) 1960

Dean (£2,000).
Very Rev. Noel Charles Christopherson, M.C., M.A 1943

Canons Residentiary (each £1,200).
Archd. Millard ..... 1946 | H. G. G. Herklots, M.A. 1959
J. L. Cartwright, M.A., 1951

Master of the Music, W. S. Vann, Mus. Bac. F.R.C.O. [1953

Archdeacons.
Northampton, Ven. R. C. O Goodchild M.A. .. 1959
Oakham, Ven. E. N. Millard, M.A. 1946
Beneficed Clergy, 250; *Curates, &c.* 30.
Chancellor, T. R. Fitzwalter Butler, O.B.E. 1962
Joint Registrars, A. F. Percival, M.A., and E. T. Channell, 37 Priestgate, Peterborough.

PORTSMOUTH.

5th Bishop, Rt. Rev. John Henry Lawrence Phillips, D.D. (Bishopswood, Fareham, Hants.) [Signs John Portsmouth] 1960
Assistant Bishops, Rt. Rev. Bryan Percival Robin, M.A. (*cons.* 1941) 1959
Rt. Rev. Frank Noel Chamberlain, C.B., O.B.E., M.A. (*cons.* 1957) 1961
Provost, Very Rev. Eric Noel Porter Goff, M.A. 1939
Organist, M. G. Menzies.

Canons Residentiary.
The Provost ...... 1939 | E. C. S. Lowman, M.A. 1962
C. Foster, Ph.D. ... 1959

Archdeacons.
Portsmouth, Ven. M. D. S. Peck, M.A. 1956
I. of Wight, Ven. G. L. Tiarks, M.A. 1961
Beneficed Clergy, 110; *Curates, &c.*, 69.
Chancellor W. S. Wigglesworth, M.A., LL.B. ... 1940
Registrar and Legal Sec., T. B. Birkett, 132 High Street, Portsmouth 1957

ROCHESTER. £2,500

104th Bishop, Rt. Rev. Richard David Say, D.D. (Bishopscourt, Rochester), [Signs David Roffen:] [1961

Bishop Suffragan.
Tonbridge, Rt. Rev. Russell Berridge White, M.A. 1959
Assistant Bishop, Rt. Rev. John Charles Mann, D.D. (*cons.* 1935) 1953

Dean (£2,000).
Rt. Rev Robert William Stannard, M.A. 1959

Canons Residentiary.
Archdeacon Harland 1951 | S. Y. Blanch, M.A. . 1960
A. G. G. C. Pentreath, M.A. .... 1958 | R. S. Hook, M.C., M.A. 1961

Organist, R. J. Ashfield, D.Mus., F.R.C.O. 1956

Archdeacons.

Rochester, Ven. L. W. Harland, M.B.E., M.A. ..1951
Tonbridge, Ven. E. E. Maples Earle, M.A. 1952
Bromley, Ven. R. G. H. McCahearty, M.A....1955

Beneficed Clergy, 223; *Curates, &c.*, 76.

Chancellor P. C. Lamb, Q.C., M.A. 1955
Registrars, H. S. Wharton (1949) and O. R. Woodfield (1955), Rochester.
Sec. D. W. Faull, 1 The Sanctuary, S.W.1....1963

ST. ALBANS. £2,500.

6th Bishop, Rt. Rev. Edward Michael Gresford Jones, D.D. (*High Almoner to Her Majesty the Queen*) (Abbey Gate House, St. Albans.) [Signs Michael St. Albans] (*cons.* 1942).....1950
Assistant Bishop, Rt. Rev. John Boys, B.A. (*cons.* 1948).................................1961

Bishop Suffragan.

Bedford, Rt. Rev. Albert John Trillo, M.Th., B.D., A.K.C. (Long Croft, 32 Couch Hall Lane, Redbourn) 1963

Dean (£1,500) (vacant).
Organist, P. Hurford, M.A., Mus.B., F.R.C.O., A.R.C.M. [1958

Archdeacons.

St. Albans, Ven. B. C. Snell, M.A. 1962
Bedford, Ven. J. T. H. Hare, M.A. 1962

Beneficed Clergy, 269; *Curates, &c.*, 95.

Chancellor, G. H. Newsom, Q.C., M.A. 1958
Registrar and Legal Sec., D. W. Faull, 1 The Sanctuary, S.W.1......................1963

ST. EDMUNDSBURY AND IPSWICH. £2,200.

5th Bishop, Rt. Rev. Arthur Harold Morris, D.D. (Bishop's House, Ipswich), *cons.* 1949, *trans.* 1954. [Signs Harold St. Edm. & Ipswich].......1954

Bishop Suffragan.

Dunwich, Rt. Rev. Thomas Herbert Cashmore, B.A. (Stonham Aspal Rectory, Stowmarket). 1955
Provost, Very Rev. John Albert Henry Waddington, M.B.E., T.D., M.A. 1958
Canon Residentiary, Archd. Norton 1958

Archdeacons.

Ipswich, Ven. C. G. Hooper, M.A. 1963
Suffolk, Ven. C. S. Scott, M.A. 1961
Sudbury, Ven, H. D. Barton, M.A. 1962

Organist, T. F. H. Oxley, B.A., B.Mus., F.R.C.O...1957

Beneficed Clergy, 285; *Curates, &c.*, 15.

Chancellor, D. C. Bain, M.C., Q.C., M.A. 1955
Registrar, G. P. V. Creagh, M.A., 80 Guildhall Street, Bury St. Edmunds.

SALISBURY. £2,200.

74th Bishop, Right Rev. Joseph Edward Fison, D.D. (South Canonry, The Close, Salisbury.) [Signs Joseph Sarum.]..........................1963

Bishop Suffragan.

Sherborne, Rt. Rev. Victor Joseph Pike, C.B., C.B.E., D.D. (69 The Close, Salisbury)............1960

Dean (£1,200).

Very Rev. Kenneth William Haworth, M.A...1960

Canons Residentiary (each £600).

C. Jackson.......1947	J. S. Maples, M.A...1960
R. S. Dawson, M.A. 1958	

Organist, C. Dearnley, M.A., B.Mus., F.R.C.O....1957

Archdeacons.

Dorset, Ven. E. L. Seager, M.A. 1956
Wilts, Ven. C. A. Plaxton, M.A. 1951
Sarum, Ven. F. McGowan, M.B.E., M.A. 1951
Sherborne, Ven. D. R. Maddock, M.A. 1961

Beneficed Clergy, 330; *Curates, &c.*, 83.

Chancellor, J. H. Ellison, M.A. 1955
Registrar and Legal Secretary, Alan M. Barker, B.A., Bishop's Walk, The Close, Salisbury.

SOUTHWARK. £2,500.

6th Bishop, Rt. Rev. Arthur Mervyn Stockwood, D.D. (Bishop's House, 38 Tooting Bec Gardens, S.W.16) [Signs Mervyn Southwark].......1959

Bishops Suffragan.

Kingston on Thames, Rt. Rev. William Percy Gilpin, M.A. (89 North Side, Clapham Common, S.W.4).................................1952
Woolwich, Rt. Rev. John Arthur Thomas Robinson, M.A., Ph.D. (17 Manor Way, Blackheath, S.E.3) 1959
Provost, Very Rev. Ernest William Southcott, B.A. 1961

Canons Residentiary.

I. G. Davies, B.A., B.D. 1957	D. A. Rhymes, B.A. 1961
S. G. Evans, M.A....1960	D. M. P. Tasker, B.A. 1961
F. Colquhoun, M.A. 1961	J. D. Pearce-Higgins, M.A. 1963

Organist, H. Dexter, M.A., Mus.B. 1956

Archdeacons.

Southwark, Ven. H. H. A. Sands, M.A. 1955
Lewisham, Ven. W. S. Hayman, M.A. 1960
Kingston, Ven. P. D. Robb M.A. 1953

Beneficed Clergy, 309; *Curates, &c.*, 351.

Chancellor, Rev. E. Garth Moore, M.A. 1948
Secretary and Registrar, D. W. Faull, 1 The Sanctuary, S.W.1...............................1963

TRURO. £2,360.

10th Bishop, Rt. Rev. John Maurice Key, D.D. (Lis Escop, Truro) (*cons.* 1947, *trans.* 1960) [Signs Maurice Truron:].......................1960
Assistant Bishop, Rt. Rev. William Quinlan Lash, M.A. (*cons.* 1947)..........................1962

Dean

Very Rev. Henry Morgan Lloyd, D.S.O., O.B.E., M.A. 1960

Canons Residentiary.

Archd. Boreham ..1947	H. A. Blair, M.A., B.D. 1960
J. A. Simcock.....1952	

Archdeacons.

Cornwall, Ven. F. Boreham, M.A. 1949
Bodmin, Ven. A. C. Williams. 1962
Organist, F. G. Ormond, B.A. 1929

Beneficed Clergy, 200; *Curates, &c.*, 19.

Chancellor, P. T. S. Boydell..................1957
Registrar and Secretary, R. W. Money, 2 Princes Street, Truro.

WORCESTER. £2,200

109th Bishop, Rt. Rev. Lewis Mervyn Charles-Edwards, D.D. (Froxmere Court, Crowle, Worcester) [Signs Mervyn Worcester].....1956
Assistant Bishop, Right Rev. Cyril Edgar Stuart, M.A. (*cons.* 1932)............................1953

Dean (£1,750).

Very Rev. Robert Leslie Pollington Milburn, M.A. 1957

Canons (each £875).

A.P. Shepherd, D.D. 1945	Bishop Stuart 1956
C. B. Armstrong, M.A., B.D. 1947	G. C. B. Davies, D.D. 1963

Organist, C. J. Robinson, M.A., B.Mus., F.R.C.O.. 1963

Archdeacons.

Dudley, Ven. A. V. Hurley, C.B.E., T.D., M.A... 1951
Worcester, Ven. P. C. Eliot, M.A. 1961

Beneficed Clergy, 175; *Curates, &c.*, 106.

Chancellor, P. T. S. Boydell..................1959
Secretary and Registrar, R. C. March, Diocesan Registry, Worcester.

Province of York

YORK. £6 000.

93rd Archbishop and Primate of England, Right Hon. and Most Rev. Frederick Donald Coggan, D.D., *cons.* 1956, *trs.* 1961. (Bishopthorpe, York.) [Signs Donald Ebor:] 1961

Bishops Suffragan.

Selby, Rt. Rev. Douglas Noel Sargent, M.A. (Tollgarth, Tadcaster Road, York) 1962
Whitby, Rt. Rev. George D'Oyly Snow, M.A. (The Old Rectory, South Kilvington, Thirsk) 1961
Hull, Rt. Rev. George Frederick Townley, M.A. (222 Park Avenue, Hull) 1957
Dean (£2,000) (vacant).

Canons Residentiary (each £800).

T. H. Tardrew, LL.B. 1954
R. E. Cant, M.A. 1957
B. A. Smith, M.A. 1963
Organist, Francis Jackson, MUS.D., F.R.C.O.

Archdeacons.

York, Ven. C. R. Forder, M.A. 1957
East Riding, Ven. F. E. Ford, M.A. 1957
Cleveland, Ven. W. Palin, M.A. 1947

Beneficed Clergy, 363; *Curates, &c.*, 54.

Official Principal and Auditor of the Chancery Court, Rt. Hon. Sir Henry Willink, Bt., M.C., Q.C., D.C.L.
Vicar-General of the Province, and Chancellor of the Diocese, W. S. Wigglesworth, M.A., LL.B. 1944
Registrar and Secretary, I. N. Ware, O.B.E., T.D. .. 1940

DURHAM. £4,000.

89th Bishop, Rt. Rev. Maurice Henry Harland, D.D. (*cons.* 1942, *trans.* 1947 and 1956). (Auckland Castle, Bishop Auckland.) [Signs Maurice Dunelm.] 1956

Bishop Suffragan.

Jarrow, Rt. Rev. Mervyn Armstrong, O.B.E., M.A. (Melkridge, Gilesgate, Durham) 1958

Dean (£3,000).

Very Rev. John Herbert Severn Wild, M.A. .. 1951

Canons Residentiary (each £1,000).

H. E. W. Turner, D.D. 1950	Archd. Stranks 1954
Archd. Cobham ... 1953	A. H. Couratin, M.A. .. 1962
	R. P. C. Hanson, B.D. 1962

Organist, C. W. Eden, MUS.B., A.R.C.O. 1936

Archdeacons.

Durham Ven. J. O. Cobham, M.A. 1953
Auckland, Ven. C. J. Stranks, M.A. 1958

Beneficed Clergy, 230; *Curates, &c.*, 85.

Chancellor, E. Garth Moore, M.A. 1954
Registrar (1948) *and Legal Secretary* (1929), H. C. Ferens, M.A. (The College, Durham).

BLACKBURN. £2,700.

4th Bishop, Rt. Rev. Charles Robert Claxton, D.D., *cons.* 1946, *trans.* 1960 (Bishop's House, Blackburn) [Signs Charles Blackburn] 1960

Bishops Suffragan.

Lancaster, Rt. Rev. Anthony Leigh Egerton Hoskyns-Abrahall (Pedders Wood, Scorton) 1955
Burnley, Rt. Rev. George Edward Holderness, M.A. (Palace House, Burnley) 1955
Provost, Very Rev. Norman Robinson, B.SC. .. 1961

Canons Residentiary.

W. R. F. Browning, M.A., B.D. 1959	G. Jackson, B.A. 1959

Archdeacons (each £500).

Lancaster, Ven. C. H. Lambert, M.A. 1959
Blackburn, Ven. H. N. Hodd, M.A. 1962
Organist, T. L. Duerden, MUS.BAC. 1939

Beneficed Clergy, 267; *Curates, &c.*, 51.

Chancellor, R. A. Forrester, M.A. 1949
Registrar, Leslie Ranson, LL.B., Cathedral Close, Blackburn 1954

BRADFORD. £3,000.

4th Bishop, Rt. Rev. Clement George St. Michael Parker, M.A. (Bishopscroft, Ashwell Road, Heaton, Bradford) *cons.* 1954 [Signs Michael Bradford 1961
Provost, Very Rev. William Hugh Alan Cooper, M.A. 1962
Organist (vacant).

Archdeacons.

Bradford, Ven. H. L. Higgs, M.A. 1957
Craven, Ven. A. Sephton, M.A. 1956

Beneficed Clergy, 142; *Curates, &c.*, 29.

Chancellor, H. C. Scott, Q.C., M.A. 1957
Registrar and Secretary, H. Firth, Martins Bank Chambers, Tyrrel Street, Bradford.

CARLISLE. £2,600.

62nd Bishop, Rt. Rev. Thomas Bloomer, D.D. (Rose Castle, Dalston, Carlisle.) [Signs Thomas Carliol] 1946

Bishop Suffragan.

Penrith, Rt. Rev. Sydney Cyril Bulley, M.A. (Fox How, Ambleside, Westmorland) 1959

Dean (about £1,800).

Very Rev. Lionel Meiring Spafford du Toit, M.A. 1960

Canons Residentiary (about £900).

Archd. Nurse 1958	T. R. Hare, M.A. .. 1959
R. T. Holtby, M.A. 1958	

Organist, R. A. Sievewright, M.A., A.R.C.O. ... 1960

Archdeacons.

Westmorland and Furness, Bishop of Penrith ... 1959
West Cumberland, Ven. W. E. A. Pugh, M.A. .. 1959
Carlisle, Ven. C. E. Nurse, M.A. 1958

Beneficed Clergy, 280; *Curates, &c.*, 57.

Chancellor, His Hon. R. H. Mais, M.A. 1950
Registrar and Sec., G. W. Graham-Bowman, O.B.E., M.C., Carlisle 1929

CHESTER. £2,500.

37th Bishop, Rt. Rev. Gerald Alexander Ellison, D.D. (Bishop's House, Chester.) *cons.* 1950 [Signs Gerald Cestr:] 1955

Bishop Suffragan.

Stockport, Rt. Rev. David Henry Saunders-Davies, M.A. (Toft House Gough's Lane, Knutsford) 1950

Assistant Bishop.

Rt. Rev. Tom Greenwood, D.D. (The Vicarage, Whitegate, Northwich) (*cons.* 1952) 1962

Dean (£1,500).

Very Rev. George William Outram Addleshaw, M.A., B.D., F.S.A. 1963

Canons Residentiary (each £900).

Archdn. Burne 1940	B. A. Hardy, M.A. .. 1946
C. E. Jarman 1943	

Organist, J. D. Sanders, M.A., MUS.B., F.R.C.O., A.R.C.M. 1963

Archdeacons.

Chester, Ven. R. V. H. Burne, M.A. 1937
Macclesfield, Ven. T. Clarke 1958

Beneficed Clergy, 272; *Curates, &c.*, 76.

Chancellor, K. J. T. Elphinstone, M.A. 1950
Legal Secretaries, Gamon & Co., 2 White Friars, Chester.

LIVERPOOL. £2,200.

4th Bishop, Rt. Rev. Clifford Arthur Martin, D.D., LL.D. (Bishop's Lodge, Woolton Park, Liverpool 25.) [Signs Clifford Liverpool] 1944

Bishop Suffragan.

Warrington Rt. Rev. Laurence Ambrose Brown, M.A. 1960
Dean (£1,500) (vacant).

Canons Residentiary.

C. B. Naylor, M.A. .. 1956	H. Ellis, M.A. 1962
F. A. Redwood, M.A. 1960	

Organist, Noel Rawsthorne, F.R.C.O. 1955

Archdeacons (each £300).
Liverpool, Ven. H. S. Wilkinson, M.A. 1951
Warrington, Ven. E. H. Evans 1959
Beneficed Clergy, 227; *Curates, &c.*, 103.
Chancellor, His Hon. E. Steel, LL.B. 1957
Registrar, E. C. Arden, 1 Hanover Street, Liverpool, 1.

MANCHESTER. £2,200.
7th Bishop, Rt. Rev. William Derrick Lindsay Greer, D.D. (Bishop's House, 26 Singleton Road, Manchester 7). [Signs William Manchester] 1947
Bishops Suffragan.
Hulme, Rt. Rev. Kenneth Venner Ramsey, B.D. (Westholme, 22 Pine Road, Didsbury, Manchester 20) 1953
Middleton, Rt. Rev. Edward Ralph Wickham, B.D. (1 Portland Road, Eccles, Manchester) 1959
Dean (£2,000) (vacant).
Canons Residentiary (each £1,000).
Archdn. Bean . . . . . 1934 | R. H. Preston, M.A. 1958
H. Hodkin, M.A. . . . 1957 | S. H. Price, M.A. . . . 1960
Organist, D. E. Cantrell, M.A., B.MUS., F.R.C.O. . . 1961
Archdeacons.
Manchester, Ven. A. Selwyn Bean, M.B.E., B.D. . 1934
Rochdale, Ven. L. G. Tyler, M.A. 1962
Beneficed Clergy, 383; *Curates, &c.*, 65.
Chancellor, His Hon. R. H. Mais, M.A. 1948
Registrar and Bishop's Secretary, L. H. Orford, M.A., LL.B., 90 Deansgate, Manchester 1933

NEWCASTLE. £2,500.
8th Bishop, Rt. Rev. Hugh Edward Ashdown, D.D. (The Bishop's House, Gosforth, Newcastle-upon-Tyne, 3) [Signs Hugh Newcastle] 1957
Provost, Very Rev. Conrad Clifton Wolters, M.A. 1962
Canons Residentiary.
The Provost . . . . . . 1958 | G. Suthers, M.A. . . . 1961
Archdeacons
Northumberland, Ven. C. P. Unwin, B.A. 1963
Lindisfarne, Ven. L. S. Hawkes, M.A. 1960
Organist, Colin A. C. Ross, F.R.C.O. 1956
Beneficed Clergy, 187; *Curates, &c.*, 52.
Chancellor, K. M. Macmorran, Q.C., LL.B. 1942
Registrar and Sec., Ian Dickinson, Cross House, Westgate Road, Newcastle-on-Tyne.

RIPON. £2,500.
9th Bishop, Rt. Rev. John Richard Humpidge Moorman, D.D. (Bishop Mount, Ripon.) [Signs John Ripon] 1959
Bishop Suffragan.
Knaresborough, Rt. Rev. Henry Handley Vully de Candole, M.A. (21 Brunswick Drive, Harrogate) 1949
Dean (£1,200)
Very Rev. Frederick Llewelyn Hughes, C.B.E., M.C., M.A. 1951
Canons Residentiary (each £900)
W. E. Wilkinson, B.A. 1948 | C. B. Sampson, M.A. 1961
| Archd. Turnbull . . . 1962
Organist, Philip Marshall, MUS. DOC., F.R.C.O. . . 1959

Archdeacons
Leeds, Ven. C. O. Ellison, B.SC. 1950
Richmond, Ven. J. W. Turnbull, B.A. 1962
Beneficed Clergy, 179; *Curates, &c.*, 58
Chancellor, H. C. Scott, Q.C., M.A. 1957
Registrar and Secretary, O. Errington Wilson, Central Bank Chambers, Leeds.

SHEFFIELD. £2,200.
3rd Bishop, Rt. Rev. Francis John Taylor, M.A. (Ranmoor Grange, Sheffield, 10.). [Signs John Sheffield] 1962
Asst. Bishops, Rt. Rev. George Vincent Gerard, C.B.E., M.C., M.A. (*cons.* 1938) 1947
Rt. Rev. Arthur Michael Hollis, M.A. B.D. (*cons.* 1942) 1963
Provost, Very Rev. John Howard Cruse, M.A. . 1949
Archdeacons
Doncaster, Ven. P. G. Bostock, M.A. 1959
Sheffield, Ven. H. Johnson, M.A. 1963
Organist, R. Tustin Baker, MUS.D.
Beneficed Clergy, 175; *Curates, &c.*, 61
Chancellor, His Hon. R. H. Mais, M.A. 1950
Registrar and Legal Sec., V. H. Sandford, M.A., 30 Bank Street, Sheffield.

SODOR AND MAN. £3,000 *gross*.
75th Bishop, Rt. Rev. Benjamin Pollard, T.D., D.D., M.SC. (Bishop's Court, Kirk-Michael, Isle of Man) (*cons.* 1936). [Signs Benjamin Sodor and Man] 1954
Archdeacon, Ven. E. H. Stenning, M.B.E., T.D., M.A., Q.H.C. 1958
Beneficed Clergy, 31; *Curates, &c.*, 17
Vicar-General, Sec. and Registrar, Frank Barnes Johnson, M.A., 24 Athol Street, Douglas.

SOUTHWELL. £2,200.
Bishop (vacant).
Asst. Bishops, Rt. Rev. Alfred Morris Gelsthorpe, C.M.G., D.S.O., D.D. (*cons.* 1933) 1952
Rt. Rev. Wilfrid Lewis Mark Way, M.A. (*cons.* 1962) 1960
Provost, Very Rev. Hugh Christopher Lempriere Heywood, M.A. 1945
Archdeacons
Newark, Ven. K. G. Thompson, M.A. 1962
Nottingham, Ven. M. R. W. Brown, M.A. 1960
Organist, K. B. Beard 1959
Beneficed Clergy, 205; *Curates, &c.*, 88.
Chancellor, B. T. Buckle 1959
Registrar, R. M. Beaumont.

WAKEFIELD. £3,000.
7th Bishop, Rt. Rev. John Alexander Ramsbotham, D.D. (Bishop's Lodge, Woodthorpe, Wakefield.) (*cons.* 1950) [Signs John Wakefield] 1958
Provost, Very Rev. Philip Norris Pare, M.A. 1961
Bishop Suffragan
Pontefract, Rt. Rev. Eric Treacy, M.B.E. 1961
Archdeacons
Pontefract, Bishop of Pontefract 1961
Halifax, Ven. J. F. Lister, M.A. 1961
Organist, P. G. Saunders, MUS.D., F.R.C.O.
Beneficed Clergy, 212; *Curates, &c.*, 44
Chancellor, G. B. Graham, LL.B. 1959
Registrar and Sec., C. E. Coles, Burton Street, Wakefield 1963

The Church Assembly, Church House, Dean's Yard, S.W.1.—*Chairman*, The Archbishop of Canterbury; *Vice-Chairman*, The Archbishop of York; *Secretary*, J. A. Guillum Scott, D.C.L. THE HOUSE OF BISHOPS.—*Chairman*, The Archbishop of Canterbury; *Vice-Chairman*, The Archbishop of York. THE HOUSE OF CLERGY.—*Chairman*, Rev. Canon J. Brierley, M.A.; *Vice-Chairman*, Rt. Rev. G. V. Gerard. THE HOUSE OF LAITY.—*Chairman*, Sir Kenneth Grubb, C.M.G.; *Vice-Chairman*, Brig. H. Miller, O.B.E.

Convocation. Canterbury, Upper House.—*President*, The Archbishop of Canterbury; *Registrar*, D. M. M. Carey, M.A.; *Apparitor-General*, Lt.-Col. J. B. Barron, O.B.E., M.C. Lower House.—*Prolocutor*, The Archdeacon of Taunton; *Actuary*, R. M. Hollis, M.A. York, Upper House.—*President*, The Archbishop of York; *Registrar*, I. N. Ware, O.B.E., Minster Yard, York; Lower House.—*Prolocutor*, The Archdeacon of Manchester; *Synodal Secretary*, Rev. H. R. Wilson, M.A.

THE CHURCH IN WALES

MONMOUTH. £2,000.

4th Bishop of Monmouth and *5th Archbishop of Wales*, Most Rev. Alfred Edwin Morris, D.D., *b.* 1894, *cons.* Bishop of Monmouth, 1945; *elected* Archbishop of Wales, 1957 (Bishopstow, Stow Hill, Newport, Mon.). [Signs Edwin Cambrensis] 1945

BANGOR. £2,100.

78th Bishop, Rt. Rev. Gwilym Owen Williams, D.D., *b.* 1913. (Llys Esgob, Menai Bridge, Anglesey.) [Signs Gwilym Bangor]......1957

LLANDAFF. £2,000.

98th Bishop, Rt. Rev. William Glyn Hughes Simon, D.D., *b.* 1903, *cons.* Bishop of Swansea and Brecon 1954, *translated* 1957 (Llys-Esgob, The Green, Llandaff, Cardiff.) [Signs Glyn Landav:]

ST. ASAPH. £2,100. [1957

72nd Bishop, Rt. Rev. David Daniel Bartlett, D.D., *b.* 1900. (Palace, St. Asaph). [Signs David St. Asaph]..............................1950

ST. DAVID'S £2,100.

122nd Bishop, Rt. Rev. John Richards Richards, D.D., *b.* 1901 (The Palace, Abergwili, Carmarthen) [Signs John St. Davids]..........1956

SWANSEA AND BRECON. £2,000.

5th Bishop, Rt. Rev. John James Absalom Thomas, D.D., *b.* 1908 (Ely Tower, Brecon). [Signs John Swansea & Brecon]....................1958

BISHOPS ABROAD

CANADA

Primate of All Canada.

The Most Rev. Howard Hewlett Clark, *b.* 1903, *cons.* Bp. of Edmonton 1954, Elected Primate of All Canada 1959. Elected Metropolitan of Rupert's Land and translated to see of Rupert's Land, 1961.

Sees.	Apptd.	Clgy.
Province of Canada.		
The Most Rev. Archbishop.		
Fredericton, Alexander Henry O'Neil (*cons.* 1957), *Archbishop and Metropolitan*	1963	80
The Rt. Rev. Bishops.		
Fredericton (*see* above).		
Montreal, R. K. Maguire, *b.* 1923	1963	113
Newfoundland, J. A. Meaden	1956	68
Asst. Bp. R. L. Seaborn. *b.* 1911	1957	
Nova Scotia, W. W. Davis (*cons.* 1958)	1963	119
Quebec, R. F. Brown, *b.* 1900	1960	60
Province of Ruperts Land.		
The Most Rev. Archbishop.		
Rupert's Land (*see* above).		
The Rt. Rev. Bishops.		
Arctic, D. B. Marsh, *b.* 1903	1950	29
Bp. Suff., H. G. Cook	1963	
Athabasca, R. J. Pierce, *b.* 1909	1950	19
Brandon, I. A. Norris, *b.* 1901	1950	34
Calgary, G. R. Calvert, *b.* 1900	1952	64
Edmonton, W. G. Burch (*cons.* 1960)	1961	49
Keewatin, H. E. Hives, *b.* 1901	1954	20
Qu' Appelle, G. F. C. Jackson, *b.* 1907	1960	63
Rupert's Land (*see* above)		64
Bp. Suff., J. O. Anderson	1963	
Saskatchewan, W. H. H. Crump, *b.* 1903	1960	30
Saskatoon, S. C. Steer, *b.* 1900	1950	32
Province of Ontario.		
The Most Rev. Archbishop.		
Algoma, William Lockridge Wright, *b.* 1904 (*cons.* 1944), *Archbishop and Metropolitan*	1955	66
The Rt. Rev. Bishops.		
Toronto, F. H. Wilkinson, *b.* 1896 (*cons.* 1953)	1955	304
Bp. Coadj., G. B. Snell.		
Bp. Suff., H. R. Hunt.		
Huron, G. N. Luxton, *b.* 1901	1948	150
Bps. Suff., H. F. Appleyard; W. A. Townshend.		
Moosonee, J. A. Watton	1963	30
Bp. Suff. (*James Bay*), N. R. Clarke.		
Niagara, W. E. Bagnall, *b.* 1903	1949	90
Ontario, K. C. Evans, *b.* 1903	1952	67
Ottawa, E. S. Reed	1954	78
Province of British Columbia.		
The Most Rev. Archbishop.		
British Columbia, Harold E. Sexton, *b.* 1888 (*cons.* 1935) *Archbishop and Metropolitan*, 1952	1936	52
The Rt. Rev. Bishops.		
Caledonia, E. G. Munn, *b.* 1903	1960	19
Cariboo, R. S. Dean, *b.* 1915	1956	14
Kootenay, W. R. Coleman, *b.* 1917	1961	30
New Westminster, G. P. Gower, *b.* 1900	1951	84
Yukon, H. H. Marsh, *b.* 1899	1962	9

INDIA, PAKISTAN, BURMA AND CEYLON

Metropolitan Bishop.

Calcutta, The Most Rev. Hiyanirinda Lakdasa Jacob de Mel, *b.* 1902 (*cons.* 1945)	1962	100
Asst. Bp., J. Richardson, *b.* 1894	1950	
The Rt. Rev. Bishops		
Amritsar, K. D. W. Anand	1960	
Assam (vacant).		25
Barrackpore, R. W. Bryan (*cons.* 1951)	1956	
Bhagalpur, P. Parmar	1955	19
Bombay, C. J. G. Robinson, *b.* 1903 (*cons.* 1947)	1962	65
Chota Nagpur, S. A. B. Dilbar Hans	1957	51
Colombo, A. R. Graham-Campbell, *b.* 1903	1948	99
Dacca, J. D. Blair, *b.* 1906 (*cons.* 1951)	1956	
Delhi, F. R. Willis, *b.* 1900	1951	18
Karachi, C. Ray	1960	
Lahore, L. H. Woolmer, *b.* 1906	1949	85
Lucknow, J. Amritanand (*cons.* 1949)	1962	
Nagpur, J. W. Sadiq	1957	
Nandyal, C. Venkataramiah	1963	
Nasik, A. W. Luther	1957	
Rangoon, V. G. Shearburn, *b.* 1901	1955	49
Asst. Bps., F. Ah Mya; J. Aung Hla, M.B.E.	1949	

AUSTRALIA

Primate of Australia

The Most Rev. the Lord Archbishop of Sydney	1959	
Province of New South Wales.		
Archbishop and Metropolitan.		
Sydney. The Most Rev. Hugh Rowlands Gough, O.B.E., *b.* 1905 (*cons.* 1948)	1958	302
Bp. Coadj., R. C. Kerle, *b.* 1915	1956	
Do., M. L. Loane, *b.* 1911	1958	
Do., A. W. G. Hudson, *b.* 1915	1960	
The Rt. Rev. Bishops.		
Armidale, J. S. Moyes, C.M.G., *b.* 1884	1929	43
Bathurst, E. K. Leslie, *b.* 1911	1958	43
Canberra and Goulburn, K. J. Clements, *b.* 1905 (*cons.* 1949)	1961	63
Grafton, R. G. Arthur, *b.* 1909 (*cons.* 1956)	1961	41
Newcastle, J. A. G. Housden, *b.* 1904	1958	85
Riverina, H. G. Robinson. *b.* 1899	1951	25
Province of Victoria.		
Archbishop and Metropolitan		
Melbourne, The Most Rev. Frank Woods, *b.* 1907 (*cons.* 1952)	1957	292

Sees. Apptd. Clgy.

Bps. Coadj., G. T. Sambell, *b.* 1914.... 1962
F. R. Arnott, *b.* 1911 1963

The Rt. Rev. Bishops.

Ballarat, W. A. Hardie, *b.* 1904........ 1960 60
Bendigo, R. E. Richards, *b.* 1908........ 1957 31
Gippsland, D. A. Garnsey, *b.* 1909 .... 1959 37
St. Arnaud. A. E. Winter, *b.* 1903...... 1951 26
Wangaratta, T. B. McCall, *b.* 1911 (*cons.* 1959).......... 1963 34

Province of Queensland

Archbishop and Metropolitan

Brisbane, The Most Rev. Philip Nigel Warrington Strong, C.M.G., *b.* 1899 (*cons.* 1936).......... 1962
Bp. Coadj., W. J. Hudson, *b.* 1904 (*cons.* 1950).......... 1960

The Rt. Rev. Bishops.

Carpentaria, S. J. Matthews, *b.* 1900..... 1960 14
New Guinea, G. D. Hand, *b.* 1918 (*cons.* 1950).......... 1963 16
Asst. Bp., G. Ambo.......... 1960
N. Queensland, I. W. A. Shevill, *b.* 1917. 1953 30
Rockhampton (vacant).

Province of Western Australia.

Archbishop and Metropolitan

Perth, The Most Rev. George Appleton, M.B.E., *b.* 1902.......... 1963 120

The Rt. Rev. Bishops.

Bunbury, R. G. Hawkins, *b.* 1911....... 1957 34
Kalgoorlie, C. E. B. Muschamp, *b.* 1902.. 1950 8
N.W. Australia, J. Frewer, C.B.E., *b.* 1883. 1929 4

Extra-Provincial Dioceses.

The Rt. Rev. Bishops.

Adelaide, T. T. Reed, *b.* 1902.......... 1957 126
Tasmania, R. E. Davies, *b.* 1913 (*cons.* 1960).......... 1963 78
Bp. Coadj., W. R. Barrett, *b.* 1893... 1957
Willochra, T. E. Jones, *b.* 1903... 1958 19

PROVINCE OF NEW ZEALAND

Archbishop and Primate

Waiapu, The Most Rev. Norman Alfred Lesser. *b.* 1902 (*cons.* 1947).......... 1961 65
Bp. Suff. (*Aoteroa*), W. N. Panapa, C.B.E., *b.* 1898.......... 1951

The Rt. Rev. Bishops

Auckland, E. A. Gowing. *b.* 1913....... 1960 112
Asst. Bp., S. G. Caulton.
Christchurch, A. K. Warren, *b.* 1900..... 1951 112
Dunedin, A. H. Johnston, *b.* 1912...... 1953 42
Melanesia, A. T. Hill, C.M.G., M.B.E., *b.* 1901.......... 1953 75
Asst. Bps., D. Tuti (1963); L. Alufarai (1963)
Nelson, F. O. Hulme-Moir, *b.* 1910 .... 1953 32
Polynesia, J. C. Vockler, *b.* 1925 (*cons.* 1959).......... 1962 9
Waikato, J. T. Holland, *b.* 1912....... 1951 42
Wellington, H. W. Baines, *b.* 1905 (*cons.* 1949).......... 1960 116
Asst. Bp., G. M. McKenzie, O.B.E...... 1962

PROVINCE OF SOUTH AFRICA

Archbishop and Metropolitan

Cape Town, The Most Rev. Joost de Blank, *b.* 1908 (*cons.* 1952).......... 1957 171
Bp. Suff., R. W. F. Cowdry, *b.* 1915.. 1958
Basutoland, J. A. Arrowsmith Maund, *b.* 1909.......... 1950 30
Bloemfontein, B. B. Burnett, *b.* 1917.... 1957 46
Damaraland, R. H. Mize.......... 1960 13
George, J. Hunter, *b.* 1897 (*cons.* 1943).. 1951 24
Grahamstown, R. S. Taylor, *b.* 1909 (*cons.* 1941).......... 1959 99
Johannesburg, L. E. Stradling, *b.* 1908 (*cons.* 1945).......... 1961 146
Kimberley & Kuruman, P. W. Wheeldon O.B.E., *b.* 1913 (*cons.* 1954).......... 1961 32

Sees. Apptd. Clgy.

Lebombo, S. C. Pickard, *b.* 1910........ 1958 30
Natal, T. G. V. Inman, *b.* 1904........ 1951 109
Pretoria, E. G. Knapp-Fisher, *b.* 1915.... 1960 57
St. Helena, H. Beardmore, *b.* 1898. .... 1960 4
St. John's, J. L. Schuster, *b.* 1912........ 1956 95
Asst. Bp., A. H. Zulu.......... 1960
Zululand and Swaziland, T. J. Savage, *b.* 1900.......... 1958 70

PROVINCE OF THE WEST INDIES

Archbishop of West Indies

Guiana, The Most Rev. Alan John Knight, C.M.G., *Archbp. & Metropolitan*, *b.* 1902 (*cons.* 1937).......... 1950 36

The Rt. Rev. Bishops

Antigua, D. R. Knowles, O.B.E., *b.* 1898. 1953 25
Barbados, E. L. Evans, *b.* 1904 (*cons.* 1957). 1960 58
Honduras, G. H. Brooks, *b.* 1905...... 1950 7
Jamaica, P. W. Gibson, C.B.E., *b.* 1893 (*cons.* 1947).......... 1955 90
Bp. Suff. (*Kingston*), J. C. E. Swaby... 1961
Bp. Suff. (*Mandeville*), B. N. Y. Vaughan.......... 1961
Nassau and the Bahamas, B. Markham... 1962 33
Trinidad, W. J. Hughes, *b.* 1894 (*cons.* 1944).......... 1962 34
Windward Islds., H. G. Pigott.......... 1962 17

PROVINCE OF WEST AFRICA

Archbishop

Onitsha, Eastern Nigeria, The Most Rev. Cecil John Patterson, C.M.G., C.B.E., *b.* 1908, *cons.* 1942, *elected Archp. of West Africa*, 1961.......... 65
Asst. Bp., L. Uzodike.......... 1961

The Rt. Rev. Bishops

Accra, R. R. Roseveare. *b.* 1902....... 1956 42
Asst. Bp., I. M. S. Le Maire.......... 1963
Benin, A. Iwe.......... 1962
Gambia and Rio Pongas (vacant). 6
Ibadan, S. O. Odutola, O.B.E. (*cons.* 1952). 1960
Lagos, S. I. Kale.......... 1963 65
Niger Delta, R. N. Bara Hart.......... 1962
Asst. Bp., H. I. J. Aonya.......... 1957
Northern Nigeria, J. E. L. Mort, *b.* 1915.. 1952 19
Ondo, D. O. Awosika (*cons.* 1957) 1961
Owerri, G. E. I. Cockin, *b.* 1908........ 1959
Sierra Leone, M. N. C. O. Scott........ 1962 36
Asst. Bp., P. J. Jones.......... 1948

PROVINCE OF CENTRAL AFRICA

Archbishop

Northern Rhodesia, The Most Rev. Oliver Green-Wilkinson, C.B.E., *b.* 1913, *elected Archbp. of Central Africa*, 1962.. 1951 55

The Rt. Rev. Bishops

Mashonaland, C. W. Alderson, *b.* 1900 (*cons.* 1949).......... 1957 80
Matabeleland, K. J. F. Skelton.......... 1962 51
Nyasaland, D. S. Arden.......... 1961 32

PROVINCE OF EAST AFRICA

Archbishop

Mombasa, The Most Rev. Leonard James Beecher, C.M.G., *b.* 1906 (*cons.* 1950), *elected Archbishop of East Africa*, 1960.......... 1953 48

The Rt. Rev. Bishops

Central Tanganyika, A. Stanway, *b.* 1908.......... 1951 94
Asst. Bps. Y. Omari (1955); M. Kahuranganga, *b.* 1921 (1962)
Fort Hall, O. Kariuki (*cons.* 1955)....... 1961 41
Masasi, E. U. T. Huddleston, *b.* 1913... 1960 69
Asst. Bp., M. D. Soseleje.......... 1963
Maseno, F. H. Olang' (*cons.* 1955)...... 1961 45
Nakuru, N. Langford-Smith (*cons.* 1960). 1961 27
South West Tanganyika, J. R. W. Poole-Hughes.......... 1962 38
Victoria Nyanza, M. L. Wiggins (*cons.* 1959).......... 1963 25

Sees.	Apptd.	Clgy.
Zanzibar, W. Scott Baker, *b.* 1902	1943	64
Asst. Bps., Y. Lukindo (1963); R. N. Russell (1963); J. Sepeku (1963)		

PROVINCE OF UGANDA, RWANDA AND BURUNDI

Archbishop

Namirembe, The Most Rev. Leslie Wilfrid Brown, *b.* 1912, *cons.* 1953	1961	

Bishops

Mbale, L. C. Usher-Wilson, C.B.E., *b.* 1903 (*cons.* 1936)	1961	
Nkore-Kigezi, K. Shalita (*cons.* 1957)	1961	
Northern Uganda, J. K. Russell, *b.* 1916 (*cons.* 1955)	1961	
Ruanda-Urundi, P. J. Brazier (*cons.* 1951)	1961	
Ruwenzori, E. Sabiti (*cons.* 1960)	1961	
Soroti, S. S. Tomusange (*cons.* 1952)	1961	
West Buganda, F. Lutaya (*cons.* 1952)	1961	

UNDER THE ARCHBISHOP OF CANTERBURY

The Rt. Rev. Bishops

Sees.	Apptd.	Clgy.
Argentina and E. S. America with the Falkland Is. C. J. Tucker	1963	
Bermuda, J. Armstrong, C.B., O.B.E., *b.* 1905	1963	
Chile and Bolivia, K. W. Howell	1963	
Gibraltar, S. A. H. Eley, *b.* 1899	1960	30
Hong Kong, R. O. Hall, M.C., *b.* 1895	1932	44
Iran, H. B. Dehqani	1961	12
Jerusalem, A. C. MacInnes, C.M.G. (*Archbishop*), *b.* 1901 (*cons.* 1953)	1957	24
Jesselton, J. C. L. Wong (*cons.* 1960)	1962	
Jordan, Lebanon and Syria, N. A. Cub'ain	1958	
Korea, J. C. S. Daly, *b.* 1903 (*cons.* 1935)	1955	15
Asst. Bp. A. E. Chadwell, *b.* 1892	1951	
Kuching, D. H. N. Allenby	1962	
Madagascar, J. Marcel (*cons.* 1956)	1961	61
Asst. Bp., J. Seth	1961	
Mauritius, A. F. B. Rogers, *b.* 1907	1959	19
Singapore and Malaya, C. K. Sansbury, *b.* 1905	1961	
Bp. Suff. (Kuala Lumpur), R. P. Koh (*cons.* 1958)	1961	
Sudan, O. C. Allison, *b.* 1908 (*cons.* 1948)	1953	
Asst. Bps., E. J. Ngalamu (1962); J. K. Dotiro	1962	

CHURCH OF ENGLAND ARCHBISHOPS AND BISHOPS WHO HAVE RESIGNED THEIR SEES OR SUFFRAGAN BISHOPRICS

Name and Diocese	Cons.	Res.
A. B. Akinyele, *b.* 1875; *Ibadan*	1933	1956
W. L. Anderson, *b.* 1892; *Salisbury*	1937	1962
J. W. Ashton, *b.* 1866; *Grafton*	1921	1938
C. A. W Aylen, *b.* 1882; *St. Helena*	1930	1939
D. Baker, *b.* 1882; *Bendigo*	1921	1937
W. F. Barfoot, *b.* 1893; *Rupertsland*	1941	1958
F. R. Barry, *b.* 1890; *Southwell*	1941	1963
H. Beevor, *b.* 1903; *Lebombo*	1952	1957
D. W. Bentley, *b.* 1882; *Barbados*	1919	1945
K. G. Bevan, *b.* 1898; *E. Szechwan*	1940	1950
S. A. Bill, *b.* 1884; *Lucknow*	1939	1947
D. B. Blackwood, *b.* 1884; *Gippsland*	1942	1955
J. J. Booth, *b.* 1886; *Melbourne*	1934	1957
J. Boys, *b.* 1900; *Kimberley and Kuruman*	1948	1960
R. Brook, *b.* 1880; *St. E. and Ipswich*	1940	1953
S. Burton, *b.* 1881; *Nassau and Bahamas*	1942	1961
H. J. Buxton, *b.* 1880; *Gibraltar*	1933	1947
M. R. Carpenter-Garnier, *b.* 1881; *Colombo*	1924	1938
P. Carrington, *b.* 1892; *Quebec*	1935	1960
S. G. Caulton, *b.* 1895; *Melanesia*	1947	1953
F. N. Chamberlain, *b.* 1900; *Trinidad*	1957	1961
G. A. Chambers, *b.* 1879; *Tanganyika*	1927	1947
G. A. Chase, *b.* 1886; *Ripon*	1946	1959
N. H. Clarke, *b.* 1892; *Plymouth*	1950	1962
G. W. Clarkson, *b.* 1897; *Pontefract*	1954	1961
F A. Cockin, *b.* 1888; *Bristol*	1946	1958
M. E. Coleman, *b.* 1902; *Qu' Appelle*	1950	1960
A. C. Cooper, *b.* 1881; *Korea*	1931	1954
B. C. Corfield, *b.* 1890; *Travancore*	1938	1945
N. E. Cornwall, *b.* 1903; *Borneo*	1949	1962
R. P. Crabbe *b.* 1883; *Mombasa*	1936	1953
G. F. Cranswick, *b.* 1894; *Tasmania*	1944	1963
F. W. T. Craske, *b.* 1901; *Gibraltar*	1953	1959
D. H. Crick, *b.* 1885; *Chester*	1934	1955
A. H. Cullen, *b.* 1887; *Grahamstown*	1931	1959
B. M. Dale, *b.* 1905; *Jamaica*	1950	1955
J. H. Dickinson, *b.* 1901; *Melanesia*	1932	1937
J. H. Dixon, *b.* 1888; *Montreal*	1943	1962
D. C. Dunlop, *b.* 1897; *Jarrow*	1944	1949
C. J. Ferguson-Davie, *b.* 1872; *Singapore*	1909	1927
Lord Fisher of Lambeth, *b.* 1887; *Canterbury*	1932	1961
R. S. Fyffe, *b.* 1869; *Rangoon*	1910	1928
A. M. Gelsthorpe, *b.* 1892; *Sudan*	1933	1952
G. V. Gerard, *b.* 1898; *Waiapu*	1938	1944
T. Greenwood, *b.* 1907; *Yukon*	1952	1961
L. D. Hammond, *b.* 1881; *Stafford*	1939	1958
A. O. Hardy; *Nagpur*	1937	1948
F. O. T. Hawkes, *b.* 1878; *Kingston*	1927	1952
R. M. Hay, *b.* 1884; *Buckingham*	1944	1960
P. M. Herbert, *b*, 1885; *Norwich*	1922	1959
H. St. B. Holland, *b.* 1882; *Wellington*	1936	1946
C. R. Hone, *b.* 1873; *Wakefield*	1931	1945
H. L. Hornby, *b.* 1888; *Hulme*	1945	1953
J. L. C. Horstead, *b.* 1898; *Sierra Leone*	1936	1961
F. Houghton, *b.* 1891; *E. Szechwan*	1937	1940
L. S. Hunter, *b.* 1890; *Sheffield*	1939	1962
F. M. Jackson, *b.* 1902; *Trinidad*	1946	1949
F. F. Johnston, *b.* 1891; *Egypt*	1952	1958
T. S. Jones, *b.* 1872; *Hulme*	1930	1945
A. B. L. Karney, *b.* 1874; *Southampton*	1922	1943
E. H. Knowles, *b.* 1874; *Qu' Appelle*	1935	1950
C. F. Knyvett, *b.* 1885; *Selby*	1941	1962
L. H. Lang, *b.* 1889; *Woolwich*	1936	1947
B. Lasbrey; *Niger*	1922	1945
W. Q. Lash, *b.* 1904; *Bombay*	1947	1961
T. Longworth, *b.* 1891; *Hereford*	1939	1961
G. L. G. Mandeville, *b.* 1894; *Barbados*	1951	1960
J. C. Mann, *b.* 1880; *Kyushu*	1935	1941
H. D. Martin, *b.* 1889; *Saskatchewan*	1939	1959
R. H. Moberly, *b.* 1884; *Stepney*	1936	1952
R. W. H. Moline, *b.* 1889; *Perth*	1947	1962
H. C. Montgomery-Campbell, *b.* 1887; *London*	1940	1961
E. R. Morgan, *b.* 1888; *Truro*	1943	1959
E. W. Mowll, *b.* 1881; *Middleton*	1943	1951
S. C. Neill, *b.* 1901; *Tinnevelly*	1939	1945
N. W. Newnham Davis, *b.* 1903; *Antigua*	1944	1952
R. S. M. O'Ferrall, *b.* 1890; *Madagascar*	1926	1961
H. van L. Otter-Barry, *b.* 1887; *Mauritius*	1931	1959
E. F. Paget, *b.* 1886; *Mashonaland*	1925	1957
T. R. Parfitt, *b.* 1911; *Madagascar*	1952	1961
W. Parker *b.* 1883; *Pretoria*	1933	1951
St. J. S. Pike, *b.* 1909; *Gambia*	1958	1963
H. R. Ragg, *b.* 1889; *Calgary*	1943	1951
R. A. Reeves, *b.* 1899; *Johannesburg*	1949	1961
C. L. Riley, *b.* 1888; *Bendigo*	1938	1956
B. P. Robin, *b.* 1887; *Adelaide*	1941	1956
A. C. W. Rose, *b.* 1887; *Dover*	1935	1956
C. J. G. Saunders, *b.* 1888; *Lucknow*	1928	1938
W. J. Simkin, *b.* 1883; *Auckland*	1940	1960
B. F. Simpson, *b.* 1883; *Southwark*	1932	1958
G. Sinker, *b.* 1900; *Nagpur*	1949	1954
A. H. Sovereign, *b.* 1881; *Athabasca*	1932	1950
R. W. Stannard, *b.* 1895; *Woolwich*	1947	1959
P. Stevens, *b.* 1882; *Kwangsi and Hunan*	1933	1950
W. H. Stewart, *b.* 1888; *Jerusalem*	1943	1957

Name and Diocese	Cons.	Res.
C. E. Storrs, *b.* 1889; *Grafton*	1946	1955
C. E. Stuart, *b.* 1893; *Uganda*	1932	1952
W. J. Thompson, *b.* 1885; *Iran*	1935	1960
F. O. Thorne, *b.* 1892; *Nyasaland*	1936	1961
G. W. R. Tobias, *b.* 1882; *Damaraland*	1939	1949
E. J. Trapp, *b.* 1910; *Zululand*	1947	1957
N. H. Tubbs, *b.* 1879; *Rangoon*	1923	1934
H. V. Turner, *b.* 1888; *Penrith*	1944	1958
G. J. Walsh, *b.* 1880; *Hokkaido*	1927	1941
J. W. C. Wand, *b.* 1885; *London*	1934	1955
G. H. Warde, *b.* 1889; *Lewes*	1946	1959
R. H. Waterman, *b.* 1897; *Nova Scotia*	1948	1963
W. L. M. Way, *b.* 1905; *Masasi*	1952	1959
J. R. Weller, *b.* 1880; *Argentina*	1934	1946
J. Wellington, *b.* 1890; *Shantung*	1940	1950
G. A. Wells, *b.* 1877; *Cariboo*	1934	1940
G. A. West, *b.* 1893; *Rangoon*	1935	1954
A. L. E. Williams, *b.* 1892; *Bermuda*	1956	1962
A. T. P. Williams, *b.* 1888; *Winchester*	1939	1961
D. J. Wilson, *b.* 1903; *Trinidad*	1938	1956

ARCHBISHOPS OF CANTERBURY SINCE 1454

1454 Thomas Bourchier
1486 John Morton
1501 Henry Dean
1503 William Warham
1533 Thomas Cranmer
1556 Cardinal Pole
1559 Matthew Parker
1576 Edmund Grindall
1583 John Whitgift
1604 Richard Bancroft
1610 George Abbot
1633 William Laud
1660 William Juxon
1663 Gilbert Sheldon
1678 William Sancroft
1691 John Tillotson
1695 Thomas Tenison
1716 William Wake
1737 John Potter
1747 Thomas Herring
1757 Matthew Hutton
1758 Thomas Secker
1758 Hon. Frederick Cornwallis
1783 John Moore
1805 Charles Manners Sutton
1828 William Howley
1848 John Bird Sumner
1862 Charles Thomas Longley
1868 Archibald Campbell Tait
1883 Edward White Benson
1896 Frederick Temple
1903 Randall Thomas Davidson
1928 Cosmo Gordon Lang
1942 William Temple
1945 Geoffrey Francis Fisher
1961 Arthur Michael Ramsey

ARCHBISHOPS OF YORK SINCE 1660

1660 Accepted Frewen
1664 Richard Sterne
1683 John Dolben
1688 Thomas Lamplugh
1691 John Sharp
1714 William Dawes
1724 Launcelot Blackburn
1743 Thomas Herring
1747 Matthew Hutton
1757 John Gilbert
1761 Robert Hay Drummond
1777 William Markham
1808 Edward Venables Vernon Harcourt
1848 Thomas Musgrave
1860 Charles Thomas Longley
1862 William Thomson
1891 William Connor Magee
1891 William Dalrymple Maclagan
1909 Cosmo Gordon Lang
1929 William Temple
1942 Cyril Forster Garbett
1956 Arthur Michael Ramsey
1961 Frederick Donald Coggan

THE CHURCH OF SCOTLAND

THE CHURCH OF SCOTLAND is Presbyterian in constitution, and is governed by Kirk Sessions, Presbyteries, Synods, and the General Assembly, which consists of both clerical and lay representatives from each of the Presbyteries. It is presided over by a Moderator (chosen annually by the Assembly), to whom Her Majesty the Queen has granted precedence in Scotland, during his term of office, next after the Lord Chancellor of Great Britain. The Sovereign is represented by a Lord High Commissioner (appointed each year by the Crown), who receives the sum of £4,000 towards his expenses. The country, for Church purposes, was, before the union of the Church of Scotland with the United Free Church of Scotland, which was effected at a joint meeting of the General Assemblies of both Churches on October 2, 1929, divided into 16 Synods and 66 Presbyteries, and there were about 2,600 ministers and licentiates engaged in ministerial and other work. There have since been added: (1) The Presbytery of England and (2) The Presbyteries of (*a*) Northern Europe, (*b*) Southern Europe, (*c*) Spain and Portugal, making 66 in all. The figures at Dec. 31, 1962, are:—Congregations, 2,220; total membership 1,281,559; Sunday Schools, 2,710, with 278,221 scholars and 39,527 teachers. In 19 Foreign Mission fields, there are 257 European missionaries (and in addition many missionaries' wives, most of whom are doing mission work in the various fields) and over 15,000 evangelists and teachers, including in both cases those of the Women's Foreign Mission.

The total amount of Christian Liberality received by Parishes and Charges in 1962 was £5,244,413.

LORD HIGH COMMISSIONER TO THE GENERAL ASSEMBLY OF THE CHURCH OF SCOTLAND (1963), H.R.H. The Duke of Gloucester.

MODERATOR OF THE ASSEMBLY (1963-64), Right Rev. J. S. Stewart, D.D.

Principal Clerk, Rev. J. B. Longmuir, T.D., M.A., B.L.

Deputy Clerk, Rev. D. F. M. Macdonald, M.A., LL.B.

Procurator, T. P. McDonald, Q.C.

Agent of the Church, D. B. Bogle, W.S.

Solicitor of the Church, G. Mercer Robertson, S.S.C.

Parliamentary Solicitor, H. L. P. Myles (London).

General Treasurer, Hay Downie, C.A.

Church Office, 121 George Street, Edinburgh 2.

Other Presbyterian Churches

(1) *The Presbyterian Church in Ireland*.—The largest of the Presbyterian churches in Ireland consists of 22 presbyteries, 566 ministers, 560 congregations, with 140,395 communicants, 128,351 families and 7,690 Sabbath-school teachers. During the 12 months ended Dec. 31, 1962, this branch contributed by congregational effort £237,081 for religious, charitable, and missionary purposes. The total income for the period for all purposes was £1,522,245—*Moderator* (1963–64), Rt. Rev. W. A. Montgomery, M.A., D.D. *General Sec.*, Rev. A. J. Gailey, B.A., D.D., Church House, Belfast.

(2) *The Presbyterian Church of England* has 15 presbyteries, 319 congregations, 14 preaching stations, 70,298 members, and 8,643 office-bearers. It has a Theological College (Westminster College, Cambridge), and supports 32 missionaries abroad, including 12 women. In 1962 the amount raised for all purposes was £797,094.

Moderator (1963–64), Rt. Rev. P. McCall, M.A.

Gen. Sec., Rev. A. L. Macarthur, M.A., M.Litt., Church House, 86 Tavistock Place, W.C.1.

THE CHURCH OF IRELAND

Sees	Archbishops.	Apptd.	Clergy.	Income of See.
*Armagh**	Most Rev. James McCann, D.D., Ph.D., *b.* 1897 (*cons.* 1945)	1959	62	£2,500
Dublin	Most Rev. George Otto Simms, D.D., Ph.D., *b.* 1910 (*cons.* 1952)	1956	113	2,500
	Bishops.			
Meath	Most Rev. Robert Bonsall Pike, M.A., D.D., *b.* 1905	1959	24	1,500
Cashel	Rt. Rev. William Cecil de Pauley, D.D., *b.* 1893	1958	21	1,458
Clogher	Rt. Rev. Alan Alexander Buchanan, M.A., D.D., *b.* 1907	1958	50	1,443
Connor	Rt. Rev. Robert Cyril Hamilton Glover Elliott, D.D., *b.* 1890	1956	109	1,750
Cork, Cloyne & Ross	Rt. Rev. Richard Gordon Perdue, D.D., *b.* 1910 (*cons.* 1954)	1957	45	1,703
Derry & Raphoe	Rt. Rev. Charles John Tyndall, D.D., *b.* 1900 (*cons.* 1956)	1958	72	2,140
Down & Dromore	Rt. Rev. Frederick Julian Mitchell, D.D., *b.* 1901 (*cons.* 1950)	1955	91	1,500
Killaloe	Rt. Rev. Henry Arthur Stanistreet, D.D., *b.* 1901	1957	21	1,500
Kilmore	Rt. Rev. Edward Francis Butler Moore, D.D., Ph.D., *b.* 1906	1958	42	2,000
Limerick	Rt. Rev. Robert Wyse Jackson, D.D., *b.* 1908	1961	21	1,461
Ossory	Rt. Rev. Henry Robert McAdoo, Ph.D., D.D., *b.* 1916	1962	52	1,535
Tuam	Rt. Rev. Arthur Hamilton Butler, M.B.E., D.D., *b.* 1912	1958	18	1,493

* *Primate.*

St. Patrick's National Cathedral, Dublin.
Dean and Ordinary, Very Rev. J. W. Armstrong, B.D.

GENERAL SYNOD

Consisting of House of Bishops (14) and House of Representatives (viz., 216 clerical and 432 lay).
Honorary Secretaries, Ven. R. G. F. Jenkins, B.D.; Very Rev. C. I. Peacocke, M.A.;
M. F. E. Dobbin; Senator W. A. W. Sheldon, T.D.
Chief Officer and Secretary to the Representative Church Body (Incorporated 1870), D. W. Pratt.
52 St. Stephen's Green E., Dublin 2; *Deputy Chief Officer and Accountant*, D. M. Hudson.
Asst. Sec., E. Taylor.

By the Act of Union, 1800, the Church of Ireland was united with the Church of England, the Sovereign, as one of its members, being supreme governor on earth. By the Act of 1869 this union was severed, and on Jan. 1, 1871, the Church of Ireland resumed her independent position. The Act of 1869 not only disestablished the Irish Church, but also took away her endowments, nothing being left but the right to the life services of the annuitant Bishops and Clergy (the annuities provided were commuted for a capital sum), the right to claim churches in use for divine service, the right to buy the See and Glebe Houses (with garden and curtilage), and £500,000 in lieu of private endowments.

The supreme governing body of the Church of Ireland is the General Synod, which meets annually.

Subject to the General Synod are 19 *Diocesan Synods*, which are assisted by smaller elected bodies called Diocesan Councils.

The Bishop of the Diocese was formerly chosen by the clerical and lay members of the *Diocesan Synod*, but since Dec. 1, 1959, has been chosen by an Electoral College. The Primate is chosen by the House of Bishops from amongst their own number.

The incumbent of the Parish is appointed by a *Board of Nomination*, consisting of 7 persons, viz.:—The Bishop, 3 diocesan nominators (2 clerical and 1 lay) appointed by the Diocesan Synod, and 3 parochial nominators (lay) appointed by the registered vestrymen of the parish.

The financial trustees of the Church are the Representative Body, composed of the Archbishops and Bishops, 14 clergymen and 28 laymen, chosen by the Diocesan Synods, with 14 co-opted members (clerical or lay). This body holds the property of the Church, and administers its funds, subject to the General Synod.

The first property it held was the capital sum £7,581,075, representing the life annuities of the Bishops and Clergy paid over as commutation money by the Church Commissioners, and also £500,000 compensation for private endowments. The funds, however, in the custody of the Representative Body amount in all to £15,309,935, made up of *Parochial Sustentation* £10,393,355, *General Synod Funds* £938,753, *Miscellaneous purposes* £3,977,727.

Since 1869 members of the Church have paid in to the Representative Body a total sum of £17,117,384. The interest of the Diocesan and Parochial Sustentation and other Funds is approximately £511,120.

THE EPISCOPAL CHURCH IN SCOTLAND

Sees. The Rt. Rev. Bishops.	Cons.	Clgy.	Stipd.
Aberdeen and Orkney, Edward Frederick Easson, D.D., *b.* 1905	1956	40	£*1,250
Argyll and the Isles, Richard Knyvet Wimbush, M.A., *b.* 1909	1963	12	*1,379
Brechin, John Chappell Sprott, M.A., *b.* 1903	1959	24	*1,250
Edinburgh, Kenneth Moir Carey, M.A., *b.* 1908	1961	74	*2,000
Glasgow and Galloway, Francis Hamilton Moncreiff, M.A. (*Most Rev. Primus*, 1962), *b.* 1907	1952	78	£*2,392
Moray, Ross and Caithness, Duncan Macinnes, M.B.E., M.C., *b.* 1897	1953	21	*1,190
St. Andrews, Dunkeld and Dunblane, John William Alexander Howe, M.A., B.D., *b.* 1920	1955	38	*1,364

* With residence.

Registrar of the Episcopal Synod, Donald B. Sinclair, W.S., 43 Castle Street, Edinburgh, 2.
Churches, Mission Stations, &c., 361. Clergy, 334. Communicants, 56,769

THE METHODIST CHURCH

UNDER the general designation of METHODISTS are included all those religious bodies which owe their existence, directly or indirectly, to the efforts of the Revd. John Wesley (*born* June 17, 1703; *died* March 2, 1791) and his brother, Revd. Charles Wesley (*born* Dec. 18, 1707; *died* March 29, 1788).

THE METHODIST CHURCH

On September 20, 1932, the Wesleyan Methodist Church, the Primitive Methodist Church and the United Methodist Church, were united and became "The Methodist Church."

The Methodist Church is governed primarily by the Conference, secondarily by the District Synods (held in September and May), consisting of all the ministers and of selected laymen in each district, over which a chairman is appointed by the Conference; and thirdly by circuit quarterly meeting of the ministers and lay officers of each circuit. The authority of both Synods and Quarterly Meetings is subordinate to the Conference, which has the supreme legislative and judicial power in Methodism.

President of the Conference (July, 1963–64), Rev. F. Greeves, M.A., LL.D.

Vice-President of the Conference (July, 1963–64), D. F. Nash.

Secretary of the Conference, Rev. E. W. Baker, M.A., D.D., Ph.D., 1 Central Buildings, Westminster, S.W.1.

President Designate (1964–5), Rev. A. K. Lloyd.
Vice-President Designate (1964–5), D. V. Brown.

Statistics.—In 1962 in association with the Conference in Great Britain (at home and abroad) there were 4,950 Ministers, 33,800 Local Preachers, 928,274 Members and Probationers. 17,209 Churches, 11,401 Sunday Schools, 108,510 Sunday School Officers and Teachers, and 661,806 Sunday Scholars.

The World Methodist Council, founded 1881, reorganized 1951, associates Methodism throughout the world in 82 countries.

The Methodist Church was founded in 1739 by the two brothers Wesley and rapidly spread throughout the British Isles and to America before 1770. The Methodist Church in Great Britain was united in 1932 by the fusion of the Wesleyan Methodist Church which was the original section, the Primitive Methodist Church, which arose through the evangelists Hugh Bourne and William Clowes in 1810, and the United Methodist Church, itself a fusion in 1907 of the Methodist New Connexion which dated from 1797, the Bible Christian Methodist Church, which dates from 1815 and the United Methodist Free Churches which originated in controversies in 1828 and 1849. The Methodist Church of America was formed by a union of three great Methodist denominations in 1939. Australasia, New Zealand, South Africa, Ghana, Nigeria and Italy have separate autonomous Methodist Churches, and other branches throughout the world have originated from the Methodist Church either in Great Britain or in America.

METHODIST CHURCH IN IRELAND

The Methodist Church in Ireland has 241 Ministers, 350 Lay Preachers, 31,763 Adult and 17,929 Junior Members, 1,939 Sunday School Teachers and 13,938 Scholars.

President (1963–4), Rev. F. E. Hill, B.A.

Secretary, Rev. R. D. E. Gallagher, M.A., B.D., The Grosvenor Hall, Belfast, 12.

THE UNITED CHURCH OF CANADA

The United Church of Canada is the result of the union (1925) of Methodist, Presbyterian and Congregational Churches in Canada. *Sec. of General Council*, Rev. Ernest E. Long, B.A., D.D., LL.D., The United Church House, 85 St. Clair E., Toronto.

INDEPENDENT METHODISTS

Independent Methodists.—This body is Congregational in its organization, with an unpaid Ministry. Its first Conference was held in 1805. In 1963 there were in Great Britain 270 Ministers, 8,111 Members, 150 Chapels and 9,146 Sunday School Scholars. *Secretary*, W. Drummond Brown, 21 Ashley Drive, Swinton, Lancs.

WESLEYAN REFORM UNION

This Union is Methodist in doctrine, Congregational in government, with, if any church desires it, a paid ministry. It is the remnant of the original Reformers expelled from Wesleyan Methodism in 1849. The adherents are mainly in the Midland and Northern counties. In 1963 there were in Great Britain 22 Ministers, 276 Lay Preachers, 5,571 Members, 158 Chapels and 7,114 Sunday Scholars. —*President* (1963–4), A. Fisher, Sheffield. *General Secretary and Connexional Editor*, Rev. A. Halladay, Wesleyan Reform Church House, 123 Queen Street, Sheffield, 1.

THE CALVINISTIC METHODIST CHURCH OF WALES

The CALVINISTIC METHODIST OR PRESBYTERIAN CHURCH OF WALES is the only Church of purely Welsh origin, and embraces a very large section of the Welsh-speaking population. Its form of government being Presbyterian, it is a constituent of the Pan-Presbyterian Council or Alliance. It is also a member of the British Council of Churches and the World Council of Churches. It has foreign missions in Assam and India.

In 1962 the body numbered—chapels and other buildings 1,400; ministers in pastoral charge, 449; elders, 7,024; communicants 131,316; Sunday-school teachers and officers 10,183, Sunday-school scholars 67,058. Contributions for various religious purposes (including the ministry), £969,531.

One of the features of the Welsh churches is the Sunday-school, which is attended by adults as well as children.

The *Eastern Association*, which now includes nine of the English Presbyteries, was formed in 1947 and has 344 chapels and 25,384 communicants.

On 18 July, 1933, the Calvinistic Methodist or Presbyterian Church of Wales Act, 1933, received the Royal Assent. By this measure the autonomy of the Church in matters spiritual and the establishment of a Properties Board have been secured.

The Welsh Mission in Assam and East Pakistan numbers over 200,000 members.

Moderator of General Assembly (1963–64), Rev. E. Howells, Bridgend.

Moderators of Associations (1963–64)—*South Wales*, Rev. W. Lloyd Jones, M.A., B.D., Skewen; *North Wales*, Sir David Hughes Parry, Q.C., LL.D., Llannwchllyn, Bala; *The East*, Rev. R. Howell Williams, B.A., Upton, Wirral.

Chief Secretary, Rev. J. Melville Jones, B.A., B.D., Neuaddwen, Tregaron, Cardiganshire.

THE INDEPENDENTS AND THE BAPTISTS

The INDEPENDENTS, or CONGREGATIONALISTS, are the most ancient community of Dissenters. In 1831 the majority of their churches united to form the Congregational Union of England and Wales, incorporated in 1902, and in 1920 nine provinces were formed, each with a Moderator. There are 51 county and other Associations in the British Isles, with 2,941 churches and preaching stations with 1,809 ministers and 210,268 members in England and Wales. *Chairman of the Congregational Union of England and Wales* (1963–64), Rev. John Marsh, M.A., D.D., D.Phil. *Secretary*, Rev. H. S. Stanley, M.A. *Office and Publication Department*, Memorial Hall, Farringdon Street, E.C.4.

The *Countess of Huntingdon's Connexion*, with 37 chapels and mission stations, is governed by nine trustees assisted by an annual conference of ministers and delegates. Most of the churches are affiliated with the Congregational Union. *Secretary*, B. Touch. *Offices*, 73 Selsea Avenue, Herne Bay, Kent.

THE CONGREGATIONAL UNION OF SCOTLAND. In 1795 James and Robert Haldane left the Church of Scotland and the churches which they founded formed the *Congregational Union* in 1812, which in 1896 united with the *Evangelical Union* (founded in 1843 by James Morison). There are 139 Churches of the *Congregational Union of Scotland* with a membership of 32,194. Of the 160 Ministers, 121 are Pastors. *President*, G. R. Green, M.A., Glasgow. *Secretary*, Rev. J. T. George, 217 West George Street, Glasgow, C.2.

The BAPTISTS have over 23,000,000 members in all countries. Like the Congregationalists, they are for the most part grouped in associations of churches, and the majority of these belong to the Baptist Union, which was formed in 1812–13. In the British Isles there were, in 1962, 2,110 pastors and deaconesses. The members numbered 310,437, young people (14–20), 58,665 and children under 14,196,733. *President of the Baptist Union* (1963–64), Rev. H. L. Watson. *Secretary*, Rev. E. A. Payne, M.A., D.D., Ll.D. *Office*, 4 Southampton Row, W.C.1.

Other Religious Denominations.

The **General Assembly of Unitarian and Free Christian Churches** has about 243 ministers, 330 chapels and other places of worship in Great Britain and Ireland. *Gen. Sec.*, Rev. John Kielty, Essex Hall, Essex Street, W.C.2.

The Salvation Army, first known as the Christian Mission, was founded by William Booth, in the East End of London in 1865. In 1878 it took its present name and adopted a quasi-military method of government. Since then it has become established in all parts of the world. The head of the denomination, known as the General, is elected by a High Council consisting of all the Commissioners of the Army. In 1962 there were, in Great Britain, 1,241 Corps (Churches), 2,986 Officers engaged in evangelistic work and 31,568 Local Officers (lay workers). The latest statistics for the world (1962) are 16,659 Corps and 25,427 Officers. *General*, (vacant).

International Headquarters:—101 Queen Victoria Street, E.C.4.

The **Brethren** number about 80,000, of whom five-eighths belong to the "Open" body. The **Society of Friends (Quakers)** consists of 21,179 members in Great Britain, and has 437 places of worship (*Recording Clerk*, Stephen J. Thorne). The total number in the world is about 160,000 (110,000 are in U.S.A. and Canada). *Central Offices* (*Great Britain*), Friends House, Euston Road, N.W.1. (*Ireland*), 6 Eustace Street, Dublin. The **Oxford Group** ("Moral Re-Armament"), *Hdqrs.*, 4 Hays Mews, Berkeley Square, W.1. The **First Church of Christ, Scientist**, in Boston, Massachusetts, U.S.A. (District Manager, Committees on Publication for Great Britain and Ireland, 30 Norfolk Street, Strand, W.C.2), has 332 branch churches and societies in Great Britain and Ireland. The **Moravian Church**, 5 Muswell Hill, N.10, has in the U.K. 40 congregations and preaching stations, with 2,936 communicants. **The Free Church of England** (otherwise called The Reformed Episcopal Church) has 37 churches in England. *Gen. Sec.*, Rev. W. C. Watkins, 8 Brassey Avenue, Broadstairs, Kent. **The Seventh Day Adventists** (*Hdqrs.*, Stanborough Park, Watford, Herts.), have 115 organized churches, 42 companies and 9,848 members in the British Isles. At Woking, Surrey, is the Shah Jehan Mosque for Moslems, built in 1889. There are also Mosques at Southfield, S.W.18, Commercial Road E.1, Birmingham, Manchester, Cardiff, South Shields, Coventry and Glasgow.

THE JEWS

It is estimated that about 450,000 Jews are resident in the British Isles, some 280,000 being domiciled in Greater London. Of the total number in Great Britain about 90 per cent. are described as adhering to orthodox views.

The *Board of Deputies of British Jews*, established in 1760, is the representative body of British Jewry and is recognized by H.M. Government. The basis of representation is primarily synagogal, but secular organizations are now also represented. It is a deliberative body and its objects are to watch over the interests of British Jewry, to protect Jews against any disability which they may suffer by reason of their creed and to take such action as may be conducive to their welfare.

President of the Board of Deputies (Woburn House, Upper Woburn Place, W.C.1), Sir Barnett Janner, M.P. *Secretary*, A. G. Brotman.

CHIEF RABBI—The Very Rev. Dr. Israel Brodie, *born* 1895, *appointed* 1948.

Secretary, Rabbi A. Rose, *Office*, 85 Hamilton Terrace, N.W.8.

The *Beth Din* (Court of Judgment) is a rabbinic body consisting of *Dayanim* (Assessors) and the Chief Rabbi, who is President of the Court. The Court arbitrates when requested in cases between Jew and Jew and gives decisions on religious questions. The decisions are based on Jewish Law and practice and do not conflict with the law of the land. The *Beth Din* also deals with matters concerning dietary laws and marriages and divorces, according to Jewish Law.

Dayanim, L. Grossnass; A. Rapoport; Dr. M. Lew; M. Steinberg; M. Swift.

Clerk to the Court, Marcus Carr, Adler House, Tavistock Square, W.C.1.

Chief Rabbi of the Community of Spanish and Portuguese Jews in London (Established 1657), Dr. Solomon Gaon.

THE ROMAN CATHOLIC CHURCH

HIS HOLINESS POPE PAUL VI (Giovanni Battista Montini), Roman Pontiff, *born* in Concesio, Italy, September 26, 1897; *ordained priest* May 29, 1920; nominated *Archbishop of Milan*, November 1, 1954; *Cardinal*, December 15, 1958; *elected Pope* June 21, 1963; *crowned* June 30, 1963.

THE SACRED COLLEGE OF CARDINALS, when complete, consists of six Cardinal Bishops, fifty Cardinal Priests and fourteen Cardinal Deacons. This number was fixed by Pope Sixtus V in 1586. Pope John XXIII created 23 new Cardinals on December 15, 1958, a further 8 new Cardinals on December 14, 1959, 7 on March 28, 1960, 4 more on Jan. 16, 1961, and 10 on Mar. 19, 1962. In August, 1963 there were 80 Cardinals. The Cardinals are the advisers and assistants of the Sovereign Pontiff and form the supreme council or Senate of the Church. On the death of the Pope they elect his successor. The assembly of the Cardinals at the Vatican for the election of a new Pope is known as the Conclave in which, in complete seclusion, the Cardinals elect by secret ballot; a two-thirds majority is necessary before the vote can be accepted as final. When a Cardinal receives the necessary votes the Dean of the Sacred College formally asks him if he will accept election and the name by which he wishes to be known. On his acceptance of the office the Conclave is dissolved and the First Cardinal Deacon announces the election to the assembled crowd in St. Peter's Square. On the first Sunday or Holyday following the election the new Pope is crowned with the tiara, the triple crown, the symbol of his supreme spiritual authority. A new pontificate is dated from the coronation.

The *Catholic Directory* estimates the Roman Catholic population of England and Wales at 3,726,500, Scotland (1962) 792,640, Republic of Ireland (1955) 2,786,033, Northern Ireland (1960) 484,214. The figures for Canada (1961) are 8,532,480, Australia (1961) 2,563,479, New Zealand (1962) 314,655, India (1961) 6,282,409, Pakistan (1961) 317,976, Ceylon (1957) 609,928, Malta (1958) 290,600, Federation of Malaya (1962) 111,426, State of Singapore (1962) 47,600. Trinidad (1961) 299,649, Jamaica (1962) 126,819, Tanganyika (1962) 1,750,528, Uganda (1962) 2,095,000, Nigeria (1962) 1,936,816, Ghana (1962) 655,138; world total (estimated) 550,357,000.

FORMS OF ADDRESS: *Cardinal*, "His Eminence Cardinal . . ." (if an Archbishop, "His Eminence the Cardinal Archbishop of . . . "); *Archbishop*, "The Most Rev. Archbishop of . . . ."; *Bishop*, "The Rt. Rev. the Bishop of . . . "

ENGLAND AND WALES

Apostolic Delegate to Gt. Britain, Malta, Gibraltar and Bermuda (vacant).

The Most Revd. Archbishops	CONS.	CLERGY*
Westminster, John Heenan (1963)	1951	887
Auxil., George Craven, M.C.	1947	
Auxil., David Cashman	1958	
Birmingham, Francis J. Grimshaw (1954)	1947	663
Auxil., Humphrey Bright	1944	
Cardiff, John A. Murphy (1961)	1948	212
Liverpool (vacant)		703
The Rt. Revd. Bishops		
Brentwood, Bernard Wall	1956	200
Clifton, Joseph Rudderham	1949	297
Hexham and Newcastle, James Cunningham (1958)	1957	432
Lancaster, Brian C. Foley	1962	278
Auxil., Thomas Pearson	1949	
Leeds, George Dwyer	1957	398
Menevia (Wales), John E. Petit	1947	204
Middlesbrough, George Brunner (1956)	1946	229
Northampton, Thomas L. Parker	1941	249
Auxil., Charles Grant	1961	
Nottingham, Edward Ellis	1944	351
Plymouth, Cyril Restieaux	1955	218
Portsmouth, *Archbishop* John H. King (1941)	1938	357
Coadj., Thomas Holland	1961	
Salford, Andrew Beck (1955)	1948	609
Shrewsbury, William Eric Grasar	1962	259
Southwark, Cyril Cowderoy	1949	666

SCOTLAND

The Most Revd. Archbishops		
St. Andrews & Edinburgh, Gordon Gray	1951	273
Glasgow (vacant)		364
Auxil., James Ward	1960	
The Rt. Revd. Bishops		
Aberdeen, Francis Walsh	1951	80
Argyll & Isles, Steven McGill	1960	37
Dunkeld, William Hart	1955	81
Galloway, Joseph McGee	1952	92
Motherwell, James D. Scanlan (1955)	1946	220
Paisley, James Black	1948	117

* In addition there are 80 priests serving as regular chaplains in H.M. Forces. The Most Rev. David Mathew, *Abp.* of *Apamea*, was appointed Bishop-in-Ordinary to H.M. Forces in 1954.

NORTHERN IRELAND†

The Most Revd. Archbishop	CONS.	CLERGY.
Armagh (vacant)		303
The Rt. Revd. Bishops		
Clogher, Eugene O'Callaghan	1943	157
Derry, Neil Farren	1939	149
Down & Connor, William Philbin	1962	315
Dromore, Eugene O'Doherty	1944	67
Kilmore, Austin Quinn	1950	140

BRITISH COMMONWEALTH

Europe

The Most Revd. Archbishop	CONS.
Malta, Michael Gonzi, K.B.E. (1943)	1924
The Rt. Revd. Bishops	
Gozo, Joseph Pace	1944
Gibraltar, John F. Healy	1956

America

Apostolic Delegate to Canada, Most Rev. Sebastiano Baggio (*Archbishop of Ephesus*).

The Most Revd. Archbishops	CONS.
Edmonton, John MacDonald (1938)	1934
Coadj.-Abp. Anthony Jordan (1955)	1945
Halifax, Gerald Berry (1953)	1945
Kingston, Joseph O'Sullivan (1944)	1931
Moncton, Norbert Robichaud	1942
Montreal, H. E. Cardinal Paul Emile Leger	1950
Ottawa, Joseph Lemieux (1953)	1936
Port of Spain, Finbar Ryan (1940)	1937
Quebec, Maurice L. Roy, O.B.E. (1947)	1946
Regina, Michael C. O'Neill	1948
Rimouski, Charles Parent (1951)	1944
St. Boniface, Maurice Baudoux (1955)	1948
St. John's, Newfoundland, Patrick Skinner (1951)	1950
Sherbrooke, George Cabana (1952)	1941
Toronto, His Eminence Cardinal James McGuigan (1934)	1930
Coadj-Abp., Philip F. Pocock (1961)	1951
Vancouver, B.C., William Duke (1931)	1928
Coadj.-Abp., Martin Johnson (1954)	1936
Winnipeg, George Flahiff (1961)	1961
Winnipeg (Byzantine Rite), Maxim Hermaniuk (1956)	1951

† There is one hierarchy for the whole of Ireland. Several of the Dioceses listed above have territory partly in the Republic of Ireland and partly in Northern Ireland.

CONS.

The Rt. Revd. Bishops

Alexandria, Rosario Brodeur ... 1941
Amos, Joseph Desmarais (1939) ... 1931
Antigonish, William Power ... 1960
Bahamas, Leonard Hagarty, V. A. ... 1950
Bathurst in Canada, Camille LeBlanc ... 1942
Belize, Robert Hodapp ... 1958
Bermuda Islands, Robert Dehler, V. A. ... 1956
Calgary, Francis Carroll ... 1936
Castries, B.W.I. Charles Gachet ... 1957
Charlottetown, Malcolm A. MacEachern ... 1955
Chicoutimi, Mario Paré ... 1956
Edmundston, Joseph Gagnon ... 1949
Edmonton (Byzantine Rite), Nicholas Sawaryn (1943) ... 1956
Fort William, Edward Jennings (1952) ... 1941
Gaspé, Archbishop Paul Bernier (1957) ... 1952
Georgetown, Richard Guilly, O.B.E. (1956) ... 1954
Gravelbourg, Aimé Decosse ... 1953
Grouard, Henry Routhier, V. A. (1953) ... 1945
Gulf of St. Lawrence, Gerard Couturier ... 1957
Hamilton, Joseph Ryan ... 1937
Harbour Grace-Grand Falls, John M. O'Neill. 1940
Hearst, Louis Levesque ... 1952
Hudson Bay. Mark Lacroix, V. A. ... 1943
Hull, Paul Charbonneau (1963) ... 1961
James Bay, Henri Belleau, V. A. ... 1940
Joliette, Joseph Papineau ... 1928
Kamloops, B.C., Michael A. Harrington ... 1952
Keewatin, Paul Dumouchel, V. A. ... 1955
Kingston (Jamaica), John McEleney (1956) ... 1950
Labrador, Lionel Scheffer, V. A. ... 1946
London, John Cody (1950) ... 1937
Mackenzie, Paul Piché, V. A. ... 1959
Mont Laurier, Abp. Joseph Eugène Limoges .. 1922
Nelson, William Doyle ... 1958
Nicolet, Albert Martin ... 1950
Pembroke, William Smith ... 1945
Peterboro', Benjamin Webster (1954) ... 1946
Prince Albert, Lawrence Morin (1959) ... 1955
Prince Rupert, Fergus J. O'Grady, V. A. ... 1956
Roseau (Dominica), Arnold Boghaert ... 1957
St. Anne de la Pocatière, Bruno Desrochers ... 1951
St. Catharines, Thomas J. McCarthy (1958) ... 1955
St. George's, N.F., Michael O'Reilly ... 1941
St. George's (Grenada), James Field ... 1957
St. Hyacinthe, Arthur Douville (1942) ... 1940
St. Jean de Quebec, Gerard Coderre (1955) ... 1951
St. Jerome, Emil Frenette ... 1951
St. John in Canada, Alfred Leverman (1953) .. 1948
St. Paul in Alberta, Louis Philip Lussier ... 1955
Saskatoon, Francis Klein ... 1952
Saskatoon (Byzantine Rite), Andrew Roborecki (1956) ... 1948
Sault Ste. Marie, Alexander Carter (1958) ... 1956
Timmins, Maxim Tessier (1955) ... 1951
Toronto (Byzantine Rite), Isidore Borecky (1956) ... 1948
Trois Rivières, Georges L. Pelletier (1947) .. 1943
Valleyfield, Alfred Langlois (1926) ... 1924
Victoria, B.C., Remi De Roo ... 1962
Whitehorse, John L. Coudert, V. A. ... 1936
Yarmouth, Albert Leménger ... 1953

Africa

Apostolic Delegate to South Africa, Most Rev. Guiseppe McGeough.
Apostolic Delegate to British East Africa, Most Rev. Guido Del Mestri.
Apostolic Delegate to West Central Africa, Most Rev. Sergio Pignedoli.
Apostolic Delegate to West Africa, Most Rev. Giovanni Maury.

The Most Revd. Archbishops

Blantyre, John Baptist Theunissen (1959) ... 1950
Bloemfontein, William P. Whelan (1954) ... 1948
Cape Coast, John Kodwo Amissah (1960) ... 1957

CONS.

Capetown, Owen McCann (1951) ... 1950
Dar-es-Salaam, Edgar Maranta (1953) ... 1930
Durban, Denis E. Hurley (1951) ... 1947
Kaduna, John McCarthy (1959) ... 1954
Lagos, Leo H. Taylor, C.B.E. (1950) ... 1934
Lusaka, Adam Kozlowiecki (1959) ... 1955
Maseru, Emmanuel Mabathoana (1961) ... 1953
Nairobi, John McCarthy (1953) ... 1946
Onitsha, Charles Heerey (1950) ... 1927
Pretoria, John Garner (1951) ... 1948
Rubaga, Joseph Kiwanuka (1961) ... 1939
Salisbury, Francis Markall ... 1950

The Rt. Revd. Bishops

Abercorn, Adolf Furstenberg ... 1959
Accra, Joseph Bowers ... 1953
Aliwal, John Lueck (1951) ... 1947
Arua, Angelo Tarantino ... 1958
Bathurst in Gambia, Michael Molony, C.B.E. . 1959
Benin City, Patrick J. Kelly (1950) ... 1940
Bethlehem, Peter Kelleter (1951) ... 1950
Bremersdorp, Constantine Barneschi (1951) ... 1939
Buea, Guilo Peeters ... 1962
Bukoba, H.E. Cardinal Laurence Rugambwa (1961) ... 1952
Bulawayo. Adolf Schmitt (1953) ... 1951
Calabar, James Moynagh (1950) ... 1947
Dedza, Cornelius Citsulu (1959) ... 1957
Dodoma, Anthony Pesce (1953) ... 1951
Eldoret, Joseph Houlihan ... 1960
Enugu, John Anyogu (1957) ... 1963
Eshowe, Aurelius Bilgeri (1951) ... 1947
Fort Jameson, Firmin Coutemanche (1959) .. 1953
Fort Portal, Vincent McCauley ... 1961
Fort Rosebery, René Pailloux ... 1961
Freetown and Bo, Thomas Brosnahan ... 1953
Gulu, John B. Cesana (1953) ... 1951
Gwelo, Louis Haene (1955) ... 1950
Ibadan, Richard Finn ... 1959
Iringa, Attilio Beltramino (1953) ... 1948
Johannesburg, Hugh Boyle (1954) ... 1949
Jos, John Redington ... 1954
Kampala, Vincent Billington (1953) ... 1948
Karema, Charles Msakila ... 1958
Kasama, Marcel Daubechies (1959) ... 1950
Keetmanshoop, Edward Schlotterbuck, V. A.. 1956
Keimoes, Henry J. Thunemann (1951) ... 1940
Keta, Antony Konings ... 1954
Kigoma, James Holmes Siedle (1958) ... 1946
Kimberley, John Boekenfohr ... 1953
Kisii, Maurice Otunga (1960) ... 1957
Kisumu, Frederick Hall (1953) ... 1948
Kokstad, Evangelist McBride (1951) ... 1949
Kroonstad, Gerard van Velsen (1951) ... 1950
Kumasi, Joseph Amihere Essuah ... 1962
Leribe, Ignazio Phakoe (1961) ... 1961
Lilongwe, Joseph Fady (1959) ... 1951
Livingstone, Phelim O'Shea (1959) ... 1950
Lydenburg, Anthony Rieterer ... 1956
Makeni, Augusto Azzolini ... 1962
Makurdi, James Hagan ... 1960
Mariannhill, Alphonsus Streit ... 1951
Masaka, Adrian Ddungu ... 1962
Mbarara, John Ogez ... 1957
Mbeya, Anthony van Oorschot (1953) ... 1950
Mbulu, Patrick Winters (1953) ... 1952
Meru, Laurence Bessone ... 1954
Mombasa-Zanzibar, Eugene Butler ... 1957
Monze, James Corboy ... 1962
Morogoro, Herman van Elswijk ... 1954
Moshi, Joseph Kilasara ... 1960
Musoma, John Rudin ... 1957
Mwanza, Joseph Blomjous (1953) ... 1946
Mzuzu, Jean Jobidon ... 1961
Navrorgo, Gerard Bertrand (1957) ... 1948
Ndanda, Victor Haelg (1961) ... 1949
Ndola, Francesco Mazzieri, O.B.E. (1949) ... 1959

Cons.

Nyeri, Kenya, Carlo Cavallera (1953) 1947
Ogoja, Thomas McGettrick.............. 1955
Ondo, William Field................ 1958
Oudtshoorn, Bruno Hippel (1951).......... 1943
Owerri, Joseph Whelan (1950)............ 1943
Oyo, Owen McCoy 1963
Peramiho, Herman Spies (1961)........... 1953
Port Elizabeth, Ernest Green 1955
Port Harcourt, Goffredo Okoye 1961
Port Louis, Daniel Liston (1949) 1947
Port Victoria, Marcel Maradan, C.B.E....... 1937
Qacha'snek, Joseph Delfine des Rosieres (1961) 1948
Queenstown, John B. Rosenthal (1951)...... 1943
Rulenge, Alfred Lanctot (1961) 1950
Shinyanga, Edward McGurkin............ 1956
Tamale, Gabriel Champagne 1957
Tanga, Eugène Arthurs.............. 1958
Tororo, John Grief, C.B.E. (1953) 1951
Umtali, Daniel Lamont 1957
Umtata Joseph Grueter (1951)............ 1941
Umuahia, Antony Nwedo, O.B.E. 1959
Umzimkulu, Pius B. Dlamini.............. 1954
Wa, Peter P. Dery 1960
Windhoek, Rudolph Koppmann, O.M.I. (1957) 1962
Yola, Patrick Dalton 1962
Zomba, Lawrence Hardman (1959)......... 1952

Asia

Internuncio to India, Most Rev. James R. Knox (*Archbishop of Melitene*)
Internuncio to Pakistan, Most Rev. Joseph Seusi

The Most Revd. Archbishops

Agra, Domenic Athaide.............. 1956
Bangalore, Thomas Pothacamury (1953)..... 1940
Bombay, H. E. Cardinal Valerian Gracias (1950) 1946
Calcutta, Albert D'Souza (1959).......... 1962
Changanacherry, Matthaw Kavakat (1956)... 1950
Colombo, Thomas Cooray (1947)........... 1946
Dacca, Lawrence Graner (1950)........... 1947
Delhi, Joseph A. Fernandes (1951) 1949
Abp.-Coadj, Angelo Fernandes.......... 1959
Ernakulam, Joseph Parecattil (1956) 1953
Hyderabad (India), Joseph Mark Gopu (1953).. 1948
Karachi, Joseph Cordeiro............... 1958
Madhurai, Peter Leonard (1953)........... 1936
Madras and Mylapore, Louis Mathias (1952).. 1934
Malacca–Singapore, Michel Olcomendy (1953) 1947
Nagpur, Eugene Louis D'Souza (1953)...... 1951
Pondicherry, Ambrose Rayappan (1955)..... 1953
Ranchi, Pio Kerketta (1961) 1961
Trivandrum (Syro-Malankara Rite), Gregorios Thangalathil (1955) 1953
Verapoly, Joseph Attipetty (1934)......... 1933

The Rt. Revd. Bishops

Ahmedabad, Edwin Pinto................ 1949
Ajmer and Jaipur, Leo de Mello........... 1949
Allahabad, Leonard Raymond............. 1947
Alleppey, Michael Arattukulam........... 1954
Amravati, Joseph A. Rosario 1955
Arabia, Irzio Magliacani, V. A............ 1950
Belgaum, Michel Rodrigues.............. 1953
Bellary (vacant).......................
Calicut, Aldo Patroni................... 1948
Chilaw, Edmund Peiris................. 1940
Chittagong, Raymond Larose............. 1952
Cochin, Alexander Edezhath 1952
Coimbatore, Savari Muthu Muthappa....... 1950
Cuttack, Paolo Gonzalez................. 1950
Cyprus, Elias Farah................... 1954
Darjeeling, Enrico Benjamin.............. 1962
Dibrugarh, Orestes Marengo............. 1951
Dinajpur, Giuseppe Obert............... 1949
Dumka, Leone Tigga.................. 1962
Galle, Nicholas M. Laudadio.............. 1934
Guntur, Ignatius Mummadi.............. 1943
Hong Kong, Laurenzo Bianchi (1951)....... 1949

Cons.

Hyderabad in Pakistan, Archbishop James van Miltenburg (1958)................ 1948
Indore, Francis Simons.................. 1952
Jabalpur, Conrad Dubbelman 1954
Jaffna, Emile Pillai (1950)............... 1949
Jalpaiguri, Ambrogio Galbiati............ 1952
Jamshedpur, Lorenzo Picachy 1962
Jesselton, James Buis, C.B.E., V. A.......... 1952
Jhansi, Francis Fenech................. 1954
Kandy, Leo Nanayakkara................ 1959
Khulna, Dante Battaglierin 1956
Kothamangalam, Matthew Potanamuzhi..... 1956
Kottar, Thomas R. Agniswami............ 1939
Kottayam, Thomas Tharayil (1951)......... 1945
Krishnagar, Luis La Ravoire Morrow....... 1939
Kuala Lumpur, Dominic Vendargon....... 1955
Kuching, John Vos, V. A................ 1952
Kumbakonam, Daniel Arulswami........... 1955
Kuwait, Theophane Stella, V. A........... 1955
Lahore, Roger Buyse.................. 1947
Lucknow, Conrad de Vito 1947
Lyallpur, Francis Cialeo (1960)............ 1939
Mangalore, Raymond D'Mello............ 1959
Meerut, Archbishop Joseph B. Evangelisti (1956) 1952
Miri, Anthony Galvin.................. 1960
Mysore (vacant) ....
Multan, Louis Scheerer................. 1960
Nellore, William Bouter................. 1929
Ootacamund, Anthony Padiyara........... 1955
Palai, Sebastian Vayalil................. 1950
Patna, Augustine Wildermuth............. 1947
Penang, Francis Chan.................. 1955
Poona, Andrew Alex De Souza............ 1949
Quilon, Jerome Fernandez............... 1937
Raigarh-Ambikapur, Stanislaus Tigga (1957). 1956
Rawalpindi, Nicholas Hettinga............ 1947
Salem, Lurdu Selvanden................ 1949
Sambalpur, Herman Westermann.......... 1951
Shillong, Stephen Ferrando (1935).......... 1934
Simla, John Burke 1959
Tanjore, Arokiaswami R. Sundaram 1953
Tellicherry, Sebastian Valloppilly.......... 1956
Tiruchirapally, James Mendonca.......... 1938
Tiruvalla, Cheriyan Polachirakal (1955) 1954
Trichur, George Alapatt 1944
Trincomalee, Ignatius Glennie 1947
Trivandrum (Latin Rite), Vincent Dereere (1937)........................ 1936
Tuticorin, Thomas Fernando (1953).......... 1950
Vellore, David Pillai................... 1956
Vijayapuram, Juan Abasolo y Leuce......... 1950
Vijayavada, Ambrogio De Battista.......... 1952
Visakhapatnam, Joseph Baud (1947)......... 1942
Warangal, Alfonso Berreta (1951) 1953

Australia

Apostolic Delegate to Australasia, Most Rev. Domenico Enrici

The Most Revd. Archbishops

Adelaide, Matthew Boevich............... 1940
Brisbane, James Duhig, K.C.M.G. (1912) 1905
Abp.-Coadj., Patrick O'Donnell 1949
Canberra-Goulburn, Eris M. O'Brien, C.M.G. (1954) 1948
Hobart, Guilford Young (1955)............ 1948
Melbourne, Daniel Mannix (1917) 1912
Abp.-Coadj., Justin Simonds (1942) 1937
Perth, Redmond Prendiville (1935).......... 1933
Sydney, H.E. Cardinal Norman Gilroy (1940) 1935

The Rt. Revd. Bishops

Armidale, Edward J. Doody.............. 1948
Australia (Byzantine Rite), John Prasko...... 1958
Ballarat, James O'Collins (1941) 1930
Bathurst (vacant) ....
Bunbury, Lancelot Goody (1954) 1951
Cairns, Thomas Cahill.................. 1949
Darwin, John O'Loughlin................ 1949

	Cons.
Geraldton, Francis Thomas	1962
Kimberleys, John Jobst, V. A.	1959
Lismore, Patrick Farrelly (1949)	1931
Maitland, John Toohey (1956)	1948
Port Pirie, Bryan Gallagher.	1952
Rockhampton, Francis Rush (1961)	1961
Sale, Patrick Lyons (1957)	1944
Sandhurst, Bernard Stewart (1950)	1947
Toowoomba, William Brennan	1953
Townsville, Hugh Edward Ryan	1938
Wagga-Wagga, Francis Henschke (1939)	1937
Wilcannia-Forbes, Thomas Martin Fox	1931
Wollongong, Thomas McCabe (1939)	1951

New Zealand

The Most Revd. Archbishop

Wellington, Peter McKeefry (1954)	1947

The Rt. Revd. Bishops

	Cons.
Aitape, Ignatius Doggett, V. A.	1957
Alexishafen, Adolf Noser, V. A. (1953)	1947
Auckland, *Archbishop* James Liston (1953)	1920
Christchurch, Edward Joyce	1950
Dunedin, John Kavanagh (1957)	1949
Fiji Islands, Victor Foley, V. A.	1944
Gilbert Islands, Pietro Guichet	1961
Goroka, Bernard Schilling, V. A.	1960
Kavieng, Alfred Stemper, V. A.	1957
Mount Hagan, George Bernarding, V. A.	1960
New Hebrides, Louis Julliard, V. A.	1950
N. Solomon Islands, Leo Lemay, V. A.	1935
Port Moresby, Virgil Copas, V. A.	1960
Rabaul, Isidore Scharmach, V. A.	1930
Samarai, Francis Doyle, V.A.	1959
Samoa and Tokelau Is., George Pearce, V. A.	1957
S. Solomon Islands, Daniel Stuyvenberg, V. A.	1936
Tonga and Niue Islands, John Rodgers, V. A.	1955
Western Solomon Islands, John Crawford, V. A.	1963
Wewak, Leo Arkfield, V. A.	1940
Yule Island, Eugene Klein, V.A.	1968

LONDON CATHEDRALS, CHURCHES, ETC.

St. Paul's Cathedral, City of London, E.C.4 (1675–1710), cost £747,660. The cross on the dome is 365 ft. above the ground level, the inner cupola 218 ft. above the floor. "Great Paul," in S.W. tower, weighs 17 tons. Organ by Father Smith (enlarged by Willis) in case carved by Grinling Gibbons (who also carved the choir stalls). The choir and high altar were restored in 1958 after war damage and the North Transept in 1962. The American War Memorial Chapel was consecrated in November, 1958. The Chapel of the Most Excellent Order of the British Empire in the Crypt of the Cathedral was dedicated on May 20, 1960. Nave and transepts free; Fees to the following parts (on weekdays only, 11 a.m. to 3.30 p.m. and—during Summer Time only—4.45 p.m. to 5.30 p.m.); Crypt, 6*d.* Library, whispering gallery, and stone gallery, 1*s.*; golden gallery 1*s.*; ball, 1*s.*; total, 3*s.* 6*d.* Service on Sundays at 8, *10.30, *3.15, and *6.30. Weekdays at 8, *10, *4. Also Wednesdays, *12.30 p.m., Litany; Fridays, *12.30 p.m. short mid-day service. (*Services are choral.) To the S. are remains of the Chapter House and Cloisters of "Old St. Paul's," destroyed by the Fire of London in 1666.

Westminster Abbey, S.W.1 (built A.D. 1050–1760).—Open on weekdays at 8 a.m. Admission to Royal Chapels by fee of 2*s.* (children 6*d.*) (weekdays) except on Fridays (open free). Transepts and Nave open on Sundays only between services. Holy Communion at 8; matins at 10.30; Holy Communion at 11.30. Evensong at 3. Evening service with Sermon at 6.30; Daily—Holy Communion at 8 a.m.; Westminster School Service at 9 a.m.; matins, 10 a.m.; evensong (choral), 5.0 p.m. (Saturday and Bank Holidays, 3 p.m.). Chapel of Henry VII, Chapter House and Cloisters; King Edward the Confessor's shrine, A.D. 1269, tombs of kings (Edward I, Edward III, Henry V, Mary, Queen of Scots, Queen Elizabeth I), and many other monuments and objects of interest, including the grave of "An Unknown Warrior" and St. George's Chapel at the W. end of Nave (1920), and Poets' Corner. The Coronation Chair encloses the "Stone of Scone" brought from Scotland by Edward I in 1297.

Southwark Cathedral, south side of the Thames, near London Bridge, S.E.1.—Mainly 13th century, but the nave is largely rebuilt. Known as St. Mary Overie before 1540. Open 7.30 a.m. to 6.30 p.m., free. Sunday services, Holy Communion, 8.30 and 11 a.m., Morning Prayer, 10.15 a.m., Evening Prayer, 3 p.m., Nave Service, 6.30 p.m. Weekdays: Matins, 8 a.m.; Evensong, 5.30 p.m. (choral except Thursdays) (5 p.m. on Saturdays). Holy Communion, 8.15 a.m., also 7.30 a.m. and 5.45 p.m., Thursdays and 1.10 p.m. Fridays. Lunch Hour Service, 1.20 p.m., Wednesdays. The tomb of John Gower (1330–1408) is between the Bunyan and Chaucer memorial windows, in the N. aisle; Shakespeare effigy backed by view of Southwark and Globe Theatre in S. aisle; the altar screen (erected 1520) has been restored; the tomb of Bishop Andrewes (died 1626) is near screen. The Early English Lady Chapel (behind the choir), restored 1930, is the scene of the Consistory Courts of the reign of Mary (Gardiner and Bonner); and is still used for this purpose. John Harvard, founder of Harvard University, was baptised here in 1607.

All Saints, Margaret Street, W.1.—Built by Butterfield in 1859. Anglo-Catholic and noted for its music.

St. Andrew Undershaft, St. Mary Axe, Leadenhall Street, E.C.3.—An early 16th-century church, contains a monument of Stow, the London antiquary (a new quill-pen being placed in his hand at an annual Commemoration Service), and a memorial of Holbein. The organ is by Renatus Harris the rival of Father Smith.

St. Bartholomew's Priory Church, Smithfield, E.C.1, the oldest parish church in London (A.D. 1123).—*Rector*, Rev. N. E. Wallbank, Mus.D. Fine old Norman building, with tomb of the first prior Rahere. N. transept restored and re-opened in June, 1893. Crypt, Lady Chapel and Cloisters opened 1905–1928. Open daily. Sunday services 9 a.m., 11 a.m. and 6.30 p.m.

St. Bride, Fleet Street, E.C.4.—Rebuilt by Wren. Restored after being gutted during Second World War and rededicated, Dec. 1957. Recent excavations have revealed remains of earlier churches on site.

St. Clement Danes, Strand, W.C.2.—Gutted in Second World War, rebuilt as Royal Air Force Church, and reconsecrated, 1958.

St. Ethelburga, Bishopsgate, E.C.2 (14th and 15th century) with two "Hudson" windows.—On April 19, 1607, Henry Hudson (the navigator who gave his name to Hudson's Bay and to the Hudson River), his son John, and his ten sailors took communion in St. Ethelburga's, "purposing to goe to sea foure days after."

St. George, Hanover Square, W.1 (18th century; famous for fashionable marriages).

St. George, Borough High Street, Southwark, S.E.—(Rebuilt 1736) contains the tombs of Bishop Bonner (1497–1569) and Edward Cocker (1631–1675), the author of Cocker's "Arithmetik."

(The expression "according to Cocker" refers to this book.)

ST. HELEN, Bishopsgate, E.C.2.—The "Westminster Abbey of the City" from its numerous monuments; building dates from 13th century. Contains a Shakespeare memorial window presented by Mr. William Prentice, an American.

ST. KATHERINE CREE, Leadenhall Street, E.C.3.—Rebuilt in early 17th century and ascribed to Inigo Jones. Contains a Catherine wheel E. window, an organ by Father Smith, Archbishop Laud's Prayer Book and Bible, and a monument of Sir Nicholas Throgmorton.

ST. MARGARET, WESTMINSTER, S.W.1.—Founded 11th or 12th century; buildings date from 15th century, with frequent "restorations." Since 1614 the parish church of the House of Commons.

ST. MARTIN-IN-THE-FIELDS, Trafalgar Square, S.W.1.—Built by James Gibbs (1721–6) in place of earlier church on same site. In register of burials are the names of Nell Gwynne (1687), Farquhar the dramatist (1707), and Roubiliac the sculptor (1672). A bust of James Gibbs by Rysbrack is in the church. Famous for its broadcast services.

ST. MARY-LE-BOW, Cheapside, E.C.2.—The famous Bow Bells were rung again for the first time on Dec. 20, 1961, more than 20 years after the church was bombed. The bells were recast from the old metal.

ST. MICHAEL, PATERNOSTER ROYAL, College Hill, Upper Thames Street, E.C.4.—Rebuilt after the Fire by Strong (a pupil of Wren's), the former church contained the tomb of "Dick Whittington" and a Grinling Gibbons altarpiece.

ST. PAUL, Covent Garden, W.C.2.—Built by Inigo Jones. The tombstones round the exterior of the church record the burial places of Samuel Butler (Hudibras), Sir Peter Lely (painter), Wycherley (dramatist), Grinling Gibbons (woodcarver), Dr. Arne ("Rule, Britannia"), and Macklin (actor); Ellen Terry memorial.

SAVOY CHAPEL, Savoy Street, Strand, W.C.2 (rebuilt about 1505, on site of 13th-century Savoy Palace, restored after disastrous fire in 1864).—Graves of Gavin Douglas and George Wither, and memorials of D'Oyly Carte, Laurence Irving.

TEMPLE CHURCH, The Temple, E.C.4.—The nave forms one of five remaining round churches in England, the others being at Cambridge, Northampton, Little Maplestead (Essex), and Ludlow Castle. Rebuilding of the church was completed in 1958. Sunday morning services, open to the public, 11.15 a.m., except in August and September. *Master of the Temple*, Rev. Canon T. R. Milford, M.A.

Church of Scotland

CROWN COURT CHURCH, Russell Street, Covent Garden, W.C.2.—Sundays, 11.15 and 6.30. *Minister*, Rev. J. M. Scott, M.A., B.D., F.S.A.Scot.

ST. COLUMBA'S, Pont Street, S.W.1. Sundays, 11 and 6.30. *Minister*, Rev. J. F. McLuskey, M.C., D.D.

Congregational

CITY TEMPLE, Holborn Viaduct, E.C.1.—Sundays 11 and 6.30. *Minister*, Rev. A. L. Griffith.

WESTMINSTER CHAPEL (CONGREGATIONAL), Buckingham Gate, S.W.1.—Sundays, 11 and 6.30. *Minister*, Rev. D. M. Lloyd-Jones.

Methodist

WESLEY'S CHAPEL, City Road, E.C.1. Contains many relics of John and Charles Wesley and other great founders of Methodism. As the "Mother Church of Methodism" visitors attend from all parts of the world.—Sunday morning at 11; evening at 6.30. Wednesday, 7.30 a.m., Holy Communion. Thursday lunch time, 1.15—1.45. John Wesley's tomb in graveyard behind chapel. In front is Wesley's House and Museum. *Minister*, Rev. M. W. Woodward, 49 City Road, E.C.1. Opposite Wesley's Chapel is *Bunhill Fields Burial Ground*, City Road, the burial place of Dr. John Owen (1583), John Bunyan (1688), Daniel Defoe (1731), Dr. Watts (1748), William Blake (1828), and Susanna Wesley (1742). To the west of the cemetery is the *Friends' Burial Ground*, with the grave of George Fox, founder of the Society of Friends.

CENTRAL HALL, Westminster, S.W.1.—Sunday Services, 11 a.m. and 6.30 p.m. *Minister*, Rev. D. A. Greeves, M.A.

KINGSWAY HALL, Kingsway and Great Queen Street, W.C.2.—Sundays at 10, 11, and 6.30. *Minister*, Rev. Donald O. Soper, M.A., Ph.D.

Baptist

BLOOMSBURY CENTRAL BAPTIST CHURCH, Junction of Shaftesbury Avenue and New Oxford Street, W.C.2.—Sundays, 11 and 6.30. *Minister*, Rev. H. Howard Williams, Ph.D.

Society of Friends

FRIENDS' HOUSE, Euston Road, N.W.1.

Roman Catholic

WESTMINSTER CATHEDRAL, Ashley Place, Westminster, S.W.1 (close to Victoria Station), built 1895–1903 from the designs of J. F. Bentley (the campanile is 283 feet high—open to public by lift, 1s.).—*Sundays*. Low Masses with short sermon, 6, 7, 8, 9; Capitular High Mass with short sermon, 10.30; Low Masses with sermon, 12 noon, 5.30 p.m. and 7 p.m.; Solemn Vespers and Benediction, 3.30; Compline, 6.30. *Weekdays*. Matins and Lauds, 8.30 a.m. Low Masses, 6.30, 7, 7.30, 8, 8.30, 9; Capitular High Mass, 10.30, Low Masses, 12.30 and 6 p.m.; Vespers, Compline and Benediction, 5 p.m.; Night prayers, 7.45. Confessions at all times. *Holydays of Obligation*. Low Masses, 6, 6.30, 7, 7.30, 8, 8.30, 9; Capitular High Mass, 10.30; Low Masses, 12 noon, 12.30, 6 and 8 p.m. Cathedral open 6 a.m. to 9 p.m. (Bank Holidays, 6 p.m.). Cardinals Wiseman, Manning, Griffin and Godfrey buried in Crypt; Cardinal Hinsley buried in St. Joseph's Chapel; Bishop Challoner in St. Gregory's Chapel; Shrine of Blessed John Southworth in the Chapel of St. George and the English Martyrs. The Arch over the High Altar and the Tympanum beneath it have been covered with a rich mosaic showing Christ in Glory, with groups of the XII Apostles. Recently completed mosaics by Boris Anrep in Blessed Sacrament Chapel, and noteworthy mosaics in Lady Chapel and elsewhere. Exhibition of Treasures daily in Sacristy (weekdays, 11.30–12.30, 2–3. Sundays, 2–3, 5.30–6.30).

THE ORATORY, Brompton, S.W.7.—Sundays: Masses, 6.15, 7, 8, 9, 10; 10.45 (High Mass); 12 (with Sermon), 4.30; Vespers and Benediction, 3.30; Night Service, 7. Weekdays: Masses, 6.30, 7, 8, 8.30 daily; 12.30, 6.30 p.m., Mon to Fri.; 10, Sat. only. Service daily at 8 p.m., except Saturday. Saturday, Benediction, 4.30. Holy days: Masses 6.30, 7, 7.30, 8, 8.30, 9. 10, 10.45 (High Mass); 12.30 and 6.30 p.m.; Vespers and Benediction, 5.30.

Principal Jewish Synagogues

SPANISH AND PORTUGUESE SYNAGOGUE, Bevis Marks, E.C.3.

GREAT SYNAGOGUE, Creechurch Place, Aldgate, E.C.3.

WEST LONDON SYNAGOGUE, Upper Berkeley Street, W.1.

LIBERAL JEWISH SYNAGOGUE, St. John's Wood Road, N.W.8.

Education

ENGLAND AND WALES

Education in England and Wales is organized under the *Education Act*, 1944 (Butler Act). Minor amending Acts were passed in 1946, 1948 and 1953. The main features of the system are (*a*) that the State school system is highly decentralized, education being the responsibility of 146 *local education authorities* (61 administrative counties, 83 county boroughs, 1 joint board and London). The County Authorities exercise their powers in many instances through Divisional Executive Committees and the Education Committees of Excepted Districts: (*b*) that voluntary agencies play an important part in educational provision often in co-operation with the State. The Ministry of Education controls the system mainly through the scheme of inspection and with power derived from statute. The expenditure of local education authorities is met partly from rates and partly from central government grants. The latter are paid mainly in the form of a general grant from the Ministry of Housing and Local Government covering local health and other services as well as education. Detailed suggestions to L.E.A's. are issued in Ministry of Education circulars and administrative memoranda. There are central advisory councils dealing with education in England and in Wales respectively.

A statutory report and two volumes of full statistical tables are published yearly by the Ministry.

The State System

The State system is in transition as the 1944 Act is being implemented. The administrative system has been reorganized and the school-leaving age raised (April 1, 1947) to 15. The major problem at present is the provision of teachers and accommodation for the increased number of children at school between 1952 and 1962. Special attention is being paid to the development of technical education. About 6,200 students were enrolled for courses leading to the Diploma in Technology in the 1961–62 session (5,000 in the preceding year). In 1961, 619 students gained the diploma as compared with 215 in 1960 and during 1961–62, 37 had been accepted as candidates for the new higher award of Membership of the College of Technologists. There are 10 Colleges of Advanced Technology. These have now been given the status of direct grant institutions, independently governed (i.e., no longer controlled by the local education authority) and financed by the Ministry. In 1960–61 about 7,500 students were taking full-time and sandwich courses leading to qualifications at university level, including degrees, diplomas in technology, and various professional qualifications. Over 5,000 were enrolled in advanced part-time day courses and 3,890 in evening courses. It is expected that by the early 1970's the number of places in these colleges will have increased to 26,000–27,000.

Education is envisaged in the 1944 Act in three stages:—

Primary Stage (for children up to 11 years). *Nursery Schools* to age 5 (must be provided by Local Education Authority for all parents who desire them); *Infant Schools*—from age 5 (compulsory school age); *Junior Schools*—from age 8 to 11.

About the age of 11 all children are to go to a secondary school. The suitability of the school may be reviewed at age 13.

Secondary Stage (11 years to 15 years, later to be raised to 16)—*Secondary Grammar Schools* (giving an academic education); *Secondary Technical Schools* (for those whose abilities are of a more practical character); *Secondary Modern Schools* (giving a general and practical education).

These Secondary Schools are intended to be of equal status and can be combined into a single multi-lateral or "comprehensive" school. The prevailing tendency is to foster wide experiment and flexibility in the organization of secondary schools. Education in Primary and Secondary Schools is ree.

Pupils in Secondary Schools may sit for the examinations leading to the award of the General Certificate of Education. The nine examining bodies set papers at three levels, ordinary, advanced and scholarship. Entrance to the Universities and to many courses of professional training depends on the results in these examinations. In accordance with the Third Report of the Secondary School Examinations Council a new and uniform system of grading and presentation of results of G.C.E. examinations at A level will be used by all examining bodies. There will be five grades of pass awards on main or "basic" papers and two "supplementary" gradings (Distinction and Merit) for abler candidates who take "S" papers in addition to main papers: the existing Scholarship papers will be discontinued.

Since 1944 various bodies have set up examinations to meet the needs of pupils for whom the G.C.E. is not suitable. The Minister has accepted in principle the recommendation made by the Secondary School Examinations Council in its 1961 report, *The Certificate of Secondary Education*, that new school-leaving examinations leading to such a certificate should be nationally established on a regional basis, and in Sept., 1962 the Council announced that the examinations will probably start by 1965. The Council proposes that pupils should have completed five years of secondary education, that the examinations should be on a "subject" basis—*i.e.*, that candidates should be free to enter for any subject or combination of subjects—and should be conducted largely under the control of teachers, but should be co-ordinated by the Council itself, which would advise the Minister on questions of recognition and standards, and should have the help of an examinations research and development unit. This follows the main recommendation of the Beloe Committee.

Further Stage. [Includes all types of provision for education after 15 (later 16).] *County Colleges* which, when established, all children not receiving full-time education will attend for the equivalent of one day a week from age 15 (later 16) to age 16 (later to be raised to 18); *Technical Colleges and Colleges of Art and Commerce* (providing specialist studies); *Evening Institutes* (evening classes in vocational and other subjects); *Service of youth* (recreational and other services for youth provided in co-operation with voluntary bodies); *Adult Education* (liberal education for adults provided in co-operation with voluntary bodies); *Community Centres, etc.*

In January, 1962, 7,168,287 children were present in the primary or secondary schools maintained, aided or controlled by Local Education Authorities. Of these 1,675,957 were in modern schools, 708,343 in grammar, 97,411 in technical, 45,248 in bilateral and multilateral and 157,477 in comprehensive.

The number of pupils aged 15 and over rose to 444,845 in maintained schools and 39,211 in direct grant schools. The number in sixth forms in grammar and other schools was 121,669. There were 123,310 (19,383 in sixth forms) in all direct grant schools, 304,227 in independent schools recognized as efficient, and 190,732 in other independent schools. The number of pupils in all special schools, including hospital, was 63,826. The number of children in all-age schools in 1962 was 170,465. The percentage of primary school children in classes of over 40 had gone down from 19·4 to 18·9. The percentage of children in senior classes of over 30 in all types of school was 56·6, a decrease of 5 per cent. The average size of class in primary schools was 32·3 and in secondary 29·0. In grant-aided establishments for further education, in 1961 full-time and sandwich students numbered 818,600 and part-time day-release students 556,000, evening students numbering 1,746,400.

Total net expenditure on revenue account of local education authorities, during the year ending March, 1962 (excluding meals and milk) amounted to approximately £781,198,000, compared with £704,553 the previous year.

The Youth Service

The Minister has issued regulations for the recognition by the Ministry of Qualified Youth Leaders, on a salary scale of £680 by £35(8) and £40 to £1,000: L.E.A.'s may pay £100–350 a year extra for posts of greater responsibility. Such leaders must *either* hold a university diploma *or* a degree in social science, *or* have completed five years' satisfactory service by Aug. 1, 1963 as full-time leaders employed by a local education authority or by a national voluntary grant-aided organization, *or* complete a course of training for full-time leadership provided by the National College, Leicester; Westhill Training College, Birmingham; University College, Swansea; the N.A.B.C. in co-operation with Liverpool University; or the National Council of Y.M.C.A.'s. In cases of existing full-time leaders who cannot fulfil either of these conditions the Minister will consider with the Joint Negotiating Committee what further training they will need for qualification. Unqualified full-time leaders may be paid on the scale £500 by £30(6) to £680. It is proposed to double the number of full-time leaders in five years but the Youth Service must continue to rely upon the participation of many thousand part-time workers, who should have adequate opportunity for training, and such training in all areas should reach the same high standard. The Ministry has established a register of youth leaders, qualified and unqualified, which at the end of 1962 contained particulars of 737 full-time leaders—about 85 per cent. of those at work.

Towards the target of 1,300 full-time youth leaders by 1966 (compared with some 700 when the Albemarle Committee reported) the number of recruits was increased in 1962 by 84 who had completed the first course at the National College, while at the end of the year 208 students were in training there and in the other four full-time courses.

Grants to national voluntary organizations for headquarters and training expenses increased in 1962 from £229,100 to £235,700. Offers of grants towards the cost of local capital projects under the Social and Physical Training Grant Regulations decreased from £863,369 for 318 projects in 1961 to £387,242 for 157 projects, but this was due to new arrangements with local authorities regarding submission of grants: the work and proposals of voluntary bodies continued in fact to grow, and co-operation between these and local authorities is developing very favourably. Proposals for building projects costing £13,500,000 in the next few years are under consideration.

Voluntary Agencies

The school system is complicated by voluntary agencies which have assisted greatly in educational development. A number of the primary and secondary schools are still provided by voluntary bodies, mainly religious, but have long been maintained by L.E.A.'s. Under the 1944 Act, the managers of such schools could obtain half of the funds required for rebuilding to modern standards, the schools remaining under their partial control as "aided schools" and the cost of running the schools being met by the Local Education Authority. Under the Act of 1959 the building grant has been increased to 75 per cent. in respect of existing schools and of new secondary schools where these are required to accommodate pupils from existing primary schools. If the managers cannot raise money necessary for rebuilding, schools become "controlled schools" under the management of the Local Education Authority, though with provisions enabling denominational religious instruction to be given. In January, 1962, there were 827,452 pupils in Church of England schools, 582,217 in Roman Catholic, and 149,261 in others; of these 962,768 were in aided schools, 531,756 in controlled and 63,909 in special agreement schools. Since 1945, grants of £31,886,560 and loan advances of £9,323,059 have been made for building. Of the 10,115 voluntary schools or departments (primary and secondary) in January, 1962, 4,652 had been given controlled, 5,352 aided and 149 special agreement status.

The Direct Grant Grammar Schools (non-profit-making and with some non-local characteristics) occupy a semi-independent position, getting grants direct from the Ministry. They are run by Boards of Governors with Local Education Authority representatives and take fee-paying pupils chosen by themselves. For these pupils fees are graded according to parent's means. At least 25 per cent. of the places must be free, and Local Authorities may claim up to a further 25 per cent. of places, for which no further fees are paid by parents. In Jan., 1961 there were 179 such schools with 111,634 pupils (9,092 being boarders). There were also 5 Direct Grant Secondary Technical Schools with 829 pupils.

About 90 *Public Boarding Schools* and 4,036 *Private Schools* remain independent of the State system, except that many Public Schools give a limited number of places to nominees of Local Education Authorities. Under the 1944 Act all schools are being inspected by the Ministry and can be closed if found inefficient. (*See also* p. 541).

The number of students in further education rose steadily between 1961–62—full-time students from 119,000 to 140,000; sandwich course students from 12,900 to 16,000; part-time day students from 556,000 to 602,000 and evening students from 784,000 to 818,000. For the first time figures have been given of grants to students for courses in establishments of further education "comparable" to those in universities and training colleges. These rose from 7,200 in 1959–60 to 10,200 in 1961–62.

In the field of Further Education many private bodies, often receiving grants of money from Local Education Authorities and from the Ministry, are associated with the public authorities.

Teachers

The number of teachers in the maintained primary and secondary schools must be further raised from 278,463, of whom 20 per cent. are graduates (March, 1962), to deal with the increasing child population. In particular there is a shortage of women teachers. The total number of teachers in grant-aided establishments is 321,274, of whom 22.8 per cent. are graduates. Teachers are trained in a total of 186 institutions of various types. These include 24 University Departments of Education providing a one-year course for graduates. In 1962–63 these had 3,260 students. The remainder provide a three-year course for non-graduates and, in certain instances, a one-year course for graduates, the number of whom is to be increased. In 1962–63, these had 47,577 students. 110 general colleges are provided by Local Education Authorities and 49 by voluntary bodies. A large-scale plan of expansion has now been initiated, providing for a student population of 80,000 in the training colleges by 1970–71. The voluntary colleges receive from the Government 75 per cent. of the building costs involved. Day training colleges, mainly for older and more mature students, have already been established in 8 areas and in Sept. 1962 had 1,750 students. Teachers, other than graduates, must have satisfactorily completed a course of training. A degree or its equivalent entitles the holder to be given qualified teacher status but the National Advisory Council on the Training and Supply of Teachers has recommended the Minister to make training compulsory after 1968 for graduates who wish to teach in maintained schools. In 1962 there were 5,263 teachers (3·7 per cent.) in maintained primary schools who were graduates, 13,673 (17·9 per cent.) in secondary modern and 28,551 (77·8 per cent.) in grammar. In direct grant grammar schools there were 4,192 (70 per cent.). In March, 1962, there were 1,275 non-qualified men teachers in maintained primary and secondary schools and 5,211 women.

Payment of teachers is regulated by the *Burnham Scale* which, on January 1, 1962, provided (for primary and secondary schools) from £600–1,200 for a non-graduate 3-year-trained teacher to £890–1,490 for a good honours graduate with six years' degree study, research and professional training. In these scales are added allowances for posts of special responsibility ranging from £100 for a graded post of assistant teacher to £1,670 for heads of the largest secondary schools. Salaries of men and women teachers are now equal.

The Commonwealth and Education

Resulting in many respects from the two recent Commonwealth Education Conferences (one at Delhi and one at Oxford) major developments have occurred in teaching about the Commonwealth in British schools (which the Commonwealth Institute assists in many ways) and co-operating with Commonwealth countries in the training and exchange of teachers. In 1961, 336 and in 1962, 390 bursaries were awarded for one or two (exceptionally three) year courses of study in this country to serving teachers, training college lecturers, inspectors and organizers from developing countries. In the summer of 1961, 80, and in 1962, 60 British teachers headed by one of Her Majesty's Inspectors conducted vacation courses in Nigeria for over 800 African teachers. The recruitment of teachers for service overseas (about 600 each year) has been considerably facilitated with the co-operation of local education authorities and teachers' associations.

EDUCATION IN SCOTLAND

The educational system of Scotland has developed independently of that of England and presents a number of distinctive features. The Scottish Education Department is the central body and the Education Authorities are the local bodies concerned in administering the provisions of the Education (Scotland) Act, 1962, which consolidates the enactments relating to education in Scotland. These authorities are the councils of the four cities (Aberdeen, Dundee, Edinburgh and Glasgow) and 31 county councils or joint county councils. Educational facilities of various kinds are also provided by the governing bodies of grant-aided schools, independent schools, central institutions providing advanced technical education and national voluntary organizations in the field of informal further education. The "Scottish solution" of the question of denominational schools arrived at in 1918 provided for the transfer of any denominational voluntary school to the management of the Education Authority subject to certain conditions relating to religious observances and the appointment of staff designed to preserve the denominational character of the school. Denominational schools provided by Education Authorities are subject to the same conditions.

Schools in Scotland fall into three main classes, *viz.* public schools, which in Scotland means schools managed by Education Authorities: grant-aided schools, conducted by voluntary managers who receive grants direct from the Department: and independent schools which receive no direct grant, but which are subject to inspection and registration. In the year ended July 31, 1962, there were 3,241 public schools, with a roll of 884,945, 48 grant-aided schools, with a roll of 21,973 and 139 independent schools, attended by 17,883 pupils.

The primary course normally lasts for seven years. At age 11½ to 12½ each pupil is allocated to the secondary course from which he seems most likely to profit in the light of his aptitude and ability, assessed on the basis of his teachers' estimates and of intelligence and other tests. [The wishes of the parents must be considered also, and a pupil may be transferred to another course if his progress in the secondary school shows that this is desirable.] In order to suit the varying needs of the pupils, secondary courses differ in length and in the subjects included. For pupils likely to leave school at 15 the course normally lasts three years. For those aiming at the Scottish Certificate of Education a variety of courses extending to four, five or six years is available. About 35 per cent. of secondary entrants are admitted to Certificate courses. Courses of all types, lasting from three to six years, are provided at comprehensive secondary schools, attended by all the pupils in the area they serve. Junior secondary schools normally provide only three-year courses, but a number now provide for their abler pupils a four-year course leading to the Ordinary grade of the Certificate. Senior secondary schools provide only courses leading to the Certificate.

The Scottish Certificate of Education (formerly the Scottish Leaving Certificate) is awarded by the Department and is normally taken at the end of senior secondary courses of four or five years' duration. Pupils may take as many of a wide range of subjects as they are capable of attempting on either the Ordinary grade, corresponding to the G.C.E. Ordinary Level, or on the Higher, which, because there is less specialized study in sixth forms as understood in England, is not of so high a standard as the G.C.E. Advanced. In the award of a pass on either grade the teacher's estimate is taken into account as well as performance in the written examination.

Facilities for further education are provided by 16 Central Institutions (advanced colleges administered by independent Boards of Governors) and by further education centres managed by Education Authorities. The Central Institutions provide the highest form of specialized and fully organized instruction in science and technology, agriculture, commerce, domestic science and the arts. These colleges issue their own Diplomas and Associateships which are, in certain cases, equivalent in academic status to honours degrees and ordinary degrees.

The further education centres provide less advanced courses which are mainly part-time covering vocational and non-vocational subjects. The vocational courses normally lead to Craft certificates, certificates of the City and Guilds of London

Institute or National Certificates. Courses are provided in any subject for which there is a reasonable demand.

There are seven Colleges of Education in Scotland. Six of the colleges (of which two are Roman Catholic residential colleges for women) provide both one- and three-year courses and are associated with a university. The seventh is a residential college of physical education for women. All men teachers must possess a university degree (except in certain "practical" subjects) and take a year's professional training at a College of Education. A considerable proportion of women teachers take a degree or diploma and a year's training, but those who do not must take three years' training. The basic scales of teachers' salaries are non-graduate, graduate and honours graduate, with additional payment for posts of special responsibility.

EDUCATION IN NORTHERN IRELAND

The statutory system of education in Northern Ireland is broadly similar to the system in Great Britain. Under the 1947 Act primary education is provided in primary schools for children up to 11½ years of age or thereabouts when they are transferred to one or other of the types of secondary schools. Those who pass to secondary intermediate schools follow a practical curriculum and the remainder, most of whom have attained a qualifying standard at an examination conducted by the Ministry of Education, proceed to secondary grammar schools. A child who is successful at the qualifying test for entry to a grammar school is awarded a scholarship by the local education authority of the area in which he is normally resident. Reciprocal arrangements between local education authorities in the United Kingdom ensure that in the event of a change of residence of the parents of a pupil who has passed the necessary test either in Great Britain or in Northern Ireland, the pupil's grammar school education will be continued.

On December 31, 1962, there were 1,526 Primary (including Nursery and Special) Schools with 191,731 pupils, 82 Grammar Schools with 40,160 pupils, 122 Secondary Intermediate Schools with 55,820 pupils and 28 Technical Intermediate Schools with 4,048 pupils. There were also 171 Institutions of Further Education (including 62 non-permanent Centres) with 5,277 full-time and 41,508 part-time students enrolled. The Queen's University of Belfast had 55 Professors, 24 Readers, 303 Lecturers, Assistant Lecturers and University Tutors, and 4,319 students. Magee University College, Londonderry, had 5 Professors, 25 Lecturers, and 357 students. The estimated cost to the Exchequer for 1963–64, of education provided by the Ministry of Education, is £21,989,150, and from rates £6,374,458.

THE UNIVERSITIES

There are twenty-one degree-giving universities in England (Birmingham, Bristol, Cambridge, Durham, East Anglia, Exeter, Hull, Keele, Leeds, Leicester, Liverpool, London, Manchester, Newcastle-upon-Tyne, Nottingham, Oxford, Reading, Sheffield, Southampton, Sussex and York): one in Wales (the University of Wales with Colleges at Aberystwyth, Bangor, Cardiff and Swansea): four in Scotland (Aberdeen, Edinburgh, Glasgow and St. Andrews): and one in Northern Ireland (the Queen's University, Belfast). In addition the Manchester College of Science and Technology and the Royal College of Science and Technology, Glasgow, receive Treasury grants on the recommendation of the University Grants Committee. An arrangement was concluded in 1961 under which St. David's College, Lampeter, under the sponsorship and through the University College of South Wales and Monmouthshire (Cardiff) is also financially assisted by the Exchequer. All these institutions are self-governing. The University of Sussex admitted its first students in October, 1961; and two other new foundations the Universities of East Anglia and York, admitted their first students in October, 1963. Plans are in hand for the establishment of other new Universities of Essex (at Colchester), of Kent (at Canterbury), of Lancaster, of Warwick (at Coventry). The total number of full-time students in the existing universities and colleges (excluding the Queen's University, Belfast) receiving grants from the University Grant Committee in the session 1961–62 was 113,143 of whom 28,781 were women (compared with a total of 107,699 in the previous year and just over 50,000 in 1939). The Government's aim is to continue the expansion of the universities to about 170,000 places by 1973–74. 87·1 per cent. of the students were assisted in whole or in part by scholarships or other awards from public or private funds. The Government has accepted the recommendation of the Anderson Committee that an award from public funds should be made available to all students admitted to degree courses who have two G.C.E. passes at A level or the equivalent. The recurrent expenditure of university institutions in Great Britain in 1961–62 amounted to £74,118,152. Grants for capital expenditure in 1963–64 are estimated at some £38,000,000.

STUDENTS FROM OVERSEAS AT UNITED KINGDOM UNIVERSITIES, 1962–63.

Full-time Students.—A total of 14,020 students from other countries, including 1,937 women, enrolled for full-time study at British Universities in 1962–63, compared with 13,385 in 1961–62 and 12,410 in 1960-61. Of these, 8,380 came from other parts of the British Commonwealth and 5,640 from foreign countries. The largest numbers of students came from India (1,746), United States (1,186), Nigeria (1,090), Canada (657), Pakistan (619), Iraq (483), Egypt (464), Kenya (445), South Africa (438), Australia (401), Ghana (330) and Malaya (322). 6,447 students were known to hold an award of some kind (fellowship, scholarship, grant, etc.).

Categories of subjects studied, with total numbers of students, and distribution of 6,642 students working for higher degrees, certain higher diplomas or other post-graduate work were: Agriculture and Forestry, 332 (*156*); Arts, 3,334 (*1,651*); Dentistry, 165 (*71*); Medicine, 2,211 (*1,056*); Pure Science, 2,274 (*1,445*); Social Studies, 2,371 (*1,020*); Technology, 3,209 (*1,229*); Veterinary Science, 124 (*14*).

Overseas students were distributed at the universities and colleges as follows: Birmingham, 525; Bristol, 216; Cambridge, 888; Durham, 426 (King's College, Newcastle, 353); Exeter, 135; Hull, 111; Keele, 27; Leeds, 632; Leicester, 93; Liverpool, 286; London, 5,795; Manchester, 843; Nottingham, 145; Oxford, 1,050; Reading, 175; Sheffield, 223; Southampton, 123; Wales, 504 (Aberystwyth, 87; Bangor, 108; Cardiff, 121; Swansea, 158; St. David's College, Lampeter, 19; National School of Medicine, 11); Aberdeen, 208; Edinburgh, 623; Glasgow, 337; Royal College of Science and Technology, Glasgow, 174; St Andrews, 248; Belfast, 225.

Part-time Students.—A further 1,800 students, including 487 women, enrolled for part-time study or research in U.K. universities in 1962–63.

UNIVERSITIES, COLLEGES AND SCHOOLS

THE UNIVERSITY OF OXFORD

FULL TERMS, 1964
Hilary, Jan. 19 to March 14
Trinity, April 26 to June 20
Michaelmas, Oct. 11 to Dec. 5

NUMBER OF UNDERGRADUATES IN RESIDENCE
Michaelmas Term, 1962, 8,803

UNIVERSITY OFFICES, &c.	Elect.
Chancellor, Rt. Hon. Harold Macmillan, M.P., *Balliol*	1960
High Steward, The Viscount Simonds, P.C., M.A., *New College*	1954
Vice-Chancellor, W. F. Oakeshott, M.A., Rector of *Lincoln*	1962
Proctors, J. D. Davies, B.C.L., M.A., *St. Catherine's*; J. B. McLeod, M.A., D.Phil., *Wadham*	1963
Assessor, Miss M. L. Tomlinson, M.A., D.Phil., D.SC., *St. Hilda's*	1963
Assessor of the Chancellor's Court, Sir Humphrey Waldock, D.C.L., *All Souls*	1947
Public Orator, A. N. Bryan-Brown, M.A., *Worcester*	1958
Bodley's Librarian, J. N. L. Myres, M.A., *Ch. Ch.*	1947
Keeper of Archives, W. A. Pantin, M.A., *Oriel*	1940
Keeper of the Ashmolean Museum, R. W. Hamilton, M.A., *Magdalen*	1962
Keeper of the Dept. of Western Art, I. G. Robertson, M.A., *Worcester*	1962
Keeper of Dept. of Antiquities, R. W. Hamilton, M.A., *Magdalen*	1957
Keeper of Dept. of Eastern Art, P. C. Swann, M.A., *St. Edmund Hall*	1961
Curator of the Museum of the History of Science, C. H. Josten, M.A., *B.N.C.*	1950
Registrar of the University, Sir Folliott Sandford, K.B.E., C.M.G., M.A. *New College*	1958
Deputy Registrars, B. G. Campbell, M.A., *Merton* (1961); A. L. Fleet, M.A., *Pembroke*	1963
Senior Assistant Registrar, H. W. Deane, M.A., *St. Catherine's*	1963
Assistant Registrars, Mrs. C. P. Dorey, M.A., *St. Anne's* (1959); R. A. Malyn, M.A., *St. Peter's* (1961); Miss E. R. M. Noyce, M.A., *L.M.H.* (1961); A. J. Dorey, M.A., *Pembroke*	1962
Secretary of Faculties, C. H. Paterson, M.A., *Corpus*	1957
Assist. do. H. W. Deane, M.A., *St. Catherine's*	1961
Secretary to the Curators of the University Chest, H. H. Keen, M.A., *Balliol*	1946
Deputy do., J. A. Cochrane, M.A., *St. Edmund Hall*	1962
Chief Accountant, H. Barrett, M.A., *Balliol*	
Acting Curator of Sheldonian Theatre, J. T. Christie, M.A., *Principal of Jesus*	1955
Acting Curator of the Schools, M. G. Brock, M.A., *Corpus*	1961
Registrar of the Chancellor's Court, H. S. Clemons, M.A., *Corpus*	1947
University Counsel, Sir Milner Holland, Q.C., B.C.L., M.A., *Hertford*	1960
Summoner of Preachers, J. A. C. Ward	1952
Clerk of the Schools, W. H. Miller	1950
Land Agent to the University, J. R. Mills, M.A., *Pembroke*	1961
Surveyor to the University, J. Lankester, M.A., *Univ.*	1956
Director, Department of Education, A. D. C. Peterson, O.B.E., M.A., *Balliol*	1957
Acting Adviser to Overseas Students, B. G. Campbell, M.A., *Merton*.	

SECRETARY TO DELEGATES OF—
Examination of Schools, G. J. R. Potter, M.A., *Ch. Ch.*
Extra-Mural Studies, F. W. Jessup, M.A., *St. John's*
Local Exams., J. R. Cummings, B.Litt., M.A., *B.N.C.*
University Museum, G. E. S. Turner, M.A., *St. Catherine's.*
University Press, C. H. Roberts, M.A., *St. John's.*

SECRETARY OF—
Committee for Appointments, C. E. Escritt, M.A., *Keble.*
The Rhodes Trustees, E. T. Williams, C.B., C.B.E., D.S.O., M.A., *Balliol.*

HEBDOMADAL COUNCIL

Ex-Officio Members, the Chancellor; the Vice-Chancellor; the Rector of *Exeter*; the Proctors; the Assessor.
Elected by Congregation—
The Provost of *Oriel*; the Principal of *Lady Margaret Hall*; the Warden of *Wadham*; the Master of *St. Catherine's*; the Principal of *Linacre House*; the Principal of *St. Anne's*; the President of *Trinity*; G. E. F. Chilver, M.A., D.Phil.; A. B. Brown, B.C.L., M.A.; E. T. Williams, C.B., C.B.E., D.S.O., M.A.; B. G. Mitchell, M.A.; R. N. W. Blake, M.A.; M. W. Dick, M.A.; R. P. Bell, M.A.; Sir George Pickering, D.M.; Sir Lindor Brown, C.B.E., M.A., F.R.S., *Magd.*; G. D. G. Hall, Ph.D., *Exeter*; W. E. van Heyningen, M.A., D.SC., Ph.D., *Exeter*.

Oxford Colleges, Halls and Societies

(*With date of foundations*)

All Souls (1438), J. H. A. Sparrow, M.A., *Warden* (1952).
Balliol (1263), Sir David Lindsay Keir, M.A., *Master* (1949).
Brasenose (1509) Sir Noel Hall, M.A., *Principal* (1960).
Christ Church (1546), Very Rev. C. A. Simpson, D.D., *Dean* (1959).
Corpus Christi (1517), W. F. R. Hardie, M.A., *President* (1950).
Exeter (1314), K. C. Wheare, M.A., D.Litt., *Rector* (1956)
Hertford (1874), W. L. Ferrar, M.A., D.SC., *Principal* (1959).
Jesus (1571), J. T. Christie, M.A., *Principal* (1950).
Keble (1868), Rev. A. M. Farrer, D.D., *Warden* (1960).
Lincoln (1427), W. F. Oakeshott, M.A., F.S.A., *Rector* (1953).
Magdalen (1458), T. S. R. Boase, M.A., *President* (1947).
Merton (1264), A. R. W. Harrison, C.B.E., M.A., *Warden* (1963).
New College (1379), Sir William Hayter, K.C.M.G., M.A., *Warden* (1958).
Oriel (1326), K. C. Turpin, B.Litt., M.A. *Provost* (1957).
Pembroke (1624), R. B. McCallum, M.A., *Master* (1955).
Queen's (1340), Sir Howard Florey, B.SC., M.A., F.R.S., *Provost* (1962).
St. Catherine's (1962), A. L. C. Bullock, M.A., *Master* (1962).
St. Edmund Hall (1270), Rev. Canon J. N. D. Kelly, D.D., *Principal* (1951).
St. John's (1555), J. D. Mabbott, C.M.G., B.Litt., M.A., *President* (1963).
Trinity (1554), A. L. P. Norrington, M.A., *President* (1954).

University (1249), Sir John Maud, G.C.B., C.B.E., *Master* (1963).
Wadham (1612), Sir Maurice Bowra, M.A., D.Litt., *Warden* (1938).
Worcester (1714), The Lord Franks, P.C., G.C.M.G., K.C.B., C.B.E., M.A., *Provost* (1962).
St. Peter's (1929), Rev. J. P. Thornton-Duesbery, M.A., *Master* (1955).
St. Antony's (1950), F. W. D. Deakin, M.A., *Warden* (1950).
Nuffield (1937), D. N. Chester, M.A., *Warden* (1954).
Linacre House (1962), J. B. Bamborough, M.A., *Principal* (1962).
Campion Hall, Rev. H. D. Hanshell, M.A., *Master* (1962).
St. Benet's Hall, Rev. F. G. Sitwell, M.A., *Master* (1947).
Mansfield (1886), Rev. J. Marsh, M.A., D.Phil., D.D., *Principal* (1953).
Regent's Park, Rev. G. H. Davies, B.Litt., M.A., *Principal* (1958).
Greyfriars Hall, Very Rev. P. L. Peacock, M.A., D.Mus., *Warden*, (1953).

Lady Margaret Hall (1878), Miss L. S. Sutherland, C.B.E., M.A., D.Litt., *Principal* (1945).
Somerville (1879), Dame Janet Vaughan, D.B.E., D.M., F.R.C.P., *Principal* (1945).
St. Hugh's (1886), Miss K. M. Kenyon, C.B.E., D. Litt., F.B.A., *Principal* (1962).
St. Hilda's (1893), Miss K. Major, B.Litt., M.A., *Principal* (1955).
St. Anne's (1952) (Originally *Society of Oxford Home-Students* (1879)) Lady Ogilvie, M.A., *Principal* (1953).

UNIVERSITY PROFESSORS	Elect.
American History (*Harmsworth*), F. E. Vandiver, M.A., *Queen's*	1963
Anatomy (*Lee's*), G. W. Harris, D.M., F.R.S., *Hertford*	1962
Anæsthetics (*Nuffield*) Sir Robert R. Macintosh, D.M., *Pemb.*	1937
Anglo-Saxon, A. Campbell, B.Litt., M.A.	1963
Anthropology, Social, E. E. Evans-Pritchard, M.A., F.B.A., *All Souls*	1946
Arabic (*Laudian*), A. F. L. Beeston, M.A., D.Phil., *St. John's*	1955
Archæology, European, C. F. C. Hawkes, M.A., *Keble*	1946
Archæology (*Lincoln*), C. M. Robertson, M.A., *Linc.*	1961
Archæology of the Roman Empire, I. A. Richmond, C.B.E., M.A., *Corpus*	1956
Astronomy (*Savilian*), D. E. Blackwell, M.A., *New Coll.*	1960
Biochemistry, Sir Hans A. Krebs, M.A., F.R.S., *Trin.*	1954
Botany (*Sherardian*), C. D. Darlington, M.A., D.Sc., F.R.S., *Magd.*	1953
Byzantine and Modern Greek Lang. and Lit., C. A. Trypanis, M.A., *Exeter*	1947
Celtic, I. Ll. Foster, M.A., *Jesus*	1947
Chemical Microbiology (*Iveagh*), D. D. Woods, M.A., F.R.S., *Trinity*	1955
Chemistry, Inorganic, J. S. Anderson, M.A.	1963
Chemistry (*Lee's*), Sir Cyril Hinshelwood, O.M., M.A., D.Sc., F.R.S., *Exeter*	1937
Chemistry (*Waynflete*), Sir Ewart Jones, D.Sc., Ph.D., F.R.S., *Magd.*	1955
Chinese, D. Hawkes, M.A., D.Phil., *Ch. Ch.*	1959
Civil Law (*Regius*), D. Daube, D.C.L., *All Souls*	1955
Colonial Economic Affairs, S. H. Frankel, M.A., *Nuffield*	1946
Comparative Philology, L. R. Palmer, M.A., *Worcester*	1952
Comparative Slavonic Philology, B. O. Unbegaun, M.A., *B. N. C.*	1953
Divinity (*Regius*), Rev. Canon H. Chadwick, D.D., *Ch. Ch.*	1958
Divinity (*Margaret*), Rev. Canon F. L. Cross, D.Phil., D.D., *Ch. Ch.*	1944
Eastern Religions and Ethics (*Spalding*), R. C. Zaehner, M.A., *All Souls*	1952
Ecclesiastical History (*Regius*), Rev. Canon S. L. Greenslade, D.D., *Ch. Ch.*	1959
Economic History (*Chichele*), H. J. Habakkuk, M.A., *All Souls*	1950
Economic Organization, J. Jewkes, M.A., *Merton*	1948
Economics, W. M. Gorman, M.A., *Nuffield*	1961
Egyptology, J. Cerný, M.A., *Queen's*	1951
Engineering Science, D. W. Holder, M.A., F.R.S., *B.N.C.*	1961
English Language, E. J. Dobson, M.A., D.Phil., *Jesus*	1961
English Language and Literature (*Merton*), N. Davis, M.A., *Merton*	1959
English Literature (*Merton*), N. H. K. A. Coghill, M.A., *Merton*	1957
English Literature (*Goldsmiths'*), Lord David Cecil, C.H., M.A., *New College*	1948
Exegesis (*Ireland*), Rev. G. D. Kilpatrick, D.D., *Queen's*	1949
Experimental Philosophy (*Lee's*), B. Bleaney, M.A., D.Phil., F.R.S., *Wadham*	1957
Fine Art (*Slade*), T. S. R. Boase, M.A., *President of Magdalen*	1963
Forestry, M. V. Laurie, M.A., *St. John's*	1959
French (*Foch*), J. J. Seznec, M.A., F.B.A., *All Souls*	1950
Geography, E. W. Gilbert, B.Litt., M.A., *Hertford*	1953
Geology, L. R. Wager, M.A., F.R.S., *Univ.*	1950
Geometry (*Savilian*), M. F. Atiyah, M.A., F.R.S., *New Coll.*	1963
George Eastman Visiting, J. F. Bonner, M.A., *Balliol*	1963
German Language and Literature, E. L. Stahl, M.A., *Ch. Ch.*	1959
Government and Public Administration (*Gladstone*), M. Beloff, B.Litt., M.A., *All Souls*	1957
Greek (*Regius*), P. H. J. Lloyd-Jones, M.A., *Ch. Ch.*	1960
Hebrew (*Regius*), W. D. McHardy, M.A., D.Phil., *St. John's*	1960
History, Ancient (*Camden*), Sir Ronald Syme, M.A., *B.N.C.*	1949
History, Ancient (*Wykeham*), A. Andrewes, M.A., *New Coll.*	1953
History of Art, E. Wind, M.A., *Trin.*	1955
History of the British Commonwealth (*Beit*), J. A. Gallagher, M.A., *Balliol*	1962
History of War (*Chichele*), N. H. Gibbs, M.A., D.Phil., *All Souls*	1953
Icelandic Literature and Antiquities (*Vigfusson*), E. O. G. Turville-Petre, B.Litt., M.A., *Ch. Ch.*	1953
International Relations (*Montague Burton*), Miss A. Headlam-Morley, B.Litt., M.A., *St. Hugh's*	1948
Interpretation of Holy Scripture, Rev. H. F. D. Sparks, D.D., F.B.A., *Oriel*	1952
Italian (*Serena*), C. Grayson, M.A., *Magdalen*	1958
Jurisprudence, H. L. A. Hart., M.A., *University*	1952
Latin (*Corpus*), Sir Roger Mynors, M.A., F.B.A., *Corpus*	1953
Law (*Comparative*), F. H. Lawson, D.C.L., F.B.A., *B.N.C.*	1948
Law (*English*), H. W. R. Wade, D.C.L., *St. John's*	1961

	Elect.
Law (Vinerian), H. G. Hanbury, Q.C., D.C.L., *All Souls*	1949
Logic (Wykeham), A. J. Ayer, M.A., *New Coll.*	1959
Mathematics (Rouse Ball), C. A. Coulson, M.A., F.R.S., *Wadham*	1952
Medicine (Regius), Sir George Pickering, D.M., F.R.S., *Ch. Ch.*	1956
Medicine, Clinical (Nuffield), L. J. Witts, C.B.E., D.M., *Magd.*	1938
Metallurgy (Wolfson), W. Hume-Rothery, M.A., D.SC., F.R.S., *St. Edmund Hall*	1958
Metaphysical Philosophy (Waynflete), G. Ryle, M.A., *Magd.*	1945
Modern History (Chichele), R. W. Southern, M.A., *All Souls*	1961
Modern History (Regius), H. R. Trevor-Roper, M.A., *Oriel*	1957
Modern History, R. B. Wernham, M.A., *Worcester*	1951
Moral and Pastoral Theology (Regius), Rev. Canon V. A. Demant, M.A., D.Litt., *Ch. Ch.*	1949
Moral Philosophy (Whites), W. C. Kneale, M.A., *Exeter*	1960
Music, Sir Jack Westrup, B.MUS., M.A., HON.D.MUS., *Wadham*	1947
Natural Philosophy (Sedleian), G. F. J. Temple, C.B.E., M.A., F.R.S., *Queen's*	1953
Obstetrics and Gynæcology (Nuffield), J. C. Moir, C.B.E., D.M., *Oriel*	1937
Orthopædic Surgery (Nuffield), J. A. Trueta, M.A., HON.D.SC., *Worcester*	1949
Pathology, H. Harris, M.A., D.Phil., *Lincoln*	1963
Pharmacology, W. D. M. Paton, D.M., F.R.S., *New Coll.*	1959
Philosophy of the Christian Religion (Nolloth), Rev. Canon I. T. Ramsey, M.A., *Oriel*	1951
Physics (Wykeham), R. Peierls, M.A., *New College*	1963
Physics (Experimental), D. H. Wilkinson, M.A., F.R.S., *Ch. Ch.*	1957
Physics (Theoretical Plasma), W. B. Thompson, M.A.	1963
Physiology (Waynflete), Sir Lindor Brown, M.A., F.R.S., *Magdalen*	1960
Poetry, R. R. Graves, B.Litt., M.A., *St. John's*	1961
Political Economy (Drummond), J. R. Hicks, B.Litt., M.A., *All Souls*	1952
Psychology, R. C. Oldfield, M.A., *Magd.*	1956
Public International Law (Chichele), Sir Humphrey Waldock, Q.C., D.C.L., *All Souls*	1947
Pure Mathematics (Waynflete), G. Higman, M.A., D.Phil., F.R.S., *Magdalen*	1960
Race Relations (Rhodes), K. Kirkwood, M.A., *St. Ant.*	1954
Romance Languages, T. B. W. Reid, M.A., *Trinity*	1958
Rural Economy (Sibthorpian), G. E. Blackman, M.A., F.R.S., *St. John's*	1945
Russian, S. Konovalov, B.Litt., M.A., *New Coll.*	1954
Russian and Balkan History, D. Obolensky, M.A., *Ch. Ch.*	1961
Sanskrit (Boden), T. Burrow, M.A., *Balliol*	1944
Social and Political Theory (Chichele), Sir Isaiah Berlin, M.A., *All Souls*	1957
Spanish Studies (King Alfonso XIII), P. E. L. R. Russell, M.A., *Queen's*	1953
Surgery (Nuffield), P. R. Allison, D.M., *Balliol*	1954
Zoological Field Studies, Sir Alister Hardy, M.A., D.SC., F.R.S., *Merton*	1946
Zoology (Entomology), G. C. Varley, M.A., *Jesus*	1948
Zoology (Linacre), J. W. S. Pringle, M.A., D.SC., F.R.S., *Merton*	1961

THE UNIVERSITY OF CAMBRIDGE

FULL TERMS, 1964

Lent. Jan. 14 to Mar. 13; *Easter*, Apr. 21 to June 12; *Michaelmas*, Oct. 6 to Dec. 4.

NUMBER OF STUDENTS IN RESIDENCE

1962–63: Men, 8,177; Women, 863.

	Elect.
Chancellor, Marshal of the Royal Air Force the Lord Tedder, G.C.B., HON.LL.D., *Magd.*	1950
Vice-Chancellor, Rev. J. S. Boys Smith, M.A., Master of *St. John's*	1963
High Steward, Rt. Hon. R. A. Butler, C.H., M.A., HON. LL.D., M.P., *Pemb.* and *Corp.*	1958
Deputy High Steward, The Lord Morton of Henryton, P.C., M.C., M.A., HON.LL.D., *Joh.*	1954
Commissary, The Lord McNair, C.B.E., Q.C., LL.D., *Cai*	1955
Orator, L. P. Wilkinson, M.A., *King's*.	
†*Registrary*, R. M. Rattenbury, M.A., *Trin.*	1953
†*Deputy Registrary*, P. C. Melville, M.A., *Selw.*	1961
Librarian, H. R. Creswick, M.A., *Jes.*	1949
Treasurer, R. E. Macpherson, M.A., *King's*	1962
Deputy Treasurer, C. K. Phillips, M.A., *Chur.*	1961
Secretary General of the Faculties, W. J. Sartain, M.A., *Selw.*	1961
Deputy Secretary General of the Faculties, L. M. Harvey, M.A., *Cath.*	1963
Esquire Bedells, N. S. Wilson, M.A., *Pemb*	1946
P. T. Sinker, M.A., *Cla.*	1960
Proctors, R. F. Bennett, M.A., *Magd.*; S. E. Abbott, M.A., *Trin. H.*	1963
Organist, D. V. Willcocks, M.C., M.A., MUS.B., F.R.C.O., *King's*	1958
Director of the Observatories, Prof. R. O. Redman, M.A., Ph.D., F.R.S., *Joh.*	1947
Director of the Fitzwilliam Museum and Marlay Curator, C. Winter, M.A., *Trin.*	1946
Director of the Museum of Zoology, F. R. Parrington, SC.D., *Sid.*	1938
Curator of the Museum of Archaeology and Ethnology, G. H. S. Bushnell, M.A., Ph.D., *Down.*	1938
Curator of the Museum of Classical Archæology Prof. R. M. Cook, M.A., *Cla.*	1962
Curator of the Sedgwick Museum of Geology, A. G. Brighton, M.A., *Chr.*	1931
Director of the Botanic Garden, J. S. L. Gilmour, M.A., *Cla.*	1950
Representative on General Medical Council, Prof. A. L. Banks, M.A., *Cai*	1957
Head of the Department of Education, Prof. W. Arnold Lloyd, Ph.D., *Trin.*	1959

SECRETARY TO

Local Examinations Syndicate, T. S. Wyatt, M.A., M.Litt., *Sid.*, Syndicate Buildings	1961
Board of Extra-mural Studies, G. F. Hickson, M.A., *Cla.*, Stuart House	1928
Highest Grade Schools Examination Syndicate, A. E. E. McKenzie, M.A., *Trin.*, 10 Trumpington Street	1945
Appointments Board, J. G. W. Davies, M.A., *Joh.*	1952
University Library, A. Tillotson, M.A., *Pet.*	1949
University Press, R. W. David, M.A., *Corp.*	1963

COUNCIL OF THE SENATE

(*Secretary*, The Registrary)

Ex-officio Members, The Chancellor; Vice-Chancellor.

Heads of Colleges, The Master of *Downing*; The Master of *St. Catharine's*; The Mistress of *Girton*; The Master of *Clare*.

† Correspondence for the *Registrary* and *Deputy Registrary* should be sent to the *University Registrary*, The Old Schools, Cambridge.

Professors and Readers, Sir Joseph Hutchinson, SC.D., *Joh.*: R. B. Braithwaite, M.A., *King's*; W. O. Chadwick, D.D., *Selw.*; A. H. Cottrell, M.A., *Chr.*

Elected as Members of the Regent House, W. Hagenbuch, M.A., *Qu.*; Miss M. B. Hesse, M.A., *Girton*; T. C. Thomas, M.A., LL.B., *Joh.*; F. Wild, M.A., Ph.D., *Down.*; W. W. Grave, M.A., Ph.D., *Fitzw.*; W. A. Camps, M.A., *Pemb.*; R. C. Evans, M.A. Ph.D., *Cath.*; Prof. D. M. MacKinnon, M.A., *Corp.*

Cambridge Colleges

(*With date of foundation*)

Christ's (1505), The Lord Todd, M.A., D.SC., D.Phil., F.R.S., *Master* (1963).

Churchill (1960), Sir John Cockcroft, O.M., K.C.B., C.B.E., M.A., Ph.D., F.R.S., *Master* (1959).

Clare (1326), Sir Eric Ashby, M.A., F.R.S., *Master* (1958).

Corpus Christi (1352), Rt. Hon. Sir Frank Lee, G.C.M.G., K.C.B., M.A., *Master* (1962).

Downing (1800), W. K. C. Guthrie, Litt.D., F.B.A., *Master* (1957).

Emmanuel (1584), E. Welbourne, M.C., M.A., *Master* (1951).

Gonville & Caius (1348), Sir Nevill Mott, M.A., F.R.S., *Master* (1959).

Jesus (1496), D. L. Page, Litt.D., F.B.A., *Master* (1959).

King's (1441), N. G. Annan, O.B.E., M.A., *Provost* (1956).

Magdalene (1542), Rt. Hon. Sir Henry Willink, Bt., M.C., Q.C., M.A., *Master* (1948).

Pembroke (1347), Sir William Hodge, SC.D., F.R.S., *Master* (1958).

Peterhouse (1284), H. Butterfield, M.A., *Master*, (1955).

Queens' (1448), A. Ll. Armitage, M.A., Ll.B., *President* (1958).

St. Catharine's (1473), E. E. Rich, Litt.D., *Master* (1957).

St. John's (1511), Rev. J. S. Boys Smith, M.A., *Master* (1959).

Selwyn (1882), Rev. W. O. Chadwick, D.D., F.B.A., *Master* (1956).

Sidney Sussex (1596), D. Thomson, M.A., Ph.D., *Master* (1957).

Trinity (1546), The Lord Adrian, O.M., M.D., F.R.S., *Master* (1951).

Trinity Hall (1350), Sir Ivor Jennings, K.B.E., Q.C., Litt.D., F.B.A., *Master* (1954).

Fitzwilliam House (*Non-Collegiate Students*) (1869), W. W. Grave, C.M.G., M.A., Ph.D., *Censor* (1959).

Colleges for Women

Girton (1869), Miss M. L. Cartwright, SC.D., F.R.S., *Mistress* (1949).

Newnham (1871), Miss R. L. Cohen, M.A., *Principal* (1954).

Hughes Hall (*formerly Cambridge T.C.* (1885), *post-graduate students in training for teaching*) Miss M. A. Wileman, M.A., *Principal* (1953).

New Hall (1954), Miss A. R. Murray, M.A., *Tutor.*

University Professors

	Elect.
Aeronautical Engineering (*Francis Mond*), W. A. Mair, M.A., *Down.*	1952
Agriculture (*Drapers*), Sir Joseph Hutchinson, C.M.G., SC.D., F.R.S., *Joh*	1957
American History and Institutions (*Pitt*), J. M. Blum, M.A., *Qu.* (for 1963–64)	
Anatomy, J. D. Boyd, M.A., *Cla.*	1951
Ancient History, A. H. M. Jones, M.A., F.B.A., *Jes.*	1951
Ancient Philosophy (*Laurence*), W. K. C. Guthrie, Litt.D., F.B.A., *Down.*	1952
Anglo-Saxon (*Elrington and Bosworth*), Miss D. Whitelock, Litt.D., F.B.A., *Newn.*	1957
Animal Pathology, W. I. B. Beveridge, M.A., *Jesus*	1947
Applied Thermodynamics (*Hopkinson and Imperial Chemical Industries*), W. R. Hawthorne, C.B.E., M.A., F.R.S., *Trin.*	1951
Arabic (*Sir T. Adams's*), A. J. Arberry, Litt.D., F.B.A. *Pemb.*	1947
Archæology (*Disney*), J. G. D. Clark, SC.D., F.B.A., *Pet.*	1952
Architecture, Sir Leslie Martin, M.A., F.R.I.B.A., *Jes*	1956
Astronomy and Experimental Philosophy (*Plumian*), F. Hoyle, M.A., F.R.S., *Joh.*	1958
Astronomy and Geometry (*Lowndean*), Sir William Hodge, SC.D., F.R.S., *Pemb.*	1936
Astrophysics, R. O. Redman, M.A., Ph.D., F.R.S., *Joh*	1947
Biochemistry (*Sir William Dunn*), F. G. Young, M.A., F.R.S., *Trin. H*	1949
Biology (*Quick*), V. B. Wigglesworth, M.D., F.R.S., *Cai*	1952
Botany, H. Godwin, SC.D., F.R.S., *Cla.*	1960
Chemical Engineering (*Shell*), P. V. Danckwerts, G.C., M.B.E., M.A., *Pemb.*	1959
Chemical Microbiology, E. F. Gale, SC.D., F.R.S., *Joh.*	1960
Chinese, E. G. Pulleyblank, M.A., *Down.*	1953
Civil Law (*Regius*), P. W. Duff, M.A., *Trin.*	1945
Classical Archæology (*Laurence*), R. M. Cook, M.A., *Cla.*	1962
Colloid Science (*John Humphrey Plummer*), F. J. W. Roughton, M.A., Ph.D., F.R.S., *Trin.*	1947
Comparative Law, C. J. Hamson, M.A., LL.M., *Trin.*	1953
Comparative Philology, W. S. Allen, M.A., Ph.D., *Trin*	1955
Criminology (*Wolfson*), L. Radzinowicz, LL.D., *Trin.*	1959
Divinity (*Ely*), Rev. Canon, G. W. H. Lampe, M.C., D.D., *Cai.*	1960
„ (*Lady Margaret's*), Rev. C. F. D. Moule, M.A., *Cla.*	1951
„ (*Norris-Hulse*), D. M. MacKinnon, M.A., *Corp.*	1960
„ (*Regius*), Rev. E. C. Ratcliff, M.A., *Joh.*	1958
Ecclesiastical History (*Dixie*), Rev. W. O. Chadwick, D.D., F.B.A., *Selw.*	1958
Economic History, M. M. Postan, M.A., F.B.A., *Pet.*	1938
Economics, E. A. G. Robinson, C.M.G., O.B.E., M.A., F.B.A., *Sid.*	1950
Economics, R. F. Kahn, C.B.E., M.A., *King's*	1951
Education, W. Arnold Lloyd, Ph.D., *Trin.*	1959
Egyptology (*Herbert Thompson*), Rev. J. M. Plumley, M.A., *Selw.*	1957
Electrical Engineering, C. W. Oatley, M.A., *Trin.*	1960
English Law (*Rouse Ball*), S. J. Bailey, LL.D., *Joh.*	1950
English Literature (*King Edward VII*), B. Willey, M.A., F.B.A., *Pemb.*	1946
Experimental Medicine, R. A. McCance, C.B.E., M.D., F.R.S., *Sid.*	1945
Experimental Physics (*Cavendish*), Sir Nevill Mott, M.A., F.R.S., *Cai.*	1954
Experimental Psychology, O. L. Zangwill, M.A., *King's*	1952
Finance and Accounting (*P.D. Leake*), J. R. N. Stone, C.B.E., SC.D., F.B.A., *King's*	1955
Fine Art (*Slade*), M. V. Levey, M.A., *King's* (for 1963–64)	1963
French (*Drapers*), L. C. Harmer, M.A., Ph.D., *Trin.*	1951

	Elect.
French Literature, J. B. M. Barrère, M.A., *Joh.*	1954
Genetics (*Arthur Balfour*), J. M. Thoday, Ph.D., *Emm*	1959
Geography, J. A. Steers, M.A., *Cath*	1949
Geology (*Woodwardian*), O. M. B. Bulman, SC.D., F.R.S., *Sid*	1955
German (*Schröder*), L. W. Forster, M.A., *Selw.*	1961
Greek (*Regius*), D. L. Page, Litt.D., F.B.A., *Trin*	1950
Hebrew (*Regius*), D. W. Thomas, M.A., *Cath*	1938
History of the British Commonwealth (*Smuts*), P. N. S. Mansergh, O.B.E., Ph.D., *Joh*	1953
Human Ecology, A. L. Banks, M.A., *Cai*	1949
Imperial and Naval History (*Vere Harmsworth*), E. E. Rich, Litt.D., *Cath*	1951
Industrial Relations (*Montague Burton*), H. A. Turner, M.A.	1963
Inorganic Chemistry, H. J. Emeléus, C.B.E., M.A., F.R.S., *Sid*	1946
International Law (*Whewell*), R. Y. Jennings, M.A., LL.B., *Jes*	1955
Italian, U. Limentani, M.A., *Corp*	1962
Latin (*Kennedy*), C. O. Brink, M.A., *Cai*	1954
Laws of England (*Downing*), Sir Ivor Jennings, K.B.E., Q.C., Litt.D., F.B.A., *Trin. H*	1962
Mathematical Statistics, D. G. Kendall, M.A., *Chur*	1962
Mathematics (*Lucasian*), P. A. M. Dirac, Ph.D., F.R.S., *Joh*	1932
Mathematics (*Rouse Ball*), H. Davenport, SC.D., F.R.S., *Trin*	1958
Mechanical Sciences, Sir John Baker, O.B.E., SC.D., F.R.S., *Cla*	1943
Mechanics, D. C. Johnson, M.A., *Trin. H*	1962
Medicine, I. H. Mills, M.D., *Trin*	1963
Medieval and Renaissance English, C. S. Lewis, M.A., F.B.A., *Magd*	1954
Medieval History, C. R. Cheney, M.A., F.B.A., *Corp*	1955
Metallurgy (*Goldsmiths'*), A. H. Cottrell, M.A., F.R.S., *Chr*	1958
Mineralogy and Petrology, W. A. Deer, Ph.D., F.R.S., *Joh*	1961
Modern History (vacant).	
Modern History (*Regius*), H. Butterfield, M.A., *Pet*	1963
Moral Philosophy (*Knightsbridge*), R. B. Braithwaite, M.A., F.B.A., *King's*	1953
Music, R. T. Dart, M.A., *Jes*	1962
Natural Philosophy (*Jacksonian*), O. R. Frisch, O.B.E., M.A., F.R.S., *Trin*	1947
Organic Chemistry, The Lord Todd, M.A., F.R.S., *Chr*	1944
Pathology, R. I. N. Greaves, M.D., *Cai*	1962
Pharmacology (*Sheild*), A. S. V. Burgen, M.A., *Down*	1962
Philosophy, A. J. T. D. Wisdom, M.A., *Trin*	1952
Physic (*Regius*), J. S. Mitchell, M.D., F.R.S., *Joh*	1957
Physical Chemistry, R. G. W. Norrish, SC.D., F.R.S., *Emm*	1937
Physics (*John Humphrey Plummer*), A. B. Pippard, M.A., Ph.D., F.R.S., *Cla*	1960
Physiology, Sir Bryan Matthews, C.B.E., SC.D., F.R.S., *King's*	1952
Physiology of Reproduction (*Mary Marshall*), A. S. Parkes, C.B.E., SC.D., F.R.S., *Chr*	1960
Political Economy, J. E. Meade, C.B., M.A., F.B.A., *Chr*	1957
Political Science, Sir Denis Brogan, M.A., F.B.A., *Pet*	1939
Pure Mathematics (*Sadleirian*), P. Hall, M.A., F.R.S., *King's*	1953
Radio Astronomy, M. Ryle, M.A., F.R.S., *Trin.*	1959
Sanskrit, Sir Harold Bailey, M.A., F.B.A., *Qu.*	1936
Slavonic Studies, Miss E. M. Hill, M.A., *Girton*	1948
Social Anthropology (*William Wyse*), M. Fortes, M.A., *King's*	1950
Spanish, E. M. Wilson, M.A., Ph.D., *Emm.*	1953
Theoretical Chemistry (*John Humphrey Plummer*), H. C. Longuet-Higgins, M.A., F.R.S., *Corp*	1954
Veterinary Clinical Studies, A. T. Phillipson, M.A., Ph.D., *Chur*	1963
Zoology, C. F. A. Pantin, SC.D., F.R.S., *Trin*	1959

THE UNIVERSITY OF LONDON, 1836

Senate House, W.C.1

TERMS, 1964

Spring, Jan. 8 to March 18; *Summer*, April 22 to July 1; *Autumn*, Oct. 7 to Dec. 16.

Internal Students (1961-62), 27,323. Registered External Students, 24,816.

Visitor, H.M. the Queen in Council.

Chancellor, H.M. Queen Elizabeth the Queen Mother.

Vice-Chancellor, P. S. Noble, M.A., LL.D.

Chairman of the Court, Prof. Sir David Hughes Parry, Q.C., M.A., LL.D., D.C.L.

Chairman of Convocation, C. F. Harris, M.D., F.R.C.P.

Principal, Sir Douglas Logan, M.A., D.Phil., D.C.L., LL.D. (1947).

THE COURT

Ex Officio, The Chancellor, The Vice-Chancellor, The Chairman of Convocation.

Appointed by the Senate, Sir Ifor Evans; Sir John Lockwood; Prof. Sir David Hughes Parry, Q.C.; Lord Piercy, C.B.E.; Prof. O. A. Saunders, F.R.S.; Prof. J. G. Semple; *By Her Majesty in Council*, Sir John Cockcroft, O.M., K.C.B., C.B.E., F.R.S.; J. C. Gridley, C.B.E.; The Lord Shawcross, Q.C. *By the L.C.C.*, Sir Isaac Hayward; Rt. Hon. A. G. F. Rippon, M.P.; *Home Counties Member* Sir Archer Hoare, C.B.E.; *Co-opted*, The Viscount Radcliffe, P.C., G.B.E.

THE SENATE

Ex Officio, The Chancellor, The Vice-Chancellor, The Chairman of Convocation, The Principal.

Heads of the following Schools—University College, King's College, Bedford College, Birkbeck College, the Imperial College of Science and Technology, London School of Economics and Political Science, Queen Mary College, Royal Holloway College, School of Oriental and African Studies, Westfield College. *Appointed by Convocation*—(*Arts*), Miss J. P. Bremner; H. A. L. Cockerell; E. G. M. Fletcher, M.P.; V. I. Gaster, O.B.E.; Miss M. C. Grobel; (*Economics*), Lord Piercy, C.B.E.; (*Engineering*), F. E. A. Manning, C.B.E., M.C., T.D.; B. G. Robbins; (*Laws*), S. R. Speller, O.B.E.; (*Medicine*), J. B. Hume; E. C. Warner; (*Music*), R. H. Hunt; (*Science*), J. S. Cook; C. C. Hentschel; W. W. Hill; W. C. Peck; W. R. Wooldridge; (*Theology*), Rev. G. Huelin. *Appointed by the Faculties*—(*Arts*), Prof. F. Norman, O.B.E.; Prof. A. C. Taylor; Prof. H. Tredennick; Prof. E. H. Warmington; (*Economics*), Prof. R. O. Buchanan; (*Engineering*), Prof. J. Greig; Prof. O. A. Saunders, F.R.S.; (*Laws*), Prof. R. H. Graveson; (*Medicine*), E. R. Boland, C.B.E.; M. I. A. Hunter; H. B. May; Prof. M. L. Rosenheim, C.B.E.; (*Music*), E. H. Thiman; (*Science*), R. E. Gibbs; Prof. C. T. Ingold; Prof. J. G. Semple; Prof. J. E. Smith; (*Theology*), Rev. Prof. D. E. Nineham. *Appointed by General Medical Schools*, V. F. Hall; Prof. W. J. Hamilton. *By King's College Theological*

THE SENATE—contd.
Dept., Rev. Canon S. H. Evans. *By University College*, Sir Bernard Waley-Cohen, Bt. *Director of the British Post-Graduate Medical Federation*, Prof. Sir James Paterson Ross. *Co-opted Members*, Dr. P. Dunsheath, C.B.E.; L. A. Jordan, C.B.E.; Prof. Sir David Hughes Parry, Q.C.; D. Skilbeck, C.B.E.

Principal Officers

Clerk of the Court, J. R. Stewart, M.A.
Secretary to the Senate, J. Hood Phillips, M.A.
Registrars: (Academic) J. Henderson, B.SC., M.A., Ph.D.; *(External)* L. E. Ball, O.B.E., B.SC.
Director, Extra-Mural Studies Dept., W. Burmeister, M.A.
Secretary to University Entrance and School Examinations Council, G. Bruce, M.A.
Goldsmiths' Librarian, J. H. P. Pafford, D.Lit., F.S.A.
Accountant, A. B. Waterfield, B.A.
Supt. of Examinations, G. S. Congreve. B.A.
Secretary to the Appointments Board, E. H. K. Dibden, B.SC., M.A.
Secretary to the Athlone Press, W. D. Hogarth, O.B.E., M.A.

University Institutes

Courtauld Institute of Art, 20 Portman Square, W.1, Prof. Sir Anthony Blunt, K.C.V.O., Ph.D., *Dir.*
Institute of Advanced Legal Studies, 25 Russell Square, W.C.1, Prof. J. N. D. Anderson, O.B.E., M.A., LL.D., *Dir.*
Institute of Archæology, 31–34 Gordon Square, W.C.1, Prof. W. F. Grimes, C.B.E., D.Litt., F.S.A., *Dir.*
Institute of Classical Studies 31–34 Gordon Square, W.C.1.
Institute of Commonwealth Studies, 27 Russell Square, W.C.1, Prof. K. Robinson, M.A., *Dir.*
Institute of Education, Malet Street, W.C.1, H. L. Elvin, M.A., *Dir.*
Institute of Germanic Languages and Literature, 29 Russell Square, W.C.1, Prof. F. Norman, F.S.A., O.B.E., M.A., *Dir.*
Institute of Historical Research, W.C.1, Prof. F. Wormald, Litt.D., F.B.A., F.S.A., *Dir.*
School of Slavonic and E. European Studies, W.C.1, G. H. Bolsover, O.B.E., Ph.D., *Dir.*
Warburg Institute, Woburn Square, W.C.1, Prof. E. H. J. Gombrich, M.A., Ph.D., F.B.A., F.S.A., *Dir.*

Schools of the University*

Bedford College, Miss N. L. Penston, B.A., D.Phil., *Principal* (1951).
Birkbeck College, Sir John Lockwood, M.A., Ph.D., LL.D., *Master* (1951).
Imperial College of Science and Technology, Sir Patrick Linstead, C.B.E., D.SC., F.R.S., *Rector* (1955).
King's College, P. S. Noble, M.A., LL.D., *Principal* (1952).
London School of Economics and Political Science, Sir Sydney Caine, K.C.M.G., B.SC.(ECON.), LL.D., *Director* (1957).
Queen Elizabeth College, Miss M. J. Sargeaunt, B.Litt., M.A., *Principal* (1947).
Queen Mary College, Sir Thomas Creed, K.B.E., M.C., Q.C., M.A., *Principal* (1952).
Royal Holloway College, Miss E. Marjorie Williamson, M.SC., Ph.D., *Principal* (1962).
School of Oriental and African Studies, Prof. C. H. Philips, M.A., Ph.D., *Director* (1957).
School of Pharmacy, F. Hartley, B.SC., Ph.D., *Dean.*
University College, Sir Ifor Evans, D.Lit., *Provost* (1951).
Westfield College, Mrs. P. Matthews, B.SC.(ECON.), *Principal* (1962).
Wye College, D. Skilbeck, C.B.E., M.A., *Principal* (1945).
King's College Theological Department, Rev. Canon S. H. Evans, B.D., M.A., *Dean* (1956).
New College, 527 Finchley Road, N.W.3, Rev. W. J. F. Huxtable, M.A., *Principal* (1953).
Richmond College, Rev. Harold Roberts, M.A., Ph.D., D.D., *Principal* (1955).
Lister Institute of Preventive Medicine, Chelsea Bridge Road, S.W.1., Prof. A. A. Miles, C.B.E., M.A., M.D., F.R.C.P., F.R.S., *Director* (1952).

* For Medical Schools, Training Colleges and Veterinary Colleges, *see under* Professional Education.

THE UNIVERSITY OF DURHAM

(Founded 1832; re-organized 1908, 1937 and 1963)
Old Shire Hall, Durham

TERMS, 1964

Epiphany, Jan. 21 to Mar. 21; *Easter*, April 28 to June 27; *Michaelmas*, Oct. 6 to Dec. 12.
Students (1962–63), 1,775
Chancellor, The Earl of Scarbrough, K.G., P.C., G.C.S.I., G.C.I.E., G.C.V.O., T.D. (1958).
Vice-Chancellor and Warden, D. G. Christopherson, O.B.E., D.Phil., F.R.S.
Pro-Vice-Chancellor, Rev. W. A. Whitehouse, D.D.
Registrar and Secretary, I. E. Graham
Treas., Col. J. C. R. Fitzgerald-Lombard, O.B.E.
Director of Institute of Education, J. J. Grant, C.B.E., D.C.L.

Colleges

University L. Slater, M.A., *Master.*
Hatfield, T. Whitworth, M.A., D.Phil., *Master.*
Grey, S. Holgate, M.A., Ph.D., *Master.*
St. Chad's, Rev. Canon T. S. Wetherall, M.A., *Principal.*
St. John's, Rev. Canon J. P. Hickinbotham, M.A., *Principal.*
St. Mary's, Mrs. M. Holdsworth, M.A., *Principal.*
St. Aidan's College, Dame Enid Russell-Smith, D.B.E., *Principal.*
Bede, K. G. Collier, M.A., *Principal.*
**St. Hild's*, Nina Mary Elizabeth Joachim, M.A., *Principal.*
**Neville's Cross*, Mary Whitley, B.A., *Principal.*
St. Cuthbert's Society, J. L. Brooks.

* Halls of Residence.

DEPARTMENT OF EDUCATION (*M.* and *W.*).

Professor of Education, Professor E. J. R. Eaglesham, M.A., B.Ed., LL.B.

THE UNIVERSITY OF NEWCASTLE

(Founded 1852; re-organized 1908, 1937 and 1963)
Newcastle-upon-Tyne 1

TERMS, 1964

Epiphany, Jan. 13 to Mar. 20; *Easter*, Apr. 20 to June 26; *Michaelmas*, Oct. 5 to Dec. 18.
Students (1962–63), 4,145.
Chancellor, The Duke of Northumberland, K.G., T.D.
Vice-Chancellor, C. I. C. Bosanquet, M.A., D.C.L.
Pro-Vice-Chancellor, Prof. G. H. J. Daysh.
Dean of Medicine, Prof. A. G. R. Lowdon, O.B.E., M.A., M.B., Ch.B., F.R.C.S.
Registrar, E. M. Bettenson, M.A.

DEPARTMENT OF EDUCATION (*M.* and *W.*)

Professor of Education, Prof. J. P. Tuck, M.A.

THE UNIVERSITY OF MANCHESTER

Oxford Road, Manchester
(Founded 1851; re-organized 1880 and 1903)

TERMS, 1963–64

Michaelmas, Sept. 30 to Dec. 13; *Lent*, Jan. 14 to Mar. 20; *Summer*, Apr. 28 to June 20.
Students (1962–63)—*Men*, 6,063; *Women*, 1,990.

Chancellor, The Earl of Woolton, P.C., C.H., M.A., B.SC. (1945).
Vice-Chancellor, Prof. Sir Mansfield Cooper, LL.M. (1956).
Registrar, Vincent Knowles, M.A. (1951).
Director of Extra-Mural Studies (vacant).
Bursar, R. A. Rainford, M.A.
Adviser to Women Students, Margaret L. M. Young, M.A., L. ès L., Ph.D. (1954).
Chairman of Convocation, R. F. Leslie, M.A., Ph.D.
Clerk of Convocation, Barbara M. Moor, Mus.B.
Librarian, M. Tyson, M.A., Ph.D. (1935).

DEPARTMENT OF EDUCATION

Professor and Director of Dept., Professor R. A. C. Oliver, M.A., B.Ed., Ph.D. (1938).
Professor and Director of the School of Education, Prof. S. Wiseman, B.SC., M.Ed., Ph.D. (1961).

THE UNIVERSITY OF BIRMINGHAM, 1900

Edgbaston, Birmingham 15

TERMS, 1963–64

Autumn, Sept. 30 to Dec. 14; *Spring*, Jan. 13 to Mar. 21; *Summer*, April 27 to July 4.
Full-time Students (1962–63)—4,759.
Chancellor, The Earl of Avon, K.G., P.C., M.C. (1945).
Pro-Chancellor, S. F. Burman, C.B.E.
Vice-Chancellor and Principal, Sir Robert Aitken, M.D., D.Phil., D.C.L., LL.D., D.SC., F.R.C.P., F.R.C.P. Ed., F.R.A.C.P. (1953).
Pro-Vice-Chancellor and Vice-Principal, Prof. K. Mather, C.B.E., M.SC., D.SC., F.R.S.
Deputy Principal, T. Alty, D.SC., Ph.D., D.C.L., LL.D.
Secretary, G. L. Barnes, M.A. (1954).
Registrar, Sir George Cartland, C.M.G.
Librarian, K. W. Humphreys, B.Litt., M.A.

DEPARTMENT OF EDUCATION

Professor of Education and Director of University Institute of Education, Prof. M. V. C. Jeffreys, C.B.E., M.A. (1946).
Professor of Education and Head of the Education Dept., Prof. E. A. Peel, D.Lit., M.A., Ph.D.

THE UNIVERSITY OF LIVERPOOL, 1903

Brownlow Hill, Liverpool 3

TERMS, 1963–64

Autumn, Oct. 1 to Dec. 13; *Lent*, Jan. 7 to Mar. 20; *Summer*, April 21 to July 4.
Students (1962)—5,057.
Chancellor, The Marquess of Salisbury, K.G., P.C. (1951).
Pro-Chancellors, D. Norman, M.C., M.A., LL.D.; The Viscount Leverhulme, T.D., B.A. (*President of the Council*).
Vice-Chancellor, W. H. F. Barnes, M.A. (1963).
Treasurer, E. A. G. Caröe, C.B.E., B.A.
Pro-Vice-Chancellors, Prof. F. E. Hyde, M.A., Ph.D. (1960); Prof. L. Rosenhead, C.B.E., Ph.D., D.SC., F.R.S. (1961).
Registrar, H. H. Burchnall, M.A. (1962).
Librarian, D. A. Clarke, M.A. (1961).
Head, Dept. of Education (vacant).
Director, Institute of Education, Prof. N. R. Tempest, M.A., Ed.M. (1954).

THE UNIVERSITY OF LEEDS, 1904

TERMS, 1963–64

Autumn, Oct. 1 to Dec. 13; *Spring*, Jan. 14 to Mar. 20; *Summer*, Apr. 21 to July 3.
Full-time Students (1963), 5,663.
Chancellor, H.R.H. the Princess Royal, C.I., G.C.V.O., G.B.E., R.R.C. (1951).
Pro-Chancellor, Brig. J. N. Tetley, D.S.O., T.D., LL.D., A.D.C. (1956).
Vice-Chancellor, Sir Roger Stevens, K.C.M.G., M.A. (1963).
Registrar, J. V. Loach, B.SC., Ph.D., F.R.I.C. (1945).
Bursar, E. Williamson, T.D., B.SC.(ECON.) (1956).
Librarian, B. S. Page, M.A. (1947).
Tutor of Women Students, Miss J. Bloxham, M.B.E., B.A.
Dept. of Education, W. E. Walsh, M.A. (1957), *Professor*.
Director, Institute of Education, B. A. Fletcher, B.A. (1961)

THE UNIVERSITY OF SHEFFIELD, 1905

Sheffield 10

TERMS, 1963–64

Michaelmas, Oct. 7 to Dec. 14; *Lent*, Jan. 6 to Mar. 14; *Easter*, Apr. 20 to June 27.
Full-time Students (1963)—Men, 2,652, Women, 872.
Chancellor, Rt. Hon. R. A. Butler, C.H., M.A., LL.D. (1959).
Pro-Chancellors, Gerard Young (1951); W. H. Olivier, T.D., M.A. (1956).
Vice-Chancellor, J. M. Whittaker, M.A., D.SC., F.R.S. (1952).
Pro-Vice-Chancellors, Prof. H. W. Lawton, M.A. (1959); Prof. D. H. Smyth, M.SC., M.D., Ph.D. (1962).
Treasurer, A. H. Connell, M.A., LL.B. (1956).
Registrar, G. Clark, M.A., B.SC. (1963).
Bursar, R. M. Urquhart, M.A. (1952).
Librarian, J. E. Tolson, M.A. (1956).
Director, Institute of Education (vacant).
Director, Training Dept., Prof. W. H. G. Armytage, M.A. (1954).

THE UNIVERSITY OF BRISTOL, 1909

Bristol 8

TERMS, 1963–64

Autumn, Oct. 3 to Dec. 13; *Spring*, Jan. 10 to Mar. 20; *Summer*, Apr. 17 to July 1.
Full-time Students—Men, 2,407; Women, 1,235.
Chancellor, The Rt. Hon. Sir Winston Churchill, K.G., O.M., C.H., F.R.S., M.P. (1929).
Vice-Chancellor, Sir Philip Morris, K.C.M.G., C.B.E., M.A., LL.D. (1946).
Treasurer, B. Clark (1957).
Librarian, J. S. Cox, M.A. (1951).
Registrar and Secretary, H. C. Butterfield, M.A. (1950).
Bursar, C. M. Singer, B.A. (1948).
Finance Officer, D. C. A. Smith, M.A. (1938).
Director, Institute of Education, Prof. B. S. Morris, B.SC., B.Ed. (1956).

THE UNIVERSITY OF READING, 1926

London Road, Reading

TERMS, 1963–64

Autumn, Oct. 4 to Dec. 12; *Lent*, Jan. 10 to Mar. 19; *Summer*, Apr. 24 to July 2.
Number of Students (1962)—1,784.
Chancellor, The Lord Bridges, P.C., G.C.B., G.C.V.O., M.C., F.R.S. (1959).
Vice-Chancellor (vacant).
President of the Council, Sir George R. Mowbray, Bt., K.B.E., D.Litt., M.A. (1933).
Registrar, J. F. Johnson, B.A. (1955).
Director, Dept. of Education, C. H. Dobinson, M.A., B.SC. (1951).

THE UNIVERSITY OF NOTTINGHAM, 1938

University Park, Nottingham

TERMS, 1963–64

Oct. 4 to Dec. 12; Jan. 8 to Mar. 17; Apr. 22 to July 2.
Undergraduates (1962)—2,386.
Chancellor, The Duke of Portland, K.G. (1955).
Vice-Chancellor, B. L. Hallward, M.A. (1948).
Deputy Vice-Chancellor, Prof. N. Haycocks, M.A. (1962).

Registrar, A. Plumb, M.A. (1958).
Bursar, A. Hendry, M.A. (1958).
Librarian, R. S. Smith, B.A. (1958).

THE UNIVERSITY OF SOUTHAMPTON, 1952

TERMS, 1963–64

Autumn, Oct. 7 to Dec. 14; *Spring*, Jan. 13 to Mar. 21; *Summer*, April 27 to July 4.
Undergraduate and Graduate Students (1962–63), Men, 1,349; Women, 551.
Chancellor (vacant).
Vice-Chancellor, D. G. James, M.A., LL.D., D.Litt. (1952).
Secretary and Registrar, R. N. M. Robertson, M.A., LL.B.
Academic Registrar, Miss M. W. Price White, B.A.
Director, Inst. of Education, Prof. F. W. Wagner, M.A., B.Sc.

THE UNIVERSITY OF HULL, 1954

TERMS, 1963–64

Autumn, Oct. 8 to Dec. 13; *Spring*, Jan. 13 to Mar. 13; *Summer*, Apr. 20 to June 27.
Full-time Students (1962–63)—Men 1,386; Women, 563.
Chancellor, The Lord Middleton, K.G., M.C., T.D. (1954).
Vice-Chancellor, B. R. Jones, Ph.D., Sc.D. (1956).
Registrar, W. D. Craig, B.L., (1954).
Professor of Education, Prof. F. W. Land, M.Sc., Ph.D.

THE UNIVERSITY OF EXETER, 1955

TERMS, 1963–64

Michaelmas, Oct. 7, to Dec. 18. *Lent*, Jan. 15 to Mar 25; *Trinity*, Apr. 22 to July 1.
Undergraduates (1963), 1,768.
Chancellor, The Dowager Duchess of Devonshire, G.C.V.O., C.B.E.
Vice-Chancellor, Sir James Cook, D.Sc., Ph.D., Sc.D., F.R.S.
Secretary, Roderick Ross, M.A.
Academic Registrar, A. G. Bartlett, M.A.

TEACHERS' TRAINING DEPARTMENT

Head of Dept., Prof. R. D'Aeth, M.A., Ph.D.

THE UNIVERSITY OF LEICESTER, 1957

TERMS, 1964

Spring, Jan. 18 to Mar. 17; *Summer*, Apr. 22 to June 25; *Autumn*, Oct. 7 to Dec. 15.
Full-time Students (1962–63), 1,730.
Chancellor, The Lord Adrian, O.M., M.D., F.R.S. (1957).
Vice-Chancellor, T. A. F. Noble, M.B.E., M.A. (1962).
Registrar, H. B. Martin, B.Com. (1947).

SCHOOL OF EDUCATION

Director, Prof. J. W. Tibble, M.A., M.Ed. (1946).

THE UNIVERSITY OF KEELE, 1962

Keele, Staffordshire

TERMS, 1963–64

Autumn, Oct. 11 to Dec. 18; *Spring*, Jan. 10 to March 19; *Summer*, April 24 to July 1.
Undergraduates (1963), 813.
Chancellor, H.R.H. the Princess Margaret, Countess of Snowdon (1962).
Vice-Chancellor, H. M. Taylor, C.B.E., T.D., M.Sc., M.A., Ph.D., F.S.A. (1962).
Registrar, J. F. N. Hodgkinson, M.A.
Director, Teachers' Training Department, Prof. W. A. C. Stewart, M.A., Ph.D.

THE UNIVERSITY OF SUSSEX, 1961

Stanmer House, Stanmer, Brighton

TERMS, 1963–64

Autumn, Oct. 4 to Dec. 14; *Spring*, Jan. 13 to March 21; *Summer*, April 20 to June 25.
Full-time Students (1962–63), 432.
Chancellor, The Viscount Monckton of Brenchley, P.C., K.C.M.G., K.C.V.O., M.C., Q.C., M.A.
Vice-Chancellor, J. S. Fulton, M.A.
Registrar, A. E. Shields, M.B.E., M.A.

THE UNIVERSITY OF EAST ANGLIA, 1963

Earlham Hall, Norwich.

Undergraduates (1963), 100 (English and Biological Sciences).
Chancellor, The Viscount Mackintosh of Halifax.
Vice-Chancellor, F. Thistlethwaite.
Registrar, G. A. Chadwick.

THE UNIVERSITY OF YORK, 1963

Heslington, York

Undergraduates (1963), 200 (Arts and Social Studies).
Chancellor, The Earl of Harewood.
Vice-Chancellor, The Lord James of Rusholme.
Registrar, J. P. West-Taylor.

THE MANCHESTER COLLEGE OF SCIENCE AND TECHNOLOGY (1955)

Sackville Street, Manchester

TERMS, 1963–64

Michaelmas, Sept. 30 to Dec. 13; *Lent*, Jan. 14 to Mar. 20; *Summer*, Apr. 28 to June 20.
Undergraduates (1963), 1,630; Post-graduate Students (1963), 514.
Principal, B. V. Bowden, M.A., Ph.D., M.I.E.E.
Registrar, J. Burgess, M.A.

The University of Wales, 1893

University Registry, Cardiff

Chancellor, H.R.H. The Prince Philip, Duke of Edinburgh, K.G., P.C., K.T., G.B.E. (1948).
Pro-Chancellor, The Lord Morris of Borth-y-Gest, P.C., C.B.E., M.C., LL.D. (1956).
Vice-Chancellor, Principal J. H. Parry, C.M.G., M.B.E., M.A., Ph.D. (1963).
Registrar, J. Gareth Thomas, M.A. (1962).
Secretary, University Council (vacant).
Treasurer, Guild of Graduates, W. H. Evans, M.Sc. (1952).

COLLEGES

Aberystwyth, T. Parry, D.Litt., F.B.A., *Principal* (1958).
Bangor, C. Evans, M.A. D.Sc., F.R.C.S., *Principal* (1958).
Cardiff, A. Steel, O.B.E., Litt.D., *Principal* (1949).
Swansea, J. H. Parry, C.M.G., M.B.E., M.A., Ph.D. *Principal* (1960).
Cardiff (National Sch. of Medicine) A. Trevor Jones, M.D., F.R.C.P., D.P.H., *Provost*.

TRAINING DEPARTMENTS

Aberystwyth, Prof. J. L. Williams, Ph.D.
Bangor, Prof. D. W. T. Jenkins, M.A.
Cardiff, Prof. Eric Evans, M.A.
Swansea, Prof. C. E. Gittins, M.A.

LAMPETER

ST. DAVID'S COLLEGE (1827)

Principal, Rev. Canon J. R. Lloyd-Thomas, M.A. (1953).

[Lampeter possesses by Charter the privilege of conferring degrees B.A. and B.D., and is affiliated to Oxford and Cambridge.]

Scotland

UNIVERSITY OF ST. ANDREWS, 1411

TERMS, 1963–64

Martinmas, Oct. 6 to Dec. 13; *Candlemas*, Jan. 6 to Mar. 13, *Whitsun*, Apr. 6 to June 5.

Students enrolled (1962–63), Men 1,979, Women 1,005.
Chancellor, The Duke of Hamilton, P.C., K.T., G.C.V.O., A.F.C. (1948).
Principal and Vice-Chancellor, Sir Malcolm Knox, M.A., LL.D. (1953).
Rector, Sir Charles Snow, C.B.E., LL.D., D.Litt. (1962).
Registrar and Secretary, A. N. Mitchell, O.B.E., M.A. (1961).
Librarians, D. MacArthur, M.A., B.Sc. (*St. Andrews*); J. R. Barker, M.A. (*Dundee*).
Factor, J. Duncan (1945).

COLLEGES

United College of St. Salvator and St. Leonard, Prof. J. N. Wright, M.A., *Master* (1959).
College of St. Mary Rev. Prof. M. Black, M.A., B.D., D.Phil., D.Litt., D.D., D.Theol., F.B.A., *Principal* (1954).
Queen's College, Dundee, Prof. A. A. Matheson, Q.C., *Master* (1958).

UNIVERSITY OF GLASGOW, 1451

Gilmorehill, Glasgow

TERMS, 1963–64

Martinmas, Oct. 3 to Dec. 14; *Candlemas*, Jan. 7 to Mar. 14; *Whitsun*, Apr. 14 to June 20.
Students enrolled (1963), Men 5,577; Women 1,944.
Chancellor, Lord Boyd-Orr, D.S.O., M.C., M.A., M.D., D.Sc., LL.D., F.R.S., F.R.S.E. (1946).
Vice-Chancellor, The Principal (1961).
Rector, A. J. Lutuli (1962).
Principal, C. H. Wilson, M.A., LL.D. (1961).
Secretary to the University Court and Registrar, Robert T. Hutcheson, O.B.E., M.A., Ph.D. (1942).

UNIVERSITY OF ABERDEEN, 1494

TERMS, 1963–64

Winter, Oct. 8 to Dec. 13; *Spring*, Jan. 14 to Mar. 20; *Summer*, Apr. 21 to June 26.
Number of Undergraduates (1963), 2,692.
Chancellor, The Rt. Hon. Thomas Johnston, C.H. (1950).
Principal, E. M. Wright, M.A., D.Phil., LL.D., F.R.S.E. (1962).
Vice-Principal, Prof. T. C. Phemister, D.Sc., Ph.D.
Secretary, W. S. Angus, M.A., LL.B. (1952).
Librarian, W. Douglas Simpson, C.B.E., M.A., D.Litt., LL.D., F.S.A. (1926).

UNIVERSITY OF EDINBURGH, 1582

Old College, South Bridge, Edinburgh 8

TERMS, 1963–64

Autumn, Oct. 8 to Dec. 13; *Spring*, Jan. 7 to Mar. 13; *Summer*, Apr. 14 to June 12.
Number of Students (1961–62), 7,509.
Chancellor, H.R.H. The Prince Philip, Duke of Edinburgh, K.G., P.C., K.T., G.B.E. (1952).
Rector, Rt. Hon. Joseph Grimond, T.D., M.A., M.P. (1960).
Vice-Chancellor and Principal, Sir Edward V. Appleton, G.B.E., K.C.B., M.A., D.Sc., Sc.D., LL.D., F.R.S. (1948).
Sec. to University, C. H. Stewart, O.B.E., M.A., LL.B. (1948).
Education Dept., Prof. J. G. Pilley, M.A. (1951).

ROYAL COLLEGE OF SCIENCE AND TECHNOLOGY (1796)

George Street, Glasgow

Full-time students (1962), 2,004.
Principal, S. C. Curran, Ph.D., D.Sc., F.R.S. (1959).
Secretary, G. H. Thomson, B.Com. (1947).

Northern Ireland

THE QUEEN'S UNIVERSITY OF BELFAST, 1908

LECTURE TERMS, 1963–64

Oct. 8 to Dec. 13; Jan. 14 to Mar. 13; Apr. 14 to May 15.
Number of Undergraduates (1963), 4,225.
Chancellor (vacant).
President and Vice-Chancellor, Michael Grant, C.B.E., M.A., Litt.D., F.S.A.
Vice-President, Prof. C. Kemball, M.A., Sc.D. (1962).
Secretary, G. R. Cowie, M.A., LL.B. (1948).
Secretary to the Academic Council, Prof. F. H. Newark, C.B.E., B.C.L., M.A. (1947).
Bursar, G. D. Burland, B.A. (1948).
Librarian, P. Harvard-Williams, M.A. (1961).

MAGEE UNIVERSITY COLLEGE, LONDONDERRY, 1865

(Associated college of University of Dublin since 1909; recognized college of the Queen's University of Belfast since 1951.)

TERMS 1963–64

Michaelmas, Oct. 9 to Dec. 14; *Hilary*, Jan. 14 to Mar. 14; *Trinity*, Apr. 14 to May 30.
President, Prof. W. G. Guthrie, M.A., Ph.D., F.R.S.E., F.R.A.S. (1959).
Vice-President, Prof. A. J. Warner, M.A., Ph.D. (1960).
Secretary of Faculty, Prof. F. G. Healey, M.A., Ph.D. (1960).
Bursar, Prof. J. L. McCracken, M.A., Ph.D. (1957).
Registrar, F. Smyth, LL.B. (1963).
Librarian, Miss A. M. McAulay, B.A. (1960).

Republic of Ireland

UNIVERSITY OF DUBLIN TRINITY COLLEGE, 1591

Undergraduates (1962–63), 3,156.

Chancellor (vacant).
Vice-Chancellor, The Earl of Rosse, LL.D. (1949).
Provost, A. J. McConnell, Sc.D. (1952).
Vice-Provost, H. W. Parke, Litt.D. (1960).
Senior Dean, F. La T. Godfrey, M.A. (1952).
Senior Lecturer, T. W. Moody, Ph.D. (1958).
Registrar, G. F. Mitchell, M.A. (1952).
Senior Proctor, W. F. Pyle, Ph.D. (1962).
Bursar, W. S. L. Ryan, Ph.D. (1962).

REGISTRARS OF THE SCHOOLS

Law (vacant).
Physic (*Dean of the Faculty*), W. J. E. Jessop, M.D. (1959).
Engineering, W. Wright, Ph.D. (1957).
Music, B. P. Boydell, Mus.D. (1962).
Agriculture, A. A. Pakenham-Walsh, M.A. (1959).
Education, Rev. E. A. Crawford, Ph.D. (1950).
Social Studies, Mrs. M. S. Crotty, M.A. (1959).
Business Studies, W. J. L. Ryan, Ph.D. (1962).
Dean of Women Students, Miss A. E. R. Brambell, M.A. (1959).

Appointments Officer, D. N. K. E. Montgomery, B.A. (1957).

NATIONAL UNIVERSITY OF IRELAND, DUBLIN, 1908

Ollscoil na h-Éireann

49 Merrion Square, Dublin

Chancellor, Éamonn de Valera, Ph.D., LL.D., Sc.D. (1921).
Vice-Chancellor, M. Tierney, M.A., D.Litt.
Registrar, Séamus Wilmot B.A., B.Comm., LL.D.

CONSTITUENT COLLEGES

Univ. Coll., Dublin, M. Tierney, M.A., D.Litt., *President* (1947).

Univ. Coll., Cork, H. St. J. Atkins, D.Sc., *President* (1954).
Univ. Coll., Galway, M. Ó. Tnúthail, D.Sc., *President* (1960).

RECOGNIZED COLLEGE

St. Patrick's Coll. Maynooth, Right Rev. Mgr. G. Mitchell, D.D., *President* (1959).

APPOINTMENTS BOARDS

The Appointments Boards of all Universities invite enquiries from Professional and Business employers in need of men or women graduates as Assistants, Secretaries, &c. The Boards are the official agencies of the Universities and are in close touch with Professors and Tutors in the Colleges of the Universities. Employers with a vacancy should write to "The Secretary of the Appointments Board,————University."

THE ASSOCIATION OF COMMONWEALTH UNIVERSITIES

36 Gordon Square, W.C.1
(Branch Office: Marlborough House, Pall Mall, S.W.1.)

The Association holds quinquennial Congresses of the Universities of the Commonwealth and other meetings in the intervening years, publishes the *Commonwealth Universities Yearbook*, etc., acts as a general information centre, and provides an advisory service for the filling of university teaching staff appointments overseas. It also supplies the secretariat for the Committee of Vice-Chancellors and Principals of the Universities of the United Kingdom, for the Commonwealth Scholarship Commission in the United Kingdom and for the Marshall Aid Commemoration Commission. *Secretary*, J. F. Foster, LL.D.

ADULT EDUCATION

Adult Education is carried on in the United Kingdom by universities and university colleges (pp. 502–510), local education authorities (pp. 512–16) and by a wide variety of voluntary organizations.

The Universities Council for Adult Education, consisting of two representatives from each university, was constituted in 1946 for interchange of ideas and formulation of common policy on extra-mural education.—*Hon. Secretary*, T. Kelly, M.A., Ph.D., Dept. of Extra-Mural Studies, The University, Liverpool.

The National Institute of Adult Education (England and Wales), 35 Queen Anne Street, W.1 (*Sec.*, E. M. Hutchinson, O.B.E.,) and the Scottish Institute of Adult Education, Education Offices, Alloa, Clackmannan, exist to provide a means of consultation and co-operation between the various forces in adult education.

UNIVERSITY DEPARTMENTS OF EXTRAMURAL STUDIES AND ADULT EDUCATION

OXFORD, Delegacy for Extra-Mural Studies, Rewley House, Wellington Square, Oxford.—*Sec.*, F. W. Jessup.

CAMBRIDGE, Board of Extra-Mural Studies, Stuart House, Cambridge.—*Sec.*, G. F. Hickson.

LONDON, Department of Extra-Mural Studies, University of London, Senate House, W.C.1.—*Dir.*, W. Burmeister.

DURHAM, Board for Extra-Mural Studies, 32 Old Elvet, Durham.—*Dir.*, T. F. Daveney.

BIRMINGHAM, Department of Extra-Mural Studies, The University, Edgbaston, Birmingham, 15.—*Dir.*, A. M. Parker.

BRISTOL, Department of Extra-Mural Studies, The University, Bristol.—*Dir.*, W. E. Salt, O.B.E.

EXETER, Department of Extra-Mural Studies, The University, Exeter.—*Head*, Prof. H. Sellon.

HULL, Department of Adult Education, The University, Hull.—*Dir.*, W. E. Styler.

KEELE, Department of Extra-Mural Studies, The University, Keele, Staffs.—*Dir.*, R. Shaw.

LEEDS, Department of Adult Education and Extra-Mural Studies, The University, Leeds, 2.—*Head of Dept.*, Prof. S. G. Raybould, Ph.D.

LEICESTER, Department of Adult Education, The University, Leicester.—*Head of Dept.*, Prof. A. J. Allaway.

LIVERPOOL, Department of Extra-Mural Studies, 9 Abercromby Square, Liverpool.—*Dir.*, T. Kelly, Ph.D.

MANCHESTER, Department of Extra-Mural Studies, The University, Manchester.—*Dir.* (vacant).

NEWCASTLE, Department of Extra-Mural Studies, The University, Newcastle-upon-Tyne.—*Dir.*, B. W. Abrahart.

NOTTINGHAM, Department of Adult Education, 14–22 Shakespeare Street, Nottingham.—*Dir.*, H. C. Wiltshire.

READING, The University, Reading.—*Registrar*, J. F. Johnson.

SHEFFIELD, Department of Extramural Studies, The University, Sheffield.—*Dir.*, M. Bruce.

SOUTHAMPTON, Department of Adult Education, University of Southampton.—*Dir.*, H. J. Trump.

WALES, The University Extension Board, University Registry, Cathays Park, Cardiff.—*Sec.*, J. Gareth Thomas.

ABERYSTWYTH, University College, Aberystwyth.—*Dir.*, A. D. Rees.

BANGOR, University College, Bangor.—*Dir.*, A. Llywelyn-Williams.

CARDIFF, University College, Cardiff, Department of Extra-Mural Studies, 31 Corbett Road, Cathays Park, Cardiff.—*Tutor-in-Charge*, I. Morgan.

SWANSEA, University College, Swansea.—*Dir.*, I. M. Williams.

EDINBURGH, Department of Extra-Mural Studies, The University, Edinburgh.—*Dir.*, J. Hossack.

GLASGOW, Department of Extra-Mural Education. 57–9, Oakfield Avenue, Glasgow, W.2.—*Dir.*, N. Dees.

ST. ANDREWS, Extra-Mural Committee, The University, St. Andrews.—*Dir.*, A. G. Robertson.

ABERDEEN, Department of Extra-Mural Studies, The University, Aberdeen.—*Dir.*, N. T. Walker, O.B.E. Ph.D.

BELFAST, Queen's University, Department of Extra-Mural Studies and Adult Education.—*Dir.*, R. H. Semple.

EDUCATIONAL CENTRES

Residential Colleges for Adult Education
(Offering courses for a year or longer)

England

CATHOLIC WORKERS' COLLEGE, Plater Hall, Boars Hill, Oxford (Men and Women).—*Principal*, J. R. Kirwan.

CO-OPERATIVE COLLEGE, Stanford Hall, Loughborough, Leics. (Men and Women).—*Principal*, R. L. Marshall, O.B.E.

FIRCROFT COLLEGE, Selly Oak, Birmingham 29 (Men) (38).—*Principal*, P. G. H. Hopkins.

HILLCROFT RESIDENTIAL COLLEGE FOR WOMEN, Surbiton, Surrey (50).—*Principal*, Mrs. C. M. Dyson.

RUSKIN COLLEGE, Oxford (Men and Women) (132). *Principal*, H. D. Hughes.

WOODBROOKE COLLEGE, Selly Oak, Birmingham, 29. Quaker Foundation for Religious, Social and International Studies (Men and Women). Shorter Courses also available.—*Warden*, W. R. Fraser.

Wales

COLEG HARLECH, Harlech, Merioneth (Men and Women) (100).—*Warden*, T. I. Jeffreys-Jones.

Scotland

NEWBATTLE ABBEY COLLEGE, Dalkeith, Midlothian (Men and Women)—*Warden*, C. L. Rigg.

Residential Colleges
(Offering Shorter Courses)

ATTINGHAM PARK, nr. Shrewsbury (Shropshire Adult College).—*Warden*, Sir George Trevelyan, Bt.

AVONCROFT COLLEGE, Stoke Prior, nr. Bromsgrove, Worcs.—*Warden*, A. Gregg.

BELSTEAD HOUSE, nr. Ipswich, Suffolk.—*Warden*, G. E. Curtis.

BRAZIERS PARK, Ipsden, Oxon.—*Convener of Board of Studies*, R. G. Faithfull, Ph.D.

BURTON MANOR, Neston, Wirral, Cheshire.—*Warden*, John Newton.

CHESHUNT COLLEGE, Cambridge. (10 places reserved each term for Y.M.C.A. students drawn from industry and commerce. 2 months general cultural course).—*Tutor*, G. F. Palmer.

DEBDEN HOUSE, Debden Green, Loughton, Essex (East Ham Education Cttee.).—*Warden*, Mrs. H. R. Dernis.

DENMAN COLLEGE, Marcham, Abingdon, Berks. (N.F.W.I.).—*Warden*, Miss M. Moller.

DILLINGTON HOUSE, near Ilminster, Somerset.—*Warden*, T. Harvey Sheppard.

DUNFORD HOUSE, Midhurst, Sussex (Y.M.C.A. College for Adults).—*Director*, Rev. F. Welbourn.

GRANTLEY HALL, nr. Ripon, Yorks.—*Warden*, Dr. H. C. Strick.

HOLLY ROYDE COLLEGE (Of Manchester University Extra-Mural Dept.), 30 Palatine Road, West Didsbury, Manchester 20.—*Warden*, D. Garside.

KINGSGATE COLLEGE, Broadstairs, Kent (Y.M.C.A. College for Adults).—*Principal*, D. Raymond.

KNUSTON HALL, Irchester, Wellingborough, Northants.—*Warden*, Miss E. Smith.

MISSENDEN ABBEY, Great Missenden, Bucks.—*Warden*, G. T. Griffith.

MOOR PARK COLLEGE, Farnham, Surrey.—*Warden*, F. S. Grimwood, D.Phil.

OFFLEY PLACE, nr. Hitchin, Herts.—*Warden*, W. P. M. Doody.

PENDRELL HALL COLLEGE, Codsall Wood, nr. Wolverhampton (L.E.A.).—*Warden*, L. N. A. Davies.

ROFFEY PARK INSTITUTE, Horsham, Sussex.—*Director*.—H. W. Clark.

URCHFONT MANOR, Devizes, Wilts.—*Warden*, M. Price, D.Phil.

WANSFELL, Theydon Bois, Epping (Essex Adult College).—*Warden*, W. Down, Ph.D.

WEDGWOOD MEMORIAL COLLEGE, Barlaston, nr. Stoke-on-Trent—*Warden*, W. E. Lloyd.

WESTHAM HOUSE, Barford, nr. Warwick.—*Principal*, F. Owen, T.D.

LOCAL EDUCATION AUTHORITIES

Full particulars regarding public provision for education can be obtained from the Local Education Authority.

English and Welsh Counties

ANGLESEY, Shire Hall, Llangefni.—*Director*, D. Jones-Davies.

BEDFORDSHIRE, Shire Hall, Bedford.—*Director*, T. S. Lucking.

BERKSHIRE, 1–5 Abbot's Walk, Reading.—*Director*, T. D. W. Whitfield.

BRECKNOCKSHIRE, Watton Mount, Brecon.—*Chief Education Officer*, D. Williams.

BUCKINGHAMSHIRE, County Offices, Aylesbury.—*Chief Education Officer*, F. J. North.

CAERNARVONSHIRE, 4 Castle Street, Caernarvon.—*Director*, M. Williams.

CAMBRIDGESHIRE, Shire Hall, Cambridge.—*Chief Education Officer*, G. D. Edwards.

CARDIGANSHIRE, Swyddfa'r Sir, Marine Terrace, Aberystwyth.—*Director*, J. H. Jones, Ph.D.

CARMARTHENSHIRE, County Hall, Carmarthen.—*Director*, I. Howells.

CHESHIRE, County Hall, Chester.—*Director*, J. G. Kellett, Ph.D.

CORNWALL, County Hall, Truro.—*Secretary*, J. G. Harries, M.B.E.

CUMBERLAND, 5 Portland Square, Carlisle.—*Director*, G. S. Bessey.

DENBIGHSHIRE, Ruthin.—*Director*, T. G. Davies.

DERBYSHIRE, County Offices, Matlock.—*Director*, J. L. Longland.

DEVONSHIRE, County Hall, Exeter.—*Chief Education Officer*, W. E. Philip.

DORSET, County Hall, Dorchester.—*County Education Officer*, J. R. Bradshaw.

DURHAM, County Hall, Durham.—*Director*, G. H. Metcalfe.

ESSEX, County Gardens, Rainsford Road, Chelmsford.—*Chief Education Officer*, B. E. Lawrence, C.B.E. Ph.D.

FLINTSHIRE, County Buildings, Mold.—*Secretary and Director*, B. Haydn Williams, Ph.D.

GLAMORGAN, County Hall, Cardiff.—*Director*, T. Jenkins.

GLOUCESTERSHIRE, Shire Hall, Gloucester.—*Chief Education Officer*, C. P. Milroy.

HAMPSHIRE, The Castle, Winchester.—*County Education Officer*, R. M. Marsh.

HEREFORDSHIRE, County Offices, Bath Street, Hereford.—*Director*, M. L. Edge.

HERTFORDSHIRE, County Hall, Hertford.—*County Education Officer*, S. T. Broad.

HUNTINGDONSHIRE, Gazeley House, Huntingdon.—*Director*, I. C. Currey.

ISLE OF ELY, County Hall, March.—*Chief Education Officer*, T. G. Fendick.

ISLE OF WIGHT, County Hall, Newport.—*County Education Officer*, A. L. Hutchinson.

KENT, Springfield, Maidstone.—*County Education Officer*, J. Haynes.

LANCASHIRE, County Hall, Preston.—*Chief Education Officer*, P. Lord.

LEICESTERSHIRE, Grey Friars, Leicester.—*Director*, S. C. Mason.

LINCOLNSHIRE (Holland), Boston.—*County Education Officer*, A. W. Newsom.

LINCOLNSHIRE (Kesteven), Sleaford.—*Director*, T. W. P. Golby, Ph.D.

LINCOLNSHIRE (Lindsey), Lincoln.—*Director*, F. J. Birkbeck.

LONDON, The County Hall, Westminster Bridge, S.E.1—*Education Officer*, W. F. Houghton.

MERIONETHSHIRE, County Offices, Penarlag, Dolgelley.—*Director*, W. E. Jones.

MIDDLESEX, 10 Great George Street, S.W.1.—*Chief Education Officer*, C. E. Gurr, Ph.D.

MONMOUTHSHIRE, County Hall, Newport, Mon.—*Director*, T. M. Morgan.

MONTGOMERYSHIRE, County Offices, Newtown.—*Director*, J. A. Davies.
NORFOLK, Stracey Road, Norwich.—*Chief Education Officer*, F. L. Ralphs, Ph.D.
NORTHAMPTONSHIRE, County Hall, Northampton.—*Chief Education Officer*, G. E. Churchill.
NORTHUMBERLAND, County Hall, Newcastle upon Tyne.—*Director*, C. L. Mellowes.
NOTTINGHAMSHIRE, County Hall, West Bridgford.—*Director*, W. G. Lawson.
OXFORDSHIRE, County Offices, New Road, Oxford.—*Director*, A. R. Chorlton.
PEMBROKESHIRE, County Offices, Haverfordwest.—*Director*, W. Davies.
PETERBOROUGH, Town Hall, Peterborough.—*Chief Education Officer*, L. Tait.
RADNORSHIRE, County Hall, Llandrindod Wells.—*Director*, M. W. Cole.
RUTLAND, County Offices, Oakham.—*Chief Education Officer*, J. A. Simmonds.
SHROPSHIRE, County Buildings, Shrewsbury.—*Secretary*, H. M. Wilson, C.B.E.
SOMERSET, Belmont, Trull Road, Taunton.—*Chief Education Officer*, W. J. Deacon.
STAFFORDSHIRE, Earl Street, Stafford.—*Director*, J. H. P. Oxspring, M.B.E.
SUFFOLK (East), Rope Walk, Ipswich.—*Chief Education Officer*, J. H. Aldham, M.C.
SUFFOLK (West), 5–6 St. Mary's Square, Bury St. Edmunds.—*Chief Education Officer*, F. J. Hill.
SURREY, County Hall, Kingston on Thames.—*Chief Education Officer*. A. M. Baird.
SUSSEX (East), School Hill House, Lewes.—*Chief Education Officer*, B. S. Braithwaite.
SUSSEX (West), County Hall, Chichester.—*Chief Education Officer*, C. W. W. Read, Ph.D.
WARWICKSHIRE, 22 Northgate Street, Warwick.—*County Education Officer*, N. A. Y. Yorke-Lodge.
WESTMORLAND, County Hall, Kendal.—*Director*, E. L. Clarke.
WILTSHIRE, County Hall, Trowbridge.—*Chief Education Officer*, J. H. Bradley.
WORCESTERSHIRE, 17 Castle Street, Worcester.—*County Education Officer*, J. C. Brooke.
YORKSHIRE, E.R., County Hall, Beverley.—*Chief Education Officer*, V. Clark.
YORKSHIRE, N.R., County Hall, Northallerton.—*Secretary*, F. Barraclough, C.B.E.
YORKSHIRE, W.R., County Education Office, Bond Street, Wakefield.—*Chief Education Officer*, A. B. Clegg.

English and Welsh County Boroughs

BARNSLEY.—*Director*, H. A. Redburn, O.B.E., T.D.
BARROW IN FURNESS, John Whinnerah Institute, Abbey Road.—*Chief Education Officer*, W. G. Bate.
BATH, Guildhall.—*Director*, H. W. Brand.
BIRKENHEAD, 63 Hamilton Square.—*Director*, H. G. Wilkinson.
BIRMINGHAM, Margaret Street, Birmingham, 3.—*Chief Education Officer*, Sir Lionel Russell, C.B.E.
BLACKBURN, Library Street—*Chief Education Officer*, D. G. Hartley.
BLACKPOOL, 3 Caunce Street.—*Chief Education Officer*, R. E. Hodd.
BOLTON, Nelson Square.—*Chief Education Officer*, W. T. Selley.
BOOTLE, 53 Balliol Road.—*Director*, W. R. J. Coe.
BOURNEMOUTH, Town Hall.—*Education Officer*, W. R. Smedley.
BRADFORD, Town Hall.—*Director*, A. Spalding.
BRIGHTON, 54 Old Steine.—*Director*, W. G. Stone.
BRISTOL, The Council House, College Green.—*Chief Education Officer*, G. H. Sylvester.
BURNLEY, 111 Manchester Road.—*Director*, R. O. Beeston.
BURTON UPON TRENT, Guild Street.—*Director*, A. H. Blake.
BURY, Town Hall.—*Director*, F. Dawson.
CANTERBURY, 78 London Road.—*Chief Education Officer*, N. Polmear.
CARDIFF, City Hall.—*Director*, R. E. Presswood.
CARLISLE, 19 Fisher Street.—*Director*, L. Charnley.
CHESTER, Town Hall.—*Director*, H. J. Hack.
COVENTRY, New Council Offices, Earl Street.—*Director*, W. L. Chinn, O.B.E.
CROYDON, 19 Katharine Street.—*Chief Education Officer*, R. W. King.
DARLINGTON, North Lodge.—*Chief Education Officer*, D. Peter.
DERBY, Becket Street.—*Director*, C. Middleton.
DEWSBURY, Halifax Road.—*Chief Education Officer*, J. D. Ridge.
DONCASTER, Whitaker Street.—*Chief Education Officer*, M. J. Pass.
DUDLEY, 3 St. James's Road.—*Chief Education Officer*, H. W. C. Eisel.
EASTBOURNE, 14 Upperton Road.—*Chief Education Officer*, J. C. Aspden.
EAST HAM, Town Hall Annexe, Barking Road, E.6.—*Chief Education Officer*, W. T. Davies.
EXETER, 32 St. David's Hill.—*Director*, J. L. Howard.
GATESHEAD, Prince Consort Road South.—*Director*, W. N. Howard.
GLOUCESTER, Belsize House, Brunswick Square.—*Education Officer*, R. Turner.
GRIMSBY, Eleanor Street.—*Director*, R. E. Richardson, Ph.D.
HALIFAX, West House.—*Chief Education Officer*, L. T. Jackson.
HASTINGS, 18–20 Wellington Square.—*Chief Education Officer*, M. O. Palmer.
HUDDERSFIELD, Ramsden Street.—*Chief Education Officer*, H. Gray.
IPSWICH, 17 Tower Street.—*Chief Education Officer*, J. T. Hill.
KINGSTON UPON HULL, Guildhall, Hull.—*Chief Education Officer*, S. W. Hobson.
LEEDS, Municipal Buildings, Calverley Street.—*Director*, G. Taylor.
LEICESTER, Newarke Street.—*Director*, E. Thomas, Ph.D.
LINCOLN, 4 Lindum Road.—*Chief Education Officer*, A. Sutcliffe.
LIVERPOOL, 14 Sir Thomas Street.—*Director*, H. S. Magnay.
MANCHESTER, Deansgate.—*Chief Education Officer*, J. K. Elliot.
MERTHYR TYDFIL, Pontmorlais.—*Director*, D. A. Davies.
MIDDLESBROUGH, Woodlands Road.—*Director*. E. D. Mason.
NEWCASTLE UPON TYNE, Northumberland Road.—*Director*, H. V. Lightfoot.
NEWPORT, Mon., Educ. Dept., Civic Centre.—*Chief Education Officer*, J. H. Fussell.
NORTHAMPTON, Springfield, Cliftonville.—*Chief Education Officer*, H. A. Skerrett, M.B.E.
NORWICH, Education Office, City Hall.—*Director*, J. W. Beeson.
NOTTINGHAM, Exchange Buildings.—*Director*, W. G. Jackson.
OLDHAM, Union Street West.—*Director*, M. Harrison.
OXFORD, Education Office, City Chambers, Queen Street.—*Chief Education Officer*, J. Garne, M.C.
PLYMOUTH. Cobourg Street.—*Director*, A. Scotland, D.Ph.

PORTSMOUTH, 1 Western Parade, Southsea.—*Chief Education Officer*, E. G. Barnard.

PRESTON, Municipal Building.—*Chief Education Officer*, W. R. Tuson.

READING Blagrave Street.—*Chief Education Officer*, W. L. Thomas.

ROCHDALE, Fleece Street.—*Chief Education Officer*, H. L. Robinson.

ROTHERHAM, 21 Moorgate Road.—*Director*, R. Bloomer.

ST. HELENS, 17 Cotham Street.—*Director*, N. F. Newbury.

SALFORD, Chapel Street, Salford, 3.—*Director*, F. A. J. Rivett.

SHEFFIELD, Leopold Street.—*Director*, T. H. Tunn.

SMETHWICK, 215 High Street.—*Chief Education Officer*, C. E. Robin.

SOUTHAMPTON, Civic Centre.—*Chief Education Officer*, J. J. B. Dempster, O.B.E., Ph.D.

SOUTHEND ON SEA, Warrior Square—*Chief Education Officer*, D. B. Bartlett.

SOUTHPORT, 99–105 Lord St.—*Chief Education Officer*, S. R. Hutton.

SOUTH SHIELDS, Westoe Hall.—*Director*, D. R. Barraclough.

STOCKPORT, Town Hall.—*Director*, E. G. Thomas, Ph.D.

STOKE ON TRENT, Town Hall, Hanley.—*Chief Education Officer*, H. Dibden.

SUNDERLAND, 15 John Street.—*Director*, W. Thompson.

SWANSEA, The Guildhall.—*Director*, L. J. Drew.

TYNEMOUTH, The Chase, North Shields.—*Chief Education Officer*, G. Wilson.

WAKEFIELD, 27 King Street.—*Director*, D. Broadhurst.

WALLASEY, Town Hall Annexe.—*Director*, K. A. Rowland.

WALSALL, Darwall Street.—*Director*, V. Millson.

WARRINGTON, Sankey Street.—*Chief Education Officer*, H. M. Phillipson.

WEST BROMWICH, Highfields.—*Director*, J. H. Turner.

WEST HAM, 95 The Grove, Stratford, E.15.—*Chief Education Officer*, R. Openshaw.

WEST HARTLEPOOL, Park Road.—*Chief Education Officer*, L. Dowsland.

WIGAN, Town Hall.—*Director*, K. H. R. Edwards.

WOLVERHAMPTON, North Street.—*Director*. G. W. Randall Lines.

WORCESTER, 5–6 Barbourne Terrace.—*Director*, T. A. Ireland.

YARMOUTH, 22 Euston Road.—*Chief Education Officer*, D. G. Farrow, O.B.E.

YORK, 5 St. Leonard's Place.—*Chief Education Officer*, H. Oldman.

Channel Islands, etc.

JERSEY, 5 Library Place, St. Helier.—*Director* H. C. A. Wimberley.

GUERNSEY, Elm Grove, St. Peter Port.—*Education Officer*, L. K. Redford.

ISLE OF MAN, Strand Street, Douglas.—*Director*, H. C. Wilkinson.

ISLES OF SCILLY, Town Hall, St. Mary's.—*Clerk*, R. Phillips.

Scotland

ABERDEEN (City), Castle Street.—*Director*, J. R. Clark.

ABERDEENSHIRE, 22 Union Terrace, Aberdeen.—*Director*, A. L. Young.

ANGUS, 50 East High Street, Forfar.—*Director*, J. Eadie.

ARGYLL (County), Education Offices, Dunoon.—*Director*, T. G. Henderson.

AYRSHIRE, County Buildings, Ayr.—*Director*, W. T. H. Inglis.

BANFF (County), Education Offices, Keith.—*Director*, J. McNaught.

BERWICK (County), Education Office, Southfield, Duns.—*Director*, R. D. Birch.

BUTE (County), Education Office, Colbeck Place, Rothesay.—*Director*, J. E. Harrison.

CAITHNESS, Education Office, Rhind House, Wick.—*Director*, H. R. Stewart.

CLACKMANNAN (County), Education Offices, Ludgate, Alloa.—*Director*, T. E. M. Landsborough.

DUMFRIESSHIRE, Huntingdon, Moffat Road, Dumfries.—*Director*, J. L. Brown.

DUNBARTON, 18 Park Circus, Glasgow, C.3.—*Director*, A. B. Cameron.

DUNDEE, 14 City Square.—*Director*, J. D. Collins.

EAST LOTHIAN, Education Offices, Haddington.—*Director*, Dr. J. Meiklejohn.

EDINBURGH, St. Giles Street, Edinburgh.—*Director*, G. Reith, Ph.D.

ELGIN. *See* MORAY AND NAIRN.

FIFE, County Offices, Wemyssfield, Kirkcaldy.—*Director*, D. M. McIntosh, C.B.E., Ph.D.

GLASGOW, Education Offices, 129 Bath Street and 25 Bothwell Street, Glasgow, C.2.—*Director*, H. S. Mackintosh, C.B.E., Ph.D.

INVERNESS (County), Ardross Street, Inverness.—*Director*, J. A. Maclean, Ph.D.

KINCARDINESHIRE, Education Office, Stonehaven.—*Director*, B. B. Smith.

KINROSS. *See* PERTHSHIRE.

STEWARTRY OF KIRKCUDBRIGHT, Castle-Douglas.—*Director*, J. Laird.

LANARKSHIRE, 118 Queen Street, Hamilton.—*Director*, J. S. McEwan.

MIDLOTHIAN, 9 Drumsheugh Gardens, Edinburgh, 3.—*Director*, T. Henderson.

MORAY AND NAIRN, County Buildings, Elgin.—*Director*, W. F. Lindsay.

ORKNEY (County), Albert Street, Kirkwall.—*Director*, R. Mack.

PEEBLES (County), County Buildings, Peebles.—*Director*, Lt.-Col. J. Jamieson, T.D.

PERTHSHIRE and KINROSS-SHIRE, County Offices, York Place, Perth.—*Director*, L. B. Young.

RENFREWSHIRE, 16 Glasgow Road, Paisley.—*Director*, J. Crawford, O.B.E.

ROSS and CROMARTY, High Street, Dingwall.—*Director*, G. Thomson, Ph.D.

ROXBURGH (County), Newtown St. Boswells.—*Director*, J. B. Baxter.

SELKIRK (County) Technical Coll., Galashiels.—*Director*, J. M. Urquhart.

STIRLING (County), Spittal Street.—*Director*, J. S. Meldrum.

SUTHERLAND (County), Brora.—*Director*, J. Mc Lellan.

WEST LOTHIAN, Linlithgow.—*Director*, J. W. Taylor.

WIGTOWNSHIRE, 10 Market Street, Stranraer.—*Director*, H. K. C. Mair.

ZETLAND (County), Brentham Place, Lerwick.—*Director*, J. H. Spence.

Northern Ireland

ANTRIM COUNTY, Education Office, 475–7 Antrim Road, Belfast, 15.—*Director*, K. A. McCormac.

ARMAGH COUNTY, Education Office, Courthouse, Armagh.—*Director*, W. J. Dickson.

BELFAST (County Borough), Education Office, Academy Street, Belfast, 1.—*Director*, J. S. Hawnt, O.B.E., Ph.D.

DOWN COUNTY, Education Office, 18 Windsor Avenue, Belfast 9.—*Director*, F. H. Ebbitt.

FERMANAGH COUNTY, Education Office, East Bridge Street, Enniskillen.—*Chief Education Officer*, J. Malone.

LONDONDERRY COUNTY, Education Office, New Row, Coleraine.—*Director*, R. B. Hunter.

LONDONDERRY (County Borough), Education Office, Brooke Park, Londonderry.—*Director*, H. M. D. McWilliam, M.B.E., T.D.

TYRONE COUNTY, Education Office, Omagh.—*Chief Education Officer*, A. Gibson.

Professional Education

ACCOUNTANCY

The main bodies granting membership on examination after a period of practical work are:

INSTITUTE OF CHARTERED ACCOUNTANTS IN ENGLAND AND WALES, Moorgate Place, E.C.2.

INSTITUTE OF CHARTERED ACCOUNTANTS OF SCOTLAND, 27 Queen Street, Edinburgh, 2, and 218 St. Vincent Street, Glasgow, C.2.

ASSOCIATION OF CERTIFIED AND CORPORATE ACCOUNTANTS, 22 Bedford Square, W.C.1.

INSTITUTE OF MUNICIPAL TREASURERS AND ACCOUNTANTS, 1 Buckingham Place, S.W.1.

INSTITUTE OF COST AND WORKS ACCOUNTANTS, 63 Portland Place, W.1.

The following Universities provide a special degree course in association with the Institute of Chartered Accountants in England and Wales and the Association of Certified and Corporate Accountants: Birmingham, Bristol, Durham, Hull, Leeds, Liverpool, London, Manchester, Nottingham, Sheffield, Southampton and Wales.

There are Accountant Student Societies at Bedford, Birmingham, Blackpool, Bournemouth, Bradford, Brighton, Bristol, Carlisle, Exeter, Grimsby, Ipswich, Hull, Leeds, Leicester, Lincoln, Liverpool, London, Manchester, Newcastle upon Tyne, Newport (I.o.W.), Nottingham, Oxford, Portsmouth, Preston, Reading, Sheffield, Southampton, Stockton-on-Tees, Truro, Cardiff and Swansea.

There are Accountant Students' Societies in Edinburgh, Glasgow and Aberdeen, and in these cities the Institute of Chartered Accountants of Scotland provides professional libraries.

ACTUARIES

Two professional organizations grant qualifications after examination:

INSTITUTE OF ACTUARIES, Staple Inn Buildings, W.C.1.

THE FACULTY OF ACTUARIES IN SCOTLAND, *Hall and Library*, 23 St. Andrew Square, Edinburgh.

ADMINISTRATION AND MANAGEMENT

ADMINISTRATIVE STAFF COLLEGE, Greenlands, Henley-on-Thames, Oxon.—*Princ.*, J. P. Martin-Bates (1961).

ROYAL INSTITUTE OF PUBLIC ADMINISTRATION, 76A New Cavendish Street, W.1.

THE INSTITUTE OF GENERAL MANAGERS, 86 Eccleston Square, S.W.1.

THE INSTITUTE OF HOSPITAL ADMINISTRATORS, 75 Portland Place, W.1.

THE INSTITUTE OF PERSONNEL MANAGEMENT, 80 Fetter Lane, E.C.4.

INSTITUTION OF WORKS MANAGERS, 196 Shaftesbury Avenue, W.C.2.

INSTITUTE OF HOUSING, 50 Tufton Street, S.W.1.

INSTITUTE OF OFFICE MANAGEMENT, 58 Victoria Street, S.W.1.

SOCIETY OF HOUSING MANAGERS, 13 Suffolk Street, Pall Mall East, S.W.1.

AERONAUTICS

(*See also* Engineering, Aeronautical)

ROYAL AIR FORCE STAFF COLLEGES

Bracknell

Commandant, Air Vice-Marshal D. J. P. Lee, C.B., C.B.E. (1962).

Andover

Commandant, Air Commodore C. V. D. Willis, D.S.O., O.B.E., D.F.C.

ROYAL AIR FORCE COLLEGE

Cranwell

Founded in 1920, the College provides permanent officers for the General Duties, Equipment and Secretarial Branches of the Royal Air Force.

Commandant, Air Commodore, M. D. Lyne, A.F.C.

Director of Studies, J. A. Boyes, M.A.

ROYAL AIR FORCE TECHNICAL COLLEGE

Henlow, Bedfordshire.

Provides professional training for cadets and officers of the Technical Branch of the Royal Air Force, including specialist training at post-graduate level.

Commandant, Air Commodore, E. M. T. Howell, C.B.E.

Director of Studies, Group Captain C. E. P. Suttle.

ROYAL AIR FORCE SCHOOL OF EDUCATION

Uxbridge, Middx.

Commanding Officer, Group Capt. D. M. B. Pitt, M.B.E.

THE COLLEGE OF AERONAUTICS

Cranfield, Bedfordshire

For post-graduate instruction in aeronautical and other branches of science and engineering.

Principal, Prof. A. J. Murphy, M.SC.

OTHER COLLEGES

COLLEGE OF AIR TRAINING Hamble, Southampton.

DE HAVILLAND AERONAUTICAL TECHNICAL SCHOOL, Astwick Manor, Hatfield, Herts.

COLLEGE OF AERONAUTICAL AND AUTOMOBILE ENGINEERING, Sydney Street, Chelsea, S.W.3, and Redhill Aerodrome, Surrey.

AGRICULTURE

The following Universities and Agricultural Colleges give Degree or Diploma courses in Agriculture and Horticulture.

ABERDEEN UNIVERSITY (Degree).

ABERDEEN (North of Scotland College of Agriculture, 41½ Union Street).—*Sec.*, H. Munro.

ABERYSTWYTH UNIVERSITY COLLEGE.

BANGOR UNIVERSITY COLLEGE (Degree and Diploma).

BELFAST, Queen's University (Degree).

CAMBRIDGE UNIVERSITY (Degree and Diploma).

CIRENCESTER, Royal Agricultural College.—*Principal*, F. H. Garner.

DURHAM UNIVERSITY, King's College, Newcastle on Tyne (Degree).

EDINBURGH UNIVERSITY (Degree and Diploma).

EDINBURGH SCHOOL OF AGRICULTURE, THE, West Mains Road, Edinburgh, 9.—*Principal*, Prof. S. J. Watson, C.B.E., D.SC., F.R.I.C., F.R.S.E.

GLASGOW UNIVERSITY (Degree).

HARPER ADAMS AGRICULTURAL COLLEGE, Newport, Salop.—*Principal*, R. Kenney, B.SC.

LEEDS UNIVERSITY (Degree and Diploma).

OXFORD UNIVERSITY (Degree and Diploma).

READING UNIVERSITY (Degree and Diploma).

SEALE-HAYNE AGRICULTURAL COLLEGE, Newton

Abbot, S. Devon.—*Principal*, Prof. H. I. Moore, M.Sc., Ph.D.

SHUTTLEWORTH AGRICULTURAL COLLEGE, Old Warden Park, Biggleswade, Bedfordshire.—*Principal*, K. N. Russell, B.Sc.

STUDLEY COLLEGE, Warwickshire (Agricultural and Horticultural College for Women).—*Principal*, Miss E. Hess.

UNIVERSITY COLLEGE OF WALES.

UNIVERSITY OF NOTTINGHAM SCHOOL OF AGRICULTURE, Sutton Bonington, nr. Loughborough.

WEST OF SCOTLAND AGRICULTURAL COLLEGE, 6 Blythswood Square, Glasgow and Auchincruive, Ayr.—*Sec.*, Nigel B. Bain, B.L.

WYE COLLEGE, Ashford, Kent (University of London).—*Principal*, Dunstan Skilbeck, C.B.E., M.A.

There are in addition over twenty county Agricultural Institutes giving a one-year course.

ARBITRATION

THE INSTITUTE OF ARBITRATORS, 39 Bedford Square, W.C.1, conducts examinations and maintains a Register of Fellows and Associates.—*Secretary*, D. Reid.

ARCHITECTURE

ARCHITECTS REGISTRATION COUNCIL OF THE U.K., 68 Portland Place, W.1.—*Chairman*, D. C. Hall; *Registrar*, D. D. Benton.

Constituted under the Architects (Registration) Acts 1931 to 1938. The Council's main duties are to maintain and publish a Register of Architects, to maintain and enforce correct standards of professional conduct, and to award scholarships and maintenance grants to architectural students of insufficient means. To qualify for admission to the Register, a person must pass one of the examinations in architecture recognized under the Acts for that purpose.

THE ROYAL INSTITUTE OF BRITISH ARCHITECTS, 66 Portland Place, W.1, has three classes of members, Fellows, Associates and Licentiates. The R.I.B.A. Board of Architectural Education controls and guides the whole system of architectural education throughout Great Britain. The following Schools are recognized by the R.I.B.A. for the purpose of exemption from its Intermediate Examination and in the case of those Schools marked "*" from its Final Examination.

SCHOOLS OF ARCHITECTURE

*Brighton College of Art and Crafts, Architectural Dept. (five years' full-time course).

*Bristol, Royal West of England Academy School of Architecture (five years' full-time course).

*Cambridge University, School of Architecture (five years' Diploma course).

*Dundee College of Art, School of Architecture (five years' full-time course).

*Hull Regional College of Art, School of Architecture (five years' full-time day course for Diploma).

*Leicester College of Art, School of Architecture (five years' full-time course).

*Oxford College of Technology, School of Architecture (five years' full-time day course).

*Portsmouth, School of Architecture, Southern College of Art (five years' full-time day course).

*Southend-on-Sea Municipal College, Department of Architecture (five years' full-time day course).

*Aberdeen, Scott Sutherland School of Architecture, Robert Gordon's Technical College (five years' full-time Diploma course and two years' part-time course concurrent with practical experience in architects' office, followed by four years' full-time).

*Birmingham School of Architecture College of Arts and Crafts (five years' full-time course).

*City of Canterbury College of Art (five years' full-time course).

*Cardiff, Welsh School of Architecture, Welsh College of Advanced Technology (five years' Diploma and six years' Degree course).

*Dublin, University College School of Architecture (five years' Degree course).

*Edinburgh University, School of Architecture (five years' full-time course).

*Edinburgh College of Art, School of Architecture (Diploma course).

*Glasgow School of Architecture, Royal College of Science and Technology (Diploma course or Degree course).

*Kingston-upon-Thames School of Art, Dept. of Architecture (five-year Diploma course).

*Leeds School of Architecture and Town Planning (five years' Diploma course and seven years' composite course).

*Liverpool School of Architecture, University of Liverpool (five-year Degree course).

*London, Architectural Association, School of Architecture (five years' full-time Diploma course).

*London University, Bartlett School of Architecture (five years' Degree course).

*London, The Polytechnic, Regent Street School of Architecture (five years' full-time day course and eight years' evening course).

*London, Northern Polytechnic, Department of Architecture (five years' full-time day course and eight years' evening course).

*London, Hammersmith College of Art and Building, Dept. of Architecture (five years' full-time course).

London, The L.C.C. School of Building, Brixton, S.W.4. (three years' full-time course).

*Manchester University, School of Architecture (five years' Degree course or five years' Diploma course).

Manchester, Regional College of Art, Dept. of Architecture.

*Newcastle upon Tyne University, School of Architecture (five years' Degree course or five years' Diploma course).

*Nottingham College of Arts and Crafts, School of Architecture (five years' Diploma course).

*Sheffield University, Department of Architecture (five years' Degree course or five years' Diploma course).

ART

(*See also* Technical Education)

Diplomas and Degrees in Art.—London University awards a diploma in Art and an honours degree and diploma in the History of Art. Reading, Leeds, Durham, Edinburgh and Glasgow Universities award degrees in Art. Other main qualifications for practical Art Teaching are the Ministry of Education Art Teachers' Diploma (involving study in an Art School or College and in a recognized Teacher Training Institution) and the Associateship of the Royal College of Art.

NATIONAL COUNCIL FOR DIPLOMAS IN ART AND DESIGN (24 Park Crescent, W.1). Set up by the Minister of Education in March, 1961, as an independent body to administer the award of diplomas available to students in Colleges of art and design who successfully complete courses approved by the Council.

Chairman, Sir John Summerson, C.B.E., F.B.A.
Secretary, F. Walsh.

Institutions concerned with the History and Appreciation of Art:—

THE COURTAULD INSTITUTE OF ART (20 Portman Square, W.1.) and THE WARBURG INSTITUTE (Imperial Institute Road, S.W.7.)—*See* University of London.

THE BARBER INSTITUTE OF FINE ARTS, University of Birmingham, Edgbaston, Birmingham 15.—*Director*, E. K. Waterhouse, C.B.E., M.A.

COLLEGES OF ART

There are about 200 Art Establishments recognized by the Ministry of Education, besides 6 University Art Schools (London (2), Oxford, Reading, Durham and Aberystwyth), the Royal Academy Schools and some old established private Schools.

LONDON.—Royal Academy Schools of Painting, Sculpture and Architecture, Burlington Gardens, W.1. (65).—*Keeper*, Henry Rushbury, C.V.O., R.A.; *Secretary*, Humphrey Brooke, M.V.O., B.A., B.Litt.; *Curator*, Walter Woodington; *Registrar*, C. W. Tanner, M.V.O.

LONDON.—The Slade School of Fine Art, University College, W.C.1, provides courses in Drawing, Painting and Sculpture, Etching, Engraving, Stage Design and Lithography. Facilities available for the Study of Film.—*Slade Professor*, Sir William Coldstream, C.B.E.; *Sec.*, I. E. T. Jenkin, M.A.

LONDON.—Royal Drawing Society, 6 Queen Square, W.C.1.—*Pres.*, R. R. Tomlinson, O.B.E., A.R.C.A., R.B.A.

LONDON.—Royal College of Art, Kensington Gore, S.W.7.—*Principal*, Robin Darwin, C.B.E.; *Registrar*, J. R. P. Moon, M.A.

OXFORD, The Ruskin School of Drawing and Fine Art, at The Ashmolean Museum (90).—*Principal*, Percy Horton, M.A., A.R.C.A. (Ruskin Master of Drawing). Courses in Drawing, Painting and Design. The University awards a Certificate in Fine Art.

GLASGOW, School of Art, 167 Renfrew Street.—*Chairman*, J. D. Kelly, C.B.E.; *Director*, D. P. Bliss, M.A., A.R.C.A.; *Sec. & Treas.* D. C. Black.

BANKING

Professional organizations granting qualifications after examination:—

THE INSTITUTE OF BANKERS, 10 Lombard Street, E.C.3.

THE INSTITUTE OF BANKERS IN SCOTLAND, 62 George Street, Edinburgh.

BREWING

FULL-TIME COURSES for brewers are conducted *for those in possession of an approved University Degree in Science* (*with Chemistry as a main subject*), at The British School of Malting and Brewing, University of *Birmingham*, and at Heriot-Watt College, *Edinburgh*.

Professional qualifications are awarded after examination by:—

THE INSTITUTE OF BREWING, 33 Clarges Street, W.1; *Sec.*, G. E. R. Sandars, C.M.G., M.B.E.

BUILDING

(*See also* under Technical Schools)

Courses leading to a degree in Building are available at the Universities of Manchester and Wales.

Ordinary and National Diplomas and Ordinary and Higher Certificates in Building are awarded by Technical Schools in agreement with the Ministry of Education, the Scottish Education Department and The Institute of Builders.

Diplomas are also awarded after examination by:—

THE INSTITUTE OF BUILDERS, 48 Bedford Square, W.C.1.

THE INSTITUTE OF CLERKS OF WORKS OF GREAT BRITAIN, Liverpool House, 15–17 Eldon Street, E.C.2.—*Sec.*, E. W. Hazell.

THE INSTITUTION OF MUNICIPAL ENGINEERS, 84 Eccleston Square, S.W.1. (Building Inspector's Certificate).

CHEMISTRY, PHYSICS, METALLURGY

Degrees and diplomas are granted by Universities. Technical College courses lead to diplomas and to National Certificates. Professional qualifications are awarded by:—

THE INSTITUTE OF PHYSICS, 47 Belgrave Square, S.W.1.

THE ROYAL INSTITUTE OF CHEMISTRY 30 Russell Square, W.C.1.—*President*, Prof. H. J. Emeléus, C.B.E., D.SC., F.R.S.; *Sec. and Registrar*, R. E. Parker, Ph.D.

THE INSTITUTION OF METALLURGISTS, 4 Grosvenor Gardens, S.W.1.—*Registrar-Secretary*, R. G. S. Ludlam.

COMMERCIAL EDUCATION

NATIONAL ASSOCIATION FOR BUSINESS EDUCATION.—*Hon. Sec.*, Dr. W. Bonney Rust, B.SC., West London College of Commerce, Airlie Gardens, W.8.

BRITISH ASSOCIATION FOR COMMERCIAL AND INDUSTRIAL EDUCATION (BACIE), 26a Buckingham Palace Road, S.W.1—*Dir.*, P. J. C. Perry.

Degrees in Commerce are awarded by Birmingham, Leeds, Liverpool, Manchester and Edinburgh Universities. A post-graduate diploma (1 yr.) is granted by the University of Birmingham.

COLLEGES OF COMMERCE

BIRMINGHAM.—The City of Birmingham College of Commerce, Gosta Green.—*Principal*, R. G. W. Bragg.

BRISTOL.—College of Commerce, Unity Street, Bristol, 1. *Principal*, W. B. Armstrong.

GLASGOW.—Scottish College of Commerce, *Principal*, Eric Thompson, Ph.D.

HULL.—The College of Commerce, Brunswick Avenue, *Principal*, T. E. Berry.

LEEDS.—The College of Commerce, 43 Woodhouse Lane. *Principal*, E. V. Roberts.

LIVERPOOL.—City of Liverpool College of Commerce, Tithebarn Street, Liverpool. 2. *Principal*, T. Gore.

LONDON.—The City of London College, Moorgate, E.C.2. *Principal*, A. J. McIntosh, Ph.D.; *Sec.*, F. W. Walker.

LONDON.—The Polytechnic School of Commerce and Social Studies, 309 Regent Street, W.1. *Head*, V. W. J. Pendred.

MANCHESTER.—College of Commerce, 103 Princess Street. *Principal*, F. Tellwright.

NEWCASTLE UPON TYNE.—College of Commerce. *Principal*, A. Bell.

WEDNESBURY.—Staffordshire College of Commerce.—*Principal*, H. Harman.

These colleges provide advanced training in most branches of commerce and prepare for examinations of the recognized professional organizations as well as for the National Certificate in Commerce.

In London the London County Council maintains colleges of commerce at Balham and Tooting, Catford, Clapham Junction, E. London, Greenwich, Holborn, N. London, Peckham, W. London and

Westminster. Some of the London polytechnics have Departments of Commerce. Particulars may be obtained from the Education Officer, County Hall, S.E.1.

Throughout the country commercial education at a lower level is provided at *Evening Institutes*, particulars of which may be obtained from the Local Education Authority.

There are also numbers of well-established private schools awarding certificates which are widely accepted.

Institutions awarding Professional Qualifications in Commerce:—

A. GENERAL

THE ROYAL SOCIETY OF ARTS (Examinations Dept.), 18 Adam Street, Adelphi, W.C.2.

THE LONDON CHAMBER OF COMMERCE, 69 Cannon Street, E.C.4.

THE NATIONAL COMMITTEE (SCOTLAND) FOR COMMERCIAL CERTIFICATES, 173 Pitt Street, Glasgow, C.2.

THE EAST MIDLAND EDUCATIONAL UNION, 1 Clinton Terrace, Derby Road, Nottingham.

THE NORTHERN COUNTIES TECHNICAL EXAMINATIONS COUNCIL, 5 Grosvenor Villas, Grosvenor Road, Newcastle upon Tyne, 2.

THE UNION OF EDUCATIONAL INSTITUTIONS, 25a Paradise Street, Birmingham.

B. SPECIALIZED

THE CHARTERED INSTITUTE OF SECRETARIES, 14 New Bridge Street, E.C.4.

THE CORPORATION OF SECRETARIES, Devonshire House, 13 Devonshire Street, W.1.

CRIPPLEGATE SECRETARIAL COLLEGE, Golden Lane, E.C.1.

THE FACULTY OF SECRETARIES, 6 Austin House Chambers, Guildford, Surrey.

THE INSTITUTE OF EXPORT, Export House, 14 Hallam Street, W.1.

THE INSTITUTE OF CHARTERED SHIPBROKERS, 25 Bury Street, E. C.3.

THE INCORPORATED SALES MANAGERS' ASSOCN., 51 Palace Street, S.W.1.

THE INSTITUTE OF TRANSPORT, 80 Portland Place, W.1.

THE INSTITUTE OF LINGUISTS, 3 Craven Hill, W.2.

THE ADVERTISING ASSOCIATION, 1 Bell Yard, W.C.2.

INSTITUTE OF PRACTITIONERS IN ADVERTISING, 44 Belgrave Square, S.W.1.

PURCHASING OFFICERS ASSOCIATION, Wardrobe Court, 146A Queen Victoria Street, E.C.4.

DANCING

THE ROYAL ACADEMY OF DANCING (incorporated by Royal Charter), 15 Holland Park Gardens, W.14 (trains students of exceptional promise in Ballet, 3 years' teachers' course and conducts examinations).

THE IMPERIAL SOCIETY OF TEACHERS OF DANCING INC., 70 Gloucester Place, W.1

THE ROYAL BALLET SCHOOL, 155 Talgarth Road, W.14, and White Lodge, Richmond Park.—*Director*, Arnold L. Haskell, C.B.E., M.A.

DENTAL

Any person is entitled to be registered in the Dentists Register if he holds the degree or diploma in dental surgery of a University in the United Kingdom or Republic of Ireland or the diploma of any of the Licensing Authorities (The Royal College of Surgeons of England, of Edinburgh and in Ireland, and the Royal Faculty of Physicians and Surgeons of Glasgow).

The Dentists Register is kept by the General Dental Council, 37 Wimpole Street, W.1.—*Pres.*, Sir Wilfred Fish, C.B.E., M.D., F.D.S.R.C.S. *Registrar*, D. Hindley-Smith.

Dental Schools in the United Kingdom

BELFAST, Queen's University.
BIRMINGHAM, The University.
BRISTOL, The University.
DUNDEE, The Dental School (St. Andrew's University).
EDINBURGH, The University.
GLASGOW, The University.
LEEDS, The University.
LIVERPOOL, The University.
LONDON, Guy's Hospital Dental School, London Bridge, S.E.1.
„ King's College Hospital Medical School, Denmark Hill, S.E.5.
„ London Hospital Dental School, Turner Street, Whitechapel, E.1.
„ Royal Dental Hospital School of Dental Surgery, Leicester Square, W.C.2.
„ University College Hospital Medical School, University Street, Gower Street, W.C.1.
See also Teaching Hospitals, pp. 521-3.
MANCHESTER, The University.
NEWCASTLE-UPON-TYNE, The University.
SHEFFIELD, The University.

DOMESTIC SCIENCE, ETC.

The main occupations to which a training in Domestic Science can lead are Domestic Subject Teaching, Institutional Management, Hotel and Restaurant Work, Industrial Catering and Electrical, Gas or Food Product Demonstrating.

A degree of B.SC. (Household and Social Science) is granted by London University and B.SC. (Domestic Science) by Bristol University. There is a Diploma course at Sheffield University.

Schools and Colleges of Domestic Subjects

Those preceded by an asterisk * are recognized by the Ministry of Education or the Scottish Education Department for the Training of Teachers.

ABERDEEN, *Robert Gordon's Technical College.
BANGOR, *Normal College.
BATH, *Bath College of Domestic Science.
BELFAST, College of Technology, Belfast.
CARDIFF, *College of Domestic Arts, Llandaff.
CLACTON, St. Osyth's Training College, Marine Parade.
DOUGLAS, Isle of Man, College of Domestic Science.
EDINBURGH, *College of Domestic Science, Atholl Crescent.
GLASGOW, *Glasgow and West of Scotland College of Domestic Science, 1 Park Drive, C.3.
„ Scottish College of Commerce, Scottish Hotel School, Ross Hall, 197 Crookston Road, Glasgow, S.W.2.
GLOUCESTER, *Gloucestershire Training College of Domestic Science, Oxstalls Lane.
ILKLEY, *College of Housecraft, Wells Road.
LEEDS, *Yorkshire Training College of Housecraft, Vernon Road.
LEICESTER, *Domestic Science Training College, Knighton Fields.
LIVERPOOL, *F. L. Calder College of Domestic Science, Dowsefield Lane, Liverpool, 18.
LONDON, *L.C.C. Battersea Training College of Domestic Science, Manor House, 58 North Side, Clapham Common, S.W.4.
„ *Digby Stuart College, Roehampton Lane, S.W.15.
„ *National Society's Training College of Domestic Subjects, Fortune Green Road, N.W.6.

LONDON, L.C.C. South-East London Technical College, Lewisham Way, S.E.4.
„ Westminster Technical College, Hotel School, Vincent Square, S.W.1.
MANCHESTER, *Elizabeth Gaskell College, Hathersage Road, Manchester 13.
NEWCASTLE-UNDER-LYME, *County of Stafford Training College, Madeley, Newcastle, Staffs.
NEWCASTLE-UPON-TYNE, *Northern Counties' College, 54 Northumberland Road.
SEAFORD, *Training College of Housecraft, Cricketfield Road.
SHEFFIELD, *Totley Hall Training College of Housecraft.
SHREWSBURY, Redbrook Training College.
WORCESTER, City of Worcester Training College, Henwick Grove, Worcester.

Other Bodies

INSTITUTIONAL MANAGEMENT ASSOCIATION, Swinton House, 324 Gray's Inn Road, W.C.1 (awards certificates in Institutional Management).
HOTEL AND CATERING INSTITUTE, 24 Portman Square, W.1.
THE BRITISH HOTELS AND RESTAURANTS ASSOCIATION, 88 Brook Street, W.1.
CATERERS' ASSOCIATION OF GREAT BRITAIN (1917), Victoria House, Vernon Place, Southampton Row, W.C.1.
NATIONAL CATERERS' FEDERATION, 156 Camden High Street, N.W.1.
INDUSTRIAL CATERING ASSOCIATION, 53-54 King William Street, E.C.4.
ELECTRICAL ASSOCIATION FOR WOMEN, 25 Foubert's Place, W.1.

DRAMA

A Diploma in Dramatic Art is awarded by the University of London as well as a Certificate of Proficiency in Diction and Drama. The chief Training Institutions in Drama are:—
GUILDHALL SCHOOL OF MUSIC AND DRAMA (*see* p. 527).
ROYAL ACADEMY OF DRAMATIC ART (founded by Sir Herbert Beerbohm Tree, 1904), 62–64 Gower Street, and Malet Street, W.C.1.—*Principal*, John Fernald.
BRITISH DRAMA LEAGUE, 9, Fitzroy Square, W.1.
CENTRAL SCHOOL OF SPEECH AND DRAMA, Embassy Theatre, Swiss Cottage, N.W.3.
LONDON ACADEMY OF MUSIC AND DRAMATIC ART (L.A.M.D.A.), Tower House, Cromwell Road. S.W.5.—*Principal*, Michael MacOwan.
ROSE BRUFORD TRAINING COLLEGE OF SPEECH AND DRAMA, Lamorbey Park, Sidcup, Kent.—*Principal*, Rose Bruford.
ROYAL SCOTTISH ACADEMY OF MUSIC, Coll. of Dramatic Art, St. George's Place, Glasgow, C.2. *Director*, Colin Chandler.

ENGINEERING

Degree Courses. The Universities of Oxford and Cambridge provide a general course in Engineering Science, leading to an honours degree. Cambridge and other Universities provide more specialized courses. Training leading to the national certificates and diplomas, to qualification through professional Institutes and to external degrees, is available at most Technical Schools and Colleges and at a few private Engineering Colleges.

Aeronautical Engineering

Degree courses available at Belfast, Bristol, Cambridge, Glasgow, London and Southampton Universities. Diploma courses are available at Hatfield and Hull Technical Colleges; Loughborough College; Northampton College of Advanced Technology, London; and the College of Aeronautics, Cranfield, Bedfordshire.

Agricultural Engineering

M.Sc. degree courses are available at University of Durham. Undergraduate type courses are available at National College of Agricultural Engineering, Silsoe, Beds.

Chemical Engineering

Degree courses are available at the Universities of Birmingham, Cambridge, Durham, Edinburgh, Glasgow, Leeds, London, Manchester, Sheffield and Wales.

Civil Engineering

Degree courses are available at most Universities.

Electrical Engineering

Degree courses are available at many of the Universities and at some University Colleges.

Marine Engineering and Naval Architecture

Degree courses in Marine Engineering and Naval Architecture are available at Durham and Glasgow Universities.

Mechanical Engineering

Degree courses available at all universities in U.K. except Reading and Hull.

ESTATE MANAGEMENT, AUCTIONEERING AND SURVEYING

Degrees are granted by Cambridge University —B.A. (Estate Management); and by London University—B.Sc. (Estate Management).

THE CHARTERED AUCTIONEERS AND ESTATE AGENTS INSTITUTE, 29 Lincoln's Inn Fields, W.C.2.
THE INCORPORATED SOCIETY OF AUCTIONEERS AND LANDED PROPERTY AGENTS, 34 Queen's Gate. S.W.7.
RATING AND VALUATION ASSOCIATION, 29 Belgrave Square, S.W.1.
VALUERS INSTITUTION, 3 Cadogan Gate, S.W.1.
THE INCORPORATED ASSOCIATION OF ARCHITECTS AND SURVEYORS, 29 Belgrave Square, S.W.1.
THE ROYAL INSTITUTE OF BRITISH ARCHITECTS, 66 Portland Place, W.1.
THE INSTITUTE OF QUANTITY SURVEYORS, 98 Gloucester Place, W.1.

THE COLLEGE OF ESTATE MANAGEMENT, St. Alban's Grove, Kensington, W.8.

FORESTRY

Degrees in Forestry are granted by Oxford University (B.A., Honours), by Edinburgh and Aberdeen Universities and the University College of North Wales, Bangor (B.Sc., Forestry).

A Diploma Course is available at Oxford University.

Professional Organizations

THE EMPIRE FORESTRY ASSOCIATION, Royal Commonwealth Society, Northumberland Avenue, W.C.2.
THE ROYAL FORESTRY SOCIETY OF ENGLAND AND WALES, 49 Russell Square, W.C.1.
THE ROYAL SCOTTISH FORESTRY SOCIETY, 7 Albyn Place, Edinburgh, 2.
THE SOCIETY OF FORESTERS OF GREAT BRITAIN, 7 Albyn Place, Edinburgh, 2.

FUEL TECHNOLOGY

Degree and Diploma Courses are available at Birmingham, Edinburgh, Leeds, London and Sheffield, Universities and the University of Wales.

Courses leading to certificates and qualifications by professional bodies are available at many Technical Colleges.

The principal professional bodies are:—

THE INSTITUTION OF GAS ENGINEERS, 17 Grosvenor Crescent, S.W.1.

THE INSTITUTE OF FUEL, 18 Devonshire Street, Portland Place, W.1.

THE INSTITUTE OF PETROLEUM, 26 Portland Place, W.1.

INSURANCE

Organizations conducting examinations and awarding diplomas:—

THE CHARTERED INSURANCE INSTITUTE, 20 Aldermanbury, E.C.2.

THE CORPORATION OF INSURANCE BROKERS, 3 St. Helen's Place, E.C.3.

THE ASSOCIATION OF AVERAGE ADJUSTERS, Burley House, 5 Theobalds Road, W.C.1.

THE ASSOCIATION OF FIRE LOSS ADJUSTERS, 13-14 Union Court, Old Broad Street, E.C.3.

JOURNALISM

The principal professional organizations are:—

THE INSTITUTE OF JOURNALISTS, 2 & 4 Tudor Street, E.C.4.

THE NATIONAL UNION OF JOURNALISTS (NUJ), 22 Great Windmill Street, W.1.

NATIONAL COUNCIL FOR THE TRAINING OF JOURNALISTS, 6 Carmelite Street, E.C.4.

The Polytechnic (309 Regent Street, W.1.) conducts a Diploma Course in Journalism.

LEGAL

Degree Courses.—The Universities giving Degree Courses in *Law* (which do not entitle the holder to practise either as Barrister or Solicitor) are Oxford, Cambridge, London, Bristol, Durham, Birmingham, Hull, Liverpool, Manchester, Leeds, Sheffield, Nottingham, Wales, Aberdeen, Edinburgh, Glasgow, St. Andrews, Belfast and Dublin. Qualifications for Barrister are obtainable only at one of the Inns of Court or Faculty of Advocates; for Solicitor, from the Law Society or its equivalent in Scotland or Ireland.

THE INNS OF COURT
EXECUTIVE COUNCIL
South Square, W.C.1

THE INNER TEMPLE, E.C.4

Treasurer (1963), G. D. Johnston.
Sub-Treasurer, Cdr. R. S. Flynn, R.N.
Chief Clerk, Miss J. Morris.

THE MIDDLE TEMPLE, E.C.4

Treasurer (1963), F. E. Skone James.
Under-Treasurer, R. H. Williams.
Chief Clerk and Accountant, H. W. Challoner.

LINCOLN'S INN, W.C.2

Treasurer (1963), Rt. Hon. Sir John Beaumont, Q.C.
Master of the Library, The Lord Denning, P.C.
Under-Treasurer and Steward, H. C. H. Fairchild.
Chief Clerk, F. C. Coales.

GRAY'S INN, W.C.1

Treasurer (till Dec. 31, 1963), The Lord Devlin, P.C.
Vice-Treasurer, His Honour P. C. Lamb, Q.C.
Master of Library, N. L. C. Macaskie, Q.C.
Under-Treasurer, Oswald Terry.
Chief Clerk, C. R. G. Hughes.

GENERAL COUNCIL OF THE BAR
(Carpmael Building, Temple, E.C.4.)

The Council is the accredited representative of the English Bar, and its duty is to deal with all matters affecting the profession, and to take such action thereon as may be deemed expedient.

Chairman, J. T. Molony, Q.C.
Vice-Chairman, R. J. A. Temple, Q.C.
Hon. Treasurer, H. E. Francis, Q.C.
Secretary, W. W. Boulton, C.B.E., T.D.

BAR AND PROBATE COURT LIBRARIES AND LIBRARIES OF THE SUPREME COURT
(Royal Courts of Justice)

Librarian, R. A. Riches, O.B.E.

COUNCIL OF LEGAL EDUCATION
(Gray's Inn Place, W.C.1.)

Established by the four Inns of Court to superintend the Education and Examination of Students for the English Bar.

Chairman, Sir Henry Wynn-Parry.
Vice-Chairman and Chairman of the Board of Studies, Hon. Mr. Justice Lloyd-Jacob.
Chairman of the Finance Committee, G. D. Johnston.
Director and Head of Inns of Court School of Law, Sir Fred E. Pritchard, M.B.E., LL.D.
Secretary to the Council and Deputy Director, T. Harvatt, C.M.G.

FACULTY OF ADVOCATES
(Parliament Square, Edinburgh)

Admission as an Advocate of the Scottish Bar is by petition to the Court of Session. The candidate is remitted for examination to the Faculty of Advocates.

Dean of Faculty, W. I. R. Fraser, Q.C.
Vice-Dean, T. P. McDonald, Q.C.
Treasurer, G. E. O. Walker, M.B.E., T.D., Q.C.
Clerk of Faculty, T. W. Strachan.
Keeper of the Library, Miss M. H. Kidd, Q.C.
Agent, Sir Hugh Watson.

NORTHERN IRELAND

Admission to the Bar of Northern Ireland is controlled by the Honourable Society of the Inn of Court of Northern Ireland (established Jan. 11, 1926), the Royal Courts of Justice (Ulster), Belfast.

Treasurer (until Dec. 31, 1963), Hon. Mr. Justice Sheil.
Under-Treasurer and Librarian, J. Ritchie.

THE LAW SOCIETY
(Chancery Lane, W.C.2)

The Society controls the education and examination of articled clerks, and the admission of solicitors in England and Wales. Number of members, 18,306.

President of the Society (1963–64), R. Long.
Vice-President (1963–64), R. J. F. Burrows.
Secretary, Sir Thomas Lund, C.B.E.
Under-Secs., G. T. Cruickshank (*Finance Officer*); H. Horsfall Turner, J. F. Warren, E. H. Matthews, T.D.; H. M. Lloyd; W. G. M Ballantyne, T.D.; P. A. Leach.

THE COLLEGE OF LAW

The College of Law, established by The Law Society, provides a complete scheme of education in legal subjects; the classes are open to all students whether articled clerks or otherwise, on payment of the prescribed fees.

Chairman, Board of Management, Sir Thomas Lund, C.B.E.

SOCIETY OF WRITERS TO H.M. SIGNET

(Parliament Square, Edinburgh)

Writers to the Signet are authorized to append to their names the letters W.S.

Deputy Keeper of the Signet, Sir Hugh Watson, M.A., LL.B.

Sub-Keeper and Clerk, R. C. Notman, M.B.E., B.L.

SOLICITORS IN THE SUPREME COURTS, SCOTLAND

President, T. S. McGregor, 24 Alva Street, Edinburgh 2.

Secretary, Stewart H. Greig, 24 Hill Street, Edinburgh 2.

LAW SOCIETY OF SCOTLAND

Law Society's Hall, North Bank Street, Edinburgh

The Society comprises all practising solicitors in Scotland. It controls the examination of legal apprentices and the admission of solicitors in Scotland and acts as registrar of solicitors under the Solicitors (Scotland) Acts, 1933 to 1958.

The Law Society of Scotland administers the Legal Aid and Advice Scheme set up under the Legal Aid (Scotland) Act, 1949.

President, (1962–63), N. Watson, LL.B.

Secretary, R. B. Laurie, W.S.

SCOTTISH LAW AGENTS SOCIETY

Secretary and Treasurer, J. W. Barty, Dunblane, Perthshire.

LIBRARIANSHIP AND ARCHIVE ADMINISTRATION

The Library Association, Chaucer House, Malet Place, W.C.1, maintains the professional register of Chartered Librarians (Fellows and Associates), for which examinations are held twice yearly.

Schools of Librarianship conducting full-time courses of instruction in preparation for the examinations of the Library Association: Birmingham College of Commerce, Birmingham 4; Brighton Technical College, Brighton 7; Ealing Technical College, W.5; College of Commerce, Leeds 2; North Western Polytechnic, N.W.5; College of Further Education, Loughborough, Leics.; College of Commerce, Manchester 1; Municipal College of Commerce, Newcastle-upon-Tyne; Scottish College of Commerce, Glasgow, C.3.

Post-graduate diploma courses are available at London University (*Dir.*, Prof. R. Irwin), Sheffield University (*Dir.*, W. L. Saunders) and at Queen's University, Belfast (*Dir.*, P. Havard-Williams) where a non-graduate diploma course is also available.

Archive Administration

The University of London offers a Post graduate Diploma in Archive Administration, intended primarily for candidates hoping to obtain appointments in local record offices and similar institutions. The full time course lasts one year, and a first or second class honours degree in an arts subject is required. Information may be obtained from the Director, School of Librarianship and Archives, University College London, Gower Street, W.C.1. The University of Liverpool (Department of History) offers a rather similar Diploma in the Study of Records and the Administration of Archives, and the University College of Wales, Aberystwyth, offers a post graduate Diploma in Palaeography and Archive Administration. The L.C.C. provide a course in palaeography and one also in archive repair work each year.

MEDICAL

Medical Study may be followed at most of the Universities and all the recognized Medical Schools in the British Isles. Medical and Surgical Degrees are conferred by nearly every University, and other medical qualifications by the various Medical Colleges and Corporations.

GENERAL MEDICAL COUNCIL, 44 Hallam Street, W.1.—*President*, The Lord Cohen of Birkenhead, M.D.; *Registrars* (*General Council and England and Wales*) W. K. Pyke-Lees, M.A.; (*Scotland*), A. B. Brown, M.C., 8 Queen Street, Edinburgh, 2; *Ireland*, Miss G. McMeekin, 20 Fitzwilliam Square, Dublin.

The Council is responsible for the standard of medical education and for keeping the Medical Register.

TEACHING HOSPITALS IN LONDON

Under the National Health Service (Designation of Teaching Hospitals) Order, 1957, and subsequent amendments, the following were designated Teaching Hospitals for the *University of London*.

CHARING CROSS HOSPITAL, Agar Street, Strand, W.C.2.—Number of beds, 323; In-patients, 1962, 5,776; New out-patients, 1962, 12,998. 24 house appointments open annually. *House Governor and Secretary*, Frank Hart. Medical School, 62 Chandos Place, W.C.2. *Dean*, S. J. R. Reynolds, M.A., M.B., B.Ch. *Secretary*, B. S. Drewe, M.A., LL.B. Charing Cross Hospital Group: Fulham (377 beds); Fulham Maternity (379 beds); Kingsbury Maternity (56 beds); West London (230 beds).

GUY'S HOSPITAL, St. Thomas's Street, S.E.1.—Number of beds, 971 (in Group); In-patients 1962, 16,635; New out-patients, 1962, 55,937; Casualty Dept. attendances, 1962, 63,750. *Chairman, Board of Governors*, The Lord Cunliffe; *Secretary*, A. H. Burfoot. Medical School, *Dean*, E. R. Boland, C.B.E., M.D., F.R.C.P. *Sub-Dean (Medical)*, J. C. Houston, M.D., F.R.C.P. *Sub-Dean (Dental)*, F. S. Warner, F.D.S., L.R.C.P., M.R.C.S. *Secretary*, W. F. Cook, Guy's Hospital Group: Evelina Hospital for Sick Children, Southwark Bridge Road, S.E.1.

KING'S COLLEGE HOSPITAL, Denmark Hill, S.E.5.—Number of beds, 509; In-patients, 1962, 12,857; New out-patients, 1962, 48,964; Casualty attendances, 1962, 82,079. *Chairman, Board of Governors*, The Marquess of Normanby, M.B.E. *House Governor and Secretary*, J. D. Banks, M.A. Medical School. *Dean*, V. F. Hall, C.V.O., L.R.C.P., M.R.C.S., I.F.A.R.C.S. *Secretary*, W. F. Gunn, LL.B. King's College Hospital Group: Belgrave Hospital for Children, Clapham Road (53 beds). *Annexes*, Walton-on-Thames (30 beds); Camberley (40 beds). The Group complement of 632 beds includes 50 for private patients.

THE LONDON HOSPITAL, Whitechapel, E.1.—Number of beds, 997; In-patients, 1962, 20,427; New out-patients, 1962, 130,852. *House Governor*, Hon. J. L. Scarlett; *Deputy House Governor*, M. J. Fairey, Medical College and Dental School, Turner Street, E.1. *Dean*, H. B. May, M.D., F.R.C.P. *Sub-Dean (Medical)*, J. V. Crawford, M.B.E., M.B., B.S., F.R.C.S. *Sub-Dean (Dental)*, N. Livingstone Ward, L.D.S., D.D.S. *Secretary*, H. P. Laird. London Hospital Group: Queen Mary's Maternity Home, Hampstead, N.W.3; *Annexes* at Banstead, Brentwood, Hayes and Reigate.

MIDDLESEX HOSPITAL, Mortimer Street, W.1.—Number of beds in Group, 990; In-patients, 1962, 19,550; New out-patients, 1962, 75,040. *Chairman, Board of Governors*, The Lord Cobbold, P.C., G.C.V.O. *Secretary-Superintendent*, Brig. G. P.

Hardy-Roberts, C.B., C.B.E. **Medical School.** *Dean*, Prof. Sir Brian Windeyer, D.SC., F.R.C.P., F.R.C.S. *Secretary*, Miss E. M. Walton. **Middlesex Hospital Group:** St. Luke's-Woodside Hospital, N.10; Hospital for Women, Soho Square, W.1.; The Arthur Stanley Institute, N.W.1.; Recovery Unit, Highgate, N.6.; Convalescent Home, Clacton-on-Sea.

ROYAL DENTAL HOSPITAL OF LONDON, Leicester Square, W.C.2.—Number of beds, 12; In-patients, 1962, 723; New out-patients, 1962, 55,808. House appointments open twice yearly, 11. *Hospital Secretary*, Miss L. J. M. Brace. School of Dental Surgery: Scholarships and Prizes open, 1; value £100. *Dean*, Prof. R. B. Lucas, M.D., M.R.C.P. *Secretary*, K. R. McK. Biggs, B.A.

ROYAL FREE HOSPITAL, Gray's Inn Road, W.C.1.—Number of beds, 746 (in Group); In-patients, 1962, 14,866; New out-patients, 1962, 32,231; Casualty attendances, 1962, 92,248. *Chairman, Board of Governors*, Hon. P. Samuel, M.C. *Secretary to the Board of Governors*, R. G. Heppell. **School of Medicine**, Hunter Street, Brunswick Square, W.C.1. *Dean*, Miss F. Gardner, M.D., F.R.C.P. *Warden and Secretary*, Mrs. S. C. Robinson, M.A. **Royal Free Hospital Group:** The North-Western Branch and the Liverpool Road Branch; Hampstead General Hospital, N.W.3.

ST. BARTHOLOMEW'S HOSPITAL, Smithfield, E.C.1. Number of beds, 814; In-patients, 1962, 15,002; New out-patients, 1962, 77,979; 57 resident appointments open annually. *Chairman, Board of Governors*, M. W. Perrin, C.B.E.; *Clerk*. J. W. Gooddy. Medical College, *Dean*, J. W. Cope. *Secretary*, C. E. Morris.

ST. GEORGE'S HOSPITAL, Hyde Park Corner, S.W.1.—Number of beds, 304; In-patients, 1962, 7,891. Clinic attendances, 1962, 109,418; Casualty Dept., 46,954. 20 resident appointments open annually. *House Governor and Secretary*, R. Ellis. Medical School. Number of scholarships and prizes open, 15; value, £1,425. *Dean*, A. Hunter, M.D. *Secretary*, C. R. Cuthbert. St. George's Hospital Group: Victoria Hospital for Children (109 beds); Atkinson Morley Hospital (112 beds); St. George's, Tooting Grove (393 beds); Royal Dental Hospital (*q.v.*).

ST. MARY'S HOSPITAL, Praed Street, W.2.—Number of beds, 887 (in Group); In-patients, 1962, 20,224; New out-patients, 1962, 61,764. *House Governor and Secretary to the Board of Governors*, A. Powditch, M.C. Medical School, Norfolk Place, W.2. Scholarships and Prizes: Entrance, 1 of £100 and 5 of £40 p.a. for 5 years; University, for Clinical students, 1 of £100, 2 of £50 p.a. for 3 years, 1 of £40 a year for 3 years. *Dean*, G. B. Mitchell-Heggs, O.B.E., T.D., M.D., F.R.C.P. *Secretary*, J. E. Stevenson, LL.B. **St. Mary's Hospital Group:** Paddington Green Children's Hospital, W.2.; Princess Louise Kensington Hospital for Children, St. Quintin Avenue, W.10; Samaritan Hospital for Women, N.W.1; St. Luke's Hospital, Bayswater, W.2.; Western Ophthalmic Hospital, N.W.1.

ST. THOMAS' HOSPITAL, S.E.1.—Number of beds, 957 (in Group); In-patients, 1962, 21,199; New out-patients 1962, 109,689. The Hospital, which was founded in Southwark, was rebuilt on its present site in 1868–71. The main hospital buildings were extensively damaged during the war of 1939–45 and a comprehensive reconstruction scheme is in progress. *Treasurer and Chairman, Board of Governors*, Hon. Sir Arthur Howard, K.B.E., C.V.O. *Clerk of the Governors*, B. A. McSwiney. Medical School, Albert Embankment, S.E.1. *Dean*, R. W. Nevin, T.D., M.A., F.R.C.S. *Medical Secretary*, A. L. Crockford, C.B.E., D.S.O., M.C., T.D. **St. Thomas's Hospital Group:** Royal Waterloo Hospital, S.E.1.; General Lying-in Hospital, S.E.1; Grosvenor Hospital, S.W.1; St. Thomas' Babies Hostel, S.E.11.

UNIVERSITY COLLEGE HOSPITAL, Gower Street, W.C.1.—Number of beds, 1,123; In-patients, 1962, 19,985; New out-patients, 1962, 50,826. *Chairman, Board of Governors*, A. D. Bonham-Carter. *Secretary*, O. R. Cross. Medical School, University Street, W.C.1. *Dean*, C. W. Flemming, O.B.E., M.Ch., F.R.C.S. *Secretary*, D. H. L. Morgan. **University College Hospital Group:** St. Pancras Hospital, N.W.1; Hospital for Tropical Diseases, N.W.1.

WESTMINSTER HOSPITAL, St. John's Gardens, S.W.1.—Number of beds, 429; In-patients, 1962, 9,615; New out-patients, 1962, 33,884. *House Governor and Secretary*, R. P. MacMahon, M.A. **Medical School.** *Dean*, R. I. S. Bayliss, M.A., M.D., F.R.C.P. *Secretary*, W. R. Moule, M.A. **Westminster Hospital Group:** Queen Mary's Hospital, Roehampton (333 beds); Westminster Hospital Chest Clinic; Westminster Children's Hospital (106 beds), Vincent Square, S.W.1; The Gordon Hospital (102 beds), Vauxhall Bridge Road, S.W.1; All Saints Hospital (52 beds), Austral Street, S.E.11. *Annexe*, Swanley, Kent (106 beds).

Post Graduate Teaching Hospitals

HAMMERSMITH HOSPITAL, W.12; St. Mark's Hospital for Diseases of the Rectum and Colon, E.C.1. HOSPITAL FOR SICK CHILDREN, W.C.1: NATIONAL HOSPITAL, Queen Square, W.C.1; Maida Vale Hospital for Nervous Diseases, W.9. ROYAL NATIONAL THROAT, NOSE AND EAR HOSPITAL (including Cent. London Hospital Division, W.C.1; Golden Sq. Hospital Division, W.1.). MOORFIELDS EYE HOSPITALS, City Road, E.C.1 and High Holborn, W.C.1. BETHLEM ROYAL HOSPITAL AND MAUDSLEY HOSPITAL. ST. JOHN'S HOSPITAL FOR DISEASES OF THE SKIN, W.C.2. HOSPITAL FOR CONSUMPTION AND DISEASES OF THE CHEST, S.W.3; London Chest Hospital, E.2. ROYAL NATIONAL ORTHOPAEDIC HOSPITAL, W.1. NATIONAL HEART HOSPITAL, W.1. ST. PETER'S, ST. PAUL'S, and ST. PHILIP'S HOSPITALS, W.C.2. ROYAL MARSDEN HOSPITAL, S.W.3. QUEEN CHARLOTTE'S MATERNITY HOSPITAL, W.6; Chelsea Hospital for Women, S.W.3. EASTMAN DENTAL HOSPITAL, W.C.1.

POST-GRADUATE MEDICAL SCHOOLS OF THE UNIVERSITY OF LONDON

London School of Hygiene and Tropical Medicine, Keppel Street, W.C.1. E. T. C. Spooner, *Dean*.

British Postgraduate Medical Federation, 18 Guilford Street, W.C.1. Prof. Sir James Paterson Ross, K.C.V.O., LL.D., M.S., F.R.C.S., *Director*.

Comprises:—

POST GRADUATE MEDICAL SCHOOL OF LONDON, Ducane Road, Shepherds Bush, W.12. C. E. Newman, M.D., F.R.C.P., *Dean*.

INSTITUTE OF BASIC MEDICAL SCIENCES, Royal College of Surgeons, Lincoln's Inn Fields, W.C.2. E. G. Muir, M.S., F.R.C.S., *Dean*.

INSTITUTE OF CANCER RESEARCH, Royal Marsden Hospital, Fulham Road, S.W.3. Prof. F. Bergel, D.SC., F.R.S., *Dean*.

INSTITUTE OF CARDIOLOGY, 35 Wimpole Street, W.1. A. G. Leatham, F.R.C.P., *Dean*.

INSTITUTE OF CHILD HEALTH, Hospital for Sick Children, Great Ormond Street, W.C.1. G. H. Newns, M.D., F.R.C.P., *Dean*.

INSTITUTE OF DENTAL SURGERY, Eastman Dental Hospital, Gray's Inn Road, W.C.1. Prof. R. V. Bradlaw, C.B.E., D.D.SC., F.R.C.S., F.D.S.R.C.S., *Dean*.

INSTITUTE OF DERMATOLOGY, St. John's Hospital for Diseases of the Skin, Lisle Street, W.C.2. B. F. Russell, M.D., F.R.C.P., *Dean*.

INSTITUTE OF DISEASES OF THE CHEST, Brompton Hospital, S.W.3. J. R. Bignall, M.D., F.R.C.P., *Dean*.

INSTITUTE OF LARYNGOLOGY AND OTOLOGY, Royal National Throat, Nose and Ear Hospital, 330–332 Gray's Inn Road, W.C.1. J. C. Hogg, C.V.O., F.R.C.S., *Dean*.

INSTITUTE OF NEUROLOGY, National Hospital, Queen Square, W.C.1. J. W. D. Bull, M.A., M.D., F.R.C.P., *Dean*.

INSTITUTE OF OBSTETRICS AND GYNÆCOLOGY, Chelsea Hospital for Women, Dovehouse Street, S.W.3. R. M. Feroze, M.D., F.R.C.S., F.R.C.O.G., *Dean*.

INSTITUTE OF OPHTHALMOLOGY, Judd Street, W.C.1. T. Keith Lyle, C.B.E., M.D., M.Ch., F.R.C.P. F.R.C.S., *Dean*.

INSTITUTE OF ORTHOPÆDICS, Royal National Orthopædic Hospital, 234 Great Portland Street, W.1. H. Jackson Burrows, M.A., M.D., F.R.C.S., F.R.A.C.S., *Dean*.

INSTITUTE OF PSYCHIATRY, Maudsley Hospital, Denmark Hill, S.E.5. D. L. Davies, M.A., D.M., *Dean*.

INSTITUTE OF UROLOGY, 10 Henrietta Street, W.C.2. A R. C. Higham, F.R.C.S., *Dean*.

ROYAL ARMY MEDICAL COLLEGE, Millbank, S.W.1. —*Commandant*, Maj.-Gen. A. N. T. Meneces, C.B., C.B.E., D.S.O., Q.H.P., M.D., F.R.C.P.

OTHER TEACHING HOSPITALS

Under the National Health Service Designation of Teaching Hospitals Order, 1959, the following have been designated teaching hospitals in the 10 university medical centres outside London:

University of Durham.—United Newcastle upon Tyne Hospitals: Royal Victoria Infirmary, Newcastle upon Tyne; Princess Mary Maternity Hospital, Newcastle upon Tyne; Babies' Hospital, Newcastle upon Tyne: Newcastle upon Tyne Dental Hospital: Castle Hill Convalescent Home.

University of Leeds.—United Leeds Hospitals: General Infirmary, Leeds; Maternity Hospital, Leeds; Hospital for Women, Leeds; Leeds Dental Hospital; The Ida and Robert Arthington Branch Hospital.

University of Sheffield.—United Sheffield Hospitals; Royal Infirmary, Sheffield; Royal Hospital, Sheffield and Annexe; Jessop Hospital for Women, Sheffield, including Firth Auxiliary Hospital, Sheffield; Children's Hospital, Sheffield and Annexes; Edgar Allen Physical Treatment Centre; Charles Clifford Dental Hospital.

University of Cambridge.—United Cambridge Hospitals; Addenbrooke's Hospital, Cambridge; Maternity Hospital, Cambridge; Brookfields Hospital; Chesterton Hospital, Cambridge.

University of Oxford.—United Oxford Hospitals: Radcliffe Infirmary; Churchill Hospital; Oxford Eye Hospital; Osler Hospital; Cowley Road Hospital; Slade Hospital.

Chairman of Board of Governors, Lord Franks, P.C., G.C.M.G., K.C.B., C.B.E., Medical School. *Regius Professor of Medicine*, Prof. Sir George Pickering, D.M., F.R.C.P. *Director of Clinical Studies*, J. Badenoch, D.M., F.R.C.P. *Director of Post-Graduate Medical Studies, and Secretary of Medical School*, A. W. Williams, D.M., F.R.C.P. *Pre-Clinical Adviser*, J. M. Walker, D.M.

University of Bristol.—United Bristol Hospitals: Bristol Royal Hospital (including Bristol Royal Infirmary and Bristol General Hospital); Bristol Maternity Hospital; Bristol Royal Hospital for Sick Children; Bristol Eye Hospital.

University of Wales.—United Cardiff Hospitals; Cardiff Royal Infirmary; Llandough Hospital, Penarth; the Lord Pontypridd Hospital, Dulwich House, Cardiff; The Maternity Hospital, Cardiff; St. David's Hospital, Cardiff; Whitchurch Hospital, Cardiff; Lansdowne Hospital, Cardiff; Prince of Wales Hospital, Cardiff; Sully Hospital, Sully.

University of Birmingham.—United Birmingham Hospitals: Birmingham United Hospital; Children's Hospital, Birmingham, including St. Cuthbert's Hospital, Malvern; Midland Nerve Hospital, Birmingham; Birmingham Dental Hospital; Birmingham and Midland Hospitals for Women.

University of Manchester.—United Manchester Hospitals: Manchester Royal Infirmary and Annexes; St. Mary's Hospitals for Women and Children, Manchester; Manchester Royal Eye Hospital; Dental Hospital of Manchester; Manchester Foot Hospital.

University of Liverpool.—United Liverpool Hospitals: Royal Liverpool United Hospital; Women's Hospital, Liverpool; Liverpool Maternity Hospital; Royal Liverpool Children's Hospitals, Liverpool and Heswall (Cheshire); Liverpool Ear, Nose and Throat Infirmary; St. Paul's Eye Hospital, Liverpool; Liverpool Dental Hospital.

DEANS OF UNIVERSITY MEDICAL SCHOOLS

England and Wales

BIRMINGHAM—Prof. D. V. Hubble, M.D., F.R.C.P.

BRISTOL—Prof. A. I. Darling, D.D.SC.

CAMBRIDGE—L. B. Cole, M.D., F.R.C.P.

DURHAM—Prof. A. G. R. Lowdon, O.B.E., M.A., M.B., Ch.B., F.R.C.S.

LEEDS—A. B. Pain, T.D., Ch.M., F.R.C.S.

LIVERPOOL—J. M. Leggate, M.B., Ch.B., F.R.C.S.

MANCHESTER—Prof. W. Schlapp, M.B., Ch.B., B.SC., Ph.D., M.SC.

OXFORD—J. Badenoch, D.M., F.R.C.P. (*Director of Clinical Studies*).

SHEFFIELD—J. G. McCrie, O.B.E., T.D., F.R.C.P.Ed.

WALES—A. Trevor Jones, M.D., F.R.C.P. (*Provost*).

Scotland

ABERDEEN—Prof. Sir Dugald Baird, D.SC., M.D., LL.D.

EDINBURGH—Prof. J. H. F. Brotherston, M.A., M.D., F.R.C.P.E., F.R.S.E.

GLASGOW—C. M. Fleming, M.A., M.D., F.R.C.P.

ST. ANDREWS—Prof. G. H. Bell, M.D., F.R.C.P.

Other Licensing Corporations granting Diplomas

THE ROYAL COLLEGE OF PHYSICIANS OF LONDON AND THE ROYAL COLLEGE OF SURGEONS OF ENGLAND, Examining Board in England, Examination Hall, Queen Square, W.C.1.

THE SOCIETY OF APOTHECARIES, Black Friars Lane, E.C.4.

ROYAL COLLEGE OF OBSTETRICIANS AND GYNÆCOLOGISTS, Sussex Place, Regent's Park, N.W.1.

THE ROYAL COLLEGE OF PHYSICIANS AND THE ROYAL COLLEGE OF SURGEONS, Edinburgh.

THE ROYAL COLLEGE OF PHYSICIANS AND SURGEONS OF GLASGOW.

THE SCOTTISH CONJOINT BOARD, 18 Nicolson Street, Edinburgh 8, and 242 St. Vincent Street, Glasgow, C.2.

NURSING

Three-year courses for State Registration in general, sick children's, mental and mental deficiency nursing. Two-year course for State enrolment. Training schools in many parts of Great Britain. University Diploma in nursing awarded by London University and Diplomas for nurse teachers by the Universities of London, Hull and Edinburgh.

NURSING RECRUITMENT SERVICE, 6 Cavendish Square, W.1. Information about a nursing career and advice about hospital training schools on application. *Secretary*, Miss L. M. Darnell, S.R.N., S.C.M.

GENERAL NURSING COUNCIL
for England and Wales
P.O. Box 803, 23 Portland Place, W.1.

The Council was established by the Nurses Registration Act of 1919. State registration is given to applicants who fulfil prescribed conditions, including a 3-year training in hospitals approved by the Council; the Nurses Act, 1943, gave similar power to the Council in relation to enrolled nurses. There are several hundred of these training schools in different parts of the country.
Chairman, Miss C. A. Smaldon, S.R.N.
Registrar, Miss M. Henry, S.R.N.

GENERAL NURSING COUNCIL
for Scotland
5 Darnaway Street, Edinburgh, 3
Registrar, Mabel Wilson, R.G.N.

THE ROYAL COLLEGE OF NURSING
AND NATIONAL COUNCIL OF NURSES OF THE UNITED KINGDOM
Education Division, 1a Henrietta Place, W.1.

The Royal College of Nursing Education Division provides instruction at post-registration level in both hospital and public health fields. Full-time courses are held in preparation for senior posts in administration and teaching as well as training courses for health visitors, occupational health nurses, ward sisters, clinical instructors and teachers of pupil nurses.
Director, Miss M. F. Carpenter, S.R.N.

CENTRAL MIDWIVES BOARD
39 Harrington Gardens, S.W.7
Chairman, Arnold L. Walker, C.B.E., M.A., M.B., B.Ch., F.R.C.S., F.R.C.O.G.
Secretary, R. J. Fenney, M.B.E., B.A. (Admin.).

CENTRAL MIDWIVES BOARD
for Scotland
7 Hill Square, Edinburgh, 8.
Chairman, J. Bruce Dewar, M.B., F.R.C.S., F.R.C.O.G.
Secretary, Miss D. S. Young, M.A.

PROFESSIONS SUPPLEMENTARY TO MEDICINE

Promotion of a high standard of professional education in chiropody, dietetics, medical laboratory technology, occupational therapy, physiotherapy, radiography and remedial gymnastics is the responsibility of the:
COUNCIL FOR PROFESSIONS SUPPLEMENTARY TO MEDICINE, York House, Westminster Bridge Road, S.E.1.—*Chairman*, Sir Sydney Littlewood; *Registrar*, J. S. Tapsfield;
and of 7 professional Boards appointed by the Council. The Registrar of the Council also serves as Registrar of each professional Board.

CHIROPODY

Professional qualifications are granted by the Society of Chiropodists, 8 Wimpole Street, W.1, to students who have passed the qualifying examinations after attending a course of full-time training for three years at one of the following recognized schools. Qualifications granted by the Society are approved for the employment of chiropodists within the National Health Service.

CHELSEA SCHOOL OF CHIROPODY, 250 King's Road, S.W.3.
THE LONDON FOOT HOSPITAL AND SCHOOL OF CHIROPODY, 33 Fitzroy Square, W.1.
BIRMINGHAM GENERAL DISPENSARY SCHOOL OF CHIROPODY, 41 Newhall Street, Birmingham 3.
MANCHESTER FOOT HOSPITAL AND SCHOOL OF CHIROPODY, Anson Road, Victoria Park, Manchester.
SALFORD SCHOOL OF CHIROPODY, Salford Technical College, 28–9 The Crescent, Salford.
CARDIFF SCHOOL OF CHIROPODY, Llandaff Technical College, Cardiff.
EDINBURGH FOOT CLINIC AND SCHOOL OF CHIROPODY, 81 Newington Road, Edinburgh.
GLASGOW FOOT CLINICS AND COLLEGE OF CHIROPODY, 22 Windsor Terrace and 48 Cumberland Street, Glasgow.

DIETETICS
(*See also* Domestic Science and Nursing)

The professional association which exercises general supervision over training is the British Dietetic Association, 251 Brompton Road, S.W.3, membership of which is open to qualified dietitians who have completed a recognized training. Particulars of training may be obtained from the Secretary.

MEDICAL LABORATORY TECHNOLOGY

Professional examinations are conducted and lecture courses arranged in approved hospitals and Technical Institutes by the Institute of Medical Laboratory Technology, 74 New Cavendish Street, W.1.

OCCUPATIONAL THERAPY

Professional qualifications are awarded after examination by the Association of Occupational Therapists, 251 Brompton Road, S.W.3.

Principal Training Centres

DORSET HOUSE SCHOOL OF OCCUPATIONAL THERAPY, LTD., Churchill Hospital, Oxford.
THE OCCUPATIONAL THERAPY CENTRE AND TRAINING SCHOOL, 12–14 Merton Rise, N.W.3.
ST. ANDREW'S HOSPITAL, Northampton.
ST. LOYES SCHOOL OF OCCUPATIONAL THERAPY, Millbrook House, Topsham Road, Exeter.
THE COLLEGE OF OCCUPATIONAL THERAPY (LIVERPOOL), LTD., Victoria Road, Huyton, nr. Liverpool.
DERBY SCHOOL OF OCCUPATIONAL THERAPY, 403 Burton Road, Derby.
SCHOOL OF OCCUPATIONAL THERAPY, Botley's Park Hospital, Chertsey, Surrey.
YORK SCHOOL OF OCCUPATIONAL THERAPY, The Military Hospital, York.

Training courses leading to a professional qualification in Scotland are available at The Astley Ainslie Hospital, Grange Loan, Edinburgh and the Glasgow School of Occupational Therapy, 29 Sherbrooke Avenue, Glasgow, S.1.

PHYSIOTHERAPY

Examinations leading to qualification are conducted by the Chartered Society of Physiotherapy, Tavistock House (South), Tavistock Square, W.C.1 and by the Faculty of Physiotherapists, 29 Waterloo Street, Glasgow, C.2, at the following schools:

BATH, *School of Physiotherapy, The Manor House, Combe Park.
BELFAST, N. Ireland School of Physiotherapy, Royal Victoria Hospital.

BIRMINGHAM, Queen Elizabeth Hospital, Edgbaston.
„ Royal Orthopædic Hospital.
BRADFORD, *Royal Infirmary.
BRISTOL, Royal Hospital (Infirmary Branch).
CARDIFF, Royal Infirmary.
COVENTRY, Coventry and Warwickshire Hospital.
EDINBURGH, Royal Infirmary.
GLASGOW, *Royal Infirmary.
„ Western Infirmary.
LEEDS, *General Infirmary.
LIVERPOOL, School of Physiotherapy, 40 Upper Parliament Street.
LONDON, *West Middlesex Hospital, Isleworth, Middlesex.
„ Guy's Hospital, S.E.1.
„ King's College Hospital, Denmark Hill, S.E.5.
„ London Hospital, Whitechapel, E.1.
„ Middlesex Hospital, W.1.
„ *Royal National Institute for the Blind, 204–6 Gt. Portland Street, W.1.
„ St. Mary's Hospital School of Physiotherapy (Swedish Institute), 108 Cromwell Road, S.W.7.
„ St. Thomas's Hospital, S.E.1.
„ *Prince of Wales's General Hospital School of Physiotherapy, 50 Chepstow Villas, W.11.
MANCHESTER, Ancoats Hospital; Royal Infirmary; Withington Hospital.
NEWCASTLE-UPON-TYNE, Royal Victoria Infirmary.
OSWESTRY, Robert Jones and Agnes Hunt Orthopædic Hospital.
SALFORD, *Salford Hospital Group. School of Physiotherapy, Hope Hospital, Salford 6.
SHEFFIELD, *United Sheffield Hospitals, Gell Street, Sheffield 3.
WOLVERHAMPTON, *The Royal Hospital.

Training for a limited number of civilian students is also available at the Service Schools:—

*Royal Naval School of Physiotherapy, Royal Naval Hospital, Haslar, Gosport, Hants.
*Army School of Physiotherapy, Royal Herbert Hospital, Woolwich, S.E.18.
*R.A.F. School of Physiotherapy, Princess Mary's R.A.F. Hospital, Halton, Aylesbury, Bucks.

* Training for male students available at schools marked thus.

RADIOGRAPHY AND RADIOTHERAPY

Examinations leading to qualification are conducted by the Society of Radiographers, 32 Welbeck Street, W.1.

There are recognized training centres in radiography and radiotherapy at 49 cities and towns in England and Wales; in Scotland at Aberdeen, Dundee, Edinburgh and Glasgow Royal Infirmaries and (for women students only) at Glasgow Western Infirmary; in Northern Ireland at the Royal Victoria Hospital, Belfast, and at Londonderry.

In London courses are available at the London Teaching Hospitals listed on pp. 521-3 (courses at Guy's, King's College, London, Middlesex, Royal Free and St. George's Hospitals for women students only); and at the Hammersmith, Lambeth and Royal Northern Hospitals, at Oldchurch County Hospital, Romford, Essex and at Woolwich.

Courses in radiotherapy only are held at Sheffield National Centre for Radiotherapy, Cardiff Radiotherapy Centre, Oxford (Churchill Hospital), Liverpool (Liverpool Radium Institute), Manchester (Christie Hospital and Holt Radium Institute), Scunthorpe and District War Memorial Hospital; and in N. Ireland at Belfast (N. Ireland Radiotherapy Centre).

REMEDIAL GYMNASTICS

Examinations leading to qualification are conducted by the Society of Remedial Gymnasts, Physical Medical Dept., Northampton General Hospital, Northampton. The recognized training centre is the School of Remedial Gymnastics and Recreational Therapy, Pinderfields Hospital, Wakefield, Yorks.

OTHER MEDICAL SERVICES

SPEECH THERAPY

The Register of qualified Speech Therapists is published by the College of Speech Therapists, 68 Queen's Gardens, W.2.

Diploma courses are available at:—

THE CENTRAL SCHOOL OF SPEECH AND DRAMA (Department of Speech Therapy), Embassy Theatre, Swiss Cottage, N.W.3.
THE KINGDON-WARD SCHOOL OF SPEECH THERAPY, 26 Lower Sloane Street, S.W.1.
THE OLDREY-FLEMING SCHOOL OF SPEECH THERAPY, 16 Harley Street, W.1.
THE WEST END HOSPITAL SCHOOL OF SPEECH THERAPY, 59 Portland Place, W.1.
ELIZABETH GASKELL COLLEGE, SCHOOL OF SPEECH THERAPY, Hathersage Road, Manchester 13.
THE LEICESTER SCHOOL OF SPEECH THERAPY, Pelham House, 100 Welford Road, Leicester.
THE EDINBURGH SCHOOL OF SPEECH THERAPY, 7 Buccleuch Place, Edinburgh, 8.
THE GLASGOW SCHOOL OF SPEECH THERAPY, 25 Athole Gardens, Glasgow, W.2.

ALMONERS

Training of almoners is organized by The Institute of Almoners, 42 Bedford Square, W.C.1.

PSYCHIATRIC SOCIAL WORKERS

One year courses in Psychiatric Social Work are conducted by the London School of Economics, Houghton Street, W.C.2.; Edinburgh University, Department of Social Science, 59 George Square, Edinburgh 8; Manchester University, Department of Psychiatry, Royal Infirmary, Oxford Road, Manchester 13; and Liverpool University, Department of Studies in Psychological Medicine, 6 Abercromby Square, Liverpool 7. Sixteen-month courses in applied social studies with a psychiatric social work specialization are run at King's College, School of Social Studies, Newcastle upon Tyne; University of Southampton, Department of Social Studies, Southampton, Hants.; and University College of South Wales and Monmouthshire, Department of Social Studies, Cathays Park, Cardiff.

The Association of Psychiatric Social Workers, 71 Albany Street, N.W.1, maintains a register of Associates.

PHARMACY

Qualification may be achieved by obtaining the Pharmaceutical Chemist Diploma on a university degree in pharmacy, followed by the Qualifying Examination of the Pharmaceutical Society in forensic pharmacy only. Further information may be obtained from the Universities and The Registrar, The Pharmaceutical Society of Great Britain, 17 Bloomsbury Square, W.C.1.

OPTICS

GENERAL OPTICAL COUNCIL, 41 Harley Street, W.1. —*Chairman*, G. R. Rougier, Q.C.; *Registrar*, A. T. Gerard.

Examining bodies granting qualifications as an ophthalmic or dispensing optician:—

THE BRITISH OPTICAL ASSOCIATION, 65 Brook Street, W.1.

THE WORSHIPFUL COMPANY OF SPECTACLE-MAKERS, Apothecaries Hall, Black Friars Lane, E.C.4.

THE INSTITUTE OF OPTICAL SCIENCE, 23 Southampton Place, W.C.1.

THE ASSOCIATION OF DISPENSING OPTICIANS, 50 Nottingham Place, W.1 (qualification as dispensing optician).

THE SCOTTISH ASSOCIATION OF OPTICIANS, 116 West Regent Street, Glasgow, C.2 (qualification as ophthalmic optician).

Recognized Training Institutions

NORTHAMPTON COLL. OF ADVANCED TECHNOLOGY (London Refraction Hospital, 58–62 Newington Causeway, S.E.1.).

MANCHESTER COLLEGE OF SCIENCE AND TECHNOLOGY, Sackville Street, Manchester, 1.

BRADFORD INSTITUTE OF TECHNOLOGY.

BIRMINGHAM COLLEGE OF ADVANCED TECHNOLOGY, Gosta Green, Birmingham 4.

CARDIFF: WELSH COLLEGE OF ADVANCED TECHNOLOGY.

STOW COLLEGE OF ENGINEERING (Glasgow Refraction Hospital, 8 Clairmont Gardens, Glasgow, C.3).

ORTHOPTICS

Orthoptists undertake the diagnosis and treatment of all types of squint and other anomalies of binocular vision, under the direction of an ophthalmic surgeon or a recognized ophthalmic medical practitioner. The training and qualification of Orthoptists are the responsibility of the Faculty of Ophthalmologists advised by the British Orthoptic Board. Training consists of a two-years and three months' course at one of the approved Orthoptic Schools. There is a post-graduate training for the Teacher's Certificate.

The Professional Association is the British Orthoptic Society and the recognized qualifying body, The British Orthoptic Board, Tavistock House, North, Tavistock Square, W.C.1.

Recognized Training Schools

THE CHILDREN'S HOSPITAL, Ladywood Road, Birmingham, 16.

BIRMINGHAM AND MIDLAND EYE HOSPITAL, Church Street, Birmingham, 3.

GENERAL, EYE AND CHILDREN'S HOSPITAL, Cheltenham.

ROYAL INFIRMARY, Chester.

COVENTRY AND WARWICKSHIRE HOSPITAL, Coventry.

GLASGOW EYE INFIRMARY, Berkeley Street, Glasgow, C.3.

MOORFIELDS EYE HOSPITAL, City Road, E.C.1 and High Holborn, W.C.1.

MANCHESTER ROYAL EYE HOSPITAL, Oxford Road, Manchester.

EYE HOSPITAL, Oxford.

UNITED SHEFFIELD HOSPITALS, West Street, Sheffield, 1.

(*See also* under Optics.)

Other recognized qualifying bodies are:

Operating Theatre, The Association of Operating Theatre Technicians, 23 Salmons Road, Lower Edmonton, N.9.

Venereology, Institute of Technicians in Venereology, 21 Crescent Avenue, Hornchurch, Essex.

OSTEOPATHY

LONDON COLLEGE OF OSTEOPATHY, 24–25 Dorset Square, N.W.1.

Dean, J. R. Lester, M.B., Ch.B.

Sec., Maj. A. F. Lockwood, E.R.D.

BRITISH SCHOOL OF OSTEOPATHY, 16 Buckingham Gate, S.W.1.—*Principal*, S. Webster-Jones.

MILITARY

STAFF COLLEGE, CAMBERLEY

Officers who graduate at the college have the letters *p.s.c.* after their names in Service Lists.

Commandant, Maj.-Gen. J. F. Worsley, C.B., O.B.E., M.C.

Assistant Commandant, Brig. A. F. Stanton, O.B.E.

Librarian, Lt.-Col. F. W. Young, M.B.E. (*ret.*).

ROYAL MILITARY ACADEMY SANDHURST

Camberley, Surrey.

The Royal Military Academy, Woolwich, founded in 1741, and the Royal Military College, Sandhurst, founded in 1799, were amalgamated in 1946 under the above title.

The object of the Academy is to train officer cadets for regular commissions in the Army. Length of course 2 years. Entrance from school by Civil Service Commissioners' Examination, or from Welbeck College, or from the ranks of the Regular Army.

Commandant, Maj.-Gen. H. J. Mogg, C.B.E., D.S.O.

ROYAL MILITARY COLLEGE OF SCIENCE

Shrivenham, nr. Swindon, Wilts.

The College was founded at Woolwich in 1864 and transferred to Shrivenham in 1946. Officer (and a few civilian) students are prepared for degrees in engineering and science of London University; Technical Staff Officers for the Home and Commonwealth armies take post-graduate courses and officers of the three Services take more advanced courses.

Commandant, Maj.-Gen. R. W. Ewbank, C.B., C.B.E., D.S.O.

Dean, Sir Donald Bailey, O.B.E.

Registrar, D. J. Chapman, B.A.

WELBECK COLLEGE

Worksop, Notts.

Headmaster, D. A. Rickards, C.B.E., M.A.

Bursar, Brig. J. M. F. Cartwright, C.B.E.

R.A.C. SCHOOL OF TANK TECHNOLOGY, R.A.C. CENTRE

Allenby Barracks, Bovington Camp, nr. Wareham, Dorset

Commandant and Chief Instructor, Col. B. S. Heath.

DUKE OF YORK'S ROYAL MILITARY SCHOOL, Dover

Commandant, Brig. G. Laing, C.B.E. (*ret.*)

Secretary, F. C. Jones.

Headmaster, Lt.-Col. R. V. M. Benn, R.A.E.C.

QUEEN VICTORIA SCHOOL

Dunblane, Perthshire, Scotland (250)

Commandant, Brig. A. M. Finlaison, C.B.E., D.S.O., (*ret*).

Headmaster, Lt.-Col. P. B. Clarke.

INSTITUTE OF ARMY EDUCATION

Eltham Palace, S.E.9 (90)

Commandant, Col. F. H. Frankcom, C.B.E.

MINING AND MINING ENGINEERING

Degree and Diploma courses in Mining, Mining Engineering and Mining Surveying are available at the Universities of Birmingham, Durham, Edinburgh (University and Heriot-Watt College),

Glasgow (Royal College of Science and Technology), Leeds, Sheffield, London (Royal School of Mines), Nottingham, and Wales, and, in Metalliferous Mining, at the School of Metalliferous Mining, Camborne, Cornwall. Courses in Oil Engineering, etc., are available at the Universities of London (Imperial College of Science and Technology) and Birmingham. Courses of study in preparation for certificates of competence in Mining and Mining Engineering awarded by the Board for Mining Examinations and the Institution of Mining Engineers are available at these universities together with most Technical Colleges in mining districts.

Miscellaneous Authorities

MINING QUALIFICATIONS BOARD, Ministry of Power, Thames House South, Millbank, S.W.1.

THE INSTITUTION OF MINING ENGINEERS, 3 Grosvenor Crescent, S.W.1.

THE INSTITUTION OF MINING AND METALLURGY, 44 Portland Place, W.1.

MUSIC

Degrees in Music are granted by the *Universities of Oxford, Cambridge, Birmingham, Bristol, Durham, London, Hull, Manchester, Sheffield* and *Nottingham*; the *University of Wales*; the *University of Edinburgh*; *Dublin University* and the *National University of Ireland*.

ASSOCIATED BOARD OF THE ROYAL SCHOOLS OF MUSIC, 14 Bedford Square, W.C.1.

Instituted in 1889 to conduct the local examinations in music of the Royal Academy of Music and the Royal College of Music, which were joined in 1947 by the Royal Manchester College of Music and the Royal Scottish Academy of Music, Glasgow.

Secretary, W. Cole, D.MUS., F.R.A.M., F.R.C.O.

ROYAL ACADEMY OF MUSIC

Marylebone Road, N.W.1

The R.A.M. was founded in 1822.

Fellows (F.R.A.M.), Honorary Fellows (HON. F.R.A.M.) and Associates (A.R.A.M.) are elected by the Directors, and Honorary Members (HON. R.A.M.) by the Committee of Management. Licentiates (L.R.A.M.) are elected by an examination held three times a year.

A complete training is offered to students of both sexes intending to take up music as a profession. Scholarships are offered for competition in March. The particulars are available in January. All students must take the full curriculum. No. of Students, 800.

Patrons, H. M. The Queen; H. M. Queen Elizabeth the Queen Mother.

President, H.R.H. The Duchess of Gloucester.

Chairman of Committee, Maj.-Gen. R. L. Bond, C.B., C.B.E., D.S.O., M.C.

Principal, Sir Thomas Armstrong, M.A., D.MUS.

Warden, Myers Foggin, F.R.A.M.

Secretary, S. Creber.

Lady Superintendent, Mrs. Deller, O.B.E.

ROYAL COLLEGE OF MUSIC

Prince Consort Road, South Kensington, S.W.7

Founded in 1883 by King Edward VII, then Prince of Wales. Fellows (F.R.C.M.), and Honorary Members (HON. R.C.M.) are elected by the Council. A.R.C.M., G.R.S.M. and M.MUS.R.C.M. awarded by examination. No. of Students (1962), 550.

Patron, H.M. The Queen.

Patron and President, H.M. Queen Elizabeth, the Queen Mother.

Director, K. Falkner, F.R.C.M.

Registrar, J. R. Stainer, B.A., MUS.B., F.R.C.M., F.R.C.O.

Bursar, Capt. J. Shrimpton, C.B.E., R.N.

GUILDHALL SCHOOL OF MUSIC AND DRAMA

John Carpenter Street, E.C.4

(Founded in 1880 by the Corporation of London)

Full-time and part-time courses in Music, Speech and Drama. Awards Diplomas of Associateship (A.G.S.M.) and Licentiateship (L.G.S.M.). The Diploma of Graduateship (G.G.S.M. Lond.) confers graduate addition to salary.

Principal, G. Thorne, M.A., MUS.B., F.R.C.O.

Secretary, E. H. Day, M.A.

Registrar, John Isard.

ROYAL COLLEGE OF ORGANISTS

Kensington Gore, S.W.7

Founded in 1864 for the promotion of the highest standard in organ playing and church musicianship. Awards Diplomas of Associateship (A.R.C.O.) and Fellowship (F.R.C.O.) and Diploma (CHM), also a certificate in choir training.

President, W. Greenhouse Allt, C.B.E., D.MUS.

Hon. Treas., W. S. Lloyd Webber, D.MUS.

Hon. Secretary, Sir William McKie, M.V.O., D.MUS.

BIRMINGHAM SCHOOL OF MUSIC

1–18 Paradise Street, Birmingham 1 (729).

Principal, G. Clinton, A.R.C.M.

TONIC SOL-FA COLLEGE OF MUSIC

Curwen Memorial Building,

9 Queensborough Terrace W.2. (1863) (60)

International examining and teaching body for dual notation.

President, Sir Malcolm Sargent, MUS.D.

Director, W. Irwin Hunt.

Secretary, J. A. Achner.

DARTINGTON MUSIC SCHOOL

Dartington College of Arts,

Totnes, S. Devon (50)

Director of Music, R. Hall.

Registrar, N. Amherst.

LONDON COLLEGE OF MUSIC

Great Marlborough Street, W.1 (500)

Complete training in music and courses in speech. Awards diplomas of Graduateship (G.L.C.M.) and Licentiateship (L.L.C.M.). Courses recognized by the Ministry of Education and Burnham Committee.

Director, Reginald Hunt, D.MUS., F.R.C.O.

Secretary, J. F. Holmes.

ROYAL SCHOOL OF CHURCH MUSIC

Addington Palace, Croydon, Surrey

Founded (1927) for the advancement of good music in the Church

Patrons, H. M. The Queen; H. M. Queen Elizabeth the Queen Mother.

President, The Archbishop of Canterbury.

Director, Gerald H. Knight, M.A., D.MUS., F.R.C.O.

Warden, Rev. G. E. Sage, M.A.

General Secretary, H. L. A. Green.

ROYAL MANCHESTER COLLEGE OF MUSIC

Devas Street, Oxford Road, Manchester, 15 (332).

Awards diplomas of Graduateship and Associateship.

President, The Earl of Harewood.

Principal, F. R. Cox, O.B.E., M.A.

Warden, N. Andrew, MUS.D., F.R.C.O.

NORTHERN SCHOOL OF MUSIC

91 Oxford Road, Manchester, 1 (800).

Principal, Miss I. Carroll.

ROYAL MILITARY SCHOOL OF MUSIC

Kneller Hall, Twickenham (42)

Commandant, Col. A. A. N. Tuck, M.B.E.
Chief Instructor, Lt.-Col. B. H. Brown, M.B.E.

ROYAL MARINES SCHOOL OF MUSIC

Deal, Kent (250)

Commandant, Col. F. N. Grant.
Principal Director of Music, Royal Marines, Lt.-Col. F. V. Dunn, C.V.O., O.B.E., F.R.A.M., R.M.
(Twenty-one Bands in commission in 1963).

ROYAL SCOTTISH ACADEMY OF MUSIC

St. George's Place, Glasgow, C.2 (900)

Curriculum provides for all branches of study necessary for entry into the musical profession. Special Diploma Course for those who wish to teach music in schools.
Principal, H. Havergal, M.A., D.Mus.

NAVAL

ROYAL NAVAL COLLEGE, Greenwich

President, Rear-Admiral M. C. M. Giles.
Secretary, Store Officer and Librarian, G. W. Fisher.

ROYAL NAVAL STAFF COLLEGE

Greenwich

Director, Capt. A. W. F. Sutton, D.S.C., R.N.

ROYAL NAVAL MEDICAL SCHOOL

Alverstoke, Hants.

Medical Officer in Charge, Surgeon Capt. S. Miles.

BRITANNIA ROYAL NAVAL COLLEGE

Dartmouth (340)

Captain, W. J. Parker, O.B.E., D.S.C., R.N.
Commander, J. W. M. Pertwee, R.N.
Dir. of Studies, G. W. E. Ghey, M.B.E., M.A.
Captain's Secretary, Lt.-Cdr. G. J. Shore, R.N.

ROYAL NAVAL ENGINEERING COLLEGE

H.M.S. *Thunderer*.

Manadon, Plymouth (338)

Captain, W. T. C. Ridley, O.B.E., R.N.
Commander, Cdr. B. P. McConnell, O.B.E., R.N.
Dir. of Engineering, Cdr. C. P. H. Gibbon, R.N.
Dean, Instr. Capt. H. E. Dykes, Ph.D., R.N.

JOINT ANTI-SUBMARINE SCHOOL

Londonderry, N. Ireland

Director, R.N., Capt. J. C. Cartwright, D.S.C., R.N.
Director, R.A.F., Group Capt. P. A. Hughes, D.F.C.
Deputy Directors, Cdr. M. L. Stacey, R.N.; Wing Comdr. J. R. Saunders, R.A.F.

ROYAL HOSPITAL SCHOOL

Holbrook, nr. Ipswich, Suffolk (660)

Headmaster, N. A. York, M.A.
Chief Naval Instructor, Cdr. J. R. Lamb, R.N. (*ret.*).

ROYAL MERCHANT NAVY SCHOOL

Bear Wood, Wokingham, Berks.

Foundationers—children of Merchant Navy officers and men. Otherwise an independent boarding school.
Headmaster, P. M. Cunningham.

TRAINING SHIPS

Merchant Navy

For Officers

H.M.S. CONWAY (1859) Merchant Navy Cadet School, Llanfair P.G., Anglesey (Training Officers for Royal and Merchant Navies) (310). *Capt. Supt.*, Capt. E. Hewitt, R.D., R.N.R.

THAMES NAUTICAL TRAINING COLLEGE (INCORPORATED).—H.M.S. *Worcester* (1862) (250). *Capt. Supt.*, Capt. L. W. L. Argles, C.B.E., D.S.C., R.N.; *Dir. of Studies*, L. H. Roberson; *Sec.*, I. A. Borland; *Offices*, Ingress Abbey, Greenhithe, Kent.

TRAINING SHIP *Mercury* (1885), Hamble, Southampton (160).—(Normal G.C.E. curriculum, including Navigation and Seamanship. Age on entry 13–14½).—*Capt. Supt.*, Cdr. R. F. Hoyle, R.D., R.N.R.

DEVITT AND MOORE NAUTICAL COLLEGE, LTD. (1917) (280).—For training officers for the Royal Navy and Merchant Navy. Particulars from *Captain's Secretary*, The Nautical College, Pangbourne, Berks. *Capt. Supt.*, Capt. A. F. P. Lewis, C.B.E., R.N. (*ret.*).

UNIVERSITY OF SOUTHAMPTON (School of Navigation), Warsash, Southampton (1935). Provides courses for candidates for Ministry of Transport certificates (200), mid-apprenticeship release courses; and trains boys who wish to become officers in the Merchant Navy. *Director*, Capt. G. W. Wakeford, M.B.E.

For Seamen

INDEFATIGABLE AND NATIONAL SEA TRAINING SCHOOL, Plas Llanfair, Anglesey, N. Wales (136). For boys between 14½ and 15¼ years of age at entry and of good character only. *Capt. Supt.*, Capt. G. W. Irvin. *Sec.*, V. G. Winfield, c/o Liverpool Sailors' Home, Canning Place, Liverpool, 1.

TRAINING SHIP *Arethusa* (1866), off Upnor in the Medway, Kent (Shaftesbury Homes and "Arethusa" Training Ship). 240 fit boys of good character educated and trained for Royal Navy and Merchant Navy. Priority to boys who are in need of help. Age of entry 13–14½ years. *Captain*, Cdr. M. H. Le Mare, R.N.

NATIONAL SEA TRAINING SCHOOLS, 146–150 Minories, E.C.3.—Schools at Sharpness, Gloucestershire (T.S. *Vindicatrix*), and Gravesend, Kent (training establishments for deck boys and junior catering ratings); for boys of 15½ to 17½ years at entry and of good character only. Numbers according to Merchant Navy requirements. *Secretary*, L. H. Tite, M.B.E.

NURSING

(*See* Medical)

ORIENTAL AND AFRICAN STUDIES

SCHOOL OF ORIENTAL AND AFRICAN STUDIES

University of London, W.C.1

No. of Students (1962–63), 802.

Chairman of Governing Body, The Viscount Radcliffe, P.C., G.B.E.
Director, Prof. C. H. Philips, Ph.D.

PERCIVAL DAVID FOUNDATION OF CHINESE ART, *see* Public and Private Buildings in London, p. 649.

PATENT AGENCY

The Register of Patent Agents is kept, under the authority of the Board of Trade, by the Chartered Institute of Patent Agents. Qualification is by examination; Intermediate and Final Examinations are held each year. Details can be obtained from the Institute.

CHARTERED INSTITUTE OF PATENT AGENTS, Staple Inn Buildings, W.C.1.—*Sec. and Registrar*, P. E. Lincroft, M.B.E.

PHOTOGRAPHY

INSTITUTE OF BRITISH PHOTOGRAPHERS (1901), 38 Bedford Square, W.C.1.—*Gen. Sec.*, J. L. A. Hunt.

Examinations in Industrial and Commercial, Scientific and Technical, Medical, Portrait,

Advertising and Publicity, Cinematography (non-theatrical) and Architectural Photography, for Associateships.

PHYSICAL EDUCATION

CENTRAL COUNCIL OF PHYSICAL RECREATION (6 Bedford Square, W.C.1).—*President*, H.R.H. the Prince Philip, Duke of Edinburgh, K.G., K.T.; *Secretary*, W. Winterbottom. Brings together about 200 national organizations in England, Wales and N. Ireland concerned with outdoor and indoor physical recreation; advises local authorities, youth organizations and industry, trains coaches and leaders, administers National Recreation Centres at Bisham Abbey, Berks, Lilleshall Hall, Salop and Plas y Brenin, Capel Curig, N. Wales.

Training Colleges

M.=For Men; *W.*=For Women

ABERDEEN (Dunfermline College of Physical Education, Woolmanhill). *W.* (220). *Principal*, Miss N. Blunden.

BEDFORD (College of Physical Education, Lansdowne Road, Bedford). *W.* (250).—*Principal*, Miss E. Alexander.

BIRMINGHAM UNIVERSITY. *M. & W.* (24).

DARTFORD, Kent (Dartford College of Physical Education) (Bergman Osterberg Trust). *W.* (180).—*Principal*, Miss M. J. Buckerfield.

DOVER (Nonington College of Physical Education, Dover). *W.* (140).—*Principal*, Miss E. M. Hinks.

EASTBOURNE (Chelsea College of Physical Education, Carlisle Road). *W.* (287).—*Principal*, Miss A. J. Bambra.

EXETER (St. Luke's College). *See p.* 530.

LEEDS (Carnegie College of Physical Education, Beckett Park, Leeds, 6). *M.* (200).—*Principal*, E. Bouffler.

LIVERPOOL (I. M. Marsh College of Physical Education, Barkhill Road, Liverpool, 17). Lancashire Education Committee. *W.* (300).—*Principal*, Miss M. T. Crabbe, C.B.E.

LONDON (L.C.C. Coll. of Physical Education, 16 Paddington Street, W.1). *M. & W.*—*Principal*, P. C. McIntosh.

LOUGHBOROUGH, Leics. (Loughborough T.C.). *See p.* 530.

SUTTON COLDFIELD, Warwickshire (Anstey College of Physical Education, Chester Road). Staffordshire Education Committee. *W.* (105).—*Joint Principals*, Miss A. K. Hobbs; Miss C. M. Webster.

WENTWORTH WOODHOUSE, Yorks. (Lady Mabel College of Physical Education). *W.* (190).—*Principal*, Miss E. F. Casson.

YORK (St. John's College). *M. & W.*—*see* p. 531.

SECRETARIAL
(*See* COMMERCIAL)

SOCIAL WORK

Degree courses in Social Studies are available at Birmingham, Exeter, Hull, Leeds, Leicester, Liverpool, London, Manchester, Nottingham and Southampton Universities and diploma courses at Belfast, Bristol, Edinburgh, Glasgow, Oxford, Sheffield and the University of Wales.

The following are among the associations awarding professional qualifications and (or) providing training:—

ASSOCIATION OF FAMILY CASE WORKERS, 296 Vauxhall Bridge Road, S.W.1.—*Hon Sec.*, Miss K. Wells.

THE INSTITUTE OF ALMONERS INC., 42 Bedford Square, W.C.1.

THE NATIONAL ASSOCIATION FOR MENTAL HEALTH, 39 Queen Anne Street, W.1.—*Gen. Sec.*, Miss Mary Applebey, O.B.E.

THE SOCIETY OF HOUSING MANAGERS, 13 Suffolk Street, Pall Mall East, S.W.1.—*Sec.*, Miss M. S. Cleaver.

THE INSTITUTE OF HOUSING (INC.), 50 Tufton Street, S.W.1.

JOSEPHINE BUTLER MEMORIAL HOUSE, 34 Alexandra Drive, Liverpool, 17.

TEACHING
TRAINING COLLEGES

(For Training Colleges in Housecraft, *see* pp. 518–19, in Physical Education, *see* col. 1.)

M.=For Men; *W.*=For Women; L.E.A.=Local Education Authority; C. of E.=Church of England; R.C.=Roman Catholic; T.C.=Training College.

ABERDEEN (Aberdeen College of Education, St. Andrew Street), *M. & W.* (750).—*Principal*, J. Scotland.

ABINGDON, Berks. (Culham T.C.). C. of E. *M.* (320).—J. V. Barnett.

ALNWICK (Northumberland College). L.E.A. *W.* (260).—Miss W. Taylor.

ALSAGER (Cheshire County T.C.) L.E.A. *M. & W.* (560).—R. Wesley.

AMBLESIDE, Westmorland (Charlotte Mason T.C.). *W.* (150).—Miss M. Boulton.

BANGOR, Caernarvonshire (S. Mary's College, Bangor). Church in Wales. *W.* (250).—Miss H. M. Stevens.

„ (Normal College, Bangor). L.E.A. *M. & W.* (420).—E. Rees.

BARNET, Herts. (Trent Park T.C.). L.E.A. *M. & W.* (700).—T. R. Theakston.

BARNSLEY, Yorks. (Wentworth Castle T.C.). L.E.A. *W.* (144).—Miss J. Richardson.

BARRY, S. Wales (Glamorgan T.C.). L.E.A. *M. & W.* (420).—E. D. Lewis, D.SC.

BATH, Somerset, (Newton Park). L.E.A. *M. & W.* (425).—Miss A. M. Dawson.

BEDFORD (T.C., 14 The Crescent, Bedford). L.E.A. *W.* (185).—Mrs. M. P. G. Taylor.

BINGLEY, YORKS. L.E.A. *M. & W.* (450).—Mrs. G. M. Gunn.

BIRMINGHAM (City of Birmingham T.C.). L.E.A. *M. & W.* (550).—Miss M. M. Rigg.

„ (St. Peter's College, Saltley). C. of E. *M.* (385).—Rev. Canon T. G. Platten.

„ (Westhill T.C., Selly Oak). *M. & W.* (300).—Rev. R. T. Newman.

BISHOP'S STORTFORD, Herts (Hockerill T.C.). *W.* (250). C. of E.—Miss A. Eden.

BLETCHLEY, Bucks (Bletchley Park T.C.). L.E.A. *W.* (154).—Miss D. G. Cohen.

BOGNOR REGIS, Sussex (Bognor Regis T.C., Upper Bognor Road). L.E.A. *M. & W.* (250).—W. R. Macklin.

BOLTON (Bolton Technical T. C., Chadwick Street). L.E.A. *M. & W.* (300).—J. P. Parry.

BRADFORD (Margaret McMillan T.C.). L.E.A. *W.* (330).—Miss M. Morrison.

BRENTWOOD, Essex (Brentwood T.C., Sawyers Hall Lane). L.E.A. *M & W.* (390).—Dr. D. W. Shave.

BRIGHTON (Brighton T. C., 8 Eastern Terrace). L.E.A. *M. & W.* (380).—A. Steward.

BRISTOL (The College of St. Matthias, Fishponds). C. of E. *W.* (440).—Miss M. M. Graham.

„ (Redland T.C., Redland Hill). L.E.A. *M. & W.* (450).—J. T. Wharton.

BROMSGROVE, Worcs. (Shenstone T.C., Burcot Lane). L.E.A. *M. & W.* (340).—Miss M. D. Wood.

CAERLEON (Monmouthshire T.C.). L.E.A. *M. & W.* (408).—G. P. Ambrose.
CAMBRIDGE (Homerton College) *W.* (375).—Miss B. Paston Brown.
CANTERBURY (Christ Church T.C.). C. of E. *M. & W.* (220).—Rev. F. Mason.
CARDIFF (City of Cardiff T.C., Cyncoed). *M. & W.* (450).—W. T. Jones.
CARMARTHEN (Trinity College). Church in Wales. *M. & W.* (480).—Rev. Canon T. Halliwell.
CHALFONT ST. GILES, Bucks (Newland Park T.C.). L.E.A. *M.* (298).—A. H. Ensor.
CHELTENHAM, Glos. (St. Mary's T.C.). *W.* (470). C. of E.—Miss V. N. Hall.
„ (St. Paul's T.C.). *M.* (480). C. of E.—E. L. Bradby.
CHESTER (Chester College). *M. & W.* (450). C. of E.—Rev. A. J. Price.
CHICHESTER, Sussex (Bishop Otter T.C.). *M. & W.* (450). C. of E.—Miss K. M. E. Murray.
CHORLEY, Lancs. (Chorley Day T.C., Union Street). L.E.A. *M. & W.*—L. Kenworthy.
CLACTON-ON-SEA, Essex (St. Osyth's T.C., Marine Parade). L.E.A. *W.* (510).—Miss M. Parsons.
COVENTRY, Warwicks. (City of Coventry T.C.). L.E.A. *M. & W.* (700).—Miss J. D. Browne.
CREWE (Cheshire County T.C.). L.E.A. *W.* (500).—Miss M. J. P. Laurence.
DARLINGTON (Darlington T.C.). Voluntary. *W.*—Miss P. M. Steele.
DERBY (Diocesan T.C., Western Road, Mickleover). *M. & W.* (480). C. of E.—Miss A. E. G. Sephton.
DONCASTER (Doncaster T.C., High Melton Hall), L.E.A. *W.* (320).—Miss G. A. Williams.
DUDLEY, Worcs. (Dudley T.C., Castle View). L.E.A. *M. & W.* (478).—D. Jordan.
DUNDEE (College of Education, Park Place). *M. & W.* (600).
DURHAM (Neville's Cross T.C.) L.E.A. *W.* (400).—Miss M. Whitley.
„ (St. Hild's). *W.* (300). C. of E.—Miss N. M. E. Joachim.
„ (The Venerable Bede). *M.* (430). C. of E.—K. G. Collier.
EASTBOURNE, Sussex. (Eastbourne T.C., Darley Road). L.E.A. *W.* (285).—Miss T. S. Hichens.
EDINBURGH (Craiglockhart College of Education). R.C. *W.* (240).—Mother Veronica Blount.
„ (Moray House College of Education), *M. & W.* (1,600).—W. B. Inglis, O.B.E., Ph.D.
EXETER (St. Luke's College). *M.* (700). C. of E.—J. L. Smeall.
EXMOUTH, Devon (Rolle T. C.). L.E.A. *W.* (430).—Miss D. E. L. Spicer.
GLASGOW (Jordanhill College of Education). *M. & W.* (2,000).—H. P. Wood.
„ (Notre Dame College of Education, Dowanhill). R.C. *W.* (630).
HEREFORD (County T.C.). L.E.A. *W.* (400).—Miss M. E. Hipwell.
HERTFORD (Balls Park). L.E.A. *W.* (320).—Miss M. M. Wingate.
HUDDERSFIELD (Technical T.C.). L.E.A. *M. & W.* (350).—A. MacLennan.
HULL (Endsleigh T.C.). R.C. *W.* (420).—Sister Mary Madeleine.
„ (T. C., Cottingham Road). L.E.A. *M. & W.* (460).—Dr. C. Bibby.
KINGSTON-ON-THAMES, Surrey (Gipsy Hill T.C., Kenry House, Kingston Hill). L.E.A. *W.* (360).—Miss F. D. Batstone.
LEEDS (City of Leeds T.C., Beckett Park). L.E.A. *M. & W.* (650).—L. Connell, Ph.D.
„ (James Graham T.C., Chapel Lane, Farnley). L.E.A. *M. & W.* (Day students only) (300).—T. H. B. Hollins.
LEICESTER (City of Leicester T.C., Scraptoft). L.E.A. *M. & W.* (570).—F. C. A. Cammaerts.
LINCOLN (Bishop Grosseteste College). *W.* (345). C. of E.—Miss E. L. Butcher.
LIVERPOOL (City of Liverpool, C. F. Mott T.C., Prescot), L.E.A. *M. & W.* (450).—Miss D. M. Farr, Ph.D.
„ (St. Katharine's College). *W.* (420). C. of E.—Miss M. A. B. Jones.
„ (Mount Pleasant T.C.) *W.* (440). R.C.—Miss A. Rawcliffe.
LONDON (Avery Hill T.C., Eltham, S.E.9). L.E.A. *M. & W.* (700).—Mrs. K. E. Jones.
„ (Borough Road College, Isleworth, Middx.). *M.* (525).—K. E. Priestley.
„ (Cavendish Square Postgraduate T.C., W.1). *W.* (120). R.C.—Miss M. Braun.
„ (Philippa Fawcett T.C., 94-100 Leigham Court Road, S.W.16.) L.E.A. *W.* (240)—Miss A. C. Shrubsole.
„ (College of S. Mark and S. John, King's Road, Chelsea, S.W.10). *M.* (460). C. of E.—A. A. Evans.
„ (Digby Stuart College, Roehampton, S.W.15). *W.* (550). R.C.—Mother Mary Richardson.
„ (Froebel Educational Institute, Grove House, Roehampton Lane, S.W.15). *W.* (450).—Miss M. Brearley.
„ (Furzedown T.C., Welham Road, S.W.17). L.E.A. *W.* (375).—Miss C. Fletcher.
„ (Garnett Technical T.C., Downshire House, Roehampton Lane, S.W.15.). L.E.A. *M. & W.* (300).—C. Jameson.
„ (Goldsmiths' Coll. Training Dept., New Cross, S.E.14). London Univ. *M. & W.* (1,170).—Dr. D. R. Chesterman.
„ (Maria Assumpta, 23 Kensington Square, W.8) *W.* (300). R.C.—Mother Augustine Mary.
„ (Maria Grey T.C., 300 St. Margaret's Road, Twickenham). L.E.A. *W.* (350).—Miss B. E. Deayton.
„ (Rachel McMillan T.C., Deptford, S.E.8). *W.* (175).—Miss E. M. Puddephat.
„ (Shoreditch T.C., Cooper's Hill, Englefield Green, Surrey). L.E.A. *M.* (550).—E. F. Marshall.
„ (St. Gabriel's College, Cormont Road, Camberwell, S.E.5). *W.* (310). C. of E.—Miss M. B. Atkinson.
„ (St. Katharine's College, Tottenham, N.17). C. of E. *W.* (260).—Dr. K. H. Nahapiet.
„ (St. Mary's College, Strawberry Hill, Twickenham). *M.* (610). R.C.—Very Rev. K. Cronin, C.B.E.
„ (Sidney Webb Day T.C., 130 Horseferry Road, S.W.1). L.E.A. *M. & W.*—Miss R. Beresford.
„ (Southlands College, 65 Wimbledon Parkside, S.W.19). *W.* (450). Methodist.—Miss M. S. Johnson.
„ (Stockwell T.C., Bromley, Kent). L.E.A. *W.* (500).—Miss R. F. Carr.
„ (Whitelands College, West Hill, Putney. S.W.15). C. of E. *W.* (450).—Miss M. M. Saunders.
LOUGHBOROUGH, Leics. (Loughborough T.C.). L.E.A. *M.* (750).—J. W. S. Hardie.
MADELEY, Staffs. (County of Stafford T.C., Madeley, nr. Crewe). L.E.A. *M. & W.* (520). Miss E. G. Malloch.

MANCHESTER (Manchester T.C., Long Millgate). L.E.A. *W.* (300).—Miss M. S. Valentine.
„ (Didsbury T.C., Wilmslow Road, Didsbury). *M. & W.* (650).—A. H. Body, O.B.E.
MATLOCK, Derbyshire. L.E.A. *M. & W.* (400).—Miss G. E. Allen.
MEXBOROUGH, Yorks. (Swinton Day T.C.). L.E.A. *M. & W.* (250).—Miss E. M. Goodjohn.
MIDDLETON, Manchester (De la Salle College). *M.* (660). R.C.—The Rev. Brother Augustine.
NEWCASTLE-UPON-TYNE (Day T.C.). L.E.A. *M. & W.* (285)—Dr. R. D. Bramwell.
„ (St. Mary's T.C.). *W.* (310). R.C.—Madame P. Baker.
„ (Kenton Lodge T.C., Gosforth). L.E.A. *W.* (270).—Miss N. I. Chelton.
NORWICH (Norwich T.C.). *M. & W.* (430). C. of E.—Miss M. G. Duff.
NOTTINGHAM (Nottingham T.C., Clifton). L.E.A. *M. & W.* (700).—K. A. Baird.
ORMSKIRK, Lancs. (Edge Hill T.C., St. Helens Road). L.E.A. *M. & W.* (565).—Dr. M. I. Bain.
OXFORD (Westminster T.C., North Hinksey). *M. & W.* (430). Methodist.—Rev. H. T. Hughes.
PORTSMOUTH (City of Portsmouth T. C., Milton). L.E.A. *M. & W.* (565).—Mrs. D. J. Williams.
PRESTWICH, Lancs. (Sedgley Park College). *W.* (320). R.C.—Madame P. Grogan.
RETFORD, Notts (Notts County T.C., Eaton Hall). L.E.A. *M. & W.* (315).—E. L. Ableson.
RIPON, Yorks. (Ripon, Wakefield and Bradford Diocesan T.C.). *W.* (375). C. of E.—Miss M. D. Gage.
RUGBY, Warwicks. (St. Paul's T.C., Newbold Revel, Stretton-under-Fosse). *W.* (310). R.C.—Sister Agnes.
SAFFRON WALDEN, Essex (British and Foreign School Society). *W.* (170).—Miss M. M. Sellens.
SALISBURY, Wilts. (Church T.C.). C. of E. *W.* (330).—*Principal*, Miss A. M. D. Ashley.
SCARBOROUGH, Yorks. (North Riding T.C.). L.E.A. *W.* (180).—Miss E. L. Madge.
SHEFFIELD (City T.C., Collegiate Crescent). *M. & W.* (800).—Dr. H. D. Wing.
„ (Thornbridge Hall, Ashford-in-the-Water, nr. Bakewell, Derbyshire). L.E.A. *W.* (150).—Miss P. H. Whittaker.
SOUTHAMPTON (College of the Immaculate Conception, The Avenue). *W.* (400). R.C.—Miss M. E. Ward.
STOKE ROCHFORD, Lincs. (Kesteven T.C.). L.E.A. *M. & W.* (300).—W. V. Warmington.
SUNDERLAND (Sunderland T.C.). L.E.A. *M. & W.* (430).—Miss J. T. Tasker.
SWANSEA (Swansea T.C., Townhill). L.E.A. *M. & W.* (450).—Miss M. R. Smith.
WAKEFIELD, Yorks. (Bretton Hall T.C.). L.E.A. *M. & W.* (340).—J. F. Friend.
WARRINGTON, Lancs. (Padgate T.C., Fearnhead). L.E.A. *M. & W.* (520).—J. L. Dobson, Ph.D.
WATFORD, Herts. (Wall Hall T.C., Aldenham). L.E.A. *W.* (320).—Miss I. N. Dickinson.
WEST WICKHAM, Kent (Coloma Coll., Wickham Court). *W.* (400). R.C.—Mother Mary Benignus.
WEYMOUTH, Dorset. (Weymouth T.C., Dorchester Road). L.E.A. *W.* (280).—Miss M. B. Weinstock.
WINCHESTER, Hants. (King Alfred's College). *M. & W.* (570). C. of E.—J. A. Stripe.
WOKINGHAM, Berks. (Easthampstead Park College). L.E.A. *W.* (220).—Miss H. M. S. Wylie.
WOLVERHAMPTON (Day T.C., Walsall Street). L.E.A. *M. & W.* (300).—R. H. Durham.
„ (Technical Teachers T.C., Compton Road West). L.E.A. *M. & W.* (100).—C. L. Heywood.
WORCESTER (City of Worcester T.C., Henwick Grove). L.E.A. *M. & W.* (580).—E. G. Peirson.
WREXHAM (Cartrefle T.C.). L.E.A. *W.* (375).—Miss M. Taylor.
YORK (St. John's College). *M. & W.* (600). C. of E.—Rev. Canon P. J. Lamb.

For Teachers of the Deaf

DEPARTMENT OF AUDIOLOGY AND EDUCATION OF THE DEAF, Manchester University. *M. & W.* (85).—*Director*, Prof. Sir Alexander Ewing.
NATIONAL COLLEGE OF TEACHERS OF THE DEAF (Longwill Deaf School), Bell Hill, Northfield, Birmingham 31.—*Hon. Sec.*, H. H. Shorrock.

For Teachers of the Blind

THE COLLEGE OF THE TEACHERS OF THE BLIND (School for the Blind, Westbury on Trym, Bristol). *Hon. Registrar*, E. H. Getliff, O.B.E. Awards certificates after examination to home teachers, school teachers and craft instructors of the Blind.

Courses of training are also available at:

THE BIRMINGHAM ROYAL INSTITUTION FOR THE BLIND (190).
THE NORTH REGIONAL ASSOCIATION FOR THE BLIND. *M. & W.* (47), Headingley Castle, 72 Headingley Lane, Leeds 6.

TECHNICAL EDUCATION

See also "Commercial Education" and "Engineering"

National Advisory Council on Education for Industry and Commerce

Established in 1948 to advise the Minister on national educational policy relating to industry and commerce.

Chairman, Sir Harry Pilkington.

National Council for Technological Awards

24 Park Crescent, W.1.

Established by the Minister of Education in 1955 to create and administer awards for students who successfully complete courses in technical colleges. The Council offers two awards, a Diploma in Technology and Membership of the College of Technologists.

Chairman, Sir Harold Cox, D.Sc., Ph.D.
Sec., F. R. Hornby, M.B.E.

Regional Advisory Councils

Set up in 1947 (i) to bring education and industry together to find out the needs of young workers and advise on the provision required, and (ii) to secure reasonable economy of provision. They also have certain responsibilities in connection with the procedure for the approval by the Ministry of Education of advanced courses, and issue handbooks, etc., giving, for the guidance of students and teachers, information about the facilities available within a region or district for various types of training (*e.g.* electrical engineering, textiles, building and chemistry). There are ten Regional Advisory Councils, in England and Wales:—

REGION 1 (LONDON AND HOME COUNTIES).—Regional Advisory Council for Technological Education, Tavistock House South, Tavistock Square, W.C.1.

REGION 2 (SOUTHERN).—Regional Council for Further Education, 9 Bath Road, Reading.
3 (SOUTH-WEST).—Regional Council for Further Education, 12 Lower Castle Street, Bristol, 1.
4 (WEST MIDLANDS).—Advisory Council for Further Education, Pitman Buildings, 161 Corporation Street, Birmingham, 4.
5 (EAST MIDLANDS).—Regional Advisory Council for the Organization of Further Education, 12 King John's Chambers, Bridlesmith Gate, Nottingham.
6 (EAST ANGLIA).—Regional Advisory Council for Further Education, County Education Offices, Stracey Road, Norwich.
7 (YORKSHIRE).—Council for Further Education, Bowling Green Terrace, Jack Lane, Leeds, 1.
8 (NORTH-WEST).—Regional Advisory Council for Further Education, Africa House, 54 Whitworth Street, Manchester, 1.
9 (NORTHERN).—Advisory Council for Further Education, 5 Grosvenor Villas, Grosvenor Road, Newcastle-upon-Tyne, 2.
10 (WALES).—Welsh Joint Education Committee, 30 Cathedral Road, Cardiff.

City and Guilds of London Institute

76 Portland Place, W.1.

Dir.-Gen., Maj.-Gen. C. Lloyd, C.B., C.B.E., T.D.
(1.) *City and Guilds College* (*see* Imperial College of Science and Technology under University of London).
(2.) *City and Guilds Art School*, 122 to 124 Kennington Park Road, S.E.11.

Technical Colleges

The majority of the technical colleges in England and Wales are maintained or assisted by local education authorities. There are four main types.

Colleges of Advanced Technology. These provide a broad range and substantial volume of work exclusively at advanced level (whether in full-time, sandwich or part-time courses), including post-graduate and research work. Since April 1, 1962, all these colleges have been administered by independent governing bodies receiving grants direct from the Ministry of Education. Up to the present, ten establishments have been formally designated by the Minister as colleges of advanced technology:—

BIRMINGHAM COLLEGE OF ADVANCED TECHNOLOGY.—*Princ.*, Sir Percy Venables, Ph.D.
BRADFORD INSTITUTE OF TECHNOLOGY.—*Princ.*, E. G. Edwards, Ph.D.
BRISTOL COLLEGE OF SCIENCE AND TECHNOLOGY, Ashley Down.—*Princ.*, G. H. Moore.
LONDON: BATTERSEA COLLEGE OF TECHNOLOGY, Battersea Park Road, S.W.11.—*Princ.*, D. M. A. Leggett, M.A., Ph.D., D.Sc.
LONDON: BRUNEL COLLEGE OF ADVANCED TECHNOLOGY, Acton, Middx.—*Princ.*, J. Topping, Ph.D.
LONDON: CHELSEA COLLEGE OF SCIENCE AND TECHNOLOGY, Manresa Road, S.W.3.—*Princ.*, C. C. Hentschel.
LONDON: NORTHAMPTON COLLEGE OF ADVANCED TECHNOLOGY, St. John Street, E.C.1.—*Princ.*, J. S. Tait, Ph.D.
LOUGHBOROUGH COLLEGE OF TECHNOLOGY.—*Princ.*, H. L. Haslegrave, Ph.D.
SALFORD: ROYAL COLLEGE OF ADVANCED TECHNOLOGY.—*Princ.*, C. Whitworth, Ph.D.
CARDIFF: WELSH COLLEGE OF ADVANCED TECHNOLOGY.—*Princ.*, A. Harvey, Ph.D.

Regional Colleges. These are colleges which do a substantial amount of advanced work, including in particular, full-time and sandwich courses, but in which the volume and character of the advanced work are not such as to make it realistic for the colleges to concentrate entirely on such work. There are at present 25 regional colleges:—

BRIGHTON COLLEGE OF TECHNOLOGY.—*Princ.*, G. E. Watts, C.B.E., Ph.D.
COVENTRY: LANCHESTER COLLEGE OF TECHNOLOGY Priory Street.—*Princ.*, A. J. Richmond, Ph.D.
DAGENHAM, Essex: S.E. ESSEX TECHNICAL COLLEGE AND SCHOOL OF ART, Longbridge Road.—*Princ.*, F. Heathcoat, Ph.D.
HATFIELD COLLEGE OF TECHNOLOGY, Roe Green.—*Princ.*, W. A. J. Chapman, Ph.D.
HUDDERSFIELD COLLEGE OF TECHNOLOGY.—*Princ.*, W. E. Scott, M.B.E., Ph.D.
KINGSTON-UPON-THAMES COLLEGE OF TECHNOLOGY.—*Princ.*, J. R. I. Hepburn, D.Sc., Ph.D.
LEEDS COLLEGE OF TECHNOLOGY, Calverley Street.—*Princ.*, C. Chew.
LEICESTER COLLEGE OF TECHNOLOGY.—*Princ.*, R. E. Wood.
LIVERPOOL: CITY OF LIVERPOOL COLLEGE OF TECHNOLOGY, Byrom Street —*Princ.*, S. A. J. Parsons.
" CITY OF LIVERPOOL COLLEGE OF BUILDING, Clarence Street, Liverpool, 3.—*Princ.*, T. E. Hall.
LONDON: BOROUGH POLYTECHNIC, Borough Road, S.E.1.—*Princ.*, J. E. Garside, Ph.D.
" BRIXTON L.C.C. SCHOOL OF BUILDING, Ferndale Road, S.W.4.—*Princ.*, D. A. G. Reid.
" NORTHERN POLYTECHNIC, Holloway Road, N.7.—*Princ.*, J. Leicester.
" THE POLYTECHNIC, 309 Regent Street, W.1.—*Director of Education*, J. E. Richardson, C.B.E., Ph.D.
" SIR JOHN CASS COLLEGE, Jewry Street, E.C.3.—*Princ.*, A. M. Ward, D.Sc., Ph.D.
" WOOLWICH POLYTECHNIC, Thomas Street, S.E.18.—*Princ.*, H. Heywood, D.Sc., Ph.D.
NEWCASTLE UPON TYNE: RUTHERFORD COLLEGE OF TECHNOLOGY.—*Princ.*, J. S. Elliot.
NOTTINGHAM AND DISTRICT TECHNICAL COLLEGE.—*Princ.*, D. A. R. Clark.
PLYMOUTH COLLEGE OF TECHNOLOGY.—*Princ.*, E. Bailey.
PORTSMOUTH COLLEGE OF TECHNOLOGY.—*Princ.*, W. Davey, Ph.D.
RUGBY COLLEGE OF ENGINEERING TECHNOLOGY.—*Princ.*, G. S. Atkinson, Ph.D.
STOKE-ON-TRENT: NORTH STAFFORDSHIRE COLLEGE OF TECHNOLOGY.—*Princ.*, E. R. Patrick, Ph.D.
SUNDERLAND TECHNICAL COLLEGE.—*Princ.*, M. Hutton.
TREFOREST: GLAMORGAN COLLEGE OF TECHNOLOGY.—*Princ.*, D. P. Evans, Ph.D.
WEST HAM COLLEGE OF TECHNOLOGY.—*Princ.*, G. Bulmer, Ph.D.

Area Colleges. There are about 160 of these, providing mainly part-time courses up to the level of Higher National Certificate or its equivalent.

Local Colleges, of which there are about 270, provide on the vocational side a wide range of mainly part-time courses up to Ordinary National Certificate level or its equivalent.

In addition to these four main categories of technical college, there are some 8,500 *Evening Institutes* ranging in size from those with a few classes for adults in such subjects as music and arts and crafts to those catering for thousands of students in a wide variety of vocational as well as non-vocational classes.

There are also six *National Colleges* providing advanced and post-graduate courses for the comparatively few students from certain highly specialized industries for whom it would be impracticable to provide the highest level of training on a local basis. These colleges, which are financed partly by contributions from the industries concerned but, principally by means of grant from the Minister of Education are:—

NATIONAL COLLEGE FOR HEATING, VENTILATING, REFRIGERATION AND FAN ENGINEERING, Borough Polytechnic, Borough Road, S.E.1.—*Dir.*, J. E. Garside, Ph.D.

NATIONAL COLLEGE OF FOOD TECHNOLOGY, St. George's Avenue, Weybridge, Surrey.—*Principal*, J. D. Mounfield, Ph.D.

NATIONAL COLLEGE OF RUBBER TECHNOLOGY, Northern Polytechnic, Holloway Road, N.7.—*Principal*, F. H. Cotton, Ph.D.

NATIONAL FOUNDRY COLLEGE, Stafford Street, Wolverhampton.—*Principal*, J. Bamford.

NATIONAL LEATHERSELLERS COLLEGE, Tower Bridge Road, S.E.1.—*Principal*, J. P. Danby, Ph.D., B.Sc.

NATIONAL COLLEGE OF AGRICULTURAL ENGINEERING, Silsoe, Bedford.—*Princ.*, P. C. J. Payne, Ph.D.

SCOTLAND

Scottish Technical Education Consultative Council

The Consultative Council represents both sides of industry and educational interests. The Council's object is "to secure the widest possible measure of consultation on vocational further education between employers, employees and those responsible for its provision, and to advise, and generally to promote, the development of such education".—*Sec.*, Miss E. C. G. Wilson, Scottish Education Department, St. Andrew's House, Edinburgh, 1.

Technical Colleges

Technical education is available at 96 day-course schools and colleges in Scotland, including those which specialize in a particular subject. The following are among those recognized by the Scottish Education Department as "central institutions" (colleges for higher technical learning); other Scottish central institutions appear under Agriculture, Art, Commerce, Domestic Science and Music.

ABERDEEN: ROBERT GORDON'S TECHNICAL COLLEGE, Aberdeen.—*Director*, A. C. West, Ph.D.

DUNDEE INSTITUTE OF ART AND TECHNOLOGY, 40 Bell Street, Dundee.—*Principal (Technical)*, J. R. Whittaker, Ph.D.

EDINBURGH: HERIOT-WATT COLLEGE, Edinburgh, 1.—*Principal*, H. B. Nisbet, Ph.D., D.Sc.

GALASHIELS: SCOTTISH WOOLLEN TECHNICAL COLLEGE, Market Street, Galashiels, Selkirkshire.—*Principal*, J. G. Martindale, Ph.D.

LEITH NAUTICAL COLLEGE, 59 Commercial Street, Leith.—*Principal*, W. A. Fisher.

PAISLEY TECHNICAL COLLEGE, 28–40 George Street, Paisley, Renfrewshire.—*Princ.*, H. N. Henry.

NORTHERN IRELAND

BELFAST (College of Technology).—*Principal*, D. H. Alexander, O.B.E.

LONDONDERRY (Municipal Tech. Coll.).—*Princ.*, T. Williams.

TEXTILES

THE TEXTILE INSTITUTE, 10 Blackfriars Street, Manchester, 3, is the responsible authority under Royal Charter for the supervision of professional status in the textile industry.—*Gen. Sec.*, D. B. Moore, B.A.

THEOLOGICAL

Church of England and Church in Wales

BANGOR (Church Hostel) (25).—*Warden*, Rev. R. G. Williams.

BIRKENHEAD (St. Aidan's) (64).—*Princ.*, Rev. Canon A. G. Widdess.

BIRMINGHAM (Queen's Coll., Somerset Road, Edgbaston) (42).—*Princ.*, Rev. Canon A. S. Gribble.

CAMBRIDGE (Ridley Hall) (60).—*Princ.*, Rev. M. M. Hennell.

„ (Westcott House, Jesus Lane) (45).—*Princ.*, Rev. P. K. Walker.

CANTERBURY (St. Augustine's Central College of the Anglican Communion) (50).—*Warden*, Rev. Canon A. K. Cragg, D.Phil.

CHESHUNT (Bishops' College) (55).—*Princ.*, Rev. P. H. Cecil.

CHICHESTER (45).—*Princ.*, Rev. C. P. M. Jones.

CLIFTON, BRISTOL (Tyndale Hall) (60).—*Princ.*, Rev J. Stafford Wright.

CLIFTON THEOLOGICAL COLLEGE, Stoke Bishop, Bristol, 9 (45).—*Princ.*, Rev. T. Anscombe.

CUDDESDON, Oxon. (54)—*Princ.*, Rev. R. A. K. Runcie, M.C.

DURHAM. *See* University of Durham—St. Chad's; St. John's.

ELY (40).—*Princ.*, Rev. Canon D. G. Hill.

KELHAM (House of the Sacred Mission) (90).—*Warden*, Rev. P. S. Mein.

LAMPETER (St. David's Coll., Bishop Burgess Theological Hall) (35).—*Warden*, Rev. Canon J. R. L. Thomas.

LICHFIELD (50).—*Princ.*, Rev. J. C. Fenton.

LINCOLN (Theological College) (48).—*Warden*, Rev. A. B. Webster.

LLANDAFF, Cardiff (St. Michael's) (48).—*Warden*, Rev. O. G. Rees.

LONDON (King's College, W.C.2).—*See* London University.

LONDON COLLEGE OF DIVINITY, St. John's Hall, Northwood, Middlesex. (78).—*Princ.*, Rev. Preb. H. Jordan.

MIRFIELD (College of the Resurrection) (52).—*Princ.*, Rev. H. Bishop.

OAK HILL (Southgate, N.14) (78).—*Princ.*, Rev. M. A. P. Wood, D.S.C.

OXFORD (Ripon Hall) (46).—*Princ.*, Rev. W. G. Fallows.

„ (St. Stephen's House) (40).—*Princ.*, Rev. D. W. Allen.

„ (Wycliffe Hall) (55).—*Princ.*, Rev. D. Anderson.

SALISBURY (45).—*Princ.*, Rev. Canon F. C. Tindall.

WELLS (55).—*Princ.*, Rev. Preb. T. G. A. Baker.

Church of Scotland

ABERDEEN (Christ's Coll.).—*Master*, Rev. Prof. A. M. Hunter, Ph.D., D.Phil., D.D.

EDINBURGH (New Coll.) (196).—*Princ.*, Very Rev. Prof. J. H. S. Burleigh, D.D.

GLASGOW (Trinity Coll.) (96).—*Princ.*, Rev. Prof. J. Mauchline, D.D.

ST. ANDREWS (College of St. Mary). *See* University of St. Andrews.

Scottish Episcopal Church

EDINBURGH (30).—*Princ.*, Rev. Canon K. J. Woollcombe.

Presbyterian

BELFAST (Presbyterian Coll.).—*Princ.*, Very Rev. Prof. R. J. Wilson.

CAMBRIDGE (Westminster Coll., Presbyterian Church of England) (30).—*Princ.*, Rev. A. G. MacLeod.

LONDONDERRY (Magee Coll.).—*See* Irish University Colleges.

Calvinistic Methodists, or Presbyterian Church of Wales

ABERYSTWYTH (31).—*Princ.* (vacant).

BALA (Preparatory Theological) (25).—*Princ. and Librarian*, Rev. R. H. Evans.

Methodist

BELFAST (Edgehill Coll.) (25).—*Princ.*, Rev. R. Greenwood.

BRISTOL (Didsbury Coll., Westbury-on-Trym) (58).—*Princ.*, Rev. F. Greeves.

CAMBRIDGE (Wesley House) (23).—*Princ.*, Rev. W. F. Flemington.

HANDSWORTH (66).—*Princ.*, Rev. C. L. Mitton, Ph.D.

HEADINGLEY, Leeds, 6 (Wesley College) (60).—*Princ.*, Rev. A. R. George.

MANCHESTER (Hartley Victoria College, Alexandra Road, South) (102).—*Princ.*, Rev. P. Scott.

RICHMOND.—*See* London University.

Congregational

BANGOR (Bala-Bangor Independent Coll., 1841) (6).—*Princ.*, Rev. G. Bowyer.

BRISTOL (Western College, 1 Cotham Road) (26).—*Princ.*, Rev. B. H. Sims.

CAMBRIDGE (Cheshunt College) (36).—*Pres.*, Rev. E. H. Pyle.

EDINBURGH (Scottish Congregational College, Hope Terrace) (17).—*Princ.*, Rev. C. S. Duthie, D.D.

LONDON (New College).—*See* London University.

MANCHESTER (Northern Congregational College) (66).—*Princ.*, Rev. W. G. Robinson, Ph.D.

NOTTINGHAM (Paton Congregational College) (24).—*Princ.*, Rev. M. Charles, Ph.D.

OXFORD (Mansfield College) (50).—*Princ.*, Rev. J. Marsh, D.Phil., D.D.

SWANSEA (40).—*Princ.*, Prof. W. T. Pennar Davies, Ph.D.

Roman Catholic

(Colleges for the Diocesan Clergy)

ABERYSTWYTH (St. Mary's College (for late vocations, secular and regular)) (30).—*Prior*, Very Rev. D. C. Flanagan, O.Carm.

BLAIRS, Aberdeen (St. Mary's) (190).—*Rector*, Very Rev. F. Thomson, S.T.L.

COTTON, N. Staffs. (Cotton College) (210).—*Headmaster*, Very Rev. Mgr. W. Doran.

GLASGOW (St. Peter's Coll., Cardross, Dunbartonshire) (33).—*Rector*, Very Rev. M. J. C. Connolly, D.D., Ph.D.

KIRKBY LONSDALE (Viâ Carnforth, Lancs.) (St. Michael's Minor Seminary, Underley Hall) (130).—*Rector*, Very Rev. Canon B. Kershaw.

MARK CROSS, Crowborough, Sussex (St. Joseph's Diocesan College) (100).—*Rector*, Rt. Rev. Mgr. W. J. Westlake.

OSCOTT COLL., Sutton Coldfield, Warwicks. (110).—*Rector*, Rt. Rev. Mgr. R. J. Foster.

OSTERLEY, Middlesex (Campion House, 112 Thornbury Road) (150).—*Superior*, Rev. C. Tigar, S.J.

UP HOLLAND, nr. Wigan, Lancs. (St. Joseph's Diocesan College) (280).—*Rector*, Rt. Rev. Mgr. S. F. Breen.

USHAW (Durham) (380).—*Pres.*, Rt. Rev. Mgr. Canon P Grant.

WARE (Old Hall Green) (122).—*Pres.*, Rt. Rev. Mgr. R. Butcher.

WONERSH, Guildford (St. John's) (114).—*Rector*, Rt. Rev. Mgr. A. Iggleden.

Baptist

BANGOR (North Wales Baptist Coll.) (22).—*Princ.*, Rev. T. Ellis Jones.

BRISTOL (1679) (34).—*Pres.*, Rev. L. G. Champion.

CARDIFF (S. Wales Baptist Coll.) (30).—*Princ.*, J. Ithel Jones.

GLASGOW (The Baptist Theol. Coll. of Scotland) (23).—*Princ.*, Rev. A B. Miller, Ph.D.

LONDON (Spurgeon's Coll., South Norwood Hill, S.E.25) (55).—*Princ.*, Rev. G. R. Beasley-Murray, Ph.D.

MANCHESTER, Rusholme, Manchester, 14 (affiliated to Manchester Univ.) (25).—*Pres.*, Rev. K. C. Dykes.

OXFORD (Regent's Park Baptist Coll., Pusey Street) (48).—*Princ.*, Rev. G. Henton Davies, D.D.

RAWDON, Leeds (31).—*Pres.*, Rev. D. S. Russell.

Unitarian

MANCHESTER (Unitarian College, Victoria Park) (14).—*Princ.*, Rev. F. Kenworthy.

Interdenominational

CARMARTHEN PRESBYTERIAN COLLEGE (14).—*Princ.*, Rev. T. G. Davies.

OXFORD (Manchester Coll.).—*Princ.*, Rev. L. A. Garrard, LL.D.

Jewish

JEWS' COLLEGE (and Institute for the Training of Teachers), Montagu Place, W.1.—*Princ.*, The Very Rev. The Chief Rabbi, Dr. Israel Brodie (*acting*).

LEO BAECK COLLEGE, 33 Seymour Place, W.1.—*Princ.*, W. Van Der Zyl, Ph.D., D.D.

VETERINARY

ROYAL COLLEGE OF VETERINARY SURGEONS (1844)

32 Belgrave Square, S.W.1.

President, Prof. W. L. Weipers.

Registrar, W. G. R. Oates.

Admission to the Register of Veterinary Surgeons may be obtained under the Veterinary Surgeons Act, 1948, by obtaining the registrable veterinary degree of a recognized University. The College is in general responsible for the supervision of veterinary education in the United Kingdom.

The following Universities present their students for registrable veterinary degrees:—

CAMBRIDGE UNIVERSITY, School of Veterinary Medicine, Madingley Road, Cambridge.

ROYAL VETERINARY COLLEGE, University of London, Camden Town, N.W.1. (408).—*Principal and Dean*, Prof. R. E. Glover, D.Sc.

LIVERPOOL UNIVERSITY, Faculty of Veterinary Science (161).—*Dean*, Prof. E. G. White.

BRISTOL UNIVERSITY, School of Veterinary Science —*Chairman, Board of Veterinary Studies*, Prof. C. W. Ottaway.

ROYAL (DICK) SCHOOL OF VETERINARY STUDIES, University of Edinburgh (275).—*Director*, Prof. A. Robertson, Ph.D., F.R.S.E.

GLASGOW UNIVERSITY VETERINARY SCHOOL, 83 Buccleuch Street, Glasgow, C.3.; VETERINARY HOSPITAL, Bearsden Road, Glasgow. (266).—*Director of Veterinary Education*, Prof. W. L. Weipers.

EDUCATIONAL TRUSTS

BOEKE TRUST, care of Messrs. Cadbury Brothers, Bournville, Birmingham. (Applications by individuals for financial assistance not considered.) —*Sec.*, J. P. Bartlett.

CARNEGIE TRUST FOR THE UNIVERSITIES OF SCOTLAND, The Merchants Hall, Hanover Street, Edinburgh.—*Sec. and Treasurer*, T. E. Wright.

CASSEL EDUCATIONAL TRUST, 21 Hassocks Road, Hurstpierpoint, Sussex.—*Sec.*, D. Hardman.

DARTINGTON HALL TRUST, Totnes, Devon.—*Chairman*, L. K. Elmhirst.

EDUCATION SERVICES, Little Brooms, Rotherfield, Crowborough, Sussex.—*Hon. Sec.*, J. B. Annand.

GILCHRIST EDUCATIONAL TRUST, 1 York Street, W.1.—*Sec.*, S. J. Worsley, D.S.O., M.C., LL.D.

HARKNESS FELLOWSHIPS OF THE COMMONWEALTH FUND, Harkness House, 38 Upper Brook Street, W.1.—*Warden*, S. G. Putt.

KING GEORGE'S JUBILEE TRUST, 166 Piccadilly, W.1.—*Sec.*, D. S. Miller, C.B.E.

LORD KITCHENER NATIONAL MEMORIAL FUND, 50 Pall Mall, S.W.1.—*Sec.*, C. G. M. Broom. Awards annually for university courses 30 to 40 scholarships established to reward long and distinguished service, and especially war service, in H.M. Armed Forces. Competition is open to (*a*) sons of members or ex-members (men or women) of the British Navy, Army or Air Force, aged over 17 and under 20 on 1st January of year of competing, and (*b*) male applicants aged under 30, who have served in war in the British Navy, Army or Air Force (National Service not normally a qualification). Administers also six Kitchener Medical Services Scholarships, and six Dental Services Scholarships, awarded annually for applicants qualified as (*a*) above, desiring to be trained for commissions in the Medical or Dental branches of the Forces. Application forms, available after Jan. 1, are returnable by Feb. 28.

MITCHELL CITY OF LONDON CHARITY AND EDUCATIONAL FOUNDATION, 31 Bedford Row, W.C.1. —*Clerk*, A. E. L. Cox.

NUFFIELD FOUNDATION, Nuffield Lodge, Regent's Park, N.W.1.—*Dir.*, L. Farrer-Brown, C.B.E.

ROYAL COMMISSION FOR THE EXHIBITION OF 1851, 1 Lowther Gardens, Exhibition Road, S.W.7.—*Sec.*, W. D. Sturch.

SIR RICHARD STAPLEY EDUCATIONAL TRUST, 121 Gloucester Place, Portman Square, W.1.—*Sec.*, Miss J. Brown.

TRUSTEES OF THE LONDON PAROCHIAL CHARITIES, 3 Temple Gardens, E.C.4.

Income 1962, £416,203. Grants made for the maintenance of City Churches and for the welfare of the poorer classes of the Metropolis.

Clerk to the Trustees, Sir Donald Allen.

THOMAS WALL TRUST, 1 York Street, W.1. *Sec.*, Miss A. F. Bowlby.

S. C. WITTING TRUST, Friends House, Euston Road, N.W.1.—*Sec.*, Miss E. M. Faram.

PRINCIPAL UNIVERSITY SETTLEMENTS AND ADULT EDUCATION CENTRES

BEDFORD INSTITUTE ASSOCIATION, 128A Hoxton Street, N.1. (6 Friends' centres at Barking, Bethnal Green, Clerkenwell, Hoxton, Ratcliff, Walthamstow).—*Gen. Sec.*, J. E. Hoare.

BERMONDSEY SETTLEMENT, Scott Lidgett Crescent, S.E.16.—*Warden*, Rev. C. D. Johnson.

BERNHARD BARON ST. GEORGE'S JEWISH SETTLEMENT, Henriques Street, E.1.—*Warden*, M. Sopel.

BIRMINGHAM SETTLEMENT, 318 Summer Lane, Birmingham, 19.—*Warden*, Miss S. de C. Forster; and 610 Kingstanding Road, Birmingham, 22.—*Warden*, C. J. Blamire.

BLACKFRIARS SETTLEMENT (formerly Women's University Settlement), 44 Nelson Square, S.E.1. —*Warden*, D. W. A. Collett.

BOSTON, Extra-Mural Department, University of Nottingham, Pilgrim College.—*Warden and Resident Tutor*, A. Champion.

BRISTOL, The Folk House, College Green.—*Warden*, R. C. Terry.

BRISTOL (Headquarters, 43 Ducie Road, Barton Hill).—*Warden*, Miss M. E. Jones.

CAMBRIDGE HOUSE, 131–139 Camberwell Road, S.E.5.—*Warden*, R. I. L. Guthrie.

CITY LITERARY INSTITUTE, Stukeley Street, W.C.2. —*Principal*, H. A. Jones.

DOCKLAND SETTLEMENTS, branches at Isle of Dogs, E.14; Bristol; Rotherhithe, S.E.16; Devonport; Dagenham Docks; Stratford, E.15; Hainault, Essex, etc.—*Gen. Sec.*, R. W. Logan-Hunt, 164 Romford Road, Stratford, E.15.

DUNDEE, Grey Lodge Settlement, Wellington Street.—*Warden*, Miss B. B. Whitton.

EDINBURGH UNIVERSITY SETTLEMENT, Cameron House, Prestonfield.—*Warden*, J. R. Waddington; *Adult Education Centre*, Kirk o' Field College, Morton House, Blackfriars Street, Edinburgh, 1.—*Sec.*, Miss E. Wood.

GOLDSMITHS' COLLEGE, New Cross, S.E.14.—*Head, Adult Educ. Dept.*, J. A. Gulland.

LEEDS, Swarthmore Educational Centre, 3–5 Woodhouse Square, Leeds 3.—*Warden*, G. B. Stapleton.

LEICESTER, Vaughan College.—*Warden*, D. J. Rice.

LIVERPOOL, Nile Street.—*Warden*, D. M. Lowson.

LIVERPOOL, Victoria Settlement, 294 Netherfield Road, N., Liverpool 5.—*Warden*, Miss D. M. Bouckley.

LOUGHBOROUGH, Quest House College of Further Education.—*Warden*, P. J. Madgwick, Dept. of Adult Education, University of Nottingham.

MANCHESTER, Round House, 20 Every Street, Ancoats, Manchester 4.—*Warden*, K. Hill.

MANSFIELD HOUSE, Fairbairn Hall, E.13.—*Warden*, Rev. E. A. Shipman.

MIDDLESBROUGH SETTLEMENT COMMUNITY CENTRE, 132 Newport Road, Middlesbrough.—*Warden* (vacant).

MIDDLESBROUGH UNIVERSITY ADULT EDUCATION CENTRE, 37 Harrow Road, Linthorpe, Middlesbrough. (Department of Extra-Mural Studies, University of Leeds).—*Warden*, J. W. Saunders.

MORLEY COLLEGE, 61 Westminster Bridge Road, S.E.1.—*Principal*, D. G. Richards.

OXFORD HOUSE IN BETHNAL GREEN, INC., Mape Street, E.2.—*Head*, Rev. J. R. G. Ragg.

PILGRIM HOUSE, Dace Road, E.3.—*Warden* (vacant).

POPLAR HOUSE PRESBYTERIAN SETTLEMENT AND TRAINING CENTRE, 56–58 East India Dock Road, E.14.

ROBERT BROWNING SETTLEMENT, Browning Street, Walworth, S.E.17.—*Warden*, Rev. H. Rathbone Dunnico, LL.D.

ROLAND HOUSE (Scout Settlement), 29 Stepney Green, E.1.—*Warden*, Wing Cdr. D. H. Montgomery.

ST. ANNE'S CATHOLIC SETTLEMENT, 46 Harleyford Road, S.E.11.—*Warden* (vacant).

ST. MARGARET'S HOUSE SETTLEMENT, 21 Old Ford Road, Bethnal Green, E.2

SPENNYMOOR SETTLEMENT, King Street, Spennymoor, Co. Durham (*Hon. Sec.*, 66 St. Paul's Gardens, Spennymoor).

TOYNBEE HALL UNIVERSITY SETTLEMENT, 28 Commercial Street, Whitechapel, E.1.—*Warden*, E. St. J. Catchpool, C.B.E.

WHITECHAPEL MISSION: WORKING LADS' INSTITUTE, 279 Whitechapel Road, E.1.—*Superintendent*, Rev. A. E. D. Clipson.

WILMSLOW, The Wilmslow Guild, 1 Bourne Street, Wilmslow, Cheshire.—*Warden*, W. Carter.

WORKING MEN'S COLLEGE, Crowndale Road, N.W.1.—*Principal*, F. M. Maurice.

YORK EDUCATIONAL SETTLEMENT, Holgate Hill, *Warden*, A. J. Peacock.

HEADMASTERS' CONFERENCE SCHOOLS

THE HEADMASTERS' CONFERENCE.—*Chairman*, D. R. Wigram (*Monkton Combe*); *Sec.*, F. L. Allan, M.B.E., M.C., 29 Gordon Square, W.C.1. The annual meetings are, as a rule, held early in October.

In considering applications for election to membership the Committee will have regard to the scheme or other instrument under which the school is administered (taking particularly into consideration the degree of independence enjoyed by the Headmaster and the Governing Body); the number of boys over thirteen years of age in the school; the number of boys in proportion to the size of the school who are in the sixth form, *i.e.* engaged on studies above the standard of the Ordinary level of the General Certificate Examination; and the connection with the Universities, as indicated by the number of undergraduates from the school at British universities.

Name of School	F'ded.	No. of Boys	Annual Fees D=Day Boys	Headmaster (*With date of Appointment*)
England and Wales				
Abingdon, Berks	1256	560	£267......D£90	J. M. Cobban, T.D. (1947)
Aldenham, Elstree, Herts	1597	326	£435......D£201	P. Griffin, M.B.E. (1962)
Alleyn's School, S.E.22	1619	830	..........D£87	C. W. Lloyd (1963)
Allhallows, Rousdon	1515	270	£408......D£150	V. A. L. Hill (1948)
Ampleforth College (*R.C.*), York	1802	702	£432......D£165	Rev. D. W. M. Price, O.S.B. (1954)
Ardingly Coll., Sussex	1858	425	£450..........	C. H. Bulteel, M.C. (1962)
Arnold School, Blackpool	1870	690	£249......D£84	F. W. Holdgate (1938)
Ashville College, Harrogate	1877	425	£262......D£90	G. R. Southam (1958)
Bablake, Coventry	1560	800	..........D£58	E. H. Burrough, T.D. (1962)
Bancroft's, Woodford Green	1737	430	£234......D£90	S. Adams (1944)
Barnard Castle	1883	475	£234......D£90	H. E. Birkbeck (1935)
Battersea Grammar, Battersea	1700	620	..........D*nil*	W. J. Langford, C.B.E. (1945)
Beaumont Coll. (*R.C.*), Old Windsor	1861	270	£396..........	Rev. J. P. Costigan, S.J. (1958)
Bedford School	1552	1000	£390......D£180	W. M. Brown (1955)
Bedford Modern School	1566	960	£246......D£63	Rev. J. E. Taylor (1946)
Berkhamsted, Herts	1541	835	£378......D£168	B. H. Garnons-Williams (1953)
Birkenhead, Cheshire	1860	650	£243......D£84	J. A. Gwilliam (1963)
Bishop's Stortford Coll., Herts	1868	420	£405......D£162	P. W. Rowe (1957)
Bloxham School, Oxon	1860	268	£420..........	R. S. Thompson (1952)
Blundell's, Tiverton	1604	400	£396......D£160	Rev. J. M. Stanton (1959)
Bolton	1524	936	..........£89	F. R. Poskitt, C.B.E. (1933)
Bootham, York	1823	250	£426..........	A. F. Lindley (1961)
Bradfield College, Berks	1850	420	£456..........	B. M. S. Hoban (1964)
Bradford Gr., Yorks	1548	1000	..........D£71	K. D. Robinson (1963)
Brentwood Sch., Essex	1557	1045	£274......D£88	C. R. Allison (1945)
Brighton College, Sussex	1845	380	£429......D£249	C. H. Christie (1963)
Bristol Grammar	1532	970	..........D£64	J. Mackay, D.Phil. (1960)
Bromsgrove, Worcs	1553	335	£420......D£231	L. M. Carey, T.D. (1953)
Bryanston School, Blandford	1928	450	£492..........	F. G. R. Fisher (1959)
Bury Grammar, Lancs	1600	650	..........D£80	J. T. Hansford (1960)
Canford, Wimborne, Dorset	1923	444	£462......D£249	I. A. Wallace (1961)
Caterham, Surrey	1811	475	£290......D£97	T. R. Leathem (1950)
Charterhouse, Godalming	1611	650	£492..........	B. W. M. Young (1952)
Cheltenham College	1841	465	£474......D£252	D. Ashcroft (1959)
Chigwell, Essex	1629	500	£357......D£165	D. H. Thompson (1947)
Christ Coll., Brecon	1541	230	£378......D£220	J. Sharp, D.Phil. (1962)
Christ's Hospital, Horsham	1252	810	*Nil*–£200..........	C. M. E. Seaman (1955)
City of London, E.C.4	1442	824	......D£154–168	A. W. Barton, Ph.D. (1950)
Clayesmore, Iwerne Minster, Blandford	1896	220	£420..........	D. P. M. Burke (*Master*) (1945)
Clifton College, Bristol	1862	700	£450......D£230	S. J. McWatters (1963)
Cranleigh, Surrey	1863	428	£444......D£255	D. A. Emms (1960)
Culford Sch., Bury St. Edmunds	1881	440	£309......D£99	C. Storey, Ph.D. (1951)
Dame Allan's School, Newcastle on Tyne	1705	430	..........D£85	B. C. Harvey (1953)
Dauntsey's, Devizes	1543	371	£301......D£115	D. J. Forbes (1956)
Dean Close, Cheltenham	1884	340	£426......D£234	Rev. D. L. Graham (1954)
Denstone College, Staffs	1868	383	£400..........	B. M. W. Trapnell, Ph.D. (1957)
Douai (*R.C.*), Woolhampton	1615	235	£360..........	Rev. F. A. Tierney, O.S.B. (1952)
Dover College, Kent	1871	340	£411......D£180	T. H. Cobb (1958)
Downside (*R.C.*), Bath	1607	547	£511...... various	Rev. C. A. Watkin (1962)
Dulwich College, S.E. 21	1619	1550	£360......D£180	R. Groves (*Master*) (1954)
Durham	1414	257	£393......D£198	J. A. Brett (1958)
Eastbourne College, Sussex	1867	461	£450......D£235	M. P. Birley (1956)
Elizabeth Coll., Guernsey	1563	500	£256......D£85	J. K. Day, T.D. (1958)
Ellesmere Coll., Shropshire	1879	390	£370......D£150	I. D. S. Beer (1961)
Eltham College, S.E. 9	1842	440	£314......D£98	C. Porteous (1959)
Emanuel Sch., S.W.11	1594	760	..........D*nil*	J. B. C. Grundy, T.D., Ph.D. (1953)

Name of School	F'ded.	No. of Boys	Annual Fees D=Day Boys	Headmaster (*With date of Appointment*)
Epsom College, Surrey	1853	520	£475......D£260	A. D. D. McCallum, T.D. (1962)
Eton College, Windsor	1440	1190	£535	A. Chenevix-Trench (1964)
Exeter, Devon	1633	435	£267......D£87	F. K. Paul, T.D. (1950)
Felsted, Essex	1564	446	£441......D£189	H. E. Reekie (1951)
Forest Sch., Walthamstow, E.17	1834	482	£340......D£186	D. A. Foxall (1960)
Framlingham Coll., Suffolk	1864	440	£282......D£93	W. S. Porter, T.D. (1955)
Giggleswick, Yorks	1512	270	£405......D£228	O. J. T. Rowe (1961)
Gresham's, Holt, Norfolk	1555	450	£480......D£255	L. Bruce Lockhart (1955)
Haberdashers' Aske's, Elstree, Herts	1690	1030	£309...D£87–114	T. W. Taylor, Ph.D. (1946)
Haileybury & Imperial Service Coll., Herts	1862 / 1912	560	£429	W. Stewart, M.C. (*Master*) (1963)
Harrow, Middlesex	1571	650	£498......D£249	R. L. James, Ph.D. (1953)
Harrow, Lower School	1876	400	......D£147	R. F. B. Campbell (1951)
Hereford, Cathedral Sch.	1381	358	£231......D£81	J. R. Peebles (1957) [(1955)
Highgate, N.6	1565	670	£365......D£171	A. J. F. Doulton, O.B.E., T.D.
High Wycombe (Royal Gr.)	1567	1096	£185......D*nil*	E. R. Tucker (1933)
Hulme Gr. Sch., Oldham	1611	600	......D£77	H. B. Shaw, M.B.E.(1931)
Hurstpierpoint College, Sussex	1849	336	£429	Rev. Canon R. C. Howard
Hymers Coll., Hull	1889	625	......D£78	H. R. Roach (1951) [(1945)
Ipswich, Suffolk	1400	650	£366......D£198	P. H. F. Mermagen, T.D. (1951)
Kelly College, Tavistock	1867	152	£378......D£214	J. T. Melvin, T.D. (1959)
Kent College, Canterbury	1885	450	£279......D£99	D. E. Norfolk (1960)
King Edward's, Birmingham	1552	700	......D£83	Rev. R. G. Lunt, M.C. (*Chief Master*) (1952)
King Henry VIII, Coventry	1545	900	......D£75	H. Walker (1950)
King's Coll., Taunton	1522	319	£408......D£177	R. C. Unmack (1937)
King's College Sch., Wimbledon, S.W.19	1829	560	£375......D£180	F. H. Shaw, M.B.E., T.D. (1960)
King's Sch., Bruton	1519	295	£360......D£204	R. C. Davey (1957)
King's Sch., Canterbury	600	668	£450......D£201	Rev. J. P. Newell (1962)
King's Sch., Chester	1541	500	......D£77	Rev. Canon L. F. Harvey (1947)
Kings' Sch., Ely	1541	359	£399......D£199	B. E. N. Fawcett (1955)
King's Sch., Macclesfield	1502	1000	......D£120	T. T. Shaw (1933)
King's Sch., Rochester	604	476	£330–360..D£150	Rev. Canon D. R. Vicary (1957)
King's Sch., Worcester	1541	604	£240......D£86	D. M. Annett (1959)
Kingston Grammar, Kingston-upon-Thames	1561	570	......D£95	P. W. Rundle (1950)
Kingswood Sch., Bath	1748	450	£441......D£240	A. L. Creed (1959)
Lancing College, Sussex	1848	420	£441	E. W. Gladstone (1961)
Latymer Upper, Hammersmith, W.6	1624	1100	......D£90	K. E. Sutcliffe (1958)
Leeds Gr. Sch.	1552	1102	......D£87	E. E. Sabben-Clare (1963)
Leighton Park Sch., Reading	1890	260	£441......D£294	J. Ounsted (1948)
The Leys Sch., Cambridge	1875	350	£450	W. A. Barker (1958)
Liverpool College	1840	724	£312......D£186	L. H. Collison, T.D. (1952)
Llandovery Coll.	1848	250	£312......D£141	Rev. R. J. Tree (1957)
Lord Wandsworth Coll., Basingstoke, Hants	1912	290	£414	A. Henderson (1943)
Loughborough Grammar	1496	760	£270......D£90	N. S. Walter (1959)
Lytham (King Edward VII School)	1908	570	......D£66	C. D. A. Baggley (1957)
Magdalen Coll. Sch., Oxford	1478	464	£255......D£84	R. S. Stanier (*Master*) (1944)
Maidstone Gr. School	1549	873	......D*nil*	W. A. Claydon, C.B.E. (1941)
Malvern Coll., Worcs	1865	600	£492......D£273	D. D. Lindsay (1953)
Manchester Gr. Sch.	1515	1440	......D£87	P. G. Mason, M.B.E. (*High Master*) (1962)
Manchester, Wm. Hulme's Gr.	1887	700	......D£81	J. G. Bird, M.B.E., T.D. (1947)
Marlborough Coll., Wilts	1843	815	£495–540	J. C. Dancy (*Master*) (1961)
Merchant Taylors', Northwood	1561	600	£381......D£243	H. Elder (1946)
Merchant Taylors', Crosby, Lancs.	1620	740	£235......D£90	Rev. H. M. Luft (1963)
Mill Hill, N.W.7	1807	430	£435......D£225	R. Moore, C.B.E. (1950)
Monkton Combe, Bath	1868	305	£435......D£276	D. R. Wigram (1946)
Monmouth	1615	440	£201......D£55	R. F. Glover (1959)
Mount St. Mary's Coll., Spinkhill, Derbyshire (*R.C.*)	1842	315	£321......D£96	Rev. J. F. Colliston, S.J. (1954)
Newcastle on Tyne (Royal Gr. Sch.)	1545	788	......D£89	W. D. Haden, T.D. (1960)
Norwich Sch.	1240	594	£237......D£81	A. Stephenson (1943)
Nottingham High Sch.	1513	920	......D£132	K. R. Imeson (1954)
Oakham, Rutland	1584	470	£320......D£97	J. D. Buchanan, M.B.E. (1958)
Oratory, Woodcote, Reading	1859	250	£405......D£180	Rev. A. Morey, O.S.B., D.Phil. (1953)
Oundle, Peterborough, Northants	1556	680	£480	R. J. Knight (1956)
Perse Sch. for Boys, Cambridge	1615	570	£283......D£93	S. Stubbs (1945)

Name of School	F'ded.	No. of Boys	Annual Fees D=Day Boys	Headmaster (*With date of Appointment*)
Plymouth College	1877	600	£246...... D£81	C. M. Meade-King (1955)
Pocklington Sch., E. Yorks.	1514	506	£282.......D£96	R. St. J. Pitts-Tucker (1945)
Portsmouth Gr. Sch.	1732	720	.... D£90	D. H. Hibbert, C.B.E. (1954)
Queen Elizabeth's Gr., Blackburn	1509	880	............D£79	B. H. Kemball-Cook (1956)
Queen Elizabeth Gr. Sch., Wakefield	1591	750	£228 ......D£81	E. J. Baggaley (1956)
Radley Coll., Abingdon	1847	475	£489	W. M. M. Milligan, M.B.E., T.D. (*Warden*) (1954)
Ratcliffe Coll. (*R.C.*), Leicester	1847	320	£390............	Very Rev. J. F. Morris (1963)
Reading School	1125	590	£195........ D*nil*	C. E. Kemp (1939)
Repton Sch., Derby	1557	480	£489...........	J. L. Thorn (1961)
Rossall, Fleetwood, Lancs.	1844	536	£460......D£240	G. S. Sale (1957)
Royal Masonic School, Bushey	1789	400	.... D*nil*	H. G. Mullens, T.D. (1957)
Rugby, Warwickshire	1567	730	£501......D£195	W. Hamilton (1957)
Rydal, Colwyn Bay	1885	287	£396...........	D. W. Hughes (1946)
St. Albans, Herts.	948	650	....D£77	W. T. Marsh, O.B.E. (1931)
St. Bees, Cumberland	1583	260	£432 .....D£210	G. W. Lees (1963)
St. Benedict's, Ealing, W.5 (*R.C.*)	1902	520	...... D£165–180	Rev. G. G. Brown, O.S.B. (1961)
St. Dunstan's, Catford, S.E.6	1446	800	..........D£150	W. R. Hecker, C.B.E. (1938)
St. Edmund's, Canterbury	1749	310	£420......D£225	(vacant)
St. Edward's, Oxford	1863	492	£450......D£250	Hon. F. F. Fisher, M.C. (*Warden*) (1954)
St. John's, Leatherhead	1851	345	£429 .....D£240	I. Sutherland (1960)
St. Lawrence Coll., Ramsgate	1879	337	£430......D£215	Rev. Canon R. Perfect (1938)
St. Olave's, S.E.1	1571	650	............D*nil*	R. C. Carrington, D.Ph. (1937)
St. Paul's, W.14	1509	665	£395......D£229	T. E. B. Howarth, M.C., T.D. (*High Master*) (1962)
St. Peter's, York	627	400	£430......D£200	J. Dronfield (1937)
Sebright Sch., Wolverley	1620	256	£345......D£160	A. C. S. Gimson (1963)
Sedbergh, Yorks	1525	423	£447 .....D£194	G. M. C. Thornely (1954)
Sevenoaks School, Kent	1418	589	£393 .....D£204	L. C. Taylor (1954)
Sherborne, Dorset	1550	594	£426......D£213	R. W. Powell (1950)
Shrewsbury School	1552	530	£465	A. R. D. Wright (1963)
Silcoates School, Wakefield, Yorks.	1820	280	£339..... D£180	R. J. M. Evans, Ph.D. (1960)
Solihull, Warwicks	1560	854	£360 .....D£186	(vacant)
Stamford, Lincs.	1532	650	£280 ......D£90	B. L. Deed, O.B.E., T.D. (1947)
Stockport Gr. Sch.	1487	446	...........D£90	F. W. Scott (1962)
Stonyhurst Coll. (*R.C.*), Blackburn	1593	360	£414..........	Rev. F. J. Turner (1961)
Stowe, Bucks	1923	600	£503..........	R. Q. Drayson (1963)
Sutton Valence, Maidstone	1576	350	£429 .....D£180	C. R. Evers (1953)
Taunton, Somerset	1847	730	£348..... D£174	J. G. Leathem (1945)
Tonbridge, Kent	1553	522	£468......D£252	M. W. McCrum (1962)
Trent College, Long Eaton, Derbyshire	1866	235	£405...........	R. G. Ikin (1936)
Truro, Cornwall	1879	650	£252.......D£93	D. W. Burrell (1959)
University Coll. Sch., N.W.3	1830	500	...........D£174	C. D. Black-Hawkins (1956)
Uppingham, Rutland	1584	590	£456...........	M. Lloyd (1944)
Victoria Coll., Jersey	1852	385	£282.......D£90	R. Postill, T.D. (1945)
Warwick	914	737	£306–339 D£120–153	P. W. Martin, T.D. (1962)
Wellingborough, Northants	1595	414	£417......D£210	H. J. C. Bashford (1956)
Wellington Coll., Berks.	1859	685	£453–474..D£270	G. H. Stainforth (*Master*) (1956)
Wellington Sch., Somerset	1842	400	£273.......D£96	J. C. Stredder (1957)
Westminster, S.W.1	1560	427	£498 .....D£315	J. D. Carleton (1957)
Whitgift, Croydon	1596	850	...........D£158	M. J. Hugill (1961)
Whitgift Trinity Sch., Croydon	1596	630	............D£63	O. C. Berthoud (1952)
Winchester College	1394	525	£498...........	Sir Desmond Lee (1954)
Wolverhampton Gr. Sch., Staffs.	1512	580	............D*nil*	E. R. Taylor (1956)
Woodhouse Grove Sch., Bradford	1812	423	£280......D£101	F. C. Pritchard, Ph.D. (1950)
Worcester College for the Blind	1866	68	£550............	R. C. Fletcher (1959)
Worcester (Royal Gr.)	1291	831	£183 ......D*nil*	A. G. K. Brown (1950)
Worksop College, Notts	1895	420	£420......D£230	R. J. Northcote-Green, M.C., T.D. (1952)
Wrekin Coll., Wellington, Salop	1880	390	£435............	R. H. Dahl, T.D. (1952)
Wycliffe Coll., Stonehouse, Glos	1882	260	£417 .....D£207	S. G. H. Loosley, M.C. (1947)
Scotland				[(1946)
Daniel Stewart's, Edinburgh	1855	945	£288...... D£78	H. J. L. Robbie, C.B.E., Ph.D.
The Edinburgh Academy	1824	620	£327......D£156	H. H. Mills, M.C., Ph.D. (*Rector*) (1962)
Fettes College, Edinburgh	1870	450	£405...........	I. D. McIntosh, Ll.D. (1958)
George Heriot's, Edinburgh	1628	1500	.... D£52	W. McL. Dewar, O.B.E. (1947)
George Watson's Coll., Edinburgh	1723	1490	£288 ... D£63–78	R. W. Young (1958)

Name of School	F'ded.	No. of Boys	Annual Fees D=Day Boys	Headmaster (*With date of Appointment*)
Glasgow Academy	1846	910	£305-397 D£75-162	B. M. Holden (*Rector*) (1959)
Gordonstoun, Elgin, Morayshire	1934	398	£594 .. D£249	F. R. G. Chew (1959)
Kelvinside Academy, Glasgow	1878	407	D £72-138	C. J. R. Mair (1958)
Loretto Sch., near Edinburgh	1827	240	£430	R. B. Bruce Lockhart (1960)
Merchiston Castle, Edinburgh	1833	280	£405	A. Bush, M.C. (1958)
Robert Gordon's Coll., Aberdeen	1729	1094	£266 D£62	J. Marshall (1960)
Strathallan, Forgandenny, Perthshire	1912	335	£435	W. N. S. Hoare, T.D. (1951)
Trinity Coll., Glenalmond, Perthshire	1847	360	£450	R. M. M. Barlow (*Warden*) (1948)
Northern Ireland				
Campbell Coll., Belfast	1894	468	£334 D£136	F. J. G. Cook (1954)
Portora Royal, Enniskillen	1608	461	£299 D£110	Rev. P. H. Rogers, M.B.E. [(1954)
Royal Academical Instn., Belfast	1810	1110	D£81	S. V. Peskett (*Principal*) (1959)
Isle of Man				
King William's College	1668	390	£381 D£138	G. R. Rees-Jones (*Principal*) (1958)
Republic of Ireland				
St. Columba's College, Rathfarnham	1843	178	£315	Rev. F. M. Argyle (*Warden*) [(1949)

With a few exceptions the schools listed above are members of the Association of Governing Bodies of Public Schools (G.B.A.). Other schools in membership of G.B.A. but not of the Headmasters' Conference are:—ABBOTSHOLME; *Ackworth*, Pontefract, Yorks; Adams' Grammar School, Newport, Salop; Archbishop Holgate's Grammar School, York; *Bedales*, Petersfield, Hants; Cannon Slade Grammar School, Bolton; Carmel College, Wallingford; CATHEDRAL, Truro; Cheadle Hulme School, Cheshire; Churchers, Petersfield, Hants; COLSTON'S BOYS' SCHOOL, Bristol; Kimbolton School, Hunts; King Edward Sch., Bath; KING'S SCHOOL, Gloucester; Melville College; MILTON ABBEY, Dorset; Morrison's Academy, Edinburgh; PRIOR PARK, Bath; Queen Elizabeth's Hospital, Bristol; Queen's College, Taunton; Reed's School, Cobham, Surrey; RENDCOMB, Glos.; RISHWORTH, Yorks; Royal Nautical College, Pangbourne, Berks.; Ruthin, Denbighshire; St. Bede's College, Manchester; St. Brendan's College, Bristol; *St. George's*, Harpenden, Herts. St. George's College, Weybridge; St. John's College, Southsea, Hants; Scarborough College; Shebbear; College, Beaworthy, N. Devon; Wakefield Grammar School; West Buckland, Devon; Woodbridge, Suffolk; *Dollar Academy*, Clackmannanshire. Co-educational Schools are shown in *italic* type. For details of schools printed in CAPITAL LETTERS, see table below.

SOCIETY OF HEADMASTERS OF INDEPENDENT SCHOOLS

THE SOCIETY OF HEADMASTERS OF INDEPENDENT SCHOOLS.—*Hon. Sec.*, M. W. Pitt, Rishworth School, Nr. Halifax.—The Society was founded in 1961 to maintain high standards of education in member schools; to improve relations with preparatory schools and universities; to ensure the genuine independence of member schools and to build up an association of schools which will contribute to the whole independent sector of education by its distinctive character, high standards and flexibility. Regular meetings of headmasters are held three times a year.

Name of School	F'ded.	No. of Boys	Annual Fees D=Day Boys	Headmaster (*With date of Appointment*)
Abbotsholme, Rocester, Uttoxeter, Staffs	1889	200	£444-471	R. A. Hodgkin (1956)
Bembridge, Isle of Wight	1919	265	£345 D£174	P. G. Rendall (1959)
Carmel College, Wallingford, Berks	1948	318	£495 D£165	D. M. Stamler (1962)
Colston's, Stapleton, Bristol	1710	281	£330 D£160	R. E. Snaith (1939)
King's, Gloucester	1541	472	£339 D£144	T. W. Brown (1951)
King's, Tynemouth, Northumberland	1860	400	D£120	Rev. J. M. Nicholson (1959)
Lindisfarne College, Ruabon, Denbighshire	1891	304	£345 £D114	R. Carrington (1963)
Milton Abbey, Nr. Blandford, Dorset	1954	250	£450	Cdr. R. H. Hodgkinson, D.S.C. (1955)
Prior Park College, Bath, Som.	1830	270	£336	Rev. J. P. Hooper (1962)
Queen's College, Taunton, Som.	1843	315	£339 D£141	S. J. Haynes (1953)
Reed's, Cobham, Surrey	1813	270	£335	(vacant)
Rendcomb College, Cirencester, Glos.	1920	112	£320	A. O. H. Quick (1961)
Rishworth, Nr. Halifax, Yorks	1724	220	£375 D£160	M. W. Pitt (1956)
Ryde, Isle of Wight	1921	235	£312-342 D£87-117	R. McIsaac (1953)
St. Edmund's College, Ware, Herts	1759	240	£300 D£110	Rev. D. Britt-Compton (1949)
St. George's College, Weybridge, Surrey	1869	490	£330 D£150	Rev. B. P. Murtough (1958)
Scarborough College, Yorks	1898	338	£390 D£165	D. K. Crews, M.B.E., T.D. (1959)
Seaford College, Petworth, Sussex	1884	310	£441	Rev. C. E. Johnson (1946)
Tettenhall College, Staffs	1863	249	£375 D£222	F. D. Field-Hyde (1942)
Truro Cathedral, Cornwall	1549	308	£294 D£129	S. M. Mischler, M.B.E. (1937)
Wells Cathedral, Som.	1140	253	£330 D£45	F. G. Commings (1954)

PUBLIC SCHOOLS OVERSEAS

NOTE.—Headmasters of Schools marked (*) are Members of the *Headmasters' Conference*; marked (†) of the *Headmasters' Conference of Australia*.

Name of School	F'ded.	No. of Boys	Annual Fees D=Day Boys	Headmaster (*With date of Appointment*)
South America				
*St. George's Coll., Quilmes, Argentine	1898	300	£450...........	Rev. E. J. Colville (1962)
*Queen's Coll., Georgetown, Brit. Guiana	1844	640	...........D£16	V. J. Sanger-Davies, T.D. (1952)
*Grange School, Santiago, Chile......	1928	620	£300......D£150	I. M. Richardson (1959)
India				
*Mayo College, Ajmer	1873	550	Rs.2,100	J. T. M. Gibson, O.B.E. (1954)
*Cathedral and John Connon Boys', Bombay	1860	722	..... DRs.420–875	B. Gunnery (1953)
St. Joseph's Coll., Darjeeling..........	1887	401	£540.....D£114	M. Stanford, S.J. (1950)
*St. Paul's, Darjeeling................	1823	300	Rs.3,600.........	L. J. Goddard, O.B.E. (*Rector*) (1934)
*Doon Sch., Dehra Dun	1935	386	Rs.2,750DRs.1,925	J. A. K. Martyn, O.B.E. (1948)
*Scindia Sch., Gwalior	1897	600	Rs.2,400. .DRs. 75	K. C. Shukla (*Principal*) (1944)
Canada				
*Ashbury Coll., Ottawa.............	1891	285	$1,700.....D $800	R. H. Perry (1950)
Hillfield, Hamilton, Ont.............	1901	350	.......D $800–950	Lt.-Col. J. P. Page, E.D. (1950)
Lower Canada Coll., Montreal......	1909	250	.......D $550–750	D. S. Penton, Ll.D. (1941)
*Ridley Coll., St. Catharines, Ont. ...	1889	414	$2,100.....D $800	E. V. B. Pilgrim (1962)
*St. Andrew's Coll., Aurora, Ont. ...	1899	300	$2,150 . . .D $1,025	J. R. Coulter (1958)
*Trinity Coll. Sch., Port Hope, Ont. .	1865	281	$2,090	A. C. Scott (1962)
*Upper Canada Coll., Toronto.......	1829	790	$2,000....D $1,000	Rev. C. W. Sowby, D.D. (*Principal*) (1949)
Australia				
N.S.W.:—				
*†Armidale Sch., Armidale...........	1894	312	£454 .....D£105	A. H. Cash (1962)
†Barker Coll., Hornsby	1890	656	£480......D£180	T. J. McGaskill (1963)
*†Sydney C. of E. Gr. Sch., North Sydney	1889	945	£486 ..... D£183	B. H. Travers, O.B.E. (1959)
*†Cranbrook Sch., Sydney...........	1918	455	£510......D£195	M. Bishop (1963)
*†The King's Sch., Parramatta........	1831	858	£525......D£210	H. D. Hake, O.B.E. (1939)
†Knox Gr. Sch., Wahroonga........	1924	700	£375-450 D£102–171	T. R. McKenzie, Ed.D. (1956)
†Newington Coll., Stanmore........	1863	1010	£495.....D£195	Rev. D. A. Trathen (1963)
†St. Aloysius Coll. (*R.C.*), Sydney...	1879	585	..........D£102	Rev. V. F. Conway, S.J. (1961)
†St. Ignatius Coll. (*R.C.*), Sydney....	1880	575	£375.....D£114	Rev. F. J. Gorman, S.J. (1961)
†St. Joseph's Coll. (*R.C.*), Hunter's Hill	1881	593	£300............	Rev. Br. Elias (1962)
*Scots Coll., Sydney...............	1893	1093	£495 ...D£198	A. E. McLucas (1956)
*†Sydney Gr. Sch., Sydney..........	1857	1050	£498......D£198	C. O. Healey, O.B.E., T.D. (1951)
†Trinity Gr. Sch., Sydney...........	1913	964	£465......D£170	J. W. Hogg (1944)
Victoria:—				
†Ballarat Coll......................	1864	344	£444–83D£93–128	A. D. P. Dyer (1960)
†Ballarat C. of E. Gr. Sch...........	1910	210	£475......D£150	G. F. J. Dart (1942)
†Carey Baptist Gr. Sch., Kew.......	1923	1230	.... D£200	S. L. Hickman (1948)
†Caulfield Gr. Sch.................	1881	1147	£437–496 D£116–175	Rev. S. W. Kurrle (1954)
*†Geelong Coll., Geelong............	1861	731	£555......D£216	P. N. Thwaites (1960)
*†Geelong C. of E. Gr. Sch., Corio...	1857	1110	£645..... D£261	T. R. Garnett (1961)
*†Haileybury Coll., E. Brighton	1892	1128	£500......D£170	D. M. Bradshaw (1954)
†Ivanhoe Gr. Sch..................	1915	600	£429–480 D£120–309	V. R. C. Brown (1948)
*†Melbourne, C. of E. Gr. Sch........	1858	1520	£550.. D£175–225	B. W. Hone (1951)
*†Scotch Coll., Melbourne...........	1851	1386	£537..... D£201	R. Selby Smith (1953)
†Trinity Gr. Sch., Kew.............	1902	830	£453..D£132–174	J. J. J. Leppitt (1959)
†Wesley Coll., Melbourne..........	1865	965	£550......D£210	T. H. Coates, Ph.D. (1957)
†Xavier Coll. (*R.C.*), Melbourne....	1878	722	£360......D£135	Very Rev. P. Keenan, S.J. (1959)
Queensland:—				
†All Souls' Sch., Charters Towers ...	1920	310	£279.......D£60	M. A. P. Mattingley (1958)
†Brisbane Boys' Coll., Toowong.....	1902	650	£285–315 D£75–105	A. J. Birtles (1956)
*Brisbane C. of E. Grammar Sch.....	1912	1175	£336.....D£112	H. E. Roberts (1947)
†Brisbane Grammar Sch.	1868	886	£240....... D£60	H. F. Newell (1956)
†The Southport Sch................	1901	560	£350	C. G. Pearce (1951)
†Toowoomba Gr. Sch...............	1876	345	£300.......D£90	C. E. Olsen (1962)
South Australia:—				
*†St. Peter's Coll., Adelaide..........	1847	580	£480 ......D£180	Rev. J. S. C. Miller (1961)
*†Prince Alfred Coll., Kent Town....	1869	885	£468......D£168	J. A. Dunning (1949)
*†Scotch Coll., Mitcham.............	1919	670	£486......D£180	C. D. Fisher (1962)
Western Australia:—				
*†Christ Church Gr. Sch., Claremont .	1910	719	£416......D£170	P. M. Moyes (1951)
†Guildford C. of E. Gr. Sch.	1896	440	£399......D£156	D. A. L. Davies (1957)

Name of School	F'ded.	No. of Boys	Annual Fees D=Days	Headmaster (*With date of Appointment*)
†Hale School, Perth................	1858	570	£420.....D£165	J. R. Prince (1960)
†Scotch Coll., Swanbourne.........	1897	560	£369-420D£90-174	G. Maxwell Keys (1947)
†Wesley Coll., Perth...............	1923	550	£360-399D£96-153	N. R. Collins (1953)
Tasmania:—				
†Launceston Church Gr. Sch........	1846	488	£325-460D£57-174	D. V. Selth (1959)
†Hutchins Sch., Hobart.............	1846	462	£465......D£180	G. H. Newman (1959)
†Scotch College, Launceston.........	1900	300	£450......D£150	Rev. R. H. Dean (1950)
New Zealand				
*Auckland, Gr. Sch.................	1869	1287	£165.......D*nil*	W. H. Cooper (1954)
*Auckland, King's Coll., Otahuhu...	1896	550	£360......D£126	G. N. T. Greenbank (1946)
*Canterbury, Timaru Boys' High Sch.	1880	690	£214............	M. A. Bull (1947)
*Christchurch Boys' High..........	1881	1085	£150......D*nil*	C. F. S. Caldwell (1959)
*Christchurch, Christ's Coll.........	1850	587	£310......D£128	N. A. H. Creese (1963)
Nelson College, Nelson............	1856	987	£174.......D*nil*	B. H. Wakelin (1957)
New Plymouth Boys' High School..	1881	1060	£150.......D*nil*	J. S. Webster (1958)
Waitaki Boys' High Sch., Oamaru..	1883	783	£200.......D*nil*	J. H. Donaldson (1961)
*Wanganui Collegiate..............	1852	435	£330......D£114	T. U. Wells (1960)
Wellington Coll., Wellington......	1874	1000	£180.......D*nil*	S. H. W. Hill (1963)
South Africa				
*St. Andrew's Coll., Grahamstown...	1855	475	£288......D£103	J. L. Cawse (1962)
*Diocesan Coll., Rondebosch........	1849	600	£265.....D£120	A. W. H. Mallett (1964)
*St. John's Coll., Johannesburg......	1898	700	£280......D£140	D. Yates (1954)
*Michaelhouse, Balgowan, Natal.....	1896	424	£330............	R. T. S. Norwood (1960)
Southern Rhodesia				
*Peterhouse School, Marandellas.....	1954	360	£360............	F. R. Snell (1954)
*St. George's College, Salisbury......	1896	630	£225.......D£90	Rev. E. P. Ennis, S.J. (1961)
Kenya				
*Prince of Wales, Nairobi..........	1931	608	£156-384D£44-186	O. C. Wigmore (1960)
West Indies				
*Harrison Coll., Barbados...........	1729	662	............D£20	J. C. Hammond, O.B.E. (1949)
*Lodge School, St. John, Barbados...	1721	400	£350.......D*nil*	A. R. V. Newsam (1954)
*Wolmer's Sch., Jamaica............	1729	607	............D£36	N. S. Jackson (1953)
Malta				
*St. Edward's College............	1929	230	£150............	Rev. J. R. Brookes, O.S.B., O.B.E., M.C. (1956)
S. Rhodesia				
Falcon College, Essexvale, S. Rhodesia	1954	310	£300...........	D. E. Turner (1962)
Mauritius				
Royal College, Curepipe, Mauritius...	1800	620	...........D£60	H. B. Bullen (1960)

INDEPENDENT SCHOOLS IN 1962

At the end of 1962, there were 2,324 finally registered independent schools on the register in England and Wales. During the year 54 schools were provisionally registered, including 25 schools which had come into existence in 1962. A further 1,526 independent schools in England and Wales were recognized as efficient at the end of the year (1961, *1,508*). 31 additional schools were recognized as efficient during the year and recognition was withdrawn from 3.

Pupils at all independent schools in England and Wales numbered 494,959 (boys, 251,766; girls, 243,193). Boarding pupils numbered 142,058 (boys, 92,613; girls, 49,445). There were 31,044 full-time teachers including 18,524 women, and 13,189 part-time teachers. In independent schools recognized as efficient there were 13·1 pupils per teacher and in all other independent schools 15·2 pupils per teacher. Direct grant grammar schools had 21·2 lower school pupils per teacher and 17·0 upper school. All maintained schools had 23·9 pupils per teacher—primary, 28·5, with an average class of 32·3 pupils; secondary 19·7, with an average of 29·0.

Scotland.—At the end of 1962 there were 139 registered independent schools in Scotland, 5 being registered during the year and 6 removed on closing. 132 schools had been finally registered.

UNIVERSITY SCHOLARSHIPS

A total of 26,050 students received State scholarships or local education authority awards tenable at universities in 1962–63 compared with 24,796 in 1961–62. In the latter year the total value of these awards was £5,000,000 from the Exchequer and £40,000,000 from local authorities. In addition, 153 awards were made to technical state scholars under a scheme terminating in 1962.

In 1962–63, State scholarships (G.C.E., technical and mature) numbered 1,936, and supplemental State scholarships, 1539; 22,182 full value awards, intended to cover the full cost of tuition and maintenance, were made by local authorities, compared with 20,975 in 1961–62, and 73 lesser value awards. There were thus 25,730 undergraduate awards during the academic year, compared with 24,551 taken up in 1961–62. 320 State studentships (for advanced postgraduate study in art subjects) were awarded and taken up (1961–62, *245*).

Scotland.—19,404 awards tenable at universities (9,843), central institutions (4,425), colleges of education (4,234) and other institutions (902), were current during the academic year 1961–62. 9,400 new awards of students' allowances were taken up. Cost to public funds, 1961–62, £4,453,018.

PRINCIPAL GIRLS' SCHOOLS

NOTES:—(*a*) "Annual Fees" represent the average amount payable annually, *exclusive* of fees for optional subjects. (*b*) "Headmistress." In certain Schools other titles prevail, *e.g.*, St. Paul's, "High Mistress."

School	F'ded.	No. of Girls	Annual Fees See note (*a*) D=Day Girls	Headmistress See note (*b*)
Abbey Sch., Malvern Wells	1880	265	£405	J. F. Jones (1963)
Abbey Sch., Reading	1887	550	D£87	S. M. Hardcastle (1960)
Abbots Hill, Hemel Hempstead	1912	65	£480	M. E. P. Yeo (1944)
The Alice Ottley Sch., Worcester	1883	620	£378..D£117-170	E. D. Millest (1964)
Ashford, Middlesex, Welsh Girls School	1718	210	£315 .....D£163	J. D. Alderson (1956)
Ashford Sch. for Girls, Kent	1910	674	£273-312D£81-150	M. Nightingale (1955)
Badminton Sch., Bristol	1858	339	£414......D£207	B. M. Sanderson (1947)
Bath, Royal Sch. for Daughters of Officers of the Army	1864	263	£165-384..D£150	M. K. Goss (1950)
Bedford High Sch.	1882	620	£366......D£156	M. G. Watkins (1949)
Bedford, Dame Alice Harpur School	1882	838	£249.......D£60	H. Lawson Brown (1955)
Benenden, Kent	1924	310	£525	E. B. Clarke (1954)
Berkhamsted, Herts	1888	480	£336......D£150	B. W. Russell (1950)
Beverley High Sch., East Yorks	1908	423	D*nil*	Mrs. R. Noble (1960)
Bilston Girls' High, Staffs	1919	360	D*nil*	H. E. Mottershead (1961)
Bishop's Stortford, Herts. & Essex H.S.	1909	590	£230.......D*nil*	J. R. F. Wilks (1951)
Blackpool, Elmslie Girls' Sch.	1918	410	D£87-120	E. L. Oldham (1952)
Bolton, Lancs	1877	830	D£89	M. D. Higginson (1954)
Bradford Girls' Gr. Sch.	1875	745	D£84-95	M. M. Black (1955)
Brentwood, Ursuline Convent High (*R.C.*)	1900	620	£250.......D£88	Mother Joseph Howley (1947)
Bridlington High Sch.	1905	580	£200.......D*nil*	D. I. Matthews (1956)
Bruton School for Girls, Som	1900	408	£315..... D£129	E. L. Chappell (1950)
Burgess Hill, Sussex (P.N.E.U.)	1900	210	£330...D£90-150	M. A. Morris (1955)
Burton-on-Trent High Sch.	1872	540	D*nil*	E. Lloyd (1952)
Bury St. Edmunds, East Anglian Sch.	1935	300	£348......D£180	M. Tuck (1949)
Casterton, Carnforth	1823	206	£342......D£145	R. Willson (1963)
Chatham, Grammar Sch. for Girls	1907	580	D*nil*	H. Evans (1962)
Chelmsford County High Sch.	1907	624	D*nil*	P. Pattison (1961)
Cheltenham Ladies' College	1853	800	£410......D£222	J. A. Tredgold (*Princ.*) (1953)
Chester, Ursuline Convent Sch. (*R.C.*)	1850	450	D£216	Mother Mary Paul Flood, O.S.U. (1951)
Christ's Hospital, Hertford	1552	294	Various	D. R. West (1942)
Church Education Corporation (35 Denison House, Westminster, S.W.1):				
Bedgebury Park, Goudhurst, Kent	1920	134	£378	E. Bickersteth (1932)
Uplands, Sandecotes, Parkstone	1903	145	£353......D£202	K. A. Hewitt (1963)
Church Schools Company (29 Euston Road, N.W.1):				
Guildford High Sch.	1888	500	D£92-126	E. S. Bryce (1960)
Hull High Sch., Tranby Croft	1890	414	£164-234D£56-126	H. W. Thompson (1956)
Southampton (Atherley Sch.)	1926	350	D£63-142	U. V. Laidlaw (1950)
Sunderland Church High Sch.	1884	390	D£88-113	J. L. Wisbach (1957)
Surbiton High Sch.	1884	390	D£113-129	S. A. Kerr (1947)
York College	1908	285	D£63-142	H. C. Randall (1944)
Clevedon, St. Brandon's School	1831	295	£345......D£135	A. K. Forster (1950)
Clifton High School for Girls	1877	730	£351......D£150	S. L. McKillop (1962)
Cobham Hall, Kent	1962	108	£480.....D£255	D. B. Hancock (1961)
Colston's, Bristol	1891	650	D*nil*	A. M. S. Dunn (1953)
Cranborne Chase Sch., Tisbury, Wilts.	1946	160	£447	C. B. Galton (1946)
Croham Hurst, South Croydon, Surrey	1899	420	D£63-168	Miss M. E. Ayre (1959)
Derby High Sch.	1892	350	D£60-159	D. M. Hatch (1957)
Dolgellau, Dr. Williams' School	1878	370	£275..... D£102	D. B. Lickes (1946)
Doncaster, High School for Girls	1905	575	D*nil*	H. V. Mellor (1949)
Downe Hse., Cold Ash, Newbury, Berks.	1907	270	£420	Mrs. T. Bourdillon (1963)
Durham High Sch.	1884	327	D£135	C. I. Salter (1958)
Edgbaston High, Birmingham	1876	460	D£78-150	E. A. Hopkins (1954)
Edgbaston C. of E. Coll.	1886	498	£258-277D£76-142	M. Going (1947)
Edgehill, Bideford, N. Devon	1884	536	£301.......D£99	A. M. Shaw (1955)
Ely High School	1905	380	D*nil*	B. Tilly, Ph.D. (1936)
Eothen, Caterham, Surrey	1892	320	D£170	J. Harrison (1955)
Exeter, Maynard's Girls' Sch	1658	500	D£88	Miss J. M. Bradley (1963)
Farnborough Hill, Hants.	1889	350	£360..... D£150	Mother R. Alexander (1958)
Farringtons, Chislehurst, Kent	1911	254	£369..... D£228	F. E. Wilson (1957)
Faversham, Wm. Gibbs School	1883	311	D*nil*	B. Saunders (1957)
Felixstowe College, Suffolk	1929	300	£400	R. M. Jones (1943)

School	F'ded.	No. of Girls	Annual Fees See note (a) D=Day Girls	Headmistress See note (b)
Frinton-on-Sea, Essex, Hawthorns Sch.	1921	120	£232-280 D£60-90	E. M. Regge (1921)
Girls' Public Day School Trust (Broadway Court, Westminster, S.W.1.):				
Bath High	1875	525	£243-261D£90-99	G. S. Blackburn (1942)
Birkenhead High	1901	641	D£90-99	I. Hindmarsh (1964)
Blackheath High	1880	522	D£93-102	F. M. Abraham (1961)
Brighton and Hove High	1876	563	£261-279D£90-99	J. Ashcroft (1950)
Bromley High	1883	600	D£93-102	M. E. Hardwick (1963)
Croydon High	1874	900	D£93-102	E. B. J. Cameron (1960)
Ipswich High	1878	525	D£90-99	B. Strong (1960)
Liverpool (Belvedere)	1880	510	D£90-99	M. C. L. Ward (1961)
Newcastle (Central) High	1895	650	D £90-99	C. Russell (1962)
Norwich High	1875	610	D£90-99	D. F. Bartholomew (1954)
Nottingham High	1875	870	D£90-99	F. M. Mitford (1950)
Notting Hill and Ealing High	1873	610	D£93-102	J. M. S. Hendry (1960)
Oxford High	1875	522	£249-267D£90-99	M. E. A. Hancock (1959)
Portsmouth High	1882	550	D£90-99	E. M. Thorn (1941)
Putney High	1893	650	D£93-102	R. Smith (1963)
Sheffield High	1878	540	D£90-99	M. C. Lutz (1959)
Shrewsbury High	1885	475	D£90-99	M. Crane (1963)
South Hampstead High	1876	570	D£93-102	P. R. Bodington (1954)
Streatham Hill and Clapham High	1887	440	D£93-102	I. A. Wulff (1963)
Sutton High	1884	850	D£93-102	J. R. Glover (1959)
Sydenham High	1887	530	D£93-102	M. D. Yardley (1942)
Wimbledon High	1880	650	D£93-102	A. A. Piper (1962)
Godolphin, Salisbury	1726	307	£399......D£195	G. Engledow (1959)
Gravesend County Grammar School	1914	600	Dnil	M. H. White (1950)
Gt. Crosby, Lancs., Seafield Gr. School, Sacred Heart of Mary (R.C.)	1908	590	D£60	Mother Françoise (1959)
Greenacre, Banstead, Surrey	1933	275	£235 . . D£78-113	G. W. Steele (1962)
Harrogate College, Harrogate	1893	380	£435	M. W. S. Todd (1952)
Haslemere, Royal Naval School	1840	240	£354-369D£165-180	Mrs. C. McClenaghan (1960)
Hawnes, Haynes Park, Beds	1929	230	£347	M. E. Twist (1961)
Headington School, Oxford	1915	282	£378 408D£69-204	P. A. Dunn (1959)
Hollington Park, St. Leonards, Sussex	1860	200	£394	A. M. Amos (1960)
Howells', Denbigh	1859	430	£366......D£135	M. K. Stone, O.B.E. (1950)
Howells', Llandaff	1860	540	£233.......D£80	M. Ll. Lewis (1941)
Hulme Gr. Sch., Oldham	1895	430	D£77	K. M. L. Jewsbury (1947)
Hunmanby Hall, Yks.	1928	310	£372	H. M. Darby (1955)
Ilford, Ursuline High Sch. (R.C.)	1903	400	D£87	Mother E. Ryan, O.S.U. (1952)
Ipswich, Northgate Gr.	1906	600	Dnil	E. J. Atkinson (1957)
Keighley Girls' Grammar Sch.	1872	700	Dnil	J. A. Evans (1942)
King Edward VI High Sch., B'ham	1883	500	D£74	D. S. Lloyd-Williams (1953)
King's High Sch., Warwick	1879	585	D£69	F. W. Hare (1948)
Lady Eleanor Holles, Hampton, Middx.	1711	630	£331......D£164	R. G. Scott (1949)
Leamington, Kingsley Sch.	1884	388	£327-348 D£108-165	N. K. Jones (1961)
Leeds, Girls' High	1876	451	D£87	M. G. Sykes (1949)
Lewes, County Grammar School	1913	553	Dnil	M. L. Medcalf (1962)
Lillesden School, Hawkhurst, Kent	1901	200	£444	Mrs. S. M. White (1962)
Lincoln, Christ's Hosp. Girls' High Sch.	1893	560	£187.......Dnil	I. V. Cleave (1943)
Liverpool Girls' College, Liverpool	1856	300	Dnil	B. R. Palmer (1945)
Liverpool, Huyton College	1893	458	£396......D£201	E. C. Fenton (1958)
Liverpool (Everton Valley), Notre Dame Collegiate (R.C.)	1902	500	D£63	Sister Francis, S.N.D. (1938)
Liverpool (Mt. Pleasant), Notre Dame High Sch. (R.C.)	1851	400	Dnil	M. M. Taylor (1963)
*London**:				
Henrietta Barnett, Hampstead, N.W.11	1911	540	Dnil	M. M. N. McLaughlan (1958)
C. E. Brooke Sch., Camberwell, S.E.5	1898	300	Dnil	J. L. Hay (1956)
Burlington, Wood Lane, W.12	1699	550	Dnil	M. E. Field (1949)
Camden, Sandall Road, N.W.5	1871	700	Dnil	D. Burchell (1947)
Channing School, Highgate, N.6	1885	360	£411....D£90-201	M. G. Lloyd Thomas (1952)
City of London, E.C.4	1894	400	D£129	G. M. Colton (1949)
Godolphin and Latymer, W.6	1905	660	Dnil	M. C. Gray (1963)
Haberdashers' Aske's, Acton, W.3	1690	720	D£81-96	Miss E. G. Harold (1944)
Haberdashers' Aske's, Hatcham, S.E.1	1896	560	Dnil	J. A. Kirby (1958)
Francis Holland, Clarence Gate, N.W.	1878	250	D£102-162	J. M. Eagles (1959)
Francis Holland, Graham Terr., S.W.1	1881	265	D£107-170	M. W. Bowden (1945)
James Allen's Girls', Dulwich, S.E.	1741	500	D£141	J. I. Leiper (1957)

* See also: Girls' Public Day School Trust, and Church Schools Company.

School	F'ded.	No. of Girls	Annual Fees See note (*a*) D=Day Girls	Headmistress See note (*b*)
London—continued*				
Lady Margaret, Parsons Green, S.W.6	1917	420	............D*nil*	F. E. Marshall (1947)
Mary Datchelor, Camberwell Green, S.E.5	1877	650	............D*nil*	R. N. Pearse, O.B.E. (1951)
North London Collegiate, Canons, Edgware	1850	860	...........D£84	Dame Kitty Anderson, D.B.E., Ph.D. (1944)
Prendergast Grammar, Catford, S.E.6	1890	600	............D*nil*	C. M. Johnson (1957)
Queen's College, Harley Street, W.1.	1848	230	..........D£180	A. M. Kynaston (*Principal*) (1942)
St. Angela's, Ursuline Convent Sch., Forest Gate, E.7 (*R.C.*)	1862	820	............D*nil*	[O.S.U. (1962) Mother J. Mary Campbell,
St. Paul's Girls' Sch., Brook Green, W.	1904	459	...........D£174	Mrs. A. Munro (*High Mistress*) [(1963)
St. Saviour's and St. Olave's Gr., New Kent Road, S.E.1	1903	550	............D*nil*	E. J. M. Wilson (1959)
Loughborough High Sch., Leicestershire	1850	662	£217.......D£57	P. J. Hadley (1963)
Loughton High School	1906	600	............D*nil*	M. E. Heald (1945)
Lowther College, nr. Rhyl	1900	271	£450...........	G. E. Kelly (1963)
Luckley-Oakfield, Wokingham, Berks.	1894	156	£330 .....D£168	E. A. S. Randle (1949)
Malvern Girls' College	1893	530	£435......D£204	M. M. Burgess (1954)
Manchester High Sch. for Girls	1874	700	.... D£80	K. L. Cottrell (1959)
Manchester, Withington Girls' Sch.	1890	520	...........D£69	M. Hulme (1961)
Merchant Taylors', Gt. Crosby	1888	415	.... D£95	M. E. Walsh (1963)
Monmouth Sch. for Girls	1894	464	£218.......D£59	A. Page (1960)
Newcastle upon Tyne Church High Sch.	1885	600	..........D£114	Mrs. M. R. Pybus (1945)
Northampton High Sch.	1878	740	...........D£80	R. M. Marsden (1937)
North Foreland Lodge, Sherfield-on-Loddon, Hants.	1909	98	£441...........	F. M. Gammell (1937)
Northwood Coll., Northwood, Middx.	1878	385	£324-354D£93-177	D. J. Worger (1938)
Norwich, Blyth	1889	830	............D*nil*	E. P. Ayles (1954)
Oakdene, Beaconsfield	1911	280	£312......D£126	A. J. Havard (1959)
Orme Girls' Sch., Newcastle under Lyme	1876	600	............D*nil*	S. M. Smith (1952)
Overstone Sch., Northampton	1929	215	£417.....D£222	Mrs. E. J. Taylor (1963)
Oxford, Milham Ford Sch.	1906	560	...........D*nil*	M. R. Price (1950)
Palmer's Girls' School, Grays, Essex	1706	545	............D*nil*	K. W. H. Jackson (1962)
Pate's Gr. Sch., Cheltenham	1905	782	............D*nil*	M. E. Lambrick (1962)
Penrhos, Colwyn Bay	1880	320	£324-450........	C. Smith (1938)
Penzance, W. Cornwall Sch.	1884	239	£306......D£147	J. Marshall (1960)
Perse Sch. for Girls, Cambridge	1881	560	....	M. A. Scott (1947)
Plymouth, Notre Dame High (*R.C.*)	1860	390	...........D£72	Sister Mary Xavier (1960)
Polam Hall, Darlington	1880	243	£345......D£156	Mrs. K. M. Davies (1963)
Preston, Winckley Sq. Convent (*R.C.*)	1875	850	...........D£63	Mother Mary Edwina (1952)
Princess Helena Coll., Temple Dinsley, Hitchin, Herts.	1820	130	£360...........	C. J. Stratford (1960)
Queen Anne's, Caversham	1894	300	£408...........	M. J. Challis (1958)
Queen Ethelburga's, Harrogate	1912	212	£408...........	E. Kerr (1950)
Queen Margaret's, Escrick Park, York	1901	245	£372...........	B. D. Snape (1960)
Queen Mary, Lytham	1930	775	.... Various	J. L. Harley (1952)
Queen's Sch., Chester	1878	546	............D£78	E. N. MacLean (1947)
Queenswood, Hatfield, Herts	1894	400	£459...........	E. M. Essame (1943)
Redland High Sch., Bristol	1882	566	...........D£78	S. Peters (1945)
Red Maids', Bristol	1634	258	£222.......D£88	D. D. Dakin (1961)
Rochester Gr. School, Kent	1888	520	...........D*nil*	N. C. Day (1962)
Roedean, Brighton	1885	400	£525...........	Mrs. J. Fort (1961)
Rosemead, Littlehampton	1919	200	£345...........	Mrs. N. Willitts (1960)
Royal Masonic Sch., Rickmansworth Pk.	1788	400	*Nil*...........	Mrs. U. J. Campbell (1959)
Runton Hill, W. Runton, Norfolk	1911	108	£360 ......D£242	M. L. Kilvert (1958)
St. Albans High School, Herts	1907	460	........D£96-165	M. H. Gent (1951)
St. Audries, West Quantoxhead, Nr. Taunton, Som.	1906	220	£384...........	C. A. M. Havergal (1947)
St. Catherine's, Bramley, Guildford	1885	273	£405...D£87-162	C. E. Stoner (1947)
St. Clare, Polwithen, Penzance	1889	184	£345......D£134	M. F. C. Harvey (1962)
St. Dominic's High Sch., Stoke-on-Trent (*R.C.*)	1857	820	...........D£62	Sister Mary Laurence (1957)
St. Elphin's, Darley Dale, Matlock	1844	347	£300......D£105	P. M. Robinson (1958)
St. Felix, Southwold, Suffolk	1897	332	£390..... D£135	M. Oakeley (1958)
St. Helen and St. Katharine, Abingdon	1903	337	£253..... D£83	Sister J. Benedict, C.S.M.V. (1962)
St. Helen's, Northwood	1899	556	£330-360D£96-180	G. A. Mackenzie (1947)
St. James's School, West Malvern	1896	206	£447...........	M. C. I. Southgate (1960)
St. Joseph's Coll., Bradford (*R.C.*)	1908	953	£134.......D£62	C. M. Shanahan (1956)
St. Margaret's, Bushey, Herts	1749	320	£375 .....D£204	E. F. Birney (1936)
St. Mary & St. Anne, Abbots Bromley	1874	496	£342 .....D£172	M. E. S. Roch (1953)

* See also: Girls' Public Day School Trust, and Church Schools Company.

School	F'ded.	No. of Girls	Annual Fees See note (*a*) D = Day Girls	Headmistress See note (*b*)
St. Mary Sch., Baldslow, St. Leonards ..	1913	200	£285......D£128	Sister B. Allen (1958)
St. Mary's, Calne, Wilts............	1873	204	£420......D£120	E. M. Gibbins (1946)
St. Mary's Convent Sch., Cambridge (*R.C.*)............	1908	436	£245......D£110	Sister M. Christopher (1949)
St. Mary's Hall, Brighton...........	1836	260	£341......D£171	D. Conrady (1950)
St. Mary's Sch., Gerrard's Cross, Bucks.	1872	264	£375 .D£138-165	W. J. Chalk (1942)
St. Mary's School, Wantage, Berks....	1873	200	£375...........	Sister Brigitta, C.S.M.V. (1958)
S. Michael's, Burton Park, Petworth, Sussex............	1844	235	£450...........	P. M. Lancaster (1962)
St. Monica's, Clacton-on-Sea.........	1936	225	£384......D£198	M. M. Parker (1960)
St. Stephen's College, Broadstairs	1867	150	£360......D£150	Sister Catherine (1960)
St. Swithun's, Winchester	1884	438	£339-412D£87-201	P. M. C. Evans (1953)
S. Winifred's, Llanfairfechan	1887	199	£323 ...... D£91	M. J. Taylor (1952)
Salford, Adelphi House (*R.C.*)........	1852	650	............D£57	A. M. Dempsey (1947)
Sheffield, Notre Dame High (*R.C.*)....	1855	700	............D£70	Sister Monica, S.N.D. (1958)
Sherborne Sch. for Girls, Dorset.......	1899	450	£450......D£225	D. Reader Harris (1950)
Shillingstone, Dorset, Croft House Sch.	1941	226	£375......D£171	Mrs. O. M. Torkington (1941)
Southend-on-Sea High Sch...........	1913	800	.... D*nil*	H. M. Cowell (1937)
Stamford High Sch., Lincs...........	1876	700	£265...... D£90	J. C. Lomax (1947)
Stockton-on-Tees, Queen Victoria High	1883	280	............D£65	E. K. Wallen (1959)
Stover Sch., Newton Abbot	1932	139	£384......D£171	L. C. J. Hill (1963)
Talbot Heath Sch., Bournemouth.....	1886	586	£257.......D£77	A. L. Macpherson, Ph.D. (1956)
Tormead, Cranley Road, Guildford...	1905	427	£315-333 .D£157	M. C. Shackleton (1959)
Truro High Sch..................	1880	508	£266-281D£91-106	S. M. Peatfield (1959)
Upper Chine, Shanklin, I.O.W........	1799	250	£345..... D£165	P. M. Gifford (1955)
Wadhurst, The College	1930	188	£357 .....D£186	M. E. Carter (1946)
Walsall, Qn. Mary's High Sch.........	1893	375	............D*nil*	E. B. Godwin (1964)
Walthamstow Hall, Sevenoaks, Kent...	1838	391	£266......D£101	E. A. Blackburn (1946)
Watford Gr. Sch., Herts.............	1704	815	............D*nil*	J. Tennet (1957)
Wentworth Milton Mount, Bournemouth............	1899	210	£375......D£180	N. A. E. Hibbert (1961)
Westcliff-on-Sea High Sch...........	1926	850	............D*nil*	J. K. Raeburn (1952)
Westonbirt, Tetbury, Glos...........	1928	303	£465...........	C. M. Scott-Smith (1955)
Westwood House, Peterborough......	1936	375	£294 .....D£130	Mrs. G. J. Bowis (1961)
Wheelwright Gr. Sch., Dewsbury.....	1888	400	............D*nil*	D. M. Levitt (1963)
Wigan Girls' High Sch., Lancs	1887	560	............D*nil*	G. Holland (1952)
Worthing Girls' High Sch., Sussex.....	1905	660	............D*nil*	A. M. Hedley (1960)
Wycombe Abbey, Bucks.............	1896	399	£501...........	P. A. Fisher (1962)
Wycombe High Sch., Bucks..........	1901	1020	............D*nil*	Mrs. B. M. Miller (1961)
Wyggeston Girls' Sch., Leicester......	1878	800	............D*nil*	M. E. Pedley (1948)
York, The Mount School............	1831	250	£402...........	J. Blake (1960)
Scotland				
Craigholme, Glasgow...............	1891	350	........D£66-88	G. M. MacLean (1962)
Esdaile, Edinburgh................	1863	140	£198 ......D£84	H. M. Ewan (1962)
Girls' School Company, Ltd. (142 St. Vincent St., Glasgow, C.2.):—				
Glasgow, Park Sch., 25 Lynedoch St.	1879	455	........D£60-102	J. Lightwood (1962)
Helensburgh, St. Bride's...........	1895	330	£300-315D£60-102	R. Drever Smith (1953)
Kilmacolm, St. Columba's..........	1897	425	£303-315D£62-110	K. C. MacArthur (1945)
George Watson's Ladies', Edinburgh..	1871	980	.... D£63-78	H. Fleming (1958)
High School, Glasgow..............	1878	520	............D£49	F. Barker (1947)
Hutcheson's Girls' Gr. Sch., Glasgow ..	1876	940	............D£63	I. G. McIver (1947)
James Gillespie's, Edinburgh.........	1803	1300	............D£30	M. D. Steel (1956)
Mary Erskine, Edinburgh............	1694	960	.........D£63-78	M. M. Jennings (1946)
Morrison's Academy, Crieff..........	1860	421	£295.......D£80	M. R. P. Muirie (1957)
St. Denis', Edinburgh..............	1858	370	£360......D£150	J. O. Ramsay (1950)
St. George's, Garscube Terr., Edinburgh	1888	447	£315-339D£84-150	Mrs. J. O. Lindsay, Ph.D. (1960)
St. Leonards, St. Andrews, Fife........	1877	390	£501......D£204	J. S. A. Macaulay (1950)
Isle of Man				
Buchan Sch., Castletown............	1875	187	£285.......D£99	Mrs. J. M. Watkin (1961)
Jersey				
Jersey College for Girls	1880	480	.... D£80	E. M. Farewell (1960)
Switzerland				
Chatelard Sch., Les Avants, Montreux .	192	210	£437-487........	J. M. Blacklock (1960)

PREPARATORY SCHOOLS

500 preparatory schools in England and Wales are members of the Incorporated Association of Preparatory Schools, 138 Church Street, W.8, recognition by the Ministry of Education as efficient being a condition of membership. The Association has a Joint Standing Committee with the Headmasters' Conference, and the Common Examination for entry to public schools is conducted by a committee of the Headmasters' Conference and I.A.P.S. *Secretary*, I.A.P.S., L. P. Dealtry.

READY RECKONER OR MARKETING TABLE

No.	¼d.		½d.		¾d.		1d.		2d.		3d.		4d.		5d.		6d.		7d.		8d.		9d.		10d.		11d.		No.
1	0	0¼	0	0½	0	0¾	0	1	0	2	0	3	0	4	0	5	0	6	0	7	0	8	0	9	0	10	0	11	1
2	0	0½	0	1	0	1½	0	2	0	4	0	6	0	8	0	10	1	0	1	2	1	4	1	6	1	8	1	10	2
3	0	0¾	0	1½	0	2¼	0	3	0	6	0	9	1	0	1	3	1	6	1	9	2	0	2	3	2	6	2	9	3
4	0	1	0	2	0	3	0	4	0	8	1	0	1	4	1	8	2	0	2	4	2	8	3	0	3	4	3	8	4
5	0	1¼	0	2½	0	3¾	0	5	0	10	1	3	1	8	2	1	2	6	2	11	3	4	3	9	4	2	4	7	5
6	0	1½	0	3	0	4½	0	6	1	0	1	6	2	0	2	6	3	0	3	6	4	0	4	6	5	0	5	6	6
7	0	1¾	0	3½	0	5¼	0	7	1	2	1	9	2	4	2	11	3	6	4	1	4	8	5	3	5	10	6	5	7
8	0	2	0	4	0	6	0	8	1	4	2	0	2	8	3	4	4	0	4	8	5	4	6	0	6	8	7	4	8
9	0	2¼	0	4½	0	6¾	0	9	1	6	2	3	3	0	3	9	4	6	5	3	6	0	6	9	7	6	8	3	9
10	0	2½	0	5	0	7½	0	10	1	8	2	6	3	4	4	2	5	0	5	10	6	8	7	6	8	4	9	2	10
11	0	2¾	0	5½	0	8¼	0	11	1	10	2	9	3	8	4	7	5	6	6	5	7	4	8	3	9	2	10	1	11
12	0	3	0	6	0	9	1	0	2	0	3	0	4	0	5	0	6	0	7	0	8	0	9	0	10	0	11	0	12
13	0	3¼	0	6½	0	9¾	1	1	2	2	3	3	4	4	5	5	6	6	7	7	8	8	9	9	10	10	11	11	13
14	0	3½	0	7	0	10½	1	2	2	4	3	6	4	8	5	10	7	0	8	2	9	4	10	6	11	8	12	10	14
15	0	3¾	0	7½	0	11¼	1	3	2	6	3	9	5	0	6	3	7	6	8	9	10	0	11	3	12	6	13	9	15
16	0	4	0	8	1	0	1	4	2	8	4	0	5	4	6	8	8	0	9	4	10	8	12	0	13	4	14	8	16
17	0	4¼	0	8½	1	0¾	1	5	2	10	4	3	5	8	7	1	8	6	9	11	11	4	12	9	14	2	15	7	17
18	0	4½	0	9	1	1½	1	6	3	0	4	6	6	0	7	6	9	0	10	6	12	0	13	6	15	0	16	6	18
19	0	4¾	0	9½	1	2¼	1	7	3	2	4	9	6	4	7	11	9	6	11	1	12	8	14	3	15	10	17	5	19
20	0	5	0	10	1	3	1	8	3	4	5	0	6	8	8	4	10	0	11	8	13	4	15	0	16	8	18	4	20
21	0	5¼	0	10½	1	3¾	1	9	3	6	5	3	7	0	8	9	10	6	12	3	14	0	15	9	17	6	19	3	21
22	0	5½	0	11	1	4½	1	10	3	8	5	6	7	4	9	2	11	0	12	10	14	8	16	6	18	4	20	2	22
23	0	5¾	0	11½	1	5¼	1	11	3	10	5	9	7	8	9	7	11	6	13	5	15	4	17	3	19	2	21	1	23
24	0	6	1	0	1	6	2	0	4	0	6	0	8	0	10	0	12	0	14	0	16	0	18	0	20	0	22	0	24
25	0	6¼	1	0½	1	6¾	2	1	4	2	6	3	8	4	10	5	12	6	14	7	16	8	18	9	20	10	22	11	25
26	0	6½	1	1	1	7½	2	2	4	4	6	6	8	8	10	10	13	0	15	2	17	4	19	6	21	8	23	10	26
27	0	6¾	1	1½	1	8¼	2	3	4	6	6	9	9	0	11	3	13	6	15	9	18	0	20	3	22	6	24	9	27
28	0	7	1	2	1	9	2	4	4	8	7	0	9	4	11	8	14	0	16	4	18	8	21	0	23	4	25	8	28
29	0	7¼	1	2½	1	9¾	2	5	4	10	7	3	9	8	12	1	14	6	16	11	19	4	21	9	24	2	26	7	29
30	0	7½	1	3	1	10½	2	6	5	0	7	6	10	0	12	6	15	0	17	6	20	0	22	6	25	0	27	6	30
31	0	7¾	1	3½	1	11¼	2	7	5	2	7	9	10	4	12	11	15	6	18	1	20	8	23	3	25	10	28	5	31
32	0	8	1	4	2	0	2	8	5	4	8	0	10	8	13	4	16	0	18	8	21	4	24	0	26	8	29	4	32
33	0	8¼	1	4½	2	0¾	2	9	5	6	8	3	11	0	13	9	16	6	19	3	22	0	24	9	27	6	30	3	33
34	0	8½	1	5	2	1½	2	10	5	8	8	6	11	4	14	2	17	0	19	10	22	8	25	6	28	4	31	2	34
35	0	8¾	1	5½	2	2¼	2	11	5	10	8	9	11	8	14	7	17	6	20	5	23	4	26	3	29	2	32	1	35
36	0	9	1	6	2	3	3	0	6	0	9	0	12	0	15	0	18	0	21	0	24	0	27	0	30	0	33	0	36
37	0	9¼	1	6½	2	3¾	3	1	6	2	9	3	12	4	15	5	18	6	21	7	24	8	27	9	30	10	33	11	37
38	0	9½	1	7	2	4½	3	2	6	4	9	6	12	8	15	10	19	0	22	2	25	4	28	6	31	8	34	10	38
39	0	9¾	1	7½	2	5¼	3	3	6	6	9	9	13	0	16	3	19	6	22	9	26	0	29	3	32	6	35	9	39
40	0	10	1	8	2	6	3	4	6	8	10	0	13	4	16	8	20	0	23	4	26	8	30	0	33	4	36	8	40
41	0	10¼	1	8½	2	6¾	3	5	6	10	10	3	13	8	17	1	20	6	23	11	27	4	30	9	34	2	37	7	41
42	0	10½	1	9	2	7½	3	6	7	0	10	6	14	0	17	6	21	0	24	6	28	0	31	6	35	0	38	6	42
43	0	10¾	1	9½	2	8¼	3	7	7	2	10	9	14	4	17	11	21	6	25	1	28	8	32	3	35	10	39	5	43
44	0	11	1	10	2	9	3	8	7	4	11	0	14	8	18	4	22	0	25	8	29	4	33	0	36	8	40	4	44
45	0	11¼	1	10½	2	9¾	3	9	7	6	11	3	15	0	18	9	22	6	26	3	30	0	33	9	37	6	41	3	45
46	0	11½	1	11	2	10½	3	10	7	8	11	6	15	4	19	2	23	0	26	10	30	8	34	6	38	4	42	2	46
47	0	11¾	1	11½	2	11¼	3	11	7	10	11	9	15	8	19	7	23	6	27	5	31	4	35	3	39	2	43	1	47
48	1	0	2	0	3	0	4	0	8	0	12	0	16	0	20	0	24	0	28	0	32	0	36	0	40	0	44	0	48
49	1	0¼	2	0½	3	0¾	4	1	8	2	12	3	16	4	20	5	24	6	28	7	32	8	36	9	40	10	44	11	49
50	1	0½	2	1	3	1½	4	2	8	4	12	6	16	8	20	10	25	0	29	2	33	4	37	6	41	8	45	10	50
51	1	0¾	2	1½	3	2¼	4	3	8	6	12	9	17	0	21	3	25	6	29	9	34	0	38	3	42	6	46	9	51
52	1	1	2	2	3	3	4	4	8	8	13	0	17	4	21	8	26	0	30	4	34	8	39	0	43	4	47	8	52
53	1	1¼	2	2½	3	3¾	4	5	8	10	13	3	17	8	22	1	26	6	30	11	35	4	39	9	44	2	48	7	53
54	1	1½	2	3	3	4½	4	6	9	0	13	6	18	0	22	6	27	0	31	6	36	0	40	6	45	0	49	6	54
56	1	2	2	4	3	6	4	8	9	4	14	0	18	8	23	4	28	0	32	8	37	4	42	0	46	8	51	4	56
58	1	2½	2	5	3	7½	4	10	9	8	14	6	19	4	24	2	29	0	33	10	38	8	43	6	48	4	53	2	58
60	1	3	2	6	3	9	5	0	10	0	15	0	20	0	25	0	30	0	35	0	40	0	45	0	50	0	55	0	60
63	1	3¾	2	7½	3	11¼	5	3	10	6	15	9	21	0	26	3	31	6	36	9	42	0	47	3	52	6	57	9	63
66	1	4½	2	9	4	1½	5	6	11	0	16	6	22	0	27	6	33	0	38	6	44	0	49	6	55	0	60	6	66
69	1	5¼	2	10½	4	3¾	5	9	11	6	17	3	23	0	28	9	34	6	40	3	46	0	51	9	57	6	63	3	69
70	1	5½	2	11	4	4½	5	10	11	8	17	6	23	4	29	2	35	0	40	10	46	8	52	6	58	4	64	2	70
72	1	6	3	0	4	6	6	0	12	0	18	0	24	0	30	0	36	0	42	0	48	0	54	0	60	0	66	0	72
78	1	7½	3	3	4	10½	6	6	13	0	19	6	26	0	32	6	39	0	45	6	52	0	58	6	65	0	71	6	78
80	1	8	3	4	5	0	6	8	13	4	20	0	26	8	33	4	40	0	46	8	53	4	60	0	66	8	73	4	80
84	1	9	3	6	5	3	7	0	14	0	21	0	28	0	35	0	42	0	49	0	56	0	63	0	70	0	77	0	84
90	1	10½	3	9	5	7½	7	6	15	0	22	6	30	0	37	6	45	0	52	6	60	0	67	6	75	0	82	6	90
100	2	1	4	2	6	3	8	4	16	8	25	0	33	4	41	8	50	0	58	4	66	8	75	0	83	4	91	8	100

EVENTS OF THE YEAR, OCT. 1, 1962—SEPT. 30, 1963

THE ROYAL HOUSE

(**1962**). **Oct. 7.** The Duke of Kent, accompanied by the Duchess, arrived at Kampala to represent the Queen at Uganda independence celebrations. **12.** Princess Alexandra attended centenary celebrations of Clifton College. **15.** The Queen and the Duke of Edinburgh, Queen Elizabeth the Queen Mother and the Duke and Duchess of Gloucester arrived at Holyroodhouse. The Queen appointed Lord Home a Knight of the Thistle and invested him with insignia of Order. **16.** The King of Norway began State visit to Scotland. The Duke of Gloucester welcomed him on Norwegian royal yacht *Norge* at Leith, and they travelled to Princes Street station, where they were met by the Queen, the Duke of Edinburgh and other members of the Royal Family and representatives of the Government. The Queen, the King of Norway and the Duke of Edinburgh then drove in procession down the Royal Mile to Holyroodhouse. Later, the Duke of Edinburgh, as Chancellor of Edinburgh University, conferred an honorary degree on King Olav in the McEwan Hall, and in the evening the Queen and the Duke entertained their royal visitor at a State banquet. **17.** King Olav received freedom of City of Edinburgh in the Usher Hall; in afternoon he visited Queensferry and sailed past ships of Royal Navy, anchored in Firth of Forth, and in evening, with the Queen, the Duke of Edinburgh and other members of the Royal Family, he attended gala performance of *Rob Roy* in Lyceum Theatre. **18.** King Olav and the Earl of Home were installed at St. Giles as Knights of the Thistle; in afternoon the King visited Glasgow, and in the evening gave banquet in honour of the Queen and the Duke of Edinburgh on board the *Norge* at Leith. **19.** King Olav sailed for Norway. The Duke and Duchess of Kent returned to London Airport from East Africa. **22.** The Queen returned to Buckingham Palace. The Duke of Edinburgh visited Manchester and later flew to London. **23.** Princess Margaret visited Redditch and Malvern. **26.** The Queen and the Duke of Edinburgh travelled to Monmouthshire, visiting Newport and Llanwern, where Her Majesty opened the Spencer steel works. **29.** The Duchess of Kent underwent minor operation in University College Hospital. **30.** The Queen opened new session of Parliament.

Nov. 2. The Queen and the Duke of Edinburgh visited Luton, and Haileybury and Imperial Service College. Queen Elizabeth the Queen Mother opened Fairfield House, new arts centre at Croydon, and attended inaugural concert there. **6.** The Queen, who was accompanied by the Duke of Edinburgh, opened new Commonwealth Institute building in Kensington. **7.** The Queen and the Duke of Edinburgh visited Royal College of Surgeons, where Her Majesty declared open the new buildings. **11.** The Queen led Two Minutes' Silence at Cenotaph. **12.** The Duke left London Airport for U.S.A. **14.** The Duke spoke at banquet in San Francisco for delegates to world conference of English-Speaking Unions. **20.** His Royal Highness arrived at Canberra, and was later admitted as first royal fellow of Australian Academy of Science. **22.** The Queen conferred Order of Merit on Sir Basil Spence and Sir Geoffrey de Havilland. The Duke of Edinburgh opened Commonwealth Games at Perth, Western Australia. **29.** The engagement of Princess Alexandra of Kent to the Hon. Angus Ogilvy, son of the Earl of Airlie, was announced.

Dec. 5. The Duchess of Kent, with the Earl of St. Andrews, left by air to join the Duke in Hong Kong, where he was stationed. **8.** The Duke of Edinburgh arrived back at London Airport. **10.** The Queen and the Duke of Edinburgh attended *première* of film *Lawrence of Arabia*. **14.** The Queen opened new Langton river entrance at Liverpool Docks. **22.** Her Majesty, with other members of the Royal Family, arrived at Sandringham for Christmas. **25.** Her Majesty's Christmas message, which had been recorded previously at Buckingham Palace, was televised and broadcast throughout the Commonwealth.

(**1963**). **Jan. 1.** New Year Honours List included Earldom for Viscount Alexander of Hillsborough, 2 baronies, one life barony, and Companionship of Honour for Mr. Holyoake, Prime Minister of New Zealand. **10.** Fire did considerable damage to roof of home of Princess Marina, Duchess of Kent, in Kensington Palace. **26.** The Queen returned to Buckingham Palace from Sandringham. **31.** The Queen and the Duke of Edinburgh left London Airport for Fiji on first stage of their Australasian tour; owing to snowstorms they made unscheduled landing at Nisku airport, near Edmonton.

Feb. 1. After further delays by weather had caused stop for night at Vancouver, the Queen and the Duke arrived at Honolulu. **3.** The Queen and the Duke spent five hours in Suva, Fiji, before sailing in *Britannia* for New Zealand. **4.** The Princess Royal opened International Gifts Fair at Blackpool. **6.** The Queen and the Duke of Edinburgh landed at Waitangi, in the Bay of Islands, New Zealand, where they were greeted by the Maori and European population on Waitangi Day, anniversary of signing of treaty of 1840, by which Maori chiefs acknowledged submission to Queen Victoria. **7.** The Queen and the Duke attended a regatta at Auckland, and in evening, from stage of St. James's Theatre, Her Majesty inaugurated the Queen Elizabeth II Arts Council of New Zealand. It was announced from Buckingham Palace that proposed visit of Princess Margaret and the Earl of Snowdon to Paris on March 9 had been cancelled. **11.** The Queen and the Duke of Edinburgh landed at Wellington, where on following day Her Majesty opened special session of New Zealand Parliament. **13.** The Queen and the Duke arrived in South Island, where the Duke visited the Outward Bound School at Anakiwa. **14.** Queen Elizabeth the Queen Mother opened new extensions at Royal Northern Hospital, Islington. **16.** The Queen and the Duke arrived at Christchurch, whence they left for Australia on Feb. 18, and after 24-hour stay in Canberra, flew to Adelaide on following day. **23.** *Britannia*, with the Queen and the Duke on board, berthed in River Yarra at Melbourne. **25.** The Queen opened Royal Children's Hospital at Parkville. Later she and the Duke sailed for Hobart, where they arrived on Feb. 27, and in evening, from *Britannia*, watched firework display from new Tasman Bridge. **26.** Queen Elizabeth the Queen Mother opened Commonwealth Hall, Cartwright Gardens, new Hall of Residence of London University. **28.** The Queen and the Duke of Edinburgh attended Hobart's 125th royal regatta.

March 1. The Queen and the Duke arrived in *Britannia* at Sydney. **4.** Her Majesty opened new Medical School at University of New South Wales and later sailed with the Duke for Brisbane, where they arrived on March 6 for 2-day visit to Queensland. **5.** Princess Alexandra opened new Out-Patients' Department at Kingston-upon-Thames Hospital. **8.** The Queen and the Duke of Edinburgh flew to Cooma airport, and drove to Cabramurra, in the Snowy Mountains, the highest town in Australia, spending week-end in small cottage near Island Bend. Queen Elizabeth the Queen Mother attended 150th anniversary concert of Royal Philharmonic Society in Festival Hall. Princess Margaret and Lord Snowdon moved into their new home in Kensington Palace. **11.** The Queen and the Duke of Edinburgh returned to Canberra, where on following day they attended ceremonies marking jubilee of Canberra's foundation. Mr. Menzies, on whom it was announced that the Queen was conferring Order of Thistle, said that to commemorate jubilee, Australian Government was establishing 10 post-graduate fellowships in physical and biological science, to be called Queen Elizabeth II Fellowships. **13.** Her Majesty opened new R. G. Menzies Library at Australian National University. **14.** The Queen and the Duke flew to Alice Springs, and on following day visited a cattle station at Hamilton Downs. **15.** The Duke and Duchess of Gloucester left London Airport for Jordan and Cyprus. **17.** The Queen and the Duke of Edinburgh flew from Darwin to Kununurra to see Ord River irrigation project. **20.** The Queen and the Duke landed at Yampi Sound, Western Australia, where they visited the iron-mining community. **21.** *Britannia* sailed to Roebuck Bay, and the Queen and the Duke saw pearls and cultured pearls gathered by divers at Broome. Princess Margaret and Lord Snowdon attended ceremony in Jerusalem Chamber, Westminster Abbey, at which Church of St. John, Smith Square, was handed over to the Friends of St. John's to be restored as educational, artistic and religious centre. **24.** The Queen opened new civic centre at Geraldton. **25.** The Queen and the Duke arrived at Perth. **26.** From her study on board *Britannia*, the Queen broadcast farewell message to people of Australia. Princess Margaret, as Colonel-in-Chief of 15th/19th King's Royal Hussars, began 2-day visit to the regiment in Münster. **27.** The Queen and the Duke of Edinburgh left Sydney by air on their return journey. Princess Margaret and Lord Snowdon began holiday at Davos. **28.** The Queen and the Duke of Edinburgh arrived back at London Airport after their Australasian tour. **29.** The Princess Royal presented new Colours to the Green Howards at Richmond Castle, Yorkshire.

April 3. The Queen and the Duke of Edinburgh were entertained to luncheon at Guildhall by the Lord Mayor and City Corporation on return from their tour. **12.** The Queen, accompanied by the Duke of Edinburgh, visited Chelmsford, where Her Majesty distributed the Royal Maundy in the Cathedral. **16.** The Duke of Edinburgh and Princess Anne left for short private holiday in Germany. **24.** In Westminster Abbey, in the presence of the Queen and many members of the Royal Family, Princess Alexandra was married by the Archbishop of Canterbury to the Hon. Angus Ogilvy. The bride and bridegroom later left by air for first part of their honeymoon at Birkhall. **29.** The Queen and the Duke of Edinburgh visited the Royal Agricultural College at Cirencester.

May 1. The Duke of Edinburgh began 2-day visit to Scotland. **3.** It was announced that the Queen had approved appointment of Mr. Lester Pearson, who had been visiting England, as Privy Councillor. **8.** Queen Elizabeth the Queen Mother left in *Britannia* for visit to Channel Islands. **9.** The Queen, who was accompanied by the Duke of Edinburgh, opened new New Zealand House. **10.** The Queen and the Duke of Edinburgh visited Monmouthshire and Brecon. **14.** King Baudouin of the Belgians and Queen Fabiola arrived for their State visit, being met at Gatwick Airport by Princess Margaret and Lord Snowdon. On reaching Victoria, they were met by the Queen and the Duke of Edinburgh, with whom they drove to Buckingham Palace. The Queen conferred the Order of the Garter on King Baudouin, who gave the Queen and the Duke of Edinburgh the Grand Cordon of the Order of Leopold. M. Spaak was made an honorary Companion of Honour. During afternoon, the royal visitors laid wreath on Tomb of Unknown Warrior in Westminster Abbey and were received by Queen Elizabeth the Queen Mother at Clarence House. In evening, they were entertained by the Queen and the Duke of Edinburgh at State banquet at Buckingham Palace. **15.** The King and Queen of the Belgians went from Westminster to the Tower by barge, and were entertained to luncheon in Guildhall by the Lord Mayor and Corporation. In the evening, with the Queen, the Duke of Edinburgh, and many other members of the Royal Family, they attended gala ballet performance at Covent Garden. **16.** King Baudouin visited Royal Aircraft Establishment at Farnborough and Queen Fabiola went to the National Gallery; in evening they entertained the Queen, the Duke of Edinburgh and other members of the Royal Family at Belgian Embassy. **17.** The King and Queen of the Belgians left Buckingham Palace upon conclusion of their visit. **24.** The Queen and the Duke of Edinburgh visited Birmingham. **25.** The Queen and the Duke watched F.A. Cup Final at Wembley. **29.** The Queen conferred Order of Merit on Sir Owen Dixon, Chief Justice of Australia. Her Majesty, accompanied by the Duke of Edinburgh, Queen Elizabeth the Queen Mother and the Princess Royal, watched the Derby at Epsom.

June 6. The Queen, who was accompanied by the Duke of Edinburgh, presented standards to the Household Cavalry on Horse Guards Parade. Princess Margaret and Lord Snowdon left for visit to Northern Ireland. **8.** On the Queen's official birthday, the Queen's Colour of the 2nd Battalion Grenadier Guards was trooped on Horse Guards Parade in the presence of Her Majesty. The Duke of Edinburgh rode beside the Queen, and the ceremony was watched by Queen Elizabeth the Queen Mother and Princess Anne. Birthday Honours list included life peerages for Dr. Charles Hill and Sir Alick Buchanan-Smith. **12.** President Radhakrishnan of India arrived in London and drove from Victoria to Buckingham Palace with the Queen and the Duke of Edinburgh, who gave a banquet for him in the evening; it was announced that Her Majesty had appointed him to be honorary member of Order of Merit. Queen Elizabeth the Queen Mother opened 50th annual congress of National Association for Maternal and Child Welfare, at Church House. **13.** The Queen and the Duke of Edinburgh visited Commonwealth Institute with President Radhakrishnan, who in evening entertained them to dinner at Indian High Commissioner's residence. **17.** Order of the Garter service took place in St. George's Chapel, Windsor, the Queen and the Duke of Edinburgh walking in procession with the Knights to the Chapel. **24.** The Queen and the Duke watched Second Test between England and West Indies at Lord's. **26.** The Queen presented to the Duke of Edinburgh the Gold Albert Medal of the Royal Society of Arts for 1963. **27.** The Queen and the Duke left for Scotland; on following day, after visiting Clackmannanshire, they went into residence at Holyroodhouse.

July 1. The Queen and the Duke of Edinburgh attended installation of Sir Robert Menzies as Knight of the Thistle in St. Giles'. **3.** The Queen and the Duke visited Paisley and Glasgow; on following day they travelled in royal train to

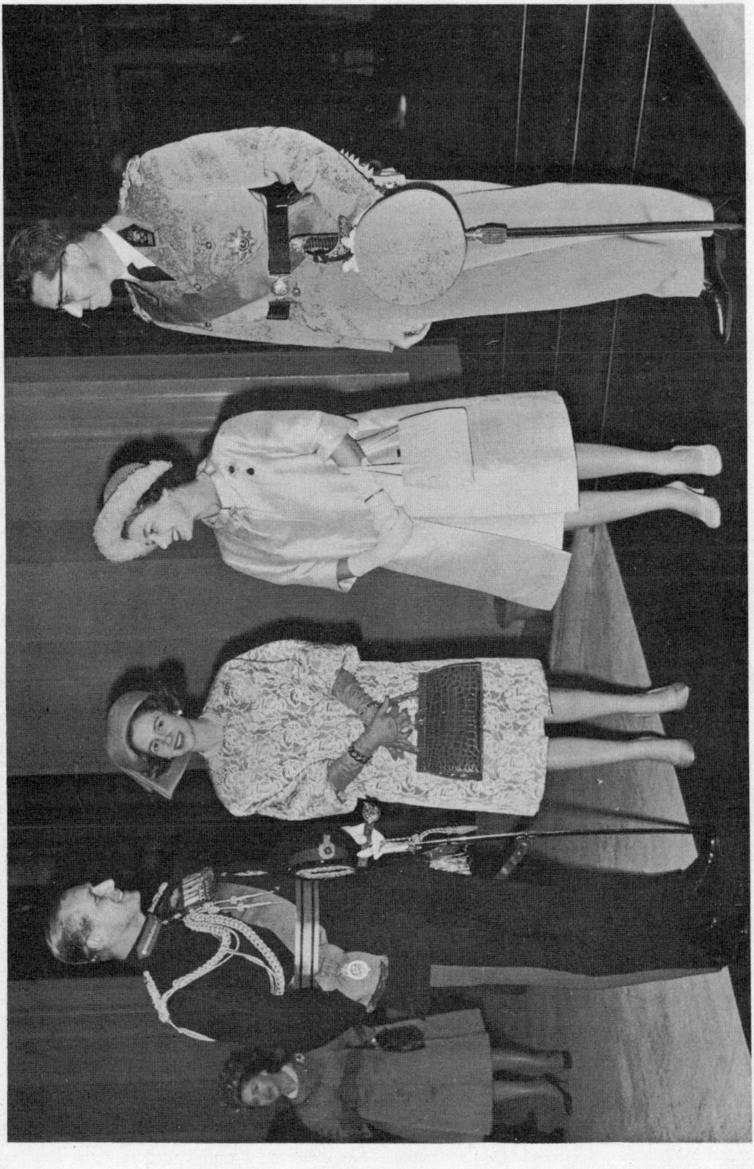

King Baudouin and Queen Fabiola of the Belgians photographed with the Queen and the Duke of Edinburgh during their State visit in May.

During the spring the Queen and the Duke of Edinburgh made a tour of Australasia. Her Majesty is shown with Sir Robert Menzies when she opened the R.G. Menzies Library at the Australian National University, Canberra, on March 13.

THE KING AND QUEEN OF THE HELLENES

King Paul and Queen Frederika of the Hellenes arrived in England for their State visit on July 9, and were greeted by the Duke of Edinburgh at Gatwick Airport.

PRINCESS ALEXANDRA'S WEDDING

Princess Alexandra was married in Westminster Abbey on April 24 to the Hon. Angus Ogilvy, son of the Earl of Airlie. The wedding-group includes, in the row behind the bride and bridegroom, from left to right: Prince Michael of Kent, the Countess and Earl of Airlie, Princess Marina, Duchess of Kent,

Mr. Dean Rusk (*left*), Mr. Gromyko (*centre*) and the Earl of Home (*right*) sign the nuclear test ban treaty at a ceremony in the Kremlin on August 5. Mr. Khrushchev is standing behind Lord Home.

THE SKOPJE EARTHQUAKE

On July 26 an earthquake devastated the town of Skopje in Yugoslavia, some 1,200 people being killed and 100,000 made homeless. The illustration shows the ruins of the Hotel Makedonija, Skopje's leading hotel, in which many tourists were staying; seven survivors were found in the basement 55 hours after the earthquake.

For the first three months of 1963 Britain suffered from a spell of intensely cold weather. A view of Whitstable Harbour, covered with large blocks of ice, and the frozen sea beyond.

WOMAN ASTRONAUT

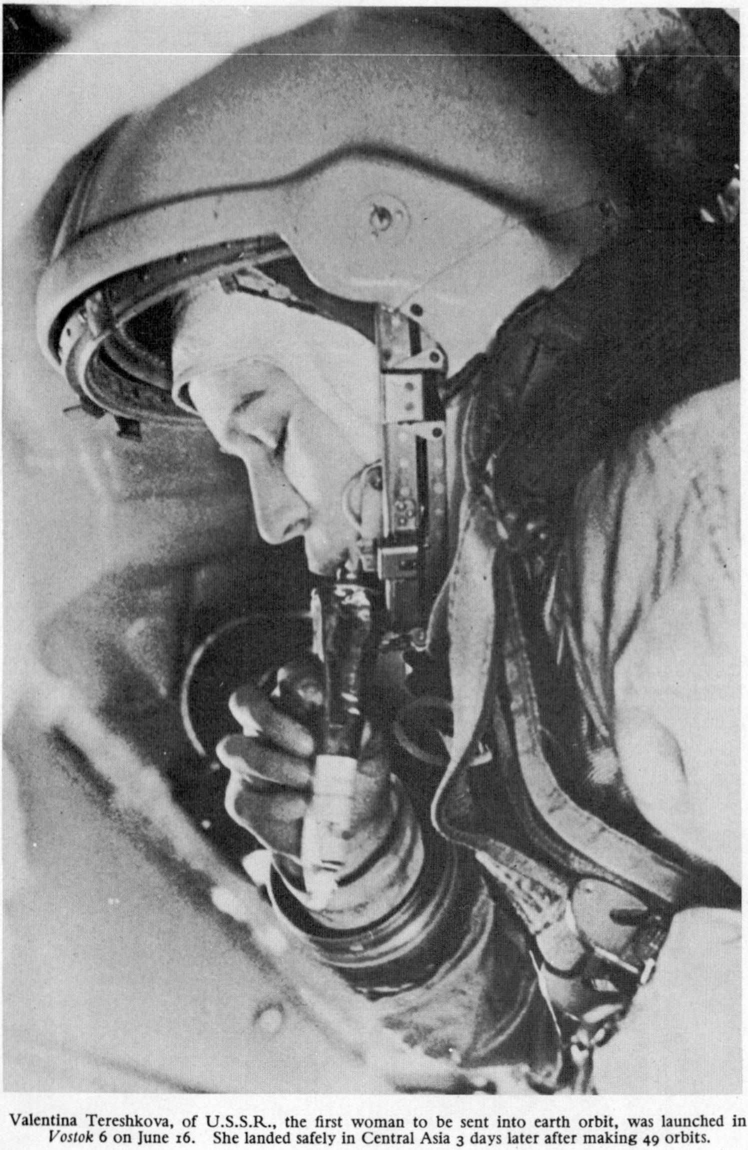

Valentina Tereshkova, of U.S.S.R., the first woman to be sent into earth orbit, was launched in *Vostok* 6 on June 16. She landed safely in Central Asia 3 days later after making 49 orbits.

H.M.S. *DREADNOUGHT*

H.M.S. *Dreadnought*, Britain's first atomic submarine, sailing up the Firth of Clyde on January 28 during her trials.

DEMONSTRATION IN WASHINGTON

An aerial view of part of the vast crowd of negroes and white sympathisers gathering round the Lincoln Memorial in Washington during the demonstration on August 28 for civil rights for negroes. It was estimated that 200,000 people took part in the march, which took place without disorderly incident.

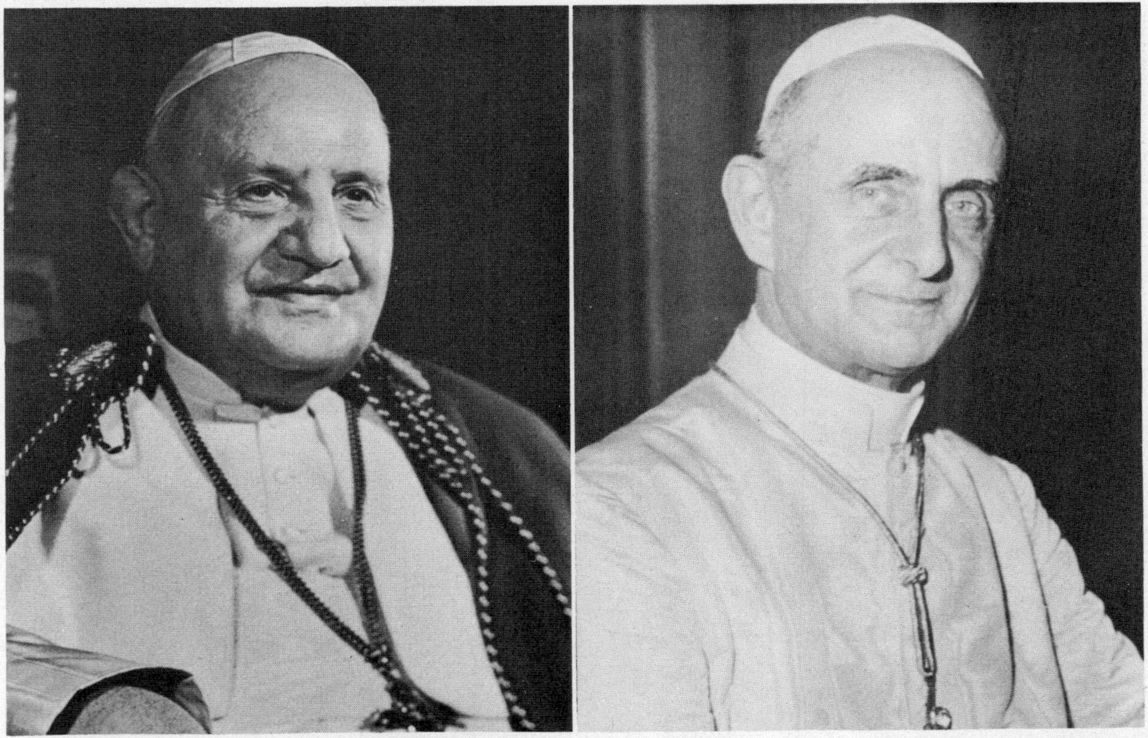

Pope John XXIII (*left*) died on June 3, at the age of 81. His Holiness, whose work for peace and unity had won world-wide acclaim, had been Pope since 1958. His successor, Cardinal Montini, Archbishop of Milan, was elected on June 21 and took the name of Paul VI.

Two of Britain's greatest leaders in the Second World War and colleagues on the Chiefs of Staff Committee, died within a week of each other during June. Admiral of the Fleet Viscount Cunningham of Hyndhope (*left*) was First Sea Lord from [illegible]

During the year the deaths took place of Mr. Hugh Gaitskell (*right*), Leader of the Labour Party and of the Opposition since 1955, who died on January 18 aged 56; and Viscount Nuffield, the great industrialist and philanthropist, whose death, at the age of 85, occurred on August 22.

HONOURED IN 1963

Among those honoured in 1963 were Mr. R. G. Menzies (*top right*), who was made a Knight of the Thistle, Mr. K. J. Holyoake, Prime Minister of New Zealand (*top left*), who became a Companion of Honour, Dr. Richard Woolley, Astronomer Royal (*bottom left*) who received a knighthood, and Alicia Markova who was appointed a D.B.E.

The West Indies won a memorable test series by beating England in the final Test Match at the Oval amid scenes of great enthusiasm on the part of their supporters. The West Indies thus became first holders of the Wisden Trophy for the winners of successive England *v.* West Indies series. The Trophy (*inset*) was given by Wisdens to commemorate the publication of the 100th edition of *Wisden's Cricketers' Almanack*.

THE ITALIAN DAM DISASTER

On Oct. 10 an avalanche from Mt. Toc fell into the Vaiont Dam in the Veneto region of Italy, forcing a vast quantity of water into the Piave Valley, where

Kenilworth and went to the Royal Show in Stoneleigh Abbey Park. **4.** Queen Elizabeth the Queen Mother, who had sailed in *Britannia* from Holyhead, began visit to Isle of Man; on July 5 Her Majesty presided at ceremony of the Tynwald and held investiture on behalf of the Queen. **9.** The King and Queen of the Hellenes arrived for State visit, being greeted at Gatwick Airport by the Duke of Edinburgh. They drove in procession from Victoria to Buckingham Palace with the Queen and the Duke of Edinburgh. The Queen conferred Order of the Garter on King Paul, and in afternoon he and Queen Frederika laid wreath on Tomb of Unknown Warrior in Westminster Abbey and later visited Queen Elizabeth the Queen Mother at Clarence House. In evening, the Queen and the Duke of Edinburgh gave State banquet at Buckingham Palace in honour of their visitors. **10.** The King and Queen of the Hellenes went by river to the City, where they were entertained to luncheon in Guildhall by the Lord Mayor and Corporation; in evening, with the Queen and the Duke of Edinburgh, they attended State gala performance of *A Midsummer Night's Dream* at Aldwych Theatre. **11.** King Paul spent day with Home Fleet at Portsmouth and Queen Frederika visited Lord Mayor Treloar College at Froyle and Radio Research Station at Winkfield; in evening, they entertained the Queen and the Duke of Edinburgh to dinner at Claridge's. **12.** The King and Queen of the Hellenes left Buckingham Palace on conclusion of their visit. **18.** It was announced that Princess Anne would enter Benenden School in autumn. **22.** The Queen opened new Welwyn and Hatfield Hospital. **24.** Her Majesty visited International Horse Show at White City. **28.** It was stated that Princess Alexandra was expecting baby in New Year, and would undertake no further official engagements.

Aug. 8. The Queen approved appointment of Major Francis Jones to new office of Wales Herald Extraordinary. **9.** The Queen and the Duke of Edinburgh visited the Eisteddfod at Llandudno and later went to Conway, Bangor and Caernarvon, where Her Majesty declared the town a royal borough. **10.** The Queen and the Duke visited Merionethshire. Later, Her Majesty left for Balmoral. **15.** The Queen appointed Dr. G. P. Gooch and Mr. Henry Moore to be members of the Order of Merit. **19.** The Duke of Edinburgh arrived at Balmoral after cruising in Scottish waters in *Bloodhound* with the Prince of Wales and Princess Anne. **27.** It was announced from Buckingham Palace that proposed state visit of President Ayub Khan of Pakistan, in October, had been postponed at his request.

Sept. 5. The Queen, with the Duke of Edinburgh, Queen Elizabeth the Queen Mother, the Prince of Wales and Princess Anne, attended Highland Games at Braemar. **11.** Queen Elizabeth the Queen Mother opened restored Tolbooth at Stonehaven. **15.** The Queen appointed Field-Marshal Sir Gerald Templer to be a Knight of the Garter. **16.** It was announced that the Queen was expecting a baby in the New Year and would undertake no further engagements after she left Balmoral in October. **20.** The Queen, who had travelled from Balmoral with Princess Anne, went with the Princess to Benenden School, where the latter began her first term. Later, Her Majesty returned to Balmoral.

IMPERIAL POLITICS (**1962**) **Oct. 1.** Labour Party conference opened at Brighton, Mr. Geoffrey Lawrence, Q.C., was appointed full-time chairman of National Incomes Commission. **2.** Mr. Callaghan was displaced by Lord Stansgate in voting for Labour Party executive. **3.** Labour conference supported executive policy statement on Common Market. Mr. D. H. Davies was elected chairman of Labour Party for ensuing year. Mr. Maudling said that Parliamentary approval would be sought for repayment of post-war credits to men at 60 and women at 55, instead of 63 and 58, at estimated cost of £42,000,000; he also said that Government had authorised increased public investment of about £70,000,000 over next 18 months. **4.** Government decided not to join U.S.A. in shipping boycott of Cuba. **5.** Labour Party Conference unanimously passed motion opposing nuclear weapon testing by any country. **7.** Mr. Macmillan issued statement explaining Government's reasons for negotiating to join Common Market. **10.** Conservative Party conference opened at Llandudno, and on following day carried by very large majority resolution approving Government's Common Market policy. **12.** It was announced that Mr. Selwyn Lloyd would undertake survey of Conservative Party organisation. Mr. I. H. Shearer, Q.C., was appointed Lord Advocate, and it was stated that he would be sworn a Privy Councillor. **19.** Reviewing Committee on Export of Works of Art recommended that Government should set up Treasury fund of £1,000,000 to finance special purchases, the fund to be replenished when it fell below £500,000. **22.** It was announced that Prime Minister had set up committee of inquiry under chairmanship of Sir Charles Cunningham to determine what breaches of security arrangements there may have been to enable the ex-Admiralty clerk Vassall to supply information to U.S.S.R., and whether there was any neglect of duty by persons responsible for his employment or conduct, and to draw attention to any weaknesses in existing security arrangements which might come to committee's notice. **23.** Foreign Office said that Soviet Union had been guilty of deception over Cuba and of deliberately opening up new area of instability and that Government was supporting U.S. request to Security Council to make recommendations to end danger. Conference on independence for British Guiana opened in London. **25.** Parliament met after Summer recess, and after statement by Mr. Macmillan in Commons on Cuba situation, was prorogued till following week. Ministry of Labour figures showed more than 500,000 unemployed in Great Britain for first time since winter of 1958–59. **30.** New session of Parliament opened; Queen's Speech contained proposals for legislation for local government reorganisation in London, setting up consumer council and creating new water authorities. Mr. B. R. Z. de Ferranti, Parliamentary Secretary to Ministry of Aviation since July, resigned for business reasons.

Nov. 1. Sir Winston Churchill fulfilled dinner engagement, leaving his home for first time since he returned from hospital in August. **5.** Mr. Maudling announced cut in purchase tax on cars from 45 to 25 per cent., and increased investment allowances on capital expenditure. **6.** Prime Minister told Commons that after the committee of inquiry on Vassall case had reported to him, he would invite Lord Radcliffe to advise him on its conclusions. British Guiana constitutional conference ended without agreement being reached. **7.** White Paper contained estimate that Government and local authority investment expenditure would rise by more than 25 per cent. by 1963–64 compared with 1960–61. At request of Prime Minister, committee considering Vassall case produced interim report, saying that letters received by Vassall from Mr. Galbraith, former Civil Lord of the Admiralty, and his wife, did not, *prima facie*, appear to contain any implication of relationship constituting security risk. **8.** Mr. Macmillan announced that he had accepted resignation of Mr. Galbraith from post of Under-Secretary for Scotland. Mr. George Brown was re-elected deputy leader of Parliamentary Labour Party by 133 votes against 103 cast for Mr. Harold Wilson. **12.** Mr. Thorneycroft said that Britain would proceed to carry out further underground test of nuclear device in Nevada. Nyasaland constitutional conference opened in London. **13.** Mr. Macmillan told Commons that inquiry would be set up under Tribunals of Inquiry (Evidence) Act, 1921, to investigate Vassall case and rumours and allegations which had arisen from it. On following day, he said that tribunal would consist of Lord Radcliffe (chairman), Mr. Justice Barry and Sir Milner Holland, Q.C. **14.** Anglo-Japanese Commercial Treaty was signed. **21.** Government confirmed proposal to demolish large block between Parliament Street and Embankment to provide more accommodation for M.P.s. **22.** Labour gained seats from Government in by-elections in Woodside division of Glasgow and in South Dorset, where Independent anti-Common Market Conservative obtained over 5,000 votes, but forfeited his deposit. At Chippenham, Conservative was returned with majority of 1,588 compared with 8,785 at General Election, Liberal candidate being in second place. **23.** Results of by-elections in Central Norfolk and South Northants. showed that Conservatives had been elected with majority reduced from 6,787 to 220 in first instance and from 5,934 to 917 in second. Nyasaland conference ended with agreement to amend constitution to permit full cabinet government under Prime Minister not later than beginning of Feb. 1963. **27.** Government agreed to supply arms and equipment to India for use against China free of payment. **29.** Police Council agreed to increased pay for all ranks of police of 3½ per cent. back dated to Sept. 1, with further increase of 2½ per cent. from Feb. 1, 1963. **30.** Minister of Labour said that he proposed to adopt March 1, 1963, as date from which payment of wages by cheque would be authorised under Payment of Wages Act, 1960.

Dec. 3. Lady Tweedsmuir was appointed to succeed Mr. Galbraith as Joint Under-Secretary at Scottish Office. Mr. H. N. Marten became Parliamentary Secretary at Ministry of Aviation and Lord Hastings, Joint Parliamentary Secretary at Ministry of Housing and Local Government. **11.** Chancellor of Exchequer referred to National Incomes Commission, for retrospective examination and report, agreements reached between Scottish builders' and plumbers' employers and trade unions for reduction of hours without loss of pay. **14.** The Prime Minister and Lady Dorothy Macmillan left for week-end visit to President and Mme. de Gaulle. **17.** Mr. Macmillan left for talks with President Kennedy in Bahamas. **18.** Five civil Supplementary Estimates totalling £49,918,000 and Supplementary Estimate of £12,000,000 for air services were published. White Paper on broadcasting said that Government proposed legislation to give I.T.A. more control over contracting companies and also intended to allow experimental pay-television services for 2 or 3 years. Home Secretary said that Select Committee would be set up to consider question of service candidates standing at elections. Government spokesman said that weekly amount which retirement and widow pensioners could earn without deduction from pension would be raised from £3 10*s.* to £4 5*s.*, and from £5 to £6 in case of widowed mothers. **19.** Mr. Butler said that Government accepted in principle that Nyasaland should be allowed to secede from Federation of Rhodesia and Nyasaland. In House of Lords, after several speakers had suggested that Government's decision violated pledges contained in confidential documents in 1953, Lord Hailsham said that Cabinet would have to consider publication of those documents in full. **20.** Lord Hailsham said that Government rejected proposal of Wolfenden committee that sports development council should be established. **27.** Government announced decision to make additional annual grant of £3,500,000 for university teachers' salaries, and referred question of those salaries to National Incomes Commission for advice on future settlements. **29.** Foreign Office statement called for resumption of negotiations in Katanga and spoke of futility of trying to impose political settlement on Congo by force. **31.** Mr. Maudling reduced from 45 to 25 per cent. purchase tax on television sets, radios, gramophones and records, perfumery and cosmetics.

(1963). Jan. 3. Bank Rate was reduced by ½ per cent. to 4 per cent. Central Electricity Generating Board announced increase in its charge for electricity to area boards of 4 per cent. from April 1. Claim was submitted for 3½ per cent. wage increase for 450,000 civil servants. **9.** Mr. Macmillan appointed Lord Hailsham to advise Cabinet on reviving industrial activity in North-East England and creating more work there. **10.** National Coal Board reported surplus for 1962 of about £1,000,000, being first annual surplus since 1956. **11.** Council of Building Societies Association recommended reduction in mortgage rate from 6½ to 6 per cent. from Feb. 1. **14.** Mr. Heath rejected idea of British association with Common Market instead of full membership, as suggested by President de Gaulle. **15.** After many sittings in private, Vassall Tribunal held its first public session. **16.** British and Saudi Arabian Governments agreed to resume diplomatic relations, broken off by Saudi Arabia in 1956. **17.** Lord Radcliffe, Chairman of Vassall Tribunal, said that he would report to High Court that two journalists had refused to comply with his direction to answer questions about their sources of information. **18.** Death of Mr. Hugh Gaitskell, Leader of the Opposition. **22.** Parliament resumed after recess, and both Houses adjourned, as mark of respect to memory of Mr. Gaitskell, after tributes had been paid to him. In consequence of cold weather, South-Western Gas Board banned use of gas in its area between 9 p.m. and 6 a.m. and between 2 p.m. and 6 p.m., until further notice. Wales Gas Board cut supplies to industry. **23.** Minister of Pensions and National Insurance said that payments to unemployed, widows and war pensioners, and sickness and disability benefits, were to be increased by 10*s.* a week; insurance contributions by both employers and employees would go up by 1*s.* 1*d.* a week, and there would be payment by Exchequer of more than £40,000,000 a year. British Government and Government of Outer Mongolia agreed to establish diplomatic relations. **24.** Unemployment figures for Jan. 14 were highest since 1947, totalling 814,632; rise over December figures was 248,474, of whom 144,361 were temporarily stopped. House of Lords passed Government amendment to Children and Young Persons Bill fixing age of criminal responsibility at 10. **28.** Government announced guillotine procedure for London Government Bill. **30.** Mr. Macmillan, broadcasting on breakdown of Common Market negotiations, blamed French Government and said that what had happened was "bad for us, bad for Europe and bad for the whole free world"; he said that British Government had no ready-made alternative plan.

Feb. 4. Minister of Labour said that Admiralty had placed order for 3 replenishment tankers, to be built on Tyneside. **5.** Draft Order was laid for dissolution of Prison Commission and its integration with Home Office. **7.** Mr. Brooke said that abolition of prison sentences for persons under 17 and lowering of minimum age for Borstal training to 15 would take effect on Aug. 1. In first ballot for Labour Party leadership, 115 votes were cast for Mr. Wilson, 88 for Mr. Brown and 41 for Mr. Callaghan, first two going forward to second ballot. **11.** Commons Select Committee recommended that applications from Servicemen for release to contest parliamentary elections should be submitted by Service departments to outside advisory committee to consider whether requests were *bona fide*. **13.** National Incomes Commission held its first public sitting; no trades union representatives were present. **14.** On second ballot, Mr. Wilson was elected Leader of Parliamentary Labour Party by 144 votes, against 103 for Mr. Brown. Mr. Sandys announced new Council of Administration, under chairmanship of Sir Eric Millbourn, to take control of Malta dockyard. **15.** Estimates showed increase of expenditure of £527,000,000, or nearly 10 per cent., on previous year. **20.** Defence White Paper spoke of development of new type of British nuclear bomb to bridge gap before Polaris became effective. Anglo-Danish talks on Faroes fishing dispute ended in deadlock. **21.** Mr. Brown agreed to continue to act as Deputy Leader of Labour Party. Unemployment figures for Feb. 11 showed total of 878,356, increase of 63,724 in month. **22.** Mr. Charles Fletcher-Cooke resigned from post of Joint Under-Secretary at Home Office. **25.** Text of Town and Country Planning Bill was published, proposing stricter control of office redevelopment, particularly in London and other large cities. Postmaster-General outlined Government's proposals to increase rentals paid by Independent Television programme contractors.

March 1. Miss Mervyn Pike became Joint Under-Secretary at Home Office and was succeeded as Assistant Postmaster-General by Mr. R. L. Mawby. **4.** Mr. Thorneycroft announced Government proposals to set up unified Ministry of Defence, with abolition of Admiralty, War Office and Air Ministry, First Lord of Admiralty and Secretaries of State for War and Air would be equivalent of Ministers of State and directly subordinate to Defence Minister. **6.** Government accepted recommendation of Rochdale Committee that National Ports Council should be set up. London Electricity Board announced further large increases in charges from April 1. **7.** Sir Keith Joseph, in Commons, rejected suggestions for modification of, or inquiry into, rating system. **11.** Treasury announced loan of over £2,000,000 to Ghana to buy 2 cargo ships in Britain. **14.** Civil Estimates showed that there would be increase of 14,764 non-industrial civil servants in ensuing year. **15.** Mr. Brooke told Commons that he had decided to deport Chief Enahoro, who faced charges of treasonable felony in Nigeria; later, after anxiety had been shown on both sides of House, Mr. Macleod, Leader of the House, agreed to debate on case, and it was stated that Chief Enahoro's deportation would meanwhile be delayed. **19.** Mr. Bevins imposed many increases in Post Office charges, including additional 3*d.* to 1*s.* on parcels over 6 lbs., minimum cost of 5*s.* per 12 words and charge of 5d. a word on inland telegrams, increase of about 30 per cent. on overseas telegtams, and higher charges for many telephone calls. **21.** After Home Secretary had again refused to grant asylum in Britain to Chief Enahoro, Opposition gave notice of censure and Mr. Brooke agreed to delay deportation pending discussion of motion, provided matter could be brought to early decision. Unemployment figures for March 11 totalled 701,930, fall of 176,426 since Feb. 11. **22.** Result of Colne Valley by-election showed that Labour had retained seat with majority of 2,039 as against 6,254 over Conservative at General Election; on this occasion Conservative was third, 11,795 behind Labour and 9,756 behind Liberal. **25.** Lord Brookeborough, owing to ill-health, resigned Premiership of Northern Ireland, which he had held for 20 years, and was succeeded by Capt. Terence O'Neill, Minister of Finance, At first meeting with Mr. Butler, Northern Rhodesian delegation walked out in absence of categorical assurance in advance that Northern Rhodesia could secede from Federation. Prime Minister announced that Government had agreed to general increase of 14 per cent. in doctors' and dentists' pay, with effect from following week. **26.** After Mr. George Brown, in debate on case of Chief Enahoro, had said that one charge against the Chief might carry death penalty, Mr. Macmillan intervened and gave assurance that the Chief would not be deported until it was established that he would face no charge which might incur death penalty. **28.** Labour retained seats in East Swansea and Rotherham by-elections. At East Swansea, Labour candidate had majority of 14,014 over Liberal, compared with 20,130 over Conservative at General Election. Independent, Conservative, Welsh Nationalist and Communist candidates forfeited deposits. At Rotherham, Labour majority over Conservative was increased from 11,539 to 13,232. Government decided to set up small committee of inquiry to establish impact of rates on different sectors of community and different income groups. **29.** Mr. Butler conceded Northern Rhodesia's right to secede from Federation; Sir Roy Welensky described action as "yielding to threats", and Mr. Winston Field said that issue of independence of Southern Rhodesia had become integral part of any future conference and he and his colleagues could make no decision to attend such conference until they had been satisfied in that respect. Immediate increase of pay by 3 per cent. was awarded to about 450,000 civil servants at annual cost of approximately £13,000,000.

April 3. Mr. Maudling introduced his Budget, which included proposals for abolition of Schedule A, income-tax reliefs by means of increased allowances, and reductions of certain stamp duties; the Chancellor proposed to inquire further into possibilities of turnover tax and taxation of gambling. **8.** Government spokesman said that Board of Trade would build 13 more small advance factories in development areas. **9.** Mr. Macmillan told Commons that time was not opportune for increase in M.P.s' pay; Mr. Wilson described statement as dismally unsatisfactory. **10.** Government carried motion in Commons approving deportation of Chief Enahoro. **11.** Mr. Butler said that all territories of Central African Federation would proceed through usual processes to independence, but that Southern Rhodesia could not expect full independence until after discussions on future relations between the territories and on transitional arrangements. **17.** Lord Poole was appointed Joint Chairman, with Mr. Macleod, of Conservative Party. **22.** First report of National Incomes Commission said that 40-hour week agreement in Scottish building industry could result only in excessive and inflationary increase in wages and was therefore contrary to national interest. Unemployment figures in Great Britain for April 8 showed total of 604,637, 97,293 fewer than on March 11. **24.** It was announced that British Polaris submarines would operate from base at Faslane in Gare Loch. **25.** Radcliffe tribunal report on Vassall case was published. Tribunal found that there was not at the time sufficiently close control at British Embassy in Moscow of association between staff and locally recruited employees, and that system by which Vassall was selected for post in Moscow was inadequate; it said that there was nothing improper in relationship between Mr. Galbraith and Vassall, and that there was no truth in allegation that Lord Carrington, First Lord of the Admiralty, and his Service chiefs knew of existence of another spy in Admiralty for 18 months before Vassall's arrest.

May 1. Sir Winston Churchill announced decision, owing to decreased mobility since his accident in 1962, not to stand for Parliament at following general election. **3.** Mr. John Hay was appointed Civil Lord of Admiralty on resignation of Mr. Orr-Ewing, and was succeeded as Joint Parliamentary Secretary at Ministry of Transport by Mr. Galbraith. **7.** In Commons debate on Vassall Tribunal report, Mr. Macmillan suggested that permanent security commission should be set up to investigate background of cases of espionage. President of Board of Trade announced decision to schedule whole Tyneside area as development district. **8.** Mr. Vosper, Secretary for Department of Technical Co-operation, resigned through ill-health and was succeeded by Mr. L. R. Carr, who became a Privy Councillor. It was announced that 2 Polaris submarines would be built by Cammell Laird at Birkenhead. Home Office said that pending further application on behalf of Chief Enahoro for writ of *habeas corpus* on grounds of fresh evidence, the Chief was not being sent back to Nigeria. **14.** House of Lords concluded its longest recorded sitting, of 12 hours, 5 minutes, sitting till 2.35 a.m. on committee stage of London Government Bill. Admiralty spokesman announced that undersea anti-submarine test centre was to be set up in Bahamas for use by Royal Navy and U.S.A. Sir Winston Churchill attended House of Commons for first time since his accident. **15.** In emergency debate on case of Chief Enahoro, Government majority fell to 57; some 8 Conservatives voted with Opposition and about same number were understood to have deliberately abstained from voting; Chief Enahoro was flown to Nigeria from Gatwick Airport in early hours of following morning. President of Board of Trade said that he had referred supply of household detergents and supply and processing of colour film to Monopolies Commission. **23.** Opposition tabled motion of censure on Mr. Brooke after he had told Commons that he had been confidentially informed by Nigerian Government that Mr. Dingle Foot and Mr. Gratiaen would not be allowed into Nigeria to defend Chief Enahoro. **28.** Government announced intention to set up housing corporation, with funds of £100,000,000 from Treasury, to assist in providing mortgages on houses. **29.** Motion tabled, signed by M.P.s of all parties, including Mr. Wilson and Mr. Grimond, urging increase in M.P.'s and ministers' salaries. Mr. Soames announced that Sugar Board would, on following day, begin payment of subsidy to trade of 6*d.* a pound on refined sugar in order to bring sugar prices back to normal level. Government spokesman said that £30,000,000 would be made immediately available to finance new orders for British owners for ships to be built in British yards. Labour Party restored whip to 5 M.P.s who had sat as Independent Labour members since 1961. **30.** Text of Peerage Bill issued. It proposed to allow hereditary peers to renounce peerages for themselves, to abolish Scottish Representative Peers and to allow hereditary peeresses to sit in House of Lords.

June 5. Mr. Profumo, Secretary of State for War, resigned; in letter to Prime Minister he said that he had misled House of Commons in personal statement in March about his association with Miss Christine Keeler. **6.** It was announced that Government was placing order with British Aircraft Corporation for all-British earth satellite which would be launched in 3 or 4 years' time. **10.** It was stated that as result of correspondence between President Kennedy, Mr. Khruschev and Mr. Macmillan it had been agreed that special representations would go to Moscow in following month to discuss nuclear test ban treaty; Lord Hailsham was appointed British representative. It was made known that before Whitsun recess Mr. Macmillan had asked the Lord Chancellor to examine security aspects of Profumo case. **17.** Parliament reassembled after Whitsun recess. In debate arising from Profumo case, Government had majority of 69; about 27 Conservative M.P.s were understood to have abstained deliberately from voting. On behalf of Government, Mr. Macleod offered to consult Opposition on methods of further investigation. **20.** In by-election at South Leeds, Mr. Gaitskell's former constituency, Labour retained seat with majority of 12,789, 1,303 more than at General Election; Communist candidate lost his deposit. **21.** Mr. Macmillan announced in Commons that Lord Denning had been appointed to inquire into security side of Profumo case and said that investigation would cover inquiry into truth or falsehood of rumours which were circulating and that if Lord Denning had difficulty in obtaining evidence, the House could consider if he needed further powers. **24.** Foreign Office said that a Third Secretary at Czechoslovak Embassy in London had been expelled for attempted spying. **26.** Mr. Profumo was removed from Privy Council at his own request. **27.** Mr. J. B. Godber was appointed Secretary of State for War and was succeeded as Minister of State for Foreign Affairs by Mr. P. J. M. Thomas. **28.** Mr. Macmillan said in television interview that all being well, if he kept his health and strength, he hoped to lead his party into next election. **29.** President Kennedy arrived for short visit to Mr. Macmillan at Birch Grove.

July 1. Mr. Heath told House of Commons that Harold Philby, former Foreign Office official who had disappeared from Beirut in March and was thought to be behind Iron Curtain, was "third man" who had warned Burgess and Maclean in time for them to escape. **2.** Mr. Sandys told Commons that Kenya would become independent on Dec. 12. Government rejected recommendation of committee on noise that grants should be paid towards cost of sound-proofing private houses near London Airport. **3.** Select Committee on Nationalised Industries reported that Britain would probably continue to suffer from electricity supply breakdowns during very cold spells till at least 1967. **4.** Labour retained seats in three-cornered contests at Deptford and West Bromwich by-elections; in former, where only 44·2 per cent. of electorate voted, Labour majority fell by 705 to 7,483, Liberal candidate coming second; at West Bromwich, Labour majority increased from 6,893 to 12,264; in neither case had there been Liberal candidate at General Election. **8.** Agreement was reached on new Federation of Malaysia, to include Malaya, Singapore, North Borneo and Sarawak; Brunei declined to join Federation. **10.** Commons Committee on Estimates reported increase of 34,500, or more than 9 per cent., in numbers of non-industrial civil servants since 1959–60, rate of increase having grown each year and increase in 1962–63 being more than double that of previous year. **12.** It was confirmed that Russian agent, whose name was later stated to be Dolnytsin, had defected to the West about 18 months previously, and was now in Britain. **18.** Minister of Power stated that he had decided to allow application by United Kingdom Oil Pipelines Ltd. to construct major oil pipelines between Thames and Mersey. **22.** Conference on constitution of British Honduras ended in London; it was agreed that ministerial system should be established on Jan. 1, 1964. During Commons debate on property profiteering, Minister of Housing and Local Government agreed to consider granting summary powers of compulsory purchase of houses to local authorities; he also announced that Sir Milner Holland would be chairman of committee to investigate housing, and particularly rented property, in London. **23.** Post Office annual report said that profits had been halved over last 2 years. South-Eastern Gas Board announced increased charges of about 8 per cent. **24.** Labour Party decided to oppose Speaker in Cities of London and Westminster constituency at next election. **30.** Mr. Malcolm St. Clair, who had been declared M.P. for South-East Bristol 2 years earlier when Mr. Wedgwood Benn had been disqualified, said that he would resign seat upon Royal Assent being given to Peerage Bill; this took place on following day and Mr. Wedgwood Benn (Lord Stansgate) and Lord Altrincham disclaimed their peerages.

Aug. 1. Mr. Sandys said that Malta would become independent not later than May 31, 1964. **2.** Parliament adjourned for summer recess. **15.** Mr. W. G. Leburn, Joint Under-Secretary of State for Scotland, died on holiday. **16.** Result of by-election for Mr. Profumo's former seat at Stratford-upon-Avon, in which 5 candidates took part, showed that Conservative had been returned with majority of 3,470; Mr. Profumo's majority in straight contest with Labour at General Election had been 14,129. **20.** Mr. Wedgwood Benn was elected with majority of 15,479 in Bristol South-East by-election, in which he was not opposed by official Conservative candidate.

Sept. 11. Liberal Party Assembly opened at Brighton. **17.** Chairman of Electricity Council and Central Electricity Generating Board forecast probability of power cuts during winter and of further increases in charges. North Thames Gas Board announced increased charges from Sept. 30. **18.** Treasury said that over 6,000 higher civil servants would receive pay increases ranging from 15 to 18 per cent. dated from Aug. 1. Mr. J. A. Stodart was appointed Under-Secretary of State for Scotland in succession to late Mr. W. G. Leburn. **20.** Zanzibar independence conference began at Lancaster House. **23.** Report of committee of inquiry on decimal currency recommended by majority a pound divided into 100 cents. **24.** Dec. 10 was agreed upon as independence date for Zanzibar. **25.** Lord Denning's report on Profumo affair was published; it rejected all rumours involving other Ministers and prominent persons, said that there was no security leakage and attached no blame to security services. Report said that it was sole responsibility of Prime Minister and his colleagues to deal with situation, and they did not succeed in doing so. Lord Denning quoted directive of 1952, still in force, which said that head of security service was responsible directly to Home Secretary and not, in ordinary way, to Prime Minister. Kenya independence conference opened in London; Jomo Kenyatta called for changes in constitution. **26.** It was stated that Nyasaland would become independent on July 6, 1964. **30.** Labour Party conference opened at Scarborough and carried motion demanding survey of all inland transport before further rail closures.

LOCAL AFFAIRS.—**(1962). Oct. 23.** It was announced that Mayor of Oxford would be henceforth styled Lord Mayor. **Nov. 1.** Court of Common Council agreed to scheme to enlarge Central Criminal Court, extending number of courts from 6 to 10, at cost of £3,652,000. **10.** Sir Ralth Perring was installed as Lord Mayor of London. **25.** It was agreed to demolish City church of St. Mary Aldermanbury and rebuild it in U.S.A. **27.** Sir Keith Joseph declined to approve preservation of 3 Georgian houses in Adelphi. **Dec. 20.** Minister of Housing and Local Government announced that Luton would become County borough on April 1, 1964. **21.** New rating assessment figures were made public; Ministry of Housing spokesman said that figure was almost trebled—from £736,616,000 to £2,013,000,000. **28.** Annual report of L.C.C. Medical Officer of Health said that one child in 8 born in London in 1961 was illegitimate.

(1963) Jan. 9. Minister of Housing and Local Government approved plan for new town at Cramlington, Northumberland. **10.** Westminster City Council bought Dolphin Square for £4,500,000. **28.** Mr. Marples announced modifications of proposals for lorry route through Highgate. **Feb. 5.** Local Government Commission recommended County borough status for Cheltenham, and a new county borough of Torbay, Paignton and Brixham; it also proposed that Lyme Regis should be transferred to Devonshire, saying that it could not accept that wishes of majority of inhabitants should be more than one of many factors to be taken into account. **19.** It was announced that new towns would be set up at Redditch and Runcorn. **25.** White Paper published contemplating encroachments in London Green Belt; in Commons on following day Sir Keith Joseph said that he had asked authorities to consider possibilities of Lea Valley as new housing area. **March 7.** Minister rejected East Sussex County Council's proposal to create Green Belt to prevent merging of East Grinstead, Crawley and Haywards Heath. **11.** Local Government Commission recommended reduction of Welsh counties from 13 to 7 and abolition of Merthyr Tydfil's county borough status. **May 9.** Labour made net gain of more than 540 seats in borough elections and won control of nearly 40 boroughs. **13.** Local Government Commission, in review of Lincolnshire and East Anglia, proposed amalgamation of Holland and Kesteven, and recommended that Yarmouth should cease to be county borough. **23.** In report to Oxford University, Sir William Holford recommended erection of additional science buildings on Merton College Cricket Ground. **June 4.** A number of cases of typhoid were confirmed at Harlow New Town. **23.** Typhoid outbreak was reported at South Shields. **27.** Scottish Office issued White Paper proposing reduction of Scottish counties from 33 to between 10 and 15 and large-scale amalgamation of small burghs and rural districts. **July 1.** Minister decided not to confirm preservation order on 9 Georgian houses at Blackheath. **24.** Sir Keith Joseph approved building of Ford Motor Company engineering and research centre and testing ground on about 267 acres in Green Belt at Basildon. **Aug. 1.** It was announced that Government had decided not to accept Local Government Commission's recommendation for merger of Rutland with Leicestershire, but would proceed with amalgamation of Soke of Peterborough with Huntingdonshire and Isle of Ely with Cambridgeshire; proposal that Burton-on-Trent should lose county borough status was also accepted. **25.** Pay agreement for 180,000 local government officers was announced, whereby they would receive 3 per cent. increase in each of three following years. **Sept. 2.** Ministers of Housing and Local Government and of Transport rejected Sir William Holford's proposals for redevelopment of Piccadilly Circus, drawn up for L.C.C. in 1961, on grounds that they did not make enough provision for expected increase in road traffic. They suggested that proposals should be re-examined. **28.** Alderman C. J. Harman was elected Lord Mayor of London for ensuing year.

ACCIDENTS.—**(1962) Oct. 18.** Ten people were killed and 6 injured in crash involving 3 vehicles at Berkeley, Glos. **Nov. 4.** Four men and a girl were killed in collision between R.A.F. training machine and light aircraft over Reading. **16.** Lord Windlesham and an R.A.F. officer were lost when naval helicopter crashed into sea near South Bishop lighthouse off St. David's Head. **17.** Seaham Harbour lifeboat, with crew of 5, capsized in storm at entrance to port after rescuing 4 men and a boy from coble which was adrift; only one man out of 10 on board, a member of coble's crew, survived. Two R.A.F. climbers were found dead under snow in blizzard in Snowdonia. **19.** Five men were killed by leak of super-heated steam in boiler room of aircraft-carrier *Centaur* off Anglesey coast. **22.** Nine people were injured when two trains collided on District Line between Victoria and St. James's Park. **Dec. 15–16.** Severe gales in many parts of Britain caused 8 deaths. **26.** Eighteen persons were killed and more than 60 injured when Midday Scot from Glasgow hit rear of stationary Liverpool–Birmingham express 5 miles north of Crewe, rear coach of latter train being telescoped.

(1963) Jan. 1. Three terrace houses collapsed in West Gorton, Manchester, in explosion thought to have been caused by gas; 2 persons lost their lives. **17.** Eight West Indians, including 6 young children, died in fire in house at West Croydon. **25.** Two persons lost their lives and a number were injured when diesel train collided with steam locomotive at Lincoln. **May 29.** The two occupants of an Auster aircraft were killed when it crashed into roof of block of flats at Willesden. **July 11.** Gas explosion in Old Town at Hastings caused injury to over 30 persons. **Aug. 9.** Fire on railway bridge at Lambeth Road, which was put out in 5 minutes, damaged signalling wires and points motors, and caused Waterloo Station to be closed for many hours during peak of rush-hour and holiday traffic; effects were still felt on following day, when many expresses were cancelled. **Sept. 12.** Viking aircraft, carrying British holidaymakers from Gatwick to Perpignan, crashed in Pyrenees, with loss of all 36 passengers together with French crew of 4. **22.** Four women lost their lives in fire at Bayswater hotel.

CRIMES AND TRIALS.—**(1962) Oct. 22.** William John Christopher Vassall, clerk at Admiralty, was sentenced by Lord Chief Justice at Central Criminal Court to total of 18 years' imprisonment for offences under Official Secrets Act. **Nov. 5.** Three men were sentenced to 14 years', 12 years' and 8 years' imprisonment respectively for their share in robbery outside bank at Mitcham. **8.** Gang attacked guard of Paddington–Cheltenham express near West Drayton, and stopped train, throwing chests containing money to accomplices near line; they secured only one chest containing £760. **17.** Driver of milk lorry was shot in hold-up at Co-operative Society depôt at Mitcham and died in hospital. George Frederick Thatcher was later charged with his capital murder and 3 others with non-capital murder. All were found guilty at Central Criminal Court on March 12, 1963. Thatcher, who at time of crime was living in hostel while still under sentence for robbery with aggravation, was sentenced to death, and the others to life imprisonment. On April 5, Court of Criminal Appeal quashed conviction of Charles Connelly, and in Thatcher's case substituted conviction of murder, with life imprisonment, for conviction of capital murder. Later, Connelly was sentenced to 15 years' imprisonment for armed robbery; on Sept. 30 his appeal against conviction was dismissed, but sentence was reduced to 10 years. **27.** Gang seized £62,000 wages money at London Airport. **Dec. 7.** Miss Barbara Fell, a senior official in Central Office of Information, was sentenced to 2 years' imprisonment for offences under Official Secrets Act.

(1963) Jan. 10. Four men stole £30,000 in raid on bank car at Gillingham. **Feb. 7.** Figures of crime in Metropolitan Police district for 1962 showed total of 214,120 indictable offences, increase of 8.8 per cent. over record figure of 1961, and more than twice the total for 1938. **20.** Gang overpowered guard of Irish Mail train between Watford and Hemel Hempstead and escaped after communication cord had been pulled. **March 29.** At Lewes Assizes, Harvey Holford, Brighton club proprietor, was found not guilty of murder of his wife but guilty of manslaughter, and sentenced to 3 years' imprisonment. **May 24.** Three men attacked and bound guard at bullion brokers' warehouse in Finsbury and stole 40 bars of gold, valued at £200,000. **July 30.** Court of Criminal Appeal quashed conviction of Aloysius Gordon who had been found guilty at Central Criminal Court of assaulting Christine Keeler. **31.** Stephen Ward was found guilty at Central Criminal Court on two charges of living on immoral earnings; earlier in day, Ward had been taken to hospital in coma, and Mr. Justice Marshall postponed passing sentence, but Ward never recovered consciousness and died on Aug. 3. **Aug. 8.** Scotland to London overnight post office express was ambushed and robbed after signals had been tampered with near Cheddington, Buckinghamshire. Sum of £2,626,000 was finally found to have been stolen. On Aug. 13, empty mailbags and 3 abandoned vehicles were found at unoccupied farm at Oakley, Buckinghamshire, about 20 miles from Cheddington; on Aug. 15, 3 men and 2 women were arrested and charged with offences connected with the robbery, and it was stated that notes to value of £102,000 had been found; on Aug. 16 further £101,000 was found in wood near Dorking and on Aug. 21 another £30,000 was discovered concealed in caravan which police moved from site at Box Hill. Further arrests were made and case was opened against 13 people at Linslade on Sept. 26. **Sept. 19.** Criminal statistics for England and Wales showed increase of 11.1 per cent. of indictable offences in 1962 over 1961, and decrease in number of offences cleared up, which amounted in 1962 to 43.9 per cent. **27.** Bank van was ambushed near Longfield, Kent, and £90,000 stolen.

LABOUR **(1962). Oct. 1.** More than 120 members of Boilermakers' Society working at Sizewell, Suffolk, were given week's notice. Mr. Marples, in intervention on television programme, arranged meeting between Mr. Greene, General Secretary of N.U.R., and Dr. Beeching, in attempt to avert rail strike. **2.** Talks between B.T.C. and railway unions proved unsuccessful. **3.** Official strike by N.U.R. members throughout country. **4.** Three hundred Coventry car delivery drivers decided to strike. **7.** Demarcation dispute between steelworkers and bricklayers over placing of dolomite bricks in furnaces spread to involve works in Scotland and Wales. **8.** T.U.C. intervened in steelworks demarcation dispute. **9** Bricklayers' and steel workers' unions agreed to arbitration on demarcation dispute, and that arbitrator's findings should be binding; bricklayers' strike was called off. **12.** Busmen from 5 London garages went on one-day strike over new winter schedules. Ford Motor Company announced that its 45,000 employees would receive pay increase of 10*s.* a week in hope of better labour relations. **15.** Dr. Beeching had informal talks with railway union leaders. **18.** N.U.R. executive decided, by small majority, in favour of negotiations with B.T.C. on railway workshop closures, and against immediate 6-day strike. After dismissal of shop steward at Ford works at Dagenham, 1,200 men failed to report for work, and further 5,000 were sent home, all car assembly stopping. **19.** London busmen's leaders agreed provisionally to larger buses and to introduction of one-man operated buses on certain outer suburban services; L.T.E. offered crews 45 per cent. of savings effected. **25.** Union leaders recommended strikers at Ford works, Dagenham, to return to work. They decided to do so on following day, Company saying that they would have to sign letter undertaking to comply with rules, regulations and agreements. **30.** Executives of building workers' unions decided to make pay claim for additional 1*s.* 6*d.* an hour.

Nov. 2. Proposed introduction of larger buses in London area, estimated to save £1,000,000 a year, was postponed. **5.** Ford Company said that all but about 70 employees at Dagenham, including 12 shop stewards, would be re-employed; trade union side of company's national joint negotiating committee recommended official strike at Dagenham to begin on Nov. 17. Dr. Beeching offered further 5 per cent. pay rise to members of railway unions; executive committee of A.S.L.E.F. rejected offer as inadequate. **7.** Dr. Beeching increased his offer to 6 per cent. and this was accepted by unions. A.E.U. doubled its political levy, from 2*s.* to 4*s.* a quarter. **9.** Industrial Court awarded 3 per cent. pay increase to 150,000 workers in cotton industry. **13.** Agreement was reached for increase of 6 per cent. in wages of railway workshop employees. **14.** Unions decided to suspend contemplated strike at Ford works at Dagenham and to seek negotiations with management. **19.** Joint statement by Fords and unions said that number of men who would not be re-employed had been reduced to about 40. **22.** Civil Service Arbitration Tribunal awarded pay increase of 5 to 6 per cent., backdated to July, to about 54,000 Post Office engineers. **26.** Sir Patrick Hennessy, chairman of Fords, said that in view of labour troubles on site of new Ford factory at Halewood, near Liverpool, his company was hesitating about proceeding with extensions there. **27.** Three strikes on Halewood site were settled, but on following day 70 members of Constructional Engineering Union went on strike again. **29.** Ford spokesman said that 84,226 man-days had been lost at Halewood up to end of October as result of disputes.

Dec. 5. Last unofficial dispute at Halewood was settled, but on Dec. 7 strike by 54 men in air conditioning plant began again. **16.** Strike of 360 bricklayers at Port Talbot works of Steel Company of Wales caused about 7,000 men to be laid off; strike lasted till Dec. 19. E.T.U. rejected Electricity Council's offer of annual increase of 3 per cent. for 3 years with additional productivity bonus. **22.** T.G.W.U. submitted claims for further substantial wage increase for London bus drivers and conductors and for reduction of working hours from 42 to 40.

(1963) Jan. 1. Last unofficial strike at Ford site at Halewood ended. Unofficial work to rule began at 9 power stations in London area and 3 elsewhere, and on following day at two more. **3.** Strike at Davy and United Engineering Co. at Sheffield ended after 5 weeks, following Company's announcement that those who did not return would be held to have discharged themselves. Strike of men installing conveyor lines on Ford site at Halewood. **8.** E.T.U. instructed its members in electricity supply industry to stop overtime from Jan. 16 unless wage claim was settled. **9.** Rolls-Royce announced that 16,000 of their 33,000 employees would be put on short-time from Jan. 28; it was hoped that all departments would be back to normal by middle of year. B.B.C. and British Actors' Equity Association signed agreement for increase in actors' T.V. fees. **10.** Engineering and shipbuilding unions decided to press for substantial increase in minimum wage rates. **16.** Electricity Board offered pay increase of 2½*d.* an hour from Feb. 1, and same amount in each of two ensuing years, together with productivity bonus of about 4*s.* 6*d.* a week. E.T.U. representative said that his union was not satisfied, and that overtime ban, which had been made official by E.T.U. earlier in day, would continue. National Federation of Building Trade Operatives lodged claim for additional 1*s.* 6*d.* an hour for members. **17.** Most extensive power black-out in London area since go-slow started. **22.** Unofficial strike of electricians began on Ford's Halewood site. **23.** T.U.C. General Council advised building unions not to submit evidence to National Incomes Commission nor to co-operate with Commission in inquiry into Scottish 40-hour week agreement. **30.** Trade union representatives recommended official strike at Ford works, Dagenham, arising from Company's refusal to take back 17 men whom it described as trouble makers. **31.** Ballot showed large majority in favour of merger between Boilermakers' Society and Shipwrights' Association.

Feb. 3. Strike of B.E.A. loaders at London Airport. **5.** Negotiations for further wage increases for London bus drivers and conductors ended in disagreement. **12.** Ballot of N.U.G.M.W. workers at Fords' Dagenham factory showed clear majority against strike. **13.** Minister of Labour decided to set up court of inquiry into Ford dispute. **14.** Ford Company said that if proposed strike were called off they would continue *ex gratia* payments to 17 dismissed men for another two months; on following day unions called off strike.

March 3. Electrical Trades Union secured 3-year agreement for contracting electricians providing, *inter alia*, for 40-hour week from September 1964; on following day it was announced that Government would refer the agreement to National Incomes Commission. **4.** Court of Inquiry into dismissal of 17 Fords' employees at Dagenham opened; Fords' spokesman said that since their discharge there had been industrial peace which had permitted uninterrupted operation of factory. **5.** National joint council for exhibition industry reached agreement for 40-hour week, to become operative immediately. **6.** A.E.U. members at new Ford works at Halewood banned overtime. Sign and Display Trades Union announced 40-hour week agreement for members under settlement with Display Producers' and Screen Printers' Association.

12. A.E.U. and T.G.W.U. recognised unofficial strikes which had been in progress for nearly a fortnight at Dunlop factory at Coventry, and which made nearly 6,000 B.M.C. employees idle at Longbridge and Cowley.

April 2. London bus drivers and conductors accepted immediate pay increase of 10*s.* a week, having rejected offer of 14*s.* per week attached to measures aimed at securing greater productivity. **3.** National Coal Board and National Union of Mineworkers agreed pay increases up to 14*s.* a week to 285,000 day-wage miners at annual cost of £10,000,000 a year. **8.** Tally clerks at Tilbury Docks went on strike, causing work to stop on 17 ships and more than 1,000 dockers to be idle. **10.** Report of inquiry by Mr. D. T. Jack into Ford dispute was published; he recommended that details of 17 men who were dismissed should be supplied to unions concerned and that Fords should have regard to unions' observations on them; he also suggested that unions involved should combine to appoint full-time paid official to supervise shop stewards and see that agreements were kept. **18.** Provisional agreement was reached for weekly wage increase of 8*s.* 9*d.* for 66,000 employees of municipal bus undertakings.

May 1. Wage increase of 5*s.* 9*d.* a week was agreed for 150,000 workers on spinning and weaving sector of Lancashire cotton industry. **2.** Production lines at Morris works at Cowley were stopped for second day in succession by unofficial strike in paintshop. **3.** Number of electricians in B.B.C. television studios went on strike. **9.** Agreement was reached on immediate pay increase of 8*s.* 9*d.* a week for about 100,000 employees of private bus companies. **10.** Dismissal of 67 electricians at Vickers-Armstrong shipyard, Barrow, arising from demarcation dispute between electricians and sheet metal workers. Port of Hull was brought to standstill by strike of tally clerks. **13.** All electricians employed by Vickers-Armstrong at Barrow came out on strike in sympathy with those dismissed. **16.** Production workers at Morris Motors radiators branch at Oxford walked out after refusing to handle work from subsidiary factory at Llanelly, where strike had been going on for over 5 weeks. **21.** Pay increases were agreed for about 6,000 engineering and maintenance men at British airports. **23.** Ford Company again told unions that they would not employ the 17 dismissed men. **24.** Nearly 6,000 production employees at Standard-Triumph Coventry factory were sent home because of strike of maintenance men and external transport drivers. **26.** T.G.W.U. members at Ford works at Dagenham decided at meeting against official strike in support of dismissed men. **27.** Jaguar car factory at Coventry was brought to standstill because of strike of 750 key workers.

July 9. Building union leaders rejected employers' offer of increased pay and shorter working hours. **16.** Steel Company of Wales announced that short-time working would be introduced at some of its plants at Abbey Works, Margam, because of shortage of orders. **18.** Members of Civil Service Union decided on Sunday strike at Tower of London and 20 national museums and art galleries, which, it was stated, would remain closed on Sundays until further notice.

Aug. 14. National Federation of Building Trade Operatives instructed about 150,000 workers at many large building and civil engineering sites to strike for a week from Aug. 19; all members of building unions were instructed to stop overtime and incentive working. **19.** Nearly 500 large building sites throughout country were closed by strike. **20.** Ministry of Labour declined to intervene in building dispute on grounds that unions had gone on strike before complying wholly with agreed negotiating procedure. **23** Strike of 20 body shop workers at Jaguar factory, Coventry, which had begun on previous day, was joined by about 1,500 assembly workers, and also caused nearly 200 workers at Pressed Steel factory, Cowley, to be laid off. **26.** Treasury agreed pay increase for 90,000 Government engineering and dockyard workers. Strike delayed finishing work on 3 large cargo vessels at shipyards at Port-Glasgow. **27.** Building employers agreed to pay wage increases for employees in each of ensuing 3 years and to reduce hours to 41 per week in November, 1964; strikes were called off. **28.** Two thousand workers were laid off at Pressed Steel works at Paisley as result of strike of 200, which had lasted since Aug. 23; further 550 men were laid off on Aug. 29.

Sept. 2. T.U.C. met at Brighton; Mr. Woodcock said that General Council intended to take initiative in coming talks with unions on amalgamation and closer co-operation. Two-day unofficial strike of dockers began at Southampton. Coventry car delivery drivers went on strike. More than 100 toolroom workers staged unofficial strike at B.M.C. factory at Washwood Heath. **3.** T.U.C. passed motion in favour of immediate increase in pensions and benefits for sick, injured, widowed and retired persons. **4.** T.U.C. voted in support of General Council's revised report opposing participation in N.E.D.C., but also approved two motions, one saying that any wage restraint must be accompanied by enforceable measures to control profits and capital gains, and the other declaring complete opposition to any form of wage restraint. Another motion, which was also carried, said that movement would refuse to accept any decision by National Incomes Commission on matters arbitrarily referred to it. **5.** T.U.C. passed resolution in favour of popular control of key enterprises and of nationalisation of road transport, steel, shipbulding and general engineering. **6.** T.U.C. concluded; General Council elected Mr. G. H. Lowthian as chairman for ensuing year. **7.** Agricultural Wages Board proposed 7*s.* a week wage increases for farm workers and reduction of hours from 46 to 45. Wage increases were agreed for 200,000 workers in clothing industry. Mr. L. Cannon, an anti-Communist, was elected President of E.T.U.; about a quarter of union's members voted. **16.** Trade unions rejected proposal in Jack report that smaller union negotiating teams should be set up at Ford works at Dagenham.

LEGAL.—**(1962) Oct. 30.** Restrictive Practices Court held that restrictions in Net Book Agreement were not contrary to public interest. **Dec. 20.** Nine Commonwealth judges were appointed Privy Councillors to enable them to assist with work of Judicial Committee. **27.** Mr. N. M. G. Faulks, Q.C., Recorder of Norwich, was appointed a Judge of the High Court upon retirement of Mr. Justice Collingwood, and was assigned to Probate, Divorce and Admiralty Division.

(1963)—Jan. 24. In High Court, Lord Chief Justice found Mr. Desmond Clough, a journalist, guilty of contempt for refusing to disclose source of information to Vassall tribunal, and on following day sentenced him to 6 months' imprisonment; later, Mr. Clough's informant came forward and he was not sent to prison. On Feb. 4, Mr. Justice Gorman sentenced two other journalists, Mr. Brendan Mulholland and Mr. Reginald Foster, to

6 and 3 months' imprisonment respectively; the Court of Appeal dismissed their appeals on Feb. 13, and the House of Lords refused them leave to appeal on March 6. **March 26.** House of Lords dismissed appeals by Mr. John Lewis and Rubber Improvement Ltd. against ordering by Court of Appeal of new trial in their libel actions against Daily Telegraph and Associated Newspapers, in which juries had awarded damages totalling £217,000. **May 27.** Judicial Committee of Privy Council held that Chief Akintola was validly dismissed from office as Premier of Western Nigeria by their Governor. **July. 4.** Mr. Justice Wilberforce, in Chancery Division, held that retain and transfer system which had been in force in Football League had been illegal, as being unreasonable restraint of trade.

SPORT.—**(1962) Oct. 7.** British drivers, J. Clark and G. Hill, took first two places in U.S. Grand Prix. **17.** New York Yacht Club rejected U.K. challenge for America's Cup series to be sailed in 1963. **25.** Alf Ramsey, manager of Ipswich Town, former Tottenham Hotspur and England footballer, was appointed manager of England team. **Nov. 7.** N. Sellwood, Australian rider of 1962 Derby winner Larkspur, was killed when his mount fell on him in race at Maisons Laffitte. **10.** M.C.C.'s score of 633 for 7 (declared) *v.* an Australian XI, was highest total ever had by an English team at Melbourne. **23.** Australian men's and women's swimming relay teams both broke world records in Commonwealth Games at Perth, W.A. **26.** Advisory County Cricket Committee recommended ending of amateur status, and also abolition of bonus points and restoration of follow-on in County Championship. England and West Indies accepted offer by Wisdens to provide perpetual trophy for winners of England—West Indies Series; the offer marked centenary, in 1964, of *Wisden's Cricketers' Almanack.* **28.** Anita Lonsbrough, the swimmer, and Brian Phelps, the diver, each won second gold medal in Commonwealth Games; Miss Lonsbrough gained third "gold" on Nov. 30. **Dec. 24.** M. C. Cowdrey, on his 30th birthday, completed innings of 307 for M.C.C. *v.* South Australia, highest innings ever played by English cricketer in Australia. **29.** G. Hill, who won South African Grand Prix at East London in a B.R.M., became champion world driver for 1962.

(1963) Jan. 3. England beat Australia by 7 wickets in Second Test at Melbourne, thus being successful in a Test in Australia for first time for 8 years; takings were a record. **26.** In Fourth Test at Adelaide, J. B. Statham overtook A. V. Bedser's record of 236 wickets in Test cricket. **27.** F. A. extended football season to May 19, because of many matches postponed through bad weather. (Season was later extended for further week.) **30.** Death of Sir Pelham Warner, great cricketer and cricket administrator. **31.** M.C.C. Committee endorsed Advisory County Cricket Committee's proposal to abolish distinction between amateurs and professionals, and also agreed to do away with bonus points in county championship and with covering of pitch except before matches and at week-ends. **Feb. 7.** Indonesia was barred from Olympic Games because of her exclusion of Formosa and Israel from Asian Games in Jakarta. **20.** Fifth Test, at Sydney, ended in draw, Australia thus retaining Ashes. **March 4.** M. C. Cowdrey, in scoring 128 not out in Second Test against New Zealand, became first England cricketer to score century against every other Test-playing country. **11.** Professional Footballers' Association decided to make Football League a "closed shop" from Sept. 1. **25.** Davey Moore, U.S. boxer, who had been knocked out while defending his world featherweight title at Los Angeles, died after being in coma for 4 days. **April 4.** Betting Levy Board listed 20 racecourses which were to receive immediate financial support and 10 others which would receive no support after 1966. **May 1.** Stirling Moss announced his retirement from motor racing. **8.** At Hampden Park, referee, who had previously sent 2 Austrian players off field, abandoned Scotland *v.* Austria match 15 minutes before end. **15.** Tottenham Hotspur won European Cup Holders' Cup, beating Athletico Madrid 5-1 in final at Rotterdam. **June 8.** Michael Lunt won Amateur Golf Championship at St. Andrews in first all-English final for 30 years; he was also first non-American to win Championship in year when Walker Cup was being held in Britain. **17.** For first time in history of County Championship, umpires declared innings to be closed when Middlesex players were not present to resume batting against Kent at Tunbridge Wells. **25.** England needed 6 runs to win with one wicket standing when Second Test Match against West Indies ended in draw at Lord's. **July 6.** For first time since 1927, weather prevented play on final day at Wimbledon; programme was postponed till July 8. **13.** R. J. Charles won Open Golf Championship, being first New Zealander and first left-hander to do so. **31.** Minister of Housing and Local Government said that appeal against refusal of planning permission to build on Sandown Park racecourse had been rejected. **Aug. 5.** Great Britain beat Sweden in Davis Cup to win European Zone for first time since war. **26.** West Indies won final Test Match at the Oval by 8 wickets, thus being successful in rubber by 3 matches to 1. **Sept. 17.** It was announced that new 12-metre yacht, to be named *Kurrewa V*, would be built to compete against *Sovereign* to be challenger for America's Cup. **28.** British athletes beat U.S.S.R. by 168/161 at Volgograd; British men won by 13 points, women losing by six.

TRANSPORT (*See also* Labour).—**(1962). Oct. 8.** B.O.A.C. reported loss for year of £14,378,201, highest ever recorded, and accumulated deficit of £64,000,000, which Corporation proposed to ask Government to be allowed to write off. **25.** British Railways announced higher fares to Channel Islands in 1963, and on Nov. 1 said that car ferry fares between mainland and Isle of Wight would be increased. **Nov. 6.** Mr. Amery, in Commons, moved second reading of Air Corporations Bill, providing for increase in borrowing limits of B.O.A.C. and B.E.A. **16.** B.E.A. asked Minister of Aviation for permission to transfer all their services at Gatwick to London Airport. **18.** Demolition began of more than £500,000 worth of new building and renovation done since the war at Euston. **23.** British Railways said that no trains would run on Western Region and Marylebone suburban line on Christmas Day, and that services on Southern Region would stop after midday; it was later learnt that a number of Christmas Eve trains on Western Region would also be cancelled. **28.** B.E.A., and 7 independent airlines, said that they would apply for authority to increase their fares between London and Glasgow, Edinburgh and Belfast. **29.** Britain and France signed agreement for joint development of 1,450 m.p.h. supersonic airliner. **Dec. 4.** It was stated that 4-car multiple-unit diesel sets on St. Pancras to St. Albans and Bedford Service were being withdrawn for modification owing to high incidence of repairs and need to correct faults; their replacement by slower diesel-hauled rolling-stock caused delays of up to 20 minutes in 60-minute run. **6.** Dr. Beeching said that commuters into London travelled at sub-normal fares. **12.** Minister of Transport said that regulations would be brought into effect from Dec. 20 requiring courts to take into consideration evidence of results of chemical tests on drivers for alcohol. British Transport Commission announced that it would go into association with 19 property development companies to exploit use of railway land. **27.** British Transport Commission announced revised plans for closure of railway workshops, reducing number of redundancies in 1963 from 8,300 to 5,300.

(1963) Jan. 1. British Railways took over Pullman Car Company. **8.** British Railways said that Sunday services would be withdrawn on former Great Central main line between Aylesbury and Sheffield from March. **11.** British Railways reported drop in receipts for freight services of £14,000,000 in 1962 compared with 1961. **Feb. 4.** Government spokesman said that work on Tay road bridge would begin in spring. **8.** Air Transport Licensing Board granted many applications by B.E.A. and independent operators for permission to increase fares from about 5 to 20 per cent. in domestic air services. **11.** Minister of Transport issued proposals for extension of M1 motorway to North Circular Road. **15.** Mr. Marples said that he could not understand why some people were worried about the proposed rail closures. **26.** British Railways announced immediate closure to passengers of 6 stations on former Great Central line. **28.** Order was passed reducing from 6 to 5 years the age for compulsory testing of cars. **March 27.** Dr. Beeching's proposals for British Railways included closure of 5,000 miles of passenger track and 2,128 stations and further substantial increases of fares in London area. Speaking after publication of report, Dr. Beeching said that he expected reduction of railwaymen employed would amount to 70,000. Mr. Marples said that roads might need to be widened to take extra traffic arising from rail closures. **28.** A.S.L.E.F. executive issued statement repudiating remarks of its general secretary on Beeching report, and pointing out that its 1962 delegate conference had expressed view that branch line closures and withdrawals of services should be strongly opposed, by industrial action if necessary. **29.** Ministry of Aviation supported proposal to raise tourist-class fares on North Atlantic and Pacific air routes. **April 2.** N.U.R. negotiating committee recommended strike against Dr. Beeching's plans, and on following day executive agreed to meeting with two other railway unions to consider action. **4.** Union leaders, after talks with Dr. Beeching, said that no progress had been made. **8.** N.U.R., A.S.L.E.F. and Confederation of Shipbuilding and Engineering Unions agreed on joint strike if they found it necessary. **10.** Annual report of Central Transport Consultative Committee said that there was urgent need for study of costs of all forms of transport, including social costs of road congestion and accidents. Committee said that negative policy of closing down railways was not a panacea and that without radical improvement in speed, comfort and punctuality of passenger and freight train services, Railways Board would not stop making losses. **11.** N.U.R. decided to call 3-day national railway strike within ensuing 4 weeks. **23.** Mr. Marples informed T.U.C. that Beeching plan would go ahead on lines proposed, and N.U.R. said that 3-day strike would take place from May 14-16. **24.** Labour Party executive called for deferment of Beeching plan until general survey of national transport had been carried out. Confederation of Shipbuilding and Engineering Unions recommended its unions to support rail strike. **25.** Scottish T.U.C. expressed opposition to Beeching plan. Number of N.U.R. branches passed resolutions asking for their members on London Underground to be called out during proposed strike. It was announced that road haulage costs would go up by 5 per cent. from June 1. **28.** Scottish Tourist Board expressed fear that Beeching plan would cause whole Highland communities to wither away. **29.** Minister of Transport told Commons that Government intended to set up independent inquiry into system of licensing road haulage vehicles. **May 1.** Leaders of A.S.L.E.F. decided that their members should not join proposed strike. **2.** It was stated that during ensuing 4 years B.O.A.C. would be reducing its fleet and staff. **9.** In consequence of promises by British Railways of better terms for redundant men, N.U.R. called off its strike. **12.** Ministry of Aviation sent message to Pan American and Trans World airlines asking whether they intended to comply with British requirements to increase Transatlantic air fares, and saying that if they failed to do so they would render their aircraft liable to detention. **June 5.** It was announced that further large increases in London bus, underground and rail fares would take place on June 23; spokesman said that this might be only interim step. **26.** English Electric Company said that owing to sudden and unexpected interruption of flow of orders from British Railways combined with steady falling-off in volume of locomotive business in general, it would be necessary to close down its locomotive works at Darlington at or soon after end of 1963, throwing 900 people out of work. **July 5.** British Railways and London Transport asked Transport Tribunal for authority to cut discount on quarterly and longer period season tickets in London area. **8.** Mr. Harold Wilson, addressing a T.G.W.U. conference, said that a Labour Government would halt Beeching "surgery" until complete survey had been made of Britain's transport needs. **19.** Dr. Beeching said that proposals under his plan were unlikely to be changed by examination of roads and other questions and that cuts need not wait until everything had been taken into account. **24.** Minister of Transport directed that proposal by British Railways to end passenger service between Haltwhistle and Alston should not be carried out. **31.** British Railways announced increase in charges for second-class sleeping berths. **Aug. 7.** Confederation of Shipbuilding and Engineering Unions agreed to concert efforts to delay railway closures until after general election. **20.** New B.A.C. One-Eleven aircraft made successful 28-minute trial flight from Hurn Airport. **Sept. 3.** London Transport announced further reduction in week-end bus routes from mid-October. **5.** T.U.C. passed unanimously resolution calling on Government to defer major rail closures proposed by Dr. Beeching until thorough survey of other transport services had been completed and national transport plan devised. **30.** Ministry of Aviation proposed increased airport charges to British and overseas airlines, totalling more than £2,000,000 a year, from April 1964. Labour Party Conference carried motion demanding survey of all inland transport before further railway closures.

BRITISH COMMONWEALTH

(*see also* under Africa)

(1962) Oct. 3. Three Supreme Court judges in Ceylon, appointed by Minister of Justice to try persons alleged to have taken part in attempted *coup d'état* in January, held unanimously that they had no jurisdiction to do so. **10.** Clashes between Indian and Chinese troops in Southern Tibet were reported. **12.** Mr. Nehru said that talks with China were no longer possible and that Indian Army had been ordered to clear Chinese from territory south of McMahon line. **21.** Indian troops were forced back with heavy losses by Chinese infantry on north-east frontier. **22.** Official spokesman said that Indian troops were still yielding ground, and it was also reported that Chinese tanks had been in action, overwhelming Indian posts. Yemen bomber and 2 fighters attacked town in Aden Amirate of Baihan, 2 houses being destroyed and a child killed. **23.** Chinese made new thrusts in Ladakh area, but Chinese Government made proposals to India for settlement by negotiation. British troops were sent to Baihan. **24.** Indian Government said that it would only consider negotiations if China withdrew north of McMahon line; Indian troops continued to fall back before Chinese assaults. **25.** Roadhead village of Towang was captured by Chinese; Indian report acknowledged heavy casualties. **26.** President of India declared state of emergency for whole country. **29.** Indian Government accepted U.S. offer of military assistance. **31.** Mr. Nehru took over post of Minister of Defence, Mr. Krishna Menon becoming head of new Ministry of Defence Production. Pakistan declined to give assurance to keep peace on Indian borders unless India agreed to plebiscite in Kashmir under U.N. auspices.

Nov. 5. Indian Government disclosed that strategic frontier post of Daulet Beg Oldi had been evacuated some days earlier. **7.** Mr. Nehru accepted resignation of Mr. Krishna Menon from Indian Cabinet. **15.** Chinese resumed attack on Indian frontier. **18.** It was reported that U.S.S.R. had promised to supply 12 MIG fighters to India and to open aircraft factory there. Chinese attacked successfully in force at both ends of North East Frontier Agency. **19.** Chinese overran important Indian position on 14,000 ft. Se La ridge. Indian Ambassador in Washington delivered message from Mr. Nehru to President Kennedy, calling urgently for U.S. aid. **21.** Chinese Government announced that its troops would cease fire from midnight and that from Dec. 1 they would be withdrawn behind lines of control which existed on Nov. 7, 1959. Mr. Nehru said that Indian position continued to be that situation on frontier before Sept. 8, 1962, should be restored. More than 200 members of Indian Communist Party were arrested, including leaders of Opposition in West Bengal, Kerala and Andhra Pradesh. **23.** Both sides ceased fire on Indian frontier. Many more Indian Communists were arrested. **29.** Mr. Nehru and President Ayub Khan of Pakistan agreed to meet in attempt to solve Kashmir question.

Dec. 3. It was announced that inhabitants of Tristan de Cunha had decided in secret ballot, by 148 votes to 5, to return to their island. **9.** Oil town of Seria, in Brunei, was reported captured by rebels; Government sent for reinforcements of British and Gurkha troops, which on following day were reported to have secured airstrip and to be advancing on town. **11.** Whole of Seria was captured except for police station, where 50 rebels remained with hostages. Tunku Abdul Rahman, Prime Minister of Malaya, said that Brunei rebel movement had begun in Indonesia. **12.** In recapture from rebels of Limbang, town in North Sarawak near Brunei frontier, 5 Royal Marines were killed. Seria police station was also recaptured and 45 persons, including 14 Britons, freed. **21.** After 3-day meeting of President Kennedy and Mr. Macmillan in Bahamas, it was announced that Skybolt missile was being abandoned and that U.S.A. would provide Polaris missiles without warheads for British submarines, to be used for international defence of Western alliance; President de Gaulle would be invited to accept similar offer. Mr. Diefenbaker arrived from Canada and took part in discussions. **31.** Leaders of Turkish Cypriots said that they would defy Government and set up separate municipal authorities in the 5 main towns.

(1963). Jan. 16. Britain and South Arabian Federation signed treaty for accession of Aden to the Federation. **28.** It was announced that British paratroops had been sent to Brunei; Tunku Abdul Rahman said that 2,000 British troops were being sent to Far East "in connexion with mounting tension in Brunei and Sarawak". **31.** Mr. Diefenbaker attacked U.S. State Department for "unprecedented and unwarranted intrusion in Canadian affairs," in suggesting that without nuclear warheads Canada was not fulfilling her proper role in North American defence.

Feb. 4. Mr. Harkness, Canadian Defence Minister, resigned because of difference with Mr. Diefenbaker over nuclear arms policy. Admiralty said that placing of R.N. contracts with Bailey (Malta) Ltd. had been temporarily suspended. **5.** Canadian Government was defeated twice on votes of no confidence in House of Commons, by 31 votes on each occasion; on following day Mr. Diefenbaker announced that Parliament had been dissolved and general election fixed for April 8. **7.** I. F. Skripov, First Secretary at Soviet Embassy in Canberra, was ordered to leave Australia within 7 days for engaging in elaborate preparations for espionage. **9.** Two more members of Mr. Diefenbaker's Ministry resigned. **26.** South Arabian Federation troops, under British Officers, fired on Yemen Republican troops which had crossed Aden border and ignored ultimatum to withdraw. **27.** Yemen Republicans machine-gunned military medical post in Beihan.

March 3. Terms of agreement fixing border between Pakistan and China were published. **28.** After unions representing railway and Government workers in East Pakistan had declared intention of defying Government's order banning proposed strike, more than 300 leaders were arrested and East Pakistan newspapers were forbidden to publish reports about strike.

April 1. Seventeen Cuban exiles were detained by police on island in Bahamas and taken by H.M.S. *Londonderry* to Nassau. **5.** Riots, with loss of life, caused by inter-union rivalry, took place in Georgetown, British Guiana. **14.** Mr. Diefenbaker conceded defeat after results in Canadian general election had given figures of 130 seats for Liberals, 94 for Conservatives, 24 for Social Credit and 17 for New Democrats. **16.** British troops were flown to Sarawak-Indonesia border after raid had taken place on police post. **17.** Mr. Diefenbaker resigned and Mr. Lester Pearson, Canadian Liberal leader, accepted Governor-General's invitation to form Cabinet. **18.** A British officer was killed in action against rebels in Brunei. **22.** Mr. Pearson was sworn in as Prime Minister of Canada, and named members of his Cabinet.

May 9. State of emergency was again declared in British Guiana by Governor at request of Dr. Jagan. **13.** Pakistan Supreme Court held that President Ayub Khan's order amending constitution to allow Ministers to retain seats in legislatures was unconstitutional; 6 out of 8 Ministers in central Government and many more in provincial Ministries were deemed ineligible to continue to sit in legislatures. **28.** More than 10,000 persons lost their lives in cyclone which struck Chittagong and adjoining areas in Bay of Bengal. **29.** After Speaker of British Guiana Parliament had called for apologies from Dr. Jagan and 3 other Government M.P.s for disrespect towards Chair, they refused to apologise or to leave House when motion for suspension was carried by 15–13; the Speaker said that as Serjeant at Arms was on strike he had no one available to remove the 4 members forcibly, and he adjourned Parliament indefinitely. **30.** Forty-eight people were arrested during pro-Yemen demonstrations in Aden.

June 3. All 29 persons on board were killed when Indian air-liner, flying holiday-makers to Srinagar, crashed near Pathankot. **4.** About 120 persons were killed in clash between Shia and Sunni Moslems at village near Khairpur in West Pakistan. **12.** Further rioting on considerable scale took place in Georgetown, British Guiana; on following day police fired on crowd which was stated to be trying to trap Dr. Jagan and his colleagues in Parliament building. **26.** Thousands of people demonstrated in Georgetown against Government; tear-gas was used to disperse the crowds.

July 2. One man was shot dead and 12 injured in further fighting in Georgetown. **4.** A company of 2nd Battalion, Green Jackets, was sent to reinforce British troops in British Guiana; 2 more persons were killed in renewed clashes. **7.** General strike in British Guiana was called off, but in further rioting, British troops opened fire after repeated warnings had been ignored and 2 persons were killed. **12.** Convicts in open gaol near Singapore hacked to death British prison superintendent and 3 guards and wounded 28 warders.

Aug. 11. British Government agreed to U Thant's representatives ascertaining wishes of people of North Borneo and Sarawak on entry into new Federation of Malaysia. **15.** Cuban armed troops from two warships and a helicopter landed on British island in Cay Sul group, seized two fishing boats and captured 19 Cuban refugees. **18.** Fighting took place between Indonesian-based guerillas and Gurkha troops on Sarawak border; a British officer was killed. **20.** British naval units arrested 5 armed Cuban exiles on another island in Bahamas. **24.** Mr. Nehru accepted resignations of 6 members of his Cabinet and 6 chief ministers of states. **31.** Singapore, North Borneo and Sarawak proclaimed *de facto* independence, although establishment of Malaysia had been deferred till Sept. 16; Prime Minister of Singapore proclaimed island to be self-governing.

Sept. 8. Pakistan Government accused air adviser to Indian High Commission, and 3 other members of staff, of espionage, and called for their withdrawal from Pakistan. **9.** Pakistan newspapers held one-day strike in protest against restrictive Government press ordinance. Commonwealth Relations Office announced agreement for re-imposition of Maldivian Government authority over Addu Atoll. **10.** President Ayub Khan suspended Pakistan press ordinance for one month. **15.** U Thant approved report of investigating team which had found general support in Sarawak and North Borneo for incorporation in Federation of Malaysia. **16.** Federation of Malaysia was officially inaugurated. **17.** Malaysia broke off diplomatic relations with Indonesia. On following day, Malaysian Cabinet decided to call up reserves. **18.** Australian Government announced that in view of opposition to name "royal" as main unit of currency under projected decimal system, "dollar" would be substituted. **26.** Progressive Conservative Government made many gains in Ontario provincial elections, winning 78 seats out of 108; Liberal leader of Opposition lost his seat.

UNITED NATIONS

(1962). Oct. 11. Sir Hugh Foot, British representative at U.N. on colonial and trusteeship questions, resigned from British delegation. **17.** In General Assembly, Nigeria was defeated by Morocco in voting for place on Security Council. **23.** Security Council began consideration of resolutions by U.S.A. and U.S.S.R., and complaint by Cuba, on Cuban crisis. **24.** U Thant sent personal appeal to President Kennedy and Mr. Khrushchev. **25.** President Kennedy said that he had authorised Mr. Adlai Stevenson to discuss with U Thant proposals for removing threat to peace, and Mr. Khrushchev said that he agreed with U Thant's proposals. General Assembly unanimously approved admission of Uganda to United Nations membership. **30.** U Thant flew to Cuba for talks with Dr. Castro. General Assembly rejected, by 56–42, with 12 abstentions, Soviet proposal to replace Nationalist China by Communist China as U.N. member. **31.** U Thant returned to New York after failing to secure acceptance from Dr. Castro of U.N. inspection to verify removal of Soviet missiles from Cuba. **Nov. 6.** General Assembly, by 67 to 16, with 23 abstentions, condemned South Africa's *apartheid* policy, recommended member states to break off diplomatic relations with South Africa and apply economic sanctions and requested Security Council if necessary to consider action under Article 6 of United Nations Charter, which provides for expulsion from U.N. **29.** United Nations plan for Congo proposed, including economic measures amounting to sanctions against Katanga to bring about its acceptance of plan. **30.** General Assembly unanimously elected U Thant Secretary-General till Nov. 1966. **Dec. 17.** General Assembly called on all member nations to stop selling arms and military equipment to Portuguese Government.

(1963). Jan. 2. U Thant declined to renew negotiations with President Tshombe of Katanga. **11.** Statement of U.N. accounts at end of 1962 showed that member nations owed about £43,000,000. **29.** U Thant said that United Nations forces in Congo would be reduced from 19,000 to 12,000 by end of March. **April 30.** U Thant said that U.N. observation team would be sent to patrol border between Saudi Arabia and Yemen and maintain demilitarised buffer zone. **May 10.** Security Council decided to leave settlement of dispute between Haiti and Dominican Republic to Organisation of American States. **22.** U.S.S.R. informed U.N. that she would continue to refuse to pay any part of costs of operations in Congo or Middle East and would not pay that part of assessment for regular budget directed towards amortizing recent issue of U.N. bonds. **28.** U Thant said that if parties concerned did not agree to bear whole cost of U.N. observation mission to Yemen, estimated at about £357,000, balance would be met from U.N. funds. **July 31.** By 8 votes to 0, with 3 abstentions, Security Council passed motion asking member states to impose partial embargo on sale and supply of arms and military equipment to Portugal. **Aug. 2.** Mr. Adlai Stevenson told Security Council that at end of year U.S.A. would put embargo on sale of all arms and military equipment to South Africa. **7.** Security Council, by 9 votes to 0, with U.K. and France abstaining, called on all states to cease forthwith sale and shipment of arms, ammunition and military vehicles to South Africa. **Sept. 3.** U.S.S.R. vetoed resolution in Security Council condemning Syrian actions on Israel frontier, for which 8 out of 11 members had voted. **13.** Great Britain exercised veto in Security Council for first time since 1956 to defeat Afro-Asian motion which sought to prevent Britain transferring armed forces and aircraft to control of Southern Rhodesia after Federation of Rhodesia and Nyasaland was dissolved. **18.** *Apartheid* committee recommended expulsion of South Africa from U.N. and blockade of the country if necessary. **19.** U.S.S.R. proposed to General Assembly that summit meeting should be held in first part of 1964 for 18 member-nations of disarmament conference.

UNITED STATES

(1962) Oct. 1. After fighting on university campus at Oxford, Mississippi, in which 2 persons were killed, Federal marshals, troops and military police restored order in early morning; nearly 200 persons were arrested including former Major-Gen. E. A. Walker, who had commanded Federal troops at Little Rock in 1957; James Meredith, the Negro applicant, was duly enrolled in University. **2.** U.S. Court of Appeals in New Orleans postponed decision in contempt proceedings against Governor Barnett of Mississippi. **3.** State Department proposed that other N.A.T.O. countries should accept restrictions on use of their shipping in Cuban trade. Commander Walter Schirra was sent into orbit from Cape Canaveral and successfully recovered from Pacific Ocean 9 hours later after making 6 circuits of earth. **9.** International Longshoremen's Association in New York recommended its members to refuse to handle cargoes to and from Russia and Cuba, including those of any ships which called at Cuban ports. **12–13.** Violent storms on Pacific Coast caused deaths of 45 people. **15.** Thor rocket had to be destroyed in unsuccessful high-altitude nuclear test over Pacific; small pieces of radioactive débris fell back on Johnston Island. **18.** President Kennedy and Mr. Gromyko held talks for 2½ hours at White House. **19.** It was announced that moon rocket launched from Cape Canaveral on previous day had become dead, its instruments having failed. **21.** High-altitude nuclear test was unsuccessfully carried out over Johnston Island. **22.** President Kennedy, in television broadcast to nation, said that nuclear missile sites had been observed in Cuba and that jet bombers capable of carrying nuclear weapons, were being assembled there, while air bases were being prepared. He said that he had ordered blockade to prevent supplies of offensive military equipment reaching Cuba, and that all ships of any kind, from whatever nation, would be turned back if found to contain cargoes of offensive weapons. The President's address was made after meetings of National Security Council and Cabinet. It was stated that divisions of 18th Airborne Corps were already on alert, as well as 2nd Marine Division and all forces at Guantanamo base in Cuba. **23.** President Kennedy signed declaration formally establishing arms blockade of Cuba from following day and saying that force would be used if vessels refused to comply with instructions. U.S. Secretary of Defence said that about 25 Soviet cargo ships were moving towards Cuba. Government published photographic evidence of missile bases in Cuba. **24.** Government spokesman said that no ships had been intercepted approaching Cuba; some Communist ships had apparently changed course, but some were still steering towards Cuba. Voluntary censorship on military news came into force. It was announced that President Kennedy had withheld his signature to Bill which would have doubled tariff on about half the cycles imported into U.S.A. **25.** Government officials said that construction of Soviet missile bases in Cuba was continuing; U.S. naval units allowed Soviet tanker to proceed through blockade. **26.** President Kennedy, in letter to U Thant, said that U.S. vessels in Caribbean would do everything possible in ensuing days to avoid direct confrontation with Soviet ships in order to minimise risk of untoward incident. First boarding of ship took place when U.S. Navy units intercepted cargo vessel flying Lebanese flag, but under Soviet charter; boarding was completed without incident. Statement from White House said that development of ballistic missile sites on Cuba was continuing at rapid pace apparently with objective of achieving full operational capacity as soon as possible. **28.** President Kennedy, in a statement and a personal message to Mr. Khrushchev, welcomed latter's decision to dismantle missile bases in Cuba. **29.** The President ordered lifting of U.S. naval blockade of Cuba for two days during visit of U Thant.

Nov. 1. Naval blockade of Cuba and aerial watch on missile bases were resumed. **2.** President Kennedy said that air reconnaissance had shown that missile sites in Cuba were being broken up. **4.** The President announced that latest series of U.S. atmospheric nuclear tests had been completed, but that underground tests would continue. **7.** Results of elections showed that Democrats had gained 4 seats in Senate and lost 4 in House of Representatives; Mr. Edward Kennedy, who won in Massachusetts, became youngest member of Senate; Mr. Nixon was defeated in California. Mrs. Eleanor Roosevelt died in New York. **9.** Defence Department spokesman said that U.S. naval units had intercepted, without incident, 5 Soviet ships returning from Cuba, and were satisfied that 3 carried ballistic missiles. **17.** Member of Cuban delegation to U.N., whose diplomatic immunity had not yet become effective, together with two other Cubans resident in New York, were arrested on charges of conspiring to commit sabotage in U.S.A. U.S. Government called for removal from country of 2 other Cuban U.N. delegates, who were diplomatically immune. **20.** President Kennedy said that he had ordered lifting of blockade of Cuba after Mr. Krushchev had informed him that all Soviet bombers would be withdrawn within 30 days. **21.** The President signed order prohibiting racial discrimination in housing built or purchased with Federal assistance.

Dec. 3. State Department said that Soviet bombers had been photographed in ships leaving Cuba. **5.** Mr. Dean Acheson, adviser to President Kennedy and former Secretary of State, said in speech at West Point that Britain's independent role was about to be played out, and that her policy seemed as weak as her military power. **6.** U.S. Government refused to allow New York representative of Katanga information service to remain in U.S.A. **7.** U.S.A. and Britain tested low-yield British underground nuclear device on site in Nevada. **14.** *Mariner II*, unmanned U.S. spacecraft, established contact between itself, Venus and the earth. **17.** President Kennedy said that U.S.A. did not need Skybolt missile and that she hoped that Europe would make greater effort on its own. Congressional committee accused State Department of misusing its visa power to silence Mr. Struelens, head of Katanga information services, when he criticised U.N. military action in Congo in 1961. **19.** U.S.A. recognised Republic of Yemen. **20.** State Department said that U.S. military mission was being sent to Congo. **24.** Strike of dockers in Atlantic and Gulf coast ports began after International Longshoremen's Association had rejected President Kennedy's proposal that it should be postponed for 90 days.

(1963) Jan. 4. State Department issued statement calling on President Tshombe to end Katanga secession promptly. **16.** President Kennedy appointed 3-man board to mediate in dock strike.

17. The President's Budget message forecast deficit of $8,800,000,000 in current financial year and $11,900,000,000 in ensuing one. **22.** Settlement was reached in East coast dock strike.

Feb. 6. It was announced that U.S. Government cargoes would no longer be shipped on foreign vessels trading with Cuba. **8.** U.S.A. suspended economic and technical assistance to Ceylon because of Ceylon Government's failure to compensate U.S. oil companies for expropriated property. **21.** In consequence of attack by 2 MIG jet fighters from Cuba on U.S. shrimping-boat in Florida Straits, President Kennedy ordered armed forces to take all necessary action against repetition of incident. **28.** Civil Aeronautics Board forbade Bonanza Airlines to buy 3 British-made B.A.C. One-Eleven jet aircraft.

March 17. Printers' union decided by small majority to reject leaders' advice for settlement of New York newspaper strike on terms proposed by Mayor Wagner. **19.** New A 3 model Polaris met with sixth failure in 8 test launches at Cape Canaveral. **24.** Special Presidential committee advised President to reduce amount and scope of foreign aid. New York printers agreed to Mayor Wagner's recommendations. **30.** Departments of State and Justice, in joint statement, said that action was being taken to prevent further raids on Cuba by Cuban exiles.

April 1. New York newspapers were published after strike lasting 114 days. **3.** Police in Greenwood, Mississippi, arrested 15 negroes who were marching to register as voters. **9.** In ceremony at White House attended by Mr. Randolph Churchill, Sir Winston Churchill was declared an honorary citizen of U.S.A. **10.** Nuclear submarine *Thresher*, with 130 men on board, was reported overdue and presumed missing in Atlantic. On April 12 all hope of saving crew was abandoned. **17.** President Kennedy's commission on civil rights advised him to consider cutting off Federal funds to State of Mississippi.

May 3. During demonstration at Birmingham, Alabama, 750 negroes were arrested. **7.** Second Telstar communication satellite was launched from Cape Canaveral. Government ordered withdrawal of all dependants of U.S. diplomatic and military staffs from Haiti. **12.** After race riots at Birmingham, Alabama, President Kennedy announced that he had ordered troops to the area. **14.** Government informed Pan American Airlines and Trans World Airlines that they could increase transatlantic fares as agreed by International Air Transport Association. President Kennedy also sent Bill to Congress proposing to give Civil Aeronautics Board authority to enforce its own fares on foreign lines. **15.** Major Gordon Cooper was successfully launched into orbit from Cape Canaveral; after circling earth 22 times he was safely recovered from Pacific on following day, having descended in sight of waiting aircraft carrier. **19.** U.S. Government instructed its representatives in Haiti to avoid all contact with Haitian Government. **20.** Supreme Court reversed number of convictions connected with negro attempts to desegregate luncheon counters by organising sit-in demonstrations. **21.** Governor Wallace of Alabama said that he would personally bar any negro from entering University of Alabama. **22.** Results of referendum showed that farmers had rejected Administration's proposals for controls designed to stop over-production of wheat and to stabilise prices.

June 5. Governor Wallace was ordered by Federal judge to refrain from interfering in any manner with enrolment of negroes at University of Alabama. **7.** A man was killed during racial rioting at Lexington, North Carolina. **11.** Two negroes were admitted as students to University of Alabama at Tuscaloosa after Governor Wallace had yielded; several hundred National Guardsmen were present under Presidential orders. Mr. Averill Harriman was appointed to lead U.S. delegation at nuclear test ban talks in Moscow. **12.** Mr. Medgar Evers, field secretary of National Association for Advancement of Coloured People, was shot dead outside his home in Jackson, Mississippi. **17.** Supreme Court voted that use of Lord's Prayer and Bible at devotinal exercises in state-supported schools was unconstitutional. **19.** President Kennedy proposed extensive civil rights legislation and asked Congress to sit until Bill was passed.

July 1. State Department demanded immediate recall of Gennadiy Sevastyanov, *attaché* in Soviet Embassy in Washington, who was said to have attempted to recruit U.S. Government official as spy. **2.** Four persons were arrested on charges of conspiring to spy for Soviet Union. **9.** It was announced that U.S. Government had rejected request for economic aid to British Guiana. **11 & 12.** Racial fighting took place in Cambridge, Maryland and Savannah, Georgia. **26.** President Kennedy appealed to President de Gaulle to sign nuclear test ban treaty and abandon French testing programme.

Aug. 1. President Kennedy said that he had approached President de Gaulle with view to discussions on how interests of U.S.A., U.K. and France could best be protected in light of nuclear test ban agreement. **6.** Government announced that retaliatory measures would be taken against imports from E.E.C. countries because of their failure to reduce tariff on U.S. chickens. **7.** Mr. Averill Harriman said that Mr. Khrushchev had turned down suggestions for exchange of mobile observers at missile sites. **16.** State Department announced that agreement had been signed with Soviet on joint programme of experiments with weather and communications satellites. **23.** House of Representatives reduced President's proposed foreign aid appropriation by $585,000,000. **28.** Demonstration of negroes and white sympathisers took place in Washington; more than 200,000 persons were estimated to have taken part in march, which took place entirely peacefully. Eight hours before national rail strike was due to begin, Congress passed emergency legislation to prohibit a strike for 180 days and to compel both sides in dispute to accept arbitration. **30.** U.S.A. suspended loan to Pakistan of $4,300,000 for new airport at Dacca.

Sept. 2. Governor Wallace of Alabama, in face of Federal court order, sent 100 state troopers to Tuskegee, where he ordered closure for week of school which had been directed to admit 13 negro children. **4.** Two negro children entered elementary school in Birmingham, Alabama and two more entered high school at Mobile; they were the first negroes to register in hitherto white schools in Alabama. **5.** In rioting at Birmingham a negro was killed, and at Governor Wallace's request the schools in which desegregation was being attempted were closed. **6.** U.S. circuit court in Alabama rejected petition to stay order to integrate schools; state troopers temporarily closed more schools in Huntsville and Mobile. **9.** Governor Wallace ordered prohibition of racial integration in public schools of Birmingham, Mobile and Tuskegee; the schools were opened, but negroes were refused admission. Department of Justice obtained court order instructing Mr. Wallace to cease interference. **10.** President Kennedy placed National Guard in Alabama under Federal command and authorised Secretary of Defence to use Army troops if necessary to enforce court orders;

20 negro children were admitted into previously all-white schools; rioting developed in Birmingham. **15.** Four negro schoolgirls were killed and 23 injured by bomb planted in church at Birmingham; during rioting which followed 16-year-old negro youth was shot dead. **20.** President Kennedy, addressing U.N. General Assembly, suggested that U.S.A. and U.S.S.R. should sponsor joint expedition to moon.

FRANCE

(1962) Oct. 4. In television broadcast to nation, President de Gaulle said that he might resign if forthcoming referendum on presidency was not favourable to his views. **5.** After 12-hour debate, motion of censure was carried against M. Pompidou's Ministry in early hours of morning. **6.** M. Pompidou tendered his resignation to President de Gaulle, who announced dissolution of National Assembly, asking M. Pompidou to remain in office meanwhile. **18.** President de Gaulle, in another television broadcast, re-affirmed that he would resign if referendum on presidency failed to support his views or majority in favour of them was inadequate. French television announcers, journalists and technicians went on strike against alleged misuse by Government of State broadcasting in referendum campaign. **19.** Council of State held military Court of justice, established by presidential decree to try O.A.S. members, to be unconstitutional and ordered its dissolution. **28.** Referendum on presidency showed 61·76 per cent. of valid votes cast to be in favour of President de Gaulle's view; there were 22·75 per cent. abstentions or spoiled papers. **Nov. 19.** Results of first ballot in general election, in which 66·56 per cent. valid votes were cast showed election of 50 Gaullist candidates out of 97 successful on first ballot. **22.** M. René Coty, last President of Fourth Republic, died at age of 80. **23.** All 21 persons in Hungarian airliner were killed when it crashed and burst into flames in field while attempting to land in fog at Le Bourget airport. **25.** Second ballot in general election confirmed victory for Gaullists, who with their allies won 265 seats, and obtained clear majority; Communists increased their number of seats from 10 to 42. **28.** President de Gaulle commuted to life imprisonment sentence of death passed on ex-General Jouhaud. **Dec. 6.** M. Pompidou named members of his new Cabinet.

(1963) Jan. 13. Legislation was approved setting up new state security court; its powers included detention of suspects for up to 10 days without preferment of charges. **14.** President de Gaulle held press conference, at which he said that Britain was not yet ready to join Common Market and rejected U.S. offer of Polaris missiles. He suggested possibility of form of association with Common Market for Britain instead of full membership. **21.** Dr. Adenauer arrived in Paris, and on following day President de Gaulle and he signed Franco-German treaty of co-operation. **Feb. 6.** Military court, trying men accused of attempting to assassinate President de Gaulle, suspended leading defence counsel from practising for 3 years. **15.** Three officers and a woman were arrested on allegations of complicity in another plot to assassinate President de Gaulle. **March 1.** French miners went on 48-hour strike; Government issued requisition order on them to take effect on March 4, subjecting them to penalties if they did not report for work; many miners continued to strike on March 4. **4.** Military court sentenced to death 6 persons (3 of them in their absence) on charges of attempting to assassinate President de Gaulle; 8 others, 2 of whom were absent, were sentenced to long terms of imprisonment. M. Bidault broadcast from London in B.B.C. television programme, which had been recorded some time earlier. **5.** Strike in French mines became almost total. **11.** Former Colonel Bastien-Thiry, who had been sentenced to death by military court, was executed; two others had death sentences commuted. **15.** Twenty-four hour railway strike took place throughout France. **25.** Talks between coal board and miners' unions broke down. **April 5.** Miners returned to work after strike lasting 35 days. **July 29.** President de Gaulle rejected Moscow test ban treaty, but said that he would invite the other nuclear powers to join in studying disarmament before the end of year. **Aug. 29.** President de Gaulle offered cordial French co-operation to South Vietnamese in any national effort they made to surmount crisis in their country. **Sept. 1.** Riot police were called in at Calais to keep order when British tourists without reservations tried to get on to car ferries. **3.** General Vanuxem and several others accused of conspiracy against state as leading members of O.A.S., were put on trial after almost two years in custody. **4.** Death of M. Robert Schuman, for many years French Foreign Minister, and great worker for unity of Europe. **7.** General Vanuxem was acquitted; two others were sentenced to 10 years' and 6 years' imprisonment respectively.

SOVIET

(1962) Oct. 17. Tass Agency reported that Russia had carried out tests in Pacific with new type of rocket. Mr. Khrushchev asked U.S.A. for resumption of talks on Berlin. **23.** Soviet Government issued warning to U.S.A. on policy in Cuba, and stopped all leave for armed forces. **24.** Mr. Khrushchev said that Soviet Government would take no rash decisions over Cuba and thought Summit conference would be useful. Foreign Ministry rejected U.S. Note about measures against Cuba. **26.** In letter to U Thant, Mr. Krushchev said that he had ordered Russian ships to stay out of interception area round Cuba as purely temporary move. **28.** Mr. Krushchev agreed to dismantle offensive missile bases in Cuba under U.N. supervision. **Nov 1.** Spacecraft was launched on 7-month journey towards Mars. **4.** Soviet authorities demanded recall of U.S. Embassy official after allegation of espionage. **7.** Mr. Khrushchev said that current Russian series of nuclear tests would end on Nov. 20. **15.** Mr. G. M. Wynne, British business-man who was arrested in Budapest on Nov. 2, was reported to have been handed over to Soviet officials. **Dec. 11.** Arrest was announced of Soviet scientific worker said to have had links with Western intelligence services through Mr. Wynne. **23.** Mr. Zorin was removed from his post as permanent representative of U.S.S.R. at U.N.

(1963) Jan. 20. Letter from Mr. Krushchev to President Kennedy was published, in which he said that Soviet would agree to 2 or 3 inspectors on territory of nuclear powers in seismic areas where suspicious earth tremors occurred. **Feb. 12.** Soviet Government ordered U.S. National Broadcasting Company to close Moscow offices and withdraw its correspondent. **19.** Government informed U.S.A. that several thousand Soviet troops would be withdrawn from Cuba by March 15. **22.** Marshal Malinovsky said that U.S. attack on Cuba would mean third world war in which whole capitalist system would be buried once and for all. **March 7.** Foreign Office reported attempt by Soviet intelligence agents to force member of British Embassy staff in Moscow to work for them. **April 2.** Fourth unmanned Soviet moon rocket was launched; it passed 5,300 miles from moon. **5.** Soviet delegate at disarmament conference said that his Government would agree to immediate establishment of direct communications link with U.S.A. for use in emergency. **May 7.** Trial began in Moscow of Mr. Wynne who pleaded guilty "with certain reservations" to spying for British and American intelligence, and of Oleg Penkovsky, senior Soviet scientific official, who pleaded guilty to high treason; allegations of spying were made against members of British Embassy; on May 11 Penkovsky was sentenced to death and Mr. Wynne to 8 years' detention, 3 in prison and 5 in labour camp. On May 13, Soviet Government declared a number of British and American diplomats mentioned during trial *personae non gratae*, on May 16 it was announced that Penkovsky had been shot. **14.** Lt.-Col. Valery Bykovsky was launched into orbit for prolonged flight; on June 16 Valentina Tereshkova, first woman to be sent into orbit, began joint flight programme with Lt.-Col. Bykovsky; they both landed safely in Central Asia on June 19, having made 82 and 49 orbits respectively. **July 15.** Nuclear test ban talks opened in Moscow, Mr. Khrushchev personally leading Soviet delegation. **19.** Mr. Khrushchev, speaking in Moscow, said that he was hopeful of reaching nuclear test ban agreement, and again offered to allow inspection of troops on Soviet soil to prevent surprise attack. **25.** Representatives of Russia, U.S.A. and Great Britain initialled agreement in Moscow providing that all nuclear tests above ground should be banned. **30.** It was announced that Harold Philby had been granted political asylum and Soviet citizenship. **Aug. 5.** Lord Home, Mr. Rusk and Mr. Gromyko signed nuclear test ban treaty in Moscow. **30.** Guy Burgess died in Moscow.

AFRICA

(1962). Oct. 2. Mr. Nkomo, leader of banned Zapu party, returned to Southern Rhodesia from East Africa and was served with restriction order for 3 months to native reserve near Bulawayo, to which he was later flown. **9.** Uganda became independent; Mr. Obote, the Prime Minister, said at press conference that Uganda would not recognise South Africa nor Federation of Rhodesia and Nyasaland. President Tshombe of Katanga said that U.N. troops had surrounded Post Office and Treasury Office in Elisabethville. **15.** Trial of Nelson Mandela, former Transvaal president of banned African National Congress, began in Pretoria. **16.** Mr. Adoula announced new federal constitution for Congolese Republic. Cease-fire was signed in Katanga. **18.** Mr. Adoula said that central Congolese Government would not accept any further delays in application of U.N. plan to reintegrate Katanga with Congolese Republic. **19.** It was announced that Ghana newspaper, *Ashanti Pioneer*, which had been an opposition paper until put under Government supervision, had been taken over by Ghana Government; it was also stated that two private insurance companies had been taken over. **20.** South African Minister of Justice banned, till April 1963, all meetings protesting against arrest, custody, trial or conviction of any person. **21.** Fighting broke out again in North Katanga. **25.** Representatives of 10 tribes in Somali Republic petitioned Ethiopian Government for acceptance as Ethiopian nationals.

Nov. 1. Two Katanga policemen were reported shot dead in centre of Elisabethville by Tunisian U.N. troops. **2.** It was announced that in consequence of inconclusive results of Northern Rhodesia elections, caretaker Government of civil servants would hold office till after by-elections in mid-December. Chief Awolowo, leader of opposition Action Group, and former Prime Minister of Western Region of Nigeria, and 27 other persons, were charged in High Court at Lagos with treasonable felony. **4.** Bishop Roseveare of Accra said that he had been authorised to return to Ghana. **5.** South African Government spokesman said that it had been decided that there should be no mixed membership in scientific and professional organisations, and that where it existed, separation should take place immediately. **6.** Liberal Party in Northern Rhodesia, which had failed to win a seat in elections, announced its disbandment. **7.** Nelson Mundela, nationalist leader, was sentenced in Pretoria to 5 years' imprisonment for inciting Africans to stay away from work and for leaving the country without valid documents. **8.** Mr. E. F. N. Gratiaen, Q.C., was refused permission to enter Nigeria to defend Chief Awolowo. **11.** South African Minister of Justice placed 5 more persons under house arrest; 2 of them were ordered to remain in their houses for 5 years and to receive no visitors except doctors or ministers of religion. **12.** Fifty persons were arrested after demonstration outside Lagos court where Chief Awolowo and others were on trial. **17.** Sir Patrick Renison was replaced by Mr. Malcolm MacDonald as Governor of Kenya. **19.** Ben Bella said that power, mines and foreign trade in Algeria would be nationalised. **30.** 337 Africans were arrested on murder charges arising from riots at Paarl on Nov. 22, when 2 white people were killed.

Dec. 4. U.S. Senator Ellender, who was reported to have said that Africans were not yet ready for self-government, was banned from entering Tanganyika. **9.** Tanganyika became a republic with Mr. Nyerere as first presdient. **12.** Mr. Adoula wrote to 17 countries asking them to put immediate embargo on all Katanga copper and cobalt exports. **14.** Governor of Northern Rhodesia announced names of new Ministers, 11 out of 14 being Africans. **15.** Results of elections in Southern Rhodesia showed that Sir Edgar Whitehead's Government had been defeated by Mr. Winston Field's right-wing Rhodesia Front. **17.** Senegal National Assembly, meeting at private house of its President, overthrew Mamadou Dia's Government after latter's forces had seized control of Assembly building. About 200 alleged terrorists were detained in Transkei. **19.** President Tshombe said that he would if necessary order scorched earth policy in Katanga. Sir Roy Welensky, at extraordinary session of Federal Parliament in Salisbury, said that in granting Nyasaland's right to secede from Federation, British Government was acting in defiance of solemn undertakings of 1953. **20.** Students stoned U.N. consulate in Elisabethville. **23.** Mr. Appiah and 3 other political detainees in Ghana were released. **27.** Judge in Johannesburg Supreme Court declared invalid Minister's order placing Mr. P. J. Hodgson under 24 hours' house arrest. **28.** Fighting broke out round Elisabethville between Katangan and U.N. troops, and by Dec. 30 latter had captured the city. Many African civilians were reported as killed; U.N. casualties were given as 4 dead and 27 wounded. **30.** U.N. claimed that resistance by Katanga was at an end, but on following day it was known to be continuing. **31.** President Tshombe returned to Kolwezi after visit to Sir Roy Welensky in Salisbury.

(1963). Jan. 3. U.N. troops captured Jadotville in Katanga, where Indian soldiers were reported to have killed 2 Belgian ladies in a car; U.N. in New York said that there had been serious breakdown of communications and co-ordination between New York headquarters and Leopoldville office of United Nations. **6.** Federal Government protested against flights by U.N. aircraft over Rhodesian territory. Ghana demanded extradition of political refugees from Togo. **8.** Bomb was thrown among crowd as President Nkrumah was leaving political rally in Accra; it was stated that 4 people had been killed. **9.** Leopoldville Government refused offer of British economic aid. **13.** President Sylvanus Olimpio of Togo was assassinated in Lomé; provisional Government took over. **14.** President Nyerere said that steps would be taken towards statutory establishment of one-party system in Tanganyika. Southern Rhodesian Government announced that all Africans under restriction were being released. **15.** President Tshombe told U.N. that he was ready to end secession of Katanga. Mob attacked British Embassy in Leopoldville. Crowd of 20,000 at Usumbura watched hanging of 5 men who had been convicted of complicity in murder of a former Burundi Prime Minister; they had been condemned to death after a second trial, having received lesser sentences at first trial. **17.** Thirteen persons were sentenced to death in Tunis on allegations of participation in plot to kill President Bourguiba; on following day the President announced recall of Tunisian Ambassador from Algeria, where, it was alleged, the plot had been encouraged. **21.** U.N. troops entered Kolwezi, in Katanga, without resistance. **24.** Leaders of U.N.I.P. and African National Congress in Northern Rhodesia asked Mr. Butler, who was visiting Central Africa, to allow Northern Rhodesia to secede from Federation of Rhodesia and Nyasaland.

Feb. 1. Nyasaland became self-governing, with Dr. Banda as Prime Minister. **5.** Five Europeans, including 2 young girls and their parents, were murdered at road camp in Transkei. **9.** Mr. Nkomo, former leader of Zimbabwe African People's Union in Southern Rhodesia, was arrested, together with several colleagues.

March 2. Tension was reported to be rising among inhabitants of Northern Frontier District in Kenya, who wished to secede to Somali Republic. The 3 battalions of K.A.R. in Kenya, with other British supporting units, were placed on 12-hour stand-by basis. **8.** Mr. Sandys announced in Nairobi that elections would be held in Kenya in May and that the country would thereafter be self-governing; Northern Frontier District populated largely by Somalis would become additional region. **10.** At Hargeisa, in Somalia, British Council premises were ransacked and British consulate stoned; 19 Britons, including women and children, were flown from Somalia at British Government's request. Fighting broke out between Kanu and Kadu supporters at Kitale in Kenya; Jomo Kenyatta and Mr. Mboya were stoned and police used tear-gas; there were some injuries and 10 persons were arrested. **11.** Government of Somalia announced intention to break off diplomatic relations with Britain; more Britons were evacuated from the country. Large numbers of Somalis took part in anti-British demonstrations in Northern Frontier District of Kenya. Disturbances broke out in Northern Rhodesia between members of U.N.I.P. and A.N.C., the two parties in Coalition Government. **13.** After further days of rioting in Northern Frontier District of Kenya, District Commissioner at Moyale was wounded by a spear. **2.** Commission of inquiry into riots at Paarl, Cape Province, in Nov. 1962, named underground organisation, Poqo, which it alleged was financed from other African countries, including Ghana. **23.** Police arrested 42 Africans, suspected of membership of Poqo, in Pretoria native townships. **24.** Thirty-three Somali chiefs in Northern Frontier District of Kenya resigned their posts and refused to see Governor of Kenya, who had arrived in the district. **25.** Kenya Government ordered suspension of Kenya Regiment on financial grounds. **28.** Federal Government Chief Whip in Nigeria said that Nigerian Government would give no undertaking to Britain on Chief Enahoro.

April 6. Mr. Atta, Ghana Minister of Justice, said that disregard of the party line in Ghana should be regarded as treason. **14.** After 4 days of fighting between rival groups at Jadotville, in Congo, death roll had risen to 52. **17.** Special criminal court in Ghana sentenced to death for treason 5 persons, who had not been represented by counsel. **18.** Kenya's new constitution was published by Order in Council, providing for phase of full internal self-government, the Governor retaining reserve powers in defence, external relations and internal security. **25.** Tanganyika Government accepted motion in National Assembly calling for immediate independence for Southern Rhodesia with majority government elected on universal adult suffrage. **29.** South African General Law Amendment Bill received third reading with only one vote against; Bill provided, *inter alia*, authority for Minister to keep persons convicted of offences against state in prison after their sentences had expired and power to detain suspected plotters against state for repeated periods of 3 months. South African Foreign Minister announced that from July 1 movement of all people between Basutoland, Bechuanaland, Swaziland and South Africa would be subject to passport control.

May 15. Congolese troops raided town of Kakona in Katanga; 3 Africans were reported killed. **17.** Nigerian Government refused permission to Mr. Dingle Foot and Mr. Gratiaen to enter Nigeria to defend Chief Enahoro. **23.** At conference of African leaders at Addis Ababa, Mr. Obote, Prime Minister of Uganda, offered his country as anti-colonial training ground for African "liberation forces". **26.** Conference at Addis Ababa agreed to set up Organisation for African Unity. **27.** Following ruling of Judicial Committee of Privy Council that Chief Akintola had been validly dismissed in 1962 by Governor from Premiership of Western Nigeria, Western Nigerian Government carried through House of Assembly retrospective amendment to constitution laying down that Governor could remove Premier only in consequence of majority decision by provincial legislature. Six journalists were detained for 2 hours by police in Johannesburg after photographing multiracial demonstration outside police station in which detainees were being held; on following day they were charged with taking pictures in contravention of Prisons Act. **28.** Results of voting for Kenya House of Representatives showed that K.A.N.U. had won by 64 seats out of 112. **31.** Governor of Kenya formally proclaimed internal self-government; on following day Jomo Kenyatta was sworn in as Prime Minister.

June 7. A British economic adviser in Buganda was ordered to be deported for criticising Mr. Obote. **13.** At request of authorities in Swaziland, where general strike had been taking place since May 20, 1st Battalion Gordon Highlanders was sent from Nairobi to assist in keeping order; on June 17 they cordoned off Havelock asbestos mine, where 1,500 miners were on strike. **24.** Zanzibar obtained internal self-government. **25.** Congolese Parliament in Leopoldville passed law creating new province of East Katanga.

July 1. The Sultan of Zanzibar died after emergency operation. **2.** Conference at Victoria Falls reached agreement that Federation of Rhodesia and

Nyasaland should end on Dec. 31. **15.** Statement issued by Kenya Minister of Information warned press that its freedom after independence would be conditional on its compliance with Government's requirements. Dr. Verwoerd said that South Africa had decided to withdraw from U.N. Economic Commission for Africa. **22.** Nigerian Government banned public meetings and processions, except in connexion with religion and sport, for two months. **24.** Governor of Kenya said that British Government had invited Government of Somali Republic to take part in talks on future of Somali area of Kenya. **26.** It was stated that new constitution of Nigeria would abolish appeals to Judicial Committee of Privy Council. **30.** Rhodesian Federal Minister of Law said that rule of law in Nyasaland had been seriously eroded and called on British Government to take immediate and effective measures to ensure its restoration and preservation.

Aug. 10. Congolese troops entered town of Kasenga near Rhodesian border, which had previously been held by former members of Katanga *gendarmerie*. **13.** Rioters in Brazzaville, where general strike was taking place, set fire to prison and released prisoners; on following day French tanks and paratroops intervened at request of President Youlou and helped to restore order. **14.** Ferhat Abbas resigned from Presidency of Algerian National Assembly, accusing Ben Bella of seeking to push constitution through Parliament to give himself absolute power. **15.** President Youlou of Congo Republic resigned; power was stated to have been entrusted to the Army. **20.** Kenneth Abrahams, coloured doctor, who claimed that he had been kidnapped in Bechuanaland by South African police, was granted *habeas corpus* hearing by South African Supreme Court. **30.** South African Minister for Justice said that Dr. Abrahams and 3 companions would be released and returned to Bechuanaland.

Sept. 2. Kenya Government announced ban on all non-essential travel to North-Eastern Region and those parts of Eastern Region coming within Northern Frontier District. **7.** Chief Enahoro was sentenced by Lagos High Court to 15 years' imprisonment. **9.** Results of referendum in Algeria showed that 5,000,000 had voted for one-party rule, with all other political parties banned; 1,000,000 abstained. **11.** Chief Awolowo was sentenced in Lagos to 10 years' imprisonment; 17 others received terms varying from 2 to 7 years; police used tear-gas to disperse crowds outside court. **13.** South African Government said that international scheduled services operated by East African Airways from Nairobi to Durban and Johannesburg would be ended on Oct. 13. **15.** Ben Bella, who was the only candidate, was elected first President of Algeria; in television interview after election he said that Government intended to take over all French settlers' lands. **18.** Last 3 privately owned newspapers in Algeria were nationalized. **30.** Ben Bella said that Moroccan troops were massing on Algerian frontier and despatched forces to surround Berber capital of Tizi Ouzou, where revolt had occurred.

OTHER COUNTRIES

(*See also* under Africa)

(1962). Oct. 1. It was disclosed that Egyptian arms, ammunition and military experts were being flown into Yemen. **3.** It was stated that the Imam of Yemen, whose death had been announced after his palace had been attacked on Sept. 26, was still alive. **7.** Fighting between Yemen republican troops and tribal forces was reported in north of country. U.S. military forces completed withdrawal from Laos. **10.** It was reported that 3 Soviet officers had been captured with republican garrison when royalist troops seized Yemen fortress of Maarab. Members of Cuban exile organisation claimed to have made raid earlier in week on Cuban port of Isabela de Sagua and to have killed 20 people, including some Russians living in military camp. **11.** Ecumenical Council opened in St. Peter's, Rome. Republican Government in Yemen said that it regarded Yemen as in state of war with Saudi Arabia. **14.** Many people were hurt in clashes between Flemish nationalists and Walloons in Brussels. **18.** 280 Turkish political prisoners, sentenced at Yassiada trials in 1961, were released. **23.** Armed forces in Cuba were put on war footing. **24.** Dr. Castro rejected any proposal for inspection of arms bases in Cuba. Organisation of American States, with one abstention owing to lack of instructions, agreed to help U.S.A. in blockade of Cuba. **25.** E.E.C. in Brussels set out principles governing adaptation of British agriculture to Common Market; Mr. Heath condemned proposals and expressed disappointment. **28.** Dr. Castro issued a number of demands to U.S.A., including one for U.S. withdrawal from naval base at Guantanamo. Communists blew up power-station of U.S.-controlled Creole Petroleum Corporation in Venezuela. Two Britons were murdered by bandits in Sardinia. **29.** Common Market Commission announced from Brussels its intention of establishing Customs Union by January 1967 if general economic situation should permit. **31.** Fierce fighting between royalist and republican tribesmen in North Yemen was reported.

Nov. 4. Egyptian aircraft were reported to have attacked Saudi Arabian villages. **5.** Anton Yugov, Prime Minister of Bulgaria and Georgi Tsankov, a deputy Prime Minister, were expelled from Communist Party central committee and relieved of their posts. **6.** After further sea and air attacks by Egyptian forces, Saudi Arabia severed relations with U.A.R. **10.** Parents of child born without arms after its mother had taken thalidomide, were acquitted at Liège, together with other members of family and doctor, of murder of the child. **15.** German Federal Republic agreed to buy tank guns and ammunition from Britain to value of £24,000,000. **22.** Demonstrations took place against Archbishop Makarios when he drove into Ankara at beginning of his state visit to Turkey. **25.** Guatemalan Air Force staged unsuccessful *coup* against Government. **26.** Cuban Government said that international inspection of missile sites in Cuba might be allowed if U.N. carried out similar inspection of areas in U.S.A., Puerto Rico and elsewhere, where it was alleged aggression against Cuba was being prepared. **28.** Princess Wilhelmina, Queen of the Netherlands from 1890 to 1948, died aged 82. Hungarian Government said that case of Mr. Wynne, British businessman arrested in Budapest on Nov. 2, was now beyond its competence. **30.** Herr Strauss, West German Minister of Defence since 1956, said that he would not be a member of a new Coalition Government.

Dec. 7. West German Christian Democratic Party parliamentary leader said that Dr. Adenauer would retire in autumn of 1963. **8.** First session of Ecumenical Council closed in Rome. **11.** Composition of Dr. Adenauer's new Coalition Government was announced. **17.** New constitution was promulgated for Monaco, which could only be modified with approval of elected National Council and replaced that of 1911 which could be suspended, abrogated or modified at will of Ruler. **23.** Release of prisoners captured in attempted invasion of Cuba in 1961, and their despatch to U.S.A. began.

(1963). Jan. 1. Saudi Arabia reported continued Egyptian air raids on her territory. **5.** Military Government in Peru declared state of siege throughout country and arrested large number of persons stated to be involved in Communist plot. **8.** Irish naval corvette arrested and brought into Waterford Harbour Soviet vessel alleged to have been fishing in Republic of Ireland territorial waters. **15.** Spokesmen for West German, Belgian, Dutch and Italian Governments expressed opposition to President de Gaulle's views on British entry into Common Market. **17.** French representatives at Common Market discussions in Brussels called for suspension of negotiations *sine die*, but on following day it was agreed to re-open talks later in month. **19.** After gunfight in Caracas, Venezuelan police recovered 5 valuable French paintings which had been stolen from exhibition in the city; several students were arrested. **23.** Turkish Foreign Minister said that dismantling of U.S. Jupiter missiles in Turkey, which were to be replaced by Polaris missiles in ships, would begin shortly. **24.** Belgian Senate voted unanimously in favour of continuing negotiations on British entry into Common Market. **26.** Mr. Krag, Danish Prime Minister, said that President de Gaulle had suggested to him that Denmark might, without Britain, apply for full membership of Common Market. **29.** Negotiations in Brussels on British entry into Common Market collapsed. **30.** Mr. Krag said it was inconceivable that Denmark, in present situation, should join Common Market without Britain.

Feb. 1. Mr. Macmillan arrived in Rome for talks with members of Italian Government. **8.** *Coup d'état* took place in Baghdad, and it was later confirmed that General Kassim had been put to death; Revolutionary Council, which was set up, said that its aim was " to complete Arab unity ". **10.** Yemen Government asked Britain to close British Legation in Taiz within 7 days; it was closed on Feb. 17. **11.** New régime in Iraq was recognised by U.K. and many other Governments. **21.** More than 300 people were killed by earthquake at Barce in Libya.

March 7. President of Yemen Republic called on Saudi Arabians to revolt and " take revenge against British ". **8.** Pro-Egyptian elements of Syrian Army staged successful *coup d'état*. **10.** M. Bidault was detained by police in village near Munich and undertook to remain in house where he was found. **20.** After it had flown King Saud to Nice, his private aircraft was found wrecked near Italian-French border; 18 persons were killed, including British pilot and other British members of crew. The King attributed disaster to bomb explosion. **22.** Renewed eruption of Mount Agung, volcano on island of Bali, killed about 1,100 persons. **23.** Ex-President Bayar of Turkey, who had been released from prison because of ill-health, was received in Ankara with demonstrations in his favour; on March 28 he was taken into custody again. **25.** It was announced that all hotels and restaurants in Zermatt would be closed after many cases of typhoid linked with the town had been reported. **31.** Armed forces took over control of Government in Guatemala, President Fuentes being flown into exile.

April 2. Soviet aircraft fired at British registered private aircraft in Berlin air corridor. **8.** M. Bidault left Portugal for Brazil. **10.** Egypt, Syria and Iraq agreed to form new federal state, to be called United Arab Republic. **20.** Julian Grimau, Spanish Communist leader, who had been sentenced to death by military court, was executed. **21.** After fighting in Jerusalem, pro-Nasser deputies in Jordan Parliament carried vote of no confidence in Government; on following day King Hussein caused new Government to be formed and dissolved Parliament. **23.** Christian Democratic Party chose Professor Ludwig Erhard to succeed Dr. Adenauer as next West German Chancellor. **28.** Dr. Scharf was re-elected President of Austria. Dominican Republic issued ultimatum to Haiti and called urgent meeting of Council of Organisation of American States after Haitian militiamen had forced entry into Dominican Embassy in Port-au-Prince. **29.** Dominican Republic and Haiti agreed to accept mediation by Organisation of American States. State of emergency and curfew were imposed on all border areas in Jordan. **30.** Results of Italian general election showed considerable gains for Communists and Liberals; Christian Democrats, though remaining largest party, received smaller percentage of total vote.

May 1. Two members of U.S. expedition reached summit of Mt. Everest. **3.** Martial law was declared in Haiti. **4.** More than 170 persons were drowned when ferry boat sank in Nile near Karara, Upper Egypt. **5.** Dominican Republic moved reinforcements of tanks and troops to Haitian border. **6.** Haiti asked for urgent meeting of U.N. Security Council to examine situation. **19.** Dr. Sukarno was made life head of state of Indonesia. **21.** Fighting took place in Ankara when attempted *coup* by army elements took place; Government said that revolt had been crushed. Later in day martial law was imposed for one month in Ankara, Izmir and Istanbul, and it was announced that 9 former army officers had been arrested. **23.** Two more teams in U.S. expedition reached summit of Mt. Everest, one pair making first ascent by West Ridge. **25.** Ten Army captains and another man, said to be supporters of General Kassim, were executed in Baghdad. **28.** Over 50 persons were killed when roof collapsed on platform at station in Lisbon. **31.** In discussions among Common Market Ministers in Brussels, French delegates blocked proposals for continuing regular exchanges of views between Common Market countries and Britain.

June 3. His Holiness Pope John XXIII died in the Vatican. **4–6.** Rioting took place in Tehran; 86 people were reported to have lost their lives. **11.** King Paul of the Hellenes accepted resignation of M. Karamanlis, Greek Prime Minister; in proclamation, the King expressed his disagreement with M. Karamanlis' advice that royal visit to Britain in July should be cancelled. **16.** Mr. Ben-Gurion, Prime Minister of Israel, resigned. **18.** Signor Nenni resigned from secretaryship of Italian Socialist party. **20.** Sacred College began election of new Pope, and on following day chose Cardinal Giovanni Battista Montini, Archbishop of Milan, who took the name of Paul VI. **21.** International Labour conference at Geneva expelled South African workers' delegate on grounds that he did not truly represent workers of his country. **22.** Three British soldiers and a Royal Marine were killed and others wounded when a party of 45 British Service men and women inadvertently walked into Yemen territory and were attacked; 20 of the party were seized, 4 of them women. The women were released on June 24, and remaining 16 members on July 4. **23.** Signor Leone, new Italian Prime Minister, and members of his minority Christian Democrat Government, were sworn in. President Kennedy arrived in Cologne and later drove to Bonn, where on following day he had talks with Dr. Adenauer; the President subsequently said that he hoped nuclear test ban would be agreed upon in 1963. **25.** Col. Stig Wennerström, former Swedish air attaché in Moscow, was committed for trial on charges of spying for Russia for over 15 years. President Kennedy addressed large audience, including members of Bundestag, in Frankfurt. **26.** President Kennedy spent 8 hours in West Berlin, where he was enthusiastically greeted; later he flew to Dublin and on following day visited Co. Wexford, from which his great-grandfather had emigrated to U.S.A. **30.** Pope Paul VI was crowned on steps of Basilica, after procession and Papal Mass had taken place in St. Peter's Square.

July 1. Mr. Khrushchev, speaking in East Berlin, offered to conclude treaty on banning of nuclear tests in the atmosphere, space and under water. President Kennedy, who had been visiting Italy, was received at the Vatican by the new Pope; the President later returned to Washington by air. **11.** Army leaders secured control in Ecuador, deposing President Arosemena. **18.** Pro-Nasser rising in Damascus was reported to have been crushed. **24.** Seventy days after resignation of previous Government, Mr. Marijnen formed new Coalition Cabinet in Netherlands. Guatemalan Government announced that it was breaking off diplomatic relations with Great Britain. **26.** Some 1,200 people were killed and many more injured by earthquake in Skopje, Yugoslavia; about 100,000 were made homeless.

Aug. 5. Body of exiles invaded Haiti in attempt to overthrow President Duvalier's régime; on Aug. 7 Haitian Government said that attempt had been defeated. **6.** Mr. Macmillan arrived in Helsinki for 4-day official visit to Finland. **19.** Syrian troops were reported to have crossed Israeli frontier and killed two persons. **21.** President Ngo Dinh Diem of South Vietnam took action against Buddhist opponents of régime, imposing martial law, putting Saigon under curfew and sending troops to occupy Buddhist pagodas and drive out monks who resisted. **23.** Norwegian Labour Government was defeated on motion of no confidence and resigned on following day; at request of the King, Mr. John Lyng, Conservative Party leader, formed Government.

Sept. 2. U.S. Embassy in Saigon granted sanctuary to Buddhist leader, Thich Tri Quang. **4.** Caravelle jet air liner of Swissair crashed 5 minutes after leaving Zürich airport for Geneva *en route* for Rome; all 80 passengers and crew were killed. **5.** Turkish military court passed sentence of death on 7 persons charged with complicity in attempted *coup* in May; 29 were sentenced to life imprisonment and 70 to lesser terms. **10.** Church of Scotland School in Tel Aviv and French Convent and Finnish Mission School in Jerusalem were attacked by campaigners against teaching of Jewish children in mission schools. **12.** It was reported that revolt of Brazilian Navy and Air Force units in Brasilia had been quelled. **16.** Demonstrators against new Federation of Malaysia attacked British Embassy in Djakarta, breaking windows and burning Ambassador's car. **17.** Left-wing labour unions in Djakarta began expropriation of British commercial firms. **18.** Rioters in Djakarta sacked and destroyed British Embassy, injured British occupants of it, wrecked and looted British homes and burnt cars. **19.** British and Australian women and children were evacuated by air from Djakarta to Singapore. **20.** President Sukarno ordered British firms in Indonesia to be taken over by Government in the interests of their own safety. Mr. Lyng's Government in Norway was defeated by 2 votes and Labour Party Party leaders agreed to form Government. **22.** Indonesian Government refused permission to Malayan Airways to land aircraft at Djakarta and Medan. Mr. Siroky, Prime Minister of Czechoslovakia since 1953, was relieved of his post and his position in Communist Party. **23.** Indonessian Government banned shipment of oil and natural gas to Malaysia and smelting of Indonesian tin there. **25.** Indonesian paratroops were flown to border of North Borneo. Armed forces of Dominican Republic overthrew President Bosch and his Government and assumed power; on following day they handed over control to provisional Government of 3 civilians. **26.** King Paul dissolved Greek Parliament and announced that general election would be held on Nov. 3. **29.** Pope Paul VI inaugurated second session of Vatican Ecumenical Council at ceremony in St. Peter's. British Consul called for immediate evacuation of about 140 British women and children from Shell oil plant at Balikpapan, in Indonesian Borneo.

OBITUARY, OCT. 1, 1962—SEPT. 30, 1963

Abraham, James Johnston, C.B.E., D.S.O., Surgeon and author, aged 86—*Aug.* 9.

Alanbrooke, *Field Marshal* Alan Francis Brooke, 1st Viscount, K.G., G.C.B., O.M., G.C.V.O., D.S.O., Chief of Imperial General Staff in Second World War, aged 79—*June* 17.

Ashcroft, Alec Hutchinson, D.S.O., former headmaster of Fettes, aged 75—*April* 18.

Austen, *General* Sir Reade Godwin, K.C.S.I., C.B., O.B.E., M.C., Corps Commander in Second World War, aged 73—*March* 20.

Barthelmess, Richard, well-known star of silent films, aged 68—*Aug.* 17.

Barton, Sir Harold Montague, prominent chartered accountant, aged 80—*Oct.* 20, 1962.

Bax, Clifford, distinguished playwright, aged 76—*Nov.* 18, 1962.

Bellman, Sir Harold, M.B.E., Chairman of Abbey National Building Society, aged 77—*June* 1.

Bemelmans, Ludwig, humorous writer and artist, aged 64—*Oct.* 1, 1962.

Ben-Zvi, Itzhak, President of Israel since 1952, aged 78—*April* 23.

Bernard, Anthony, conductor and accompanist, aged 72—*April* 6.

Beveridge, William Henry Beveridge, K.C.B., 1st and last Baron, civil servant, economist and protagonist of Welfare State, aged 84—*March* 16.

Blackburne, *Very Rev.* Harry William, D.S.O., M.C., former Dean of Bristol, aged 85—*June* 1.

Bohr, *Prof.* Niels, Danish physicist and Nobel prize-winner, aged 77—*Nov.* 18, 1962.

Bolton, Nigel Amyas Orde-Powlett, 6th Baron, forestry expert, aged 63—*June* 15.

Bone, James, C.H., distinguished journalist, aged 90—*Nov.* 23, 1962.

Bordeaux, Henry, French novelist, aged 93—*March* 29.

Bottome, Phyllis (Mrs. A. E. Forbes Dennis) novelist, aged 79—*Aug.* 22.

Brand, Robert Henry Brand, C.M.G., 1st and last Baron, banker and writer on politics and economics, aged 84—*Aug.* 23.

Braque, Georges, French Cubist painter, aged 81—*Aug.* 31.

Brooke, Sir Charles Vyner, G.C.M.G., last Rajah of Sarawak, aged 88—*May* 9.

Brooks, Van Wyck, U.S. librarian historian and critic, aged 77—*May* 2.

Bulman, *Group-Capt.* Paul Ward Spencer, C.B.E., M.C., pioneer test pilot, aged 67—*May* 6.

Burnham, *Maj.-Gen.* Edward Frederick Lawson, 4th Baron, C.B., D.S.O., M.C., former managing director of *Daily Telegraph* and Director of Public Relations at War Office, aged 73—*July* 4.

Bury, *Lt.-Col.* Charles Kenneth Howard, leader of

1921 Everest expedition and subsequently Conservative M.P., aged 80—*Sept.* 20.

Campbell, *Rt. Hon.* Sir David Callender, K.B.E., C.M.G., Ulster Unionist M.P. for Belfast South since 1952, aged 72—*June* 12.

Carr. Arthur William, former England and Nottinghamshire cricket captain, aged 69—*Feb.* 7.

Carton de Wiart, *Lt.-Gen.* Sir Adrian, V.C., K.B.E., C.B., C.M.G., D.S.O., distinguished soldier in two wars, aged 83—*June* 5.

Chapman, *Col.* Sir Robert, Bt., C.B., C.M.G., C.B.E., D.S.O., former Conservative M.P. and leading public figure in North-East England, aged 83—*July* 31.

Christiansen, Arthur, former editor of *Daily Express*, aged 59—*Sept.* 27.

Clarke, Sir Charles Noble Arden-, G.C.M.G., former Governor-General of Ghana, aged 64—*Dec.* 16, 1962.

Coade, Thorold Francis, former headmaster of Bryanston School, aged 66—*Feb.* 1.

Cole, Walton Adamson, general manager of Reuters, aged 50—*Jan.* 25.

Coty, René, President of French Republic, 1954–59, aged 80—*Nov* 22, 1962.

Crawford, John Neville, great all-round cricketer, aged 76—*May* 2.

Critchley, *Brig.-Gen.* Alfred Cecil, C.M.G., C.B.E., D.S.O., industrialist and sportsman, aged 72—*Feb.* 9.

Crocker, *General* Sir John Tredinnick, G.C.B., K.B.E., D.S.O., M.C., Corps Commander in World War II and later Adjutant-General. Lord-Lieutenant of Middlesex since 1961, aged 67—*March* 9.

Cudlipp, Percy, former editor of *Evening Standard* and *Daily Herald*, aged 57—*Nov.* 5, 1962

Cunliffe, Sir Herbert, K.B.E., Q.C., former Chairman of Bar Council, aged 95—*April* 9.

Cunningham of Hyndhope, *Admiral of the Fleet* Andrew Browne Cunningham, 1st and last Viscount, K.T., G.C.B., O.M., D.S.O., outstanding naval leader of Second World War, aged 80—*June* 12.

Cunningham *Admiral of the Fleet* Sir John Henry Dacres, G.C.B., M.V.O., naval leader in Second World War and First Sea Lord 1946–48, aged 77—*Dec.* 13, 1962.

D'Alton, Cardinal John, Archbishop of Armagh and R.C. Primate of All Ireland, aged 80—*Feb.* 1.

Daniell, John, famous rugby football and cricket player and selector, aged 84—*Jan.* 24.

Dartmouth, Humphrey Legge, C.V.O., D.S.O., 8th Earl of, aged 74—*Oct.* 16, 1962.

Darwin, Sir Charles Galton, K.B.E., M.C., F.R.S., former director of National Physical Laboratory, aged 75—*Dec.* 31, 1962.

de Silva, *Rt. Hon.* Lucien Macull Dominic, Q.C., member of Judicial Committee of Privy Council, aged 69—*Nov.* 28, 1962.

Dobson, Frank, C.B.E., R.A., distinguished sculptor, aged 74—*July* 22.

Doggart, Alexander Graham, Chairman of Football Association, aged 66—*June* 7.

Dollan, Sir Patrick Joseph, prominent Glasgow Labour leader, aged 78—*Jan.* 30.

Dugdale, Rt. Hon. John, Labour M.P. for West Bromwich since 1941 and former junior Minister, aged 57—*March* 12.

Dynevor, Charles Arthur Uryan Rhys, C.B.E., M.C., 8th Baron, former Conservative M.P., aged 63—*Dec.* 15, 1962.

Edwards, *Admiral* Sir Ralph Alan Bevan, K.C.B., C.B.E., former C.-in-C., Mediterranean, aged 61—*Feb.* 4.

Elibank, Arthur Cecil Murray, C.M.G., D.S.O., 3rd and last Viscount and 12th Baron, former Liberal M.P., aged 83—*Dec.* 5, 1962

Elliott, G. H., famous music-hall artist, aged 78—*Nov.* 19, 1962.

Elsie, Lily, celebrated actress of Edwardian era—*Dec.* 16, 1962.

Ennisdale, Henry Edward Lyons, O.B.E., 1st and last Baron, former leading member of Liberal National party, aged 84—*Aug.* 17.

Erskine, *Col.* Sir Arthur, G.C.V.O., D.S.O., extra equerry to the Queen and secretary and registrar of Order of Merit, aged 81—*July* 24.

Ferguson, Sir Donald, G.C.B., civil servant, aged 71—*March* 4.

Feversham, Charles William Slingsby Duncombe, D.S.O., T.D., 3rd and last Earl of, former junior Minister, aged 56—*Sept.* 4.

Flagstad, Kirsten, great operatic soprano, aged 67—*Dec.* 7, 1962.

Foyle, William Alfred, joint founder of famous bookselling firm, aged 78—*June* 4.

Freyberg, Bernard Cyril, 1st Lord, V.C., G.C.M.G., K.C.B., K.B.E., D.S.O., hero of two wars and former Governor-General of New Zealand, aged 74—*July* 4.

Frost, Robert, leading poet in U.S.A., aged 88—*Jan.* 29.

Fullerton, *Admiral* Sir Eric John Arthur, K.C.B., D.S.O., former C.-in-C., Plymouth, aged 83—*Nov.* 9, 1962.

Gaitskell, *Rt. Hon.* Hugh Todd Naylor, C.B.E., M.P., Leader of the Opposition since 1955 and former Labour Chancellor of the Exchequer, aged 56.—*Jan.* 18.

Gater, Sir George Henry, G.C.M.G., K.C.B., D.S.O., former Clerk of L.C.C. and Permanent Under-Secretary, Colonial Office, aged 76—*Jan.* 14.

Godfrey, *Cardinal* William, Archbishop of Westminster since 1956, aged 73—*Jan.* 22.

Gorell, Ronald Gorell Barnes, C.B.E., M.C., 3rd Baron, author and former junior Minister, aged 79—*May* 2.

Gough, *General* Sir Hubert de la Poer, G.C.B., G.C.M.G., K.C.V.O., Fifth Army Commander in First World War, aged 92—*March* 18.

Graham, Rose, C.B.E., D.Litt., F.S.A., mediaeval historian, aged 87—*July* 29.

Grey, Charles Robert Grey, 5th Earl, leading churchman, aged 83—*April* 2.

Grimsdell, Arthur, great Tottenham Hotspur and England footballer, aged 68—*March* 13.

Griswold, A. Whitney, Ph.D. President of Yale University since 1950, aged 56—*April* 19.

Gunn, John, notable all-round cricketer, aged 87—*Aug.* 22.

Hall, *Rt. Hon.* William Glenvil, Labour M.P. for Colne Valley and former junior Minister, aged 75—*Oct.* 13, 1962.

Hambro, Sir Charles Jocelyn, K.B.E., M.C., merchant banker and Governor of Bank of England, aged 65—*Aug.* 28.

Hankey, Maurice Pascal Alers Hankey, P.C., G.C.B., G.C.M.G., G.C.V.O., F.R.S., first Baron, Secretary to War Cabinet in First World War, British Secretary to Paris Peace Conference and for many years Secretary to the Cabinet, aged 85—*Jan.* 25.

Hannon, Sir Patrick Joseph Henry, industrialist and former Conservative M.P.—*Jan.* 10.

Harrison, Julius, conductor and composer, aged 78—*April* 5.

Hassall, Christopher Vernon, author, aged 51—*April* 25.

Hendren, Elias ("Patsy"), great Middlesex and England batsman, aged 73—*Oct.* 4, 1962.

Hodgson, Ralph, poet, aged 91—*Nov.* 3, 1962.
Hollis, *General* Sir Leslie Chasemore, K.C.B., K.B.E., R.M., senior military assistant Secretary to War Cabinet, and later Commandant-General, Royal Marines, aged 66—*Aug.* 9.
Hudd, Walter, actor and producer, aged 64—*Jan.* 20.
Humphery, George Edward Woods-, former managing director of Imperial Airways, aged 70—*Jan.* 25.
Hurst, Sir Cecil James Barrington, G.C.M.G. K.C.B., international jurist, aged 92—*March* 27.
Hyndley, John Scott Hindley, G.B.E., 1st and last Viscount, former Chairman of National Coal Board, aged 79—*Jan.* 5.
Ingram, Sir Bruce Stirling, O.B.E., M.C., Editor of *Illustrated London News* for over 60 years, connoisseur, art collector and philanthropist, aged 85—*Jan.* 8.
Irving, Ethel, leading comedy actress, aged 93—*May* 3.
Jacobsson, Dr. Per, Director of International Monetary Fund since 1956, aged 69—*May* 5.
Jameson, Sir Wilson, G.B.E., K.C.B., former Chief Medical Officer at Ministry of Health, aged 77—*Oct.* 18, 1962.
Jeayes, Allan, veteran actor, aged 78—*Sept.* 20.
Jones, John Henry, Labour M.P. for Rotherham and former junior Minister, aged 68—(*in car accident*) *Oct.* 31, 1962.
Kefauver, Estes, U.S. Senator and former Democratic nominee for Vice-Presidency, aged 60—*Aug.* 10.
Keown, Eric, dramatic critic of *Punch*, aged 58—*Feb.* 15.
King, Johnny, British bantamweight champion for many years, aged 50—*March* 7.
Laughton, Charles, English-born stage and film actor, aged 63—*Dec.* 15, 1962.
Leburn, William Gilmour, T.D., Conservative M.P. for Kinross and West Perthshire since 1955 and Joint Under-Secretary for Scotland since 1959, aged 50—*Aug.* 15.
Legg, Leopold George Wickham, former editor of *Dictionary of National Biography*, aged 85—*Dec.* 19, 1962.
Lewis, John Spedan, founder and former chairman of John Lewis Partnership, aged 77—*Feb.* 21.
Littlewood, Samuel Robinson, dramatic critic, aged 88—*Aug.* 10.
Lloyd, Cyril Edward, midland industrialist and former Conservative M.P., aged 86—*Feb.* 19.
Low, Sir David, famous cartoonist, aged 72—*Sept.* 19.
Macassey, Sir Lynden Livingston, K.B.E., Q.C., leading industrial lawyer, aged 86—*Feb.* 23.
MacGeagh, *Col.* Sir Henry Davies Foster, G.C.V.O., K.C.B., K.B.E., Q.C., former Judge Advocate-General to the Forces, aged 79—*Dec.* 29, 1962.
MacNeice, Louis, C.B.E., poet and dramatist, aged 55—*Sept.* 3.
Malan, *Group Capt.* Adolph Gysbert ("Sailor"), D.S.O., D.F.C., famous fighter pilot of Second World War, aged 52—*Sept.* 17.
Mann, Sir James Gow, K.C.V.O., F.B.A., F.S.A., Director of Wallace Collection, Surveyor of the Royal Works of Art and Master of Armouries, Tower of London, aged 65—*Dec.* 5, 1962.
Marshall, Eric Stewart, C.B.E., M.C., member of Shackleton's 1907–09 expedition, aged 83—*Feb.* 26.
Martindale, *Rev.* Cyril Charlie, S. J., theologian and preacher, aged 83.—*March* 18.
Masson, Sir Irvine, M.B.E., D.Sc., F.R.S., former Vice-Chancellor of Sheffield University, aged 75—*Oct.* 22, 1962.
Matania, Chevalier Fortunino, portrait-painter and illustrator, aged 81—*Feb.* 8.
Mattei, Enrico, president of Italian state oil corporation, aged 56—(*in air crash*) *Oct.* 27, 1962.
Mattingly, *Prof.* Garrett, distinguished U.S. historian, aged 62—*Dec.* 18, 1962.
Maxwell, Sir Alexander, G.C.B., K.B.E., former Permanent Secretary at Home Office and Chairman of Prison Commissioners, aged 83—*July* 1.
Middleton, James Smith, Secretary of Labour Party, 1934–44, aged 84—*Nov.* 18, 1962.
Miles, Sir John Charles, former Warden of Merton College, Oxford, aged 92—*Jan.* 12.
Milford, Lawrence Richard Philipps, 1st Baron, leader of shipping industry, aged 88—*Dec.* 7, 1962.
Miller, Max, music-hall comedian, aged 68—*May* 7.
Moiseiwitsch, Benno, C.B.E., great pianist, aged 73—*April* 9.
Montagu, Hon. Lilian Helen, C.B.E., prominent social worker for many years and leader of Liberal Judaism, aged 89—*Jan.* 22.
Mort, David Llewellyn, Labour M.P. for East Swansea from 1940, aged 74—*Jan.* 1.
Mottistone, John Alexander Seely, O.B.E., F.R.I.B.A., 2nd Baron, distinguished architect, aged 63.—*Jan.* 18.
Moyes, Alban George (Johnny), Australian cricket authority, aged 70.—*Jan.* 19.
Nichols, Sir Philip Bouverie Bowyer, K.C.M.G., M.C., former Ambassador in Prague and The Hague, aged 68—*Dec.* 6, 1962.
Normand, Wilfred Guild Normand, Lord, P.C. (life peer), former Lord Justice General of Scotland and Lord of Appeal in Ordinary, aged 78—*Oct.* 5, 1962.
Nuffield, William Richard Morris, 1st and last Viscount, G.B.E., C.H., F.R.S., great industrialist and philanthropist, aged 85—*Aug.* 22.
Odets, Clifford, U.S. dramatist, aged 57—*Aug.* 15.
O'Hara, *Most Rev.* Gerald Patrick, Apostolic Delegate to Great Britain, aged 68—*July* 16.
Olimpio, Sylvanus, President of Togo, aged 60 (*assassinated*)—*Jan.* 13.
Osborne, Malcolm, C.B.E., R.A., former Professor of Engraving at Royal College of Art, aged 83—*Sept.* 22.
Ovey, Sir Esmond, G.C.M.G., M.V.O., former Ambassador in Moscow, Brussels and Buenos Aires, aged 83—*May* 30.
Owen, *Lt.-Col.* Sir Goronwy, D.S.O., former Liberal Chief Whip, aged 82—*Sept.* 26.
Paulhan, Louis, pioneer French aviator, aged 79—*Feb.* 11.
Peacock, Sir Edward Robert, G.C.V.O., financier; for many years a director of Bank of England, aged 91—*Nov.* 19, 1962.
Penson, Dame Lillian Margery, D.B.E., Ph.D., historian and former Vice-Chancellor of London University, aged 66—*April* 17.
Phillips, Morgan, former secretary of Labour Party, aged 60—*Jan.* 15.
Piccard, *Prof.* Jean Felix, explorer of stratosphere, aged 79—*Jan.* 28.
Pitts, Zasu, popular Hollywood film actress, aged 63—*June* 7.
Plummer, Sir Leslie Arthur, K.B.E., Labour M.P. for Deptford since 1951, aged 61—*April* 15.
Poole, Austin Lane, mediaeval historian and former President of St. John's College, Oxford, aged 73—*Feb.* 22.
Pope John XXIII, *His Holiness* (Angelo Guiseppe Roncalli), 262nd Sovereign Pontiff, aged 81—*June* 3.

Poulenc, Francis, distinguished French composer, aged 64—*Jan.* 30.
Powicke, Sir (Frederick) Maurice, great mediaeval historian, aged 83—*May* 19.
Powys, John Cowper, novelist and essayist, aged 90—*June* 17.
Prasad, Rajendra, Ll.D., first President of Indian Republic, aged 78—*Feb.* 28.
Prentice, *Lt.-Col.* Frank Douglas, secretary of Rugby Football Union since 1947, aged 64—*Oct.* 3, 1962.
Rann, Ernest Hilbourne, science correspondent; contributor to WHITAKER'S ALMANACK for 50 years, aged 92—*May* 15.
Robertson, Sir Dennis Holme, C.M.G., F.B.A., economist, aged 72—*April* 21.
Robertson, Sir Howard Morley, M.C., R.A., distinguished architect, aged 74—*May* 5.
Robertson, Jean Forbes-, distinguished actress, aged 57—*Dec.* 24, 1962.
Romer, *General* Sir Cecil Francis, G.C.B., K.B.E., C.M.G., former Adjutant-General, aged 92—*Oct.* 1, 1962.
Roosevelt, Mrs. Eleanor, widow of President F. D. Roosevelt, and worker for social causes, commentator and politician, aged 78—*Nov.* 7, 1962.
Samuel, Herbert Louis Samuel, P.C., G.C.B., O.M., G.B.E., 1st Visct., veteran Liberal Statesman and philosopher, aged 92—*Feb.* 5.
Sargent, Sir Orme Garton, G.C.M.G., K.C.B., former Permanent Under-Secretary of State for Foreign Affairs, aged 77—*Oct.* 23, 1962.
Sarraut, Albert, former French Prime Minister, aged 90—*Nov.* 26, 1962.
Schuman, Robert, French Statesman and great worker for European Unity, aged 77—*Sept.* 4.
Scott, Adrian Gilbert, C.B.E., M.C., distinguished architect, aged 80—*April* 23.
Scott, John William Robertson, C.H., veteran journalist and founder of *The Countryman*, aged 96—*Dec.* 21, 1962
Seymour, Charles, U.S. historian and former President of Yale, aged 78—*Aug.* 11.
Siepmann, Harry Arthur, banking expert, aged 73—*Sept.* 16.
Simner, *Col.* Sir Percy Reginald Owen Abel, K.C.B., D.S.O., former Senior Master of King's Bench Division, aged 84—*Jan.* 11.
Simpson, Percy, D.Litt., English Scholar; editor of Ben Jonson, aged 97—*Nov.* 14, 1962.
Spens, Sir Will, C.B.E., former Master of Corpus Christi College, Cambridge, administrator and educationalist, aged 80—*Nov.* 1, 1962.
Squire, William Henry, cellist and composer of ballads, aged 91—*March* 17.
Strachey, *Rt. Hon.* Evelyn John St. Loe, Labour M.P. for West Dundee and former Minister, aged 61—*July* 15.
Stuart, Dorothy Margaret, popular author, aged 74—*Sept.* 14.
Sugden, *General* Sir Cecil Stanway, G.B.E., K.C.B. former Quartermaster-General, aged 59—*March* 25.
Sutherland, George Granville Sutherland-Leveson-Gower, 5th Duke of, K.T., P.C., aged 74—*Feb.* 1.
Taylor, John Henry, great golfer, aged 91—*Feb.* 10.
Tennant, *Admiral* Sir William George, K.C.B., C.B.E., M.V.O., Naval leader in Second World War and Lord Lieutenant of Worcestershire, aged 73—*July* 26.
Tucker, Sir James Millard, Q.C., expert on law of taxation, aged 70—*Sept.* 10.
Vyse, *Maj.-Gen.* Sir Richard Howard-, K.C.M.G., D.S.O., former President of British Legion, aged 79—*Dec.* 5, 1962.
Wakelam, *Lt.-Col.* Henry Blythe Thornhill, T. D., pioneer B.B.C. sports commentator, aged 70—*July* 10.
Wallace, Sir William, C.B.E., marine engineer and naval architect, aged 81—*May* 27.
Warner, Sir Pelham Francis, M.B.E., great cricketer and cricket administrator, aged 89—*Jan.* 30.
Warwick, Walter Curry, leading member of shipping industry, aged 85—*May* 20.
Weldon, George, distinguished conductor, aged 55—*Aug.* 16.
Wells, Cyril Mowbray, distinguished cricketer and schoolmaster, aged 92—*Aug.* 22.
Whistler, *Gen.* Sir Lashmer Gordon, G.C.B., K.B.E., D.S.O., aged 64—*July* 4.
White, *Very Rev.* Eric Milner-, C.B.E., D.S.O., D.D., Dean of York since 1941, aged 79—*June* 15.
Whiting, John, dramatist, aged 45—*June* 16.
Wilhelmina, Queen of the Netherlands from 1890 to 1945, aged 82—*Nov.* 28, 1962.
Williams, *Rt. Hon.* Sir Edward John, K.C.M.G., former Labour M.P. and High Commissioner in Australia, aged 72—*May* 16.
Williams, William Richard, Labour M.P. for Openshaw Division of Manchester, aged 68—*Sept.* 11.
Wilson, *Prof.* Frank Percy, Elizabethan scholar, aged 73—*May* 29.
Wilson, John Gideon, C.B.E., famous bookseller, aged 87—*Sept.* 6.
Windlesham, James Brian George Hennessy, 2nd Baron, Liberal peer, aged 59 (*in air accident*)—*Nov.* 16, 1962.
Wood, Sir Robert Stanford, K.B.E., C.B., first Vice-Chancellor of Southampton University, aged 76—*May* 18.
Woods, Sir John Harold Edmund, G.C.B., M.V.O., former Permanent Secretary at Board of Trade, aged 68—*Dec.* 1, 1962.
Worthington, Sir Hubert, O.B.E., R.A., distinguished architect, aged 77—*July* 26.
Zanzibar, *His Highness* Seyyid Sir Abdulla bin Khalifa bin Harub, Sultan of, aged 53—*July* 1.

THE CENTENARIES OF 1964

In December 1863, German troops had occupied Holstein without resistance by the Danes, and early in the new year Bismarck, acting in conjunction with Austria, decided on further aggression. The joint Prusso-Austrian plan was to send an ultimatum to Denmark calling for the revocation within 48 hours of the new Constitution; if, as was expected, the ultimatum was rejected, the two powers were to seize Schleswig as a pledge for the fulfilment of Denmark's obligations. The ultimatum was duly sent on Jan. 16, and duly rejected, and on Feb. 1 the allies crossed the frontier of Schleswig. On this occasion the Danes resisted, but after a few days were compelled to evacuate the Dannewerke, the line of forts in the south of Schleswig, and by the end of February Schleswig had been overrun and the invaders had penetrated into Jutland. The strongly fortified position of Düppel, however, continued to hold out, and was not taken until April 18, after a lengthy siege.

Meanwhile Lord Palmerston (who in the previous year had already expressed himself strongly in favour of Denmark) and Lord Russell were anxious to intervene. They were however in a minority in the Cabinet and were also opposed by the Queen. It was agreed to order the Channel Fleet home in case of possible contingencies, but an attempt to stage a naval demonstration in the Baltic, jointly with France and Russia, fell through.

British policy therefore proved ineffective. A conference of the Powers which had signed the Treaty of 1852 was proposed by Lord Russell, and finally met in London on April 25, but by that time nearly the whole of the disputed territory was in German hands, and though an armistice was brought about, and various attempts at compromise were made, the conference was abortive. The armistice came to an end and on June 29 the Prussians landed on Alsen and drove the Danes out of the island, subsequently occupying the whole of Jutland. The Danes were forced to yield completely and to sign a treaty at Vienna on Oct. 30, ceding the whole of Schleswig and Holstein and paying the cost of the war. Queen Victoria's part in the proceedings had been much criticized, Lord Ellenborough, in the House of Lords in May, making pointed reference to her pro-German attitude.

The differences in the Cabinet on Schleswig-Holstein were repeated in a number of domestic matters. In a speech on a Bill, introduced by Mr. Baines, to lower the borough franchise, Mr. Gladstone, Chancellor of the Exchequer, expressed himself in favour of a wide extension and said that every man not incapacitated by personal unfitness or political danger "was morally entitled to come within the pale of the Constitution". For these views he was reprimanded by Lord Palmerston. Mr. Baines' Bill was defeated, as was an attempt by the same member to introduce voting by secret ballot at general elections, Lord Palmerston opposing the latter suggestion as inconsistent with the character of Englishmen.

The American Civil War continued during the year. The Federal army was driven back from Richmond on March 1, and on May 3 the Confederate generals Lee and Longstreet, marching towards Fredericksburg, encountered General Grant (who had been appointed Federal Commander-in-Chief on March 12) and a number of fierce engagements with heavy losses on both sides took place. During June and July Grant was also repulsed in a number of attacks on Petersburg but by the end of the year Confederate resistance seemed to be weakening. On Dec. 20 Sherman completed his famous thirty days' raid through Georgia by appearing at Savannah. In June the war had made an incursion into Europe, when the Confederate raider *Alabama* was destroyed off Cherbourg by the Federal ship *Kearsarge*. On Nov. 4 Abraham Lincoln was re-elected President.

The ill-fated adventure of the Grand Duke Maximilian in Mexico began during the year; he proclaimed himself Emperor on May 28.

During the spring, Garibaldi paid a three weeks' visit to England and was received on all sides with tremendous enthusiasm. A contemporary writer said that his arrival in London on April 11 "partook of the character of a Royal progress, work being in a great measure suspended in the metropolis, and deputations and societies of all kinds following in his train". At a demonstration at the Crystal Palace on April 16 he spoke to an audience estimated at 30,000. During his stay he was entertained by Lord Palmerston and Lord Russell and visited by the Prince of Wales.

Prince Albert Victor (later the Duke of Clarence), the first child of the Prince and Princess of Wales, was born on Jan. 8. The Queen visited a flower-show at the Horticultural Gardens, Kensington, on March 30, but for the greater part of the year continued to live in seclusion, a fact which caused some popular criticism and two leading articles in *The Times* remonstrating with Her Majesty.

The 300th anniversary of the birth of Shakespeare on April 23 was commemorated by many special celebrations, both at Stratford-on-Avon and in other parts of the country.

On March 11 a disastrous flood took place in the Sheffield area, owing to the bursting of the Bradfield Reservoir, eight miles above the town. No fewer than 270 persons were drowned, the loss of life being heaviest at Malin Bridge and Rotherham and in the lower parts of Sheffield itself. An enquiry found that the reservoir had been defectively built and inadequately inspected.

In London, the Savoy Chapel was gutted by fire on July 7 and the ancient Haberdashers' Hall in Gresham Street burnt down on Sept. 19. The new Southwark Street, made between Borough High Street and Blackfriars Road, was opened on New Year's Day, and on July 8, the foundation stone of the Victoria Embankment was laid. A former London landmark, the Hungerford Bridge, was re-opened over the Avon as the Clifton Suspension Bridge on Dec. 8.

The controversy between Newman and Charles Kingsley during the year resulted in the publication of the former's *Apologia pro Vita Sua*. Other works to appear in 1864 included Browning's *Dramatis Personae*, Tennyson's *Enoch Arden* and *The Northern Farmer* and Trollope's *Small House at Allington*. Dickens began the serial publication of *Our Mutual Friend*.

THE CENTENARIES OF 1964

The following is a list of the principal centenaries which will be commemorated in 1964.

Died 1864

Jan. 3.	William Behnes. Sculptor.
Feb. 14.	William Dyce. Painter.
March 16.	R. S. Surtees. Novelist.
May 1.	Jacob Meyerbeer. Composer.
May 19.	Nathaniel Hawthorne. American novelist.
May 20.	John Clare. Poet.
June 4.	Nassau Senior. Economist.
June 18.	William Smith O'Brien. Irish nationalist.
July 31.	Louis Hachette. Publisher.
Sept. 17.	Walter Savage Landor. Poet and man of letters.
Oct. 18.	Duke of Newcastle. Cabinet Minister.
Oct. 29.	John Leech. Humorous artist.

Born 1864

Jan. 9.	Sir Donald Maclean. Liberal leader.
Jan. 10.	John Bailey. Critic and essayist.
Jan. 24.	Beatrice Harraden. Novelist.
Feb. 2.	Margot, Countess of Oxford and Asquith.
Feb. 13.	Stephen Gwynn. Author and Irish nationalist.
Feb. 20.	Henry Seymour, Lord Rawlinson. General.
March 9.	Viscount Dawson of Penn. Physician.
March 12.	Gabriele d'Annunzio. Italian writer and politician.
April 7.	R. D. Blumenfeld. Journalist.
April 12.	Lord Wester Wemyss. Admiral.
April 22.	Phil May. Humorous artist.
May 3.	Sir Henry Wilson. Field-Marshal.
May 10.	Léon Gaumont. Pioneer of the cinema.
May 13.	Vesta Tilley. Actress.
June 11.	Richard Strauss. Composer.

June 24. Sir Stanley Maude. British commander in Mesopotamia.
July 2. William Le Queux. Novelist.
July 15. Dame Marie Tempest. Actress.
July 18. Philip, Viscount Snowden. Statesman.
July 28. Stephen Phillips. Dramatist.
July 30. Sir Eyre Crowe. Diplomat.
August 23. Eleutherios Venizelos. Greek statesman.
Sept. 14 Robert, Viscount Cecil of Chelwood, Statesman and worker for peace.
Sept. 25 William Morris Hughes. Australian statesman.
Sept. 28. Barry Pain. Humorous writer.
Oct. 17. Eleanor Glyn. Novelist.
Oct. 31. Cosmo Gordon Lang (Lord Lang of Lambeth). Archbishop of Canterbury.
Nov. 4. Sir Robert Lorimer. Architect.
Nov. 6. Sir Abe Bailey, Bt. South African financier.
Nov. 14. Robert Hichens. Novelist.
Nov. 20. Sir Percy Cox. British administrator in Near East.
Dec. 31. William Clive, Viscount Bridgeman. Conservative politician.

1764
Died April 15. Marquise de Pompadour.
Oct. 26. William Hogarth. Painter.
Born April 3. John Abernethy. Surgeon.
July 21. Sir Sidney Smith. Admiral.

1664
Born July 21. Matthew Prior. Poet and diplomat.

1564
Died May 27. John Calvin.
Born Feb. 6. Christopher Marlowe.
April 23. William Shakespeare.

THE CENTENARIES OF 1965

The following is a list of the principal centenaries which will be commemorated in 1965.

Died 1865
Jan. 18. Charles Greville. Clerk of Privy Council and diarist.
Jan. 19. Pierre Joseph Proudhon. Pioneer French Socialist.
Feb. 15. Cardinal Nicholas Wiseman. First Archbishop of Westminster.
Feb. 21. Field Marshal Visct. Combermere (Sir Stapleton Cotton). Peninsular general.
March 2. John Cassell. Publisher.
March 10. Duc de Morny. French statesman.
April 2. Richard Cobden. Politician and economist.
April 14. Abraham Lincoln. President of U.S.A.
May 26. Charles Waterton. Traveller and naturalist.
June 8. Sir Joseph Paxton. Designer of Crystal Palace.
Aug. 12. Sir William Hooker. Botanist and Director of Kew Gardens.
Sept. 22. John Frederick Herring. Painter of animals.
Oct. 18. Viscount Palmerston. Prime Minister.
Nov. 8. Tom Sayers. Pugilist.
Nov. 12. Mrs. Elizabeth Gaskell. Novelist.
Dec. 10. Leopold I. First King of the Belgians.
Dec. 24. Sir Charles Eastlake. President of the Royal Academy.

Born 1865
Jan. 3. Sir Henry Lytton. Actor.
Jan. 3. Sir Richard Runciman Terry. Musical historian.
Feb. 9. Mrs. Patrick Campbell. Actress.
Feb. 19. Sven Hedin. Explorer.
Feb. 28. Sir Wilfred Grenfell. Medical missionary to Labrador.
Feb. 28. Arthur Symons. Poet and critic.
March 21. H.A.L. Fisher. Historian and Cabinet Minister.
April 1. Lord Snell. Labour politician.
April 4. Earl of Derby. Conservative politician.
May 7. A.E.W. Mason. Novelist.
May 7. C. J. Cutcliffe Hyne. Novelist.
May 25. Lord Riddell. Newspaper proprietor.
June 2. A. G. Gardiner. Journalist.
June 3. George V, King of England.
June 13. William Butler Yeats. Poet and playwright.
June 23. William Joynson-Hicks, Visct. Brentford. Politician.
June 24. Harry Plunket Greene. Singer.
June 27. Sir John Monash. Australian general.
June 28. Sir David Young Cameron. Painter and etcher.
July 15. Visct. Northcliffe. Newspaper proprietor.
July 16. George A. Birmingham (Canon J. O. Hannay). Novelist.
Aug. 25. Cardinal Arthur Hinsley. Archbishop of Westminster.
Sept. 3. H. A. Gwynne. Journalist.
Sept. 13. Lord Birdwood. Field Marshal.
Sept. 23. Baroness Orczy. Novelist.
Oct. 1. Paul Dukas. French composer.
Oct. 2. Lord Moynihan. Surgeon.
Oct. 16. Earl of Cavan. Field Marshal.
Oct. 18. Logan Pearsall Smith. Man of letters.
Nov. 11. Sir Walter Braithwaite. General.
Dec. 4. Nurse Edith Cavell.
Dec. 8. Jan Sibelius. Finnish composer.
Dec. 16. Elsie Fogerty. Teacher of drama.
Dec. 30. Rudyard Kipling. Author.

LIVE BIRTHS, MARRIAGES AND DEATHS IN THE UNITED KINGDOM

Year	Live Births	Rate per 1,000	Marriages	Rate per 1,000	Deaths	Rate per 1,000
1938	735,573	15·5	409,101	17·2	559,598	11·8
1953	804,000	15·9	395,316	15·6	577,220	11·4
1954	795,000	15·6	392,859	15·5	578,400	11·5
1955	789,000	15·4	410,630	16·0	595,916	11·6
1956	825,000	16·0	406,266	15·8	597,981	11·7
1957	851,000	16·5	398,955	15·5	591,200	11·1
1958	871,000	16·8	390,356	15·1	604,000	11·7
1959	879,000	16·9	390,178	15·0	606,200	11·7
1960	915,000	17·5	393,596	15·0	603,300	11·5
1961	936,900	17·7	397,000	15·0	631,800	12·0
1962	977,800	18·3	397,800	15·0	626,100	11·9

ALIENS AND NATURALIZATION

Aliens.—Figures in the following table show the number of aliens registered with the police in the United Kingdom on Dec. 31, 1962. These figures exclude among others children under 16, diplomatic and consular officials, certain officials of international organizations and visitors spending less than three months in the country. Under the Aliens Order, 1960, aliens to whose stay in this country no conditions are attached are exempt from registration with the police.

Naturalization.—In the years 1946–1962, 107,408 certificates of naturalization were issued by the Home Department, an average of 10,621 each year in 1946–1950 and of 4,525 in 1951–1962. Numbers of persons naturalized by principal countries of origin are shown below.

	Aliens in U.K.			Certificates of Naturalization granted				
	Male	Female	Total	1958	1959	1960	1961	1962
Europe	42,184	69 309	111,493	3,086	4,523	6,157	4,635	3,829
Austria	591	2,345	2,936	57	58	93	67	51
Belgium	291	344	635	9	13	28	29	17
Czechoslovakia	59	37	96	83	76	115	69	77
Denmark	603	2,507	3,110	15	12	16	11	16
Finland	130	1,046	1,176	2	3	7	4	3
France	2,334	6,759	9,093	22	35	33	33	34
Germany	4,142	12,480	16,622	255	362	516	329	276
Greece	1,220	1,334	2,554	27	9	19	28	37
Hungary	106	119	225	101	97	89	86	506
Italy	18,180	12,768	30,948	129	172	215	144	128
Netherlands	1,315	2 461	3,776	45	65	68	57	44
Norway	964	1,544	2,508	7	10	7	7	11
Poland	353	619	972	1,746	2,860	4,115	3,139	2,161
Portugal	926	1,374	2,300	2	3	6	11	11
Roumania	21	10	31	35	46	49	40	28
Russia (Including White Russia)	189	139	328	371	445	86	64	41
Spain	7,182	14,770	21,952	26	24	62	55	56
Sweden	398	1,674	2 072	2	1	2	5	1
Switzerland	2,211	5,881	8,092	10	4	16	9	11
Turkey	604	311	915	4	4	7	6	3
Yugoslavia	251	614	865	134	216	212	166	134
Other Countries	114	173	287	4	8	396	276	183
Africa	2,516	798	3,314	6	17	31	32	33
United Arab Republic	1,335	480	1,815	—	10	18	24	21
Other African Countries	1,181	318	1,499	—	7	13	8	12
America	8,186	5,553	13,739	20	23	37	41	24
Argentine Republic	158	186	344		1	4	6	—
Brazil	95	101	196		—	—	1	—
United States	7,264	4,602	11,866	16	18	29	33	23
Other American Countries	669	664	1,333		4	4	1	1
Asia	8,617	3,717	12,334	81	72	119	165	149
Burma	303	91	394		3	7	3	9
China	567	384	951		25	26	39	42
Iraq	2,493	364	2,857		5	17	9	10
Israel	771	621	1,392		20	44	88	62
Japan	652	324	976		—	—	1	1
Persia	1,941	1,151	3,092		8	12	8	8
Other Asian Countries	1,890	782	2,672		11	13	17	17
Australasia	—	1	1	—	—	—	—	—
Western Samoa	—	1	1	—	—	—	—	—
Other Countries	237	129	366		159	243	224	193
Stateless	99	74	173	47	48	58	51	49
Nationality uncertain	138	55	193	73	109	181	169	138
British Protected Persons	—	—	—	1	2	4	4	6
Total	61,740	79,507	141,247	3,315	4,794	6,587	5,097	4,228

IMMIGRATION AND EMIGRATION, 1962

Immigration.—In the year 1962, a total of 58,800 persons from Commonwealth countries arrived in the United Kingdom for a stay of one year or more, compared with 70,500 in 1961. Arrivals from the principal countries (with 1961 figures in brackets) were: Canada 7,400 (*10,300*); Australia, 12,300 (*11,800*); New Zealand, 3,900 (*4,000*); Rhodesia and Nyasaland, 2,200 (*3,000*); East and West Africa, 7,800 (*6,700*); India, Pakistan and Ceylon, 6,400 (*8,200*); Malaya and Singapore, 3,300 (*3,900*); West Indies and Bermuda, 11,300 (*18,000*); Other Commonwealth Countries, 4,200 (*4,700*). 4,600 persons arrived from the United States (1960, *4,600*), and 4,600 from other foreign countries (1961, *8,600*). Total immigration from all countries in 1962, 68,000 (1961, *83,700*).

Emigration.—In the year 1962, 78,400 persons left the United Kingdom for Commonwealth Countries for a stay of one year or more, compared with 78,500 in 1961: to Canada 10,700 (*9,300*); Australia 35,500 (*40,600*); New Zealand 10,800 (*9,100*); Rhodesia and Nyasaland, 1,600 (*1,400*); East and

West Africa, 5,500 (*5,200*); India, Pakistan and Ceylon, 3,300 (*3,600*); Malaya and Singapore, 2,100 (*3,400*); West Indies and Bermuda, 6,400 (*3,800*); Other Commonwealth Countries, 2,600 (*2,200*). 7,900 persons emigrated to the United States (1961, *7,100*) and 4,900 to other foreign countries (1961, *5,300*). Total emigrants from U.K. to all countries in 1962, 91,200 (*91,000*).

CAUSES OF DEATH IN ENGLAND AND WALES, 1961 AND 1962

Cause of Death	1961	1962
Natural Causes		
Tuberculosis	3,334	3,087
Syphilitic Disease	900	821
Whooping Cough	27	24
Meningococcal Infections	130	136
Poliomyelitis	59	18
Measles	152	40
Other Infective, etc., Diseases	1,037	1,047
Malignant Neoplasm:		
Stomach	13,788	13,587
Intestines, etc.	14,718	14,779
Other digestive organs	8,854	9,089
Respiratory Organs	23,941	24,863
Breast	9,367	9,426
Uterus	3,981	4,012
Leukæmia and aleukæmia	2,645	2,707
Other	22,621	23,107
Other Neoplasms	1,318	1,268
Anæmias	1,709	1,680
Diabetes	3,869	3,810
Vascular Lesions of Nervous System	77,023	78,308
Heart Diseases	168,140	172,746
Hypertension	6,269	5,617
Hypertension with Heart Disease	11,225	10,527
Other Circulatory Diseases	19,021	19,561
Influenza	7,102	3,308
Pneumonia	29,275	30,911
Bronchitis	31,363	33,288

Cause of Death	1961	1962
Natural Causes		
Other Diseases of Respiratory System	5,364	5,282
Ulcer of Stomach and Duodenum	4,405	4,686
Appendicitis	645	606
Intestinal obstruction and hernia	3,189	3,145
Gastritis, Enteritis and Colitis	2,582	2,555
Nephritis and Nephrosis	3,498	3,432
Hyperplasia of Prostate	3,075	2,892
Pregnancy, Childbirth, Abortion	274	300
Congenital Malformations	5,196	5,428
Other Diseases	38,342	37,874
TOTAL (Natural causes)	528,438	533,732
Deaths by Violence		
Accidents:		
Motor accidents	6,634	6,303
Other transport accidents	649	621
Poisoning	1,478	1,831
Falls	5,376	5,496
Burning, etc.	783	906
Other	2,887	2,844
Suicide, etc.	5,201	5,588
Homicide and Operations of War	306	308
Total (By Violence)	23,314	23,897
TOTAL, ALL CAUSES	551,752	557,629

DRUNKENNESS IN ENGLAND AND WALES, 1938–1962

Offences of drunkenness proved. Offences under Sections 6 and 11 of the Road Traffic Act, 1960 (drunk in charge, etc. of road vehicles, are not included). *Figures for 1961 and 1962 vary from those quoted on p. 592 since they include convictions where a person is found guilty of drunkenness and at the same time of some other and more serious offence.*

Year	Males	Females	Total	Number per 10,000†	Year	Males	Females	Total	Number per 10,000†
1938	46,832	7,686	54,518	16·84	1951	48,335	5,341	53,676	15·76
1939	45,846	7,083	52,929	16·17	1952	48,694	5,194	53,888	15·78
1940	40,287	6,711	46,998	15·02	1953	48,539	5,035	53,574	15.65
1941	35,359	5,605	40,964	13·56	1954	48,377	4,900	53,277	15·52
1942	22,772	4,663	27,435	9·23	1955	49,654	4,556	54,210	15·75
1943	22,069	5,294	27,363	9·36	1956	55,573	4,609	60,182	17·44
1944	18,125	4,503	22,628	7·77	1957	62,042	4,960	67,002	19·34
1945	16,375	4,294	20,669	7·09	1958	60,216	4,842	65,058	18·71
1946	17,090	3,455	20,545	6·04	1959	60,685	4,502	65,187	18·63
1947	21,354	3,816	25,170	7·38	1960	63,861	4,248	68,109	19·31
1948	28,305	4,566	32,871	9·62	1961	69,991	4,703	74,694	20·99
1949	31,278	4,455	35,733	10·42	1962	79,199	4,793	83,992	23·26
1950	42,642	5,075	47,717	13·05					

† Of population of England and Wales aged 15 years and over (mid-year estimate).

CRIMINAL STATISTICS
ENGLAND AND WALES

In 1962 the total number of persons found guilty of offences of all kinds was 1,266,596, of whom 203,775 were found guilty of indictable offences, 1,062,821 of non-indictable offences. The most numerous offences in 1961 and 1962 are listed below. In addition, 25,308 persons (19,492 under 17 years) were cautioned by the police in 1962, for indictable offences and 45,049 (16,700 juveniles) for non-indictable (other than motoring) offences.

Ages of Offenders.—The 29,570 persons found guilty of indictable offences by the *higher courts* in 1962 included 1,275 persons under 17 years of age (36 persons under 14), 8,322 persons aged 17 and under 21, and 19,973 persons aged 21 and over. In *magistrates' courts*, of 174,205 persons convicted of indictable offences in 1962, 31,853 were under 14 years of age, 33,094 were aged 14 and under 17, 27,031 persons were aged 17 and under 21 and 82,227 were aged 21 years and over.

Persons Convicted of Indictable Offences

	1938		1961		1960	
	Total	Juveniles*	Total	Juveniles*	Total	Juveniles*
Larceny	56,092	19,750	107,235	37,340	119,034	38,220
Breaking and Entering	10,853	6,793	36,240	18,944	42,760	19,592
Receiving, Frauds and False Pretences	5,333	602	13,589	3,207	15,310	3,304
Sexual Offences	2,321	475	6,150	1,180	6,068	1,166
Violence against the Person	1,583	116	11,519	1,727	11,986	1,787
ALL INDICTABLE OFFENCES	78,463	28,116	182,217	64,284	203,775	66,222

* Persons under 17 years of age.

Disposal.—In all courts in 1962, 28,702 persons aged 17 and over (females, 1,081) were sentenced to *imprisonment, corrective training* or *preventive detention*, compared with 25,629 (females, 1,041) in 1961. Of the 1962 total, 1,832 persons (females, 62) were aged under 21. A total of 80,893 persons (females, 12,434) were *fined* in all courts, including 29,974 persons under 21 years of age (females, 2,578). 41,657 persons (females 7,048) were placed on *probation*, including 30,353 persons under 21 (females, 4,021).

Non-Indictable Offences

	Persons Convicted 1961	1962
Traffic Offences	712,584	785,816
Drunkenness	71,614	80,798
Revenue Offences	29,286	34,259
Railway Offences	20,757	20,425
Breach of local and other regulations	9,788	9,784
Disorderly Behaviour	15,074	15,714
Betting and Gaming	4,901	2,556
Assaults	11,937	10,645
Education Acts Offences	5,280	5 544
Malicious Damage	15,123	15,585
Offences by Prostitutes	2,259	2,482
Vagrancy Acts Offences	6,324	7,468
Wireless Telegraphy Acts Offences	9,516	14,776
Cruelty to, or neglect of, children	772	851
Other Offences	54,965	56,118
TOTAL	970,180	1,062,821

The main types of non-indictable offence of which persons under 17 were found guilty were:—

	Persons Convicted 1961	1962
Traffic Offences:—		
Obstruction and Nuisance other than by vehicle	2,235	2,057
Offences with Pedal Cycles	8,600	7,993
Others	19,305	19,307
Malicious Damage	7,121	7,113
Railway Offences	6,076	5,646
Stealing and Receiving	745	914
Playing Games in Street	131	131
Gaming (Vagrancy Acts)	6	—
Other Offences	11,695	11,564
TOTAL	55,914	54,725

Cases of Murder

The Homicide Act, 1957, in operation from March 21, 1957, removed from the category of murder homicides (*a*) which were previously murder only by doctrine of constructive malice; (*b*) under severe provocation by words alone; (*c*) in pursuance of a suicide pact. It provided that a person charged with murder should not be found guilty of that offence if at the time of the offence he was suffering from diminished responsibility, but instead should be found guilty of manslaughter. The death penalty should not be imposed for murders other than capital murders* except where the murderer had committed another murder on a different occasion.

In 1962, 148 cases of murder of persons aged one year or over were known to the police. In 15 cases the offence was reduced to manslaughter. *Capital murder.**—18 victims were murdered by 19 known murderers or suspects. Of these, 11 victims were murdered by 9 persons who committed suicide before arrest. Proceedings were taken against 6 persons for the murder of 6 victims and for the murder of one victim proceedings were taken against 4 persons, 3 of whom were charged with non-capital murder. In one case which appeared to be of capital murder, the murderer was undetected at the time of going to press. In proceedings involving 7 victims, 3 persons committed for trial were found guilty but insane. Of 3 persons convicted, 2 involved in the murder of one victim were sentenced to life imprisonment and one sentence was quashed. Of 4 persons convicted and sentenced to death, 2 were executed; in one case the Court of Criminal Appeal substituted a conviction of manslaughter and in another a conviction of non-capital murder with life imprisonment. *Non-Capital Murder.*—In 6 cases which appeared to be of non-capital murder, the murderers were not yet detected. 108 victims were murdered by 108 known murderers or suspects. Of these, 42 victims were murdered by 35 persons who committed suicide before arrest; 2 victims were murdered by 2 persons who died before arrest. In proceedings taken against 71 persons for the murder of 64 victims, 2 died while awaiting trial.

* Murder committed in the course of or in furtherance of theft; in resisting or avoiding arrest or escaping from legal custody; murder of police officers or prison officers or persons assisting them: and murder by shooting or causing explosions.

Of 69 persons committed for trial 8 persons were found insane on arraignment and 18 were acquitted. 4 persons were found guilty but insane. 37 persons were sentenced to life imprisonment and 2 were detained during H.M. pleasure (under 18).

Suicide

Coroners' returns show that 5,583 persons (female, 2,320) committed suicide in 1962, compared with 5,212 in 1961 and 5,119 in 1960.

Magistrates Courts
Non-Criminal Proceedings

54,548 orders were made in magistrates courts in 1962 in respect of 63,968 applications, mainly in separation, maintenance and child welfare cases: Affiliation orders, 6,050; Maintenance orders, 4,459; Matrimonial orders, 18,082; Guardianship of infants, 4,995; Committals to approved schools, 5,704; to care of fit persons, 4,061; Supervision orders, 4,126; Adoption orders, 6,999 (including interim orders, 52).

SCOTLAND
Persons proceeded against

Indictable Offences	Average 1935–39	1959	1960	1961	1962
Crimes					
Against the person	2,545	2,141	2,415	2,412	2,576
Against property:—					
with violence	3,473	8,720	8,420	9,976	10,681
without violence	12,186	15,093	15,559	16,959	18,671
malicious injuries to property	3,639	238	260	2 5	307
forgery, etc.	79	132	126	179	216
Other Crimes	406	404	435	439	450
Total	22,328	26,728	27,215	30 220	32,901
Miscellaneous Offences					
Breach of Peace	20,706	23,998	26,239	29 170	29 455
Against Intoxicating Liquor Laws	16,953	14,091	14,393	16 030	15 964
Against Police Acts, etc.	11,048	11,396	11,924	12,604	19,113
Against Road Acts, etc.	43,905	57,670	*63,097	65,030	62 063
Other (including war legislation)	15,790	34,645	34,468	19,402	18 739
Total	108,402	141,800	150,121	142 236	145 334
TOTAL, ALL CRIMES AND OFFENCES	130,730	168,528	177,336	172 456	178,230

* Vehicle licences in force in the September quarter, excluding trade licences and Services vehicles, 728,600.

Cases of Murder.—In 1962, 27 cases of murder were known to the police. Ten of the 30 victims were under 10 years of age and 2 women victims were over 60. Of 4 persons proceeded against for capital murder one was found not guilty and in one case the charge was not proven; one person was ordered to be detained during Her Majesty's Pleasure and one to be detained (insane). Fifteen persons were proceeded against for non-capital murder, of whom 6 were sentenced to life imprisonment, 8 were detained (insane) and one charge was not proven. At the end of the year three cases were unsolved and proceedings were pending in four cases.

Juvenile Crime.—In 1962, 23,128 juveniles were proceeded against for crimes and offences of all kinds. 890 of these were acquitted or the charge against them was withdrawn. In 5,514 cases the charge was proved and an order made without a finding of guilt, 2,169 young persons being discharged absolutely and 3,246 placed on probation. In 16,497 cases where charges were proved with a finding of guilt, 6,083 juveniles were admonished, etc; 278 were cautioned (with or without surety); and 17 were found mentally defective. 793 juveniles were committed to approved schools, 688 to remand homes, 139 for Borstal training and 62 to the care of fit persons. Ten were placed on probation. 7,665 offenders were fined, and in 762 cases fines were imposed on the parent or guardian of the offender. 326 juveniles were discharged without trial.

PRISON POPULATIONS IN 1961 AND 1962

The daily average population of all British prisons and Borstal institutions in 1961 was 33,992, compared with 32,205 in 1961. Figures of receptions by Prisons and Borstal institutions in 1961 and 1962 were:—

Prison and Borstal Receptions	England and Wales		Scotland		Northern Ireland		United Kingdom
	1961	1962	1961	1962	1961	1962	1962
Convicted Prisoners: —							
Imprisonment (Total)	39,993†	45 579	12 373	13 300‡	1,040	1.092	59 971
under 3 years	37,812	43,278	12,221	13 158	1,012	1,071	57,507
3 years and over	2,181	2,301	152	142	28	21	2,464
Borstal Training	3,715	3,858	424	478	75	67	4,403
Corrective Training	369	263	6	8	12	13	284
Preventive Detention	218	138	—	2	6	2	142
Untried Prisoners	33 545	30 306	4,718	6 214	245	262	36,782
Civil Prisoners	9,671	11,603	4	2	454	569	12,174
DAILY AVERAGE POPULATION	28,563	30,309	2,997	3,238	445	445	34,992

† Including court martial prisoners (1962), 112; (1961), 140. In addition to figures in this table, 11,649 convicted prisoners were remanded to prison for inquiry, to await sentence, etc. in 1962 and 2 were serving other forms of sentences. ‡ Including court martial prisoners, 15; other, 1.

DETENTION CENTRES.—In the year 1962 there was a daily average population at detention centres of 754 (Scotland, 64) and a total of 3,603 receptions during the year (Scotland, 317).

FUEL AND POWER

NATIONAL COAL BOARD FINANCIAL RESULTS

£ million

	1958	1959	1960	1961	1962
Income					
From Sales (Net)	913·0	841·7	823·8	852·4	889·0
Principal Items:—					
Coal	869·1	806·1	784·6	815·8	851·7
Coke	48·7	42·4	42·6	39·5	33·1
Gas, Benzole, Crude Tar and Tar Products, etc.	22·8	21·8	22·6	21·0	20·2
Briquettes and Manufactured Fuel	13·1	11·0	9·4	11·6	13·3
Other Receipts	8·8	9·3	9·9	10·9	11·2
NET INCOME	921·8	851·0	833·7	863·3	900·2
Expenditure					
Wages, Salaries, Pensions, etc.	575·9	537·9	512·1	518·7	522·6
Payments to Open-cast Contractors	37·7	29·7	21·9	24·0	21·0
Materials, Stores, Power and Repairs	190·7	169·0	169·4	178·9	178·7
Payments for Imported Coal	7·1	0·8	—	—	—
Other Expenses and Depreciation	91·3	100·4	110·1	113·1	132·5
TOTAL EXPENDITURE	902·7	837·8	813·5	834·7	854·8
PROFIT	19·1	13·2	20·2	28·6	45·4
Adjustments relating to earlier years	*10·0*	—	—	*1·2*	—
BALANCE	29·1	13·2	20·2	27·4	45·4
Deduct Interest Payable, etc.	32·6	37·2	41·5	42·4	44·0
SURPLUS or *DEFICIENCY*	*3·5*	*24·0*	*21·3*	*15·0*	1·4

Coal Production, etc.

PRODUCTION AND DISTRIBUTION

Year	Saleable Mined Coal	Open Cast Coal	Total
1938	226,993,000	—	226,993,000
1956	209,925,000	12,106,000	222,006,000
1957	210,059,000	13,569,000	223,628,000
1958	201,475,000	14,347,000	215,822,000
1959	195,273,000	10,833,000	206,106,000
1960	186,051,000	7,553,000	193,604,000
1961	181,936,000	8,528,000	190,464,000
1962	190,135,000	7,301,000	197,436,000

Coal Distribution.—Of the 191,150,000 tons consumed at home in 1962, Industry used 27,435,000 tons, domestic users 28,621,000 tons, electricity generating stations 60,380,000 tons, gas works 22,086,000 tons, coke ovens 23,528,000 tons, railways 6,200,000 tons, and miners' coal and colliery consumption 8,900,000 tons.

Average Earnings.—Estimated average earnings, including value of Allowances in Kind, of all adult male workers in 1962 was £17 17*s.* 9*d.* per week.

GAS PRODUCTION

Total gas available in 1962/63 showed an increase of 7 per cent. compared with 1961/62 and is 90 per cent. above the pre-war level.

(Million therms)

	1960/61	1961/62	1962/63
Gas made at gasworks:			
Total*	2,211·4	2,263·1	2,403.9
Coal gas	1,705·7	1,704·9	1,684·0
Water gas	416·2	436·4	534·2
Gas bought from coke ovens, etc.	678·1	720·0	801·8
Total gas available	2,889·5	2,983·1	3,205·7

* Including producer gas, oil gas, etc., in addition to coal and water gas.

Consumption of coal in the production of gas rose from 19·1 million tons in 1938 to 22·2 million tons in 1962–63. Oil for gasmaking rose from 124,000 tons in 1938 to 1,214,000 tons in 1962–63

GAS INDUSTRY FINANCIAL RESULTS

£ million

	1958/59	1959/60	1960/61	1961/62	1962/63
Gross Revenue					
Sales—Gas	225·6	224·9	236·8	251·5	273·7
By-Products	109·6	101·0	106·2	109·5	112·0
Appliances	37·0	45·4	40·8	44·5	52·0
Other Revenue	17·4	17·8	18·1	17·6	18·2
TOTAL REVENUE	389·6	389·1	401·9	423·1	455·9
Gross Expenditure					
Process Materials:					
Coal	139·4	127·1	128·0	133·1	133·7
Coke	9·5	9·4	9·8	9·8	11·0
Oil	8·4	8·9	8·5	9·1	12·1
Gas (purchased)	14·1	16·3	18·7	20·6	23·3
Salaries and Wages	87·4	87·3	90·3	93·4	99·5
Cost of Appliances	26·0	31·6	27·7	29·7	34·5
Depreciation	26·2	28·1	29·8	30·1	31·3
Interest	21·6	23·0	24·6	25·6	26·2
Other materials, services and general expenses	58·5	59·8	62·5	68·4	79·4
TOTAL EXPENDITURE	391·1	391·5	399·9	419·8	451·0
SURPLUS	−1·5	−2·4	2·0	3·3	4·9

ELECTRICITY PRODUCTION AND FINANCE

England and Wales

In the year ended March 31, 1963, the industry sold more electricity than ever before, 11·4 per cent. more units than in 1961–62 and 138·9 per cent. more than the total sales ten years ago, income from sales reaching £754,000,000 and from contracting, £69,300,000. 115,517,000,000 units were sold to 16,363,513 consumers during the year at an average price of 1·566*d*. per unit. The maximum output capacity of the industry, 31,687mW at the end of the year, was 9·4 per cent. higher than in March, 1962. Mains operated by Area Boards were extended by 8,910 miles during the year and 18,028 new substations came into use. Transmission lines of the Electricity Generating Board were extended by 573 circuit-miles and 35 new Grid Substations came into use. The average thermal efficiency of Electricity Generating Board power stations in 1962-63 was 27·44 per cent. compared with 27·32 per cent. in 1961–62. In March, 1963, 205,910 persons were employed in the industry compared with 199,153 in 1962. The following results are those of the Electricity Council and Area Boards in England and Wales, the figures being rounded off.

Financial Results, 1962–63

	£ million	
	1961–62	1962–63
Revenue		
Sales of Electricity	670·4	756·3
Contracting	3·6	3·7
Other	13·2	13·5
TOTAL	687·2	773·5
Expenditure		
Generation and purchases	314·6	349·0
Distribution	38·9	42·6
Consumer Service	18·1	19·0
Administration, Collection of Accounts, etc.	39·1	42·0
Rates	27·6	30·8
Depreciation	114·0	127·1
Other	15·3	17·5
TOTAL	567·7	628·1
Trading Surplus	119·5	145·4
Deduct Interest payable	92·5	102·9
SURPLUS	26·9	42·5

PETROLEUM PRODUCTION AND DELIVERIES, 1961–62

Product	Production†		Deliveries*	
	1961	1962	1961	1962
Motor and Aviation Spirit	8,337,052	8,492,871	10,299,688	10,673,636
Industrial Spirits	8,637	9,552	209,093	192,763
White Spirit	148,050	140,541	149,801	142,569
Burning Oil	2,513,723	2,556,019	1,230,922	1,431,126
Vaporising Oil	170,624	53,856	261,447	212,468
Gas/Diesel Oil	8,610,572	9,966,079	3,947,520	4,619,296
Fuel Oil	21,150,183	21,961,719	18,816,964	21,329,440
Refinery Fuel Consumption (ex own production)	3,469,571	3,619,421	3,515,473	3,698,870
Bitumen	1,133,441	1,220,464	1,165,919	1,237,874
Paraffin Wax, Scale and Slack Wax	38,630	36,931	51,663	51,806
Lubricating Oil	957,587	899,123	979,614	968,087
Propane and Butane	200,825	288,339	206,285	294,163
Miscellaneous Products and Loss	2,365,820	3,052,089	2,342,136	3,007,751
TOTAL	49,104,715	52,297,004	46,014,950	50,900,433

† From imported and home-produced crude and process oils including shale.
* In addition 6,650 tons of motor spirit were produced in 1962 and 260,373 tons of refined benzole from other home-produced sources other than shale and indigenous crude oil.

Estimated end use of Motor Spirit (thousand tons)

	1961	1962
Cars and Motor Cycles	5,300	5,763
Taxis	25	23
Public Service Vehicles	77	74
Goods Vehicles	2,075	2,050
Industrial Use	215	215
Agricultural Use (incl. Agricultural Vans)	225	226
Services and Other Government	190	180
Petroleum Industry Own Use	14	12
Miscellaneous	22	22
TOTAL	8,143	8,565

NEW U.K. CAPITAL ISSUES

Year	Amount	Year	Amount
1954	£471,130,000	1959	£480,343,000
1955	567,192,000	1960	556,663,000
1956	295,952,000	1961	608,729,000
1957	383,357,000	1962	605,034,000
1958	316,452,000		

GOLD AND CONVERTIBLE CURRENCY RESERVES

£ million

1956, Dec. 31	799	1961, Dec. 31	1,185
1957, Dec. 31	812	1962, Dec. 31	1,002
1958, Dec. 31	1,096	1963, April 30	1,017
1959, Dec. 31	977	May 31	1,046
1960, Dec. 31	1,154	June 30	969

POST WAR BUILDING PROGRESS

Permanent Houses and Flats completed

Year	For Local Authorities	For Private Owners	Other†	TOTAL
	England and Wales			
1945–55 . .	1,429,502	464,731	85,775	1,983,008
1956.	139,977	119,585	9,162	268,724
1957.	137,584	122,942	8,127	268,653
1958.	113,146	124,087	4,292	241,525
1959.	99,456	146,476	3,449	249,381
1960.	103,235	162,100	3,891	269,226
1961.	92,880	170 366	5,586	268,832
1962.	105,302	167,016	6,349	278,667
1963* . . .	13,737	27,363	1,019	42,119
	Scotland			
1945–55 . .	233,274	17,330	6,638	257,242
1956.	26,290	4,576	1,035	31,901
1957.	28,326	3,513	598	32,437
1958.	27,373	4,061	736	32,170
1959.	22,709	4,232	352	27,293
1960.	21,503	6,529	560	28,592
1961.	19 541	7,147	542	27,230
1962.	18,788	7,784	189	26,761
1963*. . . .	3,433	1,332	77	4,842
	Northern Ireland			
1945–55 . .	37,611	19,737	1,061	58,399
1956.	4,443	2,270	336	7,049
1957.	3,719	2,329	452	6,500
1958.	2,764	2,072	102	4,938
1959.	2,380	2,458	56	4,894
1960.	3,478	2,776	183	6,437
1961.	3,697	3,214	188	7,099
1962.	4,487	3,411	317	8 215
1963*. . . .	890	642	61	1,593
	United Kingdom			
1945–63*	2,702,525	177,286	1,563,826	4 443 737

† Incl. housing associations (other than the Scottish Special Housing Association and the N. Ireland Housing Trust) and accommodation for families of police, prison staff, H.M. Forces, etc.

* To March 31, 1963, only.

New Houses and Flats

Of the 105,302 new dwellings completed by local authorities in 1962, 44·9 per cent. were flats. 38·3 per cent. of the new dwellings had 3 bedrooms, 32·3 had 2 bedrooms, 27·5 per cent. had 1 bedroom and 1·9 per cent. 4 or more bedrooms.

Cost.—In the first quarter of 1952, the average tender approved by the Ministry of Housing and Local Government was £1,380 (or 28*s.* 0½*d.* per square foot) for a traditional three-bedroom house of an average floor area of 984 sq. feet (including out-buildings). The average tender price for this type of house at the beginning of 1956 was £1,448 (or 31*s.* 6½*d.* per square foot), with a smaller average floor area of 918 square feet. In the last quarter of 1962, the average tender price for all types of three-bedroom houses (including new traditional houses) was £1,967 or 43*s.* 4½*d.* per sq. ft., providing an average floor area per house of 907 sq. ft.

Conversions and Improvements

In 1962, applications for grants under the Housing Acts for the improvement or conversion of 110,506 houses were approved, including applications made by local authorities and housing associations for the conversion of 1,486 dwellings, for improvements to 9,893 dwellings and for provision of standard amenities in 20,498 dwellings. Applications by private persons and housing associations were approved for 3,447 conversions, improvements in 26,942 dwellings and provision of standard amenities in 48,240 dwellings.

Slum Clearance and Repair

In 1962, 64,841 houses were demolished or closed in England and Wales, including 38,118 in scheduled clearance areas, and 168,809 persons were moved to other housing in consequence. At the end of 1962, a total of 35,271 unfit houses were retained in temporary occupation. As a result of informal action by local authorities, 141,335 dwellings were made fit or had defects remedied; in formal proceedings under the Health or Housing Acts, a further 81,485 dwellings were made fit or brought up to standard by their owners or by local authorities in default of action by the owners. 399 houses were reconstructed, enlarged or improved under the Housing Act, 1957.

Cost of the Housing Programme, 1945–62

England and Wales

The following table shows the Exchequer contributions in the post-war period towards the construction of new permanent houses and flats under the Housing Acts and the conversion or improvement of existing houses under the Housing (Financial Provisions) Act, 1958, and the Housing and House Purchase Act, 1959.

Year	Construction of new permanent houses				Conversions and improvements	
	Under pre-war legislation	Under post-war legislation	Capital grants for post-war houses*	Total	By local authorities	By private owners
	£	£	£	£	£	£
1945–48 . .	40,638,362	1,703,161	4,409,651	46,931,556	—	—
1948–49 . .	12,855,195	5,355,058	15,056,635	33,266,888	—	—
1949–50 . .	12,199,882	7,872,198	4,537,503	24,609,583	—	—
1950–51 . .	12,039,143	10,160,944	898,414	23,098,501	—	179
1951–52 . .	11,842,840	13,223,748	330,073	25,396,661	1,178	1,138
1952–53 . .	11,737,457	18,025,777	265,053	30,028,287	5,060	8,007
1953–54 . .	11,682,585	23,759,610	52,307	35,494,502	9,836	22,382
1954–55 . .	11,644,205	30,410,953	22,195	42,077,353	15,256	43,488
1955–56 . .	11,582,081	36,593,094	24,555	48,199,730	32,930	182,089
1956–57 . .	11,095,451	39,240,028	9,250	50,344,729	55,440	491,101
1957–58 . .	11,045,881	41,966,550	4,500	53,016,931	83,753	856,137
1958–59 . .	10,991,878	46,701,859	10,847	57,704,584	139,852	1,480,958
1959–60 . .	10,886,112	49,199,125	450	60,085,687	218,230	1,811,420
1960–61 . .	10,834,182	50,155,200	—	60,989,412	253,888	2,142,805
1961–62 . .	10,848,030	52,797,973	—	63,646,003	534,719	3,260,681

* Houses constructed by new tradition methods (Housing Act, 1946).

UNITED KINGDOM REVENUE AND EXPENDITURE

Year	Ordinary Revenue	Ordinary Expenditure	Surplus+ or Deficit−
1945-46 (Two Budgets)	£3,284,450,000	£5,484,333,000	− £2,199,883,000
1946-47	3,341,200,000	3,910,300,000	− 569,100,000
1947-48	3,844,800,000	3,209,500,000	+ 635,300,000
1948-49	4,006,600,000	3,175,600,000	+ 831,000,000
1949-50	3,924,000,000	3,375,300,000	+ 548,700,000
1950-51	3,977,800,000	3,257,300,000	+ 720,500,000
1951-52	4,433,400,000	4,053,600,000	+ 379,800,000
1952-53	4,438,700,000	4,350,600,000	+ 88,100,000
1953-54	4,368,100,000	4,274,500,000	+ 93,600,000
1954-55	4,737,893,000	4,304,726,000	+ 433,167,000
1955-56 (Two Budgets)	4,893,142,000	4,496,040,000	+ 397,102,000
1956-57	5,157,813,000	4,868,031,000	+ 289,782,000
1957-58	5,342,584,450	4,919,581,891	+ 423,002,559
1958-59	5,479,709,000	5,102,513,000	+ 377,196,000
1959-60	5,630,529,000	5,243,912,000	+ 386,617,000
1960-61	5,933,665,000	5,786,561,000	+ 147,104,000
1961-62	6,644,922,000	6,234,846,000	+ 410,076,000
1962-63	6,794,071,000	6,441,306,000	+ 352,765,000
1963-64*	*7,108,000,000*	*6,929,000,000*	+ *179,000,000*

* Budget Estimate, April, 3, 1963. *See also* Civil and Defence Estimates.

ORDINARY REVENUE OF THE UNITED KINGDOM. DISTRIBUTION

Following are summary details of Ordinary United Kingdom revenue, totals of which appear "above the line" in the *Financial Statement* presented to Parliament in the Budget annually. Items shown "below the line" are concerned with capital expenditure of the State (*See* p. 602).

Revenue	1960-61 Net Receipts £	1961-62 Net Receipts £	1962-63 Provisional Receipts £	1963-64 Budget Estimate £
INLAND REVENUE	3,208,889,891	3,636,240,863	3,751,000,000	3,729,000,000
Income Tax	2,428,945,436	2,719,786,925	2,818,000,000	2,789,000,000
Surtax	189,734,806	223,865,845	184,000,000	190,000,000
Profits Tax, Excess Profits Tax and Excess Profits Levy	262,805,602	335,539,303	383,000,000	398,000,000
Death Duties	236,021,230	261,176,195	270,000,000	279,000,000
Stamp Duties	90,943,916	95,486,615	96,000,000	73,000,000
Other Inland Revenue Duties	538,901	385,980	—	—
CUSTOMS	1,461,392,953	1,607,261,821	1,640,000,000	1,718,000,000
Spirits	34,770,713	37,077,779	42,000,000	44,000,000
Beer	12,069,278	13,266,891	13,000,000	13,000,000
Wine	17,782,936	20,045,897	22,000,000	24,000,000
Tea, Coffee, Cocoa, Chicory	2,035,891	2,400,442	—	—
Sugar, Molasses, Glucose, Saccharin	8,170,365	9,070,062	—	—
Tobacco	825,217,805	869,612,824	878,000,000	900,000,000
Matches and Mechanical Lighters	4,715,460	4,661,258	4,000,000	4,000,000
Hydrocarbon Oils	401,052,859	500,900,990	535,000,000	580,000,000
1958 Act Import Duties	155,427,352	149,565,627	145,000,000	153,000,000
EXCISE	927,697,753	974,660,599	1,028,000,000	1,014,000,000
Spirits	128,090,919	135,459,482	143,000,000	146,000,000
Beer	210,149,208	233,510,250	241,000,000	249,000,000
British Wines	4,164,287	4,118,932	4,000,000	5,000,000
Sugar, Molasses, Glucose, Saccharin	5,385,485	5,667,724	—	—
Matches and Mechanical Lighters	7,966,017	7,957,160	8,000,000	8,000,000
Hydrocarbon Oils	7,720,895	9,400,287	10,000,000	10,000,000
Entertainments	405,753	§	—	—
Television (Licences) Duty	11,145,876	11,734,250	12,000,000	5,000,000
(Advertisement) Duty	—	6,113,458	8,000,000	8,000,000
Liquor and Other Licences	1,249,690	1,420,987	—	—
Purchase Tax	510,251,104	521,356,848	571,000,000	545,000,000
Betting Duty	41,165,367	37,844,395	31,000,000	37,000,000
MISCELLANEOUS REVENUE				
Motor Vehicle Duties	123,942,410	144,844,905	153,000,000	160,000,000
Broadcast Receiving Licences	37,860,209	39,321,491	41,000,000	41,100,000
Other Miscellaneous Revenue	168,165,361	224,645,846	181,564,000	—

U+

§ Duty repealed April 10, 1960.

UNITED KINGDOM EXPENDITURE, 1962-63 AND 1963-64

Following is a summary of the Estimates for 1963–64, compared with the Budget Estimates and Net Total Estimates for 1962–63:

	1962–63 Net Budget Estimate	1962–63 Net Total Estimate*	1963–64 Net Budget Estimate
			£ million
CIVIL ESTIMATES...	4,227·1	4,399·3	4,677·5
DEFENCE ESTIMATES†	1,384·5	1,426·0	1,461·2
TOTAL ESTIMATES	5,611·6	5,825·3	6,138·7

* Including Supplementary Estimates. † Including Ministry of Defence and Royal Ordnance Factories Estimates.

Following are notes on some major groups of expenditure, items of which are included in several classes of the Estimates.

Public Service Remuneration

Total cost of public service remuneration in 1963–64 was estimated at £2,552m., including Forces Pay, fees for professional services, indirect remuneration in grants to local authorities, universities and Territorial and Auxiliary Forces organizations, and retirement pensions. The comparable expenditure in 1962–63 was £2,460m. Staff of the non-industrial civil service at home was estimated to number 418,045 (1962-63, *403,281*), excluding the Post Office. In addition 1,523 Forces personnel are employed in civil departments. Salaries, etc. of the non-industrial civil service, £404,042,000 (*£391,855,000*); superannuation and compensation allowances, including gratuities, injury grants, etc., £52,605,000 (*£47,049,000*, total estimate).

Agricultural and Food Subsidies

Provision was made in the Civil Estimates for 1963–64 for Agricultural Support Subsidies totalling £364·3 m. (including Administration, £8·9 m.), compared with £348·6 m. in 1962–63 (original 1962 Budget Estimate, £341·7 m.). The estimated net effect of the changes following the Annual Review of Guarantees, 1963, together with the proposed increase in the retail price of milk is a reduction of about £14 m. in the total provision (above) for agricultural support in 1963–64.

The Ministry of Education and Scottish Education Dept. Votes provide for the cost of school meals (less charges) and milk.

	1962–63	1963–64
School Meals		
England & Wales...	£53,930,000	£56,150,000
Scotland...........	6,103,000	6,309,000
Milk in Schools		
England & Wales...	12,040,000	11,985,000
Scotland...........	1,680,000	1,744,000
TOTAL...........	£73,753,000	£76,188,000

Votes for Miscellaneous Health and Welfare Services provide for the cost of the National Milk Scheme (mothers and young children), National Dried Milk and other welfare foods (including cost of Agency services):

	1962–63	1963–64
England & Wales.....	£28,910,000	£29,826,000
Scotland.............	3,669,000	3,693,000
TOTAL...........	£32,579,000	£33,519,000

Information Services

Total cost of United Kingdom information services on all Votes in 1963–64 was estimated at £30·9m., excluding expenditure on commercial publicity and £17,500 recoverable from the National Insurance and Industrial Injuries Funds. This total included £25,780,000 for overseas information (B.B.C. Colonial, Commonwealth and Foreign Offices, British Council) and £5,156,000 for home information (Defence Departments, £2,604,800).

U.K. Membership of International Organizations

Subscriptions by the United Kingdom to international organizations numbered 83 in 1963–64, at an estimated cost of £12,000,000:

To Political and Military Organizations.—Caribbean Organization, £4,315; Central Rhine Commission, £6,000; Central Treaty Organization, £39,000; C.E.N.T.O. Military Agencies, £16,000; Council of Europe, £295,000; International Supervisory Commissions on Indo-China, £713,000; North Atlantic Council, £550,000; N.A.T.O. Military Agencies, £3,500,000 (1962–63, £2,600,000); South East Asia Treaty Organization, £50,000 (Military Agencies, £8,000); South Pacific Commission, £37,757; United Nations Organization, £2,660,681; Western European Union, £103,000.

To Economic and Social Organizations.—European Free Trade Association, £73,000; General Agreement on Tariffs and Trade, £53,300; International Bureaux (Protection of Industrial, Literary and Artistic Property, Weights and Measures), £16,355; Colombo Plan Bureau, £1,900; Commission for Technical Co-operation in Africa, £13,500; Commonwealth Economic Committee, £33,103; Customs Co-operation Council, £33,000; International Criminal Police Organization, £7,200; International Labour Organization, £470,000; Organization for Economic Co-operation and Development, £691,000*; UNESCO, £490,490; World Health Organization, £763,300.

To Scientific Organizations.—Commonwealth Institutes: Biological Control, £15,470; Entomology, £20,001; Mycology, £16,231; European Launcher Development Organization, £9,500,010†; European Nuclear Energy Agency, £39,000; European Organization for Nuclear Research, £1,980,000; European Organization for Space Research, £1,100,000; International Atomic Energy Agency, £228,000; N.A.T.O. and O.E.C.D. Scientific Schemes, £242,000*; World Meteorological Organization, £18,822.

To Transport Organizations.—Eurocontrol (traffic control of high-flying aircraft), £550,000; Inter-Governmental Maritime Consultative Organization, £29,000; International Civil Aviation Organization, £154,000; and smaller subscriptions to shipping, road and railway congresses, etc., £9,280.

To Agricultural, Fishery and Food Organizations.—Commonwealth Agricultural Bureaux, £65,005; International Sugar Council, £5,880; Wheat Commission, £9,500; U.N. Food and Agriculture Organization, £738,000; and a number of smaller subscriptions.

* Partly offset by receipts.

† Estimated £6,200,010 to to be paid to the Exchequer on this head (Extra Receipts).

CIVIL ESTIMATES

Class I: Government and Exchequer

	1962–63	1963–64
House of Lords......	£271,000	£291,000
House of Commons‡.	1,703,000	1,752,000
Treasury and Subordinate Departments.	4,149,000	4,179,000
Privy Council Office.	48,000	52,000
Post Office Ministers.	7,500	7,500

	1962–3	1963–4
Customs and Excise..	£21,287,000	£21,802,000
Inland Revenue.....	60,979,000	62,885,000
Exchequer and Audit Department.......	650,000	680,000
Civil Service Commission...........	665,000	718,000
Royal Commissions, etc..............	542,000	672,000
TOTAL..	£90,301,500	£93,038,500

‡ Including Members' Salaries, £1,035,000 (1962–63, *£1,031,000*); Travelling Allowances, £138,000 (1962–63, *£128,000*).

Class II: Commonwealth and Foreign

	1962–63	1963–64
Foreign Service......	£24,320,000	£27,283,000
Foreign Grants and Loans*...	24,794,000	24,563,000
British Council......	3,952,000	4,660,000
Commonwealth Relations Office......	14,901,000	22,592,000
do. Grants and Loans†.........	21,097,000	18,265,000
Colonial Office......	9,747,688	8,569,000
do. Grants and Loans..........	13,718,000	11,999,000
do. Development and Welfare.....	20,950,000	17,500,000
Department of Technical Co-operation.	28,920,312	32,924,000
Central African Office	1,796,000	1,954,000
do. Development and Welfare....	1,700,000	1,300,000
Commonwealth War Graves Commission	1,239,000	1,215,000
TOTAL..... ...	£167,135,000	£172,824,000

* Direct assistance to foreign countries, £17,625,010 (1962-63, *£12,204,241*). † Grants (1963–64): Cyprus, £1,700,000; Federation of Nigeria, £1,006,400; Sierra Leone, £500,000; Tanganyika, Grants, £1,968,000; Loans, £2,200,000; Uganda, Grants, £1,276,000; Loans, £1,310,000; Indus Basin Development Grant, £6,500,000.

Class III: Home and Justice

	1962–63	1963–64
Home Office	£9,418,000	£10,543,000
Scottish Home and Health Dept......	1,862,990	1,981,000
Civil Defence:—		
England & Wales .	11,164,000	12,854,000
Scotland..........	1,285,990	1,398,000
Police:—		
England & Wales..	69,137,000	75,705,000
Scotland..........	7,191,000	7,767,000
Prisons:—		
England & Wales..	21,612,000	24,211,000
Scotland..........	2,137,000	2,405,000
Child Care:—		
England & Wales..	4,247,000	4,962,000
Scotland	560,000	599,000
Supreme Court......	2,000	1,000
County Courts......	498,000	649,000
Legal Aid Fund	3,594,000	3,792,000
Law Charges........	850,000	859,000
do. and Courts of Law, Scotland...	510,000	332,000
Supreme Court, N. Ireland...........	92,000	93,000
TOTAL..........	£134,160,980	£148,151,000

Class IV: Industry, Trade and Transport

	1962–63	1963–64
Board of Trade......	£6,751,000	£6,691,000
do. Trade Promotion Services....	6,905,000	8,109,000
do Promotion of Local Employment...........	41,001,000	24,525,000
Ministry of Labour ..	24,565,000	26,884,000
Ministry of Aviation.	245,650,000	270,670,000
do. Purchasing (Repayment) Services	28,000,000	37,500,000
Civil Aerodromes and Air Navigation Services..............	8,750,000	11,300,000
Ministry of Transport	5,240,000	4,794,000
Roads:—		
England & Wales..	133,557,000	151,261,000
Scotland..........	20,212,000	21,653,000
Shipping and Special Services..........	1,363,000	968,000
Railways & Waterways Boards......	20,125,000	145,882,000
Ministry of Power...	3,013,000	3,299,000
TOTAL..........	£679,534,000	£713,528,000

(Total includes nominal net estimates for Export Credits and Export Credits Special Guarantees.)

Class V: Agriculture

	1962–63	1963–64
Ministry of Agriculture, Fisheries and Food.............	£22,837,000	£22,627,000
Dept. of Agriculture and Fisheries for Scotland..........	8,011,000	9,052,000
Grants and Subsidies:—		
England & Wales..	100,388,000	98,990,000
Scotland..........	13,581,000	12,942,000
Price Guarantees:—		
England & Wales..	201,300,000	219,630,000
Scotland..........	24,397,000	24,140,000
Agricultural and Food Services..........	21,254,000	14,371,000
Food (Strategic Reserves)............	2,274,000	2,253,000
Fishery Grants and Services..........	6,395,000	5,494,000
Fisheries (Scotland) and Herring Industry ..	2,642,000	2,760,000
Forestry Commission	12,000,000	12,400,000
TOTAL..........	£415,079,000	£424,659,000

Class VI: Local Government, Housing and Social Services

	1962–63	1963–64
Ministry of Housing & Local Government.	17,290,000	17,961,000
Scottish Development Dept.	2,606,020	2,721,000
Housing:—		
England & Wales..	72,639,000	77,422,000
Scotland..........	18,375,000	17,920,000
Grants to Local Revenues:—		
England & Wales..	526,231,000	565,988,000
Scotland..........	62,938,000	65,471,000
Rate Deficiency Grants (England & Wales).	116,250,000	141,377,000

	1962–3	1963–4
Equalization and Transitional Grants to Local Revenues (Scotland)........	£20,230,000	£20,950,000
Ministry of Education	127,658,000	133,993,000
Scottish Education Dept.............	21,295,000	23,689,000
Ministry of Health...	4,005,000	4,223,000
National Health Service (England & Wales):—		
Hospital, etc., Services...........	426,946,000	451,324,000
Executive Council Services........	170,227,000	171,699,000
Miscellaneous Health and Welfare Services (England & Wales)	39,616,000	40,428,000
National Health Service (Scotland).........	81,010,000	85,426,000
Ministry of Pensions and National Insurance.............	7,832,000	7,867,000
National Insurance...	201,600,000	225,201,000
Family Allowances...	135,477,000	140,975,000
National Assistance Board...........	213,821,000	226,247,000
War Pensions, etc.* ..	102,512,000	111,998,000
TOTAL......	£2,368,564,020	£2,532,883,000

* PENSIONS, ETC. (1962–63).—(Widows' and dependants' pensions included).—*War of* 1914–18: Officers and Nurses (14,410), £3,600,000; N.C.O.'s and other Ranks (220,530), £39,020,000. Merchant Navy, Officers (350), £109,000; Seamen and Fishermen (392), £98,000. *War of* 1939–45 *and later service*: Officers and Nurses (33,510), £9,940,000; N.C.O.'s and other Ranks (356,700), £52,270,000. Merchant Navy, Officers (4,460), £1,140,000; Seamen (6,940), £1,600,000. Civilians (19,200), £3,500,000.

Class VII: Universities and Scientific Research

	1962–63	1963–64
Universities and Colleges (Gt. Britain)..	£90,203,000	£105,452,000
Office of the Minister for Science........	134,000	154,000
Atomic Energy......	68,114,000	60,471,000
Dept. of Scientific and Industrial Research	17,944,000	20,609,000
Medical Research Council..........	5,871,000	6,908,000
Agricultural Research Council..........	6,508,000	7,387,000
Nature Conservancy .	651,000	701,000
Grants for Science....	289,000	406,000
TOTAL.........	£189,714,000	£202,088,000

Class VII: Museums, Galleries and the Arts

	1962–63	1963–64
British Museum.....	£909,000	£1,122,000
British Museum (Natural History).......	603,000	657,000
Science Museum.....	346,000	360,000
Victoria and Albert Museum..........	595,000	620,000
Imperial War Museum	65,000	77,000
London Museum....	56,000	59,000
National Gallery.....	242,000	256,000
National Maritime Museum..........	136,000	114,000
National Portrait Gallery.............	47,000	47,000
Tate Gallery........	122,000	116,000
Wallace Collection...	50,000	57,000
Royal Scottish Museum..........	115,000	126,000
National Galleries of Scotland..........	£99,000	£93,000
National Library of Scotland.........	106,000	119,000
National Museum of Antiquities of Scotland..........	27,000	30,000
Grants for the Arts...	3,308,000	3,903,000
TOTAL.........	£6,826,000	£7,756,000

Class IX: Public Buildings and Common Services

	1962–63	1963–64
Ministry of Public Building & Works	£25,627,000	£26,340,000
Public Buildings (U.K.)	36,640,000	40,650,000
do. (Overseas).....	4,718,000	5,318,000
Works and Buildings for:—		
Admiralty........	18,405,000	19,522,000
War Office.......	50,102,000	61,192,000
Air Ministry......	45,398,000	47,445,000
Houses of Parliament	400,000	475,000
Royal Palaces.......	812,000	781,000
Royal Parks and Pleasure Gardens......	1,170,000	1,371,000
Historic Buildings and Ancient Monuments	1,250,000	1,328,000
Rates on Government Property..........	21,000,000	25,505,000
Stationery and Printing..............	18,699,000	20,378,000
Central Office of Inmation...........	5,574,000	6,203,000
Government Actuary	43,000	42,000
Government Hospitality.............	130,000	145,000
Civil Superannuation, etc...............	39,385,000	43,780,000
TOTAL.........	£269,355,000	£300,485,000

Class X: Smaller Public Departments

	1962–63	1963–64
Charity Commission.	£245,000	£283,000
Crown Estate Office .	171,000	175,000
Friendly Societies Registry............	123,000	124,000
War Damage Commission...........	298,000	266,000
Registrar of Restrictive Trading Agreements	159,000	149,000
Ordnance Survey....	3,727,000	3,757,000
Public Record Office.	166,000	186,000
Scottish Record Office	57,000	62,000
Registrar-General's Office..........	827,000	790,000
do. Scotland......	93,000	91,000
National Savings Committee............	1,371,000	1,439,000
TOTAL	£7,246,000	£7,328,000

(Totals include nominal net estimates for: Royal Mint, National Debt Office, Public Works Loan Commission, Public Trustee, Land Registry and Dept. of the Registers of Scotland).

Class XI: Miscellaneous

	1962–63	1963–64
Broadcasting........	£48,769,000	£52,121,000
Pensions, etc. (India, Pakistan & Burma)	7,140,000	8,749,960
Pension Supplements (Overseas Services)	812,000	1,816,000
Royal Irish Constabulary Pensions......	1,049,000	1,135,000
Irish Land Purchase Services..........	1,145,000	1,107,000
Development Fund ..	1,406,000	1,386,000

Class XI—*continued*	1962–63	1963–64
Secret Service.......	£7,000,000	£8,000,000
Miscellaneous Expenses	546,000	480,000
TOTAL..........	£68.016,000	£74.796,000

(Totals include nominal net estimates for State Management Districts.)

DEFENCE ESTIMATES

The full cost of Defence of the United Kingdom in 1963–64 was estimated at £1,904,000,000, compared with a total estimate of £1,830,000,000 in 1962–63. These figures include the Service and Ministry of Defence Votes shown below; the cost of defence services of the Ministry of Aviation (£231,000,000); Ministry of Public Building and Works (£147,000,000); Atomic Energy Authority (£5,000,000) and Civil Defence (£21,000,000).

	1962–63	1963–64
Ministry of Defence..	£18,421,000	£19,980,000
Royal Navy........	408,989,000	440,959,000
Army and Royal Ordnance Factories....	472,480,455	491,031,000
Royal Air Force.....	519,007 000	503,200,000

ROYAL NAVY.—Pay, etc. of the Royal Navy and Royal Marines, £75,581,000 (1962–63, *£72,107,000*); Admiralty Office, £10,519,000 (*11,073,000*); Research and Development and other Scientific Services, £25,895,000 (*£24,206,000*); Medical Services, Education and Civilians on Fleet Services, £13,139,000 (*£12,295,000*); Naval Stores, Armament, Victualling and other Supply Services, £16,884,000 (*£121,601,000*); H.M. Ships, Aircraft and Weapons, New Construction and Repairs, £139,657,000 (*£130,807,000*); with other smaller items.

Maximum Numbers.—Royal Navy: Officers, 10,320; Petty Officers, Seamen and Juniors, 76,500. R.M., Commissioned Officers, 630; Other Ranks, 8,820. W.R.N.S., Officers, 250; Ratings, 3,000. Q.A.R.N.N.S., Officers, 180; Other nurses, 300. Total, all ranks, 100,000.

ARMY.—Pay, etc. of the Army, £145,200,000 (1962–63, *£138,430,000*); Reserve Forces, Territorial Army and Cadet Forces, £20,710,000 (*£19,990,000*); War Office, £6,600,000 (*£6,795,705*); Civiliansat Outstations, £111,020,00 (*£107,831,650*); Movements, £27,480,000 (*£26,818,000*), Supplies, £41,520,000 (*£40,346,000*) Stores and Equipment, £87,300,000 (*£80,528,000*); with other smaller items.

Maximum Numbers.—(Male) Officers, 20,000; Other Ranks, 180,000; (Female) Officers, 1,000; Other Ranks, 6,600. Total, all ranks, 219,100.

ROYAL AIR FORCE.—Pay, etc. of the Air Force, £128,120,000 (1962–63, *£123,930,000*); Air Ministry, £4,700,000 (*£4,792,000*); Civilians at Outstations and Meteorological Office, £42,050,000 (*£41,891,000*); Movements, £13,760,000 (*£13,155,000*);Supplies, £52,600,000(*£60,490,000*) Aircraft and Stores, £244,000,000 (*£257,950,000*); with other smaller items.

Maximum Numbers.—R.A.F. Officers, 20,800; Airmen, 117,500. Princess Mary's Nursing Service, 400. W.R.A.F., Officers, 450; Airwomen, 6,850. Other officers, 350; Airmen and airwomen, 1,650. Total, all ranks, 148,000.

DISTRIBUTION OF PERSONAL INCOMES

Tables showing estimated distribution of personal incomes in the United Kingdom by ranges of income in 1962. Tax figures include both income tax and surtax.

Before Taxation

Range of Total Income	Number of Incomes	Total Income Before Tax	Income Tax and Surtax *	Net Income After Tax
£ £		£	£	£
50 to under 250	4,370,000	754,000,000	1,000,000	753,000,000
250 ,, ,, 300	1,220,000	338,000,000	3,000,000	335 000,000
300 ,, ,, 400	2,170,000	756,000,000	24,000,000	732,000,000
400 ,, ,, 500	2,190,000	988,000,000	46,000,000	942,000,000
500 ,, ,, 600	2,270,000	1,251,000,000	75,000,000	1,176.000,000
600 ,, ,, 700	2,340,000	1,523,000,000	103,000,000	1,420,000,000
700 ,, ,, 800	2,490,000	1,862,000,000	134,000,000	1,728,000,000
800 ,, ,, 1,000	4.520,000	4,042,000,000	313,000,000	3,729,000,000
1,000 ,, ,, 1,500	4,280,000	5 063,000,000	536,000,000	4 527,000,000
1,500 ,, ,, 2,000	693,000	1,179.000,000	182,000,000	997,000,000
2,000 ,, ,, 3,000	348,000	836,000,000	202,000,000	634,000,000
3,000 ,, ,, 5,000	194,000	732,000,000	219,000,000	513,000,000
5,000 ,, ,, 10,000	90,000	599,000,000	236,000,000	363,000,000
10,000 ,, ,, 20,000	20,000	269,000,000	151,000,000	118,000,000
£20,000 and over	5,000	153,000,000	118,000,000	35,000,000
TOTAL ..	27,200,000	£20,345,000,000	£2 343,000,000	£18 002,000,000

After Taxation

Range of Net Income	Number of Incomes	Total Income Before Tax	Income Tax and Surtax*	Net Income After Tax
£ £		£	£	£
50 to under 250	4,630,000	810,000,000	1,000,000	809,000,000
250 ,, ,, 500	6,310,000	2,518.000,000	103,000,000	2.415,000,000
500 ,, ,, 750	6,560,000	4.405,000,000	282,000,000	4,123,000,000
750 ,, ,, 1,000	5,810,000	5,475,000,000	424,000,000	5,051,000,000
1,000 ,, ,, 2,000	3,500,000	5,161,000,000	754,000,000	4,407,000,000
2,000 ,, ,, 4,000	320,000	1,225,000,000	394,000,000	831,000,000
4,000 ,, ,, 6,000	54,000	451,000,000	195,000,000	256,000,000
£6,000 and over	16,000	300,000,000	190,000,000	110,000,000
TOTAL..	27,200,000	£20,345,000,000	£2.343,000,000	£18,002,000,000

* At rates current in 1962–63.

UNITED KINGDOM CAPITAL EXPENDITURE

Items referred to as expenditure " below the line " in the *Financial Statement* presented to Parliament annually at the Budget consist largely of repayable advances to (i) the nationalized industries; (ii) local authorities, New Towns Corporations and other public bodies; (iii) private industry;* (iv) Colonial governments and the Colonial Development Corporation, and foreign governments. Loans to foreign governments are made under the Export Guarantees Acts, 1949–59, and may only be drawn upon to finance payments to, or for the benefit of, United Kingdom companies. Other payments below the line arise from war-time liabilities, *e.g.* war damage payments, post-war refunds of Excess Profits Tax and repayment of post-war credits. Finally, advances may also be made under Statute for central government expenditure where it is desired to spread out the capital payments concerned over a period of years, *e.g.* loans for married quarters for H.M. Forces, planning compensation, tithe redemption, etc., to be repaid by Vote provision over a specified period. Advances for the provision of temporary houses at the end of the Second World War were repaid by annuities borne on the Votes of the Housing departments, terminating in 1961–62.

Interest is charged on repayable advances made below the line at rates related to those at which the Government can borrow at the time the advance is made, with some exceptions. Each advance results in a corresponding increase in the National Debt and statutes provide that interest received on repayable advances shall be applied to the payment of an equivalent amount of interest on the National Debt.

In the three years to March 31, 1963, about 80 per cent. of the total net issues below the line has consisted of loans to the nationalized industries which may borrow through the appropriate Minister for capital purposes. Statutes under which these advances are made are the Electricity (Borrowing Powers) Acts, 1959 and 1962; Gas Act, 1962; Transport Act, 1962; Air Corporations Act, 1962; Coal Industry Acts, 1946–62; and the Post Office Act, 1961.

* Most of the Government assistance to private industry is provided " above the line " on Votes.

EXCHEQUER LOANS IN 1963 AND ESTIMATES FOR 1963–64

Position at March 31, 1963 £ million

(i) *Nationalized Industries*	Current Statutory Limit*	Net Exchequer Advances	Borrowing by Stock Issues	Temporary Borrowing	Total Loans Outstanding	Estimated Borrowing 1963–64
Electricity Council	2,300	1,120	820	69	2,009	270·8
North of Scotland Hydro-Electric Board	240	95	109	3	207	13·4
South of Scotland Electricity Board	175	127	8	6	141	37·7
Gas Council	500	157	286	27	470	21·8
British Railways Board	1,100	1,575	—	6	1,581	39·0
London Transport Board	200	162	—	1	163	6·8
British Transport Docks Board	120	85	—	—	85	2·8
British Waterways Board	30	20	—	—	20	1·5
Transport Holding Company	30	125	—	3	3	—
B.O.A.C.	260	115	54	4	173	22·8
B.E.A.	110	69	16	—	85	9·2
National Coal Board	720	561	—	—	606	—
The Post Office	910	866	—	—	866	69·0
TOTAL	6,280	5,077	1,293	—	6,534	495·0

* Further increases permissible by Order: N. of Scotland Board, £60m.; Gas Council, £25m.; National Coal Board, £50m.; Post Office, £80m.; British Railways Board, £300m.; London Transport Board, £70m.; B.O.A.C., £40m.; B.E.A., £15m. † Including provision for loans to successor bodies. ‡ The figure of £622m. counts against the statutory borrowing limit; approximately £40m. has been repaid by the National Coal Board since nationalization in respect of compensation for vested assets.

(ii) Other Public Bodies	Exchequer Loans Outstanding March 31, 1963	£ million Estimated Exchequer Loans, 1963–64
Local Authorities	2,632·7	- 55·7
Northern Ireland Exchequer	23·0	3·9
New Towns Corporations and Commission	331·0	33·9
Scottish Special Housing Association	89·0	7·7
Iron and Steel: Richard Thomas & Baldwins Ltd	70·0	—
Covent Garden Market Authority	4·0	0·1
Sugar Board	27·1	—
National Research Development Corporation	4·5	0·7
National Film Industry Corporation	—	0.6
NET TOTAL	3 181·9	– 10·0

(iii) Loans to Private Industry, etc.	Exchequer Loans Outstanding March 31, 1963	£ million Estimated Exchequer Loans, 1963–64
Colvilles Ltd	47·5	2·5
Building Societies	92·0	– 2·8
Housing Associations	—	6·2
NET TOTAL	139·5	5·9

(iv) Loans for Overseas Assistance

	Exchequer Loans Outstanding March 31, 1962	£ million Estimated Exchequer Loans, 1963-64
Colonial Governments	64·0	18·8
Colonial Development Corporation......	87.0	3·7
Export Guarantees† ..	135·0	54·3
NET TOTAL.....	286·0	76·8

† *Limit under Loan Agreements*, £315·5m. Ceylon, £2.5m.; Chile, £2·om.; Cyprus, £2·om.; Ghana, £7.2m.; India, £175·5m.; Persia, £10·1m.; Iraq, £3.om.; Malaya, £2·3m.; Nigeria, £22·om.; Pakistan, £40·om.; Rhodesia and Nyasaland, £5·om.; Sierra Leone, £3·5m.; Sudan, £5.om.; Uganda, £2·4m.; U.A.R., £3·6m.; Yugoslavia, £23·6m.

THE NATIONAL DEBT

On March 31, 1963, the National Debt was approximately £29,856,000,000, of which £27,394,000,000 was internal debt, £587,000,000 external debt payable in Sterling, and £1,875,000,000 external debt payable in other currencies. The list which follows shows the distribution under these heads. Amounts shown are those outstanding on March 31, 1962 and March 31, 1963 (in millions of £).

Internal Debt

MARKETABLE SECURITIES

£ million	1962	1963
Final Redemption Date up to 5 years		
5½% Treasury Bonds, 1962........	300	—
3% Exchequer Stock, 1962–63.....	341	341
4¾% Conversion Stock, 1963......	653	653
4½% Conversion Stock, 1964......	505	505
2½% Exchequer Stock, 1963–64....	274	274
4% Treasury Stock, 1965.........	—	391
3% Saving Bonds, 1955–65	713	709
5½% Exchequer Stock, 1966.......	984	978
2½% Funding Loan, 1956–61......	—	750
5% Exchequer Stock, 1967........	—	400
Redemption 5–15 years		
2½% Savings Bonds, 1964–67......	752	—
3% Funding Stock, 1966–68.......	540	533
3½% Conversion Stock, 1969......	341	335
3% Funding Loan 1959–69........	243	231
4% Victory Bonds...............	87	77
3% Savings Bonds, 1960–70.......	1,024	1,018
5% Conversion Stock, 1971.......	414	409
6% Conversion Stock, 1972.......	301	301
British Transport 3% Stock:—		
1967–72.....................	—	13
1968–73.....................	—	136
5¼% Conversion Stock, 1974......	299	299
3% Savings Bonds, 1965–75.......	1,073	1,073
Brit. Transport 4% Stock, 1972–77	—	242
Redemption over 15 years		
3½% Treasury Stock, 1977–80.....	262	262
3½% Treasury Stock, 1979–81.....	483	483
5½% Funding Stock, 1982–84......	500	500
Brit. Transport 3% Stock, 1978–88	—	1,052
5% Treasury Stock, 1986–89......	302	602
4% Funding Loan, 1960–90†......	181	169
3½% Funding Stock, 1999–2004....	443	443
5½% Treasury Stock, 2008–12.....	500	1,000
2½% Treasury Stock, 1986–2016...	78	78
Undated £ million	1962	1963
4% Consolidated Loan...........	376	375
3½% War Loan..................	1,909	1,909
3½% Conversion Loan...........	546	527
3% Treasury Stock, 1966 or after..	58	58
2¾% Annuities..................	2	2
2½% Annuities..................	21	21
2½% Consols...................	276	276
2½% Treasury Stock, 1975 or after.	482	482
Total Marketable Securities...	15,263	17,907
OTHER INTERNAL DEBT		
Terminable Annuities due to National Debt Commissioners......	1,026	952
Life Annuities..................	8	8
Debt to Bank of England and Bank of Ireland..................	14	14
National Savings Securities:—		
National Savings Certificates....	2,119	2,140
Defence Bonds................	1,076	1,124
Premium Savings Bonds........	353	395
National Savings Stamps and Gift Tokens..................	23	26
Tax Reserve Certificates........	397	352
Floating Debt:—		
Treasury Bills.................	5,330	4,237
Ways and Means Advances......	261	239
Total Internal Debt	25,870	27,394

External Debt

PAYABLE IN STERLING	£ million 1962	1963
Interest-free notes: I.M.F. and International Development Association......................	816	532
Government of Portugal..........	50	46
Miscellaneous (Sterling Loan Agreements 1951–53, with U.S.A.; Govts. of India, Pakistan and Jamaica)....................	10	9
Total Payable in Sterling..........	876	587
PAYABLE IN OTHER CURRENCIES		
United States Loans..............	1,479	1,453
Government of Canada...........	349	335
Debts created on liquidation of European Payments Union:—		
Government of Belgium...... Federal Republic of Germany. Government of Italy......... Government of Netherlands... Government of Sweden......	77	69
Government of Switzerland...	18	18
Total Payable in other Currencies.	1,923	1,875
Total National Debt...	28,669	29,856

Loans Guaranteed

The Nominal Net Liability of the State in respect of loans guaranteed by the British Government was stated on March 31, 1962, to be as follows:—

Sudan Loans, £2,686,100; Irish Land Purchase Stock, £10,997; Northern Ireland 4½% Bonds, £5,136,040; Northern Ireland 2¾% Stock, £15,886,460; Northern Ireland 3% Stock, £32,921,605; Irish Free State 4½% Land Bonds, £20,236,370; Ulster Savings Certificates, £53,313; 24½ per cent. of the Austrian Guaranteed Loan, secured on the gross receipts of Austrian Customs and Tobacco monopoly, certain liabilities in external currencies; Palestine Loan, £559,452; Tanganyika Loan, £155,048; Nyasaland, £521,246; Newfoundland, £4,230,148; 3 per cent. Redemption Stock (1986–96) to provide compensation in respect of *Tithe Rent Charge*, £54,184,591; and liabilities in external currencies in respect of U.S. loans to Northern and Southern Rhodesia, to the East Africa High Commission, Kenya and Nigeria.

Cost of the Debt, 1961–62

The interest on the National Debt in 1961–62 amounted to £1,002,265,330, of which £324,939,169 was met from interest received on capital advances (below the line) and £677,326,161 from the Consolidated Fund. Management charges for the year were £9,347,631 and expenses, which included £13,987,800 paid as prizes on Premium Savings Bonds, issue, conversion and redemption expenses, printing and other costs, totalled £24,212,178. The total cost of the service of the National Debt in 1961–62 was therefore £33,559,809.

Repayments, 1961–62

Reductions in the Debt are by means of Sinking Funds, including the Terminable Annuities, the capital value of which is deducted from the Debt upon the expiry of the term for which the annuities are payable. Exchequer issues to the National Debt Commissioners in 1961–62 were:—

Repayment of Terminable Annuities (Principal)	£762,623
For 3% Funding Loan, 1959–69	8,183,366
For 4% Funding Loan, 1960–90	10,735,598
For 4% Victory Bonds	9,155,131
For 3½% Conversion Loan	11,232,602
Total Sinking Funds	£40,069,320

Estimated Exchequer Assets, 1962

Exchequer assets on March 31, 1962, were summarized as follows:

Repayable Advances	£8,135,791,185
Other Issues constituting assets	1,653,740,317
Liabilities of Overseas Governments, etc.	175,856,214
Other Assets	16,335,833
Total	£9,981,723,549

Repayable Advances	
Land Settlement Acts (1919 and 1921)	£5,122,922
Export Guarantees Acts (1949–57)	135,057,000
Housing (Scotland) Acts (1950–57)	83,511,812
Building Societies	90,284,776
Local Authorities Loans Act (1945)	2,632,957,273
Finance Act, 1935 (3 p.c. Local Loans Stock)	429,196,622
Northern Ireland Exchequer (Acts of 1950 and 1955)	21,629,663
New Town Corporations and Commission	294,473,461
Loans to Nationalized Industries:—	
National Coal Board	975,270,373
Electricity Council	927,440,000
Gas Council	135,800,000
British Transport Commission:—	
Capital Borrowing	626,705,600
Railway Deficit Financing	302,164,134
British Overseas Airways Corporation	103,057,143
British European Airways Corporation	65,485,714
N. of Scotland Hydro-Electric Board	83,513,333
S. of Scotland Electricity Board	100,270,000
Post Office	831,102,000
Iron and Steel (Richard Thomas and Baldwins Ltd.)	67,300,000
(Colvilles Ltd.)	35,000,000
Raw Cotton Commission	8,270,397
National Research Development Corporation	4,764,500
Colonial Development Corporation	£135,057,000
Loans to Colonial Governments	88,853,595
National Film Finance Corporation	6,000,000
Sugar Board	29,285,000
Other Issues	
Civil Contingencies Fund (capital)	10,000,000
Subscriptions to International financial organizations:—	
International Bank	92,857,143
International Monetary Fund	696,428,571
International Finance Corporation	5,142,857
European Fund	2,819,286
International Development Association	19,788,089
European Payments Union Act (1950):—	
Debts due from Iceland	95,495
Debts due from Norway	814,822
Debts due from Turkey	794,054
Finance Act (1932) and Currency Act (1939) (Exchange Equalization Account)	825,000,000

Liabilities of Overseas Goverments, etc,

Balances totalling £72,095,639 were outstanding on March 31, 1962. The amounts (with term and total of original advance) were: Argentina, £13,448,423 (1956–66, £19,359,312); Brazil, £1,200,000 (1965–67, £2,500,000); Jordan, £866,667; Turkey, £6,955,000 (1957–60, £6,955,000); Aden Colony and Protectorate, £3,505,610 (1955–58, £3,998,892); British Guiana, £5,180,106 (1959–84, £5,500,000); British Honduras, £193,592 (1962–84, £193,672); Dominica, £9,353 (£30,777); East Africa C.S.O., £1,776,522 (1956–78, £2,390,000); Grenada, £1,493,370 (1962–85, £1,500,000); Hong Kong, £2,800,000 (1961–75); Jamaica, £595,975 (1951–72, £2,242,970); Kenya, £6,050,000 (1962–87, £6,050,000); Malaya and Singapore, £10,161,803 (1956–75, £14,850,194); Mauritius, £867,294 (1948–1980, £1,883,626); St. Lucia, £53,939 (1958–81, £61,203); Tanganyika, £1,191,448 (1921–26, £8,002,415); Nauru and Ocean Islands, £1,331,793 (1951–85, £1,843,312); Federation of Rhodesia and Nyasaland, £2,049,423 (1952–65, £5,773,000); Nyasaland, £1,412,000 (1953–90, £1,974,000); Federation of Nigeria, £2,706,134; Swaziland, £1,122 (1952–61, £12,000).

In addition advances to allied governments arising during 1939–45, outstanding on March 31, 1962, were: China, £12,237,395; Czechoslovakia, £19,747,398; Poland, £51,766,669; U.S.S.R., £7,805,211; a total of £91,556,673. Amounts outstanding from Germany (£691,428); and from Austria, £3,031,396; total £3,722,824. A further £8,330,502 was outstanding under agreements with Israel, Jordan, Ceylon and other countries.

Other Assets

The total of £16,335,833 at March 31, 1962, consisted of a balance in the Victory Bonds Sinking Fund, £4,688,112; Exchequer borrowings included in the National Debt but not brought to account, £8,573,051; and balances at the Banks of England and Ireland, £3,094,217. Additional assets not currently evaluated:—British Petroleum Co. Stock, £112,500,000; Dividend 1961–62, £13,125,000; Cable & Wireless Shares, £30,000,000; Dividend, £1,650,000; Suez Finance Company Shares (*New Frs.* 3,891,090) and 106,428 5% Bonds of *New Frs.* 285·85. Dividends of *New Frs.* 2,062,278 were received in 1962 and interest on bonds, *New Frs.* 1,496,492.

BRITAIN'S OVERSEAS TRADE

Class and Division‡	Imports		Exports	
	1961	1962	1961	1962
	£	£	£	£
A. *Food, Beverages and Tobacco—*				
Live animals for food	44,036,189	37,716,442	12,494,648	9,604,776
Meat and meat preparations	311,358,831	318,940,410	5,843,811	5,963,577
Dairy products, eggs and honey	157,971,613	167,905,997	10,906,493	10,890,151
Fish and fish preparations	42,859,979	60,295,916	6,366,683	7,069,331
Cereal and cereal preparations	213,067,304	245,361,376	15,553,569	19,411,576
Fruits and vegetables	249,730,824	294,002,246	9,267,411	9,200,069
Sugar and sugar preparations	75,285,158	62,945,581	21,346,155	20,006,205
Coffee, tea and cocoa	167,034,693	169,712,207	11,095,440	11,532,293
Feedingstuffs for animals	55,477,727	69,500,721	2,196,550	3,273,591
Miscellaneous food preparations	17,491,746	17,822,259	8,059,390	7,911,136
Beverages	46,909,862	45,336,621	85,547,700	92,198,528
Tobacco and tobacco manufactures	100,605,223	80,808,470	18,664,756	16,912,874
Total Class A	1,481,829,149	1,570,348,246	207,342,606	213,974,107
B. *Basic Materials—*				
Hides, skins and fur skins, undressed	46,842,246	46,416,159	4,146,658	4,978,495
Oil-seeds, oil nuts and oil kernels	48,878,069	53,380,955	110,700	66,345
Rubber, including synthetic, etc.	71,980,999	61,509,725	6,814,884	8,209,525
Wood and cork	177,055,341	156,771,853	971,385	1,051,217
Pulp and waste paper	117,906,841	105,107,763	1,992,501	1,705,358
Silk	1,078,180	1,046,834	4,253	1,941
Wool and other animal hair	144,402,983	136,928,384	70,890,452	61,380,206
Cotton	62,200,895	59,831,319	1,639,692	1,321,481
Textile fibres and waste	37,902,746	41,844,428	19,190,484	21,928,888
Crude fertilizers & minerals, excl. fuels	43,609,857	39,066,090	14,892,044	14,979,050
Metalliferous ores and metal scrap	143,706,405	120,687,938	4,718,965	19,725,417
Misc. animal & vegetable crude materials	37,658,286	37,431,127	2,963,617	2,954,062
Animal and vegetable oils, fats, etc.	50,703,298	41,630,869	6,130,116	6,696,311
Total Class B	983,926,146	901,653,444	134,465,751	144,998,296
C. *Mineral Fuels and Lubricants—*				
Coal, coke and briquettes	804,490	688,878	29,289,025	31,172,372
Petroleum and petroleum products	481,316,937	533,299,882	94,205,748	114,944,765
Total Class C	482,121,427	533,988,760	123,494,773	146,117,137
D. *Manufactured Goods—*				
Chemicals	167,320,755	171,617,802	324,900,646	341,430,704
Leather and manufactures and dressed furs	27,966,749	25,126,701	24,502,090	24,988,705
Rubber manufactures	6,749,917	6,740,112	47,835,674	48,440,268
Wood and cork manufactures	57,312,020	59,552,909	3,926,796	4,249,405
Paper, paperboard and manufactures	90,246,956	96,478,063	41,156,595	42,438,345
Woollen & worsted yarns, woven fabrics	14,585,927	13,562,496	81,803,851	80,381,247
Cotton yarns and woven fabrics	72,539,996	57,231,674	56,524,209	46,461,644
Synthetic fibre yarns and woven fabrics	15,281,202	17,902,655	31,606,420	39,070,025
Miscellaneous textile manufactures	43,987,360	45,459,615	79,367,650	81,546,345
Misc. non-metallic mineral manufactures	21,420,285	22,018,629	69,503,029	69,176,678
Silver, platinum and jewellery	28,233,492	21,847,354	19,739,570	22,827,449
Iron and steel	49,004,305	53,651,022	211,517,466	200,412,512
Non-ferrous base metals	245,428,081	242,564,702	102,766,480	110,416,517
Manufactures of metals	37,810,361	37,601,521	159,293,548	156,796,111
Machinery, other than electric	251,524,048	251,648,171	816,559,472	839,899,963
Electric machinery, apparatus, appliances	65,482,310	75,810,995	259,010,460	272,617,051
Railway vehicles	1,045,968	1,229,530	14,009,274	20,055,300
Road vehicles and aircraft	35,835,484	38,561,382	439,747,274	485,714,312
Ships and boats	11,956,121	27,729,382	88,643,004	36,350,125
Sanitary, plumbing, heating and light fixtures, etc.; prefab. buildings; furniture	9,521,656	10,188,358	26,653,309	26,046,973
Clothing, footwear, travel goods, etc.	67,158,896	74,162,279	45,972,056	47,561,896
Scientific instruments; photographic and optical goods, watches and clocks	43,018,138	44,649,200	56,108,120	62,916,898
Miscellaneous manufactured articles	64,914,830	71,439,887	116,003,157	122,838,950
Total Class D	1,428,344,857	1,466,774,439	3,117,177,150	3,182,687,423
E.—Postal packages	8,730,845	8,989,458	91,207,855	96,067,231
Live animals not for food	10,188,462	10,236,585	7,808,001	7,931,970
Total Class E	18,919,307	19,226,043	99,015,856	103,999,201
Total, All Classes	4,395,140,886	4,491,990,932	3,681,496,136	3,791,776,164

‡ Standard International Trade Classification of the United Nations.

POSTAL REGULATIONS

For full conditions, exceptions, &c., *see* Post Office Guide, price 2*s.* 6*d.*, Associated volumes are London Post Offices and Streets 2*s.*, Post Offices in the United Kingdom 4*s.* and Postal Addresses 1*s.* 6*d.*

CHIEF POSTAL SERVICES

LETTERS

Inland (U.K. and Irish Republic):—

Not exceeding 1 oz. ....3*d.*
Not exceeding 2 oz. ....4½*d.*
For every further 2 oz., or less ....1½*d.*

British Commonwealth and Foreign:—

(*a*) *British Commonwealth, Territories under British Trusteeship; British Postal Agencies in Bahrain, Muscat, Qatar and the Trucial States:*

Not exceeding 1 oz. ....3*d.*
For each further oz., or less ....1½*d.*

(*b*) *Elsewhere:—*

Not exceeding 1 oz. ....6*d.*
For each further oz., or less ....4*d.*

WEIGHT LIMITS:—Inland, none. Elsewhere, 4 lb.

SIZE LIMITS: (A) If in roll form:—Inland and elsewhere (32 in. for the greatest dimension); length + twice diameter, 39 in. (B) not in roll form:—(i) United Kingdom, Irish Republic, British Commonwealth, territories under British Trusteeship; British Postal Agencies in Bahrain, Muscat, Qatar and the Trucial States; 24 × 18 × 18 in.; (ii) Elsewhere, length 24 in. length + width + depth. 36 in. Envelopes must be at least 4 × 2¾ in. for inland destinations. To all overseas destinations the minimum limits for letters in the form of a roll are 6¾ inches for the length and twice the diameter combined (at least 4 inches for the greatest dimension), unless provided with a strong address label at least 6½ inches in length and width combined and 1½ inches in width. For letters other than in the form of a roll the minimum limits are one surface 4 inches in length, 2¾ inches in width, unless provided with a strong address label of the dimensions mentioned above.

POST CARDS (p. 611).

Inland, British Commonwealth etc. in (*a*) *above:—*

Single ....2½*d.*
Reply paid (2½*d.* stamp on each part) ....5*d.*

Elsewhere abroad:—

Single ....4*d.*
Reply paid ....8*d.*

Limit of size for all destinations, inland or abroad: maximum, 5⅞ inches in length, 4⅛ inches in width; minimum, 4 inches in length, 2¾ inches in width.

PRINTED PAPERS, BOOKS (p. 611).

Inland:—

Not exceeding 2 oz. ....2½*d.*
Not exceeding 4 oz. ....4*d.*
For each further 2 oz., or less ....1*d.*

British Commonwealth and Foreign:—

For first 2 oz. ....2½*d.*
For each further 2 oz., or less ....1½*d.*

Exceptionally, newspapers, periodicals, books, pamphlets, maps and sheets of music which comply with the conditions shown in the Post Office Guide under *Printed Papers at Reduced Rates* may be sent abroad at the prepaid rate of 2*d.* for the first 2 ounces and 1½*d.* for each additional 2 ounces or fraction thereof.

LIMITS: Size, as for Letters; Weight: Inland, 2 lb. All destinations abroad, 6½ lb.; but a packet of books or booklets up to 11 lb. may be sent abroad.

Unless stamped at least 3*d.*, printed papers posted after a prescribed hour are liable to be held over until next day.

COMMERCIAL PAPERS

British Commonwealth and Foreign only:—

Not exceeding 8 oz. ....7*d.* (minimum charge)
Every further 2 oz., or less ....1½*d.*

Limits: Size, as for Printed Papers; Weight, Brit. Commonwealth, Territories under British Trusteeship; British Postal Agencies in Bahrain, Muscat, Qatar and the Trucial States 5 lb.; *Elsewhere*, 4 lb.

NEWSPAPERS

(*See also* p. 611).

Inland (Newspapers "Registered at G.P.O."):—

Not exceeding 6 oz. .... per copy 3*d.*
Every further 6 oz., or less ...... per copy 1½*d.*
Limits: 2 lb. in weight; in size as *Letters*.

Inland: Newspapers registered at the G.P.O. may be sent at printed paper rate; newspapers not registered are sent at the printed paper rate.

British Commonwealth and Foreign: See printed papers.

SAMPLES (*See also* p. 611).

Inland (not to Irish Republic):—

Not exceeding 2 oz. ....2½*d.*
Not exceeding 4 oz. ....4*d.*
Every additional 2 oz. or less ....1*d.*

British Commonwealth and Foreign:—

Not exceeding 2 oz. ....2½*d.*
For each further 2 oz. or less ....1½*d.*

LIMITS: Inland: As for letters, weight 8 oz.; Abroad: British Commonwealth, territories under British Trusteeship and British Postal Agencies in Bahrain, Muscat, Qatar and the Trucial States, 24 × 12 × 12 in., 5 lb. Elsewhere: as for Letters B ii, 1 lb. If in form of roll, everywhere as for letters, A. To all overseas destinations the minimum limits of size are as for letters.

SMALL PACKETS (*See also* p. 611).

(*British Commonwealth and Foreign*—certain countries only)

Not exceeding 10 oz. 1*s.* 0½*d* (minimum charge)
For each further 2 oz. or less ....2½*d.*

LIMITS: Maximum size, as for letters A and Bii. Minimum limits of size as for letters; Weight, 2 lb.

INSURED BOXES (*See also* p. 610).

(*British Commonwealth and Foreign*—certain countries only)

Not over 10 oz. ....1*s.* 8*d.* (minimum charge)
For each further 2 oz. or less ....4*d.*
Plus appropriate fee for insurance.

LIMITS: Maximum size, 12 × 8 × 4 in. Minimum size limits as for letters other than in the form of a roll; weight, 2 lb.

PARCELS

Should be marked "Parcel Post," and must be handed across the counter; postage must be prepaid by stamps, affixed by the sender. On Sundays parcels are not accepted or (except during Christmas) delivered. The name and address of sender should be inside and (not too prominent) on the outside of every parcel, and preferably be to the left of and at right angles to the name and address of the addressee.

A rural postman will accept any packets he can conveniently carry, except overseas letters intended for insurance or any parcels for abroad; but if on foot or cycle not more, without notice, than 22 lb. from one person. He may weigh parcels on request. Mail-drivers need not accept between regular stopping points.

Parcels to or from Irish Republic Channel Is. or I. of Man are liable to customs duty: except in last case, the sender must declare contents when posting. Addressee must pay clearance fees (1s. or 2s.) if any duty be payable. Senders can undertake to pay customs charges of Irish Republic and some overseas countries (a deposit is required). The sender of a parcel from the Channel Islands may also pay the customs charges etc., at the time of posting.

Inland:—(Limit of size: length, 3 ft. 6 in.; length and girth combined, 6 ft.):—

U.K. and Irish Republic:—

Not over 2 lb. . . . 2*s.* 0*d.*	Not over 10 lb. . . 4*s.* 0*d.*
" " 3 lb. . . . 2*s.* 3*d.*	" " 12 lb. . . 4*s.* 6*d.*
" " 4 lb. . . . 2*s.* 6*d.*	" " 15 lb. . . 5*s.* 0*d.*
" " 5 lb. . . . 2*s.* 9*d.*	" " 18 lb. . . 5*s.* 9*d.*
" " 6 lb. . . . 3*s.* 0*d.*	" 22 lb. (limit) 6*s.* 6*d.*
" " 8 lb. . . . 3*s.* 0*d.*	

AIR MAIL SERVICES

For mode of packing, prohibitions, limits of size, &c., see Post Office Guide.

Normal regulations as to make-up and acceptance of various categories of postal packets and parcels apply equally to air mail items. A blue air-mail label, obtainable free from post offices, must be affixed to each air mail item except letters, letter packets and postcards for Europe. Air mail labels should not be fixed to these latter items or delay will result. Special air-mail rates apply to correspondence for members of H.M. Forces overseas (*see* leaflet PL89).

Air Letters, postage 6*d.*, written on special Air Letter forms may be sent to all countries outside Europe. The special forms may be obtained at post offices.

SECOND CLASS MAIL. Printed papers, Commercial Papers, Samples, Small Packets may be sent by air to countries outside Europe at the rates shown in col. 4 below. Minimum charges: Commercial Papers, 7*d.* Small Packets, 1*s.* 0½*d.* NEWSPAPERS. Publications registered at the G.P.O. as newspapers may be sent at the reduced rates indicated in the footnote below. There is no Second Class air mail service to Europe.

European Countries

Letters, letter packets and postcards for all European countries, prepaid at the ordinary international postage rates, are in general despatched daily by air or surface transport, whichever offers earlier delivery. The rates are:—

Letters, 6*d.* for the first ounce,
4*d.* for each additional ounce.
Postcards, 4*d.*

For *Gibraltar* and *Malta* the rates are:
Letters, 3*d.* for the first ounce,
1½*d.* for each additional ounce.
Postcards, 2½*d.*

Air mail labels should not be used.

Air Parcel Post to Europe. Rates are included in the Overseas Parcel Post tables, see pp. 615–7

Countries Outside Europe

Rates for letters, postcards and second class mail appear below; for air parcel rates, see pp. 615–7

COUNTRIES OUTSIDE EUROPE

For air mail services to Europe, see above; Air Parcel Rates, pp. 615–7. For details of insurance and times of posting at London Chief Office and of transmission to principal cities, consult G.P.O. Air Mail Leaflet at any Post Office.

Destination	Rates of Postage: Letters per ½-oz.		Post Cards	2nd class* mail per ½ oz.
	s.	*d.*	*d.*	*d.*
Aden	0	9	5	5
Afghanistan	1	3	8	6
Alaska	1	3	8	6
Algeria	0	9	5	5
Antigua	1	3	8	6
Argentine Republic	1	3	8	6
Australia	1	6	9	7
Azores‡	—		—	—
Bahamas	1	3	8	6
Bahrain	0	9	5	5
Banks Islands	1	6	9	7
Barbados	1	3	8	6
Bermuda	1	3	8	6
Bolivia	1	3	8	6
Brazil	1	3	8	6
British Guiana	1	3	8	6
British Honduras	1	3	8	6
Brunei	1	3	8	6
Burma	1	3	8	6
Cambodia	1	3	8	6
Cameroons	1	3	8	6
Canada	1	3	8	6
Cape Verde Islands‡	—		—	—
Caroline Islands	1	6	9	7
Cayman Islands	1	3	8	6
Ceylon	1	3	8	6
Chile	1	3	8	6
China	1	6	9	7
Cocos (Keeling) Islds	1	3	8	6

Destination	Rates of Postage: Letters per ½-oz.		Post Cards	2nd class* mail per ½-oz
	s.	*d.*	*d.*	*d.*
Colombia	1	3	8	6
Congolese Republic	1	3	8	6
Cook Islands	1	6	9	7
Costa Rica	1	3	8	6
Cuba	1	3	8	6
Cyprus	0	9	5	5
Dahomey	1	3	8	6
Doha, *see* Qatar.				
Dominica	1	3	8	6
Dominican Republic	1	3	8	6
Dubai	0	9	5	5
Ecuador	1	3	8	6
Egypt	0	9	5	5
Equatorial Africa †	1	3	8	6
Eritrea	0	9	5	5
Ethiopia (Abyssinia)	0	9	5	5
Falkland Islands	1	3	8	6
Fanning Island	1	6	9	7
Fiji Islands	1	6	9	7
Formosa (Taiwan)	1	6	9	7
French Guiana	1	3	8	6
French Polynesia	1	6	9	7
French Somali Coast	0	9	5	5
French West Indies	1	3	8	6
Gambia	1	3	8	6
Gaza and Khan Yunis	0	9	5	5
Ghana	1	3	8	6
Gilbert and Ellice Islds.	1	6	9	7
Greenland	1	3	8	6

*Newspapers 2*d.* per ½ oz. less in each case.
‡ Rates as for Europe, see above.

† Central African Republic and Republics of Chad, Congo, and Gabon.

For mode of packing, prohibitions, limits of size, &c., see Post Office Guide.

Destination	Rates of Postage: Letters per ½-oz. s.	d.	Post Cards d.	2nd class* mail per ½-oz d.
Grenada	1	3	8	6
Guatemala	1	3	8	6
Guinea (Republic of)	1	3	8	6
Gwadur	1	3	8	6
Haiti (Republic)	1	3	8	6
Hawaii	1	3	8	6
Honduras (Republic)	1	3	8	6
Hong Kong	1	3	8	6
India	1	3	8	6
Indonesia	1	3	8	6
Iraq	0	9	5	5
Israel	0	9	5	5
Ivory Coast	1	3	8	6
Jamaica	1	3	8	6
Japan	1	6	9	7
Jordan	0	9	5	5
Kenya	1	3	8	6
Korea, all parts	1	6	9	7
Kuwait	0	9	5	5
Laos	1	3	8	6
Lebanon	0	9	5	5
Liberia	1	3	8	6
Libya	0	9	5	5
Macao	1	3	8	6
Madagascar	1	3	8	6
Madeira‡	—		—	—
Malaya (Federation)	1	3	8	6
Marian Islands	1	6	9	7
Marshall Islands	1	6	9	7
Mauritania (Republic)	1	3	8	6
Mauritius	1	3	8	6
Mexico	1	3	8	6
Montserrat	1	3	8	6
Morocco	0	9	5	5
Muscat	0	9	5	5
Nepal	1	3	8	6
Netherlands Antilles or New Guinea	1	3	8	6
New Caledonia	1	6	9	7
New Guinea Territory	1	6	9	7
New Hebrides	1	6	9	7
New Zealand	1	6	9	7
Nicaragua	1	3	8	6
Niger (Republic of)	1	3	8	6
Nigeria	1	3	8	6
Norfolk Island	1	6	9	7
North Borneo (Sabah)	1	3	8	6
Northern Rhodesia	1	3	8	6
Nyasaland	1	3	8	6
Pakistan	1	3	8	6
Panama (Republic of) } Panama Canal Zone }	1	3	8	6
Papua	1	6	9	7
Paraguay	1	3	8	6
Persia	0	9	5	5
Peru	1	3	8	6
Philippines	1	6	9	7
Pitcairn Island	1	6	9	7
Portuguese, E. Africa	1	3	8	6
Timor	1	6	9	7
West Africa	1	3	8	6
Puerto Rico	1	3	8	6
Qatar	0	9	5	5
Réunion	1	3	8	6
Rhodesia	1	3	8	6
St. Helena	1	3	8	6
St. Kitts-Nevis-Anguilla	1	3	8	6
St. Lucia	1	3	8	6
St. Pierre and Miquelon	1	3	8	6
St. Vincent	1	3	8	6
El Salvador	1	3	8	6
Samoa	1	6	9	7
Sarawak	1	3	8	6
Saudi Arabia	0	9	5	5
Sénégal (Republic)	1	3	8	6
Seychelles	1	3	8	6
Sharjah	0	9	5	5
Sierra Leone	1	3	8	6
Singapore	1	3	8	6
Solomon Islands	1	6	9	7
Somalia (Republic)	1	3	8	6
South Africa	1	3	8	6
Southern Rhodesia	1	3	8	6
Spanish Guinea	1	3	8	6
West Africa	0	9	5	5
Sudan (Republic)	0	9	5	5
Sudanese Republic, W. Africa	1	3	8	6
Surinam (Neth. Guiana)	1	3	8	6
Syria	0	9	5	5
Tanganyika	1	3	8	6
Thailand (Siam)	1	3	8	6
Tibet	1	3	8	6
Togo (Republic)	1	3	8	6
Tonga	1	6	9	7
Tortola, W. Indies	1	3	8	6
Trinidad and Tobago	1	3	8	6
Tunisia	0	9	5	5
Turks and Caicos Is.	1	3	8	6
Uganda	1	3	8	6
United States	1	3	8	6
Uruguay	1	3	8	6
U.S.S.R. (Asia)‡	—		—	—
Venezuela	1	3	8	6
Vietnam	1	3	8	6
Virgin Islands of U.S.A.	1	3	8	6
Voltaic Republic	1	3	8	6
Wake Island	1	6	9	7
Zanzibar	1	3	8	6

* Newspapers 2*d.* per ½ oz. less in each case. ‡ Rates as for Europe, see above.

GENERAL REGULATIONS

EXPORT RESTRICTIONS.—Under Board of Trade regulations many kinds of goods, including certain foodstuffs, may be sent abroad (including Irish Republic) only under the authority of an export licence. Enquiries in the matter should be addressed to the Controller, Export Licensing Branch, Board of Trade, Gavrelle House, 14, Bunhill Row, London, E.C.1.

Under the Defence (Finance) Regulations, senders of trade letter packets or parcels exceeding £2,000 in value to most foreign countries, including the U.S.A., and also to Canada (including Newfoundland), must furnish with the parcel a currency declaration (form C.D.3) which, together with explanatory notices, may be obtained from banks.

Senders of private gift packets or parcels exceeding £100 in value must furnish with the packet or parcel a currency declaration C.D.3.

PROHIBITED AND DUTIABLE ARTICLES.—Among prohibitions are offensive or dangerous things, packets likely to impede the P.O. sorters, and certain kinds of advertisement. To Channel Islands, and I. of Man dutiable articles must be sent in Parcels. Abroad generally they may be sent in Parcels, in Insured Boxes and Small Packets (to those countries which accept them) or (where the "Green Label" system applies) in Letters and in some cases sample packets.

CERTIFICATE OF POSTING.—Given as a matter of course for registered and insured items. May also be obtained for ordinary parcels (no charge) and other unregistered packets (fee, 1*d.*).

RECORDED DELIVERY (inland, *not to Irish Republic*).—This service provides for a record of posting and delivery. Money and jewellery are not allowed, and contents must not exceed £2 in value. The service does not apply to parcels.

UNPAID PACKETS, except Business Reply packets and redirected parcels are charged *double postage* on delivery; UNDERPAID PACKETS, *double the deficiency*.

UNDELIVERABLE POSTAL PACKETS.—*Inland packets chargeable with a postage of* 3*d. or more*, undelivered, are returned to sender without charge, if his address is found either outside or inside. If the sender's address is not available, letters containing nothing of importance are destroyed; packet containing anything of importance, and parcels, if not applied for, are generally disposed of after 3 months, or if perishable are dealt with as requisite. *Packets chargeable with postage not exceeding* 2½*d.* are returned to sender only on payment of a second postage, and if name, address and request for return appear on outside; those without such request are disposed of. *British packets undelivered abroad* are returned to sender here on payment of charges due; printed papers of no value only if request for return appears outside in a language known in the country of destination. Parcels further incur other charges unless abandonment is requested *at the time of posting*.

REPLY COUPONS, for the purpose of prepaying replies to letters, are exchangeable abroad for stamps representing the minimum letter postage rate from the country concerned to the U.K. Price (valid in all countries of the Universal Postal Union), 1*s.*: (valid within the Commonwealth and Irish Republic only), 5*d.* Sold at Chief offices.

POSTE RESTANTE (solely for the accommodation of travellers, and for three months only in any one town).—A packet may be addressed as a rule to any Post Office except Town Sub-Offices, and should have the words "Poste Restante" or "to be called for" in the address. If addressed to initials, fictitious names, or Christian name only, it is treated as undeliverable. Applicants must furnish sufficient particulars to ensure delivery to the proper owner. Redirection from a Poste Restante is not undertaken for more than 14 days unless longer (up to 3 months) is applied for. Letters at a seaport for an expected ship are kept 2 months; otherwise letters are kept for 2 weeks—or for 1 month if originating from abroad—at the end of which time they are treated as undeliverable, unless bearing a request for return at or before the end of the period.

REDIRECTION.—(1) By agent of addressee: *Packets other than parcels and business reply* may be reposted free not later than the day after delivery (not counting Sundays and public holidays) if unopened and not tampered with, and if original addressee's name is unobscured. *Parcels* may be redirected free of charge, within the same time limits, only if the original and the corrected addresses are both within the same Town Delivery Area (or within the London Postal Area). *Registered packets*, which must be taken to a Post Office, are *re-registered* free only up to day after delivery. (2) By the Post Office (not undertaken when other persons remain at the address). Requests for redirection of *letters*, &c., should be on printed forms, obtainable from the postmaster, and must be signed by the persons to whom the letters are to be addressed. Redirection is free for 3 months (except for parcels re-directed to a different Town Delivery Area, see above); thereafter for each different surname and each new address costs 5*s.* for 12 months, and 10*s.* for each subsequent year. Separate forms must be filled in for the forwarding of *telegrams*.

REGISTRATION, INLAND.—All kinds of postal packets intended for registration should be marked "Registered" in bottom left-hand corner, and *must be handed to an officer of the Post Office, and a receipt taken.* The packets must be made up in a reasonably strong cover appropriate to their contents. Parcels (or the string with which they are tied) and letters must be fastened with adhesive (if tape is used it must be transparent and each piece must be signed or distinctively marked), or sealed with wax, lead, &c. Minimum fee 1*s.* 9*d.*, exclusive of postage. Advice of delivery, a further 6*d.* The latest time for registering is usually half an hour before the latest time for posting ordinary packets. Compulsory registration is applied to (*a*) any packet apparently meant for registration and wrongly posted (1*s.* 9*d.* less any prepaid excess postage); (*b*) packets found open (or undeliverable) and containing any bank or currency note, coin, jewellery, stamps, uncrossed bearer cheques, uncrossed postal orders without payee's name, &c., in each case 10*s.* or more in value (1*s.* 9*d.*).

COMPENSATION, INLAND.—Subject to certain prescribed regulations which are fully set forth in the Post Office Guide, the Post Office pays compensation for (i) loss of or damage to registered letters, parcels and recorded delivery packets (ii) though not as a legal right, for loss of or damage to unregistered parcels and for unregistered packets conveyed by Express Messenger all the way. The onus of making up properly any packet sent by post and of packing adequately any article or articles enclosed therein lies on the sender, and the Post Office does not accept any responsibility for loss arising from faulty or inadequate packing. No compensation is paid for consequential injury or damage arising in respect of anything sent by post. *Registered letters and parcels (including items sent to the Irish Republic):* The fees for registration are 1*s.* 9*d.* covering compensation up to £20; 1*s.* 10*d.*, £40; and 1*d.* for each additional £20 up to the maximum of 3*s.* 4*d.* for £400. (No legal right to compensation exists in respect of registered letters and parcels sent to and from Irish Republic.) *Unregistered parcels and unregistered packets:* Maximum compensation £5 (£4 for unregistered parcels sent to or received from Irish Republic).

Compensation in respect of money of any kind (coin, notes, orders, cheques, stamps, etc.) is only given if the money is sent by *registered letter* post in one of the special envelopes sold officially (see p. 611) and, in the case of paper money, if particulars (for identification) are kept; the maximum compensation for coin, which must be packed so as not to move about, is £5.

Compensation cannot be paid for loss or damage in the case of any packet containing anything not legally transmissible by post; and for fragile articles only if they have been adequately packed and the cover is conspicuously marked "Fragile, with care." No compensation is paid for deterioration due to delay of perishable articles or for damage to exceptionally fragile articles, liquids or semi-liquids sent by letter or parcel post to or from Irish Republic whether registered or not.

REGISTRATION, BRITISH COMMONWEALTH AND FOREIGN (except for parcels), is in force to all countries with the exception of Chagos Islands, North Korea and North Viet-Nam. Valuable articles may not be sent in unregistered letters. Fee, 1*s.* 9*d.* If claimed within a year, compensation (in the U.K., £2 18*s.*) is paid to the sender for entire loss of registered packets while in the custody of a country in the Universal Postal Union, subject to certain conditions.

INSURANCE, BRITISH COMMONWEALTH AND FOREIGN, may be effected on packets to many countries at the following rates:—1*s.* 11*d.* for £24; 2*d.* each further £12 up to 7*s.* 1*d.* for £396 and 7*s.* 3*d.* for £400 (lower maxima in many countries). For *H.M. Ships abroad and also members of H.M. Army and Air Force overseas using closed Forces addresses* (e.g. British Forces Post Office followed by a number) only parcels are insurable, up to £50. Packets containing no articles (besides correspondence) but valuable papers (banknotes, &c.) or valuable documents (plans, &c.) can be insured as *letters*; other valuable articles should be sent as insured parcels, or as "insured boxes."

COMPENSATION up to a maximum of 93*s.* may be given for loss or damage in the U.K. to *uninsured* parcels to or from most Commonwealth and Foreign Countries, if certificate of posting is produced.

No compensation will be paid for any loss or damage due to the act of the Queen's Enemies.

INSURED BOX POST.—Jewellery and precious articles (*not* letters or paper valuables) may be sent in insured boxes to certain countries. Customs declarations must be filled in.

CASH ON DELIVERY SERVICE, INLAND (*not* to or from Irish Republic, nor to H.M. Ships.)—A sum (Trade Charge) up to £40 can, under certain conditions, be collected from addressee and remitted to sender of a parcel or registered letter posted at a Money Order Office, or of goods consigned by railway. Fees (extra to usual postal or rail charges): For Trade Charge up to £1, 2*s.* 2*d*; £2, 2*s.* 4*d.*; £5, 2*s.* 6*d.*; and for each further £5 or part thereof, 2*d.* An additional charge of 1*s.* is made on consignments sent by rail.

CASH ON DELIVERY, BRITISH COMMONWEALTH AND FOREIGN.—Applicable to parcels only, but not to all countries, nor to H.M. Naval and Military Forces and R.A.F. serving overseas. Fees for collection: 4½*d.* for Trade Charge (amount to be collected) not exceeding £1, with 2½*d.* extra for each additional £1 of Trade Charge up to the maximum, which is usually £40 (fee 8*s.* 6*d.*), but in some countries less. Addressee has also to pay on delivery, besides Customs, if any, a further fee (4*d.* in U.K.) not prepayable. If Trade Charge cannot be collected, the rules for undeliverable parcels apply.

EXPRESS and SPECIAL SERVICES (INLAND).—In general the express services are limited to the hours of telegraph business, but the times vary according to the service used and local conditions. (1) *All the way*, by P.O. messenger, of packets, conspicuously marked "Express" above the address, handed over the counter. Inclusive charge, 1*s.* per mile, or part of a mile, with 3*d.* on each *separate* packet after the first. Live animals, liquids, and money may be delivered by this service. Waiting fees: 10 minutes free, each further 10 minutes or less, 4*d.*:—(2) *After transmission by post*, on *addressee's* application (1*s.* per mile, or part of a mile, and 2*d.* for every ten or less additional packets). (3) *After transmission by post*, at *sender's* request "Special Delivery" from the ordinary delivery office, if messengers are available (1*s.*+postage). Packets must be marked "Express," and letters bear a broad blue or black vertical line back and front. A similar line must be drawn completely round a packet or parcel. (4) *Special delivery on Sunday of postal packets* (*except parcels*) *handed in on Saturdays.* Limited inter-city services, for London, Belfast, and certain provincial cities (except that the service is not in operation from Southampton to Belfast) are available *only*: (1) Sundays: reciprocally between certain towns as shown in the Post Office Guide; (2) Good Friday: *to* London only *from* towns in (1). Delivery is made from offices only during periods when they are open for telegraphic business. The handing-in offices in London are:—The London Chief Office, King Edward St., E.C.1., W. and S.W. District Offices, and (Branch Offices) Camberwell Green, Clapham Common, Hammersmith Broadway, Holloway, Trafalgar Square, Stratford, and Swiss Cottage. Packets, marked "Express: Sunday Delivery," must be handed in in time to catch *preceding* night mails (in London 4.15 p.m.—6.30 p.m. for provincial towns). The latest time of posting to Belfast should be ascertained at selected office of posting. Fee is 3*s.* 0*d.* in addition to postage. Not available for parcels. (5) (*Railex.*) Postal packets not liable to registration are despatched by rail, met, and specially delivered in Great Britain, Douglas (I.O.M.), Northern Ireland, Jersey and Guernsey. Inclusive charges 2 oz., 6*s.*; 1 lb. (maximum) 7*s.* 0*d.*; but packets handed in in Northern Ireland or forwarded from Jersey and Guernsey to Great Britain, Douglas or N. Ireland may not exceed 2 oz. (6) *A Railway Parcel* is similarly accelerated at the cost of a telegram, of railway charges, and of Service (1) at both ends of its journey. It should be marked "Railway Parcel, to be handed to Post Office messenger at .... Station."

RAILWAY LETTERS, &c.—A letter, not liable to registration, may be handed in at the parcel or passenger booking office of a railway station, at any time when the station is open to the public, for conveyance by the next available train. A railway letter may either be addressed to be called for at a station, or to the residence of the addressee in which case it is posted at the station named in the address. The service is available between any two stations in Great Britain and Northern Ireland, between Great Britain and Jersey, Guernsey and Douglas (I.O.M.), and from Great Britain and Northern Ireland to the Irish Republic. It is not available at or to stations of the London Transport Executive. Fees (besides postage): at stations in Great Britain, Jersey, Guernsey and Douglas (I.O.M.), 2 oz., 1*s.* 0*d.*; 4 oz., 1*s.* 8*d.*; 1 lb. (maximum), 2*s.* 7*d.*; at stations in Northern Ireland, 2 oz. (maximum), 7*d.* The maximum weight for letters to the Irish Republic is 2 oz. Except on Sundays, or in Irish Republic, the letter can be delivered Express under Service (3), or directly from the station (Service (1)) by wiring for messenger to meet it. For other combinations of rail and express, *see* preceding paragraph, Services (5) and (6).

AIRWAY LETTERS.— On certain internal air routes operated by the British European Airways Corporation, letters may be handed in at the airport or town terminal for conveyance by the next available direct air service to be transferred to the post at the distant airport or town terminal or to be called for at the airport or town terminal. Fees (besides postage): 2 oz., 1*s*.; 4 oz., 1*s*. 8*d*.; 1 lb. (maximum), 2*s*. 7*d*. The conditions on which this service operates are, in general, similar to those applying to the Railway Letter Service. The service is not available to the Irish Republic or to any country overseas. Full information can be obtained from any office of B.E.A.C.

INTERNATIONAL EXPRESS SERVICE.—From the office of delivery by special messenger is available to or from certain countries. In some countries the service is restricted to certain towns. 1*s*. is paid by the sender, the rest, if any, by addressee, according to the local regulations. (*See* P.O. Guide.)

POST CARDS.—Minimum size 4 × 2¾ in., maximum 5⅞ × 4⅛ in. The left-hand half of the address side may be used for correspondence, inland or abroad. Plain cards, if as stiff as official cards and not under 1/100th inch thick, may also be used both inland and abroad.

Reply Post Cards for abroad must have the heading *Carte Postale avec réponse payée* on first part, and on the second part (valid only to country of origin) *Carte Postale—Réponse*.

BUSINESS REPLY SERVICE (Inland, excluding Irish Republic). This service enables a person or firm to receive cards, letters, etc. from clients without prepayment of postage, the postage together with a fee of 1*d*. being paid by the addressee on each card or letter delivered.

A licence to use the service must be obtained from the Post Office.

POSTAGE FORWARD PARCEL SERVICE.—This service enables firms to receive parcels from clients without prepayment of postage. A special label is used for this service and a licence to do this must be obtained from the local Head Postmaster.

PRINTED PAPER POST.—For certain printed or written matter (p. 606).

By this post may be sent books and other works of a literary character, with or without written dedications, and in the inland service any other *written, typed* or *printed* matter not being *in the nature of a letter*, drawings, paintings, photographic prints, engravings, maps, &c., together with normal non-fragile binding and anything necessary for safe transmission. Commercial printed forms, legal documents, printers' copy and proofs, examination papers, answers and corrections, the writing on which refers solely to the subject matter of the document, Christmas and picture cards with date, names and addresses of sender and addressee, and with conventional formulas not exceeding 5 words or initials, are also admitted, and circulars (if in characters resembling typewriting, only under special conditions). Written chess-moves and puzzle-solutions, also blank stationery, are inadmissible. To overseas, only printed matter in general is admitted as Printed Papers; items written or drawn, such as receipts, invoices and statements of account, admissible in the inland printed post service, go only as Commercial Papers, and there are other differences. Printed papers being subject to examination in the post, the cover, if any, must be capable of easy removal and replacement for purposes of examination, *i.e.* without breaking, tearing, ungumming, or cutting. (For full conditions see the Post Office Guide or free leaflet P. 386.)

ARTICLES FOR THE BLIND (Inland, including Irish Republic). Books, papers, literature and specified articles specially adapted for the use of the blind are admissible subject to certain conditions. A packet should bear on the outside the indication "Articles for the Blind" and the name and address of the sender. Packets must be capable of easy examination in the post. Rate:—2 lb., ½*d*.; 5 lb., 1*d*.; 8 lb., 1½*d*.; 11 lb., 2*d*.; 15 lb., 2½*d*. Limits: weight, 15 lb.; size, as for letters.

BLIND LITERATURE, COMMONWEALTH AND FOREIGN (in other respects treated as Printed Papers):—Papers, periodicals and books, if printed in special type (also plates for embossing blind literature, and voice recordings and special paper intended solely for the use of the blind) subject to certain conditions of posting, marked outside "Literature for the Blind", with name and address of sender. Packets must be capable of easy examination in the post. They may be sent post free by surface route to all parts.

SAMPLE POST (not to Irish Republic).—Restricted to bona-fide *Trade* Samples, without saleable value; but keys sent unaccompanied, printers' blocks, fresh cut flowers, and certain scientific specimens can be sent *abroad* by Sample Post. Packets must be capable of easy examination in the post. (*See* p. 606.)

SMALL PACKETS POST (Commonwealth & Foreign).—For small articles of merchandise by Printed Paper mails. Registration is allowed; not insurance. Available only to certain countries. A green Customs label must be affixed and, in certain cases, Customs declarations prepared. (*See* p. 606.)

NEWSPAPER POST (INLAND).—For newspapers "registered at the G.P.O." (p. 606).

The cover, if any, must be open at both ends and easily removable, and copies should be folded so that title is readily inspected. No writing or additional printing is permitted, other than the words "with compliments" name and address of sender, request for return if undelivered and a reference to a page.

Newspapers not "registered at G.P.O." or supplements to registered newspapers despatched apart from their ordinary publications should be sent at printed paper rate.

STAMPS, ENVELOPES, POST CARDS, &c.

Stamps of reigns before that of King George V are no longer valid.

POSTAGE STAMPS (used also for receipts, telegrams, and certain Inland Revenue duties) are sold for the respective values of ½*d*., 1*d*., 1½*d*., 2*d*., 2½*d*., 3*d*., 4*d*., 4½*d*., 5*d*., 6*d*., 7*d*., 8*d*., 9*d*., 10*d*., 11*d*., 1*s*., 1*s*. 3*d*., 1*s*. 6*d*., 2*s*. 6*d*., 5*s*., 10*s*., and £1. Books containing 4 each at 3*d*., 1½*d*., 1*d*., ½*d*. 2*s*.; 6 3*d*., 6 1½*d*., 6 1*d*. and 6 ½*d*. stamps, 3*s*.; 18 3*d*. stamps, 4*s*. 6*d*.; 12 3*d*. and 6 each of 2½*d*., 1*d*. and ½*d*. stamps, 5*s*.; and 30 3*d*., and 6 each of 2½*d*., 1½*d*., and 1*d*., 10*s*. Rolls of ½*d*., 1*d*., 1½*d*., 2*d*., 2½*d*., 3*d*. or 4*d*. stamps are also sold, joined lengthwise or sideways and rolls of 6*d*. stamps joined lengthwise.

REGISTERED LETTER ENVELOPES with a 2*s*. 0*d*. embossed stamp (1*s*. 9*d*. for registration and 3*d*. for postage), are of four sizes: F. 5¼ in. × 3¼ in. or G. 6⅛ in. × 3⅞ in., 2*s*. 1½*d*. each; H. 8 in. × 5 in., 2*s*. 2*d*. each; K. 11½ in. × 6 in., 2*s*. 4½d.

FORCES AIR LETTER FORMS issued against purchase of 3*d*. stamp.

LETTER CARDS with 3*d*. stamp: 4*d*. each.

POST CARDS, with impressed 2½*d*. stamp: 3*d*. each.

EMBOSSED ENVELOPES with 3*d*. stamp: "A" (4⅝ × 3⅝ in.) or "B" (6·4 × 4·5 in.), 4*d*. each. Air Letter Forms impressed with 6*d*. stamp, 6*d*. each.

Embossed or impressed postage stamps cut out of envelopes, post cards letter cards, air letter forms or newspaper-wrappers may be used as adhesive stamps in payment of postage or telegrams provided they are not imperfect, mutilated, or defaced in any way.

MONEY ORDERS

Advice of Payment: 6*d*. inland (and to Irish Republic), 6*d*. overseas orders (to certain countries). Payment may be stopped (fee 9*d*.); or deferred up to 10 days in case of Ordinary Inland Money Orders. Inland orders (including those for Irish Republic) may be crossed for payment through a bank.

Inland Ordinary Money Orders (and to Irish Republic).

The poundage charged is, for sums not exceeding £10, 2*s.* 0*d.*; and for each additional £10, 2*d.*, to £50 (maximum), 2*s.* 8*d.* No order may contain a fractional part of 1*d.* The rules and regulations are on the forms issued. No poundage is charged for M.O. in payment of many Revenues (*e.g.*, Income Tax) if demand note is produced.

Inland Telegraph Money Orders (and to Irish Republic).

Money may be transmitted by this means from most Money Order offices which despatch telegrams, and paid at most of those which also deliver telegrams, and at some other offices. On Sundays, Christmas Day, Boxing Day and Good Friday special arrangements apply (see Post Office Guide).

Poundage at the following rate, *plus* cost of official Telegram of Advice, 5*s.* for Inland Orders and 6*s.* for Irish Republic Orders.

	Poundage
Up to £10	2*s.* 6*d.*
Over £10 and up to £20	2*s.* 8*d.*
Over £20 and up to £30	2*s.* 10*d.*
Over £30 and up to £40	3*s.* 0*d.*
Over £40 and up to £50	3*s.* 2*d.*

Ordinary Money Orders for Abroad.

Poundage, up to £2, 2*s*; £5, 3*s.*; £10, 4*s.*, and thereafter 2*s.* per £10 or part thereof. Limits of amount vary according to destination but in any case may not exceed £40; validity, normally 12 months.

Telegraph Money Orders for Abroad.

Poundage as below, *plus* cost of official Telegram of Advice (at Letter Telegram rate, if desired, to certain countries).

	Poundage
Up to £2	3*s.* 6*d.*
Over £2 and up to £5	4*s.* 6*d.*
Over £15 and up to £10	5*s.* 6*d.*
Over £10 and up to £20	7*s.* 6*d.*
Over £20 and up to £30	9*s.* 6*d.*
Over £30 and up to £40	11*s.* 6*d.*

Application to remit money orders to countries outside the Scheduled Territories (formerly known as the sterling area) must be made on a special declaration form upon which the purpose of the remittance must be stated. This form is obtainable at any money order office, where it may be ascertained whether any particular country with which a money order service is in operation is outside the Scheduled Territories.

POSTAL ORDERS

Postal Orders (British pattern) are issued and paid at nearly all post offices in the United Kingdom during the ordinary hours of business on weekdays. They are also issued and paid in most countries within the Commonwealth. Transmission of postal orders to Canada or any other country outside the Scheduled Territories (formerly known as the Sterling Area) is prohibited except to members of H.M. Forces under special arrangements, particulars of which may be obtained at any Post Office transacting Postal Order business. They are *paid* (but not *issued*) in Irish Republic. They are printed with a counterfoil, for every multiple of 6*d.* up to 5*s.*, for 6*s.*, and by 1*s.* steps up to £1 1*s.* then for £2 and every multiple of £1 up to £5. Adhesive, unmarked current British Postage Stamps not exceeding two in number, if affixed in the 2 spaces provided, increase the value of an Order by not more than 5*d.* (orders up to 4*s.* 6*d.*) or 11*d.* (orders of 5*s.* and upwards). Poundage: 6*d* and 1*s.*, 2*d.*; 1*s.* 6*d.* to £1 1*s.*, 3*d.*; £2 to £5, 6*d.* The name of payee must be inserted. If not presented within six months of the last day of the month of issue, Orders must be sent to the local Head Postmaster, or in London to the District Postmaster, for verification, and commission equal to the original poundage will be charged.

INLAND TELEGRAMS

Telegrams are accepted during counter business hours at any post office or railway station at which telegraph business is transacted. They may also be handed with the necessary payment to messengers delivering telegrams or express letters. Telegrams may be tendered by telephone at all times. Rate, 12 words or less 5*s.* 0*d.* (to Irish Republic 12 words or less 6*s.* 0*d.*), each further word 5*d.* Standard Greetings telegrams on appropriately designed forms in golden decorative envelopes cost 5*s.* 6*d.* for 12 words or less, each extra word 5*d.* Greetings telegrams for special occasions on a large *de luxe* folded card with matching envelope cost 7*s.* 0*d.* for 12 words or less, each extra word 5*d.* Greetings telegrams may be tendered by telephone or handed in any day prior to day of delivery. Priority rate (not available to or from Irish Republic) 2*s.* extra. A redirection charge of 5*s.* 0*d.* per telegram is made if the original and new addresses are in the same delivery area or London Postal District. In all other cases the redirection charge is at the ordinary inland rate. Telegrams, except Press telegrams, handed in on *Sundays* and (exc. Scotland) *Good Friday* or *Christmas Day* are charged 2*s.* 6*d.* extra. Replies may be prepaid up to £1; the reply vouchers may be used in payment or part payment of any Post Office telegram or any telegraph, telex or telephone account rendered by the Post Office, or its value refunded to sender of original telegram. Receipt for charges free on request. Certified copy 2*s.* 6*d.* There is no charge for delivery in the United Kingdom. In the Irish Republic delivery is free to addresses within 1 mile of the delivery office; beyond that any necessary charge will be collected on delivery.

TELEGRAPH OFFICES ALWAYS OPEN IN LONDON:—Chief Office (King Edward Street, E.C.1). Trafalgar Sq., 24–28 William IV Street, W.C.2.

OVERSEAS TELEGRAMS

The charges for ordinary or FULL RATE telegrams from the United Kingdom to places abroad are shown below and on pp. 615–7. The minimum charge for an ordinary telegram is as for 7 words. To any place in the British Commonwealth the full rate does not exceed 1*s.* 10*d.* per word. Urgent telegrams may be sent at double the ordinary rate.

For telegrams of a social character the GLT (Commonwealth Social Telegram) service is available to Commonwealth countries. The charge is 9*s.* 2*d.* for 11 words or less (including the indicator =GLT=), and 11*d.* for each word after 11 except to Canada, Cyprus, the British West Indies, Bermuda, British Guiana, and British Honduras to which lower charges apply.

Most countries admit Letter Telegrams at half the full rate but there is a minimum charge as for 22 words. Letter Telegrams, which must be written in plain language, are subject to delay in transmission in favour of ordinary telegrams.

Phototelegrams, i.e. pictures, photographs, drawings, plans, printed, typed or written documents may be telegraphed in facsimile to many places in the world. Full particulars of all telegraph charges and services available to any country will be given on enquiry at any Postal Telegraph or Post Office Cable & Wireless Office.

RADIOTELEGRAMS

Radiotelegrams for transmission to ships at sea in any part of the world may be handed in at any

Postal Telegraph Office or dictated over the telephone. The standard rate of charge for messages sent to ships through coast stations in the British Isles is 1*s*. 8*d*. a word; there is a reduced rate of 1*s*. a word for messages to ships regularly engaged on short voyages to or from ports in the British Isles. The address should contain (1) the name and/or rank of the addressee, (2) the name of the ship, and (3) (a) the name of a coast station in the British Isles if the sender knows that the ship is within range of that station; or (b) the name of a foreign coast station if the message is to be routed through such a station; or (c) if the sender does not know the name of the appropriate coast station, standard rate messages should be addressed to *Portishead Radio*, and reduced rate messages to *Wick Radio*.

Radiotelegrams may be sent to service personnel on board H.M. Ships in foreign waters at a charge of 1*s*. 1*d*. a word and in the Home Fleet at a charge of 8½*d*. a word. The address should contain (1) the name of the addressee and his rank or rating, (2) the word "Warship" (or "Submarine") (3) the name of the ship (or identifying letters and number) and (4) the word "Admiraltyradio" (or, in the case of the Home Fleet, the words "Homewaters Admiraltyradio").

Radiotelegrams may also be sent to R.A.F. vessels in Home Waters at a reduced rate of 8½*d*. per word. Such radiotelegrams should be addressed in the same way as for commercial vessels and in addition should include the words R.A.F. Vessel before the name of the ship.

The minimum charge is as for seven words.

INLAND TELEPHONES

The quarterly rental for single exclusive lines for residential subscribers is £3 10*s*., for business subscribers it is £4. Shared service, in which two subscribers use one line but enjoy nearly all the facilities of exclusive line service, is offered under certain conditions. For this service a rebate of 10*s*. 0*d*. is allowed from the normal quarterly rental for a single exclusive line. Calls to exchanges within the local call area are charged 2½*d*. from residence telephones and 3*d*. from business telephones (4*d*. from a call office). Trunk call charges (*viz*., to exchanges outside the local call area) vary with distance but do not exceed 4*s*. 0*d*. by day (for 3 minutes) and 2*s*. 3*d*. during the cheap rate period which is 6 p.m. to 6 a.m. every night and all day Sunday (6*s*. 9*d*. and 3*s*. 9*d*. to Irish Republic). Call office charge 3*d*. extra. Personal calls (to specified person) 1*s*. 6*d*. extra (cheap rate period 9*d*.); if the person cannot be found nothing further is charged. Where subscriber trunk dialling facilities are provided local and dialled trunk calls are charged in 2*d*. units (3*d*. from a call office); the length of time per unit depends on the distance of the call, from 6 minutes for local calls to 10 seconds for distances over 50 miles (the time allowance is increased during the cheap rate period). For fuller information see Preface to Telephone Directory.

TELEX SERVICE

Annual rental of teleprinter, associated equipment and line to Telex exchange is £160 per annum in most cases. Where nearest Telex exchange is more than 30 miles distant an additional rental based on the excess mileage applies. Charges for inland calls between exchanges 35 miles or more apart are about half equivalent charges for daytime telephone calls. International calls to European countries are about two-thirds of equivalent charges for telephone calls: to United States of America and to the Republic of South Africa charges are the same as for telephone calls, *i.e.* £1 per minute (minimum three minutes). Automatic equipment allowing messages to be sent at the maximum speed of 66 words per minute can be rented in addition. Descriptive booklet available from all Telephone Managers; for local address see telephone directory.

GENERAL SUNDAY AND HOLIDAY ARRANGEMENTS

(For Express Services see p. 610)

On SUNDAY *THROUGHOUT THE U.K.* there is no delivery of letters, &c. There is a collection for night despatch in most places. *IN LONDON*, the Chief Office and Trafalgar Square Branch Office are open always, and some other offices are open from 9 a.m. to 1 p.m. for stamps, telegrams, and with some exceptions telegraph money orders up to £5, savings bank withdrawals up to £10, and National Savings Stamps encashment up to £3. *OUTSIDE LONDON*, some Head Offices and a few country telegraph Sub-offices open 9–10.30 a.m. (Scotland 9–10 a.m.) for stamps, telegrams, registration and with some exceptions telegraph money orders up to £5, Savings Bank withdrawals up to £10, and National Savings Stamps encashment up to £3; all other offices are closed.

Christmas Day, Boxing Day and Good Friday

London: One delivery of letters and parcels on Christmas Day; none on Boxing Day and Good Friday. All offices except London Chief Office and Trafagar Square Branch office are closed on Christmas Day. Selected offices open from 9 a.m. to 1 p.m. for all classes of business on Boxing Day and for "Sunday" business on Good Friday.

Outside London: In Scotland, normal weekday deliveries; offices open as usual on Boxing Day and Good Friday; on Christmas Day some town sub-offices are shut, and after 1 p.m. many chief offices are open only for telegraph business. In England, Wales and Northern Ireland one delivery of letters and parcels on Christmas Day and Good Friday; none on Boxing Day; offices are closed on Christmas Day; head offices and some country telegraph sub-offices are open from 9 a.m. to 10.30 a.m. for all classes of business on Boxing Day and for "Sunday" business on Good Friday.

Other Public Holidays

In Scotland on New Year's Day office hours and classes of business are as on Sundays; no delivery of letters and parcels and no collection. Post Office counter and postal services on other public holidays in the U.K. vary in accordance with local conditions—details may be obtained from the local Head Postmaster.

OVERSEAS TELEPHONES

The caller should ask for CONTINENTAL or INTERNATIONAL Service. Callers in London with Dial Telephones with letters should dial "104" or "108." The charges shown are minimum rates for a call of three minutes duration, each further minute or part thereof costing one-third of this charge. Transferred charge calls are possible with certain countries. Details of countries and rates will be advised by the Continental and International Exchange.

Continental Service.

The rates quoted are for calls from all places in Great Britain, Northern Ireland, the Isle of Man and the Channel Islands to the first zone of the country concerned. For *Personal Calls* an additional charge equivalent to one minute's conversation is made.

International Service.

Minimum rates, the same from all parts of Great Britain, Northern Ireland, the Isle of Man and the Channel Islands are shown below. Hours of Service to most countries are limited. A *person to person call* may be booked without extra charge; if it fails (or call is cancelled) a *Report Charge* is made (4*s.* to 8*s.* 6*d.*) but not if call matures. On Radio Services a time allowance is made for interruption by adverse conditions. A *limited duration* facility (minimum 3 mins.) is available enabling connection to be terminated after a specified period of effective conversation. *A reduced rate* (10 p.m. to 10 a.m. on weekdays and all day on Sundays) is available on services with Canada, U.S.A., the West Indies, some South American and other countries.

Ships Services

Long, Medium and Short Range Ships' Services are also available between telephone subscribers in the United Kingdom and suitably equipped ships (*see* Post Office Guide).

OVERSEAS TELEPHONE CHARGES

(Continental Services are marked (A); remaining countries are on the International Service (*See* above)

Country	*Minimum* s.	d.
Aden	75	0
Afghanistan	75	0
Alaska★	75	0
Algeria (A)	25	0
Argentine Republic	60	0
Ascension	60	0
Australia	60	0
Austria (A)	18	0
Azores (A)	31	6
Bahamas★	75	0
Balearic Islands (A)	27	0
Barbados	60	0
Belgium (A)	7	0
Bermuda	60	0
Bolivia	75	0
Brazil (Rio de Janeiro 60*s.*)	75	0
British Guiana	60	0
Bulgaria (A)	24	0
Cameroon (Republic)	67	6
Canada†	60	0
Canary Islands (A)	32	0
Cape Verde Islands	60	0
Central African Republic	60	0
Ceylon	60	0
Chad (Republic)	60	0
Chile★	75	0
Colombia★	75	0
Congo (Republic of)	60	0
Congolese Republic	60	0
Costa Rica★	75	0
Cuba†	75	0
Cyprus (Republic)	45	0
Czechoslovakia (A)	18	0
Dahomey (Republic)	67	6
Denmark (A)	12	6
Dominican Republic★	75	0
Ecuador★	75	0
Egypt (U.A.R.)	60	0
Ethiopia	60	0
Faroë (A)	15	0
Fiji Islands	75	0
Finland (A)	21	0
France (A)	7	0
French Guiana	67	6
French Somaliland	67	6
Gaboon Republic	60	0
Gambia	60	0
Germany (A)	10	0
Gibraltar (A)	18	6
Greece (A)	30	0
Guadeloupe	67	6
Guatemala★	75	0
Guinea (Republic)	67	6
Haiti★	75	0
Hawaii★	75	0
Honduras★	75	0
Hong Kong	75	0
Hungary (A)	20	0
Iceland (A)	27	0
India (Republic)	60	0
Indonesia	75	0
Iraq (incl. W. Irian)	60	0
Israel	60	0
Italy (A)	13	6
Ivory Coast (Republic)	67	6
Jamaica	60	0
Japan★	75	0
Jordan	60	0
Kenya	60	0
Lebanon	67	6
Leeward Islands	60	0
Libya	37	6
Luxemburg (A)	8	0
Madagascar	67	6
Madeira (A)	31	6
Malaya	75	0
Malta (A)	30	0
Marian Islands★	75	0
Martinique	67	6
Mauritana	67	6
Mauritius	75	0
Mexico†	75	0
Morocco (A)	27	0
Mozambique	60	0
Netherlands (A)	7	0
Netherlands Antilles	60	0
New Britain	60	0
New Guinea (British)	60	0
New Zealand	60	0
Nicaragua★	75	0
Niger (Republic)	67	6
Nigeria	60	0
North Borneo (Sabah)	75	0
Norway (A)	16	0
Nyasaland	60	0
Pakistan (Republic)	60	0
Panama★	75	0
Papua	60	0
Persia	60	0
Persian Gulf	60	0
Peru★	75	0
Philippines★	75	0
Poland (A)	18	6
Portugal (A)	22	0
Portuguese Guinea	60	0
Puerto Rico★	75	0
Réunion	67	6
Rhodesia	60	0
Roumania (A)	24	0
Ryukyu Islands★	75	0
Sahara (A)	27	0
St. Helena	60	0
St. Tomé and Principé	60	0
El Salvador★	75	0
Senegal (Republic)	67	6
Sierra Leone	60	0
Singapore	75	0
South and S.W. Africa	60	0
Spain (A)	18	6
Sudan	60	0
Sudanese Republic	67	6
Sweden (A)	16	0
Switzerland (A)	10	0
Syria (A.R.)	75	0
Tanganyika	60	0
Tangier (A)	27	0
Tasmania	60	0
Thailand	75	0
Togo (Republic)	67	6
Trinidad and Tobago	60	0
Tunisia (A)	27	0
Turkey (A)	35	0
Uganda	60	0
Uruguay★	75	0
U.S.A.†	60	0
U.S.S.R. (A)	21*s.* to 105	0
Vatican City (A)	13	6
Venezuela★	75	0
Virgin Islands (British and U.S.)★	75	0
Voltaic Republic	67	6
Windward Islands	60	0
Yugoslavia (A)	20	0

★ Sundays only, 15*s.* less. † Night and Sundays, 15*s.* less.

Recorded local weather forecasts for the cities listed below and the surrounding areas, and in London forecasts for the nearest coastal areas, may be obtained by telephoning the number shown below. The charge will be that for a call to a central exchange in the city concerned.

London	WEA 2211
Essex Coast	WEA 3311
Kent Coast	WEA 4411
Sussex Coast	WEA 5511
Birmingham	ASK 8091
Glasgow	ASK 8091
Liverpool	ASK 8091
Lancs. Coast	ASK 8092
Manchester	ASK 8091
Lancs. Coast	ASK 8092
Belfast	8091
Blackpool (Lancs. Coast)	8091
Brighton (Sussex Coast)	18
Bristol	8091
Canterbury (Kent Coast forecast)	831
Cardiff	8091
Colchester (Essex Coast)	8091
Edinburgh	932
Southern Hampshire (including I.O.W. and Poole Harbour) Portsmouth	8091
Southampton	8091
Southport (Lancs. Coast)	9541

Limit of size—as for Inland. For mode of packing, prohibitions, &c., see Post Office Guide.

Telegrams (see p.612) s. d.	DESTINATION	SURFACE MAIL 2 lb. s. d.	3 lb. s. d.	7 lb. s. d.	11 lb. s. d.	22 lb. s. d.	AIR MAIL Each ½ lb. or First lb.*	Each 1 lb. after 1st (Europe)
1 10	Aden	—	9 0	11 9	14 3	21 9	4 0	—
2 2	Afghanistan (Sea Direct)	13 0	—	16 9	21 6	35 0	7 6	—
	(Via U.S.S.R.)	15 3	—	20 9	26 3	47 0		
2 2	Alaska	—	9 3	14 9	21 6	35 6	5 6	—
1 0	Albania	12 0	—	14 9	17 9	27 3	8 6*	3 0
8	Algeria	8 9	—	11 6	14 3	22 0	2 3	—
1 5	Antigua	—	6 9	10 0	12 9	18 9	7 3	—
2 11	Argentine Republic	10 0	—	13 6	17 9	27 6	9 9	—
1 10	Ascension	—	7 9	10 3	12 9	18 3	—	—
1 10	Australia (b)	—	—	—	—	—	13 0	—
10	Austria	9 9	—	12 6	15 3	24 3	7 3*	2 0
9	Azores	9 3	—	11 6	14 0	22 6	3 6	—
1 5	Bahamas (Sea Direct)	—	6 3	8 9	11 6	15 9	5 0	—
	(Via U.S.A.)	—	11 3	19 0	28 6	47 9		
2 3	Bahrain (B.P.A.) (Sea Direct)	—	10 6	14 3	18 6	28 0	4 0	—
	(Via Lebanon)	—	14 6	20 0	26 0	44 9		
9	Balearic Islands	10 6	—	13 0	15 9	24 3	8 9*	3 3
1 5	Barbados	—	7 0	10 0	13 3	18 3	7 3	—
1 10	Basutoland (a)	—	—	—	—	—	6 9	—
1 10	Bechuanaland (c)	—	—	—	—	—	6 9	—
	Kazungula and Kasane only (d)	—	—	—	—	—	6 6	—
7	Belgium	7 0	—	8 9	11 0	16 0	5 6*	1 0
1 5	Bermuda (Sea Direct)	—	7 6	10 0	13 3	18 0	4 0	—
	(Via U.S.A.)	—	10 9	15 6	21 9	34 3		
3 5	Bolivia	9 9	—	13 6	18 0	29 0	—	—
2 8	Brazil	11 3	—	14 6	19 0	28 3	7 6	—
1 5	British Guiana	—	7 3	9 6	12 6	18 9	7 9	—
1 5	British Honduras (Via U.S.A.)	—	12 6	20 6	30 3	52 6	6 3	—
	(Via Jamaica and Direct)	—	8 0	11 0	14 0	22 3		
1 10	Brunei	—	8 3	11 9	16 0	25 0	10 6	—
1 0	Bulgaria	11 6	—	14 6	17 9	28 6	7 3*	2 9
2 2	Burma	10 0	—	13 9	18 0	28 0	7 6	—
2 0§	Burundi	11 0	—	15 9	21 3	32 9	7 0	—
3 3	Cambodia	11 3	—	14 9	18 3	29 3	10 6	—
2 8	Cameroon (Fed. Repub.)	8 6	—	11 3	14 0	20 3	5 3	—
1 5	Canada	—	11 0	14 9	19 0	26 3	5 6†	—
1 1	Canary Islands	9 0	—	11 9	14 6	21 3	8 9*	3 3
1 10	Cape Verde Islands	10 3	—	13 0	15 6	24 3	4 3	—
3 7	Caroline Islands	—	12 3	22 3	34 9	60 6	12 0	—
1 5	Cayman Islands	—	9 3	12 9	16 9	24 3	6 9	—
4 1	Central African Republic	10 0	—	13 0	16 3	25 3	5 6	—
1 10	Ceylon	9 9	—	13 9	19 0	28 6	6 9	—
4 1	Chad	10 0	—	13 0	16 3	25 3	5 6	—
2 11	Chile	13 0	—	16 9	20 6	32 0	10 0	—
3 7	China (Sea Direct)	8 3	—	12 6	17 6	28 3	7 9	—
	(Via U.S.S.R.)	13 9	—	20 3	26 9	47 0		—
1 10	Christmas Island	—	11 3	17 6	24 9	35 9	—	—
3 3	Colombia ‡(Sea Direct)	12 3	—	19 9	27 9	48 6	10 0	—
	‡(Via U.S.A.)	13 3	—	22 9	33 6	60 0		
4 1	Congo (Republic of)	10 0	—	13 0	16 3	25 3	5 6	—
2 0	Congolese Republic	10 0	—	14 9	19 0	32 0	7 0	—
7	Corsica	7 9	—	10 0	12 6	19 0	6 0*	1 6
3 3‡	Costa Rica	10 3	—	14 9	20 6	34 6	6 9	—
2 0‡	Cuba (Via Canada)	12 3	—	18 6	26 3	44 3	5 9	—
	Guantanamo Bay U.S.N. Sta.	9 9	—	16 0	23 6	39 6		
1 6	Cyprus (Sea Direct)	—	10 6	12 9	15 6	22 6	2 9	—
	(Via France and Italy)	—	12 0	15 6	18 0	27 3		
9	Czechoslovakia	10 0	—	12 9	15 0	24 3	6 6*	2 6
2 1	Dahomey	9 9	—	12 6	15 9	24 6	4 6	—
7	Denmark (Sea Direct)	6 9	—	8 6	10 6	15 0	6 0*	1 9
	(Via Netherlands)	9 0	—	11 3	13 6	21 3		
1 5	Dominica	—	7 0	9 3	12 0	18 3	7 0	—
3 5‡	Dominican Republic (Sea Direct)	7 6	—	10 3	13 0	19 0	6 6	—
	(Via U.S.A.)	10 9	—	15 9	21 6	35 3		
3 11‡	Ecuador (Sea Direct)	11 9	—	14 6	17 0	24 9	—	—
	(Via U.S.A.)	12 3	—	16 9	22 3	35 0		
1 10	Ethiopia	11 3	—	15 3	19 6	30 6	5 6	—
1 10	Falkland Islands and Dependencies	—	8 0	11 3	15 3	23 0	—	—
7	Faroes	6 9	—	8 6	10 6	15 0	—	—
1 10	Fiji Islands	—	11 0	15 9	21 9	32 3	14 3	—
11	Finland	7 6	—	10 3	12 9	18 9	7 9*	3 0
3 5	Formosa	10 6	—	14 3	18 9	29 9	11 0	—
7	France	7 3	—	9 6	12 0	17 3	6 0*	1 3
2 10	French Guiana	9 0	—	11 9	14 6	22 3	8 3	—
3 2	French Polynesia	12 9	—	20 9	30 3	51 9	17 9	—
2 2	French Somali Coast	9 9	—	12 6	15 3	23 3	5 9	—
2 10	French West Indies	8 9	—	11 3	14 0	21 6	7 0	—
4 1	Gaboon	10 0	—	13 0	16 3	25 3	5 6	—
1 10	Gambia	—	8 3	11 3	14 9	22 0	4 0	—

Rates per lb. or fraction thereof: (a) 2s. 0d. (b) 2s. 1d. (c) 2s. 6d. (d) 2s. 9d.

* Rate for first lb. † Newfoundland only, 5s. 0d. ‡ Variable rates for some parts. (§) Via Belgium, 3s. 2d.

Limit of size—as for Inland. For mode of packing, prohibitions, &c., see Post Office Guide.

Telegrams (see p. 612) s. d.	DESTINATION	SURFACE MAIL 2 lb. s. d.	3 lb. s. d.	7 lb. s. d.	11 lb. s. d.	22 lb. s. d.	AIR MAIL Each ½ lb. or First lb.*	Each 1 lb. after 1st (Europe)
8	Germany (All parts)	7 9	—	9 9	12 0	18 6	6 0*	1 6
1 10	Ghana	—	8 6	11 9	15 3	23 6	4 0	—
7	Gibraltar	—	7 6	9 9	11 9	16 3	6 6*	2 9
1 10	Gilbert and Ellice, Line and Phoenix Islands	—	8 3	13 0	19 9	32 0	13 0	—
	Ocean Island	—	10 3	15 6	22 9	35 6		
1 0	Greece (*Sea Direct*)	8 6	—	12 6	15 0	22 3	8 3*	4 0
	(*Via* France)	10 0	—	14 6	17 9	27 9		
1 6	Greenland (*Sea Direct*)	6 9	—	8 6	10 6	15 0	5 0	—
	(*Via* Netherlands)	9 0	—	11 3	13 6	21 3		
1 5	Grenada	—	7 3	9 9	12 9	17 0	7 3	—
3 3‡	Guatemala (*Sea Direct*)	10 0	—	13 6	17 6	27 3	7	—
	(*Via* U.S.A.)	14 6	—	22 6	32 0	54 3		
	(*Via* Panama)	11 9	—	17 6	24 6	41 0		
2 4	Guinea	10 0	—	12 6	15 3	24 9	4 6	—
3 5‡	Haiti (*Via* U.S.A.)	12 0	—	17 0	23 0	38 0	6 6	—
	(*Via* Dominican Repub.)	9 9	—	12 9	16 0	24 9		
2 2	Hawaii	—	9 3	14 9	21 6	35 6	10 0	—
3 7	Honduras (Repub.) (*Via* U.S.A.)	13 3	—	21 3	30 9	53 0	7 0	—
	(*Via* Panama)	11 6	—	17 6	24 9	42 9		—
1 10	Hong Kong	—	7 0	10 3	14 3	22 6	8 6	—
1 0	Hungary	11 0	—	14 0	17 0	27 9	6 9*	2 6
10	Iceland	9 9	—	12 0	14 9	22 6	9 3*	3 9
1 10	India (including Andaman and Nicobar Islands)	8 9	—	13 6	19 3	28 6	6 6	—
2 7	Indonesia	10 9	—	14 6	19 3	30 9	10 6	—
2 4	Iraq (*Sea Direct*)	—	12 6	17 6	22 6	36 3	4 0	—
	(*Via* Lebanon)	—	13 0	19 9	26 0	44 0		
1 10	Israel	9 3	—	12 9	17 9	26 0	3 3	—
9	Italy (including Sardinia and Sicily)	8 3	—	10 9	13 6	21 3	7 0*	2 0
2 1	Ivory Coast	9 9	—	12 6	15 9	24 6	4 6	—
1 5	Jamaica	—	7 6	10 6	13 9	18 6	6 0	—
3 5	Japan (*Sea Direct*)	9 3	—	12 9	16 6	26 3	10 0	—
	(*Via* U.S.A.)	13 3	—	21 3	31 0	53 3		
1 10	Jordan	10 6	—	14 0	17 9	29 0	3 0	—
1 10	Kenya	—	9 0	13 3	18 3	26 6	5 0	—
3 5	Korea (*f*)	9 9	—	13 6	17 6	28 3	11 0	—
2 4	Kuwait (*Sea Direct*)	10 9	—	14 6	19 0	27 3	4 0	—
	(*Via* Lebanon)	15 9	—	21 9	28 3	46 9		
3 3	Laos	11 3	—	15 6	20 6	33 9	—	—
1 5	Lebanon	8 6	—	11 6	14 9	23 0	3 0	—
3 0‡	Liberia	8 6	—	11 6	14 9	23 0	—	—
1 3	Libya	9 6	—	13 0	16 6	25 6	1 9	—
7	Luxemburg	7 3	—	9 3	11 0	16 3	5 6*	1 0
2 6	Madagascar	10 3	—	13 9	17 3	27 0	8 0	—
9	Madeira	7 6	—	10 3	12 9	19 6	3 6	—
1 10	Malaya and Singapore	—	8 0	11 3	15 9	23 9	8 9	—
—	Maldive Islands	10 6	—	16 6	23 3	35 0	—	—
2 1	Mali (Republic of)	9 9	—	12 6	15 9	24 6	4 6	—
8	Malta	—	7 6	10 0	13 0	19 3	7 0*	3 3
2 2‡	Mariana Islands	—	12 3	22 0	34 3	59 6	12 0	—
3 7	Marshall Islands	—	12 3	22 3	34 9	60 6	12 0	—
2 1	Mauritania	8 9	—	11 3	13 9	20 9	4 6	—
1 10	Mauritius (*Sea Direct*)	—	7 6	10 9	15 3	23 3	8 0	—
	(*Via* France)	—	9 9	13 0	16 9	25 6		
2 6	Mexico (*Sea Direct*)	8 6	—	11 3	14 6	22 6	8 0	—
	(All places except Chetumal, *via* U.S.A.)	12 6	—	19 3	27 6	46 3		
1 5	Montserrat	—	7 6	10 6	14 0	19 0	7 6	—
1 3	Morocco	9 0	—	11 9	14 9	22 3	2 6	—
2 3	Muscat	—	10 6	14 3	18 6	28 0	4 0	—
1 10	Nauru Island	—	11 3	17 0	24 6	39 0	13 0	—
1 10	Nepal	8 9	—	13 6	19 3†	—	6 6	—
7	Netherlands	7 0	—	8 9	10 9	16 0	5 6*	1 0
3 2	New Caledonia	—	11 3	16 6	23 9	37 0	15 0	—
1 10	New Guinea Territory	—	11 3	17 0	24 6	39 0	13 0	—
3 2	New Hebrides	—	10 3	15 3	21 9	34 3	16 6	—
1 10	New Zealand	—	9 6	13 6	18 9	28 6	13 0§	—
3 3‡	Nicaragua (*Via* U.S.A.)	12 0	—	16 6	22 3	36 3	6 9	—
	(*Via* Panama)	9 3	—	12 3	16 0	24 9		
2 1	Niger	9 9	—	12 6	15 9	24 6	4 6	—
1 10	Nigeria	—	9 9	13 3	17 0	24 3	4 0	—
1 10	Norfolk Island	—	11 3	17 0	24 6	39 0	13 0	—
1 10	North Borneo (Sabah)	—	9 0	13 0	17 9	27 3	10 3	—
8	Norway	7 9	—	10 0	12 6	18 6	6 6*	2 3
1 10	Nyasaland (*Via* S. Africa)(*e*)	—	—	—	—	—	6 6	—
	(*Via* Beira)	—	8 3	12 3	17 6	28 3		—
1 10	Pakistan	11 0	—	15 6	19 9	32 6	6 6	—
3 1‡	Panama (Republic of)	10 0	—	13 6	17 3	27 0	6 0	—
3 1‡	Panama Canal Zone (*Sea Direct*)	—	7 3	11 9	17 3	28 3	6 0	—
	(*Via* U.S.A.)	—	9 9	16 0	23 6	39 6		

* Rate for first lb. §16*s.* 9*d.* to Island Territories. ‡ Variable rates for some parts. Weight limit 11 lb. † Weight limit 10 lb. (*e*) 3*s.* 0*d.* per lb. or fraction thereof. (*f*) Parcels, S. Korea only.

Limit of size—as for Inland. For mode of packing, prohibitions, &c., see Post Office Guide.

Telegrams (see p. 612) s. d.	DESTINATION	SURFACE MAIL 2 lb. s. d	3 lb. s. d	7 lb. s. d.	11 lb. s. d.	22 lb. s. d.	AIR MAIL Each ½ lb. or First lb.*	Each 1 lb. after 1st. (Europe)
1 10	Papua	—	11 3	17 0	24 6	39 0	13 0	—
3 6	Paraguay	9 6	—	13 3	17 6	28 6	9 6	—
1 11	Persia	10 0	—	13 6	18 3	30 3	4 0	—
2 11‡	Peru	12 9	—	16 0	19 0	28 3	} 7 9	—
	(All Departments except Loreto, *via* U.S.A.)	13 0	—	17 9	23 6	37 3		
3 1‡	Philippines	—	10 3	14 0	18 9	26 6	9 9	—
1 10	Pitcairn Island	—	6 6	10 0	14 9	23 0	13 0	—
10	Poland	7 6	—	9 6	12 0	17 3	8 0*	2 6
9	Portugal	8 3	—	10 6	12 6	19 3	7 6*	2 6
1 11	Portuguese East Africa	8 3	—	11 6	15 6	24 6	8 0	—
2 11	Portuguese Timor	10 0	—	14 0	18 9	30 9	17 9	—
1 10	Portuguese West Africa	10 9	—	13 9	16 6	26 6	7 3(e)	—
2 2	Puerto Rico	—	9 3	14 9	21 6	35 6	6 6	—
2 7	Qatar B.P.A.	—	10 6	14 3	18 6	28 0	4 0	—
2 4	Réunion	9 3	—	12 6	15 6	24 0	8 3	—
1 10	Rhodesia, N. & S. (*Via* S. Africa)(*d*)	—	—	—	—	—	—	—
	(*Via* Beira)	—	8 3	12 3	17 6	28 3	6 6	—
1 1	Roumania	11 0	—	14 0	17 0	27 9	—	—
2 0§	Ruanda	11 0	—	15 9	21 3	32 9	7 0	—
1 10	St. Helena	—	6 3	9 0	12 0	17 3	—	—
1 5	St. Kitts-Nevis-Anguilla	—	6 3	9 0	11 6	17 0	7 3	—
1 5	St. Lucia	—	8 3	11 3	13 9	19 3	7 3	—
1 5	St. Pierre and Miquelon	—	12 9	16 6	20 9	28 0	5 6	—
1 5	St. Vincent	—	7 3	9 9	12 9	17 0	7 3	—
3 11	Salvador (*Sea Direct*)	8 3	—	11 9	15 9	25 6	} 7 0	—
	(*Via* U.S.A.)	17 9	—	26 0	36 0	59 9		
	(*Via* Panama)	11 9	—	17 6	24 6	41 0		
2 2	Samoa (U.S.) (*See also* Western Samoa)	—	11 9	20 9	32 0	55 6	15 9	—
1 10	Sarawak	—	9 6	13 6	18 3	27 9	9 3	—
2 0‡	Saudi Arabia	11 6	—	14 9	18 6	30 0	4 0	—
2 1	Senegal	8 9	—	11 3	13 9	20 9	4 6	—
1 10	Seychelles	—	9 0	13 0	18 0	28 0	6 9	—
1 10	Sierra Leone	—	9 9	13 0	16 9	23 0	4 0	—
1 10	Solomon Islands	—	7 3	10 9	15 9	25 3	17 9	—
1 10	Somalia	—	10 6	14 0	17 0	27 0	4 6†	—
1 10	South Africa (*a*)	—	—	—	—	—	6 9	—
1 10	South-west Africa (*c*)	—	—	—	—	—	6 9	—
9	Spain	10 0	—	12 6	15 3	23 0	8 9*	3 3
3 7	Spanish Guinea	10 0	—	13 3	16 6	26 6	6 0	—
9	Spanish N. Africa (Ceuta, Chafarinas, Jadu, Melilla)	10 6	—	13 0	15 9	24 3	3 0	—
1 5	Spanish West Africa	9 3	—	12 3	15 3	24 3	4 0	—
8	Spitsbergen (Svalbard) (Summer)	7 9	—	10 0	12 6	18 6	—	—
1 7	Sudan	10 9	—	14 6	18 0	29 6	4 0	—
2 10	Surinam	8 0	—	10 9	14 0	21 3	8 0	—
1 10	Swaziland (*a*)	—	—	—	—	—	6 9	—
8	Sweden	7 6	—	9 3	11 9	16 6	7 0*	2 3
8	Switzerland (and Liechtenstein)	7 9	—	9 9	12 3	19 0	6 0*	1 6
1 5	Syria	9 6	—	12 9	16 3	26 0	2 9	—
1 10	Tanganyika	—	9 0	13 3	18 3	26 6	5 0	—
2 8	Thailand	11 6	—	15 6	20 3	32 0	8 3	—
3 7	Tibet (*No Service*)	—	—	—	—	—	—	—
2 6	Togo	9 9	—	12 6	15 9	24 6	4 6	—
1 10	Tonga	—	9 3	14 0	20 6	32 0	15 6	—
1 5	Tortola (British Virgin Islands)	—	9 6	14 6	20 0	33 3	6 9	—
1 5	Trinidad and Tobago	—	7 9	10 3	13 3	17 6	7 3	—
—	Tristan da Cunha	—	7 3	13 0	19 6	31 0	—	—
2 11‡	Trucial States (B.P.A.) (*Sea Direct*)	—	10 6	14 3	18 6	28 0	} 4 0	—
	(*Via* Lebanon)	—	14 6	20 0	26 0	44 9		—
8	Tunisia	8 9	—	11 6	14 3	22 0	2 3	—
1 3	Turkey (*Sea Direct*)	9 9	—	12 6	15 0	23 3	} 8 3*	4 3
	(*Via* France)	12 0	—	15 3	18 6	30 9		
1 5	Turks and Caicos Islands	—	9 3	12 9	16 9	24 3	6 3	—
1 10	Uganda	—	9 0	13 3	18 3	26 6	5 0	—
1 4	United Arab Republic	8 6	—	11 6	14 9	23 0	2 9	—
1 3	U.S.S.R.—in Europe	8 6	—	11 9	15 0	24 0	16 3*	6 3
1 3	U.S.S.R.—in Asia	11 0	—	15 3	19 6	33 6	6 9	—
1 5	United States (*See also* Alaska; Hawaii)	—	9 3	14 9	21 6	35 6	5 6	—
3 7	Uruguay	9 9	—	13 3	17 6	27 3	9 0	—
9	Vatican City State	9 3	—	11 9	14 6	22 6	7 0*	2 0
3 8	Venezuela	10 0	—	13 0	15 6	21 6	7 9	—
3 3	Vietnam	11 3	—	14 9	18 3	29 3	10 6	—
2 2	Virgin Islands (U.S.)	—	9 3	14 9	21 6	35 6	6 9	—
2 1	Voltaic Republic	9 9	—	12 6	15 9	24 6	4 6	—
2 2	Wake Island	—	11 9	20 9	32 0	55 6	11 0	—
1 10	Western Samoa (*Via* N.Z.)	—	9 6	13 6	18 9	28 6	} 15 9	—
	(*Via* U.S.A.)	—	13 6	21 3	30 9	51 0		—
11	Yugoslavia	10 0	—	12 9	15 6	24 9	8 0*	3 6
1 10	Zanzibar	—	8 6	12 3	17 0	25 3	5 3	—

Rates per lb. or fraction thereof: (*a*) 2*s.* 0*d.*; (*c*) 2*s.* 6*d.*; (*d*) 2*s.* 9*d.* * Rate for first lb. ‡ Variable rates for some parts.
(†) Southern Region, 6*s.* 0*d.* (§) *Via* Belgium 3*s.* 2*d.* (*e*) Portuguese Guinea 5*s.* 9*d.*

THE POST OFFICE

Crown services for the conveyance of Government letters and despatches by posts or stages were set up under a Master of the Posts about 1516. Public correspondence was officially accepted for the first time for conveyance by these services at fixed postage rates in 1635, but they were still under direct Crown control. In 1657 a Post Office was created under a Postmaster-General by Oliver Cromwell, and responsibility for the carrying of all letters was thus transferred to Parliament, Charles II ratified this arrangement by statute in 1660.

The Money Order Office was inaugurated in 1792, uniform Penny Post in 1840, the Book Post in 1848, the Post Office Savings Bank in 1861, Post Office Telegraphs in 1870, Postal Orders and the Post Office Telephone Service in 1881 and the Parcel Post in 1883.

The Post Office also acts as agent for many Government Departments in the collection and payment of money.

New financial arrangements brought into effect by the Post Office Act, 1961, separated Post Office finances from the Exchequer and established the Post Office Fund on April 1, 1961.

The following table shows the income and expenditure of the Post Office, in the first year of operation of the Post Office Fund with comparable figures for the last financial year.

POST OFFICE FINANCIAL RESULTS

£ million

	1961–62			1962–63		
	Postal	Tele-communications	Combined	Postal	Tele-communications	Combined
Income						
Main services	188·2	253·6	441·8	192·8	277·8	470·6
Remittance services	10·8	—	10·8	10·1	—	10·1
Agency services	33·4	3·0	36·4	38·3	3·0	41·3
Miscellaneous	0·6	5·7	6·3	0·3	8·0	8·3
TOTAL INCOME	233·0	262·3	495·3	241·5	288·8	530·3
Expenditure						
Operating	204·4	126·7	331·1	219·6	133·1	352·7
Engineering	2·3	56·9	59·2	2·6	63·3	65·9
Supply departments	0·8	6·1	6·9	0·8	5·8	6·6
Motor transport	7·2	3·8	11·0	7·7	4·2	11·9
Accommodation	8·6	13·3	21·9	9·5	15·0	24·5
Incidental expenses	3·6	3·7	7·3	4·3	3·9	8·2
Administration	4·9	4·7	9·6	4·9	5·3	10·2
Interest	0·2	34·5	34·7	0·2	38·0	38·2
TOTAL EXPENDITURE	232·0	249·7	481·7	249·6	268·6	518·2
PROFIT	1·0	12·6	13·6	—8·1	20·2	12·1
Taxation			0·5			—
PROFIT AFTER TAXATION			13·1			12·1

MAIL SERVICES

A total of 10,600,000,000 items of correspondence was posted in the United Kingdom in 1962–63, compared with 10,500,000,000 in 1961–62. Parcels handled by the Post Office during the year numbered 224,200,000, a decrease of 9·2 million compared with 1961–62.

Inland services conveyed 5,619,000,000 letters (excluding 271,000,000 items of pools post), 245,000,000 postcards, 3,546,000,000 printed papers and samples (excluding 318,000,000 pools post), 137,000,000 newspapers and 211,400,000 parcels. These figures include 68,100,000 registered items, 11,900,000 recorded delivery items and 88,400,000 business replies.

Overseas services conveyed 291,000,000 letters, postcards and printed papers at surface mail rates and 173,000,000 at air mail rates. 10,900,000 overseas parcels were handled at surface rates and 1,890,000 at air mail rates. In the overseas services 7,000,000 registered and insured items were conveyed.

TELEPHONE SERVICES

At March 31	1961–62	1962–63
	'000	'000
Number of Local Exchanges		
Automatic	5,277	5,383
Manual	733	628
Number of Auto-Manual and Separate Trunk Exchanges	321	321
Number of Exchange Connections		
On automatic exchanges	4,358	4,596
On manual exchanges	852	758
TOTAL	5,210	5,354
(*including*)		
At Business Rate	1,956	1,985
At Residence Rate	3,113	3,223
Post Office Service	67	71
Call Office	74	75
Number of stations (telephones in use)	8,624	8,927
Applications for exchange connections during year	423	432
Outstanding, 31/3/63	147	161

Traffic

	1961–62	1962–63
Inland	'000	'000
Trunk Calls	477,000	545,000
Local Calls	4,500,000	4,750,000
Overseas		
European Cable Services	6,855	7,974
Radiotelephone and Extra-European Cable Services	759	877
Short-Range Radiotelephone calls with Ships	138	148

TELEGRAPH SERVICES

	'000	'000
Inland Telegrams	13,282	12,702
Ordinary	8,589	8,040
Greetings	3,179	3,135
Overnight	551	552
Press	135	131
Railway Pass	828	844
Inland Telex Calls	7,800	10,000
Irish Republic Telegrams	879	839
Overseas Telegrams (Including Ship to Shore Radio-telegrams, 1961–62, 812; 1962–63, 803)	19,848	19,553
Overseas Telex Calls (outward)	4,200	5,500

COUNTER SERVICES

At March 31, 1963 there were 1,822 Crown Post Offices and 23,232 Sub-Post Offices. Postage Stamps to the value of £109.3 million were sold in 1962-63 compared with £108·6 million in 1961–62. 192·9 million Family Allowances to the value of £141·3 million were paid in 1962–63 (1961–62, 188·0 million worth £139·9 million) and 52·7 million Service Allowances to the value of £153·2 million (1961–62: 53·9 million worth £155·3 million). 22·9 million licences were issued in 1962–63 compared with 22·1 million in 1961–62 (Broadcast Receiving Licences, Sound £3·2 million: Combined Sound and Television £50·1 million (including Excise Duty) and other licences to the value of £29·2 million).

Savings Business.—Savings Stamps to the value of £59·3 million were sold in both years. Savings Bank; Deposits £529·4 million (£525·9 million). Withdrawals £402·6 million (£394·3 million); Savings Certificates issued £104·4 million (£102·2 million); Repaid, £92·7 million (£97·8 million); Premium Savings Bonds; Sold £53·5 million (£52·1 million); Repaid £30·95 million (£28·97 million). Prizes Paid £15·63 million (£14·0 million).

Remittance Services.—25·1 million Inland Money Orders to the Value of £335·3 million were paid compared with 25·4 million (£325·9 million) in 1961–62. Overseas Money Orders numbered 2·4 million (£11·2 million) compared with 3·0 million (£12·4 million) in 1961–62. 591·3 million Postal Orders were issued to the Value of £437·6 million compared with 659·7 million in 1961–62 to the value of £444·6 million.

STAFF

On March 31, 1963, the staff of the Post Office numbered 371,744, compared with 366,007 in March, 1962. The total includes 27,000 part-time workers counted as a half each. Staff were divided as follows:—Administration, 7,661; Postal Operating, 170,578; Telecommunications Operating 84,972; Engineering, 96,019; Supply Departments, 7,029; Motor Transport, 5,485.

In addition 22,972 Sub-postmasters are employed on an agency basis.

DEVELOPMENT PLANS, 1963–64

Postal.—The building programme provides for a start to be made on 52 new post offices and 26 sorting or delivery offices and further modernization or replacement of the older post offices. Projects for the further mechanization of postal services include provision of overhead chain conveyors to carry mail in both directions between sorting offices and adjacent railway stations. Development and trials of new types of mail handling machinery will continue.

Inland Telecommunication.—Plans have been made to increase the number of trunk circuits from about 36,000 to about 41,000 during the year, by means of new cables and radio links and by modifying existing cable systems to give greater capacity. The total number of telephone connections at April 1, 1963, approximately 5,209,000, was expected to be increased to 5,459,000 by March 31, 1964 (new connections, 510,000; cessations, 260,000). Estimated number of telephones in use at end of year, 9,257,000. The telephone waiting list was approximately 44,000 on April 1, 1963.

Development of the telephone service to fully automatic standard is planned to be complete by 1970. During 1963–64 a further 100 manual exchanges were due to be converted to automatic working, when nearly 90 per cent. of subscribers will then have automatic service. There are plans for the building of 147 new telephone exchanges and 30 engineering centres and workshops. Subscriber Trunk Dialling—the service which enables subscribers to dial Trunk calls for themselves—is rapidly being introduced throughout the country. It is already available in most of the large towns and cities and by March, 1964, approximately two-fifths of subscribers in the country on about 650 exchanges should have the facility. A new type of coinbox, permitting call office users to dial their own trunk calls, is also being installed. It was planned to introduce about 1,900 new Telex lines during the year, bringing the total to 12,150.

A 580 feet radio tower under construction in Central London was expected to be ready for the installation of equipment early in 1964. The tower will be the tallest building in the U.K. and will have public observation platforms and a rotating restaurant at the top. A 500 feet radio tower of very different design was due to be started in Birmingham during 1963. This would have no public facilities.

Overseas Telecommunications.—In the overseas telegraph service, operators in London can now dial a large number of offices in Western Europe on the Gentex network and teleprint messages straight through. Installation of a "torn tape" message relay unit in London has commenced and improved services and economy in staffing is expected to be achieved as mechanization in this field develops. Direct dialling facilities for U.K. telex subscribers to Europe are being extended and already more than 80 per cent. of British telex calls to Europe are dialled to the distant telex installation by the caller.

The installation of equipment to enable London telephone subscribers to dial calls direct to European numbers continued in preparation for the general introduction of the facility in 1964. Already subscribers on STD equipped exchanges in London can dial calls direct to Paris exchanges. The laying of a further transatlantic cable (TAT3) has started and it was expected to be in service by November, 1963. Work, too, has started on the laying of five new North Sea cables. By December, 1964, there will be two new cables to Germany, one to Denmark and one to Holland. A further cable to Holland is planned for 1966.

EMPLOYMENT IN 1963

Distribution of total manpower in Great Britain

The total working population of Great Britain in mid-June, 1963, was 24,805,000 (males, 16,375,000; females, 8,430,000), compared with 24,818,000 at mid-June, 1962. Included in the total were 15,619,000 males and 8,298,000 females (total, 23,917,000) in civil employment; 461,000 persons wholly unemployed; and 427,000 in H.M. Forces and Women's Services (17,000).

Numbers in Civil Employment, June 1963

Agriculture and Fisheries	893,000	Clothing and Footwear	565,000
Mining and Quarrying	685,000	Other Manufactures	1,647,000
Food, Drink, Tobacco	826,000	Construction	1,657,000
Chemicals and Allied Industries	508,000	Gas, Electricity and Water	397,000
Metal Manufacture	583,000	Transport and Communications	1,658,000
Engineering and Electrical Goods	2,137,000	Distributive Trades	3,350,000
Shipbuilding and Marine Engineering	209,000	Financial, Professional, Scientific, Miscellaneous Services	5,273,000
Vehicles	870,000	National Government Service	535,000
Metal Goods	556,000	Local Government Service	776,000
Textiles	792,000		

UNEMPLOYMENT

Annual average numbers registered as unemployed, 1954–62 and mid-year figure for 1963.

	Great Britain					United Kingdom Total
	Wholly Unemployed (including Casuals)		Temporarily Stopped		Total	
	Males	Females	Males	Females		
1954	176,500	95,100	7,900	5,300	284,800	317,800
1955	137,400	75,700	9,300	9,800	232,200	264,500
1956	151,000	78,600	17,800	9,600	257,000	287,100
1957	204.300	90,200	12,300	5,700	312,500	347,200
1958	293,800	116,300	27,600	19,700	457,400	500,900
1959	322,600	121,900	21,200	9,500	475,200	512,100
1960	248,200	97,500	11,600	3,100	360,400	392,800
1961	226,300	85,800	23,300	5,300	340,700	376,800
1962	321,900	110 000	23,000	8,300	463 200	499 900
1963 (June 10)	*345 666*	*115 036*	*14,226*	*4,785*	*479,713*	*516,135*

Unemployment at July 15, 1963

Classification	Not more than 2 weeks	Wholly Unemployed (including Casuals) Duration of Unemployment: More than 2 weeks but not more than 5 weeks	More than 5 weeks but not more than 8 weeks	More than 8 weeks	Total
Men 18 and over	50,624	39,105	23,766	193,394	306,889
Boys under 18	8,730	4,572	1,680	6,014	20,996
Women 18 and over	16,062	13,978	8,916	54,277	93,233
Girls under 18	6,823	3,135	1,148	3,765	14,871
Total	82,239	60,790	35,510	257,450	435,989

The total includes 52,462 married women.

INDUSTRIAL STOPPAGES IN THE UNITED KINGDOM, 1942–1962

The year 1957 saw the highest number ever recorded of stoppages of work due to industrial disputes, a total of 2,859, involving 1,275,000 workers directly, 81,000 indirectly, and a loss of 8,412,000 working days. In 1962, about 3,785,000 days were lost through two national stoppages of engineering and shipbuilding workers and a stoppage in the railway industry.

Stoppages in progress:—	No. of Workers Involved	Working Days Lost	Stoppages in progress:—	No. of Workers Involved	Working Days Lost
1942	457,000	1,527,000	1953	1,374,000	2,184,000
1943	559,000	1 808,000	1954	450,000	2,457,000
1944	826,000	3,714,000	1955	671,000	3,781,000
1945	532,000	2,835,000	1956	508,000	2,083,000
1946	529,000	2,158,000	1957	1,359,000	8,412,000
1947	623,000	2,433,000	1958	524,000	3,462,000
1948	426,000	1,944,000	1959	646,000	5,270,000
1949	434,000	1,807,000	1960	819,000	3,024,000
1950	303,000	1,389,000	1961	779,000	3,046,000
1951	379,000	1,694,000	1962	4,423,000	5,798,000
1952	416,000	1,792,000			

STOPPAGES OF WORK IN 1962

In the United Kingdom in 1962, there were 2,449 new stoppages of work and a further 16 which had been in progress at the beginning of the year, a total of 2,465 compared with 2,701, stoppages in progress in 1961. 4,423,000 workers were involved in these stoppages, of whom approximately 124,000 were thrown out of work at the establishments where the stoppages occurred, but were not parties to the dispute. The comparable figures for 1961 were 680,000 and 99,000.

In all stoppages in progress in 1962, those involving the greatest numbers of workers and working days lost were as follows:—

	All Stoppages, 1962 Workers Involved	All Stoppages, 1962 Days Lost	New Stoppages 1962
Coal Mining....	154,500	308,000	1,205
Iron and Steel ...	222,100	261,000	65
Engineering*....	1,377,900	1,613,000	159
Shipbuilding....	322,800	46,500	78
Electrical Trades .	672,100	706,000	53
Motor vehicles and cycles.....	508,300	747,000	116
Other metal goods	211,500	239,000	54
Railways........	238,700	239,000	8
All Stoppages....	4,422,700	5,798,000	2,449

AVERAGE EARNINGS AND HOURS OF WORK

Particulars of the earnings of manual wage-earners and hours worked in manufacturing industries generally and in some of the non-manufacturing industries and services are collected periodically by the Ministry of Labour. The average weekly hours of work and average weekly earnings of workers in the United Kingdom in 1938 and in 1957–1963 were as follows:—

	Men (21 years and over)		Women (18 years and over)			
			Full-time		Part-time	
	Hours	Wages s. d.	Hours	Wages s. d.	Hours	Wages s. d.
1938 October†	47·7	69 0	43·5	32 6	—	—
1957 October†	48·2	251 7	41·0	129 9	21·4	64 2
1958 October†	47·7	256 8	41·0	134 1	21·5	66 5
1959 October‡	48·5	271 1	41·4	140 8	21·6	69 0
1960 October‡	48·0	290 8	40·5	148 4	21·7	74 10
1961 April‡	47·9	301 4	39·9	152 7	21·7	78 1
October	47·4	306 10	39·7	154 6	21·8	79 7
1962 April	47·3	312 10	39·6	157 2	21·7	81 0
October	47·0	317 3	39·4	160 10	21·8	83 1
1963 April	46·9	323 1	39·5	163 9	21·7	84 7

† Figures up to 1958 based on (1948) Standard Industrial Classification. ‡ Figures from 1959 on (1958) Classification.

PAY AS YOU EARN, 1960–61

Item	*England and Wales*	*Scotland*	*Northern Ireland*	*United Kingdom*
No. of Employers*	863,000	91,000	20,000	974,000
No. of Employees (millions)	19·55	1·95	0·4	22·85
Total Remuneration (£ million)	12,232	1,090	211	14,170
Total Tax Deducted (£ million)	1,082·4	82·3	14·5	1,245·4

*Approximate: figures are of tax remitting points which report at least one tax deduction card in the current year.

†Excluding £66,200,000 tax paid on remuneration of £637,000,000 by employees not allocated to a particular region.

BRITISH MOTOR VEHICLE PRODUCTION AND EXPORTS

Year	Passenger Cars (including Taxis)		Goods Vehicles		Omnibus Coaches, and Trolleybuses	
	Production	Exports	Production	Exports	Production	Exports
1958	1,051,551	483,877	297,785	105,877	15,071	5,752
1959	1,189,943	568,846	353,105	122,628	17,379	4,832
1960	1,352,728	569,916	438,924	139,139	19,048	6,386
1961	1,003,967	370,758	443,117	160,042	17,050	6,912
1962	1,249,426	544,792	408,514	140,728	16,590	7,413
1963 1st qr.	382,203	150,305	97,431	36,944	4,985	1,882
2nd qr.	420,896	156,372	96,589	39,926	4,607	2,133

Weekly Average Production

The highest average weekly production of cars in a recent year was achieved in 1960 with an average of 26,014. In 1962 average weekly production was again increasing and reached 32,377 in the second quarter of 1963. Average weekly production of goods vehicles reached its highest level in 1961 with 8,521 per week declining to 7,430 per week in the second quarter of 1963. Average weekly production of omnibuses, coaches and trolleybuses was 366 in 1960, 319 in 1962, rising again to 354 in the first quarter of 1963.

AGRICULTURE

Agricultural Holdings

The number of agricultural holdings in Great Britain, excluding rough grazing and holdings consisting solely of mountain and heathland, is:—

	England and Wales	Scotland	Great Britain
Under 5 acres	70,061	13,992	84,053
5 to 50 „	135,511	24,461	159,972
50 to 100 „	56,886	8,581	65,467
100 to 150 „	29,092	5,201	34,293
150 to 300 „	32,646	6,365	39,011
Over 300 „	14,099	2,708	16 807
TOTAL NUMBER	338,295	61,308	399 603

NOTE.—A *farm* may consist of more than one *holding*. It is estimated that there are about 300,000 full-time farmers in Great Britain, and, in addition, about 55,500 part-time or "hobby" farmers.

According to the latest available figures, of the total number of agricultural holdings in Great Britain 78 per cent. were of 100 acres or less in area. In England, the average size was 76 acres, compared with Scotland's 71 acres and an average of 52 acres in Wales. In England and Wales, 95 per cent. of all rural dwellings now have access to a piped water supply, and by 1962, 86·9 per cent. of all farms were provided with a mains supply of electricity. The number of farm horses has fallen by 82 per cent. since 1939 and Britain now has one of the highest tractor densities in the world.

United Kingdom Crop Acreage and Production

Commodity	Acreage (thousand acres)		Estimated harvest (thousand tons)	
	June, 1962	June, 1963	1961	1962
Wheat	2,256	1,926	2,573	3,631
Barley	3,980	4,707	4,974	5,764
Oats	1,519	1,307	1,822	1,747
Mixed Corn	125	97	171	154
Rye (threshed)	17	23	18	17
Potatoes	737	767	6,258	6,658
Sugar Beet	424	422	5,936	—
Fodder Crops:				
Beans	73	} 60	—	—
Peas	8		—	—
Turnips and swedes	393	368	7,723	7,617
Mangolds	105	90	2,719	2,661
Other fodder crops	495	439	—	—
Fruit	271	267	607	—
Vegetables	383	424	2,443	2,790
Temporary Grassland	6,948	6,975		
Permanent Grassland	12,563	12,386		
TOTAL ARABLE LAND	18,093	18,255		

Production of *Straw* in 1962 was: Wheat, 2,097,000 tons (1939, *1,990,000* tons); Oats, 1,557,000 tons (*2,610,000* tons); Barley, 2,812,000 tons (*842,000* tons).

Livestock

There were small decreases in the population of cattle and sheep during 1962–63 and increases in the numbers of pigs and poultry.

Livestock in U.K.	June, 1962 thousands	June, 1963 thousands
Cattle: total	11,859	11,747
Cows and heifers in milk	3 681	3 685
Cows in calf but not in milk	587	587
Heifers in calf with first calf	802	747
Sheep	29 498	29 367
Pigs	6 722	6,920
Poultry	109 030	111,033

Crop Prices, 1962–63

Guaranteed prices for the 1961 and 1962 Harvests

Commodity	1962		1963	
	s.	*d.*	*s.*	*d.*
Wheat, millable; average price per cwt. (*a*)	26	11	26	6
Barley, price per cwt. (*a*) (*b*)	27	7	26	8
Oats, price per cwt. (*b*)	27	5	27	5
Rye, millable, price per cwt.	21	7	21	7
Sugar Beet, 16 per cent. sugar content, per ton	124	8	124	8
Potatoes, standard ware, average per ton	265	0	275	0

(*a*) Subject to seasonal variation. (*b*) Price of merchantable grain only.

Livestock Prices, 1963–64

A list of Guaranteed Prices in 1963–64 of Livestock and Livestock products. Changes from Guaranteed Prices in 1962–63 are indicated where applicable.

	s.	*d.*
FAT CATTLE.—Steers, heifers and special young cows, per live cwt., gross weight, including quality premiums	167	0
FAT SHEEP AND LAMBS.—1st grade, average of shorn and unshorn, and including any headage payments or other bonuses: per lb. estimated dressed carcase weight, excluding caul fat (−1*d.*)	3	2
FAT PIGS.—Clean pigs in quality premium range. Per score dead weight, including quality premiums	44	11*

Livestock Products

	s.	*d.*
MILK.—Average wholesale price, plus production bonus and quality premiums, per gallon (+0·5*d.*)	3	2·35
HEN EGGS.—Sold through packing stations, guaranteed average support price for 1st quality eggs, average per dozen (−1·50*d.*)	3	8·53*
DUCK EGGS.—Sold through packing stations, guaranteed average support price for 1st quality eggs, average per doz.	2	4 46*

WOOL.—Average per lb. greasy for fleece wool, inclusive of increase in marketing cost........................ s. 4 d. 5¼

* Prices shown are standard prices related to a standard feed price. Adjustments are made to take account of changes in the price of feed over the year: fat pig price, 1963–64 is related to a feed price of 25s. 11d. per cwt.; hen and duck egg price, 1963–64 to a feed price of 25s.1d. per cwt.

Estimated Gross Value of Agricultural Output of the United Kingdom

(£ million)

Commodity	Pre-war	1960–61	1961–62
Grain	19·2	153·4	147·9
Potatoes	14·6	64·5	82·5
Sugar Beet	4·7	39·4	32·6
Other farm crops	4·4	13·3	13·4
Livestock (meat)	89·1	429·8	484·3
Milk and milk products	79·9	352·6	364·8
Eggs	31·5	170·9	169·3
Wool	4·2	16·1	17·1
Other livestock products	9·6	77·0	81·7
Fruit	8·5	37·0	52·0
Vegetables	18·9	78·1	85·8
Flowers	6·5	24·7	26·6
Other receipts and valuation changes	9·7	46·0	52·5
Total	300·7	1502·8	1 610·5

Index of Agricultural Prices

Average of 1954/55 to 1956/57 = 100

Commodity	1960*	1961*	1962*
Wheat	89·0	88·0	87·2
Potatoes	92·8	85·2	132·5
Cattle	106·3	106·8	113·6
Bacon Pigs	86·7	84·8	85·5
Milk	95·7	92·3	90·5
Eggs	84·2	87·0	78·6
Materials			
Fertilizers	89·2	86·7	87·4
Compound feeding stuffs	91·1	88·2	89·7

* Gross-price series index, after addition of subsidies paid to producers.

Agricultural Price Guarantees, 1963

In the Annual Review and Determination of Guarantees presented to Parliament in March, 1963, the Government forecast a further substantial increase in the net agricultural output for 1962–63. Taking the average net agricultural output of the years 1954–55 to 1956–57 as 100, the forecast for net output in 1962–63 is 122, compared with revised figures of 117 for 1961–62 and 119 for 1960–61.

The cold spring of 1962 delayed germination but crop yields generally were high. In spite of difficult conditions at harvest time, production of wheat and barley was at a record level. The numbers of sheep and cattle marketed were expected to be broadly the same as in the previous year but there was a notable increase in the number of pigs to be marketed—12,500,000 in 1962–63, compared with 11,250,000 in 1961–62. After the 1962 harvest, tillage operations made excellent progress but the prolonged period of exceptionally severe weather early in 1963 caused many difficulties for farmers. In particular there were losses of ewes in some parts of the country and lambing prospects suffered.

The revised estimate of the net income of the industry in 1961–62 (adjusted for normal weather conditions) is £413,000,000 and the estimate for 1962–63 on the same basis is £407,000,000. Actual net income is forecast at £408,000,000, compared with the revised estimate for 1961–62 of £423,500,000.

The price of goods and services used in agriculture have in general continued to rise. The main items are again the increase in the cost of labour and in rents, but this year there have been substantial reductions in the cost of fertilizers and interest charges. The Exchequer cost in 1961–62 reached £342,600,000. Expenditure in 1962–63 is expected to be down to £321,000,000, but the Estimates for 1963–64 presented to Parliament (which do not take into account the 1963 Determinations) show a further increase to a new high figure of £364,000,000.

The cereals acreage reached a total of nearly 8,000,000 acres in 1962, compared with less than 7,500,000 acres in 1957. Acreage figures show a sharply rising barley acreage, a decline in oats and mixed corn and a wheat acreage fluctuating around 2,000,000 acres. Yields of wheat and barley continue to rise. During the five years to 1962 home barley production rose from 3,000,000 tons to 5,800,000 tons and wheat production from 2,700,000 to 3,600,000 tons, with a general downward turn in market prices. Prices for 1962 cereal crops have been particularly low and the estimated cost of Exchequer support in the financial year 1963–64 is £83,000,000 (1962–63, £64,000,000). Accordingly the guaranteed price of wheat has been reduced by 5d. per cwt. and of barley by 11d. per cwt. Guaranteed prices for other cereals remain unchanged.

The 1962 potato acreage was 30,000 greater than the previous year's but even so was still on the low side. A further increase was considered desirable and the guaranteed price had been raised by 10s. per ton. The present level of the guaranteed price for sugar beet is maintained. Arrangements for the 1963 crop are expected to provide a larger incentive for the production of beet of a higher sugar content.

It was considered unlikely that there would be any significant increase in home production of fat cattle in the near future and no change was made in the guaranteed price. Similarly no change was made in the guaranteed prices for sheep and wool.

The pig breeding herd has been on the increase and is now at a very high level. A basic guaranteed price related to a level of marketings of 10·3 to 10·8 million pigs a year was introduced at the 1961 Review. The present size of the pig herd leads to a forecast of marketings of about 12,500,000 pigs a year. The basic guaranteed price remained unchanged, but it was decided to amend the arrangements for adjusting it according to changes in forecasts of marketings.

The guaranteed price for milk was raised by ½d. a gallon. The increase in production of milk exceeded the increase in consumption of liquid milk by 20,000,000 gallons in 1962–63, compared with an excess of 140,000,000 gallons as recently as 1960–61. This trend is expected to continue, since returns show a levelling-off in the size of the dairy herd and a significant reduction in the numbers of dairy heifers in calf.

The 1963 Review introduced new guarantee arrangements for hen eggs incorporating features analogous to a standard quantity system. They provide for an "indicator price" representing the price that the Egg Marketing Board might expect to receive from a market that was not over-supplied. No change was made in the guaranteed price for eggs.

The Crops of 1963

The following table shows the condition of the principal crops in Great Britain on September 1, compared with the previous five years and with the 10-year averages (1953–62) at the same date:—

	Wheat	Barley	Oats	Potatoes	Sugar Beet	Grass
1958....	89	87	84	76	89	102
1959....	99	96	91	88	87	70
1960....	95	92	90	95	99	99
1961....	92	92	89	87	88	89
1962....	96	94	91	91	94	93
1963....	95	93	92	94	94	98
10-year averages	94	93	90	89	92	92

FISHERIES

Quantity and Value of Fish of British taking landed in Great Britain during 1962*

Kind of Fish	Weight and Value	
	Cwt.	£
Cod	6,298,578	19,176,558
Haddock	2,704,895	9,673,694
Hake	229,786	1,876,194
Plaice	708,363	4,603,143
Skate and Ray	268,845	1,028,483
Whiting	874,805	2,109,076
Herring	1,758,676	2,731,340
Mackerel	86,871	187,941
Other	2,640,692	7,333,342
Total	15,571,511	48,719,771
Shell Fish	—	2,387,315
Grand Total	—	51,107,086

*In 1962, 21,339 Fishermen were regularly, and 5,804 occasionally employed.

LOCAL GOVERNMENT IN THE UNITED KINGDOM

ENGLAND AND WALES

Local government is carried on by directly elected councils whose powers and duties are defined by statute, under the general supervision of various departments of the central government. Departments principally concerned are the Ministries of Housing and Local Government, Education, Health and Transport; and, in matters affecting law and order, police, fire services, care of children, civil defence preparations, etc., the Home Office. Supervision is by means of inspections and enquiries, issue of Regulations and Orders, approval of bye-laws, loan sanctions for capital expenditure, examination of accounts and the administration of government grants.

County Councils.—Constituted by the Local Government Act, 1888, they were made responsible for administrative duties which were previously performed by the justices of the peace in quarter sessions. In the main their functions relate to the more important services. In most cases the area of the administrative county is that of the geographical county, excluding county boroughs. Lincolnshire, Suffolk, Sussex and Yorkshire are exceptions, being divided into parts, each with a separate council, for administrative convenience. Councils consist of a chairman, aldermen and councillors. The chairman, who may receive remuneration, is elected annually by the council, either from among the aldermen or councillors or from persons eligible for election as aldermen or councillors. The aldermen form a quarter of the council; they are elected by the councillors from among themselves or persons eligible to be councillors and hold office for six years, half retiring every three years. Councillors are elected by local government electors for three years. Excluding London there are 61 county councils in England and Wales (*see* pp. 631–3; Wales, pp. 676–7).

County Borough Councils.—Boroughs with populations of 50,000 or more in 1888 and some ancient counties of cities were constituted by the Local Government Act, 1888, as county boroughs; their councils were given the same powers and duties as county councils, but they are also governed by the general law affecting boroughs and have the same constitution. Until 1926 other boroughs reaching 50,000 population could seek county borough status, but the figure was then raised to 75,000. The Local Government Act, 1958, again raised the figure to 100,000, and placed a 15-year prohibition on Private Bills for this purpose. (Although important, level of population is only one factor in the attainment of county borough status.) Luton (Bedfordshire), with a population of approximately 135,000, is constituted a county borough from April 1, 1964. In 1963 there were 83 county borough councils in England and Wales (*see* pp. 664–71; Wales, p. 676).

The district councils within a county are borough councils (other than county borough councils), urban district councils and rural district councils.

Borough Councils.—Constituted in their present form by the Municipal Corporations Act, 1882. Urban district councils may by royal charter be incorporated as boroughs. Borough councils consist of a mayor, aldermen and councillors. The mayor, who presides at council meetings and may be paid, and the aldermen, are elected and hold office for the same terms as chairmen and aldermen of county councils (*see* above). Councillors are elected by the burgesses (local government electors of the borough) for a term of three years, one-third of the council retiring each year. The lists on pp. 672–4 indicate how the political parties were represented on the councils of the more important boroughs in 1963. There are 317 non-county boroughs in England and Wales (*see* pp. 664–71; Wales, p. 676).

Urban and Rural District Councils.—The Public Health Act, 1875, consolidated legislation on public health and conferred various powers and duties on local sanitary authorities and these bodies were reconstituted by the Local Government Act, 1894, as urban and rural district councils. They are corporate bodies and have a common seal. District councils consist of a chairman, elected annually by the council, and councillors elected for a term of three years. The chairman may receive an allowance. An important part of their responsibility is in the local administration of the Public Health Acts and Housing Acts. Urban district councils are also highway authorities. Both types of authority levy rates; they may raise loans for various purposes and make bye-laws with the sanction of the central Government. There are 564 urban district councils and 474 rural district councils in England and Wales.

Parish Councils and Parish Meetings.—Local government responsibility is for the area of the *civil* parish in rural areas and for purely secular matters. Parish meetings consist of all the local government electors of the parish under a chairman chosen by the meeting and must be held at least twice a year where there is no parish council. Parish councils consist of a chairman and a number of councillors which may vary from five to twenty-one, elected for three years. Parishes with a population of more than 300 must have a parish council. A parish meeting must be held annually and is presided over by the chairman of the parish council. Rates to meet the expenses of the parish council are levied by the rural district council.

London.—Local government is carried on by London County Council (*see* pp. 641-4), the Corporation of the City of London (pp. 635-41) and by the councils of the 28 metropolitan boroughs listed on p. 634. The recommendations of a Royal Commission set up to review local government in London, made in October, 1960, were accepted in large part by the Government, legislation being introduced in 1962. The London Government Act (1963) establishing 12 inner and 20 outer London boroughs and a Greater London Council, received the Royal Assent on July 31, 1963. The City of London, besides retaining its present functions, will have the powers of a London borough.

With effect from April 1, 1965, the administrative areas and their councils of the counties of London and Middlesex, together with the metropolitan boroughs and any existing county borough, borough (with its municipal corporation), county district or parish whose area falls wholly within Greater London, will cease to exist. The urban district of Potters Bar will become part of Hertfordshire and the urban districts of Staines and Sunbury-on-Thames part of the county of Surrey.

The following list describes the area of each new London borough by reference to existing areas and shows the initial numbers of councillors to represent the new boroughs on the Greater London Council. Unless otherwise stated, areas named as part of new boroughs are those of existing metropolitan boroughs. Names for nine of the new boroughs (supported by all existing Councils concerned) were agreed by the Minister of Housing and Local Government in September, 1963, and are shown below in capital letters.

Inner London Boroughs

WESTMINSTER (4).—Westminster, Paddington and St. Marylebone.

CAMDEN (3).—Hampstead, Holborn and St. Pancras.

———(3).—Finsbury and Islington.

———(3).—Hackney, Shoreditch and Stoke Newington.

TOWER HAMLETS (2).—Bethnal Green, Poplar and Stepney.

*CHARLTON** (3).—Greenwich and part of Woolwich (south of the Thames).

———(4).—Deptford and Lewisham.

———(4).—Bermondsey, Camberwell and Southwark.

———(4).—Lambeth and part of Wandsworth.

———(4).—Battersea and part of Wandsworth.

———(3).—Fulham and Hammersmith.

———(3).—Chelsea and Kensington.

Outer London Boroughs

———(3).—The boroughs of Chingford, Leyton and Walthamstow.

REDBRIDGE (3).—Ilford and Wanstead and Woodford, with parts of Dagenham and Chigwell.

———(3).—Borough of Romford; Urban District of Hornchurch.

* Agreed in principle—final decision deferred.

———(2).—Parts of boroughs of Barking and Dagenham.

NEWHAM (3).—County boroughs of East Ham and West Ham; part of boroughs of Barking and Woolwich (north of Thames).

———(3).—Boroughs of Bexley and Erith; Urban District of Crayford; part of the Urban District of Chislehurst and Sidcup.

———(4).—Boroughs of Beckenham and Bromley; Urban Districts of Orpington and Penge; part of Urban District of Chislehurst and Sidcup.

CROYDON (4).—County borough of Croydon; Urban District of Coulsdon and Purley.

———(2).—Boroughs of Beddington and Wallington; Sutton and Cheam; Urban District of Carshalton.

———(2).—Boroughs of Mitcham and Wimbledon; Urban District of Merton and Morden.

KINGSTON-UPON-THAMES.—Boroughs of Kingston-upon-Thames; Malden and Coombe; Surbiton.

———(2).—Boroughs of Barnes, Richmond and Twickenham.

———(3).—Boroughs of Brentford and Chiswick; Heston and Isleworth; Urban District of Feltham.

———(3).—Borough of Uxbridge; Urban Districts of Hayes and Harlington; Ruislip-Northwood; Yiewsley and West Drayton.

EALING.(4)—Boroughs of Acton, Ealing and Southall.

———(4).—Boroughs of Wembley & Willesden.

———(3).—Borough of Harrow.

———(4).—Boroughs of Finchley and Hendon; Urban Districts of Barnet, East Barnet and Friern Barnet.

HARINGEY (3).—Boroughs of Hornsey, Tottenham and Wood Green.

———(3).—Boroughs of Edmonton, Enfield and Southgate.

It was announced that Mayors of the new boroughs will be elected in March, 1965, to take office on April 1. The new borough councils will be elected in May, 1964, and will be presided over by elected chairmen during the transitional period from April, 1964 to April, 1965, to avoid confusion while mayors of present boroughs are in office.

Local Government Act, 1958.—The Act provides machinery for the review of areas and status of local authorities in the rest of England and Wales and for making changes where necessary in the interests of effective and convenient administration.

Local Government Elections

Generally speaking all British subjects or citizens of the Republic of Ireland of 21 years or over resident on the qualifying date in the area for which the election is being held are entitled to vote at local government elections. There is also a non-resident qualification (*see* p. 1173). A register of electors is prepared and published annually by local electoral registration officers. There are 9,194,674 local government electors in county boroughs, 15,946,245 in municipal boroughs, urban districts, the City of London and the metropolitan boroughs, and 6,137,585 in rural districts. These figures exclude "Y" voters, *i.e.* persons having their 21st birthday between Oct. 12 and June 16, who are entitled to vote at elections held after Oct. 1 following. County council elections are held triennially, usually in April, and elections for other authorities annually or triennially in May.

Voting takes place at polling stations arranged by the local authority and under the supervision of a presiding officer specially appointed for the purpose. Candidates, who are subject to various statutory qualifications and disqualifications designed to secure that they are suitable persons to hold office, must be nominated by two electors and, except in metropolitan borough, rural district or parish council elections, must secure the assent of eight other electors to the nomination. County council elections are based on divisions of the county regulated by the Home Secretary, each of which returns a single member; most boroughs, including county and metropolitan boroughs, are divided into wards, each electing its own members; other authorities may be so divided or may remain as single units depending upon their sizes.

Local Government Services

Local authorities must in their areas provide the services and carry out the functions required by various Acts of Parliament. They may provide additional services under general permissive legislation or under "local" Acts of Parliament which they have promoted as Private Bills. The nature of the duties imposed on local authorities and the scope of the services which they provide vary according to the type of authority. The only all-purpose council is that of the county borough. In the counties functions are divided between the county council and the borough and district councils and there is considerable delegation of functions by the county council to these other authorities, *e.g.* in education and planning matters. Principal subjects of local government administration are:—

Public health services (prevention of epidemics, abatement of sanitary nuisances, etc.) under the Public Health Act, 1936; local health services under the National Health Service; Care of deprived children; Welfare services for the aged and infirm and for the handicapped, under the National Assistance Act, 1948.

Housing; Land drainage; Water supply; Sewerage; Refuse collection and disposal; Baths and washhouses; Cemeteries.

Town and country planning; Parks and recreation grounds; Smallholdings and allotments.

Roads and bridges; Road safety; Street lighting; Harbours, docks and piers; Passenger transport.

Education; Public libraries, museums and art galleries; Municipal entertainments; Civic restaurants; Information centres.

Police; Fire services; Civil defence services.

Food and drugs inspection; Weights and measures.

Local Government Committees and Staff

Detailed administration of local government services is commonly carried out by committees, matters of policy being decided by the council as a whole; the appointment of certain committees is made compulsory by Act of Parliament. Committees may be executive or advisory; they may be constituted on a permanent basis as Standing Committees or as Special Committees set up for a limited period to deal with a particular subject; their powers and duties are laid down in the Standing Orders of the Council (subject in some cases to special statutory provisions). Where services such as water supply and sewerage are shared between two or more authorities, Joint Committees or Boards of representatives of the authorities concerned are set up to administer the service Police forces of counties are administered in this way by the Standing Joint Committee of members drawn in equal numbers from the county council and the justices in quarter sessions.

The executive policy of the local authority is carried out by a salaried staff varying in number according to the type of authority. The chief official is, in boroughs, the Town Clerk, and elsewhere the Clerk of the Council, and these appointments, together with those of certain other executive officers, are compulsory. Appointments of staff (including professional, technical and clerical classes, and manual workers) are made to a set establishment.

Local Government Finance

Local government is financed from various sources. (1) *Rates.*—Levied by county borough, borough and district councils and in London by the City Corporation and the metropolitan boroughs. Sums required by county councils are included in the rates levied by metropolitan and non-county borough and district councils. Rates are levied by a poundage tax on the rateable value of property in the area of the rating authority. New valuation lists, prepared by valuation officers of the Board of Inland Revenue, came into force on April 1, 1963. All *de-rating* then ceased (apart from the exemption of agricultural land and buildings) and all rateable property was assessed at its current rental value. (2) *Government Grants.*—From 1948–49 to 1958–59, the Exchequer made annual equalization grants to counties and county boroughs whose rateable value was below the average rateable value per head of weighted population in England and Wales to bring their respective rateable values up to the average level. Equalization grants replaced the former "block" grants paid to local authorities until 1948, which included an element of compensation for loss of revenue through de-rating. Percentage grants covered an agreed proportion of expenditure on approved services such as education, health, police and fire services. Special grants were also made.

The Local Government Act, 1958, provided for a new general grant, payable from 1959–60 onwards, in replacement of a number of specific grants, of which the largest were for the education, local health, fire and child care services. The amount of the general grant is fixed in advance for a period of not less than two years though not necessarily at the same level for each year of the period and it may subsequently be increased if there is an unforeseen increase in the level of prices, costs and remuneration. This general grant is distributed to all County and County Borough Councils by reference to objective factors (such as population and numbers of school children) which are readily ascertainable and afford a fair and reasonable measure of the relative needs of each authority.

The equalization grant mentioned above ceased to be payable after 1958–59, except for balances due in respect of previous years, and was replaced for 1959–60 onwards by a rate deficiency grant based on rate products instead of rateable values as hitherto. This is paid direct to County District Councils and to Counties and County Boroughs whose resources in terms of rate product per head of population are below the average.

(3) *Loans.*—Local authorities may raise loans on the security of the rates, with the sanction of the central Government department directly concerned, for capital expenditure on housing, roads, markets, municipal transport services, sewerage works, etc. On March 31, 1961, there were outstanding loans in England and Wales to the amount of

£6,018,921,000; against this total the sum of £29,758,000 stood at the credit of various sinking funds.

Income of Local Authorities, 1960–61

Revenue from:—	
Rates (including payments by Transport and Electricity Services)	£696,667,000
Government Grants	755,963,000
Private Improvements	7,777,000
Housing (Rents, etc.)	216 106,000
Town and Country Planning	3 082,000
Small Holdings and Allotments	2 216,000
Trading Services:—	
Water Supply	62 064,000
Passenger Transport	78,166,000
Cemeteries, Crematoria	3,956,000
Harbours, Docks, Piers, etc.	46 008,000
Other‡	30 445,000
Miscellaneous Income†	188 437,000
Total	£2,090 887,000
Capital Receipts:—	
Loans	£530 425,000
Government Grants	19 289,000
Repayment of Advances	36,369,000
Sales and other sources	24,218,000
Total	£610 301,000
Total Receipts	£2,701,188,000

‡ Including corporation estates, ferries, markets and civic restaurants.

† Including certain tolls, fees, rents and interest.

Expenditure	1960–61
Education	£752 438,000
Libraries and Museums	21 799,000
Local Health Services (N.H.S.)	72 484,000
Public Health Services:—	
Sewers and Sewage Disposal	43,902,000
House and Trade Refuse	40 970,000
Baths and Washhouses	9,809,000
Parks, Pleasure Grounds, etc.	28,929,000
Other	18 549,000
Care of the Aged, Handicapped and Homeless	38 908,000
Protection of Children	23,175,000
Housing	301,184,000
Town and Country Planning	13 574,000
Allotments and Small Holdings	4 068,000
Land Drainage, etc.	13,050,000
Highways and Bridges	119,853 000
Private Street Works	7,896,000
Public Lighting	18 634 000
Fire Service	29,199,000
Police	122,210,000
Administration of Justice	11 503,000
Civil Defence	5 591,000
Trading Services.—	
Water Supply	67 668,000
Passenger Transport	78 693,000
Cemeteries, Crematoria	8,020,000
Harbours, Docks and Piers	45 756,000
Other Trading Services	30 630,000
Other Works and Purposes	32 459,000
Unallotted	57,100 000
Total	£2 018,451,000
Capital Expenditure	620,754,000
Total Expenditure	£2,639 205,000

Rates and Rateable Values

Year	Total Receipts from Rates	Value on which levied	Average per £ of Rateable Value	
	£	£	s.	d.
1952–53	334,254,000	340,991,000	19	7
1953–54	375,048,000	347,278,000	21	7
1954–55	391,130,000	353,924,000	22	1
1955–56	400,707,000	361,818,000	22	2
1956–57	492,466,000	629,444,000	15	3
1957–58	528,115,000	601,873,000	17	7
1958–59	551,678 000	610,240,000	18	2
1959–60	646 608 000	687,618,000	18	10
1960–61	694,097,000	702,373,000	19	9
1961–62*	746,000,000	719,817,000	20	9
1962–63*	828,000,000	736,616,000	22	6

* Provisional.

Average Rates

	1962–63		1963–64	
	s.	d.	s.	d.
County Boroughs	23	5	9	11
Metropolitan Boroughs	20	3	7	9
Non-County Boroughs	24	1	9	10
Urban Districts	23	7	9	7
Rural Districts	21	2	8	7

Product of 1d. Rate and amount raised per Head of Population in 1963–64

	Product of 1*d.* Rate (Net)	Rates Raised per Head, 1963–64 (Net Rates)	
	£	s.	d.
Westminster	275,000	5,237	6
Birmingham	200,300	445	6
Manchester	104,100	435	5
Liverpool	101,268	372	4
St. Marylebone	95,000	2,372	7
Sheffield	81,629	369	3
Bristol	80,500	433	9
Leeds	80,175	373	11
St. Pancras	79,975	770	11
Kensington	71,200	687	1
Wandsworth	65,200	352	5
Croydon	58,806	445	1
Nottingham	57,400	346	11
Leicester	53,750	481	3
Lambeth	53,000	417	7
Ealing	50,500	451	10
Coventry	50,000	405	7
Cardiff	47,500	401	8
Newcastle	46,850	442	0
Holborn	44,700	395	1
Hendon	44,500	484	3
Brighton	43,350	481	1
Harrow	43,350	364	0
Southampton	41,550	456	4
Willesden	39,500	433	8
Wembley	39,000	505	10
Islington	38,600	311	8
Bournemouth	37,700	483	1
Paddington	37,200	576	4
Bradford	37,000	307	3
West Ham	36,500	474	5

The figures above are from the *Annual Return of Rates* issued by The Institute of Municipal Treasurers and Accountants (Incorporated), 1 Buckingham Place, Westminster, S.W.1.

SCOTLAND

Scotland is divided for local government purposes into counties, burghs and districts, and local authorities are similar to those in England and Wales.

County Councils.—First constituted in 1889, they are responsible for local government of the geographical area of the county excluding for most purposes the large burghs. For certain purposes the counties of Perth and Kinross, and Moray and Nairn are combined. County councils include representatives from the landward areas and from all the burghs which are within the county for any purpose, town councils electing representatives from among their own members. Councillors are elected triennially. The chairman of the county council is the convener of the County. There are 33 county councils in Scotland (*see* pp. 680–1).

Town Councils.—The town councils of the counties of cities (Edinburgh, Glasgow, Aberdeen and Dundee) are all-purpose authorities similar to the county borough councils in England and Wales and are presided over by the Lord Provost.

Scottish burghs are Royal burghs (incorporated by Royal Charter, 69), Parliamentary burghs (created by the Reform Act, 1832, with the right to send members to Parliament, 14) and Police burghs (all other burghs with a population of 7,000 or more, 115). Town councils consist of a provost (chairman), bailies and councillors. The provost and bailies (the equivalent of aldermen in England) are elected by the councillors from among themselves and hold office for three years; they are the magistrates of the burgh.

Large burghs, other than the counties of cities, are independent for all purposes except that for valuation, electoral registration, education and, in some cases, police, they are included in the county; small burghs are within the county not only for these purposes but also for such purposes as classified roads, planning, etc.

There are 199 town councils in Scotland (counties of cities, 4; other large burghs, 20; small burghs, 175). (*See* pp. 681–2; 684–5.)

District Councils.—Outside the burghs the county council is responsible for most local government functions but district councils have statutory functions with regard to recreation grounds, rights of way, allotments, bus shelters and other local matters. Two counties—Kinross and Nairn—are not divided into districts. District councils consist of elected members and the county councillors for the district *ex officio*. There are 199 district councils in Scotland.

Local Government Electors—In Scotland there are 1,244,902 electors in counties of cities, 56,568 in other large burghs, 620,687 in small burghs and 963,682 in landward areas—Total 3,397,839.

Rates and Rateable Values

Year	Total Receipts from Rates	Value on which levied	Average per £ of Rateable Value	
	£	£	s.	d.
1956–57...	63,118,000	57,806,000	21	10
1957–58...	66,700,000	58,396,000	22	10
1958–59...	70,953,000	60,278,000	23	7
1959–60...	74,621,000	63,564,000	23	6
1960–61 ..	77,372,000	65,226,000	23	9
1961–62‡..	93,656,000	96,718,000	19	4
1962–63†..	97,776,000	96,734,000	20	3

‡ Provisional.

Product of 1d. rate in Scottish Cities

The estimated product of 1*d.* in Glasgow in 1962–63 was £85,918; in Dundee, £16,300; and in Aberdeen, £14,756. Amounts of rates raised per head were: Glasgow 23*s.* 7*d.*; Dundee, 410*s.* 10*d.*; and Aberdeen, 407*s.* 3*d.*

NORTHERN IRELAND

The structure of local government in Northern Ireland is similar to that of England and Wales. Types of local authority are: county councils, 6; county boroughs, 2; non-county boroughs or municipal councils, 9; urban district councils, 25; and rural district councils, 31. (*See* p. 691.)

Electors.—The register published on Feb. 15, 1961, contained the names of 645,461 local government electors. Of this total, 198,639 related to the County Borough of Belfast and 22,414 to Londonderry County Borough. A new electoral register will be published on Feb. 15, 1964.

Local Government Debts.—The total amount of outstanding loans and capitalized annuities in Northern Ireland on March 31, 1962, was £127,550,255 (excluding Hospitals).

POLICE

The Police of England and Wales are administered by the Home Office, those of Scotland by the Scottish Home and Health Department and those of Northern Ireland by the Ministry of Home Affairs.

Strength of the Police Force.

Year	England & Wales	Scotland
1957................	69,882	7,933
1958................	71,514	8,106
1959................	72,685	8,307
1960................	72,396	8,39[illegible]
1961	75,324	8,730
1962................	75,365	9,227

In 1962 there were 2,346 women police in England and Wales; in Scotland there were 300.

On Dec. 31, 1961, the number of special constables enrolled in England and Wales was: Men, 45,730; Women, 1,022; Scotland (May, 1963): Men, 7,112; Women, 101.

On May 31, 1963, the Metropolitan Police had a total strength of 18,276; including 447 women; City Police, 779, including 17 women.

LONDON FIRE BRIGADE

Headquarters: Albert Embankment, S.E.1.

The former Metropolitan Fire Brigade (founded 1866) was taken over by London County Council under the Local Government Act, 1888, and in 1904 the title " London Fire Brigade " was adopted. The Brigade was considerably augmented during the 1939–45 war, when it was part of the National Fire Service (1941–March 31, 1948).

The number of calls to which the Brigade responded during the year ending December 31, 1962, totalled 28,926, the fires numbered 13,330, chimney fires 3,404, false alarms 8,618 (including 4,195 malicious false alarms), and the calls to perform special services numbered 3,574. The Brigade has 58 land and 2 river stations and an establishment of 2,983 men and 233 appliances in commission.

Under the provisions of the Civil Defence Act, 1948, an Auxiliary Fire Service was re-established.

Chief Officer, L. W. T. Leete, M.B.E.
Deputy Chief Officer, J. K. H. Cunningham, M.B.E.
Assistant Chief Officers, A. S. Shawyer, M.B.E.; F. R. Trust, M.B.E.
Administrative Officer.—E. W. Parker.

THE KINGDOM OF ENGLAND

Position and Extent.—The Kingdom of England occupies the southern portion of the island of Great Britain and lies between 55° 46′ and 49° 57′ 30″ N. latitude (from the mouth of the Tweed to the Lizard), and between 1° 46′ E. and 5° 43′ W. (from Lowestoft to Land's End). England is bounded on the north by the summit of the Cheviot Hills, which form a natural boundary with the Kingdom of Scotland; on the south by the English Channel; on the east by the Straits of Dover (Pas de Calais) and the North Sea; and on the west by the Atlantic Ocean, Wales and the Irish Sea. It has a total area of 50,332 sq. miles (land, 50,056; inland water, 276) and a population estimated (June 30, 1962) of 44,017,660.

Relief.—There is a natural orographic division into the hilly districts of the north, west and south-west, and the undulating downs and low-lying plains of the east and south-east. In the extreme north the *Cheviot Hills* run from east to west, culminating in the Cheviot, 2,676 feet above mean sea level. Divided from the Cheviots by the Tyne Gap is the *Pennine Chain*, running N. by W. to S. by E., with its highest point in Cross Fell, 2,930 feet above mean sea level. West of the Pennines are the *Cumbrian Mountains*, which contain in *Scafell Pike* (3,210 feet) the highest land in England, and east of the Pennines are the *Yorkshire Moors*, their highest point being Urra Moor (1,489 feet). South of the Pennines are the *Peak of Derbyshire* (2,088 feet) and *Dartmoor* (High Willhays, 2,039 feet). In the western county of Shropshire are the isolated Wrekin (1,335 feet), Longmynd (1,696 feet), and Brown Clee (1,792 feet); in Herefordshire the Black Mountain (2,310 feet), in Worcestershire the Malvern Hills (1,395 feet), in Monmouthshire (now usually grouped with Wales) the Sugar Loaf (1,955 feet) and Coity (1,905 feet), and the Cotswold Hills of Gloucestershire contain Cleeve Cloud (1,134 feet).

Hydrography.—The *Thames* is the longest and most important river of England, with a total length of 210 miles from its source in the Cotswold Hills to its outflow into the North Sea, and is navigable by ocean-going steamers to London Bridge. The Thames is tidal to Teddington (69 miles from its mouth) and forms county boundaries almost throughout its course; on its banks are situated London, the capital of the British Commonwealth; Windsor Castle, the home of the Sovereign, Eton College, the first of the public schools, and Oxford, the oldest university in the kingdom. The *Severn* is the longest river in Great Britain, rising in the north-eastern slopes of Plinlimmon (Wales) and entering England in Shropshire, with a total length of 220 miles from its source to its outflow into the Bristol Channel, where it receives on the left the Bristol Avon, and on the right the Wye, its other tributaries being the Vyrnwy, Tern, Stour, Teme and Upper (or Warwickshire) Avon. The Severn is tidal below Gloucester, and a high bore or tidal wave sometimes reverses the flow as high as Tewkesbury (13½ miles above Gloucester). The scenery of the greater part of the river is very picturesque and beautiful, and the Severn is a noted salmon river, some of its tributaries being famous for trout. Navigation is assisted by the Gloucester and Berkeley Ship Canal (16¾ miles), which admits vessels of 350 tons to Gloucester. The *Severn Tunnel*, 14 miles below the Sharpness Bridge, begun in 1873 and completed in 1886 (at a cost of £2,000,000) after many difficulties from flooding is 4 miles 624 yards in length (of which 2¼ miles are under the river). A road bridge over the Severn estuary, between Haysgate, Mon., and Almondsbury, Glos., (which will be the largest in Europe and the third largest in the world, with a centre span of 3,300 ft.) was under construction in 1963. Of the remaining English rivers those flowing into the North Sea are the Tyne, Wear, Tees, Ouse and Trent from the Pennine Range, the Great Ouse (160 miles) from the Central Plain, and the Orwell and Stour from the hills of East Anglia. Flowing into the English Channel are the Sussex Ouse from the Weald, the Itchen from the Wiltshire and Hampshire Hills, and the Axe, Teign, Dart, Tamar and Exe from the Devonian Hills; and flowing into the Irish Sea are the Mersey, Ribble and Eden from the western slopes of the Pennines and the Derwent from the Cumbrian Mountains. The *English Lakes* are noteworthy rather for their picturesque scenery and poetic associations than for their size. These lie mainly in Cumberland, but partly in Westmorland and Lancashire, the largest being Windermere (10 miles long), Ullswater and Derwentwater.

Islands.—The *Isle of Wight* is separated from Hampshire by the Solent; total area 147 sq. miles, population (estimated, 1962), 93,090. The climate is mild and healthy, and many watering places have grown up during the last century. Capital, Newport, at the head of the estuary of the Medina, Cowes (at the mouth) being the chief port; other centres are Ryde, Sandown, Shanklin, Ventnor, Freshwater, Yarmouth, Totland Bay, Seaview and Bembridge. The *Scilly Islands*, 25 miles from Land's End, consist of about 40 islands, with a total area of about 4,000 acres, only St. Mary's Tresco, St. Martin's, St. Agnes and Bryher being inhabited. The capital is Hugh Town, in St. Mary's. The climate is unusually mild, and vegetation luxuriant, semi-tropical plants flourishing in the open. *Lundy* (=Island), 11 miles N.W. of Hartland Point, Devon, is about 2 miles long and about ½ mile broad (average), with a total area of about 1,050 acres (mainly picturesque), and a population of about 20; it contains the seat of the proprietor of the island and 3 lighthouses (one disused).

Climate.—The *mean annual air temperature* reduced to sea-level varies from 52° F. at Penzance and the Scilly Islands to 48° F. near Berwick-on-Tweed. In January the south and west are warmer than the east, the mean temperature reduced to sea-level being less than 40° F. over the eastern half of the country. In July the warmest districts are more definitely in the south and inland, the range being from 63° F. around London to less than 59° F. in the extreme north. The decrease of mean temperature with height is about 1° F. per 300 ft. The coldest month of the year is January and the warmest July. Sea temperature reaches its maximum rather later than air temperature. The average annual *rainfall* decreases from west to east, owing to the preponderance of south-west winds, and also increases with altitude. Of the total area 55 per cent. has an average less than 30 in., 29 per cent. between 30 in. and 40 in. and 16 per cent. more than 40 in. In the neighbourhood of the Thames Estuary the average is only 20 in.; at Seathwaite, Cumberland, 122 in.; and at the wettest spot in the Lake District 185 in. The months of least rain are March to June and the wettest months October to January. September is on the average drier than July and August. The mean annual number of hours of bright *sunshine* varies from 1,750 hours along the south-east coast to less than 1,300 hours in the neighbourhood of the Pennine range. June is the sunniest month followed by May, July, August and September in that order.

EARLY INHABITANTS

Prehistoric Man.—Palæolithic and Neolithic remains are abundantly found throughout England. The Neolithic period is held to have merged into the Bronze Age about 2000 to 1500 B.C., and a date between these years has been given to *Stonehenge* (10 miles N. of Salisbury, Wiltshire) which consists of two circles of menhirs (the largest monolith being 22½ feet in height). The village of *Avebury* and its surroundings were scheduled in 1937, and in 1943 about 1,000 acres at Avebury were purchased by the National Trust, thus preserving the Circle of megalithic monuments, the Avenue, Silbury Hill, etc., relics of Stone Age culture of 1900–1800 B.C., which make this one of the most important archæological sites in Europe. The *Devil's Arrows*, near Boroughbridge, Yorkshire, are regarded as the finest remaining megalithic monoliths in northern Europe; the tallest arrow is 30 ft. 6 in. high and its greatest circumference is 16 ft. In the latter part of the Bronze Age the *Goidels*, a people of Celtic race, and in the Iron Age other Celtic races of *Brythons* and *Belgae*, invaded the country and brought with them Celtic civilization and dialects, place names in England bearing witness to the spread of the invasion over the whole kingdom.

The Roman Conquest.—Julius Cæsar raided Britain in 55 B.C. and 54 B.C. The Emperor Claudius, nearly 100 years later (A.D. 42), dispatched Aulus Plautius, with a well-equipped force of 40,000 all arms, and himself followed with reinforcements in the same year. The British leader from A.D. 48–51 was *Caratacus* (Caractacus), who was finally captured and sent to Rome. By A.D. 70 the conquest of South Britain was completed, a great revolt under *Boadicea*, Queen of the Icĕni, being crushed in A.D. 61. In A.D. 122, the Emperor Hadrian visited Britain and built a continuous rampart, since known as *Hadrian's Wall*, from Wallsend to Bowness (Tyne to Solway). The work was entrusted by the Emperor Hadrian to Aulus Platorius Nepos, legate of Britain from 122 to 126, the work being now regarded as "the greatest and most impressive relic of the Roman frontier system in Europe." The Romans administered Britain as a Province under a Governor, with a well-defined system of local government, each Roman municipality ruling itself and the surrounding territory. Colchester, Lincoln, York, Gloucester and St. Albans stand on the sites of five Roman municipalities, while London was the centre of the road system and the seat of the financial officials of the Province of Britain. Well-preserved Roman towns have been uncovered at (or near) *Silchester* (Calleva Atrebatum), 10 miles south of Reading, *Wroxeter* (Viroconium), near Shrewsbury, and *St. Albans* (Verulamium) in Hertfordshire. Four main groups of roads radiated from London, and a fifth (the Fosse) ran obliquely from Ermine Street (at Lincoln), through Leicester, Cirencester and Bath to Exeter. Of the four groups radiating from London one ran S.E. to Canterbury and the coast of Kent, a second to Silchester and thence to parts of Western Britain and South Wales, a third (now known as *Watling Street*) ran through Verulamium to Chester, with various branches, and the fourth reached Colchester, Lincoln, York and the eastern counties. *Christianity* reached the Roman province of Britain from Gaul in the 3rd century (or possibly earlier), *Alban*, "the protomartyr of Britain," being put to death as a Christian during the persecution of Diocletian (June 22, 303), at his native town Verulamium. The Bishops of Londinium, Eboracum (York), and Lindum (Lincoln) attended the Council of Arles in 314. The Roman garrison of Britain was much harassed in the 4th century by Saxon pirates, who invaded the eastern counties. A system of coast defence was organized from the Wash to Southampton Water, with forts at Brancaster, Burgh Castle (Yarmouth), Walton (Felixstowe), Bradwell, Reculver, Richborough, Dover, Stutfall, Pevensey and Porchester (Portsmouth). About A.D. 350 incursions in the north of Irish (Scoti) and Picts became most formidable, and towards the end of the 4th century many troops were removed from Britain for service in other parts of the Roman Empire. Early in the 5th century Gaul was taken from the Romans by Teutonic invaders and Britain was cut off from Rome. The last Roman garrison was withdrawn from Britain in A.D. 442 and the S.E. portion was conquered by the Saxons. The Latin-speaking Celts of England were replaced by their heathen and Teutonic conquerors, to the submergence of the Christian religion and the loss of Latin speech. According to legend, the British King *Vortigern* called in the Saxons to defend him against the Picts, the Saxon chieftains being *Hengist* and *Horsa*, who landed at Ebbsfleet, Kent, and established themselves in the Isle of Thanet. Bede, a Northumbrian monk, author of the Ecclesiastical History at the opening of the 8th century, described these settlers as Jutes, and there are traces of differences in Kentish customs from those of other Anglo-Saxon kingdoms.

Anglo-Saxons and Normans.—What happened in Britain during the 150 years which elapsed between the final break with Rome and the coming of St. Augustine is shrouded in the deepest mystery. The Jutes, the Saxons and the Angles (whose gods Twi, Woden, Thunor and Frigg are commemorated in "Tuesday, Wednesday, Thursday and Friday") were converted to Christianity by a mission under Augustine (dispatched by Pope Gregory in 597), which established Archbishoprics at Canterbury and York, and England appears to have been again converted by the end of the 7th century. In the 8th century Offa, King of Mercia, is stated to have built a wall and rampart, afterwards known as *Offa's Dike*, from the mouth of the Dee to that of the Wye, as a protection against the Welsh. The greatest of the English kingdoms was *Wessex*, with its capital at Winchester, and the greatest of the Wessex kings was *Alfred the Great* (871–901), who resisted the incursions of the Northmen (Danes) and fixed a limit to their advance by the Treaty of Wedmore (878). In the 10th century the Kings of Wessex recovered the whole of England from the Danes, but subsequent rulers were unable to resist the invaders, and England paid tribute (*Danegelt*) for many years, and was ruled by Danish Kings from 1016 to 1042, when Edward the Confessor was recalled from exile. In 1066 Harold (brother-in-law of Edward and son of Earl Godwin of Wessex) was chosen King of England, but after defeating (at Stamford Bridge, Yorkshire, Sept. 25) an invading army under Harald Hadraada, King of Norway (aided by the outlawed Earl Tostig, of Northumbria, younger son of Earl Godwin), he was himself defeated at the *Battle of Hastings* on Oct. 14, 1066, and the Norman Conquest secured the throne of England for Duke William of Normandy.

AREA AND POPULATION OF ENGLISH COUNTIES.

County or Shire and Administrative Headquarters	Acreage 1961	Population of Counties, Estimated, 1962		Rateable Value April, 1962 (c) £	Average Rates 1962–63 s. d.
		Administrative (a)	Geographical (b)		
Bedfordshire (Bedford)	302,941	395,990	395,990	5,711,409	23 1
Berkshire (Reading)	463,830	405,900	527,320	5,660,271	23 11
Buckinghamshire (Aylesbury)	479,407	505,130	505,130	8,334,762	24 5
Cambridgeshire (Cambridge)	315,168	193,390	193,390	2,863,260	24 8
Cheshire (Chester)	649,525	944,190	1,392,220	12,807,159	22 8
Cornwall (Truro)	868,260	340,880	340,880	3,921,778	24 6
Cumberland (The Courts, Carlisle)	973,147	223,330	294,130	2,328,653	24 5
Derbyshire (Matlock)	643,572	758,270	890,180	8,797,079	22 8
Devonshire (The Castle, Exeter)	1,671,572	536,490	825,340	7,648,811	22 10
Dorset (Dorchester)	623,746	319,800	319,800	4,245,352	25 1
Durham (Durham)	649,431	964,550	1,530,170	10,596,904	23 2
Ely, Isle of (March)	239,950	89,420	89,420	1,006,614	24 6
Essex (Chelmsford)	978,091	1,895,600	2,324,120	28,007,639	25 0
Gloucestershire (Gloucester)	804,932	509,300	1,013,740	6,471,328	23 11
Hampshire (The Castle, Winchester)	962,192	801,740	1,384,030	11,508,718	21 1
Herefordshire (Hereford)	538,924	132,670	132,670	1,387,320	27 0
Hertfordshire (Hertford)	404,525	857,200	857,200	14,339,399	24 0
Huntingdonshire (Huntingdon)	233,985	85,520	85,520	1,014,922	22 1
Kent (Maidstone)	975,923	1,695,560	1,726,280	26,871,508	23 0
Lancashire (Preston)	1,201,851	2,237,810	5,160,660	27,016,162	23 7
Leicestershire (Grey Friars, Leicester)	532,387	419,030	691,530	5,087,769	21 3
Lincolnshire:—					
Holland (Boston)	267,847	104,030	104,030	1,011,589	22 1
Kesteven (Sleaford)	462,100	140,260	140,260	1,482,942	22 8
Lindsey (Lincoln)	974,438	338,500	512,210	4,917,637	21 3
London (County Hall, S.E.1)	74,898	3,185,770	3,185,770	110,896,291	..
Middlesex (Guildhall, S.W.1)	148,684	2,239,770	2,239,770	46,319,112	20 8
Norfolk (Thorpe Road, Norwich)	1,314,331	396,210	568,420	3,821,715	21 4
Northamptonshire (Northampton)	585,148	300,960	405,870	3,741,444	25 3
Northumberland (Newcastle on Tyne)	1,291,977	487,170	825,650	5,529,825	22 7
Nottinghamshire (Nottingham)	540,016	602,160	916,520	7,455,468	22 1
Oxfordshire (Oxford)	479,177	211,320	317,880	2,502,740	21 5
Peterborough, Soke of (Peterborough)	53,464	77,400	77,400	1,074,218	24 3
Rutland (Catmose, Oakham)	97,273	26,390	26,390	287,772	18 11
Shropshire (Shrewsbury)	861,800	306,150	306,150	3,482,328	24 3
Somerset (Taunton)	1,032,325	527,240	609,410	6,565,385	22 6
Staffordshire (Stafford)	738,248	1,013,670	1,765,550	11,525,061	22 8
Suffolk:—					
East Suffolk (Ipswich)	557,354	234,880	353,290	2,603,878	23 4
West Suffolk (Bury St. Edmunds)	390,917	135,080	135,080	1,338,414	21 6
Surrey (Kingston on Thames)	461,833	1,491,000	1,744,690	28,749,714	21 2
Sussex:—					
East Sussex (Lewes)	527,210	383,100	673,190	6,783,905	21 1
West Sussex (Chichester)	405,349	418,470	418,470	8,317,407	19 9
Warwickshire (Warwick)	628,969	633,230	2,058,950	8,850,771	24 4
Westmorland (Kendal)	504,917	32,550	32,550	859,665	22 9
Wight, Isle of (Newport, I. of W.)	94,141	93,090	93,090	1,520,222	26 3
Wiltshire (Trowbridge)	860,611	439,260	439,260	5,378,441	22 7
Worcestershire (Worcester)	447,943	450,400	581,270	5,635,114	22 10
Yorkshire:—					
East Riding (Beverley)	750,385	228,530	530,170	2,782,963	21 4
North Riding (Northallerton)	1,361,788	407,390	565,080	5,524,328	22 5
West Riding (Wakefield)	1,785,767	1,677,260	3,677,220	17,072,404	22 5

(*a*) Administrative Counties, excluding County Boroughs, named in the First Schedule of the Local Government Act, 1933; (*b*) Geographical Counties, including County Boroughs; in each case as at the Census of April, 1961 (preliminary figures); (*c*) includes value of property occupied by the Crown for public purposes upon which contributions in lieu of rates are paid.

Lords Lieutenant of Counties.—The actual words used in the Letters Patent relative to these appointments are "Her Majesty's Lieutenant of and in the County of . . ." and this is the official title whether the individual appointed be a Peer or a Commoner. In documents of the highest formality the proper term is therefore "Her Majesty's Lieutenant." In less formal and informal documents and colloquially, the style "Lord Lieutenant" has been applied to H. M. Lieutenants, Peers and Commoners alike, for a great many years. The duties of the Lord Lieutenant are to advise the Lord Chancellor as to the appointment of magistrates to the county bench, to appoint Deputy Lieutenants and to raise the militia, if need be, in time of riot or invasion. The Lord Lieutenant is usually a peer or a baronet and a large landowner and is often appointed *custos rotulorum* (keeper of the records).

LORDS LIEUTENANT, HIGH SHERIFFS, AND CHAIRMEN OF QUARTER SESSIONS

County or Shire	Lord Lieutenant	*High Sheriff 1963–64	Chairman of Q.S.
(1) Bedford	Maj. Simon Whitbread.	W. W. S. Robertson, C.B.E.	W. W. Stabb.
(2) Berks	Maj. the Hon. David Smith.	Hon. H. W. Astor.	Rt. Hon. Sir Malcolm Hilbery.
(3) Bucks	Brig. Sir Henry Floyd, Bt., C.B., C.B.E.	D. J. Robarts.	The Rt. Hon. Lord Justice Davies.
(4) Cambridge	R. H. Parker, C.B.E., M.C.	Col. G. T. Hurrell, O.B.E.	W. Lawson Campbell.
(5) Isle of Ely			
(6) Cheshire	The Viscount Leverhulme, T.D.	Maj. J. N. Davies-Colley, M.C.	His Hon. Judge G. G. Lind-Smith.
(7) Cornwall	Col. Sir John C. Pole, Bt., D.S.O., [T.D.	Cdr. R. M. Favell, R.N. (*ret.*).	Hon. Mr. Justice Marshall.
(8) Cumberland	Sir Fergus Graham, Bt., K.B.E., T.D.	W. Walker.	J. M. Davies, Q.C.
(9) Derby	Lt.-Col. Sir Ian Walker-Okeover, Bt., D.S.O., T.D.	S. D. Player.	His Hon. Judge H. G. Talbot.
(10) Devon	The Lord Roborough.	P. D. Tuckett.	His Hon. Judge H. MacD. Pratt.
(11) Dorset	Col. the Lord Digby, K.G., D.S.O., M.C., T.D.	Col. R. J. Longfield.	G. D. Squibb, Q.C.
(12) Durham	The Lord Barnard, C.M.G., O.B.E., [M.C., T.D.	Cdr. S. Stevenson, R.N. (*ret.*)	W. L. Burn.
(13) Essex	Col. Sir John Ruggles-Brise, Bt., C.B., O.B.E., T.D.	Col. H. E. H. Jones, M.C., T.D.	J. R. Adams, Q.C.
(14) Gloucester	The Duke of Beaufort, K.G., P.C., [G.C.V.O.	W. P. Cripps.	R. C. Hutton.
(15) Hampshire	The Lord Ashburton, K.C.V.O.	Sir Francis Portal, Bt.	Hon. Mr. Justice Roskill.
(16) Isle of Wight			N. J. Skelhorn, Q.C.
(17) Hereford	Col. J. F. Maclean.	R. F. N. Aldrich-Blake.	His Hon. Judge Harington.
(18) Hertford	Maj.-Gen. Sir George Burns, K.C.V.O., C.B., D.S.O., O.B.E., M.C.	D. Cory-Wright.	Sir Henry Wynn-Parry: St. Albans—F. P. Crowder, M.P.
(19) Huntingdon	The Lord de Ramsey, T.D.	Col. G. T. Hurrell, O.B.E.	His Hon. Judge C. H. Gage.
(20) Kent	The Lord Cornwallis, K.B.E., M.C.	C. E. C. Hussey, C.B.E.	M. L. Berryman, Q.C.
(21) Lancashire	The Earl of Derby, M.C.	Sir Frank Lord, K.B.E.	W. H. Openshaw.
(22) Leicester	The Lord Cromwell, D.S.O., M.C.	Maj. S. G. Holland.	Lt.-Col. C. E. J. Freer.
Lincoln:			
(23) Lindsey	The Earl of Ancaster, T.D.	Capt. H. N. Nevile.	His Hon. W. K. Carter, Q.C.
(24) Kesteven			His Hon. W. K. Carter, Q.C.
(25) Holland			His Hon. Judge E. D. Lewis.
(26) London	Fd.-Marshal The Earl Alexander of Tunis, K.G., O.M., P.C., G.C.B., G.C.M.G., C.S.I., D.S.O., M.C.	Sir Cyril Hawker.	R. E. Seaton.
(27) Middlesex	Lt.-Gen. G. C. Bucknall, C.B., M.C.	Col. Sir Joseph Haygarth, C.B.E.	Hon. E. E. S. Montagu, C.B.E., Q.C.
(28) Norfolk	Col. Sir Edmund Bacon, Bt., O.B.E., T.D.	Maj. W. F. Batt, M.B.E.	The Lord Evershed, P.C. (East); R. North (W. Norfolk).
(29) Northampton	The Earl Spencer, T.D., F.S.A.	Capt. J. M. Buchanan, M.C.	His Hon. Judge N. A. Carr.
(30) Peterborough, Soke of			Sir Arthur Craig.
(31) Northumberland	The Duke of Northumberland, K.G., T.D.	J. J. Straker, M.C.	His Hon. Judge J. F. Drabble, Q.C.
(32) Nottingham	Maj.-Gen. Sir Robert Laycock, K.C.M.G., C.B., D.S.O.	Col. P. J. D. McCraith, M.C., T.D.	(vacant).
(33) Oxford	Col. J. Thomson, T.D.	Lt.-Col. A. D. Taylor, D.S.O., M.C.	Hon. Mr. Justice Phillimore O.B.E.
(34) Rutland	Col. T. C. S. Haywood, O.B.E.	Maj. R. Hoare, M.C.	G. D. Lane, A.F.C., Q.C.
(35) Salop	Maj.-Gen. The Viscount Bridgeman, K.B.E., C.B., D.S.O., M.C.	Maj. E. F. P. Gage.	Hon. Mr. Justice Stable, M.C.
(36) Somerset	Lt.-Col. the Lord Hylton.	Col. C. T. Mitford-Slade.	His Hon. Judge A. H. Armstrong.
(37) Stafford	Col. Harold Wallace-Copland.	W. A. Adams.	Hon. Mr. Justice Ashworth, M.B.E.
(38) Suffolk, E	Cdr. the Earl of Stradbroke, R.N. (*ret.*).	J. S. Schreiber.	His Hon. Judge T. F. Southall.
(39) Suffolk, W			
(40) Surrey	The Earl of Munster, P.C., K.B.E.	Sir George Erskine, C.B.E.	Brig. A. C. C. Willway, C.B., C.B.E., T.D.
(41) Sussex, E	The Duke of Norfolk, K.G. P.C., G.C.V.O.	Maj. W. L. Baxendale.	The Lord Denning.
(42) Sussex, W			Sir Geoffrey Lawrence, Q.C.
(43) Warwick	The Lord Willoughby de Broke, M.C., A.F.C.	A. Chamberlain, M.C., T.D.	Hon. Mr. Justice Finnemore.
(44) Westmorland	H. Hornyold-Strickland, F.S.A.	P. F. Scott.	The Lord Chorley, Q.C.
(45) Wilts	Capt. the Earl of Pembroke and Montgomery, C.V.O.	Lt.-Col. P. T. W. Sykes, O.B.E.	The Lord Devlin.
(46) Worcester	(vacant).	Maj. M. J. Webb.	J. F. Bourke.
(47) Yorks—E.R.	Col. The Lord Middleton, K.G., [M.C., T.D.	Sir Kenneth Wade Parkinson.	H. C. Scott.
(48) Yorks—N.R.	Col. Sir William Worsley, Bt.		P. S. Price, Q.C.
(49) Yorks—W.R.	The Earl of Scarbrough, K.G., P.C. G.C.S.I., G.C.I.E., G.C.V.O., T.D.		His Hon. Judge D. O. McKee.

* High Sheriffs are nominated by the Queen on November 12 and come into office after Hilary Term.

ENGLISH COUNTIES AND SHIRES

CHAIRMEN OF C.C., CLERKS OF THE PEACE, CHIEF CONSTABLES AND M.O.H.

Chairman of C.C.	Clerk of the Peace and Clerk of the Council*	Chief Constable	Medical Officer
(1) E. K. Martell.	G. O. Brewis.	H. R. Pratt.	W. C. V. Brothwood, M.D.
(2) Sir George Mowbray, Bt., K.B.E.	E. R. Davies.	T. C. B. Hodgson.	E. C. H. Huddy, M.D.
(3) A. E. Ward.	R. E. Millard.	Brig. J. N. Cheney, O.B.E.	G. W. H. Townsend, C.B.E.
(4) M. C. Burkitt.	C. Phythian.	(vacant)	P. A. Tyser, M.D.
(5) Cdr. A. F. Gray, R.D.	R. F. G. Thurlow.	T. C. Williams.	M. E. Hocken.
(6) Sir Wesley Emberton.	A. C. Hetherington, M.B.E.	H. Watson.	A. Brown.
(7) K. G. Foster.	E. T. Verger.	R. B. Matthews.	R. N. Curnow, O.B.E.
(8) J. Westoll.	G. N. C. Swift.	F. Williamson.	J. Leiper, M.B.E., T.D.
(9) N. Gratton.	D. G. Gilman.	W. E. Pitts, C.B.E.	J. B. S. Morgan.
(10) Sir George Hayter-Hames, C.B.E.	H. G. Godsall.	R. B. Greenwood, O.B.E.	(vacant)
(11) Cdr. H. K. B. Mitchell.	A. C. Templeman.	A. Hambleton, M.C.	(vacant)
(12) A. Cunningham.	J. T. Brockbank.	A. A. Muir.	S. Ludkin, M.D.
(13) Sir George Chaplin, C.B.E. [T.D.	W. J. Piper. C. Berridge.	J. C. Nightingale, B.E.M.	G. G. Stewart.
(14) Col. G. P. Shakerley, M.C.,	G. H. Davis.	E. P. B. White.	G. F. Bramley, M.D.
(15) Sir Alan Lubbock.	G. A. Wheatley, C.B.E.	D. Osmond, O.B.E.	I. A. MacDougall, M.B.E.
(16) Capt. H. J. Ward.	L. H. Baines.		R. K. Machell.
(17) Maj. R. E. Combe, O.B.E., M.C.	R. C. Hansen.	R. McCartney.	J. S. Cookson, M.D.
(18) J. Cockram.	N. Moon.	Lt.-Col. A. F. Wilcox, O.B.E.	G. W. Knight, M.D.
(19) The Lord Hemingford.	A. C. Aylward.	T. C. Williams.	Jean D. McKellar.
(20) R. W. Rule, O.B.E.	G. T. Heckels.	R. D. Lemon, C.B.E.	A. Elliott, M.D.
(21) Sir Alfred Bates, M.C.	C. P. H. McCall, M.B.E., T.D.	Col. T. E. St. Johnston, C.B.E.	S. C. Gawne, M.D.
(22) Col. P. H. Lloyd, T.D.	J. A. Chatterton.	J. A. Taylor, M.B.E.	G. H. Gibson.
(23) Lt.-Col. Sir Weston Cracroft-Amcotts, M.C.	W. E. Lane.	J. W. Barnett.	C. D. Cormac.
(24) Capt. H. W. N. Fane.	J. E. Blow.		T. J. O'Sullivan.
(25) Lt.-Col. G. A. Grounds, C.B.E., D.S.O., T.D.	H. A. H. Walter.		J. Fielding, M.D.
(26) A. R. Stamp.	C. L. Burgess, C.B.E. Sir William Hart, C.M.G.	(Metrop. Police Area).	J. A. Scott, O.B.E., M.D.
(27) Mrs. F. Timpson.	K. Goodacre, T.D.	(Metrop. Police Area).	G. S. Wigley.
(28) Col. Sir Bartle Edwards, C.V.O., M.C.	F. P. Boyce.	F. P. C. Garland.	A. G. Scott.
(29) E. Marlow, C.B.E., M.C.	J. A. Turner, O.B.E.	J. A. H. Gott, M.B.E., G.M.	J. J. A. Reid, T.D., M.D.
(30) Dr. J. Hunt.	E. F. Smith.	F. G. Markin.	G. Nisbet.
(31) N. Garrow, O.B.E.	E. P. Harvey.	C. H. Cooksley.	J. B. Tilley, M.D.
(32) F. A. Small, C.B.E.	A. R. Davis.	J. E. S. Browne, O.B.E.	A. R. C. Margetts.
(33) The Earl of Macclesfield.	G. G. Burkitt.	J. E. Bailey.	M. J. Pleydell, M.C., M.D.
(34) Sir Kenneth Ruddle, T.D.	A. Bond, O.B.E.	J. A. Taylor, M.B.E.	A. D. Whitelaw, M.D.
(35) W. M. W. Fell.	G. C. Godber, C.B.E.	R. G. Fenwick.	T. S. Hall, M.B.E., T.D., M.D.
(36) Brig. E. H. C. Frith, C.B.E.	E. S. Rickards.	K. W. L. Steele.	J. F. Davidson, O.B.E.
(37) J. F. Amery, O.B.E.	T. H. Evans, C.B.E.	S. E. Peck, B.E.M.	G. Ramage, M.D.
(38) Col. Sir Robert Gooch, Bt., D.S.O.	G. C. Lightfoot.	(vacant)	S. T. G. Gray.
(39) Maj.-Gen. P. G. Whitefoord, O.B.E., M.C.	A. F. Skinner, O.B.E.	W. J. Ridd, O.B.E.	D. A. McCracken, M.D.
(40) Lt.-Col. H. J. Wells, C.B.E., M.C.	G. A. Nops; W. W. Ruff.	H. G. Rutherford.	K. A. Soutar.
(41) Sir William Lindsay, C.B.E.	J. Atkinson.	R. E. Breffit, O.B.E.	F. Langford.
(42) P. Mursell, M.B.E.	T. C. Hayward, C.B.E.	R. P. Wilson, O.B.E.	T. McL. Galloway.
(43) A. H. Schmiegelow.	Sir Edgar Stephens, C.B.E.	P. E. Brodie, O.B.E.	S. W. Savage, M.D.
(44) R. S. Crossfield.	K. S. Himsworth.	F. Williamson.	J. A. Guy, M.D.
(45) Maj. S. V. Christie-Miller.	R. P. Harries.	G. R. Glendinning, O.B.E.	C. D. L. Lycett, M.D.
(46) J. M. C. Higgs.	W. R. Scurfield.	J. A. Willison.	J. W. Pickup, M.D.
(47) Lt.-Col. Sir John Dunnington-Jefferson, Bt., D.S.O.	R. A. Whitley.	J. W. P. Blenkin.	R. Watson.
(48) J. T. Fletcher.	R. A. Wotherspoon.	J. R. Archer-Burton, O.B.E.	J. A. Fraser.
(49) W. M. Hyman.	Sir Bernard Kenyon.	G. E. Scott, C.B.E.	R. W. Elliott, M.D.

* In the counties of Essex, London and Surrey, the appointments of Clerk of the Council and Clerk of the Peace are not combined in one person.

THE GOVERNMENT OF LONDON

LONDON, the capital of England and of the British Commonwealth of Nations, is situated on both banks of the River Thames, 50 miles from the North Sea.

Greater London includes the administrative counties of LONDON (the City of London and 28 metropolitan boroughs); MIDDLESEX (18 boroughs and 8 *urban districts*); and parts of SURREY (the County Borough of Croydon, the 10 Boroughs of Barnes, Beddington and Wallington, Epsom and Ewell, Kingston-upon-Thames, Malden and Coombe, Mitcham, Richmond, Surbiton, Sutton and Cheam, and Wimbledon; and the 5 *Urban Districts* of *Banstead, Carshalton, Coulsdon and Purley, Esher*, and *Merton and Morden*); parts of KENT (the 4 Boroughs of Beckenham, Bexley, Bromley, and Erith; and the 4 *Urban Districts* of *Chislehurst and Sidcup, Crayford, Orpington* and *Penge*); parts of HERTFORDSHIRE (the 4 *Urban Districts* of *Barnet, Bushey, Cheshunt* and *East Barnet*; and the Elstree Rural District); parts of ESSEX (the County Boroughs of East Ham and West Ham, the 7 Boroughs of Barking, Chingford, Dagenham, Ilford, Leyton, Walthamstow, and Wanstead and Woodford; and 2 *Urban Districts, Chigwell* and *Waltham Holy Cross*). It covers an area of 461,882 acres (722 sq. miles) and in April, 1961, had a population of 8,171,902 (within the County of London, 3,195,114; within Middlesex and the Home Counties, 4,976,788); estimated total (June 30, 1962), 8,176,810.

The City of London (*see* pp. 635-41) represents London within its ancient boundaries.

The City of Westminster, which is bounded by the City of London on the east, by Chelsea and Kensington on the west, by Paddington, St. Marylebone and Holborn on the north, and by the Thames and Chelsea on the south, was formed into a borough by the London Government Act of 1899, and was created a city by Royal Charter of Oct. 29, 1900, the Council consisting of a Mayor, 10 Aldermen and 60 Councillors. Extending from the eastern end of the Strand to Kensington Gardens, and from Oxford Street to the Thames, it includes within its boundaries a large number of the finest buildings in London. The Abbey and the Roman Catholic Cathedral, the Houses of Parliament and the Law Courts, Buckingham Palace and St. James's, and the principal government offices, clubs and theatres are situated in Westminster.

Metropolitan Boroughs.—Under the London Government Act of 1899, the administrative functions of the various vestries in the Metropolitan districts surrounding the City of London were transferred to 28 Metropolitan Boroughs, of which one became afterwards the City of Westminster. The area covered by these boroughs extends northwards to include Stoke Newington, southwards to Wandsworth and Lewisham, eastwards to Woolwich, and westwards to Hammersmith.

London County Council.—For County purposes the affairs of London are administered by the London County Council (*see* pp. 641-4), which was created by the Local Government Act of 1888.

Miscellaneous Authorities.—For Police purposes the administration is invested in the Corporation of London as to the *City Police* and in the Home

LONDON CITIES AND BOROUGHS

	Population Estimated 1962	Rate per 1,000		Rateable Value April 1, 1963	Rates 1963–64	Town Clerk	Mayor, 1963–64
		Births	Deaths				
				£	s. d.		
CITY OF LONDON ..	4,610	5·8	10·0	43,610,745	6 9	E. H. Nichols, T.D.	*See* Events of the Year.
WESTMINSTER.....	86,110	12·3	12·0	64,590,307	6 10	A. G. Dawtry, M.B.E., T.D.	L. Farmiloe, M.C.
Battersea.........	104,020	20·8	11·9	4,653,988	8 3	C. M. W. S. Freeman	J. Parker.
Bermondsey......	51,000	16·7	11·5	4,088,666	8 6	J. S. Lambert.	E. A. Rowe.
Bethnal Green.....	46,230	17·9	12·2	2,409,396	8 10	F. H. Bristow.	R. H. Rosamond.
Camberwell	173,720	20·2	11·4	7,269,737	8 4	F. D. Ward.	H. G. Lamborn.
Chelsea...........	48,550	12·9	14·6	6,984,745	7 0	J. C. Kitchin.	Lady Heath.
Deptford..........	68,980	23·0	11·7	2,831,170	7 8	K. J. Meader.	F. W. Bullion.
Finsbury..........	32,540	16·1	11·6	9,026,542	7 6	M. Casey.	A. A. Goldshaw.
Fulham...........	110,570	17·3	12·4	5,747,996	8 0	C. F. Thatcher.	A. H. Little.
Greenwich.........	84,730	15·3	12·5	4,974,845	8 0	G. C. Turk.	Mrs. I. M. Scales.
Hackney..........	163,400	23·1	11·7	8,128,085	8 0	L. G. Huddy.	J. Kotz.
Hammersmith.....	108,120	21·9	11·9	7,688,681	7 6	C. Randall.	S. M. Atkins.
Hampstead........	98,240	18·1	10·7	7,559,461	7 9	B. H. Wilson, M.B.E.	N. Oatway
Holborn...........	20,640	9·2	13·1	10,899,996	6 11	G. T. Lloyd.	H. Bright.
Islington..........	227,870	23·4	11·0	9,702,311	7 8	H. D. Clark.	G. A. Barnard.
Kensington (Royal Borough).......	172,020	19·7	10·2	17,995,813	6 11	J. W. Sainsbury.	Mrs. J. Walford.
Lambeth..........	223,370	19·9	11·7	12,887,700	7 4	J. E. Fishwick.	G. F. S. Light.
Lewisham........	222,170	16·3	11·2	8,788,421	8 0	A. M. Smith, O.B.E.	F. B. Page.
Paddington.......	113,600	22·6	11·0	9,027,848	7 4	W. H. Bentley.	Maj. J. Collins.
Poplar............	67,340	20·8	11·6	4,639,831	7 10	S. A. Hamilton.	R. Gillender.
St. Marylebone....	68,070	11·2	16·7	23,623,598	7 1	S. J. Rutty.	L. Pearl.
St. Pancras.......	124,470	20·4	11·5	12,959,759	8 0	R. C. E. Austin.	Mrs. H. Chandler.
Shoreditch........	39,580	16·1	11·3	3,907,994	8 2	C. A. James.	Rev. M. Davies, M.B.E., T.D.
Southwark........	86,440	19·1	14·2	5,871,954	7 8	E. J. Pitt.	Mrs. C. M. Clun.
Stepney...........	90,480	20·5	12·5	7,332,038	7 8	W. Reeve.	E. W. Hill.
Stoke Newington ..	52,950	24·0	10·6	2,089,578	7 6	A. J. Hazal.	Mrs. G. M. Shanager.
Wandsworth......	347,810	18·1	14·4	15,831,182	7 10	J. N. Martin.	G. F. Rowe.
Woolwich.........	148,140	15·0	10·7	7,992,632	7 10	R. L. Doble.	D. S. Ramsey.

Office as to the *Metropolitan Police.* The water authority is the *Metropolitan Water Board*; while the River Thames is administered as to its tidal portion by the *Port of London Authority* and above Teddington by the *Thames Conservancy*; the *Port Health Committee* of the Corporation is the Health Authority for the River, the lighthouse and pilotage authority being *Trinity House*. The bridges are maintained in the City of London by the *Bridge House Estates* Committee of the Corporation and in the remaining area by the London County Council.

THE CORPORATION OF LONDON

The City of London is the historic centre at the heart of London known as "the square mile" around which the vast metropolis has grown over the centuries. The civic government is carried on by the Corporation of London through the Court of Common Council, a body consisting of the Lord Mayor, 25 other Aldermen and 159 Common Councilmen. The legal title of the Corporation is "the Mayor and Commonalty and Citizens of the City of London."

The City is the financial and business centre of London and includes the head offices of the principal banks, insurance companies and mercantile houses, in addition to buildings ranging from the historic interest of the Roman Wall and the 15th century Guildhall, to the massive splendour of St. Paul's Cathedral and the architectural beauty of Wren's spires.

The City of London at the time of the revolt of the Iceni (A.D. 61) was described by Tacitus (*born* A.D. 55; *died* A.D. 120) as "a busy emporium for trade and traders." In Saxon times it was, in reality, a small independent federated State of Wards (holding *wardmotes*) with a *folkmote*, predecessor of the present Common Council, for general affairs. Its burgesses maintained their independence even after the Battle of Hastings. William the Norman only gained possession of their city by means of a treaty with them, and granted a charter, which is still preserved. The mayoralty was established on the recognition of the corporate unity of the citizens by Prince John in 1191, the first Mayor being Henry Fitz Ailwyn, who filled the office for 21 years and was succeeded by Fitz Alan (1212–15). A new charter was granted by King John in 1215, directing the Mayor to be chosen annually, which has ever since been done, though in early times the same individual often held the office more than once. A familiar instance is that of "Whittington, thrice Lord Mayor of London" (in reality four times, A.D. 1397, 1398, 1406, 1419); and many modern cases have occurred. The earliest instance of the phrase "Lord Mayor" in English is in 1414. It is used more generally in the latter part of the 15th century and becomes invariable from 1535 onwards. At Michaelmas the Liverymen in Common Hall choose two Aldermen who have served the office of Sheriff for presentation to the Court of Aldermen, and one is chosen to be Lord Mayor for the ensuing mayoral year. The Lord Mayor is presented to the Lord Chief Justice at the Royal Courts of Justice on the second Saturday in November to make the final declaration of office, having been sworn in at Guildhall on the preceding day. The procession to the Royal Courts of Justice is popularly known as the *Lord Mayor's Show*.

Aldermen are mentioned in the 11th century and their office is of Saxon origin. They were elected annually between 1377 and 1394, when a charter of Richard II. directed them to be chosen for life. The *Common Council*, elected annually on St. Thomas's Day (Dec. 21), was, at an early date, substituted for a popular assembly called the Folkmote. At first only two representatives were sent from each ward, but the number has since been greatly increased, some wards having at present as many as 12 members, and none fewer than four.

Sheriffs were Saxon officers; their predecessors were the *wic-reeves* and *portreeves* of London and Middlesex. At first they were officers of the Crown, and were named by the Barons of the Exchequer; but Henry I. (in 1132) gave the citizens permission to choose their own Sheriffs, and the annual election of Sheriffs became fully operative under King John's charter of 1199. The citizens lost this privilege, as far as the election of Sheriff of Middlesex is concerned, by the Local Government Act, 1888; but the Liverymen continue, as heretofore, to choose two Sheriffs of the City of London, who are appointed on Midsummer Day, and take office at Michaelmas.

Officers.—The Recorder was first appointed in 1298. The office of Chamberlain is an ancient one,

THE CITY'S ESTATE, 1962–1963

NET INCOME	£	s.	d.	£	s.	d.
Estates Revenue				751,677	4	3
Market Revenue Accounts:						
London Central Markets	£72,361	3	11			
Leadenhall Market	3,292	19	0			
	75,654	2	11			
Less: Metropolitan Cattle Market	£15,531	10	1			
Billingsgate Market	16,609	18	0			
	32,141	8	1	43,512	14	10
				795,189	19	1
Gresham Revenue (Moiety)				14,091	0	7
Contribution in respect of Officers' Establishments				184,120	19	3
				£993,329	18	11

NET EXPENDITURE	£	s.	d.	£	s.	d.
Magistracy	15,992	14	6			
Civil Government	133,136	11	9			
Open Spaces	82,246	11	1			
				231,375	17	4
Officers' Establishments				288,243	15	5
Administration of Criminal Justice				27,831	13	0
City of London Schools				102,471	12	5
Guildhall School of Music and Drama				30,393	1	2
Income Tax				110,332	4	1
Expenses not allocated to Departments				7,110	13	8
Charitable and Public Donations				14,401	11	5
Expenses of Honorary Votes				235	0	0
Receptions				25,292	5	8
City of London Freemen's Houses				5,106	5	10
Contribution to Staff Compassionate Fund				7,500	0	0
Sundries				11,473	2	3
Balance				131,562	16	8
				£993,329	18	11

the first contemporary record of which is 1276. The Town Clerk (or Common Clerk) is mentioned in 1274 and the Common Serjeant in 1291.

Activities.—The work is assigned to a number of committees which present reports to the Court of Common Council. These Committees are:—City Lands, Bridge House Estates, Coal and Corn and Finance, Rates Finance, Improvements and Town Planning, Streets, Central Markets, Cattle Markets, Billingsgate and Leadenhall Markets, Spitalfields Market, Police, Port and City of London Health, Library (Library, Records, Art Gallery and Museum), City of London Schools, Freemen's School, Music (Guildhall School of Music and Drama), General Purposes, Establishment, Civil Defence, Housing, Gresham (City side), Epping Forest, West Ham Park, Special, Privileges, Special (Guildhall Reconstruction), Barbican and Licensing Planning.

The Honourable the *Irish Society*, which manages the Corporation's Estates in Ulster, consists of a Governor and 5 other Aldermen, the Recorder, and 19 Common Councilmen, of whom one is elected Deputy Governor.

The *City's Estate*, in the possession of which the Corporation of London differs from other municipalities, is managed by the City Lands Committee, the Chairmanship of which carries with it the title of "Chief Commoner."

The *Coal and Corn and Finance Committee* manages the funds derived from the City's Estate and other sources and receives accounts of the Bridge House Estates (which are employed in the provision and maintenance of London, Blackfriars, Southwark and Tower Bridges). The cost of certain public services, including the upkeep of the Mayoralty and the Mansion House, the provision of hospitality, maintenance of open spaces outside the City such as Epping Forest, West Ham Park, Burnham Beeches and some of the Kent and Surrey commons and the net expense of the City of London School, the City of London School for Girls, the City of London Freemen's School, and the Guildhall School of Music and Drama is met from City's Cash.

The *Rates Finance Committee* supervises the collection of rates and the expenditure of money so collected, two rates being levied by the Corporation, a Poor Rate and a General Rate. The Poor Rate is levied mainly to satisfy the precept served on the Corporation by the London County Council for the City's share of rate-borne expenditure of the County, and also to meet the contribution the Corporation is required to make under the London Rates Equalization Scheme. The General Rate is levied to meet the net cost of the services which the Corporation as a local authority is required to maintain (*see below*).

EXPENDITURE AND INCOME ON RATE ACCOUNTS, 1962–1963

Service	Expenditure (including Debt Charge)	Income (other than Exchequer Grants)	Exchequer Grants	Net Expenditure falling upon Rates
POOR RATE—	£	£	£	£
London County Council Precept including contribution under Section 10, Local Government Act, 1948)	9,272,965	—	—	9,272,965
Other Services	46,702	76,774	—	*CR.* 30,072
Total for Poor Rate	9,319,667	76,774	—	9,242,893
GENERAL RATE—				
Library, Museum and Art Gallery	114,204	888	—	113,316
Public Health (including Port Health) Services	731,672	85,425	78,352	567,895
Town and Country Planning	1,677,289	1,023,703	139,020	514,566
Barbican Redevelopment Scheme	25,099	8,465	—	16,634
Highways, Bridges and Footpaths	887,986	124,716	81,223	682,047
Public Lighting	75,820	44	—	75,776
City Police	1,663,572	86,730	539,555	1,037,287
Civil Defence	15,965	309	9,829	5,827
Administration of Justice	156,461	35,210	—	121,251
Housing	520,468	312,546	67,341	140,581
City of London Cemetery	132,401	97,205	—	35,196
Spitalfields Market	224,894	225,998	—	*CR.* 1,104
Blackfriars Bridgehead	9,175	—	—	9,175
Other Services	321,106	69,351	—	251,755
Total for General Rate	6,556,112	2,070,590	915,320	3,570,202
SUMMARY—				
Poor Rate	9,319,667	76,774	—	9,242,893
General Rate	6,556,112	2,070,590	915,320	3,570,202
	£15,875,779	£2,147,364	£915,320	£12,813,095

The Right Honourable the Lord Mayor 1962–1963*

Sir Ralph Edgar Perring, *born* 1905; Alderman of *Langbourn*, 1951; *Sheriff of London*, 1958; *Lord Mayor* 1962 .... £15,000

Private Secretary, Col. N. F. B. Shaw, C.B.E., D.S.O.

The Aldermen

Aldermen.	*Ward*	*Born.*	*C.C.*	*Ald.*	*Shff.*	*Lord Mayor*
Sir Frank Newson-Smith, Bt.	*Farringdon Within* (1938), *Bridge Without* (1954)	1879	1911	1938	1939	1943
Sir Bracewell Smith, Bt., K.C.V.O.	*Lime Street*	1884	1935	1938	1943	1946
Sir Frederick Michael Wells, Bt.	*Bread Street*	1884	1939	1941	1945	1947
Sir Denys Lowson, Bt.	*Vintry*	1906	1940	1942	1939	1950
Sir Rupert de la Bère, Bt., K.C.V.O.	*Tower*	1893	1941	1943	1941	1952
Sir Noel Vansittart Bowater, Bt., G.B.E., M.C.	*Castle Baynard*	1892	1937	1944	1948	1953
Sir Cuthbert Lowell Ackroyd, Bt.	*Cordwainer*	1892	1940	1945	1949	1955
Col. Sir George James Cullum Welch, Bt., O.B.E., M.C.	*Bridge*	1895	1931	1947	1950	1956
Sir Denis Henry Truscott, G.B.E., T.D.	*Dowgate*	1908	1938	1947	1951	1957
Sir (Sydney) Harold Gillett, Bt., M.C.	*Bassishaw*	1890	1930	1948	1952	1958
Sir Bernard Nathaniel Waley-Cohen, Bt.	*Portsoken*	1914	....	1949	1955	1960
Sir Frederick Alfred Hoare, Bt.	*Farringdon Without*	1913	1948	1950	1956	1961
Sir Ralph Edgar Perring	*Langbourn*	1905	1948	1951	1958	1962
All the above have passed the Civic Chair.						
Clement James Harman	*Candlewick*	1894	1949	1952	1951	....
Sir James Miller	*Bishopsgate*	1905	....	1957	1956	....
Sir (Jonathan) Lionel (Percy) Denny, M.C.	*Billingsgate*	1897	1941	1957	1961	....
Robert Ian Bellinger	*Cheap*	1910	1953	1958	1962	....
Gilbert Samuel Inglefield, T.D.	*Aldersgate*	1909	....	1959	1963	....
Arnold Charles Trinder	*Aldgate*	1906	1951	1959	....	....
Lt.-Col. Ian Frank Bowater, D.S.O., T.D.	*Coleman Street*	1904	....	1960	....	....
The Lord Wardington	*Broad Street*	1924	....	1960	....	....
Douglas Rowland Holdsworth Hill	*Queenhithe*	1904	1947	1960	....	....
Peter Malden Studd	*Cripplegate*	1916	....	1960	....	....
Hamilton Edward de Coucey Howard	*Cornhill*	1915	1951	1963	....	....
Lt.-Col. Geoffrey Sturdy Incledon-Webber	*Farringdon Within*	1904	....	1963	....	....
Col. Alan Raymond Mais, O.B.E., T.D., E.R.D.	*Walbrook*	1911	....	1963	..	....

The Sheriffs 1963–1964

Alderman Gilbert Samuel Inglefield, T.D. (*see above*), and Gilbert Harold Samuel Edgar, C.B.E.; elected June 24 *and assumed office* September 28, 1963.

THE COMMON COUNCIL OF LONDON

Allcard, *Deputy* V. (1922) .... *Broad St.*
Amies, T. H. C. (1961) .... *Bridge.*
Anderson, F. C. (1950) .... *Langbourn.*
Artaud, H. F. J. (1963) .... *Cornhill.*
Arthur, B. G., C.B.E. (1954) .... *Walbrook.*
Bailey, *Deputy* J. A. (1941) .... *Farringdon Wn.*
Baker, C. W. (1957) .... *Cripplegate Wt.*
Bales, E. W. (1952) .... *Farringdon Wt.*
Barratt, *Deputy* T. E. C., C.B.E. (1944) .... *Candlewick.*
Bartlett, *Deputy* S. (1945) .... *Cornhill.*
Beecroft, H. C. H. (1942) .... *Cripplegate Wn.*
Beer, *Deputy* G. Allison- (1942) .. *Cordwainer.*
Bell, *Deputy* A. S. (1937) .... *Tower.*
Bennison, C. (1950) .... *Portsoken.*
Bianchi, V. C. (1961) .... *Bassishaw.*
Blankley, *Deputy* W. H. R. (1946) *Lime St.*
Blyth, *Deputy* H. C. (1945) .... *Vintry.*
Bradley, A. W. (1947) .... *Billingsgate.*
Brookhouse, *Lt.-Col.* H., M.V.O. (1947) .... *Dowgate.*
Burston, N. B. (1961) .... *Portsoken.*
Calder, *Deputy* H. W. K., C.B.E. (1936) .... *Bridge.*
Champness, R. F. (1954) .... *Farringdon Wn.*
Clackson, *Deputy* D. L., M.B.E. (1951) .... *Farrington Wt.*
Cleary, F. E., M.B.E. (1959) .... *Coleman St.*
Clements, G. E. I. (1961) .... *Farringdon Wt.*
Cohen, S. E. (1951) .... *Farringdon Wt.*
Collens, F. J., T.D. (1946) .... *Castle Baynard.*
Collett, Sir Henry, Bt. (1958) .... *Bridge.*
Collett, T. K., C.B.E. (1945) .... *Bridge.*
Cook, J. E. Evan (1959) .... *Lime St.*
Cope, Dr. G. (1963) .... *Farringdon Wt.*
Cork, K. R. (1951) .... *Billingsgate.*
Coulson, A. G. (1961) .... *Broad St.*
Creswell, P. H. (1958) .... *Aldgate.*
Davis, Sir Gilbert, Bt. (1946) .... *Broad St.*
Dean, H. R. (1958) .... *Cordwainer.*
Deith, R. C. (1944) .... *Farringdon Wn.*
Dennis, *Capt.* H. W., M.C. (1942) *Candlewick.*
Dickson, *Deputy* C. G. (1932) .... *Aldersgate.*
Dove, *Lt.-Col.* W. W., C.B.E., T.D. (1942) .... *Coleman St.*
Duckworth, *Maj.* H. (1961) .... *Lime St.*
Dyter, P. J. (1959) .... *Queenhithe.*
Ebbisham, The Lord, T.D. (1947) .. *Candlewick.*
Erlebach, *Deputy* D. E. (1943) .... *Aldgate.*
Evans, D. I., T.D. (1952) .... *Vintry.*
Fairweather, C. H. F. (1958) .... *Queenhithe.*
Fell, C. A. (1947) .... *Langbourn.*
Fish, H. I. (1961) .... *Farringdon Wt.*
Fisher, D. G. (1958) .... *Cornhill.*
Fox, H. M. (1962) .... *Cripplegate Wn.*
Game, *Deputy* D. S. (1950) .... *Farringdon Wt.*
Gapp, J. G. (1956) .... *Cheap.*
Glenny, *Deputy* C. F., M.V.O. (1946) .... *Bishopsgate.*
Goldman, *Deputy* H. L. (1932) ... *Portsoken.*

* The Lord Mayor for 1963–64 was elected on Michaelmas Day. *See* Events of the Year.

Goodinge, W. (1933) . . . . *Aldersgate.*
Gorman, R. W. (1956) . . . . *Aldersgate.*
Graham, G. B. (1961) . . . . *Farringdon Wt.*
Greenaway, A. P. (1952) . . . . *Bishopsgate.*
Greenland, S. R. (1938) . . . . *Broad St.*
Gregory, L. W. (1959) . . . . *Queenhithe.*
Griffiths, P. J. (1961) . . . . *Dowgate.*
Grose, G. P. (1942–46 and 1950) . . *Farringdon Wn.*
Gunton, W. H. (1932) . . . . *Aldersgate.*
Hall, N. L., M.B.E. (1952) . . . . *Farringdon Wt.*
Harris, H. Wylie (1957) . . . . *Farringdon Wn.*
Harrowing, *Deputy* T. C. (1940) . . *Bishopsgate*
Hayes, C. G. (1947) . . . . *Bishopsgate.*
Hayman, L. C. R. (1954) . . . . *Aldersgate.*
Hayter, The Lord (1919) . . . . *Castle Baynard.*
Hayward, *Deputy* R. J., C.B.E. (1943) . . . . *Walbrook.*
Henderson, *Deputy* A. S. (1941) . . . *Cripplegate Wn.*
Henderson, J. S. (1962) . . . . *Cripplegate Wn.*
Hill, E. W. F. (1962) . . . . *Tower.*
Hodge, G. D. (1947) . . . . *Tower.*
Holden, W. B. (1951) . . . . *Walbrook.*
Howes, A. C. (1949) . . . . *Bishopsgate.*
Hughes. C. J. G. (1956) . . . . *Cripplegate Wt.*
Hunt, G. W. (1952) . . . . *Bassishaw*
Hunt, W. G. G. (1962) . . . . *Cripplegate Wt.*
Jacobs, H. R. (1946) . . . . *Portsoken.*
Jacobs, T. C. (1944) . . . . *Aldgate.*
Johnson, H. B. (1951) . . . . *Cornhill.*
Jones, Lt.-Col. O. Campbell-, T.D. (1961) . . . . *Dowgate.*
Lamboll. A. S. (1949) . . . . *Langbourn.*
Last, A. W. (1948) . . . . *Bridge.*
Lester, H. E. (1946) . . . . *Castle Baynard.*
Lewis, *Deputy* C. F., C.B.E. (1936) . *Coleman St.*
Link, C. E. (1961) . . . . *Farringdon Wt.*
Lovely, P. T. (1949) . . . . *Tower.*
Loweth, *Col.* W. E., C.B.E. (1946) . *Bishopsgate.*
Lowrie, W. E. (1952) . . . . *Farringdon Wn.*
McAuley, C. (1957) . . . . *Bread St.*
Meldrum, R. (1932) . . . . *Cripplegate Wt.*
Mills, D. G. (1954) . . . . *Billingsgate.*
Monkhouse, F. J. (1952) . . . . *Cheap.*
Morgan, B. L., M.B.E. (1963) . . . . . *Bishopsgate.*
Oram, M. H. (1963) . . . . *Cordwainer.*
Osborn. A. J. (1947) . . . . *Broad St.*
Parker, *Deputy* E. A. (1952) . . . . . . *Cripplegate Wt.*
Parkin, A. M. (1961) . . . . *Cheap.*
Paul, A. N. (1946) . . . . *Portsoken.*
Peacock, R. W. (1956) . . . . *Vintry.*
Perkins, G. K. (1951) . . . . *Aldgate.*
Pike, *Deputy* H. T. (1946) . . . . *Cornhill.*
Pinker, C. L. (1948) . . . . *Bishopsgate.*
Pinnell, H.M. (1954) . . . . *Bassishaw.*
Prince, L. B. (1950) . . . . *Bishopsgate.*
Pritchard, F. S. (1961) . . . . *Walbrook.*
Pryke, Sir David, Bt. (1961) . . . . . . *Queenhithe.*
Rawson, C. L. P. (1963) . . . . *Bread St.*
Rayner, N. (1961) . . . . *Farringdon Wt.*
Read, H. S. (1958) . . . . *Aldgate.*
Richardson, *Deputy Maj.* T. G. F. (1944) . . . . *Castle Baynard.*
Rowland, Sir Wentworth, Bt. (1951) . . . . *Coleman St.*
Rowlandson, Sir Graham, M.B.E. (1961) . . . . *Coleman St.*
Rutherford, A. J. B. (1950) . . . . . . *Tower.*
Samuels, W. (1950) . . . . *Portsoken.*
Sanders, H. C. H. (1946) . . . . *Bishopsgate.*
Sheppard, S. (1957) . . . . *Billingsgate.*
Shill, Lt.-Col. C. G. S. (1956) . . . . *Castle Baynard.*
Simon, R. M. (1961) . . . . *Bread St.*
Skilbeck, *Deputy* C. (1948) . . . . *Queenhithe.*
Skinner. R. W. (1948) . . . . *Billingsgate.*
Smith, F. S., T.D. (1958) . . . . *Cordwainer.*
Smith, L. J. W. (1958) . . . . *Cripplegate Wt.*
Smith, *Deputy* J. K. Newson- (1945) . . . . *Bassishaw.*
Smith, P. A. Revell- (1959) . . . . . . *Vintry.*
Stanham, *Deputy* A. F. G. (1943) . . *Dowgate.*
Steiner, F. N. (1962) . . . . *Bread St.*
Stephens, *Deputy* R. (1940) . . . . *Langbourn*
Stoneham, R. T. (1962) . . . . *Candlewick.*
Street, S. V. (1961) . . . . *Aldgate.*
Sudbury, Col. F. A., O.B.E., E.R.D. (1963) . . . . *Tower.*
Sunderland *Deputy* O. G. (1944) . . *Billingsgate.*
Tallon, C. R. (1962) . . . . *Dowgate.*
Thompson, H. F. (1946) . . . . *Cheap.*
Tremellen, N. C. (1951) . . . . *Langbourn.*
Trentham, G. D. (1941) . . . . *Bread St.*
Turner, *Deputy* C. (1932) . . . . *Farringdon Wn.*
Utting, F. W. (1952) . . . . *Castle Baynard.*
Vine, G. M. (1955) . . . . *Farringdon Wt.*
Walker, *Deputy* S.R., C.B.E. (1937) *Bread Street.*
Watts, E. W. (1950) . . . . *Walbrook.*
Wells, A. D. (1961) . . . . *Cripplegate Wn.*
Wells, *Maj.* S. W., M.B.E. (1949) . . *Cripplegate Wn.*
Wheeler, E. (1948) . . . . *Lime St.*
Whitby, M. J. B. (1937) . . . . *Langbourn.*
Whittington, C. R., M.C. (1939) . . . *Broad St.*
Wilkins, *Deputy* E. F. (1946) . . . . . *Cheap.*
Wilson, A. B. (1961) . . . . *Aldersgate.*
Wingfield, E. H. (1943) . . . . *Cordwainer.*
Yates, J. T., M.B.E. (1959) . . . . *Cheap.*
Young, A. G. (1945) . . . . *Farringdon Wn.*
Young, D. S. (1939) . . . . *Farringdon Wn.*

THE CITY GUILDS (LIVERY COMPANIES)

The Livery Companies of the City of London derive their name from the assumption of a distinctive dress or livery by their members in the 14th century.

The order of precedence (according to 2nd Report of Municipal Corporations' Commissioners, 1837) and omitting extinct companies, is given in parentheses after the name of each Company. There are 83 Guilds in existence. The Combmakers, Silk-throwers, Silkmen, Pinmakers, Soapmakers, Hatbandmakers, Long-bow Stringmakers, Woodmongers, Starchmakers and Fishermen are extinct.

About 10,000 Liverymen of the Guilds are entitled to vote at elections in *Common Hall.*

The liveries of the Shipwrights (500), Horners (440), Carmen (406), Stationers and Newspaper Makers (406), and Apothecaries (379), are the most numerous, the Ironmongers (35) the smallest.

MERCERS (*1*). *Hall*, Ironmonger Lane, E.C.2. *Livery*, 194.—*Clerk*, G. E. Logsdon, C.B.E.; *Master*, The Lord Ebbisham, T.D.

GROCERS (*2*). *Hall*, Princes St., E.C.2. *Livery*, 201.—*Clerk*, J. A. M. Ellison-Macartney; *Master*, Lt.-Col. K. B. Hicks, O.B.E.

DRAPERS (*3*). *Hall*, Throgmorton Street, E.C.2. *Livery*, 200.—*Clerk*, H. Farmar; *Master*, H. C. Boddington.

FISHMONGERS (*4*). *Hall*, London Bridge, E.C.4. *Livery*, 285.—*Clerk*, J. S. Barclay, T.D.; *Prime Warden*, Sir Colin Anderson.

GOLDSMITHS (*5*). *Hall*, Foster Lane, E.C.2. *Livery*, 240.—*Clerk*, W. A. Prideaux, M.C.; *Prime Warden*, The Viscount Runciman of Doxford, O.B.E., A.F.C.

SKINNERS (*6* and *7*). *Hall*, 8 Dowgate Hill, E.C.4. *Livery*, 265—*Clerk*, M. H. Glover; *Master*, G. P. Pirie-Gordon.

MERCHANT TAYLORS (*6* and *7*). *Hall*, 30 Threadneedle Street, E.C.2. *Livery*, 345.—*Clerk*, J. M. Woolley, M.B.E., T.D.; *Master*, Sir James Ritchie, Bt., T.D.

HABERDASHERS (*8*). *Hall*, Staining Lane, E.C.2. *Livery*, 310.—*Clerk*, Cdr. H. Prevett, O.B.E., R.N.; *Master*, Rev. A. W. G. Cope.

SALTERS (*9*). *Livery*, 140.—*Clerk*, W. R. Nichols, T.D., 36 Portland Place, W.1.; *Master*, Rear-Adm. W. K. Weston, C.B., O.B.E.

IRONMONGERS (*10*). *Hall*, Shaftesbury Place, Aldersgate, E.C.1. *Livery*, 35.—*Clerk*, J. M. Adams Beck; *Master*, P. A. Hudson.

VINTNERS (*11*). *Hall*, Upper Thames Street, E.C.4. *Livery*, 300.—*Clerk*, W. H. Lloyd Mead; *Master*, J. M. Symmons.

CLOTHWORKERS (*12*). *Hall*, Dunster Court, Mincing Lane, E.C.3. *Livery*, 180.—*Clerk*, E. J. Reed; *Master*, P. M. S. Latham.

The above are the Twelve " Great " London Companies in order of Civic precedence.

AIR PILOTS AND AIR NAVIGATORS, GUILD OF (*81*). *Grand Master*, H.R.H. the Prince Philip, Duke of Edinburgh, K.G. *Hon. Clerk*, V. C. Varcoe, 14 South Street, W.1; *Master*, A. M. A. Majendie.

APOTHECARIES, SOCIETY OF (*58*). *Hall*, Black Friars Lane, E.C.4. *Livery*, 379.—*Clerk*, E. Busby; *Master*, R. N. Ironside.

ARMOURERS AND BRASIERS (*22*). *Hall*, 81 Coleman Street, E.C.2. *Livery*, 93.—*Clerk*, S. H. Pitt, M.C.; *Master*, C. B. Christy.

BAKERS (*19*). *Livery*, 260.—*Clerk*, H. M. Collinson, 116 Cannon Street, E.C.4.; *Master*, O. G. Sunderland.

BARBERS (*17*). *Livery*, 148.—*Clerk*, J. H. L. Trustram, M.B.E., 31 Bedford Street, W.C.2.; *Master*, Dr. G. Graham.

BASKETMAKERS (*52*). *Livery*, 239—*Clerk*, C. A., Rust, 9–10 Fenchurch Street, E.C.3.; *Prime Warden*, V. A. Ercolani.

BLACKSMITHS (*40*). *Livery*, 170.—*Clerk*, J. J. Perkin, 70 Old Broad Street, E.C.2.; *Prime Warden*, P. M. Herring.

BOWYERS (*38*). *Livery*, 44.—*Clerk*, A. T. Reed, Provincial House, 98–106 Cannon Street, E.C.4.; *Master*, B. Wood (July, 1962–64).

BREWERS (*14*). *Hall*, Aldermanbury Square, E.C.2. *Livery*, 45.—*Clerk*, R. C. Stanley-Baker; *Master*, F. O. A. G. Bennett, T.D.

BRODERERS (*48*). *Livery*, 59.—*Clerk*, S. G. B. Underwood, 80 Bishopsgate, E.C.2.; *Master*, R. I. Bellinger.

BUTCHERS (*24*). *Hall*, Bartholomew Close, E.C.1. *Livery*, 387.—*Clerk*, H. T. Kennedy; *Master*, A. W. Hedges.

CARMEN (*77*). *Livery*, 406.—*Clerk*, O. G. Sunderland, 15 Eastcheap, E.C.3; *Master*, H. F. Randall.

CARPENTERS (*26*). *Hall*, Throgmorton Avenue, E.C.2. *Livery*, 150.—*Clerk*, Capt. G. B. Barstow, R.N (*ret.*.); *Master*, D. L. Jacob.

CITY OF LONDON SOLICITORS (*79*). *Livery*, 342.—*Clerk*, W. Gillham, 5 Botolph Alley, E.C.3. *Master*, Sir Charles Norton, M.B.E., M.C.

CLOCKMAKERS (*61*). *Livery*, 246.—*Clerk*, R. C. Pennefather, M.B.E., 116 Cannon Street, E.C.4.; *Master*, C. J. Harman.

COACHMAKERS (*72*). *Livery*, 356.—*Clerk*, R. J. D. Smith, 9 Lincoln's Inn Fields, W.C.2.; *Master*, Lt.-Col. R. T. Harris.

COOKS (*35*). *Livery*, 70.—*Clerk*, C. E. Messent, 83 Clarence Street, Kingston-on-Thames; *Master*, W. Goodinge.

COOPERS (*36*). *Livery*, 192.—*Clerk*, D. J. Methven, 13 Devonshire Square, E.C.2; *Master*, R. C. Chapman.

CORDWAINERS (*27*). *Livery*, 108.—*Clerk*, E. J. Mander, 329 High Holborn, W.C.1.; *Master*, A. H. Bartley.

CURRIERS (*29*). *Livery*, 64.—*Clerk*, E. J. Mander, 329 High Holborn, W.C.1.; *Master*, R. Ashworth.

CUTLERS (*18*). *Hall*, 4 Warwick Lane, E.C.4. *Livery*, 88.—*Clerk*, G. H. Mitchell; *Master*, W. E. J. McDonnell.

DISTILLERS (*69*) *Livery*, 130.—*Clerk*, H. B. Dehn, Compter House, Wood Street, E.C.2.; *Master*, A. R. Guillet.

DYERS (*13*). *Hall*, 10 Dowgate Hill, E.C.4. *Livery*, 110.—*Clerk*, D. R. B. Park; *Prime Warden*, J. Blair.

FAN MAKERS (*76*). *Livery*, 163.—*Clerk*, E. J. H. Geffen, 3 Temple Gardens, Middle Temple Lane, E.C.4.; *Master*, H. Young, O.B.E.

FARMERS (*80*). *Office*, 15 Eastcheap, E.C.3. *Livery*, 245.—*Clerk*, O. G. Sunderland; *Master*, E. G. Parsons, C.B.E.

FARRIERS (*55*). *Livery*, 270.—*Clerk*, E. H. N. Wright, 29 Martin Lane, Cannon Street, E.C.4.; *Master*, J. E. Lines.

FELTMAKERS (*63*). *Livery*, 350.—*Clerk*, M. J. Williamson, Arundel House, W.C.2.; *Master*. Col. R. J. Cotterell, T.D.

FLETCHERS (*39*). *Livery*, 62.—*Clerk*, J. N. Gallagher, 2/3 Hind Court, Fleet Street, E.C.4.; *Master*, E. V. Smith.

FOUNDERS (*33*). *Hall*, St. Swithin's Lane, E.C.4. *Livery*, 135.—*Clerk*, H. W. Wiley; *Master*, S. R. Walker, C.B.E.

FRAMEWORK KNITTERS (*64*). *Livery*, 225.—*Clerk*, K. Mountfort, Albany Court Yard, W.1.; *Master*, T. E. Toller.

FRUITERERS (*45*). *Livery*, 206.—*Clerk*, J. J. Moreton, 199 Piccadilly, W.1.; *Master*, Col. F. S. Eiloart, O.B.E.

FURNITURE MAKERS (*83*). *Livery*, 99.—*Clerk*, J. R. Welch, The Rectory, 29 Martin Lane, E.C.4.; *Master*, K. E. Hughes.

GARDENERS (*66*). *Livery*, 180.—*Clerk*, F. N. Steiner, 4-9 Wood Street, E.C.2.; *Master*, Hon. R. C. M. Nathan.

GIRDLERS (*23*). *Livery*, 80.—*Clerk*, J. A. M. Rutherford, 22 St. Andrew Street, E.C.4.; *Master*, H. C. Westall.

GLASS-SELLERS (*71*). *Livery*, 152.—*Hon. Clerk*, H. K. S. Clark, Rowland House, 6 Eldon Street, E.C.2.; *Master*, Marshal of the R.A.F. Sir William Dickson, G.C.B., K.B.E., D.S.O., A.F.C.

GLAZIERS (*53*). *Livery*, 251.—*Clerk*, R. C. Pennefather, M.B.E., 116 Cannon Street, E.C.4.; *Master*, Sir William Beale, O.B.E.

GLOVERS (*62*). *Livery*, 175.—*Clerk*, H. M. Collinson, 116 Cannon Street, E.C.4.; *Master*, A. W. West.

GOLD AND SILVER WYREDRAWERS (*74*). *Livery*, 350.—*Clerk*, P. H. Cresswell, C.C., 5 Lloyds Avenue, E.C.3.; *Master*, G. E. Baker.

GUNMAKERS (*73*). *Livery*, 84.—*Clerk*, F. B. Brandt, 77 Bishopsgate, E.C.2.; *Master*, C. H. Lawrence, M.B.E.

HORNERS (*54*). *Livery*, 440.—*Clerk*, T. F. Clarke, 3 Laurence Pountney Hill, E.C.4.; *Master*, H. H. Woolveridge.

INNHOLDERS (*32*). *Hall*, College Street, Dowgate Hill, E.C.4. *Livery*, 107.—*Clerk*, J. H. Bentley, O.B.E.; *Master*, Rev. E. G. Turner.

JOINERS (*41*). *Livery*, 44.—*Clerk*, B. J. Turner, 12 Devonshire Square, E.C.2.; *Master*, H. F. A. Turner.

LEATHERSELLERS (*15*). *Hall*, 15 St. Helens Place, E.C.3. *Livery*, 150.—*Clerk*, J. Hingston; *Master*, W. R. H. Walker.

LORINERS (*57*). *Livery*, 260.—*Clerk*, F. C. Algar, 31 High Holborn, W.C.1.; *Master*, C. T. Fitzgerald.

MASONS (*30*). *Livery*, 91.—*Clerk*, A. F. Phillpotts. 9 New Square, W.C.2.; *Master*, G. L. Coates.

MASTER MARINERS, HONOURABLE COMPANY OF (*78*). H.Q.S. *Wellington*, Temple Stairs, W.C.2. *Livery*, 200.—*Clerk*, M. H. Disney; *Admiral*, H.R.H. the Prince Philip, Duke of Edinburgh, K.G.; *Master*, Capt. J. D. F. Elvish, C.B.E.

MUSICIANS (*50*). *Livery*, 215.—*Clerk*, Brig. H. A. F. Crewdson, T.D., 1 New Court, Lincoln's Inn, W.C.2.; *Master*, A. R. Stock.

NEEDLEMAKERS (*65*). *Livery*, 230.—*Clerk*, R. H. Lane, 108A Cannon Street, E.C.4.; *Master*, L. H. Beare.

PAINTER STAINERS (*28*). *Hall*, 9 Little Trinity Lane, E.C.4. *Livery*, 270.—*Clerk* (vacant); *Master*, E. L. Giles.

PATTENMAKERS (*70*). *Livery*, 138.—*Clerk*, J. R. Greenop, 66 Gloucester Place, W.1.; *Master*, Col. A. E. Henson, T.D.

PAVIORS (*56*). *Livery*, 225.—*Clerk*, L. McGillivray, 130 Mount Street, W.1.; *Master*, N. F. Foster.

PEWTERERS (*16*). *Hall*, Pewterer's Hall, Oat Lane, E.C.2.; *Livery*, 85.—*Clerk*, A. Stanley Grant; *Master*, A. F. Peacock.

PLAISTERERS (*46*). *Livery*, 111.—*Clerk*, H. Mott, 73 Southampton Row, W.C.1.; *Master*, W. Horrocks.

PLAYING CARD MAKERS (*75*). *Livery*, 150.—*Clerk*, E. K. King, 21A Northampton Square, E.C.1.; *Master*, N. B. Maurice, Ph.D.

PLUMBERS (*31*). *Livery*, 240.—*Clerk*. A. J. Young, 8 Staple Inn, Holborn, W.C.1.; *Master*, B. A. Holroyd.

POULTERS (*34*). *Livery*, 150.—*Clerk*, W. S. Pitt, 22 St. Andrew St., E.C.4.; *Master*, D. C. Sproat.

SADDLERS (*25*). *Hall*, Gutter Lane, Cheapside, E.C.2. *Livery*, 85.—*Clerk*, Capt. R. C. Medley, D.S.O., O.B.E., R.N. (*ret.*); *Master*, D. A. Welch.

SCRIVENERS (*44*). *Livery*, 97.—*Clerk*, H. S. S. Trotter, D.F.C., 79–80 Petty France, S.W.1.; *Master*, B. G. C. Brooks.

SHIPWRIGHTS (*59*). *Livery*, 500.—*Hon. Clerk*, J. E. Walker, 14–20 St. Mary Axe, E.C.3.; *Master*, H.R.H. the Prince Philip, Duke of Edinburgh, K.G.; *Prime Warden*, Sir Ralph Metcalfe.

SPECTACLEMAKERS (*60*). *Livery*, 186.—*Clerk*, R. Champness, Apothecaries' Hall, E.C.4.; *Master*, The Lord Crook.

STATIONERS AND NEWSPAPER MAKERS (*47*). *Hall*, Stationers' Hall, E.C.4. *Livery*, 380.—*Clerk*, G. St. P. Wells; *Master*, J. M. Rivington.

TALLOWCHANDLERS (*21*). *Hall*, 4 Dowgate Hill, E.C.4. *Livery*, 125.—*Clerk*, R. H. Monier-Williams; *Master*, J. C. N. Roberts.

TIN PLATE WORKERS (*67*). *Livery*, 181.—*Clerk*, H. B. Dehn, Compter House, Wood Street, E.C.2.; *Master*, Maj. S. H. Short, O.B.E.

TOBACCO PIPE MAKERS AND TOBACCO BLENDERS (*82*). *Livery*, 200.—*Clerk*, W. M. Wilson, 38 Finsbury Square, E.C.2.; *Master*, W. A. Williamson-Barling.

TURNERS (*51*). *Livery*, 138.—*Clerk*, R. S. Ouvry, 53 Romney Street, S.W.1.; *Master*, J. D. I. Cowper.

TYLERS AND BRICKLAYERS (*37*). *Livery*, 93.—*Clerk*, A. J. Bird, 6 Bedford Row, W.C.1.; *Master*, N. Christopherson, M.C., T.D.

UPHOLDERS (*49*). *Livery*, 150.—*Clerk*, G. E, Graham, 73 Basinghall Street, E.C.2; *Master*, P. T. Woodstock.

WAXCHANDLERS (*20*). *Hall*, Gresham Street, E.C.2. *Livery*, 50.—*Clerk*, C. G. Todd; *Master*, Lt.-Col. T. H. Winterborn.

WEAVERS (*42*). *Livery*, 120.—*Clerk*, R. S. Ouvry, 53 Romney Street, S.W.1.; *Upper Bailiff*, L. E. Tanner, C.V.O., F.S.A.

WHEELWRIGHTS (*68*). *Livery*, 290.—*Clerk*, H. W. K. Calder, C.B.E., 41–42 King William Street, E.C.4.; *Master*, A. W. White.

WOOLMEN (*43*). *Livery*, 96.—*Clerk*, H. A. Harris, 3 Albany Court Yard, W.1.; *Master*, B. Foskett, M.C.

PARISH CLERKS (*No livery*) (*Members*, 46).—*Clerk*, J. H. L. Trustram, M.B.E., 31 Bedford Street, W.C.2.; *Master*, Ald. Sir Ralph Perring.

WATERMEN AND LIGHTERMEN (*No livery*).—*Hall*, 18 St. Mary-at-Hill, E.C.3.—*Clerk*, B. G. Wilson; *Master*, H. P. Robottom.

SCIENTIFIC INSTRUMENT MAKERS (*No livery*)(*Members*, 105).—*Clerk*, H. Mott, 73 Southampton Row, W.C.1.; *Master*, F. W. Dawe.

LAUNDERERS (*No livery*).—*Clerk*, D. K. Rollit, O.B.E., 5 Oak Road, Rochford, Essex, *Master*, L. E. Brown.

NOTE.—In certain companies the election of Master or Prime Warden for the year does not take place till the autumn. In such cases the Master or Prime Warden for 1962–63 is given.

OFFICERS OF THE CITY OF LONDON

		Elect.
Recorder, Sir (Edward) Anthony Hawke	£6,500	1959
Chamberlain, Ean Kendal Stewart-Smith	4,175	1962
Town Clerk, Edward Henry Nichols, T.D.	6,115	1954
Common Serjeant, Carl Douglas Aarvold, O.B.E., T.D.	5,500	1959
Judges of Mayor's and City of London Court. John Cyril Maude, Q.C.	4,750	1954
Col. Graham Rogers, T.D.	4,750	1961
Assistant Judge of the Mayor's and City of London Court, Leslie Kenneth Allen Block D.S.C.	4,400	1953
Commissioner of City Police, Col. A. E. Young, C.M.G., C.V.O.	5,175	1950
Comptroller and City Solicitor, Desmond Heap	5,175	1947
Assistant Solicitor, C. J. Thackery	3,040	1944
Remembrancer, Paul Christopher Davie	4,800	1953

		Elect.
Secondary and High Bailiff of Southwark, Capt. Charles Bettesworth Sanders, C.B.E., V.R.D., R.N.V.R. (*ret.*)	£2,545	1947
Medical Officer for the Port and City of London, J. G. Wilson, M.D., F.R.C.P.	4,800	1954
Coroner, James Milner Helme	700	1940
Steward of Southwark, The Recorder	79 7*s.*	1959
Clerk of the Peace, Leslie Boyd	250	1955
Surveyor, Robert Scott Walker	4,800	1954
Engineer, F. J. Forty, O.B.E.	4,800	1938
City Architect, E. G. Chandler, F.R.I.B.A.	4,430	1961
Swordbearer, Brig. R. H. S. Popham, O.B.E.	1,655	1961
Common Cryer and Serjeant-at-Arms, Brig. P. J. E. Clapham	1,395	1960
Marshal, Col. G. E. P. Hutchins, D.S.O.	1,270	1961
Accountant Auditor, W. F. Moore	3,475	1956
Head Master of City of London School, A. W. Barton, Ph.D.	3,600	1950
Head Master of City of London Freemen's School (vacant)		

		Elect.
Head Mistress, City of London School for Girls, Miss G. M. Colton ...	£2,800	1949
Principal, Guildhall School of Music and Drama, G. Thorne..........	3,520	1959
Librarian and Curator and Director of the Art Gallery, A. H. Hall......	3,055	1956
Deputy-Keeper of the Records, P. E. Jones..........................	2,780	1945
Registrar and High Bailiff of Mayor's and City of London Court and Clerk of the Seal, Eric Ernest Stammers	3,550	1945
Keeper of the Guildhall, F. R. Tomkins..........................	1,765	1955
Principal Clerks:—		
Chamberlain's Dept., H. P. Greenhill..........................	3,105	1958

		Elect.
Principal Clerks—continued.		
Town Clerk's Office, C. C. Taylor, O.B.E..........................	£3,205	1951
Remembrancer's Office, E. H. Mould, O.B.E..........................	3,040	1939
Market Superintendents:—		
Central, E. A. Hornsby..........	3,155	1940
Cattle, E. F. McCleery..........	3,105	1946
Billingsgate and Leadenhall, C. A. Wiard..........................	2,855	1956
Spitalfields, D. Allchin..........	2,855	1957
Superintending Engineer, Tower Bridge, Capt. C. G. Gosling, O.B.E., R.N. (ret.)..........................	2,655	1959
Superintendent, Epping Forest and Burnham Beeches, A. Qvist.......	2,620	1960

THE LONDON COUNTY COUNCIL

Offices, The County Hall, Westminster Bridge, S.E.1.

THE London County Council was constituted under the Local Government Act of 1888. London is an *administrative* county, covering an area of 117 square miles, with a population (1962 est.) of 3,185,770.

The City of London is a county for *non-administrative* purposes, such as justices, &c., and the Metropolis outside the City is also a county for *non-administrative* purposes, by name the County of London. The offices of Clerk of the Council and Clerk of the Peace are not held jointly in the County.

The Council comprises 21 aldermen, and 126 councillors, together 147, or, if the chairman of the Council be also an elected member or alderman, 146. The term of office for aldermen is 6 years, and half their number retires every 3 years. The councillors are elected for 3 years, and they elect the aldermen. The position of aldermen and councillors is the same, except as to the method of election and the term of office.

Meetings of the Council are held fortnightly in session time, and the standing committees meet fortnightly, except a few which meet monthly.

The *Finance Committee* has important statutory powers. No costs, debt or liability exceeding £100 may be incurred by the Council except upon a resolution passed on an estimate submitted by the Finance Committee. The Council has a net debt, according to the latest returns of £382,680,000 (£288 980 000 represents debt incurred for housing). Its annual expenditure on revenue account is about £161,000,000 and on capital account about £45,000,000. Advances amounting to over £20 000,000 have been made on loan under the Housing and Small Dwellings Acquisition Acts to people who wish to buy a home.

The *General Purposes Committee* is responsible for advising the Council on the more important general questions, allocation of duties to Committees and heads of departments, consultation with other local authorities and government departments, matters relating to legislation, senior staff appointments, the development of the South Bank and the Crystal Palace site and the management of the Royal Festival Hall, and civil defence.

The *Children's Committee* is charged with the care of nearly 10,000 deprived and neglected children.

The *Education Committee* comprises thirty-eight members of the Council and twelve co-opted members. Women as well as men must be included (*see* p. 644).

The *Establishment Committee* is responsible for the efficient and economical use of manpower and for a general control over numbers, grading, pay and conditions of staff (except teachers). The Council employs over 65,000 staff of all grades.

The *Fire Brigade Committee* is responsible for carrying out the duties laid on the Council by the Fire Services Act, 1947.

The *Health Committee*, set up under the National Health Service Act, 1946, is responsible for health services provided under that Act and for discharging the functions of the Council under the Mental Health Acts and the Clean Air Act, 1956. Under this committee are nine Divisional Health Committees, the majority of whose members are drawn from the Corporation of the City of London and the Metropolitan Borough Councils. These divisional committees are entrusted with considerable responsibilities for the day-to-day administration of the personal health services.

The *Housing Committee* performs the duties placed upon the Council by the various Housing Acts, including the clearance of insanitary areas and the relief of overcrowding. The total capital expenditure incurred up to March 31, 1963, in respect of all schemes was £340,000,000. The income (rents &c.) for 1963–64 in respect of dwellings and housing estates of the Council is estimated at over £28,000,000. The total of the Exchequer subsidy in respect of the Council's housing operations is estimated at £5,210,000.

The *Supplies Committee* is responsible for supplying stores, etc., arranging contracts for printing etc., sale and disposal of old or surplus materials and general oversight of transport.

The *Rivers and Drainage Committee* administers the Metropolitan Main Drainage system which covers about 179 square miles, including certain districts outside the county, and comprises about 420 miles of main, storm-relief, intercepting and outfall sewers, twelve pumping stations, two sewage outfalls, and three sludge vessels. The total capital outlay on main drainage is over £30,000,000, and further work is in progress. This committee is also responsible for Thames flood prevention, the upkeep of the Thames tunnels, most of the Thames bridges and Woolwich Ferry.

The *Town Planning Committee* deals with questions relating to town-planning, the carrying out of street improvements and construction of bridges, tunnels and ferries, the naming of streets and numbering of houses, the maintenance of historic buildings and monuments, and also regulates under statute such matters as the construction and safety of buildings, building lines, space about buildings, and means of escape in case of fire.

The *Welfare Committee* provides residential accommodation for the aged and infirm and for other people in need of care and attention, including homeless families. They are also charged with the welfare of blind and other handicapped persons.

The *Parks Committee* is responsible for the acquisition and maintenance of parks and open spaces, and the provision of facilities for sport, open-air entertainment and exhibitions in them; the *Public Control Committee* is responsible for the control of storage of explosive substances and petroleum; testing weights and measures; the granting of licences for music, dancing, boxing and wrestling; administration of the Shops Acts; licensing and inspection of employment agencies, nurses' agencies and massage establishments; licensing of premises under the Cinematograph Acts; registration of motor cars; collection of duties on motor cars, dog, game, gun and certain other local taxation licences.

The *expenditure* of the Council, including loans to other local authorities, is met by two chief sources of supply—capital money raised by external borrowing, or by the use of the Sinking Fund of the Council's debt, the Superannuation Fund, etc., and current income raised in a county rate or by the revenue of undertakings. Substantial contributions are received from the Exchequer by way of housing subsidies, the General Grant, grants in respect of school meals and capital grants towards the cost of road improvements. All borrowings by the Council are subject to the provision of a sinking fund, under Treasury approval, sufficient to repay all expenditure generally within a period of 60 years (in a few cases the limit is 80 years). The total stock outstanding at March 31, 1963, was £204,243,000 and in addition over £200,000,000 had been borrowed from the Public Works Loan Board and other sources.

The *Rating* for the year 1963–64, as shown by the statement below (which relates to rate accounts only), amounted to 4*s*. 2½*d*. in the pound over the whole county, including the City, and a further rate over the county outside the City of ½*d*. in the pound, together 4*s*. 3*d*. (equivalent rate poundage based on old valuation levels was 12*s*. 5½*d*.). The total rate for 1962–63 was 11*s*. 3*d*. The *Rateable Value* of the County of London, on April 6, 1963, was estimated to be approximately £332,908,134—a 1*d*. rate over the whole county producing £1,360,000.

ESTIMATED EXPENDITURE AND AMOUNTS REQUIRED TO BE RAISED BY RATE 1963–64

Rate Account	Expenditure	Income	Net Expenditure	Relief from Balances	Produce of the County Rate		
					Amount	Rate in £	
	£	£	£	£	£	*s.*	*d.*
General County....	124,907,180	54,827,950	70,079,230	1,399,230	68,680,000	4	2½
Special County	576,650	19,700	556,950	*Cr.* 37,050	594,000		0½
	125,483,830	54,847,650	70,636,180	1,362,180	69,274,000	4	3
Corresponding figures for 1962–63.....	112,050,400	50,681,350	61,369,050	166,050	61,203,000	11	3

ESTIMATED EXPENDITURE ON RATE ACCOUNTS IN 1963–64

Service	Expenditure, including Debt Charges £	Income (other than Exchequer Grants) £	Exchequer Grants £	Net Expenditure falling on Rate £	Equivalent Rate in £	
					s.	*d.*
Children's services.............	5,243,720	410,760	—	4,832,960		3·55
Education..........................	73,862,315	9,053,500	—	64,808,815	3	11·66
Fire Service.......................	4,372,010	413,500	—	3,958,510		2·91
Local health services.............	8,345,540	629,320	—	7,716,220		5·67
Main drainage.....................	4,703,510	807,840	—	3,895,670		2·86
Roads	1,804,560	687,500	—	1,117,060		0·82
Parks and open spaces..........	3,146,770	409,250	—	2,737,520		2·01
Town planning and building control...........................	2,303,730	580,000	—	1,723,730		1·27
Welfare services.................	5,488,540	1,580,170	—	3,908,370		2·87
Other services....................	4,998,475	1,336,430	—	3,662,045		2·73
Special provision for:—						
Capital Expenditure...........	3,000,000	—	—	3,000,000		2·21
Contingencies..................	2,500,000	—	—	2,500,000		1·84
	119,769,170	15,908,270	—	103,860,900	6	4·40
Net deficiencies:—						
Housing........................	10,782,110	—	5,210,000	5,572,110		4·12
Royal Festival Hall...........	142,550	—	—	142,550		0·11
General Grant......................	—	—	33,500,000	*Cr.*33,500,000	*Cr.* 2	0·63
Other Govt. grants in aid of services..........................	—	—	5,439,380	*Cr.* 5,439,380	*Cr.*	4·00
	130,693,830	15,908,270	44,149,380	70,636,180	4	4·00
Relief from Balances............	—	1,362,180	—	*Cr.*1,362,180	*Cr.*	1·00
	130,693,830	17,270,450	44,1[illegible],380	69,274,000	4	3·00

ALPHABETICAL LIST OF THE 21 ALDERMEN AND 126 COUNCILLORS

The Twenty-second London County Council was elected April 13, 1961, for *three* years; the electors returned 84 *Labour* representatives and 42 representatives of the *Conservative* Party. The Aldermen (14 *Labour*, 7 *Conservative*) gave a Labour majority of 49. One Labour member has since joined the Liberal Party.

The Right Honourable the Chairman (1963–64)........... A. R. Stamp.
Vice-Chairman (1963–64)........................... A. E. Wicks.
Deputy Chairman (1963–64)........................... Mrs U. Lister, O.B.E.
Leader of the Council............................ Sir Isaac Hayward.
Leader of the Opposition.......................... Sir Percy Rugg.

Name	*Electoral Division*
Abbott, F. L. (*C.*)..........	*Battersea, S.*
*Allen, W. R. (*Lab.*)........	*Peckham.*
*e**Andrews, J. W. (*Lab.*)......	*Woolwich, E.*
*Avery, E. (*Lab.*)...........	*Paddington, N.*
*Bagnari, B. A. (*Lab.*).......	*Islington, E.*
*Banfield, F. W. (*Lab.*)......	*Barons Court.*
Banks, N. D. (*C.*)..........	*Lewisham, W.*
†Barton, S. J. (*Lab.*).........	*Alderman until 1964.*
*Bayliss, E., O.B.E. (*Lab.*)....	*Islington, E.*
*Begley, W. W. (*Lab.*)......	*Vauxhall.*
*Bennett, F. E., C.B.E. (*C.*)...	*Hampstead.*
e†Bentwich, Mrs. H. C. (*Lab.*).	*Alderman until 1964.*
Bird, C. W. J. (*Lab.*).......	*Stepney.*
Blackman, A. J. (*Lab.*)......	*Deptford.*
†Bolton, Mrs. D. (*Lab.*).....	*Alderman until 1964.*
*Bondy, L. W. (*Lab.*).......	*Holborn and St. Pancras, S.*
Bowen, Miss M. (*C.*).......	*Battersea, S.*
Bowman, E. T. (*C.*)........	*Holborn and St. Pancras, S.*
*Bradfield, G. R. D. (*C.*)....	*Lewisham, W.*
Bramall, E. A. (*Lab.*).......	*Bethnal Green.*
*e**Branagan, J. P. (*Lab.*)	*Poplar.*
*e*Brooks, J. E. (*C.*)..........	*Chelsea.*
Browne, H. E. (*Lab.*).......	*Paddington, N.*
*Bull, Mrs. E. E. (*Lab.*)......	*Islington, N.*
*Campbell, Mrs. L. (*Lab.*)....	*Holborn and St. Pancras, S.*
Carr, E. G. (*Lab.*)..........	*Vauxhall.*
*e*Carr, W. C., M.P. (*C.*)	*Alderman until 1967.*
*Cayford, Mrs. F. E. (*Lab.*)..	*Shoreditch and Finsbury.*
*e**Chaplin, Mrs. I. (*Lab.*).....	*Islington, E.*
*e**Chesworth, D. P. (*Lab.*)....	*Kensington, N.*
*e**Chrisp, A. C. (*Lab.*)........	*Greenwich.*
*e**Clarke, Lady Selwyn- (*Lab.*)	*Fulham.*
*Cleaver, R. J. (*C.*).........	*Hampstead.*
e†Cole, Mrs. M. (*Lab.*).......	*Alderman until 1964.*
†Coppock, Sir Richard, C.B.E. (*Lab.*)..................	*Alderman until 1967.*
*Corbet, Mrs. F. K., M.P. (*Lab.*)	*Peckham.*
*Corry, M. W. Lowry- (*C.*).	*Paddington, S.*
*Dartmouth, The Countess of (*C.*)	*Lewisham, W.*
*Deer, Mrs. O. G. (*Lab.*)....	*Shoreditch and Finsbury.*
*Denington, Mrs. E. J. (*Lab.*).	*St. Pancras, N.*
*Drapkin, W. (*C.*)..........	*St. Marylebone.*
*Edmonds, R. (*Lab.*)........	*Fulham.*
Emden, W. W. (*C.*).......	*Clapham.*
†Faringdon, Lord (*Lab.*)......	*Alderman until 1967.*
*Farmer, N. W., C.B.E. (*C.*)..	*Lewisham, N.*
*Fiske, W. G.. C.B.E. (*Lab.*) ...	*Barons Court.*
Fletcher, A. T. R. (*C.*).....	*Lewisham, N.*
*Gale, P. V. (*C.*)............	*Streatham.*
Gardiner, G. A., Q.C. (*Lab.*).	*Alderman until 1967.*
Gates, A. J. (*Lab.*)..........	*Southwark.*
*Gillinder, T. W. (*Lab.*).....	*Lewisham, S.*
*Gluckstein, Sir Louis, T.D., Q.C. (*C.*)................	*St. Marylebone.*
†Goodwin, R. E., C.B.E. (*Lab.*)	*Alderman until 1967.*
†Greenwood, Sir James, C.B.E. (*C.*)	*Alderman until 1967.*
*Grieves, Mrs. A. Ll. (*Lab.*)..	*Kensington, N.*
*Guy, W. H. (*Lab.*).........	*Poplar.*
*Hambly, E. H. (*Lib.*)	*Lewisham, S.*
†Hastings, S. (*Lab.*)..........	*Alderman until 1964.*
*Hawes, F. E. G. (*Lab.*)......	*Lewisham, S.*
†Hayward, Sir Isaac (*Lab.*)...	*Alderman until 1964.*
*e*Highett, L. T. (*C.*).........	*Clapham.*
†Hillman, E. S. (*Lab.*).......	*Hackney, Cent.*
Hoare, Mrs. E. M. R. (*C.*)..	*Putney.*
*e**Holman, Mrs. D. M. (*Lab.*).	*Bethnal Green.*
Iremonger, Mrs. L. D. (*C.*)..	*Norwood.*
†Jay, Mrs. P. (*Lab.*).........	*Battersea, N.*
*Jenkins, H. G. (*Lab.*).......	*Stoke Newington and Hackney N.*
*e**Johnson, Mrs. J. A. (*Lab.*)...	*Greenwich.*
*e**Keen, J. J. (*Lab.*)...........	*Southwark.*
*Kemp, A. J. (*Lab.*)..........	*Bermondsey.*
*Kerr, Mrs. A. (*Lab.*)........	*Putney.*
*Kerr, D. L. (*Lab.*)...........	*Wandsworth, Cent.*
*e**Kiely, Mrs. H. (*Lab.*).......	*Battersea, N.*
*Kirby, A. D. (*Lab.*).........	*Stepney.*
*Lamborn, H. G. (*Lab.*).....	*Dulwich.*
*Lawrence, Sir Frederick (*C.*)	*Paddington, S.*
*Lee, Mrs. G. F. (*Lab.*)......	*St. Pancras, N.*
*e**Lees, Mrs. S. L. (*Lab.*)......	*Barons Court.*
Lestor, Miss Joan (*Lab.*)......	*Wandsworth, C.*
Lister, Mrs. U., O.B.E. (*C.*)..	*Woolwich, W.*
*e*Livingston, W. W. (*C.*).....	*Norwood.*
Lowe, G. (*Lab.*).............	*Paddington, N.*
*Lygoe, H. J. L., O.B.E., M.S.M. (*Lab.*)....................	*Islington, S.W.*
e†McIntosh, Mrs. M. (*Lab.*)...	*Alderman until 1964.*
McLaughlin, A. (*Lab.*)......	*Bethnal Green.*
Mansel, Miss, I. C. (*C.*)......	*Alderman until 1967.*
Marock, N. (*Lab.*)..........	*Brixton.*
*Melman, S. A. (*Lab.*).......	*Vauxhall.*
*Mersey, Viscount (*C.*)......	*Paddington, S.*
*e*Middleton, Mrs. E. R. M. (*C.*)..................	*Woolwich, W.*
*Middleton, Mrs. P. A. (*Lab.*)	*Greenwich.*
*Miller, Sir James (*C.*).......	*Cities of London and Westminster.*
*Mishcon, C. J. V. (*Lab.*)....	*Brixton.*
†Montefiore, H. H. Sebag-(*C.*)	*Alderman until 1967.*
*e**Murray, A. J. (*Lab.*)........	*Dulwich.*
e†Nathan, Lady (*Lab.*)........	*Alderman until 1964.*
*Niederman, A. C. (*Lab.*)....	*Poplar.*
Patten, E. J. K. (*C.*)........	*Norwood.*
*Payton, B. A. (*Lab.*).......	*Stoke Newington and Hackney, N.*
†Pepler, Lady (*C.*)..........	*Alderman until 1967.*

Name	Electoral Division
*Petrie, Lady (*C.*)	*Kensington, S.*
*e**Phillips, Mrs. I. L. (*Lab.*)	*Hammersmith, N.*
Pitt, D. T. (*Lab.*)	*Stoke Newington and Hackney, N.*
*Plummer, A. D. H. (*C.*)	*St. Marylebone.*
*Pope, C. W. (*Lab.*)	*Islington, N.*
*Powe, F. W. (*Lab.*)	*Islington, S.W.*
*Prichard, N. G. M. (*Lab.*)	*Hammersmith, N.*
*Rankin, W. (*Lab.*)	*Fulham.*
*e**Reed, E. E. (*Lab.*)	*Dulwich.*
*Rezler, Dr. H. (*Lab.*)	*Hackney, Cent.*
*Rose, Mrs. H. (*Lab.*)	*Islington, N.*
Rose, Hon. Mrs. T. (*C.*)	*Lewisham, N.*
*Rowe, G. F. (*Lab.*)	*Wandsworth, Cent.*
†Rugg, Sir Percy (*C.*)	*Chelsea.*
*Salmon, Sir Samuel (*C.*)	*Cities of London and Westminster.*
Samuel, I. N. (*C.*)	*Battersea, S.*
†Samuels, A. E. (*Lab.*)	*Bermondsey.*
Samuels, J. S. (*Lab.*)	*Battersea, N.*
*Sargood, R. (*Lab.*)	*Peckham.*
*e**Serota, Mrs. B. (*Lab.*)	*Brixton.*
*e**Shearman, H. C. (*Lab.*)	*Deptford.*
Sherman, L. (*Lab.*)	*Hackney, Cent.*
*Simons, A. S. (*Lab.*)	*Deptford.*
Smith, J. I. Tweedie- (*C.*)	*Putney.*
†Soper, Rev. Dr. D. O. (*Lab.*)	*Alderman until 1964.*
*Stamp, A. R. (*Lab.*)	*Islington, S.W.*
*Stein, W. O. (*Lab.*)	*Woolwich, E.*
*Stillman, H. E. (*Lab.*)	*Southwark.*
Sullivan, W. (*Lab.*)	*Stepney.*
*e*Tennant, Miss A. M. (*C.*)	*Cities of London and Westminster.*
*e**Thomas, J. R. (*Lab.*)	*Bermondsey.*
*e**Tonge, F. L. (*Lab.*)	*St. Pancras, N.*
*e**Townend, Lt.-Col. H. S., O.B.E. (*C.*)	*Chelsea.*
*e**Townsend, Mrs. L. M. (*C.*)	*Hampstead.*
Tracey, Mrs. U. (*C.*)	*Clapham.*
Udal, J. O. (*C.*)	*Kensington, S.*
†Vaughan, Dr. G. F. (*C.*)	*Streatham.*
*Vigars, R. L. (*C.*)	*Kensington, S.*
e†Walton, Lady (*C.*)	*Alderman until 1967.*
Warren, Dr. Brian (*C.*)	*Alderman until 1967.*
Wayman, M. G. (*C.*)	*Woolwich, W.*
*e*Weyer, F. W. (*C.*)	*Streatham.*
*Wicks, A. E. (*Lab.*)	*Shoreditch and Finsbury.*
*Wilson, Mrs. O. M. (*Lab.*)	*Kensington, N.*
*Woods, E. E., O.B.E. (*Lab.*)	*Hammersmith, N.*
†Wright, G. P. (*Lab.*)	*Alderman until 1964.*
*e**Young, J. (*Lab.*)	*Woolwich, E.*

NOTE.—The letters in parentheses stand for the Party whose candidate the Member was at the election—*viz.* (*Lab.*) Labour; (*C.*) Conservative. * Denotes member of the last Council for the same division. † Denotes other members of the last Council.

The Council meets on alternate Tuesdays at 3 p.m.

PARTY STRENGTH

From 1949 until April, 1955, 129 Councillors represented 43 Divisions. In the Twentieth, Twenty-first and Twenty-second Councils, 126 Councillors represent 42 Divisions.

Party	*18th Council*	*19th Council*	*20th Council*	*21st Council*	*22nd Council*
Labour	64	92	74	101	84*
Conservative	64	37	52	25	42
Liberal	1	*Nil*	*Nil*	*Nil*	*Nil*†
	129	129	126	126	126

*Now 83. †Now 1.

Votes cast in 1961	
Labour (126 candidates)	1,177,658
Conservative (126 candidates)	987,494
Others (87 candidates)	152,804
Total (339 candidates)	2,317,956

EDUCATION COMMITTEE (*Chairman*, Mrs. M. McIntosh; *Vice-Chairman*, J. Young)—Members whose names are marked *e* form the Education Committee, together with the Chairman, Vice-Chairman and Deputy-Chairman of the Council, and the following co-opted members—Mrs. I. M. C. Bonham, J. P. Carruthers, Mrs. C. Cole, Mrs. E. K. Goodrich, D. Grant, Mrs. M. Griffith, Lady Hendy, Hon. Mrs. D. Moore-Brabazon, K. Payne, C. Pearce, Mrs. B. Vernon, R. McKinnon Wood.

CHIEF OFFICERS OF THE LONDON COUNTY COUNCIL

Clerk of the Council, Sir William Hart, C.M.G. £7,100

Deputy Clerk of the Council, T. G. Randall, C.B.E. £4,320 to £5,000

Comptroller of the Council, F. Holland £6,575

Chief Engineer and County Surveyor (vacant).

Architect to the Council and Superintending Architect of Metropolitan Buildings, H. Bennett £6,575

Solicitor and Parliamentary Officer, J. G. Barr £6,575

Chief Officer of the Fire Brigade, L. W. T. Leete, M.B.E. £4,550

Medical Officer of Health and Principal School Medical Officer, J. A. Scott, O.B.E., M.D., £6,575

Valuer, H. T. Woolcott £5,075

Director of Housing, J. P. Macey £5,075

Chief Officer, Public Control Dept., E. W. Newberry, M.B.E. £4,350

Chief Officer, Parks Department, F. Hallowes £4,650

Education Officer, W. F. Houghton £6,575

Chief Officer of Supplies, A. Morrison £5,475

Chief Officer, Welfare Department, W. Johnston £4,350

Chief Officer, School Meals and Catering Dept., H. R. Duffield-Harding £4,350

Children's Officer, T. G. Randall, C.B.E. (*see* above)

Hours, (Monday to Thursday) 9.15 to 5.15; (Friday) 9.15 to 5.30; (Saturday) 9.15 to 12.15.

Public and Private Buildings in London

ADELPHI, Strand, W.C.2.—Adelphi Terrace and district commemorate the four architect brothers, James, John, Robert and William ADAM, who laid out the district (formerly Durham House) at the close of the 18th century. Four of the streets in the Adelphi were formerly called James, John, Robert, and William Streets to commemorate these founders of the Adam style of architecture and internal decoration. They are now Adam Street, John Adam Street, Robert Street and Durham House Street. Extensive rebuilding took place between the two World Wars, and there are now few 18th-century houses left in the district. In the neighbourhood of the Adelphi was York House, built by the Duke of Buckingham in 1625 (the Water Gate of which still stands in Embankment Gardens), the commemorative streets being *Charles* Street, *Villiers* Street, *Duke* Street, *Of* Lane, *Buckingham* Street (Of Lane is now "York Buildings").

AUSTRALIA HOUSE, Strand, W.C.2.—A handsome and imposing building, erected 1911–14 by the Commonwealth of Australia as the offices of the High Commissioner for the Commonwealth. NEW SOUTH WALES, QUEENSLAND, VICTORIA and WESTERN AUSTRALIA have separate offices in the Strand; TASMANIA at Golden Cross House, Charing Cross, and SOUTH AUSTRALIA at S.A. House, Marble Arch.

BALTIC EXCHANGE, St. Mary Axe, E.C.3.—The world market for the chartering of cargo ships. The Exchange was built in 1903 and the new wing opened by Her Majesty the Queen on Nov. 21, 1956.

BANK OF ENGLAND, Threadneedle Street, E.C.2. (Not open to sightseers.)—The Bank of England, founded in 1694, has always been closely connected with the Government. The present building, completed in 1940 to the designs of Sir Herbert Baker, incorporates features reminiscent of the earlier architects, Sampson (1734), Sir Robert Taylor (1765) and Sir John Soane (1788). A Bank picquet is mounted every evening by the Brigade of Guards.

BRIDGES.—The bridges over the Thames (from East to West) are the *Tower Bridge* (built by the Corporation of London and opened in 1894), with its bascules, affording a fine view of the Pool and of the metropolis; *London Bridge* (opened after rebuilding in 1831, and until 1750 the only bridge over the Thames in London), with the London Monument (*q.v.*) and Fishmongers' Hall; *Southwark Bridge* (opened in 1819, and rebuilt by the Corporation of London, 1922); *Blackfriars Bridge* (opened in 1869 and widened by the Corporation of London in 1908); width, 105 ft.; *Waterloo Bridge* (Rennie), width, 42 ft. 6 ins. (opened in 1817) commanding a fine view of western London (rebuilt by L.C.C. and re-opened 1944); *Hungerford Bridge* (railway bridge with a footbridge); *Westminster Bridge* (built in 1750 and then presenting a view that inspired Wordsworth's sonnet; rebuilt and re-opened in 1862; width, 84 ft.) with Thornycroft's *Boadicea* at the north-eastern end; this bridge leads from Westminster Abbey and the Houses of Parliament to the County Hall (*q.v.*) and St. Thomas's Hospital; *Lambeth Bridge* (rebuilt by L.C.C. and opened in 1932) leading from Lambeth Palace to Millbank; *Vauxhall* Bridge (rebuilt in 1906) leading to Kennington Oval; *Chelsea Bridge*, leading from Chelsea Hospital to Battersea Park (reconstructed and widened 1937); and *Albert Bridge* (1873); *Battersea Bridge* (opened in 1890); *Wandsworth Bridge* (opened in 1873; rebuilt and re-opened in 1940); *Putney Bridge* (opened in 1886 and widened in 1933) where the Oxford and Cambridge Boat Race is started for Mortlake; *Hammersmith Bridge* (rebuilt 1887); *Barnes Bridge* (for pedestrians only, 1933); *Chiswick Bridge* (opened in 1933); *King Edward VII Bridge, Kew* (rebuilt in 1902), leading to the Royal Botanic Gardens, Kew; *Twickenham Lock Bridge*; *Twickenham Bridge* (opened in 1933); *Richmond Bridge* (opened in 1777); *Kingston Bridge* and *Hampton Court Bridge* (rebuilt, 1933).

BUCKINGHAM PALACE, St. James's Park, S.W.1. (Not open to the public.)—Was purchased by King George III. in 1762 from the heir of the Duke of Buckingham, and was altered by Nash for King George IV. The London home of the Sovereign since Queen Victoria's accession in 1837. Refronted in stone (part of the Queen Victoria Memorial) by Sir Aston Webb in 1913.

The Queen's Gallery, containing a selection of the finest pictures and works of art from all parts of the royal collection, was opened to the public on July 25, 1962. Open: Tues.–Sat., 11–6 p.m.; Sundays, 2–5 p.m.; Bank Holiday Mondays, 11–6 p.m. (Closed on other Mondays). Admission, 2*s.* 6*d.*, entering from Buckingham Palace Road.

The Royal Mews is open to visitors on Wednesday afternoons only. Applications for tickets should be addressed in writing to the Superintendent, accompanied by an addressed envelope. The following charges, the proceeds of which are devoted to charities, are payable on admission: *Adults*, 1*s.*; *Children under* 16, 6*d.*; *Children in arms*, free.

CANADA HOUSE, Trafalgar Square, S.W.1.—A conspicuous building on the Western side of the Square, in which are the Offices of the High Comissioner of the Dominion and Officials dealing with Trade, Emigration, etc. Designed by Sir Robert Smirke in 1820, it was renovated and embellished when vacated by the Union Club. Certain interior features of the original building are preserved, and the spacious, richly furnished room now occupied by the High Commissioner is much admired. Surrounded by Offices of Canadian Banks, Steamship, Railway and other Dominion Companies, the Canadian Building is one of London's landmarks. It was opened by H.M. King George V. in June, 1925.

CANONBURY TOWER, Canonbury, N.1.—Till recently a club for boys and girls from the vicinity (in the remains of the 16th-century house of the Priors of St. Bartholomew), but at the moment partly in use as headquarters of a theatre company. Contains the "Spencer" and "Compton" oak-panelled rooms. Other relics of Canonbury House can be seen nearby.

CARLYLE'S HOUSE, 24 Cheyne Row, Chelsea, S.W.3. The home of Thomas Carlyle for 47 years until his death in 1881, and containing much of his furniture, etc. Now the property of the National Trust. Open daily, except Tuesdays, 10–1, 2–6, or dusk, if earlier. Sundays, 2–6. Admission, 2*s.*; Children and Students, 1*s.*

CATHOLIC CENTRAL LIBRARY, St. Francis Friary, 47 Francis Street, S.W.1.—Founded as a private library in 1914, it was taken over in 1959 by the Franciscan Friars of the Atonement. Stock of 45,000 volumes for lending and reference, on many aspects of religion (devotional, Church history, doctrine, etc.), sociology, fine arts, literature, history, travel, biography and fiction. Books are sent by post when required. Hours of opening: Mon.–Fri. 11–7; Sat. 11–5.

CEMETERIES.—For *Bunhill Fields*, see p. 497. In *Kensal Green Cemetery*, North Kensington, W.10 (70 acres), are tombs of W. M. Thackeray, Anthony Trollope, Sydney Smith, Shirley Brooks, Wilkie Collins, Tom Hood, W. Mulready, George Cruikshank, John Leech, Leigh Hunt, Brunel ("Great Eastern"), Ross (Arctic), Charles Kemble and Charles Mathews (Actors). In *Highgate Cemetery*, N.6., are the tombs of George Eliot, Herbert Spencer, Michael Faraday, and G. J. Holyoake. In *Abney Park Cemetery*, Stoke Newington, N.16, are the tomb of General Booth, founder of the Salvation Army, and memorials to many Nonconformist Divines. In the *South Metropolitan Cemetery*, Norwood, S.E.27, are the tombs of C. H. Spurgeon, Lord Alverstone, Douglas Jerrold, John Belcher, R.A., Theodore Watts-Dunton, Dr. Moffat (Missionary), Sir H. Bessemer, Sir H. Maxim, Sir J. Barnby, Sir A. Manns, and J. Whitaker, F.S.A. (*Whitaker's Almanack*). In the churchyard of the former *Marylebone Chapel* are buried Allan Ramsay (poet), Hoyle (whist), Ferguson (astronomer), Charles Wesley (hymn writer) and his son Samuel Wesley (musician). The chapel itself was demolished in 1949. CREMATORIA.—*Ilford* (City of London); *Norwood; Hendon; Streatham Park; Finchley* (St. Marylebone) and *Golder's Green* (12 acres), near Hampstead Heath, with "Garden of Rest" and memorials to famous men and women.

CENOTAPH, Whitehall, S.W.1. — (Literally "empty tomb"). Monument erected "To the Glorious Dead," as a memorial to all ranks of the Sea, Land and Air Forces who gave their lives in the service of the Empire during the First World War. Erected as a temporary memorial in 1919 and replaced by a permanent structure in 1920. Unveiled by King George V. on Armistice Day, 1920. An additional inscription was added after the 1939–45 War, to commemorate those who gave their lives in that conflict.

CHARTERHOUSE, Charterhouse Square, E.C.1. (*Master*, Rev. T. S. Nevill, M.A.; *Registrar and Clerk to the Governors*, N. Long-Brown, M.A., LL.B.), a Carthusian monastery until 1538, purchased from the Earl of Suffolk in 1611 by Thomas Sutton as a home for aged "Brothers" and a School (at Godalming since 1872). The buildings are partly 14th (but mainly 16th) century. They suffered much damage during the 1939–45 War but are now restored and can accommodate 40 "Brothers." Visitors must apply to the Registrar for permission to see the Hall, etc. (Charge for admission, 4*s*. 9*d*. per person). Roger Williams, the founder and governor of Rhode Island, U.S.A., was on June 25, 1621, elected a scholar of Sutton's Hospital. Other famous Carthusians are John Wesley; the poets Crashaw and Lovelace; Addison and Steele; Sir William Blackstone and Thackeray, who described "Greyfriars School" (Charterhouse) in "The Newcomes."

CHELSEA PHYSIC GARDEN, Royal Hospital Road, S.W.3.—A garden of general botanical research, established in latter part of 17th century by the Society of Apothecaries, occupies site presented in 1722 by Sir Hans Sloane. Transferred in 1899 to the Trustees of the London Parochial Charities. Tickets of admission for approved students obtainable from the Clerk to the Trustees, 3 Temple Gardens, E.C.4.

CHELSEA ROYAL HOSPITAL (founded by Charles II, in 1682, and built by Wren; opened in 1694), Royal Hospital Road, Chelsea, S.W.3. for old and disabled soldiers. Great Hall now used as Dining Hall for in-pensioners. Much damaged by bombs in the Second World War. The extensive grounds include the former Ranelagh Gardens. Open daily 10 to 12 and 2 to 4, and on Sunday afternoons. *Governor*, General Sir Frank Simpson, G.B.E., K.C.B., D.S.O.; *Lieut-Governor and Secretary*, Major-Gen. R. G. S. Hobbs, C.B., D.S.O., O.B.E.

COLLEGE OF ARMS OR HERALDS' COLLEGE, Queen Victoria Street, E.C.4.—Her Majesty's Officers of Arms (Kings, Heralds and Pursuivants of Arms) were incorporated by Richard III., and granted Derby House on the site of the present College building by Philip and Mary. The building now in use was built after the Fire of London. The powers vested by the Crown in the Earl Marshal (The Duke of Norfolk) with regard to full State ceremonial, and the granting and use of Armorial Bearings, are largely exercised through this College. Enquiry may be made to the Officer on duty in the Public Office every day between 10 a.m. and 4 p.m. Saturdays, 10 to 1.

COMMONWEALTH INSTITUTE, Holland Park, S. Kensington W.11.—A permanent exhibition in a new building opened on Nov. 6, 1962, by Her Majesty the Queen, replacing the former Imperial Institute opened in 1893 in S. Kensington. An interesting feature of the new building is its paraboloid copper-sheathed roof. The Institute contains, in 60,000 square feet arranged in 3 galleries, a visual representation of the history and geography of the Commonwealth countries and dependencies: on the ground floor, exhibits of Canada, Australia, New Zealand, India, Pakistan and Ceylon; on the middle gallery, the African territories; and on the upper gallery, the island territories of the Commonwealth.

Open, week-days, 10–5.30; Sundays, 2.30–6. Admission free. Closed Good Friday, Christmas Eve and Christmas Day.

COUNTY HALL, Westminster Bridge, S.E.1.—The Headquarters of the London County Council (*see* pp. 641–4) built on the Pedlar's Acre, Lambeth, from the designs of Ralph Knott, with a river façade of 750 ft. Foundation stone laid by His late Majesty King George V., March 9, 1912, and the ceremonial opening of the first three sections of the building by His late Majesty, July 17, 1922. In 1939 the two central sections of the north and south blocks were completed on a site to the east of the main building. The extension to the north block was completed in 1957. The main building contains, in addition to office accommodation, the council chamber, a conference hall, committee and conference rooms; education library for teachers; county record office; and a members' library with maps, prints, drawings, books and manuscripts on London, which is open to the public for reference purposes. *Librarian*, Miss I. Darlington, M.A., F.L.A. The Council, when in session, meets in public in the council chamber fortnightly on Tuesday afternoons at 3 p.m. The times for public inspection of the building are, on Saturdays from 10.30 a.m. to 12 noon and from 1.30 p.m. to 3.30 p.m.; and on Easter Monday, Whit Monday and August Bank Holiday, from 10.30 a.m. to 12 noon and from 1.30 p.m. to 4.30 p.m. Admission free.

CUSTOM HOUSE, Lower Thames Street, E.C.3.—Built early in 19th century, with a wide quay on Thames. The *Long Room* is about 190 ft. long.

DICKENS HOUSE, 48 Doughty Street, W.C.1.—In this house Charles Dickens lived from 1837 to 1839, and here he completed *Pickwick Papers*. It is the headquarters of The Dickens Fellowship, and contains many relics of the novelist. It is open to the public daily, 10 to 12.30 and 2 to 5 (Sundays and Bank Holidays excepted); admission 1*s*. 6*d*.; children, 6*d*.

DR. JOHNSON'S HOUSE, Gough Square, Fleet Street, E.C.4.—An imposing late 17th-century house, in the garret of which, with the aid of six amanuenses, Samuel Johnson compiled his Dictionary. Open daily (except Sundays and Bank Holidays) from 10.30 to 4.30 or 5 (according to season). Admission 2s.

ELY PLACE, Holborn Circus, E.C.1.—The site of the London house of former Bishops of Ely, Ely Place is a private street whose affairs are administered by Commissioners under a special Act of Parliament. The 14th-century chapel, now St. Etheldreda's (R.C.) Church, is open daily until dusk.

FULHAM PALACE, Bishop's Avenue, Fulham, S.W.6.—The courtyard is 15th century, remainder 18th century. Residence of the Bishop of London. Grounds of 37 acres, surrounded by ancient moat. Previous application to visit should be made to the Bishop's Secretary.

GEFFRYE MUSEUM, Kingsland Road, E.2.—Open on Tuesdays to Saturdays 10 to 5, Sundays 2 to 5. Closed on Christmas Day and on Mondays except Bank Holidays. Admission free.

The Museum is housed in a building erected originally as almshouses in 1715. It was eventually purchased by the London County Council and opened as a museum in 1914. The exhibits are shown in a series of period rooms dating from 1600 to the present day, each containing furniture and domestic equipment of a middle-class English home. Photographic enlargements illustrate the costume of each period. Architectural features, mainly 18th century, an 18th century woodworker's shop and a downhearth kitchen are also shown. Temporary exhibitions and periodic series of evening lectures and recitals are held in the Lecture Hall. There is a reference library of books on furniture, social history and art. Special arrangements for children visiting the Museum in school parties and in their leisure time. *Curator*, Mrs. M. Harrison.

GEORGE INN, Southwark.—Near London Bridge Station. Given to National Trust in 1937. Last galleried inn in London, built in 1677.

GUILDHALL, King Street, City, E.C.2 (dating from early 15th century).—Burnt out by incendiary bombs, 1940. The main hall and crypt have been restored. The Library, Museum and Art Gallery adjoining mainly escaped damage, and are in part open to the public. Admission free. The Library (with Commercial Reference Room adjoining) contains Plan of London, 1570; Deed of Sale with Shakespeare's signature; first, second and fourth folios of Shakespeare's plays, etc. Open free on week-days, 9.30 a.m. to 5 p.m. and Sundays (May–Sept.), 2 p.m. to 5 p.m. *Keeper of the Guildhall*, F. R. Tomkins.

HONOURABLE ARTILLERY COMPANY'S HEADQUARTERS, City Road, E.C.1.—The H.A.C. (*Sec.*, Brig. E. Foster Hall, M.C.) received its charter of incorporation from Henry VIII. in 1537, and has occupied its present ground since 1641. The Armoury House dates from 1735. Four of its members who emigrated in the 17th century, founded in 1638 the Ancient and Honorable Artillery Company of Massachusetts. The H.A.C. is the senior regiment of the Territorial Army, and maintains a Headquarters with an Officer Training Wing, an Artillery Regiment and an Infantry Battalion.

HORNIMAN MUSEUM AND LIBRARY, London Road, Forest Hill, S.E.23. Open daily except Mondays and Christmas Day, 10.30 to 6, Sundays 2 to 6. Admission free. The Museum was presented in 1901 to the London County Council by the founder, Mr. F. J. Horniman, M.P. The Museum has three main departments, ethnology, musical instruments and zoology. In the ethnology department the large collections include exhibits illustrating man's progress in the arts and crafts from prehistoric times. The Zoological department includes an aquarium. The reference library contains forty thousand volumes dealing with the subjects represented in the Museum. *Curator*, O. W. Samson.

HORSE GUARDS, Whitehall, S.W.1.—Archway and offices built about 1753. The mounting of the guard (Life Guards, or Royal Horse Guards) at 11 a.m. (10 a.m. on Sundays) and the dismounting at 4 p.m. are picturesque ceremonies. Only those on the Lord Chamberlain's list may drive through the gates and archway into *Horse Guards' Parade* (230,000 sq. ft.), where the Colour is "trooped" on the Queen's Official Birthday. (Trafalgar Square is 168,850 sq. ft.; Parliament Square, 136,900 sq. ft.; Leicester Square, 100,000 sq. ft.).

HOUSES OF PARLIAMENT, Westminster, S.W.1. —The Palace of Westminster was re-built in 1840–68 from the designs of Sir Charles Barry and Augustus Welby Pugin, at a cost of over £2,000,000.—Open to visitors on Saturdays, on Mondays in August and on Easter and Whit Mondays and Tuesdays if neither House be sitting. Admission at the Sovereign's Entrance, House of Lords, on the above-mentioned days, from 10 a.m. to 4.30 p.m. Closed to visitors on Christmas Day, Boxing Day and Good Friday. Admission to the Strangers' Gallery of the House of Commons, during session, by member's order, or order obtained on personal application at the Admission Order Office in St. Stephen's Hall. The present House of Commons was used for the first time on October 26, 1950, the original Chamber having been destroyed by bombs in 1941. The Victoria Tower (House of Lords) is about 330 ft. high, and when Parliament is sitting the Union Jack flies by day from its flagstaff. The Clock Tower of the House of Commons is about 320 ft. high and contains "Big Ben", the Hour Bell, named after Sir Benjamin Hall, First Commissioner of Works when the original bell was cast in 1856. This bell which weighed 16 tons 11 cwt., was found cracked in 1857. The present bell (13½ tons) is a recasting of the original and was first brought into use in July, 1859. A light is displayed from this tower at night when Parliament is sitting.

INNS OF COURT.—The *Inner* and *Middle Temple*, S. of Fleet Street, E.C.4, and N. of Victoria Embankment, to which the gardens extend, have occupied (since early 14th century) the site of the buildings of the Order of Knights Templars. *Inner Temple Hall* is open to the public on Monday–Friday, 10–11.30 a.m. and 2.30–4 p.m., except during Vacations. *Temple Church*, restored in 1958 after severe damage by bombing, is open on weekdays 10–5 p.m. and the public are admitted to Sunday services (see p. 498). *Middle Temple Hall* (sixteenth century) is open to the public, Monday–Friday, 10–12 and 3–5 p.m.; Saturday, 10–4.30. Closed 1–2 p.m. and Sundays. In Middle Temple Gardens Shakespeare (Henry VI., Part I.) places the incident which led to the "Wars of the Roses" (1455–85). *Lincoln's Inn*, from Chancery Lane to Lincoln's Inn Fields, W.C.2, occupies the site of the palace of a former Bishop of Chichester and of a Black Friars monastery. It was founded early in the 14th century. The new Hall and Library are modern, and the old Hall early 16th century, the Chapel (Inigo Jones) early 17th century. *Lincoln's Inn Fields* (7 acres); the Square contains many fine old houses with handsome interiors. *Gray's Inn*, Gray's Inn Road, W.C.1, was founded in the late 14th century. The squares and roadways are open to the public during the day and the gardens from 12–2 p.m. (May–July) (August and Sept., 9 a.m.–5 p.m.). The 16th-century Hall, where the "Comedy of Errors" was performed in 1594, was reduced to a shell by bombs, but has been rebuilt. The Gardens were laid out (according to tradition) by Lord Chancellor Bacon (died 1626). No other "Inns" are active, but what remains of *Staple Inn* is worth visiting as a relic of Elizabethan London; though heavy damage was done by a flying-bomb, it retains a picturesque gabled front on Holborn (opposite Gray's Inn Road). *Clement's Inn* (near St. Clement Danes' Church), *Clifford's Inn*, Fleet Street, and *Thavies Inn*, Holborn Circus, are all rebuilt. *Serjeants' Inn*, Fleet Street (damaged by bombing), and another (now demolished) of the same name in Chancery Lane, were composed of Serjeants-at-Law, the last of whom died in 1922.

JEWISH MUSEUM, Woburn House, Upper Woburn Place, W.C.1.—Opened in 1932, the Museum contains a comprehensive collection of Jewish antiquities, liturgical paraphernalia and "Anglo-Judaica." Open free (Mon.–Thurs.), 2.30–5; (Fri. and Sun.), 10.30–12.45. Closed on Saturdays, Jewish Holy days and Bank Holidays. Conducted tours of parties by arrangement with the Secretary/Curator.

KEATS HOUSE AND MUSEUM, Keats Grove, Hampstead, N.W.3.—In one of two houses here, now made into one, John Keats lived at various times between 1818 and 1820. The house and the museum are open free, weekdays. 10 a.m. to 6 p.m. The Keats Memorial Library (5,000 volumes) in the adjoining building is open free on weekdays 9 a.m. to 7 p.m. (Monday and Thursday to 8 p.m.)

KENSINGTON PALACE, W.8.—Enlarged by Christopher Wren for King William III. (1691), and continued as a royal residence until 1760. The birthplace of Queen Victoria in 1819. State apartments, re-opened to the public in 1956 under administrative control of the London Museum, contain pictures from the royal collections, royal costumes and furniture formerly belonging to Queen Mary. *Hours of Opening:* (March 1–Sept. 30) 10 a.m.–6 p.m.; Sundays, 2–6 p.m.; (Oct. 1–Feb. 28) 10–4; Sundays, 2–4 p.m. *Kensington Gardens* (*q.v.*) adjoin.

KING HENRY VIII WINE CELLAR, Horse Guards Avenue, Whitehall, S.W.1.—Built in Cardinal Wolsey's time, the Cellar is one of the few remains of the Tudor Palace of Whitehall which King Henry VIII appropriated from the See of York when the Cardinal was deprived of the Great Seal in 1529. The Wine Cellar is open to the public on Saturdays at 2.30 p.m. from Easter Saturday to mid-December. Admission is free but is by appointment only and application for a pass must be made in advance to the Secretary, Ministry of Public Buildings and Works (A.S.8.L.), Lambeth Bridge House, Albert Embankment, S.E.1.

LAMBETH PALACE, S.E.1.—The official residence of the Archbishop of Canterbury, on south bank of Thames; the oldest part is 13th century, the house itself is early 19th century. For leave to visit the historical portions, applications should be made by letter to the Archbishop's Secretary.

LIVERY COMPANIES' HALLS.—The Principal Companies (see pp. 638–40) have magnificent halls, but admission to view them has generally to be arranged beforehand. Among the finest or more interesting may be mentioned the following: Goldsmiths' Hall, Foster Lane. The present hall was completed in 1835, and contains some magnificent rooms. Exhibitions of plate have been shown here periodically in recent years. Fishmongers' Hall, London Bridge (built 1831–3), now admirably restored after severe bomb damage, also contains fine rooms. Apothecaries' Hall, Water Lane, was rebuilt in 1670, after the Great Fire, and has library, hall and kitchen which are good examples of this period, together with a pleasant courtyard. Vintners' Hall, Upper Thames Street, was also rebuilt after the Great Fire, and its hall has very fine late 17th century panelling. The Watermen and Lightermen's Company is not, strictly speaking, a Livery Company, but its hall, in St. Mary at Hill, is a good example of a smaller 18th century building, with pilastered façade. It was completed in 1780. Stationers' Hall, in Stationers' Hall Court, behind Ludgate Hill, another post-Fire Hall, standing in its own court, has a particularly finely carved screen. Barbers' Hall, Monkwell Street, with a Hall attributed to Inigo Jones, was completely destroyed by bombing, but is to be rebuilt. The new hall is to be built some 30 ft. from the old site to enable one of the bastions and part of the wall of the Roman fort to remain exposed to view. Mercers' Hall, Cheapside, built to replace the hall destroyed by bombing, was opened in 1958.

LLOYD'S, Lime Street, E.C.3.—Housed in the Royal Exchange for 150 years and in Leadenhall Street from 1928–1957. The present building was opened by H.M. Queen Elizabeth the Queen Mother on Nov. 14, 1957. The underwriting space has an area of 44,250 sq. ft.

LORD'S CRICKET GROUND, St. John's Wood Road, N.W.8.—The headquarters (since 1814) of the Marylebone Cricket Club, the premier cricket club in England and the governing body of cricket, the scene of some of the principal matches of the season and Middlesex County headquarters. Tennis court in building behind members' pavilion.

MANSION HOUSE, City, E.C.4.—(Reconstructed 1930–31.) The official residence of the Lord Mayor; the Egyptian Hall and Ballroom are the chief attractions. Admission by order from the Lord Mayor's Secretary.

MARKETS.—The London markets (administered by the Corporation of the City of London) provide foodstuffs for 8,500,000 to 9,000,000 people. The dead meat market at Smithfield is the largest in the world, the supplies marketed amounting to nearly 500,000 tons annually. *Central Meat, Fish, Fruit, Vegetable, and Poultry Markets*, Smithfield (the Poultry Market was gutted by fire in January, 1958); *Leadenhall Market* (Meat and Poultry); *Billingsgate* (Fish), Thames Street; *Spitalfields*, E.1 (Vegetables, Fruit, etc.), enlarged 1928, and opened by the late Queen Mary; *London Fruit Exchange*, Brushfield Street (built by Corporation of London 1928–29) faces Spitalfields Market. Other markets are—*Covent Garden*, W.C.2 (established under a charter of Charles II, in 1661) and *Borough Market*, S.E.1, for vegetables, fruit, flowers, etc.

MARLBOROUGH HOUSE, Pall Mall, S.W.1.—The London home of Queen Mary until her death in 1953. Built by Wren for the great Duke of Marlborough about 1710, and purchased by the Crown in 1817. Prince Leopold lived there until 1831, and Queen Adelaide from 1837 until her death in 1849. In 1863 it became the London house of the Prince of Wales. The Queen's Chapel, Marlborough Gate, begun in 1623 from the designs of Inigo Jones for the Infanta Maria of Spain, and completed for Queen Henrietta Maria, is open to the public for services during part of the year. In 1959 Marlborough House was given by the Queen as a Commonwealth centre for Government conferences and it was opened as such in March, 1962. It is open to the public at certain times when conferences are not taking place.

LONDON MONUMENT, (commonly called "The Monument"), Monument Street, E.C.3.—Built from designs of Wren, 1671–77, to commemorate the *Great Fire of London*, which broke out in Pudding Lane, Sept. 2, 1666. The fluted Doric column is 120 ft. high (the moulded cylinder above the balcony supporting a flaming vase of gilt bronze is 42 ft. in addition), and is based on a square plinth

40 ft. high, with fine carvings on W. face (making a total height of 202 ft.). Splendid views of London from gallery at top of column (311 steps) Admission 6*d*., Monday to Saturday, 9 a.m. to 6 p.m. (Oct.–March to 4 p.m.). Sundays—May to Sept., 2–6 p.m. Closed Christmas Day, Boxing Day and Good Friday. Parties of 30 or more school children in charge of an adult 3*d*. each.

MONUMENTS.—VICTORIA MEMORIAL in front of Buckingham Palace; ALBERT MEMORIAL, South Kensington; AIR, Victoria Embankment; BEACONSFIELD, Parliament Square; BEATTY and JELLICOE, Trafalgar Square; BELGIAN, Victoria Embankment; BOADICEA (or "Boudicca"), Queen of the Iceni, E. Anglia, Westminster Bridge; BURNS, Embankment Gardens; BURGHERS OF CALAIS (replica of Rodin's statue), Victoria Tower Gardens, Westminster; CAVALRY, Hyde Park; CAVELL, St. Martin's Place; CENOTAPH, Whitehall; CHARLES I. (erected Jan. 29, 1675), Trafalgar Square; CHARLES II. (Grinling Gibbons), inside the Royal Exchange; CLEOPATRA'S NEEDLE (68½ ft. high, erected 1878), Thames Embankment (the Sphinx, W. of pedestal, and the surrounding stonework, bear scars from an air raid); CAPTAIN COOK (Brock), the Mall; CRIMEAN, Broad Sanctuary; OLIVER CROMWELL (Thornycroft), outside Westminster Hall; DUKE OF CAMBRIDGE, Whitehall; DUKE OF YORK (124 ft.). St. James's Park; EDWARD VII. (Mackennal), Waterloo Place; EROS (Shaftesbury Memorial) (Gilbert), Piccadilly Circus; MARECHAL FOCH, Grosvenor Gardens; GEORGE III., Cockspur Street; GEORGE IV. (Chantrey), riding without stirrups, Trafalgar Square; GEORGE V., Abingdon Street; GEORGE VI, Carlton Gardens; GLADSTONE, facing Australia House, Strand; GUARDS' (Crimea), Waterloo Place; (Great War), Horse Guards' Parade; HAIG (Hardiman), Whitehall; IRVING (Brock), N. side of National Portrait Gallery; KITCHENER, Horse Guards' Parade; ABRAHAM LINCOLN (St. Gaudens), Parliament Square; LONDON TROOPS, Royal Exchange; MILTON, St. Giles, Cripplegate; MONUMENT, THE (*see above*); NELSON (170 ft. 1½ in.), Trafalgar Square, with Landseer's lions (cast from guns recovered from the wreck of the *Royal George*); FLORENCE NIGHTINGALE, Waterloo Place; "PETER PAN" (Frampton), Kensington Gardens; RALEIGH, Whitehall; RICHARD CŒUR DE LION (Marochetti), Old Palace Yard; ROBERTS, Horse Guards' Parade; FRANKLIN D. ROOSEVELT, Grosvenor Square; ROYAL ARTILLERY (South Africa), The Mall; (Great War), Hyde Park Corner; ROYAL MARINES, The Mall; CAPTAIN SCOTT, Waterloo Place; SHAKESPEARE (Fontana), Leicester Square; SMUTS (Epstein), Parliament Square; TRENCHARD, Victoria Embankment; GEORGE WASHINGTON (Houdon), Trafalgar Square; WELLINGTON, Hyde Park Corner; WELLINGTON (Chantrey) riding without stirrups, Royal Exchange; JOHN WESLEY, City Road; WOLSELEY, Horse Guards' Parade.

PERCIVAL DAVID FOUNDATION OF CHINESE ART, 53 Gordon Square, W.C.1.—Set up in 1950 to promote the study and teaching of the art and culture of China and the surrounding regions, and provide facilities necessary to that end. The Foundation contains the collection of Chinese ceramics formed by Sir Percival David and his important library of books on Chinese art. To these was added a gift from the Hon. Mountstuart Elphinstone of part of his collection of Chinese monochrome porcelains. The galleries were opened to the public in 1952. The Foundation is administered on behalf of the University of London by the School of Oriental and African Studies. *Hours of opening:* Galleries, Mon. 2 to 5 p.m.; Tues. to Fri. 10.30 a.m. to 5 p.m.; Sat. 10.30 a.m. to 1 p.m.; Library, Mon. 2.30 to 4.30 p.m.; Tues. to Fri. 10.30 a.m. to 12.30 p.m.; 1.30 to 4.30 p.m.; Sat. 10.30 a.m. to 12.30 p.m. *Secretary-Librarian*, Miss B. W. D. Martin.

PORT OF LONDON.—The Port of London comprises the tidal portion of the River Thames from Teddington to the sea, a distance of 69 miles and five dock systems covering an area of 3,988 acres, of which 666 acres are water. The governing body is the Port of London Authority, whose Head Offices in Trinity Square, E.C.3, were designed by Sir Edwin Cooper. Particulars of the docks are as follows:—*London & St. Katharine Docks, E.1.*—Area 127 acres including 45 acres water. Chief commodities handled are wool, ivory, spices, shells, tea, rubber, wine, marble, canned goods, hides, perfumes, etc., and general cargo from Continental and coastwise ports. *Surrey Commercial Docks, S.E.16.*—Area 390 acres, including 136 acres water. The chief centre of the London and Provincial Soft-wood Trade. Also handles Hardwood, Grain and general cargo. *India & Millwall Docks, E.14.*—Area 455 acres including 127 acres water. Principal commodities handled are Rum, Sugar, Grain, Hardwood, Fruit, Plywood and Wood pulp. In Millwall Dock a special feature is the Granary. *East India Dock, E.14.*—Area 47 acres including 23 acres water. *Royal Victoria & Albert & King George V. Docks, E.16.*—Area 1,056 acres including 230 acres water—have special facilites for handling Frozen and Chilled Meat, Grain, Tobacco and Bananas. Large quantities of Wool, Fruit, Dairy Produce and general cargo are also dealt with. The *King George V. Dock*, opened in 1921, provides accommodation for vessels up to 30,000 tons. *Tilbury Docks, Essex.*—Area 725 acres, including 105 acres water. These docks are 26 miles below London Bridge and are used principally by vessels plying on the Australian, Indian and other Eastern routes. The Cargo Jetty in the River at Tilbury is available for vessels to discharge or load part cargoes. Tilbury Passenger Landing Stage provides accommodation for liners at all states of the tide and adjoins Tilbury Riverside Station, giving direct rail connection with London, the Midlands and the North.

PRINCE HENRY'S ROOM, 17 Fleet Street, E.C.4.—Early 17th century timber-framed house containing fine room on first floor with panelling and modelled plaster ceiling. Open Mon. to Fri. 1.45 p.m. to 5 p.m.; Sat. to 4.30 p.m. Closed Christmas Day and Good Friday. Available for evening lettings to societies, etc. on application to the Architect, County Hall, S.E.1.

ROMAN LONDON.—Though visible remains are very few, almost every excavation for the foundations of new buildings in the City reveals Roman remains. Sections of the City wall, often however merely a mediæval re-build on the Roman foundations, are the most striking remains still to be seen. Fragments may be seen near the White Tower in the Tower of London, Trinity Square, No. 1 Crutched Friars, All Hallows, London Wall—its semi-circular vestry being built on the remains of a round bastion—St. Alphage, London Wall, recently restored by the Corporation of London and showing a striking succession of building and repairs from Roman till later mediæval times, St. Giles, Cripplegate and, by permission only, the great bastion beneath the pavement of the yard of the G.P.O. in Giltspur Street. Recent excavations in the Cripplegate area have revealed that a fort was built in this area and later incorporated in the town wall in this north-west corner of the City. Evidence from these excavations proves that the fort was not built until about 100–120 A.D., and the date of the town wall must therefore be considerably later. Remains of a bath building are preserved beneath the Coal Exchange in Lower Thames Street and other foundations may be seen in the Crypt of All Hallows Barking by the Tower. The governmental headquarters of the town was a great basilica, more than 400 ft. long from east to west, the massive walls of which have been encountered, extending from Leadenhall Market across Gracechurch Street as far as St. Michael's, Cornhill. Excavations during the past few years have shown that buildings over the river front were erected on huge oaken piles and a framework of timber for a considerable distance both east and west of the present London Bridge. The "Roman Bath," in Strand Lane, which is not now held by most authorities to be of Roman origin, is maintained by the L.C.C. on behalf of the National Trust, and is open to the public on weekdays from 10 a.m. to 12.30 p.m. (*Admission*, 1s.). Excavations since 1948 on a bombed site in Walbrook, on the banks of the old Wall Brook, have produced many interesting discoveries, including a Temple of Mithras, from which the splendid marble statues have been placed in Guildhall Museum, now in the Royal Exchange, where many other relics from the Roman City may be seen.

ROYAL EXCHANGE, E.C.3 (founded by Sir Thomas Gresham, 1566, opened as "The Bourse" and proclaimed "The Royal Exchange" by Queen Elizabeth I., 1571, rebuilt 1667–69 and 1842–44).—Open to the public, free. Statues of Queen Elizabeth I., Charles II., Queen Victoria, Sir Thomas Gresham, and others; mural paintings in the ambulatory by Leighton, Abbey, Brangwyn, Wyllie, and others. Part of the Guildhall Museum is now housed in the building and from time to time various exhibitions are held there. The carillon of the Royal Exchange (reinstated 1950) plays English, Scottish, Irish, Welsh, Canadian and Australian melodies at 9 a.m., 12 noon and 3 and 6 p.m. With the exception of the courtyard ambulatory and the shops the whole of the building is now occupied by the Royal Exchange Assurance (which has had its head office there since 1720) and is administered by the Gresham Committee (*Clerk*, Mercers' Hall, Ironmonger Lane, E.C.2.).

ROYAL GEOGRAPHICAL SOCIETY, Kensington Gore, S.W.7.—Map Room open to public, *free*.

ROYAL MINT, Tower Hill, E.C.3 (building erected 1811), where coins for the United Kingdom and abroad are struck. Admission by order only, application for which should be made to the Deputy Master of the Mint, at least 6 weeks in advance of intended visit. Hours of admission, 9.20 a.m. to 2.50 p.m., Mon. to Fri., except Bank Holidays, etc., when the Mint is closed.

ST. JAMES'S PALACE, in Pall Mall, S.W.1.—(Not open to the public.) Built by Henry VIII.; the Gatehouse and Presence Chamber remain, and part of the Chapel Royal, which in 1955 was reopened to the public for services during part of the year. A royal residence from 1697 to 1837. Representatives of Foreign Powers are still accredited "to the Court of St. James's" and (by the permission of the Crown) the Conference of the Allies (1921) and later conferences have been held here.

ST. JOHN'S GATE, Clerkenwell, E.C.1.—Now the Chancery of the Order of St. John of Jerusalem, and formerly the gate of the Priory of that Order, of which the gate house (early 16th century) and crypt of Church (12th century) alone survive. The gatehouse may be inspected on application to the Secretary at the Chancery.

SIR JOHN SOANE'S MUSEUM, 13 Lincoln's Inn Fields, W.C.2. The house and galleries, built 1812–24, are the work of the founder, Sir John Soane (1753–1837) and contain his collections, arranged as he left them, in pursuance of an Act procured by him in 1833. Exhibits include the Sarcophagus of Seti I. (c. 1290 B.C.), classical vases and marbles, Hogarth's *Rake's Progress* and *Election* series, paintings by Canaletto, Reynolds, Turner, Lawrence, etc., and sculpture by Chantrey, Flaxman, etc. Soane's library of 8,000 vols. and a collection of 20,000 architectural drawings are available for study. Open Tues.–Sat. inclusive, 10 a.m. to 5 p.m. Closed Bank Holidays and throughout August. *Curator*, Sir John Summerson, C.B.E., F.B.A. *Inspectress*, Miss D. Stroud, F.S.A.

SOMERSET HOUSE, Strand, W.C.2, and Victoria Embankment, W.C.2.—The beautiful river façade (600 ft. long) was built at the close of the 18th century from the designs of Sir W. Chambers; the remainder of the building is early 19th century. Somerset House was the property of Lord Protector Somerset, at whose attainder in 1552 the palace passed to the Crown, and it was a royal residence until about the close of the 17th century. The building is now occupied by the *Board of Inland Revenue* and other branches of the Civil Service and by the *Principal Probate Registry*. All departments close at noon on Saturdays. In the Probate Registry (Central Hall) are the wills of (*inter alios*) Shakespeare, Newton, Van Dyck, Pitt, Dr. Johnson, Nelson, Wellington and Burke.

STOCK EXCHANGE, E.C.2.—The foundation stone of the present building was laid in 1801, but the building was almost entirely reconstructed in 1854 from the designs of Thomas Allason. The most notable alteration since that date occurred in 1885 when an east wing was added: this is surmounted by a dome, the apex of which is more than 100 feet above the floor. The area of the floor is about 25,000 square feet. The Stock Exchange provides a market for the purchase and sale of about 9,000 securities quoted in the Stock Exchange Daily Official List and valued at over £35,000,000,000 and also securities listed on other Exchanges. At present the members of the Stock Exchange, who consist of brokers (agents for clients) and jobbers (dealers in specific securities) number about 3,500. Visitors' Gallery (entrance, 8 Throgmorton Street) open between 10.30 a.m. and 3 p.m. from Monday to Friday. Admission free and without ticket. Film show.

THAMES EMBANKMENTS.—The Victoria Embankment, on the N. side (from Westminster to Blackfriars), was constructed by Sir J. W. Bazalgette for the Metropolitan Board of Works, 1864–70 (the seats, of which the supports of some are a kneeling camel, laden with spicery, and of others a winged sphinx, were presented by the Grocers' Company, and by Rt. Hon. W. H. Smith, M.P., in 1874); the Albert Embankment on the S. side (from Westminster Bridge to Vauxhall), 1866–69; the Chelsea Embankment, 1871–74. The total cost exceeded £2,000,000. Sir J. W. Bazalgette (1819–91) also inaugurated the London main drainage system, 1858–65. A medallion has been placed on a pier of the Victoria Embankment to commemorate the engineer of the Thames waterside improvements ("Flumini vincula posuit"). The County Hall of the L.C.C. includes an embankment on the Surrey side.

THAMES TUNNELS.—The *Rotherhithe Tunnel* (foot passengers and vehicles), constructed by the L.C.C. and opened in 1908, connects Commercial Road East, with Lower Road, Rotherhithe; the total length is 1 mile 332 yards, of which 474 yards are under the river. The cost of the tunnel and its approaches was £1,506,914. The *Blackwall Tunnel* (foot passengers and vehicles), constructed by the L.C.C. and opened in 1897, connects East India Dock Road, Poplar, with Blackwall Lane, East Greenwich. The total length of the tunnel is 1 mile 279 yards, of which 377 yards are under the river. The cost of the tunnel with its approaches was about £1,323,663. *Greenwich Tunnel* (foot passengers only), constructed by the L.C.C. and opened in 1902, connects the Isle of Dogs, Poplar, with Greenwich. The length of the subway is 406 yards, and the cost was about £180,000. The *Woolwich Tunnel* (foot passengers only), constructed by the L.C.C. and opened in 1912, connects North and South Woolwich below the passenger and vehicular ferry from North Woolwich Station, E.16, to High Street, Woolwich, S.E.18. The length of the subway is 552 yards, and its cost was about £86,000. The *Thames Tunnel* (1,300 feet) was opened in 1843 to connect Wapping (N.) with Rotherhithe (S.). In 1866 it was closed to the public, and purchased by the East London Railway Company. The *Tower Subway* for foot passengers was opened in 1870, and has long been closed.

TOWER HILL, E.C.1 and E.C.3, was formerly the place of execution for condemned prisoners from the Tower, the site of the scaffold being marked in the gardens of Trinity Square. A movement, sponsored by the Council for Tower Hill Improvement, aims at creating more open space around the Tower by the demolition of encroaching buildings and by opening Trinity Square Gardens to the public, thus restoring to Tower Hill its ancient title to be the City's pleasance, or "Board-room."

TOWER OF LONDON, E.C.3.—Admission to a general view of the Tower, the White Tower (Armouries), the Beauchamp and Bloody Towers and the Chapels Royal—1*s.* 6*d*; children, 9*d*.; to Jewel House—1*s*. Half-price for children. The Tower of London is closed on Sundays during the Winter period and on the mornings of the Summer time period, Good Friday and Christmas Day. On Sundays throughout the year the public is admitted to Holy Communion, 8.15 a.m. and Morning Service, 11.15 a.m. Open on weekdays, May 1 to Sept. 30, 10 a.m. to 5.30 p.m.; Oct. 1 to mid-March, 10 a.m. to 4 p.m.; mid-March to April 30, 10 a.m. to 4.30 p.m.; Sundays, first Sunday in April to last in Oct., 2 to 5 p.m. CONSTABLE, Field-Marshal The Earl Alexander of Tunis, K.G., P.C., G.C.B., O.M., G.C.M.G., C.S.I., D.S.O., M.C.; LIEUTENANT, Lieut.-General Sir William Pike, K.C.B., C.B.E., D.S.O.; MAJOR AND RESIDENT GOVERNOR, Col. Sir Thomas Butler, Bt., D.S.O., O.B.E.; KEEPER OF THE JEWEL HOUSE, Maj.-General H. D. W. Sitwell, C.B., M.C., F.S.A.; MASTER OF THE ARMOURIES, A. R. Dufty.

The White Tower is the oldest and central building in Her Majesty's Royal Palace and Fortress of the Tower of London. It was built at the order of William I. and constructed by Gundulph, Bishop of Rochester, in the years 1078–98. The Inner Wall, with thirteen towers, was constructed by Henry III. in the 12th century. The Moat was extended and completed by Richard I. and the Wharf first mentioned in 1228. The Outer Wall was completed in the reign of Edward I. and now incorporates 6 towers and 2 bastions. The last Monarch to reside in the Tower of London was James I. The Crown Jewels came to the Tower in the reign of Henry III. All coinage used in Great Britain was minted in the Outer Ward of the Tower of London until 1810 when the Royal Mint was formed. The Tower of London has had a military garrison since 1078.

WELLINGTON MUSEUM, Apsley House, Hyde Park Corner, W.1.—Admission on weekdays and Bank Holidays, 10 to 6; Sundays, 2.30 to 6. Closed Good Friday and Christmas Day. Adults 1*s*., Children, 6*d*. Organized School parties admitted free. Apsley House was designed by Robert Adam for Lord Bathurst and built 1771–8. It was bought in 1817 by the Duke of Wellington, who in 1828–29 employed Benjamin Wyatt to enlarge it, face it with Bath stone and add the Corinthian portico. The Museum contains many fine paintings, services of porcelain and silver plate and personal relics formerly belonging to the 1st Duke of Wellington (1769–1852) and was given to the Nation by the present Duke. It was first opened to the public in 1952, under the administration of the Victoria and Albert Museum.

WESTMINSTER HALL, S.W.1 (built by William Rufus, A.D. 1087–1100 and altered by Richard II., 1377–99), adjacent to and incorporated in the Houses of Parliament.—Westminster Hall is part of the old Palace of Westminster and survived the fire, which destroyed most of the remainder of the Palace (Oct. 16, 1834). The Hall is about 240 ft. long, 68 ft. wide, and 90 ft. high. The hammer beam roof of carved oak, dating from 1399, is one of the principal attractions. King Charles I. was tried in the Hall. Extensive repairs to the Hall have recently been carried out. Admission: During sessions—Mon. to Thurs., 10 a.m. until 1.30 p.m. Sat., 10 a.m.–5 p.m. During Recess—Mon. to Fri., except Good Friday, Christmas Day and Boxing Day, 10 a.m.–4 p.m.; Sat., 10 a.m.–5 p.m.

WHITECHAPEL ART GALLERY, High Street, E.1. Charitable institution founded in 1901 for the organization of temporary exhibitions of the Fine Arts and Architecture. There is no permanent collection. Open: Tuesdays to Saturdays 11–6, Sundays 2–6, closed Mondays. Admission Free. *Director*, Bryan Robertson, O.B.E.

PARKS, SPACES AND GARDENS

The principal Parks and Open Spaces in the Metropolitan area are maintained as under:—

By the Crown

BUSHY PARK (1,100 acres), see p. 653.

GREEN PARK (49 acres), W.1.—Between Piccadilly and St. James's Park with *Constitution Hill*, leading to Hyde Park Corner

GREENWICH PARK (196½ acres), S.E.10, see p. 653.

HAMPTON COURT GARDENS (54 acres).

HAMPTON COURT GREEN (17 acres).

HAMPTON COURT PARK (622 acres).

HYDE PARK (342 acres).—From Park Lane, W.1, to Kensington Gardens, W.2, containing the Serpentine. Fine gateway at Hyde Park Corner, with Apsley House, the Achilles Statue, Rotten Row and the Ladies' Mile. To the north-east is the *Marble Arch*, originally erected by George IV. at the entrance to Buckingham Palace and re-erected in present position in 1851.

KENSINGTON GARDENS (275 acres), W.2.—From western boundary of Hyde Park to Kensington Palace, containing the Albert Memorial.

KEW, ROYAL BOTANIC GARDENS (300 acres).—Accessible by railway and omnibus. Open daily, except Christmas Day, from 10 a.m. The closing hour varies from 4 p.m. in mid-winter to 8 p.m. in mid-summer. Admission, 3*d*. Houses and museums, 1 p.m. to dusk or 4.50 p.m. (week-days); 1 p.m. to dusk or 5.50 p.m. (Sundays). Dogs not admitted.

REGENT'S PARK and PRIMROSE HILL (464 acres), N.W.1.—From Marylebone Road to Primrose Hill surrounded by the Outer Circle and divided by the *Broad Walk* leading to Zoological Gardens.

RICHMOND GREEN (10 acres).

RICHMOND PARK (2,469 acres).

ST. JAMES'S PARK (93 acres), S.W.1.—From Whitehall to Buckingham Palace. Ornamental lake of 12 acres. The original suspension bridge built in 1857 was replaced in 1957. The *Mall* leads from the Admiralty Arch to the Queen Victoria Memorial and Buckingham Palace. *Birdcage Walk* from Storey's Gate, past Wellington Barracks, to Buckingham Palace. *Master Gunner of St. James's Park*, General Sir Robert Mansergh, G.C.B., K.B.E., M.C.

By the Corporation of London

BURNHAM BEECHES and FLEET WOOD (494 acres), see p. 653.

COULSDON COMMON, Surrey (111 acres).

EPPING FOREST (6,000 acres), see p. 653.

FARTHINGDOWN, Surrey (121 acres).

HIGHGATE WOOD (70 acres).

KENLEY COMMON, Surrey (80 acres).

QUEEN'S PARK, Kilburn (30 acres).

RIDDLESDOWN, Surrey (87 acres).

SPRING PARK, West Wickham (51 acres)

WEST HAM PARK (77 acres).

WEST WICKHAM COMMON, Kent (25 acres).

And a number of smaller open spaces within the City of London, including FINSBURY CIRCUS GARDENS.

By the London County Council

AVERY HILL (87 acres), S.E.9, with newly-restored Winter Garden.

BATTERSEA PARK (200 acres), S.W.8 to S.W.11.

BECKENHAM PLACE PARK (214 acres), Beckenham, Kent, has an 18-hole public golf course.

BLACKHEATH (271 acres), S.E.3.—*Morden College*, founded in 1695 as a home for "decayed Turkey merchants," is near the S.E. corner. The building was designed by Wren and its Chapel doors have carvings attributed to Grinling Gibbons.

BOSTALL HEATH AND WOODS (158 acres), S.E.2.

BROCKWELL PARK (127 acres), with Brockwell Hall, Herne Hill, S.E.24.

CLAPHAM COMMON (205 acres), S.W.4.

CRYSTAL PALACE (199 acres), S.E.19, with motor-racing circuit.

DULWICH PARK (72 acres), with lake, S.E.21.

FINSBURY PARK (115 acres), N.4.

GOLDER'S HILL (36 acres), adjoining West Heath, Hampstead.

HACKNEY MARSH (343 acres), E.5, E.9 and E.10. 110 football pitches.

HAINAULT FOREST (1,108 acres), Hainault, Essex, has two 18-hole public golf courses.

HAMMERSMITH PARK (8 acres), W.12.

HAMPSTEAD HEATH and Extension (294 acres), N.W.3.

HOLLAND PARK (55 acres), W.8.

HORNIMAN GARDENS (21 acres), S.E.23. Adjoining Horniman Museum.

HURLINGHAM PARK (20 acres). Includes a stadium where important athletics meetings and major hockey matches take place.

KENNINGTON PARK (28 acres), S.E.11.

KEN WOOD (200 acres), adjoining Parliament Hill Fields, and including Nightingale Valley. Part purchased in 1922 by public subscription opened and dedicated by King George V., July 18, 1925. Ken Wood House, an 18th-century Mansion (open to the public), contains a fine Adam library and valuable art treasures from the Iveagh Bequest.

LESNES ABBEY WOODS (215 acres), Erith.—Ruins of an Augustinian abbey.

LINCOLN'S INN FIELDS (7 acres), W.C.2.

MARBLE HILL (66 acres).—Twickenham, Middlesex.—A beautiful park, running down to the riverside, on the left bank of the Thames; includes a mansion, formerly the residence of Mrs. Fitzherbert, morganatic wife of George IV.

OXLEAS WOOD (221 acres), S.E.9.

PARLIAMENT HILL (271 acres)—adjoining Hampstead Heath.

PECKHAM RYE and PARK (113 acres), S.E.15, and S.E.22.

PLUMSTEAD COMMON (103 acres), S.E.18.

RAVENSCOURT PARK (34 acres), Hammersmith, W.6.

SOUTHWARK PARK (63 acres), near Surrey Commercial Docks, Rotherhithe, S E.16.

STREATHAM COMMON (68 acres), S.W.16, including Rookery Gardens.

TOOTING COMMON (221 acres), S.W.12, S.W.16 and S.W.17.

VICTORIA EMBANKMENT GARDENS (10 acres), W.C.2, a popular centre for band concerts.

VICTORIA PARK (217 acres), E.9.

WANDSWORTH COMMON (175 acres), S. W.18.

WANDSWORTH PARK (20 acres), on the right bank of the Thames, opposite the ground of Hurlingham Club.

WATERLOW PARK (26 acres), on the southern slopes of Highgate Hill, N.6, containing *Lauderdale House*, formerly occupied by Nell Gwynne.

WORMWOOD SCRUBS (215 acres), Hammersmith, W.12 and N.W.10, including Little Wormwood Scrubs.

EXHIBITIONS ETC., IN LONDON

MADAME TUSSAUD'S EXHIBITION, Marylebone Road, N.W.1. Open daily (including Sunday), Winter, from 10 a.m. to 6 p.m.; Summer, 10 a.m. to 7 p.m. Admission, 4*s*. 6*d*.; children under fourteen, 2*s*. 6*d*.

LONDON PLANETARIUM, Marylebone Road, N.W.1. Performances from 11 a.m. on weekdays; from 1.45 p.m. on Sundays. Admission, 4*s*.; children under fourteen, 2*s*. 6*d*.

ROYAL HORTICULTURAL SOCIETY, Vincent Square, S.W.1, holds fortnightly exhibitions at its Halls in Greycoat Street and in Vincent Square, S.W.1, and the Chelsea Flower Show at the Royal Hospital Grounds, Chelsea (May).

ZOOLOGICAL GARDENS, Regent's Park, N.W.1.—Opened 1828. Admission from 9 a.m. (10 a.m. in Winter) till 7 p.m., or sunset, whichever is the earlier. Sundays before 1 p.m., summer 7*s*. winter, 5*s*.; Mondays throughout year (except Bank Holidays), 3*s*.; other week-days and Sunday afternoon, summer 5*s*., winter, 3*s*. (winter = Oct. 16–March 15). Children, under 14, half-price. Additional charge for admission to the Aquarium and the Children's Zoo.

WHIPSNADE ZOOLOGICAL PARK, Whipsnade Park, nr. Dunstable, Beds. (34 miles from London, 8½ miles from Luton and 3 miles from Dunstable). Opened 1931. Admission on Sundays and week-days, from 10 a.m. to 7 p.m. (7.30 p.m. on Sundays), or sunset, whichever is the earlier. Mondays, throughout year (except Bank Holidays) 3*s*. All other days: summer 5*s*., winter 3*s*. Children under 14, half-price.

MUSIC

ROYAL OPERA HOUSE, Covent Garden, W.C.2. —Opera and Ballet throughout the year. The (third) Covent Garden Theatre was opened May 15, 1858 (the first was opened Dec. 7, 1732). *General Administrator*, Sir David Webster, Royal Opera House, Covent Garden, W.C.2.

BACH CHOIR.—The Bach Choir was formed in 1876 to give the first performance in England of Bach's Mass in B Minor. The conductor was Otto Goldschmidt and his wife Jenny Lind, the famous soprano, herself trained the lady members of the Choir. *Musical Director*, David Willcocks. *Secretary*, Miss J. Meaker, 9 Bradbrook House, Kinnerton Street, S.W.1.

London Bach Group.—Formed in 1950 and specializes in the performance of the choral and instrumental works of J. S. Bach. *Musical Director*, J. Minchinton; *Sec.*, Miss J. Norris, 45 Evelyn Gardens, S.W.7.

Royal Festival Hall, South Bank, S.E.1.—Opened for the Festival of Britain, 1951, and administered by London County Council. Concerts and regular ballet seasons. *General Manager*, T. E. Bean, C.B.E.

Kneller Hall, Twickenham.—Royal Military School of Music. The full band of 250 instrumentalists holds concerts in the grounds on Wednesdays throughout the summer season, commencing at 8 p.m. Members of the public are welcome to attend; admission, 1*s*.

Jacques Orchestra.—Founded 1936. String and Chamber Orchestra. Annual performances of the St. Matthew Passion at Festival Hall. *Secretary*, W. Ganiford, 9 Langley Park, N.W.7.

ENVIRONS OF LONDON

Barnet and Hadley Green.—Scene of Battle, A.D. 1471. Hadley Woods.

Burnham Beeches and Fleet Wood, Bucks.—Magnificent wooded scenery (425 acres), purchased by the Corporation of London for the benefit of the public in 1879; Fleet Wood (65 acres) presented in 1921. During summer omnibus runs daily, Sundays included, from Slough Station (Western Region), passing within 250 yards of "Gray's Elegy" Church. *See* "Stoke Poges."

Bushy Park (1,100 acres).—Adjoining Hampton Court, contains many fine trees and avenue of horse-chestnuts enclosed in a fourfold avenue of limes, planted by King William III. "Chestnut Sunday" (when the trees are in full bloom with their "candles") is usually about 1st to 15th May.

Chequers, a country residence for Prime Ministers, was presented to the Nation (with an endowment to maintain the estate, etc.) by Lord and Lady Lee of Fareham, as the official country residence for the Prime Minister of the day, and the gift was approved by Parliament in the *Chequers Estate Act*, 1917. In 1921 the Chequers Estate of 700 acres was added to the gift by Lord Lee. Chequers is a mansion in Tudor style in the Chilterns, about 3 miles from Princes Risborough, Bucks, and contains a collection of Cromwellian portraits and relics.

Chiltern Hundreds (Stoke, Burnham and Desborough, in Buckinghamshire).—No duly elected member of the Commons can resign his seat; he must apply for some office of profit under the Crown, and so vacate his seat under the Act of Settlement, 1707 (6 Anne, c. 7), and the usual practice is to apply for the Stewardship of the *Chiltern Hundreds*, or of the Manor of Northstead, whereupon the seat is declared vacant (under the Place Act of 1742, which expressly permitted acceptance of such offices to serve as an excuse for resignation) and a new writ is issued by the Speaker.

Darwin and Down House, Downe, Farnborough, Kent.—Where Charles Darwin thought and worked for 40 years and died in 1882. Maintained by the Royal College of Surgeons. Open daily (except Fridays and Christmas Day) 11 to 5. (Spring and summer, 10 to 5). Admission, 2*s.*; Children, 6*d.*

Dorneywood, country house in 215 acres, near Burnham Beeches, Bucks., was bequeathed to the nation by Lord Courtauld-Thomson (died 1954) as an official residence for any Minister of the Crown chosen by the Prime Minister during office. Administered by the National Trust. Open to the public, August and September, Saturdays, 2.15–6 p.m. Admission, 1*s.*; children, 6*d.*

Dulwich, S.E.21 (5 miles from London), contains *Dulwich College* (founded by Edward Alleyn in 1619), the *Horniman Museum* and *Dulwich Park* (72 acres). The *Dulwich Picture Gallery*, built by Sir John Soane to house the collection bequeathed by the artist, Sir Francis Bourgeois, was damaged by enemy action in the Second World War. The pictures, however, were saved, and the gallery has been rebuilt with the aid of a grant from the Pilgrim Trust. It was reopened by Queen Elizabeth the Queen Mother on April 27, 1953. In *Dulwich Village* the rural characteristics of the pre-suburban period are preserved.

Eltham, Kent (10 miles from London by Southern Region). Remains of 13th–15th century Eltham Palace, the birthplace of John of Eltham (1316), son of Edward II. The hall, built by Edward IV., contains fine hammer-beam roof of chestnut. In the churchyard of St. John the Baptist is the tomb of Thomas Doggett, the comedian and founder of the Thames Watermen's championship (Doggett's Coat and Badge).

Epping Forest (6,000 acres, originally purchased by the Corporation of London for £250,000 and thrown open to the public in 1882; the present forest is 12 miles long by 1 to 2 miles wide, about one-tenth of its original area). Loughton, Buckhurst Hill, Chingford, High Beech (London Transport and Eastern Region). Beautiful forest scenery.

Eton College.—22 miles from London. The most famous of English schools, founded by Henry VI. in 1440, the scholars numbering 1,182 in July, 1963. Buildings date from 1442.

Greenwich, S.E.10.—A south-eastern metropolitan borough with a frontage of 4½ miles on the Thames. *Greenwich Hospital* (since 1873, the Royal Naval College) was built by Charles II., from designs by Inigo Jones, and by Queen Anne and William III., from designs by Wren, on the site of an ancient royal palace, and of the more recent *Placentia*, an enlarged edition of the palace, constructed by Humphrey, Duke of Gloucester (1391–1447), son of Henry IV. Henry VIII., Queen Mary I. and Queen Elizabeth I were born in the Royal Palace (which reverted to the Crown in 1447) and King Edward VI. died there. In the principal quadrangle is a marble statue of George II., by Rysbraeck. (For *National Maritime Museum*, see pp. 405–6.) *Painted Hall* and *Chapel* open daily except Thursdays from 2.30 p.m. to 5 p.m. (closed on Sundays, Oct.–April inclusive). Visitors are also admitted to Morning Service in the Chapel at 11 a.m., summer and winter, except during College vacations. *Greenwich Park* (185 acres) was enclosed by Humphrey, Duke of Gloucester, and laid out by Charles II., from the designs of Le Nôtre. On a hill in Greenwich Park is the old *Royal Observatory* (founded 1675), which is now removed to Herstmonceux Castle, Sussex (see p. 409). Part of its buildings at Greenwich have been taken over by the Maritime Museum and named Flamsteed House, after John Flamsteed, the first Astronomer Royal. The parish church of Greenwich (*St. Alfege*) was rebuilt by Hawksmoor (Wren's pupil) in 1728, and restored after severe damage during the Second World War. General Wolfe (Heights of Abraham) and Tallis ("the father of Church Music") are buried in the church. Henry VIII. was christened in the former church. The Ministerial *Whitebait Dinners* at the "Ship" and "Trafalgar" Hotels, were held throughout the 19th century. *Charlton House*: built in the early 17th century (1607–1612) for Adam Newton, tutor to Prince Henry, brother to Charles I. The house is largely in the Jacobean style of architecture. *Cutty Sark*, the last of the famous tea clippers, which has been preserved as a memorial to ships and men of a past era. The ship is fully restored and re-rigged, with a museum of sail on board, Open to visitors: weekdays, 11 to 6, Sundays. 2.30 to 6.

HAM HOUSE, Richmond.—A notable example of 17th-century domestic architecture, long the home of the Tollemache family (Earls of Dysart). Now the property of the National Trust, which has let it on a long lease to the Ministry of Public Building and Works. The contents, described as "probably the finest and most varied collection of Charles II.'s reign to survive," were purchased for the Victoria and Albert Museum which now administers the house. Opened to the public in May 1950, Ham House may be seen on Tues.–Sun. inclusive and on Bank Holidays, 2–6 p.m., April–Oct., 12–4 p.m., Nov.–March. Closed Mon. (except Bank Holidays), Christmas Day and Good Friday. Admission, 1*s*., Children, 6*d*.

HAMPTON COURT.—Sixteenth-century Palace built by Cardinal Wolsey, with additions by Sir Christopher Wren for William and Mary, 15 miles from London. Fine view of river. Beautiful gardens with maze and prolific grape vine (planted in 1769). Old Royal Apartments and collection of pictures. Tennis Court, built by King Henry VIII. in 1530. The Palace is *closed* on Christmas Day, Boxing Day and Good Friday. Comprehensive ticket for all parts of the Palace open to the public, 2*s*.; children under 15, 1*s*. Individual tickets for Vine (2*d*.) and Maze (3*d*.) also available. Admission, Oct.–March, when the Tudor Tennis Court and the Banqueting House are closed, Adults, 1*s*. 6*d*.; Children, 1*s*. Refreshments can be obtained in the Tilt Yard gardens during the summer season. *Bushy Park* adjoins the Lion Gates of Hampton Court Palace.

Grace and Favour Residences.—Hampton Court contains a total of 57 residences occupied by favour of Her Majesty the Queen. The Minister of Public Building and Works reported in Parliament on April 17, 1962, that, of 140 grace and favour residences, the remainder were situated at Windsor Castle (46), Kensington Palace (16), St. James's Palace (8), Marlborough House Mews (9), Bushy Park (2), Kew Palace (1) and Hyde Park (1).

HARROW-ON-THE-HILL.—10 miles by Metropolitan and other railways. Large public school founded by John Lyon in 1571. The "Fourth Form Room" dates from 1608.

HUGHENDEN MANOR, High Wycombe, Bucks.—The home of Disraeli from 1847 till his death and contains much of his furniture, books, etc. Conveyed to the National Trust in 1947. Open daily including Sundays and Monday Bank Holidays (but not other Mondays and not the day after a Monday Bank Holiday), 2–6 or till dusk. Open also Saturdays and Sundays, 10–1. Closed all January. Admission (non-members), 2*s*. 6*d*.; children, 1*s*.; parties of 20 or more, 2*s*.

JORDANS AND CHALFONT ST. GILES, near Beaconsfield, Bucks, contain the Old *Quaker Meeting House* (1688) at Jordans, in the burial ground of which lies William Penn (Pennsylvania); a barn built out of the timbers of the *Mayflower* by the 17th-century owner of Jordans (Gardener). At Chalfont St. Giles is the cottage where Milton lived during the Great Plague (1665–1666).

KEW, Surrey, a parish contained since 1892 in the borough of Richmond, was a favourite home of the early Hanoverian monarchs. Kew House, the residence of Frederick, Prince of Wales, and later of his son, George III., was pulled down in 1803, but the earlier Dutch House, now known as Kew Palace, survives. It was built in 1631 and acquired by George III. as an annexe to Kew House in 1781. The famous Kew Gardens (*see* p. 651) were originally laid out as a private garden for Kew House for George III.'s mother in 1759 and were much enlarged in the nineteenth century, notably by the inclusion of the grounds of the former Richmond Lodge. Kew Green, between the Gardens and Kew Bridge, is very attractive and on the Green stands the parish church, built in 1714 and several times enlarged. Princess Mary of Cambridge and the Duke of Teck, the parents of the late Queen Mary, were married here in 1866 and the Church contains many reminders of Royal connections with Kew.

KINGSTON-UPON-THAMES, Surrey (about 12 miles from London), is the ancient place of coronation of the Kings of Saxon England. The Coronation Stone (hence the name "King's Stone") is preserved within railings adjoining the Guildhall.

NATIONAL ARMY MUSEUM, Royal Military Academy, Sandhurst, Camberley, Surrey.—Opened by H.M. the Queen on July 15, 1960. Official museum for British Army, Indian Army and colonial forces. There is a special section for the disbanded Irish regiments.

OSTERLEY PARK, Isleworth.—House and park of 300 acres given to the National Trust by the Earl of Jersey in 1949. Part of the Elizabethan house, built in 1577 for Sir Thomas Gresham, remains, but it was largely remodelled by Robert Adam, and the staterooms are among the best examples of Adam decoration. Open daily, except Mondays, (April–Sept.) 2–6 p.m.; (Oct.–March) 12 noon–4 p.m. Closed Monday (except Bank Holidays), Christmas Day and Good Friday. Admission 1*s*., children 6*d*.

RICHMOND, Surrey, contains the red brick gateway of *Richmond Palace* (Henry VII., 1485–1509) and buildings of the Jacobean, Queen Anne, and early Georgian periods, including *White Lodge* in Richmond Park, the former home of Queen Mary's mother (the Duke of Windsor was born there, June 23, 1894). The *Star and Garter* Home for Disabled Soldiers, Sailors, and Airmen (the Women's Memorial of the Great War) was opened by Queen Mary in 1924. *Richmond Park* (2,358 acres) contains herds of fallow and red deer. From the *Terrace Gardens*, Richmond Hill, can be obtained a wonderful view of the Valley of the Thames.

RUNNIMEDE.—A meadow of about 100 acres, on S. bank of Thames (part of the Crown Lands), between Windsor and Staines. From June 15–23, 1215, the hostile Barons encamped on this meadow during negotiations with King John, who rode over each day from Windsor. The 48 "Articles of the Barons" were accepted by the King on June 15, and were subsequently embodied in a charter, since known as *Magna Carta*, of which several copies were sealed on June 19. About half a mile N.E. of the meadow is *Magna Carta Island* (claimed as the actual site of the sealing), presented to the National Trust in 1930 by Lady Fairhaven and her sons.

A memorial at *Cooper's Hill*, near Runnimede, to members of the Commonwealth air forces who lost their lives in the Second World War while serving from bases in the United Kingdom and north-western Europe and have no known grave, was unveiled by the Queen on October 17, 1953.

ST. ALBANS.—A city in Hertfordshire, on the river Ver, 22 miles N.W. of London. The abbey church, built partly of materials from the old Roman city of Verulamium by Paul of Caen, was consecrated in 1115. Parts still remain of the Norman structure. The city was the scene of the overthrow of Henry VI. in 1455, and of the Earl of Warwick in 1461. On a printing press set up in the abbey the first English translation of the Bible was printed. The site of the pre-Roman city of King Tasciovanus and the remains of the ancient City of Verulamium, with well preserved theatre and many other features, excavated in recent years. St. Michael's Church, with tomb of Sir Francis Bacon.

STOKE POGES (2 miles from Slough station, Western Region) contains the 14th-century Church with the Churchyard of Gray's "Elegy" and "Ode on a Distant Prospect of Eton College." The poet was buried in the church in 1771.

SYON HOUSE, Brentford.—The town seat of the Duke of Northumberland. The house is part of the buildings of the Nunnery of Syon, erected by permission of Henry VI. in 1431. At the Dissolution of the Nunnery the Estate reverted to the Crown. In 1578 it was granted to the 9th Earl of Northumberland and in 1632 the house was repaired under superintendence of Inigo Jones. In 1766 the interior was transformed by Robert Adam, who also built the entrance gateway. The lion on the river-front was brought here in 1874 on the demolition of Northumberland House in the Strand. Open (*April, May, June*), Wed.-Sat., also Easter Monday, Whit Sunday and Whit Monday; (*July-Sept.*), Wed.-Sun. 1 p.m. to 4.30 p.m. Admission 2*s.* 6*d.*; children, 1*s.*

WALTHAM ABBEY (or WALTHAM HOLY CROSS), 13 miles from London (Eastern Region).—The Abbey ruins, Harold's Bridge (11th century), the Nave of the former cruciform Abbey Church (the oldest Norman building in England (consecrated May 3, 1060) and the traditional burial place of King Harold II. (1066), and a Lady Chapel of Edward II., with crypt below. New evidence of the position and style of several buildings, which once stood on the site of the Augustinian monastery, were revealed by the prolonged drought in the summer of 1933. At Waltham Cross, 1 mile from the Abbey, is one of the crosses (partly restored) erected by Edward I. to mark a resting place of the corpse of Queen Eleanor on its way to Westminster Abbey. (Ten crosses were erected, but only those at Geddington, Northampton and Waltham remain; "Charing" Cross originally stood on the spot now occupied by the statue of Charles I. at Whitehall.)

WINDSOR CASTLE (begun by William the Conqueror, A.D. 1066–87).—22 miles from London, by Western and Southern Regions. The Castle Precincts are open daily, free of charge, from 10 a.m. to sunset. When the Court is not in residence, the *State Apartments* of Windsor Castle are open to the public, during Her Majesty's pleasure, on every weekday and on certain Sunday afternoons during the summer months. When the State Apartments are open, the charges for admission are for Adults, 2*s.* and for Children, 6*d.* By the Queen's command, the net proceeds go to charities. An authorized guide book can be obtained at the office, price 1*s.* 6*d.* The hours of admission to the State Apartments are from April 1 to May 31, and Oct. 1 to 31 between 11 and 4; June 1 to Sept. 30, 11 to 5; and from Nov. 1 to March 31, between 11 and 3 and on certain Sundays during the summer between 1.30 and 5. *Queen Mary's Doll's House* and the *Old Master Drawings* can be seen on the same days and hours as the State Apartments, admission 6*d.* each person to each. The *Albert Memorial Chapel* is open throughout the year from 10–4.45 (Nov.–Feb., 4 p.m.), *except* between 1 and 2 p.m. Closed on Sundays; the *Round Tower* or *Keep* is open from April 1 to Sept. 30 (except when the Royal Standard is flying) the same days and hours as the State Apartments. Admission free. By permission of the Dean and Chapter, *St George's Chapel* may be viewed on Mon.–Thurs., between 11 a.m. and 3.45 p.m.; Fridays, 1 p.m. to 3.45 p.m.; Sundays, 2.30 to 4 p.m. Admission 2*s.* per person, except at service times. The chapel is usually closed during January. The Daily Services in the Chapel are open to the public. The *Curfew Tower* may be seen under the guidance of the Keeper to whom application must be made at the entrance (admission 6*d.*). The *Royal Mausoleum*, Frogmore Gardens, Home Park, is open only on Whit Monday, from 11 a.m. to 4 p.m. Admission free.

HOUSES OPEN TO THE PUBLIC

Times of summer opening and admission fees shown are those which obtained in 1963, and are subject to modification. Space permits only a selection of some of the more noteworthy houses in England which are open to the public. A fuller description of some houses in or near London will be found on pp. 645–51.

ALBURY PARK, nr. Guildford.—Daily, 1.30–5. Admission 2*s.* 6*d.*

ALNWICK CASTLE, Northumberland. Seat of the Duke of Northumberland.—May, June and Sept., Wed., Thurs., Fri., Sat. and Whit Monday and Tuesday, 1–5. July and Aug., daily except Sun. Admission, 2*s.* 6*d.*

ALTHORP, nr. Northampton. Seat of Earl Spencer.—May-Sept., Sun., Tues., Thurs., and Bank Holidays (also Easter Sun. and Mon.) 2.30–6, Admission, 3*s.* 6*d.*

*ARLINGTON COURT, nr. Barnstaple.—April–Sept., daily, except Sat., 11–6. Admission, 2*s.* 6*d.*

ARUNDEL CASTLE, Sussex. Seat of the Duke of Norfolk.—Mid-May to first week in July, Mon.–Thurs., 1–4.30; first week in July to end of Sept., Mon.–Fri., 12–4.30. Admission 2*s.* 6*d.*

*ASCOTT, Wing, Bucks.—Including Anthony de Rothschild collection of pictures. April-Sept. Thurs. and Bank Holidays and some Sats. and Suns., 2–6. Admission, 2*s.* 6*d.*

AUDLEY END, Saffron Walden.—Daily, except Mon. (but including Bank Holidays), 11.30–5.30. Admission, 2*s.* 6*d.*

AVEBURY MANOR, Wiltshire. (Adjoining the famous Avebury stone circle, which is also on public view).—April, June, July and Sept., Sat. and Sun.; May and August, daily except Tues., 2–6, Bank Holidays, 10–6. Admission, 2*s.* 6*d.*

BELVOIR CASTLE, nr. Grantham. Seat of the Duke of Rutland.—April–Sept., Wed., Thurs., Sat., 12–6; Bank Holidays and day following, 11–8; Sundays, 2–7. Admission, 2*s.* 6*d.*

BERKELEY CASTLE, Glos.—April-Sept., daily, except Mon., (but including Bank Holidays), 2–5.30; Bank Holidays, 11–5.30. Admission, 2*s.* 6*d.*

BLENHEIM PALACE, Woodstock. Seat of the Duke of Marlborough and birthplace of Sir Winston Churchill.—April–July and third week in Sept. till end of Oct., Mon.–Thurs. (closed Whit Monday); August and first three weeks of Sept., daily except Fri., 1–6. Admission, 3*s.* 6*d.*

* Property of the National Trust.

*BLICKLING HALL, Norfolk.—May–Sept., Wed., Thurs., Sun. and Bank Holidays, 2–5.30. Admission, 3*s*.

*BUCKLAND ABBEY, Tavistock.—Including Drake relics. Easter–Sept. 30, weekdays and Bank Holidays, 11–6. Sun. 2–6. Admission, 1*s*.

CARISBROOKE CASTLE, Isle of Wight. Former house of Governor of Isle of Wight and place of Charles I.'s captivity.—Weekdays, 9.30–7, Sundays, 2–5.30. Admission, 2*s*.

CASTLE ASHBY, nr. Northampton. A home of the Marquess of Northampton.—Thurs., Sat. and Bank Holidays, 2–6. Sundays in June, July and August, 2–6. Admission, 3*s*. 6*d*.

CASTLE HOWARD, Yorkshire.—Easter–Whitsun, Suns. only; from Whitsun, Tues., Wed., Thurs., Sat., Sun., 1.45–5.15; Bank Holidays, 11.30–5.30. Admission, 2*s*. 6*d*.

*CHARLECOTE PARK, Warwicks. Associations with Shakespeare.—Daily, except Mon., but incl. Bank Holidays, 11.15–5.45. Admission, 2*s*. 6*d*.

CHASTLETON HOUSE, Oxon.—Daily, except Wed., 10–1, 2–6; Sundays 2–4. Admission, 2*s*. 6*d*.

CHATSWORTH, Derbyshire. Seat of the Duke of Devonshire.—Wed. and Thurs., 11.30–4; Sat. and Sun., 2–5.30; Bank Holidays, 11.30–5.30; Tuesday after Bank Holidays, 11.30–4. Admission, 3*s*. 6*d*.

*CLANDON PARK, nr. Guildford.—Mon., Wed., Sat., Sun., 2–6; Bank Holidays, 11–6. Admission, 2*s*. 6*d*.

*CLAYDON HOUSE, Bucks.—Daily except Mondays, and Tuesdays after Bank Holidays, but including Bank Holiday, 2–6. Admission, 3*s*.

*COMPTON CASTLE nr. Paignton.—Fortified manor house. Mon., Wed. and Thurs., 10–12, 2 to 5. Admission, 1*s*.

COMPTON WYNYATES, Warwickshire. A home of the Marquess of Northampton.—Wed., Sat. and Bank Holidays and Sundays (June–August only), 2–6. Admission, 3*s*. 6*d*.

CORSHAM COURT, Wilts.—April to mid-July, and mid-Sept. to Oct., Wed., Thurs., Sun. and Bank Holidays; mid-July to mid-Sept., daily except Monday, 11–12.30, 2–6. Admission, 2*s*. 6*d*.

*COTEHELE, nr. Calstock, Cornwall.—April, Wed., Sat., Sun. and Bank Holidays, 2–6. May–Sept., daily except Mon. (but including Bank Holidays), 10–6. Admission, 3*s*.

HADDON HALL, Derbyshire.—Daily, except Sunday, 11–6 (Oct., 11–4). Admission, 3*s*.

HARDWICK HALL, Derbyshire.—Wed., Thurs., Sat., Sun., Bank Holidays and Tues. after Bank Holidays, 2–5. Admission, 3*s*.

HAREWOOD HOUSE, Yorks. Seat of the Earl of Harewood.—Wed. and Thurs. (also Bank Holidays, Tuesdays following Bank Holidays, and Tuesdays, June–August), 10–6; Sundays, 12–6 (Oct., 12–5). Admission, 3*s*. 6*d*.

HATFIELD HOUSE, Hertfordshire. Seat of the Marquess of Salisbury.—April–May, weekdays and Easter and Whit Sundays. June–first week in Oct., daily, except Mon., but incl. Bank Holiday. Weekdays, 12–5. Sun., 2.30–5.30. Admission, 3*s*. 6*d*.

HAYES BARTON, nr. Budleigh Salterton.—Probable birthplace of Sir Walter Raleigh. June–Sept., weekdays, 10.30–1 2.15–6. Admission, 1*s*.

HEDINGHAM CASTLE, Essex.—Easter–Sept., Tues., Thurs. and Sat., 2–6. Bank Holidays 10–6. Admission, 2*s*.

HEVER CASTLE. Kent,—Wed., Sat. and Sun., 1–7. Bank Holidays, 11–7. Admission, 5*s*.

KINGSTON LACY, Wimborne.—May–Sept., Sat., Sun., and Bank Holidays (also Easter Sun. and Mon.) 2–6. Admission, 2*s*. 6*d*.

KNEBWORTH HOUSE, Herts.—May–Sept. Sat., Sun. and Bank Holidays, 2–5. Admission, 2*s*. 6*d*.

*KNOLE, Sevenoaks.—Wed.–Sat. and Bank Holidays, 10–12, 2–4.30. Admission, 3*s*. (Fridays, 5*s*.)

*LACOCK ABBEY, Wilts.—House: Wed., Thurs. and Bank Holidays, 2–6. Admission, 2*s*. Monastic remains: Daily except Friday, 2–6. Admission, 2*s*. 6*d*.

*LITTLE MORETON HALL, Cheshire. Famous example of "black and white" timbering.—Daily except Friday, 2–8, or dusk if earlier. Admission, 2*s*.

LONGLEAT HOUSE, Wilts. Seat of the Marquess of Bath.—Daily, 10–6. Admission, 2*s*. 6*d*.

LOSELEY HOUSE, nr. Guildford.—June–Sept., Wed., Thurs., Sat. and Sun., 2–5. Whit. Mon. and August Bank Holiday, 11–5. Admission, 2*s*. 6*d*.

LUTON HOO, Beds.—Mon., Wed., Thurs., Sat. and Bank Holidays, 11–6; Sundays, 2–6. Admission, 3*s*.

*LYME PARK, Cheshire.—Daily, 1–7. Admission, 2*s*.

*LYTES CARY, Ilchester, Somerset.—Thurs. and Sat., 2–6. Admission, 2*s*. 6*d*.

MILTON MANOR HOUSE, nr. Abingdon.—May–Sept., Sat., Sun., and Bank Holidays, 2.30–6. Admission, 2*s*. 6*d*.

*MONTACUTE HOUSE, Yeovil.—Daily, except Tuesday, 11–6 (Oct., 11–12.45, 2–4) Admission, 3*s*.

OSBORNE HOUSE, Isle of Wight. State and Private Apartments are shown, including the room in which Queen Victoria died.—Mon., Wed. and Fri. (also Thursday from Whitsun), 11–5. Admission, 2*s*.

PARHAM, Pulborough, Sussex.—Wed., Thurs., Sun. and Bank Holidays, 2–5.30. Admission, 2*s*. 6*d*. (last Sunday of each month, 5*s*.)

*PAYCOCKE'S, Coggeshall, Essex. Tudor wool-merchant's town house.—Wed., Thurs., Sun. and Bank Holidays, 2–5.30. Admission, 1*s*. 6*d*.

*PECKOVER HOUSE, Wisbech, Cambs.—Wed., Thurs. and Sat., 2–5. Sun., April–Sept., 2–5. Admission 1*s*. 6*d*.

PENSHURST PLACE, Kent. Seat of Visct. De L'Isle, V.C., and the birthplace of his ancestor Sir Philip Sidney.—Easter to first week in Oct., Wed., Thurs., Sat. and Bank Holidays, 2–5. Admission, 3*s*. 6*d*. Sun. July–Sept. and some Sun. April–June, 5*s*.

*PETWORTH HOUSE, Sussex.—Tues., Thurs., Sat. and Bank Holidays, 2–6. Admission, 3*s*. First Wednesday in each month, 2–6. Admission, 5*s*.

POWDERHAM CASTLE, Devonshire. Seat of the Earl of Devon.—Mid-May to mid-Sept., daily, except Sat., 2–6. Admission, 2*s*. 6*d*.

*QUEBEC HOUSE, Westerham. Birthplace of General Wolfe.—Tues., Wed. and Sat., 2–5. Bank Holidays, 10–1, 2–6. Admission, 1*s*. 6*d*.

RAGLEY HALL, Warwickshire. Seat of the Marquess of Hertford.—Tues., Wed., Thurs. and Sat., 2–6. Sun. and Bank Holidays, 11.30–6. Admission, 3*s*. 6*d*.

*ST. MICHAEL'S MOUNT. Situated on island off Marazion, Cornwall.—Wed. and Fri. Also Mon. from June–Sept., 10.30–4.30. Admission, Wed. and Fri., 1*s*., Mon., 2*s*.

*SALTRAM HOUSE, nr. Plymouth.—April–Sept., daily except Tues., 2–6. Admission 3*s*. (Fri. 6*s*.).

SAWSTON HALL, nr. Cambridge.—Sun. and Bank Holidays, also Sat., July–Sept., 2.30–5.30. Admission, 3*s*. 6*d*.

*SNOWSHILL MANOR, nr. Broadway.—Sun. and Bank Holidays 11–1, 2–6. Wed., Thurs. and Sat., 2–6. (April, Sun. and Bank Holidays only). Admission, 2*s*. 6*d*.

STOKESAY CASTLE, Salop.—Daily, except Tuesdays, 9–6. Admission, 1*s*.

*STOURHEAD, Wiltshire.—Wed., Thurs., Sat., Sun. and Bank Holidays, 2.30–6. Admission, 5*s*.

* Property of the National Trust.

SULGRAVE MANOR, Northamptonshire. Former home of members of the Washington family.—Daily, except Fridays, 11–12, 1–6. Admission, 2*s*. 6*d*.

*UPPARK, nr. Petersfield.—Wed., Thurs., Sun. and Bank Holidays, 2.30–5.30. Admission, 2*s*. 6*d*.

*UPTON HOUSE, nr. Banbury. Including famous collection of paintings formed by 2nd Visct. Bearsted. July–Sept., Wed. and Sat. Other months, Wed. only, 2–6. Admission, 2*s*. 6*d*.

*THE VYNE, Basingstoke.—April–Sept., Wed. and Bank Holidays, 11–6. Sundays 1–6. Admission, 3*s*.

*WADDESDON MANOR, Bucks.—Wed.–Sun., 2–6, Bank Holidays, 11–6. Admission, 3*s*. (Fri., 6*s*.).

WARWICK CASTLE. Seat of the Earl of Warwick, —Weekdays, 10–5.30; Sun. (May–Oct.), 1–5. Admission, 4*s*.

WOBURN ABBEY (and Zoo Park). Seat of the Duke of Bedford. Daily from 1.30. Admission, 4*s*. 6*d*.

MUSEUMS AND ART GALLERIES OUTSIDE LONDON

BOWES MUSEUM, Barnard Castle. Important paintings of Italian, Dutch, French and Spanish schools. Fine porcelain and pottery, tapestries and furniture. Open, weekdays, May–Sept., 10–5.30; March, April and October, 10–5; Nov.–Feb., 10–4. Sundays, 2–5 (Summer); 2–4 (Winter). Admission, 1*s*.

BRIGHTON.—The Royal Pavilion. Palace of George IV. Annual Regency Exhibition, early July to end of Sept. Open daily, 10–5 (10–8 during Regency Exhibition). Closed on Christmas Day and 4th Thursday in May.

Art Gallery and Museum. Housed in buildings which were once part of Stables of Royal Pavilion. Open 10–7 (Sundays: Summer 2–7; Winter 2–6).

Thomas-Stanford Museum. In 18th-century Preston Manor. Open weekdays (except Tues.), 10–1, 2–5 (Oct.–May); 10–1, 2–7 (June–Sept.); Sundays 2.30–5. Admission 1*s*. Gardens open, free.

The Grange, Rottingdean. Includes Sussex Room and Kipling Room, latter with original Kipling letters, etc. Open, 10–7; Sundays 2–6.

BRISTOL.—*City Art Gallery*. Collection of Old Masters, 19th cent. and modern paintings, English watercolours, Chinese ceramics, glass, English silver, glass, porcelain and delftware, English and foreign embroideries. Open weekdays, 10–6. *Red Lodge*, Park Row. Furnished in style of Elizabethan period. Open weekdays, 1–5. *Georgian House*, Great George Street. Furnished in style of period. Open weekdays, 11–5.

CAMBRIDGE.—Fitzwilliam Museum. Maintained by the University, of which it is a department, but the collections are solely due to private benefaction. The chief collections comprise Egyptian, Greek and Roman antiquities, coins and medals, medieval manuscripts, paintings and drawings, prints, pottery and porcelain, textiles, arms and armour, medieval and renaissance objects of art, and a library which includes a music collection and literary autographs. Open, free, weekdays, May–Aug., 10–5; Sept.–April, 10–4; Sundays 2 till above times. Closed on first Wed. of every month, Christmas Day, Boxing Day and Good Friday.

CANTERBURY.—Royal Museum. Collections include archæology, geology and natural history. Much Roman material from post-war excavations of Canterbury. Temporary exhibitions on view in Art Gallery or the permanent collection of porcelain and paintings. Open weekdays, 9.30–6. Admission free.

CARISBROOKE.—Castle Museum. Former home in Carisbrooke Castle of Governor of Isle of Wight. Collections cover archæology and history of Isle of Wight, and personal relics of Charles I, who was imprisoned in Castle from 1647 to 1648. Open, weekdays, March–April and Oct. 9.30–5.30; May–Sept. 9.30–7; Nov.–Feb. 9.30–4. Sundays, May–Sept. only, 2–5.30. Admission (to Castle and Museum) 2*s*.

COLCHESTER.—Colchester and Essex Museum, The Castle. The Norman Castle contains collections of the Stone, Bronze and Iron Ages and the Roman and Saxon periods of the county. Medieval pottery and 19th-century coaches, looms, etc. The Holly Trees Mansion covers the activities of social life of the 18th and 19th centuries. Open, weekdays 10–5; Sundays 2.30–5, April–Sept. only. Holly Trees Mansion (1716) closed Sunday and 1–2 p.m. Tour of Castle, 1*s*. All Saints Museum of Natural History of Essex. Hours as for Holly Trees. Admission to all museums free.

DERBY.—Museum and Art Gallery, Wardwick. Important collections of works by Joseph Wright of Derby, A.R.A., 1734–1797; Derby porcelain, 1750–1848. Unique exhibit illustrating the history of the Midland Railway including a working model layout. Exhibits illustrating Derbyshire archaeology and natural history. "Prince Charlie" Room commemorating the 1745 rebellion. Open, weekdays, 10–6; Sundays, 2.30–4.30.

GUILDFORD.—Guildford Museum and Muniment Room, Castle Arch. Local museum for archæology and history of Surrey, especially West Surrey and Guildford Borough; based on collections of the Surrey Archæological Society. Record Office for Borough records, Guildford Diocese parish records, and private records of West Surrey. Open every day except Sunday 11–5.

HULL.—Ferens Art Gallery. The collection has been built up over the last fifty years. It includes a few foreign paintings (notably a fine portrait by Frans Hals), British 18th and 19th-century works especially sea-pieces and pictures by the Hull marine painters, but the bulk of the collection is 20th century, including paintings or sculpture by most of the best known modern British painters. Open, weekdays 10–5; Sundays, 2.30–4.30.

IPSWICH.—*Ipswich Museum*. Specialises in archaeology, geology and natural history of Suffolk. Open weekdays, 10–5, Sundays, 3–5. Closed Good Friday and Christmas Day. *Christchurch Mansion*. Built in 1548 on site of Augustinian Priory. Domestic nature of house is retained and collections include furniture, etc., from Suffolk houses, portraits of Suffolk families and pictures by local artists, including Gainsborough and Constable. Open weekdays and Sunday afternoons. Hours according to season. Closed Good Friday and Christmas Day.

LEEDS.—*City Art Gallery*. Important collection of early English watercolours. British and European painting, modern sculpture, Leeds pottery, silver, etc. Print Room and Art library contains study collection of drawings and prints. Open weekdays, 10–6.30, Sundays, 2.30–5. (Print Room and Art library 9–9, closed Sundays). *Temple Newsam House*. Tudor/Jacobean house altered in mid-18th cent. to make suite of state rooms. Collection of English furniture mostly of 17th and 18th cents., silver, Chinese and European porcelain, pictures, etc. Open daily. May-Sept. 10.30–6.15 (Weds. 10.30–8). Oct.-April 11.30–6.15 or dusk. Admission 1*s*. Leeds residents, 3*d*.

LEWES.—Barbican House, near Castle (Sussex Archæological Society). Large prehistoric and

Roman collections relating to Sussex; Sussex pottery, medieval and Saxon antiquities; pictures and prints relating to the county, etc. Open weekdays, 10–6 (or dusk).

Anne of Cleves' House, Southover (Sussex Archæological Society). 16th century house. Ten rooms are on view and contain the Society's large collection of furniture and bygones; the John Every Ironwork Collections; English and Flemish tapestries, etc. Open weekdays 10–6 (or dusk).

LINCOLN.—*Usher Art Gallery.* Collection of watches, miniatures, porcelain, silver, etc., Peter de Wint collection of oils and water colours, Tennyson collection of manuscripts, etc. associated with Alfred Lord Tennyson, collection of pictures relating to the city of Lincoln and small general collection of works of art. Open weekdays, 10–5.30, Sundays 2.30–5. *City and County Museum.* In the Greyfriars, a 13th cent. Franciscan building. Collections include local archaeology with special emphasis on Romano-British collections from the city and county and coins and tokens, also collections illustrating natural history of Lincolnshire. Open weekdays, 10–5, Sundays 2.30–5.

LIVERPOOL.—Walker Art Gallery. Early Italian and English schools of primary importance. Early Flemish, Dutch, German and later Italian paintings. British 19th century academic paintings with strong Pre-Raphaelite group. British and foreign modern paintings. Open, weekdays, 10–6 (10–5 Oct. to May); Sundays, 2–5. Closed on Good Friday, Christmas Day and Boxing Day.

MANCHESTER.—City Art Galleries. Comprising: *City Art Gallery*, Mosley Street, Manchester 2; *Annexe*, Princess Street, and five branches: *Heaton Hall; Platt Hall (Gallery of English Costume); Wythenshawe Hall; Queen's Park Art Gallery; Fletcher Moss Museum.* The City Art Gallery (architect, Sir Charles Barry) was built for the Royal Manchester Institution and opened in 1829. It was presented to the city in 1882. Heaton Hall, a Georgian mansion designed by James Wyatt, was bought by the Corporation in 1901 and has served as a country house museum since 1906. Other buildings were taken over at later dates up to 1938. Principal collection of paintings is at the City Art Gallery; ceramics at Annexe; costume at Platt Hall; water colours at Fletcher Moss Museum; furniture at Heaton Hall and Wythenshawe Hall; Rutherston Loan Collection, Queen's Park Art Gallery. *Hours of opening*—City Art Gallery: weekdays 10–6, Sundays 2.30–5. Other galleries: weekdays 10–8 (May–Aug.); 10–4 (Nov–Feb.); 10–6 (other months). Sunday opening at 2 p.m. Admission free except to certain temporary exhibitions. Closed Good Friday and Christmas Day.

NEWCASTLE UPON TYNE.—*Laing Art Gallery and Museum*, Higham Place. British oil paintings and water colours from 17th century to the present day; etchings and engravings; Japanese prints; sculpture; Egyptian, Greek and Roman antiquities; pottery and porcelain; glass; silver; wrought ironwork; European and Oriental arms and armour; costumes; textiles; and exhibits illustrative of the artistic industries of Tyneside. Open, weekdays, 10–6; Tues. and Thurs., 10–8; Sundays, 2.30–5.30.

NORWICH.—*Castle Museum.* Exhibits illustrating local archæology, art and natural history. Open, weekdays 10–5; Sundays 2.30–5. *Strangers' Hall (Museum of Domestic Life, Charing Cross).* Late medieval mansion furnished as a museum of urban domestic life, 16th–19th centuries. Open, weekdays 10–1, 2–5. *Bridewell Museum*, Bridewell Alley. Exhibits illustrating trade, transport, crafts and industries of Norwich, Norfolk and North Suffolk. Open, weekdays 10–1, 2–5. *St. Peter Hungate Church Museum*, Princes Street. 15th century church used for display of East Anglian church art and antiquities. Open, weekdays, 10–1, 2–5.

OXFORD, Ashmolean Museum.—Department of Western Art, Department of Antiquities, Heberden Coin Room, Department of Eastern Art, Cast Gallery. Open weekdays, 10–4, Sundays, 2–4 (Heberden Coin Room, weekdays, 2–4; Cast Gallery closed from 1 p.m. Saturdays and all day Sunday).

PLYMOUTH.—*City Museum and Art Gallery.* Collection of ceramics, including Cookworthy's Plymouth and Bristol hand paste porcelain, collections of paintings, drawings and prints, archaeological and natural history collection. Temporary exhibitions arranged. Open weekdays, 10–6 (Fridays, 10–8), Sundays 3–5. Admission free. *Elizabethan House*, New Street. Restored Elizabethan house, furnished according to period. Open 10–1, 2.15–6 (till dusk in winter). Admission free.

PORT SUNLIGHT, Cheshire. *Lady Lever Art Gallery.* Paintings by artists, mainly of British School, British water-colours, antique, Renaissance and British sculpture, English furniture, mainly 18th cent., Chinese pottery and porcelain, and comprehensive collection of old Wedgwood. Open weekdays 10–5, Sundays 2–5.

SHEFFIELD.—*City Museum.* Founded in 1875, the present building was erected in 1937. Eight galleries are normally open to the public, and the reference library and students' collections may be consulted on request. The exhibits cover a wide range of subjects, and include the Bateman Collection of antiquities from the Bronze Age barrows of the Peak District. The cutlery and old Sheffield Plate collections are considered to be the finest of their kind in the world. Open, weekdays, Sept.–May, 10–5; June–Aug. 10–8.30; Sundays 1–4 (Closed Christmas Eve and Christmas Day). *Graves Art Gallery* (opened 1934). Collections of English watercolours, including works by Constable, Cotman, Gainsborough, Girtin and Turner. Oil paintings:—English portraits from the 17th to the 20th century; English landscape of the 18th and 19th century, including examples by Constable, Turner and Wilson. Small representative selection of Dutch 17th century art, with examples by Hobbema and Van Goyen. 20th century British art is represented by works of Paul Nash, John Nash, Matthew Smith and Stanley Spencer and others. Open, weekdays, 10–8; Sundays, 2–5.

SOUTHAMPTON.—*Southampton Art Gallery.* British painting from 18th cent., particularly 20th cent. artists; work of some 14th to 17th cent. Italian, Flemish, Dutch and French painters; a few late 19th and early 20th cent. French paintings and sculpture. Frequent temporary exhibitions. Open weekdays 10–7, Sundays 2–5. (Closed Christmas Day and Good Friday). Admission free.

THE PRINCIPAL ENGLISH CITIES

BIRMINGHAM

BIRMINGHAM (Warwickshire) is the second City n Britain and the chief centre of the hardware rade. The municipal area is 51,147 acres (about o square miles), with a population (estimated 1962) f 1,115,080. It is estimated that over 1,500 istinct trades are carried on in the city, the chief ndustries being the manufacture of buttons, bed-teads, plastic goods, chocolate, chemicals, cycles, lectro-plate, guns, machine tools, glass, motor-ars and motor cycles, motor tyres, nuts and bolts, ens and nibs, tubes, paint and enamels, tools, toys, lectrical apparatus, wire, jewellery and brass vorking, etc.

Water is supplied by the City Corporation, which also owns the transport undertaking, airport, narkets and Municipal Bank. The first section of Birmingham's new Queen Elizabeth Hospital, rected at Edgbaston at a cost of approximately £1,000,000, is claimed to be the finest of its type in Europe. The city has started work on the con-truction of an inner ring road round the centre of he city, with many improvements in the shopping entre and a redevelopment of industrial areas.

The principal buildings are the Town Hall, built in 1832–1834; the Council House and Cor-oration Museum and Art Gallery (1878); Victoria Law Courts (1891); the University (1909); the Central Library; the 13th century Church of St. Martin (rebuilt 1873); the Cathedral (formerly St. Philip's Church); the Roman Catholic Cathedral of St. Chad (Pugin) and the Methodist Central Hall. Birmingham was incorporated as a borough in 1838, and was created a city in 1889; it is governed by a Lord Mayor and City Council of 39 Aldermen and 117 Councillors. The generally accepted derivation of "Birmingham" is the *ham* or dwelling-place of the *ing* or the family of *Beorma* presumed to have been a Saxon. Between the 11th and 16th centuries the de Berminghams were Lords of the Manor.

Lord Mayor and Principal City Officers.

The Lord Mayor (1963–64), L. Glass.
Recorder, J. A. Grieves, Q.C. (1960).
Stipendiary Magistrate, J. F. Milward (1951).
Town Clerk, T. H. Parkinson (1960).
Clerk of the Peace, G. M. Butts.

LIVERPOOL

LIVERPOOL (Lancashire), on the right bank of the river Mersey, 3 miles from the Irish Sea and 194 miles N.W. of London, is one of the greatest trading centres of the world and the principal port in the United Kingdom for the Atlantic trade. The municipal area is 27,819 acres (which includes 2,840 acres in the bed of the river Mersey) (about 43 square miles, excluding the bed of the river), with a population (1962 Registrar-General's estimate) of 745,230. Quays on both sides of the river are about 38 miles long, and the Gladstone Dock can accommodate the largest vessels afloat. Net tonnage of ships entering and leaving the port in the year to July 1, 1963, reached the record figure of 60,575,388. The chief import is grain, those next in importance being sugar, fruit, oil, timber, cotton and provisions.

The Corporation owns large industrial estates at Speke, Kirkby and Aintree, on which many modern factories have been built. Speke and Aintree are now almost fully developed, and at Kirkby new land is constantly being leased, bringing many new industries into the area. In 1943 a lease for 99 years was taken of the Elizabethan mansion at *Speke Hall* at a nominal rent.

The principal buildings are the Cathedral, erected from the designs of Sir Giles Gilbert Scott and consecrated in 1924; when completed this will be the largest ecclesiastical building in England; St. George's Hall, erected 1838–1854, and regarded as one of the finest modern examples of classical architecture; the Town Hall, erected 1754 from the designs of Wood; the Walker Art Gallery; the University; the Royal Infirmary; the Municipal Offices; and the Philharmonic Hall. The Roman Catholic Cathedral is in course of erection at Brownlow Hill.

The *Mersey Tunnel* connecting Liverpool and Birkenhead is one of the most important engineering achievements of recent years; begun in 1925, it was opened to traffic on July 18, 1934, the total cost being estimated at £7,077,800. In 1962–63 14,973,008 vehicles passed through it.

Liverpool was incorporated as a borough early in the 13th century and was created a city in 1880. The Corporation consists of a Lord Mayor and a City Council of 40 Aldermen and 120 Councillors.

Principal City Officers.

The Lord Mayor (1963–64), J. McMillan.
Recorder, S. Chapman, Q.C. (1963).
Stipendiary Magistrate, Arthur McFarland (1947).
Presiding Judge, Court of Passage, G. Glynn Blackledge, M.C., Q.C. (1950).
Town Clerk, T. Alker, C.B.E. (1947).

MANCHESTER

MANCHESTER (Lancashire) (the *Mancunium* of the Romans, who occupied it in A.D. 78) is 189 miles N.W. of London. The municipal area is 27,255 acres (about 43 square miles), the population (1962, Registrar-General's estimate), 659,170.

Manchester is a commercial rather than an industrial centre, the industries being largely in the neighbouring towns. Within 25 miles radius, lives a population of 4,500,000 engaged in engineering, chemical, clothing, food processing and textile industries and in providing the packing, transport, banking, insurance and other distributive facilities for those industries. The city is connected with the sea by the Manchester Ship Canal, opened in 1894, 35½ miles long, and accommodating ships up to 15,000 tons. Manchester Airport handled over 1,000,000 terminal passengers in 1962.

The principal buildings are the Town Hall, erected in 1877 from the designs of Alfred Waterhouse, R.A., together with a large extension; the Royal Exchange, built in 1869 and enlarged in 1921; the Central Library (1934); the Art Gallery; Heaton Hall; the Gallery of English Costume; the 17th century Chetham Library; the Rylands Library (1899), which includes the Althorp collection; the University (Owens College); the 15th century Cathedral (formerly the parish church) and the Free Trade Hall. Manchester is one of the principal centres of political, literary and scientific advancement, and the Hallé Concerts have placed the city in the forefront of musical development. The *Guardian* newspaper exercises a widespread influence throughout the English-speaking world.

The town received a charter of incorporation in 1838 and was created a city in 1853. The City Council consists of 38 Aldermen and 114 Councillors.

Principal City Officers.

The Lord Mayor (1963–64), R. C. Rodgers, M.B.E.
Recorder, Judge J. R. D. Crichton, Q.C. (1960).
Stipendiary Magistrate, F. B. Turner (1951)
Town Clerk, P. B. Dingle, C.B.E. (1944).

SHEFFIELD

SHEFFIELD (Yorkshire, West Riding), the centre of the special steel and cutlery trades, is situated 159 miles N.N.W. of London, at the junction of the

Sheaf, Porter, Rivelin and Loxley with the river Don. The city is set in a beautiful countryside, its residential suburbs penetrating the Peak District of Derbyshire.

Sheffield has an area of 39,598 acres (nearly 62 square miles), including 3,367 acres of publicly owned parks and woodland, and a population (estimated, 1962) of 495,240. Though its cutlery, silverware and plate have long been famous, Sheffield has other and now more important industries—special and alloy steels, engineering and tools in great variety. Titanium is one of the city's latest products. Refractory materials, silver refining, brush making, the manufacture of confectionery, canning, typefounding and the making of snuff are other contrasting industries in Sheffield. In addition to those associated with the staple industries, important institutions are concerned with research in mining, fuel, glass technology and radiotherapy.

The parish church of St. Peter and St. Paul, founded in the twelfth century, became the Cathedral Church of the Diocese of Sheffield in 1914. Parts of the present building date from about 1435. The principal modern buildings are the Town Hall (1897 and 1923), the Cutlers' Hall (1832), the University (1905 and recent extensions), City Hall (1932), Central Library and Graves Art Gallery (1934), Castle Market Building (1959) and the City Museum (1937).

Sheffield was created a borough on Aug. 24, 1843, a county borough in 1888 and a city in 1893, the Mayor becoming a Lord Mayor in 1897. It was made an Assize Town in 1955. The Corporation consists of 25 Aldermen and 75 Councillors.

Principal City Officers.

The Lord Mayor (1963–64), I. Lewis.
Recorder, R. Lyons, Q.C. (1961).
Master Cutler (1963–64) (*340th Master of the Company of Cutlers in Hallamshire*), H. P. Forder.
Town Clerk, S. Hilton (1963).
Clerk of the Peace, P. T. Ward.

LEEDS

LEEDS (Yorkshire, West Riding) is a junction for road, rail and canal services and an important commercial centre, situated 185 miles N.N.W. of London. It is a centre of the wholesale clothing trade. The city has large foundries; engineering works producing textile machinery, machine tools, etc.; printing works, tanneries, and chemical works producing dyestuffs and related products.

The municipal area is 40,619 acres, the population (estimated, 1962), 514,640.

The principal buildings are the Civic Hall (opened by King George V. in 1933), the Town Hall (1858), the Philosophical Hall, the Municipal Buildings and Art Gallery (1884) and the University. The Parish Church (St. Peter's) was rebuilt in 1840; the 17th century St. John's Church has a fine interior with a famous Renaissance screen; the 17th century Mill Hill Chapel was rebuilt in 1848. Kirkstall Abbey (about 3 miles from the centre of the city), founded by Henry de Lacy in 1152, is one of the most complete examples of Cistercian houses now remaining. Temple Newsam, birthplace of Lord Darnley, was acquired by the Corporation in 1922. The present house, a stately building in red brick, was largely re-built by Sir Arthur Ingram in about 1620. Adel Church, about 5 miles from the centre of the city, is a fine Norman structure.

Leeds was first incorporated by Charles I. in 1626, made a county borough in 1889, and was created a city in 1893. The Lord Mayor presides over a Council of 28 Aldermen and 84 Councillors. The earliest forms of the name are *Loidis* or *Ledes*, the origin of which is obscure.

Principal City Officers.

The Lord Mayor (1963–64), E. J. L. Wooler, M.B.E.
Recorder, G. S. Waller, O.B.E., Q.C. (1961).
Stipendiary Magistrate, R. Cleworth, Q.C. (1950).
Town Clerk, R. Crute (1952).
Clerk of the Peace, T. A. Whittington (1952).

BRISTOL

BRISTOL, situated on the borders of Gloucestershire and Somerset, is a City and County of itself, and is 119 miles W. of London. The present municipal area is 26,350 acres, with a population (estimated, 1962), 434,260.

Among the various industries are aircraft and aero-engine construction, general and nuclear engineering, boot and shoe manufacture, chocolate and cocoa, tobacco, pottery, paper bags, cardboard and allied products, printing, chemical industry and shipbuilding and repairing. Bristol is noted for its maritime history and the docks within the Port are the City Docks, 6 miles from the entrance to the river Avon; the Royal Edward and Avonmouth Docks, at the mouth of the river; and the Portishead Docks, to the west of the river entrance. The principal imports are grain, cereal products, cocoa, molasses, feeding stuffs, bananas and other fruit, provisions, frozen meat, sugar, metals, ores, phosphates, oil-seeds, paper, petroleum and petroleum spirit, timber, tobacco, wines and spirits, wood pulp and general merchandise, and the chief exports are machinery, chemicals, strontia, unmanufactured clay, motor vehicles and parts, coke, carbon black, prefabricated buildings and manufactured goods. A new municipal airport was opened at Lulsgate in May, 1957.

The chief buildings, in addition to the 14th century Cathedral (with later additions), with Norman Chapter House and gateway, the 14th century Church of St. Mary, Redcliffe (described by Queen Elizabeth I. as "the fairest, goodliest, and most famous parish church in England"), and Wesley's Chapel, Broadmead, are the Merchant Venturers' Almshouses, the Council House (opened by H.M. The Queen in April, 1956), Guildhall, Exchange (erected from the designs of John Wood in 1743), Art Gallery, Central Library, Cabot Tower, the University and Clifton College, Red Lodge (Tudor), Georgian House, and Blaise Castle and Mansion with Folk Museum. The *Clifton Suspension Bridge*, with a span of 702 feet over the Avon, was projected by Brunel in 1836 but was not completed until 1864. The beautiful *Clifton Down* adjoins *Durdham Down* (making a total of 442 acres), with *Leigh Woods* and *Nightingale Valley* on the opposite side of the river; *Ashton Court Estate* (840 acres) was acquired by Bristol Corporation in Jan., 1960.

Bristol was a Royal Borough before the Norman Conquest. In 1373 it received from Edward III. a charter granting it county status and in 1899 its Mayor became a Lord Mayor. The Corporation includes 28 Aldermen and 84 Councillors. The earliest forms of the name are *Brigstowe* and *Bristow*.

Principal City Officers.

The Lord Mayor (1963–64), Mrs. F. M. Brown.
Sheriff (1963–64), A. A. Baker, C.B.E.
Recorder, N. R. Fox-Andrews, Q.C. (1961).
Town Clerk, T. J. Urwin.
Clerk of the Peace, T. D. Corpe, O.B.E.

KINGSTON UPON HULL

HULL (officially "Kingston upon Hull") is situated in the East Riding of Yorkshire, at the junction of the Hull with the Humber, 22 miles from the North Sea and 205 miles N. of London. The municipal area is 14,493 acres, with a population (estimated, 1962) of 301,640.

Hull is one of the great seaports of the United Kingdom. It has docks covering a water area of 200 acres, well equipped for the rapid handling of cargoes of every kind, and its many industries include oil-extracting, saw-milling, flour-milling, engineering and chemical industries. It also claims to be the premier fishing port.

The City, restored after very heavy air raid damage during World War II, is well laid out with fine thoroughfares. It has good office and administrative buildings; its municipal centre being the Guildhall; its educational centre the University of Hull and its religious centre the Parish Church of the Holy Trinity, 272 feet in length.

Kingston upon Hull (anciently known as *Wyke*) was so named by Edward I, who granted the first of its Charter privileges in 1299. Later privileges included the creation of the office of Mayor (1331); Charter of Incorporation—the creation of the county of the town, with the power, annually exercised, to elect a Sheriff (1440); county area extended (1447); power given to elect a High Steward (1598); City status accorded (1897) and the office of Mayor raised to the dignity of Lord Mayor (1914). The City Council consists of a Lord Mayor, 21 Aldermen and 63 Councillors, representing the 21 wards of the City.

The Lord Mayor (1963–64), J. G. E. Teskey-King.
Recorder, P. Stanley-Price, Q.C. (1958).
Sheriff, D. J. Taylor.
Stipendiary Magistrate, D. N. O'Sullivan (1952).
Town Clerk and Clerk of the Peace, J. H. W. Glen.

NEWCASTLE UPON TYNE

NEWCASTLE UPON TYNE (Northumberland) a City and a County on the north bank of the Tyne estuary, 8 miles from the North Sea and 272 miles N. of London, has an area of 11,094 acres (18 square miles) and a population (estimated, 1962) of 267, 090.

The city is conveniently placed on the estuary, in the centre of the Northumberland and Durham coalfields and is the principal seaport in north-east England. It is an important manufacturing centre with a wide variety of industries.

The principal buildings include the (11th century) "New" Castle, of which the walls, keep and chapel are well preserved, the Cathedral (St. Nicholas), St. Andrew's Church (11th century), St. John's (12th century), St. George's, Jesmond, the Roman Catholic Cathedral of Hexham and Newcastle, Holy Trinity War Memorial, Guildhall (1658) Moot Hall (1810), Exchange (1860), Central Public Library and Laing Art Gallery and Museum, Wood Memorial Hall (1870), and the Custom House. The beauty of Jesmond Dene (gift of Lord Armstrong) is much appreciated by visitors, as well as the Town Moor, a tract of over 900 acres of open grassland. The city is connected with the south bank of the Tyne by six bridges.

The pre-Norman borough of *Monkchester* was re-named Newcastle in the 11th century when the castle was erected as a defence against the Scots. In 1400 it was made a county and in 1589 was incorporated. The City Corporation now comprises a Lord Mayor (1906), 20 Aldermen and 60 Councillors.

The Lord Mayor (1963–64), H. Simm.
Recorder, A. B. Boyle, C.B.E., Q.C. (1961).
Town Clerk and Clerk of the Peace, J. Atkinson (1937).

NORWICH

Norwich (Norfolk) is an ancient City and County 110 miles N.E. of London and the largest town within a radius of 100 miles. It grew from an early Anglo-Saxon settlement near the confluence of the Rivers Yare and Wensum, and now serves as provincial capital for the predominantly agricultural region of East Anglia. The name is thought to relate to the most northerly of a group of Anglo-Saxon villages or "wics." The present City comprises an area of 8,165 acres, with a population (estimated, 1962) of 119,760.

Norwich serves its surrounding area as a market town and commercial centre, banking and insurance being prominent among the City's businesses. Continuously from the fourteenth century, however (when Flemish immigrants helped to establish Norwich as the centre of the woollen industry until the Industrial Revolution) it has combined industry with commerce, and manufactures of a wide variety are now produced in the City. The biggest single industry is the manufacture of shoes and other principal trades are engineering, printing, and the production of clothing, confectionery and other foodstuffs. Norwich is accessible to seagoing vessels by means of the River Yare, entered at Great Yarmouth, 20 miles to the east.

Among many historic buildings are the Cathedral (completed in the twelfth century and surmounted by a fifteenth century spire 315 feet in height), the Keep of the Norman Castle (now serving as a museum and also housing the Colman Collection of works by the Norwich School of painters), the fifteenth century flint-walled Guildhall, some thirty mediaeval parish churches, St. Andrew's and Blackfriars' Halls, the Tudor houses preserved in Elm Hill and the Georgian Assembly House. The administrative centre of the City is the City Hall, built in 1938 and now adjoined by the new central library, opened in 1963. The University of East Anglia has been established in Norwich and received its first students in 1963. The buildings of the University will occupy a spacious site at Earlham on the City's western boundary.

The City's first known Charter was granted in 1158 by Henry II and its privileges and form of self government were prescribed successively by later Charters until the enactment of the Municipal Corporations Act, 1835. The City Council now consists of the Lord Mayor, 16 Aldermen and 48 Councillors representing the sixteen wards into which the City is divided.

The Lord Mayor (1963–64), L. A. Howes.
Sheriff (1963–64), W. J. Roe.
Recorder, P. C. Duncan, M.C., Q.C.
Judge of the Guildhall Court of Record, R. Ives.
Town Clerk, G. G. Tilsley.
Clerk of the Peace, B. O. L. Prior, T.D.

NOTTINGHAM

NOTTINGHAM (Nottinghamshire) stands on the River Trent, 124 miles N.N.W. of London in one of the most valuable coalfields of the country with excellent railway, water (being connected by canal with the Atlantic and the North Sea), and road facilities. The municipal area is 18,370 acres and population (estimated, 1962), 314,360.

The principal industries are hosiery, lace, bleaching, dyeing and spinning, tanning, engineering and cycle works, brewing, the manufacture of tobacco, chemicals, furniture, typewriters and mechanical products.

The chief buildings are the 11th century Nottingham Castle (restored in 1878, and now the City Museum and Gallery of Art), Wollaton Hall (1580–88) owned by the Corporation and now a Natural History Museum, St. Mary's, St. Peter's, and St. Nicholas's Churches, the Roman Catholic

Cathedral (Pugin, 1842–4), the Council House (1929), the Guildhall and Court House (1888), Shire Hall, Albert Hall, the University and Newstead Abbey, home of Lord Byron.

Snotengaham or *Notingeham*, "the home of the sons of Snod" (the Wise), is the Anglo-Saxon name for the Celtic *Tuigogobauc*, "Cave Homes." The city possesses a Charter of Henry II., and was created a city in 1897. The Corporation consists of 17 Aldermen and 51 Councillors (including the Lord Mayor).

The Lord Mayor (1963–64), C. Cameron, C.B.E.
Recorder, M. A. L. Cripps, D.S.O., T.D., Q.C. (1961).
Town Clerk, T. J. Owen.
Clerk of the Peace, G. A. Wharton, M.B.E., T.D.

BRADFORD

BRADFORD (Yorkshire, West Riding), 192 miles N.N.W. of London and 8 miles W. of Leeds, in the coal and iron district, is a centre of the woollen and worsted trade. The city is connected with the Mersey in the west and with the Humber in the east by canals, and is an important railway centre. The municipal area is 25,504 acres (about 40 square miles), with a population (estimated, 1962) of 296,220.

The principal textile industries are worsteds, woollens, silks and cottons, and there are also important engineering and iron works and quarries of freestone.

The chief public buildings, in addition to the 15th century Cathedral (formerly the Parish Church) and Bolling Hall (14th century), are the Town Hall (1873), the tower of which contains a clock with dials, chimes and a carillon, Cartwright Memorial Hall (1904) commemorating the inventor of the power loom, the Windsor Baths and Public Halls (1905), Grammar School (Charter, 1662), St. George's Hall (Concert Hall, 1853), Technical College (1882), the Mechanics' Institute (1832), Wool Exchange (1867), Kirkgate Market Hall (1872), Britannia House (1933) and Bradford Institute of Technology.

The Saxon township was created a parliamentary borough in 1832, a borough in 1847, a county borough in 1889, and a city in 1897. The title of Lord Mayor was conferred on the Chief Magistrate in 1907. The Corporation consists of a Lord Mayor, 20 Aldermen and 60 Councillors.

The Lord Mayor (1963–64), T. Wood.
Recorder, B. B. Gillis, Q.C. (1958).
Town Clerk, H. Patten (1960).
Clerk of the Peace, P. Denny.

OXFORD

OXFORD is a University City, an important industrial centre, and a county, assize, and market town.

It has been a City from time immemorial and a County Borough since 1889. It has an area of 8,785 acres and a population (estimated, 1962) of 106,560. Oxford is a parliamentary constituency returning one member and is governed by a Council of 68 members of whom 12 are, by special enactment, elected by the University.

The University (see also pp. 502–4) has 27 Colleges, 5 Private Halls, 3 New Foundations and 1 Society.

Industry, consisting of printing and bookbinding, and the making of agricultural implements and marmalade, played a minor part in Oxford until the motor industry was established in 1912. To-day this and the adjoining pressed steel works employ about 15,000.

It is for its architecture that Oxford is of most interest to the visitor, its oldest specimens being the reputed Saxon tower of St. Michael's church, the remains of the Norman castle and city walls and the Norman church at Iffley. It is chiefly famous however, for its Gothic buildings, such as the Divinity Schools, the Old Library at Merton College, William of Wykeham's New College, Magdalen College and Christ Church and many other college buildings. Later centuries are not represented by so many examples, but mention can be made of the exquisite Laudian quadrangle at St. John's College, the renaissance Sheldonian Theatre by Wren, Trinity College chapel, and All Saints Church; Hawksmoor's mock-Gothic at All Souls College, and the superb example of eighteenth century architecture afforded by Queen's College. In addition to individual buildings, High Street and Radcliffe Square, just off it, both form architectural compositions of great beauty. Most of the Colleges have gardens, those of Magdalen, New College, St. John's (designed by "Capability" Brown) and Worcester being the largest.

The visitor will always find some of the college chapels, halls and gardens open for public inspection between 10 a.m. and 5 p.m.

Lord Mayor (1963–64), A. P. Parker.
Recorder, J. G. Foster, Q.C., M.P. (1956). [C.B.E.
Town Clerk and Clerk of the Peace, H. Plowman,

CAMBRIDGE

CAMBRIDGE, a settlement far older than its ancient University, lies on the Cam or Granta, 51 miles north of London and 65 miles south-west of Norwich. It has an area of 10,060 acres and a population (estimated, 1962) of 95,380.

The city is a parliamentary and quarter sessions borough, county town and regional headquarters. Its industries, which include radio and electronics, flour milling, cement making and the manufacture of scientific instruments, are extensive but nowhere obtrusive. Among its open spaces are Jesus Green, Sheep's Green, Coe Fen, Parker's Piece, Christ's Pieces, the University Botanic Garden, and the Backs, or lawns and gardens through which the Cam winds behind the principal line of college buildings. East of the Cam, King's Parade, upon which stand Great St. Mary's Church, Gibbs' Senate House and King's College Chapel with Wilkins' screen, joins Trumpington Street to form one of the most beautiful thoroughfares in Europe.

University and College buildings provide the outstanding features of Cambridge architecture but several churches (especially St. Benet's, the oldest building in the City, and St. Sepulchre's, the Round Church) also make notable contributions. The modern Guildhall (1939) stands on a site of which at least part has held municipal buildings since 1224.

The City Council consists of a Mayor, 14 Aldermen and 42 Councillors. Four of the Councillors are elected by the Colleges and Halls and two by Grace of the Senate of the University. Two of the Aldermen are elected by the Council from the University and College representatives.

Mayor (1963–64), J. B. Collins.
Recorder (vacant).
Town Clerk, P. M. Vine.
Clerk of the Peace, C. H. Parker.

CANTERBURY

CANTERBURY, the Metropolitan City of the Anglican Communion, has an unbroken history going back to prehistoric times. It was the Roman Durovernum and the Saxon Cantwaraburg (stronghold of the men of Kent). Here in 597 St. Augustine began the conversion of the English race to Christianity, when Ethelbert, King of Kent, was baptized. In 1170 the rivalry of Church and State culminated in the murder in Canterbury Cathedral, by Henry II.'s knights, of Archbishop

Thomas Becket, whose shrine became a great centre of pilgrimage as described by Chaucer in his *Canterbury Tales*. After the Reformation pilgrimages ceased, but the prosperity of the City was strengthened by an influx of Huguenot refugees, who introduced weaving. In the first Elizabethan era Christopher Marlowe, the poetic genius and precursor of Shakespeare, was born and reared in Canterbury, and there are literary associations also with Defoe, Dickens and Barham, author of the *Ingoldsby Legends*. In the last war the City received severe damage from air attacks, particularly in the great "Baedeker" raid of June 1, 1942. Fortunately the Cathedral (apart from the modern Library) was not severely harmed. Great progress has been made in re-building, before which the opportunity has been taken to excavate archæologically the main areas of damage. As a result part of the street plan of Roman Canterbury has been recovered and many Roman buildings, including a large theatre, identified.

The Cathedral, with its glorious architecture ranging from the eleventh to the fifteenth centuries, is world-famous. Modern pilgrims are attracted particularly to the Martyrdom, the Black Prince's Tomb and other historic monuments, the Warriors' Chapel and the many examples of mediæval stained glass.

Of the Benedictine St. Augustine's Abbey, burial place of the Jutish Kings of Kent (whose capital Canterbury was) only extensive ruins remain. St. Martin's Church, on the eastern outskirts of the City, is stated by Bede to have been the place of worship of Queen Bertha, the Christian wife of King Ethelbert, before the advent of St. Augustine.

The mediæval City Walls are built on Roman foundations and the fourteenth century West Gate is one of the finest buildings of its kind in the country.

The city is a county borough and county of itself, with an area of 4,810 acres and a population (1962 Registrar-General's estimate) of 30,720. Before the institution of the Mayoralty in 1448 it was governed by bailiffs and earlier still by prefects or provosts.

Mayor (1963–64), E. E. Kingsman.
Recorder, Hon. H. A. P. Fisher, Q.C. (1962).
Sheriff (1963–64), C. A. L. Ash.
Town Clerk and Clerk of the Peace, J. Boyle.

YORK

YORK is a county borough, an archiepiscopal seat, the county town of Yorkshire and a county in its own right, its correct designation being "The City and County of the City of York", and it stands at the junction of the three Ridings. York has an area of 6,933 acres, and a population (1962 Registrar-General's estimate) of 104,890. The city returns one member to Parliament and is governed by a Lord Mayor, who has the title of "Right Honourable," 13 Aldermen and 39 Councillors. The City Sheriff, who is the Sovereign's representative, is elected annually with the Lord Mayor.

The recorded history of York dates from A.D. 71, when the Roman Ninth Legion established a base which later became the fortress of Eboracum. Here Constantine the Great was proclaimed Emperor in A.D. 306. Under Edwin, in the 7th century, York became the capital of the Kingdom of Northumbria. Under the Danes it became a trading centre but suffered severely at the Norman Conquest. It is mentioned in the Domesday Book. By the 14th century the city had become prosperous and was used as the chief base against the Scots. It became a great mercantile centre, chiefly owing to its control of the wool trade, but under the Tudors its fortunes declined, though Henry VIII made it the headquarters of the Council of the North, so preserving its status as the Northern capital. During the Civil War York suffered heavily in the Royalist cause, but in the 18th century it became a social centre for the northern nobility and gentry.

With its development as a railway centre in the 19th century the commercial life of York expanded and it is now a flourishing modern city.

It is rich in examples of architecture of all periods, but its finest features are the Minster with its stained glass, and the mediæval city walls and gateways, guildhalls and churches. There are many examples of domestic architecture of the Tudor and Stuart periods, but perhaps more notable are the Georgian mansions of The Mount, Micklegate and Bootham. Its museums are world-famous, and its Art Gallery is now greatly enriched by the Lycett Green collection of Old Masters.

Lord Mayor (1963–64), A. Kirk.
Recorder, H. C. Scott, Q.C. (1961).
Sheriff, W. E. Hargrave.
Town Clerk and Clerk of the Peace, T. C. Benfield.

WINCHESTER

WINCHESTER, the ancient capital of England, is situated on the River Itchen 65 miles S.W. of London and 12 miles north of Southampton. The City has an area of 3,888 acres and a population (1962 Registrar-General's estimate) of 28,650; it is a parliamentary and quarter session borough, an assize town and the county town of Hampshire.

Occupation of the city area can be traced back to 1800 B.C. but organized settlements appeared later, as at St. Catherine's Hill which was an Iron Age settlement from the 6th to 2nd century B.C. Winchester was known as Caer Gwent to the Celts and Venta Belgarum to the Romans; to the latter it was an important centre as the five roads radiating from the city testified. Saxon history is somewhat obscure but Winchester became the capital of Wessex and in the 9th century capital of all England. Alfred the Great made Winchester a centre of education. In the Saxon Cathedral there took place the coronation of Edward the Confessor. William the Conqueror marched straight from his victory at Hastings to Winchester where he established a new Castle, his Treasury and his capital. Here he compiled Doomsday Book as the returns came in from the shires. Winchester remained the capital for many years, but its decline as a capital began with the civil war between Stephen and Matilda; and with the loss of Normandy in 1204, and the sack of Southampton in 1338, Winchester had lost its favourable position. Further damage to the city occurred in the Civil War. In the latter half of the 18th century many of the city's historic buildings, including four of the six gates and much of the city wall, were destroyed. Winchester is rich in architecture of all types but the Cathedral takes first place. The longest Gothic cathedral in the world, it was rebuilt in 1079–1093 and exhibits splendid examples of Norman, Early English and Perpendicular styles. Winchester College, founded in 1393, is one of the most famous public schools, the original building remaining almost unaltered. The Hospital of St. Cross founded in 1136 by Henry de Blois, is a fine mediæval almshouse. The Great Hall, completed in 1235, is a part of the ancient castle built by William the Conqueror.

It is not certain when Winchester was first designated a city but it is probable that the term was applied between 650 and 700. Winchester is one of the oldest corporations in the country; the first written record of a Mayor occurs in 1200.

Mayor (1963–64), Mrs. D. L. Richards.
Recorder, D. P. Croom-Johnson, D.S.C., Q.C. (1962).
Town Clerk and Clerk of the Peace, R. H. McCall.

MUNICIPAL DIRECTORY OF ENGLAND

A list of all CITIES (in SMALL CAPITALS) and Boroughs (in ordinary type), and of *Urban Districts* with a population exceeding 20,000 (in *italics*); the County Boroughs named in the First Schedule of the Local Government Act, 1933, are distinguished by having § prefixed. The first figures in parentheses show the County in which the City, Borough or U.D.C. is situated (*see* p. 632). The second figures in parentheses given in the case of cities and boroughs, show the date of the first recorded Charter of Incorporation.

CITIES, Boroughs and *Urban Districts*	Population, 1962 Estimated	Rate per 1,000 Births	Rate per 1,000 Deaths	Rateable Value 1963 £	Rate levied 1963–64 s.	d.	Town Clerk (or Clerk U.D.C.)	Mayor, 1963–64 ★Lord Mayor †Chairman U.D.C.
Abingdon (2) (1556).....	14,940	16 8	12·7	576,266	10	4	E. W. J. Nicholson.	J. H. Stanley.
Accrington (21) (1878)...	38,940	15·8	15·7	1,100,202	9	10	K. Yates.	J. Riley.
Acton (27) (1921).......	64,960	17·2	11·4	7,175,060	7	4	H. C. Lockyer.	J. H. G. Martin.
Aireborough (49)........	27,920	16·8	12·0	802,873	10	6	W. H. Leathem.	†D. Gibbon.
Aldeburgh (38) (1529)...	2,920	18·9	16·5	109,989	10	4	D. J. Owen.	E. R. Garrod.
Aldershot (15) (1922)....	32,810	21·9	12·7	1,204,156	9	4	H. B. Sales.	A. W. Symonds.
Aldridge (37)...........	54,840	20·0	6·5	1,742,190	9	0	H. G. G. Nichols.	†D. A. Coombe.
Alfreton (9)............	23,050	14·6	11·6	584,137	9	8	H. Taylor.	†G. H. Cowham
Altrincham (6) (1937)...	41,300	15·2	11·5	1,625,691	10	0	E. G. Thomas.	R. Street.
Andover (15) (1175).....	17,960	19·1	10·6	760,663	9	6	J. Whatley.	J. H. Gardner.
Appleby (44) (1179).....	1,770	14·2	12·7	64,628	10	8	H. A. Jones.	Miss N. J. Hodgson.
Arnold (32)............	27,940	20·4	9·9	1,007,761	8	7	A. H. James.	†T. H. Leivers.
Arundel (42) (1586).....	2,650	14·7	16·6	112,650	8	10	G. Campbell.	G. H. Stevens.
Ashford (20)...........	28,450	14·7	12·5	1,035,759	9	6	G. H. Redfern.	†C. R. Doe.
Ashington (31)..........	27,170	15·7	11·5	693,214	10	6	J. Kent.	†Mrs. L. Robson.
Ashton (Lyne) (21) (1847)	49,810	16·0	16·6	1,546,241	9	9	G. A. Malone.	T. Shaw.
Aylesbury (3) (1916).....	29,090	19·9	11·2	1,687,825	9	11	R. D. W. Maxwell.	H. W. Poole.
Bacup (21) (1882).......	17,240	17·1	15·2	364,462	12	0	W. B. Wolfe.	Mrs. A. Stocks.
Banbury (33) (1554).....	21,410	19·7	10·2	1,057,245	10	6	F. G. E. Boys.	J. E. Ryan.
Banstead (40)...........	41,370	12·8	12·8	2,046,230	8	8	F. L. Shaw.	†Mrs. S. M. Crabtree.
Barking (13) (1931).....	72,440	14·2	10·1	4,073,682	10	8	E. R. Farr.	L. F. Henstock.
Barnes (40) (1932)......	38,950	14·5	11·4	2,407,950	8	5	L. John.	J. B. Armstrong.
Barnet (18)	27,460	14·9	11·2	1,520,034	9	7	A. S. Mays, O.B.E.	†E. Cheason.
§Barnsley (49) (1869)....	74,910	18·8	14·0	2,135,616	11	9	A. E. Gilfillan, O.B.E.	T. R. Brown, B.E.M.
Barnstaple (10).........	15,650	19·0	11·8	623.711	9	8	F. J. Broad, O.B.E.	A. S. Williams.
§Barrow-in-Furness (21) (1867)...............	64,890	18·3	13·7	2,088,767	10	6	A. M. Woll.	H. Bannister.
Basildon (13)...........	95,360	18·9	9·6	3,605,489	9	3	A. Hatt.	†A. T. Dove.
Basingstoke (15) (1392)..	26,990	20·8	12·4	1,297,228	23	4	R. J. Purvis.	J. W. Downs.
§BATH (36) (1590)......	82.170	16·4	11·0	2,999,304	10	6	J. E. Dixon.	R. Tucker.
Batley (49) (1868).......	39,890	18·5	12·8	823,482	10	10	L. O. Bottomley.	J. Laughlin.
Bebington (6) (1937)....	52,980	16·4	13·8	2,458,164	8	10	G. Chappell, O.B.E.	J. H. Ward.
Beccles (38) (1584)......	7,400	16·2	11·5	232,865	10	10	F. W. Leah.	E. G. Gilbert.
Beckenham (20) (1935)..	76,930	13·6	12·3	4,281,973	9	5	R. W. Storr.	Mrs. D. E. L. West, M.B.E.
Beddington and Wallington (40) (1937).	32,600	15·2	11·0	2,253,441	8	2	A. B. Bateman.	H. Haydon.
Bedford (Town) (1166)...	64,740	21·7	10·3	3,471,695	8	9	G. F. Simmonds.	G. R. Bailey.
Bedlingtonshire (31).....	30,110	18·1	10·7	942,872	10	6	F. S. Forster.	†W. Baron.
Bedworth (43)...........	33,380	17·3	13·6	934,617	9	10	S. G. Deeming..	†K. S. Tyler.
Beeston and Stapleford (32)................	57,380	18·9	13·9	2,316,652	8	3	H. D. Jeffries.	†F. E. Bradley.
Benfleet (13)...........	34,520	19·5	11·8	1,151,312	9	4	(vacant).	†R. M. Williams.
Bentley with Arksey (49)..	23,160	20·2	14·5	511,066	10	3	W. H. M. Alexander.	†E. Rose.
Berwick (Tweed) (1302)..	12,280	23·4	13·6	355,255	10	6	R. B. Davison.	Mrs. M. Wright.
Beverley (47) (1573).....	16,010	16·6	12·0	500,984	9	0	E. Bailey.	K. J. Bateman.
Bewdley (46) (1462).....	5,140	18·9	14·4	125,645	9	6	W. O. E. Bryan.	J. H. Garbett.
Bexhill (41) (1902)......	30,680	8·8	21·9	1,628,619	10	8	R. S. Robinson.	E. H. Corke.
Bexley (20) (1937)......	89,910	15·0	9·5	3,643,664	9	0	A. Goldfinch.	F. W. Archer.
Bideford (10) (1573).....	10,820	13·8	15·9	311,124	10	6	L. B. Galliford.	Lt.-Col. R. D. D. Birdwood, M.C.
Billingham (12).........	32,480	19·3	13·7	2,787,316	9	0	F. M. Dawson, O.B.E.	†R. Duncan.
Bilston (37) (1933)......	33,340	19·4	11·2	1,493,592	9	6	S. C. Redhead.	E. W. Bold.
Bingley (49)............	22,990	20·0	5·1	683,235	11	0	F. M. Dunwell.	†E. K. Eckersley.
§Birkenhead (6) (1877)...	142,940	19·4	13·5	4,661,114	8	5	D. P. Heath.	Mrs. E. F. Gardner.
§BIRMINGHAM (1838)....	1,115,080	19·5	11·4	49,603,319	10	4	(*See* p. 659).	★(*See* p. 659).
Bishop Auckland (12)...	35,410	18·1	14·2	911,286	10	0	J. R. Passey.	†R. Hindmarch.
Bishop's Castle (35) (1609)	1,220	14·8	9·8	31,976	11	6	G. A. Rogers.	J. H. Scales.
§Blackburn (21) (1851)...	105,740	16·9	16·2	3,086,459	11	0	F. Squires.	F. Wilkinson.
§Blackpool (21) (1876)...	151,250	14·6	14·8	7,811,971	8	11	R. O. F. Hickman.	J. H. Smythe.
Blandford Forum (11) (1605)...............	3,490	18·9	12·8	143,851	10	6	C. K. Lavington.	Mrs. G. F. Lane.
Blaydon (12)...........	31,120	16·5	12·5	727,959	9	6	C. H. Matthews.	†Miss V. Ledger.

Cities, Boroughs and *Urban Districts*	Population 1962 Estimated	Rate per 1,000 Births	Rate per 1,000 Deaths	Rateable Value 1963 £	Rate levied 1963–64 s.	d.	Town Clerk (or Clerk U.D.C.)	Mayor, 1963–64 ★Lord Mayor †Chairman U.D.C.
Blyth (31) (1922).....	36,400	17·2	9·9	937,573	9	7	E. W. Carter.	A. Rutherford.
Bodmin (7) (1798)......	6,170	12·8	9·0	155,340	10	8	I. Whiting.	L. G. Hill.
Bognor Regis (42).......	28,070	14·2	13·1	1,826,264	8	8	R. W. J. Hill.	†E. T. Bryant.
Boldon (12)............	23,280	19·2	11·1	630,176	10	9	J. McGillivray, M.B.E.	†M. Hannah.
§Bolton (21) (1838)......	160,650	17·2	14·9	5,316,581	10	4	P. S. Rennison.	T. Connor.
§Bootle (21) (1868)......	83,220	24·1	9·9	2,730,321	9	11	A. J. E. Taylor.	J. Morley.
Boston (25) (1545)......	24,930	16·6	10·6	936,279	10	2	C. L. H. Griffiths.	A. A. Goodson.
§Bournemouth (15) (1890)	149,830	12·2	17·1	9,580,874	8	0	A. L. Clegg.	H. P. E. Mears, O.B.E.
Brackley (29) (1260).....	3,520	23·8	14·4	104,737	9	0	J. M. Wild.	J. Tweedale.
§BRADFORD (1847)......	296,220	19·6	13·8	9,187,824	10	3	(*See* p. 662).	★(*See* p. 662).
Braintree and Bocking (13)..............	20,760	17·7	11·1	943,402	9	6	K. S. Rogers.	†G. A. Warne.
Bredbury and Romiley (6)	23,020	16·3	11·0	804,784	8	10	D. W. Tattersall.	†Mrs. H. Frank.
Brentford and Chiswick (27) (1932)...........	55,200	17·7	12·0	4,451,614	6	10	W. F. J. Church.	C. A. Pocock.
Bridgnorth (35) (1157)...	7,840	19·3	12·1	311,443	10	2	J. K. Banks.	C. P. Hathaway.
Bridgwater (36) (1200)...	25,930	18·7	11·2	1,003,899	10	11	J. L. Turner.	G. C. Harris.
Bridlington (47) (1899)..	25,730	17·3	12·7	952,911	10	3	S. Briggs.	H. Dixon.
Bridport (11) (1253).....	6,520	12·1	13·6	258,519	11	9	(vacant).	J. Hayne.
Brierley Hill (37).......	57,430	18·5	9·2	2,471,812	8	4	H. Hex.	†S. J. Husselbee.
Brighouse (49) (1893)....	31,260	17·0	12·4	785,923	11	2	J. R. Liddle.	L. Hulme.
§Brighton (41) (1854)....	162,200	14·4	15·7	10,821,213	7	6	W. O. Dodd.	S. D. Deason.
§BRISTOL (1188).........	434,260	16·7	12·7	19,432,000	9	9	(*See* p. 660).	★(*See* p. 660).
Bromley (20) (1903).....	68,730	14·9	12·1	4,012,883	9	3	L. Kaye.	J. L. Hunt.
Bromsgrove (46).........	35,300	17·0	12·1	1,198,025	9	0	G. A. Hall, D.F.C.	†E. H. Longney.
Brownhills (37).........	27,450	20·2	15·3	694,793	7	6	N. Waine, M.B.E.	†J. G. Cooper.
Buckingham (1554)......	4,390	20·5	9·1	195,772	9	4	A. Archdeacon.	J. Edmonds.
§Burnley (21) (1861).....	80,540	17·3	15·7	2,336,159	11	0	C. V. Thornley.	J. Lord.
§Burton-on-Trent (37) (1878).............	50,610	19·5	13·1	2,216,893	10	4	H. T. Meades.	C. J. Badcock.
§Bury (21) (1876)........	61,120	18·8	14·8	1,897,735	8	8	E. S. Smith.	Mrs. D. Butler.
Bury St. Edmunds (39) (1606)...............	21,680	17·6	10·4	891,444	10	4	R. R. Hiles.	A. G. T. Shearing.
Bushey (18).............	22,080	15·8	8·5	1,096,204	8	10	C. G. Everatt.	†P. P. Levey.
Buxton (9) (1917).......	19,370	17·7	16·6	570,567	11	0	G. D. Jones.	T. G. Gill.
Calne (45) (1565).......	6,680	18·5	10·1	219,103	10	8	L. Cave.	A. A. Rengert.
Camborne-Redruth (7)....	36,000	15·6	13·2	922,840	10	0	S. C. Wilson, M.B.E.	†D. W. Bray.
CAMBRIDGE (1207).......	95,380	15·1	10·0	5,155,780	10	0	(*See* p. 662).	(*See* p. 662).
Cannock (37)...........	43,160	17·1	10·5	1,275,086	9	8	H. C. Allen.	†I. J. Jacques.
§CANTERBURY (20) (1448)	30,720	16·1	13·6	1,334,332	8	8	J. Boyle.	E. E. Kingsman.
§CARLISLE (8) (1158).....	70,800	19·2	12·7	2,460,000	9	10	H. D. A. Robertson.	D. M. Hamilton.
Carlton (32)............	38,950	16·9	12·5	1,406,280	8	2	A. E. F. Walker.	†A. A. Hackett.
Carshalton (40)..........	56,380	10·6	12·1	2,220,807	8	9	P. W. Goddard.	†J. McMahon.
Castleford (49) (1955)....	40,420	17·2	15·2	1,069,043	12	6	E. Hutchinson.	H. Astbury.
Caterham and Warlingham (40)......	35,110	17·7	10·1	1,348,409	8	2	B. J. Smerdon.	†G. H. Thaine.
Chadderton (21)..........	32,930	17·8	15·1	1,304,633	9	0	L. Stott.	†S. G. W. Jacobs.
Chard (36) (1570).......	6,020	15·2	10·9	208,101	10	4	F. W. Searle.	L. Fisher.
Chatham (20) (1891)....	49,520	21·5	9·9	721,131	10	6	R. W. E. Hill.	T. H. Hill.
Cheadle and Gatley (6)....	47,940	20·8	13·1	2,013,318	8	9	R. Roberts.	†J. Unsworth.
Chelmsford (13) (1888).	51,180	20·7	9·0	3,003,268	9	0	B. A. Francis.	F. L. Richardson.
Cheltenham (14) (1876)..	73,770	19·2	12·9	3,099,901	10	8	F. D. Littlewood, O.B.E.	A. E. Trigg.
Chertsey (40)...........	41,790	19·8	11·0	1,600,569	8	4	L. W. Way.	†G. L. Hyde, O.B.E.
Cheshunt (18)...........	36,630	18·3	11·4	1,671,506	9	8	G. S. Newnham.	†D. T. Hickman.
§CHESTER (1506)........	59,030	19·1	12·0	2,709,864	9	10	G. Burkinshaw.	T. Sarl-Williams.
Chesterfield (9) (1598)...	68,000	13·6	13·0	2,819,073	9	6	R. Clegg, O.B.E.	J. Anderson.
CHICHESTER (42)........	19,540	14·2	10·1	973,994	9	0	E. Banks.	W. Brookes.
Chigwell (13)...........	62,070	10·9	11·6	2,903,689	8	10	B. R. Ostler.	†C. T. Davie.
Chingford (13) (1938)....	46,350	13·1	9·7	2,130,648	9	6	C. G. Dennis.	J. W. R. Nation.
Chippenham (45) (1554)..	17,930	20·6	13·3	677,217	10	0	S. F. A. Clarke.	Mrs. G. E. Moss.
Chipping Norton (33) (1606)...............	4,200	18·9	10·5	130,722	10	4	R. A. Ingram.	F. Brown.
Chislehurst and Sidcup (20)................	88,560	14·4	11·7	3,961,489	9	2	T. W. Fagg, D.F.C.	†Miss B. H. James.
Chorley (21) (1881)......	31,210			922,000	9	3	R. Potter.	D. Dunn.
Christchurch (15) (1886).	26,640	12·6	15·1	1,393,613	8	10	J. Macfadyen, D.F.C.	J. R. Bell.
Clacton (13)............	28,390	14·4	15·7	1,474,715	10	8	R. B Sayers.	†D. H. R. Moody.
Cleethorpes (23) (1936)..	32,990	19·3	10·5	917,551	9	6	G. Sutcliffe.	J. Winn.
Clitheroe (21) (1147).....	12,300	21·3	15·6	145,838	9	9	H. L. Sagar.	E. Crossley.
Coalville (22)...........	26,510	15·4	12·2	809,553	8	10	H. B. Chynoweth.	†G. A. Peacey.

CITIES, Boroughs and *Urban Districts*	Population, 1962 Estimated	Rate per 1,000 Births	Rate per 1,000 Deaths	Rateable Value 1963 £	Rate levied 1963–64 s.	Rate levied 1963–64 d.	Town Clerk (or Clerk U.D.C.)	Mayor, 1963–64 ★Lord Mayor †Chairman U.D.C.
Colchester (13) (1189)....	67,010	18·5	10·9	2,365,051	9	7	N. Catchpole.	R. A. Harrison.
Colne (21) (1895)........	19,410	17·6	15·6	501,562	10	9	A. Haigh.	J. Whalley.
Colne Valley (49)........	21,250	16·2	15·4	457,655	11	3	J. W. Lomas.	†E. Fielding.
Congleton (6) (1272).....	17,020	15·9	13·4	576,435	9	11	J. Mee.	G. A. Campbell.
Consett (12)............	38,780	16·5	11·9	1,579,682	10	6	J. Quinn.	†J. Redshaw.
Corby (29).............	39,460	25·5	4·9	2,001,689	10	0	G. B. Blackall, M.B.E.	†C. Stewart.
Coseley (37)............	40,620	17·2	13·6	1,819,668	8	10	J. C. Roper.	†J. C. Pointon.
Coulsdon and Purley (40).	74,260	13·9	13·3	3,739,172	8	6	E. F. J. Felix.	†Mrs. E. E. Bray.
§COVENTRY (43) (1345)...	310,640	20·5	9·5	12,201,246	10	6	C. Barratt.	★Mrs. E. Allen.
Crawley (42)............	55,360	21·8	5·4	3,147,781	9	1	R. W. J. Tridgell.	†R. May.
Crayford (20)...........	31,980	16·8	8·0	1,458,808	9	9	G. B. Hodgson.	†Mrs. E. M. White.
Crewe (6) (1877)........	53,580	17·1	13·1	1,849,826	9	6	A. Brook.	J. Golding.
Crook and Willington (12)	25,050	14·5	15·6	537,578	10	6	R. Coates.	†R. W. Oxley.
Crosby (21) (1937).......	59,490	17·9	14·0	1,861,777	10	0	H. O. Roberts.	D. I. Sawyer.
§Croydon (40) (1883)....	253,690	17·3	11·8	13,782,853	8	0	A. Blakemore.	F. T. Cole.
Cuckfield (41)...........	20,840	15·0	10·3	1,011,583	9	6	J. A. Evans.	†C. T. Evans, C.M.G.
Dagenham (13) (1938)...	109,470	13·3	14·7	6,289,609	9	4	K. Lauder.	J. S. Thomas.
Darlaston (37)..........	21,920	15·1	10·6	265,439	9	6	G. R. Rowlands.	†A. J. Foster.
§Darlington (12) (1867)..	84,400	17·1	12·2	1,395,788	9	0	C. N. S. Nicholson.	J. A. Bird.
Dartford (20) (1933).....	46,180	16·6	10·6	1,811,687	10	0	T. Armstrong.	L. H. T. Mayne.
Dartmouth (10) (1341)...	6,360	13·9	11·8	182,301	9	6	A. H. Wright.	Cdr. E. S. Rimmer.
Darwen (21) (1878)......	29,570	16·8	14·3	810,556	10	6	J. C. Fielding.	G. W. Snape.
Daventry (29) (1595)....	5,980	18·7	17·1	270,837	10	6	A. E. Moore.	E. H. Beech.
Deal (20) (1699)........	25,510	17·6	13·8	717,697	9	8	I. E. Ashworth.	N. U. Cavell.
Dearne (49)............	26,640	19·1	13·7	526,198	10	9	A. R. Neighbour.	†G. Copeland.
Denton (21)............	31,840	21·2	15·0	1,024,195	9	11	J. Smith.	†P. H. Armstrong.
§Derby (1154)..........	131,910	17·8	12·7	6,532,939	9	6	N. S. Fisher.	Mrs. E. J. Mack.
Devizes (45) (1605)......	8,680	18·1	9·1	117,918	10	4	R. W. Wells.	W. F. Greenaway.
§Dewsbury (49) (1862)...	53,520	18·9	15·6	1,477,709	11	2	A. N. James.	Mrs. V. Ferrari.
§Doncaster (49) (1194)...	86,460	17·0	13·0	3,662,657	10	8	H. R. Wormald.	W. E. Whittington.
Dorchester (11) (1324)...	12,750	16·8	11·9	593,740	10	4	F. P. L. Sydenham.	W. E. Bowering.
Dorking (40)...........	22,540	16·7	13·8	1,051,104	8	9	F. G. Sutherland.	†O. Nicholson-Florence.
Dover (20) (1278).......	35,650	17·5	12·2	1,219,575	9	10	J. A. Johnson.	C. C. H. Chilton.
Droitwich (46) (1215)....	8,100	15·5	12·3	304,225	9	7	R. W. Russell.	A. G. I. Cardno.
Droylsden (21)..........	25,650	18·1	15·6	251,026	10	2	G. S. Hepton.	†C. S. Bussin.
§Dudley (46) (1865).....	63,820	16·5	14·2	2,677,523	9	8	P. D. Wadsworth.	W. H. W. Poulton.
Dukinfield (6) (1899)....	17,410	15·8	15·6	487,699	9	0	D. W. Yates.	J. Cook.
Dunstable (1) (1864)....	26,480	19·1	11·2	2,209,327	7	4	J. Smith.	M. L. Kilby.
DURHAM (1602).........	22,010	13·3	13·4	850,118	10	0	D. B. Martin-Jones.	N. Richardson.
Ealing (27) (1901).......	183,300	16·0	11·0	12,184,819	6	10	E. J. Cope-Brown.	R. A. Turner.
East Barnet (18)........	40,890	14·5	10·9	748,525	9	8	R. G. Winch.	†W. Seagroatt.
§Eastbourne (41) (1883)..	61,250	11·3	18·4	3,269,476	9	2	F. H. Busby.	B. Raven.
§East Ham (13) (1904)...	105,430	17·6	11·5	4,017,361	10	0	R. H. Buckley.	L. L. Griffiths.
Eastleigh (15) (1936)....	38,080	17·6	9·7	1,500,340	9	4	R. J. Roddis.	R. A. L. Lofting.
East Retford (32) (1246).	18,020	15·9	12·2	494,674	8	10	K. D. Hanna.	G. M. B. Pearson.
Eccles (21) (1892).......	43,060	16·6	15·0	1,376,435	10	3	N. Mitchell.	D. W. Anderson.
Edmonton (27) (1937)...	91,440	15·0	11·0	5,339,230	7	10	H. Backhouse.	E. J. C. Smythe.
Egham (40)............	31,150	15·2	10·8	1,503,343	9	0	A. E. Villars.	†S. J. Wilson.
Ellesmere Port (6) (1955).	46,120	21·5	12·4	3,204,704	8	5	R. J. Bernie.	Miss V. Crutchley.
Enfield (27) (1955)......	109,670	15.4	10·7	7,364,562	7	6	C. E. C. R. Platten.	A. H. Chambers.
Epsom and Ewell (40) (1937)..............	70,380	12.5	15.4	3,554,318	8	10	E. Moore.	W. A. Glover.
Erith (20) (1938)......	45,300	17·4	10.5	2,676,137	8	11	E. M. Bennett.	Mrs. M. E. Barron.
Esher (40).............	60,970	14·0	10·7	3,756,629	8	1	A. G. Chamberlin.	†J. K. Badcock.
Eston (48).............	37,410	24·2	10.0	2,803,192	8	10	T. M. Baker.	†E. Buxton.
Evesham (46) (1604).....	12,600	19·1	10·7	509,815	10	0	N. F. Davies.	F. H. George.
§EXETER (10) (1156).....	78,950	15·6	10·9	4,375,501	10	4	W. A. McSkimming.	W. G. Daw.
Eye (38) (1206).........	1,550	18·5	7·9	40,482	9	0	S. T. Andrew.	R. Bailey.
Failsworth (21).........	20,530	19·3	13·8	607,240	9	6	J. Walton.	†C. E. Tucker.
Falmouth (7) (1661).....	17,330	14·6	12·5	839,704	11	10	E. J. K. Gibbons.	F. J. Offord.
Fareham (15)...........	63,170	20·1	10·5	2,335,095	9	2	B. W. Rands.	†J. H. W. Simpson.
Farnborough (15).......	33,430	22·4	11·2	1,183,936	8	8	D. S. Jones.	†H. C. B. Mackey.
Farnham (40)..........	27,520	16·1	14·2	533,066	8	0	H. W. Underdown.	†E. R. Gudge.
Farnworth (21) (1939)...	27,290	19·7	17·2	725,904	9	0	T. Hitchen.	P. Norfield.
Faversham (20) (1252)...	13,130	16·4	18·0	451,959	10	6	F. G. Bishop.	G. C. Ely.
Felling (12)............	37,100	21·4	9·9	919,419	11	3	J. Donkin.	†M. McGarry.
Feltham (27)...........	51,710	18·8	13·2	3,576,553	6	10	M. W. Coupe.	†E. J. Pauling.
Finchley (27) (1933).....	69,150	16·2	11·8	5,100,991	7	6	R. M. Franklin.	F. Davis.
Fleetwood (21) (1933)...	28,330	19·1	13·7	857,774	11	3	J. R. Barnes.	J. Longton.
Folkestone (20) (1313)...	44,390	16·2	12·5	1,915,619	10	11	N. C. Scragg.	Mrs. D. H. Moody.

Cities, Boroughs and *Urban Districts*	Population, 1962 Estimated	Rate per 1,000 Births	Rate per 1,000 Deaths	Rateable Value 1963 £	Rate levied 1963–64 s.	d.	Town Clerk (or Clerk U.D.C.)	Mayor, 1963–64 ★Lord Mayor †Chairman U.D.C.
Fowey (7) (1912)........	2,090	12·6	16·0	34,739	10	2	S. N. Penhale.	L. G. Trembath.
Friern Barnet (27).......	28,370	13·8	11·0	1,264,119	7	3	R. S. Clothier.	†K. J. Norman.
Frimley and Camberley (40).................	31,650	..	..	1,628,128	8	10	K. S. Harvey.	†Capt. J. R. Jeffrey
§Gateshead (12) (1835)...	103,120	19·5	11·7	3,161,760	11	10	C. D. Jackson.	T. Wilkinson.
Gillingham (20) (1903)...	73,970	18·4	11·3	2,162,129	9	4	R. Newnes.	R. A. Burns.
Glastonbury (36) (1705)..	5,940	16·1	9·7	221,764	9	10	G. H. Harland.	W. J. Chislett.
Glossop (9) (1866)........	17,440	18·0	16·1	194,220	11	8	D. E. Smith.	H. Turner.
§Gloucester (1483)......	70,180	19·9	11·2	2,559,607	12	6	A. G. W. Boggon.	B. J. Cooke.
Godalming (40) (1575)...	16,940	17·5	9·6	766,851	9	0	R. C. Hodgins.	J. I. Blackburn.
Golborne (21)............	22,240	20·1	14·5	592,715	8	6	F. Martland.	†T. H. Ralphs.
Goole (49) (1933)........	18,860	18·7	15·6	435,880	11	2	P. D. Green.	F. W. Gosney, B.E.M.
Gosforth (31)............	26,780	17·7	11·9	964,897	8	10	C. S. Perkins, O.B.E.	†T. E. Bramwell.
Gosport (15) (1922)......	68,850	21·5	11·0	2,125,052	9	0	E. G. J. Addenbrooke.	J. F. Fairhall.
Grantham (24) (1463)...	25,170	17·1	12·4	845,932	9	3	J. F. Guile.	R. Briggs.
Gravesend (20) (1562)...	51,950	22·7	10·1	1,841,058	9	8	F. W. Harrison.	C. A. White.
§Grimsby (23) (1201)....	96,780	21·0	11·9	3,420,677	10	7	F. W. Ward.	C. J. Moody.
Guildford (40) (1257)....	54,100	14·9	11·6	3,603,293	8	0	H. C. Weller.	G. O. Swayne, O.B.E.
Halesowen (46) (1936)...	44,510	16·9	11·1	1,877,840	9	4	J. B. McCooke.	D. C. Herbert.
§Halifax (49) (1848)......	96,250	17·1	14·8	2,578,574	10	6	R. De Z. Hall.	W. Haigh.
Haltemprice (47).........	43,650	16·3	11·6	1,361,205	8	10	A. B. Glasspool.	†G. Fletcher.
Harlow (13).............	58,180	26·6	4·2	3,112,123	10	0	D. F. Bull.	†R. J. Ward.
Harrogate (49) (1884)..	56,790	15·6	11·3	2,216,427	10	0	J. N. Knox.	H. S. C. Tomkinson.
Harrow (27) (1954).......	209,600	15·4	10·4	10,640,917	7	4	D. Pritchard.	G. F. Gibbons.
Hartlepool (12) (1201)...	17,990	9·1	13·8	593,689	9	6	L. O. Williams.	T. I. Boagey.
Harwich (13) (1603)......	13,570	19·0	13·0	413,596	10	2	T. B. A. Moonlight.	H. Gochin.
Haslingden (21) (1891)...	14,300	16·5	15·3	380,665	9	6	L. M. Burton.	T. Waller.
§Hastings (41) (1588)....	66,640	13·9	12·3	2,619,585	10	0	N. P. Lester.	D. W. Wilshin, M.B.E.
Havant and Waterloo (15)	78,120	18·7	12·2	2,781,197	9	0	B. R. W. Gofton, V.R.D.	†M. Spero.
Hayes and Harlington (27)	68,310	17·9	7·5	4,314,331	7	6	G. Hooper.	†W. C. Mongor.
Hazel Grove and Bramhall (6)...................	30,800	16·4	12·4	1,521,244	8	2	D. W. West.	†H. Hardern.
Heanor (9)..............	24,200	18·1	10·8	611,781	9	6	P. M. Robinson.	†E. Whitehouse.
Hebburn (12)............	25,020	19·9	11·7	1,022,075	10	2	W. Kinghorn.	†G. Watson.
Hedon (47) (1154)........	2,380	19·2	17·1	..	..		B. R. Roberts.	..
Helston (7) (1201)........	7,130	27·3	12·4	197,784	11	0	E. R. Crawshaw.	A. E. Lee.
Hemel Hempstead (18) (1898).................	58,270	20·9	7·2	3,214,287	9	0	C. W. G. T. Kirk.	F. G. Edwards.
Hendon (27) (1932).......	150,720	14·2	10·8	11,060,440	6	10	R. H. Williams.	Mrs. C. Thubrun.
Henley (33) (1526).......	9,270	18·1	13·6	371,000	9	11	G. Caldecott.	R. H. Brackston.
Hereford (1189)........	41,300	17·8	12·3	1,939,582	12	2	J. A. Weston.	J. Harding.
Herne Bay (20)..........	21,100	11·3	21·4	831,286	10	4	G. A. Bagnall.	†Mrs. G. E. Fortune.
Hertford (1555)..........	16,670	16·4	..	297,610	8	9	A. I. Clough.	G. W. Dale.
Heston and Isleworth (27) (1932)............	102,680	13·8	10·9	6,670,521	7	0	D. Mathieson.	F. J. Jansen.
Heywood (21) (1881).....	24,220	17·6	15·4	665,329	10	3	W. R. Parker.	A. Sherwin.
Higham Ferrers (29) (1251)................	3,830	12·5	10·4	135,097	10	6	G. H. Crapper.	Mrs. G. E. Woodley.
High Wycombe (3) (1237)	52,880	19·8	19·3	3,239,984	9	4	N. M. Fowler.	T. McLellan.
Hinckley (22)...........	41,480	18·1	9·9	1,493,817	8	8	J. Hilton.	†M. McCarthy.
Hindley (21)............	20,090	17·5	12·4	475,775	9	6	J. Marsden.	†R. Ollerton.
Hitchin (18)............	24,070	20·3	13·4	1,292,989	7	0	W. Wilson.	†A. R. G. Price.
Honiton (10) (1846)......	4,550	19·7	10·5	165,982	10	6	H. V. Custance.	H. E. Hansford.
Hornchurch (13).........	132,400	17·2	11·2	6,096,798	9	6	P. L. Cox.	†L. W. Carroll.
Hornsey (27) (1903)......	97,720	21·9	10·7	4,172,083	7	4	W. B. Murgatroyd.	P. P. Rigby.
Horsham (42)...........	21,950	16·4	12·3	1,211,729	8	2	S. A. Stray.	†B. N. Piggott.
Houghton-le-Spring (12)..	30,760	19·7	11·9	602,205	9	8	G. F. Lamb.	†J. McKinley.
Hove (41) (1898).........	71,980	12·5	12·8	5,704,292	9	0	J. E. Stevens.	T. Benson.
Hoylake (6)............	32,220	16·0	13·4	1,237,337	8	10	H. R. Keighley.	†Mrs. D. M. C. Higginbottom.
Hucknall (32)...........	23,800	18·8	13·2	732,119	8	3	H. Sharp.	†S. S. Greenhalgh.
§Huddersfield (49) (1868).	131,050	17·4	14·2	4,001,644	11	9	H. Bann.	Mrs. M. L. M. Haigh, M.B.E.
§Hull (47) (1440).......	301,640	19·9	11·0	8,711,799	11	8	(*See* p. 661).	★(*See* p. 661).
Huntingdon and Godmanchester.......	9,800	25·2	9·2	397,731	10	2	F. J. E. Dyer.	G. E. Terrill.
Huyton with Roby (21)...	65,630	22·9	7·9	1,610,464	9	3	D. Willgoose.	†G. W. Sealey.
Hyde (6) (1881).........	31,960	17·1	13·9	1,032,207	10	0	J. Binns.	E. F. Myles.
Hythe (20) (1575).......	10,000	14·0	15·0	435,168	10	3	J. Nowell.	Rear-Adm. D. H. Hall-Thompson.

Cities, Boroughs and *Urban Districts*	Population, 1962 Estimated	Rate per 1,000		Rateable Value 1963	Rate levied 1963–64		Town Clerk (or Clerk U.D.C.)	Mayor, 1963–64 ★Lord Mayor †Chairman U.D.C.
		Births	Deaths	£	s.	d.		
Ilford (13) (1926)........	177,460	14·3	12·1	8,760,974	9	6	K. F. B. Nicholls.	F. H. James.
Ilkeston (9) (1887)......	34,960	17·0	9·9	1,102,366	8	8	J. Yates.	R. L. Cook.
§Ipswich (38) (1200).....	118,410	18·2	11·0	4,928,949	9	0	J. C. Nelson.	J. M. Stewart.
Jarrow (12) (1875)......	28,370	19·1	13·8	871,114	10	2	M. L. Rothfield.	A. M. Campbell.
Keighley (49) (1882).....	56,070	18·4	14·4	1,568,821	11	0	J. A. Caesar.	G. W. Dale, B.E.M.
Kendal (44) (1575)....	18,630	14.2	12.7	688,721	10	0	F. J. Pearson.	Miss E. Reed.
Kettering (29) (1938)..	38,650	18.1	11.0	1,433,049	11	4	D. D. Price.	J. P. Slarke.
Kidderminster (46) (1636)	42,470	18·5	12·2	1,781,071	9	6	J. L. Evans.	R. Oakley.
Kidsgrove (37)..........	20,150	18·1	12·6	433,263	9	6	B. V. Taylor.	†A. N. Bloor.
King's Lynn (28) (1204)..	27,460	17·5	11·1	1,476,016	9	0	E. W. Gocher.	A. Bacon.
Kingston (40) (1204)....	35,990	17·0	12·8	3,398,518	8	2	L. V. Powell.	W. J. Marshall.
Kingswood (14).........	26,410	22·8	8·1	849,513	10	0	I. H. Dearnley.	†G. L. Staples.
Kirkby (21)............	54,900	18·5	12·4	1,794,404	9	3	W. Byron.	†J. O'Neill.
Kirkby-in-Ashfield (32)..	21,820	18·9	13·7	541,732	8	10	E. J. Thomas	†J. W. Aldridge.
LANCASTER (21) (1193)...	48,480	18·1	14·2	1,615,225	10	0	J. D. Waddell.	C. Preston.
Launceston (7) (1199)...	4,510	16·0	11·1	155,681	12	5	C. W. Parsons.	W. R. Bennett.
Leamington Spa (43) (1875)...............	42,950	21·7	12·5	1,815,596	10	10	J. N. Stothert.	F. I. Eaton.
Leatherhead (40)........	36,650	14·9	8·6	1,946,948	8	3	L. A. Stray.	†H. J. Killick.
§LEEDS (49) (1626)......	514,640	18·4	12·0	20,115,000	10	0	(*See* p. 660).	★(*See* p. 660).
§LEICESTER (1589)......	272,500	18·7	12·8	13,230,000	10	2	G. C. Ogden.	★Mrs. C. E. Jackson.
Leigh (21) (1899)........	46,500	17·1	16·1	1,334,786	9	6	A. Jones.	S. Jones.
Leominster (17) (1554) ..	6,430	13·6	8·2	202,561	10	8	K. Downs.	H. E. Powell.
Letchworth (18).........	26,230	17·0	9·0	2,109,262	8	10	M. Kelly.	†J. A. Talbot.
Lewes (41) (1881).......	13,810	15·2	10·8	695,062	10	6	G. K. Waddell.	Miss A. Dumbrell.
Leyton (13) (1926)......	92,970	15·0	15·0	3,708,649	10	11	D. J. Osborne.	A. L. Chamberlain.
LICHFIELD (37) (1549)...	15,350	20·0	9·5	555,072	9	10	H. J. Callender, M.B.E.	B. A. Garman, T.D.
§LINCOLN (23) (1154)....	76,930	17·9	12·2	2,504,274	10	2	J. H. Smith, O.B.E.	G. W. Colls.
Liskeard (7) (1240)......	4,560	12·9	9·4	138,788	10	8	H. J. Timbrell.	T. Phipps.
Litherland (21).........	25,020	19·4	14·3	658,165	8	8	W. Boys.	†W. Lawrenson.
§LIVERPOOL (21) (1207)..	745,230	22·1	12·3	26,083,822	11	5	(*See* p. 659).	★(*See* p. 659).
Longbenton (31).........	47,460	18·0	9·4	1,118,570	9	6	G. Harrison.	†G. E. Short.
Long Eaton (9)..........	31,230	17·7	13·0	1,108,526	9	2	G. F. Clegg.	†J. Bramley.
Lostwithiel (7) (1885)....	1,900	17·4	13·7	45,228	9	2	W. G. Scown.	P. C. Ough.
Loughborough (22) (1888)	38,730	16·9	10·5	1,707,052	10	0	A. Usher.	R. C. Fletcher.
Louth (23) (1551).......	11,390	16·2	14·0	348,704	9	9	W. Holt.	N. J. Nicholson.
Lowestoft (38) (1885)....	46,340	15·8	12·6	1,629,930	10	6	F. B. Nunney.	C. R. V. Ramm.
Ludlow (35) (1189)......	6,760	16·1	15·7	204,114	11	0	J. P. Molony.	Mrs. G. M. Potter.
§†Luton (1) (1876),.....	134,820	22·5	9·6	8,377,366	7	8	A. D. Harvey.	L. G. Bowles.
Lydd (20) (1885)........	3,440	15·0	11·6	151,352	9	3	C. L. Winkfield.	B. Prior.
Lyme Regis (11) (1284)..	3,510	11·4	15·7	136,682	11	2	H. Williams.	E. J. Hallett.
Lymington (15) (1150)...	29,220	13·9	12·1	1,393,705	9	8	A. L. Slater.	F. C. Price.
Lytham St. Annes (21) (1922)...............	36,110	13·8	16·8	1,945,380	9	6	R. A. Cork.	J. W. H. Lloyd.
Macclesfield (6) (1261)...	37,610	16·1	15·0	1,216,460	9	9	W. Isaac.	T. Barnes.
Maidenhead (2) (1582)...	35,850	17·7	11·5	2,043,160	9	6	S. Platt.	W. E. Hopgood.
Maidstone (20) (1549)....	60,570	17·6	10·6	2,545,086	10	5	T. Scholes, M.C.	J. E. Evans.
Malden and Coombe (40) (1936)...............	46,750	12·3	12·1	2,311,802	8	6	H. E. Barrett.	L. W. Hawkins.
Maldon (13) (1171)......	10,720	21·2	14·9	464,291	9	3	K. C. Robertson.	Mrs. W. R. Keeble.
Malmesbury (45) (1885)..	2,600	13·3	13·7	35,050	10	8	F. J. Weston.	R. K. M. Lush.
Malvern (46)...........	27,040	16·2	10·4	858,769	9	6	L. J. Martin.	†A. L. Surtees.
§MANCHESTER (21) (1838)	659,170	20·6	13·3	27,377,289	11	6	(*See* p. 659).	★(*See* p. 659).
Mangotsfield (14).......	24,230	..	..	771,324	10	0	R. L. Smith.	W. B. Powell.
Mansfield (32) (1891)....	53,610	17·2	12·4	1,871,151	9	4	S. W. R. Christmas.	A. H. Bailey.
Mansfield Woodhouse (32)	21,220	23·5	9·9	489,304	8	6	C. J. R. Johnson.	†C. W. Ellis.
Margate (20) (1857).....	44,930	13·8	13·6	2,146,876	11	6	T. F. Sidnell.	R. L. A. Freebairn-Smith.
Marlborough (45) (1575).	5,650	20·2	11·8	210,079	9	8	L. C. Bell.	J. W. Seamer.
Merton and Morden (40)..	67,560	12·1	11·8	3,949,706	7	8	S. Astin.	†E. K. Clarke.
§Middlesbrough(48)(1853)	157,690	22·2	10·6	4,927,908	9	6	E. C. Parr.	E. H. Barrass.
Middleton (21) (1886)....	58,460	17·3	13·6	1,547,412	10	0	F. Johnston.	Miss O. Taylor.
Mitcham (40) (1934).....	63,660	14·4	12·4	3,264,543	8	10	R. H. White.	W. H. Sanderson.
Morecambe and Heysham (21) (1902)...........	40,100	16·0	13·7	1,682,110	12	4	C. E. Bottomley.	T. F. Higginson.
Morley (49) (1885).......	41,400	18·8	11·7	907,028	10	10	E. V. Finnigan.	Mrs. M. J. Baston.
Morpeth (31) (1662).....	13,160	20·1	11·6	396,643	10	0	S. Rutherford.	J. Temple.
Mossley (21) (1885).....	9,860	18·9	13·3	276,768	10	9	I. A. Pugh.	H. Hunt.
Nelson (21) (1890).......	32,000	18·2	18·2	856,662	11	0	F. W. Roberts.	S. Cox.

†County Borough from April 1, 1964.

Cities, Boroughs and *Urban Districts*	Population, 1962 Estimated	Rate per 1,000 Births	Rate per 1,000 Deaths	Rateable Value 1963 £	Rate levied 1963–64 s.	d.	Town Clerk (or Clerk U.D.C.)	Mayor, 1963–64 ★Lord Mayor †Chairman U.D.C.
Newark (32) (1549)	24,580	19·5	12·9	862,821	9	0	J. H. M. Greaves.	D. P. Blatherwick,
Newburn (31)	29,000	17·1	13·8	891,883	9	2	C. H. Walker.	†C. H. Woods. [O.B.E.
Newbury (2) (1506)	20,700	20·1	11·7	1,004,026	9	6	L. Southern.	J. Marshall.
Newcastle (Lyme) (37) (1173)	77,210	17·8	11·0	2,222,557	23	6	C. J. Morton.	T. Bethell.
Newcastle (Tyne) (31) (1157)	267,090	17·3	14·0	11,911,280	10	6	(*See* p. 661).	★(*See* p. 661).
Newport (16)	18,950	13·6	18·2	658,199	10	6	W. R. Wilks.	D. J. Cartwright.
New Romney (20) (1563)	2,740	14·2	7·6	115,456	10	0	D. E. Collins.	E. Ellis.
Newton-le-Willows (21)	21,910	17·5	11·1	600,333	8	10	J. Roberts.	†J. C. Noon.
Northampton (1189)	104,910	18·5	12·9	4,317,817	9	5	C. E. V. Rowe.	G. J. Hackett.
Northfleet (20)	22,960	19·7	12·3	1,209,809	9	4	D. F. Bunkall.	†L. Curd.
Norwich (1194)	119,760	15·8	12·1	5,061,878	11	0	G. G. Tilsley.	★L. Howes.
Nottingham (1155)	314,360	19·9	12·1	14,140,402	7	11	(*See* p. 661).	★(*See* p. 661).
Nuneaton (43) (1907)	58,770	17·1	9·8	2,025,378	9	10	A. A. Crabtree.	E. S. Reekie.
Okehampton (10) (1272)	3,800	12·8	15·3	108,163	10	4	C. A. Orsler.	C. E. W. White.
Oldbury (46) (1935)	54,420	14·5	13·6	2,295,476	8	10	K. Pearce.	Mrs. M. E. Garratt.
Oldham (21) (1849)	114,680	17·8	14·2	3,180,566	11	5	E. Haines.	J. H. Broadbent.
Ormskirk (21)	22,880	16·7	12·2	846,951	9	5	G. Williams.	†S. C. Jones.
Orpington (20)	80,950	16·7	10·3	3,851,103	9	1	S. King.	†A. B. Howard.
Ossett (49) (1890)	15,180	21·5	11·7	343,443	10	0	B. C. H. Freeman.	J. Spurr.
Oswestry (35) (1398)	11,520	19·1	10·0	444,755	10	4	R. S. Cubitt.	D. J. Howells.
Oxford	106,560	15·9	10·9	6,306,234	10	0	(*See* p. 662).	★(*See* p. 662).
Paignton (10)	29,810	13·5	12·7	1,542,089	10	4	F. Charlesworth.	†F. E. Martin.
Penge (20)	26,020	24·8	11·2	968,585	9	7	P. J. Bunting.	†Mrs M. M. Blackburn.
Penryn (7) (1275)	4,780	10·0	5·0	118,128	10	6	L. F. Campbell.	W. G. Beswetherick.
Penzance (7) (1614)	18,960	12·9	15·2	637,099	10	2	E. O. Wheale.	Mrs. L. Garstin.
Peterborough (1874)	63,430	17·4	12·0	2,378,636	10	0	C. P. Clarke.	C. E. Hall.
Plymouth (10) (1439)	209,900	17·9	12·2	7,952,337	9	5	S. Lloyd Jones.	★H. M. Pattinson, C.B.E.
Pontefract (49) (1194)	27,960	19·2	9·8	733,964	11	0	J. F. Rook.	H. Sherwood.
Poole (11) (1248)	92,920	15·1	12·8	4,738,213	10	0	J. G. Hillier. [T.D.	H. C. R. Ballam.
Portsmouth (15) (1194)	226,670	17·4	13·1	8,664,705	9	4	J. R. Haslegrave, O.B.E.,	★H. Sotnick.
Potters Bar (27)	23,530	14·9	11·5	1,229,341	7	9	W. A. Stevens.	†A. L. Springall.
Preston (21) (1179)	112,130	19·7	14·4	4,256,961	10	1	W. E. E. Lockley.	C. E. Molyneux.
Prestwich (21) (1939)	34,160	15·5	13·0	1,052,531	9	4	C. A. Cross.	F. I. Airey.
Pudsey (49) (1899)	35,980	19·9	12·5	966,643	10	7	W. R. Cruse.	F. Ambler.
Queenborough (20) (1885)	3,080	24·5	12·7	204,889	10	0	P. I. Warters.	R. D. Sharrock.
Radcliffe (21) (1935)	26,860	17·3	14·8	853,026	10	0	H. A. Fox.	F. Whewell.
Ramsgate (20) (1884)	37,380	16·5	13·7	556,011	11	0	K. F. Speakman.	J. Barnett.
Rawtenstall (21) (1891)	23,860	16·5	15·2	594,820	11	0	C. Campbell.	W. H. Nuttall.
Reading (2) (1253)	121,420	18·2	12·4	2,269,598	7	6	G. F. Darlow, C.B.E.	J. C. H. Butcher.
Redcar (48) (1922)	32,520	18·4	11·9	1,695,528	10	4	H. Caldwell.	S. Brotton.
Redditch (46)	34,780	19·4	13·3	1,352,297	10	4	P. Smith.	†E. Harris.
Reigate (40) (1863)	54,680	15·3	12·9	2,667,790	8	2	H. Davies.	H. G. Daniels.
Richmond (40) (1890)	40,680	14·9	10·4	1,037,150	9	9	C. Heyworth.	H. A. Taylor.
Richmond (48) (1093)	6,570	14·6	12·3	177,994	12	0	J. K. Alldred.	R. W. Waldie.
Rickmansworth (18)	29,320	15·5	9·2	2,040,070	8	8	C. G. R. Williams.	†C. R. Fenton.
Ripon (49) (886)	10,540	18·4	12·0	302,967	11	4	J. A. Berry.	W. H. Parnaby.
Rochdale (21) (1856)	86,130	18·7	14·8	2,534,502	10	4	K. B. Moore.	B. C. Bowden.
Rochester (20) (1189)	51,010	18·6	11·5	1,926,854	9	8	P. H. Bartlett.	E. M. Griffin.
Romford (13) (1937)	115,600	13·9	10·9	5,233,805	9	10	J. E. Symons.	A. Hawkesworth, B.E.M.
Romsey (15) (1607)	6,400	13·6	16·3	263,976	9	8	K. C. E. Holmes.	Mrs. P. A. Wellington.
Rotherham (49) (1871)	86,220	18·8	11·8	3,301,895	10	2	J. S. Wall.	C. Duffield.
Rothwell (49)	26,030	16·1	11·5	730,698	11	2	A. T. S. Robertson.	†A. Newton.
Rowley Regis (37) (1933)	49,030	13·6	10·7	2,130,217	9	4	G. C. Cookson.	J. Adams.
Rugby (43) (1932)	53,510	23·1	13·7	834,892	10	0	T. L. Duffy.	A. Taylor.
Ruislip-Northwood (27)	74,820	14·5	9·2	4,198,487	6	10	E. S. Saywell.	†C. A. Smith.
Runcorn (6)	26,640	22·1	10·7	1,227,756	8	9	T. J. Lewis.	†T. Clare.
Ryde (16) (1868)	19,690	14·2	13·6	700,301	11	2	E. S. Sheppard.	W. G. F. Sutton.
Rye (4) (1289)	4,360	11·8	13·8	170,651	12	6	J. I. Billington.	W. S. Macer.
Saffron Walden (13) (1513)	8,110	15·9	7·5	391,646	8	7	H. C. Stacey.	Mrs. D. J. Hawkins.
St. Albans (18) (1553)	50,450	18·4	10·8	2,903,780	9	0	Miss B. V. Entwistle.	F. J. Lavery.
St. Austell (7)	25,140	15·1	14·8	760,461	11	4	L. E. Saunders.	†C. M. T. Follett.
St. Helens (21) (1868)	108,260	18·3	11·8	3,304,557	9	6	T. Taylor, M.C.	J. Hand.
St. Ives (7) (1639)	8,870	13·1	18·3	215,867	10	6	W. Rainey-Edwards.	E. H. Curnow.
St. Ives (19) (1874)	4,320	23·1	9·3	194,642	8	6	J. D. Crompton.	R. A. Singfield.
Sale (6) (1935)	52,160	17·9	12·8	1,788,822	9	3	B. Finch.	T. A. Winnington.
Salford (21) (1835)	154,000	19·5	14·0	4,607,256	11	6	R. R. Thornton.	W. Petrie.
Salisbury (45) (1227)	35,440	17·2	16·2	1,614,947	11	0	G. Richardson.	H. G. Batt.

CITIES, Boroughs and *Urban Districts*	Population, 1962 Estimated	Rate per 1,000 Births	Rate per 1,000 Deaths	Rateable Value 1963 £	Rate levied 1963–64 s.	d.	Town Clerk (or Clerk U.D.C.)	Mayor, 1963–64 ★Lord Mayor †Chairman U.D.C.
Saltash (7)	7,450	16·9	10·9	215,461	10	1	A. G. Bellingham.	P. W. Skinnard.
Sandwich (20) (1226)	4,370	13·6	9·3	262,052	8	10	B. Roberts.	A. H. Jutson.
Scarborough (48) (1181)	41,900	15·2	11·9	1,872,508	10	10	E. H. Turner.	W. H. Smith.
Scunthorpe (23) (1936)	68,130	21·2	8·4	5,122,144	8	4	T. M. Lister.	L. Hornsby.
Seaham (12)	25,630	18·2	10·5	518,170	10	0	F. A. Alderson.	†Mrs. M. I. Robinson.
Seaton Valley (31)	25,950	14·8	13·8	561,021	9	6	H. Brummitt.	†J. May.
Sedgley (37)	29,940	17·5	11·4	915,790	8	6	K. R. F. Newton.	†A. Oakley.
Shaftesbury (11) (1604)	3,280	14·9	11·6	124,816	10	5	H. Orman.	R. G. White.
§SHEFFIELD (49) (1843)	495,240	16·5	13·1	19,935,246	9	4	(*See* p. 660)	★(*See* p. 660).
Shipley (49)	29,880	15·9	14·1	851,121	12	0	E. Pears.	†T. M. Duggan.
Shrewsbury (35) (1189)	50,120	17·3	12·6	2,187,652	10	9	S. R. H. Loxton, O.B.E.	T. C. Bowdler.
Sittingbourne and Milton (20)	24,270	17·4	11·8	1,162,883	9	6	D. Allen.	†Mrs. M. M. Boulding.
Slough (3) (1938)	82,700	18·3	11·1	7,047,193	9	4	N. T. Berry.	A. Simpson.
§Smethwick (37) (1899)	68,680	19·0	13·2	2,633,051	9	6	E. L. Twycross.	H. Bone.
Solihull (43) (1954)	98,670	18·6	8·0	4,348,897	9	11	W. M. Mell.	H. B. Shaw.
Southall (27) (1936)	54,120	2·1	13·6	3,296,972	7	6	J. S. Syrett.	E. J. Sheil.
§Southampton (15) (1447)	205,790	18·9	10·6	10,288,817	9	5	A. N. Schofield.	R. F. Pugh.
§Southend (13) (1892)	166,130	15·3	12·1	7,617,227	10	2	A. Glen.	E. J. Trevett.
Southgate (27) (1933)	71,370	14·4	11·6	4,262,602	7	3	G. H. Taylor.	F. S. Furneaux, M.B.E., T.D.
South Molton (10) (1590)	2,950	13·6	25·4	78,292	10	2	C. N. B. Willey.	J. Carter.
§Southport (21) (1867)	80,730	14·9	12·7	3,795,645	8	7	R. E. Perrins.	S. Goldberg.
§South Shields (12) (1550)	109,300	18·4	12·0	2,992,069	9	2	R. S. Young.	Mrs. L. Glover.
Southwold (38) (1489)	2,200	12·0	9·5	103,792	9	10	H. Townsend.	Lt.-Col. J. B. Jarvis.
Spenborough (49) (1955)	37,160	17·7	14·5	909,907	10	6	K. H. Chorlton.	J. Smith.
Stafford (1206)	48,280	18·2	11·7	2,051,520	9	4	T. B. Nowell.	A. E. Collins.
Staines (27)	51,000	17·2	10·3	2,922,216	7	11	F. Entwistle.	†J. J. Hill.
Stalybridge (6) (1857)	22,140	17·4	16·2	622,465	9	6	P. W. Musther.	J. D. Lilley.
Stamford (24) (1461)	12,310	16·7	10·5	389,520	9	6	H. Bedford.	J. W. L. Whincup.
Stanley (12)	46,480	16·1	12·4	888,128	10	0	J. J. Shipston.	†Mrs. O. Alderson.
Stevenage (18)	46,710	27·3	4·1	3,053,340	8	8	E. J. Bowers.	†K. B. Ellis.
§Stockport (6) (1220)	142,570	19·1	13·4	5,039,195	8	5	D. W. Hay.	H. Hope.
Stockton-on-Tees (12)	82,890	21·0	12·8	2,617,264	9	8	J. B. Haworth.	Mrs. M. Scott.
§STOKE-ON-TRENT (37) (1910)	266,130	16·7	11·6	8,674,643	11	0	H. Taylor.	★J. Westwood.
Stourbridge (46) (1914)	44,010	17·9	11·0	1,632,523	9	0	A. P. Drury.	H. Hardwick.
Stratford-upon-Avon (43) (1553)	16,700	15·0	12·0	941,958	10	4	D. M. Balmford.	C. G. Kemp.
Stretford (21) (1933)	60,610	18·9	13·7	3,438,568	9	9	W. G. Hatton.	Mrs. E. M. Macpherson.
Sudbury (39) (1554)	6,550	17·2	13·7	231,393	9	8	G. C. Mountstephen.	Mrs. K. M. Hitchcock.
Sunbury on Thames (27)	34,540	18·7	11·2	2,061,804	7	8	T. L. Watts.	†Mrs. E. M. Flagg.
§Sunderland (12) (1634)	190,580	20·3	11·1	6,446,722	9	8	J. Storey.	Mrs. J. E. Hedley.
Surbiton (40) (1936)	63,170	15·5	10·4	3,537,979	8	7	J. H. A. Crundell.	H. W. Edwards.
Sutton and Cheam (40) (1934)	78,430	15·0	13·0	4,443,145	9	0	A. Priestley.	D. P. Thomas.
Sutton Coldfield (43) (1528)	75,220	19·7	8·3	3,263,467	9	10	J. P. Holden.	C. H. Smith.
Sutton in Ashfield (32)	40,540	17·2	13·7	1,043,671	9	2	W. Laughton.	†C. E. Holland.
Swindon (45) (1900)	94,560	22·4	8·7	3,403,273	10	3	D. M. John, O.B.E.	C. W. J. Streetly.
Swinton and Pendlebury (21) (1934)	41,020	16·6	15·9	1,480,642	10	0	J. W. Blomeley.	†T. H. Jones.
Tamworth (37) (1560)	13,780	15·5	13·0	597,080	10	6	H. B. Leake.	P. J. Dix.
Taunton (36) (1627)	36,230	16·0	11·3	1,343,593	11	6	K. A. Horne.	W. F. Haywood.
Tenterden (20) (1449)	4,970	15·2	11·2	160,372	9	6	C. A. Saunders.	F. W. Foreman.
Tewkesbury (14) (1574)	5,880	15·5	12·0	200,952	10	6	K. E. S. Smale.	L. G. Marston.
Thetford (28) (1573)	5,920	26·9	10·1	231,540	8	8	W. E. Clarke.	The Lord Fisher, D.S.C.
Thornaby-on-Tees (48) (1892)	22,950	20·3	16·8	611,096	9	8	A. Stockwell.	J. Kidd.
Thornton Cleveleys (21)	20,890	14·4	16·0	1,227,966	8	9	J. R. Wylde.	†A. L. Simpson.
Thurrock (13)	115,430	14·7	11·8	6,666,172	9	6	A. E. Poole.	†T. A. L. Hutson.
Tipton (37) (1938)	38,300	19·3	10·7	1,728,023	9	6	K. W. Madin.	F. A. Chamberlain.
Tiverton (10) (1615)	12,770	19·2	12·7	452,861	10	0	W. F. Pugsley.	W. H. Dunsford.
Todmorden (49) (1896)	17,300	15·3	16·4	372,383	11	3	J. D. Moys.	H. Iveson.
Tonbridge (20)	23,310	20·5	12·4	957,416	11	0	L. W. Henderson.	†Mrs. E. J. Burke.
Torquay (10) (1892)	51,700	13·2	11·9	2,529,978	10	4	T. E. Williams.	R. W. Kellow.
Torrington (10) (1554)	2,880	15·3	14·1	38,175	9	6	S. J. Parkes.	H. H. Wightman.
Totnes (10) (1206)	5,880	13·0	10·4	199,128	10	8	A. N. Buckmaster, T.D.	A. C. E. Heal.
Tottenham (27) (1934)	113,020	19·8	12·6	6,368,470	8	6	K. W. Robbins.	D. Clark.
TRURO (7) (1589)	13,620	9·6	20·4	565,873	11	0	T. H. Johnson.	E. A. Brown.

Cities, Boroughs and *Urban Districts*	Population, 1962 Estimated	Rate per 1,000 Births	Rate per 1,000 Deaths	Rateable Value 1963 £	Rate levied 1963–64 s.	d.	Town Clerk (or Clerk U.D.C.)	Mayor 1963–64 ★Lord Mayor †Chairman U.D.C.
Tunbridge Wells (20) (1889)	40,340	14·5	17·0	1,791,227	11	0	M. J. H. Girling.	J. T. Spare.
Twickenham (27) (1926)	102,500	15·8	11·8	5,029,097	7	6	W. H. Jones.	J. A. Denham.
§Tynemouth (31) (1849)	71,390	20·7	11·4	2,393,619	8	0	F. G. Egner, O.B.E.	J. Coe.
Urmston (21)	43,110	19·1	13·2	2,814,087	9	0	L. Watkins.	†Mrs. R. V. Royle-Higginson.
Uxbridge (27) (1955)	64,470	18·2	9·8	3,433,673	7	3	E. R. West.	N. Holland.
§WAKEFIELD (49) (1848)	60,560	16·1	13·6	851,478	10	6	W. S. des Forges.	H. S. Grainger.
§Wallasey (6) (1910)	103,490	18·9	13·3	3,485,063	10	2	A. G. Harrison, D.S.C.	A. E. Martin.
Wallingford (2) (1155)	5,100	20·8	8·0	269,055	10	2	L. Bullen.	O. C. Wilkinson.
Wallsend (31) (1901)	49,690	18·6	11·2	1,708,126	9	6	J. Stoker.	Mrs. E. M. A. Brown.
§Walsall (37) (1159)	119,700	19·6	10·9	4,157,960	8	6	W. S. Brookes.	R. D. Talbot.
Walthamstow (13) (1929)	108,190	14·4	11·8	5,582,856	10	4	G. A. Blakeley.	Mrs. W. M. Palethorpe.
Walton and Weybridge (40)	45,910	14·8	11·0	2,915,072	7	10	E. G. Hubbard.	†J. A. Shaw.
Wanstead and Woodford (13) (1937)	61,410	13·8	12·5	1,090,447	9	6	A. McC. Findlay.	E. V. Gardner.
Wareham (11) (1211)	3,110	15·6	11·3	108,361	9	5	H. Kirk.	R. Dixon.
§Warrington (21) (1847)	76,200	19·1	12·1	3,068,782	8	9	J. P. Aspden.	W. Mullen.
Warwick (1545)	16,300	17·2	12·6	805,611	11	0	H. B. Dolphin.	E. Lloyd-Averns.
Watford (18) (1922)	75,540	17·9	11·4	5,491,329	8	7	G. H. Hall.	G. W. Knox.
Wednesbury (37) (1886)	34,930	18·5	10·1	1,439,732	8	10	G. F. Thompson.	M. Allen.
Wellingborough (29)	31,050	17·1	13·3	1,072,643	10	4	W. G. Palmer.	†C. F. Robinson.
WELLS (36) (1201)	6,960	18·2	17·0	268,950	10	10	H. J. Dodd.	Mrs. L. M. Osmond.
Welwyn Garden City (18)	36,860	15·7	11·2	2,988,356	7	8	L. J. Slocombe.	†H. W. Dorton.
Wembley (27) (1937)	124,900	13·9	11·9	9,384,170	6	9	N. Cumpsty.	F. E. Pratt.
Wenlock (35) (1468)	14,970	14·5	12·5	128,950	10	1	A. G. Matthews.	R. W. Smith.
West Bridgford (32)	26,950	17·0	11·4	1,146,965	8	6	A. G. Mansfield.	†H. H. Sanders.
§West Bromwich (37) (1882)	97,050	19·2	8·5	4,015,883	10	0	J. M. Day.	J. Evans.
§West Ham (13) (1886)	156,960	18·8	12·9	9,328,509	8	6	G. E. Smith.	Mrs. M. Scott.
§West Hartlepool (12) (1887)	78,220	21·5	10·6	2,276,039	8	6	E. J. Waggott, O.B.E.	J. Addison.
Weston Super Mare (36) (1937)	42,750	16·8	11·2	1,852,375	11	10	R. G. Lickfold.	N. W. Haskins.
Weymouth and Melcombe Regis (11) (1280)	41,390	17·9	12·9	1,699,824	10	6	E. J. Jones.	S. V. J. Porter.
Whitehaven (8) (1894)	27,610	21·8	11·2	848,369	10	8	W. H. J. Browne.	J. McMean.
Whitley Bay (31) (1954)	36,730	15·9	14·2	1,387,600	9	8	F. S. Watson.	C. F. Michaels.
Widnes (21) (1892)	53,300	23·1	14·2	1,859,163	10	0	F. Howarth	H. Scholes
§Wigan (21) (1246)	78,910	16·6	12·6	2,743,944	10	0	A. Royle.	J. Johnson.
Wigston (22)	22,990	23·6	8·1	843,562	8	4	W. H. Gunning.	†O. D. Lucas.
Willenhall (37)	33,750	17·1	13·1	1,345,265	9	0	J. R. Riding.	†R. A. C. Wrighton.
Willesden (27) (1933)	171,230	24·8	11·1	9,716,000	7	10	R. S. Forster.	I. W. Davies.
Wilmslow (6)	22,420	16·9	13·0	1,048,825	10	2	J. H. Morris.	†W. H. Leigh.
Wilton (45) (1100)	3,930	16·2	8·2	120,792	8	4	G. L. Lush.	A. J. Tocknell.
Wimbledon (40) (1905)	56,850	15·8	11·3	3,567,436	8	9	F. J. O'Dowd.	G. Waller.
WINCHESTER (15) (1155)	28,650	14·5	11·5	1,395,672	9	6	(*See* p. 663).	(*See* p. 663).
Windsor (2) (1277)	28,350	19·7	8·6	1,177,305	9	3	G. N. Waldram.	Mrs. M. M. Pressey.
Wirral (6)	22,070	16·7	10·3	857,517	9	10	W. F. Roberts.	†R. R. Stewart.
Wisbech (5) (1549)	17,550	17·7	14·6	833,621	11	0	W. G. E. Lewis.	L. H. Rands.
Woking (40)	70,610	17·9	11·1	3,168,252	8	6	M. Shawcross.	†Mrs. R. McGaw.
Wokingham (2) (1583)	12,260	17·9	16·0	693,100	9	4	L. G. Smalley.	Mrs. P. P. Pigott.
§Wolverhampton (37) (1848)	149,710	20·9	11·3	7,245,301	8	6	R. J. Meddings.	H. Preece.
Wood Green (27) (1933)	47,510	17·1	12·2	2,482,243	8	3	G. W. Plater.	Mrs. L. Angell.
Woodstock (33) (1453)	1,820	26·3	17·1	54,463	10	9	V. N. Tolley.	Mrs. M. E. Bowley.
§WORCESTER (1189)	67,050	16·9	12·1	2,846,681	9	6	B. Webster, M.C.	Mrs. H. M. Lettice.
Workington (8) (1888)	29,710	17·0	14·5	1,068,510	10	10	G. McK. Porter.	J. C. Moore, M.B.E.
Worksop (32) (1931)	34,840	19·1	10·0	1,103,416	9	0	R. C. Pharaoh.	G. K. Boardman.
Worsley (21)	41,820	16·5	11·5	1,366,460	9	11	E. R. Huband.	†E. Harper.
Worthing (42) (1890)	79,750	11·7	14·7	4,957,399	9	2	T. Foord.	L. E. Tomlin.
§Yarmouth (28) (1208)	52,450	15·5	10·5	2,226,196	11	4	K. C. Bibby-Cheshire.	J. P. Winter.
Yeovil (36) (1854)	24,550	15·3	11·3	1,110,994	10	6	T. S. Jewels.	C. E. Hawes.
Yiewsley and West Drayton (27)	23,930	17·3	12·7	2,575,847	6	3	E. T. Bradford.	†S. J. Orme.
§YORK (1396)	104,890	15·9	12·2	3,438,773	11	10	(*See* p. 663)	★(*See* p. 663).

PARTY REPRESENTATION IN ENGLISH CITIES AND BOROUGHS

The representation of parties in English cities and boroughs after the municipal elections of May, 1963, was as follows: (*C.*=Conservative; *Ind.*=Independent, including Ratepayers' Association, etc.; *Lab.*=Labour; *Lib.*=Liberal).

Abingdon	*Lab.* 9, *Ind.* 8, *C.* 6, *Lib.* 1.
Accrington	*Lab.* 18, *C.* 13, *Lib.* 4, *Ind.* 1.
Acton	*Lab.* 25, *C.* 7.
Aldeburgh	*Ind.* 16.
Aldershot	*Lib.* 16, *C.* 13, *Ind.* 2, *Lab.* 1.
Altrincham	*C.* 10, *Lab.* 10, *Lib.* 9, *Ind.* 3.
Andover	*Ind.* 7, *C.* 4, *Lab.* 4, *Lib.* 1.
Appleby	*Ind.* 16.
Arundel	*Ind.* 16.
Ashton under Lyne	*Lab.* 32, *C.* 11, *Lib.* 1.
Aylesbury	*Lab.* 13. *C.* 10, *Ind.* 1.
Bacup	*Lab.* 9, *Lib.* 9, *C.* 5, *Ind.* 1.
Banbury	*C.* 13, *Lab.* 10, *Ind.* 1.
Barking	*Lab.* 26, *C.* 6.
Barnes	*C.* 22, *Lab.* 8, *Lib.* 2.
Barnsley	*Lab.* 32, *Ind.* 6, *Lib.* 2.
Barnstaple	*Ind.* 10, *Lib.* 7, *Lav.* 5, *C.* 2.
Barrow in Furness	*Lab.* 26, *C.* 6.
Basingstoke	*C.* 14, *Lab.* 9, *Lib.* 1.
Bath	*Lab.* 20, *C.* 16, *Lib.* 12, *Ind.* 8.
Batley	*Lab.* 21, *Ind.* 6, *Lib.* 3, *C.* 2.
Bebington	*C.* 23, *Lab.* 14, *Lib.* 2, *Ind.* 1.
Beccles	*Lab.* 11, *C.* 4, *Ind.* 1.
Beckenham	*C.* 19, *Lib.* 6, *Ind.* 5, *Lab.* 2.
Beddington and Wallington	*Ind.* 20, *Lab.* 5, *Lib.* 3.
Bedford Town	*C.* 15, *Lab.* 8, *Ind.* 5.
Beverley	*Ind.* 20, *Lab.* 4.
Bewdley	*Ind.* 11, *C.* 1.
Bexhill	*C.* 16, *Lab.* 5, *Ind.* 2, *Lib.* 1.
Bexley	*Lab.* 17, *C.* 13, *Lib.* 2.
Bideford	*Ind.* 15, *Lab.* 1.
Bilston	*Lab.* 18, *C.* 2.
Birkenhead	*Lab.* 42, *C.* 21, *Lib.* 1.
Birmingham	*Lab.* 93, *C.* 61, *Lib.* 1.
Bishops Castle	*Ind.* 16
Blackburn	*Lab.* 36, *C.* 15, *Ind.* 3, *Lib.* 2.
Blackpool	*C.* 31, *Lib.* 31, *Lab.* 5, *Ind.* 1.
Blandford	*Ind.* 15, *Lab.* 1.
Blyth	*Lab.* 25, *Ind.* 15.
Bodmin	*Ind.* 16.
Bolton	*Lab.* 47, *C.* 27, *Lib.* 18.
Bootle	*Lab.* 43, *C.* 13.
Boston	*C.* 10, *Lab.* 9, *Lib.* 7, *Ind.* 2.
Bournemouth	*C.* 37, *Ind.* 9, *Lab.* 9, *Lib.* 9.
Brackley	*Ind.* 16.
Bradford	*Lab.* 42, *C.* 28, *Lib.* 9.
Brentford and Chiswick	*C.* 20, *Lab.* 16.
Bridgnorth	*Ind.* 16.
Bridgwater	*Lab.* 16, *Ind.* 6, *Lib.* 2.
Bridlington	*Ind.* 24.
Bridport	*Ind.* 15, *Lab.* 9.
Brighouse	*Lab.* 18, *C.* 12, *Lib.* 2.
Brighton	*C.* 49, *Lab.* 23, *Ind.* 2, *Lib.* 2.
Bristol	*Lab.* 59, *Ind.* 51.
Bromley	*C.* 14, *Ind.* 6, *Lab.* 4, *Lib.* 4.
Buckingham	*Ind.* 11, *Lab.* 5.
Burnley	*Lab.* 34, *C.* 10, *Lib.* 4.
Burton on Trent	*Lab.* 17, *C.* 11, *Ind.* 4.
Bury	*C.* 21, *Lib.* 12, *Lab.* 10, *Ind.* 1.
Bury St. Edmunds	*Ind.* 17, *C.* 4, *Lab.* 3.
Buxton	*Lab.* 9, *C.* 5, *Ind.* 5, *Lib.* 5.
Calne	*Ind.* 13, *Lab.* 2,, *Lib.* 1.
Cambridge	*C.* 23, *Lab.* 15, *Ind.* 8, *Lib.* 8.
Canterbury	*C.* 23, *Ind.* 1.
Carlisle	*Lab.* 28, *C.* 10, *Ind.* 1, *Lib.* 1.
Castleford	*Lab.* 35, *C.* 3, *Ind.* 2.
Chard	*Lab.* 9, *Ind.* 6, *Lib.* 1.
Chatham	*Lab.* 15, *C.* 9.
Chelmsford	*C.* 17, *Lab.* 14, *Lib.* 1.
Cheltenham	*C.* 20, *Lab.* 8, *Lib.* 6, *Ind.* 1.
Chester	*Lab.* 29, *C.* 19, *Lib.* 8.
Chesterfield	*Lab.* 29, *C.* 13, *Ind.* 6.
Chichester	*Ind.* 21, *Lib.* 3.
Chingford	*Ind.* 19, *Lab.* 6, *Lib.* 3.
Chippenham	*Ind.* 7, *Lib.* 7, *Lab.* 6, *C.* 4.
Chipping Norton	*Ind.* 8, *C.* 5, *Lab.* 3.
Chorley	*Lab.* 17, *C.* 15.
Christchurch	*Ind.* 12, *C.* 5, *Lib.* 3, *Lab.* 2.
Cleethorpes	*C.* 10, *Lab.* 5, *Ind.* 3, *Lib.* 2.
Clitheroe	*C.* 9, *Lab.* 7.
Colchester	*Lab.* 19, *C.* 14. *Lib.* 3.
Colne	*Lab.* 14, *C.* 8, *Ind.* 1, *Lib.* 1.
Congleton	*Lab.* 13, *C.* 11, *Lib.* 3, *Ind.* 1.
Coventry	*Lab.* 43, *C.* 20.
Crewe	*Lab.* 29, *Ind.* 3.
Crosby	*C.* 23, *Ind.* 11, *Lab.* 6.
Croydon	*Ind.* 33, *Lab.* 29, *C.* 2.
Dagenham	*Lab.* 23, *Ind.* 3, *Lib.* 2.
Darlington	*Lab.* 22, *C.* 10, *Ind.* 10, *Lib.* 2.
Dartford	*Lab.* 17, *C.* 4, *Ind.* 3.
Dartmouth	*Ind.* 16.
Darwen	*Lab.* 12 *Lib.* 9, *Ind.* 2, *C.* 1.
Daventry	*Ind.* 9, *Lab.* 7.
Deal	*C.* 23. *Lab.* 8, *Lib.* 1.
Derby	*Lab.* 43, *C.* 21.
Devizes	*C.* 10, *Ind.* 7, *Lib.* 4, *Lab.* 3.
Dewsbury	*Lab.* 21, *Ind.* 15.
Doncaster	*Lab.* 38, *C.* 5, *Ind.* 5.
Dorchester	*Ind.* 17, *Lab.* 7.
Dover	*Lab.* 14, *C.* 10.
Droitwich	*Ind.* 16.
Dudley	*C.* 24, *Lab.* 17, *Ind.* 2, *Lib.* 1.
Dukinfield	*Lab.* 19, *Lib.* 3, *C.* 2.
Dunstable	*Lab.* 11, *C.* 7, *Ind.* 6.
Durham	*Ind.* 21, *Lab.* 7.
Ealing	*C.* 39, *Lab.* 24, *Lib.* 1.
Eastbourne	*C.* 20, *Lib.* 12, *Lab.* 8.
East Ham	*Lab.* 30, *Ind.* 10.
East Retford	*Ind.* 12, *Lab.* 6, *Lib.* 4, *C.* 2.
Eastleigh	*Lab.* 23, *C.* 3, *Ind.* 2.
Eccles	*Lab.* 23, *Lib.* 5, *C.* 4.
Edmonton	*Lab.* 21, *C.* 9, *Ind.* 2.
Ellesmere Port	*Lab.* 18, *C.* 9, *Ind.* 5.
Enfield	*Lab.* 24, *C.* 13, *Lib.* 2.
Epsom and Ewell	*Ind.* 34, *Lab.* 4, *Lib.* 2.
Erith	*Lab.* 22, *Lib.* 2.
Evesham	*Ind.* 20.
Exeter	*C.* 32, *Lab.* 17, *Lib.* 7, *Ind.* 2.
Eye	*Ind.* 15.
Falmouth	*Ind.* 8, *Lab.* 5, *C.* 2, *Lib.* 1.
Farnworth	*Lab.* 23, *C.* 1.
Faversham	*Lab.* 11, *C.* 3, *Ind.* 2.
Finchley	*Lib.* 19, *C.* 13,
Fleetwood	*Ind.* 11, *C.* 9, *Lab.* 4.
Folkestone	*C.* 23, *Lab.* 11, *Ind.* 2.
Fowey	*Ind.* 16.
Gateshead	*Lab.* 35, *Ind.* 13.
Gillingham	*C.* 18, *Lab.* 14.
Glastonbury	*C.* 10, *Lab.* 5, *Lib.* 1.
Glossop	*Lib.* 7, *Ind.* 6, *Lab.* 6, *C.* 5.
Gloucester	*Lab.* 25, *C.* 9, *Ind.* 3, *Lib.* 3.
Godalming	*C.* 11, *Lib.* 7, *Ind.* 4, *Lab.* 2.
Goole	*Lab.* 14, *Ind.* 9. *C.* 1.
Gosport	*C.* 18, *Lab.* 17. *Ind.* 4, *Lib.* 1.
Grantham	*Lab.* 15, *C.* 5, *Ind.* 4.
Gravesend	*C.* 18, *Lab.* 14.
Grimsby	*Lab.* 31, *C.* 25.
Guildford	*C.* 10, *Lab.* 9, *Ind.* 8, *Lib.* 5.
Halesowen	*C.* 7, *Lib.* 7, *Lab.* 4, *Ind.* 2.
Halifax	*C.* 22, *Lab.* 22, *Lib.* 16.
Harrogate	*C.* 26, *Lib.* 9, *Lab.* 1.
Harrow	*C.* 33, *Lab.* 18, *Lib.* 9.

Hartlepool	*Lab.* 15, *Ind.* 5, *C.* 4.
Harwich	*Ind.* 13, *Lab.* 2, *Lib.* 1.
Haslingden	*Lab.* 11, *C.* 7, *Lib.* 6.
Hastings	*C.* 21, *Lab.* 11, *Lib.* 6, *Ind.* 2.
Helston	*Ind.* 16.
Hemel Hempstead	*Lab.* 19, *Ind.* 3, *C.* 2.
Hendon	*C.* 20, *Lib.* 9, *Lab.* 7.
Henley	*Ind.* 14, *Lab.* 2.
Hereford	*Lab.* 10, *C.* 6, *Ind.* 6, *Lib.* 2.
Hertford	*C.* 8, *Ind.* 6, *Lab.* 3, *Lib.* 3.
Heston and Isleworth	*Lab.* 19, *C.* 16, *Lib.* 1.
Heywood	*Lab.* 20, *C.* 9, *Lib.* 7.
Higham Ferrers	*Lab.* 8, *Ind.* 4, *C.* 3, *Lib.* 1.
High Wycombe	*Lab.* 18, *C.* 8, *Ind.* 4, *Lib.* 1.
Honiton	*Ind.* 24.
Hornsey	*C.* 30, *Lab.* 18.
Hove	*C.* 33, *Ind.* 3, *Lab.* 3, *Lib.* 1.
Huddersfield	*Lab.* 25, *C.* 19, *Lib.* 15.
Hull	*Lab.* 62, *C.* 18, *Lib.* 3, *Ind.* 1.
Hyde	*Lab.* 11, *Lib.* 5, *C.* 4, *Ind.* 4.
Hythe	*C.* 9, *Lab.* 4, *Ind.* 3.
Ilford	*C.* 24, *Lab.* 14, *Lib.* 10.
Ilkeston	*Lab.* 18, *Lib.* 3, *C.* 2, *Ind.* 1.
Ipswich	*Lab.* 25, *C.* 24, *Lib.* 7.
Jarrow	*Lab.* 22, *C.* 6.
Keighley	*C.* 16, *Lab.* 16, *Lib.* 8.
Kettering	*Lab.* 15, *Lib* 8, *Ind.* 7, *C.* 6.
Kidderminster	*C.* 12, *Lab.* 10, *Lib.* 6.
King's Lynn	*C.* 12, *Lab.* 12
Kingston	*C.* 18, *Lab.* 9, *Lib.* 4, *Ind.* 1.
Lancaster	*Lab.* 19, *C.* 13, *Ind.* 4.
Launceston	*Ind.* 15, *Lab.* 1.
Leamington Spa	*C.* 22, *Lab.* 6, *Lib.* 4.
Leeds	*Lab.* 70, *C.* 41.
Leicester	*Lab.* 34, *C.* 23, *Lib.* 7.
Leigh	*Lab.* 25, *C.* 4, *Lib.* 3.
Leominster	*C.* 9, *Ind.* 5, *Lab.* 2.
Lewes	*Lab.* 13, *C.* 8, *Ind.* 3.
Leyton	*Lab.* 37, *Lib.* 2, *C.* 1.
Lichfield	*Ind.* 15, *Lab.* 4, *Lib.* 4, *C.* 1.
Lincoln	*Lab.* 18, *C.* 5, *Ind.* 5.
Liskeard	*Ind.* 15, *Lib.* 1.
Liverpool	*Lab.* 86, *C.* 67, *Ind.* 3, *Lib.* 3.
Lostwithiel	*Ind.* 15.
Loughborough	*Lab.* 17, *C.* 7, *Lib.* 3, *Ind.* 1.
Louth	*Ind.* 18, *Lab.* 4, *Lib.* 1.
Lowestoft	*Lab.* 21, *C.* 12, *Ind.* 5, *Lib.* 2.
Ludlow	*C.* 7, *Ind.* 5, *Lab.* 2, *Lib.* 2.
Luton	*Lab.* 22, *C.* 14.
Lydd	*Ind.* 16.
Lyme Regis	*Ind.* 16.
Lymington	*Ind.* 35, *Lib.* 1.
Lytham St. Annes	*C.* 25, *Lib.* 5, *Ind.* 1, *Lab.* 1.
Macclesfield	*C.* 20, *Lab.* 17, *Lib.* 11.
Maidenhead	*Lib.* 14, *C.* 4, *Ind.* 2.
Maidstone	*C.* 16, *Lab.* 6, *Lib.* 6.
Malden and Coombe	*C.* 27, *Lab.* 7, *Ind.* 2.
Maldon	*Lab.* 10, *C.* 9, *Ind.* 1.
Malmesbury	*Ind.* 14, *Lab.* 2.
Manchester	*Lab.* 89, *C.* 54, *Lib.* 9.
Mansfield	*Lab.* 17, *C.* 7.
Margate	*C.* 23, *Lab.* 8, *Ind.* 7, *Lib.* 2.
Marlborough	*Ind.* 14, *Lab.* 2.
Middlesbrough	*Lab.* 48, *C.* 15, *Ind.* 3, *Lib.* 2.
Middleton	*Lab.* 20, *C.* 12, *Lib.* 3, *Ind.* 1.
Mitcham	*Lab.* 21, *Ind.* 8, *C.* 7.
Morecambe and Heysham	*C.* 17, *Ind.* 12, *Lab.* 5, *Lib.* 2.
Morley	*Lab.* 24, *Ind.* 18, *C.* 2.
Morpeth	*Ind.* 13, *Lab.* 3.
Mossley	*Lib.* 14, *C.* 8, *Lab.* 2.
Nelson	*Lab.* 32.
Newark	*C.* 10, *Lab.* 8, *Ind.* 6.
Newbury	*Ind.* 13, *Lib.* 8, *Lab.* 3.
Newcastle (Lyme)	*Lab.* 27, *Ind.* 11, *C.* 6, *Lib.* 4.
Newcastle (Tyne)	*Lab.* 53, *C.* 27.
Newport (I.O.W.)	*Ind.* 11, *C.* 6, *Lab.* 6, *Lib.* 1.
New Romney	*Ind.* 16.
Northampton	*C.* 26, *Lab.* 22.
Nottingham	*Lab.* 36, *C.* 30, *Lib.* 1.
Nuneaton	*Lab.* 20, *C.* 11, *Lib.* 1.
Okehampton	*Ind.* 16.
Oldbury	*Lab.* 16, *C.* 6, *Lib.* 6.
Oldham	*Lab.* 39, *C.* 10, *Lib.* 3.
Ossett	*Ind.* 10, *Lab.* 5, *Lib.* 1.
Oswestry	*Ind.* 17, *Lab.* 7.
Oxford	*C.* 26, *Lab.* 25, *Ind.* 12, *Lib.* 5.
Penryn	*Ind.* 9, *Lab.* 7.
Penzance	*Ind.* 31, *Lab.* 1.
Peterborough	*Lab.* 21, *C.* 13, *Lib.* 2.
Plymouth	*Lab.* 45, *C.* 32, *Lib.* 3.
Pontefract	*Lab.* 20, *C.* 3, *Ind.* 1.
Poole	*C.* 23, *Lib.* 11, *Lab.* 6.
Portsmouth	*C.* 37, *Lab.* 27.
Preston	*Lab.* 34, *C.* 12, *Ind.* 2
Prestwich	*C.* 16, *Ind.* 5, *Lib.* 2, *Lab.* 1.
Pudsey	*Lib.* 17, *C.* 8, *Lab.* 7.
Queenborough	*Lab.* 11, *C.* 3, *Ind.* 2.
Radcliffe	*Lab.* 20, *Ind.* 16.
Ramsgate	*Lab.* 15, *Ind.* 10, *C.* 6, *Lib.* 1.
Rawtenstall	*Lab.* 14, *C.* 8, *Ind.* 1, *Lib.* 1.
Reading	*Lab.* 27, *C.* 24, *Lib.* 1.
Redcar	*Lab.* 13, *Ind.* 6, *Lib.* 5, *C.* 3.
Reigate	*C.* 18, *Lab.* 10.
Richmond (Surrey)	*C.* 19, *Lab.* 9, *Lib.* 7, *Ind.* 5.
Richmond (Yorks)	*Ind.* 16.
Ripon	*C.* 10, *Ind.* 3, *Lab.* 2, *Lib.* 1.
Rochdale	*Lab.* 26, *Lib.* 14, *C.* 7, *Ind.* 1.
Rochester	*Lab.* 16, *C.* 11, *Lib.* 1.
Romford	*Lab.* 26, *C.* 10.
Romsey	*C.* 12, *Lab.* 3, *Ind.* 1.
Rotherham	*Lab.* 38, *Ind.* 2, *Lib.* 2, *C.* 1.
Rowley Regis	*Lab.* 25, *Lib.* 5, *Ind.* 1.
Rugby	*Lab.* 17, *C.* 9, *Lib.* 7, *Ind.* 3.
Ryde	*Ind.* 13, *C.* 12, *Lib.* 3.
Rye	*Ind.* 16.
Saffron Walden	*Ind.* 6, *C.* 5, *Lab.* 5.
St. Albans	*C.* 16, *Lab.* 11, *Lib.* 1.
St. Helens	*Lab.* 32, *C.* 6, *Lib.* 2.
St. Ives (Cornwall)	*Ind.* 15, *Lab.* 1.
St. Ives (Hunts.)	*Ind.* 16.
Sale	*Lib.* 15, *C.* 12, *Lab.* 5.
Salford	*Lab.* 51, *C.* 10, *Lib.* 3.
Salisbury	*Ind.* 13, *Lab.* 10, *C.* 8, *Lib.* 1.
Saltash	*Ind.* 16.
Sandwich	*C.* 6, *Ind.* 6, *Lib.* 3, *Lab.* 1.
Scarborough	*Lib.* 10, *C.* 9, *Lab.* 3, *Ind.* 2.
Scunthorpe	*Lab.* 33, *C.* 7.
Shaftesbury	*Ind.* 16.
Sheffield	*Lab.* 72, *C.* 28.
Shrewsbury	*Lab.* 22, *C.* 19, *Lib.* 2, *Ind.* 1.
Slough	*Lab.* 31, *C.* 11, *Ind.* 1, *Lib.* 1.
Smethwick	*Lab.* 17, *C.* 15.
Solihull	*Ind.* 29, *Lab.* 5, *C.* 4, *Lib.* 2.
Southall	*Lab.* 17, *C.* 7.
Southampton	*Lab.* 45, *C.* 27.
Southend	*C.* 24, *Lib.* 19, *Lab.* 18, *Ind.* 3.
Southgate	*Ind.* 21, *C.* 7.
South Molton	*Ind.* 16.
Southport	*Lib.* 27, *C.* 23, *Lab.* 9, *Ind.* 1.
South Shields	*Lab.* 40, *Ind.* 20.
Southwold	*Ind.* 16.
Spenborough	*Lab.* 23, *C.* 12, *Ind.* 4, *Lib.* 1.
Stafford	*Lab.* 18, *Ind.* 16, *Lib.* 2.
Stalybridge	*Lab.* 18, *C.* 13, *Lib.* 1.
Stamford	*C.* 13, *Lab.* 7, *Ind.* 3, *Lib.* 1.
Stockport	*Lab.* 45, *C.* 18, *Lib.* 9.
Stockton-on-Tees	*Lab.* 32, *C.* 11, *Lib.* 1.
Stoke on Trent	*Lab.* 76, *C.* 11, *Ind.* 9.
Stourbridge	*C.* 12, *Lab.* 11, *Lib.* 1.
Stratford upon Avon	*Ind.* 26, *Lab.* 1, *Lib.* 1.
Stretford	*C.* 15, *Lab.* 15, *Lib.* 2.
Sudbury	*Ind.* 12, *Lab.* 3, *C.* 1.
Sunderland	*Lab.* 51, *C.* 19, *Ind.* 2.

Surbiton..........*C.* 26, *Lab.* 9, *Ind.* 1.
Sutton and Cheam..*C.* 24, *Lib.* 7, *Lab.* 5.
Sutton Coldfield....*C.* 24, *Ind.* 8, *Lib.* 8
Swindon..........*Lab.* 28, *Ind.* 17, *C.* 3.
Swinton and Pendlebury......*Lab.* 20, *C.* 7, *Ind.* 1.
Tamworth.........*Lab.* 17, *C.* 4, *Ind.* 3.
Taunton..........*Lab.* 11, *Ind.* 7, *C.* 5, *Lib.* 5.
Tewkesbury.......*Lib.* 10, *C.* 6.
Thetford..........*C.* 7, *Ind.* 5, *Lab.* 4.
Thornaby-on-Tees..*Lab.* 19, *C.* 3, *Lib.* 1, *Ind.* 1.
Tipton............*Lab.* 14, *C.* 7, *Ind.* 3.
Tiverton..........*Ind.* 15, *Lab.* 4, *Lib.* 3, *C.* 2.
Todmorden........*Lab.* 14, *Ind.* 8, *C.* 2.
Torquay..........*C.* 16, *Ind.* 10, *Lib.* 9.
Totnes...........*Ind.* 12, *Lab.* 4.
Tottenham.........*Lab.* 42, *C.* 2.
Truro............*Ind.* 18, *C.* 5, *Lab.* 1.
Tunbridge Wells...*C.* 23, *Lab.* 6, *Lib.* 2, *Ind.* 1.
Twickenham.......*C.* 30, *Lib.* 10, *Lab.* 4.
Tynemouth........*Ind.* 24, *Lab.* 11.
Uxbridge..........*Lab.* 19, *C.* 11, *Ind.* 6.
Wakefield.........*Lab.* 25, *C.* 18, *Lib.* 1.
Wallasey..........*Lab.* 26, *C.* 22, *Lib.* 11, *Ind.* 5.
Wallingford.......*Ind.* 12, *Lab.* 3, *Lib.* 1.
Wallsend..........*Lab.* 32, *Ind.* 4.
Walsall...........*Lab.* 23, *Ind.* 15, *C.* 6.
Walthamstow......*Lab.* 37, *C.* 11.
Wanstead and Woodford.......*C.* 18, *Lib.* 7, *Ind.* 5, *Lab.* 2.
Warrington........*Lab.* 28, *C.* 8.
Warwick..........*C.* 12, *Lab.* 9, *Ind.* 2, *Lib.* 1.
Watford..........*Lab.* 26, *C.* 18.
Wednesbury.......*Lab.* 16, *C.* 4.
Wells............*Ind.* 12, *Lab.* 2, *Lib.* 2.
Wembley.........*C.* 31, *Lab.* 9, *Lib.* 7, *Ind.* 1.
Wenlock.........*Ind.* 21, *Lab.* 11.
West Bromwich....*Lab.* 25, *C.* 17, *Ind.* 2.
West Ham.........*Lab.* 59, *Lib.* 5.
West Hartlepool....*Lab.* 19, *C.* 17.
Weston-s-Mare.....*C.* 16, *Ind.* 7, *Lab.* 5, *Lib.* 4.
Weymouth........*C.* 14, *Ind.* 12, *Lab.* 11, *Lib.* 3.
Whitehaven........*Lab.* 18, *C.* 6.
Whitley Bay.......*C.* 26, *Ind.* 4, *Lab.* 2.
Widnes...........*Lab.* 21, *C.* 10, *Ind.* 1.
Wigan............*Lab.* 49, *C.* 7.
Willesden..........*Lab.* 44, *C.* 11, *Lib.* 1.
Wilton............*Ind.* 13, *Lab.* 3.
Wimbledon........*C.* 21, *Lab.* 9, *Lib.* 2.
Winchester........*C.* 10, *Ind.* 10, *Lab.* 4.
Windsor...........*C.* 19, *Lab.* 16, *Lib.* 5.
Wisbech..........*C.* 16, *Lab.* 8, *Ind.* 5, *Lib.* 1.
Wokingham.......*C.* 8, *Ind.* 8, *Lib.* 5, *Lab.* 3.
Wolverhampton....*Lab.* 34, *C.* 26.
Wood Green.......*Lab.* 18, *C.* 6.
Worcester.........*Ind.* 16, *Lab.* 16, *C.* 13, *Lib.* 3.
Workington.......*Lab.* 24, *C.* 4, *Ind.* 4.
Worksop..........*Lab.* 18, *Ind.* 5, *Lib.* 1.
Worthing..........*C.* 22, *Ind.* 11, *Lib.* 7.
Yarmouth.........*Lab.* 26, *C.* 17, *Lib.* 3, *Ind.* 2.
Yeovil............*Lab.* 13, *Ind.* 8, *Lib.* 3.
York.............*Lab.* 26, *C.* 25, *Lib.* 1.

Welsh Cities and Boroughs

Abergavenny.......*C.* 7, *Lab.* 6, *Ind.* 2, *Lib.* 1.
Aberystwyth.......*Ind.* 19, *Lab.* 5.
Bangor...........*Ind.* 24, *Lab.* 4.
Barry............*Lab.* 20, *Ind.* 7, *C.* 1.
Brecon...........*Ind.* 7, *Lab.* 5, *C.* 4.
Caernarvon........*Ind.* 22, *Lab.* 2.
Cardiff...........*Lab.* 37, *C.* 27, *Lib.* 3.
Cardigan..........*Ind.* 16.
Carmarthen........*Ind.* 15, *Lab.* 9.
Colwyn Bay.......*Ind.* 19, *C.* 7, *Lab.* 2.
Conway...........*Ind.* 17, *Lab.* 3.
Cowbridge........*Ind.* 12, *C.* 2, *Lab.* 2.
Denbigh...........*Ind.* 16.
Flint.............*Ind.* 10, *Lab.* 8, *C.* 6.
Haverfordwest.....*Ind.* 14, *Lab.* 2.
Kidwelly..........*Ind.* 8, *Lab.* 8.
Lampeter..........*Ind.* 16.
Llandovery........*Ind.* 16.
Llanelly...........*Lab.* 20, *Ind.* 2, *Lib.* 2.
Llanidloes.........*Ind.* 12, *Lab.* 4.
Merthyr Tydfil.....*Lab.* 31, *Ind.* 1.
Monmouth........*C.* 7, *Lib.* 4, *Ind.* 3, *Lab.* 2.
Neath............*Lab.* 17, *Ind.* 7.
Newport..........*Lab.* 28, *C.* 15, *Lib.* 3, *Ind.* 2.
Pembroke.........*Ind.* 24.
Port Talbot........*Lab.* 32.
Pwllheli..........*Ind.* 16.
Ruthin............*Ind.* 16.
Swansea...........*Lab.* 42, *Ind.* 16, *C.* 2.
Tenby............*Ind.* 16.
Welshpool.........*Ind.* 12, *Lab.* 3, *C.* 1.
Wrexham.........*Ind.* 14, *Lab.* 10, *Lib.* 10, *C.* 2.

FREEMEN'S GUILDS

London.—Guild of Freemen of the City of London, 4 Dowgate Hill, E.C.4. *Clerk*, D. Reid.
Berwick upon Tweed.—Freemen's Guild of Berwick upon Tweed. *Sec.*, W. Herriott, 65 Walkergate.
Chester.—Chester City Guilds. *Secretary*, W. E. Dutton, 51 Brook Lane, Chester.
Coventry.—City of Coventry Freemen's Guild. *Clerk*, F. White, 187 Leamington Road.
Gloucester.—Gloucester Freemen's Committee. *Secretary*, B. W. Barrett, 46 Howard Street.
Grimsby.—Enrolled Freemen of Grimsby. *Clerk*, W. J. Savage, St. Mary's Chambers, Grimsby.
Lincoln.—Lincoln Freemen's Committee. *Clerk*, E. Mason, St. Swithin's Square, Lincoln.
Newcastle upon Tyne.—Freemen of Newcastle upon Tyne. *Secretary*, T. A. B. Forster, Lloyds Bank Chambers, Collingwood Street, Newcastle, 1.
Oxford.—Oxford Freemen's Committee. *Chairman*, Dr. T. W. Chaundy, 23 Sandfield Road.
Shrewsbury.—Association of Shrewsbury Freemen. *President*, M. Peele, Dogpole, Shrewsbury.
York.—Gild of Freemen of the City of York. *Clerk*, D. Lyth, 38A Coney Street, York.

THE PRINCIPALITY OF WALES AND MONMOUTHSHIRE

Position and Extent.—Wales and Monmouthshire occupy the extreme west of the central southern portion of the island of Great Britain, with a total area of 8,006 sq. miles (5,130,107 acres); they are bounded on the N. by the Irish Sea, on the S. by the Bristol Channel, on the E. by the English counties of Cheshire, Salop, and Hereford, and on the W. by St. George's Channel. Across the Menai Straits is the Welsh island-county of *Anglesey* or Môn (276 sq. miles), communication with which is facilitated by the Menai Suspension Bridge (1,000 ft. long), built by Telford in 1826 (freed from toll as from Jan. 1, 1941) and by the tubular railway bridge (1,100 ft. long) of the former L.M. & S. Railway, built by Stephenson in 1850. Holyhead harbour, on Holy Isle (N.W. of Anglesey), provides accommodation for a fast steam packet service to Kingstown and Dublin (70 miles).

Population.—The population at the *Census* of 1961 was 2,641,000 (inclusive of Monmouthshire); Registrar-General's estimate (June 30, 1962), 2,651,340.

Relief.—Wales is mostly mountainous, the chief systems being those of North Wales (Snowdon 3,560 ft., Carnedd Llywelyn 3,484 ft., Carnedd Dafydd 3,426 ft.); Berwyn (Aran-mawddwy 2,970 ft.); Powys (Plinlimmon 2,468 ft., Drygan Fawr 2,115 ft., Radnor 2,163 ft.); and the Black Mountain, Brecknock Beacons and Black Forest ranges (Carmarthen Van 2,632 ft., Brecon Beacon 2,906 ft., Pen-y-gader fawr 2,660 ft.).

Hydrography.—The principal river of those rising in Wales is the *Severn* (*see* England), which flows from the slopes of Plinlimmon to the English border, dividing Montgomeryshire on its way. The *Wye* (130 miles) also rises in the slopes of Plinlimmon, and flows between Radnor and Brecon on its course to England. The *Usk* (56 miles) flows into the Bristol Channel, through Monmouthshire. The *Dee* (70 miles) rises in Bala lake and flows through the Vale of Llangollen, where an aqueduct (built by Telford in 1805) carries the Pontcysyllte branch of the Shropshire Union Canal across the valley. The estuary of the Dee is the navigable portion, 14 miles in length and about 5 miles in breadth, and the tide rushes in with dangerous speed over the "Sands of Dee." The *Towy* (68 miles), *Teifi* (50 miles), *Taff* (40 miles), *Dovey* (30 miles), *Taf* (25 miles), and *Conway* (24 miles), the last named broad and navigable, are wholly Welsh rivers.

The largest natural lake in Wales is *Bala* (Llyn Tegid) in Merionethshire, 4 miles long and about 1 mile wide; *Lake Vyrnwy* is an artificial reservoir, about the size of Bala, and forms the water supply of Liverpool, and Birmingham is supplied from a chain of reservoirs in the Elan and Claerwen valleys.

The Welsh Language.—Statistics published on Sept. 11, 1962, show that only 656,000 persons (of three years and over) in Wales and Monmouthshire were able to speak Welsh at the time of the 1961 Census, compared with 715,000 at the 1951 Census. One per cent. of the population could speak Welsh only, compared with 4 per cent. in 1931. The proportion of people speaking Welsh fell from 28·9 per cent. in 1951 to 26 per cent in 1961. As in 1951, the Western Counties, Anglesey, Caernarvon, Merioneth (75.9 per cent.), Cardigan and Carmarthen had the highest proportion of Welsh speakers.

Flag.—A red dragon on a green and white field (per fess argent and vert a dragon passant gules). The flag was augmented in 1953 by a royal badge on a shield encircled with a riband bearing the words *Ddraig Goch Ddyry Cychwyn* and imperially crowned. Only the unaugmented flag is flown on Government offices in Wales and, where appropriate, in London. Both flags continue to be used elsewhere.

EARLY HISTORY

Celts and Romans.—The earliest inhabitants of whom there is any record appear to have been subdued or exterminated by the *Goidels* (a people of Celtic race) in the Bronze Age, and a further invasion of Celtic *Brythons* and *Belgae* followed in the ensuing Iron Age. The *Roman* conquest of South Britain and Wales was for some time successfully opposed by *Caratacus* (Caractacus or Caradog), Chieftain of the Catuvellauni and son of *Cunobelinus* (Cymbeline) King of the Trinobantes. In A.D. 78 the conquest of Wales was completed under Julius Frontinus, and communications were opened up by the construction of military roads from Chester to Carleon-on-Usk and Caerwent, and from Chester to Conway (and thence to Carmarthen and Neath). *Christianity* was introduced (during the Roman occupation) in the 4th century.

The Anglo-Saxon Attacks.—The Anglo-Saxon invaders of South Britain drove the Celtic Goidels and Brythons into the mountain fastnesses of Wales, and into Strathclyde (Cumberland and S.W. Scotland) and Cornwall, giving them the name of *Waelisc*, or Welsh (=Foreign). The West Saxons' victory of Deorham (577) isolated Wales from Cornwall and the battle of Chester (613) cut off communication with Strathclyde. In the 8th century the boundaries of the Welsh were further restricted by the annexations of Offa, King of Mercia, and counter-attacks were largely prevented by the construction of an artificial boundary from the Dee to the Wye (Offa's Dike). In the 9th century Rhodri Mawr united the country against further incursions of the Saxons by land and against the raids of Norse and Danish pirates by sea, but at his death his three provinces of *Gwynedd* (N.), *Powys* (Mid.) and *Dehenbarth* (S.) were divided among his three sons—Anarawd, Mervyn and Cadell—the son of the last named being Howel Dda who codified the laws of the country, while Lewelyn ap Seissyllt (husband of the heiress of Gwynedd) again united the provinces and reigned as Prince from 1015 to 1022.

The Norman Conquest.—After the Norman conquest of England, William I. created Palatine counties along the Welsh frontier, and Robert FitzHamon, the Norman Earl of Gloucester, raided South Wales and erected fortresses from the Wye to Milford Haven. Henry I. introduced Flemish settlers into South Wales, but after his death the Welsh rose under the leadership of Griffith ap Rhys and routed the Norman-Flemish forces at the fords of the Teifi (Cardigan) in 1136. From the early years of the 13th century the house of Gwynedd, in the north, gained an ascendancy over the whole of Wales, and Llywelyn ap Iorwerth was in constant strife with England for recognition as an independent sovereign. Llywelyn ap Grufydd (grandson of Llywelyn ap Iorwerth), the last native prince, was killed in 1282 during hostilities between the Welsh and English. On Feb. 7, 1301, Edward of Caernarvon, son of Edward I., was created *Prince of Wales*.

The Welsh are a distinct nationality, with a language and literature of their own, and the national bardic festival (Eisteddfod), instituted by Prince Rhys ap Griffith in 1176, is annually maintained. These *Eisteddfodau* (sessions) form part of the *Gorsedd* (assembly), which is believed to date from the time of Prydian, a ruling prince in an age many centuries before the Christian era.

County or Shire with Administrative Headquarters (*a*), (*b*), (*c*) See notes, p. 632	Acreage	Population of Counties		Rateable Value 1962 (*c*)	Average Rates, 1962–63
		Administrative (*a*)	Geographical (*b*)		
				£	s. d.
(1) Anglesey (Llangefni)............	176,694	51,430	51,430	500,757	31 2
(2) Brecknockshire (Brecon)........	469,285	54,460	54,460	557,192	28 8
(3) Caernarvonshire (Caernarvon)...	364,108	120,460	120,460	1,540,678	27 6
(4) Cardiganshire (Aberystwyth)....	443,189	53,390	53,390	511,134	28 0
(5) Carmarthenshire (Carmarthen)...	588,472	167,110	167,110	1,720,738	29 1
(6) Denbighshire (Ruthin)	427,977	174,180	174,180	2,030,951	25 1
(7) Flintshire (Mold)...............	163,707	150,430	150,430	2,534,588	21 4
(8) Glamorgan (Cardiff)............	523,244	748,700	1,236,980	8,503,530	25 3
(9) Merioneth (Dolgellau)...........	422,372	38,360	38,360	374,044	25 1
(10) Monmouthshire (Newport)......	346,781	340,820	449,370	3,306,909	27 9
(11) Montgomeryshire (Welshpool) ..	510,110	43,690	43,690	359,792	27 2
(12) Pembrokeshire (Haverfordwest)..	393,007	93,050	93,050	1,008,319	29 10
(13) Radnorshire (Llandrindod Wells).	301,165	18,430	18,430	242,608	25 1

MUNICIPAL DIRECTORY OF WALES AND MONMOUTH

The figures in parentheses show the County (*see above*) and the year that of incorporation as a borough. See also notes on p. 664.

CITIES, Boroughs, and *Urban Districts*	Population. 1962 Estimated	Rate per 1,000		Rateable Value 1963 £	Rate levied 1963–64 s. d.	Town Clerk (or Clerk U.D.C.)	Mayor, 1963–64 * Lord Mayor † Chairman U.D.C.
		Births	Deaths				
Aberdare (8)............	39,030	16·0	16·0	797,417	12 6	D. G. James.	†S. Wilcox.
Abergavenny (10) (1542).	9,700	16·4	12·4	261,877	12 6	T. G. Hardwick.	J. F. Thurston.
Abertillery (10)..........	25,020	18·5	11·8	399,957	13 0	J. Evans.	†J. J. Owen.
Aberystwyth (4) (1277)..	10,480	13·5	12·5	381,179	12 2	W. P. Davies.	R. K. Clues.
BANGOR (3) (1883)......	14,420	16·3	12·2	440,290	11 0	W. E. E. Jones.	E. W. Edwards.
Barry (8) (1939).........	42,040	18·2	10·6	1,206,189	11 6	J. C. Colley.	B. Williams.
Beaumaris (1) (1294)....	1,920	14·1	10·6	66,776	14 10	D. Senogles.	G. J. Dixon.
Bedwellty (10)..........	27,470	17·6	11·1	567,517	11 0	J. E. Rogers.	†G. H. Thomas.
Brecon (1412)..........	5,830	14·1	12·2	160,823	14 1	E. F. Jones.	G. W. Davies.
Caernarvon (Royal Borough) (1284)......	9,030	17·9	9·5	262,814	11 4	J. O. Smith.	F. K. White-Phillips.
Caerphilly (8)...........	36,230	18·7	15·1	799,498	13 2	J. L. J. Price.	†T. Watkins.
§CARDIFF (8) (1608).....	260,160	19·1	11·5	11,317,520	9 2	(*See* p. 677).	*(*See* p. 677).
Cardigan (1230).........	3,700	19·1	12·0	101,873	9 11	E. A. Harper.	Mrs. D. M. Adams.
Carmarthen (1313)......	12,910	..	..	504,341	11 6	W. J. Owen.	..
Colwyn Bay (6) (1934)...	22,400	15·5	12·6	469,925	12 6	G. Edwards.	R. A. Hughes.
Conway (3) (1284)......	11,100	14·6	16·8	175,225	11 7	R. C. Greensmith.	F. Sharps.
Cowbridge (8)..........	1,100	17·0	14·2	38,719	10 8	J. T. Taylor.	E. John.
Cwmbran (10)..........	23,190	15·5	13·1	722,438	10 8	K. G. S. Gunn.	†D. B. Richards, B.E.M.
Denbigh (1290).........	8,130	17·1	9·8	203,839	10 2	W. T. Williams.	T. J. Davies.
Ebbw Vale (10).........	28,350	16·9	12·0	1,480,552	11 6	H. J. Williams.	†C. C. Weston.
Flint (1284).............	13,790	19·1	10·6	436,464	10 8	R. Scott.	J. R. S. Lloyd.
Gelligaer (8)......	34,990	20·3	15·2	622,297	13 1	D. W. C. Morgan.	†H. V. Edwards.
Haverfordwest (12)(1479)	8,710	20·3	13·0	313,628	12 5	R. I. Rees.	C. T. Price.
Lampeter (4) (1884)....	2,010	13·3	13·4	66,385	12 6	W. R. Lloyd.	W. S. Watkins.
Llandovery (5) (1485)...	1,990	14·6	13·6	46,764	12 6	V. M. Williams.	B. G. Petley.
Llanelly (5) (1913)......	29,800	14·7	14·0	1,008,513	13 6	S. Samuel, O.B.E.	R. E. Bonnell.
Llanidloes (11) (1280)...	2,360	11·9	12·3	49,625	12 0	J. E. Thomas.	Mrs. A. M. Shimmin.
Llwchwr (8)...........	25,050	14·9	15·0	940,941	10 6	E. Pate.	†T. S. Edwards.
§Merthyr Tydfil (8) (1905)	58,940	17·2	14·0	1,264,083	12 6	T. S. Evans.	M. McGinty.
Monmouth (1447).......	5,780	17·3	11·4	155,898	10 6	R. Wallis.	R. H. George.
Montgomery (1885).....	950	17·9	14·7	14,276	9 4	N. O. Davies.	R. B. Jones.
Mountain Ash (8).......	29,520	16·3	12·4	436,712	11 6	R. G. Richards.	†G. F. Davies.
Neath (8)..............	30,670	14·5	16·4	1,021,502	11 6	D. K. Davies.	J. A. Rees.
§Newport (10) (1623)....	108,550	20·3	12·7	4,626,065	10 4	J. G. Iles.	W. T. Vaughan.
Ogmore and Garw (8)....	21,050	16·8	13·7	334,294	11 0	R. Hunter. [T.D.	†T. J. Fisher.
Pembroke (1100).......	12,220	22·2	13·2	323,521	12 3	R. D. Lowless, M.B.E.,	W. Carr.
Penarth (8)............	20,680	16·7	13·0	627,983	12 0	P. Metcalf.	†W. R. Jeffcott.
Pontypool (10).........	39,750	15·9	12·1	1,049,520	11 0	H. Cook.	†Mrs. F. M. Prosser.
Pontypridd (8)..........	35,480	16·2	14·5	1,022,246	12 4	B. M. Murphy.	†Mrs. G. M. Williams.
Port Talbot (8) (1921)...	51,150	19·1	9·8	4,261,708	11 6	W. E. Griffiths.	D. J. Richards.
Pwllheli (3) (1355)......	3,610	16·3	25·4	90,867	11 0	C. C. Davies.	D. S. Davies.
Rhondda (8) (1955).....	100,390	16·6	13·4	1,575,067	11 8	W. N. Thomas.	J. Gwyn.
Rhyl (7)...............	21,290	16·3	16·3	1,214,766	10 6	F. J. K. Davies.	†V. Davies.
§Swansea (8) (1169).....	169,180	16·6	12·3	6,590,745	9 4	(*See* p. 677).	(*See* p. 677).
Tenby (12) (1402).......	4,480	16·7	15·0	229,783	13 0	J. L. A. Morris.	D. C. Williams.
Welshpool (11).........	6,420	15·1	10·9	161,449	11 0	J. B. Davies, M.B.E.	J. H. Lloyd.
Wrexham (6) (1857).....	35,800	17·4	12·2	1,151,242	10 10	P. J. Walters, M.B.E.	R. S. Craig.

LORDS LIEUTENANT, HIGH SHERIFFS AND CHAIRMEN OF Q.S.

County or Shire	Lord Lieutenant	High Sheriff, 1963–64	Chairman of Q.S.
(1) Anglesey	Sir R. H. D. Williams-Bulkeley, Bt.	F. J. W. Williams, Q.C.	F. J. W. Williams, Q.C.
(2) Brecon	Sir William Parker, Bt., O.B.E.	D. M. M. Rees.	His Hon. Judge Rowe Harding.
(3) Caernarvon	Sir Michael Duff, Bt.	E. S. Evans.	The Lord Morris of Borth-y-Gest, P.C., C.B.E., M.C.
(4) Cardigan	Capt. J. H. Lewes, O.B.E., R.N. (*ret.*)	E. G. Davies, O.B.E.	His Hon. Judge D. M. Evans.
(5) Carmarthen	Lt.-Col. Sir Grismond P. Philipps, C.V.O.	Maj. T. V. Fisher-Hoch.	His Hon. Judge H. T. Morgan, M.C., Q.C.
(6) Denbigh	Col. J. C. Wynne Finch, C.B.E., M.C.	C. E. I. Wynne Finch.	Hon. Mr. Justice Davies.
(7) Flint	Brig. H. S. K. Mainwaring, C.B., C.B.E., D.S.O., T.D.	Lt.-Col. H. M. C. Jones-Mortimer.	F. J. W. Williams, Q.C.
(8) Glamorgan	Col. C. G. Traherne, T.D.	D. W. Vaughan.	W. M. Davies, Q.C.
(9) Merioneth	Col. J. F. Williams-Wynne, D.S.O.	R. C. M. V. Wynn, D.S.C.	Hon. Mr. Justice Stable, M.C.
(10) Monmouth	The Lord Raglan.	Col. Sir Godfrey Llewellyn, Bt., C.B., C.B.E., M.C., T.D.	His Hon. Judge O. Temple-Morris, Q.C.
(11) Montgomery	Col. J. L. Corbett-Winder, O.B.E., M.C.	C. L. J. Humphreys.	E. R. Bowen, Q.C., M.P.
(12) Pembroke	Hon. R. H. Philipps, M.B.E.	M. R. L. Hayes.	The Lord Merthyr, T.D.
(13) Radnor	Brig. Sir C. M. Dillwyn-Venables-Llewelyn, Bt., M.V.O.	W. H. Edwards.	His Hon. Judge D. E. T. Pennant.

WELSH COUNTY OFFICIALS

County &c.	Chairman of C.C.	Clerk of the Peace and Clerk of the Council	Chief Constable	Medical Officer
(1) Anglesey	Capt. A. Robertson.	I. Davies.	(*See* Caernarvon.)	T. A. I. Rees.
(2) Brecon	G. H. Wood.	C. M. S. Wells.	(vacant).	R. G. Evans.
(3) Caernarvon	Mrs. E. Chamberlain, M.B.E.	J. E. Owen-Jones.	Lt.-Col. W. Jones Williams, O.B.E.	D. E. Parry Pritchard, O.B.E., M.D.
(4) Cardigan	B. J. Davies.	J. E. R. Carson.	} J. R. Jones.	{ I. M. Watkin, Ph.D.
(5) Carmarthen	D. J. Jones.	W. S. Thomas.		D. G. G. Jones.
(6) Denbigh	A. R. Coates.	W. E. Bufton.	A. M. Rees, O.B.E.	M. T. Islwyn Jones, M.D.
(7) Flint	L. Schwarz.	W. H. Jones.	R. Atkins.	G. W. Roberts.
(8) Glamorgan	T. Evans.	R. John. [T.D.	M. Thomas.	W. E. Thomas.
(9) Merioneth	E. E. Jones.	D. W. J. Williams, M.C.,	(*See* Caernarvon.)	E. F. W. Richards.
(10) Monmouth	C. Rawlings.	V. Lawrence, C.B.E.	N. Galbraith.	G. G. Rocyn-Jones, M.D.
(11) Montgomery	D. Jones, O.B.E.	P. E. White.	(*See* Brecon.)	D. F. Richards.
(12) Pembroke	J. R. Williams.	H. L. Underwood.	G. W. R. Terry.	D. J. Davies, M.B.E. M.D.
(13) Radnor	G. R. Davies, C.B.E.	D. C. S. Lane.	(*See* Brecon.)	F. J. H. Crawford, M.D.

CARDIFF

CARDIFF (Glamorgan), at the mouth of the rivers Taff (Caer Taff), Rhymney and Ely, the capital of Wales and the port of the South Wales coalfields, has an area of 18,066 acres, and a population (estimated, 1962) of 260,160. Within the city there is a great variety of industry including iron and steel works, rolling mills and foundries, patent fuel works, engine wagon works, motor vehicle factories, flour mills, breweries, jam, vinegar and ice factories, enamel-ware and hollow-ware, paint works, furniture and bedding, clothing and foot-wear, sweets and confectionery, tobacco, electrical goods and appliances, food products and building materials.

The principal buildings are Cardiff Castle, built in the 11th century, Llandaff Cathedral, the National Museum of Wales, Public Library, the University College of South Wales and Monmouthshire, the Registry of the University of Wales, the Welsh College of Advanced Technology, City Hall, Law Courts, Glamorgan County Hall, Offices of Government Departments, and "The Temple of Peace and Health." The city returns 3 members to Parliament.

The Lord Mayor (1963–64), C. A. Horwood.
Stipendiary Magistrate, P. G. D. Sixsmith (1948).
Recorder, F. Elwyn Jones, Q.C., M.P. (1960).
Town Clerk and Clerk of Peace, S. Tapper-Jones.

SWANSEA

SWANSEA (in Welsh, Abertawe), a seaport of Glamorgan, is a County Borough, at the mouth of the River Tawe. It is the chief centre of the copper, tinplate and spelter industry of Wales and of the United Kingdom. The trade of the port also includes coal, patent fuel, ores, and the import and export of oil. There is also a large ship-repairing industry. The municipal airport is situated at Fairwood Common, Gower, a few miles away from the town. The municipal area is 21,600 acres, with a population (estimated, 1962) of 169,180.

The principal buildings are the Norman Castle (rebuilt in 1330), the Royal Institution of South Wales, founded in 1835 (containing Museum and Library), the University College at Singleton and the Guildhall, containing Brangwyn panels. Swansea was chartered by the Earl of Warwick, *circa* 1158–1184, and further charters were granted by King John, Henry III., Edward II., Edward III., and James II., 2 from Cromwell and 1 Lord Marcher. The borough returns 2 members to Parliament.

Mayor (1963–64), F. Slail.
Stipendiary Magistrate, H. Ll. Williams, Q.C. (1952).
Recorder, E. R. Bowen, Q.C., M.P. (1960).
Town Clerk, I. J. Watkins.

THE KINGDOM OF SCOTLAND

Position and Extent.—The Kingdom of Scotland occupies the northern portion of the main island of Great Britain and includes the Inner and Outer Hebrides, and the Orkney, Shetland, and many other islands. The Kingdom lies between 60° 51′ 30″ and 54° 38′ N. latitude and between 1° 45′ 32″ and 6° 14′ W. longitude, its southern neighbour being the Kingdom of England, with the Atlantic Ocean on the N. and W., and the North Sea on the E. The greatest length of the mainland (Cape Wrath to the Mull of Galloway) is 274 miles, and the greatest breadth (Buchan Ness to Applecross) is 154 miles. The total area of the Kingdom is 29,795 square miles (or 19,068,724 acres) exclusive of inland water, tidal water and foreshore. The population (1961 Census) was 5,178,490, an increase of 82,075 or 1·6 per cent. since the census of 1951; Registrar-General's estimate (June 30, 1962), 5,196,600. The average density of the population in 1961 was 174 persons per square mile, compared with 171 persons per sq. mile in 1951.

Land's End to John o' Groats.—The customary measurement of the Island of Great Britain is from the site of John o' Groat's house, near Duncansby Head, Caithness (at the N.E. extremity of the island) to Land's End, Cornwall (at the S.W. extremity), a total distance of 603 miles in a straight line and (approximately) 900 by road. But the site of the house of John de Groot (with its 8 doors and octagonal table, to solve the question of precedence between John and his 7 brothers) is about 4 miles S.W. of Duncansby Head, while Dunnet Head (also in Caithness) extends farther N. than Duncansby. John de Groot is believed to have obtained permission to settle in Caithness (from the Netherlands) in the reign of James IV. (1488–1513).

Relief.—There are three natural orographic divisions of Scotland. The *Southern Uplands* have their highest points in Merrick (2,764 feet), Rinns of Kells (2,668 feet), and Cairnsmuir of Carsphairn (2,612 feet), in Kirkcudbright; Hartfell (2,651 feet) in Dumfries; and Broad Law (2,754 feet) in Peebles. The *Central Lowlands* include the valleys of the Tay, Forth and Clyde, and the cities of Edinburgh, the capital of the Kingdom, and Glasgow, its principal seaport. The heather-clad *Northern Highlands* extend almost from the extreme north of the mainland to the central lowlands, and are divided into a northern and southern system by the *Great Glen*; they contain, in the central Grampian Hills, *Ben Nevis* (4,406 feet), the highest point in the British Isles, and Ben Muich Dhui (4,296 feet). The *Cheviot Hills* form a natural boundary between Scotland and England, their highest point being The Cheviot (2,676 feet).

Hydrography.—The principal river of Scotland is the *Clyde* (106 miles), one of the most important rivers in the world, with the greatest commercial estuary in Scotland. The Clyde is formed by the junction of Daer and Portrail water, and flows through the city and port of Glasgow to the Firth of Clyde. During its course it passes over the picturesque *Falls of Clyde*, Bonnington Linn (30 feet), Corra Linn (84 feet), Dundaff Linn (10 feet), and Stonebyres Linn (80 feet), above and below Lanark. The *Tweed* (96 miles) has important woollen industries ("Tweeds") in its valley. The *Tay*, noted for its salmon, and the longest river in Scotland (117 miles), flows into the North Sea, with Dundee (the centre of the jute industry) on the estuary, which is spanned by the *Tay Bridge* (2 miles 73 yards), opened in 1887 to replace that destroyed by a gale (Dec. 28, 1879). The *Dee* (90 miles), a noted salmon river, flows through scenery of unequalled beauty to the North Sea at Aberdeen, The *Spey* (110 miles), the swiftest flowing river in the British Isles, and also noted for its salmon and its scenery, flows into the Moray Firth. The *Forth* (66 miles), navigable to Stirling, is spanned by the *Forth* (*Railway*) *Bridge*, constructed 1882–9 at a cost of £3,000,000, with a length of 5,330 ft. (with approaches 8,295 ft.).

The *Falls of Glomach* in Ross-shire, with a drop of 370 feet, are the highest in the British Isles; the *Grey Mare's Tail* (Dumfriesshire) is 200 feet.

The *lochs* are the principal hydrographic feature of the Kingdom, both on the mainland and in many of the Islands. The largest in the Kingdom and in Great Britain is *Loch Lomond* (24 miles long), with Lochs Awe, Tay, Rannoch and Ericht in the Grampian valleys; *Loch Ness* (24 miles long and 800 feet deep), with Lochs Oich and Lochy, in the Great Glen; and Lochs Shin (20 miles) and Maree in the northern Highlands.

Climate.—The general climatic values for Scotland are given below, together with the corresponding values for England and Wales within brackets—mean air temperature reduced to sea level 47·1° F. (49·7); *rainfall*, 50·3 inches (35·2); number of days with rain 217 (188); mean hours per day of bright sunshine, 3·36 (3·96).

Gaelic Language.—The preliminary report on the 1961 Census of Scotland showed that 76,587 persons were Gaelic speakers, compared with 95,447 in 1951. 1,079 persons spoke Gaelic only and not English (compared with 2,178 in 1951), though it was considered from experience that this figure would be reduced after full examination of the Census returns. The majority of Gaelic speakers lived in the counties of Ross and Cromarty (38·29 per cent.) and Inverness (24·44 per cent.). 75,508 persons spoke both Gaelic and English, compared with 93,269 in 1951.

Commerce.—The principal exports are machinery, ships and vehicles, iron and steel manufactures, non-ferrous metals, woollen and worsted yarns and products, food and drink and textile materials. Whisky continues to be the leading export to dollar countries.

THE SCOTTISH ISLANDS

There were 147 inhabited islands in the Kingdom at the time of the 1951 Census, with a total population of 141,972, the number of inhabited islands having fallen by 18 since the census of 1931. Preliminary indications from the 1961 Census were of relatively large decreases in the populations of the islands since 1951. Among the islands showing a decline in population were Islay 3,866 (9·5 per cent. decrease); Mull (including Iona, etc.), 1,674 (14·6); Coll and Tiree, 1,143 (20·0); Harris Group, 3,285 (17·7); Skye, Raasay, etc., 7,765 (10·0); Barra Group, 1,467 (22·1); N. Uist Group, 1,921 (13·5).

Orkney.—About 6 miles N. of the Caithness coast, separated from the mainland by the *Pentland Firth*, is the island county of Orkney, a group of 90 islands and islets ("holms" and "skerries"), of which one-third are inhabited. The total area of the group is 375½ square miles, with a population (1961) of 18,743, a decrease of 11·8 per cent. compared with 1951. Kirkwall, in *Mainland*, the largest island of the group, is the capital of the county. Many of the Orkney (and Shetland) Islands contain *brochs* (Pictish towers) and other Pictish and Scandinavian remains. *Scapa Flow*, between *Mainland* and *Hoy*, was the war station of the Grand Fleet from 1914–19 and the scene of the scuttling of the surrendered German High Seas Fleet (June 21, 1919).

Zetland.—About 50 miles N. of Orkney (with the detached Fair Isle at 25 miles N.) is the island county of Zetland or Shetland, a group of about

100 islands and islets, of which one-fifth are inhabited. The total area of the group is 551 square miles, with a population (1961 Census, prelim.) of 17,809. Lerwick, in *Mainland* (the largest and principal island), is the capital of the county. *Fair Isle*, the southernmost of the group, is famous for handknitted hosiery, and *Unst* for the finest of the Shetland woollen work, for which the country is famous. *Muckle Flugga*, about 1 mile N. of Unst, is the most northerly of the group and of the British Isles (60° 51′ 30″ N. lat.).

Western Islands.—Off the W. coast, at varying distances, and extending from Sutherland to Argyll, are over 500 islands and islets, of which 102 are inhabited. The total area of these Western Islands is 2,812 square miles, with a population of close on 80,000, but owing to the mountainous surface of the land only about 300 square miles are under cultivation. *The Hebrides.*—Until the closing years of the 13th century "The Hebrides" included other Scottish islands in the Firth of Clyde, the peninsula of Kintyre (Argyllshire), the Isle of Man, and the (Irish) Isle of Rathlin. The origin of the name is stated to be the Greek *Eboudai*, latinized as *Hebudes* by Pliny, and corrupted to its present form. The Norwegian name *Sudreyjar* (Southern Islands) was latinized as *Sodorenses*, a name that survives in the Anglican bishopric of "Sodor and Man." The *Inner Hebrides* include the island of *Skye* (643 square miles—capital, Portree, famous as the refuge of Prince Charlie after his defeat at Culloden, Inverness-shire, in 1746), which contains the *Cuillins* (Sgurr Alasdair 3,309 feet), *Red Hills* (Ben Caillich, 2,403 feet), and many other picturesque mountains; *Mull* (367 square miles), containing *Ben More* (3,169 feet), *Ben Buy* (2,354 feet), and *Ben Creach* (2,289 feet); *Jura* (160 square miles), with a chain of hills culminating in the *Paps of Jura* (Beinn-an-Oir, 2,571 feet and Beinn Chaolais, 2,407 feet); *Islay* (235 square miles), and many smaller islands. The *Outer Hebrides*, separated from the mainland by the *Minch*, include *Lewis with Harris* (770 square miles), celebrated for its homespun "Tweeds," *North Uist*, *South Uist*, *Barra* and other islands. Thirteen miles W. of *Stornoway* (the largest town of Lewis and of the Hebrides) are the "Druidical" remains of *Callanish*, a well-preserved series of monolithic circles, cruciform in general arrangement, but usually regarded as a heathen monument of the remote Stone Age.

EARLY HISTORY

Prehistoric Man.—The *Picts*, believed to be of non-Aryan origin, and stated to have been named *Picti* by the Romans on account of the tribal habit of painting the body, seem to have inhabited the whole of North Britain and to have spread over the north of Ireland. *Picts' Houses* are most frequent in the northern counties of Caithness and Sutherland and in the Orkney Islands. Celtic *Goidels*, *Brythons* and *Belgae* arrived from Belgic Gaul during the latter part of the Bronze Age and in the early Iron Age, and except in the extreme north of the mainland and in the islands the civilization and speech of the people were definitely Celtic at the time of the Roman Invasion of Britain.

The Roman Invasion.—In A.D. 80 Julius Agricola extended the Roman conquests in Britain by advancing into *Caledonia* as far as the "Grampian" Hills, but after a victory at *Mons Graupius* (since corrupted to "Grampius") he was recalled, and no further advance was made for about 60 years, when the Roman frontier was carried to the isthmus between the Forth and Clyde and marked by the *Wall of Pius*, towards which ran military roads from the Cheviots. The Roman occupation of Southern Caledonia was not so effective as that of South Britain, and before the close of the second century the northern limit of Roman Britain had receded to *Hadrian's Wall* (Tyne to Solway Firth).

The Scots.—During the later years of the Roman occupation the garrison was continually harassed by Pictish tribes north of the Wall, aided by Scots (the Gaelic tribe then dominant in Ireland), and when the garrison was withdrawn these *Picts* and *Scots* were the principal enemies of the Celtic Brythons, who are believed to have called in the Saxons to protect them from the invasions of their neighbours. A relic of the struggle between Pict and Brython is still to be seen in the *Catrail*, or Picts' Work Dyke, of Roxburgh (from Torwoodle, near Galashiels, to Peel Fell in the Cheviots). *Christianity* was introduced into Southern Caledonia about 380 by missionaries from Romanized Britain, who penetrated to the northern districts and islands. After the withdrawal (or absorption) of the Roman garrison of Britain there were many years of tribal warfare between the Picts and Scots, the Brythonic Waelisc (Welsh) of Strathclyde (South-west Scotland and Cumberland), and the Anglo-Saxons of the Lothians. The Waelisc were isolated from their kinsmen in Wales by the victory of the West Saxons at Chester (613), and towards the close of the 9th century the Scots under *Kenneth Macalpine* became the dominant power in Caledonia. In the reign of Malcolm I. (943–954) the Brythons or Waelisc (Welsh) of Strathclyde were brought into subjection, the lowland kingdom of the English (Lothian) being conquered by Malcolm II. (1005–1034). From the close of the 11th century until the middle of the 16th there were constant wars between Scotland and England, the outstanding figures in the struggle being *William Wallace*, who defeated the English at Stirling Bridge (1297), and *Robert Bruce*, who won the victory of Bannockburn (1314). James IV. and many of his nobles fell at the disastrous battle of *Flodden* (1513), and in 1603 James VI., the Stuart King of Scotland and the heir to the Tudor line of England (his mother, Mary "Queen of Scots," was the great-granddaughter of Henry VII.), succeeded Queen Elizabeth I. on the throne, his successors reigning as Sovereigns of Great Britain. After the abdication (by flight) of James VII. and II., the crown devolved upon William III. (grandson of Charles I.) and Mary (daughter of James VII. and II.) and, their issue failing, upon Anne (second daughter of James VII. and II.). Anne's children died young, and the throne devolved upon George I. (great-grandson of James VI. and I.) In 1689 Graham of Claverhouse "roused the Highlands" on behalf of James VII. and II., but died after a military success at Killiecrankie. In 1715, armed risings led to the indecisive battle of Sherriffmuir, but the movement died down until 1745, when Prince Charles Edward defeated the Royalist troops under Sir John Cope at Prestonpans and advanced to Derby in England (1746). From Derby, the adherents of "James VIII. and III." (the title claimed for his father by Prince Charles Edward) fell back on the defensive, and the *Jacobite* movement was finally crushed by the Royalist troops under the Duke of Cumberland at *Culloden* (April 16, 1746).

The Hebrides did not become part of the Kingdom of Scotland until 1266, when they were ceded to Alexander III. by Magnus of Norway. Orkney and Shetland fell to the Scottish Crown as a pledge for the unpaid dowry of Margaret of Denmark, wife of James III., in 1468, the Danish suzerainty being formally relinquished in 1590.

Scotland is represented in the *Imperial Parliament* by 71 members, of whom 39 represent Counties, and 32 represent Burghs. The election in Orkney and Shetland is exempted from the rule that all polls must be held on the same day.

AREA AND POPULATION OF SCOTTISH COUNTIES, ETC.

Counties and Headquarters	Acres	Population (Estimated 1962)	Rateable Value, 1963 £	Average Rates, 1962–63 s.	d.	Lord Lieutenant
(1) ‡Aberdeen (Aberdeen)	1,252,267	134,707	1,267,399	17	3¾	Sir Ian Forbes-Leith, Bt., M.B.E.
(2) ‡Angus (Forfar)	546,861	95,582	545,310	19	5	The Earl of Airlie, K.T., G.C.V.O., M.C.
(3) Argyll (Lochgilphead)	1,990,521	60,226	516,530	17	11¼	Maj. Sir Charles H. F. Maclean, Bt.
(4) Ayr (Ayr)	724,234	343,367	2,281,039	18	6	Cdr. Sir Geoffrey Hughes-Onslow, K.B.E., D.S.C., R.N.
(5) Banff (Banff)	403,054	45,893	280,514	17	4¾	Col. Sir G. W. Abercromby, Bt., D.S.O.
(6) Berwick (Duns)	292,535	21,956	235,764	19	2¼	The Earl of Haddington, K.T., M.C., T.D.
(7) Bute (Rothesay)	139,711	14,157	109,579	19	4¾	Air Vice-Marshal R. Graham, C.B., C.B.E., D.S.O., D.F.C.
(8) Caithness (Wick)	438,833	28,108	150,035	15	7½	The Viscount Thurso, P.C., K.T., C.M.G., T.D.
(9) Clackmannan (Alloa)	34,937	41,636	356,991	23	8½	Capt. Sir James Younger, C.B.E.
(10) Dumfries (Dumfries)	688,112	88,113	694,993	20	4¾	Maj.-Gen. J. Scott-Elliot, C.B., C.B.E., D.S.O.
(11) Dunbarton (Dumbarton)	154,362	190,138	1,179,451	23	10½	Adm. Sir Angus E. M. B. Cunninghame-Graham, K.B.E., C.B.
(12) East Lothian (Haddington)	170,971	51,814	392,602	17	2½	The Marquess of Tweeddale.
(13) Elgin or Moray (Elgin)	304,931	50,322	445,900	12	5¼	Sir Henry W. Houldsworth, K.B.E., D.S.O., M.C.
(14) Fife (Cupar)	322,878	323,478	2,023,536	19	6	The Earl of Elgin, K.T., C.M.G., T.D.
(15) Inverness (Inverness)	2,695,094	82,264	665,982	18	6¾	The Lord Macdonald, M.B.E., T.D.
(16) Kincardine (Stonehaven)	242,460	25,538	222,349	15	8½	Maj.-Gen. the Visct. Arbuthnott, C.B., C.B.E., D.S.O., M.C.
(17) Kinross (Kinross)	52,392	6,579	112,834	15	7¼	Capt. C. K. Adam, D.S.O., R.N. (*ret.*).
(18) Kirkcudbright (Kirkcudbright).	574,024	28,305	277,670	16	4½	Lt.-Col. The Earl of Galloway.
(19) ‡Lanark (Glasgow)	535,862	577,672	5,732,735	18	10	The Lord Clydesmuir, M.B.E., T.D.
(20) ‡Midlothian (Edinburgh)	201,046	115,091	1,191,618	18	11¼	The Earl of Rosebery, P.C., K.T., D.S.O., M.C.
(21) Nairn (Nairn)	104,251	8,296	46,291	13	6¾	Brig. J. E. Stirling, D.S.O.
(22) Orkney (Kirkwall)	240,848	18,531	91,872	13	7½	Lt.-Col. R. Scarth, O.B.E.
(23) Peebles (Peebles)	222,240	13,352	138,770	17	3	Sir Ronald Thomson.
(24) Perth (Perth)	1,595,804	124,441	1,015,404	17	11¼	The Earl of Mansfield and Mansfield.
(25) Renfrew (Paisley)	143,829	342,938	1,889,472	17	3½	Lt.-Col. Sir Guy Shaw Stewart, Bt., M.C.
(26) Ross and Cromarty (Dingwall).	1,977,254	57,388	393,859	19	10¼	Gen. Sir Richard O'Connor, G.C.B., D.S.O., M.C.
(27) Roxburgh (Newtown St. Boswells).	425,564	42,518	247,211	21	1¼	The Duke of Buccleuch, P.C., K.T., G.C.V.O.
(28) Selkirk (Selkirk)	171,209	20,741	44,423	19	0¾	Vice-Adm. Sir Conolly Abel Smith, G.C.V.O., C.B.
(29) Stirling (Stirling)	288,349	195,258	1,486,392	21	5¼	Capt. Sir Ian Bolton, Bt., K.B.E.
(30) Sutherland (Golspie)	1,297,913	13,243	135,622	21	1	Lord Migdale.
(31) West Lothian (Linlithgow)	76,859	94,935	808,494	23	1½	Col. H. M. Cadell, O.B.E.
(32) Wigtown (Stranraer)	311,984	28,785	190,509	19	7½	The Earl of Stair, M.B.E.
(33) Zetland (Lerwick)	352,337	17,537	49,049	21	7¾	R. H. W. Bruce.

‡ The Cities of Edinburgh, Glasgow, Dundee and Aberdeen are each a County of a City, and the Lord Provost of each is entitled, by virtue of his office, to be appointed Lord Lieutenant; population estimates given above exclude the four cities.

CONVENERS AND COUNTY OFFICIALS

Convener	County Clerk	Clerk of the Peace
(1) Rev. P. C. MacQuoid	J. L. Craig	W. L. Richards.
(2) R.W. L. McCaig, C.B.E.	I. A. MacKnight	T. J. M. Whitson.
(3) J. G. Mathieson, C.B.E., M.C.	A. D. Jackson	J. Harvey.
(4) D. Sim	I. McCaig	H. G. McFadzean.
(5) Col. T. R. G. Duff, M.C.	F. G. Armstrong	J. L. McNaughton, M.B.E., V.D.
(6) Maj. J. M. Askew	J. B. Smith	G. S. Morrison.
(7) T. R. McArthur	A. H. Wood	W. Skelton.
(8) Brig. Sir Keith Murray, O.B.E., M.C., T.D.	J. L. Russell	J. L. Russell.
(9) T. R. Millar	A. Stewart	V. E. Cuthbert.
(10) Sir Arthur Duncan	L. T. Carnegie	J. B. McGowan.
(11) H. Gillies	J. F. Miller	D. M'Intosh.
(12) J. Rattray	T. Gibb	A. C. Stevenson.
(13) Lt.-Col. K. Mackessack	R. McGill	G. M. Spence.
(14) J. McWilliam	M. Pollock	C. D. Pagan, W.S.
(15) Sir Francis Walker, C.B.E.	R. Wallace	G. H. Munro.
(16) W. Hunter, O.B.E.	J. Slevin	F. W. Robertson.
(17) R. Tullis	H. R. W. Gardner, W.S.	D. A. R. Cuthbert, M.C.
(18) Maj.-Gen. Sir Aymer Maxwell, C.B.E., M.C.	R. C. Monteath	J. D. Sturrock.
(19) E. Daly, C.B.E.	I. V. Paterson	T. Rodger.
(20) J. G. Methven	A. A. L. Evans	J. McBoyle, C.B.E.
(21) The Earl Cawdor	C. Paterson	G. S. Storm.
(22) Col. H. W. Scarth	D. M. Wood	C. E. S. Walls.
(23) J. D. Dundas, O.B.E.	W. Geddes, M.B.E.	R. W. Goodburn.
(24) Sir George McGlashan, C.B.E.	A. L. Bushnell, C.B.E.	H. Cruickshank.
(25) Lt.-Col. Sir Guy Shaw Stewart, Bt., M.C.	R. Urquhart, C.B.E.	J. C. T. MacRobert.
(26) Capt. A. F. Matheson, R.N. (*ret.*)	J. M. Dunlop	D. S. Dewar.
(27) The Lord Stratheden and Campbell	J. Kyle	R. B. Anderson.
(28) J. Harrison	W. T. Dundas	A. T. Little.
(29) A. K. Davidson, C.B.E.	J. D. Kennedy	G. Barras.
(30) Rev. W. MacLeod	A. J. Macrae	D. Macdonald.
(31) P. Walker	J. Calder	J. T. Kidd, W.S.
(32) J. F. Niven	D. R. Wilson	S. Thomson.
(33) W. R. T. Hamilton	W. A. Scott	R. A. Johnson.

CHIEF CONSTABLES.—*Aberdeen, Banff, Moray, Kincardine and Nairn*, T. W. Chasser; *Angus*, J. J. Dingwall; *Argyll*, K. MacKinnon, M.B.E.; *Ayr*, R. Adamson, O.B.E.; *Berwick, Roxburgh and Selkirk*, T. McCallum; *Caithness*, J. W. Georgeson, O.B.E.; *Dunbarton*, W. Kerr; *Dumfries, Kirkcudbright and Wigtown*, S. A. Berry, O.B.E.; *Fife*, A. Meldrum, C.B.E.; *Inverness*, A. L. McLure; *Lanark*, J. Wilson, M.B.E.; *Midlothian, East Lothian, West Lothian and Peebles*, W. Merrilees, O.B.E.; *Orkney*, J. Cormack, B.E.M.; *Perth and Kinross* (vacant); *Renfrew and Bute*, R. S. Allan, O.B.E., B.E.M.; *Ross and Cromarty*, K. Ross; *Stirling and Clackmannan*, D. Gray; *Sutherland*, K. Ross; *Zetland*, R. Bruce, O.B.E.

PRINCIPAL SCOTTISH CITIES

EDINBURGH

EDINBURGH, the Capital of the Kingdom, has a municipal area of 34,781 acres, and a population (estimated, 1962) of 475,338. The city is built on a group of hills and contains in Princes Street one of the most beautiful thoroughfares in the world. The principal buildings are the Castle, which includes St. Margaret's Chapel, the oldest building in Edinburgh, and near it, the Scottish National War Memorial; the Palace of Holyroodhouse; Parliament House, the present seat of the judicature; the University; St. Giles' Church (restored 1879–83); St. Mary's (Scottish Episcopal) Cathedral (Sir Gilbert Scott); the General Register House (Robert Adam); the National and the Signet Libraries; the Royal Scottish Academy; and the National Portrait Gallery. The city is governed by a town council of 71 Members, and sends 7 Members to Parliament.

Rt. Hon. Lord Provost, D. M. Weatherstone, M.C., T.D.
Town Clerk, W. Borland.
City Chamberlain, A. L. Imrie, C.B.E.

GLASGOW

GLASGOW, a Royal Burgh, City and County of a City, and the principal commercial centre in Scotland, has a municipal area of 39,725 acres and a population (estimated, 1962) of 1,049,115. The city occupies the north and south banks of the Clyde, one of the chief commercial estuaries in the world. The tonnage of shipping using the harbour in 1962–63 was 14,285,461. The principal industries are iron and steel works, ship-building, chemicals, leather, woollens, muslin-weaving, distilling, tobacco,cotton-mills and furniture. The chief buildings are the Early English former Cathedral built during the first half of the 13th century, and incorporating part of an earlier structure, the University (Sir Gilbert Scott), the City Chambers, the Royal Infirmary and the Western and Victoria Infirmaries, the Art Galleries and the Mitchell Library. The city is governed by a town council of 113 Members, and sends 15 Members to Parliament.

Rt. Hon. Lord Provost, P. L. Meldrum.
Town Clerk, A. Rooke.
City Chamberlain, G. B. Esslemont. C.B.E.

ABERDEEN

ABERDEEN, a City and a Royal, Municipal and Parliamentary Burgh, 130 miles N.E. of Edinburgh, received its charter as a Royal Burgh from William the Lion in 1179. The municipal area is 11,034 acres, with a population (estimated, 1962) of 185,678. The chief industries are tourist traffic, quarrying and granite working, white fish, salmon and herring fisheries, engineering, chemicals, ship-building, paper-making, woollen and linen manufacture. From an architectural point of view, Aberdeen is truly famous for its many beautiful buildings, including Marischal College, reputed to be the most imposing white granite building in the world, King's College (1494), St. Machar Church (1378), the Auld Brig o'Balgownie (1320) and the Municipal Buildings. There is a sea beach promenade, which stretches for fully two and a half miles along golden sands, and at Hazlehead an open public park of 800 acres, of which 200 are wooded, with one of the finest public golf courses in Scotland. The climate is bracing and healthy. The city is governed by a Town Council of 37 Members, and sends 2 Members to Parliament.

The Lord Provost (May 1961–May 1964), J. M. Graham, C.B.E., D.D.
Town Clerk, J. C. Rennie.
City Chamberlain, W. G. A. McInnes.

DUNDEE

DUNDEE, a City and Royal Burgh, on the left bank of the River Tay, 42 miles N. of Edinburgh, has a municipal area of 12,229 acres, and a population (estimated, 1962) of 183,560. Principal buildings are Queen's College (St. Andrews University), the Institute of Art and Technology, High School, Albert Institute and the Caird Hall Buildings. There is a magnificent public park of 400 acres at Camperdown and other parks of 646 acres and an observatory at Balgay Park. The principal industries are jute manufacture in all its branches, and various forms of linen weaving, the making of preserves, ship-building, engineering, dyeing, fruit, etc., canning, linoleum manufacturing, watch and clock making, and brewing. The city is governed by a Town Council of 37 members and sends 2 Members to Parliament.

The Lord Provost (1963–64), M. McManus.
Town Clerk, R. Lyle.
City Chamberlain, J. C. Milne.

CHIEFS OF CLANS AND NAMES IN SCOTLAND

The following list of Chiefs comprises the persons officially recognized as such by inheritance of the ancestral arms "without brisur or mark of cadency" under the Act 1672 c. 47, and/or relative supporters, under decree of the Lyon Court. It does not include selfstyled, or Society-selected "chiefs", but the hereditary Heads of Families who conform to the evidence that "clan and family mean exactly the same thing"; and the definitions of Sir George Mackenzie of Rosehaugh, Lord Advocate to Charles II, that the undifferenced arms denote the "Chief for so we call the Representative of the Family . . . and in the Erse (Gaelic) with us the Chief of the Family is called the Head of the Clan,"—and the unanimous opinions of the Law Lords in *Seaforth* v. *Allangrange*, 1921, to the same effect that the undifferenced shield of arms denotes the Chief of the Clan; which in this hereditary familial sense of parental organization or *kin*, is denoted by the determination of armorial succession by decree of the Court of the Lord Lyon. These organizations were termed "Names" in the Lowlands, where all members bore the same basic surname, and "Clans" in the Border and Highland areas where surnames were a later development and evolved from complicated genealogical descriptions, the "clan name" being normally that of the chief.

THE ROYAL HOUSE: H.M. The Queen.

ARBUTHNOTT: Viscount of Arbuthnott, Arbuthnott House, Laurencekirk, Kincardineshire.
BARCLAY: Theodore B. de Tollie Barclay, 90 Divisadero Street, San Francisco, 17.
BORTHWICK: Maj. J. H. S. Borthwick of Borthwick, Crookston, Midlothian.
BRODIE: Ninian Brodie of Brodie, Brodie Castle, Forres.
BRUCE: Earl of Elgin and Kincardine, K.T., Culross Abbey House, Culross by Dunfermline, Fife.
BUCHAN: David S. Buchan of Auchmacoy, Auchmacoy, Ellon, Aberdeenshire.
CAMERON: Col. Donald Cameron of Lochiel, Achnacarry, Spean Bridge, Inverness.
CAMPBELL: Duke of Argyll, Inveraray, Argyll.
CARNEGIE: Earl of Southesk, K.C.V.O., Kinnaird Castle, Brechin.
CHISHOLM: Alastair Chisholm of Chisholm (*The Chisholm*), Silver Willows, Bury St. Edmunds.
CLAN CHATTAN: D. A. E. Mackintosh of Mackintosh-Torcastle and Clan Chattan, Fairburn, Felixburg, S. Rhodesia.
COCHRANE: Earl of Dundonald, Auchans, Dundonald, Ayrshire.
COLQUHOUN: Sir Ivar Colquhoun of Luss, Bt., Rossdhu, Luss, Dunbartonshire.
CRAWFORD: Hugh E. G. Crawford of Auchinames.
DARROCH: Lt.-Col. D. Darroch of Gourock.
DRUMMOND: Earl of Perth, Stobhall, Perth.
DUNBAR: Sir Adrian I. Dunbar of Mochrum, Bt., Mochrum Park, Wigtownshire.
DUNDAS: Ian H. Dundas of that Ilk and Inchgarvie, Fort Portal, Toro, Uganda.
ELIOTT: Sir Arthur Eliott of Stobs, Bt., Redheugh, Newcastleton, Roxburghshire.
ERSKINE: Earl of Mar and Kellie, Claremount House, Alloa.
FARQUHARSON: Capt. A. A. C. Farquharson of Invercauld, Invercauld, Braemar.
FERGUSSON: Sir James Fergusson of Kilkerran, Bt.
FORBES: Lord Forbes, Balforbes, Alford, Aberdeenshire.
FRASER (OF LOVAT)*: Lord Lovat, D.S.O., M.C., T.D., Beaufort Castle, Beauly, Inverness-shire.
GORDON: Marquess of Huntly, Aboyne Castle, Aberdeenshire.
GRAHAM: Duke of Montrose, Auchmar, Drymen, Stirlingshire.
GRANT: Lord Strathspey, Two Gates, Stoke d'Abernon, Surrey.
GUTHRIE: Ivan Guthrie of Guthrie, M.C., Guthrie Castle, Angus.
HAIG: Earl Haig of Bemersyde, Bemersyde, Melrose, Roxburgh.
HAY: Countess of Erroll, Easter Moncreiffe, Bridge of Earn, Perthshire.
KENNEDY: Marquess of Ailsa, Cassilis House, Maybole, Ayrshire.
KERR: Marquess of Lothian, Monteviot, Ancrum, Roxburgh.
KINCAID: A. C. Kincaid of Kincaid, Murarashi, Kenya.
LAMONT: Noel B. Lamont of that Ilk, 58 Flushcombe Road, Blocktown, Sydney, N.S.W.
LESLIE: Earl of Rothes, Strawberry House, Chiswick Mall, W.4.
LINDSAY: Earl of Crawford and Balcarres, K.T., G.B.E., Balcarres, Colinsburgh, Fife.
MACALISTER: Charles G S. MacAlister of Loup.
MCBAIN: H. M. McBain of McBain.
MACBRAYNE: John O. MacBrayne of Glenbranter.
MALCOLM (MACCALLUM): Col. George Malcolm of Poltalloch, Duntrune Castle, Argyll.
MACDONALD: Lord MacDonald (*The MacDonald of MacDonald*), Armadale Castle, Skye.

MACDONALD OF CLANRANALD*: Ranald A. MacDonald of Clanranald, 3 Lyall Street, S.W.1.
MACDONALD OF SLEATE (CLAN HUSTEAIN)*: Sir Ian Bosville-MacDonald of Sleate, Bt., Thorpe Hall, Rudston, Driffield, Yorks.
MACDONELL OF GLENGARRY*: Air Cdre. Aeneas R. MacDonell of Glengarry, D.F.C., Rockwood, Fairwarp, Uckfield, Sussex.
MACDOUGALL: Madame Coline MacDougall of MacDougall, Barcaldine, Argyll.
MACGREGOR: Sir Gregor MacGregor of MacGregor, Bt., Edinchip, Lochearnhead.
MACKAY: Lord Reay, Langlee House, Galashiels.
MACKINNON: The Mackinnon of Mackinnon, O.B.E., The Oast House, Broad St., Maidstone.
MACKINTOSH: The Mackintosh of Mackintosh, Moy Hall, Inverness.
MACLACHLAN: Madam Marjorie MacLachlan of MacLachlan, Castle Lachlan, Argyll.
MACLAREN: Maj. Donald MacLaren of MacLaren & Achleskine; Reform Club, S.W.1
MACLEAN: Sir Charles Maclean of Duart, Bt., Duart Castle, Mull.
MACLEOD: Dame Flora Macleod of Macleod, D.B.E., Dunvegan Castle, Skye.
MACMILLAN: Lt.-Gen. Sir Gordon MacMillan of MacMillan, K.C.B., Langbank, Renfrewshire.
MACNAB: A. C. Macnab of Macnab (*The Macnab*), C.I.E., Kinnell House, Killin, Perthshire.
MACNAGHTEN: Sir Antony Macnaghten of Macnaghten and Dundarave, Bt., Dundarave, Bushmills, Co. Antrim.
MACNEIL OF BARRA: Robert L. Macneil of Barra (*The Macneil of Barra*) Kismull Castle, Barra.
MACPHERSON: Ewen George Macpherson of Cluny (*Cluny Macpherson*).
MENZIES: David R. Menzies of Menzies, Arndilly, Banffshire.
MONCREIFFE: Sir Iain Moncreiffe of that Ilk, Bt., E. Moncreiffe, Bridge of Earn.
MONTGOMERIE: Earl of Eglinton, Skelmorlie Castle, Ayrshire.
MUNRO: Patrick G. Munro of Foulis, Foulis Castle, Ross.
NICOLSON OF SCORRYBRECK: Norman A. Nicolson of Scorrybreck, Campbell Town, Tasmania.
OGILVY: Earl of Airlie, K.T., Airlie Castle, Kirriemuir, Angus.
RAMSAY: Earl of Dalhousie, Brechin Castle, Angus.
RATTRAY: James S. Rattray of Rattray, Craighall, Rattray, Perthshire.
ROBERTSON: Langton Robertson of Struan (*Struan-Robertson*), Knox College. Spaldings, Jamaica.
ROSE: Miss Elizabeth Rose of Kilravock, Kilravock Castle, Nairn.
ROSS: Miss Ross of Pitcalnie, The Cottage, Tain.
RUTHVEN: Earl of Gowrie, Dunlewy House. Gweedore, Co. Donegal.
SINCLAIR: Earl of Caithness, C.B.E., D.S.O., Girnigoe Castle, Caithness.
SWINTON: W. F. H. Swinton of that Ilk, 11729, 97 Street, Edmonton, Alta., Canada.
URQUHART: W. F. Urquhart of that Ilk, 507 Jefferson Park Avenue, New Orleans, U.S.A.
WALLACE: Robert F. H. Wallace of that Ilk, Corsee, Nairn.
WEMYSS: Michael Wemyss of that Ilk, Wemyss Castle, Fife.

Only chiefs of *whole* Names or Clans are included (except certain special instances (marked *), who though not chiefs of a " whole name ", were, or are, for some reason, *e.g.* the Macdonald forfeiture, independent). Under decision (*Campbell-Gray*, 1950) that a bearer of a "double or triple-barrelled " surname, cannot be held chief of a part thereof, several others cannot be included in the list at present.

PRECEDENCE IN SCOTLAND

The Sovereign.
The Prince Philip, Duke of Edinburgh.
The Lord High Commissioner to the General Assembly (while that Assembly *is sitting*).
The Duke of Rothesay (eldest son of the Sovereign). H.R.H. Prince Andrew.
The Duke of Gloucester, the Duke of Windsor, Uncles of the Sovereign.
Lords Lieutenant of Counties, Lord Provosts of Counties of Cities, and Sheriffs Principal (successively — within their own localities and during holding of office).
Lord Chancellor of Great Britain.
Moderator of the Assembly of the Church of Scotland.
The Prime Minister.
Keepers of the Great Seal and of the Privy Seal (successively —if Peers).
Hereditary Lord High Constable of Scotland.
Hereditary Master of the Household.
Dukes (successively) of England, Scotland, Great Britain and United Kingdom (including Ireland since date of Union).
Eldest sons of Royal Dukes.
Marquesses, in same order as Dukes.
Dukes' eldest sons.
Earls, in order as Dukes.
Younger sons of Dukes of Blood Royal.
Marquesses' eldest sons.
Dukes' younger sons.
Keepers of the Great Seal and of the Privy Seal (successively —if not Peers).
Lord Justice General.
Lord Clerk Register.
Lord Advocate.
Lord Justice Clerk.
Viscounts, in order as Dukes.
Earls' eldest sons.
Marquesses' younger sons.
Lord-Barons, in order as Dukes.
Viscounts' eldest sons.
Earls' younger sons.
Lord-Barons' eldest sons.
Knights of the Garter.
Privy Councillors not included in above ranks.
Senators of Coll. of Justice (Lords of Session).
Viscounts' younger sons.
Lord-Barons' younger sons.
Sons of Life Peers.
Baronets.
Knights of the Thistle.
Knights of St. Patrick.
Knights of other Orders as in England.
Solicitor General for Scotland.
Lord Lyon King of Arms.
Sheriffs Principal (except as shown in column 1).
Knights Bachelor.
Sheriffs Substitute.
Companions of Orders as in England.
Commanders of Royal Victorian and British Empire Orders.
Eldest sons of younger sons of Peers.
Companions of Distinguished Service Order.
Members (Class 4) Royal Victorian Order.
Officers of British Empire Order.
Baronets' eldest sons.
Knights' eldest sons successively (from Garter to Bachelor).
Members of Class 5 of Royal Victorian Order.
Members of British Empire Order.
Baronets' younger sons.
Knights' younger sons.
Queen's Counsel.
Barons-feudal.
Esquires.
Gentlemen.

SCOTTISH BURGH DIRECTORY

The figures in parentheses following the name of the Burgh show the County in which it is situated (*see* p. 680). Burghs of population less than 3,000 are excluded, except where they are the headquarters of the county administration—Banff, Duns, Kinross, Kirkcudbright, and Lochgilphead.

Burghs (★Royal Burgh)	Population Estimated June 30, 1962	Rate per 1,000 Births	Rate per 1,000 Deaths	Rateable Value £	Rate levied 1963–64 s.	d.	Town Clerk	Provost †Lord Provost
ABERDEEN★ (1)	185,678	17·6	12·1	3,464,378	21	6	(*See* p. 682).	†(*See* p. 682).
Airdrie (19)	33,950	25·2	10·6	566,816	20	0	J. Taylor.	A. Campbell.
Alloa (9)	13,902	20·0	11·5	312,120	21	6	W. Maltman.	R. A. R. Grant.
Alva (9)	3,941	23·1	18·2	57,715	21	1	I. A. Grant.	J. B. Hunter.
Annan★ (10)	5,696	27·0	12·9	86,039	19	4	A. Knox.	J. L. Wallace.
Arbroath★ (2)	19,679	18·1	15·4	355,135	19	1	W. D. Smith.	D. A. Gardner.
Ardrossan (4)	9,683	19·4	11·4	198,659	20	1	W. N. M. McDermont.	W. S. Currie.
Armadale (31)	6,256	18·1	10·4	90,000	23	7	H. H. K. Clarkson.	C. King.
Ayr★	44,941	18·4	12·7	952,609	16	3	R. C. Brown.	W. Cowan.
Banff★ (5)	3,233	15·5	17·3	58,219	18	0	R. G. Halley.	W. C. Smith.
Barrhead (25)	14,959	23·5	11·5	244,015	16	0	A. Douglas.	P. L. W. Wright.
Bathgate (31)	12,967	20·0	9·5	220,104	21	2	H. T. B. Hall.	J. Davidson.
Bearsden (11)	18,456	19·5	10·7	464,000	18	9	D. L. Cuthbert.	J. O. Lennox.
Blairgowrie and Rattray (24)	5,120	15·8	18·0	95,896	19	10	A. D. Paterson.	R. G. McLean.
Bo'ness (31)	10,246	19·2	8·9	143,059	18	0	J. A. McKittrick.	A. Buchanan.
Bonnyrigg and Lasswade (20)	6,597	20·7	11·4	110,224	16	0	E. H. Thomson.	J. Moffat.
Brechin★ (2)	7,172	17·2	16·0	129,000	17	2	A. O. Small.	J. Millar.
Buckhaven and Methil (14)	21,147	20·8	14·0	353,531	19	4	D. S. Davidson.	J. Maxwell.
Buckie (5)	7,688	17·8	14·7	115,582	20	0	J. L. McNaughton.	J. F. Cameron.
Burntisland★ (14)	6,132	19·4	16·4	108,065	18	10	G. Maclachlan.	..
Campbeltown★ (3)	6,410	18·8	15·5	125,554	18	3	R. N. O'Sullivan.	A. P. MacGrory.
Carnoustie (2)	5,564	15·4	16·7	113,608	18	9	E. H. R. Kerr.	D. R. Paton.
Castle Douglas (18)	3,227	13·0	11·8	62,186	17	0	R. I. Hewat; J. K. Welsh (*Joint*).	T. M. Donald.
Clydebank (11)	50,369	22·1	10·0	975,077	24	3	R. A. Nixon.	D. Paterson.
Coatbridge (19)	54,594	25·5	10·6	924,946	22	9	L. A. Runciman.	C. W. V. Thom.
Cockenzie and Port Seton (12)	3,496	14·4	9·8	45,087	17	0	T. M. Walker.	D. H. Flockhart.
Cowdenbeath (14)	11,872	16·7	12·0	207,953	21	4	P. S. Williamson.	W. Taylor.
Crieff (24)	5,401	15·8	19·2	103,263	16	8	R. G. Mickel.	R. K. Fletcher.
Cumnock and Holmhead (4)	5,522	25·7	12·4	82,362	16	9	R. D. Hunter, M.B.E.	J. K. H. McTurk.
Cupar★ (14)	5,861	16·0	11·0	159,701	14	0	A. M. Scott.	T. E. G. Sinclair.
Dalbeattie (18)	3,080	19·7	13·2	42,857	14	10	J. M. Little.	Miss A. Jack.
Dalkeith (20)	9,037	19·9	14·4	165,341	17	0	J. F. Kerr.	J. Quinn.
Darvel (4)	3,251	15·4	13·9	61,285	15	1	G. W. More.	C. Murdoch.
Denny and Dunipace (29)	7,831	18·3	11·9	113,971	19	4	A. T. H. Craig.	T. C. Hyslop.
Dingwall★ (26)	3,851	19·5	12·4	64,881	19	2	D. S. Dewar.	A. Macrae, C.B.E., B.E.M.
Dumbarton★ (11)	26,461	22·4	11·3	565,973	26	6	J. D. Smith.	J. Campbell.
Dumfries★ (10)	27,042	19·2	13·1	508,506	24	3	G. D. Grant.	E. Watt.
Dunbar★ (12)	3,926	14·2	16·8	83,932	20	9	S. W. Brown.	H. G. More.
DUNDEE★ (2)	183,560	20·1	11·8	3,864,222	19	6	(*See* p. 682).	†(*See* p. 682).
Dunfermline★ (14)	48,863	19·4	10·8	1,135,572	21	0	J. Douglas.	Mrs. J. H. Mackie.
Dunoon (3)	9,437	9·0	16·8	172,350	19	3	D. W. Anderson.	H. A. Christie.
Duns (6)	1,812	17·6	20·4	43,753	16	4	W. Renton.	Rev. M. McCallum.
EDINBURGH★ (20)	475,338	17·7	13·1	11,757,700	14	5	(*See* p. 681).	†(*See* p. 681).
ELGIN★ (13)	12,198	19·7	10·8	236,892	17	4	H. G. Tait.	†Miss I. A. Duncan.
Falkirk (29)	37,916	20·2	11·9	797,413	22	6	J. G. Morris.	J. Maxwell.
Forfar★ (2)	10,319	15·4	14·9	203,049	19	8	W. S. McCulloch.	C. W. Renilson.
Forres★ (13)	4,828	15·6	13·3	80,264	12	11	A. H. Macdonald.	P. J. F. McKenzie.
Fraserburgh (1)	10,418	18·7	11·4	178,258	16	0	J. M. Boyle.	A. W. Noble.
Galashiels (28)	12,262	15·5	16·1	226,916	21	10	J. A. G. Hastings.	C. S. Kemp.
Galston (4)	3,992	18·3	17·5	51,712	15	0	D. C. Stewart.	J. Richmond.
Girvan (4)	6,020	20·0	14·8	114,713	19	0	J. H. Cummingham.	J. M. Kerr.
Glasgow★ (19)	1,049,115	21·6	12·7	21,609,526	24	0	(*See* p. 681).	†(*See* p. 681).
Gourock (25)	9,875	17·3	13·4	166,680	17	0	S. R. Cunmming.	A. K. Davidson.
Grangemouth (29)	19,249	22·1	9·6	1,079,854	14	0	W. B. Johnston.	J. H. Tennant.
Greenock (25)	74,607	22·7	12·1	1,117,595	23	0	J. Liddell, M.B.E.	S. Stevenson.
Haddington★ (12)	5,636	19·6	12·5	106,980	20	6	J. McVie, W.S.	H. M. Gardiner.
Hamilton (19)	42,679	20·2	11·2	741,707	20	4	M. Gallagher.	J. Marshall.
Hawick (27)	15,984	15·8	16·9	287,059	20	9	R. Barbour.	J. A. Henderson.

Burghs (*Royal Burgh)	Population Estimated June 30, 1962	Rate per 1,000 Births	Rate per 1,000 Deaths	Rateable Value £	Rate levied 1963–64 s.	d.	Town Clerk	Provost †Lord Provost
Helensburgh (11).......	9,795	19·4	14·6	216,278	20	0	T. G. Wright, M.C., T.D.	J. McL. Williamson.
Huntly (1)............	3,852	12·9	12·4	63,761	16	0	C. N. D. Yule.	W. Watson.
Inverkeithing (14)......	4,146	14·3	10·9	78,807	20	0	R. Mitchell.	C. Morris.
Inverness* (15).........	29,603	17·1	11·4	635,795	20	7	J. Cameron.	A. Ross.
Inverurie* (1)..........	5,209	13·1	13·1	74,922	16	6	G. D. Kellas.	A. McNab.
Irvine* (4).............	17,731	20·4	12·2	293,697	18	8	R. Whyte.	J. R. Anderson.
Jedburgh* (27).........	3,630	17·6	17·4	66,465	20	6	L. S. Prentice.	S. G. Ewing.
Johnstone (25).........	19,254	26·6	9·9	240,845	15	0	R. S. Macrae.	G. T. Houston. [T.D.
Keith (5)..............	4,160	16·1	15·1	75,209	18	8	W. J. G. Sutherland.	G. B. Kynoch, C.B.E.,
Kelso (27).............	3,895	17·1	15·0	84,968	20	6	J. Pennie; J. Cook (*Joint*).	D. J. Ferguson.
Kilmarnock (4).........	48,027	21·2	11·7	967,776	23	10	W. L. Walker.	D. B. Cunningham.
Kilsyth (29)...........	9,779	17·7	11·8	114,038	15	0	A. D. Mathie.	R. Smith.
Kilwinning (4).........	7,285	19·6	10·2	101,335	14	10	D. J. M. Bolton.	J. Kerr.
Kinross (17)...........	2,345	14·0	18·6	32,286	15	8	G. Wilson.	J. McWilliam.
Kirkcaldy* (14)........	52,697	18·6	11·3	1,237,674	24	0	C. S. Chapman.	H. A. Nicholson.
Kirkcudbright* (18).....	2,421	21·4	17·3	45,485	18	6	A. C. Watson.	W. F. Maxwell.
Kirkintilloch (11).......	18,743	22·8	9·6	301,743	19	6	R. Kyle.	W. J. Scott.
Kirkwall* (22).........	4,414	14·6	11·9	63,287	18	3	A. R. Buchan.	J. Scott.
Kirriemuir (2)..........	3,477	13·2	19·9	66,091	15	1	D. Smith.	Maj.-Gen. T. Menzies, C.B., O.B.E.
Lanark* (19)...........	8,406	16·4	15·8	168,204	18	6	T. G. Good.	J. Whyte.
Largs (4)..............	8,634	11·6	23·3	190,096	18	10	J. G. Young.	H. I. Acheson.
Lerwick (33)...........	5,977	16·0	13·0	66,278	20	6	R. L. C. Manson.	H. Gray.
Leslie (14)............	3,418	17·2	13·7	62,550	20	0	D. Dunn.	E. V. Anderson.
Leven (14).............	8,923	19·4	14·5	213,108	17	5	J. T. Leslie.	W. Laing.
Linlithgow* (31)........	4,562	18·8	10·3	80,431	20	4	G. Brown.	J. R. Lawrie.
Loanhead (20)..........	5,142	15·1	13·5	76,000	17	0	C. K. Brown, M.B.E.	D. M. Bowes.
Lochgelly (14)..........	9,108	21·8	10·2	128,520	17	8	G. Johnston.	D. Campbell.
Lochgilphead (3)........	1,182	15·1	21·0	19,830	17	0	W. K. B. Kinnis.	D. MacBrayne.
Lossiemouth and Branderburgh (13)....	5,975	27·1	9·9	68,965	16	6	W. Gilmour.	R. G. Tulloch.
Macduff (5)............	3,495	19·9	15·9	52,300	17	6	W. S. Knox.	R. Henry.
Maybole (4)............	4,607	16·7	14·9	60,403	16	10	D. Briggs.	J. McDowall.
Milngavie (11)..........	8,937	18·5	12·1	202,339	20	7	W. A. Morton.	R. H. M. Kennedy.
Montrose* (2)..........	10,834	15·5	16·2	212,306	18	0	J. S. Richardson.	W. Johnston.
Motherwell and Wishaw (19)..............	73,483	21·4	11·1	1,560,960	19	6	A. McIntosh.	E. Lawson.
Musselburgh (20).......	17,592	17·2	12·7	308,137	18	3	D. Taylor.	R. Arthur.
Nairn* (21)............	4,867	17·4	16·1	86,530	15	4	G. S. Storm.	G. Borwick.
Newmilns and Greenholm (4)................	3,486	14·9	15·2	57,248	18	2	G. Mair.	G. Girvan.
Newport-on-Tay (14)....	3,295	15·1	18·2	73,345	15	10	A. Gilruth.	A. C. Newell.
North Berwick (12).....	3,727	9·9	20·1	103,740	19	6	R. S. Wotherspoon.	J. R. Wishart.
Oban (3)...............	6,758	18·6	16·8	130,736	18	6	A. MacInnes.	N. Cameron.
Paisley (25)...........	96,670	21·5	12·6	1,607,645	20	0	A. Cochran.	I. H. Leishman.
Peebles* (23)..........	5,305	14·1	21·8	108,402	23	1	E. Laverock. [T.D.	J. R. Lawrie, M.B.E.
Penicuik (20)..........	6,134	17·4	10·8	114,696	14	4	Col. J. J. Lamb, O.B.E.,	A. A. Livie.
PERTH* (24)...........	40,940	17·4	13·4	837,153	24	0	A. H. Martin.	†R. Ritchie.
Peterhead (1)..........	12,698	23·4	10·5	202,111	16	6	A. Craig.	R. Forman, O.B.E.
Port-Glasgow (25).......	22,633	22·8	9·9	298,771	17	8	J. Wooler.	W. P. Lucas.
Prestonpans (12).......	3,115	24·2	10·3	43,763	19	6	R. S. Wilson.	Mrs. M. Frame.
Prestwick (4)..........	12,467	16·7	14·6	231,373	17	0	A. Inglis.	W. I. Foulds.
Renfrew*..............	18,064	23·9	11·6	662,685	17	3	H. D-M. McCutcheon.	J. H. Mason.
Rothesay* (7)..........	7,370	14·9	20·5	166,209	24	9	A. Lindsay.	W. R. Lyle.
Rutherglen* (19)........	25,518	21·5	13·4	435,767	22	6	R. F. Pollock.	J. F. MacKay.
St. Andrews* (14)......	10,149	14·8	12·8	282,860	14	8	N. C. H. Mackenzie.	T. T. Fordyce.
Saltcoats (4)...........	14,113	24·2	13·2	210,789	17	4	W. F. McAllum.	C. Martin.
Selkirk* (28)...........	5,640	13·4	17·1	96,000	21	6	J. C. Robertson.	J. R. Dalgleish.
Stevenston (4)..........	10,386	22·8	10·0	131,500	19	0	J. Campbell.	J. Clements.
Stirling* (29)...........	27,599	20·0	12·5	559,380	19	8	C. W. Norman.	W. MacF. Gray, O.B.E.
Stonehaven (16)........	4,536	13·5	16·5	76,608	17	0	F. W. Robertson, M.B.E.; I. B. Robertson (*Joint*).	T. Christie.
Stornoway (26).........	5,355	13·6	13·8	98,373	18	9	A. Macleod.	D. J. Stewart.
Stranraer* (32).........	9,319	19·4	13·4	146 835	19	6	R. M. F. Thomson.	A. Murray.
Tayport (14)...........	3,146	14·9	13·3	56,079	17	3	H. G. Wilson.	W. Jack.
Thurso (8).............	8,713	28·0	7·9	94,027	20	0	G. L. Robertson.	D. K. Sutherland.
Tillicoultry (9).........	3,970	21·2	12·6	64,230	20	7	J. C. Donaldson.	C. Eccles.
Tranent (12)...........	6,388	22·3	10·7	80,360	18	10	R. M. Sorbie.	G. F. McNeill.
Troon (4)..............	9,741	13·7	13·6	199,719	17	5	A. R. Macleod.	D. P. Anderson.
Whitburn (31)..........	6,070	23·3	8·1	71,000	21	6	J. A. Macreadie.	H. F. Stewart.
Wick* (8)..............	7,555	20·9	12·1	88,548	15	3	W. C. Hogg.	W. F. Dunnett.

MISCELLANEOUS STATISTICS

Fuel and Power

Coal.—A total of 18,525,000 tons of coal was produced in Scotland in 1962, including 731,000 tons of opencast coal and 371,000 tons of anthracite. In addition, 854,000 tons of coal were imported from the rest of the United Kingdom. 15,956,000 tons of coal was consumed in Scotland during the year: 3,840,000 tons by domestic users, 3,347,000 tons by industrial consumers and 6,687,000 tons by gas and electricity undertakings and by British Railways.

Electricity.—The installed capacity of the Electricity Boards in 1962 was 3,289 megawatts. 11,413 million kilowatt hours were generated and 10,924 million kWh. sent out. Imports and purchases from the U.K. Atomic Energy Authority totalled 1,880 million kWh. and sales to Boards' consumers amounted to 11,393 million kWh., valued at £74,816,000.

Gas.—A total of 39,872,000,000 cubic feet of gas was produced at gasworks in 1962, using 1,526,000 tons of coal, 83,000 tons of coke (1961–62) and 32,000 tons of oil. An average of 171·6 therms was sold to 1,042,000 consumers, total sales amounting to 178,819,000 therms (domestic users, 97,192,000; industrial users (including farms), 46,464,000; commercial users, 30,669,000). Net proceeds from gas, made at a net cost of £19,865,000, were £19,983,000.

Petroleum.—3,925,000 tons of oil were processed in Scotland in 1962. Output of refined fuel during the year included fuel oil, 1,630,000 tons; aviation, motor, industrial and white spirits, 740,000 tons; gas and diesel oils, 891,000 tons and kerosene, 151,000 tons. Lubricating and other oils and petroleum products totalled 509,000 tons.

Manufacturing Industries

Shipbuilding.—During the year 1962, construction of merchant vessels (100 gross tons and over) totalling 376,000 gross tons was completed, including 70,000 tons for overseas owners, and a further 304,000 gross tons laid down (overseas owners, 70,000 gross tons). Orders were received in 1962 for a total of 200,000 gross tons (overseas owners, 13,000) and at the end of the year orders were on hand for 706,000 gross tons (overseas owners, 13,000), with 405,000 gross tons under construction.

Textiles, etc.—Manufacturers' deliveries in 1962 included: Cotton yarns, 38,986,000 lbs.; cotton cloth 28,435,000 yards; Blankets, 1,217,000 lbs.; Woollen fabrics, 17,767,000 sq. yds.; Worsted fabrics, 4,903,000 sq. yds.; Linen and union fabrics, 24,277,000 sq. yds.; Carpets and rugs, 20,725,000 sq. yds.; Jute yarn and piece goods, 203,000 tons.

Metal Manufactures.—Production in 1962 included: *Iron and Steel:* Pig iron, 866,000 tons, Iron Castings, 301,000 tons; Crude steel, 1,895,000 tons (including alloys, 147,000); Finished steel products—Plates, 414,000 tons; Rails and heavy rolled products, 332,000 tons; Light rolled products, 295,000 tons; Tubes, pipes and fittings, 151,000 tons; Sheets (under 3 mm. thick), 8,000 tons; Steel castings, 48,000 tons; Forgings, tyres, wheels and axles, 19,000 tons: *Aluminium:* Virgin aluminium, 34,000 tons; Aluminium castings, 3,700 tons.

Engineering and Electrical Goods.—Total production in 1962 was valued at £284,000,000, of which £87,000,000 was for exported goods. Production included agricultural machinery, £8,800,000; metal working machine tools, £6,200,000; contractors' plant and quarrying machinery, £14,200,000; pumps and industrial valves, £15,700,000; mining machinery, £11,600,000; refrigerating machinery, £11,600,000; mechanical handling equipment, £9,800,000; electrical machinery, £11,900,000; other electrical goods, £21,300,000 (domestic appliances, £9,000,000); and office machinery, £28,200,000. Scientific and industrial instruments and apparatus valued at £8,300,000 and watches and clocks, £5,700,000, were also manufactured in 1962.

Other Manufactures.—457,000 tons of paper and board were manufactured in 1962, 23,119,000 square yards of linoleum and 30,900,000 tons of printed felt base. A total of 701,000,000 building bricks were produced in 1962 and 379,000 tons of refractory goods. Pottery to the value of £67,000 was produced. Output of Scottish sawmills included 3,842,000 cubic feet of softwood and 1,189,000 cu. ft. of hardwood, all homegrown timber. Value of sports equipment produced was £1,448,000. Sales of bedding were valued at £1,480,000.

Food, Drink and Tobacco

Food.—Animals slaughtered in 1962 were: Cattle, 635,000; Calves, 117,000; Sheep and lambs, 2,479,000; Pigs, 564,000. 14,500 tons of bacon and ham were produced. 136·3 million gallons of milk were sold for liquid consumption and 108·3 million gallons for other uses. 540·1 million eggs were sold through packing stations. Manufacture of milk products included 5,500,000 tons of butter and 18,400 tons of cheese. Other agricultural products: Wheat (milled), 399,300 tons; Oats (processed), 72,700 tons; Compound feeding stuffs, 734,700 tons. 237,200 tons of sugar was refined, including 21,800 tons from beet. Manufactured foods produced in 1962 included: Chocolate and sugar confectionery, 29,700 tons; Jam and marmalade, 27,500 tons; Biscuits, 91,000 tons; Margarine, 18,200 tons; Compound fat, 13,500 tons; Canned foods (fruit, vegetables, fish and soups), 68,900 tons. 91,000 tons of fish (mainly herring) were cured in 1962.

Drink and Tobacco.—81,800,000 proof gallons of spirits, mainly whisky were produced. The total United Kingdom exports of whisky (mainly Scotch) amounted to 30,100,000 proof gallons in 1962 and were valued at £80,900,000. 2,501,000 bulk barrels of beer and 27,000,000 gallons of soft drinks were produced during the year. Tobacco manufactured in Scotland in 1962 totalled 21,700,000 lbs.

Transport

Railways.—On January 1, 1963, the Scottish Region of British Railways had 3,134 route miles in use (running track, 4,839 miles; sidings, 1,782 miles). 809 steam and 578 diesel locomotives were in use in Scotland. In 1962, 72,300,000 passenger journeys were made and 24,700,000 tons of freight carried. Receipts for the year totalled £43,550,000 compared with £45,212,000 in 1961.

Air Transport.—In 1962, 1,854,900 passengers, 10,460 short tons (2,000 lbs.) of freight and 3,353 short tons of mail were carried to or from the 19 Scottish airfields.

Roads.—On the 28,320 miles of roads in Scotland, motor vehicles licensed in 1962 totalled 774,700—private cars, 490,700; public conveyances, 11,800; motor cycles, etc., 84,500; goods vehicles, 110,900; other vehicles, mainly tractors, 76,600. New registrations of vehicles during the year numbered 86,498. In 141,300 driving tests conducted, 72,600 failures were recorded. Net receipts from vehicle and driving licences were £12,566,000.

Public Transport.—11,800 public road passenger vehicles were licensed in Scotland at the beginning of 1963, including those of Glasgow Corporation (1,678), Edinburgh Corporation (708), Aberdeen Corporation (236) and Dundee Corporation (245).

Accidents.—In 1962, 26,703 persons (5,686 children under 15) were involved in road accidents. 664 persons were killed (children, 120), 7,052 seriously injured (children, 1,339) and 18,987 slightly injured (children, 4,227).

Inland Waterways.—The Caledonian and Crinan Canals were in use for freight traffic in 1962, carrying respectively 16,000 and 25,000 tons during the year. Vehicles passing through all Scottish canals in 1962 numbered 3,291 (Caledonian, 785; Crinan, 2,180; Forth and Clyde, 326).

Shipping.—(All Scottish seaports in 1962). Foreign trade, entered, 9,397,000 tons (net); cleared, 5,645,000 tons (net). Coasting trade, entered, 5,346,000 tons (net); cleared, 5,234,000 tons (net).

NEW TOWNS IN GREAT BRITAIN

Commission for the New Towns, Glen House, Stag Place, S.W.1.—The Commission was established on October 1, 1961, under the New Towns Act, 1959, to take over new towns in England and Wales from development corporations whose purposes have been achieved or substantially achieved. The assets and liabilities of the Crawley and Hemel Hempstead Development Corporations were transferred to the Commission on April 1, 1962. In each town, the management of residential property is conducted by a local committee appointed by the Commission in accordance with the 1959 Act and administration of all property is carried out through the Commission's local executive staff.

Chairman, Sir Duncan Anderson, K.B.E., T.D.
Deputy Chairman, H. W. Wells, C.B.E.
Members, Gen. Sir Nevil Brownjohn, G.B.E., K.C.B., C.M.G., M.C.; Mrs. B. F. R. Paterson; J. D. Russell; J. M. A. Smith.
Secretary, B. J. Collins, C.B.E.

CRAWLEY, Sussex.—*Chairman*, Gen. Sir Nevil Brownjohn, G.B.E., K.C.B., C.M.G., M.C. *Manager*, R. M. Clarke, M.C. *Offices*, Broadfield, Crawley, Sussex. Area, 6,047 acres. Population (estimated, 1962), 55,360. Estimated eventual population, 70,000 (1980). *See also Crawley Urban District Council.*

HEMEL HEMPSTEAD, Herts.—*Chairman*, H. W. Wells, C.B.E. *Manager*, A. W. Thomas. *Offices*, Swan Court, Waterhouse Street, Hemel Hempstead, Herts. Area, 5,910 acres. Population (estimated, 1962), 58,270. *See also Borough of Hemel Hempstead.*

Development Corporations

AYCLIFFE, Co. Durham.—Formed 1947. *Chairman*, Col. H. H. Peile, O.B.E., T.D. *General Manager*, A. V. Williams. *Offices*, Churchill House, Newton Aycliffe, nr. Darlington, Co. Durham. Area, 865 acres. Population (estimated, 1962), 13,803. Estimated eventual population 20,000.

BASILDON, Essex.—Formed 1949. *Chairman*, Lt.-Gen. Sir Humfrey Gale, K.B.E., C.B., C.V.O., M.C. *General Manager*, R. C. C. Boniface. *Offices*, Gifford House, Basildon, Essex. Area, 7,818 acres. Population (estimated, 1962), 95,360. Estimated eventual population, 106,000. *See also Basildon Urban District Council.*

BRACKNELL, Berks.—Formed 1949. *Chairman*, Sir Ambrose Flux Dundas, K.C.I.E., C.S.I. *General Manager*, J. V. Rowley. *Offices*, Farley Hall, Bracknell, Berks. Area, 3,296 acres. Population (estimated, 1962), 22,626. Estimated eventual population, 54,000.

CORBY, Northants.—Formed 1950. *Chairman*, H. Chisholm. *General Manager*, R. F. Brooks Grundy. *Offices*, Spencer House, Corporation Street, Corby, Northants. Area, 4,296 acres. Population (estimated, 1962), 39,460. Estimated eventual population, 75,000. *See also Corby Urban District Council.*

CRAMLINGTON, Northumberland.—A further site for a new town, 8 miles north of Newcastle-upon-Tyne, was approved on Jan. 9, 1963. Estimated eventual population, 48,000.

CWMBRAN, Mon.—Formed 1949. *Chairman*, Rear-Adm. St. J. A. Micklethwait, C.B., D.S.O. *General Manager*, J. E. McComb, D.F.C. *Offices*, Victoria Street, Cwmbran, Mon. Area, 3,157 acres. Population (estimated, 1962), 23,190. Estimated eventual population, 55,000.

DAWLEY, Shropshire.—Formed 1963. *Chairman*, Sir Reginald Pearson, O.B.E.; *General Manager*, R. P. Owen; *Offices*, Hatfield House, Dawley. *Area*, 9,100 acres. Estimated eventual population, 90,000.

HARLOW, Essex.—Formed 1947. *Chairman*, Sir Richard Costain, C.B.E. *General Manager*, B. Hyde Harvey. *Offices*, Gate House, The High, Harlow, Essex. Area 6,395 acres. Population (estimated, 1962), 58,180. Estimated eventual population, 80,000. *See also Harlow Urban District Council.*

HATFIELD AND WELWYN GARDEN CITY, Herts.—Formed 1948. *Chairman*, C. G. Maynard, C.B.E. *General Manager*, Brig. G. B. S. Hindley, C.B.E. *Offices*, Church Road, Welwyn Garden City, Herts. Area, Hatfield, 2,349 acres, Welwyn Garden City, 4,317 acres. Population (estimated, 1962), Hatfield, 21,800, Welwyn Garden City, 36,860. Estimated eventual population: Hatfield, 25,000; Welwyn Garden City, 50,000. *See also Welwyn Garden City Urban District Council.*

PETERLEE, Co. Durham.—Formed 1948. *Chairman*, Col. H. H. Peile, O.B.E., T.D. *General Manager*, A. V. Williams. *Offices*, Shotton Hall, Peterlee, Co. Durham. Area, 2,336 acres. Population (estimated, 1962), 14,000. Estimated eventual population, 30,000.

SKELMERSDALE, Lancs.—Formed 1962. *Chairman* A. J. Kentish-Barnes; *General Manager*, G. G. Watson. Area, 4,029 acres (site). Estimated eventual population, 80,000.

STEVENAGE, Herts.—Formed 1946. *Chairman*, Sir Arthur Rucker, K.C.M.G., C.B., C.B.E. *General Manager*, R. S. McDougall, C.B.E. *Offices*, Daneshill House, Stevenage, Herts. Area, 6,156 acres. Population (estimated, 1962), 46,710. Estimated eventual population, 80,000. *See also Stevenage Urban District Council.*

Scotland

CUMBERNAULD, Dunbartonshire.—Formed 1956. *Chairman*, Gen. Sir Gordon MacMillan, K.C.B., K.C.V.O., C.B.E., D.S.O., M.C. *General Manager*, G. R. B. MacGill. *Headquarters*, Cumbernauld House, Cumbernauld, Glasgow. Population (estimated, 1962), 9,100. Estimated eventual population, 70,000.

EAST KILBRIDE, Lanarkshire.—Formed 1947. *Chairman*, Prof. R. Browning, C.B.E. *General Manager*, D. Kirby, M.V.O., M.B.E. *Offices*, Torrance House, East Kilbride, Lanarkshire. Population (estimated, 1962), 33,950. Estimated eventual population, 70,000.

GLENROTHES, Fife.—Formed 1948. *Chairman*, The Lord Hughes, C.B.E. *General Manager*, Brig. R. S. Doyle, C.B.E. *Offices*, Glenrothes. Population (estimated, 1962), 13,950. Estimated eventual population, 55,000.

LIVINGSTONE, West Lothian. *Chairman*, D. Lowe.—A further site for a new town was designated on April 16, 1962.

Northern Ireland

(For geographical and historical notes on Ireland, see Index)

A Census of Population was held in Northern Ireland on April 23, 1961. Preliminary figures showed a total population of 1,425,462 (*males*, 694,768; *females*, 730,694) an increase of 54,541 over the total at the Census of 1951. Expressed as percentages of the total population, the number of persons in the various religious denominations were: Roman Catholic, 34·9; Presbyterian, 29; Church of Ireland, 24·2; Methodist, 5; others 4·9; not stated, 2. Northern Ireland has a total area of 5,462 sq. miles (land, 5,206 sq. miles; inland water and tideways 256 sq. miles) with a density of population of 272 persons per sq. mile in 1961.

Constitution and Government.—Under the Government of Ireland Act, 1920, a separate Parliament and Executive Government were established for Northern Ireland. Under the Constitution certain legislative and fiscal powers are reserved to the Parliament of the United Kingdom.

The Northern Ireland Parliament consists of a *House of Commons* of 52 elected members (who receive an allowance) and a *Senate* of 2 *ex-officio* Senators and 24 Senators elected by the members of the House of Commons on the proportional representation system. At the General Election of May, 1962, there were elected, Unionists 34, Northern Ireland Labour 4, Nationalists 9, Republican Labour 1, Independent Labour 1, Independent 1, *Eire* Labour 1, Liberal 1. Northern Ireland continues under the Act of 1920 to return 12 members to the House of Commons at Westminster.

The *Executive* power is vested in the Governor on behalf of Her Majesty the Queen; he holds office for 6 years, and is advised by 9 Ministers responsible to Parliament.

Governor, His Excellency THE LORD WAKEHURST, K.G., K.C.M.G., *born* 1895; *appointed Governor*, December 1, 1952, *re-appointed* Dec. 1, 1958 (Government House, Hillsborough, Northern Ireland) £8,000

Private Secretary and Principal A.D.C., Maj. R. Stephens, E.R.D.

Asst. Private Secretary, Mrs. F. W. Haslett, O.B.E.

The Privy Council

J. L. O. Andrews, M.P. (1957); Sir Anthony Babington, Q.C. (1926); Arthur Black (*Lord Justice*) (1947); The Viscount Brookeborough, C.B.E., M.C., M.P. (1933); Senator the Very Revd. R. Corkey (1943); W. Craig, M.P. (1963); L. E. Curran (*Lord Justice*) (1957); A. B. D. Faulkner, M.P. (1959); Senator Col. the Lord Glentoran, H.M.L. (1953); Senator Lt.Col. A. R. G. Gordon, C.B.E., D.S.O. (1951); J. F. Gordon (1938); Judge G. B. Hanna (1953); H. V. Kirk, M.P. (1962); The Lord MacDermott, M.C. (*Lord Chief Justice*) (1940); W. B Maginess, Q.C., M.P. (1945); W. J. Morgan, M.P. (1961); Hon. Sir Henry Mulholland, Bt. (1930); Ivan Neill, M.P. (1950); Capt. Hon. Terence O'Neill, M.P. (1956); Dame Dehra Parker, G.B.E. (1949); The Lord Rathcavan (1922); Capt. Sir Norman Stronge, Bt., M.C., H.M.L., M.P. (1946); Judge W. W. B. Topping (1957); J. E. Warnock, Q.C., M.P. (1944); H. W. West, M.P. (1960).

Clerk of the Privy Council, C. J. Bateman, M.B.E., Stormont Castle, Belfast.

The Senate

J. Bailie (*U.*); J. E. N. Barnhill; Rt. Hon. the Lord Mayor of Belfast (*U.*); S. W. Boyd (*U.*); Sir G. A. Clark, Bt. (*U.*); V. A. Cooke (*U.*); Very Rev and Rt. Hon. Prof. R.Corkey, Phil.D. (*U.*); Lt.-Col. J. G. Cunningham, O.B.E. (*U.*); J. Cunningham, C.B.E. (*U.*); J. C. Drennan, C.B.E.; J. P. Donaghy (*N.*); J. Fisher (*U.*); Col. the Lord Glentoran, P.C., H.M.L. (*U.*); Lt.-Col. Rt. Hon. A. R. G. Gordon, C.B.E., D.S.O. (*U.*); Mrs. M. J. Greeves, M.B.E. (*U.*); J. S. Johnston (*U.*); J. G. Lennon (*N.*); The Mayor of Londonderry (*U.*), P. F. McGill (*N.*); J. A. McGlade (*N.*); D. R. McGladdery (*U.*); P. J. O'Hare (*A-P.*); H. Quin, C.B.E., LL.D. (*U.*); S. Rodgers; A. P. Schofield; W. Stewart (*U.*); A. J. Walmsley (*U.*); (one vacancy).

The House of Commons

Belfast (16 Members).—D. W. Bleakley (*Lab.*); D. Boal (*Ind. U.*); W. R. Boyd (*Lab.*); T. W. Boyd (*Lab.*); H. Diamond (*Repub. Lab.*); G. Fitt (*Eire Lab.*); W. K. Fitzsimmons (*U.*); F. Hanna (*Ind. Lab.*); W. S. Hinds (*U.*); Rt. Hon. H. V. Kirk (*U.*); J. W. Kennedy (*U.*); Rt. Hon. W. J. Morgan (*U.*); Rt. Hon. I. Neill (*U.*); W. Scott (*U.*); F. V. Simpson (*Lab.*); Rt. Hon. J. E. Warnock, Q.C. (*U.*).

Antrim (7 Members).—Rt. Hon. W. Craig (*U.*); A. Hunter (*U.*); R. W. B. McConnell (*U.*); N. O. Minford (*U.*); Hon. P. R. H. O'Neill (*U*); Capt. Rt. Hon. T. O'Neill (*U.*); R. Simpson (*U.*).

Armagh (4 Members).—I. G. Hawthorne (*U.*); Mrs. D. McNabb, O.B.E. (*U.*); E. G. Richardson (*Ind. N.*); Capt. Rt. Hon. Sir C. N. L. Stronge, Bt., M.C., H.M.L. (*U.*).

Queen's University (4 Members).—H. E. McClure (*U.*); Miss B. H. Maconachie (*U.*); Miss S. M. Murnaghan (*Lib.*); C. Stewart, Q.C. (*N.*).

Down (8 Members).—Rt. Hon. J. L. O. Andrews (*U.*); J. Connellan (*N.*); Rt. Hon. A. B. D. Faulkner (*U.*); D. J. Little (*U.*); Capt. W. J. Long (*U.*); Rt. Hon. W. B. Maginess, Q.C., LL.D. (*U.*); R. S. Nixon (*U.*); J. O'Reilly (*N.*).

Fermanagh (3 Members).—The Viscount Brookeborough, P.C., C.B.E., M.C. (*U.*); C. Healy (*N.*); Rt. Hon. H. W. West (*U.*).

Londonderry City (1 Member).—E. W. Jones, Q.C. (*U.*).

Londonderry County (4 Members).—J. Burns (*U.*); Maj. J. D. Chichester-Clark (*U.*); P. J. Gormley (*N.*) E. G. McAteer (*N.*).

Tyrone (5 Members).—T. C. Gormley (*N.*) T. Lyons (*U.*); W. F. McCoy, Q.C. (*U.*); R. H. O'Connor (*N.*); J. F. Stewart (*N.*);

A-P. = Anti-Partition. *Ind.* = Independent. *Lab.* = Labour. *Lib.* = Liberal. *N.* = Nationalist. *U.* = Unionist.

Officers of Parliament

Speaker of the Senate, Lt.-Col. Rt. Hon. A. R. G. Gordon, C.B.E., D.S.O.

Speaker of the House of Commons, Capt. Rt. Hon. Sir Norman Stronge, Bt., M.C., H.M.L.

Chairman of Ways and Means and Deputy-Speaker, T. Lyons.

Deputy Chairman, W. R. Boyd.

Temporary Chairman, Hon. P. R. H. O'Neill.

Serjeant-at-Arms, Brig. N. Russell, C.B., D.S.O., M.C.

Black Rod and Deputy Serjeant-at-Arms, Brig. J. Y. Calwell, C.B.E., M.V.O.

Clerk of the Parliaments, J. S. F. Cooke.

Clerk Assistant, R. H. A. Blackburn.

Librarian, T. Hamilton.

Editor of Official Report, J. F. Burns.

The Cabinet

Prime Minister, Capt. Rt. Hon. Terence Marne O'Neill, M.P. (*b.* 1915); *appointed* 1963 *£4,000
Minister of Finance, Rt. Hon. J. L. O. Andrews, M.P.
Home Affairs, Rt. Hon. W. Craig, M.P.
Labour and National Insurance, Rt. Hon. H. V. Kirk, M.P.
Education, Rt. Hon. Ivan Neill, M.P.
Agriculture, Rt. Hon. H. W. West, M.P.
Commerce, Rt. Hon. A. B. D. Faulkner, M.P.
Health and Local Government, Rt. Hon. W. J. Morgan, M.P.
Minister in the Senate, Col. the Lord Glentoran, P.C., H.M.L.
Ministers, each £2,500 and Expenses, £300.

PARLIAMENTARY SECRETARIES.

Prime Minister's Department, Senator D. R. McGladdery.
Ministry of Finance, Maj. J. D. Chichester-Clark, M.P.
Ministry of Home Affairs, W. K. Fitzsimmons, M.P.
Ministry of Health and Local Government, R. W. B. McConnell, M.P.

CABINET SECRETARIAT.

Secretary, C. J. Bateman, M.B.E.
Assistant Secretary (vacant).

Government Offices

MINISTRY OF FINANCE.

Permanent Secretary, R. F. R. Dunbar, C.B., O.B.E.
Second Secretary, D. C. B. Holden, C.B., E.R.D.
First Parliamentary Draftsman, W. A. Leitch, C.B.
Second Parliamentary Draftsman, A. G. Donaldson.
Director of Establishments, H. Black.
Assistant Secretaries, W. W. Arthur; R. H. Kidd; J. Reid; P. Shea.
Registrar-General, A. J. Park.

MINISTRY OF HOME AFFAIRS.

Permanent Secretary, W. F. Stout.
Assistant Secretaries, A. Alexander, O.B.E.; J. W. E. Cathcart, O.B.E.; J. G. Hill; J. F. Irvine.
Attorney-General, Rt. Hon. W. B. Maginess, Q.C., M.P.
Chief Crown Solicitor, T. H. Goligher.

MINISTRY OF LABOUR AND NATIONAL INSURANCE.

Permanent Secretary, J. E. Greeves.
Sen. Asst. Secretary, H. A. Lowry.
Assistant Secretaries, J. E. Aiken; L. B. Jagoe; W. Slinger.

MINISTRY OF EDUCATION.
(Dundonald House, Upper Newtownards Road, Belfast, 4.)

Permanent Secretary, A. C. Williams, C.B.
Senior Assistant Secretary, J. M. Benn.
Assistant Secretaries, L. Arndell; J. Scott, O.B.E.

MINISTRY OF AGRICULTURE.

Permanent Secretary, J. C. Baird.
Senior Assistant Secretary, W. H. Elliott.
Assistant Secretaries, J. V. Bateman; W. G. Malcolm, M.B.E.; W. A. V. Sanderson, C.B.E.

MINISTRY OF COMMERCE.
(Chichester Street, Belfast, 1.)

Permanent Secretary, H. E. Jones, C.B.E.
Senior Assistant Secretaries, A. C. Brooke; K. R. Shimeld.
Assistant Secretaries, W. E. Bell; H. Ruben, O.B.E.
Director of Industrial and Forensic Science, A. J. Howard.
Registrar of Joint Stock Companies and of Business Names, Registrar of Friendly Societies and Industrial Assurance Commissioner, E. Simpson.

MINISTRY OF HEALTH AND LOCAL GOVERNMENT.

Permanent Secretary, R. F. Green, C.B.
Second Secretary, J. A. Oliver.
Senior Assistant Secretary, N. Dugdale.
Assistant Secretaries, A. P. Fitzgerald, O.B.E.; C. D. Hoey; P. A. Sythes.
Chief Medical Officer, F. F. Main.

EXCHEQUER AND AUDIT DEPARTMENT
(Arnotts Building, Belfast, 2)

Comptroller and Auditor-General, W. J. Thompson.
Chief Auditor, J. W. Acheson, O.B.E.

CIVIL SERVICE COMMISSION.

Secretary, H. Black.

NATIONAL ASSISTANCE BOARD.
(Ormeau Avenue, Belfast, 2).

Chairman, Sir Robin Kinahan.
Secretary, W. J. Arthurs.

ROYAL ULSTER CONSTABULARY.
(Knock Road, Belfast 5).

Inspector General, A. H. Kennedy.
Deputy Inspector General, J. A. Peacocke, O.B.E.

NORTHERN IRELAND AGENT IN LONDON
13 Regent Street, S.W.1.

Agent, Sir Francis Evans, G.B.E. K.C.M.G.

THE JUDICATURE

SUPREME COURT OF JUDICATURE, THE ROYAL COURTS OF JUSTICE (ULSTER), BELFAST.

The Rt. Hon. the Lord MacDermott, Lord Chief Justice of Northern Ireland £7,500
The Rt. Hon. Lord Justice (Arthur) Black; The Rt. Hon. Lord Justice (Lancelot E.) Curran; The Hon. Mr. Justice (Charles Leo) Sheil; The Hon. Mr. Justice (Herbert Andrew) McVeigh. each £6,500

Secretariat

Permanent Secretary to Supreme Court and Clerk of the Crown for Northern Ireland, J. Ritchie.
Assistant Secretary to the Supreme Court and Private Secretary to the Lord Chief Justice, J. A. L. McLean.

Registrar's Department

Registrar, W. McC. Sharpe, C.B.E., D.S.O.
Assistant Registrar, G. J. Cairns.
Deputy Assistant Registrar, V. A. Care.

Chief Clerk's Department

Chief Clerk (and Registrar in Lunacy), J. K. Davis.
Assistant Chief Clerk, R. L. G. Davison.
Assistant Registrar in Lunacy, R. L. G. Davison.

Official Assignee's Department

Official Assignee, A. K. Pryde.

Taxing Office

Master, Alfred E. Anderson.

Principal Probate Registry

Chief Registrar, James R. Lindsay, O.B.E.
Assistant Registrar (vacant).

District Probate Registry, Londonderry.

Registrar, J. J. Gibson.

Accountant-General's Office

Accountant-General, R. A. Guiler.
Chief Clerk, J. N. Bell.

Recorders

Belfast, Rt. Hon. W. W. B. Topping, Q.C..£4,900
Londonderry, I. Copeland, Q.C.............£4,400

Chairmen of Quarter Sessions

Antrim, The Recorder of Belfast.
Armagh and Fermanagh, J. G. Agnew, Q.C....£4,400
Down, Rt. Hon. G. B. Hanna, Q.C.........£4,400
Londonderry, The Recorder of Londonderry.
Tyrone, W. Johnson, Q.C.................£4,400

Bankruptcy and Chancery Registrar's Department

Registrar, J. M. Hunter.
Deputy Assistant Registrar, V. G. Bridges.

EDUCATION

Statistics of education in Northern Ireland will be found in the introduction to the Education Directory, p. 501.

FINANCE

The greater part of the taxation in Northern Ireland is imposed and collected by the United Kingdom Government. After deducting the cost of collection, certain services reserved to the United Kingdom Parliament, and the Imperial Contribution, the balance is paid over to Northern Ireland's Exchequer. The Contribution so made by Northern Ireland to the cost of United Kingdom services, *i.e.* Navy, Army and Air Force, National Debt, etc., for the period from 1921 to March 31, 1962, amounted to £433,674,344. The United Kingdom contribution has been provisionally fixed at £7,500,000 for 1962–63 and £3,500,000 for 1963–64.

	1963–64
Estimated Public Income	£140,540,000
Estimated Public Expenditure (including Imperial contribution)	£140,466,485

EXTERNAL TRADE†

	1960	1961
Total Imports	£378,301,000	£378,879,000
Total Exports	£335,117,000	£344,205,000

† Including cross-Channel trade with Great Britain.

PRODUCTION

Industries.—The total value of the industrial production of Northern Ireland in 1961 was approximately £661,000,000, and employment on industrial production was given to about 215,000 persons. The products of the engineering, shipbuilding and aircraft industries, which employed 53,000 persons, were valued at £88,000,000. The textile industries, employing 50,000 persons, produced yarns, fabrics, household textiles, handkerchiefs, carpets, hosiery, ropes and a wide variety of other products valued at approximately £99,000,000. The food, drink and tobacco industries, giving employment to 27,000 persons, produced goods valued at £312,000,000 and clothing to the value of £30,000,000 was manufactured in 1961, of which £10,800,000 represented shirts and collars, which are manufactured principally in Londonderry. Other industries of importance to the economy of Northern Ireland are synthetic rubber, cardboard boxes and packing cases, furniture, toys, pottery, and cement.

Minerals.—About 2,418 persons were employed in mining and quarrying operations in Northern Ireland in 1962, and the minerals raised were valued at some £2,954,585.

Fisheries.—The total value of sea and freshwater fish caught in 1962 was £704,000.

COMMUNICATIONS

Seaports.—The amount of shipping using the principal ports in 1962 was about 9,550,000 tons. *Belfast.*—Nightly passenger and freight services operate to Glasgow, Heysham and Liverpool. Regular vehicle ferry services are maintained to Preston and general cargo services operate to the major ports in Great Britain and to foreign ports. *Larne.*—A twice daily passenger, vehicle ferry and general cargo service to Stranraer, a regular vehicle ferry service to Preston and a cargo service to Ardrossan are operated. *Londonderry.*—A passenger and cargo service is maintained to Glasgow and freight services operate to Heysham, Liverpool and Preston.

Road and Rail Transport.—The Ulster Transport Authority provides all road passenger and freight services outside Belfast and Londonderry and provides all rail services. The gross receipts of the Authority in 1962 were over £10 million. The Authority operates over 1,100 omnibuses and 2,100 goods motor vehicles. In 1962 it carried approximately 94,000,000 passengers and over 2,500,000 tons of freight by road and rail and over 1,000,000 head of livestock by road.

Airport.—Passenger and freight services are in operation between Belfast Airport and airports throughout Great Britain. During 1962 over 585,000 passengers, over 6,000 short tons of freight and almost 3,000 short tons of mail were carried.

THE ARMS OF NORTHERN IRELAND

ARMS.—*Argent*, a Cross *gules*, over all on a 6-pointed Star of the field ensigned by an Imperial Crown *proper*, a dexter Hand couped at the wrist of the second.

COUNTIES OF NORTHERN IRELAND

Counties and *County Boroughs*	Population, 1962	Lord Lieutenant	High Sheriff, 1963–64
(1) Antrim	278,600	Capt. R. A. F. Dobbs.	J. Young.
Belfast County Borough	413,900	Col. the Lord Glentoran, P.C.	J. F. Cairns.
(2) Armagh	117,900	Capt. Rt. Hon. Sir Norman Stronge, Bt., M.C., M.Z.	Lt.-Col. A. H. Glendinning, O.B.E., T.D.
(3) Down	270,200	The Earl of Clanwilliam.	Lt.-Col. J. D. Ferguson, O.B.E., E.R.D.
(4) Fermanagh	52,400	The Visct. Brookeborough, P.C., C.B.E., M.C., M.P.	J. A. Livingstone.
(5) Londonderry†	113,600	Rt. Hon. Sir Henry Mulholland, Bt.	J. Bullick.
Londonderry County Borough	54,300	Col. Sir Basil McFarland, Bt., C.B.E.	Dr. J. A. L. Johnston, O.B.E.
(6) Tyrone	134,500	The Duke of Abercorn.	Capt. J. H. H. Pollock, C.M.G., O.B.E.

† Excluding Londonderry County Borough.

Chairmen of County Councils.—*Antrim*, J. H. Lindsay, M.B.E.; *Armagh*, A. D. Gibson; *Down*, G. McSpadden, O.B.E.; *Fermanagh*, Capt. Hon. J. W. Brooke; *Londonderry*, D. H. Christie, C.B.E.; *Tyrone*, J. P. Duff, C.B.E.

MUNICIPAL DIRECTORY OF NORTHERN IRELAND

The figures in parentheses following the name of the town show the County in which it is situated (*see* p. 690).

CITIES, Boroughs, and *Urban Districts*	Population, 1962 Estimated	Rate per 1,000 Births	Rate per 1,000 Deaths	Rateable Value £	Rate levied 1963–64 s.	d.	Town Clerk (or Clerk U.D.C.)	Mayor 1963–64 ★ Lord Mayor † Chairman U.D.C.
Armagh (2)	9,950	23·4	10·8	143,911	23	6	V. M. Conran.	†J. Gray.
Ballymena (1)	14,680	19·8	10·7	151,697	26	8	J. Simpson.	J. D. Henry.
Banbridge (3)	6,200	21·0	11·1	47,419	32	4	R. J. Weatherall.	†C. Creighton.
Bangor (3)	24,630	17·1	14·3	343,539	26	6	T. B. Graham.	C. F. Milligan.
BELFAST (1)	413,900	20·9	11·1	5,027,791	23	5	J. Dunlop, C.B.E.	★W. M. Jenkins.
Carrickfergus (1)	10,120	23·5	11·3	127,452	24	6	T. B. McVea, M.B.E.	T. J. Patterson, O.B.E.
Coleraine (5)	12,550	21·1	8·4	133,229	24	0	W. E. Henry, M.B.E.	Lt.-Col. D. J. Christie, C.B.E., E.R.D.
Enniskillen (4)	7,530	22·0	11·0	67,163	25	4	N. J. Connor.	W. F. Bryson, M.B.E.
Holywood (3)	7,983	19·0	8·9	74,702	28	0	A. Gamble.	†W. P. M. Dunn.
Larne (1)	16,460	25·7	10·1	154,721	27	0	R. Lyttle, M.C.	J. W. Sandford, M.B.E.
Lisburn (1)	17,690	19·2	9·2	151,438	27	0	R. C. Newell.	†J. Howard.
LONDONDERRY	54,300	30·4	9·6	420,927	23	0	R. H. Henderson.	A. W. Anderson, V.R.D.
Lurgan (2)	18,240	25·0	12·2	128,363	30	10	W. G. Best.	A. H. C. Greer.
Newry (3)	12,230	29·3	12·1	99,935	29	0	G. Cronin.	†T. Markey.
Newtownards (3)	13,090	18·6	10·5	97,565	30	0	W. C. Scott.	J. Algie.
Omagh (6)	8,240	27·3	10·1	74,155	24	8	J. McGale.	†T. McClay.
Portadown (2)	18,770	23·1	9·0	209,557	27	6	G. McGowan, M.B.E.	C. Cooper.

BELFAST

BELFAST, a City, the seat of Government of Northern Ireland, situated at the mouth of the River Lagan at its entrance to Belfast Lough, has a municipal area of 15,357 acres, exclusive of tidal water (1,223) and a population (June 30, 1962) of 413,900. The city received its first charter of incorporation in 1613 and has since grown, owing to its easy access by sea to Scottish coal and iron, to be a great industrial centre. The chief industries are ship-building and the manufacture of aircraft, machinery, textiles, ropes and tobacco. Belfast is an important seaport with extensive docks.

The principal buildings are of a relatively recent date and include the Parliament Buildings at Stormont, the City Hall, the Law Courts, the Public Library and the Museum and Art Gallery. The Queen's University (previously Queen's College) was chartered in 1908.

The city returns 16 members to the Parliament of Northern Ireland and 4 members to the House of Commons at Westminster. Belfast was created a city in 1888 and the title of Lord Mayor was conferred in 1897.

Lord Mayor (1963–64), W. M. Jenkins.
Town Clerk, J. Dunlop, C.B.E.

LONDONDERRY

LONDONDERRY, a City and County Borough, situated on the River Foyle, has a population (estimated, 1962) of 54,300 and was reputedly founded in 546 by St. Columba. Londonderry (formerly *Derry*) has important associations with the City of London. The Irish Society, under its royal charter of 1613, fortified the city and was for a long period closely associated with its administration.

Famous for the great siege of 1688–89, when for 105 days the town held out against the forces of James II. until relieved by sea, Londonderry was an important naval base throughout the Second World War. Interesting buildings are the Protestant Cathedral of St. Columb's (1633) and the Guildhall reconstructed in 1912 and containing a number of beautiful stained glass windows, many of which were presented by the livery companies of London. The famous Walls are still intact and form a circuit of almost a mile around the old city. The manufacture of shirts and collars is the staple industry. Other industries include motor and mechanical engineering and fancy box making. A large part of Ulster's agricultural export trade passes through the port.

Mayor (1963–64), A. W. Anderson, V.R.D.
Town Clerk, R. H. Henderson.

THE ISLE OF MAN (MONA)

an island in the Irish Sea, in lat. 54° 3′–54° 25′ N., and long 4° 18′–4° 47′ W., nearly equidistant from England, Scotland, and Ireland. The total land area is 145,325 acres (227 sq. miles), of which 77,558 acres are under cultivation. Population (1961 Census, prelim.), 48,150 (males, 22,059; females, 26,091). In 1962 the births numbered 675 and the deaths 793. 355 persons were returned at the Census of 1951 as able to speak the Manx language, compared with 4,657 in 1901 and 529 in 1931. The Island's main industry is catering for holidaymakers (numbering about 500,000 in the year) from all parts of the British Isles. Some agricultural produce is exported.

There are forty-seven miles of railway and about 25 miles of electric tram road.

Government.—The Isle of Man is governed by a Legislature, called the Tynwald, consisting of two branches—the Legislative Council and the House of Keys. The Council consists of the Lieutenant-Governor, the Bishop of Sodor and Man, the two Deemsters, the Attorney-General, 2 members appointed by the Lieutenant-Governor, and 5 members appointed by the House of Keys. The House of Keys (possibly from the Scandinavian *keise*=chosen) is one of the most ancient legislative assemblies in the world. It consists of 24 members, elected by the adult male and female population, 13 from the six *sheadings*, 7 from Douglas, 2 from Ramsey, and 1 each from Castletown and Peel. Bills after having passed both Houses are signed by the members, and then sent for the Royal Assent. After receiving the Royal Assent, a Bill does not become law unless promulgated within the ensuing twelve months, and on the first "Tynwald Day" (July 5) following it is announced in the English and Manx languages on the Tynwald Hill. On the promulgation taking place a certificate thereof is signed by the Lieutenant-Governor and the Speaker of the House of Keys.

Finance.—An annual contribution of 5 per cent. of the net "Common Purse" Receipts amounting to approximately £115,000 is made to the Imperial Government. In 1921 Tynwald accepted liability for the redemption of £250,000 War Stock, and in 1927 liability for a further sum of £500,000 of War Stock was accepted in final settlement of all responsibility to the Imperial Government in respect of the cost of the War (1914–18). The Isle of Man has made, in all, free gifts of £1,250,000 to the British Government and has lent £1,000,000 free of interest, £500,000 of the latter being converted into a free gift on June 15, 1948; of the balance of £500,000, a sum of £250,000 was repaid by the Treasury in October, 1961, and interest has since that date been paid on the remaining £250,000 invested in 3 p.c. Savings Bonds, 1960/70.

The chief source of revenue is found in the customs duties, the only direct taxation being income tax. Income tax ranges from 1*s.* 9*d.* in the £ on the first £60 of taxable income. There are no surtax or death duties, surtax having been abolished from April 6, 1961. There are 31 primary, 4 secondary schools, a school of technology, arts and crafts and a domestic science college, in addition to King William's College and the Buchan School for Girls; the gross expenditure on public education in 1962–63 was £831,362 (provisional). Public revenue and expenditure are roughly in balance at approximately £4,250,000, excluding capital expenditure which is financed out of borrowings.

CAPITAL, ΨDouglas. Population (1951) 20,288 ΨCastletown (1,749) is the ancient capital; the other towns are ΨPeel (2,582), and ΨRamsay (4,607).

Lieutenant-Governor, His Excellency Sir Ronald Herbert Garvey, K.C.M.G., K.C.V.O., M.B.E., (1959) (*plus allowances, tax free* £2,000) £3,000
Government Secretary, E. R. St.A. Davies, M.B.E. 2,500
Government Treasurer, K. W. Carney 2,500
First Deemster, His Hon. S. J. Kneale, C.B.E. (*plus allce. £100 as Deputy Governor*)...... 2,500
Second Deemster, His Hon. B. W. Macpherson. 2,350
Attorney-General, G. E. Moore.............. 2,350
Speaker, House of Keys, H. C. Kerruish.
Judge of Appeal, J. D. Cantley, O.B.E., Q.C.

THE CHANNEL ISLANDS

Situated off the north-west coast of France (at distances of from ten to thirty miles), are the only portions of the *Dukedom of Normandy* now belonging to the Crown, to which they have been attached ever since the Conquest. They consist of Jersey (28,717 acres), Guernsey (15,654 acres), Alderney (1,962 acres), Brechou (74), Great Sark (1,035), Little Sark (239), Herm (320), Jethou (44), and Lihou (38), a total of 48,083 acres, or 75 square miles. At the 1961 census the population of Jersey was 57,200, and of Guernsey, etc. 47,198 (Guernsey, 45,150; Alderney, 1,449; Sark, 560).

The climate is mild, and the soil exceptionally productive. The land under cultivation in 1961 was 40,252 vergées (2¼ vergées=1 acre) in Jersey, and about 16,500 vergées (2½ vergées=1 acre) in Guernsey, the principal product of the soil of Jersey being potatoes and tomatoes, and of Guernsey tomatoes, flowers and fern. The famous Jersey and Guernsey breeds of cows have earned a well-deserved celebrity. The Lieutenant-Governors and Commanders-in-Chief of Jersey and Guernsey are the Personal Representatives of the Sovereign and the channel of communication between H.M. Government and the Insular Governments. The Bailiffs of Jersey and Guernsey, appointed by the Crown, are Presidents both of the Assembly of the States (the Insular Legislature) and of the Royal Court in their respective Bailiwicks.

The official language is English and a Norman-French *patois* is also in use (except in Alderney). The principal imports are coal and coke, building material and groceries and provisions, and the chief exports potatoes, tomatoes, grapes, flowers, granite and cattle. The chief town of Jersey is St. Helier, on the south coast; the principal town of Guernsey is St. Peter Port, on the east coast, and of Alderney is St. Anne's A telephone exchange was opened on Alderney in May, 1949 and there is one in Sark. Herm is also connected to Guernsey by telephone.

JERSEY

Lieutenant-Governor and Commander-in-Chief of Jersey, His Excellency Vice-Adm. Sir (John) Michael Villiers, K.C.B., O.B.E. (1963) £3,500
Secretary and A.D.C., Lt.-Comdr. O. M. B. de Las Casas, R.N. (*ret.*).
Bailiff of Jersey, R. H. Le Masurier, D.S.C.
Dean of Jersey, Very Rev. A. S. Giles, C.B., C.B.E.
Attorney-General and Receiver-General, H. F. C. Ereaut.
Solicitor-General, P. L. Crill.
States Treasurer, F. N. Padgham.
Chief Aliens Officer, A. J. Le Brun.
Head Postmaster, J. Anderson.

Year to Jan. 31:	1962	1963
Revenue............	£5,982,469	£5,852,760
Expenditure..........	5,272,655	5,615,737
Public Debt..........	2,707,977	2,639,872

The standard rate of Income Tax is 4*s.* in the £. No super tax or death duties are levied.

GUERNSEY AND DEPENDENCIES

Lieutenant-Governor and Commander-in-Chief of Guernsey, His Excellency Lt.-Gen. Sir (Cyril Frederick) Charles Coleman, K.C.B., C.M.G., D.S.O., O.B.E. (1963).................. £3,500
Secretary and A.D.C., Capt. M. H. T. Mellish, E.R.D.
Bailiff of Guernsey, Sir William Arnold, C.B.E.
Dean of Guernsey, Very Rev. Edward Louis Frossard, M.A.
President of Board of Administration, E. D. Collas.
Attorney General, J. H. Loveridge, M.B.E.
Solicitor General, E. P. Shanks.
Stipendiary Magistrate, F. Gahan, Q.C.
Receiver General, R. H. Collenette.
States Supervisor, L. A. Guillemette, O.B.E.
President, Education Council, Rev. S. W. Gerhold, M.B.E.
Immigration Officer, R. W. Le Lacheur.
Postmaster, A. G. Williams.

	1961	1962
Revenue............	£2,687,415	£2,853,933†
Expenditure.........	2,281,582	2,889,680†
States Funded Debt...	4,455,460	4,634,884
Note Issue..........	560,568	632,283

† Including £91,181 and £83,622 respectively for Alderney.

ALDERNEY

President, Cmdr. S. P. Herivel, C.B.E., D.S.C.
Clerk of the States and Court, P. W. Radice.

SARK

La Dame de Sercq, Mrs. R. W. Hathaway, O.B.E.
Seneschal, W. Baker, M.B.E.

The British Commonwealth of Nations

AREA AND POPULATION.—The total area of the British Commonwealth is estimated to be about 14 million square miles. Details of the areas and populations of the member states and dependencies appear in the following pages and are also tabulated on pp. 196–200. The total population of the British Commonwealth was estimated in 1963 at 740,000,000.

GOVERNMENT.—The Commonwealth is a free association of sovereign independent states, the United Kingdom, Canada, Australia, New Zealand, Ceylon, the Federation of Malaya*, the Federation of Nigeria, Sierra Leone, Jamaica, Trinidad and Tobago, Uganda and the Republics of India, Pakistan, Ghana, Cyprus, Tanganyika and Nigeria, together with their dependencies.

The Commonwealth has no written constitution but its members are bound together by a community of ideals and interest which springs from a common historical background and a common political heritage which in spite of diversities of race and tradition has given rise to a broadly common pattern of institutions, legislative, executive and judicial. Most members of the Commonwealth have certain constitutional features in common. They are parliamentary democracies, their laws being made with the consent of a freely elected parliament after discussion in that parliament, the executive government holding office by virtue of the support of a majority in parliament. Ministers, who must be members of parliament, are collectively responsible for the actions of the executive. With the exception of New Zealand, Pakistan, Ghana, Cyprus, Sierra Leone, Tanganyika and Uganda, the Parliaments of the Commonwealth have two chambers, but in the case of the upper house the method of choosing members varies. Although legislation can be initiated in them, the upper houses are principally revising bodies and the lower houses, elected by secret ballot on a basis of adult suffrage, are dominant. The office of Speaker of the lower house is a feature of all Commonwealth parliaments.

At the head of each of the Parliaments of the Commonwealth (except those of the Federation of Malaya and the Republics) is the Queen, in whose name the administration is carried on. In all member countries of the Commonwealth except the Federation of Malaya and the Republics, Her Majesty is represented by the Governor-General, who in all essential respects holds the same position in relation to the administration of public affairs as is held by the Sovereign in Great Britain. The Governor-General is appointed by the Queen on the recommendation of the Government of the country concerned and is wholly independent of the Government of the United Kingdom. He is in many cases a national of the country in which he holds office. Her Majesty is Queen of the United Kingdom, Canada, Australia, New Zealand, Ceylon, Sierra Leone, Jamaica, Trinidad and Tobago, and Uganda, all of whom owe common allegiance to her, and is the symbol of their free association in the Commonwealth. Those countries which are Republics with Presidents as head of the state and the Federation of Malaya which has one of the Malay Rulers as Head of State, do not owe allegiance to the Queen.

*It was expected that the States of Sabah (British N. Borneo), Sarawak and Singapore would join the Federation of Malaya in a new Federation to be known as Malaysia in the autumn of 1963. British sovereignty and jurisdiction over the former colonies would then terminate.

All members accept her as the symbol of the free association of member nations of the Commonwealth and as such as Head of the Commonwealth.

The status of member nations was defined by the Imperial Conference of 1926 and given legal substance by the *Statute of Westminster*, 1931, in which the Commonwealth nations were described as "autonomous communities within the British Empire, equal in status in no way subordinate one to another, but united by a common allegiance to the Crown and freely associated as members of the British Commonwealth of Nations." (*See above* for modifications as regards Republics and the Federation of Malaya). Other parts of the Commonwealth, such as Colonies, while they may be described as "Commonwealth countries," are not *members* of the Commonwealth.

FEDERATION OF RHODESIA AND NYASALAND.—Following a conference on Central African Federation held in London in January, 1953, and a referendum held in Southern Rhodesia on April 9, the *Rhodesia and Nyasaland Federation Act* was passed by the United Kingdom Parliament on July 14, 1953, and the Federation of Rhodesia and Nyasaland, consisting of the self-governing Colony of Southern Rhodesia and the Protectorates of Northern Rhodesia and Nyasaland, established. It remained in being until 1963.

In December, 1962, as a result of sustained African opposition to the Federation, the British Government accepted the principle that Nyasaland (by that time a self-governing Protectorate) should be allowed to secede. This was followed in April, 1963, by acceptance of the principle that any of the Territories constituting the Federation should be allowed to secede. On June 27, 1963, a conference was held at Victoria Falls to make arrangements for the orderly dissolution of the Federation. It was expected that the Federation would dissolve on December 31, 1963.

WESTERN SAMOA.—Previously administered by New Zealand under a trusteeship agreement with the United Nations, Western Samoa became independent in January, 1962. It has been agreed that the New Zealand Government will assist Western Samoa in the conduct of its international relations. The Commonwealth Prime Ministers have agreed that the territory should be treated as a Commonwealth country pending a decision on whether it will become a member.

CONSULTATION.—Before the Second World War it was customary for an Imperial Conference, a formal gathering of delegates from the Commonwealth nations headed by their Prime Ministers, to meet every few years for discussion of a wide range of common problems. Its functions were purely advisory or consultative, and, as it had neither legislative nor executive authority, its resolutions were not binding on the participating Governments, though normally these Governments conformed to resolutions adopted unanimously. The last Imperial Conference was held in 1937. During the War informal meetings of Ministers were substituted. Imperial Conferences have now been replaced by Commonwealth Prime Ministers' Meetings. There have also been frequent Commonwealth ministerial meetings and conferences on Defence, Finance, etc.

CITIZENSHIP AND NATIONALITY.—Each member of the Commonwealth of Nations defines the citizenship and nationality of its own people and determines the status of other Commonwealth nationals within its own boundaries. In most cases, though not in all, they possess a common status as British subjects (or Commonwealth citizens). Even where there is no such provision for a common status, the Members of the Commonwealth differentiate, in greater or less degree, as regards the grant of privileges, between citizens of the Commonwealth and aliens. The Republic of Ireland, which in 1949 ceased to be a member of the Commonwealth, is not regarded by the other Commonwealth nations as a foreign country or her citizens as foreigners. Although Ambassadors instead of High Commissioners are now exchanged between the Republic of Ireland and Commonwealth countries, her relations with the United Kingdom are conducted through the Commonwealth Relations Office and not through the Foreign Office.

THE JUDICATURE.—The Supreme Judicial Authority of dependencies in the Commonwealth is the Judicial Committee of the Privy Council, before which appeals may be brought (in the form of a petition to the Crown) from Consular Courts and Courts of Vice-Admiralty, and also from the Courts of certain members of the Commonwealth (Australia, New Zealand, Ceylon, the Federation of Nigeria, Sierra Leone, Jamaica, Trinidad and Tobago, and Uganda). Arrangements have been made under which appeals to the Head of the Federation of Malaya may be entertained by the Committee. The Committee consists of such members of the Privy Council as have held or are holding high judicial office, provision being made for the inclusion of judges of other Commonwealth countries. The members of the Commonwealth have each a broadly similar judicial system, judges (except in the Republics, where they are appointed by the President) being appointed by the Governor-General on the advice of the Government concerned. In the Federation of Malaya, puisne judges are appointed by the Head of State on the recommendation of the Judicial and Legal Service Commission. The Supreme Judicial Authority for Great Britain and Northern Ireland is the House of Lords.

DEFENCE.—Each of the independent members of the Commonwealth is completely responsible for its own defence. Although there is no central organization to co-ordinate the defence strategy and resources of the Commonwealth, there is close liaison between the responsible governments and considerable day to day practical co-operation by the Services. This includes ministerial conferences, meetings between High Commissioners and the Governments to which they are accredited, constant exchange of information and correspondence, exchange and training of Service personnel and personal contacts between Service advisers and officials. During the Second World War collaboration between Commonwealth countries was comprehensive and continuous—each of the then members (except the Republic of Ireland) entered the war in 1939.

The territories for whose defence the United Kingdom is responsible play their part and make their contribution to Commonwealth defence as far as their means allow. While the United Kingdom safeguards sea and air communications, using bases in the territories and providing some garrisons, the dependencies are in general responsible for the forces necessary for their own local security (although in some cases the United Kingdom meets the cost).

Membership of the Commonwealth imposes no formal collective security commitment, but individual members may of course assume special international obligations for the maintenance of peace and security. All are members of the United Nations. The United Kingdom and Canada belong to N.A.T.O.; the United Kingdom and Pakistan are in C.E.N.T.O.; the United Kingdom, Australia, New Zealand and Pakistan are members of S.E.A.T.O.; Australia and New Zealand are signatories of the Pacific Security Treaty. The United Kingdom, Australia and New Zealand coordinate their defence plans in South East Asia and the South West Pacific through a joint defence machinery specially devised for this purpose.

COLONIES AND PROTECTORATES.—The United Kingdom, Australia and New Zealand have dependencies for which they are independently responsible. The United Kingdom is responsible for the following colonies, protectorates, protected states, condominiums and leased territories:—

- Aden—colony and the Protectorate of South Arabia. The High Commisioner for Aden and the Protectorate of South Arabia is responsible for Kamaran Island.
- Antigua—colony.
- Bahamas—colony.
- Barbados—colony.
- Basutoland‡—colony.
- Bechuanaland Protectorate‡—protectorate.
- Bermuda—colony.
- British Antarctic Territory—colony.
- British Guiana—colony (with internal self-government).
- British Honduras—colony.
- British Virgin Islands—colony.
- Brunei—protected state.
- Cayman Islands—colony.
- Dominica—colony.
- Falkland Islands—colony with dependencies of South Georgia and South Sandwich.
- Fiji—colony. The Governor of Fiji is also Governor of the Pitcairn Islands Group.
- Gambia—colony and protectorate (with internal self-government).
- Gibraltar—colony.
- Grenada—colony.
- Hong Kong—colony and leased territories.
- Kenya—colony and protectorate (with internal self-government).
- Malta, State of (with internal self-government).
- Mauritius—colony.
- Montserrat—colony.
- North Borneo—colony*.
- St. Christopher—Nevis—Anguilla—colony.
- St. Helena—colony with dependencies (Ascension Island and Tristan da Cunha are the principal).
- St. Lucia—colony.
- St. Vincent—colony.
- Sarawak—colony*.
- Seychelles—colony.
- Singapore, State of.*
- Swaziland‡—protectorate.
- Tonga—protected state.
- Turks and Caicos Islands—colony.
- Western Pacific High Commission—the British Solomon Islands Protectorate, the Gilbert and Ellice Islands Colony†, the Central and Southern Line Islands, and the New Hebrides Condominium, which share a High Commissioner.
- Zanzibar—protectorate (with internal self-government, from June 24, 1963).

* *See* note on Malaysia, p. 693.

† Canton and Enderbury Islands, which are part of the Colony, are administered as an Anglo-American condominium under a 50-year agreement having effect from 1939.

‡ Basutoland, Bechuanaland Protectorate and Swaziland in South Africa are administered by the United Kingdom, through the Commonwealth Relations Office and H.M. High Commissioner in Pretoria.

The Maldive Islands, a protected state, consisting of groups of coral atolls in the Indian Ocean.

Colony (or Settlement): a territory belonging by settlement, conquest or annexation to the British Crown.

Protectorate: a territory not formally annexed, but in respect of which, by treaty, grant, usage, sufferance, and other lawful means, Her Majesty has power and jurisdiction.

Protected State: a territory under a ruler which enjoys Her Majesty's protection, over whose foreign affairs she exercises control but in respect of whose internal affairs she does not exercise jurisdiction.

Condominium: a territory over which responsibility is shared by two administering powers.

Leased Territories: this term applies only to that part of the mainland of China which was in 1893 leased to Great Britain for 99 years and is administered by the Government of Hong Kong.

Other Commonwealth Dependencies.—Australia is responsible for Papua, the trust territory of New Guinea and (jointly with U.K. and New Zealand) Nauru Island. In addition Australia and New Zealand administer a number of island territories and extensive Antarctic areas.

DEVELOPMENT AND FINANCE.—Complete financial autonomy is enjoyed by all members of the Commonwealth. In some countries, customs tariffs are lower for merchandise of Commonwealth origin than for importations from foreign countries. The British Government provides guarantees for the capital issues made by dependent territories and also provides budgetary assistance in many cases as well as direct loans and grants to assist development.

Under the *Colonial Development and Welfare Act*, 1940, annual sums of £5,000,000 for Development and £500,000 for Research were made available from United Kingdom Funds for 10 years from 1941. An Act passed in 1945 extended the grant period from 1951 to 1956, making £120,000,000 available in that period subject to a maximum of £17,500,000 in any one year, of which not more than £1,000,000 might be spent on research. A further Act in 1950 increased the annual amount to £25,000,000 of which not more than £2,500,000 could be drawn in any one year for research and increased the total provision to £140,00,000 over the period 1946–56. *The Colonial Development and Welfare Act*, 1955, extended the life of the previous Acts to March 31, 1960, and provided an additional sum of £80,000,000, which, added to unspent balances remaining, made available for expenditure nearly £120,000,000, during 1955–60. In 1959 these Acts were extended to March 31, 1964, and a further £95,000,000 was made available. With the unspent balance this provides over £140,000,000 for 1959–64.

The *Commonwealth Development Act*, 1963, provides a further total of £25,000,000 for Colonial development and welfare, in addition to the unspent balance outstanding of £43,000,000, making a total of £68,000,000 available for the period 1963–1966. The Act provides also Exchequer loan funds of £5,000,000 in addition to £38,000,000 still outstanding under previous development and welfare legislation.

COMMONWEALTH SCIENTIFIC LIAISON OFFICES (LONDON)

Africa House, Kingsway, W.C.2

The Commonwealth Scientific Liaison Offices exist to keep in touch with scientific developments in the United Kingdom, to deal with scientific enquiries from and to their home countries and to act as scientific advisers to the Commonwealth High Commissioners and Governments concerned.

Joint headquarters were set up in May, 1948. Liaison offices of the various countries continue to act as separate autonomous units but share common services to the cost of which the Commonwealth countries contribute in agreed proportions. B.C.S.O. (London) serves as a headquarters for Commonwealth scientists visiting the United Kingdom. *Secretary*, E. D. A. Davies.

Countries represented (with names of their Chief Scientific Liaison Officers):
UNITED KINGDOM.—M. A. Vernon (D.S.I.R.). CANADA.—J. B. Marshall. AUSTRALIA.—W. Hartley. NEW ZEALAND.—V. Armstrong. INDIA.—A. M. D'Rozario. PAKISTAN.—C. K. Reheem. RHODESIA AND NYASALAND.—J. E. C. Coventry.

BRITISH TRADE COMMISSIONERS

CANADA.—*Ottawa* (56 Sparks Street), A. Currall.
Montreal (635 Dorchester Boulevard W.), A. Heckle.
Toronto (119 Adelaide Street W.), J. R. W. Wilby, C.M.G.
Vancouver (602 W. Hastings Street), W. K. Ward.
Winnipeg (333 Broadwav Avenue), R. Fox.
Regina (Derrick Building, 2431 11th Avenue), M. W. R. Mustoe.
Edmonton (Bank of Montreal Building, Jasper Avenue), G. R. Latham.
Halifax (5425 Spring Garden Road), H. F. Codling.

AUSTRALIA.—*Canberra* (Commonwealth Avenue), H. W. Woodruff.
Sydney (London Assurance House), M. J. Marshall.
Melbourne (The Colonial Mutual Life Building, 330 Collins Street), J. W. Stoodley.
Brisbane (M. L. C. Building), N. A. Pinch.
Perth (189 St. George's Terrace), B. A. F. Pennock.
Adelaide (15 Franklin Street), M. E. Browne.

NEW ZEALAND.—*Wellington* (Customhouse Quay), J. L. Reading, C.M.G.
Auckland (56 Shotland Street), J. D. Leithead.
Christchurch (112 Hereford Street), A. Vine.

CEYLON.—*Colombo* (Prince Street), J. F. Saunders, M.B.E.

FEDERATION OF MALAYA.—*Kuala Lumpur* (1 Suleiman Road), J. R. Cross.

FEDERATION OF NIGERIA.—*Lagos* (Private Mail Bag 2060), C. E. Dymond.
Enugu (P.O. Box 324, Garden Avenue), D. H. Mather.
Ibadan (Co-operative Bank Building), J. R. Bolton.
Kaduna (5 Ahmadu Bello Way), G. J. Swaffield.

INDIA.—*Delhi* (Chanakyapuri, New Delhi), H. Bailey, C.M.G.
Calcutta (1 Harington Street) (vacant).
Madras (6 Armenian Street), F. F. D. Ward, M.B.E.
Bombay (Mercantile Bank Building) (vacant).

PAKISTAN.—*Karachi* (Finlay House), R. W. B. Carter.
Lahore (1st Floor, Gardee Trust Building, Napier Road, P.O. Box 287), J. Stafford.
Chittagong (Quaid-e-Azam Road), K. W. Chesterman.
Dacca (Adamjee Court), W. J. Cheesman.

JAMAICA.—*Kingston* (Barclay's Bank Building), J. N. McKelvie.

HONG KONG.—(P.O. Box 528), A. Wooller.

IRISH REPUBLIC.—*Dublin* (30 Merrion Square), G. L. Pearson, M.C.

RHODESIA AND NYASALAND.—*Salisbury* (P.O. Box 984), G. W. Brazendale, C.M.G.

TRINIDAD.—*Port of Spain* (P.O. Box 225), G. Booth.

Canada

AREA AND POPULATION

Provinces or Territories and Capitals	Area (English Sq. Miles). Land and Water	Population	
		Census, 1956	Census, 1961
Alberta (Edmonton)	255,285	1,123,116	1,331 944
British Columbia (Victoria)	366,255	1,398,464	1,629,082
Manitoba (Winnipeg)	251,000	850,040	921,686
New Brunswick (Fredericton)	28,354	554,616	597,936
Newfoundland (St. John's)	156,185	415,074	457,853
Nova Scotia (Halifax)	21,425	694,717	737,007
Ontario (Toronto)	412,582	5,404,933	6,236,092
Prince Edward Island (Charlottetown)	2,184	99,285	104,629
Quebec (Quebec)	594,860	4,628,378	5,259,211
Saskatchewan (Regina)	251,700	880,665	925,181
Yukon Territory (Whitehorse)	207,076	12,190	14,628
North West Territories (*Ottawa*)	1,304,903	19,313	22,998
Total	3,851,809	16,080,791	18,238,247

Land Area, 3,560,238 square miles; Water Area, 291,571 square miles.

Of the total immigration of 74,586 in 1962, 15,603 were from the British Isles, 11,643 from the United States and 47,340 from over 60 other countries.

Increase of the People

Census Year	Population			Decennial Increase	Immigrants during Census Year
	Males	Females	Total		
1861	..	..	3,229,633	..	13,589
1871	1,869,264	1,819,993	3,689,257	459,624	27,773
1881	2,188,854	2,135,956	4,324,810	635,553	47,991
1891	2,460,471	2,372,768	4,833,239	508,429	82,165
1901	2,751,708	2,619,607	5,371,315	538,076	55,747
1911	3,821,995	3,384,648	7,206,643	1,835,328	331,288
1921	4,529,643	4,258,306	8,787,949	1,581,306	91,728
1931	5,374,541	5,002,245	10,376,786	1,588,837	27,530
1941	5,900,536	5,606,119	11,506,655	1,129,869	9,329
1951	7,088,873	6,920,556	14,009,429	2,502,774	194,391
1956	8,151,879	7,928,912	16,080,791	..	164,857
1961	9,218,893	9,019,354	18,238,247	4,228,818	71,689

Origins	1951	1961
British Races	6,709,685	7,996,669
English	3,630,344	4,195,175
Scottish	1,547,470	1,902,302
Irish	1,439,635	1,753,351
Other	92,236	145,841
European Races	6,872,889	9,657,195
French	4,319,167	5,540,346
Austrian	32,231	106,535
Belgian	35,148	61,382
Czech and Slovak	63,959	73,061
Finnish	43,745	59,436
German	619,995	1,049 599
Hungarian	60,460	126,220
Italian	152,245	450,351
Jewish	181,670	173,344
Netherland	264,267	429,679
Polish	219,845	323,517
Roumanian	23,601	43,805
Russian	91,279	119 168
Scandinavian	283,024	386,534
Ukrainian	395,043	473,337
Other	87,210	240,881
Asiatic Races	72,827	121,753
Chinese	32,528	58,197
Japanese	21,663	29,157
Other	18,636	34,399
Indian and Eskimo	165,607	220,121
All other	188,421	242,509
Totals	14,009,429	18,238,247

Religions	1951	1961
Roman Catholic	6,069,496	8,342,826
United Church of Canada	2,867,271	3,664,008
Anglican Church of Canada	2,060,720	2,409,068
Presbyterian	781,747	818,558
Baptist	519,585	593,553
Lutheran	444,923	662,744
Jewish	204,836	254,368
Ukrainian (Greek) Catholic	190,831	189,653
Greek Orthodox	172,271	239,766
Mennonite	125 938	152,452
Pentecostal	95,131	143,877
Salvation Army	70,275	92,054
Mormon	32,888	50,016
Church of Christ, Disciples	14,920	19,512
Christian Science	20,795	19,466
Adventist	21,398	25,999
Confucian and Buddhist	13,975	16,700
Others	302 429	543,627
Totals	14,009,429	18,238,247

Indian population (1951) 155,874; (1961), 208,286. Eskimo population (1951) 9,733; (1961), 11,835.

Canada was originally discovered by Cabot in 1497, but its history dates only from 1534, when the French took possession of the country. The first permanent settlement at Port Royal (now Annapolis), Nova Scotia, was founded in 1605, and Quebec was founded in 1608. In 1759 Quebec was captured by the British forces under General Wolfe, and in 1763 the whole territory of Canada became a possession of Great Britain by the Treaty of Paris of that year. Nova Scotia was ceded in 1713 by the Treaty of Utrecht, the Provinces of New Brunswick and Prince Edward Island being subsequently formed out of it. British Columbia was formed into a Crown colony in 1858 having previously been a part of the Hudson Bay Territory, and was united to Vancouver Island in 1866.

Canada occupies the whole of the northern part of the North American Continent (with the exception of Alaska), from 49° North latitude to the North Pole, and from the Pacific to the Atlantic Ocean. In Eastern Canada, the southernmost point is Pelee Island in Lake Erie, at 41° 41'.

Relief.—The relief of Canada is dominated by the mountain ranges running north and south on the west side of the Continent, by the Pre-Cambrian shield on the east, with, in between, the northern extension of the North American Plain. From the physiographic point of view Canada has six main divisions. These are: (1) Appalachian-Acadian Region, (2) the Canadian Shield, (3) the St. Lawrence-Great Lakes Lowland, (4) the Interior Plains, (5) the Cordilleran Region and (6) the Arctic Archipelago. The first region occupies all that part of Canada lying southeast of the St. Lawrence. In general, the relief is an alternation of highlands and lowlands, and is hilly rather than mountainous. The lowlands area seldom rises over 600 feet above sea level. The great Canadian Shield comprises more than half of the area. The interior as a whole, is an undulating, low plateau (general level 1,000 to 1,500 feet), with the more rugged relief lying along the southern border in Northern Quebec and Labrador. Throughout the whole area water or muskeg-filled depressions separate irregular hills and ridges, 150 to 200 feet in elevation. Newfoundland as an outlying portion of the shield consists of glaciated, low rolling terrain broken here and there by mountains. The flat relief of the St. Lawrence-Great Lakes lowland varies from 500 feet in the east to 1,700 feet south of Georgian Bay. The whole area in the western part slopes gently to the Great Lakes. The most striking relief is provided by the eastward facing scarp of the Niagara escarpment (elevation 250 to 300 feet). The Interior plains, comprising the Prairie Provinces, slope eastward and northward a few feet per mile. The descent from west to east is made from 5,000 feet to less than 1,000 feet, in three distinct levels, with each new level being marked by an eastward facing coteau or scarp. Horizontal strata and peneplanation make for slight relief of the level to rolling type. Five fairly well-developed topographic divisions mark out the Cordilleran region of western Canada. These are: (1) coastal ranges, largely above 5,000 feet with deep fiords and glaciated valleys, (2) the interior plateau, around 3,500 feet and comparatively level, (3) the Selkirk ranges, largely above 5,000 feet, (4) the Rocky Mountains with their chain of 10,000 to 12,000-feet peaks, and (5) the Peace River or Tramontane region with its rolling diversified country. The Arctic Archipelago, with its plateau-like character has an elevation between 500 and 1,000 feet, though in Baffin Land and Ellesmere Island the mountain ranges rise to nearly 7,000 feet. Two tremendous waterway systems, the St. Lawrence and the Mackenzie, providing thousands of miles of water highway, occupy a broad area of lowland with their dominant axis following the edge of the shield.

Climate.—The climate in the eastern and central portions presents greater extremes than in corresponding latitudes in Europe, but in the south-western portion of the Prairie Region and the southern portions of the Pacific slope the climate is milder. Spring, summer, and autumn are of about seven to eight months' duration, and the winter four to five months.

GOVERNMENT

The Constitution of Canada has its source in the British North America Act of 1867 which formed a Dominion, under the name of Canada, of the four provinces: Ontario, Quebec, New Brunswick and Nova Scotia; to this Federation the other Provinces have subsequently been admitted. Under this Act Canada came into being on July 1, 1867 (Dominion Day), and under the Statute of Westminster, which received the royal assent on Dec. 11, 1931, Canada and the Provinces were exempted (in common with other self-governing Dominions of the Commonwealth of Nations) from the operation of the Colonial Laws Validity Act, the Statute of Westminster having removed all limitations with regard to the legislative autonomy of the Dominions. Provinces admitted since 1867 are: Manitoba (1870), British Columbia (1871), Prince Edward Island (1873), Alberta and Saskatchewan (1905) and Newfoundland (1949).

The Executive power is vested in a Governor-General appointed by the Sovereign on the advice of the Canadian Ministry and aided by a Privy Council

FLAG.—Red shield with coat of arms of Canada in fly; Union Jack in first quarter next to staff.

GOVERNOR-GENERAL AND STAFF

Governor-General and Commander-in-Chief, His Excellency Major-General the Right Hon. GEORGES PHILIAS VANIER, D.S.O., M.C., *born* April 23, 1888, *appointed* Aug. 1, 1959.

Secretary to the Governor-General, E. U. Butler.

Assistant Secretary, Col. A. G. Cherrier, O.B.E., C.D.

Comptroller of the Household, Commander F. J. D. Pemberton, C.D., R.C.N.

Press Secretary, G. Robillard.

Attaché, M. Pitfield.

Aides-de-Camp, Lieut R. de C. Nantal, R.C.N.; Flight Lieut. P. V. Glasheen; Capt. S. C. Ross, R.C.E.

THE CANADIAN MINISTRY

THE FEDERAL CABINET

(As at July 16, 1963)

Prime Minister, Rt. Hon. Lester Bowles Pearson .... † $25,000

Minister of Justice and Attorney General, Hon. Lionel Chevrier 15,000

Secretary of State for External Affairs, Hon. Paul J. J. Martin 15,000

Minister without Portfolio and Leader of the Government in the Senate, Hon. William Ross Macdonald $15,000

Secretary of State of Canada, Hon. John Whitney Pickersgill 15,000

Minister of National Defence, Hon. Paul Theodore Hellyer 15,000

Minister of Finance and Receiver General, Hon. Walter Lockhart Gordon 15,000

Trade and Commerce, Hon. Mitchell Sharp 15,000

Postmaster General, Hon. Azellus Denis...	$15,000
Minister of Transport, Hon. George James McIlraith	15,000
Mines and Technical Surveys, Hon. William Moore Benidickson	15,000
Northern Affairs and National Resources, Hon. Arthur Laing	15,000
President of the Queen's Privy Council for Canada, Hon. Maurice Lamontagne	15,000
Minister of National Revenue, Hon. John Richard Garland	15,000
Associate Minister of National Defence, Hon. Lucien Cardin	15,000
Minister of Labour, Hon. Allan Joseph MacEachen	15,000
Public Works, Hon. Jean Paul Deschatelets	15,000
Fisheries, Hon. Hedard Robichaud	15,000
Solicitor General, Hon. J. Watson MacNaught	15,000
Minister of Veterans' Affairs, Hon. Roger Teillet	15,000
National Health and Welfare, Hon. Judy LaMarsh	15,000
Defence Production, Hon. Charles Mills Drury	15,000
Citizenship and Immigration, Hon. Guy Favreau	15,000
Forestry, Hon. John Robert Nicholson	15,000
Agriculture, Hon. Harry Hays	15,000
Minister without Portfolio, Hon. René Tremblay	15,000

Leader of the Opposition, Rt. Hon. John George Diefenbaker, Q.C.	15,000

CANADIAN REPRESENTATION ABROAD

High Commissioners

United Kingdom.—Hon. George Drew, Q.C., Canada House, Trafalgar Square, London, S.W.1.
Australia.—E. W. T. Gill.
Ceylon.—J. George
Cyprus.—A. J. Andrew.
Ghana.—D. M. Cornett.
India.—C. A. Ronning.
Jamaica.—G. C. McInnes.
Malaya.—C. E. McGaughey.
New Zealand.—K. J. Burbridge.
Nigeria and Sierra Leone.—T. Carter, M.C.
Pakistan.—(vacant).
Tanganyika and Uganda.—N. F. H. Berlis.
Trinidad and Tobago.—E. H. Gilmour.

Ambassadors

Argentina, Paraguay and Uruguay.—L. Mayrand.
Austria.—Miss R. M. Meagher.
Belgium and Luxemburg.—S. D. Pierce.
Brazil.—J. A. Chapdelaine.
Cameroon, Central African Republic, Congo, Chad, Gaboon.—F. Charpentier, M.B.E.
Chile, G. B. Summers.
Colombia and Ecuador.—T. F. M. Newton.
Costa Rica, Honduras, Nicaragua, Panama and Salvador.—J. L. Délisle.
Cuba and Haiti.—G. P. Kidd.
Czechoslovakia.—J. A. McCordick.
Denmark.—H. Allard.
Finland.—J. H. Cleveland.
France.—P. Dupuy, C.M.G.
German Federal Republic.—J. K. Starnes.
Greece.—A. Barrette.
Indonesia.—J. P. Sigvaldason.
Irish Republic.—A. Rive.
Israel.—A. J. Andrew.
Italy.—J. Léger.
Japan.—R. P. Bower.
Lebanon and Iraq.—P. A. Beaulieu, Q.C.
Mexico and Guatemala.—W. A. Irwin.
Netherlands.—W. F. Bull.
Norway and Iceland.—J. L. E. Couillard.
Persia.—T. P. Malone.
Peru and Bolivia.—F. M. Tovell.
Poland.—J. A. Irwin.
Portugal.—J. Morin.
S. Africa.—J. J. Hurley, O.B.E., E.D.
Spain and Morocco.—J. Bruchési.
Sweden.—A. K. Graham. Q.C.
Switzerland and Tunisia.—H. F. Feaver.
Turkey.—B. M. Williams.
U.S.S.R..—R. A. D. Forde.
United Arab Republic and Sudan.—(vacant).
U.S.A.—C. S. A. Ritchie.
Venezuela.—Y. Beaulue.
Yugoslavia.—G. G. Crean.

REPRESENTATIVES IN CANADA

High Commissioners

UNITED KINGDOM

High Commissioner, Sir Henry Lintott, K.C.M.G., Earnscliffe, Ottawa (1963).
Deputy High Commissioner, L. J. D. Wakely, O.B.E.
Economic Adviser and Senior Trade Commissioner, A. Currall.
Counsellor, B. J. Greenhill.
Naval Adviser, Capt. T. L. Martin. R.N.
Army Adviser, Brig. R. K. Jones, M.B.E.
Air Force Adviser, Air Commodore R. J. B. Burns, C.B.E.
Director, U.K. Information Service, R. McC. Samples, D.S.O., O.B.E.
1st Secretary (Agriculture and Food), C. H. Wake, I.S.O.
Adviser (Pensions), R. A. E. Tow.
Adviser (Defence Research and Supply), C. J. Francis.

Australia.—D. O. Hay, C.B.E., D.S.O.
Ceylon.—Sir Senarat Gunawardena.
Ghana.—C. T. Nylander.
India.—C. S. Jha.
Jamaica.—E. A. Maynier, O.B.E.
New Zealand.—J. S. Reid.
Pakistan.—S. M. Khan.
Trinidad and Tobago.—W. A. Rose.

Ambassadors

Argentina.—E. M. Villa.
Austria.—Dr. E. F. Buresch.
Belgium.—G. D. de la Chevalerie.
Brazil.—S. Correa da Costa.
Burma.—J. Barrington.
Cameroon.—J. Kuoh-Moukouri.
Chile.—M. Rodriguez.
China.—S. Hsuh.
Colombia.—Dr. F. J. Ocampo.
Cuba.—Dr. A. Cruz.
Czechoslovakia.—Dr. J. Tauer.
Denmark.—J. Knox.
Dominican Republic.—Dr. A. Rincon-Jaquez.
Finland.—A. Lehtinen.
France.—R. Bousquet.
German Federal Republic.—H. Siegfried.

---

† NOTE.—In every case—including the Prime Minister's—a sessional allowance of $8,000 *per annum* is paid to a Minister of the Crown as a member of either the Senate or the House of Commons of Canada. A motor-car allowance of $2,000 *per annum* is paid to Ministers holding portfolios. Since 1945 an expense allowance of $2,000 has been paid to Members of Parliament including Ministers of the Crown.

Greece.—J. D. Kalergis.
Guatemala.—Dr. C. Garcia-Bauer.
Haiti.—H. Hippolyte.
Iceland.—T. Thors.
Indonesia.—R. M. Soenarso (*Chargé d' Affaires*).
Iraq.—A. H. Sulaiman.
Irish Republic.—W. P. Fay.
Israel.—Y. D. Herzog.
Italy.—Baron C. de Ferrariis Salzano.
Japan.—N. Ushiba.
Lebanon.—E. Khayat.
Luxemburg.—G. Heisbourg.
Mexico.—Dr. R. Urdaueta de la Tour.
Morocco.—A. Bengelloun.
Netherlands.—A. H. J. Lovink.
Nicaragua.—Dr. G. Sevilla-Sacusa.
Norway.—B. Stabell.
Panama.—A. G. Arango.
Persia.—N. Kia.
Peru.—M. de la Fuente.
Poland.—Z. L. Wolniak.
Portugal.—Dr. E. Brazao.
S. Africa.—W. Dirkse van Schalkwyk.
Spain.—F. de Iturriaga, Marqués del Romeral.
Sweden.—R. Bagge.
Switzerland.—H. W. Gasser.
Tunisia.—T. Slim.
Turkey.—T. Carim.
U.S.S.R.—I. F. Shpedko.
United Arab Republic.—Adbel Hamid Ibrahim Seoud.
U.S.A.—W. W. Butterworth.
Uruguay.—E. Benavides (*Chargé d'Affaires*).
Venezuela.—Dr. M. R. Egana.
Yugoslavia.—D. Belovski.

THE LEGISLATURE

Parliament consists of a Senate and a House of Commons. The *Senate* consists of 102 members, nominated for life by the Governor-General, distributed between the various provinces thus: 24 for *Ontario*, 24 for *Quebec*, 10 for *Nova Scotia*, 10 for *New Brunswick*, 4 for *Prince Edward Island*, 6 for *Newfoundland*, 6 for *British Columbia*, 6 for *Manitoba*, 6 for *Alberta*, and 6 for *Saskatchewan*; each Senator must be thirty years old, a resident in the province for which he is appointed, a natural-born or naturalized subject of the Queen, and the owner of a property qualification amounting to $4,000. The Speaker of the Senate is chosen by the Government of the day. The *House of Commons* is elected every five years at longest.

The House of Commons has 265 members. Representation by provinces is as follows: Newfoundland 7, Prince Edward Island 4, Nova Scotia 12, New Brunswick 10, Quebec 75, Ontario 85, Manitoba 14, Saskatchewan 17, Alberta 17, British Columbia 22, Yukon 1, Northwest Territories 1.

The Senate.

Speaker of the Senate, Hon. Maurice Bourget (*with Member's annual indemnity $8,000, residence allowance $3,000, expence allowance $2,000, and motor-car allowance $1,000*) $9,000
Clerk of the Senate & Clerk of the Parliaments, John F. MacNeill, Q.C. $18,000

The House of Commons.

Speaker of the House of Commons, Hon. Alan A. Macnaughton, Q.C. (*with Member's annual indemnity $8,000, expense allowance $2,000, car allowance $1,000 and in lieu of residence $3,000*) . . . $9,000
Deputy Speaker, Lucien Lamoureux (*with Member's annual indemnity $8,000, expense allowance $2,000, and residence allowance, $1,500*) $6,000
Clerk of the House of Commons, Leon J. Raymond, O.B.E $18,000

THE JUDICATURE

The Judicature.—Justice is administered, as in England, by judges, police magistrates, and justices of the peace, of whom the first-named are appointed by the Governor-General, for life, from among the foremost men at the Bar in the several provinces. The highest court is the Supreme Court of Canada, composed of a Chief Justice and eight puisne judges, and holding three sessions in the year at Ottawa. The only other Dominion Court, viz., the Exchequer Court of Canada, is presided over by separate judges, and its sittings may be held anywhere in Canada. The Provincial Courts include the Court of Chancery, Court of Queen's Bench, Court of Error and Appeal, Superior Courts, County Courts, General Sessions, and Division Courts. The duties of coroners are generally analogous to those in force in England, as are also methods of civil and criminal procedure, while trial by jury prevails.

Supreme Court of Canada.

Chief Justice of Canada, Hon. R. Taschereau, P.C. $27,500
Puisne Judges, Hon. J. R. Cartwright; Hon. G. Fauteux; Hon. D. C. Abbott, P.C.; Hon. R. Martland; Hon. W. Judson; Hon. R. A. Ritchie; Hon. E. M. Hall; Hon. W. Spence . . . . . each $22,500
Registrar of the Supreme Court, K. J. Matheson, Q.C. $11,500

Exchequer Court of Canada.

President of the Exchequer Court of Canada, Hon. J. T. Thorson, P.C. $18,500
Puisne Judges, Hon. J. C. A. Cameron; Hon. J. D. Kearney; Hon. J. Dumoulin; Hon. A. L. Thurlow; Hon. C. Noel; Hon. A. A. Cattanach $16,900
Registrar, G. Belleau, Q.C $9,000

NATIONAL DEFENCE

All matters relating to defence are the responsibility of the Minister of National Defence. Under his direction the Chiefs of Staff for the Navy, the Army and the Air Force are responsible for the control and administration of their respective Services. The Chairman of the Defence Research Board is responsible to the Minister for defence research and related matters.

Navy.—The Royal Canadian Navy is administered by Naval Headquarters in Ottawa through principal commands at Halifax, N.S., and Esquimalt, B.C., and the Royal Canadian Naval Reserve through a naval command at Hamilton, Ontario.

In March, 1963, the R.C.N. had 59 ships in commission, including one light fleet carrier, 23 destroyer escorts, 18 frigates, 10 minesweepers, 2 escort maintenance ships, 3 patrol craft, one submarine and one diving depot ship. On March 31, 1963, the strength of the Regular Force was 21,476, and that of the Reserves was 3,583.

Army.—The Canadian Army comprises the Canadian Army (Regular) and the Reserves. The Regular Army consists of a field force of four Infantry Brigade Groups, and training, logistic support and headquarters units. One Infantry Brigade Group is stationed in Europe as part of NATO forces. Forces in Canada are organized into four Commands and ten Military Areas, with Army Headquarters at Ottawa, Ontario. The Reserves include the Canadian Army (Militia), the Regular Reserve, the Supplementary Reserve, the Canadian Officers' Training Corps, the Cadet Services of Canada and the Reserve Militia. Additional to, but not an integral part of, the Canadian Army are services colleges, officially authorised cadet corps, rifle associations and clubs. The strength of the Canadian Army (Regular), at 31 Mar, 1963, was 49,760 officers and men and that of the Canadian Army (Militia), 53,872.

Air Force.—The Royal Canadian Air Force is administered by Air Force Headquarters at Ottawa through: Air Defence Command, St. Hubert, P.Q.: 5 Air Division, Victoria, B.C.; 1 Air Division, Metz, France; Air Transport Command, Trenton, Ont.; Air Material Command, Rockcliffe, Ont.; Maritime Air Command, Halifax, N.S.; Training Command, Winnipeg, Man. On March 31, 1963, the R.C.A.F. had 32 squadrons in service, 21 being regular and 11 auxiliary. The strength of the R.C.A.F. (Regular) was 52,458 and of the R.C.A.F. (Auxiliary) 2,223.

EDUCATION AND LANGUAGE

Education is under the control of the Provincial Governments, the cost of the publicly controlled schools being met by local taxation, aided by provincial grants. There were (1962–63) 23 730 publicly controlled schools with 4 350,105 pupils. In addition there were 182 818 pupils in private elementary, secondary and commercial schools. There are special schools for Indians with 32,031 pupils (1962–63). At December 1, 1962, there were 39 universities and about 361 other institutions of higher education with an estimated full-time university grade enrolment of 143,188.

Canada has two official languages, English and French. At the last census about 59 per cent. of the total population gave English and about 28 per cent. gave French as their native tongue. Some 2,231,000 (or 12 per cent.) are bilingual. Owing to the spread of education the percentage of illiterates is very low: 232,447 were unable to speak English or French.

VITAL STATISTICS

BIRTHS, DEATHS AND MARRIAGES, 1962.

Province	Births	Deaths	Marriages
Alberta	38,804	9,264	10,423
British Columbia	38,128	14,912	11,196
Manitoba	22,918	7,453	6,354
New Brunswick	16,467	4,788	4,382
Newfoundland	15,064	3,198	3,274
Nova Scotia	19,432	6,342	5,256
Ontario	156,053	52 156	44,454
P.E.I.	2,805	1,056	677
Quebec	135 000	37,142	37,038
Saskatchewan	23,341	7,004	6,044
Yukon	547	75	109
N.W. Territories	1,134	309	174
	469,693	143,699	129,381

Canada's Birth Rate per 1,000 population (1962) 25·3; Death Rate 7·7; Marriage Rate 7·0; Divorces (1962) 6,709.

FINANCE

During 1962 the average market rate for the U.S. dollar was 106.89 cents in terms of Canadian funds. On May 2, 1962, the Canadian dollar was devalued to 92.5 U.S. cents.

Year ended March 31	Total Revenue	Total Expenditure
	$	$
1960	5,289,751 209	5,702,861,053
1961	5,617,679,854	5,958,100,946
1962	5,729 623 724	6,520 645 674
1963	5,876,100,000	6,585,100,000

TRADE BY COUNTRIES, 1962

Country	To Canada	From Canada
	$	$
United Kingdom	563,062,214	909 040,688
Australia	45,215,786	104 964,922
New Zealand	12,001,963	26 784,149
South Africa	16,952,196	37,524,663
Ghana	7,036,212	8,3[illegible]9,561
India	43,478 980	29 632,823
Pakistan	2,500 994	10 754,951
Ceylon	14,763,056	2,006,639
Malaya	27,739,841	5,453,061
British Guiana	23,374,663	5,102,146
Barbados	3,169 994	4,481,307
Jamaica	39,720,565	21,890,962
Leeward and Windward Is.	1,686,138	5,642,212
Trinidad and Tobago	14,100,091	14,816,647
U.S.A.	4,299,539,303	3,608,438,506
Arabia (Saudi)	40,550,538	3,256,840
Argentina	5,649,195	22,546,089
Austria	7,971,327	7,315,630
Belgium and Luxemburg	48 682 009	68,168,982
Brazil	31,599,504	28,481,474
Chile	1,116,578	13,277,984
China (except Taiwan)	4,521,079	147,430,240
China (Taiwan)	2,909 523	4,3[illegible]7,281
Colombia	15 658,040	19,887,351
Costa Rica	6,2[illegible]9,423	3,473,170
Cuba	2,803,112	10,877,648
Czechoslovakia	9 032,805	3,522,188
Denmark	13,278,312	6,086,985
Dominican Republic	1,911,896	8,488,111
Ecuador	8,611,[illegible]35	3,776,771
Finland	1,939 393	5,239,899
France	56,159,700	57,560,620
Germany:		
Fed. Republic	141,199,476	177,700,289
Eastern	880,755	148,117
Greece	1,093,568	9,234,920
Guatemala	1,795,697	2,705,275
Haiti	565,763	1,276,672
Honduras	7,617,065	898,632
Rep. of Ireland	4,82[illegible],810	10,329,471
Israel	5,646,141	6 231,683
Italy	51,859,249	74 521,434
Japan	125,358 920	214,573,193
Kuwait	10,033 659	1,040,242
Mexico	24,443 757	41,266,656
Netherlands	37,048,844	76,940,367
Neth. Antilles	35,856,105	1,793,182
Norway	16,109,105	69 054,095
Panama	8,321,443	5,645,409
Persia	31,736,182	5,293,093
Peru	3,224,845	8,139,711
Philippines	1,446,836	18,544,977
Portugal	5,998,302	2,562,698
Puerto Rico	2,712 734	12,710,978
Spain	8,463,253	15,416,359
Sweden	25,873,388	18,230,315
Switzerland	28,040,275	23 890,676
Thailand	1,031,358	3,471,659
Turkey	1,472 2[illegible]8	977,772
U.S.S.R.	1,776,711	3,296,596
Venezuela	224,274,858	42,327,984
Commonwealth Countries	881,562,996	1,240,036,457
For. Countries	5,376,250,551	4,938,594,622
Totals	6,257,813,547	6,178,631,079

DEBT

Year ended March 31	Gross Public Debt	Net Public Debt
	$	$
1957	18,335,797,515	11,007,651,158
1958	18,418,541,848	11,046,273,890
1959	20,246,773,669	11,678,389,860
1960	20,086,367,010	12,089,194,003
1961	21,602,836,960	12,437,115,095
1962	22,907,814,464	13,228,137,045
1963	24,811,900,000	13,937,100,000

The net amount of Canada Savings Bonds of all series outstanding was $4,619,000,000 on Dec. 31, 1962, compared with $4,080,000,000 on Dec. 31, 1961.

Banking.—There were 8 chartered banks on June 30, 1963. The balance of undrawn deposits in the Post Office Savings Bank on March 31, 1963 was $25,880,479. The deposits in the Quebec savings banks on March 31, 1963, were $335,560,105.

CANADIAN PRODUCTION

Agriculture.—About 8 per cent. of the total land area of Canada is classified as farm land and approximately half of this is under cultivation, the remainder being woodland or suitable only for grazing purposes. Three quarters of the land at present cultivated is found in the prairie region of Western Canada. In 1962 there were 172,551,051 acres under cultivation and 11·7 per cent. of the population of Canada were engaged in farming.

The total gross farm value of principal field crops produced on 60,860,000 acres in 1962 was $1,437,587,000.

Canadian grain crops (in thousands of bushels):

ALL CANADA	1960	1961	1962
Wheat.......	518,379	283,394	557,554
Oats.........	398,505	283 65	493,010
Barley.......	193,473	112,640	165,888
Rye.........	10,221	6,519	12,644
Flaxseed......	22,477	14,318	10,685

Live Stock.—On June 1, 1962, the live stock included 1,477,200 horses, 12,075,000 cattle, 1,433,000 sheep, 4,973,000 swine and 72,922,000 poultry. The total milk production in 1962 was 19,277,755,000 lb.; creamery butter, 361,498,000 lb.; cheddar cheese, 116,558,000 lb.; evaporated whole milk, 287,395,000 lb.

Fur farming.—There were 2,173 fur farms in Canada in 1961, 61 of which were fox farms, and 1,578 mink farms, the remainder being divided between raccoon, marten, fisher, fitch, lynx, chinchilla, nutria, ermine and skunk.

Fisheries.—The total value of the catch marketed in 1961 was $222,879,000, including Atlantic Coast $124,810,000; Pacific Coast $66,668,000; inland $19,311,000. The number of fishermen in 1961 was 78,360.

Newsprint.—Newsprint produced (1961) amounted to 6,718,000 tons valued at $809,602,000.

Imports.—The principal imports in 1962 were machinery (non-farm) and parts ($676,077,000); automobile parts ($392,687,000); crude petroleum ($304,898,000); electrical apparatus ($325,316,000); rolling mill products ($111,486,000); farm implements and machinery ($253,738,000); fruits ($171,327,000); tractors and parts ($140,287,000); passenger automobiles ($151,245,000); engines and boilers ($178,878,000); aircraft and parts ($201,741,000); cotton products ($95,925,000); plastics and products ($119,708,000); aluminium and products ($102,927,000).

Exports.—The principal exports in 1962 were newsprint paper ($753,060,000); planks and boards ($296,747,000); wheat ($601,756,000); wood pulp ($369,902,000); aluminium and products ($293,007,000); nickel ($317,352,000); copper and products ($210,951,000); iron ore ($220,522,000); uranium ores and concentrates ($166,009,000); asbestos and products ($136,808,000); machinery, except farm ($122,528,000); crude petroleum ($232,497,000); aircraft and parts ($111,420,000); farm implements ($85,323,000).

Principal Exports to the United Kingdom in 1962 were wheat ($140,134,000); aluminium and products ($82,502,000); copper and products ($60,662,000); nickel and products ($85,668,000); newsprint paper ($63,452,000); planks and boards ($47,854,000); wood pulp ($27,723,000); wheat flour ($22,776,000); flaxseed ($16,760,000); tobacco ($26,629,000); radioactive ores and concentrates ($16,598,000); plywood ($16,452,000); soya bean oil and cake meal ($17,523,000); zinc and products ($17,470,000); plastics and products ($15,288,000).

Minerals.—Canada is the world's greatest producer of nickel, asbestos and platinum, and ranks second in uranium, gold and gypsum, third in silver and zinc, fourth in lead, fifth in copper and iron ore and seventh in petroleum. The principal minerals produced in 1962 were: petroleum, crude 244,007,849 barrels ($583,592,912); copper ($283,133,249); nickel ($385,224,707); iron ore ($264,608,450); gold ($155,446,407); zinc ($110,628,845); asbestos ($132,060,7[illegible]0); coal, 10,257,092 tons ($68,527,159); lead ($3[illegible],816,785); uranium ($151,425,006); silver ($36,077,604); natural gas 955,526,300 M. cu. ft. ($97,912,9[illegible]0). The total value of mineral output in 1962 was $2,844,164,195.

COMMUNICATIONS

Railways.—The total first main track mileage of railways in operation on Dec. 31, 1961, was 43,689 miles, the capital liability of the railways being $4,982,854,654 (1961), earnings $1,156,480,700, the operating expenses $1,114,432,523. In 1961 the passengers carried on railways numbered 18,783,732, and freight 183,337,077 tons. Passengers carried by other transit systems totalled 1,987,319,165, operating income being $138,440,041 and expenses $137,257,702.

Name	Total Miles operated 1961	Capital 1961
Canadian National Railway System in Canada (single track).	22,995	$3,586,979,031
Canadian Pacific single track..............	16,483	1,083,818,421
Other Lines single track.	4,211	312,057,202
		$4,982,854,654

Shipping.—The registered shipping on Dec. 31, 1962, including inland vessels, was 22,000 vessels with gross tonnage 2,810,111.

Canals.—In 1961 the vessels passing through the Canadian sections of the St. Lawrence Seaway numbered 10,257 of 23,672,825 tons of freight. In addition to the Seaway, there were seven canal systems under control of the Federal Government. During 1961, 57,222,696 tons of freight passed through all Canadian canals in 25,980 vessels.

Civil Aviation.—The number of revenue-producing passengers carried in 1962 was 6,065,033 compared with 5,740,577 in 1961. Revenue freight was 260,487,202 lb. or an increase of 10,418,132 lb. from 1961. Mail carried increased from 39,015,215 lb. in 1961 to 41,639,976 lb. in 1962.

Motor Vehicles.—Total motor vehicle registrations numbered 5,517,023 in 1961.

Post.—There were 11,401 post offices on March 31, 1962. The net postal revenue was $213,517,994 in the fiscal year 1961–62. On March 31, 1962, there were 5,637 rural mail delivery routes on which were situated 635,009 boxes.

YUKON TERRITORY

The Yukon Act, 1955, as amended, provides for the administration of the Territory by a Commissioner acting under instructions from time to time given by the Governor in Council or the Minister of Northern Affairs and National Resources. Legislative powers, analogous to those of a provincial government, are exercised by the Commissioner in Council. The Council comprises seven members elected from electoral districts in the Territory. The area of the Territory is 207,076 square miles with an estimated population (1961) of 14,628, including 1,900 Indians and a few Eskimos. Mining is the chief industry, though trapping remains important and there is considerable timber production. Oil has been discovered in the Peel Plateau area.

SEAT OF GOVERNMENT, Whitehorse. Pop. (1961) 5,031.

Commissioner, Gordon R. Cameron.

NORTHWEST TERRITORIES.

Area 1,304,903 square miles; population (1961 census) 22,998, including approximately 12,000 Indians and Eskimos.

The Northwest Territories are subdivided into the districts of Mackenzie, Keewatin and Franklin.

The Northwest Territories Act, 1952, as amended, provides for the government of the Territories by a Commissioner (who is responsible to the Government through the Minister of Northern Affairs and National Resources), and a council of nine (comprising 4 members elected in the district of Mackenzie and 5 appointed members). Legislative powers, analogous to those of a provincial government, are exercised by the Commissioner in Council.

The chief industry of the Northwest Territories is mining, with a total value of $17,701,145 in 1962. The value of gold production in 1962 was $14,718,329; crude petroleum $892,500; silver $84,590; copper $188,928; nickel $1,791,298; natural gas $25,500. Fur produced in 1960–61 was valued at $1,319,748.

SEAT OF GOVERNMENT, Ottawa. The Commissioner in Council holds two sessions each year, one in Ottawa and the other in the Territories.

Commissioner, R. Gordon Robertson.

PROVINCES OF THE DOMINION OF CANADA

ALBERTA

Area and Population.—The Province of Alberta has an area of 255,285 square miles, including about 6,485 square miles of water, with a population (estimated March 1, 1963) of 1,400,000.

Government.—The Government is vested in a Lieutenant-Governor and Legislative Assembly composed of 63 members, elected for five years, representing 63 electoral districts into which the Province is divided. The present representation of parties is 61 Social Credit Party and 2 Liberal. The Executive Council consists of 15 members.

Lieut.-Governor, His Honour J. Percy Page (1950) $9,000

Executive.

Premier, President of Council and Attorney-General, Hon. Ernest Charles Manning	$14,000
Public Health, Hon. J. D. Ross, M.D.	11,000
Public Welfare, Hon. L. C. Halmrast	11,000
Municipal Affairs, Hon. A. J. Hooke	11,000
Public Works, Hon. F. C. Colborne	11,000
Agriculture, Hon. H. E. Strom	11,000
Lands and Forests, Hon. N. A. Willmore	11,000
Education, Hon. A. O. Aalborg	11,000
Labour and Telephones, Hon. R. Reierson	11,000
Railways and Highways, Hon. G. E. Taylor	11,000
Provincial Treasurer, Hon. E. W. Hinman	11,000
Industry and Development and Mines and Minerals, Hon. A. R. Patrick	11,000
Provincial Secretary, Hon. A. Holowach	11,000
Without Portfolio, Hon. I. McLaughlin; Hon. Mrs. E. S. Wilson	*special allowance*
Clerk of the Executive Council and Clerk of the Legislative Assembly, R. A. Crevolin	$9,000
Speaker of the Legislative Assembly, Hon. A. J. Dixon	7,000

The Judicature.

The Supreme Court of Alberta.

Appelate Division, Hon. S. B. Smith	$18,500
Judges, Hons. H. J. Macdonald; M. M. Porter; H. G. Johnson; E. W. S. Kane each	16,900
Trial Division, Hon. C. C. McLaurin (*C.J.*)	18,500
Judges, Hons. N. Primrose; J. M. Cairns; P. Greschuk; H. W. Riley; J. V. H. Milvain; M. E. Manning; H. C. Farthing; W. J. C. Kirby each	16,900

Agent-General in London, R. A. McMullen, 37 Hill Street, W.1.

Agriculture and Live Stock.—The area in field crops, 1962, was—under wheat 5,807,000 acres, producing 112,000,000 bushels; oats, 3,308,000 acres (123,000,000 bushels); barley 2,839,000 acres (89,000,000 bushels). The live stock production (1962) included 1,995,000 cattle, 980,000 calves, 299,000 sheep and lambs and 1,200,000 hogs.

The Department of Agriculture in the Provincial Government conducts free schools of agriculture at three points in the Province.

Finance.—Net Funded Debt, Mar. 31, 1961 $24,171,583, Revenue (1963–64 estimated) $373,847,650. Expenditure, $373,822,938.

Manufactures.—The gross value of the output in 1962 was estimated at $970,000,000, the principal manufacturing centres being Calgary, Edmonton, Medicine Hat and Lethbridge.

CAPITAL, EDMONTON. Population (estimated 1963) 437,000. Other centres are Calgary (323,000). Lethbridge (35,722), Medicine Hat (24,621), Red Deer, Grande Prairie, Camrose and Wetaskiwin.

BRITISH COLUMBIA

Area and Population.—British Columbia has a total area estimated at 366,255 square miles, with a population (census of June 1, 1962) of 1,659,000.

Government.—The Government consists of a Lieutenant-Governor and an Executive Council together with a Legislative Assembly of 52 members.

Lieut.-Governor, Maj.-Gen. the Hon. G. R. Pearkes, V.C., P.C., C.B., D.S.O., M.C. $9,000
Secretary, Cmdr. C. G. Dixon 8,000

Executive Council.
(Elected Sept. 12, 1960)

Premier, President of the Council and Minister of Finance, Hon. W. A. C. Bennett $17,500
Provincial Secretary and Minister of Municipal Affairs and of Social Welfare, Hon. W. D. Black 15,000
Attorney-General and Minister of Industrial Development, Trade and Commerce, Hon. R. W. Bonner, Q.C. 15,000
Lands, Forests and Water Resources, Hon. R. G. Williston 15,000
Agriculture, Hon. F. X. Richter 15,000
Mines and Petroleum Resources, Hon. W. K. Kiernan 15,000
Highways, Hon. P. A. Gaglardi 15,000
Education and Labour, Hon. L. R. Peterson, Q.C. 15,000
Health Services and Hospital Insurance, Hon. E. C. F. Martin 15,000
Public Works, Hon. W. N. Chant 15,000
Recreation and Conservation, and Commercial Transport, Hon. E. C. Westwood 15,000

Speaker, Legislative Assembly, Hon. L. H. Shantz 5,000

The Judicature.

Court of Appeal—Chief Justice of British Columbia, Hon. A. C. Des Brisay $18,500
Justices of Appeal, Hons. C. H. O'Halloran; H. I. Bird; H. W. Davey; J. M. Coady; F. A. Sheppard; T. G. Norris; C. W. Tysoe; J. O. Wilson 16,900
Supreme Court—Chief Justice, Hon. S. Lett 18,500
Puisne Judges, Hons. N. W. Whittaker; H. W. McInnes; A. E. Lord; H. T. Sullivan; J. G. Ruttan; T. W. Brown; H. A. Maclean; F. K. Collins; D. R. Verchere; R. A. Wootton; J. G. A. Hutcheson; F. C. Munroe; J. S. Aikens each 16,900
District Judge in Admiralty, Hon. T. G. Norris 1,000

Agent-General in London, J. V. Fisher, British Columbia House, 1 Regent Street, S.W.1.

Finances.—Estimated Revenue for 1963–64, $379,907,415. Estimated ordinary Expenditure $303,940,565. There is no direct debt.

Production and Industry.—The production levels of the four leading industries were estimated for 1962 as follows: forestry, $780,000,000; mining, $217,000,000; agriculture, $151,087,000; fishing, $94,673,000. Manufacturing activity is based largely on the processing of products of the four main basic industries. The total selling value of factory shipments was estimated for 1962 at $2,132,642,000. The principal manufacturing centres are Vancouver, Burnaby, Trail, Victoria, Kitimat, New Westminster, North Vancouver, Richmond, Port Moody, Powell River and Prince Rupert. Forestry and forest-based industries form the most important economic activity accounting for approximately 40 per cent. of total production. British Columbia is the leading province of Canada in the quantity and value of its timber and sawmill products. Mining, the second most important economic activity, is based on zinc, lead, iron, asbestos, copper, natural gas and crude petroleum. Lead production is approximately 83 per cent. of the Canadian total. The most important products of agriculture are livestock, poultry, fruits, and dairy products. Salmon accounts for approximately 73 per cent. of the value of fisheries. Other species include halibut, herring, soles, cod, and crab. The climate is healthy, quite moderate on the coast and continental east of the coast mountains. The economy is dependent upon markets outside the province for the disposal of most of the products of her industry. Canadian markets receive lumber, plywood, canned salmon, zinc, and fruit. World markets receive lumber, newsprint, woodpulp, aluminium, zinc, canned salmon, lead, and fruit.

Transport.—The province has deep water harbours which are well serviced by railways and modern paved highways. Vancouver is the base for regular scheduled air routes to other parts of Canada, the United States, Europe, Mexico, South America, Hawaii, Australia, and Japan.

Principal Cities.—CAPITAL, VICTORIA. Metropolitan population (1961 census) 154,152. ΨVancouver (founded in 1886), the largest city in the Province, metropolitan population (1961 census) 790,165. is the western terminus of the C.P.R. and the C.N.R. (the C.N.R. also has a terminus at Prince Rupert) and the southern terminus of the P.G.E., and possesses one of the finest natural harbours in the world. Other main trading centres are Chilliwack (8,259), Nanaimo (14,135), Penticton (13,859), Prince George (13,877), Prince Rupert (11,987), Kamloops (10,076), Dawson Creek (10,946), Trail (11,580), and Kelowna (13,188).

MANITOBA

Area and Population.—Manitoba, originally the Red River settlement, is the central province of Canada. The Province has a considerable area of prairieland but is also a land of wide diversity combining 400 miles of sea-coast, large lakes and rivers covering an area of 39,225 square miles and Precambrian rock which covers about three-fifths of the Province. The total area is 251,000 square miles with a population of 921,686 (1961).

Government.—The Government is administered by a Lieutenant-Governor, assisted by an Executive Council of 11 Ministers, who are members of the Legislative Assembly of 57 members. Each member of the Legislative Assembly receives an annual sessional indemnity of $4,000.

Lieut.-Governor, His Honour Errick French Willis, Q.C. (1960) $9,000

Executive (June 30, 1958)

Premier and President of the Council, Acting Provincial Treasurer and Minister of Dominion-Provincial Relations, Hon. D. Roblin $14,500
Agriculture, Hon. G. Hutton 12,500

Public Works and Highways, Hon. W. G. Weir.......................... $12,500
Industry and Commerce, Hon. E. G. V. Evans 12,500
Mines and Natural Resources, Hon. C. H. Witney.......................... 12,500
Education, Hon. S. E. McLean, Q.C....... 12,500
Attorney-General, Hon. S. R. Lyon, Q.C... 12,500
Health, Dr. Hon. G. Johnson.......... 12,500
Labour, Hon. O. Baizley 12,500
Municipal Affairs, Hon. R. C. Smellie, Q.C. 12,500
Public Welfare, Hon. J. Carroll........... 12,500
Public Utilities, Hon. M. B. Steinkopf, Q.C. 12,500
Without Portfolio, Hon. A. W. Harrison.. 3,000

Speaker of the Legislative Assembly, Hon. Mrs. Thelma Forbes................ 9,600

The Judicature.

Court of Appeal:—
Chief Justice of Manitoba, Hon. C. C. Miller 18,500
Puisne Judges, Hons. I. Schultz; S. Freedman; R. D. Guy; A. M. Monnin....................each 16,900
Queen's Bench:—
Chief Justice, Q.B.D., Hon. G. E. Tritschler........................ 18,500
Puisne Judges, Hons. R. Maybank; F. M. Bastin; W. G. Ferguson; I. Nitikman; C. R. Smith..................each 16,900

AGENT-GENERAL FOR MANITOBA.—R. M. Armstrong, Bucklersbury House, 83 Cannon Street. London, E.C.4.

Finances.—The revenues of the provincial government for the year ended March 31, 1962, were $112.600,000, and the expenditure $105,021,000.

Agriculture and Live Stock.—The total land area in Manitoba is 135.536,000 acres, of which 7,694,000 acres were under field crops in 1961. The gross value of agricultural production in 1961 was estimated at $262,675,000, of which field crops represented $108,724,000. Farm animals in 1961 numbered 966,000 cattle, 453,000 pigs, 90,000 sheep, 52,000 horses and 7,545,000 poultry.

Manufactures.—The gross value of manufactured products in 1961 was estimated at $770,459,000. Manufacturing enterprises employed about 45,000 persons. The chief industrial centres are Winnipeg, St. Boniface, St. James, Brandon and Selkirk. The largest manufacturing industry is the food and beverage industry, followed by iron and steel products. Petroleum has grown into one of the most important industries in Manitoba.

Principal Cities.—CAPITAL, WINNIPEG, population (1961), 265,429. Other centres are St. Boniface (37,600), St. James (33,977), Brandon (27,787), Portage La Prairie (12,223).

NEW BRUNSWICK

Area and Population.—NEW BRUNSWICK is situated between 45°–48° N. lat. and 63° 47′–69° W. long. and comprises an area of 27,985 square miles, with a population (estimated at March, 1961) of 608,000. It was first colonized by British subjects in 1761, and in 1783 by the inhabitants of New England, who were dispossessed of their property in consequence of their loyalty to the British Crown.

Government.—The Government is administered by a Lieutenant-Governor, assisted by an Executive Council, and a Legislative Assembly of 52 members elected by the people. At the General Election of April 22, 1963, 31 Liberal and 21 Conservative members were returned.

Lieutenant-Governor, His Honour J. Leonard O'Brien (1958)................. $9,000

Executive (July 12, 1960)

Premier and Attorney-General, Hon. L. J. Robichaud, Q.C.................... $17,500
Finance, Hon. L. G. Des Brisay......... 10,000
Public Works, Hon. A. F. Richard....... 10,000
Health and Social Services, Hon. G. Dumont, M.D....................... 10,000
Education, Hon. H. G. Irwin........... 10,000
Industry and Development (vacant)........ 10,000
Lands and Mines, Hon. H. G. Crocker... 10,000
Labour, Hon. K. J. Webber............ 10,000
Agriculture, Hon. J. A. Levesque......... 10,000
Chairman, New Brunswick Electric Power Commission, Hon. D. Harper......... 10,000
Municipal Affairs, Hon. J. E. Le Blanc..... 10,000
Youth and Welfare, Hon. W. R. Duffie... 10,000

Speaker of the House, Hon. B. L. Jean.... 4,000

The Judicature.

Court of Appeal and Chancery Division.

Chief Justice, Hon. J. B. McNair......... $16,000
Judges of Appeal, Hon. G. F. G. Bridges; Hon. L. McC. Ritchie; Hon. W. J. West.......................... 14,400

Queen's Bench Division.

Chief Justice, Q.B.D., Hon. J. E. Michaud $16,000
Judges, Hons. A. Robichaud; W. A. I. Anglin; C. J. Jones..............each 14,400

Court of Vice-Admiralty.

Judge, Hon. W. A. I. Anglin............ $1,000

Court of Divorce and Matrimonial Causes.

Judge, Hon. W. J. West............... $500

Finance.—The estimated revenue for the year ending March 31, 1964 is $117,149,170, and the ordinary expenditure $123,300,994.

Agriculture and Live Stock.—The total land area is 17,582,720 acres, of which 549,000 were under field crops in 1961. The live stock in 1962 included 8,000 horses, 139,000 cattle, 25,500 sheep, 40,000 hogs and 816,000 poultry. Settlement is encouraged and improved farms are obtainable at reasonable rates. The chief commercial fish are lobsters, sardines, herring, cod and salmon. The value of production of the fisheries in 1961 was $7,593,700. The cheese factories in operation produced 526,000 lb. of cheese and the creameries 8,418,000 lb. of butter in 1961.

Manufactures.—The principal manufacturing centre is Saint John. Extensive copper, lead and zinc deposits are being developed in Restigouche County. Coal is found (output, 1961, 887,903 tons, value $7,544,885), also silver, antimony, manganese, and other minerals.

Principal Cities.—CAPITAL Ψ FREDERICTON: population (1961), 19,683. Ψ Saint John (pop. 55,153) is one of the principal winter ports of Canada and is connected by C.P.R. and Canadian National Railways with Montreal: Moncton (43,840); Lancaster (13,848); Edmundston (12,791); Campbellton (9,873).

NEWFOUNDLAND

Area and Population.—THE ISLAND OF NEWFOUNDLAND is situated between 46° 37′–51° 37′ N. latitude and 52° 44′–59° 30′ W. longitude, on the north-east side of the Gulf of St. Lawrence, and is separated from the North American Continent by the Straits of Belle Isle on the N.W. and by Cabot Strait on the S.W. The island is about 317 miles long and 316 miles broad and is triangular in shape, with Cape Bauld (N.), Cape Race (S.E.) and Cape Ray (S.W.) at the angles. It comprises an area of 156,185 sq. miles (inclusive of Labrador) with a population (estimated 1961) of 462,000.

Government.—On March 31, 1949, the island, with its dependency in Labrador, became the 10th

Province of the Dominion of Canada. The Government is administered by a Lieutenant-Governor, aided by an Executive Council and a Legislative Assembly of 36 members.

Lieutenant-Governor, Hon. Fabian Odea (March 1, 1963) $9,000

Executive.

Premier and Minister of Economic Development, Hon. J. R. Smallwood, D.C.L., LL.D.
Attorney-General, Hon. L. R. Curtis, Q.C.
Mines, Agriculture and Resources, Hon. W. J. Keough.
Labour, Hon. C. H. Ballam.
Provincial Affairs and Solicitor General, Hon. M. P. Murray, Q.C.
Public Works, Hon. J. R. Chalker.
Fisheries, Hon. J. T. Cheeseman.
Municipal Affairs and Supply, Hon. B. J. Abbott.
Finance, Hon. E. S. Spencer.
Health, Hon. J. M. McGrath, M.D.
Highways, Hon. F. W. Rowe.
Education, Hon. G. A. Frecker, D.C.L., LL.D.
Public Welfare, Hon. C. M. Lane.
Without Portfolio, Hon. P. J. Lewis, Q.C.

Clerk of the Executive Council, J. G. Channing.
Leader of the Opposition, J. J. Greene.

The Judicature.

Chief Justice, Hon. R. S. Furlong $18,500
Judges, Hon. Sir Brian Dunfield; Hon. H. A. Winter each $16,900

The Legislature.

A General Election was held on Nov. 19, 1962. The present state of parties is: *Liberal*, 34; *Progressive Conservative*, 7; *Independent*, 1.

Speaker of the House of Assembly, Hon. J. R. Courage.

Finance.—The revenue in 1961–62 was $82,142,000 and the expenditure $80,550,000. The estimated revenue for 1962–63 was $90,658,000 and expenditure $90,531,000.

Production and Industry.—With the exception of Gander, Bishop's Falls, Badger, Millertown, Buchans, Howley, Deer Lake and that portion of the West Coast between St. George's and Port aux Basques the inhabitants are chiefly located on the coast-line of the shore and bays. Eleven mines are in operation: three iron ore, one limestone, one lead, zinc and copper, two fluorspar and four copper. Two pulp and paper mills are in operation with a total production of 544,892 tons of newsprint and 44,780 tons of sulphite pulp.

The value in 1961, of products of the forests was estimated at $90,000,000; fishery products were valued at $14,900,000 and the estimated value of agricultural products was $12,000,000. The value in 1961 of mineral products was $92,700,000. Lead, zinc and copper production in 1961 was 84,500 short tons, valued at $20,900,000; iron ore production was 7,853,973 tons valued at $59,800,000 and the value of fluorspar and gold production was $1,900,000 and $548,000 respectively.

Railways.—The main line of the railway extends from St. John's on the east coast to Port aux Basques on the west coast—a distance of 547 miles—with branches connecting with the ports of Argentia, Carbonear, Bonavista and Lewisporte, a total mileage of 705. There are also 56 miles of private line. Communication between various points on the coast and between Port aux Basques and North Sydney, Nova Scotia, is maintained by a fleet of 20 motor vessels and 5 steam vessels, operated by the Railway.

Posts and Telegraphs.—There were 658 post offices open in 1961. The number of telegraph and telephone offices was 662.

Civil Aviation.—Trans-Canada, British Overseas and 10 other lines (2 of them for local traffic only) operate from Gander Airport.

Shipping.—On Dec. 31. 1961, ships registered in Newfoundland consisted of 54 sailing vessels of 4,243 gross tons, 12 steam vessels of 10,380 gross tons and 742 motor vessels of 54,243 gross tons.

Principal Cities.—The Capital, ΨST. JOHN'S (population 1961 census, 88,690) contains two cathedrals, several banks and numerous public buildings. Other towns are Corner Brook (25,004), Wabana (8,013), Grand Falls (6,569), Carbonear (4,195), Windsor (5,478), Bonavista (4,126), Stephenville (6,001) and Deer Lake (3,923).

LABRADOR

Labrador, the most northerly district in the Province of Newfoundland, forms the most easterly part of the North American continent, and extends from Blanc Sablon, at the north-east entrance to the Straits of Belle Isle, on the south, to Cape Chidley, at the eastern entrance to Hudson's Straits on the north. The territory under the jurisdiction of Newfoundland has an area estimated at 110,000 square miles, with a population (1962) of 13,534. Labrador is noted for its cod fisheries. It also possesses valuable salmon, herring, trout and seal fisheries.

NOVA SCOTIA

Area and Population.—NOVA SCOTIA is a peninsula between 43° 25′–47° N. lat and 59° 40′–66° 25′ W. long., and is connected with New Brunswick by a low fertile isthmus about thirteen miles wide. It comprises an area (with Cape Breton Island) of 21,068 square miles (325 miles of which consists of lakes, rivers and inlets of the sea) with a total population (estimated 1960) of 723,000.

Government.—The Government is administered by a Lieutenant-Governor, aided by an Executive Council and a Legislative Assembly of 43 members.

Lieutenant-Governor, Hon. H. P. MacKeen (1963) $9,000

Executive.

Premier and Minister of Education, Hon. R. L. Stanfield, Q.C. $12,000
Highways and Public Works, Hon. S. T. Pyke 10,000
Attorney-General and Minister of Public Health, Hon. R. A. Donahoe, Q.C. 10,000
Labour and Municipal Affairs, Hon. N. L. Fergusson, Q.C. 10,000
Agriculture, Marketing, Lands and Forests, Hon. E. D. Haliburton 10,000
Mines, Hon. D. M. Smith 10,000
Trade and Industry, Hon. E. A. Manson ... 10,000
Provincial Secretary and Minister of Public Welfare, Hon. W. S. Kennedy Jones, Q.C. 10,000
Finance and Economics, Hon. G. I. Smith, Q.C. 10,000
Minister without Portfolio, Hon. G. A. Burridge 10,000

The Judicature.
Supreme Court.

Chief Justice, Rt. Hon. J. L. Ilsley $18,500
Judges, Hons. Josiah H. MacQuarrie; L. D. Currie; V. C. MacDonald; F. W. Bissett; F. H. Patterson; T. H. Coffin each 16,900

Finance.—The revenue in 1960–61 was $92,888,043 and the expenditure $92,816,389; the funded debt (March 31, 1961) was $295,860,000.

Agriculture and Live Stock.—According to the 1961 census Nova Scotia has a total land area of 13,275,000 acres, of which 2,230,395 acres are held as farm land. At the same census, the total number of occupied farms was listed at 12,518. Of the total area in farm land, 330,000 acres are devoted to the production of principal field crops.

The Annapolis Valley section of Nova Scotia is famous for its fruit production, with an average crop of nearly 2,500,000 bushels annually.

The number of live stock is estimated (1960) as follows: horses, 12,000; cattle and calves, 160,000; sheep and lambs, 73,000; hogs, 52,000; poultry, 2,272,000.

Manufactures.—In 1960 there were 1,278 establishments employing 28,606 people. The selling value of factory shipments was $406,182,088. Iron and steel, food and beverages, wood and paper products, petroleum and coal products, and transportation equipment accounted for the larger proportion of this amount. The principal industrial centres are Sydney, Halifax, Trenton, Amherst, Truro and Yarmouth.

Fisheries.—The total landed value of the fisheries in 1960 was $26,094,400. About 17,000 people are employed in fishing and fish processing.

Minerals.—4,300,759 tons of coal were produced in 1961. Gypsum production was 3,982,837 tons, barite totalled 171,335 tons, salt output was 235,885 tons, and anhydrite 173,777 tons. Silver, lead and zinc production recommenced in 1961 after 5 years with no base metal output. Total value of mineral output was just over $60,000,000 in 1961, slightly below the five-year average.

Principal Cities.—CAPITAL, ΨHALIFAX, population of Metropolitan area (1961) 179,000, one of the terminals of the Canadian National Railway, with a magnificent harbour, is one of the principal winter ports of Canada, and the *entrepôt* of a large trade with the West Indies, South America and Europe. One of the largest bridges in the British Commonwealth spans the harbour and connects the city of Dartmouth and surrounding area with the city of Halifax. A shipyard for the building of large ocean-going steamers, with a dry dock, is one of the leading industries; other cities and towns are Sydney, Glace Bay and New Waterford (*see below*), Dartmouth (45,276), Truro (12,098), New Glasgow (9,564) Amherst (10,569), Sydney Mines (8,948) and Yarmouth (8,455).

CAPE BRETON ISLAND.

Cape Breton Island, formerly a distinct Colony, was incorporated with Nova Scotia in 1819. It contains an area of 3,975 sq. miles, population (1961) 163,754. The chief city, Sydney (pop. 33,201), on the eastern coast, has valuable collieries in the neighbourhood and is the site of the third largest steel works in Canada. Glace Bay and New Waterford, also coal mining centres, have populations of 23,653 and 10,592 respectively. The Canadian National Railway provides service to the island. Construction of a large rail-highway causeway from mainland to island was completed in 1955.

ONTARIO

Area and Population.—The Province of Ontario contains a total area of 412,582 square miles, with a population (estimated April 1, 1962) of 6,321,000.

Government.—The Government is vested in a Lieutenant-Governor and a Legislative Assembly of 98 members elected for five years. The state of the parties in Dec. 1962, was 67 Progressive Conservatives, 24 Liberals, 5 New Democratic Party and 2 vacancies.

Lieutenant-Governor, His Honour J. K. Mackay, D.S.O., V.D., Q.C. $11,000

Executive Council.

President of the Council, Hon. J. Parmentar Robarts, Q.C.	$16,000
Attorney-General and Minister for Dept. of Insurance, Hon. F. M. Cass, Q.C.	12,000
Provincial Secretary and Minister of Citizenship, Hon. J. Yaremko, Q.C.	12,000
Labour, Hon. W. K. Warrender, Q.C.	12,000
Municipal Affairs, Hon. J. W. Spooner	12,000
Travel and Publicity, Hon. B. L. Cathcart	12,000
Public Welfare, Hon. L. P. Cecile, Q.C.	12,000
Reform Institutions, Hon. I. Haskett	12,000
Provincial Treasurer, Hon. J. N. Allan	12,000
Agriculture, Hon. W. A. Stewart	12,000
Health, Hon. M. B. Dymond, M.D.	12,000
Lands and Forests, Hon. A. K. Roberts, Q.C.	12,000
Highways, Hon. C. S. McNaughton	12,000
Public Works, Hon. T. R. Connell	12,000
Transport, Hon. J. C. C. Auld	12,000
Energy Resources and Economics and Development, Hon. R. Macaulay, Q.C.	12,000
Mines, Hon. G. C. Wardrope	12,000
Education, Hon. W. G. Davis	12,000
Ministers without Portfolio, Hon. W. A. Goodfellow; Hon. A. Grossman; J. R. Simonette	2,500

Speaker, Legislative Assembly, Hon. W. Murdoch $3,000

SUPREME COURT OF ONTARIO

Chief Justice of Ontario, Court of Appeal, Hon. D. H. Porter.

Chief Justice of the High Court Division, Hon. J. C. McRuer.

Justices of Appeal, Hon R. E. Laidlaw; Hon. W. D. Roach; Hon. J. B. Aylesworth; Hon. C. W. G. Gibson, M.C., V.D.; Hon. F. G. MacKay; Hon. W. F. Schroeder; Hon. G. A. McGillivray; Hon. A. Kelly; Hon. J. L. McLennan.

Hon. Court Judges, Hon. D. P. J. Kelly; Hon. D. C. Wells; Hon. P. E. F. Smily; Hon. G. A. Gale; Hon. R. I. Ferguson; Hon. J. M. King; Hon. H. A. Aylen; Hon. C. D. Stewart; Hon. E. G. Moorhouse; Hon. E. G. Thompson; Hon. L. A. Landreville; Hon. S. N. Schatz; Hon. J. F. Donnelly; Hon. D. R. Morand; Hon. W. D. Parker; Hon. E. A. Richardson; Hon. N. C. Fraser; Hon. C. Grant; Hon. S. H. S. Hughes; Hon. E. L. Haines.

AGENT-GENERAL FOR ONTARIO IN U.K., J. S. P. Armstrong, 13 Charles II Street, London, S.W.1 .... $12,500

Finance.—The estimated Net Ordinary Revenue of the Ontario Government for 1961–62 was $813,691,000 and the estimated Net Ordinary Expenditure was $813,259,000. The estimated Gross Capital Debt was $1,870,378,000 on March 31, 1962, and the Net Capital Debt was estimated at $1,240,729,000.

Agriculture and Live Stock.—The total land area of Ontario is about 220,219,000 acres. There are about 12,572,000 acres of improved land, of which 7,819,100 acres were under field crops in 1961. These included wheat (winter and spring) 564,000 acres; oats 1,700,000 acres; mixed grains, 735,000 acres and hay, 3,400,000 acres.

In 1961 the numbers of live stock included—

horses, 90,000; cattle, 3,210,000; sheep and lambs, 388,000; swine, 1,870,000, and poultry, 30,027 000.

Forestry.—Productive forested lands comprise 106,074,000 acres or about 48 per cent. of the land area of the Province. The total value of forest production in the Province in 1960 was estimated at $154,500,000. Pulp and paper is one of the most important manufacturing industries in the Province.

Manufactures.—Ontario is the chief manufacturing province of Canada. In 1961 the selling value of factory shipments was estimated at $11,750,000,000 and the number of employees at 593,000.

Minerals.—Ontario leads the other Provinces in mineral production, the estimated output in 1961 being $948,256,000. The principal metals produced and their value were: gold, $92,048,000; nickel, $301,435,000; copper, $122,509,000; platinum and other platinum metals, $23,829,000; iron ore, $47,868,000; uranium, $209,568,000 and cobalt, $5,235,000.

Principal Cities (with population at June 1, 1961) —CAPITAL, ΨTORONTO (Metropolitan area, 1,618,787), with extensive shipping interests on the Great Lakes, and the chief centre of industrial, commercial and financial activity; ΨHamilton, the "Birmingham of Canada" (273,991); Ottawa, the national capital (268,206); London (169,569); Brantford (55,201) ΨKingston (53,526); Peterborough (47,185); ΨWindsor, connected by tunnel and bridge with Detroit, Mich., U.S.A. (114,367); Fort William (45,214); Kitchener (74,485); Guelph (39,838); St. Catharine's (84,472); ΨSault Ste. Marie (43,088); Oshawa (62,415); Sudbury (80,120); ΨPort Arthur (45,276); Sarnia (50,976); Cornwall (43,639).

FEDERAL CAPITAL

OTTAWA, the Federal Capital, 111 miles west of Montreal and 247 miles north of Toronto, is a city on the right bank of the Ottawa river. The city was chosen as the Capital of the Province of Canada in 1858 and was later selected as the site of the Dominion capital. Ottawa contains the Parliamentary Buildings, the Public Archives, Royal Mint, National Museum, National Art Gallery and the Dominion Observatory. Manufacturing is also carried on, food production, printing and publishing being of greatest importance. Ottawa is connected with Lake Ontario by the Rideau Canal. The population of the Federal Capital was 268,206 at the Census of 1961 and of Metropolitan Ottawa, 429,750.

PRINCE EDWARD ISLAND

Area and Population.—Prince Edward Island lies in the southern part of the Gulf of St. Lawrence, between 46°–47° N. lat. and 62°–64° 30′ W. long. It is about 130 miles in length, and from 4 to 34 miles in breadth; its area is 2,184 square miles (rather larger than that of the English county of Norfolk), and its population (estimated, 1958) 100,000.

Government.—The Government is vested in a Lieut.-Governor and an Executive Council, and Legislative Assembly of 30 members elected by the people, 15 as Councillors (with a property qualification) and 15 as Assembly-men (on general suffrage).

Lieutenant-Governor, His Honour W. J. MacDonald (1963) $8,000

Executive.

Premier and President of the Executive Council, Hon. W. R. Shaw $8,000
Provincial Secretary, Tourist Development and Municipal Affairs, Hon. J. D. Stewart 5,000
Health, Hon. H. B. McNeill, M.D. 5,000
Industry and Natural Resources, and Fisheries, Hon. L. F. Rossiter 5,000
Education, Hon. L. G. Dewar, M.D. 5,000
Welfare and Labour, Hon. H. W. Wedge 5,000
Highways and Public Works, Hon. P. Matheson 5,000
Attorney and Advocate-General and Provincial Treasurer, Hon. M. A. Farmer 5,000
Agriculture, Hon. A. B. MacRae 5,000

Speaker of the Legislative Assembly, Hon. J. R. MacLean.

The Judicature.

Chief Justice, Thane A. Campbell $18,000
Assistant Judges, Hon. G. J. Tweedy; Hon. M. R. McGuigan; Hon. R. R. Bell each 16,900

Finance.—The revenue in 1961–62 was $22,782,700 and the expenditure was $24,789,100.

Principal Cities.—CAPITAL, ΨCHARLOTTETOWN (pop. 17,956), on the shore of Hillsborough Bay, which forms a good harbour. Other towns are Summerside (8,387), Souris (1,479), and Montague (1,100).

QUEBEC

Area and Population.—The Province of Quebec contains an area estimated at 594,860 square miles, with a population (estimated 1962) of 5,366,000.

Government.—The Government of the Province is vested in a Lieutenant-Governor, the Council of Ministers, a Legislative Council consisting of 24 members appointed for life, and a Legislative Assembly of 95 members elected for five years. The General Election of Nov. 14, 1962, returned 63 Liberals, 31 *Union Nationale*, and 1 Independent.

Lieut.-Governor, The Hon. Paul Comtois, P.C. (Oct. 6, 1961) $14,000

Executive.

Prime Minister and Minister of Finance and of Federal and Provincial Affairs, Hon. Jean Lesage $18,000
Attorney-General and Minister of Cultural Affairs, Hon. G. Lapalme 12,000
Labour, Hon. R. Hamel 12,000
Youth, Hon. P. Gérin-Lajoie 12,000
Agriculture and Colonization, Hon. A. Courcy 12,000
Natural Resources, Hon. R. Levesque 12,000
Provincial Revenue, Hon. E. Kierans 12,000
Transport and Communications, Hon. G. Cournoyer 12,000
Roads, Hon. B. Pinard 12,000
Family and Social Welfare, Hon. E. Lafrance 12,000
Provincial Secretary, Hon. B. Arsenault . 12,000
Health, Hon. A. Couturier 12,000
Tourist, Fish and Game, Hon. L. Bertrand. 12,000
Trade and Commerce, Hon. G. D. Levesque 12,000
Minister without Portfolio and Leader of Legislative Council, Hon. G. C. Marler. 12,000
Lands and Forests, Hon. L. Cliché 12,000
Public Works, Hon. R. Saint-Pierre 12,000
Municipal Affairs, Hon. P. Laporte 12,000
Without Portfolio, Hon. Mrs. C. Kirkland-Cosgrain; Hon. C. Fortin 8,000

The Judicature

Queen's Bench (Montreal):—

Chief Justice, Hon. L. Tremblay...... 18,500

Puisne Judges (Montreal)—Hons. B. Bissonnette; P. C. Casey; G. Miller Hyde; G. E. Rinfret; G. R. W. Owen; G. H. Montgomery; P. A. Badeaux.. .... each $16,900

Puisne Judges (Quebec)—Hons. G. Pratte; A. Taschereau; F. Choquette; A. Rivard ....each 16,900

Superior Court:—

Chief Justice—Hon. William B. Scott.. 18,500

Associate Chief Justice (Quebec)—Hon. Frédéric Dorion................. 18,500

Finance.—The revenue for the year 1961–62 was $754,144,484; ordinary expenditure amounted to $713,587,762. The bonded debt (March 31, 1962) was $620,975,000 and the net funded debt and Treasury bills $516,065,794.

Production and Industry.—The gross value of manufactured products in 1961 was $7,389,506,000 from 11,960 industrial establishments, employing 450,900 persons with salaries and wages totalling $1,670,544,000, the principal manufacturing centres being Montreal, Montreal East, Quebec, Trois-Rivières, Sherbrooke, Shawinigan Falls, Drummondville and Lachine. Forest lands cover 378,013 sq. miles, of which 220,275 sq. miles are productive, 143,428 sq. miles with merchantable softwood, mixed wood and hardwood, and 76,847 sq. miles with young growth. In 1960, 3,906,000 tons of paper were manufactured, valued at $501,597,000. The total area under cultivation in 1962 was 7,187,000 acres, the value of field crops being $167,894,000; 6,320,000 tons of hay and alfalfa were produced. In 1962 there were 91,000 horses, 1,956,000 cattle, 171,000 sheep, 970,000 swine and 12,680,000 poultry. The production of factory cheese was 45,190,000 lb. (valued at $15,004,000) and creamery butter 144,527,000 lb. (valued at $81,082,000).

The mineral production was valued at $510,146,000 in 1962, including gold 999,000 fine oz. ($37,354,000).

Principal Cities.—CAPITAL, Ψ QUEBEC (1961 census population, 171,979), historic city visited annually by thousands of tourists, and one of the great seaport towns of Canada; and Ψ Montreal (population, 1,191,062), the commercial metropolis, and the principal centre of the Canadian grain export trade, founded by the French at the confluence of the Ottawa and St. Lawrence Rivers, May 16, 1642. Other important cities are Verdun (78,317), Hull (56,929), Sherbrooke (66,554), Trois Rivières (53,477), Outremont (30,753), Westmount (25,012) and Lachine (38,630).

SASKATCHEWAN

Area and Population.—The Province of Saskatchewan lies between Manitoba on the east and Alberta on the west and has an area of 251,700 square miles, with a population (1962 estimate) of 930,000. Saskatchewan extends along the Canada-U.S.A. boundary for 393 miles and northwards for 761 miles.

Government.—The Government is vested in the Lieutenant-Governor, with a Legislative Assembly of 55 members. There is an Executive Council of 15 members.

Lieut.-Governor, His Honour R. L. Hanbridge (1963)........................ $9,000

Executive Council.

Premier and President of the Council, Hon. W. S. Lloyd $13,000

Attorney-General and Provincial Secretary, Hon. R. A. Walker................. $10,000

Provincial Treasurer and Deputy Premier, Hon. J. H. Brockelbank............. 10,000

Labour and Telephones, Hon. C. C. Williams 10,000

Mineral Resources, Hon. A. G. Kuziak.... 10,000

Natural Resources, Hon. E. Kramer...... 10,000

Highways and Transportation, Hon. C. G. Willis........................... 10,000

Education, Hon. O. A. Turnbull......... 10,000

Social Welfare and Rehabilitation, Hon. A. M. Nicholson.................. 10,000

Municipal Affairs, Hon. E. I. Wood...... 10,000

Public Works, Hon. W. G. Davies....... 10,000

Agriculture, Hon. I. C. Nollet 10,000

Public Health, Hon. A. E. Blakeney...... 10,000

Industry and Information, Hon. R. Brown.. 10,000

Co-operation and Co-operative Development, Hon. F. Meakes 10,000

Speaker of the Legislative Assembly, Hon. F. W. Dewhurst 3,000

NOTE.—Salaries do not include sessional indemnity of $6,000.

Agent-General in London, Graham Spry.

The Judicature.

Chief Justice of Saskatchewan, Hon. E. M. Culliton $18,500

Judges of Appeal, Hons. M. J. Woods; R. L. Brownridge; P. H. Maguire; R. N. Hall....................... 16,900

Chief Justice, Queen's Bench, Hon. A. H. Bence........................... 18,500

Puisne Judges, Hons. A. Doiron; S. McKercher; C. S. Davis; D. C. Disbery; M. A. MacPherson, jr.; R. M. Balfour.......................each 16,900

Finance.—The estimated revenue for the year ended March 31, 1964, was $195,453,000, and the expenditure $185,500,000. The net public debt (March 31, 1963) was $23,391,000.

Agriculture and Live Stock.—Saskatchewan produced more than 60 per cent. of the wheat grown in Canada in 1962. Wheat production in 1962 was 344,000,000 bushels from 17,388,000 acres. Total production of principal field crops (wheat, oats, barley, rye, flax) was 511,100,000 bushels from 22,397,000 acres. Cash income from the sale of farm products in 1962 was $685,000,000. Total livestock population in Saskatchewan in 1962 was 2,683,000, including 2,080,000 cattle, 429,000 hogs and 174,000 sheep. Income from livestock and livestock products was $185,000,000. The agricultural labour force numbered 136,000, or about 40 per cent. of her province's labour force.

Industries.—In 1962 there were about 2,000 industrial plants in the province. The non-agricultural labour force totalled 205,000. The gross value of industrial production in 1962 was $1,028,000,000. Manufacturing production was estimated at $366,000,000.

In 1962 the value of mineral production was $236,578,000. Oil accounted for nearly $150,000,000 and copper, zinc and uranium $68,000,000. Principal industrial centres are Regina, Saskatoon, Moose Jaw and Prince Albert.

CAPITAL—REGINA. Population (1961 census), 112,141. Other cities: Saskatoon (95,526), Moose Jaw (33,206), Prince Albert (24,168), Swift Current (12,186), North Battleford (11,230), Estevan (7,728), Yorkton (9,995), Weyburn (9,101), Lloydminster (5,667), Melville (5,191).

The Commonwealth of Australia

AREA AND POPULATION

States and Capitals	Area (English Sq. Miles)	Population*			
		Census June 30, 1933	Census June 30, 1947	Census June 30, 1954	Census June 30, 1961
States.					
New South Wales (Sydney).....	309,433	2,600,847	2,984,838	3,423,529	3 917,013
Queensland (Brisbane)..........	667,000	947,534	1,106,415	1,318,259	1,518 828
South Australia (Adelaide).......	380,070	580,949	646,073	797,094	969,340
Tasmania (Hobart)..............	26,215	227,599	257,073	308,752	350,340
Victoria (Melbourne)	87,884	1,820,261	2,054,701	2,452,341	2,930 113
Western Australia (Perth)	975,920	438,852	502,480	639,771	736,629
Territories.					
Australian Capital Territory (Canberra)......................	939	8,947	16,905	30,315	58 828
Northern Territory (Darwin)....	523,620	4,850	10,868	16,469	27,095
Total................	2,971,081	6,629,839	7,579,358	8,986,530	10,508,186

* Exclusive of full-blood Australian aboriginals.

Increase of the People

Year	Increase			Decrease			Net Increase†	Marriages
	Births	‡Oversea Arrivals	Total	Deaths	Oversea Departures	Total		
1938	120,415	77, 28	198,343	66,451	68,791	135,242	64,417	62,411
1959	226,976	253,896	480,872	89,212	177,105	266,317	213,610	74,363
1960	230,326	299,161	529,487	88,464	209,026	297,490	230,952	75 428
1961	239 936	313,090	553,076	88,961	251,567	340,528	212,014	76,685
1962	237,081	332,324	569,405	93,163	269 802	362 965	206,440	79,090

‡ Including the following arrivals under the Commonwealth Government's various schemes for assisted immigration;—1959, 64,146; 1960, 68,254; 1961, 55,685; 1962, 45,276 (preliminary figures).

† Includes adjustments for differences disclosed by results of periodic Censuses.

Inter-Censal Increases, 1881-1961

Year of Census	Population at Census			Intercensal Increase	Net Immigration during Period
	Males	Females	Total		
1891	1,705,835	1,471,988	3,177,823	927,629	1881–1890 .. 382,741
1901	1,977,928	1,795,873	3,773,801	595,978	1891–1900 .. 24,879
1911	2,313,035	2,141,970	4,455,005	681,204	1901–1910 .. 40,485
1921	2,762,870	2,672,864	5,435,734	980,729	1911–1920 .. 207,571
1933	3,367,111	3,262,728	6,629,839	1,194,105	1921–1932 .. 290,882
1947	3,797,370	3,781,988	7,579,358	949,519	1933–1946 .. 37,994
1954	4,546,118	4,440,412	8,986,530	1,407,172	1947–1953 .. 616,534
1961	5,312,252	5,195,934	10,508 186	1,521,656	1954–1960 .. 570,434

Races and Religions

Races	1947	1954	Religions	1954	1961
European	7,524,129	8,921,691	Church of England	3,408,850	3,668,931
Chinese, incld. half-caste..	12,094	15,558	Roman Catholics*	2,060,986	2,620,011
Japanese do.	335	785	Methodists	977 933	1,076,395
Indians and Cingalese do. .	3,154	3,038	Presbyterians	870,242	976,518
Aborigines	..	‡39,300	Other Christians ..	715,743	932,271
Do. half-caste	27,179	31,359	Hebrews.........	48,436	59,343
Other Races............	12,469	14,099	Other†	904,340	1,174,717

* Including Catholics, so described, 1,299,884 in 1954 and 1,480,353 in 1961.

† Including 855,819 and 1,102,930 who did not state their religion at the 1954 and 1961 Censuses respectively.

‡ Estimated as at June 30, 1954.

PHYSICAL FEATURES

Australia was separated from the other great land surfaces at a remote period, and exhibits therefore some very archaic types of fauna and flora. It may be regarded as the largest island or the smallest continent, being surrounded by the following waters:—*North*, the Timor and Arafura Seas and Torres Strait; *East*, Pacific Ocean; *South*, Bass Strait (which separates Tasmania from the Continent) and Southern Ocean; and *West*, Indian Ocean. The total area of the country is 2,944,866 English square miles, the island of Tasmania having an area of 26,215 square miles, and making a total area for the Commonwealth of 2,971,081 square miles. The coast-line of Australia is approximately 12,210 miles (including Tasmania, 900 miles), and its geographical position is between 10° 41′–39° 8′ (43° 39′, including Tasmania) South latitude and 113° 9′–153° 39′ East longitude; the greatest length East to West is 2,400 miles, and from North to South 1,971 miles. Its nearest distance from England is about 11,000 miles.

From a physical standpoint the continent of Australia is divisible into an eastern and a western area, the former containing a regular coast-line with a good harbourage, roadsteads, rivers, and inland waterways, and a greater development of fauna and flora; the latter a broken coast-line with estuaries rather than rivers, and but little inland water communication. The whole continent is, roughly speaking, a vast irregular, and undulating plateau, part of which is below the level of the sea, surrounded by a mountainous coast-line, with frequent intervals of low and sandy shore on the north, west and south. The Great Barrier Reef extends parallel with the East coast of Queensland for 1,200 miles, at a distance of about 60 miles from the mainland. A large part of the interior, particularly in the west, consists of sandy and stony desert, covered with spinifex, and containing numerous salt-marshes, though reaches of grass-land occur here and there. The geological formation of Australia is remarkable for its simplicity and regularity; the *strike* of the rocks is, with a single exception, coincident with the direction of the mountain-chains, from N. to S.; and the tertiary formation to be found in the N., S., and W. develops in the S.E. into a gigantic tertiary plain, watered by the Darling and the Murray Rivers. Nearly all round the coast, however, and in eastern and south-eastern Australia, stretching far inland from the coastal range, is a fertile area devoted partly to agriculture, partly to dairying, while the inland districts particularly are admirably adapted to the rearing of sheep. The most extensive mountain system takes its rise near the S.E. point, and includes a number of ranges known by different names in different places, none of them being of any great height. The highest peak, Mount Kosciusko, in New South Wales, reaches an elevation of 7,328 feet. The principal rivers are the Murray, which debouches on the south coast, after receiving the waters of its tributaries the Murrumbidgee, Lachlan, and Darling, in the S.E. part of the continent; on the east coast, the Hawkesbury, Hunter, Clarence, Richmond, Brisbane, Mary, Burnett, Fitzroy, and Burdekin; on the west, the Swan, Murchison, Gascoyne, Ashburton, Fortescue, De Grey, and Fitzroy; on the north, the Drysdale, Ord, Victoria, and Daly: and the Roper, the Flinders and Mitchell, which debouch into the Gulf of Carpentaria. The scarcity of the natural water supply in the inland has been, however, mitigated by successful borings and by the construction of large dams. The work of conserving the vast quantities of water which run to waste in the wet season is being vigorously prosecuted by a system of locks and weirs on some of the rivers. A major development work in progress is the use of the waters of the Snowy River in south-eastern New South Wales for hydro-electricity generation and irrigation. Minerals comprise bauxite, coal, copper, gold, gypsum, iron, lead, limestone, mineral sand, pyrite, silver, uranium, and zinc in large quantities, antimony, asbestos, barite, beryllium, chromite, dolomite, felspar, magnesite, manganese, mica, salt, silica, talc, tantelite-columbium, tin, tungsten, &c., and there are abundant supplies of building stones, clays, &c. The potentialities of the country in regard to its supplies of metals and minerals have not yet been fully tested. Traces of oil have been discovered in several places, but the commercial possibilities of these have yet to be proved.

Climate.—The seasons are: summer, December to February; autumn, March to May; winter, June to August; spring September to November. The climate generally is extremely dry, but, except in the tropical coast-land of the north, the continent is everywhere highly beneficial to Europeans, the range of temperature being smaller than that of the countries similarly situated.

GOVERNMENT

The Commonwealth of Australia was constituted by an Act of the Imperial Parliament dated July 9, 1900, and was inaugurated Jan. 1, 1901. The Government is that of a Federal Commonwealth within the British Commonwealth of Nations, the executive power being vested in the Sovereign (through the Governor-General), assisted by a Federal Ministry of twenty-two Ministers of State. Under the Constitution the Federal Government has acquired and may acquire certain defined powers as surrendered by the States, residuary legislative power remaining with the States. Trade and customs passed under Federal control immediately on the establishment of the Commonwealth; posts, telegraphs and telephones, naval and military defence, lighthouses and quarantine on proclaimed dates. The Federal Government also controls such matters as social services, patents and copyrights, naturalization, navigation, &c. The right of a State to legislate is not abrogated except in connection with matters exclusively under Federal controls but where a State law is inconsistent with a law of the Commonwealth the latter prevails to the extent of the inconsistency.

FLAG.—Blue ground, with Union Jack in top corner of hoist above large seven pointed star; Southern Constellation on fly.

GOVERNOR-GENERAL AND STAFF

Governor-General, His Excellency the Viscount DE L'ISLE, V.C., P.C., G.C.M.G., G.C.V.O., *born* 1909; *assumed office* Aug. 3, 1961 .... £10,000
Official Secretary, M. L. Tyrrell, C.V.O., C.B.E.
Military Secretary, Lt.-Col. W. E. Crowder, M.V.O., Irish Guards.
Comptroller, Lt.-Col T. A. Rodriguez, M.V.O., O.B.E., M.C.
Aides-de-Camp, Lt. D. A. Harries, R.A.N.; Flt. Lt. S. C. K. Mitchell, R.A.A.F.; Capt. P. N. de Bunsen, Coldstseam Guards.

THE COMMONWEALTH MINISTRY

(Jan. 12, 1956, as since re-constructed)

During 1961–62, the total amount provided for Ministers' salaries under the Ministers of State Acts, 1952–59, was £A99,100.

Prime Minister, Rt. Hon. Sir Robert Menzies, K.T., C.H., Q.C.
Treasurer, Rt. Hon. H. E. Holt.
Minister for Labour and National Service, Hon. W. McMahon.
Trade, Rt. Hon. J. McEwen.
Defence, Hon. A. G. Townley.
Minister for External Affairs and Attorney-General, Hon. Sir Garfield Barwick, Q.C.
Vice-President of the Executive Council and Minister for National Development, Senator Hon. Sir William Spooner, K.C.M.G., M.M.
Territories, Hon. P. M. C. Hasluck.
Civil Aviation, Senator Hon. S. D. Paltridge.
Postmaster-General, Hon. C. W. Davidson, O.B.E.
Immigration, Hon. A. R. Downer.
Primary Industry, Hon. C. F. Adermann.

The above form the Cabinet.

Repatriation, Hon. R. W. C. Swartz, M.B.E., E.D.
Health, Senator Hon. H. W. Wade.
Army, Hon. J. O. Cramer.
Air, Hon. D. E. Fairbairn, D.F.C.
Interior and Works, Hon. G. Freeth.
Social Services, Hon. H. S. Roberton.
Customs and Excise, Senator Hon. N. H. D. Henty.
Supply, Hon. A. Fairhall.
Navy, Senator Hon. J. G. Gorton.
Shipping and Transport, Hon. H. F. Opperman, O.B.E.

AUSTRALIAN REPRESENTATION ABROAD

ARGENTINA

Chargé d'Affaires, H. W. Bullock (Calle Rivadavia, Piso 5, Buenos Aires).

BELGIUM

Ambassador, W. R. Crocker, C.B.E. (*see* Netherlands).

BRAZIL

Ambassador, O. L. Davis (Rua Barao do Flamengo 22 Apto, 202, Rio de Janeiro).

BURMA

Ambassador, L. H. Border, M.V.O. (88 Strand Road, Rangoon).

CAMBODIA

Ambassador, N. St. C. Deschamps (94 Moha Vithei Preah Norodom, Phnom Penh).

CANADA

High Commissioner, D. O. Hay, C.B.E., D.S.O. (Royal Bank Chambers, 100 Sparks Street, Ottawa).

CEYLON

High Commissioner, B. C. Ballard (3 Cambridge Place, Colombo).

FRANCE

Ambassador, Sir Ronald Walker, C.B.E. (13 Rue las Cases, Paris, 7e).

GERMANY

Ambassador, F. J. Blakeney Kölnerstrasse 157, Bad-Godesberg).

GHANA

High Commissioner, B. G. Dexter (*acting*) (Ghana House, Accra).

INDIA AND NEPAL

High Commissioner, Sir James Plimsoll, C.B.E. (Communication Building, Connaught Place, New Delhi).

INDONESIA

Ambassador, K. C. O. Shann (Pengangsaan Barat 14, Djakarta).

REPUBLIC OF IRELAND

Chargé d'Affaires, H. D. White (33 Fitzwilliam Square, Dublin).

ISRAEL

Ambassador, J. D. L. Hood, C.B.E. (145 Hayarkon Street, Tel-Aviv).

ITALY

Ambassador, A. T. Stirling, C.B.E. (Via Sallustiana 26, Rome).

JAPAN

Ambassador, Sir Laurence McIntyre, C.B.E. (9 Mita, Tsuna-Machi Minato-Ku, Tokyo).

KOREA

Chargé d'Affaires, J.D. Petherbridge (32–10 Songwol-dong, Sudae Moon-Koo, Seoul).

LAOS

Ambassador, A. M. Morris (Quartier Phone Xay, Vientiane).

MALAYA

High Commissioner, T. K. Critchley (44 Ampang Road, Kuala Lumpur).

NETHERLANDS

Ambassador, W. R. Crocker, C.B.E. (18 Lange Voorhout, The Hague).

NEW ZEALAND

High Commissioner, Dr. Hon. D. A. Cameron, O.B.E. (Government Life Insurance Building, Wellington).

NIGERIA

High Commissioner, L. E. Phillips (*acting*) (P.O. Box 2427, Lagos).

PAKISTAN

High Commissioner, D. W. McNicol (9 Kutchery Road, Karachi).

PHILIPPINES

Ambassador, T. W. Cutts (L. & S. Building, 1414 Dewey Boulevard, Manila).

SINGAPORE

Commissioner, R. A. Woolcott (*acting*) (MacDonald House, Orchard Road, Singapore).

SOUTH AFRICA

Ambassador, J. C. G. Kevin (227 Vermeulen Street, Pretoria).

SWEDEN

Chargé d'Affaires, F. R. Gullick (Sergels Torg 12, Stockholm).

TANGANYIKA

High Commissioner, H. Gilchrist (Mercury House, 4 Suliman bin Nasser Street, Dar-es-Salaam).

THAILAND

Ambassador, A. H. Loomes, O.B.E. (323 Silom Road, Bangkok).

UNITED ARAB REPUBLIC

Ambassador, F. H. Stuart (1097 Corniche el Nil, Garden City, Cairo).

UNITED KINGDOM

High Commissioner, Rt. Hon. Sir Eric Harrison, K.C.M.G., K.C.V.O. (Australia House, Strand, London, W.C.2).

UNITED STATES

Ambassador, Hon. Sir Howard Beale, K.B.E., Q.C, (1700 Massachusetts Avenue, Washington, D.C.).

UNITED NATIONS

Ambassador, D. O. Hay, C.B.E., D.S.O. (750 Third Avenue, New York).

U.S.S.R.

Ambassador, S. Jamieson (13 Kropotkinsky Pereulok, Moscow).

VIETNAM

Ambassador, B. C. Hill (Caravelle Building, Place Lam Son, Saigon).

REPRESENTATIVES IN AUSTRALIA

AUSTRIA

Chargé d'Affaires, Dr. W. de Comtes.

BELGIUM

Ambassador, W. van Cauwenberg.

BRAZIL

Chargé d'Affaires, P. Leao de Moura.

BURMA
Ambassador, U Aung Shwe.
CAMBODIA
Ambassador, Poc Thieun.
CANADA
High Commissioner, E. W. T. Gill.
CEYLON
High Commissioner, Maj.-Gen. A. M. Muttukumaru.
CHILE
Chargé d'Affaires, G. Bucchi.
CHINA
Ambassador, Dr. Chen Chih-Mai.
DENMARK
Chargé d'Affaires, N. C. Stenderup.
FINLAND
Chargé d'Affaires, K. J. O. Wanne.
FRANCE
Ambassador, F. J. L. F. Brière.
GERMAN FEDERAL REPUBLIC
Ambassador, Dr. J. F. Ritter.
GREECE
Ambassador, P. A. Cavalierato.
INDIA
High Commissioner, K. R. Menon (*acting*).
INDONESIA
Ambassador, Brig.-Gen. S. Suromihardjo.
REPUBLIC OF IRELAND
Chargé d'Affaires, S. Kennan.
ISRAEL
Ambassador, D. Z. Tesher.
ITALY
Ambassador, R. Della Chiesa d'Isasca.
JAPAN
Ambassador, S. Ohta.
KOREA
Ambassador, Dong Whan Lee.
MALAYA
High Commissioner, Dato Suleiman bin Dato Abdul Rahman.
NETHERLANDS
Chargé d'Affaires, D. Ketel.
NEW ZEALAND
High Commissioner, J. Shepherd (*acting*).
PAKISTAN
High Commissioner, K. M. Kaiser.
PHILIPPINES
Ambassador, M. Ezpeleta.
PORTUGAL
Chargé d'Affaires, I. J. R. de Andrade.
SOUTH AFRICA
Ambassador, H. H. Woodward.
SWEDEN
Chargé d'Affaires, C.-J. Groth.
THAILAND
Ambassador, V. Isarabhakdi.
UNITED ARAB REPUBLIC
Ambassador, Mustafa Yusef.
UNITED KINGDOM
High Commissioner, Lieut.-Gen. Sir William Oliver, K.C.B., K.C.M.G., O.B.E.
Deputy High Commissioner, G. Kimber, C.M.G.
Counsellor and Official Secretary, E. N. Larmour.
First Secs., W. R. Bickford; E. V. Vines; S. W. F. Martin; A. E. Huttly.
Director, U.K. Information Services, D. D. Condon.
Head of U.K. Defence Liaison Staff, Rear Admiral A. Davies.
Economic Adviser and Senior Trade Commissioner, F. B. Arnold, C.M.G., O.B.E.
Agricultural Adviser, W. J. Kinghorn.
Scientific Adviser, T. M. Wilson.
Naval Adviser, Capt. T. W. Stocker.
Military Adviser, Col. A. G. Hewitt, M.B.E., M.C.
Air Adviser, Group Capt. F. B. Sutton, D.F.C.
British Council Representative, N. E. Williams, O.B.E.
UNITED STATES
Ambassador, William C. Battle.
U.S.S.R.
Ambassador, U. A. Loginov.
VIETNAM
Ambassador, Tran Van Lam.

THE LEGISLATURE

The Parliament of the Commonwealth of Australia consists of the Queen, a Senate and a House of Representatives. An Act, assented to on May 18, 1948, provided for an increase in the number of members of the Senate from thirty-six to sixty, and for the number of members of the House of Representatives to be increased from seventy-four to as nearly as practicable twice the number of Senators. There are now 124 members in the House of Representatives, including the two members, with restricted voting powers, representing the two internal territories. Members of the Senate are elected for six years by universal suffrage, half the members retiring every third year and each of the six States returning an equal number. The House of Representatives, similarly elected for a maximum of three years, contains members proportionate to the population, with a minimum of five members for each State. The present state of parties in the House of Representatives (excluding two Labour members for the internal territories) is Liberal 45, Country Party 17 and Labour 60. Members of both Houses receive £A2,750 per annum, with allowances and free air and rail travel on parliamentary business.

President of the Senate, Senator Hon. Sir Alister McMullin, K.C.M.G.
Clerk of the Senate, R. H. C. Loof, C.B.E. £5,025
Speaker, House of Representatives, Hon. Sir John McLeay, K.C.M.G., M.M.
Clerk of the House, A. G. Turner £5,025

THE JUDICATURE

HIGH COURT OF AUSTRALIA

There is a Federal High Court with a Chief Justice and 6 Justices having original and appellate jurisdiction. Appeals from the High Court may go to the Judicial Committee of the Privy Council by special leave of the Committee except in certain constitutional cases, where the certificate of the High Court is necessary. The principal seat of the Court is at Melbourne, Victoria.

Chief Justice, Rt. Hon. Sir Owen Dixon, O.M., G.C.M.G. £10,000
Justices, Rt. Hon. Sir Edward Aloysius McTiernan, K.B.E.; Rt. Hon. Sir Frank Waters Kitto, K.B.E.; Rt. Hon. Sir Alan Russell Taylor, K.B.E.; Rt. Hon. Sir Douglas Ian Menzies, K.B.E.; Rt. Hon. Sir (William John) Victor Windeyer, K.B.E., C.B., D.S.O.; Rt. Hon. Sir William Owen, C.B.E. £8,500
Principal Registrar, A. N. Gamble.

COMMONWEALTH INDUSTRIAL COURT

Chief Judge, Hon. Sir John Spicer £8,000
Judges, Hons. E. A. Dunphy; P. E. Joske; R. M. Eggleston.................each £7,000

COMMONWEALTH CONCILIATION AND ARBITRATION COMMISSION

President, Hon. Sir Richard Kirby....... £8,000
Deputy Presidents, Hons. S. C. G. Wright; F. H. Gallagher; J. C. Moore...........each £7,000

FEDERAL COURT OF BANKRUPTCY

Judge, Hon. Sir Thomas Stuart Clyne...... £7,000

SUPREME COURT OF THE AUSTRALIAN CAPITAL TERRITORY

Judges, Hon. E. A. Dunphy; Hon. P. E. Joske; Hon. R. M. Eggleston.

SUPREME COURT OF THE NORTHERN TERRITORY
Judge, Hon. A. B. K. I. Bridge.
Additional Judges, Hon. E. A. Dunphy; Hon. P. E. Joske.................each £7,000

DEFENCE

Subject to the authority of Cabinet the Minister and Department of Defence are responsible for the formulation and general application of a unified defence policy relating to the Defence Forces and their requirements. Separate Ministers and Departments of the Navy, Army and Air are responsible for the administration of their respective Services in accordance with defence policy. The Minister and Department of Supply are responsible for the supply, manufacture and overhaul of services and goods, including munitions, for the Defence Forces and for defence research and development, in accordance with approved policy.

Royal Australian Navy

Under the Naval Defence Acts, 1910–52, the naval forces of the Commonwealth are administered by a Naval Board of Administration responsible to the Minister of the Navy.

The Royal Australian Navy consists of an aircraft carrier, a fast troop transport, 4 destroyers, 3 anti-submarine frigates, 4 frigates, 4 auxiliary vessels, a fleet replenishment ship, 6 minesweepers and a variety of support craft. In addition, 3 submarines are on loan from the Royal Navy for anti-submarine training. In reserve there are 2 destroyers, 1 frigate, 4 boom working vessels, 1 fleet tug and several support craft.

Two anti-submarine frigates and a survey ship are completing in Australian dockyards. Two destroyers are being built in the U.S.A., and a third has been ordered. Initial tenders have been invited for 4 submarines.

The strength of the Royal Australian Navy on June 1, 1963, was 1,330 officers and 10,398 ratings.

Army

The Military Forces of the Commonwealth are administered by a Military Board, with the Minister for the Army as President and 7 members. There are three elements—the Australian Regular Army, the Citizen Military Forces and the Cadet Corps.

For the financial year 1962–63 the authorized strength of the Australian Regular Army was 22,500 soldiers and 5,000 civilians. This includes a Field Force, Regular Army cadres for duty with the Citizen Military Forces, administrative staff for schools, training installations and headquarters and maintenance units, in addition to the Pacific Islands Regiment comprising European officers and non-commissioned officers and native troops. The Women's Royal Australian Army Corps forms part of the Australian Regular Army, being employed in direct substitution for male soldiers in mainland units. The Royal Australian Army Nursing Corps is also an important element of the Regular Army.

The strength of the Australian Regular Army on April 30, 1963, was 22,847 all ranks, of whom 2,522 were serving outside Australia.

The strength of the Citizen Military Forces on April 30, 1963, was 27,581. The two Women's Services are also represented in the Citizen Military Forces, the strength at April 30, 1963, being 667.

The Australian Cadet Corps, composed of students at educational establishments, had a strength of 37,626 on March 31, 1963.

Air

The total strength of the R.A.A.F. on May 1, 1963, was 15,843. There were 14 flying squadrons, one ground squadron (surface air missile), 6 maintainance squadrons, 22 training units, 5 auxiliary squadrons, 6 university squadrons and 7 A.T.C. squadrons. 4 flying squadrons and one maintenance squadron were serving outside Australia.

War Losses

Australian battle casualties in the 1939–45 War:—

Killed (including died of wounds, died while P.O.W., and "missing, presumed dead")	27,073
P.O.W escaped, recovered or repatriated	22,264
Wounded and injured	23,477
	72,814

Total Non-battle casualties—7,210 killed, 157,650 injured.

COMMONWEALTH FINANCE*

Consolidated Reserve Fund

Years.	Revenue	Expenditure.	Loan Fund Expenditure.
	£A,000	£A,000	£A,000
1955–56	1,138,358	1,138,358	69,823
1956–57	1,311,835	1,311,835	49,366
1957–58	1,323,771	1,323,771	59,698
1958–59	1,296,050	1,296,050	93,613
1959–60	1,438,286	1,438,286	59,607
1960–61	1,638,279	1.638,279	41,640
1961–62	1,641,542	1,641,542	91,165

The above particulars do not include the interest payable on loans to the States, which amount is recoverable from the States concerned.

* Australian currency—£100=£A125.

DEBT

The total of the Commonwealth Debt on December 31, 1962, was £1,686,200,000. Adding the indebtedness of the States. viz. £3,051,000,000 the "face" or "book" value of Australian government securities on issue amounted (December 31, 1962) to £4,737,200,000.

The Debt per head of population at Dec. 31, 1961, was £438 4*s*. 2*d*.

COMMONWEALTH EXPENDITURE ON SOCIAL AND HEALTH SERVICES

Service	1960–61	1961–62
	£A	£A
Age and Invalid Pensions	157,900,000	180,245,000
Child Endowment	74,000,000	66,378,000
Commonwealth Rehabilitation Service	693.000	723,000
Funeral Benefits	367,000	376,000
Maternity Allowances	3,898,000	3,908,000
Unemployment, Sickness and Special Benefits	7,140,000	15,905,000
Widows' Pensions	13,468,000	15,094,000
Hospital Benefits	20,668,000	22,197,000
Medical Benefits	14,176,000	15,315,000
Nutrition of Children	3,560,000	3,742,000
Pharmaceutical Benefits	27,881,000	35,189,000
Tuberculosis Campaign	5,126,000	5,206,000
Miscellaneous	1,046,000	848,000
Rental Rebates	352,000	65,000
Total	330,604,000	365,191,000

Current Rates

Age Pension: £5 5*s*. per week.

Invalid Pension (weekly rates): Pensioner, £5 5*s*.; wife, £2 7*s*. 6*d*.; first child under 16 years 15*s*.; each child under 16 years except first, 10*s*.

Widows' Pensions (weekly rates): "A" class widows having one or more children under 16 years, £5 10*s*.; "B" class, a widow of not less than

50 years of age, without dependent children, or who, after reaching the age of 45 years, no longer has a child under 16 years, £4 12*s*. 6*d*.; "C" class, widows who at the time of death of husband are less than 50 years of age without dependent children and are in necessitous circumstances, within 26 weeks following her husband's death, or until the birth of her child if she is pregnant, £4 12*s*. 6*d*.

Maternity Allowances.—Where there are no other children under 16 years of age, £15; where there are one or two other children, £16; where there are three or more other children, £17 10*s*. Where more than one child is born at a birth, the rate is £5 for each additional child.

Child Endowment.—(For children under 16). Rate: 5*s*. per week for the first child in a family, 10*s*. per week for each other child in a family, and 10*s*. for each child in an institution.

Unemployment, Sickness and Special Benefits.—Rate: £4 2*s*. 6*d*. per week for married person or unmarried adult, plus £3 for dependent spouse or unpaid housekeeper and 15*s*. for each dependent child. For unmarried juveniles the rate is £1 15*s*. if under 18 years of age, and £2 7*s*. 6*d*. if 18 and under 21 years of age.

Hospital Benefits.—Rate: 8*s*. per day in public or private hospitals registered for the purpose. An additional 12*s*. per day is payable in respect of contributors to registered hospital benefit organisations.

Tuberculosis Benefits: Single person, £7 7*s*. 6*d*. per week. Married person £12 2*s*. 6*d*. per week plus 15*s*. per week for the first child under 16 years and 10*s*. per week for each other child under 16 years.

COMMONWEALTH AND STATE FINANCE AND BANKING.

Banking.—The average Australian liabilities and assets (excluding shareholders' funds, interbranch accounts and contingencies) of the 7 major private Trading Banks operating in the Commonwealth, together with the amount of deposits with Savings Banks, are shown below.

Private Trading Banks

Quarter ended.	Liabilities in Australia.	Assets in Australia.
March, 1962	£1,613,346,000	£1,627,327,000
June, 1962	1,580,182,000	1,598,666,000
March, 1963	1,697,333,000	1,698,355,000

Savings Banks Amount on Deposit

Date.	Amount.	Per Head.		
March, 1962	£1,670 099,000	£ 156	13	2
June, 1962	1,734 886,000	162	1	3
March, 1963	1,887,713,000	174	12	5

Finance

Consolidated Reserve Funds

State, etc.	1961-62		
	Rev. £A,000 omitted	Exp. £A,000 omitted	Surplus (+) or Deficit (−)
N.S.W.	295,612	298,745	− 3,133
Victoria	196,309	196,298	+ 11
Queensland	117,325	117,215	+ 110
S. Australia	89,102	88,596	+ 506
W. Australia	74,926	75,890	− 964
Tasmania	31,293	31,651	− 358
Total, Six States	804,567	808,395	− 3,828
Commonwealth	1,641,542	1,641,542	..
Grand Total (*a*)	2,102,583	2,106,411	− 3,828

(*a*) To avoid duplication in aggregating particulars for the Commonwealth and States, the grand totals exclude payments by the Commonwealth to the States included in State consolidated revenue funds in respect of interest on States' debts, special grants, financial assistance, grants to Universities, tuberculosis capital expenditure and National Welfare Fund payments, and payments by the States to the Commonwealth in respect of Commonwealth Pay-roll tax.

PRODUCTION AND INDUSTRY
(Commonwealth)

The estimated net values of production:—

	1960-61	1961-62 (*a*)
Agricultural	£A391 861,000	£A367,395,000
Pastoral	458,169,000	479 277,000
Dairying, &c.	183 853,000	172,920,000
Forests and Fisheries	64,870,000	63,382,000
Mining	139 027,000	138 051,000
Manufacturing	2,169 804,000	2,197,211,000
	£A3,407,584,000	£A3,418,236,000

(*a*) Subject to revision.

PRIMARY PRODUCTION

Years	Wool (million lb.)	Wheat (million (bushels)	Butter ('000 tons)
1957–58	1,434	98	176
1958–59	1,591	215	194
1959–60	1,680	199	198
1960–61	1,625	274	182
1961–62	1,699	247	199
†1962–63	1,670	307	..

† Estimated.

Agriculture and Live Stock.—The total area of rural holdings in 1961–62 was 1,172,435,000 acres. The principal crops were:—

Crop	Acreage	*Bushels*
*Wheat	14,723,000	247,178,000
Oats	3,097,000	55,130,000
Barley	2,383,000	41,504,000
Maize	211,000	7,307,000
Hay	2,274,000	*Tons*..3,693,000
Sugar-cane	387,000	*Tons*..9,577,000

*Wheat estimate (1962–63) 307,210,000 *bushels*.

Live Stock (in thousands).

	1958	1959	1960	1961	1962
Sheep	149,315	152,685	155,174	152,679	157,712
Cattle	16,892	16,257	16,503	17,332	18,033
Horses	694	671	640	598	562
Pigs	1,423	1,289	1,424	1,615	1,653

In 1961–62 Australia produced 1,698,543,000 lb. of wool (as in the grease), estimated value, £A370,394,000; 444,911,000 lb. of butter; 124,380,000 lb. of cheese; and 90,141,000 lb. (cured weight) of bacon and hams. The total meat production (beef, mutton, lamb, pork, bacon and hams) in terms of fresh meat was estimated at 1,498,332 tons.

Mines and Minerals.—In 1962 the mine production of gold was 1,073,147 fine oz. and of black coal 24,481,323 tons. Smelter and refinery production of principal metals in 1962 was: pig iron, 3,433,809 tons; copper (blister), 87,337 tons; lead, 263,326 tons; tin, 2,740 tons; zinc, 168,245 tons; silver, 7,451,196 fine oz. Value of output of all mining and quarrying in 1961, £181,378,000.

Manufactures.—In 1961–62 there were in Australia 58,450 industrial establishments, employing 1,120,666 persons; wages paid amounted to

£A1,142,002,000; value of plant and machinery £A1,524 787,000; land and buildings £A1 403 838,000; of materials, fuel, etc., used £A2 835 386,000; value added by manufacture £A2,197 211,000; and value of total output £A5,244 364,000.

Trade Unions.—In 1962 there were 347 separate Trade Unions in Australia with a total membership of 1,950,484.

TOTAL EXTERNAL TRADE

(including Bullion and Specie.)

Years	Imports £A	Exports £A
1957–58	791,940,000	817,946,000
1958–59	796,599,000	811,463,000
1959–60	927,091,000	937,682,000
1960–61	1,087,577,000	968,813,000
1961–62	884,746,000	1,077,284,000

Country	Imports from 1961–62	Exports to 1961–62
United Kingdom	£A265,917,000	£A206,374,000
Canada	34,158,000	17,524,000
Ceylon	9,821,000	8,947,000
India	16 070,000	25 222,000
Pakistan	5,663,000	3,329,000
Fed. of Malaya	11,098,000	11,560,000
New Zealand	13 548,000	58 767,000
South Africa	7,843,000	9 699,000
Hong Kong	6,418,000	20,282,000
Belgium and Luxemburg	6,810,000	22,981,000
China (mainland)	3,811,000	65 956,000
France	11,085,000	52,056,000
Germany (Fed. Rep.)	51 832,000	40 834,000
Indonesia	26,510,000	3 548,000
Italy	14 028,000	52 180 000
Japan	49,495,000	186,905,000
Netherlands	13,142,000	10,151,000
Norway	3,332,000	2,153,000
Persia	510,000	4,669,000
Poland	425,000	9,468,000
Saudi Arabia and Yemen	12,057,000	1,179,000
Sweden	16,655,000	2,124,000
Switzerland	13,761,000	1,542,000
U.S.A.	174,080,000	109 007,000
U.S.S.R.	850,000	11,767,000

IMPORTS FROM ALL COUNTRIES	1961–62
Fish Preserved in Tins	£A4,086,000
Tea	12,914,000
Tobacco, Cigars, and Cigarettes	9,744,000
Whisky	3,784,000
Aluminium and alloys	5,348,000
Trimmings and Ornaments	1,337,000
Piece-goods:—	
Hessians and Jute	3,292,000
Cotton and Linen	36,214,000
Rayon and Silk	7,239,000
Woollen, or containing Wool	1,455,000
Other	6,316,000
Carpets and Carpeting	4,532,000
Linoleums	2,746,000
Bags and Sacks	10 380,000
Yarns, Cotton, Artificial Silk, &c.	10 414 000
Sewing Silk, Cottons, &c.	2 228,000
Hides and Skins	1,481,000
Agricultural, etc., Machinery	2 463,000
Metal-working Machinery	11,678,000
Office and Accounting Machinery	11 712,000
Electrical Appliances, etc.	47,862,000
Motive-power Machinery (except Electric)	37,578,000
Tools of Trade	£A3,660,000
Vehicles and Parts:—	
Aircraft and Parts	12 174,000
Motor	47,686,000
Other Vehicles and Parts	9,115,000
Oils in bulk:—	
Kerosene	5,020,000
Lubricating (Mineral)	6,453,000
Petroleum	88,225,000
Residual and Solar	2,757,000
Glass and Glassware	7,928,000
Plated Ware and Cutlery	2,579,000
Paints and Varnishes	5,456,000
Paper and Printing	38,471,000
Stationery, Books, &c.	19,382,000
Seeds	1,883,000
Copra	1,998,000
Fertilizers	7,836,000
Arms, Ammunition, Explosives	(*a*) 8 140,000
Drugs, Chemicals, &c.	50 320,000
Bullion and Specie	2,200,000
Iron and Steel	20,403,000
Copper	3,140,000
Rubber and Manufactures	17,772,000
Timber, dressed and undressed	11,741,000

(*a*) Including military stores and equipment, £5,603,000.

EXPORTS TO ALL COUNTRIES	1961–62
Wool	£A372,531,000
Biscuits	370,000
Butter	23,537,000
Eggs	4,192,000
Meat	89 658,000
Milk and Cream	8,307,000
Cheese	5,203,000
Fruit (Fresh)	13 363,000
Fruit (Dried)	10 357,000
Fruit (Preserved in containers)	11,919,000
Wheat	142,446,000
Flour (Wheaten), plain white	17 397,000
Barley	14 954,000
Hides and Skins	32,147,000
Soap	502,000
Timber	3,021,000
Sugar and Sugar Syrups	33 940,000
Jams and Jellies	473,000
Wine	1,393,000
Tobacco (manufactures)	564,000
Pearlshell	385,000
Ores and Concentrates	24,665,000
Lead—Pig	14,253,000
Lead and Silver Lead Bullion	4,183,000
Iron and Steel	43,152,000
Zinc Bars and Blocks	6,387,000
Piece-goods	789,000
Arms, Ammunition and Explosives	(*a*) 3 494,000
Bullion and Specie	9,399,000

(*a*) Including military stores and equipment, £2,421,000.

AUSTRALIA'S TRADE WITH U.K.

1955–62

Year	Value of Merchandise From U.K.	Value of Merchandise To U.K.
1955–56	£A355,913,000	£A257,181,000
1956–57	290,251,000	275,637,000
1957–58	325,007,000	221,421,000
1958–59	307,437,000	256,935,000
1959–60	330,302,000	247,321,000
1960–61	340,531,000	231,591,000
1961–62	265,917,000	206,374,000

FOOD EXPORTS TO BRITAIN, 1961–62

Item	Value
Butter	£A19,950,000

Cheese	£A3,427,000
Eggs	3,253,000
Meats:—	
Preserved by cold process.	15,095,000
Preserved in airtight containers.	6,959,000
Jams and Jellies	83,000
Milk and Cream	305,000
Currants	86,000
Raisins and Sultanas	4,989,000
Fresh Fruits	7,517,000
Fruits (Preserved in tins)	10,723,000
Flour (wheaten), plain white	1,943,000
Wheat	16,438,000
Sugar and Sugar Syrups	18,604,000

COMMUNICATIONS

Railways.—Total length of Commonwealth-owned and State-owned railways open for general traffic at June 30, 1961:—

State-owned	Route miles	Gross Receipts
New South Wales	6,062	£88,351,021 (*a*)
Victoria	4,291	42,557,136 (*a*)
Queensland	6,077	36,158,803
South Australia	2,532	13,923,747 (*a*)
Western Australia	3,851	17,549,402
Tasmania	516	2,703,210
Commonwealth-owned		
Trans-Australian	1,108	4,146,104
Central Australia	822	1,887,855
Northern Territory	317	159,120
Capital Territory	5	48,347
Total	25,582	£207,484,745

(*a*) Excludes certain government subsidies aggregating £5,914,566.

The *Trans-Australia* (Government) *Railway*, 4 ft. 8½ in. gauge, connects Kalgoorlie, W.A.. with Port Pirie, S.A. (1,108 miles) and so forms a link (including Kalgoorlie–Perth 372 miles) between Perth and Brisbane, Q., a total length of 3,308 miles.

The gross earnings of all Government lines in 1961–62 were £207,484,745, working expenses £202,246,734, and net profit £5,238,011. In 1961–62 passenger journeys numbered 443,319,351 and 55,564,902 tons of goods and live stock were carried. There are 233 miles of electrified line in New South Wales and 264 miles in Victoria.

Tramways, Trolley-buses and Omnibuses.—The total route mileage on June 30, 1962, under Government and semi-Government control was 229 for trams, 71 for trolley-buses and 5,929 for omnibuses.

Shipping.—The entrances and clearances (one entrance and one clearance per voyage, irrespective of the number of ports visited) of vessels engaged in overseas trade at the various Australian ports in 1961–62 were: entered 3,599 (18,858,000 tons); cleared 3,611 (18,804,000 tons). Of the vessels entered, 1,776 of 9,045,000 tons were under the British flag and 1,823 of 9,812,000 tons under foreign flags.

The total, including local shipping, entering the ports of the capital cities during 1961–62 was: Sydney 4,395 vessels of 14,715,000 tons, Melbourne 2,852 (11,094,000), Brisbane 1,406 (4,870,000), Adelaide 2,496 (5,871,000), Fremantle 1,491 (8,017,000) and Hobart 577 (1,520,000). At December 31, 1962, there were 1,610 vessels of a total net tonnage of 316,876 on the shipping registers of the several States.

Posts and Telegraphs.—In the year ended June 30, 1962, there were 8,001 post offices dealing with 1,748,054,000 letters, 324,694,000 packets and newspapers, 12,357,000 registered articles and 15,854,000 parcels. 18,739,000 internal telegrams were despatched and 2,850,000 international telegrams received and despatched. At June 30, 1962, there were 7,056 telephone exchanges with 1,719,000 services and 2,382,000 instruments.

Broadcasting.—On June 30, 1962, the National Broadcasting and Television Service operated 77 stations, including 16 short-wave stations. Privately owned commercial broadcasting stations totalled 110. On June 30, 1962, there were in force in Australia 2,220,462 listeners' licences. Television transmissions commenced in September, 1956. On June 30, 1962, 26 television stations were in operation, 16 in the various State capitals, and 10 in country areas. Television licences in force at June 30, 1962, numbered 1,424,435.

Motor Vehicles.—At June 30, 1962, there were 3,138,091 motor vehicles registered in the several States. These comprised 2,184,727 cars, 85,000 motor cycles, and 868,364 commercial vehicles; revenue derived from motor registration fees and motor tax, &c., in 1961–62 was £52,778,000.

Civil Aviation.—At June 30, 1962, there were 483 recognized landing grounds, including 359 licensed public aerodromes, in the various States and Territories, and 13 flying boat bases and alighting areas. Aircraft on the Australian Register at Dec. 31, 1962, numbered 1,600. Mileage flown on regular internal air services in 1961–62 was 41,176,000 and on overseas services owned or partly-owned by Australia, 19,240,000.

CAPITAL

CANBERRA, the Capital of the Australian Commonwealth, is 203 miles by rail (153 by air) from Sydney, N.S.W. and was acquired in 1911 from the State of N.S.W. for the Australian Capital. The original area was 911 sq. miles, increased in 1917 by the acquisition of 28 sq. miles at Jervis Bay. Canberra contains the Australian (1914–18 and 1939–45) War Memorial, Parliament House, Commonwealth Offices, and the Australian National University, and is connected with the N.S.W. railway system by a line (5 miles) to Queanbeyan and by good roads to Melbourne and Sydney. Frequent air services also link it with the State capitals. The estimated population of Canberra city area at June 30, 1962, was 63,313. Total population of the Australian Capital Territory (estimated, June 30, 1962) 65,692.

THE NORTHERN TERRITORY

The Northern Territory has a total area of 523,620 square miles, and lies between 129°–138° East longitude and 11°—26° South latitude. The administration was taken over by the Commonwealth on January 1, 1911, from the government of the State of South Australia. The headquarters of the Administrator are at Darwin. The Commonwealth Parliament in May, 1959, amended the Northern Territory (Administration) Act in order to enlarge the membership of the Council. The new Council consists of six official members, three non-official members and eight elected members. The official and non-official members are appointed by the Governor-General on the recommendation of the Administrator, and the elected members are elected by adult franchise. Under the amending legislation, procedures in connection with assent were changed. Ordinances passed by the Council must be presented to the Administrator who may declare his assent, withhold his assent or reserve the ordinance for the Governor-General's pleasure. The Administrator may return an ordinance to the Legislative Council with recommended amendments; but the ordinance with or without amendments must be again presented to the Administrator for assent. Certain ordinances must be reserved for the Governor-General's pleasure. The Governor-General may return an ordinance with recommended amendments and this ordinance with or without amendments shall again be presented to the Administrator, who shall reserve it for the Governor-General's pleasure. Ordinances assented to by the Administrator may be disallowed by the Governor-General, and the Governor-General may recommend to the Administrator amendments to laws of the Territory. The new Act also sets up an Administrator's Council to advise the Administrator. The Council consists of the Administrator, two official members of the Legislative Council and three other members of the Legislative Council not being official members, and of whom at least two shall be elected members.

The population of the Northern Territory (excluding full-blooded aboriginals) at June 30, 1962, was estimated to be:—males 16,571. females 11,219, total 27,790. The number of full-blooded aboriginals was estimated (June 30, 1962) at 18,270.

Beef cattle raising is the chief pastoral activity, and the staple industry of the Territory. On June 30, 1962, there were 1,054,669 cattle, 39,835 horses and 8 976 sheep in the Territory. Importations of livestock for the year ending June 30, 1962, were: bulls 1,740, other cattle 9,559, horses 234, sheep 4,716. 134,901 cattle were exported during the same period. The Territory is capable under improved conditions of carrying successfully and profitably a great expansion of the beef cattle industry. Hides and skins exported from the Northern Territory during the year ended June 30, 1962, were as follows:—cattle 5,896, sheep 3,952, crocodile 11,891 and buffalo 653.

Agriculture in the Northern Territory hitherto has been confined to small farm settlements in the Darwin, Katherine, Daly River, Alice Springs, Adelaide River and Pine Creek areas. Principal crops grown are peanuts, grain sorghum, vegetables and fruit (pineapples, paw-paws, bananas and citrus). However, extensive experiments are being carried out particularly in the area between Darwin and Katherine to determine what crops can be successfully grown in the Northern Territory on a commercial scale. Experimental work on pastures is also being undertaken. In recent years interest has been shown in the possibility of rice production on the sub-coastal plains areas of the Territory.

Out of a total of about 335,117,000 acres in the Northern Territory, 376,000 acres are freehold, 158,026,000 acres are held in various forms of leasehold tenure, 21,623,000 acres are under annual licence, 59,590,000 acres are aboriginal and other reserves and 96,102,000 acres are unoccupied and unreserved.

The mineral industry has always contributed largely to the income of the Northern Territory and the value of mineral production exceeds that of the beef cattle industry. The principal minerals produced are copper, gold, uranium, manganese, mica and wolfram. In 1962, the total value of minerals produced (excluding uranium) was £3,688,580.

The chief rivers of the Territory are Victoria, Adelaide, Daly, Roper, South Alligator, McArthur, Liverpool, and Goyder. The first six are navigable, from 40 to 100 miles from their entrance, for boats drawing 4 feet. Mother-of-pearl fishing is carried on round the coast, the shell being of good quality.

The railway extends from Darwin to Larrimah (316 miles) and Alice Springs is connected by rail with Adelaide. A good bitumen road links Darwin with Alice Springs (954 miles) and another bitumen road runs from this road near Tennant Creek to Mt. Isa in Queensland (403 miles). The Commonwealth Government is carrying out a five-year plan to maintain and improve this highway and the Barkly highway to the Queensland border. As part of a special programme for the development of North Australia, five roads in the Northern Territory are being reconstructed to a higher standard to facilitate the movement of beef cattle by large road trains.

ΨDarwin occupies an elevated site 97 feet above sea level, overlooking Port Darwin. Alice Springs is situated in the MacDonnell Ranges. Climate of the Northern Territory ranges from dry in the south to wet-monsoonal in the north.

Administrator of the Northern Territory (Darwin), Hon. R. B. Nott.............. £4,725

Assistant Administrators, A. V. Atkins (*Economic and Social Affairs*); L. L. Gillespie (*Administration, Services and Finance*)..... £3,650

Judges, Supreme Court, Hons. A. B. K. I. Bridge; E. A. Dunphy; P. E. Joski.

TERRITORY OF PAPUA AND NEW GUINEA

The Papua and New Guinea Act, 1949, which came into force on July 1, 1949, approved the placing of the Territory of New Guinea under the International Trusteeship system and provides for the Government of the Territory of Papua and the Territory of New Guinea in an Administrative Union.

By an amendment of the *Papua and New Guinea Act* passed by the Australian Parliament in May, 1963, the Legislative Council is to be replaced by a House of Assembly consisting of 44 members elected on a common roll in single member constituencies known as open electorates; 10 non-indigenous members elected on a common roll in single-member constituencies known as reserved electorates, which will be made up of one or more open electorates; and 10 official members appointed by the Governor-General on the nomination of the Administrator. The Administrator, who is President of the present Legislative Council, will not be a member of the House of Assembly, which will elect one of its members to be the Speaker.

The Administrator's Council has also been reconstituted by amendments to the *Papua and New Guinea Act* and when the new House of Assembly has been elected the Administrator's Council will consist of the Administrator, 3 official members, and 7 elected members.

The Territory of Papua, which was placed under the authority of the Commonwealth of Australia in 1906, comprises the south eastern portion of the island of New Guinea, together with the Trobriands Woodlark, D'Entrecasteaux and Louisiade groups of islands and is separated from Australia by Torres Strait. The Territory lies wholly within the Tropics, between the 141st and the 155th meridians of east longitude and the 5th and 12th parallels of south latitude. The total area is 90,540 sq. miles, of which 87,540 are on the mainland. The non-indigenous population of Papua and New Guinea is 26,544; the indigenous population is estimated at 1,998,176. Owing to heavy rainfall Papua is well watered in most parts and possesses a large number of streams. The best-known rivers are the Fly (730 miles long, including its tributary, the Strickland, and navigable by vessels with a draught of up to 6 ft. for 580 miles) and the Purari. The climate is favourable to the cultivation of tropical products.

The German possessions on the mainland of New Guinea and certain adjacent islands were occupied by Australian forces on Sept. 12, 1914, and on Dec. 17, 1920, a mandate of the Supreme Council of the Allies entrusted the administration to the Australian Government which established its administration on May 9, 1921.

The Trust Territory includes (1) *North-Eastern New Guinea*, the northern section of east New Guinea between 2° 35′–8° S. lat., and 141°–148° E. long., with a total area of 69,700 sq. miles. This includes adjacent islands (Manam, Karkar, Long, Bagabag, Schouten and D'Urville or Kairiru Island). The chief centres are Lae, Bulolo, Finschhafen, Wau, Madang, Wewak, Goroka and Mount Hagen. (2) *Bismarck Archipelago* (19,200 sq. miles), including New Britain, New Ireland, and islands adjacent to both, and (3) *Admiralty Islands* (chief town, Lorengau, in Manus Island); and (4) the two northernmost *Solomon Islands* (4,100 sq. miles) (Bougainville and Buka with adjacent islands). The total estimated area is thus 93,000 square miles.

The principal river in N.E. New Guinea is the Sepik, 690 miles long, and navigable for 580 miles by vessels with a draught of up to 6 ft.

A road to the coast over rugged country serves the areas of the Lower Watut, Sunshine, Bulolo, Wau and Edie Creek, and a farming, timber and gold district at Wau, and another road system has been extended from Lae to Goroka and other centres in the Highlands, where a thriving coffee industry is established, and work is taking place to link Goroka by road with Lae.

Trans-Australian Airlines and Ansett-A.N.A. operate regular air services from Australia to Papua and New Guinea. There are also fortnightly T.A.A. and K.L.M. services from Lae to Hollandia, Netherlands New Guinea, and internal services run by T.A.A., Ansett Mandated Airlines and other companies.

Overseas vessels call at various ports and a regular service is maintained with Australia.

The climate is hot and moist along the coast, with a steady drop as the higher altitudes are reached. It is suitable to the growth of all tropical products. The major output of gold is still from the Morobe District, but the yield is decreasing. In the Bulolo valley a new plywood industry has been developed with an annual output of more than £A1,250,000 in value.

Trusteeship.—The Commonwealth Government has placed the Territory of New Guinea under the Trusteeship system established under the United Nations Charter and the agreement under which Australia became the sole administering authority was approved by the General Assembly of the United Nations on Dec. 13, 1946.

SEAT OF ADMINISTRATION.—Administrative Headquarters of the combined territories of Papua and New Guinea is ΨPort Moresby, the principal port and town of Papua. ΨRabaul (in New Britain), is the largest port in the combined territories and second town, while ΨLae (in Morobe District) is the third port and town of the combined territories, being the outlet for the Morobe plywood and gold mining district and for the Highlands region, and one of the principal air centres in the territories.

FINANCE AND TRADE
(Papua and New Guinea)

	1961–62	1962–63*
Revenue...	£A24,999,000 (a)	(c) £A28,680,000 (b) (d)
Expenditure..	25,001,000	28,680,000
Imports......	25,929,476	..
Exports......	15,901,043	..

*Estimated.

(a) Includes £A17,299,000; and (b) £A20,000,000 Australian Commonwealth grant; (c) Includes £A496,766 and (d) £A900,000 loan receipts.

Administrator of the Government of Papua and New Guinea, Sir Donald Cleland, C.B.E.

Port Moresby is distant from Sydney, N.S.W., 1,800 miles.

NORFOLK ISLAND

This island is about 930 miles from Sydney and 400 miles from New Zealand. It is about five miles in length by three in breadth, and was discovered by Capt. Cook in 1774. Its area is 8,528 acres and circumference 20 miles. The climate is mild, with a mean temperature of 68° and an annual rainfall of 53 inches. The descendants of the mutineers of the *Bounty* were brought here from Pitcairn Island in 1856. A modern whaling station was established on the island in 1955. The estimated population on June 30, 1962, was 1,877.

Seat of Government and Administration Offices, Kingston. Local government was established in June, 1960, by the creation of the Norfolk Island Council with power to control roads, electricity, lighterage and other municipal services.

The construction of an airfield was completed in 1943, and weekly air services are now in operation from Australia and New Zealand.

Administrator, Maj.-Gen. R. H. Wordsworth, C.B., C.B.E.

President, Norfolk Island Council, F. J. Needham.

NAURU ISLAND

This island, situated in 166° 55 East longitude and 32 minutes south of the Equator, was discovered by Capt. Fearn, R.N., in 1798, and was annexed by Germany in 1888. It surrendered to H.M.A.S. *Melbourne* in November, 1914, and is now administered by Britain, Australia and New Zealand. Under an international trusteeship agreement approved by the General Assembly of U.N. on Nov. 1, 1947, this agreement supersedes the League of Nations' Mandate, but Australia continues to be responsible for the administration of the Island on behalf of the grantor Governments. The island has an area of approximately 8 square miles, with a population (June 30, 1962) of 4,849, of whom 3,516 were Nauruans, 1,173 other Pacific Islanders, 748 Chinese and 412 Europeans. Administrative and legislative powers of government are vested in the Administrator. The Judiciary consists of a District Court, a Central Court and an Appeal Court. Expenses of the Administration so far as they exceed revenue are met by the British Phosphate Commissioners under an agreement made between the three administering Governments. There are valuable deposits of phosphates on the island, which were purchased from the Pacific Phosphate Company in 1919 by the Governments of Great Britain, Australia and New Zealand for £3,500,000, and vested in the British Phosphate Commissioners.

Nauru was occupied by the Japanese from Aug. 26, 1942, to Sept. 13, 1945. Since re-occupation the buildings and plant of the Administration and the British Phosphate Commissioners have been restored. Services provided by the Administration for the Nauruan people include medical and dental services, hospitalization, maternity and infant welfare, and education services up to fourth year secondary school standard, beyond which overseas scholarships and public service cadetships are available. Exports of phosphates for the 12 months ended June 30, 1962, totalled 1,541,652 tons.

Administrator, R. S. Leydin, O.B.E.

COCOS (KEELING) ISLANDS

The Cocos (Keeling) Islands were declared a British possession in 1857, and in 1878 were placed under the control of the Governor of Ceylon and were later annexed to the Straits Settlements and incorporated with the Settlement (now the Colony) of Singapore. On Nov. 23, 1955, their administration was transferred to the Commonwealth of Australia. They are two separate atolls comprising some 27 small coral islands with a total area of about five square miles, situated in the Indian Ocean in latitude 12° 5′ South and longitude 96° 53′ East. The main islands are West Island (the largest, about 6 miles from north to south) on which is the aerodrome and the administrative centre, and most of the European community; Home Island, the headquarters of the Clunies Ross Estate; Direction Island, on which is situated the Cable and Wireless Station and the Department of Civil Aviation's marine base; and Horsburgh. North Keeling Island, which forms part of the Territory, lies about 15 miles to the north of the group and has no inhabitants. The climate is equable and pleasant, being usually under the influence of the south-east trade winds for about three-quarters of the year. The population (June 30, 1962) was 615.

CHRISTMAS ISLAND

Until the end of 1957 a part of the Colony of Singapore, Christmas Island was administered as a separate colony until October 1, 1958, when it became Australian territory by Order in Council. It is situated in the Indian Ocean about 190 miles S. of Java Head and 529 miles E. of the Cocos (Keeling) Islds. Area, 64 sq. miles. Population (June 30, 1962), 3,200. The island is densely wooded and contains extensive deposits of phosphate of lime.

THE ANTARCTIC CONTINENT

The area of the Antarctic Continent is estimated at approximately 5 million square miles. The greater part of the coastline has been charted with varying degrees of accuracy, but considerable portions of the interior have not been visited, or at best have been seen only from the air.

The question of territorial rights is complicated and there is no general international agreement thereon. Argentina has 3 Antarctic bases in the zone claimed as "Argentine Territory," one being on Deception Island in the South Shetlands, which is part of the British Falkland Islands; another in Scotia Bay, and a third on Gamma Island, in the Melchior Archipelago.

The *Australian Antarctic Territory* was established by an Order in Council, dated February 7, 1933, and the Australian Antarctic Territory Acceptance Act of June 13, 1933, which placed under the government of the Commonwealth of Australia all the islands and territories, other than Adélie Land, which are situated south of the latitude 60°S. and lying between the 160th and 45th meridians of East longitude.

The exception of Adélie Land from the Order in Council is due to French claims based on rights of discovery and occupation.

The area administered by the Commonwealth of Australia is estimated at 2,472,000 square miles. It adjoins that belonging to New Zealand. There is an Australian research station on Macquarie Island (north of the Antarctic Convergence and sub-Antarctic), which is about 1,000 miles south-east of Hobart and has been a dependency of Tasmania since the nineteenth century.

Heard Island, about 2,500 miles south-west of Fremantle, was transferred from United Kingdom to Australian control on December 26, 1947.

In February, 1954, a base known as Mawson, was established on the coast of the Antarctic continent at lat. 67° 36′ S. and long. 62° 53′ E. Meteorological and other research is being conducted at this station. A second base, named Davis, was established in Jan. 1957 at 68° 35′ S., 77° 59′ E, and in February, 1959, Australia took over the United States base at Wilkes (lat. 66° 15′ S., long. 110° 33′ E.).

For other British dependencies in the Antarctic *see* p. 735.

STATES OF THE COMMONWEALTH OF AUSTRALIA

NEW SOUTH WALES

The State of New South Wales is situated almost entirely between the 29th and 36th parallels of S. lat. and 141st and 154th meridians of E. long., and comprises an area of 309,433 square miles (exclusive of 939 square miles of Australian Commonwealth Territory which lies within its borders).

POPULATION.—The estimated population at December 31, 1962, was: Males, 2,015,081; Females, 2,001,554. Total, 4,016,635.

Births, Deaths and Marriages.

Year	Births	Deaths	Marriages
1959	80,866	35,249	28,201
1960	81,983	35,030	29,328
1961	86,392	35,048	29 773
1962	85,439	36,681	30 360

Vital Statistics.—Annual rate per 1,000 of mean population in 1962:—Births, 21·46; Deaths, 9·26; Marriages, 7·63. Deaths under 1 year per 1,000 live births, 21·36.

Religions.

The members of the Church of England in New South Wales, according to the Census of 1961, number 1,556,965. Roman Catholic 1,031,782, Presbyterian 333,635, Methodist 294,280, Congregational 21,743, Baptist 50,805, Greek Orthodox 57,822, Lutheran 27,533, Salvation Army 15,642, and Hebrew 24,026. The religion of 388,024 persons was not stated in the census schedules.

PHYSIOGRAPHY.

Natural features divide the State into four strips of territory extending from north to south, viz., the Coastal Divisions; the Tablelands, which form the Great Dividing Range between the coastal districts and the plains; the Western Slopes of the Dividing Range; and the Western Plains. The highest points are Mount Kosciusko, 7,328 feet, and Townsend, 7,266 feet. The coastal district is well watered by numerous rivers flowing from the ranges into fertile flats which form their lower basins. The western portion of the State is watered by the rivers of the Murray-Darling system and immense reservoirs have been constructed for irrigation purposes, and there are many artesian bores. The Darling, 1,702 miles, and the Murrumbidgee, 981 miles, are both tributaries of the Murray, part of which forms the boundary between the States of New South Wales and Victoria. Other inland rivers are: Lachlan, Bogan, Macquarie Castlereagh, Namoi and Gwydir.

Climate.—New South Wales is situated entirely in the Temperate Zone. The climate is equable and very healthy. At the capital (Sydney) the average mean shade temperature is 63·7°. The mean (shade) temperature ranges for the various divisions of the State as follows: coastal, 60° in the south to 67° in the north; northern and central tableland, 53° to 60°; southern tableland, 44° to 57°; and for the rest of the State (western slope, central plains, Riverina and western), 60° in the south to 69° in the north.

GOVERNMENT.

New South Wales was first colonized as a British possession in 1788, and after progressive settlement a partly elective legislature was established in 1843. In 1855 Responsible Government was granted, the present Constitution being founded on the Constitution Act of 1902. New South Wales federated with the other States of Australia in 1901. The executive authority of the State is vested in a Governor (appointed by the Crown), assisted by a Council of Ministers.

GOVERNOR.

Governor of New South Wales, Lieutenant-General Sir Eric Winslow Woodward, K.C.M.G., K.C.V.O., C.B., C.B.E., D.S.O., *assumed office* August 1, 1957 .... £6,000

Lieutenant-Governor, Hon. Sir Kenneth Whistler Street, K.C.M.G. (1950).

THE MINISTRY:
(May 31, 1960)

Premier, Robert James Heffron, M.L.A.
Deputy Premier, Treasurer and Minister for Industrial Development and Decentralisation, Hon. John Brophy Renshaw, M.L.A.
Attorney-General and Vice-President of the Executive Council, Hon. Robert Reginald Downing, M.L.C.
Chief Secretary and Minister for Tourist Activities, Hon. Christopher Augustus Kelly, M.L.A.
Local Government and Highways, Hon. P. D. Hills, M.L.A.
Health, Hon. W. F. Sheahan, Q.C., M.L.A.
Child Welfare and Social Welfare, Hon. F. H. Hawkins, M.L.A.
Agriculture and Conservation, Hon. A. G. Enticknap, M.L.A.
Housing and Co-operative Societies, Hon. A. Landa, M.L.A.
Education, Hon. E. Wetherell, M.L.A.
Labour and Industry, Hon. J. J. Maloney, M.L.C.
Mines, Hon. J. B. Simpson, M.L.A.
Transport, Hon. J. M. A. McMahon, M.L.A.
Public Works, Hon. P. N. Ryan, M.L.A.
Justice, Hon. N. J. Mannix, M.L.A.
Lands, Hon. K. C. Compton, M.L.A.

The annual salaries of Ministers are: Premier, £4,850; Deputy Premier, £4,100; other Ministers, £3,600 each. Ministers also receive an expense allowance (Premier, £1,500, and other Ministers, £500 each) and the Vice-President of the Executive Council a further special allowance of £400. In addition, Ministers who are members of the Legislative Assembly receive an electoral allowance (ranging from £650 to £950 according to the location of the electorate).

N.S.W. GOVERNMENT OFFICES IN LONDON,
56–57 Strand, W.C.2.

Agent-General, Hon. Francis Patrick Buckley, C.B.E. (1954).

THE LEGISLATURE.

The Legislature consists of the Sovereign and the two Houses of Parliament (the Legislative Council and the Legislative Assembly). The *Legislative Council* consists of 60 members, elected jointly by both Houses of Parliament. Membership is for 12 years, 15 members retiring in rotation triennially. Members receive an annual allowance of £500 and three guineas a day attendance allowance for members living outside the metropolitan area. The *Legislative Assembly* consists of 94 members. Each member of the Legislative Assembly receives £2,350 per annum, plus an electoral allowance (£650 to £950, according to location of electorate). The Women's Legal Status Act, 1918, removed disqualification regarding the election of women to be members of the Legislative Assembly. A provident fund for members of the Legislative Assembly was established in 1946; a pension is payable to those who on ceasing to be members have served in three parliaments. Natural-born or naturalized persons 21 years of age, who have resided 6 months in the Commonwealth, 3 months in the State and 1 month in the electoral district are entitled to the franchise. Voting is compulsory. At the State General Elections in March, 1962, there were 1,060,658 men and 1,113,110 women electors, making a total of 2,173,768 enrolled; in contested electorates 94 per cent. of the eligible electors voted.

President of the Legislative Council, Hon. W. E. Dickson (incl. *allce.*) £2,300
Chairman of Committees, Legislative Council, Hon. E. G. Wright (incl. *allce.*) 1,500
Speaker, Legislative Assembly, Hon. R. S. Maher (excl. *allce.*) 3,250
Chairman of Committees, Legislative Assembly, H. T. Fowles (excl. *allce.*) ... 2,750
Leader of Opposition, Legislative Assembly, R. H. Askin (excl. *allce.*) 3,350

THE JUDICATURE.

The judicial system includes a Supreme Court (with a Chief Justice and twenty-four Puisne Judges), Land and Valuation Court, Industrial Commission, District Courts, Workers' Compensation Commission, Courts of Quarter Sessions, Petty Sessions and Children's Courts.

Supreme Court

Chief Justice, Hon. L. J. Herron (+*allce.* £350) £6,900
Puisne Judges, Hon. J. S. J. Clancy; Hon. B. Sugerman; Hon. E. P. Kinsella; Hon. J. H. McClemens; Hon. C. McLelland; Hon. A. R. Richardson; Hon. R. Le G. Brereton; Hon. W. R. Dovey; Hon. H. Maguire; Hon. F. G. Myers; Hon. C. A. Walsh; Hon. K. A. Ferguson; Hon. M. F. Hardie; Hon. J. K. Manning; Hon. W. H. Collins; Hon. R. Chambers; Hon. R. Else-Mitchell; Hon. B. P. Macfarlan, O.B.E.; Hon. G. Wallace; Hon. K. S. Jacobs; Hon. J. F. Nagle; Hon. R. L. Taylor; Hon. D. M. Selby; Hon. A. R. Moffitt (+*allce.* £250) £6,250

Industrial Commission

President, Hon. Mr. Justice Taylor (+*allce.* £250) 6,500
Members, Hons. Mr. Justice Richards; Mr. Justice Cook; Mr. Justice McKeon; Mr. Justice Beattie; Mr. Justice Kelleher; Mr. Justice Perrignon; Mr. Justice Sheehy (+*allce.* £250) .... each 6,250
Land and Valuation Court Judges, Hons. Mr. Justice Hardie; Mr. Justice Else-Mitchell.
Crown Solicitor, R. J. McKay 5,500
Workers' Compensation Commission, Chairman, His Honour Judge Conybeare (+ *allce.* £250) 5,550
Members, His Honour Judge Rainbow; His Honour Judge Dignam; His Honour Judge Wall (+*allce.* £100) 5,000
District Court, Chairman, His Honour Judge Monahan (+*allce.* £250) 5,550

EDUCATION.

Education.—Education is compulsory between the ages of 6 and 15 years. It is non-sectarian and free at all state schools. The average weekly enrolment in 1962 in 2,747 state schools was 616,841 and the average daily attendance during the year was 565,067. In addition to the state schools there were, in 1962, 839 private colleges and schools, with an average weekly enrolment of 203,765 scholars, 702 being Roman Catholic schools with 175,549 scholars. The three universities had an enrolment of 15,573 full-time students in 1963; 11,039 at Sydney (incorporated 1850), 3,574 at the University of New South Wales (1948) and 960 at New England (1954). The State expenditure on Education was £78,268,000 in the year 1961–62. Students attending the State Agricultural Colleges and Farm schools numbered 1,936 in 1962.

FINANCE.

Year ended June 30th	Revenue*	Expenditure*
	£A	£A
1959	239,769,340	239,726,798
1960	262,533,020	262,463,298
1961	282,363,517	282,701,492
1962	295,611,731	298,744,601

* Excluding the self-balancing Road Transport and Traffic Fund.

The Public Debt of New South Wales at June 30, 1962, was £A1,028,309,826, of which an amount of £139,093,174 was repayable in London (interest £5,844,965), £33,645,536 was repayable in New York (interest £1,600,711) £2,179,551 was repayable in Canada (interest £125,324), £1,616,354 was repayable in Switzerland (interest £72,736), £1,230,461 was repayable in the Netherlands (interest £64,023) and £850,494,750 was held in Australia, with an annual interest bill of £37,332,945.

Banking, &c.—There were (April 1963) 12 trading banks with deposits of £839,725,000. Savings bank deposits amounted to £678,532,000, representing £169 per head of the population. The amount assured in New South Wales in *Life Assurance* Societies in 1961 was £1,272,653 000 ordinary and £135,418,000 industrial. The membership of *Friendly Societies* was 144,472, and the funds at June 30, 1961, were £9,856,000. Members of *Trade Unions* at Dec. 31, 1961, numbered 658,877 the funds of 206 Unions being £2,683,000. Balances outstanding on *Instalment Credit* for retail sales on June 30, 1962, were £235,181,000.

PRODUCTION AND INDUSTRY.

Value of Production.—In 1961–62 the net value of production of the primary and manufacturing industries was £1,385,583,000–primary £416,130,000 and manufacturing £969,453,000. The values for the principal primary industries were: pastoral £183,002,000, agricultural £93,832,000, dairying and farmyard, £58,902,000 and mining and quarrying, £60,869,000.

Agriculture.—During the year to Mar. 31, 1962, 8,058,626 acres were under cultivation.

The total area under wheat was 4,744,714 acres, of which 4,498,244 acres were harvested for grain, and 90,490 acres for hay. The production of wheat was 78,350,205 bushels of grain and 115,660 tons of hay. Other important crops in 1961–62 were 2,349,096 bushels of maize, 13,224,966 bushels of oats, 7,045,333 bushels of rice, besides other kinds of grain, 83,301 tons of potatoes, and 27,826 cwt. of dried leaf tobacco. Sugar-cane to the extent of 555,858 tons was crushed; while 4,165,596 bushels of bananas were obtained; almost every kind of fruit and vegetable is grown. There were 17,607 acres of vineyards, of which 15,809 acres were bearing.

Land Tenure.—The total extent of land alienated and in process of alienation from the Crown on June 30, 1962, was 66,303,469 acres, while the area of land under lease, &c., from the Crown was 113,778,862 acres, and the balance 17,954,789 acres, consisted of reserve and other lands neither alienated nor leased; the total area of the State, exclusive of the Australian Capital Territory, is 198,037,120 acres.

Pastoral, etc.—The country is admirably adapted for sheep farming, the principal breed of sheep being the celebrated merino, which was introduced in 1797. On Mar. 31, 1962, there were 167,868 horses, 4,398,678 cattle, 69,498,000 sheep and lambs, 471,579 pigs. In 1961–62, 701,168,000 lb. (stated as in the grease) of wool were produced, 88,375,198 lb. of butter, 13,335,558 lb. of cheese, and 27,384,000 lb. of bacon and ham.

Forests.—The estimated forest area is 19,107,000 acres, of which State forests cover 6,664,000 acres and 1,402,000 have been set aside as timber reserves.

Mining Industry.—The principal minerals are coal, silver, lead, zinc, zircon and rutile. The total value of minerals won in 1962 was £79,600,000; the value of output of the coal-mining industry was £44,600,000, and of the silver-lead-zinc industry, £19,700,000. The mining industry gave employment to 21,798 miners during 1961. In 1962, 19,030,000 tons of coal were produced.

Factories.—In 1961–62 there were 23,629 factories. The average number of persons employed during the year was 461,087. The value of production, *i.e.* value added to raw materials, was £968,694,000. Large iron and steel works with subsidiary factories are in operation at Newcastle and Port Kembla in proximity to the coalfields. The products include iron and steel of various grades, pipes, boilers, steel wire and wire netting, copper wire, copper and brass cables and tin-plate. The production (1961–62) of pig-iron was 3,082,000 tons, and of steel ingots 4,055,000 tons.

OVERSEAS TRADE.

Year ended June 30	Oversea Imports £A (f.o.b.)	Oversea Exports £A (f.o.b.)
1959	352,711,936	221,372,019
1960	414,645,823	281,164,483
1961	479,484,226	282,420,065
1962	412,910,196	322,762,351

The chief exports in 1961–62 were foodstuffs, wool, hides and skins, minerals, metals, machinery, leather, and drugs and chemicals. Chief imports were tea, tobacco, textiles and apparel, petrol, metals, motor vehicles, aircraft and parts, machinery, timber, paper, rubber, drugs and chemicals, and plastic materials.

TRANSPORT AND COMMUNICATIONS.

Shipping.—Excluding coastal trade, 3,969 vessels entered ports of N.S.W. during the year ended June 30, 1962, the net tonnage being 16,631,000. The shipping entries at Sydney, including coastal, were 4,128 vessels of 12,323,000 net tonnage.

Roads and Bridges.—There are 130,000 miles of roads and streets in New South Wales, including 38,000 miles of natural surface and cleared only. The total expenditure by the Government and the local councils on roads, bridges, &c., in 1960–61 was £54 633,000. The construction of an arch bridge of Sydney Harbour was completed and the bridge opened for traffic in March, 1932. This bridge carries eight lanes of roadway with a total width of 84 ft., two footways each 10 ft. wide, and two lines of railway. At mean high water there is a headway of 172½ ft.

Motor Vehicles.—At April 30, 1963, there were 1,115,886 registered motor vehicles (cars, 736,406).

Railways.—The railways of New South Wales are controlled by the State, which also operates omnibus services. Tramway services ceased in February, 1961. At June 30, 1962, the mileage of the State railways open for traffic was 6,063, earnings in the year 1961-62 being £88,351,000.

Aviation.—Sydney is the principal oversea terminal in Australia. Traffic movements at Sydney airport in 1961–62 were: passengers 1,719,063 (1,513,820 domestic, 205,243 international); freight, 24,614 short tons (19,456 domestic, 5,158 international); aircraft, 52,759 (46,708 domestic, 5,871 international).

Posts, Telegraphs and Telephones.—The postal telegraphic, telephonic and radio services are administered by the Commonwealth Government. At June 30, 1962, there were 2,472 post offices in New South Wales. The postal matter carried during 1961-62 included 599,751,000 letters and registered articles and 120,580,000 newspapers and parcels posted for delivery in Australia. The overseas mails consisted of 37,676,000 registered articles and letters and 10,386,000 newspapers and parcels despatched, 50,843,000 registered articles and letters and 33,399,000 newspapers and parcels received. During the year 6,884,000 telegrams were despatched to places within Australia and 671,000 cablegrams were despatched and 731,000 received. Transit time between Sydney and London is approximately 2½ days for airborne mail and between 4 and 6 weeks for seaborne mail. The telephone services in operation numbered 665,334.

Radio and Television.—In June, 1962, there were 20 National Broadcasting Stations in New South Wales and 38 commercial stations operating under licence. The number of broadcast listeners' licences was 812,350. Regular transmission of television programmes in New South Wales began in September, 1956. At June 30, 1962, there were 8 television stations (one national, 7 commercial) in operation and the number of viewers' annual licences was 554,640.

Towns.

ΨSydney, the chief city and capital, stands on the shores of Port Jackson, with a water frontage of 152 miles; the depth of water at the Heads is not less than 80 feet, and at the wharves up to 40 ft. There are extensive facilities for handling cargo, and for storing and loading grain in bulk or bags; also for replenishing coal and oil bunkers. For 20 miles Sydney Harbour extends inland, the finest harbour in the world, and is surrounded by scenery of surpassing beauty. The principal wharves are situated in close proximity to the business centre of the city. The total area of water in the harbour is 13,600 acres, or about 21 square miles, of which approximately one-half has a depth of not less than 30 ft.: the rise and fall of the tide is from 3 to 6 ft. The metropolis contains approximately 671 square miles, with a population of 2,215,970 (estimated, June 30, 1962).

The parks in or adjacent to the metropolitan area include the Royal National Park which measures about 34,000 acres, Kuring-gai Chase 38,300 acres, Kurnell 250 acres and Centennial Park 470 acres.

Other cities and towns over 12,000 are ΨNewcastle (urban area) 212,510; Wollongong (Greater) 135,640; Broken Hill 30,810; Blue Mountains 28,980; Maitland 27,600; Goulburn 20,510; Wagga Wagga 22,440; Penrith 35,990; Lismore 19,010; Lithgow 14,100; Albury 23,240; Orange 19,120; Cessnock (Greater) 34,970; Tamworth 19,390; Grafton 15,600; Bathurst 17,030; Dubbo 14,500; Campbelltown 21,000; and Shellharbour 14,760.

Dependency of New South Wales.

Lord Howe Island (436 miles north-east of Sydney). Lat. 31° 33′ 4″ S., Long. 159° 4′ 26″ E. Area 3,200 acres. Pop. June 30, 1962, 287. The island is of volcanic origin and Mount Gower reaches an altitude of 2,840 ft. The affairs of the Island and the supervision of the Kentia palm seed industry are controlled by an elected Island Committee and a Board at Sydney. *Office*, Chief Secretary's Department, Sydney.

QUEENSLAND

This State, situated in lat. 10° 40′–29° S. and long. 138°–153° 30′ E., comprises the whole north-eastern portion of the Australian continent.

Queensland possesses an area of 667,000 square miles (*i.e.*, equal to more than 5½ times the area of the British Isles).

Population.—At June 30, 1962, the population numbered 1,542,629 persons (787,822 males and 754,807 females).

The total number of aborigines (estimated June 30, 1961) was 10,325 full blood and 7,944 half-caste, exclusive of Torres Strait Islanders.

Increase of the People.

Year	Births	Deaths	Marriages
1960	35,213	12,370	10,227
1961	36,637	12,756	10,392
1962	35,690	13,182	10,642

Infant mortality rate (1962) 21·1 per 1,000 live births.

Religion.

At the Census of 1961 there were 486,316 Church of England, 372,350 Roman Catholics (including Catholics undefined), 173,316 Presbyterians, 165,556 Methodists, 35,123 Lutherans, 22,253 Baptists, 11,777 Greek Orthodox, 9,166 Congregationalists, 57,306 other Christians, and 1,334 Hebrews.

Physiography.

The Great Dividing Range on the eastern coast of the continent produces a similar formation to that of New South Wales, the eastern side having a narrow slope to the coast and the western a long and gradual slope to the central plains, where the Selwyn and Kirby Ranges divide the land into a northern and southern watershed. The Brisbane, Burnett, Fitzroy, and Burdekin rise in the eastern ranges and flow into the Pacific, the Flinders, Mitchell, and Leichhardt into the Gulf of Carpentaria, and the Barcoo and Warrego rise in the central ranges and flow southwards.

Climate.—At Brisbane the mean temperature for 1962 was 68·7°, the maximum and minimum shade temperatures being 94·0° and 39·3°; mean barometer, 30·03 inches. The coastal regions are warm and moist, but the rainfall decreases away from the coast and is scanty in the far west. The rainfall in Brisbane during 1962 was 41·4 inches, compared with average rainfall of 40·1 inches.

Government.

Queensland was constituted a separate colony with Responsible Government in 1859, having previously formed part of New South Wales. The executive authority is vested in a Governor (appointed by the Crown), aided by an Executive Council of 11 members.

Governor.

Governor of Queensland, Col. Sir Henry Abel Smith, K.C.M.G., K.C.V.O., D.S.O., *appointed* March 18, 1958 .... £A6,500

Aide-de-Camp, Capt. G. F. Richmond-Brown.

EXECUTIVE COUNCIL.
(H.E. the Governor presides.)
(Aug. 12, 1957, as re-constructed)

Premier and Chief Secretary, Hon. G. F. R. Nicklin, M.M £5,202
Deputy Premier and Minister for Justice and Attorney-General, Hon. A. W. Munro... 4,102
Education and Migration, Hon. J. C. A. Pizzey........ 3,852
Treasurer and Housing, Hon. T. A. Hiley.. 3,852
Development, Mines, Main Roads and Electricity, Hon. E. Evans........ 3,852
Public Lands and Irrigation, Hon. A. R. Fletcher........ 3,852
Health and Home Affairs, Dr. Hon. H. W. Noble........ 3,852
Public Works and Local Government, Hon. H. Richter........ 3,852
Transport, Hon. G. W. W. Chalk........ 3,852
Labour and Industry, Hon. A. T. Dewar... 3,852
Agriculture and Forestry, Hon. J. A. Row... 3,852

AGENT-GENERAL IN LONDON.

Agent-General for Queensland, Sir David Muir, C.M.G., 409–410 Strand, W.C.2.
Official Secretary, M. McAully.

THE LEGISLATURE.

Parliament consists of a *Legislative Assembly* of 78 members, elected by universal adult suffrage. Members of the Assembly receive £2,502 per annum and an electorate allowance ranging from £325 to £1,175 p.a. The Assembly was, on June 1, 1963, composed of Liberal and Country Parties 46, Australian Labour Party 26, Queensland Labour Party 1, Independents 5.

Speaker, Hon. D. E. Nicholson........ £3,252
Chairman of Committees, K. W. Hooper. 2,752
Clerk of the Parliament, R. L. Dunlop... 3,884

THE JUDICATURE.

There is a Supreme Court, with a Chief Justice, a Senior Puisne Judge and ten Puisne Judges; District Courts, with six Judges; an Industrial Court, with a Supreme Court Judge as President and three other Members; and Inferior Courts at all the principal towns, presided over by Stipendiary Magistrates.

Chief Justice, Supreme Court, Hon. Sir Alan Mansfield, K.C.M.G. £6,400
Senior Puisne Judge, Hon. Sir Roslyn Philp, K.B.E. 5,900
Puisne Judges, Hons. E. J. D. Stanley; J. A. Sheehy; W. G. Mack; M. Hanger; B. J. Jeffriess; C. G. Wanstall; N. S. Stable; H. T. Gibbs; G. L. Hart each 5,900
District Court Judges, D. G. Andrews; W. M. Grant-Taylor; R. F. J. Cormack; R. F. Carter; G. Seaman; E. J. Moynahan each 4,500

EDUCATION.

Primary education is compulsory, secular and free. On Aug. 1, 1961, there were 1,501 state schools, including 110 providing secondary education, in operation, with 9,053 teachers and an enrolment of 243,977 children and 313 private and 8 grammar schools, with an enrolment of 72,823. There were 15 state technical colleges with 864 teachers and 34,880 students and a state agricultural college with an enrolment of 851. The state-aided University had an enrolment of 5,175 full-time students in 1963. State expenditure on education in 1960–61 was £22,591,596.

FINANCE.

Receipts and Expenditure of the Consolidated Revenue Fund and Debt of Queensland for four years ended June 30:—

Year	Revenue	Expenditure	Debt (Gross)
	£A	£A	£A
1959...	93,795,802	94,986,459	285,947,364
1960...	101,912,092	102,076,767	303,470,019
1961...	108,816,921	109,435,164	322,424,113
1962...	117,325,027	117,215,308	363,820,873

Banking.—Advances made by Trading Banks (including the Commonwealth Trading Bank of Australia) at June 30, 1962, totalled £157,919,000. The deposits at the same date amounted to £253,048,000. Depositors' balances in Queensland savings banks at June 30, 1962, £205,852,000, averaged £133 for each inhabitant. There were 1,251,000 operative accounts.

PRODUCTION AND INDUSTRY.

The gross value of primary production in 1961–62 was £300,792,000 (agriculture £105,275,000, dairying £33,012,000, pastoral £106,198,000, poultry and bee-keeping £4,730,000, mining £41,550,000, forestry, £7,914,000, fisheries £1,834,000, hunting and trapping £279,000), and net value of manufacturing £175,298,000.

Agriculture and Live Stock.—Of the total area of 426,880,000 acres 28,379,000 acres were alienated or in process of alienation at Dec. 31, 1962, and 367,105,000 acres were held under Crown leases.

The total area under crop in 1961–62 was 3,202,572 acres. The most important crop was sugar-cane, under which there were 472,393 acres, producing 1,315,393 tons of raw sugar, 749,682 acres were under wheat (yielding 12,017,907 bushels), 155,780 under maize (4,766,103 bushels), and 176,885 under barley (3,531,609 bushels). The live stock on March 31, 1962, included 7,097,862 cattle, 1,208,177 being dairy cattle, 22,125,298 sheep, 217,343 horses, and 432,609 pigs.

Forestry.—At June 30, 1962, 8,203,000 acres were reserved for State forests and timber reserves and there were 2,060,000 acres of permanent forestry plots. Total Australian grown timber processed amounted to 389,000,000 super feet.

Minerals.—There are rich deposits of bauxite, copper, lead, silver, uranium and zinc, and deposits of gold, tin, limestone, ironstone, wolfram and mineral sands. Coal is mined in the Ipswich (near Brisbane) and some northern districts, and there is extensive production by open-cut method in Central Queensland. Oil was discovered at Moonie in South Queensland in 1961. The output in 1961 included gold, £910,000; coal, £8,079,000; copper, £18,571,000; tin, £1,320,000; silver, £1,367,000; lead, £3,415,000; zinc, £2,574,000; uranium, £8,525,000.

Factories.—In 1961–62, 5,824 factories employed 101,637 persons. Value of production (value added to raw materials) was £175,298,000. Much production was the processing of primary products, e.g. sugar, butter, timber, and minerals. Included in other factory production were the products from engineering, railway and metal works, cement, and woollen mills.

Communications.—The State is served by 6,077 miles of railways, practically all 3 ft. 6 in. in gauge. During 1961–62, 26,701,000 passengers and 8,153,000 tons of goods and live stock were carried. At June 30, 1962, there were 72,131 miles of formed roads and 48,985 miles of unconstructed roads in the State, and 435,257 motor vehicles were on the register.

Aviation.—Regular services operate between Brisbane, the main Queensland coastal and inland towns and the southern capitals. Brisbane is also a port of call on a service to and from London.

Radio and Television.—On June 30, 1962, 15 national and 21 commercial stations were broadcasting in Queensland, and 1 national and 2 commercial television stations operated in Brisbane.

OVERSEAS TRADE.

Year	Imports	Exports
1959-60	£A50,858,448	£A181,321,439
1960-61	61,277,254	163,777,896
1961-62	48,861,315	172,443,180

The chief overseas exports are wool, meat, sugar, minerals and butter.

TOWNS.

CAPITAL, Ψ BRISBANE, is situated on the Brisbane River, which is navigable by large vessels to the city, over 10 miles from Moreton Bay. The City Hall is a notable building, and there are fine Government and private buildings. The estimated population of the Metropolitan Area at June 30, 1962, was 635,500. Of the 474 square miles in the Metropolitan Area, 385 square miles are under the control of the City Council, presided over by a Lord Mayor.

Ψ The main ports in their order along the coast are Brisbane, Maryborough (19,200), Bundaberg (23,100), Gladstone (7,250), Rockhampton (44,500), Mackay (21,750), Bowen (5,180), Townsville (52,600), Lucinda Point, Mourilyan, Cairns (25,700) and Thursday Island.

Other towns are Ipswich (50,000), Gold Coast (35,000), Gympie (11,200), Nambour (5,400) and Kingaroy (4,950) in the south-east; Toowoomba (51,000), Warwick (9,900) and Dalby (7,750) on the Darling Downs; Roma (5,700) and Charleville (5,240) in the south-west; Mt. Morgan (4,000), in Central Queensland; Ayr (8,120), Innisfail (6,950), Charters Towers (7,700) and Ingham (4,900) in the north-east; and Mount Isa (14,000) in the north-west.

Transmission of mails from London to Brisbane, by air, 2 days; by sea (approximate), 30 days.

SOUTH AUSTRALIA

The State of South Australia is situated between 26° and 38° S. lat. and 129° and 141° E. long., the total area being 380,070 sq. miles

POPULATION.—At Dec. 31, 1962, the population was estimated at 999,603 (504,571 males and 495,122 females), excluding full-blooded aboriginals, estimated at fewer than 3,000.

Increase of the People.

Year	Births	Deaths	Marriages
1959	20,372	7,943	6,614
1960	20,965	7,804	6,607
1961	22,399	7,815	6,804
1962	21,361	8,232	7,021

Religion.

Religion is free and receives no State aid. At the Census, 1961, the persons belonging to the principal religious denominations were as follows: Church of England, 255,054; Methodists, 216,770; Congregationalists, 17,867; Baptists, 21,032; Lutherans, 53,947; Roman Catholics, 183,053; Presbyterians, 37,911: and Churches of Christ, 23,905.

PHYSIOGRAPHY.

The most important physical features of South Australia are broad plains, divided longitudinally by four great secondary features, which form barriers to east-west movement, and which have thus largely determined the direction of roads and railways, the sites of towns and villages and the manner of distribution of the population. These four barriers are Spencer Gulf, St. Vincent Gulf, the Mt. Lofty-Flinders Ranges and the River Murray. The long, deeply-indented coastline, which provides a few major, and a multitude of lesser harbours, trends generally south-eastward. Pleasant weather conditions and good rainfall are experienced in most coastal areas.

The north-western portion of the State is mostly desert, while north of latitude 32°S. the country is unpromising by comparison with the fertile land which surrounds the hill country of the east. The Murray, which flows for some 400 miles through the south-eastern corner, is the only river of importance.

The lack of rivers and fresh-water lakes in the settled areas has necessitated the building of a number of reservoirs, which have been supplemented since 1941 by the construction of pipelines from the River Murray.

Climate.—The mean annual temperature at Adelaide is 63°, the winter temperature (July-August) averaging 53°, and the summer (November-March) 71°. During the summer months the maximum temperature at times exceeds 100°, but owing to the purity and dryness of the atmosphere the inconvenience is comparatively slight. The average annual rainfall at Adelaide, derived from over 100 years' record is 21 inches. This total is rather higher than the approximate average annual rainfall over the whole of the agricultural areas. In the Mount Lofty Ranges the mean yearly rainfall in places exceeds 40 inches, while in Adelaide the precipitation has fallen as low as 11·32 inches.

GOVERNMENT.

South Australia was proclaimed a British Province in 1836, and in 1851 a partially elective legislature was established. The present Constitution rests upon a Law of Oct. 24, 1856, the executive authority being vested in a Governor appointed by the Crown, aided by a Council of 8 Ministers.

GOVERNOR.

Governor of South Australia, His Excellency Lieut.-Gen. Sir Edric Montague Bastyan, K.C.M.G., K.C.V.O., K.B.E., C.B. (1961). £A5,000

Aides-de-Camp, Capt. A. E. O. Bastyan, Devonshire and Dorset Regt.; Capt. E. C. W. Morrison, 5 Innis. D.G.

Lieut.-Governor, Hon. Sir (John) Mellis Napier, K.C.M.G. (1942).

THE MINISTRY.

(May 15, 1944.)

(£37,450 is allotted as salaries to Ministers.)

Premier, Treasurer and Minister of Immigration, Hon. Sir Thomas Playford, G.C.M.G.

Chief Secretary, Minister of Mines and of Health, Hon. Sir (Alexander) Lyell McEwin, K.B.E., M.L.C.

Attorney-General and Minister of Labour and Industry, Hon. C. D. Rowe, M.L.C.

Lands, Repatriation and Irrigation, Hon. P. H. Quirke.

Works, Marine, and Aboriginal Affairs, Hon. G. G. Pearson.

Agriculture and Forests, Hon. D. N. Brookman.

Education, Hon. Sir Baden Pattinson, K.B.E.

Local Government, Roads and Railways, Hon. N. L Jude, M.L.C.

AGENT-GENERAL IN LONDON.

Agent-General and Trade Commissioner for South Australia, M. A. F. Pearce, C.V.O., C.B.E., South Australia House, 50 Strand, W.C.2.

Official Secretary, M. A. G. Wildy.

THE LEGISLATURE.

Parliament consists of a *Legislative Council* of 20 members elected for 6 years, one-half retiring every 3 years; and a *House of Assembly* of 39 members, elected for a maximum duration of 3 years. Election is by ballot, with universal adult suffrage for the House of Assembly for all British subjects, male and female, subject to some residential qualifications; there are certain property or war service qualifications for electors to the Legislative Council, who numbered 204,390 in 1962 those for the Assembly numbering 530,542.

The triennial elections to the House of Assembly in March, 1962, returned 18 Liberals (Government party), 19 Labour (Opposition) and 2 independents. One Independent subsequently joined the Liberal Party.

President of the Legislative Council, Hon. L. H. Densley £3,750

Speaker of the House of Assembly, Hon. T. C. Stott 3,750

THE JUDICATURE.

Law and Justice.—The Supreme Court is presided over by the Chief Justice and five Puisne Judges there are Courts of Vice-Admiralt and Insolvency, as well as Local Civil Courts with stipendiary magistrates, and the usual Police Courts.

Chief Justice and Judge of Vice-Admiralty, Hon. Sir (John) Mellis Napier, K.C.M.G. £6,250

Judges, Hon. Sir Herbert Mayo; Hon. R. R. St. C. Chamberlain; Hon. V. R. Millhouse; Hon. J. L. Travers; Hon. D. S. Hogarth 5,500

EDUCATION.

Public Education (Primary, Secondary and Technical) is provided by the State and controlled by a responsible Minister; it is secular, compulsory, and free. In 1961 there were 687 State schools, with 197 662 scholars; State expenditure in 1961–62 was £20,154 000, including grants to University, Libraries, &c. The Government grants Exhibitions and Scholarships, carrying the holders to higher schools and the University. Private schools number 174 with 42 182 scholars. There is an endowed University at Adelaide, founded in 1874, with 4,285 full-time students in 1963. A State Institute of Technology has also been established, and there are technical schools at 16 country centres and also special trade schools for apprentices and domestic art centres. The public library, museum, art gallery and local institutes are supported or assisted by the State.

STATE FINANCE.
(For years ended June 30)

Year	Revenue	Expenditure	Debt
	£A	£A	£A
1959	72,680,000	73,707,000	317,702,000
1960	80,277,000	80,539,000	339,105,000
1961	86 279 000	85,091 000	361,019,000
1962	93,202,000	92 690,000	381 699,000

Banking.—There are 9 trading banks in Adelaide, including the Commonwealth Government Bank and the State Bank of South Australia, having total average deposits of £139,318,000 in December quarter, 1962. The eight savings banks had deposits of £192,520,000 at Dec. 31, 1962.

PRODUCTION AND INDUSTRY

The gross value of primary production in 1961–1962 was: crops £62,011,000, pastoral £55,925,000, dairying £14,924,000, fisheries, game and poultry, and forestry £9,729,000.

Land Tenure.—Of the total area of the State (243,000,000 acres), 16,300,000 acres have been sold or are in the process of alienation by the Crown under systems of deferred payment; 123,200,000 acres are held under pastoral leases and 23,700,000 under other miscellaneous leases.

Agriculture.—The total area cultivated is 10,941,000 acres—under wheat, 1961–62, 2,229,000 acres, hay 209,000, oats 324,000, barley 1,271,000. Wheat harvest 1961–62, 33,854,000 bushels: barley, 21,292,000 bushels. Oranges, lemons, apples, apricots, peaches, and all stone fruits and olives are successfully grown, and fruit drying is profitable. In 1961–62, there were 58,000 acres of vines with a production of 30,831,000 gallons of wine, 55,000 cwt. of dried currants and 213,000 cwt. of sultanas and raisins. Considerable quantities of fruits (fresh and dried), wine and brandy, are annually sent to overseas countries, principally the United Kingdom, and to other Australian States. Some areas of the State, particularly near Adelaide, are also very suitable for growing all kinds of root crops and vegetables.

Live Stock (March 31, 1962).—There were 16,415,000 sheep, 659,000 cattle, 25,000 horses, 170,000 pigs. Wool production (1961–62), 206,984,000 lb.

Minerals.—Iron, pyrite, gypsum, salt, coal, limestone, clay, &c., are found. The total mineral output was valued at £A26,979,000 in 1962, including iron ore valued by the South Australian Director of Mines at £15,600,000.

Manufactures.—In 1961–62 there were 5,519 factories, employing 99,094 hands, the gross value of the output being £401,797,000. Plant machinery, land and buildings were valued at £224,800,000.

Transport and Communications.—There were (1962) 3,883 miles of railway in South Australia, 142 miles of tram and bus routes and 63,000 miles of roads. The railway mileage includes the South Australian part of the Transcontinental Railway from Port Pirie (South Australia) to Kalgoorlie (Western Australia) which forms a link in the system from Brisbane to Fremantle; and also part of the Commonwealth line from Port Augusta to the Northern Territory. There are a number of excellent harbours, of which Port Adelaide is the most important. In 1961–62, 1,958 vessels with net tonnage of 7,646,000 entered South Australian ports direct from overseas or interstate. Nationality of these vessels was—Australian 823, United Kingdom, 514, other Commonwealth 117 and foreign 504. There are 924 post offices in the State.

Civil Aviation.—There are 27 Government or licensed aerodromes, and 446,111 passengers and 8,591 tons of freight were carried in 1961–62.

Motor Vehicles.—The registrations in December, 1962, were 332,734, equal to 1 per 3·0 persons.

Wireless and Television (1962)—Broadcasting stations 16; listeners' licences 246,228. Television stations 3; viewers' licences 143,794.

OVERSEAS TRADE.

Year	Imports	Exports
	£A	£A
1958–59	45,346,000	90,916,000
1959–60	59 747,000	90,826,000
1960–61	71,382,000	99 279,000
1961–62	51,693,000	121,988,000

The principal exports are wool and other pastoral and dairying products, grain, metals and minerals, fruit and wine.

TOWNS.

Ψ ADELAIDE, the chief city and capital, population (estimated, Dec. 31, 1962), 596,800, inclusive of suburbs. Other centres (with 1962 populations) are: Port Pirie (15,500), Kadina (3,300), Moonta (2,100), and Wallaroo (2,300) in the Lower North; Port Augusta (10,100) and Peterborough (3,500) in the Upper North; Salisbury-Elizabeth (41,800) and Gawler (7,200) on the Adelaide Plains; Victor Harbor (2,600) on the South Coast; Whyalla (16,350) and Port Lincoln (8,000) on Eyre Peninsula; Murray Bridge (6,300), Renmark (6,200), and Berri (4,600) on the River Murray; and Mount Gambier (16,500), Naracoorte (5,000), and Millicent (4,100) in the South East.

Transit.—Transmission of mails from London to Adelaide, approximate, 29 days by sea and 4 days by air.

TASMANIA

Tasmania is an island in the South Pacific Ocean off the southern extremity of Australia, from which it is separated by Bass Strait, about 140 miles wide, in which are situated the Furneaux Group and King Island, included within the State. It lies between 40° 33′–43° 39′ S. lat. and 144° 39′–148° 23′ E. long., and contains an area of 26,215 square miles.

POPULATION.—At June 30, 1962, the estimated population numbered 356,937 (180,956 males and 175,981 females).

Year	Births	Deaths	Marriages
1959	8,625	2,780	2,567
1960	8,853	2,670	2,713
1961	8,982	2,789	2,677
1962	8,894	2,870	2,485

The birth rate in 1962 was 24·75, death rate 7·99, marriage rate 6·91 per 1,000. Infant mortality (1962) 20·7 per 1,000 births.

Religion.

In 1961 there were 159,101 members of the Church of England, 63,993 Roman Catholics, 42,236 Methodists, 16,757 Presbyterians, 4,193 Congregationalists and Independents, and 7,227 Baptists.

PHYSIOGRAPHY.

The surface of the country is generally hilly and timbered, with mountains from 1,500 to 5,000 ft. in height, and expanses of level, open plains. There are numerous streams, the Derwent and the Tamar being the largest. The climate is fine and salubrious, and well suited to European constitutions; the hot winds of Australia do not reach the island. At Hobart the mean annual temperature averages 53·9°, the mean temperature for Dec., Jan., and Feb. being 60·2°, and that of June, July and Aug. 47·1°. The western side of the island is very wet, the eastern side having a rainfall similar to that of eastern England; the average rainfall varies from 20 inches to 100 inches in different parts.

GOVERNMENT.

The island was first settled by the British in 1803 as an appendage to New South Wales, from which it was separated in 1825. In 1851 a partly elective legislature was inaugurated, and in 1856 Responsible Government was established. In 1901 Tasmania became a State of the Australian Commonwealth. The State executive authority is vested in a Governor (appointed by the Crown), aided by an Executive Council of Ministers responsible to the Legislature.

GOVERNOR.

Governor of Tasmania, His Excellency Lieut.-Gen. Sir Charles Gairdner, K.C.M.G., K.C.V.O., K.B.E., C.B., *apptd.* Aug. 31, 1962.

THE MINISTRY.

Premier, Treasurer and Minister for Mines, Hon. E. E. Reece.
Deputy Premier and Attorney-General, Hon. R. F. Fagan.
Lands and Works, Hon. D. A. Cashion.
Chief Secretary, Hon. J. B. Connolly.
Agriculture, Hon. A. C. Atkins.
Education, Hon. W. A. Neilson.
Housing, Hon. S. V. Ward.
Transport, Hon. H. J. McLoughlin.
Health, Hon. W. D. McNeil.

AGENT-GENERAL IN LONDON.

Agent-General for Tasmania, Hon. A. J. White.
Address, 457 Strand, Charing Cross, W.C.2.

THE LEGISLATURE.

Parliament consists of two Houses, a *Legislative Council* of 19 members, elected for six years (3 retiring annually, in rotation, except in every sixth year, when four retire) and a *House of Assembly* of 35 members, elected by proportional representation for five years, the electors for the latter being all adult Tasmanians who have resided continuously in the State for 6 months; the electorate for the Council is smaller, having a property or educational qualification for both sexes, but war service is a qualification for enrolment. The composition of the House of Assembly in 1963 was: 18 Labour, 14 Liberal, 2 Independent Liberal and 1 Independent.

President of the Legislative Council, Hon. Sir Henry Baker, K.C.M.G., D.S.O.
Clerk of the Council, E. C. Briggs.
Speaker of the House of Assembly, Hon. C. B. Aylett.
Clerk of the House, C. K. Murphy, C.B.E.

THE JUDICATURE.

The Supreme Court of Tasmania, with civil, criminal, ecclesiastical, admiralty and matrimonial jurisdiction, was established by Royal Charter on October 13, 1823.
Chief Justice, Hon. Sir Stanley Burbury, K.B.E.
Puisne Judges, Hon. M. G. Gibson; Hon. M. P. Crisp; Hon. G. H. Crawford; Hon. F. M. Neasey.

Local Courts established under the Local Courts Acts, 1896, are held before Commissioners who are legal practitioners, with a jurisdiction up to £250. Courts of General Sessions, constituted by a chairman who is a Justice of the Peace and at least one other Justice, are established in the municipalities for the recovery of debts and demands not exceeding £50. Courts of Petty Sessions are established under the Justices Act, 1959, constituted by Police Magistrates sitting alone, or any two or more justices. A single justice may hear and determine certain matters.

EDUCATION.

State schools are divided into Primary, Area, High and Technical High Schools, with a net enrolment of 68,592 scholars in 1961. There were 66 private schools with an enrolment of 13,436. The University of Tasmania at Hobart, established 1890, had 937 full-time students in 1963; there are technical schools at Hobart, Launceston, Burnie, Devonport, Queenstown, Rosebery, Ulverston, Smithton and Zeehan.

FINANCE.

Year	Revenue	Expenditure	Debt
	£A	£A	£A
1959–60	24,296 249	25,328,254	165,522,348
1960–61	26 885,193	27,083,666	177,279,340
1961–62	30,317,657	30,676,074	189,626,448

Banking.—The average weekly deposits of cheque-paying banks during December, 1962 were £41,703,000; the savings bank deposits, December 31, 1962, were £53,795,000 or £145 12*s.* 5*d.* per head of population.

PRODUCTION AND INDUSTRY.

The net value of production in 1961–62 was £100,901,000—agriculture and pastoral £18,200,000, mines and quarries £5,203,000, other primary industries £13,517,000 and manufactures £63,981,000.

Agriculture and Live Stock.—Of the total area of 16,778,000 acres there were, in 1961–62, 386,000 acres under crops. The principal crops are potatoes, apples and other fruit, hay, hops, oats, peas, turnips, barley and wheat. The live stock included (March 31, 1962) 425,000 cattle, 3,532,000 sheep, 76,000 pigs and 9,000 horses. The wool production (1961–62) was 34,443,000 lb.

Electrical Energy.—The Hydro-Electric Commission of Tasmania has effected important water-power developments at the Great Lake (Waddamana and Shannon), Lake St. Clair—River Derwent (Tarraleah, Butler's Gorge, Wayatinah and Catagunya), Nive River (Tungatinah and Liapootah) and at Trevallyn. In June, 1963, the total installed capacity of the 11 hydro-electric power stations was: turbines, 867,700 h.p.; generators, 617,050 K.W. The network extends to practically all parts of the State and the advantages of cheap electric power exercise continued attraction for new establishment of manufacturing industries.

Forestry.—State forest areas in 1961–62, 2,154,624 acres. The quantity of timber (excluding firewood) of various species cut on Crown Land forests in 1961–62 was 283,606,000 super feet, including 72,874,000 super feet for wood-pulp.

Minerals.—The chief ores mined are those containing copper, zinc, tin, silver and lead. The value of output of all mines and quarries in 1961 was £7,959,000.

Manufactures.—The chief manufactures for export are: refined metals, preserved fruit and vegetables, butter, woollen manufactures, paper, confectionery and sawn timber; the net value of production in 1961–62 was £63,981,000, the value of land, buildings, plant and machinery for the 1,760 establishments being £140,369,000.

CAPITAL, ΨHOBART, which was founded in 1804. Population (June 30, 1961) (with suburbs) 118,828.

Other towns (with population at June 30, 1962) are ΨLaunceston and suburbs (pop. 57,740), ΨDevonport (13,390), Burnie (14,590), Ulverstone (6,070) and New Norfolk (5,480).

Transmission of mails, 34 days by sea; 5 days by air.

VICTORIA

The State of Victoria comprises the south-east corner of Australia, at that part where its mainland territory projects farthest into the southern latitudes; it lies between the 34th and 39th parallels of South latitude, and the 141st and 150th meridians of East longitude. Its extreme length from east to west is about 493 miles, its greatest breadth is about 290 miles, and its extent of coast-line is about 980 geographical miles, including the length around Port Phillip Bay, Western Port and Corner Inlet, the entire area being 87,884 square miles.

Population.—The population at Dec. 31, 1962 was 3,013,447 (1,514,612 males and 1,498,835 females).

Increase of the People.

Year	Births	Deaths	Marriages
1959	62,245	25,078	20,456
1960	64,025	24,547	20,617
1961	65,886	24,500	21,264
1962	65,890	25,847	22,393

Vital Statistics.—Annual rate per 1,000 of population in 1962:—Births, 22·04; Deaths, 8·64; Marriages, 7·49. Deaths under 1 year per 1,000 births, 18·50.

Religion.

Members of the Church of England at the date of the census in 1961 numbered 893,160, Roman Catholics 762,734, Presbyterians 367,346, Methodists 275,205, Greek Orthodox 54,823, Baptists 38,627, Church of Christ 37,939, Lutheran 35,368 and Hebrew 29,932. The number of persons who did not state their religion was 315,050.

PHYSIOGRAPHY.

The *Australian Alps* and the *Great Dividing Range* pass through the centre of the State, and divide it into a northern and southern watershed, the latter sloping down to the ocean and containing, especially in the south-east, well-wooded valleys. The length of the Murray River, which forms part of the northern boundary of Victoria, is about 1,200 miles along the Victorian bank. Melbourne, the capital city, stands upon the Yarra-Yarra, which rises in the southern slopes of the Dividing Range.

Climate.—The climate of Victoria is characterized by warm summers, rather cold winters, and rain in all months with a maximum in winter or spring. Prevailing winds are southerly from November to February inclusive, with a moderate percentage of northerlies often associated with high temperatures. Northerly or westerly winds predominate from March to October inclusive. Rain on an average falls in Melbourne on 143 days per year, the annual average being 25·91 inches.

GOVERNMENT.

Victoria was originally known as the Port Phillip District of New South Wales and was created a separate colony in 1851, with a partially elective legislature. In 1855 Responsible Government was conferred. The executive authority is vested in a Governor, appointed by the Crown, aided by an Executive Council of Ministers.

Governor of the State of Victoria, His Excellency Maj.-Gen. Sir Rohan Delacombe, K.B.E., C.B., D.S.O., *born* Oct. 25, 1906, *assumed office* May 8, 1963 ...... £7,500

Lieutenant-Governor, Lieut-General Hon. Sir Edmund Herring, K.C.M.G., K.B.E., D.S.O., M.C., E.D.

THE MINISTRY.

(Sworn in, June, 1955.)

Premier and Treasurer, Hon. H. E. Bolte.

Chief Secretary and Attorney-General, Hon. A. G. Rylah.

Agriculture, Hon. G. L. Chandler, C.M.G.

Commissioner of Public Works (vacant).

Housing and Forests, Hon. L. H. S. Thompson.

Education, Hon. J. S. Bloomfield.

Labour and Industry and Electrical Undertakings, Hon. G. O. Reid.

Commissioner of Crown Lands and Survey, and Minister of Soldier Settlement and for Conservation, Hon. K. H. Turnbull.

State Development, Hon. A. J. Fraser, M.C.
Health, Hon. R. W. Mack.
Water Supply and Mines, Hon. W. J. Mibus.
Transport, Hon. E. R. Meagher.
Local Government, Hon. M. V. Porter.
Immigration, Hon. R. J. Hamer.

Agent-General in London

Agent-General for Victoria, Hon. H. R. Petty. *Address*, Victoria House, Melbourne Place, Strand, W.C.2.

The Legislature.

Parliament consists of a *Legislative Council* of 34 members, elected for the 17 Provinces for 6 years, one-half retiring every 3 years; and a *Legislative Assembly* of 66 members, elected for a maximum duration of 3 years. Voting is compulsory. The electors on the rolls at July 15, 1961, numbered 1,554,856.

President of the Legislative Council, Hon. Sir Gordon McArthur.................. £3,000
Speaker of the Legislative Assembly, Hon. Sir William McDonald............... 3,100

The Judicature

There are petty sessions courts, and general sessions and county courts; and a Supreme Court with a Chief Justice and twelve Puisne Judges.

Supreme Court.

Chief Justice, Lieutenant-General Hon. Sir Edmund Herring, K.C.M.G., K.B.E., D.S.O., M.C., E.D. (1944)...................... £7,250
Puisne Judges, Hon. Sir Norman O'Bryan; Hon. Sir John Barry; Hon. Sir Arthur Dean; Hon. Sir Reginald Sholl; Hon. T. W. Smith; Hon. E. H. Hudson; Hon. R. V. Monahan; Hon. G. A. Pape; Hon. A. D. G. Adam; Hon. D. M. Little; Hon. G. V. Gowans; Hon. O. J. Gillard; Hon. J. A. Nimmo (*acting*) ....each 6,500

County Court.

Judges, Their Honours L. E. B. Stretton, C.M.G.; A. L. Read; N. F. Mitchell; G. L. Dethridge; C. McT. Stafford; J. F. Mulvany; F. R. Nelson; J. G. Norris; B. J. Dunn; A. M. Fraser; E. H. E. Barber; T. G. Rapke; M. L. Cussen (*acting*); S. H. Z. Woinarski; J. Bourke (*acting*); G. Gunson (*acting*); H. Frederico; N. Vickery; D. Corson; A. Adams ...each 4,800
Senior County Court Judge....... 5,100
Masters of the Supreme Court, E. H. Coghill; C. P. Jacobs; S. H. Collie.........each 3,800

Crown Law Department.

Attorney-General, Hon. A. G. Rylah, E.D.
Secretary to the Law Department, R. A. W. Burns........................... 4,400
Solicitor-General, Sir Henry Winneke, O.B.E., Q.C........................... 6,500
Crown Solicitor, T. F. E. Mornane........ 4,791

Education.

Primary Education is compulsory, secular and free between the ages of 6 and 14. At December 31, 1961, there were 1,931 Primary Schools (including one Correspondence School) attended by 301,514 pupils; 291 Secondary Schools (including one Correspondence School) with an enrolment of 101,507; and 76 Technical Schools (70 of which possess a junior section with 36,719 pupils in attendance) with a roll call of 60,477 senior students.

During 1961, 165,865 pupils attended 551 independent schools, 447 of which are Roman Catholic, as the Roman Catholic Church in the State maintains an independent scholastic organization.

There are two State-aided Universities. Melbourne University has seven affiliated colleges—Trinity and Janet Clarke Hall (Anglican), Ormond (Presbyterian), Queen's (Methodist), Newman (Roman Catholic), St. Hilda's (Presbyterian and Methodist), and the University Women's College, which is not a Church foundation. Application has also been granted for a college to be instituted by the Baptist Church. The University had 8,089 full-time students in 1963. The Monash University, recently established in the eastern suburbs of Melbourne to provide for the increasing numbers of university students, at present accepts only a limited number of students of specified faculties (1,450 full-time students in 1963).

Finance.

The revenue and expenditure of the Consolidated Revenue Fund and the State Debt for those years are given as follows:—

Year	Revenue	Expenditure	Debt
	£A	£A	£A
1959–60	168,310,347	167,996,810	612,003,000
1960–61	185,101,402	184,931,572	653,756,000
1961–62	196,308,813	196,298,277	696,270,000

Banking, &c.— The state savings bank deposits at June 30, 1962, amounted to £331,835,000; in addition, deposits in the Commonwealth savings bank (in the State of Victoria) amounted to £142,562,000 and in other savings banks, £96,506,000.

Insurance (other than Life).—There were 213 companies or other bodies transacting business in Victoria during the year 1961–62. Total revenue amounted to £68,716,038, made up of premium income £64,850,742 and other income £3,865,296. Expenditure totalled £60,086,711, comprising claims £39,095,014, commission and agents' charges £6,566,964 and other expenditure £14,424,733.

Production and Industry.

The gross value of primary production in 1961–62 was £399,468,000—agricultural £115,123,000, pastoral £143,879,000, dairying £73,502,000, poultry and bee keeping £24,593,000, trapping £3,024,000, forestry £16,077,000, mining and quarries £21,254,000, fisheries £2,016,000. The net value of production of primary industries was £301,556,000. Wool, wheat, flour, butter, live stock, fruits, milk and cream, meats, poultry and eggs are staple products.

Agriculture.—Of the 6,819,000 acres under cultivation in 1961–62, 2,849,000 were wheat crops and 774,000 oats and 922,000 acres were cut for hay. In 1961–62, 3,605,000 gallons of wine were produced.

Live Stock.—There were in March, 1962, 27,533,000 sheep, 1,824,000 dairy cattle, 1,332,000 beef cattle, 325,000 pigs and 62,000 horses. The quantity of wool produced in 1961–62 was 330,639,000 lb., valued at £74,219,000.

Minerals.—Production of gold in 1962 was 28,134 ozs. Other minerals raised consisted principally of coal (black and brown), limestone, kaolin, fireclay, white clay, gypsum and bauxite. Production of brown coal in 1962 amounted to 16,687,000 tons.

Motor Vehicle Registrations.—The number of vehicles on the register at Dec. 31, 1962, was: private cars, 752,160; commercial, 110,633; hire

5,735; primary producers, 72,234; omnibuses, 1,050 and motor cycles, 16,250.

Victoria State Railways.—At June 30, 1962, there were 4,291 miles of railway open for traffic. The revenue and expenditure for the year ended June 30, 1962, were £42,571,702 and £42,906,123 respectively. Total traffic mileage was 18,902,419 and passenger journeys numbered 152,767,611. The tonnage of goods and live stock carried was 10,350,291.

Shipping.—During the year ended June 30, 1962, 3,545 vessels with net tonnage 14,909,058 entered Victorian ports and 3,537 vessels with total net tonnage of 14,872,144 cleared.

Trade and Industry.—In 1961–62 there were 273,435 males and 104,310 females (including working proprietors) employed in Victorian factories. Salaries and wages paid totalled £384,433,000. The total cost of materials used, containers, tools replaced and repairs to plant was £907,804,000 and of power, fuel and light, lubricants and water £49,529,000. Gross value of output was £1,674,660,000 and added value (net value of production) £717,327,000. The export trade (excluding inter-state trade) consists largely of agricultural and pastoral products. The principal oversea imports of the State are textiles, manufactured fibres, machines and machinery, electrical machinery and appliances, metals and metal manufactures, rubber and rubber manufactures, crude petroleum, paper, drugs and chemicals, and foodstuffs of vegetable origin.

OVERSEAS TRADE.

Year	Imports	Exports
	£A	£A
1957–58	282,712,758	219,577,919
1958–59	291,297,017	219,550,771
1959–60	339,349,389	244,070,363
1960–61	399,972,049	246,[illegible]71,035
1961–62	303,292,370	[illegible]86,800,048

CITIES, TOWNS AND BOROUGHS.

ΨMELBOURNE, the capital city, which is an episcopal see, was originally laid out in the year 1837 with wisdom and foresight; its wide streets, park lands, public gardens, university, public library, museum and large churches are the principal features of the city. Melbourne and suburbs cover an area of 519,791 acres and contained on June 30, 1962, a population estimated at 1,956,400. Other cities and towns are ΨGeelong, 94,350; Ballarat, 55,670; Bendigo, 40,980; ΨWarrnambool, 16,160; Mildura, 12,600; Hamilton, 9,620; Shepparton, 14,500; Maryborough, 7,240; Colac, 9,490; Horsham, 9,330; Castlemaine, 7,230; Ararat, 8,010; Wangaratta, 14,160; Echuca, 6,660; Sale, 8,190; Swan Hill, 6,440; Benalla, 8,490; Moe, 15,870 and ΨPortland 6,190.

WESTERN AUSTRALIA

Includes all that portion of the continent west of 129° E. long., the most westerly point being in 112° 52′ E. long., and from 13° 30′ to 35° 8′ S. lat. Its extreme length is 1,500 miles, and 1,000 miles from east to west; total area 975,920 sq. miles.

POPULATION.—At December 31, 1962, the population was 765,715 (389,304 males and 376,411 females).

The estimated number of full-blood aboriginals on June 30, 1961, was 10,000.

Year	Births	Deaths	Marriages
1959	17,111	5,497	5,387
1960	16,926	5,697	5,323
1961	17,078	5,729	5,150
1962	17,064	5,810	5,466

Religions.—Census of 1951—289,863 Church of England, 180,184 Roman Catholics, 76,465 Methodists, and 40,573 Presbyterians.

Physical Features.—Large areas of the State, for some hundreds of miles inland, are hilly and even mountainous, although the altitude, so far as ascertained, rises nowhere above that of Mount Bruce (4,024 ft.) in the north-west division or that of Bluff Knoll (3,640 ft.) in the Stirling Range in the south-west. The coastal regions are undulating, with an interior slope to the unsettled central portion of Australia. The Darling and Hamersley ranges of the west have a seaward slope to the Indian Ocean, into which flow many streams, notably the Preston, Collie, Murray, Swan, Murchison, Gascoyne, Ashburton, Fortescue, and De Grey. In the north the Fitzroy flows from the King Leopold ranges into the Indian Ocean, and the Drysdale and Ord into the Timor Sea. The greater portion of the State may be described as an immense tableland, with an altitude of from 1,000 to 2,000 ft. above sea-level, the surface of which varies from stretches of clayey soils to the sand dunes of the far interior. The climate is one of the most temperate in the world. The total rainfall at Perth during 1962 was 28·75 inches, the average for the past 86 years 34·78. Of the total area two-thirds is suitable for pastoral purposes.

GOVERNMENT.

Western Australia was first settled by the British in 1829, and in 1870 it was granted a partially elective legislature. In 1890 Responsible Government was granted, and the Administration vested in a Governor, a Legislative Council, and a Legislative Assembly. The present constitution rests upon an Amending Act of 1899, further amended by the Constitution Acts Amendment Acts of 1911, 1934 and 1955; the Executive is vested in a Governor appointed by the Crown and aided by a Council of responsible Ministers.

The Legislative Assembly (elected March, 1962) is composed of Labour Party 24, Liberal and Country League 18, Country Party 8.

GOVERNOR.

Governor of Western Australia, His Excellency Major.-General Sir Douglas Anthony Kendrew, K.C.M.G., C.B., C.B.E., D.S.O., *appointed* 1963 .... £5,250

Lieut.-Governor, Hon. Sir John Dwyer, K.C.M.G.

EXECUTIVE COUNCIL.

(Sworn in April 2, 1959)

Premier, Treasurer and Minister for Tourists, Hon. D. Brand £5,800

Deputy Premier, Minister for Agriculture and Electricity, Hon. C. D. Nalder 5,050

Industrial Development, Railways and the North-West, Hon. C. W. M. Court, O.B.E. 4,600

Education and Native Welfare, Hon. E. H. M. Lewis 4,800

Works, Water Supplies and Labour, Hon. G. P. Wild, M.B.E. 4,800

Mines Housing and Justice, Hon. A. F. Griffith 4,850

Lands, Forests and Immigration, Hon. W. S. Bovell.............................. £4,800
Chief Secretary and Minister for Health and Fisheries, Hon. R. Hutchinson, D.F.C. .. 4,600
Local Government, Town Planning and Child Welfare, Hon. L. A. Logan....... 4,800
Transport and Police, Hon. J. F. Craig..... 4,800

AGENT-GENERAL IN LONDON.

Offices. Savoy House, 115–116, Strand, W.C.2.
Agent-General, Hon. E. K. Hoar £3,000

THE LEGISLATURE.

Parliament consists of a *Legislative Council* of 30 members elected for 6 years, and a *Legislative Assembly* of 50 members elected for 3 years by universal adult suffrage; the electorate of the Council is restricted by a property qualification, that of the Assembly being subject to residence and registration.

President of the Legislative Council, Hon. L. C. Diver......................... £3,900
Speaker of the Legislative Assembly, Hon. J. M. Hearman..................... 3,900

THE JUDICATURE.

Chief Justice, Hon. Sir Albert Wolff, K.C.M.G................................ £6,400
Senior Puisne Judge, Hon. L. W. Jackson .. 5,750
Puisne Judges, Hons. J. E. Virtue; R. V. Nevile; G. B. D'Arcy; J. Hale, O. J. Negus..........................each 5,600

EDUCATION.

Education.—In 1962 there were 532 government schools and 195 non-government schools (excluding kindergartens) with 129,455 and 34,736 pupils respectively. The total amount expended on education (from Revenue) during the year ended June 30, 1962, was £12,645,380, including grants of £934,039 to the University of Western Australia (2,347 full-time students in 1963).

PRODUCTION AND INDUSTRY.

The gross value of primary production in 1961–62 was: agricultural £74,382,648; pastoral and trapping £52,910,424; dairying, poultry farming and bee-keeping £13,200,059; forestry £5,551,788; fisheries £5,344,446; mining £24,267,521.

Crops and Live Stock.—Of the total area under crop (6,975,879 acres), 4,379,751 acres were under wheat for grain, the 1961–62 production being 65,700,000 bushels. On March 31, 1962 the livestock included 1,218,432 cattle, 18,313,879 sheep, 174,182 pigs and 39,635 horses. In 1961–62 there were 9,017 acres of vineyards and 24,077 acres of orchards. The wool clip in 1961-62 was 180,000,000 lb. in the grease.

Manufacturing Industries.—There were in the year ending June 30, 1962, a total of 4,418 industrial establishments in the State employing either machinery or at least four hands. The average number of persons employed in them during the year was 51,033.

Forestry.—The forests contain some of the very finest hardwoods in the world. The total quantity of timber sawn and hewn during 1961–62 was 213,947,731 super feet.

Minerals.—The mines of the East Coolgardie and adjacent goldfields, which cover a vast portion of the interior and extend to the 125th meridian, and of the northern fields, are being constantly worked. The refinery production of gold in the State for 1962, was 859,368 fine oz. (£A14,057,303). The total amount produced from 1886 to Dec. 31, 1962, is 63,366,483 fine oz. (£A475,204,181). Magnetic iron, lead, copper, tin and manganese ores and coal, asbestos, bauxite, gypsum and ilmenite exist in large quantities.

Communications.—On June 30, 1962, there were 3,851 miles of State government railway (though operations on 570 miles have been suspended); 277 miles of private lines open for general and passenger traffic; and 454 miles of the Commonwealth line (Kalgoorlie–Port Pirie Junction). On Dec. 31, 1962, there were on the State register 397 vessels, of 19,994 tons, of which 186 were steam or motor vessels (16,555 tons) and 211 sailing vessels (3,439 tons).

FINANCE.

Revenue and Expenditure and net public Debt for 3 years ended June 30:—

Year	Revenue	Expenditure	Debt
	£A	£A	£A
1960	64,387,912	65,793,726	246,701,763
1961	69,332,710	70,537,280	261,488,118
1962	74,925,785	75,889,798	277,454,012

INTER-STATE AND OVERSEAS TRADE.

Year	Imports	Exports
	£A	£A
1959–60	169,529,312	158,998,460
1960–61	178,002,435	204,769,120
1961–62	172,692,838	190,811,727

The principal exports in 1961–62 were gold bullion (£A7,097,361), wool (£A43,834,746), wheat (£A52,178,050), wheat flour (£A2,943,981), hides and skins (£A2,289,826), oats (£A3,957,022), beef (£A3,149,718), mutton and lamb (£A1,217,874), crayfish tails (£A4,888,904), whale oil (£A632,317), raw asbestos (£A1,375,541), iron ore (£A1,243,526), barley (£A2,621,020), petroleum oils and spirits (£A25,819,703), iron and steel (£A6,909,915), machines and machinery (£A4,340,920).

TOWNS.

CAPITAL, ♆PERTH. Estimated population at June 30, 1962, of Metropolitan area, including the port of Fremantle, 431,000.

Perth, the capital, stands on the right bank of the Swan River estuary, 12 miles from Fremantle. Other towns are ♆Fremantle (31,200), Kalgoorlie—Boulder and environs (21,750), ♆Bunbury (13,600), Northam (7,300), ♆Albany (10,900), ♆Geraldton (11,400) and Collie (8,500).

PRINCIPAL LAND AREAS OF THE WORLD BELOW SEA LEVEL

(With approx. greatest depth in feet below Mean Sea Level.)

Europe: Netherlands coastal areas (15).
Asia: Jordan Valley, Dead Sea (1290).*
China: Sinkiang, Turfan Basin (980).
U.S.S.R.–Persia: Caspian Sea (85).*
Arabia: Trucial Oman-Qatar (70).
Africa: Libyan Desert Depressions:—
Qattara (440), Faiyum (150).
Wadi Rayan (140), Sittra (110).
Africa: Libyan Desert Depressions (*continued*) —
Areg (80), Wadi Natrun (75).
Melfa (60), Siwa (55), Bahrein (50).
Eritrea: Salt Plains depression (385).
Algeria–Tunisia: Shott Melghir and El Gharsa (90).*
America: Death Valley (275), Salton Sea (245).
Australia: Lake Eyre (40).

* Water surface.

New Zealand

AREA AND POPULATION

Islands	Area (English) Sq. Miles)	Population	
		Census, April 17, 1956*	Census, April 18, 1961†
(a) *Exclusive of Island Territories:*			
North Island (including Maoris)	44,281	1,497,353	1,684,775
South Island (including Maoris)	58,093	675,626	729,161
Stewart Island (including Maoris)	670	541	542
Chatham Islands (including Maoris)	372	524	487
Minor Islands:			
Inhabited—			
Kermadec Islands	13	11	10
Campbell Island	44	7	9
Uninhabited—			
Three Kings	3	..	..
Snares	1	..	..
Solander	½	..	..
Antipodes	24	..	..
Bounty	½	..	..
Auckland	234	..	..
Total exclusive of Island Territories	103,736	2,174,063	2,414,984
(b) *Island Territories:*			
Tokelau Islands	4	1,619§	1,870**
Cook Islands and Niue	199	21,387§	23,237**
Total, inclusive of Island Territories	103,939	2,197,068	2,440,091
Ross Dependency	175,000	166	198

* Excluding 2,162 members of the Armed Forces overseas.
† Excluding 2,559 members of the Armed Forces overseas.
§ Census of Sept. 25, 1956. **Census of Sept. 25, 1961.

Maori Population included in the totals for New Zealand proper—(1956) 137,151 (males 70,089, females 67,062); (1961) 167,086 (males 84,970, females 82,116).

Increase of the People.

Year	Increase			Decrease			Net Increase	Marriages
	Births	Arrivals	Total	Deaths	Departures	Total		
1958	53,774	172,791	226,565	19,014	159,930	178,944	47,621	18,305
1959	61,869	175,771	237,640	21,128	172,569	193,697	43,943	18,305
1960	62,850	195,741	258,591	20,892	193,551	214,443	44,148	18,909
1961	65,476	238,467	303,943	21,782	221,935	243,717	59,226	19,426

Birth rate (1962) 26·17; death rate 8·87; marriage rate 7·86; infant mortality 20·33 per 1,000.

Inter-censal Increases.

Year	Results of Census			Numerical Increase	Net Passenger Arrivals over inter-censal periods
	Males	Females	Total		
*1951	973,968	965,504	1,939,472	232,696	+27,486
*1956	1,093,211	1,080,851	2,174,062	234,590	+68,726
*1961	1,213,376	1,201,608	2,414,984	240,922	+39,792

* Excluding 1,894 members of the Armed Forces overseas at the time of the 1951 census, 2,162 at the 1956 census, and 2,559 at the 1961 census.

Races and Religions

Races	1956	1961	Religions	1956	1961
				Per cent.	Per cent.
Europeans	2,016,287	2,216,886	Church of England	35·92	34·60
Maoris	137,151	167,086	Presbyterians	22·26	22·30
Chinese	6,667	8,333	Roman Catholics	14·29	15·10
Other races	13,957	22,679	Methodists	7·44	7·20
			Baptists	1·56	1·70

PHYSIOGRAPHY

New Zealand consists of a number of islands of varying size in the South Pacific Ocean, and has also administrative responsibilty for a large tract in the Antarctic Ocean. The two larger and most important islands, the North and South Islands of New Zealand, are separated by only a relatively narrow strait. The remaining islands are very much smaller and, in general, are widely dispersed over a considerable expanse of ocean. The boundaries, inclusive of the most outlying islands and dependencies, range from 8° South latitude to South of 60° South latitude, and from 160° East longitude to 150° West longitude.

Geographical Features.—The two principal islands have a total length of 1,040 miles, and a combined area of 102,374 square miles. A large portion of the surface is mountainous in character. The principal range is that of the Southern Alps, extending over the entire length of the South Island and having its culminating point in Mount Cook (12.349 ft.). The North Island mountains include several volcanoes, two of which are active, others being dormant or extinct. Mt. Ruapehu (9,175 ft.) and Mt. Ngauruhoe (7,515 ft.) are the most important. Of the numerous glaciers in the South Island, the Tasman (18 miles long by 1¼ wide), the Franz Josef and the Fox are the best known. The North island is noted for its hot springs and geysers. For the most part the rivers are too short and rapid for use in navigation. The more important include the Waikato (270 miles in length); Wanganui (180), and Clutha (210). Lakes (Taupo, 238 sq. miles in area; Wakatipu, 112; and Te Anau, 132) are abundant, many of them of great beauty.

Climate.—New Zealand has a moist-temperate marine climate, but with abundant sunshine. A very important feature is the small annual range of temperature which permits of some growth of vegetation, including pasture, all the year round. Very little snow falls on the low levels even in the South Island. The mean temperature ranges from 59° F. in the North to about 49° F. in the South. Rainfall over the more settled areas in the North Island ranges from 35 to 70 inches and in the South Island from 25 to 45 inches. The total range is from approximately 13 to over 250 inches. The number of rainy days is generally in the neighbourhood of 160 to 180 in the North Island and between 110 and 140 in the South, except in the southern portion of the west coast. The amount of sunshine is generally over 2,000 hours per annum and ranges between 1,600 and 2,500 hours.

GOVERNMENT

The west coast of the South Island of New Zealand was discovered by Abel Janszoon Tasman, the navigator (voyaging under the direction of the Netherlands' East India Company), on December 13, 1642. The islands were visited, and charted, in 1769 by Captain Cook, who returned to them in 1773, 1774 and 1777. From 1800 onwards sealers and whalers settled along the coasts, and trade in timber and flax followed. Christianity was introduced in 1814, and in 1832 a British Resident was appointed. In 1840 British sovereignty was proclaimed, and on May 3, 1841, New Zealand was, by letters patent, created a separate colony distinct from New South Wales. Organized colonization on a large scale commenced in 1840 with the New Zealand Company's settlement at Wellington. On Sept. 26, 1907, the designation was changed to *The Dominion of New Zealand.* The Constitution rests upon the Imperial Act of 1852, and on the New Zealand Constitution (Amendment) Act of Dec. 10, 1947. The Statute of Westminster was formally adopted by New Zealand in 1947. The executive authority is entrusted to a Governor-General appointed by the Crown and aided by an Executive Council, within a Legislature consisting of one chamber, the House of Representatives.

FLAG: Blue ground, with Union Jack in top left quarter, four five-pointed red stars with white borders on the fly.

Governor-General and Staff.

Governor-General and Commander-in-Chief of New Zealand (1962–67), His Excellency Brigadier Sir Bernard Edward FERGUSSON, G.C.M.G., G.C.V.O., D.S.O., O.B.E., *born* 1911. (Salary £7,500, and allowances £5,500) £13,000

Official Secretary, D. C. Williams.
Comptroller, Maj. M. B. Reynolds, R.M.
Aides-de-Camp, Lt. Cdr. P. C. D. Gibaut, R.N.; Capt. T. G. Usher, The Black Watch.
Lady-in-Waiting, Miss Virginia Lucas.

§ THE EXECUTIVE COUNCIL.

His Excellency the GOVERNOR-GENERAL.
(December 12, 1960.)

Prime Minister and Minister of External Affairs, Rt. Hon. K. J. Holyoake, C.H.
Deputy Prime Minister, Minister of Industries and Commerce and Overseas Trade, Hon. J. R. Marshall.
Attorney-General, Minister of Justice and Maori Affairs, Hon. J. R. Hanan.
Transport, Railways and Civil Aviation, Hon. J. K. McAlpine.
Labour, Immigration, and Mines, Hon. T. P. Shand.
Works and Electricity, Hon. W. S. Goosman.
Finance, Hon. H. R. Lake.
Defence, Hon. D. J. Eyre.
Agriculture, Hon. B. E. Talboys.
Lands, Forests, Marine and Valuation, Hon. R. G. Gerard.
Internal Affairs, Civil Defence and Island Territories, Hon. Sir Leon Gotz, K.C.V.O.
Housing, Hon. J. Rae.
Education, Hon. W. B. Tennent.
Health, Social Security, and Minister for the Welfare of Women and Children, Hon. D. N. McKay.
Postmaster-General and Broadcasting, Hon. A. E. Kinsella.
Customs, Hon. N. L. Shelton.
Minister without Portfolio, Hon. D. C. Seath.

§ Members of the Executive Council travelling within the country on public service are entitled to an allowance not exceeding £4 4*s. per diem* when so engaged, but not during attendance at a session of the General Assembly. The Prime Minister receives £4,750 per annum with a tax-free allowance of £1,600 for expenses of his office and the Ministerial residence. The salary of each Minister holding a portfolio is £3,150 with tax-free expense allowance of £550, and that of each Minister without portfolio £2,500, with £450 tax-free expense allowance.

NEW ZEALAND REPRESENTATIVES OVERSEAS.

AUSTRALIA.
High Commissioner, J. Shepherd (*acting*).

CANADA.
High Commissioner, J. S. Reid.

INDIA AND CEYLON.
High Commissioner, F. H. T. de Malmanche.
MALAYA.
High Commissioner, R. H. Wade.
U.K.
High Commissioner for New Zealand, Hon. Sir Thomas Macdonald, K.C.M.G., New Zealand House, 415 Strand, W.C.2.
FRANCE.
Ambassador, C. E. Beeby C.M.G.
INDONESIA.
Chargé d'Affaires, D. M. Rae, C.M.G.
JAPAN AND KOREA.
Ambassador, E. B. E. Taylor.
LAOS, THAILAND AND VIETNAM.
Ambassador, Sir Stephen Weir, K.B.E., C.B., D.S.O.,
U.S.A.
Ambassador, G. R. Laking.

OVERSEAS REPRESENTATIVES IN N.Z.

Envoys Extraordinary and Ministers Plenipotentiary.

AUSTRIA.
Dr. W. de Comtes.
BELGIUM.
L. Van den Berghe.
DENMARK.
Dr. A. Serup.
FRANCE.
Ambassador, L. A. Félix.
GERMAN FEDERAL REPUBLIC.
Dr. H. Nöhring.
GREECE.
Ambassador, P. A. Cavalierato.
ITALY.
Chargé d'Affaires, C. Bonetti.
JAPAN.
Ambassador, K. Hara.
NETHERLANDS.
Chargé d'Affaires, C. G. van Geest.
SWITZERLAND.
Ambassador, Dr. F. Gygax.
U.S.A.
Ambassador, A. B. Akers.
U.S.S.R.
Chargé d'Affaires, N. V. Ivanov.

HIGH COMMISSIONERS IN N.Z.

AUSTRALIA.
Hon. D. A. Cameron, O.B.E.
CANADA.
K. J. Burbridge.
CEYLON.
Maj.-Gen. A. M. Muttukamaru, O.B.E.
INDIA.
B. K. Massand.
MALAYA.
Dato Suleiman bin Dato Abdul Rahman.
PAKISTAN.
K. M. Kaiser.
U.K.
High Commissioner, Sir Ian Maclennan, K.C.M.G.
Deputy High Commissioner, F. A. K. Harrison.
Economic Adviser, J. L. Reading, C.M.G.
First Secretaries, L. G. Heptinstall; P. L. Bourdillon; J. Eaton (*Agriculture and Food*); J. H. Reiss (*Information*).
Naval Adviser, Capt. T. G. V. Percy, O.B.E., D.S.C., R.N.
Army Adviser, Col. H. N. Hoare.
Air Adviser, Group Capt. G. B. Warner, C.B.E., D.F.C., A.F.C.

British Council Liaison Officer, R. N. Hollyer, O.B.E.

THE LEGISLATURE

Parliament consists of a House of Representatives consisting of 80 members elected for 3 years. The General Election of November, 1960, returned 46 National Party members and 34 Labour. Four of the members are Maoris elected by the Maori electors. Women have been entitled to vote since 1893, and to be elected Members of the House of Representatives since the passing of the Women's Parliamentary Rights Act, 1919. There are at present 4 women members. Members of the House receive £1,550 *per annum*, with an allowance of £370–675 *per annum* for expenses, depending on size of electorate. The Leader of the Opposition receives £2,600 *per annum* and £550 *per annum* for expenses, plus travelling allowance of £215.

Speaker of the House of Representatives, Hon. R. M. Algie (*plus expense allowance of £675 per annum and residential quarters in Parliament House*) £2,700

THE JUDICATURE

The judicial system comprises a Supreme Court and a Court of Appeal; also Magistrates' Courts having both civil and criminal jurisdiction.

Chief Justice, Rt. Hon. Sir Harold Eric Barrowclough, K.C.M.G., C.B., D.S.O., M.C., E.D. £4,750
Court of Appeal, Rt. Hon. Sir Kenneth Gresson, K.B.E. (*President*) 4,500
Hon. Sir Alfred North; Hon. Sir Alexander Turner 4,250
Supreme Court Puisne Judges, Hons. Sir James D. Hutchison; G. I. McGregor; T. E. Henry; T. A. Gresson; T. P. McCarthy; A. L. Haslam; R. Hardie Boys; I. H. Macarthur; C. P. Richmond; W. E. Leicester; A. O. Woodhouse; A. C. Perry; J. N. Wilson 4,250
Judge, Court of Arbitration, Hon. Sir Arthur Tyndall, C.M.G. 4,250
Judge, Compensation Court, D. J. Dalglish .. 4,000
Judge, Land Valuation Court, K. G. Archer .. 4,250

POLICE

On March 31, 1963, the strength of the Police Force was 2,575 of all ranks, equivalent to 1 for every 971 of the population. The total cost of police protection in 1962–3 was £3,861,521.

DEFENCE

Navy.

The Royal New Zealand Navy was greatly expanded during the Second World War and a number of small vessels were built in New Zealand. The naval forces include the Women's Royal New Zealand Naval Service, and Volunteer Reserve forces in four divisions. The strength is 1 cruiser, 4 frigates, 1 survey ship, 1 Antarctic support ship and 9 other vessels in commission; 2 frigates, and 4 ocean minesweepers in reserve. Active naval personnel numbers 310 officers and 2,514 ratings. A cruiser or a frigate is normally attached to the Far East Station.

Naval expenditure in 1962–63 amounted to £7,037,287.

Army.

The New Zealand Army consists of the Regular Force, the Territorial Force, the Army Reserve and the Cadet Corps. The establishment of the Regular Force is 6,250 and of the Territorial Force 10,000, and recruiting is in progress to raise the strength of the Army to this figure.

In 1962 selective national service was introduced to build the Territorial Force up to 10,000. The Army is now organized on the basis of one Regular Brigade Group, supported by three Territorial Brigade Groups. One battalion of the Regular Brigade Group is stationed as part of the Commonwealth Far East Strategic Reserve in Malaya.

Army expenditure for the year 1962–63 was £9,817,292.

Air.

The Royal New Zealand Air Force was constituted as a separate defence service in 1937. The Air Force now consists of the Regular Air Force, the Air Force Reserve, the Women's Royal New Zealand Air Force and the Air Training Corps. One Air Force unit is based outside New Zealand, in the Fiji islands. The strength of the Regular Force at March 31, 1963, was 4,107.

Air Force Expenditure in 1962–63 was £9,053,654.

FINANCE

Figures of the Consolidated Fund shown in this table are quoted on a gross basis, *i.e.* credits have not been deducted from departmental expenditure, but have been included as receipts. The Finance Act, 1959, provided for payment into the Social Security Fund of an annual amount from the money received as income tax. This amount is computed at 1*s.* 6*d.* in the £ of the national private income for the preceding year.

Year ended March 31	Revenue	Expenditure
	£(N.Z.)	£(N.Z.)
1959	241,310,000	240,888,000
1960	317,174,000	316,543,000
1961	284,354,000	283,958,000
1962	300,637,000	300,313,000
1963	287,025,000	290,962,000*

* Includes £133,697,000 for the social services, £23,324,000 for development of primary and secondary industries and £28,085,000 for defence.

Revenue from taxation in 1962–63 amounted to £342,014,000, of which £235,792,000 was receipts into the Consolidated Fund, £23,958,000 receipts into the National Roads Fund and £82,328,000 was paid as social security income tax.

Debt.

The gross *Public Debt* amounted on March 31, 1963, to £967,143,000, of which £136,240,000 was domiciled in London.

Banking.

There are five trading banks (with numerous branches) doing business, two of which are predominantly New Zealand banks. Of these the Bank of New Zealand is owned by the State. At April 24, 1963, total assets of all trading banks in New Zealand amounted to £353,336,000; liabilities, £356,149,000; and the value of notes in circulation amounted to £69,596,000. The Reserve Bank of New Zealand commenced business on August 1, 1934. The note-issuing powers of other banks have since been withdrawn and the Reserve Bank notes are legal tender. Net overseas assets of banks (on account of New Zealand business only) at April 24, 1963, amounted to £94,119,000, of which £45,949,000 and £22,132,000 represented the Reserve Bank's holdings of sterling exchange and overseas investments respectively. Trading banks' advances, including discounts, at the end of March, 1963, totalled £205,166,000 compared with £217,203,000 in the previous year. Deposits with trading banks at the end of March, 1962, amounted to £313,597,000.

Post-office and trustee savings banks had, at the close of the year 1962–63, 2,494,000 depositors having £430,556,000 to their credit. This amount does not include National Savings Accounts in which depositors had £52,300,000 to their credit at March 31, 1963.

As from Aug. 20, 1948, New Zealand restore[d] her currency to parity with sterling, in place of th[e] depreciated rate of £N.Z.125=£100 adopted i[n] 1933.

EDUCATION

The State system of education is free, secular, an[d] compulsory. The school-leaving age is 15 years In 1961 there were 2,063 public primary schools with 373,422 scholars; there were also 339 registere[d] private primary schools with 55,296 scholars, secondary schools with lower departmentss with 9[…] scholars and 150 Maori primary schools with 11,93[…] scholars, of whom 10,953 were Maoris. There wer[e] also 36,386 Maori children attending public primar[y] schools. The secondary education of boys and girl[s] in the cities and large towns is carried on in 16[…] state secondary schools, 92 state secondary depart[-] ments of district high schools, 100 private secondar[y] schools and 10 Maori private secondary schools The total number of pupils receiving full-tim[e] secondary education in July 1962 was 141,318 an[d] in addition there were 54,454 part-time studen[ts] attending technical classes, 2,021 receiving part-time tuition from the Correspondence School an[d] 6,678 from the Technical Correspondence School The university system consists of the University o[f] Auckland, Massey University of Manawatu Victoria University of Wellington, the Universit[y] of Canterbury and the University of Otago. Th[e] Lincoln university college of agriculture is associated with the Universities. The Universities ha[d] a total of 10,493 full-time students in 1963.

The total expenditure on Education out of publi[c] funds in 1962–63 was £51,416,000.

PRODUCTION AND INDUSTRY

Details of the estimated value of production are

	1960–61 £(N.Z.)	1961–62 £(N.Z.)
Agricultural	31,200,000	
Pastoral	216,700,000	352,000,00[0]
Dairying, etc.	109,400,000	
Forestry	27,700,000	51,000,00[0]
Fisheries	3,100,000	
Mining	20,500,000	
Factory	244,300,000	265,000,00[0]
Buildings and miscellaneous:	85,000,000	81,000,00[0]
	£737,900,000	£749,000,00[0]

Agricultural and Pastoral Production

		1961–62	1962–63
Wheat	bushels	8,250,000	9,240,00[0]
Wool	lb.	588,000,000	605,000,00[0]
Butter	tons	209,900	207,500.00[0]
Cheese	tons	99,100	100,20[0]
Stock slaughtered—			
Lambs	No.	19,846,000	21,534,000
Sheep	No.	7,289,000	7,934,000
Cattle	No.	995,000	1,259,000
Calves	No.	1,299,000	1,390,000
Pigs	No.	839,000	835,000

Agriculture and Forestry.—The total area of New Zealand (excluding its Island Territories) i[s] 66,390,700 acres, of this, approximately 43,000,00[0] acres are in holdings of one acre or more. Th[e] greater part of this is pasture land, about 53 pe[r] cent. being unimproved land used for pasturage and an additional 39 per cent. sown pasture. Th[e] output of sawn timber for 1962–63 was 643,400,00[0] board feet, of which 375,500,000 board fee[t] represented exotic varieties, mainly pine.

Live Stock.—Cattle at January 31, 1962, numbere[d] 6,598,000, including 1,968,000 dairy cows in milk pigs 686,000, including 84,000 breeding sows. A

June 30, 1962, sheep numbered 48,988,000, including 33,945,000 breeding ewes.

Manufactures.—Statistics of factory production show (1961–62) 8,981 factories in operation, employing 187,579 persons. Salaries and wages amounted to £161,532,207; cost of materials used, £488,489,840. Total value of output, £806,507,593.

Minerals.—Coal output in 1962 was 2,550,196 tons. Gold-mining was formerly an important industry, but production has declined greatly in recent years, gold produced in 1962 totalling 21,742 oz. Other minerals produced on a relatively small scale are silver, iron ore, manganese ore, tungsten and asbestos.

EXTERNAL TRADE, £N.Z.

Year	Imports	Exports	Total
1960	251,811,000	302,508,000	554,310,000
1961	322,097,000	283,679,000	605,776,000
1962	270,887,000	287,137,000	558,024,000

New Zealand produce exported to the U.K. in 1962 was valued at £N.Z.139,853,000 and included butter, 3,102,000 cwt., valued at £NZ.39,840,000, cheese, 1,630,000 cwt. (£N.Z.16,501,000); frozen and chilled beef, 630,000 cwt. (£N.Z.1,204,000); milk (dried) 538,000 cwt. (£N.Z.1,812,000) and wool 152,440,000 lb. (£N.Z.27,224,000).

Railways.—In March, 1963, there were 3,263 route miles of Government railway in operation. The number of passengers carried on Government lines in 1962–63, including season-ticket holders, was 25,666,000. Goods railed amounted to 10,044,000 tons. Railway total revenue and expenditure were £36,443,000 and £38,294,000 in 1962–63.

Motor Vehicles.—On March 31, 1963, there were 593,085 cars, and 156,118 other motor vehicles licensed, in addition to 45,816 motor cycles and power cycles.

Shipping.—During 1961 the vessels entered from overseas ports numbered 1,038 (net tonnage 4,954,000) and those cleared for overseas 1,031 (net tonnage 4,923,000).

Post Office Statistics.—(1962–63):—239,935,000 letters, letter cards and postcards, 268,954,000 printed and commercial papers, and newspapers, 7,992,000 packets and 7,174,000 parcels. Inland telegrams, 7,118,000; telephones 851,000.

Civil Aviation.—In 1961–62 domestic scheduled services flew 10,367,000 miles and carried 843,300 passengers. Freight carried amounted to 68,400 tons. International services to and from New Zealand carried 147,000 passengers, 1,265 tons of freight and 691 tons of mail.

CAPITAL, ΨWellington, in the North Island (pop. 1963, 155,400).

Other large centres:—ΨAuckland, 482,300; ΨChristchurch, 232,700; ΨDunedin, 107,400; ΨHutt, 105,600; Palmerston North, 45,800; Hamilton, 55,600; ΨInvercargill, 43,900; ΨWanganui, 37,200; ΨNew Plymouth, 34,100; ΨNapier, 35,100; Hastings, 35,000; ΨTimaru, 27,300; Rotorua, 28,100; Tauranga, 27,900; ΨNelson, 26,900; ΨGisborne, 25,900.

THE ISLANDS OF NEW ZEALAND

In addition to North, South, Stewart and Chatham Islands:—

The Three Kings (discovered by Tasman on the Feast of the Epiphany), in 34° 9′ S. lat. and 172° 8′ 8″ E. long. (uninhabited). *Auckland Islands*, about 290 miles south of Bluff Harbour, in 50° 32′ S. lat. and 166° 13′ E. long. The islands contain several good harbours, but are uninhabited. *Campbell Island* (population 9 at April 18, 1961). *Antipodes Group* (40° 41′ 15″ S. lat. and 178° 43′ E. long.) uninhabited. *Bounty Islands* (47° 4′ 43″ S. lat., 170° 0′ 30″ E. long.). *Snares Islands and Solander* (uninhabited).

The Kermadec Group (population 10 at 1961 Census), between 29° 10′ to 31° 30′ S. lat., and 177° 45′ to 179° W. long., includes Raoul or Sunday, Macaulay, Curtis Islands, L'Esperance, and some islets.

Cook and other Islands, included in the boundaries of New Zealand since June, 1901, consist of the islands of Rarotonga (8,676). Aitutaki (2,582), Mangaia (1,877), Atiu (1,266), Mauke (785), Mitiaro (307), Manuae (18), Takutea (uninhabited), Palmerston (86), Penrhyn or Tongareva (628), Manihiki (1,006), Rakahanga (319), Pukapuka or Danger (718), Suwarrow (1), Nassau (109). The population figures are from the Census of Sept. 1961, the total for the Group being 18,378 (9,454 males and 8,924 females). Niue, which is geographically part of the Cook Islands, but which is administered separately, had a population of 4,863. The chief exports are citrus fruits, fruit juice, tomatoes, pineapples, copra, pearl shell and manufactured apparel. The trade is chiefly with New Zealand and the U.S.A. The exports (1962) were valued at £N.Z.710,653, imports at £N.Z.937,273 for Cook Islands, and at £N.Z.30,753 and £N.Z.183,875 for Niue Island.

The Resident Commissioner of the Cook Islands, stationed at Rarotonga, and assisted in the other inhabited islands by Resident Agents, is responsible for the executive government of the Group. He is assisted by the Legislative Assembly of the Cook Islands, which has an elected majority of Maori members, and has full budgetary control over all Cook Islands finances (including grants from the New Zealand Government). An Executive Committee of the Assembly confers with the Resident Commissioner and advises him on executive government. A Resident Commissioner is also stationed at Niue and is assisted in the executive government of that island by the Niue Island Assembly.

The revenue of the Cook Islands in 1962–63, exclusive of grants from the New Zealand Government of £N.Z.736,900, was £N.Z.530,943, and expenditure, £N.Z.1,091,588. Revenue of Niue, exclusive of grants £N.Z.272,000, was £N.Z.181,206, and expenditure £N.Z.422,642.

Tokelau (or *Union*) *Islands.*—A group of atolls (Fakaofo, Nukunono and Atafu) (population 1,870 at the census of Sept. 1961), proclaimed part of New Zealand as from Jan. 1, 1948.

THE ROSS DEPENDENCY, ETC.

(1) The *Ross Dependency*, placed under the jurisdiction of New Zealand by Order in Council dated July 30, 1923, and defined as all the islands and territories between the 160th meridian of east longitude and the 150th meridian of west longitude which are situated south of the 60th parallel of south latitude. The Ross Dependency includes Edward VII Land and portions of Victoria Land. For some years there have been permanent bases in the area, staffed by survey and scientific personnel.

(2) The *Falkland Islands Dependencies—South Georgia* and *South Sandwich Islands.*

South Georgia is permanently inhabited and is an important seat of the whaling industry.

So far as is known the total areas of these Dependencies have not been officially estimated.

(3) *British Antarctic Territory.*—Formerly part of the Falkland Islands Dependencies, the *South Shetland* and *South Orkney Islands* and Graham's Land were constituted a separate Colony on March 3, 1962.

Ceylon

AREA AND POPULATION

Ceylon is an island in the Indian Ocean, off the southern tip of the peninsula of India and separated from it by a narrow strip of shallow water, the Palk Strait. Situated between 5° 55′–9° 50′ N. latitude and 79° 42′–81° 52′ E. longitude, it has an area of 25,332 square miles, including 296 square miles of inland water. Its greatest length is from north to south, 270 miles; and its greatest width 140 miles, no point in Ceylon being more than 80 miles from the sea.

At the Census of 1953, the population was 8,097,895, an increase of 21·7 per cent. over the last Census in 1946. The estimated population in 1960 was 9,896,000.

Races and Religions

The races of Ceylon are low-country Sinhalese, Kandyan Sinhalese, Ceylon Tamils, Indian Tamils, Ceylon Moors, Indian Moors, Burghers and Eurasians, Malays and Veddahs. Generally Sinhalese who trace their descent to a low-country district are classified as low-country Sinhalese, others as Kandyan Sinhalese. The Western and Southern Provinces, the Chilaw District and the Western part of Puttalam District are low-country areas; the Central and North Central Provinces, Uva, Sabaragamuwa, Kurunegala and the Sinhalese divisions of the districts of Batticaloa, Trincomalee and Vavuniya are regarded as Kandyan districts. At the 1953 Census 42·8 per cent of the population were low-country Sinhalese, 26·6 per cent. Kandyan Sinhalese. The religion of the great majority of inhabitants is Buddhism, introduced from India, according to ancient Sinhalese chronicles, in 300 B.C. Next to Buddhism, Hinduism has a large following.

PHYSIOGRAPHY

Ceylon is a compact area, except for the Island of Mannar and an almost detached portion in the north, the Jaffna Peninsula and its satellite islands of Delft, Kayts, etc. The relief of the island includes a mountainous area in the south-central region of 3,000 to 7,000 feet above sea level, surrounded by an upland belt of about 1,000 to 3,000 feet and a narrow coastal plain broadening out to a vast tract in the north. The coastal plain continues for a distance out to sea as a continental shelf and a coral reef, for the most part submerged, lies close to the coast. On the Central Ridge of the hill country are some of the highest peaks in Ceylon, Pidurutalagala (8,291 ft.), Kirigalpotta (7,856 ft.) and Totapola (7,741 ft.) and the high plains Nuwara Eliya (over 6,000 ft.), Elk Plains (6,000 ft.) and Horton Plains (over 7,000 ft.). The other principal peaks are Adam's Peak (7,360 ft.), Namunukula (6,679 ft.), Knuckles (6,112 ft.) and Haycock (2,167 ft.). The Peninsula of Jaffna and the Island of Mannar are featureless level stretches.

The Mahaveli-ganga, 206 miles long, is the largest river of Ceylon. Rising on the western side of the central hilly ridge, it flows north and east to empty into the Koddiyar Bay on the east coast. Other rivers are the Kelaniganga (90 miles), Aruvi-aru (104), Kala-oya (97), Yam-oya (94) and Deduru-oya (87). Waterfalls girdle the central mountainous massif and offer some of the best scenic features in the island; Dunhinda (Badulla), Diyaluma (Koslanda), Elgin (Hatton Plateau) and Perawella are among the outstanding falls. Forests, jungle and scrub cover the greater part of the island, often being intermingled. The forests, of varying species, extend from fairly near the coast right into the hill country. In areas over 2,000 feet above sea level grasslands (*patanas* or *talawas*) are found. Their total area is some 250 square miles, principally in the Province of Uva.

Climate.—The climate of Ceylon is warm throughout the year, with a high relative humidity. Temperatures average 80° F. during the year and few areas record less than 60° F. Humidity is over 75 per cent, Temperature ranges vary little between wet and dry seasons. In hilly areas, frost, mist and hail occur occasionally, but snow is completely absent. Rainfall is generally heavy, with marked regional variations; fall on the south-west slopes of the hill country (200–250 inches) being heaviest. Some cyclonic activity of the tropical variety experienced in the Bay of Bengal occurs, generally during the north-east monsoon period.

GOVERNMENT

Early in the sixteenth century the Portuguese landed in Ceylon and founded settlements, eventually conquering much of the country. Portuguese rule in Ceylon lasted 150 years during which the Roman Catholic religion was established among the Sinhalese inhabitants and to some extent Portuguese modes of living adopted. In 1658, following a twenty-year period of decline, Portuguese rule gave place to that of the Dutch East India Company which was to exploit Ceylon with varying fortunes until 1796.

The Maritime Provinces of Ceylon were ceded by the Dutch to the British on February 16, 1798, becoming a British Crown Colony in 1802 under the terms of the Treaty of Amiens. With the annexation of the Kingdom of Kandy in 1815 all Ceylon came under British rule.

On February 4, 1948, Ceylon became a self-governing Dominion of the British Commonwealth of Nations under the *Ceylon Independence Act*, 1947. The Parliament of Ceylon consists of (*a*) The Queen (represented by the Governor-General) and (*b*) two houses, namely, the Senate and the House of Representatives. The Executive consists of the Prime Minister and a Cabinet chosen from the party which has the majority in the House of Representatives.

FLAG.—Yellow lion of Kandy on a maroon ground; Sinhalese pinnacle on corners; yellow border; two vertical stripes at staff side.

Governor-General and Staff

Governor-General, His Excellency WILLIAM GOPALLAWA, M.B.E., *b.* 1897 (March 2, 1962)...... £8,000

Secretary to the Governor-General, N. W. Atukorala, C.M.G., C.B.E.

THE CABINET

Prime Minister and Minister of Defence and External Affairs, Hon. Mrs. S. D. Bandaranaike.................... Rs.18,000

Home and Local Government, Senator Hon. A. P. Jayasuriya 18,000

Justice, Senator Hon. S. P. C. Fernando. 18,000

Finance, Hon. T. B. Ilangaratne........ Rs.18,000

Education and Culture, Hon. P. B. G. Kalugalla...................... 18,000

Lands, Irrigation and Power, Hon. C. P. de Silva......................... 18,000

Labour, Hon. D. S. Gunesekara........ 18,000

Health and Housing, Hon. Badiuddin Mahmud........................ Rs.18,000
Commerce and Industries, Hon. Maitripala Senanayake........................ 18,000
Communications, Hon. Mahanama Samaraweera........................ 18,000
Agriculture, Food and Co-operative Development, Hon. F. D. Bandaranaike. 18,000
Public Works and Posts, Hon. M. P. Siriwardene........................ 18,000

U.K. High Commissioner in Ceylon

High Commissioner, Sir Michael Walker, K.C.M.G.

Deputy High Commissioner, G. D. Anderson.

First Secretaries, J. B. Howes, O.B.E.; M. A. Conville, M.B.E.; W. J. Watts; P. W. Heap; C. J. Scott, O.B.E. (*Information*); J. H. Chaplin, D.S.O., D.F.C. (*Information*).

Second Secretaries, A. G. L. Turner; L. W. Cooper.

Economic Adviser, J. F. Saunders, M.B.E.

Services Adviser, Capt. R. D. Henderson, R.N.

Cultural Adviser and British Council Representative, R. K. Brady.

Ceylon has diplomatic representatives in the following countries: Australia, Burma, Canada, China, France, West Germany, Ghana, India, Indonesia, Italy, Japan, Federation of Malaya, Netherlands, Pakistan, United Arab Republic, U.K., U.S.A. and U.S.S.R.

High Commissioner in U.K., G. P. Malalasekara, 13 Hyde Park Gardens, W.2.

THE LEGISLATURE

Parliament consists of the House of Representatives and the Senate. The House of Representatives is composed of 157 members, of whom 151 are elected by universal suffrage and 6 nominated. The Senate consists of 30 members, 15 of whom are elected by the House of Representatives and 15 by the Governor-General. One-third of the Senators retire every second year.

President of the Senate, Hon. C. Wijesinghe, O.B.E.
Clerk to the Senate, E. V. R. Samarawickrame, C.B.E........................ Rs.23,250
Speaker of the House of Representatives, Hon. R. S. Pelpola................ 18,000
Clerk of the House of Representatives, R. St. L. P. Deraniyagala, O.B.E.... 23,250

THE JUDICATURE

The Judicial System includes a Supreme Court composed of a Chief Justice and eight Puisne Judges, Court of Criminal Appeal, District Courts, Magistrates' Courts, Courts of Request, Municipal Courts, Rural Courts. Trial by jury obtains in the Supreme Court.

DEFENCE

Army.—The Ceylon Army Act provides for a Regular Force, a Regular Reserve, a Volunteer Force and a Volunteer Reserve. Steady progress has been made in the formation of the Regular and Volunteer Forces.

Navy.—The Royal Ceylon Navy, with headquarters in Colombo, mans 2 frigates, 2 minesweepers a seaward defence boat and several patrol craft. The vessels are based on Colombo, Trincomalee and Karainagar.

Air Force.—The Ceylon Air Force Act came into force on October 10, 1950, and the Ceylon Air Force was established on that date.

PRODUCTION

Agriculture.—The staple products of the island are agricultural. The most important for home consumption is rice in its two forms of paddy and husked grain. The areas under cultivation in 1961 (provisional figures) in acres, were:—Paddy, 1,160,000; tea, 587,401; rubber, 670,830; coconuts, 1,070,942; areca nuts, 53,057; cinnamon, 29,000; tobacco, 33,607; cocoa, 34,522. Production in 1961 (provisional figures) was: tea, 455,228,682 lb.; rubber, 96,046 tons; coconuts, 2,377,799,000; areca nuts, 2,966,595 cwt.; cinnamon, 40,086 cwt.; tobacco, 1,091,698 cwt.; paddy, 43,200,000 bushels. The livestock in 1961 included 1,517,191 cattle, 771,607 buffaloes, 491,810 goats, 58,237 pigs and 3,841,091 poultry.

Industry.—Factories are established for the manufacture of processing of ceramic work, vegetable oils and by-products, paper, tanning and leather goods, plywood, cement, chemicals, sugar, salt, textiles and ilmenite.

FINANCE

	1961-62
Revenue	*Rs*.1,632,319,000*
Expenditure	2,239,088,000*
Gross public debt:	
(Sept. 30, 1961)	*Rs*.2,651,000,000

* Provisional. R.1 = 1*s*. 6*d*.

Banking

In 1961 there were 13 commercial banks doing business in the island with total deposits (Dec. 31, 1961) of *Rs*. 1,155,445,372. The Ceylon Savings Bank had (Dec. 31, 1961) deposits of *Rs*.73,477,312. Depositors in the Post Office Savings Bank had *Rs*.345,326,211 to their credit at Dec. 31, 1961.

TRADE

	1960	1961
Total imports	*Rs*.1,959,622,686	*Rs*.1,703,337,595
Total exports	1,774,785,862	1,680,532,529

DISTRIBUTION OF TRADE, 1961

(Total imports from and Domestic Exports to)

Country	From	To
U.K.	*Rs*.361,975 000	*Rs*.490 561,000
Australia	81 497 000	109 869,000
Canada	206 821 000	36 361,000
India	13 019 000	88 976,000
Pakistan	22 960 000	23 359,000
New Zealand	4,633,000	39,237,000
South Africa	14 786 000	84 103,000
Belgium	26 224,000	3,344 000
Burma	185 341,000	11,157,000
China	34 870 000	82,812,000
Egypt	10 495 000	8 900,000
France	33 537 000	17 204,000
West Germany	61 410 000	51 494,000
Italy	16 380 000	33 256 000
Japan	156 755 000	40 426,000
Netherlands	40 140 000	36,628,000
Thailand	24 730 000	62,000

EDUCATION

In 1961, there were 8,265 Government and Managed schools. The total State expenditure on primary and secondary education was *Rs*.267,453,584 for 1960–61. The University of Ceylon was established on July 1, 1942, by the incorporation of the Ceylon Medical College (founded 1870) and the Ceylon University College (founded 1921) into the University, which in 1963 had 5,114 full-time students on the roll. In 1963 the Vidyalankara and Vidyodaya Universities, established in 1959, had respectively 802 and 351 full-time students.

COMMUNICATIONS

There are about 10,850 miles of motorable roads in Ceylon, of which 7,520 miles are bitumen surfaced. On Dec. 31, 1961, there were 142,970 motor vehicles on the register (83,799 private cars and cabs, 6,506 coaches, 26,500 lorries, 5,492 tractors, 3,160 trailers and 17,504 motor cycles).

In 1961, 2.364 ocean going merchant vessels of a total net register tonnage of 9,574,360 entered the port of Colombo.

In 1961 there were 1,666 money-order offices and 1,025 telegraph offices and 22,539 telephones. A commercial wireless telegraph station has a range of 500 miles by day and about 1,000 to 1,500 miles by night and handles ship-to-shore traffic.

Air Ceylon operates an international air service from Amsterdam — London — Cairo — Bahrain — Karachi — Bombay — Colombo and Singapore-Colombo. Air Ceylon also operates regional services from Colombo to Amparai and Jaffna, with branches to Madras and Tiruchirapalli, and Colombo to Trincomalee. Other services are *B.O.A.C.*, *Indian Airlines Corporation*, *K.L.M. Royal Dutch Airlines*, *Quantas Empire Airways* and *T.W.A.*

CAPITAL OF CEYLON

CAPITAL.—Ψ Colombo (estimated population 1960, 502,700). Other centres are Ψ Jaffna (85,800) Ψ Galle (66,300) and Kandy (70,400).

Colombo is distant from London 5,700 miles; transit 17 days; by air 1½ to 2 days.

Malaya

THE FEDERATION OF MALAYA

The Federation of Malaya is situated at the southern end of the Kra Peninsula between latitudes 1° and 7° North and longitudes 100° and 105° East. The country is bounded by Thailand on the north, the Johore Straits and the island of Singapore on the South, the China Sea on the East and the Straits of Malacca on the West. The total area is just over 50,000 square miles of which about 70 per cent. is still under forest and undeveloped. The climate is tropical, characterized by high humidity. Average temperatures at the lower altitudes vary between approximately 70° and 90°. The annual rainfall is about 90 inches, distributed fairly evenly throughout the year.

FEDERAL CAPITAL.—Kuala Lumpur, capital of Selangor (population, 316,230).

LANGUAGE.—Malay is the national language, with English permitted for official use for a minimum of 10 years after Independence Day. RELIGION.—Islam is the religion of the Federation, each Ruler being the head of the religion in his State; the Supreme Head of the Federation is the head of the religion in Malacca and Penang. The Federation is, however, a secular State.

FLAG.—Equal horizontal stripes of red (6) and white (5); yellow star and crescent in blue canton.

AREA AND POPULATION (Dec. 31, 1961)

State (with Capital)	Area (sq. miles)	Population	
		Total	Per sq. mile
Johore (Johore Bahru)	7,360	1,084,351	147
Kedah (Alor Star)	3,660	794 086	217
Kelantan (Kota Bharu)	5,780	579 246	100
Malacca (Malacca)	640	341,319	533
Negri Sembilan (Seremban)	2,590	430 227	166
Pahang (Kuantan)	13,920	359 739	25
Penang (George Town)	400	651 899	1,629
Perak (Ipoh)	8,030	1,404 952	175
Perlis (Kangar)	310	102 726	331
Selangor (Kuala Lumpur)	3,150	1,180,413	374
Trengganu (Kuala Trengganu)	5,000	320,431	64
Total	50,840	7,250,289	142

GOVERNMENT

The Federation of Malaya became an independent country within the Commonwealth on August 31, 1957, as a result of an agreement between H.M. the Queen and the Rulers of the Malay States, whereby Her Majesty relinquished all powers and jurisdiction over the Malay States and over the Settlements of Penang and Malacca which then became States of the Federation.

The Constitution, which came into force on Independence Day, is designed to ensure the existence of a strong Federal Government and also a measure of autonomy for the eleven State Governments. It provides for a constitutional Supreme Head of the Federation (His Majesty the *Yang di-Pertuan Agong*) to be elected for a term of 5 years by the Malay Rulers from among their number, and for a Deputy Supreme Head (His Highness the *Timbalan Yang di-Pertuan Agong*) to be similarly elected. Save in certain instances provided in the Constitution, the Supreme Head acts in accordance with the advice of a Cabinet appointed by him from among the members of Parliament on the advice of the Prime Minister. The Supreme Head appoints as Prime Minister the person who in his judgment is likely to command the confidence of the majority of the members of the House of Representatives.

There is a Conference of Rulers consisting of the Rulers of the nine States and the Governors of Malacca and Penang, presided over by the Supreme Head of the Federation. The Conference is empowered to elect the Supreme Head and Deputy Supreme Head and has certain other powers, notably in matters of religion; it has authority to deliberate on any subject.

A Federation of Malaysia, to incorporate Malaya, Singapore, North Borneo and Sarawak, was expected to be set up in the autumn of 1963.

SUPREME HEAD OF THE FEDERATION

His Majesty Syed Putra (*Raja of Perlis*).
Deputy Supreme Head, His Highness Ismail Nasiruddin Shah (*Sultan of Trengganu*).

Prime Minister and Minister of External Affairs and of Information and Broadcasting, Tunku Abdul Rahman Putra al-Haj, C.H.
Deputy Prime Minister and Minister of Defence and of Rural Development, Tun Haji Abdul Razak bin Hussein.
Finance, Tan Siew Sin.
Commerce and Industry, Lim Swee Aun.
Agricultural and Co-operatives, Mohamed Khir Johari.
Works, Posts and Telecommunications, V. T. Sambanthan.
Labour and Social Welfare, Bahaman bin Samsuddin.
Education, Capt. Abdul Hamid Khan bin Sakhawat Ali Khan.
Transport, Sardon bin Haji Jubir.
Interior and Internal Security, Dr. Ismail bin Abdul Rahman.
Health, Abdul Rahman bin Haji Talib.
Minister without Portfolio, Khaw Kai Boh.

HIGH COMMISSIONER IN LONDON

Tunku Ya'acob ibni Al-Marhum Sultan Abdul Hamid Halim Shah, 45 Portland Place, W.1.

UNITED KINGDOM HIGH COMMISSIONER IN MALAYA

Police Co-operative Building, 1 Suleiman Road, Kuala Lumpur.

High Commissioner, His Excellency Viscount Head, P.C., G.C.M.G., C.B.E., M.C.
Deputy High Commissioner, J. R. A. Bottomley.

British Council Representative, H. R. Mills, O.B.E., Victory Avenue, Kuala Lumpur.

LEGISLATURE

The Federal Parliament consists of two houses, the Senate and the House of Representatives. The Senate (*Dewan Negara*) consists of 38 members, under a President (*Yang di-Pertua Dewan Negara*), 22 elected by the Legislative Assemblies of the States (2 from each) and 16 appointed by the *Yang di-Pertuan Agong* from persons who have achieved distinction in major fields of activity or are representative of racial minorities, including the Aborigines. The first House of Representatives (*Dewan Ra'ayat*), consisting of 104 members elected on the principle of universal adult suffrage with a common electoral roll, was elected on Aug. 19, 1959, and met on Sept. 11.

Speaker, Haji Mohamad Noah bin Omar.

The Constitution provides that each State shall have a simplified version of the Federal Constitution, with the Ruler or Governor acting on the advice of an Executive Council appointed on the advice of the *Mentri Besar* or Chief Minister and a single chamber Legislative Assembly Three *ex officio* members are to sit in the Executive Council besides these elected members. They are the State Secretary, the State Legal Adviser and the State Financial Officer. The State Constitutions provide for the Ruler or Governor to appoint as *Mentri Besar* or Chief Minister, to preside over the Executive Council, a member of the Legislative Assembly who in his judgment is likely to command the confidence of the majority of the members of the Assembly. The Legislative Assemblies are fully elected on the same basis as the Federal Parliament.

Legislative powers are divided into a Federal List, a State List and a Concurrent List, with residual powers vested in the State Legislatures. The Federal List comprises broadly, external affairs, defence, civil and criminal law and justice, the machinery of government, finance, commerce and industry, communications and transport, power, education, medicine and labour and social security. The State List includes land, agriculture and forestry, local government and services and the machinery of state government. In the Concurrent List are, *inter alia*, social welfare, wild-life, animal husbandry, town and country planning, public health and drainage and irrigation.

There is provision for formal consultation between the Federal Government and the States in a National Finance Council and a National Land Council.

JUDICATURE

The Judicial System includes a Supreme Court, composed of a Court of Appeal and a High Court, and subordinate courts consisting of Sessions Courts, Magistrates' Courts and Local Courts, called Penghulus' Courts. The Supreme Court consists of a Chief Justice and up to 15 Puisne Judges.

Chief Justice, Sir James Thomson.

DEFENCE

The Armed Forces of the Federation consist of the Army, Navy and Air Force, together with volunteer and auxiliary forces for each arm. The responsibility for command, discipline and administration, under the general authority of the Supreme Head of the Federation, rests with the Armed Forces Council under the Chairmanship of the Minister of Defence. The Council is not responsible for the operational use of the Forces. The Chief of the Armed Forces Staff is the senior military member of the Council.

An agreement exists between the Government of the United Kingdom and the Government of the Federation of Malaya on external defence and mutual assistance under which the United Kingdom has the right to maintain in the Federation such military forces, including a Commonwealth Strategic Reserve, as are agreed to be necessary for the fulfilment of Commonwealth and international obligations. The United Kingdom Government, on the other hand, has agreed to provide personnel, facilities, advice and assistance in the development of the Federation Armed Forces in addition to the financial assistance already granted towards the capital cost of their expansion.

FINANCE

	1960	1961
Revenue....	M$1,069,021,000	M$1,081,007,000
Expenditure.	835,587,000	939,473,000

PRODUCTION AND TRADE

The Federation of Malaya is primarily a producer of raw materials, the chief of which are rubber and tin (of which it is the world's biggest individual supplier) iron ore, palm oil and kernels, coconut oil and copra and other agricultural products. These constitute nearly four-fifths of the total export trade, the other one-fifth being *entrepôt* trade consisting of re-export of raw materials and produce of neighbouring countries and manufactured and industrial goods of foreign countries. Imports consist mainly of foodstuffs, beverages and tobacco, minerals, fuels and lubricants, chemicals, textiles, manufactured and capital goods and raw products of neighbouring countries. The chief suppliers are the United Kingdom, Australia, the United States of America, Netherlands, W. Germany, Hong Kong, India, Japan, China, Thailand and Indonesia. Domestic rice production totalled 605,000 tons in the 1960–61 season. The balance was imported mainly from Thailand and Burma. Domestic industry includes manufacture of rubber goods, tobacco, cigarettes, pottery, cement, matches, pewter-ware, furniture, timber, bricks, tiles, soap, biscuits, aerated waters, textiles, paints, metal containers and toothpaste.

	1961	1962
Imports........	\$2,227,600,000	\$2,447,400,000
Exports........	2,626,300,000	2,625,700,000
Imports from U.K..........	£39,776 458	£44,711,178
Exports to U.K.	37,907,574	29,088,899

Federation of Nigeria

Area and Population.—The Federation of Nigeria is situated on the west coast of Africa. It is bounded on the south by the Gulf of Guinea, on the west and north by Dahomey and Niger and on the east by the Cameroon Republic. It has an area of 356,669 square miles with a population of approximately 40,000,000. The population is almost entirely African. There are some 28,000 Europeans, Americans, Lebanese and others engaged in Government posts, commerce and Missionary work.

A belt of mangrove swamp forest 10–60 miles in width lies along the entire coastline. North of this there is a zone 50–100 miles wide of tropical rain forest and oil-palm bush. North of this the country rises and the vegetation changes to open woodland and savannah. In the extreme north the country is almost desert. There are few mountains, but in Northern Nigeria the central plateau rises to an average level of 4,000 feet. The Niger, Benue, and Cross are the main rivers.

The climate varies with the types of country described above, but Nigeria lies entirely within the tropics and temperatures are high. Temperatures of over 100° in the north are common while coast temperatures are seldom over 90°. The humidity at the coast, however, is much higher than in the north. The rainy season is from about May to October; rainfall varies from under 25 inches a year in the extreme north to 150 inches on the eastern coast line. During the dry season the *harmattan* wind blows from the desert; it is laden with fine particles of dust.

Government.—Nigeria is divided into three Regions, the Northern Region, the Eastern Region and the Western Region (with Regional Headquarters at Kaduna, Enugu and Ibadan respectively) and the Federal, Capital of Lagos. A fourth Region (Mid-West) is planned. Eastern and Western Nigeria became self-governing in 1957 and Nothern Nigeria in 1959. The Federation of Nigeria became fully independent on October 1, 1960, continuing as a member state of the Commonwealth. It was expected to become a Republic in October 1963.

The Federal Parliament consists of the *Senate* and the *House of Representatives* and its authority includes subjects as external affairs, aviation, banks, census, customs, defence, police, shipping, mines and minerals, posts and telegraphs, trunk roads and railways.

Each Region has an Executive Council presided over by a Premier, a House of Assembly and a House of Chiefs. The Governor of each Region acts on the advice of his ministers. Regional Governments have administrative and executive responsibility for regional legislation, development plans, health, education, local government, agriculture, justice, finance, natural resources, regional public works, communications (other than those under Federal control), regional trade, industry and production and welfare.

Governor-General

Governor General and Commander-in-Chief, His Excellency the Rt. Hon. Nnamdi Azikiwe, LL.D., *born* 1904, *assumed office*, November 16, 1960.

Secretary to the Governor-General, A. K. Disu.

FEDERAL CABINET

Prime Minister. Rt. Hon. Sir Abubakar Tafawa Balewa, K.B.E.

Minister of Foreign Affairs and Commonwealth Relations, Hon. Jaja Wachuku (*N.C.N.C.*).

Defence, Alhaji the Hon. Muhammadu Ribadu, M.B.E. (*N.P.C.*).

Finance, Chief the Hon. Festus Okotie-Eboh, C.M.G. (*N.C.N.C.*).

Transport and Aviation, Hon. R. A. Njoku (*N.C.N.C.*).

Works and Surveys, Alhaji the Hon. Muhammadu Inuwa Wada (*N.P.C.*).

Labour, Hon. J. M. Johnson (*N.C.N.C.*).

Commerce and Industry, Alhaji the Hon. Zanna Bukar Dipcharima (*N.P.C.*).

Education, Hon. Aja Nwachuku (*N.C.N.C.*).

Establishments, Hon. J. C. Obande (*N.P.C.*).

Internal Affairs, Aljahi the Hon. Shehu Shagari (*N.P.C.*).

Mines and Power, Hon. Malam Maitama Sule (*N.P.C.*).

Information, Hon. T. O. S. Benson (*N.C.N.C.*).

Economic Development, Alhaji the Hon. Waziri Ibrahim (*N.P.C.*).

Communications, Hon. Olu Akinfosile (*N.C.N.C.*).

Lagos Affairs, Hon. Mallam Musa Yaradua (*N.P.C.*),

Health, Senator the Hon. M. A. Majekodunmi, C.M.G.

Attorney-General and Minister of Justice, Dr. Hon. T. O. Elias.

Ministers of State, Senator the Hon. Nuhu Bamalli; Senator Dr. Hon. E. A. Esin; Hon. M. T. Mbu; Hon. M. A. Olarewaju.

N.P.C.—Northern Peoples Congress.

N.C.N.C.—National Council of Nigeria Citizens.

President of the Senate, Chief the Hon. D. C. Osadebay (*N.C.N.C.*).

Speaker. House of Representatives, Mallam Ibrahim Jalo Waziri (*N.P.C.*).

NORTHERN REGION

Governor, Northern Region, His Excellency Kashim Ibrahim.

Premier, Sir Ahmadu Bello.

Eastern Region

Governor, Eastern Region, Sir Francis Ibiam, K.C.M.G., K.B.E.

Premier, M. I. Okpara.

Western Region

Governor, Chief Sir Joseph Fadahunsi, K.C.M.G.

Premier, Chief S. L. Akintola.

U.K. HIGH COMMISSIONER

Kajola House, 62–64 Campbell Street, Lagos.

High Commissioner, His Excellency Hon. Sir Francis Cumming-Bruce, K.C.M.G.

Deputy High Commissioner, R. W D. Fowler, C.M.G.

Counsellors, J. O. Moreton, M.C.; K. C. Christofas, M.B.E.

Military Adviser, Col. A. J. M. Flint, M.B.E.

Economic Adviser and Senior Trade Commissioner, C. E. Dymond.

Director, U.K. Information Services, A. C. Hall.

Deputy High Commissioners, R. L. Jasper (*Ibadan*); W. S. Bates (*Kaduna*); R. G. Chisholm (*Enugu*).

British Council Representative in Nigeria, J. A. O'Brien, 227 Herbert Macaulay Street, Lagos.

NIGERIAN HIGH COMMISSIONER IN LONDON

Nigeria House, 9 Northumberland Avenue, W.C.1 [Trafalgar: 1244]

High Commissioner, His Excellency Alhaji Abdulmaliki, C.B.E.

Regional Agents-General

Northern Nigeria, Abba Jiddun Gana.

Eastern Nigeria, J. C. Achara.

Western Nigeria, Prince Odubanjo, 178 Great Portland Street, W.1.

NIGERIAN REPRESENTATIVES ABROAD

Cameroon Republic.—M. B. Malabu (*Ambassador*).
Germany.—Chief M. E. Egimofor (*Ambassador*).
Ghana.—L. O. Harriman (*Acting High Commissioner*).
Guinea.—Chief Hon. O. Oweh (*Ambassador*).
Ivory Coast.—Alhaji Koguna (*Ambassador*).
Liberia.—N. A. Martins (*Ambassador*).
Sierra Leone.—A. B. Oyediran (*High Commissioner*).
Sudan.—Mallam Waziri (*Ambassador*).
U.A.R.—Alhaji Muhammad Ngileruma (*Ambassador*).
U.S.A.—J. M. Udochi (*Ambassador*).
United Nations.—Chief S. O. Adebo (*Permanent Delegate*).

Judicature

Chief Justice, Federal Supreme Court, Rt. Hon. Sir Adetokunbo Ademola.

Chief Justice, High Court of Lagos, Sir Marie de Lestang.

Chief Justice, Northern Region High Court, Sir Wilfred Hurley.

Chief Justice, Eastern Region High Court, Sir Louis Mbanafo.

Chief Justice, Western Region High Court, S. O. Quashie-Idun.

Education.—Education is the responsibility of the Regional Governments, the Federal Government retaining responsibility for education in Lagos and for those institutions of higher learning which have Nigerian significance, such as the Universities at Ibadan, Lagos, Ife and Kano, and the Man o' War Training Centre. University College, Ibadan, became a full independent university on Oct. 1, 1962 (1,778 full-time students in 1963). The University at Nsukka, E. Region (1960), had 1,248 full-time students in 1963. The Universities of Lagos, Kano and Ife were formally established in 1962. Free and universal primary education for all children within the 6–12 year age group is now available in West and East Nigeria and in the Federal Territory of Lagos. Over 3,000,000 pupils were enrolled at primary and higher schools in 1962.

Railways.—The Nigerian railway system, which is controlled by the Nigerian Railway Corporation, is the most extensive in Africa. There are 1,870 route miles of lines. There are two major bridges, one over the Niger at Jebba and one over the Benue at Makurdi. The latter is 2,624 ft. long, and it is believed to be the second longest in Africa. The North-western main line runs from Lagos to Kano (700 miles) through the important towns of Abeokuta, Ibadan, Ilorin, Jebba, Minna, Kaduna and Zaria. From Kano the line continues for another 143 miles in a north-easterly direction to its terminus at Nguru, and there is a branch line from Zaria *viâ* Gusau to Kaura Namoda to serve north-western Nigeria. This line is also linked with Sokoto by a scheduled railway road service from Gusau. The eastern line runs from Port Harcourt deep-water quay on the Bonny river through the thickly populated oil palm area to Enugu, where it serves the collieries. It then crosses the Benue and joins the north-western line at Kaduna, 569 miles from Port Harcourt. A branch line of 63 miles from Kafanchan serves the tin mines at Jos. The railway hauled 2,724,000 tons of freight in 1960-61, and its passenger traffic totalled 9,828,000 passengers.

Roads.—There are 45,000 miles of motorable road. Most of the roads have gravelled or earth surfaces, but about 7,000 miles are tarred. An extensive programme of bituminous surfacing is now being carried out and work has begun on the construction of a road bridge over the lower Niger between Onitsha and Asaba to provide a through trunk road between East and West Nigeria.

Civil Aviation.—Trunk route services operated by Nigerian and the principal international airlines bring Nigeria within less than 12 hours of the Western European capitals and South Africa. There are also services to other parts of Africa and to the United States. A network of internal air services connects the main centres. Comprehensive radio navigational aids are installed at Kano and Lagos airports, and basic radio navigational facilities are provided at the twelve other aerodromes in regular use. Several flying strips are also in use by light aircraft. There is a network of meteorological reporting stations.

Production and Industry.—Nigeria is mainly an agricultural country. Four of the country's main agricultural products, *viz.* palm-oil and palm kernels, cocoa, cotton and ground nuts are of the greatest importance in Nigeria's export trade (see figures under "Trade" below). Other crops include benniseed, capsicums, cassava, coffee, copra, guinea-corn, gum arabic, kola-nuts, maize, millet, piassava, rice, rubber, tobacco and yams. There are important tin and coal-mining industries, at Jos and Enugu respectively. The coal is mainly used within the country. Nigeria is the principal source of supply of the world's requirements of columbite. Timber and hides and skins are other major exports. Industrial products include soap, cigarettes, beer, margarine, groundnut oil, meal and cake, concentrated fruit juices, soft drinks, canned food, metal containers, plywood, textiles, ceramic products, cotton cloth, rubber shoes, boat building, car and cycle assembly, plastics, concrete and cement manufacturers and printing. A steel rolling mill has begun operations.

Trade.—The principal imports (1961) were cotton piece goods (£26,435,000), unmanufactured tobacco and cigarettes (£1,490,746), jute bags and sacks (£4 322,310), artificial silk piece-goods (£7,360,000), motor-vehicles and spares (£16,902,000), bicycles and spare parts (£1,154,800), other machinery (£32,328,584), cement £3,664,448), corrugated iron sheets (£2,690,063), stockfish (£7,564,055), and petroleum products (£11 668 000). The principal exports were cocoa (£33 746,456), groundnuts (£32,232,698), palm-kernels (£19 888 699), palm oil (£13,226,855), timber, sawn and logs (£6,721,922), hides and skins (£4 119,820), cotton (£11,120,055), columbite (£1,164,575), tin ore (£6,642,691), and rubber (£10,966,656).

	1960	1961
Total imports......	£215,195,000	£222,013,000
Total exports.......	164,879,000	173,496,000

Exports to the U.K. include about one-third of the U.K.'s total cocoa imports, one-quarter of her tin imports, one-quarter of her dry hides, and 10 per cent. of her hardwoods.

	1961	1962
Imports from U.K. .	£85,192,152	£63,264,869
Exports to U.K.....	76,217,961	73,063,247

Revenue and Expenditure figures include statutory appropriations from Federal to Regional revenues.

Finance

	1961–62	1962–63*
Revenue............	£112,126,641	£124,768,071
Expenditure.........	108,704,080	113,272,710

* Estimated.

CAPITAL.—ΨLAGOS, estimated population, 450,000. Other important towns are Ibadan (600,000), Kano (130,000), Iwo (100,000), Ogbomosho (140,000), Oyo (72,000), Oshogbo (123,000). Onitsha (77,000), Ife (111,000), Abeokuta (84,000), Ilesha (72,000), Enugu (63,000), Aba (58,000), Yerwa (57,000), Katsina (53,000), Port Harcourt (72,000), Sokoto (48,000), Zaria (54,000).

FLAG.—Three equal vertical bands, green, white, green.

Sierra Leone

Area and Population, etc.—The peninsula of Sierra Leone, situated on the West Coast of Africa, was ceded to Great Britain in 1787 by the native chiefs to be used as an asylum for the many destitute negroes then in England. At a somewhat later date the Colony was used as a settlement for Africans from North America and the West Indies, and great numbers of Africans rescued from slave ships have from time to time been liberated and settled there. The total area of Sierra Leone is about 27,925 sq. miles, and the total population was estimated in 1961 at 2,400,000. For administrative purposes, the interior portion of Sierra Leone is divided into 3 Provinces covering 12 Districts, each administered by a Resident Minister. The principal peoples are the Limbas and Korankos in the north, the Temnes in the centre, and the Mendis in the south.

Government.—Sierra Leone became a fully independent state and a member of the British Commonwealth on April 27, 1961. Under the 1961 Constitution, Her Majesty the Queen's representative is the Governor-General, who is appointed on the advice of the Prime Minister. The House of Representatives consists of a Speaker and 74 members, elected from constituencies established by an Electoral Commission. The House has full power to legislate. The Governor-General is advised by a Cabinet consisting of the Prime Minister and not less than 7 other ministers, who must be elected members of the House of Representatives. The Ministers are appointed by the Governor-General on the recommendation of the Prime Minister. Eighteen members of the Cabinet hold ministerial portfolios, and the remaining two are Ministers without portfolio.

Governor-General

Governor-General, His Excellency Sir Henry Josiah Lightfoot Boston, G.C.M.G., *born* August 19, 1898, *assumed office*, May 5, 1962.

Adviser to the Government, Sir Alfred Newns, K.C.M.G., C.V.O.

CABINET

Prime Minister and Minister of Internal Affairs and Defence, Rt. Hon. Sir Milton Margai, M.B.E.

Minister of Finance, A. M. Margai.

Minister of External Affairs, Dr. J. Karefa-Smart.

Education, A. Wurie, M.B.E.

Lands, Mines and Labour, A. J. Demby.

Development, R. G. O. King, M.B.E.

Health, D. L. Sumner.

Trade and Industry, M. S. Mustapha, C.B.E.

Communications, Kande Bureh.

Works, M. J. Kamanda-Bongay.

Natural Resources, S. J. Sheriff.

Information and Broadcasting, J. Nelson-Williams.

Social Welfare, G. Dickson-Thomas.

Housing and Country Planning, C. B. Rogers-Wright.

Eastern Province, T. Ngobeh.

Southern Province, R. B. Kowa, M.B.E.

Northern Province, Y. D. Sisay.

Ministers without Portfolio, Paramount Chief Madam E. K. Gulama, M.B.E.; Paramount Chief Bai Sherbro Yumkella II.

U.K. HIGH COMMISSIONER

Bank of West Africa Building, Oxford Street, Freetown.

High Commissioner, His Excellency D. J. C. Crawley, C.V.O.

Deputy High Commissioner, B. G. Smallman.

First Secretaries, J. N. Allan; T. N. Rosser, O.B.E., D.F.C.

First Secretary (Information) and Director of U.K Information Services, G. W. Baker, V.R.D.

SIERRA LEONE HIGH COMMISSIONER IN LONDON

33 Portland Place, W.1.
[Museum: 6483–6]

High Commissioner, His Excellency Dr. W. H. Fitzjohn.

Counsellor, S. C. A. Forster.

JUDICATURE

Chief Justice, Sir Salako A. Benka-Coker, O.B.E.

Puisne Judges, R. B. Marke, C.B.E.; S. B. Jones; C. O. E. Cole; J. B. Marcus Jones; S. C. W. Betts.

Communications.—A railway runs inland from Freetown to Pendembu (227½ miles) and a branch line of 83 miles extends in a north-easterly direction from Bauya to Makeni. A mining company, the Sierra Leone Development Company, owns a railway which runs for 57 miles from the iron ore deposits at Marampa to the shipping port of Pepel. There are about 3,000 miles of road in the country, of which about 200 miles are bitumen-surfaced. There is a trunk line network of 951 miles of telephone and telegraph routes connecting Freetown with most of the more important centres and towns.

The Freetown international airport is situated at Lungi, across the Sierra Leone River from Freetown. The main port is Freetown, which has one of the largest natural harbours in the world, and where a deep water quay, capable of berthing two medium-sized ships, came into operation in 1954. There are smaller ports at Pepel, Bonthe and Sulima. Inland waterways total some 493 miles, but several are only navigable for about three to four months of the year. The Sierra Leone Broadcasting Service operates a direct service, and is responsible for the Freetown Rediffusion System. Broadcasts are made daily in several of the more important indigenous languages, in addition to English.

Education.—In 1962 primary education was provided in a total of 629 schools, of which all but 24 were assisted from public funds. The total enrolment was 98,088. Primary education is neither free nor compulsory, but the rate of fee is low and equipment is provided free of charge. The percentage of children attending school is higher in the Freetown area than in the Provinces. There are 39 secondary schools in the country. One school provides a secondary technical education; the remainder are grammar schools. Technical education is provided in the two Government Technical Institutes, situated in Freetown and Kenema, and in the technical training establishments of the two mining companies. Teacher training is carried out in two Government and three Church/Mission training colleges in the Provinces, and in the Freetown Training College. The total number of teachers in training in 1961 was 659. The University College (Fourah Bay College) was founded by the Church Missionary Society and is affiliated to the University of Durham. It has a number of departments and faculties.

Trade.—In the Colony area, farming is largely confined to the production of cassava and garden crops, such as maize and vegetables, for local consumption. In the Protectorate, the principal agricultural product is rice, which is the staple food of the country, with cassava as a supplementary item of diet. In 1961 the most valuable exports were:

Diamonds £13,911,698; iron ore £3,396,476; palm kernels £1,766,141.

Other agricultural exports were: coffee (£577,495) cocoa (£415,799), piassava (£231,238), kola nuts (£80,290) and ginger (£80,272). The only other mineral export of importance was chrome ore (£90,362). The principal imports were food (including rice to the value of £39,930 in 1961), tobacco, drink, apparel, cotton and synthetic piece goods, hardware, machinery, motor vehicles, patent fuel and oils.

	1960	1961
Total Imports....	£26,342,213	£24,554,545*
Total Exports....	29,630,668	24,650,064*
	1961	1962
Imports from U.K.	£13,127,365	£11,012,789
Exports to U.K...	5,067,447	4,992,974

* As at Sept. 30, 1961.

FINANCE.

	1961–62	1962–63
Public revenue...	£13,924,401	£14,200,114
Public expenditure	13,785,953	14,052,202

The net public debt of Sierra Leone on March 31, 1962, amounted to £9,620,152.

The unit of currency is the pound sterling.

CAPITAL.—ΨFREETOWN (population 85,000). Freetown, which possesses the finest and most important harbour in West Africa, is 3,078 miles from Liverpool; transit, 9 days by sea; 2 days by air; there are also air connections with most of the capital cities of the world, and an internal air service between Freetown and some of the more important towns in Sierra Leone.

British Council Representative, J. Sanderson.

FLAG.—Three horizontal stripes of leaf green, white and cobalt blue.

India and Pakistan

THE *Indian Independence Act*, 1947, which received the Royal Assent on July 18, 1947, brought to an end the whole structure of British Government in India and the handing over of power was completed by August 15, 1947. The Indian Empire, which extended over a territory larger than the Continent of Europe without Russia, is now represented by the *Republic of India*, the *Republic of Pakistan*, and Territories of Indian Rulers formerly under the suzerainty of the King-Emperor. Certain tracts of Tr bal Territory on the North West and North East Frontiers are under the political influence, though not under the administrative rule, of the Government of Pakistan.

GEOGRAPHICAL INDIA

Physical Features.—The country may be broadly divided into three sections, viz. the Himalayan region, the northern river-plains, and the southern tableland.

The Himalayas.—The Himalayas (which lie partly beyond the frontier), with their southern offshoots, form the natural northern boundary of India. The Himalayan range runs for 1,500 miles from N.W. to S.E., with a varying breadth of 150 to 200 miles, and attains a general height of 20,000 feet above the plain, culminating in the loftiest peaks yet measured on the globe—Mount Everest, 29.002 feet, Kunchinjunga, 28,146 feet, and Dhaulagiri, 26,826 feet, near the centre of the range; and K. 2, 28,250 feet, near its junction with the Hindu Kush. The line of perpetual snow is at about 16,000 feet, The Himalayas collect and store up water for the plains below. The slopes give a representation of the tropical zone (especially on the southern slopes to the E.), the temperate zone (particularly to the S.W. of the range), and the arctic zone as the upward journey is taken from the plains. In the Himalayas are several sanatoria, including Murree, Simla, Mussoorie, Naini Tal, and Darjiling. Himalayan vegetation includes such varied species as the tree-fern, ilex, pine, oak, fir, deodar (cedar), rhododendron, barley, oats, millet, and many domestic vegetables. The fauna are as varied as the flora, and include the bison, musk-deer, yak, wild sheep and goat, bear, elephant, monkey, and tiger, with eagles, partridges, and pheasants.

The Great Plain.—The northern river-plains, lying at the foot of the Himalayas, comprise the rich alluvial plains watered by the Indus, the Ganges, the Lower Brahmaputra, and their tributaries. At no great distance from one another, four rivers take their rise in the Himalayas. The sources of two are on the north side—the Indus, which flows westward for 1,800 miles, and the Tsan-po or Brahmaputra, which flows eastward for nearly 1,500 miles. The other two, on the southern slope, are the Sutlej, which, after flowing W. and S.W. for 900 miles and collecting various other streams, joins the Indus; and the Ganges, which, during a journey S.E. and E. of about 1,550 miles, drains almost all the Bengal plain. The Brahmaputra, after flowing along the northern side as far as the eastern extremity of the Himalayas, turns sharply to the S., then to the W., and finally joins the Ganges, 75 miles from where their combined streams enter the Bay of Bengal. Thus the Himalayas supply India with the water gathered on both slopes. The Indus and Ganges, with their tributaries, are the source of an extensive system of irrigation by canals. The richest, most populous, and most historically famous part of India lies in the basins of these great rivers. Formerly the Ganges was the only great highway of Bengal; it is still the fertiliser and the water-carrier. But a close network of railways is increasingly used for transport. In Northern India there are two harvests, *rabi* (spring) crops being reaped in March and April, *kharif* (autumn) crops in October to December. In the north we find wheat, pulse, maize, millet, barley, and tea; while in the south, indigo, cotton, sugar-cane, jute, oilseeds, tobacco, opium, and spices are produced. Among the fauna are monkeys, panthers, tigers, leopards, hyenas, jackals, squirrels, elephants, deer, crocodiles, and snakes. Salt, mica, and coal are the chief minerals. The Ganges delta yields rice, bamboos, and a large variety of palms. The Aravalli range, the primeval chain of India, divides Rajputana from the Central India States. To the N.W. of the peninsula lies the mountainous, barren, and thinly populated region of Baluchistan.

The Deccan.—Just as the Himalayas on the N. and the Hindu Kush and Suleiman Mountains on the N.W. form natural barriers of defence for Hindustan, so do the Vindhya Mountains, running almost due E. from the head of the Gulf of Cambay, north of the Nerbudda River, form a firm southern boundary to the river-plains of Northern India. Southern India, or the Deccan, is a plateau of triangular shape and very old geological formation, bounded on two sides by the Malabar and Coromandel coasts, which converge at Cape Comorin, and on the third by the Vindhyas. The Eastern and Western Ghauts all but complete this environing triangle of mountain ranges. In the extreme N.W., south of the Vindhyas, and parallel to them, but north of the Western Ghauts, we find the Nerbudda and the Tapti flowing westwards, their basins being sharply defined by the Satpura Mountains, which lie midway between them. As the Western Ghauts lie close to the coast, and afford no exit for rivers, there are no streams on the Malabar coast south of the Tapti; all the rivers flow eastwards, through defiles in the Eastern Ghauts, into the Bay of Bengal. The four chief rivers are the Mahanuddy, in the extreme N.E. (520 m.), the Godavery (900 m.), the Kistna (800 m.), and the Cauvery (472 m.), at intervals further to the south. The physical geography of Southern India has shaped its history: the S.W. coast, shut in by mountains, is very primitive and moves slowly; the S.E., open and easy of access by sea and towards the interior, has made great progress. The mountain slopes of this region, especially those of the Western Ghauts, which rise to 8,000 feet in the Nilgiris, are still covered with the splendid vegetation of primeval forests. Teak, ebony, satinwood, sandalwood, palm, and bamboo abound. The jungles in the E. are very deadly. The tiger, bison, leopard, deer, and various small game afford sport. Snakes are found everywhere. In the valleys and on the higher plains many valuable crops are raised, chiefly rice, millet, cotton, oilseeds, coffee, tea, indigo, tobacco, and chinchona. The southern tableland has furnished considerable supplies of minerals. At present the minerals principally worked are coal, manganese ore, mica, monazite, and gold.

Climate.—About half of India is within the tropics, but the greatest extremes of heat and cold are in the N.W. In the Himalayas the climate is moist and cold. In Northern India it is dry, and the winters are rather cold. In tropical Southern India the climate is more equable. Calcutta, Bombay, and Madras all have an equable climate, owing to proximity to the sea. India depends for its fertility upon the monsoon rains. The S.W. monsoon brings moisture from the ocean south of the Equator, and reaches the west coast early in June and the northern provinces late in June. The mountains arrest these currents and precipitate rainfall, which averages 60 inches in the sub-Himalayan region, 39 inches in the Indo-Gangetic plain, and 30 inches in the Deccan, but is small in Sind and Rajputana. Madras benefits by the N.E. monsoon in the autumn.

Jammu and Kashmir.—The Kashmir territory, area 82,258 sq. miles, population 4,021,616 (census 1941), of whom some 880,000 are non-Moslems, may be divided physically into two areas, the north-eastern and south-western areas, The dividing line is formed by the great Himalayan chain which runs from the northern boundary of the Chamba State to where Nanga Parbat towers 26,600 feet above the Indus. The smaller, more populous south-western area may be divided geographically into three sections; the region of the outer hills, the middle mountains and the Kashmir Valley. The north-eastern section is comprised between the great central chain on the south and the Karakoram range and its continuation on the north. The chief characteristic of this region is the great altitude of the rivers and plains. The Indus near the Kashmir-Tibet boundary runs at a height of 13,800 feet above sea level. Hand made products of wool and silk are produced. Chief towns are Srinagar (Kashmir), Jammu and Leh (Ladakh).

Portuguese India.—On December 18–19, 1961, the Portuguese possessions of *Goa*, *Daman* (Damao) and the island of *Diu* were invaded and occupied by the Indian Army. The three territories were absorbed into the Indian Union, legislation enacted on March 14, 1961, providing for their administration by the Central Government.

Indian System of Notation.—The Indian numerical notation system differs from the European. Large numbers are punctuated as crores and lakhs and not in hundreds, thousands and millions. A *lakh* is one hundred thousand (written 1,00,000), and a *crore* is one hundred lakhs or ten millions (1,00,00,000) Thus, 1,68,00,000 is read as 1 crore 68 lakhs.

Currency.—The principal unit of currency in both India and Pakistan is the *rupee* (=1*s.* 6*d.*), formerly divided into *annas* (16), *pice* (64) or *pies* (192). India adopted the decimal system of coinage from April 1, 1957, using the *rupee* of 100 *Naye Paise*, and Pakistan from Jan. 1, 1961, using the rupee of 100 *pice* with coins for decimal parts of the *rupee*.

India

AREA AND POPULATION

State/Territory	Land Area (in sq. miles)	Population Census, 1961
States		
Andhra Pradesh	105,858	35,983,447
Assam	84,899*	11,872,722
Bihar	67,198	46,455,610
Gujarat	72,226	20,633,350
Kerala	15,005	16,903,715
Madhya Pradesh	171,210	32,372,408
Madras	50,132	33,686,953
Maharashtra	118,741	39,553,718
Mysore	74,[illegible]91	23,586,772
Orissa	60,136	17,548,846
Punjab	47,304	20,306,812
Rajasthan	132,150	20,155,602
Uttar Pradesh	113,654	73,746,401
West Bengal	33,829	34,926,279
Union Territories		
Andaman and Nicobar Islands	3,215	63,548
Delhi	573	2,658,612
Himachal Pradesh	10,879	1,351,144
Laccadive, Minicoy and Amindivi Islands	11	24,108
Manipur	8,628	780,037
Tripura	4,036	1,142,005
Total Indian Union:	1,173,971	434,677,056

* Including North East Frontier area and Naga Hills–Tuensing area.

FLAG.—The National Flag is a horizontal tricolour with bands of deep saffron, white and dark green in equal proportions. On the centre of the white band appears an Asoka wheel in navy blue.

VITAL STATISTICS.—The provisional birth rate in 1961 was 27·8 per 1,000, the death rate 12·2 per 1,000.

CAPITAL.—Delhi (2,344,051, including Delhi, New Delhi and Cantonment).

PRESIDENT

President of the Republic of India, Dr. Sarvepalli Radhakrishnan, O.M., *elected* May 11, 1962.

Vice-President, Dr. Zakir Husain.

MINISTERS

Cabinet.

Prime Minister and Minister of External Affairs and of Atomic Energy, Jawaharlal Nehru.

Minister of Home Affairs, Gulzarilal Nanda.

Minister of Finance, T. T. Krishnamachari.

Minister of Transport and Communications (vacant).

Minister of Food, Agriculture and Railways, Swaran Singh.

Minister of Planning, Labour and Employment (vacant).

Minister of Irrigation and Power, K. L. Rao.

Minister of Commerce and Industry (vacant).

Minister of Steel and Heavy Industries, C. Subramaniam.

Minister of Law, A. K. Sen.

Minister of Education (vacant).

Minister of Information and Broadcasting (vacant).

Minister of Mines and Fuel, O. V. Alagesan.

Minister of Scientific Research and Cultural Affairs, Humayun Kabir.

Minister of Parliamentary Affairs, Satya Narayan Sinha.

Minister of Defence, Y. B. Chavan.

Minister of Defence Production, K. Ragha Ramaiah.

Ministers of State

Minister of Community Development and Co-operation, S. K. Dey.

Minister of Works, Housing and Supply, Mehr Chand Khanna.

Minister of International Trade, Manubhai Shah.

Minister of Shipping, Raj Bahadur.

Minister of Health, Sushila Nayar.

Minister of State for Food and Agriculture, Ram Subhag Singh.

Minister of State for Home Affairs, B. N. Datar.

Minister of State for Industry, Nityanand Kanungo.

Minister of State for Labour, Jai Sukh Lal Hathi.

Minister of State for External Affairs, Lakshmi N. Menon.

R*s. per mensem*, each, R*s*. 2,250, *plus residence*.

OFFICE OF THE HIGH COMMISSIONER FOR THE UNITED KINGDOM IN INDIA

Chanakyapuri, New Delhi, 21.

High Commissioner, His Excellency Sir Paul Gore-Booth, K.C.M.G., K.C.V.O.

Deputy High Commissioner, R. H. Belcher, C.M.G.

Economic Adviser and British Senior Trade Commissioner in India, H. Bailey, C.M.G.; *Financial Adviser and British Treasury Representative in S. Asia*, A. Mackay; *Naval Adviser*, Capt. C. J. Cunningham, D.S.O., R.N.; *Military Adviser*, Brig. I. M. Christie; *Air Adviser*, Air Cdre. W. J. Burnett, D.S.O., D.F.C., A.F.C.; *Director of British Information Services*, M. Scott, M.V.O.

Deputy High Commissioners, E. G. Norris, C.M.G. (*Calcutta*); P. Gautrey, C.V.O. (*Bombay*); W. J. M. Paterson, C.M.G. (*Madras*).

BRITISH COUNCIL

Representative in India, H. P. Croom-Johnson, C.B.E., 21 Jor Bagh, New Delhi.

REPUBLIC OF INDIA
REPRESENTATIVES ABROAD

High Commissioners

Australia and New Zealand, B. K. Massand.
Canada, C. S. Jha.
Ceylon, B. K. Kapur.
Cyprus, I. S. Chopra.
Ghana and Sierra Leone, J. C. Kakar.
Federation of Malaya, Y. K. Puri.
Nigeria, P. N. Haksar.
Pakistan, G. Parthasarathi.
Tanganyika, R. D. Sathe.
United Kingdom (vacant), India House, Aldwych, W.C.2.

Ambassadors

AFGHANISTAN—J. N. Dhamija.
ARGENTINA AND PARAGUAY—Tara Singh Bal.
AUSTRIA—A. S. Lall.
BELGIUM AND LUXEMBURG—K. B. Lall.
BOLIVIA, CHILE AND COLOMBIA—P. Ratnam.
BRAZIL—V. H. Coelho.
BURMA—R. S. Mani.
CAMBODIA—R. R. Sinha.
DENMARK—K. K. Menon.
ETHIOPIA—J. K. Atal.
FRANCE—Ali Yavar Jung.
WEST GERMANY—P. A. Menon.
GREECE, BULGARIA AND YUGOSLAVIA—J. N. Khosla.
INDONESIA—A. B. Pant.
IRAQ—Sadat Ali Khan.
ITALY—S. N. Haksar.
JAPAN—Lalji Mehrotra.
JORDAN AND LEBANON—I. S. Chopra.
LAOS—M. S. Sair.
MALAGASY REPUBLC—S. G. Ramachandran.
MEXICO AND PANAMA—P. L. Bhandari.
MOROCCO AND TUNISIA—B. K. Acharya.
NEPAL—R. Dayal.
NETHERLANDS—R. K. Tandon.
NORWAY—V. M. M. Nair.
PERSIA—M. R. A. Baig.
POLAND—L. R. S. Singh.
ROUMANIA AND CZECHOSLOVAKIA—M. P. Mathur.
SAUDI ARABIA—M. N. Masud.
SENEGAL AND UPPER VOLTA—N. V. Rajkumar.
SUDAN—S. S. Ansari.
SWEDEN AND FINLAND—Khub Chand.
SWITZERLAND—M. A. Rauf.
THAILAND—N. S. Gill.
TURKEY—V. L. Mehta.
UNITED ARAB REPUBLIC AND LIBYA—M. A. Hussain.
U.S.A.—B. K. Nehru.
U.S.S.R.—T. N. Kaul.

CONSTITUTION

The Constitution of India came into force on January 26, 1950. The Constitution provides for a single and uniform citizenship for the whole of India, with the right of vote for every adult citizen.

EXECUTIVE

The executive of the Indian Union consists of the President (Rashtrapati), the Vice-President and the Council of Ministers. The President is elected for five years by an electoral college consisting of all elected members of Parliament and of the various State Legislative Assemblies. The Vice-President is also elected for five years by members of the two Houses of Parliament. As head of the State the President exercises his functions with the aid and advice of the Council of Ministers headed by the Prime Minister. The Council is collectively responsible to the House of the People.

LEGISLATURE

The Legislature of the Union is called Parliament. It consists of two Houses known as the Council of States (Rajya Sabha) and the House of the People (Lok Sabha). The Council of States consists of not more than 250 members, of whom 12 are nominated by the President and the rest are indirectly elected by the Legislative Assemblies of the various States. The Council is not subject to dissolution, one-third of its members retiring every two years. The House of the People consists of not more than 500 members directly elected from territorial constituencies in the States and on the basis of adult franchise and not more than 20 members to represent the Union Territories, chosen in such manner as Parliament provides. The House has a maximum duration of five years.

Subject to the provisions of the Constitution the Union Parliament can make laws for the whole of India and the State legislatures for their respective units. The distribution of legislative powers is governed by a system of three lists—the Union, the State and the Concurrent—under which all legislative activity has been mapped out. The Union Parliament has exclusive powers to legislate on 97 subjects of all-India importance, such as defence, foreign affairs, communications, railways, currency and banking, insurance, customs duties, etc. The State List contains 66 headings, e.g. public order and police, justice, education, public health, local government, agriculture, etc. The Concurrent List contains 47 subjects of common interest to the Union and the States.

OFFICIAL LANGUAGE

The Constitution (Art. 343) provides that the official language of the Union shall be Hindi in the Devanagari script and the form of numerals for official purposes shall be the international form of Indian numerals. English will, however, continue to be the official language for a period of 15 years from the commencement of the Constitution (January 1950).

THE JUDICATURE

The Supreme Court of India, consisting of a Chief Justice and 13 associate judges, is the highest court in respect of constitutional matters. It is also the final Court of Appeal in the country.

Chief Justice, B. P. Sinha. Rs. 60,000.

Judges, J. Imam; S. K. Das; P. B. Gajendragadkar; A. K. Sarkar; K. Subba Rao; K. N. Wanchoo; M. Hidayatullah; K. C. Das Gupta; J. C. Shah; Raghubar Dayal; N. Rajagopala Ayyangar; J. R. Mudholkar. Rs. 48,000.

TRADE

DISTRIBUTION OF TRADE, 1961

	Imports Rs. lakhs	*Exports* Rs. lakhs
U.K.	20,026	16,291
U.S.A.	24,000	11,443
U.S.S.R.	2,542	3,100
Western Germany	12,253	2,128
Italy	2,401	963
Netherlands	1,173	912
France	1.636	820
Japan	6,070	4,027
Australia	1,760	1,657
Canada	1,746	1,738
Pakistan	1,154	985
Kenya	1,014	553
Czechoslovakia	1,428	915
Egypt	1,030	1,213

Imports from All Countries 1961	Rs. lakhs
Machinery other than electric	23,098
Cotton, raw	6,932
Iron and steel	10,216
Chemical elements and compounds	3,577
Petroleum products	4,789
Textile yarn and thread	1,338
Transport equipment	5,738
Electrical machinery and appliances	6,345
Wheat, unmilled	7,306
Copper	2,053
Manufactures of metals	1,761
Petroleum, crude and partly refined	3,577

Exports to All Countries 1961	Rs. lakhs
Tea	12,445
Cotton fabrics	5 054
Textile fabrics other than cotton	8,398
Textile articles (other than clothing and footwear)	6,977
Cotton, raw	1,869
Leather	2,599
Fresh fruits and nuts	2 112
Iron ore and concentrates	1,806
Non-ferrous base metal ores and concentrates	1,341
Crude vegetable materials (inedible)	1,595

PRODUCTION

About 70 per cent. of the inhabitants of India are dependent on agricultural pursuits. Most of the agricultural holdings are less than 5 acres. Food crops occupy four-fifths of the cultivated land. There are about 159,000,000 cattle, or about a quarter of the world's cattle population.

Area and Production of Principal Crops, 1960-61

Crop	Area (lakh acres)	Production (lakh tons)
Rice	833·3	337·0
Jowar	421·1	90·8
Bajra	280·6	31·3
Maize	107·6	39·1
Wheat	317·5	106·5
Barley	79·2	27·3
Ragi	57·6	16·4
Small millets	122·4	19·5
Pulses	576·7	124·7
Total foodgrains	2,796·0	792·7
Groundnut	154·5	43·5
Castorseed	11·3	1·0
Sesamum	48·6	2·9
Rape and mustard	72·6	13·8
Linseed	42·3	4·1
Cotton	189·7	53·9*
Jute	15·3	40·3*
Sugarcane	57·3	850 4
Tobacco	9·7	2·9
Tea (1959)	7·9	6,990†
Coffee (1959)	2·7	930†
Rubber (1960)	3·0	520†

* lakh bales † lakh lbs.

Industrial

The output of coal in 1961 was 55,800,000 tons. Production of finished steel in 1961 was 2,840,000 tons. Cement 8,200,000 tons (metric) in 1961 against 7,835,000 tons in 1960. Paper production 364,000 tons, cotton cloth 5,127 mill. yards in 1961 and yarn 1,887 mill. lbs. as compared with 5,048 mill. yards and 1,737 mill. lbs. in 1960.

In 1961 21,042 metric tons of aluminium were produced. The yield of gold in 1960 was 4,995 kgs. Manganese ores have taken an important place among the minerals produced in India.

BANKS AND BANKING

The number of scheduled banks was 84 and the number of offices of scheduled banks was 4,329 in Oct., 1961. Advances by scheduled banks totalled Rs. 12,014 mill. at April 27, 1962.

COMMUNICATIONS

Civil Aviation.—India occupies an important place in civil aviation among the nations of the world. All air lines were nationalized in 1953 and two corporations formed, Indian Airlines Corporation and Air India International (now Air India). During 1961, Indian aircraft flew about 33,100,000 miles, carrying about 1,060,000 passengers and nearly 182,200,000 lbs. of cargo and mail on scheduled and non-scheduled services together. At the end of 1961, 86 aerodromes were maintained by the Civil Aviation Department of the Government.

Railways.—The railways are grouped into eight administrative zones, Southern, Central, Western, Northern, North-Eastern, North-East Frontier, Eastern and South-Eastern.

In 1960–61, passengers "originating" were 1,615,894,000, passenger mileage 48 580 975,000, goods traffic freight-ton miles 53 714 893,000.

Gross Traffic Receipts (1960-61) Rs. 4,568 million. Working expenses, Rs. 3,639 million. Net railway revenues, Rs. 879 million.

Roads.—At the end of March, 1961, it was estimated that there were 144,000 miles of surfaced roads and over 250,000 miles of unsurfaced roads. The national highway system covers about 14,880 miles.

Ports.—The chief seaports are ΨBombay, Calcutta, Madras, Cochin, Visakhapatanam and Kandla (Kutch). There are over 150 minor working ports with varying capacity.

Shipping.—At the end of November, 1961, 175 ships totalling 905,000 gross tons were on the Indian Register.

Postal.—In 1960-61 there were 76,862 post offices, 11,229 telegraph offices, and 481,000 telephones.

DEFENCE

The supreme command of the armed forces is vested in the President. Administrative and operational control resides in the Army, Navy and Air Headquarters under the supervision of the Ministry of Defence.

The Army has 3 Commands, Southern, Eastern and Western, with headquarters at Poona, Lucknow and Simla respectively. A Territorial Force was inaugurated in Oct. 1949. A National Cadet Corps, with senior, junior, and girls' divisions, has also been raised.

The *Indian Navy* consists of an aircraft-carrier, two cruisers and a number of destroyers, frigates, minesweepers and auxiliary vessels. A Naval aviation wing and a hydrographic office have also been set up. The Navy's air station is at Cochin.

The *Indian Air Force* is organised in four formations, the Operational Command at Palam, the Training Command at Bangalore, the Maintenance Command at Kanpur and the Eastern Air Command. It also has seven Auxiliary Squadrons.

EDUCATION

In 1959-60, there were 1.351 pre-primary schools, 320 586 primary schools, 57 863 secondary schools, 3,836 vocational and technical schools, 56 434 special education schools, 946 arts and science colleges, 728 professional colleges, 177 special education colleges, 42 research institutions and 40 universities. 62·1 per cent. of children between the ages of 6 and 11 were estimated to have been at school in 1960–61, 22·8 per cent. between 11 and 14 and 11·5 per cent. between 14 and 17.

REVENUE AND EXPENDITURE OF THE GOVERNMENT OF INDIA
(On Revenue Account)

	(In Lakhs of Rupees)			
	1960–61 Accounts	1961–62 Budget	1961–62 Revised	1962–63 Budget
Revenue				
Customs	170,03	189,64	199,60	199,60 +7,80*
Union Excise Duties	416,35	432,63	470,95	492,28 +30,80*
Corporation Tax	111,05	141,00	160,00	168,00 +10,50*
Taxes on Income	167,38	133,00	142,00	148,00 +15,40*
Estate Duty	3,09	3,00	4,00	4,00
Taxes on Wealth	8,15	7,00	7,50	7,00 +2,00*
Taxes on Railway Fares	15,89	—	—	
Expenditure Tax	91	80	80	80 −70*
Gift Tax	88	80	85	85
Other Heads	15.57	14,32	15,46	15,83
Debt Services	14,81	13,84	11,58	167,51
Administrative Services	66	97	1,11	6,11
Social and Development Services	53.11	44.70	45.55	35.29
Multi-purpose River Schemes, etc.	3	−1	−1	36
Public Works, etc.	3.27	3.76	3.74	4,02
Transport and Communications	2,17	2,46	2,38	6,30
Currency and Mint	58,10	60,63	53,15	69 53
Miscellaneous	25.35	20,99	22,92	24,56
Contributions and Miscellaneous Adjustments	5,22	22,12	21,68	24,41
Extraordinary Items	3.72	10,00	13,00	40,00
Deduct—Share of Income Tax payable to States	−87,37	−80,79	−93,27	−89,70 −5,00*
Deduct—Share of Estate Duty payable to States	−2,91	−2,91	−3,88	−3,88
Deduct—Share of Taxes on Railway Fares payable to States	−13.79	—	—	—
Total Revenue	971,67	1,017,95	1,079,11	1,320,87 +60,80*
Deficit on Revenue Account	—	5.57	—	—
Expenditure				
Collection of Taxes and Duties	97.53	21,24	21,15	22,58
Debt Services	77,09	81,90	86,10	247.90
Administrative Services	58,66	58,37	60,00	70,31
Social and Development Services	209,79	167,78	155.72	163,24
Multi-purpose River Schemes, etc.	1,11	1,26	1,23	1,57
Public Works, etc.	20,46	20,62	21,92	21,88
Transport and Communications	5,06	5,68	6,22	8,75
Currency and Mint	10,15	11,96	11,62	20,23
Miscellaneous	140,38	73.76	81,77	109,45
Contributions and Miscellaneous Adjustments	48,55	287,26	283,70	330,97
Extraordinary Items	4,09	10,87	13,79	41,40
Defence Services (Net)	247.55	282,92	301,93	343.37
Total Expenditure	920,42	1,023,52	1,045,15	1,381,65
Surplus on Revenue Account	51,25	—	33,96	2*

* Effect of Budget proposals.

STATES AND ADMINISTRATIONS OF THE REPUBLIC OF INDIA

MADRAS

Madras (area, 50,132 sq. miles; population 33,686,953) was not only the oldest, but the most important of the three original Presidencies before Clive's conquest of Bengal, though it was small in extent until the annexation of the Carnatic in 1801. The state has no good natural harbour, but an artificial harbour has been constructed at Madras at great expense. The state is not naturally fertile, though irrigation systems in the river deltas have enormously increased the produce of the soil, and have yielded a large profit to the State. Rice, millet, and other food grains, oilseeds, cotton, indigo, spices, tobacco, tea, etc., are cultivated. Madras is served by the Southern Railway. About 91 per cent. of the people are Hindus. The language principally spoken is Tamil, though Telugu, Malayalam and Kannada are also spoken. Madurai (424 975) and Tiruchinopoly (249,933), famous for their Hindu temples, are the chief cities after the capital.

CHIEF CITY, ΨMadras. Population, 1,725,216. *Governor*, Bisnuram Medhi.

CABINET.

M. Bhaktavatsalam; C. Subramaniam; M. A. Manickavelu; R. Venkataraman; P. Kakkan; V. Ramaiah; S. L. Simon.

LEGISLATIVE ASSEMBLY.

Speaker (vacant).

HIGH COURT OF JUDICATURE.

Chief Justice, P. V. Rajamannar.

MAHARASHTRA

The State of Maharashtra was formed on May 1, 1960 as a result of the bifurcation of the former Bombay State.

It stretches on the west coast of India between 22·1° and 16·4° north latitude and 72·6° and 80·9° east longitude. The State is bounded by the Arabian Sea on the west, Gujarat in the north-west, Madhya Pradesh in the north, Andhra Pradesh in the south-east and Mysore and Goa in the south. The region is drained by a number of rivers, large and small, most of them forming tributaries of the Tapi, Godavari, Bhima, Krishna, Wardha and Waiganga. The relief of the land shows high plateaux with plains on the western coast and along the river basins.

Maharashtra State contains 118,741 square miles with a population of 39,504,294 (provisional figures of the 1961 census). It is a predominantly urban and industrial State. According to the 1961 Census, 28·2 per cent. of the population is urban. Marathi is the principal language. 63·98 per cent. of the population are dependent on agriculture. The railway systems running through Maharashtra State are the Western Railway running from Bombay to the north, the Central Railway to the north-east and south-east and the Southern Railway running from Poona to the south and the South-East Railway. According to provisional estimates of the 1961 population census the following 12 cities in the State have a population of more than 100,000. Greater Bombay (4,152,056), Poona (597,562), Nagpur (643,659), Sholapur (337,583), Kolhapur (187,442), Amravati (137,875), Nasik (131,103), Malegaon (121,408), Nagar (119,020), Akola (115,760), Ulhasnagar (107,760) and Thana (101,107).

CABINET MINISTERS.

M. S. Kannamwar (*Chief Minister*); S. H. Shah; V. P. Naik; G. B. Khedkar; S. K. Wankhede; D. S. Desai; P. K. Savant; S. B. Chavan; S. G. Barve; H. J. H. Taleyarkhan; D. S. Palaspagar; Salebhoy Abdul Kadar; N. R. Bhosale; M. D. Choudhari; M. G. Mane; K. S. Sonawane.

LEGISLATIVE COUNCIL.

Chairman, V. S. Page.

LEGISLATIVE ASSEMBLY.

Speaker, T. S. Bharde.

GUJARAT

On May 1, 1960, the new state of Gujarat, consisting of the northern part of Bombay State, was set up with a temporary capital at Ahmedabad, the remainder of the former Bombay state adopting the name of Maharashtra (*see above*). Gujarat, consisting of the districts of Kutch, Banaskantha, Mehsana, Sabarkantha, Ahmedabad, Kaira, Panchmahal, Baroda, Broach, Surat, Rajkot, Surendranagar, Junagadh, Jamnagar, Bhavnagar, Amreli and Dangs has a total area of 72,226 square miles and a population of 20,633,350 (1961 census).

Governor of Gujarat, Nawab Mehdi Nawaz Jung, *Chief Minister*, Dr. Jivraj Mehta.

WEST BENGAL

West Bengal has an area of 33,829 sq. miles and a population (1961 census) of 34,926,279. The old Bengal Presidency included practically all Northern and Central India, but subsequently Bengal Province consisted of part of Bengal proper with Bihar, Orissa and Chota Nagpur. This Province of Bengal ceased to exist in 1947 when it was divided, West Bengal forming part of India and East Bengal part of Pakistan. The state of Cooch Behar was merged with West Bengal on Jan. 1, 1950, and the French settlement of Chandernagore, which came under Indian administration on May 2, 1950, was merged with West Bengal on Oct. 2, 1954. On Nov. 1, 1956, certain territories of Bihar were transferred to West Bengal.

The chief products are rice, oilseeds, sugar cane, tobacco, jute, silk, tea, coal, mesta and potatoes. West Bengal is now served by three State Railways, the Eastern Railway, the South-Eastern Railway and the North-Eastern Railway. The Eastern Railway is the great artery of the Ganges Valley.

Howrah (pop. District. 2,038,477; Town, 512,598), the great jute manufacturing centre, adjoins Calcutta.

CHIEF CITY ΨCalcutta. Population (including Howrah) 3,439 887; Calcutta proper 2,927,289. *Governor*, Shrimati Padmaja Naidu.

CABINET.

P. C. Sen (*Chief Minister*); K. N. Das Gupta; A. K. Mukherjee; I. D. Jalan; H. N. Choudhuri; T. K. Ghosh; S. D. Banerjee; P. Mukhopadhyay; S. Bhattacharyya; J. Kolay; S. Mukherjee; A. Maiti; S. M. F. Rahaman; B. S. Nahar.

THE LEGISLATURE.

The Legislature is bicameral, consisting of a Legislative Assembly of 252 elected members from 252 constituencies, and 4 members from the Anglo-Indian community nominated by the Governor, and a Legislative Council of 75 members, including 9 nominated by the Governor.

CALCUTTA

HIGH COURT OF JUDICATURE.

Chief Justice, H. K. Bose.

UTTAR PRADESH

Uttar Pradesh, called the United Provinces until 1949 (formerly the United Provinces of Agra and Oudh) (area, 113,654 sq. miles; etc. pop. (1961) 73,746,401), forms the upper part of the great Ganga plain to the W. of Bengal, lying between the Himalayas and the hilly border of the central plateau. The Province is now a State in which the former three princely States, Rampur, Tehri-Garhwal and Benares have been merged and certain areas of the Vindhya Pradesh and Rajasthan

States have also been absorbed. Agriculture employs 72 per cent. of the population, the chief products being wheat, rice, barley, pulse, tobacco, millet, cotton, sugar, and oilseeds. About 84·7 per cent. of the population are Hindus and 14·6 per cent. Muslims. Hindi is the chief language. The State is served by the Northern Railway and the North-Eastern Railway. Among the important cities may be named the ancient city of Agra (462,020), containing the Taj Mahal and other great works of architecture, the sacred Hindu city of Varanasi (Benares) (471,258), the great manufacturing centre, Kanpur (Cawnpore) (881,177), Lucknow (595,440) the capital, Bareilly (254,409), and Allahabad (411,955).

Governor, Dr. Burugala Ramakrishna Rao
Rs. *per mensem*, 5,500

COUNCIL OF MINISTERS.

H. S. Visen; Charan Singh; A. J. Kishore; S. Kripalani; Hargovind Singh; G. Lal; Syed Ali Zaheer; K. Tripathi; V. N. Sharma; Muzaffar Hasan; R. Murti; A. R. Shastri; C. Sharma; J. S. Negi; Phool Singh; M. P. Srivastava.

LEGISLATIVE COUNCIL.

Chairman, R. V. Dhulekar.

LEGISLATIVE ASSEMBLY.

Speaker, M. M. Verma.

HIGH COURT OF JUDICATURE.

Chief Justice, M. C. Desai.

PUNJAB

The Punjab, the eastern part of the old Punjab Province and Patiala and East Punjab States Union, has an area of 47,304 sq. miles and a population (1961 census) of 20,306,812.

CHIEF CITY, Chandigarh.

Governor, Pattom A. Thanu Pillai......Rs. 66,000

BIHAR

This state has an area of 67,197 sq. miles and a population (1961 census) of 46,455,610. It comprises 4 administrative divisions, Patna, Bhagalpur, Tirhut and Chota-Nagpur. The state is liable to extreme temperatures. The population is exceedingly dense, being 691 to the square mile in 1961. The highlands of Chota-Nagpur are thinly peopled and contain a large aboriginal population. Rice, wheat, barley, jute, oilseeds, sugar cane and tobacco are cultivated. 84·7 per cent. of the people are Hindus. The majority of the population speak Hindi, of which there are various dialects. The railway systems are the Eastern, North-Eastern, South-Eastern and North-East Frontier Railways.

CHIEF CITY, Patna. Population 364,594 (1961).

Governor, M. A. Ayyangar (May 1962)
Rs. *per mensen* 5,500

CABINET.

D. N. Sinha; B. Paswan; B. Patel; S. N. Sinha; B. N. Verma; M. P. Sinha; H. N. Misra; A. Q. Ansari; K. B. Sahay; S. C. Tubid.

LEGISLATIVE COUNCIL.

Chairman, Ravaneshwar Mishra.

LEGISLATIVE ASSEMBLY.

Speaker, Dr. Lakshmi Narain Sudhanshu.

HIGH COURT OF JUDICATURE.

Chief Justice, V. Ramaswami.

MADHYA PRADESH

The State of Madhya Pradesh was formed on November 1, 1956. Madhya Pradesh has an area of 171,210 sq. miles and a population of 32,372,408. It is composed of the former Madhya Bharat, Vindhya Pradesh and Bhopal States together with the 17 Hindi districts of former Madhya Pradesh, and the Sironj sub-division of Kotah district of Rajasthan excluding the Sunel enclave of Mandsaur district in former Madhya Bharat.

The chief crops are wheat, paddy, cotton, sugar cane, oilseeds, pulses, juwar and bajra. Nearly 31 per cent. of the State's area is covered by forests. Hindi is the chief language.

The State has extensive belts of mineral deposits, possessing coal, iron ore, manganese, bauxite, diamond and limestone. A small quantity of diamonds is found near Panna. The State is rich in forest and agricultural resources.

There are 19 textile mills, 3 cement factories, 5 sugar mills, a newsprint mill, steel plant, and several other large and small industries.

STATE CAPITAL, Bhopal.

Governor, H. V. Pataskar.

CABINET.

Takhtmal; S. N. Shukla; Dr. S. D. Sharma; Mishrilal Gangwal; V. V. Dravid; Raja Naresh Chandra Singh; Narsinghrao Dixit; Kesholal Gumashta; Jagmohan Das; M. P. Dube.

LEGISLATIVE ASSEMBLY.

Speaker, Kunjilal Dube.

HIGH COURT OF JUDICATURE.

Chief Justice, P. V. Dixit.

ASSAM

Assam, which has an area of 47,098 sq. miles (exclusive of the North-East Frontier and Naga Hills—Tuensing areas); pop. 11,872,722 (1961 census) first became a British territory in 1826 and was constituted a separate administration in 1874. It was combined in 1905 with part of Bengal to form a new province, Eastern Bengal and Assam, but again became a separate administration in 1912. By the terms of the Indian Independence Act, 1947, the district of Sylhet was detached from Assam and amalgamated with East Bengal (Pakistan). A range of mountains divides Assam into the Surma and Brahmaputra valleys, of which the chief towns are Silchar and Gauhati respectively. The people are mainly Hindus, Muslims and Tribals. The North-East Frontier railway serves the state. Tea, petroleum, coal, timber, jute and rice are the principal products.

CHIEF CITY, Shillong.

Governor, Vishnu Sahay.....Rs. *per mensem* 5,500

CABINET.

B. P. Chaliha (*Chief Minister*); F. A. Ahmed; R. Brahma; K. P. Tripathy; M. N. Hazarika; M. H. Choudhury; S. N. Sorma; B. Mukherjee; C. Teron; D. K. Barorah.

LEGISLATIVE ASSEMBLY.

Speaker, M. M. Choudhury.

HIGH COURT.

Chief Justice, Gopalji Mehrotra.

Judge, S. K. Dutta.

ORISSA

Area, 60,136 sq. miles; pop. (1961) 17,548,846, constituted on April 1, 1936, comprises the Orissa Division, transferred from the Province of Bihar and Orissa and areas transferred from the Central Provinces and Madras. 24 States were merged with Orissa in 1948 and 1949. A large majority of the population is Hindu. It is an agricultural State with few towns. The Hirakud dam across the Mahanadi river is now irrigating 3·80 lakh acres of land and generating about 100 Mw. of power. Paradeep is being developed as a port.

CAPITAL, Bhubaneswar.

Governor, Dr. Ajudhia Nath Khosla.
Rs. *per mensem* 5,500

COUNCIL OF MINISTERS.

Biren Mitra; Sadasiva Tripathy; P. M. Pradhan; Nilamani Routray; P. V. Jaganath Rao; Harihar Singh Mardaraj.

LEGISLATIVE ASSEMBLY.

Speaker, Lingaraj Panigrahi.

HIGH COURT OF JUSTICE.

Chief Justice, R. L. Narasimham.

HIMACHAL PRADESH

Himachal Pradesh was set up as a Union Territory in 1956. Its area is 10,879 sq. miles and population (1961 census) 1,351,144. The territory is divided into six administrative districts, Mahasu, Sirmoor, Mandi, Chamba, Bilaspur and Kinnaur.

CAPITAL, Simla.

Lieut.-Governor, Bajrang Bahadur Singh.

DELHI

The Union Territory of Delhi (area 573 sq. miles; pop. (census 1961) 2,658,612), has been administered directly since November 1, 1956 by the Government of India (Ministry of Home Affairs). An Advisory Council has also been set up.

Chief Commissioner.—Bhagwan Sahay.

ANDAMAN AND NICOBAR ISLANDS

The Andamans are a group of 204 islands of various sizes, lying between the 6th and 14th parallels in the Bay of Bengal. The northern-most "Landfall Island" is 560 miles from the mouth of Hooghly River. The main part of the group is composed of five large islands, *viz*., North Andaman, Middle Andaman, South Andaman, Baratang and Rutland Islands, generally known as the Great Andamans. To the south of Great Andamans is the island of Little Andaman. The extreme length of the Great Andaman Islands is 290 miles and the extreme breadth 32 miles, the total land area being approximately 2,580 sq. miles. These islands consist mostly of a mass of hills covered with dense tropical forests and separated by three straits and several creeks; there are several very good harbours—Port Blair, Port Cornwallis, Mayabunder and Port Elphinstone.

The Nicobar Islands, numbering 19 from Car Nicobar in the North to Great Nicobar in the South, lie between Little Andaman and Sumatra. The southern island of Great Nicobar is about 100 miles from Pulo Brassee off Achin Head in Sumatra and the northern island of Car Nicobar 75 miles from Little Andaman. The extreme length of the sea space occupied by the Nicobars is 163 miles and the extreme width 36 miles. The most important harbour in the area is Nancowrie.

The total area of the Territory is 3,215 sq. miles, with a population of 63,548. Some 77 per cent. of the total area is covered by forests, from which 23,349 tons of timber were exported in 1961–62. Plywood is produced in the islands. Other important products are coconuts and rice, about 16,721 acres being under paddy cultivation in 1962–63. Budget estimates for 1963–64 were: Revenue, Rs. 18,105,200; Expenditure, Rs. 64,426,900.

The Andaman Islands are administered by the President acting through a Chief Commissioner.

CHIEF CITY, Port Blair. Population, 14,075.

Chief Commissioner, B. N. Maheshwari.

ANDHRA PRADESH

The State of Andhra, consisting of the Telugu-speaking areas of the old Madras State, with Kurnool as capital, was inaugurated on Oct. 1, 1953. The Telangana area of Hyderabad State was added in 1956, when the enlarged State, comprising 20 districts, assumed the name of Andhra Pradesh.

Andhra Pradesh has an area of 105,858 sq. miles with a population of 35,983,447.

The Legislature consists of two chambers, the Legislative Assembly and the Legislative Council.

CHIEF CITY, Hyderabad. Population 2,062,995.

Governor, Gen. S. M. Shrinagesh.

Chief Minister, S. Reddy.

KERALA

The State of Kerala, constituted in 1956, consists of most of the territories of Travancore-Cochin and the Malabar district of Madras. Bounded by Madras and Mysore, the State brings together the majority of the Malayalam speaking peoples. The North-Eastern part of Kerala is rich in plantations producing rubber, tea and pepper. Area, 15,005 sq. miles. Population, 16,903,715.

CAPITAL, Trivandrum.

Governor, V. V. Giri.

Chief Minister, R. Sankar.

MYSORE

The Mysore State, formed in 1956, consists of territories of the former State of Mysore, part of Coorg and parts of the former Madras, Bombay and Hyderabad States. The State brings together the Kannada speaking people, previously distributed in five States. Its area is 74,191 sq. miles and population (1961 census) 23,586,772. The State consists largely of an elevated table land. It is rich in hydro-electric power and fairly rich in minerals; it is the major gold producing State of the Indian Union.

CAPITAL, Bangalore.

Governor, Jaya Chamaraja Wadiyar.

RAJASTHAN

The State of Rajasthan was formed between March 1948 and Jan. 1950 through the integration of 22 former princely States, including Alwar, Jaipur, Jodhpur, Mewar, Bikaner, Jaisalmer, Dholpur and Bharatpur. The former state of Ajmer and parts of the fomer States of Bombay and Madhya Bharat were added in 1956. The State has an area of 132,150 sq. miles and a population of 20,155,602.

CAPITAL, Jaipur.

Governor, Sampuranand.

Pakistan

The Republic of Pakistan consists of two geographical units of West Pakistan and East Pakistan situated respectively to the north-west and north-east of the Republic of India and separated by about 1,100 miles of Indian territory.

GOVERNMENT

Pakistan was constituted as a Dominion under the Indian Independence Act, 1947, which received the Royal Assent on July 18, 1947.

In terms of the Act the Dominion of Pakistan consisted of former territories of British India. The Punjab States of Bahawalpur and Khairpur, with a Muslim population of almost 80 per cent. and with Muslim rulers, acceded to Pakistan in October, 1947. Boundaries of the Provinces of East Bengal and of Punjab (West Punjab) were defined by a Boundary Commission presided over by Sir Cyril Radcliffe, K.B.E., Q.C. (now Viscount Radcliffe). The following States have also acceded to Pakistan: the Baluchistan State of Kalat, Mekran, Las Bela and Kharan, and the North-West Frontier States of Amb, Chitral, Dir and Swat. The States of Junagadh and Manavadar which had acceded to Pakistan, were occupied by India on November 8, 1947.

The Constitution of Pakistan was passed on February 29, 1956. Pakistan became a Republic on March 23, 1956, when the provisions of the Constitution came into force. On October 7, 1958, however, this Constitution was abrogated and Pakistan came under martial law. General (now Field Marshal) Mohammed Ayub Khan, Commander-in-Chief of the Pakistan Army, was appointed the Chief Martial Law Administrator. On October 28, 1958, General Mohammed Ayub Khan also became President of Pakistan. On March 1, 1962, the President announced a new Constitution, setting up a system of Government in which all executive authority vests in the President. Elections for the National Assembly took place in April, and the new Assembly met at Rawalpindi on June 8, 1962.

AREA AND POPULATION

Province	Area (English sq. miles)	Population	
		Total	Per sq. mile
West Pakistan	310,403	42,880 378	138
East Pakistan	55,126	50,840,235	922
Total†	365,529	93 720,613	257

† Excluding Jammu and Kashmir, Gilgit and Baltistan, Junagadh and Manavadar.

FLAG.—The National Flag of Pakistan is dark green, with white vertical part at the mast, the green portion bearing a white crescent in the centre and a five-pointed heraldic star.

COUNCIL OF MINISTERS

President and Minister for Defence, Field Marshal Mohammed Ayub Khan.
Law and Parliamentary Affairs, Khursheed Ahmad.
Communications, Abdus Sabur Khan.
External Affairs and Natural Resources, Z. A. Bhutto.
Commerce, Wahid-uz-Zaman.
Finance, Mohammad Shoaib.
Health, Works and Rehabilitation, Rana Abdul Hamid.
Education, Food and Agriculture, Labour and Social Welfare, Fazalul Qader Chaudhry.
Home and Kashmir Affairs, Habibullah Khan.

U.K. HIGH COMMISSIONER

Chamber of Commerce Building, Wood Street, Karachi.

High Commissioner, His Excellency, Sir (John) Morrice (Cairns) James, K.C.M.G., C.V.O., M.B.E.
Deputy High Commissioner, R. C. C. Hunt.
Deputy High Commissioner (Lahore), R. G. Britten.
Deputy High Commissioner (Dacca), A. R. Adair, C.V.O., M.B.E.
Deputy High Commissioner (Peshawar), K. R. Crook.
British Council Representative, J. B. S. Jardine, C.B.E.

PAKISTAN HIGH COMMISSIONER IN LONDON

35 Lowndes Square, S.W.1.

High Commissioner, Agha Hillaly.

PAKISTAN HIGH COMMISSIONERS, AMBASSADORS AND MINISTERS ABROAD

AUSTRALIA AND NEW ZEALAND (*High Commissioner*)—K. M. Kaiser.
BELGIUM AND LUXEMBURG—Abdur Rahman Khan.
BURMA AND CAMBODIA—P. M. Chaudhuri.
CANADA (*High Commissioner*)—S. M. Khan.
CEYLON (*High Commissioner*)—Zafrul Islam (*acting*).
CHINA—Maj.-Gen. N. A. M. Raza.
FRANCE AND MOROCCO—J. A. Rahim.
GERMANY—M. Ayub.
GHANA (*High Commissioner*)—A. H. B. Tayabji (*acting*).
INDIA (*High Commissioner*)—(vacant).
INDONESIA—Sultanuddin Ahmad.
IRAQ—Sajjad Hyder.
ITALY AND TUNISIA—Begum Ra'ana Liaquat Ali Khan.
JAPAN—Lt.-Gen. K. M. Shaikh.
LEBANON AND JORDAN—Hamid Nawaz Khan.
FEDERATION OF MALAYA (*High Commissioner*)—Maj.-Gen. Nawabzada Sher Ali Khan.
NETHERLANDS(*Chargé d'Affaires*)—Jamiluddin Hasan.
PERSIA—Akhtar Husain.
PHILIPPINES—Dr. A. M. Malik.
SAUDI ARABIA AND SOMALIA—Abdul Fatah Memon.
SPAIN—J. G. Kharas.
SUDAN AND ETHIOPIA—S. A. A. K. Durrani.
SWEDEN, NORWAY, DENMARK AND FINLAND—Lt.-Gen. W. A. Burki.
SWITZERLAND, AUSTRIA, HOLY SEE—Habibur Rahman.
THAILAND AND LAOS—M. S. A. Baig.
TUNISIA (*Chargé d'Affaires*)—H. Imam.
TURKEY AND GREECE—Air Commodore M. Rabb.
UNITED ARAB REPUBLIC, LIBYA AND YEMEN—S. Tayyeb Husain.
U.S.A., MEXICO, CUBA AND VENEZUELA—G. Ahmed.
U.S.S.R., CZECHOSLOVAKIA AND POLAND—Arshad Husain.

THE JUDICATURE

There is a Supreme Court of Pakistan. In addition the High Court of West Pakistan sits at Lahore, Karachi and Peshawar, and the High Court of East Pakistan at Dacca.

DEFENCE

Army.—8 Infantry Regiments, 6 Armoured Corps units, 8½ Artillery Regiments and 34 Engineer units.

Navy—The Navy consists of 1 cruiser, 5 destroyers, 2 frigates, 6 minesweepers, 1 survey ship, 1 salvage vessel, 1 harbour oiler, and auxiliary vessels.

EDUCATION

The latest census (1961) shows that 19·2 per cent. of the total population of Pakistan is literate. The Commission on National Education set up in 1959, recommended far-reaching changes in the organizational structure, content and methods of education. Most of the recommendations of the Commission have been carried out. Two Engineering and two Agricultural universities were established in both the wings of the country in 1961, thereby raising the number of universities to 10.

The University of the Punjab, founded in 1882, is the oldest university in the country. It undertakes teaching at the honours and post-graduate level, and several colleges are affiliated to it. During 1963 it had a total of 56,335 full-time students including those at affiliated colleges. The University of Dacca, established in 1921, as a unitary residential university, assumed, after independence, the additional function of an affiliating university for colleges in East Pakistan. During 1963, it had 17,290 full-time students. The University of Sind was established at Karachi in 1947. In 1952 it was moved to Hyderabad. It is an affiliating as well as a teaching university. In 1963, it had 3,960 students. The University of Peshawar was founded in 1950. It is a teaching residential and affiliating university. The number of full-time students on the roll of the University was 2,280 during 1963. The University of Karachi was set up during 1950–51. It provides for teaching at honours and post-graduate levels. All the colleges in the Karachi division are affiliated to the University. There were 2,065 students in 1963. The University of Rajshahi, established in 1953, is also a teaching and affiliating University with 7,386 students in 1963.

The number of educational institutions in Pakistan in 1961–62 was: Primary Schools, 51,678; Secondary Schools, 6,559; Colleges of Arts and Science, 233; Medical Colleges, 13; Law Colleges, 10; Engineering Colleges, 3.

LANGUAGE

Urdu and Bengali are the two main languages of Pakistan. English is the official language.

IRRIGATION

Pakistan has one of the longest irrigation systems in the world. The total area irrigated is about 23,000,000 acres.

PRODUCTION

Pakistan's economy is chiefly based on agriculture, which is the occupation of about 85 per cent. of the population. Estimated acreage (000's omitted) of principal crops in 1962–63 was: rice 23,009, wheat 11,991, sugar cane 1,381, rapeseed and mustard 1,648, cotton 3,282, jute 1,723, tea 81 and tobacco (1961–62) 219.

FOREIGN TRADE

Year	Exports	Imports	Balance
	Mill. Rupees		
1958	1,416·9	1,887·8	−470·9
1959	1,527·1	1,681·0	−153·9
1960	1,873·1	3,106·2	−1,233·1
1962	1,760·0	2,615·0	−855·0

COMMERCE

The chief exports of the country are raw jute, cotton, hides and skins, oil-seeds and tea. Industrial machinery and mill work, metals and ores, chemicals and drugs, mineral oils and hardware and instruments are the principal imports.

FINANCE

The Pakistan rupee was revalued on Aug. 1, 1955. Exchange rates are now Rs.100=£7·5 sterling or U.S. $21.

The State Bank, established July 1, 1948, has a capital of Rs.30,000,000, 51 per cent. of which is held by the Government. Deposits at all banks in the country on June 30, 1960 amounted to Rs. 3,082,300,000. There are 73 insurance companies operating in the country, of which 28 are Pakistani businesses. Total life insurance in force in Pakistan at the end of 1959 was Rs.941,250,000. New life insurance business during the year amounted to Rs.257,990,000.

Revenue and Expenditure since 1958–59 are as follows:—

Revenue: (1958–59) (15 months) Rs. 2,070·2 million; (1959–60) Rs. 1,887·7 million; (1960–61) Rs. 1,970·4 million; (1961–62, revised estimate) Rs. 2,155·3 million; (1962–63, Budget estimate) Rs. 2,143 million.

Expenditure met from Revenue: (1958–9)(15 months) Rs. 2,067·7 million; (1959–60) Rs. 1,733·8 million; (1960–61) Rs. 1,740·1 million; (1961–61, revised estimate) Rs. 1,919·0 million; (1962–63, Budget estimate) Rs. 1,958·8 million.

COMMUNICATIONS

There are 7,044 miles of railway line in the country. Of this total mileage, West Pakistan has 5,335 miles of railway line and East Pakistan has 1,709 miles. The Pakistan railways comprise two independent railway systems—the Pakistan Western Railway in West Pakistan and the Pakistan Eastern Railway in East Pakistan—managed and owned by the State.

ΨThe principal sea ports are Karachi and Chittagong in West and East Pakistan respectively. These two ports handled in 1961–62 about 4,970,000 tons and 2,890,000 tons of traffic respectively. The anchorage of Chalna, established in Dec. 1950, on the river Pussur in East Bengal to relieve congestion of traffic at Chittagong, now has nine moorings.

Karachi is the main air port, and being situated on the trunk air routes of the world, holds an important position. Pakistan International Airlines is the chief air transport company in Pakistan.

Post and telegraph facilities are available to every country in the world.

PROVINCES OF PAKISTAN

PROVINCES OF THE ISLAMIC REPUBLIC OF PAKISTAN

1. West Pakistan

The Establishment of West Pakistan Act, 1955, came into force on October 3, 1955, and incorporated: (1) the former Governors' Provinces of the Punjab, North-West Frontier and Sind; (2) the former Chief Commissioners' Provinces of Baluchistan and Karachi; (3) the States of Bahawalpur and Khairpur and the Baluchistan States Union; (4) the Tribal Areas of Baluchistan, the Punjab and the North-West Frontier and the States of Amb, Chitral, Dir and Swat, into the Province of *West Pakistan* with effect from October 14, 1955.

At the 1961 Census the total population, excluding the Federal Territory of Karachi, was 40,815,000 (preliminary figures).

West Pakistan (including the Federal Territory), has an area of 310,403 square miles; 97·1 per cent. of the population are Muslim; 0·5 per cent. Caste Hindu; 1·1 per cent. Scheduled Caste Hindu and 1·3 per cent. Christian. Running through West Pakistan are five great rivers, the Indus, and its tributaries, Jhelum, Chenab, Ravi, and Sutlej. The upper reaches of these rivers are in Kashmir and their sources are in the lofty Himilayas.

West Pakistan is one of the richest wheat-producing areas populated by a hardy peasantry with great martial traditions. Of the other crops grown, cotton, rice, gram, jowar and oil-seeds are the most important. There are large deposits of rock salt, which with cotton forms the principal exports. The Province is served by the Pakistan Western Railway.

Chief City and Headquarters of West Pakistan: Lahore (population, 1961 census preliminary, 1,297,000).

Governor, Malik Amir Mohammad Khan of Kalabagh.

2. EAST PAKISTAN

The Province of East Pakistan: area, 55,126 sq. miles, population (1961 census), 50,840,235 (of whom 80·4 per cent. are Muslim; 8·6 per cent. Caste Hindu; 9·8 per cent. Scheduled Caste Hindu; 0·3 per cent. Christian and 0·9 per cent. others), comprises the Eastern territories of the partitioned province of Bengal and Sylhet, formerly a district of Assam (excluding certain thanas in the Karimganj sub-division), and the Chittagong Hill tracts.

CHIEF CITY (and Headquarters of East Pakistan): Dacca. Population 556,712 (1961 census).

Governor, Abdul Monem Khan.

CAPITAL OF PAKISTAN

An executive order was issued on Aug. 2, 1960, proclaiming Rawalpindi (340,175) as Capital of Pakistan in place of Karachi, and providing that Karachi would in future be known as the Federal Territory of Karachi. Pakistan's new Federal Capital, Islamabad, is being built near Rawalpindi. Karachi Territory had a population of 2,153,000 (preliminary figures) at the 1961 Census; Metropolitan population 1,916,000.

Ghana

Ghana (formerly the British Colony of the Gold Coast) is situated on the Gulf of Guinea, between 3° 15′ W. long. and 1° 12′ E. long. It is bounded on the west by the Republic of Ivory Coast, on the east by the Republic of Togo, and on the south by the sea. It extends about 334 miles along the coast-line and inland to an average distance of 440 miles or to 11° N. lat. Although a tropical country, Ghana is cooler than many countries within similar latitudes.

Area and Population.—Ghana has a total area of 92,100 sq. miles with a total population at the Census of 1960 of 6,690,730. Distribution by Administrative regions was as follows:—

Region	*Area Sq. miles*	*Population Census, 1960*
Eastern	8,750	1,088,843
Western	9,494	1,348,844
Central	3,656	..
Ashanti	9,700	1,108,548
Brong Ahafo	14,900	588,724
Volta	8,000	782,547
Northern	27,122	1,282,164
Upper	10,478	..
	92,100	6,690,730

Figures for the Eastern Region exclude the population of the capital district, Accra, which with Adangbe-Shai, Tema and the Accra Rural Areas had a population in 1960 of 491,060.

GOVERNMENT

The Gold Coast region of West Africa was first visited by European traders in the fifteenth century. The Gold Coast Colony, Ashanti, the Northern Territories and Transvolta-Togoland, the constituent parts of the new State, came under British administration at various times, the original Gold Coast Colony, the coastal and Southern areas, being first constituted in 1874; Ashanti in 1901; and the Northern Territories Protectorate in 1902. The territory of Transvolta-Togoland, part of Togo, a former German colony, was mandated to Britain by the League of Nations after the First World War, and remained under British administration as a United Nations Trusteeship after the Second World War. After a plebiscite in May, 1956, under the auspices of the United Nations, the territory was integrated with the Gold Coast Colony.

The former Gold Coast Colony and associated territories became the independent state of Ghana and a member of the British Commonwealth on March 6, 1957, under the *Ghana Independence Act*, 1957 and adopted a Republican constitution on July 1, 1960.

President of the Republic, Dr. Kwame Nkrumah (July 1, 1960)
(+*tax-free allce.* £2,500) £12,000.

CABINET

Prime Minister and Secretary for African Affairs, Dr. Kwame Nkrumah.
Minister for Foreign Affairs, Kojo Botsio.
Minister of Finance and Trade, F. D. K. Goka.
Agriculture, Krobo Edusei.
Interior, Kwaku Boateng.
Health, A. E. Inkumsah.
Communications and Works, E. K. Bensah.
Education, A. J. Dowuona-Hammond.
Information and Broadcasting, L. R. Abavana.
Justice, K. A. Ofori-Atta.
Social Welfare, O. Owusu-Afriyie.
Industries, Imoru Egala.
Defence, Kofi Baako.

SALARIES.—The salaries of Cabinet Ministers are £3,000 p.a.; their annual allowances total £2,100.

GHANAIAN COMMISSIONER IN U.K.

UNITED KINGDOM (*High Commissioner*), Kwesi Armah, 13 Belgrave Square, London, S.W.1.

UNITED KINGDOM HIGH COMMISSIONER

P.O. Box 296, High Street, Accra.

High Commissioner (vacant).
Deputy High Commissioner, D. L. Cole, M.C.

British Council Representative, F. H. Cawson, O.B.E.

LEGISLATURE

The Republican constitution of Ghana came into effect on July 1, 1960. It provides for a parliament consisting of the President and the National Assembly of 104 members, with a maximum term of 5 years. A further 10 seats have been created for representatives of the women of Ghana. At least one session of a month's duration is held each quarter. Electoral constituencies remained as for the Legislative Assembly and voting is on a basis of adult suffrage.

Houses of Chiefs

The Constitution guarantees the office of Chief in Ghana as existing by customary law and usage and provides for the establishment of Houses of Chiefs. Houses of Chiefs have power under the Constitution to consider any matters referred to them by a Minister and may at any time offer advice to any Minister.

JUDICATURE

There are: (*a*) 9 Supreme Court Judges, including the Chief Justice; (*b*) 15 High Court Judges: (*c*) 8 Circuit Court Judges and (*d*) 8 Circuit Courts; (*e*) 20 District Magistrates and (*f*) 25 District Magistrates' Courts. Appeals from Local Courts go straight to Circuit Courts.

COMMUNICATIONS

There are four aerodromes in Ghana, situated at Accra, Takoradi, Kumasi and Tamale. Accra Airport is an international airport and is the terminus for services from the United Kingdom, the Northern Region, Ashanti and the Western Province. There is a National Meteorological Service, providing forecasting, climatological and agro-meteorological services.

Railway communications consist of a main line running from Takoradi to Kumasi thence to Accra, a distance of 357 miles, with branches from Kojokrom to Sekondi (3 miles), Tarkwa to Preslea (18 miles) and Achimota to Tema (16 miles). A link of 51 miles between the Huni-Valley–Kade line at Achiasi Junction and the Accra–Kumasi line at Kotoku was opened in 1956. Total route mileage is 591 miles 3′ 6″ gauge track. On Dec. 31, 1961, the mileage of all-weather roads was 4,792, comprising 2,014 miles of bitumen surface and 2,778 miles gravel surface. In addition there are 700 miles of roads at present maintained by the regional organization and local authorities.

Takoradi Harbour consists of two breakwaters enclosing a water area of 220 acres. Seven quay berths are situated on the lee breakwater—five are used for the handling of general cargo, one is leased specially for manganese exports and one is used for shallow draft colliers. The first stage is now being completed on the construction of Tema, Africa's largest artificial harbour and a prospective major port of the South Atlantic. Tema Harbour was opened in Feb. 1962. There are 10 berths for larger ocean going vessels, and 2 more are being built. An oil berth is also being built to serve the Ghaip refinery, which is under construction at Tema. As part of the Tema Harbour project a new town, Tema, is being built, its ultimate population now envisaged at 50,000. Many light industries are already operating there.

FINANCE

	1961–62 £G	1962–63† £G
Revenue............	94,000,000	101,000,000
Expenditure.........	128,000,000	127,700,000

At Dec. 31, 1961, the public debt amounted to £G87,800,000.

† Estimates. Financial year, Oct. 1–Sept. 30.

TRADE

	1961	1962
Total imports....	£G142,735,000	£G119,101,830
Total exports....	115,203,000	115,036,389
Imports from U.K.	£49,527,082	£36,571,500
Exports to U.K...	19,880,015	21,860,627

In 1961 imports of non-durable consumers' goods amounted to 41·1 per cent. of total imports; of these, the most important commodities were textiles, food, drink, tobacco and footwear.

Imports of durable producers' goods amounted to 32·5 per cent. of the total. Fuels and lubricants, mainly petroleum products, amounted to 4·2 per cent. of total imports.

FLAG.—Horizontal bands of red, gold and green, bearing a black star on a gold band.

CAPITAL.—Ψ ACCRA. Population of the Capital District (including Accra Municipal Council area, Adangbe-Tema Development Area and Accra Rural area) at the Census of 1960, 491,060. Other towns are Kumasi, Tamale, Sekondi-Takoradi, Cape Coast, Koforidua, Tarkwa and Winneba.

Accra is sea distant from Liverpool, 3,920 miles; transit 12 to 30 days. A 14 hours air service operates to and from the U.K. four times a week.

Cyprus

Area and Population.—Cyprus is a large island in the Mediterranean Sea, between N. lat. 34° 33′ and 35° 41′, and E. long. 32° 20′ and 34° 35′. It is about 40 miles distant from the nearest point of Asia Minor, and 60 miles from Latakia on the Syrian coast. The distance to Port Said, at the entrance of the Suez Canal, is 238 miles. The larger part of the island is an irregular parallelogram 100 miles long and 60 to 30 broad, from which a narrow peninsula, 5 or 6 miles wide, runs out for 40 miles towards the north-east. The area is 3,572 square miles. In 1962 the estimated population was 584,000. There are two major communities, Greek Cypriots (77·1 per cent.) and Turkish Cypriots (18·2 per cent.); and minorities of Armenians, Maronites and others.

President, Archbishop Makarios, *elected* Dec. 14, 1959; *assumed office* Aug. 16, 1960.

Vice-President, Dr. Fazil Kuchuk.

CABINET

Minister of Foreign Affairs, Spyros Kyprianou.
Interior, Polykarpos Georgadjis.
Justice, Mme Stella Souliotou.
Communications and Works, Andreas Papadopoulos.
Labour and Social Insurance, Tassos Papadopoulos.
Commerce and Industry, Andreas Araouzos.
Finance, Renos Solomides.
Agriculture and Natural Resources, Fazil Plümer.
Health, Dr. Niazi Maniera.
Defence, Osman Orek.

HIGH COMMISSIONER OF CYPRUS IN LONDON

A. Soteriades, Ulster Chambers, 168 Regent Street, W.1.

U.K. HIGH COMMISSIONER

Alexander Pallis Street, Nicosia.

High Commissioner, His Excellency Sir William Arthur Weir Clark, K.C.M.G., C.B.E.
Deputy High Commissioner, D. M. Cleary.

Representative of the British Council, B. C. D. Jones.

GOVERNMENT

Cyprus was formally annexed to Great Britain on Nov. 5, 1914, on the outbreak of war with Turkey. From 1925–60 it was a crown colony administered by a Governor, assisted by an Executive Council and also for a time by a partly-elected Legislative Council. A state of emergency was declared in November, 1955, and Archbishop Makarios was deported. Further proposals for a workable constitution made in 1956 and a seven-year-plan for the government of Cyprus in association with Greece and Turkey were rejected by the Greek Government and Greek Cypriots. Archbishop Makarios was released in March, 1957, but was not allowed to return immediately to Cyprus. Following a meeting at Zürich between the Prime Ministers of Greece and Turkey, a conference was held in London and an agreement was signed on February 19, 1959, between the United Kingdom, Greece and Turkey, which provided that Cyprus would be a Republic.

Constitution.—Under the Cyprus Act, 1960, the island became an independent sovereign republic on August 16, 1960. The constitution provides for a Greek Cypriot President and a Turkish Cypriot Vice-President elected for a five-year term by the Greek and Turkish communities respectively. A Council of Ministers (7 Greek, 3 Turkish) is designated by the President and Vice-President, and a House of Representatives, elected for five years by universal suffrage of each community separately, consists of 35 Greek and 15 Turkish members. The number of representatives is fixed by agreement between the communities. Matters of religion, education and culture and matters of purely communal character are looked after by two Communal Chambers, one Greek and one Turkish.

British Sovereign Areas.—The United Kingdom retained full sovereignty and jurisdiction over two areas—Akrotiri–Episkopi–Paramali and Dhekelia–Pergamos–Ayios Nikalaos–Xylophagou—and use of roads and other facilities. The British Administrator of these areas is appointed by the Queen and is responsible to the Secretary of State for Air.

Production and Industries.—About 40 per cent. of those gainfully employed take part in agriculture, the chief agricultural products being:—cereals, vine products, potatoes, carobs, carrots, citrus and other fresh and dried fruit, tobacco and legumes. Various kinds of livestock are raised, donkeys and mules being the principal exports. The value of agricultural and livestock exports in 1962 was £9,915,500. Mining is an important industry in Cyprus; the value of minerals exported in 1962 was £7,702,000.

Education.—Each religious denomination has its own elementary schools. In 1962–63 there were 763 elementary schools (536 Greek and 227 Turkish) and 55 secondary schools (39 Greek and 16 Turkish). There are also two teachers' training colleges (one Greek and one Turkish) and 7 technical schools (3 Greek and 4 Turkish).

Communications.—Ψ Famagusta is the main seaport. In 1962 2,211 steamships (tonnage 4,616,545) and 382 sailing vessels (tonnage 18,650) engaged in the foreign trade. Air passenger traffic in, out and through Nicosia totalled 152,468 persons and freight amounted to 1,413 metric tons. Nicosia Flight Information Centre controls and safeguards movements of civil aircraft through the Eastern Mediterranean.

FINANCE

	1961	1962
Ordinary Revenue....	£19,069,170	£20,128,719
Ordinary Expenditure.	18,339,523	18,543,668

TRADE

	1961	1962
Imports.............	£38,331,000	£44,953,000
Exports.............	17,780,000	20,797,000
Imports from U.K....	£13,312,167	£14,892,754
Exports to U.K......	8,015,929	11,954,691

CAPITAL.—Nicosia, near the centre of the island, with a population of 95,343 (1960 census figures) (including suburbs); the other principal towns are ΨLimassol (population 43,561), ΨFamagusta (34,752), ΨLarnaca (19,807), Paphos (9,079) and Kyrenia (3,441). Nicosia is distant from London 2,028 miles by air.

FLAG.—Gold map of Cyprus on a white ground, surmounting crossed olive branches (green).

Tanganyika

Tanganyika occupies the east central portion of the African continent, between 1°–11° 45′ S. lat. and 29° 20′–40° 38′ E. long. It is bounded on the N. by Kenya and Uganda; on the S.W. by Lake Nyasa, Nyasaland and N. Rhodesia; on the S. by Portuguese E. Africa; on the W. it is bounded by Ruanda, Burundi and the Congolese Republic; on the E. the boundary is the Indian Ocean. Tanganyika has a coastline of about 500 miles and an area of 362,688 sq. miles (including 20,650 sq miles of water). The greater part of the country is occupied by the Central African plateau from which rise, among others, Mt. Kilimanjaro, the highest point on the continent of Africa (19,340 ft.) and Mt. Meru (14,979 ft). The Serengeti National Park, which covers an area of 6,000 sq. miles in the Northern and Lake Provinces is famous for its variety and number of species of game.

The native population consists mostly of tribes of mixed Bantu race. The total population of Tanganyika is estimated at 9,403,700, including approximately 22,700 Europeans and 123,000 other non-Africans (mainly Asians). Swahili, the language of the coastal people, is understood throughout the country and has been adopted as the basic standard dialect for literature, both for educational and general purposes.

President, Julius Kambarage Nyerere, *b.* 1922; *elected* Nov. 1962; *took office* Dec. 9, 1962.

GOVERNMENT

Following a constitutional conference held in Dar es Salaam in March, 1961, Tanganyika became an independent state and a member of the British Commonwealth on December 9, 1961.

Tanganyika became a Republic, within the Commonwealth, on December 9, 1962, with an executive President, elected by universal suffrage, who is both the Head of State and Head of the Government. A presidential election will be held whenever Parliament is dissolved, and the presidency is closely linked with the majority party in the National Assembly. The National Assembly comprises 71 elected members and up to a maximum of 10 members nominated by the President. To assist him in carrying out his functions the President appoints a Vice-President, who must be an elected member of the National Assembly and is the leader of Government business in the Assembly. The Vice-President and ministers comprise the Cabinet, which is presided over by the President.

CABINET

Vice-President, R. M. Kawawa.
Minister of Finance, P. Bomani.
Justice, Sheik Amri Abedi.
Labour, M. M. Kamaliza.
Home Affairs, J. M. Lusinde.
Communications, Power and Works, A. H. Jamal.
Agriculture, D. N. M. Bryceson.
Commerce and Industry, C. G. Kahama.
Education, S. N. Eliufoo.
Lands, Forest and Wildlife, Alhaj T. S. Tewa.
Local Government, A. K. E. Shaba.
Co-operative and Community Development, J. S. Kasambala.
Development Planning, A. Z. N. Swai.
External Affairs and Defence, O. S. Kambona.
Health, S. A. Maswanya.
National Culture and Youth, L. N. Sijaona.

TANGANYIKA HIGH COMMISSIONER IN U.K.

S. Ntiro, Grand Buildings, Trafalgar Square, S.W.1.

U.K. HIGH COMMISSIONER IN TANGANYIKA

Permanent House, Independence Avenue, Dar es Salaam.
High Commissioner (vacant).
Deputy High Commissioner, F. S. Miles.

Chief Justice of Tanganyika, Hon. Sir Ralph Windham.

EDUCATION.—In 1962, there were 2,733 primary schools, mostly co-educational, 369 middle schools, 12 State secondary schools and 17 voluntary secondary schools. There are separate facilities for the education of Europeans and of Indians, both largely financed by non-Government sources. A technical college in Dar es Salaam with over 300 full-time and about 1,000 part-time students provides technical and commercial education for both sexes of all races. Financial assitance for students going overseas is provided by the Government. There are also 3 mission schools mainly for Goans and one school run by the Goan community.

FINANCE.—Total revenue for 1962–63 was estimated at £31,237,000 and expenditure, £31,482,000, compared with £28,768,000 and £29,161,000 respectively in 1961–62.

PRODUCTION.—The economy is based mainly on the production and export of primary produce and the growing of foodstuffs for local consumption. The chief commercial crops are sisal, cotton, coffee and oilseeds. The most important minerals are diamonds, gold, lead and mica. Hides and skins are another valuable export. Industry is at present largely concerned with the processing of raw materials for either export or local consumption. There is also a healthy growth of secondary manufacturing industries, including factories for the manufacture of leather and rubber footwear, knitwear, razor blades, cigarettes and textiles, and a wheat flour mill.

Live Stock.—In 1961 there were about 8,016,000 cattle, 2,986,000 sheep, 4,448,000 goats and 23,000 pigs in the country.

Minerals.—The provisional value of mineral sales in 1961 was £7,976,000, mainly: diamonds, £5,780,000; gold, silver, copper and lead, £1,333,000; mica sheet, £88,000; salt, £271,000; building minerals, £293,000; tin concentrates, £152,000; other, £59,000.

TRADE.—The value of Tanganyika's principal exports in 1961 was: sisal, £14,028,000; coffee, £6,762,000; cotton, £6,794,000; diamonds, £5,762,000; oilseeds, nuts and kernels, £1,943,000; cashew nuts, £1,805,000; hides and skins, £1,759,000; meat and meat preparations, £2,054,000. Other exports include gold, metalliferous ores, tea, beans, peas and pulses, animal feeding stuffs, cassava flour, beeswax, papain, wood and timber, lead and unmanufactured tobacco. Total value of trade in 1961 was: Exports, £48,649,000; Imports, £39,686,000; Exports to U.K., 1961, £11,852,904; Imports from U.K., £10,364,750.

CAPITAL.—Ψ Dar es Salaam (population, Census 1957, 128,742). Other towns are ΨTanga (38,053); Mwanza (19,877); Tabora (15,361); and ΨMtwara (10,459).

FLAG.—Broad horizontal stripes of green, black and green, separated by 2 narrow stripes of gold.

British Council Representative.—W. R. Keight, M.B.E., Dar es Salaam.

Uganda

Situated in East Central Africa, Uganda is flanked by the Congolese Republic, the Sudan, Kenya and on the south by Tanganyika and Ruanda. Large parts of Lakes Victoria, Edward and Albert are within its boundaries, as are Lakes Kyoga and Salisbury and the course of the River Nile from its outlet from Lake Victoria to the Sudan frontier post at Nimule. Uganda has an area of 93,981 sq. miles (water, 13,600 sq. miles) and a population estimated (1959) at 6,538,175. The total includes some 10,000 Europeans, 72,000 Asians and some smaller racial groups. About 2,500,000 Africans who occupy Central and Southern parts speak Bantu languages, the most important being Luganda. Ki-Swahili in a debased form is also spoken as a trading language and is used by the police. Peoples of Northern Uganda are akin to various tribes in the South of the Sudan. The official language of Uganda is English. CAPITAL.—Kampala (population, 12,000).

Government.—Uganda became a fully independent member of the Commonwealth on October 9, 1962. Full sovereign status was granted by the Uganda Independence Act, 1962, and the Constitution is now embodied in the Uganda (Independence) Order in Council, 1962. This Constitution provides for a Governor-General, representing the Queen, a Prime Minister, a Cabinet of Ministers and a National Assembly. The National Assembly consists of the Speaker and 92 members, who are 82 elected members, 9 specially elected members and the Attorney-General (*ex officio*). Elections to the National Assembly were held on April 25, 1962. The Uganda People's Congress obtained 37 seats, the *Kabaka Yekka* Movement in Buganda, 21 seats and the Democratic Party 24 seats. The Coalition Government of Uganda People's Congress and *Kabaka Yekka* took office immediately following the election and the Hon. M. A. Obote became Prime Minister of independent Uganda. The Constitution also provides for a federal relationship between Buganda and the Central Government. The precise terms of this federal relationship are set out in schedules to the Uganda Constitution. *It was announced in the autumn of 1963 that Uganda would become a republic on October 9, 1963, remaining within the Commonwealth, and that a President would then be elected in place of the Governor-General.*

CABINET
(October 9, 1962)

Prime Minister, Minister of Defence and of Foreign Affairs, A. Milton Obote.
Minister of Internal Affairs, F. K. Onama.
Finance, A. Kalule Sempa.
Justice, G. S. K. Ibingara.
Attorney-General, G. L. Binaisa, Q.C.
Health, Dr. E. B. S. Lumu.
Information, Broadcasting and Tourism, A. A. Nekyon.
Industry and Communications, L. Kalule Settala.
Commerce, J. S. Mananja-Nkangi.
Works, B. K. Kirya.
Agriculture and Co-operatives, M. M. Ngobi.
Mineral and Water Resources, J. W. Lwamafa.
Community Development and Labour, A. A. Ojera.
Animal Industry, Game and Fisheries, J. K. Babiiha.
Regional Administrations, C. J. Obwangor.
Education, Dr. J. S. Luyimba-Zake.

British High Commissioner in Uganda, His Excellency D. W. S. Hunt, C.M.G., O.B.E., 5 Shimoui Road, P.O. Box 2894, Kampala.
Uganda High Commissioner in U.K., His Excellency T. B. Bazarrabusa, M.B.E., Uganda House Trafalgar Square, W.C.2.

British Council Representative in Uganda, P. Marsh.

Education.—Local authorities in both urban and rural areas are responsible for primary and junior secondary education. The Ministry retains responsibility for policy, school curricula and examinations, for secondary education and teachers' training. The contribution of religious voluntary agencies, in co-operation with the local authorities, is still of great importance. At the end of 1961, these were 2,315 grant-aided primary schools (African, 2,223; Asian, 80; European, 12) and 107 unaided; 312 grant-aided African junior secondary schools and 28 senior secondary schools taking both African and Asian pupils. There were 427,055 pupils at schools of all types. Other institutions with numbers of pupils were: a technical institute (444 students); junior technical schools, 12 (1,056); rural trade schools, 36 (1,277); farm schools, 7 (114); and homecraft centres, 13 (393). Makerere University College (Kampala) established in 1939, draws students from all the East African territories. Students at the College in 1962 (951), included 278 from Uganda. A further 800 students from Uganda were attending courses of higher education overseas.

Communications.—There is a first-class international airport at Entebbe, with direct flights to Europe, W. Africa, S. Rhodesia, Sudan, Kenya, Tanganyika and the Congolese Republic by B.O.A.C., B.U.A., Sudan Airways, Air Congo and Sabena. 83,000 passengers used the airport in 1962. There are 10 other state airports in Uganda. There are 3,342 miles of all-weather and 8,300 miles of other roads. Lake, marine, road and rail services are operated by the E. African Railways and Harbours Administration.

Production and Trade.—The principal export crops are coffee and cotton, value of exports in 1961 being £30,695,063. Production of cash crops in 1961 was: coffee, 91,000 tons (clean); cotton, 72,067,000 lbs.; tea, 11,278,000 lbs.; tobacco, 3,612,000 lbs. Ground-nuts, maize, castor-seed, sugar, sisal and various oil seeds are also grown. Freshwater fish from Uganda's extensive lakes and rivers had a retail value of over £3,000,000 in 1961. Production of sawn timber, mostly hardwood, in 1961—June, 1962 totalled 20,000 tons.

Minerals exported in 1961 were blister copper, 15,535 tons (£3,441,000); beryl, 1,063 tons (£130,000); and tin, 94 tons (£60,800). The Owen Falls hydro-electric power scheme will have an eventual capacity of 150,000 kWh. It is now exporting 7,500,000 units per month to Kenya. Kampala, the capital is the principal commercial centre. Other towns of importance are Entebbe (8,000), Jinja and Mbale.

TRADE WITH U.K.

	1961	1962
Imports from U.K....	£4,973,727	£4,470,699
Exports to U.K.......	5,397,176	6,477,534

Finance. Revenue Budget.

	1961—June, 1962	1962—June, 1963*
Revenue............	£17,641,968	£19,831,765
Expenditure..........	20,344,359	20,390,380

Estimated revenue on capital account in 1962–63 was £2,149,050; expenditure, £6,381,[illegible]50.

Dominions, Colonies and Protectorates

NOTE.—*Canada, Australia, New Zealand, Ceylon, Malaya, Nigeria, Sierra Leone, India, Pakistan, Ghana, Cyprus, Tanganyika and Uganda* are shown separately in the preceding pages.

ADEN

(*Aden Colony and Protectorate*)

The area of Aden Colony is 75 sq. miles and of the Protectorate about 112,000 sq. miles. The estimated population of the Colony (1963) is 210,000. The estimated population of the Protectorate is about 1,000,000.

The peninsula of Aden, situated on the southern coast of Arabia and lying on the Red Sea trade-route between Europe and the East, was first occupied by the British in 1839. Aden was always an important centre. Its trade decayed after the Portuguese discovery of the Cape route, but with the opening of the Suez Canal it regained more than its old importance and is now a great oil bunkering and coaling station and port of call, and an emporium for the trade of the adjacent African and Arabian coasts. Aden is a free port. The chief industries are fishing, salt, soap and cigarette manufacture, aluminium pressing of domestic utensils and dyeing and printing of cloth. The traffic in arms and ammunition is subject to special regulations. The British Government has treaty engagements with, and subsidises, the neighbouring Arab tribes, both inland and along the coast, from the Straits of Bab-al-Mandeb to Muscat territory at Ras Darbhat 'Ali.

Perim.—A small unfortified island with an area of 5 square miles was occupied in 1857 and is administratively attached to Aden. The port has been closed since November, 1936, on the withdrawal of the Perim Coal Company from the island. Population, 283.

Kamaran.—The island of Kamaran in the Red Sea about 200 miles north of Perim was taken by the British from the Turks in 1915, and is administered under the control of the Governor of Aden. It has an area of 88 square miles and a population of about 2,200.

The Aden Protectorate to the West of approximate longitude 46° is bounded on the East by the Qara country, which is part of the dominions of the Sultan of Muscat and Oman, and by Saudi

Arabia, and on the North and West by the Great Desert and the Kingdom of Yemen, whose Southern boundary was temporarily fixed by Article III of the Treaty of San'a (February, 1934) by which His Majesty's Government and the Yemen Government agreed to maintain the *status quo* frontier as it was on the date of the signing of the treaty. The coastline of the Aden Protectorate, which is about 750 miles long, starts in the West from Husn Murad, opposite the island of Perim, and it runs eastward to Ras Dharbat 'Ali, where it meets the Sultanate of Muscat and Oman.

The Aden Protectorate is divided into two parts, the Western Aden Protectorate and the Eastern Aden Protectorate. The former consists of 18 Sultanates, the chiefs of which are all in protective treaty relations with Her Majesty's Government.

On February 11, 1959, "The Federation of Arab Amirates of the South" (now known as the "Federation of South Arabia") was inaugurated in the West Aden Protectorate, composed of the Sultanates of Audhali, Lower Yafai, and Fadhli, the Amirates of Baihan and Dhala, and the Sheikdom of Upper Aulaqi. They were joined later by five other States—Lahej, Lower Aulaqi, Dathina and Aqrabi from the Western Aden Protectorate and the Wahidi Sultanate from the Eastern Aden Protectorate. The Federation, which is governed by a constitution providing for a Supreme Council and a Federal Council, is open to other States in the Protectorate. Under a related treaty with Her Majesty's Government, the Federation continues to receive advice and financial and technical assistance from Her Majesty's Government. The treaty also provides for assistance and co-operation in defence and security. The objects of the Federation include concerted resistance to repeated incursions from the Yemen and the promotion of economic development programmes. The flag adopted by the Federation consists of an Islamic crescent moon with a central star and five horizontal stripes (black, yellow, green, yellow, blue). The Colony of Aden acceded to the Federation in Jan. 1963.

The Eastern Aden Protectorate comprises the Hadhramaut (consisting of the Quaiti State of Shihr and Mukalla and the Kathiri State of Seiyun), and the Mahri Sultanate of Qishn and Socotra, all of which are in protective treaty relations with Her Majesty's Government. His Highness the Sultan of Shihr and Mukalla is the premier chief of the Eastern Aden Protectorate, and the Hadhramaut is the most important and best organised of these areas. It is bounded on the west by the Wahidi Sultanates and on the east by the Mahri Sultanate.

The Mahri Sultanate of Qishn and Socotra is the most easterly area in the Aden Protectorate, for it is bounded on the East by the Sultanate of Muscat and Oman. The Sultan of Qishn and Socotra resides on the island of Socotra (area 1,400 square miles) which lies 150 miles from Cape Guardafui. The island was occupied by the East India Company in 1834 and it came under British protection in 1886 when the treaty with the Mahri Sultan was concluded. It contains about 12,000 inhabitants principally engaged in livestock husbandry.

Finance

Colony

	1961-62	1962-63
Revenue............	£4,697,110	£5,552,563
Expenditure.........	£4,713,818	£5,475,281

Trade

	1960	1961
Total imports.......	£76,580,601	£82,886,404
Total exports........	60,035,136	64,929,355

	1961	1962
Imports from U.K....	£10,904,373	£11,251,895
Exports to U.K......	7,245,546	11,118,640

Government

Amendments to the Constitution were agreed in Dec. 1962. They included the following: the maximum term of the Legislative Council was extended from 4 to 5 years; 4 additional members of the Legislative Council would be elected by the Council itself; all the *ex officio* members, except the Attorney-General, would retire from the Executive and Legislative Councils; the Governor would appoint as Chief Minister the member of the Legislative Council who appeared to him most likely to command the support of the majority of the Council; the Executive Council would be renamed the Council of Ministers and be composed of the Chief Minister, Attorney-General and not fewer than 6 members appointed by the Governor on the Chief Minister's advice; the Governor would act on the advice of the Council of Ministers, subject to the retention of his reserved powers and his responsibility for external affairs, defence, internal security, police and staffing of the public service. It was further provided that the title of Governor should be changed to that of High Commissioner.

High Commissioner, Sir Gerald Trevaskis, K.C.M.G., O.B.E. (1963)

Council of Ministers
(July 9, 1963)

Chief Minister, Zain Abdo Baharoon.
Finance, Abdullah Salem Basendwah.
Labour, Welfare and Immigration, Ali Salem Ali.
Local Government and Prisons, Mustafa Abdullah Abdo.
Works and Water, Hasson Ismail Khodabux Khan.
Religious Endowments, Abdul Hamid Muhammad Ghanem.
Minister of State, Ali Abdullah Basahai.
Lands and Antiquities, Joseph A. Salole.
Attorney-General, T. Maloney.

British Council Representative, W. E. N. Kensdale.

Aden is distant from London 4,654 miles; transit by sea 13 days, and by air 12 hours.

ASCENSION
(*See* St. Helena)

THE BAHAMAS

The Bahamas (or Lucayos) are an archipelago near the British West Indies, lying between 20° 56′—27° 22′ N. lat. and 72° 40′—79° 20′; W. long., and extending from the coast of Florida on the north-west to Haiti on the south-east. The group consists of twenty-two inhabited islands, and an immense number of islets and rocks, comprising an area of about 4,403 square miles, and a population estimated (1962) at 112 556, the most part being descendants of liberated Africans. The principal islands are: New Providence (containing the capital Nassau), Cat Island, Abaco, Grand Bahama, Long Island, Eleuthera, Exuma, Harbour Island, Inagua, Andros Island, San Salvador (at one time known as Watling's Island), Rum Cay, Long Cay, Ragged Island and Bimini. Watling's Island was the first landfall in the New World made (October 12, 1492) by *Christopher Columbus*, who gave it the name of San Salvador, which has been restored by an Act of the Bahamas Legislature. Originally settled by Englishmen, the Bahamas were, in 1782, surprised by the Spanish, but at the Peace of Versailles were restored to the English. The climate is salubrious and in the winter Nassau, which is outside the tropics, is frequented by many visitors from all parts of the world.

Industries.—Tomatoes and okra are cultivated in large quantities for shipment to Canada and the United States. Lumbering and salt raking are the chief national industries.

Education.—Education is compulsory between the ages of 6 and 14. There are 148 state-maintained schools with a total roll of 19,762; there are also 53 denominational and private schools with a total roll of 8,850. There are 5 Government and 5 denominational secondary schools and 1 private secondary school.

Civil Aviation.—Facilities for external traffic are provided by Pan-American Airways, B.O.A.C., Trans-Canada Air Lines, Cunard Eagle and Mackey Air Lines, while Bahamas Airways and Bahamas Air Traders provide internal schedule and charter flights to the outlying islands. There are several daily air services between Nassau, Miami, Palm Beach, Fort Lauderdale, Tampa and St. Petersburg (Florida), and a regular service between Nassau and Montego Bay, Jamaica, besides regular trunk communication with London, New York, Toronto, Montreal, Bermuda and Kingston.

Communications.—There is a General Post Office in Nassau, 4 branch offices in New Providence and 106 sub-offices in the Out Islands. In 1962, 13,300,000 letters and prints were handled. Wireless and telephone services are in operation to all parts of the world. There are 64 radio stations among the islands.

FINANCE AND TRADE

	1961	1962
Public revenue	£8,563,582	£8,689,155
Expenditure	8,574,914	9,042,292
Public debt	..	1,610,526
Total imports	30,431,511	24,524,492
Total exports	2,959,719	3,222,613
Imports from U.K.	6,619,807	4,288,977
Exports to U.K.	280,099	355,778

The imports are chiefly foodstuffs, tobacco, spirits, automobiles, machinery, electrical items and lumber. The chief exports in 1962 were tomatoes, crawfish, salt, pulpwood and cucumbers.

GOVERNMENT

The Government is vested in a Governor, aided by an Executive Council of 9 members, a nominated Legislative Council of 11 members and an elective Representative Assembly of 33 members.

Governor and Commander-in-Chief, His Excellency Sir Robert de Stapeldon Stapledon, K.C.M.G., C.B.E. (1960) £6,500
Chief Justice, Hon. Sir Ralph Campbell .. 3,640
Puisne Judge, Hon. J. G. F. Scarr 2,680
Colonial Secretary, Hon. K. M. Walmsley, C.M.G., O.B.E. 3,200
Attorney-General, Hon. K. G. L. Isaacs ... 2,850
Receiver-General, Hon. W. H. Sweeting, C.B.E. 2,850
President, Legislative Council, Hon. Sir George Roberts, C.B.E. 520
Speaker, House of Assembly, Hon. R. H. Symonette 650
Chairman, Civil Service Commission, J. G. MacKenzie, C.M.G. 3,425
Director of Education, T. P. Lightbody 2,680
Comptroller of Customs, E. H. McKinney, O.B.E. 2,680
Chief Medical Officer, E. H. Murcott, M.D. 2,680
Director of Public Works, R. G. Rae 2,680
Director of Telecommunications, R. E. Knowles 2,680
Director of Civil Aviation, H. H. Thompson 2,680
Crown Lands Officer, R. E. Sweetman 2,680
Chief Industrial Officer, M. Pounder 2,680
Parliamentary Registrar, M. J. Thompson .. £2,680
Postmaster, C. Saunders 2,550
Inspector of Imperial Lighthouses, Cdr. T. A. Pack-Beresford, R.N.

CAPITAL. ΨNassau. Estimated population (1962), 57,858. Nassau is distant from Liverpool 4,000 miles; transit, 8 to 14 days, *viâ* the Azores.

BARBADOS

(*See* WEST INDIES)

BASUTOLAND, BECHUANALAND PROTECTORATE AND SWAZILAND

H.M. High Commissioner for Basutoland, Bechuanaland Protectorate and Swaziland, Sir Hugh Stephenson, K.C.M.G., C.I.E., C.V.O., O.B.E. £7,000
Chief Secretary, C. R. Latimer, C.B.E. ... 3,600
Administrative Secretary, J. A. Steward, C.B.E. 2,970
Secretary of Finance, F. W. Essex, C.M.G. 2,970
Director of Audit, D. E. Bragg 2,760
Chief-Justice, Sir Peter Watkin-Williams 3,240
Attorney-General and Legal Adviser to the High Commissioner, C. B. O'Beirne, Q.C. 3,060

The Ambassador in South Africa for Her Majesty's Government in the United Kingdom holds office concurrently as Her Majesty's High Commissioner for Basutoland, the Bechuanaland Protectorate and Swaziland.

HIGH COMMISSION TERRITORIES

Trade with U.K.

	1961	1962
Imports from U.K.	£436,394	£271,583
Exports to U.K.	3,779,055	3,641,559

BASUTOLAND

(*The Territory of Basutoland*)

Basutoland is an enclave within the Republic of South Africa and is bounded north and west by the Orange Free State, east by Natal and East Griqualand, and south by the Cape Province, with an area of 11,716 square miles. The land, which is mountainous, rising to over 11,000 ft. in places, is held in trust for the Basotho by the Paramount Chief and is not made available for settlement. Sites are granted, however, for missions, schools, trading and commercial enterprises. The figures of the April, 1956 Census showed a population of 641,674 (638,857 Africans 1,926 Europeans, 247 Asiatics and 644 persons of mixed race).

The economy of the Territory is predominantly agrarian.

The livestock census for 1960 gave the following figures:—

Cattle, 331,203; horses, 83,910; mules, 5,022; donkeys, 48,564; sheep, 1,037,372; goats, 579,166.

During 1961, 7,356,026 lb. of wool were exported to the value of £804,656. The total quantity of mohair exported during 1961 was 1,226,125 lb. valued at £360,310.

Education.—In 1961 there were 1,074 primary schools and 21 secondary schools. The total enrolment of all schools was 144,600.

Communications.—There are no railways in Basutoland with the exception of 1 mile of the South African Railways which enters Basutoland at Maseru from the Orange Free State. A main road runs from Butha Buthe in Northern Basutoland to Quthing in the South. It connects all the Government Stations with the exception of Qacha's Nek and Mokhotlong. Qacha's Nek is accessible by road from Matatiele in East Griqualand and there is a jeep service up the Sani Pass to Mokhotlong. There are 28 air-strips in the

Territory, of which 5 are used by a regular internal air service, which carries mail and goods to and from otherwise inaccessible mountain regions. The remaining strips are used mainly by traders and Missions.

FINANCE

Basutoland is an extremely poor and unproductive country. The principal sources of revenue are customs and excise duty, taxes, and wool and mohair export duty.

Total estimated revenue for 1961-62 was £2,000,000, and expenditure £2,700,000, the difference being met by a grant from the U.K. Government. There is no direct trade between the Territory and the U.K.

GOVERNMENT

Basutoland is an African territory without white settlers or landowners. It has a British administration which functions in conjunction with a hereditary chieftainship. As a result of recent constitutional reforms there are now an Executive Council and a Legislative Council. At the head of the administration is the Resident Commissioner, who works under the direction of the High Commissioner for Basutoland, the Bechuanaland Protectorate and Swaziland, and who is also the British Ambassador to the Republic of South Africa. For administrative purposes the territory is divided into nine districts each with a District Commissioner who works in close co-operation with the Principal and Ward Chiefs. The local authority in each district is the District Council which has certain local powers. Its members are elected from a single roll for Basotho and non-Basotho British subjects and British protected persons. As a result of constitutional reforms, which came into operation in March, 1960, the territory has an Executive Council, which is the main policy making body, and a Legislative Council known as the *Basutoland National Council*. The Executive Council consists of the Resident Commissioner, who acts as Chairman, the Government Secretary, Financial Secretary, Legal Secretary, three persons chosen by the Basutoland National Council from among their own number, and one person nominated by the Paramount Chief. The Basutoland National Council consists of 80 members, divided equally between elected and non-elected members. The former are elected by District Councils sitting as electoral colleges for that purpose. The non-elected element is made up of three of the official members of the Executive Council (excluding the Chairman), the Commissioner for Local Government, the 22 Principal and Ward Chiefs, and 14 persons nominated by the Paramount Chief. The Basutoland National Council has power to legislate for all persons in Basutoland in respect of all matters, save the following, which are the High Commissioner's matters: External Affairs and Defence, Internal Security, Currency, Public Loans, Customs and Excise, Copyright, Posts and Telegraphs and the recruitment, etc., of officers to the Public Service. The Basutoland courts of law consist of: (*a*) The Court of Appeal, (*b*) The High Court, (*c*) the Subordinate Courts, including the Courts of Judicial Commissioners and (*d*) Basotho Courts. Appeals lie to the Privy Council by leave of the Chief Justice of the High Commission Territories who is also President of the Court of Appeal, and has jurisdiction in all cases, both civil and criminal, which arise in the Territory

Resident Commissioner, A. F. Giles, C.M.G., M.B.E. £3,600
Deputy Resident Commissioner and Government Secretary, G. M. Hector, C.B.E. 2,970
Finance Secretary, E. C. de Chazel 2,760
Chief Justice, Sir Peter Watkin-William... £3,240
Puisne Judge, I. V. Elyan.............. 2,970
Assistant Attorney-General, B. L. O'Leary, M.B.E. 2,760
Director of Audit, D. E. Bragg.......... 2,760
Director of Health, Dr. R. E. J. Clarke.... 2,760
Director of Livestock and Agricultural Services, D. D. Campbell, M.C. 2,760
Director of Public Works, M. S. Barnes.... 2,760
Director of Education, G. I. Michael....... 2,760

CAPITAL, Maseru, Pop., 9,000.

Maseru is distant from London 7,668 miles; transit, through the Cape, about 20 days and by air 3 days.

BECHUANALAND PROTECTORATE

The Bechuanaland Protectorate is bounded on the south and east by the Cape and Transvaal Provinces of the Union, on the north and north-east by Southern Rhodesia, the Zambesi and Chobe (Linyanti) Rivers, and on the west by South-West Africa. It is about 500 miles long and 550 miles broad, with a total area of about 222,000 square miles. The population at the census of 1956, was 320,665, of whom 3,173 were whites and the remainder Africans with a few Indians and coloured.

The climate is healthy during part of the year. Malarial fever is prevalent in some districts during February, March, and April, but with ordinary precautions is not seriously detrimental to health. The country is essentially pastoral, although sorghum, maize, beans, pumpkins and melons are sown. Cattle thrive, and numbered 1,271,838 on Dec. 31, 1960. The population is almost entirely a native one, the principal tribes being those of Linchwe (Bakgatla), of Kgari Sechele, O.B.E. (Bakwena), of Bathoen, C.B.E. (Bangwaketse), of Mokgosi (Bamalete), of Elizabeth Pulane Moremi, Regent during the minority of Letsholatebe Moremi (Batawana), of Kgosi Matala (Batlokwa) and of Kebalepile (Barolong). The chieftainship of the largest tribe, the Bamangwato, is in abeyance.

Schemes for improvements in agriculture, medical services, education and communications, and schemes for combating soil erosion, investigating mineral resources, improving water supplies, irrigation dams, tribal granaries and roads and for improving living conditions are being carried out.

In 1962, there were 214 primary schools with enrolment of 38,067 and 6 secondary schools with enrolment of 817.

The railway from Kimberley to Vryburg and Mafeking traverses the Protectorate on its way to the Rhodesias. There is a telegraph line from Cape Province through from Mafeking, *viâ* Gaberones and Francistown to Bulawayo and Salisbury. The chief European centres are Lobatsi, Gaberones, Francistown, and Serowe.

FINANCE AND TRADE

	1961-62	1962-63*
Revenue..........	£3,385,016	£3,191,301
Total expenditure....	3,407,646	3,191,301

*Estimated

Exports during 1960 totalled £2,716,219, of which animals and animal products accounted for £2,334,770. Imports were valued at £3,282,692.

TRADE WITH U.K.

See Basutoland.

GOVERNMENT

Orders in Council for a new Constitution were published at the end of 1960, providing for an Executive Council and for a Legislative Council with equal numbers of European and African unofficial members and one Asian elected member.

Resident Commissioner, R. P. Fawcus, C.M.G., O.B.E. £3,000
Deputy Resident Commissioner and Government Secretary, S. V. Lawrenson, C.B.E. 2,500
First Assistant Secretaries, J. A. Allison, O.B.E. (*Finance*); A. J. A. Douglas, O.B.E. (*Administration*) 2,200
Development Secretary, R. A. R. Bent, O.B.E. 2,200
Senior District Officers, A. N. W. Matthews; N. B. Rutherford, O.B.E. 2,200
Director of Medical Services, Dr. W. R. Gemmell 2,300
Director of Education, C. J. Hunter 2,300
Director of Public Works, W. O. Davies 2,300
Director of Agriculture, J. S. de Beer, M.B.E. 2,200
Director of Geological Survey, C. Boocock, M.B.E. 2,200
Commissioner of Police, Lt.-Col. J. T. A. Bailey, O.B.E. 2,200
Treasurer, A. J. Beeby, M.B.E. 2,200

The headquarters of the Protectorate Administration are at MAFEKING.

SWAZILAND

(*The Swaziland Protectorate*)

Swaziland is the smallest of the three High Commission Territories in Southern Africa. Geographically and climatically, it is divisible into four physiographic provinces; the broken mountainous Highveld of the west, adjacent to the Drakensburg, with altitudes averaging over 4,000 ft., the Middleveld which is mostly mixed farming country, about 2,000 ft. lower, and the Lowveld, a hot woodland region, bounded on the east by the Lubombo mountains, with an average altitude of 1,500 ft. The Lubombo mountains form the fourth physiographic province. Four rivers, the Komati, Usutu, Umbuluzi and Ingwavuma, flow from west to east, cutting their way through the Lubombo mountains to the Indian Ocean. The exploitation of these rivers is particularly important to the agricultural development of the middle and bush veld, where irrigation projects are giving the scenery a different aspect. The total area is 6,705 sq. miles and the estimated population figure in 1961 was 269,500 (260,000 Swazis, 7,500 Europeans and 2,000 Eurafricans).

Cotton, tobacco, citrus, sugar and rice are the main exported agricultural products. Two mills in the lowveld were constructed in 1959 and are capable of crushing 80,000 tons of raw sugar a year. The Usutu Pulp Company with an initial capital of £5,000,000 was formed in 1959 and a mill to exploit Usutu forests was completed in 1961. There are rich asbestos and iron deposits in the west and asbestos is still the most valuable export of the territory.

In 1961 there were 341 African schools (181 Government-maintained) with a total enrolment of 39,660 pupils; 12 European schools, 11 of which were Government-aided and one private, with 1,552 pupils; and 5 Eurafrican Government-aided schools had 672 pupils.

A contract for the construction of Swaziland's first railway has been signed. Work began in mid-1962. The railway, which is scheduled to be completed by the end of 1964, will be about 140 miles long, starting at Ngwenya, 13 miles north-west of Mbabane, and connecting at the Mozambique frontier with an extension to the existing line between Lourenço Marques and Goba. Principal export traffic on the railway will be the iron ore mined at Bomvu Ridge, near Ngwenya, by the Swaziland Iron Ore Development Company.

There is a daily South African Railway motor omnibus service between Breyten and Mbabane (89 miles); Mbabane and Manzini (27 miles); Manzini and Stegi (43 miles); Manzini and Balegane (42 miles); Manzini and Piet Retief (72 miles); Piet Retief and Hlatikulu (50 miles); Goedgegun and Hluti (33 miles) and Hluti and Gollel (26 miles). There are post offices and telegraph and telephone offices at all the chief centres.

FINANCE

	1961–62	1962–63
Revenue	£1,970 628	£2,554,770
Expenditure	2,077 628	2,554,317
Public debt (March 31, 1962)	1,401,000	...

GOVERNMENT

The High Commissioner has the power of making laws by proclamation for the Protectorate, where he is represented by a Resident Commissioner. Following a constitutional conference in March, 1963, at which no agreement was reached, the Colonial Secretary proposed, in May, an imposed constitution for Swaziland, whereby the country would be divided into 4 constituencies, each returning 3 members, one of whom must be white, 4 Europeans would be elected by their own community, and 8 Swazis would for the time being be nominated. There would be an Executive Council, with the Resident Commissioner in the chair, 3 *ex officio* members and 5 elected members. The President would be called Her Majesty's Commissioner for Swaziland. The High Commissioner would retain power to give directions.

Resident Commissioner, Sir Brian Marwick, K.B.E., C.M.G. £3,000
Deputy Resident Commissioner and Government Secretary, A. C. E. Long, M.B.E. 2,500
Treasurer, G. H. O'Farrell 2,200
Secretaries, H. J. Steward, O.B.E.; J. C. Martin, O.B.E.; M. J. Fairlie, O.B.E.; J. F. B. Purcell, O.B.E. 2,200
Senior District Officer, F. Fleck 2,200
Director of Medical Services, B. D. Whitworth, O.B.E. 2,300
Director of Land Utilization, J. M. G. King, C.M.G. 2,300
Director of Education, W. E. C. Pitcher, O.B.E. 2,300
Director of Public Works, P. St. C. Ballenden, O.B.E. 2,300
Commissioner of Police, Maj. P. C. Temple. 2,200
Director of Geological Survey and Mines, D. N. Davies, O.B.E. 2,300

Mbabane (European population, 1,092), the headquarters of the Administration, is situated on the hills at an altitude of 4,000 feet. There are townships in the districts at Manzini, formerly Bremersdorp (European population, 652), Hlatikulu, Stegi, Goedgegun, Emlembe, Pigg's Peak, Mankaiana and Mhlambamyati.

BERMUDA

The Bermudas, or Somers Islands, are a cluster of about 100 small islands (about 20 only of which are inhabited) situated in the west of the Atlantic Ocean, in 32° 15′ N. lat. and 64° 51′ W. long., the nearest point of the mainland being Cape Hatteras in North Carolina, about 570 miles distant. The total area is now approximately 20·59 sq. miles which includes 2·3 sq. miles leased to, or reclaimed by, the U.S. authorities between 1941 and 1957 under the terms of the 99 year lease. The civil population (1962) was 46,342 (16,803 white and 29,539 coloured and others). The colony derives its name from Juan Bermudez, a Spaniard, who sighted it before 1515, but no settlement was made until 1609 when Sir George Somers, who was shipwrecked here on his way to Virginia, colonized the islands.

Vegetation is prolific, the principal trees being the Bermuda cedar (juniper), formerly of great importance for shipbuilding, but since 1943 almost entirely destroyed by blight. At one time the islands enjoyed a flourishing export in onions, potatoes, and green vegetables, but the imposition of tariffs in U.S.A. made further growing for export unprofitable. The lily bud trade with Canada and U.S.A. and locally manufactured concentrates and pharmaceuticals are now the Colony's leading exports. Little food is produced except vegetables and fish, other foodstuffs being imported.

The Colony's economic structure is based on its importance as a tourist resort and as an air and naval base and from these sources most of its revenue is derived. It is now within two hours' air travel from New York, and in 1962, 3,407 arriving and departing aircraft carried a combined total of about 353,000 passengers. The island landing ground is used by B.O.A.C., Pan-American Airways, Trans-Canada, Eastern and Iberian air lines.

Education cost £729,128 in 1962. Free elementary education was introduced in May, 1949. In secondary schools, fees may reach £70 per annum, excluding books and stationery.

There is a broadcasting and television service, and overseas telephone and telegraph services are maintained. The use of motor cars was banned in the island from 1908 until 1946.

CAPITAL, ΨHamilton. Population (1960) 2,814.

FINANCE AND TRADE

	1961	1962
Public revenue	£5,148,022	£5,601,641
Public expenditure	5,115,759	5,691,315
Public debt, Dec. 31	108,000	14,400
Total imports	21,955,457	20,305,055
Total exports	9,534,387	9,385,369
Imports from U.K.	11,234,847	7,260,177
Exports to U.K.	431,509	394,542

GOVERNMENT

The Government is administered by a Governor, who is advised by an Executive Council of 9 members, appointed by the Crown. There is also a Legislative Council, composed of 11 members appointed by the Crown; and a representative House of Assembly consisting of 36 members who are elected every five years. Voters must be British subjects of twenty-five years of age or older at the time of registration, and if they do not possess Bermudian status, they must have been ordinarily resident in Bermuda for the whole of the period of three years immediately before registration. Registration is held every year during the months of February and March. Candidates for election must qualify as electors and must possess Bermudian status. Electors who own the freehold estate in land in Bermuda of an area of not less than 2,000 square feet qualify for an additional vote.

Governor and Commander-in-Chief, His Excellency Major-General Sir Julian Alvery Gascoigne, K.C.M.G., K.C.V.O., C.B., D.S.O. (1959) (*excluding allowances*) . . . £6,100
Chief Justice, M. J. Abbott . . . 4,500
Colonial Secretary, Hon. J. W. Sykes, C.M.G., C.V.O. . . . 4,400
Attorney-General, Hon. J. C. Summerfield, O.B.E., Q.C. . . . 4,000
Colonial Treasurer, Hon. W. W. Davidson, C.B.E. . . . £4,200
Speaker of the House of Assembly, Hon. Sir John Cox, C.B.E. (*in lieu of fees*) . . . 450
Assistant Judge, Hon. Sir Allan Smith, M.C. Fees
Director of Education, D. J. Williams . . . 2,900
Director of Health Services, S. M. Frazer . . . 2,900
Colonial Postmaster, W. A. Manuel, M.B.E. . . 2,730
Director of Works, C. H. Smith, O.B.E. . . . 3,045
Commissioner of Police, G. R. Robins, M.B.E. . . . 2,900
Colonial Auditor, C. W. Kempe . . . 2,500
Director of Agriculture, G. R. Groves, O.B.E. 2,600
Collector of Customs, R. L. Gauntlett . . . 2,205

NOTE.—A 25 per cent. non-pensionable bonus is at present added to the above salaries, except those of Chief Justice, Colonial Secretary, Attorney-General and Colonial Treasurer.

Hamilton, 2,970 nautical miles (3,420 statute miles); transit, 10 days.

BRITISH BORNEO

Borneo is a large island in the Eastern Archipelago, extending from lat. 7° 4′ N. to 4° 10′ S. and from long. 108° 50′ to 119° 20′ E. It is about 850 miles in length and 600 in breadth, and contains an area of 284,000 square miles, divided by the equatorial line into two nearly equal portions. The population is probably about 2,750,000. It is thought that the island was discovered by the Portuguese in 1521. About 202,000 sq. miles are included within Indonesia. Of the remainder of the island (the North Coast) approximately 50,000 sq. miles form the Colony of Sarawak and 30,000 sq. miles the Colony of North Borneo (including Labuan), all British.

NORTH BORNEO

The former State of North Borneo was governed by the British North Borneo (Chartered) Company, the last Chartered Company to administer an area of the British Empire, from 1882 to 1942, and became part of the new Crown Colony of North Borneo on July 15, 1946. North Borneo is to enter (as the State of Sabah) the new Federation of Malaysia, which was expected to be set up in the autumn of 1963, and would then cease to be a British colony.

North Borneo occupies the northern part of the island of Borneo, and has an area of 29,388 square miles with a coast-line of approximately 900 miles. The interior is mountainous. Mt. Kinabalu, sacred to the Dusuns Kadazans, is the highest mountain in the East Indies, rising to 13,455 feet. Most of the Colony is densely timbered. On the west coast there is a narrow coastal plain which supports the main agricultural and rubber production of the Colony.

The seventh census of the population was held on August 10, 1960. Since 1951, the year in which the last census was held, the total population of the Colony had increased by 36 per cent. from 334,141 to 454,421 and the native population by 26·1 per cent. from 243,009 to 306,498. The Chinese population had increased by 40·6 per cent. from 74,374 to 104,542. The number of Europeans, including Eurasians, had increased from 1,213 to 1,896. The native population comprises Dusuns Kadazans (mainly agricultural), Bajaus and Bruneis (fishing and agricultural), Muruts and Suluks and several smaller tribes. The main towns of the Colony are Sandakan (29,291) and Jesselton (21,497).

Climate.—North Borneo is favoured by a relatively cool climate for a place situated so near the Equator. The average mean temperature varies between a maximum of 88° and a minimum of 66° F. The annual rainfall varies from 60 to 180 inches according to locality

Communications.—The only railway is a metre gauge line running from Jesselton on the coast through Beaufort (57 miles) to Melalap in the interior, a distance of 96 miles, with a branch line from Beaufort to Weston (20 miles), which is shortly to be removed when the new road joining those towns is completed. There are 243 miles of bituminous surfaced roads, 221 miles of gravel surfaced road and 570 miles of earth roads. Work is proceeding on the construction of a road system to connect the main centres of population. The internal air services of North Borneo, Brunei and Sarawak are operated by Borneo Airways Ltd. using DC3 Twin Pioneer aircraft. Aerodromes are established at Jesselton, Labuan, Kudat, Keningau, Ranau, Sandakan, Lahad Datu and Tawau. Jesselton has a daily service in each direction with Singapore, Sarawak and Brunei, provided by Viscount and DC3 aircraft of Malayan Airways; and a twice weekly service in each direction with Hong Kong (one service *viâ* Manila) by Electric aircraft of Cathay Pacific Airways Ltd.

Production.—The main industries of the Colony are timber extraction and the cultivation of rubber (estimated at 187,500 acres), rice (86 800 acres), coconuts (78,800 acres), tobacco (1,800 acres) and Manila hemp (4,400 acres). The cultivation of cocoa and oil palms is increasing. Fishing gives employment to a large number of local natives and Chinese. About four-fifths of the territory is still heavily timbered with many valuable species of hardwoods and soft hardwoods, of which the more important are seraya (Borneo cedar) and camphor.

Trade.—North Borneo is primarily a producer of raw materials, the principal exports of which, during 1962, were: timber, valued at £14,247,374; rubber, valued at £4,282,380; and copra, valued at £2,158,693, with exports of hemp and tobacco being of lesser importance. Imports consist mainly of tobacco manufactures, petroleum products, foodstuffs (of which the largest single item is rice), textiles and clothing, machinery, metal manufactures and building materials.

FINANCE	1962 Revised estimates
Revenue—	
Ordinary	$80.336 236
Special	28.573 606*
	$108,909,842
Expenditure—	
Ordinary	$78 262.814
Development	25 026 548†
	$103.289 362

* Includes $20.004.172 contribution to Development account from Ordinary Budget.

† Includes $5.805,934 on Colonial Development and Welfare Schemes.

TRADE		1962
Imports		$27.874 556
Exports		27 389 633
	1961	1962
Imports from U.K.	£3,138,178	£2,829,874
Exports to U.K.	2,045,108	1,212,847

Governor and Commander-in-Chief, His Excellency Sir William Allmond Codrington Goode, G.C.M.G. (1960) (*and duty allce.* £2,500) ... £4,500
Chief Secretary, R. N. Turner, C.M.G. ... 3,178
Financial Secretary, H. W. Davidson, C.M.G., M.B.E. ... 2,856
Deputy Financial Secretary, M. V. Saville ... £2,422
Secretary for Local Government, J. H. Macartney ... 2,856
Under Secretary, A. M. Grier, C.M.G. ... 2,618
Residents, W. K. C. Wookey; E. J. K. Wicksteed (£2,618); W. S. Holley; G. R. Hedley; P. G. Edge ... each 2,422
Chief Justice of Sarawak, North Borneo and Brunei, Sir Campbell Wylie, E.D. ... 3,388
Attorney-General, W. K. H. Jones ... 2,856
Commissioner of Labour and Welfare, J. P. Rutherford (*acting*) ... 2,618
Conservator of Forests, G. L. Carson ... 2,618
Director of Agriculture, E. J. H. Berwick ... 2,618
Director of Medical Services, Dr. L. J. Clapham, C.B.E. ... 2,613
Director of Public Works, L. Jackson ... 2,618
Director of Education, G. D. Muir ... 2,618
Director of Posts and Telegraphs, C. J. Fenton, O.B.E. ... 2,422
Director of Civil Aviation (*British Borneo Territories*), R. L. Milton ... 2,422
Commissioner of Police, D. Matheson ... 2,422
Accountant-General, H. V. I. Jones ... 2,422
Director of Audit, P. P. Wise, O.B.E. ... 2,422
Director of Lands and Surveys, B. A. Reeves 2,422
General Manager, Railway, A. F. Lucarrotti, D.F.C., T.D. ... 2,422
Commissioner of Trade and Customs, R. Knowles, O.B.E. ... 2,422
Commissioner of Inland Revenue, A. R. Wilkey, M.B.E., T.D. ... 2,422
Director of Geological Survey, British Territories in Borneo, Dr. F. H. Fitch ... 2,422
British Council Representative, R. B. Lodge, Gaya Street, Jesselton.

Headquarters of the Government, Jesselton (population 21,497).

BRUNEI

Sultan, H. H. Sir Omar Ali Saifuddin Wasa'dul Khairi Waddin, K.C.M.G., *acceded* 1950.

High Commissioner, A. MacK. MacKintosh, C.M.G.

Brunei is a British Protected State on the north-west coast of the island of Borneo, total area about 2,226 sq. miles, population (1960 census figure) 83,877 of whom 59,203 were of Malay or other indigenous race and 21,795 Chinese. The chief town, Brunei, with its rural area, has a population of about 37,000. The country has a humid tropical climate.

On September 29, 1959, His Highness the Sultan of Brunei promulgated the first written constitution. The Constitution provides for a Privy Council, an Executive Council, and a Legislative Council. The post of British Resident has been abolished, and there is instead a *Mentri Besar* (Chief Minister) appointed by the Sultan and responsible to him for the exercise of executive authority. The Sultan presides over the Privy Council and the Executive Council, and the Chief Minister over the Legislative Council. Under a new agreement concluded between Her Majesty The Queen and His Highness the Sultan, the United Kingdom Government continues to be responsible for defence and external affairs. The agreement provides for a High Commissioner to advise the Sultan on such matters.

FINANCE	1962
Revenue	$109.879,467
Expenditure	47,017,590

BRITISH GUIANA

Area and Population.—British Guiana, which includes the Counties of Demerara, Essequibo, and

Berbice, is situated on the north-east coast of South America and has a total area of 83,000 square miles with a seaboard of more than 500 miles. The population at December 31, 1962, was estimated at 602,660. There are about 27,520 aboriginal Indians. The colony is bounded on the south by Brazil, on the east by Surinam, on the west by Venezuela, and on the north and N.E. by the Atlantic. The coastland is very like the Netherlands, below the level of the sea, and intersected with canals constructed by its former Dutch owners. At the junction of the British Guiana-Venezuela-Brazil boundaries is Mt. Roraima, a flat topped mountain 9,000 feet above sea-level. There are many beautiful waterfalls in British Guiana: on the Potaro River (a tributary of the Essequibo) is the *Kaieteur Fall*, with a clear drop of 741 feet and a total fall of 822 feet, and on the Essequibo, the *Horse Shoe Falls* (discovered in 1934); a fall, with a drop of some 500 feet discovered in 1934 on the Ipobe River, a tributary of the Kuribrong, has been named the *Marina Fall* and other falls were discovered in 1938 on the Kamarang River, 80 miles north-east of Mt. Roraima. The seasons are divided into dry and wet, the two dry seasons lasting from the middle of February to the end of April, and from the middle of August to the end of November. The climate on the coast, for the greater part of the year, is pleasant and healthy. In the Aug.-Oct. period it is hot. The mean temperature is 80·3°, its extremes during 86 years ranging between 68° and 96°, but these are very rare, the usual extremes being 70° and 90°. In the interior the mean temperature is higher—82·6°, its extremes ranging from 66° to 103°. The yearly rainfall is subject to marked variation, its mean on the coast lands averaging about 90 inches with an average of 58 inches on the savannahs. The daily average sunshine is a little over 6 hours and, except when rain is falling, dull and cloudy weather is rarely experienced.

Production, etc.—Much of the country is forest. The cultivated portion (about 280,000 acres, of which 86,700 are under sugar-cane and 179,200 in rice) is largely confined to the narrow coastal alluvial belt. There are extensive deposits of gold, diamonds, manganese, bauxite and mica.

Communications.—There were 9,066 telephones in use in 1961; 275 sub-exchanges, call offices and private branch exchanges are in operation. 36 land-line telegraph stations are maintained at coastal post offices and 4 wireless telegraph stations in the interior, providing communications with the coast. In Georgetown, a central radio station provides radio-telephone communication with 4 branch offices, 9 stations operated by other Government departments, 39 by private concerns, and 8 coastal ships and launches. Overseas radio and telephone services are provided by Cable and Wireless (W.I.) Ltd., in association with the Post Office telephone system. There are 137 post offices and postal agencies. There are two broadcasting stations, which are operated on a commercial basis by private enterprise. There are 95 miles of railway, and the British Guiana Airways (a government company) provides internal air-services.

Education.—On August 31, 1961, there were 337 Government-owned and Government-aided primary schools in the colony; 346 of these had an enrolment of 129,373 pupils. The 3 Government-owned and 12 of the 14 Government-aided secondary schools had an enrolment of 7,220 students, while there were about 30 private secondary schools with an estimated 3,500 students. At the Government Training College and the 3 vocational schools there were 150 and 588 full-time students respectively.

Finance and Trade

	1960	1961
Public revenue.....	$56,197,587	$59,670,271
Public expenditure..	50,691,393	56,127,398
Public debt (Dec. 31)	5,764,804	5,179,054
Total imports......	147,598,723	146,549,911
Total exports.......	127,003,450	147,653,950

Trade with U.K.

	1961	1962
Imports............	£10,477,396	£8,640,817
Exports............	6,852,644	6,483,430

The leading exports are sugar ($56,846,260 in 1961), rum, molasses, diamonds, gold, timber, balata, bauxite and rice.

Government

The constitution of British Guiana, which came into effect on July 18, 1961, provides for a bicameral legislature—a Legislative Assembly of 35 members, elected by universal adult suffrage, and a nominated Senate of 13 members, eight appointed on the advice of the Premier, three after consultation with such persons as can speak for the differing political views of opposition groups in the Assembly, and two by the Governor in his discretion. The life of the Legislative Assembly is four years unless dissolved before this time. The Legislative Assembly is presided over by a Speaker, who may or may not be a member of the assembly. The senate is presided over by a President, chosen by members from amongst their own number. The Senate has delaying powers only. The executive body, called the Council of Ministers, consists of ten, presided over by the Premier, one of whom is the Attorney-General.

The Premier is the member of the Legislative Assembly who, in the judgment of the Governor, is best able to command the confidence of a majority of the members of that Chamber. At least one and not more than three members of the Council must be members of the Senate. The Council of Ministers is responsible to the Legislative Assembly.

The Governor must exercise all his powers in accordance with the advice of the Council of Ministers except where otherwise expressly stated (the notable exceptions are in respect of defence and external affairs).

Governor, His Excellency Sir Ralph Francis Alnwick Grey, K.C.M.G., K.C.V.O., O.B.E. (1959)...............(+ £2,000 *allces.*) £7,000

Ministry

Dr. C. B. Jagan (*Prime Minister and Development and Planning*); Ranji Chaudi Singh (*Labour, Health and Housing*); R. Ramkarran (*Works and Hydraulics*); Mrs. J. Jagan (*Home Affairs*); B. Benn (*Natural Resources*); J. Hubbard (*Trade and Industry*); Dr. C. Jacob (*Finance*); C. V. Nunes (*Education and Social Development*); Dr. F. Ramsahoye (*Attorney-General*); E. M. G. Wilson (*Communications*).

Chief Justice, Sir Joseph Luckhoo........ £2,500

Puisne Judges, W. A. Date; R. S. Miller; H. B. S. Bollers; H. A. Fraser; G. Persand; B. O. Adams (*acting*); A. Khan (*acting*); A. Chung (*acting*)........... 2,000

British Council Representative (*Georgetown*), W. E. Roach.

Capital. ΨGeorgetown, Population (1960 census), 72,991. ΨNew Amsterdam has a population (1960) of 14,046.

Georgetown is 16–21 days distant from London by sea, and 3 days by air *viâ* New York or Brazil.

BRITISH HONDURAS

British Honduras, in Central America, lies within 18° 29′ 50″ to 15° 53′ 12″ N. latitude and 89° 13′ 28′ to 88° 05′ 11″ W. longitude. Its extreme length and breadth are approximately 186 m. and 64 m. respectively; it is bounded on the north and north-west by Mexico (Quintana Roo Province, formerly Yucatan); on the west and south by Guatemala; and on the east by the Caribbean Sea. The total area (including offshore islands) is about 8,867 sq. miles, with a population (Census 1960) of 90,343 (44,586 males and 45,757 females). The climate generally is damp and hot, but not unhealthy. The temperature ranges from 59° to 92° F. The average lies between 75° and 80°, but this is considerably tempered by the prevailing sea-breezes.

The greater part of the country is covered by forest, of which 72 per cent. is high rain forest, 15·5 pine forest and dry savannah, 5·5 wet savannah and mangrove forest, the remaining 7 per cent. being existing or recently abandoned cultivation. The wire grass and sedges of the dry savannahs make very poor pasturage for cattle. The north of the territory and the southern coastal plain (8 to 20 miles wide) is nearly flat, and near the sea is low and swampy. The central mountain mass has a general altitude of 2,000 to 3,000 feet and 20 per cent. of the area of the territory is over 1,000 feet in elevation above mean sea-level.

The staple products are obtained from the forests, and include mahogany, cedar, and *chicle* (the basis of chewing-gum). Agricultural crops which grow readily include sugar cane, coconuts, citrus fruit, plantains, pineapples, mangoes, maize, rice, varieties of beans and peas. Bananas also grow well in certain localities. All varieties of citrus fruits flourish, and in particular grape-fruit, of which a very high grade is exported.

In 1962 there were 131 Government and grant-aided and 27 private elementary schools in the country, the total enrolment being 22,768. There are also 14 secondary schools with a total enrolment of 1,864 students.

There are 34 post offices, dealing in 1962 with 2,105,820 articles of mail. There is a radio-telegraph station for external communications at Belize. Air services are scheduled twice weekly to and from the capitals of Panama, Honduras, Mexico, Salvador, Guatemala, Nicaragua and Costa Rica. A weekly service exists from and to the capitals of the West Indian islands *viâ* Jamaica. There is a four times weekly service from and to New Orleans and a twice weekly service from and to Miami. A local scheduled air service links five of the six districts into which the country is divided.

CAPITAL, ΨBelize. Population (1960 Census) 32,867 (Belize District, 40,084); other towns ΨCorozal (9,730), El Cayo (11,764), ΨStann Creek (10,906), Orange Walk (10,306), Toledo (7,553).

FINANCE AND TRADE

	1961	1962
Public revenue	$10,328,302	$8,730 945
Public expenditure	9,579,271	8,730,945

TRADE WITH U.K.	1961	1962
Imports from U.K.	£1,554,466	£2,040,812
Exports (domestic) to U.K.	2,238,613	1,050,561

GOVERNMENT

The Constitution of 1960 provides for a Legislative Assembly of 25 members, 18 of whom are elected, 5 nominated and 2 *ex officio* members. The Assembly elects its Speaker and provision is made for the appointment of a First Minister. The life of the Assembly is 4 years, but the Governor has power to prorogue or dissolve it by proclamation. Certain other powers are reserved to the Governor. A full ministerial system has been introduced and portfolios allotted by the Governor, on the advice of the First Minister.

Governor and Commander-in-Chief, His Excellency Sir Peter Hyla Gawne Stallard, K.C.M.G., C.V.O., M.B.E. (1961) $12,000
Chief Justice, Sir Clifford Inniss 8,800
Colonial Secretary, M. S. Porcher, C.M.G., O.B.E. 8,600
Speaker of the Legislative Assembly, W. H. Courtenay, O.B.E. 2,400
First Minister and Minister of Finance and Development, G. C. Price 6,600
Minister of Public Works, Power and Communications, A. E. Cattouse 6,000
Minister of Natural Resources, Commerce, Industry and Tourism, A. A. Hunter 6,000
Minister of Labour, Prisons and Cinemas, C. L. B. Rogers 6,000
Minister of Local Government, Social Welfare and Co-operatives, L. S. Sylvestre 6,000
Minister of Education, Health, Housing, Information and Broadcasting, J. W. Macmillan, O.B.E. 6,000

British Council Representative, J. M. Miller, M.B.E.

Belize is distant from London about 4,700 miles; transit, 17 days by sea, 2 to 4 days by air.

THE BRITISH VIRGIN ISLANDS

The Virgin Islands are a group of islands at the eastern extremity of the Greater Antilles, divided between Great Britain and the U.S.A. Those of the group which are British number about 42, of which 11 are inhabited, and have a total area of about 59 square miles. The principal are Tortola, the largest (situate in 18° 27′ N. lat. and 64° 40′ W. long.), Virgin Gorda, Anegada and Jost Van Dykes. The population is 7,338 (1961). Communication is by daily launch service to St. Thomas; also an external telephone service linking Tortola with St Thomas and Puerto Rico by which messages may be sent to all parts of the world, and one linking Tortola with Antigua. An airfield on Beef Island is used by small planes. The principal exports are livestock, fish, charcoal, vegetables and fruit, for which the principal market is St. Thomas. Rum is distilled on a small scale.

Finance and Trade

	1960	1961
Revenue	£260 062	£277,843
Expenditure	276,036	355,606
Imports	305,927	473,240
Exports	65,142	87,897

Government

The administration is headed by an Administrator assisted by an Executive Council, two members of which are chosen by the unofficial members of the Legislative Council. The Legislature consists of the Administrator, as President, four nominated members (two being unofficials) and six elected members.

Administrator, His Honour M. S. Staveley, C.B.E. .... (+*allce.*) £2,150
Crown Attorney, O. M. Browne 1,200
Superintendent of Medical Services, M. M. Parker 900
Treasurer and Postmaster, D. S. Mordecai ... 900–960

Superintendent of Agriculture, J. L. M. Winter, M.B.E. £900–960

Administrative Secretary, N. E. A. Harrigan, M.B.E. 900–960

Superintendent of Public Works, C. W. D. Taylor 900–960

CAPITAL. ΨRoad Town (on the south-east of Tortola). Population, about 900.

FALKLAND ISLANDS

These, the only considerable group in the South Atlantic, lie about 300 miles east of the Straits of Magellan, between 52° 15′–53° S. lat. and 57° 40′–62° W. long. They consist of East Falkland (area 2,610 sq. miles), West Falkland (2,090 sq. miles) and upwards of 100 small islands in the aggregate, the total population at the census of 1962 being 2,172. Mount Usborne, the loftiest peak, rises 2,312 feet above the level of the sea. The Falklands were discovered by Davis in 1592, and visited by Hawkins in 1594. A settlement was made by France in 1764; this was subsequently sold to Spain, but the latter country recognized Great Britain's title to a part at least of the group in 1771. The settlement was destroyed by the Americans in 1831. In 1833 occupation was resumed by the British for the protection of the seal-fisheries, and the islands were permanently colonized as the most southerly organized colony of the British Empire. The climate is cool, the thermometer ranging in winter from 20° to 50°, and in summer from 46° to 70° Fahrenheit; it is notably windy. The islands are chiefly moorland. The population is almost totally British, and is principally engaged in sheep-farming, to which practically all the land in the colony is devoted, 618,561 sheep being carried in 1962. Wool, hides and sheepskins are exported. The only important settlement is Stanley, on the coast of East Falkland.

FINANCE AND TRADE

	1960–61	1961–62
Public revenue........	£266,586	£275,982
Expenditure..........	275,172	320,613
	1961	1962
Total imports........	£467,655	£412,549
Total exports	984,457	940,433

Trade with U.K., *see* below

GOVERNMENT

The Governor is assisted by a Legislative Council of 11 members, with the Governor as Chairman, 3 *ex officio* (Colonial Secretary, Senior Medical Officer and Colonial Treasurer), 2 official and 2 non-official members (nominated by the Governor) and 4 representatives elected by the people.

Governor and Commander-in-Chief, His Excellency Sir Edwin Porter Arrowsmith, K.C.M.G. (1957) ..... (+*duty allce.* £550) £2,800

Colonial Secretary, R. H. D. Manders, O.B.E. 2,000

Senior Medical Officer, R. S. Slessor, O.B.E. 1,950

Colonial Treasurer, L. C. Gleadell........ 1,680

CHIEF TOWN, ΨStanley. Estimated population 1,074.

DEPENDENCIES.—*South Georgia*, an island 800 miles east-south-east of the Falkland Group, with an area of 1,450 square miles. An Administrative Officer and other officials reside there. The South Sandwich Islands group, which is uninhabited and lies some 470 miles S.E. of South Georgia, is the only other dependency. No whaling companies operated during the 1962–63 season. 6,500 tons of whale and seal oil were exported in 1962.

A chain of meteorological stations is maintained in the Dependencies.

Trade of the Dependencies

	1961	1962
Total imports......	£1,071,801	£687,000
Total exports.........	2,234,355	593,237

Ψ Stanley, the capital of the Falkland Islands, is distant from England about 8,103 miles; transit by steamer *viâ* Montevideo. Telegrams by wireless U.K. direct. The journey from U.K. to Falkland Isles can be accomplished in 5 days travelling to Montevideo by air and thence by local steamer to the Falklands.

British Antarctic Territory

Those territories south of latitude 60° S. which were formerly part of the Falkland Islands Dependencies were constituted a separate Colony on March 3, 1962. The principal units of the new Colony are the South Shetlands, the South Orkneys and Graham's Land (a peninsula of the Antarctic Continent) and that part of the Antarctic Continent lying between 20° W. and 80° W. long. The climate is inhospitable and the territory is covered with snow and ice and almost destitute of plant life. A chain of meteorological scientific and survey stations is maintained in the territory.

High Commissioner, His Excellency Sir Edwin Porter Arrowsmith, K.C.M.G. (1962).

Falkland Islds. and Dependencies

TRADE WITH U.K.

	1961	1962
Imports from U.K....	£551,723	£434,563
Exports to U.K.......	2,181,648	1,440,068

FIJI

This is a group of 322 islands (of which only 106 are inhabited) in the South Pacific Ocean, about 1,100 miles north of New Zealand. The gross area of the group, which extends 300 miles from east to west, and 300 north to south, between 15′ 45′—21° 10′ S. lat. and 176° E.—178° W. long. is 7,083 square miles. Many of the islands are of volcanic origin, with lofty mountains, and well wooded. The principal are Viti Levu, Vanua Levu, Taveuni and Kandavu. The climate is oceanic. Shade temperatures seldom rise above 93°F. or fall below 60° except in the mountains. On the windward sides of the larger islands rainfall is copious and vegetation luxuriant; on the leeward (or dry) sides the vegetation is sparse and scattered. The chief products are coconuts, sugar cane, gold, rice, bananas, pineapples, yams, and dalo or taro (colocasia).

The population (estimated 1962) was 427,851 (212,829 Indians, 177,770 Fijians, 9,226 part Europeans, 10,553 Europeans, 12,296 other Pacific races, 5,177 Chinese and 91 others).

FINANCE

	1961	1962
Public income........	£F7,445,265	£F8,069,923
Public expenditure....	7,413,694	8,110,910
Public debt (Dec. 31)..	6,756,808	6,846,143

TRADE

	1961	1962
Total imports	£F17,228,039	£F17,358,318
Total exports.	13,126,662	15,596,090
Imports from U.K....	£3,505,406	£3,908,634
Exports to U.K.......	3,717,279	3,316,419

Fijian currency—£111 Fiji=£100 sterling.

The principal exports are sugar, coconut oil, gold, copra, bananas, biscuits, trocas shell and manganese ore. The chief imports are drapery, machinery, motor vehicles, petroleum products, timber, foodstuffs and electrical goods. The tourist industry is growing.

Government

The Governor is appointed by the Crown, and is assisted by an Executive Council. Laws are passed by a Legislative Council (of which the Governor is president) containing 19 official members, 6 European members (4 elected, 2 nominated), 6 Fijian members (4 elected, 2 nominated by the Council of Chiefs), 6 Indian members (4 elected and 2 nominated), and a Speaker (H. M. Scott, C.B.E., D.F.C.).

The executive officer for the native administration is the Secretary for Fijian Affairs, who is responsible to the Governor and, in appropriate matters, to the Legislative Council. The controlling financial authority is the Fijian Affairs Board whose members are the Secretary for Fijian Affairs (Chairman), the six Fijian members of Legislative Council, a legal adviser, and a financial adviser. The Board has power to make regulations affecting the Fijians, but such regulations are subject to approval by the Legislative Council.

Governor of Fiji, His Excellency Francis Derek Jakeway, C.M.G., O.B.E., *apptd.* 1963 (+*duty allowance* £1,750)	£5,000
Chief Justice (vacant)	3,400
Colonial Secretary, P. D. Macdonald, C.M.G., C.V.O. (+*duty allowance* £150)	3,300
Secretary for Fijian Affairs, A. C. Reid, C.M.G.	2,900
Attorney-General, J. Lewis	3,000
Financial Secretary, H. P. Ritchie	3,000
Assistant Colonial Secretary, K. R. Bain	2,500
Controller of Organization and Establishments, J. B. Claydon (*acting*)	2,500
Director of Lands, Mines and Surveys, D. T. Lloyd	2,800
Director of Public Works, J. H. Common, O.B.E.	2,800
Commissioner of Police, R. H. T. Beaumont, M.V.O.	2,800
Director of Agriculture, J. A. Sandys	2,800
Director of Medical Services (+£650 *as Inspector-General, South Pacific Health Services*), Dr. C. H. Gurd, O.B.E.	2,900
Conservator of Forests, J. R. B. Angus	2,500
Comptroller of Customs, E. T. J. Mabbs	2,500
Director of Education, J. G. Rodger	2,800
Postmaster-General, W. G. J. Cruickshank	2,500
Director of Audit, K. A. W. Johnson	2,500
Accountant-General, J. F. Griffiths	2,500
Registrar-General, B. L. Gregg	2,500
Commissioner of Inland Revenue, D. J. Barnes	2,500
Commissioner of Labour, J. Amputch, M.B.E.	2,500
Government Printer, R. L. Gribble	1,900
Supt. of Prisons, B. M. Sellers, M.B.E.	1,900
Public Relations Officer, E. J. F. Hackett	1,900
Commerce and Industries Officer, R. W. Parkinson	2,100
Government Storekeeper, R. H. Baines	2,100
Registrar of Co-operative Societies, F. M. Warner, M.B.E.	2,100
Puisne Judge, C. J. Hammett	2,900
Deputy Financial Secretary, R. M. Major	2,500
British Council Representative, Suva, J. T. Harrison.	

CAPITAL. Ψ Suva, in the island of Viti Levu. Population (1958), 37,371.

Suva is 11,000 miles from London; transit from London, *viâ* Auckland, about 30 days; *viâ* Vancouver or San Francisco, about 30 days; *viâ* Panama, about 30 days; by air, *viâ* Canada, U.S.A., or Sydney, about 4 days. Fiji is on the main air route between North America and Australia and New Zealand. It is a base for South Pacific regional air services, covering New Zealand, Western Samoa, New Caledonia, Tahiti, Cook and Norfolk Islands.

GAMBIA

The West African river Gambia, which is navigable for some 300 miles from its mouth, was discovered by the Portuguese in 1447; and in 1588, the year of the Spanish Armada, Queen Elizabeth I. being then at war with Spain and Portugal, gave a charter to a British Company to trade with the Gambia, and as early as 1618 an effort to do so was made, but it was not successful. In 1686 a fort was built upon a rocky island, and, in honour of the new King, was named Fort James; but the English merchants had formidable rivals in the Portuguese and French, and it was not until 1783 that the river was recognized, by the *Treaty of Versailles*, as British. The Colony had no regular political institutions until 1807, when it was put under the Government of Sierra Leone. The Colony of the Gambia was created in 1843, and was constituted a separate government in 1888. It now consists of a narrow strip of land, estimated at 4,003 sq. miles, lying on both sides of the River Gambia to a distance of about 350 miles, mainly between 13° 15′–13° 45′ N. and 13° 45′–13° 65′ W. The river is navigable to ocean-going vessels for 150 miles and to river steamers up to 300 miles from its mouth. The capital, Bathurst, is situated on the island of St. Mary at the mouth of the River and, together with a small adjoining district and some outlying areas, constitutes the "Colony". The remainder of Gambia constitutes the "Protectorate". The latter is, in future, to be known as the provinces. The total population of the territory is about 316,000. The climate of Bathurst is extremely pleasant except during the rainy season from June to October, when it sometimes becomes uncomfortably warm. Conditions in the country generally are healthy. The rainfall varies between 30 and 60 inches a year.

Communications.—Bathurst is 2,600 miles from London; the mail boat from Liverpool takes seven days. There is one direct air service weekly *viâ* Las Palmas and three weekly, changing at Dakar. Ocean-going vessels entering the ports in 1962 totalled 181 (tonnage 532,289). Civil aviation movements at the international aerodrome of Yundum near Bathurst numbered 1,133. Internal communication is by road and river. There are some 845 miles of motor road, including about 70 miles of bituminous surface road communicating between Bathurst and areas on South Bank. There are eight Government wireless stations and a V.H.F. telephone service linking Bathurst with the principal towns in the provinces. In 1962 a broadcasting service was started.

Education.—There are 67 primary schools (50 Government and 17 Mission), 8 post-primary schools or departments, and 5 secondary schools, three of which are recognized for School Certificate Examination. The total school enrolment in 1962 was 12,193 pupils, including 3,300 girls. The technical trade school in Bathurst offers courses in carpentry and metal work. Yundum College provides training for teachers.

Production.—Most of the population is engaged in agriculture, the chief product being ground-nut which is the single important cash crop. Other crops are rice, millet and various kinds of fruit and vegetables. Fishing and livestock production are considerable. No minerals are at present being exploited and there are practically no manufactures other than ground-nut processing.

FINANCE

	1962 (Revised Estimate)	1963 (Budget)
Recurrent revenue....	£1,737,963	£1,926,570
Recurrent expenditure.	2,313,383	2,517,151
Development expenditure...............	957,583	1,031,129
Public debt (actual) ...	238,760	200,000

For 1963 the recurrent revenue is supplemented by grant-in-aid from the United Kingdom Treasury.

TRADE

	1961	1962
Total imports........	£4,572,466	£4,481,054
Total exports........	3 232,350	3,568 670
Imports from U.K....	1,837 511	1,548 567
Exports to U.K.......	1,091,010	1,286 193

The chief export is decorticated ground-nuts, which account for over 90 per cent. of total exports, the main markets being Italy and United Kingdom. Other exports are palm kernels, dried fish and hides. Foodstuff imports include rice, sugar, flour and kola nuts. Manufactured goods of all kinds are imported, the chief being textiles and apparel, vehicles, machinery, metal goods and petroleum products.

CHIEF TOWN, Ψ Bathurst. Population, 28,000.

GOVERNMENT

The Gambia has a representative Government with a Speaker, Deputy Speaker and 32 elected members: 7 from the Colony and 25 from the Protectorate. In addition, there are 4 Chiefs elected to the House of Representatives by the Chiefs in Assembly and 2 members nominated by the Governor, who are without votes. The Governor is President of the Executive Council, which is composed of the Premier and 8 Ministers drawn from the Legislature. It was announced in July, 1963, that Gambia would become fully self-governing as soon as the necessary procedures were completed.

Governor and Commander-in-Chief, His Excellency Sir John Warburton Paul, K.C.M.G., O.B.E., M.C. (1962)........... £4,100
Deputy Governor, P. A. Gore, C.V.O....... 3,000
Chief Justice, J. A. L. Wiseham.......... 2,800
Attorney-General, H. S. S. Few, Q.C....... 2,650

MINISTERS

D. K. Jawara (*Premier*); S. S. Sisay (*Finance*); S. M. Dibba (*Local Government and Lands*); P. L. Baldeh (*Education*); Musa Dabo (*Agriculture*); A. B. N'Jie, M.B.E. (*Works and Services*); J. L. B. Daffeh (*Health*); Seyfu O. M. M'Baki (*Communications*); Y. S. Samba (*Labour and Social Welfare*).

British Council Representative, Bathurst, E. B. Evans.

LONDON OFFICE

Gayfere House, Great Peter Street, S.W.1.

GIBRALTAR,

a rocky promontory, 3¾ miles in length, ¾ of a mile in breadth and 1,396 feet high at its greatest elevation near the southern extremity of Spain, with which it is connected by a low isthmus. It is about 14 miles distant from the opposite coast of Africa. The population at the census of Oct. 1961 was 24,502.

Ψ Gibraltar is a naval base of vital strategic importance to Great Britain. It was captured in 1704, during the war of the Spanish Succession, by a combined Dutch and English force, under Sir George Rooke, and was ceded to Great Britain by the Treaty of Utrecht, 1713. Several attempts have been made to retake it, the most celebrated being the great siege in 1779–83, when General Elliot, afterwards Lord Heathfield, held it for 3 years and 7 months against a combined French and Spanish force. The town stands at the foot of the promontory on the W. side. Gibraltar is a free port, and enjoys the advantages of an extensive shipping trade. It is a popular tourist centre. The chief sources of revenue are the port dues, the rent of the Crown estate in the town, and duties on wine, spirits, tobacco, beer, motor spirit, perfumery, coffee, fuel oil, motor vehicles, radios, cameras and cinematograph projectors, mechanical lighters, razor blades, watches and clocks.

The Department of Education runs 8 secondary schools and 16 primary and infant schools. There are also 3 private infant schools. Teacher training and University Scholarships have been provided, 4,550 pupils are at present in Government schools, and the Government expenditure on education in 1962 was £171,270.

FINANCE AND TRADE

	1961	1962
Revenue.............	£2,144,962	£2,096,585
Expenditure..........	2,134,460	2,086,294
Imports from U.K.....	4,719,034	4,390,943

GOVERNMENT

Under the Constitution promulgated in 1950 and amended in July, 1956, the Governor is assisted by a Legislative Council and an Executive Council. The Governor is the President of the Legislative Council, which has 3 *ex officio* members, 7 elected and 2 nominated members (of whom both may, and one must, be unofficial). An independent Speaker for the Legislative Council was appointed on May 24, 1958, and normally presides over sittings of the Council.

Governor and Commander-in-Chief, His Excellency General Sir Dudley Ward, G.C.B., K.B.E., D.S.O. (1962) (*including £750 entertainment allowance and £500 from Army funds*) £6,250
Flag Officer, Gibraltar, and Admiral Supt., H.M. Dockyard, Gibraltar, Rear Admiral E. N. Sinclair, D.S.C.
Deputy Fortress Commander and O.C. Troops, Brigadier H. E. Boulter, D.S.O.

Chief Justice, Sir Hubert Flaxman, C.M.G... £2,600
Speaker, Sir Joseph Patron, O.B.E., M.C....
Chief Secretary, J. D. Bates, C.M.G., C.V.O. 2,600
Chief Asst. Sec., J. J. Clinton, M.B.E...... 1,750
Financial Secretary, C. J. Gomez, O.B.E.... 2,200
Accountant General, J. H. Romero........ 1,700
Captain of the Port, R. L. Rickard........ 1,700
Commissioner of Lands and Works, C. MGrail, O.B.E..................... 1,750
Commissioner of Police, L. Hannon, M.B.E. 1,750
Colonial Postmaster, J. A. Giraldi........ 1,650
Medical Administrator, R. Scott-Stevenson, M.D.................................. 1,900
Attorney-General, A. M. Greenwood, Q.C. 2,200
Registrar, Supreme Court, J. E. Alcantara.. 1,650
Stipendiary Magistrate, W. D. Carew..... 1,750
Principal Auditor, J. A. Frost............ 1,700
Inspector of Schools and Planning Officer, M. Campbell........................ 1,750
Director of Labour and Social Security, E. H. Davis, O.B.E...................... 1,750

Distance, 1,209 miles; transit, 3½ days. B.E.A. have an air service from U.K. on Tuesdays and Thursdays *viâ* Madrid (transit time 4 hrs. 25 mins.).

HONG KONG

The Crown Colony of Hong Kong, consisting of a number of islands and of a portion of the mainland, on the south-eastern coast of China, is situated at the eastern side of the mouth of the Pearl River, between 22° 9′ and 22° 37′ N. lat. and 113° 52′–114° 30′ E. long.

The capital city, Victoria, situated on the island of Hong Kong, is 91 miles S.E. of Canton and 40 miles E. of the Portuguese colony of Macao at the other side of the Pearl River. It lies along the northern shore of the island and faces the mainland; the harbour (23 sq. miles water area) lies between the city and the mainland, on which is situated Kowloon with a population equalling that of Victoria. The total area of the Colony is 398¼ sq. miles with a population which has varied considerably during recent years owing to unsettled conditions in China. In Dec. 1962 it was thought to be about 3,526,500.

The island of *Hong Kong* is about 11 miles long and from 2 to 5 miles broad, with a total area of 29 square miles; at the eastern entrance to the harbour it is only separated from the mainland by a narrow strait (Lei Yue Mun), 500–900 yards in width. It was first occupied by Great Britain in January, 1841, and formally ceded by the Treaty of Nanking in 1842; *Kowloon* was subsequently acquired by the Peking Convention of 1860; and the *New Territories*, consisting of a peninsula in the southern part of the Kwangtung province, together with adjacent islands, by a 99-year lease signed June 9, 1898.

The island is broken in shape and mountainous, the highest point being Victoria Peak, which is 1,805 feet high. The New Territories contain several peaks higher than this, the highest being Tai Mo Shan, 3,140 feet. The summer weather is continuously hot and humid and often cloudy and showery. During the winter months, from November to March, the climate is cooler, drier, and more invigorating. The mean monthly temperature ranges from 59°F. in February to 82°F. in July, the average for the year being 72°F. The temperature rarely exceeds 95°F. in summer or falls below 40°F. in winter. The average annual rainfall is 84·76 in., of which no less than 75 per cent. falls between May and September, when the S.W. monsoon prevails.

Communications.—Hong Kong, one of the world's finest natural harbours, possesses excellent wharves and dry docks, capable of holding vessels up to 750 ft. in length. Shipping tonnage for the year ending March, 1963, was 41,751,152. A railway, 22 miles in length, owned by the Government, runs between Kowloon and the Chinese frontier. It forms a direct overland communication with Canton, Hankow and Shanghai, but since October, 1949, all through passenger traffic has been suspended.

Hong Kong (Kai Tak) Airport, is on the north shore of Kowloon Bay, some 4 miles from the centre of Kowloon. Some 20 airlines operate scheduled services to the Colony in addition to numerous charter flights by other operators. The Colony, with its modern runway of 8,350 ft., is an important link on the main air routes of the Far East, with frequent services to Europe, America and neighbouring territories, China excepted. B.O.A.C. operates 12 services per week to London, 9 *viâ* Europe and 3 *viâ* U.S.A., in addition to 2 services to Sydney and 8 services to Japan each week. Full night flying facilities, precision approach radar, and an instrument landing system are available at the airport, and a seaplane alighting area exists alongside the runway promontory.

Education.—In March, 1963, there were 2,098 schools with 770,762 pupils. 46·6 per cent. of the pupils are financed wholly or in part by the Government. The University of Hong Kong has a full-time residential student strength of 1,426 (including 391 women) in Faculties of Arts, Science, Medicine, Engineering and Architecture. There are also an Institute of Oriental Studies and a Department of Extra-Mural Studies.

Finance

	1961–62	1962–63
Public revenue....	\$1,030,447 880	\$1,253 064.583
Public expenditure.	953,205.237	1,113,276,099

\$=Hong Kong Dollar=1*s.* 3*d.*

Trade

Since the United Nations embargo on trade with China imposed severe limitations on Hong Kong's traditional *entrepôt* economy, the pattern and direction of the Colony's trade have changed fundamentally. A different type of *entrepôt* trade has developed on a smaller scale, involving all countries in the Far East, with Hong Kong as an intermediary. However, re-exports now represent under 25 per cent. of total exports. This has been due to the rapid growth of domestic industry, mainly manufacturing for consumers, which now provides the bulk of goods for the export trade. The Colony's products include a wide range of cotton piecegoods, cotton yarn, rayon and silk brocades, clothing, household enamel and aluminium ware, plastic articles (including toys and artificial flowers), rattan and hardwood furniture, foodstuffs and beverages, jade, jewellery and ivory, and an extensive range of metal products.

Diversification of manufacture is a feature of recent industrial developments. New products include wool and wool fabrics. The marked improvement in both quality and output of items for which precision engineering is required, notably cameras, binoculars and transistor radios, has continued.

The adverse balance on visible trade is offset by a favourable balance on invisible account—remittances from overseas Chinese, investments, exchange, shipping and insurance profits, and the spending of tourists, etc. In 1962 Hong Kong's principal customers for its domestic products, in order of value of trade, were U.S.A., the United Kingdom, Malaya, the Federal Republic of Germany, Canada, Australia and Japan. China continued to be the Colony's principal supplier, followed by Japan, U.S.A., the United Kingdom, Thailand, Australia and the Federal Republic of Germany.

Imports and Exports

Total Exports (1962).........H.K.\$4,387,328,638
Total Imports (1962).........H.K.\$6,657,240,435

	1961	1962
Imports from U.K.	£43,735,793	£46,440,711
Exports to U.K.	45,289,948	54,816,225

Government

Hong Kong is administered as a Crown colony with a Governor, aided by an Executive Council, consisting of 6 official and 6 unofficial members, and a Legislative Council, which consists of nine official and eight unofficial members. There is also an Urban Council in which is vested, *inter alia*, power of making bye-laws in respect of certain matters of public health and sanitation.

Governor, His Excellency Sir Robert Brown Black, G.C.M.G., O.B.E. (1958) (+*allce.* £3,500) £6,500
General Officer Commander-in-Chief, Lieut.-General Sir Richard Craddock, K.B.E., C.B., C.B.E., D.S.O..................
Chief Justice, Sir Michael Hogan, C.M.G.... 6,000
Colonial Secretary, E. B. Teesdale, M.C.... 6,000
Deputy Colonial Secretary, G. C. Hamilton 4,425
Senior Puisne Judge, I. C. C. Rigby...... 4,425
Puisne Judges, A. D. Scholes; W. A. Blair-Kerr; R. H. Mills-Owens............ 4,425

Attorney-General, M. Heenan, Q.C. £4,725
Secretary for Chinese Affairs, J. C. McDouall 4,725
Financial Secretary, J. J. Cowperthwaite, O.B.E. 4,725
Commissioner of Labour, P. C. M. Sedgwick 4,425
Chairman, Urban Council and Director of Urban Services, K. S. Kinghorn 4,425
Director of Medical and Health Services, Dr. D. J. M. Mackenzie, C.M.G., O.B.E. 4,425
Director of Public Works, A. M. J. Wright 4,425
Commissioner of Police, H. W. E. Heath, C.M.G. 4,425
Director of Marine, J. P. Hewitt 4,425
Manager and Chief Engineer, Kowloon-Canton Railway, Lam Po-hon 4,050
Director of Education, P. Donohue 4,425
District Commissioner, New Territories, J. P. Aserappa 4,425
Director of Commerce and Industry, D. R. Holmes, C.B.E., M.C., E.D. 4,425
Commissioner for Resettlement, C. G. M. Morrison 4,425
Director of Social Welfare, D. W. B. Baron 4,425
British Council Representative, R. E. Lawry.

LONDON OFFICE

Hong Kong Government Office, 54 Pall Mall, S.W.1.—*Dir.*, E. G. A. Grimwood, O.B.E.

JAMAICA

An island situated in the Caribbean Sea, about 90 miles to the south of Cuba, within 17° 43′—18° 32′ North lat, and 76° 11′—78° 21′ W. long., Jamaica was discovered on May 4, 1494, by Columbus. It was taken possession of by the Spaniards in 1509, and called St. Jago; but in 1655 a British expedition, sent out by Oliver Cromwell, under Penn and Venables, attacked the island, which capitulated after a trifling resistance. In 1670 it was formally ceded to England by the *Treaty of Madrid*.

Area and Population.—Jamaica is 146 miles in length and 51 in extreme breadth, containing an area of 4,411 square miles. The island is divided into 3 counties (Surrey, Middlesex and Cornwall) and 14 parishes. The census taken in April, 1960, showed a total population of 1,613,148.

The climate attracts many winter visitors, mainly from U.S.A. Value of the tourist trade in 1961 was £14,600,000. Visitors numbered 206,838 in 1962.

Physical Features.—From the sea-level on all sides of Jamaica a series of ridges gradually ascends towards the central ranges, dividing the larger rivers, and attaining, in the culminating Blue Mountain Peak, in the eastern part of the island, an elevation of 7,402 feet. From these mountains at least 70 streams descend to the north and south shores, but none is navigable except the Black River, and that only for small craft.

Capital.—The seat of government is ΨKingston, the largest town and seaport (estimated population of Kingston and St. Andrews, 1962, 445,797). Other towns are ΨMontego Bay (24,758) and Spanish Town (15,116).

GOVERNMENT

After more than three centuries of British rule, Jamaica became an independent state on August 6, 1962, and was recognized as a member of the British Commonwealth. The legislature consists of a *Senate* of 21 nominated members and a *House of Representatives* consisting of 45 members elected by universal adult suffrage. The number of members may vary up to 60. The Senate has no power to delay money bills for longer than one month or other bills for longer than seven months against the wishes of the House of Representatives.

Governor-General, His Excellency Sir Clifford Clarence Campbell, G.C.M.G. (1962).

CABINET
(August 6, 1962)

Premier, Hon. Sir Alexander Bustamante.
Deputy Prime Minister and Minister of Finance, Hon. D. B. Sangster.
Education, Hon. E. L. Allen.
Labour, Hon. L. G. Newland.
Trade and Industry, Hon. R. C. Lightbourne.
Health. Dr. Hon. H. W. Eldemire.
Development and Welfare, Hon. E. Seaga.
Agriculture and Lands, Hon. J. P. Gyles.
Home Affairs, Hon. R. A. McNeill.
Housing, Hon. D. C. Tavares.
Communications and Works, Hon. K. A. Jones.
Local Government, Hon. L. A. Lynch.
Attorney-General, Senator Hon. V. B. Grant, Q.C.
Withour Portfolio, Senator Hon. W. O. Hill; Senator Hon. H. Shearer (*Leader of Government Business in Senate*).

Speaker, House of Representatives, Hon. T. N. Golding.

U.K. HIGH COMMISSIONER IN JAMAICA

High Commissioner, His Excellency Sir Alexander Morley, K.C.M.G., C.B.E.
Deputy High Commissioner, C. E. Diggines.

JAMAICAN HIGH COMMISSIONER IN LONDON

High Commissioner, His Excellency H. L. Lindo, C.M.G., 6–10 Bruton Street, W.1.

JUDICATURE

Chief Justice and Keeper of Records, Hon. R. A. Phillips.
Judges of the Court of Appeal, Hon. H. G. H. Duffus; Hon. J. A. M. Lewis; Hon. Sir Cyril Henriques.
Senior Puisne Judge, Hon. A. R. Cools-Lartigue.
Puisne Judges, Hon. R. H. Small; Hon. G. E. Waddington; Hon. L. T. Moody; Hon. H. Shelly; Hon. A. Douglas.

COMMUNICATIONS

There are several excellent harbours, and the island is intersected by good roads. There are 249 miles of railway open. Telegraph stations and post offices are established in every town and in very many villages. The Palisadoes Airport at Kingston (now capable of handling the largest civil jet aircraft) is used by British West Indian Airways Ltd., British Overseas Airways Corporation, Pan-American Airways, K.L.M., Trans-Canada Air Lines, RANSA, DELTA, Mexicana, VIASA and Aerovias Panama Airways, which provide air communications with Europe, North, Central and South America an the Caribbean Islands. The Montego Bay Airport is also used by many airlines. In June 1963 Jamaica Airlines, Ltd., was formed. This airline provides a morning and afternoon service between Kingston and the principal towns of the north-east. A number of non-scheduled airlines operate through the island for non-traffic purposes in accordance with the provisions of International Air Services Transit Agreement.

PRODUCTION

Most of the staple products of tropical climates are raised. Sugar and rum are manufactured and exported; the latter is still counted the best in the world, and the coffee raised in certain districts of the Blue Mountains is of fine quality and fetches a high price. Sugar production in 1962 amounted to 437,067 tons processed from 4,105,784 tons of cane. There is an extensive trade in fruits, chiefly bananas, with the U.K. Citrus (and juices), cocoa and pimento are important export crops. Jamaica has developed a breed of dairy cattle known as the Jamaica Hope which is being exported to other tropical countries on an increasing scale. Good beef cattle are also raised. Jamaica is now the largest producer of bauxite in the world. The bauxite deposits are worked by one Canadian and three American companies; the Canadian company processes bauxite into alumina. Exports in 1962 amounted to: Alumina, 628,000 tons (£14,400,000); Bauxite, 5,987,000 tons (£15,700,000).

Gypsum is also mined, production for 1962 being 216,000 tons. Cement is manufactured locally, the output of the factory being 196,000 tons in 1962.

There is a textile mill and local factories also manufacture garments, knitted fabrics, shoes, paints, corrugated cardboard containers, small plastic articles, drugs, aluminium furniture and hollow-ware, gin, corn meal, soap, condensed milk, beer, baseballs, typewriters, radio sets, brake linings and brake shoes and electric light fittings.

Finance

The financial settlement with the United Kingdom prior to independence included grants to Jamaica amounting to £1,000,000 (portion of Colonial Welfare and Development Funds) and an Exchequer loan of £1,250,000 towards the island's capital Budget for 1962–63.

	1962–63	1963–64
Revenue	£49,752,444	£47,858,942*
Expenditure	51,314,670	50,618,914*
Public Debt (March 31)	37,865,592	45,451,408

*Estimated

Trade

	1961	1962
Total imports	£75,395,637	£61,557,111
Total exports	79,578,519	64,499,614

	1961	1962
Imports from U.K.	£23,053,780	£22,802,518
Exports to U.K.	18,223,819	18,489,711

Chief exports (1962): bauxite, £15,700,000; sugar, £14,571,000; rum, £1,032,000; bananas, £4,200,000; raw coffee, £297,000; pimento, £1,184,000; alumina, £14,400,000; fruit juices, £643,000; prepared and preserved fruits, £899,000; raw cocoa, £457,000.

British Council Representative in Kingston, C. Hentschel.

KENYA

The Colony and Protectorate of Kenya is bisected by the equator and extends approximately from latitude 4° N. to latitude 4° S. and from longitude 34° E. to 41° E. From the coast of the Indian Ocean in the east, the borders of Kenya are with Somaliland in the east and Ethiopia and Sudan in the north and north-west. To the west lie the Uganda Protectorate and Lake Victoria. On the south is Tanganyika Territory. The total area is 224,960 square miles (including 5,224 square miles of water). The total estimated population in mid 1961 was 7,287,000, including 66,000 Europeans, 178,000 Indo-Pakistans and Goans, and 45,000 other non-Africans. The African population is estimated at 7,000,000.

The Territory is divided into 6 Provinces (Nyanza, Rift Valley, Central, Coast, Southern and Northern) and an Extra-Provincial District (Nairobi).

Kenya Protectorate consists of a strip extending 10 miles inland along the coast from the Tanganyika mandated territory frontier to Kipini and the islands of the Lamu Archipelago. The Protectorate also includes the Witu Protectorate, a small tract of country at the mouth of the Tana River.

Production.—Agriculture provides about 85 per cent. of the national income; the principal exports in 1961 included: coffee, £10,624,891; tea, £4,004,198; sisal, £4,191,840; pyrethrum, £808,483; hides and skins £1,556,282; meat preparations (tinned), £1,350,360. The great variation in altitude and ecology provide conditions suitable for the production of a wide range of crops including coffee, tea, pyrethrum, sisal, coconuts, cotton, maize, wheat and fruit of all varieties. Legislation in 1961 abolished the Highlands Order in Council which reserved for European agriculture an area of 12,733 sq. miles, about 5·8 per cent. of the total land area of Kenya. Anyone is now able to purchase land in the Highlands. Settlement schemes for Africans are being started in the Highlands on land of high potential which has been purchased from European farmers by the Settlement Board. European agriculture provided about 80 per cent. of the total exportable surplus of agricultural products for the Colony in 1961, in addition to considerable quantities of food for areas devastated by famine and flood. African tribal lands, which remain exclusively reserved for the use of the indigenous people, amount to some 191,214 sq. miles, about 87 per cent. of the land area. Of this area only 63·5 per cent. is of agricultural use, the rest being semi-desert and waterless country. Production from the African areas is now increasing rapidly. Forest reserves cover 6,137 sq. miles, and provide valuable timber for building, fuel, and an assortment of purposes.

Prospecting and mining are carried on in many parts of the Colony, the principal minerals at present produced being copper, carbon dioxide gas (natural), diatomite, gold, limestone, salt and soda-ash. The value of the production of main minerals in 1961 was as follows: refined gold, £153,481; soda-ash £1,584,938, cement £2,559,385, salt £183,492, diatomite £47,584, carbon dioxide gas (natural) £44,151, limestone £106,092.

Hydro-electric power has been developed, particularly on the Upper Tana River and electricity is now available in Nairobi from the Owen Falls Dam scheme in Uganda.

Since the war there has been a great increase in industrial activity and particularly in the number of secondary industries. Many of these are engaged in processing agricultural produce but there is now manufactured an increasing range of products from local and imported materials and there has been a very sharp increase in the manufacture of consumer goods. The market served is that of all the East African territories. Industrial areas have been developed in all the principal towns and light industrial areas are being developed in rural areas.

The main imports are manufactured goods, classified chiefly as materials, machinery and transport equipment, mineral fuels, lubricants and related materials, food and chemicals.

Communications.—There were 230 post offices in operation in Kenya at Dec. 31, 1961. It is estimated that 72,300,000 letters, postcards and printed papers were handled during 1961. The number of parcels handled was 599,087. The Post Office operates a Savings Bank on behalf of the Kenya Government. During 1961, withdrawals exceeded deposits by £618,789. The number of deposit accounts increased by 29,000 to 401,710 by the end of 1961. The total amount held on behalf of depositors in Kenya was approximately £6,507,000. 23,421 exchange lines and 44,137 telephones (including extensions) were in service at the end of 1961. There are 144 telegraph offices in Kenya. A teleprinter service, provided by means of private wires between the users' offices in the various towns, gives direct and exclusive communication. There were 99 such circuits in operation at the end of 1961. An International Telex Service was introduced in July 1960.

The East African Railways and Harbours are a self-contained and self-financing service of the East African Common Services Organization; the railway, which is metre gauge, has a total route mileage of open line of 3,490 miles, made up as follows: Kenya and Uganda Section—Main Line: Mombasa–Kampala–Kasese (1,036 miles); Principal Lines: Nakuru Junction–Kisumu (131), Tororo–Soroti (100), Voi–Kahe Junction (94); Minor and Branch Lines: Rongai–Solai (27), Kisumu–Buture (43), Leseru–Kitale (41), Mbulamuti–Namasagali (19), Kampala–Port Bell (6), Gilgil–Thomson's Falls (48), Nairobi–Nanyuki (145). The Konza–Lake Magadi Line (91 miles) is worked but not owned by East African Railways and Harbours. Tanganyika Section—Main Line: Dar-es-Salaam–Kigoma (779 miles); Principal Line: Tabora–Mwanza (236); Branch Lines: Kaliuwa–Mpanda (131); Kilosa–Mikumi (44). The Tanga Line runs from Tanga to Arusha (273 miles). Southern Province Railway: Mtwara–Nachingwea–Masasi (154 miles). In addition the Administration operates a marine service on Lakes Victoria, Kioga, Albert and Tanganyika, and also on the River Nile with a route mileage of 4,194 miles. There are also 2,685 miles of road services connecting the Central and Tanga Lines and providing regular transport to the Southern Highlands, with subsidiary road services in Kenya and Uganda. East African Railways and Harbours control the five seaports of Mombasa, Tanga, Dar-es-Salaam, Lindi and Mtwara. Mombasa, Dar-es-Salaam and Mtwara have deep-water berths and Tanga and Lindi are lighterage ports.

Scheduled trunk airline services during 1961 were operated to or through Kenya, from Nairobi airport, by East African Airways Corporation, B.O.A.C., Air India, South African Airways, Air France, Central African Airways, Scandinavian Air System, British United Airways and Alitalia, while regional scheduled services were also run by East African Airways Corporation, Sabena, Ethiopian Air Lines, Aden Airways and Alitalia.

Roads policy and the administration of the Road Fund are under the control of the Road Authority. The Colony has approximately 26,000 miles of road including 3,750 miles of trunk roads, 6,500 miles of secondary roads. There is a total of 920 miles of bitumen-surfaced roads. During 1961, 84,540 vehicles were licensed, a decrease of 4,965 in comparison and the previous year.

FINANCE

	1961–62	1962–63*
Revenue	£41,373,000	£48,075,000
Expenditure	45,599,000	50,340,000

* Estimated.

The funded public debt at June 30, 1961, was £69,171,000.

TRADE

	1961
Imports	£68,937,000
Exports	41,736,000

TRADE WITH U.K.

	1961	1962
Imports from U.K.	£28,921,242	£29,593,439
Exports to U.K.	12,443,912	15,219,652

Since 1949 the Customs Departments of Kenya, Uganda and Tanganyika have been amalgamated under the title of the East African Customs and Excise Department under the East Africa Common Services Organization.

GOVERNMENT

In 1963, a transitional constitution was promulgated, providing for the period before Kenya attains full independence. The Governor retains reserve powers only in the case of defence, external relations and internal security. Each region has a regional assembly. After the elections in May, 1963, a Prime Minister and Cabinet took office.

Governor and Commander-in-Chief, His Excellency Rt. Hon. Malcolm MacDonald (1962) (*and allowances*) £10,500

CABINET
(June 1, 1963)

Prime Minister, Jomo Kenyatta.
Justice and Constitutional Affairs, Tom Mboya.
Home Affairs, Oginga Odinga.
Finance and Economic Planning, James Gichuru.
Education, Joseph Otiende.
Local Government and Regional Affairs, S. O. Ayodo.
Commerce and Industry, Dr. Gikonyo Kiano.
Works, Communications and Power, D. Mwanyumba.
Labour and Social Services, N. Mwenda.
Lands, Game, Fisheries, Water and Natural Resources, L. G. Sagini.
Health and Housing, Dr. Njoroge Mungai.
Information, Broadcasting and Tourism, Achieng Oneko.
Ministers of State, Joseph Murumbi (*Prime Minister's Office*); Peter Koinange (*Pan-African Affairs*).

Chief Justice, Sir John Ainley, M.C.
Puisne Judges, G. B. W. Rudd; C. P. Connell; T. H. Mayers; E. A. J. Edmonds; J. P. Murphy; J. S. Templeton; B. S. Miles; A. D. Farrell; J. Wicks; P. N. Dalton.
British Council Representative, A. Ross, O.B.E.

Public Relations Office in U.K., Kenya House, 172 Strand, W.C.2.

Nairobi, the Capital City and seat of Government is situated at latitude 2° S. and longitude 36° 8′ E. at 5,500 feet above sea level, and has a population of about 297,000. It is 307 miles by road from Mombasa, the Colony's port. Mombasa possesses what is perhaps the finest harbour on the East Coast of Africa and is well served by shipping lines from Europe and Asia besides a frequent coastal service. Other centres are Eldoret, Kisumu, Lamu, Nakuru and Nyeri.

Nairobi: transit from London about 16 days by sea; by air, 1 day.

THE MALDIVE ISLANDS

The Maldive Islands are a chain of coral atolls, some 400 miles to the South West of Ceylon, stretching from just south of the equator for about 600 miles to the north. There are 12 clearly defined atolls, separated from each other by deep channels, through which the currents run strongly. The total number of islands is over 7,000, some being very small indeed; about 200 of them are inhabited. The islands are thickly covered with coconut palms, and coir and copra are exported. The principal industry is fishing, and considerable quantities of dried fish are exported to Ceylon, where it is in great demand. The population of the islands is about 90,000. The people are Moslems, and the Maldivian language is akin to Elu or old Sinhalese. They are highly civilized and are great navigators and traders.

The Maldive Islands is a Sultanate, which is elective. The present Sultan, His Highness Al Amir Sir Mohamed Farid Didi, K.C.M.G., was installed on March 7, 1954. There is a Parliament (the Majlis) with representatives elected from all the atolls. The life of the Majlis is 5 years. The Government consists of the Prime Minister (Ibrahim Nasir) and the Cabinet, who are responsible to the Majlis.

The Islands are a Protected State, and their international relations are conducted by, or in accordance with the advice of, the British Government.

With the agreement of the Maldivian Government, an R.A.F. Staging Post has been constructed on Gan Island, in Addu Atoll, the most southerly atoll, lying just south of the equator.

The capital of the Islands is Malé (population about 10,000). Communications are by steam or sailing ship, and a small air-strip has been constructed on Hulule Island, about 1 mile from Malé.

British Representative, H. A. Arthington-Davy, M.B.E. (1960).

MALTA, G.C.

an island in the Mediterranean Sea, 58 miles from Sicily and about 180 from the African coast, about 17 miles in length and 9 in breadth, and having an area of 94·9 square miles. The colony includes also the adjoining island of *Gozo* (area 25·9 sq. miles): *Comino* and several islets. The estimated population on Dec. 30, 1962 was 329,285.

The island of Malta is said to have been converted to Christianity on the occasion of the shipwreck of St. Paul in A.D. 58. In 870 it was taken by the Arabs, its commerce was destroyed, and it was used mainly as a base for piratical expeditions. In 1090 it was again brought under Christian rule, being conquered by the Norman Count Roger of Normandy. It passed successively under the rule of the Angevins and Aragonese, and followed the fortunes of their kingdoms. In 1530 it was handed over to the Knights of St. John, who made of it a stronghold of Christianity. In 1565 it sustained the famous siege, when the last great effort of the Turks was successfully withstood by Grandmaster La Vallette. The Knights expended large sums in fortifying the island and carrying out many magnificent works, until they were expelled by Napoleon in 1798. The Maltese rose against the French garrison soon afterwards, and, with the assistance of some British and Neapolitan troops, compelled the French to capitulate in 1800. The islands were then, at their own wish, admitted into the British Empire, the act being confirmed by the Treaty of Paris in 1814.

Malta was again closely besieged in the last war and again withstood the attacks of all its enemies. From June, 1940, to the end of the war, 432 members of the garrison and 1,540 civilians were killed by enemy aircraft, and about 35,000 houses were destroyed or damaged. In recognition of the part played by the Maltese people, King George VI awarded the George Cross to the island.

The Parliament of the United Kingdom made a free grant of £10,000,000 for restoring war damage, and a further grant of £20,000,000 was subsequently made for the same purpose and for general construction and replanning.

The climate, although not tropical, is hot in summer. The islands are intensively cultivated. The chief export crops are potatoes and onions. Wheat, barley, clover and tomatoes are extensively grown on dry lands, while on irrigated land all the usual temperate climate and sub-tropical vegetables are grown. Tomatoes are grown on irrigated and non-irrigated land. Agriculture and fishing are among the principal occupations of the inhabitants.

Mdina (Notabile), the former capital of the island, contains the ancient palace of the courts of justice, the Cathedral, and the Old Seminary; its population has now dwindled to 836, but its suburb, Rabat, has 13,501 inhabitants. Notabile has been entirely eclipsed in importance by the modern capital, ♆Valletta, which was founded in 1566. The Grand Harbour is one of the finest in the world; it is very deep, and large vessels can anchor alongside the shore. It is an important port of call for vessels passing to and from the East and Suez Canal, being about half-way between Gibraltar and Port Said.

Malta possesses a University, 6 grammar schools (3,831 pupils); 112 primary schools (50,932 pupils); 5 technical schools (1,111 pupils)and 89 private schools (18,818 pupils). There are also 2 industrial training centres and a College of Arts, Science and Technology. Adult education classes had an attendance of 857 in 1962. English and Maltese are taught in all classes in Government primary schools. In religion the Maltese are Roman Catholics. The Maltese language is of Semitic origin, and is held by some to be derived from the Carthaginian and the Phœnician tongues. There is a Maltese order of nobility, recognized by the Crown, consisting of 28 families.

English and Maltese are the official languages of administration and Maltese is the official language in all the Courts of Law and the language of general use in the islands. The Court may order the use of the English language in any proceedings before it where any party or any accused person does not speak Maltese as the principal language to which he is accustomed; but when all parties or accused persons are English-speaking, the use of English is obligatory. Where the proceedings are in a language not known to the party or parties or to the accused they are translated. In 1934, Maltese was substituted for Italian as the principal language of the Courts of Law.

FINANCE

	1961–62	1962–63
Public revenue.......	£13,124,950	£13,012,369
Ordinary expenditure.	12,923,725	13,086 459
Capital expenditure...	3,672,205	3,552,765

Only notes issued by the Commissioners of Currency are now legal tender. In addition, British coins, including silver, cupro-nickel and bronze coins, are legal tender.

TRADE WITH U.K.

	1961	1962
Imports from U.K.....	£11,666,752	£10,576,210
Exports to U.K.......	1,377,050	1,501,504

The principal imports for home consumption are foodstuffs—mainly wheat, meat and bullocks, milk and fruit—fodder, beverages and tobacco, fuels, chemicals, textiles and machinery (industrial, agricultural and transport). The chief domestic exports are scrap-metal, hides and skins, potatoes and onions, smoking requisites, gloves, hosiery, buttons, beer, mineral waters, canned fruits, edible oil, tallow, fresh flowers and flower-cuttings.

CAPITAL, ♆Valletta. Population (estimated June 30, 1962) 17,993.

GOVERNMENT

After the war Malta was granted a measure of self-Government (subject to the reservation of certain powers to the Governor) under a Constitution introduced by Letters Patent dated September 5, 1947. On April 30, 1958, a state of emergency was declared and the direct administration of the Island was assumed by the Governor. On April 15, 1959, the state of emergency was brought to an end, and the 1947 Constitution was revoked and replaced by an interim Constitution established by the Malta (Constitution) Order in Council, 1959, and the Malta Royal Instructions, 1959.

Following the report of a Constitutional Commission under the chairmanship of Sir Hilary Blood, a new Constitution for Malta was introduced by the Malta (Constitution) Order in Council, 1961, under which the Island is now known as " the State of Malta". The Constitution provides *inter alia* for the protection of fundamental rights and freedoms of the individual; the United Kingdom Government still retains final responsibility for defence and external affairs; the Governor and Commander-in-Chief is required to consult with the Cabinet composed of a Prime Minister and 7 Maltese Ministers, in exercising all his powers, with certain exceptions; a United Kingdom Commissioner is appointed to represent the Government of the United Kingdom in Malta. There is also provision for the appointment of a Consultative Council composed of the Governor as Chairman, the Prime Minister, the United Kingdom Commissioner, not more than 3 members appointed by a Secretary of State and not more than 3 members appointed by the Prime Minister, providing for consultation on policy relating to defence and external affairs, and on any matters affecting the relations between the United Kingdom Government and the Government of Malta as may be referred to it by either Government.

Elections for the 50 seats in the Legislative Assembly, as opposed to 40 seats under the 1947 Constitution, were held in February 1962. The present state of the parties is as follows: Nationalist Party, 26 seats; Malta Labour Party, 16; Christian Workers Party, 4; Democratic Nationalist Party, 3; Progressive Constitutional Party, 1.

Governor and Commander-in-Chief, His Excellency Sir Maurice Dorman, G.C.M.G., G.C.V.O. (1962) £7,000

CABINET
(March 5, 1962)

Prime Minister and Minister of Economic Planning and Finance, G. Borg Olivier, LL.D.
Minister of Industrial Development and Tourism, G. Felice, LL.D.
Minister of Education, A. Paris, M.D.
Minister of Agriculture, Power and Communications, C. Caruana, LL.D.
Minister of Justice, T. Caruana Demajo, LL.D.
Minister of Works and Housing, J. Spiteri, LL.D.
Minister of Labour and Social Welfare, A. Cachia Zammit, M.D.
Minister of Health, P. Borg Olivier, M.D.

THE JUDICATURE

Chief Justice and President of the Court of Appeal, His Honour Sir Anthony Mamo, O.B.E. £2,250
Judges, Dr. A. J. Montanaro Gauci, C.B.E.; Dr. W. Harding, C.B.E.; Dr. T. E. Gouder; Dr. A. V. Camilleri; Dr. J. Caruana Colombo; Dr. J. H. Xuereb; Dr. J. Flores .... each £1,750

BRITISH COUNCIL

Representative, H. G. Ellis.

U.K. COMMISSIONER IN MALTA

Sir Edward Wakefield, C.I.E. (+*allce.* £1,565) £4,115

COMMISSIONER-GENERAL IN LONDON

Malta House, Haymarket, S.W.1.
[Trafalgar: 5033]
Commissioner-General, J. Axisa, M.B.E.

MAURITIUS

Mauritius is an island lying in the Indian Ocean, 550 miles east of Madagascar, between 57° 17′–57° 46′ E. long. and S. lat. 19° 58′–20° 33′, and comprising with its dependencies an area of 805 square miles. The resident population at the census of 1962 (preliminary figures) was 680,300, made up of Europeans (mainly of French extraction), Asiatic races and persons of mixed descent. The total population, including dependencies, was estimated (Dec. 31, 1962) at 691,000.

Mauritius was discovered in 1511 by the Portuguese, but they never formed any settlement on it. The Dutch visited it in 1598, and named it Mauritius, in honour of the Stadtholder, Prince Maurice of Nassau. In 1638 they established a small colony on the shore, but in 1710 they abandoned the island, and in 1715 the French took possession of it and changed the name to Isle de France, but did not settle it until 1721. Under the French it became a great centre of trade. In 1789 the seat of French Government in the East was removed to it from Pondicherry, and it was taken by a British force in 1810. A British garrison remained on the island until its withdrawal in June 1960. There is a Naval Volunteer Force, and a special internal security force was set up in 1960. The French language and French law have been preserved under British rule though the ancient name, Mauritius, was restored. There are 4 bi-lingual French-English daily papers and 5 Chinese daily papers.

Of the total cultivable area of about 230,000 acres, 214,000 are under sugar, about 400 under aloe (regular plantations), 300 under maize, 4,900 under tea, 700 under tobacco and the rest under other foodcrops and mixed farming. The sugar crop of 1962 was about 533,000 metric tons.

Mauritius enjoys a sub-tropical maritime climate, with sufficient difference between summer and winter to avoid monotony: further variation is introduced by the wide range of rainfall and temperature resulting from the mountainous nature of the island. Humidity is rather high throughout the year and rainfall is sufficient to maintain a green cover of vegetation, except for a brief period in the driest districts.

The pleasantest months are April–June and September–November, the winter months having persistent winds and being colder and wetter especially on the plateau and the summer months hotter especially near the coast. Tropical cyclones, when they occur, are most likely to be encountered in the January–March period, their incidence being otherwise rare. At times, as in 1892, 1931, 1945, 1960 and 1962 they are very severe and do much damage to crops and buildings.

Railways and Shipping.—There is an excellent harbour on the N.W. coast, on which the capital, Port Louis, stands, and the annual trade of the island passes entirely through Port Louis. The shipping entered in 1962 amounted to 1,543,336 tons, and the shipping cleared to 1,540,234 tons. In 1962 there were 67 miles of railway (4 ft. 8½ in. gauge), 77 post-offices and postal agencies, 50 telegraph offices and 15 telephone-exchange offices in the island, with 210 miles of telegraph, including block telegraph of the railway and 11,140 miles of underground and overhead (Government) telephone wires and 9,973 telephone installations.

Civil Aviation.—Air services are operated by: (1) *B.O.A.C.* to Nairobi, Khartoum, Rome and London; (2) *Air France* to Réunion, Madagascar, Dar-es-Salaam, Nairobi, Athens, Nice and Paris; (3) *South African Airways* to Johannesburg, Cocos Islands and Perth (West Australia); (4) *QANTAS* to Johannesburg, Cocos Islands, Perth and Sydney; (5) Rhodesian Air Services to Salisbury.

Education.—The inhabitants of European descent are mostly Roman Catholic. Educational facilities are available up to University entrance level. Primary education is provided in 357 schools, of which 124 are Government and 75 aided. Secondary education is given in 4 Government, 13 aided and 88 private schools. There are also 2 central schools, a technical institute and a teacher training college. Current expenditure on education in 1961–62 totalled Rs.20,655,161.

FINANCE

	1961–62	1962–63*
Public revenue....	Rs.158,603,800	Rs.165,442,700
Public expenditure.	157,759,560	164,965,460

*Estimated.

The Public Debt, at June 30, 1962, was Rs.152,150,916.

Currency—Rs.=Rupee=1*s.* 6*d.*

TRADE

	1961	1962
Total imports.....	Rs.323,960,507	Rs.332,727,118
Total exports......	287,208,110	299 408,109
Imports from U.K.	£6,575,576	£6,040,981
Exports to U.K....	11,183,079	12,004,339

The necessities of life have all to be imported from abroad.

GOVERNMENT

The Government is vested in a Governor with an Executive and Legislative Council. The Mauritius (Constitution) Orders in Council, 1958 to 1962, provide for a Legislative Council consisting of the Speaker (appointed by the Governor from outside the Council) three *ex officio* members (the Chief Secretary, the Attorney-General and the Financial Secretary), forty elected members and such nominated members, not exceeding 12, as the Governor may appoint.

The Colony is divided into 40 single member Constituencies and every person (male or female) has the right to vote who—(*a*) is a British subject of the age of 21 years or upwards; and (*b*) has resided in the Colony for a period of at least 2 years immediately before the date of registration or is domiciled in the Colony and is residing therein at that date; and (*c*) has resided in the constituency in which he is entitled to be registered as a voter for a period of at least 6 months immediately before the date of registration.

The Executive Council consists of the 3 *ex officio* members above mentioned and 10 members appointed by the Governor from elected or nominated members of the Legislative Council. The *ex officio* members and the appointed members are styled Ministers.

Governor and Commander-in-Chief, His Excellency Sir John Shaw Rennie, K.C.M.G., O.B.E. (1962) Rs.80,000
Chief Minister and Minister of Finance, Dr. Hon. S. Ramgoolam............... 36,000
Chief Justice, Sir Ramparsad Neerunjun, O.B.E............................ 41,200
Speaker, Legislative Council, H. R. Vaghjee.......................... 36,000
Chief Secretary, T. D. Vickers, C.M.G..... 40,000
Financial Secretary, A. F. Bates, C.M.G.... 36,000
Attorney-General, J. J. M. Lavoipierre, Q.C.............................. 36,000
Minister of Education and Cultural Affairs, Hon. A. Beejadhur................. Rs.36,000
Minister of Agriculture and Natural Resources, Hon. S. Boolell............ 36,000
Minister of Health and Reform Institutions, Hon. J. G. Forget................. 36,000
Minister of Local Government and Co-operative Development, Hon. F. Laventure.............................. 36,000
Minister of Housing, Lands and Town and Country Planning, Hon. A. R. Mohamed.......................... 36,000
Minister of Industry, Commerce and External Communications, Hon. Sir André Nairac, C.B.E., Q.C......................... 36,000
Minister of Labour and Social Security, Hon. V. Ringadoo..................... 36,000
Minister of Works and Internal Communications, Hon. H. E. Walter.......... 36,000
Minister of Information, Posts and Telegraphs and Telecommunications, Hon. A. H. M. Osman................. 36,000
Senior Puisne Judge, M. J. J. L. Rivalland, M.B.E............................. 34,000
Puisne Judges, J. G. H. Glover; M. J. G. Lalouette......................each 32,000

CAPITAL, ΨPort Louis. Population (1961), 92,400; other centres are Curepipe (38,300), Beau Bassin and Rose Hill (37,300), Vacoas and Phoenix (37,000), Quatre Bornes (23,150) and ΨMahebourg (12,250).

British Council Representative, G. de G. Sells, D.S.O., D.F.C.

DEPENDENCIES OF MAURITIUS

Rodrigues, 350 miles east-north-east of Mauritius, area, 40 square miles. Population (1962 Census) 18,300. Cattle, beans, salt fish, sheep and goats are the principal exports. The island is under the administration of a Magistrate and Civil Commissioner from Mauritius, who takes his orders from the Governor of Mauritius. *Magistrate*, P. Lefébure.

Trade with Mauritius

	1961	1962
Total imports.....	Rs.3,508,587	Rs.4,225,580
Total exports......	1,400,081	1,641,111

Other Dependencies.—Most of the scattered groups of coral islands belonging to Great Britain in the Indian Ocean are administered by the Mauritius Government, being visited periodically by two magistrates, whose duty it is to inquire into the condition of the labourers, and settle any disputes which may be referred to them. The chief product is coconut oil. The most important are the Oil Islands Group, the largest of which, Ψ*Diego Garcia* (pop. 1962, 600), lies on the direct route from the Red Sea to Australia, and possesses a good harbour; other islands are Six Islands, Peros Banhos, Agalega, St. Brandon, Salomon, and Trois Frères. The total area of the "Other Dependencies" is about 47½ square miles, with a population (1962) of 1,900.

Trade with Mauritius

	1961	1962
Imports..........	Rs.720,782	Rs.411,586
Exports..	1,495,993	1,533,634

THE NEW HEBRIDES

The New Hebrides Group, in the South Pacific Ocean, situated between the 13th and 21st degrees of South latitude and the 166th and 170th degrees of East longitude, of an area of roughly 5,700 square miles, is administered by a British-French Condominium Government.

The principal islands are Espiritu Santo, Malekula, Epi, Ambrym, Efate, Erromanga. Tanna, Aneityum, Aoba, Maewo and Pentecost. The British Resident Commissioner, exercising powers delegated to him by the High Commissioner for the Western Pacific, and the French Resident Commissioner, representing the High Commissioner for France in the Pacific Ocean, are the joint heads of the Administration. They each have staffs of national officers who assist them in general administrative work and the running of social services (health and education) financed from national funds, part of which come from the Metropolitan Governments. In addition they control the "joint" public services (posts and telegraphs, public works, mines, meteorology, etc.) which are financed from funds raised in the Territory. The population (1960) was 60,374, of which 55,428 is the estimated number of native inhabitants. Principal products are copra, coffee, cocoa, frozen fish, manganese, kauri timber, sandalwood and shell. Imports for 1962 totalled £2,239,368, of which £1,120,420 was the value of imports from Australia. Exports in 1962 were valued at £1,982,330, £818,444 being the value of exports to France. Joint revenue, 1962, £752,977; expenditure on joint services, £760,304.

Attached to the New Hebrides are the Banks (309 sq. miles, pop. 2,475) and Torres (40 sq. miles, pop. 164) Islands.

Seat of New Hebrides Administration—Ψ Vila, Efate, pop. about 4,000.

British High Commissioner, Sir David Trench, K.C.M.G., M.C.

French High Commissioner, M. Biros.

British Resident Commissioner, A. M. Wilkie, C.M.G.

French Resident Commissioner, M. Delauney.

PACIFIC ISLANDS

(*Western Pacific High Commission*)

High Commissioner, His Excellency Sir David Clive Crosbie Trench, K.C.M.G., M.C., (1961) . . . . . . (+*allce.* £A1,625) £A5,000

Chief Justice, G. G. Briggs 4,374

Chief Secretary, M. D. I. Gass, C.M.G. 4,374

Financial Sec., L. M. Davies, O.B.E. 3,954

Secretary for Protectorate Affairs, R. Davies, O.B.E. 3,714

Establishment Secretary, M. A. Andrew . . . 3,414

Deputy Financial Secretary, T. Russell, O.B.E. 3,414

The principal groups under the High Commissioner in, over, and for the Western Pacific Islands are (1) The Gilbert and Ellice Islands Colony; (2) The British Solomon Islands Protectorate; (3) The New Hebrides; (4) The Central and Southern Line Islands. The headquarters of the High Commissioner are at Honiara in the British Solomon Islands Protectorate.

The Gilbert and Ellice Islands Colony, which includes Ocean, Christmas, Fanning and Washington Islands, besides the Gilbert, Ellice and Phoenix Groups, was formerly a Protectorate, and was formally annexed to the Empire in November, 1915. The total land area of the Colony is about 360 sq. miles with a population (Census, 1947) of 36,000 (304 Europeans, 142 Chinese, 29,923 Micronesians and 5,066 Polynesians), estimated at 47,508 at the end of 1961. Expressed in Australian currency, the estimated revenue of the Colony in 1962 was £753,435; expenditure £752,567.

The Government maintains one boys' and one girls' boarding school and 27 primary schools. Village school primary education is mainly run by missionary societies, with financial assistance from the Government, and at the end of 1961 these schools were attended by 8,831 pupils. Missions have in recent years entered the field of secondary education, and supported 5 secondary schools at the end of 1961.

The Gilbert Group, situated between 4° N. and 3° S. latitude and 172° and 177° E. longitude, consists of 16 islands, Makin, Makin Meang, Marakei, Abaiang, Tarawa (Headquarters of the Colony), Maiana, Abemama, Kuria, Aranuka, Nonouti, Tabiteuea, Beru, Nukunau, Onotoa, Tamana and Arorae. The area of the group is 114 sq. miles and the population (estimated 1961) 36,168. The *Ellice Group* of 9 islands (Nanumea, Nanumanga, Niutao, Nui, Vaitupu, Nukufetau, Funafuti, Nukulaelae and Niulakita) lies between lat. 5° 30′ and 11° SE. and long. 176° E. and 180° E. The area of the group is 9½ sq. miles and the population (estimated 1961) 5,120. *Ocean Island* (or Banaba), in lat. 0° 52′ S. and long. 169° 35′ E. was proclaimed British in 1900. The *Line Islands* between lat. 4° 40′ and 2° N. and long. 160° 20′ and 157° W. include Fanning, Washington and Christmas Islands. *Fanning* and *Washington Islands* were included in the Colony in 1916, *Christmas Island* in 1919. Christmas Island is the largest atoll in the Pacific. The boundaries of the Colony were extended (March 18, 1937) to include the *Phœnix Islands* (Birnie, Canton, Enderbury, Gardner, Hull, McKean, Phœnix and Sydney Islands), between 3° and 5° S. and 170° and 175° W. Enderbury and Canton Islands are for common use of Gt. Britain and U.S.A. for aviation and communications, under an agreement made on April 6, 1939. Canton Island is an international airport on the Trans-Pacific route between Fiji and Honolulu, although, with the development of long-range jet aircraft, it has lost much of its former importance.

In each island of the Gilbert and Ellice Groups (except Nurakita) and in two islands in the Phœnix Group there is a native Government under an appointed native magistrate whose court administers a code of native laws. The Colony is administered by the High Commissioner through a Resident Commissioner.

Resident Commissioner, Gilbert and Ellice Islands, Valdemar Jens Andersen, O.B.E., (1962) . . . . (+*allce.* £175) £A3,645

The British Solomon Islands Protectorate, established in 1893, now includes all the islands in the Solomons Archipelago S. and S.E. of the large island of Bougainville. The main islands in the Protectorate are Choiseul, Santa Isabel, Shortland Group, Vella Lavella, Kolombangara, Ganongga, Gizo, the New Georgia Group, the Florida Group, Guadalcanal, the Russell Islands, Malaita and San Cristobal, and the outlying islands of Bellona, Rennell, Santa Cruz, Vanikoro, Tikopia, Swallow (or Reef Islands) and Duff Groups, the Stewart Islands and the Ontong Java Atoll. The Protectorate is situated between 5°–13° S. lat. and 155°–170° 20′ E. long. It has a total land area of about 11,500 sq. miles. The latest population figures are: 850 Europeans, 400 Chinese, 123,000 Melanesians, 5,000 Polynesians; total 130,000. Estimated revenue (1963) £A2,300,916 (including Colonial Development and Welfare Funds (£A490,860) and Grant-in-Aid from the United Kingdom (£A625,316); estimated expenditure (1963) £A2,300,916; imports (1962) £A2,233,611; domestic exports £A1,589,184. The main imports are foodstuffs, consumer goods and building materials. Principal exports are copra, timber and trochus shell. A small export of cocoa has recently begun. On October 18, 1960, the British Solomon Islands (Constitution) Order in Council, 1960, came into operation. An Executive Council and a Legislative Council were established for the Protectorate, replacing the former Advisory Council. The Legislative Council has an official majority with 11 *ex officio* and 10 unofficials, all of whom are appointed by the High Commissioner. The High Commissioner presides over both Councils.

The High Commissioner's Court for the Western Pacific was reconstituted by the Western Pacific (Courts) Order in Council 1961, which came into operation in April 1962, as the High Court of the Western Pacific with the powers and jurisdiction of a Superior Court of Record exercised by the Chief Justice and puisne judges.

SOUTH PACIFIC COMMISSION

The South Pacific Commission, an advisory and consultative body set up by the Governments responsible for the administration of island territories in the South Pacific region, recommends to the member Governments means for promoting the well-being of the peoples of these territories. It is concerned with social, economic and health matters. *Headquarters*, Nouméa, New Caledonia.

The Commission was established by an Agreement between the Governments of Australia, France, the Netherlands, New Zealand, the United Kingdom and the United States of America, signed at Canberra in 1947 and ratified on July 29, 1948. Until November 7, 1951, the area of the Commission's activities comprised territories lying generally south of the Equator from and including Netherlands New Guinea in the west to the French Establishments in Oceania and Pitcairn in the east. On November 7, 1951, an additional Agreement was signed extending the scope of the Commission to include Guam and the Trust Territory of the Pacific Islands under United States administration. Netherlands membership ceased on Dec. 31, 1962. The Commission consists of ten Commissioners, two from each Government, and normally holds one session each year.

There are two auxiliary bodies, the Research Council and the South Pacific Conference. There is a Research Council meeting yearly, which may be either a meeting of the full Council, or of one or other of its three main sections, specializing in health, economic development and social development. Members of the Council are appointed by the Commission and are selected for their special knowledge of the questions with which the Commission is concerned, and the problems of the Territories in these fields. The chief function of the Research Council is to advise the Commission what investigations and projects are necessary. Arrangements to carry out those which are approved are the responsibility of the Secretary-General and other principal officers. The South Pacific Conference, which meets at intervals not exceeding three years, consists of delegates from the territories who may be accompanied by advisers. The first Conference was held in Fiji in April, 1950, the second in New Caledonia in April, 1953, the third in Fiji in April–May, 1956, and the fourth in New Britain in April–May, 1959. The fifth South Pacific Conference was held in American Samoa in July, 1962.

Secretary-General, W. D. Forsyth.

Executive Officers, Dr. J. Barrau (*Economic Development*); Dr. R. Seddon (*Social Development*); Dr. G. Loison (*Health*).

FEDERATION OF RHODESIA AND NYASALAND

AREA AND POPULATION

The Federation of Rhodesia and Nyasaland covers an area of 486,942 square miles (S. Rhodesia, 150,333; N. Rhodesia 288,130; and Nyasaland 36,879 square miles), including approximately 12,298 square miles of water.

Population.—The estimated population of the Federation (May, 1962) is 9,274,600 of all races (S. Rhodesia 3,838,800; N. Rhodesia 2,514,800; Nyasaland 2,921,000).

PHYSIOGRAPHY

Boundaries.—The Federation extends from latitude 22° 30′ South to latitude 8° 15′ South. On the South it is bordered by the Republic of South Africa, on the West by the Bechuanaland Protectorate, and Portuguese West Africa, on the North-West and North by the Congolese Republic, on the North by Tanganyika and on the East by Portuguese East Africa.

Relief.—Most of Rhodesia is at an altitude of between 3,000 and 5,000 feet above sea level, the highest land lying on the eastern border of Southern Rhodesia where some mountains rise above 8,000 feet above sea level (Mt. Inyangani 8,541 feet). In the large river valleys, the Zambezi, Sabi, Kafue and Luangwa, the level of the land falls below 2,000 feet.

In Nyasaland, the level of the littoral of Lake Nyasa and of parts of the Shire River Valley is 1,500 feet above sea level. Elsewhere the altitude varies between 2,000 and 8,000 feet with the crest of the Mlanje Mountain massif rising to 10,000 feet above sea level. Lake Nyasa itself, the greatest depth of which is about 2,500 feet, is a southward extension of the Great Rift Valley.

Rivers.—Portions of the Zambezi River, Lake Nyasa, Lake Bangweulu, the Luapula River and the Chambeshi River are navigable and are extensively used by waterborne transport. The Federation has, however, no great natural waterways, either to provide access to the sea or to connect major industrial centres, but there are a number of large rivers which could be brought into the service of agriculture for irrigation and of power supplies for hydro-electric schemes. The recently completed Kariba Dam, on the Zambezi, is 175 miles long and 2,000 sq. miles in area, provides hydro-electric power from the Copper Belt to Bulawayo. The principal rivers, in addition to the Zambezi, are—in Southern Rhodesia: the Sabi River and its tributaries (irrigation and power potentialities); the Hunyani River (already dammed at several points); and the Umfuli River (irrigation potentialities). In Northern Rhodesia: the Kafue River (power potentialities); the Mulungushi and Lunsemfwa Rivers (already supplying hydro-electric power to Broken Hill mine and town); and the Zambezi River at the Victoria Falls (supplying hydro-electric power to Livingstone). In Nyasaland: the Shire River (power and irrigation potentialities).

Climate.—Though the entire Federal area lies within the tropics most of it is at an altitude which gives climatic conditions favouring permanent European settlement. The main rainfall throughout the area is concentrated into a season extending from about November to March. Average rainfall (except for certain somewhat arid low-lying regions on the one hand and some high altitude areas of very heavy rainfall on the other) is 25 to 30 inches a year.

GOVERNMENT

The Federation of Rhodesia and Nyasaland came into being on September 4, 1953, when the first Governor-General assumed office. The Order-in-Council authorizing the setting up of the Federation was approved by Her Majesty the Queen on August 1, 1953. An interim Ministry was sworn in on September 7. The first elections to the Federal Assembly took place on December 15, 1953. In the first months of the Federation only the minimum administrative machine was created and the Federal Government assumed its functions from the territories by degrees. By July 1, 1954, the Federal Ministries had taken over most of their duties.

GOVERNOR-GENERAL AND STAFF

Acting Governor-General, His Excellency Hon. Sir Humphrey Vicary Gibbs, K.C.M.G., O.B.E.; *born* 1902; *assumed office*, May 7, 1963 (+£3,500 *allce.*) £5,000
Official Secretary and Comptroller, Commander J. P. P. Michell, M.V.O., O.B.E., R.N. (*ret.*).

THE FEDERAL MINISTRY

(November, 1956, as since reconstructed)

Prime Minister and Minister of External Affairs, Rt. Hon. Sir Roy Welensky, K.C.M.G. (+£1,000 *tax free allce.*) £4,000
Minister of Law and of Home Affairs, Hon. J. M. Greenfield, C.M.G., Q.C. *£3,250
Minister of Transport and of Posts, Hon. F. S. Owen, C.B.E. *£3,250
Minister of Commerce and Industry, Hon. J. A. Clark *£3,250
Minister of Finance, Hon. J. M. Caldicott, C.M.G. *£3,250
Minister of Agriculture, Hon. J. C. Graylin *£3,250
Minister of Education and Minister for the Public Service, Hon. J. P. G. Duncan, M.B.E. *£3,250
Minister of Health, Hon. B. D. Goldberg, C.M.G. *£3,250
Minister of Economic Affairs, of Defence and of Power, and Deputy Prime Minister, Hon. Sir Malcolm Barrow, C.B.E. *£3,250
Minister of Works, Hon. G. N. R. L'Ange, C.B.E. *£3,250
Secretary, Office of the Prime Minister and External Affairs, F. H. N. Parry, C.B.E.
Secretary for Defence, M. B. Benoy, C.B.E.
Secretary for Transport, T. S. Bell.
Secretary for Commerce and Industry, D. H. Cummings, O.B.E.
Secretary for Home Affairs, Sir Athol Evans, K.B.E.
Attorney-General, R. A. Yates, Q.C.
Postmaster-General, Lt.-Col. C. R. Dickenson.
Secretary for Education, D. C. Ferrer.
Secretary for Agriculture, C. A. Murray, O.B.E.
Secretary for Health, Dr. D. M. Blair, O.B.E.
Under Secretary for Power, E. R. Fothergill, O.B.E., M.C., E.D.
Government Solicitor, E. Morris.
Secretary for Economic Affairs, Dr. F. T. Russell, M.B.E.
Secretary for the Public Service Commission, D. R. Allen.
Secretary for Finance, H. M. McDowell, C.B.E.
Under Secretary for Works, R. W. Petheram, M.B.E.
Comptroller and Auditor General, D. J. Morris.

* *Plus* £500 tax free allowance.

REPRESENTATIVES ABROAD

United Kingdom

Rhodesia House, 429 Strand, W.C.2

High Commissioner (vacant).
Deputy High Commissioner, M. J. Lamb.

Nigeria, Lagos (*High Commissioner*).—M. M. Hove, M.B.E.
South Africa, Pretoria (*Head of Mission*)—J. W. M. Fitt, O.B.E.
U.S.A., Washington (*Minister*).—O. B. Bennett, C.B.E.

U.K. HIGH COMMISSIONER IN SALISBURY

High Commissioner, His Excellency J. B. Johnston, C.M.G.
Deputy High Commissioner, D. A. Scott.
Military Adviser, Brig. C. V. Halden, M.B.E., T.D.
Air Adviser, Group Capt. H. G. Slade, A.F.C.
Economic Adviser, G. W. Brazendale, C.M.G.

LEGISLATURE

The Federal Assembly consists of 59 members and is composed as follows: forty-four elected members (Southern Rhodesia, 24; Northern Rhodesia, 14; Nyasaland, 6); eight African elected members (Southern Rhodesia, 4; Northern Rhodesia, 2; Nyasaland, 2); 4 specially elected African members (Northern Rhodesia, 2; Nyasaland, 2); and three European members charged with special responsiblity for African interests, of whom one is elected in Southern Rhodesia and the other two appointed, one each by the Governors of Northern Rhodesia and Nyasaland.

The main matters on which the Federal Legislature has power to make laws are external affairs, defence, immigration, financial and economic affairs, inter-territorial roads, railways, European agriculture in the Rhodesias, posts and telegraphs, education except African primary and secondary education and Federal courts. In addition, there are a number of matters on which both the Federal and Territorial Legislatures have powers to make laws. They include the development of industries, electricity, scientific and industrial research, health, town planning, archives, census and statistics.

African Affairs Board

A Standing Committee of the Federal Assembly, known as the African Affairs Board, consists of the three European members representing African interests and one of the elected African members from each territory. The Board makes representations to the Federal Government on matters within the authority of the Federation in the interests of Africans; to assist a Territorial Government, at its request, in the study of matters affecting Africans, and to draw attention to any Federal legislation of a differentiating character and to ask that it should be reserved for the signification of Her Majesty's pleasure.

Speaker of the Federal Assembly, Hon. T. I. F. Wilson, C.M.G.
Clerk of the House, E. Grant-Dalton.

FEDERAL SUPREME COURT

The Court, constituted under the Federal Constitution of 1953, came into being on July 1, 1955.

Chief Justice of the Federation, Rt. Hon. Sir John Clayden.
Federal Justices, Hon. Sir Vincent Quénet; Hon. Sir Alastair Forbes.

The Chief Justices of Southern Rhodesia, Northern Rhodesia and Nyasaland are *ex officio* members of the Court.

DEFENCE

The Army of Rhodesia and Nyasaland, with headquarters in Salisbury is comprised of regular and territorial forces. The regular forces include a battalion of the Rhodesia Light Infantry, a battalion of The Rhodesian African Rifles, a battalion of the Northern Rhodesia Regiment and two battalions of the King's African Rifles, units of the Rhodesia and Nyasaland Corps of Engineers, the Rhodesia and Nyasaland Corps of Signals, the Rhodesia and Nyasaland Army Service Corps, the Rhodesia and Nyasaland Medical Corps and the Rhodesia and Nyasaland Army Pay Corps. The Territorial Force comprises three active force battalions and four reserve battalions of the Royal Rhodesia Regiment, with headquarters at Salisbury, Bulawayo and Kitwe. There are also three major training establishments. The Federation has its own regular air force, the Royal Rhodesian Air

Force, which is equipped with Canberra and Vampire jet aircraft, as well as trainers, transport aircraft and helicopters.

EDUCATION

The Federal Government is responsible for all education other than that of Africans, that is for European, Asian and Coloured children. In July, 1962, the numbers of such children at school were as follows: Southern Rhodesia, 51,623 (186 schools); Northern Rhodesia, 18,486 (72 schools); Nyasaland, 5,522 (36 schools). In addition to the Government Schools, there are 67 State-aided private schools, attended by a further 11,909 children.

FINANCE

The tenth Federal Budget was presented on June 27, 1963.

Expenditure and revenue for the year ending June 30, 1964 was estimated as follows:

Revenue	£71,295,000
Expenditure from revenue funds	£70,619 588
Expenditure from loan funds	£3,946,497

The public debt amounted to £282,380,000 at June 30, 1963.

Currency.—Federal currency is linked to British sterling and currency backing is held in London in balances, in British Treasury Bills and in Government securities issued in the United Kingdom. The Bank of Rhodesia and Nyasaland, which was established by an Act of the Federal Assembly in 1960, is responsible for the issue of the currency.

PRODUCTION, TRADE AND INDUSTRY

Agriculture.—European agriculture in Southern and Northern Rhodesia is the administrative responsibility of the Federal Government, the remainder of the agricultural industry of the Federal area being in the charge of the various Territorial Governments. Production of principal crops in 1961 was:

	Southern Rhodesia '000 lb.	Northern Rhodesia '000 lb.	Nyasaland '000 lb.	Total '000 lb.
Tobacco‡	215,693	17,790	36,146	269,629
Cotton	1,286	330	38,060	39,676
Tea	2,840	—	29,410	32,250

‡ All types except Turkish. Production of flue-cured tobacco, mainly in Southern Rhodesia, totalled 234,454,000 lb. and of all fire-cured tobacco mainly in Nyasaland, 25,272,000 lb.

NUMBERS OF LIVESTOCK, 1962

	Southern Rhodesia	Northern Rhodesia	Nyasaland	Total
Cattle	3,717,000	1,271,000	380,000	5,368,000
Sheep	388,000	37,000	76,000	501,000
Goats	501,000	162,000	493,000	1,156,000
Pigs	133,000	72,000	105,000	310,000

MINERAL PRODUCTION, 1962

	Quantity	Value
Copper	618,000 tons	£114,901,000
Gold	555 000 oz.	6,946,000
Asbestos	142,000 tons	7,310,000
Chrome	508,000 tons	2,708,000
Zinc	45,000 tons	2,345,000
Lead	16,000 tons	753,000
Cobalt	—	973,000
Manganese	51,000 tons	433,000

Manufactures.—Since 1955–56, the census of industrial production has been held on a federal basis, giving a gross output of £180,800,000 and a net output of £74,600,000 for the year 1961. Tobacco, textiles and garments, foodstuffs and metal products remain the most important groups, drawing largely for their materials on local sources.

EXTERNAL TRADE

In 1962, the ninth year for which statistics of external trade were available for the Federation as a single trading entity, total external trade was valued at £352,571,000.

With exports valued at £209,516,000 and imports at £142,995,000, there was a favourable balance of trade of £73,366,000 (including net gold sales of £6,845,000).

About 67 per cent. of the exports consisted of minerals—copper, gold, asbestos, lead, zinc, chrome being the most important. About 20 per cent. of all exports consisted of tobacco.

The remaining 13 per cent. was made up of a wide range of products, including manufactured articles of which textiles are the most important.

About 23 per cent. of imports in 1962 were metals and machinery, a high proportion being mining, electrical and agricultural machinery, railway materials and other durable producers' goods required for the growth of industry, agriculture and basic services such as communications and the provision of electric power.

The most important market for the Federation's products was the United Kingdom. Exports to the United Kingdom in 1962 were made up mainly of copper (£48,242,000), tobacco (£22,695,000), asbestos and tea. The most important supplier of the Federation's requirements in 1962 was the United Kingdom.

Total	1961	1962
Imports from U.K.	£47,254,070	£41,350,879
Exports to U.K.	101,793,692	95,541,529

COMMUNICATIONS

Railways.—The two Rhodesias are served by the Rhodesia Railways which connect with the South African Railways at Mafeking. The main line forks at Bulawayo; the northern section runs *viâ* the Victoria Falls through Northern Rhodesia to the Copperbelt and on to the Congo Border where it connects with the Katanga system. The eastern section runs along the watershed of Southern Rhodesia to serve the main centres and ends at Umtali where it joins the Portuguese system to provide access to Beira. With branch lines, the total mileage of the Rhodesia Railways is over 2,600 miles, including the line linking the Midlands of Southern Rhodesia with the port of Lourenço Marques in Portuguese East Africa, which was completed in 1955.

Nyasaland is served by a Railway system (the Trans-Zambezia Railway, the Central Africa Railway and the Nyasaland Railways) which connects Beira with Nyasaland. The total length of the system is nearly 500 miles.

Roads.—Main roads, which are in process of modernization, connect all the main centres of the Federation with one another and with adjacent territories, and secondary roads serve rural areas. The total route mileage of roads is about 62,000 miles (36,000 miles in Southern Rhodesia, 20,000 miles in Northern Rhodesia and nearly 6,000 miles in Nyasaland) of which some 11,600 miles are designated as main or principal roads (5,000 miles in Southern Rhodesia, 3,700 miles in Northern Rhodesia and 2,900 miles in Nyasaland, excluding roads within municipal areas). Major bridges, many of which were the gift of the Beit Trustees, span the larger rivers on main roads, the Beit Bridge over the Limpopo, the Ottobeit Bridge at Chirundu over the Zambezi and the Birchenough Bridge over the Sabi River being noteworthy.

Air Services.—Civil aviation has made rapid progress in the Federal area since the war. The existing airline was reconstituted in partnership between the three territories as the Central African Airways Corporation. Flying Viscount, Dakota and Beaver aircraft, Central African Airways provide daily services between the major towns of the Federation as well as services to Nairobi, Johannesburg, Lourenço Marques, Durban, Elisabethville and Beira. Beaver aircraft provide services between many of the smaller centres in Northern Rhodesia and Nyasaland. Links to overseas countries are provided by a number of the major world airlines which operate through the international airport at Salisbury. The travelling time between the Federation and London is 17 hours by B.O.A.C. Comet and 15½ hours by S.A.A. Boeing 707's.

CAPITAL

SALISBURY, the Federal capital, is also the principal city of Southern Rhodesia. It is built round the site where the Pioneer Column ended its march into Mashonaland in 1890. Situated in the north-east of Southern Rhodesia, it is on the main railway line which traverses the more closely settled areas of the Colony. Branch railway lines run north-east and north-west. It is the centre of the tobacco industry—the tobacco auction sales at Salisbury are the largest in the world—and an industrial centre of considerable importance. Estimated population, including townships on the periphery of Salisbury: Europeans, 91,000; Africans, 217,000; Asians and Coloured, 6,200. Total: 314,200.

FLAG

Shield bearing emblems of the colonies, with dovetailing to show their unification, gold sun rising on blue sky, lion red on white, 13 black and white wavy bars—all on a Blue Ensign.

SOUTHERN RHODESIA

Southern Rhodesia, comprising Matabeleland, Mashonaland and Manicaland, is that part of the territory named after Cecil Rhodes lying south of the Zambesi River, its political neighbours being Northern Rhodesia and Portuguese East Africa on the N.; the Transvaal and Bechuanaland on the S. and W.; and Portuguese East Africa on the E. The total area is 150,333 square miles. The estimated population, at Dec. 31, 1962, numbered 223,000 Europeans, 18,700 Asiatics and Coloureds and 3,690,000 Africans, giving a combined total of approximately 3,931,700. In 1962 the birth-rate was 23 per thousand and the death-rate 6.

The majority of the natives of Southen Rhodesia (members of the so-called Bantu race), are known as Mashona. In the Western portion of the Colony are the descendants of the Amandebele who conquered and settled down among the Mashona, and from whom the Province of Matabeleland derives its name.

Southern Rhodesia was administered by the British South Africa Company from the date of occupation (1890) to 1923, when responsible government was granted. On this latter date the Company relinquished all rights and interests in the land of Southern Rhodesia except in those estates which it was already developing on July 10, 1923. A Land and Agricultural Bank grants loans for farm development and acquisition of residential property on easy terms of repayment. Of the Colony's 97,184,000 acres, 21,020,000 have been allocated for Native Reserves, 8,052,000 for Native Purchase Areas and 12,878,000 for Special Native Areas.

FINANCE

	1961–62	1962–63*
Revenue	£25,273,000	£25,462,000
Expenditure from revenue funds	24,938,000	25,960,000
Expenditure from loan funds	4,605,000	3,688,000

*Estimated.

(A large proportion of the Public Debt has been taken over by the Federal Government.)

EDUCATION

African education comes under the Minister of African Education in the Southern Rhodesia Government. Expenditure in 1962–63 was £5,155,000. There are 3,387 schools of all types including 52 teacher training schools, 50 secondary schools, 15 post-primary industrial schools and 5 schools catering for the blind, the deaf and the dumb. The total enrolment for all types of schools is 654,555 and there are 15,635 African teachers in employment; European teachers number 608. Secondary schools provide education up to Southern Rhodesia Junior Certificate level, while 28 of them go as far as Cambridge School Certificate and 2 schools prepare pupils for Higher School Certificate. It is estimated that nearly 90 per cent. of children of school going age are able to find a place in school.

GOVERNMENT

The Colony obtained self-government in 1923 and has a Parliament of 65 members and a Cabinet of 8 members. The Queen is represented by a Governor who presides over the Executive Council. The Southern Rhodesian Government is responsible for native affairs, bridges, irrigation, roads, power, local government, labour, housing and social welfare. All discriminatory legislation is reserved for the consent of the British Government.

Municipal self-government has been established in the city of Salisbury, the city of Bulawayo, and in the towns of Umtali, Gwelo, Gatooma, Que Que and Fort Victoria. Smaller areas are administered by Town Management Boards. Over the past ten years local self-government among the Africans has been encouraged and by the end of 1962 there were 57 Native Councils raising their own rates.

Governor, His Excellency Hon. Sir Humphrey Vicary Gibbs, K.C.M.G., O.B.E. (1959).

MINISTRY
(Dec. 17, 1962)

Prime Minister and Minister of the Public Service, Hon. W. J. Field, C.M.G., M.B.E.

Deputy Prime Minister, Minister of the Treasury, and Leader of the House, Hon. I. D. Smith.

Minister of Justice and of Law and Order, Hon. C. W. Dupont.

Minister of Mines and Industrial Development, Hon. J. Gaunt.

Minister of Agriculture and of Lands and Natural Resources, The Duke of Montrose.

Minister of Irrigation and of Roads and Road Traffic, Hon. W. J. Harper.

Minister of Internal Affairs, Local Government, and African Education: Hon. J. H. Howman.

Minister of Labour and Social Welfare, Hon. I. F. McLean.

Speaker, Legislative Assembly, Dr. Hon. W. Alexander, C.M.G.

Secretary, Department of the Prime Minister and Cabinet Office, G. B. Clarke, I.S.O.

Secretarial Head, Division of Justice, J. W. Pithey, C.B.E.

Secretary for Internal Affairs, S. E. Morris, C.M.G.
Director of Mines, Dr. F. L. Amm.
Secretary to Treasury, C. E. M. Greenfield, C.M.G., M.B.E.
Secretary for Law and Order, A. M. Bruce Brand.
Secretary for Lands and Natural Resources, K. K. Parker.
Secretarial Head, Ministry of Labour and Social Welfare, J. Armstrong, I.S.O.
Secretarial Head, Division of Local Government, S. G. A. Hinde.
Secretarial Head, Ministry of Water Development, J. H. R. Savory.
Secretary for Agriculture, F. C. Wisdom.

SALISBURY, the capital, is situated on the Mashonaland plateau, altitude 4,850 ft., population (estimated) 314,200, including 91,000 Europeans. BULAWAYO, the largest town in Matabeleland, altitude 4,450 ft., estimated population 210,900, including 50,000 Europeans. Other centres are Umtali, Gwelo, Gatooma, Que Que and Fort Victoria.

Salisbury is 5,600 miles from London (air route) transit 17 hours; by sea, *viâ* Cape Town, 17 days (approx.).

NORTHERN RHODESIA

The Protectorate of Northern Rhodesia lies on the plateau of Central Africa between the longitudes 22° E. and 33° 33′ E. and between the latitudes 8° 15′ S. and 18° S. Its area is 288,130 square miles, and its boundaries are 3,515 miles in length.

With the exception of the valleys of the Zambezi, the Luapula, the Kafue and the Luangwa Rivers, and the Luana valley, the greater part of Northern Rhodesia has a flat to rolling topography, with elevations varying from 3,000 to 5,000 feet above sea level, but in the north-eastern districts the plateau rises to occasional altitudes of over 6,000 feet. In many localities the evenness of the plateau is broken by hills, sometimes occurring as chains which develop into areas of broken country.

Although Northern Rhodesia lies within the tropics, and fairly centrally in the great land mass of the African continent, its elevation relieves it from the extremely high temperatures and humidity usually associated with tropical countries. The lower reaches of the Zambezi, Luangwa and Kafue rivers in deeper valleys do experience high humidity and trying extremes of heat, but these areas are remote and sparsely populated.

At Dec. 31, 1961, the estimated population of Northern Rhodesia was 75,000 Europeans, 7,900 Asiatics, 1,900 mixed races and 2,430,000 Africans.

FINANCE

	1962–63	1963–64*
Revenue	£20,667,450	£19,584,000
Expenditure	21,060,659	21,745,000

* Estimated.

With the coming into being of the Federation of Rhodesia and Nyasaland, the Federal Government assumed, under the Constitution, powers to impose certain important taxes formerly enjoyed by the Northern Rhodesia Government and also took over responsibility for the administration of various departments and services.

GOVERNMENT

Government is carried on by a Governor appointed by the Crown, assisted by an Executive Council of four officials and six unofficial members, of whom two must be Africans. The Legislative Council consists of 38 elected members, 4 officials and 4 nominated members. The Legislative Council is presided over by a Speaker who is a member of the Council, and who is appointed by the Governor on behalf of Her Majesty the Queen.

Governor of Northern Rhodesia, His Excellency Sir Evelyn Dennison Hone, K.C.M.G., C.V.O., O.B.E. (1958).

EXECUTIVE COUNCIL

Chief Secretary, R. E. Luyt, C.M.G., D.C.M.	£3,450
Legal Affairs, B. A. Doyle, Q.C. (*Attorney-General*)	3,200
Finance, T. C. Gardner, C.B.E.	3,200
Native Affairs and Chief Commissioner, F. M. Thomas, C.M.G.	3,200
Local Government and Social Welfare, K. D. Kaunda	3,200
Transport and Works, F. N. Stubbs	3,200
Lands and Natural Resources, C. E. Cousins, C.B.E.	3,200
African Education, H. M. Nkumbula	3,200
African Agriculture, S. M. Kapwepwe	3,200
Labour and Mines, R. C. Kamanga	3,200

Speaker, T. Williams, O.B.E., E.D.

JUDICATURE

Chief Justice of the High Court, Sir Diarmaid Conroy, C.M.G., O.B.E., T.D.	£3,550
Puisne Judges, W. E. Evans; M. W. D. Dennison, M.C.; T. Pickett; W. E. Windham; J. R. Blagden	2,900

PROVINCIAL COMMISSIONERS

Provincial Commissioners, A. St. J. Sugg; E. L. Button, M.B.E.; G. C. M. Heathcote; P. C. Middleton; D. C. Goodfellow, M.B.E.; J. E. Madocks, M.B.E.; P. G. D. Clark; J. H. R. Davies, M.B.E.	2,900

British Council Representative in N. Rhodesia, R. P. R. Sangster.

CAPITAL AND SEAT OF GOVERNMENT, Lusaka, situated in the Midlands (1956 Census, European pop. 9,440). Other centres are Livingstone, Broken Hill, Fort Jameson, Mazabuka, Abercorn, Kasama, Mongu, Ndola, Luanshya, Mufulira, Chingola, Bancroft and Kitwe (the main copper mining town of the copper belt—European pop. 9,680).

Commissioner in London, J. P. Murray, C.M.G., 57 Haymarket, S.W.1.

NYASALAND PROTECTORATE

The Nyasaland Protectorate comprises Lake Nyasa and its western shore, with the high tableland separating it from the basin of the Luangwa River, the watershed forming the western frontier with Northern Rhodesia; south of the lake the Protectorate reaches almost to the Zambezi and is surrounded by Portuguese East Africa (Mozambique) the frontier lying on the west on the watershed of the Zambezi and Shire Rivers and to the east on the Ruo, a tributary of the Shire, and Lakes Chiuta and Chilwa. This boundary reaches the eastern shore of Lake Nyasa and extends up the mid-point of the lake for about half its length where it returns to the eastern and northern shores to form a frontier with Tanganyika.

Nyasaland has a total area of 45 747 sq. miles (land area, 36,481) with an estimated population at the end of 1961 of 2,921,100 (2,900,000 Africans, 8,800 Europeans and 12,300 Asians and other non-Africans).

The seat of Government is Zomba (estimated population 1961, 7,500), the other main centres being Blantyre/Limbe, the commercial and indsutrial centre and headquarters of the Southern Province; Lilongwe, headquarters of the Central Province; Mzuzu, headquarters of the Northern Province; Cholo, Mlanje, Fort Johnston and Mzimba. A single-track railway runs from the south end of the lake (itself served by one passenger and a number of cargo boats) through Blantyre/Limbe to the southern frontier, whence, crossing the Zambezi by a bridge 12,050 feet long, it reaches the coast at the Mozambique port of Beira, which handles the bulk of the Territory's imports and exports. A good-class earth road system covers the whole country and is already tar-macadamized from Mlanje through Blantyre/Limbe and Zomba to the Shire River 30 miles further north, and also from Lilongwe to the lake-shore at Salima, northern terminus of the railway.

Finance

	1961–62	1962–63†
Revenue	£7,194,910	£7,699,006
Expenditure	7,930,953	9,203,818
Development Fund Expenditure.*	3,393,742	4,106,802

†Estimated.

* Financed by loans, grants under the Colonial Development and Welfare Acts, contributions from recurrent revenue, etc.

In 1953, the Government of the Federation of Rhodesia and Nyasaland assumed responsibility for the servicing of the public debt of the Protectorate, then amounting to £6,228,488. The Nyasaland Government is responsible for the servicing of the Public Debt raised since Oct. 23, 1953, totalling (at June 30, 1962) £9,476,718.

Government

The constitution of Nyasaland, which came into effect on May 10, 1963, provides for a Legislative Assembly of 28 elected members, 8 elected by the Higher Roll and 20 by the Lower Roll and an *ex officio* Minister of Finance. The Cabinet is presided over by the Prime Minister and consists of the Prime Minister, the Attorney General, the Minister of Finance and seven other Ministers. The Cabinet is collectively responsible to the Legislative Assembly. The Governor normally acts in accordance with the advice of the Cabinet except in the case of certain expressly reserved subjects.

Governor, His Excellency Sir Glyn Smallwood Jones, K.C.M.G., M.B.E., *apptd.* 1961 (+*allce.* £2,250) £5,800
Deputy Governor, R. S. Foster, C.M.G. 3,250

Cabinet

Prime Minister, and Minister of Natural Resources and Surveys, Dr. Hon. H. K. Banda £4,500
Minister of Education, Social Development and Information, Hon. M. W. K. Chiume 3,000
Minister of Local Government, Hon. H. B. M. Chipembere 3,000
Minister of Justice, Hon. O. E. C. Chirwa 3,000
Financial Secretary and Minister of Finance, Hon. H. E. I. Phillips, C.M.G., M.B.E. 3,000
Minister of Works and Housing, Hon. A. W. Bwanausi 3,000
Minister of Transport and Communications, Hon. C. Cameron 3,000
Minister of State, Hon. M. Mkandawire .. 2,000
Minister of Labour, Hon. W. Chokani 3,000
Minister of Trade and Industry, Hon. J. D. Msonthi 3,000

Chief Justice, Sir Edgar Unsworth, C.M.G. .. £3,350

Provincial Commissioners

Central Province, Maj. P. F. C. Nicholson. £2,800
Northern Province, M. A. Sharpe, M.B.E. ... 2,800
Southern Province, D. A. G. Reeve, O.B.E. .. 2,300

British Council Representative, R. P. K. Harrison, M.B.E., Sharrers Road, Blantyre.

ST. HELENA

probably the best known of all the solitary islands in the world, is situated in the South Atlantic Ocean, 955 miles S. of the Equator, 760 S.E. of Ascension, 1,140 from the nearest point of the African Continent, 1,800 from the coast of S. America and 4,477 from Southampton, in 15° 55′ S. lat. and 5° 42′ W. long. It is 10½ miles long, 6½ broad, and encloses an area of 47 square miles, with an estimated population at Dec. 31, 1962, of 4,624. St. Helena is of volcanic origin, and consists of numerous rugged mountains, the highest rising to 2,700 feet, interspersed with picturesque ravines. Although within the tropics, the south-east "trades" keep the temperature mild and equable. St. Helena was discovered by the Portuguese navigator, João de Nova, in 1502 (probably on St. Helena's Day) and remained unknown to other European nations until 1588. It was used as a port of call for vessels of all nations trading to the East until it was annexed by the Dutch in 1633. It was never occupied by them, however, and the English East India Company seized it in 1659. In 1834 it was ceded to the Crown. During the period 1815 to 1821 the island was lent to the British Government as a place of exile for the Emperor Napoleon Bonaparte who died in St. Helena on May 5, 1821. It was formerly an important station on the route to India, but its prosperity decreased after the construction of the Suez Canal. A phormium (flax fibre) and lacemaking industry has been established. ♆St. James's Bay, on the north-west of the Island, possesses a good anchorage.

Government

The government of St. Helena is administered by a Governor, with the aid of an Executive Council of up to 4 official and 3 unofficial members. The Governor is also assisted by an Advisory Council of up to 10 unofficial members chosen to represent, as far as possible, all unofficial sections of the community, the Governor alone making all ordinances.

Capital, ♆Jamestown, population (1956), 1,568.

Governor, His Excellency Sir John Osbaldiston Field, C.M.G. (1962) (+*allce.*) £2,000
Government Secretary, A. F. B. Glennie, C.M.G. £1,400
Colonial Treasurer and Collector of Customs, J. O. Talbot-Phibbs 1,200
Senior Medical Officer, Dr. J. S. Noaks 2,500
Agricultural and Forestry Officer, A. G. Brightman .... (+*allce.*) 1,150

Distance from London: 4,472 miles; transit 14 days.

Finance and Trade

	1961	1962
Public revenue	£258,132	£303,105
Expenditure	291,541	290,477
Total imports	258,432	244,988
Total exports	69,454	101,066
Imports from U.K.	271,270	261,535
Exports to U.K.	53,964	47,318

ASCENSION

An isolated island in the South Atlantic (3,417 miles from Plymouth, 760 from St. Helena, and

900 from Cape Palmas on the African coast), is of volcanic origin, the peak rising to the height of 2,820 feet, situated 7° 55′ 55″ S. lat. and 14° 25′ 55′ W. long. It is said to have been discovered by João de Nova, on Ascension Day, 1501, and two years later was visited by Alphonse d'Albuquerque, who gave the island its present name. Its extreme length is 7½ miles, and extreme breadth 6 miles, with an area of about 38 square miles, and, being situated in the heart of the S.E. trade winds, its climate is dry and salubrious up to 1,800 feet, but above that height to its limit it is damp and foggy. It remained uninhabitated till 1815, when the English took possession of it; on Dec. 31, 1961, the population was 336. Ascension was administered by the Board of Admiralty until 1922, when by Royal Letters Patent it became a Dependency of St. Helena, and was transferred to the Colonial Office. Ψ Georgetown, the capital, is situated in a small bay on the N.W. coast. Ascension is visited from January to May by the sea-turtle, which lay their eggs in the sand; the sooty tern, or "wide-awake," use the island as a nesting-place about every eighth month.

Resident Magistrate, J. R. Bruce.

TRISTAN DA CUNHA

Is the chief of a group of islands of volcanic origin lying in lat. 37° 6′ S. and long. 12° 2′ W., discovered in 1506 by a Portuguese admiral (Tristão da Cunha), after whom they are named. They have a total area of 45 square miles and in 1921 the inhabitants numbered 127, increased in 1959 to 292. The main island is about 1,800 miles W. of the Cape of Good Hope, 3,600 miles N.E. of Cape Horn, and about 1,320 miles S.S.W. of St. Helena. It was the resort of British and American sealers from the middle of the 18th century, and in 1760 a British naval officer visited the group and gave his name to Nightingale Island. On August 14, 1816, the group was annexed to the British Crown and a garrison was placed on Tristan da Cunha, but this force was withdrawn in 1817, William Glass, a corporal of artillery (*died* 1853), remaining at his own request, with his wife and two children. This party, with two ex-Navy men, Alexander Cotton and John Mooney, and three masons imported for the purpose of housing the garrison, formed a settlement. In 1827 five coloured women from St. Helena, and afterwards, others from Cape Colony, joined the party.

In 1961 the population numbered 280 persons, the islands being administered by the Colonial Office through a resident Administrator, with headquarters at the settlement of Edinburgh.

In October, 1961, a volcano, believed to have been extinct for thousands of years, erupted and mounds of earth were thrown up in some cases to a height of 35 feet. In view of the danger of further volcanic activity, the inhabitants were evacuated on Oct. 10 to Nightingale Island and taken by a Dutch liner to Cape Town. The British Government assumed responsibility for the transport and resettlement of the party which reached the United Kingdom on Nov. 23, 1961, where they remained for nearly two years. An advance party returned to Tristan da Cunha in the spring of 1963, and the main body of islanders was expected to go back in the autumn.

Administrator, P. A. Day.

Chaplain, Rev. J. E. K. Flint.

INACCESSIBLE ISLAND is a lofty mass of rock with sides 2 miles in length; the island is the resort of penguins and sea-fowl. Cultivation was started in 1937.

THE NIGHTINGALE ISLANDS are three in number, of which the largest is 1 mile long and ¾ mile wide, and rises in two peaks, 960 and 1,105 ft. above the sea-level respectively. The smaller islands, Stoltenhoff and Middle Isle, are little more than huge rocks. Seals, innumerable penguins, and vast numbers of sea-fowl visit these islands.

GOUGH ISLAND (or Diego Alvarez), in 40° 20′ S. and 9° 44′ W., lies about 250 miles S.S.E. of Tristan da Cunha. The island is about 8 miles long and 4 miles broad, with a total area of 40 square miles, and has been a British possession since 1816. The island is the resort of penguins and sea-elephants and has valuable guano deposits. There is no permanent population, but there is a meteorological station maintained on the island by the South African Government and manned by South Africans.

By Letters Patent dated January 12, 1938, the Islands of *Tristan da Cunha*, *Gough*, *Nightingale* and *Inaccessible* in the South Atlantic were made Dependencies of the Island of St. Helena.

SARAWAK

Sarawak is a British Colony on the north-west coast of the island of Borneo, with a seaboard of about 500 miles, an area of 48,250 square miles, and a population (1962 census) of 776,990, composed of various races, of whom the Sea Dyaks (Ibans), Malays, Chinese, Land Dyaks, Melanaus, Kayans and Kenyahs are the most numerous. The government of Sarawak was granted in 1841 by the Sultan of Brunei to Sir James Brooke, who became well known as Rajah Brooke of Sarawak. Other concessions were made in 1861, 1882, 1885, and 1890, when the Limbang River was obtained. The Lawas River was added in 1905. In 1864 Great Britain recognized Sarawak as an independent State, and under an agreement of 1888 the State was placed under British protection. In 1941 the centenary of Brooke rule was celebrated throughout the State.

Sarawak was ceded to Great Britain by the Rajah on July 1, 1946. It was due to become part of the new Federation of Malaysia on the latter's inception in the autumn of 1963.

The territory of Sarawak extends from Cape Datu in the south to the Lawas District, where it touches the boundary of North Borneo. The southern boundary is, except for a few short stretches, formed by outstanding ridges of hills; the eastern boundary is a broken range of mountains with peaks rising to over 5,000 feet. The principal rivers are the Rejang (navigable for about 160 miles), the Baram (navigable for about 100 miles), the Batang-Lupar, and the Limbang. Kuching, the capital, stands on a small river (the Sarawak) which is navigable from its mouth to Kuching (23 miles).

The country produces rubber, oil, bauxite, timber, sago, rice, illipe nuts, birds' nests, gold, pepper, rattans and jungle produce. There are also known coal deposits.

FINANCE	1962 (Estimated)
Revenue	$80,260,000
Expenditure (Recurrent)	77,652,000*
Expenditure (Capital)	35,400,000

* Including $10,852,000 to Capital Account.

TRADE WITH U.K.

	1961	1962
Imports from U.K.	£1,464,673	£2,270,707
Exports to U.K.	5,421,149	6,717,278

Governor and Commander-in-Chief, His Excellency Sir Alexander Nicol Anton Waddell, K.C.M.G., D.S.C. (1959) (*duty allowance* £2,500) £4,500

Chief Justice of Sarawak, North Borneo and Brunei, Sir Campbell Wylie	$29,040
Chief Secretary (vacant)	
Attorney-General, P. E. H. Pike, Q.C.	24,480
Financial Secretary, B. A. St. J. Hepburn, C.M.G.	24,480
Deputy Chief Secretary, A. R. Snelus, C.M.G.	23,040
Chairman, Public Service Commission, R. L. V. Wilkes, C.M.G.	22,440
Senior Residents, J. C. B. Fisher, C.M.G., O.B.E.; A. F. R. Griffin	22,440
Residents, J. F. Drake-Brockman; R. H. Morris, O.B.E.; M. M. McSporran	20,760
Senior Puisne Judge, L. D. Smith	22,440
Puisne Judges, A. H. Simpson; E. R. Harley; D. B. McGilligan	20,760
Director of Public Works, J. K. Wardzala	22,440
Commissioner of Constabulary, P. E. Turnbull	22,440
Director of Agriculture, J. Cook, C.B.E.	22,440
Director of Education, M. G. Dickson, C.M.G.	22,440
Director of Medical Services, Dr. D. A. Baird, C.B.E.	22,440
British Council Representative, H. R. Crooke.	

Chief Town, Ψ Kuching; population of municipal area, 51,403. Distance from London 8,700 miles; distance from Singapore 400 miles.

SEYCHELLES

The Colony of Seychelles, in the Indian Ocean, consists of two distinct collections of islands—the Mahé group, 32 islands in all, granitic with high hills and mountains (highest point 2,971 feet) and the Out-lying Islands, the Coralline group, numbering 60 more and, for the most part, only a little above sea-level. Proclaimed as French territory in 1756, the Mahé group began to be settled as a dependency of Mauritius from 1770, was captured by a British ship in 1794 and was finally assigned to Great Britain in 1810. By Letters Patent of September, 1903, these islands, together with the Coralline group, were erected into a separate Colony. The total area of the Granitic group is 87 square miles, of which Mahé, the largest island and the seat of Government, claims 55. The next largest island is Praslin, home of the unique double coconut, Coco de Mer. Islands of the Coralline group lie at distances from Mahé varying between 60 to 612 miles and. exclusive of the Aldabra lagoon (50 sq. miles), have a total area of approximately 13 sq. miles. Aldabra is famous for the gigantic land tortoises. These islands have no permanent population and, where worked, are supplied by contract labour from the Granitic group. The population on June 30, 1962, was 43,748. Although only 4° S. of the Equator, the islands are healthy; the death and birth rates in 1962 were 11·5 and 39·6 per 1,000 respectively. There are 30 primary schools, 9 secondary schools and a teachers' training college.

The Governor is assisted by an Executive Council of 4 *ex officio* members and 4 unofficial members appointed by the Governor, and by a Legislative Council of 4 *ex officio*, 5 elected and 3 nominated members. One of the nominated members is an unofficial.

FINANCE

Recurrent	1961	1962
Revenue	Rs.5,804,513	Rs.6,829,392
Expenditure	7,037,550	7,164,092

Rs=Rupees.

Exchange rate 1 Rupee=*1s. 6d.* The colony is grant-aided; expenditure from Colonial Office funds in 1961 was *Rs.*2,730,057; in 1962 *Rs.*2,337,820.

TRADE

	1961	1962
Imports	Rs.12,011,349	Rs.12,781,410
Exports	6,643,394	7,301,886
Imports from U.K.	£284,315	£265,445
Exports to U.K.	60,208	91,317

The principal imports are cereals, sugar, cotton piece goods and manufactures. The chief exports are copra, essential oils, vanilla, cinnamon bark, patchouli leaves, guano and dried fish.

CAPITAL, Ψ Victoria (population 1960, 10,500), on the N.E. side of Mahé, has an excellent harbour.

Governor and Commander-in-Chief, His Excellency the Earl of Oxford and Asquith, C.M.G. (1961)	Rs.36,000
Chief Justice, N. P. F. Bonnetard, Q.C.	26,000
Colonial Secretary, G. P. Lloyd	25,000
Attorney-General, A. F. M. A. Sauzier, O.B.E.	23,500
Administrative Secretary, J. W. Jeffrey, M.B.E., D.S.C.	23,500
Financial Secretary (vacant)	23,500
Principal Auditor, W. A. Peel, M.B.E.	20,000
Director of Medical Services, A. G. Penrose	23,000
Chief Police Officer (vacant)	22,000
Director of Public Works, K. B. Thomas, M.C.	22,000
Director of Education, F. J. F. Tingay	22,000
Director of Agriculture, G. Lionnet, M.B.E.	22,000
Director of Tourism and Information, D. Knox	20,000

Letters to and from London—2 to 6 weeks.

SINGAPORE

The State of Singapore consists of the island of Singapore and the adjacent islets with a total area of 224·5 sq. miles. It was due to become part of the new Federation of Malaysia on the latter's inception in the autumn of 1963.

Singapore Island is situated off the southern extremity of the Malay Peninsula, to which it is joined by a causeway, carrying a road and a railway, across the Straits of Johore, which are about three-quarters of a mile in width; its length is 26 miles and its breadth 14 miles; its population at June 30, 1962 was estimated at 1,732,800, comprising 1,302,500 Chinese, 243,400 Malaysians, 143,700 Indians and Pakistanis, 13,700 Eurasians, 14,300 Europeans and 15,290 others.

FINANCE

	1962*
Revenue	$391,109,000
Expenditure	394,026,200

*Estimated.

The currency is linked to sterling and the rate of exchange is $1.00=2s. 4d.

PRODUCTION AND TRADE

In 1962 Singapore handled foreign trade valued at M$7,452,900,000 brought by 39,190 ships of a total net tonnage of 76,913,945 from all parts of the world. Trade with the Federation of Malaya was valued at $1,669,700,000.

Manufactures comprise a wide range of industries including the processing of rubber, pineapples, coconut oil, shipbuilding and repairing, sawmilling, steelrolling, motor assembly, printing and the manufacture of rubber foot-wear, soap, dry cell batteries, beer, soft drinks, tin containers, glassware, shoe polish, yarn, aluminium utensils, bricks, tiles and metal windows. The traditional concentration on the processing of primary products (rubber, tin, rattan), the provision of shipbuilding, docking and facilities, light engineering works and motor assembly plants have been supplemented in recent years by various industrial projects relating to chemical, mechanical, electrical, metal working, engineering, building materials and food industries.

TRADE WITH U.K.

	1961	1962
Imports from U.K.....	£37,439,727	£34,825,822
Exports to U.K.......	19,171,194	15,771,407

Head of State, The Yang di-Pertuan Negara, Inche Yusof bin Ishak (Dec. 3, 1959).

U.K. High Commissioner, The Earl of Selkirk, P.C., G.C.M.G., O.B.E., A.F.C.

Deputy High Commissioner, P. C. B. Moore.

Prime Minister, Lee Kuan Yew.

British Council Representative, D. Hardwick, M.B.E.

SWAZILAND

(*See* BASUTOLAND)

TONGA

The Tongan or *Friendly Islands* form a self-governing State under the protection of Great Britain, in accordance with the terms of the revised Treaty of Friendship signed at Nuku'alofa on Aug. 26, 1958. These islands are situated in the Southern Pacific some 300 miles to the E.S.E. of Fiji, with an area of 270 square miles, and population (1961) of 65,620. The largest island, Tongatapu, was discovered by Tasman in 1643. Most of the islands are of coral formation, but some are volcanic (Tofua, Kao and Niuafoou or " Tin Can " Island). The limits of the group are between 15° and 23° 30' S., and 173° and 177° W. Nukualofa, on the island of Tongatapu, is the seat of government. The present Queen Salote Tubou, G.C.V.O., G.B.E., succeeded her father the late King George Tubou II on April 12, 1918. The constitution provides for a Government consisting of the Sovereign, a privy council and cabinet, a legislative assembly and a judiciary. The legislative assembly has 21 members, with a Speaker, and includes the Ministers of the Crown, the two Governors of island groups, and the representatives of the Nobles and of the people (seven of each), who are elected triennially. In 1960, women were allowed to vote for the first time. Soil generally is fertile, the principal export is copra. Revenue 1961 £T728,374; expenditure £T811,092. There is no debt. Total imports (1961) £T1,424,201; total exports £T1,374,658. The total shipping cleared in 1961 was 176,101 tons. Tongan currency is on parity with Australian currency in relation to sterling.

British Commissioner and Consul, E. J. Coode (1960) (*and duty allowance* £200) £2,100.

TRINIDAD AND TOBAGO

AREA AND POPULATION

Trinidad, the second largest and most southerly of the West Indian Islands, lies close to the north coast of the continent of S. America, the nearest point of Venezuela being 7 miles distant. The island is situated between 10° 2'—10° 50' N. lat. and 60° 55'—61° 56' W. long., and is about 50 miles in length by 37 in breadth, with an area of 1,864 square miles, and a population (Census of 1960) of 827,957 (including Tobago). The racial groups at the 1960 census were: African 43 per cent., East Indian 36 per cent., Mixed or Coloured 16 per cent., European 2 per cent., Chinese 1 per cent. The island was discovered by Columbus in 1498, was colonized in 1532 by the Spaniards, capitulated to the British under Abercromby in 1797, and was ceded to Britain under the Treaty of Amiens (March 25, 1802). Two mountain systems, the Northern and Southern Ranges, stretch across almost its entire width and a third, the Central Range, lies somewhat diagonally across its middle portion; otherwise the island is mostly flat. The highest peaks are in the Northern Range (Aripo 3,085 ft., E. Tucuche 3,072 ft.). The climate is tropical with temperatures ranging from 70° to 90°F. and a rainfall ranging from 100 inches in the north east to 50 inches in the west. There is a well-marked dry season from January to May and a wet season from June to December. The nights are invariably cool. The main tourist season is from December to April.

Tobago lies between 11° 8' and 11° 21' N. lat. and between 60° 30' and 60° 50' W. long., about 75 miles south-east of Grenada, 19 miles north-east of Trinidad, and 120 miles S.W. of Barbados. It was ceded to the British Crown in 1814 and amalgamated with Trinidad in 1888. The island is 26 miles long, and 7½ broad, and has an area of 116 square miles, with a population (Census of 1960) of 33,333. It is one of the healthiest of the West Indies and a popular tourist resort. The main town is ♆Scarborough.

Other Islands.—Corozal Point and Icacos Point, the N.W. and S.W. extremities of Trinidad, enclose the Gulf of Paria, and west of Corozal Point lie several islands, of which Chacachacare, Huevos, Monos and Gaspar Grande are the most important. On Chacachacare is a leper settlement, the Medical Superintendent of which appeals for Sunday and weekly editions of British newspapers.

CAPITAL.—♆Port of Spain (pop. 93,954), one of the finest towns in the West Indies, with sewerage, electric lighting, omnibus and telephone services. Other towns of importance are ♆San Fernando (pop. 39,830), about 33 miles south of the capital, and Arima (pop. 10,982).

GOVERNMENT

The Territory of Trinidad and Tobago became an independent state and a member of the British Commonwealth on August 31, 1962, under the Trinidad and Tobago Independence Act, 1962. There is a Parliament consisting of a Senate and a House of Representatives with an elected Speaker. The Senate has 24 members nominated by the Governor-General, 14 appointed on the advice of the Premier, 4 on the advice of the Leader of the Opposition, and 7 to represent religious, economic or social interests, chosen after consultation with appropriate organizations.

Governor-General, His Excellency Sir Solomon Hochoy, G.C.M.G., O.B.E. (1962).

CABINET

(August 31, 1961)

Prime Minister and Minister of External Affairs, Dr. Hon. E. E. Williams.

Deputy Prime Minister and Minister of Home Affairs, Dr. Hon. P. V. J. Solomon.

Education and Culture, Senator Hon. D. Pierre.

Health and Housing, Hon. Mrs. I. Teshea.

Public Utilities, Hon. K. Mohammed.

Agriculture, Industry and Commerce, Hon. I. M. Robinson.

Local Government and Community Development, Hon. S. Mohammed.

Labour, Hon. R. E. Wallace.

Finance, Hon. A. N. R. Robinson.

Works, Hon. G. Montano.

Attorney-General, Senator Hon. G. A. Richards.

Petroleum and Mines, Hon. J. O'Halloran.

Without Portfolio, Hon. W. W. J. Alexander; Hon. A. A. Thompson; Hon. A. C. Alexis.

President, Senate, Hon. J. H. Maurice.
Speaker, House of Representatives, Hon. C. A. Thomasos.

JUDICATURE

Chief Justice, Hon. Sir Hugh Wooding, C.B.E.
Justices of Appeal, Hons. A. H. McShine; I. E. Hyatali; C. E. G. Phillips.
Puisne Judges, Hons. M. H. A. Corbin; N. A. M. Peterkin; K. P. de la Bastide; E. A. Rees; H. A. Fraser; C. E. Achong; P. T. Georges; G. M. Scott.

COMMONWEALTH REPRESENTATION

Port-of-Spain

United Kingdom High Commissioner, His Excellency Sir Norman Costar, K.C.M.G.
Deputy High Commissioner, S. J. G. Fingland.

London

High Commissioner for Trinidad and Tobago, His Excellency Sir Learie Constantine, M.B.E., 51 South Audley Street, W.1.

British Council Representative (Port-of-Spain), J. Makin, M.B.E.

EDUCATION

The system of education has been reformed to co-ordinate more closely the interlocking levels—primary, post-primary/secondary and higher. The system provides for education of the pupils from 5 to 12 in primary schools—453 at present—and from 12 plus to 18 in a present total of 36 Government and assisted secondary schools—grammar, modern and 2 technical schools. There are also about 42 recognized private secondary schools. Figures for 1962 of primary enrolment amount to 195,162, with an average attendance of 158,647. The Government Polytechnic Institute was established in 1959 and has an enrolment of 607.

TRANSPORT AND COMMUNICATIONS

There are 109 miles of public railway and the total mileage of main and local roads maintained during 1961 was 2,527. There are 198 post offices and postal agencies, 56 of which transact savings bank and money order business. There are an internal telegraph system and two local broadcasting stations.

Trinidad is well served by steamship lines and there are deep water wharf facilities at Port of Spain. Eleven international scheduled airlines operate to and through Trinidad (Piarco), which acts as a focal point for air traffic between the Americas. There were 11,961 movements of aircraft in 1961. A domestic air service between Trinidad and Tobago is operated by B.W.I.A. Flights in 1961 averaged three per day. Air transit to London, 16½ hrs.; to New York, 8 hrs.

PRODUCTION

Oil is the principal export. A remarkable phenomenon is the asphalt lake, 114 acres in extent, near the village of La Brea, from which in 1962 162,613 tons of natural asphalt were removed. The soil of Trinidad is rich and productive, the most important products being sugar, molasses, rum, cocoa, coconuts and coconut products, citrus and coffee. Agricultural exports totalled $50,072,000 in 1961.

FINANCE

	1961	1962
Revenue	$147,941,000	$213,202,000
Expenditure	212,793,000	225,562,000
Gross public debt	98,868,000	120,381,000

TRADE

	1961	1962
Imports	$575,789,000	$605,982,600
Exports	593,934,000	593,279,000

	1961	1962
Imports from U.K.	£25,328,756	£24,418,637
Exports to U.K.	34,000,057	30,959,134

THE WEST INDIES

Trade Enquiry Office in London, Trade Commissioner for the British West Indies, British Guiana and British Honduras, 6–10 Bruton Street, W.1.

The West Indies are a number of islands and islets, some of them mere rocks, situated between 10° to 27° North and 59° 30′ to 85° West. The whole archipelago extends in a curve from the Florida Channel (North America) to within 7 miles of the coast of Venezuela (South America), and is divided into three main groups: I. GREATER ANTILLES, which contain the largest islands, *Cuba* (44,000 sq. miles) and *Hispaniola* (Haiti and the Dominican Republic) (30,000 sq. miles), Jamaica and Puerto Rico; II. BAHAMAS, which are entirely British. III. LESSER ANTILLES, which are divided among the United Kingdom, France, Netherlands, the United States and Venezuela; the British colonies in the Lesser Antilles are Barbados, Leeward and Windward Islands and Trinidad and Tobago. The total area of the archipelago is nearly 100,000 square miles, of which 72,000 square miles are *Independent*, 12,300 *British*, 3,890 *United States*, 1,350 *French*, 430 *Netherlands*, and 90 *Venezuelan*.

The West India Islands that lie nearest the East have been called the *Windward Islands*; the others the *Leeward Islands*, on account of the winds blowing generally from the eastern point in those quarters.

CARIBBEAN ORGANIZATION

Established in September, 1961, by agreement between the Governments of France, the Netherlands, the United Kingdom and the United States, as the successor to the Caribbean Commission, the organization gives advice on social, cultural and economic matters of common interest to the Caribbean area, particularly agriculture, communications, education, fisheries, health, housing, industry, labour, music and the arts, social welfare and trade.

The members of the Organization are France for the Departments of French Guiana, Guadeloupe and Martinique; the Netherlands Antilles; Surinam; British Guiana; the British Virgin Islands; The West Indies; the Commonwealth of Puerto Rico; and the Virgin Islands of the U.S. The Organization is governed by a Council, the Caribbean Council, on which each member country is represented.

The Central Secretariat of the Organization is situated at Hato Rey, Puerto Rico.

Secretary-General, C. F. Beauregard.

The Federation of the West Indies, set up on January 3, 1958, under the British Caribbean (Federation) Act, 1956, of ten colonies with dependencies, came to an end in 1962. Jamaica became an independent state on August 6, 1962, and Trinidad and Tobago on August 31, 1962. (*See* separate articles.) The United Kingdom Government is empowered under the West Indies Act, 1962, to make provision for the administration of the remaining West Indian Colonies and for the establishment of common courts. Agreement was reached at a conference in London in May, 1962, on the formation of a new *West Indies Federation* of eight members—Barbados, the Leeward Islands (Antigua, St. Kitts-Nevis-Anguilla, Montserrat) and the Windward Islands (Dominica, Grenada, St. Lucia and St. Vincent), with the Federal Capital in Barbados.

TERRITORIES

	Area sq. miles	Population
Antigua	171	57,000
Barbados	166	235,132
Cayman Islands	100	7,616
Dominica	290	59,479
Grenada	133	88,677
Jamaica*	4,411	1,613,418
Montserrat	32	12,157
St. Kitts-Nevis-Anguilla	153	56,644
St. Lucia	238	94,718
St. Vincent	150	80,000
Trinidad and Tobago*	1,984	827,957
Turks and Caicos Islands	166	5,714

* For Jamaica and Trinidad and Tobago, *see* separate articles.

ANTIGUA

Antigua lies in 17° 6′ N. lat. and 61°45′ W. long., and is nearly 108 square miles in area with a coast-line of about 70 miles. Antigua was first settled by the English in 1632, and was granted to Lord Willoughby by Charles II. It is much less hilly and wooded than the other Leeward Islands, and is largely given up to the cultivation of sugar, for which one central sugar factory has been erected. Cotton is now planted on a large scale and the island also exports molasses, tomatoes and rum. The population, with Barbuda, is estimated at 57,000.

Finance and Trade

	1961	1962
Revenue	£2,020,115	£1,900,301
Expenditure	2,074,284	1,715,289
Public debt	619,417	627,458
Total imports	4,067,855	4,507,040
Total exports	948,353	1,099,909

Government

A new constitution, which came into effect on January 1, 1960, provides for the office of Chief Minister and three other Ministers making the number four in all as against three formerly. All the members of the new Executive Council are unofficials except the Attorney-General, who is an official. The Administrator continues to preside in Executive Council.

Administrator, His Hon. I. G. Turbott, C.M.G. (*plus £300 allce. and house*) £3,000
Attorney-General, Hon. W. Macintyre... 1,750
Financial Secretary, J. F. Booth, M.B.E..... 1,650
Senior Medical Officer, K. H. Uttley, M.D... 1,750
Director of Agriculture, H. A. L. Francis .. 1,600

Barbuda, formerly a possession of the Codrington family, is situated 30 miles N. of Antigua, of which it is a dependency, in lat. 17° 35′ N., long. 61° 42′ W. Area, 62 square miles. Population, 1,000. The island is flat and mostly stony, producing cotton, corn and ground-nuts. Wild deer are found, and there is good tarpon and other fishing.

Warden, A. Dyer (*and quarters*), £825 to £937.

Redonda is uninhabited.

CAPITAL ♆St. John. Population (1960), 21,000.

BARBADOS,

the most easterly of the West India Islands, is situated in 13° 4′ N., and longitude 59° 37′ W. It is nearly 21 English miles long by 14 broad at the widest part, and comprises an area of 166 sq. miles, about 68,875 acres being cultivated. The estimated population on Dec. 31, 1962, was 235,132. The principal exports are sugar, molasses, rum, margarine, lard and laundry soap, and the imports meat, rice, salted fish, dairy products, flour, corn meal, lumber, textiles, animal foods and chemical fertilizers.

FINANCE

	1961–62	1962–63
Revenue	$26,209,316	$28,107,495
Expenditure	27,157,008	28,361,497
Public debt	27,237,728	34,398,978

TRADE

	1961	1962
Total imports	$80,282,100	$83,905,000
Total exports	43,176,800	42,443,900

TRADE WITH U.K.

	1961	1962
Imports from U.K.	£5,272,453	£5,304,695
Exports to U.K.	3,695,816	3,117,096

Barbados $=4*s.* 2*d.*

Net tonnage of merchant shipping entered and cleared in 1962, 3,349,412 tons.

GOVERNMENT

Barbados has always remained in the possession of Great Britain, by which it was settled in 1627. The Crown has a veto on legislation. The Legislature consists of the Governor, a Legislative Council of 14 members appointed by the Sovereign, and a House of Assembly of 24 members elected every five years by adult suffrage.

A ministerial system of Government was introduced in 1954 and a cabinet system in Jan. 1958. There are a Premier and five other Ministers, responsible for the executive functions of Government except defence and security, personnel, establishment and external affairs. Since the attainment of full internal self-government on Oct. 16, 1961, the Executive Council has been replaced by a Privy Council and the Judicial and Legal Service Commission and the Public Service Commission have full executive powers of appointment and discipline.

Governor, Sir John Montague Stow, K.C.M.G. (1959) (+*duty allowance* $7,200) $26,400

Premier and Minister of Finance, Hon. E. W. Barrow.
Minister of Social Services, Hon. A. da C. Edwards.
Minister of Development, Trade, Industry, Labour and Tourism, Hon. A. W. Crawford.
Minister of Communications, Works and Housing, Hon. G. G. Fergusson.
Minister of Agriculture, Lands and Fisheries, Hon. C. E. Talma.
Minister of Education, Hon. J. C. Tudor.
Minister without Portfolio, Hon. H. A. Vaughan.

Chief Judge, Sir Kenneth Stoby......... $13,200
President of Legislative Council, Hon. Sir Grey Massiah, C.B.E.
Speaker, House of Assembly, J. E. T. Brancker, Q.C.
Attorney-General, Hon. W. E. Jacobs, Q.C. (*acting*)............ 11,340
Financial Secretary, E. S. S. Burrowes, C.M.G. 11,340
Auditor-General, C. D. Gittens, O.B.E. 9,480
Chief Agricultural Officer, A. de K. Frampton, C.M.G.......... 10,200
Director of Medical Services, Dr. M. A. Byer, O.B.E.......... 10,200
Chief Education Officer, R. A. Jordan.... 9,480

The CAPITAL and port is ♆Bridgetown (estimated pop., 11,452). A new deep-water harbour with berths for 8 ships was opened in July, 1961.

THE CAYMAN ISLANDS

The Cayman Islands, between 79° 44′ and 81° 26′ W. and 19° 15′ and 19° 46′ N., consist of three islands, Grand Cayman, Cayman Brac, and Little Cayman, with a total area of 100 square miles. Population (1960 Census), 7,616. The constitution provides for an Administrator, Legislative Assembly and an Executive Council. The Legislative Assembly consists of the Administrator, not less than two nor more than three nominated members, not less than two nor more than three official members and 12 elected members. The Executive Council consists of the Administrator and two official members appointed from among the official members of the Assembly, one nominated member appointed from among the nominated members of the Assembly and two elected members, elected by the non-official members of the Assembly from among the elected members of the Assembly. The normal life of the Assembly is three years. Supervisory powers over the government of the islands exercised by the Government of Jamaica came to an end in August, 1962.

The principal town is ♆George Town, in Grand Cayman, population (1960 census) 2,558.

FINANCE

	1960–61	1961–62
Revenue	£151,517	£211,286
Expenditure	144,664	193,570
Public Debt	80,000	77,055

TRADE

	1960	1961
Total imports	£750,000	£796,845
Total exports	31,988	32,974

Administrator, His Hon. Jack Rose, C.M.G., M.B.E. D.F.C. ....(+*allce.* £300) £2,000

Stipendiary Magistrate and Judge of the Grand Court, Lt.-Col. R. C. Laming, M.B.E. .... £1,200 to £1,400

MONTSERRAT

is situated in 16° 45′ N. lat. and 61° 15′ W. long., 27 miles S.W. of Antigua. It is about 11 miles in length and 7 in breadth, comprising an area of 32½ square miles, population (1960 census), 12,157. Discovered by Columbus in 1493, it was settled by Irishmen, conquered and held by the French for some time, and finally assigned to Great Britain in 1783. It is justly considered one of the most healthy and beautiful of the Antilles; it contains three active soufrières and several hot springs, while the scenery is charmingly diversified. About two-thirds of the island is mountainous, the rest capable of cultivation. The chief exports are sea island cotton, tomatoes, carrots, onions, limes and lime products, bananas and livestock.

Administrator, His Hon. D. A. Wiles, O.B.E. (1960) (+*allowances of £300 and £200 and quarters*) £2,250

CHIEF TOWN. ♆Plymouth (3,500).

ST. KITTS-NEVIS-ANGUILLA

The islands of St. Kitts, Nevis, and Anguilla are united to form one Territory, and taken together they have a population (1960) of 56,644, and a total area of about 153 square miles. The climate is decidedly healthy for the tropics, the temperature being from 66° to 88°.

St. Kitts (population 1960, 38,291), the principal island, was the first possession of the British West Indies to be colonized (1623); it is situated in lat. 17° 18′ N. and long. 62° 48′ W., and comprises an area of 68 square miles, its greatest length being 28 miles, and greatest breadth about 5 miles. It is one of the most effectively cultivated sugar islands in the West Indies, a continuous line of green sugar estates sweeping up all round the coast from the sea towards the central range, which rises to a height of 3,792 feet (Mount Misery). Cotton is also grown to a considerable extent. The capital, ♆Basseterre, is a port of registry.

Nevis (population 1960, 12,761) is separated from St. Kitts by a strait 3 miles wide and has an area of 50 sq. miles. Cotton is exported and coconuts are now processed for the oil-extraction plant. The raising of livestock and cultivation of vegetables are also important features of the island's economy. Its greatest elevation is 3,596 feet. The chief town, ♆Charlestown, is a port of entry.

Anguilla (population 1960, 5,592) is about 60 miles N.W. of St. Kitts, 16 miles in length, and varies in breadth from 1 to 3 miles, containing an area of 35 square miles. There are no hills. Salt is the principal product, and small stock are raised.

Administrator, Lt.-Col. Hon. H. A. C. Howard. C.M.G. (1957) (+*allce.*) $10,800

CAPITAL, ♆Basseterre (St. Kitts). Population (1960), 15,897.

TURKS AND CAICOS ISLANDS

These West India islands geographically form part of the Bahamas group, from which Government they were separated in 1848. From 1873 until 1962 they were annexed to Jamaica, from which they are distant about 450 miles, reverting to U.K. administration on August 6, 1962, upon Jamaica's attainment of independence. They have an area of about 166 square miles, and a population (1960 census) of 5,714, of which the principal island, Grand Turk, contains 2,339. ♆Grand Turk is an important cable station. The islands are celebrated for producing some of the finest salt in the world. Other exports are sisal, crawfish and conches. A considerable number of men are employed overseas in the Bahamas. There is a U.S. Air Force base and a Naval facility at Grand Turk, and a government-owned airstrip at South Caicos, at which refuelling but no other facilities are provided.

FINANCE

	1961	1962*
Revenue	£256,915	£234,482
Expenditure	239,027	259,640

*Revised Estimate.

TRADE

	1961	1962
Total imports	£225,914	£249,902
Total exports	57,503	64,827

The Constitution provides for an Administrator, a Legislative Assembly and an Executive Council. The Legislative Assembly consists of the Administrator, not less than two nor more than three official members, not less than two nor more than three nominated members and nine elected members. The Executive Council consists of the Administrator, two official members from among the official members of the Assembly, one nominated member from among the nominated members of the Assembly and two elected members, elected by the non-official members of the Assembly from among the elected members of the Assembly. The normal life of the Assembly is three years.

Administrator, His Hon. Geoffrey Colin Guy, O.B.E. (+*duty allce.* £300) £2,150

THE WINDWARD ISLANDS

The Windward Islands consist of the four colonies of Grenada, St. Vincent, St. Lucia and Dominica with their dependencies; the Grenadines being divided between Grenada and St. Vincent. The total area is 821 square miles, with a population estimated (1958) at 328,625. There is an Administrator in each of the four islands and an elected majority in each of the four Legislative Councils. The ministerial form of government was introduced in 1956.

Grenada and the Grenadines

Grenada is situated between the parallels of 12° 13'–11° 58' N. lat. and 61° 20'–61° 35' W. long., and is about 21 miles in length and 12 miles in breadth; it is about 96 miles north of Trinidad, 68 miles S.S.W. of St. Vincent, and 100 miles S.W. of Barbados. Area, about 133 square miles: estimated population (including some of the Grenadines), 88,677 (1960). The country is mountainous and very picturesque, and the climate is healthy. Grenada was discovered by Colombus in 1498, and named Conception. It was originally colonized by the French, and was ceded to Great Britain by the Treaty of Versailles in 1783.

The soil is very fertile, and cocoa, spices, sugar cane, cotton, coconuts, limes and fruit are grown. The imports chiefly comprise dry goods, wheat flour, dried fish, bread-stuffs, hardware, etc.

ΨSt. George's (population approximately 26,894), on the south-west coast, is the chief town, and possesses a good harbour.

Finance

	1961	1962
Public revenue	$8,053,480	$6,615,432
Expenditure	8,190,395	8,023,583
Public debt	12,713,650	12,615,618

Trade

	1962
Total imports	$5,930,027
Total exports	5,828,000

Government

Under the Constitution which came into force on Jan. 1, 1960, Grenada is administered by an Administrator who is advised by an Executive Council consisting of the Chief Minister, 3 other ministers, a member without portfolio and one official (the Principal Law Officer). The Administrator is President of the Executive Council. There is also a Legislative Council which comprises a Speaker, 10 elected members, 2 nominated members and one *ex officio* member (the Principal Law Officer).

Administrator, His Honour L. A. Pinard, O.B.E. £2,500
Financial Secretary, E. H. Towner 1,650
Senior Medical Officer and Registrar-General, F. C. Alexis 1,750
Magistrates, S. J. Bain (*S. District*); G. A. Redhead (*E. District*); J. A. P. Compton (*N. and W. Districts*) .... £975 to £1,400
Secretary to Government, H. H. Williams .. £1,650
Chief of Police, J. H. Holley, M.B.E. £1,250 to £1,500
Attorney-General, N. A. Berridge £1,750

The Grenadines are a chain of small islands lying between Grenada and St. Vincent within which Governments they are included. The largest island is Carriacou, attached to the Government of Grenada, with area of 13 sq. miles and population of 6,431.

St. Lucia,

the second largest and the most picturesque of the Windward group, situated in 13° 54' N. lat. and 60° 50' W. long., at a distance of about 90 miles W.N.W. of Barbados, 21 miles N. of St. Vincent, and 24 miles S. of Martinique, is 27 miles in length, with an extreme breadth of 14 miles. It comprises an area of 238 square miles with a population (1960) of 94,718. About 56,000 acres are devoted to agriculture. It possesses perhaps the most interesting history of all the smaller islands. Fights raged hotly around it, and it constantly changed hands between the English and the French. It is mountainous, its highest point being 3,145 feet above the sea, and for the most part it is covered with forest and tropical vegetation. The principal exports are bananas, sugar, copra, coconuts, cocoa, edible oil, lime oil, fresh fruit and vegetables. The chief imports are flour, machinery, cotton-piece goods, sacks and bags.

ΨCastries, the capital (estimated population, 24,500) is recognized as being one of the finest ports in the West Indies on account of its reputation as a safe anchorage in the hurricane season. In 1961, 1,475 vessels with a total gross tonnage of 1,395,041 called at Castries.

Government

There is an Executive Council over which the Administrator presides, consisting of a Chief Minister, three other ministers, one other member and one *ex officio* member, (the Principal Law Officer). There is a Legislative Council consisting of one *ex officio* member (the Principal Law Officer), 2 nominated members and 10 elected members.

Administrator, G. J. Bryan, O.B.E., M.C. (*acting*) (+*allce.* $2,880) $12,000
Chief Minister, G. F. L. Charles 8,160
Attorney-General, W. Cenac (*acting*) 7,440
Chief Secretary, G. S. Da Breo 7,200
Financial Secretary, Col. A. G. Tubb, C.B.E. 7,200

St. Vincent,

an island about 95 miles west of Barbados, situate in 13° 10' N. lat. and 60° 57' W. long., is 18 miles in length and 11 in breadth, comprising an area, with its dependencies, of 150 sq. miles, and a population (1960) of 80,000. In 1846, a large number of Portuguese labourers, amounting to 2,400, entered the island, and proved a valuable acquisition. St. Vincent is more thoroughly English than the three other islands of the group. In 1783 it was secured to Great Britain.

The chief products are bananas, arrowroot, cotton, copra, coconuts, cassava, cocoa, ground provisions, and spices. Its chief imports are food-stuffs (including canned and pickled meat, salted and pickled fish, butter, rice and flour), cotton and woollen piece goods, hardware, lumber, iron and steel manufactures, cement and fertilizers.

There were 56 primary schools with 22,966 pupils in 1962, and 2 Government secondary schools with an attendance of 590. In addition, there are 3 grant-aided secondary schools with an attendance of 687.

Capital, ΨKingstown. Population (1960), 16,141.

Finance and Trade

	1961	1962
Revenue (incl. Grants)	$7,294,525	$5,673,878
Expenditure (do.)	7,089,756	5,671,870
Public debt	465,741	493,170
Total imports	12,631,200	12,477,200
Total exports	5,778,200	6,098,900

Government

There is a Legislative Council of 1 *ex officio* member, 2 nominated and 9 elected members, and a Speaker elected from outside the House.

Administrator, S. H. Graham, O.B.E. $12,000
Attorney General, B. F. Dias $8,400
Financial Secretary, C. A. Jacobs $7,920
Senior Medical Officer, R. R. Japal $8,400
Magistrates, C. A. E. Rawle; K. Lewis $5,280 to $6,720
Registrar and Additional Magistrate, H. M. Squires .... $5,280 to $6,720

DOMINICA

Dominica, the loftiest of the Lesser Antilles, was transferred from the Leeward to the Windward Group on Jan. 1, 1940. It is situated between 15° 20′—15° 45′ N. lat. and 61° 13′—61° 30′ W. long., 95 miles S. of Antigua, and is about 29 miles long and 15 broad comprising an area of 290 sq. miles, of which about 37,000 acres are under cultivation. The island is of volcanic origin and very mountainous and picturesque, abounding in streams fairly well stocked with fish, and the soil is very fertile. The temperature varies, according to the altitude, from 55° to 85°. The climate is healthy, and during the winter months very pleasant. The exports consist almost entirely of agricultural produce, principally bananas, lime oil, lime juice, oranges, bay oil, cocoa, copra and vanilla. Population (census 1960, 59,124). The principal towns are ♆Roseau, on the south-west coast, population (1960), 12,577 and Portsmouth, population (1960), 2,209.

Education.—There are 52 elementary schools, of which 49 are Government and 3 assisted. Of the 4 secondary schools, 3 receive a grant-in-aid and one is maintained by the Government.

Finance and Trade

	1962	1963*
Revenue (incl. Grants).	$6,775,161	$6,192,673
Expenditure (do.).....	6,462,606	5,775,323
Public debt..........	136,861	147,210
	1960	1961
Imports.............	$10,022,000	$10,577,000
Exports.............	6,230,000	7,252,000

*Estimated

Government

There is an Executive Council composed of one official and five unofficial members, and a Legislative Council consisting of one official, 2 nominated and 11 elected members. Four of the elected members of the Executive Council are styled Ministers and control departments representing the major part of the Government's activity.

Administrator, Col. A. Lovelace, C.M.G., M.B.E., M.C. (1960).

Chief Secretary, L. A. Roberts.

WESTERN SAMOA

Head of State, H.H. Malietoa Tanumafili II, C.B.E.

Prime Minister, Hon. Fiame Mata'afa Faumuina Mulinu'u II, C.B.E.

Formerly administered by New Zealand (latterly with internal self-government), Western Samoa became, on January 1, 1962, the first fully-independent Polynesian State. It is for the present being treated as a member country of the British Commonwealth, pending a final decision by the Government.

Western Samoa consists of the islands of Savai'i (703 sq. miles) and of Upolo, which with its adjacent islands, has an area of 430 sq. miles. All the islands are mountainous. Upolo, the most fertile, contains the harbours of ♆Apia and ♆Saluafata. The islanders are mostly Christians of different denominations. A census held on Sept. 25, 1961, showed a total population of 114,427, of whom 101,288 were Samoans and 11,813 part-Samoans, 522 other Pacific Islanders and 668 Europeans.

The chief exports are copra, cocoa and bananas. In 1962, the total trade was valued at: exports £2,806,495 (copra £908,098, cocoa £1,165,802 and bananas £908,098); imports £2,861,737.

CAPITAL.—♆Apia (population 25,000).

FLAG.—Five white stars (depicting the Southern Cross) on a quarter royal blue at top next staff, and three quarters red.

ZANZIBAR

(*The Zanzibar Protectorate*)

Sultan, H. H. Seyyid Jamshid bin Abdulla, *born* Sept. 16, 1929; *succeeded* July 2, 1963.

The Zanzibar dominions became independent in 1856 under the rule of Seyyid Majid, a son of Seyyid Said, Sultan of Muscat and Zanzibar. They formerly extended along the mainland as far south as Tunghi Bay and north to Warskeikh; but they are now confined to the islands of Zanzibar and Pemba, a coastal strip from Vanga to Ras Kiamboni (Dick's Head) and the islands of Lamu, Manda, Patta, and Siu.

Zanzibar has an area of 640 square miles with a population of 165,253 (1958 Census); Pemba (380 square miles) population, 133,858; total area, 1,020 square miles; total population, 299,111.

Production, etc.—The islands produce a large percentage of the world's supply of cloves and clove oil (cloves exported in 1962 were valued at £2,079,635 and clove bud and stem oil at £98,437). They also exported £212,371 of coconut oil, £387,710 of copra, £73,547 of coconuts and £103,148 of coir fibre in 1962. Clove and coconut products constituted 95 per cent. of the Protectorate's total exports.

Education.—In 1962 there were 74 primary schools, of which 62 were government schools, 10 grant-aided and 2 private. There were 5 approved secondary schools and 6 private post-primary schools, open to all pupils from all communities. There are government training colleges for men and women primary teachers. The total enrolment in all government and grant-aided primary and secondary schools and private schools in October, 1962, was 23,260. The total expenditure from local revenue in 1962 was £422,338.

Communications.—There are 341 miles of road suitable for motor traffic in Zanzibar and 107 miles in Pemba. Radio telephone communication is available from Zanzibar to the three mainland territories and to Pemba, though it is not yet possible to telephone from Pemba to the mainland. The town of ♆Zanzibar, on the island of the same name, has a population of 45,284. It possesses a good anchorage, which provides facilities for shipping and trade generally. Two Government-owned vessels maintain a weekly service between Zanzibar and Pemba and a monthly coastal service to the mainland ports of Mombasa and Mtwara.

The civil aerodrome is situated 5 miles south-east of the town, linked with Tanganyika and Kenya by charter and daily scheduled services. There is also a civil aerodrome in Pemba linking the island with Zanzibar, Kenya and Tanganyika by regular services with the East African Airways Corporation.

FINANCE

	1961–2	1962–3*
Revenue............	£2,618,222	£2,674,077
Expenditure.........	3,142,200	2,958,328

*Estimated

TRADE

The principal imports are rice, grain, groceries, sugar, tobacco, ivory, petroleum and piece-goods; the exports are cloves, copra, marine products, clove oil, coconut oil, oil cakes and coir fibre in addition to re-exports of previously imported ivory and piece-goods.

	1961	1962
Imports.............	£6,318,091	£6,658,533
Exports.............	5,226,932	5,858,835

	1961	1962
Imports from U.K....	£788,476	£668,014
Exports to U.K......	300,389	222,200

GOVERNMENT

Zanzibar is a British Protectorate which attained internal self-government in June, 1963. The ministerial system of government was introduced in January, 1961 and the cabinet system in June, 1963. There are a Prime Minister and seven other ministers responsible for the executive functions of Government except those relating to external affairs, defence and internal security for which a British Resident retains responsibility. There is a National Assembly of 31 elected members presided over by a Speaker. His Highness the Sultan presides over a Privy Council, consisting of the British Resident, Deputy British Resident, the Heir Apparent, the Prime Minister, the Attorney-General, and not more than three other persons appointed by the Sultan.

British Resident, Sir George Mooring, K.C.M.G. (1959) £3,500

Chief Justice, Sir Gerard Mahon £3,000

Deputy British Resident, Hon. P. A. P. Robertson, C.M.G. 2,800

Speaker, National Assembly, Hon. K. S. Madon, M.B.E. 1,200

Prime Minister, Hon. Muhammed Shamte Hamadi, M.B.E. 1,750

Home and Legal Affairs, Hon. Ali Muhsin 1,600

Finance, Hon. Juma Aley 1,600

Health, Hon. Ahmad Abdulrahman Baalawy 1,600

Commerce and Industry, Hon. Ibuni Saleh 1,600

Education and Welfare, Hon. Maulidi Mshangama Haji 1,600

Works, Communications and Land, Hon. Salim Kombo Saleh 1,600

Agriculture, Hon. Abadhar Juma Khatib 1,600

Trade Enquiry Office in London, Grand Buildings, Trafalgar Square, W.C.2.

UNIVERSITIES OF THE BRITISH COMMONWEALTH

With date of foundation, number of full-time students and name of Executive Head (*Vice-Chancellor*, *President* or *Principal*)

Australia

ADELAIDE (1874). (Full-time students, 4,285).—*Vice-Chancellor*, H. B. Basten, C.M.G.

AUSTRALIAN NATIONAL (1946), Canberra. (843).—*Vice-Chancellor*, L. G. H. Huxley, D.Phil., D.Sc.

MELBOURNE (1853). (8,089).—*Vice-Chancellor*, Prof. Sir George Paton, LL.D., D.C.L.

MONASH (1958), Melbourne. (1,450).—*Vice-Chancellor*, J. A. L. Matheson, M.B.E., Ph.D.

NEW ENGLAND (1954), Armidale. (960).—*Vice-Chancellor*, R. B. Madgwick, O.B.E., D.Phil., D.Litt., LL.D.

NEW SOUTH WALES (1949), Sydney. (2,982).—*Vice-Chancellor*, J. P. Baxter, C.M.G., O.B.E., Ph.D.

NEWCASTLE UNIV. COLL. (1951). (560).—*Warden*, J. J. Auchmuty, Ph.D.

WOLLONGONG UNIV. COLL. (1961). (32) *Warden*, Prof. C. A. M. Gray.

QUEENSLAND (1909), Brisbane. (5,002).—*Vice-Chancellor* Prof. Sir Fred Schonell, Ph.D., D.Lit.

UNIV. COLL. OF TOWNSVILLE (1961). (173).—*Warden*, K. J. C. Back, Ph.D.

SYDNEY (1850). (11,039).—*Vice-Chancellor*, Prof. S. H. Roberts, C.M.G., Litt.D., LL.D., D.Sc.(Econ.), D.C.L., D.Litt.

TASMANIA (1890), Hobart. (937).—*Vice-Chancellor*, K. S. Isles.

WESTERN AUSTRALIA (1911), Perth. (2,347).—*Vice-Chancellor*, S. L. Prescott, O.B.E.

Basutoland

BASUTOLAND, BECHUANALAND PROTECTORATE AND SWAZILAND (1964), Roma.

Canada

ACADIA (1838), Wolfville. (Full-time students, 1,189).—*President*, W. Kirkconnell, Ph.D., LL.D., D.P.Ec., D.Litt., Litt. D., L.H.D., D.ès.L.

ALBERTA (1906), Edmonton. (8,502).—*President*, W. H. Johns, Ph.D., LL.D.

BISHOP'S (1843), Lennoxville. (513).—*Vice-Chancellor*, C. L. O. Glass, D.C.L.

BRITISH COLUMBIA (1908), Vancouver. (13,264).—*President*, J. B. Macdonald, D.D.S., Ph.D., LL.D.

CARLETON (1942), Ottawa. (1,956)—*President*, A. Davidson Dunton, D.Sc., LL.D.

DALHOUSIE (1818), Halifax. (2,521)—*President*, H. D. Hicks, LL.D., D.Ed., D.C.L.

UNIV. OF KING'S COLL. (1789), Halifax. (217).—*President* (vacant).

LAVAL (1852), Quebec. (14,230). — *Rector Magnificus*, Mgr. L.-A. Vachon, D.Th., D.Ph.

MCGILL (1821), Montreal. (9,003)—*Principal*, H. R. Robertson, M.D., D.C.L.

MCMASTER (1887), Hamilton. (2,488).—*President*, H. G. Thode, M.B.E., Ph.D., LL.D., D.Sc.

MANITOBA (1877), Winnipeg. (7,607).—*President*, H. H. Saunderson, Ph.D., LL.D., D.Sc.

BRANDON COLL. (1899). (465).—*President*, J. E. Robbins, Ph.D., LL.D.

ST. PAUL'S COLL. (1926), Winnipeg.—*Rector*, Very Rev. H. Kierans.

UNITED COLL. (1938), Winnipeg.—*Principal*, W. C. Lockhart, Ph.D., D.D.

MEMORIAL, NEWFOUNDLAND (1949), St. John's. (1,998).—*President*, R. Gushue, C.B.E., LL.D., D.Cn.L.

MONCTON (1963). (467).—*President* (vacant).

MONTREAL (1876). (20,635).—*Rector*, Mgr. I. Lussier, LL.D.

COLL. JEAN-DE-BRÉBEUF, Montreal.—*Rector*, Rev. Fr. R. Fortin.

LOYOLA COLL., Montreal.—*Rector*, Rev. P. G. Malone.

MARIANOPOLIS COLL., Montreal.—*Dean*, Sr. St. Madeleine of Charity.

MOUNT ALLISON (1858), Sackville. (1,208).—*President*, L. H. Cragg, Ph.D., D.C.L.

MOUNT ST. VINCENT COLL. (1925), Halifax. (452).—*President*, Sister Francis d'Assisi, Ph.D.

NEW BRUNSWICK (1785), Fredericton. (2,367).—*President*, C. B. Mackay, D.C.L., LL.D.

NOVA SCOTIA AGRICULTURAL COLL. (1905), Truro. (165).—*Principal*, K. Cox.

NOVA SCOTIA TECHNICAL COLL. (1909), Halifax. (384).—*President*, G. W. Holbrook, Ph.D.

OTTAWA (1848). (3,520).—*Rector*, Very Rev. H. Légaré, D.Soc.Sc., LL.D.

QUEEN'S, KINGSTON (1841). (3,451).—*Vice-Chancellor*, W. A. Mackintosh, C.M.G., Ph.D., LL.D., D.C.L.

ROYAL MILITARY COLL. OF CANADA (1876), Kingston. (491).—*Commandant*, Air Commodore L. J. Birchall, O.B.E., D.F.C., C.D.

ST. DUNSTAN'S (1855), Charlottetown. (429).—*President*, Very Rev. G. A. Macdonald.

ST. FRANCIS XAVIER (1853), Antigonish. (1,604).—*President*, Rt. Rev. H. J. Somers, Ph.D., D.Litt.

ST. MARY'S (1841), Halifax. (656).—*President*, Very Rev. C. J. Fischer.
SASKATCHEWAN (1907), Saskatoon. (6,710).—*President*, J. W. T. Spinks, M.B.E., Ph.D., D.Sc., LL.D.
SHERBROOKE (1954). (2,827).—*Rector*, Mgr. I. Pinard.
SIR GEORGE WILLIAMS (1929), Montreal. (2,420).—*Principal*, R. C. Rae.
TORONTO (1827). (13,765).—*President*, C. T. Bissell, Ph.D., D.Litt., LL.D.
UNIV. OF ST. MICHAEL'S COLL. (1852), Toronto. (1,224).—*President*, Rev. J. M. Kelly, Ph.D.
UNIV. OF TRINITY COLL. (1851), Toronto. (725).—*Vice-Chancellor*, Rev. D. R. G. Owen, Ph.D., D.D.
VICTORIA (1836), Toronto. (2,179).—*President*, Rev. A. B. B. Moore, D.D., LL.D.
YORK (1959), Toronto. (305).—*President*, M. G. Ross, Ed.D., D.C.L.
FEDERATED COLLEGES (1862, 1874, 1902), Guelph.—(1,658).—*President*, J. D. MacLachlan, Ph.D.
WATERLOO (1959). (1,687). *Vice-Chancellor*, J. G. Hagey, LL.D.
WATERLOO LUTHERAN (1960). (1,275).—*President*, Rev. W. J. Villaume, Ph.D.
WESTERN ONTARIO (1878), London. (5,096).—*President*, G. E. Hall, A.F.C., M.D., Ph.D., D.Sc., LL.D.
HURON COLL. (1863), London.—*Principal*, Rev. J. G. Morden.
WINDSOR (1963). (1,587).—*Vice-Chancellor*, Rev. E. C. LeBel, LL.D.

Ceylon

CEYLON (1942), Peradeniya. (Full-time students, 5,114).—*Vice-Chancellor*, Sir Nicholas Attygalle, D.Sc., LL.D.
VIDYALANKARA (1959), Kelaniya. (802).—*Vice-Chancellor*, Ven. K. Pannasara, D.Litt.
VIDYODAYA (1959), Gangodawila. (351).—*Vice-Chancellor*, Ven. W. Sorata, D.Litt.

East Africa

EAST AFRICA (1963), Entebbe, Uganda.—*Vice-Chancellor*, Sir Bernard de Bunsen, C.M.G., LL.D.
ROYAL COLL., NAIROBI (1961), Kenya. (Full-time students, (460).—*Principal*, (vacant).
UNIVERSITY COLL., DAR ES SALAAM (1961), Tanganyika (47).—*Principal*, R. C. Pratt.
MAKERERE UNIV. COLL. (1949), Kampala, Uganda. (951).—*Principal*, vacant.

Ghana

GHANA (1961), Legon. (Full-time students, 1,174).—*Vice-Chancellor*, C. C. O'Brien, Ph.D.
UNIV. COLL. OF CAPE COAST (1962). (152).—*Principal*, C. A. Ackah, Ph.D.
KWAME NKRUMAH UNIV. OF SCIENCE AND TECHNOLOGY (1961), Kumasi (736).—*Vice-Chancellor*, R. P. Baffour, O.B.E., D.Sc.

Hong Kong

HONG KONG (1911). (Full-time students, 1,597).—*Vice-Chancellor*, Sir Lindsay Ride, C.B.E., D.M., LL.D.

India

AGRA (1927). (Full-time students, 48,576).—*Vice-Chancellor*, P. D. Gupta.
ALIGARH MUSLIM (1920). (5,128).—*Vice-Chancellor*, B. H. Zaidi.
ALLAHABAD (1887). (6,783). — *Vice-Chancellor*, B. Prasad, D.Sc.
ANDHRA (1926), Waltair. (28,214).—*Vice-Chancellor*, A. L. Narayan, D.Sc.
ANNAMALAI (1928), Annamalainagar. (3,371).—*Vice-Chancellor*, C. P. Ramaswami Aiyar, LL.D., D.Litt.
BANARAS HINDU (1915). (6,905). *Vice-Chancellor*—N. H. Bhagwati.
BARODA (1949). (9,598).—*Vice-Chancellor*, J. M. Mehta, Ph.D.
BIHAR (1952), Muzaffarpur. (24,121).—*Vice-Chancellor*, P. L. Shrivastava, D.Phil.
BOMBAY (1857). (52,138).—*Vice-Chancellor*, V. R. Khanolkar, M.D.
BURDWAN (1960). (21,962).—*Vice-Chancellor*, B. K. Guha.
CALCUTTA (1857). (97,454).—*Vice-Chancellor*, B. Malik.
DELHI (1922). (4,309).—*Vice-Chancellor*, C. D. Deshmukh.
GAUHATI (1948). (30,350).—*Vice-Chancellor*, H. J. Taylor, Ph.D.
GORAKHPUR (1956). (14,243).—*Vice-Chancellor*, A. C. Chatterji, D.Sc., Dr.Ing.
GUJARAT (1949), Ahmedabad. (27,456).—*Vice-Chancellor*, L. R. Desai.
INDIAN INST. OF TECHNOLOGY, BOMBAY (1958). (1,148).—*Director*, S. K. Bose.
INDIAN INST. OF TECHNOLOGY, KANPUR (1960). (288) —*Director*, P. K. Kelkar, Ph.D.
INDIAN INST. OF TECHNOLOGY, KHARAGPUR (1951). (1,882).—*Director*, S. R. Sen Gupta, Ph.D.
INDIAN INST. OF TECHNOLOGY, MADRAS (1959). (603). —*Director*. Prof. B. Sengupto.
JABALPUR (1957). (10,259).—*Vice-Chancellor*, V. R. Sen.
JADAVPUR (1955), Calcutta. (3,234).—*Rector*, T. Sen, Dr. Ing.
JAMMU AND KASHMIR (1948), Srinigar. (10,410).—*Vice-Chancellor*, T. M. Advani, Ph.D.
KARNATAK (1949), Dharwar. (17,121).—*Vice-Chancellor*, D. C. Pavate.
KERALA (1937), Trivandrum. (49,990).—*Vice-Chancellor*, K. C. K. E. Raja.
KURUKSHETRA (1956). (819).—*Vice-Chancellor*, S. Bhan.
LUCKNOW (1921). (12,928).—*Vice-Chancellor*, A. V. Rao, Ph.D.
MADRAS (1857). (61,300).—*Vice-Chancellor*, Sir A. L. Mudaliar, M.D., LL.D., D.Sc., D.C.L.
MARATHWADA (1958), Aurangabad. (8,377).—*Vice-Chancellor*, S. R. Dongerkery.
MYSORE (1916). (40,341).—*Vice-Chancellor*, M. Rahmathulla.
NAGPUR (1923). (28,522).—*Vice-Chancellor*, S. P. Kotval.
OSMANIA (1918), Hyderabad. (21,684).—*Vice-Chancellor*, D. S. Reddi, D.Litt.
PANJAB (1947), Chandigarh. (54,753).—*Vice-Chancellor*, A. C. Joshi, D.Sc.
PATNA (1917). (11,402).—*Vice-Chancellor*, G. Jacob, Ph.D.
POONA (1948). (36,874).—*Vice-Chancellor*, D. V. Potdar.
RAJASTHAN (1947), Jaipur. (30,624).—*Vice-Chancellor*, M. S. Mehta, Ph.D.
ROORKEE (1949). (1,823).—*Vice-Chancellor*, G. Pande.
SARDAR VALLABHBHAI VIDYAPEETH (1955), Anand. (6,051).—*Vice-Chancellor*, M. D. Patel, Ph.D.
SAUGAR (1946), Sagar. (17,895).—*Vice-Chancellor*, G. P. Bhutt.
SHREEMATI N. D. THACKERSEY WOMEN'S (1951), Bombay. (7,641).—*Vice-Chancellor*, Mrs. P. V. Thackersey, D.Litt.
SRI VENKATESWARA (1954), Tirupati. (10,379).—*Vice-Chancellor*, S. Govindarajulu.
U. P. AGRICULTURAL (1960), Pantnagar.
UTKAL (1943), Bhubaneswar. (17,907).—*Vice-Chancellor*, P. Parija, O.B.E., D.Sc.
VIKRAM (1957), Ujjain (19,192).—*Vice-Chancellor*, G. L. Datta, Ph.D.

VISVA-BHARATI (1951), Santiniketan. (384).—*Vice-Chancellor*, S. R. Das.

Malaya

MALAYA (1962), Kuala Lumpur. (Full-time students, 1,341).—*Vice-Chancellor*, Sir Alexander Oppenheim, O.B.E., D.SC., Ph.D., LL.D.

Malta

ROYAL UNIV. OF MALTA (1769), Valletta. (365). —*Vice-Chancellor*, J. A. Manché, C.B.E., M.D., LL.D.

New Zealand

AUCKLAND (1882). (Full-time students 2,716).—*Vice-Chancellor*, K. J. Maidment.

CANTERBURY (1873), Christchurch. (2,264).—*Vice-Chancellor*, L. L. Pownall, Ph.D.

LINCOLN COLL. (1873), Christchurch. (406).—*Principal*, M. M. Burns, C.B.E., Ph.D.

MASSEY UNIV. OF MANAWATU (1964), Palmerston North. (646).—*Vice-Chancellor*, A. Stewart, D.Phil.

OTAGO (1869), Dunedin. (2,443).—*Vice-Chancellor*, A. Beachamp, O.B.E., Ph.D.

VICTORIA, WELLINGTON (1897). (2,068).—*Vice-Chancellor*, J. Williams, Ph.D., LL.D.

Nigeria

AHMADU BELLO (1962), Zaria. (Full-time students, 425).—*Vice-Chancellor*, N. S. Alexander, C.B.E., Ph.D., D.Sc.

IBADAN (1948). (1,778).—*Vice-Chancellor*, K. O. Dike, Ph.D., LL.D., D.Litt., D.Sc.

IFE (1961).—*Vice-Chancellor*, O. A. Ajose, O.B.E., M.D.

LAGOS (1962) (72).—*Vice-Chancellor*, E. Njoku, Ph.D.

NIGERIA (1960), Nsukka. (1,248).—*Vice-Chancellor*, G. M. Johnson, J.S.D.

Pakistan

DACCA (1921). (Full-time students, 17,290).—*Vice-Chancellor*, M. O. Ghani, Ph.D.

E. PAKISTAN AGRICULTURAL (1961), Mymensingh. (524).—*Vice-Chancellor*, S. D. Choudhuri, Ph.D.

E. PAKISTAN U. OF ENGINEERING & TECHNOLOGY (1961), Dacca. (1,026).—*Vice-Chancellor*, M. A. Rashid, D.Sc.

KARACHI (1950). (2,065).—*Vice-Chancellor*, I. H. Qureshi, Ph.D.

PANJAB (1882), Lahore. (22,238).—*Vice-Chancellor*, M. Sharif.

PESHAWAR (1950). (2,280).—*Vice-Chancellor*, M. Ali.

RAJSHAHI (1953). (7 386).—*Vice-Chancellor*, M. Ahmed, Ph.D.

SIND (1947), Hyderabad. (3,960).—*Vice-Chancellor*, M. Raziuddin Siddiqi, Ph.D., D.Sc.

W. PAKISTAN AGRICULTURAL (1961), Lyallpur. (1,037).—*Vice-Chancellor*, Z. A. Hashmi, D.V.M.

W. PAKISTAN U. OF ENGINEERING & TECHNOLOGY (1961), Lahore. (722).—*Vice-Chancellor*, A. G. Asghar, Ph.D.

Rhodesia and Nyasaland

UNIV. COLL. OF RHODESIA AND NYASALAND (1955), Salisbury. (Full-time students, 480).—*Principal*, W. Adams, C.M.G., O.B.E., LL.D.

Sierra Leone

FOURAH BAY COLL., THE UNIV. COLL. OF SIERRA LEONE (1960), Freetown. (Full-time students, 426).—*Principal*, D. S. H. W. Nicol, M.D., Ph.D.

Singapore

NANYANG (1953), Singapore. (Full-time students 2,109).—*Vice-Chancellor*, C. L. Chuang, Ph.D.

SINGAPORE (1962). (2,014).—*Vice-Chancellor*, B. R. Sreenivasan, LL.D.

West Indies

UNIV. OF THE WEST INDIES (1962), Jamaica. (Full-time students, 1,268).—*Vice-Chancellor*, P. M. Sherlock, C.B.E., LL.D.

THE ARCTIC OCEAN

The Arctic Ocean consists of a deep sea over 2,000 fathoms, on the southern margin of which there is a broad continental shelf with numerous islands. Into this deeper sea there is only one broad channel, about 700 miles, between Greenland and Scandinavia. Behring Strait is only 49 miles wide and 27 fathoms deep. The southern boundary of the Arctic Ocean is the Wyville-Thomson and Faeroe-Icelandic submarine ridge, which separates the North Atlantic from the Norwegian and Greenland Seas. The Norwegian Deep lies between Norway and Jan Mayen and Iceland; it exceeds 1,500 fathoms. The Greenland Deep, of similar depth, lies between Spitsbergen and Greenland. These two depressions are separated by a somewhat deeply submerged ridge from the east of Jan Mayen to Bear Island, south of Spitsbergen. A shallow ridge from the north-west of Spitsbergen to Greenland separates the Greenland Sea from the deep North Polar Basin. This extends from the north of Spitsbergen and Franz Josef Land to the north of the New Siberia Islands and of the North American Arctic Archipelago.

Another more shallow depression is Baffin Bay, less than 1,000 fathoms. This is separated from the North Atlantic by a submarine ridge. Barent's Sea, between Spitsbergen, Norway and Novaya Zemlya, and the Kara Sea, between Novaya Zemlya and the Siberian coast, are respectively below 200 and 100 fathoms.

The total area of the Arctic Sea is about 5·5 million square miles, of which 2·3 million square miles are probably covered with floating ice.

BRITISH EMPIRE CASUALTIES, 1939–1945

Casualties to all ranks of the British Commonwealth and Empire Forces (excluding death from natural causes) from Sept. 3, 1939, to Aug. 14, 1945:—

Division	Killed	Missing	Wounded	Prisoners of War	Total
United Kingdom	244,723	53,039	277,090	180,405	755,257
Canada	37,476	1,843	53,174	9,045	101,538
Australia	23,365	6,030	39,803	26,363	95,561
New Zealand	10,033	2,129	19,314	8,453	39,929
South Africa	6,840	1,841	14,363	14,589	37,633
India	24,338	11,754	64,354	79,489	179,935
Colonies	6,877	14,208	6,972	8,115	36,172
Total	353,652	90,844	475,070	326,459	1,246,025

NOTES.—The figures in the above table exclude (i) civilian casualties due to enemy action; (ii) casualties to merchant seamen: and (iii) casualties to members of the Home Guard while on duty.

Ireland

See also Northern Ireland, pp. 688–91; Republic of Ireland, pp. 796–8.

Position and Extent.—Ireland lies in the Atlantic Ocean, to the West of Great Britain, and is separated from Scotland by the North Channel and from Wales by the Irish Sea and St. George's Channel. The land area of the island is 32,408 sq. miles and its geographical position between 51° 26′ and 55° 21′ N. latitude and from 5° 25′ to 10° 30′ W. longitude. The greatest length of the island, from N.E. to S.W. (Torr Head to Mizen Head), is 302 miles, and the greatest breadth, from E. to W. (Dundrum Bay to Annagh Head), is 174 miles. On the N. coast of *Achill Island* (Co. Mayo) are the highest cliffs in the British Islands, 2,000 feet sheer above the sea. Ireland is occupied for the greater part of its area by the *Central Plain*, with an elevation of 50 to 350 ft. above mean sea level, with isolated mountain ranges near the coast-line. The principal mountains, with their highest points, are the *Sperrin Mountains* (Sawel 2,240 ft.) of County Tyrone; the *Mountains of Mourne* (Slieve Donard 2,796 ft.) of County Down, and the *Wicklow Mountains* (Lugnaquilla 3,039 ft.); the *Derryveagh Mountains* (Errigal 2,466 ft.) of County Donegal; the *Connemara Mountains* (Twelve Pins 2,695 ft.) of County Galway; *Macgillicuddy's Reeks* (Carrantuohill 3,414 ft., the highest point in Ireland); and the *Galtee Mountains* (3,018 ft.) of County Tipperary, and the *Knockmealdown* (2,609 ft.) and *Comeragh Mountains* (2,470 ft.) of County Waterford. The principal river of Ireland (and the longest in the British Isles) is the *Shannon* (240 miles), rising in County Cavan and draining the central plain. The Shannon flows through a chain of loughs to the city of Limerick, and thence to an estuary on the western Atlantic seaboard. The *Slaney* flows into Wexford Harbour, the *Liffey* to Dublin Bay, the *Boyne* to Drogheda, the *Lee* to Cork Harbour, the *Blackwater* to Youghal Harbour, and the *Suir*, *Barrow* and *Nore*, to Waterford Harbour. As in Scotland, the principal hydrographic feature is the *Loughs*, of which Lough *Neagh* (150 sq. miles) in the north-east is the largest in Ireland and the British Isles, others being the Shannon Chain of *Allen*, *Boderg*, *Forbes*, *Ree* and *Derg*, and the Erne Chain of *Gowna*, *Oughter*, *Lower Erne*, and *Erne*; *Melvin*, *Gill*, *Gara* and *Conn* in the north-west; and *Corrib* and *Mask* (joined by a hidden channel) in the west. In County Kerry, to the east of Macgillicuddy's Reeks, are the famous *Lakes of Killarney*. The climate of Ireland is more equable than that of Great Britain, the extreme range of temperature readings being from 2° F. to 90° F. (compared with — 17° F. to 100° F. over Great Britain). The average annual rainfall varies from 27 inches at Dublin to more than 100 inches in the mountains of Connemara. The rainfall is also more uniform from year to year than in Great Britain.

Primitive Man.—Although little is known concerning the earliest inhabitants of Ireland, there are many traces of neolithic man throughout the island; a grave containing a polished stone axehead assigned to 2,500 B.C. was found at Linkardstown, Co. Carlow, in 1944, and the use of bronze implements appears to have become known about the middle of the 17th century B.C. In the later Bronze Age a Celtic race of *Goidels* appear to have invaded the island, and in the early Iron Age *Brythons* from South Britain are believed to have effected settlements in the south-east, while *Picts* from North Britain established similar settlements in the north. Towards the close of the Roman occupation of Britain, the dominant tribe in the island was that of the *Scoti*, who afterwards established themselves in Scotland.

History.—According to Irish legends, the island of Ierne was settled by a Milesian race, who came from Scythia by way of Spain, and established the *Kingdom of Tara*, about 500 B.C. The supremacy of the *Ardri* (high king) of Tara was acknowledged by eight lesser kingdoms (Munster, Connaught, Ailech, Oriel, Ulidia, Meath, Leinster and Ossory) ruled by descendants of the eight sons of Miled. The basalt columns on the coast of Antrim, eight miles from Portrush, known as the *Giant's Causeway*, are connected with the legendary history of Ireland as the remnants of a bridge built in the time of Finn M'Coul (Fingal) to connect Antrim with Scotland (Staffa).

Hibernia was visited by Roman merchants but never by Roman legions, and little is known of the history of the country until the invasions of *Northmen* (Norwegians and Danes) towards the close of the 8th century A.D. The Norwegians were distinguished as Findgaill (White Strangers) and the Danes as Dubgaill (Black Strangers), names which survive in "Fingall," "MacDougall" and "MacDowell," while the name of the island itself is held to be derived from the Scandinavian *Ira-land* (land of the Irish), the names of the Provinces being survivals of Norse dialect forms (Ulaids-tir, Laigins-tir, Mumans-tir and Kunnak-tir). The outstanding events in the encounters with the Northmen are the *Battle of Tara* (980), at which the Hy Neill king Maelsechlainn II. defeated the Scandinavians of Dublin and the Hebrides under their king Amlaib Cuarán; and the *Battle of Clontarf* (1014) by which the Scandinavian power was completely broken. After Clontarf the supreme power was disputed by the O'Brians of Munster, the O'Neills of Ulster, and the O'Connors of Connaught, with varying fortunes. In 1152 Dermod MacMurrough (Diarmait MacMurchada), the deposed king of Leinster, sought assistance in his struggle with Ruaidhri O'Connor (the high king of Ireland), and visited Henry II., the Norman king of England. Henry authorized him to obtain armed support in England for the recovery of his kingdom, and Dermod enlisted the services of Richard de Clare, the Norman Earl of Pembroke, afterwards known as *Strongbow*, who landed at Waterford (Aug. 23, 1170) with 200 knights and 1,000 other troops for the reconquest of Leinster, where he eventually settled, after marriage with Dermod's daughter. In 1172 (Oct. 18) Henry II. himself landed in Ireland. He received homage from the Irish kings and established his capital at Dublin. The invaders subsequently conquered most of the island and a feudal government was created. In the 14th and 15th centuries, the Irish recovered most of their lands, while many Anglo-Irish lords became virtually independent, royal authority being confined to the "Pale," a small district round Dublin. Though under Henry VII., Sir Edward Poynings, as Lord Deputy had passed at the *Parliament of Drogheda* (1494) the act later known as *Poynings' Law*, subordinating the Irish Legislature to the Crown, the Earls of Kildare retained effective power until, in 1534, Henry VIII. began the reconquest of Ireland. Parliament in 1541 recognized him as King of Ireland and by 1603 English authority was supreme.

Christianity.—Christianity did not become general until the advent of St. Patrick. *St. Patrick* was born in Britain about 389, and was taken to Ireland as a slave about sixteen years later. escaping to Gaul at the age of 22. In 432 he was consecrated Bishop at Auxerre and landed in Wicklow to establish and organize the Christian religion throughout the island.

Republic of Ireland

Area and Population.—The Republic has a land area of 26,600 sq. miles, divided into the four Provinces of LEINSTER (Carlow, Dublin, Kildare, Kilkenny, Laoighis, Longford, Louth, Meath, Offaly, Westmeath, Wexford and Wicklow); MUNSTER (Clare, Cork, Kerry, Limerick, Tipperary and Waterford); CONNACHT (Galway, Leitrim, Mayo, Roscommon and Sligo); and part of ULSTER (Cavan, Donegal and Monaghan). Total population of the Republic at the Census held on April 9, 1961 was 2,818,341 (males, 1,416,549; females, 1,401,792), a density of 106 persons per sq. mile. Provisional figures showed 61,611 births, 15,409 marriages and 33,643 deaths in the year 1962.

THE PRESIDENT

Uachtaran na hÉireann (President), Éamon de Valéra, *born* 1882, *assumed office* June 25, 1959.

MEMBERS OF THE GOVERNMENT

Taoiseach, Seán F. Lemass	£3,000
Tánaiste and Minister for Health, Seán Mac an tSaoi (Seán MacEntee)	2,000
Finance, An Dr. Seámas ó Riain (Dr. James Ryan)	2,000
External Affairs, Proinsias Mac Aogáin (Frank Aiken)	2,000
Agriculture, Pádraig Mac Gabhann (Patrick Smith)	2,000
Transport and Power, Erskine H. Childers	2,000
Industry and Commerce, Seán ó Loinsigh (John Lynch)	2,000
Local Government, Niall Bléine (Neil T. Blaney)	2,000
Social Welfare, Caoimhghin Ó Beoláin (Kevin Boland)	2,000
Lands and the Gaeltacht, Micheál Ó Móráin (Michael Moran)	2,000
Posts and Telegraphs, Micheál Hilliard (Michael Hilliard)	2,000
Education, An Dr. Pádraig Ó hIrighile (Dr. Patrick J. Hillery)	2,000
Defence, Gearóid Mac Pharthaláin (Gerald Bartley)	2,000
Justice, Cathal Ó hEochaidh (Charles Haughey)	2,000

GOVERNMENT

The Constitution.—The Constitution approved by a plebiscite on July 1, 1937, came into operation on December 29, 1937.

The Constitution declares that Ireland is a sovereign independent democratic State and affirms the right of the Irish Nation to choose its own form of Government, to determine its relations with other nations, and to develop its life, political, economic and cultural, in accordance with its own genius and traditions. The national territory is declared to be the whole island of Ireland, its islands and the territorial seas. Pending the re-integration of the national territory, and without prejudice to the right of the Parliament and the Government established by the Constitution to exercise jurisdiction over the whole of the national territory, the laws enacted by that Parliament shall have the like area and extent of application as those of the Irish Free State, which did not include the six counties of Northern Ireland. The national flag is the tricolour of green, white and orange. The Irish language, being the national language, is the first official language. The English language is recognized as a second official language.

The President.—The President—*Uachtarán na hÉireann*—is elected by direct vote of the people for a period of seven years. A former or retiring President is eligible for a second term. The President summons and dissolves Dáil Éireann on the advice of the *Taoiseach* (Head of the Government). He signs and promulgates laws. The supreme command of the Defence Forces is vested in him, its exercise being regulated by law. He has the power of pardon. The President, in the exercise and performance of certain of his constitutional powers and functions, is aided and advised by a Council of State.

The Legislature.—The Parliament—*Oireachtas*—consists of the President and two Houses: a House of Representatives—*Dáil Éireann*—and a Senate—*Seanad Éireann.*

Dáil Éireann is composed of 144 members elected by adult suffrage on a basis of proportional representation.

Seanad Éireann is composed of 60 members, of whom 11 are nominated by the Taoiseach and 49 are elected; three by the National University of Ireland, three by the University of Dublin, and 43 from panels of candidates, established on a vocational basis.

The Executive.—The executive authority is exercised by the Government subject to the Constitution. The Government is responsible to Dáil Éireann, meets and acts as a collective authority, and is collectively responsible for the Departments of State administered by the Ministers.

The Taoiseach is appointed by the President on the nomination of Dáil Éireann. The other members of the Government are appointed by the President on the nomination of the Taoiseach with the previous approval of Dáil Éireann. The Taoiseach appoints a member of the Government to be the *Tánaiste* who acts for all purposes in the place of the Taoiseach in the event of the death, permanent incapacitation, or temporary absence of the Taoiseach. The Taoiseach, the Tánaiste and the Minister for Finance must be members of Dáil Éireann. The other members of the Government must be members of Dáil Éireann or Seanad Éireann, but not more than two may be members of Seanad Éireann.

THE LEGISLATURE

The Legislature (*Oireachtas*) consists of the President and two Houses—a House of Representatives (*Dáil Éireann*) and a Senate (*Seanad Éireann*). Dáil Eireann is composed of 144 Members, elected on the system of Proportional Representation by means of the single transferable vote. All citizens who have reached the age of 21 years and are not disqualified by law have the right to vote. The same Dáil does not continue for a longer period than seven years, but a shorter period of five years has been fixed by existing legislation. The present (17th) Dail was elected on October 4, 1961, and met on October 11, 1961.

Party Strength (Dáil Éireann)

	1961	1962	1963
Fianna Fáil	75	70	70
Fine Gael	41	47	47
Labour	11	15	15
Farmers (Clann na Talmhan)	3	2	2
Independent	7	6	6
Clann na Poblachta	1	1	1
Sinn Féin	4	0	0
National Progressive Democrats	2	2	2
Speaker	1	1	1
Vacancies	2	—	—
Total	147	144	144

*** Members of Dáil Éireann are paid an allowance of £1,000 per annum (and members of Seanad Éireann £750); are allowed free travelling facilities between Dublin and their constituencies and are, subject to certain restrictions, granted free telephone and postal facilities from Leinster House and allowances for overnight stays in Dublin.

Parliamentary Secretaries.

Parliamentary Secretary to the Taoiseach and to the Minister of Defence, Seosamh Ó Braonáin (Joseph Brennan).

Do. to the Minister for Finance, Donnchadh Ó Máille (Donogh Brendan O'Malley).

Do. to the Minister for Lands, Brian Ó Luineacháin (Brian Joseph Lenihan).

Attorney-General, Aindrias Ó Caoimh, S.C.

Secretary to the Government, Nioclás Ó Nualláin, Ph.D. (Nicholas G. Nolan).

Assistant Secretary to the Government, Tadhg Ó Cearbhaill (Tadhg O'Carroll).

United Kingdom Ambassador to the Republic of Ireland

H.E. Sir Geofroy Tory, K.C.M.G. (1963), 39 Merrion Square, Dublin.

Counsellor, G. E. Crombie, C.M.G.

First Secretary, C. A. Lovitt.

Military Attache, Brig. R. N. Thicknesse.

Trade Commissioner, G. L. Pearson, M.C.

Diplomatic Representatives Abroad

The Holy See: T. V. Commins (*Ambassador*).

Argentina: M. L. Skentelbery (*Minister*).

Australia: S. Kennan (*Chargé d'Affaires*).

Austria: W. Warnock (*Ambassador*).

Belgium and Luxemburg: F. Biggar (*Ambassador*).

Canada: W. P. Fay (*Ambassador*).

Finland, J. A. Belton (*Minister*).

France: D. R. McDonald (*Ambassador*).

Federal Republic of Germany: B. Gallagher (*Ambassador*).

Great Britain: C. C. Cremin (*Ambassador*), 17 Grosvenor Place, London, S.W.1.

Italy: J. F. Shields (*Ambassador*).

Netherlands: J. W. Lennon (*Ambassador*).

Federation of Nigeria: E. L. Kennedy (*Ambassador*).

Norway: J. A. Belton (*Ambassador*).

Portugal: Count G. O'Kelly (*Chargé d'Affaires*).

Spain: T. J. Horan (*Ambassador*).

Sweden: J. A. Belton (*Ambassador*).

Switzerland: W. Warnock (*Ambassador*).

Turkey: J. F. Shields (*Ambassador*).

U.S.A.: T. J. Kiernan (*Ambassador*).

THE JUDICIARY

The Judiciary consists of Courts of First Instance and a Court of Final Appeal called the Supreme Court—*Cúirt Uachtarach.* The Courts of First Instance include a High Court—*Ard-Chúirt*—invested with full original jurisdiction in and power to determine all matters and questions, whether of law or fact, civil or criminal, and also Courts of local and limited jurisdiction, with a right of appeal as determined by law. The High Court alone has original jurisdiction to entertain the question of the validity of any law having regard to the provisions of the Constitution. The Supreme Court has appellate jurisdiction from all decisions of the High Court, subject to exceptions and regulations prescribed by law. No law may, however, be enacted excepting the question of the validity of any law from the appellate jurisdiction of the Supreme Court.

Chief Justice, Hon. Cearbhaill Ó Dalaigh (Daly) £6,000

President of the High Court, Hon. Cahir Davitt 4,500

Judges, Supreme Court, Hon. Cecil Lavery; Hon. T. C. Kingsmill Moore; Hon. Kevin Haugh; Hon. Brian Walsh £4,500

Judges, High Court, Hon. F. G. O. Budd; Hon. R. McLoughlin; Hon. Thomas Teevan; Hon. George Murnaghan; Hon. Seán Kenny; Hon. Seamus Henchy; Hon. Barra O'Brien (*ex officio*) .... each 3,250

Master of High Court, John O. Leary, S.C.

DEFENCE

Under the direction of the President, and subject to the provisions of the Defence Act, 1954, the military command of the Defence Forces is exercisable by the Government through the Minister for Defence. To aid and counsel the Minister for Defence on all matters in relation to the business of the Department of Defence on which he may consult it, there is a Council of Defence consisting of the Parliamentary Secretary to the Minister, the Secretary of the Department of Defence, the Chief of Staff, the Adjutant-General and the Quartermaster-General. Establishments provide at present for a Permanent Defence Force of approximately 13,000 all ranks, including the Air Corps and the Naval Service. The Defence Estimates for the year ending March 31, 1963, provide for approximately 26,000 all ranks of the Reserve Defence Force. Recruitment is on a voluntary basis. Minimum term of enlistment for the Army is three years in the Permanent Defence Force with, in most cases, nine years in the Reserve Defence Force. Suitable men may complete twenty-one years service in the Permanent Defence Force. For the Naval Service, enlistment is for six years in the Permanent Defence Force and six years in the Reserve Defence Force. The Naval Service comprises three corvettes and three tenders. The Defence Estimates for the year ending March 31, 1963, provide for an expenditure of £8,848,100.

FINANCE

	1962–63 (Actual)	1963–64 (Estimated)
Revenue	£163,480,000	£181,570,000
Expenditure	193,279,000	208,032,000

The expenditure figures include certain services of a capital nature regarded as proper to be met from borrowing. Issues for these services in 1962–63 amounted to £24,949,000 and for 1963–64 are estimated at £26,462,000.

The estimated *Revenue* for 1963–64 includes Customs £48,360,000; Excise, £36,890,000; Estate, etc., Duties, £3,200,000; Income Tax, Sur-tax and Super-tax, £40,050,000; Corporation Profits Tax, etc., £7,800,000; Motor Vehicle Duties, £7,700,000; Stamp Duties, £2,830,000; Post Office Services, £12,150,000.

The principal items of estimated *Expenditure* for 1963–64 are Debt Service, £38,289,000; Agriculture, etc., £26,228,000; Army, £9,159,000; Police, £4,988,000; Education, £19,765,000; Social Insurance, £8,130,000; Social Assistance, £21,987,000; Health Services, £11,258,000; Postal Services, £9,842,000; Superannuation, £7,713,000.

The *Gross Debt* on March 31, 1963 was, £589,000,000 with *Assets* £310,000,000, leaving the *net* total of the debt at £279,000,000.

RELIGION

(Census of 1946)

Catholics	2,786,033
Protestant Episcopalians	124,829
Presbyterians	23,870
Methodists	8,355
Others	12,020
Total	2,955,107

EDUCATION

Primary education is directed by the State (4,867 schools with an enrolment of 484,618 and average daily attendance 87.0 per cent). Secondary education is in private hands and is largely conducted by Religious Orders (557 recognised schools with 84,916 pupils 12–20 years of age). Vocational (continuation and technical) education is conducted by 38 local Committees in 294 permanent schools (excluding 12 residential schools of domestic training and one day trades preparatory school) and a large number of temporary centres (28,325 whole-time day students and 68,576 other students).*

The estimated State expenditure on education in 1963–64, excluding administration and inspection, is Primary £12,659,500; Secondary £3,745,000; Vocational £2,255,200; Science and Art £287,170. The vote for Universities and Colleges for 1963–64 amounts to £2,366,170 while in addition grants of £260,684 are provided in respect of the Faculties of General Agriculture and Dairy Science.

* There are two Universities in Dublin, of which the National University has 3 constituent colleges (Dublin, Cork and Galway) with 693 Professors, etc., and 8,639 students; and Trinity College, Dublin, with 233 Professors, etc., and 3,156 students in the academic year 1961–62.

PRODUCTION AND INDUSTRY

Agriculture and Live Stock.—In 1962 there were 1,074,000 acres under corn crops, 502,400 under root and green crops, 11,000 under fruit and 1,853,100 under hay, a total of 3,440,500 acres. The principal produce in 1962 was: oats, 390,100 tons; wheat, 432,000 tons; barley, 593,600 tons; turnips, 2,117,000 tons; potatoes, 2,083,700 tons; sugar beet, 916,300 tons; and hay, 3,642,700 tons. The *Live Stock* included 4,741,800 cattle, 4,670,600 sheep, 1,110,600 pigs and 195,900 horses.

Minerals.—1,300 persons were employed in the coal mines in 1961 and 198,000 tons of coal won.

Sea Fisheries.—5,697 persons were employed in the fisheries in 1962, the total value of all fish (excluding salmon) landed being £1,499,000.

COMMUNICATIONS

Railways.—In the year ended March 31, 1962, there were 1,655 miles of railway all of standard (5 ft. 3 in.) gauge; 10,156,568 passengers and 2,372,169 tons of merchandise were conveyed; the receipts were £8,424,277 and expenditure £10,017,516. These figures are in respect of railway working by *Coras Iompair Éireann*, the national transport undertaking which is now the only concern operating a rail service in the State.

Road Motor Services.—In 1962 road motor vehicles carried 298,208,529 passengers, the gross receipts being £7,236,650.

Shipping.—In 1962 the number of ships with cargoes and in ballast entered at the various Ψ ports, Cobh, Cork, Drogheda, Dublin, Dundalk, Dún Laoghaire, Galway, Limerick, Rosslare, Waterford, Whitegate, etc. was 10,196 of 10,388,286 tons, of which 1,748 (1,417,971 tons) were Republic of Ireland flag, and 4,728 (5,745,884 tons) British.

Civil Aviation

Shannon Airport, 15 miles W. of Limerick, is on the main transatlantic air route. In 1962 the airport handled 370,101 passengers, 20,772 tons of cargo and 1,590 tons of mail.

Dublin Airport, 6 miles N. of Dublin, serves the cross-channel and European services operated by the Irish national airline *Aer Lingus* and other airlines. During 1962 the airport handled 987,190 passengers, 15,989 tons of cargo and 1,843 tons of mail.

Licensed private aerodromes include: Weston, 9 miles W. of Dublin; Dunmore East, 10 miles S.E. of Waterford; Coonagh, 2 miles W. of Limerick; Oranmore, 5 miles E. of Galway; Killarney Racecourse. 1 mile S. of Killarney; Rosapenna Strand, 16 miles N. of Letterkenny and Headfort, 1½ miles E.N.E. of Kells.

OVERSEAS TRADE

Year	Imports	Exports	Trade Balance
	£	£	£
1950	159,393,975	72,390,761	− 87,003,214
1951	204,595,585	81,520,383	− 123,075,202
1952	172,309,040	101,599,437	− 70,709,603
1953	182,480,351	114,097,405	− 68,382,946
1954	179,890,195	115,341,682	− 64,548,513
1955	207,663,264	110,851,440	− 96,811,824
1956	182,848,621	108,126,933	− 74,721,688
1957	184,171,966	131,340,964	− 52,831,002
1958	198,957,116	131,293,044	− 67,664,072
1959	212,646,748	130,706,519	− 81,940,229
1960	226,228,389	152,703,014	− 73,525,375
1961	261,402,920	180,473,121	− 80,929,799
1962	273,657,234	174,005,194	− 99,652,040

Principal Articles

Imports (1962)

The principal groups were: machinery and electrical goods, £39,340,024; textiles, £26,508,322; vehicles £25,052,581; oilseeds, oils, fats, resins and gums, £20,818,938; chemicals, perfumery, dyes and creams, £15,286,201; iron and steel, £13,586,100; cereals and feeding-stuffs, £13,537,464; live animals, £12,858,344; non-metalliferous mine and quarry products, £12,680,987; fruit, nuts and vegetables, £8,330,007; paper and cardboard, £7,710,011; fertilizers, £6,953,347,

Domestic Exports (1962)

Principally live animals £47,553,575; food-stuffs of animal origin, £42,448,444; textiles, £13,135,776; drink, £7,242,972; clothing and footwear, £6,159,848.

CAPITAL

Dublin (*Baile Atha Cliath*) is a City and County Borough on the River Liffey at the head of Dublin Bay. In April, 1961, its population was 537,448. There are many notable public buildings in the City, among them the two Cathedrals of Christ Church and St. Patrick, the Bank of Ireland (formerly the House of Parliament) and Trinity College (the only constituent College of the University of Dublin). University College is a constituent college of the National University of Ireland. A large export trade of agricultural products passes through the city and there is a considerable brewing industry, while there is an increasing amount of light manufacturing.

Other cities and towns are Ψ Cork (pop. 77,980), Ψ Limerick (50,786), Ψ Dún Laoghaire (47,792), Ψ Waterford (28,216), Ψ Galway (22,028), Ψ Dundalk (19,790), Ψ Drogheda (17,085), Sligo (13,145), Wexford (11,328), Bray (11,688), Kilkenny (10,159), Tralee (10,723), Clonmel (10,640) and Athlone (9,624).

ARMS OF IRELAND

Azure a harp *or* stringed *argent*.

FLAG

Equal vertical stripes of green, white and orange.

The United States of America

Area and Population

	Land Area, 1960 (sq. miles)	Population	
		Census 1950	Census 1960
The United States*	3,548,974	151,325,798	179,323,175
Commonwealth of Puerto Rico	3,421	2,210,703	2,349,544
Possessions	450	106,219	123,151
Guam	209	59,498	67,044
Virgin Islands of U.S.	132	26,665	32,099
American Samoa	76	18,937	20,051
Midway Islands	2	416	2,356
Wake Island	3	349	1,097
Canton Island and Enderbury Island	27	272†	320†
Johnston Island and Sand Island	—	46†	156†
Swan Islands	1	36†	28†
Other Outlying areas:			
Panama Canal Zone	362	52,822	42,122
Corn Islands	4	1,304	1,872
Pacific Islands Trust Territory	687	54,843	70,724‡
Population Abroad		*481,455*	1,374,421
Total	3,553,898	154,233,234	183,285,009

* The 50 States and the Federal *District of Columbia* (*see* p. 801).
† The islands of Enderbury, Sand, Little Swan and Little Corn were uninhabited at the time of enumeration.
‡ Census held 1958. *Italic* figures are estimates.

REGISTERED BIRTHS AND DEATHS

Calendar Year	Live Births		Deaths	
	Number	Rate per 1,000	Number	Rate per 1,000
*1952	3,846,986	24·7	1,496,838	9·6
*1953	3,902,120	24·6	1,517,541	9·6
*1954	4,017,362	24·9	1,481,091	9·2
1955	4,047 295	24·6	1,528,717	9·3
*1956	4,163,090	24 9	1,564,476	9·4
*1957	4,254,784	25·0	1,633,128	9·6
*1958	4,203,812	24·3	1,647,886	9·5
*1959	4,244,796	24·0	1,656,814	9 4
*1960	4,257,850	23·7	1,711,982	9·5
*1961	4,268,326	23·3	1,701,522	9·3
§1962	4,167,000	22·4	1,757,000	9.5

* Births based on 50 per cent. sample. § Estimated.

Note.—Figures tabulated are for the United States, including (from 1959) Alaska and (from 1960) Hawaii. Deaths exclude fœtal deaths. Except for 1960, birth and death rates are based on the population as estimated on July 1. 1960 figures are based on the Census taken on April 1.

IMMIGRATION AND NATURALIZATION

From 1820 to 1962, 42,396,068 immigrants were admitted to the United States. Of those admitted in 1962, 21,189 were born in the United Kingdom; 24,088 in Germany; 1,633 in Austria; 5,783 in Scandinavia; 21,442 in Italy; 3,732 in France; 1,355 in Hungary; 22,105 in Asia; 30,377 in Canada; and 55,291 in Mexico. The total number of immigrants admitted in 1962, was 283,763. 127,307 alien residents of the United States became naturalized citizens during that year.

MARRIAGE AND DIVORCE

Laws of marriage and of divorce are within the exclusive jurisdiction of each State. Each State legislature enacts its own laws prescribing rules and qualifications pertaining to marriage and its dissolution.

Year	Marriages	Per 1,000 Pop.	Estimated Divorces	Per 1,000 Pop.
1952	1,539,000	9·9	392,000	2·5
1953	1,546,000	9·8	390,000	2·5
1954	1,490,000	9·2	379,000	2·4
1955	1,531,000	9·3	377,000	2·3
1956	1,585,000	9·5	382,000	2 3
1957	1,518,000	8·9	381,000	2·2
1958	1,451,000	8·4	368,000	2 1
1959	1,494,000	8·5	395,000	2 2
1960	1,523,000	8·5	393,000	2·2
1961	1,548,000	8·5	..	*2·2
*1962	1,580,000	8·5	..	*2·2

* Provisional estimate.

Note.—Figures include Alaska (from 1959) and Hawaii (from 1960). Rates are based on population as estimated on July 1, except for the Census year of 1960.

Increase of the People.

Year of Census	Total Population				Increase over preceding census	Inter-Censal Immigrants*
	White	Negro	Other Races	Total		
1890	55,101,258	7,488,676	357,780	62,947,714	12,791,931	5,246,613
1900	66,809,196	8,833,994	351,385	75,994,575	13,046,861	3,687,564
1910	81,731,957	9,827,763	412,546	91,972,266	15,977,691	8,795,386
1920	94,820,915	10,463,131	426,574	105,710,620	13,738,354	5,735,811
1930	110,286,740	11,891,143	597,163	122,775,046	17,064,420	4,107,209
1940	118,214,870	12,865,518	588,887	131,669,275	8,894,229	528,431
1950	134,942,028	15,042,286	713,047	150,697,361	19,028,086	1,035,039
1960	158,831,732	18,871,831	1,619,612	179,323,175	28,625,814	2,515,479†

* Includes immigrants to territorial possessions, etc. † Total for 10 years to June 30, 1960

National Origins of the Population

In 1960, of a total white population of 158,837,671, 5·9 per cent, were foreign born; of the total non-white population of 20,488,000, 2·2 per cent. were foreign born. 34,050,406 persons in the United States were of foreign stock, the countries of origin being:

Country	Number	Country	Number	Country	Number	Country	Number
United Kingdom...	2,884,651	France........	351,681	Finland.......	240,827	Canada.......	3,181,051
Eire..........	1,773,312	Germany.....	4,320,664	Roumania....	233,805	Mexico.......	1,735,992
Norway......	774,754	Poland.......	2,780,026	Greece.......	378,586	Other American Countries...	580,679
Sweden......	1,046,942	Czechoslovakia	917,830	Italy.........	4,543,935	All other.....	140,309
Denmark.....	399,350	Austria.......	1,098,630	Portugal......	277,402		
Netherlands...	398,658	Hungary.....	701,637	Other European Countries...	492,386		
Switzerland...	263,054	Yugoslavia....	448,503	Asia.........	1,141,839		
		U.S.S.R......	2,693,113				

Nineteen per cent. of the U.S. population are first or second generation Americans. Of the above, 9,738,143 persons were foreign born and 24,312,263 born in the United States with one or both parents foreign born. Third and subsequent generation Americans (native born of native parents) numbered 145,275,265 in 1960.

PHYSIOGRAPHY

The conterminous States of the Republic occupy nearly all that portion of the North American Continent between the Atlantic and Pacific Oceans, in latitude 25° 07′–49° 23′ North and longitude 66° 57′–124° 44′ West, its northern boundary being Canada and the southern boundary Mexico. The separate State of Alaska reaches a latitude of 71° 23′ N., at Point Barrow, a distance of 2,504 miles from the geographic centre of the United States.

Its coast-line has an estimated length of about 2,069 miles on the Atlantic, 7,623 miles on the Pacific (Alaska, 5,580), 1,631 miles on the Gulf of Mexico, 3,586 miles on the Great Lakes and 1,060 miles on the Arctic Ocean. The principal river is the mighty Mississippi-Missouri-Red Rock, traversing the whole country from north to south, and having a course of 3,710 miles to its mouth in the Gulf of Mexico, with many large affluents, the chief of which are the Yellowstone, Platte, Arkansas, Ohio, and Red Rivers. The rivers flowing into the Atlantic and Pacific Oceans are comparatively small; among the former may be noticed the Hudson, Delaware, Susquehanna, Potomac, James, and Savannah; of the latter, the Columbia, Sacramento, and Colorado. The Alabama and Colorado of Texas fall into the Gulf of Mexico, also the Rio Grande, a long river partly forming the boundary with Mexico. The areas of the water-basins have been estimated as follows:—Rivers flowing to the Pacific, 644,040 square miles; to the Atlantic, 488,877; and to the Gulf of Mexico, 1,683,325 square miles, of which 1,257,547 are drained by the Mississippi-Missouri-Red Rock. The chain of the Rocky Mountains separates the western portion of the country from the remainder, all communication being carried on over certain elevated passes, several of which are now traversed by railroads; west of these, bordering the Pacific coast, the Cascade Mountains and Sierra Nevada form the outer edge of a high tableland, consisting in part of stony and sandy desert and partly of grazing land and forested mountains, and including the Great Salt Lake, which extends to the Rocky Mountains. Eastward the country is a vast, gently undulating plain, with a general slope southwards towards the partly marshy flats of the Gulf of Mexico, extending to the Atlantic, interrupted only by the Appalachian Highlands, of inferior elevation, in the Eastern States. Nearly the whole of this plain, from the Rocky Mountains to some distance beyond the Mississippi, consists of immense prairies. In the Eastern States (which form the more settled and most thickly inhabited portion of the country) large forests of valuable timber, as beech, birch, maple, oak, pine, spruce, elm, ash, walnut; and in the south, live oak, water-oak, magnolia, palmetto, tulip-tree, cypress, etc., still exist, the remnants of the forests which formerly extended over all the Atlantic slope, but into which great inroads have been made by the advance of civilization. The Mississippi valley is eminently fertile. The mineral kingdom produces much ore of iron, copper, lead, zinc, and aluminium, the non-metallic minerals include immense quantities of coal, anthracite, petroleum, stone, cement, phosphate rock, and salt. Precious metals include gold and silver, mined chiefly in Colorado, California, Montana, Utah, and Idaho. The highest point is Mount McKinley (Alaska), 20,320 feet above sea level, and the lowest point of dry land is in Death Valley (Inyo, California), 282 feet below sea-level. The mean elevation of the United States is approximately 2,500 feet.

GOVERNMENT

The United States of America is a Federal Republic consisting of 50 States and 1 Federal District (of which 13 are Original States, 7 were admitted without previous organization as Territories, and 30 were admitted after such organization), and of 1 organized Territory. Hawaii formally entered the Union as the 50th State on Aug. 21, 1959, from which date the flag of the United States has 13 stripes and 50 stars in 9 horizontal rows of six and five alternately.

THE CONSTITUTION.—By the Constitution of Sept. 17, 1787 (to which ten amendments were added on Dec. 15, 1791, and eleventh to twenty-third Jan. 8, 1798, Sept. 25, 1804, Dec. 18, 1865, July 28, 1868, March 30, 1870, Feb. 25, 1913, May 31, 1913, Jan. 16, 1920, Aug. 26, 1920, Feb. 6, 1933, Dec. 5, 1933, Feb. 26, 1951 and March 29, 1961), the government of the United States is entrusted to three separate authorities—the Executive, the Legislative, and the Judicial.

THE EXECUTIVE

THE *Executive* power is vested in a President, who is elected every four years, and is eligible for re-election to one additional term. The mode of electing the President is as follows:—Each State appoints, in such manner as the Legislature thereof directs (they are now elected by popular vote on the *first Tuesday after the first Monday in November* of the year preceding the year in which the Presidential term expires), a number of electors, equal to the whole number of Senators and Representives to which the State may be entitled in the Congress; but no Senator or Representative, or anyone holding office under Government, shall be appointed an elector. The electors for each State meet in their respective States on the *first Monday after the second Wednesday in December* following, and there vote for a President by ballot. The ballots are then sent to Washington, and opened on the *sixth day of January* by the President of Senate in presence of Congress, and the candidate who has received a majority of the whole number of electoral votes cast is declared President for the ensuing term. If no one has a majority, then from the highest on the list (not exceeding three) the House of Representatives elects a President, the votes being taken by States, the representation from each State having one vote. There is also a Vice President, who, on the death of the President, becomes President for the remainder of the term. Under the XXth Amendment to the Constitution the terms of the President and Vice President end at noon on the 20th day of January of the years in which such terms would have ended if the Amendment had not been ratified, and the terms of their successors then begin. In case of the removal or death of both President and Vice President, a statute provides for the succession.

The President must be at least 35 years of age and a native citizen of the United States. He receives a taxable salary of $100,000 with a taxable expense allowance of $50,000 and a non-taxable travelling allowance of not exceeding $40,000. Under the XXIInd Amendment to the Constitution, the tenure of the Presidency is limited to two terms. Executive duties:—

(1) He is Commander-in-Chief of the Army and of the Navy (and of the Militias when they are in Federal service), and he commissions all officers therein.

(2) With the consent of the Senate, he appoints the Cabinet officers and all the chief (and many minor) officials.

(3) He exercises a general supervision over the whole Federal Administration and sees that the Federal Laws are duly carried out. Should disorder arise in any State which the authorities thereof are unable to suppress, the aid of the President may be invoked.

(4) He conducts the Foreign Policy of the Republic, and has power, "by and with the Advice and Consent of the Senate, to make Treaties, provided two thirds of the Senators present concur." The Declaration of War rests with Congress.

(5) He makes recommendations of a general nature to Congress, and when laws are passed by Congress he may return them to Congress with a veto. But if a measure so vetoed is again passed by both Houses of Congress by a two-thirds majority in each House, it becomes law, notwithstanding the objections of the President.

THE PRESIDENT

President of the United States (January 20, 1961, to January 20, 1965), JOHN FITZGERALD KENNEDY, *born* May 29, 1917, *sworn in as President* (in succession to Dwight D. Eisenhower), January 20, 1961. *Democrat.*

Vice-President, Lyndon Baines Johnson, of Texas, *born* Aug. 27, 1908, *elected* Nov. 8, 1960. *Democrat.*

THE CABINET

(Each $25,000)

Secretary of State, Dean Rusk, of New York (*born* Feb. 9, 1909), *appointed* Jan. 21, 1961.
Secretary of Treasury, Douglas Dillon, of New Jersey (*born* Aug. 21, 1909), *appointed* Jan. 21, 1961.
Secretary of Defence, Robert S. McNamara, of Michigan (*born* June 9, 1916), *appointed* Jan. 21, 1961.
Attorney-General, Robert F. Kennedy. of Massachusetts (*born* Nov. 20, 1925), *appointed* Jan. 21, 1961.
Postmaster-General, John Gronouski, of Wisconsin (*born* 1920), *appointed* Sept. 9, 1963.
Secretary of Interior, Stewart L. Udall, of Arizona (*born* Jan. 31, 1920), *appointed* Jan. 21, 1961.
Secretary of Agriculture, Orville L. Freeman, of Minnesota (*born* May 9, 1918), *appointed* Jan. 21, 1961.
Secretary of Commerce, Luther H. Hodges, of N. Carolina (*born* Mar. 8, 1898), *appointed* Jan. 21, 1961.
Secretary of Labour, W. Willard Wirtz, of Ohio (*born* Mar. 14, 1912), *appointed* Aug. 30, 1962.
Secretary of Health, Education and Welfare, Anthony J. Celebrezze, of Ohio (*born* Sept. 4, 1910), *appointed* July 31, 1962.

THE CONGRESS

The Legislative power is vested in two Houses, the Senate and the House of Representatives, the President having a *veto* power, which may be overcome by a two-thirds vote of each House. The Senate is composed of two Senators from each State, elected by the people thereof for the term of six years, and each Senator has one vote; and Representatives are chosen in each State, by popular vote, for two years The number of Representatives for each State is allotted in proportion to its population—at present 1 for 301,164. The *Senate* consists of 100 members. The salary of a Senator is $22,500 per annum, with mileage at 20 cents per mile each session. The *House of Representatives* consists of 435 Representatives and a resident commissioner from Puerto Rico. The salary of a Representative is $22,500 per annum with mileage as for Senators. By the XIXth Amendment, sex is no disqualification for the franchise. On July 1, 1950, there were 47,860,228 men and 49,556,137 women of voting age, excluding members of the armed forced overseas.

THE EIGHTY-EIGHTH CONGRESS

Noon of Jan. 3, 1963, to Noon of Jan. 3, 1965.*

President of the Senate, Lyndon B. Johnson, *Texas* $30,000
Speaker of the House of Representatives, John W. McCormack, *Mass.* $30,000
Secretary of the Senate, Felton M. Johnston, *Miss.*
Clerk of the House of Representatives, Ralph R. Roberts, *Ind.*

Members of the 88th Congress were elected on Nov. 6, 1962.

The 88th Congress is constituted as follows:

Senate.—Democrats, 67; Republicans, 33. Total, 100.

House of Representatives.—Democrats, 257; Republicans, 177. Total 435.

CAPITAL OF THE U.S.

In 1790 Congress ratified the cession of 100 sq. miles by the States of Maryland and Virginia as a site for a Federal City to be the national capital of the United States. In 1791 it was decided to name the capital *Washington* and in 1793 the foundation-stone of the Capitol building was laid. In 1800 the seat of government was removed to Washington, which was chartered as a city in 1802. In 1846 the Virginia portion was retroceded and the present area of the *District of Columbia* (with which the City of Washington is considered co-extensive) is 69·245 square miles, with a population at the Census of 1960 of 763,956.

The District of Columbia is ruled directly by the President and Congress through a Board of Commissioners appointed by the President.

The *City of Washington*, is situated on the west central edge of Maryland, opposite the State of Virginia, on the left bank of the Potomac at its confluence with the Anacostia, 107 miles from Chesapeake Bay and 186 from the Atlantic Ocean.

THE JUDICATURE

The *Federal Judiciary* consists of three sets of Federal Courts: (1) The *Supreme Court* at

Washington, D.C., consisting of a Chief Justice and eight Associate Justices, with original jurisdiction in cases affecting Ambassadors, &c., or where a State is a party to the suit, and with appellate jurisdiction from inferior Federal Courts and from the decisions of the highest Courts of the States. (2) The *United States Courts of Appeals*, dealing with appeals from District Courts, and consisting of the Justice of the Supreme Court for the Circuit and all the Circuit and District Judges within the circuit. (3) The 93 *District Courts*, served by 199 District Court Judges.

THE SUPREME COURT

(U.S. Supreme Court Building, Washington, D.C.)
Chief Justice, Earl Warren, *Cal.*, *born* March 19, 1891, *appointed* Sept. 30, 1953.......... $35,500

Associate Justices (each $35,000)

Name.	Born.	Apptd.
Hugo L. Black, *Ala.*	1886	1937
Wm. O. Douglas, *Conn.*	1898	1939
Tom C. Clark, *Texas*	1899	1949
John M. Harlan, *N.Y.*	1899	1955
William J. Brennan, Jr., *N.J.*	1906	1956
Potter Stewart, *Ohio*	1915	1958
Byron R. White, *Colo*	1917	1962
Arthur J. Goldberg, *Ill.*	1908	1962

Supreme Court Officers.

Clerk, John F. Davis.
Chief Deputy Clerk, Edmund P. Cullinan.
Marshal, T. Perry Lippitt.
Reporter of Decisions, Walter Wyatt.
Librarian, Helen Newman.

CRIMINAL STATISTICS, U.S.

(Crime Index, 1958)

Crime	No. of Offences 1960	1961
Murder	9,140	8,600
Rape	15,560	16,010
Robbery	88,970	91,660
Aggravated Assault	130,230	133,020
Burglary	821,100	852,500
Larceny ($50 and over)	474,900	498,100
Thefts of Automobiles	321,400	326,200
Total	1,861,300	1,926,090

DEFENCE

Department of Defence.

Secretary of Defence (*in the Cabinet*), Robert S. McNamara (Jan. 21, 1961).
Secretary of the Army (*not in the Cabinet*), Cyrus R. Vance.
Secretary of the Navy (*not in the Cabinet*), Fred Korth.
Secretary of the Air Force (*not in the Cabinet*). Eugene Zuchert.

The Defence Reorganization Act, making important changes in the organization of the United States armed forces, came into effect on Jan. 1, 1959. It provided for unified command of the three services and their central control by the Defence Department, which also became responsible for research and development of new weapons. The Secretary of each service, Army, Navy and Air Force, became responsible to the Secretary of Defence for the operation and efficiency of his department. Existing practice by which service chiefs and individual departments might approach Congress on their own initiative was, however, continued. The Secretary of Defence assumed powers under the Act to abolish, merge or transfer functions of the individual services, provision being made for proposals of this kind to be laid before Congress and the Senate for thirty days, with the possibility of a veto if objections were raised.

Unified Defence Commands

U.S. European Command, Paris.—*Cdr.*, Gen. Lyman L. Lemnitzer (concurrently *NATO Supreme Allied Commander*).
Caribbean, Panama Canal Zone.—*Cdr.*, Lt.-Gen. Andrew P. O'Meara (*U.S. Army*).
Atlantic, Norfolk, Virginia—*Cdr.*, Adm. Robert L. Dennison (*U.S. Navy*) (concurrently *NATO Supreme Allied Commander, Atlantic*).
Pacific, Hawaii.—*Cdr.*, Adm. Harry D. Felt (*U.S. Navy*).
E. Atlantic and Mediterranean, London.—*Cdr.*, Vice-Adm. D. L. McDonald (*U.S. Navy*).
Continental Air Defence Command, Colorado Springs —*Cdr.*, Lt.-Gen. John K. Gerhart (*U.S.A.F.*).
Strategic Air Command, Omaha.—*Cdr.*, Gen. Thomas S. Power (*U.S.A.F.*).
Alaska Command, Anchorage, Alaska.—*Cdr.*, Lt.-Gen. G. W. Mundy (*U.S.A.F.*)

Army.—The Army of U.S. had a strength of 8,291,336 on V.E. Day, reduced by June 30, 1959, to 591,700 (excluding Air Corps). The strength on April 30, 1962 was 1,080,847. Stationed in Europe were five divisions and other large combat elements of less than division size. There were two divisions in Korea and one in Hawaii. Strong combat units were on duty in the Caribbean area and in Alaska and units of approximately brigade strength were in Italy. The need for flexibility in combined-arms forces capable of rapid deployment to areas threatened by aggression prompted the inclusion of the Strategic Army Corps (STRAC) in a new unified command, the U.S. Strike Force. Some 5,600 fixed-wing and helicopter aircraft were in Army service, including helicopters of observation, utility and transport types. Under a 10-year modernization programme, the Army expects to reduce the number of aircraft models in service, but the number of Army aircraft is to rise to about 8,000 by 1970.

Navy.—The peak strength of the Navy (including Marine Corps) in the summer of 1945 was 3,855,497. The strength on April 20, 1962, was 670,412. Strength of the Marine Corps, 189,891.

The U.S. Navy had in service in June, 1962, approximately 900 vessels including attack carriers (16), anti-submarine carriers (10), cruiser types (13), destroyer types (238), command ship (1), submarines, including 25 nuclear submarines (9 of the *Polaris* type) (118), minecraft (84), patrol craft (70), amphibians (130) and auxiliaries (218).

Air.—The U.S. Air Force was formerly the Army Air Corps and directly under command of the War Department. In 1947 an independent Department of the Air Force was established under a Secretary of the Air Force. The Navy and Marine Corps retained separate air organizations. Strength of the Air Force (March 31, 1962), 888,737.

In 1961, the Air Force assumed new and significant responsibilities in the field of military space systems and its requirements for both manned and unmanned weapons were extended. Early in the year provision was made to increase production capacity for the *Minuteman* missile. The proportion of the strategic bomber force maintained on a 15-minute ground alert was raised from one-third to one-half. Steps were also taken to strengthen the air defence command and control systems.

A new command, the Air Force Communications Service, was established to operate and maintain inter-base communications and flight and air traffic control. The initial strength of the Command was 30,000.

FINANCE

The following table shows administrative budget receipts and expenditure on an actual fiscal year basis. The U.S. Consolidated Cash Budget, which is more comprehensive than the administrative budget, includes the transactions of funds held in trust by the Federal Government for programmes such as social security, federal aided highway construction and veterans life insurance (totalling $25,000,000,000 in the fiscal year 1963). Consolidated Cash receipts in the fiscal year 1963 were $109,800,000,000; payments were $113,900,000,000; deficit, $4,100,000,000.

ADMINISTRATIVE BUDGET RECEIPTS AND EXPENDITURES

Fiscal Years	1962 actual	1963 actual
ADMINISTRATIVE BUDGET RECEIPTS		
Individual income taxes	$45,571,000,000	$47,596,000,000
Corporation income taxes	20,523,000,000	21,567,000,000
Excise taxes	9,585,000,000	9,914,000,000
Customs	1,142,000,000	1,205,000,000
Estate and gift taxes	2,016,000,000	2,165,000,000
Miscellaneous receipts	3,204,000,000	4,424,000,000
TOTAL	82,041,000,000	86,871,000,000
Deduct interfund transactions	*633,000,000*	*513,000,000*
NET TOTAL	81,409,000,000	86,357,000,000
ADMINISTRATIVE BUDGET EXPENDITURES		
National defence	51,103,000,000	52,743,000,000
International affairs and finance	2,817,000,000	2,545,000,000
Space research and technology	1,257,000,000	2,552,000,000
Agriculture and agricultural resources	5,895,000,000	7,028,000,000
Natural resources	2,147,000,000	2,352,000,000
Commerce and transportation	2,774,000,000	2,816,000,000
Housing and community development	349,000,000	*−78,000,000*
Health, labour, and welfare	4,524,000,000	4,761,000,000
Education	1,076,000,000	1,244,000,000
Veterans, benefits and services	5,403,000,000	5,187,000,000
Interest	9,198,000,000	9,976,000,000
General government	1,875,000,000	1,978,000,000
TOTAL	88,420,000,000	93,103,000,000
Deduct interfund transactions	*633,000,000*	*513,000,000*
NET TOTAL	87,787,000,000	92,590,000,000

PUBLIC DEBT

On June 30, 1962, the *Federal Public Debt* of the United States stood at $298,201,000,000; the level at the end of the fiscal year 1961 was $288,971,000,000.

COST OF LIVING IN U.S.A.

The Consumer Price Index (for city wage-earner and clerical worker families in 46 cities representative of all cities in the United States) showed a monthly average during the calendar year 1962 of 105·4 (the basic figure of 100 being the 1957–59 average). The average of consumer prices for the first four months of 1963 was: January, 106·0, February, 106·1, March, April and May, 106·2.

According to figures prepared by the Bureau of Labour Statistics, the index of consumer prices (all items) rose from 105·2 to 105·8 during the calendar year 1962, displaying price stability. In the year to May, 1963, food rose from 103·2 to 104·2 and all other commodities from 102·6 to 103·0. The Index for services rose from 109·4 to 111·1 (rent, 105·5 to 106·6); all other services, 110·1 to 111·9).

The wholesale price index of all commodities showed a monthly average during 1959 of 100·6 (the average for the years 1957–59 = 100). The monthly average fell to 100·3 in 1961 and the provisional figure for 1962 is 100·6. Wholesale prices for farm products rose from 96·0 in 1961 to 100·6 in Sept., 1962, and fell to 94·4 in May, 1963. Industrial prices maintained an average of 100·8 in 1961 and 1962, falling to 100·5 in May, 1963.

PERSONAL INCOMES IN U.S.A.

Personal incomes in the United States rose from $401·3 billion in 1960 to $417·4 in 1961 and further to $442·1 in 1962. In the year 1962, labour income rose by $19·0 billion, business and professional income by $1·2 billion and personal interest income by $2·3 billion. Dividend income rose by $1·3 billion to $16·6 billion. Personal incomes from all sources other than agriculture rose by $24·2 billion. Preliminary estimates for June, 1963 (seasonally adjusted annual rate) showed personal income at $462·1 billion, an increase of $20·0 billion over the 1962 level. Labour income rose from $309·2 billion in 1962 to $325·1 billion in June, 1963, an increase of $15·9 billion. Business and professional incomes rose from $36·5 billion in 1962 to $37·5 billion in June, 1963, and personal interest income rose from $30·0 billion in 1962 to $32·3 billion in June, 1963.

Disposition of personal incomes.—Of the total of $442·1 billion gross personal income, $57·7 billion was taken by personal taxes and $355·4 billion was consumed on durable goods ($48·2 billion), non-durable goods ($161·4 billion) and services ($145·7 billion), showing personal saving totalling $29·1 billion out of $384·4 billion disposable personal income. At current prices the latter showed an average of $2,060 per head. Savings amounted to 7·6 per cent. of disposable personal income.

Private Domestic Investment.—The total gross private investment rose from $49·9 billion in 1952 to $78·8 billion in 1962. Fixed investment in new residential construction (excluding farm investment) rose to $23·2 billion (1952, $12·8 billion) and other new construction to $21·2 billion (1952, $12·7 billion). Investment in producers' durable equipment (excluding farm equipment) rose from $18·6 billion in 1952 to $26·0 billion in 1962.

PRODUCTION

AGRICULTURE AND LIVE STOCK

Agriculture.—The total land surface, excluding island possessions and Alaska, is 1,901,680,000 acres of which about 59 per cent. is in farms. The total number of farms in 1959 (1959 Census of Agriculture) was 3,703,642. The cash income from crops in 1957 was $12,461,000,000; in 1958, $14,182,000,000; in 1959, $14,656,000,000; in 1960, $15,103,000,000; in 1961, $15,495,000,000 and in 1962, $15,935,000,000. Cash income from livestock and livestock products in 1957, $17,363,000,000; in 1958, $19,223,000,000; in 1959, $18,856,000,000; in 1960, $18,909,000,000 in 1961, $19,416,000,000 and in 1962, $19,986,000,000.

Record high yields per acre for many crops lifted total production of crops in the United States to the record level of 1960, The all-crop production index at 108 (1957–59 = 100) was the same as 1960 but up 1 per cent from the 1961 level of 107. Crop acreage was 3 per cent smaller than in 1961, largely the result of farmers' participation in the Government Feed Grain and Wheat Programmes. Favourable growing weather in the central part of the United States helped corn and other feed grains to reach record yields per acre.

Live Stock on Farms, Jan. 1.

	1961	1962	1963
All cattle...	97,534,000	100,002,000	103,754,000
Cows......	46,463,000	47,472,000	48,690,000
Hogs.......	55,506,000	57,000,000	58,695,000
Sheep......	32,982,000	31,320,000	30,170,000
Stock Sheep	28,571,000	27,065,000	26,129,000
Chickens...	361,685,000	368,452,000	365,217,000
Turkeys....	6,770,000	6,488,000	6,598,000

MINERALS

The value of mineral production in continental United States in 1962 totalled an estimated $18·7 billion. The comparable value for 1961 was $18·1 billion and for 1959 was $17·9 billion.

Nearly 68 per cent. of the mineral production of the United States (in value) consists of fuels. In 1962 U.S. production of crude petroleum amounted to 2,670 million barrels, about 48,000,000 barrels more than in 1961.

Bituminous coal and lignite produced in 1962 totalled 420 million tons, 17,000,000 tons less than in 1961. The average value of soft coal at the mine was estimated at $4·54 a ton, compared with $4·58 in 1961.

Despite a slight drop in anthracite output, solid fuels as a group enjoyed their best year since 1957 as the combined effects of exports and expanding electrical power generation overcame continued losses in domestic space-heating markets. The combined solid-fuels output has held steady or increased modestly for several years but the value of the output had continued to drop until 1962. Reports at the end of 1962 indicated continued improvements. Within the mineral fuels group the largest dollar increases were estimated for petroleum, natural gas, bituminous coal and lignite, and helium, in that order. The greatest percentage gain over 1961 was scored by helium, followed by carbon dioxide, peat, and asphalt and related bitumens.

MANUFACTURES

The leading five States according to value added by manufacture (adjusted) at the 1961 Annual Survey were: New York ($18,039,754,000), California ($14,305,061,000); Ohio ($13,302,845,000); Illinois ($12,752,785,000); and Pennsylvania ($12,364,605,000).

The average number of employees in 1961 for the United States as a whole was 16,341,022, salaries and wages totalling $88,141,489,000. The value added by manufacture (value of output less cost of materials and supplies, plus value created by merchandising operations, etc.) was $164,292,449,000.

LABOUR IN THE UNITED STATES

Organized Labour.—On December 5, 1955, the American Federation of Labour (AFL), founded in 1881, and the Congress of Industrial Organizations (CIO), formerly established in 1938, merged into an organization called the American Federation of Labour and Congress of Industrial Organizations. The combined membership is now 15,072,000 (including 927,000 members in Canada). There are

MAJOR INDUSTRY GROUPS, 1961 (Adjusted)

Group	No. of Employees	Payroll	Value added by Manufacture
Food and kindred products.......	1,703,535	$8,368,113,000	$20,194,869,000
Tobacco products...............	78,709	323,357,000	1,595,608,000
Textile mill products............	871,453	3,171,234,000	5,613,161,000
Apparel and related products......	1,211,610	3,864,828,000	6,697,239,000
Lumber and wood products......	553,306	2,066,522,000	3,395,331,000
Furniture and fixtures...........	349,599	1,492,432,000	2,543,215,000
Paper and allied products.........	573,246	3,192,435,000	6,647,182,000
Printing and publishing..........	923,324	5,226,726,000	9,491,960,000
Chemicals and allied products.....	714,657	4,528,008,000	14,767,606,000
Petroleum and coal products......	163,198	1,142,479,000	3,438,052,000
Rubber and plastics products......	372,983	2,025,698,000	3,929,023,000
Leather and leather products......	350,351	1,225,305,000	2,041,979,000
Stone, clay and glass products.....	569,924	2,947,956,000	6,335,635,000
Primary metal industries..........	1,105,346	7,089,730,000	12,834,211,000
Fabricated metal products.........	1,050,517	5,810,282,000	10,282,655,000
Machinery, except electrical.......	1,374,469	8,367,424,000	14,147,685.000
Electrical machinery.............	1,364,450	7,689,294,000	13,758,559,000
Transportation equipment........	1,505,956	10,130,443,000	17,584,567,000
Instruments....................	342,642	2,099,100,000	3,911,107,000
Miscellaneous manufacturing......	557,903	2,903,586,000	5,064,516,000
Administrative and auxiliary......	602,934	4,471,384,000	—
Total......................	16,341,022	$88,141,489,000	$164,292,449,000

also 3,045,000 members of unions not affiliated to the AFL-CIO.

Approximately one-third of the non-agricultural labour force of the United States is estimated to be organized.

Work Stoppages.—There were 3,614 stoppages recorded in 1962, involving 1,230,000 workers. There were 18,600,000 man-days of idleness, representing 0·16 per cent. of estimated working time of all workers.

Employment and Unemployment.—The civilian labour force (working population) was 73,127,000 in May, 1963. This includes self-employed, wage and salary-earners, and unpaid family workers, employed and unemployed. Unemployment was estimated at 4,066,000 (5·6 per cent.). In addition there were 25,000 temporarily stopped, and 13,016,000 working fewer than 35 hours a week.

Wages

March 1963	Average Weekly Earnings	Hours Per Week	Average Hourly Earnings
Manufacturing.......	$98·09	40·2	$2·44
Durable..........	106·49	40·8	2·61
Non-durable......	87·07	39·4	2·21
Coal Mining........	114·87	36·7	3·13
Bituminous.......	115·29	36·6	3·15
Building construction	121·99	36·2	3·37
Gas, Electricity and Sanitary Services...	119·43	40·9	2·92
Wholesale trade.....	98·58	40·4	2·44
Retail trade......... (except eating and drinking places)	66·93	37·6	1·78
Laundries, cleaning and dyeing plants......	50·95	38·6	1·32

In March, 1963, gross average weekly earnings by industry ranged from $147·70 per week in special dies, tools, jigs and fixtures to $39·36 in the limited price variety stores (32·0 hours and $1·23 average hourly earnings). The average for all manufacturing was $97·76, almost a four-fold increase since 1939 but in terms of 1947-49 purchasing power, the increase was 1·88 times.

On Sept. 3, 1961, the minimum wage set by federal law became $1·15 an hour for employees engaged in interstate commerce or in the production of goods for interstate commerce, or in activities closely related and directly essential to such production. The law requires at least time and a half of an employee's regular rate of pay for all hours over 40 a week. From September 3, 1963, the minimum wage for these employees became $1·25 an hour.

Other employees employed in certain large enterprises having some employees engaged in commerce or the production of goods for commerce, on September 3, 1961, became entitled to a minimum wage of $1·00 an hour. Overtime premium pay did not become due to these workers until September 3, 1963, and then only after 44 hours in a week. The minimum wage and overtime premium pay for these employees will gradually be changed until on September 3, 1965, all employees to whom the law applies will have a minimum wage of $1.25 an hour and overtime premium pay after 40 hours in a week.

There are certain exemptions from these monetary requirements in specific occupations and industries.

In addition to cash wages, most workers receive some type of "fringe" benefits—the most common forms being paid vacations, and public holidays, various types of insurance and health funds financed by the employer or by employer and employees jointly.

RECLAMATION

Bureau of Reclamation, Department of the Interior, Interior Building, 18th and 19th Streets (between C and E streets), N.W., Washington, D.C. *Commissioner*, Floyd E. Dominy.

The Bureau of Reclamation constructs and operates multiple-purpose water resource development projects for irrigation, municipal and industrial water supply, hydro-electric power, flood control, fish and wildlife conservation, recreation, and other beneficial purposes in the area of the United States west of the 97th meridian. It is the Federal agency with principal responsibility for water conservation in this region, roughly the western half of the country. Irrigation facilities completed by the Bureau of Reclamation were capable of serving more than 8,600,000 acres of land, of which 7,200,000 acres were irrigated in 1962. The total farm value of crops grown on all Reclamation projects in 1962 was $1·22 billion. Forty-four power plants in operation on Reclamation multi-purpose projects, at December 31, 1962, had an installed capacity of 5,300,000 kilowatts. Power revenue in Fiscal Year 1962 totalled almost $77,300,000.

In June, 1963, the Bureau had 135 irrigation and multiple-purpose projects in operation, under construction, or authorized. Among them are the ten-state Missouri River Basin Project; the Central Valley Project, California; the Columbia Basin Project, Washington; and the five-state Colorado River Storage Project. Pre-construction work has started on the Fryingpan-Arkansas and San Juan-Chuama Projects, both of which will divert water from the western to the eastern slope of the Continental Divide. Storage was initiated during 1963 at Flaming Gorge Dam and Glen Canyon Dam, two of the four main units of the Colorado River Storage Project. Navajo Dam was completed during 1962, and construction is continuing on the Curecanti Unit structures. Major dams on which the Bureau began construction during 1963 include: San Luis Dam, where over 2,000,000 acre-feet of water will be stored for irrigation and municipal use in central and southern California; Morrow Point Dam, to be 465 feet high and 720 feet long, on the Gunnison River in Colorado; Glen Elder Dam, to be 130 feet high and 14,380 feet long, on the Solomon River in Kansas; and Joes Valley Dam, to be 195 feet high and 740 feet long, on a tributary of the San Rafael River, Utah.

MAJOR DAMS IN U.S.A.

Name of Dam	State	River	Height (feet)	Length (feet)	Power Capacity (kw)
Grand Coulee	Washington	Columbia	550	4,173	1,974,000
Hoover	Arizona/Nevada	Colorado	726	1,244	1,344,800
Glen Canyon	Arizona	,,	710	1,550	900,000
Flaming George	Utah	Green	502	1,180	108,000
Shasta	California	Sacramento	602	3,460	379,000
Hungry Horse	Montana	S. Fork/Flathead	564	2,115	285,000
Trinity	California	Trinity	537	2,450	100,000

EXTERNAL TRADE OF THE UNITED STATES

Figures for all periods shown have been adjusted to include imports of uranium ore and exports of uranium and other nuclear fuels.

Year	General Imports	Total Exports and Re-exports	Excess of Non-military Exports over Imports
1956	$12,774,000,000	$19,095,000,000	+ $4,564,000,000
1957	13,255,000,000	20,862,000,000	+ 6,252,000,000
1958	13,255,000,000	17,916,000,000	+ 3,118,000,000
1959	15,627,000,000	17,633,000,000	+ 779,000,000
1960	15,017,000,000	20,558,000,000	+ 4,592,000,000
1961	14,713,000,000	20,962,000,000	+ 5,439,000,000
1962	16,396,000,000	21,628,000,000	+ 4,505,000,000

EXPORTS BY PRINCIPAL COMMODITIES OF DOMESTIC ORIGIN, 1962

Commodity	Value
Animals and animal products	$660,000,000
Vegetable food products	2,824,000,000
Wheat	1,058,500,000
Coarse grains	785.700,000
Vegetables	143,600,000
Fruits	285,500,000
Vegetable products (inedible)	1,448,600,000
Rubber and manufactures	335,300,000
Synthetic rubber	169,500,000
Tobacco	491,000,000
Textile fibres and manufactures	1,238,900,000
Raw Cotton	527,900,000
Wood and paper	655,200,000
Coal and products	385,200,000
Petroleum and products	442.800,000
Metals and manufactures	1,622,100,000
Machinery and vehicles	6,614,200,000
Electrical apparatus	916,000,000
Industrial machinery	3,017,900,000
Automobiles, parts, etc.	1,220,900,000
Aircraft and engines	342,800,000
Chemicals and related products	1,773,600,000
Miscellaneous	1,207,600,000

UNITED STATES IMPORTS FOR CONSUMPTION, BY PRINCIPAL COMMODITIES, 1962

Commodity	Value
Cocoa	$131,400,000
Coffee	989,600,000
Cane sugar	509,300,000
Whisky	248,000,000
Crude rubber	216,600,000
Vegetable oils	$134,000,000
Tobacco	101,300,000
Textiles	1,413,900,000
Wood	438,000,000
Pulp, Paper and Products	1,144,300,000
Petroleum and Products	1,767,700,000
Diamonds	242.700,000
Iron Ore, etc.	324.700,000
Uranium Ore	252,300,000
Iron and Steel Mill products	536,800,000
Iron and Steel Manufactures	148,700,000
Non-ferrous metals	1,152,500,000
Aluminium	323,000,000
Copper	272,700,000
Lead	70,000,000
Nickel	186,500,000
Tin	117,500,000
Chemicals, etc.	412,100,000
Machinery and vehicles	1,690,700,000
Miscellaneous	1,007,600,000

UNITED STATES FOREIGN TRADE BY ECONOMIC CLASS, 1962

Class	Imports (1)	Exports (2)
Crude materials	$3,341,600,000	$2,234,000,000
Crude foodstuffs	1,776,700,000	2,008,000,000
Manufactured do.	1,797,200,000	1,366,100,000
Semi-manufactures	3,392,900,000	3,044,900,000
Finished manuf.	5,950,700,000	12,706,100,000
Total	$16,259,100,000	$21,359,100,000

(1) Imports for consumption.
(2) Exports of United States merchandise, including civilian supplies sent to occupied areas.

UNITED STATES FOREIGN TRADE BY PRINCIPAL COUNTRIES, 1962

Country	Exports and Re-exports to	General Imports from
Argentina	$374,500,000	$106,200,000
Australia	399,900,000	290,400,000
Belgium and Luxemburg	448,100,000	386,300,000
Brazil	424,800,000	541,100,000
Canada	3,829,700,000	3,656,700,000
Colombia	226,600,000	275,100,000
France	585,400,000	428,400,000
Germany, West	1,075,900,000	961,200,000
India	668,800,000	255,100,000
Italy	$767,500,000	$452,000,000
Japan	1,413,800,000	1,357,600,000
Mexico	790,200,000	578,300,000
Netherlands	752,200,000	221,100,000
Philippines	268,300,000	327,300,000
S. Africa	222,900,000	256,700,000
Spain	233,400,000	90,500,000
Sweden	260,000,000	170,400,000
Switzerland	298,800,000	227,100,000
U.K.	1,074,800,000	1,004,600,000
Venezuela	468,300,000	975,600,000

UNITED STATES STOCK OF MONEY

$ million

June 30	Gold*	Standard Silver Dollars	Subsidiary Silver	Federal Reserve Notes	National Bank Notes	TOTAL
1958	21,356·1	488·2	1,448·8	27,498·4	59·9	54,058·1
1959	19,704·6	488·0	1,496·9	28,276·4	57·7	53,260·4
1960	19,322·2	487·8	1,552·1	28,394·2	56·0	53,070·9
1961	17,550·2	487·6	1,608·7	28,960·3	54·4	51,947·1
1962	16,435·2	487·4	1,710·8	30,161·6	53·2	52,194·9

*Held by U.S. Treasury only.

COMMUNICATIONS

Railways

Data pertaining to Class I and II Carriers and their non-operating subsidiaries:—

	1961
Capital Stock outstanding	$6,737,812,856
Funded Debt outstanding	8,440,936,258
Total Railway capital actually outstanding	15,178,749,114
Dividends declared	*385,017,043
Interest accrued	386,823,296
Total dividends and interest	771,840,339
Railway operating revenues	9,309,696,468
Railway operating expenses	7,361,751,372
	Number
Number of passengers carried earning revenue	318,358,751
Number of passenger-train cars in service	24,426
Number of freight-train cars in service	1,639,148
Number of railway employees	727,148
Miles operated	229,369

*Includes $1,890,200 stock dividend.

Roads

In 1961 there were 3,573,046 miles of roads and streets in the United States, of which 3,127,225 miles were in rural areas and 445,821 miles were in municipal areas. Surfaced roads and streets account for 2,587,921 miles of the total; 985,125 miles were unimproved and graded and drained. State primary roads, including extensions in municipal areas, total 450,056 miles (444,536 surfaced). Other roads under State control total 268,765 miles (232,217 surfaced); 2,738,402 miles are under local control (1,882,334 surfaced); and 115,823 miles (28,834 surfaced) are under Federal control (in National forests and parks).

An estimated total of $11,453,000,000 was spent in 1962 for roads and streets in the United States. Of this total $7,588,000,000 was spent for State highways, $1,896,000,000 was spent for county and local rural roads, $1,734,000,000 was spent for city streets, and $235,000,000 was spent on roads in Federal areas. Capital outlay accounted for 62·7 per cent of the total expenditure; 25·3 per cent was spent for maintenance; and 4·8 per cent for administration; 3·3 per cent for highway police and safety; and 3·9 per cent for interest on highway bonds.

Motor Vehicles and Taxation.—The number of motor vehicles registered in 1962 in the United States was 79,022,916, an increase of 4·2 per cent over the 1961 total of 75,826,514. In 1941 the registrations in the U.S.A. were 34,894,134. The State Governments received $1,468,554,000 in 1941 and $2,065,263,000 (est.) in 1962, respectively, from motor-fuel, motor-vehicle, and motor-carrier taxes. In 1962 the Federal Government received $4,864,869,000 from excise taxes on motor vehicles and parts, tyres and tubes, gasoline, diesel and special fuels and lubricating oils.

Accidents.—In 1961 there were 38,000 deaths caused by motor vehicle accidents. The death rate per 100,000,000 miles of travel was 5·2 in 1961, compared with 5·3 in 1960.

Shipping

The active ocean-going Merchant Marine of the U.S. on July 1, 1963, consisted of 919 vessels of 1,000 gross tons and over, of which 901 were privately owned and 18 were government-owned ships under charter or general agency agreement with private companies. There were 1,827 government-owned vessels in the reserve fleets. Of the active vessels, 627 were dry cargo ships, 31 were combination passenger and cargo and 261 were tankers.

Air Transport

United States domestic and international scheduled airlines in 1961 were estimated to have carried 58,441,000 passengers over 39,827,000,000 passenger miles, over half of which were flown in jets. The freight flown by the scheduled airliners during 1961 totalled 732,946,000 ton-miles, and express 61,167,000 ton-miles. In addition, the airliners flew 299,216,000 ton-miles of mail, an increase of 24·4 per cent. over 1960.

Total operating revenues of all U.S. scheduled airlines reached the record figure of $3,073,292,000 in 1961, an increase of 6·5 per cent. over 1960. Similarly, total operating expenses rose to a record high total of $3,016,537,000 last year, or 7·45 per cent. more than the previous year. The net operating income (*i.e.* before deduction of taxes, interest, etc.) was $56,755,000, a decrease of 26·76 per cent. from the previous year, resulting in a loss of $36,887,000 compared with a profit of $8,604,000 in 1960.

Nine principal classes of commercial air carriers can be distinguished in the United States, (*a*) The Domestic Trunk Lines (11); (*b*) Local Service Lines, operating the low-density traffic routes between the smaller traffic centres and between small and large centres (13); (*c*) The International and Territorial Group, including all U.S. flag air carriers authorized to operate between the U.S.A. and foreign countries, between foreign countries and into Mexico, the Caribbean and to Alaska and Hawaii (18); (*d*) Intra-Hawaiian Air Carriers, operating in Hawaii (2); (*e*) Intra-Alaskan Carriers, providing service within Alaska (12); other classes are (*f*) Certified All Cargo Lines (6); (*g*) Helicopter Operators (3); (*h*) Supplemental transport carriers (29); and (*i*) air freight forwarders (75) and air taxi operators, of which there are 2,618 authorized.

In 1961, 171,610 persons were employed by the domestic and international airlines, 2·4 per cent. more than in 1960.

U.S. Scheduled Airline Industry Statistics, 1961 (Thousands)

	Domestic Trunk Lines	Local Service Airlines	Intra-Hawaian Airlines	Helicopter Airlines	Intern'l & Territorial Airlines	Intra-Alaskan Airlines	All Cargo Carriers
Revenue passengers	44,781	6,478	838	430	5,698	216	—
Revenue passenger miles	29,534,800	1,343,800	125,600	8,604	8,768,500	46,000	—
Air-mail ton miles	144,690	3,356	96	93	135,712	2,208	13,061
Express ton miles	56,745	3,019	NA	40	605	NA	758
Freight ton miles	384,161	5,491	1,847	7	216,561	2,829	122,050
Revenue ton miles	3,435,200	142,400	12,500	969	1,362,400	11,800	428,200
Revenue plane miles	676,800	103,300	5,200	2,157	161,400	7,400	13,200

EDUCATION

State School Systems

Almost every State in the Union has a compulsory school attendance law. In general, children are obliged to attend school from 7 to 16 years of age, and those from 14 to 16 must attend school or be lawfully employed. In the States there are, connected with the local administrative units, officers charged with enforcing the compulsory attendance law, known in the majority of States as the truant or attendance officers.

In the autumn of 1962 the total number of children in the United States of 5 to 17 years of age was 47,400,000, of whom 38,837,000 were enrolled in public elementary and secondary schools. The average daily attendance in the public schools was 34,953,000, the average length of school term was estimated at 178 days, and the average number of days attended by each pupil enrolled at 160. In 1962, 1,511,251 teachers were employed. The average annual salary of all teachers was $5,735.

The total revenue receipts for school purposes, excluding balances on hand, was about $18,548,161,000. Of this amount, about $667,981,000 was received from Federal sources, $7,313,472,000 from State sources and $10,566,708,000 from county and local sources. current expenditure was $15,833,835,000. $3,083,132,000 was expended for sites, buildings, furniture and equipment and $626,725,000 for interest.

Institutions of Higher Education

In the autumn of 1962 enrolment in institutions of higher education numbered 4,207,000.

Institutions of higher education include universities, colleges, professional schools, teachers' colleges and normal schools, and junior colleges. The 1962 survey of enrolments covered 2,043 institutions classified as follows: 1,479 universities, colleges and professional schools enrolling 3,615,000 students; and 564 junior colleges enrolling 592,000 students. There are 105 institutions of higher education attended predominantly by Negroes, enrolling 103,500 students included in the foregoing figures.

During the school year 1961–62, 420,485 bachelor's degrees were conferred, 262,015 to men and 158,470 to women; 84,889 masters' degrees, 58,705 to men and 26,184 to women; and 11,622 doctorates, 10,377 to men and 1,245 to women. Education, Social Science and Business and Commerce were, in that order, the fields in which most students received baccalaureate degrees. There were 97,507 bachelors' degrees in Education, 59,346 in Social Science and 48,909 in Business and Commerce. The three leading fields of study for the master's degree were Education (35,921), Engineering (8,909) and Social Sciences (7,319). The most popular fields of study on the doctorate level were Physical Sciences (2,122), Education (1,900), and Social Sciences (1,365).

Particulars of some of the Universities are: Harvard (12,413 students, including 1,022 women in 1962), founded at Cambridge, Mass., on Oct. 28, 1636, and named after John Harvard of Emmanuel College, Cambridge, England, who bequeathed to it his library and a sum of money in 1638; Yale (8,364 students, including 649 women, in 1962), founded at New Haven, Connecticut, in 1701; Bowdoin, Brunswick, Me. (founded 1794) (817 men); Brown, Providence, R.I. (founded 1764; 4,281 students, including 1,151 women, in 1962); Columbia, New York, N.Y. (founded 1754; 24,000 students, including 9,650 women, in 1961); Cornell (founded at Ithaca, N.Y., 1865; 12,687 students, including 3,206 women, in 1962); Dartmouth, Hanover, N.H. (founded 1769, 3,404 students including 6 women in 1962); Georgetown, Washington, D.C. (founded 1789; 6,791 students, including 1,166 women, in 1962); North Carolina, Chapel Hill, N.C. (founded in 1789; 10,517 students including 2,563 women, in 1962); Pennsylvania, Philadelphia, Pa. (founded 1740; 18,347 students, including 5,038 women, in 1962); Pittsburgh, Pittsburgh, Pa. (founded 1787; 13,938 students, including 4,201 women in 1962); Princeton, Princeton, N.J. (founded 1746; 4,196 men and 15 women); Tennessee, Knoxville, Tenn. (founded 1794; 17,394 students, including 5,[illegible]03 women, in 1962); William and Mary, Williamsburg, Va. (founded 1693; 5,889 students, including 2,665 women, in 1962); New York University, founded in 1831 at New York, had 33,232 students, including 8,972 women, in 1962.

Private Schools and Colleges

In the autumn of 1962 it was estimated that there were about 5,400,000 pupils in private kindergarten and elementary schools, 1,300,000 pupils in private high schools and academies and 1,540,000 students in privately controlled institutions of higher education. In addition there were some 21,000 pupils enrolled in privately controlled elementary and secondary schools for exceptional children.

WEIGHTS, MEASURES AND CURRENCY

The *Weights and Measures* in the United States in common use are of British origin and in the case of weights and linear units correspond in large part with those now employed in Great Britain. The *short ton* of 2,000 pounds (20 hundred weight of 100 pounds each) is generally used instead of the *long ton* of 2,240 pounds. The old "Winchester" bushel and the wine gallon and their subdivisions are used instead of the British Imperial units of capacity; 1 U.S. bushel=0·9689 British bushel, and 1 U.S. gallon=0·83267 British gallon. The U.S. *liquid quart* is divided into 32 fluid ounces.

The metric system was made lawful in the United States by Congress in 1866. It is used almost universally in scientific work and by the majority of companies in the pharmaceutical industry in U.S.A. A *decimal inch* is regularly used in the automotive and other large industries and a *decimal pound* is also in use in industry and increasingly so in retail food stores. The unit of currency is the *dollar* of 100 *cents*. The rate of exchange with sterling will be found on p. 84.

MAJOR RELIGIONS IN U.S., 1960

	Members
Baptist	21,000,000
Lutheran	8,021,000
Methodist	12,358,000
Presbyterian	4,203,000
Protestant Episcopal	3,127,000
Jewish	5,500,000
Roman Catholic	40,871,000
Eastern Orthodox	2,807,000
Other Denominations	5,161,000

INDIAN POPULATION

According to the last Census the Indian population of the United States on April 1, 1960, was 523,000. This includes 14,400 persons of Indian blood among the 43,000 natives of Alaska. There are many persons of Indian blood who are not enrolled with any recognized tribe, have no rights in tribal property, and receive no services from the Government. The States with the largest estimated number of Indians still residing in reservation areas and receiving some services from the Government are: Arizona, 83,387; Oklahoma, 64,689; New Mexico, 56,225; South Dakota, 25,794; Montana, 21,181.

THE UNITED STATES

State (with date and *order* of admission)	Area Sq. M.‡	Census Population 1960	Capital	Governor (term of office in yrs. and date of completion*)	
Alabama (Ala.) (1819) (*22*)	51,609	3,266,740	Montgomery	George C. Wallace, *D.* (4—1967)	$25,000
Alaska (1959) (*49*)	586,400	226,167	Juneau	William A. Egan, *D.* (4—1967)	25,000
Arizona (Ariz.) (1912) (*48*)	113,909	1,302,161	Phoenix	Paul Fannin, *R.* (2—1965)	22,500
Arkansas (Ark.) (1836) (*25*)	53,104	1,786,222	Little Rock	Orval E. Faubus, *D.* (2—1965)	10,000
California (Cal.) (1850) (*31*)	158,693	15,717,204	Sacramento	Edmund G. Brown, *D.* (4—1967)	44,100
Colorado (Colo.) (1876) (*38*)	104,247	1,753,947	Denver	John A. Love, *R.* (4—1967)	20,000
Connecticut (Conn.) § (1788) (*5*)	5,009	2,535,354	Hartford	John N. Dempsey, *D.* (4—1967)	15,000
Delaware (Del.) § (1787) (*1*)	2,057	446,292	Dover	Elbert N. Carvel, *D.* (4—1965)	17,500
Dist. of Columbia (D.C.) (1791)	69	763,956	..	†	..
Florida (Fla.) (1845) (*27*)	58,560	4,951,560	Tallahassee	Farris Bryant, *D.* (4—1965)	22,500
Georgia (Ga.) § (1788) (*4*)	58,876	3,943,116	Atlanta	Carl E. Sanders, *D.* (4-1967)	12,000
Hawaii (1959) (*50*)	6,423	632,772	Honolulu	John A. Burns, *D.* (4—1966)	27,500
Idaho (1890) (*43*)	83,557	667,191	Boise	Robert E. Smylie, *R.* (4—1967) (*c*)	15,000
Illinois (Ill.) (1818) (*21*)	56,400	10,081,158	Springfield	Otto Kerner, *D.* (4—1965)	30,000
Indiana (Ind.) (1816) (*19*)	36,291	4,662,498	Indianapolis	Matthew E. Welsh, *D.* (4—1965)	15,000
Iowa (1846) (*29*)	56,290	2,757,537	Des Moines	Harold E. Hughes, *D.* (2—1965)	17,500
Kansas (Kan.) (1861) (*34*)	82,276	2,178,611	Topeka	John Anderson, Jr., *R.* (2—1965)	20,000
Kentucky (Ky.) (1792) (*15*)	40,395	3,038,156	Frankfort	Bert Combs, *D.* (4—1963, Dec.)	18,000
Louisiana (La.) (1812) (*18*)	48,523	3,257,022	Baton Rouge	Jimmie H. Davis, *D.* (4—1964, May)	20,000
Maine (Me.) (1820) (*23*)	33,215	969,265	Augusta	John H. Reed, *R.* (4—1967)	15,000
Maryland (Md.) § (1788) (*7*)	10,577	3,100,689	Annapolis	J. Millard Tawes, *R.* (4—1967)	15,000
Massachusetts (Mass.) § (1788) (*6*)	8,257	5,148,578	Boston	Endicott Peabody, *D.* (2—1965)	20,000
Michigan (Mich.) (1837) (*26*)	58,216	7,823,194	Lansing	George W. Romney, *R.* (2—1964)	27,500
Minnesota (Minn.) (1858) (*32*)	84,068	3,413,864	St. Paul	Elmer L. Anderson, *R.* (4—1967)	19,000
Mississippi (Miss.) (1817) (*20*)	47,716	2,178,141	Jackson	Ross R. Barnett, *D.* (4—1964)	25,000
Missouri (Mo.) (1821) (*24*)	69,674	4,319,813	Jefferson City	John M. Dalton, *D.* (4—1965)	25,000
Montana (Mont.) (1889) (*41*)	141,138	674,767	Helena	Tim M. Babcock, *R.* (4—1965)	14,000
Nebraska (Nebr.) (1867) (*37*)	77,227	1,411,330	Lincoln	Frank B. Morrison, *D.* (2—1965)	1,4000
Nevada (Nev.) (1863) (*36*)	110,540	285,278	Carson City	Grant Sawyer, *D.* (4—1967)	20,000
New Hampshire (N.H.)§(1788)(*9*)	9,304	606,921	Concord	John W. King, *D.* (2—1965)	16,587
New Jersey (N.J.) § (1787) (*3*)	7,836	6,066,782	Trenton	Richard J. Hughes, *D.* (4—1966)	35,000
New Mexico (N.Mex.) (1912) (*47*)	121,666	951,023	Santa Fe	Jack M. Campbell, *D.* (2—1964)	17,500
New York (N.Y.) § (1788) (*11*)	49,576	16,782,304	Albany	Nelson A. Rockefeller, *R.* (4—1966)	50,000
North Carolina (N.C.) § (1789) (*12*)	52,712	4,556,155	Raleigh	Terry Sanford, *D.* (4—1965)	25,000
North Dakota (N.Dak.) (1889)(*39*)	70,665	632,446	Bismarck	William L. Guy, *D.* (2—1965)	10,000
Ohio (1803) (*17*)	41,222	9,706,397	Columbus	James A. Rhodes, *R.* (4—1967)	25,000
Oklahoma (Okla.) (1907) (*46*)	69,919	2,328,284	Oklahoma City	Henry Bellmon, *R.* (4—1967)	25,000
Oregon (Oreg.) (1859) (*33*)	96,981	1,768,687	Salem	Mark O. Hatfield, *R.* (4—1967) [(*a*)	20,000
Pennsylvania (Pa.)§(1787)(*2*)	45,333	11,319,366	Harrisburg	William W. Scranton, *R.* (4—1967)	35,000
Rhode Island (R.I.)§(1790)(*13*)	1,214	859,488	Providence	John H. Chafee, *R.* (2—1965)	25,000
South Carolina (S.C.) § (1788) (*8*)	31,055	2,382,594	Columbia	Donald S. Russell, *D.* (4—1967) (*c*)	22,000
South Dakota (S.Dak.) (1889) (*40*)	77,047	680,514	Pierre	Archie Gubbrud, *R.* (2—1965)	15,000
Tennessee (Tenn.) (1796) (*16*)	42,244	3,567,089	Nashville	Frank G. Clement, *D.* (4—1967) (*c*)	18,500
Texas (Tex.) (1845) (*28*)	267,339	9,579,677	Austin	John B. Connally, *D.* (2—1965)	25,000
Utah (1896) (*45*)	84,916	890,627	Salt Lake City	George D. Clyde, *R.* (4—1965)	13,200
Vermont (Vt.) (1791) (*14*)	9,609	389,881	Montpelier	Philip H. Hoff, *D.* (2—1965)	13,750
Virginia (Va.) § (1788) (*10*)	40,815	3,966,949	Richmond	Albertis S. Harrison, Jr., *D.* (4—1966)	25,000
Washington (Wash.) (1889) (*42*)	68,192	2,853,214	Olympia	Albert D. Rosellini, *D.* (4—1965)	22,500
West Virginia (W.Va.) (1863)(*35*)	24,181	1,860,421	Charleston	William W. Barron, *D.* (4—1965)	17,500
Wisconsin (Wis.) (1848) (*30*)	56,154	3,951,777	Madison	John W. Reynolds, *D.* (2—1965)	20,000
Wyoming (Wyo.) (1890) (*44*)	97,914	330,066	Cheyenne	Clifford P. Hansen, *R.* (4—1967)	20,000
OUTLYING TERRITORIES AND POSSESSIONS					
Puerto Rico (1899)	3,435	2,349,544	San Juan	L.Muñoz-Marin, *Pop.Dem.*(4—1965)(*b*)	10,600
Guam (1899)	206	66,910	Agaña	M. F. Leon Guerrero (4—1965)	19,000
Panama Canal Zone (1904)	553	41,684	Balboa Heights	Maj-Gen. W. E. Potter (*Pres. and Gov.*)	..
Samoa (1900)	76	20,040	Pago Pago	H. Rex Lee, *D.* (*e*)	19,000
Virgin Islands (1917)	133	31,904	Charlotte Amalie	Ralph M. Paiewonsky, *D.* (*e*)	19,000

D.—Democratic Party. *R.*—Republican Party

* Term expires in January of the year unless otherwise stated. § The 13 Original States. † The capital territory is governed by Congress through a three-member Commission (*see* p. 803). ‡ Gross area, including water.

(*a*) plus expenses $9,000. (*b*) plus expenses $4,800. (*c*) plus residence. (*e*) term appointed by the President.

Largest Cities

With populations from the Census of 1960

Ψ New York, N.Y.	7,781,984	San Antonio, Texas	587,718	Ψ Oakland, Calif.	367,548
Chicago, Ill.	3,550,404	Ψ San Diego, Calif.	573,224	Fort Worth, Texas	356,268
Ψ Los Angeles, Calif.	2,479,015	Ψ Seattle, Wash.	557,087	Ψ Long Beach, Calif.	344,168
Ψ Philadelphia, Pa.	2,002,512	Buffalo, N.Y.	532,759	Birmingham, Ala.	340,887
Detroit, Mich.	1,670,144	Cincinnati, Ohio	502,550	Oklahoma City, Okla.	324,253
Ψ Baltimore, Md.	939,024	Memphis, Tenn.	497,524	Rochester, N.Y.	318,611
Ψ Houston, Texas	938,219	Denver, Colo.	493,887	Toledo, Ohio	318,003
Cleveland, Ohio	876,050	Atlanta, Ga.	487,455	St. Paul, Minn.	313,411
WASHINGTON, D.C.	763,956	Minneapolis, Minn.	482,872	Ψ Norfolk, Va.	305,872
St. Louis, Mo.	750,026	Kansas City, Mo.	475,539	Omaha, Nebr.	301,598
Milwaukee, Wis.	741,324	Indianapolis, Ind.	476,258	Ψ Honolulu, Hawaii	294,144
Ψ San Francisco, Calif.	740,316	Columbus, Ohio	471,316	Ψ Miami, Fla.	291,688
Ψ Boston, Mass.	697,197	Phoenix, Ariz.	439,170	Akron, Ohio	290,351
Dallas, Texas	679,684	Newark, N.J.	405,220	El Paso, Texas	276,687
Ψ New Orleans, La.	627,525	Louisville, Ky.	390,639	Jersey City, N.J.	276,101
Pittsburgh, Pa.	604,332	Ψ Portland, Ore.	372,676	Tampa, Fla.	274,970

Ψ Seaport.

THE PRESIDENTS OF THE UNITED STATES OF AMERICA

Name (*with Native State*)	Party	Born	Inaug.	Died	Age
1. GEORGE WASHINGTON, *Va*.	Fed.	1732, Feb. 22	1789	1799, Dec. 14	67
2. John Adams, *Mass*.	,,	1735, Oct. 30	1797	1826, July 4	90
3. Thomas Jefferson, *Va*.	Rep.	1743, April 13	1801	1826, July 4	83
4. James Madison, *Va*.	,,	1751, Mar. 16	1809	1836, June 28	85
5. James Monroe, *Va*.	,,	1758, April 28	1817	1831, July 4	73
6. John Quincy Adams. *Mass*.	,,	1767, July 11	1825	1848, Feb. 23	80
7. Andrew Jackson, *S.C*.	Dem.	1767, Mar. 15	1829	1845, June 8	78
8. Martin Van Buren, *N.Y*.	,,	1782, Dec. 5	1837	1862, July 24	79
9. William Henry Harrison†, *Va*.	Whig	1773, Feb. 9	1841	1841, April 4	68
10. John Tyler (*a*), *Va*.	,,	1790, Mar. 29	1841	1862, Jan. 17	71
11. James Knox Polk, *N.C*.	Dem.	1795, Nov. 2	1845	1849, June 15	53
12. Zachary Taylor† *Va*.	Whig	1784, Nov. 24	1849	1850, July 9	65
13. Millard Fillmore (*a*), *N.Y*.	,,	1800, Jan. 7	1850	1874, Mar. 8	74
14. Franklin Pierce, *N.H*.	Dem.	1804, Nov. 23	1853	1869, Oct. 8	64
15. James Buchanan, *Pa*.	,,	1791, April 23	1857	1868, June 1	77
16. Abraham Lincoln†§, *Ky*.	Rep.	1809, Feb. 12	1861	1865, April 15	56
17. Andrew Johnson (*a*), *N.C*.	,,	1808, Dec. 29	1865	1875, July 31	66
18. Ulysses Simpson Grant, *Ohio*	,,	1822, April 27	1869	1885, July 23	63
19. Rutherford Birchard Hayes, *Ohio*	,,	1822, Oct. 4	1877	1893, Jan. 17	70
20. James Abram Garfield†§, *Ohio*	,,	1831, Nov. 19	1881	1881, Sept. 19	49
21. Chester Alan Arthur (*a*), *Vt*.	,,	1830, Oct. 5	1881	1886, Nov. 18	56
22. Grover Cleveland, *N.J*.	Dem.	1837, Mar. 18	1885	1908, June 24	71
23. Benjamin Harrison, *Ohio*	Rep.	1833, Aug. 20	1889	1901, Mar. 13	67
Grover Cleveland, *N.J*.	Dem.	1837, Mar. 18	1893	1908, June 24	71
24. William McKinley†§, *Ohio*	Rep.	1843, Jan. 29	1897	1901, Sept. 14	58
25. Theodore Roosevelt (*a*), *N.Y*.	,,	1858, Oct. 27	1901	1919, Jan. 6	60
26. William Howard Taft, *Ohio*	,,	1857, Sept. 8	1909	1930, Mar. 8	72
27. Woodrow Wilson, *Va*.	Dem.	1856, Dec. 28	1913	1924, Feb. 3	67
28. Warren Gamaliel Harding†, *Ohio*	Rep.	1865, Nov. 2	1921	1923, Aug. 2	57
29. Calvin Coolidge (*a*), *Vt*.	,,	1872, July 4	1923	1933, Jan. 5	60
30. Herbert C. Hoover, *Iowa*	,,	1874, Aug. 10	1929	..	..
31. Franklin Delano Roosevelt†‡, *N.Y*.	Dem.	1882, Jan. 30	1933	1945, April 12	63
32. Harry S. Truman, (*a*), *Missouri*	,,	1884, May 8	1945	..	..
33. Dwight D. Eisenhower, *Texas*	Rep.	1890, Oct. 14	1953	..	..
34. John F. Kennedy, *Mass*.	Dem.	1917, May 29	1961	..	..

† Died in office. § Assassinated. (*a*) Elected as Vice-President.
‡ Re-elected Nov. 5, 1940, the first case of a third term; re-elected for a fourth term Nov. 7, 1944.

TERRITORIES AND PRINCIPAL ISLAND POSSESSIONS OF THE UNITED STATES

The territories and the principal islands and island groups under the sovereignty of the United States of America comprise: Palmyra Island; Kingman Reef (about 1 sq. mile); Johnston (or Cornwallis) Island and Sand Island (about 1 sq. mile in all); Canton and Enderbury Islands (jointly administered with Great Britain); Midway Islands; Wake Island; Guam; Howland, Baker and Jarvis Islands (about 3 sq. miles in all); American Samoa (including the island of Tutuila, the Manua Islands, and all other Islands of the Samoan group east of longitude 171° west of Greenwich together with Swains Island); the Commonwealth of Puerto Rico; the Virgin Islands of the United States, and Navassa Island (2 sq. miles).

The Canal Zone is under the jurisdiction of the United States.

The Trust Territory of the Pacific Islands is under the jurisdiction of the United States pursuant to a trusteeship agreement between the U.S. Government and the Security Council of the United Nations. It consists of the Mariana (except Guam), Caroline and Marshall Islands, with a land area of 687 square miles and a population of 80,980 in 1962. Nine individual languages are spoken in the Territory. Copra is the principal export of importance.

There are certain small guano islands, rocks, or keys which, in pursuance of action taken under the Act of Congress, August 18, 1856, subsequently embodied in Sections 5570–5578 of the Revised Statutes, are considered as appertaining to the United States. Responsibility for territorial affairs generally is centred in the Office of Territories, Dept. of the Interior, Washington, D.C.

CANTON AND ENDERBURY

Under the Anglo-American Pact of Aug. 10, 1938, Canton and Enderbury (of the Phoenix Island Group in the Central Pacific) were declared to be for the common use of Gt. Britain and U.S.A. for aviation and communications. The islands, which are about midway between Hawaii and Australia, extend to a total of 27 sq. miles with a population of 391 in 1962.

On April 6, 1939, the U.S. and Great Britain agreed to set up a joint regime for Canton and Enderbury Islands. Provision for the joint control of these islands was made by exchange of notes between the two Governments on April 6, 1939.

GUAM

Guam, the largest of the Ladrone or Mariana Islands in the North Pacific Ocean, lies in 13° 26′ N. lat. and 144° 39′ E. long., at a distance of about 1,506 miles east of Manila. The area of the island is estimated at 209 square miles, with a population of 67,044 at the 1960 Census. The Guamanians are of Chamorro stock mingled with Filipino and Spanish blood. The Chamorro language belongs to the Malayo-Polynesian family, but has had considerable admixture of Spanish. English is the language used throughout the island, although Chamorro is also used in Guamanian homes.

Guam was occupied by Japanese in Dec., 1941, but was recaptured and occupied throughout by U.S. forces before the end of August, 1944. Under the Organic Act of Guam of August 1, 1950 (Public Law 630 of the 81st Congress), Guam has statutory powers of self-government, and Guamanians are United States citizens. A governor is appointed for a four-year term. A 21-member unicameral legislature is elected biennially. There is also a District Court of Guam, with original jurisdiction in cases under federal law.

Governor, Manuel F. Leon Guerrero.

Secretary (vacant).

CAPITAL, Agaña. Port of entry, ♆Apra.

WAKE AND MIDWAY ISLANDS

Wake Island, annexed in 1898, has an area of about 3 sq. miles and lies in the N. Pacific about 2,300 miles from Hawaii on the direct route to Hong Kong. Wake Island was occupied by Japanese Dec. 27, 1941; it was re-occupied by U.S. on Sept. 15, 1945. Population (1960), 1,097.

Midway Islands, with a total area of 28 sq. miles and a population (1960) of 2,356, lie in the N. Pacific about 1,300 miles from Hawaii. There is no indigenous population. The group is under the jurisdiction of the U.S. Navy.

PUERTO RICO

Puerto Rico (Rich Port) is an island of the Greater Antilles group in the West Indies, and lies between 17° 50′–18° 30′ N. lat. and 65° 30′–67° 15′ W. long., with a total area of 3,435 square miles and a population of 2,349,544 (1960 Census). The majority of the inhabitants are of Spanish descent and Spanish and English are the official languages. The island is about 100 miles from west to east, and 40 miles from north to south at the western end, narrowing towards the eastern extremity. The capital is 1,399 miles distant from New York, and 963 miles from Key West. Puerto Rico was discovered in 1493 by Christopher Columbus. It was explored by Ponce de León in 1508. It continued a Spanish possession until Oct. 18, 1898, when the United States took formal possession as a result of the Spanish-American War. It was ceded by Spain to the United States by the Treaty ratified on April 11, 1899. Sugar is grown along the coastal plain and tobacco and coffee on the slopes of the hills; fruits, cotton, maize, sweet potatoes, and yams are also grown. The trade is principally with the U.S. 4,536 miles of paved roads were in use in 1958. There are good harbours at San Juan and Ponce. The Constitution approved by the Congress and the President of the United States, which came into force on July 25, 1952, establishes the Commonwealth of Puerto Rico with full powers of local self-government. Legislative functions are vested in the Legislative Assembly, which consists of 2 elected houses; the Senate of 27 members (2 from each of 8 senatorial districts and 11 at large) and the House of Representatives of 51 members (1 from each of 40 representative districts and 11 at large). Membership of each house may be increased slightly to accommodate minority representatives. The term of the Legislative Assembly is 4 years. The Governor is popularly elected for a term of 4 years. A Supreme Court of 9 members is appointed by the Governor, with the advice and consent of the Senate. There are 9 similarly appointed Secretaries at the head of permanent departments, but the selection of the Secretary of State must be approved also by the House of Representatives. The Governor appoints all judges. Puerto Rico is represented in Congress by a Resident Commissioner, elected for a term of 4 years, who has a seat in the House of Representatives, but not a vote. Great improvement has been made in the progress, industrialization and welfare of the island during the last two decades. A programme of tax exemption has raised income from industry to a level higher than that from agriculture. Public schools are established throughout—enrolment in 1961 reached 626,420. The capital, ♆ San Juan, had 588,805 inhabitants in 1960, other major towns being ♆ Ponce 145,586, ♆ Mayaguez 83,850, Caguas 65,098, ♆ Arecibo 69,879 and Bayamón 72,221.

♆ Seaport.

FINANCE

	1961	1962
Revenue	$273,000,000	$298,512,000
Expenditure	318,000,000	320,000,000

TRADE

	1961	1962
Total Imports	$930,000,000	$1,081,000,000
Total Exports	674,000,000	740,300,000

TRADE WITH U.K.

	1961	1962
Imports from U.K.	£2,087,087	£2,751,070
Exports to U.K.	370,401	297,591

Governor, Luis Muñoz Marín, *elected* 1948; *re-elected* 1952, 1956 and 1960.

Resident Commissioner, Antonio Fernós Isern.

AMERICAN SAMOA

American Samoa consists of the island of Tutuila, Aunu'u, Ofu, Olosega, Ta'u, Rose and Swains Islands, with a total area of 76·5 square miles and a population of 20,051 in 1960, distributed as follows:—Tutuila and Aunu'u 17,250; Rose Island, uninhabited; Manu'a Group (Ofu, Ta'u and Olosega Islands) 2,695; and Swain's Island.

Tutuila, the largest of the group, has an area of 52 square miles and contains a magnificent harbour at ♆Pago Pago (pop. 1960, 1,251), the capital and seat of government. The remaining islands have an area of about 24 square miles. Tuna and copra are the chief exports.

Under an Executive Order of the President, which became effective on July 1, 1951, civilian administration under the Department of the Interior replaced the Naval administration which had existed since 1900. At present the Government consists of an executive, a bicameral legislature and a judiciary. Most of the Samoans are U.S. nationals, but some have acquired citizenship through service in the United States armed forces.

Governor, H. Rex Lee.

Secretary, Owen S. Aspinall.

TRUST TERRITORY OF THE PACIFIC ISLANDS

The Trust Territory of the Pacific Islands consists of the Mariana (excluding Guam), Caroline and Marshall Islands which extend from latitude 1° to 20° north and from longitude 130° to 172° east. They cover an ocean area of 3,000,000 square miles but have a total land area of only 687 square miles. There are 96 separate islands and island groups in the Trust Territory. The population in 1962 was 80,980. The inhabitants of the Trust Territory are broadly classed as Micronesians. The native cultures vary markedly among island groups and even more among islands and atolls in the same geographic area. Nine mutually unintelligible languages are spoken in the territory.

The Trust Territory is administered by the United States pursuant to a Trusteeship Agreement with the Security Council of the United Nations of July 18, 1947, administration being under the general jurisdiction of the Secretary of the Interior.

For administrative purposes, the territory is divided into six districts: The Marianas, Palau, Yap, Truk, Ponape and the Marshalls. Local governments exist within each district.

High Commissioner, M. Wilfred Goding.

Deputy High Commissioner, José A. Benitez.

CAPITAL (Provisional).—Saipan, Mariana Islands.

VIRGIN ISLANDS

Purchased by the United States from Denmark for the sum of $25,000,000, and proclaimed, January 25, 1917. The total area of the islands is 133 sq. miles, with a population of 32,099 (1960 Census). *St. Thomas* (28 sq. miles) has a population of 16,201; *St. Croix* (84 sq. miles) has a population of 14,973; *St. John* (20 sq. miles) has a population of 925. St. Croix exports sugar and rum; ΨSt. Thomas is famous for its harbour.

CAPITAL, ΨCharlotte Amalie (11,000) contains one of the finest harbours in the West Indies, accommodating vessels of large draught, and has a large coaling and oil refuelling station. The climate of the Virgin Islands is delightful at all times, and particularly so during the winter months.

Governor, Ralph M. Paiewonsky.

Government Secretary, Cyril E. King.

THE PANAMA CANAL

The Panama Canal and its adjuncts, including the related commercial enterprises in the Canal Zone, are operated by the Panama Canal Company, which was formed on July 1, 1951, under the provisions of the Panama Canal Company Act. The Canal Zone is governed by the Canal Zone Government, which was established simultaneously with the new Canal Company. Both organizations are headed by Major-General Robert J. Fleming, Jr., U.S.A., who holds the joint title of Governor of the Canal Zone and President of the Panama Canal Company.

In 1523, Charles V of Spain ordered an investigation as to the possibility of a canal through the Isthmus of Panama. From then until 1904, the principal maritime nations of the world gave earnest consideration to the project. In 1876 a concession for the construction of a canal was granted to a French promotion corporation which conducted surveys during a period of two years, and reported to an international congress held at Paris in May, 1879, over which Ferdinand de Lesseps presided. This congress advised the construction of a canal at sea-level, and in 1881 the work was undertaken by the Universal Interoceanic Panama Canal Company, of which de Lesseps was nominal head. For various reasons, including those of finance and an inability to master the health problems on the humid isthmus, the initial effort failed. A receiver was appointed in 1889 and a second French company undertook the last project, with excavation work resuming in 1894. This was continued until the United States Government acquired the effects of the French company in Panama on May 4, 1904.

Congress authorized the President in 1902 to purchase the rights and property of the French company for $40,000,000. Meanwhile, a treaty was negotiated with the Government of Colombia for the cession, upon payment of $10,000,000, of the territory through which the canal was to be constructed. The failure of the Colombian Government to ratify this treaty led to the secession of Panama on November 3, 1903. The new Government was immediately recognized by the United States, and a treaty was ratified on February 26, 1904, in which rights of sovereignty over a strip of land ten miles in width, extending across the isthmus, were ceded to the United States. The U.S. guaranteed the Republic of Panama's independence and agreed to pay it $10,000,000 and an annuity which was to begin nine years after the ratification of the treaty. The canal is built through the centre of this territory. Under the terms of a treaty between Panama and the United States, signed at Panama in January, 1955, the United States increased its annuity to Panama from $430,000 to $1,930,000 and agreed to hand over to the Republic land and railroad yards valued at $25,000,000, to construct a high-level bridge over the Pacific entrance to the Canal which cost $20,000,000 and to extend various commercial and other privileges to the Republic. The Canal Zone has an area of 533 sq. miles (land area, 362 sq. miles) and a population of 42,122 (Census 1960).

Ψ Seaport.

The canal is fifty statute miles long (44·08 nautical miles), and the channel is from 300 to 1,000 feet wide at bottom. It contains 12 locks in twin flights; 3 steps at Gatun on the Atlantic side, 1 step at Pedro Miguel and 2 at Miraflores on the Pacific side. Each lock chamber is 1,000 feet long and 110 feet wide. Transit from sea to sea takes on average 16 hours. The least width is in Gaillard Cut, and the greatest in Gatun Lake, where the channel can be made much broader at any time by the cutting down of trees and a small amount of dredging. The Panama Canal Company is engaged in a $60,000,000 Canal improvement programme which will result in a minimum channel width of 500 feet in the Cut. Gatun Lake is 85 feet above sea-level. The Canal's minimum channel depth, including Gaillard Cut, is 42 feet.

Including only ocean-going commercial vessels, 300 Panama Canal net tons measurement or over, against which tolls were collected, the volume of commercial traffic passing through the Canal during each of the last 23 fiscal years is shown below:—

Fiscal Year	No. of Transits	Canal. * Net Tons	Cargo Tons
1945	1,939	8,380,959	8,603,607
1946	3,747	17,516,517	14,977,940
1947	4,260	20,233,043	21,670,518
1948	4,678	22,902,064	24,117,788
1949	4,793	23,473,236	25,305,158
1950	5,448	28,013,236	28,872,293
1951	5,593	27,180,425	30,073,022
1952	6,524	30,674,302	33,610,509
1953	7,410	36,678,636	36,095,349
1954	7,784	38,027,812	39,095,067
1955	7,997	38,643,797	40,646,301
1956	8,209	41,273,020	45,119,042
1957	8,579	43,714,264	49,702,200
1958	9,187	47,968,018	48,124,809
1959	9,718	52,216,061	51,153,096
1960	10,795	58,301,926	59,258,219
1961	10,866	61,826,002	63,669,738
1962	11,149	65,378,845	67,524,552
1963	11,017	64,438,115	62,247,094

* Net Tonnage figures are estimated figures based on revised measurement rules which became effective March 1, 1938.

Distance from New York to Various Points (Nautical Miles.)

	Via Panama	*Via* Suez	*Via* Cape Town
Yokohama	9,699	13,056	15,099
Manila	11,364	11,521	—
Hong Kong	11,691	11,605	—
Melbourne	9,945	12,933	13,162
Sydney	9,691	13,437	13,402
Wellington	8,522	14,355 (*a*)	14,129
Colon	1,974	—	—
Valparaiso	4,633 (*b*)	—	—
San Francisco	5,262	—	—
Seattle	6,038	—	—

(*a*) *Via* Strait of Magellan 11,344.
(*b*) *Via* Strait of Magellan 8,380.

Distance from Liverpool to Various Points

(Nautical Mile.)	Via Panama	Via Suez	Via Cape Town
Colon	4,548	—	—
Valparaiso	7,207	—	—
Sydney	12,385	12,201	—
Wellington	11,096	12,461	13,353
Melbourne	12,519	11,084	12,157
Yokohama	12,273	11,536	—
Manila	14,129	9,649	—
Hong Kong	13,764	9,743	—

BRITISH REPRESENTATIVES IN U.S.

BRITISH EMBASSY

3100 Massachusetts Ave., N.W. Washington 8, D.C.

Ambassador Extraordinary and Plenipotentiary, His Excellency the Rt. Hon. Sir (William) David Ormsby-Gore, K.C.M.G. (1961) £7,015

Minister, D. A. Greenhill, C.M.G., O.B.E.

Minister (Economic), Sir Eric Roll, K.C.M.G., C.B.

Minister (Commercial), J. E. Chadwick, C.M.G.

Minister (Information), M. A. M. Robb, C.M.G.

Minister (Rhodesia and Nyasaland Affairs), O. B. Bennett.

Defence and NATO Adviser, Gen. Sir Michael West, K.C.B., D.S.O.

Naval Attaché, Rear Adm. J. F. D. Bush, C.B., D.S.C.

Military Attaché, Maj.-Gen. R. E. T. St. John, M.C.

Air Attaché, Air Vice Marshal I. G. Esplin, C.B., O.B.E., D.F.C.

Attaché for Defence Research, Dr. H. M. Wilson, M.B.E.

Counsellors, J. E. Killick; S. J. L. Olver, M.B.E.; R. H. Mason, O.B.E.; N. C. C. Trench; P. S. Rankine, C.B.E.; J. A. McCall Judson; M. Oldfield, C.B.E.; A. J. P. Crick, O.B.E.; M. Gale, M.B.E. (*Commercial*); J. B. Cullen (*Commercial*); N. M. P. Reilly, C.M.G. (*Financial*); H. F. B. Fane, O.B.E. (*Labour*); P. F. Barrett, O.B.E. (*Rhodesia and Nyasaland Affairs*); J. F. Bowles (*Rhodesia and Nyasaland Affairs*).

1st Secretaries, P. Wilkinson; I. J. M. Sutherland; H. C. M. Stone; J. A. Thomson; R. W. H. du Boulay; A. S. Clark; P. R. H. Wright; C. R. E. Brooke; O. G. Forster, M.V.O.; R. Arculus (*Commercial*); F. H. Jackson (*Commercial*); F. J. Pelly, M.B.E. (*Commercial*); D. M. Day (*Information*); C. Wilson (*Information*); F. Mitchell, O.B.E. (*Press*); Miss J. M. Forsyth (*Financial*); H. Christie (*Financial*); R. A. G. Clark (*Administration*); H. N. Walmsley (*Consul*); Kingsley Dube (*Rhodesia and Nyasaland Affairs*).

2nd Secretaries, P. G. de Courcy-Ireland; Miss B. M. Hutchinson; Miss H. H. Sheppard; G. Hay, M.B.E.; G. T. Burgess (*Commercial*); H. C. L. Fassnidge (*Commercial*); Miss C. J. Tasch; W. R. Mills (*Administration*).

3rd Secretary, J. K. E. Broadley.

Attachés, E. I. R. MacGregor (*Civil Air*); G. R. W. Brigstocke (*Shipping*); J. D. Hennings (*Colonial*); S. F. Nicholls, M.B.E.; Group Captain J. S. Rowlands, G.C., O.B.E.; L. W. Osborne (*Agricultural*); R. G. Barratt (*Ministry of Public Building and Works*); A. B. Powell (*Petroleum*); J. Stephenson (*Atomic Energy*); R. H. Parker; Dr. J. A. Saxton (*Scientific*); Miss J. V. Thom.

UNITED STATES REPRESENTATIVES IN GREAT BRITAIN

EMBASSY—1 Grosvenor Square, W.1 [GROsvenor 9000]

Ambassador Extraordinary and Plenipotentiary in London, His Excellency David K. E. Bruce, C.B.E. (1961).

Minister and Deputy Chief of Mission, Hon. G. Lewis Jones.

Minister for Economic Affairs, Hon. Wilson T. M. Beale, Jr.

Counsellors, Elim O'Shaughnessy (*Political*); T. Eliot Weil (*Consular*); William L. Clark (*Public Affairs*); Nathaniel Knowles (*Commercial*); Findley Burns, Jr. (*Administration*).

1st Secretaries, Walter A. Radius; Raymond F. Courtney; John F. Correll (*Labour*); Joseph J. Wagner; Albert E. Irving; Edward T. Lampson; George R. Jacobs (*Econ.*); Oscar V. Armstrong; Hermann F. Eilts; Sam L. Yates (*Commercial*); Paul R. S. Brumby; Arthur A. Hartmann (*Econ.*); Charles Gilbert; Lewis M. Purnell.

2nd Secretaries, Henry J. Lilienfield; Charles W. Lyons (*Econ.*); Roger G. Gifford; Alice D. Westbrook (*Admin.*); Henry H. McKee (*Admin.*); Roberta McKay; Paul J. Hoylen; Jack L. Vrooman (*Admin.*); Henry W. Kemp (*Admin.*); Malcolm Lawrence (*Commercial*); Helen M. Bailey; Ray E. White; Raymond J. Swanson; Alfred Harding; J. Marshall Pifer; Bernice M. Kelly (*Admin.*); James Stromayer; David P. Banowetz; Mark C. Lissfelt (*Admin.*); James L. Tull.

Air Attaché, Brig.-Gen. William K. Skaer, U.S.A.F.

Naval Attaché and Naval Attaché for Air, Rear-Admiral Richard B. Lynch, U.S.N.

Army Attaché, Col. Kenneth R. Dyer, G.S., U.S.A.

Senior Assistant Air Attaché, Col. George L. Newton, Jr., U.S.A.F.

Senior Assistant Army Attaché, Col. John H. Voegtly. G.S., U.S.A.

Attachés, Robert N. Anderson (*Agriculture*); Sam Y. Cross, Jr. (*Financial*); Dr. William W. Greulich (*Science*); Archibald B. Roosevelt, Jr.; Samuel G. Nordlinger (*Atomic Energy*); Dr. Edward D. Myers, Jr. (*Cultural*); John N. Hutchison (*Public Affairs*); James C. Graham; Morton J. Schwartz (*Economic*); Duncan N. Scott (*Public Affairs*); Paul J. Findlen (*Agriculture*); Karl G. Shoemaker (*Agriculture*); Virgil M. Barr; Edward J. McHale (*Public Affairs*); Francis S. Mason, Jr. (*Public Affairs*); James T. Pettus, Jr. (*Public Affairs*); Stephen Namisnak (*Econ.*); Heinz L. Herz (*Customs*); Eva May Morris (*Administration*).

FASTEST ATLANTIC PASSAGES

Year	Days	Ship	Tons	Year	Days	Ship	Tons
1862*a*	9	*Scotia*	3,871	1932*c*	4*d*. 15*h*. 56*m*.	*Europa*	51,656
1869*a*	8	*City of Brussels*	3,081	1933*c*	4*d*. 17*h*. 43*m*.	*Bremen*	51,650
1882*a*	7	*Alaska*	6,400	1934*d*	4*d*. 6*h*. 58*m*.	*Emp. of Britain*	42,348
1889*a*	6	*City of Paris*	10,669	1935*f*	4*d*. 3*h*. 2*m*.	*Normandie*	80,000
1894*a*	5⅓	*Lucania*	12,950	1936*f*	4*d*. 0*h*. 27*m*.	*Queen Mary*	81,237
1897*b*	6	*Kaiser Wilhelm*	14,349	1936*g*	3*d*. 23*h*. 57*m*.	*Queen Mary*	81,237
1903*c*	5½	*Deutschland*	16,502	1937*f*	3*d*. 23*h*. 2*m*.	*Normandie*	80,000
1909*a*	4*d*. 10*h*. 41*m*.	*Mauretania*	30,696	1938*f*	3*d*. 21*h*. 45*m*.	*Queen Mary*	81,237
1924*e*	5*d*. 1*h*. 49*m*.	*Mauretania*	30,696	1938*g*	3*d*. 20*h*. 42*m*.	*Queen Mary*	81,237
1929*c*	4*d*. 18*h*. 17*m*.	*Bremen*	51,650	1952*f*	3*d*. 12*h*. 12*m*.	*United States*	51,500
1930*c*	4*d*. 17*h*. 6*m*.	*Europa*	51,656	1952*g*	3*d*. 10*h*. 40*m*.	*United States*	51,500

a From Queenstown; *b* from Southampton; *c* from Cherbourg; *d* Quebec to Cherbourg; *e* to Cherbourg; *f* Bishop Rock to Ambrose Light (2,907 miles); *g* Ambrose Light to Bishop Rock (2,938 miles).

The United Nations

CHARTER OF THE UNITED NATIONS

The foundations of the Charter of the United Nations were laid at the Conference of Foreign Ministers in Moscow in 1943, and upon those foundations a structure was built at the meetings at Dumbarton Oaks, Washington, D.C., Aug. 21–Oct. 7, 1944. The design was discussed and criticized at San Francisco from April 25 to June 26, 1945, on which date representatives of 50 Allied Nations appended their signatures to the Charter.

The United Nations formally came into existence on October 24, 1945. It was later decided that its seat should be in the United States. Permanent headquarters have been erected at Manhattan, New York.

The following 111 states are members of the United Nations:—

Afghanistan, Albania, Algeria, Argentina, Australia, Austria, Belgium, Bolivia, Brazil, Bulgaria, Burma, Burundi, Byelorussian Soviet Socialist Republic, Cambodia, Cameroon, Canada, Central African Republic, Ceylon, Chad, Chile, China, Colombia, Congo (Brazzaville), Congolese Republic (Leopoldville), Costa Rica, Cuba, Cyprus, Czechoslovakia, Dahomey, Denmark, Dominican Republic, Ecuador, Ethiopia, Finland, France, Gaboon, Ghana, Greece, Guatemala, Guinea, Haiti, Honduras, Hungary, Iceland, India, Indonesia, Iraq, Republic of Ireland, Israel, Italy, Ivory Coast, Jamaica, Japan, Jordan, Kuwait, Laos, Lebanon, Liberia, Libya, Luxemburg, Madagascar, Malaya, Mali, Mauritania, Mexico, Mongolia, Morocco, Nepal, Netherlands, New Zealand, Nicaragua, Niger, Nigeria, Norway, Pakistan, Panama, Paraguay, Persia, Peru, Philippines, Poland, Portugal, Roumania, Ruanda, Salvador, Saudi Arabia, Senegal, Sierra Leone, Somalia, South Africa, Spain, Sudan, Sweden, Syria, Tanganyika, Thailand, Togo, Trinidad and Tobago, Tunisia, Turkey, Uganda, Ukrainian Soviet Socialist Republic, Union of Soviet Socialist Republics, United Arab Republic, United Kingdom, United States of America, Uruguay, Venezuela, Voltaic Republic, Yemen, Yugoslavia.

The principal organs of the United Nations are:—(1) The General Assembly; (2) The Security Council; (3) The Economic and Social Council; (4) The Trusteeship Council; (5) The International Court of Justice; (6) The Secretariat.

1. The General Assembly

The General Assembly consists of all the Members of the United Nations. Each Member is entitled to be represented at its meetings by five representatives, but has only one vote. The General Assembly meets once a year in regular session normally beginning on the third Tuesday in September. Special Sessions may also be held.

The work of the General Assembly is divided between seven Main Committees, on each of which every Member has the right to be represented:—(1) Political and Security (including the regulation of armaments); (2) Economic and Financial; (3) Social, Humanitarian and Cultural; (4) Trusteeship (including Non-Self Governing Territories); (5) Administrative and Budgetary; (6) Legal. There is also a Special Political Committee, to relieve the burden on the first Committee.

The Main Committees consider items referred to them by the General Assembly and recommend draft resolutions for submission to the Assembly's plenary meetings.

The Assembly has two procedural committees—a General Committee and a Credentials Committee; and three standing committees—an Advisory Committee on Administrative and Budgetary Questions, a Committee on Contributions and a Disarmament Commission.

The General Assembly appoints such *ad hoc* committees as may be required from time to time for special purposes. The Assembly is also assisted in its work by subsidiary bodies such as a Board of Auditors, an Investments Committee, a United Nations Staff Benefit Committee, and an International Law Commission.

2. The Security Council

The Security Council consists of eleven Members, each of which has one representative and one vote. There are five *permanent Members* (China, France, U.K., U.S.A., U.S.S.R.) and six non-permanent Members elected for a two-year term.

The Security Council bears the primary responsibility for the maintenance of peace and security. Decisions on procedural questions are made by an affirmative vote of seven Members. On all other matters the affirmative vote of seven Members must include the concurring votes of the *permanent Members*, and it is this clause which makes the *Veto* possible. The only exception to this rule is that in regard to measures for peaceful settlement a party to a dispute must refrain from voting.

The General Assembly, any member of the United Nations, or the Secretary-General, can bring to the Council's attention any matter considered to threaten international peace and security. A non-member State can bring a dispute before the Council provided it accepts in advance the U.N. Charter obligations for peaceful settlement.

A *Committee on the Admission of New Members* was set up by the Security Council on May 17, 1946, for the purpose of examining applications for admission to membership in the United Nations which may be referred to it by the Security Council. It is composed of a representative of each of the members of the Security Council.

The Security Council also establishes *ad hoc* committees and commissions which may be required from time to time for special purposes.

3. The Economic and Social Council

This body is responsible under the General Assembly for carrying out the functions of the United Nations with regard to international economic, social, cultural, educational, health and related matters.

It has established the following Commissions: Statistical, Human Rights, Social, Status of Women, Narcotic Drugs, Population, International Commodity Trade, Regional Economic Commissions for Europe, Asia and the Far East, Latin America and Africa. The Council also supervises and co-ordinates the work of fourteen related agencies.

United Nations Children's Fund (UNICEF), London Office, 14–15 Stratford Place, W.1.—Established by the United Nations in 1946, to meet the emergency needs of children, particularly in war-devastated countries. UNICEF is financed by voluntary contributions from Governments and from the public, which amounted to $29,697,000 in 1962 and assisted 501 projects in 116 countries and territories.

4. Trusteeship Council

The establishment of a Trusteeship Council in connection with territories placed under United Nations supervision through individual Trusteeship Agreements was made possible after the General

Assembly on December 13, 1946, approved the following eight Trusteeship Agreements: *New Guinea* (with Australia); *Ruanda-Urundi* (Belgium); *French Cameroons and French Togoland* (France); *Western Samoa* (New Zealand); *British Cameroons, British Togoland*, and *Tanganyika* (the United Kingdom); a ninth agreement was afterwards approved concerning *Nauru* (administered by Australia on behalf of Australia, New Zealand and U.K.). The Trusteeship Agreement for British Togoland ceased to have effect in March, 1957, when that country was united with Ghana. The trusteeships in the French Cameroons and French Togoland came to an end in 1960 with the achievement of full independence by these States. The Trusteeship Agreements for the British Cameroons, Tanganyika and W. Samoa ended in 1961 and for Ruanda-Urundi in 1962.

A Trusteeship Agreement for the former Japanese mandated islands, the *Marshalls, Marianas* and *Carolinas*, was submitted by the United States to the United Nations, and after approval by the Security Council, came into force on July 18, 1947.

A Trusteeship Agreement for the former Italian Colony of *Somaliland*, in force from Dec. 2, 1950, ended on July 1, 1960.

The Trusteeship Council is composed of countries administering Trust Territories, permanent members of the Security Council, and enough other countries (elected by the General Assembly for three-year terms) to make an equal division between countries which administer Trust Territories and countries which do not.

The Trusteeship Council considers reports from administering authorities; examines petitions in consultation with the administering authority; makes periodic inspection visits; and checks conditions with an annual questionnaire on the political, economic, social, and educational advancement of the inhabitants of trust territories.

5. International Court of Justice

The International Court of Justice is the principal judicial organ of the United Nations. The Statute of the court is an integral part of the Charter and all Members of the United Nations are *ipso facto* parties to it. The Court is composed of 15 judges, no two of whom may be nationals of the same State, and meets at The Hague.

If any party to a case fails to adhere to the judgment of the Court, the other party may have recourse to the Security Council.

THE SECRETARIAT

Secretary-General, U. Thant (*Burma*).

Under Secretaries

Special Political Affairs, Ralph J. Bunche (*U.S.A.*).
Chef de Cabinet, C. V. Narasimham (*India*).
Conference Services, Jiri Nosek (*Czechoslovakia*).
Economic and Social Affairs, P. de Seynes (*France*).
Trusteeship and Information from Non-Self-Governing Territories, D. Protitch (*Yugoslavia*).
Political and Security Council Affairs, V. P. Suslov (*U.S.S.R.*).
Personnel, Sir Alexander McFarquhar (*U.K.*).
Public Information, H. Tavares de Sa (*Brazil*).

U.N. Information Centre, 14–15, Stratford Place, W1.

BUDGET OF THE UNITED NATIONS

The financial year coincides with the calendar year. On February 13, 1946, the General Assembly established a Working Capital Fund of $25,000,000 (U.S.).

For the year 1962, the gross appropriation was $72,969,300 (£26,000,000). The scale of assessments for 1962–64 budget for the British Commonwealth countries was: Australia, 1·66 per cent.; Canada, 3·12 per cent.; Ghana, 0·09 per cent.; India, 2·03 per cent.; Malaya, 0·13 per cent.; New Zealand, 0·41 per cent.; Pakistan, 0·42 per cent.; United Kingdom, 7·58 per cent. The United States contribution was 32·02 per cent.; U.S.S.R. was 14·97 per cent.; France was 5·94 per cent.; Italy was 2·24 per cent.; Japan was 2·27 per cent.; and China was 4·57 per cent.

UNITED KINDOM REPRESENTATIVES

New York

Permanent Representative to the Security Council and Representative to the United Nations, Sir Patrick Dean, G.C.M.G. £7,015
Deputy Permanent Representative, R. W. Jackling, C.M.G.
Ministers, C. E. King, C.M.G. (*Trusteeship Affairs*); K. Unwin, C.M.G., O.B.E. (*Adviser for Economic and Social Affairs*); J. Gibson (*Treasury Adviser*).
Counsellors, A. H. Campbell (*Head of Chancery*); Miss J. A. C. Gutteridge, C.B.E. (*Legal Adviser*).
1st Secretaries, H. P. L. Attlee; W. R. Haydon; D. J. Swan; P. A. H. Hodgson; W. E. H. Whyte; S. J. G. Cambridge; A. A. Acland; E. G. White; J. A. Sankey (*Colonial Affairs*); J. A. Scott (*Commonwealth Relations*).
Permanent Representative to the U.N. European Office, C. P. Scott, O.B.E.

INTERNATIONAL ATOMIC ENERGY AGENCY

Kärntnerring 11–13, Vienna I.

Set up on July 29, 1957, to accelerate and enlarge the contribution of atomic energy to peace, health and prosperity throughout the world and to ensure that assistance provided by it is not used to further any military purpose. Agreements have been reached concerning the Agency's working relationship with the United Nations and some of the specialized agencies. In 1963, 81 states were members.

A General Conference of all members meets in regular annual session and in such special session as may be necessary. A Board of Governors (25 members) carries out the functions of the Agency.

Director-General, Sigvard Eklund (*Sweden*).

INTERNATIONAL AGENCIES

Twelve other international organizations, having wide responsibilities in economic, social, cultural, educational and other related fields, carry out their functions in co-operation with the United Nations under agreements made with a standing committee of the Economic and Social Council.

International Labour Organisation (ILO) Geneva (London Office, 38–39 Parliament Street, S.W.1).—Established in 1919 as an autonomous institution connected with the League of Nations, in 1946 it became the first specialized agency associated with the United Nations. The ILO exists to contribute to the establishment of lasting peace by promoting social justice and by international action to improve labour conditions and living standards, and to promote economic and social stability. In June, 1963, the Organisation had 108 member States.

A *General Conference*, composed of national delegations of two government delegates, one delegate representing management and a fourth representing labour, meets annually and formulates international social standards.

A 48-member *Governing Body*, composed of the representatives of 20 Governments, 12 worker members and 12 employer members, supervises the work of the *International Labour Office* and of the various committees and commissions. Ten Governments hold seats on the Governing Body because of their industrial importance. These are at present Canada, China, France, Federal Republic of Germany, India, Italy, Japan, U.S.S.R., the United Kingdom and the United States.

The International Labour Office provides the Secretariat of the Organisation, collects and distributes information, assists governments upon request in drafting legislation on the basis of decisions of the Conference, directs technical co-operation activities and issues publications.

Director-General, David A. Morse (*U.S.A.*).

Food and Agriculture Organization of the United Nations (FAO), Viale delle Terme di Caracalla, Rome.—Established on October 16, 1945, to raise levels of nutrition and standards of living, to secure improvements in the efficiency of the production and distribution of all food and agricultural products and to better the condition of rural populations, thus contributing to the expansion of world economy. Among its many activities the Organization promotes the global exchange of new types of plants, combats epidemics of animal diseases in many countries and provides technical assistance in such fields as nutrition and food management, soil erosion control, re-afforestation, irrigation engineering, control of infestation of stored foods, production of fertilizers, control of crop pests and diseases, and improvement of fishing vessels, fish distribution and marketing. A world-wide Freedom from Hunger Campaign will continue until 1965, and a World Food Congress was held at Washington in 1963. Current work of the Organization includes a $100,000,000 World Food Programme. The 1961 Conference approved a budget of $31,185,000 for the 1962–63 biennium. In addition to these funds, the UN Special Fund and the Expanded Technical Assistance Program (ETAP) have allocated $25,868,719 to FAO.

The policy of the Organization is directed by a two-yearly Conference of the 105 members and associates. A council (27 members) acts for the Conference between its sessions.

Director-General, B. R. Sen (*India*).

United Nations Educational, Scientific and Cultural Organization (UNESCO), 9 Place de Fontenoy, Paris, 7 éme.—Unesco was established on Nov. 4, 1946, to contribute to peace and security by promoting collaboration among the nations through education, science and culture in order to further universal respect for justice, for the rule of law and for the human rights and fundamental freedoms which are affirmed for the peoples of the world, without distinction of race, sex, language or religion, by the Charter of the United Nations; to collaborate in the work of advancing the mutual knowledge and understanding of peoples, . . . to give fresh impulse to popular education and to the spread of culture, . . . to maintain, increase and diffuse knowledge.

The three main bodies of the Organization are: a *General Conference* which meets every two years to approve the programme and budget, an *Executive Board* of 24 members and the *Secretariat*. In addition, National Commissions are set up in Member States to serve as a link with Unesco and carry out the programme of the Organization.

This programme is essentially designed to stimulate and expand international co-operation and national efforts in the fields of education, natural sciences, social sciences, cultural activities, mass communication and exchange of persons for study and educational travel abroad. Current activities of the Organization focus on development of international co-operation among specialists and non-governmental organizations, the collection and dissemination of information, direct action to promote education and science in under-developed countries and the preparation of international agreements related to Unesco's interests. Member States at July 1, 1963, 113. Approved budget for 1963–64, U.S.$39,000,000.

Director-General, René Maheu (*France*) (*acting*).

World Health Organization (WHO), Palais des Nations, Geneva. Established on April 7, 1948, the World Health Organization exists to forward the attainment by all peoples of the highest possible level of health. Its services are of two kinds—advisory, to spread knowledge, help to train personnel and assist countries on such subjects as malaria, tuberculosis, venereal diseases and other communicable diseases, maternal and child health, nutrition, and environmental health—and technical services of world wide interest such as biological standardization and unification of pharmacopœias, collection and dissemination of epidemiological intelligence, medical research and publication of technical and scientific works. Revised budget estimates for 1963 amount to $30,394,100 and the approved working budget for 1964 is $34,065,100. Membership (May, 1963), 120, including 3 Associate Members.

Organs are a *World Health Assembly* meeting annually to frame policy, an *Executive Board* (24 members), meeting at least twice a year, and a *Secretariat*. Operations in member countries are entrusted to six regional organizations.

Director-General, Dr. M. G. Candau (*Brazil*).

International Bank for Reconstruction and Development (*The World Bank*), 1818 H Street, Washington 25 D.C.—Established on Dec. 27, 1945, to assist in the reconstruction and development of territories of members by facilitating the investment of capital for productive purposes; to promote private foreign investment and, when private capital is not readily available on reasonable terms, to supplement private investment by providing loans for productive purposes out of its own capital, funds raised by it, and its other resources; and to promote the balanced growth of international trade and the maintenance of equilibrium in balances of payments by encouraging international investment for the development of the productive resources of the International Bank's members. Loans made by the Bank since its inception to June 30, 1963, totalled $6,983,000,000. Subscribed capital, July 1, 1963, $20,709,800,000.

The *Board of Governors* consists of one Governor and one alternate appointed by each of the 85 member countries.

Eighteen *Executive Directors* exercise all powers of the Bank except those reserved to the Board of Governors. The *President*, selected by the Executive Directors, conducts the business of the Bank, with the assistance of an international staff.

President, George D. Woods (*U.S.A.*).

International Finance Corporation (IFC), 1818 H Street, Washington 25, D.C.—The IFC is an international institution created in July 1956 to assist the industrial development of its less developed member countries. While IFC is an affiliate of the International Bank for Reconstruction and Development (*The World Bank*), it is a separate legal entity and it has its own funds and staff. Membership, which now numbers 73 nations, is open only to those countries that are members of the World Bank. The purposes of IFC—all in aid of the private sector—are to promote the flow of private capital internationally, to stimulate the development of capital markets within its member countries, and to promote the establishment of new private enterprises and the development of private investment opportunities. By and large, IFC's activities fall under four main heads: first, investment in manufacturing enterprises, usually on a mixed loan and equity basis; second, standby and underwriting arrangements; third, work with development banks, in which connection IFC renders certain services to the World Bank and to the International Development Association (IDA); fourth, the sale of participations in its investments.

By May 31, 1963, IFC had made 59 investments including underwritings, totalling $82,300,000 in 24 member countries.

IFC is controlled by a *Board of Directors* consisting of those Executive Directors of the World Bank who represent at least one government which is also a member of IFC.

The President of the World Bank serves as Chairman of IFC's Board of Directors, which has selected him to serve also as President of IFC.
Preisdent, George D. Woods (*U.S.A.*).

International Monetary Fund, 19 and H Streets, Washington 25, D.C.—Established on Dec. 27, 1945, the Fund exists to promote international monetary co-operation and the expansion of international trade; to promote exchange stability, maintain orderly exchange arrangements and avoid competitive exchange depreciations; and to assist in the establishment of a multilateral system of payments in respect of current transactions between members and in the elimination of foreign exchange restrictions which hamper world trade. Total drawings from the Fund up to April 30, 1963, amounted to $6,854,400,000.
Managing Director, Pierre-Paul Schweitzer (*France*).

International Civil Aviation Organization (ICAO), 1080 University Street, Montreal, 3—Established on April 4, 1947, to study problems of international civil aviation and the establishment of international standards and regulations for civil aviation, ICAO encourages the use of safety measures, uniform regulations for operation, and simpler procedures at international borders. It promotes the use of new technical methods and equipment. With the co-operation of members, it has evolved a pattern for meteorological services, traffic control, communications, radio beacons and ranges, search and rescue organization, and other facilities required for safe international flight. It has secured much simplification of government customs, immigration, and public health regulations as they apply to international air transport. 101 states are now members of ICAO. The net budget for 1963 was $U.S. 4,663,234.

An *Assembly* of delegates from member states meets annually. A *Council* of 27 members is elected by the Assembly, taking into account the countries of chief importance in air transport and the need for representation of the main geographical areas of the world. The Council is the executive body, working through subsidiary committees.
Secretary-General, R. M. Macdonnell (*Canada*).

Universal Postal Union (UPU), Schosshaldenstrasse 46, Berne.—Established on October 9, 1874, by the postal Convention of Berne and in operation from July 1, 1875, UPU exists to form a single postal territory of all the countries, members of the Union, for the reciprocal exchange of correspondence in order to secure the organization and improvement of the various postal services and to promote in this sphere the development of international collaboration. Every member agrees to transmit the mail of all other members by the best means used for its own mail. The Union comprises all the countries of the world with the exception of the Maldive and Laccadive Islands. Budget, 1963, about $940,000.

A *Universal Postal Congress* meets at five-yearly intervals.
Director, Dr. Edouard Weber (*Switzerland*).

International Telecommunication Union (ITU), Place des Nations, Geneva.—Founded at Paris in 1865 as the International Telegraph Union, ITU was re-organized in 1947 and since 1961 has been governed by the Convention adopted by the Geneva Conference held in 1959. ITU exists to set up international regulations for telegraph, telephone, and radio services to further their development and extend their utilization by the public, at the lowest possible rates; to promote international co-operation for the improvement and rational use of telecommunications of all kinds; the development of technical facilities and their most efficient operation. ITU allocates the radio frequency spectrum and registers radio frequency assignments. It studies, recommends, and collects and publishes information on telecommunication matters. The budget for 1963 was $4,205,810.
Secretary-General, Gerald C. Gross (*U.S.A.*).

World Meteorological Organization (WMO), Geneva.—Established on March 23, 1950. WMO exists to facilitate world-wide co-operation in establishing networks of stations making observations related to meteorology, and to promote the establishment and maintenance of centres providing meteorological services; to promote the establishment of systems for the rapid exchange of weather information; to promote standarization of meteorological observations and to ensure their uniform publication; to further the application of meteorology to aviation, shipping, agriculture, and other human activities; to encourage research and training in meteorology and to coordinate their international aspects. The budget for 1964–67 is $U.S. 5,373,000 and a sund for meteorological development of $U.S. 1,500,000

A *World Meteorological Congress* meets at least once every four years. An *Executive Committee* (21 members), meeting at least annually, carries out the resolutions of the Congress, initiates studies and makes recommendations on matters requiring international action. Other organs are six *Regional Meteorological Associations* (Africa, Asia, S. America, N. and Central America, Europe and South-West Pacific), technical commissions and a Secretariat.
Secretary-General, D. A. Davies (*U.K.*).

Inter-Governmental Maritime Consultative Organization (IMCO), Chancery House, Chancery Lane, W.C.2.—Established on March 17, 1958, to provide machinery for cooperation among governments in the field of governmental regulation and practices relating to technical matters, including those concerning safety at sea; to encourage the removal of discriminatory action and of unnecessary restrictions by governments; to consider matters concerning unfair restrictive practices by shipping concerns; to consider any matters concerning shipping that might be referred to it by any organ or specialized agency of the United Nations; and to provide for the exchange of information among governments. In June, 1963, membership consisted of 55 nations. Budget, 1962–63, $892,350.

An *Assembly* of all members meets every two years. A *Council* (16 members) acts for the Assembly between sessions.
Secretary-General, J. Roullier.

International Trade.—A draft charter for an international trade organization was completed in 1948, but it became clear that the leading trading powers would not ratify it without considerable delay. The organization has not yet been established.

An international treaty to which 50 countries are parties, the *General Agreement on Tariffs and Trade* (GATT) was signed in 1947, with the object of lowering and stabilizing tariffs, expanding international trade and promoting economic development. Five tariff conferences have since been held at which members have reduced or frozen their tariffs on thousands of items.
Executive Secretary, E. W. White (*U.K.*)

Foreign Countries

THE following Articles have been revised under the direction of the various Governments or of the British Representatives at Foreign Courts, to whom the Editor desires to express his warmest thanks. The Editor is also greatly indebted to the Embassies, Legations, and Consulates-General in London for various corrections and additions.

Salaries and Allowances.

The Salaries of Officers of Branch " A " of H.M. Foreign Service are shown below. In addition foreign allowances and furnished accommodation (or rent allowances in lieu thereof) are assigned to Officers serving abroad:—

Grade I—£7,015.	Grade VI—£2,865 to £3,565.
Grade II—£5,015.	Grade VII—£1,959 to £2,711.
Grade IV—£4,115.	Grade VIII—£1,498 to £1,837.
Grade V—£3,565.	

Grade IX—£846 to £1,369.

NOTE.—Salaries of Ambassadors and of Ministers Plenipotentiary at British Embassies and Legations abroad shown in the following articles are in each case the maximum salary for the post and exclude *Frais de Représentation.*

Diplomatic Status in U.K.

At the end of 1962, 6,020 persons were entitled to full diplomatic immunity in the United Kingdom: Heads and members of 83 foreign diplomatic missions (including 1,025 wives), 3,439; of Commonwealth missions (770 wives), 2,581. 464 persons have immunity restricted to their official acts; and a further 306 persons enjoy certain legal immunities.

ABYSSINIA. *See* Ethiopia.

AFGHANISTAN

(Afghānistān)

King of Afghanistan, H.M. Zahir Shah, *born* Oct. 15, 1914, *acceded* Nov. 8, 1933 (on the assassination of his father, Nadir Shah); *married* Nov. 7, 1931, Humaira, daughter of Sardar Ahmad Shah Khan, and has surviving issue four sons and two daughters: H.R.H. Prince Ahmed Shah Khan, *b.* Sept. 23, 1934; H.R.H. Prince Mohammad Nadir, *b.* 1941; H.R.H. Prince Daud, *b.* 1949; H.R.H. Prince Mir Wais, *b.* 1957; and H.R.H. Princess Bilqis, *b.* 1931; H.R.H. Princess Maryam, *b.* 1936.

EMBASSY IN LONDON
31 Princes Gate, S.W.7.
[Kensington: 8891]

Ambassador in London, His Excellency Mohammed Kabir Ludin.
1st Secretary, Faiz Ahmad Zikria.
2nd Secretary, Ghulam Farouk.

Afghanistan lies to the N. and W. of Western Pakistan. Its ancient name was Aryana, by which title it is referred to by Strabo, the Greek geographer who lived in the 1st century B.C. The estimated area is 250,000 sq. miles, and the population is estimated at about 10 to 12 millions. The population is very mixed. The most numerous race is the Pathan which predominates in the South and West, the main divisions being the Durranis, from whom the Royal family springs, and the Ghilzais. Then come the Tajiks, an Iranian people mainly cultivators and small traders. There are also Uzbeks and Turkomen in the North, Hazaras in the centre, Baluchis in the South-West and the Nuristanis who live near the Chitral border. All are Sunni Moslems, except the Hazaras and Kizilbashes, who belong to the Shia sect.

Afghanistan is bounded on the W. by Persia (boundary fixed 1857 and 1904), on the S. by Baluchistan (now W. Pakistan) (boundary fixed 1896–7), on the N. by Asiatic Russia (boundary fixed 1886–7 and 1893–5), and on the E. by the N.W. Frontier Province (now W. Pakistan) (boundary fixed 1895). The northern boundary runs from Zulfikar on the Persian frontier to Kushk, the Russian railway terminus, to the Oxus (or Amu Darya, "Mother of Rivers") which forms the boundary from Khamiab to Lake Victoria, whence the line to the Chinese frontier on the branch line from Merv, and thence N.E. was fixed by the Pamir agreement of 1895. The Russo-Afghan frontier was demarcated by the Tashkent Boundary Commission in 1948. The Indo-Afghan frontier was settled by the Durand agreement of 1893. On this frontier from the Pamirs to the Gomal Pass are many Pathan tribes, who have a strong tradition of independence and are much influenced by mullahs.

Mountains, chief among which are the Hindu Kush, cover three-fourths of the country, the elevation being generally over 4,000 feet. There are three great river basins, the Oxus, Helmand, and Kabul. The climate is dry, with extreme temperatures.

Afghanistan is divided into seven major provinces, Kabul, Mazar-i-Sharif, Kandahar, Herat, Nengrahar (formerly Eastern), Paktya (formerly Southern) and Qataghan, and eleven minor provinces, Parwan, Ghazni, Farah-Chakhansur, Girishk, Maimana, Badakhshan, Shibarghan, Ghore, Bamian, Talegan and Uruzgan. Each province is under a Governor (called in major provinces *Naib-ul-Hakmuah*, and in minor provinces *Hakim-i-Ala*).

Government.—Amir Abdurrahman (1880–1901) established a strong central government, with a regular civil and military organization, including offices for public works, posts, police, finance, trade, &c. The Army has been reorganized and is recruited by annual calls; service is for two years with the colours and eight with the reserve. The peace strength is about 64,000. A military academy and military colleges are located in Kabul; and provision is made for training of regular officers abroad. A small Air Force is maintained. All military and air force equipment is now of Russian pattern. Factories for munitions and for various commercial products have been erected in Kabul and elsewhere.

As the result of a British mission to Kabul in 1904–5, the engagements which had existed with the Amir Abdurrahman since 1880 were renewed by the treaty of March 21, 1905. By the Anglo-Russian Convention of August, 1907, Russia declared Afghanistan outside the Russian sphere of influence. Afghan troops crossed the Indian frontier on May 2, 1919, on which the Indian Government took immediate steps to expel them; fighting followed and Dakka was occupied by British troops, but overtures were made by King Amanulla of Afghanistan and a treaty of peace was signed in August. By this treaty Afghanistan is left formally free and independent. By treaty of Nov. 22, 1921 (renewed in 1930), Great Britain and Afghanistan agreed to respect one another's internal and external independence; to recognize boundaries then existent, subject to a slight re-adjustment near the Khyber; and to establish Legations and consular offices. As successor state to the British Government, Pakistan has agreed that her relations with Afghanistan shall be based on the 1921 treaty.

Under the Constitution of Oct. 31, 1931, there is a Senate of 43 nominated members and a National Council of 171 elected members, with a Grand Assembly (*Loe Jirgeh*) which is summoned on important occasions. The administration is entrusted to a Council of Ministers.

The laws of Afghanistan are based on the "Shariat," or Islamic law, and tribal custom.

Production.—Agriculture and sheep raising are the principal industries. There are generally two crops a year, one of wheat (the staple food), barley, or lentils, the other of rice, millet, maize, and *dal*. Sugar beet and cotton are grown. Afghanistan is rich in fruits. Sheep, including the Karakuli, and transport animals are bred. Silk, woollen and hair cloths and carpets are manufactured. Salt, silver, copper, coal, iron, lead, rubies, lapis lazuli, gold, chrome and talc are found.

The following main roads are open to motor traffic. (*a*) Internal: Kabul–Kandahar (310 miles); Kandahar–Farrah–Herat (400 miles); Herat–Maimana to Mazar-i-Sharif (500 miles); Mazar-i-Sharif–Kabul (380 miles). Also Kabul–Khanabad–Faizabad (450 miles); Kabul–Gardez (80 miles); Kabul–Bamian (140 miles). The road from Kabul to the North is being shortened by cutting through the Salang pass. (*b*) Roads to the frontiers: Kabul–Khyber (175 miles); Kandahar–Chaman (70 miles) and roads from Herat to the Russian and Persian borders. Work on the metalling of the Kabul–Khyber road by American engineers is now almost complete and a new metalled road from Kabul to Kandahar and Spin Baldak is being constructed under an I.C.A. contract. An agreement has recently been signed with the Soviet Government for the construction of a road from the Russian border at Kushk to Herat and Kandahar. Otherwise roads are unmetalled. A network of minor roads fit for motor traffic in fine weather links up all important towns and districts.

Goods are still conveyed by pack animals, but motor transport is rapidly taking the place of pack transport as the chief means of conveyance. The chief trade routes to Pakistan and India are the Khyber Pass route, from Kabul to Peshawar (190 miles), and the road from Kandahar to Chaman (70 miles).

Language and Literature.—The languages of the country are Persian and Pushtu and Turki (spoken by Uzbeks and Turkoman tribes in the North). The Turki language is unwritten in Afghanistan. All schoolchildren learn both Persian and Pushtu. The Government is encouraging the spread of Pushtu, the language of the Pathans. Education is free and nominally compulsory, elementary schools having been established in most centres; there are secondary schools in large urban areas and a university (established in 1932) at the capital.

The annual revenue, of some 2,000,000,000 *Afghanis*, consists largely of payments in kind. There are taxes on land, sales of animals, a grazing tax, customs duties, stamps, fines, receipts from State lands, monopolies, and factories and mining royalties; in addition certain businesses and individuals have now become eligible for income-tax.

The official rate for the *Afghani* is 45 = $U.S. 1. The free rates fluctuate by 20 per cent. or more but in May, 1963, were approximately as follows: 700 *Afghanis* = 100 Indian *Rupees*; 550 *Afghanis* = 100 Pakistani *Rupees*; 150 *Afghanis* = £1; 52 *Afghanis* = $1.

Trade with U.K.

	1961	1962
Imports from U.K.	£459,128	£756,232
Exports to U.K.	3,701,410	4,230,772

Exports are mainly Persian lambskins (Karakuli), fruits, cotton, raw wool, carpets and spices, while the imports are chiefly cotton yarn and piece goods, metals, leather goods, tea, sugar, jute manufactures, paper and cement.

CAPITAL, Kabul (about 300,000). The chief commercial centres are Kabul and Kandahar (77,000). Other provincial capitals are Herat (75,000), Mazar-i-Sharif (42,000), Jalalabad (22,000) and Khanabad (18,000).

FLAG. Vertical stripes of black, red and green, with white device in centre.

BRITISH EMBASSY
(Kabul)

Ambassador Extraordinary and Plenipotentiary, His Excellency Arthur James de la Mare, C.M.G. (1963) £4,115

1st Secretary, J. M. Heath.

Military and Air Attaché, Col. R. V. Hawker, M.B.E.

2nd Secretaries, H. H. Hale; J. A. Erskine-Young (*Consul*).

3rd Secretary, R. J. Alston.

Kabul is distant 7,500 miles from London, transit 21 days; by air 2–4 days.

ALBANIA

Head of the State, Hadji Lechi, *assumed office*, July 24, 1953.

Prime Minister, General Enver Hodja.

Situated on the Adriatic Sea, Albania is bounded on the north and east by Yugoslavia and on the south by Greece. The area of the Republic is estimated at 10,700 sq. miles, with a population (1955) of 1,394,000.

On Nov. 10, 1945, the British, U.S.A. and U.S.S.R. governments decided to recognize the Albanian administration under Colonel-General Enver Hodja as the provisional government of Albania on the understanding that free elections would be held at an early date, in order that a truly representative government could be formed. Elections were held in December, 1945, on Jan. 11, 1946, the Constituent Assembly declared Albania an independent Republic, and on Aug. 7, 1946, Albania applied for admission to the United Nations, but its entry was vetoed by Great Britain and the U.S.A. It was admitted in 1955. United Kingdom diplomatic relations with Albania ceased in 1946.

Albania is almost entirely an agricultural country and the staple crops are wheat and maize.

CAPITAL, Tirana (pop. 50,000).

FLAG.—Black two-headed eagle surmounted by yellow outline star, all on a red field.

ALGERIA
(Republic of Algeria)

President and Prime Minister, Ahmed Ben Bella, *elected* Sept. 26, 1962.

CABINET
(July 1, 1963)

Minister of Justice, Hadj Smail.

Interior, Ahmed Medeghri.

National Defence, Haouari Boumedienne (*First Deputy Prime Minister*).

Foreign Affairs, Abdelaziz Bouteflika.

Finance, Ahmed Francis.

Agriculture, Ali Mahsas.

Public Works, Ahmed Boumendjel.

National Economy, Bachi Boumaza.

National Education, Abder Benhamida.

Labour, Health and Social Affairs, Mohamed Seghir Nekkache.

Minister of Posts and Transport, Abdel Kader Zaibek.
War Pensioners, Mohammedi Said (*Deputy Prime Minister*).
Tourism, Ahmed Caid.
Religious Affairs, Tewfik el Madani.
Without Portfolio, Amar Ouzegane.

ALGERIAN EMBASSY IN LONDON
4 Halkin Place, S.W. 1
[Belgravia: 6200, 6209]

Ambassador Extraordinary and Plenipotentiary, His Excellency Mohammed Kellou (1963).
Counsellor, Said Chellal.

Algeria lies between 8° 45′ W. to 12° E. longitude, 37° 6′ N. to a southern limit about 19° N. Area, 855,900 sq. miles (estimated). Population (1963), about 7,500,000.

Government.—Algiers surrendered to a French force on July 5, 1830, and Algeria was annexed to France in Feb. 1842. From 1881 the three northern departments of Algiers, Oran and Constantine formed an integral part of France. Between 1955 and 1960 these were re-organized to form 13 departments: Algiers, Tizi-Ouzou, Orleansville, Médéa, Constantine, Bône, Setif, Batna, Oran, Tlemcen, Mostaganem, Saida and Tiaret. An armed rebellion led by the Moslem *Front de Libération Nationale* (*F.L.N.*) against French rule broke out on Nov. 1, 1954. On September 16, 1959, General de Gaulle announced plans for the self-determination of Algeria, but the Moslem Nationalist Revolution continued. After various attempts by the European population of Algeria aided by a section of the French Army, to retain control in Algeria, peace talks between representatives of the French Government and the Nationalists opened at Evian on May 30, 1961, and agreement was finally reached between the two parties on March 19, 1962. A Referendum held in France on April 8, 1962, and a second one held in Algeria on July 1, confirmed the choice of the Algerian people for independence with continued co-operation with France. President de Gaulle declared Algeria independent on July 4, 1962. The Ben Bella Government took office in September, 1962. Algerian independence and the aftermath of the European insurrection in Algiers led to the flight of more than four-fifths of the French population. In a series of decrees the Algerian Government took over a large number of properties and organized their running by committees of workers. In March, 1963, some large properties still held by French landlords were expropriated and this process has continued. Considerable amounts in aid to sustain the Algerian economy are still being provided by the French Government.

Trade with U.K.

	1961	1962
Imports from U.K. ..	£3,009,829	£1,758,815
Exports to U.K.	9,242,920	9,732,887

Exports are mainly wine, barley and other cereals, skins, olives, fruits, iron and zinc ores, phosphate rock, corkwood, esparto grass, manufactured tobacco, vegetables and crude petroleum. The principal imports from the United Kingdom are tractors and agricultural machinery, engines, machine tools, rubber manufactures and metal manufactures. Natural gas from the Sahara is being supplied to the coastal area and exported in specially-designed tankers. Imports into the U.K. of this methene gas were planned to begin in 1964 under a 15-year contract agreed between the Gas Council and the companies marketing the Algerian natural gas. Imports are expected to amount to 300,000,000 therms in 1964, rising to 350,000,000 therms by 1966. Two special tankers to carry this gas are being built in the U.K. A £500,000 loan was offered by the British Government in June, 1963, for the purchase of British equipment and a technical assistance programme was arranged between the two Governments.

In 1961 there were 2,580 miles of railways open for traffic, and in 1961 the number of ships in foreign trade entering Algerian ports was 24,863. 34,473 commercial aircraft arrived at or departed from Algerian airports in 1961.

The territories of Ain Sefra, Ghardaia, Touggourt and the Saharan Oasis, formerly a separate colony, became an integral part of Algeria on independence.

Oil, natural gas and iron ore are found in quantities in the Saharan regions. Substantial oil and gas deposits are now being worked. In 1962, about 16,000,000 tons of crude oil were exported. In 1963 this figure was expected to rise to about 20,000,000 tons when the present pipelines reached saturation point. A new pipeline to take surplus is planned.

CAPITAL.—Ψ Algiers, population (estimated 1963) 850,000. The large numbers of French inhabitants who left the country have largely been replaced by an influx of Algerians. Other towns include Ψ Oran (430,000), Constantine (400,000), Ψ Bône (144,000), Sidi-Bel-Abbes (101,000), Tlemcen (80,000), Ψ Philippeville (85,000), Blida (87,000), Mostaganem (64,000), Tizi Oyzou (40,000).

Flag.—Red crescent and star on a divided green and white background.

BRITISH EMBASSY
Immeuble Cassiopée, Chemin des Glycines, Algiers.

Ambassador Extraordinary and Plenipotentiary and Consul-General, His Excellency Trefor Ellis Evans, C.M.G., O.B.E. (1963)......... £4,115
Counsellor and Consul, C. T. E. Ewart-Biggs, O.B.E.
1st Secretaries, S. H. Dearden, M.B.E. (*Information*). N. D. Clive, O.B.E., M.C., T.D.; W. R. Thomson (*Labour*); W. H. Lawson, M.B.E. (*Commercial*).
Military Attaché, Colonel W. L. Slingsby, M.B.E.
British Council Representative, C. W. Fyfield.

ANDORRA

A small, neutral principality situated on the southern slopes of the Pyrenees, between Spain and France, with an approximate area of 180 square miles and population of approximately 6,000. It is surrounded by mountains which attain an altitude of from 6,500 to 10,000 feet. Historians place the origin between the eighth and ninth centuries. Andorra is divided into six Parishes each of which has four Councillors elected by vote to the Valleys of Andorra Council of Twenty-four (Heads of families only may vote). The nominal heads of the state are the Bishop of Urgel, Spain, and the President of the French Republic. These two "co-princes" can veto certain decisions of the Council of the Valleys but cannot impose their own decisions without the consent of the Council. Each co-prince nominates his own representative and has a Permanent Delegation and a Supreme Tribune for the hearing of civil causes. These two Tribunes together form the Supreme Courts. The official language of the country is Catalan. Spanish *pesetas* and French *francs* are the accepted currency. A good road crossing the Valleys from Spain to France is open most of the year. Andorra has deposits of iron and quantities of alum and lead, stone quarries, granite, jasper and marble. Slate is abundant. Timber includes pine, fir, oak, birch and box-tree. Potatoes and cereals are produced in the highlands and tobacco in the plains. The climate is naturally cold for six months, but mild in spring and summer. The mountain slopes are suitable for skiing, and it is estimated that 400,000 tourists visit the Valleys during the year. The imports from U.K. during 1962 were £34,771.

There are two radio stations in Andorra, one privately-owned and one operated by a French Government corporation. Both pay dues to the Council of the Valleys.

CAPITAL: Andorra la Vella (population 2,200).

FLAG.—Three vertical bands, blue, yellow, red; Andorran coat of arms frequently imposed on central (yellow) band but not essential.

H.M. Consul-General, B. C. A. Cook, C.M.G., O.B.E. (*Resident at Barcelona*).

ARABIA

Arabia is a peninsula in the south-west of the Asiatic continent, forming the connecting link between Asia and Africa, and lies between 30° 30′—60° E. long. and 12° 45′—34° 50′ N. lat. The north-western limit is generally taken from Akaba at the head of the Gulf of Akaba, to a point in the Syrian Desert about 150 miles north-east, and thence northwards to a point about 50 miles due east of Damascus. The remaining land boundaries are in the form of a horse-shoe, encompassing the Syrian Desert, and descending in a south-easterly direction to the head of the Persian Gulf, and thus excluding the whole of Mesopotamia and the Euphrates Valley. The other boundaries of Arabia are the Red Sea and Gulf of Aden, the Arabian Sea, and the Persian Gulf and Gulf of Oman. Generally speaking, the peninsula consists of a plateau sloping from south-west to north-east towards the Euphrates Valley, except that the broad south-eastern promontory, which encloses the Persian Gulf, contains a coastal range in the Sultanate of Muscat and Oman.

The total area is estimated at 1,200,000 sq. miles (of which nearly one-half is occupied by the Syrian, Nafud, Dahana, and Rub Al Khali deserts), and the total population is believed to be about 10,000,000.

Language and Literature.—Arabic is spoken not only in Arabia, but in many other countries, either as the principal or auxiliary tongue, notably in Egypt and the Sudan, Libya, Morocco, Algeria, Iraq, Jordan, Syria, Lebanon; and to some extent also in Nigeria, Madagascar and Zanzibar. Owing to Moorish incursions it was formerly spoken in Spain, the Balearic Islands and Sicily. There are anthologies of pre- and post-Islamic poetry and a considerable prose literature, including popular romances and story cycles (such as "The Thousand Nights and One Night"), historical and biographical studies, and, resulting from the westernizing movement, there is a general revival of learning among Arabic speaking peoples. Many daily newspapers are published in Arabic and there is a native Arabic drama.

See also.—BAHRAIN; KUWAIT; MUSCAT AND OMAN; QATAR; SAUDI ARABIA; TRUCIAL STATES; YEMEN.

ARGENTINE REPUBLIC

(República Argentina.)

President, Dr. Arturo Illia, *elected* July 28, 1963.

CABINET

Minister of the Interior, Gen. Osiris Guillermo Villegas.

Foreign Affairs and Worship, Gen. Juan Carlos Cordini.
Economy, Dr. José Alfredo Martinez de Hoz.
Education and Justice and National Defence, Dr. José Mariano Astigueta.
Social Assistance and Public Health, Dr. Horacio Castells.
Labour and Social Security, Dr. Bernardo Bas.
Works and Public Services, and (Interim) Transport, Ing. Horacio Jorge Zubiri.
Secretary for:
Navy, Contralmirante Carlos Kolungia.
War, Gen. Hector Alberto Repetto.
Air, Brig. Eduardo McLoughlin.
Treasury, Dr. Eduardo Tiscornia.
Communications, Gen. Miguel Angel Perez Tort.
Agriculture, Dr. Carlos Lopez Saubidet.
Fuel and Power, Dr. Jorge Bermudez Emparanza.
Industry and Mines, Dr. Luis Gottheil.

EMBASSY IN LONDON.

9 Wilton Crescent, S.W.1.

[Belgravia: 3717]

Ambassador (vacant).
Chargé d'Affaires (Minister-Counsellor), Miguel M. Padilla.
Counsellors, José A. Prando; Andrés G. Ceustermans.
Military and Air Attaché, Commodore Egidio José Eyherabide.
Economic Counsellors, Raúl E. Dejean del Castillo; Dr. Alfredo Louro.
Financial Counsellor, Dr. Carlos C. Helbling.
First Secretary, Frederico Diego Erhart del Campo.
Third Secretaries, Roberto Dellepiane Rawson; Guillermo Jorge McGough.
Consul-General, Raúl Eduardo Sidders.
Consulate-General, 53 Hans Place, S.W. 1 (Knightsbridge: 1701).

There are also Consulates in *Liverpool* and *Cardiff*.

Argentina is a wedge-shaped country, occupying the greater portion of the southern part of the South American Continent, and extending from Bolivia to Cape Horn, a total distance of nearly 2,300 miles; its greatest breadth is about 930 miles. It is bounded on the north by Bolivia, on the north-east by Paraguay, Brazil, and Uruguay, on the south-east and south by the Atlantic, and on the west by Chile, from which Republic it is separated by the Cordillera de los Andes. On the west the mountainous Cordilleras, with their plateaux, extend from the northern to the southern boundaries: on the east are the great plains. Those in the north are thickly wooded and are known as *El Gran Chaco*, and further south lie the treeless pampas extending from the Bolivian boundary in the north to the Río Negro; and south of the Río Negro are the vast plains of Patagonia. Argentina thus contains a succession of level plains, broken only in Córdoba by the San Luis and Córdoba ranges, in the north-western states by the eastern spurs of the Andes, and in the southern portion of the Province of Buenos Aires by the Tandil Hills (about 1,000 ft.) and the Sierra Ventana, near Bahia Blanca (about 3,000 ft.). The Paraná River, formed by the junction of the Upper Paraná with the Paraguay River, flows through the north-eastern states into the Atlantic, and is navigable throughout its course in Argentina; the Pilcomayo, Bermejo, and Salado del Norte are also navigable for some distance from their confluence with the Paraná. In the Province of Buenos Aires the Salado del Sud flows south-east for some 300 miles into Samborombon Bay (Atlantic). In the south the Colorado and Río Negro rise in the extreme west and flow across the pampas into the Atlantic, many similar streams in Patagonia (notably the Chubut and Santa Cruz) traversing the country from the Andes to the Atlantic. The climate ranges from sub-tropical to cold temperate.

The Republic consists of 22 provinces and one federal district (Buenos Aires), comprising in all an area of 1,079,965 square miles, with an estimated population of 20,959,100 (June 30, 1960).

In 1959 births numbered 467,300 and deaths 165,000, and in Jan.–June, 1960, 228,700 and 81,500 respectively.

Government.—The estuary of La Plata was discovered in 1515 by Juan Díaz de Solís, but it was not until 1534 that Pedro de Mendoza founded Buenos Aires. This city was abandoned and later founded once more by Don Juan de Garay in 1580. In 1810 (May 25) Spanish rule was defied, and in 1816 (July 9), after a long campaign of liberation conducted by General José de San Martín, the independence of Argentina was declared by the Congress of Tucumán. A revolt in September, 1955, overthrew the Government under the presidency of General Juan D. Perón and an interim Provisional Government was formed by the late General Eduardo Lonardi. This Provisional presidency passed to General Pedro Aramburu in November, 1955.

A Constituent Assembly, elected on July 28, 1957, decided that the country should revert to the 1853 Constitution, in accordance with which, on February 23, 1958, general elections were held and Dr. Arturo Frondizi was elected President and Dr. Alejandro F. Gomez, Vice-President, for the normal period of six years. They assumed office on May 1, 1958, but several months later, owing to dissensions, Dr. Alejandro Gomez, the Vice-President, was forced to resign. The vice-presidency has not since been filled. Following Peronist victories in the partial elections of March, 1962, the armed forces arrested Dr. Frondizi and the Chairman of the Senate, Dr. Guido, then assumed the Presidency, holding office until July, 1963. Following general elections of July 7, Dr. Arturo Illia was elected President on July 28, 1963.

Agriculture.—Of a total land area of approximately 700,000,000 acres, farms occupy about 425,000,000. About 60 per cent. of the farmland is in pasture, 10 per cent. in annual crops, 5 per cent. in permanent crops and the remaining 25 per cent. in forest and wasteland. A large proportion of the land is still held in large estates devoted to cattle raising but the number of small farms is increasing. The principal crops are wheat, maize, oats, barley, rye, linseed, sunflower seed, alfalfa, sugar and cotton. Argentina is pre-eminent in the production of beef, mutton and wool, being self-sufficient in basic foodstuffs and conducting a large export trade in many others. Pastoral and agricultural products provide more than 90 per cent. of Argentina's exports and they originate mainly from the pampas or rich central plain which embraces the provinces of Buenos Aires, Santa Fé, Entre Rios, Córdoba and La Pampa.

The following table shows the yield of the more important crops:

Crop	1961–2 Tons
Wheat	5,100,000
Maize	2,200,000
Linseed	818,000
Oats	700,000
Barley	800,000
Rye	510,000
Sunflower seed	834,000
Rice	190,000
Canary seed	37,400
Cotton (gross bulk production)	364,400
Sugar cane	8,637,000
Millet	215,000
Tobacco	40,000

Livestock.—Livestock population in 1960 was: cattle, 43,250,000; sheep, 48,000,000; and pigs, 3,750,000. Meat exports to U.K. in 1962 were 226,015 tons, compared with 185,773 in 1961. In 1961 total exports of meat (with 1960 totals in brackets) were: beef, 224,000 tons (*221,000*); mutton and lamb, 26,000 tons (*26,700*); and pork, 5,250 tons (*11,500*). 11,250,000 cattle were slaughtered in 1961.

Mineral Production.—Oil is found in various parts of the Republic and is obtained to a considerable extent at Comodoro Rivadavia (Chubut), Mendoza, Plaza Huincul (Neuquen), Tartagal (Salta) and in other districts. A natural gas pipeline between Comodoro Rivadavia and Buenos Aires has been in operation since 1949. An oil pipeline from Campo Duran (Salta) to a refinery in San Lorenzo (Santa Fé) was put in service in March, 1960, as was also a natural gas pipeline from the same source to the outskirts of Buenos Aires. The production of oil is of first importance to Argentina's rapidly expanding industries and, to some extent, to her economic and financial development. Total petroleum output for 1962 was 15,600,000 cubic metres compared with 13,428,000 cubic metres in 1961 and 10,152,900 in 1960.

Coal, lead, zinc, tungsten, iron ore, sulphur, mica and salt are the other chief minerals being exploited. There are small worked deposits of beryllium, manganese, bismuth, uranium, antimony, copper, kaolin, arsenate, gold and silver. Coal production is approximately 300,000 tons per year (1961, 342,000 tons); this is produced at the Rio Turbio mine in the province of Santa Cruz. The output of other materials is not large but greater attention is now being paid to the development of these natural resources.

Industries.—Meat-packing is one of the principal Industries; flour-milling, sugar-refining, and the wine industry are also important. In recent years great strides have been made by the textile industry and in engineering, especially in the production of motor vehicles and steel manufactures.

Communications.—There are 27,874 miles of railways of which 15,604 miles are broad gauge (5′ 6″), 1,940 miles standard (4′ 8½″), 9,664 miles of 1 metre, 537 miles of 0.75 metre and 129 miles of 0.60 metre. They are all State property. Plans are in hand for complete re-organization of the railways which is expected to bring a substantial reduction in the lengths of lines operated. The combined national and provincial road network totals approximately 91,500 miles of which 7,500 miles are surfaced. World Bank and other important loans are to be used for a considerable extension and surfacing improvement. There are air services between Argentina and all the neighbouring republics, Europe, Canada and the U.S.A.

Total tonnage entering Argentine ports was 9,418,876 in 1961. Of the latter figure, 1,287,713 tons were Argentine; 1,482,788 British; 932,316 Norwegian; 789,357 Italian; 782,404 U.S.A.; 649,694 Netherlands; 504,430 Panamanian; 414,506 German; 395,493 French; 317,509 Swedish; 308,798 Liberian; 304,801 Greek; 351,015 Spanish and 203,897 Danish.

There are now 13 short-wave broadcasting stations, 67 medium wave (of which 17 are official), 4 television stations in Buenos Aires, 1 each in Mar del Plata, Mendoza and Córdoba. Television receivers numbered 800,000 at the end of 1960.

Defence.—The Army is organized in four corps in which are combined four infantry divisions, one motorized infantry division and one motorized infantry brigade, one mounted infantry division, one armoured division and one cavalry division and numbers about 5,000 officers, 15,000 N.C.O.s and 65–70,000 men on a peace footing.

The Navy consists of 2 cruisers, 1 aircraft carrier, 9 destroyers, 7 frigates, 1 ice-breaker, 8 minesweepers, 9 motor torpedo boats, 2 submarines, 23 landing craft, 7 oilers, 8 transports, 2 survey ships and auxiliary vessels; 4 squadrons Naval Air Arm. Strength about 2,000 officers and 25,000 men.

The Air Force consists of 5 brigades and a training force, with a strength of 1,700 officers, 11,000 other ranks and 19,000 civilians. The aircraft include Meteor IV, Lincoln, Lancaster, Viking, Bristol 170 and Dove.

Education.—Primary Education is free and compulsory for four years between the ages of 6 and 14. The scattered population of the country districts constitutes a problem in attendance which is being gradually solved. Illiteracy of adults has fallen in the last 20 years; it is now almost non-existent except in the north and far south, where it is still about 42 per cent. *Secondary* Education is controlled by the National Government in National Colleges, in Normal Schools, and in Special Institutes for Commerce, Arts and Crafts, Mining, Agriculture, &c. There are *National Universities* at Córdoba, Buenos Aires, San Miguel de Tucumán, Santa Fé, Mendoza, La Plata and Bahia Blanca.

Language and Literature.—Spanish is the language of the Republic and the literature of Spain is accepted as an inheritance by the people. There is little indigenous literature before the break from Spain, but all branches have flourished since the latter half of the nineteenth century, particularly journalism. Under the Perón régime many newspapers and reviews were closed down and others turned into Government mouthpieces. Since the 1955 revolution the traditional freedoms have been restored. About 200 daily newspapers are published in Argentina, including 50 in the city of Buenos Aires. The English language newspaper is the *Buenos Aires Herald* (daily). There are numerous other foreign language newspapers.

TRADE

	1961	1962
	Dollars U.S.	
Total Imports....	1,460,325,000	1,350,118,000
Total Exports....	964,116,000	1,209,531,000

Trade with U.K.

	1961	1962
Imports from U.K....	£50,477,278	£46,919,464
Exports to U.K.......	75,000,775	93,197,113

For Exchange Rates *see* p. 83.

Capital, ΨBuenos Aires, Pop. (Dec. 1958), 4,500,000. Other large towns are: ΨRosario de Santa Fé (720,000), Córdoba (635,000), ΨLa Plata (410,000), Avellaneda (380,000), Santa Fé (275,000), ΨMar del Plata (270,000), San Miguel de Tucumán (251,000) and Mendoza (165,000).

NATIONAL COLOURS: Blue and White (War Flag.—3 horizontal bands, blue, white, blue, with rising sun on white band).

NATIONAL DAYS.—May 25, July 9 and July 20.

BRITISH EMBASSY

Edificio Británico, Calle Reconquista 314, Buenos Aires.

British Ambassador, His Excellency Sir George Humphrey Middleton, K.C.M.G. (1961)... £5,015
Minister, T. E. Rogers, C.M.G., M.B.E.
Counsellor and Consul General, F. C. Ogden, C.B.E.
1st Secretaries, S. M. Mackenzie, C.B.E., D.S.C.; C. J. Audland; C. W. Wallace (*Commercial*); J. M. Carlin, D.F.C. (*Labour*).
2nd Secretaries, M. A. Cafferty (*Commercial*); G. C. Tout, M.B.E. (*Commercial*); M. W. Atkinson (*Information*).
3rd Secretaries, K. G. MacInnes; E. C. F. Macpherson.
Junior Attachés, R. P. Breakspear; A. E. Daley.
Naval and Military Attaché, Capt. P. E. I. Bailey, R.N.
Air Attaché, Gp. Capt. G. F. Lerwill, D.F.C.
Agricultural and Food Attaché, A. G. Mill.
Veterinary Attaché, R. H. Ewart.
Consul, A. G. Battle.
Vice-Consuls, B. Kelly, M.B.E.; C. R. MacCorquodale (*acting*).

BRITISH CONSULAR OFFICES

There are British Consular Offices at *Buenos Aires*, *Comodoro Rivadavia*, *Córdoba*, *La Plata*, *Puerto Deseado*, *Rio Gallegos*, *Rio Grande*, *Rosario de Santa Fé* and *Trelew*.

BRITISH COUNCIL

Representative in Argentine, Dr. N. A. R. MacKay, O.B.E., Lavalle 190, Buenos Aires.

BRITISH CHAMBER OF COMMERCE

Calle Bartolomé Mitre 441. (6 Piso), Buenos Aires.

Buenos Aires is 7,160 miles from Southampton; transit, 19 days by steamship; 1 day by air.

AUSTRIA

President of the Austrian Republic, Dr. Adolf Schaerf, *born* 1890; *elected* May 5, 1957; *re-elected* April 28, 1963.

CABINET.
(April 11, 1961)

Chancellor, Dr. Alfons Gorbach (*Austrian People's Party*).
Vice-Chancellor, Dr. Bruno Pittermann (*Socialist*).
Foreign Affairs, Dr. Bruno Kreisky (*Socialist*).
Interior, Franz Olah (*Socialist*).
Justice, Dr. Christian Broda (*Socialist*).
Defence, Dr. Ing. Karl Schleinzer (*Austrian People's Party*).
Finance, Dr. Franz Korinek (*Austrian People's Party*).
Education, Dr. Heinrich Drimmel (*Austrian People's Party*).
Commerce and Reconstruction, Dr. Fritz Bock (*Austrian People's Party*).
Agriculture and Forestry, Ing. Eduard Hartmann (*Austrian People's Party*).
Transport and Electricity Industry, Otto Probst (*Socialist*).
Social Welfare, Anton Proksch (*Socialist*).

AUSTRIAN EMBASSY IN LONDON.
18 Belgrave Square, S.W.1.
[Belgravia: 3731]

Ambassador in London, His Excellency Dr. Johannes Schwarzenberg (1955).
Counsellor, Dr. Friedrich Kudernatsch.
1st Secretary, Dr. Egon Libsch.
2nd Secretary, Dr. Heinrich Blechner.
Military and Air Attaché, Col. Franz Attems-Petzenstein.
3rd Secretaries, Dr. Peter Jankowitsch; Dr. Franz Parak.

Austria is a country of Central Europe bounded on the north by Czechoslovakia, on the south by Italy and Yugoslavia, on the east by Hungary, on the north-west by Germany and on the west by Switzerland. Its area is 32,376 square miles and its population (estimated July, 1962), 7,128,000.

Government.—The Austrian Federal Republic comprises nine States (Vienna, Lower Austria, Upper Austria, Salzburg, Tyrol, Vorarlberg, Carinthia, Styria and Burgenland) and was established in 1918 on the break-up of the Austro-Hungarian Empire. On March 13, 1938, as a result of the *Anschluss*, Austria (*Oesterreich*) was incorporated into the German *Reich* under the name *Ostmark*. After the liberation of Vienna in 1945, the Austrian Republic was reconstituted within the frontiers of 1937 and, after a period of provisional government, a freely elected Government took office on December 20, 1945. The country was divided at this time into four zones occupied respectively by the U.K., U.S.A., U.S.S.R. and France, while Vienna was jointly occupied by the four Powers. On May 15, 1955, the Austrian State Treaty was signed in Vienna by the Foreign Ministers of the four Powers and of Austria. This Treaty recognized the re-establishment of Austria as a sovereign, independent and democratic state, having the same frontiers as on January 1, 1938. It entered into force on July 27, 1955.

There is a National Assembly of 165 Deputies. At the last general elections in November, 1962, the Austrian People's Party gained two seats from the Socialist Party. The present state of the parties is as follows:

Austrian People's Party	81
Socialist Party	76
Freedom Party (right wing)	8

Religion and Education.—The predominant religion is Roman Catholic. Elementary education is free and compulsory between the ages of 6 and 14, and there are good facilities for secondary, technical and professional education. There are Universities at Vienna, Graz and Innsbruck.

Language and Literature.—The language of Austria is German, but the rights of the Slovene- and Croat-speaking minorities in Carinthia, Styria and Burgenland are protected. The press is free. There are now 10 daily papers in Vienna and 23 in the provinces, as well as numerous weeklies and monthlies.

Communications.—Internal communications in Austria are partly restricted because of the mountainous nature of the country, and road and rail routes must, of necessity, follow the river valleys. The railways in Austria are state-owned and have approximately 4,000 miles of track. Much progress in electrification has been made in recent years and 70 per cent. of the railway system is now electrified. While road surfaces in many cases are not up to British standards, the main roads linking the major towns are generally good and relatively fast. Progress is being made in the construction of the Autobahn Salzburg-Linz-Vienna, which joins the Munich-Salzburg Autobahn and some sections are already in use. An internal air service between the major towns of Austria was inaugurated in May, 1963.

Production and Industry.—Agriculture is the most important industry, the arable land producing wheat, rye, barley, oats, maize, potatoes, sugar beet, turnips, and miscellaneous crops. Many varieties of fruit trees flourish and the vineyards produce excellent wine. The pastures support horses, cattle and pigs. Timber forms a valuable source of Austria's indigenous wealth with about 35 per cent. of the total land area consisting of forest areas. Coniferous species predominate and account for more than 80 per cent. of the timber under cultivation. Hard-wood trees are mainly confined to Lower Austria. Spruce is the most common among the conifers (about 60 per cent. of the total) and beech is the most prevalent of the broad leaf trees.

Austria has important heavy industries. Production figures for 1962 include (in thousands of metric tons): pig iron 2,118, crude steel 2,970, rolled products 2,097. Raw magnesite, nitrogenous fertilizers, paper and chemical pulp are produced in quantity. In addition, motor cycles and motor-scooters, tractors and motor lorries are produced.

Hydro-electric power offers great possibilities in Austria. Much has already been done to develop it, and a long-term plan has been evolved for further development including greater export of electric current to surrounding countries. Production in 1962 was 17,807 million kWh.

Minerals.—There are large iron ore deposits and, in Eastern Austria, large oil deposits. In addition there are useful deposits of brown coal, magnesite, salt and lead. There are also limited deposits of copper.

FINANCE.

Budget	1962 (*Schillings*)
Ordinary Budget:	
Expenditure	52,634,000,000
Revenue	52,370,000,000
Extraordinary Budget:	
Expenditure	1,444,000,000
Revenue	44,000,000

Trade with U.K.

	1961	1962
Imports from U.K.	£21,942,101	£24,634,525
Exports to U.K.	14,144,975	13,608,789

Currency.—The unit of currency is the *Schilling* of 100 *Groschen*, reintroduced in December, 1945. The official rate of exchange was fixed in May, 1953, at 72·80 Austrian schillings=£1, for all purposes.

CAPITAL, Vienna, on the Danube, population 1,627,566. Other towns are Graz (237,080), Linz (195,978), Salzburg (108,114), Innsbruck (100,695) and Klagenfurt (69,218).

FLAG.—Horizontal stripes of red, white, red, with eagle crest on white stripe.

BRITISH EMBASSY.

Vienna.

British Ambassador Extraordinary and Envoy Plenipotentiary, His Excellency Sir Malcolm Siborne Henderson, K.C.M.G. (1961) £4,115

Minister Counsellor and Consul-General, H. C. Hainworth, C.M.G.

Counsellor (Commercial), A. C. Maby, C.B.E.

There are British Consular Offices at *Vienna* and *Innsbruck*.

British Council Representative, C. R. Hewer, O.B.E., Freyung 1, Vienna 1.

BAHRAIN

Ruler, H. H. Shaikh Isa bin Sulman Al Khalifah, *born* 1932; *acceded* Nov. 2, 1961.

Bahrain consists of a group of low-lying islands situated halfway down the Persian Gulf some 20 miles off the east coast of Arabia. The largest of these, Bahrain Island itself, is about 30 miles long and 10 miles wide at its broadest. The two most important towns are Manama (61,726) and Muharraq (32,302). The latter is situated on a separate island of the same name which is connected with Bahrain Island by a causeway 1½ miles long. The population of the islands at the Census held in 1959 was 143,135, of whom about half are the original inhabitants belonging to the Shia Sect, the remainder, including the ruling family, being Sunnis. There are 2,815 Europeans and Americans (about 75 per cent. of whom live at the Bahrain Petroleum Company's town of Awali) and 21,586 non-Bahrainis of whom about half are Iranians, Indians and Pakistanis. The standard of living is high among the large and influential merchant class and steadily rising among the lower social groups.

Bahrain enjoys a typical Persian Gulf climate with long, mild winters and an annual rainfall of about 3″. Summer extends from May to October, with temperatures between 90° F and 100° F and humidity often approaching 100 per cent. The surrounding sea abounds in a variety of fish, and some of the best prawns in the world inhabit the warm sheltered waters.

The ruling family (Al Khalifah) came originally from the neighbourhood of Kuwait and occupied Bahrain, which was then in the hands of the Persians, in 1782. The state is administered under the Ruler by a number of departmental heads whose activities are co-ordinated by the Secretariat. A small Administration Council consisting of members of the ruling family and heads of departments has been created by the Ruler to consider and advise on general matters; Health, Education, Port, Agriculture and Water Councils exist to advise the respective departments. Local government is the responsibility of six municipalities and the Rural Affairs Department which cares for the villages. Half of the members of four of the municipal councils (Manama, Muharraq, Rifaa and Hidd) are elected by the public and half nominated by the Government; all the members of the other two, which were created later (Sitra and Jidhafs) are nominated by the Government. In addition to the Department of Rural Affairs, there is a Department of Social Affairs, a Labour Department, a Lands Department and a Public Works Department. There is free primary and secondary education and free medical treatment.

In earlier days the only industry was the pearl trade, of which Bahrain was an important centre, but this has declined since the advent of the cultured pearl and petroleum dominates the scene. Oil was discovered in 1932 and The Bahrain Petroleum Company, Limited (BAPCO), has its headquarters in Awali, some eleven miles from Manama. The company also operates a refinery and about 80 per cent. of the oil refined is piped from Saudi Arabia.

The second source of revenue is that of Bahrain's traditional *entrepôt* trade. The island is conveniently situated to handle goods in transit to the mainland and it is estimated that not less than 70 per cent. of the imports unloaded at Bahrain were, up to a few years ago, destined for onward movement. A decline in this *entrepôt* trade has, however, occurred as there is a growing tendency, as new developments occur, for eastern Saudi Arabia, Qatar and other places in the Gulf to import direct. (In 1960 Bahrain re-exported 36·45 per cent. of its imports and in 1962, 35·21 per cent.) To counteract this trend and to encourage the *entrepôt* trade, free transit facilities were introduced in the port of Bahrain on January 1, 1958, and a new harbour, named the Mina Sulman after the late Ruler, was opened in May, 1962.

The principal imports and re-exports are household goods, foodstuffs, piece-goods, timber and building materials (especially cement), vehicles and machinery.

Manama, the capital and commercial centre, extends for two miles along the northern shore of Bahrain Island and is a regular port of call for thirty steamship lines. Bahrain is also a port of call for B.O.A.C. and other international airlines, with a newly-opened air terminal and facilities for jet airlines. Banking services are provided by the Bank of Bahrain and by branches of the Eastern Bank, the British Bank of the Middle East and of the Arab Bank. There is a radio-telephone service to the United Kingdom and many other parts of the world. The electricity supply system is being extended over the island and piped water supplies are being introduced into the principal towns and villages.

The principal coin in use is a rupee introduced especially by the Reserve Bank of India for circulation in the Persian Gulf States. The value of this special rupee is the same as that of the Indian rupee (Rs. 13·285=£1).

FLAG: Red, with vertical straight or serrated white bar next to staff.

CAPITAL, Ψ Manama; population, 61,726.

Secretary to the Government, G. W. R. Smith, M.B.E.
H.M. Political Agent, J. P. Tripp (1963).

Bahrain is the headquarters of *H.M. Political Resident in the Persian Gulf*, Sir William Luce, G.B.E., K.C.M.G. £5,015

BELGIUM

(Royaume de Belgique.)

King of the Belgians, H.M. King Baudouin, K.G., *born* Sept. 7, 1930; *succeeded* July 17, 1951, on the abdication of his father, King Leopold III, after having acted as Head of the State since August 11, 1950; *married* Dec. 15, 1960, Doña Fabiola de Mora y Aragòn.

Heir Presumptive, H.R.H. Prince Albert, *born* June 6, 1934, *brother* of the King; *married* July 2, 1959, Donna Paola Ruffo di Calabria, and has *issue* Prince Philippe Léopold Louis Marie, *b.* April 15, 1960; Princess Astrid Josephine-Charlotte Fabrizia Elisabeth Paola Marie, *b.* June 5, 1962.

CABINET.

(April 25, 1961)

Prime Minister, M. Théo Lefevre (*CS*).
Assistant Prime Minister and Foreign and African Affairs, M. Paul-Henri Spaak, C.H. (*Soc.*).
National Defence, M. P. W. Segers (*CS*).
Justice, M. P. Vermeylen (*Soc.*).
Interior, M. A. Gilson (*CS*).
Economic Affairs, M. A. Spinoy (*Soc.*).
Finance, M. A. Dequae (*CS*).
Social Security, M. E. Leburton (*Soc.*).
Agriculture, M. C. Heger (*CS*).
Public Works, M. G. Bohy (*Soc.*).
Public Health and Family, M. J. Custers (*CS*).
Labour, M. L. Servais (*CS*).
Foreign Trade and Aid to Underdeveloped Countries, M. M. Brasseur (*CS*).
Education and Culture, M. V. Larock (*Soc.*).
Assistant Foreign Affairs, M. H. Fayat (*Soc.*).
Communications, M. A. Bertrand (*CS*).
Posts and Telegraphs, M. E. Anseele (*Soc.*).
Middle Classes, M. A.-M. Declerck (*CS*).
Assistant Finance, M. H. Dervelles (*Soc.*).
Assistant National Education and Culture, M. R. van Elslande (*CS*).

CS=Christian Social Party. *Soc.*=Socialist.

BELGIAN EMBASSY IN LONDON.

Chancery and Passport Office, 103 Eaton Square, S.W.1.

[Belgravia: 5422]

Ambassador Extraordinary and Plenipotentiary, His Excellency Monsieur Jacques de Thier (1961).
Minister Counsellor, M. Jacques Graeffe.
Counsellor (Commercial), M. Charles Michel Werck.
Naval, Military and Air Attaché, Col. Yves van Strydonck de Burkel.
Counsellors, M. Guy Stuyck; M. Robert Thissen.
1st Secretaries, M. Hedwig Coessens; M. J. Blancquaert.
Shipping Counsellor, Baron Philippe de Gerlache de Gomery.
Asst. Naval, Military and Air Attaché, Comdt. Georges Cuissart de Grelle, M.B.E.
Agricultural Attaché, M. Maurice Cammaerts.

Attachés, M. J. Fobe; M. Maurice Carmen; Mlle. F. van Haelewyck.

A Kingdom of Western Europe, with a total area of 11,775 square miles and a population, Dec. 31, 1962 (including Eupen and Malmedy) of 9,251,414. The Kingdom of Belgium is bounded on the N. by the Kingdom of the Netherlands, on the S. by France, on the E. by Germany and Luxemburg, and on the W. by the North Sea.

Belgium has a frontier of 831 miles, and a sea-board of 42 miles. The Meuse and its tributary, the Sambre, divide it into two distinct regions, that in the west being generally level and fertile, while the table-land of the Ardennes, in the east, has for the most part a poor soil. The "polders" near the coast, which are protected by dykes against floods, cover an area of 193 sq. miles. The highest hill, Baraque Michel, rises to a height of 2,230 feet, but the mean elevation of the whole country does not exceed 526 feet. The principal rivers are the Scheldt and the Meuse. Brussels has a mean temperature of 49° F. (summer 65°, winter 37°).

Belgium is inhabited by two distinct races, the Flemish, of Germanic stock, and the Walloons, of Latin stock. Since 1938 there has been an increase in the Flemish population of almost 517,000 and in the Walloon population of about 100,000. Nearly all the inhabitants are Roman Catholics.

Government.—The kingdom formed part of the "Low Countries" (Netherlands) from 1815 until Oct. 14, 1830, when a National Congress proclaimed its independence, and on June 4, 1831, Prince Leopold of Coburg was chosen hereditary king. The separation from the Netherlands and the neutrality and inviolability of Belgium were guaranteed by a Conference of the European Powers, and by the *Treaty of London* (April 19, 1839), the famous "Scrap of Paper," signed by Austria, France, Great Britain, Prussia, The Netherlands, and Russia. On Aug. 4, 1914, the Germans invaded Belgium, in violation of the terms of the treaty.

The Kingdom was again invaded by Germany on May 10, 1940. The whole Kingdom eventually fell into enemy hands and was occupied by Nazi troops until the victorious advance of the Allies in September, 1944. A monument at Hertain in the province of Hainault (where British forces crossed the frontier on Sept. 3, 1944), set up by the Anglo-Belgian Union, was unveiled on St. George's Day, 1949.

According to the Constitution of 1831 the form of government is a constitutional representative and hereditary monarchy with a bicameral legislature, consisting of the King, the Senate and the Chamber of Representatives. The Senate is partly directly and partly indirectly elected (or co-opted) for 4 years. 106 members out of 175 are directly elected. The Chamber of Representatives consists of not more than 1 per 40,000 inhabitants and is elected directly by all adult nationals.

The elections of March 26, 1961, returned to the Senate 81 Social Christians (Catholics), 73 Socialists, 17 Liberals, 1 Communist and 3 others, total, 175; and to the Chamber of Representatives 96 Social Christians (Catholics), 84 Socialists, 20 Liberals, 5 Communists and 7 others, total 212.

Production.—Belgium is essentially a manufacturing country. With no natural resources except coal, annual production of which formerly averaged some 30,000,000 tons but which dropped to 21,228,000 tons in 1962 following the closing of uneconomic pits, industry is based largely on the processing for re-export of imported raw materials. A large proportion of the population is engaged in agriculture and forestry, the former supplying four-fifths of the population's needs. Principal industries are coal, steel and metal products (Mons, Charleroi, Liège, Namur, Hainault, Brabant and Limburg), textiles (Ghent, Bruges, Courtrai, Verviers, etc.), glass, nitrogen, heavy chemicals, sugar, breweries, etc. Steel output in 1962 was 7,356,000 metric tons.

EDUCATION.—Schools are maintained by communal taxation, with provincial and State grants, while many are under ecclesiastical control, Roman Catholic largely predominating. There are 261 State grammar and high schools. In addition there are 83 elementary schools under the control of the State and 296 under the control of local government authorities. There are 1,037 private colleges and secondary schools. The Universities of Ghent and Liège are maintained by the State; those of Brussels and Louvain are independent institutions. After considerable opposition, Ghent University was in 1930 turned into a purely Flemish institution.

Language and Literature.—Flemish is spoken in the provinces of West Flanders, East Flanders, Antwerp, Limburg, and the northern half of Brabant, and French in the provinces of Hainault, Namur, Luxemburg, Liège and the southern half of Brabant. Legislation enacted on Feb. 15, 1962, provided for a fixed linguistic border between the Flemish-speaking and French-speaking areas of Belgium. Flemish is recognized as the official language in the northern areas and French in the southern (Walloon) area and there are guarantees for the respective linguistic minorities. The City of Brussels and the University of Louvain are bilingual, though the latter is situated in a Flemish-speaking area. The linguistic border runs from a point south of Ypres and on the French frontier, to a point south of Brussels, then to a point north of Liège and east to the German frontier south of Aachen.

The literature of France and the Netherlands is supplemented by a current of indigenous Belgian literary activity, in both French and Flemish. Maurice Maeterlinck (1862–1949) was awarded the Nobel Prize for Literature in 1911. Louvain library, which ranked among the great libraries of the world, was destroyed by German invaders in the war of 1914–18; reconstructed, mainly by American funds, after peace was declared, it was again destroyed in May, 1940, by German invaders. There are 64 daily newspapers (French, Flemish and some German) in Belgium.

FINANCE.	*Francs*
Revenue (1963 Ordinary Budget estimate)	139,760,000,000
Expenditure (1963 Ordinary Budget estimate)	139,600,000,000
Budget Estimate (1963) Extraordinary:	
Revenue	435,000,000
Expenditure	17,990,000,000

The unit of currency is the Belgian *franc*. On July 1, 1962, the Bank of England official rate of exchange was 140 *francs*=£1. (*See also* p. 83.)

TRADE.

	1961	1962
Total Imports	*Fr*.210,951,736,000	*Fr*.227,770,943,000
Total Exports	196,219,720,000	216,179,285,000

Trade with U.K.

	1961	1962
Imports from U.K.	£77,170,859	£91,928,609
Exports to U.K.	64,808,556	72,581,528

COMMUNICATIONS.—On Dec. 31, 1961, there were 4,620 kilometres of normal gauge railways operated by the Belgian National Railways, of which 956 kilometres were electrified; the length of light railways operated in 1961 was 821 kilometres (of which 708 were electrified). Belgian National Railways also operate 9,202 kilometres of regular bus routes. On Dec. 31, 1961, there were 823,643 telephone subscribers in Belgium.

Ship canals include *Ghent-Terneuzen* (18 miles, of which half is in Belgium and half in the Netherlands; constructed 1825–27) which, under the terms of an agreement recently signed by the Belgian and Netherlands Governments is to be improved to permit the passage to Ghent of ships up to 50,000 tons; *Roupel* (20 miles, by which ships drawing 18 ft. reach Brussels from the sea; opened in 1922); and *Bruges* (from Zeebrugge on the North Sea to Bruges, 6½ miles; opened in 1922). The *Albert Canal* (79 miles), which figured prominently in the fighting (Sept. 1944), for the relief of Belgium and the Netherlands and for the invasion of Germany, links Liège with Antwerp; it was completed in 1939 at the cost of £13,500,000, and accommodates barges up to 1,350 tons. The modernization of the port of Antwerp begun in 1956 is now well advanced, Inland waterway approaches to Antwerp are also to be improved. The river Meuse from the Dutch to the French frontiers, the river Sambre between Namur and Monceau, the river Scheldt from Antwerp-Ghent and the Brussels-Charleroi Canal will be widened or deepened to take barges up to 1,350 tons. These improvements are expected to be completed in 1966 and to cost £78,500,000. There are 10,169 kilometres of State roads and 1,288 kilometres of provincial roads. Most of the maritime trade of Belgium is carried on in foreign bottoms, the mercantile marine consisting (1961) of 91 vessels (625,667 tons), in addition to which there are 412 fishing boats (29,580 tons).

The Belgian National Airline operates regular services between Brussels and London, Manchester and many continental centres, as well as overseas services to the United States, the Congo and the U.S.S.R. A passenger and mail-carrying helicopter service, the first of its kind in the world, was inaugurated in 1953. Many foreign air-lines call at Brussels.

CITIES AND TOWNS.

The Capital, BRUSSELS, had a population (Dec. 31, 1962) of 1,029,693 (with suburbs). Other towns are ΨAntwerp, the chief port (647,060); ΨGhent (228,986), which has large cotton and flax spinning mills, and is the second port of importance after Antwerp, while its flower shows are famous; Liège (446,414), the centre of the iron industry, and Charleroi (280,666), the important coal-mining and metallurgical centre; Malines (64,847); ΨOstend (56,811); ΨBruges (52,463). Brussels is 224 miles from London; transit, by rail and sea, 8 hrs.; by air, 1 hr.

NATIONAL FLAG.—3 vertical banks, black, yellow, red.

BELGIAN INDEPENDENCE DAY—July 21.

BRITISH EMBASSY.

2 Rue de Spa, Brussels.

Consular and Information Sections, Service and Labour Attachés, 68 Rue Joseph II, Brussels.

Ambassador Extraordinary and Plenipotentiary, His Excellency Sir Roderick Edward Barclay, K.C.M.G., K.C.V.O. (1963) £5,015

Counsellor, C. O. I. Ramsden.

Commercial Counsellor, J. B. Wraight, C.M.G.

Military and Naval Attaché, Brig. P. R. Ashburner, M.C.

Air Attaché, Group-Capt. J. R. Gard'ner.

1st Secretaries, F. W. Stockwell; H. Carr; R. A. Hibbert (*Commercial*); G. R. Boon (*Consul*); G. R. Coate (*Information*); R. O. Barritt (*Labour Attaché*).

2nd Secretaries, A. B. Milne; P. R. Springett.

3rd Secretary, A. D. Brighty (*Commercial*).

Junior Attachés, K. O. Kenneth; A. H. B. Tyrell; R. O. Barnes.

Archivist, D. H. Hugill.

BRITISH CONSULAR OFFICES.

There are British Consular Offices at *Brussels*, *Antwerp* and *Ostend*.

BRITISH COUNCIL.

23 Avenue Marnix, Brussels.

Representative, M. H. Cardiff, O.B.E

BRITISH CHAMBER OF COMMERCE, 204 Rue Royale, Brussels.

BHUTAN

Bhutan (area, about 18,000 sq. miles; pop. about 700,000, mainly Buddhists) is an independent State bounded on the North and East by Tibet, on the South by India, and on the West by Sikkim, which is now a Protectorate of the Republic of India. In 1949, a treaty was concluded with the Government of India under which the Kingdom of Bhutan agreed to be guided by the Government of India in regard to its external relations, but it still retains complete independence, issues its own passports and has diplomatic representatives in Tibet as well as in India. It also receives from the Government of India an annual payment of about £35,000 as compensation for portions of its territory annexed by the British Government in India in 1864. The principal cottage industries are weaving, metal works and crafts, and the main exports are timber, rice and wheat. The first motor road in Bhutan, 107 miles long, from Paro, the winter capital, to Phuntsholing in W. Bengal, was completed in February, 1962. The road took 2 years to build and reaches a height of 8,500 feet above sea level. Three other roads linking Bhutan with India are under construction or projected. The present Ruler is Maharaja Jigme Dorji Wangchuk who was born in 1929 and succeeded his father in March, 1952. The Government of India has a diplomatic representative whose headquarters are situated at Gangtok, capital of the neighbouring State of Sikkim.

CAPITAL, Punakha.

BOKHARA. *See* U.S.S.R.

BOLIVIA

(República de Bolivia)

President of the Republic, Señor Victor Paz Estenssoro, *assumed office*, August 6, 1960.

EMBASSY IN LONDON.

106 Eaton Square, S.W.1

[Belgravia: 4248]

Ambassador, His Excellency Don Manuel Barrau Pelaez (1959).

Consulate, 106 Eccleston Mews, S.W.1.

Hon. Consul, Reginald Bird.

There are Bolivian Consular Offices in *Liverpool*, *Birmingham*, *Hull*, *Cardiff* and *Glasgow*.

The Republic of Bolivia extends between lat. 10° and 23° S. and long. 57° 30′ and 69° 45′ W., and its area is estimated at 415,000 square miles with an estimated population (1960) of 3,462,002. The Republic derives its name from its liberator, Simon Bolivar (born 1783, died 1830).

The executive power is vested in a President elected for 4 years by direct popular vote. Under the 1961 Constitution, a President may be re-elected for a second term; after this 4 years must elapse before he is again eligible for election. A Vice-President is elected for 4 years and may be re-elected for a second term or as President; after a total of two terms, 4 years must elapse before he is again eligible for election. Since 1952 the National Revolutionary Movement has been in power. Dr. Paz was President from 1952 to 1956, Dr. Hernan Siles Zuazo from 1956 to 1960 and Dr. Paz was re-elected in 1960.

The National Congress consists of a Senate of 27 members elected for 6 years, with one-third renewable every two years and a Chamber of Deputies of 68 members elected for four years, one-half renewable every two years.

The chief topographical feature is the great central plateau (65,000 square miles) over 500 miles in length, at an average altitude of 12,500 feet above sea level, between the two great chains of the Andes, which traverse the country from south to north, and contain, in Illampu, Illimani, and Sajama, three of the highest peaks of the western hemisphere. The total length of the navigable streams is about 12,000 miles, the principal rivers being the Itenes, Beni, Mamore, and Madre de Dios.

Mining, petroleum and agriculture are the principal industries. The ancient silver mines of Potosi are now worked chiefly for tin, but gold, partly dug and partly washed, is obtained on the Eastern Cordillera of the Andes; the tin output is, after that of Malaya, the largest in the world, 20,735 metric tons being exported in 1961: copper, antimony, lead, zinc, asbestos, wolfram, bismuth, salt and sulphur are found, and petroleum is also produced. The Republic has been self-supporting in most petroleum products since January, 1954, and crude petroleum exports in 1961 to neighbouring countries, mainly Argentina, were valued at over $U.S. 2,138,000. Its agricultural produce consists chiefly of rice, barley, oats, sugar-cane, maize, cotton, indigo, rubber, cacao, potatoes, cinchona bark, medicinal herbs, brazil nuts, &c. Manufactures are in a very undeveloped state, but the Government plans to encourage their development under a policy of "diversification of the economy". There are 1,454 miles of railways in operation. New lines are under construction from Corumbá to Santa Cruz (405 miles) and from Yacuiba to Santa Cruz (312), both of which are virtually completed. Work on a third new line, from Cochabamba to Santa Cruz, was suspended some years ago. Another railway project from La Paz to Coroico is partially completed. There are about 10,950 miles of telegraphs, and wireless services between Riberalta, La Paz, Cobija, Capitandi (Chaco). There is direct railway communication to the sea at Antofagasta (32 hours), Arica (10 hours), and Mollendo (2 days), and also to Buenos Aires (3½ days); branch lines run from Oruro to Cochabamba, and from Rio Mulato to Potosi, and from Potosi to Sucre, the legal capital. The principal railway line is the Antofagasta and Bolivia railroad (749 miles), which is under British administration on behalf of the Bolivian Government. Communication with Peru is effected by rail to Guaqui and thence by steamer across Lake Titicaca to the railroad at Puno.

Commercial Aviation in Bolivia is conducted by Pan American-Grace Airways and Braniff International Airways (American) and Lloyd Aereo Boliviano (Bolivian), the two former providing international connections with U.S.A., West coast South American countries, Canal Zone, Brazil and Argentina; Lloyd Aereo Boliviano, maintaining a service to Lima and Buenos Aires and attending to local flights, links La Paz with Oruro, Cochabamba, Santa Cruz and Trinidad, &c., and connects with LAN of Chile, Argentine Airlines and Cruzeiro do Sul of Brazil. There is a new line from La Paz to Asuncion and Buenos Aires, also operated by Lloyd Aereo Boliviano.

Bolivia is without a sea-coast, having been deprived of the ports of Tocopilla, Cobija, Mejillones and Antofagasta by the "Pacific War" of 1879–1882.

Language and Literature.—The official language of the country is Spanish, but the Indian inhabitants (about two-thirds of the population) speak either Quechua or Aymará, the two races being more or less equal in numbers.

The Roman Catholic religion was disestablished in 1961 but relations between it and the State are good. Elementary education is compulsory and free and there are secondary schools in urban centres. The high percentage of illiterates is yielding to modern methods; all illiterates under 21 are nominally compelled to attend school. Provision is also made for higher education; in addition to St. Francisco Xavier's University at Sucre, founded in 1624, there are seven other universities, the largest being the University of San Andres at La Paz. Bolivian literature has not yet produced authors of world-wide renown. There are seven principal daily newspapers in Bolivia, with an estimated daily circulation of 80,000–100,000.

FINANCE.

The 1962 figure for estimated revenue and expenditure is *Bs.* 464,000,000,000.

On December 15, 1956, the *Boliviano* was made freely convertible for all purposes without restriction and from Jan. 1, 1963, the *Boliviano* is replaced by the *Péso Boliviano* at the rate of *Bs.* 1,000 = *Peso* 1 ($b.1). (*See also* p. 83.)

Trade with U.K.

	1961	1962
Imports from U.K.	£1,081,095	£1,579,633
Exports to U.K...	12,511,837	12,556,509

The principal exports are tin (almost all of which is exported to the U.K.), lead and antimony ores, silver, copper, wolfram, zinc, gold, nuts, hides and skins, vicuña wool and coffee; Bolivia also ranks as the second rubber-exporting country in South America after Brazil. The chief imports are wheat and flour, sugar, iron and steel products, machinery, vehicles and textiles.

SEAT OF GOVERNMENT, La Paz. Population (estimated 1960) 347,394. Other large centres are Cochabamba (90,037), Oruro (81,553), Santa Cruz (66,548), Sucre, the legal capital and seat of the judiciary (60,092), Potosi (53,528), and Tarija (20,127).

FLAG: Three horizontal bands; Red, yellow, green; device on yellow band.

BRITISH EMBASSY.

(2732, 2740 and 2754 Avenida Arce, La Paz.)

British Ambassador, His Excellency Leonard Gibson Holliday, C.M.G. (1960)..............£4,115
1st Secretary and Consul, E. A. W. Bullock.
Air Attaché, Group Capt. J. F. C. Melrose, D.F.C. (*resident in Lima, Peru*).
1st Secretary (Labour), F. E. Sharples.
2nd Secretary (Commercial), S. W. Martin.
Vice-Consul, D. F. C. Ridgway.

BRITISH CONSULAR OFFICES.

There are British Consular Offices at *La Paz* and *Cochabamba*.

BRAZIL

(República dos Estados Unidos do Brasil.)

President, Sr. João Belchior Marques Goulart, *assumed office* Sept., 1961.

CABINET
(June 20, 1963)

Foreign Affairs, Dr. Evandro Lins e Silva.
Finance, Prof. Carlos Alberto de Carvalho Pinto.
Justice and Interior, Sr. Abelardo Araújo Jurema (*P.S.D.*)
Industry and Commerce, Sr. Egydio Michaelsen (*P.T.B.*)
Mines and Energy, Sr. Antônio Ferreira de Oliveira Brito (*P.S.D.*).
Transport and Public Works, Sr. Espidito Machado Ponte (*P.S.D.*).
Agriculture, Sr. Oswaldo Cavalcanti Costa Lima Filho (*P.T.B.*)
Labour and Social Security, Sr. Amaury de Oliveira e Silva (*P.T.B.*).
Education and Culture, Sr. Paulo de Tarso Santos (*P.D.C.*).
Health, Dr. Wilson Fadul (*P.T.B.*).
War, Gen. Jair Dantas Ribeiro.
Air Force, Lt.-Gen. Anísio Botelho.
Navy, Adm. Sylvio Borges de Souza Motta.
Administrative Reforms, Sr. Ernani do Amaral Peixoto (*P.S.D.*).
Chiefs of President's Household, Prof. Darcy Ribeiro (*Civil*); Col. João Sarmento (*Military*).

P.S.D.=Social Democrat; *P.T.B.*=Labour; *P.D.C.*=Christian Democrat.

BRAZILIAN EMBASSY IN LONDON.
54 Mount Street, W.1.
[Mayfair: 0155]

Ambassador, His Excellency Senhor José Cochrane de Alencar (1961).
Minister-Counsellor, Senhor G. E. Nascimento e Silva.
Minister for Economic Affairs, Sr. Miguel Franchini-Netto.
Naval and Military Attaché, Capt. Alexandrino Ramos de Alencar.
First Secretary, Senhor F. J. Novaes Coelho.
Second Secretaries, Sr. Guilherme Weinschenck; Sr. R. F. Leite Ribeiro; Sr. L. P. Lindenberg Sette; Sr. Luiz Carlos Barreto Thedim; Sr. Francesco Thompson Flôres.
Commercial Attaché, Sr. Antonio Marinho.

CONSULATE-GENERAL IN LONDON.

Consul-General, Senhora Beata Vettori.
Consul, Senhor Heitor Soares de Moura.

There are also Brazilian Consular offices at *Liverpool*, *Newcastle-on-Tyne*, *Southampton*, *Cardiff* and *Glasgow*.

POSITION AND EXTENT.

Brazil, the most extensive State of South America, discovered in 1500 by Pedro Alvares Cabral, Portuguese navigator, is bounded on the north by the Atlantic Ocean, the Guianas, Colombia and Venezuela; on the west by Peru, Bolivia, Paraguay, and Argentina; on the south by Uruguay; and on the east by the Atlantic Ocean. Brazil extends between lat. 5° 16′ N. and 33° 45′ S. and long. 34° 45′ and 73° 59′ 22″ W., being 2,685 miles from north to south, and 2,690 from west to east, with a coast-line on the Atlantic of 4,604 miles. The Republic comprises an area of 3,289,440 square miles with a population (estimated December, 1960) of 66,302,000.

The northern States of Amazonas and Pará are mainly wide, low-lying, forest-clad plains. The central state of the Mato Grosso is principally plateau land and the eastern and southern States are traversed by successive mountain ranges interspersed with fertile valleys. The principal ranges are *Serra do Mar* in São Paulo; the *Serra Geral* (Caparao 9,393 feet) between Minas Gerais and Espirito Santo, the *Serra da Mantiqueira* (Itatiaia, 9,163 feet), and the *Serra do Espinhaço* (Itacolumi, 5,748 feet), in the south-east of Minas Gerais; the *Serra do Paraná*, between Goiás and Minas Gerais, the *Serra dos Aimorés*, which divide Espirito Santo from Minas Gerais; and the *Serra do Gurgueia*, *Branca* and *Araripe*, which envelop Piaui.

Brazil is unequalled for its rivers. The River *Amazon* has tributaries which are themselves great rivers, and flows from the Peruvian Andes to the Atlantic, with a total length of some 4,000 miles. Its principal northern tributaries are the *Rio Branco*, *Rio Negro*, and *Japurá*; its southern tributaries are the *Juruá*, *Purus*, *Madeira* and *Tapajós*, while the *Xingú* meets it within 200 miles of its outflow into the Atlantic. The *Tocantins* and *Araguaia* flow northwards from the Plateau of Mato Grosso and the mountains of Goiás to the Gulf of Pará. The *Parnaiba* flows from the encircling mountains of Piaui into the Atlantic. The *São Francisco* rises in the South of Minas Gerais and traverses Bahia on its way to the eastern coast, between Alagoas and Sergipe. The *Paraguai*, rising in the south-west of Mato Grosso, flows through Paraguay to its confluence with the *Paraná*, which rises in the mountains of that name and divides Brazil from Paraguay. On the *Iguaçú* or *Iguassú*, which unites with the Upper Parana at the Brazil-Argentine-Paraguay boundary, are the majestic *Falls of the Iguassu* (200 ft.), and on the *São Francisco* are the no less famous falls of *Paulo Afonso* (260 ft.).

Government.—Brazil was colonized by Portugal in the early part of the sixteenth century, and in 1822 became an independent empire under Dom Pedro, son of the refugee King João VI. of Portugal. On Nov. 15, 1889, Dom Pedro II., second of the line, was dethroned and a republic was proclaimed. Constitutional Government, under the Constitution of 1891, was suspended after the revolution of 1930. Dr. Getulio Vargas, who had been Chief of the Provisional Government since 1930, was elected President and assumed office on July 20, 1934. By a *coup d'état* of Nov. 10, 1937, he closed Congress, abolished the old political parties and issued a new Constitution. On Sept. 18, 1946, the *Estado Novo* established by Vargas was superseded by a new constitution, limiting the Presidential term to 5 years (in place of 7) and restoring a Congress of two chambers. In October, 1960, elections took place in which Sr. Jânio Quadros was elected President to succeed Dr. Kubitschek. Sr. Quadros resigned in August, 1961, and was succeeded by the Vice-President, Sr. Goulart.

As a result of a referendum held on Jan. 6, 1963, the *Ato Adicional* instituting the office of Prime Minister was revoked. President Goulart reorganized his Cabinet between June 14–20, 1963, associating the Christian Democrats with the Administration to obtain wider political support for his fiscal reform programme and plans for economic development.

Production.—There are large and valuable mineral deposits including among others, iron ore (hematite), manganese, bauxite, beryllium, chrome, nickel, tungsten, cassiterite, lead, gold, monazite (containing rare earths and thorium) and zirconium. Diamonds and precious and semi-precious stones are also found. The mineral wealth is still exploited to only a very limited extent. Production is increasing, but is capable of great further development. The iron ore deposits are particularly rich. The estimated production of iron ore in 1962 was 9,782,000 metric tons. Oil production in 1962 was 33,401,000 barrels. Coal production in 1962 was estimated at 2,390,000 metric tons. 2,335,000 metric tons of steel ingots and 101,036,000 barrels of refined petroleum products were produced in 1962. Licences for new foreign investments amounting to U.S.$20,263,000 were issued in 1962 bringing the total value of licences issued since 1955 to U.S. $510,063,000. Investment has been particularly marked in the motor, tractor, shipbuilding and engineering industries.

Brazil's agricultural and vegetable produce is abundant, coffee, cotton, maize, sugar, cocoa, rice, citrus fruits and bananas being the main agricultural products, and rubber, carnauba wax, maté, jute and other fibres being the main vegetable extracts. Timber is also important.

The main exports of agricultural produce in 1962 were:

	Metric Tons	Value $U.S.
Coffee	982,506	642,671,000
Cotton	215,915	112,166,000
Cocoa beans.....	55,341	24,227,000

Coffee is grown mainly in the States of São Paulo and Paraná and to a lesser extent in Minas Gerais and Espirito Santo.

Defence.—The peace-time strength of the Army is 120,000, with an immediate reserve of 250,000. The Navy consists of 1 aircraft carrier, 2 cruisers, 19 destroyers and escorts, 11 corvettes, 3 submarines, 15 submarine chasers, 1 sail training ship, 3 ocean-going tugs, 3 survey vessels, 2 river monitors and various auxiliaries. The strength of the Navy is about 30,000 all ranks. The Air Force is the largest in South America, with 650 aircraft and a strength of 35,000 all ranks.

Education.—*Primary* education is carried out by State governments and municipalities and private initiative, in some cases with a Federal subsidy. In 1958 there were 82,953 primary schools (not including kindergartens) with an enrolment at the beginning of the school year (March) of 5,775,000 pupils. There were 182,602 teachers in the primary schools.

Secondary education is carried out by the Federal Government, State and Municipal Governments and by private schools. In 1959, there were 3,435 schools and 794,690 pupils. Other establishments classified at an intermediate level are: 1,256 commercial schools with an enrolment of 171,994 pupils; 1,149 normal schools with 81,526 scholars; 420 industrial training schools with 22,312 pupils; 88 agricultural schools with 5,679 students.

A total of 89,586 students attended 20 Federal and State Universities and other establishments offering courses at a university level in 1959. There were 544 faculties in all the universities of Brazil, and also 502 isolated faculties. Of this total (1,046), there were 331 federal, 138 State, 23 municipal and 554 private faculties.

Language and Literature.—Portuguese is the language of the country, but Italian, Spanish, German, Japanese and Arabic are spoken by immigrant minorities, and newspapers of considerable circulation are produced in those languages. English and French are currently spoken by educated Brazilians.

Until the second quarter of the nineteenth century Brazilian literature was dominated by Portugal. French influence is traceable for the next half century, since when a national school has come into existence and there are many modern authors of high standing. Public libraries have been established in urban centres and there is a flourishing national press with widely circulated daily and weekly newspapers; 25 daily newspapers are published at Rio de Janeiro.

Communications.—In 1961 there were about 37,287 kilometres of railways in service, largely of 1 metre gauge, but including some 4,000 kilometres of other gauges. Traffic carried in 1961 was—Passengers, 456,563,000; Freight, 41,125,000 metric tons; Livestock, 4,092,000 head. During 1962 the ports of Rio de Janeiro and Santos together were used by 7,247 vessels representing 28,612,000 registered tons.

Nine foreign airlines, Air France, B.O.A.C., SAS, KLM, Aerolinas Argentinas, Swissair, Iberia, Alitalia and Lufthansa (in addition to Panir do Brasil) operate services between Brazil and Europe. Pan American World Airways, Braniff and Varig operate services between Brazil and U.S.A., and there are connections with all Latin American countries. Eight major domestic airlines, as well as the Brazilian Air Force, maintain services throughout the country. During 1962, 5,471,878 passengers passed through Brazilian airports; 39,736 tons of cargo were received and 46,328 despatched. The airports of Rio de Janeiro and São Paulo alone recorded 128,940 aircraft arrivals and departures in 1962.

Postal facilities in Brazil include approximately 5,750 post offices and 50,000 miles of telegraph. In 1959, 874,000 telephones were in use, of which a large proportion are dial operated.

FINANCE.

	1961 (millions of Cruzeiros)	1962* (millions of Cruzeiros)
Revenue........	511,829,000	737,348,005
Expenditure.....	726,694,000	1,024,527,628

*Estimated

The total external debt of Brazil on December 31, 1962, was U.S.$2,988,415,000. The total internal debt of the Union in 1962 amounted to *Crs*.31,293,545,000; States (1961) *Crs*.43,019,070,000. The average for the year 1962 of the Bank of Brazil's free selling rate of exchange was *Crs*. 386·35 to $U.S. 1 or *Crs*.1,083·06 to £1.

TRADE (1962)

Total Imports.............	$U.S.1,475,047,000*
Total Exports..............	$U.S.1,214,184,000*

*Converted at official exchange rate.

Trade with U.K.

	1961	1962
Imports from U.K...	£16,092,504	£16,547,107
Exports to U.K.....	29 512,786	25 990,950

The principal imports are fuel oils, machinery, wheat, chemicals, industrial raw materials and newsprint. The principal exports are coffee (about 70 per cent. of the total value of exports), cocoa, timber, iron ore, sugar, fruit, tobacco, wax, hides and skins and fibre.

CAPITAL.—Brasilia (inaugurated on April 21 1960). Population (estimated 1960), 142,000. Other important centres are São Paulo 3,850,000; the former capital ΨRio de Janeiro, with a population (est. 1960) of 3,288,000; ΨRecife (Pernambuco) 784,000; ΨSalvador (Bahia) 656,000; ΨPorto Alegre (Rio Grande do Sul) 643,000; ΨBelo Horizonte (Minas Gerais) 600,000; ΨFortaleza (Ceará) 514,000; Curitiba (Paraná) 362,000; ΨNiteroi (Rio de Janeiro) 245,000.

FLAG.—Green, with yellow lozenge in centre; blue sphere with white band and stars in centre of lozenge.

BRITISH EMBASSY.
Rio de Janeiro

Residence, Rua São Clemente 360.
Chancery, Praia do Flamengo 284, 2° andar.
Ambassador Extraordinary and Plenipotentiary, His Excellency Sir Leslie Alfred Charles Fry, K.C.M.G., O.B.E. (1963)...................... £5,015

Minister (Commercial), J. H. Wardle-Smith, C.M.G.
Counsellor, R. A. Burroughs.
1st Secretaries, C. de Salis; J. A. L. Morgan (*Commercial*); R. L. Morris (*Labour*); G. S. L. Cook (*Information*); P. I. Lake (*Consular*); R. J. D. Evans (*Information*).
2nd Secretaries, T. G. Simon (*Commercial*); Miss Z. M. Hawson (*Consular*).
3rd Secretary, D. S. Ruxton.
Naval, Military and Air Attaché, Capt J. T. Checketts, R.N.

BRITISH CONSULAR OFFICES.

There are British Consular Offices at *Rio de Janeiro, São Paulo, Belém (Para), Belo Horizonte, Vitoria, Salvador (Bahia), Manaus, Fortaleza, Porto Alegre, Rio Grande, Curitiba, Santos* and *Recife*.

BRITISH COUNCIL.—*Representative of the British Council in Brazil*, J. A. Cayton, O.B.E., Avenida Portugal, 360, Rio de Janeiro.

BRITISH CHAMBER OF COMMERCE IN BRAZIL, Rua da Conceição 105, 22nd Floor, Caixa Postal 56, Rio de Janeiro.

BRITISH AND COMMONWEALTH CHAMBER OF COMMERCE IN SÃO PAULO, Rua Barão de Itapetininga 275, Caixa Postal 1621, São Paulo. (Correspondents at *Santos* and *Porto Alegre*.)

Rio de Janeiro, 5,750 miles distant from London; transit, 15 days.

BULGARIA

(Bulgariya.)

President of the Presidium of the National Assembly, Dimiter Ganev.

COUNCIL OF MINISTERS (1962)

President, Todor Zhivkov.
First Vice-Presidents, Georgi Traikov; Raiko Damyanov.
Vice-Presidents, Ivan Mihailov (*Army General*); Stanko Todorov; Tano Zolov; Pencho Kudabinski.
Minister of Education and Culture, Gancho Ganchev.
National Defence, Dobri Dzhurov (*Army General*).
Internal Trade, Peko Takov.
Foreign Trade, Ivan Budinov.
Transport and Communications, M. Kudabinski.
Foreign Affairs, Ivan Bazhev.
Interior, Diko Dikov.
Farm Production, Marin Vachkóv.
Health and Social Welfare, Dr. Kiryl Ignatov.
Finance, Dimiter Popov.
Justice, Peter Tanchev.
Chairman of the State Planning Committee, Apostol Pashev.
Chairman of the Committee for Party and State Control, Boris Velchev.
Industry, Atanas Dimitrov.
Labour and Prices, Stoyan Tonchev.
Technical Progress, Nacho Papazov.
Construction, Marin Grashnov.

LEGATION AND CONSULATE IN LONDON.
12 Queen's Gate Gardens, S.W.7.
[Knightsbridge: 9400]

Minister, His Excellency Radenko Grigorov (1962).

The Republic of Bulgaria is bounded on the north by Roumania, on the west by Yugoslavia, on the east by the Black Sea, and on the south by Greece and Turkey. The total area is approximately 43,000 square miles, with a population (Census of 1959) of 7,797,800. The largest religion of the Bulgarians is the Eastern Orthodox Church. For secular purposes the Gregorian (Western) Calendar is in use.

A Principality of Bulgaria was created by the *Treaty of Berlin* (July 13, 1878) and in 1885 Eastern Roumelia was added to the newly-created principality. In 1908 the country was declared to be an independent kingdom, the area at that date being 37,202 square miles, with a population of 4,337,500. In 1912–13 a successful war of the *Balkan League* against Turkey increased the size of the kingdom, but in August, 1913, a short campaign against the remaining members of the League reduced the acquired area, and led to the surrender of Southern Dobrudja to Roumania. On Oct. 12, 1915, Bulgaria entered the War on the side of the Central Powers by declaring war on Serbia. She thus became involved in the defeats of 1918, and on Sept. 29, 1918, made an unconditional surrender to the Allied Powers. On Nov. 29, 1919, she signed the *Treaty of Neuilly*, which ceded to the Allies her Thracian territories (later handed over to Greece) and some territory on the western frontier to Yugoslavia.

Nazi troops entered the country on March 3, 1941, and occupied Black Sea ports, but Bulgaria was not officially at war with the Soviet Union. On August 26, 1944, the government declared Bulgaria to be "neutral in the Russo-German war" and delegates to Cairo sought terms of peace from Great Britain and the United States. The Soviet Union refused to recognize the so-called "neutrality" and called upon Bulgaria to declare war against Germany, and no satisfactory reply being received on Sept. 5, 1944, the U.S.S.R. declared war on Bulgaria. Bulgaria then asked for an armistice and on Sept. 7 declared war on Germany, hostilities with U.S.S.R. ending on Sept. 10. The armistice with the Allies was signed in Moscow, Oct. 28. On Sept. 9 a *coup d'état* gave power to the Fatherland Front, a coalition of Communists, Agrarians, Social Democrats and Republican officers and intellectuals. In August, 1945, the main body of Agrarians and Social Democrats left the Government. The Peace Treaty with Bulgaria was signed on Feb. 22, 1947, and came into force on Sept. 15, 1947. It recognized the return of Southern Dobrudja to Bulgaria.

GOVERNMENT.—On Sept. 8, 1946, a referendum was held, at which, according to the published results, an overwhelming majority declared for the abolition of the Monarchy and the setting up of a Republic. On Oct. 27, a general election to a Grand National Assembly (with power to make a constitution) was held; the Opposition won 101 seats out of 465. According to the present Constitution the legislature is a single chamber National Assembly or *Subranie* elected by adult suffrage on the basis of one deputy to every 25,000 inhabitants for a maximum term of four years. The opposition Agrarian Party was suppressed on Aug. 24, 1947, following the pronouncement of the death sentence on its leader, Nikola Petkov. The opposition newspapers ceased to appear after April, 1947. Nine opposition Social Democrats continued to sit in the National Assembly until they were placed under restraint in July, 1948. The Government Social Democratic Party fused with the Workers' (Communist) Party on Aug. 11, 1948.

Bulgaria linked herself to the other countries of Eastern Europe by a series of treaties of friendship, collaboration and mutual aid, the first of which was signed with Yugoslavia on November 27, 1947. This was followed by similar treaties with Roumania (January 16, 1948), the Soviet Union (March 18), Czechoslovakia (April 26), Poland (May 30) and Hungary (July 6). The treaty with Yugoslavia was abrogated in 1949.

PRODUCTION.—Bulgaria is essentially an agricultural country, but is engaged upon an elaborate programme of industrialization. Over 90 per cent. of the country's agriculture has been collectivized, and a much smaller proportion mechanized. The principal crops are wheat, maize, beet, tomatoes, tobacco, oleaginous seeds, fruit, vegetables and cotton. The live-stock includes sheep, goats, cattle, pigs, horses, asses, mules and water buffaloes.

In 1961 electricity generating capacity totalled 5,406 million kWh., compared with 4,675 million kWh. in 1960. Much of this increase is from hydro-electric stations. The considerable progress which has been made in the exploitation of Bulgaria's mineral resources, is shown by the following production figures:—

	Production 1961	Percentage increase over 1960
Coal	18,600,000	109
Lead	41,000	101
Zinc	22,000	131
Copper concentrate (20 per cent. copper base)	82,000	115
Steel	340,000	134

There are other mineral deposits of varying importance, but no production figures are available. There are also a number of thermal and mineral springs, several of which have been modernized. Bulgaria's newly acquired heavy industry includes an iron and steel works which inaugurated its first blast furnace in 1957, a nitrogenous fertilizer plant and other chemical works.

DEFENCE.—Under the Peace Treaty signed between Bulgaria and the Allies, the Bulgarian Army is limited to 55,000 men, but it is believed at present to be at least 200,000 strong.

EDUCATION.—Free basic education is compulsory for children from 7 to 15 years inclusive. The Bulgarian educational system was reorganized on Soviet lines in September, 1950, and in 1960–61 there were 2,408 elementary schools, 93 secondary schools, 3,060 combined elementary and secondary schools, 144 grammar schools (gymnasia), 172 schools for all levels and 231 vocational training schools; there were 1,306,327 pupils and 56,414 teachers.

There are 20 universities (known as Higher Educational Establishments and including universities proper and Academies of Music, Science, etc.), including those of Sofia, Plovdiv and Varna. In 1960–61 there were stated to be 54,965 students at higher educational establishments.

LANGUAGE AND LITERATURE.—Bulgarian is a Southern Slavonic tongue, closely allied to Russian (*see* U.S.S.R.) with local admixtures of modern Greek, Albanian and Turkish words. There is a modern literature, chiefly educational and popular. The alphabet is Cyrillic, as in Russia. In 1960 there were 6 daily newspapers in Sofia.

FINANCE.—It is estimated that budget revenue and expenditure in 1963 were roughly balanced at about *leva* 37,500,000,000. Currency of Bulgaria is the *lev*, the rate of exchange in 1963 being approximately *leva* 3·29=£1 (see also p. 83.)

TRADE.

The principal imports are wool, industrial and agricultural machinery, metals, tools, chemicals, dyestuffs, drugs, rubber, paper. The principal exports are cereals, tobacco, fruit, vegetables, oil seeds, oils, fats, textiles, eggs, chemicals, essential oils including attar of roses, hardwoods, non-ferrous metals, and livestock. In 1960, 82 per cent. of Bulgaria's foreign trade was with the Soviet bloc, including 54 per cent. with the Soviet Union.

Trade with U.K.

	1961	1962
Imports from U.K.	£1,804,532	£1,218,433
Exports to U.K.	3,265,240	3,338,854

CAPITAL, Sofia. Pop. (1956), 725,756, at the foot of the Vitosha Range, the capital and commercial centre, is on the main railway line to Istanbul, 338 miles from the Black Sea port of ΨVarna (119,769) and 125 miles from Lom (23,015), on the Danube; ΨBurgas (72,795) is also a Black Sea Port, those on the Danube being ΨRusé (83,472), ΨSvishtov (18,537), ΨVidin (23,984). Other important trading and industrial centres are Plovdiv (162,518) and Pleven (57,758).

FLAG.—3 horizontal bands, white, green, red; national emblem on white stripe near hoist.

BRITISH LEGATION.

Residence, 69 Boulevard Tolbuhin, Sofia.

British Minister, His Excellency William Harpham, C.M.G., O.B.E. (1963) £4,115

1st Secretary and Consul, M. E. Heath.

Military Attaché, Col. J. B. Sanderson.

2nd Secretary (Consular and Commercial), Miss D. G. Hammond.

BURMA

(Republic of the Union of Burma.)

Revolutionary Government

Chairman and Member for Defence, National Planning, Finance, Judicial Affairs, General Ne Win.

BURMESE EMBASSY AND CONSULATE

19A Charles St., Berkeley Square, W.1.

Ambassador, His Excellency U Hla Maung (1961).

Consul-General, Khin Maung.

Area and Population.—Burma forms the western portion of the Indo-Chinese district of the continent of Asia, lying between 9° 58′ and 28° N. latitude and 92° 11′ and 101° 9′ E. longitude, with an extreme length of approximately 1,200 miles and an extreme width of 575 miles. It has a sea coast on the Bay of Bengal to the south and west and a frontier with Pakistan and India to the north-west; in the north and east the frontier with China was determined by a treaty with the People's Republic in October, 1960, and has since been demarcated; there is a short frontier with Laos in the east, while the long finger of Tenasserim stretches southward along the west coast of the Malay Peninsula, forming a frontier with Thailand to the east. The total area of the Union is about 262,000 square miles, with an officially estimated population of 21,526,824—about 82 persons to the square mile.

Political Divisions.—The Union of Burma comprises Burma proper (at about 145,000 sq. miles by far the largest unit), administered direct by the Central Government, and also the Shan State (about 57,500 sq. miles), Kachin State (about 29,500 sq. miles), Karen State (about 11,600 sq. miles) and Kayah State (about 4,600 sq. miles) each with their own State Governments. There is also the Special Division of the Chins (about 14,000 sq. miles).

Physical Features.—Burma falls into four natural divisions, Arakan (with the Chin Hills region), the Irrawaddy basin, the old Province of Tenasserim, including the Salween basin and extending southwards to the Burma-Siam peninsula, and the elevated plateau on the east made up of the Shan States. Mountains enclose Burma on three sides, the highest point being Hka-kabo Razi (19,296 ft.) in the northern Kachin hills. Mt. Popa, 4,981 ft., in the Myingyan district is an extinct volcano and a well-known landmark in Central Burma. The principal river systems are the Kaladan-Lemro in Arakan, the Irrawaddy-Chindwin and the Sittang in Central Burma, and the Salween which flows through the Shan Plateau.

Races, Language and Religions.—The indigenous inhabitants who entered Burma from the north and east are of similar racial types and speak languages of the Tibeto-Burman, Mon-Khmer and Tai groups. The three important non-indigenous elements are Indians and Pakistanis (about 800,000), Chinese (about 300,000), with Europeans and Anglo-Burmans numbering less than 10,000. Burmese is the official language, but minority languages include Shan, Karen, Chin, and the various Kachin dialects. English is still spoken in educated circles in Rangoon and elsewhere. Buddhism is the religion of 85 per cent. of the people, with 5 per cent. Animists, 4 per cent. Moslems, 4 per cent. Hindus and rather less than 3 per cent. Christians.

Government.—Burma became an independent republic outside the British Commonwealth on January 4, 1948. It was a bicameral parliamentary democracy with an elected Head of State. For the first ten years of independence the ruling party was the Anti-Fascist People's Freedom League under the Leadership of U Nu. After a split in the A.F.P.F.L. in 1958, General Ne Win and his Caretaker Government were invited to take office. General Elections in February, 1960, resulted in a victory for U Nu's new party, The Union Party (161 out of 250 seats).

On March 2, 1962, the army staged a *coup d'etat*, abolished parliament, suspended the Constitution and imprisoned most of the Cabinet. The Revolutionary Council of senior officers under General Ne Win have since taken a number of measures to establish state socialism in Burma in line with the policy statement "The Burmese Way to Socialism". A new political party is projected to take over the government under a one-party system. The problem of insurgency (minority and Communist groups) remains an important one for the country.

Education.—The literacy rate is high compared with other Asiatic countries, there is no caste system and woman engage freely in social intercourse and play an important part in agriculture and retail trade.

There are four Universities: The University of Rangoon, founded in 1920; the University of Mandalay, formerly an Intermediate College, granted university status in 1958; and the universities of Moulmein and Bassein, formerly intermediate colleges affiliated to Rangoon University, granted university status in 1963. Rangoon University has two attached medical colleges, a veterinary college and an institute of technology. Mandalay has an attached medical college. Affiliated to Mandalay University are three intermediate colleges at Taunggyi, Magwe and Myitkyina. The intermediate college at Kyaukpyu, which was affiliated to Rangoon University, was closed down in 1963.

There are state teachers training colleges in Rangoon and Mandalay, which train both junior assistant and primary assistant teachers, and four state teachers training institutes at Kyaukpyu, Bassein, Moulmein and Meiktila, which train primary assistant teachers only. The Faculty of Education in Rangoon University trains senior assistant teachers and awards degrees. There are two Government technical institutes at Insein (near Rangoon) and Mandalay and Government technical high schools at Rangoon and Mandalay. The Government is now reorganizing the educational system.

Finance.—The chief sources of revenue are profits on state trading, income-tax, customs duties, commercial taxes and excise duties; the chief heads of expenditure are general administration, defence, education, police and development. The budget estimates for 1962–63 were (in terms of sterling): receipts £118,170,000; expenditure £125,510,000.

Production, Industry and Commerce.—Three-quarters of the population depend on agriculture; the chief products are rice, oilseeds (sesamum and groundnut), maize, millet, cotton, beans, wheat and grain. Rice is the mainstay of Burma's economy; before the war Burma was the world's largest exporter of rice, her total production of over 7,000,000 tons a year being derived from 12,000,000 acres or 70 per cent. of the country's total cropped area. The pre-war yearly average of rice exports was over 3,000,000 tons. In 1962 exports were 1,720,364 tons. The net area sown to all crops in 1961–62 was 18,660,000 acres and reserved forests covered 22,264,960 acres. The principal export after rice is teak, of which some 200,000 tons were exported annually before the war. The 1962 figure was 119,019 tons. Burma is rich in minerals, including petroleum, lead, silver, tungsten, zinc, tin, wolfram and gemstones. Of these, petroleum is the most important. Production in 1962 was 153,389,000 gallons. There is a refinery at the main oilfield, Chauk, and an output of 685,000 gallons per day is planned for the Syriam refinery near Rangoon. Their combined output of petroleum products is sufficient for most of Burma's needs. The production and distribution of petroleum and the importation of oil products is a monopoly of the Burma Oil Company (1954), Ltd., which is now fully owned by the Government of Burma.

Under the Government's development plan, a steel rolling mill, a jute bag and twine mill, two cotton spinning and weaving mills, a pharmaceutical plant, a large hydro-electric scheme and three sugar factories are in production. Other industrial projects are being considered in connection with the £30,000,000 loan from the Chinese Communist Government and a West German loan of £3,150,000. Japanese reparations are to be increased by £50,000,000 beginning in 1965, together with an additional £10,700,000 in commercial loans at 6 per cent. interest.

Trade with U.K.

	1961	1962
Imports from U.K.	£12,128,824	£11,828,042
Exports to U.K.	9,994,398	11,277,914

Burma joined the Colombo Plan in 1952 and is now receiving important assistance from member countries.

Communications.—The Irrawaddy and its chief tributary, the Chindwin, form important waterways, the main stream being navigable beyond Bhamo (900 miles from its mouth) and carrying much traffic.

Ψ The chief seaports are Rangoon, Moulmein, Akyab and Bassein. Transit from London to Rangoon: by sea, 26–35 days; by air, 1 day.

The Burma Railways had a total length in 1940 of 2,300 miles, extending to Mytikyina, on the Upper Irrawaddy. The first diesel locomotives were introduced in 1958 and a further 50 diesel-electric locomotives have been purchased with a recent World Bank loan. There are about 5,472 miles of main roads. Since the war a considerable network of internal air services has come into being. The airport at Mingaladon, about 9 miles north of Rangoon, has been reconstructed and handles much international traffic.

Chief Towns.—The chief city of Lower Burma, and the seat of the government of the Union is Rangoon, on the left bank of the Rangoon river, about 21 miles from the sea. The city contains the Shwe Dagon pagoda, much venerated by Burmese Buddhists. Population (1953), about 740,000. Mandalay, the chief city of Upper Burma had a population of (1953) 186,000, Moulmein one of 103,000 and Bassein 78,000. Pagan, on the Irrawaddy, S.W. of Mandalay, contains many sacred buildings of interest to antiquaries.

NATIONAL FLAG.

The Union flag is red, with a canton of blue bearing a large white five-pointed star surrounded by 5 smaller stars.

BRITISH EMBASSY.

(80 Strand Road, Rangoon.)

British Ambassador, His Excellency Gordon Coligny Whitteridge, C.M.G., O.B.E. (1962)...... £4,115
Counsellor, S. H. Hebblethwaite.
Counsellor (Commercial), A. R. K. Mackenzie.
Consul, A. C. Dugdale.
Cultural Attaché and Representative of British Council, W. R. McAlpine, 67–69 Lewis Street, Rangoon.

BURUNDI

(Kingdom of Burundi)

Ruler, Mwambutsa IV, Mwami of Urundi.

Formerly a Belgian trusteeship under the United Nations, Burundi was proclaimed an independent State on July 1, 1962. Situated on the east side of Lake Tanganyika, the State has an area of 10,747 sq. miles and a population estimated at 2,213,000, mainly of the Bahutu and Batutsi tribes engaged in agriculture and the rearing of livestock. The chief crop is coffee much of which is exported to the United States. Other exports are livestock and hides from the large herds maintained.

CAPITAL: Kitega. The principal town and commercial centre of Burundi is Usumbura.

BRITISH EMBASSY

Usumbura

Ambassador, His Excellency William Patrick Cranston (1963).

CAMBODIA

(Kampuchea)

Queen-Dowager (symbol of the Throne), Her Majesty Kossamak Nearirat, widow of King Norodom Suramarit (*died* April, 1960).

A Government headed by Prince Norodom Kantol took office on October 6, 1962.

ROYAL CAMBODIAN EMBASSY IN LONDON

26 Townshend Road, N.W.8.

[Primrose: 8011]

Ambassador in London, His Excellency Au Chheun.
1st Secretaries, Chea San; Ky Soth.
Attaché, Chek Voun.

Area and Population.—A kingdom with an area of some 70,000 square miles and a population of 5,000,000 (estimated), Cambodia is situated between Thailand to the west and South Vietnam to the east. It is bordered on the north and south respectively by Laos and the Gulf of Siam.

History.—Once a powerful kingdom, which, as the Khmer Empire, flourished between the tenth and fourteenth centuries, Cambodia became a French protectorate in 1863 and was granted independence within the French Union as an Associate State in 1949. Two years earlier Prince (then King) Norodom Sihanouk had promulgated a constitution providing for parliamentary government. The Geneva Conference of 1954 took Cambodia further along the road to independence by ensuring the withdrawal of French and Viet-minh forces from the country, and the process was completed when, in January, 1955, Cambodia became financially and economically independent not only from France but also from Laos and Vietnam. All governments since then have been drawn from the Popular Socialist Community, a movement formed by Prince Norodom Sihanouk who abdicated from the throne in March, 1955, in favour of his parents, King Norodom Suramarit and Queen Kossamak. The community holds all 77 seats in the National Assembly as a result of the last general elections which were held in June, 1962. Following the death of King Norodom Suramarit in April, 1960, a Council of Regency was in being until June, when Prince Norodom Sihanouk assumed office as Head of State.

Geography, Economy and Communications.—Cambodia is largely underdeveloped and under-populated with an economy based on agriculture, fishing and forestry, the bulk of its people being rice-growing farmers living in the basins of the Mekong and Tonlé Sap rivers. In addition to rice, which is the staple crop, the major products are rubber, livestock, maize, timber, pepper, palm sugar, fresh and dried fish, kapok, beans, soya and tobacco. Rice and rubber are the main exports. Fifty per cent. of the total land area is forest or jungle abounding in wild life of all kinds, including big game. The climate is tropical monsoon with a rainy season from May to October.

The country has some 4,000 kilometres of roads, of which about a third are hard-surfaced and passable in the rainy season. There is one railway which runs from Phnom-Penh to the Thai border. Phnom-Penh is a river port capable of receiving ships of up to 2,500 tons all the year round The main installations of a deep water port at Sihanoukville (Kompong Som) on the Gulf of Thailand have been completed and can receive ships up to 10,000 tons. The port is linked to Phnom-Penh by a modern highway. A railway linking Sihanoukville to the capital is under construction. There is as yet no large-scale industry, but a textile mill and plywood and paper factories have been constructed with Chinese aid and a cement factory is under construction; a jute mill is also scheduled for construction under the Five Year Plan (1960–64). Cambodia receives substantial foreign aid, notably from the U.S.A., China, France, the Soviet Union, the Colombo Plan countries and Japan. Since 1956, Cambodia has sought to increase her foreign trade by the conclusion of trade exchange and payments agreements with several countries, including China, Poland, Czechoslovakia, North Vietnam, Yugoslavia, the United Arab Republic, Laos and Japan.

The Cambodian airline, Royal Air Cambodge, operates services with Air Vietnam between Phnom-Penh and Saigon and with Cathay Pacific Airways between Phnom-Penh and Hong Kong. A service to Vietnam and Hanoi is planned. There are flights also to Siemreap where the famous ruins of Ankgor Wat are situated. Cargo boats from Singapore and Hong Kong visit Phnom-Penh regularly.

Culture and Education.—Cambodian culture is predominantly Indo-Siamese and is distinct from Annamite culture which is largely derived from China. The state religion is Buddhism of the "Little Vehicle". There are fairly large Chinese (300,000) and Vietnamese (400,000) minorities. The national language is Cambodian, although French is widely spoken and is still largely the official language of government and commerce. Considerable efforts are now being devoted to the development of education and new schools, colleges and technical institutes have been established. A Buddhist University has been inaugurated in Phnom-Penh, where there are also Faculties of Medicine and Law. A residential teachers' training college is now in operation.

Trade with U.K.

	1961	1962
Imports from U.K.	£1,299,894	£795,525
Exports to U.K.	610,804	484,320

CAPITAL, Phnom-Penh. Population (estimated, 1958), 550,000.

FLAG.—Horizontal stripes of blue, wide red stripe bearing emblem (Temple of Angkor Wat in white), and blue.

BRITISH EMBASSY

96 Boulevard Préah Bat Norodom, Phnom-Penh.

Ambassador Extraordinary and Plenipotentiary and Consul General, His Excellency Peter Murray, C.M.G. (1961) £3,415
1st Secretary, R. Hanbury-Tenison (*Head of Chancery and Consul*).
2nd Secretaries, D. N. Higginbottom; L. A. Taylor (*Commercial and Information*).
Vice-Consul, P. W. Chandley.

CAMEROON REPUBLIC

(Federal Republic of Cameroon)

President, Ahmadou Ahidjo, *elected for* 5 *years*, May 5, 1960.
Vice-President, John Ngu Foncha.

CAMEROON EMBASSY

69 Eaton Place, S.W.1.
[Belgravia: 3006]

Ambassador Extraordinary and Plenipotentiary, His Excellency Martin Epie (1963).
Counsellor, Mr. NjoKLea.
1st Secretary. Mr. Nkweta.

The Federal Republic of Cameroon lies on the Gulf of Guinea between Nigeria to the west, Chad and the Central African Republic to the east and Congo to the south. It has an area of approximately 432,000 sq. miles and a population estimated (1962) at 4,907,000 (E. Cameroon 850,000). Principal products of East Cameroon are cocoa, coffee, cotton, timber, groundnuts and aluminium; of West Cameroon, bananas, rubber, timber, cocoa and palm products. There is an aluminium smelting plant at Edéa in East Cameroon with an annual capacity of 50,000 tons. East Cameroonian exports in 1962 were worth £36,900,000 (£400,000 to the U.K.), Imports were worth £36,300,000 (£855,000 from the U.K.), West Cameroonian exports in 1961 were worth £8,844,000 (£7,200,000 to the U.K.): Imports were worth £5,500,000 (£2,700,000 from the U.K.).

The whole territory was administered by Germany from 1884–1916. From 1916–1959, present-day East Cameroon was administered by France as a League of Nations (later U.N.) trusteeship. On Jan. 1, 1960 it became independent as the Republic of Cameroon. The Republic was joined on October 1, 1961, by the former British administered trust territory of the Southern Cameroons (now West Cameroon), after a plebiscite held under United Nations auspices. The Federal government consists of President, Vice President and 9 Federal Ministers. There are separate East and West Cameroon state governments.

CAPITAL.—Yaoundé (60,000). ΨDouala (120,000), is an important commercial centre.

FLAG.—Vertical stripes of green, red and yellow with two five-pointed gold stars in upper half of green band.

BRITISH EMBASSY

Yaoundé.

Ambassador Extraordinary and Plenipotentiary, His Excellency Edward Redston Warner, C.M.G., O.B.E. (1963).
1st Secretary, C. T. McGurk, M.B.E.
2nd Secretary, M. A. Goodfellow.
3rd Secretary, R. J. R. Owen.
Vice-Consul, D. J. Self.
Archivist, P. C. E. Davies.

CENTRAL AFRICAN REPULIC

President, David Dacko, *assumed office* August 17, 1960.

Formerly the French colony of Ubanghi Shari, the Republic lies just north of the Equator between the Cameroon Republic and the southern part of Sudan. It has a common boundary with the Republic of Chad in the north and with the Congolese Republic in the south. The Republic has an area of about 234,000 sq. miles and a population estimated (1961) at 1,227,000. On December 1, 1958, Ubanghi Shari elected to remain within the French Community and adopted the title of the Central African Republic. It became fully independent on August 17, 1960. Imports from U.K., 1962, £233,401; Exports to U.K., £23,629.

CAPITAL.—Bangui, near the border with the Congolese Republic (82,300).

FLAG.—Four horizontal stripes, blue, white, yellow, green, crossed by central vertical red stripe; a yellow star in centre of blue half-stripe next staff.

French Ambassador, M. Roger Barberot.
British Ambassador, His Excellency William Scott Laver, C.B.E., (1962) (*Resident at Brazzaville, Congo*).

CHAD REPUBLIC

President, François Tombalbaye, *elected* August 11, 1960.

Situated in north-central Africa, the Chad Republic extends from 23° N. latitude to 7° N. latitude and is flanked by the Republics of Niger and Cameroon on the west, by the Kingdom of Libya in the north, by the Sudan on the east and by the Central African Republic on the south. It has an area of 487,920 sq. miles and a population estimated in 1961 at 2,675,000. Chad became a member state of the French Community on Nov. 28, 1958, and was proclaimed fully independent on August 11, 1960. On April 14, 1962, a new Constitution was adopted for a presidential-type regime, Mr. Tombalbaye accepting the formal title of President on April 23, 1962. Trade with U.K., 1962: Imports, £106,053; Exports to U.K., £368,893.

CAPITAL.—Fort Lamy, south of Lake Chad (45,600).

FLAG.—Vertical stripes, blue, yellow and red.

French High Representative, M. René Millet.
British Ambassador, His Excellency William Scott Laver, C.B.E.,(1962) (*Resident at Brazzaville, Congo*).

CHILE

(República de Chile.)

President (1958–64), Jorge Alessandri Rodriguez, *assumed office*, Nov. 4, 1958.

CABINET.

Minister of the Interior, Sotero del Rio Gundian.
Foreign Affairs (vacant).
Finance, Luis Mackenna Shiel.
Education, Dr. Alejandro Garreton.
Health, Dr. Francisco Rojas.
Public Works, Ernesto Pinto.
Agriculture, Ruy Barboza.
Labour and Social Security, Miguel Schweitzer.
Economics, Julio Philippi Izquierdo.
Mines, Luis Ialacios.
Defence, Carlos Vial Infante.
Justice, Enrique Ortuzan Escobar.
Lands and Colonization, Federico Pena.

EMBASSY IN LONDON.

3, Hamilton Place, W.1.
[Mayfair: 8382.]

Ambassador in London, His Excellency Victor Santa Cruz (1959).

Minister-Counsellor, Señor Rafael Vergara.
2nd Secretary, Señor Juan José Fernandez.
Naval Attaché, Captain Quintilio Rivera.
Air Attaché, Col. Carlos Toro-Mazote.
Consul-General, J. H. Fischer.
Consul, Señor Santiago Rogers.
Consulate, 3 Hamilton Place, W.1.

A State of South America, of Spanish origin, lying between the Andes and the shores of the South Pacific, extending coastwise from just north of Arica to Cape Horn south, between lat. 17° 15′ and 55° 59′ S., and long. 66° 30′ and 75° 48′ W. Extreme length of the country is about 2,800 miles, with an average breadth, north of 41°, of 100 miles. The great chain of the Andes runs along its eastern limit, with a general elevation of 5,000 to 15,000 feet above the level of the sea; but numerous summits attain a greater height. The chain, however, lowers considerably towards its southern extremity. The Andes form a boundary with Argentina, and at the head of the pass where the international road from Chile to Argentina crosses the frontier, has been erected a statue of *Christ the Redeemer*, 26 feet high, made of bronze from old cannon, to commemorate the peaceful settlement of a boundary dispute in 1902. There are no rivers of great size, and none of them is of much service as a navigable highway. In the north the country is arid.

Among the island possessions of Chile are the *Juan Fernandez group* (3 islands) about 360 miles distant from Valparaiso, where a wireless station has been erected. One of these islands is the reputed scene of Alexander Selkirk's (Robinson Crusoe) shipwreck. *Easter Island* (27° 8′ S. and 109° 28′ W.), about 2,000 miles distant in the South Pacific Ocean, contains stone platforms and hundreds of stone figures, the origin of which has not yet been determined. The area of the island is about 45 sq. miles.

Chile is divided into 25 provinces and the total area of the Republic is estimated at 290,000 square miles, with an estimated population of 7,440,000 (April, 1959). In 1929 Chile signed a treaty ceding the province of Tacna to Peru but retained the province of Arica in return for a payment to Peru of £1,200,000. Included in the total are four racial divisions: (*a*) Spanish settlers and their descendants; (*b*) indigenous Araucanian Indians, Fuegians, and Changos; (*c*) mixed Spanish Indians; and (*d*) European immigrants.

In 1959 the registered births per thousand inhabitants numbered 35·4; marriages 7·4; and deaths 12·5.

GOVERNMENT.—Chile was discovered by Spanish adventurers in the 16th century, and remained under Spanish rule until 1810, when a revolutionary war, culminating in the *Battle of Maipú* (April 5, 1818), achieved the independence of the nation. Under the present Constitution (Aug. 30, 1925), the President is elected by direct choice of all Chilean citizens who have the right to vote. The National Congress consists of a Senate of 45 members, and of a Chamber of 147 Deputies. There is universal suffrage for persons who have attained the age of 21, can read and write, and are on the electoral roll. Chilean women obtained equal voting rights with men on Dec. 21, 1948, before which they only participated in municipal elections.

PRODUCTION, &c.—Agriculture and mining are the principal occupations, though industrial development is being actively encouraged by the Government. Wheat, maize, barley, oats, beans, peas, lentils, wines, tobacco, hemp, chili-pepper, potatoes, onions and melons are grown extensively; the vine and all European fruit-trees flourish in the central zone and fruit is an important export item. Excellent wines are produced and exported and are becoming more widely known in world markets. There are large timber tracts in the central and southern zones of Chile, some types of which were exported to Europe and the Argentine, but high production costs have caused serious difficulties to this export trade. The mineral wealth is considerable, the country being particularly rich in copper-ore, iron-ore and nitrate. Uranium is also said to have been discovered in small quantities. The production of refined copper in 1961 was 502,031 metric tons. The rainless north is the scene of the only commercial production of nitrate of soda (Chile saltpetre) from natural sources in the world. Production in 1961 (including potassium nitrate) was 1,110,405 metric tons. Chile also produces iodine, manganese ore, coal, and a small quantity of gold. 1,763,800 metric tons of coal and 5,255,468 metric tons of iron ores were produced in 1961. The country has also large deposits of high grade sulphur, but mostly around high extinct volcanoes in the Andes Cordillera, difficult of access. Production of refined sulphur has hitherto been in relatively small quantities. Annual production is between 25,000 and 50,000 metric tons. Oil was struck in Magallanes (Tierra del Fuego) in December, 1945, and the industry is now self-supporting. Production in 1961 was 1,472,703 cubic metres. An oleoduct 70 kilometres long now joins the principal field in Cerro Manantiales with Clarence Bay. Almost all the production is now being refined at Concon, a few miles north of Valparaiso. A large steel plant was completed and started operation during 1950 at Huachipato, near Concepción. In 1961 the output of steel ingots from Huachipato totalled 362,800 metric tons; rolling mill products totalled 283,800 metric tons.

In recent years a considerable cotton and woollen textile industry has developed. Minor industries include tanning, flour milling, lumbering, distilling, fish canning and whaling, brewing, and the manufacture of starch, soap, biscuits, rope, glassware, plastic goods, pottery, paint, boots and shoes, hosiery, millinery, cheese, furniture, matches, brushes, cordage, paper and newsprint, radio receivers and valves, rubber products, synthetic detergents, motor vehicle tyres and cigarettes. Domestic industries include weaving and embroidery.

COMMUNICATIONS.—Most of the country's commerce is distributed along its lengthy sea-board in Chilean ships, which have a virtual monopoly of cabotage. Foreign trade continues to be carried on mostly by foreign steamship lines operating either directly to the West Coasts of North and South America, or *viâ* the Panama Canal to Europe or *viâ* the Straits of Magellan. Chilean vessels have also been participating for many years in foreign trade with North America and Europe. The Chilean mercantile marine in May, 1962, numbered 65 vessels (of over 100 tons gross) with a total gross tonnage of 319,345. Under a law promulgated in June, 1956, 50 per cent. of Chile's foreign trade must be carried by Chilean vessels.

The first railway was opened in 1851 and there are now 6,575 miles of track, of which 5,360 miles are State owned. A metre-gauge line runs from Pisagua to La Calera, just north of Santiago. From La Calera to Puerto Montt runs the wide-gauge (1·676 metre) main line of the State railways.

With the completion of a section of 435 miles from Corumba, Brazil, to Santa Cruz, Bolivia, the Trans-Continental Line will link the Chilean Pacific port of Arica with Rio de Janeiro on the Atlantic. Another line from Antofagasta to Salta (Argentine) was opened in 1948. Further south, the Trans-

Andine Railway connects Valparaiso on the Pacific with Buenos Aires. crossing tne Andes at 11,500 ft.

Chile is served by 11 international airlines which, in 1958, carried 143,271 passengers in and out of the country. Four-fifths of the domestic traffic is carried by the State-owned Linea Aerea Nacional, which in 1960 carried 388,000 passengers over 429,900,000 passenger-miles. Chile has an extensive, system of airports which are being modernized with U.S. financial assistance.

Chile's road system is about 55,000 kilometres in length, but only an estimated 3,000 kilometres are first-class paved highways. At the end of 1960 there were registered 57,578 cars and taxis, 63,238 goods vehicles, 5,515 buses and 19,304 motor cycles and scooters.

The country had 192,000 telephone subscribers at the end of 1960. Telegrams are handled by 607 telegraph offices, mostly owned by the State.

DEFENCE.—Military service is compulsory, but not all those who are liable are required. Recruitment for the Navy is voluntary. In 1961 the Army had 6 infantry and 1 cavalry divisions with a total strength of 1,900 officers, 11,000 regular other ranks plus 11,000 conscripts. In addition there is a police force of " Carabineros " of 22,500 officers and men. The Air Force had 600 officers and 6,180 other ranks with a strength of 230 aircraft. The Navy consisted of 2 cruisers, 8 destroyers, 3 frigates, 3 corvettes, 2 submarines, all operational. There is a support force of transports, tankers, 1 submarine depôt ship and ancillary small craft. The strength of the Navy is 937 officers and 13,785 men, plus a Marine Force for coastal defence of 87 officers and 2,200 men.

EDUCATION is free, elementary education being compulsory since 1920. There are 8 Universities (3 in Santiago, 2 in Valparaiso, 1 in Antofagasta, 1 in Concepción and 1 in Valdivia). The religion is Roman Catholic.

LANGUAGE AND LITERATURE.—Spanish is the language of the country, with admixtures of local words of Indian origin. Recent efforts have reduced illiteracy and have thus afforded access to the literature of Spain, to supplement the vigorous national output. The Nobel Prize for Literature was awarded in 1945 to Señorita Gabriela Mistral, for Chilean verse and prose. There are over 100 newspapers and a large number of periodicals, including some devoted to professional, scientific and social subjects.

FINANCE.	1963 *Escudos*
Budget, 1963	
Estimated Revenue...........	1,249,900,000
Estimated Expenditure........	1,121,300,000

At the end of 1961 *bonded* debt amounted to—Internal, *E*°46,971,270, $158,956,047 and *DM* 50,000,000: External, $80,439,000; £13,047,971 and *Swiss Francs* 66,415,900.

The official rate of exchange, June 30, 1962, was about *E*° 5·20=£1. (*See also* p. 83).

EXTERNAL TRADE.

	1962
Total imports................	$U.S.517,904,000
Total exports................	532,055,000

Trade with U.K.

	1961	1962
Imports from U.K....	£12,004,891	£14,993,946
Exports to U.K.......	27,900,876	29,097,220

The principal exports are metallic and non-metallic minerals (refined copper, ingots and bars, iron ore, etc.), cereals, vegetables, fruit and wool. The principal imports are industrial oils, raw cotton, chemicals, machinery, tools, electrical and transport equipment and sugar.

CAPITAL, Santiago (December, 1956) 1,627,962 (Greater Santiago). Other large towns are:—ΨValparaiso (261,684), ΨConcepción (158,941), Temuco (109,141), Viña del Mar (107,563), Chillán (79,461), Talca (75,354), ΨAntofagasta (74,050), ΨValdivia (72,988), ΨTalcahuano (75,643), ΨIquique (47,906), ΨPunta Arenas (44,597). Punta Arenas, on the Straits of Magellan, is the southernmost city in the world.

FLAG.—2 horizontal bands, white, red; in top sixth a white star on blue square, next staff.

BRITISH EMBASSY.

Calle Bandera 227, Piso 3° Santiago (Casilla 72D).

Ambassador Extraordinary and Plenipotentiary, His Excellency Sir Robert David John Scott Fox, K.C.M.G. (1961)..................... £4,115

Chancery, Calle Bandera 227, Piso 3°, Santiago.

First Secretary, K. G. Ritchie.

First Secretary (Commercial), H. T. Kennedy.

First Secretary (Information), J. de C. Ling.

Naval Attaché, Capt. N. G. Hallett, D.S.C., R.N.

First Secretary and Consul, L. Borax, M.B.E.

First Secretary (Labour), J. M. Carlin. D.F.C.

Second Secretary (Commercial), Miss I. M. Illman.

Third Secretary (Information), N. L. Shearman.

BRITISH CONSULAR OFFICES.

There are British Consular Offices at *Santiago*, *Antofagasta*, *Arica*, *Iquique*, *Valparaiso*, *Concepción*, *Coquimbo*, *Valdivia*, *Osorno* and *Punta Arenas*.

BRITISH COUNCIL.—*Representative of the British Council in Chile*, C. H. Whistler, Teatinos 307, Santiago.

There are Anglophil Societies at Santiago, Valparaiso and Concepción.

BRITISH CHAMBER OF COMMERCE IN THE REPUBLIC OF CHILE, Calle Bandera 227 (Piso 4°) Casilla 4087, *Santiago*.

Valparaiso is distant from London 9,000 miles *viâ* Panama, and 11,000 *viâ* the Strait; transit 28 to 45 days; by air, 24 hrs.

CHINA

(Chunghua Jenmin Kunghokuo—The People's Republic of China.)

Chairman of the Central People's Government Council, Liu Shao-Ch'i, *elected* April, 1959.

Vice-Chairman, Sung Ch'ing-lin, (*Mme.* Sun Yat-sen) Tung Pi-wu.

Chairman of the Standing Committee of the 2nd National People's Congress, Chu Teh.

Prime Minister, Chou En-Lai.

Vice-Premier and Minister of Foreign Affairs, Marshal Ch'en Yi.

Vice-Premier and Minister of Defence, Marshal Lin Piao.

Chairman of the Chinese Communist Party, Mao Tse-tung.

LONDON OFFICE.

49 Portland Place, W.1.

Chargé d'Affaires, Huan Hsiang-hui.

Counsellors, Ma Chia-Chun; Chuang Yen; Li Chuo-chih (*Commercial*).

AREA AND POPULATION.—The area of China is about 4,300,000 square miles. Estimates of the present population vary considerably, but a figure of more than 700,000,000 is generally accepted. According to figures published in 1957 by the National Bureau of Statistics, the total population of China was 656,630,000, not including Chinese living in Hong Kong, Maçao or abroad. The Chinese still use the round figure of 650,000,000. According to the 1953 census the birth rate averaged 37 per thousand and the death rate 17 per thousand, producing an annual population increase of 2 per cent. In 1953 the percentage distribution of the population was as follows:

Han, 94·13; Mongolian, 0·26; Tibetan, 0·48; Manchu, 0·41; Tribal, 3·57; Others, 1·15. There is no reason to suppose that the proportions have significantly changed.

THE PROVINCES OF CHINA.

According to the National Bureau of Statistics the populations of the Chinese provinces at the end of 1957 were as follows:

Anhwei	33,560,000
Chekiang	25,280,000
Chinghai	2,050,000
Fukien	14,650,000
Heilungkiang	14,860,000
Honan	48,670,000
Hopei	44,720,000
Hunan	36,220,000
Hupeh	30,790,000
Kansu	12,800,000
Kiangsi	18,610,000
Kiangsu	45,230,000
Kirin	12,550,000
Kwangsi Chuang Autonomous Region	19,390,000
Kwangtung	37,960,000
Kweichow	16,890,000
Liaoning	24,090,000
Inner Mongolian Autonomous Region	9,200,000
Ningsia Autonomous Region	1,810,000
Shansi	15,960,000
Shantung	54,030,000
Shensi	18,130,000
Sinkiang Uighur Autonomous Region	6,640,000
Szechuan	72,160,000
Tibet	1,270,000
(Taiwan	10,100,000)
Yunnan	19,100,000

Sinkiang is the largest region or province in area (about 1/6th of the whole area of the country) and Szechuan the most populous.

Government.—On October 10, 1911, the party of reform forced the Imperial dynasty to a "voluntary" abdication, and a Republic was proclaimed at Wuchang. Events leading up to the end of the war with Japan are briefly described in earlier issues of WHITAKER'S ALMANACK.

On September 30, 1949, the Chinese People's Political Consultative Conference (C.P.P.C.C.) met in Peking and appointed the National People's Government Council under the Chairmanship of Mao Tse-tung. On October 1, Mao proclaimed the inauguration of the Chinese People's Republic. The Soviet Union broke off relations with the Nationalists and established relations with the new *régime* on October 2. The *régime* was recognised by all the Communist *bloc* countries in quick succession, and soon after by the Asian countries of the Commonwealth, the United Kingdom and by a number of other countries. The most important countries which still recognise the Nationalist *régime* in Formosa are the United States and France.

The C.P.P.C.C. continued to be the supreme legislative body of the new state until September 20, 1954, when a new constitution was adopted. It was then replaced as the highest organ of state power by the National People's Congress, which exercises legislative power. The Congress can amend the constitution and supervises its enforcement, enacts laws and decides on questions of war and peace. It approves the state budget and adopts the national economic plan. It elects and may remove from office the Chairman and Vice-Chairmen of the Republic. The National People's Congress is supposed to meet only once a year; between sessions its functions are exercised by its Standing Committee, a body made up of a Chairman, 13 Vice-Chairmen, the Secretary-General and 35 ordinary members.

With the adoption of the Constitution, the National People's Government Council was replaced by the State Council, composed of the Premier, 10 Vice-Premiers and the heads of ministries and commissions. This body is the supreme administrative body, responsible for the day-to-day running of the country.

Under the Constitution a complicated interlocking hierarchy exists from the bottom to the top. The National People's Congress is not directly elected, but is the peak of a pyramid. Direct elections occur only in rural districts, urban districts and small towns. Local Congresses have two main functions: (1) to appoint as their administrative arm a People's Council; and (2) to elect the next higher level congress, in this case county congresses or large town congresses. The County congresses have a similar twin function: to appoint County People's Councils and to elect the Provincial Congresses. The Provincial Congresses appoint Provincial People's Councils and elect the National People's Congress. The administrative organs, the People's Councils, are controlled by the next higher administrative organ. (*e.g.* a County People's Council obeys the orders of the Provincial Council immediately above it). Complications are caused by the existence of Autonomous Regions and Counties set aside for particular national minorities and by the fact that large cities such as Peking, Tientsin and Shanghai are under the Central Government and other towns under provincial governments. Since Congresses meet only rarely and the Councils are responsible for arranging elections of the next Congress, the line of control running down from the State Council through the hierarchy of local Councils is much stronger than the expression of the public will rising up from the basic level Congresses to the National People's Congress.

China is a Communist state but the position of the Communist party is not reflected in the constitution. Its complete dominance over the Government, which includes "united-front" figures from lesser parties, is achieved by ensuring that all the really important positions at whatever level are filled by Party members. Until April, 1959, Mao Tse-tung was Chairman both of the Republic and of the Communist Party. Since he stood down from his position as Head of State, Lui Shao-ch'i, the first Vice-Chairman of the Party, has been Head of State.

Defence.—An order introducing compulsory military service for all men between the ages of 18 and 40 was passed by the National People's Congress in 1955. Regulations were also approved for the creation of an officer corps with ranks similar to those of the Russian Army. Nearly 80,000,000 men were made liable for service in the Army (3 years), the Navy (5 years) or the Air Force (4 years). Naturally only a small number of these are called up and conscription is in practice selective. It was announced that the new Army would be organized in 14 combat and supporting corps, including a "political" division to serve with front-line troops.

Religion.—The indigenous religions of China are Confucianism (which includes ancestor worship), Taoism (originally a philosophy rather than a religion) and, since its introduction in the first century of the Christian era, Buddhism. There are also Chinese Moslems and Christians. Since 1949, the practice of all religions has been severely curtailed, although not actually prohibited.

Education.—Although primary education was compulsory under the Nationalists, mass education did not become a fact until after the Communists had taken over. In 1958, according to official figures, 85 per cent. of all children of school age were actually attending primary school. There were 8,500,000 students in middle schools and 1,470,000 students in technical middle schools. The number of students in higher educational institutes reached 660,000 (four times the number of the pre-1949 peak). The majority of the 27 provinces have provincial universities in addition to national institutions. In August, 1950, the Government took over all schools previously run by foreign missions and in October, 1950, closed the Roman Catholic University in Peking.

Language and Literature.—The Chinese language has many dialects, Cantonese, Hakka, Swatow, Foochow, Wenchow, Ning-po and Wu (Shanghai), and, most important, Pekinese. Pekinese is the basis of the Common Speech (*P'ut'unghua*). The Communists, when they came into power, continued the Kuomintang policy of promoting it as the national language and made much more intensive efforts to propagate it throughout the country. Since the most important aspect of this policy is the use of the spoken language in writing, the old Mandarin style of writing has fallen into disuse.

Chinese writing is ideographic and not phonetic. The number of sounds in *P'ut'unghua* is strictly limited; each sound may have a large number of different characters and meanings. Whereas originally the language was monosyllabic and confusion was avoided by the use of different characters, thus producing texts which were visually clear but ambiguous to the ear, with the increasing use of the spoken language for writing people are increasingly making use of polysyllabic compounds both in speech and writing in order to avoid confusion. In 1956, after some 4 years of study, the Government decided to introduce 230 simplified characters with a view to making reading and writing easier. The list was enlarged; there are now about 1,000 simplified characters in use. In January, 1956, all Chinese newspapers and most books began to appear with the characters printed horizontally from left to right, instead of vertically reading from right to left, as previously.

In November 1957, after some experimentation, the Government introduced a system of Romanization of the characters based on the usual 26 letters of the Latin alphabet. This is at present used only in assisting primary school children and others to learn their characters and pronounce them in *P'ut'unghua*. Hopes have been expressed that eventually the new alphabet will replace the characters entirely, but this aim is not likely to be realized for many years.

Chinese literature is one of the richest in the world. Paper has been employed for writing and printing for nearly 2,000 years. The Confucian classics which formed the basis of the traditional Chinese culture date from the Warring States period (4th–3rd centuries B.C.) as do the earliest texts of the rival tradition, Taoism. Histories, philosophical and scientific works, poetry, literary and art criticism, novels and romances survive from most periods. Many have been translated into English. In the past all this considerable literature was available only to a very small class of *literati*, but with the spread of literacy in the 20th century, a process which has received enormous impetus since the Communists took over in 1950, the old traditional literature has been largely superseded by modern works of a popular kind and by the classics of Marxism and modern developments from them.

Eight newspapers are now published in Peking, of which the most important is the People's Daily, the organ of the Chinese Communist Party.

Currency and Exchange.—The *yuan* was revalued with effect from March 1, 1955, on the basis of 10,000 old *yuan* for one new *yuan*. From the same date the official exchange rates for sterling and dollars were altered to:

6·895 *yuan*=£1; 2·46 *yuan*= $1.

Production and Industry.—China is essentially an agricultural and pastoral country. Wheat, barley, maize, millet and other cereals, with peas and beans, are grown in the northern provinces, and rice and sugar in the south. Rice is the staple food of the inhabitants. Cotton (mostly in valleys of the Yangtze and Yellow Rivers), tea (in the west and south), with hemp, jute and flax, are the most important crops.

Livestock is raised in large numbers. Silkworm culture is one of the oldest industries. Cottons, woollens and silks are manufactured in large quantities. The mineral wealth of the country is very great. Coal of excellent quality is produced. Iron ore, tin, antimony, wolfram, bismuth and molybdenum are also abundant. Oil is produced in Kansu, Sinkiang and Sining. No reliable figures for industrial production have been published since 1959. The figures given below for 1958 levels are accepted as generally accurate:

Steel, 8,000,000 tons; Pig Iron, 9,530,000 tons; Coal, 270,000,000 tons; Electric Power, 27,530,000,000 kWh.; Crude Petroleum, 2,264,000 tons; Cement, 9,300,000 tons; Timber, 35,000,000 cubic metres; Sulphuric Acid, 740,000 tons; Chemical Fertilizers, 811,000 tons; Machine Tools, 50,000; Motor Vehicles, 16,000; Paper, 1,630,000 tons; and Cotton Cloth 5,700,000,000 metres

Other production figures (with percentage increases over the year) were: Cotton, 2,410,000 tons (31 p.c.); Electricity, 41,500,000,000 kWh (51 p.c.); Cement, 12,270,000 tons (32 p.c.); Timber, 41,200,000 cu. metres (18 p.c.); Fertilizers, 1,333,000 tons (64 p.c.); Machine tools, 70,000 (40 p.c.); and Paper, 2,310,000 tons (31 p.c.).

The principal articles of export are animals and animal products; oils; textiles fibres; ores and metals and tea. The principal imports are raw cotton, cotton yarn and thread; fats and soap; motor vehicles; machinery, petrol, oil and lubricants; books, paper and paper-making materials; chemicals; metals and ores; and dyes, paints and varnishes.

Trade with U.K.

	1961	1962
Imports from U.K..	£12,892,392	£8,376,427
Exports to U.K.....	30 858 254	23,149,109

Communications.—Of the total area of China about half consists of tableland and mountainous areas where communications and travel are generally difficult. By 1949, the communications system, as a result of years of neglect and civil war, was more or less completely paralysed. In any case such roads and railways as did exist were largely confined to the eastern plains. After the Communists achieved complete control they devoted much attention to restoring and improving the communications system. By the end of 1958 the total length of railways was 19,000 miles (42 p.c. more than 1949), the total length of roads was 250,000 miles (about 5 times as much as in 1949) and of inland waterways about 100,000 miles (twice as much as 1949). In addition, internal civil aviation has been developed: routes total more than 20,000 miles. As a result the communications network now covers most of the country. In the past where roads did not exist the principal means of communications east to west was provided by the rivers, the most important of which are the Yangtze (3,400 miles long), the Yellow River (2,600 miles long) and the West River (1,650 miles). These, together with the network of canals connecting them, are still much used, but their overall importance is less than it was. In the past 10 years great progress has been made in developing postal and telecommunications. It is now claimed that 95 p.c. of all rural communes are on the telephone and that postal routes reach practically every production brigade headquarters (commune sub-division).

SPECIAL TERRITORY

Tibet, a plateau seldom lower than 10,000 feet, forms the northern frontier of India (boundary imperfectly demarcated), from Kashmir to Burma, but is separated therefrom by the Himalayas. The area is estimated at 463,000 square miles with a population (estimated, 1957) of 1,270,000. About one-fifth of the male population are monks and polyandry is common. There is an army with an establishment of 10,000 all ranks, consisting of infantry serving on a militia basis and armed with modern weapons. India imports from Tibet wool, borax, salt, and musk; musk, horn and herbs are sent to China. The imports are chiefly cotton and woollen goods, grain, hardware, glass, sugar, biscuits, dried fruits and tobacco, with silver bullion and coined rupees to balance the excess of exports. The present currency is reckoned in *sangs* (mostly paper). The 1939 value was about 8 *sangs*=1 rupee, which has risen in favour of Tibet to about 3½ *sangs*=1 rupee. Trade passes from Bengal (through Sikkim) and from the Punjab and the United Provinces.

From 1911 to 1950, Tibet was virtually an independent country but its status was never officially so defined. In October, 1950, Chinese Communist forces invaded Eastern Tibet. The Dalai Lama later left Lhasa and set up his Government at Yatung, near the Sikkim frontier. On May 23, 1951, an agreement was reached whereby the Chinese army was allowed entry into Tibet. A Communist military and administrative headquarters was set up. In 1954 the Government of India recognized that Tibet was an integral part of China, in return for the right to maintain trade and consular representation there.

A series of revolts against Chinese rule over several years culminated on March 17, 1959, in a rising in Lhasa. Heavy fighting continued for several days before the rebellion was suppressed by Chinese troops and military rule imposed. The Dalai Lama fled to India where he and his followers were granted political asylum. On May 4, the Indian Government announced that an estimated 9,000 Tibetans had entered India or the Himalayan hill states. On March 28, 1959, the Chinese Prime Minister issued an order dissolving the Tibetan Government and setting up a 16-member Preparatory Committee for the Tibetan Autonomous Region, with the Panchen Lama as Chairman and including 4 Chinese officials. Elections were held to elect local People's Congresses in Tibet, thus indicating that the governmental organization there no longer differed significantly from that of any ordinary province in China. The Dalai Lama, now exiled in India, announced a "new constitution" in March, 1963.

CAPITAL.—Peking, population (estimated, 1957), 4,010,000. The population of the other principal towns in 1957 was estimated as: ΨShanghai, 6,900,000; Tientsin, 3,220,000; Shenyang (Mukden), 2,411,000; Wuhan (*formerly* Hankow, Hanyang and Wuchang), 2,146,000; Chungking, 2,121,000; ΨCanton, 1,840,000; Harbin, 1,552,000; ΨPort Arthur (Lushun)/Dairen, 1,508,000; Nanking, 1,409,000; Sian, 1,310,000; ΨTsingtao, 1,121,000; Chengtu, 1,107,000; Taiyuan, 1,020,000.

OFFICE OF THE BRITISH CHARGÉ D'AFFAIRES
5 Kuang Hua Lu,
Chien Kuo Men Wai, Peking.

Chargé d'Affairs, His Excellency Terence Willcocks Garvey, C.M.G. (1962) £4,115
Counsellor, H. T. Morgan.
1st Secretaries, L. S. Ross (*Commercial*); R. M. Evans; D. R. A. Spankie.
2nd Secretary, T. Pidgeon.
3rd Secretaries, G. E. Clark; D. C. Wilson.
Attachés, T. Bryant; Miss M. Rudman.

H.M. Chargé d'Affaires also maintains an office in *Shanghai*.

FORMOSA
(Taiwan)

President, General Chiang Kai-shek, *born* 1886, *assumed office* 1949.

An island of some 13,800 sq. miles in the China Sea, Formosa lies 90 miles east of the Chinese mainland in latitude 21° 45′ N.—25° 38′ N. The population, principally Chinese, was 10,050,000 at the census of 1961. The territory of Formosa includes the Pescadores Islands (Quemoy and Matsu) a few miles from the mainland, area 50 sq. miles. Originally settled by the Chinese, the island has been known as Ryukyu and Taiwan. It has been colonized in part by Dutch and Spanish expeditions and latterly by Japan. Japanese administration lasted from 1894 to 1945. General Chiang Kai-shek withdrew to Formosa in 1949, towards the end of the war against the Communist régime, accompanied by 500,000 Nationalist troops, since when the territory has continued under his presidency. American forces have intervened on several occasions to maintain the status quo, the United States recognizing the Formosa *régime* as Nationalist China.

The eastern part of the main island is mountainous and forest covered. Hsinkaoshan (14,720 ft.) and Tz'ukaoshan (12,480 ft.) are the highest peaks. The western plains are watered by many rivers and the soil is very fertile, producing sugar, rice, tea, bananas, pineapples and tobacco. Formosa is a main producer of camphor. Coal, sulphur, iron, petroleum, copper and gold are mined. There are important fisheries. The principal seaports ΨTansui and ΨKeelung (145,200) are situated at the extreme north of the island. Goods to the value of £985,715 were exported to the United Kingdom in 1962; imports from U.K., £655,186.

CAPITAL.—Taipeh (population 1961, 927,400). Other towns are Kaohsiung (275,600) and Tainan (229,500).

BRITISH CONSULATES

Tamsui, R. F. McKeever (*Consul*).
Taipeh, R. Weston (*Vice-Consul*).

COLOMBIA
(República de Colombia.)

President, Sr. Guillermo-Leon Valencia, *elected* May 4, 1962, *assumed office* Aug. 7, 1962.

EMBASSY AND CONSULATE
3 Hans Crescent, S.W.1.
[Kensington: 9177]

Ambassador Extraordinary and Plenipotentiary (vacant).
Counsellor, Señor Pedro Felipe Valencia.
1st Secretary, Señor Joaquin Fonseca.

Consul-General, Señor Germán Vargas.

There is a Colombian Consular Office at *Liverpool.*

The Republic of Colombia lies in the extreme north-west of South America, having a coastline on both the Atlantic and Pacific Oceans. It is situated between 2° 40′ S. to 12° 25′ N. lat. and 68° to 79° W. long., with an estimated area of 461,606 square miles, and a population (estimated 1962) of 14,750,000.

The Colombian coast was visited in 1502 by *Christopher Columbus*, and in 1536 a Spanish expedition under Jiménez de Quesada penetrated to the interior and established on the site of the present capital a government which continued under Spanish rule until the revolt of the Spanish-American colonies of 1811–1824. In 1819 *Simon Bolivar* (born 1783, died 1830) established the Republic of Colombia, consisting of the territories now known as Colombia, Panama, Venezuela and Ecuador. In 1829–1830 Venezuela and Ecuador withdrew from the association of provinces, and in 1831 the remaining territories were formed into the Republic of New Granada. In 1858 the name was changed to the Granadine Confederation and in 1861 to the United States of Colombia. In 1886 the present title was adopted. In 1903 Panama seceded from Colombia, and is now a separate Republic.

Following a period of dictatorship and government by decree from 1953, a military junta established on May 10, 1957, prepared the way for a return to democratic government. Congressional elections were held on March 16, 1958, which yielded a Liberal majority of votes. A plebiscite voted on December 1, 1957, had made constitutional changes by which the office of president would during the next sixteen years alternate between candidates of the Liberal and Conservative parties who would hold office for terms of four years, while the two parties would have equal representation in Congress and in the national and departmental governments. On May 4, 1962, presidential elections returned Señor Guillermo-Leon Valencia.

There are three great ranges of the Andes, known as the Western, Central, and Eastern Cordilleras; the second contains the highest peaks, but the latter is the more important, as it consists of a series of vast tablelands, cool and healthy. This temperate region is the most densely peopled portion of the Republic.

The principal rivers are the Magdalena, Câuca, Atrato, Caquetá, Meta, Putumayo and Patia. The Patia flows through the famous *Minima Gorge* of the Western Cordilleras, and one of its tributaries (the Carchi, or Upper Guiatara) is spanned by the Rumichaca Arch, or *Inca's Bridge*, of natural stone. On the Rio Bogotá is the Great *Fall of Tequendama*, 482 feet in height.

The Colombian forests are extensive; among the trees are mahogany, cedar, fustic, and other dye-woods and medicinal plants. The mineral productions are emeralds, gold, silver, platinum, copper, iron, lead, and coal; in 1960 some 55 million barrels of petroleum were produced and prospecting for new sources of production is in progress in many parts of the Republic. The principal agricultural products are coffee (which accounts for 80 per cent. of total exports by value), cotton, bananas, rice, cocoa, sugar, tobacco, maize, wheat and other cereals. Manufactures, mainly for home consumption, consist of woollen, cotton and artificial silk textiles, leather goods, chemicals, asbestos-cement goods, many pharmaceutical products, rubber goods, including motor tyres, furniture, boots and shoes, confectionery, cigarettes, beer, cement, glass containers and, since the latter part of 1954, steel. Successive foreign exchange crises have led to the encouragement by the Government of the rapid development of new industries, including the local assembly and partial manufacture of motor vehicles, radio sets and office machinery.

The Navy consists of 4 destroyers, 3 frigates, some gunboats and some other small craft, with personnel about 4,500, including one battalion of marines; a battalion of the Colombian army served with the United Nations forces in Korea. The first railway was opened in 1855, about 1,914 miles being open in 1949. The "Atlantic Railway" running through the Magdalena Valley, which links the departmental lines running down to the river, and completes the connection between Bogotá and Santa Maria, was opened in July, 1961. There are about 2,200 miles of rail in use at present. There were also (1955) some 13,125 miles of metalled roads, of which 8,440 miles are national highways and the remainder departmental and municipal highways; this excludes "dirt" roads (passable by motors in dry weather only). Colombia was granted loans totalling $47,300,000 (118,500,000 *pesos*) by the International Bank, towards the total of 515,000,000 *pesos* expected to be required to complete the rehabilitation of highways which is now in progress. The national telephone and telegraph system consists primarily of wireless links between the more important centres. Large appropriations have been made for modernization of the country's telecommunication system. A large volume of traffic is carried on the River Magdalena, which is navigable for 900 miles. There are daily passenger and cargo air services between Bogotá and all the principal towns. There are daily services to the U.S.A., frequent services to other countries in South America, a direct B.O.A.C. *Britannia* service once a week to London, and other services to London daily *viâ* New York, three times a week *viâ* Jamaica and twice a week *viâ* Paris, and air mail is delivered to the United Kingdom 3 to 5 days after leaving Bogotá. There are wireless stations in the main cities, and a television station in Bogotá with relays to Manizales, Medellin, Cali and Tunja.

Roman Catholicism is the established religion.

Language and Literature.—Spanish is the language of the country and education has been free since 1870. Great efforts have been made in reducing illiteracy and it is estimated that about 60 per cent. of those over 10 years of age can read and write. In addition to the National University with headquarters at Bogotá there are 20 other universities. There is a flourishing press in urban areas and a national literature supplements the rich inheritance from the time of Spanish rule.

Finance.—Ordinary budget revenue and expenditure were roughly in balance at about *pesos* 2,600,000,000 in 1961 and *pesos* 3,500,000 in 1962. Rate of exchange, Jan. 1, 1963 was *pesos* 24·5=£1. (*See also* p. 83).

TRADE.

	1959 *pesos*	1960 *pesos*
Total imports....	2,534,031,500	3,392,284,000
Total exports.....	2,406,090,130	2,453,288,000

Trade with U.K.

	1961	1962
Imports from U.K.	£10,999 835	£9,318,070
Exports to U.K...	8,694,834	7,543,700

CAPITAL, Bogotá, pop. (estimated, 1962) 1,329,000. Bogotá is an inland city in the Eastern Cordilleras, at an elevation of 8,600 to 9,000 feet above sea level. Other centres are Medellin (690,500), Cali (693,000), Barranquilla (450,000), Bucaramanga (220,000) ♆ Cartagena (180,000), and Manizales (175,000).

FLAG.—Broad yellow band in upper half, surmounting equal bands of blue and red.

BRITISH EMBASSY.
(Carrera 8, No. 15–46, Bogotá.)

Ambassador Extraordinary and Plenipotentiary, His Excellency Alfred Stanley Fordham, C.M.G. (1960) £4,115

1st Secretary, J. A. Honeyford.

Naval Attaché, Capt. N. G. Hallett, D.S.C., R.N.

Military and Air Attaché, Group Capt. J. F. C. Melrose, D.F.C. (*resident at Lima, Peru*).

BRITISH CONSULAR OFFICES.

There are British Consular Offices at *Bogotá, Barranquilla, Medellin, Cali* and *Cartagena*.

BRITISH COUNCIL—*Representative in Colombia*, J. W. L. Gale, O.B.E. Calle 22, No. 6–21, Bogotá.

CONGO

President (vacant).

The Republic lies on the Equator between Gaboon on the west and the Congolese Republic on the east, the River Congo and its tributary the Ubanghi forming most of the eastern boundary of the state. The Congo has a short Atlantic coastline. Area of the Republic of Congo is 129,960 sq. miles, with a population (Census of 1962) of 864,000. Formerly the French colony of Middle Congo, it became a member state of the French Community on November 28, 1958, and was proclaimed fully independent on August 17, 1960.

M. Fulbert Youlou held office as President of the Republic from Aug. 7, 1960. Growing discontent with the regime culminated in riots in Brazzaville and led to the President's resignation on Aug. 15, 1963, and the dissolution by the Army of the National Assembly. A provisional Government led by M. Alphonse Massemba-Debat took office on Aug. 16, pending the establishment of a new constitution.

Trade with U.K., 1962: Imports, £415,412; Exports to U.K., £137,066.

CAPITAL.—Brazzaville (136,000); ♆ Pointe Noire (54,000).

FLAG.—Tricolour of green, yellow and red (diagonal yellow stripe).

French Ambassador, M. Jean Rossard.

British Ambassador, His Excellency William Scott Laver, C.B.E. (1962).

THE CONGOLESE REPUBLIC

President, Joseph Kasavubu, *assumed office* June 30, 1960.

CONGOLESE EMBASSY
26, Chesham Place, S.W. 1.

Chargé d'Affaires, Thomas Kanza.

The State of the Congo, founded in 1885, became a Belgian Colony on Nov. 15, 1908, and was administered by Belgium until June 30, 1960. Situated between long. 12°–31° E. and lat. 5° N.–13° S., the Congolese Republic comprises an area of 905,582 sq. miles, with a population estimated (1961) at 14,150,000. The State was divided into 21 provinces by July, 1963.

Government.—On June 30, 1960, the Belgian Congo became an independent unitary state under the Presidency of M. Kasavubu with a provisional constitution, the *Loi Fondamentale*, drawn up by the metropolitan Belgian Parliament. On July 11, M. Moise Tshombe announced the independence of the State of Katanga and although he failed to obtain international recognition he continued to act in an independent manner with the creation of a visa system, a Katanga franc, etc. Katanga did not come under the Government at Leopoldville until January 14, 1963.

The constitutional and political situation remained unsettled until 1962, United Nations mixed forces remaining in the country. (Details of events up to June, 1962, were given in WHITAKER'S ALMANACK, 1963).

In July, 1962, M. Adoula remodelled his government which he had formed, in July, 1961, excluding many of its more extreme members. His support in Parliament fell as did his popularity, especially when it became evident that the U Thant plan was not leading to a solution of the Katangan problem. This plan, which had been evolved in the summer of 1962, and accepted by MM. Adoula and Tshombe, provided for the adoption of a new constitution, the integration of the Katangan gendarmerie, an amnesty for political offenders, the equitable distribution of revenues etc. A Central Government delegation which went to Elisabethville, to discuss its implementation met, however, with continual obstruction. However, Union Minière agreed to pay its revenues to the Central Government instead of to the Katangan government, as hitherto. Continued incidents between the Katangan gendarmerie and the U.N. forces finally deteriorated into general fighting at the end of December, 1962. A swift and virtually unopposed advance by the U.N. Indian Brigade from Elisabethville to Jadotville and Kolwezi brought the end of resistance by the Katangan gendarmerie and with it the end of Katangan secession. M. Tshombe announced the "end of secession" at Kolwezi on January 14, 1963, and U.N. troops entered the town on January 21. A Minister of State for Katangan Affairs (M. Ileo) was sent to Elisabethville. Elements of the Congolese National Army entered Katanga which, by July, 1963, had been split into three provinces and integration proceeded reasonably successfully.

M. Adoula paid a successful visit to Brussels in February 1963. In April, he once again reconstructed his government, including members of the Lumumbist MNCL party and also representatives of M. Tshombe's party, the Conakat.

Climate.—Apart from the coastal district in the West which is fairly dry, the rainfall averages between 60 and 80 inches. The average temperature is about 80° F., but in the South the winter temperature can fall nearly to freezing point. There has been some increase in sleeping-sickness since independence. Malaria, formerly under control in Leopoldville and Matadi, has also begun to creep back as the former daily spraying ceased.

Extensive forest covers the central districts.

Production.—The cultivation of oil palms is widespread, palm oil now being the most important agricultural cash product, although the value of exports has declined slightly since 1958 (in 1962 exports totalled *Frs*. 2,215,000,000). Rubber (Exports in 1962, *Frs*. 1,252,345,000), coffee (*Frs*. 850,007,000) and timber (*Frs*. 432,438,000) are the next most important agricultural exports. The production of tea (*Frs*. 115,751,000) rose in 1962, but cotton, pyrethrum, copal and fibres production continues to be severely reduced. The country is rich in minerals, particularly Katanga province. Provisional production figures for 1962 are: copper 295,000 metric tons; zinc concentrates 166,900 metric tons; cobalt 9,683 metric tons; cadmium 97 metric tons; silver 49 metric tons and germanium 8 metric tons. Production of diamonds in Kasai province for 1962 is estimated at 15–16,000,000 carats. There is still no legal production of gem stones at the Tshikapa concession. Production of cassiterite, wolfram, tin and tantalite fell markedly in 1961 but increased again in 1962, cassiterite returning almost to the 1959 level. Extensive radium deposits exist near Elisabethville and reef-gold exists in the north-east of the Congo.

There is a wide variety of small but flourishing secondary industries, the main products being: cotton fabrics, blankets, sacks, footwear, beer, cigarettes, cement, paint and sugar. There are very large reserves of hydro-electric power.

The chief exports are copper, palm-oil and palm-kernels, coffee, diamonds, rubber, cobalt and cassiterite.

Trade with U.K.

	1961	1962
Imports from U.K.	£5,617,493	£4 332,231
Exports to U.K.	3,627,514	3,718,348

Language, Religion and Education.—The people are mainly of Bantu-Negro stock, divided into semi-autonomous tribes, each speaking a Bantu tongue. Swahili, a Bantu dialect with an admixture of Arabic, is the nearest approach to a common language in the East and South, and Lingala along the river. It is estimated there are 5,000,000 African Christians in the Republic (Roman Catholic 4,200,000, Protestant 800,000).

CAPITAL, Leopoldville (population, estimated 1963: 800,000–1,000,000). Principal towns, Elisabethville (182,638); Stanleyville (79,941); Jadotville (74,478); Luluabourg (59,935); ΨMatadi (59,184); Kolwezi (47,712) Coquilhatville (37,587); and ΨBoma (31,598).

FLAG.—A new flag was introduced on June 30, 1963. It has a large gold star next staff on a pale blue ground, diagonal red strip flanked by two narrow yellow strips running from bottom left corner.

BRITISH EMBASSY
Leopoldville.

Ambassador Extraordinary and Plenipotentiary, His Excellency Edward Michael Rose, C.M.G. (1963).
Counsellor, F. W. Marten, M.C.
Military Attaché, Lt.-Col. the Hon. J. R. K. Sinclair, O.B.E.
Air Attaché, Wing Commander J. C. Cogill, D.S.O., D.F.C.
1st Secretaries, B. W. Gordon (*Commercial and Consul*); D. Blyth; L. R. Kay; J. A. Stevens (*Information Officer*).
2nd Secretaries, P. J. Monk (*Vice-Consul*); W. G. Winter.
3rd Secretaries, R. A. Nielson; J. Illman; G. J. Garrett.

There are British Consulates at *Elisabethville* and at *Stanleyville*.

British Council Representative, A. W. J. Barron, M.B.E., P.O. Box 597, Leopoldville.

COSTA RICA
(República de Costa Rica.)

President (1962–66), Senor Francisco J. Orlich, *elected* February, 1962.

COSTA RICAN EMBASSY IN LONDON.
1A Inverness Terrace, W.2.

Ambassador, Señora Maria del Carmen Chittenden (1962).
1st Secretary (vacant).
Consul General, Señorita O. Rodriguez-Quirós, 4 Palace Gate, W.8.
Vice-Consul, Rafael Reig.

The Republic of Costa Rica, the most southerly State of Central America, extending across the isthmus between 8° 17′ and 11° 10′ N lat. and from 82° 30′ to 85° 45′ W. long., contains an area of 19,653 English square miles, and an estimated population (Dec., 1962) of 1,302,000. The rate of increase is about 4 per cent., one of the highest in the world. The population is basically of European stock in which Costa Rica differs from most Latin American countries. The Republic lies between Nicaragua and Panama and between the Caribbean Sea and the Pacific Ocean.

For nearly three centuries (1530–1821) Costa Rica formed part of the Spanish-American dominions, the seat of government being at Cartago. In 1821 the country joined in the War of Independence, and from 1824–1839 it was one of the United States of Central America.

On Dec. 1, 1948, the Army was abolished, the President declaring it unnecessary, as the country loved peace.

The coastal lowlands by the Caribbean Sea and Pacific have a tropical climate but the interior plateau, with a mean elevation of 4,000 feet, enjoys a temperate climate. The capital is 103 miles from the Atlantic and 72 miles from the Pacific.

The principal agricultural products are coffee (of a high quality), bananas, rice, maize, sugar-cane, potatoes, cocoa beans and hemp, the soil being extremely fertile. Increasing attention is being paid to cattle raising.

The chief ports are Limón, on the Atlantic coast, through which passes most of the coffee exported, and Puntarenas on the Pacific coast. Bananas are principally exported from Golfito, a port which has been developed on the Pacific Coast by the United Fruit Co. In 1962, 943 ships of a gross tonnage of 4,642,415 entered at Costa Rican ports. About 400 miles of railroad are open. The country is well provided with airways, and Pan-American Airways, LACSA and TACA call at San José, while feeder services link the main centres of population with the capital.

Spanish is the language of the country. Education is compulsory and free. The literacy rate is the highest in Latin America. In post-war years there has been a big advance in the provision of social services.

FINANCE.		1962
Revenue	*Colones*	386,140,363
Expenditure		433,806,435
Public debt (Dec. 1962):—		
External		224,364,145
Internal		402,772,780

Exchange rate: 6·62 *Colones* to U.S.$ and 18·53 *Colones* to the £ Sterling.

TRADE.

	1961	1962
Total imports	$U.S. 107,162,136	$U.S. 113,529,819
Total exports	79,781,562	85,443,335

Trade with U.K.

	1961	1962
Imports from U.K.	£1,684,783	£1,847,581
Exports to U.K.	345,836	423,262

The chief exports (1962) were coffee, bananas, cocoa, tunny fish, sugar, timber and rice. The imports, 46·4 per cent. from U.S.A. and 5·1 per cent. from U.K., consisted of flour, copper sulphate, textiles, mineral oils, motor vehicles, chemical products, fertilizers, lard, powdered milk, cement, bicycles, chinaware, etc.

CAPITAL, San José, pop. (March, 1963), 167,573; ΨLimon, 29,079; ΨPuntarenas, 25,979; Alajuela,

23,684; Heredia, 19,110; Cartago, 17,886; Liberia, 10,250.

FLAG.—Five horizontal bands, blue, white, red, white, blue (the red band twice the width of the others with emblem near staff).

BRITISH EMBASSY.
San José.

Ambassador Extraordinary and Plenipotentiary and Consul-General, His Excellency Frederic Francis Garner, C.M.G. (1961) £3,415
1st Secretary and Consul D. Reis, M.B.E.
3rd Secretary, E. W. Wise.
Commercial Attaché, J. M. Bowden.

There is also a British Consular Office at *Port Limon*.

San José is 5,687 miles from London; sea transit direct 18 days; *viâ* New York, 20 days; Air Mails (*viâ* New York), 3 to 10 days from London. Ocean Mail, 4 to 10 weeks.

CUBA

(Republica de Cuba.)

President, Osvaldo Dorticós Torrado, *appointed* July 17, 1959.

COUNCIL OF MINISTERS
(January 5, 1959)

Prime Minister, Dr. Fidel Castro Ruz.
Vice-Premier and Armed Forces, Major Raúl Castro Ruz.
Minister of State (Foreign Affairs), Dr. Raul Roa y Garcia.
Justice, Dr. Alfredo Yabur Maluf.
Treasury, Luis Alvarez Rom.
Interior, Maj. Ramiro Valdés.
Communications, Maj. Fauré Chomon.
Public Works, Arch. Osmani Cienfuegos.
Foreign Trade, Alberto Mora Becerro.
Internal Trade, Manuel Luzardo.
Industry, Maj. Ernesto Guevara.
Public Health, Dr. J. Ramón Machado Ventura.
Education, Armando Hart Dávalos.
Labour, Augusto R. Martinez Sánchez.
National Economy, Dr. Regino Boti.
Transport, Capt. Omar Fernández.

CUBAN EMBASSY IN LONDON
22 Mount Street, W.1.
[Mayfair: 6636]

Ambassador Extraordinary and Plenipotentiary, His Excellency Dr. Federico de Cordova Castro.
Consul, Señor Julio del Castillo, 329 High Holborn, W.C.1.

Cuba (the largest of the "West India" Islands) lies between 74° and 85° W. long., and 19° and 23° N. lat., with a total area of 44,178 sq. miles and a population (estimated, 1960) of 6,499,344.

The island of Cuba was visited by Christopher Columbus during his first voyage, on October 27, 1492, and was then believed to be part of the Western mainland of India. Early in the 16th century the island was conquered by the Spaniards, to be used later as a base of operations for the conquest of Mexico and Central America, and for almost four centuries Cuba remained under a Spanish Captain-General. [The island was under British rule for one year, 1762–1763, when it was returned to Spain in exchange for Florida.] Separatist agitation culminated in the closing years of the 19th century in a fierce and blood-thirsty war. In 1898 the government of the United States intervened and despatched the battleship *Maine* to Havana harbour, and in February of that year the vessel was sunk by an explosion, the cause of which remains an unsolved mystery. On April 20, 1898, the U.S. Government demanded the evacuation of Cuba by the Spanish forces, and a short Spanish-American war led to the abandonment of the island, which was occupied by U.S. troops. From Jan. 1, 1899, to May 20, 1902, Cuba was under U.S. military rule, and reforms of the widest and most far-reaching character were instituted. On May 20, 1902, an autonomous government was inaugurated with an elected President, and a legislature of two houses. The island was, however, again the prey of revolution from Aug. to Sept., 1906, when the U.S. Government resumed control. On Jan. 28 1909, a republican government was again inaugurated. In 1933 a revolution was followed by provisional government until May, 1936, when a constitutional government was elected. A new Constitution was promulgated in 1940, but its operation was suspended for various periods until February 24, 1955, when the Government elected on November 1, 1954, took office.

A revolution led by Dr. Fidel Castro overthrew the Government of General Batista on January 1, 1959. A provisional government was set up and elections were promised within four years. Dr. Castro has since proclaimed the revolution to be Socialist and himself to be a Marxist-Leninist.

A new communist party, the United Party of the Socialist Revolution, is in course of formation. It is the only authorized political party. Elections are no longer to be held. A new Socialist constitution has also been promised, but no date has been set for its introduction.

The Revolutionary Government has carried out programmes of land and urban reform and of nationalization of the means of production and distribution. By June, 1963, 90 per cent. of industrial production, all foreign trade and about 50 per cent of small commercial companies were in state hands. About half the cultivated land is in state farms or cooperatives. Private small-holders, who own the other half, also come under a measure of Government control.

Sugar remains the major item in the economy, although production has fallen from 5·6 million tons in 1960 to about 3·6 million tons in 1963. It accounts for 80 per cent. of Cuban exports. Tobacco provides 5 per cent. of exports. Sweet potatoes, bananas, rice, coffee, cocoa, maize, cotton and tropical fruits also flourish. There are large herds of cattle.

11,915 miles of railway are open (public service 4,880; sugar plantations and mining areas 7,035) and about 12,000 miles of telegraph line. There are about 8,291 miles of road. At present scheduled international air services run only to Mexico City, Moscow, Prague and Madrid.

Language and Literature.—Spanish is the language of the island, but English is widely understood. Education is compulsory and free. The University of Havana was founded in 1728, but until its enlargement under American auspices in the first quarter of the twentieth century no great progress was made in secondary or higher education. There are universities at Santiago de Cuba and Santa Clara. Public libraries have been established. The daily press, which has a fairly wide circulation, is under government control, as are broadcasting and television.

Finance.—The public revenue has risen from an estimated $365,247,946 in 1958 to $2,093,560,093 for 1963, including profits from State trading concerns, etc. No up-to-date figures are available for the public debt—at the end of 1958 this stood at $760,300,000.

Nominally $=U.S. $1. U.S. currency ceased to be legal tender in Cuba on June 30, 1951 (*see also* p. 84).

Trade.—Exports for 1962 were $520,728,000. No figures are available for imports, but it is known that Cuba has a trade deficit with the Communist-bloc countries.

Trade with U.K.

	1961	1962
Imports from U.K.....	£4,416,919	£2,568,017
Exports to U.K	£5,339,440	£7,115,117

The exports are principally molasses and tobacco; the imports are mainly machinery.

CAPITAL, ♆Havana (pop., Census 1953, 783,162); other towns are ♆Santiago (166,565), Holgüin (226,644), Camagüey (204,254), Santa Clara (144,630), and ♆Cienfuegos (990,00).

FLAG.—Five horizontal bands, blue and white (blue at top and bottom) with red triangle, close to staff, charged with silver.

BRITISH EMBASSY

(Chancery: Edif. Bolívar, Capdevila No. 101, 9th Floor. Postal address: Apartado 1069, Havana.)

British Ambassador Extraordinary and Plenipotentiary, His Excellency John Hugh Adam Watson, C.M.G., (1963)............................£4,115
Counsellor, P. H. Scott.
1st Secretary (*Consul*).) J. W. Pethybridge.
2nd Secretaries, B. Hitch; R. A. C. Byatt; J. R. Clube (*Commercial*).
3rd Secretary, S. D. Eccles.
Naval and Air Attaché, Group Capt. V. Rees, D.F.C. (*Resident at Caracas*).

BRITISH CONSULAR OFFICES.

There are British Consular Offices at *Havana*, *Camagüey* and *Santiago de Cuba.*

ZECHOSLOVAKIA

(Československá Socialistická Republika.)

President, Antonin Novotný, *born* December 10, 1904, *elected* November 19, 1957.

CABINET.

(Sept. 22, 1963)

Prime Minister, Josef Lenart.
Vice-Premiers, František Krajčír.; Jan Pillar; Otakar Simunek; Oldřich Cernik.
Agriculture, Forestry and Water Conservancy, Jiri Burian.
Food Industry, Vatislav Krutina.
Heavy Engineering, Josef Pešl.
Consumer Goods Industry, Mrs. Bozena Machacová-Dostálová.
General Engineering, Karel Poláček.
Finance, Richard Dvorak.
Justice, Dr. Alois Neumann.
National Defence, Gen. Bohumir Lomsky.
Internal Trade, Jindrich Uher.
Interior, Lubomir Strougal.
Health, Dr. Josef Plojhar.
Construction, Samuel Takáč.
Education and Culture, Cestmir Cisar.
Foreign Trade, František Hamouz.
Fuel and Power, Josef Odvarka.
Metallurgy and Ore Mines, Josef Krejci.
Chemical Industry, Josef Pučik.
Foreign Affairs, Václav David.
Transport, Alois Indra.
State Control and Statistics, Pavol Majling.
Central Power Administration, Josef Korčák.
Without Portfolio, Michal Chudik; Vincenc Krahulec.

CZECHOSLOVAK EMBASSY AND CONSULATE

6–7 Kensington Palace Gardens, W.8.
[Bayswater: 9191.]

Ambassador, His Excellency Zdenek Trhlik (1961).
Counsellor, Miroslav Jiráska.
Military and Air Attaché, Col. Jaroslav Mikoška.
Commercial Counsellor, Lubromír Šilhavy.
Commercial Attachés, Josef Pištora; Jiří Nováček.
3rd Secretaries, Jan Mrázek; Robert Husák.
Attachés, Milos Stepánek; Jaromír Johanes; František August (*Head of Consular Dept.*); Eduard Sevčik.

Area and Population.—Czechoslovakia, formerly part of the Austro-Hungarian Monarchy, declared its independence on Oct. 28, 1918 (Czechoslovak Independence Day), the territory thus affected having an area of 53,700 square miles.

Since the War of 1939–45 the territory and population of the Republic have undergone change. By a treaty with the Soviet Union (June 29, 1945) Ruthenia was ceded to U.S.S.R., thus reducing the area by over 4,000 square miles and the population by over 750,000. In addition, the Sudeten German minority was expelled as sanctioned at the Potsdam Conference and the preliminary results of the census of March 1, 1961, gave the population as 13,742,000.

Government—In September, 1938, Adolf Hitler demanded the cession of the Sudeten districts. On Sept. 29, 1938, a Four Power Conference at Munich acquiesced in the annexation of the territory on the understanding that no further demands would be made, but on March 14, 1939, Nazi troops invaded Czechoslovakia, in flagrant violation of the terms of the Munich Conference, and two days later Adolf Hitler proclaimed that Czechoslovakia had "ceased to exist": a "Slovak State" was established and Bohemia and Moravia were declared a Protectorate of the Reich.

On July 22, 1940, Great Britain recognized the Czechoslovak National Committee set up in London as a provisional Czechoslovak Government, and on July 18, 1941, Great Britain fully recognized the Czechoslovak Government headed by President Benés.

Following the liberation of Eastern Slovakia by Soviet forces in 1945, President Benés and most of the members of his Government left London for Moscow for discussions with the Czechoslovak *émigré* movement in the Soviet Union on the formation of a new Government which would have its seat on Czechoslovak territory. The composition and programme of this Government, which was headed by M. Z. Fierlinger, were announced at Kosice in Slovakia on April 4, 1945. The Kosice Government included equal representation of four Czech parties (Czech Socialists, Social Democrats, Communists and Popular Party) and two Slovak parties (Democrats and Communists).

The first elections in the liberated Republic were held on May 26, 1946, the Communists emerging as the leading party with 38 per cent. of the votes cast. On July 3, 1946, K. Gottwald, the Communist leader, formed a Government of parties participating in a National Front. The uneasy alliance between the parties was terminated by a crisis precipitated by the mass resignation on February 20, 1948, of Ministers representing parties opposed to the Communists in protest against the widespread introduction of Communists into the police force by the Communist Minister of the Interior. The Communist Party, with the aid of Action Committees, seized power, and on February 25 a new Government, predominantly Communist, was formed. On May 30, 1948, new elections were held, the choice lying between a single joint election list of parties in the National Front, and a blank vote. The Communist control of the country is now unqualified. On July 11, 1960, a new constitution was proclaimed, replacing that of 1948. Its purpose was to express the fact that Czechoslovakia is now deemed to have completed the construction of Socialism and to be on the road to true Communism. The official title of the State was accordingly changed to "The Czechoslovak Socialist Republic".

The first Five-Year plan which came to an end in December, 1953, was largely concerned with extending heavy industry and industrializing Slovakia. It was officially claimed that production had doubled during the plan, but it was also admitted that the economy had been thrown out of balance by poor progress in the development of ore reserves, fuel, power and agricultural production. The second Five-Year plan covered the years 1956–1960, after two interim years (1954 and 1955) devoted to correcting these faults. During the second Five-Year plan gross industrial production increased by 66 per cent., the emphasis remaining on heavy industry. Progress in hard coal production and in increasing power generating capacity, however, was less good, and agricultural production remained virtually stagnant in spite of the continued formation of agricultural co-operatives. The third Five-Year plan was abandoned in the early summer of 1962 because its targets were set too high. The economy was being run on a one-year plan in 1963, with a seven-year plan up to 1970 in preparation.

Language and Literature.—Czech and Slovak are the official languages but the literature is mainly Czech in Bohemia, Moravia and Silesia. The Reformation gave a widespread impulse to Czech literature, the writings of Jan Hus (who was martyred in 1415) familiarizing the people with Wyclif's teaching. This impulse endured to the close of the seventeenth century when Amos Komensky, or Comenius (1592–1670) was expelled from the country. Under Austrian repression, and with the outlawing of the national language, there was a period of stagnation until the national revival in the early nineteenth century. Modern prose drama and fiction are represented by several authors of international reputation, notably K. M. Capek-Chod (1860–1927), F. X. Svoboda (1860–1943), Jaroslav Hilbert (1871–1936), Viktor Dyk (1877–1931), Arnost Dvorák (1880–1933), Ivan Olbracht (*b.* 1882), K. Capek (1890–1938), and Vladimír Vancura (1891–1942). Liberty of the press ceased with the violation of independence in 1939. It was temporarily restored on the liberation of the country. After the Communist coup of February 25, 1948, however, freedom of the press was "curtailed." All papers and periodicals were forced to follow the party line and a number of publications were banned.

Education.—In 1961–62 the number of pupils in general (primary and secondary) schools was given as 2,277,954. In addition there were, in 1961–62, 254,945 pupils at technical schools, including 106,353 adults studying extra-murally. Education is compulsory and free for all children from the ages of 6 to 14, and under the 1960 Education Act the school-leaving age is being raised to 15. There are five universities in Czechoslovakia of which the most famous is Charles University in Prague (founded 1348), the others being situated at Bratislava, Brno, Olomouc and Košice. In 1961–62 the number of university students was said to be 22,360, with another 12,172 extra-mural students. Students at technical colleges of university standing totalled 38,406 (full-time) and 13,832 (extra-mural) in 1962–62. A further 1,212 full-time and 98 part-time students were attending art or music colleges and 13,337 full-time and 9,239 part-time students were at other institutions.

Finance.—The Czechoslovak currency is the Czechoslovak *Koruna* (*Kčs*=Czechoslovak crown) of 100 *heller*. From the devaluation of the pound in 1949 up to May 30, 1953, the exchange rate was *Kčs.* 139·58=£1. On June 1, 1953, the official rate was changed to *Kčs.* 20·16=£1, but a bonus of 100 per cent. was added to certain non-commercial transfers including the encashment of travellers' cheques. This change took place as the result of an internal currency reform when a new currency was issued at a basic exchange rate of *Kčs.* 1·00 of the new currency for *Kčs.* 5·00 of the old. Thre present rate is *Kcs.* 20·10=£1, with a bonus of *Kčs.* 20 for non-commercial travellers. The Budget estimates for 1963 total *Kčs.* 125,815,000,000 for expenditure and *Kčs.* 125,877,000,000 for revenue.

Trade with U.K.

	1961	1962
Imports from U.K....	£10,068,876	£12,911,299
Exports to U.K......	13,577,555	13,236,441

CAPITAL, Prague (Praha), on the Vltava (Moldau), the former capital of Bohemia with a population (1961) of 1,003,341. Other towns are Brno (Brunn), capital of Moravia (314,379), Bratislava (Pressburg), capital of Slovakia (242,091), Ostrava (234,671) and Plzen (Pilsen) (137,673).

FLAG.—Two equal horizontal stripes, white (above) and red; a blue triangle next to staff.

BRITISH EMBASSY.

Thunovská ulice 14, Prague I.

Ambassador Extraordinary and Plenipotentiary, His Excellency Cecil Cuthbert Parrott, C.M.G., O.B.E. (1960)........................£4,115
Counsellor, J. M. Hunter, M.C.
1st Secretary (Commercial) and Consul, W. N. Hillier-Fry.
Vice-Consul, G. M. Braidwood.
3rd Secretaries, J. R. Banks; D. Caccia.
Military Attaché, Col. K. A. M. Bennett, M.C.
Assistant Military Attaché, Maj. W. J. Exley.
Air Attaché, Group-Capt. M. C. Adderley, O.B.E., A.F.C.
Cultural Attaché (British Council Representative), W. G. Woods

DAHOMEY

(Republic of Dahomey)

President, Hubert Maga, *elected for five years*, December 11, 1960.
President of the National Assembly, Valentin Djibodé Aplogan.
Vice-President and Ambassador to U.K. and France, S. M. Apithy.
Foreign Affairs, Emile Zinzor.

A republic situated in West Africa, between 2° and 3° W and 6° and 12° N., Dahomey has a short coast line of 78 miles on the Gulf of Guinea but extends northwards inland for 437 miles. It is flanked on the west by Togo, on the north by the Voltaic Republic and Niger and on the east by Nigeria. It has an area of about 47,000 square miles and a population estimated in 1961 at 1,934,000. Although poor in resources, Dahomey is one of the most thickly populated areas in West Africa, with a high level of education. It is divided into four main regions running horizontally: a narrow sandy coastal strip, a succession of intercommunicating lagoons, a clay belt and a sandy plateau in the north.

The first treaty with France was signed by one of the kings of Abomey in 1851 but the country was not placed under French administration until 1892.

Dahomey became an independent republic within the French Community on Dec. 4, 1958; full independence outside the Community was proclaimed on August 1, 1960. Special agreements with France, covering financial and cultural matters, technical assistance, defence, etc., were signed in Paris on April 24, 1961. Dahomey is a member of the *Conseil de l'Entente* (*see* Ivory Coast). The official language is French.

The Constitution of Dahomey, adopted on November 25, 1961, provides for a presidential system of government, a single Chamber National Assembly and a Supreme Court. At elections held on Dec. 7, 1960 the newly-established *Parti Dahoméen de l'Unité* won a large majority.

Finance.—The currency of Dahomey is the *Franc CFA* (*Francs CFA* 50=1 French *Franc*) (*Francs CFA* 691=£1). In 1963 the Budget balanced at 6,688,188,000 an increase of *CFA* 400,000,000 on 1962.

Trade.—The principal exports are palm products (80 per cent.) followed by ground nuts, shea-nuts and coffee. Small deposits of gold, iron and chrome have been found. Trade in 1961 was valued at: Imports *Francs CFA* 6,275,345,000: Exports *Francs CFA* 3,579,000,000. Trade in 1962 (10 months) was valued at: Imports *Francs CFA* 5,380,487,000: Exports *Francs CFA* 2,483,471,000. Imports from the United Kingdom in 1962, £288,642; Exports to U.K., £21,634.

CAPITAL.—Porto Novo (58,500). Principal commercial town and port, ΨCotonou (85,845).

FLAG.—Three stripes, one vertical, green, two horizontal yellow and red.

British Ambassador (*see* Ivory Coast).

DENMARK

(Kongeriget Danmark.)

King, Frederik IX, K.G., elder son of King Christian X, *born* March 11, 1899; *suc.* April 20, 1947; *married* May 24, 1935, Princess Ingrid (born March 28, 1910), daughter of H.M. King Gustav VI Adolf, King of Sweden; and has issue Princess Margrethe, *born* April 16, 1940 (*Heir Presumptive*), Princess Benedikte, *born* April 29, 1944, and Princess Anne-Marie, *born* Aug. 30, 1946.

CABINET.
(September 3, 1962)

Prime Minister, Jens Otto Krag.
Finance, Prof. Kjeld Philip.
Foreign Affairs, Per Haekkerup.
Interior, Lars B. Jensen.
Fisheries, A. C. Normann.
Defence, Poul Hansen.
Agriculture, Karl Skytte.
Labour, Erling Dinesen.
Social Affairs, Kai Bundvad.
Education, K. Helveg Petersen.
Greenland, Mikael Gam.
Communications, Kai Lindberg.
Ecclesiastical Affairs, Mrs. Bodil Koch.
Commerce, Hilmar Baunsgaard.
Justice, Hans Hækkerup.
Economic and Nordic Affairs (vacant).
Housing, Carl P. Jensen.
Cultural Affairs, Julius Bomholt.

ROYAL DANISH EMBASSY IN LONDON.
29 Pont Street, S.W.1
[Belgravia: 4696]

Ambassador in London, His Excellency Nils T. Svenningsen, G.B.E. (1961).
Counseller, Albert W. Kœnigsfeldt.
1st Secretary, Miss I. Ammentorp.
2nd Secretary, Jørgen Abrahamsen.
Naval and Air Attaché, Lt.-Col. Einer Beck Meincke.
Military Attaché, Lt.-Col. H.H. Prince Georg of Denmark, C.V.O.
Agricultural Counsellor, P. A. Moltesen.
Asst. Agricultural Attaché, Anker Kloppenborg-Skrumsager.
Counsellor for Press and Cultural Affairs, H. Agerbak.
Press and Cultural Attaché, S. S. Oestergaard.
Fisheries Attaché, J. C. Bogstad.

Commercial and Consular Section
67 Pont St., S.W.1. [Kensington: 6656].

Consul-General, Henning Hjorth-Nielsen (*Minister Plenipotentiary and Commercial Counsellor*).
Vice-Consuls, Niels Lassen (*Commercial Secretary*); Hans Duborg (*Commercial Secretary*).
Consul, C. Jacobsen.
Vice-Consul, T. F. Germer.

AREA AND POPULATION.—A Kingdom of Northern Europe, and the smallest of the Northern States, consisting of the islands of Zeeland, Funen, Lolland, etc., the peninsula of Jutland, and the outlying island of Bornholm in the Baltic. Denmark is situated between 54° 34'–57° 45' N. lat., and 8° 5'–15° 12' E. long., with an area of 16,608 square miles, and a population estimated Sept. 26, 1960) at 4,585,256. In 1961 there were 76,439 births, 43,310 deaths and 36,364 marriages.

GOVERNMENT.—Under the Constitution of the Kingdom of Denmark Act of June 5, 1953, the legislature consists of one chamber, the *Folketing*, of not more than 179 members, including 2 for the Faröe and 2 for Greenland. The voting age is 21 years. In the 1960 elections the Social Democrats obtained 76 seats; Venstre 38; Conservatives 32; Radicals 11; Socialist People's Party 11; Faröe 2; Greenlanders 2; Slesvig Party (German Minority) 1; Independent 6.

EDUCATION is free and compulsory, the schools being maintained by taxation. Special schools are numerous, technical and agricultural predominating. There are Universities at Copenhagen (founded in 1478) and Aarhus (1933).

LANGUAGE AND LITERATURE.—The Danish language is akin to Swedish and Norwegian. Danish literature, ancient and modern, embraces all forms of expression, familiar names being Hans Christian Andersen (1805–1875), Sőren Kierkegaard (1813–1855) and Georg Brandes (1842–1927), with Henrik Pontoppidan (1857–1943) and Karl Gjellerup (1857–1919), who shared the Nobel Prize for Literature in 1917, and Johannes V. Jensen (1873–1950), who received the same award in 1944. Over 200 newspapers are published in Denmark; 10 daily papers are published in Copenhagen.

PRODUCTION AND INDUSTRY.—Twenty-one per cent. of the population live exclusively by agriculture, and about 48 per cent. by manufactures and trade. The chief products are wheat, rye, oats, barley, potatoes, seeds, cattle, horses, pigs and dairy produce; manufactures are mostly based on imported raw material but there are also considerable imports of finished goods.

COMMUNICATIONS.—Mercantile marine (ships above 100 gross tonnage) (December, 1961) 1,044 ships, with a gross tonnage of 2,411,832. On March 31, 1962, there were 4,215 kilometres of railway and 559,480 kilometres of telegraph and telephone lines.

FINANCE	1963–64
Revenue (*Budget estimate*).....	*Kr.* 10,802,662,093
Expenditure (*Budget estimate*)..	10,290,532,100
Government Debt (March 31, 1962):—	
Internal....................	6,663,000,000
External....................	1,334,000,000

Rate of Exchange—Kr. 19·34=£1 (*see also* p. 83).

TRADE	1962
Total Imports	*Kr.*14,664,800,000
Total Exports	11,253,000,000

Trade with U.K.

	1961	1962
Imports from U.K.	£ 91,938,286	£103,509,292
Exports to U.K.	142,032,666	152,140,641

The principal imports are machinery, liquid and solid fuels, base metals, vehicles, textile products, chemicals, fertilizers, cereals, feeding stuffs and wood and cork. The chief exports are agricultural produce, fish products, butter, bacon, eggs, meat and livestock, ships, machinery, pharmaceuticals and ready made clothing.

CAPITAL, ΨCopenhagen. Population (1955), 923,974. Other centres are ΨAarhus, 119,568; ΨOdense, 111,145; ΨAalborg, 85,800; ΨEsbjerg, 55,171; ΨRanders, 42,238; ΨHorsens, 37,261; ΨKolding, 35,101; Roskilde, 31,928; ΨVejle, 31,362 and ΨFredericia 29,870.

FLAG.—Red, with white cross.

Copenhagen, distant from London 728 miles; transit 36 hours by sea.

BRITISH EMBASSY.

Offices, Kastelsvej 38–40, Copenhagen.
Residence, Bredgade 26, Copenhagen.

British Ambassador, His Excellency Hon. John Patrick Edward Chandos Henniker-Major, C.M.G., M.C. (1962) £4,115

Counsellor, C. C. B. Stewart, C.M.G.

Commercial Counsellor (and H.M. Consul-General), C. B. B. Heathcote-Smith, C.B.E.

Counsellor for Scientific Questions, W. F. G. Drury (*resident in Stockholm*).

1st Secretaries, M. A. C. S. Cope; L. S. Price (*Consular*); J. Mellon (*Agriculture and Food Attaché*); K. Kenney (*Labour Attaché, Resident in Helsinki*); R. E. Jones (*Information*).

2nd Secretary, E. R. Powell.

3rd Secretaries, A. L. S. Coltman; Major C. L. Bayliss, M.B.E.

Naval Attaché, Cdr. C. S. Mosely, R.N.

Military and Air Attaché, Wing-Cdr. T. H. Hutchinson.

Assistant Military Attaché, Maj. A. Trimmer (*Resident in Stockholm*).

Assistant Air Attaché, Sqn.-Ldr. J. M. Beeby (*Resident in Stockholm*).

Chaplain, Rev. H. L. Heizler.

There are also Vice-Consulates at *Aabenraa*, *Aalborg*, *Aarhus*, *Esbjerg* and *Odense*; and at *Thorshavn* (Faroë). There is a Consular Agent at *Klaksvig* (Faroë).

BRITISH COUNCIL.

Representative, J. Sutherland (*Cultural Attaché*), c/o The British Embassy.

Outlying Parts of the Kingdom

The outlying parts of Denmark have about 69,000 inhabitants. The FARÖE, or Sheep Islands (540 sq. m. pop. (1960) 34,596), capital, Thorshavn, are governed by a *Lagting* of 25 members, and send 2 representatives to the *Folketing* at Copenhagen. On September 14, 1946, the Lagting, with the consent of the Danish Government, for its own guidance held a plebiscite on the Faröe. About one-third of the electors did not, however, take part in the voting: of the rest a little more than half the votes cast were in favour of separation from Denmark and the establishment of a republic. At a subsequent general election for the Lagting a great majority voted in favour of remaining a part of the Kingdom of Denmark with a certain extent of home rule. In 1948 the Faröe received a certain measure of home rule. Special Faröese affairs are administered by a council of 3 members. Trade with U.K. in 1962 totalled: Imports, £683,090; Exports, £1,353,812. GREENLAND (ice-free portion about 132,000 sq. m., total area about 840,000 sq. m., population, Dec. 31, 1961, 34,312), is divided into 3 provinces (West, North and East). West Greenland (capital, Godthaab) has a *Landsraad* of 14 members and sends 2 representatives to the *Folketing* at Copenhagen. The trade of Greenland is mainly under the management of the Royal Greenland Trade Department; discoveries of lead were made in 1948. The United States of America has acquired certain rights to maintain air bases in Greenland.

DOMINICAN REPUBLIC

(República Dominicana.)

Following a *coup d'état* by the armed forces on Sept. 25, 1963, the following were named as the provisional Government—Señor Emilio de los Santos, Dr. Ramon Tatia Espinal and Señor Manuel Tavares Espaillat.

EMBASSY AND CONSULATE.

4 Braemar Mansions, Cornwall Gardens, S.W.7
[Western: 1921]

Ambassador (vacant).

Consul-General, Señor Victor Cabral.

There are also Consular Offices at *Liverpool*, *Birmingham*, *Manchester*, *Nottingham*, *Grimsby*, *Sheffield*, *Southampton*, *Plymouth*, *Cardiff*, *Edinburgh*, *Glasgow* and *Belfast*.

The Dominican Republic, formerly the Spanish portion of the island of Hispaniola, is the oldest settlement of European origin in America.

The island was discovered by Christopher Columbus in December, 1492, who named it "La Española" or "Little Spain." In 1496 he ordered his brother, Bartholomew Columbus, to found the capital at the mouth of the Ozama River, on the south of the island, which city he called Santo Domingo. The island immediately became the objective for adventurous Spanish colonists, who exploited the native Indians for the sake of the gold found in the streams. African negroes were imported for the sugar and other plantations both in Santo Domingo and Haiti.

In 1821 Santo Domingo broke away from Spain and declared itself independent, but in 1822 it was invaded and subjugated by its negro neighbours from the west, the Haitians. The latter were driven out on Feb. 27, 1844, when the Dominican Republic was definitely proclaimed by the natives.

The country was occupied by American marines from 1916 until the adoption of a new Constitution in 1924. In July, 1924, a properly elected Constitutional Government was installed, with complete authority over all matters except the collection of the Customs and the redemption of foreign obligations, which continued to be administered by an American official.

From 1930 until May 30, 1961 (when he was assassinated) Generalissimo Rafael Trujillo ruled the country with an iron hand. Since January 1, 1962, legislative and executive powers have been vested temporarily in a seven-man Council of State headed by the President of the Republic. Elections for a constituent assembly to revise the constitution and later for a new President and Legislature were expected to be held before the end of 1962.

The Dominican Republic lies between Cuba on the west and Puerto Rico on the east and covers an area of about 19,322 square miles, with a population of 3,013,525 at a Census held in August, 1960. The climate is tropical in the low lands and semi-tropical to temperate in the higher altitudes. According to local classification there are 2,398 miles of first class and 2,098 miles of second class and inter-communal roads in the Republic. There is a direct road from Santo Domingo to Port-au-Prince, the capital of Haiti, enabling the journey to be made in one day. There are about 80 miles (Sánchez–La Vega) of public railway, and a telephone system connects practically all the principal towns of the republic. The Dirección General de Comunicaciones, All American Cables, and Radio Corporation of America maintain an efficient telegraph service with all parts of the world. There are more than 60 commercial broadcasting stations and there is a television station operated by Radio Santo Domingo, which with the help of relay stations provides reception of its programmes throughout the Republic. A second television station in Santo Domingo-Rahintel transmits to the local area.

Spanish is the language of the Republic.

Sugar, coffee, cocoa, and tobacco are the most important crops. Other products are peanuts, maize, rice, bananas, molasses, salt, cement, timber, cattle, iron ore, sisal products, honey and chocolate. There are several light industries producing sisal bags and rope, glass products, cotton textiles, shoes, paper, rum, matches, peanut oil and other products.

The Republic is served by five airlines, Pan-American, Caribair, Compania Brasileina de Aviacion (VARIG), Venezuelan National Airways (VIASA) and the Compania Dominicana de Aviacion. The new international airport 18 miles to the east of the capital is now in full operation.

FINANCE

Budget	1961	1962†
Revenue	RD$ 126,744,235	RD$ 128,400,000
Expenditure..	125,990,087	147,000,000

† Estimated.

One *Dominican Peso*=$1·00 U.S. (*see also* p. 84).

TRADE

	1960	1961
Imports	RD$ 87,022,913	RD$ 69,489,393
Exports	180,366,732	143,147,623

Trade with U.K.

	1961	1962
Imports from U.K.....	£1,974,449	£2,759,027
Exports to U.K.......	6,494,717	505,831

The chief imports are machinery, foodstuffs, iron and steel, cotton textiles and yarns, mineral oils (including petrol), cars and other motor vehicles, chemical and pharmaceutical products, electrical equipment and accessories, construction material, paper and paper products, and rubber and rubber products; the chief exports are sugar, coffee, cocoa, chocolate and molasses.

The principal export to U.K. over a number of years has been sugar.

CAPITAL.—Santo Domingo (recently called Ciudad Trujillo), population of the Capital District (Census, 1960), 462,192; population of Santo Domingo urban area, 367,053. Other centres are: Santiago de los Caballeros (169,139); Concepcion de la Vega (134,060); San Francisco de Macoris (100,726); San Juan de La Maguana (86,294); San Cristobal (85,657); Moca (81,839); ΨPuerto Plata (62,052); and Bani (57,945).

FLAG.—Red and blue, with white cross bearing an emblem at centre.

BRITISH EMBASSY

(Avenida Independencia, 84, Santo Domingo.)

Ambassador Extraordinary and Plenipotentiary and Consul-General, His Excellency Stephen Alexander Lockhart, C.M.G., O.B.E. (1962).

1st Secretary, G. W. Harding (*Consul*).

BRITISH CONSULAR OFFICES

There are British Consular Offices at *Santo Domingo*, *Puerto Plata* and *San Pedro de Macoris*.

ECUADOR

(Republica del Ecuador)

President of the Republic (vacant). [Military Junta *assumed power* July 11, 1963].

EMBASSY AND CONSULATE.

Flat 3B, 3 Hans Crescent, S.W.1

[Knightsbridge: 1367]

Ambassador (vacant).

Charge d'Affairs and 2nd Secretary, Dr. Manuel Andrés Borrero.

Air, Military and Naval Attaché, Lt. Col. Luis A. German.

Consul and 2nd Secretary, Señor Ing. Belisario Palacios González.

3rd Secretary, Señora Dora Paulson.

Consuls at *Liverpool*, *Birmingham* and *Glasgow*.

Area and Population.—Ecuador is an equatorial State of South America, the mainland extending from lat. 1° 38′ N. to 4° 50′ S., and between 75° 20′ and 81° W. long., comprising an area reduced by boundary settlements with Peru (Jan. 29, 1942) to about 226,000 sq. miles.

The Republic of Ecuador is divided into 20 provinces and one territory. It has a population estimated (June, 1963) at 4,500,000, mostly descendants of the Spaniards, aboriginal Indians, and Mestizoes. The territory of the Republic extends across the Western Andes, the highest peak of which is Aconcagua, in the Chilean sector (22,976 ft.), the highest peaks in Ecuador being Chimborazo (20,498 ft.), Iliniza (17,405 ft.), Carihuairazo (16,515 ft.); Cotocachi (16,301 ft.), and Pichincha (16,000 ft.) in the Western Cordillera; and Cotopaxi (19,498 ft.), Antisana (18,864 ft.), Cayambe (19,160 ft.), Altar (17,730 ft.), Sangay (17,464 ft.), Tungurahua (16,690 ft.), and Sincholagua (16,365 ft.) in the Eastern Cordillera. Ecuador is watered by the Upper Amazon, and by the rivers Guayas, Mira, Santiago, Chone, and Esmeraldas on the Pacific coast. There are extensive forests, and the cinchona bark tree is common.

The *Galápagos* (Tortoise) *Islands* forming the province of Colon, were annexed by Ecuador in 1832. The archipelago lies in the Pacific, about 500 miles from Saint Elena peninsula, the most westerly point of the mainland. There are 12 large and several hundred smaller islands with a total area of about 3,000 sq. miles and an estimated population (1959) of 1,790. The capital is San Cristobal, on Chatham Island. Although the archipelago lies on the equator, the temperature of the surrounding water is well below equatorial average owing to the *Antarctic Humboldt Current*. The islands export guano, orchilla moss and cattle. There is an increasing amount of fishing, mainly for the North American market.

Government.—The former *Kingdom of Quito* was conquered by the Incas of Peru in the latter part of the 15th century. Early in the 16th century Pizarro's conquests led to the inclusion of the present territory of Ecuador in the Spanish Viceroyalty of Peru. The independence of the country was achieved in a revolutionary war which culminated in the battle of Mount Pichincha (May 24, 1822). A new constitution was issued on Dec. 31, 1946. Dr. Carlos Arosemena, President of Ecuador from Nov. 8, 1961, was deposed by the Army on July 11, 1963, his powers being taken over by a Junta of officers.

Production and Industry.—The chief products are bananas, cocoa, coffee, rice, petroleum, straw hats, vegetable ivory and balsa wood. The petroleum is insufficient to meet the whole of Ecuador's needs. In the highlands the principal crops are maize, wheat, potatoes and other temperate products. Small amounts of gold, silver and lead are mined, and emeralds and rubies are occasionally found. There is little industry, the textile industry being the most important.

Communications.—There are about 2,000 miles of permanent roads and 2,500 miles of roads which are only open during the dry season. There are about 750 miles of railway, including the railway from Quito to Guayaquil. The laying of a new track from Ibarra to San Lorenzo has now been completed. Eight commercial arilines (Panagra, Area, Braniff, K.L.M., Avianca, Equatoriana de Aviación, Air France, Aerolíneas Panameñas and Aerovías Peruanas), operate international flights, linking Ecuador with New York, Miami, Lima, Santiago, Rio de Janeiro, etc. Area, Tame and other Ecuadorean companies operate internal services between all important towns.

Defence.—The standing Army has a strength of about 8,000. There is an Air Force of some 40 front line aircraft and a small Navy. All are being advised by U.S. missions.

Language and Literature.—Spanish is the language of the country. The electorate of Congress is confined to adult male and female citizens who can read and write, and in recent years considerable headway has been made in reducing the high figure of illiteracy. 2 daily newspapers are published at Quito and 3 at Guayaquil. Elementary education is free and compulsory. In 1957–58 there were 501,622 pupils at the 4,661 primary schools and 53,840 pupils at the 249 High Schools. The 6 Universities (at Quito, Guayaquil, Cuenca, Loja and Portoviejo) and the Polytechnic School at Quito had 6,646 students in the same year.

FINANCE

	1963
Revenue (*Budget Estimates*) ...	*Sucres* 1,994,147,000
Expenditure (*Budget Estimates*) .	1,994,147,000
Internal Debt (June 30, 1962) .	1,234,722,000
External Debt (do.)	$ U.S.47,092,000

The official rate of Exchange: *Sucres* 50·76 = £1, is used for most legal imports and exports. A free rate of exchange (buying *sucres* on June 21, 1963) was *Sucres* 58·50 = £1. *See also* p. 83.

TRADE

Import licences are required for all merchandise and these are issued by the Central Bank of Ecuador.

	1961	1962
Imports*.....	$U.S. 103,417,000	$U.S. 97,839,000
Exports*.....	101,269,000	116,918,000

*Permits cleared

Trade with U.K.

	1961	1962
Imports from U.K.....	£2,880,224	£2,074,108
Exports to U.K.......	239,810	276,805

In 1961 the United States sent about 48 per cent. of Ecuadorean imports and received about 61 per cent. of her exports.

The chief exports are bananas, coffee, and cocoa. Other exports are rice, balsa wood, castor-oil seeds, hats, pharmaceuticals, fish, ivory nuts and pyrethrum. Foodstuffs and manufactured goods are the main imports.

CAPITAL.—Quito. Population (1962), 384,151; Ψ Guayaquil (506,037) is the chief port; other centres are Cuenca (60,021); Ambato (52,713); Riobamba (41,417); Manta (33,222) and Esmeraldas (32,992).

FLAG.—Three horizontal bands, yellow, blue and red (the yellow band twice the width of the others); framed emblem in centre.

BRITISH EMBASSY

Calle G. Suarez (P.O. Box No. 314), Quito.

Ambassador Extraordinary and Plenipotentiary, His Excellency Gerard Thomas Corley Smith, C.M.G. (1962) £4,115

Secretary and Consul, D. F. Duncan.

Commercial Secretary, R. T. Anthony.

Vice-Consul, Miss E. G. Forsyth.

There are British Consular Offices at *Quito* and *Guayaquil*.

EGYPT. *See* United Arab Republic

ETHIOPIA

(Ya Ityopia Nigusa Nagast Mangist)

Emperor of Ethiopia, His Imperial Majesty Hailé Selassié I, K.G., G.C.B., G.C.M.G., G.C.V.O., LL.D., son of the late Ras Makonnen, Governor of Hara; *born* July 23, 1892; *married* in July, 1911, Woizero (*Lady*) Menan, daughter of Jantrar Asfaw of Ambassal (*who died* February, 1962) and Woizero (*Lady*) Sehin Mikael, daughter of King Mikael of Wollo, *crowned as Negus* Oct., 1928; *proclaimed Emperor* April 2, 1930; *crowned as Emperor* Nov. 2, 1930; *in exile* 1936–1940; *led his patriot army* 1940–41; *returned to his capital* May 5, 1941.

Crown Prince, H.I.H. Prince Asfa Wossen, G.C.V.O., G.B.E., eldest son of the Emperor, *born* July 27, 1916; *married* May 9, 1932, Walatta Israel daughter of Ras Siyum, whom he divorced in 1945, when he married Woizero Madferiash Worq, daughter of Major-General Ababa Damtaw.

EMBASSY IN LONDON

17 Princes Gate, S.W.7

[Kensington: 7212]

Ambassador, His Excellency Haddis Alemayehou (1961).

1st Secretary, Berhane Deneke.

2nd Secretary, Amare Gugsa.

3rd Secretary, Bahta Melles.

Position and Extent.—The Empire of Ethiopia, with which Eritrea was federated from 1952 to 1962 when it was incorporated as a province, is in North-Eastern Africa, bounded on the north west by the Sudan; on the south by Kenya; on the east by French Somaliland and the Republic of Somalia; and on the north-east by the Red Sea. The area is estimated at 400,000 square miles, with a population estimated (1961) at 21,800,000, of whom about one-third are of the ruling race of Semitic origin (Amharas and Tigres) and the remainder mainly Gallas, Guraghi, Sidama, Agao, negro tribes on the west and south frontiers, and Danakil and Somalis on the east.

Ethiopia is mainly a mountainous country, volcanic in origin, with several peaks of about 14,000 ft., notably in the centre and in the Simien range in the north; many other mountains exceed 10,000 ft. Eritrea consists of a mountainous hogs-back range up to 10,000 ft., interposed between the Red Sea and the Sudan, flanked on east and west by flatter territory. The lower country and valley gorges are very hot; the higher plateaux are well watered, with a genial climate. On the high plateaux there are two main seasons in the year, a dry winter, October to May, and a rainy summer from June to September, with a season of "small rains" occurring generally in March. The chief river is the Blue Nile, issuing from Lake Tana; the Atbara and many other tributaries of the Nile also rise in the Ethiopian highlands.

Those of Semitic origin (Amharas and Tigres), who inhabit the southern highlands of Eritrea provinces of Tigre, Begemdir, Gojjam, parts of Shoa, and many of the Gallas, are Christian (a branch of the Coptic Church). The head of the Coptic Church is the Patriarch at Alexandria. Since 1959, however, the Ethiopian Church has been autocephalous; the Patriarch ranks immediately after the Alexandrian Patriarch. Moslems predominate in some areas, notably northern Eritrea, Herar and Jimma and Arussi, the Moslem centre being at Harar. The province of Gamu Gofa and parts of Sidamo and Arussi have considerable pagan elements.

Government

Ethiopia.—The Empire is governed by a Council of Ministers, responsible to the Emperor, and a Parliament consisting of a Senate and a Chamber of Deputies, in accordance with the constitution promulgated in 1955. Elections, on a basis of universal suffrage, were held in 1957, and the Chamber of Deputies met for the first time at the end of that year. The second General Election was held in 1961. The Chamber enjoys greater fiscal control than the previous Assembly and there is a limited degree of ministerial responsibility to Parliament. The Senate continues to be nominated by the Emperor.

Eritrea.—Eritrea was administered by Great Britain from the end of the Second World War until September 15, 1952, when in accordance with a resolution of the United Nations Assembly of December 2, 1950, it was federated with Ethiopia under the Ethiopian Crown, becoming a province of Ethiopia in 1962.

Production and Industry.—The principal pursuits are agriculture and cattle breeding. In the hotter regions, sugar-cane, cotton, &c., flourish; in the middle zone maize, wheat, barley, coffee, oranges and other fruit trees, tobacco, potatoes and oil seeds are cultivated; and above 6,000 feet are excellent pastures with some corn cultivation. Coffee provided approximately 50 per cent. of the country's total exports by value in 1962. The forests are a potential source of wealth. Horses, mules, donkeys, cattle, oxen, goats, and sheep, and camels in the lowlands, form a large portion of the wealth of the people. Industry is small, the main products being textiles, foodstuffs, beer and cement.

Communications.—A railway links Addis Ababa, the capital, *viâ* Dire-Dawa, with Jibuti, 486 miles away. In Eritrea a narrow gauge line runs from Massawa to Asmara and on to Agordet. Several roads were constructed before and during the Italian occupation; the principal road runs from Addis Ababa to Dessie and on to Asmara, with a branch from Dessie to Assab on the Red Sea Coast. Gondar is linked to Asmara by a road through Axum and Adua. Others run from Addis Ababa west to Lekempti, south-west to Jimma, Gore and Gambela, south to the Kenya frontier, and in the East from Dire Dawa to Harar and the northern region of the Somali Republic. Partly financed by large loans from the International Bank for Reconstruction and Development, much further improvement and extension of roads is being undertaken. The Ethiopian Air Lines maintain regular services from Addis Ababa to most of the provincial towns. External services are operated to Jibuti, Taiz, Hodeida, Port Sudan, Cairo, Khartoum, Nairobi, Athens, Frankfurt, Madrid, Lagos, Accra, Conakry and Monrovia.

Defence.—A Ministry of Defence has been instituted. The armed forces comprise the Imperial Army, the Imperial Bodyguard, the Imperial Air Force and the Imperial Navy. The Army consists of infantry, artillery, engineers, signals, ordnance, and supply services, and has an armoured battalion of light tanks and armoured cars and a parachute battalion. The army is trained by Americans and Israelis and Swedish officers are employed in the Ministry of Defence. There is a military academy at Harar and a military academy at Holleta has a specialist training wing. The Imperial Air Force comprises a ground attack wing, a transport squadron and a flying training school The aircraft are of Swedish and American manufacture.

The Imperial Navy has a small headquarters in Addis Ababa with a naval base situated at Massawa. The training of the Navy is mainly in the hands of Norwegian instructors. The Fleet comprises one seaplane tender, four coastal cutters and two motor torpedo boats.

Education.—Elementary education is provided without religious discrimination by Government schools in the main centres of population; there are also Mission schools and cadet-schools for the Army, Air Force, and Police. Government secondary schools are found mainly in Addis Ababa, but also in most of the provincial capitals. In 1961 the Hailé Selassié I University was founded to co-ordinate the existing institutions of higher education (University College, Engineering, Building and Theological Colleges in Addis Ababa, Agricultural College at Alemaya, near Harar, and Public Health Centre in Gondar, etc.) and to provide a framework for future development. Amharic is the official language of instruction, with English as the first foreign language. Arabic is taught in Koran Schools; and Ge'ez (the ancient Ethiopic) in Christian Church Schools, which abound. Adult education is met to some extent by institutes which provide evening classes in Addis Ababa.

Finance

	1962-63 Ordinary	Extraordinary
Revenue	£29,100,000	£10,900,000
Expenditure	29,900,000	11,100,000

Currency.—The Ethiopian dollar has a value of 5·52 grains of fine gold and is divided into 100 cents. At Dec. 31, 1962, the combined note and coin issue amounted to £28,200,000; gold, silver and foreign exchange reserves amounted to £20,800,000. Eth. $7 = £1.

Trade

Total Imports (Yr. to Sept. 10, 1961)	£32,400,000
Total Exports (Yr. to Sept. 10, 1961)	26,300,000

Trade with U.K.

	1961	1962
Imports from U.K.	£2,952,838	£2,533,681
Exports to U.K.	1,632,113	1,691,993

The chief imports by value are cottons, petroleum products, machinery, motor vehicles and parts; the principal exports by value being coffee, oilseeds, hides and skins, and pulses.

Capital, Addis Ababa (population, estimated July, 1961, 449,021), also capital of the province of Shoa; Asmara (population 120,000) is the capital of the Province of Eritrea; other provincial capitals are Makale (Tigré), Gondar (Begemdir), Dessie (Wallo), Dbera Markos (Gojjam), Lekempti (Wallega), Goré (Illabobor), Jimma (Kaffa), Chencha (Gamu-Gofa), Yirgalem (Sidamo), Aselle (Arusi), Goba (Bale), and Harar (Harar). Dire Dawa is the most important commercial centre after Addis Ababa and Asmara, Ψ Massawa and Ψ Assab (recently enlarged) are the two main ports. There are ancient architectural remains at Aksum, Gondar, Lalibela and elsewhere.

Ethiopian Flag.—Three horizontal bands; green, yellow, red; bearing crowned lion at centre.

BRITISH EMBASSY
(Addis Ababa)

Ambassador, His Excellency John Wriothesley Russell, C.M.G. (1962) £4,115
Counsellor, D. R. Ashe.
Naval Attaché, Cdr. W. J. Carter, R.N.
Military Attaché, Lt.-Col. I. J. D. Stevenson-Hamilton, D.S.O.
Air Attaché, Wing-Cdr. D. B. Delany, A.F.C.
Civil Air Attaché, R. S. Swann.
1st Secretaries, Miss E. M. Dumbell, O.B.E.; N. G. Beckett (*Commercial*); R. G. Peel, M.B.E. (*Consul*).
3rd Secretary, R. H. Baker.

BRITISH CONSULAR OFFICES

There are British Consular Offices at *Addis Ababa, Asmara* and *Mega*.

BRITISH COUNCIL

Representative, P. G. Lloyd, P.O. Box 1043, Addis Ababa.

FINLAND
(Suomi)

President, Dr. Urho Kaleva Kekkonen, *born* 1900, *elected* Feb. 15, 1956; re-elected 1962, for term of six years.

CABINET
(April 13, 1962)

Prime Minister, Dr. Ahti Karjalainen.
Foreign Affairs, Prof. Veli Merikoski.
Interior, Niilo Ryhtä.
Justice, Dr. J. O. Söderhjelm.
Finance, Osmo Karttunen.
Defence, Arvo Pentti.
Education, Mrs. Armi Hosia.
Agriculture, Dr. Johannes Virolainen.
Communications, Erkki Savela.
Trade and Industry, Toivo Wiherheimo.
Social Affairs, Olavi Saarinen.
Deputy Ministers, Onni Koski (*Finance*); Verner Korsbäck (*Agriculture*); Onni Närvänen (*Communications*); Miss Kyllikki Pohjala (*Social Affairs*).

FINNISH EMBASSY AND CONSULATE
66 Chester Square, S.W.1
[Sloane: 0771]

Ambassador in London, His Excellency Leo Tuominen (1957).
Consul, A. P. J. Talvitie.

Area and Population.—A country situated on the Gulfs of Finland and Bothnia, with a total area of 130,165 square miles, of which 70 per cent. is forest, 9 per cent. cultivated, 9 per cent. lakes and 12 per cent. waste and other land, population (Jan. 1, 1962), 4,490,000. In 1961 the birth rate was 18·3, death rate 9·0 per 1,000. The infant mortality rate was 19·8 per 1,000 live births. 94·2 per cent. of the people are Lutherans, 1·5 per cent. Greek Orthodox and 5·4 per cent. others. The loss of Karelia meant resettling about 480,000 refugees mainly on some 46,000 new farms provided by the Government, partly from holdings exceeding 62 acres and partly by purchase.

The Aland Archipelago (Ahvenanmaa), a group of small islands at the entrance to the Gulf of Bothnia, covers about 572 square miles, with a population (1959) of 22,144 (97 per cent. Swedish-speaking). The islands have a semi-autonomous status.

Government.—Under the Constitution there is a single Chamber (*Eduskunta*) for which women are eligible, now composed of 200 members, elected by universal suffrage of both sexes. The legislative power is vested in the Chamber and the President. The highest executive power is held by the President who is elected for a period of 6 years.

Upon the re-election of the President, the Prime Minister, Mr. Martti Miettunen, tendered on Mar. 1, 1962, the resignation of his Government which had been in office since July 14, 1961. After prolonged negotiations Dr. Karjalainen formed a Government of all parties on April 13, 1962, supported by 113 of the 200 members of the Diet.

Defence.—By the terms of the Peace Treaty (Feb. 10, 1947) with U.K. and U.S.S.R., the army is limited to a force not exceeding 34,400. The Navy is limited to a total of 10,000 tons displacement with personnel not exceeding 4,500. The Air Force, including naval air arm, is limited to 60 machines with a personnel not exceeding 3,000. Bombers or aircraft with bomb-carrying facilities are expressly forbidden. The Defence Forces contain a cadre of regular officers and N.C.O.'s, but their bulk is provided by conscripts who serve for 8–11 months. None of the defence forces has the full complement permitted.

Education.—Primary education is compulsory and free for all children from 7 to 15 years, and in 1961 there were 625,968 in attendance at primary schools, with 214,601 in secondary schools; and 51,383 in colleges for vocational training. In 1961 there were 11 Higher Schools with 7,000 students, and 4 universities; the State University of Helsinki (about 12,000 students); 2 at Turku (one Swedish-speaking); and a new university (632 students) at Oulu. Combined enrolment at Higher Schools and Universities was 23,532.

Language and Literature.—Most Finns are bilingual. 91·2 per cent. speak Finnish as their first language, 8·6 Swedish and the remaining 0·2 per cent. other languages (mainly Lapps living a nomadic life in the North). Since 1883 Finnish has been on an equal footing with Swedish as the official language of Finland, but since independence in 1919 Finnish has slowly been displacing Swedish. In literature also, until the close of the eighteenth century, Swedish was dominant, but awakening Finnish nationalism in the early years of the nineteenth century and the establishment of an association for the promotion of Finnish literature in 1831 gave Finnish the status of a literary language. There is a vigorous modern literature. Eemil Sillanpää was awarded the Nobel Prize for Literature in 1939. There are 62 daily newspapers in Finland.

Production and Industry.—Finland has a greater area covered in forest than any other European country except the Soviet Union. Consequently the national economy is based on the timber, pulp and paper industries. These industries employ a large proportion of the working population and accounted in 1962 for 72 per cent. of Finland's foreign exchange earnings. The metal and metal working industries, producing 19 per cent. of Finland's export income in 1962, form the second important group. In the agricultural field, production is relatively low and the tendency is towards dairy farming. Exports of agricultural and dairy products amounted to 4 per cent. of total exports in 1962. The remaining export revenue came from the glass, ceramics and furniture industries. To a large extent domestic requirements in the textile, rubber, plastics, chemical and pharmaceutical, footwear and foodstuff trades, are met by local factories.

Communications.—There are 4,056 miles of railroad and a well-developed telegraph and telephone system. There is railway connection with Sweden and U.S.S.R., passenger boat connection with most of the countries of Western Europe, and telephone communication with most countries of the world. External civil air services are maintained by BEA,

Aero Oy (Finnish Airlines), Scandinavian Airlines System, Pan American Airways, Swissair, Malev and Icelandic Airlines. Aero Oy and Aeroflot each maintain a service with Moscow twice a week. Aero Oy maintains an extensive internal air service. Aeroflot maintains a service twice a week with Leningrad and Czech State Airlines twice a week with Prague. The merchant fleet (January, 1963) consists of 189 steamships (293,000 tons gross), 290 motor vessels (585,000 tons gross), and 76 sailing ships with auxiliary engine (8,000 tons gross).

FINANCE

On Jan. 1, 1963, all values expressed in Finnmarks were divided by 100, in a reform of the currency. All Finnmark figures below, including those relating to 1962, are expressed in terms of the *New Finnmark*. *New Marks* 9·03=£1 (*see also* p. 83).

	1963
Revenue (*Budget*)........*New Marks*	4,560,910,792
Expenditure (*do.*)........	4,559,807,557
Debt (March 1961)......	1,761,000,000

TRADE

	1962
Total Imports...........*New Marks*	3,930,534,000
Total Exports...........	3,533,108,000

Trade with U.K.

	1961	1962
Imports from U.K...	£51,119,399	£54,734,277
Exports to U.K.....	94,880,830	88,742,742

The principal imports are raw materials, foodstuffs, machinery and manufactured goods. The exports are principally the output of the timber mills (timber, cellulose and paper).

CAPITAL, ΨHelsinki (Helsingfors). Population (Jan., 1962), 467,500; other towns are Tampere (Tammerfors), 126,600; ΨTurku (Abo), 124,200; Lahti, 66,600; Oulu (Uleaborg) 58,300; Pori (Björneborg), 54,000; Kuopio, 45,000 and ΨVaasa (Vasa), 42,700.

FLAG.—White with blue cross.

NATIONAL DAY: December 6.

BRITISH EMBASSY
Helsinki

British Ambassador's Residence, It. Kaivopuisto 8B. *Chancery Offices*, Korkeavuorenkatu 34.

Ambassador Extraordinary and Plenipotentiary, His Excellency Anthony Edward Lambert, C.M.G. (1963) £4,115

Counsellor (Commercial), P. D. Stobart.

1st Secretaries, P. A. Rhodes; K. Kenney (*Labour*); R. F. Muston (*Information*); W. W. Wilson (*Commercial*).

Naval Attaché, Cmdr. F. S. Hope, R.N.

Military Attaché, Col. W. A. Robinson.

Air Attaché, Wing-Cdr. R. H. B. Dixon.

2nd Secretaries, R. F. Walter; F. W. Clement; Miss M. Wood (*Commercial*); W. H. Harper (*Consul*).

3rd Secretaries, H. Lester (*Vice-Consul*); M. H. Murphy.

There are British Consular offices at *Helsinki, Tampere, Turku, Pori, Kotka, Oulu, Hamina* and *Vaasa*.

British Council Representative, R. P. H. Davies, Esplanaadikatu 22, Helsinki.

FRANCE

(La République Française)

President of the French Republic (1959–66), General Charles de Gaulle, *born* 1890, *elected* Dec. 21, 1958, *assumed office*, Jan. 8, 1959.

Secretary-General of the President's Office, M. Etienne Burin des Roziers.

CABINET
(1962)

Prime Minister, M. Georges Pompidou.

Ministers of State, M. André Malraux (*Cultural Affairs*); M. Louis Jacquinot (*Overseas Departments and Territories*); M. Louis Joxe (*Administrative Reform*); M. Gaston Palewski (*Scientific Research and Atomic and Space Questions*); M. Raymond Triboulet (*Co-operation*).

Public Works and Transport, M. Marc Jacquet.

Justice, M. Jean Foyer.

Foreign Affairs, M. Maurice Couve de Murville.

Interior, M. Roger Frey.

Armed Forces, M. Pierre Messmer.

Finance and Economic Affairs, M. Valéry Giscard d'Estaing.

Education, M. Christian Fouchet.

Industry, M. Maurice Michel-Bokanowski.

Agriculture, M. Edgar Pisani.

Labour, M. Gilbert Grandval.

Health and Population, M. Raymond Marcellin.

Housing, M. Jacques Maziol.

Ex-Servicemen, M. Jean Sainteny.

Posts and Telegraphs, M. Jacques Marette.

Repatriation, M. François Missoffe.

Information, M. Alain Peyrefitte.

Secretaries of State, M. Robert Boulin (*Budget*); Prince Jean-Marie de Broglie (*Algerian Affairs*); M. Pierre Dumas (*Parliamentary Relations*); M. Michel Habib-Deloncle (*Foreign Affairs*).

FRENCH EMBASSY IN LONDON

Residence: 11 Kensington Palace Gardens, W.8
[Bayswater: 9411]

Chancery: 58 Knightsbridge, S.W.1. [Belgravia: 8080]. Consulate-General: 51 Bedford Square, W.C.1.

Ambassador Extraordinary and Plenipotentiary, His Excellency Monsieur Geoffroy de Courcel, G.C.V.O., M.C. (1962).

Minister-Counsellor, M. Arnauld Wapler, K.C.V.O.

1st Counsellor, M. Gerard André, C.V.O.

2nd Counsellor, M. Jacques Dupuy.

1st Secretaries, M. Luc La Barre de Nanteuil; Paul Henry Manière.

2nd Secretaries, M. Gérald de la Rochefordière; M. Michel Drumetz.

Attaché, M. Emmanuel Arnauld d'Andilly.

Consul-Attaché, M. Charles Nupied, M.B.E.

Naval Attaché, Contre Amiral Jean Witrand.

Assistant Naval Attaché, Capitaine de Corvette Lionel Marmier.

Military Attaché, Col. Gabriel Favreau, M.C.

Assistant Military Attachés, Lt.-Col. Guy de Barbot; Lt.-Col. Paul Lucet; Cdt. Jacques Barjou.

Air Attaché, Col. Henri de Bordas.

Assistant Air Attaché, Col. Claude Devoucoux.

Labour Counsellor, M. Henry Hauck (*Minister Plenipotentiary*).

Financial Counsellor, M. Louis Franck.

Financial Attaché, M. Daniel Deguen.

Commercial Counsellor, M. Georges Libersart (*Minister Plenipotentiary*).

Assistant Commercial Counsellor, M. François Gaudefroy Demoubynes.

Commercial Attachés, M. Jehan Dior; M. Corentin Kérouédan; M. Gérard Hibon; M. Francis Mouton.

Assistant Commercial Attachés, M. Maurice Houin; M. René Tranchant; M. Alexandre Apostol.

Press Counsellor, M. Yves Barbier.

Cultural Counsellor, M. Cyrille Arnavon.

Cultural Attaché, M. Jean Llasera.
Asst. Cultural Attaché, M. Tony Mayer.
Consul-General, François de Vial, 51 Bedford Square, W.C.1.

POPULATION OF FRENCH DEPARTMENTS

Census of 1963

Ain	327,146	Lot	149,929
Aisne	512,920	Lot et Garonne	275,028
Allier	380,221	Lozère	81,868
Alpes Basses	91,843	Maine-et-Loire	556,272
Alpes Hautes	87,436	Manche	446,878
Alpes Maritimes	618,265	Marne	442,195
Ardèche	248,516	Marne, Haute	208,446
Ardennes	300,247	Mayenne	250,030
Ariège	137,192	Meurthe-et-Moselle	678,078
Aube	255,099	Meuse	215,985
Aude	269,782	Morbihan	530,833
Aveyron	290,442	Moselle (*a*)	919,412
Bouches-du-Rhône	1,248,355	Nièvre	245,921
Calvados	480,686	Nord	2,293,112
Cantal	172,977	Oise	481,289
Charente	327,658	Orne	280,549
Charente-Maritime	470,897	Pas-de-Calais	1,366,282
Cher	293,514	Puy-de-Dôme	508,928
Corrèze	237,926	Pyrénées, Basses	466,038
Corse	275,465	Pyrénées, Hautes	211,433
Côte d'Or	387,869	Pyrénées-Orientales	251,231
Côtes du Nord	501,923	Rhin, Bas (*b*)	770,150
Creuse	163,515	Rhin, Haute (*c*)	547,920
Dordogne	375,455	Rhône	1,116,664
Doubs	384,881	Saône, Haute	208,440
Drôme	304,227	Saône-et-Loire	535,772
Eure	361,904	Sarthe	443,019
Eure-et-Loire	277,546	Savoie	266,678
Finistère	749,558	Savoie, Haute	329,230
Gard	435,482	*Seine*	5,646,446
Garonne, Haute	594,633	Seine-Maritime	1,035,844
Gers	182,264	*Seine-et-Marne*	524,486
Gironde	935,448	*Seine-et-Oise*	2,298,931
Hérault	516,658	Sèvres-Deux	321,118
Ille-et-Vilaine	614,268	Somme	488,225
Indre	251,432	Tarn	319,560
Indre-et-Loire	395,210	Tarn-et-Garonne	175,847
Isère	729,789	Var	469,557
Jura	225,682	Vaucluse	303,536
Landes	260,495	Vendée	408,928
Loir-et-Cher	250,741	Vienne	331,619
Loire	696,348	Vienne, Haute	332,514
Loire, Haute	211,036	Vosges	380,676
Loire-Atlantique	803,372	Yonne	269,826
Loiret	389,372	Belfort (Terr. de)	109,371

Departments of the *District of Paris* appear in *italic* type.

(*a*), (*b*), (*c*). These Departments correspond with the districts of Alsace and Lorraine.

Area and Population.—The most westerly State of Central Europe, extending from 42° 20′ to 51° 5′ N. lat., and from 7° 45′ E. to 4° 45′ W. long., bounded on the north by the English Channel and Straits of Dover (Pas de Calais), which separate it from England. Its circumference is estimated at about 3,000 miles, and its area (in 1939) at 212,895 square miles divided into 90 departments, including the island of Corsica, in the Mediterranean, off the west coast of Italy. The population of Metropolitan France at a national census held on March 7, 1962, was 46,520,271. During 1961 there were 829,700 live births, 538,300 deaths and 317,000 marriages.

Government.—The monarchical system of government was overthrown by the *French Revolution* (1789–1793), and the *First Republic* endured until the Great Napoleon (born Aug. 15, 1769, died May 5, 1821) founded the First Empire in 1804. The monarchy was restored in 1814, and also after the "Hundred Days" of Napoleon (March 20–June 29, 1815), until the *Second Republic* of 1848, which became the Second Empire on Nov. 22, 1852. On Sept. 4, 1870, the Emperor Napoleon III. (nephew of the Great Napoleon) was deposed, and the *Third Republic* was set up. The constitution of the Third Republic vested the legislative power in a Chamber of Deputies and a Senate. The executive was vested in the President, who was elected for 7 years by the Senate and Chamber assembled in Congress.

On Sept. 1, 1939, Germany invaded Poland, thus precipitating war with France and Great Britain, which had (March 31, 1939) given an open pledge to support Poland against aggression.

On June 17, 1940, the late Maréchal Pétain sought terms of surrender from the Germans. A number of French troops had reached British ports after the evacuation of the British Expeditionary Force from Dunkirk and St. Valéry, and on June 23, 1940, after stating that the French Government had capitulated before all means of resistance had been exhausted, General de Gaulle announced the formation of a Provisional National Committee "to defend that part of the French Empire which has not yet been conquered by Germany and to free that part of France still under the yoke of the invader."

On June 3, 1943, after prolonged negotiation, there was set up a *French Committee of National Liberation*, which was recognized by the allied nations on August 26, 1943.

Paris was liberated on August 25, 1944, and on October 13, 1944, the de Gaulle administration was recognized by the allied nations as the government of France.

Under the de Gaulle administration there was a single chamber legislature (The National Consultative Assembly) which met at Algiers until France was liberated. The enlarged Consultative Assembly met in the Luxemburg Palace (Paris), formerly the Senate House, on Nov. 7, 1944.

Following a national referendum on Oct. 21, 1945, a Constituent Assembly was elected with the task of drafting a new constitution. This was duly drawn up and adopted at a further referendum on Oct. 13, 1946. A National Assembly and Council of the Republic, elected on a territorial basis, were set up. With amendments made in 1954, the Constitution of the Fourth Republic was in force from 1946 until Oct. 5, 1958. From the liberation of Paris in 1944 until the Fourth Republic came to an end in 1958, 26 Cabinets were formed with an average life of 5½ months. The Government of M. Mollet for 16 months in 1956–57 was the longest in office, that of M. Queuille in 1950 the shortest, being in office for only three days.

Insurrections took place in Algeria and in the Metropolitan Department of Corsica in May, 1958, and, faced by a threat of imminent insurrection among the armed forces at home, President Coty warned the nation that it was on the brink of civil war and invited General de Gaulle to form a Government. M. Pflimlin formally resigned the office of Prime Minister on May 31. On June 1, by 329 votes to 224, Gen. de Gaulle was invested in the National Assembly as Prime Minister, with power to govern by decree for a period of six months during which time proposals for constitutional reform would be submitted to a national referendum.

The Fifth Republic.—The Constitution of the Fifth Republic, embodying important changes, was adopted by an overwhelming majority at a referendum held on Sept. 28 in Metropolitan France and all overseas departments and territories. (*See also* French Community *below*).

The *President* is elected for a term of 7 years by an electoral college consisting of both Houses of Parliament, the departmental general councils, overseas assemblies and elected representatives of the municipal councils. As the result of a referendum in October, 1962, future Presidents are to be elected by direct universal suffrage. Presidents are eligible for re-election. The President appoints the Prime Minister. He may dissolve the National Assembly after consultation with the Prime Minister and Presidents of both Houses, but may not do so more than once in twelve months. He may submit disputed legislation to a national referendum at the request of the Government or of both Houses of Parliament. The President may assume special powers in an emergency. At the presidential elections held on Dec. 21, 1958, General de Gaulle was elected President by an overwhelming majority and took office on Jan. 8, 1959, as first President of the Fifth French Republic.

Parliament consists of the National Assembly and the Senate. Bills may be presented in either House, except money bills, which must originate in the National Assembly. The normal session of Parliament is confined to 5½ months each year and it may also meet in extraordinary session for 12 days at the request of the Prime Minister or a majority of the Assembly. Voting rights are personal and can only be delegated in special circumstances.

The *Prime Minister* and the Cabinet are responsible only to Parliament. The Prime Minister is assumed to have the Assembly's confidence unless the Opposition moves a censure motion signed by not less than one-tenth of the deputies; such motion must be approved by an absolute majority; if defeated, its sponsors must not introduce another no-confidence motion in the same session. Ministers relinquish Parliamentary seats on joining the Cabinet.

A *Constitutional Council* is responsible for supervising all elections and referenda and must be consulted on all constitutional matters and before the President of the Republic assumes emergency powers. At the request of the Government, the *Economic and Social Council* gives advice on bills, ordinances or decrees referred to it. Any economic or social plan or bill must be submitted to it.

Production.—The chief agriculture products are wheat, barley, rye, maize, oats, potatoes, beetroot (for the manufacture of sugar), hops, &c. Rice is being grown in parts of the Camargue (Rhône delta). Fruit trees abound, and are very productive, the principal being the olive, chestnut, walnut, almond, apple, pear, citron, fig, plum, &c.

The harvest in 1962 was:—

	(Quintals)
Wheat	138,500,000
Oats	26,000,000
Barley	59,200,000
Rye	3,600,000
Maize	17,500,000

Forestry is an important industry, the principal forests being those of the Ardennes, Compiègne, Fontainebleau, and Orléans, consisting chiefly of oak, birch, pine, beech, elm, chestnut and the cork-tree in the south. The vine is cultivated to a very great extent, as the names Bordeaux, Burgundy, Champagne, &c., universally testify. Production of wine in 1962 was 64,600,000 hectolitres. Cider-making is also an important industry. The live stock (1962) included 20,583,000 cattle, 8,924,000 sheep and lambs, 9,217,000 pigs, 1,617,000 horses and 1,176,000 goats. The mineral resources include coal, oil, pig iron, bauxite, lead, silver, antimony and salt. In 1962 coal production amounted to 55,238,000 tons and oil production in the *Franc Zone* totalled 23,820,000 tons. The most important manufactures are of metals, cars, aircraft, watches, jewellery, cabinet-work, carving, pottery, glass, chemicals, dyeing, paper making, cottons, woollens, carpets, linen, silk and lace.

Language and Literature.—French is the universal language of France and of a large proportion of the people of Belgium, Luxemburg, Switzerland, Italy, Egypt, Tunisia, Algeria, Mauritius, Haiti, the Province of Quebec, Canada, and of the State of Louisiana, U.S.A., to whom the almost inexhaustible literature of France is a treasured heritage. The work of the *French Academy*, founded by Richelieu in 1635, has established *le bon usage*, equivalent to "The King's English" in Great Britain. French authors have been awarded the Nobel Prize for Literature on 10 occasions—R.F.A. Sully-Prudhomme (1901), F. Mistral (1904), Romain Rolland (1915), Anatole France (1921), Henri Bergson (1937), Roger M. du. Gard (1937), André Gide (1947), François Mauriac (1952), Albert Camus (1957) and St. John Perse (Alexis Léger) (1960).

Defence.—The *personnel* of the Defence Forces at the end of 1961 was: *Army*, 818,700 (including *Gendarmie* of 65,000); *Navy* (Oct. 1, 1961), 77,594; *Air Force*, 143,560. The French Navy included 3 aircraft carriers, 3 cruisers, 60 destroyers and frigates and 21 submarines.

Education.—The educational system is highly developed and centralized. It is administered by the Ministry of National Education, comprising (a) the *Direction de l'Administration Générale*, the *Direction de l'Enseignement Supérieur*, and the *Direction Générale de l'Organisation et des Programmes Scolaires*, the three principal administrative services; (b) the Superior Council of National Education (consultative); (c) the High Commissariat for Youth and Sports; (d) other organizations and services concerned with libraries, research, external relations whose heads are directly responsible to the Minister; and (e) the Inspectorate. *Local Administration* comprises 20 Territorial Academies, with inspecting staff for all grades, and (b) Departmental Councils presided over by the *Préfet*, and charged especially with *primary* education. Primary and secondary education are compulsory, free and secular, the school age being from 6 to 14 (6 to 16 from 1967 onwards). Schools are for boys, for girls, or mixed. (i) *Primary* education is given in *écoles maternelles* (nursery schools), *écoles primaires élémentaires* (primary schools) and *collèges d' enseignement général* (4-year secondary modern course); (ii) *Secondary* education in *collèges d'enseignement technique* and *lycées* (7-year course leading to one of the eight options of the *baccalauréat*: classic A or A'—two classical languages; classic B or C—Latin plus modern languages or science; modern—modern languages plus science and mathematics; M'—mathematics and experimental sciences; technical A or B). Many private establishments also exist in all categories. (iii) *Special schools* are numerous. (iv) There are 19 *universities* (State universities alone grant degrees, but numerous private faculties and private institutions further higher education): Aix (A.D. 1409), Besançon (1485), Bordeaux (1441), Caen (1432), Clermont-Ferrand (1808), Dijon (1772), Grenoble (1339), Lille (1530), Lyons (1808), Montpellier (1125), Nancy (1572), Nantes (re-created 1961), Paris

(1150), Poitiers (1431), Reims (1961) Rennes (1735). Strasbourg (1567) and Toulouse (1230). A new Académie of Orléans was created in 1961, but there is as yet no faculty. Higher education is also given in various branches—medicine, law, science and arts—in State institutes in Amiens, Angers, Chambéry, Le Mans, Limoges, Nice, Pau, Rouen, St. Etienne and Tours.

Archæology, etc.—There are dolmens and menhirs in Brittany, prehistoric remains in Dordogne, cave drawings in Ariège, and throughout France various megalithic monuments erected by primitive tribes, predecessors of Iberian invaders from Spain (now represented by the Basques), Ligurians from northern Italy and Celts or Gauls from the valley of the Danube. Julius Cæsar found Gaul "divided into three parts" and described three political groups—Aquitanians south of the Garonne, Celts between the Garonne and the Seine and Marne, and Belgae from the Seine to the Rhine. Roman remains are plentiful throughout France in the form of aqueducts, arenas, triumphal arches, &c., and the celebrated Norman and Gothic Cathedrals, including Notre Dame in Paris, and those of Chartres, Reims, Amiens (where Peter the Hermit preached the First Crusade for the recovery of the Holy Sepulchre), Bourges, Beauvais, Rouen, etc., have survived invasions and bombardments, with only partial damage, and many of the renaissance and XVIIth century châteaux survived the French Revolution.

Roads.—The length of the *Routes Nationales* is about 50,500 miles, and of other roads 437,500 miles. The principal rivers of France are the Seine, Loire, Garonne, and Rhône, the navigable waterways in general use having a length of 8,000 km. The Rhône is navigable for 1,200-ton vessels from the sea to Switzerland.

Railways.—The system of railroads in France is very extensive. The length of lines of general interest, exclusive of local lines, open for traffic on Jan. 1, 1962, was 38,840 km., of which 7,260 km. were electrified. The lines left open in Sept., 1944 totalled only 11,126 miles, but the work of reconstruction then begun has restored the pre-war figure. Traffic in 1961 totalled 33,480,000,000 passenger-km. and 58,836,000,000 ton-km, and in 1962, 35,760,000,000 passenger kilometres, and 61,176,000,000 ton-kilometres.

Civil Aviation.—In 1961 passenger/kilometres flown by aircraft of French airlines totalled 6,360,000,000, of which 4,773,600,000 were by *Air France*.

Shipping.—The French mercantile marine on Jan. 1, 1962, consisted of 783 ships of 4,842,397 tons gross, of which 64 were passenger vessels (585,050 tons), 171 tankers (2,022,893 tons) and 541 cargo vessels (2,098,713 tons).

FINANCE	1962
Total revenue (*Budget*).....	F. 85,000,000,000
Ordinary expenditure (*do.*).	78,000,000,000

The *Public Debt*, on November 30, 1961, amounted to *F.* 84,500,000,000, of which the external debt accounted for *F.* 3,633,000,000.

Currency.—The unit of currency is the *franc* of 100 *centimes*. On August 11, 1957, a system of exchange rates was introduced which amounted to a devaluation of the franc by 20 per cent. in certain sectors. This devaluation was made general on October 26, 1957. On Dec. 29, 1958, the franc was further devalued by 17½ per cent. to *Frs.* 1,382 = £1 (*Frs.* 492·70 = $1 U.S.). The *New Franc*, worth 100 old francs, came into use on Jan. 1, 1960, in metropolitan France and Algeria, as the basic monetary unit. Bank notes in 10, 50 and 100 *new franc* denominations and coins for 1 and 5 *new francs* were introduced. On January 1, 1963, the designation of the French currency was changed from *New Franc* to *Franc* with no change in value.

COMMERCE

The principal imports are wool, cotton, chemicals, coke, crude oil, oleaginous fruits and seeds, machinery, raw skins, timber, rubber, copper and coffee. The principal exports are chemical products, iron and steel, textiles (silk and cotton), automobiles, wine and other agricultural products, soaps and perfumes, and glass.

FRENCH FOREIGN TRADE	1962 *Francs*
Imports.........................	29,426,530,000
Exports	29,049,700,000

Trade with U.K.

	1961	1962
Imports from U.K.	£112,225,233	£138,131,158
Exports to U.K...	147,790,882	131,431,427

OVERSEAS DEPARTMENTS

With effect from Jan. 1, 1947, the colonies of Guyane (French Guiana), Martinique, Guadeloupe and La Réunion with its dependencies have been theoretically administered in exactly the same way as the Metropolitan Departments, but in practice somewhat greater discretion is allowed to the Prefects and the locally elected bodies.

La Réunion.—Formerly Ile de Bourbon, about 420 miles E. of Madagascar, Réunion has been a French possession since 1643. Area, about 1,000 sq. miles. Population (Census, 1961), 347,000. Capital, St. Denis (41,863). Assigned to the administration of Réunion are the distant islands of St. Paul (3 sq. miles), New Amsterdam (27 sq. miles) and Kerguelen containing whaling and fishing stations (1,100 sq. miles). The Crozet Islands (200 sq. miles) and Adélie Land (*see* p. 719) in the Antarctic Continent are also dependencies of Réunion.

Martinique.—An island situated in the Windward Islands group of the West Indies, between the British colonies of Dominica in the north and St. Lucia in the south. Population (Census, 1961), 291,000. Capital, ΨFort de France (60,600). Other towns are ΨTrinité (39,173) and ΨMarin (31,369).

Guadeloupe.—In the Leeward Islands of the West Indies, the island of Guadeloupe, together with Marie Galante, the Ile des Saintes, Petite Terre, St. Barthélemy and St. Martin, form the other West Indian Department of France. Population (Census, 1961), 282,000. Capital, ΨPointe à Pitre (26,200). Other towns are ΨBasse Terre (13,636) in Guadeloupe and ΨGrand Bourg (12,827) in Marie Galante.

French Guiana.—Area, 35,000 sq. miles. Population (Census, 1961), 33,000. Capital, ΨCayenne (13,300). Situated on the north-eastern coast of South America, French Guiana is flanked by Netherlands Guiana on the west and by Brazil on the south and east. Under the administration of French Guiana is a group of islands (St. Joseph, Ile Royale and Ile du Diable), known as Iles du Salut. On Devil's Isle, Captain Dreyfus was imprisoned from 1894–1899.

CAPITAL OF FRANCE. Paris, on the Seine. Population (Census of 1962), 2,790,091.

District of Paris.—Created by legislation promulgated on August 2, 1961, the District covers the areas of the Seine, Seine-et-Marne and Seine-et-Oise Departments, with a population of 8,469,863. Improvement and development of the Paris region is the responsibility of a Council of Administration consisting of 28 members, half elected by the Government from among local members of Parliament and the other half by local councils. The Council, which has its own budget and revenue, co-ordinates the development works of existing authorities and has power to initiate its own schemes. A Delegate-General appointed by the Government is the Council's executive officer. The first meeting of the Council was held on Dec. 19, 1961.

Delegate-General, M. Paul Delouvrier.

Thirty-two other French cities have populations greater than 100,000—Ψ Marseilles (783,738); Ψ Lyons (535,784); Toulouse (330,570); Ψ Nice (294,976); Ψ Bordeaux (254,122); Ψ Nantes (246,227); Strasbourg (233,549); St. Etienne (203,633); Lille (199,033); Ψ Le Havre (184,133); Ψ Toulon (172,586); Grenoble (162,764); Rennes (157,692); Ψ Brest (142,901); Dijon (141,104); Reims (138,576); Le Mans (136,083); Clermont-Ferrand (134,532); Nancy (133,532); Ψ Rouen (123,474); Montpellier (123,367); Angers (122,269); Limôges (120,596); Roubaix (113,163); Mulhouse (110,735); Amiens (109,869); Metz (109,678); Villeurbanne (107,630); Boulogne-Billancourt (107,074); Nîmes (105,199) Besançon (101,729).

The chief towns of Corsica are Ψ Ajaccio (42,282) and Ψ Bastia (50,881).

Paris is distant from London 267 miles; transit by air, 1 *hr*.

FLAG.—The "tricolour," three vertical bands, blue, white, red (blue next to flagstaff).

BRITISH EMBASSY

(35 Faubourg St. Honoré, Paris 8e)

Ambassador Extraordinary and Plenipotentiary, His Excellency Sir Pierson Dixon, G.C.M.G., C.B. (Oct, 1960) £7,015

Envoy Extraordinary and Minister Plenipotentiary, H. A. F. Hohler, C.M.G.

Minister (Economic), F. C. Everson, C.M.G.

Counsellor and Consul-General, H. Braham, C.B.E.

Counsellors, Hon. P. E. Ramsbotham; A. H. Birch, O.B.E. (*Commercial*); F. B. Richards, C.M.G., D.S.C. (*Press*); L. Hagestadt, O.B.E. (*Labour*).

1st Secretaries, R. A. Farquharson; M. D. Butler; J. B. S. Pedler; K. S. Butler; J. T. Fearnley; S. H. Anstey; R. W. P. Dawson, C.B.E., D.S.O.; J. H. Farmer, M.C.; N. Morton.

2nd Secretaries, T. Macaulay; H. Tansey; E. A. Townsend; A. H. Grey; A. J. Hannaford; M. R. Jenkins.

2nd Secretaries (Commercial), J. J. Sinclair; I. J. Benson; D. H. Bevan.

3rd Secretary, J. S. N. Drew.

Naval Attaché, Capt. C. B. H. Wake-Walker, R.N.

Asst. Naval Attaché, Cdr. E. J. Watson, R.N.

Military Attaché, Brigadier B. Wilson, D.S.O.

Asst. do. Lt.-Col. D. E. Isles.

Air Attaché, Air Commodore G. F. W. Heycock, C.B., D.F.C.

Asst. Air Attaché, Wing-Cdr. M. G. Bourdaud'hui.

Civil Air Attaché, A. Holden.

Scientific Attaché, R. V. Melville.

Agricultural Attaché, A. V. Vickery.

Chaplain of the British Embassy Church, Rev. R. J. W. Morris.

BRITISH CONSULAR OFFICES

There are British Consular Offices in Metropolitan France at *Paris*, *Ajaccio*, *Bordeaux*, *Boulogne*, *Calais*, *Cherbourg*, *Dieppe*, *Dunkirk*, *Le Havre*, *Lille*, *Lyons*, *Marseilles*, *Nice*, *St. Malo* and *Strasbourg*.

BRITISH CHAMBER OF COMMERCE

6 Rue Halévy, Paris

President, M. F. Bannerman.

Vice-Presidents, H. C. Talbot; J. W. Briant.

BRITISH COUNCIL

Representative in Paris, C. F. S. de Winton, O.B.E., 36 rue des Ecoles, Paris V.

THE FRENCH COMMUNITY

The Constitution of the Fifth French Republic promulgated on Oct. 6, 1958, envisaged the establishment of a French Community of States closely linked with common institutions. In the last four years a number of the former French States in Africa have seceded from the Community but for all practical purposes continue to enjoy the same close links with France as those that remain formally members of the French Community. The Community Institutions in fact never operated as envisaged and the major part of the mechanism is for the present at least in abeyance. Nevertheless, with the exception of Guinea, which opted out of the Community in the 1958 referendum, all the former French African colonies are closely linked to France by a series of financial, technical and economic agreements. French relations with these countries are conducted through the Quai d'Orsay and, so far as aid and technical assistance is concerned, through the Ministry of Co-operation which has been specially set up for this purpose. M. Jacques Foccart, as Secretary General to the Presidency for the Community and African and Malagasy affairs heads the President's personal secretariat which supervises and coordinates French relations with these countries.

Madagascar (République malgache).—*See* separate article.

SOMALILAND AND ISLAND TERRITORIES

French Somaliland.—Area, 9,000 sq. miles. Population (1957), 67,000. Capital, Ψ Jibuti (17,000). Situated on the N.E. African coast round the Gulf of Tajura and extending about 80 miles inland.

New Caledonia.—Area, 7,200 sq. miles. Population (1956), 68,000. Capital, Ψ Noumea (12,000). A large island in the Western Pacific, 700 miles E. of Queensland. Dependencies are the Isle of Pines, the Loyalty Islands (Mahé, Lifou, Urea, etc., the Huon Islands and Alofis). New Caledonia was discovered in 1774 and annexed by France in 1854; from 1871 to 1896 it was a convict settlement.

Wallis and Futuna Islands.—Following a request from local kings and chiefs, it was decided by referendum (Dec. 27, 1959) that the islands would become the sixth Overseas Territory of France. Population of the islands, formerly dependencies of New Caledonia, is about 9,500, mostly Polynesians.

French Polynesia.—Area, 2,500 sq. miles. Population (1956), 77,000. Capital, Ψ Papeete (15,220), in Tahiti. Includes the Society Islands (Tahiti, Moorea, Makatea, etc.), the Marquesas (Nukahiva, Hiva-oa, etc., 500 sq. miles. population, 3,000); the Leeward Isles (Huahine, Raiatea, Tahaa, Bora Bora, Maupiti, etc.): the Gambier Islands (Mangareva, etc.); the Tubuai Islands (Tubuai, Rurutu, Raivavae, Rimatara and Rapa Island; and Maiao Island).

Comoro Archipelago.—Area, 800 sq. miles. Population (1957), 177,000. Capital, Dzaoudzi. Includes the islands of Great Comoro, Anjouan, Mayotte and Mohilla and certain islets in the Indian Ocean.

St. Pierre and Miquelon.—Area, 93 sq. miles. Population (1957), 4,900. Two small groups of Islands off the coast of Newfoundland.

The former French settlements in India, Pondicherry, Mahé, Karikal and Yanaon were formally transferred to India on Aug. 16, 1962.

GABOON
(Republic of Gaboon)

President, Leon M'ba, *assumed office* August 17, 1960.
Ambassador to U.K., M. André Mintsa (*resident in Paris*).

Gaboon lies on the Atlantic coast of Africa at the Equator and is flanked on the north by the Spanish territory of Rio Muni and the Cameroon Republic and on the east and south by the Republic of Congo. It has an area of 101,400 sq. miles and a population estimated in 1961 at 440,000. Gaboon elected on Nov. 28, 1958, to remain an autonomous republic within the French Community and was proclaimed fully independent on August 17, 1960. Trade with U.K., 1962: Imports, £496,793; Exports to U.K., £906,238.

CAPITAL.—Libreville (16,700).

FLAG.—Horizontal bands, green, yellow and blue.

French High Commissioner and Ambassador, M. Paul Cousseran.

British Ambassador, His Excellency William Scott Laver, C.B.E. (*Resident at Brazzaville, Congo*).

GERMANY
* Deutsches Reich (German Realm)

THE HISTORY OF GERMANY from 1863–1945 is marked by wars of aggression. In 1864, Prussia, in company with Austria, attacked Denmark, and after a short campaign annexed the peninsula of Schleswig-Holstein. In 1866, as a result of war with Austria (the Seven Weeks' War), Prussia acquired the hegemony of the North Germanic Confederation from Austria. After the Franco-Prussian War of 1870, when Prussia wrested Alsace-Lorraine from France, the North Germanic Confederation and three South German States became the Germanic Confederation, the King of Prussia being proclaimed German Emperor at Versailles on Jan. 18, 1871.

At the outbreak of the War of 1914–1918, Germany was a Confederate League bearing the name German Empire under the hereditary presidency of the King of Prussia holding the title of German Emperor. At the close of the war, Germany lost most of the gains she had acquired since 1863, including all her colonies.

GERMANY BETWEEN THE TWO WARS.—On Nov. 9, 1918, two days before Germany sued for an Armistice from the victorious Allies, the German Emperor abdicated, and the Government of the country was taken over by the Council of the People's Commissioners in Berlin. In January, 1919, elections were held to a National Assembly on the basis of universal adult suffrage (male and female). The Assembly met at Weimar (Feb. 6, 1919), and elected Friedrich Ebert President of the Republic, a position he occupied until his death (Feb. 28, 1925) when Field Marshal Paul von Hindenburg was elected in his stead. Von Hindenburg was re-elected April 10, 1932, the rival candidate being Adolf Hitler, who was born at Braunau, Austria (April 20, 1889) and had migrated as a young man to Bavaria. A General Election of 1933 provided Hitler's party, the *Nationalsozialistische Deutsche Arbeiter Partei* (National Socialist German Workers' Party, or *Nazis*) with an absolute majority in the legislature (*Reichstag*) and Hitler became Prime Minister (Chancellor), a position which became fused with that of President at the death of von Hindenburg (Aug. 2, 1934), and Adolf Hitler exercised supreme and uncontrolled authority in the Reich.

THE WAR OF 1939–1945.—After concluding a Treaty of Non-Aggression with Soviet Russia (Aug. 24, 1939), Germany invaded Poland (Sept. 1, 1939), thus precipitating war with France and Great Britain, who had (March 31) given a pledge to support Poland against aggression.

Germany invaded and occupied Denmark and Norway (April, 1940), Belgium, the Netherlands, Luxemburg and France (May, 1940). Norway capitulated on June 9, France sued for peace in mid-June. The lightning war against Britain began on August 11, 1940, but the *Luftwaffe* attack, which was to prepare the way for invasion, was defeated. In April, 1941, Yugoslavia was invaded and Germany joined Italy in attacking Greece and Crete. On June 22, 1941, the U.S.S.R. was invaded. In 1942 the Nazi empire reached its height. The boundaries of Greater Germany included Alsace-Lorraine, Luxemburg, Eupen-Malmédy, large areas of Poland, Memelland and Slovenia; Germany and her satellites controlled all European countries except the British Isles, Spain, Portugal, Switzerland, Sweden and parts of European Russia, as well as large tracts of North Africa. The turning point came in November, 1942, with the Soviet victory at Stalingrad and the British at El Alamein. In 1943 a Soviet offensive threw the invader back almost to the Polish frontier, and the Western Allies, after defeating the Axis in North Africa, landed in Italy. In June, 1944, the Second Front opened on the Normandy beaches and by September, 1944, Germany itself was the battlefield. On May 8, 1945, the unconditional surrender of all German forces was accepted by representatives of the Western Allied and Soviet Supreme Commanders.

Hitler committed suicide on April 30, 1945.

In 1962 the Federal Statistical Office reported that during the course of the war from 1939–1945, 593,000 persons were killed during allied air attacks on Germany and 403,000 dwellings were destroyed. 537,000 civilians were killed, some 15 per cent. children under 14, and 56,000 foreign civilians, members of the police and armed forces. In the area now covered by the Federal Republic persons injured numbered 486,000, including 16,000 foreigners and prisoners of war.

THE POST WAR PERIOD.—After the surrender the Allied Powers assumed supreme authority in Germany. Power was to be exercised by the Commanders-in-Chief, each in his own zone of occupation and jointly in matters affecting Germany as a whole through a Control Council. Berlin was to be governed jointly by the four occupying powers. The guiding lines of policy were laid down in the agreement reached between the U.K., U.S. and U.S.S.R. Governments at Potsdam in August, 1945, which was to remain in force until a Peace Treaty should confirm or revise its directives. It was decided that "for the time being no Central German Government shall be established," but that central German administrative departments acting under the direction of the Control Council should be established in the fields of finance, transport,

---

* Nazi historians referred to the National Socialist régime as *Drittes Reich*. The *First* was the Holy Roman Empire, established in A.D. 962 by Otto I of Saxony, enduring until 1806. The *Second* was established by Prince Otto von Bismarck, after the Franco-Prussian war in 1871, and endured until 1918. The *Third* was established by Adolf Hitler in 1933.

communications, foreign trade and industry. The Eastern frontier of Germany was provisionally redrawn (pending final settlement in the Peace Treaty) to transfer the northern area of East Prussia, including Königsberg (now Kaliningrad), to the U.S.S.R. and the rest of East Prussia and all the area lying east of the Oder and Western Neisse rivers to Polish control. On Oct. 15, 1947, the Saar, enlarged at the expense of German territory, voted for economic union with France, but following a plebiscite was incorporated in the Federal Republic of Germany on Jan. 1, 1957. The Potsdam agreement also laid down that Germany should be disarmed and prohibited from producing armaments, that production of certain other goods should be limited to the amount needed to support a peacetime economy and that existing capital equipment surplus to these requirements should be removed as reparations and distributed by the Inter Allied Reparations Agency among the nations who had suffered war damage, in proportion to their losses. (The proportions were fixed by the Paris Conference of November, 1945.) The agreement further dealt with denazification, democratization, refugees, restitution, decartelization, etc.

Though certain details of the Potsdam agreement (not yet superseded by a Peace Treaty) have been carried out, differences in interpretation among the Allies have made it impossible to apply the provisions in full. Quadripartite control became a dead letter when the Russians withdrew from the Control Council in March, 1948.

Federal Republic of Germany

President, Dr. Heinrich Lübke, *born* Oct. 14, 1894, *elected* July 1, 1959, *for five years from* Sept. 15, 1959.

Cabinet

Federal Chancellor, Dr. Konrad Adenauer (C.D.U.).
Vice-Chancellor and Minister for Economic Affairs, Prof. Ludwig Erhard (C.D.U.).
Foreign Minister, Dr. Gerhard Schröder (C.D.U.).
Interior, Hermann Höcherl (C.S.U.).
Justice, Dr. Ewald Bucher (F.D.P.).
Finance, Dr. Rolf Dahlgrün (F.D.P.).
Defence, Kai-Uwe von Hassel (C.D.U.).
Labour, Theodor Blank (C.D.U.).
Affairs of the Federal Council and Länder, Alois Niederalt (C.D.U.).
Housing, Paul Lücke (C.D.U.).
Agriculture, Werner Schwarz (C.D.U.).
All-German Affairs, Dr. Rainer Barzel (C.D.U.).
Transport, Dr. Hans-Christoph Seebohm (C.D.U.).
Posts and Telegraphs, Richard Stücklen (C.S.U.).
Family and Youth Questions, Dr. Bruno Heck (C.D.U.).
Economic Property of the Federal Republic, Dr. Werner Dollinger (C.D.U.).
Economic Co-operation, Walter Scheel (F.D.P.).
Scientific Research, Hans Lenz (F.D.P.).
Refugees, Wolfgang Mischnick (F.D.P.).
Special Tasks, Dr. Heinrich Krone (C.D.U.).
Health, Dr. Elisabeth Schwarzhaupt (C.D.U.).
C.D.U.=Christian Democratic Union; C.S.U.=Christian Social Union; F.D.P.=Free Democrats.

Embassy in London

23 Belgrave Square, S.W.1.

[Belgravia: 5033]

Ambassador Extraordinary and Plenipotentiary, His Excellency Hasso von Etzdorf (1961).
Minister-Counsellor, Dr. Rudolf Thierfelder.
Counsellors, Dr. Franz Beer; Paul Pritz (*Legal and Consular*); Dr. Hans Scherer (*Press*); Karl-Hans Berlet (*Economic*); Frau Dr. Brigitte Lohmeyer (*Cultural*).
Consulate General, 6 Rutland Gate, S.W.7. Dr. R. Knickenberg (*Consul*).

Area and Population.—The area of the Federal Republic is approximately 95,737 sq. miles. A Census held on June 6, 1961, showed the total population of the Federal Republic as 53,975,200, excluding Western Berlin, compared with approximately 40,248,000 in 1939. Distribution of the population among the *Länder* in June, 1961, was:—

Schleswig-Holstein	2,316,600
Hamburg	1,832,400
Lower Saxony	6,641,400
Bremen	706,400
North Rhine Westphalia	15,901,700
Hessen	4,814,400
Rhineland Palatinate	3,147,100
Baden-Württemberg	7,759,000
Bavaria	9,513,900
Saarland	1,072,400

Western Berlin had a population of 2,197,600 at the Census held on June 6, 1961.

The population of the principal cities and towns in the Federal Republic in June, 1961 was:—

Hamburg	1,845,107	Münster	179,393
Munich	1,080,000	Bielefeld	175,000
Cologne	795,183	Aachen	172,000
Essen	726,000	Solingen	170,000
Frankfurt/Main	674,079	Ludwigshafen	170,000
Düsseldorf	664,000	Münchengladbach	154,216
Stuttgart	645,000	Bonn	145,000
Dortmund	630,000	Bremerhaven	142,300
Hanover	576,600	Freiburg	138,800
Bremen	557,000	Osnabrück	136,350
Duisburg	500,000	Saarbrücken	134,000
Nuremberg	454,221	Darmstadt	133,000
Wuppertal	424,552	Mainz	131,888
Gelsenkirchen	392,000	Recklinghausen	131,800
Bochum	365,000	Oldenburg	128,800
Mannheim	315,000	Heidelberg	128,000
Kiel	271,000	Remscheid	123,500
Oberhausen	261,000	Regensburg	120,900
Wiesbaden	258,500	Würzburg	117,995
Brunswick	249,000	Herne	117,500
Karlsruhe	246,000	Offenbach/Main	113,000
Lübeck	234,766	Bottrop	112,500
Augsburg	208,000	Wanne-Eickel	108,000
Krefeld	205,800	Salzgitter	107,000
Kassel	202,400	Wilhelmshaven	100,637
Hagen	195,000		
Mülheim/Ruhr	188,500		

Vital Statistics.—There were 18·3 live births per 1,000 inhabitants in the Federal Republic in 1961, compared with 19·8 per 1,000 for the same area in 1938. There was an excess of live births over deaths in 1961 of 7·4 per 1,000 and in 1938 of 8·4.

Government.—The Federal Republic grew out of the fusion of the three western zones. The economic union of the U.K. and U.S. zones followed the Fusion Agreement of December, 1946. The Bizone was later joined by the French zone and in 1948–49 a Parliamentary Council, elected by the Diets of the three zones, drafted a provisional democratic federal constitution for Germany. This Basic Law came into force in the three western zones on May 24, 1949. It provides for a President, elected for a five-year term, a Lower House, with a four-year term of office, elected by direct universal suffrage, and an Upper House composed of delegates of the *Länder*, without a fixed term of office.

The results of the elections held for the lower House (*Bundestag*) on September 17, 1961, were as follows:

Party	*Numbers*
Christian Democratic and Christian Social Unions	251
Social Democrats	203
Free Democrats	67
Total	521

These figures include a total of 22 members for Berlin (C.D.U./C.S.U., 9; S.P.D., 12). The Christian Democratic and Christian Social Unions, having no absolute majority, formed a coalition with the Free Democrats.

When the Federal Government took office the Allied Military Governors were replaced by High Commissioners. In 1952 a contractual agreement was signed between the Federal Republic and the western Allies, whereby the Republic, in return for certain promises regarding a defence contribution, a foreign debt settlement, and the continuation of allied policies concerning decartelization, democratization, restitution, etc., regained virtual sovereignty in May, 1955, after ratification by all the parties concerned. The High Commissioners then became Ambassadors.

The Prime Ministers of the *Länder* governments in May, 1963, were:—

Ministers-President

Baden-Württemberg.—Kurt-Georg Kiesinger.
Bavaria.—Alfons Goppel.
Berlin.—Willy Brandt (*Governing Mayor*).
Bremen.—Wilhelm Kaisen.
Hamburg.—Dr. Paul Nevermann.
Hessen.—Dr. Georg-August Zinn.
North Rhine-Westphalia.—Dr. Franz Meyers.
Rhineland-Palatinate.—Dr. Peter Altmeier.
Saarland.—Dr. Franz-Josef Röder.
Lower Saxony.—Dr. Georg Diederichs.
Schleswig-Holstein.—Dr. Helmut Lemke.

Economic Position.—Despite the difficulties arising from the division of Germany, which cut off from the Federal Republic the main food producing areas of Eastern Germany and some of the principal centres of light industry, German economic recovery has made rapid strides since the currency reform of 1948. As a result of United States and British economic aid and of successful economic policies pursued by the Federal Government, Germany has regained her position as the main industrial power on the Continent, and is the most economically powerful member of the European Common Market. The Gross National Product at current prices in 1961 was estimated at *DM.* 310·4 milliard, an increase of *DM.* 28 milliard or 9·9 per cent. over 1960. In accordance with the Franco-German Agreement of 1957, the economic integration of Saarland with the Federal Republic took place on July 6, 1959.

Agriculture.—The total agricultural area (in 1961) amounted to 54,825 sq. miles, of which 30,656 sq. miles were under plough. The forest area is 27,437 sq. miles. The 1961 harvest yielded 6.700,400 metric tons of bread grains, 5,687,700 metric tons of feeding grains and 21,503,800 metric tons of potatoes. The livestock population at the end of 1961 included 13,276,700 cattle, 634,100 horses, 1,009,500 sheep, 17,206,900 pigs and 65,838,100 fowls.

Industry.—The average index of industrial production per working day (excluding Saarland and Berlin) has developed as follows (1950 = 100):

	1960	1961
Mining	146	150
Manufacturing industry	260	276
(i) Basic materials	260	275
(ii) Capital goods	337	365
(iii) Consumer goods	211	220
(iv) Foodstuffs	214	223
Power (electricity and gas)	243	257
Building Industry	222	241
Total industry	249	264

Hard coal production rose from 142·3 million tons in 1960 to 142·7 million tons in 1961; brown coal rose from 96·1 million tons to 97·2 million tons; pig iron fell from 25·7 million tons to 25·4 million tons; crude steel fell from 34·1 million tons to 33·5 million tons; rolled steel products fell from 22·5 million tons to 21·9 million tons. An average of 145,991 passenger vehicles a month were produced in 1961 (1960 = 139,525), 19,562 commercial vehicles (1960 = 19,180), 211,000 tons of sulphuric acid (1960 = 216,000), 60,384 tons of chlorine (1960 = 54,817), 33,606 tons of cotton yarn (1960 = 35,079) and 9,472 tons of woollen yarn (1960 = 9,794), 564,700 new dwellings were completed in 1961 (1960 = 574,400).

Labour.—Of 20,933,600 employed in September, 1961, 13,794,900 were men. The average number of unemployed was 161,100, of whom 106,300 were men. In 1961, an average of 8,001,975 were employed in industry; coal mining absorbed 517,683; iron and steel production, 365,901; mechanical engineering and vehicle production, 1,599,624; chemicals, 479,510; and textiles and clothing, 952,622. Productivity of labour in industry (excluding electricity, gas and building industry) per working hour in 1961 reached 194 per cent. (1960 = 184) of the 1950 level.

Finance.—Under the Federal constitution the yields of indirect taxes, other than the beer tax, accrue to the Federal Government, while direct taxes accrue to the *Länder*, who are obliged to transfer part of them to the central authorities. From 1961, the financial year coincides with the calendar year instead of, as previously, ending on March 31 each year. The 1960 financial year is from April 1 to December 31, 1960, and figures are therefore valid only as to 75 per cent.

The pattern of budgetary expenditure in 1961 was: Total expenditure *DM.* 44·8 milliard (1960 = 41·9 milliard); Social expenditure (including housing and welfare), *DM.* 16·8 milliard (about 37 per cent.); Defence (including the amount spent on foreign troops in the Federal Republic), *DM.* 12·9 milliard (about 29 per cent.); Agriculture and food, *DM.* 2·3 milliard (about 5 per cent.); Transport, *DM.* 3·2 milliard (about 7 per cent.).

In 1952 an agreement was reached for the settlement of German pre-war and post-war foreign debts. An agreement was also signed whereby the Federal Republic will pay to Israel and Jewish organizations over a period of years reparations amounting to *DM.* 3·5 milliard.

Currency.—The currency of the Federal Republic is the *Deutsche Mark* of 100 *Pfennig*, the rate of exchange with sterling being *DM.* 11·22 = £1. Limited exchange fluctuations are permitted. (*See also* p. 83.)

Foreign Trade.—In 1961, imports (including West Berlin) were valued at *DM.* 44,363 million (1960 = 42,723 million); and exports at *DM.* 50,978 million (1960 = 47,946 million); 26·3 per cent. of imports consisted of foodstuffs and 20·5 per cent. of industrial raw materials; 31·1 per cent. came from the Common Market† countries; 19·4

† Common Market: W. Germany, Belgium and Luxemburg, France, Italy, Netherlands.

per cent. from the E.F.T.A.* and 15·9 per cent. from the United States and Canada. The Common Market countries took 31·7 per cent. of all exports, the E.F.T.A.* 28·3 per cent. and the United States and Canada 7·8 per cent.

Trade with U.K.

	1961	1962
Imports from U.K.	£171,243,391	£199,323,790
Exports to U.K.	194,256,504	193,638,862

Communications.—The state-owned railways of the Federal Republic measure 19,060 miles and the privately owned railways 3,229 miles, a total of 22,289 miles. In 1961 the railways handled 321,900,000 tons of goods and the inland waterways 172,000,000 tons. Railway rolling stock (*Deutsche Bundesbahn*) included, in 1961, 6,766 steam locomotives, 1,128 electric locomotives, 1,089 diesel locomotives, 19,747 passenger coaches, 887 rail buses and 273,107 goods waggons. The classified roads measure 84,668 miles. On Jan. 1, 1962, there were 5,587,599 cars and 716,835 lorries. Ocean-going shipping under the German flag in Dec., 1961, amounted to 5,274,000 tons gross.

Social Welfare.—There is compulsory insurance against sickness, accident, old age and unemployment. Children's allowances are payable in respect of the third and subsequent children. Pension schemes for widows and orphans of public servants are in operation. Public assistance is given to persons unable to earn their living, or with insufficient income to maintain a minimum standard of living.

Law and Justice.—Judicial authority is exercised by the Federal Constitutional Court, the Supreme Federal Court, and the courts of the *Länder*. Judges are independent and subject only to the law. The death sentence has been abolished.

Language and Literature.—Modern (or New High) German has developed from the time of the Reformation to the present day, with differences of dialect in Austria and Alsace and in the German-speaking cantons of Switzerland. The literary language is usually regarded as having become fixed by Luther and Zwingli at the Reformation, since which time many great names occur in all branches, notably philosophy, from Leibnitz (1646–1716) to Kant (1724–1804), Fichte (1762–1814), Schelling (1775–1854) and Hegel (1770–1831); the drama from Goethe (1749–1832) and Schiller (1759–1805) to Gerhart Hauptmann (1862–1946); and in poetry, Heine (1800–1856). German authors have received the Nobel Prize for Literature on five occasions—Theodore Mommsen (1902), R. Eucken (1908), P. Heyse (1909), Gerhart Hauptmann (1912), and Thomas Mann (1929). There are now 1,464 daily papers.

Education.—School attendance is compulsory for all children between the ages of 6 and 14. For the school year 1959–60 there were 30,000 elementary schools, with 198,000 teachers and 5,000,000 pupils in the Federal Republic. State expenditure per primary school pupil per annum amounted to *DM.* 640. In addition there were 760 intermediate schools with 310,000 pupils and 10,100 teachers, 1,550 grammar schools with 763,000 pupils and 14,000 teachers. State expenditure per pupil for intermediate schools was *D.M.* 980 and for grammar schools was *D.M.* 1,440 per annum. The grammar school leaving examination (*Abitur*) entitles the holder to a place of study at a university. The number of examinations passed in 1957 was 38,700. Children below the age of 18 who are not attending an intermediate or grammar school are obliged to take a three-year course (part-time) at a vocational school. There were 9,700 such schools with 2,300,000 pupils and 22,000 teachers. State expenditure per pupil per annum was *DM.* 1,100. In the winter term of 1959 the 18 universities, 8 technical universities, and 7 other institutions of university status, together with teacher training and other colleges in the Federal Republic registered a total of 196,000 German, and 18,800 foreign students. The largest universities are in Munich, Berlin, Cologne, Aachen (T.U.), Hamburg, Frankfurt, Heidelberg, Freiburg and Göttingen. There were 1,200 adult education centres with 3,500 rural branches. The attendance figure for 1959 was 4,400,000 and state expenditure amounted to 40,000,000 *DM.*

Religion.—At the 1950 Census there were 24,430,815 Protestants in the Republic, 21,576,179 Roman Catholics, 17,116 Jews, 142,849 agnostics and 1,528,713 others.

CAPITAL, Bonn, in North Rhine Westphalia, on the left bank of the Rhine, 15 miles distant from Cologne. Population, 145,000.

AIR TRANSIT FROM U.K.—London to Berlin, 3 *hrs.* 30 *mins.*; Cologne, 1 *hr.* 35 *mins.*; Düsseldorf, 1 *hr.* 25 *mins.*; Frankfurt, 1 *hr.* 50 *mins.*; Hamburg, 2 *hrs.*; Hanover, 3 *hrs.* 10 *mins.*; Munich, 2 *hrs.* 25 *mins.*

BRITISH EMBASSY
Friedrich-Ebert Allee, 77, Bonn

Ambassador Extraordinary and Plenipotentiary, His Excellency Sir Frank Kenyon Roberts, G.C.M.G., (1963) £7,015
Minister, E. E. Tomkins, C.M.G., C.V.O.
Counsellors, A. A. Duff, D.S.O., D.S.C. (*Head of Chancery*); A. L. Pope, O.B.E.
1st Secretaries, R. Brash; A. T. Franks; W. Cohn; Miss A. M. Warburton; J. R. Freeland; J. L. Bullard.
2nd Secretaries, C. G. Mays; A. D. S. Goodall; D. J. M. Cornwell; A. W. Rhodes; J. A. Robson.
Minister (Economic), E. Melville, C.M.G.
Counsellor (Economic), D. N. Royce.
1st Secretaries (Commercial), J. F. Croxen; R. K. Robertson; G. W. Wallington.
2nd Secretaries (Commercial), M. J. Newington; G. A. Ball; J. A. Hardman; E. L. Bailey.
Counsellor (Information), J. L. W. Price.
1st Secretaries (Information), P. W. R. C. Haley, M.B.E.; H. Berman, O.B.E.
2nd Secretaries (Information), A. H. Dartnall; Miss B. Richards.
Naval Attaché, Capt. C. C. Anderson, R.N.
Asst. do., Cdr. W. E. Grenfell, R.N.
Military Attaché, Brig. M. V. Fletcher.
Asst. do., Maj. P. L. Gudgin.
Air Attaché., Air Commodore C. A. Alldis, C.B.E., D.F.C., A.F.C.
Civil Air Attaché, A. V. Parker.
Labour Attaché, E. C. M. Cullingford, C.M.G.
Scientific Attaché, R. Ashton.
Supply Attaché, C. F. McFarlane, C.B.E.
Asst. do., F. A. Neal.
Head of Visa Section (Düsseldorf), H. M. Shone.
Counsellor (Administration), K. J. Simpson, C.M.G.
1st Secretary (Administration), E. G. Ducker.
Chaplain, Rev. M. Halliwell.
Archivist, Miss G. Lawrence.
Accountant, F. E. Greville.

There are British Consulates-General at *Berlin*, *Hamburg*, *Hanover*, *Düsseldorf*, *Frankfurt*, *Munich* and *Stuttgart*; and a British Vice-Consulate at *Bremen*.

BRITISH COUNCIL

Representative, R. Seymour, C.B.E., Hahnenstrasse 6, Cologne. There are British Council offices at Berlin, Hamburg, Frankfurt and Munich.

* E.F.T.A. (European Free Trade Association): Austria, Denmark, Norway, Portugal, Sweden, Switzerland, U.K.

BERLIN

G.O.C. British Sector, Maj.-Gen. C. I. H. Dunbar, C.B., C.B.E., D.S.O.
Deputy Commandant (Minister,) A. G. R. Rouse, C.M.G., O.B.E.
Administrative Officer, D. J. Lloyd, M.B.E.

Eastern Germany

Administration.—When the Federal Republic was formed, the People's Council of the Soviet zone, appointed in 1948, was converted into a Provisional People's Chamber. On Oct. 7, 1949, this Chamber enacted a constitution of the "German Democratic Republic," and a provisional *Land* Chamber was established, now known as *Volkskammer*. The German Democratic Republic is not recognized by the governments of western countries. A number of governmental reforms have been introduced since the original constitution was drafted. The Presidency was abolished on Sept. 12, 1960. From that date the main Government posts have been held as follows:—

Chairman, Council of State, W. Ulbricht.
Prime Minister, Otto Grotewohl.
President of the Volkskammer, Dr. Johannes Dieckmann.
Deputy Prime Minister and Foreign Affairs, Dr. Lothar Bolz.
Chairman, State Planning Commission, B. Leuschner.
Chairman, State Control Commission, F. Lange.

It was not until the summer of 1953 that the Soviet Commander-in-Chief was replaced in the civilian sphere by a High Commissioner. In September, 1953, the post of High Commissioner was combined with that of Ambassador.

Area and Population.—The area of Eastern Germany is 41,380 sq. miles and its population in October, 1946, was 17,300,000*:—

Saxony-Anhalt	4,200,000	Saxony	5,600,000
Brandenburg	2,500,000	Thuringia	2,900,000
Mecklenburg	2,100,000		

Principal cities and towns: Dresden (467,966); Leipzig (607,655); Magdeburg (236,326); Halle (222,505); Erfurt (174,633); Rostock (114,869); Zwickau (122,862), and Karlmarxstadt (Chemnitz) (250,188). Eastern Berlin, an integral part of the zone and its capital city, has a population of approximately 1,200,000.

In July, 1952, in the interests of "democratization" and the further centralization of power, the old *Länder* were abolished and replaced by 14 *Bezirke* (regions) as follows:

Land	*Bezirke*
Mecklenburg	Rostock; Schwerin; Neubrandenburg.
Brandenburg	Potsdam; Cottbus; Frankfurt.
Saxony	Karlmarxstadt; Dresden; Leipzig.
Saxony-Anhalt	Halle; Magdeburg.
Thuringia	Erfurt; Gera; Guhl.

* Figures published in 1961 by the West German Ministry of Refugees showed that 2,600,000 refugees had fled to the Federal Republic from Eastern Germany (*German Democratic Republic*) in 1949–1961, many of them crossing to the Western sector of Berlin. More than a quarter of a million persons fled to the Federal Republic in each of the years 1955–1957. In the first six months of 1961, 103,159 refugees were received in West Germany, 30,444 more in July and a further 15,000 in August, 1961, until the Berlin border was sealed by the East German authorities. Refugees crossing in 1960 included about 700 doctors, 142 professors and college lecturers and some 2,000 school teachers.

Each region has its own *Bezirkstag* (assembly) and *Bezirksrat* (council) to deal with purely regional affairs.

Economic Position.—From the economic point of view the Eastern zone is a more unbalanced area than the Federal Republic. It is more nearly self-sufficient in food, but has few industrial raw materials apart from brown coal and copper ore. Before the war its highly developed secondary industries were dependent on Ruhr coal and steel.

The Soviets claimed reparations from Germany to a value of \$(1938)10 milliard. Between 1945 and March, 1948, they removed considerable quantities of capital equipment to the U.S.S.R. and took over a number of important plants as Soviet State Concerns (S.A.G.). S.A.G.'s now account for perhaps one-eighth of all industrial production in Eastern Germany. Their products are sold partly in Germany and partly to the U.S.S.R. and other foreign countries. In addition the zone pays reparations from current production to the U.S.S.R. and, although the amounts have been reduced, the obligation continues until 1965. Economic control has been centralized, industry subjected to rigid central planning, state ownership and trading greatly expanded at the expense of private interests and the basic industries given priority over secondary industries. Large new steel plants have been erected at Fürstenberg/Oder and at Calbe, and crude steel production is now greater than before the war.

The East German Government announced on April 14, 1960, that collectivization of agriculture in East Germany had been completed, the only exceptions being a few small areas unsuitable for large-scale farming.

Trade with U.K.

	1961	1962
Imports from U.K.	£8,214,078	£7,191,374
Exports to U.K.	6,708,610	6,604,411

GREECE
(Hellas)

King of the Hellenes, Paul I, K.G., *born* Dec. 14, 1901; *acceded* (on the death of his brother King George II), April 1, 1947; *married* Jan. 8, 1938, Princess Frederika, daughter of the Duke of Brunswick (*born* April 18, 1917), and has issue:—
(i) Crown Prince (*Diadoch*) H.R.H. Prince Constantine, Duke of Sparta, *born* June 2, 1940.
(ii) H.R.H. Princess Sophia, *born* Nov. 2, 1938; *married* May 14, 1962, H.R.H. Don Juan Carlos, of Spain.
(iii) H.R.H. Princess Irene, *born* May 11, 1942.

CABINET*
(June 19, 1963)

Prime Minister, Foreign Affairs, P. Pipinelis.
Defence, P. Dragoumis.
Economic Co-ordination, C. Arliotis.
Justice (vacant).
Education, C. Stratos.
Finance, G. Sofronopoulos.
Commerce (vacant).
Industry, G. Drossopoulos.
Public Works, G. Markakis.
Communications, A. Patamianos.
Agriculture, A. Bernaris.
Welfare, J. Kyriakos.
Merchant Navy, E. Stratigis.
Labour, Mr. Stambelos.

* *A second caretaker Government headed by* Mr. Stylianos Mavromihalis *took office on Sept. 28, 1963, pending elections later in the year.*

ROYAL GREEK EMBASSY IN LONDON
51 Upper Brook Street, W.1
[Mayfair: 0694]

Ambassador Extraordinary and Plenipotentiary, His Excellency Michel Melas.
Counsellors, J. A. Dracoulis; C. J. Tsamados.
1st Secretary, N. C. Karageorgos.
2nd Secretary (Consular Affairs), C. Zepos.
Naval and Military Attaché, Captain M. Stavridis.
Minister Plenipotentiary (Press Affairs), M. Cosmetatos.
Air Attaché, Group Capt. E. Karydis.
Commercial Counsellor, E. Anagnostopoulos.
Commercial Secretary, G. Mitrofanis.
Hon. Educational Counsellor, P. Argenti.
Consulate General, Department of Information and Commercial Department, 49 Upper Brook Street, W.1., G. Kapsambelis (*Consul-General*).

There are Honorary Consulates at *Birmingham*, *Bradford*, *Bristol*, *Falmouth*, *Hull*, *Immingham*, *Liverpool*, *Newcastle*, *Plymouth*, *Portsmouth*, *Southampton* and *Yarmouth*, *Swansea* and *Glasgow*, and at *Belfast*.

A maritime Kingdom in the south-east of Europe, bounded on the N. by Albania, Yugoslavia and Bulgaria, on the S. and W. by the Libyan and Ionian seas, and on the E. by Turkey, with an estimated area of 51,182 sq. miles. A census held throughout the country on March 19, 1961, recorded a population of 8,388,553.

The area of the mainland is 41,328 sq. miles, and of the islands 9,854 sq. miles. The main divisions are: *Macedonia* (which includes Mt. Athos and the island of *Thasos*), *Thrace* (including the island of *Samothrace*), *Epirus*, *Thessaly*, *Continental Greece* (which includes the island of *Euboea* and the *Sporades*, or " scattered islands," of which the largest is *Skyros*), the *Peloponnese* (or *Morea*), the *Dodecanese* or *Southern Sporades* (12 islands occupied by Italy in 1911 during the Italo-Turkish War and ceded to Greece by Italy in 1947) consisting of Rhodes, Astypalaia, Karpathos, Kassos, Nisyros, Kalymnos, Leros, Patmos, Kos, Symi, Khalki and Tilos, the *Cyclades* (a circular group numbering about 200, with a total area of 923 sq. miles; the chief islands are Syros, Andros, Tinos, Naxos, Paros, Santorini, Milos and Serifos), the *Ionian Islands* (Corfu, Paxos, Levkas, Ithaca, Cephalonia, Zante and Cerigo), the *Aegean Islands* (Chios, Lesbos, Limnos and Samos). In *Crete* there was for over 1,500 years (3000 to 1400 B.C.) a flourishing civilization which spread its influence far and wide throughout the Aegean, and the ruins of the palace of Minos at Cnossos afford evidence of astonishing comfort and luxury. Greek civilization emerges about 1300 B.C. and the poems of Homer, the blind poet of Chios, which were probably current about 800 B.C., record the 10-year struggle between the Achaeans of Greece and the Phrygians of Troy (1194–1184 B.C.).

Government.—The Independence of Greece dates from March 25 (O.S.), 1821, and was ratified by the *Treaty of Adrianople* (Sept. 14, 1829) and the *Convention of London* (Feb. 3, 1830), after a successful insurrection against the Ottoman Empire, to which the country had been subjected since the 15th century. The first Head of State was a Greek, John Capodistrias, who was assassinated in Nauplia in 1831. The Allied Powers then chose a prince of the Wittelsbach (Bavarian) dynasty; he ruled as King Otho until his abdication in 1862. He was succeeded by King George I of the Glucksburg (Danish) dynasty. Since then Greece has had one period as a republic (1924–35) and one period of uncertainty (from the Second World War until September, 1946), but in both cases returned to the monarchical system under the Glucksburg dynasty after a plebiscite.

At the time of its independence, the Kingdom of Greece included little more than the Peloponnese, Sterea Hellas and the Cyclades, but the Ionian Islands were added in 1864, Thessaly in 1881, Macedonia, Crete and the Aegean Islands in 1913, Western Thrace in 1919 and the Dodecanese in 1947. The Treaty of Sèvres (1922), under which Greece would have received large territories round Istanbul and in Asia Minor, was nullified by the Greek defeat in the Asia Minor campaign of 1922. This was followed by a major exchange of populations which largely settled the minority problems between Greece and Turkey. The long campaign for *enosis* (union) of Cyprus with Greece was terminated in 1959 by the Zürich and London Agreements which led to the proclamation of Cyprus as an independent republic in 1960.

On October 28, 1940, Italy declared war on Greece and invaded the country from Albania, but within a month Greek troops, assisted at sea and in the air by Great Britain, expelled the invader and advanced in triumph into Albania. On April 6, 1941, Germany invaded Yugoslavia and Greece and came to the aid of the defeated Italian forces. British and Commonwealth ground forces were sent to the assistance of Greece, but the fresh onslaught led to her occupation by German, Italian and Bulgarian troops. By her own exertions and by Allied help Greece was freed in October, 1944.

There followed in December–January, 1944–5 a short period of civil war in which the Communists attempted to seize power by force. In 1947, Communist guerilla disturbances assumed the proportions of civil war, which continued with increasing damage and destruction to the country until the summer of 1949 when the Greek Army's victories overwhelmed the guerillas. Normal conditions were sufficiently restored throughout the country to enable a general election to be held on March 5, 1950. Since then, with considerable economic help from the United States, Greece has made great progress in the formidable task of rehabilitation and reconstruction. Greece acceded to the North Atlantic Treaty in Feb. 1952. In the economic field the country has made steady, if slow, progress.

At a general election held on October 29, 1961, the National Radical Union Party was for the third time returned to power. A Cabinet, formed by M. Karamanlis on Nov. 4, 1961, held office until June 11, 1963, when he resigned after the King had refused to accept his advice that the state visit to Britain should be postponed in view of incidents in London. A caretaker Government under M. Pipinelis was then appointed, and received a vote of confidence in Parliament (*see also* Note, p. 862).

Defence.—The Navy has 65 major war vessels, almost all of U.S. origin, and is mainly a fleet of landing ships supported by destroyers and other escort vessels. The strength of the Army is 120,000. The Air Force consists of 24,000 men, eight offensive squadrons and two transport squadrons, together with a few helicopters and the necessary support, training and maintenance organizations.

Production.—Though there has in recent years been a substantial measure of industrialization, Greece is still predominantly an agricultural country. Agriculture employs about half the working population, the most important product and export being tobacco, which still, despite recent difficulties in disposing of the crop abroad, accounts for one-third of the value of total visible exports from Greece. Since the war the production of wheat, cotton and rice has been greatly increased, partly in an attempt to make the country's economy less dependent upon tobacco. The most important of the fruit trees are the olive, vine, orange, lemon, fig, almond, pomegranate and currant-vine, and considerable efforts have lately been made to develop exports of Greek fresh fruit and vegetables as well as currants and other dried fruits. Currants, grown mainly around Patras, remain one of Greece's main exports, the United Kingdom being the principal purchaser.

The principal minerals mined in Greece are iron ore, iron pyrites, manganese, magnesite, chrome, bauxite, lead, zinc and emery, and prospecting for petroleum is being carried on. An oil refinery, the first in Greece, was opened near Athens early in 1958. The chief industries are textiles (cotton, woollen, silk and rayon), chemicals, cement, glass, metallurgy, shipbuilding, domestic electrical equipment and footwear. 1962 saw the opening of new factories for the production of tyres and polystyrene and of refineries for processing locally-grown sugar beet. Industrial projects, either in the course of being carried out or planned in the near future, include the erection of a second oil refinery, to be associated with a petrochemicals plant and a steel mill, the extension of existing iron and steel industries, establishment of plants for the manufacture of aluminium and of fertilizers, and a motor-vehicle manufacturing industry. The development of the country's electric power resources, irrigation and land reclamation schemes, and the exploitation of Greece's lignite resources for fuel and industrial purposes are also being carried out, and a television network is planned for the near future. Greece enjoys substantial financial assistance from the United States and has received loans from the Federal Republic of Germany. Following a decision made at the N.A.T.O. ministerial meeting in Athens in May, 1962, a consortium of 8 countries from O.E.C.D. has been formed to help Greece's economic development.

Communications.—The 2,650 kilometres of Greek railways had all been repaired by the end of 1950, in spite of delays due to the activities of guerilla bands. All are now State owned with the exception of the Athens–Piraeus Electric Railway. The railway from Athens to the Peloponnese, serving Patras and southern Greece, is metre gauge, but the other lines, except one or two minor ones, are standard gauge. Athens is linked with Istanbul, Paris (*viâ* Belgrade, Trieste and Lausanne), Ostend (*viâ* Belgrade, Salzburg, Cologne and Brussels) and Vienna by direct sleeping-car services. Greek roads total somewhat over 50,000 kilometres, of which about 30 per cent. are classified as national highways and 30,000 km. are classified as provincial roads. More than 7,000 km. of both classes are asphalt and a further 14,000 km. are macadamized. At the end of March, 1962, the Greek mercantile fleet numbered 1,287 ships with a total tonnage of 7,290,669 tons gross. A further 668 Greek-owned ships were under foreign flags (6,345,656 tons gross). The Greek national airline, Olympic Airways, flies numerous internal and external services, including Athens–London, and it and other airlines connect Athens directly with most countries in Europe and the Middle East.

Religion.—Over 97 per cent. of the people are adherents of the Greek Orthodox Church, which is the State religion, all others being tolerated and free from interference. The Church of Greece recognizes the spiritual primacy of the Œcumenical Patriarch of Constantinople, but is otherwise a self-governing body administered by the Holy Synod under the Presidency of the Archbishop of Athens and All Greece. It has no jurisdiction over the Church of Crete, which has a degree of autonomy under the Œcumenical Patriarch, nor over the Monastic Community of Mount Athos and the Church in the Dodecanese, both of which come directly under the Œcumenical Patriarch.

Education is free and compulsory from the age of 6 to 12 and is maintained by State grants. There are two Universities, Athens and Salonika.

Language and Literature.—The *spoken* language of modern Greece is descended by a process of natural development from the "Common Greek" of Alexander's empire. Official and technical matter is mostly composed in *Katharevusa*, a conservative literary dialect evolved by Adamantios Corais (Diamant Coray), who lived and died in Paris (1748–1833), but novels and poetry are mostly composed in *dimotiki*, a progressive literary dialect which owes much to John Psycharis (1854–1929). The poets Solomos, Palamas, Cavafis and Sikelianos have won a European reputation.

CURRENCY

The Greek *drachma* has an official exchange rate of 84=£1 sterling and 30=U.S. $1.
(*See also* p. 83.)

TRADE

	1961	1962
Total imports....	£255,000,000	£250,000,000
Total exports.....	70,767,000	88,780,000

Trade with U.K.

	1961	1962
Imports from U.K..	21,132,478	£25,764,416
Exports to U.K.....	7,526,262	10,416,312

CAPITAL, Athens. Population (including Ψ Piraeus and suburbs), 1,852,709. Other large towns are: Salonika (373,635); ΨPatras (95,364), ΨVolos (67,424); Larissa (55,391); and ΨCavalla (44,517); in Crete—ΨHeraklion or Candia (63,458), ΨCanea (38,467), and ΨRethymnon (14,999); in the Ionian Islands—ΨCorfu (26,991); in the Dodecanese—ΨRhodes (27,393); in the Cyclades—ΨSyros (Hermopoulos) (14,402); in Lesbos—ΨMitylene (25,758); in Chios—ΨChios (24,053).

FLAG.—9 horizontal bands, alternately blue and white, with white cross, on blue ground, in corner.

NATIONAL DAY: March 25.

BRITISH EMBASSY

(4 Odos Gennadiou, Athens)

Ambassador Extraordinary and Plenipotentiary, His Excellency Sir (Francis) Ralph (Hay) Murray, K.C.M.G., C.B. (1962) £5,015

Counsellors, R. C. Barnes; R. A. Sykes, M.C. (*Commercial*).

1st Secretaries, J. C. Moberly; H. S. Colchester, O.B.E.; E. J. C. Hare, O.B.E., T.D. (*Information*); J. D. Blakeway; C. Marshall (*Labour*) (*Resident at Tel Aviv*).

2nd Secretaries, R. H. Stockbridge, M.C.; F. G. C. Robinson (*Consul*); G. A. Fletcher (*Commercial*); K. W. Hazle (*Information*); W. H. Lamport; D. McAlindon.

3rd Secretaries, G. F. Noble (*Commercial*); S. Levicky (*Visa*).

Naval Attaché, Capt. R. H. Martin, D.S.C., R.N.

Military Attaché, Brig. W. C. G. Rogers, O.B.E., M.C.

Air Attaché, Air Commodore J. Holmes, D.F.C.

Attachés, H. Bradley (*Archivist*); E. C. Duckworth (*Commercial*).

Embassy Chaplain, Rev. J. Findlow.

Hon. Attaché, H. M. Megaw (*Director, British School of Archæology*).

BRITISH CONSULAR OFFICES

There are British Consular Offices at *Athens, Salonika, Piræus, Corfu* and *Samos*.

BRITISH COUNCIL

Representative, R. A. Close, O.B.E., 8 Ermou Street, Athens.

GUATEMALA

(República de Guatemala)

HEAD OF GOVERNMENT

Col. Enrique Peralta Azurdia, *assumed office*, March 31, 1963.

Guatemala, the most northerly of the Republican States of Central America, is situated in N. lat. from 13° 45′ to 17° 49′, and in W. long from 88° 12′ 49″ to 92° 13′ 43″, and comprises an area of 42,042 square miles, and a population (estimated, 1962) of 4,016,624. The constitutionally elected president, Gen. Miguel Ydígoras Fuentes, who had taken office on March 3, 1958, was overthrown on March 31, 1963 by the Army, which handed executive and legislative powers to the Minister of Defence, Col. Enrique Peralta Azurdia. Congress has been suspended. There is a cabinet of 10 Ministers of State. A return to constitutional government has been promised as soon as the country is ready for elections. The Republic is divided into 22 departments, and is traversed from W. to E. by an elevated mountain chain, containing several volcanic summits rising to 13,000 feet above the sea; earthquakes are frequent, and the capital (which is at an altitude of 4,800 ft.) was destroyed by an upheaval in Dec. 1917. The country is well watered by numerous rivers; the climate is hot and malarial near the coast, temperate in the higher regions. The rainfall in the capital is 57 in. per annum. The chief Ψ seaports are San José de Guatemala and Champerico on the Pacific and Livingston, Matías de Gálvez (*formerly* Santo Tomás) and Puerto Barrios on the Atlantic side.

Language and Literature.—Spanish is the language of the country, and since the establishment of the University in the capital, education has received a marked impulse and the high figure of illiteracy is being reduced. The National library contains about 80,000 volumes in the Spanish tongue.

FINANCE		1961–62
Revenue (Actual)	*Quetzales*	99,346,000
Expenditure (Actual)	"	109,567,200

At par 1 *Quetzal* = $1 U.S. Exchange rate 2·80 Q = £1. (*See also* p. 83.)

TRADE

	1961 *Quetzales*	1962 *Quetzales*
Imports (c.i.f.)	133,554,708	132,998,334
Exports (f.o.b.)	110,177,280	109,303,392

Trade with U.K.

	1961	1962
Imports from U.K.	£2,263,740	£1,903,533
Exports to U.K.	418,461	516,278

The principal export is coffee, other articles being bananas, cotton, *chicle* (chewing gum), essential oils, zinc and lead. The chief imports are textiles, petroleum, vehicles, machinery and foodstuffs.

CAPITAL, Guatemala. Pop. (1962), 417,218. *Quezaltenango* (second city of the Republic), has a pop. of 39,638. Other towns are Ψ Puerto Barrios (22,929), Mazatenango (16,179), and Antigua (15,606).

FLAG.—Three vertical bands, blue, white, blue; coat of arms on white stripe.

BRITISH EMBASSY

(Diplomatic relations suspended, July 24, 1963).

GUINEA

(Republic of Guinea)

President, Sékou Touré, *elected for a term of 7 years, January*, 1961.

President of National Assembly, Diallo Saifoulaye.

CABINET

(Oct. 2, 1958)

Prime Minister, Sékou Touré.
Minister of State, Diallo Saifoulaye.
Secretary of State, Camara Balla.
Interior and Collectives, Kaba Sinkoun.
National Defence and Security, Kéita Fodéba.
Commerce, Keita N'Famara.
Planning, Barry Ibrahima.
Finance, Diakité Moussa.
Economic Development, Touré Ismaël.
Education, Conté Saïdou.
Health and Social Affairs, Diallo Abdourahmane.
Public Administration and Labour, Touré Fodé Mamadou.
Justice, Paul Faber.
Secretary of State for Information, Diallo Alpha Amadou.
Posts and Telecommunications, Diop Alassane.
Foreign Affairs, Béavogui Louis-Lansana.
Industry and Mines, Dramé Alioune.
Rural Economy, Barry Sory.
Transport, Accab Najib Roger.
Secretary of State for Housing, Cissé Fodé.
Secretary of State for Social Affairs, Mme. Camara Loffo.

Formerly part of French West Africa, Guinea has a coastline on the Atlantic Ocean between Portuguese Guinea and Sierra Leone and in the interior is adjacent to Senegal, Mali and the Republic of Ivory Coast. Area, 96,865 sq. miles. The population was estimated in 1961 at 3,000,000, mostly of the Fullah, Malinké and Soussou tribes. It is estimated that there are about 2,000 Europeans in the country.

Government.—Guinea was separated from Senegal in 1891 and administered by France as a separate colony until 1958. In the referendum held in Metropolitan France and the overseas territories on Sept. 2, 1958, Guinea rejected the new French Constitution. Accordingly, on Sept. 28, it was declared that Guinea had separated itself from the other territories of French West Africa which had adopted the Constitution. French administrative and financial assistance was terminated; and Guinea left the French Community. On October 2, 1958, Guinea became an independent republic governed by a Constituent Assembly. M. Sékou Touré, Prime Minister in the Territorial Assembly, assumed office as head of the new Government.

A provisional constitution, adopted on Nov. 12, 1958, declared Guinea "a democratic, secular and social republic", powers of government being exercised by a president assisted by the Cabinet. The President, eligible for a term of 7 years and for re-election, is head of state and of the armed forces. M. Sékou Touré was elected President of the Republic by an overwhelming vote in an election (in which he was the sole candidate) in January, 1961. General recognition of Guinea as an independent state was followed by her admission to membership of the United Nations in December, 1958.

Guinea withdrew from the Franc Zone on March 1, 1960, and established her own currency, the *Guinea franc* (at par with the *franc C.F.A.*). This led to the rupture of commercial relations with France, hitherto her most important supplier and purchaser. Guinea is in receipt of economic aid and technical assistance from a number of countries, including the United States, Federal Republic of Germany, Yugoslavia, the Soviet Union and China. The Government's foreign policy is one of "positive neutralism." In May, 1963, Guinea signed agreements with France covering *inter alia* the settlement of Governmental claims and technical co-operation.

Production, etc.—The principal products of Guinea are alumina, iron-ore, palm kernels, millet, rice, coffee, bananas, pineapples and rubber. Principal imports are cotton goods, manufactured goods, tobacco, petroleum products, sugar, rice, flour and salt; exports, alumina, iron-ore, diamonds, coffee, hides, bananas, palm kernels and pineapples. In the mountains in the hinterland of Guinea (Fouta Djalon, 4,970 feet), where the rivers Senegal, Gambia and Niger have their sources, large deposits of bauxite (the raw material of aluminium) are worked and alumina is produced for export. Bauxite has been worked and exported from the Conakry area where there are also rich deposits of iron-ore and large-scale mining is carried on.

Trade with U.K.

	1961	1962
Imports from U.K......	£836,246	£820,507
Exports to U.K.........	840,124	400,581

CAPITAL.—Ψ Conakry (100,000). Other towns are Kankan (24,000), which is connected with Conakry by a railway, Kindia (13,000), N'Zérékoré, Mamou, Siguiri and Labé.

FLAG.—Three vertical stripes of red, yellow and green.

BRITISH EMBASSY
Conakry

Ambassador Extraordinary and Plenipotentiary and Consul General, His Excellency Hilary William King, M.B.E. (1962).
1st Secretary, J. C. C. Bennett.
2nd Secretary, P. B. Thompson.
3rd Secretary (and Vice-Consul), F. J. Clough.

British Council Representative, J. H. Grimes.

HAITI

(République d'Haiti)

President, Dr. François Duvalier, *installed* Oct. 22, 1957; *re-installed* May 22, 1961.

EMBASSY AND CONSULATE
Office: 22 Hans Road, S.W.3.; *Residence:* 63B, Cadogan Square, S.W.1.

Chargé d'Affaires, Delorme Mèhu.

The Republic of Haiti occupies the western third of the island of Hispaniola, which, next to Cuba, is the largest island in the West Indies.

The area of the Republic is about 10,000 sq. miles with a population of about 4,000,000. The people are mainly negroes but there are numbers of mulattoes and others with some admixture of European blood. About 250 British subjects, chiefly of British West Indian origin, reside in Haiti.

A French colony under the name of Saint-Domingue from 1697, the slave population, estimated at 500,000, revolted in 1791 under the leadership of Toussaint L'Ouverture, who was born a slave and made himself Governor-General of the colony. He capitulated to the French in 1802 and died in captivity in 1803. Resistance was continued by Jean Jacques Dessalines, also a former black slave, who, on January 1, 1804, declared the former French colony to be an independent state. It was at this time that the name Haiti, an aboriginal word meaning mountainous, was adopted. Dessalines became Emperor of Haiti, but was assassinated in 1806. In 1915, following a period of political upheaval, the country was occupied by a force of U.S. marines. The occupation came to an end in 1934, and U.S. control of the revenue of Haiti officially ended on October 1, 1947.

The six-year term of General Magloire having ended in December 1956, he attempted to stay in power for a further period but was forced to resign and go into exile. A period of political upheaval followed and for many months there was no effective government. A military junta took over in June, 1957, and elections were held in September, following which Dr. Duvalier was installed as the new President of the Republic.

Production, Industry, etc.—In French colonial times, Haiti was one of the most productive countries in the world and the richest French possession. Improvident methods of peasant agriculture succeeded the plantation system and resulted in the gradual impoverishment of natural resources through exhaustion of the soil, deforestation and erosion. In recent years measures for agricultural rehabilitation have been taken with the aim of a gradual restoration of the productiveness of the country. The main project now approaching completion is a scheme for the irrigation of more than 70,000 acres of the Artibonite valley for which the Import-Export Bank approved a loan of $27,000,000 and the Development Loan Fund, on May 28, 1959, a further loan of $4,300,000.

The principal products are coffee, sisal, sugar, essential oils, bananas, logwood, cocoa and cotton. Coffee accounts for about two-thirds of total exports and is the mainstay of the country's economy. Exports of bauxite began in 1957 and production of copper in the Terre Neuve area started in 1960. Industry is still on a small scale. The tourist trade expanded until 1956, since when it has fallen off owing to political upheavals.

Communications.—There are very few asphalted roads and internal communications are very bad. Air services between the capital and the principal provincial towns are maintained by the Aviation Corps of the Haitian Army. The principal towns and villages are connected by telephone and/or telegraph. The internal telephone and telegraph system is permanently out of order. The reinstallation which was being carried out by a British firm was stopped in 1957 and has not been resumed. External telegraph, telephone and postal services are normal.

Air services by Pan-American World Airways are regular and frequent, and there are passenger sailings every 10 days (approx.) for New York and Panama by the Grace Line. Freight sailings are frequent for the U.S.A., Canada and Europe. Sailings between Haiti and Jamaica are infrequent. (Air mail transit U.K./Port-au-Prince 4–7 days.)

Climate.—The climate is tropical with comparatively little difference in the temperatures between the summer (March–Oct.) and the winter (Nov.–Feb.). The temperature at Port-au-Prince rarely exceeds 95° F., but the humidity is high, especially in the autumn.

Language and Literature.—French is the language of the government and the press, but it is only understood by the educated minority. The usual language of the people is Creole. Education is free but estimates of illiteracy are as high as 90 per cent. There are 4 French daily newspapers and several weekly papers including 2 in English. The total circulation is very small.

	1958–59 $U.S.	1959–60 $U.S.
Revenue	32,740,000	23,200,000
Expenditure	37,200,000	37,200,000

5 *Gourdes*= $1 (U.S.). (*See also* p. 83.)

	1958–59 $U.S.	1959–60 $U.S.
Total Imports	29,260,000	35,000,000
Total Exports	23,000,000	42,600,000

Trade with U.K.

	1961	1962
Imports from U.K.	£599,908	£629,660
Exports to U.K.	35,767	27,524

The principal exports are listed above; the principal imports are cottons, foodstuffs, machinery, mineral oil and soap.

CAPITAL, Ψ Port-au-Prince. Population (1960 census), 250,000. Other centres are: Ψ Cap Haitien (24,957); Ψ Gonaives (13,534); Ψ Les Caves (11,835); Jérémie (11,138); Ψ St. Marc (10,485); Ψ Jacmel (8,545); Ψ Port de Paix (6,309)

FLAG.—Two horizontal bands, blue, red; in the centre, the coat-of-arms on a white square.

BRITISH EMBASSY
(Port-au-Prince)

Chargé d'Affaires, H. Niblock.

HEJAZ, *see* Saudi Arabia

HONDURAS
(Republica de Honduras)

President (vacant). (*See* Occurrences during Printing.)

HONDURAN EMBASSY AND CONSULATE
104 Great Portland Street, W.1.
[Langham: 6103]

Ambassador, His Excellency Dr. Francisco José Durón (1960).

Consul-General, Dr. Gonzalo Rodriguez-Soto.

There is a Consular Office at *Birmingham*.

Honduras, one of the five Republican States of Central America, lies between lat. 13° and 16° 30′ N. and long. 83° and 89° 41′ west, with a seaboard of about 400 miles on the Caribbean Sea and an outlet, consisting of a small strip of coast 77 miles in length on the Pacific. Its frontiers are contiguous with those of Guatemala, Nicaragua and El Salvador.

The Republic contains a total area of approximately 43,278 square miles and a population of 1,887,389 (estimate of June 30, 1959) of mixed Spanish and Indian blood. There is a strong foreign negro (British West Indian) element in Northern Honduras. The country is very mountainous, being traversed by the Cordilleras, Most of the soil is poor and acid, except for a few areas along the North coast and in the interior. There has been no recent volcanic activity. Rainfall is seasonal, May to October being wet and November to April dry. The climate varies with the altitude, being tropical throughout the year in the coastal belts and temperate and mainly healthy in the uplands.

Originally discovered and settled by the Spaniards at the beginning of the sixteenth century, Honduras formed part of the Spanish American Dominions for nearly three centuries until 1821 when independence was proclaimed.

Under the Constitution of Dec. 21, 1957, the Legislature consists of a single Congress of 64 members elected by popular vote in the ratio of approximately one per 30,000 inhabitants. The executive authority is vested in the President who is assisted by a Cabinet of nine Ministers.

The Republic is divided into 18 departments, the newest of which, Gracias a Dios, formed in Feb. 1957, covers all the territory previously known as La Mosquitia, together with portions of the Departments of Olancho and Colón. It is inhabited by Indian tribes and largely unexplored.

The chief industry is the production of bananas. Other products are coffee, tobacco, beans, maize, rice, cotton, sugar cane, cement and tropical fruits. Cattle raising is becoming an increasingly important industry, a large number of cattle being exported to the neighbouring countries every year. Honduras is also a timber producing country, the most important woods being pine, mahogany and cedar. There are large tracts of uncultivated land.

The mineral resources of the country are reputed to be considerable, but only a small portion is at present exploited owing to transport difficulties.

835 miles of railway were in operation in the year 1959, chiefly to serve the banana plantations and the Caribbean ports. The total road mileage is approximately 2,000, the greater part of which is in poor condition, but improvements are now being made and new roads built. There are 34 unpretentious airports and one large international airport in use in Honduras, and numerous small landing and emergency fields. There are three international air services (TACA Internacional, PAA and TAN) and a domestic air service (SAHSA). There are 2,979 miles of telephone lines, 4,981 miles of telegraph lines and 369 post-offices.

ΨThe chief ports are Puerto Cortes, Tela and La Ceiba on the North Coast, through which passes the bulk of the trade with the United States and Europe, and Amapala, situated on Tiger Island in the Gulf of Fonseca, on the Pacific side.

Language and Literature.—The language of the country is Spanish. Primary and secondary education is free and compulsory and, although there is still a great deal of illiteracy, it is gradually diminishing. There is no recognized native literature.

FINANCE		1963
Revenue (*Budget estimate*)	*Lempiras*	81,852,491
Expenditure	„	110,262,491
Loans	„	28,410,000

The currency is the *Lempira* (named after a native chief), value of 50 cents., U.S. and *Lps.* 5·60 to the £. (*See also* p. 83.)

The Public Debt amounted at the end of 1962 to U.S. $16,600,000 (external) and U.S. $15,200,000 (internal).

TRADE		1962 (Jan. June)
Imports	*Lempiras*	78,900,000
Exports	„	88,700,000

Trade with U.K.

	1961	1962
Imports from U.K.	£502,699	£643,736
Exports to U.K.	334,297	269,100

CAPITAL.—Tegucigalpa. Pop. (1961), 133,877 (including the contiguous town of Comayaguela); other towns are San Pedro Sula (58,931), ΨLa Ceiba (22,780), ΨTela (15,979), ΨPuerto Cortes (16,102), Choluteca (8,000), Amapala (3,000) and Trujillo (2,000).

FLAG.—Three horizontal bands, blue, white, blue (with five blue stars on white band).

BRITISH EMBASSY
(Tegucigalpa.)

Ambassador Extraordinary and Plenipotentiary and Consul-General, His Excellency John Henry Wright (1963) £3,415
1st Secretary and Consul, R. F. C. Hall.
Air Attaché, Group Capt. V. Rees (*resident in Caracas*).
Labour Attaché, J. S. Rew (*resident in Mexico City*).
Attaché, H. R. Ward.

BRITISH CONSULAR OFFICES

There are British Consular Offices at *Tegucigalpa*, *San Pedro Sula* and *Tela*.

Tegucigalpa is 5,930 miles from London; transit, *viâ* New York, 14 days; *viâ* Panama 20 days. By air *viâ* New York 2 days.

HUNGARY
(Magyarország)

President of the Presidential Council of the Republic, István Dobi, *re-elected* Feb., 1963.

COUNCIL OF MINISTERS
(Sept. 13, 1961)

Prime Minister, János Kádár.
Deputy Prime Minister, Gyula Kállai; Antal Apró; Jenö Fock; Lajos Fehér.
Minister of State, Dr. Ferenc Münnich.
Foreign Affairs, János Peter.
Home Affairs, Janos Pap.
Defence, Lajos Czinege.
Finance, Mátyás Timár.
Justice, Ferenc Nezvál.
Metallurgy and Machine Industry, Gyula Horgos.
Heavy Industry, Ferenc Lévárdi.
Light Industry, Mrs. József Nagy.
Foreign Trade, Jenö Incze.
Internal Trade, János Tausz.
Agriculture, Pál Losoncz.
Health, Dr. Frigyes Doleschall.
Food, Imre Kovács.
Education, Pal Ilku.
Construction, Rezsö Trautmann.
Labour, Jozsef Veres.
Communications and Postal Affairs, István Kossa.
President, National Planning Office, Miklos Ajtai.
President, Technical Development Committee, Arpad Kiss.

LEGATION IN LONDON
(35 Eaton Place, S.W.1)
[Belgravia: 4048]

Minister in London, His Excellency Béla Szilágyi (1959).
Consulate, 46 Eaton Place, S.W.1 (Belgravia: 4462).

Area and Population.—The area of Hungary may be stated as approximately 36,000 sq. miles with a population (Nov., 1962) of 9,961,044.

Government.—Hungary was reconstituted a kingdom in 1920 after having been declared a republic on Nov. 17, 1918. She joined the Anti-Comintern Pact on Feb. 24, 1939, and entered the 1939–45 War on the side of Germany. On Jan. 20, 1945, a Hungarian provisional government of liberation, which had been set up during the preceding December, signed an armistice with the United Nations under the terms of which the frontiers of Hungary were withdrawn to the limits existing in 1937.

For the first four years after the liberation, Hungary was governed by a coalition of the Smallholder, National Peasant, Social Democrat and Communist parties. During this time land reform was carried out, the great landowners being dispossessed and their estates partitioned among peasants; mines, heavy industry, banks and schools were nationalized. By 1949 the Communists, under the leadership of Mr. Rákosi, having compelled the Social Democrat Party to merge with them, and having disrupted the peasant parties, had succeeded in gaining a monopoly of power. Elections in that year, in which candidates for the National Assembly were drawn from a single list, resulted in 95·6 per cent. of the votes cast being obtained by the Communist-dominated People's Front. A campaign was opened to collectivize agriculture and by 1952 practically the entire economy had been "socialized."

In mid-1953 Mr. Imre Nagy replaced Mr. Rákosi as Prime Minister, though the latter continued to hold his post as First Secretary of the Party. Mr. Nagy introduced a more moderate policy based largely on the development of agriculture rather than heavy industry; but in April, 1955, Mr. Rákosi succeeded in turning the tables on his rival who was removed from his position as Prime Minister and subsequently expelled from the Party. But after the 20th Congress of the Soviet Communist Party, opposition to Mr. Rákosi within the Hungarian Communist Party mounted and on July 18, 1956, he was removed from his post as First Secretary and succeeded by Mr. Gerö, who had been one of his closest associates. The period from July to the outbreak of the national revolution on Oct. 23, 1956, was marked by growing ferment in intellectual circles and increased discord within the Party. The immediate signal for the revolt was a series of students' demonstrations, first in Szeged on Oct. 22 and in Budapest a day later. The chief demands put forward by students and other demonstrators were for the return of Mr. Nagy as Prime Minister, for the withdrawal of Soviet troops from the country and for free elections. Fighting broke out on the night of Oct. 23 between demonstrators, who had been joined by large numbers of factory workers, and the State Security Police (A.V.H.). Soviet forces intervened in strength early the next morning. By Oct. 30 Soviet troops had withdrawn from Budapest and on Nov. 3 Mr. Nagy formed an all-party coalition government. This government was overthrown and the revolution suppressed as the result of a renewed attack by Soviet forces on Budapest in the early hours of Nov. 4. Simultaneously the formation of a new Hungarian Revolutionary Worker Peasant Government under the leadership of Mr. Kádár, Mr. Gerö's successor as First Secretary of the Party, was announced. The trial and execution of Imre Nagy and three of his associates was announced on June 17, 1958. Dr. Ferenc Münnich succeeded as President of the Council on Jan. 27, 1958, and held office until Sept. 13, 1961, being replaced by Mr. Kádár. Several other Ministers were replaced at the same time.

Production, Industry, etc.—Though industrialization has made considerable progress in the last decade, agriculture still occupies an important place in the Hungarian economy and 58 per cent. of the total area of the country is arable land. About 14 per cent. of this arable land is owned by state farms and about 75 per cent. by co-operative farms. Production of the most important crops in 1961 was as follows (1,000 tons):—Wheat 1,936; rye 297; barley 984; oats 139; rice 38; maize 2,715; potatoes 1,630; sugar-beet 2,356; cattle-turnip 7,073; sunflower 105; lucerne 936; red clover 433.

Industry is mainly based on imported raw materials, but Hungary has her own coal (mostly brown), bauxite, some iron ore and oil. Output figures in 1961 (1,000 tons) were as follows:—coal 28,176; bauxite 1,358; iron ore 605; pig-iron 1,161; steel 2,100; crude oil 1,455; cement 1,601.

The output of raw materials and general industrial production were sharply reduced by the revolution of Oct., 1956, but all the ground then lost has since been made up and industrial production rose by 12 per cent. in 1961. Hungary's economic plan for 1962 provided for an increase of 8 per cent. in industrial production.

Religion and Education.—About two-thirds of the Magyars are Roman Catholics, and the remainder mostly Calvinist. There are five types of schools under the Ministry of Education—infant schools 3–6, general schools 6–14 (compulsory), vocational schools (15–18), secondary schools (15–18), universities and adult training schools (over 18). In the academic year 1960–61 there were 40,000 students at universities, 156,000 at secondary schools of all types and 1,400,000 at general schools.

Language and Literature. — Magyar, or Hungarian, is one of the Finno-Ugrian languages. Hungarian literature began to flourish in the second half of the sixteenth century. Among the greatest writers of the nineteeth and twentieth centuries are Mihály Vörösmarty (1800–1855), Sándor Petöfi (1823–1849), János Arany (1817–1882), Endre Ady (1877–1918), Attila József (1905–1937), Mihály Babits (1883–1941) and Dezsö Kosztolányi (1885–1936).

Finance.—The budget estimates for the year 1962 were: Revenue, *Forints* 84,483,000,000; Expenditure, *Forints* 83,886,000,000. The *Forint* (of 100 *Filler*) has an official exchange value of 32·87 *Forints*=£1, but travellers to Hungary are accorded a bonus of 100 per cent. when exchanging sterling and certain other foreign currencies.

Trade		1961
Imports	*Forints*	12,022,500,000
Exports		12,075,100,000

Trade with U.K.

	1961	1962
Imports from U.K.	£5,658,119	£6,782,698
Exports to U.K.	4,259,418	4,774,420

CAPITAL: Budapest, on the Danube; population (estimated, 1960) 1,807,030. Other large towns are: Miskolc (144,000); Debrecen (129,000); Pécs (115,000); and Szeged (99,000).

FLAG.—Red, white, green (horizontally).

BRITISH LEGATION
6 Harmincad Utca, Budapest V

Minister Plenipotentiary, His Excellency Sir Ivor Thomas Montague Pink, K.C.M.G. (1961) £4,115
1st Secretary and Head of Chancery, H. M. Carless.
1st Secretaries, I. M. MacPherson; A. R. Sinclair.
2nd Secretary (Information), K. H. M. Duke.
Consul, S. Relton.
Commercial Secretary, K. G. W. Frost.
Military Attaché, Col. T. A. Cave.
Air Attaché, Group Capt. R. J. H. Uprichard.
Cultural Attaché (British Council Representative), R. Bruce, O.B.E.

Budapest is distant 1,126 miles from London, transit by rail 34 hours; by air 5 hrs.

ICELAND
(Island)

President, Asgeir Asgeirsson, *elected* Aug. 1, 1952, *re-elected* Aug. 1, 1956 and Aug. 1, 1960.
Prime Minister, Olafur Thors (1959).
Foreign Affairs, Gudmundur I. Gudmundsson.

EMBASSY IN LONDON
1 Eaton Terrace, S.W.1
[Sloane: 5131–2]

Ambassador Extraordinary and Plenipotentiary, His Excellency Henrik Björnsson (1960).

Iceland is a large volcanic island in the North Atlantic Ocean, extending from 63° 23′ to 66° 33′ N. lat., and from 13° 22′ to 24° 35′ W. long., with an estimated area of 40,500 square miles, or greater than that of Ireland. The population was 183,000 on Dec. 1, 1962.

Iceland was uninhabited before the ninth century, when settlers came from Norway. For several centuries a form of republican government prevailed, with an annual assembly of leading men called the *Althing*, but in 1241 Iceland became subject to Norway, and later to Denmark. During the colonial period, Iceland maintained its cultural integrity but a deterioration in the climate, together with frequent volcanic eruptions and outbreaks of disease led to a serious fall in the standard of living and to a decline in the population to little more than 40,000. In the nineteenth century a struggle for independence began which led first to home-rule for Iceland under the Danish Crown (1918), and later to complete independence under a republican form of rule in 1944.

The Icelandic Cabinet normally consists of seven Ministers, responsible to the *Althing*, a Parliamentary assembly of 60 members. The present government, elected in June, 1963, is a coalition of Conservatives and Social Democrats, with the Progressive and Communist parties forming the Opposition.

Iceland lives very largely by her catching and export of fish, and this is held to justify an extension of exclusive fishery limits round her coast to a greater extent than that hitherto sanctioned by international law. In 1952, the Icelandic limits were extended from three to four miles, and at the same time a new method of establishing base-lines across bays and estuaries was introduced. This led to a dispute with the U.K., and the British trawler industry succeeded in imposing a ban on the landing of fish by Icelandic trawlers in England. This dispute was settled in October, 1956, by which time a considerable proportion of the Icelandic fish trade had been diverted to Russia. Conferences on the law of the sea held at Geneva in 1958 and 1960 ended without reaching a decision and it was announced on April 28, 1960, that the British Government refused to recognize Iceland's unilateral claim for a 12-mile fishery limit.

After lengthy negotiation between the Icelandic and British Governments, the dispute was settled by an Exchange of Notes on March 11, 1961, by which the United Kingdom Government agreed that it would no longer object to a 12 mile fishery zone around Iceland and the Icelandic Government agreed that United Kingdom fishing vessels could fish within certain specified zones between 6–12 miles for a period of 3 years.

The principal products of the island are fish, fish oils, whales, mutton, wool and ponies. The principal exports are fish, fish meals and oils, whale oil and meat, and sheepskins; the imports consist of almost all the necessaries of life, the chief items being petroleum, transportation equipment, textiles, machinery, base metals, wood and cork, and cereals.

At January 1, 1962, the mercantile marine consisted of 887 vessels of a gross tonnage of 140,850. There were: 47 trawlers (32,816 tons), 33 passenger and cargo vessels (47,536 tons), 111 fishing boats of over 100 tons (18,257 tons), 681 fishing boats of under 100 tons (23,577 tons), 8 coastguard and lifesaving vessels (2,622 tons), 4 oil carriers (14,882 tons), 6 pilot and customs boats (59 tons) and 5 other vessels (1,101 tons). There is a regular shipping service between Reykjavik, Leith and Copenhagen, fortnightly in summer and every three weeks in winter. Frequent but irregular services run between Reykjavik and Hull, and the Continent.

A regular thrice-weekly air service (daily in summer) is maintained between Renfrew and London and Reykjavik. There are also air services from the island to Scandinavia, U.S.A., Germany and Luxemburg. Road communications are adequate in summer but greatly restricted by snow in winter. Only roads in town centres are well surfaced. The State highways and side roads are non-metalled (gravel and lava dust). The climate and terrain make first-class surfaces for highways out of the question.

Language and Literature.—The ancient Norraena (or Northern tongue) presents close affinities to Anglo-Saxon and as spoken and written in Iceland to-day differs little from that introduced into the island in the ninth century. There is a rich literature with two distinct periods of development, from the middle of the eleventh to the end of the thirteenth century and from the beginning of the nineteenth century to the present time.

FINANCE		1961
Revenue	*Krónur*	1,672,000,000
Expenditure	"	1,509,800,000
External Debt	"	642,078,000
Internal Debt	"	206,310,000

TRADE		1962
Exports	*Krónur*	3,618,852,000
Imports	"	3,842,762,000

Trade with U.K.

	1961	1962
Imports from U.K.	£3,295,460	£4,969,884
Exports to U.K.	5,568,865	5,747,988

The Icelandic *Krona* was devalued with effect from Aug. 4, 1961, with the concurrence of the International Monetary Fund, the new par value being expressed as *Kronur* 43 = $U.S. 1. (*See also* p. 83.)

CAPITAL: Reykjavik. Population (Dec. 1, 1962) 74,664.

Other centres in approximate order of importance are Akureyri, Akranes, Hafnafjord, Kopavogur, Siglufjord, Keflavik, Isafjord and Westmann Islands.

FLAG.—Blue, with white-bordered red cross.

BRITISH EMBASSY
Laufasvegur, 49, Reykjavik

Ambassador Extraordinary and Plenipotentiary and Consul-General, His Excellency Evelyn Basil Boothby, C.M.G. (1962) £4,115
1st Secretary and Consul, A. F. Comfort.

BRITISH CONSULAR OFFICES

There are Consular Offices at *Reykjavik, Akureyri* and *Westmann Islands.*

INDONESIA

(Republic of Indonesia)

President and Prime Minister, Dr. Sukarno, *born* June 6, 1901; *assumed office as President*, December 17, 1949.
Chief Ministers, Dr. Subandrio; Dr. Johannes Leimena.

INDONESIAN EMBASSY AND CONSULATE
38 Grosvenor Square, W.1.

Ambassador Extraordinary and Plenipotentiary, His Excellency Burhanudin Mohamad Diah.
Minister Plenipotentiary, Suyoto Suryo-di-Puro.
Minister Counsellor (Economic), Haroen al Rasid Saleh.
Air Attaché, Air Commodore R. I. S. Wirjospoetro.
Military Attaché, Col. H. R. Dharsono.
Naval Attaché, Col. D. Maris.
Counsellor (Cultural), Mrs. S. Suleiman.
1st Secretaries, Mr. Soekarno (*Press and Public Relations*); Mr. Surjo-Atmono (*Economic*).
3rd Secretaries, Mr. Slamet (*Consular Affairs*); L. H. I. Sumantri (*Economic Affairs*); J. H. Siregar; J. W. Damanik.
Attaché, R. Soenarjo (*Administration*).

Situated between latitudes 6° North and 11° South and between longitudes 95° and 141° East, Indonesia comprises the islands of *Java* and *Madura*, the island of *Sumatra*, the *Riouw-Lingga Archipelago* (which with Karimon, Anambas, Natuna Islands, Tambelan, and part of Sumatra, forms the "Residency of Riouw"), the islands of *Bangka* and *Billiton*, part of the island of *Borneo*, *Celébes Island*, the *Molucca Islands* (Ternate, Halmahera, Buru, Ceram, Banda, Timor-Laut, Larat, Bachiam, Obi, Kei, Aru, Babar, Leti and Wetar), part of *Timor Island*, the islands of *Bali* and *Lombok* and the western half of the island of New Guinea (West Irian), with a total area of 887,000 sq. miles, and a population of 98,000,000.

From the early part of the 17th century much of the Indonesian Archipelago was under Netherlands rule. Following the World War, 1939–45, a strong nationalistic movement manifested itself and after sporadic fighting the formal transfer of sovereignty by the Netherlands took place on December 27, 1949. The provisional federal constitution then adopted was, on August 15, 1950, changed to a unitary Republic of Indonesia in which the separate provinces were guaranteed broad regional autonomy and on February 13, 1956, the agreement of 1949 with the Netherlands was unilaterally abrogated. As a result of the failure of the parliamentary parties to provide political and economic stability, President Sukarno as Commander-in-Chief of the Armed Forces proclaimed martial law on March 14, 1957, and appointed a temporary cabinet under a non-party Prime Minister. At the end of the year the Government, in response to popular feeling, took over control of most of the Dutch commercial concerns. The great majority of Dutch citizens left the country during the next few months. On February 15, 1958, regional discontent came to a head with the proclamation of a rival Indonesian Government in West Sumatra and North Celebes under Dr. Sjaffruddin. The Central Government resorted to military action and organized resistance had ceased in Sumatra by May, 1958, though small scale operations continued till the autumn of 1961.

On July 5, 1959, the President issued a decree dissolving the Constituent Assembly and declared the re-application of the 1945 constitution. The elected House of Representatives was dissolved by the President on March 5, 1960, and a nominated House has been set up in its place. There are also a Supreme Advisory Council and a National Planning Council with advisory powers. Under the 1945 constitution, sovereignty is vested in the Provisional People's Consultative Assembly which was inaugurated in November, 1960. This nominated Assembly is responsible for ratifying national policy, but effective authority is vested in the President himself.

Finance.—The budgetary system in Indonesia has been in deficit for some years now. The active currency circulations increased from *Rupiahs* 34·5 billion in 1959 to *Rupiahs* 48·75 billion in 1961. Gold and foreign currency cover at the end of 1960 stood at 34·6 per cent. since when no further figures have been issued. It is, however, clear that foreign exchange reserves have been seriously depleted and note issues considerably increased.

The official exchange rate of the *Rupiah* remains at 126 = £1 but since May, 1963, national importers have been able to retain certain percentages of their foreign exchange earnings for the import of goods, subject to levies and additions which create, according to the class of goods, three effective exchange rates of approximately 880, 2,250 and 4,500 = £1. Tourists and foreign residents in Indonesia are able to change currency at the first of these rates.

Production.—Nearly 70 per cent. of the population of Indonesia is engaged in agriculture and related production. Copra, kapok, nutmeg and pepper cloves are produced, mainly by smallholders; palm oil, sugar, fibres and cinchona are produced by large estate companies. Rubber, tea coffee and tobacco are also produced by both in large quantities. Rice is a traditional staple food for the people of Indonesia and the islands of Java and Madura are important producers, but production is insufficient to meet home demands and substantial imports of rice are necessary.

Indonesia is rich in minerals; petroleum, tin, coal and bauxite are the principal products; gold, silver, manganese phosphates, nickel and sulphur were produced in quantity before the Second World War and there are considerable deposits, the exploitation of which the Government is now starting.

Trade with U.K.

There has been a general cut in Indonesia's imports and proportionately the United Kingdom held its position. The rise in exports was attributable mainly to the petroleum and petroleum products sector.

	1961	1962
Imports from U.K.....	£21,390,197	£17,482,471
Exports to U.K.......	6,010,429	10,560,906

Principal exports to the United Kingdom are rubber, tea, petroleum and sugar. Imports from the United Kingdom are mainly of machinery, chemicals, electrical equipment, motor vehicles, cycles, lubricating and heavy oils, and metal goods.

Transport.—In Java a main line connects Djakarta with Surabaya in the East of Java and there are several branches, including a line from Semarang on the North coast to Djogjakarta in the South. In Sumatra the important towns of Medan, Padang and Palembang are the centres of short railway systems.

Sea communications in the archipelago are maintained by the State-run shipping companies Djakarta-Lloyd (ocean-going) and Pelni (coastal and inter-island) and other smaller concerns. In 1962 there were 13 ocean-going and 276 inter-island vessels in use by Indonesia. Transport by small craft on the rivers of the larger islands plays an important part in trade. Air services in Indonesia are operated by Garuda Indonesian Airways and Djakarta is served by various international services, including those of B.O.A.C. There were approximately 49,000 miles of roads in Indonesia at the end of 1961.

CAPITAL: Djakarta, formerly Batavia (population 3,000,000). Other important centres are: (Java) Surabaya, Semarang, Bandung, Tjeribon, Surakarta and Djogjakarta; (Madura) Pamekesan (180,000); (Sumatra) Palembang (500,000), Medan (500,000) and Padang; (Celébes) Macassar (450,000) and Menado; (Borneo) Banjermasin, Balikpapan and Pontianak; (Moluccas) Ternate (9,000); (Bali) Denpasar and Singaradja (120,000); (W. Timor) Kupang (10,000).

FLAG.—Equal bands of red over white.

NATIONAL ANTHEM: *Indonesia Raya.* August 17 is celebrated as INDEPENDENCE DAY in Indonesia.

BRITISH EMBASSY
Djakarta

Ambassador Extraordinary and Minister Plenipotentiary, His Excellency Andrew Graham Gilchrist, C.M.G. (1963)........................ £4,115
Counsellor, R. W. Selby, C.M.G.
Counsellor (Commercial), P. R. Oliver.

BRITISH CONSULAR OFFICES

There are British Consular Offices at *Djakarta, Surabaya* and *Medan*.

BRITISH COUNCIL

Representative, H. T. Lawrence, O.B.E., Medan Merdeka Barat, 2, Djakarta.

IRAN, see Persia

IRAQ

President, Marshal Abdul Salam Mohammed Arif (*assumed power*, Feb., 1963).

CABINET
(July, 1963)

Prime Minister, Major-Gen. Ahmad Hasan al-Bakr.
Deputy Prime Minister and Minister of Guidance, Ali Salih as-Sa'di.
Minister of Defence, Staff Lt.-Gen. Salih Mahdi 'Ammash.
Foreign Affairs, Talib Husain Ash-Shabib.
Communications, Staff Lt.-Col. Abdus-Sattar Abdul Latif.
Health, Dr. Izzat Mustafa.
Justice, Mahdi al Dawla'i.
Municipalities, Staff Maj.-Gen. Mahmud Sheet Kattab.
Agriculture (vacant).
Oil, Abdul Aziz al Wattari.
Education, Dr. Ahmad Abdus Sattar al Jiwari.
Finance, Dr. Mohammad Jawad al Abusi.
Works and Housing, Brigadier Rajab Abdul Mauid.
Commerce, Shukri Salih Zaki.
Agrarian Reform, Dr. Sa'dun Hammadi.
Labour and Social Affairs, Hamid Khalkhal.
Minister of State for Federal Unity Affairs, Dr. Musari ar Rawi.
Planning, Dr. Abdul Karim Ahmad al Ali.
Industry, Staff Maj.-Gen. Naji Talib.
Presidential Affairs and Acting Minister of the Interior, Hazim Jawad.

IRAQ EMBASSY IN LONDON
21–22 Queen's Gate, S.W.7
[Knightsbridge: 7141]

Ambassador Extraordinary and Plenipotentiary, His Excellency Abdul Rahman al Bazzaz (1963).
1st Secretary, Fouad Al-Rawi.
2nd Secretaries, Wissam Al-Zahawie; Mamdoh Abdul Hamid.
Air Attaché, Brig. Hamid Tawfiq.
Asst. Military Attaché, Capt. Ahmad Al-Hadithi.
Commercial Attaché, Dr. Khalid Al-Shawi.
Cultural Attaché, Abdul Malik Al-Yasin (*acting*).
Assistant Cultural Attaché, Ali Mohammed Al-Mathno.

Area. etc.—Lying between the Rivers Euphrates and Tigris, Iraq extends from Turkey on N. and N.E. to the Persian Gulf on the S. and S.E., and from Iran on E. to Syria and the Arabian Desert on W., the approximate position being between 37½° to 48½° E. long., and from 37½° to 30° N. lat.

The total area of Iraq is about 172,000 sq. miles, the distance from Basrah in the south to Mosul in the north being approximately 500 miles.

Population (1957 census):—

	Males	Females	Totals
Baghdad........	670,161	636,443	1,306,604
Hillah........	177,543	176,071	353,614
Diyala.......	166,506	163,307	329,813
Diwaniyah ...	246,467	261,081	507,548
Ramadi	119,306	114,956	234,262
Karbalah	105,347	111,668	217,015
Kut..........	137,432	152,638	290,070
Basra..........	252,382	250,502	502,884
Amarah......	162,188	167,459	329,647
Nasiriyah	210,654	244,990	455,644
Mosul	363,331	354,169	717,500
Arbil	137,602	134,924	272,526
Kirkuk.......	196,548	192,364	388,912
Sulaimaniyah	156,165	143,813	299,978
Deserts.........	37,059	31,503	68,562
Iraqi communities abroad.......	30,750	11,714	42,464
Delayed registrations.........	124,632	96,434	221,066
	3,294,073	3,244,036	6,538,109

The *Liwa* is the present Iraqi unit of administration, the *Vilayet* being the former Ottoman unit.

Of the total population there were in 1947: Moslems 4,226,974 (five-thirteenths being Sunni and eight-thirteenths Shiite), Christians 141,664, Jews 116,836, and other religions, 38,862 (Mandaeans Yazidis, Bahais, &c.). Almost the entire Jewish population has now emigrated to Israel.

The *Euphrates* (which has a total length of 1,700 miles from its source to its outflow in the Persian Gulf) is formed by two arms, of which the Murad Su (415 miles) rises in the slopes of the Ala Dagh, a mountain of Eastern Erzerum, and flows westwards to a junction with the Kara Su, or Frat Su (275 miles); the other arm rises in the north-west of Erzerum in the Dumlu Dagh. The *Tigris* has a total length of 1,150 miles from its source to its junction with the Euphrates at Qurna, 70 miles from the Persian Gulf, and rises in two arms south of the Taurus mountains, in Kurdistan, uniting at Til, where the boundaries of the districts of Diarbekir, Van and Bitlis conjoin.

Government.—Under the Treaty of Lausanne (1923), Turkey renounced the sovereignty over Mesopotamia. A provisional Arab Government was set up in Nov., 1920, and in Aug., 1921, the Emir Faisal (3rd son of ex-King Hussein of the Hejaz) was elected King of Iraq.

In 1939 King Faisal II, grandson of Faisal I, acceded to the throne at the age of 3 on the death of his father, King Ghazi, and until 1953, when Faisal II ascended the throne, Iraq was ruled by Prince Abdulillah as Regent. Faisal II, together with Prince Abdulillah, other members of the Royal family and the then Prime Minister, Gen. Nuri al-Said, was assassinated in Baghdad in July, 1958, during a *coup d'état* resulting in the formation of a republican form of government. The monarchy was succeeded by a three-man Council of Sovereignty exercising presidential powers and a republican cabinet formed by Brigadier Qasim.

On Feb. 8, 1963, the Qasim regime was overthrown by a further *coup d'état* and on Feb. 19, 1963, Qasim was executed.

Production and Industry.—Iraq is capable of supporting a considerably greater population if irrigation is developed and extended. Apart from the valuable revenues to be derived from oil the wealth of the country depends upon agricultural development, and two harvests can be gathered in the year, the chief crops being wheat, barley, beans, rice, dates and Indian corn; wheat averages 464 lb. per acre, barley 612 lb., and rice over 370 lb. Cotton growing is successful in some years. Tobacco from the northern *liwas* is sufficient for the needs of the country. Production of crude oil in Iraq totalled 962,609 long tons in 1935, rising to 4,162,939 long tons in 1938. Revised production figures for the years 1955–1962 are:

	Long Tons		Long Tons
1955	32,716,227	1959....	40,897,676
1956....	30,606,282	1960....	46,534,398
1957....	21,361,979	1961....	48,000,000
1958....	34,931,461	1962....	48,214,537

Few industries are yet established on any scale but an increasing industrialization is taking place under both private enterprise and Government action. An economic and technical co-operation agreement was signed with the Soviet Union in 1960, providing for the setting up of specified industries. Existing industries include cement, building materials, flour milling, cigarettes, soap, beer, steel fabrications including furniture, tanning, textiles, footwear and vegetable oils.

Communications and Trade.—New roads are being rapidly built, and communications between Baghdad and the provincial capitals are being improved and secured. Under the terms of the Permanent Economic Plan, 1961–66, 51 per cent. of all oil royalties is allocated for development projects. A minimum of £25,000,000 per annum is guaranteed, but oil revenues by 1962 had reached £95,137,356 for the year. The Permanent Economic Plan provides for a total expenditure of *ID*556,000,000 on industry, communications, agriculture and building construction. The industrial projects include 13 factories being supplied under the Iraq/Soviet agreement. Contracts for 9 of these were signed in 1961, and work on some has already begun.

The port of Basrah is well equipped and able to handle expeditiously all seaborne traffic. Continuous dredging of the Shatt-al-Arab has provided a navigable channel of 22½ feet at low water (as compared with 9 feet before dredging was begun) giving easy access to the Port at all times. A new channel across the Fao Bar has recently been dredged. The desert route between Baghdad and the Mediterranean carries an increasing amount of traffic, though most goods reaching Iraq are still sent *viâ* Basrah. Exceptional floods in the spring of 1954 caused serious damage in Central Iraq and interruptions to communications, but effective flood control works have since been completed and prevented severe flooding in 1957.

Airports for the use of international air traffic have been provided at Baghdad and Basrah (Maqil). BOAC provides a thrice-weekly service between London and Baghdad, which is also served by Iraqi Airways and airlines of Iran, the Lebanon, the Netherlands, Italy, West Germany, Switzerland, Czechoslovakia and Pakistan. Iraqi Airways operates a daily service to Basrah and services from Baghdad to Mosul, Kirkuk, the Persian Gulf, Amman, Beirut, Cairo, Damascus, Tehran, Athens, Istanbul, Rome, Zürich, Prague, Vienna, Frankfurt, London, Karachi and Bombay.

Iraqi Republican Railways provide a regular passenger and goods service between Baghdad and Basrah by the metre gauge line completed in 1920, which also extends northwards to Khanaqin, Kirkuk and Arbil. The railway line from Baghdad to Mosul, linking up through Syria and Turkey with the Mediterranean and the Bosphorus, is standard gauge. By July, 1963, a standard gauge line from Basra–Baghdad was 75 per cent. complete.

Language, Literature and Archæology.—The language is mainly Arabic (*see* Arabia) and English is widely used in commerce, science and the arts.

There is evidence that an advanced civilization had been reached in the alluvial valley of the Euphrates while Europe was in a state of barbarism. Astronomy, geometry, engineering and land surveying were cultivated by the Sumerians of Mesopotamia, and various arts reached a point of perfection by 3000 B.C., as investigations at Ur of the Chaldees have shown. Sumerian culture spread from Mesopotamia to Crete and Egypt and to Greece. In 1944 excavations at Tell Hassuna, near Shura (on the Tigris in North Iraq) unearthed abundant traces of culture dating back to 5000 B.C.

Excavations in 1948 at Tel Abu Shahrain, 14 miles south of "Ur of the Chaldees," confirm Eridu's claim to be the most ancient city of the Sumerian world.

Hillah, the ancient city on the left bank of the Shatt el Hillah, a branch of the Euphrates, about 70 miles south of Baghdad, is near the site of Babylon and of the "house of the lofty-head" or "gate of the god" (Tower of Babel).

Mosul *Liwa* covers a great part of the ancient kingdom of *Assyria*, the ruins of Nineveh, the Assyrian capital, being visible on the banks of the Tigris, opposite Mosul. A British archaeological expedition has been excavating at Nimrud in the same area since 1950.

Qurna, at the junction of the Tigris and Euphrates, is the traditional site of the *Garden of Eden*. The "*Tree of Knowledge*," which had stood there "from time immemorial," withered and died in December, 1946. It has been replaced by a shoot said to be from the original tree.

FINANCE

	1961–62	1962–63
Total revenue....	ID112,000,000	ID120,300,000
Total expenditure.	120,700,000	134,900,000

The Iraqi *Dinar* of 1,000 *Fils* = £1 sterling.

TRADE
(Excluding oil)

	1961	1962
Total imports....	ID145,600,000	ID128,700,000
Total exports.....	7,800,000	19,300,000

Trade with U.K.

	1961	1962
Imports from U.K....	£28,517,707	£20,176,536
Exports to U.K.......	45,017,131	53,092,191

The principal imports are iron and steel, mechanical and electrical machinery, motor cars, cotton and rayon piecegoods, sugar and tea; and the chief exports are crude petroleum, cereals, dates, raw wool, hides, live animals and raw cotton.

CAPITAL.—The chief city is Baghdad, the former capital of the Abbassid dynasty, one of the Caliphs of that dynasty being Haroun al Rashid of "the Arabian Nights." Baghdad has a population of 552,047; of the other towns Mosul has a population of 340,541 and Ψ Basrah 206,302.

FLAG.—Horizontal stripes of black, white and red, with three green stars on the white stripe.

BRITISH EMBASSY
(Saleh Al Din Street, Karkh, Baghdad)

Ambassador Extraordinary and Plenipotentiary, His Excellency Sir Roger Allen, K.C.M.G. (1961) £5,015
Counsellor, D. J. B. Robey, C.M.G.
Counsellor (*Commercial*), A. K. Rothnie.
H.M. Consul, F. J. Bradshaw.
1st Secretaries, E. F. G. Maynard; S. L. Egerton; H. St. J. B. Armitage (*Commercial*); J. F. Bradshaw (*Consul*); L. H. Barnes, M.B.E. (*Administration*).
2nd Secretary, R. C. B. Taylor (*Commercial*).
3rd Secretaries, D. K. Haskell; C. H. N. Moy; R. Long (*Information*).
Naval Attaché, Capt. H. H. Cook, R.N. (*Resident in Ankara*).
Military Attaché, Col. D. S. Carden.
Assistant Military Attaché, Maj. F. D. Carson.
Air Attaché, Wing Cdr. W. E. Hamilton, D.F.C.
Chaplain, Rev. J. R. de Chazal.
Counsellor (*Labour*), P. Archer (*Resident in Beirut*).

BRITISH CONSULAR OFFICES

There are British Consular Offices at *Baghdad* and *Basrah*.

BRITISH COUNCIL.—*Representative of the British Council in Iraq*, D.E. Frean, Rashid Street, Baghdad.

ISRAEL
(Yisrael)

President of the Republic, Zalman Shazar, *born* 1889, *elected President of Israel*, May 22, 1963.

CABINET
(June 26, 1963)

Prime Minister and Minister of Defence, Levi Eshkol (*Mapai*).
Deputy Prime Minister, Abba Eban (*Mapai*).
Foreign Affairs, Mrs. Golda Meir (*Mapai*).
Agriculture (vacant).
Labour, Yigal Allon (*A.A.*).
Finance, Commerce and Industry, Pinhas Sapir (*Mapai*).
Education and Culture, Zalman Aranne (*Mapai*).
Justice, Dr. Dov Joseph (*Mapai*).
Police, Bechor Shalom Shitreet (*Mapai*).
Interior and Health, Moshe Shapiro (*N.R.P.*).
Commerce and Industry, Pinhas Sapir (*Mapai*).
Transport and Communications, Israel Bar Yehuda (*A.A.*).
Posts (vacant).
Development and Housing, Yosef Almogi (*Mapai*).
Health, Israel Barzilai (*Mapam*).
Social Welfare, Josef Burg (*N.R.P.*).
Religious Affairs, Dr. Zerah Warhaftig (*N.R.P.*).

NOTE:—*Mapai* = Labour Party.
N.R.P. = National Religious Party.
A.A. = Ahdut Avodah (*left of Mapai*).

EMBASSY IN LONDON
2 Palace Green, Kensington, W.8.

Ambassador in London, His Excellency Arthur Lourie (1960).
Consular Section, 2A Palace Green, W.8.
Consul-General, Gideon Shomron.

Area and Population.—Israel lies on the western edge of the continent of Asia at the eastern extremity of the Mediterranean Sea, between lat. 29° 30′–33° 15′ N. and long. 34° 15′–35° 40′ E. Its political neighbours are Lebanon on the North, Syria on the North and East, Jordan on the East and the Egyptian province of Sinai on the South.

The area is estimated at 7,992 square miles out of the 10,429 square miles comprised in the whole of Palestine (the remainder being occupied by Jordan and Egypt). The population was estimated (Dec., 1962) at 2,331,800, of whom 2,068,900 were Jews, the remainder mostly Arabs. These figures result from the rapid progress of Jewish immigration since the establishment of the State. In 1912 there were only 83,790 Jews in Palestine out of a total population of 752,048. During the upheavals of 1948–49 some 600,000 Arabs left the country as refugees and settled in neighbouring countries. Since 1948 the population of Israel has more than trebled.

Hebrew is the official language of Israel. Arabic is also used extensively in Government publications and on coins and stamps. Arabs are entitled to transact all official business with Government Departments in Arabic, and provision is made in the

Knesset for the simultaneous translation of all speeches into Arabic.

Physical Features.—Israel comprises four main regions: (*a*) the hill country of Galilee and Judæa and Samaria, rising in places to heights of nearly 4,000 feet; (*b*) the coastal plain from the Gaza strip to North of Acre, including the plain of Esdraelon running from Haifa Bay to the south-east, and cutting in two the hill region; (*c*) the Negev, a semi-desert triangular-shaped region, extending from a base south of Beersheeba, to an apex at the head of the Gulf of 'Aqaba; and (*d*) parts of the Jordan valley, including the Hula Region, Tiberias and the south-western extremity of the Dead Sea. The principal river is the Jordan, which rises from three main sources in Israel, the Lebanon and Syria, and flows through the Hula valley and the canals which have replaced Lake Hula, drained in 1958. Between Hulata and Tiberias (Sea of Galilee) the river falls 926 ft. in 11 miles and becomes a turbulent stream. Lake Tiberias is 696 ft. below sea-level and liable to sudden storms. Between it and the Dead Sea the Jordan falls 591 ft. The other principal rivers are the Yarkon and Qishon. The largest lake is the *Dead Sea* (shared between Israel and Jordan); area 393 sq. miles, 1,286 feet below sea-level, 51·5 miles long, with a maximum width of 11 miles and a maximum depth of 1,309 ft.; it receives the waters of the Jordan and of six other streams, and has no outlet, the surplus being carried off by evaporation. The water contains an extra-ordinarily high concentration of mineral substances. The highest mountain peak is Mount Meron, 3,962 feet above sea-level, near Safad, Upper Galilee.

Climate.—The climate is variable, similar to that of Lower Egypt, but modified by altitude and distance from the sea. The summer is hot but is tempered in most parts by daily winds from the Mediterranean. The winter is the rainy season lasting from November to April, the period of maximum rainfall being January and February.

Antiquities.—The following are among the principal historic sites in Israel: Jerusalem: the Church of the Dormition and the Cænaculum on Mount Zion (the principal Christian and Moslem Holy Places of the Jerusalem area are in Jordan territory): Ein Karem: Church of the Visitation, Church of St. John the Baptist. Galilee: The Sea; Church and Mount of the Beatitudes, ruins of Capernaum and other sites connected with the life of Christ. Mount Tabor: Church of the Transfiguration. Nazareth: Church of the Annunciation and other Christian shrines associated with the childhood of Christ. There are also numerous sites dating from biblical and mediæval days, such as Ascalon, Cæsarea, Atlit Megiddo and Hazor.

History.—The early history of Palestine, from the time when Moses led the children of Israel from Egyptian bondage towards the *Promised Land* to the time of the *Diaspora* (Dispersion) in the second century of the Christian Era, can be found in the Books of the Old Testament and in the Works of Josephus. Before the dispersion it had become the cradle of Christianity and the *Holy Land* of the Christian World, but after the break up of the Roman Empire, into which it had been brought by Pompey in 65 B.C., it was conquered by Moslem Arabs (A.D. 634), remaining under the Crescent as part of the Ottoman Empire (except for a break from 1098 to 1187 under the Crusaders) until Allenby's victory over the Germano-Turkish forces in the plain of Armageddon (Megiddo) on September 19, 1918.

On November 2, 1917, a statement, afterwards known as The *Balfour Declaration*, was made by the British government that Britain viewed with favour the establishment in Palestine of a home for the Jewish people. This principle was incorporated in the mandate to Britain, which came officially into force on Sept. 29, 1923. From 1917 until 1948 Great Britain administered Palestine and laid the foundations of modern self-government.

The British mandate ended at midnight on May 14, 1948, when the Jewish National Council proclaimed a Jewish State of Israel, with David Ben Gurion as Prime Minister. On the following day Palestine was invaded by Syrian and Lebanese troops in the north, by the Transjordan Arab Legion and the Iraqis in the east and by the Egyptians in the south. On June 30 the last British troops left Haifa, which was taken over by Israel.

Hostilities ceased in January, 1949. The four armistice agreements signed under United Nations auspices in 1949 left Israel in occupation of various areas originally allotted to the Arab State. The situation as at present governed by the terms of the armistices has not yet been stabilized by peace treaties between Israel and any of its neighbours. The Arab parts of Palestine occupied by Jordan were formally incorporated with the latter in April, 1950. Egyptian forces occupy the "Gaza strip," a small coastal area with an Arab population.

Government.—There is a Cabinet and a single-chamber Parliament (*Knesset Israel*) of 120 members. On August 15, 1961, eleven political parties returned members to the *Knesset*, including *Mapai* (42), *Liberals* (17), *Herut* (17), *National Religious Front* (12), *Mapam* (9) and *Ahdut Avoda* (8). The General Election was followed by a long period of negotiations among the parties and it was not until November, 1961, that a new Coalition of *Mapai*, National Religious Front and *Ahdut Avoda*, with the support of three smaller groups was formed under the Premiership of Mr. Ben-Gurion. Mr. Ben-Gurion resigned on June 16, 1963, and Mr. Eshkol became Prime Minister in his place. The new Cabinet under him took office on June 26, 1963.

Immigration.—The Declaration of Independence of May 14, 1948, laid down that "the State of Israel will be open to the immigration of Jews from all countries of their dispersion." The Law of Return, passed by the *Knesset* on July 5, 1950, provides that an immigrant visa shall be granted to every Jew who expresses his desire to settle in Israel. Since the establishment of the State over 1,000,000 immigrants had entered Israel from over 100 different countries.

Education.—Elementary education for all children from 5 to 14 years is compulsory. In the 1961–62 school year the number of pupils in elementary and secondary schools was approximately 627,000, of whom about 55,000 were Arab pupils attending Arab schools, 83,000 in kindergartens, 421,000 at primary and 82,000 at post-primary and secondary schools, 14,000 at universities and comparable institutions and 27,000 elsewhere. The Hebrew University, Jerusalem, has 8,600 graduate and undergraduate students. The Israel Institute of Technology (*Technion*) at Haifa provides courses in engineering, architecture, aeronautics and other technical subjects for 3,608 students. Tel Aviv University provides courses in science and the humanities for 1,471 students. The Weizmann Institute of Science at Rehovoth is engaged in pure and applied research and has a staff of 237.

Finance.—Government expenditure for the fiscal year 1961–62 totalled I£2,098,308,219 while revenue during the same period was I£2,128,312,218.

The unit of account is the Israel pound of 100 *agorot*. The official rate of exchange (following devaluation of the I£ on Feb. 9, 1962) is I£3 = U.S. $1, which is roughly equivalent to I£8·39 = £1 sterling.

COMMUNICATIONS

Railways and Roads.—Israel State Railways started operating in August, 1949. Towns now served are Haifa, Tel Aviv, Jerusalem, Lydda, Nahariya, Beersheba, and intermediate stations. In December, 1962, the total railway network amounted to 650 kms. There were approximately 3,073 km. of paved roads and 106,402 licensed vehicles.

Shipping.—Israel's merchant marine on December 31, 1962, included 69 vessels with a total deadweight tonnage of 565,591. In 1962, 1,484 ships with a net tonnage of 3,218,000 entered Israel ports. Cargo (excluding fuel) unloaded during the year amounted to 2,401,332 tons and cargo loaded to 1,106,040 tons.

The chief ports are Ψ Haifa, a modern harbour, with a depth of 30 ft. alongside the main quay; the port on the Red Sea at ΨEilat, with an annual cargo-handling capacity of 200,000 tons, Ψ Jaffa and ΨTel Aviv, where there are harbours for small craft, and large vessels anchor at open roadstead. Ψ Acre has an anchorage for small vessels. A deep-water port at Ashdod on the Mediterranean Coast about 20 miles south of Tel Aviv is under construction and is expected to have by 1965/66 a cargo-handling capacity of 1,000,000 tons.

Civil Aviation.—The B.E.A./Olympic Airways/ Cyprus Airways consortium operates nine Comet services per week between Lydda and London, two of them *viâ* Nicosia. B.O.A.C. operates two Boeing 707 services per week on the same route and two Boeing services to Melbourne. El Al (Israel Airlines) operates six Boeing 707/720B services per week betwen Lydda and London, and other services to Amsterdam, Athens, Brussels, Zürich, Munich, Frankfurt, New York, Paris, Rome, Teheran, Nairobi, Salisbury and Johannesburg. Four Britannia services of El Al operate weekly to Istanbul, three to Nicosia, two to Vienna and one to Athens and Copenhagen. During 1962, 3,456 aircraft arrived at Lod (Lydda) Airport, carrying 161,244 passengers and 2,468,844 kilograms of freight; 159,696 passengers and 3,925,236 kilograms of freight left through the same airport.

PRODUCTION AND INDUSTRY

Agriculture.—The country is generally fertile and climatic conditions vary so widely that a large variety of crops can be grown, ranging from temperate crops, such as wheat and cherries, to sub-tropical crops such as sorghum, millet and mangoes. The famous "Jaffa" orange is produced in large quantities in the coastal plain for export; other kinds of citrus fruits are also grown and exported. The citrus yield during the 1962–63 season was 692,258 tons. Of this total, 494,458 tons were exported, of which about 158,481 tons went to the U.K. Olives are cultivated, mainly for the production of oil used for edible purposes and for the manufacture of soap. The main winter crops are wheat and barley and various kinds of pulses, while in summer sorghum, millet, maize, sesame and summer pulses are grown. Large areas of seasonal vegetables are planted; potatoes can be grown in autumn and in the winter. Since the establishment of the State of Israel, beef, cattle and poultry farming have been developed and the production of mixed vegetables and dairy produce has greatly increased. Tobacco and medium staple cotton are now grown. Fishing has also been extended, and production (mostly from fish ponds) reached 15,564 tons in 1962. All kinds of summer fruits such as figs, grapes, plums and apples are produced in increasing quantities for local consumption. Water supply for irrigation is the principal limiting factor to greater production, but the number of new deep wells is being extended and the construction of a pipeline to take water to the Negev from the River Jordan continues. A large part of the dairy industry is dependent on the production of fodder crops under irrigation; areas under fodder crops have doubled. The Israel land measure is the *dunam*, equivalent to 1,000 square metres (approximately a quarter of an acre).

Industry.—Among the more important industries are citrus and by-products, manufactured food products, pharmaceuticals, textiles and wearing apparel, artificial teeth, polished diamonds, plywood, cement, plastics, light engineering and the assembly of motor cars and trucks.

TRADE

	1961	1962
Imports	$U.S. 586,348,000	$U.S. 612,407,000
Exports	245,280,000	279,150,000

Trade with U.K.

	1961	1962
Imports from U.K.	£19,839,953	£21,911,763
Exports to U.K.	13,721,085	15,354,555

The principal imports are foodstuffs, crude oil, machinery and vehicles, iron, steel and manufactures thereof, and chemicals. The principal exports are citrus fruits and by-products, polished diamonds, plywood, cement, tyres, minerals, finished and semi-finished textiles.

CAPITAL.—Most of the Government departments are in Jerusalem, (population, estimated 1961, 166,301), which is not, however recognised as the capital by the United Nations. Other principal towns are ΨTel Aviv-Jaffa (386,612); ΨHaifa and district (182,007); Ramat Gan (90,234).

FLAG.—White, with two horizontal blue stripes, the Shield of David in the centre.

JERUSALEM

Jerusalem and District is at present divided between Israel and Jordan under the terms of the armistice arranged at the end of hostilities. The Old City, which contains 34 of the 36 recognized Holy Places, is under the control of Jordan; the New City, with 2 Holy Places, is under Jewish administration. A resolution proclaiming Jerusalem as the capital of Israel was adopted by the Israel parliament on Jan. 23, 1950.

BRITISH EMBASSY

Chancery: 192 Hayarkon Street, Tel Aviv; Consular and Visa Sections: El Al Building, 32 Ben Yehuda, Tel Aviv.

Ambassador Extraordinary and Plenipotentiary, His Excellency John Stanley Greville Beith, C.M.G. (1963) £4,535

BRITISH COUNCIL

Representative, N. Sutcliffe, 13 Idelson Street, Tel Aviv.

ITALY

(Repubblica Italiana)

PRESIDENT OF THE ITALIAN REPUBLIC, Antonio Segni, *born* at Sassari in 1895. *Elected* May 6, 1962.

COUNCIL OF MINISTERS

(June 21, 1963)

President of the Council, Signor Giovanni Leone.

Deputy President and Minister for Foreign Affairs, Senator Attilio Piccioni.

Interior, Sig. Mariano Rumor.

Justice, Senator Giacinto Bosco.
Budget, Senator Giuseppe Medici.
Finance, Sig. Mario Martinelli.
Treasury, Sig. Emilio Colombo.
Defence, Sig. Giulio Andreotti.
Education, Sig. Luigi Gui.
Public Works, Sig. Fiorentino Sullo.
Agriculture and Forests, Sig. Bernardo Mattarella.
Transport, Senator Guido Corbellini.
Posts and Communications, Sig. Carlo Russo.
Industry and Commerce, Sig. Giuseppe Togni.
Labour and Social Insurance, Sig. Umberto Delle Fave.
Foreign Trade, Senator Giuseppe Trabucchi.
Merchant Marine, Sig. Francesco Maria Domenidò.
State Participation, Senator Giorgio Bo.
Health, Senator Raffaele Jervolino.
Sport and Tourism, Sig. Alberto Folchi.
Without Portfolio, Prof. Giuseppe Codacci-Pisanelli (*Relations with Parliament*); Sig. Roberto Lucifredi (*Administrative Reform*); Sig. Giulio Pastore (*Fund for the South*).

ITALIAN EMBASSY IN LONDON
14 Three Kings Yard, Davies Street, W.1
[Mayfair: 8200]

Italian Ambassador in London, His Excellency Signor Pietro Quaroni, M.C. (1961).
Ministers Plenipotentiary, Signor Paolo Pansa-Cedronio; Signor Enso Malgeri (*Commercial*).
Counsellors, Signor Pasquale Ricciulli, C.M.G.; Signor Emilio Savorgnan; Signor Angélo Macchia (*Labour*); Signor Antonio Zecchi (*Financial*).
1st Secretaries, Signor Gianfranco Farinelli; Signor Sergio Romano.
2nd Secretary, Signor Umberto Toffano.
3rd Secretary, Signor Sergio Berlinguer.
Commercial Attaché, Signor Giovanni Battistini.
Asst. Commercial Attaché, Signor Gaetano Zucconi.
Naval Attaché, Capt. Eugenio Manca di Villahermosa.
Asst. Naval Attaché, Cdr. Raffaele de Meis.
Military Attaché, Lt.-Col. Lelio Giannangeli.
Asst. Military Attaché, Maj. Carlo Andreotti.
Air Attaché, Col. Taurico Chiantia.
Asst. Air Attaché, Capt. Elio Guarnieri.
Cultural Attaché, Prof. Filippo Donini.
Press Attaché, Signor Mario de Mandato.
Administrative Attaché, Signor Amadeo Baroni.
Italian Consulate General, 38 Eaton Place, S.W.1. (Belgravia: 4831).
Consul General, Signor Stanislao Cantono di Ceva.

Area and Population.—Italy is a Republic in the South of Europe, consisting of a peninsula, the large islands of Sicily and Sardinia, the island of Elba and about 70 islands (with certain dependencies noted below). Italy is bounded on the N. by Switzerland and Austria, on the S. by the Mediterranean, on the E. by the Adriatic and Yugoslavia, etc., and on the W. by France and the Ligurian and Tyrrhenian Seas. The total area may be estimated at 324,000 sq. kilometres, about 131,000 sq. miles, with a population (estimated June, 1962) of 50,003,000.

Live births in 1963 numbered 938,990, deaths 507,917, and marriages 406,496 (estimated figures).

Physiography.—The peninsula is for the most part mountainous, but between the Apennines, which form its spine, and the East coastline are two large fertile plains; of Emilia/Romagna in the north and of Apulia in the south. The Alps form the northern limit of Italy, dividing it from France, Switzerland Austria and Yugoslavia. *Mont Blanc* (15,782 feet), the highest peak, is in the French Pennine Alps, but partly within the Italian borders are Monte Rosa (15,217 feet), Matterhorn (14,780 feet) and several peaks from 12,000 to 14,000 feet.

The chief rivers are the Po (405 miles), which flows through Piedmont, Lombardy and the Veneto and the Adige (Trentino and Veneto) in the north, the Arno (Florentine Plain) and the Tiber (flowing through Rome to Ostia). The *Rubicon*, a small stream flowing into the Adriatic near Rimini (and now usually identified with the Fiumicino) formed the boundary between Italy and Cisalpine Gaul: "crossing the Rubicon" (as Cæsar did in 49 B.C., thus "invading" Italy in arms) is used to indicate definite committal to some course of action.

Government.—Italian unity was accomplished under the House of Savoy, after an heroic struggle from 1848 to 1870, in which the great patriots Mazzini (*born* 1805; *died* 1872), Garibaldi (*born* 1807; *died* 1882) and Cavour (*born* 1810; *died* 1861) were the principal figures. It was completed when Lombardy was ceded by Austria in 1859 and Venice in 1866, and through the evacuation of Rome by the French in 1870. In 1871 the King of Italy entered Rome, and that city was declared to be the capital.

Benito Mussolini, known as *Il Duce* (The Leader), was born July 29, 1883, and was continuously in office as Prime Minister from June 30, 1925, until July 25, 1943, when the Fascist *régime* was abolished. He was captured by Italian partisans while attempting to escape across the Swiss frontier and was put to death on April 28, 1945.

In fulfilment of a promise given in April, 1944, that he would retire when the Allies entered Rome a decree was signed on June 5, 1944, by the late King Victor Emmanuel III under which Prince Umberto, the King's son, became "Lieutenant-General of the Realm." The King remained head of the House of Savoy and retained the title of King of Italy until his abdication on May 9, 1946, when he was succeeded by the Crown Prince.

A general election was held on June 2, 1946, together with a referendum on the question of Republic or Monarchy. The Referendum resulted in 12,717,923 votes for a Republic and 10,719,284 for a Monarchy. The Royal Family left the country on June 13, and on June 28, 1946, a Provisional President was elected.

Since the General Election of 1948, governments have been formed by Signor de Gasperi (1948–53, coalition); Signor Pella (1953–54, *Christian Democrat*); Signor Scelba (1954–55, coalition); Signor Segni (July, 1955–May, 1957, coalition); Signor Zoli (June, 1957–May, 1958, *Christian Democrat*); Signor Fanfani (May, 1958–Feb., 1959, coalition); S. Segni (Feb., 1959–Feb., 1960, *Christian Democrat*, with *Liberal* support). Signor Tambroni (March 25–July 1960, *Christian Democrat*, with Neo-Fascist support); Signor Fanfani (July 27, 1960–Feb., 1962, *Christian Democrat*); Signor Fanfani (Feb. 1962–June, 1963, coalition).

Signor Fanfani's Government remained in office until June 21, 1963, when it was replaced by a single party of Christian Democrat minority administration led by the former Speaker of the Chamber of Deputies, Signor Leone. The reason for the change was the failure by Signor Moro, the Secretary General of the C.D. Party, after the general election of April 28, 1963, at which the Christian Democrat Party lost and the Communist Party gained ground, to form another Centre Left Government on the same lines as Signor Fanfani's fourth administration. Signor Moro failed because the Socialist Party could not agree to support him. As a result President Segni invited Signor Leone to form a Christian Democrat Government which was intended to be limited in programme and in time, so as to enable the annual Budget to be voted and ordinary administration to be carried out and to give the

Socialist Party time to settle its internal difficulties at a Party Congress fixed for the autumn of 1963.

The New Constitution.—On Dec. 22, 1947, the Constituent Assembly approved the new Constitution laying the foundation of the Italian Republic, Article I of which states "Italy is a Democratic Republic founded on work. Sovereignty belongs to the people who exercise it in the forms and within the limits of the Constitution."

Defence.—The *Army* consists of about 230,000 men and includes two armoured divisions, five recently reorganized infantry divisions, five Alpine brigades and five brigade groups. The *Navy* consists of 2 cruisers, 6 destroyers, 43 escorts, 7 submarines, 77 minesweepers and also coastal craft and fleet auxiliaries. The *Air Force* consists of 612 aircraft; approximate strength: officers, 5,439; men, 48,975; cadets at Air Academy, 247; in training, 2,830.

Language and Literature.—Italian is a Romance language derived from Latin. It is spoken in its purest form at Siena (Tuscany), but there are numerous dialects, showing variously French, German, Spanish and Arabic influences. Sard, the dialect of Sardinia, is accorded by some authorities the status of a distinct Romance language. Italian literature (in addition to Latin literature, which is the common inheritance of the civilized world) is one of the richest in Europe, particularly in its golden age (Dante, 1265–1321; Petrarch, 1304–1374; and Boccaccio, 1313–1375) and in the renaissance during the fifteenth and sixteenth centuries (Ariosto, 1474–1533; Machiavelli, 1469–1527; Tasso, 1544–1595). Modern Italian literature has many noted names in prose and verse, notably Manzoni (1785–1873), Carducci (1835–1907) and Gabriele d'Annunzio (1864–1938). The Nobel Prize for Literature has been awarded to Italian authors on four occasions—G. Carducci (1906), Signora G. Deledda (1926), Luigi Pirandello (1934) and Salvatore Quasimodo (1959). In 1963, there were 101 daily newspapers published in Italy, of which 18 were published in Rome and 11 in Milan.

Education.—Primary education is free and compulsory, and evening continuation classes are also compulsory for military recruits. It is maintained by local taxation and State grants. Secondary education is generally State-maintained, and schools are increasing in number. Several of the 26 Universities are of very ancient foundation, Bologna, Genoa, Macerata, Naples, Padua and Perugia in thirteenth century; Siena, Rome, Pisa, Pavia and Ferrara in fourteenth century; Catania and Turin in fifteenth century; Parma, Messina and Urbino in sixteenth century.

Production.—Agriculture is still Italy's main industry but employs a fast decreasing share of the total labour force. The principal products are cereals, fruit (especially citrus), vegetables, olives and olive oil, cheese and wine. Wheat is the most important cereal with an average annual yield of over 8,000,000 metric tons since 1948. Sugar beet is by far the most important industrial crop; tobacco is also grown. Livestock supplies large dairy and meat industries, but growing quantities of beef are imported. Fishing is carried on extensively, almost exclusively for the home market, but once again imports of fish are necessary to supplement the declining yield of Mediterranean waters.

Italy is generally poor in mineral resources but since the war large deposits of natural methane gas and smaller deposits of oil have been discovered and rapidly exploited. Production of lignite has also increased. Sulphur production, in Sicily and Calabria, is important although declining in volume. Other minerals produced in significant quantities include iron ores and pyrites, mercury (over one-quarter of world production), lead, zinc and aluminium. Marble is a traditional product of the Massa Carrara district. Salt and tobacco are Government monopolies.

The chief manufactures are textiles of all kinds, including synthetic fibres, iron and steel and their products, building materials, ships, rolling stock, motor vehicles, rubber products, leathers and footwear, chemicals, engineering products, agricultural and light machinery of all kinds, wood manufactures, especially furniture, food preserves and plastics. Numerous artisan industries produce gloves, straw products and typical Italian artistic products such as pottery, glassware, mosaics, coral and imitation jewellery.

Tourist Traffic.—A record total of nearly 21,300,000 tourists visited Italy in 1962 compared with 18,900,000 in 1961, 18,010,000 in 1960 and 16,780,000 in 1959. Out of the 1962 total by far the largest number were from Germany; the U.K. came fourth after the U.S.A. and France.

Communications.—The main railways system is State-run, but some subsidiary lines are still privately operated. Serious damage to the railway system during the war necessitated a large programme for restoring the tracks, electrification, rebuilding stations and replacing and increasing rolling stock. The electrification programme is now virtually complete, but a 5-year modernization and re-equipment plan (notably for tracks and rolling-stock) is still under way. A network of *autostrade* (motorways) is at present under construction between the major cities and steps have been taken to improve local roads particularly in the South where these were formerly very poor or non-existent. A new road tunnel under the Alps, joining Italy and France was completed in September, 1962. The Italian Mercantile Marine totalled 5,476,000 tons on March 31, 1963, compared with 3,500,000 tons before the war. *Alitalia*, the principal international and domestic airline, is State-owned. Other smaller companies operate on domestic routes.

The Economy and Foreign Trade

General Economic Conditions.—Italy's rapid economic expansion continued in 1962, although not quite at the rate achieved in 1961. The gross national product rose by 5·8 per cent., agricultural production by 1·9 per cent. and industrial production by 9·9 per cent. Industrial investment rose by 7·5 per cent. in real terms over 1961 and the Government embarked on a number of important new development plans involving investment of large sums of money in hospitals, schools, and in the island of Sardinia. Encouraged by the Government, an increasing proportion of industrial as well as agricultural investment went to the South, although most industrial activity is concentrated in the North. Steel production in 1962 was 9,500,000 metric tons, an increase of 14 per cent. over 1961. Motor vehicle production rose by 23 per cent. over 1961 to 930,000 units. The currency after remaining stable for several years lost some purchasing power in 1962. Prices rose steadily during the year and the early part of 1963, chiefly due to the effect of prolonged bad weather on food prices and to higher wages. Unemployment fell to 1,260,000 in December, 1962 (15 per cent. less than in December, 1961) and there are shortages of skilled labour. Increasing prosperity and a rising standard of living have led to a growing demand for consumer goods. Foreign exchange reserves totalled *lire* 2,078,000,000 in March, 1963.

Industrial Activity.—Of Italy's total labour force

of about 20,000,000 nearly 5,500,000 (27·8 per cent.) work on the land; 8,100,000 people (40·7 per cent.) work in industry. The North is traditionally the main industrial area, the principal centres of heavy industry being Milan, Turin and Genoa. Italy has to import most of her coal but this disadvantage has largely been overcome by the exploitation of natural gas deposits and hydroelectric power. Electricity production in 1962 was 64·8 milliard kWh. A 200 mW. nuclear power station has been completed at Latina near Rome and two others are under construction. The main industries are general engineering, motor vehicles, oil refining (41,800,000 tons were refined in 1962), textiles and clothing, food processing, consumer goods and tourism.

Foreign Trade.—Germany, the United States, France, the United Kingdom, and the Middle East oil states are the main sources of Italy's imports. The principal markets for her exports are Germany, the U.S.A., France, Switzerland and the United Kingdom. In recent years the balance of visible trade has been against Italy, but this deficit has been offset by her invisible earnings, particularly from tourism, and by a high level of foreign investment.

	1960	1961	1962
	(£'000,000)		
Total Imports........	1,696	1,876	2,174
Total Exports........	1,311	1,504	1,675

Trade with U.K.

	1961	1962
Imports from U.K...	£114,506,335	£138,815,935
Exports to U.K.....	102,066,161	112,921,029

The following table gives the percentage by value of Italy's total trade in 1962 with EEC, EFTA and United Kingdom:—

	Italian Imports	*Italian Exports*
EEC....................	31·1	34·8
EFTA (including U.K.)....	15·9	20·5
U.K....................	6·3	6·0

CURRENCY

The market rate of exchange in the first four months of 1963 stood at about *lire* 1,740 = £1.

CAPITAL, Rome, founded according to legend by Romulus in the year now known as 753 B.C., is situated on the Tiber, 15 miles from its mouth. It was the focal point of Latin civilization and dominion under the Republic and afterwards under the Roman Empire, and became the capital of Italy when the kingdom was established in 1871. Population (estimated, Oct. 1961), 2,160,773.

Estimated population of the principal cities and towns on October 15, 1961 was: Milan, 1,580,978; ΨNaples, 1,179,608; Turin, 1,019,230; ΨGenoa, 775,107; Bologna, 441,143; Florence, 438,138; ΨVenice, 336,184; ΨBari, 311,268; ΨTrieste, 273,390; Verona, 221,138; Padua, 198,403; ΨTaranto, 191,515; Brescia, 174,116; ΨLeghorn, 159,973; Ferrara, 151,145; ΨReggio Calabria, 150,334; Parma, 140,844; Modena, 139,496; ΨLa Spezia, 121,191; ΨSalerno, 118,171; Reggio Emilia, 116,515; ΨRavenna, 115,205; Bergamo, 113,512; in *Sicily*: ΨPalermo, 587,063; ΨCatania, 361,466; ΨMessina, 251,423; in *Sardinia*: ΨCagliari, 181,499.

TRIESTE.—From June 12, 1945, the area of Trieste was administered by Allied Military Government; Zone A, including Duino and the city and harbour of Trieste, by Anglo-U.S. forces and Zone B, including the towns of Capodistria, Pirano and Cittanuova by Yugoslavia. Provision for setting up a Free Territory of Trieste, included in the Italian Peace Treaty signed in Paris on Feb. 10, 1947, proved to be unworkable and military occupation of the two Zones continued until 1954, when an agreement was concluded in London on Oct. 5 between Italy, Yugoslavia, the United Kingdom and the United States, partitioning this territory between Italy and Yugoslavia along the lines of demarcation of the two Zones, with a minor frontier rectification in favour of Yugoslavia. Zone A, an area of about 90 square miles with a population of 296,229, was formally handed over to Italian administration on October 26, 1954.

Friuli—Venezia Giulia.—Legislation introduced in the Chamber of Deputies on June 19, 1962, providing for the creation of an autonomous region of Friuli-Venezia Giulia, consisting of the three provinces of Udine (population, 800,000), Gorizia (140,000) and Trieste (300,000), was passed July 24, 1962, and referred to the Senate. The city of Trieste will be the capital of this proposed new region.

ISLANDS.—*Pantelleria Island* (part of Trapani Province) in the Sicilian Narrows, has an area of 31 sq. miles and a population of 10,306. The *Pelagian Islands* (Lampedusa, Linosa and Lampione) are part of the Province of Agrigento and have an area of 8 sq. miles, pop. 4,458.

FLAG.—Vertical stripes of green, white and red.

BRITISH EMBASSY

Villa Wolkonsky, Via Conte Rosso, Rome.

British Ambassador, His Excellency Sir John Guthrie Ward, K.C.M.G. (1962).............. £7,015
Minister, D. S. Laskey, C.M.G., C.V.O.
Naval Attaché, Capt. T. N. Catlow, R.N.
Military Attaché, Col. W. M. Inglis.
Air Attaché, Group-Capt. R. J. Abrahams, O.B.E.
Counsellors, J. S. Rooke, C.M.G., O.B.E. (*Commercial*); A. G. Wallis, D.F.C. (*Labour Attaché*); Hon. E. B. C. Howard, M.V.O.
1st Secretaries, W. N. Hugh-Jones, M.V.O.; J. G. Hart, O.B.E.; J. R. Greenwood (*Information Officer*); C. L. Booth, M.V.O.; J. Dawson (*Administrative Officer*); N. R. W. Smith (*Head of Consular Section*); A. S. Auger (*Head of Visa Section*); J. A. Patterson.
2nd Secretaries, T. N. Haining; R. J. Jacques; A. J. Walker, M.B.E. (*Asst. Information Officer*).
3rd Secretaries, R. C. Samuel; A. E. D. Chamier; E. L. Glover.
Commercial Attaché, A. A. C. Nash.
Chaplain, Rev. D. J. N. Wanstall, C.B.E.

BRITISH CONSULAR OFFICES

There are British Consular Offices at *Rome*, *Naples*, *Milan*, *Genoa*, *Florence*, *Palermo*, *Turin*, *Venice*, *Trieste* and *Messina*.

THE BRITISH COUNCIL

Representative, H. Harvey Wood, O.B.E., Palazzo del Drago, Via Quattro Fontane 20, Rome.

There are *British Council Institutes* at Milan and Naples, and a *Centre* at Bologna. There are also British Institutes at Florence and Turin.

IVORY COAST

(Republic of the Ivory Coast)

President and Minister of Foreign Affairs, Félix Houphouët-Boigny, *elected* for five years on November 27, 1960.
President of National Assembly, Philippe Yacé.
President of Economic and Social Council, Mamadou Coolibaly.
President of Supreme Court, Alphonse Boni.
Minister of State, Auguste Denise.
Minister Delegate for Foreign Affairs, Camille Alliali.

IVORY COAST EMBASSY IN LONDON
2 Upper Belgrave Street, S.W.1
[Belgravia: 6991]

Ambassador Extraordinary and Plenipotentiary, His Excellency Amadou Bocoum.
Counsellor, M. Louis Guirandou N'Diaye.
Press Attaché, M. René Boissin.
1st Secretary, M. Victor Oga Agnon.
Attaché, M. Collet Vieira.

The Ivory Coast is situated on the Gulf of Guinea between 5° and 10° N and 3° and 8° W and is flanked on the West by Guinea and Liberia, on the North by Mali and the Voltaic Republic and on the East by Ghana. It has an area of about 189,029 square miles—tropical rain forest in the southern half and savannah in the northern—and a population estimated in 1961 at 3,300,000 divided into a large number of ethnic and tribal groups.

Although official French contact was made in the first half of the 19th century, the Ivory Coast became a Colony only in 1893 and was finally pacified in 1912. It decided on December 5, 1958 to remain an autonomous republic within the French Community; full independence outside the Community was proclaimed on August 7, 1960. Special agreements with France, covering financial and cultural matters, technical assistance, defence, etc., were signed in Paris on April 24, 1961. The Ivory Coast was a founder member of the *Conseil de l'Entente*, established on May 29, 1959, as a loose union embracing also, without abrogation of sovereignty, Dahomey, Niger and Upper Volta. The official (and only common) language is French.

The Ivory Coast has a presidential system of government modelled on that of the United States and the French Fifth Republic. The single Chamber National Assembly of 70 members was elected on November 27, 1960, for five years. The defence of the Constitution, which was promulgated on Nov. 3, 1960, is vested in a Supreme Court.

Finance.—The currency of the Ivory Coast is the *Franc CFA* (*Francs CFA* 50=1 *French franc*; *Francs CFA* 691=£1. In 1963, the Ivory Coast budget balanced at *Francs CFA* 27,496,000,000, a rise of 2·7 per cent. over the previous year.

Trade.—The principal exports are coffee, cocoa, timber and bananas. The United Kingdom imports Ivory Coast timber and a small quantity of her coffee. Diamonds and manganese to the value of *Francs CFA* 1,103,000,000 were exported in 1962 and there are a few deposits of other minerals. Trade in 1962 was valued at: Imports, *Francs CFA* 34,547,000,000; Exports, *Francs CFA* 44,719,000,000.

Trade with U.K.

	1961	1962
Imports from U.K....	£1,570,695	£1,341,277
Exports to U.K.......	935,185	1,416,762

CAPITAL, Ψ Abidjan (population, 1962, 212,000) which is also the main port and handled 2,503,105 tons of goods (exports and imports) in 1962.

FLAG.—3 vertical stripes, orange, white and green.

BRITISH EMBASSY
Avenue Chardy, Abidjan

Ambassador Extraordinary and Plenipotentiary, His Excellency Thomas Richard Shaw, C.M.G. (1963) £4,115
(also Ambassador to *Dahomey*, *Niger* and the *Voltaic Republic*).
1st Secretary and Consul, R. S. Faber.
1st Secretary, A. J. Warren.
2nd Secretary (Commercial) and Vice-Consul, D. M. Edwards, D.S.C.
2nd Secretary (Information), M. L. Creek.
Administration Officer and Vice-Consul, T. A. Duncan.

JAPAN

(Nippon Koku—Land of the Rising Sun)

Emperor of Japan, His Majesty Hirohito, *born* April 29, 1901; *succeeded* Dec. 25, 1926; *married* (1924) Princess Nagako (*born* March 6, 1903), daughter of the late Prince Kuniyoshi Kuni, and has issue two sons and four daughters.
Heir-Apparent, His Imperial Highness Prince Akihito, *Crown Prince*, *born* Dec. 23, 1933; *married* April 10, 1959, Miss Michiko Shoda and has issue Prince Naruhito Hironomiya, *born* Feb. 23, 1960.

CABINET
(July 18, 1960)

Prime Minister, Hayato Ikeda.
Minister for Foreign Affairs, Masayoshi Ohira.
Justice, Okinori Kaya.
Agriculture and Forestry, Munenori Akagi.
Construction, Ichiro Kono.
Labour, Takeo Ohashi.
Health and Welfare, Takeji Kobayashi.
International Trade and Industry, Hajimet Fukuda.
Education, Hirokichi Nadao.
Transport, Kentaro Ayabe.
Postal Services, Shinzo Koike.
Finance, Kakuei Tanaka.
Autonomy and Public Safety, Takashi Hayakawa.
Administrative Management Agency, Shinjiro Yamamura.
Science and Technology, Hokkaido Development, Chairman of Atomic Energy Commission, and Olympic Affairs, Eisaku Sato.
Defence Agency, Tokuyasu Fukuda.
Economic Planning Agency, Kiichi Miyasawa.
Chief Cabinet Secretary, Yasumi Kurogane.

JAPANESE EMBASSY AND CONSULATE
46 Grosvenor Street, W.1
[Hyde Park: 6030]

Ambassador, His Excellency Katsumi Ohno.
Ministers, Haruki Mori; Masato Fujisaki (*Consul-General*).
Counsellors, Maseru Fukuda (*Financial*); Shizuo Saito (*General Affairs*); Tadatomi Ishimaru (*Commercial*).
1st Secretaries, Kei Miyakawa (*Press*); Hisayoshi Terai (*Transport*); Col. Michio Utsunomiya (*Defence Attaché*); Kyo Ando (*Agricultural*); Yoshio Okawa (*Commercial*); Taro Ishibashi (*General Affairs*); Yutaka Nomura (*Gen. Affairs*); Masataka Okura (*Financial*); Toru Mori (*Gen. Affairs*); Shigefumi Tamiya (*Scientific*).
2nd Secretaries, Kazuo Adachi (*Labour*); Sosuke Hanaoka (*Commercial*); Kunihiko Murono (*Visas*); Tsuneo Tanaka (*Press*).
3rd Secretary, Genrokuro Furuhashi (*Financial*).
Attachés, Hiroyuki Yushita (*Protocol*); Masayoshi Matsumura (*Press*); Kazuo Kishi (*Accounts*); Takashi Tajma (*Commercial*); Sadayuki Hayashi (*Gen. Affairs*).

Area and Population.—Japan consists of 4 large and many small islands situated in the North Pacific Ocean between longitude 128° 6′ East and 145° 49′ East and between latitude 26° 59′ and 45° 31′ N., with a total area of 182,700 square miles and a population, Oct. 1962, of 95,180,000.

Japan Proper consists of *Honshû* (or Mainland), 230,532 sq. k. (89,011 sq. m.), *Shikoku*, 18,773 sq. k. (7,248 sq. m.), *Kyūshū*, 42,079 sq. k. (16,247 sq. m.), *Hokkaido*, 77,096 sq. k. (29,764 sq. m.). Formosa and the Kwantung Province, which had been throughout the years of Japanese expansion and aggression leased or annexed, reverted to Chinese sovereignty after the War of 1939–45.

After the unconditional surrender to the Allied Nations (Aug. 15, 1945), Japan was occupied by Allied forces under General MacArthur (Sept. 15,

1945). A Japanese peace treaty conference opened at San Francisco on Sept. 4, 1951, and on Sept. 8, 48 nations signed the treaty, which became effective on April 28, 1952. Japan then resumed her status as an independent power.

British participation in the occupation of Japan was virtually over by May, 1950. However, the outbreak of hostilities in Korea in June, 1950, resulted in the despatch to Korea of British Forces, from the United Kingdom, Australia, New Zealand and Canada to participate in the United Nations action. The main base of this force was established in Japan at Kure. On July 1, 1956, the base was moved to Inchon, Korea, and all Commonwealth troops had left Japan by the middle of 1957.

Under the terms of the Japan-U.S.A. Security Treaty of Sept. 8, 1951, United States forces remained to assist in the defence of Japan. However, as Japan's own Self Defence Forces have been built up, U.S. ground troops have been withdrawn. A revised version of the security treaty, which went into effect on June 23, 1960, was the subject of considerable controversy in the summer of that year.

Vital Statistics.—In October, 1962, Japan proper contained 95,180,000 inhabitants. The birth rate in 1962 was 17·0 per 1,000 (compared with 34·3 per 1,000 in 1947). It has been stated that a major part in reducing the birth rate to its present level was played by drastic methods, induced abortion and sterilization, the legal grounds for which had been extended by the Eugenics Law, 1948, to include economic and social hardship. The improving standard of living has also played an important part in keeping the birthrate down and over-population is not now regarded as critical.

The death rate in 1962 was 7·5 per 1,000, compared with 17 per 1,000 in pre-war years, natural increase of the population being 913,811 in 1962. It is estimated that, if present trends continue, the population of Japan will reach 102,206,000 in 1970 and 113,293,000 in 1995. The *Ainu*, remnant of the indigenous inhabitants, are dying out but are still found in small numbers in Hokkaido.

Physiography.—The coastline exceeds 17,000 miles and is deeply indented, so that few places are far from the sea. The interior is very mountainous, and crossing the mainland from the Sea of Japan to the Pacific is a group of volcanoes, mainly extinct or dormant. Mount Fuji, the loftiest and most sacred mountain of Japan, about 60 miles from Tokyo, is 12,370 ft. high and has been dormant since 1707, but there are other volcanoes which are active, including Mount Aso in Kyūshū. There are frequent earthquakes, mainly along the Pacific coast near the Bay of Tokyo. Japan proper extends from sub-tropical in the south to cool temperate in the north. Heavy snowfalls are frequent on the western slopes of Hokkaidō and Honshū, but the Pacific coasts are warmed by the Japan current. There is a plentiful rainfall and the rivers are short and swift-flowing, offering abundant opportunities for the supply of hydro-electric power.

Government.—According to Japanese tradition, Jimmu, the first Emperor of Japan, ascended the throne on Feb. 11, B.C. 660. Under the Constitution of Feb. 11, 1889, the monarchy was hereditary in the male heirs of the Imperial house. A new constitution approved by the Supreme Allied Commander was published on March 6, 1946, superseding the "*Meiji Constitution*" of 1889 and containing many radical changes based on the constitutional practices of the United Kingdom, U.S.A. and France.

The new constitution came into force on May 3, 1947. Legislative authority rests with *The Diet*, which is bicameral, consisting of a *House of Representatives* and a *House of Councillors*, both Houses being composed of elected members. Executive authority is vested in the Cabinet which is responsible to the Legislature.

A general election was held on November 20, 1960, in which the Liberal Democratic Party was once more returned to power. The strength of the parties in the House of Representatives on July 19, 1963, was: Liberal Democratic Party, 288; Socialist Party, 137; Democratic Socialist Party, 15; Communist Party, 3; Independents, 2; (22 vacancies). Strengths of the parties in the House of Councillors were: Liberal Democratic Party, 142; Socialist Party, 66; Democratic Socialist Party, 11; Independents, 11; Komeikai, 15; Communist Party 4; (one vacancy).

Agriculture and Livestock.—Owing to the mountainous nature of the country not more than one-sixth of its area is available for cultivation. There were in 1960, 24,403,023 hectares of forest, which include the Cryptomeria japonica, Pinus massoniana, Zelkowa keaki, and Pawlonia imperialis in addition to camphor trees, mulberry, vegetable wax tree and a lacquer tree which furnishes the celebrated lacquer of Japan. The soil is only moderately fertile, but intensive cultivation secures good crops. In 1961 there were 6,678,390 hectares under cereals (rice, 3,328,000 hectares). The tobacco-plant, tea-shrub, potato, rice, wheat and other cereals are all cultivated: rice is the staple food of the people, about 12,419,000 metric tons being produced in 1961. The floral kingdom is rich, beautiful, and varied, though scented flowers are comparatively few. Fruit is abundant, including the mandarin, persimmon, loquat and peach; European fruits such as apples, strawberries, pears, grapes and figs are also produced. Mulberry trees are now cultivated on only 141,700 hectares (1961) compared with 577,525 in 1935.

Minerals.—The country has mineral resources, including gold and silver, and copper, lead, zinc, iron chromite, white arsenic, coal, sulphur, petroleum, salt and uranium, but iron ore, coal and crude oil are among the principal post-war imports to supply deficiencies at home.

Industry.—Japan is the most highly industrialized nation in the Far East, with the whole range of modern light and heavy industries, including mining, metals, machinery, chemicals, textiles (cotton, silk, wool and synthetics), cement, pottery, glass, rubber, lumber, paper, oil refining and shipbuilding. The labour force of Japan in April, 1963, was 46,980,000, of which only 340,000 were unemployed. Of the total labour force, some 33,410,000 were engaged in non-agricultural industries, 13,130,000 in agriculture and forestry and 540,000 in fisheries.

Communications.—There were 27,888 kilometres of Government and private railroad (steam and electric) in 1962. The Japanese mercantile marine reached 6,000,000 gross tons in 1941, but more than three-quarters of it was sunk during the war. In March, 1963, the merchant fleet (ocean-going ships over 3,000 tons gross) consisted of 4,448 steel vessels totalling 8,344,000 tons gross. It is intended to expand to 13,350,000 tons by 1970, of which 74 per cent. will be industrial carriers.

In Japan the Maritime Safety Board has responsibility for merchant shipping and pilotage. Its strength in 1963 was about 11,187 with some 208 vessels and a few aircraft.

Armed Forces.—After the unconditional surrender of August, 1945, the land forces were disarmed and disbanded and all aircraft confiscated by the occupying forces.

Although the Constitution of Japan prohibits the maintenance of armed forces, an internal security force, known as the National Police Reserve, came into being at the end of 1950. In October. 1951, this Force was renamed the National Safety Force and together with a Coastal Safety Force was placed under a National Safety Agency. By January, 1953, the National Safety Force had reached its authorized strength of 110,000.

In March, 1954, a Mutual Defence Agreement for the supply of equipment and materials was concluded with the United States. In June, the mission of the forces was extended to include the defence of Japan against direct and indirect aggression, the Agency was renamed the Defence Agency, the forces under it, the Ground Self Defence Force and the Maritime Self Defence Force respectively, and a new arm, the Air Self Defence Force, was created.

By 1956, the authorized uniformed strength of these forces was 160,000, 22,700 and 10,350 respectively and by 1962 these figures had increased to 171,500, 33,291 and 38,337. The Combined Defence Agency vote for 1962–3 was *Yen* 205,824,000, 8·4 per cent. of the total budget.

At the end of 1962, the Maritime Self Defence Force had 18 destroyers (4 ex-U.S.), 26 frigates (20 ex-U.S.), 4 submarines (1 ex-U.S.) and 164 minor war vessels and auxiliaries. The Fleet Air Arm has 115 patrol aircraft, 33 helicopters, 4 transports, 7 flying boats and 88 trainers, all shore-based. Its strength, including 5,996 officers, 28,054 ratings and 4,787 civilians, was 38,837.

The Ground Self Defence Force is broadly organized into 12 divisions (about 9,000 strong), one armoured division and an airborne brigade. Equipment other than Japanese-made light trucks and some armoured vehicles, is largely of U.S. manufacture.

The Air Self Defence Force had at the end of 1962 467 fighter aircraft (F-104J, F-86F and F86D), 18 reconnaisance planes (RF-86F), 45 transports (C-46), 29 helicopters and 596 training planes. About 58 per cent. of these aircraft were built in Japan. Its strength was 36,432 uniformed personnel and 4,731 civilians.

Religion.—All religions are tolerated. The principal religions of Japan are Mahayana Buddhism and Shinto. The Roman Catholic Church has 1 Cardinal, 2 archbishops and 12 bishops. The Nippon Seikokai (Holy Catholic Church of Japan) has 15 Japanese bishops and is an autonomous branch of the Anglican communion. There is also an United Protestant Church.

Education.—According to the laws passed in 1947, education on elementary level (6-year course) and lower secondary level (3-year course) is free, compulsory and co-educational. Upper secondary schools (3-year course) are mainly established and maintained by prefectures, and are co-educational. They have several courses in general, agricultural, commercial, technical, mercantile marine, radio-communication and home-economics education, etc. There are 2- or 3-year junior colleges and 4-year universities. Some of the 4-year universities have graduate schools. In May, 1963, the total number of these junior colleges and universities was 565, of which 100 were established and maintained by the State, while 74 were established and maintained by prefectures and cities, and 391 were private institutions. The most prominent universities are the seven State Universities of Tokyo, Kyoto, Tohoku (Sendai), Hokkaidō (Sapporo), Kyushu (Fukuoka), Osaka and Nagoya, and the two private universities, Keio and Waseda.

Language and Literature.—Japanese is said to be one of the Uro-Altaic group of languages and remained a spoken tongue until the fifth-seventh centuries A.D., when the Chinese characters came into use. Japanese who have received school education (99·8 per cent. of the population) can read and write the Chinese characters in current use (about 1,800 characters) aad also the syllabary characters called Kana. English is the best known foreign language. It is compulsory in almost all middle and high schools. In April, 1962, there were 708 libraries open to the public (The National Diet Library and 707 public libraries) with 21,164,911 volumes. In addition there were 700 University libraries with 34,310,249 volumes in May, 1962. There were 103 daily newspapers in Japan of which 18 were published at Tokyo, 14 at Osaka and 10 in the Nagoya region (all editions included). Japan's present total newspaper circulation is estimated at 40,218,000 copies and 1·84 per household.

FINANCE

The Budget for the financial year 1963–64, ending on March 31, is estimated to balance at *Yen* 2,855,800,000,000 for revenue and expenditure on the general account, an increase of 17·6 per cent. over the preceding financial year.

The official rate of exchange of *yen* 360=1 U.S.$ was established on April 25, 1949, and (after Japan's accession to the International Monetary Fund) was confirmed by the Fund on May 11, 1953. Exchange rates of all currencies are allowed to fluctuate within IMF limits.

PRODUCTION AND TRADE

Being deficient in natural resources, Japan has had to develop a complex foreign trade. Principal imports consist of raw materials (cotton, wool, mineral oils, rubber, iron ore, coking coal, salt, wood pulp, hides), foodstuffs (wheat, barley, soya beans, sugar), petroleum, chemicals and specialized machinery. Principal exports consist of cotton and rayon textiles, machinery, ships, metals and products, canned fish, chemicals and a wide variety of manufactured goods, including chinaware, toys, bicycles, sewing machines, cameras and transistor radios.

FOREIGN TRADE

	1961	1962
	$1,000	$1,000
Total Imports	5,811,000	5,632,000
Total Visible Exports	4,235,000	4,913,000
Deficit	$1,574,000	$719,000

Trade with U.K.

	1961	1962
Imports from U.K.	£41,742,137	£43,339,360
Exports to U.K.	39,222,477	53,248,172

There was an adverse balance of U.S.$124,123,496 for the fiscal year ending March 31, 1959.

CAPITAL OF JAPAN, Tokyo. Its population in February, 1962, was estimated to be 10,003,055. The other chief cities then had the following populations:

Ψ Osaka	3,140,000
Ψ Nagoya	1,655,000
Ψ Yokohama	1,459,000
Kyoto, the ancient capital	1,299,000
Ψ Kobé	1,149,000

FLAG.—White, charged with sun (red).

Yokohama, by sea 11,260 miles distant from London, transit, 35 days; Tokyo, by air (B.O.A.C.) 9,927 miles distant from London: transit by polar route (8,382 m.), about 18 hrs.

British Embassy
(Ichiban-cho, Kojimachi, Chiyoda-ku, Tokyo.)

Ambassador Extraordinary and Plenipotentiary, His Excellency Sir Francis Brian Anthony Rundall, K.C.M.G., O.B.E. (1963) £5,015
Minister, D. J. Cheke, C.M.G.
Counsellors, C. G. Harris (*Commercial*); J. G. Figgess, C.M.G., O.B.E. (*Information*).
Naval Attaché, Capt. A. J. Petrie-Hay, R.N.
Military Attaché, Col. P. S. W. Dean.
Consul, R. J. Bray.

Consulates

Osaka-Kobé—Consul-General, J. O. Lloyd. *Consuls*, R. S. Milward (*Osaka*); J. H. Callan (*Kobé*).
Yokohama.—Consul, R. G. Brereton.

British Council

Representative and Cultural Attaché, British Embassy, E. W. F. Tomlin, O.B.E., Suzuki Building, 13 Samon-cho, Shinjuku-ku, Tokyo.

JORDAN

(The Hashemite Kingdom of The Jordan)

King of the Jordan, Hussein, G.C.V.O., *born* November 14, 1935, *succeeded* on the deposition of his father, King Talal, Aug. 11, 1952, *assumed constitutional powers*, May 2, 1953, on coming of age.
Heir Apparent, Prince Abdullah, *born* Jan. 30, 1962.

Cabinet
(July 10, 1963)

Prime Minister and Minister of Foreign Affairs, Sharif Husain bin Nasr.
Deputy Prime Minister, Said Mufti.
Finance, Abdul Rahman Khalifeh.
Interior, Saleh Majali.
Education and Justice, Hassan Kaid.
Defence, Abdul Kader Saleh.
Economy (*Acting Chief Justice*), Rashad al-Khatib.
Labour and Social Affairs, Amin Husaini.
Public Works, Abdul Latif an-Abtawi.
Health, Dr. Saleh Burkan.
Communications, Muhammad Ali Rida.
Agriculture, Kamel Muhyiddin.
Building, Yub Musallam.

Jordanian Embassy and Consulate
6 Upper Phillimore Gardens, W.8
[Western: 3685]

Ambassador, His Excellency Anastas Hanania.
1st Secretary and Consul, Zeid al-Rifa'i.
Military, Naval and Air Attaché, Col. Rageb Abu Taleb.

Area and Population.—The Hashemite Kingdom of the Jordan is made up of two areas: Western Jordan, which includes the districts of Hebron, Jerusalem and Nablus, and Eastern Jordan, which includes the districts of Ma'an, Kerak, Belqa and Ajlun. The union of East and West Jordan was effected by a decision taken unanimously by both houses of the Legislature on April 24, 1950. The union was recognized a few days later by the British Government subject to certain reservations on the subject of Jerusalem. The Kingdom is bounded on the north by Syria, on the west by Israel, on the south by Saudi Arabia and on the east by Iraq. The majority of the population are Sunni Moslems and Islam is the religion of the state. The first census of population, held in Oct.-November, 1961, disclosed a population of 1,752,095.

Government.—The Executive consists of a Council of Ministers and the legislature of a Senate (30 persons nominated by the King) and a House of Representatives, consisting of 60 elected members.

Production and Industry.—West Jordan is fertile, but severely eroded. East Jordan (the old Amirate of Transjordan), consists of a fertile mountainous area and the eastern half of the Jordan valley which are productive; the rest of the country is arid steppe. Jordan's only industrial product of note is raw phosphate, of which about 390,000 tons were exported in 1961.

Communications.—The Hejaz Railway runs (with the exception of the first few miles) through Jordan territory from Deraa to Ma'an. During the Second World War, 24 miles of line were laid from Ma'an to Ras Naqb; there are good roads to all the chief towns in the country. A new road now connects Aqaba, the country's only port, with Amman.

Finance	1963–64 (Estimates)
Expenditure	£JD43,535,000
Revenue	37,604,800
Deficit	5,930,200

Currency.—The Jordan *Dinar* of 1,000 *fils* = £1.

Trade with U.K.

	1961	1962
Imports from U.K.	£7,614,886	£7,366,483
Exports to U.K.	235,533	457,590

Capital, Amman. Population (Census of 1961), 244,599. The population of the Jordanian part of Jerusalem was 60,337.

Flag.—Black, white and green horizontal stripes, surcharged with white seven-pointed star on red triangle.

British Embassy, Amman

Ambassador, His Excellency Sir Roderick Wallis Parkes, K.C.M.G., O.B.E. (1962)......... £5,015
Counsellor, J. F. S. Phillips.
Secretaries, A. J. D. Stirling; C. de L. Herdon; P. W. E. Murdie; W. R. Tomkys.
Commercial Secretary, E. G. Rowe.

British Council

Representative, F. J. Wakelin, O.B.E., Jebel Amman, P.O Box 634, Amman.

KOREA

(Hankuk.)

Korea is situated between 124° 11″ and 130° 57″ E. long., and between 33° 7″ and 43° 1″ N. lat. It has an area of 85,256 sq. miles with an estimated population of about 28,000,000, of whom about 21,500,000 live south of the present dividing line. The southern and western coasts are fringed with innumerable islands, of which the largest, forming a province of its own, is Chejudo (Quelpart). The soil is fertile, but the arable land is limited by the mountainous nature of the country. The staple agricultural products are rice, barley, and other cereals, beans, cotton, tobacco and hemp. Fruit-growing and seri-culture are also practised. Gingseng, a medicinal root much affected by the Chinese, is largely grown at Kaesong (now in North Korean hands) but also in parts of South Korea. It forms a rich source of revenue. Gold, copper, coal, iron, graphite, tungsten and other minerals are distributed throughout the country, but are more abundant in the north. In pre-war days the south was mainly agricultural and most of the limited industries were in the north. Political necessity in recent years has led to some industrialization south of the demarcation line, but the southern portion of the peninsula remains predominantly agricultural.

History.—The last native dynasty (Yi) ruled from 1392 until 1910, in which year Japan formally annexed Korea. The country remained an integral part of the Japanese Empire until the defeat of Japan in 1945, when it was occupied by troops of the U.S.A. and the U.S.S.R.; the 38th parallel being fixed as the boundary between the two zones of occupation. The U.S. Government endeavoured to reach agreement with the Soviet Government for the creation of a Korean Government for the whole country and the withdrawal of all Russian and American troops. These efforts met with no success, and in September, 1947, the U.S. Government laid the whole question of the future of Korea before the General Assembly of the United Nations. The Assembly in November, 1947, resolved that elections should be held in Korea for a National Assembly under the supervision of a temporary Commission formed for that purpose by the United Nations and that the National Assembly when elected should set up a Government. The Soviet Government refused to allow the Commission to visit the Russian Occupied Zone and in consequence it was only able to discharge its function in that part of Korea which lies to the south of the 38th parallel.

The Korean War.—The country remained effectively divided into two along the line of the 38th parallel, until the aggression of June 25, 1950, when the North Korean forces invaded South Korea. On the same day, at an emergency meeting of the United Nations Security Council, a resolution was adopted calling for immediate cessation of hostilities, and the withdrawal of the North Korean armed forces to the 38th parallel. The Communist forces ignored this demand and continued their advance. In response to a Security Council recommendation that United Nations members should furnish assistance to repel the attack, 16 nations, including the United States of America and the United Kingdom, came to the aid of the Republic of Korea. A unified command under the leadership of the United States was established on July 8. Shortly afterwards U.S. troops were landed in Korea but were at first unable to stem the Communists' onslaught. Finally the United Nations and South Korea forces were able to stabilize a front around the Pusan perimeter. On September 15, U.S. Marines made a successful surprise landing at Inchon which was quickly followed by a break-out from the Pusan perimeter and a general advance to the north. The Communist forces had been pushed back almost to the Manchurian frontier, when, at the beginning of November, hordes of Chinese "Volunteers" began to pour over the Yalu River and by sheer weight of numbers forced the U.N. troops to withdraw once again south of Seoul. However, the latter quickly regrouped and threw the Communist forces back to approximately the old dividing line.

The fighting was ended by an armistice agreement signed by the U.N. Commander-in-Chief and the commanders of the North Korean army and the Chinese People's "Volunteers" on July 27, 1953. By this agreement (which was not accepted by the government of the Republic of Korea) the line of division between North and South Korea remained in the neighbourhood of the 38th parallel. The Geneva Conference discussed Korea from April 26 to June 15, 1954, but failed to agree on measures for reunifying the country.

Republic of Korea

Acting President, Gen. Pak Chung Hi.
Prime Minister, Kim Hyun Chul (July 11, 1962).

Korean Embassy and Consulate

36 Cadogan Square, S.W.1
[Kensington: 8025]

Ambassador Extraordinary and Plenipotentiary, His Excellency General Honkon Lee.
Counsellor, Kyu Sup Chung.
1st Secretaries and Consuls, Nam KiLee; Insoo Park.
3rd Secretary, Chong Hoon Kim.
Attaché, Jong Hong Kim.
Naval, Military and Air Attaché, Brig.-Gen. Bong Hi Chun.
Consul, Kwang Jung Song.

The Republic of Korea has been officially recognized by the Governments of the United States, France, Great Britain, and most other countries except the U.S.S.R. and its satellites. It has an area of 96,930 sq. km. (37,426 sq. miles) and a population (estimated Dec. 1, 1962) of 26,277,635.

A general election was held on May 10, 1948, and the first National Assembly met in Seoul on May 31. The Assembly passed a Constitution on July 12, and on July 20 elected Dr. Syngman Rhee as the first President of the Republic of Korea for four years. On August 15, 1948, the Republic was formally inaugurated and American Military Government came to an end. All U.S. troops were withdrawn by the end of June, 1949.

In the elections on March 15, 1960, Syngman Rhee and his nominee the late Lee Ki Poong were returned by overwhelming majorities as President and Vice-President respectively. Widespread resentment against the conduct of the elections culminated in demonstrations by University students in Seoul on April 18 and 19, renewed on April 25 and 26 after demonstrations by the professors, which finally led to the resignation of President Rhee on April 27 and the replacement of his Liberal Party Government. On May 16, 1961, a number of army officers led a revolution which overthrew the government of Dr. John M. Chang, while leaving the President in office. This movement, now re-named the Supreme Council for National Reconstruction, rules the country in place of the former House of Representatives and House of Councillors. The Supreme Council's programme calls for efficient, incorrupt government, austerity, social, moral and economic regeneration, strengthened anti-Communism and adherence to the U.N. Charter and Korea's international commitments. On March 22, 1962, President Yun resigned. General Pak Chung Hi took over as acting President, retaining his post as Chairman of the Supreme Council, pending elections and the restoration of civil government, which have both been promised for 1963. These were originally promised for May and August, 1963, respectively, but when political activities were allowed to start again at the beginning of that year there was considerable confusion, so that the military government decided to retain power until December, 1963.

The Republic of Korea has an army of about 550,000 men, a small navy mainly for coast protection duties, a small air force and a Marine Corps which includes one division trained in amphibious operations.

Finance.—The Budget for the year ending December 31, 1963, totalled *Won* 76,870,000,000, reduced in April, 1963, by *Won* 4,280,000,000. Expenditure on National Defence is estimated at *Won* 21,250,000,000.

The unit of Korean currency was changed in June, 1962, from *Hwan* to *Won*, the *Won* being ten times the value of the *Hwan*. The official rate of exchange (1963) is *Won* 130 = £1. The quotation for £1 varies slightly.

Trade.—The Republic of Korea's main exports are rice, tungsten and iron ores, graphite, anthracite, fish and fish products, agar-agar, seaweed, raw silk, textile yarns and fabric. Her main customer is

Japan. Imports greatly exceed exports. In 1962 exports totalled $56,702,000; imports amounted to $387,317,000 of which $191,472,000 were financed by American aid.

Trade with U.K.

	1961	1962
Imports from U.K.	£1,400,933	£1,743,051
Exports to U.K.	380,319	637,114

CAPITAL.—Seoul, population (1960), 2,444,883. Other main centres are ΨPusan (pop. 1,163,614), Taegu (pop. 678,277) and ΨInchon (pop. 402,009). Pusan on the south-east coast, and Inchon on the west coast, only 28 miles from Seoul, are the main ports but the development of Inchon is hampered by a tide variation of 28–30 feet.

BRITISH EMBASSY
Seoul

Ambassador, His Excellency Walter Godfrey, C.B.E. (1961) £4,115
1st Secretaries, S. J. Whitwell, M.C. (*Head of Chancery and Consul*); R. A. Kidd.
Military Attaché, Brig. C. M. M. Man, O.B.E., M.C.
2nd Secretaries, M. E. Pike; J. H. Bailey; J. R. Barnes.
Vice-Consul, Miss J. Woolrich.

Democratic Peoples' Republic of Korea.—Meanwhile in the Russian-occupied zone north of the 38th parallel the Democratic People's Republic had been set up with its capital at Pyongyang; a Supreme Peoples' Soviet was elected in September 1948, and a Soviet-style Constitution adopted. Recognition had been given by the U.S.S.R. and its satellites.

KUWAIT

(The State of Kuwait)

Amir, H.H. Shaikh Abdullah as-Salim As-Sabah, G.C.M.G., C.I.E., *born* 1895, *acceded* Feb. 25, 1950.
Prime Minister and Heir Apparent, H.H. Shaikh Sabah as-Salim as-Sabah, *appointed* Jan. 27, 1963.

KUWAIT EMBASSY IN LONDON
40 Devonshire Street, W.1
[Langham: 8471]

Ambassador, His Excellency Sayyid Khalid Mohammad Jaffar (1963).

Kuwait is an independent Arab State whose relations with the United Kingdom are governed by an exchange of letters dated June 19, 1961, in which Her Majesty's Government confirmed its recognition of Kuwait's independent status. It extends along the shore of the Persian Gulf from Iraq to Saudi Arabia, with an area of about 5,800 square miles and a population, according to a census taken in 1961, of 321,621, including 26,000 Iraquis, 20,000 Persians, 15,000 Jordanians and large numbers of Indians, Pakistanis, Saudi Arabians and Lebanese. The total European and American population was about 3,500 in 1961. Kuwait has a hot, dry climate with a summer season extending from April to September. During the coldest month (January) the temperatures range between 50° to 60°F. Shade temperatures are about 85°F; and have been known to reach 125°F.; 165°F. has been recorded in the sun. Humidity rarely exceeds 60 per cent.

The port of Ψ Kuwait, the capital (pop. 210,000), is traditionally an *entrepôt* for goods for the interior, and for the export of pearls (in diminishing quantities), skins and wool. However with the development of the oil industry, the importance of the *entrepôt* trade has diminished. Imports for the year 1962 amounted to approximately £101,865,180, while exports, including re-exports, amounted to £8,101,538, excluding oil. Kuwait was traditionally the dhow-building centre for the Persian Gulf, but the craft is declining.

The centre of the Kuwait Oil Company's production is at Burgan, south of Kuwait town. An oil port has been constructed by the company at Mina-al-Ahmadi, about five miles from Ahmadi, the company's administrative and residential centre. Production of crude oil in 1962 totalled 90,721,636 tons. The Company is jointly owned by the British Petroleum Company and the American Gulf Oil Corporation. It employs about 5,750 men, including British, Americans, Indians, Pakistanis, Kuwaitis and Arabs from neighbouring territories. In May, 1962, the Company relinquished about half of its original concession area. Oil was also struck in the Kuwait-Saudi Arabian Neutral Zone to the South of the State early in 1953. Concessions for this area are held by the American Independent Oil Co. from Kuwait and the Getty Oil Company from Saudi Arabia. Total production of crude oil in the neutral zone in 1962 was approximately 10,000,000 tons.

The Arabian Oil Company, of Japan, having been awarded in 1958 the oil concession for the Neutral Zone offshore sea-bed by Kuwait and Saudi Arabia for their respective half shares, commenced exploratory drilling in the summer of 1959 and struck oil in commercial quantity early in 1960. The first shipment of crude oil was made in March, 1961 and production rose to 2,863,398 tons in 1962. A concession covering the off-shore area of Kuwait proper was awarded to the Shell Company in November, 1960, and the concession agreement in the name of The Kuwait Shell Petroleum Development Co. was signed in Kuwait on January 15, 1961. Exploratory drilling began in 1962. The establishment of a Kuwaiti company, The Kuwait National Petroleum Co., was authorized by an Emirie Decree on October 5, 1960. This company took over the distribution of petroleum products in Kuwait from the Kuwait Oil Co., on June 1, 1961, and has been provisionally awarded the concession to exploit the area relinquished by the K.O.C. Ltd. in 1962.

As a result of the very considerable oil revenues, the Kuwait Government embarked on a large scale development scheme and plans for social services. Education and medical treatment are free. New hospitals and schools continue to be built. In 1962–63 there were 35,154 boys and 23,715 girls in 142 schools. Kuwait has a domestic water supply from a State-owned sea water plant which operates on waste natural gas from the oil fields. The plant can produce over 6,000,000 gallons of fresh water daily. For storage there are two 15,000,000 gallon reservoirs and one of 3,000,000 gallons.

In 1961 a natural source of fresh water was discovered at Raudhatain in the north of the State. This has been developed to produce 5,000,000 gallons per day for at least 20 years and a pipeline has been built to carry the water to Kuwait town. The power station has a capacity of 160,000 kW. The town is now served by a network of dual carriageway roads and more are under construction.

Ships of British, Dutch and other lines make regular calls at Kuwait. B.O.A.C., Kuwait Airways and several International and Middle Eastern airlines operate regular air services, and other companies make non-scheduled flights to Kuwait under charter. Wireless communications, telephone and postal services are conducted by the Kuwait Government. Banking is carried out by the British Bank of the Middle East, the National Bank of Kuwait, the Commercial Bank, and the Gulf Bank. The currency is the Kuwait *dinar*, equal in value to the £.

Government.—Although Kuwait had been independent for some years, the " exclusive agreement " of 1899 between the Shaikh of Kuwait and the British Government was formally abrogated by an exchange of letters dated June 19, 1961. This exchange was immediately followed by Iraqi claims to sovereignty over Kuwait and, in accordance with the terms of the exchange, the Amir requested British Military assistance to help him maintain his sovereignty and independence, which was immediately supplied. British troops were withdrawn in October, 1961, and replaced by the Arab League Security Force composed of contingents from various Arab States. The withdrawal of this Force was completed in January, 1963.

Elections were held in December, 1961, for a Constituent Assembly, which held its first meeting in January, 1962. A council of Ministers including non-members of the ruling family was formed in January, 1962, to replace the former Supreme and Joint Councils. Under the Constitution drafted by the Constituent Assembly, a 50-member National Assembly was elected in January, 1963. The Constitution provides that the Assembly must pass all laws and approve the Heir Apparent nominated by the Amir. The Prime Minister is appointed by the Amir and can appoint his Ministers from the members of the Assembly or from outside. The Assembly has the right to pass a vote of no confidence in any Minister except the Prime Minister.

FLAG.—Three horizontal stripes of green, white and red, with black trapezoid next to staff.

BRITISH EMBASSY
Kuwait

Ambassador Extraordinary and Plenipotentiary, His Excellency Gordon Noel Jackson, C.M.G., M.B.E. (1963) £4,115
1st Secretary and Consul, M. W. Errock.
1st Secretary, L. P. Fernandez.
Economic Counsellor, C. T. Gandy.
1st Secretary (Commercial), W. F. Marshall.
Vice-Consul, R. S. Ellis.
Vice-Consul (Mina al-Ahmadi), P. T. O'K. Gardner.

British Council Representative in the Persian Gulf, O. J. J. Tuckley, M.B.E., P.O. Box 345, Kuwait.

LAOS

King, Setha Khatya (. . . Savang Vatthana), *born* 1908, *succeeded* Nov. 4, 1959.
Prime Minister, Prince Souvana Phouma (Aug. 16, 1960).

EMBASSY IN LONDON
5 Palace Green, W.8

Ambassador Extraordinary and Plenipotentiary, H.R.H. Prince Souphantharangsi.
Counsellor, Khamtan Ratanavong.

Laos includes the former Kingdoms of Luang Prabang and Vientiane and the Principality of Champassac, united under King Sisavang Vong of the House of Luang Prabang, father of the present ruler. The country has an estimated area of 90,000 square miles and an estimated population of 2,500,000. The independence of the kingdom was recognized by France in July, 1949. In the Indo-China war the rebel Pathet Lao forces led by Prince Souphannouvong collaborated with the Viet Minh. The 1954 Geneva Agreements provided for the integration of the Pathet Lao forces and the re-unification of the country. Agreement was reached on these points in November, 1957 but the agreement later broke down and in 1960 elections brought a right-wing government to power.

The government was overthrown on August 9, 1960, by a *coup d'état* led by Captain Konglae. The new government of Prince Souvanna Phouma was opposed by one half of the army led by General Phoumi Nosavan who set up a Revolutionary Committee at Savannakhet under the nominal headship of Prince Boun Oum. General Phoumi retook Vientiane in December, 1960, and, Souvanna Phouma's government having fled, a government under Prince Boun Oum was approved by the National Assembly on January 4. Captain Konglae and Prince Souvanna Phouma retired to Xieng Khouang where, in collaboration with the pro-communist Pathet Lao forces and with material support from communist countries, they were able to counter-attack successfully and compel the Government forces to agree to a cease-fire. A 14-nation conference met in Geneva in May, 1961 to work out an international framework for Laotian neutrality. Agreement was held up by internal rivalries in Laos, but in June, 1962, the "three Princes" finally agreed on a coalition government under Prince Souvanna Phouma, and a new Geneva agreement to safeguard Laotian neutrality was signed on July 23.

CAPITAL.—Vientiane, population (estimated) 80,000.

FLAG.—Three-headed white elephant on 5 steps, surmounted by parasol, all on a red ground.

BRITISH EMBASSY
Vientiane

Ambassador Extraordinary and Plenipotentiary, His Excellency Donald Charles Hopson, C.M.G., D.S.O., M.C., T.D. (1962) £3,451
1st Secretaries, J. B. Denson; J. B. D. McKibbin; A. G. Trevor-Wilson, O.B.E. (*Information*); H. Docherty (*Commercial*).
Military Attaché, Lt.-Col. J. M. B. Isaac, M.C.
Asst. do., Maj. F. C. Wallerstein, M.C.
2nd Secretary, A. V. Hartley.
3rd Secretary, D. A. Campbell.

LEBANON

President of the Republic of Lebanon, General Fuad Chehab, *elected* July 31, 1958; *assumed office* September 23, 1958.

Prime Minister, Rashid Karameh.
Foreign Affairs, Phillippe Takla.

LEBANESE EMBASSY IN LONDON
(21 Kensington Palace Gardens, W.8)
[Bayswater: 7265]

Ambassador His Excellency, Shaikh Khalil Takieddinne (1962).
Counsellor, Michel Farah.
1st Secretary, Jean Riachi.
Attaché, Ibrahim Kharma.
Consular Section, 15 Palace Gardens Mews, W.8 (Bayswater: 8485).

The republic of the Lebanon is in the Levant, covering a portion of the former Ottoman Empire taken from the Turks by British forces (with a small French detachment and some Arab forces under the Emir Faisal and Colonel Lawrence) in 1918, but following the Anglo-French Convention of September, 1919, Great Britain withdrew in favour of France, to whom a Mandate was granted by the Supreme Council of Allied Powers in 1920. The French authorities granted a Constitution and the first President of the Republic (under the Mandate) was elected in 1926.

In 1941 hostilities broke out between the French troops in Syria and Lebanon and the Allied Forces in the Middle East, the latter having been directed to prevent further Nazi penetration into French

Mandated Territory. Hostilities ceased on July 11, 1941, and the French High Command agreed to remove the garrison.

In accordance with the undertaking given by the British and Free French Forces, Syria and Lebanon were declared to be independent and separate States. In 1943 the amended Constitution came into force and the first President of the independent Lebanon Republic was elected.

Under an agreement signed by General Catroux (on behalf of the French Committee of National Liberation) and by representatives of Syria and Lebanon "all powers and capacities exercised hitherto by the French under mandate" were transferred to the Syrian and Lebanese governments as from Jan. 1, 1944.

Lebanon forms a strip, about 120 miles in length and varying in width from 30 to 35 miles, along the Mediterranean littoral, and extending from the Palestine frontier on the south to the Nahr al Kebir (15 miles north of Tripoli) on the north; its eastern boundary runs down the Anti-Lebanon range and then down the Great Central depression, the *Beqaa*, in which flow the rivers Orontes and Litani. It is divided into 5 districts, North Lebanon, Mount Lebanon, Beirut, South Lebanon and Beqaa. The seaward slopes of the mountains have a Mediterranean climate and vegetation. The inland range of Anti-Lebanon has the characteristics of steppe country. There is a mixed Arabic-speaking population of Christians, Moslems and Druses.

Area and Population.—The total area of Lebanon is about 4,300 sq. miles, the population being estimated at 1,750,000 in 1963.

Production.—Fruits are the most important products and include citrus fruit, apples, bananas and olives. Industry is on a small scale, the most important industries being those connected with food and drinks (sugar refining, flour milling, confectionery, wines and beer, etc.) and the textile industry. There is little remaining of the famous cedars of Lebanon.

Railways.—A narrow-gauge railway runs from Beirut to Damascus, connecting at Rayak with a branch of the standard-gauge line which runs from Tripoli through Homs, Hama and Aleppo to the Turkish frontier, from Nusaybin to the Iraq frontier at Tel Kotchek. A standard gauge railway also runs up the coast from Nakoura on the Palestine border, through Sidon and Beirut to Tripoli, but no services were in operation south of Beirut in the summer of 1963.

Civil Aviation.—Beirut International Airport is one of the most important traffic centres in the Middle East. Numerous international air services to all parts of the world pass through it, and local services connect with all Middle Eastern capitals except Tel Aviv. There are 3 national airline companies in the Lebanon serving international as well as local routes. Of these the most important is Middle East Air Liban, which operates *Comet*, *Viscount* and *Caravelle* services.

Rivers.—The Orontes flows northwards from the Lebanon range across the northern boundary to Antioch; the Litani flows southwards from Lebanon, turns westwards round the southern extremity of the range and flows into the Mediterranean.

Archæology, etc.—Lebanon has some important historical remains, notably Baalbek (Heliopolis) which contains the ruins of I-III century Roman temples and Jubail (Biblos), one of the oldest continuously inhabited towns in the world.

Language and Literature.—Arabic is the principal language (*see* Arabia), and French is also widely used. The use of English is increasing. About 40 daily papers are published, including 3 in French, 2 in English and 4 in Armenian; and a further 30 periodicals.

Education.—There are four universities in Beirut, the American and the French (R.C.) Universities established in the last century, and the Lebanese National University and the Arab University which are recent foundations in the early stages of development. There are several institutions for vocational training and there is a good provision throughout the country of primary and secondary schools, among which are a great number of private schools.

CAPITAL.—ΨBeirut (population about 500,000). Other towns are ΨTripoli (175,000), Zahlé (40,000), ΨSidon (25,000), ΨTyre (12,000).

FINANCE

Receipts and Expenditure, 1963 (Estimated) £L425,400,000.

Currency. The monetary unit is the Lebanese £(*L*); official rate £1=£L6·13. There is also an officially recognized free market in foreign currencies, which is used for nearly all commercial transactions. The free market rate for sterling is variable, but averages about £L8·60=£1.

TRADE

Principal imports: Gold and precious metals, cereals, cotton and woollen textiles, artificial and cotton yarns, iron and steel goods, wood, pharmaceuticals, raw hides, sugar, motor-vehicles, livestock, wheat, flour, machinery, crude oil, chemicals and domestic electric appliances, and paper.

Principal exports: Gold and precious metals, citrus fruits, onions, textiles, apples and pears, scrap metal, vegetables, hides and skins, soap, butter, cereals, oilseed, cement products, wooden and steel furniture, tobacco and wines.

Trade with U.K.

	1961	1962
Imports from U.K....	£16,017,867	£11,511,978
Exports to U.K.......	1,837,183	2,946,690

There is also a considerable transit trade through Beirut, mainly in gold and crude oil. Lebanon is the terminal for two oil pipe lines, one, belonging to the Iraq Petroleum Company, debouching at Tripoli, the other belonging to the Trans-Arabian Pipeline Company, at Sidon. There are refineries at each end of the pipeline which can, to all intents and purposes, fulfil Lebanon's needs.

FLAG.—Horizontal bands of red, white and red with a green cedar of Lebanon in the centre of the white band.

BRITISH EMBASSY

Beirut

Ambassador Extraordinary and Plenipotentiary, His Excellency Sir Derek Martin Hurry Riches, K.C.M.G. (1963)........................£4,115

Counsellors, Hon. H. A. A. Hankey, C.M.G., C.V.O.; P. C. D. Archer, O.B.E. (*Labour*).

1st Secretaries, H. G. Balfour-Paul; P. N. Lunn, C.M.G.; J. M. O. Snodgrass; M. B. Eaden; E. A. McNaught; D. W. Rowley.

1st Secretary and Consul, R. G. Smedley.

Naval Attaché, Capt. P. R. C. Higham, R.N.

Military Attaché, Col. F. W. Finnigan, M.C.

Civil Air Attaché, R. S. Swann.

The British Embassy houses the Middle East Regional Information Office (*Counsellor*, G. F. N. Reddaway, M.B.E.) and the Department of Technical Co-operation (*Counsellor*, P. P. Howell, O.B.E.).

BRITISH COUNCIL

Representative, J. H. Grimes, Beit Fauzi Azar, Sharia Sidani, Beirut.

LIBERIA

(Republic of Liberia)

President, Hon. William V. S. Tubman, G.C.M.G., *elected* May 6, 1943; *installed* Jan. 1, 1944; *re-elected* in May, 1951, 1955, 1959 and 1963 *for further 4-year terms.*
Vice-President, William R. Tolbert.
Secretary of State, J. Rudolph Grimes.
Treasury, Charles D. Sherman.
Attorney-General, J. Dossen Richards (*acting*).
Postmaster-General, McKinley A. Deshield.
Defence, R. A. Brewer (*acting*).
Education, John Payne Mitchell (*acting*).
Interior, J. Samuel Melton.
Public Works and Utilities, M. A. Ketter.
Agriculture and Commerce, Stephen Tolbert.

LIBERIAN EMBASSY IN LONDON
21 Princes Gate, S.W.7
[Kensington: 9405]

Ambassador Extraordinary and Plenipotentiary, His Excellency George T. Brewer, Jr. (1959).
Consul-General, Mrs M. Reeves-Gorgla, 13 New Burlington Street, W.1.

An independent Negro Republic of Western Africa, occupying that part of the coast between Sierra Leone and the Ivory Coast, which is between the rivers Mano in the N.W. and Cavalla in the S.E., a distance of about 350 miles, with an area of about 43,000 square miles, and extending to the interior to latitude 8° 50′, a distance of 150 miles from the seaboard. It was founded by the American Colonization Society in 1822, and has been recognized since 1847 as an independent State. The population was estimated in 1961 at 1,250,000. The first national census was held in 1962.

The executive power is vested in a President elected for 4 years (8 years in the first instance) assisted by a Cabinet; there are two houses of Legislature, the Senate, with 10 members elected for six years, and the House of Representatives with 39 members elected for four years. The Army of Liberia consists of one division of 2 brigades, with a Police Constabulary Force known as the Liberian National Guard. The artificial harbour and free port of Monrovia was opened on July 26, 1948. There are 9 ports of entry, including 3 river ports.

Liberia is receiving assistance from the U.S. A.I.D. (successor to I.C.A.), particularly in the field of education, and technicians have been sent from U.S.A. to advise on various projects. UNESCO, WHO and FAO have missions in the country providing technical assistance. The U.S.A. has also made loans for the improvement of power supplies.

FINANCE	1961–62
Revenue	$36,093,262
Expenditure	41,022,000

$=U.S. Dollar.

TRADE

	1960	1961
Imports	$69,190,400	$90,667,766
Exports	82,609,200	61,906,457

Trade with U.K.

	1961	1962
Imports from U.K.	£2,928,291	£6,303,483
Exports to U.K.	2,818,608	4,228,799

The principal exports are crude rubber, iron ore, uncut diamonds, palm kernels, cocoa and coffee. Iron ore deposits have been discovered and its export is being rapidly developed. The chief imports are manufactured goods of all kinds, transport equipment and foodstuffs.

The language of the Republic is English. British weights and measures (but American dollars) are used.

CAPITAL, ΨMonrovia. Est. Pop. 70,000. Other ports are ΨBuchanan, ΨMarshall and ΨHarper (Cape Palmas).

FLAG.—Alternate horizontal stripes (5 white, 6 red), with 5-pointed white star on blue field in upper corner next to flagstaff.

BRITISH EMBASSY.
Monrovia

Ambassador Extraordinary and Plenipotentiary and Consul-General, His Excellency Malcolm Thomas Walker (1963) £3,415
1st Secretary and Consul, F. C. Hensby.

Monrovia, 3,650 miles distant; transit by English steamers from Liverpool, 11 to 20 days; also by French, Netherlands, German and U.S. vessels from Continent and U.S.A. Air France, Pan American Airways, Ghana Airways, Nigerian Airways, K.L.M., S.A.S., Ethiopian Airways and Air Liban aircraft call at Robertsfield, 50 miles from Monrovia, and Air France aircraft call at James Spriggs Payne Airfield just outside Monrovia.

LIBYA

(United Kingdom of Libya)

King, His Majesty Idris I, *born* 1890; proclaimed King of Libya, Dec. 24, 1951; sworn in March 25, 1952.

COUNCIL OF MINISTERS
(March 1963)

Prime Minister and Minister of Foreign Affairs, Muhi Al Din Fikaini.
Finance and National Economy, Mansur Qadara.
Petroleum Affairs, Wahbi Al Buri.
Planning and Development, Hamid Al Abaidi.
Interior, Wanis Al Qaddafi.
Defence, Said Al Nasr Abdul Jalil.
Industry, Muhammad Al Karaikshi.
Justice, Omar Muntasir.
Health, Ahmad Al Bishti.
Labour and Social Affairs, Mahdi Buzu.
Communications and Public Works, Muhammad Yasin Al Mabri.
Agriculture and Animal Husbandry, Hamid Abu Sraiwil.
Education, Ahmad Fuad Shenaib.
News and Guidance, Abdul Latif Shwairif.
Minister of State for Parliamentary Affairs and Conferences, Ali Al Hasumi.

LIBYAN EMBASSY IN LONDON
58 Princes Gate, S.W.7.
[Kensington: 5235[

Ambassador, His Excellency Dr. Abdussalam Busairi.
Counsellor, Hasan Bukres.
1st Secretary, Mohamed S. Sadeq.
2nd Secretary, Ali Sheneba.
Financial Secretary, Guima Turkey.
Cultural Attaché, Ahmed Ben Khayal.
Commercial Attaché, Ayad Azzabi.
Attaché, Fauzi Leguel.

Libya, on the Mediterranean coast of Africa, is bounded on the East by Egypt and the Sudan, on the South by the Republics of Chad and Niger, and on the West by Algeria and Tunisia. It consists of the three former provinces of Tripolitania, Cyrenaica and the Fezzan, with a combined area of approximately 810,000 square miles and a population estimated (1961) at 1,195,000. The people of Libya are principally Arab with some Berbers in the West and African negroes in the Fezzan, and there is a considerable Italian minority in Tripolitania. Islam is the official religion of

Libya, but all religions are tolerated. The official language is Arabic.

Vast sand and rock deserts, almost completely barren, occupy the greater part of Libya. The Southern part of the country lies within the Sahara Desert. There are no rivers and, as rainfall is precarious, a good harvest is infrequent. Agriculture is confined mainly to the coastal areas of Tripolitania and Cyrenaica, where barley, wheat, olives, almonds, citrus fruits and dates are produced, and to the areas of the oases, many of which are well supplied with springs supporting small fertile areas. Among the important oases are Ghaghbub, Gadames, Jofra, Sebha, Murzuch, Brach, Gat, Jalo, Bir Hakim and the Kufra group in the South-East. Exports from Libya include crude oil, wool, cattle, sheep and horses, esparto grass, olive oil, sponges and hides and skins. Principal imports are foodstuffs, including sugar, tea and coffee and most constructional materials and consumer goods. Twenty-two oil companies are prospecting in the country and two American companies, Esso and Oasis, have already found exploitable fields and several other companies, including British Petroleum Ltd., have had promising strikes.

Exports of crude oil officially commenced on October 25, 1962, when H.M. King Idris opened the Esso pipeline at Mersa Bregha, a newly-constructed oil terminal. The pipeline connects Esso's Zelten field with the sea some 90 miles away. The U.S. Oasis Company has also constructed a pipeline from Dahra and Mahuk in Tripolitania to the sea at Ras-es-Sidre. Further plans include a pipeline from Waha (in Cyrenaica) to Dahra (Tripolitania). Oil production in Libya amounted to approximately 300,000 barrels a day in mid-1960—exports 125,000 barrels per day. B.P. discovered oil at their concession in Southern Cyrenaica during 1962 and by mid-year tested production was over 15,000 barrels a day from 3 wells.

The ancient ruins in Cyrenaica, at Cyrene, Ptolemais (Tolmeta) and Apollonia, are outstanding, as are those at Leptis Magna near Homs, 70 miles from Tripoli and at Sabratha, 40 miles west of Tripoli. Recently an Italian expedition has found in the S.W. of the Fezzan a series of rock-paintings more than 3,000 years old which are technically in advance of any yet seen. The Museum in the Castello at Tripoli has been completely re-organized and is of great interest to visitors.

Communications in Libya are good in the coastal area, where a motor road runs from the Tunisian frontier through Tripoli to Benghazi, Tobruk and the Egyptian border, serving the needs of the main population centres. A road from the coast to Sebha, in the Fezzan, was completed in October, 1962. Elsewhere roads are poor and the transport inland is confined to caravan and occasional motor bus routes. There are airports near Tripoli (Idris el Awal) and Benghazi (Benina) regularly used by commercial airlines, and military airfields at El Adem (near Tobruk, R.A.F.), and Wheelus Field, Mellaha (near Tripoli, U.S.A.A.F.).

Government.—Libya was occupied by Italy in 1911–12 in the course of the Italo-Turkish War, and under the Treaty of Ouchy (Oct., 1912) the sovereignty of the province was transferred by Turkey to Italy. In 1939 the four Provinces of Libya (Tripoli, Misurata, Benghazi and Derna) were incorporated in the national territory of Italy as *Libia Italiana.* After the Second World War Tripolitania and Cyrenaica were placed provisionally under British and the Fezzan under French administration, and in conformity with a resolution of the General Assembly on Nov. 21, 1949, Libya became on Dec. 24, 1951, the first independent state to be created by the United Nations.

Libya has an hereditary monarchy. Government is by a two-chamber parliament. The Senate has 24 members, half of whom are nominated by the King. The House of Representatives is an elected body at present consisting of 55 members, 35 from Tripolitania, 15 from Cyrenaica and 5 from the Fezzan. Members are elected on a basis of one for every 20,000 inhabitants and elections of all members are to be held every four years. Legislation may be initiated by the King, the Senate or the House of Representatives, except laws concerning the Budget or taxation, which may not be introduced by the Senate.

Local Government.—Until the amendment of the Constitution in 1963, Libya was a Federal State, each of the three Provinces, Tripolitania, Cyrenaica and Fezzan, being administered by a Governor assisted by Executive and Legislative Councils. In April 1963, however, comprehensive unity was proclaimed and the Federal system (together with the Governors and the Executive and Legislative Councils) abolished. The country is now divided into ten divisions, each administered by a Commissioner (*Muhafidh*).

Currency.—Libya entered the Sterling Area on January 3, 1952, and a new currency was introduced on March 24, 1952. The £ Libyan is equal to the £ Sterling and is divided into 100 piastres and 1,000 millièmes. There are seven denominations of notes (£10, 5, 1, ½, and ¼, 10 piastres and 5 piastres) and five denominations of coins (1 and 2 piastres, 5, 2 and 1 millièmes).

Grants have been made by the United Kingdom, France, Italy and the United States to foster Libya's economic development and technical assistance is being provided by the United Nations and the United States.

A treaty of alliance and friendship between the United Kingdom and Libya, together with military and financial agreements, was signed at Benghazi on July 29, 1953. The United Kingdom will provide financial aid to Libya for 20 years. During the first five years £1,000,000 was paid annually for economic development, while from 1953–55 £2,750,000, in 1956 £3,000,000 and 1957 £3,250,000 was paid to the Libyan Budget. The figure for the second five-year period has been fixed at £3,250,000 for the Budget: the development aid from this source has ceased. Libya will make military facilities available to British troops (including the R.A.F.) which will be stationed in Libya under certain conditions. The United States Government is permitted under the terms of the United States–Libyan Base Rights Agreement of Oct. 30, 1954, to maintain armed forces and installations in Libya. A separate exchange of notes governs the financial assistance which the United States Government will provide for Libya's economic development during the period of this Agreement which runs until Dec. 24, 1970.

Trade with U.K.

	1961	1962
Imports from U.K....	£12,245,584	£13,528,629
Exports to U.K......	2,876,355	20,493,832

CAPITAL. Tripoli and Benghazi are the joint capitals of Libya. A new Federal capital is under construction at Beida in Cyrenaica, to which Ministers have now officially moved.

The principal towns with the latest available estimates of populations are Tripoli (170,000); Misurata (56,902); Benghazi (69,718); Homs-Cussabat (62,272); Derna (15,891); Barce (9,992); Tobruk (4,995); Sebha (7,298).

FLAG.—The Libyan National flag is a tricolour of red, black and green horizontal stripes, bearing a white crescent and star in the centre.

BRITISH EMBASSY IN LIBYA

Ambassador Extraordinary and Plenipotentiary, His Excellency Roderick Francis Gisbert Sarell, C.M.G. (1963) £4,115
Counsellor (Benghazi), R. G. Dundas, C.B.E.
1st Secretaries, Hon. I. T. M. Lucas; S. Drysdale (*Oriental*); J. McGlashan; R. McGregor (*Information*); D. R. Collard (*Commercial*).
2nd Secretary, J. D. Garner (*Commercial*).
Consul (Tripoli), D. A. R. Herridge.
Vice-Consul (Benghazi), A. J. Ward.

There are British Consular Offices at *Benghazi* and *Tripoli*.

British Council Representative, Dr. A. Craig-Bennett, O.B.E., 16 Zaviet ed Dahmani, Tripoli.

LIECHTENSTEIN

(Fürstentum Liechtenstein)

Prince, Franz Josef II., *b.* Aug. 16, 1906; *suc.* Aug. 25, 1938; *married* March 7, 1943, Countess Gina von Wilczek.

Liechtenstein is represented in diplomatic and consular matters in the United Kingdom by the Swiss Embassy, *q.v.*

A Principality on the Upper Rhine, between Vorarlberg (Austria) and Switzerland, with an area of 59·61 square miles and a population (census, Dec. 1962) of 17,800. The main industries are metal goods, cotton spinning and weaving, calculating machines, cameras, measuring instruments, coating of lenses, manufacture of vacuum apparatus, ceramics, artificial teeth and sausage casings, textiles, various apparatus, foodstuffs, leatherware and woodwork. The chief products are cotton yarn, cotton material, screws, bolts and bolt-shooting apparatus, needles, knitting machinery, ceramics, artificial teeth, precision measuring instruments, vacuum pumps, coated lenses, shoes, leather gloves, calculating machines, cameras, bed springs, conveyor belts, cooking ovens, boilers, preserves, damask cloth, socks and stockings, and furniture. Revenue (1962), *Swiss francs* 16,757,530. Expenditure (1962), *Swiss francs* 16,844,358.

Trade with U.K.

	1961	1962
Imports from U.K....	£161,836	£ 89,378
Exports to U.K.......	693,720	861,372

The language of the Principality is German.

FLAG: Blue and red (blue at the top, red at the bottom, with a gold crown in the blue part).

CAPITAL, Vaduz. Pop. (1962), 3,620.

British Consul-General, J. M. Walsh, C.M.G., O.B.E. (1962) (resides at 56 Dufourstrasse, Zürich, Switzerland). *Consul (Commercial)*, R. C. Robinson.

LUXEMBURG

(Grand-Duché de Luxembourg)

Grand Duchess, H.R.H. Charlotte, G.C.V.O., *born* Jan. 23, 1896, *succeeded* (on the abdication of her sister) Jan. 9, 1919; *married*, Nov. 6, 1919, Prince Felix of Bourbon-Parma (H.R.H. the Prince of Luxemburg, K.B.E.). *Heir Apparent* (and since May, 1961, *Lieutenant-Representative* of the Grand Duchess), The Hereditary Grand Duke (Prince Jean), *born* Jan. 5, 1921, *married*, April 9, 1953, Princess Joséphine-Charlotte of Belgium, and has issue, 3 sons and 2 daughters.
Prime Minister and Minister of Finance, M. Pierre Werner.
Deputy Prime Minister, Foreign Affairs, Defence, M. Eugène Schaus.
Labour, Social Security, Public Health, M. Emile Colling.
Public Works, Physical Education, M. Robert Schaffner.
Agriculture, Education, M. Emile Schaus.
Justice, Economic Affairs, Middle Classes, M. Paul Elvinger.
Interior, Transport, M. Pierre Grégoire.

EMBASSY AND CONSULATE
27 Wilton Crescent, S.W.1.
[Belgravia: 6961]

Ambassador Extraordinary and Plenipotentiary and Consul-General, His Excellency André J. Clasen (1955).

A Grand Duchy in Western Europe, bounded by Germany, Belgium, and France. Established as an independent State under the sovereignty of the King of the Netherlands as Grand Duke by the Congress of Vienna in 1815, it formed part of the Germanic Confederation, 1815–66, and was included in the German "Zollverein." In 1867 the Treaty of London declared it a neutral territory. On the death of the King of the Netherlands in 1890 it passed to the Duke of Nassau. The territory was invaded and overrun by the Germans at the beginning of the war in 1914, but was liberated in 1918. By the *Treaty of Versailles*, 1919, Germany renounced her former agreements with Luxemburg in respect of the customs union, etc., and in 1921 an economic union was made with Belgium (Belgolux). The Grand Duchy was again invaded and occupied by Germany on May 10, 1940. The constitution of the Grand Duchy was modified on April 28, 1948, and the stipulation of permanent neutrality was then abandoned. Luxemburg is now a fully effective member of the Western association of powers and a signatory of the Brussels and North Atlantic Treaties. She is also a member of the European Coal and Steel Community, the High Authority and Court of which have their seat in Luxemburg; of the European Economic Community and of "Euratom". Besides Belgolux, Luxemburg is also a member of the Belgium-Netherlands-Luxemburg Customs Union (Benelux).

The area is 1,000 square miles; the population (1960 census) 314,800, nearly all Roman Catholics. There is a Chamber of 52 Deputies, elected by universal adult suffrage for 5 years. Legislation is submitted to the Council of State. The Grand Duchy is rich in iron-ore and possesses an important iron and steel industry with an annual productive capacity of over 3,000,000 tons. The revenue for 1961 was estimated at *Francs* 5,763,391,000, expenditure *Francs* 5,871,955,000. The Luxemburg *franc* has at present the same value as the Belgian *franc* and the latter is legal tender in the Grand Duchy. Exchange Rate, 140 *Francs* = £1. There are approximately 260 miles of railway.

Trade with U.K.

	1961	1962
Imports from U.K....	£589,494	£751,961
Exports to U.K.......	612,390	447,769

The capital, Luxemburg, pop. (1960), 71,653, is a dismantled fortress. The country is well wooded, with many deer and wild boar. The language is Letzeburgesch but French is the official language: all speak German and many English.

FLAG.—Three horizontal bands, red, white and blue.

BRITISH EMBASSY
Luxemburg

Ambassador Extraordinary and Plenipotentiary, His Excellency Geoffrey William Aldington, C.M.G., O.B.E. (1961) £3,415
1st Secretary and Consul, F. E. B. Ide.

MADAGASCAR

(Ny Repoblika Malagasy)

President and Head of Government, M. Philibert Tsiranana (1959).
Vice-President of the Government, M. Calvin Tsiebo
Minister of Foreign Affairs, M. Albert Sylla.

MALAGASY EMBASSY IN LONDON
33 Thurloe Square, S.W.7.
[Knightsbridge: 3714]

Ambassador, His Excellency Pierre Razafy-Andriamihaingo (1961).

Area 228,000 sq. miles. Population (1962), 5,657,601. Madagascar is 240 miles distant from the S.E. coast of Africa and is the fifth largest island in the world. It became a French protectorate in 1895. In 1896 the Hova dynasty was suppressed and the administration entrusted to a Governor General. Constitutional reforms were introduced in 1957, giving the island internal autonomy and Madagascar adopted republican status on Oct., 14, 1958, while remaining within the French Community. Complete independence was proclaimed on June 26, 1960, and immediately thereafter, the President of the Republic, M. Philibert Tsiranana, signed formal agreements with the French Government confirming Madagascar's continued membership of the French Community and establishing co-operation with the French Republic on defence, monetary, judicial and educational matters, etc.

Agriculture is the mainstay of the island's economy, the principal exports in 1962 in order of value being coffee (31 per cent. of total exports), rice, vanilla, sugar, sisal, tobacco, clove, groundnuts, butter beans, raffia and pepper. Cattle raising is also an important activity. Minerals found include graphite and mica. Total exports in 1962 were *Frs. CFA* 23,285,500,000 compared with *Frs. CFA* 19,137,665,000 in 1961. The main imports in 1962 (which totalled *Frs. CFA* 30,027,800,000, compared with *Frs. CFA* 25,530,899,600 in 1961) were textiles, food products and beverages, transport equipment, chemical goods, metal products, machinery and engineering equipment, clothing and shoes, electrical appliances, petroleum products, paper and paper products.

Trade with U.K.

	1961	1962
Imports from U.K....	£506,838	£516,740
Exports to U.K.......	887,094	936,030

The average rate of exchange is *Frs. CFA* 688 = £1.

CAPITAL, Antananarivo (Tananarive) (254,271). Other towns are ΨTamative (39,627), the chief port; Fianarantsoa (36,189); ΨMajunga (34,119), the second port; Tuléar (33,850), Diego Suarez (22,887) and Antsirabe (23,129).

The former dependencies of Madagascar in the Mozambique Channel, Juan de Nova, Europa Island and Bassas da India (uninhabited), are integral parts of the French Republic and, as such, are administered by the Ministry of Overseas Territories and Departments of the French Government. The Island of Saint-Marie, off the east coast of Madagascar is recognized as a dependency of the Malgasy Republic but its inhabitants are to enjoy dual (French/Malgasy) nationality.

FLAG.—Equal horizontal bands of red (above) and green, with vertical white band by staff.

BRITISH EMBASSY
19 Rue Amiral Pierre, Tananarive
(P.O. Box 167)

Ambassador Extraordinary and Plenipotentiary, His Excellency Alan Bowes Horne.........£3,415
1st Secretary and Consul, P. P. Caruana, M.B.E.
Commercial Attaché and Vice-Consul, M. Pitchen.

There is an Honorary British Vice-Consul at *Tamatave*.

MALI

(Republic of Mali)

President, Modibo Kéita.

MALI EMBASSY
16 Lowndes Street, S.W.1
[Belgravia: 3944[

Ambassador Extraordinary and Plenipotentiary, His Excellency Gourdo Sow.

The Republic of Mali, an inland state in north-west Africa, is bounded by Mauritania in the west, by Algeria in the north, by the Republic of Niger in the east and by the Voltaic Republic, Ivory Coast and Guinea in the south. It has an area of 582,437 square miles and the population was estimated at 4,100,000 in 1961.

Formerly the French colony of Soudan, the territory elected on Nov. 24, 1958, to remain as an autonomous republic within the French Community. It associated with Senegal in the Federation of Mali which was granted full independence on June 20, 1960. The Federation was effectively dissolved on August 22 by the secession of Senegal. Dissolution of the Federation was recognized by the Sudanese Republic and the title Republic of Mali was adopted on Sept. 22, 1960. The Republic is no longer a member of the French Community. Trade with the United Kingdom in 1962 amounted to: Imports from U.K., £1,580,312; Exports £1,569,726 (Board of Trade estimates). On July 1, 1962, a Mali *franc* equal in value to the *Franc CFA* was introduced and a new State bank of issue was set up.

CAPITAL.—Bamako (110,000).

FLAG.—Vertical stripes of green (by staff), yellow and red.

BRITISH EMBASSY
Bamako

Ambassador Extraordinary and Plenipotentiary, His Excellency Charles Martin Le Quesne, C.M.G.

MAURITANIA

(Islamic Republic of Mauritania)

President and Prime Minister, Moktar Ould Daddah.

Mauritania lies on the north-west coast of Africa between Spanish Sahara and the Republic of Senegal. It is bounded on the east and south by the Republic of Mali. Area 322,340 sq. miles. The population of Mauritania was estimated at 727,000 in 1961. The Republic of Mauritania elected on November 28, 1958, to remain within the French Community as an autonomous republic. It became fully independent on Nov. 28, 1960. Mauritania's main source of potential wealth lies in rich deposits of iron ore around Fort Gouraud, in the north of the country. These are being exploited by an international company, the Société de Mines de Fer de Mauritanie, with the aid of a loan from the I.B.R.D. Exports began in June, 1963, by a new railway built to link the mine with the Mauritanian coast at Port Etienne. Exports of ore are expected to reach 4,000,000 tons annually by 1965. Mauritania imported goods to the value of £676,711 from the United Kingdom in 1962.

FLAG.—Yellow star and crescent on green ground.

CAPITAL.—Nouakchott.

British Ambassador, His Excellency John Howard Peck, C.M.G. (1962) (*Resident at Dakar*).

MEXICO

(Estados Unidos Mexicanos)

President (1958–1964), Lic. Adolfo Lopez Mateos, *assumed office*, Dec. 1, 1958.

CABINET

Minister of Interior, Lic. Gustavo Diaz Ordaz.
Foreign Affairs, Sr. Manuel Tello.
Finance, Lic. Antonio Ortiz Mena.
Communications and Transport, Ing. Walter C. Buchanan.
Public Works, Ing. Javier Barros Sierra.
Navy and Marine, Admiral Manuel Zermeno Araico.
Education, Sr. Jaime Torres Bodet.
Health and Public Welfare, Dr. José Alvarez Amezquita.
National Defence, General Augustin Olachea Aviles.
Industry and Commerce, Lic. Raul Salinas Lozano.
Labour and Social Affairs, Lic. Salomon Gonzalez Blanco Garrido.
Agriculture and Livestock, Ing. Julian Rodriguez Adame.
National Property, Lic. Eduardo Bustamante.
Hydraulic Resources, Sr. Alfredo del Mazo.
Attorney General (vacant).
Social Security, Lic. Benito Coquet.

MEXICAN EMBASSY IN LONDON
48 Belgrave Square, S.W.1
[Belgravia: 4037]

Ambassador, His Excellency Señor Lic. Don Antonio Armendariz (1961).
Counsellor, Señor Lic. Don Rubén González Sosa.
Commercial Attaché, Señor Lic. Don Julio Faesler Carlisle.
Consul, Enrique Fernandez Rivera, 48 Montrose Place, S.W.1.

Area and Population.—Mexico occupies the southern part of the continent of North America, with an extensive seaboard to both the Atlantic and Pacific Oceans, extending from 14° 33′ to 32° 43′ N. lat. and 86° 46′ to 117° 08′ W. long., and comprising one of the most varied zones in the world. It contains 29 states, 2 territories, and the federal district of Mexico, making in all 32 political divisions, covering an area of 758,000 square miles. Preliminary results of the Mexican General Census taken on June 8, 1960, showed a total population of 34,625,903; estimated (1962), 37,233,227.

The two great ranges of North America, the Sierra Nevada and Rocky Mountains, are prolonged from the north to a convergence towards the narrowing Isthmus of Tehuantepec, their course being parallel with the west and east coasts. The surface of the interior consists of an elevated plateau between the two ranges, with steep slopes both to the Pacific and Atlantic (Gulf of Mexico). In the west is the Peninsula of Lower California, with a mountainous surface, separated from the mainland by the Gulf of Lower California. The Sierra Nevada, known in Mexico as the *Sierra Madre*, terminates in a transverse series of volcanic peaks, from Colima on the west to Citlaltepetl ("El Pico de Orizaba") on the east. In February, 1943, a new volcano (*El Paricutin*) was in eruption about 250 miles from Mexico City and 20 miles from the town of Uruapan, but is no longer active. The low-lying lands of the coasts form the *Tierra Caliente*, or tropical regions (below 3,000 feet), the higher levels form the *Tierra Templada*, or temperate region (from 3,000 to 6,000 feet), and the summit of the plateau with its peaks is known as *Tierra Fria*, or cold region (above 6,000 feet). The only considerable rivers are the *Rio Grande del Norte*, which forms part of the northern boundary, and is navigable for about 70 miles from its mouth in the Gulf of Mexico, and the *Rio Grande de Santiago*, the *Rio Balsas* and *Rio Papaloapan*. The remaining streams are governed by the formation of the land, and run in mountain torrents between deep-cut cañons or "barrancas." The largest fresh-water lakes are *Chapala* (70 miles long and 20 miles wide), and *Pátzcuaro*. In the north-west are saline lakes amid bare and dry regions. The climate varies according to the altitude, the rainy season lasting from June to October.

History and Archaeology.—The present Mexico and Guatemala were once the centre of a remarkable indigenous civilization, which had unknown beginnings in the centuries before Christ, flowered in the periods from 500 to 1100 A.D. and 1300 to 1500 A.D. and collapsed before the little army of Spanish adventurers under Hernán Cortés in the years following 1519. Pre-Columbian Mexico was divided between different but connected Indian cultures, each of which has left distinctive archaeological remains: the best-known of these are Chichén Itzá, Uxmal, Bonampak and Palenque, in the States of Yucatán and Chiapas (Maya); Teotihuacán, renowned for the Pyramid of the Sun (216 feet high) in the Valley of Mexico (Teotihuacano); Monte Albán and Mitla, near Oaxaca (Zapotec); El Tajín in the State of Vera Cruz (Totonac); and Tula in the State of Hidalgo (Toltec). The last and most famous Indian culture of all, the Aztec, based on Tenochtitlán, suffered more than the others from the Spaniards and only very few Aztec monuments remain.

A few years after the Conquest, the Spaniards built Mexico City on the ruins of Tenochtitlán, and appointed a Viceroy to rule their new dominions, which they called New Spain. The country was largely converted to Christianity, and a distinctive colonial civilization, representing a marriage of Indian and Spanish traditions, developed and flourished, notably in architecture and sculpture. In 1810 a revolt began against Spanish rule. This was finally successful in 1821, when a precarious independence was proclaimed. Friction with the United States in Texas led to war from 1845–48, at the end of which Mexico was forced to cede the northern provinces of Texas, California and New Mexico. In 1862 Mexican insolvency resulted in invasion by French forces which installed Maximilian as Emperor. The empire collapsed with the execution of the Emperor in 1867 and the austere reformer, Juárez, restored the republic. Juárez's death was followed by the dictatorship of Porfirio Diaz, which saw an enormous increase of foreign, particularly British and United States, investment in the country. In 1910 began the Mexican Revolution which reformed the social structure and the land system, curbed the power of foreign companies and ushered in the independent industrial Mexico of today.

Government.—Under the Constitution of Feb. 5, 1917 (as subsequently amended), Congress consists of a Senate of 60 members, elected for six years, and of a Chamber of Deputies, at present numbering 178, elected for three years. Presidents, who wield full executive powers, are elected for six years: they cannot be re-elected.

There are five political parties registered in Mexico, of which by far the largest and most influential is the *Partido Revolucionario Institucional* (P.R.I.) which has for many years constituted the government party.

Communications.—Veracruz, Tampico and Coatzacoalcos are the chief ports on the Atlantic, and Guaymas, Mazatlán, Acapulco and Salina Cruz on the Pacific. Work is proceeding on two new ports, Matamoros on the Atlantic and Topolobampo on the Pacific. Registered merchant marine amounted at the end of 1961 to 357,195 gross tons, with 7,058 vessels (5 tons and over, 2,859; under 5 tons, 4,199). There were 23,487 kilometres of railway track open in Mexico in 1961. Work is proceeding on the reorganization, rehabilitation and re-equipment of the whole system: help in this has been forthcoming from the World Bank, the Export-Import Bank and private sources in the United States. Railway wagons are already manufactured in Mexico and it is possible that railway carriages will be manufactured before very long. Work on a track between Chihuahua and Topolobampo linking north central Mexico with the Pacific has been completed.

The total length of road at the end of 1961 was 49,309 kilometres, of which 41,957 kilometres were usable in all weathers. Mexico City may be reached by at least three excellent roads from the United States, and work is complete on roads southward from Mexico City to Yucatán and the Guatemalan border. These are already usable for all but the rainy season. The road between Durango and Mazatlán was opened in 1961.

At the end of 1961 the national telegraph system's lines were 188,327 kilometres in length. International telegraph services to the United States frontier are provided by the Government-owned Mexican Telegraph Company and then through the United States to Canada and Europe. Telephone communications are similar, with 2,864,388 km. of lines in 1961.

There is a good internal network of air services: commercial flights rose from 54,000 in 1960 to 58,000 in 1961 in the national service and fell from 16,000 to 12,000 in the foreign service. Distance covered in 1961 totalled 72,000,000 kilometres. Registered civil aircraft in 1961 numbered 773. The principal international air services are from Mexico to New York, Vancouver, Toronto, Los Angeles, Chicago, Miami, Lima, Guatemala, direct; Mexico to Houston-Montreal-Amsterdam; Mexico to Panama-Caracas; and Mexico to Miami-Paris.

Production.—The total acreage of arable land is estimated at 60,000,000 acres, though only some 25,000,000 acres are considered arable without artificial irrigation. Approximately 13,000,000 acres are under cultivation and great efforts are being made to increase this area. Grazing land is estimated at 80,000,000 acres and about 50,000,000 acres are under forest. The principal agricultural crops are maize, beans, wheat, sugar cane, coffee, cotton, tomatoes, chili, tobacco, rice, chickpeas, groundnuts, sesame, alfalfa, vanilla, cocoa and many kinds of fruit, both tropical and temperate. The maguey, or Mexican cactus yields several fermented drinks, mezcal and tequila (distilled) and pulque (undistilled). Another species of the same plant supplies sizal-hemp (herequen). The forests abound in mahogany, rosewood, ebony and chicle trees.

In 1960 there were 34,685,060 head of cattle, 4,047,239 horses, 1,549,112 mules, 2,890,539 donkeys, 5,853,233 sheep, 11,689,396 goats and 8,928,444 pigs.

The principal industries (apart from agriculture) are mining and petroleum, but during recent years there has been very considerable expansion of both light and heavy industries, 80 per cent. of all consumer goods now being made in Mexico. Most of the remaining 20 per cent. is in fact made up of bulk imports of foodstuffs and motor vehicles for assembly, so that the true figure for local manufacture of consumer goods is nearer to 92 per cent. The steel industry has expanded rapidly and produced 1,836,987 tons of steel in 1962. The mineral wealth is great, but in recent years the low world market prices have caused a slump in the mining industry. The principal minerals are gold, silver, copper, lead, zinc, quick-silver, iron and sulphur. Substantial reserves of uranium have been found. Production in 1962 amounted to (kilograms): Gold, 7,364; Silver, 1,281,796; Copper, 47,124,641; Lead, 193,297,839; and Zinc, 250,683,071.

The total petroleum reserves were said to be over 4,997 m. U.S. barrels in 1961. Total production of crude oil and natural gasoline reached 116,820,000 barrels in 1961, against 108,772,000 in 1960. During 1959 and 1960 Petroleos Mexicanos, the nationalized oil industry, received large credits from various countries for the re-equipment of the industry and the development of the petro-chemical industry.

Woollen and cotton spinning and weaving, the making of footwear and clothing and of domestic appliances of all kinds have made such progress in recent years that all these industries are protected by high import duties and import licence restrictions.

An indication of the rapid industrial expansion of Mexico is that output of electricity increased from 4,423 million kWh in 1950 to 12,507 million kWh in 1962.

Defence.—The regular army has a strength of fifty infantry battalions, one infantry brigade and a Presidential Guard of three battalions, 21 cavalry regiments, a parachute battalion and a small number of artillery and engineer units. There is also a conscript army of about 250,000 men organized into National Service divisions, each 6,000-7,000 strong. The Navy has some 36 ships of all kinds and the Air Force some 160 aircraft.

Language and Literature.—Spanish is the official language of Mexico and is spoken by about 90 per cent. of the population. About 2,500,000 inhabitants speak Indian languages, but half of these speak Spanish as well. Of those speaking indigenous languages only about 30 per cent. speak Nahuatl, 9 per cent. Maya, 8 per cent. Zapotec, 7 per cent. Otomi and 10 per cent. Mixtec, the remainder speaking other varieties of the minor linguistic families. The National Library at the capital contains about 500,000 volumes. The Press of Mexico is in a flourishing condition with many daily newspapers in the capital and in other urban centres. The first printing press and the first regularly issued newspaper in the New World were established by the Spaniards in Mexico City.

Education.—Education is divided into primary, secondary and university. Primary education is free, secular and nominally compulsory. In 1961 there were 33,233 primary schools with 5,247,282 pupils, 1,065 secondary schools with 193,314 pupils, and 847 technical and commercial secondary schools with 168,098 pupils. The National University of Mexico was founded in 1533 and reorganized in 1910. There are 34 other Universities including one exclusively for women. The prevailing religion is Roman Catholic. In 1957, only 28 per cent. of the population above 6 years old were illiterate; while progress in reducing illiteracy has been steady over the last few years, it has barely kept pace with the rapidly increasing population.

FINANCE		1963
Estimated revenue (*Budget*)...	*Pesos*	13,802,000,000
„ expenditure (*do.*)..	„	13,801,400,000
		1961
Bonded Internal Debt	„	11,783,200,000
Debts of Mexican States......	„	48,500,000
External Debt	„	257,700,000

As from April 19, 1954, by agreement with the International Monetary Fund, the Rate of Exchange has been fixed at 12·50 *pesos*=1 $U.S. (*See also* pp. 83

and 84.) Mexican gold and dollar reserves stood at $U.S.375,000,000 on March 30, 1962.

TRADE		1962
Total Imports	Pesos	14,287,500,895
Total Exports	„	12,847,572,955

Trade with U.K.

	1961	1962
Imports from U.K.	£16,114,572	£15,075,033
Exports to U.K.	6,105,189	7,154,959

The imports (mainly from U.S.A.) consist largely of machinery and implements for industry, mining and agriculture, and raw materials for industry. Principal exports are cotton, coffee, sisal (henequen), tomatoes and shrimps, lead, silver, gold, copper, zinc and other metals, tobacco, sulphur and heavy fuel oil.

CAPITAL, Mexico City, Population (Census, June 8, 1960) 4,829,402. Other towns are Guadalajara (734,346), Monterrey (600,609), Puebla (285,284), ΨMérida (177,405), San Luis Potosi (173,886), Mexicali (171,648), Chihuahua (144,653), Aguascalientes (122,809), Morelia (101,395).

FLAG.—Three vertical bands, green, white, red, with shield of Mexico in centre.

BRITISH EMBASSY

(Calle del Río Lerma 71, Colonia Cuauhtémoc, Mexico 5, D.F.)

Ambassador Extraordinary and Plenipotentiary, His Excellency Sir (Isham) Peter Garran, K.C.M.G. (1960) £4,115

Commercial Counsellor, D. H. T. Hildyard, D.F.C.

1st Secretaries, T. C. Barker (*Consul*); H. F. Bartlett (*Information*); J. D. Atkinson (*Commercial*); R. A. F. Wallis, O.B.E.

2nd Secretaries, Hon. R. E. L. Johnstone, M.V.O. (*Commercial*); A. F. Batten (*Information*).

Vice-Consuls, G. E. Rickards; R. C. Harrison.

Archivist, M. J. Copson.

There are British Consular Offices at *Mexico City, Guadalajara, Guaymas, Mazatlán, Mérida and Progreso, Monterrey, Pachuca, Tampico, Tapachula, Torreón, Veracruz*.

British Council Representative.—E. R. H. Paget, O.B.E., Calle M. Antonio Caso 127, Col. San Rafael, Mexico 4, D. F.

BRITISH CHAMBER OF COMMERCE, Plaza de la Republica 43, Mexico, D.F.—*Manager*, J. Scates.

Transit from London to Mexico City:—By sea, U.K.-New York, 5 to 10 days; New York-Mexico City, by rail, 3 days. By air, 6 hours. There is a direct freight service from Liverpool to Vera Cruz and the Pacific Coast.

MONACO

(Principauté de Monaco)

Sovereign Prince, H.S.H. Rainier III-Louis-Henri-Maxence Bertrand, *born* May 31, 1923, *succeeded his grandfather* (H.S.H. Prince Louis II), May 9, 1949; *married* April 19, 1956, Miss Grace Patricia Kelly and has issue Prince Albert Alexandre Louis Pierre, *born* March 14, 1958, and Princess Caroline Louise Marguerite, *born* January 23, 1957.

Secretary of State and Director of Prince's Household, M. Paul Noghès.

President of the National Council, M. Jean Reymond, *appointed* Aug. 16, 1963.

CONSULATE-GENERAL IN LONDON
4 Gray's Inn Square, W.C.1
[Chancery: 5323]

Consul-General, The Lord Ashcombe.
Consul, A. J. Hucker.

A small Principality on the Mediterranean, with land frontiers joining France at every point, and consisting of the old town of Monaco, La Condamine, and Monte Carlo, where is the famous casino. The Principality comprises a narrow strip of country about 2 miles long and half-a-mile broad (area approx. 360 acres), with (1956) 20,422 inhabitants (Monégasque nationals, 2,696), and a yearly average of over 650,000 visitors. The whole available ground is built over, so that there is no cultivation, though there are many public and private gardens. Monaco has a small harbour (20 ft. alongside quay), and the import duties are the same as in France. The National Council consists of 18 members and the Council of Government of the Minister of State and three State Counsellors. There is a local police force of 160 men.

A new constitution was promulgated by Prince Rainier on Dec. 17, 1962, which is subject to modification only with the approval of the elected National Council. It maintains the traditional hereditary monarchy and gives guarantees for the right of association, trade union freedom and the right to strike.

CAPITAL, Monaco-ville.

FLAG.—Red and white.

BRITISH CONSULAR OFFICE

Monaco—Consul-General, A. Hermann.

MONGOLIA

(Mongolian People's Republic)

Prime Minister, Tse Den-bal (May, 1952).

Area and Population.—Mongolia is an almost entirely unsurveyed tract in Asia, bounded by the Siberian provinces of U.S.S.R. in the north, the Chinese province of Sinkiang and the Great Wall of China in the south, by Manchuria on the east and by the Tarbagatai Mountains and the Turkestan provinces of U.S.S.R. on the west.

The total area is estimated at 1,750,000 to 2,000,000 square miles with a total population (not yet enumerated) of 3,000,000 to 5,000,000, of whom the greater number are traditionally adherents of Lamaism, a form of Buddhism.

North-West Mongolia consists of an elevated plateau bounded by the Russian Altairange (N.W.), the Sayans (N.E.), the Kentei (S.E.), and the Ektagh Altai (S.W.). The plateau contains many lakes and is watered by numerous rivers, among which are the headwaters of the Yenisei, the Irtish and the Selenga. Agriculture is almost unknown, but excellent pasture provides grazing grounds for numerous cattle and sheep, and particularly for transport animals (camels and oxen). The exports are wool, hides, skins, and gold.

The principal town of North-Western Mongolia is Ulan Bator (Ulan-Bator-Khoto, "Town of the Red Knight") which has an estimated population of 80,000 to 100,000; other centres are Uliassutai, and Kobdo, of importance as trading posts on the main caravan routes. Part of North-Western Mongolia has been incorporated in the Soviet Union as the *Tannu Tuva* autonomous Province which lies between the Sayan and Tannu Ola ranges, the capital being Kyzyl.

South-East and South Mongolia include the *Gobi* ("Desert"), or *Sha-mo* ("Sand Desert"), which covers nearly one-third of the total area, and in the extreme south-east the *Ordos* Desert, bounded on the south by the Great Wall of China, and encircled on the north by part of the main stream of the Hwangho river. Agriculture is carried on wherever Chinese influence has been exerted, but is mainly confined to the south-eastern borders. The principal industry (as in

North-West Mongolia) is sheep and cattle raising and the breeding of camels, oxen and horses for transport, in order to supply the caravan routes from China to Siberia. The centres of population depend mainly upon the overland commerce of China and Eastern Russia across the Gobi. Of recent years this trade has been organized and financed by Soviet Russia. The principal centres are: Kalgan, Kukukhoto, Kuku-erghi, Dolon-Nor and Birukhoto. In the north-east, Keru-lun (on the river of that name), is a junction of the southern routes from the Chinese province of Hopei and the western routes from Urga, in N.W. Mongolia.

Government.—In 1915 Mongolia threw off its allegiance to China, and by the Treaty of Kiakhta was recognized as an Autonomous Republic. Negotiations with Russia, after the 1917 revolution, led to an alliance, and by Treaty (May 31, 1924) the U.S.S.R. acknowledged the suveraínty of China over Outer Mongolia, but by the Russo-Chinese Treaty of Aug. 25, 1945, China recognized the complete independence of Outer Mongolia.

Diplomatic Representation.—The Government of Outer Mongolia and the British Government agreed in January, 1963, to establish diplomatic relations and exchange ambassadors. The British *Chargé d'Affaires* in China was appointed Ambassador to Outer Mongolia but continues to reside in Peking.

FLAG.—Vertical tricolour, red, blue, red and in the hoist magical symbols in gold.

MOROCCO

(Kingdom of Morocco)

King, H.M. King Hassan II, *born* July 9, 1929; *acceded* February 26, 1961, *on the death of his father*, King Mohammad V.

CHIEF MINISTERS
(June 5, 1963)

Prime Minister, Personal Representative of the King and Minister for Foreign Affairs, Haj Ahmed Balafrej.
Minister of State for African Affairs and Minister for Public Health, Abdelkrim Al Khatib.
Agriculture and Director of the Royal Cabinet, Ahmad Rida Guedira.
Interior, Ahmad Hamiani.
Finance, Driss Slaoui.
Justice, Ahmad Bahnini.
Public Works, Dr. Mohammad Benhima.
Information, Youth and Sports, Abdelhadi Boutaleb.
Education, Dr. Yusef Bel Abbes.
Commerce, Mines and Merchant Marine, Driss Debbagh.
Tourism, Fine Arts and Artisanat, Moulay Ahmad Al Alaoui.
Posts and Telegraphs, Mohammed Abdeslam Al Fassi.
Labour and Social Affairs, Abdelqadir Benjelloun.
Defence, Mahjoubi Aherdane.

MOROCCAN EMBASSY AND VICE-CONSULATE
66 Ennismore Gardens, S.W.7.
[Knightsbridge: 8827]

Ambassador, Prince Moulay Hassan Ben El Mehdi.
Secretaries, Mohamed Abderrahman El Alaoui; Abbes El Mokri.
Chancellor, Houssine Bekkali.
Vice-Consul, Mohamed Lahlou.

Area and Population.—Morocco is situated in the north-western corner of the African continent between latitude 27° 40′–36° N. and longitude 2°–11° W. with an area estimated at approximately, 180,000 sq. miles, and a population (estimated 1961) of 11,626,000. It is traversed in the north by the Riff Mountains and in a general S.W. to N.E. direction, by the Middle Atlas, the High Atlas, the Anti-Atlas and the Sarrho ranges. The northern flanks of the Middle and High Atlas Mountains are well wooded but their southern slopes, exposed to the dry desert winds, are generally arid and desolate, as are the whole of the Anti-Atlas and Sarrho ranges. The north-westerly point of Morocco is the peninsula of Ceuta which is separated from the continent of Europe by the narrow strait of Gibraltar. The Jebel Mousa dominates the promontory and, with the rocky eminence of Gibraltar, was known to the ancients as the *Pillars of Hercules*, the western gateway of the Mediterranean.

Climate.—The climate of Morocco is generally good and healthy, especially on the Atlantic coats, the country being partially sheltered by the Atlas mountains from the hot winds of the Sahara. The rainy season may last from November to April. The plains of the interior are intensely hot in summer. Average summer and winter temperatures for Rabat are 81° F. and 45° F.; for Marrakesh 101° F. and 40° F. respectively.

Government.—Under the terms of the Treaty of Fez (1912) Morocco was a French Protectorate until 1956. A Spanish "sphere of influence" extended over the northern part of the country with the exception of the Tangier Zone. The latter territory, under international administration, enjoyed a special régime involving a free monetary system and free trade, until its final integration with Morocco on April 19, 1960.

Ceuta and Melilla (*see* under Spain) are Spanish "State Territories." Ceuta, situated opposite Gibraltar, has been a Spanish possession since the close of the sixteenth century, and Melilla, further east on a rocky promontory of the Riff coast, has been a Spanish possession since 1492. The Penon (Rock) of Alhumas, Penon de Velez and the Zaffarin Islands are Spanish possessions.

Morocco became an independent sovereign state in 1956, following joint declarations made with France on March 2, 1956, and with Spain on April 7, 1956. The Sultan of Morocco, Sidi Mohammed ben Youssef, adopted the title of King Mohammed V and as Prime Minister was personally responsible for the administration until his death on Feb. 26, 1961. He was succeeded by the Crown Prince as King Hassan II.

On November 18, 1962, the King announced in a national broadcast that the Moroccan people would be called upon on December 7, 1962, to approve a draft constitution by referendum. The text was published immediately afterwards. During the referendum campaign the National Union of Popular Forces (NUPF), supported by the Moroccan Labour Union, declared they would boycott the referendum, but the referendum results showed only 15·77 per cent. abstaining, while 80·21 per cent. voted "Yes." The constitution came into force on December 14, 1962, and provides for a bi-cameral elected legislative with limited legislative powers and a considerable degree of overall control of affairs by the Monarch. It is nonetheless a considerable advance, and specific provision for amendments is written into it.

On March 20, 1963, M. Ahmad Rida Guédira, then Director of the Royal Cabinet, Minister of the Interior and of Agriculture, announced at a press conference in Casablanca the formation of a Front for the Defence of Constitutional Institutions (FDCI), which was supported by the Popular Movement led by Dr. Abdelkrim Al Khatib, by the Independent Liberals, by a number of independent personalities and, some time later, by the Constitutional Democratic Party led by M. Mohammad Hassan Al Ouezzani.

King Hassan announced on April 17 that the series of elections necessary to the establishment of the Parliamentary institutions provided for by the Constitution would begin on May 17, 1963, with an election for the Chamber of Representatives (the lower house, with 144 members). This was to be followed by elections for Chambers of Commerce and Industry, Chambers of Agriculture, Chambers of Artisans, Municipal and Communal Councils, Trade Union Representatives, and Provincial Assemblies which together are to elect indirectly the members of the Chamber of Counsellors (the upper house, whose total membership has not yet been fixed). The House of Representatives elections resulted in the election of 69 Representatives from the FDCI (of which over 50 were members of the Popular Movement), 41 from the Istiqlal Party, 28 from the NUPF, and 6 Independents. The latter afterwards declared party affiliations resulting in the FDCI being unable to form a majority Government, but over 100 results were being contested.

After some inconclusive soundings amongst the opposition after the May 17 election, the King announced the formation of a new Government on June 5, 1963, which is that listed on the previous page.

Defence.—The Moroccan army, formed in 1956, is about 40,000 strong. A Moroccan air force was also formed in 1959 and a navy in 1960. The Soviet Union agreed in November, 1960, to supply Mig 15 and 17 jet aircraft for the Moroccan air force. 14 aircraft were delivered in February, 1961. They were accompanied by a party of technicians and instructors. The Moroccan Army also received in 1962 a consignment of Russian arms. The Army already possesses quantities of French and American equipment, including aircraft.

Production and Trade.—Morocco's main sources of wealth are agricultural and mineral. The construction of dams for irrigation and for electric power is an important factor in the country's development. Its industries are in the main extractive and such as rely on local raw materials. Importance is also attached to the tourist trade.

Among agricultural, forest and animal products in sufficient quantity for export are citrus fruits, early and canned vegetables, leguminous plants, esparto, vegetable fibre, cork, skins and hides, casings, raw wool, fish (preserved and canned). Livestock in 1962 included about 14,500,000 sheep, 7,100,000 goats, 2,880,000 horned cattle and smaller numbers of donkeys, camels, horses and pigs.

Morocco's leading mineral exports are phosphates, manganese, iron ore, lead and zinc. Other minerals produced include anthracite, petroleum, cobalt, graphite, copper, molybdenum, tin, antimony, ochre and gypsum. Production of phosphates reached 8,162,000 tons in 1962 of which 7,995,000 tons were exported. There is a small oil refinery at Sidi Kacem and a new one at Mohammedia, near Casablanca, which began to operate early in 1962. Production of crude oil in 1962 amounted to 127,000 tons.

Morocco's main import requirements are petroleum products, motor vehicles and tyres, building materials, fabrics, agricultural and other machinery, chemical products, clothing, householdware, sugar, green tea and other foodstuffs.

The trade of Morocco, which is chiefly with France and the *franc* area, the U.S.A., Germany, the United Kingdom and Italy, was valued in 1962 at: Imports, £156,788,000; Exports, £125,965,000.

Trade with U.K.*

	1961	1962
Imports from U.K......	£5,047,040	£4,647,758
Exports to U.K.......	12,759,102	12,105,315

* Excluding Tangier Province

There are British Chambers of Commerce at Casablanca (101 Boulevard Mohammed el Hansali) and at Tangier (Boîte Postale 2142, Socco).

Finance and Currency.—A new unit of currency, the *dirham* (1 *DH*=*M. francs* 100) was introduced in October 1959, concurrently with the devaluation of the *M. franc* from *M. francs* 1,176=£1 to *M. francs* 1,416·8=£1. Future public accounting will be expressed in *dirhams*, the rate for which is thus: *DH* 14·168=£1.

The 1962 Ordinary Budget amounted to *DH* 2,035,000,000 and the Development Budget to *DH* 720,332,000.

Communications: Railways.—The railway runs south from Tangier to Sidi Kacem. From this junction, one line runs eastwards through Fez and Oujda to Algeria, and another continues southwards, through Rabat and Casablanca, to Marrakesh. A line running due South from Oujda skirts the Morocco-Algeria frontier and reaches Colomb-Bechar in Algeria, the beginning of the Mediterranean-Niger project. Moroccan railroads cover 1,092 miles and traction is electric or by diesel locomotives.

Roads.—In the former Southern Zone the road network is extensive (9,000 miles of road suitable for year-round traffic and some 20,000 miles of dry-season tracks). In the former Northern Zone an asphalt road links Tangier with Tetuan, branches north to Ceuta, and continues eastward through Villa San Jurjo to Mellila, and on to Oujda through Berkane. The new Route de l'Unité, connecting the road network of the former Northern Zone with the South, through Fez, was opened to traffic in 1962.

Tangier is distant from London about 1,200 miles or a matter of hours by air, 4 days by sea. There are air services between Tangier and Gibraltar connecting with B.E.A. services to London. Air-France and Royal-Air-Maroc operate internal services and many between Morocco and towns in France and Spain. There are also regular services to other European countries and to Algeria, West Africa, Equatorial Africa and the Congolese Republic.

Language.—Arabic is the official language. Berber is the vernacular mainly in the mountain regions. French and Spanish are also spoken, mainly in the towns. The European population, about 500,000 in 1954, has since been much reduced by the departure of a large part of the French community. Three Arabic, five French and one Spanish newspapers are published daily.

Education.—There are government primary, secondary and technical schools. At Fez there is a theological university of great repute in the Moslem world. There is a secular university at Rabat. Schools for special denominations, Jewish and Catholic, are permitted and may receive government grants.

CAPITAL.—ΨRabat (population 227,445). On Jan. 2, 1962, it was decreed that Tangier (141,714) would be the summer capital of Morocco, the King and the Government residing there for two months each year from 1962. Tangier was on the same date declared a "free zone" primarily for commercial purposes. The other chief towns are: ΨCasablanca (965,277); Marrakesh (243,134); Fez (216,133); Meknès (175,934); Oujda (128,645);

Tetuan (101,352). ♆Kenitra (86,000) was renamed Mina Hassan Tani (Port Hassan II) on July 9, 1962. The towns of Fez, Marrakesh and Meknès were capitals at various times in Morocco's past history.

FLAG.—Red, with green pentagram (the Seal of Solomon).

BRITISH EMBASSY

Rabat

Ambassador Extraordinary and Plenipotentiary, His Excellency Richard Ashton Beaumont, C.M.G., O.B.E. (1961) £4,115

1st Secretaries, K. M. Wilford; R. G. Giddens (*Commercial*); J. E. Morris.

2nd Secretaries, A. E. Saunders (*Oriental*); A. F. Ward.

Naval Attaché, Lt.-Cdr. L. R. Tilsley, R.N. (*resident in Gibraltar*).

Air Attaché, Wing Cdr. A. M. J. Kent (*resident in Gibraltar*).

BRITISH CONSULAR OFFICES

There are British Consular Offices at *Rabat*, *Tangier*, *Casablanca* and *Larache*.

BRITISH COUNCIL

Representative, R. J. Hilton, O.B.E., 288 Avenue Mohammed V, B.P. 427, Rabat.

MUSCAT & OMAN

(The Sultanate of Muscat and Oman)

Sultan, Said bin Taimur, *born*, Aug. 13, 1910, *succeeded his father* (as 13th of his dynasty to be Sultan of Muscat and Oman), Feb. 10, 1932.

CONSULATE IN LONDON

7, Albert Court, Kensington Gore, S.W.7

Consul, Capt. C. Kendall.

The independent State of Muscat and Oman is situated at the easterly corner of Arabia. Its seaboard is nearly 1,000 miles long and extends from near Tibat on the west coast of the Musandam Peninsula round to Ras Darbat Ali, with the exception of the stretch between Dibba and Kalba on the east coast of the peninsula which belongs to the Trucial Shaikhdom of Sharjah. Ras Darbat Ali marks the boundary between the Sultanate and the territory of the Sultan of Qishn and Socotra, a Sultanate within the Eastern Aden Protectorate. The Sultanate extends inland to the borders of the Rub'al Khali or "Empty Quarter" as the South-Eastern Arabian Desert is called. Physically, the Sultanate consists of 3 divisions, a coastal plain, a range of hills and a plateau. The coastal plain varies in width from 10 miles in the neighbourhood of Suwaiq to practically nothing in the vicinity of Matrah and Muscat towns, where the hills descend abruptly into the sea. The mountain range runs generally from north-west to south-east, reaching its greatest height in the Jebel Akhdar region where heights of over 9,000 feet occur. The hills are for the most part barren, but in the high area round Jebel Akhdar they are green and there is considerable cultivation. The plateau has an average height of 1,000 feet. With the exception of oases there is little or no cultivation. North-west of Muscat the coastal plain is known as the Batinah. It is fertile and prosperous, the date gardens extending for over 150 miles, Batinah dates (which ripen in the first half of July, well before the Basra dates) being famous for their flavour. The coast-line between Muscat and the province of Dhofar is barren and forbidding. The fertile province of Dhofar lies on the south-eastern coast of Arabia. Sugar cane is grown and cattle can be raised in this province, which is the only part of the Arabian peninsula to receive the benefit of the monsoon. Frankincense is also exported. Its principal town is Salalah on the coast, while ♆Murbat is the port. ♆*Gwadur*, situated on the Baluchistan coast, formerly belonged to the Sultanate, but was transferred to Pakistan on September 8, 1958.

The town of Muscat is the capital and seat of Government of the Sultanate of Muscat and Oman, although the Sultan himself has stayed in Salalah since 1958. Possessing a natural harbour, though exposed to the north-west wind (*Shumal*), and at one time a town of some commercial importance, it has lost most of its trade, which has been transferred to the adjacent town of Matrah. Matrah is the starting point for the trade routes into the interior. Other ports on the Gulf of Oman are Sohar, Khaburah and Sur. None, however, provides sheltered anchorage.

The area of the Sultanate has been estimated as about 82,000 square miles and the population as 550,000. The inhabitants are for the most part Arab, but there is a strong infusion of negro blood, especially along the coast. The inhabitants of the towns of Muscat (pop. 6,208) and Matrah (pop. 14,119) are mostly of Baluchi and Negro stock. The Baluchis have originally mostly migrated from Mekran and the Negroes from Zanzibar. There are few Arab residents in these two towns. In the valleys of the interior, as well as on the Batinah, date cultivation has reached a high level, and there are possibilities of agricultural development if the water supply were more certain. A Development Secretary was appointed in 1958, and under his control much progress has been made in agriculture, public health, education and roads. The inland tribes breed large numbers of camel, which are prized in Arabia for their quality. There are no industries of importance.

The only port of call for steamers is ♆Muscat (one of the ports on the mail route between Bombay and Basra). 190 vessels of all nationalities with a total tonnage of 555,168 entered the port in the foreign trade of Muscat in 1962. 120 of these were British. In addition, 14 tankers (171,101 net tons) entered Muscat to obtain medical treatment for members of their crews. The mail service between Muscat and Basra is once every two or three weeks in each direction. The G.P.O. London, operates the post office in Muscat. The postage stamps are ordinary British stamps surcharged with their value in Indian currency. Cable and Wireless, Ltd., operates the telegraph office, and an automatic telephone service in Muscat and Matrah.

Inland transport is by pack animals. The towns of Muscat and Matrah are now connected by a fairly good concrete road and the concrete road from the airfield at Bait-al-Falaj to Matrah is also complete. Outside the towns of Muscat and Matrah and the airfield there are only tracks ranging from good ones which have been cleared and graded to ravines containing large boulders or stretches of soft sand. Land Rovers and similar types of truck are the only vehicles which can be relied on. The Sultanate Development Department has completed over 500 miles of motorable tracks so far.

In December, 1951, a new treaty of friendship, to remain in force for 15 years, was signed between the United Kingdom and the Sultanate of Muscat and Oman.

FINANCE.

Annual Revenue (estimated).......... £900,000

The common medium of exchange is the Maria Theresa dollar. On the coast the Indian Gulf rupee circulates, and is the official currency of the Sultanate, although not generally in use in the interior. There are also three denominations of copper coins, twenty, ten, and five, called "baizas." The normal rate of exchange is 170 baizas = 1 M.T. dollar = Rs.3½ (approx.). The weights in use are one kiyas = the weight of six dollars or 5·9375 oz.; 24 kiyas = one Muscat maund; 10 maunds = one Farasala; 200 maunds = 1 Bahar. Rice is sold by the bag, other cereals by the following measurement: 40 Palis = one Farrah; 20 Farrahs = one Khandi.

Trade with U.K.

	1961	1962
Imports from U.K.	£1,110,401	£1,134,312
Exports to U.K.	14,684	79,652

Commerce and Trade.—Trade is mainly with India, Pakistan and the Persian Gulf States. Imports for the year 1962 amounted to £3,703,000; export figures for the same period are not available. Chief imports for the first nine months of 1962 were: rice, £462,115; wheat and wheat flour, £138,635; sugar, £69,000; cement, £37,600; pumping equipment, £70,400 (U.K., £63,000); cigarettes and tobacco, £46,943 (U.K., £43,000). (The last 2 figures are for the full year.)

CAPITAL, ΨMuscat, population (estimated), 6,208. *Muscat—British Consul-General*, J. S. R. Duncan, M.B.E.

NEJD. *See* Saudi Arabia

NEPAL

Sovereign, King Mahendra Bir Bikram Shah Deva; *succeeded*, March 13, 1955.

CABINET

(April 2, 1963)

Prime Minister, Minister of Foreign Affairs and of Palace Affairs, Dr. Tulsi Giri.
Vice-Premier, Economic Planning, Finance and Law, Surya Bahadur Thapa.
Forests and Agriculture, Bhuban Lal Pradhan.
Education, Transport and Communications, Kirtinidhi Bista.
Home Affairs and Panchayats, Khadga Bahadur Singh.
Power and Irrigation, Dr. Nageshwar Prasad Singh.
Commerce and Industries, Vedanand Jha.

ROYAL NEPALESE EMBASSY IN LONDON
12A, Kensington Palace Gardens, W.8
[Bayswater: 1594]

Ambassador, His Excellency Kali Prasad Upadhyay (1961).
1st Secretary, Bharat Raj Bhandary.
Military Attaché, Lt.-Col. S. P. Shah.
2nd Secretary, Jai Pratap Rama.

Nepal (area about 54,000 sq. miles; pop. (1961), 9,387,661) lies between India and Tibet on the slopes of the Himalayas, and includes Mt. Everest (29,002 ft.). Amid the mountains lie many fertile valleys. The lower hills and Terai Plains are covered with jungle, in which wild animals abound. Rice, wheat, maize, etc., are grown. Katmandu, the capital, is connected with India by a road, the mountain section of which was built by India under the Colombo Plan.

Nepal exports rice and other grains, hides, oilseeds, *ghi*, cattle, jute, large quantities of timber, &c., and imports cotton goods and yarn, sugar, salt, spices, petrol, metals, &c. Nepalese imports from U.K. were valued at £95,376 in 1961 and £65,542 in 1962. The revenue, realized chiefly from land rent, forests, customs, &c., is approximately £5,500,000. A State Bank was inaugurated on April 26, 1956, to issue bank notes, regulate the Nepalese currency, fix foreign exchange rates and help in the preparation of a national budget.

The inhabitants are of mixed stock with Mongolian characteristics prevailing in the north and Indian in the south, and their religions are Buddhism and Hinduism. They were originally divided into numerous hill clans and petty principalities, one of which, Gorkha or Gurkha, became predominant in 1768. During the 1914–18 and the 1939–45 wars, the Nepalese Government rendered unstinted and unconditional assistance to the British Government.

From the middle of the nineteenth century, Nepal was ruled by the Rana family which provided the hereditary prime ministers of the country. After the Second World War, a revolutionary movement in 1950 and 1951 achieved the aim of restoring to the monarchy the powers which it had lost 104 years before and of breaking the hereditary power of the Ranas. After ten years, during which various parties and individuals tried their hand at government, King Mahendra resumed direct powers on December 15, 1960, with the object of leading a united country to basic democracy. The state of emergency ended on April 13, 1963, the King having resigned the Premiership on April 2, appointing a Cabinet consisting of Dr. Giri and six other ministers. A State Council (*Raj Sabha*) of 69 members, to advise the King on state affairs, constitutional matters and on the choice of the heir to the throne was also appointed on April 2, 1963. An Act was passed at the same time maintaining the existing ban on political parties.

A new constitution, based on the Panchayat system, was introduced on April 14, 1963.

CAPITAL.—Katmandu, population (1961) 122,507.

FLAG.—Double-peaked standard of red with blue border on peaks; white moon with rays and human face in centre of top peak; white quarter sun, recumbent in centre of bottom peak.

BRITISH EMBASSY

British Ambassador, His Excellency Guy Hamilton Clarke, C.M.G. (1962) £4,115
1st Secretary, P. A. Wilde.
Military Attaché, Lt.-Col. C. G. Wylie.
Vice-Consul, Miss L. J. Corston.

British Council Representative, W. L. Clough, Adda Ghar, King's Road, Katmandu.

NETHERLANDS (or HOLLAND)
(Koninkrijk Der Nederlanden)

Queen of the Netherlands, Her Majesty JULIANA, K.G., *born* April 30, 1909; *married* January 7, 1937, Prince Bernhard of Lippe Biesterfeld, G.C.B., G.C.V.O., G.B.E. (PRINCE OF THE NETHERLANDS), *born* June 29, 1911, *succeeded*, September 4, 1948, upon the abdication of her mother Queen Wilhelmina who died Nov. 28, 1962.

(1) H.R.H. Princess Beatrix Wilhelmina Armgard, G.C.V.O., *born* Jan. 31, 1938.
(2) H.R.H. Princess Irene Emma Elizabeth, *born* Aug. 5, 1939.
(3) H.R.H. Princess Margriet Francisca, *born* (at Ottawa, Canada), Jan. 19, 1943.
(4) H.R.H. Princess Maria Christina, *born* Feb. 18, 1947.

CABINET

(July 24, 1963)

Prime Minister, V. G. M. Marijnen (*Catholic*).
Vice Premier and Minister of Agriculture and Fisheries, B. W. Biesheuvel (*Anti-Revolutionary*).
Home Affairs, E. H. Toxopeus (*Liberal*).
Foreign Affairs, J. M. A. H. Luns (*Catholic*).
Justice, Y. Scholten (*Christian Historical*).
Education, Arts and Sciences, T. H. Bot (*Catholic*).
Finance, Professor H. J. Wilteveen (*Liberal*).

Defence, P. J. S. de Jong (*Catholic*).
Economic Affairs, Professor J. E. Andriessen (*Christian Historical*).
Housing, P. C. W. M. Bogaers (*Catholic*).
Social Affairs and Public Health, G. M. J. Veldkamp (*Catholic*).
Social Welfare, Mrs. J. F. Schouwenaar (*Liberal*).
Transport and Waterways, J. van Aartsen (*Anti-Revolutionary*).

NETHERLANDS EMBASSY IN LONDON
38 Hyde Park Gate, S.W.7
[Knightsbridge: 5040]

Ambassador in London (vacant).
Minister Plenipotentiary, Baron C. W. van Boetzelaer van Asperen.
1st Secretaries, Baron R. S. N. van der Feltz; A. Mansvelt.
2nd Secretary, W. F. van Eckelen.
Naval Attaché and Naval Attaché for Air, Capt. H. A. van Oorde.
Assistant Naval Attaché and Naval Attaché for Air, Lt.-Cdr. H. J. E. van der Kop.
Air Attaché, Col. F. L. M. Focquin de Grave.
Military Attaché, Lt.-Col. J. Le Heux.
Counsellor for Press and Cultural Affairs (vacant).
1st Secretary (*Press Affairs*), B. W. N. Servatius.
Minister Plenipotentiary (*Economic Affairs*), F. J. Gerderman.
Attaché (*Commercial*), J. H. M. van den Muijsenberg.
1st Secretary (*Commercial and Financial*), P. C. Witte.
Civil Air Attaché, Dr. D. Goedhuis.
Agricultural Attaché (vacant).
Asst. Agricultural Attaché, L. W. Binkhorst.
Consular Section, 38 Hyde Park Gate, S.W.7.
Consul-General, Jhr. H. A. Teixeira de Mattos.
Consul, A. G. Jonker.

Area and Population.—The Kingdom of the Netherlands is a maritime country of Western Europe, situated on the North Sea, in lat. 50° 46′-53° 34′ N. and long. 3° 22′-7° 14′ E., consisting of 11 provinces plus the North-East Polder (reclaimed part of the Zuider Zee) and containing a total area of 34,830 sq. kms. The population on May 1, 1963 was 11,938,081. The live birth-rate in 1962 was 20·8 per 1,000 of the population, and the death-rate 7.9.

The land is generally flat and low, intersected by numerous canals and connecting rivers—in fact, a network of water courses. The principal rivers are the Rhine, Maas, and Yssel, with the mouths of the Scheldt. The chief agricultural products are potatoes, sugar beet, cattle, horses, swine, butter, wheat, rye, barley, oats, beans, peas, flax-seed, cheese, poultry, eggs, vegetables, fruit and flower bulbs and there is an important fishing industry. Among the principal industries are engineering, motors, shipbuilding, iron and steel, incandescent lamps, radio, electrical and telecommunications equipment, cotton, woollen, linen and rayon spinning and weaving, earthenware, glass, leather goods, boots and shoes, chemical and pharmaceutical products, oils, paper and board, cigars, sugar, "genever" liqueurs, beer, clothing, bicycles, tyres and rubber products. Production of coal (1962) was 11,573,000 metric tons; oil, 2,046,490 metric tons; and steel, 2,086,900 metric tons. Diamond-cutting, though still an important industry, has declined considerably in importance, now employing about 655 hands, compared with about 3,500 in 1939.

Government.—In 1815 the Netherlands became a constitutional Kingdom under King William I., a Prince of Orange-Nassau, a descendant of the house which has taken a leading part in the destiny of the nation since the 16th century. The States-General comprise the *Eerste Kamer* (First Chamber) of 75 members, elected for 6 years by the Provincial Diets: and the *Tweede Kamer* (Second Chamber) of 150 members, elected for 4 years by men and women voters of 23 years and upwards. Members of the Tweede Kamer are paid.

General elections were held on May 15, 1963, for the Second Chamber of the States-General. Party representation is: Catholic People's Party, 50; Labour Party, 43; Liberal, 16; Anti-Revolutionary, 13; Christian Historical Union, 13; Communists, 4; Pacifist Socialists, 4; Farmers' Party, 3; Reformed Political Union, 1.

The Upper House of the States General was elected by the Provincial Councils after the General Elections. Party representation is: Catholic People's Party, 26; Labour Party, 25; Liberal Party, 7; Anti-Revolutionary Party, 7; Christian Historical Union, 7; Pacifist Socialist Party, 2; Communist, 1.

Defence.—The army is a component part of the North Atlantic Treaty Organization. The Royal Netherlands Navy is being built up to a modern force of one aircraft carrier, 2 heavy cruisers, 12 modern destroyers and 6 submarines, supported by an escort force of 24 frigates and a considerable number of ancillary vessels. The Air Force, which since 1953 has been independent of the Army with the title "Royal Netherlands Air Force," has been reconstituted since the war, and now forms an integral part of the air defence of N.A.T.O. After a period of reorganization and expansion it has now attained a considerable strength consisting mainly of jet-fighters which are divided between an air defence and a tactical air command. The latter is integrated into the N.A.T.O. tactical air force.

Language and Literature.—Dutch is a West-Germanic language of Saxon origin, closely akin to Old English and Low German. It is spoken in the Netherlands and the northern part of Belgium. It is also used by many people in the Netherlands West Indies. Afrikaans, one of the two South African languages, has Dutch as its origin, but differs from it in grammar and pronunciation. There are ten national papers, four of which are morning papers, and there are many regional daily papers.

Education.—Illiteracy is practically non-existent. Primary and secondary education is given in both denominational and State schools, the denominational schools being eligible for State assistance on equal terms with the State schools. Attendance at primary school is compulsory. Secondary schools are numerous, well equipped and well attended. The principal Universities are at Amsterdam, Groningen, Leiden, Nijmegen (*R.C.*), and Utrecht, and there are technical universities at Delft (polytechnic), Rotterdam (economics), Wageningen (agriculture), Tilburg (*R.C.*) (commercial) and Eindhoven (polytechnic) (opened in Sept. 1957).

Communications.—The total extent of navigable rivers is 4,232 miles (large rivers comprising 696 miles) and of main roads approximately 4,720 miles. In December, 1962, the total length of the railway system amounted to 2,027 miles, of which 1,009 miles were electrified. The mercantile marine on July 1, 1962, consisted of 1,907 ships of total 5,166,000 gross registered tons, including vessels registered in the Netherlands Antilles and Surinam, but excluding tugs and contractors' equipment. The total length of air routes covered by K.L.M. (Royal Dutch Airlines) in the course of 1962 was 145,000 miles.

FINANCE

Budget, 1963

Current Revenue	*Fl.* 10,359,000,000
Current Expenditure	9 486,000,000
Capital Revenue	374,000,000
Capital Expenditure	2,141,000,000
Aggregate Budget Revenue	10,627,000,000
" " Expenditure	11,627,000,000
Funded Internal Debt, Feb. 28, 1963	12,837,000,000
Internal Floating Debt	5,749,000,000
Foreign Debt	766,000,000

The official rate of exchange permits of fluctuation between 9·98 and 10·20 *florins*=£1.

See also p. 83.

TRADE

During 1961, the European Economic Community, as established by the Treaty of Rome in 1957, between France, Germany, Italy and the Benelux countries, continued to reduce internal tariffs. More progress was made than had been planned in the original Treaty, with the result that duties were down by 60 per cent. by July 1, 1963. External tariffs rose correspondingly, but with practically complete liberalization, imports into the Netherlands rose in 1961. In conformity with the Treaty, the Netherlands is reducing customs duties on imports from France, West Germany and Italy. The Netherlands does not impose duties on Belgium and Luxemburg with which countries she is already in association in the Benelux Customs union.

Since the level of the Benelux tariff was below that of the other three members of the EEC, Netherlands duties on imports from countries outside the Community are in most cases being increased towards the projected final level for the Community as a whole. The Netherlands imposes very few quantitative restrictions on imports.

The rate of overall production in the Netherlands rose from 159 in 1961 to 165 in 1962 and that of production per worker rose from 138 to 142 (1953 =100).

In 1962 Dutch imports amounted to *Fl.* 19,358,077,000 and exports to *Fl.* 16,596,278,000 so that imports were covered by exports to the extent of 18·5 per cent.

Trade with U.K.

	1961	1962
Imports from U.K.	£137,561,224	£150,991,258
Exports to U.K.	172,543,227	197,497,172

SEAT OF GOVERNMENT, The Hague (Den Haag or, in full, 's-Gravenhage). Pop. (January 1, 1963, 604,112).

PRINCIPAL TOWNS, ♆ Amsterdam, 866,830; ♆ Rotterdam, 730,963; Utrecht, 261,043; Eindhoven, 174,612; Haarlem, 171,009; Groningen, 149,486; Tilburg, 141,580; Nijmegen, 136,111; Enschede, 130,256; Arnhem, 127,955; Breda, 113,193; Alpendoorn, 109,037, and Hilversum, 103,310.

FLAG.—Three horizontal bands of red, white and blue.

BRITISH EMBASSY

(Lange Voorhout, 32. The Hague)

British Ambassador Extraordinary and Plenipotentiary, His Excellency Sir Andrew Napier Noble, Bt., K.C.M.G. (1960) £5,015

Counsellor, G. A. Carey-Foster, C.M.G., D.F.C., A.F.C.

Counsellor (Commercial), E. A. Midgley, M.B.E.

Naval and Military Attaché, Capt. A. R. E. Bishop, R.N.

Air Attaché, Group-Capt. J. C. Button, D.S.O., D.F.C.

1st Secretaries, L. Sherbourne (*Commercial*); Mrs. H. de Vivenot (*Information*); A. T. Lecky.

2nd Secretaries, J. A. Edmunds (*Commercial*); J. W. D. Margetson; M. J. Wilmshurst.

Labour Attaché, R. O. Barritt.

Agricultural Attaché, J. Mellon.

BRITISH CONSULAR OFFICES

There are British Consulates-General in *Amsterdam* and *Rotterdam*, and Consular Officers at *Willemstad* and *Aruba* in the Netherlands Antilles and at *Paramaribo* in Surinam.

BRITISH COUNCIL

Representative, H. G. Wayment, 343 Keizersgracht, Amsterdam.

OVERSEAS TERRITORIES

The Netherlands West Indies comprise *Surinam* (Dutch Guiana) in South America, and certain islands in the West Indies known as the *Netherlands Antilles* (Curaçao, Bonaire, Aruba, part of St. Martin, St. Eustatius, and Saba). The area of Surinam is about 54,000 sq. miles, with a population in 1959 of about 302,372; area of Netherlands Antilles, 394·1 sq. miles, with a population of 187,041 at January 1, 1961. Under the Realm Statute which took effect on December 29, 1954, Surinam and the Netherlands Antilles received autonomy in domestic affairs, as parts of the Netherlands Realm under the Crown. Agreement on their new status was reached after prolonged negotiations between the Netherlånds Government and representatives of the territories concerned. Bauxite is an important export of Surinam.

Governor of the Netherlands Antilles, N. Debrot.

Trade with U.K.

Netherlands Antilles	1961	1962
Imports from U.K.	£5,151,609	£6,755,740
Exports to U.K.	21,983,813	21,857,951
Surinam		
Imports from U.K.	£1,514,307	£1,445,612
Exports to U.K.	91,957	155,077

The administrative capital of Surinam is Paramaribo (population, 1962, 120,000); the capital of Curaçao is ♆ Willemstad (pop. 45,000), of Aruba, ♆ Oranjestad; of Bonaire, ♆ Kralendijk; of St. Martin, Philipsburg; of Statius (St. Eustatius), Oranjestad; and of Saba, Bottom.

NICARAGUA

(República de Nicaragua)

President, Dr. René Schick Gutierrez, *elected for 4 years*, Feb. 2, 1963, *assumed office*, May 1, 1963.

Foreign Affairs, Dr. Alfonso Ortega Urbina.

NICARAGUAN EMBASSY IN LONDON

120 Roebuck House, Palace Street, S.W.1
[Victoria: 0575]

Ambassador (vacant).

Minister (Chargé d'Affaires), His Excellency Señor Don José L. Sandino (1961)

Consulate, 11 Blenheim Street, W.1.

Area and Population.—Nicaragua is the largest State of Central America, with a long seaboard on both the Atlantic and Pacific Oceans, situate between 9° 45′–15° N. lat. and 83° 40′–87° 38′ W. long., containing an area of 57,145 English square miles and a population (1963 estimate) of 1,605,000, of whom about three-quarters are of mixed blood. Another 15 per cent. are white, mostly of pure Spanish descent, and the remaining 10 per cent. are Indians or negroes. The latter group includes the

Mosquitos, who live on the Atlantic Coast and were formerly under British protection. A census of population was held in 1963.

Government.—The eastern coast of Nicaragua was touched by Columbus in 1502, and in 1519 was overrun by Spanish forces under Davila, and formed part of the Spanish Captaincy-General of Guatemala until 1821, when its independence was secured. The present constitution took effect on May 1, 1951. The President is elected by direct suffrage. Congress comprises a Senate of 16 members (together with ex-Presidents of the Republic) and a Chamber of Deputies of 42 members.

Agriculture and Industry.—The country is mainly agricultural. The major crops are coffee, cotton, sesame, sugar, rice and maize. Bananas, beans, cocoa and ipecacuanha are also important. Livestock and timber production, already considerable, are capable of unlimited expansion. Nicaragua possesses deposits of gold and silver, both of which are mined and exported by United States and Canadian concessionaires.

Communications.—There are 252 miles of railway, all on the Pacific side, 3,159 miles of telegraph and 3,721 miles of telephone and there are several powerful wireless stations and a television station at Managua. An automatic telephone system has been installed in the capital and extended to the provincial towns of León and Chinandega. Transportation, except on the Pacific slope, is still attended with difficulty but many new roads have either been opened or are under construction. The Inter-American Highway runs from the Honduras frontier in the north to the Costa Rican border in the south; the interoceanic highway, running laterally from Corinto on the Pacific coast to Rama, where there is a natural waterway to Bluefields on the Atlantic, is progressing and admits of a through passage in dry weather.

Language and Literature.—The official language of the country is Spanish. In 1963 there were 5 daily newspapers published at Managua, apart from the official Gazette (*La Gaceta*) and 2 in the provinces. Education is backward, at least 60 per cent. of the population being illiterate. There are universities at León and Managua.

FINANCE

	1960–61 *Córdobas*	1961–62 *Córdobas*
Revenue	275,237,000	284,804,000
Expenditure	274,425,000	272,104,000

Official Exchange *Córdobas* 7 = U.S. $.
London rate, C$19·60 = £1. *See also* p. 84.

TRADE

	1961	1962
Imports	U.S.$74,350,937	U.S.$100,287,884
Exports	68,356,671	87,927,894

Trade with U.K.

	1961	1962
Imports from U.K.	£981,770	£1,347,098
Exports to U.K.	885,089	1,139,133

Considerable quantities of foodstuffs are imported as well as cotton goods, jute, iron and steel, machinery and petroleum products. 49·33 per cent. of imports in 1962 were from U.S.A.; the chief exports are coffee, gold, cotton, sesame and lumber.

CAPITAL, Managua, population (1962), 241,409; León, 55,347; Granada, 36,037; Masaya, 33,445; Chinandega, 20,088; Jinotepe, 17,239; Matagalpa, 16 718; and Ψ Bluefields, 12,293. Ψ Corinto, on the Pacific, is the chief port, handling about 70 per cent. of the total trade; Bluefields and Puerto Cabezas on the E. coast are mainly concerned in the banana and timber trade to New Orleans, U.S.A.

FLAG.—Three horizontal bands, blue, white, blue (the arms of the Republic on the white band, displaying five volcanoes surmounted by a cap of liberty under a rainbow).

BRITISH EMBASSY
Managua

Ambassador Extraordinary and Plenipotentiary and Consul-General, His Excellency Roger Philip Pinsent (1963) £3,415

NIGER
(Republic of Niger)

President, Minister for Foreign Affairs and Minister of National Defence, Hamani Diori, *elected* for five years, November 9, 1960.

President, National Assembly, Boubou Hama.

President, Supreme Court, Diallo Ousmane Bassarou.

Situated in West Central Africa, between 12° and 24° N. and 0° and 16° E., Niger has common boundaries with Algeria and Libya in the north, Chad in the east, Nigeria and Dahomey in the south, and Mali and the Voltaic Republic in the west. It has an area of about 484,000 square miles with a population estimated in 1961 at 2,870,000. Apart from a small region along the Niger Valley in the south-west near the capital the country is entirely savannah or desert. The main races in Niger are the Haussas in the east, the Djermas in the south-west and the nomadic Touaregs in the north.

The first French expedition arrived in 1891 and the country was fully occupied by 1914. It decided on December 18, 1958, to remain an autonomous republic within the French Community; full independence outside the Community was proclaimed on August 3, 1960. Special agreements with France, covering financial and cultural matters, technical assistance, defence, etc., were signed in Paris on April 24, 1961.

The constitution of Niger, adopted on November 8, 1960, provides for a presidential system of government, modelled on that of the United States and the French Fifth Republic, and a single Chamber National Assembly, whose life was extended under the terms of the constitution for a further period of five years. Niger is a member of the *Conseil de l'Entente* (see Ivory Coast). The official language is French.

Finance.—The currency of Niger is the *franc CFA* (*Francs CFA* 50 = 1 *French Franc*) (*Francs CFA* 691 = £1). In 1963 the Budget balanced at *CFA* 7,127,310,000, an increase of *Francs CFA* 127,000,000 on 1962.

Trade.—The cultivation of ground nuts and the production of livestock are the main industries and provide the two main exports. There are indications of deposits of copper, uranium and iron and several companies are prospecting for petroleum. Total value of trade in 1961 was: Imports, *francs CFA* 4,653,000,000; Exports, *francs CFA* 3,824,000,000. Trade of the Republic with U.K. in 1962 was valued at: Imports, £84,464; Exports to U.K. £14,677.

CAPITAL.—Niamey (24,300).

FLAG.—Three horizontal stripes, orange, white and green with an orange disc in the middle of the white stripe.

BRITISH AMBASSADOR (*see* Ivory Coast).

NORWAY
(Norge)

King, Olav V, K.G., K.T., G.C.B., *b.* July 2, 1903; *succeeded*, Sept. 21, 1957, on death of his father King Haakon VII; *married* March 21, 1929,

Princess Märtha of Sweden (*born* March 29, 1901. *died* April 5, 1954); having issue, Harald (*see below*) and two daughters.

Heir-Apparent, H.R.H. Prince Harald, G.C.V.O., *b*. Feb. 21, 1937.

CABINET
(Sept. 25, 1963)

Prime Minister, Einar Gerhardsen.
Foreign Minister, Halvard Lange.
Defence, Gudmund Harlem.
Justice, Oscar Gundersen.
Trade, Erik Himle.
Local Affairs, Jens Haugland.
Agriculture, Leif Granli.
Fisheries, Magnus Andersen.
Finance, Andreas Cappelen.
Industries, Trygve Lie.
Communications and Transport, Trygve Brattelie.
Church and Education, Helge Sivertsen.
Prices and Incomes, Karl Trasti.
Social Affairs, Olav Gjaerevoll.
Family and Consumer Affairs, Ase Bjerkholdt.

ROYAL NORWEGIAN EMBASSY IN LONDON
Residence: 10 Palace Green, W.8
[Western: 2247]
Offices: 25 Belgrave Square, S.W.1
[Belgravia: 7151]

Ambassador in London, His Excellency Arne Skaug, G.C.V.O. (1962).
Counsellor, Egil Ulstein, D.F.C., C.V.O.
Counsellor (Press and Information), Arne Haugland.
Counsellor (Consular Affairs), Georg I. K. Thestrup.
Counsellor (Commercial, Economic and Financial), Erik Andreas Ribu.
Counsellor (Fisheries), Olaf Grönaas.
1st Secretary, Kjell Eliassen, M.V.O.
2nd Secretary, Ivar Eriksen.
Naval Attaché, Captain Eigil John Bruen, D.S.C., M.V.O.
Air and Army Attaché, Lt.-Col. Thorvald Randers, M.V.O.
Counsellor, specially attached, Herman Kristoffer Lehmkuhl, C.B.E.
Cultural Attaché, Ragnar Austad.
Press Attaché, Svenn Refshal.
Commercial Attaché, Hans B. Thomsen, 20 Pall Mall, S.W.1.
Asst. Commercial Attaché, Ole F. Knudsen; Chr. Salvesen.
Consulate, 42 Lancaster Gate, W.2.
Consul, G. F. C. Collin.
Consul, A. A. Bouston.
Vice-Consul, A. Petersen.

Area and Population.—Norway ("The Northern Way"), a kingdom in the northern and western portion of the Scandinavian peninsula, was founded in 872. It is 1,752 km. in length, its greatest width about 430 km. The length of the coastline is 2,650 km., and the frontier between Norway and the neighbouring countries is 2,555 km. (Sweden 1,643 km., Finland 716 km. and U.S.S.R. 196 km.). It is divided into 20 counties (*fylker*) and comprises an area of 323,917 sq. km. with a population (1960) of 3,604,400. In 1960 there were for every 1,000 inhabitants: 17·5 live births; 9·0 deaths; 18·7 deaths during first five years of infancy (per 1,000 live births); 6·6 marriages; 101·0 divorces.

The Norwegian coast-line is extensive, deeply indented with numerous fiords, and fringed with an immense number of rocky islands. The surface is mountainous, consisting of elevated and barren tablelands, separated by deep and narrow valleys. At the North Cape the sun does not appear to set from the second week in May to the last week in July, causing the phenomenon known as the *Midnight Sun*; conversely, there is no apparent sunrise from about Nov. 18 to Jan. 23. During the long winter nights are seen the multiple coloured *Northern Lights* or *Aurora Borealis*, which have a maximum intensity in a line crossing North America from Alaska to Labrador and Northern Europe to the Arctic coast and Siberia. A similar phenomenon occurs in the Antarctic and is known as *Aurora Australis*.

Production.—The cultivated area is about one-fortieth part of the country; forests cover nearly one-fourth; the rest consists of highland pastures or uninhabitable mountains.

The *Gulf Stream* pours from 140 to 170 million cubic feet of warm water per second into the sea around Norway and causes the temperature to be higher than the average for the latitude. It brings shoals of herring and cod into the fishing grounds and causes a warm current of air over the west coast, making it possible to cultivate potatoes and barley in latitudes which in other countries are perpetually frozen.

The chief industries are agriculture and forestry, mining, manufactures, fisheries, whaling and shipping. The most recent figures showed that 34 per cent. of the population lived on industry, 22 per cent. on agriculture and forestry, 9 per cent. on trading, 9 per cent. on transport and communications and 6 per cent. on fishery and whaling. Manufactures are aided by great resources of water power, estimated at 12,500,000 kw. at 75 per cent. efficiency, of which over 3,200,000 kw. are utilized. In normal years the quantity of fish caught by Norwegian fishing vessels is greater than that of any other European country except U.S.S.R. In 1958 the total catch amounted to 1,370,000 metric tons. Whale oil production, chiefly from pelagic whaling in the Antarctic, was 863,000 barrels in 1959.

Government.—From 1397 to 1814 Norway was united with Denmark, and from Nov. 4, 1814, with Sweden. under a personal union which was dissolved on June 7, 1905, when Norway regained complete independence. Under the constitution of May 17, 1814, the *Storting* (Parliament) itself elects one-quarter of its members to constitute the *Lagting* (Upper Chamber), the other three-quarters forming the *Odelsting* (Lower Chamber). Legislative questions alone are dealt with by both parts in separate sittings.

On April 8–9, 1940, Germany invaded Norway, and it was not until June 7, 1945, that the late King Haakon was able to return from Great Britain to Oslo.

Defence.—Norway is a member of the North Atlantic Treaty Organization, and the Headquarters of Allied Forces, Northern Europe, is situated near Oslo. Extensive reorganization of the Norwegian armed forces is in progress. In 1963 it was expected that the period of compulsory national service would be reduced to 15 months (without refresher training) in the Navy, and 12 months (with later refresher training) in the Army and Air Force. Previously the period of national service was 18 and 16 months respectively.

Education is compulsory and free between the ages of 7 and 14, schools being maintained by local taxation with State grants in aid. Secondary schools are provided by the State, by local authorities, and privately. There are many special schools and industrial and technical institutes. The University of Oslo (opened in 1811) was attended by 5,224 students and the University of Bergen (opened in 1948) by 1,000 students in 1960.

The State Institute of Technology in Trondheim possesses University status and awards degrees in engineering and architecture. In 1959 it was attended by 1,433 students.

Language and Literature.—Norwegian is one of the Scandinavian languages and is the language of the mainland and of Svalbard. Old Norse literature is among the most ancient (and the richest) in Europe. Modern Norwegian became formed in the time of the Reformation and Ludwig Holberg (1684–1754) is regarded as the founder of Norwegian literature, although modern Norwegian literature dates from the establishment of a national university at Christiania (Oslo) in 1811 and with the writings of Wergeland (1805–1845). Some of the famous names are Henrik Ibsen (1828–1906) the dramatist, Björnstjerne Björnson (1832–1910) journalist, dramatist and novelist and Nobel Prizewinner in 1903, Jonas Lie (1833–1908) novelist, Knut Hamsun (1859–1952) novelist and Nobel Prizewinner in 1920, and Sigrid Undset (1882–1949), champion of Norwegian womanhood and herself a Nobel Prizewinner in 1928. In 1958 there were 87 daily newspapers in the country with a total circulation of 1,298,000, and 90 newspapers publishing on two or three days a week with a total circulation of 335,000.

Communications.—The total length of railways open at the end of 1962 was 4,330 km., excluding private lines. The extension of the main line from Fauske to Bodö, 60 miles north of the Arctic Circle, was completed in 1962 and opened on June 7 by King Olav. The length of telegraph and telephone lines in 1960 was 88,000 km. and the number of telephones 700,000 (about 5 inhabitants per telephone). There are approximately 51,000 km. of public roads in Norway. At the end of 1961 a total of 395,767 road motor vehicles were registered, equivalent to 13·0 inhabitants per passenger car.

Civil Aviation.—Scheduled airlines are operated by Scandinavian Airlines System (SAS) on behalf of Det Norske Luftfartselskap (DNL), by Braathens South American and Far East Airtransport (SAFE), and by Wideróes Flyveselskap A.S.

Mercantile Marine.—The Mercantile Marine, March 31, 1963, consisted of 2,300 vessels of 12,767,000 gross tons (vessels above 100 gross tons, excluding fishing boats, floating whaling factories, tugs, salvage vessels, icebreakers and similar types of vessel). The fleet ranks fourth among the merchant navies of the world.

FINANCE	1962
Revenue (*Budget*)	*Kr.*7,305,000,000
Expenditure (*do.*)	6,990,000,000
National Debt (1960)	9,757,000,000

Rate of Exchange (1962, Oct.) *Kr.*20·03 = £1. *See also* p. 83.

TRADE

	1961 *Kroner*	1962 *Kroner*
Total imports	9,418,000,000	11,883,000,000
Total exports	6,207,000,000	6,957,000,000

Trade with U.K.

	1961	1962
Imports from U.K.	£85,248,738	£84,497,061
Exports to U.K.	74,812,939	66,670,961

The chief imports are raw materials, motor spirit, fuel and other oils; coal, ships and machinery: together with cereals, fruits and manufactures of silk, cotton and wool. The exports consist chiefly of fish and products of fish (as canned fish, whale oils), pulp, paper, iron ore and pyrites nitrate of lime, stone, calcium carbide, aluminium, ferroalloys, zinc, nickel, cyanamide, etc.

CAPITAL, ΨOslo (incl. Aker). Pop. (1958), 461,591. Other towns are ΨBergen 114.711, ΨTrondheim 58,915, ΨStavanger 52,848, ΨDrammen 30,704, ΨKristiansand 27,610. ΨAalesund 19,047, ΨHaugesund 26,391,* Moss 19,780.

FLAG.—Red, with white-bordered blue cross.

AIR TRANSIT FROM U.K.—London–Bergen or Oslo, 2 *hrs.* 55 *mins.*

BRITISH EMBASSY

(Drammensveien 79, Oslo; Chancery: Drammensveien 4)

Ambassador Extraordinary and Minister Plenipotentiary, His Excellency Patrick Francis Hancock, C.M.G. (1963) £4,115

Counsellor, R. A. Clinton-Thomas.

Counsellor (*Commercial*), P. J. E Male, M.C.

1st *Secretaries*, J. F. Walker, M.B.E. (*Chancery*); R. W. Bosley, O.B.E. (*Visa*); D. S. Cross (*Consular Section*).

2nd *Secretary*, J. L. W. Hobbs (*Commercial*).

Naval, Military and Air Attaché, Wing-Cdr. P. D. Bird.

Commercial Attaché, W. S. K. Millar.

Chaplain, Rev. H. Picton.

BRITISH CONSULAR OFFICES

There are British Consular Offices at *Bergen*, *Oslo* and *Tromsö*, and Honorary Vice-Consulates at *Aalesund*, *Narvik*, *Stavanger* and *Tønsberg*.

BRITISH COUNCIL

Representative, J. P. Lucas, M.C., Fridtjof Nansen Plass 5, Oslo.

SVALBARD

(*Spitsbergen and Bear Island*)

By Treaty (Feb. 3, 1920) the sovereignty of Norway over the Spitsbergen ("Pointed Mountain") Archipelago was recognized by the Great Powers and other interested nations, and on Aug. 14. 1925, the Archipelago was officially taken over by Norway. In September, 1941, Allied forces (British, Canadian and Norwegian) landed on the main island. After destruction of the accumulated stocks of coal and dismantlement of mining machinery and the wireless installation, the Norwegian inhabitants (about 600) were evacuated to a British port and the Russians (about 1,500) to the U.S.S.R. After the war the Norwegian mining plants were rebuilt. In 1956 the production of coal, the chief mineral of the archipelago, was 390,000 tons.

The Svalbard Archipelago lies between 74°–81° N. lat. and between 10°–35° E. long., with an estimated area of 24,295 square miles. The archipelago consists of a main island, known as West Spitsbergen (15,200 sq. miles); North East Land, closely adjoining and separated by Hinlopen Strait; the Wiche Islands, separated from the mainland by Olga Strait; Barents and Edge Islands, separated from the mainland by Stor Fjord (or Wybe Jansz Water); Prince Charles Foreland, to the W.; Hope Island, to the S.E.; Bear Island (68 square miles) 127 miles to the S.; with many similar islands in the neighbourhood of the main group. In addition to those engaged in coal-mining, the archipelago is also visited by hunters for seal, foxes and polar bears.

South Cape is 360 miles from the Norwegian Coast. Ice Fjord is 520 miles from Tromsö, 650 miles from Murmansk, and 1,300 miles from Aberdeen. Transit from Tromsö to Green Harbour $2\frac{1}{2}$ to 3 days; from Aberdeen 5 to 6 days.

* Boundaries extended, January 1, 1958.

JAN MAYEN, an island in the Arctic Ocean (70° 49′—71° 9′ N. lat. and 7° 53′ 9° 5′ W. long.) was joined to Norway by law of Feb. 27, 1930.

Norwegian Antarctic

BOUVET ISLAND (54° 26′ S. lat. and 3° 24′ E. long.) was declared a dependency of Norway by law of Feb. 27, 1930.

PETER THE FIRST ISLAND (68° 50′ S. lat. and 90° 35′ W. long.), was declared a dependency of Norway by resolution of Government, May 1, 1931.

PRINCESS RAGNHILD LAND (from 70° 30′ to 68° 40′ S. lat. and 24° 15′ to 33° 30′ E. long.) has been claimed as Norwegian since Feb. 17, 1931.

QUEEN MAUD LAND.—On Jan. 14, 1939, the Norwegian Government declared the area between 20° W. and 45° E., adjacent to Australian Antarctica, to be Norwegian territory.

OMAN. *See* Arabia

PANAMA

(República de Panama)

President, Dr. Roberto Chiari; *elected* May 21, 1960; *assumed office*, October 1, 1960.
Vice-Presidents, Dr. Sergio Gonzalez Ruiz; José D. Bazan.
Foreign Affairs, Dr. Galileo Solis.

EMBASSY AND CONSULATE

Ibex House, Minories, E.C.3 (*Temporary address*).
Ambassador in London (vacant).
Counsellor, Señor Elio V. Ortiz.
Attachés, Mlle. Lastenia Guillermina-Lopez; Señor Osvaldo E. Osorio.
Consul-General (London), Señora Belgica Q. de Ortiz.
Vice-Consul (London), Señorita Ann Gagliani.
Consul-General (Liverpool), Señora Carmen Lara de Paniza.

There are Consular Offices of the Republic at *Newcastle*, *Glasgow* and *Birmingham*.

Panama on the isthmus of that name which connects N. and S. America, was formerly one of the nine Departments of Colombia. After a revolt (Nov. 3, 1903) it declared its independence and established a separate Government, with a single chamber legislature elected every four years and now consisting of 53 elected members. The area of the Republic is 31,890 sq. m., the population, according to preliminary figures of the 1960 census, was 1,067,766. The birth rate in 1959 was 40·8 and the death rate 9·1 per thousand. The soil is extremely fertile, but nearly one-half of the land is uncultivated. The chief crops are bananas, coconuts, cacao, coffee and cereals. The shrimping industry plays an important rôle in the Panamanian economy. A railway 47 miles in length joins the Atlantic and Pacific oceans.

Education is compulsory and free from 7 to 15 years. In 1962–63 there were 1,321 official primary schools and 51 private primary schools; 29 official secondary and 107 private secondary schools. Primary students numbered 171,159 in 1962–63; secondary students, 42,171. There were 4,227 students at Panama University.

Language and Literature.—The official language is Spanish. There are 8 daily newspapers published in the capital, 2 of which print editions in English. There is also one English and one Spanish weekly newspaper.

FINANCE

		1963
Estimated Budget Revenue....	*Balboas*	77,202,913
Estimated Budget Expenditure .	„	77,202,913

The monetary unit is the *Balboa* (= $1 U.S.)· no Panamanian paper currency is issued, and U.S. dollar bills of all values are in circulation in the Republic and in the Canal Zone.

TRADE

	1961	1962*
Imports...........	$124,413,631	$69,938,465
Exports............	21,612,810	15,653,033

*January to June

Trade with U.K. †

	1961	1962
Imports from U.K..	£5,281,388	£4,753,652
Exports to U.K...	530,599	496,879

† Including Canal Zone.

The imports are mostly manufactured goods and foodstuffs; the exports are bananas, cacao, fresh shrimps, mahogany and cement.

CAPITAL, ΨPanama City. Population (1960), 271,425 (Panama *Province*, 369,280; Panama *District*, 292,190); Colon, 59,032 (Colon *Province*, 103,738; Colon *District*, 72,889).

FLAG.—Opposing quarters of red and blue; 2 quarters of white bearing blue star (next staff above) and red star.

Dependencies of Panama.—The Republic has a penal settlement at ΨGuardia on the Island of Coiba (or Quibo) in the Pacific and stations on the Island of Taboga. Coiba has an area of about 19 sq. miles and Taboga of about 4 sq. miles.

BRITISH EMBASSY
(120 Via España, Panama)

Ambassador Extraordinary and Plenipotentiary, His Excellency Randle Reid-Adam, C.B.E. (1963) £4,115
1st Secretary and Consul, G. L. Bullard.
2nd Secretary and Vice-Consul, Miss E. Squires.

BRITISH CONSULAR OFFICES

There are Consular Offices at *Panama City* and *Colon*.

Panama, 4,650 miles; transit from Liverpool, 15 to 19 days; from Southampton 15 days; *viâ* N.Y., 14 days.

PARAGUAY

(República del Paraguay)

President, General Alfredo Stroessner, *inaugurated* Aug. 15, 1954, *re-elected* 1958 and 1963.
Foreign Affairs, Dr. Raúl Sapena Pastor.
Finance, General Cesar Barrientos.
Interior, Dr. Edgar Ynsfrán.
Defence, General Leodegar Cabello.
Justice and Labour, Dr. Sabino A. Montanaro.
Education and Worship, Dr. Jorge B. Gorostiaga.
Public Health and Social Welfare, Dr. Dionisio Gonzales Torres.
Public Works and Communications, General Marcial Samaniego.
Agriculture and Livestock, Dr. Ezequiel González Alsina.
Industry and Commerce, Sr. José Antonio Moreno González.
Minister without Portfolio, Dr. Juan Ramón Chaves.
President of Central Bank, Dr. César Romeo Acosta.

PARAGUAYAN EMBASSY IN LONDON
51B Cornwall Gardens, S.W.7
[Western: 1253]

Ambassador in London, His Excellency Dr. Ernesto Gavilan (1963).
Consul-General, Sr. Bernardo Galeano, 29 Kensington Court, W.8.

There is also a Paraguayan Consulate in Liverpool.

Area and Population.—Paraguay is an inland subtropical State of South America, situate between Argentina, Bolivia and Brazil. The area is computed at 157,000 square miles, with an estimated population of 1,800,000.

Paraguay proper consists of a series of plains, intersected by abrupt ranges of hills, some of which reach an altitude of 2,000 to 3,000 feet above sea level. The Paraguay and Alto Paraná rivers are navigable at most seasons for vessels of 6 to 7 feet draught. Many of the tributary streams are also navigable for much of the year. The Pilcomayo river is navigable for small craft for 180 miles from Asunción. Paraguay is a country of grassy plains and dense forest, the soil being marshy in many parts and liable to floods; while the hills are covered for the most part with immense forests. The streams flowing into the Alto Paraná descend precipitously into that river. In the angle formed by the Paraná-Paraguay confluence are extensive marshes, one of which, known as "Ñeembucú," or "endless," is drained by *Lake Ypoa*, a large lagoon, south-east of the capital. The *Chaco*, lying between the rivers Paraguay and Pilcomayo and bounded on the north by Bolivia, formed the subject of a long-standing dispute with that country and led to war between Paraguay and Bolivia from 1932 to 1935. The Chaco is practically a dead level, though a slight and uniform rise westward is now known to exist; it suffers much from floods and still more from drought.

Government.—Paraguay was visited in 1527 by Sebastian Cabot, and in 1535 was settled as a Spanish possession. In 1811 Paraguay declared its independence of Spain.

The Senate was abolished under the constitution adopted in 1940 and replaced by a Council of State nominated by the government. The Chamber of Representatives comprises 60 members (Government party, 40; Opposition, 20). In 1954 women were accorded civil rights.

Production.—About three-quarters of the population are engaged in agricultural and pastoral pursuits, cattle breeding being the principal industry. In addition to canned meat, timber, quebracho extract, cotton, hides, *yerba maté*, tobacco, and *petit grain* essence (which are the principal exports), manioca, sugar, maize, rice, citrus fruits and edible oils are also produced for home consumption. Grape fruit is now exported. The production of rice, wheat and ground nuts is being encouraged by the government. The forests contain many varieties of timber, but only cedar and a few of the best known hardwoods find a market abroad.

Communications.—A railway, 985 miles in length, connects Asunción with Buenos Aires. The journey takes 55 hours. Train ferries enable the run to be accomplished without break of bulk. River steamers also connect Buenos Aires and Asunción (3 to 5 days). Direct shipping services operate regularly between Hamburg, Antwerp, Amsterdam and Asunción, and every five to six weeks between Liverpool, London and Asunción. A shipping service from New York was started early in 1955. Nine airlines operate services from Asunción. *Aerolineas Argentinas* operates a daily service between Asunción and Buenos Aires, calling at Corrientes and Rosario. *Braniff* (American) has a twice weekly service, through Asunción, from Buenos Aires to New York (calling also at Lima and La Paz). *Pan American Airways* have a weekly flight through Asunción between Buenos Aires and New York *viâ* Caracas, while their subsidiary company, *Panair do Brasil*, operates a service from Rio de Janeiro (*viâ* São Paulo and Asunción) to Santiago three times a week. *Varig/Real* (Brazilian) maintains three flights a week to Rio de Janeiro with calls at Foz do Iguazu, Curitiba and São Paulo. *Pluna* (Uruguayan) carries on a twice weekly service to Montevideo and Buenos Aires. *Lapsa* (*Lloyd Aero Paraguaya S.A.*) operates a weekly service to Curitiba, São Paulo and Rio de Janeiro, and also to Montevideo.

There are about 100 miles of asphalted roads in Paraguay, and about 600 miles of earth roads in fairly good condition, but liable to be closed or to become impassable in wet weather. Bus services connect the principal towns.

Defence.—There is a permanent military force of about 20,000 all ranks. Two gunboats and a number of small armed launches patrol inland waters.

Language and Literature.—Spanish is the official language of the country but outside the larger towns *Guaraní*, the language of the largest single unit of original Indian inhabitants, is widely spoken. Three morning and one evening newspapers are published in Asunción.

Education—Primary education is free and compulsory. There are about 300 secondary and special schools and a national university with close on 1,500 students.

FINANCE

	1961 *Guaranies*	1962 *Guaranies*
Revenue	2,842,900,000	3,424,600,000
Expenditure	2,805,400,000	3,421,600,000
External Debt	909,100,000	758,000,000
Internal Debt	469,300,000	445,200,000

Currency.—A free exchange system was introduced in August, 1957. The rate of exchange has been fairly stable at *Gs.* 347·6 = £1.

Trade.—The imports are chiefly articles of food and drink, consumer goods, textiles, vehicles and machinery. The chief articles of export are timber, tannin, cotton, hides and meat products.

Trade with U.K.

	1960	1961
Imports from U.K.	£978,104	£1,084,044
Exports to U.K.	2,298,017	2,307,176

CAPITAL, Ψ Asunción, about 1,000 miles up the River Paraguay from Buenos Aires. Pop. (estimated, 1962), 300,000; other centres being Ψ Encarnación 33,664; Concepción, 28,357; and Villarica 26,000.

FLAG.—Three horizontal bands, red, white, blue (with the Arms of the Republic on the obverse white band and the Treasury seal on the reverse white band).

BRITISH EMBASSY
(25 de Mayo 171, Asunción)

British Ambassador Extraordinary and Plenipotentiary and Consul-General, His Excellency Sir Leonard Arthur Scopes, K.C.V.O., C.M.G., O.B.E. (1962) £3,415

1st Secretary (Commercial) and Consul, C. R. Wrigley.
Naval and Military Attaché, Capt. P. E. I. Bailey, R.N.
Air Attaché, Gp.-Capt. G. F. Lerwill, D.F.C.
Labour Attaché, J. M. Carlin, D.F.C.
3rd Secretary, J. R. H. Evans.

Asunción is approximately 4,000 miles distant from London by air. Transit by sea 25 days. By air 2 days.

*PERSIA

(Keshvar-e-Shahanshahi-ye-Iran)

Shahanshah of Persia, H.I.M. Mohammed Reza Pahlevi, *born* Oct. 26, 1919; *acceded* Sept. 16, 1941 (on abdication of his father Reza Shah Pahlevi); *married* (March 15, 1939), Princess Fawzieh, sister of ex-King Farouk of Egypt (marriage dissolved Nov. 17, 1948), and has issue

* On Oct. 26, 1949, it was announced that foreigners might henceforth use the name Persia.

a daughter *born* 1940. The Shah *married* (Feb. 12, 1951) Suraya Esfandiari Bakhtiari (marriage dissolved, April 6, 1958); *married* Dec. 21, 1959, Farah Dibah (Queen Farah Pahlevi).
Heir, Prince Riza, *born* Oct. 31, 1960.

CABINET
(July, 1962)

Prime Minister, Amir Assadullah Alam.
Minister of War, Lt.-Gen. Ali Asghar Naqdi.
Ministers without Portfolio, Dr. Ghulam Husain Khusbin; Jahangir Tafazzuli; Gen. Azizi.
Foreign Affairs, Abbas Aram.
Interior, Dr. Sayyed Mehdi Pirasteh.
Finance, Abdul Husain Behnia.
P.T.T., Eng. Hushang Sami'i.
Labour, Ata'ullah Khusruvani.
Industry and Mines, Alinaqhi Alikhani.
Justice, Dr. Muhammad Baheri.
Roads, Nusratullah Mu'inian.
Agriculture, Lt.-Gen. Isma'il Riahi.
Health, Dr. Ebrahim Riahi.
Education, Dr. Parviz Natel Khanlari.

PERSIAN EMBASSY IN LONDON
26 Princes Gate, S.W.7 (Ambassador's Residence)
[Kensington: 6458]
Offices of the Embassy and Consulate:
50, Kensington Court, W.8.
[Western: 5225]
Consular Section: [Western: 6540]

Ambassador in London, His Excellency Ardeshir Zahedi (1962).
Minister, Mostafa Vassighy.
Counsellor, Dr. Abbas Nayeri.
1st Secretaries, Dr. Fereydoun Sotoudeh; Dr. Reza Hashemian; Dr. Mostafa Safavi; Seyfeddin Khalatbary.
3rd Secretaries, Parviz Safinya; Farhad Sepahbody.
Attachés, Dr. Ahmad Tehrani; Ahmad Ghaffari; Fahad Sepahbodi.
Military, Naval and Air Attaché, Col. Hossein Jahanbani.
Asst. Military, Naval and Air Attaché, Capt. Amonollah Aghevli.
Cultural Counsellor, Mas'uud Farzaad.
Assistant Cultural Counsellors, Ali Asghar Emami-Ahari; Manouchehr Mahmoudi.
Commercial Attaché, Nubar Gulbenkian.
Labour Attaché, Keighobad Zafar.
Press Attaché, Manuchehr Razmjoo.

Area and Population.—Persia comprises an area of 628,000 sq. miles, with a population estimated at 21,000,000 in January, 1962. It is mostly an arid table-land, encircled, except on the east, by mountains, the highest in the north rising to 18,700 ft. The central and eastern portion is a vast salt desert.

The Persians are mostly Shi'ah Moslems but among them are a few hundred thousand Zoroastrians, Bahais, Sunni Moslems and Armenian Christians. There is also a substantial Jewish community. Civil and Penal codes based on those of France and Switzerland are in force.

Government.—Persia was ruled from the end of the 18th century by Shahs of the Qajar Dynasty, with despotic power, subject only to the influence of interpreters of the sacred law. A nationalist movement became active in Dec., 1905, and in Aug., 1906, the Shah, Muzaffer-ud-Din, admitting the need for reforms, granted a Constitution. After the war of 1914–18, the subsequent troubles and the signature of the Soviet-Persian Treaty of 1921, a vigorous Prime Minister, Reza Khan, formerly an officer of the Persian Cossack Regiment, re-established general order. On Oct. 31, 1925, the last representative of the Qajar Dynasty, Sultan Ahmed Shah who had been absent from the country for some time, was deposed by the National Assembly, which handed over the government to the Prime Minister, Reza Khan, who was elected Shah on Dec. 13, 1925, by the Constituent Assembly, and took the title Reza Shah Pahlevi.

Owing to Nazi German penetration before and during the early part of the war of 1939–45, the Shah and his Government tended so far to favour the Axis powers that, after the German invasion of the U.S.S.R. in 1941, counter-measures became necessary; British and Soviet Forces entered the country from south and north on August 25, 1941, and expelled the agents of the Axis. On September 16, 1941, Reza Shah abdicated and left the country, nominating the Crown Prince as his successor. The Prince ascended the throne under the title of Mohammad Reza Shah Pahlevi.

Under the Anglo-Soviet-Persian Treaty of Alliance of January 29, 1942, the independence and territorial integrity of the country were guaranteed by the United Kingdom and the U.S.S.R. Evacuation by the forces of both powers was to take effect within six months of the signature of the armistice with Germany and her associates. On September 9, 1942, Persia declared war on the Axis powers and on February 28, 1945, on Japan. During the remainder of the war with Germany, Persia became one of the principal routes of aid to the Soviet Union. United States Forces, which had joined British and Soviet troops in Persia to participate in the delivery of aid to Russia, were withdrawn from the country at the end of 1945. British troops evacuated Persia, in accordance with the Anglo-Soviet-Persian agreement, by March 2, 1946, six months after the conclusion of hostilities with Japan. Soviet troops, nevertheless, remained; and when Communist disturbances took place in the north-west part of Persia known as Azerbaijan, they refused to allow Persian forces to enter the area, with the result that an autonomous government was established at Tabriz. Soviet forces, however, eventually left the country in the month of May. This belated evacuation took place in accordance with an agreement which included provision for the formation of a Perso-Soviet Oil Company to operate in the north of Persia, subsequently rejected by the Majlis, and an understanding that the question of Azerbaijan should be peaceably settled. In December, 1946, Persian Government forces entered the province, virtually unopposed by the partisans of the autonomous Government, which itself collapsed upon the flight of the revolutionary leaders into the Soviet Union.

In March, 1949, the Shah issued an Imperial Firman convoking a Constituent Assembly to make certain revisions to the Constitution and the Assembly was duly elected and convened on April 21. After this Assembly the Senate was formed for the first time.

On March 17, 1951, the Majlis adopted a Bill for the nationalization of the Persian oil industry, and on March 20, the Bill was approved by the Senate. On April 28, the Majlis agreed to a resolution, which was passed on April 30 by the Senate, recommending the immediate taking over of all installations, including those of "the late Anglo-Iranian Oil Company." On April 29 the Shah appointed Dr. Mussadiq Prime Minister. The oil company sought arbitration, but this was rejected by the Persian government, and on May 26 the British government applied to the International Court of Justice at The Hague for a declaration that this refusal to submit to arbitration was illegal. The application was not approved.

In August, 1953, after the Shah had appointed Gen. Zahedi as Prime Minister, fighting broke out between his followers and those of Dr. Mussadiq. The Shah temporarily left the country, but Gen. Zahedi's forces were successful, and Dr. Mussadiq was arrested together with a number of the members of his former Cabinet. In December, 1953, diplomatic relations with Great Britain, which Persia had broken off in October, 1952, were re-established, and in August, 1954, the oil dispute was settled by an agreement, ratified on October 29, which provided for compensation to the A.I.O.C. and for the production, refining and sale of Persian oil by a Consortium in which the A.I.O.C. have a 40 per cent. share (*Production and Industry*, below). In November, 1955, Persia joined the Baghdad Pact, later Central Treaty Organization (CENTO).

For the purposes of local government the country is divided into 11 Provinces (*Ustans*) comprising 76 Sub-Provinces (*Shahristans*), under Governors-General and Governors, respectively.

Defence.—The present strength of the Persian Army, mainly conscript, is approximately 170,000. The army, to which is attached a U.S. Advisory Mission, is well-equipped by 1939 standards and comprises 12 divisions and ancillary troops grouped under two Army headquarters with the preponderance of strength in North-West Persia. The present strength of the Air Force is approximately 10,000. It is equipped with about 120 American aircraft, including 80 jets.

The gendarmerie, to which is also attached a United States Mission, has a strength of nearly 26,000 all ranks. The Persian Navy consists of a small fleet of frigates, minesweepers and patrol boats in the Persian Gulf and some small craft in the Caspian Sea. The personnel of the Navy amounts to about 5,000 all ranks.

Education.—Since 1943 primary education has been compulsory and free. There are over 9,000 schools, 1,700,000 pupils, and also a few foreign schools in Tehran; there are Universities in Tehran and Tabriz, and University Colleges at Isfahan, Meshed and Shiraz.

Language and Literature.—Persian, or Farsi, the language of Iran, and of some other areas formerly under Persian rule, is an Indo-European tongue with many Arabic elements added; the alphabet is mainly Arabic, with writing from right to left. Among the great names in Persian literature are those of Abu'l Kásim Mansúr, or Firdausi (A.D. 939–1020), Omar Khayyám, the astronomer-poet (died A.D. 1122), Muslihu'd-Din, known as Sa-di (born A.D. 1184) and Shems-ed-Din Muhammad, or Hafiz (died A.D. 1389). The Persian Press consists of a large number of Tehran and provincial newspapers and periodicals. Two Tehran dailies and three weeklies have circulations exceeding 20,000 copies. Circulations in the provinces are very small. English and French dailies are published in Tehran.

FINANCE

	1960–61* Rials	1961–62* Rials
Revenue	82,274,000	90,432,000
Expenditure	83,177,000	93,049,000

*Estimated

The commercial rate of exchange was stabilized in 1955 as follows: Bank Melli buying rate: *Rials* 210=£1. Selling rate *Rials* 214·2=£1. The official rate of Exchange is *Rials* 210=£1; *Rials* 75=$1. (*see also* p. 84).

Production and Industry.—While petroleum is the principal product and by far the greatest export, Persia, except for its desert areas, is essentially an agricultural country and three-quarters of the inhabitants depend for their living on the land. Wheat is the principal crop, using about half the area under cultivation. Other important crops are barley, rice, cotton, sugar beet, fruits and vegetables. Wool is also produced—sheep, as well as goats, being numerous. There are extensive forests in the north and west, the conservation of which is an urgent problem. The cultivation of opium is prohibited. A certain amount of progress has been made in the development of industry. Apart from oil, the principal industrial products are carpets, textiles (mainly cotton), sugar, cement and other construction materials, ginned cotton, vegetable oil and other food products, leather and shoes, metal manufactures, matches and cigarettes. The oilfields had produced over 200,000,000 metric tons of oil from their first output to Dec. 31, 1946, and subsequent figures (in metric tons) were 1946, 19,858,471; 1947, 21,737,949; 1948, 24,871,000; 1949, 26,807,000; 1950, 35,000,000; 1951 (to Oct.) 17,000,000. Oil shipments were resumed on Oct. 30, 1954, and recent production figures have been (long tons): 1956, 25,934,000; 1957, 37,800,000; 1958, 39,800,000; 1959, 44,700,000; 1960, 51,000,000; 1961, 57,100,000; 1962, 63,461,000.

The former functions of A.I.O.C. (now renamed "British Petroleum Company") in Persia were taken over for an initial period of 25 years by a consortium of 8 oil companies (including A.I.O.C., one French, one Dutch and five U.S.), A.I.O.C. receiving from Persia £25,000,000 cash in the 10 years from Jan. 1, 1957, in compensation for its oil assets in Northern Persia and in settlement of losses since 1951; and from the other members of the consortium for their shares, about £214,000,000 payable over 20–25 years. The consortium is responsible for the production, refining and sale of Persian oil through two operating companies, while "non-basic" operations are undertaken by the National Iranian Oil Company.

Communications.—The principal roads are from the frontier of Iraq at Khusruvi to Tehran; from Tehran *viâ* Arak to Ahwaz and Khorramshahr; from Tehran *viâ* Qum, Isfahan and Shiraz to Bushire; from Tehran into Azerbaijan, through Tabriz to Julfa (on the Soviet frontier) with branch roads into Turkey and Northern Iraq; from Tehran to Meshed; three roads through the Elburz mountains to the Caspian coast and the Soviet borders east and west of the Caspian Sea; and from Isfahan, *viâ* Yezd and Kerman to Zahidan and thence to Meshed. Zahidan is connected by road with Quetta (Pakistan). Some of these roads traverse extremely difficult mountainous country; others are desert tracks. Generally speaking, Persian roads are not asphalted but gravel-surfaced, although the asphalting of main trunk routes is progressing steadily. Railways have been constructed since 1927. The *Trans-Iranian Railway*, from Bandar Shah, on the Caspian Sea, to Bandar Shahpur, on the Persian Gulf, was inaugurated in 1938; this line has a total length of 872 miles, the total cost, after eleven years' work, being approximately £30,000,000. The branch lines from Tehran to Meshed and to Tabriz have now been completed. There are also railroads from Tabriz to Julfa and from Zahidan to Mirjawa and branch lines from Ahwaz to Khorramshahr and Khorramshahr to Tanuma in Iraq (on the Shatt el Arab, opposite Basra) were opened during the war. An extension from Qum to Kashan is now in operation as is one from Bandar Shah to Gorgan.

Civil Aviation.—In May, 1946, a Department of Civil Aviation was created, subordinate to the Ministry of Roads. Progress has been made towards establishing first-class International Airports at Tehran and Abadan, with secondary airfields in accordance with ICAO standards. The

Iranian National Airlines Corporation was formed from the former *Iranian Airways* and *Persian Air Services* in February, 1962. The Company is 51 per cent. Government-owned and operates internal services and some services to the Persian Gulf states. Air France, K.L.M., S.A.S., Iraqi, M.E.A., P.A.A., Lufthansa, B.O.A.C., Alitalia and Aryana Airways operate services to Tehran.

TRADE

	1960–61	1961–62
Imports..	*Rials* 52,657,139,000	*Rials* 47,170,706,000
Exports..	8,359,875,000	9,593,450,000

These figures are calculated at the commercial rate of exchange and exclude oil exports.

Trade with U.K.

	1961	1962
Imports from U.K....	£33,568,677	£28,346,946
Exports to U.K........	48,899,776	35,329,568

The leading imports into Persia in 1961/62 were industrial and agricultural machinery, iron and steel (including manufactures), sugar, electrical machinery and goods, chemicals, and pharmaceuticals, motor vehicles, tyres and certain textile yarns and fabrics. The main exports, apart from oil, were cotton, carpets, dried fruits and nuts, hides and skins, mineral ores, wool, gums, cainar, cummin seed and animal casings. The principal countries trading with Persia were West Germany, U.S.A., U.K., U.S.S.R. and Japan.

CAPITAL: Tehran, population (1963), 1,900,000. Other large towns are Tabriz (290,000), Isfahan (254,000), Meshed (242,000), Shiraz (169,000), Resht (109,000), Kerman (62,000), Hamadan (100,000), Yezd (66,000), Kermanshah (125,000), Abadan (226,000), Ahwaz (120,000).

FLAG.—Equal horizontal bands of green, white and red; with arms (lion and sun) in centre.

BRITISH EMBASSY
Tehran

Ambassador Extraordinary and Plenipotentiary, His Excellency Sir Denis Arthur Hepworth Wright, K.C.M.G. (1962).......................£5,015
Counsellors, H. Phillips, C.M.G. (*Economic*); D. H. Clibborn (*Economic*).
1st Secretaries, B. H. C. Sykes (*Head of Chancery*); A. K. Forter, O.B.E.; I. M. Hurrell, M.V.O. (*Press*); E. N. Smith (*Commercial*); Air Vice-Marshal C. S. Moore, C.B., O.B.E. (*Technical Co-operation*); M. Kendall, M.V.O. (*H.M. Consul*).
2nd Secretaries, G. A. Morris; G. T. Winters.
3rd Secretaries, H. J. Arbuthnott; R. W. Brittain.
Naval Attaché, Capt. H. J. S. Banks, R.N.
Military Attaché, Col. S. J. Watson, M.B.E.
Air Attaché, Group Capt. J. S. Owen.

BRITISH COUNCIL

Representative, S. C. G. Bach, O.B.E., 58 Avenue Ferdowsi, Tehran.

PERU

(República del Peru)

President, Sr. Fernando Belaunde Terry, *elected* June 9, 1963, *assumed office* July 28, 1963.

COUNCIL OF MINISTERS
(July 27, 1963)

Prime Minister and Minister of the Interior, Dr. Oscar Trelles.
Finance, Javier Salazar.
Foreign Affairs, Fernando Schwalb.
Public Works, Carlos Pestana.
Labour, Miguel Cussianovich.
Public Health, Dr. Javier Arias.
Education, Francisco Miro Quesada.
Justice, Luis Deboya Reyes.
Agriculture, Enrique Torres.
War, Gen. Julio Luna Ferreccio.
Air, Lt.-Gen. Carlos Granthon.
Navy, Vice-Adm. Florencio Teixeira.

PERUVIAN EMBASSY AND CONSULATE
52, Sloane Street, S.W.1
[Belgravia: 1917/2545]

Ambassador Extraordinary and Plenipotentiary, His Excellency Señor Don Gonzalo N. de Arumburu (1962).
1st Secretary (vacant).
3rd Secretary, Señor Don Luis Solari.
Naval Attaché, Rear Admiral Carlos Monge.
Air Attaché, Maj.-Gen. C. E. Bielich.
Consul-General, Señor Don José Varela Arias.
Consul-General, Liverpool (24 Sir Thomas Street), Señor Don Guillermo Gerberding.
Vice-Consul, Señor Don Guillermo Nieto.

There are Consultates at *Hull*, *Birmingham* and *Glasgow*.

Area and Population.—Peru is a maritime Republic of South America, situated between 0° 00′ 48″ and 18° 21′ 00″ S. latitude and between 68° 39′ 27″ and 81° 20′ 13″ W. longitude. The area of the Republic including 4,440 square kilometres of the Peruvian section of Lake Titicaca and 32 square kilometres of the coastal islands, is about 531,000 square miles. The total population at the Census of July 2, 1961, was 10,364,620 (preliminary figures). In 1960 there were 376,356 births, 114,605 deaths and 43,549 marriages (final figures).

Physical Features.—The country is traversed throughout its length by the Andes, running parallel to the Pacific coast, the highest points in the Peruvian sector being *Huascaran* (22,211 feet), *Huandoy* (20,855 feet), *Ausangate* 20,235 feet), *Arequipa* (or Misti) volcano (18,364 feet), *Hualcan* (20,000 feet), *Chachani* (19,037 feet), *Antajasha* (18,020 feet), *Pichupichu* (17,724 feet), and *Mount Meiggs* (17,583 feet).

There are three main regions, the *Costa*, west of the Andes, the *Sierra* or mountain ranges of the Andes, which include the *Punas* or mountainous wastes below the region of perpetual snow and the *Montana*, or *Selva*, which is the vast area of jungle stretching from the eastern foothills of the Andes to the eastern frontiers of Peru. The coastal area, lying upon and near the Pacific, is not tropical, though close to the Equator, being cooled by the Humboldt Current; its chief products are cotton, sugar, and petroleum. It contains the capital, Lima, and most of the white population. In the mountains, where most of the Indians live, are to be found minerals in great richness and variety, and cattle, sheep, llamas and alpacas are bred there. In the mountain valleys maize, potatoes and wheat are grown. Upon the eastern slopes of the Andes are to be found very large tracts suitable for cultivation and stock raising. The main products of the jungle are timber, barbasco and leche caspi.

Government.—Peru was conquered in the early 16th century by Francisco Pizarro (born 1478, died 1541). He subjugated the Incas (the ruling caste of the Quichua Indians), who had started their rise to power some 500 years earlier, and for nearly three centuries Peru remained under Spanish rule. A revolutionary war of 1821–1824 established its independence, declared on July 28, 1821. The constitution rests upon the fundamental law of Oct. 18, 1856 (amended in 1860, 1919, 1933, 1936 and in 1939), and is that of a democratic Republic. The President is elected for six years by direct vote of the people. Congress is composed of a Senate and of a Chamber of Deputies, both Houses being elected for six years. Voting is compulsory for all Peruvian men and women between the ages of 21 and 60, for married men and women between 18 and 60 and for single men and women between the ages of 18 and 21 who are legally released from parental tutelage.

At presidential elections in July, 1962, no candidate received the necessary (one-third) proportion of the votes, but the electoral board refused to annul the election. On July 18, 1962, President Prado was arrested and all civil and political posts taken over by military personnel, led by the President of the Chiefs of Staff, Gen. Perez Godoy, who promised "clean" elections in 1963. Presidential and Congressional elections were held on June 9, 1963, and the new President, Sr. Terry, took office on July 28, Peru's day of independence.

The Congressional elections were run on a system of proportional representation. The APRA party of Sr. Haya de la Torre gained most seats in the Chamber of Deputies (57) with the alliance of Sr. Belaunde's *Acción Popular* party (39) and the Christian Democrat Party (13) having the next highest number and former-President General Odria's *Union Nacional Odriísta*, with 26, having all but five of the remainder. In the Senate, the seats are allocated to APRA—15; *Acción Popular*—14; *Union Nacional Odriista*—6; Christian Democrat—5; Peruvian Democratic Movement—2 and 3 independents.

Production.—Agriculture and mining are the principal industries, employing over 70 per cent. of the inhabitants. The chief crops in order of value are cotton, potatoes and other vegetables, sugar, fruit, maize, rice, wheat, barley, grapes and coffee. At Dec. 31, 1960, the gainfully employed population numbered 4,084,000, of whom 2,352,000 were engaged in agricultural and pastoral activities.

4,652,891 acres were under cultivation at the end of 1960 and steps are being taken to increase this area, which was probably larger in Inca times, by more intensive irrigation. Minerals produced in 1961 were valued at *soles* 6,014,037,978 and included lead, zinc, copper, iron ore, petroleum, silver, gold, tungsten, bismuth, antimony and vanadium. The islands off the Pacific coast provided guano amounting to 159,198 metric tons in 1961.

Communications.—In recent years the coastal and sierra zones have been opened up by means of roads and air routes and there is air communication, as well as communication by protracted land routes, with the tropical eastern zones, which lie east of the Andes towards the borders of Brazil, and consist mainly of unexplored or little known country inhabited by Indians in a savage state. The completion in 1944 of the trunk road of the *Andean Highway* from the Pacific port of Callao, *viâ* Lima, Oroya, Cerro de Pasco (14,700 ft.), Huanuco, Tingo Maria, to Pucallpa, the river port on the Ucayali, one of the largest tributaries of the Amazon and accessible all the year round to vessels of 3,000 tons, forms a link between the Pacific, the Amazon and the Atlantic. The trunk road runs through the *Boqueron del Padre Abad*, a pass rediscovered on July 22, 1937, in the backbone of the Blue Cordillera. The Peruvian section of the Pan American highway is complete and is asphalted throughout the major part of its length.

The first railway was opened in 1850 and of the 2,494 miles of railways now operating, Government lines account for 578 miles, the Peruvian Corporation 1,180 miles and private enterprises about 726 miles. There is also steam navigation on the eastern rivers such as the Ucayali (*see* Andean Highway, above) and Huallaga, and in the south on Lake Titicaca. Air services are maintained throughout Peru, and a number of international services call at Lima.

Defence.—The Army is recruited by voluntary enlistment, supplemented by conscription (2 years), and numbers about 30,000 of all ranks. Armoured units are equipped with American and French vehicles. Engineer units are employed on the reconstruction of roadways in North Eastern Peru using American equipment. *Navy.*—The Navy consists of 2 cruisers; 5 destroyers; 3 frigates; 4 submarines completed in the United States of America in 1954–57; 4 LST's; 7 river gunboats; 4 fleet oilers; 4 fleet auxiliaries; 2 river transports; 4 patrol boats; 4 launches; 1 floating dock; 3 tugs. There is a naval cadet school at La Punta and a submarine base at Callao. *Air Force.*—The Air Force is equipped with British Hunter and Canberra aircraft; American fighter, bomber, transport and training aircraft; French helicopters (*Alouette*) for training and rescue purposes. There are military aerodromes at Talara, Chiclayo, Las Palmas (near Lima) and Piura, and a seaplane base at Iquitos.

Education.—Elementary education is compulsory and free for both sexes between the ages of 7 and 14. In 1961 there were 1,495,047 pupils undergoing primary education, 184,849 attending ordinary secondary schools and 42,978 attending technical secondary schools. There were 13,510 state primary schools with 36,503 teachers and 450 state secondary schools with 10,900 teachers (of which 191 schools and 4,200 teachers provided technical education). In addition there were 1,350 private schools providing primary education, with 7,050 teachers, and 420 private secondary schools (of which 70 technical) with 7,490 teachers (990 technical); and 306 schools conducted by religious orders. The state provides rural agricultural schools for Indians, and mining schools and polytechnics in the more populated centres. There are now 20 universities in Peru, of which seven are private. The University of San Marcos at Lima, founded in 1551 had 1,400 students in 1962.

Language and Literature.—Spanish is the official language of the country and notably of the original Spanish stock from which the governing and professional classes are mainly recruited, but more than half the nation is composed of Indians, whose principal languages (Quichua and Aymara) are widely spoken. Before the arrival of Pizarro, the Incas had attained a high state of culture, some traces of which survived three centuries of Spanish rule. Modern Peruvian literature includes a national drama in the Spanish tongue and many Peruvian writers have attained international fame. The national library founded at Lima in 1821 was pillaged by Chileans in the Pacific War of 1879–1882, but many of the scattered manuscripts and books have since been recovered. The greater part of the historical section of the library was destroyed by fire in 1943. The first printed news-sheet in South America was issued at Lima in 1594 and in 1960 there were 5 main national daily papers, and 48 provincial ones with a small and purely local circulation. A chair of English was established in 1938 at the Universidad Mayor de San Marcos in Lima.

FINANCE

	1960 *Soles*	1961 *Soles*
Public revenue...	5,997,505,205	7,576,543,440
Public expenditure	5,519,513,709	7,326,869,679
Internal debt.....	3,468,735,198	3,454,033,481
Internal floating debt..........	670,211,609	978,874,546

Rate of Exchange (fluctuating) at April 30, 1963: *Soles* 75·16 = £1; *Soles* 26·82 = U.S. $1.00. (*See also* p. 84.)

TRADE

	1961 Soles	1962 Soles
Total imports......	12,584,137,822	14,412,601,504
Total exports......	13,306,629,778	14,478,460,194
Imports from U.S.A.	5,550,527,000	5,706,620,000
Exports to U.S.A...	4,753,629,000	4,996,440,000

Trade with U.K.

	1961	1962
Imports from U.K...	£10,505,012	£10,359,186
Exports to U.K.....	18,652,526	23,617,342

The principal imports are machinery and vehicles, foodstuffs, metal and manufactured metal goods, chemicals, and pharmaceutical products. The chief exports are cotton, sugar, lead, copper, petroleum, silver, iron ore, fish, zinc, wool and coffee.

CAPITAL, Lima. Population (Census, 1961, preliminary), 1,715,971; other large towns are Ψ Callao (161,286), Arequipa (156,657), Ψ Iquitos (55,695), Ψ Chiclayo (86,904).

FLAG.—Three vertical bands, red, white, red; coat of arms on white band.

BRITISH EMBASSY

(Offices; Edificio República, Lima; Residence: Esquina Arenales y Bermudez, Lima.)

Ambassador Extraordinary and Plenipotentiary, His Excellency Robert Hugh Kirk Marett, C.M.G., O.B.E. (1963) £4,115

1st Secretary, G. E. Hall.

Commercial Secretary, A. H. Spire.

Consul, K. C. Benton.

Naval Attaché, Capt. N. G. Hallett, D.S.C., R.N. (*Resident at Santiago*).

Air and Military Attaché, Group Capt. J. F. C. Melrose, D.F.C.

2nd Secretaries, D. J. Couvell; D. K. Urquhart (*Commercial*); D. C. Lees (*Vice-Consul*).

BRITISH CONSULAR OFFICES

There are British Consular Offices at *Lima*, *Arequipa*, *Callao*, *Iquitos*, *Trujillo* and *Mollendo*.

BRITISH COUNCIL

Representative, J. K. H. Harriman, O.B.E., Camaná 787, Lima.

Lima, 7,020 miles; transit, *viâ* New York and Colon, 21–27 days: *viâ* Liverpool and Colon, 17–30 days. Direct BOAC service Lima–London.

THE PHILIPPINES

(Repúblika ng Pilipinas)

President, Diosdado Macapagal, *b.* 1910, *elected* Nov. 14, 1961, *assumed office* Dec. 30, 1961.

Vice-President, Emmanuel Pelaez.

CABINET

Foreign Affairs (vacant).

Justice, Juan Liwag.

Finance, Rodrigo D. Perez, Jr. (*acting*).

Agriculture and Natural Resources, Benjamin Gozon.

Public Works and Communications, Brigido R. Valencia.

Education, Alejandro R. Roces.

Labour, Bernardino R. Abes (*acting*).

National Defence, Marcario Peralta, Jr.

Health, Francisco Duque.

Commerce and Industry, Rufino F. Hechanova.

Executive Secretary, Salvador L. Marino.

Economic Coordination, Manuel Cuenco.

General Services, Duma Sinsuat.

Press Secretary, Leoncio R. Paruñgao, Jr.

National Economic Council, Cornelio Balmaceda.

Chairman on Administrative Performance Efficiency, Eleuterio Adevoso.

PHILIPPINE EMBASSY AND CONSULATE

9a Palace Green, W.8

[Western: 3646]

Ambassador in London (vacant).

Consul-General, A. L. Katigbak.

Area and Population.—The Philippines are situated between 21° 20′–4° 30′ N. lat. and 116° 55′–126° 36′ E. long., and are distant about 500 miles from the south-east coast of the continent of Asia.

The total land area of the country is 114,834 square miles, of which total 106,914 square miles are contained in the eleven largest islands, the 7,079 other islands having a combined area of 7,920 square miles.

The principal islands are:—

Name	sq. miles	Name	sq. miles
Luzon.....	40,422	Mindoro.....	3,759
Mindanao..	36,538	Leyte........	2,786
Samar.....	5,050	Cebu.........	1,703
Negros....	4,906	Bohol	1,492
Palawan...	4,550	Masbate......	1,262
Panay.....	4,446		

Other groups in the Republic are the Sulu Islands (Capital, Jolo), Babuyanes and Batanes; the Catanduanes; and Culion Islands.

The population of the Philippines at the 1960 census was 27,455,199.

The inhabitants, known as Filipinos, are basically all of Malay stock, with a considerable admixture of Spanish and Chinese blood in many localities, and over 90 per cent. of them are Christians, predominantly Roman Catholics. Most of the remainder are Mohammedan Moros in the south, and Pagans, mainly in the north. There is a Chinese minority estimated at 350,000, and other much smaller foreign communities, notably Spanish, American and Indian.

Government.—The Portuguese navigator Magellan came to the Philippines in 1521 and was slain by the natives of Mactan, a small island near Cebu. In 1565 Spain undertook the conquest of the country which was named "Filipinas," after the son of the King of Spain, and in 1571 the city of Manila was founded by the conquistador Legaspi, who subdued the inhabitants of almost all the islands, their conversion from barbarism and paganism being undertaken by the Augustinian friars in Legaspi's train. In 1762 Manila was occupied by a British force, but in 1764 it was restored to Spain. In the nineteenth century there were frequent disturbances in the islands, and at the outbreak of the Spanish-American War of 1898 a rebellion under Aguinaldo, a native leader, had just died down. After the Spanish fleet had been destroyed in Manila Bay (May 1, 1898), Manila was captured by American troops with the help of Filipinos, on Aug. 13, 1898, and the Islands were ceded to the United States by the *Treaty of Paris* of Dec. 10, 1898. However, the Filipinos, under Aguinaldo, rose up in arms on Feb. 4, 1899, against the U.S. Government, maintaining a desultory rebellion until it was quelled in 1902. Following this, the Philippine Commission was established, consisting of a Governor-General and Commissioner appointed by the President of the United States, who exercised a large measure of executive and legislative authority.

A measure of local independence was granted under the Jones Act of August 29, 1916. On March 24, 1934, the Tydings-McDuffie Law, gave the Philippines a "Commonwealth" Status. The Republic of the Philippines came into existence on July 4, 1946. The Constitution provides for a President elected for a term of four years, and a bi-cameral Congress, consisting of a Senate composed of 24 senators and a House of Representatives of not more than 120 members. No person may serve as President for more than eight consecutive years. The term of office of Senators is six years and of Representatives four years.

Language and Literature.—The official languages are English, Spanish and the National language (of Malay origin) Tagalog. A majority of the people read or understand English, which is the language of instruction. The literacy rate is estimated at 75 per cent. There is a National library in the capital with branches in other urban centres, and a flourishing English press. Education accounts for about a quarter of local expenditure in the national budget. Secondary and higher education is extensive. There are 24 private universities recognized by the Government, including the Dominican University of Santo Tomas (founded in 1611), the first in the Far East and 25 years older than Harvard; there is also the State-supported University of the Philippines at Manila (1908).

Roads and Railways.—Communications suffered serious damage during the War of 1941–45 owing to the lack of proper maintenance during the Japanese occupation and destruction by bombardment. The highway system of approximately 22,747 miles of roads and streets is undergoing rehabilitation and extension. Before the war the railways, which were largely Government owned, operated approximately 845 miles of track of which some 832 miles were in operation in 1960. Rolling stock losses were also heavy, but have been largely made up, and the Manila railway, on Luzon island, has been converted to diesel traction.

Shipping.—The ports of entry are Manila, Cebu, Iloilo, Zamboanga, Davao, Jolo, Legaspi, Aparri, José Panganiban, San Fernando La Union and Tacloban. There are nearly 2,000 vessels of various types, totalling over 130,000 tons, engaged in coastwise and river traffic.

Civil Aviation.—Air transport plays a key part in inter-island travel and an important one in communications overseas. Philippine Air Lines (54 per cent. Government-owned) operate a comprehensive air service between the islands, run regular flights to Hong Kong and operate two trans-Pacific flights a week to San Francisco.

FINANCE

	1964
Estimated Receipts	P.2,164,561,560
Estimated Expenditure	2,159,832,940

P.=Philippine *Peso*=50 cents U.S. The *Peso* was decontrolled on Jan. 21, 1962. Rate of exchange for imports is P.3·82=U.S.$1; exports P.3.43=U.S.$1. (*See also* p. 84).

TRADE

	1961	1962
Total Imports	P.1,244,347,430	P.2,267,708,528
Total Exports	1,071,876,738	1,990,348,885

Trade with U.K.

	1961	1962
Imports from U.K.	£9,269,936	£9,553,061
Exports to U.K.	4,004,468	3,016,414

The Philippines is a predominantly agricultural country, the chief products being rice, coconuts, maize, sugar-cane, abaca (manila hemp), fruits, tobacco and lumber. There is, however, an increasing number of manufacturing industries and it is the policy of the Government to diversify its economy.

The principal Philippine exports in both natural and manufactured states are coconuts, sugar, abaca, base metals, lumber, pineapples, embroideries and tobacco.

CAPITAL.—ΨManila, in the island of Luzon: population (1960), including the separately administered but integral areas of Quezon City and Pasay City, 3,006,627. Quezon City has been designated as the future capital of the Philippines, but pending completion of government building projects, the Executive, Legislative and Judicial departments of the government are still located in Manila. The next largest cities are ΨCebu (259,194), Davao (231,833), ΨIloilo (150,976), ΨZamboanga (131,411) and Bacolod (119,169).

FLAG.—Equal horizontal bands of blue (above) and red; gold sun with three stars on a white triangle next staff.

BRITISH EMBASSY
Manila

British Ambassador Extraordinary and Plenipotentiary, His Excellency John Mansfield Addis, C.M.G. (1963) £4,115

CONSULAR OFFICES

There are honorary British Vice-Consuls at *Cebu*, *Davao*, and *Iloilo-Bacolod*.

POLAND

(Polska Rzeczpospolita Ludowa)

COUNCIL OF STATE

Chairman, Aleksander Zawadzki.
Deputy Chairman, S. Kulczynski; O. Lange; B. Podedworny; E. Ochab.
Secretary, J. Horodecki.

COUNCIL OF MINISTERS

Chairman, Josef Cyrankiewicz.
Vice-Chairmen, S. Ignar; P. Jaroszewicz; Z. Nowak; E. Szyr; J. Tokarski.
Foreign Affairs, Adam Rapacki.
Finance, J. Albrecht.
Agriculture, M. Jagielski.
Mining and Electric Power, Jan Mitrega.
Light Industry, Eugeniusz Stawinski.
Foreign Trade, W. Trampczynski.
Communal Economy, S. Sroka.
Internal Trade, M. Lesz.
Shipping, S. Darski.
Justice, M. Rybicki.
Education, W. Tulodziecki.
Transport, J. Popielas.
Communications, Zygmunt Moskwa.
Forestry, R. Gesing.
Health, M. Sztachelski.
Culture and Arts, Tadeusz Galinski.
Higher Education, Henryck Golanski.
Internal Affairs, Wladyslaw Wicha.
Heavy Industry, F. Waniolka.
Chemical Industry, A. Radlinski.
Food and Purchases, E. Pisula.
Building and Building Materials, M. Olewinski.
National Defence, M. Spychalski.
Health and Social Welfare, J. Sztachelski.
Chairman of Planning Commission, S. Jedrychowski.

POLISH EMBASSY IN LONDON
47 Portland Place, W.1
[Langham: 4324]

Ambassador in London, His Excellency Dr. Witold Rodzinski (1960).
Counsellor, Bohdan Tomorowicz.
1st Secretary, Stanislaw Kostarski.
2nd Secretaries, Stanislaw Konik; Dyonizy Bilinski.
Commercial Counsellor, Stanislaw Struš.
Attachés, Stanislaw Ryza; Jozef Dobrowolski; Kazimierz Ciaś; Wladyslaw Gondzik; Ryszard Guminski.
Military, Air and Naval Attaché, Col. Mierczyslaw Roman.
Assistant Military, Air and Naval Attaché, Col. Kazimierz Kopeć.

Asst. Military Attaché, Col. Zdzislaw Modrzewski.
Commercial Attachés, Jan Koscinski; Stanislaw Kurnicki.
Consulate-General in London, 19 Weymouth Street, W.1.

Area and Population.—In 1939 the area of the Polish Republic was 150,572 square miles with a population of about 35,000,000, of whom 30 per cent. were national minorities (including over 3,000,000 Jews). Frontier changes took place at the end of the war as foreshadowed at the Tehran Conference in 1943. About 69,000 square miles of territory in the east were ceded to the Soviet Union. In exchange Poland received in the west 39,000 square miles of Eastern Germany. The southern boundary was not affected except for minor adjustments to that part formerly dividing Poland from Ruthenia (Czechoslovakia). The western boundary is formed by the Rivers Oder and Neisse. Poland now has a maritime frontier stretching from west of Kaliningrad (formerly Königsberg) to west of Szczecin (formerly Stettin). As a result of the change of frontier and of very great war-time losses, at the census of December 3, 1950, the population had fallen to 24,977,000 in an area of 121,000 square miles; on Dec. 31, 1961, it was estimated at 30,133,000. In 1961 live births showed a rate of 20·7 per 1,000; deaths, 7·6 per 1,000; infant mortality, 54 per 1,000 (provisional figures). Roman Catholicism is the religion of the vast majority of the inhabitants.

Government.—The Republic of Poland (reconstituted within the limits of the old Polish Commonwealth) was proclaimed at Warsaw in November, 1918, and its independence guaranteed by the signatories of the Treaty of Versailles. The Polish Commonwealth had ceased to exist in 1795 after three successive partitions in 1772, 1793 and 1795, in which Prussia, Russia and Austria shared. During the Napoleonic wars, the small Grand Duchy of Warsaw was created but was dissolved by the final act of the Congress of Vienna. The so-called "Congress Kingdom" was then established on the Polish territory which had fallen to Russia's share and the Tsar assumed the title of King of Poland. Prussia acquired Poznania and Polish Pomerania, Austria acquired Galicia and the small Republic of Cracow came into existence under the joint control of Prussia, Russia and Austria. In 1831, after an insurrection, the Congress Kingdom was dissolved and annexed by Russia and in 1848 the Austrians absorbed the Cracow Republic, Poland as an independent state ceasing to exist until the end of the War of 1914–18, when she became independent once again, after 150 years of foreign rule.

In March, 1939, Great Britain entered into a treaty with Poland (France had done so in 1921) guaranteeing Polish territory against aggression, and on Hitler's invasion France and Britain implemented their guarantee. On September 17, 1939, Russian forces invaded eastern Poland and on September 21, 1939, Poland was declared by Germany and Russia to have ceased to exist. A line of demarcation was established between the areas occupied by German and Russian forces. At the end of the war a Coalition Government was formed in which the Polish Workers' Party played a large part. In December, 1948, the Polish Workers' Party and the Polish Socialist Party fused in the new Polish United Workers' Party. This is a Communist Party which closely controls every branch of State activity. A new Constitution modelled on the Soviet Constitution of 1936 was adopted on July 22, 1952. It changed the title of the country to the Polish People's Republic (*Polska Rzeczpospolita Ludowa*). It made no provision for a President of the Republic, whose functions were to be jointly exercised by a Council of State. Private ownership of land and freedom of religion was recognized. Church and State were to be separate.

Despite the guarantee of religious freedom in the Constitution, a campaign of encroachment in 1953 culminated in the arrest of the Primate of the Roman Catholic Church, Cardinal Wyszyński. Dissatisfaction with the régime and conditions of life led to riots in Poznań in June, 1956, and subsequently M. Władyslaw Gomułka, who had been expelled from the Party in 1949, was reinstated and elected First Secretary of the Party. At the same time Cardinal Wyszyński was allowed to resume his functions. In Jan., 1957, elections to the *Sejm* were held and in Feb., 1957, a reconstructed Government, still led by M. Cyrankiewicz, took office. Fresh elections to the *Sejm* were held in April, 1961; M. Cyrankiewicz remained Prime Minister, with the composition of the Government almost unchanged.

Education.—Elementary education is compulsory and free. In 1961–62 there were 4,994,356 pupils in elementary schools, 298,396 in secondary schools, and 977,800 students in technical, professional and trade colleges and schools. There are universities at Krakow, Warsaw, Poznań, Lodz, Wroclaw, Lublin and Toruń and a considerable number of other seats of higher study.

Language and Literature.—Polish is a western Slavonic tongue (*see* U.S.S.R.), the Latin alphabet being in use, as in Czechoslovakia. Polish literature developed rapidly after the foundation of the University of Cracow (a printing press was established there in 1474 and there Copernicus died in 1543). A national school of poetry and drama survived the dismemberment and the former era of romanticism was followed by realistic and historical fiction, including the works of Henryk Sienkiewicz (1846–1916), Nobel Prize-winner for Literature in 1905, Boleslaw Prus (1847–1912), and Stanislaw Reymont (1868–1925), Nobel Prize-winner in 1924. There are now 46 daily papers published in Poland, 11 of them in Warsaw.

Production and Industry.—On January 3, 1946, a decree was issued to provide for the nationalization of mines, petroleum resources, water, gas and electricity services, banks, textile factories and large retail stores. At present over 99 per cent. of Polish industry is stated to be "socialized", but 86 per cent. of agricultural land is privately farmed.

FINANCE	1962
Estimated revenue...........	*Zloty* 248,876,144
Estimated expenditure........	„ 245,557,548

The official exchange rate is 11·20 *zloty* = £1 but this is not used in practice. A special rate of 67·20 *zloty* = £1 has been in force since Feb. 11, 1957 for non-commercial transactions with western countries. All foreign trade is conducted in foreign currencies. (*See also* p. 84.)

Trade with U.K.

	1961	1962
Imports from U.K...	£22,460,217	£32,449,278
Exports to U.K......	36,838,875	38,491,843

CAPITAL.—Warsaw, on the Vistula, pop. (Dec., 1961) 1,171,000. Other large towns are Lodz (723,000), centre of the Polish textile industry; Wroclaw (Breslau) (443,000); Poznan (418,000); Krakow, on the Vistula, a town of great beauty and the capital of mediæval Poland (490,000); Ψ Gdansk (Danzig) (286,000); Bydgoszcz (231,000); Katowice (269,000); Czestochowa (164,000); Lublin (181,000); Ψ Gdynia (148,000); Chorzow (147,000) and Ψ Szczecin (Stettin) (269,000).

FLAG.—Equal horizontal stripes of white (above) and red.

BRITISH EMBASSY
(No. 1 Aleja Róz, Warsaw)

British Ambassador Extraordinary and Plenipotentiary, His Excellency Sir George Lisle Clutton, K.C.M.G. (1960) £4,115
Counsellor, P. G. F. Dalton, C.M.G.
Naval and Military Attaché, Col. G. D. Gill, M.B.E.
Air Attaché, Group-Capt. P. J. Halford, A.F.C.
Consul, R. N. Dawson.
Commercial Secretary, J. A. Dobbs.

BRITISH CONSULATE

There is a British Consular Office at *Gdynia*.

BRITISH COUNCIL

Representative, T. W. Morray, O.B.E., Al Jerozolimskie, 59, Warsaw.

PORTUGAL
(República Portuguesa)

President of the Republic, Rear-Admiral Americo Deus Rodrigues Tomás, *inaugurated President* August 9, 1958.

CABINET
(1932—reconstructed on a number of occasions)

Prime Minister, Dr. Antôniode Oliveira Salazar, G.C.M.G.
Minister of State, Assistant to President of the Council, Dr. José Correia de Oliveira.
Minister of the Interior, Dr. Alfredo Rodrigues dos Santos Junior.
Defence, Gen. Manvel Gomes de Aravjo.
Justice, Prof. Dr. João de Matos Antunes Varela.
Finance, Prof. Dr. António Manuel Pinto Barbosa.
Army, Colonel da Luiz Cunha.
Marine, Rear-Admiral Fernando Quintanilha Mendonça Dias.
Foreign Affairs, Dr. Alberto Franco Nogueira.
Public Works, Eng. Eduardo de Arantes e Oliveira.
Overseas, Cdr. Antonio Peixoto Correia.
Education, Prof. Dr. InnocencioGalvão Teles.
Economy, Dr. Luiz Teixeira Pinto.
Communications, Eng. Carlos Gomes da Silva Ribeiro.
Corporations and Social Security, Prof. Dr. José Gonçalves Proença.
Health, Dr. Pedro Mario Soares.

EMBASSY IN LONDON
Chancery: 11 Belgrave Square, S.W.1
[Belgravia: 5331]

Ambassador in London, His Excellency Senhor Manuel Ferrajota Rocheta, G.C.V.O. (1961).
Minister-Counsellor, Senhor Humberto Alves Morgado.
1st Secretary, Senhor António Vaz Pereira.
2nd Secretary, Senhor José Manuel de Villas-Boas de Vasconcellos Faria.
3rd Secretary, Senhor Zózimo Justo da Silva.
Economic Counsellor, Senhor António Paulo Passos de Gouveia.
Military and Air Attaché, Lt.-Col. João Tiroa.
Naval Attaché, Commander J. Pinto Pereira.
Press Counsellor, Senhor António Potier, M.V.O.
Commercial Counsellor, Senhor Luiz Leotte do Rego.
Commercial Attaché, Senhor António Bento Franco Mendes.
Asst. Commercial Attaché, Senhor José Henrique da Rocha Ramos.
Consulate-General, 103 Sloane St., S.W.1 (Belgravia: 6216).

Area and Population.—Continental Portugal occupies the western part of the Iberian Peninsula, bounded on north and east by Spain, and on south and west by the Atlantic ocean; it contains an area of 34,500 square miles, with an estimated population (including the Azores and Madeira) of 8,980,682 (1958). It lies between 36° 58′–42° 9′ 12″ N. lat. and 6° 11′ 48″–9° 29′ 45″ W. long., being 302 miles in length from N. to S., and averaging about 117 in breadth from E. to W. The Azores and Madeira Islands in North Atlantic are politically an integral part of the Republic.

In 1961 there were 217,516 live births, 99,590 deaths and 78,199 marriages in Continental Portugal.

Government.—From the eleventh century until 1910 the government of Portugal was a monarchy, and for many centuries included the Vice-Royalty of Brazil, which declared its independence in 1822. In 1910 an armed rising in Lisbon drove King Manoel II. and the Royal family into exile, and the National Assembly of Aug. 21, 1911, sanctioned a Republican form of government. The President is elected for seven years by indirect vote of the electors, who vote for members of an electoral college to select the President. He is not eligible for a second term. The Prime Minister is appointed by the President, who also appoints the other Ministers on the recommendation of the Prime Minister. The Government is responsible only to the President. There is a single Chamber Legislature (*Assembleia Nacional*) of 120 members elected by direct vote of the electors. There is also a "Corporative Chamber" consisting of representatives of local authorities and industrial, commercial, cultural and religious interests, to which all bills introduced into the Chamber must be submitted for its opinion. The Legislature is in session for three months in the year. In the recess the Government legislates by decrees or decree-laws, of which the latter only must be confirmed by the legislature. Both men and women enjoy the franchise; but there are certain educational or tax-payment qualifications.

Production.—The chief agricultural products of Portugal are cork, wheat, maize, rye, rice, oats, barley, potatoes, beans, chickpeas, onions, olives, oranges, lemons, figs, almonds, resinous products, timber and wine (including the rich red "port" shipped from Oporto). Sardine fisheries are important.

There are extensive forests of pine, oak, cork, eucalyptus and chestnut, covering about 20 per cent. of the total area of the country, and lumbering is the second largest industry.

The principal mineral products are iron pyrites, wolfram, iron ores, tin, and gold and silver. The principal manufactures are textiles, furniture, pottery, glassware, cork goods, leather, paper, cement, fertilizers and chemicals. A steel works has recently begun production.

The Second Six-Year Development Plan (1959–64) provides *inter alia* for irrigation, agricultural resettlement and afforestation, for the development of electricity generation, mainly by hydroelectric means, of the steel and chemical industries, for extensive port works including a new shipyard at Lisbon, railway electrification, a bridge over the River Tagus at Lisbon and the expansion of the fishing and merchant fleets.

Defence.—Military service is compulsory for all men who are physically fit, less than 25 per cent. being exempted each year. The peace strength of the army is: officers 2,821 (active list), and about 2,000 (reserve); other ranks—permanent cadre of 34,000 with a yearly class of 31,000. A considerable amount of modern equipment has been received from the U.S.A. The navy consists of 860 officers and 6,375 ratings, manning a total of over 60 destroyers, frigates, sloops, submarines, mine-sweepers, patrol vessels and other small craft. The destroyers are of pre-war design, and many of the others have been either built or bought abroad mainly in the U.K. or U.S.A. The frigates, minesweepers, submarines and coastal patrol vessels are all of late-war or post-war construction. The establishment of the Air Force is 500 officers and 2,000 men with 350 aircraft of all types.

Language and Literature.—Portuguese is a Romance language with admixtures of Arabic and other idioms. It is the language of Portugal and Brazil.

Portuguese language and literature reached the culminating point of their development in the *Lusiadas* (dealing with the voyage of Vasco da Gama) and other works of Camoens (Camões), born in 1524, died in 1580. Until the second quarter of the nineteenth century Portuguese literature dominated that of Brazil. Modern literature, both prose and verse, is in a flourishing condition and there are more than twenty daily newspapers, of which 9 are published in Lisbon.

Education is free and compulsory for three years from the age of 7. In 1952 a series of new measures was decreed to ensure school attendance and to reduce illiteracy, which was 30 per cent. at the time of the 1950 Census.

Secondary education is mainly conducted in State lyceums, but there are also private schools. There are also military, naval, technical and other special schools. There are Universities at Coimbra (founded in 1290), Lisbon (1911) and Oporto (1911).

Communications.—On Jan. 1, 1959 there were 2,235 miles of railway open for traffic, of which 475 miles were narrow gauge. The Lisbon-Sintra (15 miles), Lisbon–Cascais (16 miles) and Lisbon–Entroncamento (66 miles) lines are electrified and work on the Entroncamento–Oporto was expected to start in 1961.

On Dec. 31, 1959, the mercantile fleet comprised 90 long-distance vessels with a total gross registered tonnage of 427,430 tons, 19 port-to-port vessels (21,452 tons), 30 national coasters (3,791 tons) and 41 international coasters (6,351 tons). In 1959, 35,147,174 gross tons of shipping entered ports in continental Portugal and adjacent islands, including 5,890,065 gross tons under the British flag.

Civil Aviation is controlled by the Ministry of Communications. There is an international airport at Portela, about 5 miles from Lisbon, and the airport of Pedras Rubras near Oporto is also used for some international services. There is a civil airline, an inter-island service, services in Portuguese Africa and an airline running services within Portuguese India and to Karachi. British European Airways and Transportes Aereos Portugueses operate a daily service between London and Lisbon by agreement between them which calls at Oporto twice weekly in both directions. There are altogether 19 airlines operating a total of about 400 services a month through Lisbon airport.

FINANCE	1961
Revenue (*Budget*)	*Escudos* 12,463,250,000
Expenditure (*do.*)	12,460,818,000
Public Debt (Dec. 1961):—	
Internal Debt.	3,853,016,000
External Debt, Redeemable	509,783,000

The Second Six-Year Development Plan (1959–64) contemplates an expenditure of about 21,000,000,000 *Escudos* in metropolitan Portugal, and about 9,000,000,000 *Escudos* in the Overseas Provinces.

Currency.—*Escudo* (of 100 *Centavos*) = 3*d*. *Conto* (of 1,000 *escudos*) = £12 10s. Exchange Rate (stable) about 80 *escudos* = £1. (*See also* p. 83.)

TRADE

	1960 *Escudos*	1961 *Escudos*
Imports	15,685,321,000	18,867,149,000
Exports	9,408,129,000	9,372,926,000

Trade with U.K.

	1961	1962
Imports from U.K.	£35,870,824	£30,579,047
Exports to U.K.	17,951,087	18,195,419

The principal exports in 1960 were canned fish, cotton piece goods, cork manufactures, unmanufactured cork, unmanufactured or semi-manufactured wood, resins, port wine, ordinary wines and cotton thread. 25·7 per cent. (by value) of exports went to the Portuguese Overseas Provinces, 13·6 per cent. to the United Kingdom, 11·3 per cent. to the United States and 9·0 per cent. to Western Germany.

Principal imports in 1960 were iron and steel, raw cotton, crude oil, passenger cars and sugar. 14·4 per cent. (by value) of imports came from the Portuguese Overseas Provinces, 17·1 per cent. from Western Germany, 11·9 per cent. from the United Kingdom and 8·3 per cent. from France.

CAPITAL, ♆Lisbon. Population (Census, 1960) 1,397,213. ♆Oporto 284,842; ♆Setubal 44,030.

FLAG.—Green and red, with arms in centre.

Lisbon, distance 1,110 miles; transit, 50 hours; by air, 2½ hours.

BRITISH EMBASSY

Ambassador's Residence—Rua S. Francisco de Borja 63, Lisbon. *Chancery Offices*, Rua São Domingos a Lapa 37, Lisbon.

Ambassador Extraordinary and Plenipotentiary, His Excellency Sir Archibald David Manisty Ross, K.C.M.G. (1960) £4,115

Counsellor, A. L. Mayall.

Commercial Counsellor, T. C. Sharman, O.B.E.

Naval Attaché, Cdr. H. P. Westmacott, D.S.O., D.S.C., R.N.

Military Attaché, Lt.-Col. F. J. Burnaby-Atkins.

Air Attaché, Group Capt. P. H. Baldwin.

1st Secretary and Visa Officer, Mrs. M. I. Dunlop, M.B.E.

1st Secretary and Consul-General, F. C. Bishop.

1st Secretary and Information Officer, G. Stow.

2nd Secretary, D. C. Thomas.

2nd Secretaries (Commercial), W. Watson, M.B.E.; F. G. E. Walford, O.B.E.

Attaché, T. H. Froebelius, M.B.E.

BRITISH CONSULAR OFFICES

There are British Consular Offices at *Lisbon, Oporto, Setubal* and *Vila Real de Santo Antonio (Portugal), Ponta Delgada (Azores), St. Vincent (Cape Verde Islands), Funchal (Madeira), Lourenço Marques* and *Beira (Portuguese East Africa), Luanda (Portuguese West Africa)* and *Macão.*

BRITISH COUNCIL

Representative, J. G. G. Muir, O.B.E., D.S.C. The British Institute, Rua de Luis Fernandes 3, Lisbon.

There is a British Institute at *Coimbra* (Rua Alexandre Herculano 34) and an Anglo-Portuguese Association at *Oporto* (Rua de Breyner 79).

ROYAL BRITISH CLUB, rua S. Pedro d'Alcantara, 3, Lisbon.

BRITISH CHAMBER OF COMMERCE IN PORTUGAL, 4 Rua Victor Cordon, Lisbon (Branches at

Madorninha Senhora de Hora, *Oporto*, and 13*a* Rua 5 de Junho, *Funchal, Madeira*).

MADEIRA AND THE AZORES

Madeira and The Azores are administratively parts of metropolitan Portugal.

The Madeiras are a group of islands in the Atlantic Ocean about 520 miles west of Lisbon, and consist of Madeira, Porto Santo and 3 uninhabited islands (Desertas). The total area is 314 square miles, with a population of 269,769. ΨFunchal in Madeira, the largest island (270 square miles), is the capital, with a population of 37,035; Machico (4,734). Trade with U.K., 1962: Imports from U.K., £646,992; Exports, £402,640.

The Azores are a group of 9 islands (Flores, Corvo, Terceira, Sao Jorge, Pico, Fayal, Graciosa, Sao Miguel and Santa Maria) in the Atlantic Ocean, with a total area of 922 square miles and a population of 318,558. Ψ Ponta Delgada the capital of the group, has a population of 22,448. Other ports are ΨAngra, in Terceira, (10,296) and ΨHorta (8,564). Trade with U.K., 1962: Imports from U.K., £238,485; Exports, £271,148.

PORTUGUESE OVERSEAS PROVINCES

CAPE VERDE ISLANDS, off the west coast of Africa, consist of two groups of islands, Windward (Santo Antão, São Vicente, Santa Luzia, São Nicolao, Boa Vista and Sal, the last-named having a South Atlantic air base, opened in 1949) and Leeward (Maio, São Tiago, Fogo and Brava) with a total area of 1,516 square miles and a population (Census of 1950) of 148,331. Revenue (1957) *Escudos* 119,969,00; imports (1957) *Escudos* 378,361,000; exports *Escudos* 346,820,000, shipping entries (1957) 8,749,927 gross tons. Capital, ΨPraia (6,000). Vessels take coal and oil at ΨMindelo, Sao Vicente (pop. 20,000).

SÂO TOMÉ and PRÍNCIPÉ ISLANDS, in the Gulf of Guinea (area 372 square miles, population (1950), 60,159). Revenue (1957) *Escudos* 71,899,000; imports (1956) *Escudos* 137,345,000; exports, *Escudos* 173,670,000. Capital, ΨSão Tomé (3,187). The fort of St. John Baptist on the Slave Coast is a dependency of the Province of São Tomé.

ANGOLA has an area of 488,000 sq. miles, pop. 4,145,266, with present capital ΨSt. Paul de Luanda (pop. 40,000), and capital designate Nova Lisboa, and includes also Kabinda and Portuguese Zaire (N. of Congo). Angola was restored to Portugal by the Netherlands in 1648. Revenue (1957): *Contos* 2,172,394; imports (1957), *Contos* 3,565,578; exports, *Contos* 3,327,927. Shipping entries (1957) 8,991,000 gross tons.

Trade with U.K.

	1961	1962
Imports from U.K..	£4,521,449	£4,944,716
Exports to U.K....	1,393,751	1,088,176

PORTUGUESE GUINEA, area 14,000 sq. miles, pop. (1950) 510,777 (capital ΨBissau, population 6,000). Revenue (1957) *Escudos* 150,446,000; imports (1956) *Escudos* 208,082,000; exports, *Escudos* 207,359,000; shipping entries (1953), 186,783 gross tons.

A transcontinental railway from *Benguela* (Lobito Bay) in Angola, which traverses the Katanga mineral district of the Congo and then runs southwards through Rhodesia to Bulawayo and eastwards to Beira, is being developed under British, Belgian and Portuguese control. This line makes through communication from Lobito Bay on the Atlantic to Beira on the Indian Ocean.

PORTUGUESE EAST AFRICA, OR MOZAMBIQUE, Lourenço Marques, Inhambane, Quelimane, Tete, Mozambique, Cape Delgado and Nyasa, together with the territory of Manica and Sofala, has a total area of 297,657 square miles, with a population (1950) of 5,732,317. Capital ΨLourenço Marques (48,000). Revenue (1957) *Escudos* 3,131,067,000; imports (1957), *Escudos* 3,111,562,000: exports, *Escudos* 2,029,294,000; trade with U.K., 1962: Imports from U.K., £4,748,738; Exports, £2,697,293. Shipping entries (1956), 18,463,714 gross tons.

ΨMACAU, in China, on the Canton River, has an area of 5 square miles and a population (1950) of 187,772. Revenue (1957), *Escudos* 109,755,000.

PORTUGUESE TIMOR (the eastern portion of the island), in the Malay Archipelago, has an area of 7,329 square miles, with a population (1950) of 442,378. Revenue (1957) *Escudos* 71,546,000; imports (1957), *Escudos* 61,330,000; exports *Escudos* 38,880,000; shipping entries (1957), 88,587 gross tons. Capital, ΨDili, pop. 7,000.

QATAR

Ruler of Qatar, Shaik Ahmad bin Ali bin Abdullah al Thani; *succeeded* Oct. 24, 1960.

Deputy Ruler and Minister of Finance, Shaikh Khalifa bin Hamad al Thani.

Director of the Government, Dr. Hassan Kamel.

Qatar is an independent Arab Shaikhdom in special treaty relations with Her Majesty's Government. It covers the peninsula of Qatar from approximately the Northern shore of Khor al Odaid to the Eastern shore of Khor al Salwa. The area is about 4,000 sq. miles, with a population variously estimated at 45–60,000.

Oil deposits on land are being exploited by the Qatar Petroleum Company, a subsidiary of I.P.C., under a concession granted by the Ruler, and the first oil shipment was made on December 31, 1949. Oil is now being extracted at the rate of over 8,000,000 tons a year. Considerable development has resulted from this source of income. Outside Doha and the oil company's installations, conditions are primitive. The inhabitants are semi-settled tribesmen and Bedouin; apart from employment in the oil industry and on development projects, pearling, which has greatly declined in recent years, and fishing, are the only alternatives to poor grazing as a means of livelihood. Such towns as exist are merely enlarged villages, with the exception of Doha, which boasts a bazaar, a good harbour for native craft, an airport, an increasing number of modern buildings, and an expanding population. The oil company has constructed a deep water port at Umm Said on the East coast of the peninsula. The off-shore concession is held by the Shell Company of Qatar, which is at present drilling for oil in the sea bed. Regular air services connect Qatar with the other Persian Gulf Shaikhdoms (Bahrain, the Trucial States and Kuwait), Muscat, the Lebanon, Europe and the United Kingdom. The Ruler has an international staff of technical assistants. Wireless communications are managed by Cable and Wireless, Ltd. On May 24, 1963, the Qatar Government took over the management of its postal services from the British G.P.O. The currency is the Indian external *rupee*.

Foreign affairs are in the charge of the British Political Agent who lives in Doha.

CAPITAL.—Doha. Population (estimated) 40,000.

FLAG.—White and coffee-coloured, white portion nearer the mast; vertical indented line comprising 17 angles divides the colours.

British Political Agent, P. McKearney.

ROUMANIA

(Republica Populara Romina)

STATE COUNCIL

President, Gheorghe Gheorghiu-Dej.
Vice-Presidents, Ion Gheorghe Maurer; Stefan Voitec; Avram Bunaciu.

COUNCIL OF MINISTERS

(March 21, 1961)

President of the Council, Ion Gheorghe Maurer.
Vice-Presidents of the Council, Emil Bodnaras Petre Borilă; Alexandru Moghioros; Gheorghe Apostol; Alexandru Birladeanu; Alexandru Draghici; Gheorghe Gaston Marin.
Minister for Foreign Affairs, Corneliu Manescu.
Justice, Ioan Constant Manoliu.
Finance, Aurel Vijoli.
Internal Affairs, Col.-Gen. Alexandru Draghici.
Petroleum Industry and Chemicals, Mihail Florescu.
Education, Stefan Balan.
Forest Economy, Mihai Suder.
Health and Social Welfare, Voinea Marinescu.
Metallurgy and Machine Building, Constantin Tuzu.
Light Industry, Alexandru Sencovici.
Foreign Trade, Gheorghe Radulescu.
Internal Trade, Mihai Levente.
Armed Forces, Col.-Gen. Leontin Salajan.
Transport and Communications, Dumitru Simulescu.
President of State Planning Committee, Gaston Marin.
Food Industry, Janos Fazekas.
Mines and Electric Power, Bujor Almasan.
Building Industry, Dumitru Mosora.
President, Higher Council for Agriculture, Mihai Dalea.
President, State Committee for Culture and Arts, Constanta Craciun.

ROUMANIAN LEGATION IN LONDON

4 Palace Green, W.8
[Western: 9666]

Envoy Extraordinary and Minister Plenipotentiary, His Excellency Alexandru Lazareanu (1961).

Area and Population.—Roumania is a republic of South-Eastern Europe, formerly the classical *Dacia* and *Scythia Pontica*, having its origin in the union of the Danubian principalities of *Wallachia* and *Moldavia* (and the addition thereto of a strip of Southern *Bessarabia*) under the *Treaty of Paris* (April, 1856). The area in October, 1945, was estimated at 91,600 sq. miles, with a population (estimated, 1962) of 18,566,932

Government.—The principalities remained separate entities under Turkish suzerainty until 1859, when Prince Alexandru Ion Cuza was elected Prince of both, still under the suzerainty of Turkey. Prince Cuza abdicated in 1866 and was succeeded by Prince Charles of Hohenzollern-Sigmaringen, in whose successors the crown was vested. By the *Treaty of Berlin* (July 13, 1878) the Principality was recognized as an independent State, and part of the *Dobrudja* (which had been occupied by the Roumanians) was incorporated. On March 27, 1881, it was recognized as a Kingdom.

The outcome of the War of 1914–18 added Bessarabia, the Bukovina, Transylvania, The Banat and Crişana–Maramureş, these additions of territory being confirmed in the Treaty of St. Germain, 1919, and the Treaty of Petit Trianon, 1920.

On June 27, 1940, in compliance with an ultimatum from U.S.S.R., Bessarabia and Northern Bukovina were ceded to the Soviet Government, the area affected being about 20,000 sq. miles, with a population of about 4,000,000.

In August, 1940, Roumania ceded to Bulgaria the portion of Southern Dobrudja (about 3,000 sq. miles) taken from Bulgaria in 1919.

A new Constitution, modelled on the Soviet Constitution of 1936, was adopted unanimously on September 24, 1952, by the Grand National Assembly. The Assembly was later dissolved and elections were held for a new Grand National Assembly on November 30, 1952; in each constituency there was only one candidate for election, representing the People's Democratic Front. Further elections on similar lines were held in February, 1957 and in March 1961.

Agriculture.—The soil of Wallachia and Moldavia is among the richest in Europe producing wheat, maize, millet, oats, barley, rye, beans, peas and other vegetables. Grape vines and fruits are abundant. The fertile plain of Transylvania yields large crops of maize, wheat, rye, oats, flax, and hemp. Agriculture and sheep and cattle raising are the principal industries of Roumania, but the climate of this part of South-Eastern Europe is of the Continental character, and the intense winter cold and summer heat, and fierce summer drought sometimes defeat these principal industries. The forests of the mountainous regions are extensive (17,851,401 acres), and the timber industry is important. The total arable land under cultivation in 1960 was about 10,000,000 hectares.

Socialization of agriculture was completed when plans for collectivization were fulfilled in the spring of 1962, some three years ahead of the planned date.

Natural Resources and Industry.—Petroleum is the backbone of Roumanian industry and of the country's general economy. Production in 1936 (the peak pre-war year) amounted to 8,700,000 tons. In the immediate post-war period, production declined to less than half this figure, but it is now claimed that, with the discovery of new oilfields, production has recovered and reached a new peak of 11,582,000 tons in 1961. The country is also rich in other minerals, and produces in limited quantities coal, lignite, iron, gold, silver, mica and uranium. Industrialization is proceeding rapidly and at the end of the first Five-Year Plan, 1951–55, the Government claimed to have exceeded their intention of increasing industrial production by 244 per cent. compared with 1950. The subsequent Five-Year Plan was later reduced to cover a four-year period, 1956–59, during which an average annual increase in industrial production of 10 per cent. was claimed. The new Six-Year Plan (1960–65) provides for an average annual increase of industrial production of 13 per cent. An increase of 16 per cent. in industrial production was achieved in each year 1960 and 1961.

Other 1961 production figures, with 1965 targets in brackets are:

Crude oil..........	11,582,000 tons (12,200,000)
Coal.....	8,704,000 tons (11,500,000–12,500,000)
Electric power	8,631,000,000 kWh (18,500,000,000)
Natural gas..	7,197,000,000 cu. metres (13,300,000,000)
Steel..............	2,127,000 tons (3,300,000)
Pig Iron...........	1,099,000 tons (2,000,000)

Language and Literature.—Roumanian is a Romance language with many archaic forms and with admixtures of Slavonic, Turkish, Magyar and French words. The folk-songs and folklore, composed by the people themselves, and transmitted orally through many centuries (and collected in the 19th century), form one of the most interesting of such collections. The publication of all books and reviews is controlled and authorized by the *Editura de Stat*, which comes under the jurisdiction of the Council of Ministers. In 1962, 32 daily newspapers were published. The dominating religion is that of the Roumanian Orthodox Church.

Education is free and nominally compulsory, with 2,588,000 in attendance in 1960, including over 241,000 at secondary schools and 80,000 in higher education. There are four Universities, at Bucharest, Iaşi, Cluj and Timisoara. A "Marxist-Leninist" University was opened in Bucharest in 1951. There are polytechnics at Bucharest, Timisoara, Cluj, Brasov, Galatz and Iasi, two commercial academies at Bucharest and Brasov, and agricultural colleges at Bucharest, Iasi, Cluj, Craiova and Timisoara.

Communications.—In 1960 there were 6,824 miles of railway open for traffic. The mercantile marine, as a result of war losses, seizure and reparations, was reduced to a few moderate-sized sea-going steamers and a number of coastal and river craft, but is being steadily built up. The principal ports are Constantza (on the Black Sea), Giurgiu, Braila, Galati and Turnu-Severin (on the Danube), and Sulina (on the Danube Estuary). Work on a canal linking the Danube and the Black Sea just north of Constantza was abandoned in 1953 and no more was heard of the project to build a canal linking Bucharest with Danube Estuary.

FINANCE

Final figures of actual state revenue expenditure in 1961 were: Revenue, *Lei* 66,142,200,000; Expenditure, *Lei* 63,726,000,000.

	1962* *Lei*	1963* *Lei*
Revenue	78,790,000,000	84,462,000,000
Expenditure	77,790,000,000	81,462,000,000

*Budget Estimates.

Up-to-date figures of the Public Debt are not available. No foreign loans (other than short-term commercial loans) are known to have been contracted since March, 1947. The internal debt was virtually wiped out by stabilization in August, 1947; there has been no internal loan issue since that date.

The Roumanian *Leu* (of 100 *Bani*) was revalued for the third time since the war on Feb. 1, 1954, foreign exchange rates being fixed at £1=16·80 *lei* and 1 U.S. $=6·00 *lei*. On July 1, 1957, the Roumanian State Bank announced the payment of 100 per cent. premium on all "capitalist" currencies for non-commercial transactions. This premium brings the effective exchange rate to £1=33·60 *lei* and 1 U.S. $=12 *lei*. A special tourist rate is available to tourists who make their arrangements through O.N.T. CARPATI (State tourist agency): *lei* 42·0=£1.

TRADE

	1960 *Lei*	1961 *Lei*
Imports	3,886,700,000	4,886,700,000
Exports	4,303,700,000	4,757,100,000

No complete figures for foreign trade have been published since the start of the Communist régime. Imports are chiefly semi-manufactured goods, raw materials, machinery and metals; exports consist principally of maize, wheat, barley, oats, petroleum, timber and cattle. Trade with U.K., although relatively small has increased notably since the signature of an Anglo-Roumanian trade arrangement in 1960.

Trade with U.K.

	1961	1962
Imports from U.K.	£13,568,952	£8,378,680
Exports to U.K.	6,066,695	7,074,033

About 65 per cent. of Roumania's foreign trade is now with the Soviet Union and the other countries of Eastern Europe. Roumania is a member of the Soviet-sponsored "Council for Mutual Economic Assistance."

CAPITAL, Bucharest, on the Dimbovitza, population (1960) 1,225,507. Other towns with a population of over 100,000 in 1960 are: Cluj (161,931); Timisoara (146,988); Brasov (for a time called Stalin) (128,882); Ploesti (125,724); Iasi (123,172); ΨConstantza (112,993); Arad (112,457); ΨBraila (110,901); Craiova (108,773); Oradea (105,949); ΨGalati (105,048).

FLAG.—Three vertical bands, blue, yellow, red, with the emblem of the Republic in the centre band.

BRITISH LEGATION
24 Strada Jules Michelet, Bucharest 3

Minister, His Excellency James Dalton Murray, C.M.G. £4,115
1st Secretary, J. I. McGhie.
Military Attaché, Lt.-Col. A. C. F. Godwin.
2nd Secretaries and Vice-Consuls, J. J. Christie; Miss E. A. Urquhart.

RUANDA
(Republic of Ruanda)

President, Grégoire Kayibanda, *born* 1925; *elected* Oct. 26, 1961; *assumed office*, July 1, 1962.

A small state situated in North Central Africa, between Tanganyika and the Congolese Republic, Ruanda became an independent republic on July 1, 1962. Formerly part of the Belgian-administered trusteeship of Ruanda-Urundi, it has an area of 10,169 sq. miles and a population estimated at 2,634,000, mainly of the Batutsi and Bahutu tribes and some 50,000 pygmies. Coffee and cotton are grown and there is some mineral production. Cattle and hides are also exported.

At a referendum held in September, 1961, under supervision of the United Nations, a large majority voted against the retention of the monarchy which was accordingly abolished on Oct. 2, 1961. Elections for a new Legislative Assembly were also held in September, 1961, and the Assembly elected M. Kayibanda as President of the National Council, to hold office as Head of State and Head of the Government. Admission of Ruanda to membership of the United Nations was approved on July 26, 1962.

CAPITAL.—Kigali.
British Embassy.—*See* BURUNDI.

SALVADOR
(República de El Salvador)

President, Lt.-Col. Julio A. Rivera; *elected* April 29, 1962; *assumed office* July 1, 1962.
Vice-President (and Salvadorean Ambassador in Washington), Dr. Francisco Lima.
Minister of Foreign Affairs, Dr. Escobar Sorrano.

SALVADOREAN EMBASSY AND CONSULATE
6 Roland Gardens, S.W.7
[Fremantle: 2455]

Ambassador, Dr. Antonio Melendez (1958).
Secretary and Consul-General, Dr. Ricardo González.

Area and Population.—The Republic of El Salvador extends along the Pacific coast of Central America for 160 miles with a general breadth of about 50 miles, and contains an estimated area of 7,722 square miles, with a population (Census of 1961) of 2,501,278. El Salvador is therefore one of the most densely populated countries of the new world. It is divided into 14 Departments.

The surface of the country is very mountainous, many of the peaks being extinct volcanoes. The highest peaks are the Santa Ana volcano (7,700 ft.) and the San Vincente volcano (7,200 ft.). Much of the interior has an average altitude of 2,000 feet. The lowlands along the coast are generally hot, but towards the interior the altitude tempers the severity of the heat. Much has been done in recent years to improve sanitary conditions and services. There is a wet season from May to October, and a dry season from November to April. Earthquakes have been frequent in the history of El Salvador, the most recent being that of May 6, 1952, when the towns of Jucuapa and Chinameca were destroyed.

The principal river is the Rio Lempa. There is a large volcanic lake (Ilopango) a few miles to the east of the capital, while farther away and to the west lies the smaller but very picturesque lake of Coatepeque, which appears to have been formed in a vast crater flanked by the Santa Ana volcano.

Government.—Salvador was conquered in 1525 by Pedro de Alvarado, and formed part of the Spanish vice-royalty of Guatemala until 1821. In 1839 the Republic broke away from the federation of Central American States. A new Constitution was adopted in 1950. The President is elected for six years and the Legislature for two. President Lemus was elected in 1956, but was deposed in Sept., 1960. A *Junta de Gobierno* assumed power, but was itself deposed in Jan., 1961, when a Civil-Military Directory took office. The Directory enacted by decree a sweeping programme of social reforms and held elections for a Constituent Assembly on December 17, 1961. This Assembly re-enacted the 1950 Constitution with some amendments, including a reduction of the Presidential term to five years, and elected a provisional President. Presidential elections were then held on April 29, 1962, at which the only candidate was Colonel Rivera. Colonel Rivera was formerly a member of the Civil-Military Directory and had resigned in September, 1961, to lead the official *Partido Conciliación Nacional.*

Production and Industry.—The chief industry is the cultivation of coffee, which is grown under shade-trees principally on the slopes of the volcanoes; cane sugar is also produced, as well as cotton, maize, sesame, indigo, rice, balsam, etc. In the lower altitudes towards the east, sisal is produced and used in the manufacture of coffee and sugar bags.

Education.—The illiteracy rate is about 50 per cent. Primary education is nominally compulsory, but the number of schools and teachers available is too small to enable education to be given to all children of school age. In recent Budgets, however, a high percentage of the national revenue has been devoted to education and great efforts are being made to eliminate the existing shortage of schools and teachers.

Language and Literature.—The language of the country is Spanish. Indigenous literature has not yet produced work of international repute. There are 4 daily newspapers published at the capital, and 4 in the provinces.

Communications.—The Salvador Railway, nearly 100 miles in length, connects Acajutla with the capital and with the important coffee centre of Santa Ana. The International Railways of Central America have a line from the port of La Union (on the Gulf of Fonseca) to the capital and another one in the opposite direction which taps the richest coffee growing region in the country and proceeds to Zacapa (in Guatemala) thereby affording continuous railway communication between San Salvador and Guatemala City and Puerto Barrios on the Caribbean coast. The re-draining and re-paving of most of the capital has been completed, as has also the macadamizing or paving of several hundred miles of rural roads, many of which are now passable all the year round. There is a good motor road between the port of La Libertad and the capital (23 miles), while motor transportation is possible throughout the year between the capital and Guatemala City. The Pan-American Highway from the Guatemalan frontier follows this route and continues to the Honduran frontier. The highway is now completed through the country. Pan-American Airways, TACA, TAN, LANICA, SAHSA and LACSA connect El Salvador with the rest of the world.

There are post and telegraph offices throughout the country. There are many broadcasting stations and two television stations.

FINANCE

	1962 Colones	1963 Colones
Revenue (*Budget*)	183,359,000	194,000,000
Expenditure (*do.*)	184,859,000	194,863,624

Public Debt (Dec. 31, 1962):

External Debt	83,409,137
Internal Debt	53,336,350

TRADE

	1961 Colones	1962 Colones
Imports	271,100,000	312,160,737
Exports	297,700,000	340,761,981

Trade with U.K.

	1961	1962
Imports from U.K.	£1,267,197	£1,515,751
Exports to U.K.	47,988	105,684

Par of Exchange 2·50 *Colones*=$1 (U.S.), 7·00 *Colones*=£1. (*See also* p. 84.)

Coffee accounted for 55½ per cent. of the exports in 1962 and cotton for 24 per cent. The others are sisal (in the form of the bags used for exporting coffee, sugar, etc.), gold, sugar, indigo, sesame, balsam, hides and skins. The chief imports are cotton textiles, iron and steel goods, motor cars, manures, chemical products and petrol.

CAPITAL.—San Salvador. Population (Census of 1961), 248,100. Other towns are Santa Ana (73,864); San Miguel (38,330), Ψ La Union (Cutoco), Ψ La Libertad and Ψ Acajutla.

FLAG.—Three horizontal bands light blue, white, light blue; coat of arms on white band.

BRITISH EMBASSY

13A Avenida Norte (Continuación), Colonia Dueñas, San Salvador

British Ambassador Extraordinary and Plenipotentiary and Consul-General, His Excellency Geoffrey William Kirk, C.M.G. (1960).

1st Secretary and Consul, D. W. M. Pierotti.

Hon. Commercial Attaché, S. M. Stadler O.B.E.

There is a Consular Office at *La Libertad.*

San Salvador is 5,700 miles from London.

SAN MARINO

(Repubblica di San Marino)

Regents, Two "Capitani Reggenti".

CONSULATE GENERAL IN LONDON

19 St. Peter's Road, St. Margaret's, Twickenham, Middlesex [Popesgrove: 9213]

Consul General, R. E. Rudge.

A small Republic in the hills near Rimini, on the Adriatic, founded, it is stated, by a pious stonecutter of Dalmatia in the 4th century. The Republic always resisted the Papal claims and its integrity is respected by Italy. The Republic is governed by a State Congress of 10 members, under the Presidency of two Captains-Regent. The Great and General Council, a legislative body of 60 members is elected by a universal suffrage for a term of 5 years. A Council of Twelve forms in certain cases a Supreme Court of Justice. The area is approximately 23 square miles, the population about 17,000. There is an army of 180. The city of San Marino, on the slope of Monte Titano, has three castles, a fine church and Government palace, a theatre and a museum. The principal industries are wine, cereals, cattle, ceramics, lime, concrete, cotton yarns, colour and paints. A Treaty of Extradition between the Governments of Great Britain and the Republic of San Marino has been in force since 1899.

In 1962 revenue and expenditure balanced at *lire* 2,333,496,875. The capital San Marino, has a population of 2,000.

FLAG.—Two horizontal bands, white, blue (with coat of arms of the Republic in centre).

SAUDI ARABIA

(al Mamlaka al Arabiya as-Sa'udiya.)

King of Saudi Arabia, H.M. King Saud bin Abdul Aziz, G.B.E., *born* 1902, *succeeded* Nov. 9, 1953. The Saud family previously ruled in *Nejd* but was deposed by Ibn al Rashid and took refuge in Kuwait. Ibn Saud, the father of the present king, occupied *Riyadh* in 1900 and conquered the larger part of *Nejd* in 1913. In 1921 he became *Sultan of Nejd*, conquered the *Hejaz* and became King in 1926. He changed the name of his Kingdom to *Saudi Arabia* in 1932.

Crown Prince, H.R.H. Amir Faisal bin Abdul Aziz, G.B.E., *born* 1904.

Foreign Affairs, H.R.H. Amir Faisal bin Abdul Aziz.
Defence and Aviation, H.R.H. Sultan bin Abdul Aziz.
Interior, H.R.H. Fahd bin Abdul Aziz.
Agriculture, Sheikh Ibrahim al-Sewayel.
Education, Sheikh Hasan Al al-Sheikh.
Trade, Sheikh Abid Sheikh.
Communications, Dr. Omar Tawfiq.
Oil and Mineral Resources, Sheikh Ahmed Zaki Yamani.
Health, Dr. Yusuf al-Hajiri.
Labour and Social Affairs, Sheikh Abdurrahman Abu al-Khayl.
Information, Sheikh Jamil al-Hujailan.
Pilgrimage and Trusts, Dr. Husseyn Arab.

SAUDI ARABIAN EMBASSY
24 Kensington Palace Gardens, W.8
[Bayswater: 3144]

Ambassador Extraordinary and Plenipotentiary, His Excellency Shaikh Hafiz Wahba.
Counsellor, Ibrahim Bakur.
2nd Secretary, Abdullah S. Al-Fadhul.
3rd Secretaries, Said A. Jawad; Shafik Al-Sabban.

The Kingdom of Saudi Arabia, so named since Sept. 20, 1932, is a personal union of two countries, the Sultan of Nejd being also King of the Hejaz.

By the *Treaty of Jedda* (May 20, 1927) Great Britain recognized Ibn Saud as an independent ruler, King of the Hejaz and of Nejd and its Dependencies.

The total area of the Kingdom is about 927,000 sq. miles, with an estimated population of not more than 6 millions.

In the 18th century Nejd was an independent State and the stronghold of the Wahhabi sect. It subsequently fell under the Turkish yoke, but in 1913 Ibn Saud threw off Turkish rule and captured from the Turks the Province of Hasa. In 1921 he added to his dominions the territories of the Rashid family of Jebel Shammar, which he captured by force of arms; in 1925 he completed the conquest of the Hejaz, and in 1926 accepted the surrender of the greater part of Asir, the whole of which is now part of the Kingdom.

Nejd ("Plateau") has no definite frontiers, but may be said to extend over about 800,000 square miles of Central Arabia, including the Nafud and Dahana Deserts, and reaches eastward to the Persian Gulf (Hasa). The population is largely nomadic and is estimated at close on 3,000,000, the majority being Moslems of the Wahhabi movement. There is little agriculture, but wheat and barley are grown, and there is an experimental farm, irrigated from natural deep pools and covering 3,000 acres, at al-Kharj, about 50 miles south of Riyadh. The principal occupation of the bulk of the population is camel and sheep raising, but oil makes by far the largest contribution to the economy of the country. Oil was found in commercial quantities at Dammam, near Dhahran in the Hasa in 1938, and by 1962 production of crude oil from field storage amounted to over 555,000,000 barrels per annum. Exports other than oil are negligible. The capital is Riyadh (100,000), and the principal trading centres are Hofuf (the chief town of the Hasa province) (100,000), ΨAl Khobar and ΨDammam on the Persian Gulf littoral, Anaiza, Buraida, Hail (20,000), and Jauf. The old ports (Persian Gulf) were ΨQatif, ΨUqair and ΨAl Khobar, which were suitable only for sailing craft, but the Arabian-American Oil Company, which is exploiting the Hasa oil under a 60 years' lease, has built a deep-water port for its own purposes at ΨRas Tannura, and a civil deep-water port, with a pier seven miles long, was brought into use at ΨDammam in 1950. A railway is now in operation from Dammam through Hofuf to Riyadh.

The *Hejaz* ("The Boundary"—between Nejd and Tihama) extends from Asir in S. to Transjordan in N., and from the Red Sea, the Gulf of Akaba in the W. to the ill-defined boundaries of Central Arabia. The coastline on the Red Sea is about 800 miles, and the total area is about 112,500 sq. miles, with a population of from 1,000,000 to 1,500,000, including many nomad tribes. On the coast are the small ports of El Wejh, Yanbu', Rabegh, Gizan and ΨJedda, the main port of Saudi Arabia. Jedda contains the ruins of the reputed "tomb of Eve, the mother of mankind"; and inland are many settlements through which runs the course of the disused Saudi-Arabian section of the Hejaz Railway which is scheduled for reconstruction. The *Oasis of Khaibar*, east of the railway, contains a considerable population, descendants of former negro slaves, with a centre at Kasr el Yahudi. The importance of the Hejaz depends upon the pilgrimages to the holy cities of Medina and Mecca. *Medina* (*al Madinah al Munawwarah*, "The City of Light"), once the terminus of the Hejaz Railway, 820 miles from Damascus, has a permanent population of about 20,000 and is celebrated as the burial place of Muhammad, who died in the city on June 7, 632 (12 Rabia, A.H. 11). The Mosque of the Prophet (500 feet in length and over 300 in breadth) contains the sacred tomb of Muhammad. *Mecca*, the birthplace of the Prophet, is 45 miles east of the seaport of Jedda, by road, and about 200 miles south of Medina, and has a fixed population estimated at 100,000. The city contains the great mosque surrounding the *Kaaba*, or sacred shrine of the Muhammadan religion, in which is the black stone "given by Gabriel to Abraham," placed in the south-east wall of the Kaaba at such a height that it may be kissed by the devout pilgrim. Ψ*Jedda* (200,000) is the principal port and commercial centre.

Asir ("The Inaccessible") extends, geographically, from a line drawn inland from Birk on the southern limit of Hejaz to the northern boundary of the Yemen, some 12 miles N. of the port of

Meidi. Its breadth extends about 180 miles eastwards to Bisha in the north and to the boundary of the Beni Yam in the south. According to ancient Arab geographers, Asir used to be considered as a part of the Yemen. The territory includes the Farsan Islands, where prospectors have searched for oil, but without success. The maritime lowland is interspersed with fertile areas near the wadis, which afford pasturage and bear grain. Capital, Abha.

Trade and Finance.—Formerly the annual pilgrimage to the Holy Places of the Hejaz provided Saudi Arabia with virtually the whole of her means of payment for imports. It is therefore not surprising that the foreign trade of the country was largely conducted by the merchant communities of Jedda and Mecca. Industry was, and is, almost non-existent. Imports are estimated to have averaged about £2,500,000 annually before 1939, of which the United Kingdom contributed less than £100,000. India was traditionally Saudi Arabia's principal commercial connection; and indeed the legal tender of Saudi Arabia, the silver rial, is of the same weight and fineness as the old Indian rupee. Religious objections to usury have affected the development of banking in Saudi Arabia. Though paper money is widely used, it is not officially recognised as currency. It has virtually supplanted gold as a means of payment for transactions nevertheless. Exchange rates, which were formerly subject to violent fluctuations, have now been given a considerable degree of stability by the operations of the Saudi Arabian Monetary Agency. The country shared the inflationary experiences of other Middle East countries during the war years. The effect of oil developments and of investment, mainly American, in Saudi Arabia has been to revolutionize the country's foreign exchange position and greatly to increase the size of the market.

Trade with U.K.

	1961	1962
Imports from U.K....	£6,690,224	£8,719,203
Exports to U.K......	13,077,720	20,508,402

Communications.—The railway from the port of Dammam to the oilfields at Abqaiq and through Hofuf to Riyadh was opened late in 1951. A metalled road connects Mecca with its Port of Jedda, and there are new roads from Jedda–Medina (410 miles) and from Riyadh to Dhahran. The Saudi Arabian Government employs Trans-world Airlines to pilot and maintain the Government-owned Saudi Arabian Airlines with Dakota, Skymaster, Convair and Boeing 720 aircraft. Scheduled services are flown between Jedda, Taif, Riyadh, Hofuf and Dhahran. There are first-class airports at Dhahran, where a new airport was opened in 1962, and at Jedda. The other airfields named are being developed. Saudi Arabian airlines also maintain regular services to Cairo and Beirut. Services operated by Aden Airways, Arab Airways (both subsidiaries of B.O.A.C.), Middle East Airlines and Czechoslovak Airlines and Misrair call at Jedda, the route of Aden Airways including Cairo-Luxor-Jedda-Port Sudan - Asmara - Kamaran - Aden and return.

Education.—There are over 300 Government schools, mostly primary, but including seven secondary schools and one preparatory school, which prepares students who have completed their secondary course for University training, in Egypt or elsewhere. There is an Islamic University at Medina and a recently opened University at Riyadh. With three exceptions all schools are maintained by the Government.

SAUDI ARABIAN FLAG.—Green oblong, white Arabic device in centre: "There is no God but God, Muhammad is the Prophet of God," and a white scimitar beneath the lettering.

CAPITAL, Riyadh, population about 100,000.

BRITISH EMBASSY
Shari' Malik Abdul Aziz,
Jedda

Ambassador Extraordinary and Plenipotentiary, His Excellency Sir Colin Tradescant Crowe, K.C.M.G. (1963).
1st Secretaries, J. L. Christie; D. A. Hamley; C. J. Treadwell.
2nd Secretary, C. J. Burgess (*Vice-Consul*).
3rd Secretaries, P. Dow; J. H. Symons; D. G. Taylor.

SENEGAL

(Republic of Senegal)

President and Head of Government, Léopold Senghor, *elected President*, Sept. 5, 1960.
Ambassador in London, His Excellency M. Léon Boissier-Palun, 21 Portman Square, W.1. [Welbeck 0313].

Senegal lies on the west coast of Africa between Mauritania in the north and the Republic of Guinea in the south. It has an area of 77,814 sq. miles and the population was estimated at 2,973,300 in 1961.

Formerly a French colony, Senegal elected on Nov. 25, 1958, to remain within the French Community as an autonomous republic. Foundation of a Federation of Mali, to consist of the State of Senegal, (French) Soudan, Dahomey and Upper Volta, was announced in January, 1959, and the Federation came into existence on April 4, consisting of Senegal and the Sudanese Republic only, the others having meanwhile withdrawn. Mali was proclaimed fully independent by the President of the Federal Assembly, M. Léopold Senghor, on June 20, 1960. However, these arrangements proved short-lived as on August 22, 1960, the Senegal Legislative Assembly formally approved measures to secede from the Federation and continue as an independent state. In March, 1963 (after an attempted *coup d'état* by the then Prime Minister in the previous December) a new constitution was approved giving executive powers to the President, on the lines of the present French constitution. Senegal's principal exports are groundnuts (raw and processed) and phosphates. Exports to U.K. amounted in 1962 to £578,942 in value, and her imports from Great Britain amounted to £1,181,628.

CAPITAL.—Ψ Dakar (383,000).

FLAG.—Three vertical bands, green, yellow and red; a green star on the yellow band.

British Embassy: B.P. 6025, Dakar.
British Ambassador, His Excellency John Howard Peck, C.M.G. (1962) £4,115

SERBIA. *See* Yugoslavia

SIAM. *See* Thailand

SOMALIA

(Somali Republic)

President, Aden Abdulle Osman, *elected* July 6, 1961, *for a term of six years.*
Prime Minister, Dr. Abdi Rashid Ali Shirmarke.
Minister of Foreign Affairs, Abdullahi Issa.

The Somali Republic occupies part of the north-east horn of Africa, with a coast-line on the Indian Ocean extending from the boundary with Kenya (2° South latitude) to Capo Guardafui (12° N.); and on the Gulf of Aden to the boundary with French Somaliland. Somalia is bounded on the west by French Somaliland, Ethiopia and Kenya and covers an area of approximately 246,000 sq. miles. The population, of which a large proportion is nomadic, is estimated (1961) at 1,990,000. Cattle raising is the main occupation in Somalia and there is a modest export trade in cattle on the hoof, skins and hides. Italy imports the bulk of the banana crop under agreement with the Somali Government.

Government.—The Somali Republic, consisting of the former British Somaliland Protectorate and the former Italian trust territory of Somalia, was set up on July 1, 1960. British rule in Somaliland lasted from 1887 until June 26, 1960, with the exception of a short period in 1940–41 when the Protectorate was occupied by Italian forces. Somalia, formerly an Italian colony, was occupied by the United Kingdom from 1941 until the end of 1950, when it was placed under Italian administration by resolution of the United Nations. This trusteeship came to an end on July 1, 1960, when Somalia became independent and united with the former British Somaliland Protectorate under the title of the Somali Republic. The President of the Legislative Assembly of Somalia was elected provisional first President of the Republic. Aden Abdulle Osman was returned to office as the first substantive President of the Republic and a new government was formed on July 27, 1961.

Trade with U.K.

	1961	1962
Imports from U.K.	£788,226	£849,003
Exports to U.K.	51,844	127,069

CAPITAL.—ΨMogadishu, population (estimated 1956), 150,000. Other towns are Hargeisa (50,000), Kisimayu (30,000), ΨBerbera (19,000) and Burao (10,000).

FLAG.—Five-pointed white star on blue ground.

BRITISH EMBASSY
Mogadishu

(Closed, March, 1963, at interruption of diplomatic relations).

British Council Representative, R. A. F. Sherwood, Via Lungomare Duca d'Abruzzi, 5, P.O. Box 262, Mogadishu.

SOUTH AFRICA

(Republiek van Suid-Afrika)

State President, Charles Robberts Swart, *elected for a term of* 7 *years*, May 10, 1961; *assumed office* May 31, 1961.

CABINET
(May 31, 1961)

Prime Minister, Dr. Hendrik F. Verwoerd.
Minister of Foreign Affairs, E. H. Louw.
Social Welfare and Pensions. J. J. Serfontein.
Justice, B. J. Vorster.
Transport, B. J. Schoeman.
Economic Affairs and Mines, Dr. N. Diederichs.
Interior, Education, Arts and Science, J. de Klerk.
Agricultural Technical Services and Water Affairs, P. M. K. Le Roux.
Defence, J. J. Fouché.
Labour and Immigration, A. E. Trollip.
Post and Telegraphs ana Health, Dr. A. Hertzog.
Finance, Dr. T. E. Dönges.
Lands, Forests and Public Works, P. O. Sauer.
Bantu Administration and Development, M. D. C. de Wet Nel.
Bantu Education and Indian Affairs, W. A. Maree.
Agricultural Economics and Marketing, D. C. H. Uys.
Coloured Affairs, Community Development and Housing, P. W. Botha.
Information, F. W. Waring.

EMBASSY AND CONSULATE
South Africa House, Trafalgar Square, W.C.2
[Whitehall: 4488]

Ambassador Extraordinary and Plenipotentiary, His Excellency, Dr. Hilgard Muller (1961).
Consul-General, A. J. Oxley.

Area and Population.—The Republic occupies the southernmost part of the African continent from the courses of the Limpopo, Molopo and Orange Rivers (34° 50′ 22″ South latitude) to the Cape of Good Hope, with the exception of Basutoland, Bechuanaland and Swaziland, and part of Mozambique. It has a total area of 472,359 square miles, and a total population (census of 1961) of 15,982,664 (White, 3,088,492; African, 10,907,789; Coloured, 1,509,258; and Asian, 477,125). Populations of the Provinces at the 1961 census (preliminary figures) were: Cape Province (278,465 sq. miles), 5,342,720; Natal (33,578 sq. miles), 2,979,920; Transvaal (110,450 sq. miles), 6,273,477; Orange Free State (49,866 sq. miles), 1,386,547.

Zululand, annexed in 1897, comprises about two-thirds of the country formerly under Zulu kings, and is bounded on the south and south-west by the Tugela River; on the south-east by the Indian Ocean; on the north by the Portuguese possessions; and on the west by the districts of Babanango, Vryheid and Ngotshe and by Swaziland. In 1951, the appointment was confirmed of Cyprian Bekuzulu, grandson of Dinizulu and great-grandson of Cetewayo, as Paramount Chief of the Zulus in Natal.

The southernmost province contains many parallel ranges, which rise in steps towards the interior. The south-western peninsula contains the famous *Table Mountain* (3,582 feet), while the *Great Swartberg* and *Langberg* run in parallel lines from west to east of the Cape province. Between these two ranges and the *Roggeveld* and *Nuweveld* ranges to the north is the Great Karroo Plateau, which is bounded on the east by the *Sneeuberg*, containing the highest summit in the province (Kompasberg, 7,800 feet). In the east are ranges which join the *Drakensberg* (11,000 feet) between Natal and the Orange Free State.

The Orange Free State presents a succession of undulating grassy plains with good pasture-land, at a general elevation of some 3,800 feet, with occasional hills or kopjes. The Transvaal is also mainly an elevated plateau with parallel ridges in the *Magaliesberg* and *Waterberg* ranges of no great height. The veld or plains of this northernmost province is divisible into the High Veld of the south, the Bankenveld of the centre, and the Low Veld of the north and east, the first and second forming the grazing and agricultural region of the Transvaal and the last a fertile sub-tropical area. The eastern province of Natal has pastoral lowlands and rich agricultural land between the slopes of the Drakensberg and the coast, the interior rising in terraces as in the southern provinces. The *Orange*, with its tributary the *Vaal*, is the principal river of the south, rising in the Drakensberg and flowing into the Atlantic between the Territory of South West Africa and the Cape Province. The *Limpopo*, or Crocodile River, in the north, rises in the Transvaal and flows into the Indian Ocean through Portuguese East Africa. Most of the remaining rivers are furious torrents after rain, with partially dry beds at other seasons.

Government.—The self-governing colonies of the Cape of Good Hope, Natal, the Transvaal and the Orange River Colony became united on May 31, 1910, under the South Africa Act, 1909, in a legislative union unper the name of the Union of South Africa, the four colonie., becoming Provinces of the Union. The Union of South Atrica continued as a member of the British Commonwealth until 1961, the Crown being represented by a Governor-General. A referendum held among white voters on October 5, 1960, decided by a narrow majority in favour of Republican status. 1,633,772 votes were cast—a poll of 90·73 per cent.—with 52·05 per cent. in favour. The Union of South Africa became a republic on May 31, 1961, and withdrew from the Commonwealth. Mr. C. R. Swart, Governor-General of the Union from Jan. 12, 1960, resigned on April 30, 1961, and was elected the first President of the Republic on May 10, by an electoral college consisting of the members of both Houses of Parliament. The President assumed office on May 31, 1961.

The *Senate*, as reconstituted by the Senate Act, 1960, consists of 54 members, appointed or elected for a term of five years. Eleven are appointed by the Government (8 for the Republic, 2 for South West Africa and a Coloured representative). Forty-three are elected (Transvaal, 14; Cape Province, 11; Natal and Orange Free State, each 8; and South West Africa, 2). The Act of 1960 reintroduced proportional representation at elections to the Senate and excluded Native representation.

The *House of Assembly* consists of 160 elected members, 52 of whom represent the Cape of Good Hope, 16 Natal, 68 Transvaal, 14 the Orange Free State, and 6 South West Africa. There are also 4 members elected under the Separate Representation of Voters Act, 1951, to represent the electoral divisions for the coloured voters in the Cape Province. Members of both Houses must be South African citizens of white descent. White female franchise was introduced under the provision of Act No. 18 of 1930. Cape Bantu voters ceased to be entitled to elect 3 members in Nov. 1959.

After the General Election on Oct. 18, 1961, the party representation in the House of Assembly was as follows: Nationalist Party, 105; United Party, 49; National Union, 1; Progressive Party, 1; Representatives of Coloured Voters, 4. Total, 160. The National Union Party members have since joined the United Party on disbanding of the former party.

Defence.—The South Africa Defence Act, 1957, became law on Nov. 1, 1958. This Act, as amended in 1961, provides that every citizen between the ages of 17 and 65 is liable to render personal service in time of war, and those between 17 and 25 are liable to undergo a prescribed course of peace training with the Citizen Force or Commandos spread over a period of four consecutive years. Thereafter citizens are required to serve with the Reserve for a prescribed period of time.

Education.—The Provinces have been relieved of all vocational education (technical and industrial), and the Department of Education, Arts and Science under the Minister is concerned with 9 Universities, 11 technical colleges, schools of industries, reformatories and State technical, housecraft and commercial high schools, State-aided vocational schools and State and State-aided special schools for the physically handicapped. There are two non-white university colleges and three Bantu university colleges, students of these taking the examinations of the University of South Africa. The number of full-time students at the universities in June, 1960, was 26,947.

The central direction of public education (other than higher education) is exercised by the Provincial Education Department in each of the four Provinces. Each Department is controlled by a Director. The majority of schools for whites in all the Provinces are state schools. In all Provinces primary education in schools for all races is free. Secondary education in all the Provinces is also free, with an age limit of 19 years in the Cape Province. Expenditure on education in 1959–60 by the Central Government was *R*.41,823, and by provincial administrations *R*.122,667, a total for the Republic of *R*.164,490.

Communications.—The total open mileage of Government-owned railway lines at the end of June, 1963, was 14,025 miles, of which 13,642 miles were 3 ft. 6 in. gauge and 383 miles 2 ft. gauge. Working expenditure (excluding depreciation) amounted to *R*259,000,000. Internal air services are operated between all the major centres in South and South West Africa. Regional air services are operated between Johannesburg and the Federation of Rhodesia and Nyasaland, East Africa, Central Africa and Portuguese East Africa. The "Springbok Service" is operated jointly by South African Airways and the British Overseas Airways Corporation, using modern aircraft and providing a regular service between Johannesburg and London.

In the year ended December, 1962, South African ports handled 21,500,000 short tons of cargo, an increase of 2,000,000 tons over the 1961 total. The total harbour revenue in 1961–62 was *R*18,500,000, the expenditure *R*14,000,000. Ψ Durban, the most important seaport, handled 11,100,000 tons of goods in 1962. Other ports are Cape Town, Port Elizabeth, and East London; Walvis Bay and Luderitz Bay.

On March 31, 1962, there were 3,216 post and 3,506 telegraph offices open.

Production and Trade.—The principal crops produced in 1962–63 (lbs. '000) were wheat, 1,521,600; maize, 57,708; Kaffir corn, 1,942; barley, 92,250; oats, 229,050. 152,000 short tons of groundnuts were also produced. Sales of wool during the 1962–63 season amounted to 300,000,000 lbs. (1961–62, 313,000,000 lbs.).

Mineral production is of the greatest importance in the South African economy, value of production in 1962 being (*R*1,000): gold, 636,582; diamonds 36,100; coal, 65,088; copper, 19,065; tin, 2,425; silver, 1,952; asbestos, 22,133. Exports of uranium oxide amounted to *R*74,200,000 in 1962.

Value of trade in 1962 (with 1961 figures in *italic* type) was: *R*1,027,000,000 (*R*1,005,000,000); Exports *R*946,000,000 (*R*952,000,000).

Trade with U.K.*

	1961	1962
Imports from U.K.	£146,984,899	£146,397,340
Exports to U.K.	103,302,063	103,046,687

*Excluding gold bullion and specie.

Currency.—The South African £ reached parity with the £ sterling in 1946. A new decimal currency the *Rand* (*R*.) was introduced in South Africa on Feb. 14, 1961, including the British High Commission Territories of Basutoland, Bechuanaland and Swaziland. By agreement with the International Monetary Fund the par value of the *Rand* had previously been fixed at 10*s*. sterling. Five silver coins, the *crown* (50 cents); *florin* (20 cents); *shilling* (10 cents); 6*d*. (five cents); and 3*d*. (2½ cents); and bronze coins, 1 *cent* and ½-*cent* were struck for ordinary use. (*See also* p. 83.)

Finance.—Revenue of the Republic of South Africa in 1962–63 totalled *R*826,000,000 (1961–62, *R*737,800,000); expenditure, *R*798,000,000 (*R*723,400,000). The gross Public Debt of the Republic on March 31, 1963, was R2,790,000,000 (1962, *R*2,638,000,000).

CAPITAL.—The administrative seat of the Government is PRETORIA, Transvaal; population (census of 1961), 422,590; the seat of the Legislature is Ψ CAPE TOWN, population (1961), 807,211. Cape Town is 5,979 miles from Southampton; transit by mail steamship 14 days, and by air mail two days. There is a modern and well-equipped aerodrome seventeen miles by road from the centre of the city. Cape Town's harbour and docking facilities, existing and projected, are in keeping with its status as a world port of commercial and strategic importance. Other large towns are Johannesburg, Transvaal (1,110,905); ΨDurban, Natal, the largest seaport (659,934); ΨPort Elizabeth, Cape (274,180); Germiston, Transvaal (213,642); BLOEMFONTEIN, capital of Orange Free State (145,273); Springs, Transvaal (137,253); Benoni, Transvaal (136,476); ΨEast London, Cape (115,677); Welkom, O.F.S. (97,614); and PIETERMARITZBURG, capital of Natal (96,236).

FLAG.—Three horizontal stripes of equal width; from top to bottom, orange, white, blue; in the centre of the white stripe, the old Orange Free State flag hanging vertical, towards the pole the Union Jack horizontal, away from the pole the old Transvaal Vierkleur, all spread full. The national flag was adopted by the Union in 1927 and was flown side by side with the Union Jack. This practice was expected to be continued in Natal.

BRITISH EMBASSY
Hill Street, Pretoria
91 Parliament Street, Cape Town (Jan.–June)

Ambassador and High Commissioner for Basutoland, Bechuanaland and Swaziland, His Excellency Sir Hugh Southern Stephenson, K.C.M.G., C.I.E., C.V.O., O.B.E. (1963) £7,015
Minister, W. H. Young, C.M.G.
Minister (Commercial), D. A. Bryan, C.M.G., O.B.E.
Counsellor, D. McD. Gordon.
1st Secretaries, J. S. Longrigg; The Viscount Dunrossil; P. S. Ziegler; J. Walters; T. H. Gillson; B. S. Picton.
Air Attaché and Senior Service Liaison Officer, Air Comdre. C. D. Tomalin, O.B.E., D.F.C., A.F.C.
Military Attaché, Col. A. C. W. Noel, M.C.
Assistant Air Attaché, Sqn.-Ldr. J. MacDonald, D.F.C.
Assistant Military Attaché and Secretary, Major J. F. Ballard.
Cultural Attaché and British Council Representative, R. T. Butlin, O.B.E.

There are British Consular Offices at *Cape Town, Johannesburg, Durban, Port Elizabeth* and *East London*.

South West Africa

Administrator, D. T. du P. Viljoen.

SOUTH WEST AFRICA lies between S. lat. 17° 23′ and the Orange River, with a narrow strip between 17° 30′–18° 20′ S. lat. extending from 21° to 25° E long., known as the Caprivi Zipfel, and gives access to the Zambesi. Off the coast are a number of guano islands (Hollandsbird, Mercury, Ichaboe, Seal, Penguin, Halifax, Long, Possession, Albatross, Pomona, Plumpudding, Sinclair and Roastbeef Islands).

The estimated area of the country is 318,261 square miles, and the population (1961 census, preliminary) is 525,064, of whom 73,154 are whites.

South West Africa was occupied by Germany in 1884, but at the conclusion of the War of 1914–1918 the territory was mandated to the Union of South Africa in accordance with the Treaty of Versailles. Under the Union Act No. 49 of 1919, the exercise of the mandate was vested in a Governor-General, who delegated his powers to an Administrator appointed by the Union Government. A limited measure of self-government was conferred upon the inhabitants by the Union Act No. 42 of 1925. Fundamental and far-reaching changes in the constitutional position of the Territory were introduced by the passing of the South-West Africa Affairs Amendment Act, 1949 (No. 23 of 1949). The Advisory Council was abolished and all 18 members of the Legislative Assembly are now chosen by the registered voters of the Territory.

The Territory is represented in the House of Assembly of the Republic of South Africa by six members duly elected by the registered voters of the Territory and in the Senate by four Senators, of whom two are elected and two nominated by the Republican Government.

Generally speaking, only the Parliament of the Republic has the power to legislate on those matters in respect of which the Legislative Assembly is not competent to legislate, and the Legislative Assembly in respect of other matters.

On July 11, 1950, the International Court of Justice at The Hague delivered an opinion that South West Africa was still under international mandate; that international obligations resulting from the mandate were still incumbent on the Union, including obligation to submit reports on its administration; and that South Africa was not competent to modify its international status without consent of the United Nations.

The Capital of the Territory is Windhoek, which lies practically in the centre of the country at 5,500 ft. above sea-level. The ports are Ψ Walvis Bay and ΨLuderitz. The port and enclave of Walvis Bay, constitutionally and administratively, are however part of Cape Province and not of South West Africa.

SPAIN

(Estado Español)

Head of the Spanish State, Generalissimo Don Francisco Franco Bahamonde, *born* Dec. 17, 1892, *assumed office*. Oct. 1, 1936.
Vice-President of the Government and Chief of Staff, Capt.-Gen. Muñoz Grandes, *appointed* July 10, 1962.

CABINET

Minister for Foreign Affairs, Sr. Don Fernando Maria Castiella.
Interior, Teniente General Don Camilo Alonso Vega.
Army, Teniente General Don Pablo Martin Alonso.
Marine, Almirante Don Pedro Nieto Antunez.
Air, Teniente General José Lacalle Larraga.
Justice, Sr. Don Antonio Iturmendi Bañales.
Finance, Sr. Don Mariano Navarro Rubio.
Industry, Sr. Don Gregorio Lopez Bravo.
Agriculture, Sr. Don Cirilo Cánovas Garcia.
Labour, Sr. Don Jesús Romeo Gorria.
Education, Sr. Don Manuel Lora Tamayo.
Public Works, Sr. Don Jorge Vigón Suero-Diaz.
Commerce, Sr. Don Alberto Ullastres Calvo.
Information and Tourism, Sr. Don Manuel Fraga-Iribarne.
Under Secretary to the Presidency, Contralmirante Don Luis Carrero Blanco.
Minister Secretary-General of the Falange, Sr. Don José Solís Ruiz.
Minister of Housing, Sr. Don José María Martínez Sánchez-Arjona.
Minister without Portfolio and President of the Council of Economy, Sr. Don Pedro Gual Villalbi.

SPANISH EMBASSY IN LONDON
24 Belgrave Square, S.W.1
[Sloane: 6181]

Ambassador Extraordinary and Plenipotentiary, His Excellency the Marqués de Santa Cruz (1958).
Minister-Counsellor (Cultural Affairs), Don Ernesto La Orden.
Counsellor, Don Alberto López Herce.
1st Secretary, Don Santiago Martinez Caro.

2nd Secretaries, Don Francisco Javier Palazón (*Cultural Attaché*); Don Carlos Manzano; Don Salvador Bermudez de Castro; Don Gil Armangue (*Vice-Consul*).
Military Attaché, Lt.-Col. Don Francisco Mendivil.
Naval Attaché, Capt. Don Enrique Barbudo.
Air Attaché, Col. Don Felipe Gallarza.
Commercial Counsellor, Don Manuel Quintero.
Commercial Attaché, Don Manuel Barroso.
Information Counsellor, Don Tristan La Rosa.
Information Attaché, Don Luis Climent.
Agricultural Attaché, Don Claudio Rodriguez Porrero.
Labour Attaché, Don Luis Burgos Boezo.
Honorary Attachés, Don Rafael de Romero; Don Aurelio Valls Belda.
Consular Section, 3 Hans Crescent, S.W.1.
Commercial Office, 3 Hans Crescent, S.W.1.
Spanish Institute, 102 Eaton Square, S.W.1.

Area and Population.—A National State in the south-west of Europe, between 36°–43° 45′ N. lat. and 4° 25′ E.–9° 20′ W. long., bounded on the south and east by the Mediterranean, on the west by the Atlantic and Portugal, and on the north by the Bay of Biscay and France, from which it is separated by the Pyrenees. Continental Spain occupies about eleven-thirteenths of the Iberian peninsula, the remaining portion forming the Republic of Portugal. Its coast-line extends 1,317 miles—712 formed by the Mediterranean and 605 by the Atlantic—and it comprises a total area of 196,700 square miles, with an estimated population (Dec., 31, 1962) of 30,946,732. Provisional returns for 1962 gave 650,091 births, 271,591 deaths and 236,488 marriages. Infant mortality was estimated at 3·2 per 100 live births in 1962.

Physical Features.—The interior of the Iberian Peninsula consists of an elevated tableland surrounded and traversed by mountain ranges—the Pyrenees, the Cantabrian Mountains, the Sierra Guadarrama, Sierra Morena, Sierra Nevada, Montes de Toledo, &c. The principal rivers are the Douro, the Tagus, the Guadiana, the Guadalquivir, the Ebro, and the Minho.

Government.—Phoenician traders visited the peninsula more than a thousand years before the Christian era, but they were traders rather than settlers, although Cadiz has preserved its identity and claims to be "the oldest city in the world." The Roman occupation of Spain was completed after the close of the Second Punic War (202 B.C.) and *Hispania* was divided into two provinces. After the decline of the Roman Empire the Italian elements, which had partly displaced the Celts and Iberians, were in turn disturbed by settlers of Germanic origin. After the union of Aragon and Castile in the 15th century Spain was ruled by sovereigns of the Aragon, Habsburg and Bourbon lines (with the intervention of a Republic 1873–74). Alfonso XIII. succeeding at birth in 1886. On April 14, 1931, following the results of the Municipal Elections, which showed anti-monarchical feeling to be extremely high in all the chief towns of Spain, King Alfonso XIII. left the country, and the Queen and other members of the Royal Family left on the following day. A Republic was immediately proclaimed and a Provisional Government, drawn from the various Republican and Socialist parties, was formed. The Republican Assembly (*Cortes*) was a single Chamber Congress of Deputies. Each Province had an Assembly (*Diputacion Provincial*), and, with the approval of the *Cortes*, Provinces might combine to form an Autonomous Region within the Republic.

On July 18, 1936, a counter-revolution broke out in many military garrisons in Spanish Morocco and spread rapidly throughout Spain. The principal leader was General Francisco Franco Bahamonde, formerly Governor of the Canary Islands, from which office he was dismissed by the Azaña Government. The struggle, in its later phases, threatened to embroil some of the European Powers, those of Nazi-Fascist tendency lending aid to General Franco (leader of the Military-Fascist fusion, or *Falange*) while those of Communist views supported the Azaña (*Popular Front*) government. In October, 1938, many of the supporting troops were withdrawn, and on March 29, 1939, the Civil War was declared to have ended, the Popular Front Governments in Madrid and Barcelona surrendering to the *Nationalists* (as General Franco's followers were then named). On June 5, 1939, the Grand Council of the *Falange Española Tradicionalista y de las Juntas Ofensivas Nacional-Sindicalistas*, which replaced the former *Cortes*, met at Burgos to legislate for the reorganization of the country under the Presidency of General Franco, who had assumed the title of *Caudillo (Leader) of the Empire and Chief of the State*. In the Civil War of 1936–39 over 1,000,000 lives were lost.

On July 1, 1942, General Franco announced the reinstitution of the *Cortes de España*, which was composed (May, 1955) of 515 members: *ex officio members*—16 ministers, 101 National Councillors of Falange, the President of the Council of State, the President of the Supreme Court of Justice, the President of the Supreme Court of Military Justice, 12 rectors of universities, 3 presidents of Royal Academies, and 52 mayors of the provincial capitals including Ceuta and Melilla. *Elected Members*—159 representatives of national syndicates, 101 representatives of municipalities, 4 representatives of Royal Academies, and 15 representatives of professions. *Nominated Members*—50 persons of high ecclesiastical, military, administrative or social rank.

On April 1, 1947, a Law of Succession was promulgated creating two new bodies: the Council of the Realm and the Council of Regency. The main duty of the Council of the Realm is to nominate a successor to Generalissimo Franco should the latter not already have done so before the time of his decease or incapacitation. The Council of Regency is intended to rule during an interregnum and in the absence abroad of the Head of State; it has a membership of three. On July 6, 1947, a referendum asking approval of this law was announced (July 27) to have received 14,145,163 affirmative votes out of a recorded total of 15,219,563. Under this law a Regency Council of three was to be set up in the event of the death or incapacitation of the Head of the State.

Defence.—*Army*: Spain is divided into nine Military Regions, the Balearic Islands Command, North Africa Command, and Canary Islands, West Africa Command. Each Military Region contains one or more Divisions, and, with the exception of 9th Military Region, possesses a Corps H.Q. There are in Spain one Armoured, one Cavalry, four Mountain and seven Infantry Divisions of which three are mechanized. There are also an Airborne Brigade and Independent brigades of Infantry, mechanized Cavalry and Artillery in the Peninsula. The Spanish Army in North Africa consists of the strong garrisons of Ceuta, Melilla and the Spanish islands in North Africa. In Canary Islands and West Africa an Inter Service Command under an Army general, contains long service forces in which the Legion (Spain's only regular units of troops) is predominant. The Guardia Civil also forms part of the Army though it operates as a gendarmerie in the rural areas under control of the Ministry of the Interior. Marines are now wholly under Naval command.

The active *Navy* consists of 3 cruisers, 6 destroyers, 27 A/S escorts (destroyers, frigates and corvettes), 3 minelayers, 19 minesweepers, 3 landing ships, 2 squadrons of helicopters and a large number of small craft. An extensive modernization programme was completed in 1961.

The *Air Force* is divided into 5 Air Regions with 2 overseas Air Zones, and a separate, functional Air Defence Command. It consists of 5 Fighter Wings, 2 Fighter-Bomber Wings, 3 Light Bomber Wings and 2 Transport Wings, with many training and rescue aircraft.

Education.—Primary education is free, but compulsory attendance cannot be enforced because of the inadequate number of schools. Official figures of illiteracy in 1950 give a total number of illiterates, excluding children under 10, of 3,983,890, or 14·24 per cent. of the population (men, 9·86 per cent., women, 18·30 per cent.). There are 12 Universities in continental Spain and 1 at La Laguna in the Canary Islands. The University of Salamanca was founded in 1230, Valencia (1245), Oviedo (1317), Valladolid (1346), Barcelona (1450), Saragossa (1474), Santiago (1501), Seville (1502), Granada (1526), Madrid (1590), Murcia (1915). The Catholic University of Pamplona (1953) is the only University in Spain not subject to government control.

Language and Literature.—Castilian is the language of more than two-thirds of the population of Spain and is the form of Spanish spoken in Mexico, Central and (except in Brazil) Southern America. Basque, reported to have been the original language of Iberia, is spoken in the rural districts of Vizcaya, Guipuzcoa and Alava. Catalan is spoken in Provençal Spain, and Galician, spoken in the north-western provinces, is allied to Portuguese. The literature of Spain is one of the oldest and richest in the world, the *Poem of the Cid*, the earliest and best of the heroic songs of Spain, having been written about A.D. 1140. The outstanding writings of its golden age are those of Miguel de Cervantes Saavedra (1547–1616), Lope Felix de Vega Carpio (1562–1635) and Pedro Calderón de la Barca (1600–1681). The Nobel Prize for Literature has three times been awarded to Spanish authors—J. Echegaray (1904), J. Benavente (1922) and Juan Ramón Jimenez (1956).

FINANCE	1962
Revenue................. *Pesetas*	95,469,100,000
Expenditure..............	89,246,500,000

Public Debt (December 31, 1962) excluding para-statal organizations and State-guaranteed issues: *Pesetas* 94,510,960,000.

The rate of exchange for the *peseta* in October, 1962, was 168·0 *pesetas* = £1 sterling (*see also* p. 83).

Production and Industry.—The country is generally fertile, and well adapted to agriculture and the cultivation of heat-loving fruits—as olives, oranges, lemons, almonds, pomegranates, apricots and grapes. The agricultural products include wheat, barley, oats, rice, hemp and flax. In 1962 the orange crop, of which Germany, the United Kingdom and France were the chief importing countries, amounted to 1,800,000 tons but was later severely damaged by frost and export earnings were consequently affected. The wine is cultivated widely; in the south-west, Jerez, the well-known sherry and tent wines are produced.

Spain's mineral resources of coal, iron, wolfram, copper, lead and other ores are variously exploited. Many of the richer and more easily worked deposits have been exhausted, but the authorities are actively engaged in stimulating the exploitation of hitherto unworked or lower grade deposits. In 1962 the coal output amounted to 16,575,000 tons and iron ore 5,841,000 tons. The iron and steel industries produced 2,387,000 tons of pig iron and 2,225,000 tons of steel. Other production figures (in tons) included; cement, 6,761,000: lead, 75,412; zinc, 60,809; sulphuric acid, 1,438,000; paper, 395,000; cotton yarn, 88,460; and wool yarn 15,900. Production of electric power was 20,900 million kWh. The fishing industry is of importance.

The principal manufactures are textile goods of all kinds, footwear and other leather goods, ceramics, sewing machines, bicycles, chemical products and light engineering manufactures.

The tourist industry is becoming increasingly important and it is estimated that 8,669,000 tourists visited Spain in 1962.

Communications.—In 1960 there were 11,335 miles of railways in service. The sea-going mercantile marine in 1960 consisted of 1,742 vessels of 1,643,621 gross tons. Civil aviation is under the control of the Air Ministry; there are several inland and international services in operation.

TRADE

	1961 *Pesetas*	1962 *Pesetas*
Imports...........	65,537,000,000	94,162,000,000
Exports...........	42,575,000,000	43,323,000,000

Trade with U.K.

	1961	1962
Imports from U.K...	£32,207,287	£52,617,305
Exports to U.K.....	54,848,087	54,271,312

The principal imports are cotton, tobacco, cellulose, timber, coffee and cocoa, fertilizers, dyes, machinery, motor vehicles and agricultural tractors, wool and petroleum products. The principal exports include iron ore, cork, salt, vegetables, citrus fruits, wines, olive oil, potash, mercury, pyrites, tinned fruit and fish, bananas and tomatoes.

CAPITAL, Madrid. Population 2,000,000. Other large cities are ΨBarcelona (1,800,000), Valencia (543,000), ΨSeville (500,000), ΨMalaga (350,000), Zaragoza (301,000), Bilbao (281,000); Murcia (243,000).

FLAG.—Three horizontal bands, red, yellow and red, with coat of arms on yellow band.

AIR TRANSIT FROM U.K.—London–Barcelona (713 miles) 2 *hrs.* 25 *mins.*; Madrid (775 miles), 2 *hrs.* 50 *mins.*; Valencia, 2 *hrs.* 10 *mins.*

BRITISH EMBASSY

(Calle Fernando el Santo, 16, Madrid)

Ambassador Extraordinary and Plenipotentiary, His Excellency Sir George Peter Labouchere, K.C.M.G. (1960)...................... £5,015

Minister, A. C. I. Samuel, C.M.G., C.V.O.
Hon. Attaché, B. Malley, C.M.G., C.B.E.
1st Secretary, H. A. Dudgeon (*Head of Chancery*).
1st Secretary and Consul, F. B. S. Jell.
2nd Secretary, H. J. H. Maud.
Counsellor (*Commercial*), D. I. Dunnett, O.B.E.
1st Secretary (*Commercial*), N. E. Cox.
2nd Secretary (*Commercial*), E. A. Arnoux.
2nd Secretary (*Information*), E. J. Anglin.
Naval Attaché, Cdr. J. L. Rigge, R.N.
Military Attaché, Brigadier M. J. A. Paterson, D.S.O.
Air Attaché, Group Capt. P. H. Baldwin, O.B.E.
Archivist, Miss N. B. Low.
Chaplain, Rev. R. B. Ney, M.B.E.

BRITISH CONSULAR OFFICES

There are Consular Offices at *Barcelona*, *Palma de Mallorca*, *Tarragona*, *Valencia*, *Cartagena*, *Granada*, *Seville*, *Cadiz*, *Jerez*, *Algeciras*, *La Linea*, *Vigo*, *Bilbao*, *San Sebastian*, *Malaga*, *Teneriffe*, *Las Palmas*, *Orotava* (*Canary Islands*), *Ceuta* and *Melilla* (*Morocco*), and *Madrid*.

BRITISH COUNCIL

Representative, D. A. A. Traversi, O.B.E., Calle Almagro 5, Madrid, 4.

There are British Institutes at Madrid and Barcelona.

BRITISH CHAMBER OF COMMERCE OF SPAIN, Carrera San Jeronimo 28, *Madrid*; Paseo de Gracia 11 (Segundo), *Barcelona*; Pascual y Genis 22, *Valencia*.

Madrid, 1,150 miles; transit, 45 to 50 hours.

The BALEARIC ISLES are an archipelago off the east coast of Spain. There are four large islands (Majorca, Minorca, Iviza and Formentera), and seven smaller (Aire, Aucanada, Botafoch, Cabrera, Dragonera, Pinto and El Rey). The islands were occupied by the Romans after the destruction of Carthage and provided contingents of the celebrated Balearic slingers. The total area is 1,935 square miles, with a population of 441,842. The archipelago forms a province of Spain, the capital being ♆Palma in Majorca, pop. 149,921; ♆Mahon (Minorca), pop. 16,547.

The CANARY ISLANDS are an archipelago in the Atlantic, off the African coast, consisting of 7 islands and 6 uninhabited islets. The total area is 2,807 square miles, with a population of 908,718. The Canary Islands form two Provinces of Spain.—*Las Palmas* (Gran Canaria, Lanzarote, Fuerteventura and the islets of Alegranza, Roque del Este, Roque del Oeste, Graciosa, Montaña Clara and Lobos), with seat of administration at ♆Las Palmas (pop. 177,746) in Gran Canaria, where major oil companies have installations for re-fuelling shipping; and *Santa Cruz de Tenerife* (Tenerife, La Palma, Gomera and Hierro), with seat of administration at ♆Santa Cruz in Tenerife, pop. 124,462.

Trade with U.K.

	1961	1962
Imports from U.K.....	£5,667,142	£6,691,047
Exports to U.K......	13,664,602	15,312,780

ISLA DE LOS FAISANES OF ILE DE LA CONFERENCE is a Franco-Spanish condominium, under the Treaty of Bayonne Dec. 2, 1856, and March 27, 1901. It lies at the mouth of the Bidassoa in La Higuera bay. It is uninhabited.

♆CEUTA is a fortified post on the Moroccan coast, opposite Gibraltar. The total area is 5 square miles, with a population of 64,000.

♆MELILLA is a town on a rocky promontory of the Rif coast, connected with the mainland by a narrow isthmus. Melilla has been in Spanish possession since 1492. The population is 87,000. Ceuta and Melilla are parts of Metropolitan Spain.

OVERSEAS TERRITORIES

The Spanish Colonies consist of certain settlements in, and islands round the coast of, Africa, with a total area of close on 82,400 square miles, and a population estimated in 1935 at 951,000.

SPANISH GUINEA, consisting of the islands of Fernando Póo and Annobon, the Corisco Islands and Rio Muni (mainland) was divided into two provinces on April 1, 1960, each becoming a province of Metropolitan Spain under a civil governor, the inhabitants having the same rights as Spanish citizens. Since December, 1960, six deputies have represented the two provinces in the *Cortes* at Madrid. It was announced on Aug. 11, 1963, that Spain would grant autonomy to these territories. *Fernando Póo* lies in the Bight of Biafra in 3° 12′ N. lat. and 8° 48′ E. long., about 20 miles distant from the west coast of Africa, and is a mountainous island (Pico de Santa Isabel, 10,800 feet), with forests of oil palm, ebony, mahogany, and oak, and sugar-cane, cotton, and indigo. Cocoa, coffee, sugar, tobacco, vanilla, and kola nut are cultivated, and large quantities of cocoa and other products are exported. With its dependencies it has an area of about 800 square miles, and a population estimated at 34,200. The capital of Spanish Guinea is ♆Santa Isabel (pop. 9,000) on the island of Fernando Póo. The total area, mainland and islands, is about 10,000 sq. miles, with an estimated population of 204,495, of whom about 4,124 are whites.

Annobon Island (Anno Bom), in the Gulf of Guinea, in 1° 24′ S. lat. and 5° 3E. long.; population 1,410.

Corisco Islands, consisting of Corisco, Elobey Grande, and Elobey Chico, lie in Corisco Bay, and export ebony, logwood, and other forest produce.

Rio Muni (the second province) is a coastal settlement between Cameroon and Congo (1° N.—2° 10′ N. lat.), extending about 125 miles inland. The inhabitants are Bantu tribes, and the principal settlements are at the mouths of the Muni Benito and Campa rivers, and at ♆Bata (the principal town) on the coast.

WESTERN SAHARA.—Spanish possessions in the Western Sahara consist of two provinces—Ifni and Spanish Sahara. Ifni (capital, Sidi Ifni) extends on the coast from the mouth of Bou Sedra (Asif Saloguad) (approximately 29° 38′ N. lat.) to the River Assaka (Nun) which forms the S.W. boundary. The eastern boundary runs between 9° 50′ and 9° 55′ W. long. The coast line is 36 miles in length and the territory measures approximately 950 square miles. The province of Spanish Sahara extends from 27° 40′ N. lat. in the north to La Agüera (Cape Blanco) in the south, though the main southern boundary runs along latitude 21° 20′. The land area is approximately 125,000 square miles. Spanish Sahara is divided into two regions separated by latitude 26° which passes south of Cape Bojador. The northern region is the Seguia el Hamra (Rio Rojo) of which the capital is Aaiun. It extends eastward to approximately 8° 40′ W. long. The southern region is the Rio de Oro, of which the capital is Villa Cisneros. Its eastern boundary is approximately 12° W. long. Total population about 36,000.

SPANISH MOROCCO.—In addition to Ceuta and Melilla, Spain exercised until 1956 a protectorate over a part of Northern Morocco. Moroccan independence was proclaimed after negotiations with France and Spain in 1956 (*see* "Morocco"). Remaining Spanish settlements on the Moroccan seaboard are:—

Alhucemas, the bay of that name includes six islands: population 366.

Penon de la Gomera (or *Peñon de Velez*) is a fortified rocky islet about 40 miles west of Alhucemas Bay; population 450.

The Chaffarinas (or Zaffarines) are a group of three islands near the Algerian frontier, about 2 miles north of Cape del Agua; population 610.

SUDAN

(Republic of the Sudan)

Council of Ministers

President, Prime Minister, Minister of Defence and Commander-in-Chief, Ferik Ibrahim Abboud.

Minister of Education, Lewa Talaat Farid.

Agriculture, Lewa Ahmed Rida Farid.

Cabinet Affairs and Deputy Commander-in-Chief, Lewa Hassan Beshir Nasr.

Local Government, Lewa Ahmed Magdoub El Bahari.

Information and Labour, Lewa Mohammed Nasr Osman.
Interior, Lewa Mohammed Ahmed Irwa.
Commerce, Industry & Supply, Lewa Magboul el Amin El Haj.
Works, Sayed Ziada Arbab.
Finance & Economics, Sayed Abdul Magid Ahmed.
Foreign Affairs and Mineral Resources, Sayed Ahmed Kheir.
Animal Resources, Sayed Santino Deng.
Irrigation & Hydro-Electric Power, Sayed Mekki El Manna.
Health, Dr. Ahmed Ali Zaki.
Communications, Sayed Suleiman Hussein.
[The first eight Ministers are also members of the Supreme Council for the Armed Forces.]

SUDANESE EMBASSY IN LONDON
3 Cleveland Row, S.W.1.
[Trafalgar: 8080]

Ambassador Extraordinary and Plenipotentiary, His Excellency Sayed Amin Ahmed Hussein (1961).
Counsellor, Sayed Mohamed Kamal el Bakri.
2nd Secretary, Sayed Omer Abbas Agabna.
Military Attaché, Col. Muzzamil Salman Ghandour.
Press Attaché, Sayed Mutasim Ali Bereir.
Cultural Attaché, Sayed Bushra Abdul Rahman Soghayer.
Assistant Cultural Attaché, Sayed Hassan Abbas.
Commercial Attaché, Sayed Bukhari Abdullah.

Area and Population.—The Sudan extends from the southern boundary of Egypt, 22° N. lat., to the northern boundary of Uganda, 3° 36′ N. lat., and reaches from the Republic of Chad about 21° 49′ E. (at 12° 45′ N.) to the north-west boundary of Ethiopia in 38° 35′ E. (at 18° N.). The greatest length from north to south is approximately 1,300 miles, and from east to west 950 miles.

The northern boundary is the 22nd parallel of North latitude; on the east lie the Red Sea and Ethiopia; on the south lie Kenya, Uganda and the Congolese Republic; and on the west the Central African Republic, Chad and Libya.

The *White Nile* enters from Uganda at the Sudan frontier post of Nimule in Equatoria Province, as the *Bahr el Jebel*, and leaves the Sudan at Wadi Halfa. The *Blue Nile* flows from Lake Tana on the Ethiopian Plateau. Its course in the Sudan is nearly 500 miles long, before it joins the White Nile at Khartoum. The next confluence of importance is at Atbara where the main Nile is joined by the River Atbara. The total length of the Nile, now accepted as the longest river in the world, is estimated to be 4,160 miles from its source to the Mediterranean Sea. Between Khartoum and Wadi Halfa occur five of the six *Cataracts*.

The estimated area is about 976,750 sq. miles, with a population (estimated 1961) of 12,109,000, partly Arabs, partly Negroes, and partly Nubian of mixed Arab-Negro blood, with a small foreign element, including some 8,000 Europeans. The Arabs and Nubians are all Moslems. The Negroes are generally pagans, but some have been converted to Christianity and others are beginning to go over to Islam. Population of provinces at the census of 1956 was: Bahr-el-Ghazal 991,022; Blue Nile 2,069,646; Darfur 1,328,765; Equatoria 903,503; Kassala 941,039; Khartoum 504,923; Kordofan 1,761,968; Northern 873,059; Upper Nile 888,611.

Government.—By virtue of the Condominium Agreement of 1899 between H.M. Government and the Egyptian Government, and Article 11 of the Anglo-Egyptian Treaty of 1936, the Sudan was administered by a Governor-General on the joint behalf of Great Britain and of Egypt.

On February 12, 1953, an Anglo-Egyptian Agreement guaranteed to the Sudanese the right to determine their own future and reserved the sovereignty of the Sudan until the day of self-determination for the Sudanese. The first Sudanese General Election was held at the end of 1953.

The Sudan House of Representatives on Dec. 19, 1955, voted unanimously a declaration that the Sudan was a fully independent sovereign state, and on Jan. 1, 1956, the Republic was proclaimed and was recognized by Great Britain and Egypt, a Supreme Commission being sworn in to take over sovereignty. On November 17, 1958, by means of a *coup d'état*, the Army took over control of the country. The constitution was suspended, Parliament and political parties dissolved. A Supreme Council of the Armed Forces and a Council of Ministers were set up. In November, 1962, the Government announced a new electoral system comprising partly elected and partly nominated local councils, province councils and a Central Council. The local and province councils under the new system were in being by July, 1963, and the Central Council was expected to be set up before the end of the year.

Education.—Government education is free, beginning at the age of seven and passing through elementary, intermediate and secondary stages, each of four years. University degree courses vary from 4 to 6 years. Arabic is the normal language of instruction in schools throughout the Sudan, although English is still used in most subjects in secondary schools, and is the language of instruction at Khartoum University. English is taught in intermediate and secondary schools as the first foreign language.

In 1962/63 the University of Khartoum had over 1,800 students, of whom 207 graduated in 1963 in eight faculties. There were nearly 1,400 students at the Khartoum Technical Institute, the Senior Trade School and 9 other vocational schools, and there were 90 students at the newly founded Higher Teacher Training Institute at Omdurman. Non-governmental higher education was offered by Cairo University, Khartoum Branch (three faculties) with over 1,400 students, and at religious Institutes, 1 Muslim (320 students) and two Christian (40 students).

There were two training colleges for intermediate teachers with 186 boys and 40 girls, and 14 training colleges for elementary and junior elementary school teachers with 1,300 students. 26 academic secondary schools, with a total first year entry of 74 classes with 35 pupils each (60 for boys and 14 for girls, an increase in the year of 6 and 4 respectively), had an overall total of 7,400 boys and 1,200 girls. There was one secondary technical school with 4 class entry (an increase of 2 classes) and seven post-intermediate two-year technical schools, with a total of 900 boys. 6 Government religious secondary schools also had about 900 boys. 148 academic intermediate schools, with a total of 174 class entries (40 students each) for boys and 36 for girls, an increase during the year of 5 for each sex, had in all 26,400 boys and 5,000 girls. There were 41 religious intermediate schools, an increase of 9, with a little under 5,000 boys. There were 2,931 elementary and junior elementary schools with 362,000 pupils. 295 private schools, at all levels between infant and secondary, had about 48,000 pupils.

Production.—The principal grain crop is *dura* (great millet), the staple food of the people in the Sudan. Sesame and ground-nuts are other important food crops, which also yield an exportable surplus and a promising start has been made with castor seed. The principal export crop is cotton. Main production is of long-staple (Egyptian type) cotton, but smaller quantities of short-staple

(American type) cotton are also grown. Much of the high quality, long-staple cotton is provided by the Sudan Gezira Scheme, a Government-controlled project irrigated from the Sennar Dam on the Blue Nile. An extension to this known as the South West Extension (Managil Scheme) has also been producing long staple cotton since 1959. The Sudan also produces the bulk of the world's supply of gum arabic. Livestock is the mainstay of the nomadic Arab tribes of the desert and the negro tribes of the swamp and wooded grassland country in the South. New dams are under construction at Kashin El Girba and Roseires; 500,000 acres of land will be irrigated from the former.

Communications.—The railway system (3 ft. 6 in. gauge) has a route length of about 3,200 miles, linking Khartoum with Wadi Halfa, Port Sudan, Wad Medani, Sennar, Kosti, El Obeid and Nyala. A line branches out southwards to Wau from the Sennar/Nyala western line. Regular rail and Nile steamer services (operated by Sudan Railways) connect with the Egyptian State Railways to the North, and with the East African Railways and Steamers system to the South. ΨPort Sudan is a well-equipped modern seaport. Sudan Airways fly regular services from Khartoum to many parts of the Sudan and to Egypt, Greece, Italy, the Lebanon, the United Kingdom, Ethiopia, Uganda and W. Germany and are equipped with some Comet aircraft.

FINANCE

	1963–64
Revenue	£67,228,368
Expenditure	58,209,328

£S = Sudanese *Pound* of 100 *Piastres*.
Exchange Rate 97·15 *Piastres* = £1 sterling.

TRADE

	1962
Total imports	£89,333,399
Exports	78,958,563

Trade with U.K.

	1961	1962
Imports from U.K.	£19,888,453	£23,695,895
Exports to U.K.	12,737,975	12,599,504

The principal export is cotton, the value of which, together with cotton-seed, amounted in 1962 to £S48,525,726. Exports of gum arabic amounted to £S4,566,900. The chief imports are cotton piece goods, base metals, vehicles and transport equipment, machinery, petroleum products, sugar, tea, coffee, chemicals and pharmaceuticals.

CAPITAL, Khartoum. The town contains many mosques, an Anglican Cathedral, and the University, with extensive Government buildings. Estimated population, 124,000. Khartoum North and Omdurman have estimated populations of 53,000 and 154,000 respectively.

FLAG.—3 horizontal stripes of blue, yellow and green.

BRITISH EMBASSY
Khartoum

Ambassador Extraordinary and Minister Plenipotentiary, His Excellency Sir Ian Dixon Scott, K.C.M.G., C.I.E. (1961) £4,115

BRITISH COUNCIL

Representative, Dr. N. A. Daniel, Aboul Ela New Building, P.O. Box 1253, Khartoum.

SWEDEN
(Sverige)

*King of Sweden, of the Goths and the Wends**, Gustaf VI Adolf, K.G., elder son of the late King Gustaf V, *born* Nov. 11, 1882; *married* (1) June 15, 1905, H.R.H. the late Princess Margaret of Connaught (*died* May 1, 1920), (2) Nov. 3, 1923, Lady Louise Mountbatten, Princess of Battenberg, *born* July 13, 1889; *succeeded* Oct. 29, 1950.

Heir Apparent, Crown Prince Carl Gustaf, Duke of Jämtland, *grandson* of the King, *born* April 30, 1946.

CABINET

Prime Minister, Tage Erlander.
Justice, Herman Kling.
Foreign Affairs, Torsten Nilsson.
Defence, Sven Andersson.
Social Affairs, Sven Aspling.
Civil Service Affairs, Sigurd Lindholm.
Communications, Gösta Skoglund.
Finance, Gunnar Sträng.
Education and Ecclesiastical Affairs, Ragnar Edenman.
Agriculture, Eric Holmqvist.
Commerce, Gunnar Lange.
Interior, Rune B. Johansson.
Ministers without Portfolio, Mrs. U. Lindström; Sven af Geijerstam; R. Hermansson.

SWEDISH EMBASSY IN LONDON
29 Portland Place, W.1
[Langham: 2080]

Ambassador Extraordinary and Plenipotentiary, His Excellency Gunnar Hägglöf, G.C.V.O.
Counsellors, P. B. Kollberg; C. J. Rappe.
1st Secretary, R. Nyström.
2nd Secretary, J. Ölander.
Attaché, C. Bausch.
Military Attaché, Col. N. I. Carlborg.
Naval Attaché, Capt. B. Hedlund.
Air Attaché, Group Capt. N. H. Dahl.
Assistant Air and Naval Attaché, Sqn.-Ldr. L-O. Ohlson.
Press Attaché, G. Fagrell.
Assistant Press Attaché, G. Landberg.
Cultural Attaché, L. Warne.
Labour Attaché, S. Klasén.
Chaplain, Rev. S. Evander.
Consulate-General, 14 Trinity Square, E.C.3 (Royal: 1901).
Consul-General, G. F. von Otter.
Consul, H. Sköld.

Area and Population.—Sweden occupies the eastern half of the Scandinavian peninsula in N.W. Europe and comprises 25 local government districts, "Län," with an area of 173,436 sq. miles, and a population, Jan. 1, 1962, of 7,542,459. Of the 52,371 foreigners (non-Scandinavians) with permission to reside in Sweden, about 4,100 are Baltic refugees and 17,000 Germans. In 1961 there were 104,789 births (13·9 per 1,000 inhabitants), 73,800 deaths (9·8 per 1,000) and 52,444 marriages (6·9 per 1,000). In 1961 the infantile mortality rate was 16·6 per 1,000.

Government.—Under the Constitution of June 6, 1809 (with amendments) the throne is hereditary in the House of Bernadotte, Prince of Ponte Corvo, a Marshal of France, who was invited to accept the title of Crown Prince, with succession to the throne. The Marshal landed at Helsingborg on Oct. 20, 1810, and succeeded Charles XIII. in 1818. There is a Diet (*Riksdag*) of two Chambers, *Första Kammaren* of 151 members, elected for 8 years; and *Andra Kammaren* of 232 members, elected for 4 years. The Council of Ministers (*Statsråd*) is responsible to the Riksdag.

Production and Industry.—About 14 per cent. of the working population is devoted to agriculture, forestry and fisheries, about 220,000 being owners and 40,000 tenants of the land they cultivate. The country may be divided into three separate districts, the northern, forest; central, mining, industrial agricultural and forest; the southern, agricultural and industrial. The climate in the south is favourable

* This is the official title of the King of Sweden.

for producing grain. The principal articles of cultivation are oats, wheat, rye, barley, potatoes, roots, oleaginous plants and grasses. Dairy produce, however, accounts for nearly half the value of Swedish agricultural production. Sweden contains the great lakes of Vänern, Vättern, Mälaren and Hjälmaren. The forests are very extensive, covering over one-half of the surface of the country, and consisting chiefly of pine, spruce and birch; these are of great importance, supplying timber, pitch, fuel and tar, in addition to sulphite, sulphate and mechanical wood pulp for the paper-making and rayon industries. The mineral resources are extremely rich; iron ore of excellent quality; lead, zinc, sulphur, manganese, arsenic, gold, granite and marble. There are also considerable deposits of low grade uranium ore. There is a railroad opening up the rich iron-ore districts of Lapland and mineral trains run from Gällivare and Kiruna to Luleå on the Gulf of Bothnia and to Narvik on the Atlantic.

In 1960 there were 15,432 industrial establishments (including mines and quarries) employing 700,613 operatives, and 198,146 in administrative and executive posts. The fishing industry landed catches valued at *Kr.*184,300,000 in 1961.

Communications.—Railroads totalling 9,680 miles in length (of which 9,150 are the property of the State) were open on January 1, 1962. At the beginning of 1962 there were 384 telephones for every 1,000 of the population, 388 per 1,000 had obtained wireless licences and in April, 1963, the number of television licences issued had reached 1,600,000. The number of private cars in use on the same date was estimated at about 1,300,000 or 1 to every 7 of the population. The Mercantile Marine (March, 1963), consisted of a total of 1,358 ships of 4,134,000 tons gross. Civil aviation is under the control of the Ministry of Communications, under whose supervision all matters concerning civil aviation are handled by the Department of Civil Aviation. Regular domestic air traffic is maintained by the Scandinavian Airlines system (on behalf of the Swedish Airlines) and by A. B. Linjeflyg. Regular European and inter-continental air traffic is maintained within the framework of the Scandinavian Airlines System in Copenhagen by the Swedish Airlines in collaboration with the Danish and Norwegian Airlines.

Defence.—Service in the Defence Forces is universal and compulsory, between 35,000 and 40,000 being trained annually; strength of the *Army* during the war of 1939–45 was about 500,000, equipped on modern lines and principally mechanized. The *Navy* consists of 2 cruisers, 8 destroyers, 13 frigates, 38 motor torpedo boats, 21 submarines and a large number of minor craft and auxiliaries. The naval stations are Stockholm, Karlskrona and Göteborg. The *Air Force* is equipped on most modern lines and consists mainly of 20 wings of jet fighters and ground attack aircraft, many of which are supersonic.

Religion.—The State religion is Lutheran Protestant, to which over 95 per cent. of the people adhere.

Language and Literature.—Swedish is one of the Germanic languages spoken by the people of Scandinavia and is closely allied to Icelandic, Danish and Norwegian. Swedish national literature may be dated from the foundation of the University of Uppsala in 1477 and reached its golden age under Gustavus III. (1771–1792), who founded the Swedish Academy in 1786. Among modern Swedish authors who have achieved world-wide reputations are August Strindberg (1849–1912), dramatist and novelist; Selma Lagerlöf (1858–1940), who was awarded the Nobel Prize for Literature in 1900 on account of her pre-eminence as a novelist; Verner von Heidenstam (1859–1940), poet and Nobel Prize-winner (1916); Erik A. Karlfeldt (1864–1931), Nobel Prize-winner in 1931 after his death, and Par Lagerkvist, Nobel Prize-winner, 1951. In 1962 there were 176 daily newspapers in the country, 5 major papers being published at Stockholm, 4 at Göteborg and 4 at Malmö.

Education.—(i.) *Primary:* Compulsory and free. Maintained by the State and by local taxation. Attendance good. (ii.) *Secondary:* Well-developed, schools numerous and efficient. (iii.) *Special schools* make a feature of technics, commerce and navigation. (iv.) *Universities:* State Universities at Uppsala (founded 1477); Lund (founded 1668); Stockholm and Göteborg.

FINANCE

	1963–4 (Estimated) *Kronor*
Revenue (Operational Budget)...	20,034,000,000
Expenditure (Operational Budget)	19,730,000,000
Debt (April, 1963):—	
Consolidated Internal..........	15,452,643,177
Internal (Floating).............	5,035,531,294
Total Internal debt..........	20,488,174,472

The Swedish *Krona* of (100 *Ore*) exchanges at 14·37–14·6 *Kronor* = £1 sterling. (*See also* p. 83.)

TRADE

	1961 *Kronor*	1962 *Kronor*
Imports........	15,006,000,000	16,118,000,000
Exports........	14,167,000,000	15,126,900,000

Trade with U.K.

	1961	1962
Imports from U.K.	£141,174,582	£154,256,094
Exports to U.K...	160,698,704	157,230,001

The chief imports are coffee, tobacco, and other ordinary colonial produce, coal and coke, machinery, motor cars, mineral oils, cloth, cotton, wool, artificial fertilizers, chemicals, skins, copper, iron and steel. The chief exports are timber, wood pulp, paper, machinery, iron ore, iron and steel, ships, ball-bearings, matches and food products.

CAPITAL: ΨStockholm. Population (1962), 807,127. Other towns are ΨGöteborg (408,292), ΨMalmö (233,532), ΨNorrköping (91,397), ΨHälsingborg (77,027), Orebro (76,242), Borås (67,680), Västerås (79,171), Uppsala (79,308), Linköping (66,029), Eskilstuna (59,911), ΨGävle 55,882).

AIR TRANSIT: Stockholm (899 miles), 2½ *hrs.*

FLAG.—Yellow cross on a blue ground.

BRITISH EMBASSY

(*Residence*, Laboratoriegatan 8; *Chancery*, Strandvägen 82, Stockholm.)

British Ambassador, His Excellency Sir Moore Crosthwaite, K.C.M.G. (1963) £5,015

Counsellor, M. G. L. Joy, M.C.

Counsellor (Commercial), I. C. Mackenzie, C.B.E.

1st Secretaries, R. T. Eland (*Information and Press*); A. D. Thomas, O.B.E. (*British Council Representative, Cultural Attaché*); E. P. N. de Haan.

2nd Secretary, J. W. Maslen.

1st Secretary (Commercial), F. C. D. Sargeant.

2nd Secretary (Commercial), J. C. Longbotham, M.B.E.

Naval Attaché, Cdr. C. Gordon, D.S.O., R.N.

Military Attaché, Col. J. C. Johnson.

Assistant Military Attaché, Major A. Trimmer.

Air Attaché, Group Capt. J. W. Appleton.

Assistant Air Attaché, Squadron-Ldr. J. M. Beeby.

Scientific Attaché, W. F. G. Drury.

Labour Attaché, K. Kenney (*Resident in Helsinki*).

Consul, S. R. Airey.

Archivist, R. G. Rogers.

BRITISH CONSULAR OFFICES

There are British Consular Offices at *Gävle, Göteborg, Hälsingborg, Luleå, Malmö, Norrköping, Stockholm* and *Sundsvall.*

British-Swedish Chamber of Commerce in Sweden: Hovslagaregatan 5B, Stockholm.

SWITZERLAND

(Schweizerische Eidgenossenschaft—Confédération Suisse—Confederazione Svizzera.)

GOVERNMENT

**President and Minister of Transport, Communications and Power* (1963), M. Willy Spühler.
Vice-President (1963) *and Justice and Police,* M. Ludwig von Moos.
Defence, M. Paul Chaudet.
Foreign Affairs, Prof. Dr. Friedrich Traugott Wahlen.
Interior, Prof. Hans-Peter Tschudi.
Finance and Customs, M. Roger Bonvin.
Public Economy, M. Hans Schaffner.

SWISS EMBASSY IN LONDON
18 Montague Place, Bryanston Square, W.1
[Paddington: 0701]

Ambassador in London, His Excellency M. Armin Daeniker (1955).
Counsellor, Jean de Stoutz.
Military and Air Attaché, Col. Werner Koch.
Counsellor for Economic Affairs, Marcel Heimo.
Counsellor for Press and Cultural Affairs, Jean Revilliod.
Counsellor for Labour Affairs, Felix Ansermoz.
1st Secretaries, William Roch; Hans Gallusser.
3rd Secretary, François Heuer.
Asst. Military and Air Attaché, Peter Storrer.
Consular Section, 1 Montagu Place, W.1.
Consul and Head of Chancery, Enrico Tosio.

There is a Swiss Consulate in *Manchester.*

Area and Population.—The Helvetia of the Romans, a Federal Republic of Central Europe, situated between 45° 50′–47° 48′ N. lat. and 5° 58′–10° 3′ E. long. It is composed of 22 Cantons, 3 subdivided, making 25 in all, of very dissimilar size, united under a Constitution dated May 29, 1847, and comprises a total area of 15,950 square miles, with a population (Dec. 31, 1962) of 5,608,000. In 1962 there were 104,322 live births, 55,125 deaths and 44,342 marriages. The infant mortality rate was 21 per 1,000 live births. In 1960, out of a total of 5,492,061, 52·6 per cent. of the population was Protestant, 45·6 per cent. Roman Catholic and 0·4 per cent. Jewish.

Physical Features.—Switzerland is the most mountainous country in all Europe. The Alps, covered with perennial snow and from 5,000 to 15,217 feet in height, occupy its southern and eastern frontiers, and the chief part of its interior; and the Jura mountains rise in the north-west. The Alps occupy 61 per cent., and the Jura mountains 12 per cent., of the country. The *Alps* are a crescent-shaped mountain system situated in France, Italy, Switzerland, Bavaria and Austria, covering an area of 80,000 square miles from the Mediterranean to the Danube (600 miles). The highest peak, Mont Blanc, Pennine Alps (15,732 feet) is partly in France and Italy; Monte Rosa (15,217 feet) and Matterhorn (14,780 feet) are partly in Switzerland and partly in Italy. The highest wholly Swiss peaks are Finsteraarhorn (14,026), Aletschhorn (13,711), Jungfrau (13,671), Mönch (13,456), Eiger (13,040), Schreckhorn (13,385), and Wetterhorn (12,150) in the Bernese Alps, and Dom (14,918), Weisshorn (14,803) and Breithorn (13,685).

The Swiss lakes are famous for their beauty and include Lakes Maggiore, Zürich, Lucerne, Neuchâtel, Geneva, Constance, Thun, Zug, Lugano, Walensee and Brienz.

Production and Industry.—Agriculture is followed chiefly in the valleys, where wheat, oats, maize, barley, flax, hemp, and tobacco are produced, and nearly all English fruits and vegetables as well as grapes are grown. Dairying and stock-raising are the principal industries, about 3,000,000 acres being under grass for hay and 2,000,000 acres pasturage. The forests cover about one-quarter of the whole surface. The chief manufacturing industries comprise engineering and electrical engineering, metal-working, chemicals and pharmaceuticals, textiles, watchmaking, woodworking, foodstuffs and footwear. Banking, insurance and tourism are major industries.

Government.—The legislative power is vested in a Parliament, consisting of two Chambers, a National Council (*Nationalrat*) of 200 members, and a Council of States (*Ständerat*) of 44 members; both Chambers united are called the Federal Assembly, and the members of the National Council are elected for four years, an election taking place in October. The executive power is in the hands of a Federal Council (*Bundesrat*) of 7 members, elected for four years by the Federal Assembly and presided over by the President of the Confederation. The members of the Federal Council are elected for four years; each year the Federal Assembly elects from this council the President and the Vice-President; they are elected for one year. Not more than one of the same canton may be elected member of the Federal Council; on the other hand, there is a tradition that Italian and French-speaking areas should between them be represented on the Federal Council by at least two members.

Defence.—Army. Elite (ages 20 to 36), 16 yrs.; initial training, 118 days. Subsequently 8 training periods of 21 days; then Landwehr (36 to 48) and Landsturm (48 to 60). Under the proposed reorganization of the Swiss forces, the ages for military service will be reduced as follows: Elite, 20–32 years, Landwehr, 33–42, Landsturm, 43–50. *Air Force.* Ground personnel: as Army. Flying personnel: age 20 to 36. Initial training 1 year. 6 weeks with squadron each year and completion of 70 hours' flying. After 36 revert to ground duties with Air Force or Army.

Communications.—By the end of June, 1961, the electrification of the entire Swiss railway system of 3,582 miles (Swiss Federal Railways 1,809 miles, Swiss privately owned railways 1,773 miles) of track was completed. At the end of 1962, there were 41,510 miles of telegraph and telephone lines. By December, 1962, the number of telephone subscribers amounted to 1,228,274 and the network was fully automatic throughout the country. There were 1,538,283 licensed radio receivers and 273,894 television receivers. At the end of 1961, the total length of first-class roads was 10,867 miles. The number of motor vehicles licensed at the end of 1961 was 985,472 (549,778 private cars, 336,700 motor cycles, motor scooters and bicycles with auxiliary motor, 3,274 motor buses, 88,637 motor lorries, 5,904 special vehicles and 1,179 tractors). A merchant marine, established in 1940, consisted in 1962 of 33 vessels with a total displacement of 175,401 tons (gross). In addition 458 vessels with a total tonnage of 416,618 were engaged in Rhine shipping. In 1962, goods handled at the Basle Rhine Port amounted to 6,787,583 tons. 113 lake vessels transported 9,549,000 passengers and 494,709

---

* The President is elected in December and remains in office from Jan. 1 to Dec. 31; he is *generally* succeeded by the Vice-President.

tons of freight in 1961. During 1962, Swissair flew 23,000,000 miles and carried 1,648,419 passengers.

Education. Control by cantonal and communal authorities. No central organ. Illiteracy practically unknown. (i.). *Primary*: Free and compulsory. School age varies, generally 7 to 14. (ii.) *Secondary*: Age 12–15 for boys and girls. Schools numerous and well-attended, and there are many private institutions. (iii.) *Special schools* make a feature of commercial and technical instruction. (iv.) *Universities*: Basle (founded 1460), Berne (1834), Fribourg (1889), Geneva (1873), Lausanne (1890), Zürich (1832), and Neuchâtel (1909), and the technical University of Zürich and commercial University of St. Gall.

Language and Literature.—There are three official languages: French, German and Italian. In addition Romansch is recognized as a national, but not an official language. German is the dominating language in 19 of the 25 cantons; French in Fribourg. Geneva, Neuchâtel, Valais and Vaud; Italian in Ticino, and Romansch in parts of the Grisons. Many modern authors, alike in the German school and in the Suisse Romande, have achieved international fame. Karl Spitteler (1845–1924) and Hermann Hesse (1877–) were awarded the Nobel Prize for Literature, the former in 1919, the latter in 1947.

FINANCE		1962
Revenue.............	*Swiss Francs*	4,116,600,000
Expenditure..........	" "	3,684,200,000
Federal Public Debt (Dec. 31, 1962):—		
Internal consolidated	" "	54,804,00,000

Since the convertibility of sterling in December, 1958, the rate of exchange has fluctuated between Swiss *Francs* 12·10 and 12·19=£1 sterling for transactions through normal financial channels. The rate of exchange for sterling notes has fluctuated between Swiss *Francs* 12·05 and 12·25=£1 since the abolition of controls on imports of sterling notes into the United Kingdom.

TRADE

	1962	1961
Total Imports.	*Fr.*11 644 000,000	*Fr.*12,986,000,000
Total Exports.	8 822,000,000	9,580,000,000

Trade with U.K.

	1961	1962
Imports from U.K....	£52,893,138	£63,791,371
Exports to U.K.......	48,502,008	52,476,581

The principal imports are metals, machinery, instruments and apparatus; motor vehicles, chemical and pharmaceutical raw materials and products; fuel oil, petrol and coal; timber; cereals, fruit and vegetables. The principal exports are machinery, watches, chemicals and pharmaceuticals, textiles and foodstuffs.

CAPITAL, Berne. Population (estimated 1962), 168,900. Other large towns are Zürich (444,000), Basle (210,800), Geneva (181,400), Lausanne (132,500), St. Gallen (78,300), Winterthur (86,300), Lucerne (72,400), Biel (64,000) and La Chaux de Fonds (41,200).

FLAG.—Red, with white cross.

AIR TRANSIT FROM U.K.—London–Basle (446 miles), $1\frac{1}{2}$ *hrs.*; Geneva (468 miles), $1\frac{1}{2}$ *hrs.*; Zürich (491 miles), 1 *hr.* 40 *mins.*

RAIL TRANSIT FROM U.K.—London–Berne, 16 *hrs.*

BRITISH EMBASSY
(Thunstrasse 50, Berne)

Ambassador Extraordinary and Plenipotentiary, His Excellency Sir Paul Francis Grey, K.C.M.G. (1960) £4,115

Counsellor, F. G. K. Gallagher, C.M.G. (*Commercial*).
1st Secretaries, G. A. Crossley; W. Steedman, C.B.E.; C. S. R. Giffard (*Commercial*).
2nd Secretary, D. V. Morris (*H.M. Consul*).
Military and Air Attaché, Col. A. G. Rich.
Attaché, P. Arengo-Jones.

BRITISH CONSULAR OFFICES

There is a Consular Section at H.M. Embassy, Berne, and British Consular Offices at *Basle*, *Geneva*, *Lucerne*, *Montreux* and *Zürich*.

BRITISH COUNCIL

Representative, W. J. Perryman, Rämistrasse 34, Zürich, 2.

BRITISH-SWISS CHAMBER OF COMMERCE FOR SWITZERLAND, St. Peterstrasse 1, *Zürich*. (Branch at 1 Galeries Benjamin Constant, *Lausanne*.)

SWISS-BRITISH SOCIETY, Berne.—*President*, Professor R. Fricker.

SWISS-BRITISH SOCIETY, Zürich.—*President*, Dr. R. Schneebeli.

SYRIA

(Syrian Arab Republic)
[National Council of the Revolutionary Command].

Prime Minister (May 14, 1963), Sąlah al Din Bitar.

SYRIAN EMBASSY AND CONSULATE
56 Porchester Terrace, W.2.

Ambassador (vacant).
Minister-Counsellor, Abdallah F. El-Khani.
Military, Naval and Air Attaché, Brig.-Gen. Zouheir Abdullatif Akil.
Asst. Military, Naval and Air Attaché, Capt. Abdul Kerim Haddad.
1st Secretaries, Bachir El-Kotb (*Consular*); Mohammed Fayez Rifai.
3rd Secretary, Misbah Dalati.
Cultural Attaché, Nazem Tahan.
Attachés, Rafic Kheir; Mouhiddin Tayan (*Admin.*); Nour Dine Houbbi (*Admin.*); Michel Khoury (*Consular*); Chafik Fayad Ibrahim (*Admin.*).

Area and Population.—Syria is in the Levant, covering a portion of the former Ottoman Empire, with an estimated area of 70,800 sq. miles and a population of 4,500,000, Arabic speaking and mainly Moslems. It includes the districts of Damascus, Aleppo, Lattakia, Hama, Homs, Hassakeh, al Rashid, Deir-ez-Zor, Idlib, Deraa and Suweida. It is bounded on the north by Turkey, on the east by Iraq, on the south by Jordan and Israel, and on the west by the Lebanon and thence northwards by the Mediterranean to the Turkish frontier. The Orontes flows northwards from the Lebanon range across the northern boundary to Antioch (Turkey). The Euphrates crosses the northern boundary near Jerablus and flows through north-eastern Syria to the boundary of Iraq.

Archaeology, etc.—The region is rich in historical remains. Damascus (*Dimishq ash-Sham*) is the most ancient city in the world, having an existence as a city for over 4,000 years. It is situated on the river Abana (now known as Barada), in an oasis at the eastern foot of the Anti-Lebanon, and at the edge of the wide sandy desert which stretches to the Euphrates. The city contains the Omayyed Mosque, the Tomb of Saladin, and the "Street Called Straight" (Acts ix 11), while to the North-East is the Roman outpost of Dmeir and further east is Palmyra.

On the Mediterranean coast at Amrit are ruins of the Phoenician town of Marath, where the *tell* has been found and is being excavated and also ruins of Crusaders' fortresses at Markab, Sahyoun, and Krak des Chevaliers. At Tartous (also on the coast) the cathedral of Our Lady of Syria, built by the Knights Templars in the XII-XIII century has been restored as a museum.

Hittite cities, dating from 2,000 to 1,500 B.C., have recently been explored on the west bank of the Euphrates at Jerablus and Kadesh.

Government.—Syria, which had been under French mandate since the 1914–18 war, became an independent Republic during the 1939–45 war. The first independently elected Parliament met on August 17, 1943, but foreign troops were in part occupation until April, 1946. Syria remained an independent Republic until February, 1958, when it became part of the United Arab Republic. Syria seceded from the United Arab Republic on Sept. 28, 1961. Following a *coup d'etat* by the Army on March 8, 1963, Syria is governed by a Ministerial Cabinet directly responsible to the National Council of the Revolutionary Command, a body believed to consist of about 12 serving officers.

Production and Industry.—Agriculture is the principal source of production; wheat and barley are the main cereal crops, but the cotton crop is the highest in value. Tobacco is grown in the maritime plain in Sahel, the Sahyoun and the Djebleh district of Lattakia; skins and hides, leather goods, wool and silk, textiles, cement, vegetable oil and copper and brass utensils are locally produced. Mineral wealth is small but oil has been found at Karachuk in the north-eastern corner of the country and drilling is continuing. An oil refinery is in production at Homs and revenue is derived from the Kirkuk-Banias oil pipeline and the pipeline from the oilfields of Saudi-Arabia to Sidon in Lebanon (Tapline). There is a five-year industrial development plan and a 10-year economic development plan.

Language and Literature.—Arabic is the principal language (*see* Arabia), but a few villages still speak Aramaic, the language spoken by Christ and the Apostles. There are 3 daily newspapers and 2 periodicals in Arabic published in Damascus.

Education.—Education in Syria is under State control and, although many of the schools are privately owned, they all follow a common system and syllabus Elementary education is free at State Schools, and is compulsory from the age of seven. Secondary education is not compulsory and is free only at the State Schools. Because of the shortage of places, entry to these State Schools is competitive. Damascus University, founded in 1924, has faculties of law, medicine, engineering, science, arts and a Higher Teachers' Training College. The number of students has risen from a few hundred in 1943 to about 16,000 in 1963. There are also about 2,000 students at Aleppo University (founded 1961). Approximately 10 per cent. of all students receive scholarships, and at the present time Palestinian refugees are admitted free. The rest pay fees.

Communications.—A narrow-gauge railway runfrom Beirut in the Lebanon to Damascus, connecting at Rayak (Lebanon) with the standards gauge line which runs from Tripoli (in the Lebanon) through Homs, Hama and Aleppo to the Turkish frontier, from Nusaybin to the Iraq frontier at Tel Kotchek. From Damascus the Hejaz railway runs southwards to Jordan. All the principal towns in the country are connected by roads of varying quality. A small internal air service operates between Damascus and Aleppo, and between Aleppo and Qamichliyé, and Aleppo, Lattakia and Damascus. There are also flights from Damascus to Palmyra and Deir-ez-Zor.

Currency.—The monetary unit is the Syrian paper pound (*£Syr.*). The market rate of exchange for commercial transactions was approximately *£Syr* 10.65=£1 sterling in June, 1963. After a period of free exchange, exchange control was re-imposed in May, 1963, and the free money market abolished.

TRADE

Principal Imports.—Gold, textiles, petroleum products, vehicles, agricultural equipment, machinery of all kinds and electrical material, base metals and wares thereof, chemicals and pharmaceuticals, wood and its manufactures, live animals and animal products, vegetable products, rubber products.

Principal Exports.—Textile materials and manufactures (including raw cotton and wool), cereals and vegetable products, live animals and animal products, raw hides and skins, prepared foods, gold.

The value of Syria's foreign trade was:—

	1962
Imports	*£Syr.*862,280,000
Exports	617,158,000

Trade with U.K.

	1961	1962
Imports from U.K.	£6,020,268	£8,519,755
Exports to U.K.	1,141,372	1,827,466

CHIEF TOWNS.—Damascus (population 450,000) is the capital of Syria, other important towns being Aleppo (population 450,000), Homs (150,000) and Hama (100,000), and the principal port is ΨLattakia (52,000).

FLAG: Green over white over black horizontal bands, with three green stars on central white band.

BRITISH EMBASSY

Kutub Building, Adnan Maliki Street, Damascus.

Ambassador Extraordinary and Plenipotentiary, His Excellency Thomas Eardley Bromley, C.M.G. (1962).

1st Secretaries, D. A. Roberts; J. C. M. Mason (*Commercial*).

2nd Secretary (*Commercial*), F. W. J. Cooper.

3rd Secretaries, A. J. Johnstone; O. H. C. Bakes (*Consular*).

THAILAND (Siam)

King, His Majesty Bhumibol Adulyadej, *born* 1927; *succeeded his brother*, June 9, 1946; *married* Princess Sirikit Kityakara, April 28, 1950; *crowned* May 5, 1950; daughter *born*, April 6, 1951; son and heir *born*, July 28, 1952; second daughter *born* April 2, 1955; third daughter *born* July 4, 1957.

Prime Minister, Field Marshal Sarit Thanarat.
Foreign Minister, Nai Thanat Khoman.

ROYAL THAI EMBASSY IN LONDON

21–23 Ashburn Place, S.W.7 [Frobisher: 2983];
28 Princes Gate, S.W. 7 [Knightsbridge: 5421].

Ambassador in London, H.S.H. Prince Plerng Nobadol Rabibhadana (1963).

Area and Population.—The Kingdom of Thailand, or Muang Thai, formerly known as Siam, has an area of 198,247 sq. miles with a population (estimated 1963) of 30,000,000. Thailand is in South-Eastern Asia. It has a common boundary with the Federation of Malaya in the south, and is bounded on the west and north-west by the Union of Burma and in the north-east and east by the Kingdoms of Laos and Cambodia, which were formerly part of the French Colony of Indo-China. Although there is no common boundary between Thailand and China, the Chinese province of Yunnan is only separated from the Thai northern border by a narrow stretch of Burmese and Lao territory. The country slopes southwards from the north-west and from the great mountains of Tibet. The principal rivers are the Salween (which forms a boundary with Burma for 200 miles), the Menam Chao Phya with its tributary the Meping (which are Thai throughout) and the Mekong and its tributaries, which water the eastern plateau.

Government.—Thailand is a sovereign independent state. Under the interim constitution promulgated in February, 1959, following on the bloodless revolution of October, 1958, the King exercises legislative power by and with the advice and consent of a Constituent Assembly, executive power through the Council of Ministers and judicial power through the courts established by law. He is advised by a Privy Council appointed by himself. The 240 members of the Constituent Assembly, who were appointed in February, 1959, under the terms of the interim constitution, as well as acting for the time being as the national legislature, have the additional task of drafting a permanent constitution for Thailand, but no definite date has yet been set for the completion of this.

Language, Religion and Education.—Thai is basically a monosyllabic, tonal language, a branch of the Indo-Chinese linguistic family. The principal religion is Buddhism, its followers numbering over 15 millions in 1953, with about 670,000 Moslems and some 78,500 Christians. The 2,500th anniversary of the Buddhist Era was celebrated in Bangkok from May 12–15, 1957, with religious and public ceremonies. Primary education is compulsory and free and secondary education in Government Schools is free. In 1960 there were 27,314 schools of all kinds, with 4,344,689 pupils and 131,651 teachers. There are 5 Universities attended by 40,829 students, 34 training colleges and 196 vocational schools (all types).

Production and Industry.—The country's most important products are agricultural or forest; rice (about 4,500,000 tons a year), rubber (about 170,000 tons a year and increasing) and timber (about 1,300,000 cubic metres a year and decreasing). Other crops of some importance are sugar cane, tapioca, kenaf, groundnuts, tobacco, maize, soya beans and coconuts.

As regards mineral wealth, tin ore (production in 1962, 20,300 tons) is important, and small amounts of wolfram, iron and lead ores are mined, and over 100,000 tons of lignite. Upwards of 200,000 tons a year of salt is produced by sea-water evaporation, but production is declining owing to marketing difficulties.

Before the war industry was mainly confined to the basic processing industries—sawmilling, rice-milling, etc. After the war the Government set up a number of factories, run by the Civil Service or the Armed Forces. The Government still has a sizeable stake in industry—notably the tobacco monopoly and factories for the manufacture of paper, textiles, sugar and beer and spirits. The present Revolutionary Government in 1958 instituted a policy of encouraging the private sector to invest in industry, by means of tax reliefs and other incentives. This policy is beginning to produce results although the Government has interests, directly or indirectly, in some of the largest current or prospective ventures—*e.g.* two refineries, a paper mill and a fertilizer factory. The private sector industries are almost entirely of a secondary nature; soap products, gunny bags, textiles, car assembly, etc. Most of the investment has been local but a certain amount of foreign capital has been attracted, notably from the United States and Japan.

Communications.—About 2,250 miles of State-owned railways were open to traffic in 1961. The track is metre gauge. Main lines run from Bangkok to Aranya Pradet, linking up with the Cambodian state railway at this border town (160 miles E.); *viâ* Korat to Ubol (about 352 miles E.) and to Nongkhai (415 miles N.) the ferry terminal on the River Mekhong opposite Vientiane, capital of Laos; to Chiengmai (411 miles N.); and to Haadyai (600 miles S.), whence lines go down the eastern and western sides of the Malay Peninsula, *viâ* Sungei Golok and Penang respectively, to Singapore.

Thailand has about 8,900 kilometres of highways, of which only about 28 per cent. are paved. An additional 1,700 kms. of unpaved highway is under construction or planned, and appreciable lengths of the major arteries are in the process of being paved, largely with U.S. aid finance. The development of roads is being given top priority in the Government's development plans, and an eight-year plan has been adopted in 1962 to rehabilitate about 4,000 kms. of existing highway and construct some 1,500 kms. of new roads.

A loan of $35,000,000 was obtained from the International Bank for Reconstruction and Development in 1963 for the first phase of this programme. Bangkok is an international airport of importance, and services connect it with Europe, America, India, Pakistan, Japan and Australasia, as well as other parts of S.E. Asia. Thai Airways International (THAI), was formed in 1960 in association with SAS to operate international routes. There are about 14,500 miles of telegraph lines. The harbour at Bangkok can take vessels up to 10,000 tons dead weight.

FINANCE	1960	1961
Budget Estimates	Millions of *Baht*	
Total revenue.............	7,700	8,000
Total expenditure..........	7,700	8 000

Since 1953 Thailand has received a total of U.S.$106,000,000 in loans from the International Bank for rehabilitation and development of railways, the port of Bangkok, and irrigation, including the latest loan (in 1957) of $66,000,000 for the Yan-Hee hydro-electric project.

The value of United States economic and technical aid to Thailand amounted by July, 1960 (the beginning of the U.S. fiscal year) to U.S. $275,200,000 (including $46,200,000 in loans); the expected programme for 1961 being about $24,300,000. In addition, the military aid programme up to the end of the fiscal year 1959 cost $304,718,000 ($17,000,000 in 1959) and the estimate for 1960 was $24,782,000.

The exchange rate for the *Baht* is not officially fixed, but has for some time remained in the neighbourhood of *Baht* 59 = £1 sterling, with little fluctuation. Foreign exchange reserves are at present sufficient and steady, and the currency backing is 60 per cent.

TRADE

	1961 *Baht*	1962 *Baht*
Total imports.....	10,287,000,000	11,412,000,000
Total exports......	9,997,000,000	9,592,000,000

Trade with U.K.

	1961	1962
Imports from U.K....	£13,161,680	£14,466,840
Exports to U.K.......	7,233,860	8,252,017

The main exports are rice and rubber which normally account for about 60 per cent. of the total.

Principal exports in 1961 (millions of *Baht*) were: Rice, 3,598; Rubber, 2,130; Tin, 617; Maize, 597. Other exports, whose levels vary more are jute and kenaf, teak, and tapioca products. The main imports are machinery, petroleum products, iron and steel, cotton fabrics and vehicles.

CAPITAL, ΨBangkok (with Dhonburi), pop. 1960—2,318,000; in the delta of the Manam Chao Phya. Other centres are Chiengmai, Nakorn Sawan and Korat, but no other town approaches Bangkok in size or importance.

FLAG.—Five horizontal bands, red, white, dark blue, white, red (the blue band twice the width of the others).

BRITISH EMBASSY
(Bangkok)

British Ambassador Extraordinary and Minister Plenipotentiary, His Excellency Sir Dermot Francis MacDermot, K.C.M.G., C.B.E. (1961).....£4,115

CONSULAR OFFICES

There are Consular Offices at *Bangkok, Chiengmai* and *Phuket*.

BRITISH COUNCIL

Representative, H. C. Burrow, O.B.E., 122 Chakrapetr Road, Bangkok.

TOGO
(Republic of Togo)

President, Nicholas Grunitsky, *assumed office as Head of State*, May 10, 1963

Vice-President, Minister of Finance, Economy and Planning, Antoine Meatchi.

Minister of State for Foreign Affairs, Georges Apedo-Amah.

The Republic occupies a narrow strip of territory running north from a short coast-line on the Gulf of Guinea and lies between the Republics of Ghana on the west and Dahomey on the east. It has an area of 20,000 sq. miles and a population (estimated 1961) of 1,440,000, including people of several African races. The Ewe race are in a majority in the south. The economy of Togo is largely agricultural, the main exports being coffee, cocoa, palm kernels, copra, cotton and manioc. A promising start has been made in the growing of teak. Development of phosphate mines by a group of French companies began in 1955.

Trade with U.K.

	1961	1962
Imports from U.K.	£971,576	£1,011,449
Exports to U.K.	120,387	72,495

Formerly part of the German colony of Togoland surrendered in 1914, the Republic was administered by France as a mandated territory and from 1946 as a trusteeship under the auspices of the United Nations Organization. On November 14, 1958, the United Nations General Assembly voted for the cancellation of the trusteeship and for the establishment of an independent state at a date in 1960 to be agreed between Togoland and France. Accordingly, the Republic of Togo was set up as an independent state on April 27, 1960. A new constitution was adopted and a President elected on April 9, 1961.

On January 13, 1963, President Sylvanus Olympio was assassinated by a military junta which seized control of the country. The National Assembly was dissolved by decree of the provisional Government led by M. Grunitsky and the Constitution suspended. On May 5, a new Constitution was adopted and a fresh National Assembly elected. Both came into force when the President took his oath of office on May 10.

CAPITAL.—ΨLomé (70,000).

FLAG.—Green and yellow horizontal stripes; a quarter in red in one corner bearing a white star.

BRITISH EMBASSY

Ambassador Extraordinary and Plenipotentiary and Consul-General, His Excellency Oliver Kemp, O.B.E. (1962).

1st Secretary, G. Dawson (*Consul and Head of Chancery*).

2nd Secretary, K. H. Jones (*Vice-Consul*).

TRUCIAL STATES

Seven independent Shaikhdoms, known collectively as the Trucial States, have treaty relations with the British Government originating in treaties to prevent slavery and the piracy, which formerly gave the name of "The Pirate Coast" to this area, and to maintain a perpetual maritime truce. The earliest treaty dates from 1820.

The British Government, by virtue of a treaty made in 1892, is responsible for the external affairs of the states through the British Political Resident in the Persian Gulf and the British Political Agent in the Trucial States. Six of the states lie on the coast of the Gulf between the Musandam peninsula in the East and the Qatar peninsula in the West and one, Fujairah, lies on the Gulf of Oman.

Area and Population.—The approximate combined area of the states is 32,000 square miles and the estimated population is about 110,000. Security in the area is maintained by the Trucial Oman Scouts, the force having its headquarters at Sharjah. There are police forces in Dubai and Abu Dhabi.

Revenue is chiefly derived from customs dues on imports and oil concession payments. The export of dried fish is also a significant source of revenue and some pearling is still carried on. In Abu Dhabi, the onshore concession is held by Abu Dhabi Petroleum Co. and the offshore concessions by Abu Dhabi Marine Areas Ltd.; in Dubai, the onshore concession is held by Dubai Petroleum Company and the offshore concession by Dubai Marine Areas; the onshore and offshore concessions in Sharjah, Ajman and Umm al Qaiwain are held by Mecomoil Ltd. in partnership with Pure Oil. The British Government finances a Trucial States Development Scheme to contribute to the material welfare of the people; the Scheme includes an Agricultural Trials Station in the Shaikhdom of Ras al-Khaimah, Trade Schools in Sharjah and Dubai, a hospital in Ras al Khaimah and a number of dispensaries in the smaller towns and villages. The Kuwait Government also gives aid in the form of schools, clinics and mosques.

Kuwait and Qatar contribute educational assistance to the states. There are hospitals in Dubai and Ras al-Khaimah. Her Majesty's Government has jurisdiction over certain categories of foreigners. The Rulers of all the states meet together in the Trucial States Council to discuss matters of mutual interest once or twice a year. The currency is the Persian Gulf Indian *rupee*.

Abu Dhabi is the largest of the Trucial States in area, stretching from the Khor el Odaid in the West to the borders with Dubai in the region of Jebel Ali. It includes seven villages of the Buraimi oasis and a number of settlements in the series of oases known as the Liwa. Two oil companies are operating in Abu Dhabi territory, Petroleum Development (Trucial Coast) Ltd. on land and Abu Dhabi Marine Areas Ltd. in the Abu Dhabi off-shore concession area. Oil has been discovered off Das Island, where Abu Dhabi Marine Areas has its headquarters and production started in 1962. Production from the on-shore Murban oil field is expected to start in 1964. There are airfields at Abu Dhabi and at Das Island and an air strip at Buraimi. Work has started on a substantial development plan for the town of Abu Dhabi and the first stage has been completed.

Ψ *Dubai* is by far the largest town in the Trucial States and has a population estimated at about 45,000. It is the main port for the import of goods into the Trucial States and the interior of Oman, and there is also a lively *entrepôt* trade. The value of imports in the year 1962 was over £8,000,000. It has a good natural harbour, improvements to which have been carried out since 1959. The airport is being enlarged to take jet airliners and the Dubai Telephone Company commenced operations in the same year. The main source of revenue is from customs. Wireless communications are managed by Cable and Wireless Ltd. and the Post Office was handed over to the Dubai Government by the British G.P.O. in 1963.

Sharjah has a port, much silted up, and a diminishing *entrepôt* trade. It has an airport served by Gulf Aviation which connects it with Doha, Bahrain, Kuwait and Muscat. Sharjah has dependencies on the Batinah coast at Khorfakkhan, which forms a good natural harbour, Kalba and Dibba. The headquarters of the Trucial Oman Scouts is in Sharjah as well as a Royal Air Force base.

Ajman is the smallest state, having a population of only about 5,000. It has inland enclaves at Manama and Masfut. *Umm el Quwain* does a small trade in dried fish. It has an oasis at Falaj al Mu'alla where palms and some fruit are grown. *Ras al Khaimah* has a population of about 10,000, of whom about half live in the town. It is an ancient seaport near which some remains of archaeological interest have been found. Dates, vegetables, fruit and tobacco are grown. There is a plan to move the town from its present exposed position on the shore to the inland side of the Creek. *Fujairah* was recognized as one of the Trucial States in 1952. The inhabitants are hill people in the mountains of the Musandam peninsula, with a few cultivators around Fujairah itself, which is on the fertile plane of the Batinah coast. The most important export is tobacco.

British Political Agent, Trucial States, A. J. M. Craig (*resident at Dubai*).

British Political Agent, Abu Dhabi, Col. J. E. H. Boustead, C.M.G., D.S.O.

TUNISIA

(Tunisian Republic)

President, Habib Bourguiba, *elected* July 25, 1957; *re-elected* Nov. 8, 1959.

CABINET

(April 15, 1956)

Presidency of the Republic and National Defence, Bahi Ladgham.
Foreign Affairs, Mongi Slim.
Interior, Taïeb Mehiri.
Justice, Hedi Khefacha.
Plan and Finance, Ahmen ben Salah.
Education, Mahmoud Messadi.
Agriculture, Abdelmajid Chaker.
Health and Social Welfare, Moudher ben Ammar.
Posts and Telegraphs, Rachid Driss.
Public Works and Housing, Ahmed Noureddine.
Information and Culture, Chedly Klibi.

TUNISIAN EMBASSY IN LONDON

29 Princes Gate, S.W.7
[Knightsbridge: 5167]

Ambassador, His Excellency Habib Chatty (1962).
2nd Secretary, Moncef Ounaies.
Attaché, Mustapha Trabelsi.

Area and Population.—Tunisia lies between Algeria and Libya and extends southwards to the Sahara Desert, with a total area of 45,000 sq. miles and a population (estimated 1963) of 4,198,000.

Government.—A French Protectorate from 1881 to 1956, Tunisia became an independent sovereign State with the signing on March 20, 1956, of an agreement whereby France recognized Tunisia's independence and right to conduct her own foreign policy and to form a Tunisian Army. The United Kingdom formally recognized Tunisia as an independent and sovereign state on May 10, 1956. Following a first general election held on March 25, 1956, a Constituent Assembly met for the first time on April 8. On July 25, 1957, the Constituent Assembly deposed the Bey, abolished the monarchy and elected M. Bourguiba first President of the Republic. A few days later the Government was reconstructed on the "presidential" model, the Ministers becoming Secretaries of State. On June 1, 1959, the Constitution was promulgated and on December 7, 1959, the National Assembly held its first session.

Important changes in the system of local government were decreed on June 16, 1956. The country was divided into 12 regions each administered by a Governor.

Production, Trade, etc.—The valleys of the northern region support large flocks and herds, and contain rich agricultural areas, in which wheat, barley, and oats are grown. The vine and olive are extensively cultivated. The chief exports are cereals, olive oil, phosphates, iron-ore, lead and derivatives, wines, etc., dates, etc.; the chief imports are textiles, machinery, iron and steel and petroleum products. In 1962 imports totalled 90,890,000 *dinars* and exports 48,687,000 *dinars*. The greater part of the trade is with France which, in 1962, took 53 per cent. of the exports and supplied 52 per cent. of the imports.

Trade with U.K.

	1961	1962
Imports from U.K.	£2,045,003	£2,723,488
Exports to U.K.	6,234,847	3,997,201

A new currency, the Tunisian *dinar*, was adopted on Nov. 3, 1958. At the same time a new Central Bank of Tunisia became responsible for the issue of notes. Although Tunisia remains in the Franc Zone the dinar is not tied to the French franc and on June 1, 1963, stood at 1·166 to the £. Except for minor fluctuations it has been at this level for the past four years. So far as trade is concerned Tunisia was effectively part of metropolitan France until September, 1959, when she abrogated the Customs Union with the latter and a new trade and payments agreement was negotiated. This reduced or eliminated the tariff advantages enjoyed by certain French goods. Under a commercial agreement concluded in November, 1962, import quotas were established for certain French goods.

CAPITAL, ΨTunis, connected by canal with La Goulette on the coast, had a population (Municipal Council area) of 680,000 at the Census of 1956. The ruins of ancient Carthage lie a few miles from the city. Other towns of importance are ΨSfax (65,635), ΨSousse (48,172), Kairouan (33,968).

FLAG.—Red crescent and star in a white orb, all on a red ground.

BRITISH EMBASSY
Place de la Victoire, Tunis

Ambassador Extraordinary and Plenipotentiary and Consul-General, His Excellency Sir Herbert Stanley Marchant, K.C.M.G., O.B.E. (1963). £4,115
1st Secretaries, A. E. Davidson (*Consul*); D. I. Newman (*Information*); W. R. Thomson (*Labour*).
2nd Secretary, E. H. Noble (*Commercial*).
British Council Representative, A. M. Welsh.

TURKEY

(Türkiye Cümhuriyeti.)

President of the Republic, General Cemal Gürsel, *born* 1895, *assumed power* May 27, 1960; *elected President*, Oct. 26, 1961.

COUNCIL OF MINISTERS
Names as spelt in Turkish characters.

Prime Minister, Ismet Inönü.
Deputy Prime Ministers, Ekrem Alican; Hassan Dinçer; Prof. T. Feysioğlu.
Interior (vacant).
Foreign Affairs, Feridun Cemal Erkin.
Finance, Ferit Melen.
Education, Ibrahim Öktem.
Communications, Ihsan Şeref Dura.
Labour, Bulent Ecevit.
Customs and Monopolies, Orhan Oztrak.
Public Works, Ilyas Seckin.
Housing, Prof. F. K. Gokay.
Agriculture, Mehmet Izmen.
Justice (vacant).
Health and Social Services, Yusuf Azizoglu.
Press, Broadcasting and Tourism, Nurettin Ardiçoğlu.
Defence, Ilhami Sancar.
Commerce, Ahnet Oğuz.
Industry, Prof. F. Celikbas.

TURKISH EMBASSY IN LONDON
Chancery: 43 Belgrave Square, S.W.1.
[Belgravia: 5252]

Turkish Ambassador in London, His Excellency Kemal Nejat Kavur (1962).
1st Secretaries, Behic Hazar; Selçuk Korkud.
2nd Secretaries, Tanjü Ülger; Miss Betin Kuntol.
Naval Attaché, Captain Erşed Erdem.
Air Attaché, Col. Mecdet Bayar.
Military Attaché, Lt.-Col. Süreyya Yüksel.
Commercial Counsellor, Celil Vayisoğlu.
Consulate-General, 46 Rutland Gate, S.W.7.
Consul-General, Fikret Berker.
Deputy Consul-General, Lemi Kemalyeri.
Consul, Nusret Aktan.

Area and Population.—The Turks belong to the Turanian Race, which comprises the Manchus and Mongols of North China, the Finns, and the Turks of Central Asia. Their numbers probably exceed 50,000,000, with the same language, religion and culture, but the actual Turkish State occupies only a small part of the area inhabited by the Turkish Race, the remainder being in Soviet Russia, China, Afghanistan and Persia. Under the Seljuks (Turkish rulers in Anatolia) the conquest of Asia Minor was completed in the 11th century. The Seljuks were succeeded, early in the 14th century, by the Osmanli dynasty, which remained in power until the War of 1914–18.

During the 15th, 16th and 17th centuries the Ottoman Empire was one of the strongest Powers in the world, extending from the Caspian Sea to the Adriatic and Hungary, and from the Indian Ocean to Morocco and the Sudan. It comprised Asia Minor, part of Russia, the Ukraine, the Crimea, the Balkan States and the whole of Arabia. The Black Sea, the Mediterranean, the Red Sea and the Ægean were dominated by Turkish ships, and the Ottoman dominions included not only the Byzantine Empire, but the greater part of the whole Roman Empire.

Turkey now extends from Adrianople to Transcaucasia and Persia, and from the Black Sea to the Mediterranean, Syria and Iraq. The sixth general census of population was held in October 1955. The results of the last four counts are:—

Year	Population
Oct., 1945	18,790,174
Oct., 1950	20,936,524
Oct., 1955	24,111,778
Oct., 1960	27,754,820

Turkey in Europe (9,256 sq. miles, population 2,262,023 in 1955) consists of Eastern Thrace, including the cities of Istanbul (Constantinople) and Edirne (Adrianople), and is separated from Asia by the Bosphorus at Istanbul and by the *Dardanelles* (Hellespont)—about 40 miles in length with a width varying from 1 to 4 miles—the political neighbours being Greece and Bulgaria on the west.

Turkey in Asia (285,246 sq. miles, population 21,849,755 in 1955), comprises the whole of Asia Minor or *Anatolia* ("Land of the Rising Sun" or Orient), and extends from the Ægean Sea to the western boundaries of Georgia, Soviet Armenia and Persia, and from the Black Sea to the Mediterranean and the northern boundaries of Syria and Iraq. The former Turkish Sanjak of Alexandretta (latterly known as the Republic of Hatay), was ceded by France on July 23, 1939, having formed part of Mandated Syria since 1922.

Government.—For two centuries before the War of 1914–18, disintegration had reduced the power and extent of the Turkish Empire, and after that War its boundaries were still further restricted, Iraq, Syria and Arabia passing into other hands. Sultan Mehmed VI., the last of the Osmanli rulers, fled from Constantinople to Malta on Nov. 20, 1922, and the Sultanate was abolished by the National Assembly. On Oct. 29, 1923,* the National Assembly declared Turkey a Republic and elected Gazi Mustafa Kemal (later known as Kemal Atatürk) President. Following the introduction of a multi-party régime in 1945, the Democratic Party was returned to power in 1950 and re-elected in 1954 and 1957. On May 27, 1960, the D.P. Government was overthrown by the Turkish Armed Forces which ruled through the Committee of National Union, a body originally composed of 38 military officers, but reduced to 23 following an internal purge in November, 1960. The committee ruled from January to November, 1961, in conjunction with a civilian House of Representatives, the two bodies together forming the Constituent Assembly. Following a prolonged trial on multiple charges of crimes against the Constitution, Adnan Menderes, the former Democratic Party Prime Minister, was executed on Sept. 17, 1961, together with the former Foreign and Finance Ministers. Sentence of death passed on Celal Bayar, former President, was commuted to life imprisonment.

In October, 1961, general elections for a new National Assembly, composed of the Senate of the Republic (150 Senators) and the Assembly (450 Deputies) resulted in the People's Republican Party getting 173 seats in the Assembly, against 158 for the Justice Party (successor to D.P.), 54 for the Republican Peasants National Party and 65 for the New Turkey Party. In the Senate the J.P. obtained 70 seats, the P.R.P. 36, the R.P.N.P. 16 and

* TURKISH NATIONAL HOLIDAY.—Oct. 29 is observed throughout the Republic as a National Holiday.

the N.T.P. 28. The C.N.U. was dissolved (its members becoming additional life Senators), and General Cemal Gürsel was elected President of the Republic. M. Ismet Inönü, leader of the P.R.P., formed a coalition government comprising the P.R.P. and the J.P. This coalition broke up on May 31, 1962, and was replaced by a second coalition, with M. Inönü as Prime Minister again, composed of the P.R.P., N.T.P. and R.P.N.P., with the J.P. in opposition.

Turkey is divided for administrative purposes into 67 *vilayet* with subdivisions into *kaza* and *nahiye*. Each *vilayet* has a governor (*vali*) and elective council.

Religion and Education.—The majority of the inhabitants are Moslems. There are numerous Christians (of the Latin and Eastern rites) in Istanbul (Constantinople) and a considerable number of Jews. On April 10, 1928, the Grand National Assembly passed a law in virtue of which Islam ceased to be the State religion of the Republic. Education is compulsory, free, and secular. There are elementary, secondary and vocational schools.

In 1955 there were over 17,800 primary schools, with about 1,877,000 pupils. There are two universities at Istanbul (one being a Technical University), two at Ankara (including the recently-founded Middle East Technical University), one at Izmir and one at Erzerum (the Atatürk University). The expenditure allocated to education in the 1961 budget was £T1,051,974,650.

Language and Literature.—Osmanli or Ottoman Turkish is one of the Turanian languages spoken from Macedonia to Siberia. Until 1926 this language was written in Arabic script, but in that year the Roman alphabet was substituted for use in official correspondence and in 1928 for universal use, with Arabic numerals as used throughout Europe. Mainly as a consequence of this change the percentage of Turks who can read and write is rising steadily. Ancient Turkish literature aped the Arabic manner, but the revolution of 1908 was followed by a popular reaction against the writings of the past (which appealed only to a small class) and led to the introduction of a native literature free from foreign influences and adapted to the understanding of the people. The vehicle first employed was the newspaper, printed in the neo-Latin alphabet, with supplements for prose and dramatic fiction, poetry and literary criticism. The leading Turkish newspapers are centred in Ankara and Istanbul, although most provincial towns have their own daily papers. There are foreign language papers in French, Greek and English and numerous magazines and weeklies on various subjects.

Production and Industry.—Although it is estimated that 16 per cent. of the country is entirely unproductive and only 16 per cent. fully arable, agriculture provides a livelihood for 75 per cent. of the population and the economy is based extensively on the export of agricultural products. Agriculture is still largely primitive, but is being modernized at an accelerated pace. The principal crops are cereals, cotton, tobacco, sultanas and figs, pulses, oilseeds, valonea, hazel-nuts, opium, sugar beet, and many varieties of fruit. Since 1949, when there were only 4 sugar factories in Turkey, the country has become self-supporting in sugar, and has a margin for export. There are now 17 sugar factories. With the important exception of wheat, which is grown mostly on the arid Central Anatolian Plateau, most of the crops are grown on the fertile littoral. Tobacco, sultana and fig cultivation is centred at Izmir, where substantial quantities of cotton are also grown. The main cotton area is the Çukurova Plain around Adana. In 1960 it was estimated that there were more than 76,000,000 head of livestock, including horses, donkeys and mules. Animal by-products include wool, hides and skins, and mohair. The forests which lie between the littoral plain and the Anatolian Plateau, contain beech, pine, oak, elm, chestnut, lime, plane, alder, box, poplar and maple. During recent years the Government has attempted, so far not altogether successfully, to combat the depredations of peasant and goat which threatens to destroy the existing forests within the next 25 years.

Turkey's second most important industry is based on her considerable mineral wealth, which is, however, as yet comparatively unexploited. The most important developments are in coal, of which some 7,000,000 metric tons are produced annually (over 40 per cent. of which is lignite), and which is used to meet domestic needs. The main export minerals are chromite, production of which in 1962 amounted to about 450,000 metric tons and blister copper of which 25,775 metric tons were produced in 1962. Some 14,400 metric tons were exported. The most vexing problem concerning the Turkish mining industry during 1962 was the impact on Turkish chrome mines caused by increased exports of cheap Russian high-grade metallurgical chromite to Western European consumers and substantial forward sales to the U.S. ferrochrome industry. At the end of 1962 it was estimated that stocks in the hands of private and State producers of chromite exceeded 400,000 metric tons. Iron ore, boron minerals, cupreous pyrites, manganese ores and salt are the other principal mineral developments. Working mainly through the State-owned Eti Bank (Mining) and the Sümer Bank (Industry), great strides have been made during recent years in industrializing the country. The share of private industry is increasing. Developments include the expansion of the iron and steel works at Karabuk, and other factories and plans for the production of textiles, paper, pulp, cement, artificial silk, sugar, leather goods, glass-ware, heavy chemicals, artificial fertilizers, canned goods, wines and spirits, vegetable oils, soap and refined sulphur. The cement industry has recently made great progress: many new factories have been built throughout the country and annual production, which totalled 375,522 metric tons in 1949, reached the figure of 2,316,548 metric tons in 1962. Legislation was passed in 1954 to encourage the investment of foreign capital in Turkey and to permit the exploitation of Turkey's petroleum resources by foreign companies. At the end of June, 1962, 20 American British, German and Turkish companies were prospecting for oil in Turkey. Production of oil by the Turkish Petroleum Administration from the Raman-Garzan field in Eastern Turkey, amounted to 451,860 metric tons in 1962. An oil refinery at Izmit, owned jointly by the Turkish Petroleum Corporation and Caltex, went into production in August, 1961, and the construction of a refinery at Mersin, for the Socony-MobilOil-Shell-B.P. consortium, was completed in June, 1962. The combined production capacities of the Batman refinery and the two new refineries at Izmit and Mersin (which will refine imported crude oil), will be about 4,500,000 metric tons.

Turkey's first Five-Year Development Plan, for the years 1963/67, drafted by the State Planning Organization, became effective from January 1, 1963. The Plan provides for the investment from public and private sources of about £2,350,000,000 in all sectors of the economy, the main emphasis being on irrigation and agricultural machinery, investment in manufacturing industry, the construction of roads and harbours, and the improvement of housing and education. Details of projects to be undertaken within the Plan will appear in annual programmes, the first of which, the 1963 programme, was published in February, 1963. The cost of the Plan will be met mainly by Turkey herself, but it is estimated that she will require substantial external assistance. A consortium on aid to Turkey, of which the United Kingdom is a member, was set up under the auspices of O.E.C.D., and, in the first instance, co-ordinated the various forms of financial assistance which were made towards the Turkish programme for 1963. On May 1, 1963, the U.K. Government made a loan of £2,857,000 to the Turkish Government as its contribution to international aid in 1963 for Turkey: the loan, which is available to finance the projects on a wide range of capital and semi-capital goods from the United Kingdom, will be re-paid between 1970 and 1988.

COMMUNICATIONS

Railways.—The complete network became the property of the State Railways Administration in 1948. The total length in operation at the end of March, 1962, was 7,882 kilometres. In 1962, the railways carried 77,277,000 passengers, 10,310,000 tons of freight and 4,177,000 head of livestock.

Roads.—In September, 1948, a 9-year road construction programme was started, involving the construction, reconstruction, improvement and maintenance of a national highway system totalling 24,300 kilometres of all-weather standard roads. Much progress has been made with the help of mechanized road building equipment from American aid sources. By 1961, there were 23,647 kilometres of road open to traffic throughout the year. The total number of motor vehicles, excluding tractors, in use at the beginning of 1961 was 114,208.

Posts.—In 1960, the number of telephone subscribers in Turkey was 180,030. There is a considerable shortage of telephone lines in some of Turkey's major cities: consequently work began in 1961 to provide 55,700 additional lines in 15 of the main cities in the country.

Shipping.—The strength of the Turkish Merchant Navy at the beginning of 1956 was 1,510 vessels, totalling about 752,000 tons. About 35 per cent. of Turkey's commercial fleet is owned by the Denizçilik Bankasi (the Maritime Bank).

Civil Aviation.—The State Airlines (T.H.Y.) operate all internal services and have services to Athens, Beirut, Nicosia, Rome, Frankfurt and London, while most of the leading foreign airlines, including British European Airways and British Overseas Airways Corporation, operate services to Istanbul and some also to Ankara. The T.H.Y. fleet is composed of Vickers *Viscounts*, *Dakotas* and *Fokker Friendships*. The airports at Istanbul, Ankara and Adana have been improved to P.I.A.C.O. (Class B) standard and a sum of £T45,000,000 is being spent on ten other new airfields in Turkey. In addition nine military airfields, costing £T160,000,000 are being constructed by N.A.T.O.

FINANCE	1963–64
Revenue (Budget)	£T12,101,638,158
Expenditure (Budget) (Ordinary)	8,164,488,319
(Investment)	3,937,149,839
Debt (October, 1962):—	
Internal funded	£T8,285,523,000
Internal floating	603,000,000
External funded	5,794,856,000
External floating	904,755,000

The Turkish *Lira*, or £T. (of 100 *Kurus*) has a nominal value of 25·20 to the £ and 9·00 to the U.S. Dollar.

TRADE

	1961 £T'000	1962 £T'000
Total imports*	4,585,129	5,599,896
Total exports	3,120,573	3,430,683

* Including imports of wheat from the United States under P.L.480.

Trade with U.K.

	1961	1962
Imports from U.K.	£23,202,638	£20,549,663
Exports to U.K.	11,974,309	14,696,854

The imports included iron and steel, machinery and spares, petroleum products, textiles and yarn, agricultural machinery, motor vehicles and pharmaceuticals: the exports included tobacco, cotton, dried fruit, cement, sugar, livestock, chrome ore, oilseeds, opium and valonea.

The principal imports from United Kingdom in 1962 were road vehicles, machinery, apparatus and appliances, metal manufactures, chemicals and pharmaceuticals; the principal exports to United Kingdom were tobacco, mohair, nuts, figs and raisins, cotton and borax.

CAPITAL OF TURKEY, ANKARA (Angora), an inland town of Asia Minor, about 200 miles E.S.E. of Istanbul, with a population (1955 census), of 353,170 and now estimated to exceed 500,000. Ankara (or Ancyra) was the capital of the Roman Province of *Galatia Prima*, and a marble temple (now in ruins), dedicated to Augustus, contains the *Monumentum* (*Marmor*) *Ancyranum*, inscribed with a record of the reign of Augustus Caesar. A new city has been laid out on modern lines, with parks, statues and avenues. ΨISTANBUL (Constantinople), the former capital, was the Roman city of Byzantium, and was selected by Constantine the Great as the capital of the Roman Empire about A.D. 328, and renamed by him; it became capital of the Eastern Roman Empire in A.D. 364; estimated population, 1,214,616. Istanbul contains the celebrated Mosque of St. Sophia, since 1934 a museum of Byzantine and Turkish art. Other cities are ΨIzmir (Smyrna) 286,310; Adana 172,465; Bursa (Brusa) 131,366; Eskisehir 122,755; Gaziantep 97,144; Konya 93,125; Kayseri (Caesarea) 81,127 and Erzerum 69,499.

FLAG.—Red, with white crescent and star.

BRITISH EMBASSY
(Ankara)

Ambassador Extraordinary and Plenipotentiary, His Excellency Sir William Denis Allen, K.C.M.G., C.B. (1963) £5,015
Minister, M. C. G. Mann, C.M.G.
Commercial Counsellor, A. H. Ballantyne, C.V.O., C.B.E.
1st Secretaries, D. P. Aiers; H. R. Latham; W. J. A. Wilberforce; Miss M. I. Mackie, M.V.O.; H. J. Spence.
2nd Secretaries, T. L. A. Daunt; T. W. Sharp; D. J. Melliar Smith.
3rd Secretary, Miss P. M. Thomas.
Naval Attaché, Capt. H. J. S. Banks, R.N.
Military Attaché, Brigadier V. L. M. Wainwright, O.B.E., M.C.
Air Attaché, Group-Capt. I. E. Butler, D.F.C., A.F.C.
Cultural Attaché, E. L. Hancock, O.B.E.
Labour Attaché, C. W. C. Stevens.
Information Officer, W. D. Wilson.
Asst. Information Officer, J. H. Potter.
Administrative Officer and Consul, H. A. Chambers.
Asst. do., C. Scott.
Archivist, A. C. V. Onslow.
Accountant, G. L. Beattie.
Chaplain, Rev. C. W. Piper.

BRITISH CONSULAR OFFICES

There are British Consular Offices at *Istanbul*, *Izmir* (*Smyrna*) and *Iskenderun*.

BRITISH COUNCIL

Representative, E. L. Hancock, O.B.E., 27 Adakale Sokak, Yenişehir, Ankara.

There is also a centre at Istanbul.

BRITISH INSTITUTE OF ARCHAEOLOGY, Ankara.—*Director*, M. Gough.

BRITISH CHAMBER OF COMMERCE OF TURKEY, 4/5 Buldanioğlu Han, No. 246 Necati Bey Caddesi, Galata, Istanbul (Postal Address, P.K.190 Galata, Istanbul).

Chairman, R. A. Sutch. *Secretary*, N. Covey.

UNITED ARAB REPUBLIC
(Egypt)

President, Gamal Abdel Nasser (*elected* Feb. 21, 1958).

Presidency Council

Vice-Presidents, Abdul Latif Baghdadi; F.M. Abdul Hakim Amer; Zakariya Muhyiddin; Hussein el Shafei; Kemaluddin Hussein.

Other Members, Aly Sabri (*President of the Executive Council*); Anwar Sadat; Ahmed Abdul el-Sharabasi; Nurreddin Tarraf; Kamaluddin Rifaat; and Hassan Ibrahim.

Executive Council

President, Ali Sabry.
Foreign Affairs, Dr. Mahmoud Fawzi.
Treasury and Planning, Dr. Abdul Moneim Al-Kaissouni.
Industry, Aziz Sidki.
Education, Sayed Youssef.
Higher Education, Abdul Aziz el Sayed.
Culture, Information and National Guidance, Abdul Kader Hatem.
Economy, Ahmed Zendo.
Health, Mohammed el Nabawi el Muhandis.
Justice, Fathi el Sharqawi.
Public Works, Hassan Zaki.
Agrarian Reform and Land Reclamation, Abdul Muhsin Abul Nur.
Agriculture, Mohammed Neguib Hashad.
Communications, Dr. Mustafa Khalil.
Labour, Anwar Salamaa.
Supply, Dr. Kamal Ramzi Stino.
High Dam, Zedki Soliman.
Scientific Research, Salah Hedayat.
War, Abdel Wahab Elbishri.
Housing and Public Utilities, Ahmed Mohram.
Wakfs and Alazhar Affairs, Muhammed Elbahei.
Interior, Abdel Azim Fahmy.
Youth, Talaat Khairy.
Social Affairs, Mme. Hekmat Abuzeid.
Local Government, Abbas Radwan.

In addition there are Deputy Ministers for *Foreign Affairs*, *Housing*, *Education* and *Planning*.

EMBASSY IN LONDON
75 South Audley Street, W.1.
[Grosvenor: 2401]

Ambassador, His Excellency Mohamed el-Kony (1961).
Military and Air Attaché, Brig.-Gen. Saad Mohamed El Jusseiny El Shazly.
Naval Attaché, Cdre. Ahmed Fakry El Sioufi.
Cultural Attaché, Muhammed Fatthy.
Counsellors, Mohsen Abdel Khalek (*Commercial*); Fawzi Maboub (*Consular*).
1st Secretary, A. Z. Abou El-Nasr.
Press Counsellor, Ahmed Ibrahim Khabil Anis.
Consulate-General, 46 Rutland Gate, S.W.7.

AREA AND POPULATION.—The total area of Egypt is estimated at 1,000,000 square kilometres (386,110 square miles), the inhabited area being only 35,168 square kilometres (13,578 square miles), with a population (estimated 1961), 26,059,000.

There are three distinct elements in the native population. The largest, or "Egyptian" element, is a Hamito-Semite race, known in the rural districts as *Fellahin* (*fellâh*—ploughman, or tiller of the soil). The *Fellahin* have been mainly of the Moslem faith since the conquest of the country in the 7th century, but in 1947 there were more than 1,000,000 Coptic and Greek Orthodox Christians in Egypt. A second element is the *Bedouin*, or nomadic Arabs of the Libyan and Arabian deserts, of whom about one-seventh are real nomads, and the remainder semi-sedentary tent-dwellers on the outskirts of the cultivated end of the Nile Valley and the Fayûm. The third element is the *Nubian* of the Nile Valley between Aswân and Wadi-Halfa of mixed Arab and negro blood. The Bedouin and Nubians are Moslems.

The territory of Egypt comprises (1) *Egypt Proper*, forming the N.E. corner of the African continent, divisible into (*a*) the valley and delta of the Nile, (*b*) the Libyan or Western Desert, and (*c*) the Arabian or Eastern Desert; (2) *The Peninsula of Sinai*, forming part of the continent of Asia; and (3) a number of *Islands* in the Gulf of Suez and Red Sea, of which the principal are Jubal, Shadwan, Gafatin and Zeberged (or St. John's Island). This territory lies between 22° and 32° N. lat. and 24° and 37° E. long. The northern boundary is the Mediterranean, and in the south Egypt is conterminous with the Sudan. The western boundary runs from a point on the coast 10 kilometres N.W. of Sollûm to the latitude of Siwa and thence due S. along the 25th meridian to the parallel of 22° N. (the N. boundary of the Sudan) at 'Uweinat Mountain. The E. boundary follows a line drawn from Rafa on the Mediterranean (34° 15′ E. long.) to the head of the Gulf of Aqaba, from which point the remainder of the E. boundary is washed by the waters of the Gulf of Aqaba and the Red Sea. The "settled land area" is stated officially at 7,667,000 *feddâns* (12,431 square miles) and the area of lakes at 641,000 *feddâns* (1,039 square miles), a total of 8,308,000 *feddâns* (13,470 square miles).

Physical Features.—The Nile valley varies in width from less than half a mile in the southern granitic region to over 10 miles in the northern limestone region, and the cliffs in some places rise to heights of over a thousand feet above the river. The fertile lands, on which the prosperity of the country depends, occupy the floor of the valley between the river and the bounding cliffs, while to the north of Cairo they spread out into the irregular fan-shaped formation of the Delta which comprises the six provinces of Lower Egypt, with the richest soil in the country.

The *Nile* has a total length of 4,160 miles. In the 960 miles of its course through Egypt it receives not a single tributary stream. The river has a regular yearly rise and fall, attaining its maximum level about the middle of September and its minimum about the end of May. At Cairo the average rise and fall is about 13 feet. Westward from the Nile Valley into Tripoli stretches the *Libyan Desert*, an arid region, containing some depressions, whose springs irrigate small areas known as *Oases*, of which the principal, from S.E. to N.W., are known as Kharga, Dakhla, Farafra, Baharia, and Siwa.

On the eastern edge of the Libyan Desert, a few miles south-west of Cairo stand the Pyramids of Giza, of which the highest, the *Great Pyramid*, is 451 feet high. Close to the pyramids is the *Great Sphinx*, 189 feet long. In the Eastern Desert a great backbone of high and rugged mountains extends north-westwards from Ethiopia to near Suez, and reappears as a detached mass in the

Peninsula of Sinai. Flanking this mountain chain on the west, between the axis of the range and the Nile, are plateaux of sandstones and limestones, dissected by *wadis* (dry water-courses), often of great length and depth, with some wild vegetation and occasional wells and springs. The roads follow the course of the main *wadis* from well to well, and here and there are to be found small encampments of wandering Arabs.

Religions—At the Census of 1947 there were 17,397,946 Moslems, 1,346,035 Coptic Christians, 50,200 Roman Catholics, 155,600 other Christians (Protestant and Reformed Churches), and 65,639 Jews. The chief Moslem religious authorities in Egypt are the *Sheik el Gami el Azhar* and the *Mufti al Gumhuriya al Arabiya al Muttahida*.

Government.—From 30 B.C. to A.D. 639 Egypt was a province of the Roman Empire, but in A.D. 640 the Christian inhabitants were subjugated by Moslem invaders, and Egypt became a province of the Eastern Caliphate. In 1517 the country was incorporated in the Ottoman Empire and was governed by pashas sent from Constantinople until the beginning of the 18th century, when for about 100 years the ruler was chosen from among the Mamelukes, or bodyguard. *Mohammed Ali*, who was proclaimed *Pasha* in 1805, exterminated the Mamelukes in 1811 and was eventually made hereditary governor of Egypt and the Sudan by a *firman* from the Sultan of June 1, 1841.

In 1882, a military revolt, headed by an officer of the Egyptian Army (Ahmed Arâbi *Pasha*), assumed alarming proportions and a British expedition was despatched to re-establish the authority of the Khedive. Meanwhile a revolt had broken out in the southern provinces, headed by Sheikh Mohammed Ahmed of Dongola, who proclaimed himself a *Mahdi* of Islam, and the British expeditionary force, sent to quell the rebellion of 1882, remained in the country as an army of occupation until 1936 (*see* below).

During the War of 1914–18 a British Protectorate over Egypt was declared (Dec. 18, 1914) and Khedive Abbas Hilmi was deposed. He was succeeded by Hussein Kamel, with the title of Sultan, who died Oct. 9, 1917, being succeeded by his brother, Ahmed Fuad. The British Protectorate terminated on Feb. 28, 1922, and Sultan Ahmed Fuad was proclaimed King of Egypt. Following closely on the accession of King Farouk, the *Anglo-Egyptian Treaty* was signed in London (Aug. 26, 1936); the military occupation by British troops was terminated and Ambassadors were duly accredited at the Courts of St. James's and Cairo.

The security of Egypt was threatened after the outbreak of war in 1939 and reinforcements were sent from Britain and the Dominions. Axis troops invaded Egypt in 1940 and fierce fighting ensued, with Allied victories and reverses, until the decisive victory in "The Battle of Egypt" (Oct.–Nov. 1942) drove the enemy out of the country. In July, 1952, following a military *coup d'etat*, King Farouk abdicated in favour of his infant son, who became King Ahmed Fuad II. In June, 1953, however, Gen. Neguib's military council deposed the young king, and declared Egypt a Republic, Gen. Neguib himself assuming the Presidency. In November, 1954, General Neguib was deposed by Lt.-Col. Gamal Abdel Nasser and the military council. On June 23, 1956, Col. Nasser assumed office as President, after an election at which voting was compulsory, and he was the only candidate.

The United Arab Republic came into being on Feb. 1, 1958, when a union of Egypt and Syria was confirmed by a plebiscite. A provisional constitution announced on Feb. 5, provided for a Presidential régime with a National Assembly selected from the existing Egyptian and Syrian Chambers. The Government was by regional councils with a central cabinet. As a result of a coup d'état in Syria on September 28, 1961, Syria seceded from the Union, a development accepted by President Nasser. The title and flag of the U.A.R. were, however, retained for Egypt.

In November, 1961, President Nasser announced arrangements for the drafting of a new Constitution, to replace the provisional Egyptian Constitution of January, 1956, which had been superseded by the U.A.R. Constitution of 1958. On the basis of recommendations by a Preparatory Committee convened in November, 1961, for this purpose, a representative elected Assembly, the National Congress of Popular Forces, met from May 21–July 5. The Congress discharged the dual tasks of approving the National Charter presented by President Nasser, expressing the aims and ideals of the Egyptian Revolution, and the formation of an Arab Socialist Union, henceforward to be the basis of popular representation in the U.A.R., the General Congress, which would be the next stage in Constitutional development. This Congress is to decide the formation of an elected Legislative Assembly, which will in its turn be entrusted with the task of drawing up a permanent Constitution for the U.A.R.

Agriculture.—The principal crops grown during *Saifi* (summer) are cotton, rice, sugar cane, and sorgho (maize). *Nili* (flood) part of *Saifi*, has the date of its commencement fixed by the Irrigation Department according to the quantities of water available before the flood, which reaches its highest level in September—it generally begins in July; the principal crops are maize and rice. *Chitwi* (winter) begins in November and ends in June; the principal crops are cereals, bersim (a variety of clover) and—mainly in Upper Egypt—beans, lentils, onions and helba.

Railways.—The principal lines radiate from Cairo to Alexandria (and on to Rosetta), Damietta and Ismailia (continuing northwards to Port Said and southward to Suez). From Cairo the line runs southwards for a distance of 554 miles to Shellal, the First Cataract. At this point a steamer connection runs to Wadi Halfa, connecting the Egyptian Republic with the Sudan Government Railways. Westwards from Alexandria (and close to the coast) runs a line to the frontier at Sollûm, thus joining Tripoli to Egypt. The gauge is standard (4 ft. 8½ in.). There are two other State-owned lines in Egypt, namely, the Auxiliary Railways of Upper Egypt, consisting of 282 miles of standard gauge, and the Western Oases Railways, a length of 141 miles (75 centimetre gauge) connecting the oasis of Kharga with the Nile Valley.

Roads and Caravan Routes.—A sea coast motor road exists from Alexandria to Mersa Matruh, with an extension along the coast to Sollûm and thence to connect with the coast road in Libya. The principal caravan routes lead to the Oases of the Libyan Desert (though Kharga can now be reached by train), whence there is a route, known as the Darb el 'Arbain, leading to Dar Fûr and the south of the Sudan. There are many well-known routes across the Arabian Desert to the Red Sea, that from Qena to Qoseir, a metalled road, being probably the most frequently used.

Shipping.—Ψ Apart from the three great seaports of Alexandria, Port Said and Suez, Egypt has but few harbours and anchorages adapted for large craft; the principal are those of Sollûm and Matruh on the Mediterranean, Tor, Abu Zenima, Zeitia, Jemsa and Hurghada in the Gulf of Suez, and Safaga and Qoseir on the Red Sea.

Currency.—£E (Egyptian *pound* of 100 *piastres*) = £1 0s. 6½*d.* sterling. Official Rate of Exchange —(*Buying*) *Piastres* 97·50 = £1; (*Selling*) Piastres 97·60 = £1. (*See also* p. 83.)

Trade with U.K.

	1961	1962
Imports from U.K.	£22,267,516	£24,440,595
Exports to U.K.	4,864,435	10,680,263

The principal imports are metals, and manufactures thereof, coal and coke, chemicals and pharmaceuticals, capital plant and other machinery, vehicles, foodstuffs, timber and wood and paper. The exports are principally raw cotton, rice, mineral products and onions.

BRITISH EMBASSY

Kasr-el-Doubara, Garden City, Cairo

Ambassador Extraordinary and Plenipotentiary, His Excellency Sir Harold Beeley, K.C.M.G., C.B.E. (1961) £5,015
Counsellor, D. J. D. Maitland, O.B.E.
Counsellor (*Commercial*), R. A. Daniell, O.B.E.
Military Attaché, Brig. T. C. T. Mossman.
Air Attaché, Group-Capt. J. R. Gibbons, A.F.C.
Cultural Attaché, I. H. Williams.
1st Secretaries, D. F. Hawley, M.B.E. (*Head of Chancery*); M. S. Weir; M. P. V. Hannam (*Commercial*); C. T. Brant; J. W. G. Ridd; C. S. Palmer, O.B.E. (*Consul*); S. Oates (*Consul*); W. H. G. Fletcher (*Claims*); R. L. Cook (*Administration*).
2nd Secretaries, T. Quinlan (*Commercial*); H. I. Duck; P. H. Wilkinson (*Vice-Consul*); M. Sullivan (*Claims*).
Archivist, D. Jenkins.

There is a British Consulate-General in *Alexandria*.

British Council Representative, I. H. Williams.

CAPITAL.—Cairo (population 1960, 3,346,000), stands on the E. bank of the Nile, about 14 miles from the head of the Delta. Its oldest part is the fortress of Babylon in old Cairo, with its Roman bastions and Coptic churches. The earliest Arab building is the Mosque of 'Amr, dating from A.D. 643, and the most conspicuous is the Citadel, built by Saladin towards the end of the 12th century.

ΨALEXANDRIA (pop. 1960), 1,513,000, founded 332 B.C. by Alexander the Great, was for over 1,000 years the capital of Egypt and a centre of Hellenic culture which vied with Athens herself. Its great *pharos* (lighthouse), 480 feet high, with a lantern burning resinous wood, was one of the "Seven Wonders of the World." Other towns are: Ismailia (276,000); ΨPort Said (244,000); Mansura (102,709), Asyût (284,000), Faiyûm (162,000), Tanta (139,965), Mahalla el Kubra (115,509), ΨSuez (203,000), ΨDamietta (97,000).

CAIRO is 2,520 miles from London: transit *viâ* Trieste, 5 days; *viâ* Marseilles, 6 days.

URUGUAY

(República Oriental del Uruguay)

NATIONAL COUNCIL OF GOVERNMENT

Sr. Daniel Fernández Crespo (*President*, 1963–64); Ing. Luis Giannattasio; Dr. Wáshington Beltrán; Sr. Alberto Heber; Dr. Carlos Maria Peñadés; Dr. Hector Lorenzo y Losada; Dr. Amilcar Vasconcelles; Dr. Alberto Abdala; Gen. Oscar Gestido.

Minister of Interior, Dr. Felipe Gil.
Foreign Affairs, Sr. Alejandro Zorilla de San Martin.
National Defence, General Modesto Rebollo.
Finance (vacant).
Public Works, Ing. Isadoro Vejo Rodriguez.
Public Health, Dr. Aparicio Mendez.
Public Instruction and Social Welfare, Prof. Juan Pivel Devoto.
Industries and Labour, Sr Walter Santoro.
Livestock and Agriculture, Sr. Wilson Ferreira Aldunate.

EMBASSY AND CONSULATE

Chancery: 48 Lennox Gardens, S.W.1 [Kensington: 8835]

Residence: 1 Campden Hill, W.8 [Park: 6557]

Ambassador in London, His Excellence Dr. Roberto E. MacEachen (1961).
Minister-Counsellor, Dr. Jorge Barreiro.
2nd Secretaries, Señor Don Guy P. Nery; Sra. E. Risso Platero.

Area and Population.—The smallest Republic in South America, on the east coast of the Rio de la Plata, situate in lat. 30°—35° S. and long. 53° 25′—57° 42′ W., with an area of 72,180 square miles, and an estimated population of 3,000,000 (over 1,000,000 in the capital), almost entirely white and predominantly of Spanish and Italian descent. Most Uruguayans are Roman Catholics. There is complete freedom of religion and no church is established by the State.

Physical Features.—The country consists mainly (and particularly in the south and west) of undulating grassy plains. The principal chains of hills are the Cuchilla del Haedo, which cross the Brazilian boundary and extend southwards to the Cuchilla Grande of the south and east. In no case do the peaks exceed 2,000 feet. The principal river is the *Rio Negro* (with its tributary the Yi), flowing from north-east to south-west into the *Rio Uruguay*. The boundary river *Uruguay* is navigable from its estuary to Salto, about 200 miles north, and the Negro is also navigable for a considerable distance. Smaller rivers are the Cuareim, Yaguaron, Santa Lucia, Queguay, and the Cebollati. On the south-east coast are several lagoons, and the north-east boundary crosses (the Brazilian) Lake Merin. The climate is reasonably healthy. The summer is warm, but the heat is often tempered by the breezes of the Atlantic. The winter is, on the whole, mild, but cold spells, characterized by icy winds from the South Polar regions, are experienced in June, July and August. Rainfall is regular throughout the year, but there are occasional droughts.

Government.—Uruguay—or the *Banda Oriental*, as this territory lying on the eastern bank of the Uruguay River was then called—resisted all attempted invasions of the Portuguese and Spaniards until the beginning of the 17th century, and 100 years later the Portuguese settlements were captured by the Spaniards. From 1726–1814 the country formed part of Spanish South America and underwent many vicissitudes during the Wars of Independence. In 1814 the armies of the Argentine Confederation captured the capital and annexed the province, and it was afterwards annexed by Portugal and became a province of Brazil. In 1825, the country threw off the Brazilian yoke. This action led to war between Argentina and Brazil, which was settled by the mediation of the United Kingdom, Uruguay being declared an independent state in 1828. In 1830 a Republic was inaugurated.

A new Constitution was approved and brought into force on March 1, 1952, whereby the executive power is discharged by a National Council of Government composed of nine members (including six from the party which has won the elections), elected every four years and assisted by nine ministers. The members of the National Council of Government are eligible for re-election after four years have elapsed since the date on which their mandate ceased. The Legislature consists of a Chamber of 99 deputies and of a Senate of 30 members, elected for four years by all adult male and female citizens who can read and write. At the November, 1958, elections for the National Council of Government and the Legislature, the *Partido Nacional* (*Blancos*) gained power after 93 years in opposition to the *Partido Colorado*; and at the November, 1962, elections they retained power by a short head, losing control of the Municipal Government of Montevideo, however, to the *Colorados*. The new Government took office on March 1, 1963.

The Republic is divided into 19 Departments each with a chief of police and a Departmental Council. The most important cities of the interior are Salto and Paysandu, both situated on the River Uruguay, which forms the main line of division from Argentina.

Production and Industry.—Wheat, barley, maize, linseed, sunflower seed and rice are cultivated. The wealth of the country is obtained from its pasturage, which supports large herds of cattle and sheep, the wool of which is of excellent quality. The 1961 livestock census showed figures of 8,700,000 cattle, 21,500,000 sheep, 640,000 horses, 270,000 hogs, and 19,000 goats. In addition to the meat packing industry, textiles and wine and beer are of importance. The development of local industry continues and during and since the Second World War, in addition to the greatly augmented textile industry, marked expansion in local production is notable in respect of tyres, sheet-glass, three-ply wood, cement, leather-curing, beet-sugar, plastics, household consumer goods, edible oils and the refining of petroleum and petroleum products. There are no mineral deposits of importance.

Communications.—There are about 5,000 miles of national highways, and about 7,508 miles of telegraph, with 48,375 miles of telephones.

In 1955 there were about 1,828 miles of standard gauge railway in use in Uruguay. A national Corporation was formed to administer the railway systems purchased by the Government from four British companies in 1948.

Civil aviation is developing rapidly. An internal airline, PLUNA, which is now owned by the State, runs a daily passenger and limited freight service to the principal capitals of the interior, and also runs services to Southern Brazil, Paraguay and Argentina. International passenger and freight services are maintained by American, South American and European airlines. The airport of Carrasco lies 12 miles outside Montevideo.

Education and Social Services.—Uruguay is one of the most advanced of the South American states, with old-age pensions, maternity and child welfare centres, accident insurance, etc. Primary education is compulsory and free, with about 252,400 pupils in 1,879 state schools and technical and trade schools, and evening courses for adult education. In 1959 there were 54,800 pupils in secondary schools including 9,700 in the 11 State *liceos* of the capital. The University at Montevideo (founded in 1849) had, in 1961, 15,000 students enrolled in its ten faculties.

Language and Literature.—Spanish is the language of the Republic. Modern literature has provided some authors with international reputations and the literature of Spain is accessible in all public libraries. 10 daily newspapers are published in Montevideo with an estimated total circulation of 550,000. Most of them are distributed throughout the country.

FINANCE

Actual revenue and expenditure for the years 1961 and 1962 and estimated revenue and expenditure for 1963 were as follows:—

	1962 *Ur.*$'000	1963 *Ur.*$'000
Revenue	2,064,968·2	2,244,000·0
Expenditure	2,874,772·7	3,283,000·0

(May, 1963)	*Ur.*$
Internal Debt	2,986,275,632
External Debt	68,764,724

The monetary unit is the *peso*. By a law dated December 17, 1959, the nominal value of the *peso* was reduced from 0·585 grammes of fine gold to 0·17619 grammes of pure gold of a standard value of 900 milésimos of fine gold giving a parity of *pesos* 6·50 to the *U.S. dollar*.

The circulating medium is, however, the paper *peso* which at the free rate of exchange has a value of *Ur.*$ = £1. The rate for the £ in August, 1962, was about *pesos* 30·77 (buying) and for the U.S. dollar *pesos* 10·98 (buying). Moreover a draft Bill is at present before Parliament which would establish an official new parity rate of *Ur.*$ 14·99 = U.S.$1.

TRADE

	1961	1962
Total imports	$U.S.209,073,210	$U.S.230,484,000
Total exports	174,715,681	153,431,000

Trade with U.K.

	1961	1962
Imports from U.K.	£8,418,558	£7,101,249
Exports to U.K.	15,850,440	10,915,241

The exports are principally animal and agricultural products, and include chilled, frozen and canned meat, wool, hides and oleaginous products; the imports are principally machinery, motor vehicles, fuels and lubricants, raw materials, construction materials, timber and foodstuffs.

The principal imports from the U.K. are agricultural machinery, motor vehicles, tinplate, rayon fibre, hardware, road-making machinery and cellulose.

CAPITAL, Montevideo, Pop. (1959), 900,000. Other centres are ΨSalto (41,000), ΨPaysandu (42,000), Rivera (31,000), ΨMercedes (24,000), Melo (21,000) and Minas (20,000).

FLAG.—Four blue and five white horizontal stripes surcharged with sun on a white ground in the top corner, next flagstaff.

Time of transit from London to Montevideo, by air, 22 hours (B.O.A.C. Comet).

BRITISH EMBASSY

Chancery, Calle Rincon 454, 5° piso, Montevideo.

Ambassador Extraordinary and Plenipotentiary, His Excellency Sir (Henry) Norman Brain, K.B.E., C.M.G. (1961) £4,115

1st Secretary and Consul, K. Hamylton Jones.

1st Secretary (Commercial), J. L. Taylor.

2nd Secretary and Consul, A. K. Milne.

2nd Secretary and Vice-Consul, E. G. Toomer.

2nd Secretary and Information Officer, A. B. Blackwood.

Naval and Military Attaché, Capt. P. E. V. Bailey, R.N.

Air Attaché, Group-Capt. G. F. Lerwill, D.F.C.

Labour Attaché, J. M. Carlin, D.F.C.

Administration Officer, P. Robinson.

Archivist, R. T. Boyce.

BRITISH CONSULAR OFFICES

There are British Consular Offices at *Montevideo* and *Fray Bentos*.

BRITISH COUNCIL

Representative, P. J. Seccombe, Avenida Agraciada 1464 1er Piso, Montevideo.

ANGLO-URUGUAYAN CULTURAL INSTITUTE, Avenida Agraciada 1464, 1er Piso, Montevideo—*Director*, P. J. Seccombe.

There are branch Institutes at Salto, Paysandu, Fray Bentos, Rivera, Las Piedras, Melo, Trinidad and Treinta y Tres.

BRITISH CHAMBER OF COMMERCE IN URUGUAY, Edificio Banco de Londres, Calle Cerrito, *Montevideo*.

U.S.S.R.

(Soyuz Sovetskikh Sotsialisticheskikh Respublik = Union of Soviet Socialist Republics)

THE COMMUNIST PARTY OF THE SOVIET UNION

(August, 1963)

(K.P.S.S. = Kommunisticheskaya Partiya Sovetskogo Soyuza)

Constitutionally, the highest executive organ of the C.P.S.U. is its *Central Committee* which at present consists of 175 members; there are also 155 "candidates for membership" who have a consultative voice at the deliberations of the Central Committee, and 65 members of the *Central Auditing Commission*. The real power in the Party is vested, however, in the *Presidium* and *Secretariat* of the Central Committee.

Presidium of the Central Committee, L. I. Brezhnev; N. S. Khrushchev; A. P. Kirilenko; A. N. Kosygin; F. R. Kozlov; O. W. Kuusinen; A. I. Mikoyan; N. V. Podgorny; D. S. Polyansky; N. M. Shvernik; M. A. Suslov; G. I. Voronov (*full members*). L. N. Efremov; V. V. Grishin; K. T. Mazurov; V. P. Mzhavanadze; Sh. R. Rashidov; V. V. Shcherbitsky (*candidates for membership*).

Secretaries of the Central Committee, N. S. Khrushchev (1st) (*elected* September 13, 1953); Yu. P. Andropov; L. I. Brezhnev; P. N. Demichev; L. F. Ilyichev; F. R. Kozlov; O. W. Kuusinen; N. V. Podgorny; V. I. Polyakov; B. N. Ponomarev; A. P. Rudakov; A. N. Shelepin; M. A. Suslov; V. N. Titov.

Party Commission, N. M. Shvernik (*Chairman*); Z. T. Serdyuk (*1st Vice-Chairman*).

Bureaux and Commissions of the Central Committee:

Agriculture, V. I. Polyakov.
*Central Asia**, V. G. Lomonosov.
Chemical and Light Industries, P. N. Demichev.
Ideology, L. F. Ilyichev.
Industry and Building, A. P. Rudakov.
Party Organization, V. N. Titov.
R.S.F.S.R., N. S. Khrushchev.
*State and Party Control***, A. N. Shelepin.
*Transcaucasia****, G. N. Bochkarev.
Komsomol (*Young Communist League*), S. P. Pavlov (*1st Secretary*).

GOVERNMENT OF THE U.S.S.R.

The Presidium of the Supreme Soviet (= Council) of the U.S.S.R.

Chairman, Leonid Ilyich Brezhnev (*elected* May 7, 1960).

Secretary, M. P. Georgadze.

* Based in Tashkent, Uzbek SSR.

** Subordinated also to the Council of Ministers of the U.S.S.R.

*** Based in Tbilisi, Georgian SSR.

The Supreme Soviet consists of two chambers.

Chairman (= Speaker) of the Council of the Union, I. V. Spiridonov.

Chairman (= Speaker) of the Council of Nationalities, J. V. Pejve.

The Council of Ministers of the U.S.S.R.

Chairman, Nikita Sergeyevich Khrushchev (*appointed* March 27, 1958)

1st Vice-Chairmen, A. N. Kosygin; A. I. Mikoyan; D. F. Ustinov.

Vice-Chairmen, V. E. Dymshits; M. A. Lesechko; P. F. Lomako; I. T. Novikov; D. S. Polyansky; K. N. Rudnev; A. N. Shelepin; L. V. Smirnov.

MINISTERS

Agriculture, I. P. Volovchenko.
Communications, N. D. Psurtsev.
Culture, Mrs. E. A. Furtseva.
Defence, Marshal R. Ya. Malinovsky.
Finance, V. F. Garbuzov.
Foreign Affairs, A. A. Gromyko.
Foreign Trade, N. S. Patolichev.
Higher and Technical Secondary Education, V. P. Elyutin.
Merchant Marine, V. G. Bakayev.
Public Health, S. V. Kurashov.
Railways, B. P. Beshchev.
Other officials of ministerial rank, N. V. Baybakov; V. E. Boyko; B. E. Butoma; P. V. Dementyev; A. A. Etmekdjian; A. A. Goreglyad; I. A. Grishmanov; V. M. Gushchin; A. A. Ishkov; V. K. Kalamkarov; V. D. Kalmykov; L. R. Korniets; A. V. Korobov; A. A. Kortunov; L. A. Kostandov; A. I. Kostousov; E. F. Kozhevnikov; V. A. Kucherenko; V. D. Lebedev; N. V. Melnikov; P. N. Naumenko; P. S. Neporozhny; V. N. Novikov; E. S. Novoselov; N. A. Obolensky; G. M. Orlov; M. V. Posokhin; M. E. Rakovsky; A. V. Romanov; P. K. Romanov; V. M. Ryabikov; A. I. Shokin; A. V. Sidorenko; E. P. Slavsky; S. A. Stepanov; N. I. Strokin; A. I. Struyev; A. M. Tarasov; N. N. Tarasov; S. M. Tikhomirov; N. A. Tikhonov; A. V. Topchiev; F. B. Yakubovsky; V. F. Zhigalin; V. P. Zotov; S. A. Zverev.

Committees, Councils, Boards etc. subordinated directly to the Council of Ministers:

*State and Party Control**, A. N. Shelepin.
Labour and Wages, A. P. Volkov.
Press, P. K. Romanov.
Broadcasting and Television, M. A. Kharlamov.
Film Industry, A. V. Romanov.
Food Procurement, L. R. Korniets.
External Economic Relations, S. A. Skachkov.
External Cultural Relations, S. K. Romanovsky.
State Security (*K.G.B.*), V. E. Semichastny.
State Bank, A. A. Poskonov.
Central Statistical Board, V. N. Starovsky.

Supreme Council of National Economy (*V.S.N.Kh.*)
Chairman, D. F. Ustinov.
Vice-Chairmen, A. M. Tarasov; S. M. Tikhomirov.

The following administrative bodies are subordinated to the Supreme Council and, through it, to the Council of Ministers:

(1) *State Planning Committee* (*Gosplan*):
Chairman, P. F. Lomako.

The *Gosplan* in its turn supervises the *State Committees* for:

Chemical and Oil Industries, N. K. Baybakov.
Ferrous and Non-Ferrous Metal Industries, V. E. Boyko.
Fuel Industry, N. V. Melnikov.
Automation and Machinebuilding, A. I. Kostousov.
Electrical Engineering, N. A. Obolensky.

* Subordinated also to the Central Committee of the CPSU.

Auto-Tractor and Agricultural Machinery Industry, N. I. Strokin.
Timber, Paper, Woodworking Industries and Forestry, G. M. Orlov.
Light Industries, N. N. Tarasov.
Food Processing Industries, P. V. Naumenko.
Vocational and Technical Education, G. I. Zelenko.
Heavy, Power-Station and Transport Machine Building, A. V. Topchiev.
Manufacture of Instruments, Automation Panels and Control Systems, M. E. Rakovsky.
Construction of Chemical and Oil-Refining Machinery, A. L. Kostandov.
The Central *Gosplan* directs the work of Republican *Gosplans*.
(2) *State Building Committee (Gosstroy)*:
Chairman, I. T. Novikov.
The *Gosstroy* supervises the *State Committees* for:
Transport Development, E. F. Kozhevnikov.
Assembly and Erection of Special Building Projects, F. B. Yakubovsky.
Building in Central Asia, V. M. Gushchin.
Building Materials Industry, [name of chairman unknown].
Civil Construction and Architecture, M. V. Posokhin.
Construction of Building, Road-Building and Public Services Machinery, E. S. Novoselov.
The Central *Gosstroy* directs the work of Republican *Gosstroys*.
(3) *Council of National Economy (Sovnarkhoz)*:
Chairman, V. E. Dymshits.
The *Sovnarkhoz* supervises the work of the *State Committees* for:
Fisheries, A. A. Ishkov.
Trade, A. I. Struyev.
Agricultural Machinery Supply, A. A. Ezhevsky.
Cotton Cultivation in Central Asia, V. Kulikov.
The Central *Sovnarkhoz* directs the work of Republican *Sovnarkhozes*.
The *Supreme Council of National Economy* also supervises directly the *State Committees* for:
Co-ordination of Science and Research, K. N. Rudnev.
Aircraft Industry, P. V. Dementyev.
Defence Industry, S. A. Zverev.
Radio Electronics, V. D. Kalmykov.
Electronic Engineering, A. I. Shokin.
Shipbuilding, B. E. Butoma.
Atomic Energy, A. M. Petrosyants.
Geology, A. V. Sidorenko.
Standards, Measures and Measuring Appliances (vacant).
Inventions and Discoveries, Yu. F. Maksarev.
Medium Machine Building (Nuclear Weapons), E. P. Slavsky.
Power and Electrification, P. S. Neporozhny.
Gas Industry, A. K. Kortunov.

The Prime-Ministers of the 15 constituent Republics belong *ex officio* to the Council of Ministers of the U.S.S.R. (*see* their names under the individual Republics).

Chairman of the Supreme Court, A. F. Gorkin.
Prosecutor General, R. A. Rudenko.

Embassy of the U.S.S.R. in London

13 Kensington Palace Gardens, W.8.
[Bayswater: 3215; 3628; 6411]

Ambassador Extraordinary and Plenipotentiary, His Excellency Aleksandr Alekseyevich Soldatov (1960).
Counsellors, A. I. Romanov; A. A. Gromyko; V. I. Yarotsky; S. G. Voronin; N. G. Bagrichev; V. G. Kozlovsky; V. S. Safronchuk.
1st Secretaries, M. S. Almazov; V. I. Vorobyev; A. N. Gorshenev; V. S. Nesterov; M. T. Chizhov.
2nd Secretaries, L. A. Rogov; V. I. Gavryushkin; Y. P. Filimonov; M. M. Avdeyev; P. N. Filatov; L. S. Storozhilov; Mlle G. P. Tsygankova; N. A. Berdennikov; I. M. Rostov; V. I. Timofeyev; V. K. Boyarov; V. I. Voshchankin.
Military Attaché, Major-General S. A. Edemsky.
Air Attaché, Col. F. S. Roumiantsev.
Naval Attaché, Capt. 1st Rank K. N. Sukhoruchkin.
Trade Representative, V. I. Rodnov.
Deputy Trade Representatives, E. F. Manakhov, S. F. Anfimov.
Consulate, 5 Kensington Palace Gardens, W.8.

Area and Population

The U.S.S.R. is now composed of 15 Union-Republics (*see* below). Before the outbreak of the war of 1939–45 the U.S.S.R. consisted of 11 Republics—the Russian Socialist Federal Soviet Republic (R.S.F.S.R.) and the Ukrainian, Belorussian, Armenian, Azerbaidjan, Georgian, Turkmen, Uzbek, Tadjik, Kazakh and Kirghiz Soviet Socialist Republics. After the collapse of Poland in September, 1939, the Soviet Government by agreement with Germany seized five-eighths of Poland's territory, the so-called *Western Ukraine* and *Western Belorussia*, subsequently incorporated into the Ukrainian and Belorussian Republics respectively.

In March, 1940, some territories ceded by Finland under the 1940 Treaty were joined to the Karelian Autonomous Soviet Socialist Republic to form a Karelo-Finnish S.S.R. which became the 12th constituent Republic of the U.S.S.R., while others, including the town of Viipuri (Vyborg), were added to the R.S.F.S.R. Similarly, in August of the same year, the major part of *Bessarabia* ceded by Roumania in June was joined to the Moldavian A.S.S.R. to form a Moldavian S.S.R. as the 13th Soviet Republic, while a smaller part of Bessarabia, including the Danube estuary port of Izmail, and *Northern Bukovina*, also ceded by Roumania, became part of the Ukraine. The new Soviet-Roumanian frontier was confirmed by the 1947 Peace Treaty with Roumania.

In August, 1940, the three independent Baltic States, *Estonia*, *Latvia* and *Lithuania*, were forcibly incorporated into the Soviet-Union to form the 14th, 15th and 16th Republics respectively. In June, 1945, *Ruthenia* was ceded by Czechoslovakia and became part of the Ukrainian S.S.R under the name of *Transcarpathia*. After the defeat of Germany, a part of *East Prussia* with its capital Königsberg (renamed Kaliningrad in July, 1946) became part of the R.S.F.S.R., while the port and district of *Memel* (Klaipeda) was incorporated into the Lithuanian S.S.R. By the 1947 Peace Treaty with Finland, the district of *Petsamo* (Pechenga) was added to the territory of the R.S.F.S.R. In the Far East, the southern half of *Sakhalin* and the whole of the *Kurile Islands* were incorporated into the last-named Republic in 1945, after the defeat of Japan. In October, 1944, *Tannu-Tuva*, until the war of 1939–45 a nominally independent state lying to the N.W. of Outer Mongolia, became the autonomous province of *Tuva* and in 1961, the Autonomous Republic of Tuva, within the R.S.F.S.R.

In July, 1956, the Karelo-Finnish Republic reverted to the status of an Autonomous (*Karelian*) Republic within the R.S.F.S.R.

Area and population (according to the 1959 census) of the constituent Republics of the U.S.S.R. (with their capitals):—*

* By July 1, 1963, the total population of the U.S.S.R. is said to have risen to 225,000,000.

Republic	Sq. miles	Population
I. R.S.F.S.R. (Moscow)	6,593,391	117,494,000
II. Ukraine (Kiev)	232,046	41,893,000
III. Belorussia (Minsk)	80,154	8,060,000
IV. Uzbekistan (Tashkent)	158,069	8,113,000
V. Kazakhstan (Alma-Ata)	1,064,092	9,301,000
VI. Georgia (Tbilisi)	26,911	4,049,000
VII. Azerbaidjan (Baku)	33,436	3,700,000
VIII. Lithuania (Vilnius)	26,173	2,713,000
IX. Moldavia (Kishinev)	13,012	2,880,000
X. Latvia (Riga)	24,695	2,094,000
XI. Kirghizia (Frunze)	76,642	2,063,000
XII. Tadjikistan (Dushanbe)	54,019	1,982,000
XIII. Armenia (Erevan)	11,306	1,768,000
XIV. Turkmenistan (Ashkhabad)	188,417	1,520,000
XV. Estonia (Tallinn)	17,413	1,196,000
Total	8,599,776	208,826,000

The net increase of population since the 1939 census amounts to only 18,100,000. Assuming a theoretical average annual rise of 3,000,000 (at present the annual rise is 3,500,000), the net increase between 1939 and 1959 should have amounted to about 60,000,000. The deficit of 42,000,000 is the measure of direct and indirect losses suffered by the Soviet people as a result of the war and the deportation policies of the Government. The age-groups of young people born between 1942 and 1946 are abnormally thin.

Geographically, the growth of the population has been very uneven. There has been a steady shift eastwards. Thus, while the total population has increased since 1939 by 9·5 per cent., that of the Urals has risen by 32 per cent.; of Western Siberia, by 24 per cent.; of Eastern Siberia, by 34 per cent.; of the Far East, by 70 per cent.; of Central Asia and Kazakhstan, by 38 per cent. Two Republics on the Western fringes of the Union, *Belorussia and *Lithuania, have actually suffered a net loss of population (844,000 and 167,000 respectively).

Another demographic feature is the growing urbanization. While in 1939 the proportion of urban population was 32 per cent. of the total,* in 1959 it has reached 48 per cent., owing to migration into towns, growth of new towns, incorporation of villages into conurbations and a higher birth-rate in urban areas. There are now 25 towns with over 500,000 (11 in 1939).

The proportion of women to men is 55 to 45 per cent. There is a high incidence of marriages (12 per 1,000), a high birth-rate (25 per 1,000) and a low mortality-rate (7·5 per 1,000).

Ethnical Composition of the Population (millions)

Russians	114·114
Ukrainians	37·253
Belorussians	7·913
Uzbeks	6·015
Tartars	4·968
Kazakhs	3·621
Azerbaidjanis	2·940
Armenians	2·787
Georgians	2·692
Lithuanians	2·326
Jews	2·268
Moldavians	2·214
Germans	1·619
Chuvashes	1·470
Latvians	1·400
Poles	1·380
Tadjiks	1·353
Mordovians	1·285
Bashkirs	0·989
Estonians	0·989
Kirghizians	0·969
Daghestan tribes	0·945
Udmurtians	0·623
Maris	0·504
Other Nationalities	5·009

* Within present borders.

Constitution

Under the 1936 ("Stalin") Constitution, the *Union of Soviet Socialist Republics* is "a socialist state of workers and peasants" (§ 1) in which "all power belongs to the working people as represented by the Soviets [Councils] of Working People's Deputies" (§ 3), while its economy is based on "the socialist ownership of the instruments and means of production" (§ 4). "The land, its mineral wealth, waters, forests, mills, factories, mines, rail, water and air transport, banks, communications, large state-organized agricultural enterprises, as well as municipal enterprises and the bulk of dwelling-houses in the cities and industrial localities, are state property" (§ 6), while "the joint enterprises of collective farms and co-operative organizations . . . constitute the common, socialist property of the collective farms and co-operative organizations" (§ 7). "The law [also] permits the small private economy of individual peasants and handicraftsmen based on their own labour and precluding the exploitation of the labour of others" (§ 9). "The personal property right of citizens in their incomes and savings from work, in their dwelling-houses and subsidiary home enterprises, in household articles . . . as well as the right of citizens to inherit personal property, is protected by law" (§ 10). The whole economic life, however, is subordinated to the state economic plan (§ 11).

The U.S.S.R. is a federal state, "formed on the basis of a voluntary union of equal Soviet Socialist Republics" (§ 13); every Republic has "the right to secede from the U.S.S.R." (§ 17).

"The highest organ of state power in the U.S.S.R. is the Supreme Soviet of the U.S.S.R." (§ 30) which exercises exclusively the legislative power (§ 32). It consists of two Chambers, the *Soviet of the Union* (elected on the basis of one deputy for every 300,000 of the population) and the *Soviet of Nationalities* (elected at the ratio of 25 deputies from each Union Republic, 11 from each Autonomous Republic, 5 from each Autonomous Province and 1 from each National Territory) (§§ 33–35). The *Supreme Soviet* which, as a rule, meets 4 to 5 times a year for about a week, delegates most of its power to its *Presidium* which acts as a kind of collective President of the U.S.S.R. between the sessions.

"The highest executive and administrative organ of state power is the Council of Ministers of the U.S.S.R." (§ 64). It is appointed by the Supreme Soviet (§ 70) and is accountable to it, or, in the intervals between the sessions, to its Presidium (§ 65).

The Supreme Court of the U.S.S.R. and the Special Courts of the U.S.S.R. are elected by the Supreme Soviet for a term of five years (§ 104). Similarly, the Procurator-General, who exercises "supreme supervisory power to ensure the strict observance of law" (§ 113), is appointed by the Supreme Soviet for a term of seven years.

Citizens of the U.S.S.R. have the right to work, to rest and leisure, to maintenance in old age and sickness and disability relief and to education (§§ 118–121). "Women are accorded equal rights with men" (§ 122). Citizens are accorded equal rights irrespective of their nationality or race (§ 123). The citizens are also guaranteed freedom of speech, of the press, of assembly and of street processions and demonstrations, "in conformity with the interests of the working people and in order to strengthen the socialist system" (§ 125).

Section 126 of the Constitution is remarkable for containing the only reference to the real master of the country, the Communist Party. It says that "the most active and politically conscious citizens in the ranks of the working class and other sections of the working people unite in the Communist Party of the Soviet-Union, which is the vanguard of the working people in their struggle to strengthen and develop the socialist system and is the leading core of all organizations of the working people, both public and state." The draft of a new Party programme, published on July 30, 1961. envisages a great increase of the economic capacity of the country and promises the transition to "full Communism" some time after 1980.

A special Committee, with N. S. Khrushchev as its chairman, was set up by the XXIInd Party Congress in November, 1961, to draft a new Constitution.

Local Government.—The State power in regions, provinces, autonomous provinces, territories, districts, towns and rural localities is vested in the *Soviets of Working People's Deputies* (§94), elected by the working people of the respective administrative units for a term of two years (§95). The executive and administrative organ of a Soviet is its Executive Committee elected by it (§99). The Union Republics and the Autonomous Republics have Supreme Soviets and Councils of Ministers of their own (§§ 57–63 and 79–88), although their jurisdiction is severely circumscribed in favour of the central Government. Since February, 1944, the Union Republics have had the right to enter into direct relations with foreign states and to conclude agreements and exchange diplomatic and consular representatives with them (§ 18A). So far, however, the only important activity of this kind has been the individual membership of the Ukraine and of Belorussia in the United Nations Organization. Similarly, the 1944 law allowing each Union Republic to possess its own Republican military formations (§ 18B) seems to have remained a paper provision.

The Union Republics possess Ministries of their own for internal affairs, certain branches of heavy and light industry, agriculture, public health, trade, finance and the like. The work of these Ministries is co-ordinated by respective federal Ministries and/or the *Gosplan*. The Union Republics possess exclusive jurisdiction over such matters as motor transport, housing, social security, municipal affairs, local industry, education and, since 1956, inland water transport and justice. The general trend lately has been toward progressive administrative decentralization or, rather, "deconcentration," particularly in industrial matters.

Religion.—Section 124 of the Constitution lays down that "in order to ensure to citizens freedom of conscience, the church in the U.S.S.R. is separated from the state, and the school from the church," and that "freedom of religious worship and freedom of anti-religious propaganda is recognized for all citizens." Churches have remained open in virtue of contracts concluded between the congregations and the local authorities. The clergy live on voluntary donations from their parishioners. A new *modus vivendi* between the Government and the religious communities was created during the War of 1939–1945. Two administrative bodies, the Council for the Affairs of the Russian Orthodox Church and the Council for the Affairs of Religious Cults, were set up in October, 1943, to provide liaison between the Council of Ministers and the religious bodies. In September, 1943, Stalin agreed to the election of the Patriarch of Moscow and All Russia, a post which had been vacant since the death of Patriarch Tikhon in 1925. Patriarch Sergius, elected by the Council of the Russian Church in 1943, died in May, 1944, and was succeeded in February, 1945, by the present holder of the See, Patriarch Alexius. A number of seminaries for training of priests, many churches, mosques and synagogues and several big monasteries have been reopened. Several religious periodicals are now published in the U.S.S.R., but religious propaganda is still banned.

The proselytizing successes of the religious communities, notably of various sectarian bodies, have become of great concern to the authorities; there has been a great increase of anti-religious articles in the press since 1958, and a number of religious institutions was once again closed or banned.

Education.—Under the Constitution, citizens of the U.S.S.R. have the right to education. Since 1956 the entire educational course, including higher education at universities, technical colleges, etc., has been free. In view of an acute shortage of young man-power caused by the abrupt fall of the birth-rate in the years 1942–1946, the government has been discouraging secondary school graduates from going on immediately to the University. Boys and girls of school-leaving age are ordered by law to put in two years of practical work in industry and agriculture, and 80 per cent. of all vacancies in the universities are reserved for young people who have accomplished this spell of practical work.

The state controls all educational institutions, theatres, cinemas, museums, libraries and picture galleries, as well as the press and the radio. The main centre of research and learning is the Academy of Sciences of the U.S.S.R., which is in effect a vast and efficient government-controlled pool of scientists.

President, M. V. Keldysh.

Chronological System.—On February 14, 1918, the Soviet Government adopted the Gregorian (Western) Calendar, and by a decree of June 16, 1930, the Soviet Government advanced all the clocks in the Union by one hour, thus adopting permanent Summer Time. The country is divided into several time zones (Moscow time is 3 hours ahead of G.M.T.).

Language, Literature and Arts

Language and Literature.—Russian is a branch of the Slavonic family of languages which is divided into the following groups: *Eastern*, including Russian, Ukrainian and White Russian; *Western*, including Polish, Czech, Slovak and Sorbish (or Lusatian Wendish); and *Southern*, including Serbo-Croat, Slovene, Macedonian and Bulgarian. The Western group and part of the Southern group are written in the Latin alphabet, the others in the Cyrillic, said to have been instituted by SS. Cyril and Methodius in the ninth century, and largely based on the Greek alphabet. Before the Westernization of Russia under Peter the Great (1682–1725), Russian literature consisted mainly of folk ballads (*byliny*), epic songs, chronicles and works of moral theology. The eighteenth and particularly the nineteenth centuries saw a brilliant development of Russian poetry and fiction. Romantic poetry reached its zenith with Alexander Pushkin (1799–1837) and Mikhail Lermontov (1814–1841). The 20th century produced great poets like Alexander Blok (1880–1921), the Nobel Prize laureate of 1958 Boris Pasternak (1890–1960) and Vladimir Mayakovsky (1893–1930). Realistic fiction is associated with the names of Nikolai Gogol (1809–1852), Ivan Turgenev (1818–1883), Fedor Dostoyevsky (1821–1881) and Leo Tolstoy (1828–1910), and later with Anton Tchehov (1860–1904), Maxim Gorky (1868–1936) and Ivan Bunin (1870–1953).

Great names in music include Glinka (1804–1857), Mussorgsky (1839–1881), Rimsky-Korsakov (1844–1908), Rubinstein (1829–1894), Tchaikowsky (1840–1893), Rakhmaninov (1873–1949), Skriabin (1872–1915), Prokofiev (1891–1953), Stravinsky (*b.* 1882) and Shostakovich (*b.* 1906).

Finance

A new, "heavy" Rouble was introduced on January 1, 1961. Prices and wages have been changed accordingly at the rate of 10 old Roubles = 1 new Rouble. The exchange rate of the new Rouble, however, has been altered in favour of foreign currencies. The official exchange rate is now £1 = R. 2·52. New banknotes in circulation are those valuing R. 1, 3, 5, 10, 25, 50 and 100. There are also new coins valuing Kopecks 1, 2, 3, 5, 10, 15, 20, and 50 and R. 1. Old Kopeck coins are also current at the same value as new ones.

Defence

No official returns concerning the services have been made for many years. According to Western estimates, the Soviet forces (including the MVD and KGB troops) amounted in 1959 to about 3,800,000 men. The *ground forces* were estimated to number about 2,700,000 (including security forces), formed in *ca.* 140 infantry divisions (including 70 armoured), some 40 artillery divisions (including some tactical missile units), an unknown number of cavalry divisions and independent brigades and 130 cadre divisions. The *Navy* is understood to be undergoing a big reorganization. Building of larger ships of the cruiser type seems to have been halted. Some cruisers are being converted to guided missile ships. The strength of the submarine fleet is uncertain. The Soviet Navy appears to possess between six and 12 nuclear submarines and 18 conventionally-powered boats with guided missiles. The number of ordinary submarines appears to have been reduced from 450 in 1960 to 430 in 1961. The *Air Force* was estimated in 1959 to number 700,000 personnel and over 25,000 operational aircraft, having at its disposal about 1,000 airfields on the territory of the U.S.S.R. It consists of five commands, the Long Range A.F., the Frontal A.F., the Fighter A.F., the Airborne Troops A.F. and the Navy A.F. There is an unknown number of strategic missile units and of A.A. units which were made a separate arm in 1955. A Rocket Weapons Command was set up in 1960.

Length of service is fixed at two years for the Army and the MVD troops, three years for the KGB border units and the Air Force and four years for the Navy and Coastal Defence Units. The general tendency is to turn the Soviet Armed forces into a professional body.

Minister of Defence, Marshal R. Ya. Malinovsky.
Senior Vice-Minister, Marshal A. A. Grechko.
Chief of General Staff, Marshal S. S. Biryuzov.
Chief, Political Administration, Soviet Armed Forces, Army Gen. A. A. Epishev.

On May 14, 1955, a Treaty of Friendship, Cooperation and Mutual Assistance was signed in Warsaw between the Soviet Union and its European satellites (Albania, Bulgaria, Eastern Germany, Hungary, Poland, Roumania and Czecho-Slovakia) to serve as a counter-poise to NATO. A unified military command was set up in Moscow (*C.-in-C.*, Marshal A. A. Grechko).

Industry and Agriculture

One of the most remarkable aspects of Soviet economy has been the transformation of what was primarily an agricultural country into the second-strongest industrial power in the world in the course of successive *Five-Year Plans* and the current *Seven-Year Plan.* The 1962 output amounted to 55,300,000* tons of pig iron, 76,300,000* tons of steel, 59,200,000* tons of rolled metal, 517,000,000* tons of coal, 186,000,000* tons of crude oil, 57,300,000* tons of cement, 369,000,000,000 kW/h of electric power.

The area under crops increased from 292,121,000 acres in 1913 to 538,925,000 in 1963. Land under crops east of the Volga and the Caspian has greatly increased, in Kazakhstan by nearly five times, since 1913. Stock breeding has been less of a success. The *livestock* in 1962 included 86,800,000 cattle (66,800,000 in 1928), including 37,900,000 cows (33,200,000 in 1928), and 139,700,000 sheep. The level of agricultural productivity remains very low.

The lingering crisis in the field of meat and dairy production caused spectacular price increases (25–30 p.c.) in the early summer of 1962.

Two major reforms in the course of 1958 have given greater scope to the collective farms (*kolkhozy*)—the abolition of the State-owned Machine-and-Tractor Stations and the sale of their equipment to the *kolkhozy*; and the reorganization of the system of compulsory deliveries of produce by the farms to the State. On the other hand new territorial farming boards were established in 1961 to tighten up control over agricultural production.

Forests cover nearly 40 per cent. of the whole area of the Union and form a considerable source of wealth.

Trade with U.K.

	1961	1962
Imports from U.K....	£43,354,538	£41,920,538
Exports to U.K.......	85,032,621	84,114,340

Communications

Railways.—Length of railways in use:

Year	Miles	Year	Miles
1913	44,551	1950	72,637
1928	47,772	1955	74,998
1940	65,926	1957	75,265
1958	76,383		

European Russia is relatively well served by railways, Leningrad and Moscow being the two main focal points of rail routes. The centre and south have a good system of north-south and east-west lines, but the eastern part (the Volga lands) traversed as it is by trunk lines between Europe and Asia which enter Siberia *viâ* Sverdlovsk, Chelyabinsk, Magnitogorsk and Ufa, lacks north-south routes. In Asia, there are still large areas of the U.S.S.R., notably in the Far North and Siberia, with few or no railways. Railways built since 1928 include the Turkestan-Siberian line (*Turksib*) which has made possible a large-scale industrial exploitation of Kazakhstan, a number of lines within the system of the *Trans-Siberian Railway* (Magnitogorsk-Kartaly-Troitsk, Sverdlovsk-Kurgan, Novosibirsk-Proyektnaya, etc.), which are of great importance for the industrial development in the east, the Petropavlovsk-Karaganda-Balkhash line which has made possible the development of the Karaganda coal basin and of the Balkhash copper mines, and the Moscow-Donbass trunk line. Lines

* Metric.

envisaged under the new Seven Year Plan include the Stalinsk-Magnitogorsk trunk line. In the northern part of European Russia, the North Pechora Railway has been completed, while in the Far East a second Trans-Siberian line is under construction; it will follow a more northerly alignment than the existing Trans-Siberian and will terminate in the Pacific port of Sovetskaya Gavan.

Sea Ports and Inland Waterways.—The most important ports (Odessa, Nikolayev, Batum, Taganrog, Rostov, Kerch, Sebastopol and Novorossiisk) lie around the Black Sea and the Sea of Azov. The northern ports (Leningrad, Murmansk and Archangel) are, with the exception of Murmansk, icebound during winter. Several new ports have been built along the Arctic Sea route (between Murmansk and Vladivostok) and are now in regular use every summer. The great Far Eastern port of Vladivostok, the Pacific naval base of the U.S.S.R., is kept open by icebreakers all the year round. Inland waterways, both natural and artificial, are of great importance in the country, although all of them are icebound in winter (from 2½ months in the south to 6 months in the north). The great rivers of European Russia flow outwards from the centre, linking all parts of the plain with the chief ports, an immense system of navigable waterways which carries about 139,000,000 tons of freight per year. They are supplemented by a system of canals which provide a through traffic between the White, Baltic, Black and Caspian Seas. The most notable of them, built largely by forced labour, are the *White Sea-Baltic Stalin Canal*, and the *Moscow-Volga Canal*. The 63-miles long *Volga-Don* Canal, linking the Baltic and the White Seas in the North to the Caspian, the Black Sea and the Sea of Azov in the South, was completed in May, 1952.

FLAG OF THE U.S.S.R.—Red, with five-pointed star above hammer and sickle.

NATIONAL DAY OF THE U.S.S.R.—November 7 (Commemorating the Bolshevik *coup d'état* of 1917).

BRITISH EMBASSY

(Sofiiskaya Naberezhnaya 14, Moscow)

British Ambassador, His Excellency Sir Humphrey Trevelyan, K.C.M.G., C.I.E., O.B.E. (1962) £7,015

Minister, T. Brimelow, C.M.G., O.B.E.

Counsellors, H. F. T. Smith; D. L. L. Stewart (*Commercial*); T. Garrett (*Scientific*).

1st Secretaries K. A. Geary; E. Bolland; A. Brooke-Turner (*Cultural Attaché*); Miss G. M. Galbraith; K. Kirby (*H.M. Consul*); Dr. W. F. Townsend-Coles (*Medical Officer*).

2nd Secretaries, B. G. Cartledge; N. H. Marshall; M. C. C. Wheeler; D. O. Amy; E. J. Scott; G. Heffer.

3rd Secretaries, B. L. Crowe; M. D. B. Alexander; D. J. Johnson; V. B. Grogan; M. J. Long; G. D. G. Murrell; W. S. Dally; Miss R. Chaplin.

Naval Attaché, Cdr. F. S. Hope, R.N.

Assistant Naval Attachés, Lt.-Cdr. A. E. Thompson, R.N.; Lt.-Cdr. M. V. Middleton, R.N.

Military Attaché, Brig. L. Maxwell, O.B.E.

Assistant Military Attaché, Major I. M. Aylwin.

Air Attaché, Air Cdre. A. N. Davis, D.S.O., D.F.C.

Assistant Air Attachés, Sqn.-Ldr. R. A. Nash; Sqn.-Ldr. C. Wood; Flt.-Lt. N. Walsh.

There are no British Consulates in the U.S.S.R. apart from the Consular Section attached to the Embassy.

I.—R.S.F.S.R.

(The Russian Soviet Federal Socialist Republic)

Chairman of the Presidium of the Supreme Soviet, N. G. Ignatov.

Chairman of the Council of Ministers, G. I. Voronov.

Minister of Foreign Affairs, M. A. Menshikov.

Chairman of the All-Russian Economic Council, S. A. Afanasyev.

The R.S.F.S.R. has no Communist Party Central Committee of its own; there is, however, a Bureau of the Central Committee of the CPSU for the R.S.F.S.R., with N. S. Khrushchev as its Chairman, and L. N. Efremov and A. P. Kirilenko as Vice-Chairmen.

The R.S.F.S.R., the largest and the most important of the Republics, occupies the major half of the European part of the U.S.S.R. and the major northern half of its Asiatic part and makes up 77 per cent. of the total territory of the U.S.S.R. with 56 per cent. of the total population. It consists of 16 Autonomous Republics (the Bashkir, Buryat, Checheno-Ingush, Chuvash, Daghestan, Kabardin-Balkar, Kalmyk,* Karelian, Komi, Mari, Mordovian, North-Osetian, Tartar, Tuva, Udmurt and Yakut A.S.S.R.'s); 6 regions (Altai, Khabarovsk, Krasnodar, Krasnoyarsk, Maritime and Stavropol) containing in their turn 5 autonomous provinces and 4 national territories; 49 provinces (Amur, Archangel, Astrakhan, Belgorod, Bryansk, Chelyabinsk, Chita, Gorky, Irkutsk, Ivanovo, Kalinin, Kaliningrad, Kaluga, Kamchatka, Kemerovo, Kirov, Kostroma, Kuibyshev, Kurgan, Kursk, Leningrad, Lipetsk, Magadan, Moscow, Murmansk, Novgorod, Novosibirsk, Omsk, Orel, Orenburg, Penza, Perm, Pskov, Rostov, Ryazan, Sakhalin, Saratov, Smolensk, Sverdlovsk, Tambov, Tomsk, Tula, Tyumen, Ulyanovsk, Vladimir, Volgograd, Vologda, Voronezh and Yaroslavl), which in their turn include 6 national territories.

Physical Features.—The R.S.F.S.R. may be conveniently divided into three areas, a low-lying flat Western part stretching eastwards up to the Yenisei and divided in two by the Ural ridge; an eastern part, between the Yenisei and the Pacific, consisting of a number of tablelands and ridges, and a southern mountainous part. Climatically, the R.S.F.S.R. lies in all zones, except the tropics, and may be divided into the following belts (from north to south): Arctic, Tundra, Forest, Mixed Forest-Steppe, Steppe, Sub-Tropics.

The Republic has a very long coast-line, including the longest Arctic coast-line in the world (about 17,000 miles). The most important rivers in the European Part of the R.S.F.S.R. are the Volga with its tributaries Kama and Oka, the Northern Dvina and the Pechora, the short but wide Neva, the Don and the Kuban, and in the Asiatic part, the Ob with the Irtysh, the Yenisei, the Lena and the Amur, and, further north, Khatanga, Olenek, Yana, Indigirka, Kolyma and Anadyr. Lakes are abundant, particularly in the north-west. The huge Baikal Lake in Eastern Siberia is the deepest lake in the world. There are also two large artificial water reservoirs within the Greater Volga canal system, the Moscow and Rybinsk "Seas."

Minerals.—The Republic occupies one of the first places in the world for mineral wealth. Coal is mined in the Kuznetsk area, in the Urals, south of Moscow, in the Donets basin (its Eastern part lies in the R.S.F.S.R.) and in the Pechora area in the North. Oil is produced in the Northern Caucasus and in the area between the Volga and the Ural (the so-called "Second Baku"). The Ural mountains contain a unique assortment of minerals—high-quality iron ore, manganese,

* During the Second World War, the Kalmyks, a Mongolian people, were scattered to remote areas in a deportation programme. Their territory was restored as an autonomous province in 1957, and on July 30, 1958, the Supreme Soviet of the U.S.S.R. restored a Kalmyk A.S.S.R.

copper, aluminium, gold, platinum, precious stones, salt, asbestos, pyrites, coal, oil, etc. Iron ore is mined, in addition to the Urals, near Kursk, Tula, Lipetsk, Khoper, in several areas in Siberia and in the Kola Peninsula. Non-ferrous metals are found in the Altai, in Eastern Siberia, in the Northern Caucasus, in the Kuznetsk Basin, in the Far East and in the Far North. Nine-tenths of all U.S.S.R. forests are located in the R.S.F.S.R.

Production and Industry.—The vastness of the territory of the Republic and the great variety in climatic conditions cause great differences in the structure of agriculture from north to south and from west to east. In the Far North stag breeding, hunting and fishing are predominant. Further south, timber industry is combined with grain growing. In the southern half of the forest zone and in the adjacent forest-steppe zone, the acreage under grain crops is far larger and the structure of agriculture more complex. In the eastern part of this zone, between the Volga and the Urals, cericulture is predominant (particularly summer wheat), with cattle breeding next. Beyond the Urals, we find another important grain-growing and stock-breeding area in the southern part of the Western-Siberian plain. The southern steppe zone is the main wheat granary of the U.S.S.R. containing also large acreages under barley, maize and sunflower. In the extreme South (Krasnodar region, Stavropol region) cotton is now cultivated. Vine, tobacco and other Southern crops are grown on the Black Sea shore of the Caucasus.

Industrially, the R.S.F.S.R. occupies the first place among the Soviet Republics. Major changes in the location of industry have occurred since the revolution and again since the war with two new industrial areas being developed in the Urals and in the Kuznetsk basin, although Moscow and Leningrad are still the two largest industrial centres in the country. Most of the oil produced in the U.S.S.R. now comes from two areas in the R.S.F.S.R.—the Bashkir and Tartar Autonomous Republics. All industries are represented in the R.S.F.S.R., including iron and steel and engineering. Industrial centres include Magnitogorsk, Chelyabinsk, Novokuznetsk, Tula, Komsomolsk, Perm, Ufa, Irkutsk, Kuibyshev, Krasnoyarsk, Nizhny-Tagil, Novosibirsk, Omsk, Volgograd, Gorky, Saratov, Grozny, Rostov and Taganrog.

CAPITAL, MOSCOW. Population 5,032,000 (an increase of 120 per cent. since 1939). Moscow, founded about A.D. 1147 by Yuri Dolgoruki, became first the centre of the rising Moscow principality and, later, in the 15th century, the capital of the whole of Russia (Muscovy). In 1325, it became the seat of the Metropolitan of Russia. In 1703 Peter the Great transferred the capital to the newly built St. Petersburg, but on March 14, 1918, Moscow was again designated as the capital. Ψ Leningrad (before the First World War "St. Petersburg" and from 1914–1924 "Petrograd") has a population of 3,300,000.

Other cities with populations exceeding 500,000 (1959) are:—

Gorky (Nizhny-Novgorod)	942,000
Novosibirsk (Novonikolayevsk)	887,000
Kuibyshev (Samara)	806,000
Sverdlovsk (Yekaterinburg)	777,000
Chelyabinsk	688,000
Kazan	643,000
Perm (Molotov)	628,000
Ψ Rostov-on-Don	597,000
Volgograd (Stalingrad; Tsaritsyn)	591,000
Saratov	581,000
Omsk	579,000
Ufa	546,000

About 83 per cent. of the population are Russians.

Ψ Seaport.

II.—THE UKRAINE

First Secretary of the Party Central Committee, P. E. Shelest.

Chairman of the Presidium of the Supreme Soviet, D. S. Korotchenko.

Chairman of the Council of Ministers, I. P. Kazanets.

Chairman of the Economic Council, P. A. Rozenko.

Minister of Foreign Affairs, L. F. Palamarchuk.

This Republic, second largest in population, lying in the south-western part of the European half of the U.S.S.R., was formed in December, 1917. It consists of 25 provinces—Cherkasy, Chernigov, Chernovtsy, Crimea, Dnepropetrovsk, Donets, Ivan-Frankovsk, Kharkov, Kherson, Khmelnitsky, Kiev, Kirovograd, Lugansk, Lvov, Nikolayev, Odessa, Poltava, Rovno, Sumy, Ternopol, Transcarpathia, Vinnitsa, Volhynia, Zaporozhye and Zhitomir.

Physical Features.—The larger part of the Ukraine forms a plain with small elevations. The Carpathian mountains lie in the south-western part of the Republic. The climate is moderate, with relatively mild winters (particularly in the south-west) and hot summers. The main rivers are the Dnieper with its tributaries, the Southern Bug and the Northern Donets (a tributary of the Don).

Production and Industry.—The main centre of Soviet coal mining and iron and steel industry is situated in the southern part of the Ukraine. Engineering and chemical industry have been greatly developed under the Soviet régime. In 1955, the Ukraine provided 37 per cent. of the total Soviet steel, 39 per cent. of metal goods and 32 per cent. of coal. The central forest-steppe region (mainly on the right bank of the Dnieper) is the greatest sugar-producing area in the U.S.S.R. The Ukraine also leads in grain-growing and stock-raising.

There are large deposits of coal and salt in the Donets Basin, of iron ore in Krivoy Rog and near Kerch in the Crimea, of manganese in Nikopol, and of quicksilver in Nikitovka.

CAPITAL (since 1934), Kiev, the oldest city in Russia, founded in the 9th century A.D., was the capital of the Russian State from 865 to 1240. Population (1959) 1,102,000. Other cities with population over 500,000 are:—

Kharkov	930,000
Donetsk (Stalino; Yuzovka, *i.e.* Hughesovka)	701,000
Ψ Odessa	667,000
Dnepropetrovsk (Yekaterinoslav)	658,000

III.—BELORUSSIA
(White Russia)

First Secretary of the Party Central Committee, K. T. Mazurov.

Chairman of the Presidium of the Supreme Soviet, V. I. Kozlov.

Chairman of the Council of Ministers, T. Ya. Kiselev.

Minister of Foreign Affairs, K. V. Kiselev

Chairman of the Economic Council, S. M. Kishkin.

The Belorussian S.S.R., lying in the western part of the European half of the U.S.S.R., was formed early in 1919. It now consists of six provinces (Brest, Gomel, Grodno, Minsk, Mogilev and Vitebsk). It is largely a plain with many lakes, swamps and marshy land. Before the revolution of 1917 the area was one of the most backward parts of European Russia. Since then, agriculture has been greatly developed, thanks to draining of swamps. Most of the Republic's industry is also of recent growth. Woodworking is of great importance, but engineering has also been greatly extended with several major plants built in Gomel and Minsk.

The main rivers are the upper reaches of the Dnieper, of the Niemen and of the Western Dvina.

CAPITAL, Minsk. Population 509,000.

Belorussians make up four-fifths of the population, with Russians and Poles coming next.

IV.—UZBEKISTAN

First Secretary of the Party Central Committee, Sh. R. Rashidov.

Chairman of the Presidium of the Supreme Soviet, Mrs. Ya. S. Nasriddinova.

Chairman of the Council of Ministers, R. Kurbanov.

Chairman of the Central Asian Economic Council,* S. I. Kadyshev.

The Uzbek S.S.R. was formed in 1924 and consists of the Kara-Kalpak A.S.S.R. and of 8 provinces (Andizhan, Bokhara, Ferghana, Khorezm, Samarkand, Surkhan-Darya, Syr-Darya and Tashkent). It lies between the high Tienshan Mountains and the Pamir highlands in the east and south-east and sandy lowlands in the west and north-west. The major part of the territory is a plain with huge waterless deserts and several large oases, which form the main centres of population and economic life. The largest is the Ferghana valley, watered by the Syr-Darya. Other oases include Tashkent, Samarkand, Bokhara and Khorezm. The climate is continental and dry. Minerals include oil (in the Ferghana valley and in Khaudag), coal (Angren) and sulphur (Shorsu).

The Uzbeks, a Turkic people, make up 62 per cent. of the population, the Russians (14 per cent.) and Tartars (five per cent.) come next.

There is a major agricultural machinery plant at Tashkent and a chemical combine at Chirchik. Uzbekistan is the main cotton-growing area of the U.S.S.R. producing more than 60 per cent. of all Soviet cotton. Irrigation has always been of decisive importance in this area, and the Soviet Government has done much in this field, including the construction of the Great Ferghana Canal (230 miles).

CAPITAL, Tashkent. Population 911,000. Samarkand (195,000) contains the Gur-Emir (Tamerlane's Mausoleum), completed A.D. 1400 by Ulug-bek, Tamerlane's astronomer-grandson, and a 15th-century observatory, recently restored.

V.—KAZAKHSTAN.

First Secretary of the Party Central Committee, I. Yusupov.

Chairman of the Presidium of Supreme Soviet, I. Sh. Sharipov.

Chairman of the Council of Ministers, D. A. Kunayev.

Chairman of the Economic Council, Yu. P. Voronenkov.

The Kazakh S.S.R., the second-largest Union-Republic, stretching from the lower reaches of the Volga and the Caspian in the west to the Altai and Tien-shan in the east, and bordering on China, was formed in 1920 as an autonomous republic (under the name of the Kirghiz A.S.S.R.) within the R.S.F.S.R., and was constituted a Union Republic in 1936. It consists of the Virgin-land Region (*Tselinny Kray*), comprising the Kokchetav, Kustanay, North-Kazakhstan, Pavlodar and Tselinograd (formerly, Akmolinsk) Provinces; the West-Kazahkstan Region comprising the Aktyubinsk, Guryev and Uralsk Provinces; the South-Kazakhstan Region comprising the Chimkent, Djambul and Kzyl-Orda Provinces, and of four other Provinces (Alma-Ata, East-Kazakhstan, Karaganda and Semipalatinsk).

Kazakhstan is a country of arid steppes and semi-deserts, flat in the west, hilly in the east and mountainous in the south-east (Southern Altai and Tien-shan). The climate is continental and very dry. The main rivers are the (Upper) Irtysh, the Ural, the Syr-Darya and the Ili. Kazakhstan contains rich deposits of non-ferrous metals: copper in Kounrad, Djezkazgan and Boshchekul, other metals in the Altai, in the Kara-Tau Mounts, and elsewhere. It also contains an important coal-producing area (Karaganda) ranking third in the U.S.S.R. and an oil-bearing area (near Emba). Major centres of metal industry exist now in the Altai Mountains, in Chimkent, North of the Balkhash Lake and in Central Kazakhstan. Stock-raising is highly developed, particularly in the central and south-western parts of the Republic. Grain is grown in the north and north-east and cotton in the south and south-east. In 1954 an ambitious programme of development of "virgin" lands in the steppes was launched by the Government to increase grain production.

The Kazakhs (a Turkic people) are now in a minority in the Republic named after them; they constitute only 30 per cent. of its population. Russian settlers make up 43 per cent. and Ukrainians 8 per cent.

CAPITAL, Alma-Ata (formerly Verny). Population 455,000.

VI.—GEORGIA

First Secretary of the Party Central Committee, V. P. Mzhavanadze.

Chairman of the Presidium of the Supreme Soviet, G. S. Dzotenidze.

Chairman of the Council of Ministers, G. D. Djavakhishvili.

Chairman of the Economic Council, G. I. Chogovadze.

The Georgian S.S.R., occupying the north-western part of Transcaucasia, lies on the shore of the Black Sea and borders in the south-east on Turkey. It was formed in 1921; in 1922 it joined the Transcaucasian Federation which, in its turn, adhered to the U.S.S.R. in the same year. After the liquidation of the Transcaucasian S.F.S.R. in 1936 Georgia became a Union Republic. It contains two Autonomous Republics (Abkhazia and Adjaria) and the South-Osetian Autonomous Province. Georgia is a country of mountains, with the Greater Caucasus in the north and the Smaller Caucasus in the south. A relatively low-lying land between these two ridges is divided into two parts by the Sura Ridge: Western Georgia with a mild and damp climate and Eastern Georgia with a more continental and dry climate. The Black Sea shore and the Rion lowlands are sub-tropical in their climatic character. The most important mineral deposits are manganese (Chiatury), coal (Tkibuli and Tkvarcheli) and oil (Kakhetia). Georgia is leading as regards production of manganese in the U.S.S.R. There are also many oil refineries. Viniculture and tobacco-growing are the two main agricultural industries. The Black Sea coast harbours many famous holiday resorts. Georgians make up 63 per cent. of the population, the remainder being composed of Armenians, Russians, Azerbaidjani and Osetians.

CAPITAL, Tbilisi (Tiflis). Population 664,000.

VII. AZERBAIDJAN

First Secretary of the Party Central Committee, V. Yu. Akhundov.

Chairman of the Presidium of the Supreme Soviet, M. A. Iskenderov.

Chairman of the Council of Ministers, E. A. Alikhanov.

Chairman of the Economic Council, S. A. Vezirov.

The Azerbaidjan S.S.R. occupies the eastern part of Transcaucasia, on the shores of the Caspian Sea, and borders on Persia. It was formed in 1920. Between 1922–1936 it formed part of the Transcaucasian Federation. In 1936 it became a Union Republic. It contains the Nakhichevan

* For the four Central-Asian Republics.

Autonomous Republic and the Nagorno-Karabakh Autonomous Province.

The north-eastern part of the Republic is taken up by the south-eastern end of the main Caucasus ridge, its south-western part by the smaller Caucasus hills, and its south-eastern corner by the spurs of the Talysh Ridge. Its central part is a depression irrigated by the Kura and by the middle reaches of its tributary Aragva. Sheltered by the mountains from the humid west winds blowing from the Black Sea, Azerbaidjan has a continental climate. The land requires artificial irrigation. The Republic is very rich in minerals, particularly in oil. The Baku oilfields form the second-largest oil-producing area in the U.S.S.R. A large power station on the Kura (Mingechaur) was completed in 1954. Azerbaidjan is also important as a cotton growing area. The Azerbaidjani (Turks) make up two-thirds of the population of the Republic, Armenians, about 12 per cent., and Russians, about 14 per cent.

CAPITAL, ΨBaku. Population 968,000.

VIII.—LITHUANIA

First Secretary of the Party Central Committee, A. J. Sniečkus.

Chairman of the Presidium of the Supreme Soviet, J. I. Paleckis.

Chairman of the Council of Ministers, M. J. Šumauskas.

Chairman of the Economic Council, P. A. Kulvets.

Lithuania, formerly a Province of the Russian Empire, was declared an independent Republic at Vilna in 1918 and was incorporated into the U.S.S.R. in August, 1940. It was occupied by German forces from June, 1941, until the autumn of 1944. The Republic forms a plain with a large number of lakes and swamps. The forests occupy 19 per cent. of the whole area. The main river is the Niemen with its tributaries.

The chief industries are agriculture and forestry, the chief products being rye, oats, wheat, barley, flax, sugar-beet and potatoes. Before its incorporation into the Soviet Union, Lithuania exported a large quantity of meat and dairy produce.

The Lithuanians make up four-fifths of the population, Russians and Poles, 8·5 per cent. each. The majority of the Jews were exterminated by the Germans.

CAPITAL, Vilnius (Vilna, restored to Lithuania by U.S.S.R. after invasion and collapse of Poland in 1939, and recaptured by Soviet forces in July, 1944). Population 235,000.

IX.—MOLDAVIA

First Secretary of the Party Central Committee, I. I. Bodyul.

Chairman of the Presidium of the Supreme Soviet, K. F. Ilyashenko.

Chairman of the Council of Ministers. A. F. Diorditsa.

Chairman of the Economic Council, N. A. Shchelokov.

Moldavia, occupying the south-western corner of the U.S.S.R., borders in the west on Roumania with the Pruth forming the frontier. In 1918, Roumania seized the Russian Province of Bessarabia. In 1924 a Moldavian Autonomous Republic was formed within the Ukraine, and in 1940 the U.S.S.R. forced Roumania to give back Bessarabia, the major part of which was merged with the Moldavian A.S.S.R. to form a Moldavian Union Republic. Moldavia was occupied by the Germans and Roumanians between 1941–1944.

The northern part of the Republic consists of flat steppe lands, now all under plough. Some forests skirt the Dniester. Further south, around Kishinev, there are woody hills, and further south again, low-lying steppe lands. The climate is moderate. The main river is the Dniester, navigable along the whole course.

The main industry is agriculture (viniculture, fruit-growing and market-gardening). Industry is insignificant in both parts of Moldavia, but the Republic has the densest population in the U.S.S.R. A radical agrarian reform has been carried out under the Soviet régime. Moldavians make up 65 per cent. of the population, with Ukrainians, and Russians next. In the south there are colonies of Bulgarians.

CAPITAL, Kishinev (Chisinau). Population 214,000.

X.—LATVIA

First Secretary of the Party Central Committee, A. J. Pelše.

Chairman of the Presidium of the Supreme Soviet, J. E. Kalnberzin.

Chairman of the Council of Ministers, V. P. Ruben.

Chairman of the Economic Council, G. I. Gajle.

The Latvian S.S.R., lying on the shores of the Baltic and of the Gulf of Riga, was formerly a Baltic Province of the Russian Empire. It was proclaimed an independent state in 1918 and was forcibly incorporated into the U.S.S.R. in August 1940. Between 1941 and 1944 the Republic was occupied by the German forces.

The surface of the country is generally flat, interspersed by occasional chains of hills. The climate is moderately-continental. The main rivers are the lower reaches of the Western Dvina and its tributaries. Forests occupy 20 per cent. of the total territory.

The Latvians make up 62 per cent. of the Republic's population, the Russians, 27 per cent.

Latvian industry was always highly developed, with shipbuilding, engineering, chemical industry, textile industry, wood-working and dairying being the chief occupations. Both Riga and Liepaja (Libava, Liebau) are important sea-ports.

As in other newly-acquired Republics an agrarian reform was carried out in Latvia in 1940–41 and again after 1944.

CAPITAL, ΨRiga. Population 605,000.

XI.—KIRGHIZIA

First Secretary of the Party Central Committee, T. U. Usubaliyev.

Chairman of the Presidium of the Supreme Soviet, T. Kulatov.

Chairman of the Council of Ministers, B. Mambetov.

The Kirghiz S.S.R. occupies the north-eastern part of Soviet Central Asia and borders in the south-east on China. In 1924, a Kara-Kirghiz Autonomous Province was formed within the R.S.F.S.R. In 1926 it became a Kirghiz Autonomous Republic, and in 1936, a Union Republic. It contains two provinces (Osh and Tien-Shan). The Kirghiz Republic is a mountainous country, the major part being covered by the ridges of the Central Tien-Shan, while mountains of the Pamiro-Altai system occupy its southern part. There are a number of spacious mountain valleys, the Alai, Susamyr, the Issyk-kul lake and others. The majority of the population is concentrated in plains, lying at the foot of mountains—Chu, Talass, part of the Ferghana Valley. where agriculture prospers. Industry is insignificant, but some mining is done. A number of railways have been built under the Five Year Plans. The Kirghiz now constitute only 41 per cent. of the population, the Russians, 30 per cent. The Uzbeks (in Eastern Ferghana) amount to 10 per cent.

CAPITAL, Frunze (formerly Pishpek). Population 217,000.

XII.—TADJIKISTAN

First Secretary of the Party Central Committee, D. R. Rasulov.

Chairman of the Presidium of the Supreme Soviet, M. Kholov.

Chairman of the Council of Ministers, A. Kakharov.

The Tadjik S.S.R. lies in the extreme south-east of Soviet Central Asia and borders in the south on Afghanistan and in the east on China. It was originally formed in 1924 as an Autonomous Republic within the Uzbek S.S.R. and became a Union Republic in 1929. It includes the Gorno-Badakhshan Autonomous Province and the Leninabad Province.

The country is mountainous: in the east lie the Pamir highlands with the highest point in the U.S.S.R., the Stalin Peak (24,590 feet), in the centre the high ridges of the Pamir-Altai system. Plains are formed by wide stretches of the Syr-Darya valley in the north and of the Amu-Darya in the south.

Like the other Central-Asiatic Republics, Tadjikistan is a cotton-growing country. Its climatic conditions favour the cultivation of Egyptian cotton. Irrigation is of great importance. Fifty-three per cent. of the population are Tadjiks (linguistically and culturally akin to the Persians), about 23 per cent. Uzbeks, the rest Russians and Tartars.

CAPITAL, Dushanbe (formerly Stalinabad; Dyushambe). Population 224,000.

XIII.—ARMENIA

First Secretary of the Party Central Committee, Ya. N. Zarobyan.

Chairman of the Presidium of the Supreme Council, M. Kholov.

Chairman of the Council of Ministers, A. E. Kochinyan.

Chairman of the Economic Council, S. Astsatryan.

The Armenian S.S.R. occupies the south-western part of Transcaucasia; it was formed in 1920. In 1922 it joined the Transcaucasian Federation, and on its liquidation in 1936 became a Union Republic. In the south it borders on Turkey. It is a mountainous country consisting of several vast table lands surrounded by ridges. The population and the economic life are concentrated in the low-lying part of Armenia, the Aras valley and the Erevan hollow; the climate is continental, dry and cold, but the Aras valley has a long, hot and dry summer. Irrigation is essential for agriculture. At the junction of the former Turkish, Persian and Russian boundaries is *Mount Ararat* (17,160 ft.), the traditional resting place of "Noah's Ark." Industrial and fruit crops are grown in the low-lying districts, grain in the hills. Armenia is traditionally noted for her wine. There are large copper ore and molybdenum deposits and other minerals. The Armenian Church centred in Etchmiadzin is the oldest established Christian Church, Christianity having been recognized as the State religion in A.D. 300.

Nearly 90 per cent. of the population is Armenian.

CAPITAL, Erevan. Population 509,000.

XIV.—TURKMENISTAN

First Secretary of the Party Central Committee, B. O. Ovezov.

Chairman of the Presidium of the Supreme Soviet, N. Bayramov.

Chairman of the Council of Ministers, M. N. Gapurov.

Turkmenia occupies the extreme south of Soviet Central Asia, between the Caspian and the Amu-Darya and borders in the south on Iran and Afghanistan. It was formed in 1924 and contains three Provinces (Chardjou, Mary and Tashauz). The country is a low-lying plain, fringed by hills in the south. Ninety per cent. of the plain is taken up by the arid Kara-Kum desert. Of all Central-Asiatic Republics, Turkmenia is the lowest and driest. The principal industries are agriculture and stock-raising, cotton, wool, astrakan furs, carpets and horses being the principal products. Minerals include oil and sulphur. Most of the land under plough is artificially irrigated. Silk industry is of an old standing. There are also some fisheries in the Caspian.

Turkmens, nomadic in the past, make up 61 per cent. of the population, with Russians coming second, and Uzbeks, third.

CAPITAL Ashkhabad (formerly Askhabad, Poltoratsk). Population 170,000.

XV.—ESTONIA

First Secretary of the Party Central Committee, I. G. Käbin.

Chairman of the Presidium of the Supreme Council, A. A. Mürisepp.

Chairman of the Council of Ministers, W. I. Klauson.

Chairman of the Economic Council, L. T. Weimer.

Estonia, formerly a Baltic province of the Russian Empire, was proclaimed an independent Republic in 1918. In 1940, it was forcibly incorporated into the U.S.S.R. It lies on the shores of the Baltic and of the Finnish Gulf in the north and of the Gulf of Riga in the south-west. Some 800 islands, among them Dagö and Ösel, form part of Estonian territory. Between 1941–44, Estonia was occupied by the German forces.

The country forms a low-lying plain with many lakes, among them the Chud (or Pskov) Lake, on the border with the R.S.F.S.R. Forests take up about one-fifth of the territory. Agriculture and dairy-farming are the chief industries, rye, oats, barley, flax and potatoes being the chief crops, and butter, bacon and eggs the chief products of dairy farming. There are important manufactures, including textiles, engineering, shipbuilding, woodworking, etc.

The population consists of Estonians (73 per cent.) and Russians (22 per cent.).

CAPITAL, ΨTallinn (formerly Reval). Population 280,000.

THE VATICAN CITY STATE

(Stato della Città del Vaticano)

Sovereign Pontiff, His Holiness Pope Paul VI (Giovanni Battista Montini), *born* at Concesio (Brescia), Sept. 26, 1897, *elected* Pope (in succession to John XXIII), June 21, 1963.

Secretary of State, Cardinal Amleto Cicognani, *appointed* Aug. 14, 1961.

The office of the ecclesiastical head of the Roman Catholic Church (*Santa Sede* or Holy See) is vested in the Pope of Rome, the Sovereign Pontiff. For many centuries the Sovereign Pontiff exercised temporal power, and in 1859 the Papal States had an area of 17,218 square miles, with a population of 3,124,688. During the reign of Pius IX. (1846–1878), the Papal States of Romagna, Umbria and the Marches were incorporated in the Kingdom of Sardinia and with the remaining States (Rome, Comacchio, Viterbo. Civita Vecchia, Velletri and Frosinone) became part of Unified Italy in 1870. The territory of the Papacy was confined to the palaces of the Vatican and the Lateran and the Villa of Castel-Gandolfo. and the temporal power of the Pope was in suspense until the treaty of Feb. 11, 1929, which recognized the full and independent sovereignty of the Holy See in the City of the Vatican. Accompanying the treaty were conventions regulating the condition of religion and of the Catholic Church in Italy and agreeing to pay 750,000,000 *lire* in cash and the income at 5 per cent. on 1,000,000,000 *lire* State bonds as a final settlement of the claims of the Holy See against Italy for the loss of temporal power. The population of the Vatican City at the census in March, 1947, was 940.

BRITISH LEGATION

(91 Via Condotti, Rome)

British Envoy Extraordinary and Minister Plenipotentiary to the Holy See, His Excellency Sir Peter William Shelley Yorke Scarlett, K.C.M.G., K.C.V.O. (1960)............... £5,015
1st Secretary, D. Cape.
Attaché, J. D. Utley.
Archivist, Miss A. Y. Thomas.

VENEZUELA

(La Republica de Venezuela)

President (1959–March, 1964), Señor Romulo Betancourt, *assumed office* Feb. 13, 1959.

VENEZUELAN EMBASSY IN LONDON

3, Hans Crescent, S.W.1

[Knightsbridge: 4206]

Ambassador in London, His Excellency Dr. Ignacio Iribarren Borges (1959).
1st Secretary, Señor Gabriel Paoli.
3rd Secretary, Señora Mercedes Senior.
Naval and Military Attaché, Capt. Armando de Pedraza Pereira.
Air Attaché, Lt.-Col. Edgar Suarez Mier y Terán.
Special Attaché, Señora Miriam Blanco-Fombona de Hood.
Consulate-General, 3 Cadogan Square, S.W.1.
There is also a Consulate-General at *Liverpool*.

Area and Population.—The most northerly Republic of South America, situated approximately between 1° 40′ S. lat. and 12° 26′ N. lat. and 59° 52′–73° 15′ W. long. It consists of one Federal District, 20 states and 2 territories. The best authorities calculate the actual present area to be approximately 352,051 square miles. The population at the Census on February 26, 1961, was 7,523,999.

Venezuela lies on the north of the South American continent, and is bounded on the north by the Caribbean Sea, west by the Republic of Colombia, east by British Guiana, and south by Brazil. Included in the area of the Republic are over 70 islands off the coast, with a total area of about 14,650 square miles, the largest being *Margarita*, which is politically associated with Tortuga, Cubagua and Coche to form the State of *Nueva Esparta*. Margarita has an area of about 400 square miles. In 1942 Great Britain ceded to Venezuela the small island of *Patos* (170 acres) about 3 miles from the mainland.

Physical Features.—The Eastern Andes from the south-west cross the border and reach to the Caribbean Coast, where they are prolonged by the Maritime Andes of Venezuela to the Gulf of Paria on the north-east. The main range is known as the Sierra Nevada de Merida, and contains the highest peaks in the country in Picacho de la Sierra (15,420 feet) and Salado (13,878 feet), the maritime ranges containing the Silla de Caracas (8,531 feet). Near the Brazilian border the Sierras Parima and Pacaraima, and on the eastern border the Sierras de Rincote and de Usupamo, enclose the republic with parallel northward spurs, between which are valleys of the Orinoco tributaries. The Sierra Parma contains Yaparana (7,175 feet) and Duida (8,120 feet), and Para Caima contains Maraguaca (8,228 feet) and Roraima (9,000 feet), the latter being on the Venezuela-Guiana boundary. The slopes of the mountains and foothills are covered with dense forests, but the basin of the Orinoco is mainly *llanos*, or level stretches of open prairie, with occasional woods.

The principal river of Venezuela is the *Orinoco*, with innumerable affluents, the main river exceeding 1,500 miles in length from its rise in the southern highlands of the republic to its outflow in the deltaic region of the north-east.

A Franco-Venezuelan Expedition, led by Major Frank Risquez, claims to have discovered the source of the Orinoco, on Nov. 27, 1951, at 63° 15′ W. long., 2° 18′ N. lat., and about 1,100 metres above sea-level.

The Orinoco is navigable for large steamers from its mouth for 700 miles, and by smaller vessels as far as the Maipures Cataract, some 200 miles farther up-stream. Dredging operations completed at the beginning of 1954 opened the Orinoco to ocean-going ships, of up to 24 ft. draft, as far as Puerto Ordaz (about 150 miles up-stream). Among the many tributaries of the main stream are the Ventuari, Caura and Caroni from the south, and the Apure (with its tributary the Portuguesa), Arauca, Meta, and Guaviare from the west, the Meta and Guaviare being principally Colombian rivers. The upper waters of the Orinoco are united with those of the Rio Negro (a Brazilian tributary of the Amazon) by a natural river or canal, known as the *Casiquiare*. The coastal regions of Venezuela are much indented and contain many lagoons and lakes, of which *Maracaibo*, with an area exceeding 7,000 square miles, is the largest lake in South America. Other lakes are Zulia (290 square miles), south-west of Maracaibo, and Valencia (216 square miles). about 1,400 feet above sea-level in the Maritime Andes. The *llanos* also contain lakes and swamps caused by the river floods, but they are dry in the summer seasons.

The climate is tropical and, except where modified by altitude or tempered by sea breezes, is unhealthy, particularly in the coastal regions and in the neighbourhood of lowland streams and lagoons. The hot, wet season lasts from April to October the dry, cooler season from November to March.

Government.—Venezuela was visited by Columbus in 1498, and in 1499 by Alonzo de Ojeda and Amerigo Vespucci, the former naming the Gulf of Maracaibo Venezuela, or "Little Venice" (on account of the Indian pile-built settlements on the coast and shores of the lake), and the name was afterwards extended to the whole of the Orinoco basin. In 1550 the territory was formed into the captaincy-general of Caracas, and the country remained under Spanish rule until the revolt under *Simon Bolivar*, a native of Caracas, who defeated the Spanish forces in the battles of Los Taguanes (1813) and Carabobo (1821), and thus secured the independence of the country. Bolivar was an untiring hero in the cause of independence, and through his efforts (and those of his adjutant Sucre) Venezuela, Ecuador and Colombia achieved their freedom from Spain, while Peru was enabled to establish its independence in consequence of his victories. He died in 1830, at the age of 47. Venezuela formed part of the Federal Republic of Colombia from 1822–30, since which time it has been independent.

On January 23, 1958, the military dictatorship of Colonel Marcos Pérez Jiménez, which had lasted since 1953 and covered a period of remarkable economic expansion due to the Venezuelan oil boom, was overthrown by a popular and military uprising. The Government was then assumed by a provisional Junta, headed by Rear-Admiral Wolfgang Larrazábal Ugueto. General elections were held in December, 1958, and resulted in the election of Sr. Rómulo Betancourt to the Presidency. Sr. Betancourt currently presides over a Coalition Government, composed of his own political party, *Acción Democrática*, and the Social Christian Party (COPEI). The term of office of the present President and Legislature will expire in March, 1964, and elections for a succeeding Government were to be held in November, 1963.

Production and Industry.—The produce of Venezuelan forest and fields includes the following: (*a*) Tropical forest region: orchids, wild rubber, timber, mangrove bark, balata gum and tonka beans. (*b*) Agricultural areas: cocoa beans, coffee, cotton, rice, maize, sugar, sesame, groundnuts, potatoes, tomatoes, other vegetables, sisal and tobacco. Although there is an extensive beef and dairy farming industry, the country does not produce all the grain and other food products it requires. Food and drink imports were valued at *Bs.* 498,000,000 in 1961. An autonomous Government body, the Corporacion Venezolana de Fomento, and other Government agencies, are endeavouring, by loans, investment and other means, to foster agricultural and industrial development. A strong nationalist movement began in 1958 to speed up the rate of industrialization; to this end many tariffs were raised and legislation introduced to compel Governments to give preference to national manufacturers.

The principal industry is that of *Petroleum*. The production of the oilfields is shown below (in barrels of 42 gallons):—

Year	Barrels	Year	Barrels
1947	438,000,000	1955	785,237,000
1948	490,000,000	1956	899,183,000
1949	482,300,000	1957	1,014,929,190
1950	546,730,000	1958	950,057,040
1951	622,187,000	1959	1,010,873,705
1952	658,427,000	1960	1,044,520,500
1953	644,221,000	1961	1,065,743,712
1954	691,181,000	1962	1,168,000,000

Before the war of 1939–45 over 80 per cent. of the crude oil was exported to Netherlands' West Indies refineries. In 1942 small refineries were established in Venezuela, capable of handling about 200,000 barrels daily. The large Shell plant at Punta Cardon went into production in February, 1949, and the Creole refinery at Amuay a year later. Other refineries are being operated at Caripitó, San Lorenzo, Puerto La Cruz, Tucupitó, El Chaure and El Palito and 35 per cent. of the total output of crude oil was refined in Venezuela in 1962. Hitherto the Venezuelan Government has been receiving over 50 per cent. of the profits of local oil companies. As a result of income tax increases decreed in December, 1958 this percentage was raised to over 70 per cent. Rich iron ore deposits in Eastern Venezuela are being developed and production reached 13,226,000 metric tons in 1962. The government-owned steel mill at Las Matanzas in the Guayana region is now in production. It uses local iron ore and obtains its electric power from the hydro-electric installation on the Caroni River. It produces seamless steel tubes, billets and wire. The production of many more steel products is planned over the next four years.

Other industries include gold, diamonds and asbestos; cotton, wool and rayon weaving; manufacture of paper, cement, beer, tyres, cigarettes, soap, animal feeding concentrates, non-alcoholic drinks, simple steel products, shoes, tins, jewellery, rope, metal and wooden furniture, sacks, paint and motor-vehicle assembly, preparation of pharmaceutical goods, lard, powdered milk, vegetable oil, flour, biscuits and other foods; fishing and fish-canning; pearl fishing. New industries planned include petrochemicals, plate glass, and the manufacture of paper from bagasse.

Language and Literature.—Spanish is the language of the country. Some Venezuelan literature is of international repute. There are 23 daily newspapers in Venezuela, of which 8 are published in Caracas, 75 weeklies and 23 fortnightlies. There are also 233 other periodicals, mostly monthlies, but including also some appearing once, twice or three times a week.

Education is free and primary education compulsory from the age of 7 years. There were, in 1959-60, 1,074,434 primary school pupils and 149,335 secondary school pupils including those at technical schools. There are seven universities in Venezuela, three in Caracas and the others in Maracaibo, Mérida, Valencia and Ciudad Bolívar. The total number of university students is 21,292 (1960).

FINANCE

	1960 *Bolivares*	1963 *Bolivares*
Revenue	6,136,000,000	6,255,000,000
Expenditure	6,136,000,000	6,255,000,000
Direct Public Debt (Dec. 31, 1962)		1,441,087,000

The official rate of exchange of the *Bolivar* is *Bs.* 9·38 = £1. The Government-controlled free rate of exchange fluctuates around *Bs.* 12·5 = £1; and the unofficial free rate fluctuates around the same figure. There are special buying rates for petroleum, coffee and cocoa.

Communications.—There are about 17,900 miles of all-weather roads. The State has now acquired all but a very few of the railway lines, whose total length is only some 760 miles. Road and river communications have made railway development less important in Venezuela than in some other countries. Several British, U.S. and European airlines provide Venezuela with a wide range of services. There are three Venezuelan airlines (two of them state-owned) which between them have a comprehensive network of internal lines and also connect Caracas with New York, Miami, Bermuda, Havana, Lima, Bogotá, the West Indies, Lisbon, Madrid and Rome. The Venezuelan state-owned merchant fleet controls a total tonnage of about 250,000. Foreign vessels are not permitted to engage in the coast trade. The telegraph, radio-telegraph and radio-telephone services are state-owned. There are one government-controlled and 79 commercial broadcasting stations. There are five television stations in Venezuela (three in Caracas, one in Maracaibo and one in Valencia). The two Caracas commercial television stations have relay transmitters in the interior of the country, Radio Caracas T.V. having five and Venevision three.

TRADE

	1960	1961
Imports	*Bs.* 3,571,424,000	*Bs.* 3,581,450,000
Exports	8,500,216,297	8,083,726,598

The principal imports are machinery, foodstuffs, durable and non-durable consumer goods, iron, steel and chemicals. The principal exports are petroleum and petroleum products (92 per cent. in 1961), iron ore, coffee and cocoa. The value of exports of iron ore in 1961 amounted to *Bs.* 442,471,736.

Trade with U.K.

	1961	1962
Imports from U.K.	£17,934,945	£17,956,637
Exports to U.K.	67,336,552	74,876,624

CAPITAL, Caracas (3,000 ft.). Population, February, 1961, 1,257,515; other principal towns are Maracaibo (457,416), Barquisimento (231,703), Valencia (204,273), Maracay (142,192), San Cristobal (129,059), Cumaná (110,201) and Ciudad Bolivar (87,928).

FLAG.—Three horizontal bands, yellow, blue, red (with seven white stars on blue band).

BRITISH EMBASSY

Edificio La Estancia, Apartado 1246, Ciudad Comercial Tamanaco, Caracas.

Ambassador Extraordinary and Plenipotentiary, His Excellency Sir Douglas Laird Busk, K.C.M.G. (1960) £5,015

Counsellors, R. H. G. Edmonds, M.B.E.; K. D. Jamieson (*Commercial*); L. Boas, O.B.E. (*Information*).

1st Secretaries, J. G. Wills; J. Doyle (*Commercial*).

Naval, Military and Air Attaché, Group Capt. E. W. Wootten, D.F.C., A.F.C.

Consul, Miss M. B. Forrester.

Vice-Consul, D. W. Dobinson.

Do., for *W. Indian Federation* and *British Guiana*, S. S. Lutchman.

BRITISH CONSULAR OFFICES

There are British Consular Offices at *Caracas*, *El Cardon*, *Maracaibo*, *Puerto La Cruz* and *Valencia*.

BRITISH COUNCIL

Representative, K. G. Wilson, Venezuelan-British Cultural Institute, Avenida de Los Jabillos No. 21, La Florida (Apartado 1246), Caracas.

VIETNAM

President of the Republic of Vietnam, Ngo dinh Diem, *assumed office*, Oct. 26, 1955; *re-elected for 5 years*, April, 1961.

VIETNAM EMBASSY AND CONSULATE
12 Victoria Road, W.8
[Western: 3765]

Ambassador Extraordinary and Plenipotentiary, Ngo Dinh Luyen (1956).

Counsellor, Phan van Think.

1st Secretaries, Le Van Ky (*Consular*); Pham Huy Ty (*Economic*).

2nd Secretaries, Nguyen Trieu Dan; Dao Huu Tuong; Le Van Loi; Tran Manh Phuc.

3rd Secretaries, Nguyen Duc Quy (*Press*); Nguyen Trong Loc.

Attaché, Le Dinh Phuoc.

Since the Geneva Conference of July 1954, Vietnam has been divided into two zones.

SOUTHERN ZONE

The Southern Zone has an area of 66,281 sq. miles. Its population was estimated in 1960 at 14,072,000. Rice and rubber are the chief products. Total trade in 1962 was: Imports £93,500,000; Exports £19,600,000.

Trade with U.K.

	1961	1962
Imports from U.K.	£1,642,417	£1,197,667
Exports to U.K.	3,426,672	3,314,132

The rate of exchange (free market) in 1962 was *VN*\$205·5=£1. An official rate of exchange of *VN*\$98=£1 was still in use in 1963, but its operation was complicated by a tax which raised the effective rate to 168 for most transactions.

On October 23, 1955, a referendum showed a large majority in favour of the deposition of the former Chief of State, Bao Dai, and the election of Ngo dinh Diem to his place. The latter was accordingly proclaimed Chief of State on October 26, and his first act was to declare Vietnam a Republic of which he became the President. An elected constituent assembly, after two months' deliberation, set up a democratic constitution which was promulgated on October 26, 1956. This constituent assembly, on the date of the promulgation of the constitution, became the first Legislative Assembly of the Republic of Vietnam. A new national assembly was elected on August 31, 1963, President Diem having been re-elected for a second term of 5 years in April, 1961. The Government of the Republic of Vietnam in Saigon is recognized by the United Kingdom, the United States, France and other members of the United Nations as the legal government of Vietnam.

CAPITAL.—Ψ Saigon, population (1960, with Cholon), 1,400,000. Other principal towns are Hué (1960 population: 103,870) and Ψ Tourane (1960 population: 104,800). Saigon and Tourane are the main ports.

BRITISH EMBASSY
Saigon

Ambassador Extraordinary and Plenipotentiary, His Excellency Raymond Gordon Antony Etherington-Smith, C.M.G. (1963) £4,115

British Council Representative, L. S. Downes, 119 Dai-lo Nguyen-Hue, Saigon.

NORTHERN ZONE

President, Ho Chi Minh, *assumed office*, 1945; *re-elected* July 15, 1960.

Vice-President, Ton Duc Thang.

Prime Minister, Pham Van Dong (1955).

Minister of Foreign Affairs, Xuan Thuy (1963).

The Northern Zone (north of the 17th parallel) has an area of approximately 63,000 sq. miles and a population of 17,000,000 (approx.). The capital is Hanoi (800,000) and the chief port is Ψ Haiphong (367,000). The chief crop is rice, of which the production in 1961 was claimed to be 4,600,000 tons, while the chief industrial products are coal and cement. The production of apatite (phosphate) is increasing, and with Chinese and Soviet aid some new factories have been built to produce consumer goods.

The régime in the north styles itself the Government of the Democratic Republic of Vietnam, of which the President is Ho chi Minh. Power is wielded by the *Lao Dong* (or Workers') Party which is Communist in character, and which can exert its influence through another mass organization known as the Fatherland Front (which some years ago superseded the "Vietminh"). The policy of the northern régime is to work for unification of north and south, whilst in the meantime it strives to remould the political and economic life of the north on Communist lines. A five-year plan started in 1961. Elections to the "Second National Assembly" were held in the north in May 1960. The régime has diplomatic relations with the U.S.S.R., China and other states of the Sino-Soviet bloc, but very few other countries recognize it.

There is a British Consulate General at *Hanoi*.

VOLTAIC REPUBLIC
(Republic of Upper Volta)

President, Maurice Yaméogo, *re-elected for five years*, Dec. 8, 1960.

President, National Assembly, Beguon Koné.

VOLTAIC EMBASSY
60 Portland Place, W.1
[Langham: 6895]

Ambassador Extraordinary and Plenipotentiary, His Excellency Gérard Kango Ouédraogo.

President, Economic and Social Council, Victor Ouédraogo.

Minister for Foreign Affairs, Lompolo Koné.

The Voltaic Republic is an inland, savannah state in West Africa, situated between 9° and 15°N and 2°E and 5°W with an area of about 100,000 square miles and a population estimated in 1961 at 3,635,000. It has common boundaries with Mali on the west, Niger and Dahomey on the east and Togo, Ghana and the Ivory Coast on the south. The largest tribe is the Mossi whose king, the Moro Naba, still wields a certain moral influence.

Upper Volta was annexed by France in 1896 and between 1932 and 1947 was administered as part of the Colony of the Ivory Coast. It decided on December 11, 1958, to remain an autonomous republic within the French Community; full independence outside the Community was proclaimed on August 5, 1960. Special agreements with France, covering financial and cultural matters, technical assistance, etc., were signed in Paris on April 24, 1961. The Voltaic Republic is a member of the *Conseil de l'Entente*. The official language is French. The constitution, adopted by referendum on November 27, 1960, provides for a presidential form of government with a single chamber National Assembly, whose life was extended by the terms of the constitution for a further period of five years.

Finance and Trade.—The currency of the Republic is the *Franc CFA* (*Francs CFA* 50=1 *French Franc*) (*Francs CFA* 691=£). In 1963 the Budget balanced at *Francs CFA* 8,450,000,000, which represents a decrease of *Francs CFA* 300,000,000 on 1962.

The principal industry is the rearing of cattle and sheep and the chief exports are livestock, groundnuts, shea-nuts and cotton. Small deposits of gold, manganese, copper, bauxite and graphite have been found. Value of trade in 1961 amounted to: Imports, *francs CFA* 7,004,256,000; Exports, *francs CFA* 881,845,000.

Trade with U.K.

	1961	1962
Imports from U.K.	£66,085	£68,873
Exports to U.K.	21,266	300

CAPITAL.—Ouagadougou (63,000). Other principal town: Bobo-Dioulasso (46,550).

FLAG.—Three horizontal stripes, black (above) white and red.

British Ambassador, see Ivory Coast.

THE YEMEN

(The Mutawakilite Kingdom of The Yemen)

King of The Yemen Saif al Islam Muhammad al Badr*, *born* 1920, *succeeded* Sept. 19, 1962.

* Sana'a Radio announced on Sept. 27, 1962, that the King had been killed during destruction of the royal palace by Yemeni rebels led by Army officers. He was subsequently reported to be alive and conducting operations against this revolutionary government during 1963.

(Diplomatic relations suspended)

Yemen, "the land on the right hand" (of Syria) and the *Arabia Felix* of the ancients, occupies the S.W. corner of Arabia between Asir and the Aden Protectorate, with an estimated area of 74,000 square miles and a population of 4,000,000. It extends inland to the borders of the Hadramaut. The highlands and central plateau of Yemen, and the highest portions of the maritime range form the most fertile part of Arabia, with an abundant and regular rainfall. The main exports are coffee, cotton, oil-grains, salt, hides, and raisins. Trade agreements have been concluded with a number of countries. Aden is an important centre for Yemeni exports and imports. No statistics of the total British trade with the Yemen are available. Direct imports from the U.K., which in 1962 totalled £28,711 and direct exports to the U.K., which in 1962 totalled £105,475, represent only a small percentage of the actual trade between the two countries. The chief port of the Yemen is ♆Hodeida (Ahmedia) which now has deep water quays, able to accommodate ocean-going vessels.

The ruins of Marib, the ancient Sabæan capital and its dam are in the Yemen.

On March 8, 1958, an agreement was signed in Cairo whereby the Yemen joined the United Arab Republic in a federation to be known as the United Arab States. This agreement was abrogated by the U.A.R. in December, 1961.

FLAG.—Red, with horizontal Arabian sword in centre with 3 stars above and 2 below.

CAPITAL, Taiz (pop. about 20,000); Sana'a has about 60,000 inhabitants. Other cities of the Yemen are ♆Hodeida, Ibb, Mocha and Beidha.

BRITISH LEGATION

(Diplomatic relations suspended)

YUGOSLAVIA

(Socijalistička Federativna Republika Jugoslavija.)

President of the Republic, General Secretary of the League of Communists of Yugoslavia, Chairman of the National Defence Council and Supreme Commander of the Armed Forces, Josip Broz Tito, *assumed office*, Jan. 13, 1953, *re-elected for* 4 *years*, 1954, 1958 *and* June 30, 1963.

Vice-President of the Republic and President of the Socialist Alliance of the Working People of Yugoslavia, Aleksandar Ranković.

President of the Federal Assembly, Edvard Kardelj.

President of the Federal Executive Council, Petar Stambolić.

Vice-Presidents of the Federal Assembly, Mijalko Todorović; Zvonko Brkić; Strahil Gigov.

Vice-Presidents of the Federal Executive Council, Boris Krajger; Miloš Minić; Veljko Zeković.

Secretary of the Federal Executive Council, Dr. Milivoje Rukavina.

Foreign Affairs, Koča Popović.

Defence, Ivan Gošnjak.

Internal Affairs, Vojin Lukić.

Finance, Kiro Gligorov.

Internal Trade, Dragutin Kosovac.

Foreign Trade, Nikola Džuverović.

Presidents of the Republican Assemblies: Dusan Petrović-Sane (*Serbia*); Ivan Krajačić (*Croatia*); Vidoe Smilevski (*Macedonia*); Rato Dugonjić (*Bosnia and Hercegovina*); Ivan Macek (*Slovenia*); Andrija Mugoša (*Montenegro*).

President of the Constitutional Court, Blažo Jovanović.

YUGOSLAV EMBASSY IN LONDON
25 Kensington Gore, S.W.7
[Kensington: 3400]

Ambassador in London, His Excellency Srdja Prica (1960).

Counsellors, Antun Duhaček; Djuro Vukolić; Dušan Grujić.

1st Secretaries, Stevan Mladenović; Radovan Urosev.

2nd Secretary, Zivojin Jazić.

3rd Secretary, Petar Lombardić.

Military and Air Attaché, Col. Vincent Polajner.

Asst. Air Attaché, Lt.-Col. Zdravko Loucar.

Assistant Military Attaché, Maj. Stojanče Stojičić.

Asst. Commercial Attaché, Naste Calovski.
Consulate, 19 Upper Phillimore Gardens, W.8.

Area and Population.—Yugoslavia is a Federation comprising the People's Republics of Serbia, Croatia, Slovenia, Montenegro, Bosnia and Herzegovina, and Macedonia. Serbia includes the autonomous province of the Vojvodina and the autonomous region of Kosovo and Metohija (Kosmet). In July, 1946, Pelagosa and adjacent islands with all territory east of the line known as the *French Line* in Istria (including Pola and Fiume) were ceded by Italy to Yugoslavia. By an agreement concluded in London on Oct. 5. 1954, between Yugoslavia, Italy, the United Kingdom and the United States, Zone B of the Trieste Territory was transferred to the civil administration of Yugoslavia, under whose military administration it had been since 1945. Zone B, an area of 200 square miles with a population of 73,500, included the towns of Kopar (Capodistria), Piran (Pirano) and Novi Grad (Cittanuova). The area has now been divided between the Republics of Slovenia and Croatia. The area of Yugoslavia in 1953 was estimated at 255,804 square kilometres (98,725 square miles) and the population in 1962 at 18,841,000. As a result of the war there was a decrease of nearly 2,000,000 in the population of Yugoslavia, and this loss has only recently been made up.

Montenegro (*Crna-Gora*) was united to Serbia by a decision of the Montenegrin Parliament in November, 1918, when King Nicholas was deposed.

Government.—Stretching from Central Europe to the Balkans, different parts have been subjected to different historical, religious, cultural and geographical influences. *Serbia* came early under the Orthodox Church and then passed 500 fallow years of subjection to the Turkish Empire. In *Bosnia*, an outpost of the Turkish Empire, large numbers of the population were forcibly converted to Islam. *Croatia* and *Slovenia*, on the other hand, came under the Roman Catholic Church, and in later years were subjected to a civilizing influence of the Austro-Hungarian Empire. Such factors have, despite community of race, hampered the process of fusion into a united nation. In Jan. 1929, King Alexander abrogated the Constitution and instituted an absolute monarchy for two years, when it was superseded by a modified constitution. On King Alexander's assassination in 1934, his brother, Prince Paul governed as Regent, with two others, on behalf of the young King Peter. Faced with the threat of German invasion, the Government came to an accommodation with Hitler on March 25, 1941, but was overthrown two days later by a popular rising, which placed King Peter at the head of the state. The country was invaded by the German and Bulgarian armies on April 6, 1941, and the King and Government went into exile. The invaders parcelled up the country, placing Serbia under a puppet goverment, Dalmatia under Italian administration and Croatia under the so-called independent régime of Pavelić (Ustashi). Two main resistance movements developed, the Chetniks under Mihajlović, and the Partisans under Marshal Josip Broz, commonly known as Marshal Tito. The latter emerged from the turmoil of the war years as the most potent force in the country and the modified constitution was superseded by an agreement signed on November 1, 1944, by the Yugoslav Prime Minister (Dr. Ivan Subasić) and Marshal Tito as leader of the National Liberation Committee, recognizing a provisional parliament. On March 7, 1945, the agreement was confirmed by the Royal Yugoslav government in London, and a provisional government was set up in Belgrade.

On Nov. 29, 1945, the Constituent Assembly of Yugoslavia, at a joint session of the Skupshtina and the House of Nationalities, proclaimed Yugoslavia a Republic. In January, 1953, a new Constitution became effective, under which two houses (the Federal Council and Council of Producers) were established. Elections to these houses were held in November, 1953 and March, 1958.

On April 7, 1963, a new Constitution was proclaimed under which the official name of the country was changed to "The Socialist Federal Republic of Yugoslavia." A new office of Vice-President of the Republic was created. The existing two Councils of the Federal Assembly were replaced by five Chambers of 120 members each (Federal Chamber, Economic Chamber, Educational-Cultural Chamber, Social Welfare and Health Chamber, and Organizational/Political Chamber), plus a Chamber of Nationalities of 70 members. A Constitutional Court was created. Elections to the new Federal Assembly were held in June 1963.

Defence.—The Army, Navy and Air Force on a peace footing consist of 370,000 officers and men, the war strength being about 1,250,000.

Religion and Education.—The Orthodox, Roman Catholic, Protestant, Islamic and Judaic faiths are recognized by the State. According to the 1948 Census, 49·53 per cent. of the population is Orthodox, 36·7 per cent. Catholic, 1·14 per cent.Protestant and other Christian denominations 12·52 per cent. Moslem and 0·04 per cent. Jews. The Church is separated from the State. All religious instruction in schools has been forbidden since January 1952. Priests are allowed to teach in churches. Eight years elementary education is compulsory and all education is free. In 1961 there were 14,527 elementary schools with 84,279 teachers and 2,764,000 pupils and 1,699 secondary schools with 37,915 teachers and 503,000 pupils. There are five universities: Belgrade, Zagreb, Ljubljana, Sarajevo and Skoplje, with 77 faculties and 104,875 students and 11 art academies with 1,418 students.

Language and Literature.—The languages of the country are Serbo-Croat, Slovenian and Macedonian, all South Slav tongues. Serbo-Croat predominates and is the language of the Federal Government. In Serbia, Macedonia and Montenegro the Cyrillic script is used and in the rest of the country the Latin; Hungarian, Roumanian, Albanian and Italian are also used in certain districts. The desire for the political union of the South Slavs led to a cultural unity and a revival of Slav literature. There are 4 Serbian daily newspapers in Belgrade, 2 Slovene dailies in Ljubljana (Laibach), 2 Croat dailies in Zagreb, 2 dailies in Novi Sad, one in Hungarian, 2 dailies in Rijeka, one in Italian and daily papers at Skoplje, Sarajevo, Prištine, Split, Maribor and Osijek.

Production and Industry.—About 50 per cent. of the population is engaged in agriculture. although in recent years industry has expanded rapidly and industrial production has more than doubled since 1947. Since 1955 substantial new investment has been diverted from basic industry to consumer goods. In agriculture the main emphasis is on increased investment in mechanization and fertilizers. The main crops are wheat and maize, of which the average yield in 1962 was 3,510,000 and 5,270,000 tons respectively. The forest areas produced some 8,831,000 cubic metres of timber in 1961. According to Yugoslav official estimates, the livestock population during 1962 was approximately as follows: horses, 1,226,000; cattle, 5,884,000; sheep, 11,143,000; pigs, 5,161,000; poultry, 28,304,000. Minerals are a great source of wealth, particularly in the central regions. Estimated production in

1962 included the following ('000 tons); Hard coal, 1,187; brown coal, 9,319; lignite, 14,188; blistered copper, 46; electrolytic copper, 46; refined lead, 98; iron ore, 2,190; pig iron, 1,050; steel (total), 1595; aluminium, 28; zinc, 39; mercury, 0·561; and petroleum (crude), 1,525.

FINANCE

Federal Budget (estimated figures).	1961
	Dinars
Revenue	528 800,000,000
Expenditure	516,100,000,000

The Yugoslav *Dinar* has a nominal value of 1/10 penny, the official exchange rate being 2,100*D*=£1 (*see also* p. 84).

Communications.—In 1960 there were approximately 11,900 miles of standard and narrow gauge railway. There are also 20,714 miles of telephone lines and 21,560 miles of telegraph lines. Yugoslavia has a long seaboard on the Adriatic coast. The principal Yugoslav Ψ ports are Rijeka, Šibenik, Split, Zadar, Dubrovnik and Kotor (Carraro) and new ports are under construction at Ploče and Bar. The Danube forms a great commercial highway and the tributary rivers Sava and Tisa provide other shipping routes.

Trade with U.K.

	1961	1962
Imports from U.K.	£14,484,282	£16,086,531
Exports to U.K.	19,160,490	20,093,706

The chief exports to the United Kingdom are meat and meat products, furniture and timber. The main imports from the United Kingdom are machinery of all kinds, iron and steel, chemicals, wool tops and metal manufactures.

CAPITAL.—Belgrade, population (1961), 594,000. Other towns are: Zagreb (457,000), Sarajevo (198,000), Skopje (168,000), Ljubljana (157,000), Novi Sad (111,000), Rijeka (100,000), Split (99,000), and Maribor (85,000).

FLAG.—State coat of arms on a red ground.

BRITISH EMBASSY

Prvog Maja 46, Belgrade.

British Ambassador Extraordinary and Plenipotentiary, His Excellency Sir Michael Justin Creswell, K.C.M.G. (1960) £4,115

Counsellors, D. D. Brown, M.M.; C. N. Jupp (*Commercial*).

Naval Attaché, Capt. P. Weekes, C.B.E., D.S.C., R.N.

Military Attaché, Col. C. B. Welch.

Air Attaché, Group-Capt. H. W. Harrison.

1st Secretaries, M. H. Morgan; J. D. Campbell, M.B.E., M.C. (*Information*).

2nd Secretaries, E. W. Cook (*Consular*); A. A. Plummer (*Commercial*); W. G. Borman (*Visa*).

3rd Secretaries, J. M. Candlish (*Commercial*); P. R. Holmes (*Consular*); D. A. Burns; A. St. J. H. Figgis.

Attaché, D. Stingemore.

BRITISH CONSULAR OFFICES

There are British Consular Offices at *Belgrade, Zagreb,* and *Split.*

BRITISH COUNCIL

Representative, G. L. H. Hitchcock, O.B.E., Prvog Maja 34, Belgrade. There is also a centre at *Zagreb.*

PASSPORT REGULATIONS

Applications for Foreign Office passports must be made on the forms obtainable at any of the Passport Offices (addresses given below) or at any Local Office of the Ministry of Labour. Applications for passports required in less than four working days (May–July—7 working days) should not be taken to Ministry of Labour Offices.

London.—Clive House, Petty France, S.W.1. (Hours: Mon.–Fri., 9.30–4.30.)

Liverpool.—India Buildings, Water Street, Liverpool 2. (Hours: Mon.–Fri., 9.30–4.30.)

Glasgow.—14 Princes Square, 48 Buchanan Street, Glasgow. C.1. (Hours, Mon.–Fri., 9.30–4.30.)

The Passport Offices are also open for cases of special emergency only, between 4.30 p.m. and 6 p.m. (Saturdays 9.30–4) or (Glasgow 9.30–1 p.m.) and in *London* on Sundays and Public Holidays between 10 a.m. and noon.

To facilitate the issue of passports applicants are recommended to make personal application to any one of the above mentioned offices. If it is not possible to make personal application at one of the Passport Offices or Ministry of Labour Local Offices, completed forms of applications should be sent to one of the three Passport Offices, with photographs, supporting documents and the fee of £1 10*s*. Remittances sent with postal applications should be in the form of a Cheque or Postal Order which should be crossed and made payable to the Passport Office. Notes or postage stamps should not be sent in payment.

Foreign Office Passports are granted:—

(i) To citizens of the United Kingdom and Colonies.

(ii) To British subjects without citizenship.

(iii) To British Protected Persons.

Passports are available for *five years* in the first instance, unless otherwise stated. They may be renewed for a further period of 5 years for a fee of £1. They are not available *beyond ten years from the original date of issue.* Thereafter, or if at any time the Passport contains no further space for visas, a new Passport must be obtained.

A Passport including particulars of the *holder's wife* is not available for the wife's use when she is travelling alone. A wife's particulars may *only* be added at the time of issue of a passport.

Children who have reached the age of sixteen years require separate Passports. When they apply for a Passport the written consent of father or other legal guardian is necessary.

The application must be countersigned in Section 9 by a Member of Parliament, Justice of the Peace, Minister of Religion, Medical or Legal Practitioner, Bank Officer, established Civil Servant, Public Official, Police Officer or any person of similar standing personally acquainted with the applicant. The applicant's birth certificate and other evidence in support of the statements made in the application must be produced.

In the case of children under the age of 16 requiring a separate passport, an application should be made by the child's father or other legal guardian on form (B) obtainable from a Passport Office or any local office of the Ministry of Labour.

If the applicant for a Passport be a British subject by naturalization or registration, the Certificate of Naturalization or registration must be produced with the application.

British Passports are generally available for travel *to all countries.* The possession of a Passport does not, however, exempt the holder from compliance with any *Immigration Regulations* in force in British or foreign countries, or from the necessity of obtaining a *visa* where required.

A Passport cannot be issued or renewed by the Foreign Office on behalf of *a person already abroad;* such person should apply, in a foreign country, to the nearest British Mission or Consulate, or, within the British Commonwealth outside the United Kingdom of Great Britain and N. Ireland, to the nearest British Passport issuing authority.

Persons resident in *Northern Ireland* should apply in person to the Foreign Office Passport Agency, 1 May Street, Belfast, or by post to the Branch Passport Office, Liverpool; citizens of the United Kingdom and Colonies resident in the Irish Republic should make application to the Visa Section British Embassy, 30 Merrion Square, Dublin.

British Visitors' Passports

A simplified form of travel document is available for British subjects* (Citizens of the United Kingdom and Colonies) wishing to pay short visits (not exceeding three months) to certain foreign countries, *viz.*

AUSTRIA	LUXEMBURG
BELGIUM	MONACO
DENMARK†	NETHERLANDS
FINLAND†	NORWAY†
FRANCE (incl. CORSICA)	PORTUGAL (incl. MADEIRA & AZORES)
GREECE	SAN MARINO
W. GERMANY (incl. West Berlin by air only)	SPAIN (incl. BALEARIC & CANARY ISLANDS)
ICELAND	SWEDEN†
ITALY	SWITZERLAND
LIECHTENSTEIN	TURKEY

**See* Legal Notes. †Length of stay restricted to three months in any nine months in Nordic Group Countries (including Finland) as a whole. Holders may also pay short visits to Canada, Gibraltar and Malta. A British Visitor's Passport must be valid for three months beyond the last day on which the visitor will be in Canada.

A fee of 7*s.* 6*d.* is charged for the issue of a British Visitors' Passport, which is valid for 12 months, cannot be amended and is not renewable; on expiry application should be made for a new passport if required. Particulars of an applicant's wife and/or children under 16 years can be included *at the time of issue only* at no extra cost. A child of 8 years of age and over is eligible to hold a British Visitors' Passport. Applications for, or including, a person under 21 years of age (unless married or serving in H.M. Forces) must be countersigned by the legal guardian.

British Visitors' Passports are obtainable by application on Form VP (from any local office of the Ministry of Labour and from the Passport Office or Branches). Applicants in England, Scotland and Wales should take the completed form in person to any local office of the Ministry of Labour which will normally issue the passport without further delay; applicants in Northern Ireland to any office of the Ministry of Labour and National Insurance. *British Visitors' Passports are not obtainable from the Passport Office or Branches.* Two recent passport photographs will be required, of the applicant and of his wife if to be included; photographs of children are not required. Size of photographs must be 2 in. × 1½ in. *see also* (PHOTOGRAPHS below). No visas are required on British Visitors' Passports.

RENEWAL OF PASSPORTS

Applications for the renewal of Foreign Office passports must be made on Form D, obtainable at any of the Passport offices (see above) or at any local office of the Ministry of Labour.

PHOTOGRAPHS

Duplicate unmounted photographs of applicant (and his wife, if to be included in the Passport) must be sent. These photographs should be printed on *thin* paper and must not be glazed on the reverse side. They should measure not more than 2½ in. by 2 in. or less than 2 in. by 1½ in., and should be taken full face without a hat.

EXPECTATION OF LIFE IN YEARS

	England and Wales 1959		Scotland 1959		Northern Ireland 1957–59		United States* 1958		France 1952–56	
Age	Male	Female	Male	Female	Male	Female	Male	Female	Male	Female
0	68·1	73·8	66·00	71·44	67·44	71·82	66·4	72·7	65·04	71·15
1	68·8	74·3	67·16	72·22	68·55	72·77	67·5	73·5	66·78	72·44
5	65·1	70·5	63·51	68·52	64·84	69·03	63·8	69·8	63·31	68·95
10	60·2	65·6	58·65	63·63	59·97	64·15	59·0	64·9	58·48	64·09
15	55·3	60·7	53·78	58·72	55·10	59·23	54·1	60·0	53·63	59·20
20	50·6	55·8	48·97	53·84	50·31	54·35	49·4	55·2	48·90	54·36
30	41·1	46·1	39·46	44·17	40·80	44·59	40·2	45·6	39·69	44·84
40	31·6	36·6	30·13	34·71	31·42	35·15	31·1	36·2	30·68	35·58
50	22·7	27·5	21·48	25·77	22·65	26·13	22·7	27·3	22·36	26·73
60	15·1	19·0	14·24	17·56	15·16	17·83	15·6	19·1	15·24	18·54
65	12·0	15·2	11·33	13·94	12·02	14·19	12·6	15·4	12·09	14·75
70	9·3	11·7	8·90	10·63	9·41	10·91	10·1	12·1	9·26	11·31

* White population only.

THE HIGHEST BUILDINGS

	Feet
Empire State, N.Y., U.S.A.	1,472
Chrysler Building, N.Y., U.S.A.	1,046
Eiffel Tower, Paris (originally)	985
60 Wall Tower, N.Y., U.S.A.	950
Bank of Manhattan, N.Y., U.S.A.	927
Rockefeller Centre, N.Y., U.S.A.	850
Woolworth's, N.Y., U.S.A.	792
City Bank Farmers' Trust, 20 Exchange Place, N.Y., U.S.A.	741
Metropolitan Life Building, Madison Avenue, N.Y., U.S.A.	700
500 Fifth Avenue, N.Y., U.S.A.	697
Chanin, Lexington Avenue and 42nd Street N.Y., U.S.A.	680
Pyramid of Cheops, Egypt	450
Salisbury Cathedral (Spire), England	401
St. Paul's Cathedral (Cross), England	365

MONEYS OF ALL NATIONS

Country	Monetary Unit	Value of Unit in British Currency†	Denominations in Circulation	
			Notes	Coins
		£ s. d.		
Afghanistan......	*Afghani* of 100 *Puls*	0 0 2 (highest rate)	*Afghanis*, 1,000, 500, 100, 50, 20, 10, 5, 2	*Afghanis* 2; *Puls* 50, 25
Albania..........	*Lek* of 100 *Qintar*	0 0 1¾	*Leks* 1,000, 500, 100, 50, 10	*Leks* 5, 2, 1, ½
Argentina........	*Peso* of 100 *Centavos*	0 0 0¾	*Pesos* 5,000, 1,000, 500, 100, 50, 10, 5	*Peso* 10, 5, 1; *Centavos* 50, 20, 10, 5
Australia.........	*Pound* of 20 *Shillings*, or 240 *Pence*	0 16 0	*£A.* 10, 5, 1; 10*s.*	2*s.*, 1*s.*; 6*d.*, 3*d.*, 1*d.*, ½*d.*
Austria..........	*Schilling* of 100 *Groschen*	0 0 3¼	*Schillings* 1,000, 500, 100, 50, 20	*Schillings*, 50, 25, 10, 5, 1; *Groschen* 50, 10, 5, 2, 1
Belgium.........	*Franc* of 100 *Centimes*	0 0 1¾	*Frs.* 1,000, 500, 100, 50, 20	*Frs.* 100, 50, 20, 5, 1; *Centimes* 50, 25, 20
Bolivia..........	*Peso* of 100 cents or 1000 *Bolivianos*.	0 6 0¾	*Pesos* 100; 50; 20; *Bolivianos* 10,000, 5,000, 1,000, 500, 100, 50, 20	*Cents* 50, 20, 10, 5
Brazil...........	*Cruzeiro* of 100 *Centavos*	0 1 2 (100 *Cruzeiros*)	*Cruzeiros* 5,000, 1,000, 500, 200, 100, 50, 20, 10, 5, 2, 1	*Cruzeiros* 2, 1; *Centavos* 50, 20, 10
Bulgaria.........	*Lev* of 100 *Stotinki*	0 6 1	*Leva* 20, 10, 5, 2, 1	*Lev* 1; *Stotinki* 50, 20, 10, 5, 2, 1
Burma..........	*Kyat* of 100 *Pyas*	0 1 6	*Kyats* 100, 50, 20, 10, 5, 1	*Kyat* 1; *Pyas* 50, 25, 10, 5, 1
Cambodia........	*Riel* of 100 *Sen*	0 0 2½	*Riels* 500, 100, 50, 20, 10, 5, 1	*Sen* 50, 20, 10
Canada..........	*Dollar* of 100 *Cents*	0 6 7½	*Dollars* 1,000, 500, 100, 50, 25, 20, 10, 5, 2, 1	*Dollar* 1; *Cents* 50, 25, 10, 5, 1
Ceylon..........	*Rupee* of 100 *Cents*	0 1 6	*Rupees* 100, 50, 10, 5, 2, 1	*Cents* 50, 25, 10, 5, 2, 1
Chile...........	*Escudo* of 100 *Cóndores* or 100 *Centésimos* (= 1,000 *Pesos*)	0 2 4¾ (free rate)	*Escudos* 1, ½	*Centésimos* 10, 5, 2, 1 *Pesos* 10, 1
China...........	*Jenminpi* or *Yuan* of 10 *Chiao* or 100 *Fen*	0 2 10¾	*Yuan* 10, 5, 3, 2, 1; *Chiao* 5, 2, 1; *Fen* 5, 2, 1	*Fen* 5, 2, 1
Colombia........	*Peso* of 100 *Centavos*	0 0 8½ (free rate)	*Pesos* 100, 50, 20, 10, 5, 2, 1; *Centavos* 50	*Centavos* 50, 20, 10, 5, 2, 1
Congolese Republic	*Franc* of 100 *Centimes*	0 0 1¼	*Frs.* 1,000, 500, 100, 50, 20, 10, 5	*Frs.* 5, 2, 1; *Centimes* 50, 20, 10
Costa Rica.......	*Colon* of 100 *Centimos*	0 1 1	*Colones* 1,000, 500 100, 50, 20, 10, 5	*Colones* 2, 1; *Centimos* 50, 25, 10, 5
Cuba............	*Peso* of 100 *Centavos*	0 7 1½	*Pesos* 100, 50, 20, 10, 5, 1	*Centavos* 40, 20, 5, 2, 1
Curaçao.........	*Florin* of 100 *Cents*	0 3 9½	*Florins* 500, 250, 100, 50, 25, 10, 5, 2½, 1	*Florins* 2½, 1; *Cents* 25, 10, 5, 2½, 1
Cyprus..........	*Pound* of 1,000 *Mils*	1 0 0	*£5*, *£1*; *Mils* 500, 250	*Mils* 100, 50, 25, 5, 3
Czechoslovakia...	*Crown* of 100 *Halér*	0 1 0* (highest rate)	*Crowns* 100, 50, 25, 10, 5, 3	*Crowns* 1; *Halér* 25, 10, 5, 3, 1
Denmark........	*Krone* of 100 *Öre*	0 1 0½	*Kroner* 500, 100, 50, 10	*Kroners* 5, 2, 1; *Öre* 25, 10, 5, 2, 1
Dominican Republic.........	*Peso* of 100 *Centavos*	0 7 1½	*Pesos* 1,000, 500, 100, 50, 20, 10, 5, 1	*Peso* 1, ½; *Centavos* 25, 10, 5, 1
Ecuador.........	*Sucre* of 100 *Centavos*	0 0 4 (free rate)	*Sucres* 1,000, 500, 100, 50, 20, 10, 5	*Sucre* 1; *Centavos* 20, 10, 5, 1
Egypt. *See* United Arab Republic				
Ethiopia.........	*Dollar* of 100 *Cents*	0 2 10¼	*Dollars* 500, 100, 50, 20, 10, 5, 1	*Cents* 50, 25, 10, 5, 1
Finland..........	*New Markka* of 100 Penniä (1 *New Markka*=100 old *Markkas*)	0 2 2¾ (100 *Markkas*)	*Markkas* 100, 50, 10, 5, 1	*Pennies* 50, 20, 10, 5, 1
France..........	*Franc* of 100 *Centimes* (1 *Franc* = 100 old *Francs*)	0 1 5½	*Francs* 500, 100, 50, 10, 5; *Old Francs* 10,000, 5,000, 1,000, 500	*Francs* 5, 1; *Old Francs* 100, 50, 20, 10, 5, 2, 1
Germany (East)...	*Deutsche Mark* of 100 *Pfennig*	0 3 2½	*D.M.* 100, 50, 20, 10, 5, 1; *Pfennig* 50	*D.M.* 2, 1; *Pfennig* 50, 10, 5, 1
Germany (Federal Republic of)...	*Deutsche Mark* of 100 *Pfennig*	0 1 9½	*D.M.* 100, 50, 20, 10, 5	*D.M.* 5, 2, 1; *Pfennig* 50, 10, 5, 2, 1
Ghana...........	*Pound* of 20 *Shillings* or 240 *Pence*	1 0 0	*£5*, 1; 10*s.*	2*s.*, 1*s.*; 6*d.*, 3*d.*, 1*d.*, ½*d.*

* Multiple exchange rates in operation. † Sterling equivalents of currency units are approximate.

Country	Monetary Unit	Value of Unit in British Currency†	Denominations in Circulation: Notes	Denominations in Circulation: Coins
		£ s. d.		
Greece	*Drachma* of 100 *Lepta*	0 0 3	*Drachmae* 1,000, 500, 100, 50	*Drachmae* 20, 10, 5, 2, 1 *Lepta* 50, 20, 10, 5
Guatemala	*Quetzal* of 100 *Centavos*	0 7 1½	*Quetzales* 1,000, 500, 100, 20, 10, 5, 1; *Centavos* 50	*Centavos* 25, 10, 5, 2, 1
Haiti	*Gourde* of 100 *Centimes*★	0 1 5	*Gourdes* 100, 50, 10, 5, 2, 1	*Centimes* 50, 20, 10, 5
Honduras	*Lempira* of 100 *Centavos*	0 3 6¾	*Lempiras* 100, 50, 20, 10, 5, 1	*Lempira* 1; *Centavos* 50, 20, 10, 5, 2, 1
Hong Kong	*Dollar* of 100 *Cents*	0 1 3	*Dollars* 500, 100, 10, 5, *Cents* 1	*Dollar* 1; *Cents* 50, 10, 5
Hungary	*Forint* of 100 *Fillér*	0 0 7¼	*Forints* 100, 50, 20, 10	*Forints* 500, 100, 50, 25, 20, 10, 5, 2, 1; *Fillér* 50, 20, 10, 5, 2
Iceland	*Krona* of 100 *Aurar*	0 0 2	*Krone* 1,000, 500, 100, 50, 25, 10, 5	*Krone* 2, 1; *Aurar* 25, 10, 5, 2, 1
India	*Rupee* of 100 *Naye Paise*	0 1 6	*Rupees* 10,000, 5,000, 1,000, 100, 10, 5, 2, 1	*Rupee* 1, ½, ¼; *Naye Paise* 50, 25, 10, 5, 2, 1
Indonesia	*Rupiah* of 100 *Sen*	0 0 2	*Rupiahs* 2,500, 1,000, 500, 100, 50, 25, 10, 5, 2½, 1	*Sen* 50, 25, 10, 5, 1
Iraq	*Dinar* of 1,000 *Fils*	1 0 0	*Dinars* 10, 5, 1, ½, ¼	*Fils* 100, 50, 25, 10, 5, 1
Ireland (Republic of)	*Pound* of 20 *Shillings* or 240 *Pence*	1 0 0	£100, 50, 20, 10, 5, 1; 10*s.*	2*s.* 6*d.*, 2*s.*, 1*s.*; 6*d.*, 3*d.*, 1*d.*, ½*d.*, ¼*d.*
Israel	*Pound* of 100 *Agorot* (formerly 1,000 *Prutot*)	0 2 4½	*Pounds* 50, 10, 5, 1, ½; *Prutot* 500, 250	*Agorot* 25, 10, 5, 1; *Prutot* 250, 100, 50, 25, 10, 5, 1
Italy	*Lira* of 100 *Centesimi*	0 1 1¾ (100 *Lire*)	*Lire* 10,000, 5,000 1,000, 500	*Lire* 500, 100, 50, 20, 10, 5, 2, 1
Jamaica	*Pound* of 20 *Shillings* (or 240 *Pence*)	1 0 0	£J 5, 1; 10*s.* 5*s.*	5*s.*, 2*s.* 6*d.*, 2*s.*, 1*s.*, 6*d.*, 3*d.*, 1*d.*, ½*d.*, ¼*d.*
Japan	*Yen*	0 1 11½ (100 *Yen*)	*Yen* 10,000, 5,000, 1,000, 500, 100, 50, 10, 5, 1	*Yen* 100, 50, 10, 5, 1
Jordan	*Dinar* of 1,000 *Fils*	1 0 0	*Dinar* 10, 5, 1; *Fils* 500	*Fils* 100, 50, 20, 10, 5, 1
Korea	*Won* of 100 *Jeon*	0 0 6½ (10 *Won*)	*Won* 500, 100, 50, 10, 5, 1	*Won* 5, 1, *Jeon* 50, 10
Kuwait	*Dinar* of 1000 *fils*	1 0 0	*Dinar* 10, 5, 1; *Fils* 500, 250	*Fils* 100, 50, 20, 10, 5, 1
Lebanon	*Pound* (*Livre*) of 100 *Piastres*	0 2 3¼ (free rate)	*Pounds* 100, 50, 25, 10, 5, 1	*Piastres* 50, 25, 10, 5, 2½, 1
Liberia	*U.S.A.* $ of 100 *Cents*	0 7 1½	*Dollars* 20, 10, 5, 1	*Dollar* 1; *Cents* 50, 25, 10, 5, 2, 1
Libya	*Pound* of 100 *Piastres* or 1,000 *Milliemes*	1 0 0	£L 10, 5, 1, ½, ¼; *Piastres* 10, 5	*Piastres* 2, 1; *Milliemes* 5, 2, 1
Luxemburg	*Franc* of 100 *Centimes* (Belgian currency is legal tender)	0 0 1¾	*Francs* 100, 50, 20, 10	*Francs* 100, 5, 1; *Centimes* 25
Malaya, Federation of	*Malayan Dollar* of 100 *Cents*	0 2 4	*Dollars* 1,000, 100, 50 10, 5, 1	*Cents* 50, 20, 10, 5, 1
Mexico	*Peso* of 100 *Centavos*	0 0 6¾	*Pesos* 10,000, 1,000, 500, 100, 50, 20, 10, 5, 1	*Pesos* 10, 5, 1; *Centavos* 50, 25, 20, 10, 5, 1
Morocco	*Dirham* (= 100 *Francs*)	0 1 5	*Dirhams* 10, 5; *Francs* 10,000, 5,000, 1,000, 500, 100, 50	*Dirham* 1; *Francs* 500, 200, 100, 50, 20, 10, 5, 2, 1
Nepal	*Rupee* of 100 *Pice*	0 0 11¼	*Rupees* 100, 10, 5, 1	*Rupee* 1; *Pice* 50, 25, 20, 10, 5, 4, 2, 1
Netherlands	*Florin* (*Guilder*) of 100 *Cents*	0 1 11¾	*Florins* 1,000, 100, 25, 10, 2½, 1	*Florin* 2½, 1; *Cents* 25, 10, 5, 1
New Zealand	*Pound* of 20 *Shillings* or 240 *Pence*	0 19 10	£*NZ* 50, 10, 5, 1; 10*s.*	2*s.* 6*d.*, 2*s.*, 1*s.*; 6*d.*, 3*d.*, 1*d.*, ½*d.*
Nicaragua	*Córdoba* of 100 *Centavos*	0 1 0¼	*Córdobas* 1,000, 500, 100, 50, 20, 5, 2, 1	*Centavos* 50, 25, 10, 5, 1
Norway	*Krone* of 100 *Öre*	0 1 0	*Kroner* 1,000, 500, 100, 50, 10, 5	*Kroner* 5, 1; *Öre* 50, 25, 10, 5, 2, 1
Pakistan	*Rupee* of 16 *Annas* or 64 *Pice* or 192 *Pies* or 100 *Paisa*	0 1 6	*Rupees* 100, 10, 5, 2, 1	*Rupee* 1; ½, ¼; *Annas* 2 1, ½; *Pice* 1; *Pie* 1 *Paisa* 10, 5, 1
Panama	*Balboa* of 100 *Cents* (=*U.S.* $)	0 7 1½	*U.S.* $ 10,000, 5,000, 1,000, 500, 100, 50, 20, 10, 5, 2, 1	*Balboa* 1, ½, ¼, 1/10, 1/20; *Cents* 2½, 1 (U.S. coins also circulate)

† Sterling equivalents of currency units are approximate and are calculated at the rates ruling in June 1963. ★U.S.A. currency is also used.

Country	Monetary Unit	Value of Unit in British Currency† (£ s. d.)	Denominations in Circulation: Notes	Denominations in Circulation: Coins
Paraguay	*Guarani* of 100 *Céntimos*	0 0 7 (10 *Guaraníes*)	*Guaraníes* 1,000, 500, 100, 50, 10, 5, 1	*Céntimos* 50, 25, 10, 5, 1
Persia (Iran)	*Rial* of 100 *Dinars*	0 0 1	*Rials* 1,000, 500, 200, 50, 20, 10, 5	*Rials* 10, 5, 2, 1; *Dinars* 50, 25, 10, 5
Peru	*Sol* of 100 *Centavos*	0 0 3	*Soles* 500, 100, 50, 10, 5	*Sol* 1, ½; *Centavos* 20, 10, 5, 2, 1
Philippines	*Peso* of 100 *Centavos*	0 1 10 (free rate)	*Pesos* 100, 50, 20, 10, 5, 2, 1; *Centavos* 50, 20, 10, 5	*Peso* 1; *Centavos* 50, 25, 20, 10, 5, 1
Poland	*Zloty* of 100 *Groszy*	0 1 9½* (highest rate)	*Zlotys* 500, 100, 50, 20, 10	*Zlotys* 10, 5, 2, 1; *Groszy* 50, 20, 10, 5, 2, 1
Portugal	*Escudo* of 100 *Centavos*	0 0 3	*Escudos* 1,000, 500, 100, 50, 20	*Escudos* 20, 10, 5, 2½, 1; *Centavos* 50, 20, 10
Rhodesia and Nyasaland (Federation of)	*Pound* of 20 *Shillings* or 240 *Pence*	1 0 0	£10, 5, 1; 10*s.*	2*s.* 6*d.*, 2*s.*, 1*s.*; 6*d.*, 3*d.*, 1*d.*, ½*d.*
Roumania	*Leu* of 100 *Bani*	0 1 2¼ (highest rate)	*Lei* 100, 25, 10, 5, 3, 1	*Lei* 3; *Leu* 1; *Bani* 50, 25, 15, 10, 5, 3, 1
El Salvador	*Colon* of 100 *Centavos*	0 2 10	*Colones* 100, 25, 10, 5, 2, 1	*Centavos* 50, 25, 10, 5, 3, 1
Saudi Arabia	*Riyal* of 20 *Qursh* or 100 *Halalas*	0 1 7	*Riyals* 100, 50, 10, 5, 1	*Qursh* 4, 2, 1, ½
South Africa	*Rand* of 100 *Cents*	0 10 0	*Rands* 20, 10, 2, 1; £*SA* 100, 20, 10, 5, 1; 10*s.*	*Cents* 50, 20, 10, 5, 2½, 1, ½; 5*s.*, 2*s.* 6*d.*, 2*s.*, 1*s.*; 6*d.*, 3*d.*, 1*d.*, ½*d.*, ¼*d.*
Spain	*Peseta* of 100 *Céntimos*	0 0 1½	*Pesetas* 1,000, 500, 100, 50, 25, 5, 1	*Pesetas* 50, 25, 5, 2½, 1, *Céntimos* 50, 10
Sudan	*Pound* of 100 *Piastres* or 1,000 *Milliemes*	1 0 6	£*S* 10, 5, 1; *Piastres* 50, 25	*Piastres* 10, 5, 2; *Milliemes* 10, 5, 1
Surinam	*Gulden* of 100 *Cents*	0 3 9½	*Gulden* 1,000, 100, 25, 10, 5, 2½, 1	*Guilder* 1; *Cents* 25, 10, 5, 1
Sweden	*Krona* of 100 *Öre*	0 1 4½	*Kronor* 10,000, 1,000, 100, 50, 10, 5	*Kronor* 5, 2, 1; *Öre* 50, 25, 10, 5, 2, 1
Switzerland	*Franc* of 100 *Centimes*	0 1 7¾	*Francs* 1,000, 500, 100, 50, 20, 10, 5	*Francs* 50, 25, 5, 2, 1; *Centimes* 50, 20, 10, 5, 2, 1
Syria	*Pound* of 100 *Piastres*	0 1 9¾	*Pounds* 500, 100, 50, 25, 10, 5, 1	*Pound* 1; *Piastres* 50, 25, 10, 5, 2½
Thailand	*Baht* or *Tical* of 100 *Satangs*	0 0 4	*Bahts* 100, 20, 10, 5, 1	*Tical* 1; *Satangs* 50, 25, 10, 5, 1
Tunisia	*Dinar* of 1,000 *Millimes*	0 17 1½	*Dinars* 5, 1, ½	Old coins expressed in *francs* circulate; (1 *Franc*=1 *Millime*) *Francs* 100, 50, 20, 5, 2, 1; *Millimes* 100, 50, 20, 10, 5, 2, 1
Turkey	*Lira* (£) of 100 *kuruş* (*piastres*)	0 0 9½ (100 Piastres)	£*T* 1,000, 500, 100, 50, 10, 5, 2½	£*T* 10, 2½, 1; *Kuruş* 25, 10, 5, 2½, 1
United Arab Republic	*Pound* of 100 *Piastres* or 1,000 *Millièmes*	0 16 4¾	*Pounds* 10, 5, 1; *Piastres* 50, 25, 10, 5	*Piastres* 20, 10, 5, 2; *Millièmes* 20, 10, 5, 2, 1
United Kingdom (*See also* p. 445).	*Pound* of 20 *Shillings* or 240 *Pence*	1 0 0	£5, 1; 10*s.*	2*s.* 6*d.*, 2*s.*, 1*s.*; 6*d.*, 3*d.*, 1*d.*, ½*d.*
United States of America	*Dollar* of 100 *Cents*	0 7 1½	$10,000, 5,000, 1,000, 500, 100, 50, 20, 10, 5, 2, 1	$1; *Cents* 50, 25, 10, 5, 1
Uruguay	*Peso* of 100 *Centésimos*	0 0 5¼ (free rate)	*Pesos* 1,000, 500, 100, 50, 10, 5, 1	*Peso* 10, 1; *Centésimos* 50, 20, 10, 5, 2
U.S.S.R.	*Rouble* of 100 *Copecks*‡	0 7 11¼	*Roubles* 100, 50, 25, 10, 5, 3, 1 (dated 1961)	‡*Rouble* 1; *Copecks* 50, 20, 15, 10, 5, 3, 2, 1
Venezuela	*Bolivar* of 100 *Centimos*	0 1 7 (free rate)	*Bolivares* 500, 100, 50, 20, 10	*Bolivares* 5, 2, 1; *Centimos* 50, 25, 12½, 5
Vietnam (South)	*Piastre* of 100 *Cents*	0 0 2½* (highest rate)	*Piastres* 500, 200, 100, 50, 20, 10, 5, 2, 1	*Piastre* 1; *Cents* 50, 20, 10
West Indies (The) except Jamaica	*Dollar* of 100 *Cents*	0 4 2	$100, 20, 10, 5, 2, 1	*Cents* 50, 25, 10, 5, 2, 1
Yugoslavia	*Dinar* of 100 *Paras*	0 0 11½ (100 *Dinars*—Official rate)	*Dinars* 5,000, 1,000, 500, 100	*Dinars* 50, 20, 10, 5, 2, 1; *Paras* 50

* Multiple exchange rates in operation. † Sterling equivalents of currency units are approximate and are calculated at the rates ruling in June, 1963. ‡ With the exception of *Copecks* 3, 2, 1, notes and coins dated to prior 1961 are invalid.

ECONOMIC CO-OPERATION IN EUROPE

EUROPEAN COMMUNITY

ECSC Rue August-Lumière 3/5, Luxembourg.
Common Market and Euratom, Rue Ravenstein 2, Brussels.

The European Community is an economic union of six European nations, namely Belgium, France, Germany, Italy, Luxemburg and the Netherlands. It was the aim of its creators that economic union should promote political unification. The Community consists of three parts:

The European Coal and Steel Community (ECSC) was set up in 1952 to pool the six nations' resources in coal, steel, iron ore and scrap in a single market without frontier barriers.

The *Common Market* (officially the European Economic Community or EEC), whose institutions were set up at the beginning of 1958, is gradually (over 12 years) pooling these nations' other economic resources in a mass market of 170 million consumers.

Euratom (The European Atomic Energy Community or EAEC), set up at the beginning of 1958, is helping to provide the Community with a powerful atomic industry pledged to the peaceful uses of nuclear energy.

These three communities share certain institutions of government, namely the Council of Ministers, the European Parliament and the Court of Justice. The administrations are separate, however. The ECSC is administered by the High Authority, the EEC and Euratom are administered each by a Commission. There are also a number of advisory bodies, the most important of which is the Economic and Social Committee.

The Council of Ministers.—This consists of 6 ministers, one from each member government, the minister concerned depending on the subject under discussion. It is the Community's main decision-taking body but its authority is not as great in ECSC matters as in those relating to Common Market and Euratom. For coal and steel, decisions are usually by majority vote: in Common Market and Euratom matters decisions have usually to be unanimous in the early stages, but increasingly decisions are taken by a qualified majority vote, that is by twelve votes out of seventeen, the votes being weighted as follows: France, Germany and Italy, four votes each; Belgium and the Netherlands two votes each, and Luxemburg one. On Commission proposals twelve votes suffice; in other cases the twelve votes must include those of four countries. Their meetings are prepared by a committee of permanent representatives for the Common Market and Euratom and by a Co-ordinating Committee for the ECSC.

EUROPEAN PARLIAMENT

Secretariat: 19 Rue Beaumont, Luxemburg.

The European Parliament consist of 142 members elected by the national parliaments of the member countries—36 members each from France, Germany and Italy, 14 each from Belgium and the Netherlands and 6 from Luxemburg. Set up under the terms of the ECSC Treaty of 1952, its authority was extended by the Treaty of Rome 1957 to cover also the European Economic and Atomic Communities. The Parliament must be consulted on all major issues and can force the dismissal of the Commission by a vote of no-confidence. The Treaty provides for its direct election and a scheme for this was drawn up by the Parliament in May, 1960. So far no decision on this project has been taken.

President, Gaetano Martino (*Italy*) (1962).

EUROPEAN COURT OF JUSTICE

12, Rue de la Côte d'Eich, Luxemburg.

The European Court superseded the Court of Justice of ECSC and is common to the three European Communities. It exists to safeguard the law in the interpretation and application of the Community treaties, to decide on the legality of decisions of Councils of Ministers or Commissions and to determine violations of the Treaties. Cases may be brought to it by the member States, the Community institutions, firms or individuals. The seven judges of the court are appointed by the member Governments in concert and hold office for 6 years, being eligible for re-appointment. The Court was inaugurated on October 7, 1958.

President, Prof. A. M. Donner (*Netherlands*).
Judges, T. R. Lecourt (*France*); M. L. Delvaux (*Belgium*); M. Ch. L. Hammes (*Luxemburg*); O. Riese (*German Federal Republic*); R. Rossi (*Italy*); A. Trabucchi (*Italy*).
Attorneys-General, L. Lagrange (*France*); M. Roemer (*German Federal Republic*).
Registrar, A. Van Houtte (*Belgium*).

EUROPEAN COAL AND STEEL COMMUNITY

This, the first of the European Communities, was established in 1952. Since then it has abolished for coal, steel, iron ore and scrap, customs duties, quantitative restrictions, the dual pricing system whereby prices charged on exported coal or steel differed from those charged to home consumers, currency restrictions and discrimination in transport rates based on the nationality of customers and the special frontier charges which made international transport of these goods within the Community dearer than transport within national frontiers. It has applied rules for fair competition and a harmonised external tariff for the whole Community.

In the ten years 1952 to 1962 Community steel production rose rapidly from 41·9 to 72·8 million tons. The coal industry, however, after expanding initially in conditions of acute energy shortage, found that a growing share of the energy market was being won by oil. The task of the High Authority thus came to be to ensure the orderly retreat of coal at a price which would preclude social or economic dislocation. So far, since the start of the crisis in 1957, the Community's coal industry has lost a quarter of its labour force. The High Authority has been especially active in meeting the social problems raised by such changes. Its readaption aid from 1953 to mid-1962 amounted to $47 million. It has also made loans for industrial development; $2·4 million to the hard-hit Borinage in Belgium. Its housing programmes have contributed to 100,000 homes, the grants, loans, etc. involved being $154 million.

The ECSC High Authority (Place de Metz 2, Luxemburg) consists of nine members whose decisions are directly binding on the industries concerned. The High Authority now supervises the smooth working of the Common Market in ECSC products, ensures that the Treaty rules of fair competition are observed, stimulates investment and research, and aids workers threatened with unemployment. In cooperation with the other two executives, it has worked out proposals for a common energy policy.

EUROPEAN ECONOMIC COMMUNITY (THE COMMON MARKET)

Discussions were held at Messina, Sicily, in 1955 between the foreign ministers of the six member states of ECSC (*see above*) on proposals for further advances towards economic integration in Europe, and after intensive study of these proposals, a treaty was signed at Rome on March 25, 1957, setting up the European Economic Community.

The Treaty aimed to lay the foundations of an enduring and closer union between the European peoples by gradually removing the economic effects of their political frontiers. The Common Market is to be established during a transition period of twelve years. The Treaty provides for the elimination of customs duties and quotas in the trade between member states; the establishment of a common customs tariff and a common commercial policy towards third countries; the abolition of the obstacles to free movement of persons, services and capital between member states; the inauguration of common policies for agriculture and transport; the establishment of a system ensuring that competition shall not be distorted in the Common Market; the coordination of economic policies; the harmonisation of social and economic legislation to the extent necessary in order to enable the Common Market to work; the creation of a European Social Fund in order to improve the possibilities of employment for workers and to contribute to the raising of their standard of living; the establishment of a European Investment Bank intended to facilitate the economic expansion of the Community through the creation of other resources; and the association of overseas countries and territories with the Community with a view to increasing trade and to pursuing jointly this effort towards economic and social development.

Reduction of Trade Barriers.—A first 10 per cent. reduction in custom duties within the Common Market took place on January 1, 1959, and import quotas of individual member states were converted to global quotas and increased. Tariffs were again reduced by 10 per cent. on July 1, 1960. The Council of the Community resolved on May 12, 1960, to speed up the process of liberalization and to aim for complete elimination of internal tariffs by 1966. An additional 10 per cent. reduction in customs duties was accordingly made on January 1, 1961. A year later a further cut of 10 per cent. was made and at the same time quota restrictions on industrial goods were abolished. More 10 per cent. cuts were made on July 1, 1962, and July 1, 1963, by which time the total internal cuts were 60 per cent.

Common External Tariff.—The treaty visualises the achievement of a common external tariff at the end of the transitional period. The first move of 30 per cent. was taken at the end of 1960, on the basis of a tariff provisionally reduced by 20 per cent. Subsequently, in negotiations with the other members of the GATT, during 1961–62, this cut was consolidated for most products. A further move of 30 per cent. towards the Common external tariff was made on July 1, 1963. In the first four years of the Common Market intra-Community trade increased by an average of 21 per cent. per annum, and the gross product of the Community rose by some 20 per cent.

Agriculture.—Detailed provision for a common policy for the marketing of the Community's major products were agreed in January, 1962. The new arrangements came into force on July 30 that year. Free trade within the Community is to be achieved by the end of the transition period (a system of degressive levies having replaced previous national tariffs) and a system of common tariffs or variable levies is to ensure a regulation of imports from non-members. A special fund has been set up to modernise farming and improve agricultural productivity in the member countries.

Transport.—The Treaty aims to establish a common policy on transport, with common rules for international transport within the Common Market, covering road, rail and inland water transport. Rates for freight which discriminate as to the national origin or destination of goods transported are to be eliminated within the transitional period. During 1962 the Commission proposed an action programme through which this common policy is to be gradually achieved by the end of the transition period.

Labour.—By the end of the transition period workers will be able to move freely throughout the Community. At present Community workers can apply for jobs advertised anywhere in the Community on the same terms as local workers, subject only to a three-week delay intended to give priority to applicants in the country in which the vacancy occurred.

Services.—Freedom for Community citizens to engage in business or professional activities anywhere in the EEC is to be achieved by the end of the transition period. The present programme is divided into four stages, in each of which specified sectors are liberalized. Studies of how to harmonize university degrees and other qualifications are proceeding.

Capital.—So far unconditional and complete freedom of movement has been achieved for direct investments, transfers of personal funds and emigrants' remittances, short and medium term commercial loans and the buying and selling of stocks and shares. For other transactions, such as capital issues, there is conditional liberalization. Ways are being sought to equalize access to domestic capital markets within the Six.

Rules for Fair Competition.—The Common Market Treaty bans agreements which prevent, restrain or distort competition and, in particular, price-fixing, market-sharing, restriction of production or of technical development and discriminatory supply conditions if they are likely to affect trade between member-states. The abuse of a dominant position in the market by a firm or firms is also banned. The Commission has been given strong powers of inspection and control and has already caused some 40,000 restrictive agreements to be registered.

Economic Policy.—Member states are required by the Treaty to consider their economic policies as matters of common interest, and to consult with each other and the Commission in order to concert these policies. The Commission undertakes annual economic forecasts, quarterly economic surveys, and monthly business surveys to help towards this end. In its Action Programme of October 1962 it proposed that these economic programming activities should be considerably extended—especially in order to guide national economic planning within the Six.

Social Policy.—Under the Treaty member states agree upon the necessity to promote improvement of the living and working conditions of labour so as to permit the equalization of such conditions in an upward direction. They are also to cooperate closely on matters relating to employment, labour legislation and working conditions, occupational training, social security, industrial accidents and diseases, industrial hygiene and trade union law. Equal pay for men and women is also required and a regulation was agreed in December, 1961, by which all discrimination was to be abolished by the end of 1964. The Commission's most important instrument of social policy is the European Social Fund which promotes employment and the mobility of workers within the community by means of vocational retraining, resettlement and other aids. It provides 50 per cent. of expenditure undertaken by the Six governments in the productive re-employment of workers. By December 31, 1962 the Fund had paid out $12,291,798 in this way. The European Investment Bank, with a capital of $1000 million, aids investments in the Community's underdeveloped regions and helps financial modernization of new activities of general Community interest. By the end of 1962 the Bank had approved 37 loans totalling slightly over $250 million.

The Association of Overseas Territories and Countries.—The Community assumes special responsibility for the development of the overseas States associated with it which are largely in Africa. A new Association Agreement was signed in July, 1963 to last, like the first agreement, for five years. Under this Community tariffs on some exports from associated countries will be abolished immediately, while their remaining exports will continue to benefit from the progressive reduction of Community duties. In principle the associated countries' tariffs on imports from the Community will be reduced by 15 per cent. annually but in practice they will be allowed to maintain old tariffs or create new ones where these increases are required to maintain infant industries. The Community will also provide, through the European Development Fund, aid totalling $800 million over the five year period.

Budget of EEC.—Contributions to the Budget of EEC were fixed in the following proportions: France, Italy and German Federal Republic, each 28 per cent.; Belgium and the Netherlands, each 7·9 per cent.; Luxemburg 0·2 per cent. In the autumn of 1961, after consultation with members of the British Commonwealth, the United Kingdom Government made formal application for membership of the Common Market. Negotiations terminated in February, 1963, after General de Gaulle made it plain that France was opposed to British entry.

EUROPEAN ATOMIC ENERGY COMMUNITY
(Euratom)

Council of Ministers, Rue Ravenstein 2, Brussels 1.

A second treaty, arising from the Messina discussions between the ECSC powers on additional means of co-operation, was signed in Rome on March 25, 1957, setting up the European Atomic Energy Community. The task of *Euratom*, defined in detail in the Treaty, is to create within a short period the technical and industrial conditions necessary to utilize nuclear discoveries and especially to produce nuclear energy on a large scale. A five-member commission was instituted by the Treaty, to promote and co-ordinate nuclear research in member countries and to disseminate to them all the information acquired. Other sections of the Treaty cover the establishment and growth of nuclear industries, the procurement, ownership and control of nuclear materials, matters affecting health and safety, including training, and external relations. A chairman (from member countries in turn) is elected to hold office for six months.

The Euratom Commission consists of five members, who can in a number of cases issue directly binding regulations. The Commission's task is to help create within the Community a powerful industry for the peaceful use of atomic energy, to stimulate scientific research and the training of specialists, to help administer a Supply Agency through which all nuclear fuel can be channelled, to supervise the nuclear common market, to inspect and control the use of fissile material, and to safeguard both workers and the population at large by laying down basic standards for the protection of health.

Atomic Energy Commission
Rue Belliard 51, Brussels 4.

President, Pierre Chatenet (*France*).
Vice-President, E. Medi (*Italy*).
Members, M. de Groote (*Belgium*); Herr Krekeler (*German Federal Republic*); Hr. Sassen (*Netherlands*).

ECONOMIC AND SOCIAL COUNCIL

An advisory body, common to EEC and *Euratom*, the Council consists of representatives of all sections of economic and social life, including employers' associations, trade unions and similar organizations. The Council consists of 24 members each from France, Italy and the German Federal Republic; 12 each from Belgium and the Netherlands and 5 from Luxemburg.

JOINT EXECUTIVE SERVICES
of the European Communities

JOINT INFORMATION SERVICE.—*Director*, Jacques-René Rabier. *Assistant Director*, Mario Melani. There are offices of the Joint Information Service in Paris, Bonn, Rome, The Hague, London and Washington.

JOINT LEGAL SERVICE.—*Directors-General*, Michel Gaudet (*EEC Matters*); Robert Krawielicki (*ECSC matters*); Theodor Vogelaar (*Euratom matters*). *Assistant Director-General* (*EEC matters*), Marc Sohier.

EUROPEAN STATISTICAL OFFICE.—*Director-General*, Rolf Wagenführ. *Assistant Director-General*, Helmut Reum.

BRITISH AMBASSADOR TO THE EUROPEAN COMMUNITY
Brussels

Ambassador Extraordinary and Plenipotentiary, His Excellency Hon. Sir Con Douglas Walter O'Neil, K.C.M.G. (1963)

EUROPEAN FREE TRADE ASSOCIATION
(EFTA)

Early in 1956 moves were made in OEEC by the low tariff countries in Europe—Belgium, Denmark, Luxemburg, the Netherlands, Sweden and Switzerland—towards organization of a wide free trade area in Europe. Proposals were studied on a multilateral basis in 1957 and 1958 but were not acceptable to all parties. On May 27, 1959, Sweden invited Austria, Denmark, Norway, Portugal, Switzerland and the United Kingdom ("The Seven") to join with her in exploring the possibility of forming a free trade area. Discussions began in Stockholm in June, 1959, and a Convention for a European Free Trade Association, agreed by Ministers of the "Seven" on Nov. 20, 1959, became effective on May 5, 1960. On July 1, 1961, Finland became an associate member of EFTA.

The Convention defines the objects of the Association as (1) to promote economic expansion in the area of the Association and in each member state; (2) to ensure that trade between member states takes place in conditions of fair competition; (3) to prevent significant disparity between member states in the conditions of supply of raw materials produced within the area; and (4) to contribute to the harmonious development and expansion of world trade and to the progressive removal of barriers to it.

Members agreed to reduce progressively their tariffs on imports of industrial goods originating in the Area with a view to their complete elimination by January 1, 1970. They also undertook to abolish quantitative restrictions on imports of goods from the free trade area within 10 years, existing quotas being increased by at least 20 per cent. each year. Provision was made for alterations in these timetables and in May, 1963, when tariffs had been reduced to 50 per cent. of the original rates, members agreed to bring forward the date when tariffs would be finally eliminated to December 31, 1966. They undertook to abolish quantitative restrictions by the same date. There is no common external tariff for the Association, each member country being free to fix the level of its tariffs against countries outside the area. Various rules govern trading within the area of goods manufactured wholly or in part from materials originating outside the area and fair conditions of competition—such matters as government subsidies, restrictive practices, dumping, etc. Special arrangements are in force in relation to agricultural produce and fish.

The Council of EFTA consists of one ministerial or official representative from each member country. Each state has a single vote and recommendations must normally be unanimous. Decisions of the Council are binding on member countries.

DISTANCES FROM LONDON BY AIR

A list of the distances in statute miles from London to various places abroad. Distances given are those of the shortest routes in use by the British Airways Corporations—B.O.A.C. services(*O*); B.E.A.services(*E*).

To	Miles	To	Miles	To	Miles
Abadan (*O*)	3,110	Dar-es-Salaam (*O*)	4,897	Montreal (*O*)	3,402
Accra (*O*)	3,814	Darwin (*O*)	9,974	Moscow (*E*)	1,549
Aden (*O*)	3,946	Delhi (*O*)	5,203	Munich (*E*)	588
Ajaccio (*E*)	791	Detroit (*O*)	3 984	Nairobi (*O*)	4,451
Amman (*O*)	2,637	Djakarta (*O*)	8,413	Naples (*E*)	1,012
Amsterdam (*E*)	231	Doha (*O*)	3,541	Nassau (*O*)	4,429
Athens (*E*)	1,501	Düsseldorf (*E*)	311	New York (*O*)	3,500
Auckland (*O*)	13,496	Entebbe (*O*)	4,470	Nicosia (Cyprus) (*E*)	2,028
Baghdad (*O*)	2,980	Frankfurt (*E*)	406	Oslo (*E*)	722
Bahrain (*O*)	3,523	Geneva (*E*)	468	Palma (Majorca) (*E*)	834
Bangkok (*O*)	6,845	Gibraltar (*E*)	1,085	Paris (*E*)	215
Barbados (*O*)	4,888	Hamburg (*E*)	463	Rangoon (*O*)	6,622
Barcelona (*E*)	713	Hanover (*E*)	436	Rio de Janeiro (*O*)	5,973
Basle (*E*)	446	Hong Kong (*O*)	8,056	Rome (*E*)	908
Beirut (*O*)....2,292; (*E*)	2,162	Honolulu (*O*)	8,611	Salzburg (*E*)	652
Berlin (*E*)	593	Istanbul (*E*)	1,562	San Francisco (*O*)	6,161
Bermuda (*O*)	3,501	Johannesburg (*O*)	6,299	Santiago (*O*)	8,140
Biarritz (*E*)	555	Kano (*O*)	2,869	Sao Paulo (*O*)	6,270
Bogotá (*O*)	6,139	Karachi (*O*)	4,427	Singapore (*O*)	7,797
Bombay (*O*)	5,080	Khartoum (*O*)	3,241	Stavanger (*E*)	564
Bordeaux (*E*)	458	Kingston (Jamaica) (*O*)	5,200	Stockholm (*E*)	899
Boston (*O*)	3,385	Kuala Lumpur (*O*)	7,582	Sydney (*O*)	11,941
Brisbane (*O*)	12,289	Kuwait (*O*)	3,254	Teheran (*O*)	3,229
Brussels (*E*)	218	Lagos (*O*)	3,564	Tel Aviv (*E*)	2,230
Buenos Aires. (*O*)	7,406	Lima (*O*)	7,312	Tokyo (*O*)	9 927
Cairo (*O*)	2,280	Lisbon (*E*)	972	Toronto(*O*)	3,728
Calcutta (*O*)	5,835	Los Angeles (*O*)	6,462	Trinidad (*O*)	5,023
Caracas (*O*)	5,410	Madrid(*E*)	775	Tripoli (*E*)	1,520
Chicago (*O*)	4,235	Malta (*E*)	1,306	Venice (*E*)	703
Cologne (*E*)	331	Mauritius (*O*)	6,524	Vienna (*E*)	791
Colombo (*O*)	5,189	Melbourne (*O*)	13,221	Warsaw (*E*)	914
Copenhagen (*E*)	609	Milan (*E*)	581	Washington (*O*)	3,774
Dakar (*O*)	2,800	Montego Bay (*O*)	5,122	Zürich (*E*)	491
Damascus (*O*)	2,484	Montevideo (*O*)	7,390		

NORTH ATLANTIC TREATY ORGANIZATION

Headquarters: Porte Dauphine, Paris 16.

The North Atlantic Treaty was signed on April 4, 1949, by the Foreign Ministers of twelve nations. The twelve are Belgium, Canada, Denmark, France, Iceland, Italy, Luxemburg, the Netherlands, Norway, Portugal, the United Kingdom and United States. Greece and Turkey acceded to the Treaty in 1952 and the Federal Republic of Germany in 1955. Since April, 1952, the *North Atlantic Council*, principal body of the Treaty Organization, has been in continuous session in Paris. Member Governments are represented by permanent representatives, who head national delegations of advisers and experts. *Permanent U.K. Representative*, Sir Evelyn Shuckburgh, K.C.M.G., C.B. The senior military authority in NATO is the Military Committee (composed of a Chief-of-Staff of each member country), which is responsible for higher strategic direction throughout the North Atlantic Treaty area.

A Secretary-General is appointed by and is responsible to the Council. He has direct access to all NATO agencies and to member Governments, is responsible for organizing the work of the International Secretariat and serves as Chairman. Each year a Foreign Minister is President of the Council.

Secretary-General, M. Dirk U. Stikker (*Netherlands*).
Deputy Secretary-General, Sig. Guido Colonna (*Italy*).
Asst. Secretaries-General, R. Hooper (*U.K.*) (*Political Affairs*); Francois-Didier Gregh (*France*) (*Economic and Financial*); Johnson Garrett (*U.S.A.*) (*Production, etc.*); Dr. W. P. Allis (*U.S.A.*) (*Scientific*).
Executive Secretary, The Lord Coleridge, C.B.E. (*U.K.*).

Supreme Commander, Allied Powers in Europe, Gen. Lyman L. Lemnitzer (*U.S.A.*).
Allied Commander, North Atlantic, Adm. Harold Page Smith (*U.S.A.*).
Allied Commander, Channel, Adm. Sir Wilfrid Woods, K.C.B., D.S.O., (*U.K.*).

WORLD TRADE

(Value in million U.S. $)

Countries	Exports (f.o.b.)			Imports (c.i.f.)		
	1960	1961	1962	1960	1961	1962
World Total (a)	*112,700*	*117,800*	*123,700*	*118,800*	*123,900*	*131,700*
North America	*25,937*	*26,565*	*27,300*	*20,726*	*20,394*	*22,180*
Canada	5,554	5,810	5,926	5,655	5,692	5,846
United States	20,383	20,755	21,374	15,071	14,702	16,334
Latin America	*8,600*	*8,660*	*9,200*	*8,240*	*8,560*	*8,840*
Argentina	1,079	964	1,210	1,249	1,460	1,350
Brazil	1,269	1,403	1,214	1,462	1,460	1,475
Chile	490	508	532	500	585	518
Colombia	465	434	464	519	557	540
Dominican Rep.	180	143	172	87	69	123
Ecuador	144	125	140	100	94	97
Mexico	763	826	937	1,186	1,139	1,143
Peru	431	494	538	373	468	538
Venezuela	2,432	2,413	2,586	1,060	1,051	1,061
Western Europe	*51,240*	*54,870*	*57,920*	*56,770*	*60,470*	*65,800*
Austria	1,120	1,202	1,263	1,416	1,485	1,552
Belgium-Luxemburg	3,775	3,924	4,324	3,957	4,219	4,555
Denmark	1,493	1,537	1,660	1,805	1,873	2,129
Finland	989	1,054	1,104	1,063	1,153	1,228
France	6,862	7,210	7,360	6,276	6,678	7,519
Germany	11,415	12,687	13,264	10,104	10,941	12,279
Italy	3,648	4,183	4,666	4,721	5,223	6,056
Netherlands	4,028	4,307	4,585	4,531	5,112	5,348
Norway	881	931	973	1,462	1,616	1,654
Portugal	328	326	367	546	656	586
Spain (b)	725	710	722	721	1,092	1,568
Sweden	2,564	2,743	2,922	2,899	2,927	3,114
Switzerland	1,879	2,041	2,216	2,243	2,707	3,020
Turkey	321	347	381	468	509	622
Yugoslavia	566	569	690	826	910	888
Sterling Area	*23,760*	*24,520*	*25,410*	*28,850*	*28,110*	*28,940*
Australia	1,962	2,324	2,349	2,365	2,094	2,262
Ceylon	385	364	380	412	358	349
Hong Kong	689	688	768	1,026	1,045	1,165
India	1,331	1,386	1,409	2,293	2,260	2,310
Irish Republic	428	505	485	633	732	766
Malaya	956	858	856	703	728	799
New Zealand	846	793	798	790	901	753
Nigeria	475	481	467	604	623	568
Pakistan	393	400	397	654	642	738
Rhodesia and Nyasaland Fed.	576	579	587	439	434	400
Singapore	1,136	1,081	1,170	1,332	1,295	1,367
United Kingdom	9,953	10,308	10,617	12,319	11,862	12,136
South Africa (c)	1,238	1,333	1,333	1,556	1,406	1,436
West Indies (d)	1,081	1,233	..	1,192	1,263	..
Rest of World						
Algeria	394	368	..	1,265	1,024	..
U.A.R.	568	485	399	667	678	721
Indonesia	840	784	..	574	794	..
Iraq	654	662	692	391	408	363
Japan	4,055	4,236	4,916	4,491	5,810	5,637
Morocco	354	343	348	413	452	434
Philippines	560	499	551	604	611	587
Tunisia	120	110	116	191	211	216
Africa	*6,400*	*6,560*	*6,750*	*8,020*	*7,890*	*7,630*

(*a*) World total exclusive of China (Mainland), U.S.S.R., and Eastern European countries not mentioned for which data are not reported currently. (*b*) Including Canary Islands. (*c*) Including S.W. Africa. (*d*) Including Netherlands Antilles.

THE NOBEL PRIZES

The Nobel Prizes are awarded each year from the income of a trust fund established by the Swedish scientist Alfred Nobel, the inventor of dynamite, who died on December 10, 1896, leaving a fortune of £1,750,000. They are awarded to those who have contributed most to the common good in the domain of (*a*) Physics; (*b*) Chemistry; (*c*) Physiology or Medicine; (*d*) Literature; (*e*) Peace. The first awards were made in 1901 on the fifth anniversary of Nobel's death. The awarding authorities are the Swedish Academy of Sciences—(*a*) Physics; (*b*) Chemistry; the Royal Caroline Institute, Stockholm—(*c*) Physiology or Medicine; the Swedish Academy—(*d*) Literature; a committee of five persons elected by the Norwegian Storthing—(*e*) Peace. The Trust is administered by the Board of Directors of the Nobel Foundation, Stockholm. The Board consists of four members and two deputy members appointed by the awarding authorities; the Swedish Government appoints a chairman and a deputy chairman.

The nationality of prizewinners is indicated as follows: (a) Great Britain; (b) U.S.A.; (c) France; (d) Sweden; (e) Belgium; (f) U.S.S.R.; (g) Germany; (h) Netherlands; (i) Switzerland; (k) Denmark; (l) Norway; (m) Spain; (n) Poland; (o) Austria; (p) Italy; (q) India; (r) Hungary; (s) Finland; (t) Canada; (u) Chile; (v) Argentine; (w) Japan; (x) Portugal; (y) Irish Free State; (z) Republic of Ireland; (aa) South Africa; (bb) Iceland; (cc) China; (dd) Czechoslovakia; (ee) Australia; (ff) Yugoslavia. The distribution by nationalities is shown at foot of table.

For prize winners for the years 1901–1946, *see* earlier editions of WHITAKER'S ALMANACK.

Year	(*a*) PHYSICS	(*b*) CHEMISTRY	(c) PHYSIOLOGY OR MEDICINE	(*d*) LITERATURE	(*e*) PEACE
1947	Sir Edward Appleton (a)	Sir Robert Robinson (a)	Prof. and Mrs. C. F. Cori (b) and B. A. Houssay (v)	André Gide (c)	The Society of Friends.
1948	P. M. S. Blackett (a)	A. Tiselius (d)	P. H. Müller (i)	T. S. Eliot (a)	*No award*
1949	H. Yukawa (w)	W. F. Giauque (b)	W. R. Hess (i) A. E. Moniz (x)	W. Faulkner (b)	Lord Boyd Orr (a)
1950	C. F. Powell (a)	O. Diels (g) K. Alder (g)	E. C. Kendall (b) T. Reichstein (i) P. S. Hench (b)	Earl Russell (a)	R. Bunche (b)
1951	Sir John Cockcroft (a) E. T. S. Walton (z)	E. M. McMillan (b) G. T. Seaborg (b)	M. Theiler (aa)	P. Lagerkvist (d)	L. Jouhaux (c)
1952	F. Bloch (b) E. M. Purcell (b)	A. J. P. Martin (a) R. L. M. Synge (a)	S. A. Waksman (b)	F. Mauriac (c)	A. Schweitzer (c)
1953	F. Zernike (h)	H. Staudinger (g)	H. A. Krebs (a) F. A. Lipmann (b)	Sir Winston Churchill (a)	G. C. Marshall (b)
1954	M. Born (a) W. Bothe (g)	L. C. Pauling (b)	J. F. Enders (b) T. H. Weller (b) F. C. Robbins (b)	E. Hemingway (b)	Office of the U.N.H.C.R.
1955	W. E. Lamb (b) P. Kusch (b)	V. du Vigneaud (b)	A. H. T. Theorell (d)	H. K. Laxness (bb)	*No award*
1956	W. Shockley (b) J. Bardeen (b) W. H. Brattain (b)	Sir Cyril Hinshelwood (a) N. N. Semenov (f)	A. F. Cournand (b) W. Forssmann (g) D. W. Richards, Jr. (b)	J. R. Jiménez (m)	*No award*
1957	C. N. Yang (cc) T. D. Lee (cc)	Sir Alexander Todd (a)	D. Bovet (p)	A. Camus (c)	L. Pearson (t)
1958	P. A. Čerenkov (f) I. M. Frank (f) I. E. Tamm (f)	F. Sanger (a)	G. W. Beadle (b) E. L. Tatum (b) J. Lederberg (b)	B. L. Pasternak (f)	G. Pire (e)
1959	E. Segrè (b) O. Chamberlain (b)	J. Heyrovský (dd)	S. Ochoa (b) A. Kornberg (b)	S. Quasimodo (p)	P. J. Noel-Baker (a)
1960	D. A. Glaser (b)	W. F. Libby (b)	Sir Macfarlane Burnet (ee) P. B. Medawar (a)	St. J. Perse (c)	A. Luthuli (aa)
1961	R. Hofstadter (b) R. Mössbauer (g)	M. Calvin (b)	G. von Békésy (b)	I. Andric (ff)	D. Hammarskjöld (d)
1962	L. D. Landau (f)	M. F. Perutz (a) J. C. Kendrew (a)	F. H. C. Crick (a) J. D. Watson (b) M. H. F. Wilkins (a)	J. Steinbeck (b)	L. Pauling (b)

The awards have been distributed as follows:—PHYSICS:—*U.S.A.*, 20; *Gt. Britain*, 15; *Germany*, 13; *France*, 7; *Netherlands*, 5; *Austria*, 3; *U.S.S.R.*, 4; *Sweden*, 2; *Italy*, 2; *China*, 2; *India*, 1; *Denmark*, 1; *Japan*, 1; *Republic of Ireland*, 1. CHEMISTRY:—*Germany*, 20; *U.S.A.*, 13; *Gt. Britain*, 14; *France*, 6; *Sweden*, 4; *Switzerland*, 3; *Netherlands*, 2; *Hungary*, 1; *Austria*, 1; *Finland*, 1; *U.S.S.R.*, 1; *Czechoslovakia*, 1. PHYSIOLOGY OR MEDICINE:— *U.S.A.*, 27; *Gt. Britain*, 13; *Germany*, 9; *Denmark*, 4; *Switzerland*, 4; *France*, 3; *Austria*, 3; *Belgium*, 2; *Canada*, 2; *Italy*, 2; *Netherlands*, 2; *Hungary*, 2; *U.S.S.R.*, 2; *Sweden*, 2; *Spain*, 1; *Argentine*, 1; *Australia* 1; *Portugal*, 1; *South Africa*, 1. LITERATURE:—*France* 10; *Gt. Britain*, 6; *Germany*, 5; *U.S.A.*, 6; *Italy*, 4; *Sweden*, 4; *Norway*, 3; *Denmark*, 3; *Spain*, 3; *Poland*, 2; *Switzerland*, 2; *U.S.S.R.*, 2; *Belgium*, 1; *India*, 1; *Finland*, 1; *Chile*, 1; *Irish Free State*, 1; *Iceland*, 1; *Yugoslavia*, 1. PEACE:—*U.S.A.*, 13; *France*, 8; *Gt. Britain*, 7; *Sweden*, 4; *Germany*, 3; *Switzerland*, 3; *Belgium*, 3; *Norway*, 2; *Austria*, 2; *Argentina*, 1; *Canada*, 1; *Denmark*, 1; *Italy*, 1; *Netherlands*, 1; *South Africa*, 1.

RETROSPECT OF SPORT 1962–63

VIIth EMPIRE AND COMMONWEALTH GAMES

Held in PERTH, Australia, November 22–December 1, 1962

Athletics

MEN'S EVENTS

	Time h. m. s.
100 yards.—S. Antao (Kenya)	9·5
220 yards.—S. Antao (Kenya)	21·1
440 yards.—G. Kerr (Jamaica)	46·7
880 yards.—P. Snell (N.Z.)	1 47·6
Mile.—P. Snell (N.Z.)	4 04·6
3 miles.—M. Halberg (N.Z.)	13 34·2
6 miles.—B. Kidd (Canada)	28 26·6
Marathon.—B. Kilby (England)	2 21 17
120 yards Hurdles.—G. Raziq (Pakistan)	14·3
440 yards Hurdles.—K. Roche (Australia)	51·5
Steeplechase.—T. Vincent (Australia)	8 43·4
440 yards Relay—England (P. Radford, L. Carter, A. Meakin, O. Jones)	40·6
Mile Relay.—Jamaica (M. Spence, L. Kahn, Mel Spence, G. Kerr)	3 10·2

	ft.	in.
High Jump.—P. Hobson (Australia)	6	11
Pole Vault.—T. Bickle (Australia)	14	9
Long Jump.—M. Ahey (Ghana)	26	5
Triple Jump.—I. Tomlinson (Australia)	53	2
Shot.—M. Lucking (England)	59	4
Discus.—W. Selvey (Australia)	185	3½
Hammer.—A. Payne (England)	202	3
Javelin.—A. Mitchell (Australia)	256	3

WOMEN'S EVENTS

	Time m. s.
100 yards.—D. Hyman (England)	11·2
220 yards.—D. Hyman (England)	23·8
880 yards.—D. Willis (Australia)	2 03·7
Hurdles.—P. Kilborn (Australia)	10·9
440 yards Relay—Australia	46·6

	ft.	in.
High Jump.—R. Woodhouse (Australia)	5	10
Long Jump.—P. Kilborn (Australia)	20	6¾
Shot.—V. Young (N.Z.)	49	11½
Discus.—V. Young (N.Z.)	164	8½
Javelin.—S. Platt (England)	164	10½

Bowls

	Points
Singles.—D. Bryant (England)	24
Pairs.—New Zealand (R. McDonald, H. Robson)	18
Fours.—England (D. Bryant, G. Fleming, J. Watson, S. Drysdale)	16

Boxing

Flyweight.—R. Mallon (Scotland)
Bantamweight.—J. Dynevor (Australia).
Featherweight.—J. McDermott (Scotland).
Lightweight.—E. Blay (Ghana).
Light-Welterweight.—C. Quartey (Ghana).
Welterweight.—W. Coe (New Zealand).
Light-Middleweight.—H. Mann (Canada).
Middleweight.—C. Colquohoun (Jamaica).
Light-Heavyweight.—A. Madigan (Australia).
Heavyweight.—G. Oywello (Uganda).

Cycling

	Time h. m. s.
1,000 m. Sprint.—T. Harrison (Australia)	
1,000 m Time Trial.—P. Bartels (Australia)	1 12·9
4,000 m. Pursuit.—M. Langshaw (Australia)	5 08·8
10 miles Track.—D. Adams (Australia)	22 14·8
120 miles Road.—W. Mason (England)	5 20 26·2

Fencing

	Wins	Defeats
Foil (Individual).—A Leckie (Scotland)	7	1
Epée (Individual).—I. Lund (Australia)	7	1

Fencing—*continued*

	Wins	Defeats
Sabre (Individual).—A. Cooperman (England)	7	1
Foil (Team).—England (A. Cooperman, A. Jay, R. Paul, M. Howard)	4	0
Epée (Team).—England (M. Howard P. Jacobs, J. Pelling)	4	0
Sabre (Team).—England (M. Amberg, A. Cooperman, G. Birks)	4	0
Foil (Women).—M. Coleman (N.Z.)	6	1

Rowing

	Time m. s.
Single Sculls.—J. Hill (N.Z.)	7 39·7
Double Sculls.—England (G. Justicz, N. Birkmyre)	6 52·4
Pairs.—England (S. Farquharson, J. Lee Nicholson)	7 03·7
Coxed Fours.—New Zealand (W. Stephens, K. Heselwood, H. Smedley, G. Paterson, D. Pulman)	6 48·2
Coxless Fours.—England (C. Davidge, M. Clay, J. Beveridge, J. Tilbury)	6 31·1
Eights.—Australia	5 53·4

Swimming

MEN'S EVENTS

	Time m. s.
110 yards Free Style.—R. Pound (Canada)	55·8
440 yards Free Style.—M. Rose (Australia)	4 20·0
1,650 yards Free Style.—M. Rose (Australia)	17 18·1
110 yards Backstroke.—G. Sykes (England)	64·5
220 yards Backstroke.—J. Carroll (Australia)	2 20·9
110 yards Breaststroke.—I. O'Brien (Australia)	1 11·4
220 yards Breaststroke.—I. O'Brien (Australia)	2 38·2
110 yards Butterfly.—K. Berry (Australia)	59·5
220 yards Butterfly.—K. Berry (Australia)	2 10·8
440 yards Individual Relay.—A. Alexander (Australia)	5 15·3
4×*110 yards Free Style Relay.*—Australia (P. Phelps, M. Rose, P. Doak, D. Dickson)	3 43·9
4×*220 yards Free-Style Relay.*—Australia (M. Rose, A. Wood, C. Strahan, B. Windle)	8 13·4
4×*110 yards Medley Relay.*—Australia (J. Carroll, I. O'Brien, K. Berry, D. Dickson)	4 12·4

	Points
Springboard Diving.—B. Phelps (England)	154·14
Highboard Diving.—B. Phelps (England)	168·35

Swimming

WOMEN'S EVENTS

	Time min. sec.
110 yards Freestyle.—D. Fraser (Australia)	59·5
440 yards Freestyle.—D. Fraser (Australia)	4 51·4
110 yards Backstroke.—L. Ludgrove (England)	1 11·1
220 yards Backstroke.—L. Ludgrove (England)	2 35·2
110 yards Breaststroke.—A. Lonsbrough (England)	1 21·3
220 yards Breaststroke.—A. Lonsbrough (England)	2 51·7
110 yards Butterfly.—M. Stewart (Canada)	1 10·1
440 yards Individual Medley.—A. Lonsbrough (England)	5 38·6
4×*110 yards Freestyle Relay.*—Australia (L. Bell, R. Eevruss, R. Thorn, D. Fraser)	4 11·0
4×*110 Medley Relay.*—Australia (P. Sargeant, M. Ruygrok, L. McGill, D. Fraser)	4 45·9

	Points
Springboard Diving.—S. Knight (Australia)	134·72
Highboard Diving.—S. Knight (Australia)	101·15

Weightlifting	Pounds
Bantamweight.—Chua Phung Kim (Singapore)	710
Featherweight.—G. Newton (England)	720
Lightweight.—C. Goring (England)	775
Middleweight.—Tan Howe Liang (Singapore)	860
Light-Heavyweight.—P. Caira (Scotland)	900
Middle-Heavyweight.—L. Martin (England)	1,035
Heavyweight.—A. Shannos (Australia)	1,025

Wrestling

Flyweight.—M. Niaz (Pakistan).
Bantamweight.—D. Siraj (Pakistan).
Featherweight.—Ala-uddin (Pakistan).
Welterweight.—M. Bashir (Pakistan)
Middleweight.—M. Faiz (Pakistan)
Lightheavyweight.—A. Buck (England)
Heavyweight.—N. Muhammad (Pakistan)

WORLD'S ATHLETIC RECORDS

* (All the world records given below have been accepted by the International Amateur Athletic Federation with the exception of those marked thus (*) which await ratification and are likely to be accepted.)

Distance	*Time* hr. min. sec	*Name*	*Nation*	*Year*
100 yards	9·2	F. J. Budd	U.S.A.	1961
,,	9·2	H. W. Jerome	Canada	1962
,,	9·1*	R. Hayes	U.S.A.	1963
100 metres	10·0	A. Hary	Germany	1960
,,	10·0	H. W. Jerome	Canada	1960
200 metres (straight)	20·0	D. W Sime	U.S.A.	1956
,,	20·0	F. Budd	U.S.A.	1962
200 metres (curve)	20·5	P. F. Radford	G.B.	1960
,,	20·5	S. Johnson	U.S.A.	1960
,,	20·5	R. Norton	U.S.A.	1960
,,	20.5	L. Berruti	Italy	1960
,,	20·5	P. Drayton	U.S.A.	1962
,,	20·3*	H. Carr	U.S.A.	1963
220 yards (straight)	20·0	D. W. Sime	U.S.A.	1956
,,	20·0	F. Budd	U.S.A.	1962
220 yards (curve)	20·5	P. F. Radford	G.B.	1960
,,	20·5	P. Drayton	U.S.A.	1962
,,	20·3*	H. Carr	U.S.A.	1963
400 metres	44·9	O. Davis	U.S.A.	1960
,,	44·9	C. Kaufmann	Germany	1960
440 yards	45·7	G. A. Davis	U.S.A.	1958
,,	44·9*	A. Plummer	U.S.A.	1963
800 metres	1 44·3	P. G. Snell	New Zealand	1962
880 yards	1 45·1	P. G. Snell	New Zealand	1962
1,000 metres	2 16·7	S. Valentin	Germany	1960
1,500 metres	3 35·6	H. J. Elliott	Australia	1960
One Mile	3 54·4	P. G. Snell	New Zealand	1962
2,000 metres	5 01·6	M. Jazy	France	1962
3,000 metres	7 49·2	M. Jazy	France	1962
2 miles	8 29·8	J. Beatty	U.S.A.	1962
,,	8 29·6*	M. Jazy	France	1963
3 miles	13 10·0	M. G. Halberg	N.Z.	1961
5,000 metres	13 35·0	V. Kuts	U.S.S.R.	1957
6 miles	27 43·8	S. Iharos	Hungary	1960
10,000 metres	28 18·2	P. Bolotnikov	U.S.S.R.	1962
10 miles	47 47·0	B. B. Heatley	G.B.	1961
20,000 metres	59 51·8	E. Zatopek	Czechoslovakia	1951
,,	59 28·6*	W. Baillie	New Zealand	1963
15 miles	1 14 01·0	E. Zatopek	Czechoslovakia	1955
25,000 metres	1 16 36·4	E. Zatopek	Czechoslovakia	1955
30,000 metres	1 34 41·2	A. Vandendriesche	Belguim	1962
12 miles 810 yards	One hour	E. Zatopek	Czechoslovakia	1951
12 miles 960 yards	,,	W. Baillie	New Zealand	1963
3,000 metres steeplechase	8 30·4	Z. Krzyszkowiak	Poland	1961
,,	8 29·6*	G. Roelants	Belgium	1963
Hurdling				
120 yards (3 ft. 6 in.)	13·2	M. Lauer	Germany	1959
,,	13·2	L. Calhoun	U.S.A.	1960
110 metres	13·2	M. Lauer	Germany	1959
,,	13·2	L. Calhoun	U.S.A.	1960
200 metres (2 ft. 6 in.) (straight)	21·9	D. Styron	U.S.A.	1960
200 metres (curve)	22·5	M. Lauer	Germany	1959
,,	22·5	G. Davis	U.S.A.	1960
220 yards (straight)	21·9	D. Styron	U.S.A.	1960
220 yards (curve)	22·7	C. Tidewell	U.S.A.	1958
400 metres (3 ft.)	49·2	G. Davis	U.S.A.	1958
,,	49·2	S. Morale	Italy	1962

WORLD'S ATHLETIC RECORDS—*continued*

Distance	*Time*		*Nation*	*Year*
440 yards	49·7	G. Potgieter	S. Africa	1958
,,	49·3★	G. Potgieter	S. Africa	1960

Relay Racing	*Distance*	*Time*	*Nation*	*Year*
	4×100 metres	39·1	United States	1961
	4×110 yards (1 turn)	39·6	United States	1959
	4×110 yards (2 turns)	40·0	United States	1962
	,,	40·0★	Great Britain	1963
	4×200 metres	1 22·6	United States	1958
	4×220 yards	1 22·6	United States	1958
	4×400 metres	3 02·2	United States	1960
	4×440 yards	3 05·6	United States	1960
	4×800 metres	7 15·8	Belgium	1956
	4×880 yards	7 19·4	United States	1960
	4×1,500 metres	15 04·2	France	1961
	,,	14 58·0★	East German Team	1963
	4×1 mile	16 09·0	University of Japan	1962

Jumping and Throwing	ft.	in.	*Name*	*Nation*	*Year*
High Jump	7	5¾★	V. Brumel	U.S.S.R.	1963
Pole Vault	16	2½	P. Nikula	Finland	1962
,,	17	0¾★	J. Pennell	U.S.A.	1963
Long Jump	27	3	Ter Ovanesian	U.S.S.R.	1962
Triple Jump	55	10½	J. Schmidt	Poland	1960
Shot	65	10½	D. Long	U.S.A.	1962
Discus	204	10½	A. Oerter	U.S.A.	1962
,,	205	5½	A. Oerter	U.S.A.	1963
Hammer	231	10	H. V. Connolly	U.S.A.	1962
Javelin	284	7	C. Lievore	Italy	1961
Decathlon	8.683 pts		R. Johnson	U.S.A.	1960
,,	9,121★		Y. Chuan Kwang	Formosa	1963

Walking	hr. min. sec.		*Nation*	*Year*
20,000 metres	1 27 05·0	V. Golubnichiy	U.S.S.R.	1958
30,000 metres	2 17 16·8	A. Yegorov	U.S.S.R.	1959
20 miles	2 31 33·0	A. Vedyakov	U.S.S.R.	1958
30 miles	4 04 56·8	A. Pamich	Italy	1961
50,000 metres	4 14 02·4	A Pamich	Italy	1961
16 miles 743 yards	Two hours	A. Yegorov	U.S.S.R.	1959

WOMEN'S EVENTS

Running Distance	*Time* min. sec.	*Name*	*Nation*	*Year*
60 metres	7·2	B. Cuthbert	Australia	1960
,,	7·2	I. Bochkareva	U.S.S.R.	1960
100 yards	10·3	M. Mathews	Australia	1958
100 metres	11·2	W. Rudolph	U.S.A.	1961
200 metres	22·9	W. Rudolph	U.S.A.	1960
220 yards	23·2	B. Cuthbert	Australia	1960
,,	23·2★	M. Burvill	Australia	1963
400 metres	53·4	M. Itkina	U.S.S.R.	1959
,,	53·1★	B. Cuthbert	Australia	1963
440 yards	53·7	M. Itkina	U.S.S.R.	1959
,,	53·4	B. Cuthbert	Australia	1963
800 metres	2 01·2	D. Willis	Australia	1962
880 yards	2 02·0	D. Willis	Australia	1962
80 metres hurdles	10·5	G. Birkkmeyer	Germany	1960
,,	10·5	B. Moore	G.B.	1962

Relays				
	4×100 metres	44·3	United States	1961
	4×110 yards	45·3	England	1958
	,,	45·2★	Great Britain	1963
	4×200 metres	1 36·0	East Germany	1958
	,,	1 34·7	U.S.S.R.	1963
	4×220 yards	1 36·0	East Germany	1958
	3×800 metres	6 27·4	Ukraine National Team	1958
	,,	6 26·5	U.S.S.R.	1963
	3×880 yards	6 36·2	Hungarian National Team	1954

Jumping and Throwing	ft.	in.	*Name*	*Nation*	*Year*
Hign Jump	6	3¼	I. Balas	Roumania	1961
Long Jump	21	5	T. Shchelkanova	U.S.S.R.	1961
,,	21	8¾	T. Shchelkanova	U.S.S.R.	1962
Shot	60	10¼	T. Press	U.S.S.R.	1962
Discus	193	6	T. Press	U.S.S.R.	1961
,,	194·6★		T. Press	U.S.S.R.	1963
Javelin	195	2	E. Ozolina	U.S.S.R.	1960
,,	196	1½★	E. Ozolina	U.S.S.R.	1963
Pentathlon	5,137 pts		I. Press	U.S.S.R.	1961

UNITED KINGDOM (ALL COMERS') RECORDS

(Records made in the United Kingdom of Great Britain and Northern Ireland by any athlete.)

Distance	*Time*	*Name*	*Nation*	*Year*
	hr. min. sec.			
100 yards	9·4	K. A. Gardner	Jamaica	1958
„	9·4	P. F. Radford	G.B.	1960
100 metres	10·3	W. H. Dillard	U.S.A.	1948
„	10·3	P. F. Radford	G.B.	1960
200 metres (t)		P. F. Radford	G.B.	1960
220 yards (t)	20·5	P. F. Radford	G.B.	1960
400 metres	45·9	A. Seye	France	1960
„	45·9	R. I. Brightwell	G.B.	1962
440 yards	45·9	R. I. Brightwell	G.B.	1962
800 metres	1 46·8	P. G. Snell	N.Z.	1960
880 yards	1 47·3	H. J. Elliott	Australia	1958
1,500 metres	3 38·9	H. J. Elliott	Australia	1958
1 mile	3 55·4	H. J. Elliott	Australia	1958
2 miles	8 33·0	M. Halberg	N.Z.	1958
3 miles	13 12·0	M. B. S. Tulloh	G.B.	1961
5,000 metres	13 51·6	C. J. Chataway	G.B.	1954
„	13 51·6	D. A. G. Pirie	G.B.	1960
6 miles	27 49·8	H. R. Fowler	G.B.	1962
„	27 49·8	M. J. Bullivant	G.B.	1962
„		R. Hill	G.B.	1963
10,000 metres	28 52·4	D. Taylor	G'B.	1963
10 miles	47 47·0	B. B. Heatley	G.B.	1961
15 miles	1 17 10·2	D. O'Gorman	G.B.	1958
12 miles 515 yards	One hour	F. Norris	G.B.	1958
3,000 metres steeplechase	8 36·6	M. Herriott	G.B.	1963
120 yards hurdles	13·8	H. Jones	U.S.A.	1963
110 metres hurdles	13·9	W. F. Porter	U.S.A.	1948
„	13·9	H. Jones	U.S.A.	1961
220 yards hurdles (straight)	23·3	P. B. Hildreth	G.B.	1955
220 yards hurdles (curve)	23·3	E. Gilbert	U.S.A.	1957
400 metres hurdles	49·7	G. A. Potgieter	S. Africa	1958
440 yards hurdles	49·7	G. A. Potgieter	S. Africa	1958
4× 100 metres	39·8	——	G.B.	1963
4× 110 yards	40·0	——	G.B.	1963
4× 220 yards	1 26·0	——	London Team	1959
4× 400 metres	3 05·8	——	G.B. Team	1961
4× 440 yards	3 06·4	——	U.S.A.	1960
4× 880 yards	7 19·4	——	U.S.A.	1960
4× 1 mile	16 28·2	——	England Team	1961
	ft. in.			
High Jump	7·3	V. I. Brumel	U.S.S.R.	1961
Pole Vault	16 10¼	J. Pennel	U.S.A.	1963
Long Jump	25 10	R. Boston	U.S.A.	1963
Triple Jump	52 5¼	R. Malcherczyk	Poland	1962
Shot	64 9¾	W. H. Nieder	U.S.A.	1960
Discus	199 7½	J. J. Sylvester	U.S.A.	1962
Hammer	221 2	V. Rudyenkov	U.S.S.R.	1961
Javelin	271 11½	V. Kuznyetsov	U.S.S.R.	1957
Decathlon	6,985 pts	E. Kamerbeek	Netherlands	1959
Walking	hr. min. sec.			
20 miles	2 42 25·2	D. J. Thompson	G.B.	1959
30 miles	4 19 50·8	D. J. Thompson	G.B.	1956
15 miles 701 yards	Two hours	R. Bridge	G.B.	1914

WOMEN

100 yards	10·6	M. Willard	Australia	1958
„	10·6	H. J. Young	G.B.	1958
„	10·6	W. Rudolph	U.S.A.	1960
„	10·6	D. Hyman	G.B.	1962
100 metres	11·6	G. Leone	Italy	1960
200 metres	23·5	D. Hyman	G.B.	1962
220 yards	23·6	M. Willard	Australia	1958
400 metres	53·2	E. J. Grieveson	G.B.	1963
440 yards	54·2	G. Kraan	Netherlands	1962
800 metres	2 05·5	G. M. Kraan	Netherlands	1963
880 yards	2 05·5	G. M. Kraan	Netherlands	1963
4× 100 metres	45·0	——	G.B.	1963
4× 110 yards	45·2	——	G.B.	1963
4× 220 yards	1 39·3	——	G.B.	1963
3× 880 yards	6 42·4	——	Mitcham A.C.	1963

Women's United Kingdom All-Comers Records—*continued*

Distance	*Time*	*Name*	*Nation*	*Year*
80 metres hurdles	10·7	B. Moore	G.B.	1962
"	10·7	T. Ciepla	Poland	1962
"	10·7	E. Fisch	Germany	1962
	ft. in.			
High Jump	6 0	I. Balas	U.S.A.	1959
Long Jump	21 1¾	M. Rand	G.B.	1963
Shot	53 11½	T. Press	U.S.S.R.	1191
Discus	193 6	T. Press	U.S.S.R.	1961
Javelin	188 4	A. Pazera	Australia	1958
Pentathlon	4,679 pts	M. Bignal	G.B.	1959

UNITED KINGDOM (NATIONAL) RECORDS

(Records made anywhere by athletes eligible to represent Great Britain and Northern Ireland.)

100 *yards*.—9·4 sec. (P. F. Radford, 1960).
100 *metres*.—10·3 sec. (E. R. Sandstrom, 1956; P. F. Radford, 1960; D. H. Jones, 1961; T. B. Jones, 1963).
200 *metres*.—20·5 sec. (P. F. Radford, 1960).
220 *yards*.—20·5 sec. (P. F. Radford, 1960).
400 *metres*.—45·7 sec. (A. P. Metcalfe, 1961).
440 *yards*.—45·9 sec. (R. I. Brightwell, 1962).
800 *metres*.—1 min. 46·6 sec. (D. J. N. Johnson, 1957).
880 *yards*—1 min. 47·8 sec. (B. S. Hewson, 1958, J. P. Boulter, 1963).
1,000 *metres*.—2 min. 19·2 sec. (B. S. Hewson, 1958).
1,500 *metres*.—3 min. 41·1 sec. (B. S. Hewson, 1958).
1 *mile*.—3 min. 57·2 sec. (G. D. Ibbotson, 1957).
2,000 *metres*.—5 min. 08·0 sec. (A. Simpson, 1962).
3,000 *metres*.—7 min. 52·8 sec. (D. A. G. Pirie, 1956).
2 *miles*.—8 min. 34·0 sec. (M. B. S. Tulloh, 1962).
3 *miles*.—13 min. 12·0 sec. (M. B. S. Tulloh, 1961).
5,000 *metres*.—13 min. 36·8 sec. (D. A. G. Pirie, 1956).
6 *miles*.—27 min. 49·8 sec. (H. R. Fowler, M. J. Buillivant, 1962, R. Hill, 1963).
10,000 *metres*.—28 min. 52·4 (D. Taylor, 1963).
10 *miles*.—47 min. 47·0 sec. (B. B. Heatley, 1961).
20,000 *metres*.—1 hr. 01 min. 25·2 sec. (F. Norris, 1959).
15 *miles*.—1 hr. 14 min. 29·0 sec. (F. Norris, 1059).
25,000 *metres*.—1 hr. 17 min. 13·0 sec. (F. Norris, 1959).
30,000 *metres*.—1 hr. 36 min. 42·0 sec. (F. Norris, 1958).
12 *miles* 515 *yards*.—1 hr. (F. Norris, 1958).
3,000 *metres Steeplechase*.—8 min. 35·4 sec. (M. A. Herriott, 1963).
120 *yards Hurdles*.—13·9 sec. (J. M. Parker, 1963).
110 *metres Hurdles*.—14·1 sec. (J. M. Parker, 1963).
220 *yards Hurdles* (*straight*).—23·3 sec. (P. B. Hildreth, 1955).
220 *yards Hurdles* (*curve*).—23·7 sec. (P. A. L. Vine, 1955).
400 *metres Hurdles*.—50·5 sec. (J. H. Cooper, 1963).
440 *yards Hurdles*.—51·6 sec. (C. E. Goudge, 1958)
4×100 *metres Relay*.—39·7 sec. (British Team, 1963).
4×110 *yards*.—40.0 sec. (British Team, 1963).
4×220 *yards*.—1 min. 26·0 sec. (London Team, 1959).
4×400 *metres*.—3 min. 04·9 sec. (British Team, 1961).
4×440 *yards*.—3 min. 07·0 sec. (English Team, 1961).
4×880 *yards*.—7 min. 30·6 sec. (English Team, 1951).
4×1,500 *metres*.—13 min. 27·2 sec. (English Team, 1953).
4×1 *mile*.—16 min. 24·8 sec. (English Team, 1961).
Pole Vault.—14 ft. 6 in. (D. D. Stevenson, 1963).
Long Jump.—25 ft. 4 in. (L. Davies, 1963, J. M. Morbey, 1963).
Triple Jump.—52 ft. 7 in. (F. J. Alsop, 1962).
Shot.—64 ft. 2 in. (A. Rowe, 1961).
Discus.—186 ft. 0½ in. (R. A. Hollingsworth, 1963).
Hammer.—213 ft. 1 in. (M. J. Ellis, 1959).
Javelin.—260 ft. (J. V. McSorley, 1962; J. F. Greasley, 1963).
Decathlon.—6,184 pts (G. A. McLachlan, 1962).

Walking

2 *miles*.—13 min. 02·4 sec. (S. F. Vickers, 1960).
5 *miles*.—34 min. 21·2 sec. (K. J. Matthews, 1960).
10,000 *metres*.—42 min. 35·6 sec. (K. J. Matthews, 1960).
7 *miles*.—48 min. 24·0 sec. (K. J. Matthews, 1961).
10 *miles*.—1 hr. 14 min. 06·0 sec. (G. W. Coleman, 1956).
20,000 *metres*.—1 hr. 28 min. 18·0 sec. (K. J. Matthews, 1960).
20 *miles*.—2 hr. 42 min. 25·2 sec (D. J. Thompson, 1959).
30 *miles*.—4 hr. 19 min. 50·8 sec. (D. J. Thompson, 1956).
50,000 *metres*.—4 hr. 29 min. 38·6 sec. (D. J. Thompson, 1956).
8 *miles* 1,018 *yards*.—1 hr. (K. J. Matthews, 1960).
15 *miles* 701 *yards*.—2 hr. (R. Bridge, 1914).

Women

100 *yards*.—10·6 sec. (H. Young, 1958; D. Hyman, 1962).
100 *metres*.—11·3 sec. (D. Hyman, 1963).
200 *metres*.—23·2 sec. (D. Hyman, 1963).
220 *yards*.—23·8 sec. (J. Paul, 1956; D. Hyman, 1962).
400 *metres*.—53·2 sec.(E. J. Grieveson 1963).
440 *yards*.—54.4 sec. (E. J. Grieveson, 1962).
800 *metres*.—2 min. 05·0 sec. (J. Jordan, 1962).
880 *yards*.—2 min. 05·9 sec. (J. Jordan, 1962).
80 *metres Hurdles*.—10·5 sec. (B. Moore, 1962).
4×100 *metres Relay*.—44·7 sec. (National Team, 1956).
4×110 *yards Relay*.—45·2 sec. (G.B. Team, 1963).
4×200 *metres Relay*.—1 min. 38·4 sec. (National Team, 1955).
4×220 *yards Relay*.—1 min. 37·7 sec. (G.B. Team, 1962).
3×800 *metres Relay*.—6 min. 34·4 sec. (National Team, 1954).
3×880 *yards Relay*.—6 min. 42·4 sec. (Mitcham A.C., 1963).
High Jump.—5 ft. 8½ in. (T. Hopkins, 1956).
Long Jump.—21 ft. 1¾ in. (M. Rand, 1963).
Shot.—49 ft. 1½ in. (S. Allday, 1958).
Discus.—156 ft. 6 in. (S. Allday, 1958).
Pentathlon.—4,726 pts. (M. Rand, 1963).

GREAT BRITAIN *v.* U.S.A.

Held at the White City, Aug. 3 and 5, 1963

MEN'S EVENTS	Time m.	s.
100 *yards*.—R. Hayes (U.S.A.)		9·5
220 *yards*.—H. Carr (U.S.A.)		20·9
440 *yards*.—U. Williams (U.S.A.)		46·7
880 *yards*.—M. Groth (U.S.A.)	1	48·1
Mile.—T. O'Hara (U.S.A.)	4	03·0
3 *miles*.—M. Tulloh (G.B.)	13	22·4
6 *miles*.—R. Hill (G.B.)	27	56·0
4× 110 *yards Relay*.—Great Britain		*40·0
120 *yards Hurdles*.—H. Jones (U.S.A.)		13·8
440 *yards Hurdles*.—R. Cawley (U.S.A.)		51·4
Steeplechase.—M. Herriott (G.B.)	†8	40·4
	ft.	in.
High Jump.—G. Johnson (U.S.A.)	6	8
Pole Vault.—J. Pennel (U.S.A.)	*16	10½
Triple Jump.—F. Alsop (G.B.)	52	3¾
Shot.—M. Lindsay (G.B.)	59	3¾
Discus.—R. Humphreys (U.S.A.)	185	9
Hammer.—H. Payne (G.B.)	207	4
Javelin.—F. Covelli (U.S.A.)	251	10½

* World Record. † U.K. Record.

United States won by 120 points to 91.

WOMEN'S EVENTS	m.	s.
100 *yards*.—D. Hyman (G.B.)		10·7
220 *yards*.—D. Hyman (G.B.)		23·8
440 *yards*.—J. Grieveson (G.B.)		54·6
880 *yards*.—S. Knott (U.S.A.)	2	10·7
4× 110 *yards Relay*.—Great Britain		*45·7
Hurdles.—R. Bonds (U.S.A.)		11·1
	ft.	in.
High Jump.—F. Slaap (G.B.)	5	6
Long Jump.—M. Rand (G.B.)	21	1¾
Shot.—C. Wyatt (U.S.A.)	48	4½
Discus.—S. Shepherd (U.S.A.)	154	6
Javelin.—S. Platt (G.B.)	166	8½

* World Record.

Great Britain won by 65½ points to 51½.

GREAT BRITAIN *v.* WEST GERMANY

White City Stadium, August 23 and 24, 1963

MEN'S EVENTS	Time m.	s.
100 *metres*.—T. Jones (G.B.)		10·5
200 *metres*.—D. Jones (G.B.)		21·0
400 *metres*.—A. Metcalfe (G.B.)		47·9
800 *metres*.—M. Kinder (G.)	1	48·5
1,500 *metres*—S. Taylor (G.B.)	3	43·3
5,000 *metres*—H. Norpoth (G.)	14	08·6
10,000 *metres*.—D. Taylor (G.B.)	**28	52·4
400 *metres Relay*.—Great Britain		**39·7
1,600 *metres Relay*.—West Germany	3	08·7
110 *metres Hurdles*.—K. Willimczik (G.)		14·2
400 *metres Hurdles*.—J. Cooper (G.B.)		51·6
Steeplechase.—M. Herriott (G.B.)	8	45·6
	ft.	in.
High Jump.—J. Sieghart (G.)	6	6¾
Pole Vault.—W. Reinhardt (G.)	14	5¼
Long Jump.—W. Klein (G.)	25	5
Triple Jump.—H. Müller (G.)	52	1½
Shot.—M. Lindsay (G.B.)	58	1¾
Discus.—J. Reimers (G.)	180	11½
Hammer.—A. Payne (G.B.)	205	7½
Javelin.—H. Salomon (G.B.)	265	7½

West Germany won by 109 points to 101.

WOMEN'S EVENTS	Time m.	s.
100 *metres*.—D. Hyman (G.B.)		11·5
200 *metres*.—D. Hyman (G.B.)		23·8
400 *metres*.—J. Grieveson (G.B.)		54·2
800 *metres*.—M. Wörner (G.)	2	8·6
400 *metres Relay*.—Great Britain		**45·1
80 *metres Hurdles*.—I. Schell (G.)		11·0
100 *metres Hurdles*.—M. Rand (G.B.)		13·3
	ft.	in.
High Jump.—L. Knowles (G.B.)	5	4½
Long Jump.—M. Bignal (G.B.)	20	10½
Shot.—S. Kofink (G.)	50	3
Discus.—K. Hausmann (G.)	176	1½
Javelin.—A. Gerhardt (G.)	181	0½
	Points	
Pentathlon.—M. Rand (G.B.)	**4,726	

** U.K. All comers' and National Records.

Great Britain won by 75½ points to 65½.

A.A.A. CHAMPIONSHIPS

White City Stadium, July 12 and 13, 1963

MEN'S EVENTS	Time m.	s.
100 *yards*.—T. B. Jones (Birchfield H.)		9·7
220 *yards*.—D. H. Jones (Woodford Green A.C.)		22·3
440 *yards*.—A. P. Metcalfe (Leeds A.C.)		47·3
880 *yards*.—N. Carroll (Eire)	1	50·3
Mile.—A. Simpson (Rotherham A.C.)	4	04·9
3 *miles*.—M. B. S. Tulloh (Portsmouth A.C.)	13	23·8
6 *miles*.—R. Hill (Bolton United H.)	*27	49·8
10 *miles*.—(a) M. R. Batty (Thurrock)	48	13·4
Marathon.—(b) B. L. Kilby (Coventry Godiva H.)	†2 h. 16	45·0
120 *yards Hurdles*.—J. L. Taitt (Herne Hill H.)		*14·1
440 *yards Hurdles*.—W. Atterbury (U.S.A.)		51·2
Steeplechase.—M. A. Herriott (Sparkhill H.)	8	47·8
	ft.	in.
High Jump.—K. Sugioka (Japan)	6	8
Pole Vault.—J. Pennel (U.S.A.)	‡16	8¾
Long Jump.—F. J. Alsop (Hornchurch H.)	24	8¼
Triple Jump.—K. Sakurai (Japan)	51	3½
Shot.—M. R. Lindsay (Queens Park H.)	57	10¾
Discus.—D. Weill (U.S.A.)	176	10
Hammer.—T. Sugawara (Japan)	†215	1
Javelin.—C. G. Smith (Thames Valley H.)	237	9
	m.	s.
2 *miles Walk*.—K. J. Matthews (Royal Sutton Coldfield W.C.)	13	18·2
7 *miles Walk*.—(c) K. J. Matthews (R. Sutton Coldfield W.C.)	49	52·8
	Points	
Decathlon.—(d) Z. Sumich (Australia)	†6,438	
	m.	s.
4× 110 *yards Relay*.—(e) Polytechnic Harriers		†41·4
4× 440 *yards Relay*.—(e) Birchfield Harriers	†3	13·0

* Equals best championship performance.

† Best championship performance.

‡ World Record.

(a) Held at Hurlingham on April 13.
(b) Held at Coventry on August 17.
(c) Held at Hurlingham on March 31.
(d) Held at Loughborough on August 9 and 10.
(e) Held at White City on August 31.

White City Stadium, July 6, 1963

WOMEN'S EVENTS	Time m.	s.
100 *yards*.—D. Hyman (Hickleton Main Y.C.)		10·9
220 *yards*.—D. Hyman (Hickleton Main Y.C.)		24·3
440 *yards*.—J. Grieveson (Darlington H.)		55·9
880 *yards*.—P. Perkins (Ilford A.C.)	2	12·2
Mile.—P. Davies (Selsonia L.A.C.)	5	10·8
1½ *miles Walk*.—J. Farr (Trowbridge A.C.)	12	26·4
80 *metres Hurdles*.—P. Nutting (Ruislip/Northwood A.C.)		11·2
200 *metres Hurdles*—P. Nutting (Ruislip Northwood A.C.)		*28·9

	ft.	in.
High Jump.—I. Balas (Roumania)	5	7
Long Jump.—M. Rand (London Olympiades)	19	4¾
Shot.—M. Klein (West Germany)	†50	9½
Discus.—L. Manoliu (Roumania)	†162	1
Javelin.—A. Gerhards (West Germany)	165	0½

* Decided on time from heats.
† Best championship performances.

GREAT BRITAIN *v*. NETHERLANDS
Women

White City Stadium, September 13 and 14, 1963

100 metres.—D. Hyman (G.B.), 11·5 sec.
200 metres.—D. Hyman (G.B.), 23·7 sec.
400 metres.—E. J. Grieveson (G.B.). 53·2 sec. (a)
800 metres.—G. M. Kraan (Neth.), 2 min. 06·1 sec.
400 Relay.—Great Britain, 45·0 sec. (b)
80 Hurdles.—P. Nutting (G.B.), 10·9 sec.
High Jump.—F. M. Slaap G.B.), 5 ft. 6½ in.
Long Jump.—M. D. Rand (G.B.), 20 ft. 11½ in.
Shot.—S. Allday (G.B.), 48 ft. 2½ in.
Discus.—S. Allday (G.B.), 148 ft. 11½ in.
Javelin.—S. Platt (G.B.), 151 ft. 0½ in.

Great Britain won by 74 points to 43.

(a) U.K. All-comers and National Records.
(b) U.K. All-comers Record.

GREAT BRITAIN *v*. SWEDEN

White City Stadium, Friday and Saturday, September 13 and 14, 1963

100 metres.—T. B. Jones (G.B.), 10·5 sec.
200 metres.—D. H. Jones (G.B.), 21·0 sec.
400 metres.—R. I. Brightwell (G.B.), 46·9 sec.
800 metres.—M. A. Fleet (G.B.), 1 min. 48·7 sec.
1,500 metres.—S. G. Taylor (G.B.), 3 min 44·3 sec.
5,000 metres.—S. O. Larsson (Swed.) 14 min. 01·4 sec.
10,000 metres.—B. B. Heatley (G.B.) 28 min. 55·8 sec.
4×100 *Relay.*—Great Britain, 40.0 sec.
4×400 *Relay.*—Great Britain, 3 min. 08·7 sec.
110 Hurdles.—J. M. Parker (G.B.), 14·3 sec.
400 Hurdles.—J. H. Cooper (G.B.), 41·6 sec.
Steeplechase.—M. A. Herriott (G.B.), 8 min. 36·6 sec. (a)
High Jump.—K. A. Nilsson (Swed.), 6 ft. 10¾ in.
Pole Vault.—T. Mertanen (Swed.), 15 ft. 2 in.
Long Jump.—L. Davies (G.B.), 24 ft. 11¾ in.
Triple Jump.—F. J. Alsop (G.B.), 51 ft. 11½ in.
Shot.—E. Uddebom (Swed.), 56 ft. 10 in.
Discus.—R. L. Hollingsworth (G.B.), 186 ft. 0½ in. (b)
Hammer.—B. Asplund (Swed.), 214 ft. 11½ in.
Javelin.—J. R. Greasley (G.B.), 260 ft. (c)

Great Britain won by 126 points to 86.

(a) United Kingdom All Comers and National Record.
(b) United Kingdom National Record.
(c) Equals United Kingdom National Record.

GREAT BRITAIN *v*. RUSSIAN FEDERAL REPUBLIC

VOLGOGRAD, September 28 and 29, 1963
Men's Events

100 metres.—T. B. Jones (G.B.), 10·4 sec.
200 metres.—D. H. Jones (G.B.), 21·4 sec.
400 metres.—R. I. Brightwell (G.B.), 46·6 sec.
800 metres.—M. A. Fleet (G.B.), 1 min. 49·1 sec.
1,500 metres.—S. G. Taylor (G.B.), 3 min. 44·8 sec.
5,000 metres.—J. P. Anderson (G.B.), 14 min. 04·8 sec.
10,000 metres.—I. Ivanov (R.), 29 min. 18·2 sec.
400 Relay.—G.B., 39·9 sec.
1,600 Relay.—G.B., 3 min. 06·6 sec.
110 Hurdles.—J. M. Parker (G.B.), 14·1 sec.
400 Hurdles.—J. H. Cooper (G.B.), 50·5 sec.
Steeplechase.—M. Herriott (G.B.), 8 min. 36·2 sec.
High Jump.—V. Brumel (R.), 7 ft. 1¾ in.
Pole Vault.—S. R. Porter (G.B.); B. Loskov (R.), 14 ft. 1¼ in.
Long Jump.—I. Ter-Ovanesian (R.), 25 ft. 1 in.
Triple Jump.—V. Kravchenko (R.), 52 ft. 8¼ in.
Shot.—V. Lipsnis, 61 ft. 1½ in.
Discus.—V. Lyakov, 173 ft. 6 in.
Hammer.—V. Rudenkov, 213 ft. 2½ in.
Javelin.—V. Kuznetsov, 250 ft. 2 in.

Great Britain 112 points.
Russian Federal Republic 99.

Women's Events

100 metres.—D. Hyman (G.B.), 11·5 sec.
200 metres.—D. Hyman (G.B.), 23·4 sec.
400 metres.—A. Packer (G.B.), 53·3 sec.
800 metres.—Z. Skobtsova (R.), 2 min. 6·1 sec.
400 Relay.—Great Britain, 44·8 sec.
High Jump.—L. Knowles (G.B.), 5 ft. 6¾ in.
Long Jump.—M. D. Rand (G.B.), 20 ft. 10 in.
Shot.—T. Press (R.), 54 ft. 11 in.
Discus.—T. Press (R.), 180 ft. 3½ in.
Javelin.—E. Gorchakova (R.), 181 ft. 10½ in.

Russian Federal Republic 62 points.
Great Britain 56.

GREAT BRITAIN *v*. HUNGARY

BUDAPEST, October 2 and 3, 1963
Men's Events

100 metres.—T. B. Jones (G.B.), 10·3 sec.
200 metres.—D. H. Jones (G.B.), 20·9 sec.
400 metres.—A. Metcalfe (G.B.), 46·6 sec.
800 metres.—C. Carter (G.B.), I min. 48·7 sec.
1,500 metres.—P. Parsch (H.), 3 min. 45·0 sec.
5,000 metres.—J. Anderson (G.B.), 13 min. 51·6 sec.
10,000 metres.—M. Batty (G.B.), 29 min. 14·6 sec.
400 Relay.—Great Britain, 39·9 sec.
1,600 Relay.—Great Britain, 3 min. 08·3 sec.
110 Hurdles.—J. M. Parker (G.B.), 14·9 sec.
400 Hurdles.—J. H. Cooper (G.B.), 51·4 sec.
Steeplechase.—J. Macsar (H.), 8 min. 35 sec.
High Jump.—J. Medovarszky (H.), 6 ft. 7 in.
Pole Vault.—I. Tamas (H.), 14 ft. 1¼ in.
Long Jump.—L. Davies (G.B.), 24 ft. 10¼ in.
Triple Jump.—H. Kalocsai (H.), 51 ft. 6½ in.
Shot.—Z. Nagy (H.), 61 ft. 9¾ in.
Discus.— J. Szecsenyi (H.), 186 ft. 7 in.
Hammer.—G. Zsivotzky (H.), 219 ft. 8 in.
Javelin.—G. Kulcsar (H.), 258 ft. 2½ in.

Great Britain 106½ points.
Hungary 105½.

Women's Events

100 metres.—D. Hyman (G.B.), 11·3 sec.
200 metres.—D. Hyman (G.B.), 23·2 sec.
800 metres.—O. Kazi (H.), 2 min. 05·4 sec.
Relay.—Hungary, 45·5 sec.
Hurdles.—A. Kovacs (H.), 11·4 sec.
High Jump.—L. Knowles (G.B.), 5 ft. 4½ in.
Long Jump.—M. D. Rand (G.B.), 20 ft. 8½ in.
Shot.—J. Bognar (H.), 54 ft. 6¾ in.
Discus.—J. Stugner (H.), 161 ft. 11 in.
Javelin.—F. Rudas (H.), 163 ft. 7½ in.

Hungary 55 points.
Great Britain 48.

OXFORD *v*. CAMBRIDGE

Held at WHITE CITY, May 11, 1963.

	Time m.	s.
100 yards.—J. B. Cook (C.)		10·0
220 yards.—J. B. Cook (C.)		21·6
440 yards.—A. P. Metcalfe (O.)		49·0
880 yards.—M. H. Mullin (O.)	1	50·0
Mile.—J. P. Boulter (O.)	4	13·0
3 miles.—D. M. Turner (C.)	13	46·0

	m. s.
120 yards Hurdles.—T. N. Blodgett (C.)	*14·2
220 yards Hurdles.—T. N. Blodgett (C.)	*23·7
440 yards Hurdles.—J. B. Cook (C.)	†53·5
Steeplechase.—T. F. K. Johnston (C.)	†9 26·8
	ft. in.
High Jump.—C. van Dyck (O.)	6 1
Pole Vault.—T. N. Blodgett (C.)	*13 8½
Long Jump.—A. O. Oyenuga (C.)	22 11½
Triple Jump.—M. Ralph (O.)	48 1
Shot.—A. W. Ross (C.)	46 5½
Discus.—R. H. Baxter (O.)	148 7½
Javelin.—T. N. Blodgett (C.)	191 0½

* Best performance. † New event.

Cambridge beat Oxford by 86 points to 67.

The Sports were first held in 1864. To date Cambridge have won on 42 occasions, Oxford on 40, and there have been six ties.

A.A.A. JUNIOR CHAMPIONSHIPS

Held on Saturday, August 10, at Hurlingham

100 yards.—R. Frith (Poly.), 9·8 sec.*
220 yards.—A. Ronay (Poly.), 21·9 sec.
440 yards.—E. Jenkins (Doncaster), 48·7 sec.
880 yards.—D. Hogg (Sale), 1 min. 54·3 sec.
Mile.—W. Barrow (Victoria Park), 4 min. 08·9 sec.*
120 hurdles.—D. Henery (Ruislip), 14·6 sec.=
200 hurdles.—M. Bell (Walthamstow), 22·5 sec.*
Steeplechase.—M. Williams (M.T., Crosby) 4 min. 20·0 sec.
Mile walk.—M. Tolley (Sheffield), 6 min. 57·9 sec.
High Jump.—M. Selby (London), 6 ft. 2 in.
Pole Vault.—N. Foster (Shettleston), 13 ft. 0 in.*
Long Jump.—G. Beales (Border), 23 ft. 7½ in.*
Triple Jump.—J. Vernon (Becket), 45 ft. 9¾ in.
Shot.—A. Carter (Westbury), 61 ft. 4 in.*
Discus.—J. Hiller (Cambridge H.), 167 ft. 1½ in.
Hammer.—P. Aston (Woodford Green), 200 ft.*
Javelin.—W. Peet (Hornchurch), 201 ft. 9 in.

* Best Championship performance
= Equals Championship performance

NATIONAL CROSS-COUNTRY CHAMPIONSHIP

Held at CAMBRIDGE, March 2, 1963

	Time m. s.
1. B. B. Heatley (Coventry Godiva H.)	50 25
2. H. R. Fowler (N. Staffs. & Stone H.)	50 35
3. E. F. Strong (Bristol A.C.)	50 44
4. T. J. Braiult (Brighton A.C.)	50 56
5. T. F. K. Johnston (Portsmouth A.C.)	51 03
6. B. B. Craig (Blackpool & Fylde A.C.)	51 22
Team Result	Points
1. Coventry Godiva Harriers (1, 11, 17, 36, 42, 48)	155
Junior Race	m. s.
1. J. Farrington (Cheltenham & C.H.)	32 02
2. W. Adcocks (Coventry Godiva H.)	32 55
3. J. Hammond (Coventry Godiva H.)	33 01
Team Result	Points
1. Coventry Godiva Harriers (2, 3, 32, 81)	118

INTERNATIONAL CROSS-COUNTRY CHAMPIONSHIP

Held at SAN SEBASTIAN, Spain.
March 17, 1963

Individual Result	Time m. s.
1. H. R. Fowler (England)	37 19·7
2. G. Roelants (Belgium)	37 32·0
3. M. Haro (Spain)	37 41·6
4. R. Bogey (France)	37 55·6
5. T. F. K. Johnston (England)	37 38·7
6. F. Guardia (Spain)	38 09·0
Team Placings	Points
1. Blegium (2, 8, 14, 17, 29, 40)	110
2. France (4, 9, 18, 21, 28, 33)	113
3. England (1, 5, 13, 22, 35, 37)	113

INTERNATIONAL CROSS-COUNTRY

Junior Race	secm. s.
1. J. Farrington (England)	25 17·4
2. A. Zammel (Tunisia)	25 23·6
3. J. Stewart (Scotland)	25 37·6
Team Result	Points
1. England (1, 4, 7)	12

WOMEN'S NATIONAL CROSS-COUNTRY CHAMPIONSHIP

RICHMOND PARK, March 9, 1963

	Time m. s.
1. M. Ibbotson (Longwood H.)	19 20
2. P. Perkins (Ilford A.C.)	19 45
3. P. Davies (Selsonia)	19 55
Team Result	Points
1. Mitcham Athletic Club (9, 10, 15, 19)	53

TEN MILES WALKING CHAMPIONSHIP

Held at MANCHESTER, March 16, 1963

	Time m. s.
1. K. J. Matthews (R. Sutton Coldfield)	73 00
2. P. Nihill (Surrey W.C.)	73 30
3. J. Edgington (Coventry Godiva)	75 12
Team Championship	Points
1. Belgrave Harriers (4, 12, 22, 24)	62

TWENTY MILES CHAMPIONSHIP

Held at EWELL, Surrey, May 11, 1963

	Time h. m. s.
1. P. Nihill (Surrey W.C.)	2 39 43
2. C. Fogg (Enfield)	2 42 58
3. R. C. Middleton (Belgrave)	2 44 21
Team Championship	Pionts
1. Surrey Walking Club (1, 4, 9, 10)	24

50 KILOMETRES ROAD WALKING CHAMPIONSHIP

Held at BADDERSLEY, Warwickshire, June 15, 1963

	h. m. s.
1. R. C. Middleton (Belgrave)	4 16 43·2
2. D. Thompson (Metro W.C.)	4 21 43·0
3. C. Fogg (Enfield)	4 22 52·0
Team Championship	Points
1. Surrey Walking Club (3, 4, 5, 11)	23

UNIVERSITY EVENTS

Cross Country.—At Roehampton, December 8, 1962, Cambridge beat Oxford 23 points to 58.

Cambridge Freshmen beat Oxford Freshmen at Athletics by 79 points to 56 at Milton Road on November 13.

Cambridge beat Oxford by 7 events to 0 in Field Events Match at Cambridge on November 23.

Cambridge beat Oxford by 6 events to 1 in Relays at Oxford on November 29th.

THE TURF

The Turf in Great Britain is under the control of:—

Flat Racing. The *Jockey Club*, H.Q. at Newmarket. Stewards are Lt.-Gen. Sir George Collingwood, K.B.E., C.B., D.S.O.; Lord Howard de Walden; Viscount Allendale.

Steeplechasing. The *National Hunt Committee*. Stewards are: The Earl Cadogan, M.C.; The Earl of Cottenham; Maj. W. D. Gibson.

Leading Owners and Trainers, 1963
(Flat Season up to Sept. 27)

Winning Owners		Winning Trainers	
J. R. Mullion	£68,882	P. J. Prendergast (Ireland)	£125,294
Miss M. Sheriffe	36,053	J. Jarvis	51,819
M. F. Dupré	35,338	T. A. Corbett	51,375
Lord Rosebery	33,855	J. Tree	50,496
Lady Sassoon	27,215	F. Armstrong	49,066
G. A. Oldham	26,542	N. Murless	46,532
Mrs. P. A. B. Widener	22,829	Sir G. Richards	46,389
Miss J. Olin	21,046	H. Wragg	43,273
H. Loebstein	18,609	W. Elsey	42,256
Lord Carnarvon	17,970	W. R. Hern	36,342
Mrs. A. B. Biddle	17,933	S. Hall	35,945
Duke of Norfolk	16,674	F. Mathet (France)	35,338

Leading Breeders, 1963
(Up to Sept. 27)

	Horses	Races won	Value
Mr. H. F. Guggenheim	1	3	£66,011
Sassoon Studs	22	34	38,515
Hanstead Stud	3	5	35,831
M. F. Dupré	1	1	35,338
Lord Rosebery	16	29	35,338
Astor Studs	20	33	33,763
Mrs. P. A. B. Widener	1	1	27,226
Mrs. P. C. Margetts	1	2	22,829
The late Miss D. Paget	14	26	20,643
Mr. F. Tuthill	14	20	21,450
Mr. G. S. Stephens	3	6	20,909
Mrs. R. Laye	2	6	18,658
			18,180

Winning Jockeys, 1963
(Up to Sept. 27)

	1st	2nd	3rd	Unpl	Total Mts
A. Breasley	153	109	87	268	617
L. Piggott	151	90	61	269	571
D. Smith	101	81	69	342	593
R. Hutchinson	99	80	76	355	610
J. Mercer	79	66	42	223	410
J. Sime	77	43	32	226	378
R. Maddock	72	44	50	273	439
J. Lindley	70	55	47	201	373
J. Lewis	68	49	46	307	470
E. Hide	62	57	57	268	444
D. Keith	45	50	64	282	441
E. Smith	44	45	31	227	347

Winning Sires, 1963
(Up to Sept. 27)

	Horses	Races won	Value
Ribot (1952), by Tenerani	7	11	£121,288
Chanteur II (1942), by Chateau Bouscaut	19	24	80,411
Rockefella (1941), by Hyperion	14	25	40,719
March Past (1950), by Petition	24	43	39,641
Grey Sovereign (1948), by Nasrullah	27	43	36,441
Mossborough (1947), by Nearco	15	22	35,376
Tanerko (1953), by Tantième	1	1	35,338
Acropolis (1952), by Donatello II	15	19	30,138
Crepello (1954) by Donatello II	22	29	29,912
Vimy (1952), by Wild Risk	19	26	29,787
Native Dancer (1950), by Polynesian	3	4	29,473
Aureole (1950), by Hyperion	19	24	27,975

THE DERBY, 1953–1963

For particulars of the Derby from 1780–1952 see 1921-53 editions.

The *Distance* of the Derby course at Epsom is 1½ mile. Lord Egremont won Derby in 1782, 1804, 5, 7, 26 (also, 5 Oaks); Duke of Grafton, 1802, 9, 10, 15 (also, 9 Oaks); Mr. Bowes, 1835, 43, 52, 3; Sir J. Hawley, Teddington (1851), Beadsman (1858), Musjid (1859), and Blue Gown (1868), the 1st Duke of Westminster, Bend Or (1880), Shotover (1882), Ormonde (1886), and Flying Fox (1899). Lady James Douglas was the first lady to win the Derby—War Substitute at Newmarket (1918); at Epsom, Mrs. G. B. Miller (1937). First winner was Sir Charles Bunbury's Diomed in 1780. From 1940 to 1945 a substitute Derby was run at Newmarket. By winning his 5th Derby, the late Aga Khan equalled Lord Egremont's record. He also won 2 Oaks.

Year	Owner and Name of Winner	Betting	Jockey	Trainer	No. of R'n'rs.
1953	Sir V. Sassoon's Pinza	5 to 1 (Jt.F)	Sir G. Richards	N. Bertie	33
1954	Mr. R. S. Clark's Never Say Die°	33 to 1	L. Piggott	J. Lawson	33
1955	Mme. L. Volterra's Phil Drake (Fr.)	100 to 8	F. Palmer	F. Mathet	22
1956	M. P. Wertheimer's Lavandin (Fr.)	7 to 1	W.R. Johnstone	A. Head	23
1957	Sir V. Sassoon's Crepello*	6 to 4 F.	L. Piggott	N. Murless	22
1958	Sir V. Sassoon's Hard Ridden (Ir.)	18 to 1	C. Smirke	J. Rogers	20
1959	Sir H. de Trafford's Parthia	10 to 1	W. H. Carr	C. Boyd-Rochfort	20
1960	Sir V. Sassoon's St. Paddy°	7 to 1	L. Piggott	N. Murless	17
1961	Mrs. A. Plesch's Psidium	66 to 1	R. Poincelet	H. Wragg	28
1962	Mr. R. R. Guest's Larkspur (Ir.)	22 to 1	N. Sellwood	V. O'Brien	26
1963	M. F. Dupré's Relko (Fr.)	5 to 1 F.	Y. Saint-Martin	F. Mathet	26

Marked * also won the Two Thousand Guineas; ° the St. Leger.

Record times, 2 min. 34 secs. by Hyperion in 1933; Windsor Lad in 1934; 2 min. 33·8 sec. Mahmoud in 1936.

TWO THOUSAND GUINEAS. First run, 1809. Rowley Mile Newmarket. 9 st.

Year	Owner and Name of Winner	Betting	Jockey	Trainer	No. of R'n'rs.
1959	Prince Aly Khan's Taboun (Fr)	5 to 2F.	G. Moore	A. Head	13
1960	Mr. R. N. Webster's Martial (Ir)	18 to 1	R. Hutchinson	P. Prendergast	17
1961	Mr. T. C. Yuill's Rockavon	66 to 1	N. Stirk	G. Boyd	22
1962	Major G. Glover's Privy Councillor	100 to 6	W. Rickaby	T. Waugh	19
1963	Miss N. Sheriffe's Only For Life	33 to 1	J. Lindley	J. Tree	21

ONE THOUSAND GUINEAS. 1814. Rowley mile. Newmarket. Fillies 9 st.

Year	Owner and Name of Winner	Betting	Jockey	Trainer	No. of R'n'rs
1959	Prince Aly Khan's Petite Etoile	8 to 1	D. Smith	N. Murless	14
1960	Mrs. H. E. Jackson's Never Too Late II (Fr)	8 to 11F.	R. Poincelet	E. Pollet	14
1961	Mrs. S. M. Castello's Sweet Solera	4 to 1 jt F	W. Rickaby	R. Day	14
1962	Mr. R. More O'Ferrall's Abermaid	100 to 6.	W. Williamson	H. Wragg	14
1963	Mrs. P. A. B. Widener's Hula Dancer (Fr)	1 to 2 F.	R. Poincelet	E. Pollet	12

OAKS. 1779. Epsom. 1½ mile. Fillies. 9 st.

Year	Owner and Name of Winner	Betting	Jockey	Trainer	No. of R'n'rs
1959	Prince Aly Khan's Petite Etoile*	11 to 2	L. Piggott	N. Murless	11
1960	Mrs. H. E. Jackson's Never Too Late II* (Fr)	6 to 5F.	R. Poincelet	E. Pollet	10
1961	Mrs. S. M. Castello's Sweet Solera*	11 to 4 F.	W. Rickaby	R. Day	12
1962	Mr. G. P. Goulandris' Monade (Fr)	7 to 1	Y. Saint-Martin	J. Lieux.	18
1963	Mrs. J. M. Olin's Noblesse (Ir)	4 to 11 F.	G. Bougoure	P. J. Prendergast	9

* Also won 1,000 Guineas.

ST. LEGER. 1776(8). Doncaster. 1¾ mile, 132 yards.

Year	Owner and Name of Winner	Betting	Jockey	Trainer	No. of R'n'rs.
1959	Mr. W. Hill's Cantelo	100 to 7	E. Hide	C. F. Elsey	11
1960	Sir V. Sassoon's St. Paddy‡	4 to 6F.	L. Piggott	N. Murless	9
1961	Mrs. V. Lilley's Aurelius	9 to 2	L. Piggott	N. Murless	13
1962	Maj. L.B. Holliday's Hethersett	100 to 8	W. H. Carr	W. R. Hern	15
1963	Mr. J. R. Mullvon's Ragusa (Ir)	2 to 5 F.	G. Bougoure	P. J. Prendergast	7

‡ Also won Derby.

	Lincolnshire Handicap. 1 mile.	Free Handicap. Newmarket—3 yrs.—7f.	Jockey Club Stakes Newmarket 1¾ miles.	Coronation Cup. Epsom 1½ m.
1960	Mustavon 5y 6st 13lb.	Running Blue 8st. 4lb.	..	Petite Etoile 4y 8st 4lb.
1961	John's Court 6y 7st 7lb	Erudite 8st 6lb	..	Petite Etoile 5y 8st 7lb.
1962	Hill Royal 4y 7st 9lb	Privy Councillor 8st 4lb.	Pardao 4y 9st	Dicta Drake (Fr.) 4y 8st 7lb
1963	Monawin, 8y 7st. 9lb.	Ros Rock 8st. 1lb.	Darling Boy 5y 9st. 7lb	Exbury (Fr) 4y 8st. 7lb.

	Ascot Stakes. Now 2½ miles.	Gold Cup. Ascot 2½ miles.	Coventry Stakes. Ascot—2 yrs—5 furlongs	Grand Prix de Paris. 1 mile 7 furlongs.
1960	Shatter 4y 7st 9lb	Sheshoon (Fr). 4y 9st.	Typhoon (Ir.) 9st	Charlottesville
1961	Angazi 5y 8st 1lb	Pandofell 4y 9st	Xerxes 9st	Balto
1962	Trelawny 6y 9st 8lb	Balto (Fr.) 4y 9st	Crocket, 9st	Armistice
1963	Trelawny 7y 10st.	Twilight Alley 4y 9st	Showdown 9st	Sanctus

	Chester Cup. Chester—2¼m. 77yd.	Jubilee Handicap. Kempton Pk.—1¼m.	Eclipse Stakes. Sandown Pk.—1¼m.	King George VI and Queen Elizabeth Stakes. Ascot—1½ miles.
1960	Trelawny 4y 7st 11lb.	Rocky Royale 4y 7st 9lb.	Javelot (Fr.) 4y 9st	Aggressor 5y 9st 7lb.
1961	Hoy 5y 8st	Chalk Stream 6y 7st 5lb.	St. Paddy 4y 9st 7lb	Right Royal V (Fr) 3y 8st 7lb
1962	Golden Fire 4y 7st 9lb.	Water Skier 5y 7st 10lb	Henry the Seventh 4y 9st	Match III (Fr) 4y 9st 7lb.
1963	Narratus 5y 7st 5lb.	Water Skier 6y 7st. 11lb.	Khalkis (Ir.) 3y 8st 2lb	Ragusa (Ir) 3y 8st 7lb

	Nunthorpe Stakes. York 5f.	Cheveley Park Stakes. New'k't—2 yrs.—6f.	Cambridgeshire. New'k't 9 furlongs.	Middle Park Stakes. New'k't—2 yrs.—6 furlongs
1960	Bleep-Bleep 4y 9st 5lb.	Opaline II (Fr.) 8st. 12lb.	Midsummer Night II 3y. 7st 12lb	Skymaster 9 st.
1961	Floribunda (Ir.) 3y 9st.	Display (Ir.) 8st. 11lb	{ Henry the Seventh 3y 8st 4lb / Violetta III 3y 7st 8lb	Gustav 9st
1962	Gay Mairi 3y 8st 11lb.	My Goodness Me 8st 11lb.	Hidden Meaning 3y 9st	Crocket 9st
1963	Matatina 3y 8st 11lb.	Grimea II 8 st 11 lb.	Commander in Chief 4y 8st.	Showdown 9 st

	Cesarewitch. New'k't 2¼ m.	Dewhurst Stakes. New'k't 2 yrs.—7f.	Champion Stakes. New'k't 1¼ m.	Grand National. L'pool 4m. 856 yds.
1960	Alcove 3y 7st 7lb	Bounteous 8st 13lb	Marguerite Vernaut (It.) 3y 8st. 4lb.	Merryman II 9y 10st 12lb.
1961	Avon's Pride 4 y 7st 11lb.	River Chanter 9st 2lb	Bobar II (Fr.) 3y 8st 11lb	Nicolaus Silver 9y 10st 1lb.
1962	Golden Fire 4y 7st 11lb.	Follow Suit 8st 12lb.	Arctic Storm 3y 8st 7lb.	Kilmore 12y 10st. 4lb.
1963	Utrillo 6y 8st.	King's Lane 8 st 12 lb	Hula Dancer (Fr.) 3y 8st. 4st	Ayala 9y 10st

CRICKET

Cricket is played under the "Laws of Cricket" and is governed by the Committee of the Marylebone Cricket Club (1787), Lord's, N.W.1. *Pres.*—The Lord Nugent. *Sec.*, S. C. Griffith. *Asst. Secs.* J. G. Dunbar; D. B. Carr.

1963. Cricket Feats

Firsts.—1,000 runs—P. E. Richardson (Kent). 100 wickets—B. R. Knight (Essex). 1,000 runs and 100 wickets—B. R. Knight (Essex). 2,000 runs—P. E. Richardson (Kent). 3,000 runs—None. 200 wickets—None.

All round.—Three players made 1,000 runs and took 100 wickets. They were: B. R. Knight (Essex) 1,578 runs and 140 wickets; J. S. Pressdee (Glamorgan) 1,467 runs and 106 wickets; J. B. Mortimore (Gloucestershire) 1,425 runs and 102 wickets.

High Scores.—West Indies, 501 for 6 *v.* England (First Test, Manchester); Kent 475 for 6 *v.* Leicestershire; Kent, 441 for 5 *v.* Derbyshire.

Low Scores.—Nottinghamshire, 44 *v.* Glamorgan; Middlesex, 47 *v.* Yorkshire; Glamorgan, 52 *v.* Somerset; Essex, 56 *v.* West Indies; Sussex, 56 *v.* Derbyshire.

Bowling Feats.—O. S. Wheatley (Glamorgan), 8 for 40 (in innings) *v.* Worcestershire; A. Brown (Kent), 8 for 47 (in innings) *v.* Warwickshire; D. W. White (Hants.) 14 for 99 (in match) *v.* Leicestershire; F. E. Rumsey (Somerset) 12 for 59 (in match) *v.* Glamorgan; F. S. Trueman (Yorkshire) 10 for 36 (in match) *v.* Warwickshire; J. S. Pressdee (Glamorgan) 10 for 43 (in match) *v.* Nottinghamshire.

Highest Individual Scores.—D. Nicholls (Kent), 211 *v.* Derbyshire; J. B. Bolus (Nottinghamshire), 202* *v.* Glamorgan; R. M. Prideaux (Northamptonshire), 202* *v.* Oxford University.

* Denotes not out.

Wicket-Keeping.—D. L. Murray (West Indies) set up a new record for a Test series by making 24 dismissals against England. L. A. Johnson (Northamptonshire), *v.* Sussex, equalled world record by taking 10 catches in one match.

County Championship Table, 1963

County Order for 1963. 1962 in brackets	Played	Won	Lost	Drawn	No dec.	First Innings Lead in Match		Points
						L't.	Dn.	
Points Awar'd	—	10	—	—	—	2	2	—
Yorkshire (1)	28	13	3	11	1	1	6	144
Glamorgan (14)	28	11	8	8	1	1	6	124
Somerset (6)	28	10	6	11	1	2	7	118
Sussex (12)	28	10	6	12	0	1	7	116
Warwickshire (3)	28	10	3	14	1	1	7	116
Middlesex (13)	28	9	5	11	3	1	7	106
Northants.(8)	28	9	8	11	0	1	5	105
Gloucestershire (4)	28	9	7	11	1	2	3	100
Notts. (15)	28	6	8	13	1	4	7	82
Hampshire (10)	28	7	8	10	3	1	4	80
Surrey (5)	28	5	6	17	0	1	11	74
Essex (9)	28	6	4	17	1	0	5	70
Kent (11)	28	5	6	17	0	1	8	68
Worcestershire .(2)	28	4	8	13	3	2	8	60
Lancashire (16)	28	4	10	13	1	2	7	58
Leicestershire (17)	28	3	13	10	2	2	3	40
Derbyshire (7)	28	2	14	9	3	1	3	28

Northamptonshire gained five points instead of two in drawn match when scores finished level and they were batting.

County Championships

The first County Championship was in 1873 when Gloucestershire and Nottinghamshire finished equal on points. Yorkshire have won 26 times; Surrey 16; Notts 8; Lancs 8; Middlesex 5; Kent 4; Gloucester 2; Derby 2; Warwick 2; Glamorgan 1; Hampshire 1; Notts and Lancs tied in 1879 and 1882, and Notts, Lancs and Surrey were all equal in 1889. Middlesex and Yorkshire tied in 1949 and Lancashire and Surrey tied in 1950.

Minor Counties Championship, 1963

County	P.	W.	L.	First Innings W.	First Innings L.	No. res.	Pts.	Avge
Cambridgeshire	10	6	0	1	2	1	67	6·70
Wiltshire	10	5	2*	1	2	0	58	5·80
Hertfordshire	10	4	5‡	0	1	0	53	5·30
Somerset II	8	4	2	0	2	0	42	5·25
Durham	12	5	3	3	1	0	60	5·00
Lancashire II	12	5	2	2	2	1	60	5·00
Warwickshire II	8	3	0	2	2	1	40	5·00
Cheshire	10	3	1*	2	1	3	46	4·60
Berkshire	10	3	1*	3	3	0	45	4·50
Lincolnshire	10	3	2	4	1	0	43	4·30
Yorkshire II	12	4	2	0	4	2	48	4·00
Bedfordshire	10	3	5†	1	1	0	40	4·00
Devon	10	2	1	5	1	1	38	3·80
Suffolk	8	2	3*	1	1	1	29	3·62
Oxfordshire	10	2	0	3	4	1	35	3·50
Buckinghamshire	10	2	2	3	2	1	33	3·30
Cornwall	8	2	5*	1	0	0	26	3·25
Staffordshire	12	2	6†	1	1	2	34	2·83
Norfolk	12	1	3*	2	3	3	28	2·33
Dorset	10	1	5*	1	2	1	20	2·00
Shropshire	8	1	7†	0	0	0	16	2·00
Northumberland	10	0	2	3	2	3	17	1·70
Cumberland	8	0	4	0	1	3	7	0·87

* First innings points (3) in one match lost. † First innings points in two matches lost. ‡ First innings points in four matches lost.

Minor Counties Challenge Match: Abandoned owing to rain.

Second Eleven Competition, 1963

	P.	W.	L.	Drawn	First Innings only	Pts.	Avge.
Worcester	18	7	2	8	1W	92	5·11
Northants	22	8	2	11(1A)	1W	104	4·95
Surrey	14	5	1	6(1A)	2L	60	4·63
Kent	18	6	4	8(2A)	—	72	4·50
Glamorgan	14	3	5	6(4A)	—	36	3·60
Essex	16	3	6	6(2A)	1W	44	3·14
Warwickshire	20	4	2	13(2A)	1W	56	3·11
Sussex	8	2	3	3	—	24	3·00
Middlesex	12	3	3	6	—	36	3·00
Gloucester	14	2	6	4(3A)	1L. 1W.	32	2·90
Notts	14	2	3	7(1A)	1L. 1W.	32	2·46
Lancashire	8	1	—	7(3A)	—	12	2·40
Somerset	18	1	7	9(5A)*	1L	18	1·38
Derbyshire	10	1	2	7(1A)	—	12	1·33
Hampshire	10	—	3	6(2A)*	1L.	6	·75
Leicester	16	—	1	13(1A)	1W.1L.	8	·50

A denotes match abandoned without a result. Not taken into the reckoning of average. * 1 Tie.

Provisional Test Match Dates, 1964

The following are the dates provisionally arranged for the first day of each five-day Test Match between England and Australia in 1964: June 4, Nottingham; June 18, Lord's; July 2, Leeds; July 23, Manchester; Aug. 13, Oval.

Before the 1963 season, the distinction between amateur and professional cricketers was ended. In the county championship, bonus points for faster scoring in first innings were abolished, and the follow-on rule, which had been experimentally suspended, was restored.

BATTING AND BOWLING AVERAGES

English Batting Averages, 1963
(Qualification, 8 Innings)

Batsmen	Number of Innings	Times not out	Total Runs	Highest Innings	Average
M. J. K. Smith	39	6	1,566	144*	47·45
G. Boycott	43	7	1,628	165*	45·22
C. C. Inman	51	11	1,708	120*	42·70
J. B. Bolus	57	4	2,190	202*	41·32
K. F. Barrington	45	7	1,568	110*	41·26
J. H. Edrich	55	7	1,921	125	40·02
S. E. Leary	38	5	1,311	158	39·72
P. E. Richardson	56	2	2,110	172	39·07
P. H. Parfitt	53	5	1,813	135*	37.77
G. Atkinson	50	2	1,797	177	37·43
T. E. Bailey	54	12	1,568	122	37·33
D. B. Carr	10	0	368	136	36·80
K. G. Suttle	57	4	1,854	141	34·98
T. W. Graveney	50	7	1,492	100	34·69
R. E. Marshall	55	3	1,800	161*	34·61
A. Jones	58	4	1,857	187*	34·38
H. Horton	51	5	1,566	139	34·04
R. A. White	48	8	1,355	108*	33·87
K. J. Grieves	53	4	1,649	127	33·65
R. C. Wilson	43	3	1,346	159*	33·65
R. I. Jefferson	12	5	234	136	33·42
B. W. Luckhurst	52	7	1,501	126*	33·35
J. Pressdee	54	10	1,467	88*	33·34
B. L. Reynolds	60	5	1,834	145*	33·34
N. F. Horner	48	2	1,531	113	33·28
M. H. Denness	40	7	1,098	110*	33·27
E. R. Dexter	45	1	1,446	118	32·86
M. E. Norman	60	4	1,840	152	32·85
D. B. Close	50	3	1,529	161	32·53
M. J. Horton	49	0	1,583	100	32·30
Nawab of Pataudi	45	5	1,290	153	32·25
C. A. Milton	47	6	1,321	131	32·21
R. M. Prideaux	58	6	1,633	202*	31·40
R. W. Barber	47	5	1,316	113	31·33
R. E. Hitchcock	43	9	1,062	106	31·23
N. Hill	28	3	780	134	31·20
W. E. Russell	53	4	1,523	138	31·08
R. E. F. Minns	14	1	403	81	31·00
J. M. Parks	47	3	1,363	136	30·97
P. Marner	48	6	1,292	142*	30·76
M. C. Cowdrey	17	3	429	107*	30·64
M. R. Hallam	52	6	1,400	115*	30·43
J. M. Brearley	28	2	790	100	30·38
E. J. Craig	15	1	424	87	30·28
D. A. Livingstone	53	3	1,503	151	30·06
M. J. Bear	43	4	1,170	132	30·00
W. E. Alley	38	2	1,076	105	29·88
C. Milburn	53	0	1,580	123	29·81
A. R. Lewis	53	6	1,401	107*	29·80
D. M. Young	55	2	1,572	127	29·66
L. J. Lenham	49	4	1,334	191*	29·64
M. D. Willett	43	6	1,096	124	29·62
G. E. Barker	53	3	1,474	118	29·48
M. J. Stewart	41	2	1,148	169	29·43
R. G. A. Headley	55	6	1,432	108	29·22
D. C. Morgan	41	5	1,039	113*	28·86
B. Roe	45	2	1,235	99	28·72
B. R. Knight	59	4	1,578	124	28·69
D. Kenyon	49	0	1,393	166	28·42
P. J. Sharpe	55	6	1,384	138*	28·24
C. Greetham	46	4	1,186	141	28·23
R. A. E. Tindall	47	7	1,126	109*	28·15
R. A. Gale	29	3	723	105	27·80
K. Taylor	17	2	413	85	27·53
M. Hill	50	5	1,232	100*	27·37
R. A. Hutton	44	3	1,122	163*	27·36
R. W. Hooker	46	6	1,083	119*	27·07
W. B. Stott	30	2	758	143	27·07
M. G. M. Groves	21	3	485	74*	26·94
A. B. D. Parsons	37	3	915	95	26·91
R. C. White	49	0	1,318	94	26·89
J. B. Mortimore	56	3	1,425	149	26·88
J. H. Hampshire	54	4	1,342	120	26·84
F. J. Titmus	43	8	938	65	26·80
A. S. M. Oakman	59	5	1,447	108	26·79
K. E. Palmer	46	16	793	53	26·43
J. T. Murray	39	10	766	133*	26·41
W. T. Greensmith	20	7	343	59*	26·38
K. Fletcher	54	4	1,310	94	26·20
B. Hedges	56	2	1,406	96	26·03

* Denotes not out

English Bowling Averages, 1963
(Qualification, 10 Wickets in 10 Innings)

Bowlers	Overs	Maidens	Runs	Wickets	Average
F. S. Trueman	844·3	206	1,955	129	15·15
P. H. Parfitt	105	31	286	18	15·88
K. E. Palmer	1,018·5	289	2,234	139	16·07
A. E. Moss	642·5	249	1,355	84	16·13
D. A. D. Sydenham	819·1	239	1,753	108	16·23
J. B. Statham	791	168	1,874	113	16·58
D. Shackleton	1,387·3	583	2,446	146	16·75
J. W. F. Larter	821·1	226	2,028	121	16·76
A. G. Nicholson	589	180	1,189	69	17·23
A. S. M. Oakman	408·3	136	953	55	17·32
O. S. Wheatley	752·1	228	1,666	94	17·72
T. W. Cartwright	888·1	360	1,786	100	17·86
R. V. Webster	571	138	1,430	80	17·87
R. Illingworth	483·4	170	1,078	60	17·96
D. Doughty	214·1	68	635	35	18·14
E. Lewis	170·1	54	476	26	18·30
D. J. Shepherd	1,285·3	40	2,373	126	18·83
R. C. Kerslake	191·4	67	490	26	18·84
A. T. Castell	215·1	70	528	28	18·85
D. Wilson	850·4	317	1,950	102	19·11
F. J. Titmus	894·3	288	1,976	103	19·18
P. J. Watts	492·2	142	1,172	61	19·21
J. C. Laker	374	128	828	43	19·25
N. I. Thomson	1,076·2	368	2,173	112	19·40
W. E. Alley	401	148	758	39	19·43
F. E. Rumsey	794·1	176	1,989	102	19·50
N. Gifford	602	229	1,409	72	19·56
D. Bennett	287·1	63	882	42	19·57
D. N. F. Slade	712·4	307	1,402	71	19·74
G. C. Cooper	153·5	69	317	16	19·81
B. Crump	1,017·2	377	2,120	106	20·00
R. C. Smith	345·3	101	956	47	20·34
A. Buss	792·4	203	1,888	92	20·52
D. L. Bates	453	114	1,171	57	20·54
J. B. Mortimore	1,027·2	389	2,104	102	20·62
R. L. Pratt	201·3	50	538	26	20·69
C. Cook	434·3	179	935	45	20·77
D. Underwood	941·4	376	2,134	101	21·12
R. B. Edmonds	325·4	116	744	35	21·25
J. Cotton	565·3	128	1,506	70	21·51
J. Pressdee	975·5	327	2,292	166	21·62
B. R. Knight	1,123·5	207	3,042	140	21·72
S. J. Storey	172·1	44	435	20	21·75
G. Arnold	145	39	393	18	21·83
I. Davison	883·1	213	2,434	111	21·92
H. L. Jackson	790·3	241	1,515	69	21·95
D. R. Smith	790	195	1,816	82	22·14
M. J. Horton	618·3	217	1,353	61	22·18
P. J. Loader	552	133	1,379	62	22·24
D. A. Bick	256·4	71	690	31	22·25
A. Brown	762·5	190	1,940	86	22·55
J. S. Savage	924·3	272	2,400	105	22·85
J. S. Price	631	163	1,901	83	22·90
T. Greenhough	590·1	190	1,307	57	22·92
R. Harman	286·3	97	785	34	23·08
D. Gibson	693·1	137	1,795	77	23·31
M. E. Miller	333·4	130	770	33	23·33
D. W. White	730·4	141	2,224	95	23·41
J. A. Flavell	792·3	169	1,951	83	23·50
D. A. Allen	877·4	325	1,811	77	23·51
B. Langford	718·2	258	1,647	70	23·52
M. R. Dilley	178	39	427	18	23·72
A. Wassell	830	351	1,663	70	23·75
C. Milburn	296·3	69	784	33	23·75
B. D. Wells	1,078	415	2,306	97	23·77
H. J. Rhodes	736·2	174	1,786	75	23·81
R. W. Barber	508	127	1,550	65	23·84
K. Ibadulla	261	82	573	24	23·87
R. W. Hooker	409	122	1,003	42	23·88
A. B. Jackson	693·2	154	1,696	71	23·88
E. J. Fillary	217·5	40	790	33	23·93
R. M. H. Cottam	403	78	1,154	48	24·04
A. S. Brown	860·4	223	2,205	91	24·23
R. V. Bell	645·3	246	1,610	66	24·39
G. A. R. Lock	874·2	302	2,149	88	24·42
M. Ryan	704·2	194	1,547	63	24·55
J. A. Snow	254·5	44	712	29	24·55
R. C. White	71·1	14	247	10	24·70
C. Greetham	402·1	94	1,113	44	25·29

TEST MATCHES

Australia v. England, 1962–1963

First Test.—(Brisbane, Nov. 30–Dec. 5). Drawn. Australia 404 and 362 for 4 dec.; England 389 and 278 for 6.

Second Test.—(Melbourne, Dec. 29–Jan. 3). England won by 7 wickets. Australia 316 and 248; England 331 and 237 for 3.

Third Test.—(Sydney, Jan. 11–15). Australia won by 8 wickets. England 279 and 104; Australia 319 and 67 for 2.

Fourth Test.—(Adelaide, Jan. 25–30). Drawn. Australia 393 and 293; England 331 and 223 for 4.

Fifth Test.—(Sydney, Feb. 15–20). Drawn. England 321 and 268 for 8 dec.; Australia 349 and 152 for 4.

New Zealand v. England, 1963

First Test.—(Auckland, Feb. 23–27). England won by innings and 215. England 562 for 7 dec.; New Zealand 258 and 89.

Second Test.—(Wellington, March 1–4). England won by innings and 47. New Zealand 194 and 187; England 428 for 8 dec.

Third Test.—(Christchurch, March 15–19). England won by 7 wickets. New Zealand 266 and 159; England 253 and 173 for 3.

West Indies Tour of Britain, 1963

First class matches: played, 30; won, 14; lost, 2; drawn 14.

BATTING

Batsmen	Number of Innings	Times not out	Total Runs	Highest score	Average
G. S. Sobers	34	6	1,333	112	47·60
B. F. Butcher	34	5	1,294	133	44·62
C. C. Hunte	37	6	1,367	182	44·09
R. B. Kanhai	32	4	1,149	119	41·03
E. D. McMorris	29	5	878	190*	36·58
S. M. Nurse	29	2	911	116*	33·74
M. C. Carew	39	4	1,060	117	30·28
W. V. Rodriguez	18	4	413	93	29·50
J. S. Solomon	35	6	774	62	26·68
F. M. Worrell	23	2	522	74*	24·85
W. A. White	14	3	228	68*	20·72
D. L. Murray	20	4	269	67	16·81
W. W. Hall	21	2	264	102*	13·89
L. A. King	22	7	202	27*	13·46
D. W. Allan	22	5	226	34	13·29
C. C. Griffith	23	7	164	27*	10·25
L. R. Gibbs	18	6	89	31	7·41
A. L. Valentine	11	5	10	6*	1·66

* Not out.

BOWLING

Bowlers	Overs	Maidens	Runs	Wickets	Average
C. C. Griffith	701·2	192	1,527	119	12·83
S. M. Nurse	13	1	53	3	17·66
L. R. Gibbs	733	216	1,564	78	20·05
W. W. Hall	566·4	113	1,506	74	20·35
J. S. Solomon	152·5	25	540	26	20·76
C. C. Hunte	44·1	8	112	5	22·40
G. S. Sobers	758·3	182	1,844	82	22·48
W. A. White	286	83	647	28	23·10
M. C. Carew	32	7	99	4	24·75
L. A. King	493·5	100	1,284	47	27·31
A. L. Valentine	306·3	98	822	24	34·25
F. M. Worrell	204	56	480	13	36·92
W. V. Rodriguez	59	6	240	4	60·00

Also Bowled.—B. F. Butcher 2·3—0—10—1; E. D. McMorris, 3—0—26—0.

HUNDREDS

G. Sobers (4): 112 *v.* Somerset (Bath; 102 *v.* England (Leeds, 4th Test); 101 *v.* T. N. Pearce's XI (Scarborough); 100* *v.* Yorks. (Sheffield). C. C. Hunte (3): 182 *v.* England (Manchester, 1st Test); 108* *v.* England (Oval, 5th Test); 103 *v.* Middlesex (Lord's). S. M. Nurse (3): 116* *v.* Oxford Univ. (Oxford); 103* *v.* Glamorgan (Swansea); 100 *v.* T. N. Pearce's XI (Scarborough). B. F. Butcher (2): 133 *v.* England (Lord's, 2nd Test); 130 *v.* Somerset (Bath). E. D. McMorris (2): 190* *v.* Middlesex (Lord's); 100 *v.* Kent (Canterbury). M. C. Carew (1): 117 *v.* Glamorgan (Cardiff). W. W. Hall (1): 102* *v.* Cambridge Univ. (Cambridge). R. B. Kanhai (1): 119 *v.* Cambridge Univ. (Cambridge).

England v. West Indies, 1963

First Test.—Manchester (June 6–10). West Indies won by 10 wickets. West Indies 501 for 6 (dec.) and 1 for 0; England 205 and 296.

Second Test.—Lord's (June 20–25). Drawn. West Indies 301 and 229; England 297 and 228 for 9.

Third Test.—Birmingham (July 4–9). England won by 217 runs. England 216 and 278 for 9 (dec.); West Indies 186 and 91.

Fourth Test.—Leeds (July 25–29). West Indies won by 221 runs; West Indies 397 and 229; England 174 and 231.

Fifth Test.—Oval (Aug. 22–26). West Indies won by 8 wickets. England 275 and 223; West Indies 246 and 255 for 2.

TEST MATCH AVERAGES

ENGLAND (BATTING)

	Av.		Av.
P. J. Sharpe	53·40	G. A. R. Lock	19·16
E. R. Dexter	34·00	J. H. Edrich	17·16
D. B. Close	31·50	M. C. Cowdrey	13·00
K. F. Barrington	27·50	D. Shackleton	10·00
M. J. Stewart	26·37	F. S. Trueman	9·11
J. B. Bolus	26·25	J. B. Statham	7·25
J. M. Parks	23·75	D. A. Allen	4·00
F. J. Titmus	20·71		

Also batted:—K. V. Andrew, 3* and 15; P. E. Richardson 2 and 14.

ENGLAND (BOWLING)

	Wkts.	Av.		Wkts.	Av.
F. S. Trueman	34	17·47	F. J. Titmus	6	42·66
E. R. Dexter	7	32·42	D. A. Allen	4	52·00
D. Shackleton	15	34·53	J. B. Statham	3	81·00
G. A. R. Lock	6	38·33			

Also bowled:—D. B. Close 25–5–88–0.

WEST INDIES (BATTING)

	Av.		Av.
C. C. Hunte	58·87	M. C. Carew	19·00
R. B. Kanhai	55·22	D. L. Murray	15·50
B. F. Butcher	47·87	W. W. Hall	13·16
G. S. Sobers	40·25	E. D. McMorris	9·00
J. S. Solomon	25·60	C. C. Griffith	6·40
F. M. Worrell	20·28	L. R. Gibbs	3·75

Also batted:—W. V. Rodriguez, 5 and 28.

WEST INDIES (BOWLING)

	Wkts.	Av.		Wkts.	Av.
C. C. Griffith	32	16·21	W. W. Hall	16	33·37
L. R. Gibbs	26	21·30	F. M. Worrell	3	34·66
G. S. Sobers	20	28·55			

MISCELLANEOUS CRICKET RECORDS

Highest individual scores.—In first-class cricket in England: A. C. Maclaren, 424, for Lancashire v. Somerset at Taunton, July, 1895. In Australia: D. G. Bradman (Australia), 452 (not out) for N.S.W. v. Queensland, Sydney, 1929–30. In India: B. B. Nimbalkar (Maharashtra v. W. Indian States), Poona, 1948–49, 443 (not out). In Pakistan: Hanif Mohammed, 499, Karachi v. Bahawalpur, 1959. In a minor inter-county match: F. E. Lacey (Hampshire v. Norfolk), Southampton, 1887, 323 (not out). In other minor matches: A. E. J. Collins, aged 14, scored 628 (not out) in a Junior House match playing for Clarke's House v. North Town at Clifton College. This score extended over five afternoons, 1899.

Highest team innings.—Australia, Victoria 1,107 v. N.S.W., Melbourne, 1926; England, England 903 (for 7 dec.) v. Australia, 1938.

Win.—Victoria beat Tasmania by innings and 666 runs, 1922–3.

Runs in a day.—Australia v. Essex, Southend, May 15, 1948, 721.

Smallest totals.—Oxford University (one man absent), 12 v. M.C.C. at Oxford, May, 1877; Northants, 12 v. Gloucester, June 11, 1907.

Highest Aggregate.—Fifth Test, Durban, March, 1939. S. Africa 530 and 481; England 316 and 654 for 5 wickets. 1,981 (35 wkts.). India, Bombay, 651 and 714 for 8 dec. v. Maharashtra, 407, 604, Poona 1948–9. Total 2,376 (38 wkts.).

Highest Partnerships.—Gul Mahomed (319) and V. S. Hazare (288) made 577 for 4th wicket for Baroda v. Holkar (Mar. 7, 1947). Previous: C. L. Walcott and F. M. Worrell, 574 for Barbados v. Trinidad, 1946. P. Holmes and H. Sutcliffe 555 for Yorks. v. Essex, Leyton, 1932, 1st wicket highest.

Most centuries in one season.—D. C. S. Compton, 18 (1947); J. B. Hobbs, 16 (1925); W. R. Hammond, 15 (1938); H. Sutcliffe, 14 (1932); D. G. Bradman (1938), C. B. Fry (1901), W. R. Hammond (1933, 7), T. Hayward (1906), E. P. Hendren (1923, 7, 8), C. P. Mead (1928), and H. Sutcliffe (1928, 31), 13 centuries. Six consecutive—C. B. Fry, 1901; D. G. Bradman (Australia), 1938–9; five consecutive Test centuries, E. Weekes, 1949. Total centuries in career—J. B. Hobbs, 197 (175 in Eng.).

Most runs made in a year.—D. C. S. Compton (Middlesex), 3,816 (1947); W. J. Edrich (Middlesex), 3,539 (1947); T. Hayward (Surrey), 3,518 (1906). L. Hutton (Yorks), 3,429 (1949); F. E. Woolley (Kent), 3,352 (1928).

Most wickets in season.—A. P. Freeman (Kent), 304, 1928, and 298, 1933; T. Richardson (Surrey), 290, 1895.

Aggregates.—J. B. Hobbs, 61,237; W. G. Grace, 54,896, 2,876 wkts. W. R. Rhodes, 4,187 wkts. Also F. E. Woolley, 58,969; E. P. Hendren, 57,610; C. P. Mead, 55,060; W. R. Hammond, 50,493; A. P. Freeman, 3,776 wkts.

Record Benefits.—C. Washbrook (Lancs.), £14,000 (1948); D. C. S. Compton (Middlesex), £12,200 (1949); A. V. Bedser (Surrey), £12,866 (1953). J. B. Statham (Lancs.), £13,047 (1961). Sir D. G. Bradman received £A10,000 for his Testimonial match in Australia, 1948–49.

1,000 runs in May —W. G. Grace, 1895, W R. Hammond, 1927, C. Hallows, 1928, D. G. Bradman, 1930, 1938, W. J Edrich, 1938; incl. April, T. Hayward, 1900. In June, L. Hutton, 1,294, 1949. In July.—M. J. K. Smith, 1,209, 1959: August.—W. R. Hammond, 1,281, 1936.

Fastest century.—P G. H. Fender for Surrey v. Northamptonshire in 1920, 100 runs in 35 mins.

Most Sixes in Match.—17, W. J. Stewart, Warwickshire v. Lancashire, 1959.

Double.—J. H. Parks (Sussex). 3,003 runs and 101 wkts., 1937. Double centuries in match: A. E. Fagg (Kent) v. Essex, 1938, Colchester, 244 and 202 (not out).

Highest batting average in England 115·66, D. G. Bradman (S. Aust.), 1933.

Most Catches in Match —W. R. Hammond 10, Gloucestershire v. Surrey at Cheltenham, 1928.

UNIVERSITIES AND SCHOOLS, ETC.

Oxford and Cambridge

First played 1827. Played 118. Cambridge have won 50, Oxford 43, drawn 26.

1958 Cambridge (99 runs). Cambridge 101 for 7 (dec.) and 269 for 8 (dec.): Oxford 180 and 151.
1959 Oxford (85 runs). Oxford 217 and 238; Cambridge 174 and 196.
1960 Drawn. Cambridge 153 and 243 for 9; Oxford 310.
1961 Drawn. Cambridge 173 and 254 for 6; Oxford 232 for 8 (dec.).
1962 Drawn. Cambridge 259 for 6 (dec.) and 190 for 6 (dec.); Oxford 237 and 136 for 5.
1962 Drawn. Cambridge 246 and 148 for 8 (dec.); Oxford 201 for 6 (dec.) and 136 for 6.
1963 Drawn. Cambridge 246 and 148 for 8 (dec.); Oxford 201 for 6 (dec.) and 136 for 6.

Eton and Harrow

First played 1805. Played 128. Eton have won 46, Harrow 39. Drawn 42.

1956 Drawn. (Eton 157 for 8 (dec.); Harrow 94 for 1 (match abandoned)).
1957 Drawn. (Harrow 183 for 9 (dec.); Eton 204 for 6).
1958 Drawn. (Eton 170 and 110 for 7 (dec.); Harrow 96 and 81 for 7).
1959 Drawn. (Eton 270 for 5 (dec.) and 106; Harrow 175 and 157 for 8).
1960 Harrow (124 runs). (Harrow 216 and 143; Eton 153 and 82).
1961 Harrow (innings and 12). (Harrow 295 for 9 (dec.); Eton 147 and 136).
1962 Drawn. (Harrow 247; Eton 110 and 262 for 7).
1963 Drawn. (Eton 202 for 9 (dec.); Harrow 82 for 8 (match abandoned)).

School Matches. 1963

Eton and Winchester drew. Winchester 94; Eton 166 for 7 (dec.) (Rain).

Oratory beat Beaumont by 116 runs. Oratory 236 for 4 (dec.); Beaumont 120.

Tonbridge beat Clifton by 9 wickets. Clifton 152 and 89; Tonbridge 166 and 76 for 1.

Cheltenham and Haileybury and I.S.C. drew. Haileybury and I.S.C., 130; Cheltenham 107 for 7. (Rain).

Rugby beat Marlborough by 22 runs. Rugby 99 and 233; Marlborough 134 and 176.

Southern Schools beat Rest by 10 wickets. Rest 134 and 146; Southern Schools 193 and 88 for 0.

Combined Services and Public Schools drew. Public Schools 262 for 6 (dec.) and 152; Combined Services 236 for 8 (dec.) and 165 for 8.

County Knock-Out Competition

Final.—Sussex beat Worcestershire by 14 runs. Sussex 168; Worcestershire 154.

LIST OF COUNTY CHAMPIONS.

1873	Notts. and Glos.	1892	Surrey	1913	Kent	1938	Yorkshire
1874	Derbyshire	1893	Yorkshire	1914	Surrey	1939	Yorkshire
1875	Notts.	1894	Surrey	1919	Yorkshire	1946	Yorkshire
1876	Gloucester	1895	Surrey	1920	Middlesex	1947	Middlesex
1877	Gloucester	1896	Yorkshire	1921	Middlesex	1948	Glamorgan
1878	Middlesex	1897	Lancashire	1922	Yorkshire	1949	Middlesex / Yorkshire
1879	Notts. and Lancs.	1898	Yorkshire	1923	Yorkshire		
1880	Notts.	1899	Surrey	1924	Yorkshire	1950	Lancashire / Surrey
1881	Lancashire	1900	Yorkshire	1925	Yorkshire		
1882	Lancs. and Notts.	1901	Yorkshire	1926	Lancashire	1951	Warwickshire
1883	Notts.	1902	Yorkshire	1927	Lancashire	1952	Surrey
1884	Notts.	1903	Middlesex	1928	Lancashire	1953	Surrey
1885	Notts.	1904	Lancashire	1929	Notts.	1954	Surrey
1886	Notts.	1905	Yorkshire	1930	Lancashire	1955	Surrey
1887	Surrey	1906	Kent	1931	Yorkshire	1956	Surrey
1888	Surrey	1907	Notts.	1932	Yorkshire	1957	Surrey
1889	Notts. / Lancs. / Surrey	1908	Yorkshire	1933	Yorkshire	1958	Surrey
		1909	Kent	1934	Lancashire	1959	Yorkshire
		1910	Kent	1935	Yorkshire	1960	Yorkshire
1890	Surrey	1911	Warwickshire	1936	Derbyshire	1961	Hampshire
1891	Surrey	1912	Yorkshire	1937	Yorkshire	1962	Yorkshire
						1963	Yorkshire

RUGBY FOOTBALL

International Union Table, 1962-63

Country	Played	Won	Drawn	Lost	Points Scored For	Points Scored Agst.	Points
England	4	3	1	0	29	19	7
France	4	2	0	2	40	25	4
Scotland	4	2	0	2	22	22	4
Ireland	4	1	1	2	19	33	3
Wales	4	1	0	3	21	32	2

CALCUTTA CUP England *v.* Scotland		COUNTY CHAMPIONSHIP
1958	Draw 3–3	Warwickshire.
1959	Draw 3–3	Warwickshire.
1960	England 21–12	Warwickshire.
1961	England 6–0	Cheshire.
1962	Draw 3–3	Warwickshire.
1963	England 10–8	Warwickshire.

INTERNATIONAL MATCHES, 1962–63

1962

Nov. 17 Dublin. Ireland 3; Wales 3. (Postponed from 1961–62 season).

1963

Jan. 12 Paris. France 6; Scotland 11.
19 Cardiff. Wales 6; England 13.
26 Dublin. Ireland 5; France 24.
Feb. 2 Edinburgh. Scotland 0; Wales 6.
9 Dublin. Ireland 0; England 0.
23 Twickenham. England 6; France 5.
Edinburgh. Scotland 3; Ireland 0.
Mar. 9 Cardiff. Wales 6; Ireland 14.
16 Twickenham. England 10; Scotland 8.
23 Paris. France 5; Wales 3.

COUNTY CHAMPIONSHIP FINAL

Warwickshire beat Yorkshire 13–10.

OTHER CHIEF MATCHES, 1962–63

Universities. 1962.—Cambridge University beat Oxford University 14–0 at Twickenham on Dec. 11, 1962.

Hospitals Cup Final.—St. Mary's beat St. Thomas's 6–0.

Army Rugby Challenge Cup.—1st Bn. Welsh Guards beat 28 Coy. R.A.O.C. 9–6.

Services.—Army beat R.N. 11–3; R.A.F. beat R.N. 3–0; R.A.F. beat Army 19–14.

Middlesex Seven-a-Side Finals.—London Scottish beat Hawick 15–11.

ENGLISH TOUR OF AUSTRALASIA, 1963

May 25 Auckland. New Zealand 21; England 11.
June 1 Christchurch. New Zealand 9; England 6.
June 4 Sydney. Australia 18; England 9.

RUGBY FOOTBALL LEAGUE (Est. 1895)
International Matches

1962

June 9 Sydney. Great Britain 31; Australia 12.
June 30 Brisbane. Great Britain 17; Australia. 10.
July 14 Sydney. Great Britain 17; Australia 18.
July 28 Auckland. Great Britain 0; New Zealand 19.
Aug. 11 Auckland. Great Britain 8; New Zealand 27.
Dec. 2 Perpignan. Great Britain 12; France 17.

1963

April 3 Wigan. Great Britain 42; France 4.

Rugby League Challenge Cup.—Final. Wakefield Trinity beat Wigan 25–10 pts. at Wembley Stadium on May 11, 1963. Attendance 84,482. Receipts £44,521. *Semi Finals.* Wakefield Trinity beat Warrington 5–2 (at Swinton); Wigan beat Hull Kingston Rovers 18–4 (at Leeds).

County Championship.—Yorkshire.

First Division Winners.—Swinton.

Western Division Championship.—Workington Town beat Widnes 10–0.

Eastern Division Championship.—Hull Kingston Rovers beat Huddersfield 13–10.

County Cup Winners: Yorkshire Cup.—Hunslet.

Lancashire Cup.—St. Helens.

LACROSSE, 1962-63

Annual Territorial Match.—North beat South.

English Club Championship (Iroquois Cup).—Mellor beat Cambridge University.

North of England Senior Flag.—Mellor beat Heaton Mersey.

South of England Senior Flag.—Cambridge University beat Purley.

Northern Counties Championship.—Lancashire beat Cheshire.

University.—Cambridge University beat Oxford University.

ASSOCIATION FOOTBALL

International Table, 1962–63

Country	Played	Won	Drawn	Lost	Goals For	Goals Agst.	Points
Scotland	3	3	0	0	10	4	6
England	3	2	0	1	8	3	4
Wales	3	1	0	2	6	8	2
Ireland	3	0	0	3	3	12	0

ENGLAND *v.* SCOTLAND.

	g. g.
1958 England	4—0
1959 England	1—0
1960 Draw	1—1
1961 England	9—3
1962 Scotland	2—0
1963 Scotland	2—1

FOOTBALL ASSOCIATION CUP.

Bolton W. *b.* Manchester U. . 2—0
Notts F. *b.* Luton . . . 2—1
Wolverhampton W. *b.* Blackburn R. . . . 3—0
Tottenham H. *b.* Leicester C. 2—0
Tottenham H. *b.* Burnley . . . 3—1
Manchester U. *b.* Leicester C. 3—1

LEAGUE COMPETITION, 1962–63

Div. I.—Everton, 61 pts.; Tottenham Hotspur, 55 pts. Relegated: Leyton Orient, 21 pts. and Manchester City, 31 pts.

Div. II.—Promoted: Stoke City, 53 pts. and Chelsea, 52 pts. Relegated: Luton Town, 29 pts. and Walsall, 31 pts.

Div. III.—Promoted: Northampton, 62 pts. and Swindon Town, 58 pts. Relegated: Halifax Town, 30 pts., Carlisle United, 35 pts., Brighton and Hove Albion, 36 pts. and Bradford, 40 pts.

Div. IV.—Promoted: Brentford 62 pts. Oldham Athletic, 59 pts., Crewe Alexandra, 59 pts., Mansfield Town, 57 pts.

Reorganization of Sections.—Since the 1958–59 season the former Northern and Southern sections have been reorganized into National Third and Fourth Divisions. At the end of each season, the last four clubs in the Third Division are relegated to the Fourth Division and the first four clubs in the Fourth Division promoted to the Third Division.

SCOTTISH LEAGUE.—Div. 1. Champions: Rangers, 57 pts.; Div. 2. Champions: St. Johnstone, 55 pts.

REPRESENTATIVE MATCHES, 1962–63

HOME INTERNATIONALS

1962
Oct. 20 Belfast. Ireland 1; England 3.
Cardiff. Wales 2; Scotland 3.
Nov. 7 Hampden Park. Scotland 5; Ireland 1.
21 Wembley. England 4; Wales 0.
1963
Apr. 3 Belfast. Ireland 1; Wales 4.
6 Wembley. England 1; Scotland 2.

OTHER INTERNATIONALS

1962
Oct. 3 Sheffield. England 1; France 1.
1963
Feb. 27 Paris. France 5; England 2.
May 8 Wembley. England 1; Brazil 1.
May 29 Bratislava. Czechoslovakia 2; England 4.
June 2 Leipzig. E. Germany 1; England 2.
5 Basle. Switzerland 1; England 8.

INTER-LEAGUE MATCHES

1962
Oct. 31 Norwich. Football League 3; Irish League 1.
Nov. 14 Rome. Italian League 4; Scottish League 3.
28 Celtic Park. Scottish League 11; League of Ireland 0.
29 Highbury. Football League 3; Italian League 2.
1963
Mar. 18 Dublin. League of Ireland 1; Irish League 3.

UNDER 23 INTERNATIONALS

1962
Nov. 7 Plymouth. England 6; Belgium 1.
28 Birmingham. England 5; Greece 0.

1963
Mar. 21 Manchester. England 0; Yugoslavia 0.
May 29 Belgrade. Yugoslavia 2; England 4.
June 2 Bucharest. Romania 1; England 0.

CUP FINALS, 1962–63

F.A. CUP.—*S.F.:* April 27 (Villa Park), Manchester United beat Southampton 1–0. Attendance 65,000. (Hillsborough, Sheffield), Leicester City beat Liverpool 1–0. Attendance 65,000.
Final: May 25 (Wembley Stadium), Manchester United beat Leicester City 3–1. Attendance 100,000. Receipts £89,000.

F.A. AMATEUR.—*S.F.:* April 13 (Highbury). Wimbledon beat Leytonstone 2–1. (Fulham), Sutton United beat Hitchin Town 4–0.
Final: May 4 (Wembley Stadium). Wimbledon beat Sutton 4–2. Attendance 45,000.

SCOTTISH CUP.—*S.F.:* (Hampden Park), Rangers beat Dundee United 5–2. (Ibrox Park), Celtic beat Raith Rovers 5–2.
F.: Replay, May 15 (Hampden Park), Rangers beat Celtic 3–0, after draw 1–1 at Hampden Park on May 4.

SCOTTISH LEAGUE CUP.—*F.:* Hearts beat Kilmarnock 1–0.

ARTHUR DUNN CUP.—Old Reptonians beat Old Malvernians 4–0.

EUROPEAN CUP.—*S.F.:* Benfica (Portugal) beat Feyenoord (Netherlands) (on aggregate) 3–1; Milan beat Dundee (on aggregate) 6–1; *F.* Milan beat Benfica 2–1 (at Wembley).

CUP-WINNERS' CUP.—*S.F.:* Atletico (Madrid) beat Nuremberg (on aggregate) 3–2; Tottenham Hotspur beat O.F.K. Belgrade (on aggregate) 5–2. *F.* Tottenham Hotspur beat Atletico 5–1 (at Rotterdam).

AMATEUR HOME INTERNATIONALS

1962
Sept. 29 Dulwich. England 3; Ireland 2.
Nov. 17 Shrewsbury. England 3; Wales 2.
1963
Jan. 12 Wrexham. Wales 0; Ireland 2.
Mar. 15 Hampden Park. Scotland 2; England 4.
Apr. 20 Wrexham. Wales 3; Scotland 1.
May 10 Belfast. Ireland 5; Scotland 2.

HOCKEY, 1962–63

MEN'S HOCKEY

INTERNATIONAL CHAMPIONSHIP

	P.	W.	D.	L.	Goals F.	Goals A.	Pts.
England	3	3	0	0	5	1	6
Scotland	3	2	0	1	7	7	4
Ireland	3	1	0	2	7	4	2
Wales	3	0	0	3	4	11	0

INTERNATIONAL MATCHES

England beat Wales 1–0; England beat Ireland 2–1; England beat Scotland 2–0; Scotland beat Ireland 2–1; Ireland beat Wales 5–0; Scotland beat Wales 5–4.

OTHER INTERNATIONAL

Great Britain beat Spain 1–0.

Universities.—Oxford University beat Cambridge University 3–0.

Services.—Army beat R.N. 1–0; R.A.F. beat R.N. 1–0; Army beat R.A.F. 3–2.

County Championship Final.—Surrey beat Devon 4–1.

WOMEN'S HOCKEY

LEADING MATCHES, 1962–63

England beat Scotland 5–0; Wales beat England 1–0; England beat Ireland 3–0; England and Germany drew 0–0; England "B" and France drew 0–0.

SPORTS GROUND AND COURT SIZES

A *Cricket Pitch* is 22 yards (one chain) between the stumps.

A *Tennis Court* is 96 ft. × 31 ft. 8 in.

A *Lawn Tennis Court* is 78×36 feet (double) and 78×27 feet (single).

A *Badminton Court* is 44×20 ft., with net 30 ins. deep and 5 ft. high at centre.

A *Polo Ground* is 300×160 yards.

A *Football Ground* (*Association*) is 130×100 yards (full size) and 120×80 yards for international matches; (*Rugby*) 110×75 yards (full size) (with in-goal area of 25×75 yards at each end).

A *Squash Racquets Court* is 32 ft. long × 21 ft. broad.

A *Bowls Rink* is not less than 19 ft. wide, and the green is usually 42 yards long.

GOLF, 1962–63

CHAMPIONSHIPS.

OPEN (Instituted 1860.)

- 1956 P. W. Thomson (Australia), 286.
- 1957 A. D. Locke (S.A.), 279
- 1958 P. W. Thomson (Australia) after tie with D. C. Thomas in 278.
- 1959 G. Player (S.A.), 284.
- 1960 K. Nagle (Australia) 278.
- 1961 A. Palmer (U.S.A.), 284
- 1962 A. Palmer (U.S.A.), 276
- 1963 R. J. Charles (N.Z.) beat P. Rodgers (U.S.A.) after tie in 277

AMATEUR (1885.)

- 1956 J. C. Beharrell.
- 1957 R. R. Jack.
- 1958 J B. Carr.
- 1959 D. R. Beman (U.S.A.).
- 1960 J. B. Carr.
- 1961 M. F. Bonallack.
- 1962 R. D. Davies (U.S.A.)
- 1963 M. S. R. Lunt.

LADIES (1893.)

- 1956 Miss M. Smith (U.S.A.).
- 1957 Miss P. Garvey (Ireland).
- 1958 Mrs. G. Valentine.
- 1959 Miss E. Price.
- 1960 Miss B. McIntire (U.S.A.).
- 1961 Mrs. A. D. Spearman.
- 1962 Mrs. A. D. Spearman.
- 1963 Mlle. B. Varangor (France).

PROFESSIONAL MATCH PLAY TOURNAMENT (*News of the World.*)

- 1957 C. O'Connor (Ireland).
- 1958 H. Weetman.
- 1959 D. Snell.
- 1960 E. C. Brown.
- 1961 P. W. Thomson (Australia).
- 1962 E. C. Brown.
- 1963 D. C. Thomas.

WALKER CUP

(Turnberry, May 24–25, 1963)

U.S.A. won by 12 Matches to 8

Winners.—

Singles—U.S.A.: W. J. Patton (2); Dr. E. Updegraft; L. E. Harris; R. Gardner; C. Coe.
Great Britain: D. B. Sheahan (2); R. D. B. M. Shade (2); J. B. Carr; S. W. T. Murray; M. F. Bonallack.

Foursomes—U.S.A.: D. Beman and Coe (2); A. D. Gray and Harris (2); Patton and R. H. Sikes; Gardner and Updegraft.
Great Britain: Bonallack and Murray.

OTHER CHIEF GOLF EVENTS, 1962–63

Canada Cup.—(Buenos Aires, Nov. 1962). 1, U.S.A. (A. Palmer and S. Snead), 557; 2, Argentina, 559; 3, Australia, 569; 4, England, 572. *Individual:* R. de Vicenzo (Argentina), 276; 2, P. Alliss (England) and A. Palmer, 278.
President's Putter.—J. G. Blackwell.
Halford Hewitt Cup.—Repton beat Fettes 3–2.
English Amateur.—M. F. Bonallack.
Schweppes Tournament.—P. J. Butler, 306.
Penfold-Swallow.—B. J. Hunt, 272.
Brabazon Trophy.—R. D. B. M. Shade.
Daks.—N. C. Coles and P. Alliss, 280.
Yorkshire Evening News.—T. B. Haliburton, 280.
Martini.—N. C. Coles and C. O'Connor, 298.
Gevacolour.—B. J. Hunt, 273.
Assistant Professional.—G. Will.
European Amateur Team Championship.—(Falsterbö, Sweden, July).—1, England; 2, Sweden; 3, Italy and W. Germany.
Cox Moore Tournament.—B. G. C. Huggett, 276.
Grafton Tournament.—B. J. Hunt, 279.
Jeyes Tournament.—G. B. Wolstenholme, 269.
Smart Weston Tournament.—B. J. Hunt.
Welsh Amateur.—W. I. Tucker.
Welsh Professional.—H. Gould.
Welsh Ladies.—Miss P. Roberts.
Scottish Amateur.—R. D. B. M. Shade.
Scottish Ladies.—Miss J. Lawrence.
Irish Amateur.—J. B. Carr.
Irish Professional.—C. O'Connor.
Irish Ladies.—Miss P. Garvey.
Carroll Sweet Afton Tournament.—B. J. Hunt, 270.
U.S.A. Masters.—J. W. Nicklaus.
U.S.A. Open.—J. Boros.
U.S.A., P.G.A. Championship.—J. W. Nicklaus.
U.S.A. Amateur.—D. Beman.
University.—Cambridge beat Oxford 12–2.
Artisans' Championship.—F. W. Sunderland.
English County Championship.—Yorkshire.
Women's County Championship.—Warwickshire.
British Youth Open.—A. J. Low.
Golf Illustrated Gold Vase.—R. H. Mummery.
Boys' International.—Scotland beat England 9–3.
British Boys' Amateur Championship.—A. H. C. Soutar.
Dutch Open.—R. Waltman (South Africa), 279.
Girls' International.—England beat Scotland 9–3.
British Girls' Open.—Miss D. Oxley.
Home International (*Raymond Trophy*).—England, Ireland and Scotland tied.
Dunlop Masters.—B. J. Hunt, 282.
English Women's Championship.—Mrs. M. F. Bonallack.
Women's Home Internationals.—1, England; 2, Scotland; 3, Ireland; 4, Wales.
Swiss Open.—D. J. Rees (after play-off with H. R. Henning (S. Africa)).
Northern Open.—G. Will.
Northern Professional.—G. A. Caygill.
Northern Women.—Miss A. Irvin.
Southern Professional.—H. Weetman.
Midland Open.—A. Rees.
Midland Professional.—C. H. Ward.
Midland Amateur.—C. Stowe.
Midland Women.—Miss A. Higgott.
West of England Open.—E. G. Lester.
Hennessy Tournament.—C. O'Connor, 277.
Senior Service Tournament.—D. Ragan (U.S.A.), 271.
Commonwealth Women's Tournament.—Great Britain.
French Open.—B. Devlin (Australia), 273.
French Amateur.—P. Cros.
German Open.—B. G. C. Huggett (G.B.), 278
German Amateur.—J. Hood (Australia).
P.G.A. Order of Merit Table.—(Harry Vardon Trophy) 1, N. C. Coles; 2, B. J. Hunt; 3, B. G. C. Huggett.
County Amateur Champions' Tournament—M. J. Burgess (Surrey) and R. Foster (Yorkshire), 152.

LAWN TENNIS

THE DAVIS CUP CHALLENGE ROUNDS

(Founder—Dwight Filley Davis (1879–1945), First Played, 1900.)

1921 U.S.A. beat Japan 5–0	1933 Great Britain beat France ... 3–2	1951 Australia beat U.S.A. 3–1
1922 U.S.A. beat Australia 4–1	1934 Great Britain beat U.S.A. ... 4–1	1952 Australia beat U.S.A. 4–1
1923 U.S.A. beat Australia 4–1	1935 Great Britain beat U.S.A. ... 5–0	1953 Australia beat U.S.A. 3–2
1924 U.S.A. beat Australia 5–0	1936 Great Britain beat Australia . 3–2	1954 U.S.A. beat Australia 3–0
1925 U.S.A. beat France 4–1	1937 U.S.A. beat Great Britain ... 4–1	1955 Australia beat U.S.A. 5–0
1926 U.S.A. beat France 4–1	1938 U.S.A. beat Australia 3–2	1956 Australia beat U.S.A. 5–2
1927 France beat U.S.A. 3–2	1939 Australia beat U.S.A. 3–2	1957 Australia beat U.S.A. 3–2
1928 France beat U.S.A. 4–1	1946 U.S.A. beat Australia 5–0	1958 U.S.A. beat Australia 3–2
1929 France beat U.S.A. 3–2	1947 U.S.A. beat Australia 3–1	1959 Australia beat U.S.A. 3–2
1930 France beat U.S.A. 4–1	1948 U.S.A. beat Australia 5–0	1960 Australia beat Italy 4–1
1931 France beat Great Britain ... 3–2	1949 U.S.A. beat Australia 4–1	1961 Australia beat Italy 5–0
1932 France beat U.S.A. 3–2	1950 Australia beat U.S.A 4–1	1962 Australia beat Mexico 5–0

THE CHAMPIONSHIPS (WIMBLEDON) 1963

Men's Singles.—C. R. McKinley (U.S.A.) beat F. Stolle (Australia) 9–7, 6–1, 6–4.

Women's Singles.—Miss M. Smith (Australia) beat Miss B. J. Moffitt (U.S.A.) 6–3, 6–4.

Men's Doubles.—R. H. Osuna and A. Palafox (Mexico) beat J. C. Barclay and P. Darmon (France) 4–6, 6–2, 6–3, 6–2.

Women's Doubles.—Miss M. E. Bueno (Brazil) and Miss D. R. Hard (U.S.A.) beat Miss R. A. Ebbern and Miss Smith (Australia) 8–6, 9–7.

Mixed Doubles.—K. N. Fletcher and Miss Smith (Australia) beat R. A. J. Hewitt (Australia) and Miss Hard (U.S.A.) 11–9, 6–4.

All England Plate.

Men's Singles.—E. L. Scott (U.S.A.) w.o., I. S. Crookshank (N.Z.), scr.

Women's Singles.—Miss F. Durr (France) beat Miss A. Dmitrieva (U.S.S.R.) 6–1, 6–1.

Junior International Invitation Tournament.

Boys' Singles.—K. Kalogeropoulos (Greece) beat I. El Shafei (Egypt) 6–4, 6–3.

Girls' Singles.—Miss D. M. Salfati (France) beat Miss K. Denning (Australia) 6–4, 6–1.

WIGHTMAN CUP (CLEVELAND, OHIO, AUGUST)

U.S.A. won by 6 matches to 1.

Results—

Singles: Mrs P. F. Jones (G.B.) beat Miss D. R. Hard (U.S.A.) 6–1, 0–6, 8–6; Miss B. J. Moffitt (U.S.A.) beat Miss C. C. Truman 6–4, 19–17; Miss N. Richey (U.S.A.) beat Miss D. M. Catt (G.B.) 14–12, 6–3; Miss Hard beat Miss Truman 6–3, 6–0; Miss Moffitt beat Mrs. Jones. 6–4, 4–6, 6–3.

Doubles: Miss Richey and Mrs. D. Fales (U.S.A.) beat Miss Catt and Miss D. E. Starkie 6–4, 6–8, 6–2; Miss Hard and Miss Moffitt beat Mrs. Jones and Miss Truman 4–6, 7–5, 6–2.

BRITISH HARD COURT CHAMPIONSHIPS (BOURNEMOUTH)

Men's Singles.—W. A. Knight (G.B.).

Women's Singles.—Mrs. P. F. Jones (G.B.).

Doubles.—*Men's:* R. Hewitt and F. Stolle (Australia). *Women's:* Mrs. Jones and Miss A. Mortimer (G.B.). *Mixed:* A. R. Mills and Mrs. Mills (G.B.).

U.S.A. Championships:

Men's Singles.—R. H. Osuna (Mexico).

Women's Singles.—Miss M. E. Bueno (Brazil).

Men's Doubles.—C. R. McKinley and R. D. Ralston (U.S.A.).

Women's Doubles.—Miss M. Smith and Miss R. Ebbern (Australia).

Mixed Doubles.—Miss M. Smith and K. N. Fletcher (Australia).

Public Schools.—*Youll Cup:* High Wycombe R.G.S. beat Charterhouse 3–2.

D'Abernon Cup.—U.C.S. Old Boys.

County Championships.—*Men:* Middlesex; *Women* Yorkshire.

Inter-Services Tournament.—Royal Navy.

Services.—*R. Navy Championship:* Lt. G. Clarke. *Army Championship:* Capt. J. R. McManus. *R.A.F. Championship:* F/O. D. Short. *W.R.N.S: Championship:* Second Officer S. Hogg. *W.R.A.C. Championship:* Maj. N. J. Comyn. *W.R.A.F. Championship:* Cpl. P. Kemp.

Universities.—Cambridge University beat Oxford University 19–2.

Slazenger Professional Championships (Eastbourne).

Singles.—R. Becker (G.B.) beat J. W. Cawthorn (Australia) 3–2. *Doubles.*—Becker and Cawthorn beat W. Buchholz and M. Lohr (Germany) 3–0.

British Professional Championships (Eastbourne).

Singles.—J. M. Melhuish beat J. M. Watson 3–1. *Doubles:*—G. Bradley and W. J. Moss beat J. N. Draper and J. M. Melhuish 3–1; *Veterans*—B. R. Lawrence beat D. F. Roupell 2–0.

BRITISH JUNIOR CHAMPIONSHIPS (WIMBLEDON)

Boys' Singles.—G. R. Stilwell beat S. J. Matthews 6–4, 4–6, 8–6.

Girls. Singles.—Miss M. E. Greenwood beat Miss S. M. Veale 6–3, 6–3.

Boys' Doubles.—S. J. Matthews and G. R. Stilwell beat A. G. Long and P. J. Moores 6–2, 8–6.

Girls' Doubles.—Miss M. E. Greenwood and Miss S. Percival beat Miss A. F. Morris and Miss S. M. Veale 6–4, 6–3.

Mixed Doubles.—M. R. Lewinsohn and Miss S. M. Veale beat D. A. Lloyd and Miss A. F. Morris 7–5, 6–1.

TENNIS, 1963

Amateur Championships.

Singles.—G. W. T. Atkins beat D. J. Warburg 3–1.

Doubles.—J. W. Leonard and A. C. S. Tufton beat Lord Aberdare and D. J. Warburg 3–1.

Henry Leaf Cup.—Rugby beat Eton II 2–1.

M.C.C. Gold Prize.—D. J. Warburg beat P. Kershaw.

University.—Cambridge University beat Oxford University 3–0.

BADMINTON, 1963

ALL-ENGLAND CHAMPIONSHIPS, 1963

Men's Singles.—E. Kops (Denmark) beat C. Rattana-Saeng-Sueng (Thailand) 2–0.

Ladies' Singles.—Mrs. G. C. K. Hashman (U.S.A.) beat Miss A. M. Bairstow (England) 2–0.

Men's Doubles.—F. Kobbero and J. Hammergaard (Denmark) beat F. A. Sonneville and Tan Joe Hok (Indonesia) 2–1.

Ladies' Doubles.—Mrs. Hashman (U.S.A.) and Mrs. P. W. Peard (Ireland) beat Mrs. K. Jorgensen and Miss U. Rasmussen (Denmark) 2–0.

Mixed Doubles.—F. Kobbero and Miss U. Rasmussen (Denmark) beat A. D. Jordan and Mrs E. Timperley (England) 2–0.

Universities.—Cambridge University beat Oxford University 10–5.
Inter-County Championship.—Surrey beat Lancashire 12–3.
Uber Cup (Women's World Trophy). Challenge Round.—U.S.A. beat England 4–3.

SQUASH RACKETS, 1962–63

Open Championship.—Mohibullah Khan (Pakistan) beat A.F.A. Taleb (Egypt) 3–2.
Amateur Championship.—K. Hiscoe (Australia) beat T. Shafik (Egypt) 3–1.
U.K. Professional Championships.—J. H. Giles beat A. E. Catherine.
Women's Championships.—Miss H. Blundell (Australia) beat Mrs. G. E. Marshall 3–0.
Inter-County Championship.—*Men*, Surrey beat Yorkshire 4–1; *Women*, Middlesex beat Scottish Counties 5–0.
Services Championship.—*Royal Navy:* Cadet R. M. Bawtree beat Lt. E. D. Fox 3–0; *Army:* Capt. C. M. Willmot beat Capt. M. G. P. Chignell. 3–1; *R.A.F.:* S/Ldr. R. L. Lees beat F/Lt. M. H. A. Eggleton 3–0.
Inter-Services Tournament.—1, R.A.F.; 2, Royal Navy; 3, Army.
University Match.—Oxford University beat Cambridge University 3–2.
Londonderry Cup.—Old Sherbornians beat Old Merchant Taylors 3–2.
Drysdale Cup.—Sharif Khan beat C. Stiff 3–0.
Lonsdale Cup.—P. R. Goodwin and P. E. Goodwin (Lancing).

FENCING, 1962–63

Amateur Championships:
Foil.—A. L. N. Jay (Salle Paul).
Epée.—J. D. Glasswell (Grosvenor).
Sabre.—A. M. Leckie (R. C. de France).
Ladies' Foil.—Miss M. A. Pritchard (Thames).
International Cups:
C.-L. de Beaumont Cup (Ladies' Foil).—Miss E. Botbijl (Netherlands).
Miller-Hallett Cup (Epée).—S. Higginson (Oxford University).
Corble Cup (Sabre).—A. R. Cooperman (Salle Paul).
Universities.—Oxford University beat Cambridge University 15–12.
Public Schools Championships:
Foil.—R. L. Brearley (St. Paul's).
Epée.—J. S. Underwood (Brentwood).
Sabre.—R. Craig (Merchant Taylors')

RACKETS, 1962–63

World and British Open Championship.—G. W. T. Atkins beat J.W. Leonard.
Amateur Singles Championship.—G. W. T. Atkins beat J. W. Leonard 3–2.
Amateur Doubles Championships.—C. J. Swallow and J. W. Leonard beat M. R. Coulman and J. G. H. Hogben 4–0.
Public Schools Championship.—*Singles (H. K. Foster Cup):* H. R. Angus (Winchester) beat R. P. Walker (Malvern) 3–2. *Doubles;* Eton (R. A. Pilkington and M. D. T. Faber) beat Winchester (H. R. Angus and C. L. Sunter) 4–1.
Noel Bruce Cup.—Eton (J.W. Leonard and C. T. M. Pugh) beat Tonbridge (J. R. Thompson and R. M. K. Gracey) 4–3.
Universities.—Cambridge University beat Oxford University 3–0.
Army Championships.—Lt. N. J. Peto (9th/12th Lancers).

ETON FIVES, 1963

Amateur Championships.—*Kinnaird Cup.*—D. J. S. Guilford and A. Hughes beat J.W. Biggs and J. C.Wallis 3–1.
Public Schools Competition.—City of London (C. S. H. Hampton and P. A. Hall) beat Highgate (M. F. Hayes and R. B. Sumsam) 3–1.
University.—Cambridge University beat Oxford University 3–0.

RUGBY FIVES, 1963

Amateur Singles Championship.—*(Jesters' Club Cup).*—E. Marsh beat J. F. Pretlove 2–0.
Amateur Doubles Championship.—*(Cyriax Cup).*—J. Watkinson and M. Elliott beat J. F. Pretlove and H. R. Smith 15–6, 10–15, 15–8.
Schools Competition.—*Singles (Jesters' Cup):* M. S. Chesworth (Bedford) beat D. D. Braithwaite (Denstone). *Doubles (Mappin Cup):* Denstone (D. D. Braithwaite and T. Newey) beat Clifton (J. Bretten and D. W. Hasell).

POLO, 1963

Tyro Cup.—Polo Cottage beat Cowdray Park 5–4.
Cooch Behar Cup.—Cowdray Park beat Sao Silvestre 8–7½.
Queen's Cup.—Cowdray Park beat Centaurs 9–4½.
Royal Windsor Cup.—Cirencester Park beat Friar Park 5½–4.
Cowdray Gold Cup.—La Vulci beat Cowdray Park 8–7.
Cowdray Park Challenge Cup.—Sao Silvestre beat Centaurs 9–8½.
County Cup.—Cirencester Park beat Kirtlington Park 5–3½.
Harrison Cup.—Windsor Park beat Sao Silvestre 3–2.
Holden White Cup.—Quarry Hill beat Vychan 2–0.
Midhurst Town Cup.—Sao Silvestre beat Windsor Park 5–2.
Aotea Cup.—Cowdray Park beat Cholmondeley 6–5½.
Brecknock Cup.—Jersey Lilies beat Pirates 9–2½.
Argentine Ambassador's Cup.—Cowdray Park beat The Rest 7–3½.
Ruins Cup.—Jersey Lilies beat Cheshire 8–1.

TABLE TENNIS, 1963

English Open Championships (Brighton)

Singles.—*Men:* Z. Berczik (Hungary) beat J. Fahazi (Hungary) 3–1; *Women:* Miss M. Alexandru (Roumania) beat Mrs. L. Foldi (Hungary) 3–0.
Doubles.—*Men:* I. Andreadis and V. Miko (Czechoslovakia) beat Z. Berczik and J. Fahazi (Hungary) 3–0. *Women:* Miss D. Rowe and Miss M. Shannon beat Mrs. Foldi and Miss E. Hierits (Hungary) 3–2; *Mixed:* J. Fahazi and Mrs. Foldi (Hungary) beat Z. Berczik and Miss Hierits (Hungary) 3–1.

World Championships.—*Swaythling Cup (Men)*, China; *Corbillon Cup (Women)*, Japan.

WRESTLING, 1963

British Open Championships

Flyweight.—C. O'Connor (Slough); *Bantamweight.*—F. Chardhi (Persia); *Featherweight.*—H. Hall (Oldham); *Lightweight.*—C. Hill (London); *Welterweight.*—J. Barnaville (Borehamwood); *Middleweight.*— G. Farquhar (Edinburgh); *Light-Heavyweight.*—A. Buck (Liverpool); *Heavyweight.* D. McNamara (London).

Cumberland and Westmorland Championships

Lightweight.—M. Frost (Burnley); *Welterweight.*—S. Barr (Lancaster); *Heavyweight.*—J. B. Hartley (Burnley).

SWIMMING

World's Amateur Swimming Records
(as at Sept. 14, 1963)

MEN—FREE STYLE

100 *metres*.—R. B. McGregor, Gt. Britain, 54 s.
200 *metres*.—D. Schollander, U.S.A., 1 m. 58·4 s.
220 *yards*.—J. Konrads, Australia, 2 m. 1·6 s.
400 *metres*.—M. Rose, Australia, 4 m. 13·4 s.
440 *yards*.—J. Konrads, Australia, 4 m. 15·9 s.
800 *metres*.—M. Rose, Australia, 8 m. 51·5 s.
880 *yards*.—J. Konrads, Australia, 8 m. 59·6 s.
1,500 *metres*.—J. Konrads, Australia, 17 m. 11·0 s.

Free Style Relay:
4×100 *metres*.—National Team, U.S.A., 3 m. 36·1 s.
4×200 *metres*.—National Team, U.S.A., 8 m. 3·7 s.

Medley Relay:
4×100 *metres*.—National Team, U.S.A., 4 m. 0·1 s.

Individual Medley:
400 *metres*.—T. Stickles, U.S.A., 4 m. 51 s.

MEN—BACK STROKE

100 *metres*.—T. Stock, U.S.A., 1 m. 0·9 s.
200 *metres*.—T. Stock, U.S.A., 2 m. 10·9 s.

MEN—BREAST STROKE

100 *metres*.— C. Jastremski, U.S.A., 1 m. 7·5 s.
200 *metres*.—C. Jastremski, U.S.A., 2 m. 29·6 s.
220 *yards*.—M. Shigematsu, Japan, 2 m. 33·4 s.

MEN—BUTTERFLY STROKE

100 *metres*.—L. A. Nicolao, Argentina, 57 s.
200 *metres*.—C. Robie, U.S.A. 2 m. 8·2 s.
220 *yards*.—K. Berry, Australia, 2 m. 9·7 s.

WOMEN—FREE STYLE

100 *metres*.—Miss D. Fraser, Australia, 59·5 s.
200 *metres*.—Miss D. Fraser, Australia, 2 m. 11·6 s.
220 *yards*.—Miss D. Fraser, Australia, 2 m. 11·6 s.
400 *metres*.—Miss C. von Saltza, U.S.A., 4 m. 44·5 s.
440 *yards*.—Miss I. Konrads, Australia, 4 m. 45·4 s.
800 *metres*.—Miss C. House, U.S.A., 9 m. 51·6 s.
880 *yards*.—Miss I. Konrads, Australia, 10 m. 11·4 s.
1,500 *metres*.—Miss C. House, U.S.A., 18 m. 44 s.

WOMEN—BREAST STROKE

200 *metres*.—Miss K. Beyer, E. Germany, 2 m. 48 s.

WOMEN—BUTTERFLY STROKE

100 *metres*.—Miss M. Stewart, Canada, 1 m. 7·3 s.
200 *metres*.—Miss S. Finneran, U.S.A., 2 m. 30·7s.
220 *yards*.—Miss B. Collins, U.S.A., 2 m. 33·6 s.

WOMEN—BACK STROKE

100 *metres*.—Miss L. Burke, U.S.A., 1 m. 9 s.
200 *metres*.—Miss S. Tanaka, Japan, 2 m. 28·2 s.

Free Style Relay:
4×100 *metres*.—National Team, U.S.A., 4 m. 8·9 s.

Individual Medley:
400 *metres*.—Miss S. Finneran, U.S.A., 5 m. 21·9 s.

Medley Relay:
4×100 *metres*.—National Team, East Germany, 4 m. 40·1 s.

UNIVERSITY

1963

Oxford University beat Cambridge University by 45 pts. to 41 pts. *Water Polo*.—Oxford University beat Cambridge University 9–5.

AMATEUR SWIMMING ASSOCIATION CHAMPIONSHIPS
(Blackpool, Aug., 1963)

Men:
110 *yards Free Style*.—R. B. McGregor, 54·1 s.
220 *yards Back Stroke*.—R. S. G. Jones, 2 m. 25 s.
220 *yards Free Style*.—R. B. McGregor, 2 m. 4·8 s.
220 *yards Breast Stroke*.—N. Nicholson, 2 m. 42·2 s.

Men:
440 *yards Free Style*.—J. Martin-Dye, 4 m. 31·3 s.
440 *yards Medley*.—B. Jenkins, 5 m. 16·9 s.
220 *yards Butterfly*.—B. Jenkins, 2 m. 17·6 s.
Mile.—J. Martin-Dye, 20 m. 7·5 s.
110 *yards Boys' Free Style*.—S. Brambley, 59·6 s.
110 *yards Boys' Butterfly*.—E. C. Hodgson, 65·7 s.
110 *yards Boys' Back Stroke*.—G. R. Thwaites, 66·5 s.
110 *yards Boys' Breast Stroke*.—R. Roberts, 76 s.
220 *yards Boys' Free Style*.—K. Bewley, 2 m. 15·2 s.
Free Style 4×110 *yards Team Relay*.—1, York City, 3 m. 54·1 s.; 2, Southampton, 4 m. 0·3 s.; 3, Penguin, 4 m. 7·3 s.
Medley Relay.—1, York City, 4 m. 28 s.; 2, Darlington, 4 m. 28·9 s.; 3, Penguin, 4 m. 31·8 s.

Ladies:
110 *yards Free Style*.—Miss D. E. Wilkinson, 63·3 s.
110 *yards Back Stroke*.—Miss L. K. Ludgrove, 71·2 s.
110 *yards Butterfly*.—Miss M. Stewart, 68·6 s.
220 *yards Free Style*.—Miss A. Lonsbrough, 2 m. 19·7 s.
220 *yards Breast Stroke*.—Miss S. Mitchell, 2 m. 52·6 s.
440 *yards Free Style*.—Miss E. C. Long, 4 m. 52·4 s.
440 *yards Medley*.—Miss A. Lonsbrough, 5 m. 37 s.
110 *yards Girls' Butterfly*.—Miss J. Price, 74·8 s.
110 *yards Girls' Free Style*.—Miss S. Keen, 65·5 s.
110 *yards Girls' Back Stroke*.—Miss L. K. Ludgrove, 72 s.
110 *yards Girls' Breast Stroke*.—Miss S. Mitchell, 1 m. 21·1 s.
220 *yards Girls' Free Style*.—Miss P. Sillet, 2 m. 28·6 s.
Free Style 4×100 *yards Team Relay*.—1 Hampstead, 4 m. 30·3 s.; 2, Kingston, 4 m. 34·9 s.; 3, Stoke Newington, 4 m. 38·2 s.
Medley Relay.—1, Hampstead, 4 m. 58 s.; 2, Stoke Newington, 5 m. 6 s.; 3, Kingston, 5 m. 6 s.

Diving Championships
(Blackpool, August)

Men.—Springboard: K. Collin, 128·69 pts.; *High Diving:* A. A. Kitcher, 161·08 pts.
Ladies.—Springboard: J. Newman, 109·08 pts.; *High Diving:* Miss J. Newman, 103·60 pts.
Boys' Diving: K. C. O'Brien, 71·91 pts.
Girls' Diving: Miss K. Rowlett, 79·01 pts.

YACHTING

THE AMERICA'S CUP

History.—The America's Cup, originally a British trophy, was won outright by the U.S. schooner America at Cowes on August 22, 1851, and every contest since has been won by the U.S.A. There have been 17 unsuccessful attempts to take the cup out of the United States—15 by Britain and 2 by Canada. There have been 17 contests and 54 races, 48 of the races being won by the U.S.A.

Shamrock I lost to Columbia, 1899; Shamrock II lost to Columbia, 1901; Shamrock III lost to Reliance 1903; Shamrock IV lost to Resolute, 1920; Shamrock V lost to Enterprise, 1930; Endeavour lost to Rainbow, 1934; Endeavour II lost to Ranger, 1937; Sceptre lost to Columbia, 1958.

In 1962, for the first time, an Australian challenge was issued. The Royal Sydney Yacht Squadron's sloop Gretel raced against the American defender Weatherly off Newport, Rhode Island, from Sept. 15–25. Gretel became the first challenger since 1934 to win a race, but Weatherly won the series 3–1.

YACHTING, 1963

Finn Class Championship (Poole, June).—Chesapeake (J. Knights).

Universities (Poole, July).—Cambridge University beat Oxford University.

National Merlin Rocket Championship (Whitstable, June 25–28).—Rhythm IV (B. Southcott).

International Dragon Championship (*Duke of Edinburgh Cup*) (Torbay, July 1–5).—Andromeda (E. M. Parry).

International 14 ft. Dinghy (*Prince of Wales Cup*) (Torbay, July 4).—Polyester (M. Peacock and J. Allen).

Admiral's Cup (*Fastnet Race*).—Clarion of Wight (G.B.). (D. Boyer and D. Miller).

National Hornet Championship (Torbay, July 9–12).—Woof II (J. Berger).

National Flying Dutchman Championships (Whitstable, Aug. 19–23).—Lady C (K. Musto and A. Morgan).

Britannia Cup (Cowes, Aug. 6).—Staika III (Sweden).

CANOEING 1963

Devizes–Westminster Race (124 miles).—1, J. Haines and D. Arnold (R.M.), 21 hr. 58 m. 9 s.; 2, R. Seeger and H. Wiltshire (R.M.); 3, A. Havelock-Stevens and P. Flockton (R.W.F.).

THE UNIVERSITY BOAT RACE

(Putney-Mortlake, 4m. 1f. 180 yds)

Year	Winner	m.	s.	Won by
1953	Cambridge ...	19	54	8 lengths
1954	Oxford	20	23	4½ lengths
1955	Cambridge ...	19	10	16 lengths
1956	Cambridge ...	18	36	1¼ lengths
1957	Cambridge	19	1	2 lengths
1958	Cambridge ...	18	15	3½ lengths
1959	Oxford	18	52	6 lengths
1960	Oxford	18	59	1¼ lengths
1961	Cambridge ...	19	22	4¼ lengths
1962	Cambridge ...	19	46	5 lengths
1963	Oxford	20	47	5 lengths

Cambridge have won 60 times, Oxford 48, and there has been 1 dead-heat.

Race Mishaps.

1859.—Cambridge sank, Oxford won.

1912.—Cambridge sank at 1 mile, and Oxford shortly after Hammersmith Bridge, Oxford won re-row.

1925.—Oxford sank soon after Hammersmith Bridge and Cambridge paddled home to win.

1951.—Oxford sank after half a mile. Race abandoned because of weather and rowing conditions. Cambridge won the re-row.

HENLEY REGATTA, 1963

Grand Challenge Cup.—London University beat Cornell University (U.S.A.) by ¾ length, 6 m. 38 s.

Ladies' Challenge Plate.—R.M.A. (Sandhurst) beat St. Edmund Hall (Oxford) by ½ length, 6 m. 55 s.

Princess Elizabeth Cup.—Nautical College, Pangbourne beat St. Paul's by 2 lengths, 7 m. 2s.

Thames Cup.—Queens' College, Cambridge beat Argosies by 2¾ lengths, 6 m. 53 s.

Stewards' Cup.—Molesey beat Thames by ⅔ length, 7 m. 16 s.

Prince Philip Cup.—Auckland, N.Z., beat Thames easily, 7 m. 32 s.

Visitors' Cup.—Christ's College (Cambridge) beat Pembroke College (Cambridge) by ¾ length, 7 m. 32 s.

Wyfold Cup.—Nottingham and Union beat Derby by 2⅓ lengths, 7 m. 24 s.

Silver Goblets.—C. G. V. Davidge and S. A. Mackenzie (Leander) beat J. B. Amlong and T. V. Amlong (U.S.A.) by 4 lengths, 7 m. 55 s.

Double Sculls.—M. B. Alwin and W. Van Der Togt (Netherlands) beat B. Mounereau and H. Duhamel (France) by 2 lengths, 7 m. 30 s.

Diamond Sculls.—G. Kuttmann (Switzerland) beat W. L. Barry (Quintin) by 2 ft., 8 m. 9 s.

OTHER AQUATIC EVENTS

Head of the River (*Thames, Mortlake-Putney*).—1, London University, 18 m. 33 s.; 2, Barn Cottage, 18 m. 38 s.; 3, London R.C., 18 m. 41 s.

Oxford Summer Eights.—Keble College.

Cambridge Mays.—Queens' College.

Wingfield Sculls (*Putney–Mortlake*).—1, W. L. Barry (Quintin), 23 m. 10 s.; 2, K. R. Smith (London R.C.), 23 m. 25 s.; 3, J. M. Russell (Molesey), 23 m. 52 s.

Doggett's Coat and Badge (*Estab.* 1715, 249th *Race*) *London Bridge—Chelsea*, 4½ miles). 1, D. Allen (Erith), 29 m. 6·5 s.; 2, M. G. Neicho (E. Ham), 29 m. 49 s.; 3, J. S. Aldridge (E. Ham), 30 m. 55 s.

Sculling, Head of the River (*Putney–Mortlake*).—1, W. L. Barry (Quintin), 22 m. 34 s.; 2, J. M. Russell (Molesey), 22 m. 43 s.; 3, N. Tubbs (St. Thomas's Hospital), 22 m. 55 s.

SKATING, 1962–63

Men's Figure.—D. McPherson (Canada).

Ladies' Figure.—Miss S. Dijkstra (Netherlands).

Pairs.—H. J. Baumber and Miss M. Kilius (W. Germany).

Ice Dancing.—P. Roman and Miss M. E. Romanova (Czechoslovakia).

EUROPEAN CHAMPIONSHIPS
(Berlin)

Men's Figure.—A. Calmat (France).

Ladies' Figure.—Miss S. Dijkstra (Netherlands).

Pairs.—H. J. Baumler and Miss M. Kilius (W. Germany).

Ice Dancing.—M. Phillips and Miss L. Shearman (G.B.)

World Speed Skating Championship.—J. Nilsson (Sweden).

European Championship.—N. Aaness (Norway).

BRITISH CHAMPIONSHIPS (Ice)

Men's Figure.—M. R. Cannon.

Ladies' Figure.—Miss D. Clifton-Peach.

Pairs.—P. H. Webb and Miss V. A. Jeffery.

Dancing.—M. Phillips and Miss L. Shearman.

(Roller)

Men's Figure.—R. C. Balls.

Ladies' Figure.—Miss K. Choat.

Pairs.—Mr. and Mrs. C. H. Preston.

Dancing.—Mr. and Mrs. B. P. Colclough.

SKI-ING, 1962–63

British Ski-Running Championships.—Downhill, R. A. Montgomerie; *Slalom*, I. W. McCormick; *Combined*, I. W. McCormick; *Giant Slalom*, C. de Westenholz.

Roberts of Kandahar.—L. Vitt (Spain).

Duke of Kent Cup.—P. Krassel (Austria).

Duchess of Kent Cup.—Miss T. Heald.

Ladies' Ski-running Championships.—Downhill, Miss T. Heald; *Slalom*, Miss A. Asheshov; *Combined*, Miss A. Asheshov; *Giant Slalom*, Miss T. Heald.
Infante Alfonso Team Race.—Vienna.

Arlberg-Kandahar Meeting (Chamonix)

Men:
Downhill, L. Leitner (Germany); *Slalom*, F. Boulieu (France); *Combined*, F. Boulieu (France).
Ladies:
Downhill, A. Famose (France); *Slalom*, T. Hecher (Austria); *Combined*, T. Hecher (Austria).

SHOOTING—BISLEY 93rd N.R.A., 1963

Queen's Prize.—K. M. Pilcher, 283 pts.; *Runners-up*, B. H. B. Wrey and D. A. Friend, 282 pts.
St. George's Challenge Vase.—1, Group Capt. K. P. Lewis, 144 pts.; 2, Miss M. E. Foster and Capt. C. O. James, 143 pts.
Universities.—Humphry Challenge Cup.—Cambridge University, 821; Oxford University, 812.
County Championship.—1, Kent; 2, Surrey; 3, Hampshire.
Elcho Challenge Shield.—1, England, 1,628; 2, Ireland, 1,604; 3, Scotland, 1,602.
Kolapore Cup.—1, Mother Country, 1,138; 2, Canada, 1,121; 3, Guernsey, 1,106.
Universities.—Chancellor's Challenge Plate.—1, Cambridge University, 1,118; 2, Oxford University, 1,106.
Inter-Services Long Range.—1, R.N., 531; 2, R.M., 515; 3, R.A.F., 507.
Ashburton Shield.—1, Allhallows, 522; 2, Marlborough, 515; 3, Dean Close, 515.

NATIONAL SMALL-BORE RIFLE ASSOCIATION SHOOTING, 1963

British Long Range Championship (Earl Roberts Cup).—J. Hall (City of Birmingham), 574.
English Long Range Championship (Royal Society of St. George Cup).—J. Hall (City of Birmingham), 574.
British Pistol Championship (J. K. Gallie Memorial Cup).—C. H. Sexton (Totton), 284.
Bisley Grand Aggregate (Codrington Memorial Trophy).—T. P. Morgan (Addiscombe), 2,134.
Women's Open Meeting Championship (Flowers Trophy).—Mrs. B. M. Whittingham (Borough of Wandsworth), 388.
British Short Range Championship ("News of the World" Cup).—J. H. Linford (Withergate), 400.

CLAY PIGEON SHOOTING, 1963

International Cup.—1, England, 8119/9000; 2, Wales, 7791; 3, Scotland, 7781.
Mackintosh Trophy.—1, Australia, 8694/9000; 2, New Zealand, 8608; 3, South Africa, 8378.
British Open Down-the-Line Championship.—R. Flynn (Dublin), 292/300.
British Open Skeet Championship.—N. E. Sansome (Northants.), 97/100.
British Open Sporting Championship.—S. Gulyas (Suffolk), 84/100.
Coronation Cup.—J. Wheater (Hull), 367/400.
Grand Prix of Great Britain (Olympic Trench).—F. Eisenlauer (U.S.A.), 193/200.

ARCHERY, 1963

British Championships

Men.—1, R. P. Bishop, 1,895 pts.; 2, F. W. Bing, 1,866 pts.; 3, K. H. Turner, 1,797 pts.
Ladies.—1, Mrs. A. Brien, 1,866 pts.; 2, Miss S. M. Lyons, 1,857 pts.; 3, Miss S. D. Kemp, 1,829 pts.
County Championship.—(Men).—1, Warwickshire, 6,936 pts.; 2, Lancashire, 6,767 pts.; 3, Kent, 6,205 pts. *(Ladies).*—1, Yorkshire, 6,840 pts.; 2, Lancashire, 6,529 pts.; 3, Middlesex, 6,328 pts.

World Championships

(Biennial. Held in 1963)

Men.—1, C. Sandlin (U.S.A.); 2, J Thornton (U.S.A.) 3, D. Keaggy, jr. (U.S.A.). *Ladies.*—1, Miss V. Cook (U.S.A.); 2, Miss N. Vanderheide (U.S.A.); 3, Miss M. Neime (Finland). *Teams.—(Men).*—1, U.S.A.; 2, France; 3, Sweden. *(Ladies).*—1, U.S.A.; 2, Finland; 3, Great Britain.

British National Records

Flight Shooting (Distance).—490 yards, J. Flinton, 1955.
York Round (Men).—6 doz. arrows at 100 yds., 4 doz. at 80 yds. and 2 doz. at 60 yds.; J. P. Davies, 1,014 pts., 1963.
Double York Round.—R. D. Matthews, 1,933 pts. 1958.
Hereford Round (Ladies).—6 doz. arrows at 80 yds., 4 doz. at 60 yds., and 2 doz. at 50 yds.; Mrs. L. Fowler, 994 pts., 1962.
Double Hereford Round.—Miss J. Warner, 1,891 pts., 1961.

BOXING, 1963

A.B.A. Championships

(Winners)

Flyweight.—M. Land (St. Ives); *Bantam.*—B. Packer (Dartford); *Feather.*—A. J. Riley (Rootes); *Light.*—Pte. B. O'Sullivan (Army); *Light-Welter.*—R. McTaggart (Kelvin); *Welter*—J. Pritchett (Bingham, Notts.); *Light-Middle.*—A. Wyper (Scotland); *Middle.*—A. J. Matthews (Litherland, Liverpool); *Light-Heavy.*—P. Murphy (Chorley); *Heavy.*— R. Sanders (R.N.).

Universities

Cambridge University beat Oxford University by six bouts to three.

PROFESSIONAL BOXING WORLD CHAMPIONS

Title holders in Oct. 1963

Flyweight.—P. Kingpetch (Thailand); *Bantamweight.*—E. Jofre (Brazil); *Featherweight.*—S. Ramos (Cuba); *Lightweight.*—C. Ortiz (U.S.A.); *Welterweight.*—D. Tiger (Nigeria) or E. Griffith (U.S.A.); *Middleweight.*—D. Tiger (Nigeria); *Light-Heavyweight.*—W. Pastrano (U.S.A.); *Heavyweight.*—S. Liston (U.S.A.).

BRITISH CHAMPIONS

Title holders in Oct. 1963

Flyweight.—W. McGowan (Scotland); *Bantamweight.*—F. Gilroy (N. Ireland); *Featherweight.*—H. Winstone (Wales); *Lightweight.*—D. Charnley (England); *Welterweight.*—B. Curvis (Wales); *Middleweight.*—M. Leahy (England); *Light-Heavyweight.*—C. Calderwood (Scotland); *Heavyweight.*—H. Cooper (England).

BRITISH EMPIRE CHAMPIONS

Title holders in Oct. 1963

Flyweight.—W. McGowan (Scotland); *Bantamweight.*—F. Gilroy (N. Ireland); *Featherweight.*—F. Robertson (Ghana); *Lightweight.*—B. Grant (Jamaica); *Welterweight.*—B. Curvis (Wales); *Middleweight.*—D. Tiger (Nigeria); *Light-Heavyweight.*—C. Calderwood (Scotland); *Heavyweight.*—H. Cooper (England).

EUROPEAN CHAMPIONS

Title holders in Oct. 1963

Flyweight.—S. Burruni (Italy); *Bantamweight.*—P. Rollo (Italy); *Featherweight.*—H. Winstone (Wales); *Lightweight.*—C. Rudhof; *Welterweight.*—D. Loi (Italy); *Light-Heavyweight.*—G. Rinaldi (Italy); *Middleweight*—L. Papp (Hungary); *Heavyweight.*—I. Johansson (Sweden).

GREYHOUND RACING, 1963

Greyhound Derby (June 29).—Lucky Boy Boy, 29 sec.

BILLIARDS AND SNOOKER, 1962–63

English Amateur Billiards Championship.—J. H. Beetham beat N. Dagley by 4,052 to 2,759 pts.

English Amateur Snooker Championship.—G. Owen beat R. Gross by 11–3 frames.

Women (Amateur).—Billiards: Miss S. Isaacs; *Snooker:* Miss R. Holmes.

Boys' Snooker Championship.—J. Hollis.

B.A. and C.C. Youths.—Billiards: T. Matthews; *Snooker:* T. Matthews.

Record Breaks

Billiards (Professional).—W. Lindrum, 4,137 *v.* J. Davis, Jan. 19–20, 1932.

Championship (under Amended Baulk Line Rules).—J. Davis, 1,784 in 1936.

Non-Championship (under Amended Baulk Line Rules).—W. Lindrum, 3,752 (Australia 1944).

All Round Break (without Nursery Cannons).—W. Smith, 2,743 in 1928.

Spot Stroke.—W. J. Peall, 3,304 in 1890. (Note.—The whole score 3,304 was not made by the spot stroke. The break included spot-stroke runs of 92, 151, 123, 172, 120 and 400.)

Consecutive Run of Nursery Cannons.—W. Lindrum, 529 in a break of 1,164 in 1933; 529 cannons equalling 1,058 points, out of total break of 1,164.

Amateur Break.—R. Marshall (Australia), 702 in Australian Amateur Championship, 1953.

English Amateur Championship.—K. Kennerley, 549 in 1937.

English Amateur Snooker Championship Break.—G. Thompson, 115.

World Professional Snooker Break.—J. Davis, 147 in 1955.

Professional Snooker Championship Break.—J. Davis, 136 in 1946.

World Amateur Billiards Championship.—T. Cleary (Australia), 682 in 1954.

World Amateur Snooker Record Break.—G. Thompson, 115 in 1962.

BOWLS, 1963

English Bowling Association Championship (Mortlake).

Rinks.—S.F.: Aylesbury Borough beat March Conservatives 25–19; Wellingborough Town beat Mansfield 24–8. *F.:* Wellingborough Town beat Aylesbury Borough 21–12.

Triples.—S.F.: Paddington beat Banbury Chestnuts 18–7; Rookery (Suffolk) beat Poole Park 19–14. *F.:* Paddington beat Rookery 20–14.

Pairs.—S.F.: March Conservatives beat Kingsway (Sussex) 21–19; Greenhill (Dorset) beat Bristol Civil Service 27–11. *F.:* Greenhill (W. G. Reynolds and T. V. Rogers) beat March Conservatives 22–17.

Singles.—S.F.: H. Haynes (Welwyn Garden City) beat F. W. Driver (March Conservatives) 21–14; C. Graham (Edenside, Cumberland) beat C. Mason (Kettering Conservatives) 21–16. *F.:* C. Graham beat H. Haynes 21–20.

Inter-County Championship (Middleton Cup).—S.F.: Essex beat Yorkshire 119–116; Hampshire beat Warwickshire 110–106. *F.:* Hampshire beat Essex 125–114.

International Championship.—Winners.—Scotland. *Results.*—England beat Wales 105–92; Scotland beat Ireland 101–73; Scotland beat England 95–86; Wales beat Ireland 107–91; England beat Ireland 103–80; Scotland beat Wales 126–82.

BRITISH SHOW JUMPING 1963

International White City Horse Show (44th)

Prince of Wales Cup.—1, Great Britain (Miss A. Drummond-Hay on Merely-a-Minor, Miss A. Townsend on Dunfoyne, D. Barker on Mister Softee, H. Smith on Warpaint); 2, Ireland (Mrs. S. Hayes on Sweet Control, Hon. D. Connolly-Carew on Barrymore, S. Hayes on Goodbye and T. Wade on Dundrum); 3, Italy (Lt. G. Gutierrez on Mount Leinster, G. Mancinelli on The Rock, Signora L. Novo on Rahin, and Capt. R. d'Inzeo on Posilippo).

King George V Cup.—1, T. Wade (Ireland) on Dundrum; 2, G. Hobbs (G.B.) on Brandy Soda; 3, G. Mancinelli (Italy) on Rockette.

Queen Elizabeth II. Cup.—1, Miss J. Nash (G.B.) on Trigger Hill; 2, Miss A. Drummond-Hay (G.B.) on Merely-a-Minor; 3, Lady Sarah Fitzalan-Howard (G.B.) on Oorskiet.

Horse and Hound Cup.—1, D. Broome (G.B.) on Balan Silver Knight; 2, T. Wade (Ireland) on Dundrum; 3, Miss P. Smythe (G.B.) on Scorchin'.

Daily Mail Cup.—1, Miss A. Townsend (G.B.) on Dunboyne; 2, H. Mohr (Switzerland) on Troll; 3, Miss J. Nash (G.B.) on Trigger Hill.

Lonsdale Cup.—1, H. Mohr (Switzerland) on Troll; 2, F. Welch (G.B.) on Brule Tout; 3, H. Smith (G.B.) on Warpaint and K. Pritchard (G.B.) on Red Link.

ANGLING

National Championship

Year	Venue	No. of teams	Individual Winner	Weight	Team winners	Weight	Total Weight in match
				lb. oz.		lb. oz.	lb. oz.
1956	R. Witham, Lincs.	94	C. R. Lusby (Lincs.)	251 8	Coventry and District A.A.	86 4	1 ton 15 lb. 10 oz.
1957	R. Severn, Bridgnorth, Salop	96	H. Storey (Nottingham A.A.)	7 12½	Nottingham Anglers Assoc.	20 8¼	522 7
1958	R. Welland, Spalding, Lincs.	98	W. Hughes (Northern Anglers)	24 3	Coventry and District A.A.	59 15¼	1,105 0
1959	R. Nene, Peterborough	100	J. Sharpe (Bedford)	57 8½	Bedford Angling Club	86 1¼	3,240 0
1960	Rivers Ant, Bure and Thurne, Gt. Yarmouth	101	K. Smith (Norwich and Dist.)	50 14½	King's Lynn	81 15¼	1 ton 11 cwt. 1 qr. 5 lb.
1961	R. Trent, Gunthorpe, Notts	..	J. Blakey (Saltaire)	23 12¾	Coventry and District A.A.	77 6¾	1 ton 17 cwt. 9 lbs.
1962	R. Welland, Spalding, Lincs.	103	V. A. Baker (Derby)	13 11	Lincoln A.A.	56 2¾	1 ton 19 cwt. ½ lb.
1963	Gloucester Canal	105	R. Simms (N. Somerset & W. Wilts. Fed.)	14 15½	Northampton Nene	19 11½	8 cwt.

OXFORD AND CAMBRIDGE

Principal Events and Winners, 1962–63

Event	Summary of Results			Results 1962–63
	Ox.	Camb.	Drawn	
Cricket (1827)	43	50	26	Draw
Boat Race (1829)	48	60	1	Oxford
Rackets (1858)	53	31	19	Camb.
Tennis (1859)	24	51	15	Camb.
Athletics (1864)	41	42	6	Camb.
Football—				
Association (1873–4)	30	33	17	Camb.
Rugby (1871–2)	37	33	12	Camb.
Golf (1878)	31	38	4	Camb.
Lawn Tennis (1881)	25	36	—	Camb.
Hockey (1890)	21	28	11	Oxford
Boxing (1897)	21	33	6	Camb.

Other University Events and Winners 1962–63

Chess........Oxford
Cross-Country........Cambridge
Relays........Cambridge
Fencing........Oxford
Sailing........Cambridge
Lacrosse........Cambridge
Eton Fives........Cambridge
Shooting........Cambridge
Squash Rackets........Oxford
Swimming........Oxford
Ice Hockey........Cambridge
Badminton........Cambridge
Water Polo........Oxford

CYCLING, 1963

Tour de France.—J. Anquetil (France).
Tour of Britain.—P. Chisman (G.B.).
World Championships:—
Professional Sprint.—S. Gaiardoni (Italy).
Professional Pursuit.—L. Faggin (Italy).
Amateur Sprint.—P. Serçu (Belgium).
Amateur Pursuit.—J. Walschaerts (Belgium).
Amateur Road Race.—F. Vicentini (Italy).
Professional Road Race.—B. Beheyt (Belgium).
Ladies' Sprint.—G. Ermolaeva (U.S.S.R.).
Ladies' Pursuit.—B. Burton (G.B.).
Ladies' Road Race.—Y. Reynders (Belgium).
National Championships:—
Amateur Sprint.—K. Barton.
Ladies' Sprint.—J. Dunn.
Amateur Pursuit.—H. Porter.
Ladies' Pursuit.—B. Burton.
Amateur Road Race.—R. Addy.
Ladies' Road Race.—B. Burton.
National (R.T.T.C.) Time Trial Championships:—
25 *miles.*—D. Bonner, 55 m. 52 s.
50 *miles.*—R. Allsopp, 1 hr. 57 m. 17 s.
100 *miles.*—D. Woodings, 4 hr. 2 m. 38 s.
12 *hours.*—R. Spencer, 267·26 miles.
24 *hours.*—N. Carline, 475·18 miles.
Ladies' 25 *miles.*—B. Burton, 1 hr. 0 m. 55s.
Ladies' 50 *miles.*—B. Burton, 2 hr. 4 m. 53 s.
Ladies' 100 *miles.*—J. Pitchford, 4 hr. 30 m. 45 s.

MOTOR RACING, 1963

24-*hour Race (Le Mans).*—1, L. Scarfiotti and L. Bandini (Ferrari), 2,834 miles (118·1 m.p.h.); 2, E. Buerlys and G. Langlois (Ferrari), 2,700 miles; 3, M. Parkes and U. Maglioli (Ferrari), 2,699 miles.

Monaco Grand Prix.—1, G. Hill (B.R.M.), 2. hr 41 m. 49·7 s. (72·42 m.p.h.); 2, R. Ginther (B.R.M.), 2 hr. 41 m. 54·3 s.; 3, B. McLaren (Cooper), 2 hr. 42 m. 2·5 s.

French Grand Prix.—1, J. Clark (Lotus) 2 hr. 10 m. 54·3 s. (125·3 m.p.h.); 2, T. Maggs (Cooper), 2 hr. 11 m. 59·2 s.; 3, G. Hill (B.R.M.), 2 hr. 12 m. 8·2 s.

Belgian Grand Prix.—1, J. Clark (Lotus), 2 hr. 27 m. 47·6 s. (114·1 m.p.h.); 2, B. McLaren (Cooper-Climax), 2 hr. 32 m. 41·6 s.; 3, D. Gurney (Brabham-Climax).

British Grand Prix (Silverstone).—1, J. Clark (Lotus), 2 hr. 14 m. 9·6 s. (107·75 m.p.h.); 2, J. Surtees (Ferrari), 2 hr. 14 m. 35·4 s.; 3, G. Hill (B.R.M.), 2 hr. 14 m. 47·2 s.

German Grand Prix.—1, J. Surtees (Ferrari), 2 hr. 13 m. 6·8 s. (95·81 m.p.h.); 2, J. Clark (Lotus), 2 hr. 14 m. 24·3 s.; 3, R. Ginther (B.R.M.), 2 hr. 15 m. 51·7 s.

Italian Grand Prix.—1, J. Clark (Lotus), 2 hr. 24 m. 19·6 s. (127·74 m.p.h.); 2, R. Ginther (B.R.M.), 2 hr. 25 m. 54·6 s.; 3, B. McLaren (Cooper).

Dutch Grand Prix.—1, J. Clark (Lotus), 2 hr. 8 m. 13·1 s. (97·52 m.p.h.); 2, D. Gurney (Brabham-Climax); 3, J. Surtees (Ferrari).

Tourist Trophy (Goodwood).—1, G. Hill (Ferrari) 3 hr. 16 m. 45·6 s. (94·14 m.p.h.); 2, M. Parkes, (Ferrari), 3 hrs. 16 m. 46 s.; 3, R. Salvadori, (Jaguar), 3 hr. 17 m. 30·4 s.

MOTOR CYCLING 1963

Senior T.T., Isle of Man.—1, M. Hailwood (M.V. Agusta), 2 hr. 9 m. 48·4 s. (104·64 m.p.h.); 2, J. Hartle (Gilera), 2 hr. 11 m. 1·8 s. (103·67 m.p.h.); 3, P. W. Read (Gilera), 2 hr. 15 m. 42·2 s. (100·10 m.p.h.).

Junior 350 *c.c. Race, Isle of Man.*—1, J. Redman (S. Rhodesia) (Honda), 2 hr. 23 m. 8·2 s. (94·91 m.p.h.); 2, J. Hartle (Gilera), 2 hr. 29 m. 58·2 s. (90·58 m.p.h.); 3, F. Stastry (Czechoslovakia) (Jawa), 2 hr. 31 m. 20·6 s. (89·76 m.p.h.).

250 *c.c. Lightweight T.T., Isle of Man.*—1, J. Redman (S. Rhodesia) (Honda), 2 hr. 23 m. 13·2 s (94·85 m.p.h.); 2, F. Ito (Japan) (Yamaha), 2 hr.. 23 m. 40·4 s. (94·55 m.p.h.); 3, W. A. Smith (Honda), 2 hr. 29 m. 5·2 s. (91·12 m.p.h.).

Manx Grand Prix (Isle of Man).—*Senior:* 1, G. Jenkins (Norton), 2 hr. 21 m. 21·2 s. (record) (96·10 m.p.h.); 2, P. Darvill (Norton), 2 hr. 21 m. 47·2 s. (95·81 m.p.h.); 3, J. Guthrie (Norton) 2 hr. 27 m. 35·2 s. (92·04 m.p.h.). *Junior:* 1, P. Darvill (A.J.S.), 2 hr. 26 m. 53·8 s. (record) (92·48 m.p.h.); 2, R. Hunter (A.J.S.), 2 hr. 28 m. 6·6 s. (91·72 m.p.h.); 3, S. Griffiths (A.J.S.), 2 hr. 28 m. 39·2 s. (91·38 m.p.h.).

CHESS, 1963

World Championship.—T. Petrosian (U.S.S.R.) beat M. Botvinnik (U.S.S.R.) by 12½–9½.

British Championship (Whitby).—J. Penrose. *Ladies,* Mrs. R. M. Bruce; *Junior Under* 21, M. J. Basman and R. A. Harris; *Boys Under* 18, P. Jamieson; *Boys Under* 16, N. J. Patterson; *Girls* D. Dobson, G. Moore and M. Syme.

Universities.—Oxford University beat Cambridge University 4–3.

Hastings Congress.—S. Gligoric (Yugoslavia) and A. Kotov (U.S.S.R.).

County Championships.—*Senior,* Middlesex; *Junior,* Middlesex; *Correspondence,* Yorkshire.

Clare-Benedict Tournament.—W. Germany 12½; Netherlands 11; England 10; Austria 9½; Spain 9; Switzerland 8.

Glorney Cup.—England 12½; Scotland 9½; Ireland 9; Wales 5.

National Club Championship.—Manchester.

SPORTS REPRESENTATIVE BODIES

ANGLING.—National Federation of Anglers. *Hon. Sec.*, T. G. Draper, 47 Lindon Drive, Alvaston, Derby.

ARCHERY.—Grand National Archery Society. *Sec.*, Group Capt. P. H. Bragg, Wyllics, Deaks Lane, Cuckfield, Sussex.

ASSOCIATION FOOTBALL.—The Football Association. *Sec.* D. Follows, M.B.E., 22 Lancaster Gate, W.2.

ATHLETICS.—Amateur Athletic Association. *Hon. Sec.*, E. H. L. Clynes, O.B.E., 54 Torrington Place, W.C.1.

—— Women's Amateur Athletic Association. *Hon. Sec.*, Miss M. Hartman, 41 Hayward Court, Levehurst Way, S.W.4.

BADMINTON.—Badminton Association of England. *Sec.*, H. A. E. Scheele, 4 Madeira Avenue, Bromley, Kent.

BASKET BALL.—Amateur Basket Ball Association. *Sec.*, K. K. Mitchell, Dept. of Physical Education. The University, Leeds, 2.

BILLIARDS.—Billiards Association and Control Council. *Chairman*, H. A. Phillips, Maxwell House, 11 Arundel Street, W.C.2.

BOBSLEIGH.—British Bobsleigh Association. *Hon. Sec.*, N. Barclay, Rockfort, Helensburgh, Dunbartonshire.

BOWLS.—English Bowling Association. *Sec.*, E. Sussum, 2 Roseford Road, Cambridge.

BOXING.—Amateur Boxing Association. *Sec.*, W. T. Lovett, 69 Victoria Street, S.W. 1.

—— British Boxing Board of Control, 1/9 Hills Place, W.1., *Sec.*, E. J. Waltham.

CANOEING.—British Canoe Union. *Sec.*, R. W. Baker, 147A Station Road, E.4.

CLAY PIGEON SHOOTING.—Clay Pigeon Shooting Association. *Sec.*, A. P. Page, Eley Estate, Angel Road, N.18.

CRICKET.—Marylebone Cricket Club, Lord's Ground, N.W.8. *Sec.*, S. C. Griffith, D.F.C., T.D.

—— Women's Cricket Association. *Hon. Sec.*, Miss E. M. Riley, Corner Farm, Frittenden, nr. Cranbrook, Kent.

CYCLING.—British Cycling Federation, 21 Blackfriars Road, S.E.1.—*Hon. Sec.*, R. P. Itter.

FENCING.—Ladies' Amateur Fencing Union. *Sec.*, Miss M. Somerville, 58a Ridgmount Gardens, W.C.1.

GOLF.—Royal and Ancient Golf Club, St. Andrews. *Sec.*, Brig. E. Brickman, D.S.O.

—— English Golf Union. *Sec.*, Lt.-Col. K. A. Nash, 35 Broad Street, Wokingham, Berks.

—— Ladies' Golf Union, Sandilands, Sandwich Bay, Kent.

HOCKEY.—Hockey Association. *Hon. Sec.*, W. C. Longstaff, 24 St. Mary Axe, E.C.3.

—— All England Women's Hockey Association. *Sec.*, Mrs. M. Macdonald, 45 Doughty Street, W.C.1.

LACROSSE.—English Lacrosse Union. *Sec.*, K. O. Peachey, 92 Chelmsford Road, N.14.

—— All England Ladies' Lacrosse Association. *Hon. Sec.*, Mrs. D. Stokes, 108 Dereham Road, Barking, Essex.

LAWN TENNIS.—Lawn Tennis Association. *Sec.*, S. B. Reay, O.B.E., Palliser Road, Barons Court, West Kensington, W.14.

MOUNTAINEERING.—British Mountaineering Council, c/o Alpine Club, 74 South Audley Street, W.1. *Hon. Sec.*, T. H. Sinclair.

NETBALL.—All England Netball Association. *Sec.*, Miss E. L. Sanders, 12 Rochester Road, Carshalton, Surrey.

RACING (FLAT).—The Jockey Club, Newmarket. *Sec.*, E. W. Weatherby, 15 Cavendish Square, W.1.

RACING (STEEPLECHASING).—The National Hunt Committee. *Secretaries*, Messrs. Weatherby & Sons, 15 Cavendish Square, W.1.

RIFLE SHOOTING.—National Rifle Association. *Sec.*, Capt. E. K. Le Mesurier, C.B.E., M.V.O., R.N. (*ret.*), Bisley Camp, Brookwood, Woking, Surrey.

—— National Small-bore Rifle Association. *Sec.*, A. J. Palmer, Codrington House, 113 Southwark Street, S.E.1.

ROWING.—Amateur Rowing Association. *Sec.* J. H. Page, O.B.E., The Tower, The Terrace, Barnes, S.W.13.

RUGBY FIVES.—Rugby Fives Association. *Hon. Sec.*, D. E. Gardner, 51 Rafford Way, Bromley, Kent.

RUGBY FOOTBALL.—The Rugby Football Union, Whitton Road, Twickenham, Middx. *Sec.*, R. E. Prescott.

—— The Rugby Football League. *Sec.*, W. Fallowfield, O.B.E., 180 Chapeltown Road, Leeds, 7.

SKATING.—National Skating Association of Great Britain. *Sec.*, E. G. Coggins, Charterhouse, E.C.1.

SKI-ING.—Ski Club of Great Britain. *Gen. Sec.*, M. N. H. Milne, O.B.E., E.D., 118 Eaton Square, S.W.1.

SQUASH RACKETS.—Squash Rackets Association. *Sec.*, J. H. Horry, 137 Regent Street, W.1.

—— Women's Squash Rackets Association. *Hon. Sec.*, Mrs. M. Fisk, 22 Childebert Road, S.W.17.

SWIMMING.—Amateur Swimming Association. *Hon. Sec.*, H. E. Fern, C.B.E., 64 Cannon Street, E.C.4.

TABLE TENNIS.—English Table Tennis Association. *Sec.*, D. P. Lowen, 652 Grand Buildings, Trafalgar Square, W.C.2.

TOBOGANNING.—Luge Association of Great Britain. *Hon. Sec.*, N. Barclay, Rockfort, Helensburgh, Dunbartonshire.

WATER SKI-ING.—British Water Ski Federation. *Hon. Sec.*, R. C. Panton, 7 Rivermead Court, Hurlingham, S.W.6.

WRESTLING.—British Amateur Wrestling Association. *Sec.*, A. Wishart, 60 Calabria Road, N.5.

SOME BRITISH MOUNTAINEERING CLUBS

(with name of Secretary).

ACHILLE RATTI C.C.—W. F. Carter, Millfield, 4 Meadow Drive, Bolton-le-Sands, Carnforth, Lancs.

ALPINE CLUB.—A. K. Rawlinson, 74 South Audley Street, W.1.

ASSOCIATION OF BRITISH MEMBERS OF THE SWISS ALPINE CLUB.—*Hon. Sec.*, M. Bennett, 5 Savile Close, New Malden, Surrey.

CAIRNGORM CLUB.—J. Y. L. Haw, 18 Bon-Accord Square, Aberdeen.

CAVE & CRAG CLUB.—D. D. Snell, 154 Station Road, Wylde Green, Sutton Coldfield.

CEUNANT M.C.—M. E. Connelly, 22 Ashbourne Road, Birmingham, 16.

CLIMBERS' CLUB.—M. H. Westmacott, 26 Gordon Avenue, Stanmore, Middlesex.

CREAGH DHU M.C.—A. Fulton, 488 Broomfield Road, Balornock, Glasgow, N.

DERBYSHIRE PENNINE CLUB.—M. H. A. Finch, 442 Glossop Road, Sheffield 10.

FELL & ROCK CLIMBING CLUB OF THE ENGLISH LAKE DISTRICT.—C. S. Tilly, Park House, Greatham, Co. Durham.

GLOUCESTERSHIRE M.C.—P. Lewis, 24 Lansdown Place, Cheltenham.

GRAMPIAN CLUB.—A. C. Gardner, 17 Albert Gardens, Broughty Ferry, Dundee.

GRITSTONE CLUB.—E. Gudgeon, 22 The Rise, Morris Lane, Leeds 5.

INVERNESS M.C.—J. I. R. Martin, Runival, 10A Culduthel Road, Inverness.

IRISH M.C. (BELFAST SECTION).—Miss D. McMaster, Biochemistry Dept., Queen's University, Northern Ireland.

KESWICK M.C.—J. D. Oliver, 8 The Crescent, Keswick, Cumberland.

LADIES ALPINE CLUB.—Miss M. P. Darvall, Heath House, Lyndhurst Terrace, N.W.3.

LADIES SCOTTISH C.C.—Miss E. Leslie, 1 Woodburn Terrace, Edinburgh, 10

LOMOND M.C.—W. Bailey, 27 Ryedale Place, Glasgow, W.S.

MIDLAND ASSOCIATION OF MOUNTAINEERS.—D. G. Smith, 160 Maidavale Crescent, Styvechale, Coventry.

MORAY M.C.—Miss E. Soutar, 17 Petrie Crescent, Elgin.

MOUNTAINEERING SECTION OF THE CAMPING CLUB, —G. H. Watkins, 8 Bankhurst Road, S.E.6.

NORTHUMBRIAN M.C.—Miss D. Walden, 33 Springbank Road, Newcastle upon Tyne 2.

PINNACLE CLUB.—Countess D. Gravina, Rose Cottage, Frittenden, nr. Cranbrook, Kent.

RUCKSACK CLUB.—J. E. Byrom, Highfield, 3 Douglas Road, Hazel Grove, Stockport.

SCOTTISH M.C.—J. S. Stewart, Temple Cottage, Balmore, Torrance, by Glasgow.

YORKSHIRE M.C.—E. A. Shepherd, 6 Station Road, Clayton, Bradford, Yorks.

YORKSHIRE RAMBLERS' CLUB.—E. C. Downham, Bierley House, Oakenshaw, Bradford, Yorks.

In addition, most universities, colleges and branches of the armed services have mountaineering clubs open to members of the respective University, college or service.

HOMES OF SPORT

RACING

The two most famous homes of British flat racing are Newmarket and Epsom. The former, the home of the Jockey Club and the headquarters of British racing since the days of Charles II, who paid frequent visits there, is the scene of two of the "Classics", the 2,000 and 1,000 Guineas, and of many other important races, including the Cesarewitch and the Cambridgeshire, the "Autumn Double". At Epsom, with the exception of the war years, the Derby has been run since 1780 and the Oaks since 1779. The Coronation Cup also takes place during the Derby meeting. There are many trainers' establishments at both Newmarket and Epsom. The fifth classic race, the St. Leger, is run at Doncaster in September.

Two events of long-standing social, as well as racing, significance are the **Royal Ascot** meeting in June and the **Goodwood** meeting at the end of July. The latter is the only occasion during the year at which racing takes place at Goodwood, but there are a number of meetings on Ascot Heath, including that at which the very valuable King George VI and Queen Elizabeth Stakes, an important feature in the present-day racing programme, is run.

Courses near London include **Alexandra Park** (Wood Green), **Kempton Park** (Sunbury-on-Thames), **Sandown Park** (Esher) and **Windsor**. The old-established **Hurst Park** course (near Hampton Court) held its last season's racing in 1962; part of it is to be built over. Among important courses in other parts of the country may be mentioned **Lincoln** and **Manchester**, the scenes of the first and last big flat races of the season, the Lincolnshire and Manchester November Handicap, respectively, and **York** and **Chester**, the homes of the Ebor Handicap and Chester Cup. Steeplechasing and hurdling under National Hunt rules also take place during the winter at many centres of flat racing.

The Grand National steeplechase is run over a distance of 4 m. 856 yds., with 30 fences, at **Aintree** near Liverpool. Other very important races under National Hunt rules, including the Cheltenham Gold Cup and the Champion Hurdle, take place at the National Hunt meeting at **Cheltenham**, while the King George VI Steeplechase at Kempton Park on Boxing Day has in recent years been very popular.

CRICKET

Test matches are now played on six English grounds—**Lord's**, **The Oval**, **Trent Bridge** (Nottingham), **Old Trafford** (Manchester), **Headingley** (Leeds) and **Edgbaston** (Birmingham). In the normal course, five Test Matches are played against visiting teams to England and take place at Lord's, the Oval and three out of the other four test-match grounds, one dropping out each season in turn.

Lord's, the headquarters of Cricket and of the M.C.C., is the third ground of the name. Thomas Lord founded his first ground in 1787, and after two moves, established it on the present site at St. John's Wood in 1814. Middlesex play almost all their home matches at Lord's, as do Surrey at the Oval at Kennington, which has been the home of Surrey cricket since 1846.

In addition to the grounds already mentioned, others of great historic interest and current importance include, in the South, the Sussex county ground at **Hove** and the St. Lawrence ground at **Canterbury**, and in the North, **Bramall Lane** (Sheffield) and the ground at **Scarborough**, where the annual end-of-season Festival has taken place since last century.

ASSOCIATION FOOTBALL

The F.A. Cup Final has been held at **Wembley Stadium** since 1923, on the famous occasion when the crowd invaded the ground. Since then admission to the Cup Final has been by ticket only, but the Stadium can accommodate about 100,000 spectators. Many international matches and the F.A. Amateur Cup Final also take place at Wembley.

Wembley is, however, surpassed in capacity by **Hampden Park**, Glasgow, where the record for paying spectators is 149,547. England *v.* Scotland matches take place at Wembley and Hampden Park in alternate years.

London teams, with their grounds, currently playing in First Division football are as follows: Arsenal (Highbury), Chelsea (Stamford Bridge), Fulham (Craven Cottage), Tottenham Hotspur (White Hart Lane) and West Ham United (Upton Park).

RUGBY FOOTBALL

The three most famous centres of Rugby Union Football in the United Kingdom, scenes of many international matches, are **Twickenham**, the headquarters of the Rugby Union, **Cardiff Arms Park** and **Murrayfield** (Edinburgh). The University match and the games for the Services Championship are also played at Twickenham, where, in addition, most of the Harlequins' home matches take place. Of other famous London clubs, Blackheath play at the **Rectory Field, Blackheath**, Richmond and London Scottish share the **Richmond Athletic Ground** and the London Welsh occupy the nearby **Old Deer Park** Rosslyn Park, who for many years played at the latter, now have a ground of their own at **Roehampton.** The Wasps' ground is at Sudbury.

GOLF

The links at St. Andrews, the home of the Royal and Ancient Golf Club and the traditional centre of golf, remain the most famous in the world. Other great Scottish courses are at **Muirfield, Prestwick** and **Troon.**

The 1957 Ryder Cup match was played at Lindrick and the Professional Match Championship has many times taken place at Walton Heath in Surrey. Except for Sandwich, however, most of the major championship courses are now either in Scotland or in Lancashire or Cheshire (*e.g.* **Hoylake, Formby, Birkdale** and **Royal Lytham** and **St. Annes**). Other famous golfing centres are **Rye, Burnham** and **Westward Ho!** and in Wales, **Harlech and Porthcawl.**

ATHLETICS

While the number of running tracks in this country is slowly increasing and well-attended meetings are held in many centres, most of the international matches and events such as the A.A.A. Championships and the University Sports take place at the **White City Stadium** at Shepherd's Bush. The 1958 Empire Games were held at Cardiff and the 1948 Olympic Games at Wembley.

LAWN TENNIS

The All-England Lawn Tennis Championships have been played at **Wimbledon** since their inception in 1877, first on the former ground at Worple Road and more recently on the present courts of the All-England Lawn Tennis Club in Church Road. **Bournemouth** is the venue of the British Hard Court Championships, and in recent years one of the leading Professional Tournaments in this country, the Slazenger Championship, has taken place at **Devonshire Park,** Eastbourne.

TENNIS, RACKETS, ETC.

The chief centre for tennis and rackets may be said to be **Queen's Club** in West Kensington. A number of other tennis courts are still in use, notably at **Lord's**, where the M.C.C. Gold and Silver Prizes are important events, **Hampton Court** (built by Henry VIII in 1530), **Oxford, Cambridge, Canford School, Leamington and Manchester.** Many of the leading squash rackets matches take place in the courts belonging to West End Clubs.

ROWING

Most of the leading rowing events of the year are contested on the River Thames. The **Henley** Regatta continues to attract the foremost oarsmen from all over the world. Apart from the Boat Race, several other important races take place either from **Putney** to **Mortlake** or in the reverse direction, including the Thames Head of the River Race and the Wingfield Sculls. The course for Doggett's Coat and Badge, instituted in 1715, possibly the oldest sporting event still regularly contested, is from **London Bridge to Chelsea.** The rowing events in the 1958 Empire Games took place on **Lake Padarn** in Wales.

YACHTING

Cowes, the headquarters of the Royal Yacht Squadron and of the Royal London Yacht Club and the scene of the great Cowes Week at the beginning of August, is still the most famous name in British yachting, but there are many other centres of the sport. Among others on or near Spithead and the Solent are **Bembridge, Ryde, Yarmouth, Southampton** and **Hamble** and, elsewhere, **Burnham-on-Crouch, Poole Harbour, Weymouth, Plymouth, Falmouth** and **the Clyde.**

POLO

In recent years, the polo grounds at **Cowdray Park,** Midhurst, and at **Windsor** have become the two most important centres of the sport in this country, though a number of other grounds exist, among which those at **Woolmers Park,** Hertfordshire and **Cirencester** may be mentioned.

OTHER SPORTS

The National Rifle Association's annual meeting at its headquarters at **Bisley Camp,** near Brookwood, Surrey, is the chief event in the rifle-shooting programme. Since the closing of Harringay Arena, many big boxing programmes have been staged at the **Empire Pool,** Wembley, and well-known provincial centres of the sport are the **Liverpool Stadium** and the **Granby Halls, Leicester.** The Greyhound Derby is run at the White City and the Waterloo Cup, the most important coursing prize, at **Altcar,** Lancashire.

CLOSE TIMES

Wild Birds.—The *Protection of Wild Birds Act,* 1954, lays down a close season for wild birds (other than Game Birds) from February 1 to August 31 inclusive, each year. Exceptions to these dates are made for—

Capercaillie and (except Scotland) *Woodcock,* Feb. 1—Sept. 30.

Snipe, Feb. 1—Aug. 11.

Wild Duck and Wild Goose (in or over water areas), Feb. 21—Aug. 31.

Birds which may be killed or taken outside the close season (except in Scotland on Sundays, on Christmas Day or in a prescribed area) are the above and coot, curlew (other than stone curlew), bar-tailed godwit, moorhen, plover (golden or grey), common red-shank, certain wild duck (common pochard, gadwall, mallard, pintail, shoveller, teal, tufted duck, wigeon) and certain wild geese (bean, Canada, pink-footed and white-fronted).

Certain wild birds may be killed or taken at any time by authorized persons—cormorant, crow, gull (black-backed or herring), jackdaw, jay, magpie, rook, shag, sparrow, sparrowhawk, starling, stock-dove and wood pigeon; and, in Scotland only, goosander, red-breasted merganser and rock-dove. The sale of Wild Bird's Eggs is prohibited, except that gulls' eggs may be sold at any time and those of the lapwing (green or black plover) from Jan. 1—April 14 inclusive.

Game Birds—In each case the dates are inclusive:—

Black Game—Dec. 11 to Aug. 19 (Aug. 31 in Somerset, Devon, and New Forest).
**Grouse*—Dec. 11 to Aug. 11.
**Partridge*—Feb. 2 to Aug. 31.
**Pheasant*—Feb. 2 to Sept. 30.
**Ptarmigan*—(Scotland only) Dec. 11 to Aug. 11.

It is also unlawful (in *England* and *Wales*) to kill the game marked * on a Sunday or Christmas Day.

Hunting and Ground Game.—There is no statutory close-time for fox-hunting or rabbit-shooting, nor for hares: but by an Act passed in 1892 the *sale* of hares or leverets in Great Britain is prohibited from March 1 to July 31 inclusive under a penalty of a pound. The First of November is the recognized date for the opening of the *fox-hunting* season, which continues till the following April. *Otter-hunting* lasts from mid-April to Mid-September.

Deer.—The Deer Act, 1963, effective from Nov. 1, 1963, imposed the following close times. *Red Deer and Sika Deer:* Stags, May 1–July 31; Hinds, March 1–Oct. 31. *Fallow Deer and Roe Deer:* Buck, May 1–July 31; Doe, March 1–Oct. 31. Under the Act it is an offence to take or wilfully kill deer of any species from one hour after sunset to one hour before sunrise.

Principal Book Publishers and Their Addresses

More than 3,700 firms, individuals and societies have published one or more books in recent years. The list which follows is a selective one comprising, in the main, those firms whose names are most familiar to the general public. An interleaved list containing some 2,000 names and addresses is available, price 5s. od. post free, from the publishers of "Whitaker."

Abelard-Schuman, 8 King Street, W.C.2.
Aberdeen University Press, Aberdeen.
Allan (Ian), Craven House, Hampton Court, Sy.
Allen (W. H.), 43 Essex St., W.C.2.
Allen & Unwin, 40 Museum St., W.C.1
Angus & Robertson, 54 Bartholomew Close, E.C.1.
Architectural Press, 9 Queen Anne's Gate, S.W.1.
Arco, 9 Grape St., W.C.2.
Arnold (E.), & Co., 41 Maddox St., W.1
Arnold (E. J.) & Son, Butterley St., Leeds.
Arrow Books, 178 Gt. Portland St., W.1.
Arrowsmith, Winterstoke Rd., Bristol.
Athlone Press, 2 Gower St., W.C.1.
Baillière, Tindall & Cox, 8 Henrietta St., W.C.2.
Barker (Arthur), 20 New Bond St., W.1.
Barrie & Rockliff, 2 Clement's Inn, W.C.2.
Bartholomew & Son, 12 Duncan St., Edinburgh.
Batsford, 4 Fitzhardinge St., Portman Square, W.1.
Bell (Geo.) & Sons, 6 Portugal St., W.C.2.
Benn (Ernest), 154 Fleet St., E.C.4.
Black (A. & C.), 4 Soho Sq., W.1.
Blackie, Glasgow, and 5 Fitzhardinge St., W.1.
Blackwell (Basil), 49 Broad St., Oxford.
Blackwood, Edinburgh and Buckingham House, Buckingham St., W.C.2.
Blandford Press, 167 High Holborn, W.C.1.
Bles (Geoffrey), 52 Doughty St., W.C.1.
Blond (Anthony), 56 Doughty St., W.C.1.
Boardman (T. V.), 2 Portman St., W.1.
Bodley Head, 10 Earlham St., W.C.2.
Books for Pleasure, 583 Fulham Rd., S.W.6.
Bowes & Bowes, 42 Gt. Russell St., W.C.1.
Brockhampton Press, Corridor Chambers, Market Place, Leicester.
Brown, Son & Ferguson, 52 Darnley St., Glasgow.
Browne & Nolan, Clonskeagh, Dublin.
Brython Press, 9 Hackins Hey, Liverpool.
Burke Pub. Co., 14 John St., W.C.1.
Burns & Oates, 25 Ashley Place, S.W.1.
Business Dictionaries, 133–137 Fetter Lane, E.C.4.
Butterworth & Co., Bell Yard, W.C.2.
Calder (John), 17 Sackville St., W.1.
Cambridge Univ. Press, 200 Euston Rd., N.W.1, and Cambridge.
Cape (Jonathan), 30 Bedford Square, W.C.1.
Carey Kingsgate Press, 6 Southampton Row, W.C.1.
Cassell & Co., 35 Red Lion Sq., W.C.1.
Caxton Publishing Co., 44 Hill St., W.1.
Centaur Press, Fontwell, Arundel, Sx.
Chambers (W. & R.), 11 Thistle St., Edinburgh.
Chapman & Hall, 37–39 Essex Street, W.C.2.
Chatto & Windus, 40–42 William IV St., W.C.2.
C.M.S., 6 Salisbury Square, E.C.4.
Churchill (J. & A.), 104 Gloucester Place, W.1.
Clark (T. & T.), 38 George St., Edinburgh.
Clarke (Jas.) & Co., 33 Store St., W.C.1.
Cleaver-Hume Press, St. Martin's St., W.C.2.
Clonmore & Reynolds, 29 Kildare St., Dublin.
Clowes (Wm.), Little New Street, E.C.4.
Collier-Macmillan, 10 South Audley St., W.1.
Collingridge, 2–10 Tavistock St., W.C.2.
Collins, Sons & Co., 14 St. James's Place, S.W.1.
Constable & Co., 10 & 12 Orange St., W.C.2.
Country Life, 2–10 Tavistock St., W.C.2.
Cresset Press, 11 Fitzroy Square, W.1.
Dakers (Andrew), 583 Fulham Rd., S.W.6.
Darton, Longman & Todd, 64 Chiswick High Rd., W.4.
Davies (Peter), 23 Bedford Sq., W.C.1.
Davis (R. Hart-), 36 Soho Square, W.1.
Dean & Son, 43 Ludgate Hill, E.C.4.
Deane (H. F. W.), 31 Museum St., W.C.1.
Dent (J. M.) & Sons, 10 Bedford St., W.C.2.
Deutsch (A.), 105 Gt. Russell St., W.C.1.
Dobson (Dennis), 80 Kensington Church St., W.8.
Dryad Press, Northgates, Leicester.
Duckworth & Co., 3 Henrietta St., W.C.2.
Edinburgh House P., 2 Eaton Gate, S.W.1.
Educational Prodns., 17 Denbigh St., S.W.1.
Elek, 14 Gt. James St., W.C.1.
Elliot (A. G.), Kingswood Bldg., Kingswood, Surrey.
Encyclopædia Britannica, 11 Belgrave Rd., S.W.1.
English Universities Press, 102 Newgate St., E.C.1.
Epworth Press, 25 City Road, E.C.1.
Evans Bros., Montague House, Russell Sq., W.C.1.
Eyre & Spottiswoode, 22 Henrietta St., W.C.2.
Faber & Faber, 24 Russell Sq., W.C.1.
Fleetway Publications, Farringdon St., E.C.4.
Focal Press, 31 Fitzroy Square, W.1.
Foulis (G. T.) 1–5 Portpool Lane, E.C.1.
Foulsham & Co., Yeovil Rd., Slough, Bucks.
Fountain Press, 46 Chancery Lane, W.C.2.
Four Square Books, Barnard's Inn, Holborn, E.C.1.
French (Samuel), 26 Southampton St., W.C.2.
Gale & Polden, Wellington Press, Aldershot.
Gall & Inglis, 12 Newington Road, Edinburgh.
Gee & Co., 151 Strand, W.C.2.
Geographia, 114 Fleet St., E.C.4.
Gibbons (Stanley), 391 Strand, W.C.2.
Gifford (John), 125 Charing Cross Road, W.C.2.
Ginn & Co., 18 Bedford Row, W.C.1.
Gollancz (Victor), 14 Henrietta St., W.C.2.
Green (W.), 2 St. Giles St., Edinburgh.
Griffin (Charles), 42 Drury Lane, W.C.2.
H.M. Stationery Office, Atlantic Ho., Holborn Viaduct, E.C.1.
Hachette, 217 Tottenham Court Rd., W.1.
Hale (Robert), 63 Old Brompton Rd., S.W.7.
Hamilton & Co., 108 Brompton Rd., S.W.3.
Hamilton (Hamish), 90 Gt. Russell St., W.C.1.
Hamlyn (P.), 583 Fulham Rd., S.W.6.
Hammond, Hammond & Co., 87 Gower St., W.C.1.
Harrap (G. G.) & Co., 182 High Holborn, W.C.1.
Harvill Press, 23 Lower Belgrave St., S.W.1.
Heffer & Sons, 4 Petty Cury, Cambridge.
Heinemann (Wm.), 15 Queen St., W.1.
Hely Thom, 33 Botanic Rd., Dublin.
Hill (Leonard), 229 Shepherds Bush Rd., W.6.
Hodder & Stoughton, Warwick Lane, E.C.4.
Hodge & Co., 12 Bank St., Edinburgh.
Hogarth Press, 40–42 William IV St., W.C.2.
Hollis & Carter, 10 Earlham St., W.C.2.
House of Grant, 91–95 Union St., Glasgow.
Hughes & Son, 29 Rivulet Rd., Wrexham.
Hurst & Blackett, 178 Gt. Portland St., W.1.
Hutchinson & Co., 178 Gt. Portland St., W.1.
Iliffe & Sons, Dorset House, Stamford St., S.E.1.
Independent Press, Farringdon St., E.C.4.
Jarrold & Sons, Cowgate, Norwich.
Jarrolds, 178 Gt. Portland St., W.1.
Jenkins (Herbert), 3 Duke of York St., S.W.1.
Johnson Pubns., 11 Stanhope Mews West, S.W.7.
Johnston (W. & A. K.), Edina Works, Edinburgh.
Jordan & Sons, 116 Chancery Lane, W.C.2.
Joseph (Michael), 26 Bloomsbury St., W.C.1.
Kaye (N.), 194 Bishopsgate, E.C.2.
Kelly's Directories, 2 Arundel St., W.C.2.
Kimber (Wm.), 46 Wilton Place, S.W.1.
Kimpton (Henry), 134 Gt. Portland St., W.1.

Laurie (T. Werner), 10 Earlham St., W.C.2.
Lawrence & Wishart, 81 Chancery Lane, W.C.2.
Lewis (H. K.). 136 Gower St., W.C.1.
Livingstone (E. & S.), 17 Teviot Pl., Edinburgh.
Lockwood (Crosby), 26 Old Brompton Rd., S.W.7.
Long (John). 178 Gt. Portland St., W.1.
Longacre Press, 161 Fleet St. E.C.4.
Longmans, Green & Co., 48 Grosvenor St., W.1.
Low (S.), Marston & Co., Potter Row, Gt. Missenden, Bucks.
Lutterworth Press, 4 Bouverie St., E.C.4.
Macdonald & Co., 2 Portman St., W.1.
McDougall's Educational Co., 30 Royal Terrace, Edinburgh, 7.
MacGibbon & Kee, 9 Grape St., W.C.2.
McGraw-Hill, Shoppenhangers Rd., Maidenhead, Berks.
Machinery Pub. Co., 21 West St., Brighton, 1.
MacLellan (Wm.), 240 Hope St., Glasgow.
Macmillan & Co., St. Martin's St., W.C.2.
Marshall (Percival), 19 Noel St. W.1.
Marshall, Morgan & Scott, 1–5 Portpool Lane, E.C.1.
May Fair Books, 13A Old Burlington St., W.1.
Mayflower, 282 Vauxhall Bridge Rd., S.W.1.
Methuen & Co., 36 Essex St., W.C.2.
Mills & Boon, 50 Grafton Way, W.1.
Mowbray, 28 Margaret St., W.1.
Muller (F.), 110 Fleet St., E.C.4.
Murray (John), 50 Albemarle St., W.1.
Museum Press, 26 Old Brompton Rd., S.W.7.
Naldrett Press, Tadworth, Surrey.
National Magazine Co., 28–30 Grosvenor Gdns., S.W.1.
National S.S.U., 104–5 Newgate St., E.C.1.
Nelson (T.), 36 Park St., W.1.
Nevill (P.), 583 Fulham Rd., S.W.6.
New Authors, 178 Gt. Portland St., W.1.
Newman Neame, 50 Fitzroy St., W.1.
Newnes (G.), Southampton St., W.C.2.
Nisbet & Co., Digswell Pl., Welwyn, Herts.
Nonesuch Library, 10 Earlham St., W.C.2.
Novello & Co., 160 Wardour St., W.1.
Odhams Press, 67–68 Long Acre, W.C.2.
Oldbourne, 121 Fleet St., E.C.4.
Oliphants, 1–5 Portpool Lane, E.C.1.
Oliver & Boyd, Tweeddale Court, Edinburgh.
Owen (Peter), 50 Old Brompton Rd., S.W.7.
Oxford Univ. Press, Warwick Square, E.C.4.
Pan Books, 8 Headfort Place, S.W.1.
Parrish (Max). 55 Queen Anne St., W.1.
Paternoster Press, 3 Mount Radford Crescent, Exeter, Devon.
Paul (Kegan), 43 Gt. Russell St., W.C.1.
Paul (Stanley), 178 Gt. Portland St., W.1.
Pearson (C. A.), Southampton St., W.C.2.
Penguin Books, Harmondsworth, Middlesex.
Pergamon Press, Headington Hill Hall, Oxford.
Phaidon Press, 5 Cromwell Place, S.W.7.
Pharmaceutical Press, 17 Bloomsbury Sq., W.C.1.
Philip (George), 12 Long Acre, W.C.2.
Phœnix House, 10 Bedford St., W.C.2.
Pickering & Inglis, 229 Bothwell St., Glasgow.
Pitkins, 9 John St., W.C.1.
Pitman (Sir Isaac), 39–41 Parker St., W.C.2.
Playfair Books, 39–43 Battersea High St., S.W.11.
Putnam & Co., 42 Gt. Russell St., W.C.1.
Reinhardt (Max), 10 Earlham St., W.C.2.
Religious Education Press, 85 Manor Road, Wallington, Surrey.
Rider & Co., 178 Gt. Portland St., W.1.
Rivingtons, Montague House, Russell Sq., W.C.1.
Routledge & Kegan Paul, 68–74 Carter Lane, E.C.4.
Scribner's, 23 Bedford Square, W.C.1.
Scripture Union & C.S.S.M., 5 Wigmore St., W.1.
Secker & Warburg, 14 Carlisle St., W.1.
Seeley, Service, 196 Shaftesbury Av., W.C.2.
Sheed & Ward, 33 Maiden Lane, W.C.2.
Sidgwick & Jackson, 1 Tavistock Chambers, W.C.1.
Skeffington & Son, 178 Gt. Portland St., W.1.
S.P.C.K., 121 Radwinter Rd., Saffron Walden, Essex.
Souvenir Press, 34 Bloombury St., W.C.1.
Spon (E. & F. N.), 22 Henrietta St., W.C.2.
Sporting Handbooks, 13 Bedford Square, W.C.1.
Stanford (Edward), 12–14 Long Acre, W.C.2.
Staples Press, 9 Grape St., W.C.2.
Stevens & Sons, 11 New Fetter Lane, E.C.4.
Student C. M. P., 58 Bloomsbury St., W.C.1.
Studio, 161 Fleet St., E.C.4.
Sweet & Maxwell, 11 New Fetter Lane E.C.4.
Sylvan Press, 5 Museum House, Museum St., W.C.1.
Talbot Press, 89 Talbot Street, Dublin.
Technical Press, 112 Westbourne Grove, W.2.
Temple Press, Bowling Green Lane, E.C.1.
Thames & Hudson, 30 Bloomsbury St., W.C.1.
Times Publishing Co., Printing House Sq., E.C.4.
Tiranti (Alec), 72 Charlotte St., W.1.
Transworld, Park Royal Rd., N.W.10.
Tuck (Raphael), 2 Portman St., W.1.
University of London Press, Warwick Square E.C.4.
University of Wales Press, Cathays Park, Cardiff.
University Tutorial Press, Euston Rd., N.W.1.
Vallentine, Mitchell, 18 Cursitor St., E.C.4.
Virtue & Co., 53 Cannon St., E.C.4.
Vista Books, 161 Fleet St., E.C.4.
Ward, Lock, 116 Baker St., W.1.
Warne, 1–4 Bedford Court, Bedford St., W.C.2.
Watts & Co., 39 Parker St., W.C.2.
Weidenfeld & Nicolson, 20 New Bond St., W.1.
"Whitaker," 13 Bedford Square, W.C.1.
Williams & Norgate, 154 Fleet St., E.C.4.
Wills & Hepworth, Angel Press, Loughborough.
Witherby (H. F. & G.), 61–62 Watling St., E.C.4.
World Distributors, St. Luke's St., Manchester.
World's Work, Tadworth, Surrey.
Wright (John), Bath Rd., Bristol.
Wright & Brown, 18 Stukeley St., W.C.2.

Most of the principal book publishers are members of The Publishers Association, whose address is 19, Bedford Square, London, W.C.1.—*President*, John Brown (Oxford U.P.), *Secretary*, R. E. Barker.

BOOK PRODUCTION AND BOOK EXPORTS

Figures issued by The Publishers Association (based on information supplied to its Chartered Accountants by individual publishers) show a marked and continuing increase in book exports in recent years. The totals for the years 1951 to 1962 are shown below:—

Year	Total value of Books produced in U.K.	Total value of Books exported from UK.	Year	Total value of Books produced in U.K.	Total value of Books exported from U.K.
1951	£41,553,760	£13,740,323	1957	£60,456,095	£22,505,440
1952	42,790,387	14,482,036	1958	63,608,654	23,817,453
1953	44,892,291	15,566,874	1959	66,945 183	25 393,960
1954	46,270,953	16,527,054	1960	75,426,683	29,833,866
1955	49,439,087	18,156,084	1961	78,911,506	31,738,057
1956	56,659,484	20,870,594	1962	81,376,301	34,493,754

BOOKS PUBLISHED IN GREAT BRITAIN IN 1962

This Table, from *The Bookseller* of January 5, 1963, shows the books published in 1962 with the number of new editions, translations and limited editions.

Books and pamphlets priced at less than 6*d*. have been omitted, as are also all Government publications except the more important issued by H.M. Stationery Office.

	Total	Reprints and New Editions	Translations	Limited Editions
Aeronautics	176	56	2	—
Annuals and Serials	19	12	—	—
Anthropology and Ethnology	72	15	2	—
Archæology	85	15	8	—
Art and Architecture	666	88	78	7
Astronomy and Meteorology	149	27	7	—
Banking and Finance	213	64	—	—
Bibliography and Literary History	661	142	11	3
Biography and Memoirs	577	118	44	4
Botany, Horticulture and Agriculture	259	67	4	1
Calendars, Booklets and Albums	11	—	—	—
Chemistry and Physics	613	106	19	—
Children's Books	2,126	219	59	—
Classics and Translations	79	29	27	—
Dictionaries and Encyclopædias	81	17	—	—
Directories and Guide Books	400	214	7	—
Domestic Economy	198	41	2	—
Educational	2,265	348	12	—
Engineering, Electricity and Mechanics	701	127	20	—
Essays and Belles-Lettres	112	29	5	2
Facetiæ	135	28	1	—
Fiction	4,232	1,980	403	3
Geology, Mineralogy and Mining	179	41	9	—
History	605	184	28	2
Illustrated Gift Books	13	1	2	—
Law and Parliamentary	566	132	5	—
Maps and Atlases	92	33	1	—
Mathematics	271	41	11	—
Medical and Surgical	1,158	311	20	—
Music	193	39	17	—
Natural History, Biology and Zoology	516	89	13	2
Nautical	167	58	1	—
Naval and Military	284	55	8	1
Occultism	58	13	—	—
Oriental	16	3	2	—
Philately	24	7	1	1
Philosophy and Science	347	110	36	2
Poetry and Drama	716	126	59	11
Politics, Political Economy and Questions of the Day	1,078	138	40	—
Psychology	180	46	12	—
Religion and Theology	1,373	261	127	4
Sociology	566	87	12	—
Sports, Games and Pastimes	401	79	5	—
Technical Handbooks	1,013	205	9	2
Topography, Local History & Folklore	365	59	22	5
Trade, Commerce and Industry	531	114	2	—
Travel and Adventure	169	40	12	—
Veterinary Science, Farming and Stock-keeping	253	53	2	—
Wireless and Television	115	37	2	—
Totals	25,079	6,104	1,169	50

COPYRIGHT

The Government Department dealing with Copyright is the *Industrial Property Department, Board of Trade*, 25 Southampton Bldgs., W.C.2.

Subject to the provisions of the Copyright Act, 1956, copyright subsists automatically in every original literary, dramatic, musical and artistic work and continues to subsist until the end of the period of fifty years from the end of the calendar year in which the author died and shall then expire. *No registration nor other formalities are required in order to obtain the protection of the Act.* Protection is conferred not only against reproduction but also against the public performance of a work without permission. Copyright may also subsist in sound recordings, cinematograph films and television and sound broadcasts. Libraries entitled to receive free copies of books published in the United Kingdom, are the British Museum, the Bodleian Library, Oxford, University Library, Cambridge, the National Library of Wales, the National Library of Scotland and Trinity College, Dublin.

Voluntary Registration at Stationers' Hall.—Compulsory registration at Stationers' Hall terminated on Dec. 31, 1923, but in the following year the Stationers' Company established a *new* Register in which Books and Fine Arts can be registered. A copy has to be filed at Stationers' Hall and certified copies of the entries are issued, the fees being 20s. for a Book, or a Fine Art; certified copies 10s. in either case. The fee for a search is 5s.

LITERATURE OF THE YEAR

British Books in the World

The primacy of English as a world language was challenged more vigorously than in recent years. An agreement between the French and West German Governments to give teaching priority to each other's languages was concluded in January, though a spokesman for the West German Ministry of Family Affairs said that it was "not a matter of pushing out English but of extending French". Strong resistance to a Bill for the continuance of English as an associate official language was made by opposition groups in the Indian Parliament and members were ejected (April 14). In conferring American citizenship on Sir Winston Churchill, President Kennedy said that he had "mobilized the English language and sent it into battle". The militancy of English is confirmed by book trade statistics for 1962. During the year, British publishers brought out 25,079 titles of which 18,795 were new books, while 21,914 titles were issued in the United States. Introducing the House of Lords debate on the Government's Overseas Information Services in the last week of March, Lord Massereene and Ferrard said that Britain was still the greatest exporter of books in the world. Statistics released by the Publishers Association in May showed that turnover in 1962 was £81,376,301, of which 42·4 per cent. related to export sales. Home sales fell, however, by £290,902, and there was a decline in British exports to some countries, e.g., Australia, relative to their imports from America.

Home Affairs

Some publishers feared that books were being priced out of the market; Mr. David Ascoli, speaking at the annual conference of the Booksellers Association, said (June 9) that he had "a strong feeling that the law of diminishing returns is now operating with a vengeance". He warned the trade of pitfalls in the pursuit of bigger margins. Britain was not a nation of bookbuyers; it was impossible to travel round the world without becoming acutely aware of the comparative apathy towards buying and owning books in this country. Some lay critics attributed this to the disappearance of the old and alluring bookshop; a visitor to Dijon, quoted in *The Daily Telegraph* (September 12), said that there he had found a dozen, while in his English provincial university town there was only one "that you and I would call a bookshop". In an article in *The Sunday Times* (Nov. 18, 1962), Lord Francis-Williams offered "Thoughts on Laying Down a Library", a kind of cellar for one's grandson with annual expenditure, over twenty-one years, of £5 or £6, while Sir Alan Herbert's letters to the newspapers continued to press for the "Public Lending Right" as a stimulus to the trade and as an incentive to authors. That the writer's profession in Britain is hazardous was shown by details of ten personal budgets in *The Author* (June 12); a novelist and television playwright earned £4,320 and headed the list; at its foot came a poet who earned £344.

Nevertheless, there was a general feeling of strength and buoyancy in the book trade. Long uncertainties had been allayed by the declaration, in the Restrictive Practices Court (Oct. 30, 1962) that the restrictions in the Net Book Agreement, 1957, were not contrary to the public interest. The Court, consisting of Mr. Justice Buckley, Sir Stanford Cooper, Mr. W. L. Heywood and Mr. D. V. House, found that the abrogation of the Agreement (which provides that most classes of new books shall be retailed at net published prices, a discount of 10 per cent. being allowed to public libraries) would result in fewer and less well-equipped stockholding bookshops, more expensive books, and fewer published titles. The Court held that the avoidance of any of these consequences would be a sufficient justification for the continuance of the Agreement. This judgment meant, in the formula of the Restrictive Trade Practices Act, 1956, that the Agreement conferred upon the public "specific and substantial benefits or advantages", and substantiated the claim of the trade that "books *are* different". With confidence, if with caution, publishers felt able to look ahead, and plans for a 1964 Book Fair, into which they alone would put perhaps £100,000, were revealed in June.

There were other evidences of expansion. Collins' new building in Glasgow, six storeys high, six acres in extent and capable of stocking 17,000,000 volumes, was opened (26 November 1962) by Field-Marshal Viscount Montgomery. The Matthew Hodder group of companies moved into new premises in Warwick Lane, E.C.4, with 25,000 sq. ft. of floor space. They were opened by Sir John Hunt (June 5). Mr. Robert Maxwell, of Pergamon Press, announced (June 23) that he hoped to begin building a new plant of 130,000 sq. ft. at Dundee within a year. Against this, a scheme for the extension of the Central Criminal Court, announced in November 1962, will involve the demolition of the London offices, at Amen House, of the Oxford University Press.

New steps were taken towards cohesion and order in the trade. The Publishers Association, it was announced in March, has reconstituted its Net Book Agreement Defence Committee as a new Trade Practices Committee; this will keep in review remaining matters within the interest of the former Defence Committee. The Publishers Association announced at the same time that in future discount licences granted to public libraries would take the form of standard conditions laid down by the Association alone; it would be supplemented by a system of school library licences. Better educational facilities within the trade, and minima of turnover and stock, were the principal points in a Charter for Booksellers resolution carried at the annual general meeting of the Booksellers Association (June 7). Blackwell's and the Oxford University Press announced (Sept. 25) the formation of a company to serve the new universities. Their joint statement said, "The expansion of existing universities and the creation of new universities call for bookshop facilities of the highest standards". It would be the task of the new company to supply these needs, which had been discussed in correspondence in *The Times* during July and August. One letter, from Bodley's Librarian, deplored parsimonious support of university libraries, especially in their pursuit of rare books and manuscripts. Dr. Myres and other correspondents were defended by a leading article, "The Library's Place", in *The Times Literary Supplement* (August 9); but Mr. William Wiseley of Findlay, Ohio, writing in the same journal (Sept. 20), declared his resentment that new university libraries should seek prestige by "scattering into a hundred corners of the globe the materials needed by scholars, whose treks from one to another now resemble the weary travels of mediaeval students". An unnamed American university was reported in August to have offered £36,000 to its British owner for the Bible given by King Charles I, on the morning of his execution, to Bishop Juxon. But dispersion did not triumph everywhere: Georgetown University, Washington, D.C., announced (Sept. 26) that it would return to the British Museum a volume of seventeenth century pamphlets thought to have been stolen a century ago. A notable purchase by the British Museum was the autograph manuscript of Virginia Woolf's novel *Mrs. Dalloway* (April 24). Sotheby's announced (Nov. 14, 1962) that Mr. H. P. Kraus of New York had "willingly agreed to cede" to Plymouth Corporation his purchase of Drake's letters patent for the Cadiz expedition, and had donated the £360 commission to the Friends of the National Libraries. Another specially notable sale at Sotheby's was Lord Ilchester's Savonarola collection, which realised £7,747.

Festivals, Commemorations, Exhibitions

Under the headline "Boom for the Bard" *The Daily Telegraph* reported (August 22) that Shakespeare was enjoying the best season of his long career and was the fount of thirteen festivals in the United States during 1963. On the same day the *New York Times* displayed memorial notices to "Plantagenet, Richard" in which The Friends of Richard III and the Fellowship of the White Boar accused Shakespeare of malice against their patron. In London, *The Times* published polemic correspondence, during March, on this theme. This followed Dr. R. H. G. Lyne-Pirkis's paper to the Richard III Society (Feb. 27) which awarded the King a not-proven verdict as murderer of the Princes. A leader in the same newspaper (May 3) regretted that Shakespeare, not being of royal blood or a postal dignitary, would not under present rules qualify for a commemorative stamp next year, the fourth centenary of his birth. In general, however, Shakespeare remained a figure of veneration. Fourteen lectures were given during the annual Summer School (Aug. 20–29) at Stratford-upon-Avon. Dr. A. L. Rowse claimed in articles in *The Times* in September, anticipating publication of *William Shakespeare: a Biography*, to have solved many of the identification and dating problems of the Sonnets; President Nyerere of Tanganyika translated *Julius Caesar* into Swahili (announced Aug. 27), and Sir Laurence Olivier described the move to open Shakespeare's tomb as "a clod-hopping, jackbooted outrage" (Aug. 14). A Shakespeare Art Exhibition will be held at Guildhall from May 22 to June 27, 1964. It was announced (Sept. 11) that The London Marlowe Society would open with *Edward II* on Feb. 26, 1964, the anniversary of Marlowe's baptism. It would be played later at Berkeley Castle; while the poet's birthplace, Canterbury, would see *The Jew of Malta* in February and another play in August. Among literary plays at the 1963 Dublin Festival were stage treatments of James Joyce's novels, *Finnegan's Wake* and *Dubliners*. The Cheltenham Festival of Literature opened (Sept. 30) with Mr. J. B. Priestley in the chair at a discussion on the state of literature. The International Drama Conference in Edinburgh (September) barely touched on literary matters save, in the view of a speaker at the Edinburgh Presbytery of the Church of Scotland, in the use of four-letter words. The Presbytery nevertheless declined to condemn the Conference (Oct. 1). Mr. John Lehmann and Mr. Angus Wilson, delegates to the European Writers' Congress at Leningrad, flew to meet Mr. Khrushchev (Aug. 13), at his Black Sea villa. Mr. Wilson thought their host unwilling to compromise on cultural matters but to approve of the meeting of Western and Soviet writers.

Other literary landmarks were the 200th anniversary of the now defunct *Almanach de Gotha*, the centenary of *The Statesman's Year Book*, the 70th anniversary of *The Studio*, the half-centenary of *The New Statesman* and the 40th anniversary of *Time*.

Among personal anniversaries, the bi-centenary of William Cobbett was celebrated at Farnham, Surrey (March 9) and that of Wolfe Tone—author of the burlesque *Belmont Castle* as well as United Irishman—at Trinity College, Dublin (June 23). Mr. R. St. Barbe Baker planted an oak at Wotton, Surrey, to commemorate the 300th anniversary of the writing of John Evelyn's *Sylva*, or *Forest Trees*. Mr. John Masefield wrote a poem to celebrate the restoration of W. B. Yeats's house in Woburn Walk, London (Aug. 16), while an undated poem by Ben Jonson, inscribed on a paten, was displayed for the first time in Lincoln Cathedral (April 15). Sir James Barrie's birthplace at Kirriemuir, Angus, was reopened (May 3). A plaque to Thomas Moore was unveiled by the Irish Ambassador at 85 George Street, London (Sept. 11). The Bible concordancer, Alexander Cruden, was commemorated by a plaque, unveiled by Mr. John Betjeman, in Camden Passage, Islington (Nov. 13, 1962). Other literary personalities and landmarks were less fortunate: an appeal was made (May 7) for a memorial to mark the site at Twerton, Bath, of Henry Fielding's demolished house; *The Times* deplored (May 11) reports that Robert Louis Stevenson's birthplace museum in Edinburgh might close owing to lack of visitors; Rutgers University, N.J., where it stood, announced (Aug. 18) that the white oak of Joyce Kilmer's poem *Trees*, was dying and must be cut down. Dr. Margaret Murray published a book in the week of her 100th birthday (13 July).

Literary and Publishing Events

Dr. Coggan, Archbishop of York, told an Oxford audience (Feb. 17) that the growth of world literacy posed the problem not only of helping people to read but of what they should read. The Archbishop said at a Rotary conference (April 27) that millions of adults in Africa and elsewhere were learning to read and that this might be the most significant fact of the mid-century. Preaching at Doncaster (April 12) he discussed the second part of the problem. Penguin Books (April 10) had announced that *Lady Chatterley's Lover*, with 3,500,000 copies sold, had registered the highest sales of all their titles. "This fact," said Dr. Coggan, "did not say much for our tastes in literature or for our morals. Such books were a cancer". Moralists also pointed to the sales of *Lord Denning's Report*, which headed the best-seller lists in late September. But the merits of D. H. Lawrence's novel, cited by the Public Orator in June when its publisher received a doctorate at Oxford, and the standing of the *Report* as a State paper, defended some at least of their readers from the charge of vulgar curiosity. The late Pope John XXIII had warned the Press in another context (Oct. 13, 1962) of the dangers of sensationalism, and questions of ethics and censorship touched newspapers rather than books during the year. In November 1962, however, an order for the forfeiture of 15,000 paperbacked books was made by the Marylebone magistrate, while two retailers were sentenced for an offence under the Obscene Publications Act, after jury trial in March, to nine months' imprisonment. Henry Miller's novel, *Tropic of Cancer*, was published in England on April 4 and the Member of Parliament for Dulwich promptly asked the Attorney-General to set in motion proceedings against Mr. Miller and his publisher. Sir John Hobson refused. Mr. Miller's play, *Just Wild about Harry*, was presented at the Edinburgh Festival (Aug. 27) in an expurgated form to which the author gave reluctant consent. Sterner, and perhaps more surprising action was taken elsewhere. In March, a professor at the Australian National University, Canberra, was fined £16 for posting to an American colleague, interested in ballad sources, a work said to be "obscene, indecent and blasphemous". In mid-July six district attorneys in the State of New York filed charges of obscenity against John Cleland's *Fanny Hill; or Memoirs of a Woman of Pleasure*, published in England in 1749. The State Supreme Court ruled (Aug. 23) that the work could not be characterized as patently offensive when examined in the light of current community standards. In his Nobel Laureate speech (Dec. 10, 1962), Mr. John Steinbeck declared that literature was not "a game for the cloistered elect, the tinhorn mendicants of low-calory despair", and *The Sunday Times* reviewer, on publication of *Another Country* in February, counselled moralists to "read Mr. Baldwin and tremble". But its booksellers in New Orleans were arrested in July for giving currency, in the words of the City Attorney, to "the most filthy and pornographic book I have ever read". James Baldwin's *The Fire Next Time*, published in England in July, was an urgent, reasonable appeal for interracial charity. The work was a compassionate indictment of hardened hearts, economical, sensitive and homiletic.

Another sociological denunciation from abroad, from which compassion, again, is rarely absent was Danilo Dolci's *Waste:* a catalogue of religious and civic stagnation in Sicily. It was an anatomy of incompetent feudalism and gangster efficiency. A study of an environment at once less colourful and more aseptic was *The Evolution of a Community*, by Peter Willmott. Mr. Willmott found in Dagenham a transplanted East End, undisturbed since the exodus of the 'twenties, conformist, kindly, contented and so much of a vacuum of adventure and ideas that, statistics notwithstanding, *The Observer's* reviewer, for one, could not quite believe it. But a maddening national complacency was laid bare with conviction in *The Affluent Sheep: A Profile of the British Consumer*, by Robert Millar. Conformist acceptance of mechanized American bliss was derided urbanely in *A Public Happiness* by August Hecksher. A more profound and generalized study of the human condition was Denis Gabor's *Inventing the Future:* a brave, confident and convincing book which looked war, want, work and boredom squarely in the face and found them paper tigers, powerless before the millennium. "A man who wants to sacrifice his life for his nation is highly social", said Professor Gabor, "but we shall have no use for him". The wars and their heroes continued, however, to stimulate a considerable literature. John Terraine's *Haig* was documented, detached and fair. *German East*, by Brian Gardner, studied the logistic and tactical follies, and the prodigies of improvisation (these mainly on the German side) of the African campaign of 1914–1918. *The Boilerplate War*, by John Foley, was an exceptionally readable account of the early deployment and technology of the Tank Corps. Distinguished airmen wrote of another new arm in *Years of Combat*, by Lord Douglas of Kirtleside, and *Early Bird*, by W. Geoffrey Moore. *The K Boats*, by Don Everitt, told the story of the large and unlucky steam submarines of the First World War. *The Collected Poems of Wilfred Owen*, "probably the greatest poems about war in our literature", in the words of his editor, C. Day Lewis, were issued with critical notes and Edmund Blunden's memoir of 1931. *Journey from Obscurity*, by Harold Owen, dealt with the poet and was the first volume of a family biographical trilogy. *Pebbles from my Skull*, by Stuart Hood, was the introspective, sensitive, account of an escaped prisoner's role as a partisan in the last War; *The War and Colonel Warden*, by Gerald Pawle, was a study of Sir Winston Churchill's personal life from 1939 to 1945; and *The Rise of the Boffins*, by Ronald W. Clark, listed with clarity some of the achievements in that war of the technologists and scientific planners. A more distant campaign was studied, perhaps with no undue generosity to the French, in *Bonaparte in Egypt*, by J. Christopher Herold; while an unexpected charity illuminated the same period in *The Life and Letters of Emma Hamilton*, by Hugh Tours.

The English eye was cast much abroad. The publishing season opened with Viscount Montgomery's *Three Continents*, a catalogue of global travel with crisp solutions to global problems. Limited to Italy, certainly offering no solutions to anything, but a delight in ironic presentation, was Aubrey Menen's *Speaking the Language like a Native*. In *Pound Wise*, Sir Osbert Sitwell discussed treasure, taste and art from London to Peking. *The Prophet's Camel Bell*, by Margaret Laurence, was a highly literate account of her life among the Somalis, while *Oyster River*, by George Millar, was the story, well and urbanely narrated, of a voyage round the Brittany coast. Another sailor, Derek Robert, wrote entertainingly and with kindness (though with reservations towards Australia) of the South Pacific in *Look at me Now*. The eye returned introspectively in John Mander's *Great Britain or Little England*, a cool appraisal of Britain's leadership and standing in the world, and in *A State of England*, by Anthony Hartley. Mr. Hartley, sitting on the right wing of the political stage, deplored at once snobbish intellectualism, semi-literacy and the decay of individual freedom.

Practical politicians have found less time for writing than in recent years, though Sir Edward Boyle reviewed Karl Popper's *The Open Society and its Enemies* in *New Society*, Mr. Enoch Powell wrote a critical article for *The Times*, and Mr. Duncan Sandys contributed to the 100th number of *Commonwealth Today*. Lord Attlee broadcast (April 21) two of his own unpublished verses. Mr. Maurice Edelman published a novel, *The Fratricides*. It was announced (April 19) that the late Earl Winterton, sometime "Father of the House", had left his diaries to Mr. Alan Houghton Brodrick; and (July 5) that the Gladstone diaries would be prepared for publication by Mr. M. R. D. Foot. Lord Avon's memoirs, published in November 1962, threw light on many unresolved controversies and renewed one outside politics—the "50 year rule" limiting the availability of Cabinet papers to scholars. Popper's *Open Society* had another admirer within the Government—Sir Keith Joseph—who presented a copy to the Cabinet Room Library. It was announced from the White House (August 16) that the Librarian of Yale University had chosen 1,780 titles for the President's library; Mr. Kennedy himself had advised on the selection, in April, of books for a village library in Long Island. These included works by Sir Winston Churchill, Lord David Cecil, Peter Quennell and Ian Fleming.

Among biographies of statesmen were *Chaim Weizmann*, essays edited by M. W. Weisgal and Joel Carmichael, and Kenneth Young's *Arthur James Balfour*; Fenner Brockway's second volume of autobiography, *Outside the Right*, also appeared: it was a mellower work than *Inside the Left*, kindly, tolerant, yet jealously dedicated to personal dignity and liberty. Edith Simon's *The Making of Frederick the Great* related the horrendous education, and development to the age of 33, of an unloved soldier-politician; while Roberto Ridolfi's *Machiavelli* (translated by Cecil Grayson) was a "work of cleaning and restoration" of the classic political adventurer. Statecraft, industry and warfare were the intermingled themes of *Vickers: a History*, by J. D. Scott.

In one chapter of military history, *T. E. Lawrence to his Biographers*, a soldier, Captain Liddell Hart, and a poet, Mr. Robert Graves, collaborated. Mr. Graves declared in November 1962 that "nine-tenths of English poetic literature is the result either of vulgar careerism, or of a poet trying to keep his hand in. Most poets are dead by their late twenties". In a year in which the deaths of Robert Frost, Christopher Hassall, Theodore Roethke and Louis MacNeice were mourned it was heartening to see a considerable poetic output and a revival of critical interest. Among poetry readings at Kenwood House one (Sept. 15) was a tribute to Hassall. The BBC "Monitor" programme (Sept. 29) included memorial readings from MacNeice and Roethke. A Festival of Poetry opened under the direction of Patric Dickinson at the Royal Court Theatre on July 15. Dannie Abse's presentation at the Lyric Theatre, Hammersmith, *Ash on a Young Man's Sleeve* (Feb. 18), was a declaimed anthology. Roy Fuller's *Collected Poems* appeared early in the publishing season, as did two mature works, *Downstream* and *Another September* by the Irish poet, Thomas Kinsella. From San Francisco came Allen Ginsberg's *Reality Sandwiches*, 1953–60. Other poems of North American provenance were *Sestina for a Far Off Summer* by Richard Lattimore and *Collected Poems* by the Canadian, A. J. M. Smith. From Anthony Thwaite came *The Owl in the Tree*, which was particularly well received, as was *A Peopled Landscape*, by Charles Tomlinson—with its near-metaphysical imagery and short, raw words perhaps the most interesting offering of the year. One of the best anthologies was *Contemporary American Poetry*, edited by Donald Hall; individual, new, odd, English and noteworthy was Rosemary Tonks's *Notes on Cafés and Bedrooms*.

The novelists' year began with the publication, to coincide with his eightieth birthday (Jan. 17), of Sir Compton Mackenzie's *My Life and Times*, the first volume of his autobiography. *A Reader's Guide to the Contemporary English Novel* by F. R. Karl and *Postwar British Fiction* by James Gindin were two useful and crowded charts and *The Times* ran a series of valuable Thursday articles *Critics under Review*. An "East-West Symposium" of Critics in New York during August inspired a special number, *Critics Abroad*, of *The Times Literary Supplement* (Sept. 27). Novelists themselves were immensely prolific during the year. Among novels reported by booksellers and librarians as particular successes were: *Portrait of a Young Man Drawing*, by Charles Perry: *Dust*, by Yael Dayan; *The Seed and the Sower*, by Laurens Van Der Post; *The Sand Pebbles*, by Richard McKenna; *The Golden Spur*, by Dawn Powell; *Youngblood Hawk*, by Herman Wouk; two novels in one volume by Han Suyin, *Cast but one Shadow* and *Winter Love;* Zoe Oldenbourg's *Cities of the Flesh; The Gift*, by Emyr Humphreys; *Speculations about Jakob* by Uwe Johnson; *Cat and Mouse* by Günter Grass; and *The Centaur* by John Updike. *Night and Silence, who is Here?*, by Pamela Hansford-Johnson, *The Unicorn*, by Iris Murdoch and *The Girls of Slender Means*, by Muriel Spark, attracted special interest.

Honours and Awards

Companions of Literature (Royal Society of Literature awards): Dame Edith Sitwell (poet), Mr. Evelyn Waugh (novelist); *Nobel Prize for Literature*, 1962; Mr. John Steinbeck (novelist); *Prix Goncourt*, 1962: Mme. Anna Langfus, for novel *Les Bagages de Sable; Prix Femina*, 1963: M. Yves Berger, for novel *Le Sud*; *Prix Renaudot*, 1963; Mlle Simonne Jacquemard, for novel *Le Veilleur de Nuit*; *James Tait Black Memorial Prizes*, 1962: Miss Meriol Trevor, for her two volumes on Cardinal Newman, *The Pillar of Cloud* and *Light in Winter* (biography award), and Mr. Robert Hardy, for *Act of Destruction* (fiction award); *Library Association's Children's Book Awards*, 1962: Miss Pauline Clark, for *The Twelve and the Genii* (Carnegie Medal) and Mr. Brian Wildsmith, for illustrations incorporated in his own *ABC* (Kate Greenaway Medal); *Pulitzer Prizes*, 1963: the late William Faulkner, for novel *The Reivers* and Miss Barbara Tuchman, for non-fiction work *The Guns of August*; *Duff Cooper Memorial Prize*, 1962: Mr. Michael Howard, for *The Franco-Prussian War*; *Prix Formentor*, 1963: Señor Jorge Semprun; *Grand Prix de* l'Academie Française, 1963: M. Michel Mohrt; and the *William Foyle Poetry Prize*, 1963: Mr. Hugh McDiarmid.

BOOK CLUBS

The following Book Clubs are registered with the Publishers Association:—

FOLIO SOCIETY LTD., 6 Stratford Place, W.1.

FOYLE (W. & G.) LTD., 121 Charing Cross Road, W.C.2.
- The Book Club.
- Catholic Book Club.
- Children's Book Club.
- Garden Book Club.
- Quality Book Club.
- Romance Book Club.
- Scientific Book Club.
- Thriller Book Club.
- Travel Book Club.
- Western Book Club.

HUTCHINSON & CO. (PUBLISHERS) LTD., 178 Great Portland Street, W.1.
- Adventurers' Club.
- Man's Book Club.
- Mystery Book Guild.
- Soccer Book Club.
- Valentine Romance Club.

ODHAMS PRESS LTD., 67–68 Long Acre, W.C.2.
- Companion Book Club.
- *Herald Sun* Readers' Book Club (Australia).

OLDBOURNE BOOK CO. LTD., 121 Fleet Street, E.C.4,
- Scientific Book Guild

PHOENIX HOUSE LTD., 10–13 Bedford Street, Strand, W.C.2.
- Contemporary Fiction.
- Country Book Club.
- Jazz Book Club.
- Motoraces Book Club.
- Science-Fiction Book Club.
- Sportsman's Book Club.

READERS UNION LTD., 10 Bedford Street, W.C.2.
- Readers Union.

REPRINT SOCIETY LTD., High Street, Aldershot, Hants.
- World Books.

S.C.M. PRESS LTD., 56 Bloomsbury Street, W.C.1.
- S.C.M. Religious Book Club.

TOWN BOOKSHOP, Enfield, Middx.
- Sophisticated Book Club.

MUSIC AND OPERA OF 1962–63

(1962) Oct. 1. The Hamburg State Opera, as its last production on its visit to Sadler's Wells, introduced Berg's unfinished opera *Lulu* for its first performance in London. **3.** The B.B.C. Symphony Orchestra, under Antal Dorati, began a new series of concerts in the Festival Hall. **10.** The opening of the Royal Philharmonic Society's 151st season was marked by a concert at the Festival Hall given by the Hallé Orchestra, conducted by Sir John Barbirolli, with Artur Rubinstein as soloist in Beethoven's fourth piano concerto. **11.** A new production of Mozart's *Idomeneo* was presented at Sadler's Wells. **15.** The London Symphony Orchestra played at a Festival Hall concert under Jean Martinon, the French conductor. **30.** The Rotterdam Philharmonic Orchestra, on a short English tour, visited London for the first time, giving a concert at the Festival Hall.

Nov. 2. The inaugural concert was held at the new Fairfield Hall in Croydon in the presence of Queen Elizabeth the Queen Mother; the programme of Elgar, Bruch and Beethoven was given by the B.B.C. Symphony Orchestra with Yehudi Menuhin; Sir Malcolm Sargent conducted. **5.** Artur Rubinstein took part in a concert at the Festival Hall in the Philharmonia Orchestra's Brahms Festival, with Carlo Maria Giulini as conductor. **7.** At a concert at the Festival Hall in which Yehudi Menuhin and Pierre Monteux took part with the Royal Liverpool Philharmonic Orchestra, Sir Adrian Boult presented Mr. Menuhin with the Philharmonic Society's gold medal. The 90-year-old U.S. composer Clarence Dickinson, was present at the Albert Hall to hear the London *première* of his *Storm King* symphony for orchestra and organ played by the Royal Philharmonic Orchestra with Nicholas Danby as soloist. **9.** The Bournemouth Symphony Orchestra, conducted by Constantin Silvestri, appeared in a concert at the Festival Hall. **13.** David Willcocks conducted the Bach Choir in Bach's B Minor Mass at the Festival Hall, with Wilfred Brown, John Shirley-Quirk, Helen Watts and Heather Harper as soloists. **14.** The B.B.C. fortieth birthday concert in the Festival Hall, conducted by Antal Dorati, with the B.B.C. Orchestra and Chorus, consisted of works by Stravinsky, Schoenberg and Bartok, preceded by a specially commissioned work by Michael Tippett, a Praeludium for brass, bells and percussion. **20.** The annual Saint Cecilia concert took place in the Festival Hall in the presence of the Queen.

Dec. 2. George Malcolm gave a harpsichord recital of works by Bach and Scarlatti at the Festival Hall. **4.** The London Philharmonic Orchestra, conducted by Sir Adrian Boult, performed Vaughan Williams' *Sinfonia Antarctica* at the Festival Hall; Hazel Schmid was the soprano soloist. **5.** Sir Malcolm Sargent conducted the Royal Philharmonic Orchestra at the Festival Hall in Holst's *The Planets* and Dvorak's cello concerto, in which the soloist was Paul Tortelier. **6.** Britten's *War Requiem* received its first London performance, being conducted by Meredith Davies in Westminster Abbey with the B.B.C. Orchestra and Chorus, and Peter Pears, Vladimir Ruzdjak and Heather Harper as soloists. **9.** The London Choral Society and the Philomusica of London gave a concert of Christmas music at the Victoria and Albert Museum, the programme including Vaughan Williams' *The Shepherds of the Delectable Mountains*, Alan Bush's cantata *The Winter Journey*, a cycle of Argentinian songs by Albert Ginastera and three carols by John Tobin (who conducted them) based on traditional Spanish melodies. **10.** In the composer's centenary year, Delius' *A Mass of Life* was sung in English by the Royal Choral Society, conducted by Sir Malcolm Sargent, at the Albert Hall. **12.** In a B.B.C. Symphony Orchestra concert at the Festival Hall, conducted by Jean Martinon, the soloist in Schumann's concerto for cello and orchestra was the 17-year-old Jacqueline du Pré. **14.** The Royal Philharmonic Orchestra under Rudolf Kempe gave a Beethoven concert at the Festival Hall; Hans Richter-Haaser was the soloist in the Emperor concerto. **19.** The Royal Choral Society's annual carol concert took place at the Albert Hall.

(1963) Jan. 9. The Weill-Brecht opera, *The Rise and Fall of the City of Mahagonny*, first produced at Leipzig in 1930, was performed for the first time in England in a production at Stratford-upon-Avon, by Michael Geliot, with Colin Davis as conductor; on Jan. 16 the same production opened at Sadler's Wells. **25.** The Hallé Orchestra, under Sir John Barbirolli, performed Shostakovich's Fifth Symphony at the Festival Hall.

Feb. 3. The London Symphony Orchestra, conducted by George Hurst, played one of Tchaikovsky's early symphonies—the Second, or Little Russian—in a Festival Hall concert. **4.** Bruckner's *Nullte* (or Number 0) symphony was performed for the first time at a concert in this country, in Bryan Fairfax's Polyphonia series at St. Pancras Town Hall. **6.** The B.B.C. Chorus and Orchestra, conducted by Antal Dorati, with Alexander Young, Jennifer Vyvyan and Norma Procter as soloists, performed Britten's *Spring Symphony* in the Festival Hall. **8.** A concert performance of an Italian version of Donizetti's opera *Fille du Régiment* was given at the Festival Hall, with Bryan Balkwill as conductor, the Philharmonia Orchestra, the Glyndebourne Festival Chorus, and, as soloists, Giuseppe Baratti, Renato Capecchi, Jolanda Meneguzzer and Monica Sinclair. **12.** In a concert in its international series at the Festival Hall, the London Symphony Orchestra appeared under the Hungarian conductor, Istan Kertesz, in a programme of Mozart, Dvorak and Bartok. **24.** The Hungarian State Symphony Orchestra, conducted by Janos Ferencsik, appeared at the Festival Hall.

March 6. Elgar's second symphony in E flat, conducted by Sir Malcolm Sargent, was performed in a B.B.C. orchestral concert. **8.** The 150th anniversary concert of the Royal Philarmonic Society took place at the Festival Hall in the presence of Queen Elizabeth the Queen Mother. The programme included Cherubini's *Anacreon* overture (the first work heard at the first Philharmonic concert) and variations on a theme of Hindemith specially composed for the occasion by Sir William Walton, who conducted the piece, the other works being conducted by Sir Adrian Boult. **9.** The second half of the Philharmonia Concert Society's programme at the Festival Hall was devoted to Handel's cantata *Apollo e Dafne*, with Dietrich Fischer-Dieskau and Heather Harper as soloists. **15.** The Bach Choir, conducted by David Willcocks, sang the St. John Passion at the Festival Hall; the soloists were John Carol Case, John Shirley-Quirk, Wilfred Brown, Robert Tear and Helen Watts. **23.** The Bournemouth Symphony Orchestra, under Constantin Silvestri, appeared at the Festival Hall. **24.** At the Festival Hall, the Philharmonia Chorus sang *The Dream of Gerontius*, with Sir John Barbirolli as conductor and Ronald Dowd, Donald Bell and Anna Reynolds as soloists.

April 11. A Festival began at Bournemouth in honour of the 70th anniversary of the Bournemouth

Symphony Orchestra, the programme at the first concert including Schumann's seldom-performed violin concerto. **25.** The 15th anniversary concert of the National Youth Orchestra took place at the Festival Hall in the presence of Queen Elizabeth the Queen Mother.

May 5. Yehudi Menuhin played as solo violinist in Mozart's A major concerto at the Festival Hall, and afterwards conducted the London Symphony Orchestra in Beethoven's seventh symphony and Enesco's first symphony. **9.** Yehudi Menuhin and the English Chamber Orchestra under Raymond Leppard gave a concert at the Festival Hall devoted to the works of Vivaldi. **22.** Richard Strauss' last opera, *Capriccio*, was produced at the opening of the Glyndebourne opera season. **30.** Artur Rubinstein played at the Festival Hall in Brahms' F minor sonata and in works by Chopin, Debussy and Szymanowski. **31.** Maria Callas sang at the Festival Hall in a concert with the Philharmonia Orchestra.

June 4. Josef Krips and the London Philharmonic Orchestra completed their annual Beethoven cycle with a performance of the Ninth Symphony. **6.** The Bath Festival began in the restored Assembly Rooms; Yehudi Menuhin again appeared with the Festival Orchestra, and the Springhead Ring Choir. The Essex Youth Orchestra and the Zürich Chamber Orchestra all took part in the Festival. Yehudi Menuhin and his sisters, Hephzibah and Yaltah, all played in the final concert on June 16. **17.** Ralph Votapek, the young U.S. pianist, made his debut in this country, playing at the Festival Hall in Beethoven and Rachmaninov concertos with the Philharmonia Orchestra under Anatole Fistoulari. **18.** A new production of Mussorgsky's opera *Khovanschina*, by Vlado Habunek, took place at Covent Garden. **19.** The Handel Opera Society began its season at Sadler's Wells with a production of *Xerxes*. **21.** The Aldeburgh Festival opened. Among those who took part in the Festival were Benjamin Britten, Yehudi Menuhin, Maurice Gendron, Kenneth McKellar, Heather Harper, Janet Baker, Peter Pears, Bryan Drake, George Malcolm, Julian Bream, Bruno Schrecker, Percy Hart, Margaret Major, Stephen Bishop and Gervase de Peyer. The Festival included a series of concerts, presented by the B.B.C. Transcription Service, devoted to the works of John Dowland (the quatercentenary of whose birth fell in 1963) and his contemporaries. The series was organised by Imogen Holst, and among the works heard were Dowland's 7 instrumental pavanes, *Lachrymae*, anthems by Weelkes and Tallis and Tallis' motet for 40 voices, *Spem in alium*. Owing to the illness or Mstislav Rostropovich, the Festival could not, as planned, end with Benjamin Britten's new symphony for cello and orchestra, which was to have been played by Rostropovich (to whom it is dedicated) and conducted by the composer. **30.** The Cheltenham Festival opened with festal evensong sung in St. Matthew's Church by the choir of St. John's College, Oxford; on the following day the first symphony concert was given in the Town Hall by Antal Dorati and the London Symphony Orchestra. During the festival, the B.B.C. Northern Orchestra gave two concerts, at one of which they played a new sinfonia by Thea Musgrave, commissioned for the occasion. Other new works heard at the festival included a wind quintet by William Mathias, a sonata by John Joubert, a set of twelve variations for piano by David Blake, a suite of three nocturnes by Richard Rodney Bennett, Iain Hamilton's arias for small orchestra and *A Knot of Riddles*, by Sir Arthur Bliss.

July 2. Malcolm Williamson's opera, *Our Man in Havana*, was produced at Sadler's Wells. **5.** At the York Festival, the Academy of St. Martin-in-the-Fields, a string ensemble, gave a Bach concert in York Minster. During the Festival a symphony by Alexander Goehr, composed in memory of his father, Walter Goehr, was also heard. **23.** Leopold Stokowski appeared for the first time at a Promenade Concert. **29.** The Glyndebourne production of Monteverdi's opera, *L'Incoronazione di Poppea* was given at a Promenade Concert, conducted by John Pritchard, with Richard Lewis, Carlo Cava and Magda Laszlo taking part.

Aug. 5. Carlo Maria Giulini and the Philharmonia Chorus, with Richard Lewis, David Ward, Amy Shuard and Anna Reynolds as soloists, performed Verdi's *Requiem* at a Promenade Concert to commemorate the 150th anniversary of the composer's birth. **9.** At a Promenade Concert, Lennox Berkeley conducted his new Four Ronsard Sonnets, specially commissioned by the B.B.C. Peter Pears was the soloist. **18.** *Edinburgh Festival.* Berlioz' *Temptation of Faust* opened at the Usher Hall with the Covent Garden Orchestra and Chorus, directed by Georg Solti, and Nicolai Gedda, George London, Robert Savoie and Josephine Veasey as soloists. Later in the Festival the Covent Garden Orchestra performed the same composer's *Harold in Italy*. On Aug. 19, the English Opera Group produced Britten's *The Rape of Lucretia* at the King's Theatre. Morning concerts included a programme of music by John Dowland, in which Peter Pears sang a number of Dowland's songs, and a number of performances of works by Berlioz from the Tatrai Quartet. On Aug. 23, Hans Werner Henze conducted the London Symphony Orchestra in the first performance in this country of his own fifth symphony, and on the following day the London Symphony Orchestra and the Edinburgh Royal Choral Union took part, under Colin Davis, in Berlioz' Fantastic Symphony and his *Lélio*. During the Festival the San Carlo Company of Naples, appearing for the first time in Edinburgh, and for the first time in Britain since 1946, produced a number of operas, including Cilea's *Adriana Lecouvreur* and Verdi's *Luisa Miller*. On Sept. 1, the B.B.C. Symphony Orchestra, conducted by Lorin Maazel, gave the first of two concerts in the Usher Hall, and on Sept. 2, the Concertgebouw Orchestra from Amsterdam, appearing in their 75th anniversary year, presented their first concert of the Festival.

Sept. 1. The Three Choirs Festival opened at Worcester with a concert in the Cathedral conducted by Douglas Guest. On the following day, Sir Arthur Bliss conducted the first performance of his new cantata, *Mary of Magdala*, with Norma Procter in the name part. On Sept. 3 the afternoon concert contained works by Carissimi, Vaughan Williams and Stravinsky and in the evening Elgar's *Dream of Gerontius* was performed, with David Galliver, Harvey Alan and Marjorie Thomas as soloists. In the afternoon of Sept. 4, a concert of French music, by Fauré, Roussel and Poulenc, took place, and in the evening there was a performance of Britten's *War Requiem*, with Gerald English. John Shirley-Quirk and Heather Harper as soloists, On Sept. 5, an early 13th century Mass, *Missa Salve*, reconstructed by Denis Stevens, was sung and *L'Enfance du Christ*, by Berlioz, was performed. **11.** A new production, by Hans Hotter, of Wagner's *Götterdämmerung* was presented at Covent Garden. **12.** The Promenade Concert was devoted to the works of Benjamin Britten; the composer himself conducted the London Symphony Orchestra in the first performance in Britain of his latest work, the *Cantata Misericordium*, written for the centenary of the International Red Cross.

DRAMATIC SUMMARY, 1962-1963

After a long and memorable career, during which it had assisted appreciably in keeping alive all that is best and most artistic in the London Stage, the Old Vic., the famous theatre on the Surrey side of Waterloo Bridge, saw the close of its individual existence during the summer. Its final production was *Measure For Measure*, and the last night was celebrated by an enthusiastic audience whose farewell was voiced by Dame Sybil Thorndike, one of the many notable artistes who had graced the stage of the house. But the theatre had not ended its good endeavours, for only a few months later it became the temporary home of the National Theatre, and the company opened a repertory season of Shakespearean and other classic plays, with Sir Laurence Olivier, its Director, as producer, the first offering being *Hamlet*.Another interesting venture of the year was provided by the National Youth Theatre, hitherto content with an occasional performance or two but now embarking upon a four weeks' season of Shakespeare, marked by an exciting presentation of *Hamlet*, with a promising actor of 21 as the Prince. Among the new plays was Mr. Terence Rattigan's latest drama, *Man and Boy*, and the success of *Oliver* was followed by a musical, *Pickwick*, based on the still popular Dickens novel.

The following plays were produced between Oct. 1, 1962, and Sept. 30, 1963:—

ADELPHI, Strand, W.C.2.—(1963) *Sept.* 26. *Six of One*, musical show (Dora Bryan).

ALDWYCH, Aldwych, W.C.2.—(1962) Royal Shakespeare Company's productions: *Oct.* 9. *Curtmantle*, play by Christopher Fry on life of Henry II (Derek Godfrey, Alan Dobie and Maxine Audley). *Oct.* 15, *Troilus and Cressida* (Ian Holm, Michael Hordern, Max Adrian, Derek Godfrey, Patrick Allen, Roy Dotrice and Dorothy Tutin). *Oct.* 18. Revival of *The Devils*, by John Whiting (Max Adrian, Roy Dotrice, Peter McEnery, Richard Johnson and Dorothy Tutin). *Dec.* 12. *King Lear* (Paul Scofield, Alec McCowen, Brian Murray, Tom Fleming, Alan Webb, James Booth, Irene Worth, Diana Rigg and Patience Collier). (1963) *Jan.* 9. *The Physicists*, by Friedrich Dürrenmatt (Cyril Cusack, Michael Hordern, Alan Webb, Irene Worth, Diana Rigg and Patience Collier). *June* 13. *A Midsummer Night's Dream* (Ian Holm, Paul Hardwick, Ian Richardson, Tony Steedman, John Nettleton, Juliet Mills, Diana Rigg and Ann Beach). *July* 16. Revised version of *The Beggar's Opera* (Derek Godfrey, Ronald Radd, Tony Church, Dorothy Tutin, Virginia McKenna, Doris Hare and Patience Collier). *Sept.* 25. Abridged version of Rolf Hochhuth's *The Representative* (Alan Webb, Alec McCowen, Paul Hardwick, Ian Richardson, Julian Somers and Gordon Gostelow).

CAMBRIDGE, Earlham Street, W.C.2.—(1963) *March* 21. *Half a Sixpence*, musical based on H. G. Wells' *Kipps* (Tommy Steele, Arthur Blake, James Grout and Marti Webb).

COMEDY, Panton Street, S.W.1.—(1963) *Jan.* 24. *An Evening of British Rubbish*, revue (Peter Cushing, Bruce Lacey, Douglas Gray, Peter Crofton Sleigh and Joyce Grant). *May* 27. *The Umbrella*, comedy by Louis Bertrand Costelli (Everett Sloane, Alex Viespi and Sheila Allen).

CRITERION, Piccadilly. W.1.—(1963) *June* 27. *A Severed Head*, comedy by Iris Murdoch and J. B. Priestley (Paul Eddington, Robert Hardy, Heather Chasen and Monica Evans).

DUCHESS, Catherine Street,W.C.2.—(1962) *Dec.* 20. *Rule of Three*, three plays by Agatha Christie (David Langton and Betty McDowall). (1963). *March* 13. *See You Inside*, revue (Jon Pertwee, Hugh Paddick, Moyra Fraser and Amanda Barrie). *May* 8. *The Shot in Question*, by Michael Gilbert (John Carson, Archie Duncan, Derek Blomfield, Kynaston Reeves, Edith Sharpe and Andrée Melly). *May* 20. *Norma*, comedy by Frank Harvey (John Standing, David Andrews, Bernard Lee, Kathleen Harrison and Dilys Lane). *July* 22, *Alfie*, transferred from the Mermaid Theatre.

DUKE OF YORK'S, St. Martin's Lane, W.C.2.—(1962) *Oct.* 4. Two one-act plays, *Talking to You* and *Across the Board Tomorrow Morning*, by William Saroyan (Terence de Marney, Johnny Sekka, Nigel Hawthorne, Graham Payne, Harry Towb, Alexis Kanner and Rex Garner). *Nov.* 7. *Policy for Murder*, thriller by Jack Popplewell (John Slater, Dermot Walsh, Ronald Adam and Heather Chasen).

GARRICK, Charing Cross Road, W.C.2.—(1963). *Sept.* 19. *Power of Persuasion*, by Gert Hofmann (John Mills, Anthony Quayle and Joyce Redman).

HAYMARKET, Haymarket, S.W.1.—(1962) *Nov.* 29. *The Tulip Tree*, by N. C. Hunter (John Clements, Harold Scott, Celia Johnson and Lynn Redgrave). (1963). *April* 2. *Who'll Save the Plowboy?*, by Frank D. Gilroy (Harry H. Corbett, Donal Donnelly and Maxine Audley). *May* 23. Shaw's *Doctor's Dilemma* (Brian Bedford, Peter Howell, James Donald, Wilfred Hyde White, Moray Watson, Liam Redmond, Anna Massey and Madge Brindley). *Aug.* 8. *The Ides of March*, adapted by Jerome Kilty from the novel by Thornton Wilder (Sir John Gielgud. John Stride, Valerie Sarruf and Irene Worth).

LYRIC, Shaftesbury Avenue, W.1.—(1963). *Feb.* 8. *Carnival*, U.S. musical by Bob Merrill and Michael Stewart (James Mitchell, Michael Maurel and Sally Logan). *March* 19. *Ménage à Trois*, by Ronald Duncan (Marius Goring, Phylis Calvert and Elizabeth Shepherd). *May* 16. *A Shot in the Dark*, American version of comedy by Marcel Achard (George Baker and Judi Dench). *July* 2. *Windfall*, by Michael Gilbert (Alastair Sim, Garry Marsh, Hugh Latimer, Ronald Adam, Kerry Gardner, Peter Furnell, Douglas Muir, Margaret Wedlake and Merlith Sim).

LYRIC, Hammersmith, W.6.—(1962). *Oct.* 4. *Escape from Eden*, by Graeme Campbell (Geoffrey Tetlow, Earl Green, Vivienne Bennett and Madeleine Blakeney). *Nov.* 15. *Clap Hands*, Canadian revue (Eric House and Jack Creeley). (1963). *April* 24. Sheridan's *The Rivals* (Laurence Harvey, John Cairney, Fay Compton and Denise Coffey). *June* 11. *Domino*, adaptation by Adrian Brine of Marcel Achard's play (Geoffrey Chater, Peter Wyatt, Jeremy Spenser and Renee Asherson).

MAY FAIR, Stratton Street, W.1. This theatre opened on June 17, 1963 with a production of Pirandello's *Six Characters in Search of an Author* (Sir Ralph Richardson, Michael O'Sullivan, Barbara Jefford and Megs Jenkins).

MERMAID, Puddle Dock, E.C.4.—(1962) *Oct.* 17. *Eastward Ho!*, by Ben Jonson, Chapman and Marston (Brian Wright, Cardew Robinson and Aubrey Morris). *Nov.* 21. *The Witch of Edmonton* by Dekker, Ford and Rowley (William Lucas, Timothy Bateson, Melvyn Hayes and Ruby Head). (1963) *Jan.* 31. *The Bed Sitting Room*, extravaganza by John Antrobus and Spike Milligan (Graham Stark, Valentine Dyall, Spike Milligan and Marjorie Lawrence). *March* 6. *All in Good Time*, by Bill Naughton (Bernard Miles and Maureen Pryor). *April* 10. *Virtue in Danger*, musical adaptation of Vanbrugh's comedy (John Moffatt, Patricia Routledge and Patsy Byrne). *June* 19. *Alfie*, by Bill Naughton (John Neville, James Booth, Margaret Courtenay and Marcia Ashton). *July* 18. Revival of Brecht's *The Life of Galileo* (Joss Ackland, Peter Bayliss, Olaf Pooley and Brian Phelan). *Aug.* 21. *Schweyk in the Second World War*, by Brecht (Bernard Miles and Bill Fraser).

OLD VIC, Waterloo Road, S.E.1.—(1962) *Oct.* 17. *The Merchant of Venice* (Lee Montague, Esmond Knight, James Maxwell, Errol John, David William, George Howe, Sheila Allen, Judi Bloom and Rosalind Knight). *Nov.* 28. Ben Jonson's *The Alchemist*, in modern dress (Leo McKern, Lee Montague, Charles Gray, David William, Fulton Mackay and Priscilla Morgan). (1963) *Jan.* 30. *Othello* (Errol John, Leo McKern, Catherine Lacey and Adrienne Corri). *April* 3. *Measure for Measure* (James Maxwell, Lee Montague, James Kerby, Esmond Knight, Dilys Hamlett and Irene Hamilton).

PHOENIX, Charing Cross Road, W.C.2.—(1962) *Dec.* 13. *All Things Bright and Beautiful*, by Keith Waterhouse and Willis Hall (John Barrie, Griffith Davies, Peggy Mount and Juliet Cooke). (1963) *Feb.* 7. *Baal*, by Bertold Brecht (Peter O'Toole, Harry Andrews and Mary Miller).

PICCADILLY, Denman Street, W.1.—(1952) *Oct.* 8. *Fiorello!*, musical version of life of Mayor LaGuardia (Derek Smith, Bryan Blackburn, Peter Reeves, Marcon Grimaldi and Nicolette Roeg). *Dec.* 19. *The Rag Trade*, by Ronald Wolfe and Ronald Chesney (Peter Jones, Reg Varney, Miriam Karlin and Esma Cannon). (1953) *March* 18. *Comédie Française* Season opened with production of *Le Mariage de Figaro*. *July* 3. *Enrico*, Italian musical (Renato Rascel, Bryan Blackburn, Roger Delgado).

PRINCE CHARLES, Leicester Place, W.C.2. This new theatre opened on *Dec.* 26, 1962, with *Clap Hands*, a Canadian revue, transferred from the Lyric Theatre, Hammersmith. (1963) *April* 23. *Looking for the Action*, revue by Chicago Second City Company.

PRINCE OF WALES, Coventry Street, W.1.—(1963) *May* 30. *On the Town*, U.S. musical (Elliott Gould, Franklin Kiser, Don McKay, John Humphries, Andrea Jaffe, Carol Arthur, Gillian Lewis, Elspeth March and Rosamund Greenwood). *Sept.* 24. *Never Too Late*, by Sumner Arthur Long (Fred Clark, Tom Stern, Joan Bennett and Jennie Linden).

QUEEN'S, Shaftesbury Avenue, W.1.—(1962).—*Nov.* 27. *Vanity Fair*, musical based on Thackeray's book with music by Julian Slade (Naunton Wayne, George Baker, Michael Aldridge, Dame Sybil Thorndike and Frances Cuka). (1963) *Feb.* 27. *Mary, Mary*, comedy by Jean Kerr (Donald Harron. Ron Randell and Maggie Smith). *Sept.* 4. *Man and Boy*, by Terence Rattigan (Charles Boyer, Geoffrey Keen, Barry Justice and Jane Downs).

ROYAL COURT, Sloane Square, S.W.1.—(1962) *Nov.* 1. *Happy Days*, by Samuel Beckett (Peter Duguid and Brenda Bruce). *Dec.* 18. *Squat Betty* and *The Sponge Room*, by Willis Hall and Keith Waterhouse (Robert Stephens, George Cole and Jill Bennett) (1963). *Jan.* 8. Shaw's *Misalliance* (Campbell Singer, Christopher Guinee, Barbara Jefford, Alison Leggatt and Patricia Healey). *Feb.* 1. *Jackie the Jumper*, by Gwyn Thomas (Ronald Lewis, Dudley Jones, John Cole, Michael Gough and Branwen Iorworth). *April* 4. *Naked*, by Luigi Pirandello (Julian Glover, Joseph Wiseman, Diane Cilento and Freda Jackson). *May* 14. *Day of the Prince*, farce by Frank Hilton (Bernard Bresslaw, Bari Jonson, Arnold Yarrow, Christopher Sandford, Angela Baddeley, Jean Conroy and Pauline Boti). *June* 12. *Kelly's Eye*, by Henry Livings (Nicol Williamson and Sarah Miles). *July* 23. *Skyvers*, by Barry Reckord (David Hemmings, Bernard Kay, Philip Martin, Dallas Cavell and Chloe Ashcroft). *Aug.* 15. Revival of Arnold Wesker's *Chips with Everything* (Ronald Lacey, Gary Bond, Derek Fowlds and Alan Dobie). *Sept.* 12. *Exit the King*, by Ionesco (Sir Alec Guinness, Graham Growden, Peter Bayliss, Googie Withers, Eileen Atkins and Natasha Parry).

ST. MARTIN'S, West Street, W.C.2.—(1962). *Oct.* 25. *Kill Two Birds*, written by Philip Levene (Roger Livesey, Tony Britton, Peter Myers, Jerold Wells and Renée Asherson). (1963). *Feb.* 12. *Stephen D.*, by Hugh Leonard, adapted from James Joyce (Norman Rodway, T. P. McKenna, Gerard Healy, Keven Flood and Ruth Durley). *May* 28. *The Hot Tiara*, by Janet Allen (William Franklyn, Mary Kerridge and Ambrosine Phillpotts). *July* 9. *Where Angels Fear to Tread*, adaptation by Elizabeth Hart of E. M. Forster's novel (Michael Denison, Dulcie Gray and Violet Farebrother).

SAVILLE. Shaftesbury Avenue, W.C.2.—(1962). *Dec.* 5. *Semi-Detached*, by David Turner (Sir Laurence Olivier, James Bolam, John Thaw, Newton Blick, Mona Washbourne, Eileen Atkins and Patsy Rowlands). (1963). *May* 22. *Night Conspirators*, by Robert Muller (Peter Wyngarde, Patrick Troughton, Ronald Leigh-Hunt, Ralph Michael, John Robinson, Cyril Luckham and Wolfe Morris). *July* 4. *Pickwick*, musical by Wolf Mankowitz, Cyril Ornadel and Leslie Bricusse (Harry Secombe, Julian Orchard, Gerald James, Oscar Quitak, Teddy Green, Anton Rodgers and Jessie Evans).

SAVOY, Strand, W.C.2.—(1963). *March* 5. *Trap for a Lonely Man*, thriller by Robert Thomas (Michael Bryant, Patrick Newell, André Morell and Barbara Murray). *May* 29. *The Masters*, adaptation by Ronald Miller of C. P. Snow's novel (John Clements, Gerald Cross, David Bird, Peter Copley, David Dodimead, Allan Jeayes, Harold Scott, Geoffrey Lumsden, David Horne and Valerie Taylor).

SHAFTESBURY (formerly PRINCES), Shaftesbury Avenue, W.C.2.—(1963). *March* 28. *How to Succeed in Business Without Really Trying*, U.S. musical (Warren Berlinger, David Knight, Billy De Wolfe, Robert Nichols, Eileen Gourlay and Josephine Blake).

STRAND, Aldwych, W.C.2.—(1963). *March* 12. *Devil May Care*, by Alan Melville (Ian Carmichael, Ronald Radd, Moira Lister and Gladys Henson).

VAUDEVILLE, Strand, W.C.2.—(1963). *Feb.* 19. *How Are You, Johnnie?*, thriller by Philip King (Ian McShane, Derek Fowlds, Nigel Stock and Hilda Fenemore). *March* 26. *Licence to Murder*, thriller by Elaine Morgan (Alan Gifford, William Sylvester, Bruce Boa and Faith Brook). *April* 25. *All Square*, revue by Alan Melville (Naunton Wayne and Beryl Reid). *July* 24. Vanbrugh's *The Provok'd Wife* (Trevor Martin, Eileen Atkins, Ann Bell and June Brown). *Sept.* 17. *So Much to Remember*, entertainment by Fenella Fielding.

WYNDHAM'S, Charing Cross Road, W.C.2.—(1962). *Nov.* 8. *Out of Bounds*, by Arthur Watkyn (Sir Michael Redgrave, Charles Heslop and Pauline Jameson). (1963). *June* 20. *Oh What a Lovely War*, musical by Charles Chilton.

WIRELESS DEVELOPMENT AND BROADCASTING, 1962–63

GOVERNMENT AND PILKINGTON REPORT

In a second memorandum on the Pilkington report, published on Dec. 18, 1962, the Government outlined its views on the future position of I.T.A. It said that statutory powers would be taken to strengthen I.T.A.'s control over contracting companies, and that responsibility would pass to the Authority, which would approve and supervise arrangements for buying and selling programmes, and be responsible for the shape, content, balance and quality of the service as a whole. "Programmes", said the memorandum, "should achieve their position on the network through quality and merit, and if quality failed to measure up to promise then the renewal of contracts would be in peril." The Government also held that the programme companies should pay substantially higher rentals.

In the Government's view, there was little evidence of public demand for a fourth channel, to be used for a second commercial programme, and it was not satisfied that sufficient advertising revenue would be forthcoming to sustain two such programmes adequately.

The memorandum also dealt with local sound broadcasting and pay-television programmes. On the former, it said that there would be a review at a later date, but no immediate development. Experimental pay-television services for two or three years would, however, be allowed, and applications for making the experiment were invited.

TELEVISION LEGISLATION

The Government's attitude was further developed when the Postmaster General, Mr. Bevins, spoke on the second reading of the Television Bill in the Commons on Feb. 25, 1963. Mr. Bevins estimated that the revenue to the Exchequer from the increased rentals paid by programme contractors, which would be based on the gross advertising receipts of the companies, would amount to £18,000,000 a year. He also said that he had been authorised by the Chancellor of the Exchequer to announce that the television advertisements duty, which yielded about £8,000,000 a year in revenue, would be abolished in mid-1964. The new scheme would begin operating at the same time, when new contracts were awarded to the programme companies. The Government wanted a two-tier payments system, the first being reimbursement of the cost of the I.T.A., and the second an extra payment justified by the value of a public concession. The payment of the rental would go to the Exchequer. Mr. Bevins said that they should apply the incentive of profitability to the production of the best programmes and provide real competition in programme production.

Actual figures of rental increases were made known after the passing of the Television Act, when the I.T.A., on Sept. 15, invited applications for new contracts for the period beginning July 30, 1964. These applications were due to be submitted by Nov. 18, and the Authority expected to appoint contractors early in Jan. 1964.

Existing rentals from contractors brought in about £5,500,000 and the new figures anticipated a total of £23,000,000, including an estimated £15,000,000 levy related to advertising revenue. Rentals for 10 of the 14 contracts would be increased, that for Northern Ireland would remain the same and those for the Borders, North-East Scotland and the Channel Islands would be reduced. Companies would pay no levy for the first £1,500,000 of advertising revenue. For the next £6,000,000 they would pay 25 per cent. and for the amount by which receipts exceeded the aggregate of £7,500,000 they would pay 45 per cent. The I.T.A. said that for the new period it had had to increase its income to about £8,000,000 to meet costs which it would incur in the building and operation of the u.h.f. network.

The new contracts would run for three years, but would be subject to possible earlier termination or renewal depending on the timing of the introduction and extension of a possible second I.T.A. service. It was expected that most of the existing programme companies would apply for new contracts, and it was assumed that the increased rentals would be paid for out of profits, though some firms might increase their advertising rates. Some had put up their rates for the schedules for the autumn of 1963 by 10 per cent., but it was nevertheless expected that the expenditure on future advertising would continue to expand.

TELEVISION IN WALES

The areas to be covered by the new I.T.A. contracts remained broadly the same as for the existing ones, with the exception of Wales and the West of England. Here South Wales and the West of England and the existing West and North Wales area were advertised as one. The Authority said that it intended to see that the contractor appointed paid full regard to the needs and interests of Wales. In order to provide separate coverage of the Welsh and English parts of the area, the I.T.A. said that it had asked the Postmaster General whether a second v.h.f. channel could be made available to it in South Wales. Such a step would overcome the technical limitation which had hitherto made it possible to provide only a single transmission to cover both sides of the Bristol Channel. Welsh and English viewers could then be provided with separate editions of the I.T.A. service.

B.B.C. SECOND PROGRAMME

During the year B.B.C. plans for its second programe, B.B.C.-2, were announced. Trial transmissions, including films, were expected to start in January, 1964 and the full programme would begin in London and the South-East in April. The programme was due to be available for the Midland region, from the Sutton Coldfield Station, in April, 1965, and by about the end of 1965 there would be 10 u.h.f. television stations providing the new programme to between 60 and 70 per cent. of the population of Britain. B.B.C. spokesmen said that the second programme would be a planned alternative to existing schedules, with the main programmes starting at 7 p.m. or 7.30 p.m., and that on Saturdays there would be programmes for people who did not like sport or teenage record features. The B.B.C. also said, during May, that in order to operate the second programme, about 1,400 more staff would be added to the 9,600 who ran the existing television service. About 750 would be needed for the production side, administration and supporting staff; for these jobs there had been 6,000 applications, and selection boards would be held almost daily throughout the summer of 1963. Between 600 and 700 more engineers would also be required, and 300 had already been appointed, bringing the strength of the television engineering staff up to 2,000.

On Sept. 16, the B.B.C. announced that a fortnight later it would launch a campaign to make viewers aware of B.B.C.-2. The symbol chosen to publicise the network was a kangaroo. It would appear in a series of short trailers which were designed to give information about the service. These trailers would be shown in the London area on three nights a week during the peak viewing period and every night after that period. Similar campaigns were planned for each region six months before the introduction of B.B.C.-2.

The B.B.C. said that in the central London district 95 per cent. of viewers would have no reception difficulties with dual-standard sets if they used suitable aerials. For pockets where viewing would be poor because of the shadows cast by hills or high buildings, it was intended to build " fill-in " or relay stations. By April, 1964, nine of the Corporation's major production studios in London would be equipped to put B.B.C.-2 on the air. Mr. Hugh Carleton Greene, Director General of the B.B.C., said later that April 20, 1964, was the target date for the opening of the programme in the London area.

NEW B.B.C. AND I.T.A. STATIONS

Mr. Bevins, in a parliamentary answer on July 9, gave further details of new television stations which were to be built. The B.B.C. second programme would be broadcast for the London area from a new ultra-high frequency station at Crystal Palace and Mr. Bevins said that he had approved in principle the building of a further 17 high-power u.h.f. stations. Seven of the stations would be built at the site of existing B.B.C. Band I stations, at Sutton Coldfield, Wenvoe, Rowridge, Pontop Pike, Divis, Tacolneston and Llanddona. Five stations (Winter Hill, Emley Moor, Black Hill, Durris and Dover) would be built at or near the sites of existing Band III stations of the Independent Television Authority, which had agreed to play a full part in the planning and development of the u.h.f. network. New sites would have to be found for the remaining five stations (Bristol, Nottinghamshire, Suffolk, North Yorkshire and Northamptonshire) and it was therefore much less certain how soon they would be operating.

The Postmaster General also spoke of the use of Band III to improve and extend the cover of the existing B.B.C. and I.T.A. programmes. He said that he had approved in principle proposals by the B.B.C. to build additional 405-line stations, operating in Band III, to serve North-East Wales, South-West Scotland, East Lincolnshire, Mid-Lancashire and South-West Lancashire. The station in North-East Wales would complete the network transmitting the B.B.C.'s Welsh programmes. Three of the stations had been designed to improve reception in Lincolnshire and Lancashire, which was suffering from periodic interference by Continental stations operating on the same channels.

Approval had also been given to I.T.A. proposals for building additional stations, operating in Band III, to serve Bedford-Peterborough, Central Berkshire, East Lincolnshire, Scarborough, Dundee and Caithness-Orkney. These six stations would bring I.T.A. programmes to nearly a million new viewers and would improve reception for another 600,000.

Three of the stations mentioned (North-East Wales, South-West Scotland and Bedford-Peterborough) would have to use Channel 6, and this would necessitate temporary restrictions on their transmissions. A sky survey of the Northern hemisphere was being conducted by the Mullard Observatory at Cambridge, using frequencies within Channel 6. When the three stations in question started broacasting it would be generally necessary, in order to avoid interference with the radio-astronomy survey, to restrict their transmissions each day to the 12-hour period noon to midnight, until the completion of the survey at the end of 1967.

COLOUR EXPERIMENTS

After two months of testing in their 625-line experimental service, radiating purely engineering information from the Crystal Palace, the B.B.C. began, in November, 1962, to add full colour to some transmissions, and to broadcast material, including films, for 7½ hours a day from Monday to Friday. Initially the B.B.C. used the American N.T.S.C. system. In April, 1963, however, they began, in co-operation with the G.P.O., the I.T.A. and the radio industry to test, at the Crystal Palace, the French Secam colour system. It was stated that they were also interested in the Pal system, a modified version of the N.T.S.C. system produced by the Telefunken Company in Germany. Prolonged experiments were not possible because the B.B.C. needed time to prepare their two u.h.f. transmitters for broadcasting the new second television programme in black and white in April, 1964.

On July 8, full-scale demonstrations of the three possible systems began in London and were attended by delegates from many countries within the European Broadcasting Union, as well as the Organisation Internationale de Radiodiffusion et Télévision (O.I.R.T.), representing Eastern Europe, including the U.S.S.R. It was hoped that by the end of the year agreement would be reached, at least within the E.B.U., on the use of one of the three systems, and that the selected method would be adopted early in 1964 as a common standard by the International Radio Consultative Committee (C.C.I.R.). The use of a common system would make it possible to exchange live programmes in colour between one country and another over the Eurovision network. A B.B.C. spokesman said that he thought that Britain was likely to be the first country with colour television in Europe by quite a few years, and that if the N.T.S.C. system was chosen a service could be started in England early in 1965.

CONVERTING T.V. SETS

It was stated at a meeting of the British Radio Equipment Manufacturers' Association in London on August 22 that perhaps about 80 per cent. of the television sets in the London reception area would be unsuitable for the B.B.C.-2 service when it started in April, 1964. All receivers now being manufactured are of the dual-standard type. Some are being made complete and immediately ready, except for the special u.h.f. aerial system needed, to receive both 405-line and 625-line standards; others are being sold without the u.h.f. tuner section, which can be fitted at a later date. Of the receivers made during the previous two years, between 1,000,000 and 1,500,000 are of the type designed with the idea of conversion at some stage into dual-standard receivers. Older sets are unsuitable for conversion because the complexity of the operation would make it uneconomic. The Association gave a warning against having such work done without first checking with the manufacturer or an authorised dealer that the receiver was suitable for modification. It was pointed out that the older sets would, of course, still be capable of receiving transmission by the B.B.C. and I.T.A. in Bands I and III.

NEW ZEALAND HOUSE

It has been said that once in a while a building is completed which can serve as a yardstick by which we can measure our architectural conceptions. Such a building is the new headquarters of the High Commissioner for New Zealand and his staff. Designed by Robert Matthew, Johnson-Marshall & Partners, and built at a cost estimated to be in the region of £2,250,000. New Zealand House which was officially opened by the Queen in May, 1963, is now probably the finest office building in London. It stands on the site of the old Carlton Hotel, at the corner of Pall Mall and the Haymarket, upon land which has been leased from the Crown Commissioners, including Her Majesty's Theatre which will in due course be demolished to make room for the completion of the scheme. The site also includes Nash's Royal Opera Arcade, which now adjoins the new building on its west side.

The total accommodation of over 200,000 sq. ft. has been planned in two main elements—a podium block covering the whole area and rising to a height of 60 ft. and a tower block rising from within the podium to a height of 225 ft. Both dimensions were dictated by the Crown Estate Commission, the podium to conform with the general cornice level of the surrounding commercial premises and the tower block on account of what was then considered its excessive height. The main structure consists of a reinforced concrete frame with circular columns supporting the main floor beams at 27 ft. centres with secondary beams at 9 ft. centres cantilevered beyond the perimeter columns to allow uninterrupted external elevations. Centrally the tower is carried on the two-lift shaft box columns. Below ground level are a basement for storage and car parking and a deep sub-basement housing the air conditioning electrical and heating plant. Below this floor the columns are founded on piles carried down a further 80 ft. into the London clay.

A characteristic of the old New Zealand House in the Strand was its inviting friendliness which it owed partly to its "Visitors" lounge immediately inside the main entrance. This gave a cue for the new building and a spacious lounge has been provided at a slightly raised level off the main entrance hall commanding a long view down Cockspur Street towards Trafalgar Square. Slightly higher, at a mezzanine level, are a newspaper gallery with reading desks and writing tables, and a staff restaurant overlooking Pall Mall. The whole of this ground floor and mezzanine area offers a variety of spaces for social and public use. The first and second floors of the podium contain offices including departments of finance, purchasing and immigration and include a small cinema conference room to seat about 50 people. The offices of the High Commissioner himself and his deputy are situated on the third floor looking onto a wide terrace along the Pall Mall frontage. Here also are the library, the department of external affairs and dining-room for the High Commissioner. The fifteen storeys of the tower block rising above the podium, with the exception of the penthouse floor at the top, are devoted to offices occupied mainly by the administrative staff; the penthouse will eventually provide a small recreation suite with kitchen and bar.

An outstanding feature is the size of the glazing units made possible by the use of air conditioning and the consequent elimination of opening windows. The use of plate glass windows in the lower block in uninterrupted sheets measuring some 18 ft. by 9 ft., four storeys from the ground, is an innovation in building technique. The inner skin of glazing is of large sliding sheets of plate glass to facilitate cleaning. Generally natural, maintenance free, materials have been used throughout the building. The external glazing is framed in high quality silver anodised aluminium with floor depths expressed in Portland Stone. Plinth areas of the podium are clad with black Belgian fossil marble, while internally Greek White Pentellic and grey Marathon marbles are used in conjunction with a considerable amount of natural New Zealand timber.

LONDON'S SKYSCRAPERS

It is something of a shock to be reminded that at its inception during the latter part of the 1950's the 225 ft. tower of New Zealand House caused violent controversy on account of what was then considered to be its excessive height. Today this building which made London history by bursting through the old limitations of the London Building Acts and London Fire Brigade requirements, is almost dwarfed among a whole panorama of new towers. The Vickers building on the North side of the river, the Shell headquarters on the South, the Hilton Hotel overlooking Hyde Park and The Stag Brewery site at Victoria, with many others still on the drawing board, are slowly but surely changing the face of London, with the old skyline of Westminster, St. Paul's and the Wren churches trying hopelessly to keep in the picture.

London's tallest building at present is the new 387 ft. high tower block of the Millbank Development, designed by Ronald Ward & Partners for a partnership of Vickers Ltd. and the Legal & General Assurance Society. On a 3½ acre site between the Tate Gallery and Thames House, on Crown land, the developers have provided a 34 storey office building, an 8 storey Y-shape office block 97 ft. high and an 11 storey residential block 123 ft. high. These structures are interconnected by a podium providing a conference hall for 200 people, restaurants, parking space for 250 cars with circular ramp access, banking facilities and further office space. The whole group is set off by open courtyards and gardens at ground level. There is over 310,000 sq. ft. of office space and more than 50,000 sq. ft. of associated accommodation with 79 residential flats.

In terms of volume and floor area the tower block forms over half the total development. The diabolo shaped plan can be enclosed within a rectangle of 120 ft. by 110 ft., the two longer sides being convex and the shorter sides concave. The entire façade is clad in a specially developed continuous curtain walling fixed to the edge of the cantilevered floor slab. It is of stainless steel with fixed double windows and venetian blinds. This walling will be cleaned by an "Escaler" machine travelling up and down the façade on bronze track guides fixed to the face of the mullions. The unusual structural problems asscoiated with a high building were accentuated by the proximity of the Thames tidal waters, which resulted in the necessity of driving nearly 500 large diameter concrete piles to form a foundation.

The upper half of the tower is to provide office accommodation for the headquarters staff of the Vickers Group of Companies. The 29th and 30th floors will provide directors' offices, board room and dining suites. The board room is panelled in French Walnut with sections of some of the ships constructed by the company. The whole development is air conditioned from a central plant but room temperatures and humidities although also centrally controlled can be altered locally within limits by the occupants to allow for personal preferences.

C.I.S. OFFICES, MANCHESTER

Whereas London has perhaps witnessed the erection of more tower buildings than any other town or city in the British Isles, in height at least no one can dispute Manchester's claim to leadership. The service tower of the Co-operative Insurance Society's new building rises in a sheer wall of grey mosaic to a height of 400 ft., and nearly 13 acres of floor space are devoted to the service of a staff of 2,500.

In general terms, apart from the urgent need to provide an adequate centralised headquarters for a rapidly growing insurance office, C.I.S. intended that their new building should add to the prestige of the Society and the Co-operative Movement, improve the appearance of the City of Manchester and provide first class accommodation for their staff. The first steps towards planning the new building to replace the many scattered Society offices were taken in the early 1950's. Architects and specialist designers were appointed at an early stage to act in association with the C.W.S. chief architect, and architects and directors visited the U.S.A. and Italy to study design services and finishes. As a result the advisory committee recommended that the design should be for a really tall building with curtain walling in the current idiom.

The profile of the design for the tower block which emerged is perhaps the most successful aspect of the entire composition. The steel framed office building is clearly indentified from the function of the windowless shaft of the reinforced concrete service tower alongside it. The two elements comprise a T-shape plan, admirably linked together, with the " leg " of the service shaft rising elegantly above the roof line of the office block. The office structure was clad in anodised aluminium curtain walling with infiliing panels of black vitreous enamelled steel and plate glass, in contrast with the windowless structure of the service tower clad entirely in mosaic at a cost of £25,000.

Internally, since the main office floors, which are entirely air conditioned, have fully glazed walls the architects' primary concern was with the ceilings, lighting fittings and floor finishes. Mischa Black & Alexander Gibson of the Design Research Unit were called in to advise on the design of furniture and the interiors of special areas and including the entrance hall, two executive floors, the branch office, cafeteria and recreation room. The detailing of the entrance hall is impeccable and sets the standard for the internal spaces. It would indeed be difficult to nominate another building of a superior quality of interior design. The floor of rough granite, white Sicilian marble walls with a white plastic troughed ceiling and black metal sheathed columns combine to produce an atmosphere of elegant simplicity relieved by timber panelling and an exceptionally well executed mural designed by George Mitchell. This centre piece of abstract design in bronze fibre glass, cast in deep relief against a polystyrene mould is tinted to produce soft green highlights which in places accentuated by spotlights, produces a hidden sparkle and brings life to the entire area. The executive suite has walls and ceilings of teak veneer relieved by neutral close carpeting with occasional panels of white formica and thin slits of green tinted glass. The senior staff dining rooms on the floor above have natural cherry veneers with soft grey carpets and white ceilings. Throughout the building the same high standard of finish persists setting an example in quality of design which is a credit to this decade of architecture.

EDUCATION

The continued emphasis on the need for further expansion in the field of advanced education has given rise in recent years to an evolutionary study of advanced building techniques, which in the hands of an enlightened few has produced some exceptionally fine examples of modern architecture.

Liverpool University

Such a building is the recently completed Faculty of Arts Library at Liverpool University. Designed by Bryan Westwood, this building is a class library as opposed to a central one and is therefore designed to house the books currently in use in the Faculty of Arts. This has affected the planning inasmuch as really valuable books are unlikely to be in this particular collection, and expansion is not quite such an important factor as it would be in a central libary. Combined with the library, it was desired to provide nine lecture rooms for use generally in the faculty.

The site is in a densely populated semi-derelict area, and a long time was likely to elapse before the University Precinct would become fully established, and this factor gave an additional reason for the design of a building which would look inwards rather than outwards. The objection to this was an obvious tendency for the building to shut itself away from the ordinary coming and going of students. This has been overcome by placing the library at first floor, the lecture rooms at ground floor level, and allowing free circulation straight through the building.

The library becomes a square, with an open courtyard in the centre. The external walls are solid and will be covered with bookshelves, and further bookstacks will be placed at right-angles all the way round. The reading spaces are in the area adjacent to the inner courtyard and the walls here are almost entirely of glass, and the lighting through the vertical windows is supplemented by further lighting from the ceiling. The roof is a single pitch, sloping inwards, allowing for a gallery round the perimeter.

The large lecture rooms are designed to be solely illuminated artificially for geographers' slides and map studies, etc., but the smaller ones along the north side of the building have natural lighting and are so constructed that the intermediate walls can be removed so as to create an additional gallery for the library if required in later years.

The construction and materials of the building follow directly from the experience gained in designing the Mathematics Building in the same street. A special effort was made to limit the number of materials, and the exterior consists simply of dark brickwork at the base with tamped concrete vertical structural members forming the whole of the walling of the library. To give an additional degree of modelling, these vertical members (which resemble sheet piling) are inclined at various angles.

Since the building will be surrounded by higher ones in due course, the roof had to be specially designed and a new profile of asbestos roofing was evolved in conjunction with the manufacturers. This will not only give good modelling when seen from above, but it also enables the very large concrete beams which span the library to be housed within the convolutions, thus avoiding any apparent upstands.

Internally, there is very little decoration, the walls being covered in books and the ceiling being lined with sawn boarding backed by a glass wool acoustic blanket. As a relief, the windows at each end of the galleries are in stained glass with a simple pattern of vivid colours. These were designed by Miss Gillian Rees-Thomas.

Sussex University

Attention has not only been confined to the modernisation and expansion of existing universities. New centres are being established where none existed before, owing no allegiance to the past and offering unlimited scope for imaginative planning and design. Noteworthy among these is the new University of Sussex designed by Sir Basil Spence. Set in a countryside of rolling downs and woodlands, the new buildings comprising the first stage of the university which is planned to accommodate 1200 students by 1965, are Falmer House, the Physics and Arts buildings, the Library and departments of Chemistry, Engineering and Natural Sciences and Administration. The main campus around which these buildings are all grouped is planned as a pedestrian precinct. From this the students will be able to circulate up the natural valley formed by the contours of the site to reach the playing fields and halls of residence. The architect has sought to avoid in his design anything of an institutional flavour, characteristic of many modern school buildings and achieve something embodying the distinctive qualities of Sussex. He felt that with the tradition of Oxford and Cambridge as a precedent he wanted to develop the same idea of precinct courtyards. The situation in a valley precluded the use of tower buildings and the scheme for a close knit horizontal development with interlocking courtyards was evolved. The University has been planned for expansion and work will be going on somewhere on the site for about another 12 years. To help establish the unity so vital for success of such a concept a robust and sculptural form has been adopted. This owes something to the influence of Le Corbusier and perhaps even to the Colosseum, not as it was, but as it is now, a vaulted structure with great arches.

Falmer House is the focal point of the social life of the university. It is conceived as a gatehouse quadrangle and contains a hint of the architectural themes to be developed in later buildings. The main entrance is through a 36-ft. high archway giving access to the quadrangle which on three sides is set on colonnades, cut off from the pavement by a 15 ft. wide moat. Light is reflected up from the water into the shallow vaults above, giving a softening effect to the otherwise hard urban character of the courtyard itself. The building serves both students and staff provision for future expansion being provided by spaces on the upper floors in the south and east side of the building. These spaces are outlined by deep concrete beams from roof terraces in the first stage and can later be enclosed to provide more interior space at a minimum of structural alteration. The structure is mainly one of precast concrete beams and vaults spanning the full 40 foot width of the building and supporting timber floors. In contrast to the fairfaced concrete great use is made throughout of brickwork a warm pinkish brown in colour used both inside and out.

NORWICH CENTRAL LIBRARY

Norwich was described by John Evelyn as " One of the noblest cities of England ", and in its new central library contributes a fully up-to-date public building to the city's high architectural quality. Completely of its day—reported in the words of the City Architect as—" an essay in cast and precast concrete "—it nevertheless maintains a traditional link with the past, in its large-scale use of the local black knapped flint, which is an ever present feature of Norwich architecture.

The new building, officially opened by Queen Elizabeth the Queen Mother on January 19, 1963, forms a part of the new Civic Centre being developed round the City Hall, which dominates the scene from the North. To the east stands the 500 year old church of St. Peter Mancroft with a site reserved for the proposed new assembly and concert halls on the south. The library consists essentially of a low block, clad with knapped flints in precast panels, surrounding three sides of a central paved court, with a seven storey administrative block clad with white precast concrete slabs on its west side. The main entrance is under this high block, inside the courtyard, and is reached through a 30-ft. wide porch opening in the eastern side. Once within the courtyard area one is struck by the relative quietness of the place—the paving here is largely white, carrying the eye across to and up the white clad administrative block. Combined with the almost totally glazed character of the building throughout the lower levels an effect within the courtyard of great clarity and lightness has been achieved.

The main departments of the library are in the main housed at ground floor level, with ease of circulation for staff and books kept carefully in mind throughout. From the main entrance, approached through the courtyard over a bridge looking down into a second smaller paved courtyard at basement level, one passes left into the lending library. Here also are located the exhibition room and lecture theatre which cuts partly through into the basement. The children's lending library is on a mezzanine floor above the lecture theatre and is reached by a cleverly contrived, cantilevered concrete staircase. Provision has been made for a possible similar additional gallery at the other end of the lending library. Access on the right of the entrance hall is given to the American Memorial Library and into the reference section. The Memorial is to the members of the United States Air Force killed while serving in East Anglia during the war and, together with the water garden in the courtyard, has been given by the Memorial Trust of the 2nd Air Division of the U.S.A.A.F. Designed to house an American collection this room will also have provision for art exhibitions. The general appearance of the interior of the building is pleasantly luxurious despite a relatively tight budget. Good cohesion has been obtained by the restrained use of simple materials, clean uncluttered design and a good choice of furniture. The careful integration of natural and artificial lighting by means of precast concrete roof units throughout the single storey blocks is particularly interesting. The units themselves are made up of 3-ft. deep precast inverted troughs, spreading outward at the bottom and perforated at intervals on top by flat doubly glazed roof lights the spaces beetwen the troughs containing the artificial lighting. The structural frame of the building is of reinforced concrete and the cladding panels are bolted into position to facilitate removal to enable the building to be extended.

SHOPS AND OFFICES IN S.E. LONDON

During the last decade or so the building of offices and shops throughout the Greater London area has proceeded on a very large scale. It has on the whole been regarded as a profitable enterprise by the speculative developers who have converted vast sums of money into terms of bricks and mortar, but in retrospect one can only be struck by the apparent mediocrity of the resulting architecture. One of the few exceptions, indicating that good architecture can still be combined with the developers' requirements of maximum site coverage and minimum building cost, is to be found at Catford in South East London. These up-to-date office premises, shops and supermarket were designed for the Sunley Investment Trust by Owen Luder,

Dennis Drawbridge and Rodney Gordon. The low rentals in this area of South London indicated that the buildings had to be of low cost and include as many shops as possible. Accordingly the whole ground floor area was made over to shops with the supermarket building designed as a separate unit situated to the east of the offices and smaller shops. In order to provide basement storage for each shop, car parking was displaced to the first floor level, which is open on all sides, separating the shops from the offices above. Cars are parked by lift from the rear of the building, the lift being operated by the driver. The elevational treatment of the building is intended to avoid the monotony of the glass box, and create an interesting structural rhythm. Both the store and the office building owe something to the new Japanese influence in concrete architecture, most apparent in the detailing of the upturned eaves and the brick infill panels and powerful concrete detailing of the offices and lift tower. Structurally great use has been made of an in-situ concrete frame and panels with some precast units at the end of the office block. The office floor elevations are broken up into bays which project from the structure and give a varied rhythm to the façades which while adding interest do not reflect a different function behind individual bays. Each office floor is planned to be let separately, has its own metered electric under floor heating and its own source of hot water. Building costs are thus reduced by minimising plumbing and eliminating the need for a control boiler plant or flue serving the whole building. Windows are generally glazed from floor to ceiling providing a neat and sharp contrast to the rough concrete framing.

OFFICE BUILDING AT WALTON-ON-THAMES

Built to accommodate all the headquarters staff of Birds Eye Food Ltd. this large office building was erected at Walton-on-Thames in response to official appeals to move commercial buildings out of the centre of London.

Tastes in architecture and design change rapidly and a building can date within ten years. Striking advances have been made in the development of new materials for building in the last few years, however, and many of these have influenced the architect's work. No longer tied to traditional materials and techniques, he is constantly experimenting with new forms and ideas as new materials emerge.

The architects of the Birds Eye building, Sir John Burnet Tait & Partners, bearing in mind the company's brief that the building should be regarded as being modern in 20 years' time, have paid particular attention to the choice of both external and internal materials. Current architectural clichés have been avoided and the appearance of the building relies to a great extent on balanced proportions and textural contrasts using panels of a permanent colour. Externally anodised aluminium curtain walling has been used in conjunction with plate glass, the latter made thicker on the noisy side of the building to improve sound insulation. Above and below the first and second floor windows there is a raised geometric motif on a blue vitreous steel background, pairs of which are formed into a hexagonal unit. The supporting ground floor columns are bush hammered white concrete and the ancillary buildings are faced in a special white brick.

Structurally the building is 318 feet long by 170 feet deep with two internal garden courtyards. This is to enable simple, removable partitions to be used throughout the building giving a completely flexible internal layout which could if required be changed overnight without alteration to lighting, telephones or other services. The ceiling construction was also standardised in order that air conditioning plant behind the panels is readily accessible for maintenance purposes.

More than 23,500 tons of concrete were used in the building and nearly 400 men were involved in the construction programme each week. The electricity used to run the services of the building is sufficient to supply 350 houses and there are four miles of lighting troughs and 47 miles of cable altogether.

A high velocity induction system of air conditioning has been used throughout, providing both temperature and humidity control. Air is introduced through special units below each window and withdrawn through the suspended ceiling for partial re-circulation, while a separate extract system controls the kitchens, lavatories and meeting rooms. Nearly all windows are protected internally by vertically louvred plastic blinds, which have been found essential to enable the staff to work in comfort during the summer. These are very pleasant to the eye and make a notable contribution to tne effectiveness of the elevations as a whole.

The general character of the interior tends to present a slightly clinical atmosphere of quiet efficiency, the demountable partitions are faced mainly with P.V.C. throughout the building, but the long lengths of corridor faced on either side with the same unrelieved blue grey colour while pleasant enough in itself become monotonous by repetition. A welcome exception to this is achieved in the carpeted waiting area, where the cantilevered main staircase rises in a wide space over an internal pool and some very attractive views over into the courtyards are to be found.

The building is in one of the pleasant residential avenues of Walton and the area immediately surrounding the building was placed in the hands of one of Britain's leading landscape architects to ensure that full advantage would be taken of the attractive natural woodland features of the site. The main entrance paradoxically at the rear of the building faces a well developed wood of oak and Scots pine providing a variety of spring and autumn colouring enhanced by azaleas and rhododendrons. On the west side stands a group of three copper beeches 25-ft. high which were specially transplanted from a nursery in Berkshire. The avenue side of the building is graced by spacious lawns with groups of weeping willows along the sides of a large pool immediately outside. A dynamic sculpture of rising birds by John McCarthy is placed in a setting of boulders, reeds and rushes, while from the centre of the pool rises a group of perspex bubble fountains filled with colourless anti-freeze and floodlit from below. The internal courtyards were planned by the same landscape architect and each is treated differently. The east courtyard is punctuated by a series of concrete monoliths sculptured by Alan Collins, and constrasting with a variety of floor treatments, pools, fountains, grass, gravel, boulders, pavings and a 40 year old cut leaf alder tree, which was hoisted into position over the roofs on completion of the building. The other courtyard tends toward the Japanese influence of shallow concrete platforms at different levels with an interesting arrangement of pebble boulders, azaleas and waterside plants.

CONGRESS THEATRE, EASTBOURNE

The Congress Theatre was commissioned by the Eastbourne Corporation in 1956 as a building which, linked with the existing Winter Garden, could be used for conferences and entertainment purposes varying in extent from orchestral concerts to opera and ballet. The architects, Bryan & Norman Westwood & Partners, were briefed to make provision in their design for a fully equipped stage with fly tower, dressing rooms for 60 artists, foyers, bars and a restaurant seating 200 which could also cater for teas in connection with the tennis tournaments in the adjacent Devonshire Park.

The site, originally a roller skating rink, adjoins the west end of the present Winter Garden and the new building is so conceived that the two can be used as a single unit with the restaurant forming the connecting link. The prevailing level of the site some 6 feet lower than that of the surrounding road made a satisfactory solution difficult and to overcome the appearance of the building being sunk into a hole when viewed from the adjoining Wilmington Square, the auditorium was raised to first floor level. The relationship of the theatre, particularly in respect of scale and colour, to the existing typical 19th century seaside buildings was felt to be extremely important and the considerable attention devoted by the architects to solving this particular problem typifies their careful approach to the whole scheme.

The multi-purpose auditorium has a nominal seating capacity of 1,678 usable for conferences and orchestral concerts; of this number 1,400 seats lying within the optimum sight lines can be used for variety shows, plays, opera and ballet, on which occasion the remaining seats in the side galleries can be curtained off. For smaller gatherings the rear stalls under the gallery can also be curtained off leaving approximately 600 seats in the front stalls. Additional seating space is gained by raising the electrically operated orchestra lift platform to stalls floor level, conversely the first three rows of the stalls are removable to allow extra room for an orchestra of ballet or grand opera proportions. An interesting feature of the auditorium is the provision of large double glazed windows along each side. These can be blacked out when required, but it is hoped that the admission of daylight on occasions will in the long run help to combat " conference fatigue " so often noticeable in traditional halls.

Internally, the walls of the auditorium are faced with slatted teak and ribbed mahogany acoustic panelling which seen against a background of predominantly white painted but occasionally coloured plasterwork, combine with the gay red upholstery of matching gallery curtains to give an effect of quiet simplicity. The floors are in cork throughout, that of the stage being in hardwood strip.

There are spacious foyers at all levels planned as a glazed enclosure around the central mass of the auditorium. The lowered entry foyer is approached across a wide covered walkway below the building which is continued round to the west side, giving a sheltered access from cars entering or leaving the car park without impeding the pedestrian approach from the street pavement level. From the entry foyer with its paving of polished concrete slabs interspersed with blue bricks, terrazzo faced reinforced concrete stairs rise through a double height void into the main foyer at first floor level. Two galleries above are linked by further voids making this part of the building appear considerably more generous than its plan would seem to imply. Access to the auditorium for wheeled chairs is provided via the scenery ramp.

The main frame of the theatre and stage block is in-situ reinforced concrete, certain elements such as the main beams on the glazed area around the foyers and the stepping in the rear stalls, being precast. The main trusses over the auditorium are in steel, running from front to back so as to offer minimum obstruction to services and to minimise the structural loading of the side walls and stanchions.

Externally panels of blue grey brick face the theatre and stage unit at ground floor level in contrast to the exposed aggregate finish of the concrete columns and beams. Above this level, split white concrete slabs present a cladding of pronounced texture and the columns are faced with blue grey riven slate. The walls of the auditorium projecting above fourth floor level are faced with blue-grey Lumford bricks. The stage walls also are brick faced and an area of these on the north side is specially laid to give an abstract sculptured pattern designed by Eric Peskett. The stage tower projecting above the roof of the auditorium is clad with ribbed aluminium sheeting.

It is too early yet to judge the auditorium in use, but the results of the early concerts and plays were very pleasing for both the audience and the players. Quality and balance of tone were good and speeches from the stage were received clearly, without the need for amplification, in every part of the house.

PERIODS OF GESTATION AND INCUBATION

The table shows approximate periods of gestation or incubation for some common animals and birds. In some cases the periods may vary considerably from average and where doubt arises professional advice should be sought.

Species	Shortest Period. Days	Usual Period. Days	Longest Period. Days	Species	Shortest Period. Days	Usual Period. Days	Longest Period. Days
Human	240	273	313	Turkey	25	28	23
Mare	305	336	340	Duck	28	28	32
Ass	365	—	374	Goose	28	30	32
Cow	273	280	294	Pigeon	17	18	19
Ewe	140	147–50	160	Canary	12	14	14
Goat	147	151	155	Guinea Pig	63	—	70
Sow	109	112	125	Mouse	18	—	19
Bitch	55	63	70	Rat	21	—	24
Cat	53	56	63	Elephant		2 years	
Rabbit	30	32	35	Camel		45 weeks	
Hen	20	21	22	Zebra		56 weeks	

SCIENCE, DISCOVERY AND INVENTION IN 1963

British Association.—The British Association for the Advancement of Science held its 125th annual meeting at Aberdeen on August 28–September 4, 1963, under the presidency of Sir Eric Ashby, Master of Clare College Cambridge.

The subject of his presidential address was " Investment in Man."

Doubtless in the nineteenth century a three-year course in classics did set a man up for a lifetime, Sir Eric said, but that was in the days when a graduate could assume that he would grow old in a world familiar to him as a youth. We were living in the first era for which this assumption was false, and we had not yet faced the consequences of this fact.

The present generation of students would still be employed in the year 2000; but long before then their degrees and diplomas—at any rate in science, technology, and the social sciences—would have become obsolete. The only students who could be sure of escaping obsolescence were those very few who would themselves become innovators. Our investment in the rest—the great majority of our human resources—would inevitably be devalued by technological and social change. Measures to combat obsolesence therefore, became of prime importance, he said.

What measures had already been taken? There was a plentiful supply of scientific and professional journals. But that was not enough: re-education, like education, required challenge and response, an encounter between teacher and student. Refresher courses offered that; but the extent to which they were used, and the scope and duration of most of them, were pitifully inadequate to meet the need.

There was no evidence that any educational institution was planning to offer sustained courses of re-education on a massive enough scale to prevent widespread obsolescence among teachers. In technology the story was similar. Some universities and colleges put on short courses of re-education for technologists; but by no stretch of imagination could those courses be regarded as a comprehensive system to prevent obsolescence. In the training of physicists and chemists there was no sign that any provision was to be made. For medicine the University of London had set up the British Postgraduate Medical Federation, which last year offered courses for general practitioners attended by over 2,000 doctors. But most of those courses were only for weekends or single weeks; and again they could not meet the need for sustained and systematic re-education to prevent obsolescence in the medical profession.

" So this is how we stand," Sir Eric continued. " We already spend large sums, even if they are inadequate, on higher education in Britain. It is probable that we shall be asked to spend a great deal more, in a massive programme for investment in man. A large proportion of this expenditure will be devoted to science and technology. But this investment in man will inevitably depreciate as the volume of effort in science and technology increases throughout the world.

" There is need for drastic steps to prevent obsolescence. Here is an opportunity for the extramural departments of our universities (which are, in any case, seeking for a new inspiration). Of course universities and colleges cannot alone sponsor a programme to combat obsolescence. There will have to be co-operation from all forms of employers, releasing men on full pay for sustained full-time courses every few years."

" Perhaps the time may come when a degree or a professional qualification, like a passport, is valid only for a limited number of years, and is renewed only after attendance at a systematic course of re-education." The task of higher education was (in the words of the president of the Carnegie Corporation) to provide " a framework within which continuous innovation, renewal and rebirth can occur ". " In the disturbing, storm-swept, feverish 37 years remaining to this century, nothing less than this will suffice for investment in man."

Earlier in his address Sir Eric said that British policy for higher education was tenable only on certain assumptions: that the techniques for selection were efficient, reliable and satisfied social justice; that the numbers of young people selected each year for different kinds of full-time higher education were sufficient for the nation's needs, and that we offered acceptable opportunities for part-time further education to those who were not selected.

" None of these assumptions is justified ", he continued. Our methods of selection assumed that our intellectual resources were limited by genetic factors, and that when we selected candidates to go to grammar schools or to universities we were drawing from the population those with the innate ability to profit from those privileged kinds of education. Of course the intellectual resources in a population were ultimately limited by its genetic makeup; but we had abundant evidence that it was not genetics, it was the inequalities in our society and inadequacies in our educational system which at the present time limited our investment in man. That was true even in the most affluent nations.

There was now convincing evidence that thousands of children fell out of our educational system each year not through lack of ability, but from lack of motive, incentive, and opportunity. A child who succeeded in climbing the ladder of education had responded to a challenge. " If there is no challenge there can be no response; and our machinery for selection, unlike that in many countries, is in fact a machinery for distributing challenges. The trouble is that no refinement of our methods of selection will solve the problem which confronts us; for the problem we set ourselves is not to select, from among those who leave school, the candidates who are likely to profit from higher education; it is to select, from among those likely to profit from higher education, the candidates lucky enough to be offered it—which is quite a different thing."

Under those circumstances it was no adequate test of our methods of selection to follow the success or failure of those we selected; we must also follow the success or failure of those who were rejected. On the one or two occasions when that had been done we found what indeed we might have expected: that the majority of those rejected by one university got into another, or took degrees externally, and (in such statistical studies as had been made) the chance of academic success among the rejected candidates was no worse than that among the accepted candidates.

We were uneasy in our search for talent. We spent a great deal of time and energy over the problems of selection and we were tempted to believe that there must be a " right " way to select students for admission to universities, if only we could discover it. " Of course there is no right way and it is vain to seek one. It is our policy for investment in man which leads us into this Calvinism of the intellect. 'Every selection ', said the German philosopher Jaspers, 'is in some way an injustice. We delude ourselves when we think that we can avoid such injustice through rational and determined effort."

Having dealt with the first assumption, referring to investment policy, Sir Eric turned to the second, that our system of higher education was on a big enough scale to meet our future needs for scientists and technologists. That, he said, "is untenable in the light of recent studies of manpower requirements". On the third assumption, that there were acceptable alternatives for those who were not selected for full-time higher education, he found nothing inherently unsound—indeed there were great merits—in systems of part-time further education integrated with employment. "The trouble about these systems in Britain is their inefficiency."

While asserting that our policy for higher education was based on untenable assumptions, Sir Eric did not advocate a colossal proliferation of universities in Britain. But we needed to know far more than we did about the pattern of higher education which was likely to be relevant to the lives graduates were going to live. When one asked whether our universities were appropriate instruments for investment in man we lacked the data to provide an answer. "Each question we ask leads us into untested assumptions. To test whether the assumptions are valid we need to undertake a sustained programme of research on British higher education. Until this research is done the questions remain unanswered."

The presidents of sections and the subjects of their addresses were as follows:—*Mathematics and Physics:* Dr. J. S. Forrest, "High voltage insulation." *Chemistry:* Prof. J. Monteath Robertson, C.B.E., F.R.S., "A physical approach to chemical structures." *Geology:* Prof. J. H. Taylor, F.R.S., "Some aspects of diagenesis." *Zoology:* Dr. F. Fraser Darling, "The unit of ecology." *Geography:* Prof. H. C. Darby, O.B.E., "British National Parks." *Economics:* Prof. T. Wilson, O.B.E., "The price of growth." *Engineering:* Dr. S. G. Hooker, O.B.E., F.R.S., "Future of the aeroplane in civil and military fields." *Anthropology:* Peter Opie, "The tentacles of tradition." *Physiology and Biochemistry:* Prof. J. McMichael, F.R.S., "The contribution of clinical medicine to physiology." *Psychology:* Prof. O. L. Zangwill, "Cerebral localization of psychological function." *Botany:* E. J. H. Corner, F.R.S., "The tropical botanist." *Education:* Sir Charles Morris, K.C.M.G., "Personal values in education." *Agriculture:* Prof. M. Jones, "Providing food for man and beast." *Sociology:* Prof. W. J. H. Sprott, "Problems in penology." *General:* Prof. D. J. Robertson, "The present position of the city."

The 126th annual meeting will be held at Southampton from August 26 to September 2, 1964, under the presidency of Lord Brain. Future meetings are to be held at Cambridge (1965) and at Nottingham (1966).

ALLOY SCREW THERMOMETER.—Alloy screws one-eighth of an inch long, capable of measuring temperatures up to 1,000 deg. Centigrade with an accuracy of plus or minus 1 per cent, have been developed to measure the temperature of the moving parts of a machine. Many metal alloys become permanently harder or softer when heated, and the screw thermometers depend for their efficiency on the accurate measurement of the final degree of hardness. If the difference between the initial and final hardness is measured the temperature to which the screw has been subjected can be determined. Since the heat dissipated by, for instance, the radiator of a motor car, represents wasted energy, an engine which can be built to run at a higher temperature will do more work per gallon of petrol. Engineers, therefore, are eager to achieve such increases in operating temperatures, but their achievement depends upon a fairly accurate knowledge of the temperatures to which the moving parts of the engine are subjected.

ANTARCTIC EXPLORATION.—Preparations for one of the toughest Antarctic exploration missions ever undertaken have been made by a party of Britons who sailed aboard the Danish polar ship *Kista Dan*. They are to establish supply bases along the 300 treacherous miles between the British Antarctic Survey's loneliest base—Halley Bay—and the unexplored Tottan Mountains. The mountains lie beyond a floating ice shelf criss-crossed by a network of crevasses. When the bases are set up, scientists and technicians, using dog-sledge, motor toboggan and a track-laying snow vehicle, will make for the mountains, mapping as they go.

ANTARCTIC: 120-DAY JOURNEY.—A six-man expedition returned to the Australian Antarctic base of Wilkes after one of the longest and most scientifically important treks in recent Antarctic history. During their 120-day journey they travelled 900 miles by tractor train to the Russian summer base of Vostok and back across the Polar ice cap. The party, which returned two days ahead of schedule, carried out seismic tests to determine the thickness of the ice cap and the level of the rock base in the heart of Antarctica. Mr. Thomson, the 35-year-old leader of the expedition, said they had encountered blizzards and temperatures as low as −83° C. (−117° F.). The party used four tracked vehicles drawing nine sleds and two caravans. The cold caused the tracks to break frequently, and visibility was often zero. At one point members of the party suffered from altitude sickness when they reached a height of 12,400 ft. about 100 miles from Vostok. The party carried out its full scientific programme, including the setting up of seismic and magnetic stations. One discovery was that the rock base between Wilkes and Vostok was largely below sea level, in some places by as much as 4,000 ft.

Dr. F. Jacka, acting director of Australia's Antarctic division, described the expedition as a more difficult journey than that of Sir Vivian Fuchs, and scientifically more valuable. Sir Vivian Fuchs led an expedition of British, New Zealand, Australian, and South African scientists and explorers across the Antarctic in 1958. The journey, of 2,158 miles, was from Shackleton Base on the Weddell Sea, to Scott Base on the Ross Sea by way of the South Pole. The journey took 99 days.

ASTRONAUTS OF 1963.—Miss Valentina Tereshkova, a Russian and the first woman cosmonaut, and Lieutenant-Colonel Valery Bykovsky returned safely to Earth, landing in central Asia, a few hundred miles from their launching point. Miss Tereshkova said later that she had bruised her nose during re-entry into the atmosphere. The final descent for both astronauts is assumed to have been by parachute. Both were flown from the landing area in Kazakhstan to the Baikonour launching site farther south, to be examined by doctors and space scientists.

Colonel Bykovsky was launched into space in *Vostok* 5 at 1 p.m. B.S.T. on June 14. He landed at 12.06 B.S.T. on June 19 on his eighty-second orbit, having travelled about 2,060,000 miles in four days, 23 hours, 54 minutes. He was only once reported to have left his seat to carry out experiments. He was in orbit for 25 hours and 32 minutes longer than the previous record holder, Major Andrin Nikoylayev.

Miss Tereshkova, launched in *Vostok* 6 at 10.30 a.m. B.S.T. on June 16, landed at 9.20 B.S.T. on her forty-ninth orbit on June 19, having travelled about 1,250,000 miles in two days, 22 hours, 50 minutes. She was apparently strapped to the controls of *Vostok* 6 throughout the flight. Miss Tereshkova failed by only seven minutes to equal the flight time of Colonel Popovitch. The longest American space flight to date is Major Gordon Cooper's 22 orbits in one day, 10 hours and 20 minutes.

Sir Bernard Lovell, director at Jodrell Bank, said that Russia's launching of a woman in space could be part of a long-term plan to colonize another part in the solar system in about 25 years' time. Their main object, he said, would be Mars, which had the least hostile environment. The problem of living there would be no greater than living in a jet airliner at 30,000 ft.

Sir Bernard said it would be important for such a programme to establish the effects of weightlessness and radiation damage on both the female and male. Sending a woman into space was certainly not a "stunt," he added.

ASTRONOMICAL ANTI-MATTER.—The discovery of a missing link in matter—named Anti-xi-Zero—has given scientists another clue to the make-up of galaxies in space. The discovery of a long-missing member of the family of anti-particles—the direct opposite of ordinary matter known on earth—was announced by the Atomic Energy Commission here. Anti-particles are created by bombarding particles of matter with other kinds of particles, duplicating the work of cosmic rays in the atmosphere. Virtually all anti-particles have a life measured in a fraction of a second. Scientists believe the discovery lends new weight to the theory that elsewhere in the universe whole galaxies may be made up of anti-matter, the A.E.C. said.

The finding, the commission added, confirmed a fundamental theory that for every known elementary particle in the universe, there must be an anti-particle. The discovery was made by physicists from Yale University and the A.E.C.'s Brookhaven national laboratory at Upton, New York, using a huge atom-smashing machine and a bubble chamber in which sub-atomic particles form a trail of bubbles. One scientist outside the A.E.C. said that powerful radiation from distant galaxies that had long puzzled astro-physicists could conceivably be explained on the basis of clouds of matter colliding with clouds of anti-matter.

BIRD MIGRATION.—The punctuality of the spring migrants in 1963 was remarkable. Reports show that almost every species, from the chiff-chaff to the spotted flycatcher, and from the sand martin to the swift, turned up in its usual haunts at about its usual time. Cold winds affecting the Continent as well as the British Isles had been expected to slow migration, but there was little sign of any delay. This was the case even in the north of Scotland.

Observers gave duplicated dates of arrival for migrant wagtails and for wheatears. With the wheatear, however, late dates can be more interesting than early ones. Those on migration at the end of April or early in May are likely to be of the larger Greenland race, which at that time passes northward not only along the coast but by many routes inland.

BIRMINGHAM'S RADIO TOWER.—Work has started in Birmingham on a 500 ft. radio tower with a capacity for 150,000 simultaneous telephone conversations and 40 television channels. At present the main inter-city television links working on micro-wave radio systems to Birmingham terminate on a 170-ft. lattice mast on the roof of Telephone House, in the city centre. The new tower, which will be sited near by, should give adequate clearance over existing buildings and allow a margin for future higher buildings, a Post Office official said. Designed by the chief architect's division at the Ministry of Public Building and Works, it has been approved by the Royal Fine Arts Commission.

BRONZE AGE SITES EXCAVATED.—Excavations on the moors east of Derbyshire Derwent, at two Bronze Age ceremonial sites of ring-bank type and part of a large cairn group marked the beginning of a programme of organized research in the Peak District. The work will contribute to knowledge of the cairn groups and associated monuments over the whole of Britain.

At Barbrook, in the parish of Holmesfield, Mr. G. D. Lewis directed work on one of two circles associated with a concentration of cairns. The circle, whose external diameter is about 75 ft., was formed by a bank of earth with a stone capping, and definite kerbing on both sides. An entrance was found on the north-west, and just outside it a cup-marked stone was discovered *in situ* on the level of the old ground surface. Under a small cairn near the centre of the circle, a pit was located, containing charcoal, a calcined flint scraper, and pottery which is almost certain to belong to a Middle Bronze Age urn.

About half a mile from this site, at Totley, a smaller circle, about 45 ft. across, was examined under the direction of Mr. Jeffrey Radley. Its wide low bank was of similar construction to that at Barbrook, and there was again a small cairn in the middle. Below it were three cremations all associated with urns, but it was interesting that only one urn actually contained the bones. There were also two "satellite" burials, one with some traces of a pot, and the other with none. All the urns were Middle Bronze Age ones of Pennine type. A notable find at this site was the hearth in which the cremation had been carried out, where there was a depth of ash but no bones. In the area of this circle a mass of prehistoric material had been collected from the surface, including arrowheads, spindle-whorls and stone querns, suggesting the proximity of a domestic site. Samples were collected at both excavations for radio-carbon dating, and the assignation of an absolute date to the circles and the urns from them would add great value to the excavation and give a flying start to the new programme of research. More than a dozen further circles have been observed on this area of the moors.

CAERWENT RE-DEVELOPING.—For nearly 40 years the Ministry of Works has been quietly acquiring bits of the wall which once protected Caerwent (Monmouth), then a Roman city, against its foes. The last stretch has now changed hands, along with the weed infested remains of a Roman temple. This is in keeping with the intention that one day the present village will have gone to make way for the Roman remains, most of which now lie under ground. The cost of the "redevelopment" will be about £250,000 and may take 70 years. Caerwent was the only fully developed Romano-British town in Wales and remains have been found of a basilica, a forum, baths, houses and shops, though not the best of amphitheatres. About 2,000 people are believed to have lived here. It was founded, according to one theory, to subdue hostile local people by attracting them to Roman town life so that they became part of it. The war memorial stands on a base of stones, first laid by Romans, in the main village street. A stone found near by, commemorating a Roman officer, is now in the church porch.

CAERPHILLY FORT DISCOVERY.—Excavation recently completed at Caerphilly has revealed an entirely new Roman auxiliary fort, surface traces of which had been obliterated by the construction and later ramifications of the large medieval castle.

The work was carried out by the ancient monuments staff at the castle, with the co-operation of the owner of the land, which lay outside that under the guardianship of the Ministry of Public Building and Works. The original aim of the excavation was to examine and elucidate an outwork of Civil War date, and the Roman finds were completely unexpected.

This discovery follows the finding of similar forts in recent years at Llystyn, Caernarvonshire, and Trawsfynydd, Cardiganshire, and should prove an important addition to the growing fund of knowledge of the conquest and Romanization of south Wales. The new fort lies midway between the Roman forts of Cardiff and Gelligaer, on the route leading through Penydarren, Merthyr Tydfil, to Brecon Gaer, and suggests a junction here with a route from the legionary fortress of Caerleon. This latter route would have reached Caerphilly by the natural approach of the Rhymney valley, where evidence of lead working dating from the beginning of the Roman occupation is known. The new fort is a small one of some three or four acres, occupying the highest point of the basin in which Caerphilly lies.

CLEANING THE MISSISSIPPI.—The citizens of St. Louis voted to spend $95,000,000 (about £34,000,000) on cleaning up the Mississippi River, which is still as dirty and unprepossessing today as it was when Mark Twain's raftsman, defending it against the clear Ohio, claimed that the mud was nutritious and anyone who drank of it could grow corn in his stomach. Captain Marryat called it "the Great Sewer." It is more muddy than the Danube is truly blue. Moreover, St. Louis's homes, industries, business, and institutions contribute 300m. gallons of sewage to the river daily. The discharge receives no processing of any kind before flowing into the stream and its volume is Augean in proportions, being the equivalent of about 50,000 standard sized railway tank cars every day.

The $95,000,000 authorized by the voters will be used to construct a $27,067,000 sewage treatment plant on the river north of the city and an $18,953,000 plant to the south. Interceptor systems leading to the two plants will cost $46,287,000 and the instrumentation of the new system will come to $1,331,000. Twenty pumping stations must be installed, and when all is in readiness the 72 large outfall sewers now pouring material into the stream along 20 miles of riverfront will do so no longer. During the bond campaign, St. Louis was said to be the only large city in the country that lacked suitable sewage facilities. It was blamed for the fact that the fishing industry which once flourished downstream had waned, and it was held responsible for the river's lack of appeal for boating and other recreational purposes.

The United States Government has spurred research on ways of preventing, controlling, and removing contaminants. When Liguest came from New Orleans to establish St. Louis 200 years ago, the Mississippi was a more pleasant stream than it is now. The citizens of St. Louis, as they prepare to mark the bicentennial, like to think the river will regain some of its pioneer freshness.

CLEANING THE THAMES.—A recommendation to start preliminary work which could lead to a scheme estimated to cost up to £20,000,000 to keep the tidal portion of the Thames clear of pollution has come before the L.C.C.

The Rivers and Drainage Committee has recommended trial borings and surveys with a view to the possible extension of the northern outfall works to ensure that the tidal portion of the Thames will achieve the standard of freedom from nuisance advocated by the Pippard Committee on pollution. The cost of the preliminary work is estimated at £60,000. The major scheme would be to make allowances for the increase in the average daily flow from 215,000,000 gallons at present to 250,000,000 gallons expected in 1970 and for the likely increase in the flow of trade effluents. Other works would include the construction of storm-water tanks at Abbey Mills pumping station to avoid having to build an additional outfall sewer at the northern outfall; extensions to existing plant and some additional equipment. A third sludge vessel would also be needed.

CLINICAL MEDICINE AND PHYSIOLOGY.—The modern physician was increasingly using the tools and methods of the physiologist, and on the mutual efforts and understanding of their common problems the future welfare of man in health and disease depended, Professor J. McMichael said in his 1963 presidential address to the physiology and biochemistry section of the British Association.

The complete physiological experiment was seldom possible in man. Observation had to be supplemented by comparison with experience on laboratory animals. Nevertheless man could cooperate intelligently in the study of himself; he could provide background information on his life history and on his heredity which might alter his reactions to the influences under study.

"He is a large animal providing opportunities for experimental approaches not applicable, say, in the mouse. In disease, man presents a plethora of responses, the detailed physiological analysis of which has only just begun in this generation. From the pursuit of such studies by the physiological and biochemical techniques, we can reap a rich harvest of benefit to man himself, as well as to fundamental biological knowledge."

Professor McMichael said that one of the major problems of medicine today was occlusive disease of the arteries. Affecting the vessels supplying the heart, coronary disease was responsible for 100,000 deaths a year in this country, but the same vascular disorder could also affect other parts of the body, including the brain (strokes), killing about 50,000 a year, and disabling many more.

A great deal of research had been directed to the study of diet, and especially dietary fats, in causing this disease, but equally important was the problem of selective localization of the disease in the arterial system.

COAL BY PIPELINE.—An experimental system for the transfer of coal by pipeline from pit to power station was started at Wakefield last September.

The Central Electricity Generating Board said that the experiment would run for about three years, and they hoped it would help to answer one of the board's biggest problems—how to transport quickly and economically the vast amount of coal needed by modern large electricity power stations. At the Wakefield power station, chosen for the field trials because it demands relatively modest quantities of fuel, coal is taken by conveyor from pithead bunkers at Walton Colliery to a pump house. There it is magnetically screened, crushed to half-inch size, mixed with water and passed through a three-pump system into the pipeline. Flushed by the water, the coal takes four to five minutes to cover the mile and a half journey to the power station. It is then spun-dried by a centrifugal drying plant to drain off the water before being taken by conveyors to the station's coal stockyard.

COLOUR PICTURES OF THE BRAIN.—Doctors of neuro-surgery at the Foch hospital at Suresnes near Paris presented what they claim to be the first colour pictures of activities inside a living human brain.

The photographs were taken with the aid of a new instrument, the ventriculoscope. This is a 7 mm. tube which is inserted into the brain during an operation and illuminates the part to be operated on by reflecting intense light from a quartz component. With the instrument, it was claimed, the cause of hydrocephaly (" water on the brain ") in a baby had been filmed, and a completely successful operation carried out, again using the instrument, within 15 minutes, which represented a considerable advance over other treatments of hydrocephalic disturbances. In another case, the ventriculoscope helped to reveal the existence of a brain tumour in a man where other examinations had permitted no precise diagnosis.

COMPUTERS IN SCIENCE AND MEDICINE.—New uses of computers in the study of trees, vegetation patterns and bacteria were described to the British Association Botany Section. Professor W. T. Williams, of Southampton University, stated that in three test areas a computer had done as well or better than professional botanists in working out natural regions of vegetation and determining their boundaries.

Mr. A. S. Gardiner and Mr. J. N. R. Jeffers, of the Forestry Commission research station at Alice Holt Lodge, Wrecclesham, Surrey, described the use of computers to distinguish different species of birch from different characteristics of sample leaves. It had been lately suggested that more than three species of birch might be native to Britain and the use of the computer was to find out which of 13 measurements were the most useful for classifying trees on the basis of leaf characters.

A similar use of computers for the difficult job of classifying bacteria on the basis of shape was reported by Dr. P. H. A. Sneath, of the National Institute of Medical Research, Mill Hill. The result, he said, had been a considerable advance both theoretically and practically, and it was possible to imagine the use of computers to classify on the basis of patterns of other kinds whether in organisms or in trade between nations.

Prodigious calculations were called for in the three-dimensional analysis of complex molecular structures, Professor J. Monteath Robertson, F.R.S., Department of Chemistry, Glasgow University, said in a presidential address to the chemists on " A physical approach to chemical structure ".

He described one case, completed last March in less than four months after receiving the crystals, which apart from the experimental work involved some 120 million operations. Such work, he said, would be virtually impossible without a fast electronic computer.

There could be no doubt that the most striking feature of chemical science during the past 10 years, and certainly the one that had led to the greatest and most rapid development in nearly all branches, had been the increasing power of physical methods of investigation. It was hard to explain, Professor Robertson said, how that tremendously rapid surge of progress had come about. Some of it, of course, was due to new fundamental discoveries in physical science; but the basis for a great many of those advances had been well established far earlier.

He described the X-ray method of analysis as " an all-or-nothing approach ". Unlike the various other physical methods, it was not possible to isolate a part of the structure or a particular group in the molecule for separate study; but just because of that the solution was a very comprehensive one and provided an accurate determination of the position of every atom in space. " In other words, it solves the chemical structure completely, in every detail."

Very often in the course of investigation such a thorough-going and comprehensive analysis might not be necessary. It was better to reserve the more powerful X-ray method for those very important key structures that had hitherto defied the more standard methods, and upon whose solution further progress depended.

A great effort was now being made to employ those powerful methods to obtain information about the many vastly more complex biological molecules that were so vitally important in living matter. Great progress had recently been made and solutions for some of the simpler protein and enzyme molecules were now within sight."

The use of computers in compiling and storing medical information could prevent another thalidomide tragedy, a doctor told the Liberal Summer School in Oxford.

Dr. J. L. McCallum, a London general practitioner and a member of the British Medical Association Council, said: " Our hope is that centres will be set up where information can be fed into computers and be readily available to anyone who wants information on a particular drug or treatment." He said that " startling facts " would be revealed when the Birthday Trust reported on its survey of births. It had been discovered, he said, that roughly 40 per cent of the deaths at or soon after birth could be avoided. Already, Dr. McCallum said, a computer library service had been set up in London and all details of births could be sent to it.

CORONARY DISEASE STUDIES.—Mortality from coronary disease among males in the United States was about 2·6 times that among Irish males, the International Congress on Nutrition was told last year.

A study of 153 pairs of brothers showed that the brother living in Ireland ate on average 600 calories a day more than the brother living in Boston; and those living in Ireland were 8 per cent lighter. The conclusion of the doctor who conducted the study was that the Irish took more exercise than the Americans, and were thus possibly protected from the coronary disease. In prosperous countries there is no doubt that dietary excesses contribute to the increasing incidence of diseases of the cardio-vascular system. The role of animal fats in the causation of coronary artery disease was disputed. Although a high dietary intake of animal fats leads to a high level of cholesterol in the blood, which is closely associated with coronary disease, it is still uncertain whether it actually causes the pathological changes.

Dr. G. V. Mann, of Tennessee, reported a study on the Masai tribe in East Africa, when no case of coronary disease was found in a large group of men in spite of a daily intake of 175 grammes of fat derived largely from meat and milk. He attributed their immunity to the fact that Masai men were physically active, hunting and looking after their cattle. Other speakers supported the view that lack of physical exercise contributed more to the production of heart disease than did dietary excesses.

Professor J. Mayer, of Harvard, in a paper on nutrition and athletics, described a new technique, based on cinematograph records, for measuring activity during participation in various sports. He found that a group of obese young girls when playing tennis was stationary on the court for 80 per cent of the time, whereas a group of girls of normal weight were actively playing for over 70 per cent of the time.

Dr. I. Maddocks, of Australia, reported that in some tribes in New Guinea blood pressure levels fell with advancing age and high blood pressure was unknown. They had a small intake of salt which they could obtain only from one small spring. He suggested that high intakes of salt might be an important contributory cause of high blood pressure.

Professor J. F. Brock, of Cape Town, called for a foundation to inaugurate a long-term study of man from birth to 70 years of age, without which, he said, one could not expect to understand the many effects of diet on the development of degenerative diseases. On the immediately practical side Professor R. Nicolaysen, of Norway, set out a policy of moderation. Less animal fat in the diet, more physical exercise, and fewer cigarettes would lead, he was confident, to less heart disease.

DEATH-WATCH BEETLE AND WEEVIL.—The British Pest Control Conference in April was told that no cases of death-watch beetle in public buildings in this country had been reported in the last 50 years. This was explained by the fact that any beetles in buildings had been brought in with the original wood. There was no other way they could have got there, since they had never been observed to fly. It was said that the beetle colonies in the woodwork of Westminster Hall must have been there for 800 years. A possible explanation for the non-appearance of the death-watch beetle was that timber of large dimensions was no longer used in buildings. There is, however, a greater menace—the New Zealand Weevil, which, although first recorded in this country in 1937, was found during a recent survey in London to exist in 13 per cent of the houses examined.

EARLIEST ROPE FOUND.—Among interesting discoveries by archaeologists during the year, shown to members of the Council for British Archaeology, was a pottery figurine of a lady of fashion of the early sixteenth century from the Whitehall Palace site. Other discoveries are a medieval head of a priest, from Mary-le-Port, Bristol, and a small bronze horse from the Roman town of Silchester. The Tudor figurine may have formed part of the lid of a vessel used in King Henry VIII's Banqueting Hall.

An outstanding find was a short section of rope which dates back to about 1,500 B.C. and is believed to be the earliest specimen of rope ever recovered below ground in Britain. It was found at the bottom of a deep shaft at Wilsford.

EARS BY SURGERY.—A Greek boy, aged five, has returned to his home in Athens after 12 operations in an Oxford hospital which have provided him with ears. The boy, Aristides Goulielmou, was born without ears or earholes and could hear only very imperfectly. He was brought to Britain in October, 1962, by his mother and for 7 months was under the care of a plastic surgeon at the Churchill Hospital, Oxford.

The operations consisted of forming two ears from the cartilage at the front end of the boy's ribs and by grafting skin from other parts of his body. The earholes were formed in two operations carried out by an ear and throat specialist. Although operations of this kind have been carried out before, it is believed that nine months is the shortest time yet taken to complete such a series. It is normally estimated that it takes a year to complete one ear. The boy's hearing greatly improved, and he will not need to use a hearing aid.

ECOLOGICAL JUBILEE MEETING.—Ecology, the branch of biology which deals with the mutual relations between organisms and their environment, is still a word of mystery to millions, but the British Ecological Society celebrated its golden jubilee in London during the year by a meeting which attracted 400 members and visitors.

Besides invited speakers from the United States, Denmark, Malaya, and Switzerland, research workers from a dozen countries, including Czechoslovakia and New Zealand, attended. Many of them were taking time off from postgraduate studies over here.

Ecology began in Britain with the botanists as an unexpected product of the Auld Alliance. The influence of Professor Falhaud of Montpellier on Robert Smith—a young Scot who died in 1900 when only 26—started Smith on mapping his native vegetation. His brother, William, took over from there. He became a lecturer at Leeds and, on the bare moors of Yorkshire, he worked with his students on the relationship of plants to their environment.

Professor W. H. Pearsall, the chairman for the jubilee meeting, surveyed the whole development of the science from its first preoccupation with mapping, its progress to quantitative assessments of populations and its present emphasis on the productivity of biological systems.

EGYPTIAN HOME IDENTIFIED.—A sculptured stone head in Dundee Museum has been identified as that of Princess Neferure, from the ancient Egyptian temple of Deir-el-Bahari. The sculptured head was discovered by Mr. Boyd, Director of the Museum, when he was checking exhibits in the museum basement. Pencil-rubbing matches exactly the relevant hole in the wall at Deir-el-Bahari temple. It is suggested that the missing part at the temple might be replaced by a cast of the Dundee exhibit.

EXPLORERS' NEED OF WATER.—Should the traveller in a hot climate train himself to do without water? Some medical authorities say he should, others that he should not. These differences among experts were disclosed in a symposium sponsored by the Royal Geographical Society, the Medical Research Council, and the medical services of the Navy, Army, and Air Force.

Sir Raymond Priestley, president of the Royal Geographical Society, recalled that when he was with Shackleton's and Scott's expeditions between 1907 and 1913, their reading included *Hints to Travellers: Part II.* That work was out of date but it was most important that we should have more up-to-date booklets of that kind, particularly as there was a shortage of doctors for expeditions.

Dr. C. S. Leithead, of the School of Tropical Medicine, Liverpool, laid some emphasis on the medical view that a man should drink adequate quantities of water to balance increased perspiration in hot climates.

Major-General W. R. M. Drew, Commandant of the Royal Army Medical College, maintained that it was best for people travelling across a hot country to drink water freely and as they felt the need. Lieut.-General Sir Charles Richardson, Director-General of Military Training, urged that travellers should be trained to endure long spells without water. Sir Vivian Fuchs, giving the explorer's view, recalled that on journeys in Kenya he had felt it really necessary to drink water less frequently when he was not on the move. Mr. Wilfred Thesiger told of having gone for 15 days in the deserts of southern Arabia on a pint of water a day.

FALLOUT TOOTHPASTE.—Toothpaste which removes radioactive strontium from the system by way of the saliva was put on sale in Finland during the year. It is claimed to be the first of its kind in the world. The preparation is a result of research by Professor Setälä, a specialist in radiation at Helsinki University. For some years he has been working on the extraction of fallout products from living organisms, and in the case of mammals he discovered that strontium was not permanently anchored in the bone, but moved in a cycle which included the saliva. The new toothpaste uses this principle. It is claimed that regular use twice a day will eliminate most of the fallout absorbed under normal conditions, that is to say, those resulting from atomic tests already carried out. A tube costs two Finnish marks, about 4s. 6d.

FIREMEN'S NEW AID.—A new type of breathing apparatus for firemen, weighing only 25 lb., some 11 lb. less than the standard oxygen equipment, has been developed by the Vickers research centre at Sunningdale, Berkshire, in response to a request by the Fire Brigades Union for a modern, lightweight, and if possible, safer design. Among the innovations are person-to-person communication and an automatic device for signalling the wearer's whereabouts. The new apparatus was described by Dr. B. Lucas, a specialist in respiration problems at University College, London. The modern fireman going into a fire, he said, looked very much like a Christmas tree. With the new breathing set, unnecessary bulk was eliminated by building the breathing bag into the jacket so that it extended right round the man; this also meant that he compressed the bag merely by expanding his chest as he breathed, and so saved himself effort. The cooling system was more efficient, Dr. Lucas said, and still had some effect at the end of the 60 minutes for which the equipment was designed to operate. It was a physiological fact that a man could continue to work in conditions of extreme heat so long as he could breathe cool air.

FISHBOURNE ROMAN VILLA.—Last summer excavation took place at the important Roman site at Fishbourne near Chichester, on the north and west wings of the palatial building, already shown by earlier excavation to be a luxurious villa, built *c.* A.D. 75–80. Modification of the building took place around the beginning of the second century, and there were minor alterations during its use, which continued until late in the third century. The area on which this magnificent building was erected was partly occupied earlier by timber buildings belonging to a harbour settlement, and whose earliest structures date from shortly after the Claudian invasion of A.D. 43. One of these timber buildings is apparently a granary, and should fit into a military context.

Although present evidence is not nearly conclusive, the discovery is of great significance to theories that there were multiple Roman landing points, rather than a single one in Kent. A supply base in the Fishbourne area would also have been of use in the early stages of the campaigns of the Second legion, commanded by Vespasian, which conquered the Isle of Wight and subdued the south-west.

FOSSIL 200m. YEARS OLD.—Simon Stephens, aged 16, a student, of Hobart, Tasmania, found the fossil of a tortoise or turtle which is stated to be about 200 million years old. The discovery was made in Derwent Estuary in the Hobart suburb of Taroona. Professor S. W. Carey of Hobart University dated the fossil from the Triassic period and Hobart zoologists said it was of a species of tortoise or turtle new to science. It was the oldest fossil of a tortoise or turtle found in Australia and one of the oldest in the world.

The removal of superfluous stone from the fossil was a highly complex job.

FROZEN RAIL POINTS.—British winters are not cold enough, say chemists of British Railways' Western Region, who are seeking an answer to the problem of frozen rail points. Frozen water binds the points to the rail like glue, and the freezing, thawing and re-freezing cycles, usual in this country, present difficulties not found in countries where freezing is mainly continuous. Experiments have produced a de-icing mixture which releases the ice, reduces corrosion and leaves a film which will keep a point unaffected by frost for 18 hours. Following these tests, a system will be devised to treat each point with the most effective quantity of the new fluid.

HEART RESTARTED BY TAPPING.—A report of a new method of resuscitating a heart which has stopped was published in *The Lancet*. The method consists simply of tapping sharply the lower part of the chest bone, or sternum, with the edge of the hand. The report, from the London Hospital, tells of a man whose heart stopped beating. Firm tapping of the lower end of the sternum was carried out at a rate of 60 a minute, and each tap was accompanied by a beat of the heart. This was continued intermittently for an hour and a half, and whenever it was stopped the patient lost consciousness. While the tapping was performed the patient was conscious and complained of no pain. In due course a pacemaker was inserted, and the patient made an uneventful recovery. Attention is drawn to the simplicity and safety of the method and its value as an emergency method in resuscitating the heart and so maintaining it in action until more permanent measures can be taken.

HEART VALVES TRANSPLANTED.—Heart valves from young road crash victims are being " banked " by a three-man team of doctors to replace those of older people which have become diseased. The valve is the aortic—through which flows blood from the heart into the main artery of the body. Sterilized and freeze-dried, the heart valves are kept in a vacuum for up to nine months. Although the disease is quite rare, supplies are short because the " spare " valves had to be taken from young people soon after death and under the present law relatives' permission is delayed until it is too late. Between 15 and 20 people in Britain had received human aortic valves in the past year, either at the Radcliffe Hospital, Oxford, or at Guy's Hospital in London, which is cooperating in the work. No trouble has been met through the patient's body rejecting the transplanted valve—the trouble which so often defeats kidney transfer operations. This, it is thought, is because the material of which the valve is made does not provoke the immunological reaction.

HIGH ALTITUDE WIND SPEEDS.—The existence of high-speed wind currents more than 50 miles above the surface of the earth was announced by the United States National Aeronautics and Space Administration. At altitudes up to about 44 miles winds follow a global pattern, regularly reversing with the season. Between about 44 miles and 50 miles up, wind becomes erratic and unpredictable, and above 50 miles is a region where strong and highly variable winds are sandwiched between zones of relative calm. Between 56 and 68 miles, wind velocities have been observed to increase by more than 250 miles an hour and even to reverse their direction within an altitude span of three miles. Immediately above this turbulent layer wind velocities diminish almost to zero, but above 70 miles there is another region of strong winds with velocities of about 200 miles an hour. This region would appear to extend to altitudes of as much as 125 miles.

HIGHLAND POWER PLAN.—Plans for two hydro-electric stations costing nearly £9,000,000 were published in March by the North of Scotland Hydro-Electric Board. They are to be at Fada-Fionn and Loch a'Bhraoin, both in Ross and Cromarty. The two stations will provide work for about 1,000 persons and a total installed capacity of about 65,000 kilowatts—estimated annual output, 193 million units of electricity.

Fada-Fionn is designed to have an annual output of 145m. units. Precautions have been taken to avoid impairing the scenic beauty by the shores of Loch Maree. The power station is to be underground and all aqueducts are to be buried.

The scheme, by far the larger of the two, utilizes the rainfall over a catchment area of 66 sq. miles. In two dams, one 40 ft. and the other 25 ft. high, arrangements will be made for the protection and improvement of stocks of fish in the rivers and lochs.

HOMO AQUATICUS PREDICTED.—A forecast that a " new man " would be developed, probably over the next 50 years, was made by Commandant Jacques-Yves Cousteau at the second World Congress of Underwater Activities. Such a man would be able to exist without the use of his lungs, which would be filled with compressible liquid, and he would be able to withstand pressures at depths of 3,000 ft. to 5,000 ft. The development of this *Homo aquaticus* would mean that eventually hospitals would be established at the bottom of the sea and babies would undergo surgery at birth which would enable them to live thereafter under water as well as on land. There would be new nations living under water. We have good reason to believe that sea mammals are animals that have returned to the sea.

He spoke of a " village " which would be erected at varying depths in the sea. As many as two dozen people would live there, probably including himself. It would be erected with small nuclear plants to provide energy to draw respiratory gases from the sea, and would have no physical connection with a land base.

HOSPITAL TESTS BY MACHINE.—A machine similar to that used in the training and selection of astronauts has been installed in the Tyrone County Hospital at Omagh to help to trace the causes of giddiness. Selected patients sit on a platform that spins. Acceleration and deceleration phases are operated from a control panel and wire leads connected to the patient's body give a pen tracing in the same way that an electro-cardiograph registers heart beats. The machine is the first of its kind in the United Kingdom. The installation was supervised by Dr. Frank Dittrich, of the University of Geneva, who was one of its inventors.

HYDROFOIL CRAFT.—A captain's launch that can travel at nearly twice the speed of the parent ship is a feature of Ben Line's new 12,400-ton *Benarty*.

She is the first British merchant ship to carry a small hydrofoil craft for rapid ship-to-shore travel in wide Eastern rivers and estuaries.

The hydrofoil is the second craft sold by International Aquavion (G.B.) Ltd., a company formed last year by the Inchcape Group and Wallace Bros., to give Britain a foothold in the rapidly expanding market for high-speed hydrofoils.

A bigger version carrying 40 passengers at 32 knots was due to carry out trials in the Orkneys. The distance between the main town, Kirkwall, and the outlying islands is such that, with a four-hour sea journey each way, the islanders have rarely known what it is to have a day out. The hydrofoil, capable of crossing between islands in less than an hour, will allow them several hours on the mainland for market, shopping, and social visits, and still return home the same night. At £60,000 it should be able to carry passengers at under 5*d*. a mile.

ICE AGE: OCEAN-BED CLUE.—Scientists at the Lamont Geological Observatory of Columbia University believe that they have found proof that the Earth's first great Ice Age started as a sudden climatic catastrophe. They placed the onset of the Ice Age, marking the transition from Pliocene to the Pleistocene, considerably farther back in time than hitherto assumed, at least 800,000 years ago. Their conclusions are based on a study of fossil remains in sediment at the bottom of the Atlantic and Indian Oceans. With the aid of a piston corer, allowing cores of more than 36 ft. in length to be raised intact to the surface and preserved, more than 3,000 sediment cores have been raised from the oceans during 43 oceanographic expeditions organized by the observatory. Eight had probed deep enough into sediments of past ages to contain a boundary clearly defined by changes in their content of fossilized planktonic remains. The authors—Dr. Ericson, Dr. Ewing and Dr. Wollin—conclude that this boundary marks the beginning of the first Ice Age of the Pleistocene.

These micro-organisms, or rather their star shaped skeletons, are found in enormous numbers in sediments reaching back 60 million years, from the Paleocene through Pliocene Age. In the sediment cores studied, a whole series of faunal changes, including the total disappearance of disco-asters, were found to have occurred within a thickness of no more than four to six inches, indicating a profound change in climate in a brief period of no more than 6,000 years and possibly much less.

INSURANCE AGAINST HAILSTORMS.—After a bad start after the war, research on the artificial release of rain from clouds has settled down into a pattern which has provided a great deal of new knowledge of the processes that go on in clouds. It may now be possible to increase the amount of rainfall in particular areas and to reduce damage done to crops by hail-storms by modifying the structure of storm clouds. On the positive side—the production of rain where it is wanted—large-scale trials in Australia are beginning to yield conclusions. One was begun in 1955 in the Snowy Mountains of New South Wales, where natural rainfall is heavy but additional rainfall is still of value because of hydro-electric and irrigation schemes. Preliminary analysis suggests that an increase of 10 per cent. may have been achieved, though further experiments will be necessary to confirm this. The next large-scale trial was begun in 1957 in the mid-north area of South Australia, where rainfall averages about 20 in. a year and is markedly seasonal. The reason for the failure is known. Because temperature there often rises with height in the lower part of the atmosphere, instead of falling, that at cloud-top level is commonly too low: about $-2°C$, whereas seeding with silver iodine is effective only at temperatures below −6°C. The fact that the sums paid out as insurance against hail damage total some £20m. annually in both Europe and the United States suggests that the lead given will be followed up.

IRRIGATION AND FOOD.—The idea that the limit of world food production would be reached soon because all suitable land was already in use was ridiculed by Professor Martin Jones in a presidential address to the Agricultural Section of the British Association. The problem of food was how to collect the energy from life and convert that life energy into food energy either in the form of fruit and vegetables or as meat and milk. Only about a tenth of the life energy an acre was utilized now by our farm crops, even the most popular ones. He added that improvements from manuring and plant breeding were playing their part, but the limiting factor over much of the world's surface was lack of moisture. Man only needed to irrigate large areas of desert in the tropics to bring a tenfold increase in the amount of food available, particularly when modern manures were also used.

Experiments had shown that such methods were practicable. Irrigation was spreading so fast that it would soon be regarded as a waste of manures if the proper amount of water was not supplied. It might even be necessary, one day, to adjust the distribution of the human race, encouraging settlements in drier climates.

" This all adds up to limitless opportunity for an increase in our food production so as to keep pace with the increase in population for the next few hundred years. By that time even our proposed methods may again be out of date: the human being may be able to get his supply of energy through some other means than a green plant."

ISRAEL HARNESSES THE SUN.—Israel is exporting water heaters working off the sun's rays. Several thousand solar water heaters are installed each year and one successful design is being exported to Mediterranean and African countries.

The solar heating device, working off glass collector plates on the house roof are said to give an " endless supply of hot water throughout the day, and, because the tanks are well insulated, even at night ". Israel has devoted a great deal of research to trapping the energy of the sun and a national solar laboratory has been set up with 25 professors and technical staff. Part of the work is done in Israel's southern desert at the Negev institute for arid zone research, where the sun bears down day after day throughout the year, and part is conducted at the Hebrew University in Jerusalem.

Heat from sunshine is absorbed by a black surface and much fundamental research has been done on the preparation of this selective surface. The twin glass collector plates of the solar apparatus for heating can be seen on the roofs of many houses all over Israel.

LICHENS THE WORLD'S " OLDEST INHABITANTS ".—The possibility that some of the lichens of the Arctic and Antarctic, and not the giant redwoods of California, can claim to be the " world's oldest living things " was discussed by the Botany Section of the British Association.

A remarkable feature of many lichens was their ability to live for many years in extreme climates. For example, on the Antarctic continent there were only three species of flowering plants; but there were at least 450 species of lichens. They have been collected at altitudes of 27,000 ft., and in hot regions the temperature of some lichens growing on rocks might regularly rise to 60° to 70°C during the daytime. Another characteristic of most lichens was their very slow growth, sometimes increasing their diameter by little more than a millimetre or a fraction of a millimetre each year. It followed that large plants of such lichens must be of very great age, he said.

The Swiss lichenologist, Roland Beschel, attempted to estimate the age to which some lichens would live in Europe. He put the maximum age at some hundreds of years, and for one species it was put as over 1,000 years. In the Arctic Beschel claimed that lichens of the genus Rhizocarpon might have a maximum age of 4,500 years (though similar kinds of lichens in the tropics might last for only a very few years); thus the claim to be " the world's oldest living thing " might rest with some of the lichens.

How did lichens manage to live for so long under starvation conditions? Recent research had shown that they were probably very efficient at absorbing substances from dilute solutions—in some cases more efficient than very rapidly growing plants such as yeast. There was evidence that having absorbed nutrients lichens tended to store them up rather than use them straight away, as if to build up reserves for any lean periods ahead. However, when existing in conditions of atmospheric pollution, they would build up toxic quantities of pollutants inside themselves more rapidly than other kinds of plants, and that might well explain why lichens were so markedly absent from towns and cities. It might also account for the fact that lichens tended to accumulate more radioactive fallout than higher plants.

Dr. J. H. Tallis (Manchester University) said lichens were coming more and more to be used as indicators of clear air conditions. In the immediate centre of urban areas lichens were completely absent. Studies in Belfast, south Sweden, and Manchester gave distances of about five, three, and 20 miles respectively from the centre of pollution before leafy lichens appeared in any quantity. About 400 square miles of south Lancashire was thus devoid of the larger lichens and presumably heavily polluted, Dr. Tallis said.

MAP OF THE SEA BED.—A new map of 14,000 square miles of the sea bed, the product of six years' research by the Royal Society, gives firmer clues to the geological history of the English Channel and Western Approaches.

The most advanced methods employed in surveying the sea bed have been " sparkers " and " boomers " which send electrical discharges and shock waves through water to the bottom. The way they reflect from submerged rock surfaces is recorded in rather the same way as in seismic surveys for oil. The geologist, sitting in a laboratory in the ship, read the results as they were printed before him. The research is continuing in co-operation with similar projects abroad, particularly in the United States.

NATIONAL LIBRARY IN WAR FACTORY.—The National Lending Library for Science and Technology at Boston Spa, housing 350,000 volumes and 12,000 periodicals, was opened by Lord Hailsham, Minister for Science. It is intended for industrial firms, learned bodies, and individuals trying to keep up with the flow of scientific knowledge. Lord Hailsham said the library, whose intake is now 10 million words a day, was one of the wonders of modern Britain. It would serve a field in which the corpus of human knowledge was growing at the most rapid rate and the need for documentation, classification and bibliography was greater than anywhere else. Drawn from 109 countries, the collection is valued at £2m. and is said to be the largest in western Europe. Dr. D. J. Urquhart, the director, who has worked on its creation since 1956, expects to double this size in 10 years. Looking farther ahead it could expand to 15 million in a century. Traditional methods of library working have been dispensed with. The idea of having a catalogue was thrown out because it would take almost as long to catalogue the stock as to deal with borrowers. Most books will be sent to borrowers by a return of post service after being selected from the 20 miles of shelving or the 120 miles of microfilm records. The library possesses more books in the Russian language than in English. Of the £300,000 annual cost of operaton, about £140,000 is spent in translating from the Russian, with £75,000 regained from users.

NEOLITHIC AXE FIND.—Excavations at Ousethorpe, near Pocklington, in the East Riding of Yorkshire, yielded information on a hitherto unsuspected range of occupation. A bank and ditch, making a square of 100 yards side on a site sloping gently towards a stream, are the only visible signs of antiquity. They are now securely dated by green-glazed pottery resembling that encountered in York and attributed to the fourteenth century A.D.

In the north-west corner on the higher ground is a large hollow which proved to be the site of a building hitherto unknown and unrecorded. Initially it was built of stone, with doorways flanked with pillars of magnesian limestone. Later, and almost certainly in Tudor times, floors and fireplaces were added in brick. Why such an opulent building should have disappeared even from folk memory is not clear.

Outside this building were storage pits. These contained quantities of sand-tempered pottery of the post-Conquest Norman period, such as is found at Pontefract or Almondbury, as well as shell paste St. Neots ware, which is pre-Conquest in date. This carries the history of the site back almost to the period when it received its Domesday name of Ianulverstorp.

Under the medieval bank but unknown to its builders is a section of ditch or palisade-trench which seems to form an elongated oval in plan and which has yielded boars' tusks, antler picks, or hammers, a few scraps of Neolithic pottery, but, above all, three polished stone axes, one of which is indisputably a Graig Lwyd axe from the famous axe factory at Penmaenmawr and which is securely dated elsewhere to the Neolithic period *c.* 2500 B.C.

A handful of small geometric microliths hold out the possibility that the Neolithic occupants succeeded to a site previously occupied by Mesolithic hunters.

OCCUPATIONAL NOISE SURVEY.—The research team of the Medical Council and the National Physical Laboratory moved ahead with their investigation into the effects of occupational exposure to noise. The recent Wilson report echoed the Government's concern. Just before the report was published, the Government announced a £65,000 research project.

This programme entails a review of the types and groups of industry in Britain by relevant noise surveys. It is intended to cover all industries which have noisy jobs and to examine the hearing of all staff who have been on such work for an uninterrupted period, exposed to noise above a level of about 85 decibels on the A scale of a standard noise meter. This level of noise is experienced—to take a familiar example—by a person standing 50 ft. from an unmuffled drill breaking concrete.

People who have been exposed to military noise or gunfire or shooting of any kind will be excluded. So also will those who have any kind of ear defect which can be attributed to anything other than noise.

Although many thousands will be examined throughout a year, it is estimated that about a third of the 150 tested each week will be studied. Once included in the survey a person will be reviewed every nine months or so for three years.

Before the survey started a number of problems had to be overcome. Usually tests of this kind are conducted in sound-proofed audiometric testing booths in hospitals and clinics. These conditions are not to be found in a steelworks or cotton mill or any other "noisy" environment. To cope with the large number of people to be covered by the survey it was essential that the testing time was kept to a minimum. A further point was that if the comparative results of the tests were to be valid they had to be conducted in the same degree of quietness.

OIL OR GAS FROM UNDER THE SEA.—Fifteen or so vessels are surveying 30,000 sq. miles of the North Sea for the oil companies, searching for oil or natural gas in the rock formations of the sea bed.

They use the modern method of exploding charges to produce shock waves which penetrate the sea bed and—unevenly reflected—build up a clear picture of the strata. More than 20 companies altogether are now searching for oil, or natural gas, in various parts of the sea. It has been suggested that the sea bed here may be the Klondyke of the 1960s, and the North Sea hydrocarbon rush may fairly be said to be on.

Geologically the prospects must seem inviting. On one side of the sea lie the small east Midlands oilfields: on the other the great natural gas deposits in the Dutch province of Groningen which are said to be the third largest yet discovered in the world. It is thought that oil and natural gas come from marine deposits, and these have been accumulating in the North Sea since Carboniferous times. So it is reasonable to estimate that the centre of the depositional basin lies somewhere out beneath the waters. Postwar improvements in technique mean that it would be neither very difficult nor very expensive to drill in this shallow sea bed.

The BP Exploration Company announced that it has made plans to drill an offshore well on the Lulworth Bank, two and a half miles south-west of Lulworth Cove, Dorset. Drilling was expected to begin early in September. A seismic survey of the area in 1960 disclosed a potential oil-bearing structure in the sea bed of Lulworth, but it does not follow that oil is there or that it is present in commercial quantities.

PARCEL SORTING MACHINE.—A press-button parcel sorting machine, which cost nearly £150,000 was introduced at Worcester Post Office during the year. Worcester was selected for the first installation of the machine in this country because, with a large mail order firm in the district, the office has to deal with an average of 10,000 parcels a day, compared with about 2,000 for other cities of its size. The machine, which is about 100 ft. long, will deal with up to 40 parcels a minute. A conveyor-belt brings bags from the collecting vans and the parcels drop in front of the sorter, who reads the address and presses a destination button.

PLASTICS IN BUILDING.—New high-speed building techniques developed by the London County Council are likely to lead to London getting its first flats clad in reinforced plastics. The new methods involve the extensive use of steel and could bring much-needed relief to the heavy steel industry of the high unemployment areas of the North-East and Scotland.

Two years of development work on the new techniques has solved the technical problems. There remain the problems of large-scale production of the reinforced plastic units. These are being investigated by a group of companies who were considering forming a consortium for the project.

Steel framing was thought to be the best way of getting the speed and precision needed for fast multi-storey construction. One of the main problems had been that of finding a substitute for the normal method of casting the steel in concrete cast on the site. The answer was a plastic dry casing, with foam plastic used for infilling. The reinforced plastic cladding panels are each the size of the outside wall of a room. To speed construction the normal process of jointing the panels after they had been fixed in position had to be avoided. This had been achieved by the use of gaskets which sealed the joints as the panels were bolted into position.

The L.C.C. had done some preliminary costing on steel frame building as compared with conventional construction and it was found that steel framing was competitive.

The only remaining problem with the new methods was that of machinery for manufacturing the external wall panels. This was expensive, but was a practical proposition if the quantity produced was large enough.

RADIUM ON WATCH DIALS BANNED.—New Swiss regulations concerning protection against radioactivity prohibit the use on watch dials of luminous material based on radium. Tritium, which has the same luminous qualities but only slight radiation, will be used. Some time ago the New York health service banned the sale of pocket watches with radium painted dials as these could be the cause of serious lesions. Such lesions have not yet been found in people using the watches but radiation could affect the reproductive organs. In collaboration with the Swiss watch-making research department, the federal hygiene service has concluded that while the effect on the human body of radium marked dials is negligible in the case of wrist watches, the effect is greater in the case of pocket watches, these being closer to the body. Professor Joyet, the Zurich scientist, said that a person wearing a wrist watch with radium marked figures on the dial is exposed to an average dose of seven milliröntgen a year while a wearer of a pocket watch is exposed to a dose of at least double that amount.

RECORD PLAYER WITH VISION.—A young Wolverhampton design consultant said that he had invented a record player which reproduced vision as well as sound. Record enthusiasts would be able to see their favourite entertainer or orchestra as well as hear them by using this invention, which plugged into an ordinary television set.

The researches of the inventor, Mr. Colin Mason, Wolverhampton, have covered seven years and have been backed by a Wolverhampton company. The record player will need special records which will incorporate the vision. But they will not cost any more than normal records—they may, in fact, cost less. The record player is the usual size and shape and will cost about £35. It is a video player and instead of asking for an audio record fans will have to ask for a video one. Records would be no bigger than ordinary commercial types and the device would be known as a " videogram ".

REVOLUTION IN ASTRONOMY.—Sir Bernard Lovell, professor of radio-astronomy at Manchester University, said that the revolution in observation astronomy achieved through radio-telescopes was almost as great as when Galileo first looked at the heavens through a small telescope. Men were now able to observe the universe in a completely different range of the spectrum. Since the radio-telescope had come into operation in 1957, over 27,000 hours of research had been carried out. Less than 5 per cent. had been associated with any of the recent historical events in space. Nevertheless, such rocket exploration of space was most important and would give scientists vital information about the environment of the Earth. It was hoped that there would be many clues in the next five years about the evolution of the solar system itself. Every time man had looked at the heavens with a stronger telescope, the number of visible bodies had increased; the number of new extra-galactic nebulae was almost uncountable. Thousands of galaxies were being discovered. The reason for larger and more sensitive instruments was not because ultimate penetration had still to be reached, but to obtain more information and detail about the things already being recorded.

ROAD WARNINGS BY TALKING SIGN.—A talking road sign which broadcasts advance information of road hazards over a car radio was shown at the road research laboratory of the Department of Scientific and Industrial Research at Crowthorne, Berkshire. The sign works through a cable buried in the road, through which taped live messages can be broadcast and picked up on a special receiving set installed in a car or wired through its radio. An official at the establishment said that such a device in a normal saloon car would cost about £10. An extension of the device enables vehicles to be guided through fog.

ROMAN BATH-HOUSE.—Excavation at Rowe Place Farm, Eccles, Kent, has produced details of a large Romano-British villa, whose presence was established in 1961 by Mr. M. A. Ocock in an aerial survey. Lasting from Easter until the beginning of October, the work was directed by Mr. A. P. Detsicas and financed by the Carnegie United Kingdom Trust, the Kent Archæological Society, the Society of Antiquaries, and public contributions, and had the co-operation of landowners, and farmers, Messsrs. A. A. and A. C. Southwell. The main digging in 1962 was done on the bath-house. This proved to have several structural periods, and was first built about A.D. 80–100, on the site of an earlier building dating from the middle of the first century A.D. There were several hypocaust heated rooms and a small cold plunge-bath. About A.D. 115–120 at least four new heated rooms were added, and an unusually large cold plunge-bath, 44 ft. long by 11 ft. wide. The latter had a concrete floor 12 in. thick, and was surrounded on three sides by a narrow corridor, whose internal walls were faced with painted plaster, bearing multi-coloured mainly geometric designs.

ROMAN ROAD WITH CART TRACKS.—Excavations in Colliton Park, Dorchester, Dorset, have uncovered a 40 ft. length of a Roman Road, whose surface clearly preserves ruts left by vehicles which used it. Numerous sandal studs and one coin were also found embedded in the road's surface. The work has been carried out by members of the Dorset Natural History and Archaeological Society on a site within the Roman town, where work during the past two years has brought to light stone and timber buildings and a series of ovens.

The road is just inside the town's earliest rampart, a clay and chalk structure, which is known from earlier excavations to have been 80 feet wide at its base. The road has a cobbled surface, and the flints at the centre were held firm with what seems to have been a lime cement. The vehicle ruts are clearly seen, and so close is the road to the rampart that some ruts cut into rising chalk at its base, just below a cobbled walk which runs along the bottom of it. A coin of the mid-second century A.D. was found on this walk. Where the vehicle ruts can be separated into pairs, the distance between them is about 4 ft. 9 in.–4 ft. 10 in., which agrees with the axle width of known Roman carts. In places the ruts had been patched with flint and beach pebbles. Dating evidence for the road is not conclusive yet but it could well first have been in use during the first century A.D. The site has also produced what is almost certainly a well, a deep pit cut into the chalk, already excavated to a depth of 18 ft., which would probably be a little less than half its depth. It had been filled in during the third century.

SAXON PALACE AT CHEDDAR.—An excavation carried out at Cheddar by the Ministry of Works has revealed the site of a Saxon palace. Mr. P. A. Rahtz, in charge of the excavation, says that the site is of particular interest because there are very few left, most of them have remained underneath cities like London and Winchester, but the Cheddar site, once a home of the kings of Wessex, had remained open country. The excavation has revealed at least four distinct periods of occupation of English Kings. Of the first period, the most important building was a narrow " boat "-shaped hall, 80 ft. long and 18 feet wide. The second phase, dated by coins of Athelstan, Edmund, and Ethelred the Unready, brought to light a rectangular hall, to the south of the ninth-century hall. Remains were found of a corn mill and bakery of the same period, and to the east of the hall a large post hole which probably housed the base of a tall flagstaff. The most interesting find in the third period was another hall built in the reign of Henry I. The post holes showed this to have been an aisled building of posts and interlocking timbers. This hall was rebuilt by King John on a smaller scale. Later in the thirteenth-century, the whole property was given by the Crown to the Bishop of Wells. Excavations showed that the chapel, which is on the site of part of the ninth-century hall, had several stages covering a period of about A.D. 930 to A.D. 1400.

SKELETON 4,000 YEARS OLD.—A skeleton believed to be over 4,000 years old has been unearthed by archaeolgists digging at a site near Radley, in Berkshire. The dig was undertaken for the Ministry of Works under the direction of the Ashmolean Museum, Oxford. Nothing was found with the skeleton but there were traces of a Neolithic settlement about a quarter of a mile in diameter and some remnants of Neolithic pottery were found in the area. The skeleton is in small pieces and the archaeologists have been dusting earth away with light brushes to avoid further damage. It is in the " crouched burial " position with knees drawn up under the chin. The area is scheduled for building in the near future but it is hoped that most of the Neolithic settlement (about 4,500 years old) will be unearthed first.

SLEEP: TWO KINDS.—The nature of sleep is one of the mysteries of life. An interesting discovery is that there are two kinds of sleep. The two forms alternate throughout the night, and it would appear that "paradoxical" sleep occurs about every one-and-a-half hours and lasts for 10 to 50 minutes. Observations which have been made open up interesting possibilities in our understanding of dreams and of some of the abnormalities of sleep. There is evidence that paradoxical sleep becomes more common towards the end of a night's sleep—and this is the period when dreams are most liable to occur—or, at least, dreams that can be recalled on awakening. It has also been found that if an individual is awakened from paradoxical sleep he will probably say that either he has just been dreaming or that he was awake anyhow and " thinking ". Equally interesting is the suggestion that has been put forward that the rapid eye movements that occur during paradoxical sleep are related to the " dream content " and that " the dreamer was, as it were, looking at the ' dream pictures ' ". Evidence in support of this suggestion is forthcoming from some recent investigation of the sleep of blind men. This showed that men blind for only a few years had visual experiences in their dreams and still had the rapid eye movements of paradoxical sleep. Men who had been blind all their lives, or for the greater part of them, had no rapid eye movements and were unable to " visualize " their dreams. They had, and could describe, quite vivid and bizarre dreams, but they did not " see " things in their dreams.

Yet another contribution of these studies of paradoxical sleep to the elucidation of dreaming is the possible explanation they provide of those nightmares in which the dreamer is placed in some terrifying situation and is unable to get out of it because he or she cannot move. Is it possible that this petrifying paralysis is merely a dream-like translation of the increased loss of muscular tone that occurs during paradoxical sleep?

This phenomenon may provide an explanation of a condition that has been arousing considerable interest in recent years—the condition known as sleep paralysis. This is a condition in which the victim, usually on wakening, finds he cannot move voluntarily or make any sound, though he is usually fully aware of external events. He is easily aroused to full consciousness by even a slight touch. Many theories have been put forward to explain this terrifying phenomenon, but the most likely appears to be that the victim of sleep paralysis is in a state of paradoxical sleep, accompanied by dreaming and this loss of muscular tone which gives him the sensation of paralysis. This concept of paradoxical sleep may help to explain certain other of the abnormalities of sleep, such as sleep-walking (or somnambulism) and night terrors—as well as sleeping paralysis. In somnambulism and night terrors, consciousness is lost but there is no impairment of muscle tone, while in sleep paralysis the reverse holds true. It may well be that these abnormalities of sleep are due to a lack of co-ordination between the two sections of the reticular system responsible for the control of sleep.

STRAWBERRY CROPS IN THE ARCTIC.—Few people would imagine that strawberries could be grown north of the Arctic Circle, let alone on a 150 ft. layer of permafrost. Yet the Canadian Department of Agriculture reported last year that for the past three seasons good-sized berries have been cultivated at Inuvik, North-West Territory, which is 127 miles north of the circle. With adequate soil fertility, strawberry plants grow well during the long days of a brief Arctic summer. In contrast, the wild strawberry does not survive in these remote regions.

In summer months the air temperature at Inuvik can reach 80°F, though it falls during the winter to 60° below zero on occasions. On the other hand, the variation in soil temperature is comparatively small, according to Mr. F. S. Nowasad, a northern agricultural expert with the department. For instance, nine soil readings taken at a depth of 41 ft. between March and December averaged 30·6°. At 10 ft. the temperature was 29·9°, and where tested it remained unchanged for the rest of the permafrost depth.

Strawberry plants survived the savage Arctic winter under a cover of brush mulch and snow which moderated ground temperatures and gave protection from the bitterly cold air. The surface temperature under the mulch and snow from March to December averaged 31·5°, the lowest figure being 1·5° in November and the highest 85° in late July. The summer in Inuvik allows a reasonably good crop of potatoes, cabbage and other hardy vegetables to be grown without protection, the department says, but plastic shelters are needed for the more tender crops; moisture has to be carefully preserved owing to the surprisingly low precipitation at Inuvik.

SUPERSONIC AIR CONDITIONS.—A laboratory to test the air-conditioning systems of supersonic aircraft was opened by the Minister of Aviation, at the Royal Aircraft Establishment at Farnborough, Hampshire. Initially it is being used to test the systems for the projected Anglo-French Mach 2·2 (1,450 m.p.h.) airliner and the TSR 2 supersonic strike and reconnaissance aircraft now being built. Because of the high temperatures at these greater speeds stainless steel aircraft structures will have to be used. At Mach 2·2, the temperature of the outside " skin " of the aircraft goes up to 240°F at a flying height of 60,000 ft.—near the limiting temperature for light alloy structures—and for an aircraft travelling at four times the speed of sound at 80,000 ft. the temperature rise on the outer skin will be up to some 680°F. The supersonic airliner cabin is represented in the R.A.E. laboratory by a section 12 ft. in diameter and 20 ft. long, mounted in an altitude chamber. Air is supplied by refrigeration and pressurization equipment similar to that which will be installed in the aircraft. The air will be taken in through the engine-compressor, some will be tapped off and cooled in a heat-exchanger and eventually go through a refrigeration system. The cabin is fitted with 24 seats and, to avoid having too many people there doing nothing while tests are made, aluminium dummies are used. The human body gives out a heat of 100 watts—more if the person has been imbibing—and to represent the conditions created by human passengers in the cabin the dummies are fitted with electrical elements having a similar output.

SURFACE SPACE IN ICECAP.—The second of two British submarines that spent three weeks under the Polar icecap returned to H.M.S. *Dolphin*, Gosport. They had been were experimenting with new instruments for discovering polynia—holes in the ice. These are found dotted all over the Arctic ice-pack. The submarines, which went looking for polynia big enough to allow a submarine to surface, were the Grampus and the Porpoise. The experiments were successful. The submarines also set up new endurance records for underwater craft. They sailed 515 miles under ice and penetrated beneath the icecap to between 40 and 50 miles. They found ice to a thickness of 50 ft. Lieutenant-Commander P. G. W. Herbert, commanding the Porpoise, described finding the iceholes. " The water was incredibly clear. We had the periscope pointing upwards at 75° and could see the holes. We could see the ripples on the surface of the water and blocks of ice floating." The Grampus rolled as she submerged and dented her alloy fin on the ice. Her commanding officer, Lieutenant-Commander P. R. Compton-Hall, said: " It is unlikely that you would do serious structural damage in the ice." Lieutenant D. Armstrong, of the Grampus, tried to combat boredom by growing radishes and mustard and cress. The radishes were not successful, but the mustard and cress provided two meals.

TELEVISION MICROSCOPE.—Closed-circuit television at Llanfrechfa Grange Hospital, Cwmbran, enables doctors to see on a television screen what a microscope lens picks up. The hospital, after experimenting with cameras for some months, succeeded in showing a chromosome count on a television screen. This may now have practical application, in teaching for example, in showing medical students what chromosomes look like. Normally a microscope is necessary for a chromosome count. Now, it has been found possible to put a television camera to a microscope and then to project what the microscope sees on to a large screen.

TIMBER IN ITS MODERN USES.—Professor H. M. Steven, in an address to the British Association, said that although steel, concrete, plastic and other substances were being used as substitutes for forest products, new uses for wood products were continually being found and consumption of timber products was steadily rising. Consumption of timber products was expanding, not only with rising population but, in some categories, on a *per capita* basis. This fact was particularly marked in the case of wood pulp, paper and board products. The world's pulp requirements were expanding at a rate of over 5 per cent. per annum. But it should be noted that the consumption per head of forest products in the undeveloped countries of Africa and Asia was very low, about one-tenth of that of Europe, and about one-thirtieth of the requirements of North America.

" With increasing literacy in such countries, there will be a spectacular increase in paper requirements ", he said. " In developed countries the spread of the supermarket and the sale of packaged goods are steadily increasing the demand for pulp products. In another category which is expanding rapidly are board products, fibre and particle, both for insulation and decorative use. The products of the forest are not always obviously of wood."

Professor Steven's conclusion was that substantial areas should be acquired by the state in a number of upland areas in Britain to investigate and demonstrate the best ways of increasing the productive capacity of such lands by steadily developing and enriching them, instead of impoverishing them. Forestry in Britain had suffered severely from large populations of animals that caused damage to trees, and he instanced rabbits and squirrels, brown and grey. This position had arisen partly because of the undue killing of their natural predators, sometimes almost to extinction, as in the case of the polecat and the pine marten, in the interest principally of the protection of game birds.

What the forester wanted in his woodlands was a balance between predator and prey, that balance to be maintained as far as possible by natural means, but where necessary by controlled killing. With a larger area of woodland there could be both a larger and a more varied fauna without causing loss to neighbours.

TOOTH DECAY IN CHILDREN.—The Minister of Health announced in Parliament that he will approve local health authority schemes to add fluoride to water supplies. The Secretary of State will be applying the same policy in Scotland. Where this was done the incidence of dental decay in young children should be reduced by about half, Mr. Powell said. The cost of the operation would be about 10d. a head a year in the areas supplied. Sixty or 70 local authorities had said they wished to introduce fluoridation. It was a fantastically cheap way of cutting down immense pain, ill-health of all kinds, and ruination of the mouths of children. Sixty-two per cent. of children had tooth decay at the age of three; at five years only 11 per cent. were free from decay. At the age of 12 only 3 per cent. had a full complement of sound teeth and at 15 only 2 per cent. were free from dental decay. A dramatic cut in dental pain and dental ill-health had followed the introduction of fluoride in the test areas.

TRANSISTOR THAT USES LIGHT.—A new type of transistor, in which signals are carried by light instead of by electric current, has been introduced by the International Business Machines Corporation in New York. The experimental " optical transistor " can be operated at high frequencies and is relatively easy to make.

The transistor, created by Mr. Richard F. Rutz, is made of gallium arsenide. Some of the energy of the incoming electric current is converted into light. After passing through the device the light is absorbed and frees electrons on the output side, which then pass into the external circuit as output current. The advantage of this is that light moves much faster than electricity through the " base " or middle portion of the device. In a conventional transistor the base has to be made extremely thin in order to shorten the time required for electric charges to move across it, and this adds to the difficulty of manufacture. In the optical transistor extremely thin base regions are not required.

TREES IN WIND TUNNEL TEST.—Wind tunnel experiments at Farnborough may help to reduce gale destruction in British forests. Mr. A. I. Fraser, a Forestry Commission research worker, said that small trees and a model forest had been tested in the tunnel at the Royal Aircraft Establishment. These experiments showed that the margins of the forest can play an important part in modifying the air flow over the crop. A heavily thinned windward margin, he said, could cut turbulence immediately behind the margin without affecting the forces on trees well inside the crop. He added, however, that thinning was a dangerous operation on poor ground because of the sudden exposure to which trees were subjected.

TRISTAN DA CUNHA: VOLCANIC EFFECTS.—Valuable additions to knowledge of the islands towards the southern end of the mid-Atlantic ridge have been provided by the geologists and biologists who were sent to study the effects of the new volcano on Tristan da Cunha. They reported to the Royal Society that the vegetation on Tristan suffered from the noxious fumes from the volcano. The islanders' crops of flax (used for thatch) had withered and some trees like eucalyptus and avocado appeared to be dead, but there were signs of fresh growth. The outflow of rocky lava which buried the crawfish canning station and extended into the sea is crumbling fast under the sea's action and in one place had retreated 20 feet during the seven weeks the expedition was there. The dogs ran wild and probably killed 707 out of a total of 740 sheep left behind, as well as many calves. Fifty geese had disappeared but the hens and chickens seemed to be thriving. Cats and rats decreased but the donkeys, numbering about 70 seemed unaffected. They invaded the potato patches and may incidentally have helped to control the population of aphids, previously kept down by DDT. Seals—elephant and fur-bearing—which had been decimated in the early days of the settlement have begun to return and breed.

TROPICAL BIRDSONG.—Tropical birds which sing to each other in turn, first one coming in and then the other, respond more quickly to sound than does a human being, and have also a more accurate sense of timing.

For one pair of birds whose duets were recorded, the shortest interval between the start of the first bird's note and the start of the reply note was an eighth of a second; and, when 20 yards or so apart, as they often are, the response must be even quicker. Once started on their duet, the second bird keeps closely to whatever interval of time has been established by its first reply. This interval was found in another species to be constant to within about three-thousandths of a second—about eight times as accurate in timing as that of which a human being would be capable. Singing of this kind is most common in species living in dense jungle scrub or undergrowth and is thought to take the place of visual display. Pairs of birds are thought to develop individual duet patterns, through which either bird can recognize the other at a distance.

TYPE SETTING BY COMPUTER.—The *Oklahoma City Times* published one of its regular editions with type set entirely by computer. The system of type setting employed is based on the 1620 computer, a machine that can punch teletype tape at the rate of 85 column-lines a minute, a line on the *Oklahoma Times* being 11 picas of nine-point type. The rate is fast enough to feed eight linotype machines continuously. " Unjustified " perforated tape, such as might be made by a reporter working on a special tape-producing typewriter, is fed into the computer, which cuts a perforated tape. The tape is run through the linotype machine, which sets the type automatically. The computer, in producing its tape, " justifies " the lines of type to the required column width.

UNDERSEA TUNNEL STARTED.—Japan's channel tunnel project to connect the main island of Honshú with the northern island of Hokkaido was formally launched. Two vertical shafts about 18 ft. in diameter and 400 to 600 ft. deep are to be dug at Fukushima and near Tappi Saki, on Honshú, to test the geological survey.

When completed, perhaps in seven years, the tunnel will be the longest in the world under the sea—some 22·6 miles, 14 of it under the seabed. It will be known as the Seikan Tunnel. The only other undersea tunnel is also in Japan; it is two miles long joining Honshú to the southern island of Kyúshú at Shimonoseki.

Though considerably more difficult to construct than a Straits of Dover tunnel, it would boost the development of Hokkaido, which with its mere five million of a total Japanese population of 93,000,000, is an underdeveloped territory. Transport between Honshú and Hokkaido at present uses ferries. A tunnel will increase traffic fourfold. Plans include a double track for electric trains, and cars will be carried on railway trucks.

The following comparisons were made by the assistant chief of the national railways bureau in charge of the project:—

In Tsugaru Straits the maximum depth was 143 metres; Straits of Dover about 50 metres. Sixty per cent. of Tsugaru Straits more than 100 metres deep, 80 per cent more than 50 metres deep. Tsugaru Straits two-thirds tuff and mudstone, one-third volcanic rock; Straits of Dover, chalk. The Seikan tunnel could be built at 70 to 100 metres below the seabed, compared with 30 to 40 metres for a Dover-Calais tunnel. The site of the tunnel had been chosen where there was not much danger of earthquakes.

WATER TURBINE DESIGN.—A promising new approach to the design of pumps and water turbines was discussed by Dr. I. S. Pearsall, of the National Engineering Laboratory, East Kilbride, at the British Association meeting. Unlike most new developments, this begins by accepting a loss in efficiency of some 20 to 25 per cent. in return for gains in other directions.

In water turbines the gain is a reduction in size and capital cost. This, Dr. Pearsall suggested, may be an important factor in the choice of equipment for tidal power stations and in hydro-electric schemes on rivers where the head of water available is small, notably in developing countries. The gain in pumps is ability to handle liquids which with conventional pumps are either difficult or impossible. Examples range from the chemical industry to the liquid hydrogen and oxygen used as rocket fuels.

The new approach is to design for an effect—the formation and collapse of bubbles of water vapour on the surface of fast-moving blades—which has been regarded hitherto as a nuisance. Known as cavitation, this has long been a problem for designers of ships' propellers. It leads not only to a loss of energy but also, in the ordinary way, to corrosion of the metal surface of the blades. Most of the damage is done when the bubbles collapse.

The new solution is to arrange matters so that only large bubbles are formed. When this is done the bubbles break away from the surface before they collapse, as could be seen vividly in a high-speed film shown by Dr. Pearsall.

The new machines are known as supercavitating pumps and turbines. They were described by Dr. Pearsall as a logical extension of research in the United States and the Soviet Union on the use of a supercavitating hydrofoil to support high-speed boats clear of the water. The same principle has since been applied in the design of propellers for very fast marine craft.

WELSH LEGEND EXPLODED.—The centuries-old Welsh legend that under the waters of Cardigan Bay lies a once fertile and flourishing farmland area has been dismissed after three weeks' research by geologists from Aberystwyth University College. Substance for the legend was found until now in the fact that just north of Aberystwyth a ridge extends from the beach seven miles out to sea. Geologists led by Professor Alan Wood have now replied that the legend is false. "The ridge is not the remains of an old road. It is a natural accumulation of pebbles", Professor Wood said. It is not yet known why such a long ridge of pebbles, over 30 ft. high in places, has remained undisturbed for centuries by the action of the sea, and the geologists are still investigating the area. "But it is definite from our observations so far that there is no truth in the legend", Professor Wood said.

WILD LIFE IN THE COLD SPELL.—The long cold spell in the early part of the year caused many casualties among wild life in the Alps. Chamois driven down by hunger and thirst were victims of poachers, foxes and even of farm dogs. Food was dropped by helicopters in their usual haunts. Roe deer were compelled to approach farms and mountain hamlets—they were helped in some districts by their traditional foes, the hunters, who put out bread and other food. Outlying farms were besieged by jackdaws perched on window sills and roofs, waiting for housewives to throw out kitchen waste. Buzzards were seen on the outskirts of Geneva preying on mice or chickens. Lake Geneva had a large temporary population of wild duck, grebes and sea gulls as well as the usual ducks and swans. Scores of birds trying to reach titbits thrown from the promenade were frozen into the ice, some being rescued by the river police who responded to calls even during the night.

WORLD'S SMALLEST TUBE.—A British company is once again able to boast that it manufactures the world's smallest tube. It has an outside diameter of 0·000515 in., which allows the company to claim that a bundle of 19 tubes would be about equivalent to the thickness of a human hair. The bore is about 0·00013 in. This is so small that the tube had to be photographed by an electron-microscope so that the company could prove there was a hole down the middle. About 1,250,000 m. of these tubes could be placed in an average wedding ring, and 3½ oz. of the pure nickel tubing would stretch the length of the M1 motorway. It may be of no use. Other record-breaking tubes have been used to inoculate flies for medical research and to inseminate queen bees. The firm would no doubt be pleased to receive suggestions in this case. The main purpose in producing the tube, however is said to be the development of tube-making techniques.

It was reported that the British company returned an American "smallest tube in the world" with a Black Country tube threaded inside it.

YOUNG DUCKLINGS' BEHAVIOUR.—One Whit-Sunday in the 1930's a group of tourists who looked over a garden fence in Austria were alarmed to see moving through the long grass in figures of eight a crouching man, constantly looking over his shoulder and quacking like a duck. The reason for his strange behaviour, which the tourists could not see, was a group of ducklings, following behind but hidden in the long grass. This was Dr. Konrad Lorenz carrying out one of his earliest experiments, which showed that newly hatched ducklings and goslings have an innate tendency to follow the first large moving object they see, but if they are hatched in an incubator by a man who will act the part of a mother duck or goose, then the young birds will follow him instead. If Dr. Lorenz stopped quacking, shrill wails of distress broke from the ducklings, who thought they had been deserted by mother. The discovery of this process of early fixation on a mother-substitute was Lorenz's great contribution to science. When he first put forward this theory it was believed to represent a unique type of learning behaviour, confined to a very short period and also irreversible, so that once a young bird had learned to follow its mother-substitute, it would never be able to learn to follow a mother of its own kind.

It is now known, that imprinting is not an irreversible once-for-all event. Mallard ducklings after following their own mother for a day and a half, can still be induced to follow a blue balloon instead.

THE NATIONAL PARKS

The ten National Parks described below in their order of designation have been established in England and Wales—the legislation noted on p. 408 does not apply to Scotland. These areas are not public property and visitors are not free to wander over private land within the Park boundaries. They have been marked out for special planning care aimed at two prime purposes: to preserve and enhance their natural beauty, and to promote their enjoyment by the public.

Peak District National Park (542 sq. miles).—Mainly in Derbyshire but extending into Staffordshire, Cheshire, the West Riding of Yorkshire and the City of Sheffield. In the south and east are limestone uplands, and finely wooded dales with swift, clear rivers and unspoilt stone villages. Northwards, moorlands, edged by gritstone crags, attract hill walkers and climbers. There are information centres at Edale and at Buxton (just outside the Park) and an information caravan tours the Park.

Lake District National Park (866 sq. miles).—In Cumberland, Lancashire and Westmorland. Spectacular mountain scenery with wooded lower slopes enhanced by lakes and tarns. The area includes England's highest mountains (Scafell Pike, Helvellyn and Skiddaw) and largest lakes. Walking and rock-climbing are the principal recreations, but there are fishing, swimming, sailing, boating and winter sports as well. There is an information room in the public library at Windermere.

Snowdonia National Park (845 sq. miles).—In Caernarvonshire and Merioneth and a small section of Denbighshire in North Wales. A wild mountainous region, traversed by high passes, offering some of the finest rock-climbing and mountain walking for both beginner and expert. The main valleys, often finely wooded, hold a lake (or llyn) and are watered by rivers with cascading falls. There are information centres at Dolgellau, Llanrwst and Tremadoc.

Dartmoor National Park (365 sq. miles).—In Devon, the highest area of high moorland in southern England, famous for its granite "tors" often weathered into fantastic shapes. Fine hanging oak woods adorn the river valleys which lead up into the Moor. The Park is rich in prehistoric relics and offers fine walking and riding.

Pembrokeshire Coast National Park (225 sq. miles).—A spectacular section of Britain's coastline, where rocky cliffs alternate with bays and sandy coves. In the north is Mynydd Presely, abounding in prehistoric relics. The Park includes the fine estuary of Milford Haven, Tenby, the Cathedral of St. David's, and Carew and other Norman castles.

North York Moors National Park (553 sq. miles).—In the North Riding of Yorkshire, the Park stretches from the Hambleton Hills in the west to the coastline above Scarborough. On the coast sheltered bays and sandy beaches alternate with headlands harbouring villages such as Staithes and Robin Hood's Bay. The heart of the Park offers tracts of open moorland, intersected by beautiful wooded valleys. Mount Grace Priory and the abbeys of Rievaulx and Byland are within the Park.

Yorkshire Dales National Park (680 sq. miles).—An area of upland moors, cut by deep valleys, in the North and West Ridings of Yorkshire, the Park includes some of the finest limestone scenery in Britain: Kilnsey Crag in Wharfedale, Gordale Scar, and Malham Cove in Malhamdale. In the Park also are Swaledale and Wensleydale, the three peaks of Ingleborough, Whernside and Pen-y-Ghent, and many relics of the past such as the Roman fort at Bainbridge and Bolton Abbey in Wharfedale.

Exmoor National Park (265 sq. miles).—Mainly in Somerset but extending into Devonshire, this is a moorland plateau surrounded by finely wooded combes. The well-known coastline between Minehead and Combe Martin Bay is exceptionally beautiful. In the east are the Brendon Hills. There is an information centre at Minehead.

Northumberland National Park (398 sq. miles).—A region of hills and moorland, stretching from Hadrian's Roman Wall in the south to the Cheviot Hills on the Scottish Border. The area is rich in historical interest. An information office covers the National Park.

Brecon Beacons National Park (515 sq. miles).—The most recent National Park, established in 1957, is centred on "The Beacons" with its three peaks: Corn Du, Cribyn and Pen-y-Fan, rising nearly to 3,000 feet. Bounded in the east by the Black Mountain in Monmouthshire, its western boundary rests on Carmarthenshire's Black Mountains above Abergavenny. The Usk valley, Llangorse Lake, Brecon Cathedral, Carreg Cennen Castle and Llanthony Abbey are all within the Park. There is an information centre at Brecon.

AREAS OF OUTSTANDING BEAUTY

Generally these are smaller in extent than the National Parks, no special arrangements for their administration being laid down, and there is no special provision for the development of facilities for open-air recreation. The areas so far designated are:—

Gower (73 sq. miles).—Partly in the County of Glamorgan and partly in Swansea, South Wales, the area is known for its beautiful coastline, its rocky limestone cliffs, sandy bays and coves and for its wooded ravines stretching inland.

Quantock Hills (38 sq. miles).—The main feature of this area in Somerset is the range of red sandstone hills rising to a height of 1,260 feet at Will's Neck above Crow Combe.

Lleyn (60 sq. miles).—An isolated peninsula in North Wales of unique character, still largely unspoilt by the hand of man.

Surrey Hills (160 sq. miles).—The Hog's Back and the ridge of the North Downs from Guildford to Titsey in the east are within this area, as are Leith Hill, Hindhead Common, the Devil's Punch Bowl; the well-known villages of Abinger, Shere, Hambledon and Chiddingfold; Box Hill and Frensham Ponds.

Dorset (400 sq. miles).—This is the largest area so far designated. It includes the whole of the coastline between Lyme Regis and Poole, with the Isle of Portland and Weymouth omitted, and stretches inland to include the Purbeck Hills and the downs, heaths and wooded valleys of the Hardy country.

Northumberland Coast (50 sq. miles).—Low cliffs and rocky headlands with active fishing villages comprise this area which stretches from just south of Berwick to Amble. It includes Holy Island, with the oldest monastic ruins in the country; the Farne Islands, and the great castles of Bamburgh, Dunstanburgh and Warkworth.

Cannock Chase (26 sq. miles).—This is an area of high heathland in Staffordshire, relieved by varied scenery in which parklands adjoin farms, woodlands and pleasant villages. Deer continue to roam over the Chase.

Shropshire Hills (300 sq. miles).—This area includes the fine landscape around Church Stretton, with Caer Caradoc, the Long Mynd, the Stiperstones, and the long ridge of Wenlock Edge from which it extends north-east to the Wrekin and the Ercall.

Malvern Hills (40 sq. miles).—The area embodies the whole range of the Malvern Hills in the counties of Gloucester, Hereford and Worcester. Such well-known features as the Worcestershire Beacon, North Hill, the Herefordshire Beacon, and Midsummer Hill, a National Trust property, are within the area.

Cornwall (360 sq. miles).—Comprising a number of separate areas including Bodmin Moor and some of the finest and best-known coastal scenery in Britain. Most of the Land's End peninsula; the coast between St. Michaels Mount and St. Austell with Falmouth omitted; the Fowey Estuary and Rame Head are all included: in north Cornwall most of the coast to Bedruthan Steps, north of Newquay, and between Perranporth and Godrevy Towans.

North Devon (66 sq. miles).—Comprising three sections of fine coastline—the whole of the Hartland peninsula; from Bideford Bar to the western limits of Ilfracombe, and from east of Ilfracombe to the boundary of the Exmoor National Park. Clovelly, Braunton Burrows, Woolacombe and Combe Martin are all included.

South Devon (128 sq. miles).—It includes the magnificent coast between Bolt Head and Bolt Tail, a National Trust property; Salcombe, Slapton Sands and Dartmouth, and the four estuaries and valleys of the Yealm, Erme, Avon and Dart.

East Hampshire (150 sq. miles).—The area stretches from the outskirts of Winchester to the Hampshire–Sussex border at a distance of about 10 miles inland from the south coast.

THE ROYAL SOCIETY

The Royal Society received a charter from Charles II. on April 22, 1662, when it was incorporated as a body politic and corporate under the appellation of The President, Council and Fellowship of the Royal Society of London, for improving Natural Knowledge.

Presidents of the Royal Society

Sir Robert Moray	1660
Viscount Brouncker	1662
Sir Joseph Williamson	1677
Sir Christopher Wren	1680
Sir John Hoskins, Bt.	1682
Sir Cyril Wyche	1683
Samuel Pepys	1684
Earl of Carbery	1686
Earl of Pembroke	1689
Sir Robert Southwell	1690
Earl of Halifax	1695
Lord Somers	1698
Sir Isaac Newton	1703
Sir Hans Sloane, Bt.	1727
Martin Folkes	1741
Earl of Macclesfield	1752
Earl of Morton	1764
Sir James Burrow	1768
James West	1768
Sir John Pringle, Bt.	1772
Sir Joseph Banks, Bt.	1778
William Hyde Wollaston	1820
Sir Humphrey Davy, Bt.	1820
Davies Gilbert	1827
The Duke of Sussex	1830
Marquess of Northampton	1838
Earl of Rosse	1848
Lord Wrottesley	1854
Sir Benjamin Brodie, Bt.	1858
Maj.-Gen. Sir Edward Sabine	1861
Sir George Biddell Airy	1871
Sir Joseph Dalton Hooker	1873
William Spottiswoode	1878
Thomas Henry Huxley	1883
Sir George Stokes, Bt.	1885
Lord Kelvin	1890
Lord Lister	1895
Sir William Huggins	1900
Lord Rayleigh	1905
Sir Archibald Geikie	1908
Sir William Crookes	1913
Sir Joseph John Thomson	1915
Sir Charles Scott Sherrington	1920
Lord Rutherford	1925
Sir Frederick Gowland Hopkins	1930
Sir William Henry Bragg	1935
Sir Henry Hallett Dale	1940
Sir Robert Robinson	1945
Lord Adrian	1950
Sir Cyril Hinshelwood	1955
Sir Howard Florey	1960

THE ENGLISH MILE COMPARED WITH OTHER EUROPEAN MEASURES

	English Mile	English Geog. M.	French Kilom.	German Geog. M.	Russian Verst	Austrn. Mile	Dutch Ure	Norweg. Mile	Swedish Mile	Danish Mile	Swiss Stunde
English Statute Mile	1·000	0·868	1·609	0·217	1·508	0·212	0·289	0·142	0·151	0·213	0·335
English Geog. Mile	1·153	1·000	1·855	0·250	1·738	0·245	0·333	0·164	0·169	0·246	0·386
Kilometre	0·621	0·540	1·000	0·135	0·937	0·132	0·180	0·088	0·094	0·133	0·208
German Geog. Mile	4·610	4·000	7·420	1·000	6·953	0·978	1·333	0·657	0·694	0·985	1·543
Russian Verst	0·663	0·575	1·067	0·144	1·000	0·141	0·192	0·094	0·100	0·142	0·222
Austrian Mile	4·714	4·089	7·586	1·022	7·112	1·000	1·363	0·672	0·710	1·006	1·578
Dutch Ure	3·458	3·000	5·565	0·750	5·215	0·734	1·000	0·493	0·520	0·738	1·157
Norwegian Mile	7·021	6·091	11·299	1·523	10·589	1·489	2·035	1·000	1·057	1·499	2·350
Swedish Mile	6·644	5·764	10·692	1·441	10·019	1·409	1·921	0·948	1·000	1·419	2·224
Danish Mile	4·682	4·062	7·536	1·016	7·078	0·994	1·354	0·667	0·705	1·000	1·567
Swiss Stunde	2·987	2·592	4·808	0·648	4·505	0·634	0·864	0·425	0·449	0·638	1·000

NUCLEAR TESTING, 1945–1963

The *New York Times*, in its issue of July 26, 1963, gave the following chronological list of nuclear explosions which have taken place since the first experimental atomic bomb was exploded in New Mexico in 1945. The United States and U.S.S.R. have carried out nuclear tests of which no announcement was made, but before the signing by the United Kingdom, U.S.A. and U.S.S.R. on Aug. 25, 1963, of a treaty which partially bans nuclear testing, 414 nuclear tests had been announced: by U.S.A. 259; United Kingdom, 21; U.S.S.R., 126; and by France, 6.

1945

July 16—First atomic explosion (experimental bomb) at Alamogordo, New Mexico.

Aug. 6—Hiroshima destroyed.

Aug. 9—Nagasaki destroyed.

1946

July 1—United States tests atomic device at Bikini.

July 25—United States tests atomic device underwater.

1948

April—United States tests three nuclear devices at Eniwetok.

1949

Sept. 23—Soviet Union tests its first atomic bomb.

1951

Jan. 27–Feb. 7—United States conducts five tests.

April–May—United States conducts four atomic tests, one underground.

October—Soviet Union tests two atomic devices.

Oct 22–Nov. 29—United States conducts seven tests.

1952

April 1–June 5—United States conducts eight tests.

Oct. 3—Britain tests her first nuclear device near the Montebello Islands.

Oct. 31—United States tests an atomic device at Eniwetok.

Nov. 1—United States tests first thermo-nuclear (hydrogen) weapon at Eniwetok.

1953

March 17–June 4—United States tests 11 atomic devices.

Aug. 12—Soviet Union tests its first hydrogen bomb.

Aug. 23—Soviet test of an "atomic device."

October—Britain tests two atomic devices.

1954

March 1–May 14—United States tests six nuclear devices.

October—Soviet Union tests a nuclear weapon.

1955

February–May—United States conducts 15 tests, including one underwater and one underground.

August-November—Soviet Union tests four devices and weapons.

1956

March–April—Tests by Soviet Union.

May–July—Thirteen tests by United States.

May 15–June 19—Britain tests two weapons.

August–November—series of Soviet tests resumed, total of seven for year.

September–October—Britain carries out four tests.

1957

Jan. 19–April 16—Soviet conducts a series of weapons tests.

May 17—Britain tests her first hydrogen bomb at Christmas Island.

May–October—Twenty-four tests by United States in Nevada, including one underground.

August–December—Soviet Union concludes series of 13 tests for year.

September–October—Britain tests three devices.

Nov. 8—Britain explodes hydrogen device, bringing total of tests for year to seven.

1958

February–March—Ten Soviet test shots.

April–July—United States tests 29 devices, including four underground.

April 28—Britain tests atomic device.

August—United States tests two nuclear missile warheads.

August–September—Britain tests four devices.

August–September—Two high-altitude devices tested by United States.

September–October—United States tests 19 devices, including three underwater.

November—Series of 15 Soviet tests.

1960

Feb. 13—France explodes her first atomic bomb in the Sahara.

April 1—France explodes second nuclear device.

Dec. 27—France sets off third nuclear device.

1961

April 25—France sets off fourth nuclear device.

September—Soviet Union resumes testing with 31 shots, including the largest explosion in history and one underwater.

United States conducts eight undergound tests.

1962

April—United States begins series of tests in Pacific. Final American test in atmosphere takes place on Nov. 4. Total of 86 devices tested in year.

August—Soviet Union starts series of 40 tests. Shot of Dec. 24 is last known Soviet test in atmosphere.

One test conducted by France. Two underground tests conducted in Nevada by United States and Britain.

1963

June 30—United States repor s "inconclusive evidence" of Soviet test.

United States conducts 10 underground tests.

France conducts an underground test.

ROMAN NUMERALS

1	I	11	XI	30	XXX	400	CD
2	II	12	XII	40	XL	500	D
3	III	13	XIII	50	L	600	DC
4	IV	14	XIV	60	LX	700	DCC
5	V	15	XV	70	LXX	800	DCCC
6	VI	16	XVI	80	LXXX	900	CM
7	VII	17	XVII	90	XC	1000	M
8	VIII	18	XVIII	100	C	1500	MD
9	IX	19	XIX	200	CC	1900	MCM
10	X	20	XX	300	CCC	2000	MM

Other Examples: 43=XLIII; 66=LXVI; 98=XCVIII.
339=CCCXXXIX; 619=DCXIX; 988=CMLXXXVIII; 996=CMXCVI.
1674=MDCLXXIV; 1962=MCMLXII.

A bar placed over a numeral has the effect of multiplying the number by 1,000, *e.g.*:
6,000=$\overline{\text{VI}}$; 16,000=$\overline{\text{XVI}}$; 160,000=$\overline{\text{CLX}}$; 666,000=$\overline{\text{DCLXVI}}$.

WEATHER IN THE UNITED KINGDOM, 1962–1963

(1962) *August.*—Temperatures had been below average each month over the country generally since the very cold March and the weather of August continued cool, mainly cyclonic. The month began with local thunderstorms moving east across southern England. Sunshine was widespread in the south on the 2nd, but a deep depression to the north of Scotland brought rain to many districts on the 3rd. The next two days were generally sunny, especially in the south, but there was widespread rain on the 6th. Bank Holiday Monday was the coldest at Kew (Surrey) and the wettest at Birmingham, since about 1888. Rain continued in the north-east on the 7th, but there were only scattered showers on the 8th. The 9th and 11th were generally wet and stormy, with mainly south-west winds, giving flooding in the English Lake District and southern Scotland on the 11th, as much as 5 in. of rain falling at Langdale in 24 hours. Winds reached gale force over much of the country on the 11th, but became light and variable on the 12th and 13th, with sunshine in the north. Thundery rain occurred in southern England on the 14th, spreading to other parts of the country on the 15th. Temperature fell to 29° F. in the northern Pennines on the 14th. For the remainder of the month winds were mainly from the west. Temperature reached 77° F. at Gillingham (Kent) on the 19th. Thundery showers occurred on the 21st to 22nd and widespread rains, with gale force winds, on the 23rd and 26th, bringing flooding again to parts of Scotland and the Lake District on the 23rd. There were widespread sunny periods on the 24th and 25th and after the 27th. The total rainfall failed to reach the average in parts of the east, but exceeded twice the local average around the Cotswolds. Sunshine totals were below average over most of England, Wales and south-west Scotland.

September.—The weather was generally cool, wet and cyclonic, but the fine weather at the end of August continued on the 1st. Rain spread over much of the country, except the south-east, on the 2nd and 3rd. At Writtle (Essex) temperature reached 82° F. on the 3rd. Local thunderstorms interrupted sunny periods on the 4th and 6th, but the 5th, 7th and 8th were generally fine and sunny. A deep depression moving north-east across Scotland brought more than 2 in. of rain to parts of Scotland and the English Lake District on the 9th, heavy rain to southern England on the 10th and widespread rain on the 11th, especially in Wales, where locally 3 in. fell in 24 hours. After northerly winds on the 12th, the 13th was generally dry and sunny and the 14th fine in the south. A belt of rain moved across the country on the 15th. The 16th and 17th were cool and sunny. For a week dull dry weather prevailed in the south, but widespread ground frost occurred between the 17th and 22nd, temperature falling to 29° F. locally in Norfolk on the 18th. Rain spread to much of Scotland and Northern Ireland on the 22nd and to the remainder of the country by the 25th or 26th. Rain again occurred in most districts on the 27th, 28th and 29th, with widespread gales on the 29th and 30th, gusts reaching 89 m.p.h. at Stornoway on the 30th. The total rainfall exceeded the average over most of the country, with more than twice the average in places, *e.g.* parts of West Sussex, Oxfordshire and south Scotland. Mean temperature was below average over the country generally for the seventh consecutive month. Sunshine totals exceeded the average at a few places in southern England, *e.g.* Bournemouth, but at Edinburgh it was the dullest September since that of 1896.

October—The weather during the first two days was generally showery, with strong south-westerly winds in the west and north on the 1st. Afternoon temperature reached 73° F. at Gillingham (Kent) on the 2nd. From the 3rd to 24th quiet, dry, anticyclonic weather prevailed. The 6th to 9th was mainly fine and warm after the clearance of early morning fog, temperatures reaching 70° F. at Thorney Island (Hampshire) and Kinloss (Morayshire). A second anticyclone, which intensified off the north of Scotland on the 10th moved to southern England. From the 10th to 14th light winds from the North Sea brought mainly dry but cloudy weather to the east, with sunny periods in the south and west. During the 15th to 20th, with the anticyclone centred over southern England, widespread fog developed at night, which was slow to clear locally. The anticyclone moved to the southern North Sea on the 21st, and then south-eastwards to the continent. The 21st to 23rd was generally mild and dry, but some rain spread into north-west Scotland. With the approach of a depression from the Atlantic on the 24th widespread and persistent rains occurred on the 24th and 25th, with more than 1 in. in south-east England on the 25th. During the night, 26th–27th, there was widespread air-frost. Gale force winds occurred next day in north-western districts, with hail and sleet, and heavy rain in southern and eastern areas. The 29th was generally wet and temperature fell to 22° F. at Lincoln. Gales were widespread on the 30th with scattered thunderstorms and hail. The total rainfall was less than one-quarter of average near Exeter and Birmingham, and also in Monmouthshire and north-east England. Mean temperature was above the October average. At Worthing it was the sunniest October, apart from that of 1959, for 40 years.

November—The first ten days of the month were mild, the highest recorded temperature being 61° F. in Warwickshire on the 5th. Heavy rain occurred during the evening of the 1st, especially in south-east England. Thunderstorms, with hail occurred on the 2nd and persisted with decreasing frequency until the 4th. The hailstones on the 2nd were unusually large, reaching 2 in. in diameter in Cornwall. Temperatures reached 57° F. near the Isle of Wight on the 8th and 9th. With easterly winds, temperature fell abruptly and after early morning frosts on the 12th and 13th good sunshine amounts were recorded. Widespread rain occurred on the 14th. With northerly winds on the 15th, weather became brighter with snow showers in the north. As a depression moved from western Scotland across the country to northern France on the 16th and 17th stormy weather prevailed with widespread snow. Level snow reached a depth of 7 in. in parts of Scotland with drifts up to 3 ft. and many roads became blocked. For a further two days cold northerly winds persisted with widespread early morning frost. A depression moving south-east across England on the 20th gave rain in the south-west and snow in the south-east. The next two days were quiet and dull, temperature falling to 5° F. in Peeblesshire on the 21st. There was a marked rise of temperature on the 22nd–23rd with mild south-westerly winds accompanied by heavy rain. Fog became widespread on the 25th and 26th persisting all day in some areas. The remainder of the month was quiet and dull, with frequent fogs in parts of England and Wales. The total rainfall was less than half the average in parts of Wales and the Pennines, but exceeded the average in the north-east and south of England. Sunshine was generally below average, especially in the south and east, Worthing recording the dullest November since 1899.

December—Light winds, mainly from the south to south-east, predominated from the 1st to 6th with dry but foggy weather. Fog was widespread at night in central and southern England on the 1st and 2nd, and later persisted day and night over much of the country, with temperatures around freezing. The fog cleared during the night of 5th to 6th, except in the Thames Valley. Fog in the London areas from the 4th to 6th was the worst there since that of December 1952. Winds were mainly from the north-west until the 22nd, stormy weather with heavy rains alternating with fair spells. Moderate falls of snow occurred in parts of Scotland and eastern England on the 12th, being 2 in. deep in parts of Durham and Norfolk. The 15th was very wet and stormy, especially over Scotland and Northern Ireland, with gusts of 117 m.p.h. on Lowther Hill, Lanarkshire, and 90 m.p.h. at Liverpool. The 17th and 20th were dull and wet. By the 23rd a very cold easterly airstream from central Russia spread to most districts. The 23rd and 24th were sunny and cold in England and Wales, but a belt of rain in the north of Scotland on the 24th turned to snow as it moved south. On Christmas day snow lay 3 in. deep in the Glasgow area, giving the first white Christmas there since 1938. The belt of snow reached southern England on the 26th and becoming slow moving gave continuous snow for 24 hours in places. In London the Christmas period, 24th–26th, was the coldest since 1897. On the 27th much of southern England had snow to a depth of a foot, with 2 in. even in the Channel Islands. On the 29th a blizzard swept across south-west England and the Channel coast, with heavy snowfall and much drifting. Many villages in the south-west were isolated for some days, snowdrifts reaching 15–20 ft. deep in places. A thaw, with rain, reached the south-west on the 31st, but elsewhere it continued very cold with snow showers in the north.

Year 1962—The year began and ended with bitterly cold weather and widespread snow cover. Mean temperature was below the 1921–50 average in each month after February, apart from October. Over England and Wales it was the coldest year since 1919, over Scotland 1952 was colder. With easterly winds predominating during March it was the coldest March this century over much of the country. The spring over England and Wales was the coldest this century, although over Scotland the spring of 1951 was colder. Temperatures reached 80° F. locally on only a few occasions, *e.g.* June 8 and 9, July 25 and September 3. Annual rainfall amounts were more normal. Most of the country received rather less than the average, with more than 110 per cent. of the local average in parts of Scotland and less than 70 per cent. in the Vale of York. In the south-west of England the spring and early summer were unusually dry, the six months, February to July, giving less than one-quarter of the average annual amounts from east Devon to south Gloucestershire and Hampshire. Sunshine totals were generally about or somewhat above average. January, August and September were generally sunny, and March, June, July, October and November less sunny than usual. April was exceptionally sunny in parts of Scotland. Winds from the north and east were more frequent than usual. Gales were frequent and severe. Considerable damage was caused in the east of the Pennines, *e.g.* at Sheffield, during the gale of February 16, while severe gales and high seas damaged sea walls in the south-west of England and Wales on March 7. The fog in the London area from December 4 to 6 was the worst since the "Great Smog" of December 1952.

(1963) *January*—The very cold weather, with winds from the east, which set in on December 23 continued during most of the month. Mean temperature was below 32° F. nearly everywhere, apart from the extreme south-west and north-west, giving for England and Wales the coldest January since 1814 and the coldest month this century, being rather colder than February 1947. Scattered snow showers on the 1st and 2nd were followed by heavy snowfalls and drifting in the south and south-west on the 3rd, which again blocked road and rail traffic. Further slight falls of snow occurred in the south on the 5th and 6th. From the 7th to 13th weather remained generally dry, with day temperatures around freezing point and very severe frost at night, temperatures falling to 3° F. at places in the east. Over the Midlands, northern England and Clyde-Forth Valley freezing fog was widespread during the nights 11th to 14th. There was a slow day-time thaw in most districts on the 14th. Cold easterly winds returned on the 16th and from the 16th to 25th frost was continuous day and night in most places. Fog, dense at night, with spectacular rime deposits, persisted over parts of the Midlands and London area from the 23rd to 25th. The sea froze at several places, including near Herne Bay, and the Thames was frozen over in places and there were ice-floes near Tower Bridge. Temperature fell to −5° F. at Stansted (Essex) on the 23rd and to −8° F. at Braemar (Aberdeenshire) on the 18th. The night 26th–27th was the first frost-free night for three weeks over most of the Midlands and eastern England, afternoon temperatures on the 27th and 28th exceeding 40° F. in places. In spite of occasional heavy falls of snow the total precipitation was below average in most places, giving the driest January over England and Wales since 1881. Sunshine totals were appreciably above average, especially in the west, Stornoway recording its sunniest January since 1881.

February—Bitterly cold weather predominated, with almost continuous frost, often severe at night. Although over England and Wales February 1963 was not as cold as that of 1947, the winter as a whole ranked as one of the coldest since 1740, certainly in central England. On the 1st and 2nd there were frequent snow showers over most of the country, with more continuous snow on the 4th and 5th. The blizzard in the south-west on the 5th and 6th was the worst of the month, Exmoor experiencing 36 hours of continuous snow and Princetown reporting snow to a depth of 22 in. Tredegar (Monmouthshire) had an accumulated snow depth of 65 in. by the 7th and 8th, but on the 8th there was a temporary thaw in the south-west with some flooding, while widespread fog persisted all day in many places. Heavy rain occurred in Cornwall on the 9th with sleet and snow in southern England on the 10th. The 13th was generally sunny, especially in the west, but stormy weather reached south-west England late on the 13th and as it spread north-east on the 14th heavy falls of snow occurred on the Pennines and in Scotland. Cold easterly winds became re-established on the 16th, with snow in the north-west of England and south of Scotland on the 17th and in southern England on the 19th and 20th. The last week of the month was mainly fine, sunny and cold in the east, but temperatures rose to more normal values on the last day. Temperature fell to −1° F. in northern England on the 25th and 26th. Precipitation in Scotland was mainly in the form of snow, with more than the average in the east, but only 25 per cent. in the west. Some north-west and central districts of England and Wales also recorded only 25 per cent. Sunshine totals exceeded the local average over most of Scotland and north-west England.

March—The first three days were sunny with easterly winds, afternoon temperatures about normal and severe frosts at night. Snow was 2–3 in. deep in parts of the south of England until the 2nd and snow cover remained in many northern districts until the 5th. Temperatures fell to 4° F. at Braemar, Aberdeenshire, on the 2nd and 5° F. at Kielder, Northumberland, on the 1st, 3rd and 4th. A mild south-westerly air-stream brought occasional rain to many districts on the 4th and prolonged rains and gales in the west and north on the 5th. The 6th gave the first morning of the year with no reports of frost and afternoon temperatures rose to 62° F. in the London area, the warmest day there since October 25. Gales and heavy rains were widespread in southern England on the 9th and the 11th was again wet in the south. On the 12th snow showers occurred in East Anglia and good sunny periods in the south and west. The 13th was mild and wet, especially in the south-west, while the next two or three days were generally mild with afternoon temperatures reaching 60° F. in the south-east. Heavy rains occurred in the south-west on the 17th and sunny periods in the south on the 18th. By the 20th a cold easterly air-stream became established over the country, with sea-fog over much of the north-east coast. The cold spell was short, milder air from the south-west spreading over the country on the 24th. The weather of the remainder of the month was changeable and wet with average temperatures. Mean temperature for the month was slightly above the 1931–60 average over the country as a whole. There was more than three times the average March rainfall locally in western Scotland and more than twice the average over much of Scotland and the north and west of England. Sunshine was above average in Northern Ireland, but below average over England and Wales.

April—The weather was mainly cyclonic and typically showery. The first two days were mild with showers, while the 3rd brought scattered thunderstorms to eastern districts but long sunny periods to the west. Wintry showers of snow and hail were widespread on the 4th and 5th, giving snow cover in parts of southern England on the 5th. During the night, 5th–6th, rain spread from France over most of England. This was followed by dry easterly winds and fine sunny weather prevailed from the 6th to 8th. Temperature fell to 22° F. on Great Dun Fell (Westmorland) on the 8th. The next three days were dull and wet, rain being heavy in southern England on the 9th and in the Midlands on the 10th and 11th. Good Friday (12th) was sunny in the south but wintry showers persisted in the north. Easter Saturday was sunny in southern England but Easter Sunday was generally wet. Dull weather continued in southern England on Bank Holiday (15th), although it was sunny in Scotland. The 16th and 17th were dull with occasional rain and while the 18th and 19th were generally fine, thunderstorms developed locally. Another depression brought widespread rain and gales to most western districts on the 20th and 21st. As the depression moved away there was a good deal of sunshine in southern England on the 22nd and fine sunny weather predominated until the 26th. Temperature rose steadily, although patches of sea fog affected some coastal areas from the 25th to 29th. Temperatures reached 67° F. in Aberdeenshire on the 26th and 70° F. at Mickleham, Surrey, on the 27th. The 28th was mild and dull, but heavy rain spread to south-east England by the 29th. The 30th started sunny in the south but later rain spread across Scotland to most areas. The total rainfall exceeded twice the average along the Sussex and Hampshire coasts, Worthing experiencing the wettest April since 1923.

May—The first two weeks were mainly cyclonic, with changeable weather, but the last week was fine and sunny. During the 1st rain spread southwards across England. The next two days were cool, but sunny with local showers. From the 4th to 7th winds from the south-west prevailed, giving rain in the north and west, but dry weather in the south and east. Air frost occurred in south-east England and the Midlands on the 4th, and scattered snow or sleet showers over high ground in the Midlands on the 5th. Temperature fell to 25° F. near Norwich on the 4th. A gust of 90 m.p.h. was recorded at Edinburgh on the 7th. From the 8th to 14th spells of rain alternated with fairer periods, associated with the passage of a series of depressions. Rain was widespread on the 8th, 10th, 12th and 14th. The 15th to 17th were fine and sunny in the south, with occasional rain in the north; the 18th and 19th were showery with local hail and thunder; the 20th brought widespread rain; on the 21st cool northerly winds spread across the country. With a ridge of high pressure many places had 14 hours of sunshine both on the 22nd and 23rd, but heavy rain occurred in south-east England on the 23rd and in northern districts on the 24th. The remainder of the month was generally sunny, commencing the best spell of weather so far experienced during the year, although the 28th and 29th were cool in the south-east with outbreaks of thundery rain. On the 25th temperature exceeded 68° F. in many places and on the 31st temperature rose to 80° F. in south-east England and 76° F. at Prestwick (Ayrshire). The 29th was especially sunny in Scotland and Northern Ireland, while for many places the 31st was the warmest day since the summer of 1961. The total rainfall exceeded twice the average in parts of Invernessshire.

June—The warm weather at the end of May continued until the 12th, but the remainder of June was generally cool and changeable. Temperatures exceeded 80° F. on the 1st in parts of southern England and locally in northern Scotland, but the 2nd (Whit Sunday) was less warm as easterly winds spread across the country. Manchester experienced the sunniest Whitsun this century. Mainly warm sunny days persisted in western and central districts until the 11th, when, with the decline of easterly winds, warmer weather extended to eastern districts as well. The weather was mainly dry, apart from local thunderstorms *e.g.*, at Bristol on the 6th and at Kensington Palace on the 7th, where 2¼ in. fell in 35 mins., giving rise to flooding. On the 12th low cloud and sea fog persisted in many southern districts with rain in Northern Ireland, while on the 13th heavy rain occurred in southern England. Afternoon temperatures on the 14th were frequently some 14° F. lower than on the previous day. While the 14th was dry, rain spread to most districts on the 15th and subsequently a series of depressions brought changeable, cool weather until the 25th. Rain was heavy in places on the 17th and gusts exceeded 57 m.p.h. on the 18th in north-west England and also in the Channel Islands. Heavy rain also occurred in many places on the 25th. For the remainder of the month winds were mainly from the north-east with general rain on the 28th to 29th. For the month as a whole temperature was slightly above average, sunshine exceeded the average in the west and north-west of Scotland, where some places had less than half the average rainfall. Most places had more than average rainfall, and there was twice the average in parts of the south and east of England.

July—With winds from the south and south-east during the first five days frequent showers occurred, accompanied by thunderstorms. An inch or more of rain fell on the 2nd in Norfolk, on the 3rd and 4th in Cornwall, while on the 5th flooding occurred in Kilmarnock. The 6th was generally wet, with more than 1 in. over wide areas. From the 6th to 10th winds were mainly from the north to north-west with cool weather, occasional showers and good sunny periods. Temperature over grass fell to 28°F. at Benbecula, in the Outer Hebrides, on the 11th. Clear night skies on the 11th, 12th and 13th resulted in slight ground frost in parts of Scotland and the formation of early morning fog over south-east England on the 13th. From the 14th to 19th winds were mainly from the south-west, with widespread rain on the 15th, dull wet weather on the 17th and 19th, and sunny periods on the 16th and 18th. The weather improved by the 20th as an anticyclone developed over the British Isles, warm sunny weather prevailing until the 23rd, when a disturbance brought widespread rain. On the 22nd 84°F. was recorded at Littlehampton. The warm sunny weather returned on the 25th, as another anticyclone moved towards southern Ireland. The 26th to 31st were dry everywhere and daily totals of sunshine reached 15 hrs. in parts of northern England and Scotland. Temperature rose steadily, exceeding 80°F. on the afternoon of the 30th both in south-east England and eastern Scotland and reaching 84°F. at Wisley, Surrey, and Gordon Castle, Morayshire. Mean temperature for the month was nearly 2°F. below average, sunshine totals were generally slightly above average, while in most areas rainfall was appreciably less than average. Snow and sleet showers fell over high ground in Scotland on the 9th, 10th and 25th.

General Values, 1960–63 (June)

Month	Rainfall (inches)				Temperature at Sea-Level (° F.)				Bright Sunshine (Hrs. per day)			
	1960	1961	1962	1963	1960	1961	1962	1963	1960	1961	1962	1963
England and Wales												
Jan.	5.2	4.7	4.2	1.3	40.5	39.9	41.2	30.2	1.2	1.4	2.0	2.0
Feb.	3.2	2.8	1.4	1.4	40.3	45.5	41.2	32.0	2.7	2.3	2.6	2.6
March	2.0	0.6	1.8	3.9	44.1	47.7	37.9	43.9	2.2	4.8	4.0	3.4
April	1.8	3.9	2.8	3.1	48.8	50.4	46.4	47.7	5.3	3.3	5.2	4.0
May	1.8	1.6	2.7	2.1	55.5	52.5	51.1	51.6	5.9	6.8	5.4	6.2
June	2.0	1.5	0.7	3.4	60.9	59.0	57.0	58.8	8.6	7.3	8.0	6.2
July	4.5	2.7	2.5	—	59.7	59.9	58.8	—	4.9	5.4	4.3	—
Aug.	4.5	3.3	4.4	—	59.9	60.8	59.0	—	5.2	5.6	5.0	—
Sept.	4.5	3.2	4.1	—	56.7	60.1	55.8	—	4.1	4.3	3.9	—
Oct.	7.2	4.7	1.5	—	51.7	52.7	52.3	—	2.2	3.7	3.5	—
Nov.	6.0	2.5	2.9	—	46.3	44.6	43.2	—	2.1	2.1	1.4	—
Dec.	4.5	4.1	2.9	—	40.7	38.1	37.4	—	1.6	1.8	2.1	—
YEAR	47.2	35.6	31.9	—	50.4	50.9	48.6	—	3.8	4.1	4.2	—
Scotland												
Jan.	4.9	4.8	8.1	1.9	38.6	38.1	39.4	33.3	1.4	1.4	1.4	1.7
Feb.	4.7	4.9	4.4	1.5	37.4	42.8	40.3	34.3	3.2	2.2	2.4	3.1
March	2.1	3.1	2.4	5.5	42.3	46.2	36.9	42.3	2.6	2.9	3.5	3.2
April	3.9	3.8	3.0	3.2	47.7	46.6	44.2	45.5	4.4	3.8	6.5	4.4
May	2.2	2.2	3.2	4.4	53.1	50.2	49.1	48.7	6.1	6.0	5.5	6.0
June	3.0	2.7	3.0	3.8	57.9	54.7	54.7	56.1	6.7	4.9	5.7	5.2
July	4.1	4.6	3.1	—	57.4	56.5	55.6	—	4.5	3.4	4.4	—
Aug.	5.9	5.9	7.1	—	56.9	56.7	55.2	—	4.6	4.5	4.8	—
Sept.	3.5	5.7	6.1	—	53.5	55.8	52.5	—	4.3	3.5	2.5	—
Oct.	4.9	7.2	2.8	—	49.5	49.8	50.4	—	1.6	2.7	2.5	—
Nov.	5.9	4.3	4.0	—	43.0	41.7	41.5	—	1.7	1.8	1.3	—
Dec.	5.6	4.8	6.0	—	38.5	35.8	40.5	—	1.3	1.1	1.1	—
YEAR	50.7	54.0	53.2	—	48.1	47.8	46.4	—	3.5	3.3	3.5	

TEMPERATURE AND RAINFALL RECORDS

GENERAL: The *maximum shade temperature* of the air on record is 136° F. at Azizia (Uzzizia) in Tripoli on Sept. 13, 1922; the *extreme lowest recorded temperature* is in Antarctica *e.g.*—125° F. at Vostok on Aug. 25, 1958. In the upper air temperatures as low as −143° F. have been recorded —*e.g.* over Halley Bay on Aug. 9, 1959 at about 27 kms.

The *wettest place* in the world is considered to be the neighbourhood of Cherrapunji in Assam where annual averages exceeding 400 inches have been obtained, of which 90 per cent. usually falls in the six months April to September, and annual totals have reached 670 inches.

U.K.: The *maximum shade temperature* recorded in the air at 4 feet above the ground is 100° F. at Greenwich Observatory (Aug. 9, 1911).

The *lowest shade temperatures* are −17° F. at Braemar (Feb. 11, 1895) and −16° F. at Kelso (Dec. 3, 1879).

The *greatest rainfall* recorded in a day was at Martinstown, near Dorchester, 11.00 inches in the 24 hours commencing 9 a.m. (July 18, 1955). *Annual totals* exceeding 240 inches were recorded at The Stye, Borrowdale, in 1872, 1923, 1928 and 1954; at Ben Nevis Observatory in 1898 and at Llyn Llydaw, Snowdon, in 1909. The *smallest annual total* is 9.29 inches at Margate in 1921 and the *largest* may be regarded as 257 inches at Sprinkling Tarn in 1954.

TEMPERATURE, RAINFALL AND SUNSHINE AT VARIOUS PLACES IN GREAT BRITAIN

Mean Temperature of the air (° C.), Rainfall (inches) and Bright Sunshine (as mean hours per day) at representative British Health Resorts and Towns during the year July, 1962, to June 1963, and the calendar year 1962. Also height of Climatological Station above mean sea level, altitude being given in feet. Fuller details of the weather are given in the *Monthly Weather Report* published by the Meteorological Office. (To convert °C. to °F. multiply by 9/5 and add 32).

	Altitude	1962											
		July			August			September			October		
		Temp.	Rain	Sun	Temp.	Rain	Sun	Temp.	Rain	Sun	Temp.	Rain	Sun
	ft.	°C.	in.	hrs.	°C.	in.	hrs.	°C.	in.	hrs.	°C.	in.	hrs.
Aberystwyth	12	—	2·0	5·2	—	4·7	4·7	—	4·4	3·6	—	2·0	4·3
Aldergrove	217	13·3	1·7	3·6	13·3	3·5	4·9	11·7	5·7	2·3	10·3	1·4	2·9
Ambleside	151	14·1	2·5	3·5	13·4	11·9	3·2	11·9	8·6	2·0	9·5	5·5	2·7
Balmoral	927	11·1	2·4	—	10·9	3·8	—	9·4	4·9	—	8·3	1·2	—
Bath	67	16·1	1·3	5·1	15·4	5·1	5·2	13·3	4·3	4·4	10·7	0·9	3·0
Birmingham	536	14·7	2·0	3·9	14·3	4·9	4·6	12·7	4·0	3·5	10·8	0·7	3·6
Bournemouth	130	15·3	1·4	5·7	15·1	3·4	5·9	13·3	3·6	5·9	11·2	1·5	4·5
Buxton	1007	12·7	2·6	—	12·4	6·9	—	11·3	5·2	—	8·5	2·9	—
Cambridge	41	15·2	2·5	4·1	15·3	1·9	5·9	13·1	3·4	4·3	10·7	1·1	3·4
Cardiff	202	15·4	2·0	5·1	14·9	5·1	5·6	13·4	3·6	4·2	10·9	1·1	4·2
Cromer	178	13·9	4·0	5·6	14·2	3·0	6·4	13·0	4·1	4·7	11·1	1·2	4·1
Douglas	284	13·5	2·0	5·3	13·3	5·6	5·5	12·1	4·0	3·3	10·8	2·6	3·4
Dovercourt	11	15·2	3·2	5·0	15·7	1·2	6·4	12·9	2·3	4·0	11·5	1·1	4·1
Dumfries	140	13·3	2·9	4·3	13·1	6·5	4·5	11·3	6·6	2·7	9·6	2·1	3·8
Dundee	147	13·5	3·3	4·8	13·5	5·5	5·0	11·9	4·7	1·9	10·3	0·6	2·4
Durham	336	13·2	2·3	3·7	13·3	2·5	5·5	11·8	2·8	3·1	9·9	0·5	3·2
Eastbourne	23	15·5	2·1	6·4	15·6	4·2	7·2	14·3	2·5	6·1	12·1	2·0	5·1
Edinburgh	441	13·0	3·8	5·0	13·3	3·5	5·4	11·5	4·2	2·1	10·3	0·9	3·3
Falmouth	167	15·1	3·5	5·5	14·8	3·0	5·0	13·5	3·9	4·8	12·0	1·3	4·4
Glasgow	351	13·3	3·0	4·8	12·9	5·9	4·0	11·1	7·5	2·1	9·9	2·2	2·3
Hastings	149	15·3	1·6	5·7	15·7	4·3	7·0	14·1	2·3	5·6	12·5	1·9	4·8
Huddersfield	325	14·5	2·1	3·6	14·3	4·1	4·6	12·5	2·6	2·9	10·4	1·3	2·9
Hull	8	14·5	1·4	3·9	15·1	4·1	4·8	13·1	2·3	3·5	11·1	0·5	3·2
Ilfracombe	25	15·7	2·7	6·1	15·5	3·7	5·2	14·3	3·5	4·7	—	1·6	—
Inverness	13	13·1	1·8	4·8	12·9	3·6	4·6	11·6	1·6	2·2	10·5	0·8	2·5
Lincoln	22	14·2	1·1	3·6	14·3	3·8	4·7	12·5	3·7	4·0	9·7	0·7	3·1
Liverpool	198	14·7	1·1	5·1	14·3	2·6	5·2	12·7	2·3	3·3	10·9	1·6	2·6
Llandrindod Wells	772	14·0	2·4	3·7	13·5	5·7	4·3	11·7	5·4	3·4	9·1	1·5	2·8
Llandudno	12	14·6	1·1	5·2	14·6	2·3	5·2	13·3	3·2	3·4	11·5	1·0	4·2
London (Kew)	18	16·3	2·3	4·3	15·9	2·4	5·6	13·8	2·8	5·1	11·7	2·2	3·8
Manchester Airport	248	14·6	2·4	3·4	14·0	5·4	4·6	12·7	3·2	3·2	10·7	1·9	2·8
Margate	51	15·8	1·6	6·2	16·3	1·9	6·6	14·5	1·1	5·3	12·5	1·5	4·4
Marlborough	424	14·7	1·3	4·7	14·1	5·2	4·9	11·9	3·6	4·3	9·3	1·8	3·5
Morecambe	24	14·7	2·3	4·3	14·4	7·3	4·5	12·6	4·4	3·2	10·3	1·8	2·8
Newquay	176	14·9	2·7	5·9	14·8	2·1	5·0	13·5	3·3	4·9	11·5	1·2	4·7
Nottingham	192	15·0	1·0	3·2	14·7	3·6	4·3	13·1	3·2	3·6	10·5	0·6	2·6
Oxford	208	16·0	2·1	4·4	15·5	3·8	5·0	13·3	4·5	4·7	10·8	1·2	3·5
Penzance	62	15·5	3·4	6·1	14·9	3·3	4·7	13·9	3·1	5·4	12·5	1·4	4·8
Plymouth	119	15·7	1·9	5·8	15·0	3·4	5·3	13·7	3·9	5·2	12·1	1·4	4·9
Prestwick	30	13·7	3·0	4·9	13·6	5·2	5·1	12·1	6·5	3·0	10·9	1·4	2·9
Ross-on-Wye	223	15·3	1·6	4·1	14·7	3·6	4·1	12·9	3·2	3·9	10·6	0·6	3·2
Sandown	13	16·3	1·0	6·2	16·2	3·2	6·7	14·5	2·9	5·9	12·6	2·2	4·9
Scarborough	118	13·7	1·9	4·3	14·5	3·8	5·1	12·9	2·6	3·0	11·1	0·6	3·3
Scilly	158	15·5	2·6	5·9	15·2	3·3	4·8	14·6	3·4	5·9	13·2	1·3	4·5
Sheffield	429	14·3	1·6	3·2	14·3	3·7	4·7	12·6	3·3	2·9	10·7	1·3	2·8
Shrewsbury	184	14·9	1·9	3·9	14·3	3·4	4·6	13·0	3·6	3·3	10·3	0·7	2·9
Skegness	15	14·4	1·4	4·3	15·1	3·7	4·9	13·3	2·5	3·9	10·7	0·9	3·2
Southampton	65	16·5	1·6	4·7	16·2	3·2	5·5	14·1	4·2	5·1	12·1	1·5	4·5
Stornoway	11	12·0	2·1	5·9	11·7	5·7	5·1	10·5	2·8	3·2	10·1	3·4	1·8
Tiree	29	13·1	1·6	5·9	12·8	4·9	5·9	11·7	5·8	3·3	11·0	3·0	2·1
Torquay	26	15·7	2·1	6·0	15·5	3·7	6·1	13·8	3·2	6·0	12·1	1·1	4·4
Tunbridge Wells	351	14·8	2·1	5·0	14·7	2 0	6·4	12·3	3·4	4·9	10·2	1·8	4·6
Weston-s.-Mare	28	16·3	1·4	5·3	15·5	4·7	5·2	14·0	2·9	4·1	11·3	1·2	3·6
Weymouth	16	16·0	1·0	6·1	15·9	3·7	6·4	14·3	3·2	5·8	12·3	1·8	5·0
Worthing	25	15·9	2·4	5·8	15·9	3·2	6·3	14·1	3·4	5·8	12·3	1·4	5·4
York	57	14·7	1·9	3·7	14·7	4·2	4·6	12·9	3·2	3·0	10·9	0·5	3·0

TEMPERATURE, RAINFALL AND SUNSHINE AT VARIOUS PLACES IN GREAT BRITAIN

Mean Temperature of the air (°C,), Rainfall (inches) and Bright Sunshine (as mean hours per day) at representative British Health Resorts and Towns during the year July, 1962, to June, 1963, and the calendar year 1962. Fuller details of the weather are given in the *Monthly Weather Report* published by the Meteorological Office. (To convert °C. to °F. multiply by 9/5 and add 32.)

	1962						1962			1963					
	November			December			Year			January			February		
	Temp.	Rain	Sun	Temp.	Rain	Sun	Temp.	Rain	Sun	Temp.	Rain	Sun	Temp.	Rain	Sun
	°C.	in.	hrs.	°C.	in.	hrs.	°C.	in.	hrs.	°C.	in.	hrs.	°C.	in.	hrs.
Aberystwyth	8·1	2·6	1·8	5·2	2·2	2·4	—	32·9	4·2	−1·1	0·3	3·2	0·2	0·8	3·9
Aldergrove	6·0	3·0	0·9	4·0	3·3	1·1	8·3	29·2	3·6	−0·5	1·3	1·8	0·9	1·6	3·0
Ambleside	4·7	5·2	1·4	1·5	6·2	1·7	7·9	78·9	3·1	−0·1	0·6	2·4	−0·5	1·5	3·8
Balmoral	2·5	3·2	—	1·1	4·7	—	5·8	36·2	—	−4·3	2·1	—	−3·1	1·7	—
Bath	5·7	2·7	1·1	2·3	2·1	1·9	9·3	27·8	4·2	−3·2	0·8	1·7	−0·3	0·8	2·4
Birmingham	5·5	2·3	1·2	2·1	2·1	1·8	8·6	26·9	3·6	−1·9	1·0	2·2	−1·1	0·9	2·3
Bournemouth	6·5	3·7	1·5	3·0	2·7	2·9	9·2	27·2	4·8	−2·4	0·6	2·7	0·1	1·6	2·7
Buxton	3·9	2·5	—	0·9	6·0	—	6·8	49·5	—	−2·8	2·5	—	−2·7	1·7	—
Cambridge	5·3	1·5	1·1	0·9	1·7	2·2	8·7	19·5	4·1	−2·7	1·1	1·9	−0·9	0·6	2·1
Cardiff	6·3	2·6	1·6	2·9	2·8	2·0	9·3	35·3	4·4	−2·1	2·2	2·2	−0·3	1·3	2·9
Cromer	5·9	2·4	1·6	2·8	1·9	3·2	8·5	26·2	4·6	−0·9	1·5	2·3	−0·8	0·8	3·2
Douglas	7·0	5·5	1·3	5·1	3·5	1·9	8·7	38·5	4·3	1·3	1·3	2·4	1·1	1·4	3·9
Dovercourt	5·9	2·0	1·6	2·4	1·2	2·8	8·9	—	—	−1·1	0·5	1·4	−0·2	0·6	2·7
Dumfries	4·7	3·2	1·5	2·3	3·2	1·7	7·7	42·4	3·7	−0·3	0·7	2·2	−0·9	1·5	3·8
Dundee	4·9	2·9	1·8	2·8	2·3	1·6	8·3	27·5	3·7	0·3	1·7	1·8	0·5	1·9	3·6
Durham	4·6	2·9	2·2	1·3	2·7	2·2	7·8	22·6	3·9	−0·5	2·9	1·8	−1·2	2·8	2·1
Eastbourne	7·3	2·8	1·2	3·6	3·8	3·8	9·5	27·7	5·1	−0·9	0·5	2·3	0·3	0·8	3·4
Edinburgh	5·1	3·3	1·7	3·1	1·9	1·4	8·1	25·8	3·7	0·1	1·9	1·3	−0·1	0·5	3·1
Falmouth	7·9	3·2	1·9	6·5	5·2	1·8	10·0	40·7	4·4	1·1	0·8	2·2	3·3	4·8	3·1
Glasgow	4·7	2·7	1·0	2·5	4·5	1·3	7·8	43·3	3·4	−0·9	0·9	1·7	−0·7	0·7	3·5
Hastings	7·0	3·9	1·1	3·6	3·3	3·7	9·3	26·8	4·7	−1·3	0·7	2·4	0·0	0·9	3·6
Huddersfield	5·5	1·0	1·2	1·1	2·4	1·0	8·3	27·1	3·2	−1·5	1·5	1·2	−1·1	0·6	1·4
Hull	5·7	2·1	1·7	1·9	1·7	2·1	8·8	21·0	3·7	0·1	1·2	1·4	−0·9	1·3	2·2
Ilfracombe	7·9	3·0	1·4	5·5	2·2	2·2	—	32·6	—	−0·2	0·9	3·0	1·9	1·4	3·7
Inverness	5·6	1·6	1·2	4·3	3·2	0·8	8·3	25·5	3·4	0·0	0·2	1·4	0·9	0·2	3·2
Lincoln	4·7	1·7	1·7	0·5	1·2	1·5	8·0	20·2	3·6	−2·7	0·8	1·5	−1·5	0·4	2·4
Liverpool	6·3	1·6	1·7	2·9	2·2	1·8	8·9	20·5	4·1	−0·9	0·8	2·0	−0·1	0·4	3·3
Llandrindod Wells	4·3	2·4	1·2	1·1	3·1	1·7	7·6	36·5	3·4	−3·6	0·9	1·6	−2·5	1·0	2·5
Llandudno	7·4	1·9	1·8	4·3	2·4	2·1	9·4	23·6	4·3	−0·1	1·0	2·4	1·1	0·3	4·0
London (Kew)	6·7	2·0	1·2	2·8	2·3	2·2	9·7	22·3	4·1	−1·1	0·8	1·6	0·4	0·2	2·5
Manchester Airport	5·5	1·5	1·5	2·3	3·1	2·0	8·5	29·9	3·6	−1·4	0·4	2·2	−0·1	0·2	3·4
Margate	7·1	3·3	1·0	3·3	1·7	2·4	9·7	17·2	4·6	−1·1	0·2	1·4	−0·4	0·6	2·9
Marlborough	4·4	2·9	1·2	—	—	—	—	—	—	−4·3	0·7	1·9	−1·7	0·8	2·3
Morecambe	5·9	2·4	1·7	2·7	3·4	1·9	8·7	39·6	3·9	−0·4	0·6	2·3	0·4	0·4	4·1
Newquay	7·6	3·4	1·5	5·7	4·7	1·9	9·8	31·0	4·5	−0·3	1·2	3·6	3·1	4·0	3·9
Nottingham	5·7	1·3	1·3	1·9	1·2	1·6	8·8	18·4	3·3	−1·6	0·6	1·6	−0·3	0·2	1·5
Oxford	5·5	2·2	1·1	1·3	2·0	2·3	9·0	24·9	4·2	−3·0	1·1	1·9	−0·7	0·4	2·4
Penzance	8·5	4·6	1·7	7·1	5·3	2·1	10·5	40·3	4·6	1·8	1·2	2·5	3·9	4·5	3·3
Plymouth	7·2	3·1	1·6	5·5	4·3	2·5	10·1	32·8	4·7	−0·2	0·9	3·2	2·3	3·0	3·3
Prestwick	6·1	1·8	1·6	4·2	3·5	1·3	8·6	35·6	—	0·5	0·4	2·7	0·6	0·3	4·5
Ross-on-Wye	5·7	2·2	1·5	2·3	1·6	1·9	8·9	21·5	3·9	−3·1	0·8	2·4	−0·7	1·6	2·7
Sandown	7·5	2·8	1·6	4·3	3·2	3·5	10·1	24·6	5·0	−0·9	1·0	2·3	0·6	1·3	3·0
Scarborough	6·3	3·0	1·7	3·1	2·0	2·0	8·8	23·4	3·9	1·2	1·6	1·7	0·3	1·4	2·4
Scilly	9·4	2·7	2·2	7·7	3·4	1·9	11·0	30·4	4·8	3·5	0·8	2·1	5·1	4·5	3·4
Sheffield	5·3	1·5	1·0	2·3	2·1	1·5	8·5	27·1	3·4	−0·8	1·8	1·3	−1·0	1·1	1·5
Shrewsbury	5·5	1·7	1·2	1·9	2·0	1·8	8·7	23·5	3·6	−3·5	1·2	2·1	−1·0	0·6	3·1
Skegness	6·1	1·4	1·5	2·3	1·6	2·4	8·7	18·9	3·9	−0·3	1·1	1·9	−0·7	0·6	2·4
Southampton	6·7	3·0	1·2	3·3	3·1	2·8	9·9	28·0	4·3	−1·7	0·6	2·7	0·5	1·3	2·9
Stornoway	5·9	3·1	1·5	5·3	5·2	0·9	7·7	45·1	3·6	2·5	1·0	2·1	2·6	0·4	2·7
Tiree	7·3	3·5	1·5	5·9	4·6	1·2	8·7	43·3	4·2	2·3	0·7	2·2	2·5	0·8	2·9
Torquay	7·1	2·6	1·8	5·5	4·0	2·4	10·1	30·0	4·9	−0·1	1·6	2·1	1·8	3·3	3·0
Tunbridge Wells	5·2	4·0	0·9	1·3	3·2	3·3	8·1	28·0	4·4	−2·9	0·6	1·9	−1·5	0·6	2·9
Weston-super-Mare	6·6	2·7	1·4	3·1	1·7	2·2	9·7	25·2	4·4	−2·3	0·4	2·1	0·3	1·7	3·1
Weymouth	7·1	3·6	1·8	4·3	3·2	3·2	10·1	27·4	5·0	−1·1	0·8	2·9	1·3	1·9	2·8
Worthing	7·1	3·8	1·3	3·6	2·9	3·7	9·6	25·9	4·9	−1·5	0·4	2·6	0·3	0·8	3·2
York	5·0	1·6	1·7	1·3	1·2	1·6	8·7	20·2	3·6	−0·3	0·9	1·7	−0·7	1·2	2·1

TEMPERATURE, RAINFALL AND SUNSHINE AT VARIOUS PLACES IN GREAT BRITAIN

Mean Temperature of the air (° C.), Rainfall (inches) and Bright Sunshine (as mean hours per day) at representative British Health Resorts and Towns during the year July, 1962, to June, 1963, and the calendar year 1962. Fuller details of the weather are given in the *Monthly Weather Report* published by the Meteorological Office. (To convert ° C. to ° F. multiply by 9/5 and add 32.)

	1963											
	March			April			May			June		
	Temp.	Rain	Sun	Temp.	Rain	Sun	Temp.	Rain	Sun	Temp.	Rain	Sun
	° C.	in.	hrs.	° C.	in.	hrs.	° C.	in.	hrs.	C.	in.	hrs.
Aberystwyth	6·1	3·8	3·6	7·9	4·5	3·9	9·9	2·5	5·9	14·1	5·4	5·9
Aldergrove	6·2	2·3	3·4	7·9	2·1	4·5	9·3	3·1	5·9	13·7	3·5	6·1
Ambleside	5·0	11·7	3·2	8·3	5·7	3·3	9·8	5·5	5·3	14·4	4·2	5·5
Balmoral	2·9	2·9	—	5·5	2·4	—	7·1	2·0	—	11·6	4·2	—
Bath	6·7	4·2	3·9	8·7	3·6	3·4	10·9	1·5	6·1	15·3	3·0	6·8
Birmingham	5·7	3·3	2·7	8·5	2·5	3·3	10·3	1·9	5·6	14·9	3·3	7·0
Bournemouth	6·0	4·0	4·2	8·7	3·3	4·0	10·8	1·0	7·2	14·7	3·5	6·5
Buxton	3·9	4·7	2·4	6·5	3·5	3·0	8·6	4·4	5·5	13·1	4·8	6·6
Cambridge	6·3	2·0	3·3	9·2	1·8	4·2	10·9	1·6	6·1	15·5	1·7	6·7
Cardiff	6·5	5·2	3·9	8·7	3·5	3·5	11·1	1·6	6·1	15·7	4·3	6·5
Cromer	5·9	2·0	4·2	7·9	1·9	5·0	10·1	1·8	7·0	13·5	2·7	6·4
Douglas	5·7	5·5	3·9	7·5	3·2	4·7	9·3	3·4	7·1	13·7	3·3	6·4
Dovercourt	5·3	2·5	3·9	8·1	2·2	5·0	11·4	2·3	6·9	15·0	1·9	7·3
Dumfries	5·1	6·7	3·5	7·6	2·9	4·7	9·1	3·5	7·3	13·7	3·5	5·8
Dundee	5·2	3·6	3·1	7·7	2·5	4·4	10·0	1·8	6·0	13·5	2·9	5·0
Durham	4·7	1·7	3·5	7·9	1·6	4·2	9·9	1·0	5·0	13·5	3·1	4·9
Eastbourne	5·7	2·9	4·4	8·1	3·5	5·1	10·8	1·7	7·7	14·7	3·4	7·4
Edinburgh	5·8	2·2	3·2	7·4	2·2	3·6	9·4	1·7	6·0	12·8	3·6	4·6
Falmouth	7·7	5·8	3·9	9·0	3·9	5·0	10·9	1·3	7·1	14·3	2·8	6·5
Glasgow	5·1	4·3	2·9	7·4	2·4	4·3	9·3	3·5	6·5	13·7	4·1	5·7
Hastings	5·4	2·7	3·8	8·1	3·5	4·4	10·9	1·8	7·3	14·5	2·8	6·6
Huddersfield	5·6	2·5	2·7	7·7	1·9	2·9	10·3	1·4	5·0	14·4	3·5	5·9
Hull	5·6	1·9	2·9	8·1	2·4	3·5	10·7	1·6	6·2	14·3	4·0	6·5
Ilfracombe	7·5	5·6	3·9	8·7	3·1	5·0	11·3	1·7	6·8	—	—	—
Inverness	6·5	1·3	4·2	7·9	1·1	5·0	9·9	1·3	5·9	13·3	3·1	4·8
Lincoln	5·7	2·2	3·0	8·2	1·9	3·7	10·3	1·3	6·1	14·5	1·4	6·9
Liverpool	6·1	1·4	3·5	8·5	1·9	4·2	10·6	0·9	6·7	14·9	3·1	6·5
Llandrindod Wells	5·1	4·8	2·9	7·7	3·6	3·4	9·6	2·3	5·1	14·1	3·8	5·6
Llandudno	7·3	2·5	4·6	8·7	2·1	4·2	10·7	1·0	6·9	14·3	3·1	7·1
London (Kew)	6·9	2·3	3·4	9·7	1·9	4·5	11·6	1·5	6·6	15·9	1·9	6·7
Manchester Airport	6·3	2·0	3·2	8·5	2·0	3·4	10·4	1·6	5·9	15·1	3·9	6·7
Margate	6·4	2·6	4·4	8·5	1·9	4·7	11·0	2·2	6·5	14·2	2·4	6·1
Marlborough	5·3	4·9	3·2	8·2	—	—	9·9	1·6	6·2	14·3	3·8	5·6
Morecambe	5·9	4·0	3·8	8·2	3·7	4·2	10·5	1·9	6·6	15·1	—	6·8
Newquay	7·6	4·9	3·9	8·9	3·3	5·4	11·1	1·5	6·9	14·5	3·0	6·5
Nottingham	6·2	2·4	2·4	8·6	1·9	3·1	—	—	—	—	—	—
Oxford	6·5	3·0	2·8	9·5	2·0	4·0	11·3	1·7	6·2	15·5	2·6	6·7
Penzance	8·0	6·3	4·2	9·3	3·2	5·3	11·3	1·7	7·3	14·5	2·6	6·6
Plymouth	7·3	5·3	4·0	9·3	3·5	5·0	11·3	2·2	6·7	14·8	2·6	6·6
Prestwick	6·2	3·4	3·6	8·1	1·8	4·8	9·9	2·9	7·0	14·5	1·9	6·9
Ross-on-Wye	6·4	3·6	3·1	9·0	2·8	3·6	10·8	1·8	5·2	15·1	2·3	6·5
Sandown	6·1	3·5	4·6	8·5	4·1	5·0	11·8	1·8	7·5	15·1	2·6	7·3
Scarborough	5·4	1·6	3·2	7·6	1·6	3·3	10·5	1·1	6·6	13·3	3·4	5·7
Scilly	8·6	4·9	4·1	9·5	3·1	5·9	9·5	1·4	7·4	13·9	1·7	—
Sheffield	5·3	2·8	3·0	8·0	2·4	2·7	10·5	1·2	5·0	14·8	3·9	6·0
Shrewsbury	6·4	2·3	2·9	8·9	2·1	3·4	11·0	1·5	5·4	14·9	2·4	6·7
Skegness	5·3	1·9	3·6	7·9	1·8	4·2	10·1	1·6	6·3	13·9	2·6	6·5
Southampton	7·0	4·5	3·6	9·9	3·8	4·2	11·7	1·7	6·6	16·0	2·5	5·9
Stornoway	6·1	4·5	3·6	7·2	2·1	6·1	8·4	4·0	6·6	12·1	1·9	5·7
Tiree	6·1	5·3	4·1	7·3	1·7	5·4	9·0	3·7	7·3	12·9	1·9	7·7
Torquay	7·3	5·4	4·7	9·7	3·8	4·2	11·5	1·2	6·7	15·5	1·8	6·7
Tunbridge Wells	5·5	4·2	3·4	8·1	3·3	4·2	10·3	2·1	6·3	14·3	2·4	6·5
Weston-super-Mare	6·7	4·0	4·0	9·0	3·3	3·6	11·7	1·0	6·0	15·9	2·4	6·7
Weymouth	6·7	3·9	4·5	9·4	3·3	4·2	11·9	1·3	7·6	15·2	2·8	6·5
Worthing	5·4	3·0	3·9	8·3	3·4	4·8	11·1	1·8	7·1	15·3	1·9	6·8
York	5·7	2·0	3·2	8·1	1·7	3·7	10·9	1·1	6·1	14·6	4·6	6·2

Weather Record, August, 1962

Day	Temperature Max.	Temperature Min.	Mean Pressure	Wind Speed	Rainfall	Sunshine
	°C.	°C.	mb.	knots	mm.	hours
1	22·6	13·0	1019·7	4·5	0·1	6·7
2	21·8	14·2	1015·1	4·0	—	8·2
3	18·2	12·9	1010·1	10·7	3·8	1·9
4	20·1	11·2	1012·3	7·2	—	11·9
5	20·1	11·9	1010·7	5·1	—	9·7
6	15·5	11·7	1002·9	5·3	29·3	—
7	15·7	9·3	1000·4	10·0	8·3	1·7
8	17·6	9·3	1015·1	4·1	—	7·2
9	17·2	7·6	1018·1	9·0	3·1	6·7
10	21·2	14·6	1013·5	10·3	—	7·8
11	17·3	15·7	1009·3	15·5	0·2	0·2
12	20·1	13·6	1013·8	2·3	—	0·7
13	20·1	14·1	1019·9	8·1	—	4·3
14	16·7	12·4	1012·4	8·1	6·5	0·3
15	19·4	13·6	1002·7	12·0	0·1	3·2
16	18·7	12·1	1007·0	8·8	6·0	3·4
17	19·7	12·9	1005·2	8·9	—	7·2
18	21·4	12·1	1016·5	4·7	—	8·8
19	22·9	12·2	1018·7	3·2	—	7·2
20	21·2	16·0	1013·0	5·0	0·6	3·9
21	19·3	12·4	1014·2	8·2	—	5·9
22	20·3	13·7	1014·9	9·5	0·1	7·0
23	16·8	12·4	1012·6	12·4	2·2	0·4
24	19·6	15·5	1009·0	12·2	—	8·4
25	18·8	12·6	1017·2	8·1	—	10·8
26	18·3	10·2	1012·3	13·1	0·7	3·6
27	19·3	12·5	1014·8	9·0	0·6	9·5
28	20·2	12·3	1017·5	6·5	—	2·3
29	20·4	13·3	1023·1	2·5	—	8·3
30	21·5	9·9	1024·2	2·5	—	9·1
31	19·9	10·1	1023·8	3·9	—	6·5
Total ..	—	—	—	—	61·6	172·8
Mean ..	19·4	12·4	1013·5	7·6	—	—
Temp. °F	66·9	54·3	—	—	—	—
Average	70·7	55·4	1015·6	6·3	57	184

Weather Record, September, 1962

Temperature Max.	Temperature Min.	Mean Pressure	Wind Speed	Rainfall	Sunshine	Day
°C.	°C.	mb.	knots	mm.	hours	
21·3	10·6	1022·5	3·0	—	9·3	1
23·2	10·3	1017·2	2·4	—	6·8	2
20·3	14·5	1007·9	7·4	0·6	3·0	3
17·8	14·6	1001·3	8·4	9·0	5·0	4
19·6	12·8	1001·7	8·0	4·5	7·5	5
19·6	13·8	997·9	7·9	13·8	4·4	6
17·3	12·2	1006·4	4·7	—	7·3	7
16·6	9·9	1016·2	4·9	—	3·9	8
18·3	9·2	1015·8	8·1	—	11·8	9
17·3	11·7	1009·3	6·4	2·5	0·4	10
16·8	13·9	1011·6	8·7	3·1	—	11
19·5	16·1	1011·3	11·7	2·7	3·7	12
17·4	9·9	1027·0	2·9	—	9·8	13
19·0	8·4	1019·4	3·9	1·3	10·4	14
19·3	10·4	1008·2	4·0	0·1	4·3	15
15·6	9·3	1011·5	5·0	0·2	10·0	16
13·6	7·8	1012·7	5·0	0·1	8·3	17
13·7	5·4	1015·2	4·7	0·1	1·9	18
14·0	10·4	1017·1	6·4	—	1·3	19
15·1	9·5	1023·1	8·5	—	2·3	20
13·2	7·3	1030·4	4·8	—	3·7	21
15·2	9·6	1029·6	3·1	—	5·3	22
15·6	7·9	1025·3	3·8	—	3·3	23
17·0	7·5	1021·9	1·5	—	1·1	24
19·8	9·6	1010·2	5·7	7·7	8·8	25
15·8	12·4	1004·0	4·8	1·6	—	26
15·0	6·3	1008·3	6·3	1·0	8·0	27
15·9	12·3	1003·5	7·8	6·1	0·1	28
16·0	7·6	1006·4	8·1	16·7	8·7	29
15·3	13·4	999·7	13·0	1·1	1·8	30
—	—	—	—	72·2	152·2	.. Total
17·1	10·5	1013·1	6·0	—	—	.. Mean
62·8	50·9	—	—	—	—	Temp. °F
65·6	52·0	1016·8	6·3	50	137	Average

Weather Record, October, 1962

Day	Temperature Max.	Temperature Min.	Mean Pressure	Wind Speed	Rainfall	Sunshine
	°C.	°C.	mb.	knots	mm.	hours
1	17·6	12·7	1007·5	12·0	19·0	1·3
2	18·7	14·1	1013·5	5·1	0·1	4·1
3	15·3	10·3	1020·7	3·4	—	2·2
4	15·7	4·4	1024·7	3·5	—	9·4
5	17·1	9·0	1024·9	4·6	—	1·3
6	17·2	11·7	1029·0	1·0	—	0·1
7	18·7	11·6	1027·1	7·6	—	7·8
8	18·7	10·0	1022·6	6·5	—	8·4
9	18·4	11·7	1021·6	1·4	—	3·8
10	17·9	9·5	1012·6	4·2	—	5·2
11	14·7	12·1	1019·4	8·4	—	—
12	14·8	12·1	1017·2	11·1	—	1·3
13	13·4	7·9	1018·5	7·1	—	1·7
14	15·0	4·6	1023·0	2·7	—	3·5
15	15·6	6·7	1026·6	1·2	—	3·2
16	13·9	6·3	1026·0	0·3	—	4·3
17	16·2	6·3	1027·5	0·7	—	4·9
18	18·7	6·6	1026·0	2·0	—	6·6
19	14·5	10·7	1025·9	1·6	—	—
20	14·0	9·6	1028·4	5·3	—	1·3
21	15·0	12·1	1026·9	9·0	—	5·7
22	15·0	7·8	1022·9	4·7	—	7·8
23	13·3	5·6	1021·9	1·4	—	—
24	13·3	9·7	1020·0	3·3	2·2	—
25	15·3	11·2	1008·9	7·8	20·3	0·3
26	10·7	10·6	1011·6	8·3	3·4	—
27	9·7	1·3	1018·6	7·6	0·2	5·5
28	10·7	6·3	1009·9	9·5	3·6	7·1
29	9·7	2·5	1017·8	6·0	5·6	7·0
30	12·3	7·3	1003·8	11·5	0·1	5·9
31	9·8	4·6	1005·4	7·2	0·1	7·3
Total ..	—	—	—	—	54·6	117·0
Mean ..	14·9	8·6	1020·0	5·4	—	—
Temp. °F	58·8	47·5	—	—	—	—
Average	57·5	45·9	1015·3	6·6	57	95

Weather Record, November, 1962

Temperature Max.	Temperature Min.	Mean Pressure	Wind Speed	Rainfall	Sunshine	Day
°C.	°C.	mb.	knots	mm.	hours	
11·0	0·0	1002·6	8·8	8·6	0·5	1
13·6	8·3	995·2	8·8	2·2	5·1	2
12·7	6·0	999·3	4·7	2·6	1·1	3
13·1	4·0	997·7	4·6	4·6	5·5	4
13·4	10·5	988·0	4·7	0·8	—	5
12·4	9·6	991·3	5·9	0·4	0·1	6
10·4	5·1	1002·5	1·8	5·4	1·9	7
12·1	4·0	1001·9	9·0	—	—	8
12·0	10·0	1006·1	4·7	2·1	—	9
11·2	9·7	1011·9	11·5	2·3	—	10
7·0	6·6	1016·6	11·2	—	—	11
7·8	4·2	1018·1	6·9	—	3·3	12
7·6	1·9	1019·9	7·3	—	4·6	13
8·1	1·1	1016·9	5·0	1·0	0·4	14
6·4	4·2	1016·7	7·3	—	7·3	15
6·4	−1·2	1012·9	6·1	2·5	—	16
5·4	5·4	992·5	9·6	6·0	—	17
5·6	3·4	997·0	13·4	2·4	0·1	18
3·5	−0·8	1011·4	12·3	—	3·2	19
3·9	−1·1	1008·2	4·4	6·4	0·2	20
4·4	2·1	1003·7	7·3	0·1	—	21
5·3	1·0	1017·7	1·5	—	0·6	22
6·7	−1·1	1020·4	3·7	2·9	—	23
11·6	6·7	1017·0	5·0	0·3	0·6	24
11·8	7·7	1029·3	1·1	—	1·2	25
8·7	7·2	1034·6	1·9	—	0·1	26
6·9	6·0	1033·4	4·3	—	—	27
8·1	6·1	1030·2	2·2	—	—	28
8·1	6·9	1028·1	2·6	—	—	29
9·1	6·4	1030·2	2·4	—	0·9	30
—	—	—	—	50·6	36·7	.. Total
8·8	4·7	1011·7	6·1	—	—	.. Mean
47·8	40·5	—	—	—	—	Temp. °F
49·2	40·7	1013·7	7·0	63	51	Average

Entries of Maximum Temperature cover day period 9–21 h.; Minimum Temperature night period 21–9 h. and are entered to day of reading; Rainfall the 24 hours commencing at 9 h. on day of entry; Sunshine the 24 hours 0–24 h.; Mean Wind Speed in knots at 50 ft. above ground (100 knots = 110·5 m.p.h.); Pressure is at station level, the correction to M.S.L. being usually + 1·3 mb. Rainfall 1000 mm. = 39·37 in. Averages refer to the following standard periods:—Temperature, Pressure, Mean Wind Speed and Sunshine 1921–50; Rainfall, 1916–1950.

Weather Record, December, 1962

Day	Temperature Max.	Temperature Min.	Mean Pressure	Wind Speed	Rainfall	Sunshine
	°C.	°C.	mb.	knots	mm.	hours
1	7·9	1·4	1036·8	3·7	—	5·0
2	4·2	−0·5	1034·2	4·3	—	5·6
3	4·7	−2·9	1030·6	1·7	0·1	5·3
4	0·1	−4·4	1030·2	0·3	—	—
5	−0·6	−4·4	1029·4	0·5	—	—
6	0·8	−2·5	1027·0	0·2	0·1	—
7	5·6	−2·0	1025·2	2·7	0·2	2·0
8	9·9	5·5	1016·7	12·9	9·9	—
9	8·3	6·8	1007·9	13·2	—	5·2
10	8·2	4·1	1014·9	7·4	—	5·9
11	10·1	4·1	998·8	11·9	3·8	—
12	4·2	0·6	990·2	7·3	6·2	0·6
13	3·9	0·6	1005·7	11·3	—	3·8
14	8·7	0·9	1009·6	8·7	0·3	0·9
15	13·2	8·6	994·6	14·9	—	—
16	8·2	7·2	998·4	18·0	—	4·5
17	6·7	2·7	1003·2	5·5	0·5	3·5
18	8·2	4·7	1001·7	9·8	—	4·5
19	6·1	2·9	1010·9	7·1	1·9	5·3
20	10·0	−0·4	1008·0	8·0	7·3	—
21	8·0	6·2	1015·9	10·2	—	6·4
22	3·9	0·5	1035·0	4·0	—	—
23	0·1	−2·2	1043·3	10·6	—	1·9
24	0·7	−2·1	1038·5	12·9	—	5·0
25	0·8	−2·3	1029·9	10·1	—	2·9
26	0·6	−3·8	1015·7	3·3	10·0	—
27	1·3	0·0	1007·1	6·5	4·2	—
28	0·7	0·0	1006·7	5·3	—	—
29	1·1	−2·1	1003·3	14·1	6·4	—
30	0·7	−1·6	999·4	12·8	2·8	—
31	1·9	−0·3	1005·8	15·9	4·4	—
Total ..	—	—	—	—	58·1	68·3
Mean ..	4·8	0·8	1015·3	8·2	—	—
Temp. °F	40·6	33·4	—	—	—	—
Average	44·5	37·7	1015·4	7·4	52	39

Weather Record, January, 1963

Temperature Max.	Temperature Min.	Mean Pressure	Wind Speed	Rainfall	Sunshine	Day
°C.	°C.	mb.	knots	mm.	hours	
−0·3	−0·6	1010·1	13·3	0·4	—	1
0·0	−2·1	1006·2	9·2	4·2	—	2
1·3	−0·4	994·1	8·7	3·6	—	3
2·4	1·2	992·7	2·3	0·1	1·4	4
1·7	0·1	996·6	2·1	—	—	5
2·4	1·5	1004·4	10·6	0·2	—	6
0·4	−0·4	1012·2	14·8	—	0·1	7
1·3	−0·4	1017·1	10·1	—	0·5	8
0·7	−2·9	1019·0	15·8	0·1	6·5	9
1·2	−2·3	1021·1	10·9	—	3·5	10
−1·0	−3·9	1025·2	10·3	—	2·4	11
−1·3	−6·2	1028·8	4·5	—	0·2	12
−2·2	−7·8	1030·7	3·3	—	—	13
2·8	−4·6	1026·0	5·2	—	2·6	14
2·6	−1·5	1026·0	3·3	0·1	0·4	15
1·2	−0·4	1023·2	8·4	0·8	—	16
−1·4	−4·3	1031·8	15·7	—	3·9	17
−0·4	−4·1	1025·7	16·0	—	4·2	18
−1·7	−4·6	1013·8	17·9	6·1	4·9	19
−0·5	−5·2	1012·4	14·2	0·1	—	20
−0·8	−2·4	1029·1	17·3	—	6·2	21
−1·3	−6·2	1041·0	7·0	—	5·4	22
−1·3	−9·1	1040·3	0·6	—	—	23
−2·8	−7·7	1035·6	1·0	—	—	24
−2·6	−9·7	1038·1	1·9	—	3·7	25
5·5	−5·5	1038·5	5·4	—	2·9	26
3·9	2·6	1041·8	7·1	—	0·1	27
3·8	1·8	1039·3	6·8	0·9	—	28
2·3	1·8	1029·8	5·0	0·6	—	29
1·6	0·6	1020·4	6·6	0·2	—	30
1·3	−1·7	1022·5	6·4	2·1	0·4	31
—	—	—	—	19·5	49·3	.. Total
0·6	−2·7	1022·4	8·4	—	—	.. Mean
33·1	27·1	—	—	—	—	Temp. °F
44·1	37·1	1015·6	8·2	55	42	Average

Weather Record, February, 1963

Day	Temperature Max.	Temperature Min.	Mean Pressure	Wind Speed	Rainfall	Sunshine
	°C.	°C.	mb.	knots	mm.	hours
1	−0·6	−2·3	1016·7	9·3	1·7	4·6
2	−2·0	−5·4	1016·0	13·4	0·3	0·6
3	0·7	−4·1	1008·1	6·7	1·0	0·5
4	0·7	−2·7	999·9	2·6	—	0·3
5	0·4	−3·8	1003·8	9·1	—	3·8
6	1·8	−2·5	1002·4	9·4	0·6	—
7	2·9	1·6	1000·6	5·3	0·7	—
8	3·7	0·9	1010·9	3·7	—	1·8
9	2·4	0·5	1013·1	9·6	—	—
10	0·8	0·3	1002·7	13·6	1·6	—
11	0·9	0·1	1001·0	7·9	—	—
12	1·8	0·0	1004·5	4·8	0·4	—
13	3·7	1·1	1010·6	4·8	—	2·5
14	3·6	−1·7	1000·5	9·6	0·3	—
15	1·9	0·7	989·6	8·6	—	—
16	0·9	−0·1	992·3	10·7	—	—
17	2·1	−0·4	1001·6	8·2	—	2·8
18	2·4	−0·9	1002·9	7·5	—	3·8
19	0·2	−1·4	998·2	12·0	0·1	0·1
20	1·0	−1·6	1005·4	9·5	0·4	0·7
21	3·3	−1·1	1015·0	3·7	0·1	6·6
22	3·3	0·2	1020·8	1·2	—	0·1
23	2·9	0·2	1025·6	4·4	—	3·4
24	1·5	−3·3	1026·5	7·0	—	5·6
25	3·3	−6·4	1028·8	5·5	—	7·5
26	6·0	−3·3	1029·3	8·9	—	8·9
27	5·7	−2·1	1029·9	10·5	—	8·0
28	7·4	−1·8	1028·3	9·0	—	9·3
Total ..	—	—	—	—	6·3	70·9
Mean ..	2·2	−1·4	1010·2	7·7	—	—
Temp. °F	36·0	29·5	—	—	—	—
Average	45·2	36·5	1016·4	8·3	39	60

Weather Record, March, 1963

Temperature Max.	Temperature Min.	Mean Pressure	Wind Speed	Rainfall	Sunshine	Day
°C.	°C.	mb.	knots	mm.	hours	
5·4	−2·2	1029·8	8·9	—	8·9	1
8·1	−2·5	1027·9	6·2	—	9·3	2
8·9	−2·7	1025·8	5·2	—	9·3	3
11·3	−1·6	1022·1	6·5	—	3·2	4
9·0	4·0	1021·9	10·3	0·1	0·3	5
13·1	7·0	1016·8	11·5	—	4·8	6
13·0	8·4	1013·3	12·4	—	6·8	7
12·1	6·9	1002·0	13·3	2·7	2·3	8
7·7	6·7	993·5	18·6	9·8	—	9
10·8	6·4	988·2	12·6	6·1	2·2	10
10·0	4·7	928·6	9·8	3·0	0·8	11
8·7	4·2	995·6	8·0	0·1	0·7	12
10·3	0·7	1011·4	7·3	5·3	4·1	13
13·9	7·7	1007·0	12·3	1·8	4·7	14
13·2	8·6	1004·0	11·3	6·1	5·1	15
12·3	7·9	1003·7	15·7	0·3	7·8	16
11·7	5·7	1011·0	11·0	2·1	0·2	17
13·3	9·1	1003·7	9·9	1·5	0·2	18
10·9	6·7	1008·1	7·4	1·4	0·8	19
9·7	6·9	1007·4	7·9	—	—	20
5·3	2·7	1018·5	9·3	—	—	21
4·9	1·3	1025·7	13·7	—	1·4	22
6·3	1·7	1032·8	7·8	—	1·3	23
11·2	−1·4	1026·6	10·0	0·7	9·4	24
12·4	4·5	1009·8	15·9	7·2	5·5	25
9·5	5·5	1001·9	5·2	0·9	0·5	26
10·1	2·8	1003·9	7·6	0·8	4·6	27
10·4	2·9	1002·1	7·7	3·8	7·6	28
8·7	4·6	993·5	9·6	3·4	0·9	29
8·3	4·0	998·1	9·8	1·4	1·2	30
6·9	4·3	1015·5	8·2	—	—	31
—	—	—	—	58·5	103·9	.. Total
9·9	4·0	1009·8	10·0	—	—	.. Mean
49·8	39·2	—	—	—	—	Temp. °F
50·4	37·8	1016·5	7·7	37	112	Average

See footnote, p. 1038.

Weather Record, April, 1963

Day	Temperature Max.	Temperature Min.	Mean Pressure	Wind Speed	Rainfall	Sunshine
	°C.	°C.	mb.	knots	mm.	hours
1	11·3	−0·7	1021·1	5·0	1·1	2·4
2	13·8	6·1	1021·1	4·5	0·1	4·0
3	12·1	6·3	1019·8	5·4	1·0	3·2
4	7·2	4·1	1014·2	7·9	0·5	4·5
5	6·7	2·7	1011·3	9·8	1·0	1·1
6	12·4	3·1	1010·2	16·0	—	8·3
7	12·6	3·3	1009·8	12·0	—	8·1
8	14·1	3·4	1005·4	5·3	—	2·1
9	14·4	6·7	994·6	8·3	6·0	0·3
10	10·9	9·2	983·5	9·2	0·2	—
11	12·1	8·8	989·1	11·0	2·3	0·1
12	10·0	3·6	1009·7	7·3	—	11·9
13	10·2	1·6	1017·9	9·8	0·1	8·5
14	11·8	6·6	1013·6	13·6	3·4	0·9
15	12·8	7·8	1004·5	10·0	10·3	0·8
16	15·2	9·4	1001·3	6·2	·2	2·6
17	10·9	8·2	993·6	11·2	1·2	0·9
18	12·2	8·2	999·6	7·7	0·6	4·9
19	16·5	5·7	1010·9	3·0	—	6·7
20	11·8	6·2	1004·7	11·0	4·5	—
21	13·9	9·5	1004·1	14·7	1·2	7·4
22	14·6	9·1	1009·8	9·6	—	12·5
23	16·9	6·9	1011·3	8·5	—	9·2
24	13·8	7·3	1016·7	3·7	—	0·4
25	12·9	4·8	1023·7	5·3	—	7·7
26	14·4	6·3	1027·7	2·4	—	9·4
27	19·1	3·8	1027·4	4·3	—	8·6
28	19·6	11·8	1022·7	5·0	2·5	0·6
29	15·6	12·1	1017·3	4·0	4·5	—
30	15·0	7·7	1019·1	7·2	8·4	8·7
Total ..	—	—	—	—	49·1	135·8
Mean ..	13·2	6·3	1010·5	8·0	—	—
Temp. °F	55·8	44·3	—	—	—	—
Average	55·6	41·7	1014·3	8·0	46	147

Weather Record, May, 1963

Temperatures Max.	Temperatures Min.	Mean Pressure	Wind Speed	Rainfall	Sunshine	Day
°C.	°C.	mb.	knots	mm.	hours	
12·0	8·2	1003·1	9·1	4·6	0·9	1
11·2	3·8	1006·8	8·1	—	6·8	2
13·3	7·4	1007·0	8·5	0·3	8·0	3
14·9	4·5	1011·1	6·0	—	8·9	4
14·1	8·8	1009·0	10·1	—	7·1	5
14·3	5·6	1014·1	7·5	—	8·5	6
16·9	7·4	1016·9	8·0	—	10·4	7
15·9	6·5	1014·9	7·6	3·1	3·1	8
16·1	8·4	1015·5	6·4	3·2	10·9	9
13·0	8·3	1006·6	12·9	1·9	2·8	10
14·8	9·2	1013·7	11·1	—	4·7	11
12·8	8·3	1016·6	12·9	3·6	—	12
13·9	9·8	1012·1	11·1	2·6	7·5	13
12·7	7·8	1015·3	7·5	4·5	1·7	14
12·7	6·8	1019·0	8·2	—	4·8	15
17·6	5·4	1024·5	4·7	0·1	10·1	16
16·7	11·7	1023·7	5·7	—	10·7	17
15·0	7·2	1019·4	8·2	—	8·1	18
14·3	7·4	1017·6	8·3	—	8·3	19
14·1	7·9	1009·8	10·3	0·9	0·1	20
14·8	10·1	1004·2	10·9	—	9·5	21
15·4	7·3	1010·7	5·3	—	5·4	22
11·3	7·8	1015·3	7·8	5·3	—	23
15·7	7·3	1017·1	5·8	—	9·3	24
20·1	5·6	1023·5	2·5	—	8·8	25
19·2	6·9	1023·5	4·7	—	13·2	26
19·3	8·6	1024·0	8·5	2·0	11·9	27
13·3	9·9	1025·5	9·8	6·3	0·5	28
12·3	8·0	1024·3	12·5	0·1	0·1	29
23·5	9·6	1018·2	8·5	—	9·6	30
25·4	11·6	1014·6	8·2	—	13·8	31
—	—	—	—	38·5	205·5	.. Total
15·4	7·8	1015·4	8·3	—	—	.. Mean
59·7	46·0	—	—	—	—	Temp °F.
62·5	46·5	1015·6	7·2	46	192	Average

Weather Record, June, 1963

Day	Tempearture Max.	Tempearture Min.	Mean Pressure	Wind Speed	Rainfall	Sunshine
	°C.	°C.	mb.	knots	mm.	hours
1	22·6	15·1	1014·8	12·5	—	14·2
2	20·1	12·5	1014·5	14·5	—	15·0
3	18·2	11·6	1011·7	13·5	—	8·1
4	21·8	10·4	1009·0	11·8	1·3	9·4
5	20·8	9·8	1007·7	7·0	—	4·1
6	24·6	11·8	1010·8	2·5	—	11·7
7	25·6	11·7	1015·4	3·2	—	11·1
8	25·3	12·2	1018·1	6·2	—	10·5
9	24·9	12·3	1013·5	6·4	1·5	8·6
10	24·3	13·3	1010·3	9·3	—	14·7
11	24·1	10·3	1013·4	5·0	—	12·2
12	25·0	10·8	1014·7	4·2	0·6	12·8
13	17·2	12·9	1012·9	3·6	9·4	—
14	15·4	11·3	1014·3	8·7	—	0·8
15	21·5	8·4	1013·7	4·5	0·1	8·3
16	15·8	13·3	1012·0	8·7	0·1	—
17	20·4	14·1	1010·6	9·0	2·2	5·1
18	17·3	14·6	1002·4	11·6	6·3	4·2
19	14·7	10·0	1007·1	9·2	1·0	1·7
20	21·1	12·2	1001·8	9·8	—	1·6
21	19·7	14·6	1008·3	10·7	—	2·9
22	20·1	13·5	1013·3	7·7	—	9·8
23	18·4	10·5	1016·9	7·6	—	10·9
24	15·6	12·2	1009·9	12·3	0·6	1·1
25	15·9	12·4	1000·2	11·3	4·6	2·3
26	16·6	10·6	1007·6	9·0	1·0	5·1
27	19·4	10·2	1012·8	3·7	1·9	9·0
28	17·6	12·1	1012·5	2·3	10·8	1·3
29	16·7	12·0	1011·3	7·4	6·9	1·0
30	18·9	11·6	1012·1	4·7	0·8	5·7
Total ..	—	—	—	—	49·1	203·2
Mean ..	20·0	11·9	1011·2	7·9	—	—
Temp. °F	68·0	53·4	—	—	—	—
Average	68·3	52·4	1017·2	7·0	44	206

Weather Record, July, 1963

Temperature Max.	Temperature Min.	Mean Pressure	Wind Speed	Rainfall	Sunshine	Day
°C.	°C.	mb.	knots	mm.	hours	
20·0	12·4	1012·8	5·0	—	5·8	1
20·1	12·3	1015·7	1·8	0·3	5·0	2
21·6	12·2	1016·2	4·6	—	4·7	3
20·1	9·0	1018·5	3·1	0·4	6·1	4
19·6	9·5	1018·7	4·4	—	5·2	5
16·4	12·7	1014·6	4·3	20·8	0·1	6
19·9	10·6	1016·2	4·5	—	7·6	7
19·2	11·6	1017·2	4·1	—	5·8	8
20·0	11·8	1011·7	7·4	—	7·5	9
17·6	13·8	1007·9	7·9	3·1	1·0	10
18·9	13·2	1010·9	4·0	—	3·5	11
18·5	11·8	1009·6	5·7	0·3	2·9	12
18·7	10·3	1007·6	3·3	5·3	3·4	13
17·9	9·6	1014·1	10·4	0·3	5·7	14
18·0	15·1	1014·9	10·7	0·5	0·1	15
20·3	14·5	1015·4	7·0	—	6·0	16
18·8	11·8	1013·5	6·2	0·3	3·7	17
17·8	13·5	1012·6	6·1	—	—	18
18·9	14·6	1016·0	7·0	—	1·3	19
24·2	16·1	1023·8	3·4	—	5·4	20
23·4	12·6	1024·0	5·1	—	12·5	21
26·0	12·4	1018·4	1·8	—	10·4	22
26·8	15·5	1011·8	4·3	—	10·3	23
19·8	16·8	1007·4	11·3	1·1	1·5	24
19·1	13·6	1017·8	3·5	—	9·0	25
19·9	9·9	1029·0	3·3	—	14·4	26
20·6	8·4	1029·6	5·1	—	13·6	27
21·1	10·2	1026·9	7·3	—	13·8	28
26·4	11·9	1024·3	5·7	—	12·9	29
25·6	11·1	1022·2	6·0	—	12·9	30
23·5	13·8	1017·0	6·9	—	11·9	31
—	—	—	—	32·4	204·0	.. Total
20·6	12·3	1016·7	5·5	—	—	.. Mean
69·1	54·1	—	—	—	—	Temp. °F
71·8	56·2	1015·5	6·4	62	195	Average

See footnote, p. 1038.

COMPOUND INTEREST TABLES

ABLE I.—Showing the Sum to which an Annuity of £1 accumulating at Compound Interest will amount in from One to Fifty Years at Various Rates.

Table II.—Showing the Amount which £1 accumulating at Compound Interest will reach in from One to Fifty Years at Various Rates.

2½ Per Ct.	3½ Per Ct.	4½ Per Ct.	5 Per Ct.	5½ Per Ct.	6 Per Ct.	Yr.	2½ Per Ct.	3½ Per Ct.	4½ Per Ct.	5 Per Ct.	5½ Per Ct.	6 Per Ct.
1·000	1·000	1·000	1·000	1·000	1·000	1	1·0250	1·0350	1·0450	1·0500	1·0550	1·0600
2·025	2·035	2·045	2·050	2·055	2·060	2	1·0506	1·0712	1·0920	1·1025	1·1130	1·1236
3·076	3·106	3·137	3·153	3·168	3·184	3	1·0769	1·1087	1·1412	1·1576	1·1742	1·1910
4·153	4·215	4·278	4·310	4·342	4·375	4	1·1038	1·1475	1·1925	1·2155	1·2388	1·2625
5·256	5·362	5·471	5·526	5·581	5·637	5	1·1314	1·1877	1·2462	1·2763	1·3070	1·3382
6·388	6·550	6·717	6·802	6·888	6·975	6	1·1597	1·2293	1·3023	1·3401	1·3788	1·4185
7·547	7·779	8·019	8·142	8·267	8·394	7	1·1887	1·2723	1·3609	1·4071	1·4547	1·5036
8·736	9·052	9·380	9·549	9·722	9·897	8	1·2184	1·3168	1·4221	1·4775	1·5347	1·5938
9·955	10·368	10·802	11·027	11·256	11·491	9	1·2489	1·3629	1·4861	1·5513	1·6191	1·6895
11·203	11·731	12·288	12·578	12·875	13·181	10	1·2801	1·4106	1·5530	1·6289	1·7081	1·7908
12·483	13·142	13·841	14·207	14·584	14·972	11	1·3121	1·4600	1·6229	1·7103	1·8021	1·8983
13·796	14·602	15·464	15·917	16·386	16·870	12	1·3449	1·5111	1·6959	1·7959	1·9012	2·0122
15·140	16·113	17·160	17·713	18·287	18·882	13	1·3785	1·5640	1·7722	1·8856	2·0058	2·1329
16·519	17·677	18·932	19·599	20·293	21·015	14	1·4130	1·6187	1·8519	1·9799	2·1161	2·2609
17·932	19·296	20·784	21·579	22·409	23·276	15	1·4483	1·6753	1·9353	2·0789	2·2325	2·3966
19·380	20·971	22·719	23·657	24·641	25·673	16	1·4845	1·7340	2·0224	2·1829	2·3553	2·5404
20·865	22·705	24·742	25·840	26·996	28·213	17	1·5216	1·7947	2·1134	2·2920	2·4848	2·6928
22·386	24·500	26·855	28·132	29·481	30·906	18	1·5597	1·8575	2·2085	2·4066	2·6215	2·8543
23·946	26·357	29·064	30·539	32·103	33·760	19	1·5987	1·9225	2·3079	2·5270	2·7656	3·0256
25·545	28·280	31·371	33·066	34·868	36·786	20	1·6386	1·9898	2·4117	2·6533	2·9178	3·2071
27·183	30·269	33·783	35·719	37·786	39·993	21	1·6796	2·0594	2·5202	2·7860	3·0782	3·3996
28·863	32·329	36·303	38·505	40·864	43·392	22	1·7216	2·1315	2·6337	2·9253	3·2475	3·6035
30·584	34·460	38·937	41·430	44·112	46·996	23	1·7646	2·2061	2·7522	3·0715	3·4262	3·8197
32·349	36·667	41·689	44·502	47·538	50·816	24	1·8087	2·2833	2·8760	3·2251	3·6146	4·0489
34·158	38·950	44·565	47·727	51·153	54·865	25	1·8539	2·3632	3·0054	3·3864	3·8134	4·2919
36·012	41·313	47·571	51·113	54·966	59·156	26	1·9003	2·4460	3·1407	3·5557	4·0231	4·5494
37·912	43·759	50·711	54·669	58·989	63·706	27	1·9478	2·5316	3.2820	3·7335	4·2444	4·8223
39·860	46·291	53·993	58·403	63·234	68·528	28	1·9965	2·6202	3·4297	3·9201	4·4778	5·1117
41·856	48·911	57·423	62·323	67·711	73·640	29	2·0464	2·7119	3·5840	4·1161	4·7241	5·4184
43·903	51·623	61·007	66·439	72·435	79·058	30	2·0976	2·8068	3·7453	4·3219	4·9840	5·7435
46·000	54·429	64·752	70·761	77·419	84·802	31	2·1500	2·9050	3·9139	4·5380	5·2581	6·0881
48·150	57·335	68·666	75·299	82·677	90·890	32	2·2038	3·0067	4·090	4·7649	5·5473	6·4534
50·354	60·341	72·756	80·064	88·225	97·343	33	2·2589	3·1119	4·2740	5·0032	5·8524	6·8406
52·613	63·453	77·030	85·067	94·077	104·184	34	2·3153	3·2209	4·4664	5·2533	6·1742	7·2510
54·928	66·674	81·497	90·320	100·251	111·435	35	2·3732	3·3336	4·6673	5·5160	6·5138	7·6861
57·301	70·008	86·164	95·836	106·765	119·121	36	2·4325	3·4503	4·8774	5·7918	6·8721	8·1473
59·734	73·458	91·041	101·628	113·637	127·268	37	2·4933	3·5710	5·0969	6·0814	7·2501	8·6361
62·227	77·029	96·138	107·710	120·887	135·904	38	2·5557	3·6960	5·3262	6·3855	7·6488	9·1543
64·783	80·725	101·464	114·095	128·536	145·058	39	2·6196	3·8254	5·5659	6·7048	8·0695	9·7035
67·403	84·550	107·030	120·800	136·606	154·762	40	2·6851	3·9593	5·8164	7·0400	8·5133	10·2857
70·088	88·510	112·847	127·840	145·119	165·048	41	2·7522	4·0978	6·0781	7·3920	8·9815	10·9029
72·840	92·607	118·925	135·232	154·100	175·951	42	2·8210	4·2413	6·3516	7·7616	9·4755	11·5570
75·661	96·849	125·276	142·993	163·576	187·508	43	2·8915	4·3897	6·6374	8·1497	9·9967	12·2505
78·552	101·238	131·914	151·143	173·573	199·758	44	2·9638	4·5433	6·9361	8·5572	10·5465	12·9855
81·516	105·782	138·850	159·700	184·119	212·744	45	3·0379	4·7024	7·2482	8·9850	11·1266	13·7646
84·554	110·484	146·098	168·685	195·246	226·508	46	3·1139	4·8669	7·5744	9·4343	11·7385	14·5905
87·668	115·351	153·673	178·119	206·984	241·099	47	3·1917	5·0373	7·9153	9·9060	12·3841	15·4659
90·860	120·388	161·588	188·025	219·368	256·565	48	3·2715	5·2136	8·2715	10·4013	13·0653	16·3939
94·131	125·602	169·859	198·427	232·434	272·958	49	3·3533	5·3961	8·6437	10·9213	13·7838	17·3775
97·484	130·998	178·503	209·348	246·217	290·336	50	3·4371	5·5849	9·0326	11·4674	14·5420	18·4202

When the annuity is payable at the beginning instead of at the end of the year, the amount for the following r less £1, must be taken. Thus, for £1 at 2½ per cent. for 25 years, take 26 years, £36·012, and deduct —£35·012.

WIND FORCE MEASURES

The *Beaufort Scale* of wind force has been accepted internationally and is used in communicating weather onditions. Devised originally by Admiral Sir Francis Beaufort in 1805, it now consists of these umbers 0–17, each representing certain strength or velocity of wind.

Scale No.	*Wind Force*	*M.p.h.*	*Knots*	*Scale No.*	*Wind Force.*	*M.p.h.*	*Knots*
0	Calm	1	1	9	Strong gale	47–54	41–47
1	Light air	1–3	1–3	10	Whole gale	55–63	48–55
2	Slight breeze	4–7	4–6	11	Storm	64–72	56–63
3	Gentle breeze	8–12	7–10	12	Hurricane	73–82	64–71
4	Moderate breeze	13–18	11–16	13	—	83–92	72–80
5	Fresh breeze	19–24	17–21	14	—	93–103	81–89
6	Strong breeze	25–31	22–27	15	—	104–114	90–99
7	High wind	32–38	28–33	16	—	115–125	100–108
8	Gale	39–46	34–4-	17	—	126–136	109–118

NATIONAL HEALTH SERVICE

The National Health Service was inaugurated on July 5, 1948, by the Minister of Health under the *National Health Service Act*, 1946, " to promote the establishment in England and Wales of a comprehensive Health Service designed to secure improvement in the mental and physical health of the people of England and Wales and the prevention, diagnosis and treatment of illness." There are separate Acts for Scotland and Northern Ireland, where the Health Services are run on very similar lines. The Minister of Health is responsible to Parliament for seeing that Health Services of all kinds of the highest possible quality are available to all who need them. He is advised by the Central Health Services Council (and certain Standing Advisory Committees dealing with special subjects), which he appoints after consultation with the various interested bodies.

The National Health Service which covers a comprehensive range of hospital, specialist, practitioner (medical, dental, ophthalmic), pharmaceutical, appliance and local authority services, is available to every man, woman and child in the country. Everyone resident in the country is entitled to use the Service as a whole or any complete part of it. No insurance qualification is necessary. Most of the cost of running the Service is met by the Exchequer—that is from taxes. Other sources of finance are: (i) the weekly National Health Service contributions (since September, 1957), which are estimated to produce about £145,000,000, approximately ⅛th of the total cost of the Service in 1963–64. (For convenience these are collected with the National Insurance contribution in a single combined weekly stamp); (ii) local taxation, which pays for about half the cost of local health authority services; (iii) partial charges to patients for prescription items, spectacles, dentures and dental treatment, appliances, amenity beds in hospital; (iv) superannuation contributions.

Details of the way in which the National Health Service is organized, and of the services provided by its main branches are described in the following paragraphs.

THE HEALTH SERVICES

Family Doctor Service

In England and Wales the Family Doctor Service is organized by 138 Executive Councils which also organize the Dental, Pharmaceutical and Supplementary Eye Services for their areas. There is an Executive Council for each County and County Borough area, but in some cases one Council covers two areas. Members, who serve voluntarily, are appointed by local doctors, dentists and pharmacists (12), the Local Health Authority (8) and the Minister of Health (5). Any doctor may take part in the Family Doctor Scheme, provided the area in which he wishes to practise has not already an adequate number of doctors, and about 22,000 general practitioners do so. They may at the same time have private fee-paying patients. Health Service doctors are paid on a capitation basis, *i.e.* an annual fee in respect of each patient accepted.

Everyone aged 16 or over can choose his doctor (parents or guardians choose for children under 16) and the doctor is also free to accept a person or not as he chooses. A person may change his doctor if he wishes, either at once if he has changed his address or obtained permission of the doctor on whose list he is, or by informing the local Executive Council (in which case 14 days must elapse before the other doctor can accept him). When people are away from home they can still use the Family Doctor Service if they ask to be treated as " temporary residents," and in an emergency, if a person's own doctor is not available, any doctor in the service will give treatment and advice.

Patients are treated either in the doctor's surgery or when necessary, at home. Doctors may prescribe for their patients all drugs and medicines which are medically necessary for their treatment and also a certain number of surgical appliances (the more elaborate being provided through the hospitals).

Drugs, Medicines and Appliances.—The number of chemists (including drug stores and appliance suppliers) in England and Wales, within the National Health Service at December 31, 1961, was 15,681. 196,626,238 prescriptions were dispensed in 1962. Since March 1, 1961, there has been a charge of 2*s.* in respect of each item on a prescription form made out by the family doctor and presented for dispensing, except for elastic hosiery for which the charge is 5*s.* or 10*s.* for each article. In those country areas where the doctor does his own dispensing, the charge is collected by the doctor.

Dental Service

Dentists, like doctors, may take part in the Service and may also have private patients. About 10,500 of the dentists available for general practice have joined the National Health Service. They are responsible to the Executive Councils in whose areas they provide services.

Patients are free to go to any dentist taking part in the Service and willing to accept them, and do not require to register with any particular dentist. Dentists receive payment for items of treatment for individual patients, instead of the capitation fee received by doctors. There is no need for the patient to obtain a recommendation before seeking dental treatment. The dentist is able to carry out at once all normal conservative treatment (*e.g.* fillings), provision of dentures in some cases, emergency treatment and ordinary denture repairs; he seeks prior approval from the Dental Estimates Board before undertaking treatment when it involves the extraction of teeth and the provision of dentures (in some cases); extensive and prolonged treatment of the gums; inlays; crowns (in some cases); special appliances and oral surgery and certain other items.

A dentist may, with the approval of the Dental Estimates Board, charge his patient a prescribed sum for such types of treatment as crowns, inlays or metal dentures where these are not clinically necessary, if the patient wishes to have them. Where a denture supplied under the Service has to be replaced because of loss or damage the whole or part of the cost may be charged to the patient if he has been careless. In May, 1951, charges were introduced for dentures; these were increased in May, 1961, to £2 5*s.*–£2 15*s.* for the supply of one denture or up to £5 for a set. In June, 1952, a charge of £1, or the full cost of any treatment if less than £1, was introduced. No charge is made for the clinical examination of a patient's mouth. Expectant mothers or mothers who have had a child during the preceding twelve months, children under 16; or 16 or over, but still in full-time attendance at school, do not pay charges. Other patients between 16 and 20 years of age pay charges for dentures only.

Supplementary Ophthalmic Service

Supplementary Ophthalmic Services which are run by the Executive Councils, form part of the Eye Services available under the National Health Service, and provide for the testing of sight and supply of glasses only. Any ophthalmic medical practitioner or ophthalmic optician who has joined the Service may be consulted. The first time a person uses the Service he must obtain a recommendation from his doctor that his sight needs testing. After this he can use the Service direct without first obtaining a note from his doctor.

Until 1951 there were no charges under the Supplementary Ophthalmic Service except, in certain cases, for the renewal or repair of glasses or where the patient chose a more expensive spectacle frame than one of the standard frames available free, or asked to be supplied with special lenses. In May, 1951, charges to patients of 10*s*. for each lens, plus the actual cost of the frames, were introduced. As from May 16, 1961, charges to patients have been increased to 12*s*. 6*d*. for each single-vision lens or 20*s*. for each bi-focal lens. As hitherto, children's glasses in the standard type of children's frame remain free of charge. As from May, 1961, schoolchildren aged 10 years or over may be supplied with lenses without charge if any other type of N.H.S. frame is used; the charge for the frame must then be paid.

Hospitals and Specialists

On July 5, 1948, ownership of 2,688 out of 3,040 voluntary and municipal hospitals in England and Wales was vested in the Minister of Health. The Minister has a duty to provide hospital accommodation and specialist services to such an extent as he considers necessary to meet all reasonable requirements for the treatment of the acutely ill, maternity cases, the chronic sick and those suffering from tuberculosis or infectious diseases as well as the mentally disordered. Convalescent treatment is also provided for those who need it and surgical and medical appliances are supplied in appropriate cases.

In the main, this part of the Service is organized by 15 Regional Hospital Boards (*see* Index); in 14 of these regions there is a University having a teaching hospital or medical school. Hospitals are administered on behalf of the Boards by 369 Hospital Management Committees. The only hospitals in the Service outside the Regional Boards' immediate responsibility are the teaching hospitals which provide facilities for undergraduate and post-graduate medical or dental education and which are administered by Boards of Governors. There are 26 Boards of Governors in London and 10 in the rest of the country.

Specialists and consultants who take part in the Service (and nearly all of them are doing so) hold hospital appointments. They can take up whole-time or part-time service and those who have part-time appointments can still accept fee-paying patients outside the Service.

Certain hospitals have accommodation in small wards or single rooms which, if not required for patients who need privacy for medical reasons, may be made available to patients who desire it as an amenity. Amenity bed charges are fixed under Regulations and are at present 12*s*. or 24*s*. per day. In such a case the patient pays nothing for the cost of treatment or the normal cost of maintenance. In some hospitals a number of pay-beds has been placed at the disposal of part-time specialists taking part in the Service for use by private patients who agree to pay full hospital maintenance costs, and (usually) private fees to the specialist as well. The fees that may be charged by specialists to patients occupying private pay-beds are normally restricted to 75 guineas to cover everything. For exceptionally long or complicated treatment this limit may be raised to 125 guineas and special arrangements may be made in a limited proportion of pay-beds for patient and doctor to agree to fees outside these limits.

Arrangements to obtain the service or advice of a hospital specialist are made by the patient's family doctor as in the past. A specialist usually sees a patient at the hospital or clinic at which he works, but arrangements will be made for the specialist to visit the patient at home if he is unable, for medical reasons, to be taken to hospital. No charges are made to National Health Service in-patients (except for amenity beds as above or dentures or glasses of a special type supplied at the patient's request), but a charge of 2*s*. is made to out-patients for each item on a prescription form for drugs and medicines (unless administered at hospitals). Exemptions from this charge are made in the case of patients receiving National Assistance or their dependants; war pensioners receiving medicines for their accepted disability; and patients attending V.D. clinics who receive medicines as part of their treatment. Also hospital out-patients have to pay fixed charges for elastic hosiery, surgical abdominal supports, surgical footwear (and heeling and soling repairs), dentures, glasses and wigs. Exceptions are made in the case of a child under 16 years of age or at full-time attendance at school, to National Assistance recipients and their dependants and to war pensioners in respect of their accepted war disabilities.

There are at present 82 hospitals providing distribution centres where hearing aids can be obtained after recommendation by a specialist.

Local Health Authority Services

The Local Health Services, mainly concerned with the care of patients in their own homes, are the responsibility of the local health authorities—County Councils and County Borough Councils. There are 146 Local Health Authorities in England and Wales and 29 other authorities exercise delegated health and welfare functions.

Local Health Services provide such services as midwifery; ante-natal, post-natal and infant welfare clinics, and priority dental services where practicable for expectant and nursing mothers and young children; health visiting; home nursing; ambulances; provision of domestic help on health grounds; special care and after-care of the sick; health education; local mental health services; and also vaccination and immunization. Most authorities also provide a chiropody service with priority for the elderly, physically handicapped persons and expectant mothers. The provision of Health Centres is also a local Health Authority responsibility in England and Wales. In Scotland such centres are the responsibility of the Scottish Home and Health Department.

All these services are free of charge except for domestic help and, in certain cases, provision of residential accommodation, meals, chiropody, nursing requisites, bedding and other services for care and after-care, for which a charge may be made according to means. Since June, 1952, Local Health Authorities have also had power to make charges for the use of day nurseries. A charge may also be made for yellow fever vaccinations. The Local Health Authorities may only charge what is reasonable, having regard to the means of the users.

Cost of the Service

	England and Wales	Scotland	Northern Ireland
	£	£	£
1950–51...	336,559,753	40,297,713	9,416,000
1951–52...	348,457,732	43,426,325	10,091,000
1952–53...	384,155,261	47,563,768	10,863,000
1953–54...	367,947,357	46,423,240	10,848,985
1954–55...	388,860,290	49,865,376	11,772,991
1955–56 ..	423,796,657	53,271,739	13,454,000
1956–57...	468,012,590	57,894,572	14,698,000
1957–58...	480,445,973	59,462,208	15,569,138
1958–59...	486,433,921	60,057,771	17,662,974
1959–60...	558,786,397	61,327,785	17,635,009
1960–61...	626,473,951	69,323,522	19,980,921
1961–62...	623,819,858	68,585,560	21,820,430
1962–63*..	722,494,000	81,010,000	22,661,290
1963–64*..	754,474,000	87,726,000	

* Estimated.

NATIONAL INSURANCE AND ASSISTANCE

For Combined Contributions, see p. 1051.

The State insurance and assistance schemes in force since July 5, 1948, comprise schemes of national insurance and industrial injuries insurance, national assistance and non-contributory old age pensions, and family allowances. The two insurance schemes and the family allowances scheme are administered by the Ministry of Pensions and National Insurance, and the national assistance scheme and non-contributory old age pensions by the National Assistance Board.

NATIONAL INSURANCE

The National Insurance Scheme operates under the National Insurance Act, 1946, as amended by the National Insurance Acts of 1949, 1951, 1953, 1954, 1955, 1956, 1957, 1959, 1960 and 1963, the National Insurance (No. 2) Act, 1957, the Family Allowances and National Insurance Acts, 1952, 1956, 1959 and 1961, and the National Health Service Contributions Acts, 1957 and 1961, and Regulations made under these Acts.

The National Insurance Acts, 1959 and 1963, extended the existing flat-rate scheme by providing, for employed persons over 18, a system of contributions graduated according to earnings, with related graduated additions to retirement pensions. Employees with equivalent occupational pension rights may be contracted out of this graduated part of the scheme. Provision was also made for higher Exchequer supplements, and for four quinquennial increases in contribution rates beginning in 1965.

The National Insurance Act, 1963, amended the amounts of flat-rate contributions and benefits payable under the scheme.

INSURED PERSONS AND CONTRIBUTIONS

Subject to certain statutory exceptions, every person living in Great Britain who is over school leaving age and under pension age becomes insured under the Acts.

There are three classes of insured persons namely:

(*a*) Class 1. Employed persons, i.e. persons who work for an employer under a contract of service or are paid apprentices.

(*b*) Class 2. Self-employed persons, i.e. persons gainfully occupied but not working under the control of an employer.

(*c*) Class 3. Non-employed persons, i.e. persons who are not gainfully occupied.

The estimated number of persons in respect of whom contributions were payable in 1960 was as follows: employed, 22·5 million; self-employed, 1·4 million; non-employed, 0·3 million.

National Insurance contributions are payable by insured persons, by employers of employed persons, and out of moneys provided by Parliament (*see* p. 1151).

The ordinary flat-rate contributions are usually paid by means of stamps on a single insurance card; the stamp also covers the National Health Service contribution and, in the case of employed persons, the Industrial Injuries contribution.

Since June 1, 1963, employed persons over age 18 earning more than £9 in any week (who are not contracted out as members of approved occupational pension schemes) and their employers have paid, in addition to the flat rate contribution covering earnings up to £9 a week, a graduated contribution for earnings over £9 and up to £18 a week. People in class 1 who are contracted out pay a higher flat-rate contribution (*see* pp. 1147, 1051).

Regulations made under the Acts give married women and widows, upon certain conditions, the choice whether to pay the National Insurance flat-rate contribution or not.

Men aged 70 and over and women aged 65 and over in classes (1) and (2) pay no National Insurance contribution. Men aged 65 to 70 and women aged 60 to 65 in these classes, with certain exceptions, are liable to pay contributions, including any graduated contributions, if they have not retired from regular employment. Normally no contributions are payable by men over 65 or women over 60 in class (3).

Regulations state the cases in which insured persons may be excepted from paying National Insurance contributions, and the conditions upon which contributions are credited to persons who are excepted.

From April, 1961, the yearly Exchequer contribution, subject to a minimum of £170 million a year, is equal to one-quarter of the national insurance portion of the contributions paid by employers and employed persons (excluding graduated contributions) and one-third of the national insurance portion of self-employed and non-employed contributions.

BENEFITS

The Acts give the following benefits:—

- Unemployment benefit.
- Sickness benefit.
- Maternity benefits, including maternity grant, home confinement grant and maternity allowance.
- Widow's benefits, including widow's allowance, widowed mother's allowance and widow's pension.
- Child's special allowance.
- Guardian's allowance
- Retirement pension.
- Death grant.

The benefits available to the various classes of insured persons are as follows:

Employed persons....	All benefits.
Self-employed persons.	All benefits *except* unemployment benefit.
Non-employed persons	All benefits *except* unemployment and sickness benefits and maternity allowance.

There is one system of adjudication on all claims for benefit under the Acts; with certain exceptions, questions as to the right to benefit are decided by independent statutory authorities, consisting of insurance officers, local tribunals and the Commissioner and Deputy Commissioners.

UNEMPLOYMENT BENEFIT

The *standard weekly rates of benefit* are as follows:

	s.	d.
Man, single woman or widow over 18...	67	6
Married woman over 18: ordinary rate	46	0
Person under 18: ordinary rate.........	38	6

	s.	d.
Increase of benefit for only child or elder or eldest child (where payable)	20	0
Increase of benefit for each additional child (where payable)	12	0
Increase of benefit for adult dependant (where payable)	41	6

Normal Contribution Conditions.—The claimant must have paid 26 Class 1 contributions since July 5, 1948, and, to be entitled to benefit at the standard rate during a benefit year, must have paid or had credited 50 Class 1 contributions during the preceding contribution year.

Waiting Period.—Benefit is not payable for the first three days of a spell of unemployment or sickness unless the claimant has twelve days or more of unemployment or sickness within a period of 13 weeks beginning with the first of these days. Odd days of unemployment or sickness count for benefit only where any two or more of them fall within a period of six consecutive days, excluding Sundays, and such spells of two or more days are treated as "linked up" if not separated by more than 13 weeks.

Duration of Benefit.—A claimant can draw in respect of any period of interruption of employment 180 days of unemployment benefit, together with additional days of benefit, assessed on his record of contributions and benefit.

Requalification for Benefit.—A person who has exhausted his standard benefit, including any additional days, requalifies therefor when he has paid 13 Class 1 contributions.

Disqualifications.—As in the former scheme, there are disqualifications for receiving benefit, e.g. for a period not exceeding six weeks if a person has lost his employment through his misconduct, or has voluntarily left his employment without just cause, or has, without good cause, refused an offer of suitable employment.

Numbers Unemployed.—During the year 1962 the average number of persons registered as unemployed in Great Britain was 463,200. On November 6, 1961, 202,000 persons were receiving unemployment benefit.

SICKNESS BENEFIT

Standard Rates of Benefit.—Same as for unemployment benefit.

Normal Contribution Conditions.—Same as for unemployment benefit, except that Class 2 as well as Class 1 contributions are counted.

Waiting Period.—Same as for unemployment benefit. Days of sickness are "linked up" with days of unemployment falling within the same period of 13 weeks.

Duration of Benefit.—A person who has paid 156 Class 1 or Class 2 contributions receives sickness benefit of unlimited duration. If he has paid less than 156 such contributions, benefit is limited to 312 days (one year); but he will requalify for benefit when he has paid contributions for 13 weeks.

Disqualifications.—Regulations provide for disqualifying a person for receiving sickness benefit for a period not exceeding six weeks if he has become incapable of work through his own misconduct, or if he fails without good cause to attend for or submit himself to prescribed medical or other examination or treatment, or if he acts in a way which would retard his recovery.

Number of Claims.—During 1961, 9,152,000 new claims for sickness benefit were received. The number of claimants incapacitated owing to sickness varied during the year from 818,000 in July to 1,228,000 in February.

MATERNITY BENEFITS

The National Insurance Act, 1953, made changes in the structure of maternity benefits provided by the principal Act.

Maternity Grant.—A cash grant of £16 is payable on the mother's own insurance or on her husband's. Extra grants are payable, in certain circumstances, if more than one child is born. The normal contribution conditions for this grant are (i) that the mother or her husband has paid not less than 26 contributions of any class since his or her entry into insurance, and (ii) that not less than 26 contributions of any class have been paid by or credited to that person during the previous contribution year, or the mother has satisfied the contribution conditions for a maternity allowance at the standard rate or at a reduced rate.

Home Confinement Grant.—An additional grant of £6 is payable to women who are confined at home or elsewhere at their own expense.

Maternity Allowance.—A woman who is gainfully occupied receives in addition a maternity allowance of 67*s.* 6*d.* a week normally for 18 weeks beginning eleven weeks before the expected week of confinement, provided that she abstains from work. The rate of allowance is increased where the woman has dependants. The normal contribution conditions for this benefit are (i) that the claimant has paid or had credited 50 Class 1 or 2 contributions during the 52 weeks ending 13 weeks before the expected week of confinement; and (ii) that in the same 52 weeks at least 26 Class 1 or 2 contributions have been paid.

During 1961 maternity grants were paid for about 867,000 births; in addition, the home confinement grant was paid in about 326,000 cases, and about 198,000 women received weekly maternity allowances.

WIDOW'S BENEFITS

This benefit in any of its three forms is payable to the widow of any class of insured person. The normal contribution conditions to be satisfied by the husband are (*a*) that he had paid not less than 156 contributions of any class since his last entry into insurance (104 if he was married before July 5, 1948, and insured from before September 30, 1946), and (*b*) that the yearly average of the contributions paid by or credited to him since his insurance started was not less than 50.

Widow's Allowance.—A woman who at her husband's death is under 60, or, if the husband had not qualified for a retirement pension, is over 60, receives (during the first 13 weeks of widowhood) a cash allowance usually of 95*s.* a week, with an increase of 30*s.* for the first or only child and 22*s.* for each other child.

Widowed Mother's Allowance.—When the 13 weeks of widow's allowance have elapsed, a widow who is left with one or more dependent children receives a cash allowance usually of 97*s.* 6*d.* a week so long as she has a child of qualifying age, and in addition 22*s.* a week for each child other than the first. A widowed mother's personal allowance, usually 67*s.* 6*d.* a week, is payable to widows who have living with them a child under 18 who has left school and is not an apprentice.

Widow's Pension.—A widow who is under pensionable age or, being over 60 and not yet 65, has not retired from regular employment, receives a widow's pension usually of 67*s.* 6*d.* a week (i) when widow's allowance ends, if she was over 50 at the time of her husband's death and had been married for not less than three years; or, (ii) when her widowed mother's allowance comes to an end, if she is then over 50 (40 if widowed before February

4, 1957) and not less than three years have elapsed since marriage.

Widow's benefit of any form ceases upon remarriage. A 67*s*. 6*d*. widow's pension is reduced by sixpence for each shilling of any net earnings in excess of 85*s*. and a further sixpence for each shilling of net earnings in excess of 105*s*. A widowed mother's allowance is reduced by sixpence for each shilling of any net earnings in excess of 120*s*. and a further sixpence for each shilling of net earnings in excess of 140*s*.; but it must not be reduced in any week by more than 41*s*. 6*d*.

If a woman, who was married before July 5, 1948, to a man insured under the old scheme immediately before that date does not qualify for widow's benefit under the new scheme, she may qualify for a widow's basic pension, usually of 10*s*. a week.

At the end of 1961, about 568,000 widows were receiving widowed mother's allowance, widow's pension or widow's 10*s*. pension, and about 21,000 widow's allowances were current.

CHILD'S SPECIAL ALLOWANCE

The National Insurance Act, 1957, provides for a special allowance for a woman whose marriage has been dissolved or annulled and who has not remarried, to be payable on the ex-husband's death if the woman has in her family a child to whose maintenance the ex-husband had before his death been contributing at least 5*s*. a week in cash or its equivalent. The allowance is 30*s*. a week for the first or only child *plus* 22*s*. for each other child in addition to Family Allowances. The contribution conditions for the allowance are substantially the same as for widow's benefit.

GUARDIAN'S ALLOWANCE

Where the parents of a child are dead, and one at least of them was an insured person, any person who has the child in his family receives a guardian's allowance of 37*s*. 6*d*. a week while the child is of school age. At the end of 1961 about 5,500 allowances were being paid.

RETIREMENT PENSIONS

A flat-rate retirement pension is payable for life to an insured person who (*a*) is over pension age (65 for a man and 60 for a woman), (*b*) has retired from regular employment, and (*c*) has paid the prescribed number of contributions. Men aged 70 and over and women aged 65 and over are not required to satisfy condition (*b*).

The standard flat-rate pension is 67*s*. 6*d*. a week, plus 41*s*. 6*d*. for a dependent wife, plus 20*s*. for the first or only child and 12*s*. for each other child.

Where the insured person postpones retirement beyond minimum pension age, the weekly rate of pension is increased, when he or she finally retires or reaches the age of 70 (65 for women), in respect of contributions paid as an employed or self-employed person during the five years after reaching minimum pension age. After Aug. 2, 1959, the increment to pension is 1*s*. for every 12 contributions. A retirement pensioner between the ages of 65 and 70 (60 and 65 for women) can choose to be treated as not retired and thus earn pension increments by temporarily forgoing his pension and paying contributions during employment or self-employment.

A man aged 65 to 70 (or a woman aged 60 to 65) who has qualified for pension will have it reduced by sixpence for each shilling of net earnings in excess of 85*s*. and a further sixpence for each shilling of net earnings in excess of 105*s*.

The Normal Contribution Conditions are (*a*) that 156 contributions of any class have been paid (104 if insurance began before September 30, 1946), and (*b*) that the yearly average of contributions paid or credited is not less than 50.

Special Provisions as to Women.—Subject to certain conditions, a married woman on reaching 60 or a woman on marriage after that age receives by virtue of her husband's insurance a retirement pension of 41*s*. 6*d*. a week. A widow over the age of 60 when her husband dies will usually qualify for a retirement pension of 67*s*. 6*d*. a week from her husband's insurance instead of a widow's pension. A retirement pension payable to a woman by virtue of her husband's insurance is increased by 6*d*. during his lifetime and 1*s*. on widowhood for every 12 contributions paid by the husband after Aug. 2, 1959, as an employed or self-employed person while he is over 65 and under 70 and she is over 60, and her pension in widowhood is increased by 6*d*. for every 12 of these contributions paid by him on or after December 25, 1961, while she is under 60. A widow who qualifies for retirement pension on her own insurance can receive, in addition to any increments she may earn by deferring her own retirement and paying contributions beyond age 60, half of all the 1*s*. increments which her husband earns by deferring retirement and paying contributions on or after December 25, 1961. The pension of a woman under 65 is reduced by sixpence for each shilling of her net earnings in excess of 85*s*. and a further sixpence for each shilling of her net earnings in excess of 105*s*.

Unemployment and sickness benefit is payable to men between 65 and 70 and women between 60 and 65 who have not retired from regular employment at the same rate as the retirement pension they would have been entitled to had they retired from regular employment.

At the end of 1961 retirement pensions, or contributory old age pensions under the old Acts, were being paid to approximately 5,677,000 persons, about 114,000 more than a year earlier.

THE GRADUATED PENSION SCHEME

From April, 1961, when the new graduated pension scheme came into operation under the National Insurance Act, 1959, National Insurance contributions and retirement pensions are graduated, within specified limits, according to earnings. The scheme does not apply to employed persons under 18, or to self-employed or non-employed persons (see p. 1051).

Graduated contributions.—Employed persons over 18 (including men over 65 and under 70, and women over 60 and under 65, who have not retired), unless contracted out as members of occupational pension schemes satisfying certain conditions, pay a weekly flat-rate contribution covering earnings up to £9 a week, plus a graduated contribution on all earnings over £9 and up to £18 a week.

As from June 1, 1963, the flat-rate contribution, which includes the separate National Health Service and Industrial Injuries contributions, is 21*s*.4*d*. for an employed man (of which the employee pays 11*s*. 8*d*. and the employer 9*s*. 8*d*.) and 18*s*. for an employed woman (of which the employee pays 9*s*. 8*d*. and the employer 8*s*. 4*d*.) (see p. 1051).

During the period up to April, 1965, on earnings above £9 and up to £18 a week the graduated contribution will be 8½ per cent. of earnings, divided equally between employer and employee. On earnings above £18 a week the graduated contribution is the same as on earnings of £18 a week, viz., 15*s*. 4*d*., divided equally between employer and employee (*see* p. 1051).

The graduated contribution is the same for men and women. Employed married women, and widows receiving certain benefits, are still able to choose not to pay the flat-rate contribution (other than the 5*d*. Industrial Injuries contribution), but, unless contracted out, they pay their share of the graduated contribution on their earnings between £9 and £18 a week.

The graduated contributions are in general payable on the gross earnings (including overtime pay, bonus, etc.) received in each week (or month, etc.) taken separately, and not on the cumulative total over the year (see Leaflet N.I. 116, obtainable at Pensions and National Insurance Offices).

Contracted-out employees (whatever their earnings) and their employers pay flat-rate contributions which, in the case of employees aged 18 and over, are higher than those payable by employees who are not contracted out (see p. 1051).

The flat-rate contributions are usually paid by means of a combined weekly stamp. The graduated contributions are collected through the P.A.Y.E. system, in association with income tax (see Leaflet N.I. 116).

The National Insurance Acts, 1959 and 1963, provide for increases in the flat-rate contributions and the graduated contributions in April, 1965, and at five-yearly intervals thereafter up to April, 1980.

The graduated pension.—The graduated addition to the flat-rate retirement pension for each contributor is at the rate of 6*d*. a week for each unit of graduated contributions paid by him or her since the start of the new scheme. A unit of contributions during the period from April, 1961, to April, 1965, will be £7*s*. 10*s*. for men, and £9 for women, of graduated contributions paid by the employee. A widow over age 60 gets a graduated addition to her flat-rate retirement pension equal to half of any graduated addition earned by her late husband, plus any addition earned by her own graduated contributions.

Graduated additions are subject to the usual condition of retirement and initially are subject to the same earnings rules as the flat-rate retirement pension (see p. 1046). Persons who defer retirement will continue to pay graduated contributions until they retire or reach 70 (65 for women) whether retired or not, when they will qualify for graduated additions to pension in respect of graduated contributions they have paid. In addition, half of the graduated additions they have forgone by deferring retirement will be treated as extra graduated contributions paid by them and will count towards further graduated pension (see Leaflet N.I. 111).

Contracting out.—Adult employees who have retirement pension rights in an occupational pension scheme can be contracted out of the graduated part of National Insurance retirement pensions if the following conditions are satisfied:

(1) the occupational scheme is financially sound;
(2) it provides the employees contracted out with retirement pension rights at least equal to the maximum graduated pension that could have been earned in the State scheme for a corresponding period of service up to age 65 (women 60);
(3) pension rights at least up to this amount are preserved should the employee change his job (see Leaflet N.I. 114).

To be contracted out, an employee must be in an employment covered by a Certificate of Non-participation issued to his employer by the Registrar of Non-participating Employments. In general, the application for a certificate must come from the employer. An employer who wishes to contract out all or particular groups of employees must first give notice to the employees and others concerned (e.g. trustees, insurers, committee of management) and allow a period for consultation, and the Registrar can defer the issue of a certificate to allow time for further consultation. There is a right of appeal to the Adjudicator against a refusal by the Registrar to issue a certificate.

If an application was not made in sufficient time before the new scheme came into force, graduated contributions will be payable from April, 1961, until a certificate is issued and takes effect. It is open to an employer to seek the Registrar's advice as to whether a pension scheme is suitable for contracting out before a formal application is made. A leaflet R 1, which explains the arrangements for contracting out and for modifying schemes for the purpose of satisfying the contracting out conditions can be obtained from the Registrar of Non-participating Employments, Government Buildings, Monck Street, London, S.W.1.

Up to April 1, 1962, about 37,000 certificates of non-participation, covering some 4·4 million employees, had been issued.

As a consequence of the increase in the maximum graduated contributions and pensions under the National Insurance Act, 1963, equivalent pension benefits and payments in lieu are also increased. Employers are allowed until January 5, 1964, to adjust their occupational pension schemes and the new levels of equivalent pension benefits and payments in lieu will apply only to service after that date.

DEATH GRANT

A death grant is payable on the death of an insured person or of his wife, child or widow or, if the insured person is a woman, of her husband, child or widower. The normal grant is for an adult £25, a child aged 6–17 £18 15*s*., a child aged 3–5 £12 10*s*., a child under 3 £7 10*s*. For the deaths of people who on July 5, 1948, were between 55 and 65 (men) or between 50 and 60 (women) the grant is £12 10*s*.

The normal contribution conditions for death grant are that (*a*) not less than 26 contributions of any class have been paid by or credited to the deceased or the person by virtue of whose insurance the grant is claimed since July 5, 1948, and (*b*) either not less than 45 contributions of any class have been paid by or credited to him in the previous contribution year, or the yearly average of the contributions paid or credited since July 5, 1948 (or 16th birthday if later) is not less than 45. No grant is payable for deaths of persons already over pension age on July 5, 1948. For deaths in 1960 about 303,000 grants were awarded.

The grant is paid to the deceased person's executors or administrators, if any; otherwise it is paid to the person who meets the funeral expenses or to the next of kin.

FINANCE

Under the Act of 1946 two funds are set up, viz. the National Insurance Fund, and the National Insurance (Reserve) Fund. The income from contributions, Exchequer grants and interest from both funds are paid into the National Insurance Fund, and payments are made out of the Fund to meet the cost of benefits and administration. Under the National Health Service Contributions Act, 1957, payments hitherto made from the Fund towards the cost of the National Health Service, which were equivalent to 10*d*. out of each total weekly National Insurance contribution for men, 8*d*. for women, and 6*d*. for boys and girls, were discontinued; consequential reductions were made in the rates of National Insurance contributions, and provision was made for separate National Health Service contributions, yielding twice the amount of the payments previously made from the National Insurance Fund to the National Health Service, to be collected in conjunction with the National Insurance contributions. Increases in the rates of National Health Service contributions under the National Health Service Contributions Acts, 1958 and 1961, took effect as from July 7, 1958 and July 3, 1961, respectively. (*See* p. 1051).

Approximate receipts and payments of the National Insurance Fund for the year ended March 31, 1962, were as follows:—

Receipts		£'000
Balance, April 1, 1961		264,329
Flat-rate contributions from employers and insured persons		766,989
Exchequer contribution		187,381
Graduated contributions		148,021
Income from investments		10,415
Transfer from the Reserve Fund of income from investments, etc.		35,665
Other receipts		387
		1,413,187
Payments		
Benefit:—	£'000	£'000
Unemployment benefit	36,265	
Sickness benefit	154,570	
Maternity benefit	24,500	
Widow's benefit	80,000	
Guardian's allowance	480	
Child's special allowance	17	
Flate-rate retirement pension	783,904	
Graduated retirement benefit	15	
Death grant	6,160	
		1,085,911
Administration expenses		42,522
Other payments		7,279
Balance, March 31, 1962		277,475
		1,413,187

This Account reflected the increases in flat-rate contributions and in benefits, and the introduction of graduated contributions, under the National Insurance Acts, 1959 and 1960. Payments exceeded receipts during the year by £13·1 million. Compared with 1960–61, receipts increased by £211·9 million and payments by £157·5 million.

The balance in the Reserve Fund at March 31, 1962, was £1,168·0 million.

INDUSTRIAL INJURIES INSURANCE

The National Insurance (Industrial Injuries) Act, 1946, substituted for the Workmen's Compensation Acts, 1925 to 1945, a system of insurance against personal injury caused by accident arising out of and in the course of a person's employment and against prescribed diseases and injuries due to the nature of a person's employment. The scheme, which insures against personal injury caused and prescribed diseases and injuries developed on or after July 5, 1948, operates under the Act of 1946, as amended by the National Insurance (Industrial Injuries) Acts, 1948 and 1953, the National Insurance Acts, 1951, 1954, 1957, 1960 and 1963, the National Insurance (No. 2) Act, 1957, and the Family Allowances and National Insurance Acts, 1952, 1956, 1959 and 1961, and Regulations made by the Minister under those Acts. Higher rates of contributions and higher rates or amounts of benefits took effect under the National Insurance Act, 1963, from June 3, 1963.

The Workmen's Compensation Acts, including the Workmen's Compensation (Temporary Increases) Act, 1943, (which is now made permanent) continue to apply, subject to certain amendments, to cases arising before the new scheme started.

The Workmen's Compensation (Supplementation) Scheme, 1951, as amended, provides for the payment out of the Industrial Injuries Fund of allowances supplementing workmen's compensation where the accident or disease happened before 1924.

The Pneumoconiosis and Byssinosis Benefit Scheme, 1952, provides for payment of benefits out of the Industrial Injuries Fund for those totally disabled by pneumoconiosis or byssinosis, and for dependants of those who died from one of those diseases, after December 31, 1949, if they are not covered by either the Workmen's Compensation Acts or the Industrial Injuries Acts. This Scheme was extended by the Amendment Scheme, 1954, to cases of partial disablement as a result of either disease, and was further amended by the Amendment Schemes, 1957 and 1958.

The Industrial Diseases (Miscellaneous) Benefit Scheme, 1954, provides for payment of benefit out of the Industrial Injuries Fund to or in respect of certain persons who are disabled or die or have died after December 31, 1949, as a result of certain malignant and other diseases due to occupational exposure to carcinogens, in cases where neither workmen's compensation nor benefit under the Industrial Injuries Act is payable.

Under the Workmen's Compensation and Benefit (Supplementation) Act, 1956, as amended by the Family Allowances and National Insurance Act, 1961, and the National Insurance Act, 1963, a supplementary benefit of 65*s*. a week is payable out of the Industrial Injuries Fund to the classes of totally disabled persons mentioned in the 1956 Act who are receiving workmen's compensation.

INSURED PERSONS

The persons covered by the Industrial Injuries scheme correspond closely to the class of "employed persons" under the National Insurance Act, 1946 (excluding members of the Forces), and numbered in 1960 22¼ million, of whom rather more than one-third were women.

CONTRIBUTIONS

Contributions are payable by insured persons and their employers, unless exempted, and the Exchequer contributes an amount equal to one-fifth of the combined contributions of insured persons and employers.

The normal weekly rates of contributions payable by insured persons and employers respectively are 8*d*. and 9*d*. for men over 18, 5*d*. and 6*d*. for women over 18, 4*d*. and 5*d*. for boys under 18, and 3*d*. and 3*d*. for girls under 18. Normally contributions are paid by means of stamps on a single insurance card, the same stamp also covering the flat-rate National Insurance and the National Health Service contributions.

There are no contribution conditions for the payment of benefits. Persons employed in insurable employment are covered from the time of starting work, but if employed while of school age pay no contributions.

BENEFITS

Injury Benefit is payable for not more than the first 26 weeks of incapacity; no payment is made for the first three days unless there are a further nine days of incapacity within the injury benefit period. Benefit is payable to persons over 18 and to juveniles with dependant's allowances, at the weekly rate of 115*s*. (days being paid for at one-sixth of the weekly rate), *plus* 41*s*. 6*d*. for one adult dependant, *plus* 20*s*. for the first or only child and 12*s*. for each other child. Juveniles not entitled to a child or adult dependant's allowance receive benefit at half the adult rate if under 17 and at three-quarters the adult rate if 17 and under 18.

Disablement Benefit is payable if at or after the end of the injury benefit period the insured person suffers from loss of physical or mental faculty such that the resulting disablement is assessed at not less than one per cent. (In cases of pneumoconiosis and byssinosis disablement benefit is paid from the start without a period of injury benefit.) The amount of disablement benefit varies according to the degree of disablement (in the form of a percentage) assessed by a medical board or medical appeal tribunal by reference to the claimant's disabilities (incurred as a result of the loss of faculty) as compared with a normal person of the same age and sex. In cases of disablement of less than 20 per cent., benefit normally takes the form of a *gratuity* paid according to a prescribed scale, but not exceeding £380. Where the degree of disablement is 20 per cent. or more, the benefit is a weekly *pension* payable either for a limited period or for life according to the following scale:

Degree of disablement	*Weekly Rate* s.	d.
100 per cent	115	0
90 " "	103	6
80 " "	92	0
70 " "	80	6
60 " "	69	0
50 " "	57	6
40 " "	46	0
30 " "	34	6
20 " "	23	0

These are basic rates applicable to adults and to juveniles entitled to an increase for a child or adult dependant; other juveniles receive one-half the adult rate if under 17, and three-quarters of the adult rate if 17 and under 18.

Basic rates of pension are not related to the pensioner's loss of earning power, and are payable whether he is in work or not. Upon prescribed conditions, however, pension is supplemented for unemployability and in cases of special hardship. There is provision also for increases of pension during approved hospital treatment or if the pensioner requires constant attendance. An increase of 41*s*. 6*d*. for an adult dependant and of 20*s*. for the first or only child and 12*s*. for each other child is also payable where the pensioner is either entitled to an unemployability supplement or receiving approved hospital treatment. Subject to certain exceptions, a pensioner who is not in receipt of unemployability supplement can draw other national insurance benefits in full in addition to disablement pension.

Death Benefit, in the form of a pension, a gratuity or a weekly allowance for a limited period, available for widows and other dependants in fatal cases, depends in amount upon their relationship to the deceased and their circumstances at the time of death and not upon the deceased's earnings. A widow who was living with her husband at the time of his death receives a pension of 95*s*. a week for the first 13 weeks and thereafter of 75*s*. or less a week according to circumstances, *plus* 30*s*. for the first or only child and 22*s*. for each other child.

Regulations impose certain obligations on claimants and beneficiaries and on employers, including, in the case of the former, that of submitting to medical examination and treatment and attending courses of vocational training or rehabilitation approved by the Ministry of Labour.

Industrial Diseases, etc.—The Act of 1946 extends insurance to prescribed industrial diseases and prescribed personal injuries not caused by accident, which are due to the nature of an insured person's employment and developed on or after July 5, 1948.

Determination of Questions and Claims.—Provision is made for the determination of certain questions (*e.g.*, as to insurability and liability to contribute) by the Minister, and of "disablement questions" by a medical board (or a single doctor) or medical appeal tribunal or, on appeal on a point of law, by the Industrial Injuries Commissioner, subject to leave. Claims for benefit and certain questions arising in connection with a claim for or award of benefit (e.g., whether the accident arose out of and in the course of the employment) are determined by an insurance officer appointed by the Minister, or a local appeal tribunal consisting of a chairman appointed by the Minister and equal numbers of members representing employers and insured persons, or, on appeal, by the Commissioner.

About three-quarters of a million new awards of injury benefit are made each year. The number of awards of disablement benefit and of special hardship allowance has increased year by year. The number of disablement pensions in payment rose during the year ended October 31, 1960, from 164,400 to 172,800; of those in payment at the end of the period 47,500 were in respect of pneumoconiosis. During the same year the number of special hardship allowances in payment increased from 101,400 to 107,700. The annual number of awards of death benefit slightly exceeds 2,000; at the end of 1960, about 19,500 widows' pensions and 14,300 allowances to dependent children were in payment.

FINANCE

Contributions from employers, insured persons and the Exchequer are paid into, and benefits and administrative expenses are paid out of, a fund established under the Act of 1946, viz., the Industrial Injuries Fund.

Receipts, 1961-62	£'000
Balance, April 1, 1961	271,270
Contributions from employers and insured persons	57,398
Exchequer contribution	11,981
Income from investments	12,117
Other receipts	649
	353,415

Payments, 1961-62	£'000	
Benefit:—		
Injury	20,399	
Disablement (*a*)	32,900	
Death (*a*)	4,000	
Other benefits (*b*)	1,156	
		58,456
Administration expenses		6,844
Other payments		23
Balance, March 31, 1962		288,093
		353,415

(*a*) Division estimated. (*b*) Allowances paid under the Workmen's Compensation (Supplementation) Scheme, 1951, as amended, allowances and death benefit paid under the Pneumoconiosis and Byssinosis Benefit Scheme, 1952, as amended by the Pneumoconiosis and Byssinosis Benefit Amendment Scheme, 1954, or under the Industrial Diseases (Miscellaneous) Benefit Scheme, 1954, and allowances paid under the Workmen's Compensation and Benefit (Supplementation) Act, 1956.

As the Industrial Injuries scheme in general applies to cases arising after July 4, 1948, expenditure on benefits will not reach maturity for many years.

NATIONAL ASSISTANCE

The National Assistance Act, 1948, was designed, from July 5, 1948, to substitute for certain existing services provided by the State or by local authorities a unified State service of financial assistance according to need. The service is administered by the National Assistance Board, the ultimate responsibility to Parliament resting with the Minister of Pensions and National Insurance.

Application for assistance may be made by any person aged 16 or over who is not in full-time work and is in need, including a person who needs assistance in supplementation of a pension or insurance benefit. The National Assistance Acts, 1948 and 1959, and the National Assistance (Determination of Need) Regulations, 1948, as amended, lay down how the need of an applicant shall be determined, and for this purpose how his requirements and resources shall be computed.

The scale rates for requirements other than rent, prescribed by the amending Regulations which came into operation on May 27, 1963, are as follows:

	Ordinary		Special (*a*)	
	s.	*d.*	*s.*	*d.*
Husband and wife........	104	6	129	0 (*b*)
Single householder.......	63	6		
Other persons:—				
Aged 21 or over.......	55	0	88	0
Aged 18–20...........	43	0	63	0
Aged 16–17...........	37	0	53	0
Aged 11–15...........	28	0	28	0
Aged 5–10............	23	0	23	0
Aged under 5.........	19	6	19	6

(*a*) For blind and certain tuberculous persons.

(*b*) 145*s.* when both husband and wife are in the special classes.

The amount to be added for rent, if the applicant, or his wife or her husband, is a householder, or if the applicant is living alone, will be the net rent payable, or such a part thereof as is reasonable in the circumstances. If an applicant over the age of 18 is a member of a household but is not himself the householder, the amount to be added for rent will be a reasonable share of the rent payable by the householder, subject to a minimum addition of 2*s.* 6*d.* a week and a maximum of 15*s.* a week.

The rules for the computation of resources contain provisions for the treatment of capital and earnings and certain statutory disregards.

The amount to be paid by way of assistance is settled by the local officer of the Board; an applicant who is dissatisfied with the amount granted has a right of appeal to the local Appeal Tribunal, whose decision is final.

On July 5, 1948, national assistance had to be given to some 800,000 persons who had previously been receiving unemployment assistance (31,000), supplementary pensions (512,000), outdoor relief (200,000), blind domiciliary assistance (40,000), or tuberculosis treatment allowances (20,000). The number of weekly assistance allowances in payment rose from 1,011,000 at the end of 1948 to 1,810,000 in February, 1955. By the end of September, 1955, the number had fallen to 1,595,000, due mainly to the increase in benefit rates under the National Insurance Act, 1954. Subsequently, the number fluctuated, but during 1959, 1960 and 1962 there were substantial increases. At the end of 1962 the number was 2,007,000 when the needs of 2,975,000 persons were being provided for wholly or in part. At the end of 1962 about 202,000 recipients were registered at the Employment Exchange; most of the rest were old, sick or otherwise incapable of work. More than two-thirds of the allowances were paid in supplementation of insurance pensions and benefits. During 1962 the Board also made single payments amounting to £6,800,000. In addition, assistance amounting to £3,969,000 was given to meet charges raised under the National Health Service for prescriptions, spectacles, dentures and dental treatment, and surgical appliances.

The total net expenditure of the Board during 1962 was about £202,436,000, as compared with £184,766,000 in 1961 and £60,760,000 in 1948. Included in the figure for 1962 were payments of national assistance £180,900,000 and payments of non-contributory old age pensions £7,850,000.

NON-CONTRIBUTORY OLD AGE PENSIONS

The maximum non-contributory old age pension payable under the Old Age Pensions Act, 1936, to persons aged 70 and over, and under the Blind Persons Act, 1938, to blind persons aged 40 and over, was increased in October, 1946, from 10*s.* a week to 26*s.* a week for single persons of either sex and married men and 16*s.* a week for married women. Pension was payable at the maximum rate where the yearly means calculated in accordance with the provisions of the Act, did not exceed £26 5*s.* *od.* Where the yearly means were between £26 5*s.* od. and £89 5*s.* *od.* pension was payable at rates varying from 24*s.* (16*s.* for married women) to 2*s.* Where the yearly means exceeded £89 5*s.* *od.*, no pension was payable. As from Jan. 27, 1958, when, under the National Insurance (No. 2) Act, 1957, the issue of weekly tobacco tokens to pensioners ceased, non-contributory pensions were increased by an amount equal to the current value of the tokens, i.e., 2*s.* 4*d.*

The National Assistance Act, 1948, which charged the National Assistance Board with the administration of non-contributory old age pensions, assimilated the pensions procedure to the national assistance procedure, and the Board has power to supplement old age pensions by national assistance in case of need.

The number of pensions in payment fell from 453,000 at the end of 1948 to 135,000 at the end of 1961, and declined further to 114,000 by the end of 1962. At the latter date, pensions were supplemented by national assistance in 85,000 cases. The award of new non-contributory pensions (other than to blind persons) has now been brought to an end by the provisions of section 74 of the National Insurance Act, 1946, under which sighted persons do not qualify unless they reached the age of 70 before September 30, 1961.

FAMILY ALLOWANCES

The Family Allowances Act, 1945, which was brought into operation from August 6, 1946, provided for a payment by the Minister of National Insurance out of moneys provided by Parliament of an allowance of 5*s.* a week for each child in a family other than the elder or eldest. From September 2, 1952, under the Family Allowances and National Insurance Act, 1952, the allowance was increased to 8*s.* From October 2, 1956, under the Family Allowances and National Insurance Act, 1956, the allowance for the third and each younger child was increased to 10*s.* The allowance is payable (through the Post Office) while a child is of school age or, if handicapped, under 16, and up to the age of eighteen years if he or she is undergoing full-time instruction in a school or is an apprentice. Claim forms for allowances can be obtained at any post office or local Pensions and National Insurance Office. Claims are decided by the National Insurance adjudication authorities.

At the end of January 1961, about 5,764,000 allowances were in payment for over 3½ million families. It is estimated that in 1961 over £133½ million was paid in allowances (excluding administrative expenses), as compared with £63 million in 1951 and £130 million in 1960.

COMBINED WEEKLY FLAT-RATE CONTRIBUTIONS

From June 3, 1963, the main combined weekly flat-rate contributions for National Insurance, the National Health Service and, in the case of employed persons, Industrial Injuries Insurance, paid by means of stamps on a single insurance card, are as follows:—

	Employees contracted out			Employees not contracted out			Self-employed persons	Non-employed persons
	Employee	Employer	Total	Employee	Employer	Total		
	s. d.	s. d.	s. d.	s. d.	s. d.	s. d.	s. d.	s. d.
Men 18 and over...	14 1	12 1	26 2	11 8	9 8	21 4	16 2	13 0
Women 18 and over	11 2	9 10	21 0	9 8	8 4	18 0	13 2	10 0
Boys under 18.....	FLAT-RATE CONTRIBUTIONS			7 8	7 0	14 8	9 1	7 4
Girls under 18.....				6 4	5 7	11 11	7 9	6 0

Further details of the various contributions including the special rates for certain employed married women, widows and people over pension age are obtainable at all local Pensions and National Insurance Offices.

Distribution of Combined Weekly Flat-rate Contributions

	Employed Person				Employer			
	Men	Women	Boys	Girls	Men	Women	Boys	Girls
	s. d.	s. d.	s. d.	s. d.	s. d.	s. d.	s. d.	s. d.
National Insurance:								
Employees:								
Contracted out........	10 8½	8 8½			10 8½	8 8½		
Not contracted out.....	8 3½	7 2½	5 11½	4 8½	8 3½	7 2½	5 11½	4 8½
Industrial Injuries Insurance .	0 8	0 5	0 4	0 3	0 9	0 6	0 5	0 3
National Health Service....	2 8½	2 0½	1 4½	1 4½	0 7½	0 7½	0 7½	0 7½

	Self-employed Person				Non-employed Person			
	Men	Women	Boys	Girls	Men	Women	Boys	Girls
	s. d.	s. d.	s. d.	s. d.	s. d.	s. d.	s. d.	s. d.
National Insurance.........	13 4	11 0	7 7	6 3	10 2	7 10	5 10	4 6
National Health Service....	2 10	2 2	1 6	1 6	2 10	2 2	1 6	1 6

GRADUATED NATIONAL INSURANCE CONTRIBUTIONS (see pp. 1046–1047)

Employed men and women aged 18 or over who are not contracted out of the graduated pension scheme pay in addition to the ordinary flat-rate contribution a graduated contribution (collected in association with P.A.Y.E. income tax). This amounts to approximately 4¼ per cent. of that part of their pay between £9 and £18, and ranges from 1*d*. a week by employees earning £9 0*s*. 1*d*. to £9 4*s*. 11*d*. a week to 7*s*. 8*d*. a week by employees earning £18 a week or more. The employer pays the same amount.

Examples of the graduated contributions payable for weekly paid employees are given below:

Total Weekly Pay	Employee	Employer	Total
	s. d.	s. d.	s. d.
£10 to £10 4*s*. 11*d*.	0 11	0 11	1 10
£11 to £11 4*s*. 11*d*.	1 10	1 10	3 8
£12 to £12 4*s*. 11*d*.	2 8	2 8	5 4
£13 to £13 4*s*. 11*d*.	3 6	3 6	7 0

Total Weekly Pay	Employee	Employer	Total
	s. d.	s. d.	s. d.
£14 to £14 4*s*. 11*d*.	4 4	4 4	8 8
£15 to £15 4*s*. 11*d*.	5 2	5 2	10 4
£16 to £16 4*s*. 11*d*.	6 1	6 1	12 2
£17 to £17 4*s*. 11*d*.	6 11	6 11	13 10
£18 or more......	7 8	7 8	15 4

Fuller details are given in Leaflet N.I. 130, available at local Pensions and National Insurance Offices.

Principal Daily Newspapers

LONDON (showing circulations at June, 1963):—

The Times (*Ind.*) 5*d.*, Printing House Sq., E.C.4 (254,754).
Daily Express (*Ind.*) 3*d.*, Fleet St., E.C.4 (4,224,148).
Daily Herald (*Lab.*) 3*d.*, 27 Floral St., W.C.2 (1,301,631).
Daily Mail (*Ind.*) 3*d.*, Northcliffe House, E.C.4 (2,479,466).
Daily Mirror (*Ind.*) 3*d.*, Holborn Circus, E.C.1 (4,630,964).
Daily Sketch (*Ind.*) 3*d.*, New Carmelite House, E.C.4 (922,937).
Daily Telegraph and Morning Post (*Cons.*) 3*d.*, 135 Fleet St., E.C.4 (1,290,012)
Daily Worker (*Communist*) 3*d.*, 75 Farringdon Road, E.C.1.
Financial Times (*Ind.*) 5*d.*, 10 Cannon St., E.C.4 (140,864).
Lloyd's List. 6*d.*, Lloyd's, E.C.3.
Morning Advertiser (*Ind.*) 4*d.*, 18-20 St. Andrews St E.C.4.
New Daily (*Ind.*) 3*d.*, (Evening Edition 2*d.*), 175 High Holborn, W.C.1.
Evening News and Star (*Ind.*) 3*d.*, Carmelite House, E.C.4 (1,387,623).
Evening Standard (*Ind.*), 3*d.*, 47 Shoe Lane, E.C.4 (729,241).

ABERDEEN........Press and Journal (*Cons.*) 3*d.*
Evening Express (*Ind.*) 4*d.*
BARROW.........North-Western Evening Mail (*Ind.*) 3*d.*
BATH............Bath and Wilts Evening Chronicle (*Cons.*) 3*d.*
BELFAST.........News Letter (*Un.*) 3*d.*
Northern Whig (*Un.*) 2*d.*
Telegraph (*Cons.*) 3*d.*
Irish News (*Nat.*) 2*d.*
BIRMINGHAM.....Post (*Ind.*) 3*d.*
Evening Mail and Despatch (*Ind.*) 2½*d.*
BLACKBURN......Evening Teleg. (*Ind.*) 4*d.*
BLACKPOOL......W. Lancs. Ev. Gazette (*Ind.*) 3*d.*
BOLTON.........Evening News (*Ind.*) 4*d.*
BOURNEMOUTH...Evening Echo, Bournemouth (*Ind.*) 3*d.*
BRADFORD.......Telegraph and Argus (*Ind.*) 3*d.*
BRIGHTON.......Evening Argus (*Ind.*) 3*d.*
BRISTOL.........Western Daily Press (*Ind.*) 3*d.*
Evening Post (*Ind.*) 3*d.*
BURTON.........Daily Mail (*Un.*) 2½*d.*
CAMBRIDGE.......Daily News (*Ind.*) 2½*d.*
CARDIFF.........South Wales Echo and Evening Express (*Ind.*) 4*d.*
Western Mail (*Ind.*) 3*d.*
CARLISLE........Cumberland Evening News (*Cons.*) 3*d.*
CHELTENHAM.....Gloucestershire Echo (*Ind.*) 3*d.*
COVENTRY.......Coventry Evening Telegraph (*Ind.*) 3*d.*
DARLINGTON.....Northern Echo (*Ind.*) 3*d.*
Northern Despatch (*Ind.*) 3*d.*
DERBY...........Evening Telegraph and Express (*Ind.*) 3*d.*
DOUGLAS (Isle of Man). Isle of Man Daily Times (*Cons.*) 3*d.*
DUNDEE.........Courier and Advertiser (*Ind.*) 3*d.*
Evening Telegraph and Post (*Ind.*) 3*d.*
EDINBURGH......Scotsman (*Ind.*) 4*d.*
Evening Dispatch (*Ind.*) 2*d.*
Evening News (*Ind.*) 2½*d.*
Scottish Daily Mail (*Ind.*) 3*d.*
EXETER..........Express and Echo (*Ind.*) 2½*d.*
GLASGOW........Glasgow Herald (*Ind.*) 4*d.*
Daily Record and Mail (*Cons.*) 3*d.*
Evening Citizen (*Ind.*) 3*d.*
Evening Times (*Ind.*) 3*d.*
Scottish Daily Express (*Ind.*) 3*d.*
GLOUCESTER......Citizen (*Ind.*) 3*d.*
GREENOCK.......Telegraph (*Lib.*) 3*d.*
GRIMSBY.........Evening Telegraph (*Ind.*) 3*d.*
GUERNSEY.......Evening Press (*Ind.*) 3*d.*
Star (*Ind.*) 3*d.*
HALIFAX.........Daily Courier and Guardian (*Ind.*) 3*d.*
HUDDERSFIELD....Daily Examiner (*Lib.*) 3*d.*
HULL...........Daily Mail (*Ind.*) 3*d.*
IPSWICH.........East Anglian Daily Times (*Ind.*) 3*d.*
Evening Star (*Ind.*) 3*d.*
KETTERING.......Northants Ev. Tele. (*Ind.*) 3*d.*
LEAMINGTON SPA..Leamington Spa, Warwick, etc. Morning News (*Ind.*) 2*d.*
LEEDS...........Yorkshire Post (*Cons.*) 3*d.*
Yorkshire Evening News (*Ind.*) 3*d.*
Yorkshire Evening Post (*Cons.*) 3*d.*
LEICESTER........Evening Mail (*Ind.*) 2½*d.*
Mercury (*Ind.*) 3*d.*
LINCOLN.........Echo (*Ind.*) 2½*d.*
LIVERPOOL.......Echo (*Ind.*) 3*d.*
Daily Post (*Ind.*) 3*d.*
Journal of Commerce (*Ind.*) 5*d.*
MANCHESTER.....Guardian (*Lib.*) 4*d.*
Manchester Evening News & Chronicle (*Ind.*) 4*d.*
MIDDLESBROUGH..Evening Gazette (*Cons.*) 4*d.*
NEWCASTLE......Journal (*Cons.*) 3*d.*
Evening Chronicle (*Cons.*) 4*d.*
NEWPORT, MON...South Wales Argus (*Ind.*) 3*d.*
NORTHAMPTON...Chronicle and Echo (*Ind.*) 3*d.*
NORWICH........Eastern Daily Press (*Ind.*) 3*d.*
Eastern Evening News (*Ind.*) 3*d.*
NOTTINGHAM.....Guardian Journal (*Cons.*) 2½*d.*
Evening Post & News (*Ind.*) 3*d.*
NUNEATON.......Nuneaton Evening Tribune (*Ind.*) 2½*d.*
OLDHAM.........Evening Chronicle (*Lib.*) 3*d.*
OXFORD..........Mail (*Ind.*) 3*d.*
PAISLEY.........Daily Express (*Ind.*) 2½*d.*
PLYMOUTH.......Western Morn. News (*Ind.*) 2½*d.*
Western Evening Herald (*Ind.*) 2½*d.*
PORTSMOUTH.....Evening News (*Ind.*) 2½*d.*
PRESTON........Lancashire Evening Post (*Ind.*) [3*d.*
St. Helier (JERSEY). Evening Post (*Ind.*) 3*d.*
SCARBOROUGH....Evening News (*Ind.*) 2½*d.*
SHEFFIELD........Sheffield Telegraph (*Cons.*) 3*d.*
Star (*Ind.*) 3*d.*
SHIELDS..........Gazette & Shipping Telegraph (*Ind.*) 3*d.*
SOUTHAMPTON....Southern Evening Echo (*Ind.*) 2½*d.*
STOKE...........Evening Sentinel (*Ind.*) 2½*d.*
SUNDERLAND.....Echo (*Ind.*) 3*d.*
SWANSEA........South Wales Evening Post (*Ind.*) 3*d.*
SWINDON........Evening Advertiser (*Ind.*) 3*d.*
TORQUAY........Herald Express (*Ind.*) 2½*d.*
WEST HARTLEPOOL Northern Daily Mail (*Ind.*) 2½*d.*
WEYMOUTH.....Dorset Evening Echo (*Ind.*) 2½*d.*
WOLVERHAMPTON. Express and Star (*Ind.*) 3*d.*
WORCESTER......Evening News and Times (*Ind.*) 3*d.*

WORKINGTON.... Cumberland Even. Star. (*Ind.*) 3*d*.
YORK.......... Yorkshire E. Press (*Ind.*) 3*d*.

SUNDAY NEWSPAPERS

Independent—Royal Buildings, St. Andrews Cross, Plymouth. 5*d*.
News of the World (*Ind.*)—30 Bouverie St., E.C.4. 6*d*.
Observer (*Ind.*)—22 Tudor St., E.C.4. 6*d*.
People (*Ind.*)—93, Long Acre, W.C.2. 5*d*.
Sunday Citizen (*Lab.*)—Pioneer House, Wicklow St., W.C.1. 6*d*.
Sunday Express (*Ind.*)—Fleet St., E.C.4. 5*d*.
Sunday Mail (*Cons.*)—Record House, Glasgow. 5*d*.
Sunday Mercury (*Ind.*)—Corporation St., Birmingham. 5*d*.
Sunday Mirror (*Ind.*)—Holborn Circus, E.C.1. 5*d*.
Sunday Post (*Ind.*)—144 Port Dundas Road, Glasgow. 4*d*.
Sunday Sun (*Cons.*)—Chronicle Buildings, Westgate Rd., Newcastle-on-Tyne. 5*d*.
Sunday Telegraph (*Cons.*)—135 Fleet St., E.C.4. 5*d*.
Sunday Times (*Ind.*)—200 Gray's Inn Road, W.C.1. 7*d*.

RELIGIOUS PAPERS

Anglican World—29 Tufton St., Westminster, S.W.1. 3*s*. 6*d*.
Baptist Times—6 Southampton Row, W.C.1. 4*d*.
British Weekly—16 Walker St., Edinburgh. 6*d*.
Catholic Herald—67 Fleet St., E.C.4. 6*d*.
Christian—Bush House North East Wing, Aldwych, London, W.C.2. 6*d*.
Christian Endeavour—31 Lampton Rd., Hounslow, Mx. 1*s*.
Christian Herald—4 Western Esplanade, Portslade, Brighton, Sussex. 5*d*.
Church Illustrated—29 Tufton St., Westminster, S.W.1. 6*d*.
Church of England Newspaper and Record—182 Fleet St., E.C.4. 6*d*.
Church of Ireland Gazette—16–17 Mark St., Dublin. 3*d*.
Church Times—7 Portugal St., W.C.2. 5*d*.
English Churchman—69 Fleet St., E.C.4. 6*d*.
Friend—46–7 Chancery Lane, W.C.2. 9*d*.
Inquirer—14 Gordon Square, W.C.1. 4*d*.
Jewish Chronicle—25 Furnival St., London, E.C.4.
Jewish Telegraph—Levi House, Bury Old Road, Manchester, 8. 3*d*.
Life and Work—121 George St., Edinburgh 2. 6*d*.
Methodist Recorder—176 Fleet St., E.C.4. 4*d*.
Student Movement—Annandale, North End Road, N.W.11. 1*s*.
Sunday School Chronicle—104 Newgate St., E.C.1. 4*d*.
Tablet—14 Howick Place, S.W.1. 1*s*.
Universe and Catholic Times—Universe House, 21 Fleet St., E.C.4. 6*d*.
War Cry—117–121 Judd St., W.C.1. 3*d*.

PERIODICALS, MAGAZINES AND REVIEWS

Achievement—40 Chancery Lane, W.C.2. 2*s*. 6*d*.
Aeromodeller—38 Clarendon Road, Watford, Herts. 2*s*.
African World—21–2 St. Bride Institute, Bride Lane, E.C.4. 1*s*. 6*d*.
Air Pictorial—2 Bream's Bldgs., E.C.4. 1*s*. 6*d*.
Amateur Cine World—46–7 Chancery Lane, W.C.2. 1*s*. 3*d*.
Amateur Gardening—2–10 Tavistock St., W.C.2. 6*d*.
Amateur Photographer—Dorset House, Stamford St., S.E.1. 1*s*. 6*d*.
Angling Times—Newspaper House, Broadway, Peterborough. 6*d*.
Antiquaries' Journal—Oxford U. Press, Amen House, Warwick Sq., E.C.4. 20*s*.
Antique Collector—16 Strutton Gd., S.W.1. 4*s*. 6*d*.
Apollo—10 Cannon St. London, E.C.4. 7*s*. 6*d*.
Argosy—Fleetway House, Farringdon St., E.C.4. 2*s*. 6*d*.
Asian Review—191 Temple Chambers, E.C.4. 5*s*.
Audio and Record Review—4 Mill St., Hanover Square, London, W.1.
Birds and Country Magazine—17 Creechurch Lane, E.C.3. 2*s*. 6*d*.
Blackfriars—2 Serjeant's Inn, Fleet St., E.C.4. 2*s*. 6*d*.
Blackwood's Mag.—45 George St., Edinburgh. 2*s*. 6*d*.
Bowls News—19 Harcourt St., W.1. 6*d*.
Boxing News—92 Fleet St., E.C.4. 9*d*.
Boy's Own Paper—Gulf House, Portman Street, W.1. 2*s*.
Brain—St. Martin's St., W.C.2. 15*s*.
British Bee Journal—The Old Watermill, Desborough, Northants. 1*s*.
Burlington Mag.—12 Bedford Sq., W.C.1. 7*s*. 6*d*.
Cage and Aviary Birds—Dorset House, Stamford St., S.E.1. 9*d*.
Caravan—Link House, Dingwall Ave., Croydon, Surrey, 1*s* 6*d*.
Children—National Children's Home and Orphanage, Highbury Park, N.5. 2*d*.
Children's Newspaper—Fleetway House, Farringdon St., E.C.4. 5*d*.
Classical Quarterly—Oxford U. Press, Amen House, Warwick Square, E.C.4. 22*s*. 6*d*.
Classical Review—Oxford U. Press, Amen House, Warwick Square, E.C.4. 19*s*. 6*d*.
Coal News—Hobart House, Grosvenor Place, S.W.1. 3*d*.
Competitors Journal—30 Bouverie St., E.C.4. 6*d*.
Connoisseur—Chestergate House, Vauxhall Bridge Road S.W.1. 10*s*.
Contemporary Review—42, The Broadway, Westminster, S.W.1. 4*s*.
Cornhill—50 Albemarle St., W.1. 3*s*. 6*d*.
Country Life—Tower House, Southampton St., W.C.2. 3*s*.
Countryman, The—10 Bouverie St., E.C.4. 5*s*.
Courier—77 Brook St., W.1. 3*s*.
Cricketer—Kander, Blundel Lane, Stoke D'Abernon, Surrey. 2*s*.
Current Literature—13 Bedford Square, W.C.1. 10*d*.
Cycling and Mopeds—Bowling Green Lane, E.C.1. 9*d*.
Daily Sketch International Edition—New Carmelite House, E.C.4. 1*s*. 9*d*.
Dalton's Weekly House and Apartment Advertiser, 27 South Lambeth Road, S.W.8. 4*d*.
Dance and Dancers.—16 Buckingham Palace Road, London, S.W.1. 3*s*.
Dancing Times—12 Henrietta St., W.C.2. 2*s*.
Discovery—103–119 Waterloo Road, S.E.1. 2*s*. 6*d*.
Dog World—Idle, Bradford. 1*s*.
Drama—9 Fitzroy Sq., W.1. 2*s*.
Dublin Review—14 Howick Place, S.W.1. 6*s*.
Eagle—161–166 Fleet St., E.C.4. 5*d*.
East Africa—66 Great Russell St., W.C.1. 10*d*.
Economic Journal—St. Martin's St., W.C.2. 15*s*.
Economica—Lond. Sch. of Economics, Houghton St., Aldwych, W.C.2. 10*s*.
Economist—22 Ryder St., St. James's, S.W.1. 1*s*. 6*d*.
Edinburgh Gazette (*Official*)—Exchequer Chambers, Edinburgh. 1*s*. 6*d*.
Elizabethan—2 Bream's Buildings, E.C.4. 2*s*.
Encounter—Panton House, 25 Haymarket, S.W.1. 3*s*. 6*d*.
English Digest—1 Furnival St., E.C.4. 2*s*.
Eugenics Review—69 Eccleston Square, S.W.1. 10*s*.

Everywoman—6 Catherine St., W.C.2. 1*s.* 9*d.*
Exchange and Mart—24 Store St., W.C.1. 5*d.*
Family Doctor—47-51 Chalton St., N.W.1. 1*s.* 6*d.*
Farm and Country—13-15 John Adam St.Adelphi, W C.2. 2*s.*
Field (*Ind.*)—8 Stratton St., W.1. 2*s.*
Fishing Gazette—92 Park Lane, Croydon. 1*s.* 6*d.*
Folklore—87 Fetter Lane, E.C.4. 10*s.* 6*d.*
Freemason—59, Riverholme Drive, Ewell, Surrey. 2*s.*
Freethinker—103 Borough High St., S.E.1. 6*d.*
Fur and Feather—Idle, Bradford. 9*d.*
Gardeners' Chronicle Gardening Illustrated.—Printing House Square, Queen Victoria St., E.C.4. 9*d.*
Geographical Journal—Kensington Gore, S.W.7. 10*s.*
Geographical Magazine—Printing House Square, Queen Victoria St., E.C.4. 3*s.* 6*d.*
Go—52-53 Fetter Lane, E.C.4. 2*s.* 6*d.*
Golf Illustrated—8 Stratton St., W.1. 1*s.* 3*d.*
Golf Monthly—94 Hope St., Glasgow, C.2. 2*s.*
Good Housekeeping—Chestergate House, Vauxhall Bridge Road, S.W.1. 2*s.* 6*d.*
Gramophone—379 Kenton Road, Kenton, Mx. 1*s.* 6*d.*
Greece and Rome—Oxford U. Press, Amen House, Warwick Sq., E.C.4. 15*s.*
Guide—17-19 Buckingham Palace Rd., S.W.1. 5*d.*
Guider—17-19 Buckingham Palace Rd., S.W.1. 9*d.*
Harper's Bazaar—28-30 Grosvenor Gdns,, S.W.1. 3*s.* 6*d.*
Health & Strength—5 Church St., S.E.5 2*s.*
Health Education Journal—Tavistock House, Tavistock Square, W.C.1. 20*s.* p.a.
Hibbert Journal—Manchester College, Oxford. 3*s.* 6*d.*
History—68-74 Carter Lane, E.C.4. 8*s.* 6*d.*
History Today—10 Cannon St., E.C.4. 3*s*
Homefinder—199 Strand, W.C.2. 1*s.* 6*d.*
Homes and Gardens—Tower House, Southampton St., W.C.2. 2*s.* 6*d.*
Homeopathic World—Health Science Press, Rustington, Sussex. 1*s.* 3*d.*
Horse and Hound—6 Catherine St., W.C.2. 1*s.* 3*d.*
House and Garden—Vogue House, Hanover Sq., W.1. 3*s.*
Housewife—161-166, Fleet St., E.C.4. 2*s.* 3*d.*
Ideal Home—6 Catherine St., W.C.2. 2*s.* 6*d.*
Illustrated London News (*Ind.*)—13-15 John Adam St. Adelphi, W.C.2. 2*s.* 6*d.*
International Affairs—Chatham House, St. James's Square, S.W.1. 7*s.*
Kennel Gazette—1-4 Clarges St., Piccadilly, W.1. 3*s.*
King-Hall Newsletter Service—162 Buckingham Palace Rd., S.W.1. 20*s.* p.a.
Labour—23-8 Great Russell St., W.C.1. 7*s.* 6*d.* p.a.
Labour Monthly—134 Ballards Lane, N.3. 1*s.* 6*d.*
Labour News (*Ind.*)—69 Fleet St., E.C.4. 6*d.*
Lady—39 and 40 Bedford St., W.C.2. 9*d.*
Land and Liberty—177 Vauxhall Bridge Rd., S.W.1. 6*d.*
Lawn Tennis and Badminton—192 Palace Chambers, S.W.1. 1*s* 3*d.*
Liberal News—54 Victoria St., S.W.1. 6*d.*
Light (*Psychic*)—16 Queensberry Place, S.W.7. 3*s.* 6*d.*
Light and Lighting—32 VictoriaSt., S.W.1. 3*s.* 6*d.*
Light Horse—19 Charing Cross Rd., W.C.2. 1*s.* 6*d.*
Listener and B.B.C. Television Review—35 Marylebone High St., W.1. 6*d.*
Local Government Chronicle (*Ind.*)—11-12 Bury St., St. Mary Axe, E.C.3. 1*s.* 3*d.*
Local Government Journal—1 Norwich St., E.C.4. 6*d.*
London Gazette (*Official*)—3rd Floor, State House, W.C.1. 2*s.*
London Magazine—58 Frith Street, W.1. 3*s.* 6*d.*
London Quarterly—25-35 City Rd., E.C.1. 4*s.* 6*d.*
London Weekly Advertiser—163a Strand, W.C.2. 4*d.*
Man—21 Bedford Square ,W.C.1. 3*s.*
Manchester Guardian Weekly—3 Cross St., Manchester. 4*d.*
Meccano Magazine—Binns Rd., Liverpool. 1*s.* 3*d.*
Men Only—Tower House, Southampton St., W.C.2. 2*s.* 6*d.*
Meteorological Magazine—Atlantic House, Holborn Viaduct, E.C.1. 2*s.* 6*d.*
Mind—Parkside Works, Dalkeith Rd., Edinburgh. 7*s.* 6*d.*
Ministry of Labour Gazette (*Official*)—Atlantic House, Holborn Viaduct E.C.1. 2*s.* 6*d.*
Modern Language Review—Camb. U. Pr., 200 Euston Rd., N.W.1. 20*s.*
Modern Poultry Keeping—19 Compton Terrace, N.1. 5*d.*
Modern Woman—Tower House, Southampton St., W.C.2. 1*s.* 9*d.*
Monthly Digest of Statistics (*Official*)—Atlantic House, Holborn Viaduct, E.C.1. 6*s.*
Mother—6 Catherine St., W.C.2. 2*s.*
Municipal Engineering—4, Clements Inn, W.C.2. 1*s.*
Municipal Journal (*Ind.*)—3 and 4 Clement's Inn, W.C.2. 1*s.* 6*d.*
Municipal Review — Victoria Station House, S.W.1. 1*s.*
Museums Journal—33 Fitzroy St., Fitzroy Square, W.1. 10*s.*
My Home—Fleetway House, Farringdon St., E.C.4. 1*s.* 9*d.*
My Weekly—186 Fleet St., E.C.4. 4*d.*
Naturalist—148 Ossulston St., Euston Rd., N.W.1. 5*s.* 6*d.*
Nature—St. Martin's St., W.C.2. 4*s.*
Nautical Magazine—52 Darnley Street, Glasgow. 2*s.*
Navy—Grand Buildings Trafalgar Square, W.C.2. 1*s.* 6*d.*
Needlewoman and Needlecraft—34 Cannon St, Manchester. 1*s.* 6*d.*
New Scientist—Cromwell House, Fulwood Place, W.C.1. 1*s*
New Statesman (*Ind.*)—10 Great Turnstile, High Holborn, W.C.1. 9*d.*
Notes and Queries—Oxford U. Press, Amen House, Warwick Square, E.C.4. 4*s.* 6*d.*
Nursery World—Gulf House, 2 Portman St., W.1. 1*s.*
Ocean Times—Dorset House, Stamford St., S.E.1.
Opera—2 Breams Buildings, E.C.4. 2*s.* 6*d.*
Our Dogs—Oxford Road, Station Approach, Manchester. 1*s.*
Overseas Daily Mirror and Sunday Mirror—Daily Mirror Building, Holborn, E.C.1. 1*s.* 6*d.*
Oxford—Oxford U. Press, Amen House, Warwick Sq., E.C.4. 1*s.* 6*d.*
Parade—136-144 City Road, E.C.1. 1*s.*
Parents' Review (P.N.E.U.)—Murray House, Vandon St.. S.W.1. 1*s.* 6*d.*
Parliamentary Debates (Hansard)—Atlantic House, Holborn Viaduct E.C.1. 1*s.*
People's Friend—7 Bank St., Dundee. 4*d.*
Philosophy—St. Martin's St., W.C.2. 6*s.*
Photoplay—8-10 Temple Avenue, E.C.4. 1*s.* 6*d.*
Poetry Review—33 Portman Square, W.1. 3*s.* 6*d.*

Political Quarterly—11 New Fetter Lane, E.C.4. 8*s*. 6*d*.
Polytechnic Magazine—14 Bedford Row, W.C.1. 1*s*.
Pony—19 Charing Cross Rd., W.C.2. 1*s*. 6*d*.
Popular Gardening—Fleetway House, Farringdon St., E.C.4. 6*d*.
Poultry Farmer—6 Catherine St., W.C.2. 6*d*.
Poultry World—Dorset House, Stamford St., S.E.1. 6*d*.
Practical Householder—Tower House, Southampton St., W.C.2. 1*s*. 6*d*.
Progress (*Braille Type*)—224–8 Great Portland St., W.1. 5½*d*.
Punch (*Ind.*)—10 Bouverie Street, E.C.4. 1*s*.
Quarterly Rev.—50 Albemarle St., W.1. 10*s*.
Queen (*Ind.*)—52–53 Fetter Lane, E.C.4. 2*s*. 6*d*.
Raceform—39–43 Battersea High St., S.W.11 240*s* p.a.
Racing Calendar—15 Cavendish Sq., W.1. 5*s*.
Radio Times—35 Marylebone High St., W.1. 5*d*.
Reader's Digest—25 Berkeley Sq., W.1. 2*s*. 6*d*
Red Star Weekly—186 Fleet St., E.C.4. 4½*d*.
Riding—Tower House, Southampton St., W.C.2. 1*s* 9*d*.
Round Table—69 Victoria St., S.W.1. 7*s*. 6*d*.
Scotland's Magazine—7 Castle Terrace, Edinburgh. 2*s*.
Scots Independent—27 Murray Place, Stirling. 3*d*.
Scottish Field—65 Buchanan St., Glasgow. 2*s*.
Scout—Tower Hse., Southampton St., W.C.2. 6*d*.
Scouter—Tower House, Southampton St., W.C.2. 1*s*.
Sea Breezes—17 James St., Liverpool. 1*s*. 6*d*.
Seafarer—207 Balham High Rd., S.W.17. 2*s*.
She—Chestergate House, Vauxhall Bridge Road, S.W 1. 1*s*. 6*d*.
Shooting Times and Country Magazine—19–20 Noel St., W.1. 1*s*. 6*d*.
Smallholder—Tower House, Southampton St., W.C.2. 6*d*.
Socialist Leader—48 Dundas St., Glasgow, C.1. 4*d*.
Sociological Review—University College of North Staffordshire, Keele, Staffs. 30*s*. p.a.
Southern Africa (*Ind.*)—21–22 St. Bride Institute, Bride Lane, E.C.4. 9*d*.
Spectator (*Ind.*)—99 Gower Street, W.C.1. 9*d*.
Sphere (*Ind.*)—13–15 John Adam St., W.C.2. 2*s*. 6*d*.
Sporting Chronicle—Thomson House, Manchester. 4*d*.
Sporting Express & Greyhound Express, Fleet Lane House, Fleet Lane, E.C.4. 6*d*.
Sporting Life—27 Floral St., W.C.2. 9*d*.
Statist (*Ind.*)—51 Cannon St., E.C.4. 1*s*. 6*d*.
Stitchcraft—223–7 St. John St., E.C.1. 1*s*. 6*d*.
Strad—Temple House, Tallis St., E.C.4. 9*d*.
Studio—161–166 Fleet St. E.C.4. 4*s*.
Sunday Companion—Fleetway House, Farringdon St., E.C.4. 5*d*.
Sunny Stories—Tower House, Southampton St., W.C.2. 6*d*.
Tatler and Bystander (*Ind.*)—13–15 John Adam St., W.C.2. 2*s*.
Teazle's News-Letter—Kingsbury Manor, St. Albans, Herts. 20*s*. p.a.
Territorial Magazine—61 Connaught Street, W.2. 2*s*.
TheatreWorld—Dorset House, Stamford St., S.E.1. 2*s*.
Time & Tide and John o' London's (*Ind.*)—40–43 Chancery Lane, W.C.2. 1*s*.
Times Educational Suppl't.—Printing Ho. Sq., E.C.4. 6*d*.
Times Literary Suppl't.—Printing Ho. Sq., E.C.4. 9*d*.
Times Weekly Review (*Ind.*)—Printing Ho. Sq., E.C.4. 6*d*.
Tit-Bits—Tower House, Southampton St., W.C.2. 6*d*.
Toc H Journal—15 Trinity Square, E.C.3. 9*d*.
Today—189 High Holborn, W.C.1. 6*d*.
Tribune—222 Strand, W.C.2. 6*d*.
Trout & Salmon—Newspaper House, Broadway, Peterborough. 2*s*.
True Romances—8–10 Temple Ave., E.C.4. 1*s*. 6*d*.
True Story Magazine—8 Temple Ave., E.C.4. 1*s*. 6*d*.
Twentieth Century—20 Tudor St., E.C.4. 5*s*.
United Nations News—25 Charles St., W.1. 1*s*.
Universities Quarterly—10 Gt. Turnstile, W.C.1. 7*s*. 6*d*.
Vanity Fair—Chestergate House, Vauxhall Bridge Road, S.W.1. 1*s*. 6*d*.
Vogue—Vogue House, Hanover Square, W.1. 2*s*. 6*d*.
Weather—49 Cromwell Rd., S.W.7. 2*s*.
Weekend—Northcliffe House, E.C.4. 5*d*.
Welsh Nation—8 Queen St., Cardiff. 3*d*.
West Africa (*Ind.*)—9 New Fetter Lane, E.C.4. 1*s*.
West African Rev.—9 New Fetter Lane, E.C.4. 2*s*.
Wide World Magazine—Tower House, Southampton St., W.C.2. 2*s*.
Woman—6 Catherine St., W.C.2. 7*d*.
Woman and Beauty—Fleetway House, Farringdon St., E.C.4. 1*s*. 6*d*.
Woman and Home—Fleetway House, Farringdon St., E.C.4. 1*s*. 9*d*.
Woman's Journal—Fleetway House, Farringdon St., E.C.4. 3*s*.
Woman's Own—Tower House, Southampton St., W.C.2. 7*d*.
Woman's Realm—6 Catherine St., W.C.2. 5*d*.
Woman's Weekly—Fleetway House, Farringdon St., E.C.4. 5*d*.
Women's Employment—25, Ebury St., S.W.1. 6*d*.
World Today—Chatham House, St. James's Square, S.W.1. 3*s*.
Yachting Monthly—3–4 Clements Inn, W.C.2. 3*s*.
Yachting World (*Ind.*)—Dorset House, Stamford St., S.E.1. 3*s*.
Yachts and Yachting—196 Eastern Esplanade, Southend-on-Sea. 2*s*.
Yachtsman—Blenheim House, 28 Albemarle Street, W.1. 3*s*.

TRADE, PROFESSIONAL AND BUSINESS JOURNALS

Accountancy—Moorgate Place, E.C.2. 3*s*. 6*d*.
Accountant—151 Strand, W.C.2 1*s*. 9*d*.
Accountants' Journal—22 Bedford Square, W.C.1. 1*s*.
Accountants' Magazine—27 Queen St., Edinburgh. 3*s*. 6*d*.
Advertiser's Weekly—109 Waterloo Rd., S.E.1. 1*s*. 9*d*.
Aeroplane and Commercial Aviation News—Bowling Green Lane, E.C.1. 1*s*.
Agricultural Machinery Journal—1 Dorset Buildings, E.C.4. 2*s*. 6*d*.
Aircraft Engineering—12 Bloomsbury Square. W.C.1. 3*s*.
Ambassador—49 Park Lane, W.1. 65*s*. p.a.
Architect and Building News—Dorset House, Stamford St., S.E.1. 1*s*.
Architects' Journal—9–13 Queen Anne's Gate, S.W.1. 1*s*.
Architectural Review—9–13 Queen Anne's Gate, S.W.1. 5*s*.
Artist—33 Warwick Sq., S.W.1. 3*s*. 6*d*.
Author—84 Drayton Gardens, S.W.10. 2*s*.

Autocar—Dorset House, Stamford Street, S.E.1. 1s. 3d.
Automobile Engineer—Dorset House, Stamford St., S.E.1. 5s.
Baker and Confectioner—65-66 Turnmill St., E.C.1. 6d.
Bakers Review—13 Ashley Place, S.W.1. 1s.
Bank Officer—28 Old Queen St., S.W.1. 3d.
Banker—10 Cannon St., E.C.4. 3s.
Bankers' Magazine—85-6 London Wall, E.C.2. 3s. 6d.
Bedding, Upholstery and Furniture—33 Furnival St., E.C.4. 20s. p.a.
Board of Trade Journal (*Official*)—Atlantic House, Holborn Viaduct, E.C.1. 1s. 3d.
Bookseller, The—13 Bedford Square, W.C.1. 1s.
Brewers' Guardian—7 Garrick St., W.C.2. 30s. p.a.
Brewers' Journal—Eastcheap Buildings, E.C.3. 3s. 6d.
Brewing Trade Review—19 Briset St., E.C.1. 3s. 6d.
British Baker—Maclaren House, 131 Great Suffolk St., S.E.1. 6d.
British Book News—59 New Oxford St., W.C.1. 2s. 6d.
British Books—92 Park Lane, Croydon, Surrey. 3s.
British Clay Worker—4 Catherine St., Aldwych, W.C.2. 2s.
British Communications & Electronics—Drury House, Russell St., WC.2. 2s. 6d.
British Dental Journal—13 Hill St., W.1. 3s.
British Export Gazette—119 Moorgate, E.C.2. 3s. 6d.
British Farmer—26 Knightsbridge, S.W.1. 6d.
British Jeweller—27 Frederick St., Birmingham. 2s.
British Journal for Philosophy of Science—Parkside Works, Edinburgh, 9. 10s. 6d.
British Journal of Applied Physics—47 Belgrave Square, S.W.1. 12s. 6d.
British Journal of Photography—24 Wellington Street, W.C.2. 8d.
British Manufacturer—6 Holborn Viaduct, E.C.1. 2s.
British Medical Journal—Tavistock Square, W.C.1. 4s.
British Packer—311 Grays Inn Rd., W.C.1. 42s. p.a.
British Plastics—Dorset Hse., Stamford St., S.E.1. 5s.
British Printer—30 Old Burlington St., W.1. 3s. 6d.
British Stationer—Commonwealth House, New Oxford St., W.C.1. 4d.
British Steelmaker—7 Chesterfield Gdns., W.1. 2s. 6d.
British Sugar Beet Review—134 Piccadilly, W.1. 1s.
British Trade Journal and Export World—154 Fleet St., E.C.4. 3s. 6d.
British Veterinary Journal—7-8 Henrietta St., W.C.2. 7s.
Brushes—65, Turnmill St., E.C.1. 3s.
Builder—4 Catherine St., W.C.2. 1s. 6d.
Builders' Merchants' Journal—28 Essex St., W.C.2. 1s.
Building Equipment News—33 Tothill St., S.W.1.
Building Materials and Floors—The Tower, Brook Green Road, W.6. 40s. p.a.
Building Societies' Gazette—Burgon St., E.C.4. 3s. 9d.
Bus and Coach—Dorset House, Stamford St., S.E.1. 3s. 6d.
Cabinet Maker—154 Fleet St., E.C.4. 1s. 6d.
Caterer—1 Dorset Buildings, Salisbury Square, E.C.4. 1s.
Caterer's Association Bulletin—Victoria House Vernon Place, Southampton Row, W.C.1.
Caterers' Journal—7 Garrick St., W.C.2. 1s. 6d.
Catering Management—167 High Holborn, W.C.1. 1s. 6d.
Chamber of Commerce Journal—69 Cannon St., E.C.4. 1s.
Chartered Secretary—14 New Bridge St., E.C.4. 1s. 6d.
Chemical Age—154 Fleet St., E.C.4. 1s. 9d.
Chemical and Process Engineering—The Tower, Brook Green Road, W.6. 30s. p.a.
Chemical Trade Journal—26 Finsbury Square, E.C.2. 1s. 6d.
Chemist and Druggist—28 Essex St., W.C.2. 1s.
Chemistry and Industry—14 Belgrave Sq., S.W.1. 5s.
Chemo-Therapy Review—194 Bishopsgate, E.C.4. 22s. 6d. p.a.
Chief Steward—7-17 Jewry St., E.C.3. 2s.
Chiropodist—8 Wimpole St., W.1. 1s. 8d.
Cinema—93-5 Wardour St., W.1. 6d.
City Press (Non-Political)—80A Coleman St., E.C.2. 4d.
Civil Engineering—8 Buckingham St., W.C.2. 3s. 6d.
Coal and Appliances Trade Digest—8 Lloyd's Avenue, E.C.3. 25s. p.a.
Coal Merchant and Shipper—17-19 John Adam St., W.C.2. 9d.
Colliery Engineering—33 Tothill St., S.W.1. 2s. 6d.
Colliery Guardian—30 Furnival St., E.C.4. 1s. 3d.
Commercial Grower—154 Fleet St., E.C.4. 1s.
Commercial Motor—Bowling Green Lane, E.C.1. 1s. 3d.
Concrete and Constructional Engineering—60, Buckingham Gate, S.W.1. 3s.
Confectionery and Baking Craft—Maclaren House, 131 Gt. Suffolk St., S.E.1. 2s.
Confectionery Journal—Maclaren House, 131 Gt. Suffolk St., S.E.1. 4d.
Confectionery News—Drury House, Russell St., W.C.2. 4d.
Contract Journal—32 Southwark Bridge Rd., S.E.1. 2s.
Contractors' Record—Lennox House, Norfolk St., W.C.2. 1s.
Cordage, Canvas and Jute World—65, Turnmill St., E.C.1. 5s. 3d.
Corrosion Technology—The Tower, Brook Green Road, Hammersmith, London, W.6. 40s. p.a.
Corsetry and Underwear—47 Hertford St., W.1. 5s.
Cost Accountant—63 Portland Place, W.1. 1s. 10d.
Cotton—32 Barton Arcade, Deansgate, Manchester. 30s. p.a.
Daily Cinema—142 Wardour St., W.1. 6d.
Dairy Engineering—The Tower, Brook Green Road, W.6. 30s. p.a.
Dairy Industries—9 Gough Sq., E.C.4. 3s. 6d.
Decorator—17-19 John Adam St., Adelphi, W.C.2. 1s. 6d.
Director—5 Belgrave Sq., S.W.1.
Display—167 High Holborn, W.C.1. 3s.
Dock and Harbour Authority—19 Harcourt St., W.1. 3s.
Draper's Record—229-231 High Holborn, W.C.1. 1s. 6d.
Drapery and Fashion Weekly—Drury House, Russell St., W.C.2. 6d.
Dyer, Textile Printer—Drury Hse., Russell St., W.C.2. 1s. 10d.
Education—10 Queen Anne St., W.1. 7d.
Electrical and Radio Trading—Drury House, Russell Street, W.C.2. 2s.

Electrical Industries Export—33 Tothill St., S.W.1. 20s. p.a.
Electrical Review—Dorset House, Stamford St., S.E.1. 1s. 6d.
Electrical Times—Sardinia House, Kingsway, W.C.2. 1s. 6d.
Electronic Engineering—28 Essex St., W.C.2. 3s.
Embroidery—73 Wimpole St., W.1. 3s.
Engineer—28 Essex St., Strand, W.C.2. 2s.
Engineering—35-6 Bedford St., W.C.2. 2s.
Engineer's Digest—120 Wigmore St., W.1. 4s. 6d.
Estates Gazette—28 Denmark St., W.C.2. 1s. 6d.
Factory Manager—7-8 Rathbone Place, W.1. 2s.
Fairplay (Shipping)—Palmerston House, Bishopsgate, E.C.2. 2s.
Fancy Goods Trader—15 Cursitor St., E.C.4. 20s. p.a.
Far East Trade—3 Belsize Crescent, N.W.3. 3s.
Farm Implement and Machinery Review—28 Essex St., Strand, W.C.2. 2s. 6d.
Farm Mechanization—Bowling Green Lane, E.C.1. 3s.
Farmer and Stockbreeder—Dorset House, Stamford St., S.E.1. 9d.
Farmers' Weekly—161-166 Fleet St., E.C.4. 9d.
Farming Express—Old bourne Hall, Shoe Lane, E.C.4. 4d.
Farming News—65 Buchanan St., Glasgow. 6d.
F.B.I. Review—21 Tothill St., S.W.1. 5s.
Fertiliser and Feeding Stuffs Journal—Maclaren House, 131 Great Suffolk St., S.E.1. 2s.
Financial World—5 New St., Bishopsgate, E.C.2. 9d.
Fire (British Fire Service)—72 Fleet St., E.C.4. 2s.
Fire Protection Review—154 Fleet St., E.C.4. 2s.
Fish Friers' Review—City Chambers, Infirmary St., Leeds. 1s.
Fish Trades Gaz.—17-19 John Adam St., Adelphi, W.C.2. 6d.
Flight—Dorset House, Stamford St., S.E.1. 1s. 6d.
Food Manufacture—The Tower, Brook Green Road, W.6. 50s. p.a.
Food Processing and Packing—33 Tothill St., S.W.1. 2s. 6d.
Food Trade Review—7 Garrick St., W.C.2. 42s. p.a.
Foundry Trade Journal—17-19 John Adam St., Adelphi, W.C.2. 1s. 6d.
Free Trader—24 Austin Friars, E.C.2. 3s.
Fruit, Flower and Vegetable Trades Journal—6-7 Gough Square, E.C.4. 1s.
Fuel—88 Kingsway, W.C.2. 20s.
Funeral Service Journal—Hillingdon Press, Uxbridge, Mx. 15s. p.a.
Furs—1, Skinners Lane, E.C.4. 2s. 6d.
Fur Weekly News—18 Tile Yard Road, N.7. 30s. p.a.
Furnishing—Drury House, Russell St., W.C.2. 2s. 6d.
Furnishing World—109-119 Waterloo Rd., S.E.1. 1s. 3d.
Games and Toys—30-1 Knightrider St., E.C.4. 3s.
Garage and Motor Agent—62 Doughty St., W.C.1. 1s. 6d.
Gas & Coke—33 Tothill St., S.W.1. 2s. 6d.
Gas Journal—Finwell House, 26 Finsbury Sq., E.C.2. 1s. 9d.
Gas Times—65 Turnmill St., London, E.C.1. 3s. 6d.
Gas World—154 Fleet St., E.C.4. 1s. 9d.
George Broomhall's Corn Trade News—37 Victoria St., Liverpool. 294s. p.a.
Glass—9 Moor Park Rd., Northwood, Mx. 2s.
Goldsmiths' Journal—226 Latymer Ct., W.6. 1s. 3d.
Grocer—Eastcheap Buildings, E.C.3. 8d.
Grocers' Gazette—1-2 Pudding Lane, E.C.3. 6d.
Grower and Prepacker—49 Doughty St., W.C.1. 1s.
Hair and Beauty—18-20 York Bldgs., W.C.2. 3s. 9d.
Hairdressers' Journal—1-3 Pemberton Row, London E.C.4. 1s. 9d.
Handy Shipping Guide—12-16 Laystall St., E.C.1. 1s. 6d.
Hardware Trade Journal—154 Fleet St., E.C.4. 1s. 6d.
Harper's Sports and Games—8 Lloyd's Avenue, E.C.3. 25s. p.a.
Harper's Wine and Spirit Gazette—8 Lloyd's Avenue, E.C.3. 105s.
Head Teachers' Review—59 Victoria Rd., Surbiton, Surrey. 4d.
Heating—90 High Holborn W.C.1. 2s. 6d.
Heating and Air Conditioning—147 Victoria St., S.W.1. 2s.
Heating and Ventilating Engineer—11-13 Southampton Row, W.C.1. 2s. 6d.
Horological Journal—226 Latymer Ct., W.6. 1s. 6d.
Hosiery Times—134 Fleet St., E.C.4. 1s. 9d.
Hosiery Trade Journal—11 Millstone Lane, Leicester. 3s.
Hospital—75 Portland Place, W.1. 2s. 9d.
Hospital and Health Management—Victoria House, Mason's Hill, Bromley, Kent. 3s.
Hotel and Catering Review—1 Dorset Buildings, Salisbury Square, E.C.4. 2s. 6d.
Hotel and Catering Times—Finwell House, 26 Finsbury Square, E.C.2. 6d.
Hotel and Restaurant Management—167 High Holborn, W.C.1. 2s.
Ice Cream Industry—154 Fleet St., E.C.4. 1s. 6d.
Illus. Carpenter and Builder—Pioneer House, Wicklow St., Gray's Inn Rd., W.C.1. 6d.
Industria Britanica—154 Fleet St., E.C.4. 3s.
Industrial Chemist—33 Tothill St., S.W.1. 2s. 6d.
Industrial Daily News—Pear Tree Court, E.C.1. 2s.
Industrial Welfare—48 Bryanston Square, W.1. 3s.
Insurance Mail, 44 Fleet St., E.C.4., 1s. 6d.
Insurance Record—75 Carter Lane, E.C.4. 2s. 6d.
Interbuild—11 Manchester Sq., W.1. 2s. 6d.
Investor's Chronicle—110 Queen Victoria St., E.C.4. 1s. 6d.
Investors' Guardian—Guardian House, Wormwood St., E.C.2. 1s.
Investor's Review—5-7 New St., Bishopsgate, E.C.2. 1s.
Iron and Steel—Dorset Hse., Stamford St., S.E.1, 3s.
Ironmonger—28 Essex Street, W.C.2. 1s.
Jeweller and Metalworker—New House, 67, Hatton Garden, E.C.1. 8d.
Journal of Commerce and Shipping Telegraph—6-8 Fenchurch Buildings, Fenchurch St., E.C.3. 6d.
Journal of the Institute of Bankers—10 Lombard St., E.C.3. 20s. p.a.
Journal of Scientific Instruments—47 Belgrave Square, S.W.1. 120s. p.a.
Journal of the Chemical Society—Burlington House, W.1. 400s. p.a.
Journal of the Society of Dyers and Colourists—19 Piccadilly, Bradford. 140s. p.a.
Journal of the Textile Institute—10 Blackfriars St., Manchester 3. 12s.
Junior Age—167 High Holborn, W.C.1. 2s.
Justice of the Peace and Local Govt. Review—Little London, Chichester. 1s. 10d.
Jute and Canvas Review—222 Strand, W.C.2. 3s. 6d.

Kinematograph Weekly—6 Catherine St., W.C.2. 3*s.*
Lancet—7 Adam Street, W.C.2. 1*s.* 6*d.*
Land Agents Record—22 Clinton Crescent, St. Leonards-on-Sea. 6*d.*
Laundry and Cleaning—Drury House, Russell St., W.C.2.
Law Journal—88 Kingsway, W.C.2. 1*s.* 9*d.*
Law Quarterly Review—11 New Fetter Lane, E.C.4. 13*s.* 6*d.*
Law Reports. The—3 Stone Buildings, Lincoln's Inn, W.C.2. 252*s.* p.a.
Law Society's Gazette—Chancery Lane, W.C.2. 60*s.* p.a.
Law Times—88 Kingsway, W.C.2. 1*s.* 9*d.*
Leather Goods—15 Cursitor St., E.C.4. 2*s.* 6*d.*
Leather Trades Review—154 Fleet St., E.C.4. 2*s.*
Licensing World—32 Bedford Sq. W.C.1. 6*d.*
Light Metals—Bowling Green Lane, E.C.1. 2*s.* 6*d.*
Linen Trade Circular—62 Great Victoria St., Belfast. 70*s.* p.a.
Litho-Printer—97 Jermyn St., S.W.1. 2*s.*
Lloyd's Loading List—Lloyd's, E.C.3. 1*s.* 6*d.*
Lloyd's Shipping Index—Lloyd's, E.C.3. Subs. only.
Local Government Finance—1 Buckingham Place, Westminster, S.W.1. 52*s.* 6*d.* p.a.
Locomotive Journal—9 Arkwright Rd., N.W.3. 4*d.*
London Corn Circular—7 Northumberland Alley, E.C.3. 75*s.* p.a.
Machine Shop Magazine—Dorset House, Stamford St., S.E.1. 2*s.*
Machinery—Nat. House, West St., Brighton. 1*s.* 3*d.*
Machinery Lloyd—33 Tothill St., S.W.1. 50*s.* p.a.
Machinery Market—146A Queen Victoria St., E.C.4. 1*s.* 3*d.*
Maker-Up—9 Gough Square, E.C.4. 3*s.* 6*d.*
Man-made Textiles—Old Colony House, South King St., Manchester. 3*s.*
Manager—80 Fetter Lane, E.C.4. 3*s.*
Manufacturing Chemist—The Tower, Brook Green Road, W.6. 50*s.* p.a
Manufacturing Clothier—9 Gough Square, E.C.4. 3*s.* 6*d.*
Marine Engineer—9 Catherine Place, S.W.1. 3*s.* 6*d.*
Mass Production—4 Ludgate Circus, E.C.4. 2*s.* 6*d.*
Meat Marketing—1 Dorset Buildings, Salisbury Square E.C.4. 1*s.*
Meat Trades Journal—5 Charterhouse Square, E.C.1. 9*d.*
Mechanical Handling—Dorset House, Stamford St., S.E.1. 5*s.*
Mechanical World and Engineering Record—31 King St. West, Manchester. 2*s.* 6*d.*
Medical Officer—72-8 Fleet St., E.C.4. 1*s.* 3*d.*
Medico-Legal Journal—3-4 Petty Cury, Cambridge. 7*s.* 6*d.*
Melody Maker—6 Catherine St., W.C.2. 6*d.*
Members Circular (Master Printers)—11 Bedford Row, W.C.1.
Men's Wear—229-231 High Holborn, W.C.1. 6*d.*
Mercantile Guardian—52 Bishopsgate, E.C.2. 40*s.* p.a.
Metal Bulletin—46 Wigmore St., W.1. 1*s.* 10*d.*
Metal Industry—Dorset House, Stamford St., S.E.1. 1*s.* 6d.
Metal Treatment—17-19 John Adam St., Adelphi, W.C.2. 2*s.* 6*d.*
Metallurgia—31 King St. West, Manchester, 3. 2*s.* 6*d.*
Milk Producer—Milk Marketing Board, Thames Ditton, Surrey.
Milling—37 Victoria St., Liverpool. 3*s.*
Mine and Quarry Engineering—33 Tothill St., S.W.1. 2*s.* 6*d.*
Mining Journal—15 Wilson St., Moorgate, E.C.2. 1*s.*
Mining Mag.—482 Salisbury House, E.C.2. 3*s.*
Model Engineer—19-20 Noel St., W.1. 2*s.* 6*d.*
Modern Caravan—Heathcock Court, Strand, W.C.2. 1*s.* 6d.
Modern Refrigeration—Maclaren House, 131 Gt. Suffolk St., S.E.1. 2*s.* 6*d.*
Modern Transport—3-16 Woburn Place, W.C.1. 1*s.*
Motor—Bowling Green Lane, E.C.1. 1*s.* 3*d.*
Motor Boat and Yachting—Bowling Green Lane, E.C.1. 2*s.* 6*d.*
Motor Body—79 Petty France, Westminster S.W.1. 2*s.*
Motor Cycle—Dorset Hse., Stamford St., S.E.1. 9*d.*
Motor Cycle and Cycle Trader—Dorset House, Stamford Street, S.E.1. 28*s.* p.a.
Motor Cycling—Bowling Green Lane, E.C.1. 6*d.*
Motor Industry—17-19 John Adam St., Adelphi, W.C.2. 3*s.* 6*d.*
Motor Trader—Dorset House, Stamford Street, S.E.1. 55*s.* p.a.
Motor Transport—Dorset House, Stamford St., S.E.1. 9*d.*
Muck Shifter & Bulk Handler—The Tower, Brook Green Road, W.6. 30*s.* p.a.
Music Trades Review—44A Worship St., E.C.2. 2*s.* 3*d.*
Musical Times—160 Wardour St., W.1. 1*s.* 6*d.*
National Builder—82 New Cavendish St., W.1. 3*s.*
National Master Painter—40 King St., W., Manchester. Subs.
National Newsagent—107-111 Fleet St., E.C.4. 9*d.*
Nuclear Energy—147 Victoria St., S.W.1. 5*s.*
Nuclear Engineering—Bowling Green Lane, E.C.1. 3*s.* 6*d.*
Nurseryman, Seedsman and Glasshouse Grower—62 Doughty St., W.C.1. 40*s.* p.a.
Nursing Mirror—Dorset House, Stamford St., S.E.1. 8*d.*
Nursing Times—St. Martin's St., W.C.2. 6*d.*
Off Licence Journal—1 Dorset Bldgs., Salisbury Square, E.C.4. 1*s.* 3*d.*
Official Architecture—4 Catherine St., London, W.C.2. 2*s.* 6*d.*
Oil Engine—Bowling Green Lane, E.C.1. 4*s.*
Optician—69 Aldwych, W.C.2. 1*s.* 6d.
Outfitter—17-19 John Adam St., W.C.2. 9*d.*
Packaging—75 Carter Lane, E.C.4. 5*s.*
Packaging Review—Commonwealth House, New Oxford St., W.C.1.
Paint Manufacture—The Tower, Brook Green Road, W.6. 40*s.* p.a.
Paint, Oil and Colour Journal—83 Farringdon St., E.C.4. 50*s.* p.a.
Paint Technology—4 Ludgate Circus, E.C.4. 4*s.*
Painting and Decorating—30 Princes St., Southport, Lancs. 1*s.* 9*d.*
Paper Maker—50-51 Fetter Lane, E.C.4. 2*s.* 9*d.*
Passenger Transport—30 Bouverie St., London, E.C.4.
Perambulator Gazette—13 St. George St., W.1. 2*s.*
Perfumery and Essential Oil Record—33 Chiswell St., E.C.1. 6*s.* 6*d.*
Personnel Management, and Methods—103-119 Waterloo Rd., S.E.1. 35*s.* p.a.
Petroleum—Leonard Hill House, Eden St., N.W.1. 40*s.* p.a.
Petroleum Times—Bowling Green Lane, W.C.1. 3*s.*
Pharmaceutical Journal—17 Bloomsbury Square, W.C.1. 2*s.*
Philatelic Magazine—27 Maiden Lane, W.C.2. 9*d.*
Philatelic Trader—27 Maiden Lane, W.C.2. 15*s.* p.a.

Pianomaker—13 St. George St., W.1. 2s. 3d.
Plastics—Bowling Green Lane, E.C.1. 3s.
Plumbing Trade Journal—30 Princes St., Southport, Lancs. 1s. 9d.
Police Review—67 Clerkenwell Rd., E.C.1. 5d.
Policy Holder—10 Kennedy St., Manchester. 9d.
Post Mag—12-13 Henrietta St., W.C.2. 1s.
Pottery and Glass—Maclaren House, 131 Gt. Suffolk St., S.E.1. 35s. p.a.
Pottery Gazette—83 Farringdon St., E.C.4. 40s. p.a.
Power and Works Engineering—33 Tothill St., S.W.1. 2s. 6d.
Power Laundry—Dorset House, Stamford St., S.E.1. 1s. 6d.
Practical Mechanics—Tower House, Southampton St., W.C.2. 2s.
Practical Television—Tower House, Southampton St., W.C.2. 2s.
Practical Wireless—Tower House, Southampton St., W.C.2. 2s.
Practitioner—5 Bentinck St., W.1. 5s.
Print in Britain—97 Jermyn St., S.W.1. 2s.
Product Finishing—4 Ludgate Circus, E.C.4. 3s.
Public Ledger—11 Tokenhouse Yard, E.C.2. 10d.
Production Technology—Dorset House, Stamford St., S.E.1. 5s.
Quarry Manager's Journal—62-64 Baker St., W.1. 2s. 6d.
Railway Gazette—33 Tothill St., S.W.1. 2s.
Railway Magazine—33 Tothill St., S.W.1. 2s. 6d.
Railway Review—205 Euston Rd., N.W.1. 6d.
Rating and Valuation Reporter—Oyez House, Bream's Bldgs., Fetter Lane, E.C.4. 2s. 6d.
Retail Chemist—18-20 York Bldgs., Adelphi, W.C.2. 2s. 2d.
Retail Newsagent—15 Charterhouse St., E.C.1. 9d.
Review (Insurance)—10 Lincoln's Inn Fields, W.C.2. 2s.
Review of Economic Studies—39a Welbeck St., W.1. 12s. 6d.
Ridley's Wine and Spirit Trade Circular—110 Cannon St., E.C.4. 50s. p.a.
Roads and Road Construction—147 Victoria St., S.W.1. 2s.
Royal Society of Health Journal—90 Buckingham Palace Rd., S.W.1. 10s. 6d.
Rubber and Plastics Age—Gaywood House, Gt. Peter St., S.W.1. 3s. 6d.
Sales Appeal—85-87 Jermyn St., S.W.1. 3s. 6d.
School and College—18-20 York Bldgs., Adelphi, W.C.2. 1s. 8d.
School Government Chronicle and Education Review—24-26 Black Friars Lane, E.C.4. 1s.
Science and Art of Mining—Rowbottom Square, Wigan. 4d.
Scope's Factory and Office Service—85-87 Jermyn St., S.W.1. 3s. 6d.
Scotland—1 Castle St., Edinburgh. 2s.
Scottish Farmer and Farming World and Household—39 York St., Glasgow. 6d.
Scottish Grocer—34-6 North Frederick St., Glasgow 6d.
Scottish Schoolmaster—10 Atholl Crescent, Edinburgh. 3s. 6d. p.a.
Secretaries' Chronicle—Devonshire House, 12 Devonshire St., W.1. 2s.
Service Station—2 Caxton St., S.W.1. 2s.
Sheet Metal Industries—17-19 John Adam St., Adelphi, W.C.2. 2s. 6d.
Shipbuilder—39 Victoria St., S.W.1. 3s.
Shipbuilding and Shipping Record—33 Tothill St., S.W.1. 2s.
Shipping World—154 Fleet St., London, E.C.4. 2s.
Shoe and Leather News—South Place, E.C.2. 1s.
Shoe and Leather News—Spencer House, South Place, Finsbury, E.C.2. 1s.
Shoe Manufacturers' Monthly—4 Market Place, Leicester. 3d.
Skinner's Silk and Rayon Record—44 Brazennose St., Manchester. 2s.
Soap, Perfumery and Cosmetics—9 Gough Square, E.C.4. 3s. 6d.
Solicitors' Journal—Oyez House, Bream's Bldgs., Fetter Lane, E.C.4. 1s. 9d.
Sports Trader—15 Cursitor St., E.C.4. 2s.
Stage—19 Tavistock St., W.C.2. 9d.
Steam Engineer—90 High Holborn, W.C.1. 3s.
Stock Exchange Gazette—330 Gresham House, Old Broad St., E.C.2. 1s. 6d.
Stores and Shops—68 Welbeck St., W.1. 2s. 6d.
Structural Engineer—11 Upper Belgrave St., S.W.1. 5s. 3d.
Surveyor and Municipal and County Engineer—42 Russell Square, W.C.1. 1s. 6d.
Syren and Shipping—7-17 Jewry St., E.C.3. 1s. 6d.
Tailor and Cutter—42 Gerrard St., W.1. 1s.
Teacher—Hamilton House, Hasting St., London, W.C.1. 6d.
Teacher's World—Montague House, Russell Sq., W.C.1. 6d.
Textile Manufacturer—31 King St. West, Manchester. 2s. 6d.
Textile Mercury—Mercury House, Acton Sq., Salford, 5. 8d.
Textile Recorder—Old Colony House, South King St., Manchester. 3s.
Textile Weekly—33 Blackfriars St., Manchester 3. 8d.
Timber and Plywood—194-200 Bishopsgate, E.C.2. 1s. 6d.
Timber Trades Journal—154 Fleet St., E.C.4. 1s. 6d.
Times Review of Industry—Printing House Square, E.C.4. 1s.
Tobacco—17-19 John Adam St., Adelphi, W.C.2. 1s. 6d.
Tobacconist and Confectioner (*inc.* Tobacco Trade Review)—Eastcheap Buildings, E.C.3. 3d.
Tooling—4 Ludgate Circus, E.C.4. 2s.
Town and Country Planning—28 King St., W.C.2. 2s.
Toy Trader—65 Turnmill St., N.W.1. 20s. p.a.
Trade Marks Journal—25 Southampton Bldgs., W.C.2. 3s. 6d.
Transport Management—18 Kensington Gate, W.8. 1s.
Transport World—3 Fleet St., E.C.4. 25s. p.a.
Waste Trade World—Maclaren House, 131 Great Suffolk St., S.E.1. 6d.
Watchmaker, Jeweller and Silversmith—Drury House, Russell Street, W.C.2. 2s. 6d.
Water and Water Engineering—30 Furnival St., E.C.4. 2s. 6d.
Weekly Law Reports (Legal)—3 Stone Buildings, Lincoln's Inn, W.C.2. 126s. p.a.
Welding—Dorset House, Stamford St., S.E.1. 5s.
Wine and Food—28-30 Grosvenor Gardens, S.W.1. 5s.
Wine and Spirit Trade Record—7 Laurence Pountney Hill, Cannon St., E.C.4. 84s. p.a.
Wine and Spirit Trade Review—Eastcheap Buildings, E.C.3. 40s. p.a.
Wire Industry—33 Furnival St., E.C.4. 40s. p.a.
Wireless and Electrical Trader—Dorset House, Stamford St., S.E.1. 60s. p.a.
Wireless World—Dorset House, Stamford St., S.E.1. 2s. 6d.
Women's Wear News—3-5 Barrett St., W.1. 9d.
Wood—33 Tothill St., S.W.1. 2s. 6d.

Woodworker—Montague House, Russell Sq., W.C.1. 1s. 6d.
Wool Record—91 Kirkgate, Bradford. 85s. p.a.
World Crops—The Tower, Brook Green Road, W.6. 40s. p.a.
World Power Engineering—Drury House, Russell St., W.C.2. 2s. 6d.
World Sports—185 Fleet St., E.C.4. 2s.
World's Carriers—147 Victoria St., S.W.1. 1s. 6d.
World's Fair—Union St., Oldham. 6d.
World's Paper Trade Review—296–302 High Holborn, W.C.1. 1s.
World's Press News and Advertiser's Review—6–10 Old Bailey, E.C.4. 2s.

LONDON OFFICES OF COMMONWEALTH, NORTHERN IRISH AND AMERICAN NEWSPAPERS

Australia:—
Adelaide Advertiser—107 Fleet St., E.C.4.
Adelaide Chronicle—107 Fleet St., E.C.4.
Adelaide Sunday Mail—34 Ludgate Hill, E.C.4.
Adelaide News—34 Ludgate Hill, E.C.4.
Brisbane Courier-Mail—107 Fleet St., E.C.4.
Brisbane Telegraph—107 Fleet St., E.C.4.
Launceston Examiner—30 New Bri. St., E.C.4.
Melbourne Age—132 Fleet St., E.C.4.
Melbourne Australian Post—107 Fleet St., E.C.4.
Melbourne Herald—107 Fleet St., E.C.4.
Melbourne Sun News-Pictorial—107 Fleet St., E.C.4.
Melbourne Weekly Times—110 Fleet St., E.C.4.
Perth Daily News—110 Fleet St., E.C.4.
Perth West Australian—107 Fleet St., E.C.4.
Sydney Bulletin—107 Fleet St., E.C.4.
Sydney Mirror—Red Lion Court, E.C.4.
Sydney Morning Herald—85 Fleet St., E.C.4.
Sydney Sun-Herald—85 Fleet Street, E.C.4.
Sydney Telegraph—107 Fleet St., E.C.4.

Canada:—
Calgary Albertan—26 Craven St., W.C.2.
Calgary Herald—40–43 Fleet St., E.C.4.
Edmonton Journal—40–43 Fleet St., E.C.4.
Globe and Mail (Toronto)—Printing House Square, E.C.4.
Montreal Gazette—34–40 Ludgate Hill, E.C.4.
Ottawa Citizen—34–40 Ludgate Hill, E.C.4.
Ottawa Journal—56 Bloomsbury Sq., W.1.
Toronto Daily Star—83–80 Farringdon St., E.C.4.
Toronto Star Weekly—83–86 Farringdon St., E.C.4.
Toronto Telegram—40–43 Fleet St., E.C.4.
Vancouver Province—40–43 Fleet St., E.C.4.

Ceylon:—
Ceylon Daily News—302–8 Regent St., W.1.
Ceylon Observer—302–8 Regent St., W.1.
Times of Ceylon—Stuart House, 1 Tudor St., E.C.4.

India:—
Allahabad Leader—3 Salisbury Court, Fleet St., E.C.4.
Bombay Evening News of India—3 Albemarle St., W.1.
Hindu, The (Madras)—2–3 Salisbury Court, Fleet St., E.C.4.
Hindustan Standard (Calcutta)—Wheatsheaf House, Carmelite St., Fleet St., E.C.4.
Hindustan Times (New Delhi)—2 Salisbury Court, Fleet St., E.C.4.
Illustrated Weekly of India—3 Albemarle St., W.1.
Madras Mail—302–8 Regent St., W.1.
National Herald (Lucknow)—2–3 Salisbury Court, E.C.4.
Statesman (Calcutta)—41 Whitehall, S.W.1.
Times of India—3 Albemarle St., W.1.

New Zealand:—
Auckland Star—30 New Bridge St., E.C.4.
Auckland Weekly News—107 Fleet St., E.C.4.
Christchurch Press—107 Fleet St., E.C.4.
Dominion (Wellington)—34 New Bridge St., E.C.4.
Dunedin Evening Star—34 New Bridge St., E.C.4.
New Zealand Evening Post—107 Fleet St., E.C.4.
New Zealand Farmer (Auckland)—34 New Bridge St., E.C.4.
New Zealand Herald—107 Fleet St., E.C.4.
Otago Daily Times and Witness—107 Fleet St., E.C.4.
Southland Daily News (Invercargill)—34 New Bridge St., E.C.4.
Southland Times—107 Fleet St., E.C.4.
Wanganui Chronicle—34 New Bridge St., E.C.4.

Northern Ireland:—
Armagh Guardian—151 Fleet St., E.C.4.
Ballymena Observer—69 Fleet St., E.C.4.
Ballymena Weekly Tel.—112 Fleet St., E.C.4.
Banbridge Chronicle—151 Fleet St., E.C.4.
Belfast News Letter—85 Fleet St., E.C.4.
Belfast Telegraph (and Weekly Telegraph)—Thomson House, 200 Grays Inn Road, W.C.1.
Coleraine Chronicle—151 Fleet St., E.C.4.
County Down Spectator—59 Fleet St., E.C.4.
Derry Journal—69 Fleet St., E.C.4.
Derry Standard—177 Fleet St., E.C.4.
Down Recorder—69 Fleet St., E.C.4.
Impartial Reporter (Enniskillen)—69 Fleet St., E.C.4.
Irish News—177 Fleet St., E.C.4.
Irish Weekly and Ulster Examiner—177 Fleet St., E.C.4.
Londonderry Sentinel—80 Fleet St., E.C.4.
Lurgan Mail—69 Fleet St., E.C.4.
Mid Ulster Mail—177 Fleet St., E.C.4.
Newtownards Chronicle—151 Fleet St., E.C.4.
Newtownards Spectator—69 Fleet St., E.C.4.
Northern Constitution (Coleraine)—Clifford's Inn, Fleet St., E.C.4.
Northern Whig—143 Fleet St., E.C.4.
Portadown News—69 Fleet St., E.C.4.
Portadown Times—69 Fleet St., E.C.4.
Strabane Weekly News—69 Fleet St., E.C.4.
Tyrone Constitution—69 Fleet St., E.C.4.
Tyrone Courier—69 Fleet St., E.C.4.
Ulster Gazette (Armagh)—69 Fleet St., E.C.4.
Ulster Herald—120 Bank Chambers, 329 High Holborn, W.C.1.

Pakistan:—
Karachi Dawn—24–27 High Holborn, W.C.1.
Pakistan Times—118 Fleet St., E.C.4.

U.S.A.:—
Baltimore Sun—85 Fleet St., E.C.4.
Chicago Daily News—69 Fleet St., E.C.4.
Chicago Tribune—85 Fleet St., E.C.4.
Christian Science Monitor—Africa House, 64–78 Kingsway, W.C.2.
New York Daily Mirror—78 Fleet St., E.C.4.
New York Herald-Tribune—The Adelphi, W.C.2.
New York Times—Printing House Square, E.C.4.
New York Wall Street Journal—245 Oxford St., W.1.

NEWSPAPER GROUP PUBLISHERS

In recent years a large number of newspapers in London and the Provinces have been acquired by various groups of publishers, either in one company or in a series of companies associated with each other. The following is a list of the chief newspaper group publishers, with the journals controlled:

Northcliffe Group (Viscount Rothermere):

LONDON—Daily Mail, Daily Sketch, Evening News.

PROVINCES—*Cheltenham*, Gloucester Echo, Cheltenham Chronicle; *Derby*, Evening Telegraph; *Edinburgh*, Scottish Daily Mail; *Gloucester*, Citizen, Gloucester Journal; *Grimsby*, Evening Telegraph, Saturday Telegraph; *Hull*, Daily Mail, Hull Times; *Leicester*, Evening Mail; *Lincoln*, Echo; *Stoke on Trent*, Evening Sentinel, Weekly Sentinel; *Swansea*, Herald of Wales, South Wales Evening Post.

Harmsworth Group

PROVINCES—*Barnstaple*, North Devon Journal-Herald; *Bodmin*, Cornish Guardian; *Crediton*, Gazette; *Exeter*, Express & Echo, Western Times & Gazette; *Exmouth*, Chronicle; *Ilfracombe*, Chronicle; *Penzance*, Cornishman; *Plymouth*, Western Morning News, Western Evening Herald; *Tiverton*, Gazette; *Torquay*, Herald Express; *Truro*, West Briton; *Wellington*, Wellington Weekly News.

Provincial Newspapers Group

PROVINCES—*Blackburn*, Times; *Burnley*, Express and News; *Doncaster*, Gazette; *Edinburgh*, Evening News; *Leeds*, Yorkshire Evening News; *Northampton*, Chronicle and Echo, Independent, Mercury and Herald; *Nuneaton*, Observer; *Preston*, Lancashire Evening Post, Guardian.

LONDON SUBURBAN—*Balham*, News and Mercury; *Clapham*, Observer; *Merton*, News; *Mitcham*, News and Mercury; *Norbury*, News; *Norwood*, News; *Penge*, News; *Streatham*, News; *Wimbledon*, Boro News.

Berrow's Newspapers Ltd.
(WORCESTER)

PROVINCES—*Worcester*, Evening News and Times, Saturday Sports News, Berrow's Worcester Journal; *Stourport*, News; *Kidderminster*, Times; *Droitwich*, Guardian; *Malvern*, Gazette; *Ledbury*, Reporter.

Beaverbrook Group (Lord Beaverbrook):

LONDON—Daily Express, Evening Standard, Sunday Express.

PROVINCES—*Glasgow*, Scottish Daily Express, Evening Citizen.

East Midland Allied Press Ltd.

PROVINCES—*Kettering*, Northamptonshire Evening Telegraph, Northamptonshire Advertiser; *Market Harborough*, Advertiser & Midland Mail; *Peterborough*, Citizen & Advertiser; *Stamford*, Lincoln, Rutland & Stamford Mercury; *Spalding*, Guardian, Lincolnshire Free Press; *Wisbech*, Isle of Ely & Wisbech Advertiser; *King's Lynn*, Lynn News & Advertiser; *Bury St. Edmunds*, Bury Free Press; *Sudbury*, Suffolk Free Press; *Newmarket*, Journal.

Westminster Press Group

PROVINCES—*Abingdon*, North Berks Herald; *Alnwick*, Northumberland Gazette; *Auckland*, Chronicle; *Barrow*, North Western Evening Mail, News; *Bath*, Chronicle & Herald, Somerset Guardian, Wiltshire News; *Bedford*, Record, Times; *Biggleswade*, Chronicle; *Blyth*, News; *Bradford*, Telegraph and Argus, Yorkshire Sports; *Chertsey*, Surrey Herald; *Consett*, Chronicle; *Darlington*, Northern Echo, Northern Despatch, Times; *Dalton*, News; *Devizes*, Wiltshire Gazette; *Durham*, County Advertiser, Chronicle; *Ealing*, Middlesex County Times; *Harrow*, Observer; *Keighley*, News; *Kendal*, Westmorland Gazette; *Lincoln*, Chronicle; *Malton*, Gazette; *North Shields*, Weekly News; *Oxford*, Mail, Times; *South Shields*, Gazette, Sports Gazette; *Stanley*, News; *Swindon*, Evening Advertiser, Football Pink, Wilts. Gazette and Herald; *Uxbridge*, Middlesex Advertiser; *Wembley*, Observer, News; *Whitley Bay*, Chronicle & Guardian; *Woking*, Herald; *York*, Yorkshire Gazette and Herald, Yorkshire Evening Press.

Thomson Group (Roy Thomson)

LONDON—Sunday Times.

PROVINCES—*Manchester*, The Sporting Chronicle, Midday, Evening Chronicle; *Newcastle upon Tyne*, Newcastle Journal and North Mail, Evening Chronicle, Sunday Sun; *Blackburn*, Northern Evening Telegraph; *Liverpool*, Journal of Commerce and Shipping Telegraph; *Macclesfield*, Macclesfield County Express; *Middlesbrough*, Evening Gazette; *Sheffield*, Star, Sheffield Telegraph; *Stockport*, Stockport Express.

SCOTLAND—*Edinburgh*, The Scotsman; *Aberdeen*, The Press and Journal, Evening Express.

WALES—*Cardiff*, Western Mail, South Wales Echo.

Odhams Press Group

LONDON—Daily Herald, People, Sporting Life.

REPORTING AND NEWS AGENCIES

ASSOCIATED NEWS SERVICE,
30 Fleet Street, E.C.4. Fleet Street. 6280.

ASSOCIATED PRESS LTD.,
83–86 Farringdon Street, E.C.4. Fleet Street. 1515.

BRENARD PRESS LTD.,
London Airport, Hounslow, Middx. Skyport 1234.

BRITISH UNITED PRESS LTD.,
8 Bouverie Street, E.C.4. Fleet Street 7266.

CENTRAL PRESS FEATURES,
80 Fleet Street, E.C.4. Fleet Street 7792.

COMTELBURO LTD.,
85 Fleet Street, E.C.4. Fleet Street 6060.

EXCHANGE TELEGRAPH CO., LTD.,
Extel House, East Harding Street, E.C.4. Fleet Street 1080.

INFORMATION BUREAU LTD.,
11, Crane Court, E.C.4. Fleet Street 6234.

LONDON INTERNATIONAL PRESS LTD.,
3–4 Ludgate Circus Buildings, E.C.4. Central 8931.

NATIONAL PRESS AGENCY LTD.,
Newspaper House, 8–16 Great New Street, E.C.4. Fleet Street 1030.

NEWSPAPER FEATURES LTD.,
110 Fleet Street, E.C.4. Fleet Street 7888.

P.A. FEATURES LTD.,
85 Fleet Street, E.C.4. Fleet Street 7440.

PARLIAMENTARY NEWS SERVICES,
92 Fleet Street, E.C.4. Ludgate Circus 7848.

PRESS ASSOCIATION LTD.,
85 Fleet Street, E.C.4. Fleet Street 7440.

REUTERS LTD.,
85 Fleet Street, E.C.4. Fleet Street 6060.

UNIVERSAL NEWS SERVICE LTD.,
11 New Fetter Lane, E.C.4. Fleet Street 1633.

Birmingham: Cater's News Agency, 5 Digbeth, Birmingham, 5. Birmingham. Midland 7671.

Bristol: Bristol & West News Agency, Peloquin House, Pipe Lane, Bristol, 1.

Cambridge: Cambridge News Service, 44a Hills Road, Cambridge. Cambridge 52494–6.

Halifax: North Eastern Trade Press Agency, 120 Rochdale Road, Ripponden, Yorks. Ripponden 3236.

Liverpool: Gronbach (Journalists) Ltd., Chicago Buildings, 13 Whitechapel, Liverpool, 1. Liverpool Central 1388.

Manchester: General News Services, 274–278 The Corn Exchange, Fennel Street, Manchester, 4. Manchester Deansgate 4607–8.

LONDON POSTAL DISTRICTS

Central Area.—Principal streets or approximate boundaries of the postal districts are named in the area from Edgware Road and Park Lane to Bishopsgate; and from Marylebone and Euston Roads to the Thames.

E.C.1.—Clerkenwell, City Road, Old Street, Goswell Road, Aldersgate Street, St. Martin's-le-Grand, Newgate Street, Holborn Viaduct, etc.

E.C.2.—Rivington Street, Liverpool Street, Bishopsgate, Threadneedle Street, Poultry, Cheapside, Foster Lane, Finsbury Square, Tabernacle Street, Moorgate, London Wall, Gresham Street, Old Broad Street, etc.

E.C.3.—Cornhill, Houndsditch, Leadenhall Street, Aldgate, Gracechurch Street, Lombard Street, Fenchurch Street, Eastcheap, Lower Thames Street, Tower Hill, etc.

E.C.4.—Fetter Lane, Fleet Street, Temple, Farringdon Street, New Bridge Street, Old Bailey, Ludgate Hill, Paternoster Row, Queen Victoria Street, Cannon Street, Upper Thames Street, King William Street, etc.

W.C.1.—From (excl.) Tottenham Court Road to (incl.) Phoenix Place and Gray's Inn Road; from (excl.) Euston Road and (excl.) Pentonville Road to (incl.) New Oxford Street, High Holborn and Holborn.

W.C.2.—From Charing Cross Road, Leicester Square, Trafalgar Square to Chancery Lane and Essex Street; from (excl.) New Oxford Street and (excl.) Holborn to the Thames.

W.1.—From (excl.) Edgware Road and (incl.) Park Lane to (incl.) Tottenham Court Road and (incl.) Shaftesbury Avenue; from (excl.) Marylebone Road and (excl.) Euston Road to (incl.) Piccadilly.

S.W.1.—From (incl.) Pont Street, Sloane Street and Chelsea Bridge Road to Haymarket, Victoria Embankment and Millbank; from (incl.) Knightsbridge and (excl.) Piccadilly to Grosvenor Road.

Other Areas.—Boundaries of the postal districts are not necessarily the same as those of boroughs of the same name.

N.1.	Islington, Hoxton.
N.2.	East Finchley.
N.3.	Finchley, Church End.
N.4.	Finsbury Park, Harringay.
N.5.	Highbury.
N.6.	Highgate.
N.7.	Holloway.
N.8.	Hornsey.
N.9.	Lower Edmonton.
N.10.	Muswell Hill.
N.11.	New Southgate.
N.12.	North Finchley.
N.13.	Palmer's Green.
N.14.	Southgate.
N.15.	South Tottenham.
N.16.	Stoke Newington.
N.17.	Tottenham.
N.18.	Upper Edmonton.
N.19.	Upper Holloway.
N.20.	Whetstone.
N.21.	Winchmore Hill.
N.22.	Wood Green.
N.W.1.	Regent's Park, N. Camden Town, Somers Town.
N.W.2.	Cricklewood, Hampstead.
N.W.3.	Hampstead.
N.W.4.	Hendon.
N.W.5.	Kentish Town.
N.W.6.	Kilburn, Brondesbury.
N.W.7.	Mill Hill.
N.W.8.	St. John's Wood.
N.W.9.	The Hyde, Kingsbury.
N.W.10.	Willesden, Harlesden, Neasden.
N.W.11.	Golders Green.
W.2.	Paddington, Edgware Road.
W.3.	Acton
W.4	Chiswick.
W.5.	Ealing.
W.6.	Hammersmith.
W.7.	Hanwell.
W.8.	Kensington.
W.9.	Maida Hill.
W.10.	North Kensington.
W.11.	Notting Hill.
W.12.	Shepherd's Bush.
W.13.	West Ealing.
W.14.	West Kensington.
S.W.2.	Brixton, Streatham Hill.
S.W.3.	Chelsea.
S.W.4.	Clapham.
S.W.5.	Earl's Court.
S.W.6.	Fulham, Walham Green.
S.W.7.	South Kensington.
S.W.8.	South Lambeth.
S.W.9.	Stockwell.
S.W.10.	West Brompton.
S.W.11.	Battersea.
S.W.12.	Balham.
S.W.13.	Barnes.
S.W.14.	Mortlake.
S.W.15.	Putney, Roehampton.
S.W.16.	Streatham.
S.W.17.	Tooting.
S.W.18.	Wandsworth.
S.W.19.	Wimbledon.
S.W.20.	West Wimbledon.
S.E.1.	Lambeth, Southwark, Bermondsey.
S.E.2.	Abbey Wood.
S.E.3.	Blackheath.
S.E.4.	Brockley.
S.E.5.	Camberwell.
S.E.6.	Catford.
S.E.7.	Charlton.
S.E.8.	Deptford.
S.E.9.	Eltham.
S.E.10.	Greenwich.
S.E.11.	Kennington.
S.E.12.	Lee.
S.E.13.	Lewisham.
S.E.14.	New Cross.
S.E.15.	Peckham.
S.E.16.	Rotherhithe.
S.E.17.	Walworth.
S.E.18.	Woolwich, Plumstead.
S.E.19.	Norwood.
S.E.20.	Anerley, Penge.
S.E.21.	Dulwich.
S.E.22.	East Dulwich.
S.E.23.	Forest Hill.
S.E.24.	Herne Hill.
S.E.25.	South Norwood.
S.E.26.	Sydenham.
S.E.27.	West Norwood.
E.1.	Spitalfields, Mile End, Wapping, Shadwell, Stepney.
E.2.	Bethnal Green.
E.3.	Bow.
E.4.	Chingford.
E.5.	Clapton.
E.6.	East Ham.
E.7.	Forest Gate.
E.8.	Hackney, Dalston.
E.9.	Homerton, Hackney Wick, South Hackney.
E.10.	Leyton.
E.11.	Leytonstone, Wanstead.
E.12.	Manor Park.
E.13.	Plaistow.
E.14.	Limehouse, Poplar, Millwall, Isle of Dogs.
E.15.	Stratford.
E.16.	Canning Town, Victoria Docks, Silvertown, N. Woolwich.
E.17.	Walthamstow.
E.18.	Woodford.

Principal British and Irish Societies and Institutions

THE ROYAL ACADEMY OF ARTS (1768), Burlington House, W.1.—*President*, Sir Charles Wheeler, K.C.V.O., C.B.E. (1956); *Keeper*, Henry Rushbury, C.V.O., C.B.E., R.A. *Treas.*, Sir Basil Spence, O.M., O.B.E., T.D., R.A.; *Sec.*, Humphrey Brooke, M.V.O., B.A., B.LITT.; *Reg.*, C. W. Tanner, M.V.O.; *Librarian*, S. C. Hutchinson, F.S.A.

Royal Academicians

1963 Aldridge, John.
1941*Anderson, Stanley, C.B.E.
1949 Austin, Robert S.
1955 Bawden, Edward, C.B.E.
1937‡Brockhurst, G. L.
1955 Buhler, Robert.
1962 Burn, Rodney J.
1955 Charoux, Siegfried.
1958 Clark, J. Cosmo, C.B.E.
1944 Cundall, Charles.
1955 Dring, William.
1950 Dunlop, R. O.
1953 Eurich, Richard.
1954 Fitton, James.
1933*Flint, Sir W. Russell.
1942‡Frampton, Meredith.
1960 Greenham, Peter G.
1961 Gunn, Sir James.
1942*Harris, E. V., O.B.E.
1961 Hepple, Norman.
1930*Kelly, Sir Gerald F., K.C.V.O.
1936*Knight, Dame Laura, D.B.E.
1952 Lambert, Maurice.
1938 Lawrence, A. K.
1954 Le Bas, Edward, C.B.E.
1962*Lowry, L. S.
1963 McFall, David.
1955 Machin, Arnold.
1933*McMillan, W., C.V.O.
1962 McMorran Donald H.
1951*Mason, Arnold.
1947*Maufe, Sir Edward.
1959*Methuen, Lord.
1938 Monnington, W. T.
1951 Nash, John.
1943*Newton, Algernon.
1955 O'Rorke, Brian.
1953 Pitchforth, R. V.
1942 Procter, Mrs. Dod.
1944*Richardson, Sir Albert, K.C.V.O.
1936 Rushbury, Henry, C.V.O., C.B.E.
1961 Sanders, Christopher C.
1963 Sisson, Marshall A., C.B.E.
1959 Skeaping, John R.
1954 Spear, Ruskin.
1960 Spence, Sir Basil, O.M., O.B.E., T.D.
1959 Spencer, Gilbert.
1931*Taylor, L. Campbell.
1945 Thomson, A. R.
1949 Todd, A. R. Middleton.
1954 Tunnicliffe, C. F.
1955 Walker, B. Fleetwood-.
1940 Wheeler, Sir Charles, K.C.V.O., C.B.E.
1945 Woodford, James, O.B.E.

Associates

1962 Ardizzone, Edward
1959 Bratby, John R.
1963 Burra, Edward.
1957 Carr, Henry.
1962 Casson, Sir Hugh.
1957 Cowern, Raymond T.
1962 de Grey, Roger.
1959 Dunstan, Bernard.
1953†Durst, Alan L.
1962 Ehrlich, Georg.
1956 Elwes, Simon.
1959 Frith, Raymond C.
1955 Freeth, H. Andrew.
1961 Gibberd, Frederick, C.B.E.
1955 Gwynne-Jones, Allan, D.S.O.
1963 Hayes, Colin.
1963 Hermes, Miss Gertrude.
1957 Hillier, Tristram.
1961 Holford, Sir William.
1961 Mahoney, Charles.
1958 Nimptsch, Uli.
1948†Prout, Mrs. M. Fisher.
1960 Redpath, Miss Anne.
1958 Roberts, William.
1960 Rosoman, Leonard.
1957 Schilsky, Eric.
1963 Soukop, Willi.
1956 Ward, John.
1955 Weight, Carel.

Hon. Academician Extraordinary (1948), Rt. Hon. Sir Winston S. Churchill, K.G., O.M., C.H., M.P.

* Senior Academician. † Senior Associate.
‡ Honorary Retired Academician.

Former Presidents of the Royal Academy

Sir. J. Reynolds, 1768.
Benjamin West, 1792.
James Wyatt, 1805.
Benjamin West, 1806.
Sir T. Lawrence, 1820.
Sir M. A. Shee, 1830.
Sir C. Eastlake, 1850.
Sir Francis Grant, 1866.
Lord Leighton, 1878.
Sir J. Millais, 1896.
Sir E. Poynter, 1896.
Sir A. Webb, 1919.
Sir F. Dicksee, 1924.
Sir W. Llewellyn, 1928.
Sir E. Lutyens, 1938.
Sir A. J. Munnings, 1944.
Sir G. F. Kelly, 1949.
Sir A. E. Richardson, 1954.

ROYAL CAMBRIAN ACADEMY OF ART (1881), Plas Mawr, Conway.—*Hon. Sec.*, Mrs. M. della R. Whitehead; *Curator and Sec.*, Frederic Lees.

THE ROYAL SCOTTISH ACADEMY (1826), Princes Street Edinburgh.—*Pres.*, Sir William MacTaggart, R.S.A.; *Sec.*, Donald Moodie, R.S.A.; *Treas.*, W. H. Kininmonth, R.S.A.; *Librarian*, William Wilson, O.B.E., R.S.A.; *Asst. Sec.*, W. Keith.

Honorary Retired Academicians

1929 Carrick, Alex.
1937 Cursiter, Stanley, C.B.E.
1943 Orphoot, B. N. H.
1953 Henderson, A. Graham.

Royal Scottish Academicians

1958 Armour, Mrs. Mary
1958 Blyth, R. Henderson.
1944 Bone, Phyllis. M.
1962 Coia, J. A.
1956 Crawford, H. Adam
1962 Donaldson, David A.
1956 Fleming, Ian.
1947 Gillies, William G., C.B.E.
1959 Glass, W. Mervyn.
1959 Gleave, J. L.
1956 Kininmonth, W. H.
1960 Lindsay, Ian G., O.B.E.
1923 Lintott, Henry.
1957 Lorimer, Hew.
1946 MacDougall, Leslie Grahame.
1939 McGlashan, Arch. A.
1948 MacTaggart, Sir William.
1952 Moodie, Donald.
1963 Morrocco, Alberto.
1957 Patrick, J. McIntosh.
1962 Philipson, Robin.
1952 Redpath, Anne, O.B.E.
1956 Schilsky, Eric.
1937 Schotz, Benno.
1936 Sutherland, D. M.
1946 Thomson, Adam B., O.B.E.
1957 Thomson, J. Murray.
1954 Whalen, Thomas.
1949 Wilson, William, O.B.E.

Non-Resident Academician

Hutchison, Sir William.

Associates

Armour, William.
Barr, James.
Beveridge, Thomas.
Blackadder, Elizabeth.
Burns, W. A.
Cameron, Gordon S.
Clark, James H.
Crosbie, William.
Cumming, James.
Dempster, Miss Elizabeth.
Dick, Miss Alix.
Dods, Andrew.
Ewart, David S.
Forrest, Norman J.
Gordon, Esmé.
Hislop, Mrs. Margaret.
Jackson, C. d'O. Pilkington.
Johnston, Ninian.
Johnstone, Miss Dorothy.
McClure, David.
Matthew, Prof. Sir Robert H., C.B.E.
Miller, James.
Miller, John.
Peploe, Denis.
Pulsford, Charles.
Sutherland, Scott.
Thomson, Sinclair.
Wheeler, H. Anthony.
Whiston, Peter.

Non-Resident Associates

Mrs. Josephine Miller; Sir Basil Spence, O.M., O.B.E., T.D.; Ancell Stronach.

ROYAL IRISH ACADEMY (1786), 19 Dawson Street, Dublin.—*Pres.*, J. L. Synge, F.R.S.; *Treas.* V. C. Barry, D.SC.; *Sec.* B. Ó. Cuív, D.LITT.

ACCOUNTANTS, INSTITUTE OF CHARTERED, in England and Wales (1880), Moorgate Place, E.C.2.—*Pres.* (1963–64), R. P. Winter, C.B.E., M.C., T.D.; *Joint Secretaries*, F. M. Wilkinson; C. A. Evan-Jones, M.B.E.

ACCOUNTANTS, THE INSTITUTE OF COMPANY (1928), 11 Portland Road, Edgbaston, Birmingham, 16.

ACCOUNTANTS AND AUDITORS, BRITISH ASSOCIATION OF (1923), 2/4 Chiswick High Road, W.4.—*Sec.*, A. Taylor.

ACCOUNTANTS, ASSOCIATION OF CERTIFIED AND CORPORATE (1904), 22 Bedford Square, W.C.1.—*Pres.* V. R. Chennell; *Sec.*, F. C. Osbourn, M.B.E., B.A., LL.B.

ACCOUNTANTS, ASSOCIATION OF INTERNATIONAL (1932), 5–7 New Street, Bishopsgate, E.C.2.—*Sec.*, C. E. Taylor.

ACCOUNTANTS OF SCOTLAND, INSTITUTE OF CHARTERED (1854), 27 Queen Street, Edinburgh, 2.—*Pres.*, W. L. Milligan; *Sec.*, E. H. V. McDougall.

ACCOUNTANTS, ASSOCIATION OF INDUSTRIAL AND COMMERCIAL EXECUTIVE, 126 Great Cambridge Road, Tottenham, N.17.—*Sec.*, D. E. G. Wing.

ACCOUNTANTS IN IRELAND, INSTITUTE OF CHARTERED (1888), 7 Fitzwilliam Place, Dublin, and 6 Callender Street, Belfast.—*Secs.*, W. S. Orr (Dublin); T. D. Lorimer (Belfast).

ACCOUNTANTS, SOCIETY OF COMMERCIAL, 31 Stoke Grove, Westbury-on-Trym, Bristol.—*Sec.*, J. B. Haggett.

ACTORS' BENEVOLENT FUND (1882), 6 Adam Street, W.C.2.—*Sec.*, Miss A. G. Marks.

ACTORS' CHURCH UNION (1899), 4 Foster Lane, E.C.2.—*Sec.*, Rev. T. B. McKee.

ACTUARIES IN SCOTLAND, THE FACULTY OF (1856), Hall and Library, 23 St. Andrew Square, Edinburgh.—*Hon. Secs.*, H. Valentine; A. F. Ross.

ACTUARIES, INSTITUTE OF (1848), Staple Inn Hall, W.C.1.—*Pres.*, K. A. Usherwood; *Hon. Secs.*, P. R. Cox, R. S. Skerman; *Sec.*, N. J. Page, M.C.

ADDICTION (TO ALCOHOL AND OTHER DRUGS), SOCIETY FOR THE STUDY OF (1884).—*Gen. Sec.*, Rev. Benson Harrison, 4 Palace Gate, W.8.

ADDITIONAL CURATES SOCIETY; HOME MISSIONS OF CHURCH OF ENGLAND AND THE CHURCH IN WALES (1837), 14 Rothamsted Avenue, Harpenden, Herts.—*Sec.*, Rev. C. J. Read, M.A.

ADOPTION SOCIETY, NATIONAL, 47a Manchester Street, nr. Baker Street, W.1.—*Sec.*, Miss N. C. Davis.

ADVERTISING ASSOCIATION, 1 Bell Yard, W.C.2.—*Director-General*, L. E. Room, O.B.E.

ADVERTISING, ADVISORY COUNCIL FOR THE CONTROL OF OUTDOOR (*Formerly* S.C.A.P.A.), 3 Dean's Yard, S.W.1.—*Hon. Sec.*, Miss E. B. Ashford.

ADVERTISING BENEVOLENT SOCIETY, NATIONAL (1913), 27 Old Bond Street, W.1.

ADVERTISING, INSTITUTE OF PRACTITIONERS IN, 44 Belgrave Square, S.W.1.—*Dir.*, J. P. O'Connor.

ADVERTISING MANAGERS' ASSOCIATION, INCORPORATED (founded 1932, inc. 1938), Brooks House, Upper Thames Street, E.C.4.—*Gen. Sec.*, Miss D. Stevens.

AERONAUTICAL SOCIETY, ROYAL (1866) (incorporating the Institution of Aeronautical Engineers and the Helicopter Association of Great Britain), 4 Hamilton Place, W.1.—*Pres.* (1963–64), Prof. A. R. Collar; *Sec.*, Dr. A. M. Ballantyne.

AFRICAN INSTITUTE, INTERNATIONAL (1926), St. Dunstan's Chambers, 10-11 Fetter Lane, E.C.4.—*Administrative Director*, Prof. Daryll Forde; *Sec.*, Miss A. Currie.

AGED PILGRIMS' FRIEND SOCIETY (1807), 19 Ludgate Hill, E.C.4.—*Sec.*, F. R. Clifford.

AGED POOR SOCIETY (1708) AND ST. JOSEPH'S HOUSE, 39 Eccleston Square, S.W.1.—*Sec.*, Miss M. Flood.

AGRICULTURAL BENEVOLENT INSTITUTION, ROYAL, Vincent House, Vincent Square, S.W.1.—*Hon. Treas.*, Sir Evelyn Shaw, K.C.V.O., LL.D.; *Sec.*, Cdr. G. M. Pares, R.N.

AGRICULTURAL BENEVOLENT INSTITUTION, ROYAL SCOTTISH (1897), 10 Duke Street, Edinburgh.—*Sec.*, Sir Charles G. Connell, W.S.

AGRICULTURAL BOTANY, NATIONAL INSTITUTE OF (1919), Huntingdon Road, Cambridge.—*Director*, F. R. Horne, C.B.E., M.A.; *Sec.*, M. G. Tozer, M.B.E.

AGRICULTURAL ENGINEERS ASSOCIATION, LIMITED (1877), 6 Buckingham Gate, S.W.1.—*Sec. and Chief Executive*, Air Vice-Marshal F. L. Hopps, C.B., C.B.E., A.F.C.

AGRICULTURAL SOCIETY OF ENGLAND, ROYAL (1838), 35 Belgrave Square, S.W.1.—*Sec.*, C. Dadd. (The 1964 Show will be held at Stoneleigh Abbey, nr. Kenilworth, Warwicks, July 7–10).

AGRICULTURAL SOCIETY, GLASGOW, (1860).—*Sec.*, S. Gilmour, 82 Gordon Street, Glasgow, C.1.

AGRICULTURAL SOCIETY, ROYAL ULSTER (1826), The King's Hall, Balmoral, Belfast 9.—*Sec.*, J. T. Kernohan.

AGRICULTURAL SOCIETY OF THE COMMONWEALTH, ROYAL (1959)—*Sec.*, A. Hobson, C.B.E., M.V.O., Clare Cottage, Oulton, Norwich.

AGRICULTURE ASSOCIATION OF (1947), 78 Buckingham Gate, S.W.1.—*Gen. Sec.*, Alexander Hay, O.B.E.

AGRICULTURE AND HORTICULTURE, BRITISH ASSOCIATION OF CONSULTANTS IN, Horticultural Advisory Bureau, Arkley, Herts.—*Hon. Sec.*, W. E. Shewell-Cooper, M.B.E., D.Litt.

AIRBROKERS ASSOCIATION (1949), 25 Bury Street, E.C.3.—*Sec.*, J. L. Logan.

AIR LEAGUE OF THE BRITISH EMPIRE (1909), 142 Sloane Street, S.W.1.—*Sec.-Gen.*, Air Comm. G. J. C. Paul, C.B., D.F.C.

ALCOHOLICS ANONYMOUS (1935), Central Service Office, 11 Redcliffe Gardens, S.W.10.—*Sec.*, W. R. Padgett.

ALEXANDRA ROSE DAY FUND, 33 The Little Boltons, S.W.10.—*Organizer*, Mrs. Edward Day.

ALLIED CIRCLE, 46 Green Street, Park Lane, W.1.—*Sec.*, Lt. Col. F. Szystowski, O.B.E.

ALLOTMENTS AND GARDENS SOCIETY, NATIONAL (1930), Drayton House, Gordon Street, W.C.1.—*Sec.*, W. France.

ALMSHOUSES, NATIONAL ASSOCIATION OF, Billingbear Lodge, Wokingham, Berks.—*Gen. Sec.*, L. A. Hackett, O.B.E.

ANALYTICAL CHEMISTRY, THE SOCIETY FOR, 14 Belgrave Square, S.W.1.—*Hon. Sec.*, S. A. Price.

ANCHORAGE MISSION (Branch of The Children's Aid Society), 55 Leigham Court Road, S.W.16.—*Director*, Lt.-Col. H. Glanfield, O.B.E.

ANCIENT BUILDINGS, SOCIETY FOR THE PROTECTION OF (1877), 55 Great Ormond Street, W.C.1.—*Sec.*, Mrs. M. Dance, M.B.E.

ANCIENT MONUMENTS SOCIETY (1924).—*Sec.*, I. Bulmer-Thomas, 12 Edwardes Square, W.8.

ANGLO-ARAB ASSOCIATION (1961), 27 Eaton Place, S.W.1.—*Sec.*, Sir Peregrine Henniker-Heaton, Bt.

ANGLO-BELGIAN UNION (1918), 6 Belgrave Square, S.W.1.—*Hon. Sec.*, Miss M. Taylor.

ANGLO-BRAZILIAN SOCIETY (1943), 1 Hamilton Place, W.1.—*Hon. Sec.*, F. Whittle.

ANGLO-DANISH SOCIETY (1924), 5 St. Helen's Place, Bishopsgate, E.C.3.—*Chairman*, The Viscount Tenby, P.C., T.D.

ANGLO-LIBERIAN SOCIETY (1956), 70 Home Park Road, Wimbledon, S.W.19.

ANGLO-NETHERLANDS SOCIETY (1920), 3 Temple Chambers, Temple Avenue, E.C.4.—*Hon. Sec.*, F. J. P. Richter, C.B.E., M.A.

ANGLO-NORSE SOCIETY, c/o Royal Norwegian Embassy, 25 Belgrave Square, S.W.1.—*Hon. Sec.*, Mrs. B. Barnett.

ANGLO-SWEDISH SOCIETY, 4 Staple Inn, High Holborn, W.C.1.—*Sec.*, Mrs. G. Gluyas.

ANGLO-TURKISH SOCIETY (1954), 2 Temple Chambers, E.C.4.—*Hon. Sec.*, F. Richter, C.B.E.

ANIMAL HEALTH TRUST, 14 Ashley Place, S.W.1.—*Scientific Dir.*, W. R. Wooldridge.

ANTHROPOLOGICAL INSTITUTE, ROYAL (1843), 21 Bedford Square, W.C.1.—*Hon. Sec.*, A. H. Christie, M.A.

ANTHROPOSOPHICAL SOCIETY IN GREAT BRITAIN, Rudolf Steiner House, 35 Park Road, N.W.1.—*Chairman*, A. C. Harwood.

ANTIQUARIES, SOCIETY OF (1707), Burlington House, W.1.—*Pres.*, Miss Joan Evans, D.Litt., LL.D.; *Treas.*, H. L. Bradfer-Lawrence; *Director*, Prof. I. A. Richmond, C.B.E., Litt.D., F.B.A.; *Sec*, A. R. Dufty.

ANTIQUARIES OF SCOTLAND, SOCIETY OF (1780). National Museum of Antiquities of Scotland, Queen Street, Edinburgh.—*Secs.*, Angus Graham, M.A., F.S.A.; *Treas.*, James J. Lamb, O.B.E., M.A., LL.B., W.S.

ANTI-SLAVERY SOCIETY FOR THE PROTECTION OF HUMAN RIGHTS (1826), 49 Denison House, Vauxhall Bridge Road, S.W.1.

ANTI-VIVISECTION: BRITISH UNION FOR THE ABOLITION OF VIVISECTION (INC.) (1898), 47 Whitehall, S.W.1.—*Sec.*, W. Tyldesley.

ANTI-VIVISECTION SOCIETY, THE NATIONAL (1875), 27 Palace Street, S.W.1.

ANTI-VIVISECTION SOCIETY, SCOTTISH, 104 West George Street, Glasgow, C.2.—*Sec.*, E. G. Barlow.

APOSTLESHIP OF THE SEA (1921), Atlantic House, Hardman Street, Liverpool 1.—*Sec.*, Rev. F. S. Frayne.

APOTHECARIES, SOCIETY OF (1617).—Black Friars Lane, Queen Victoria Street, E.C.4.—*Clerk and Registrar*, Ernest Busby.

ARAB HORSE SOCIETY, Beechmead, Rowledge, Farnham, Surrey.—*Sec.*, Col. R. C. de V. Askin, M.B.E., M.C.

ARBITRATORS, THE INSTITUTE OF (1915), 39 Bedford Square, W.C.1.—*Sec.*, D. Reid.

ARCHÆOLOGICAL ASSOCIATION, BRITISH (1843), 20 Portman Square, W.1.—*Hon. Sec.*, P. Kidson, Ph.D., F.S.A.

ARCHÆOLOGICAL ASSOCIATION, CAMBRIAN (1846).—*Pres.* (1963–64), Prof. W. F. Grimes, C.B.E., F.S.A.; *Treas.*, W. H. Howells, District Bank, Castle Street, Cardiff; *Gen. Sec.*, W. T. Thomas, 3 Lon Cadog, Swansea.

ARCHÆOLOGICAL INSTITUTE, ROYAL (1843), c/o The London Museum, Kensington Palace, W.8.—*Hon. Sec.*, S. D. T. Spittle, M.A., F.S.A., A.R.I.B.A.

ARCHÆOLOGY, COUNCIL FOR BRITISH (1944), 10 Bolton Gardens, S.W.5.—*Pres.* (1962–64), Prof. C. F. C. Hawkes, M.A., F.B.A., F.S.A.; *Hon. Sec.*, M. W. Barley, M.A., F.S.A.; *Sec.*, Miss B. de Cardi, B.A., F.S.A.

ARCHITECTS, THE ROYAL INSTITUTE OF BRITISH (1834), 66 Portland Place, W.1.—*Pres.* (1963–64), Prof. Sir Robert Matthew, C.B.E., A.R.S.A.; *Sec.*, G. R. Ricketts, M.A.

ARCHITECTS, INSTITUTE OF REGISTERED (1933), 68 Gloucester Place, W.1.—*Pres.*, G. C. Fox; *Sec.*, A. E. Ward.

ARCHITECTS AND SURVEYORS, INCORPORATED ASSOCIATION OF (1925), 29 Belgrave Square, S.W.1.—*Pres.*, R. E. J. Harding; *Hon. Sec.*, A. C. Williamson.

ARCHITECTS' BENEVOLENT SOCIETY (1850) 66 Portland Place, W.1.—*Hon. Sec.*, Howard Lobb, C.B.E.

ARCHITECTS IN SCOTLAND, ROYAL INCORPORATION OF (1922), 15 Rutland Square, Edinburgh.—*Sec. and Treas.*, G. W. Burnet, W.S.

ARCHITECTURAL ASSOCIATION (INC.) (1847), 34–36 Bedford Square, W.C.1.—*Sec.*, G. R. Wiltshire.

ARCHIVISTS, SOCIETY OF (1946), *Hon. Sec.*, P. Walne, County Hall, Hertford.

ARMS AND ARMOUR SOCIETY (1950).—*Hon. Sec.*, F. Wilkinson, 40 Great James Street, W.C.1.

ARMY BENEVOLENT FUND (1944), 20 Grosvenor Place, S.W.1.—*Controller*, Maj.-Gen. P. N. White, C.B., C.B.E.

ARMY CADET FORCE ASSOCIATION (1930), 58 Buckingham Gate, S.W.1.—*Sec.*, W. F. L. Newcombe, O.B.E., T.D.

ARMY HISTORICAL RESEARCH, SOCIETY FOR (1921).—*Hon. Sec.*, Maj. N. P. Dawnay, c/o The Library, War Office, S.W.1.

ARMY SPORT CONTROL BOARD (1918), War Office, Whitehall, S.W.1.—*Director*, Brig. G. A. Rimbault, C.B.E., D.S.O., M.C.

ART-COLLECTIONS FUND, NATIONAL (1903), Hertford House, Manchester Square, W.1.—*Sec.*, Mrs. A. H. Meldrum, M.B.E.

ART EDUCATION, NATIONAL SOCIETY FOR (1888), Brough, Yorks.—*Gen. Sec.*, S. I. Hemming.

ART WORKERS GUILD (1884), 6 Queen Square, Bloomsbury, W.C.1—*Master*, A. Llewellyn Smith, M.B.E., F.R.I.B.A.; *Sec.*, R. Murry.

ARTISTS' GENERAL BENEVOLENT INSTITUTION (1814) AND ARTISTS' ORPHAN FUND, Burlington House, Piccadilly, W.1.—*Sec.*, Miss J. H. E. Macpherson, O.B.E.

ARTS COUNCIL OF GREAT BRITAIN, 4 St. James's Square, S.W.1.—*Chairman*, The Lord Cottesloe, G.B.E., T.D.; *Secretary-General*, N. J. Abercrombie.

ASLIB (1924). (Formerly Association of Special Libraries and Information Bureaux), 3 Belgrave Square, S.W.1.—*Director*, L. Wilson, M.A.

ASSISTANT MASTERS IN SECONDARY SCHOOLS, INCORPORATED ASSOCIATION OF (1891), 29 Gordon Square, W.C.1.—*Sec.*, A. W. S. Hutchings, M.A.

ASSISTANT MISTRESSES IN SECONDARY SCHOOLS, ASSOCIATION OF, 29 Gordon Square, W.C.1.—*Org. Sec.*, Miss S. D. Wood, B.Sc.

ASTHMA RESEARCH COUNCIL, 28 Norfolk Place, W.2.—*Chairman*, F. M. P. Maurice.

ASTRONOMICAL ASSOCIATION, BRITISH.—*Office*, 303 Bath Road, Hounslow West, Middlesex. Meetings at Burlington House, W.1.—*Pres.*, E. A. Beet, B.Sc.; *Secs.*, W. M. Baxter; N. G. Goodman; *Asst. Sec.*, Lydia A. Brown.

ASTRONOMICAL SOCIETY, ROYAL (Incorporated 1820), Burlington House, W.1.—*Pres.*, Sir Richard Woolley, O.B.E., F.R.S.; *Secs.*, Prof. H. Bondi, F.R.S.; Dr. M. W. Ovenden.

A.T.S. BENEVOLENT FUND (1941), 73 Elizabeth Street, S.W.1.—*Gen. Sec.*, Miss I. J. Perceval, M.B.E.

AUCTIONEERS' AND ESTATE AGENTS' INSTITUTE, THE CHARTERED (1886), 29 Lincoln's Inn Fields, W.C.2.—*Pres.* (1962–63), E. C. Spencer, M.B.E., M.A.; *Sec.*, R. S. Borner, O.B.E., V.R.D.

AUCTIONEERS AND LANDED PROPERTY AGENTS, INCORPORATED SOCIETY OF (1924), 34 Queen's Gate, S.W.7.—*Pres.* (1963–64), H. E. Colton; *Sec.*, A. E. Watts (*acting*).

AUDIT BUREAU OF CIRCULATIONS LTD. (1931), 19 Dunraven Street, W.1.—*Sec.*, G. S. M. Brand.

AUTHORS, PLAYWRIGHTS AND COMPOSERS, INCORPORATED SOCIETY OF, 84 Drayton Gardens, S.W.10.—*Gen. Sec.*, M. E. Barber.

AUTOMOBILE ASSESSORS, INSTITUTE OF (1939), 52–53 Jermyn Street, S.W.1.—*Sec.*, G. Williams.

AUTOMOBILE ASSOCIATION (1905), Fanum House, Leicester Square, W.C.2.—*Chairman*, The Viscount Brentford; *Joint Secretaries*, H. A. Evans; H. Cecil Orr, O.B.E.

AVICULTURAL SOCIETY (1894).—*Hon. Sec.*, A. A. Prestwich, Galley's Wood, Edenbridge, Kent.

AYRSHIRE CATTLE SOCIETY OF GREAT BRITAIN AND IRELAND (1877), 1 Racecourse Road, Ayr.—*Gen. Sec.*, J. R. Madge.

AYRSHIRE CATTLE BREEDERS ASSOCIATION OF ENGLAND AND WALES (1943), 17 Devonshire Street, W.1.—*Sec.*, S. H. Dingley.

BALTIC EXCHANGE (1903), St. Mary Axe, E.C.3.—*Chairman*, Sir Leslie Phillips, C.B.E.; *Vice-Chairman*, The Lord Kilmarnock, M.B.E.; *Sec.*, J. E. Walker.

BANKERS' ASSOCIATION, BRITISH (1920), 10 Lombard Street, E.C.3.—*Sec.*, R. H. Barkshire.

BANKERS, THE INSTITUTE OF (1879), 10 Lombard Street, E.C.3.—*Pres.*, Sir Edward Reid, Bt., O.B.E.; *Sec.*, H. Eason.

BANKERS IN SCOTLAND, THE INSTITUTE OF (1875), 62 George Street, Edinburgh.—*Sec.*, F. S. Taylor.

BAPTIST MISSIONARY SOCIETY (1792), 93-97 Gloucester Place, W.1.—*Secs.*, Rev. A. S. Clement, B.A., B.D. (*Home*); Rev. E. G. T. Madge, B.A., B.D. (*Foreign*); H. B. Glenny (*Financial*).

(DR.) BARNARDO'S HOMES (1866), National Incorporated Association. *Head Offices*, Stepney Causeway, E.1. 162,000 children have been admitted. More than 7,000 boys and girls now supported.—*Chairman of Council*, Sir Alfred Owen, C.B.E.; *Gen. Sec.*, F. J. Potter.

BARONETAGE, STANDING COUNCIL OF THE (1898), Kent House, Telegraph Street, E.C.2.—*Sec. and Regr.*, S. L. Forwood.

BARRISTERS' BENEVOLENT ASSOCIATION (1873), 7 King's Bench Walk, Temple, E.C.4.—*Hon. Secs.*, P. Browne, Q.C.; Hon. R. B. Holroyd Pearce; *Sec.*, Mrs. Rickards.

BEIT MEMORIAL FELLOWSHIPS (for Medical Research) (1909).—*Sec.*, Sir Roy Cameron, F.R.S., University College Hospital Medical School, University Street, W.C.1.

BIBLE AND MEDICAL MISSIONARY FELLOWSHIP (formerly Zenana Bible and Medical Mission) (1852), 39 Ladbroke Grove, W.11.—*Home Sec.*, R. F. S. Hills.

BIBLE CHURCHMEN'S MISSIONARY SOCIETY (1922), 47 Clapham High Street, S.W.4.—*Gen. Sec.*, Rev. A. T. Houghton M.A.

BIBLE LANDS SOCIETY (1854).—*Sec.*, C. R. Clothier, The Old Kiln, Hazlemere, High Wycombe, Bucks.

BIBLE SOCIETY, BRITISH AND FOREIGN (1804), 146 Queen Victoria Street, E.C.4.—*Secs.*. Rev. N. J. Cockburn, Ph.D.; Rev. J. T. Watson. Has published or circulated all or parts of the Bible in 870 different languages and has distributed over 700 million copies since the inception of the Society.

BIBLIOGRAPHICAL SOCIETY (1892), c/o British Academy, Burlington Gardens, W.1.—*Pres.*, S. Nowell Smith; *Hon. Secs.*, Sir Frank Francis; R. J. Roberts.

BIBLIOGRAPHICAL SOCIETY, EDINBURGH (1890), c/o National Library of Scotland, Edinburgh, 1.—*Hon. Sec.* J. R. Seaton.

BIOCHEMICAL SOCIETY, THE (1911), 20 Park Crescent, W.1.

BIOLOGISTS, ASSOCIATION OF APPLIED.—*Hon. Gen. Sec.*, F. T. Last, Ph.D., Glasshouse Crops Research Institute, Rustington, Littlehampton, Sussex.

BIOLOGY, INSTITUTE OF, 41 Queen's Gate, S.W.7.—*Pres.*, Prof. G. E. Blackman; *Gen. Sec.*, D. J. B. Copp.

BIRD PRESERVATION, INTERNATIONAL COUNCIL FOR (BRITISH SECTION), c/o Natural History Museum, Cromwell Road, S.W.7.—*Hon. Sec.*, Miss Phyllis Barclay-Smith, M.B.E.

BIRDS, ROYAL SOCIETY FOR THE PROTECTION OF, The Lodge, Sandy, Beds.—*Sec.*, P. E. Brown.

BLIND, BRISTOL ROYAL SCHOOL FOR THE (1793), Westbury-on-Trym.—*Gen. Supt.*, E. H. Getliff, O.B.E.

BLIND, GARDNER'S TRUST FOR THE (1882), 8 Bloomsbury Square, W.C.1.—*Sec.*, K. G. Lindsay, O.B.E.

BLIND, GREATER LONDON FUND FOR THE (1921) 2 Wyndham Place, W.1.—*Pres.*, The Lord Mayor of London ; *Gen. Sec.*, A. C. Jay, D.S.C.

BLIND, GUIDE DOGS FOR THE, ASSOCIATION, 83–89 Uxbridge Road, Ealing, W.5.—*Sec.*, Lt.-Col. P. P. T. McConnell.

BLIND, INCORPORATED ASSOCIATION FOR PROMOTING THE GENERAL WELFARE OF THE (1854), 257–8 Tottenham Court Road, W.1.—*Gen. Manager*, C. J. Godfrey.

BLIND, LONDON ASSOCIATION FOR THE (1857), Pelican House, 88–92 Peckham Road, S.E.15. A voluntary organization helping the Blind both in London and country. Training and employment; homes and hostels; self-contained flats; benevolent and pensions fund.—*Gen. Sec.*, G. C. Haines, F.S.A.

BLIND, METROPOLITAN SOCIETY FOR THE, AND INDIGENT BLIND VISITING SOCIETY, 51 Denison House, 296 Vauxhall Bridge Road, S.W.1.—The blind are visited in their own homes, in institutions and in hospitals. Weekly clubs. Permanent homes for blind men and women at Maldon (50) and at Worthing (54). At Worthing there are in addition 14 beds for holiday guests and for those needing recuperative care after being in hospital. Hackney House, E.8., provides 12 unfurnished flats for blind women workers—*Sec.*, Mrs. M. Davie.

BLIND, ROYAL COMMONWEALTH SOCIETY FOR THE (1950), Windsor House, 46 Victoria Street, S.W.1.—*Dir.*, J. Wilson, O.B.E.

BLIND, ROYAL NATIONAL INSTITUTE FOR THE (1868), 224 Great Portland Street, W.1.—*Director-General*, J. C. Colligan, C.B.E. Branches of the Institute: *Queen Elizabeth Homes of Recovery, Homes for Blind and Deaf Blind, School of Physiotherapy, Schools for Blind Girls and Boys, School for Shorthand-Typing and Telephony, Sunshine Home Nursery Schools, Braille and Moon Periodicals and Books, Braille Music, Talking Books, Students' Library, Professional and Industrial Placement, Vocational Assessment Centre for Blind Adolescents, Apparatus and Appliances, Personnel Services, Prevention of Blindness, etc.*

BLIND, NATIONAL LIBRARY FOR THE (1882), 35 Great Smith Street, S.W.1.—Books and music in embossed type are sent free on loan and post free to blind readers, schools and institutions in all parts of the world. Stock of volumes, 330,000.—*Librarian and Director-General*, W. A. Munford.

BLIND PENSION SOCIETY, ROYAL (1863), 9 Suffolk Street, Pall Mall, S.W.1.—*Sec.*, L. E. Watts.

BLIND, ROYAL LONDON SOCIETY FOR THE (1838), *Head Office and Workshops*, 105–9 Salusbury Road, Brondesbury, N.W.6; *School*, Dorton House,

Seal, nr. Sevenoaks, Kent.—*Hon. Sec.*, E. J. Mander.

BLIND, ROYAL NORMAL COLLEGE (1872), Albrighton Hall and Rowton Castle, nr. Shrewsbury.—*Princ. and Sec.*, J. N. Langdon, B.SC., Ph.D.

BLIND, ROYAL SCHOOL FOR THE INDIGENT (1799), Leatherhead.—*Resident Principal and Chaplain*, Rev. B. G. Bartlett, M.A.

BLIND, SOCIETY FOR GRANTING ANNUITIES TO THE POOR ADULT, c/o The Clothworkers' Company, Clothworkers' Hall, Dunster Court, Mincing Lane, E.C.3.

BLIND (LONDON) SPORTS CLUB FOR THE (1932), *Hon. Sec.*, W. E. Smedley, 61 Conway Road, Southgate, N.14.

BLOOD TRANSFUSION. *See* GREATER LONDON RED CROSS BLOOD TRANSFUSION SERVICE.

BLUE CROSS, THE (Incorporating Our Dumb Friends' League) (1897), Animals' Hospital, Hugh Street, Victoria, S.W.1.—*Joint Secs.*, Peter Carpmael; Stuart Gelder.

BODLEIAN, FRIENDS OF THE, Bodleian Library, Oxford.—*Sec.*, D. H. Merry.

BOOK-KEEPERS, INSTITUTE OF (1916), 139 Stoke Newington High Street, N.16.—*Sec.*, C. E. Hall.

BOOKMEN, THE SOCIETY OF (1921).—*Hon. Sec.*, Ian Norrie, 31 Granville Road, N.12.

BOOKSELLERS ASSOCIATION OF GREAT BRITAIN AND IRELAND (1895), 14 Buckingham Palace Garden , S.W.1.—*Gen. Sec.*, G. R. Davies.

BOOK TRADE PROVIDENT INSTITUTION, NATIONAL (1962), 19 Bedford Square, W.C.1, incorporating the Booksellers' Provident Institution (1837), Booksellers' Provident Retreat (1843) and National Book Trade Provident Society (1902). —*Pres.*, Sir Stanley Unwin, LL.D.; *Sec.*, R. E. Barker.

BOTANICAL SOCIETY OF THE BRITISH ISLES (1836), c/o Dept. of Botany, British Museum (Natural History), S.W.7.

BOTANICAL SOCIETY OF EDINBURGH, Royal Botanic Garden, Edinburgh.—*Joint Hon. Secs.*, R. Watling, B.SC., P. Watson, M.A., Ph.D.

BOY SCOUTS ASSOCIATION (INCORPORATED) (1908), *Headquarters*, 25 Buckingham Palace Road, S.W.1.—*Chief Scout*, Sir Charles Maclean, Bt.; *Chief Executive Commissioner*, A. W. Hurll, C.B.E.

BOYS' BRIGADE, THE (INCORPORATED) (1883), Abbey House, Westminster, S.W.1. Membership: British Isles, 106,368 Officers and Boys, with 76,419 in The Life Boys; Overseas 57,066 Boys' Brigade and 16,243 Life Boys in 54 countries.—*Brigade Secretary*, Maj.-Gen. D. J. Wilson-Haffenden, C.B.E.

BOYS' CLUBS, NATIONAL ASSOCIATION OF, INCORPORATED (1925), 17 Bedford Square, W.C.1. Responsible for the development and co-ordination of boys' club work throughout the country, and has affiliated to it, either directly or through local organizations, 1,950 Clubs.—*Gen. Sec.*, R. E. Goodwin, C.B.E.

BOYS' CLUBS, NORTHERN IRELAND ASSOCIATION OF, (1940), 28 Bedford Street, Belfast.—*Gen. Sec.*, V. J. Dunlop.

BREWING, INSTITUTE OF (1886), 33 Clarges Street, W.1.—*Sec.*, G. E R. Sandars, C.M.G., M.B.E.

BRIBERY PREVENTION LEAGUE (1906) (Inc.), Francis House, Francis Street, S.W.1.—*Hon. Sec.*, F. J. Hesketh-Williams.

BRIDEWELL HOSPITAL, King Edward's School, Witley, Surrey (1553).—*Treasurer*, Gerald Coke; *Clerk to the Governors*, G. J. Batten, M.B.E., T.D.

BRITISH ACADEMY, THE (1901), Burlington Gardens, W.1.—*President*, The Lord Robbins, C.B.; *Council*, Sir Harold Bailey; Rev. Prof. H. Chadwick; Sir Goronwy Edwards; Miss H. Gardner, C.B.E.; Dr. A. L. Goodhart, K.B.E., Q.C.; P. Grierson; Prof. W. K. C. Guthrie; Prof. H. L. A. Hart; Prof. J. R. Hicks; Prof. E. F. Jacob; Prof. A. R. Johnson; Dr. Kathleen M. Kenyon, C.B.E.; J. W. Pope-Hennessy, C.B.E.; Prof. H. H. Scullard; Prof. J. R. Sutherland; *Treas.*, Prof. R. G. D. Allen, C.B.E.; *Sec.*, Sir Mortimer Wheeler, C.I.E., M.C.; *Foreign Sec.*, C. H. Roberts.

BRITISH AND FOREIGN SCHOOL SOCIETY (1808), 7 Stone Buildings, Lincoln's Inn, W.C.2.—*Sec.*, G. G. G. Robb.

BRITISH ASSOCIATION FOR THE ADVANCEMENT OF SCIENCE (1831), 3 Sanctuary Buildings, Great Smith Street, S.W.1.—*President* (1964), The Lord Brain; *Gen. Secs.*, Dame Kathleen Lonsdale, D.B.E., F.R.S.; Sir Lawrence Bragg, O.B.E., M.C., F.R.S.; Sir William Slater, K.B.E., F.R.S.; *Gen. Treas.*, P. A. Macrory; *Sec.*, N. C. Wright, C.B.

BRITISH ASSOCIATION OF THE HARD OF HEARING.—*Hon. Sec.*, C. H. Mardell, Briarfield, Syke Ings, Iver, Bucks.

BRITISH BOARD OF FILM CENSORS, 3 Soho Square, W.1.—*Pres.*, The Lord Morrison of Lambeth, P.C., C.H.; *Sec.*, J. Trevelyan, O.B.E.

BRITISH COLOUR COUNCIL (1930) (for the co-ordination of Colour and Design), 13 Portman Square, W.1.—*Studio Director*, Miss K. A. Battersby; *Sec.*, H. M. Blyth.

BRITISH COMMONWEALTH EX-SERVICES LEAGUE, 92 New Bond Street, W.1.—*Sec.-Gen.*, Air Commodore B. J. R. Roberts.

BRITISH COTTON GROWING ASSOCIATION (1904), 333–350 Royal Exchange, Manchester 2.—*Sec.*, R. Derbyshire.

BRITISH COUNCIL, THE (1934), 65 Davies Street, W.1.—*President*, General Sir Ronald Forbes Adam, Bt., G.C.B., D.S.O., O.B.E.; *Chairman*, Lord Bridges, P.C., G.C.B., G.C.V.O., M.C., F.R.S.; *Director-General*, Sir Paul Sinker, K.C.M.G., C.B.

BRITISH CYCLING FEDERATION (1878), 21 Blackfriars Road, S.E.1.—*Hon. Sec.*, R. P. Itter.

BRITISH DENTAL ASSOCIATION (1880), 13 Hill Street, Berkeley Square, W.1.—*Pres.*, D. Greer Walker; *Sec.*, J. N. Peacock.

BRITISH DIABETIC ASSOCIATION (1934), 152 Harley Street, W.1.—*Sec.-Gen.*, J. G. L. Jackson.

BRITISH DRAMA LEAGUE (1919), 9–10 Fitzroy Square, W.1.—*Administrator*, W. Lucas.

BRITISH ELECTRICAL DEVELOPMENT ASSOCIATION (1919), 2 Savoy Hill, W.C.2.—*Director and Sec.*, J. I. Bernard.

BRITISH EMPIRE AND COMMONWEALTH GAMES FEDERATION.—*Hon. Sec.*, K. S. Duncan, M.B.E., 95 Mount Street, W.1.

BRITISH FIELD SPORTS SOCIETY (1930), 51 Victoria Street, S.W.1.—*Sec.*, Brig. A. H. Pepys, D.S.O.

BRITISH FILM INSTITUTE (1933), 81 Dean Street, W.1. —*Director*, James Quinn; *Sec.*, Stanley Reed. Departments include the National Film Archive (*Curator*, E. H. Lindgren, O.B.E.,) and the National Film Theatre (*Manager*, L. Hardcastle).

BRITISH GLIDING ASSOCIATION (1930), affiliated to Royal Aero Club. Artillery Mansions, Victoria Street, S.W.1.—*Sec.*, Miss F. Leighton.

BRITISH GOAT SOCIETY (1879), Palgrave, Diss, Norfolk.—*Sec.*, Miss M. F. Rigg.

BRITISH HORSE SOCIETY, 16 Bedford Square, W.C.1. —*Sec.*, R. A. Brown.

BRITISH INDUSTRIES, FEDERATION OF, 21 Tothill Street, S.W.1.—*Director-General*, Sir Norman Kipping, K.B.E.

BRITISH INSTITUTE OF ARCHÆOLOGY AT ANKARA, 16 Bryanston Street, W.1.—*Dir.*, M. R. E. Gough, F.S.A.

BRITISH INSTITUTE OF INTERNATIONAL AND COMPARATIVE LAW, 1 Temple Gardens, E.C.4.—*Sec.*, Mrs. A. J. Lang.

BRITISH INSTITUTE OF RECORDED SOUND (1955), 38 Russell Square, W.C.1.—*Sec.*, P. Saul.

BRITISH INTERPLANETARY SOCIETY (1933), 12 Bessborough Gardens, S.W.1.—*Sec.*, L. J. Carter.

BRITISH ISRAEL WORLD FEDERATION (1919), 6 Buckingham Gate, S.W.1.—*Sec.*, H. E. Stough.

BRITISH LEGION. *Headquarters*, Pall Mall, S.W.1. *President*, Lt.-Gen. Sir Oliver Leese, Bt., K.C.B., C.B.E., D.S.O.; *Gen.Sec.*, D. E. Coffer, O.B.E.—*British Legion Poppy Fund*, £1,085,000 raised on Poppy Day, 1961, exclusive of Scotland. Grand total for years 1921 to 1961, £29,377,628.

BRITISH LEGION VILLAGE (1925), British Legion Industries (Preston Hall), Incorporated, Maidstone, Kent.—*Sec.-Administrator*, A. A. Howick, M.B.E.

BRITISH LEGION, SCOTLAND, Haig House, 23 Drumsheugh Gardens, Edinburgh, 3.—*Gen. Sec.*, Col. C. S. MacLeod of Glendale, O.B.E., T.D.

BRITISH LEOPROSY RELIEF ASSOCIATION (1924), 8 Portman Street, W.1.—*Gen. Sec.*, Air Vice-Marshal W. J. Crisham, C.B., C.B.E.

BRITISH MEDICAL ASSOCIATION (1832), B.M.A. House, Tavistock Square, W.C.1.—*President*, Sir George Pickering, D.SC., M.D., F.R.C.P., F.R.S.; *Sec.*, D. P. Stevenson, M.R.C.S., L.R.C.P.

BRITISH OPTICAL ASSOCIATION, THE, 65 Brook Street, W.1.—*Sec.*, G. H. Giles, O.B.E.

BRITISH PLASTICS FEDERATION, 47–48 Piccadilly, W.1.—*Gen. Manager*, C. J. G. Stanley.

BRITISH RECORDS ASSOCIATION, The Charterhouse, Charterhouse Square, E.C.1.

BRITISH RECORD SOCIETY (1888), 38 Finsbury Square, E.C.2.—*Hon. Sec.*, P. Spufford.

BRITISH RED CROSS SOCIETY (1908). *National Headquarters*, 14–15 Grosvenor Crescent, S.W.1. —*Secretary-General*, F. H. D. Pritchard, C.B.E.

BRITISH SAILORS' SOCIETY INCORPORATED (At Home and Abroad) (1818), 680 Commercial Road, E.14. Residential Clubs and Canteens in ports throughout the world. World wide welfare service; ocean library services; chaplains and port missionaries; sea training school for boys.—*Gen. Sec.*, Stanley Heesom, O.B.E.

BRITISH SCHOOL AT ATHENS.—*Chairman of the Managing Committee*, Prof. C. M. Robertson, M.A.; *Director*, A. H. S. Megaw, C.B.E., M.A., F.S.A.; *London Sec.*, Mrs. M. J. Thornton, B.A., 31–34 Gordon Square, W.C.1.

BRITISH SCHOOL AT ROME (1901).—*President*, H.R.H. the Princess Royal; *Chairman of Executive Committee*, T. S. R. Boase, M.C., LL.D.; *Director*, J. B. Ward Perkins, C.B.E.; *Hon. Sec.*, W. D. Sturch, 1 Lowther Gardens, S.W.7.

BRITISH SCHOOL OF ARCHÆOLOGY IN IRAQ (GERTRUDE BELL MEMORIAL) (1932), 31–34 Gordon Square, W.C.1.—*Sec.*, Miss G. C. Talbot.

BRITISH SCHOOL OF ARCHÆOLOGY IN JERUSALEM (1919), 2 Hinde Mews, Marylebone Lane, W.1.—*Chairman*, Sir Mortimer Wheeler, C.I.E., M.C.

BRITISH SEAMEN'S BOYS' HOME, Rock House, Brixham.—*Supt.*, Capt. W. G. Parry, R.N.

BRITISH SHIP ADOPTION SOCIETY (1936), H.Q.S. *Wellington*, Temple Stairs, Victoria Embankment, W.C.2.—*Sec.*, Miss K. V. Friend.

BRITISH SOCIAL BIOLOGY COUNCIL, 69 Eccleston Square, S.W.1.—*Sec.*, R. Weatherall.

BRITISH SOCIETY FOR INTERNATIONAL UNDERSTANDING (1939), (Publishers of *The British Survey*), Benjamin Franklin House, 36 Craven Street, W.C.2. Also headquarters of the British Atlantic Committee, the Council for African–British Relations, European Cultural Fund (U.K.) and Atlantic Treaty Education Secretariat.—*Director*, John Eppstein, O.B.E.

BRITISH STANDARDS INSTITUTION, 2 Park Street, W.1.—*Director*, H. A. R. Binney, C.B.

BRITISH TUBERCULOSIS ASSOCIATION (1928), 59 Portland Place, W.1.—*Sec.*, L. D. Booker, M.B.E.

BRITISH UNITED PROVIDENT ASSOCIATION (1947), Essex Street, Strand, W.C.2.—*Gen. Manager*, E. F. Webb, M.B.E.

BRITISH VETERINARY ASSOCIATION (1881), 7 Mansfield Street, W.1.—*Sec.*, J. A. Anderson.

BRONTË SOCIETY, THE (1893). (Brontë Parsonage Museum and Library, Haworth, nr. Keighley, Yorks.).—*Hon. Sec.*, Mrs. E. M. Weir.

BUILDERS, INSTITUTE OF (1834), 48 Bedford Square, W.C.1.—*Sec.*, D. A. Neale, M.C.

BUILDING SOCIETIES ASSOCIATION, 14 Park Street, W.1.—*Sec.*, N. E. Griggs.

BUILDING SOCIETIES INSTITUTE, 7 Aldford Street, W.1.—*Sec.*, E. C. L. Butler.

BUILDING SURVEYORS' INSTITUTE (1952), 186–7 Temple Chambers, Temple Avenue, E.C.4.—*Gen. Sec.*, J. W. Rowley.

BUSINESS AND PROFESSIONAL WOMEN'S CLUBS OF GREAT BRITAIN AND NORTHERN IRELAND, NATIONAL FEDERATION OF (1938), 55 Russell Square, W.C.1.—*Gen. Sec.*, Mrs. I. G. Rayner.

BUSINESS ARCHIVES COUNCIL, 9 King's Bench Walk, E.C.4.—*Sec.*, Cdr. D. Doble, R.N.

BUTCHERS' CHARITABLE INSTITUTION (1828).—*Sec.*, J. A. Fordyce, 61 West Smithfield, E.C.1.

CALOUSTE GULBENKIAN FOUNDATION, LISBON, United Kingdom and British Commonwealth Branch (1956), 98 Portland Place, W.1.—*Sec.*, J. C. Thornton.

CAMBRIDGE FUND AND WILLIAM WOODMAN CHARITY, ROYAL. (Applicants must be ex-soldiers who served as Regulars before the 1914–18 War.) *Address*, The Under-Secretary of State (C.2) War Office, S.W.1.

CANADIAN CHAMBER OF COMMERCE IN GREAT BRITAIN INC. (1921), 3 Lower Regent Street, S.W.1.—*Pres.*, C. F. Wood; *Sec.*, J. V. Smelley (*acting*).

CANCER CAMPAIGN, BRITISH EMPIRE (1923), 11 Grosvenor Crescent, S.W.1. For research into the disease of cancer in all its forms.—*Sec. Gen.*, Capt. F. B. Tours, O.B.E., R.N. (*ret.*).

CANCER RELIEF, NATIONAL SOCIETY FOR (1924), 47 Victoria Street, S.W.1.—*Founder and Chairman*, D. Macmillan, M.B.E.; *Sec.*, F. H. Georgeson.

CANCER RESEARCH FUND, IMPERIAL (1902), Lincoln's Inn Fields, W.C.2.—*Sec.*, A. B. L. Clarke, O.B.E.

CANCER RESEARCH, INSTITUTE OF: ROYAL CANCER HOSPITAL (1911), Fulham Road, S.W.3.—*Sec.*, N. P. Hadow, O.B.E.

CARAVAN MISSION TO VILLAGE CHILDREN (1893), 47 Marylebone Lane, W.1.—*Sec.*, H. P. M. Warde.

CARNEGIE DUNFERMLINE TRUST (1903) (operations confined to Dunfermline).—*Sec.*, F. Mann.

CARNEGIE HERO FUND TRUST (1908). Income £26,800. Relieves hardship occasioned by the performance of acts of heroism in saving human life in peaceful pursuits within the British Isles and territorial waters.—*Sec.*, F. Mann, Abbey Park House, Dunfermline.

CARNEGIE UNITED KINGDOM TRUST (1914), Comely Park House, New Row, Dunfermline.—*Object*, The improvement of the well-being of the masses of the people of Great Britain and Ireland by means which are "charitable" in law and are to be selected by the Trustees themselves. The Trust is particularly concerned with social welfare schemes of a pioneer or experimental kind; grants are not made to individuals or in response to general appeals for subscriptions. Management—By trustees. *Sec.*, D. N. Lowe, O.B.E.; *Treas.*, J. Pirie Glen. Income (1962)—£150,000.

CATHOLIC MARRIAGE ADVISORY COUNCIL (National Office), 15 Lansdowne Road, W.11; (London Centre), 38–39 Parliament Street, S.W.1.—*Chairman*, Rev. M. O'Leary, S.T.L.

CATHOLIC RECORD SOCIETY (1904).—*Hon. Sec.*, Miss R. Rendel, 48 Lowndes Square, S.W.1.

CATHOLIC TRUTH SOCIETY (1868), 38–40 Eccleston Square, S.W.1.—*Gen. Sec.*, T. H. Rittner.

CATHOLIC UNION OF GREAT BRITAIN.—*Pres.*, The Duke of Norfolk, K.G., P.C., G.C.V.O.; *Sec.* A. F. Trappes-Lomax, 35 Coleherne Road, S.W.10.

CATTLE BREEDERS' CLUB, BRITISH (1949), c/o Weller & Co., 86 Woodbridge Road, Guildford, Surrey.—*Sec.*, C. R. Stains.

CAVALRY BENEFIT ASSOCIATION (1911), 206 Brompton Road, S.W.3.—*Sec.*, Mrs. M. L. Bernard.

CAXTON CONVALESCENT HOME (1895), The Chart, Limpsfield, Surrey. (For Printing, and Kindred Trades, Men and Women.) *London Office*, 1 Gough Square, E.C.4.—*Sec.*, S. T. Marshall.

CECIL HOUSES (Inc.), 190–192 Kensal Road, W.10.—*Sec.*, Mrs. E. Gordon Phillips.

CENTRAL AFTER-CARE ASSOCIATION, 289–299 Borough High Street, S.E.1.; (*Boys*), 2 The Abbey Garden, Great College Street, S.W.1.

CEREALS AND BALTIC FRIENDLY SOCIETY (1908), 24 St. Mary Axe, E.C.3.—*Sec.*, Charles W. Stevens, M.B.E.

CERAMIC SOCIETY, BRITISH (1900), Shelton House, Stoke Road, Shelton, Stoke-on-Trent, Staffs.—*Hon. Gen. Sec.*, N. F. Astbury, SC.D.

CERAMICS INSTITUTE OF (1955), Shelton House, Stoke Road, Shelton, Stoke-on-Trent, Staffs.—*Sec.*, G. H. Stewart.

CEYLON ASSOCIATION IN LONDON, 2/3 Crosby Square, Bishopsgate, E.C.3.—*Sec.*, N. De Saram.

CHADWICK TRUST (1895) (for the promotion of sanitary science), 90 Buckingham Palace Road, S.W.1.—*Clerk*, P. A. Wells.

CHAMBERS OF COMMERCE.—*See* COMMERCE.

CHANTREY BEQUEST (1875).—*Sec. to the Trustees*, The Secretary, Royal Academy of Arts, Burlington House, W.1.

CHARITY ORGANIZATION SOCIETY, *see* FAMILY WELFARE ASSOCIATION.

CHEMICAL ENGINEERS, INSTITUTION OF (1922), 16 Belgrave Square, S.W.1.—*Pres.* (1963–64), Prof. F. Morton; *Gen. Sec.*, Dr. J. B. Brennan, M.B.E.

CHEMICAL INDUSTRY, SOCIETY OF, 14 Belgrave Square, S.W.1.—*Pres.*, Sir Sydney Barratt; *Sec.*, F. J. Griffin, O.B.E..

CHEMICAL SOCIETY, Burlington House, Piccadilly, W.1.—*Pres.*, Prof. J. M. Robertson, F.R.S.; *Gen. Sec.*, J. R. Ruck Keene, M.B.E., T.D., M.A.

CHEMISTRY, THE ROYAL INSTITUTE OF, 30 Russell Square, W.C.1.—*Pres.*, Prof. H. J. Emeléus; *Sec. and Registrar*, R. E. Parker, Ph.D.

CHESS FEDERATION, BRITISH.—*Hon. Sec.*, A. F. Stammwitz, 5 Clifford Road, Hounslow West, Middx.

CHEST AND HEART ASSOCIATION (formerly National Association for the Prevention of Tuberculosis) (1899), Tavistock House North, Tavistock Square, W.C.1.—*Sec. Gen.*, J. H. Harley Williams, O.B.E., M.D.

CHILDREN, THOMAS CORAM FOUNDATION FOR, *see* CORAM FOUNDATION.

CHILDREN'S AID SOCIETY, THE (1856), 55 Leigham Court Road, S.W.16.—*Director*, Lt.-Col. H. Glanfield, O.B.E.

CHILDREN'S COUNTRY HOLIDAYS FUND, 1 York Street, W.1.—*Sec.*, Miss L. B. Ellis.

CHILDREN'S RELIEF INTERNATIONAL (1959), Overstream House, Cambridge.—*Sec.*, Miss S. White.

CHINA ASSOCIATION (1889), Broad Street House, 54 Old Broad Street, E.C.2.—*Sec.*, H. J. Collar, C.B.E.

CHIROPODISTS, THE SOCIETY OF, 8 Wimpole Street, W.1.—*Sec.*, G. C. Jenkins.

CHOIR SCHOOLS ASSOCIATION (1921).—*Hon. Sec.*, B. J. Rushby Smith, Minster Grammar School, Southwell, Notts.

CHOLMONDELEY CHARITIES (1830), for Clergy and their families only. All correspondence to Secretary, 4 College Hill, E.C.4.

CHRISTIAN ACTION (1949), 2 Amen Court, E.C.4.—*Sec.*, Miss F. Nuell.

CHRISTIAN EVIDENCE SOCIETY (1870), Rectory Chambers, 8 St. Mary-at-Hill, E.C.3.—*Hon. Sec.*, Rev. M. R. Parsons, M.A., B.D., M.Th.

CHRISTIAN KNOWLEDGE, SOCIETY FOR PROMOTING (1698), Holy Trinity Church, Marylebone Road, N.W.1.—*Dir.*, Rev. F. N. Davey, M.A.

CHRISTIANS AND JEWS, COUNCIL OF (1942), 41 Cadogan Gardens, S.W.3.—*Gen. Sec.*, Rev. W. W. Simpson, M.A.

CHURCH ARMY, P.O. BOX 420, 55 Bryanston Street, W.1.—*Chief Sec.*, Rev. D. M. Lynch, M.A.

CHURCH BUILDING SOCIETY, INCORPORATED (1818), 7 Queen Anne's Gate, S.W.1.—*Sec.*, R. J. McNally.

CHURCH EDUCATION CORPORATION, 35 Denison House, S.W.1.—*Sec.*, W. F. Holmes.

CHURCH HOUSE (1888), Dean's Yard, Westminster, S.W.1.—*Sec.*, H. Symons.

CHURCH LADS' BRIGADE (1891), *National Headquarters*, 58 Gloucester Place, W.1.—*General Secretary*, Rev. J. H. S. Burton, M.A.

CHURCH MISSIONARY SOCIETY (1799), Salisbury Square, E.C.4. Income, 1962 £888,913.—*Secs.*, Rev. Canon J. V. Taylor (*General*); Rev. B. J. H. de Saram (*Africa*); Rev. A. C. M. Hargreaves, M.A. (*Asia*); A. Iliff (*Medical*); Rev. L. G. Fisher, A.L.C.D. (*Home*); Miss E. Price, B.A.; H. H. Busfield (*Financial and Administrative*); Rev. Canon H. A. Wittenbach, B.A.

CHURCH OF ENGLAND CHILDREN'S SOCIETY (1881) (formerly Waifs and Strays), Old Town Hall, Kennington, S.E.11.—*Gen. Sec.*, Col. E. St. J. Birnie.

CHURCH OF ENGLAND MEN'S SOCIETY (1899), Fulham Palace, S.W.6.—*Gen. Sec.*, Rev. C. I. Pettitt, M.A.

CHURCH OF ENGLAND SOLDIERS', SAILORS' AND AIRMEN'S CLUBS, (1891), 537 Grand Buildings, Trafalgar Square, W.C.2.—*Chairman*, Maj.-Gen. H. T. Tollemache, C.B., C.B.E.; *Sec.*, Group Capt. J. A. S. Brown.

CHURCH PASTORAL AID SOCIETY (1836), Falcon Court, 32 Fleet Street, E.C.4.—*Sec.*, Rev. Canon T. G. Mohan, M.A.

CHURCH SOCIETY, 7 Wine Office Court, Fleet Street, E.C.4.—*Sec.*, Rev. J. F. Sertin.

CHURCH UNION (1859), 199 Uxbridge Road, W.12.—*Sec.*, Rev. F. P. Coleman.

CHURCHES, BRITISH COUNCIL OF (1942), 10 Eaton Gate, S.W.1.—*Gen. Sec.*, Rev. K. Slack, M.B.E.

CHURCHES, COUNCIL FOR THE CARE OF, 83 London Wall, E.C.2.—*Sec.*, Miss J. G. Scott, F.S.A.

CHURCHES, FRIENDLESS, FRIENDS OF (1957), 12 Edwardes Square, W.8.—*Hon. Dir.*, I. Bulmer-Thomas; *Hon. Sec.*, L. E. Jones.

CHURCHES MAIN COMMITTEE (1941), 2 Great Peter Street, S.W.1.—*Sec.*, Sir Griffith Williams, K.B.E., C.B.

CIRCUS PROPRIETORS OF GREAT BRITAIN, ASSOCIATION OF, 22 Bedford Row, W.C.1.—*Sec.*, Ronald R. Pickering.

CIVIL ENGINEERS, INSTITUTION OF (1818). Great George Street, S.W.1.—*Pres.*, H. J. B. Harding; *Sec.*, A. McDonald.

CIVIL LIBERTIES, NATIONAL COUNCIL FOR (1934), 4 Camden High Street, N.W.1.—*Sec.*, M. Ennals.

CIVIL SERVANTS, SOCIETY OF, 19 Surrey Street, W.C.2.—*Gen. Sec.*, J. L. Williams.

CIVIL SERVICE COUNCIL FOR FURTHER EDUCATION.—*Sec.*, T. F. Evans, LL.B., Treasury Chambers, Great George Street, S.W.1.

CLASSICAL ASSOCIATION (1903).—*Hon. Secs.*, Prof. B. R. Rees; T. W. Melluish, M.A.; *Hon. Treas.*, Prof. L. A. Moritz, D.Phil., University College, Cardiff.

CLASS TEACHERS, NATIONAL FEDERATION OF, 2 Felton Crescent, Gateshead 8.—*Sec.*, W. Coates.

CLAY TECHNOLOGY, INSTITUTE OF (1927), 7 Chesterfield Gardens, Curzon Street, W.1.—*Gen. Sec.*, J. E. Roberts, F.R.S.A.

CLERGY FRIENDLY SOCIETY (1882), 53 Tufton Street, S.W.1.—*Sec.*, Rev. R. W. P. Dale.

CLERGY ORPHAN CORPORATION (1749), 5 Verulam Buildings, Gray's Inn, W.C.1.—*Sec.*, Miss V. B. Warters.

CLERGY PENSIONS BOARD (1926), 53 Tufton Street, S.W.1.—*Sec.*, L. J. Sillito.

CLERKS OF THE PEACE OF COUNTIES AND OF CLERKS OF COUNTY COUNCILS, SOCIETY OF.—*Hon. Sec.*, G. A. Wheatley, The Castle, Winchester.

CLERKS OF THE PEACE OF SCOTLAND, ASSOCIATION OF (1908).—*Hon. Sec.*, J. B. McGowan, 135 Irish Street, Dumfries.

CLERKS OF URBAN DISTRICT COUNCILS, SOCIETY OF (1926).—*Hon. Sec.*, E. S. Saywell, Council Offices, Northwood, Middx.

CLERKS OF WORKS OF GREAT BRITAIN INCORPORATED, INSTITUTE OF (1882), Liverpool House, 15–17 Eldon Street, E.C.2.—*Sec.*, E W. Hazell.

CLYDESDALE HORSE SOCIETY OF GREAT BRITAIN AND IRELAND (1877), 19 Hillington Gardens, Glasgow, S.W.2.

COACHING CLUB (1871), 16 Bedford Square, W.C.1.—*Sec.*, R. A. Brown.

COAL TRADE BENEVOLENT ASSOCIATION (1888), 66 Mark Lane, E.C.3.—*Sec.*, H. C. F. Squire.

COAL UTILISATION COUNCIL (1932), 19 Rochester Row, S.W.1.—*Director*, Sir Campbell Hardy, K.C.B.

COKE OVEN MANAGERS' ASSOCIATION, 1 Cliff Street, Mexborough, Yorks.—*Asst. Sec.*, C. P. Tiptaft, M.C.

COLLEGE OF THE SEA (Seafarers' Education Service) (1938), Mansbridge House, 207 Balham High Road, S.W.17.

COMBINED CADET FORCE ASSOCIATION (1952), 58 Buckingham Gate, S.W.1.—*Sec.*, W. F. L. Newcombe, O.B.E., T.D.

COMMERCE, ASSOCIATION OF BRITISH CHAMBERS OF (1860).—*Pres.*, T. H. Summerson; *Sec.*, A. C. F. Hey, 68 Queen Street, E.C.4.

COMMERCE, BRITISH AND LATIN AMERICAN CHAMBER OF (Incorporated), 11–12 West Smithfield, E.C.1.—*Sec.*, A. Cutts-Watson.

COMMERCE, COUNCIL OF SCOTTISH CHAMBERS OF, 30 George Square, Glasgow, C.2.—*Chairman*, T. D. Bruce (*Dundee*); *Joint Secs.*, M. Neil (*Glasgow*); W. V. Stevens (*Edinburgh*).

COMMERCE, LONDON CHAMBER OF (1881), 69 Cannon Street, E.C.4.—*Pres.*, The Earl of Verulam; *Sec.*, W. J. Luxton, C.B.E.

COMMERCE AND MANUFACTURES, CHAMBER OF, (1783), 30 George Square, Glasgow, C.2.—*Sec.*, M. Neil.

COMMERCE AND MANUFACTURES, EDINBURGH CHAMBER OF (1786), 25 Charlotte Square, Edinburgh 2.—*Sec.*, W. V. Stevens, O.B.E.

COMMERCIAL AND INDUSTRIAL EDUCATION, BRITISH ASSOCIATION FOR (BACIE), 26A Buckingham Palace Road, S.W.1.—*Dir.*, P. J. C. Perry.

COMMERCIAL TRAVELLERS' BENEVOLENT INSTITUTION (1849), Wax Chandlers' Hall, Gresham Street, E.C.2.—*Sec.*, E. B. Auger.

COMMISSIONAIRES, THE CORPS OF (1859), founded by the late Captain Sir Edward Walter; for the employment of ex-regular Soldiers, Sailors and Airmen. *Headquarters*, Exchange Court, 410A Strand, W.C.2. *Outquarters*, 124 Donegall Street, Belfast; Room 53, Guildhall Buildings, Navigation Street, Birmingham; 90 Colston Street, Bristol; 99 Shandwick Place, Edinburgh; 230 W. Regent Street, Glasgow; Room 23, 10–12 East Parade, Leeds; 21 Dale Street, Liverpool; 2 St. John Street, Deansgate, Manchester; 8 Higham Place, Newcastle-upon-Tyne. Total strength, 4,700.—*Commandant*, Lt.-Col. R. F. Walter; *Adjutant*, Brig. J. A. S. Hopkins, D.S.O.

COMMONS, OPEN SPACES AND FOOTPATHS PRESERVATION SOCIETY (1865), 11 King's Bench Walk, E.C.4.—*Sec.*, Miss B. K. Searle.

COMMON WEALTH, 12 High Street, Hampstead, N.W.3.—*Hon. Gen. Sec.*, D. Bannister; *Political Sec.*, W. J. Taylor.

COMMONWEALTH AND CONTINENTAL CHURCH SOCIETY (1823), 7 York Buildings, Adelphi, W.C.2.—*Sec.*, Rev. J. R. Hassett.

COMMONWEALTH INDUSTRIES ASSOCIATION, 100 New Cavendish Street, W.1.—*Gen. Sec.*, E. C. F. R. MacKenzie.

COMMONWEALTH MISSIONARY SOCIETY (1836), 202 Memorial Hall, Farringdon Street, E.C.4.—*Sec.*, Rev. E. J. Edwards.

COMMONWEALTH PARLIAMENTARY ASSOCIATION—*see* page 306.

COMMONWEALTH PRESS UNION (1909), 154 Fleet Street, E.C.4.—*Sec.*, Brig. L. L. Cross. C.B.E.

COMMONWEALTH PRODUCERS' ORGANIZATION (1916), 25 Victoria Street (North Block), S.W.1.—*Dir.* P. B. Broadbent.

COMMONWEATH UNIVERSITIES, ASSOCIATION OF, *General Office*, 36 Gordon Square, W.C.1; *Commonwealth Scholarships and Appointments*, Marlborough House, Pall Mall, S.W.1.—*Sec.*, J. F. Foster, M.A., LL.D.

COMMUNIST PARTY OF GREAT BRITAIN EXECUTIVE COMMITTEE (1920), 16 King Street, W.C.2.—*Gen. Sec.*, J. Gollan.

COMPOSERS' GUILD OF GREAT BRITAIN, THE (1945), 5 Egmont House, 116 Shaftesbury Avenue, W.1.—*Sec.*, Mrs. T. Levan.

CONSERVATIVE AND UNIONIST ASSOCIATIONS, NATIONAL UNION OF (1867), 32 Smith Square, S.W.1.—*Sec.*, S. A. Cooke, M.B.E.; *Women's National Advisory Committee.*—*Sec.*, Miss D. E. Brant; *Young Conservative and Unionist National Advisory Committee.*—*Sec.*, R. A. B. Durant.

CONSERVATIVE AND UNIONIST CENTRAL OFFICE, 32 Smith Square, S.W.1.—*Joint Chairmen*, Rt. Hon. I. N. Macleod, M.P.; The Lord Poole, C.B.E., T.D.; *Personal Assistant to the Chairmen*, The Lord Aldington, P.C., K.C.M.G., C.B.E., D.S.O., T.D.; *Vice-Chairmen*, P. E. O. Bryan, D.S.O., M.C., M.P.; Dame Barbara Brooke, D.B.E.; *Treasurers*, R. A. Allan, D.S.O., O.B.E., M.P.; Hon. Richard Stanley,

M.P.; *General Director*, Sir William Urton, M.B.E., T.D.; *Chief Organization Officer*, C. F. R. Bagnall, C.B.E.; *Chief Publicity Officer*, G. Hutchinson.

CONSERVATIVE CLUBS, LTD., ASSOCIATION OF (1894), 32 Smith Square, S.W.1.—*Sec.*, Col. R. E. Fellows.

CONSULTING ENGINEERS, ASSOCIATION OF (1913), Abbey House, 2 Victoria Street, S.W.1.—*Sec.*, Rear-Adm. P. D. H. R. Pelly, C.B., D.S.O.

CO-OPERATIVE SOCIETIES AND ASSOCIATIONS:—

Agricultural Central Co-operative Association, Ltd. (1956), Agriculture House, Knightsbridge, S.W.1.—*Chief Executive Officer* and *Sec.*, J. A. E. Morley, M.B.E.

Co-operative Party, 54 Victoria Street, S.W.1.—*Sec.*, H. E. Campbell.

Co-operative Productive Federation (1882), 138 Charles Street, Leicester.—*Sec.*, J. Leonard.

Co-operative Union (1869), Holyoake House, Hanover Street, Manchester, 4.—*Gen. Sec.*, R. Southern, C.B.E., B.A.

Co-operative Wholesale Society (C.W.S.) (1863), 1 Balloon Street, Manchester, 4.—*Sec.*, H. Buckley.

Co-operative Women's Guild, Pioneer House, 348 Gray's Inn Road, W.C.1.—*Gen. Sec.*, Mrs. K. Kempton.

Fisheries Organization Society, Ltd. (1914), Minster House, 272 Vauxhall Bridge Road, S.W.1.—*Sec.*, W. J. Lord, M.B.E.

International Co-operative Alliance (1895), 11 Upper Grosvenor Street, W.1.—*Dir.*, W. P. Watkins; *Gen. Sec.*, Miss G. F. Polley, O.B.E.

Plunkett Foundation for Co-operative Studies (1919), 10 Doughty Street, W.C.1.—*Sec.*, Miss M. Digby, O.B.E.

Scottish Agricultural Organisation Society (1905), 28 Rutland Street, Edinburgh 1.—*Sec.*, C. J. M. Cadzow, O.B.E.

Welsh Agricultural Organisation Society, Ltd., (1922), P.O. Box 8, Brynawel, Great Darkgate Street, Aberystwyth.—*Dir.*, E. R. Thomas.

(THOMAS) CORAM FOUNDATION FOR CHILDREN (formerly FOUNDLING HOSPITAL) (1739) AND CORAM NURSERY. All inquiries to 40 Brunswick Square, W.C.1.—*Sec.*, F. C. Brown.

CORONERS' SOCIETY OF ENGLAND AND WALES (1846).—*Hon. Sec.*, G. Thurston, Coroner's Court, 65 Horseferry Road, S.W.1.

COST ACCOUNTANTS' ASSOCIATION (1937), Hope House, 45 Great Peter Street, S.W.1.—*Sec.*, K. D. Gilpin.

COST AND WORKS ACCOUNTANTS, INSTITUTE OF (1919), 63 Portland Place, W.1.—*Sec.*, Derek du Pré.

COUNTRY LANDOWNERS' ASSOCIATION (1907), 7 Swallow Street, W.1.—*Sec.*, Francis F. Taylor, O.B.E.

COUNTY COUNCILS ASSOCIATION (1890) Eaton House, 66A Eaton Square, S.W.1.—*Sec.*, W. L. Dacey, LL.B.

COUNTY PLANNING OFFICERS' SOCIETY, Shire Hall, Bury St. Edmunds.—*Hon. Sec.*, J. M. Gorst.

COUNTY SURVEYORS' SOCIETY (1884).—*President* (1963–64), J. H. H. Wilkes, County Hall, Taunton, Somerset; *Hon. Sec. and Treas.*, M. Milne, County Hall, Chichester.

COUNTY TREASURERS, SOCIETY OF (1903), County Hall, Chester.—*Hon. Sec.*, R. H. A. Chisholm.

CRAFTS CENTRE OF GREAT BRITAIN (1948), 16/17 Hay Hill, W.1.—*Chairman*, John Farleigh, C.B.E.; *Sec.*, Mrs. S. Pocock, M.B.E.

CRUEL SPORTS, LEAGUE AGAINST, (1924), 58 Maddox Street, W.1.

CRUEL SPORTS, NATIONAL SOCIETY FOR THE ABOLITION OF.—*Sec.*, M. Norgate, 7 Lloyd Square, W.C.1.

CRUELTY TO ANIMALS, ROYAL SOCIETY FOR THE PREVENTION OF. *See* "ROYAL."

CRUELTY TO ANIMALS, CENTRAL COUNCIL OF SOCIETIES IN SCOTLAND FOR PREVENTION OF (1950), 19 Melville Street, Edinburgh 3.—*Hon. Sec.*, L. G. Langwill.

CRUELTY TO ANIMALS, ULSTER SOCIETY FOR THE PREVENTION OF, 65–67 May Street, Belfast, 1.—*Sec.*, Miss N. Parker.

CRUELTY TO CHILDREN. *See* "NATIONAL" and "ROYAL SCOTTISH."

CURATES' AUGMENTATION FUND (1866), East Wing, Fulham Palace, S.W.6.—*Sec.*, Rev. C. M. Lamb, M.A.

CYCLISTS' TOURING CLUB (1878), 3 Craven Hill, W.2.—*Sec.*, Leslie C. Warner.

CYMMRODORION, THE HONOURABLE SOCIETY OF (1751).—*Hon. Sec.*, Sir John Cecil-Williams, M.A., LL.D., 108A Cannon Street, E.C.4.

DAIRY ASSOCIATION, UNITED KINGDOM (1950), 17 Devonshire Street, W.1.—*Sec.*, R. O. Hubl.

DAIRY TECHNOLOGY, SOCIETY OF (1943). 17 Devonshire Street, W.1.—*Sec.*, M. Sonn.

DEAF, ROYAL NATIONAL INSTITUTE FOR THE (1911) AND NATIONAL BENEVOLENT SOCIETY AND EX-SERVICEMEN'S FUND FOR THE DEAF, 105 Gower Street, W.C.1.—*Dir. Gen.* K. S. Robinson.

DEAF AND DUMB, ROYAL ASSOCIATION IN AID OF THE (Registered under the National Assistance Act, 1948), 7–11 Armstrong Road, Acton, W.3.—*Sec.*, B. R. F. MacNay.

DEAF AND DUMB WOMEN, BRITISH HOME FOR, 26 Clapton Common, E.5.—*Sec.*, Miss B. M. Ayton.

DEAF CHILDREN, ROYAL SCHOOL FOR (1792), Margate. *Office*, 90 Queen Street, E.C.4.—*Sec.*, J. Coombs.

DEAF, COMMONWEALTH SOCIETY FOR THE (1959), 31 Gloucester Place, W.1.—*Sec.*, Miss Campbell.

DEBATING SOCIETIES, ASSOCIATION OF GREATER LONDON (1961).—*Hon. Sec.*, J. F. Mason, 10 Pear Close, Kingsbury, N.W.9

DECORATORS AND INTERIOR DESIGNERS, INCORPORATED INSTITUTE OF BRITISH (1899), Alderman House, 37 Soho Square, W.1.—*Sec.*, C. W. Allen.

DELINQUENCY, INST. FOR THE STUDY AND TREATMENT OF (1932), 8 Bourdon Street, W.1.—*Gen. Sec.*, Miss E. Saville.

DENTAL HOSPITALS OF GREAT BRITAIN AND NORTHERN IRELAND, ASSOCIATION OF (1942),—*Hon. Sec.*, Miss J. Irwin, M.A., Dental Hospital, Bridgeford Street, Manchester, 15.

DESIGN AND INDUSTRIES ASSOCIATION (1915) 13 Suffolk Street, S.W.1.—*Gen. Sec.*, M. Farr.

DESIGNER CRAFTSMEN, SOCIETY OF (*formerly* Arts and Crafts Exhibition Soc.) (1888), 6 Queen Square, W.C.1.—*Sec.*, Mrs. M. Denholm.

DESTITUTE SAILORS' FUND (1827), c/o The Red Ensign Club, Dock Street, E.1.

DEVON AND CORNWALL RECORD SOCIETY (1904).—*Hon. Sec.*, Miss G. M. Jerred, M.A., Heatherbank, Thorn Cross, Bovey Tracey, Devon.

DEVONIAN ASSOCIATION, LONDON (1888).—*Hon. Sec.*, Mrs. D. Gunzi, 59 Elms Road, Clapham Common, S.W.4.

DICKENS FELLOWSHIP, Dickens House, 48 Doughty Street, W.C.1.

DIRECTORS, INSTITUTE OF (1903), 10 Belgrave Square, S.W.1.—*Dir. Gen.*, Sir Richard Powell, Bt., M.C.

DISABLED, CENTRAL COUNCIL FOR THE (1919), 34 Eccleston Square, S.W.1.—*Administrator*, J. W. Cusack, C.M.G., O.B.E.

DISCHARGED PRISONERS' AID SOCIETIES, NATIONAL ASSOCIATION OF (Incorporating the Prison Welfare Service), 289–299 Borough High Street, S.E.1.—*Gen. Sec.*, Lt.-Cdr. A. Hague, R.D., R.N.R.

DISCHARGED PRISONERS' AID SOCIETY, ROYAL LONDON (1939), 56 Stamford Street, S.E.1.—*Sec.*, H. C. Bennett.

DISPENSING OPTICIANS, ASSOCIATION OF (1925), 22 Nottingham Place, W.1.—*Sec.*, M. G. Aird.

DISTRESS, SOCIETY FOR THE RELIEF OF (1860), 5 Denison House, Vauxhall Bridge Road, S.W.1. —*Hon. Sec.*, Rev. D. H. Pateman.

DISTRESSED GENTLEFOLKS' AID ASSOCIATION (1897), (Offices and Nursing Home) Vicarage Gate House, Vicarage Gate, Kensington, W.8.

DISTRICT NURSING IN LONDON, CENTRAL COUNCIL Miss H. McKeague, B.A. (*acting*).

DITCHLEY FOUNDATION, Ditchley Park, Enstone, Oxon.—*Provost*, H. V. Hodson.

DR. GRAHAM'S HOMES, KALIMPONG (LONDON COMMITTEE) (1900), 25 Temple Chambers, Temple Avenue, E.C.4.—*Chairman*, G. W. U. Liddle, M.B.E.; *Hon. Sec.*, J. F. E. d'A Willis. O.B.E.

DOGS' HOME BATTERSEA, THE (1860), Battersea Park Road, S.W.8. *Hours:* Weekdays, 9.30 to 5.—*Sec.*, Lieut-Cdr. B. N. Knight, R.N.

DOMESTIC SERVANTS' BENEVOLENT INSTITUTION (1846), Royal Bank of Scotland, Burlington Gardens, W.1.—*Sec.*, P. M. Clements.

DOMINION STUDENTS' HALL TRUST, London House, Mecklenburgh Square, W.C.1.

DOWSERS, BRITISH SOCIETY OF (1933), York House, Portugal Street, W.C.2.—*Hon. Treas. and Sec.*, C. Somers Taylor.

DRAMATISTS, LEAGUE OF, 84 Drayton Gardens, S.W.10.—*Sec.*, M. E. Barber, M.A.

DUKE OF EDINBURGH'S AWARD OFFICE, 2 Old Queen Street, S.W.1.—*Director*, Sir John Hunt, C.B.E., D.S.O.; *Gen. Sec.*, F. A. Evans.

DUNKIRK VETERANS ASSOCIATION (1940).—*Gen. Sec.*, H. Robinson, 35 Springbank Crescent, Leeds, 6.

DYERS AND COLOURISTS, SOCIETY OF (1884), Dean House, 19 Piccadilly, Bradford, Yorks.—*Gen. Sec.*, J. W. Nicholls.

EARL HAIG'S (BRITISH LEGION) APPEAL FUND. *See* "BRITISH LEGION."

EARL HAIG FUND (SCOTLAND). Established for the relief of distress among ex-service personnel of all ranks and their dependants in Scotland. Applicants may apply to either of the following: *North, South and East Area*, 23 Drumsheugh Gardens, Edinburgh 3.—*Gen. Sec.*, Col. J. M. Grant, O.B.E., or *Glasgow and South-West Area*, 1 Fitzroy Place, Glasgow, C.3.—*Sec.*, Lt. G. B. Steel, R.N.R.

EARLY ENGLISH TEXT SOCIETY (1864).—*Hon. Director* Prof. N. Davis, M.B.E.; *Hon. Sec.*, R. W. Burchfield, M.A., 40 Walton Crescent, Oxford.

EAST AND CENTRAL AFRICAN BOARD, JOINT (1926), 25 Victoria Street (North Block), S.W.1.—*Dir.*, P. B. Broadbent.

EAST AND WEST FRIENDSHIP COUNCIL (1921) (arranges hospitality for non-European students), 101 Gower Street, W.C.1.—*Sec.*, O. H. Gibson.

EAST INDIA ASSOCIATION (India, Pakistan and Burma) (1866), 2 Temple Chambers, Temple Avenue, E.C.4.—*Hon. Sec.*, Sir Francis Low.

ECCLESIOLOGICAL SOCIETY (Founded in 1839 as the Cambridge Camden Society).—*Hon. Sec.*, H. V. Molesworth Roberts, 17 Belmont Road, Wallington, Surrey.

EDUCATION COMMITTEES, ASSOCIATION OF, 10 Queen Anne Street, W.1.—*Sec.*, Sir William Alexander, Ph.D., Ed.B., M.A., B.Sc.

EDUCATION COMMITTEE OF COUNTY COUNCILS ASSOCIATION (1890), Eaton House, 66A Eaton Square, S.W.1.—*Sec.*, W. L. Dacey, LL.B.

EDUCATION COUNCIL OF THE SOCIETY OF FRIENDS, Friends' House, Euston Road, N.W.1.—*Sec.*, Gertrude M. Ostler.

EDUCATION, INSTITUTE OF CHRISTIAN (1935), 46 Gordon Square, W.C.1.—*Org. Sec.*, Mrs. Norah Taylor.

EDUCATION LEAGUE, SECULAR, 13 Prince of Wales Terrace, W.8.—*Hon. Sec.*, M. L. Burnet.

EDUCATION, NATIONAL COMMITTEE FOR AUDIO-VISUAL AIDS IN, 33 Queen Anne Street, W.1.—*Dir.*, Dr. J. A. Harrison.

EDUCATION OFFICERS, ASSOCIATION OF CHIEF.—*Hon. Sec.*, J. J. B. Dempster, O.B.E., PH.D., Education Office, Civic Centre, Southampton.

EDUCATION, SCOTTISH COUNCIL FOR RESEARCH IN, 46 Moray Place Edinburgh, 3.—*Director*, D. A. Walker, M.A., B.Ed., Ph.D., F.R.S.E.

EDUCATION THROUGH ART, SOCIETY FOR, Morley College, 61 Westminster Bridge Road, S.E.1. —*Pres.*, Sir Herbert Read, D.S.O., M.C., D.Litt.; *Sec.*, Miss C. J. Crowther.

EDUCATIONAL CENTRES ASSOCIATION, Walthamstow Educational Settlement, Greenleaf Road, E.17.—*Hon. Sec.*, Ray Lamb.

EDUCATIONAL FOUNDATION FOR VISUAL AIDS, 33 Queen Anne Street, W.1.—*Chief Executive Officer*, Dr. J. A. Harrison.

EDUCATIONAL INSTITUTE OF SCOTLAND (1847), 46 Moray Place, Edinburgh.—*Gen. Sec.*, G. S. Bryden, M.B.E.

EDUCATIONAL RESEARCH, NATIONAL FOUNDATION FOR, 79 Wimpole Street, W.1.—*Director*, Dr. W. D. Wall.

EDUCATIONAL TELEVISION, INSTITUTE FOR (1962), 30 Portman Square, W.1.—*Secretary*, Miss M. Noble.

EDUCATIONAL VISITS AND EXCHANGES, CENTRAL BUREAU FOR, 55A Duke Street, W.1.—*Sec.*, G. Dickson (*acting*).

ELDERLY INVALIDS FUND (Incorp. 1954), 34 King Street, E.C.2.—*Hon. Gen. Sec.*, W. L. Graham.

ELECTORAL REFORM SOCIETY (founded 1884 as Proportional Representation Soc.), Albany Institute, Creek Road, S.E.8.—*Director and Sec.*, Miss E. Lakeman.

ELECTRICAL ENGINEERS, INSTITUTION OF (1871), Savoy Place, W.C.2.—*Pres.* (1963–64), A. H. Mumford, O.B.E.; *Sec.*, Dr. G. F. Gainsborough.

ELECTRONICS, INSTITUTION OF (1930), 78 Shaw Road, Rochdale, Lancs.—*Gen. Sec.*, W. Birtwistle.

EMPIRE COTTON GROWING CORPORATION (1921), 12 Chantrey House, Eccleston Street, S.W.1.—*Director*, D. F. Ruston; *Sec.*, M. H. White.

EMPIRE RHEUMATISM COUNCIL, Faraday House, 8–10 Charing Cross Road, W.C.2.—*Gen. Sec.*, M. C. G. Andrews.

EMPLOYMENT FELLOWSHIP (formerly WINTER DISTRESS LEAGUE) (1922), Drayton House, Gordon Street, W.C.1. Helps to organize work schemes, especially for the elderly.—*Organizing Sec.*, C. McKenna.

EMPLOYMENT OF REGULAR SAILORS, SOLDIERS AND AIRMEN, NATIONAL ASSOCIATION FOR (1885), 4 Buckingham Palace Mansions, Buckingham Palace Road, S.W.1.—*General Manager*, Air Vice-Marshal R. S. Blucke, C.B., C.B.E., D.S.O., A.F.C. (*ret.*).

ENGINEERING DESIGNERS, INSTITUTION OF (1945), 38 Portland Place, W.1.—*Gen. Sec.*, W. E. Walters.

ENGINEERING FEDERATION, BRITISH MECHANICAL (1912), 32 Victoria Street, S.W.1.—*Sec.*, R. K. Fenelon.

ENGINEERING INSPECTION, INSTITUTION OF (1919), 616 Grand Buildings, Trafalgar Square, W.C.2. *Sec.*, Cdr. J. Spencer, O.B.E., R.N.

ENGINEERS AND SHIPBUILDERS IN SCOTLAND, INSTITUTION OF (1857), 39 Elmbank Crescent, Glasgow, C.2.—*Pres.*, Prof. A. S. T. Thomson; *Sec.*, P. W. Thomas.

ENGINEERS AND SHIPBUILDERS, N.E. COAST INSTITUTION OF (1884), Bolbec Hall, Newcastle-on-Tyne, 1.—*Sec.*, Cdr. R. F. A. Whately, R.N.

ENGINEERS' GUILD, LTD. (for Professional Engineers), 201 High Holborn, W.C.1.—*Sec.*, J. G. Orr.

ENGINEERS, JUNIOR INSTITUTION OF (1884), 14 Rochester Row, S.W.1.—*Sec.*, G. W. Germain.

ENGINEERS, SOCIETY OF (Incorporated) (1854), Abbey House, Victoria Street, S.W.1.—*Sec.*, L. T. Griffith.

ENGLISH ASSOCIATION (1906), 8 Cromwell Place, S.W.7.—*Sec.*, Mrs. E. M. Fielding.

ENGLISH FOLK DANCE AND SONG SOCIETY (1932), Cecil Sharp House, 2 Regent's Park Road, N.W.1.—*Administrator*, S. R. S. Pratt.

ENGLISH PLACE-NAME SOCIETY (1923).—*Hon. Director*, Prof. A. H. Smith, O.B.E., Ph.D., D.Lit., University College, W.C.1.

ENGLISH-SPEAKING UNION OF THE COMMONWEALTH (1918), 37 Charles Street, Berkeley Square, W.1.—*Chairman*, The Lord Baillieu, K.B.E., C.M.G.; *Sec.*, C. Colbeck.

ENHAM-ALAMEIN VILLAGE CENTRE for disabled ex-Servicemen and Civilians (1918), Andover, Hants (Village Centres for Curative Treatment, and Training Council).—*Sec.-Gen.*, Denis Benwell, 16 Grosvenor Place, S.W.1.

ENTOMOLOGICAL SOCIETY OF LONDON, ROYAL (1833), 41 Queen's Gate, S.W.7.—*Hon. Sec.*, D. R. Ragge, Ph.D.

ENTOMOLOGY, COMMONWEALTH INSTITUTE OF (1913), c/o Natural History Museum, S.W.7. (*Publications Office and Library*, 56 Queen's Gate, S.W.7.).—*Director*, E. O. Pearson.

EPILEPSY ASSOCIATION, BRITISH, 27 Nassau Street, W.1.—*Gen. Sec.*, G. S. Burden.

EPILEPTICS, THE NATIONAL SOCIETY FOR (1892), Chalfont Colony, Chalfont St. Peter, Bucks.—*Secretary Superintendent*, E. G. England.

ESPERANTO ASSOCIATION (INC.), BRITISH (1907), 140 Holland Park Avenue, W.11.—*Sec.*, J. W. Leslie.

EUGENICS SOCIETY (1907), 69 Eccleston Square, S.W.1.—*Gen. Sec.*, Dr. G. C. L. Bertram.

EVANGELICAL ALLIANCE (1846), 30 Bedford Place, W.C.1.—*Gen. Sec.*, Rev. G. W. Kirby.

EVANGELICAL LIBRARY, THE, 78A Chiltern Street, W.1.—*Founder and Organizing Sec.*, Geoffrey Williams.

EXAMINERS UNDER SOLICITORS (SCOTLAND) ACTS (1933–1958), Law Society's Hall, North Bank Street, Edinburgh.—*Clerk*, R. B. Laurie, W.S.

EXPORT, INSTITUTE OF, Export House, 14 Hallam Street, W.1.—*Director*, A. J. Townsend.

EX-SERVICES MENTAL WELFARE SOCIETY (for ex-Service men and women suffering from war psychoses and neuroses), 37–39 Thurloe Street, S.W.7.—*Admin. Sec.*, Major J. R. Donnelly, M.B.E., T.D.

FABIAN SOCIETY (1884), 11 Dartmouth Street, S.W.1.—*Gen. Sec.*, Mrs. S. Williams.

FAIRBRIDGE SOCIETY (1909) (formerly Fairbridge Farm Schools), Creagh House, 38 Holland Villas Road, W.14.—*Dir.*, W. R. Vaughan, O.B.E.

FAIR ISLE BIRD OBSERVATORY TRUST, 21 Regent Terrace, Edinburgh.—*Hon. Sec.*, George Waterston, F.R.S.E.

FAMILY PLANNING ASSOCIATION, 231 Tottenham Court Road, W.1.—*Gen. Sec.*, Brig. R. C. Elstone, C.B.E., M.C.

FAMILY SERVICE UNITS, 207 Marylebone Road, N.W.1.—*Sec.*, A. F. Philp.

FAMILY WELFARE ASSOCIATION (Founded 1869 as CHARITY ORGANISATION SOCIETY), Denison House, Vauxhall Bridge Road, S.W.1.—*Dir.*, J. S. Burt.

FARADAY SOCIETY (1903), 6 Gray's Inn Square, W.C.1.—*Pres.*, Prof. A. R. Ubbelohde, M.A., D.Sc., F.R.S.; *Sec.*, F. C. Tompkins, D.Sc., F.R.S.

FAUNA PRESERVATION SOCIETY (1903).—*Office*, c/o Zoological Society, Regent's Park, N.W.1.—*Sec.*, R. S. R. Fitter.

FAWCETT SOCIETY (1866), 27 Wilfred Street, S.W.1.—*Sec.*, Mrs. H. V. Horton.

FEDERAL UNION, 10 Wyndham Place, W.1.—*Dir.*, R. E. Shaw.

FEDERATION OF SMALL MINES OF GREAT BRITAIN, 32 King Street, Wigan, Lancs.—*Sec.*, T. M. Broadie-Griffith.

FEEDING STUFFS TRADE BENEVOLENT SOCIETY OF GREAT BRITAIN (1923), Baltic Exchange Chambers, 24 St. Mary Axe, E.C.3.—*Sec.*, R. T. Whelans.

FELLOWSHIP HOUSES TRUST (Homes and flatlets for Aged) (1937), Clock House, Byfleet, Surrey.—*Sec.*, J. Atkinson.

FIELD LANE INSTITUTION (1841), Vine Hill, Clerkenwell Road, E.C.1; HOMES FOR OLD PEOPLE; COMMUNITY CENTRE, 32 Cubitt Street, W.C.1.—*Gen. Sec.*, A. C. Ash.

FIRE ENGINEERS, INSTITUTION OF, 94 Southwark Bridge Road, S.E.1.—*Gen. Sec.*, H. L. Oates.

FIRE PROTECTION ASSOCIATION, Aldermary House, Queen Street, E.C.4.—*Dir.*, N. C. Strother Smith.

FIRE SERVICES ASSOCIATION, BRITISH, 86 London Road, Leicester.—*Gen. Sec.*, A. W. Beevers.

FIRE SERVICES ASSOCIATION, NATIONAL (1940), 12 New Court, Lincoln's Inn, W.C.2.—*Hon. Sec.*, J. J. Ellis.

FIRE SERVICES NATIONAL BENEVOLENT FUND (1943).—*Hon. Organizing Sec.*, R. W. Greene, M.B.E., 94 Southwark Bridge Road, S.E.1.

FLAX SUPPLY ASSOCIATION (1867), 7 Donegall Square, W., Belfast, 1.—*Sec.*, G. A. E. Roberts, O.B.E.

FOLK-LORE SOCIETY, c/o University College London, Gower Street, W.C.1.—*Hon. Sec.*, A. W. Smith.

FORCES HELP SOCIETY AND LORD ROBERTS'S WORKSHOPS (1899), 118–122 Brompton Road, S.W.3.—*Comptroller*, A. M. Hankin.

FOREIGN BONDHOLDERS, COUNCIL OF (1873), 17 Moorgate, E.C.2.—*Director-General*, E. F. M. Butler.

FOREIGN PRESS ASSOCIATION IN LONDON, 11 Carlton House Terrace, S.W.1.—*Pres.*, Nasim Ahmed.

FORENSIC SCIENCES, BRITISH ACADEMY OF (1959).—*Secretary-General*, F. E. Camps, M.D., 28 Portland Place, W.1.

FORESTERS OF GREAT BRITAIN, SOCIETY OF (1925), c/o Commonwealth Forestry Institute, South Parks Road, Oxford.—*Sec. and Treas.*, J. Pitt, M.A., B.Sc.

FORESTRY ASSOCIATION, COMMONWEALTH (1921), Royal Commonwealth Society, Northumberland Avenue, W.C.2.—*Editor-Sec.*, P. C. Lancaster, O.B.E., M.A.

FORESTRY ASSOCIATION LTD., ENGLISH (1926), The Knowle Nurseries, Caversham Heights, Reading.

FORESTRY SOCIETY OF ENGLAND, WALES AND NORTHERN IRELAND, ROYAL (1882), 49 Russell Square, W.C.1.—*Sec.*, P. S. Leathart, M.B.E.

FORESTRY SOCIETY, ROYAL SCOTTISH (1854), 7 Albyn Place, Edinburgh 2.—*Sec. and Treas.*, R. Angus Galloway, O.B.E., M.C., B.SC.

FRANCO-BRITISH SOCIETY, 1 Old Burlington Street, W.1.—*Chairman*, Major-Gen. Sir Guy Salisbury-Jones, G.C.V.O., C.M.G., M.C.; *Sec.*, Miss M. Coate.

FREE CHURCH FEDERAL COUNCIL, 27 Tavistock Square, W.C.1.—*Moderator* (1963-64), Rev. J. Ithel Jones; *Gen. Sec.*, Rev. A. R. Vine, M.A., B.SC., D.D.

FREEMASONS, GRAND LODGE OF SCOTLAND (1736), Freemasons' Hall, Edinburgh.—*Grand Master Mason of Scotland*, The Lord Bruce; *Grand Sec.*, A. F. Buchan, M.B.E., B.SC., Ph.D., F.R.S.E.

FREEMASONS, UNITED GRAND LODGE OF ENGLAND, Freemasons' Hall, Great Queen Street, W.C.2.—*Grand Master*, The Earl of Scarbrough, K.G., P.C., G.C.S.I., G.C.I.E., G.C.V.O., T.D.; *Deputy Grand Master*, The Earl Cadogan, M.C.; *Assistant Grand Master*, Maj. Gen. Sir Allan Adair, Bt., C.B., C.V.O., D.S.O., M.C.; *Grand Wardens*, The Marquess Townshend; Hon. F. N. W. Cornwallis, O.B.E.; *Grand Chaplains*, The Bishop of Jarrow, O.B.E.; Rev. Canon G. T. Waldegrave, M.B.E.; *Grand Sec.*, J. W. Stubbs.

FREEMEN OF CITY OF LONDON, GUILD OF (1908), 4 Dowgate Hill, E.C.4.—*Master*, R. Ward, F.R.I.B.A.; *Clerk*, D. Reid.

FRESHWATER BIOLOGICAL ASSOCIATION (1932), The Ferry House, Far Sawrey, Ambleside, Westmorland.—*Sec. and Director of Laboratories*, H. C. Gilson, M.A.

FRIEND OF THE CLERGY CORP. (1849), 15 Henrietta Street, Strand, W.C.2.—*Sec.*, Cdr. R. A. Dudley, R.N.

FRIENDS OF THE NATIONAL LIBRARIES, c/o The British Museum, W.C.1.—*Chairman*, The Lord Kenyon; *Hon. Sec.*, T. S. Blakeney.

FRIENDS OF THE POOR & GENTLEFOLK'S HELP (1905), and DISABLED SOLDIERS EMBROIDERY INDUSTRY, 42 Ebury Street, S.W.1.—*Gen. Sec.*, Dame Dorothy Vaisey, D.C.V.O., O.B.E.

FROEBEL FOUNDATION, NATIONAL, 2 Manchester Square, W.1.—*Gen. Sec.*, Miss V. E. Nightingall.

FUEL, INSTITUTE OF (1927), 18 Devonshire Street, Portland Place, W.1.—*Sec.*, R. W. Reynolds-Davies, O.B.E., B.SC.

GARDENERS' ROYAL BENEVOLENT SOCIETY (1839), 48 Broadway, S.W.1.—*Sec.*, Miss J. Morley.

GAS ENGINEERS, INSTITUTION OF (1863), 17 Grosvenor Crescent, S.W.1.—*Sec.*, A. G. Higgins.

GEMMOLOGICAL ASSOCIATION OF GREAT BRITAIN (1931), St. Dunstan's House, Carey Lane, E.C.2.—*Sec.*, G. F. Andrews.

GENEALOGICAL RESEARCH SOCIETY, IRISH, Oak Hill, Belstead Road, Ipswich.—*Sec.*, Rev. W. Clare, F.R.S.A.

GENEALOGISTS, SOCIETY OF (1911), 37 Harrington Gardens, S.W.7.—*Sec.*, Mrs. C. M. Mackay.

GENERAL PRACTITIONERS, COLLEGE OF (1952), 14 Princes Gate, S.W.7.—*Sec.*, Cdr. A. E. P. Doran, D.S.C., R.N. (*ret.*).

GENTLEPEOPLE, GUILD OF AID FOR (1904), 280A Earls Court Road, S.W.5.—*Sec.*, Miss E. C. Ritchie.

GEOGRAPHICAL ASSOCIATION, c/o The Park Branch Library, Duke Street, Sheffield, 2.—*Hon. Sec.*, Prof. Alice Garnett.

GEOGRAPHICAL SOCIETY, ROYAL (1830), Kensington Gore, S.W.7.—*Pres.*, Prof. L. Dudley Stamp, C.B.E.; *Hon. Secs.*, Sir Christopher Summerhayes, K.B.E., C.M.G.; Prof. M. J. Wise, M.C. *Hon. Foreign Sec.*, Maj.-Gen. R. Ll. Brown, C.B., C.B.E.; *Hon. Treas.*, G. P. Pirie-Gordon; *Director and Sec.*, L. P. Kirwan, C.M.G., T.D.; *Librarian and Map Curator*, G. R. Crone.

GEOGRAPHICAL SOCIETY, MANCHESTER (1884), 16 St. Mary's Parsonage, Manchester.—*Sec.*, A. Murch.

GEOGRAPHICAL SOCIETY, ROYAL SCOTTISH (1884), 10 Randolph Crescent, Edinburgh 3.—*Sec.*, D. G. Moir.

GEOLOGICAL SOCIETY (1807), Burlington House, Piccadilly, W.1.—*Pres.*, Prof. O. M. B. Bulman, SC.D., F.R.S.; *Secs.*, W. B. Harland; P. A. Sabine, Ph.D.; *Foreign Sec.*, Prof. O. T. Jones, M.A., D.SC., F.R.S.

GEOLOGISTS' ASSOCIATION.—*Hon. Gen. Sec.*, F. H. MOORE, B.SC., Ph.D., 278 Fir Tree Road, Epsom Downs, Surrey.

GEORGIAN GROUP, 2 Chester Street, S.W.1.

GILBERT AND SULLIVAN SOCIETY.—*Hon. Sec.*, Miss C. Lambert, 273 Northfield Avenue, W.5.

GIRL GUIDES ASSOCIATION.—An organization founded by the first Lord Baden-Powell, as a sister movement to the Boy Scouts and incorporated by Royal Charter in 1922. In 1962 the total membership in Great Britain and Northern Ireland was 602,214 and the world membership was over 5,500,000. *Commonwealth Headquarters*, Box 269, 17-19 Buckingham Palace Road, S.W.1.

GIRLS' FRIENDLY SOCIETY AND TOWNSEND MEMBERS' FELLOWSHIP (1875), Townsend House, Greycoat Place, S.W.1.—*Sec.*, E. P. M. Dunbar,

GIRLS' GUILDRY, THE (1900), 212 Bath Street, Glasgow, C.2; *London Office*, 53 Victoria Street, S.W.1; *Scottish Office*, 24 Ainslie Place, Edinburgh; *Welsh Office*, 70 Wood Road, Pontypridd, Glam.

GIRLS' LIFE BRIGADE (Incorp.) (1902), 8 Upper Belgrave Street, S.W.1.—*Brigade Sec.*, Miss I. Bosworth.

GIRLS OF THE REALM GUILD (1900), Brambles, Yateley, Camberley, Surrey.—*Sec.*, Mrs. M. C. Dempsey.

GIVEN-WILSON INSTITUTE, Pelly Bridge, Pelly Road, Plaistow, E.13.—*Hon. Sec.*, Rev. A. H. Weir.

GLACIOLOGICAL SOCIETY, c/o Scott Polar Research Institute, Lensfield Road, Cambridge.

GLANVIL SOCIETY (1948), 5 Essex Court, E.C.4. For providing barrister lecturers on legal and allied topics.—*Hon. Sec.*, P. B. Calwell.

GLASS-PAINTERS, BRITISH SOCIETY OF MASTER (1921) 6 Queen Square, W.C.1.—*Hon. Sec.*, E. Liddall Armitage.

GLASS TECHNOLOGY, SOCIETY OF (1916), 20 Hallam Gate Road, Sheffield 10.—*Hon. Sec.*, T. S. Busby.

GORDON BOYS' SCHOOL (1885), West End, Woking.—*Commdt. and Sec.*, Brig. D. E. Holbrook, C.B.E.

GORDON SMITH INSTITUTE FOR SEAMEN (INCORPORATED) (1820) (Gordon Smith Seamen's Club), 96 Paradise Street, Liverpool, 1.—*Sec. and Supt.*, N. A. Williams,

GOVERNESSES' BENEVOLENT INSTITUTION, 39 Buckingham Gate, S.W.1. For the benefit of governesses and women private teachers. Annuities, temporary assistance; homes for the retired and chronic sick.—*Sec.*, J. W. Beattie.

GRAPHIC ARTISTS, SOCIETY OF (1920), 195 Piccadilly, W.1.—*Pres.*, C. S. Tresilian; *Sec.*, D. I. John.

GREATER LONDON RED CROSS BLOOD TRANSFUSION SERVICE (1921), 4 St. Andrew's Place, N.W.1. [Hunter: 2579).

GRENFELL ASSOCIATION OF GREAT BRITAIN AND IRELAND, Hope House, Great Peter Street, S.W.1. For medical and social work among the fishermen of Labrador and Northern Newfoundland.—*Sec.*, Miss Betty Seabrook.

GULBENKIAN FOUNDATION, *see* CALOUSTE.

HANDICRAFT TEACHERS, INSTITUTE OF.—*Gen. Sec.*, T. E. Atkinson, Hillside, Little Weighton, Hull.

HANSARD SOCIETY FOR PARLIAMENTARY GOVERNMENT (1944), 162 Buckingham Palace Road, S.W.1.—*Sec.*, E. Macalester.

HARLEIAN SOCIETY (1869), 79 Duke Street, Grosvenor Square, W.1.—*Hon. Sec. and Treas.*, N. H. MacMichael, F.S.A.

HARVEIAN SOCIETY OF LONDON.—*Hon. Sec.*, Dr. W. B. Thomson, 11 Chandos Street, Cavendish Square, W.1.

HEADMASTERS' CONFERENCE. *See* p. 536.

HEAD MASTERS, INCORPORATED ASSOCIATION OF, 29 Gordon Square, W.C.1.—*Pres.* (1963), J. S. Robinson; *Joint Hon. Secs.*, E. C. Axford; W. R. Hecker; *Hon. Treas.*, S. Davies; *Sec.*, F. L. Allan, M.B.E., M.C.

HEAD MISTRESSES, ASSOCIATION OF, 29 Gordon Square, W.C.1.—*President* (1962–64), Miss R. N. Pearse, O.B.E.; *Sec.*, Miss L. Spalding.

HEADMISTRESSES OF PREPARATORY SCHOOLS, ASSOCIATION OF.—*Hon. Sec.*, Mrs. J. S. Davey, Halstead, Woodham Rise, Woking, Surrey.

HEADMISTRESSES OF RECOGNIZED INDEPENDENT SCHOOLS, ASSOCIATION OF.—*Hon. Sec.*, Miss A. A. Mowat, M.B.E., Manor Grange, Tunbridge Wells, Kent.

HEAD TEACHERS, NATIONAL ASSOCIATION OF.—*Gen. Sec.*, W. J. W. Glossop, 29a The Broadway, Crawley, Sussex.

HEAD TEACHERS' ASSOCIATION, LONDON, St. Bride Institute, Bride Lane, E.C.4.—*Sec.*, Dr. T. Harper Smith, 48 Perryn Road, W.3.

HEALTH EDUCATION, CENTRAL COUNCIL FOR (1927), Tavistock House, Tavistock Square, W.C.1.—*Medical Director*, Dr. A. J. Dalzell-Ward.

HEALTH, GUILD OF (1904), Edward Wilson House, 26 Queen Anne Street, W.1.—*Chaplains*, Rev. Canon H. W. Bird; Rev. L. Maclachlan.

HEART FOUNDATION, BRITISH (1963), Tavistock House, North, Tavistock Square, W.C.1.—*Sec.*, Harley Williams, O.B.E., M.D.

HEATING AND VENTILATING ENGINEERS, INSTITUTION OF (1897), 49 Cadogan Square, S.W.1.—*Sec.*, B. A. Hodges, B.A.

HELLENIC STUDIES, SOCIETY FOR THE PROMOTION OF (1879), 31–34 Gordon Square, W.C.1.—*Pres.*, Prof. A. Andrewes, F.B.A.; *Hon. Treas.*, B. Rickatson-Hatt; *Hon. Sec.*, Prof. R. P. Winnington-Ingram, F.B.A.

HENRY GEORGE SCHOOL OF SOCIAL SCIENCE, 177 Vauxhall Bridge Road, S.W.1.—*Dir. of Studies*, V. H. Blundell.

HERALDRY SOCIETY, THE (1947), 59 Gordon Square, W.C.1.—*Sec.*, Col. C. C. Danby, O.B.E.

HERTFORD BRITISH HOSPITAL, Rue de Villiers, 48 Levallois-Perret (Seine), Paris, France.—Provides a medical service for British citizens; no British subject is ever refused admission. *Medical Superintendent*, Prof. C. Olivier; *Sec.*, H. Natanson.

HIGHWAY ENGINEERS, INSTITUTION OF (1930), 47 Victoria Street, S.W.1.—*Hon. Sec.*, J. T. C. Hatcher.

HISPANIC COUNCIL (1943), Canning House, 2 Belgrave Square, S.W.1.—*Dir.-Gen.*, Sir John Walker, K.C.M.G., O.B.E.

HISTORIC AND ARTISTIC WORKS, INTERNATIONAL INSTITUTE FOR CONSERVATION OF, c/o The National Gallery, Trafalgar Square, W.C.2.—*Pres.*, A. van Schendel, D.Phil.; *Sec.-Gen.*, N. Brommelle.

HISTORICAL ASSOCIATION (1906), 59A Kennington Park Road, S.E.11.—*Hon. Sec.*, H. L. Freakes.

HISTORICAL SOCIETY, ROYAL (1868), 96 Cheyne Walk, Chelsea, S.W.10.—*Pres.* Prof. Sir Goronwy Edwards, D.Litt., Litt.D., F.B.A., F.S.A.; *Hon. Sec.*, Prof. F. R. H. Du Boulay, M.A.,

HISTORY OF SCIENCE, BRITISH SOCIETY FOR THE.—*Pres.*, T. Martin; *Hon. Sec.*, J. A. Chaldecott, c/o Science Museum, S.W.7.

HOMELESS CHILDREN'S AID AND ADOPTION SOCIETY, and F. B. Meyer Children's Home (Incorp.) (1920), 54 Grove Avenue, Muswell Hill, N.10.—*Sec.*, Mrs. J. Simpson.

HOMES FOR WORKING BOYS IN LONDON (Incorporated) (1870).—*Office*, 15 Champion Hill, S.E.5.

HONG KONG ASSOCIATION (1961), 54 Old Broad Street, E. C. 2.—*Sec.*, H. J. Collar, C.B.E.

HORATIAN SOCIETY (1933).—*Sec.*, Miss K. L. Steele, 60 Meriden Court, Chelsea Manor Street, S.W.3.

HOROLOGICAL INSTITUTE, BRITISH (1858), 35 Northampton Square, E.C.1.—*Sec.*, F. West.

HOROLOGICAL SOCIETY, ANTIQUARIAN (1953), Northampton Square, Clerkenwell, E.C.1.—*Hon Sec.*, J. C. Stevens.

HOSPITAL ADMINISTRATORS, INSTITUTE OF (1902), 75 Portland Place, W.1.—*Sec.*, S. R. Speller, O.B.E., LL.B.

HOSPITALS CONTRIBUTORY SCHEMES ASSOCIATION, BRITISH (1948), Royal London Buildings, 42 Baldwin Street, Bristol, 1.—*Hon. Sec.*, John Dodd.

HOSPITAL SATURDAY FUND, THE (1873).—*Head Office*, 14–18 Holborn, E.C.1.—*Sec.*, L. B. Dart.

HOSPITAL SAVING ASSOCIATION, THE, 30 Lancaster Gate, W.2.—*Gen. Sec.*, A. H. Trembath.

HOSPITAL SERVICE PLAN (London Association for Hospital Services) 157 St. John's Road, Tunbridge Wells, Kent.—*Gen. Manager*, J. H. Dyter.

HOTELS AND RESTAURANTS ASSOCIATION, BRITISH, 88 Brook Street, W.1.

HOUSE OF ST. BARNABAS IN SOHO (House of Charity for Distressed Women in London) (1846), 1 Greek Street, Soho Square, W.1.—*Warden*, Mrs. Gibbs.

HOUSEWORKERS, NATIONAL INSTITUTE OF, LTD., Boston Manor House, Boston Manor Road, Brentford, Middlesex.

HOUSING AND TOWN PLANNING COUNCIL, NATIONAL (1900), 42 Devonshire Street, Portland Place, W.1.—*Sec.*, A. R. Kerrell-Vaughan.

HOUSING ASSOCIATION FOR OFFICERS' FAMILIES (1916), 41B Kensington High Street, W.8.—*Sec.*, R. Davis.

HOUSING, INSTITUTE OF (1931), 50 Tufton Street, S.W.1.

HOUSING MANAGERS (INC.), SOCIETY OF, 13 Suffolk Street, Pall Mall East, S.W.1.—*Sec.*, Miss M. S. Cleaver.

HOWARD LEAGUE FOR PENAL REFORM (1866), 6 Endsleigh Street, W.C.1. To promote the constructive treatment of delinquents and the prevention of crime.—*Sec.*, Hugh Klare.

HUGUENOT SOCIETY OF LONDON (1885), c/o Barclays Bank, Ltd., 1 Pall Mall East, S.W.1.—*Hon. Sec.*, Miss I. Scouloudi, M.SC., F.S.A.

HUNTERIAN SOCIETY.—*Secs.*, H. G. Hanley, M.D., F.R.C.S., 147 Harley Street, W.1.; H. W. Balme, M.D., F.R.C.P., 150 Harley Street, W.1.

HUNTERS' IMPROVEMENT AND NATIONAL LIGHT HORSE BREEDING SOCIETY (1885), 17 Devonshire Street, W.1.—*Sec.*, C. G. Wright.

ILLUMINATING ENGINEERING SOCIETY (1909), York House, Westminster Bridge Road, S.E.1.—*Sec.*, G. F. Cole.

INCOME TAX PAYERS' SOCIETY, Abbey House. Victoria Street, S.W.1.—*Sec.*, Miss D. G. Reid,

INDEXERS, SOCIETY OF, 3 Twyford Crescent, W.3.—*Gen. Sec.*, E. Alan Baker.

INDIA, PAKISTAN AND BURMA ASSOCIATION, Outer Temple, 222 Strand, W.C.2.—*Joint Adviser and Sec.*, G. W. Tyson, C.I.E.

INDUSTRIAL ARTISTS AND DESIGNERS, SOCIETY OF (1930), 7 Woburn Square, W.C.1.—*Sec.*, Mrs. A. Townsend.

INDUSTRIAL ASSOCIATION OF WALES AND MONMOUTHSHIRE.—*Head Office*, Aberdare House, Mount Stuart Square, Cardiff.

INDUSTRIAL CHRISTIAN FELLOWSHIP (1877), St. Katharine Cree Church, Leadenhall Street, E.C.3.—*Chairman*, The Bishop of Blackburn.

INDUSTRIAL CO-PARTNERSHIP ASSOCIATION (1884), 60 Buckingham Gate, S.W.1.—*Director*, J. Ward Daw; *Sec.*, Mrs. I. S. Ramsey, M.B.E.

INDUSTRIAL WELFARE SOCIETY (INCORPORATED) (1918), Robert Hyde House, 48 Bryanston Square, W.1.—*Dir.*, J. Garnett.

INLAND WATERWAYS ASSOCIATION LTD. 4 Emerald Street, W.C.1.—*Gen. Sec.*, P. Grahame.

INSTITUTIONAL MANAGEMENT ASSOCIATION (1938), Swinton House, 324 Gray's Inn Road, W.C.1.—*Sec.*, Mrs. B. A. Cleaver.

INSTRUMENT TECHNOLOGY, SOCIETY OF (1944), 20 Peel Street, W.8.—*Sec.*, Cdr. A. A. W. Pollard, D.S.C., R.N. (*ret.*).

INSURANCE AGENTS, CORPORATION OF (1906), 68 Gloucester Place, W.1.—*Sec.*, A. E. Ward.

INSURANCE ASSOCIATION, BRITISH (1917), Aldermary House, Queen Street, E.C.4.—*Sec.*, R. T. D. Wilmot.

INSURANCE BROKERS, CORPORATION OF (1906), 15 St. Helen's Place, E.C.3.—*Sec.*, C. E. Ovington, M.B.E., M.C., T.D.

INSURANCE INSTITUTE, CHARTERED (1897), 20 Aldermanbury, E.C.2.—*Sec.*, H. A. L. Cockerell, B.A.

INTERNATIONAL COUNCIL OF NURSES, 1 Dean Trench Street, S.W.1.—*Gen. Sec.*, Miss Helen Nussbaum.

INTERNATIONAL FOLK MUSIC COUNCIL, 35 Princess Court, Queensway, W.2.—*Sec.*, R. W. I. Band.

INTERNATIONAL LAW ASSOCIATION (1873), 3 Paper Buildings, Temple, E.C.4.—*Chairman*, The Lord Spens, K.B.E.; *Sec.-Gen.*, J. B. S. Edwards.

INTERNATIONAL POLICE ASSOCIATION (British Section).—*Sec.-Gen.*, E. C. Loats, 69 St. Anthony's Avenue, Eastbourne, Sussex.

INTERNATIONAL SHIPPING FEDERATION (1909), 146–150 Minories, E.C.3.—*President*, W. L. Denholm, T.D.; *Gen. Manager*, Sir Richard Snedden, C.B.E.; *Sec.*, H. W. Greany, C.B.E.

INTERNATIONAL UNION FOR LAND VALUE TAXATION AND FREE TRADE, 177 Vauxhall Bridge Road, S.W.1.—*Sec.*, V. H. Blundell.

INTERNATIONAL VOLUNTARY SERVICE (1920), 72 Oakley Square, N.W.1.—*Sec.*, F. Judd.

INTER-PARLIAMENTARY UNION. *See* p. 306.

INVALID CHILDREN'S AID ASSOCIATION (LONDON), INCORPORATED (1888), 4 Palace Gate, W.8.—8 area offices covering London, Middlesex, Surrey, Essex and Kent.—*Gen. Sec.*, Miss G. Rattenbury, G.M.

IRISH CHURCH MISSIONS, SOCIETY FOR (1849), 11 Buckingham Street, W.C.2.—*Irish Superintendent*, Rev. G. G. Thomson.

IRISH LINEN MERCHANTS' ASSOCIATION (1872), 7 Donegall Square West, Belfast 1.—*Sec.*, G. A. E. Roberts, O.B.E.

IRISH SOCIETY, THE HONOURABLE THE (1613), Irish Chamber, Guildhall Yard, E.C.2.—*Sec.*, E. H. Shackcloth; *Gen. Agent and Solicitor (Ireland)*, Peter W. Dickson.

IRON AND STEEL INSTITUTE (1869), 4 Grosvenor Gardens, S.W.1.—*Sec.*, K. Headlam-Morley, O.B.E.

JAPAN ASSOCIATION (1950), 54 Old Broad Street, E.C.2.—*Sec.*, H. J. Collar, C.B.E.

JAPAN SOCIETY OF LONDON (1891), 95A Chancery Lane, W.C.2.

JERUSALEM AND THE EAST MISSION (1887), 12 Warwick Square, S.W.1.—*Sec.*, J. B. Wilson.

JEWISH ASSOCIATION FOR THE PROTECTION OF GIRLS, WOMEN AND CHILDREN (administered by the Jewish Board of Guardians) (1885), 74a Charlotte Street, W.1.

JEWISH BOARD OF GUARDIANS (1859), 74A Charlotte Street, W.1.

JEWISH HISTORICAL SOCIETY OF ENGLAND, Mocatta Library, University College, W.C.1.—*Hon. Sec.*, W. M. Schwab, B.A., 33 Seymour Place, W.1.

JEWISH LADS' BRIGADE (1895), Woburn House, Upper Woburn Place, W.C.1.

JEWISH RELIGIOUS EDUCATION, CENTRAL COUNCIL OF, Woburn House, Upper Woburn Place, W.C.1.—*Secs.*, S. Cohen; Miss R. Barnett.

JEWISH YOUTH, ASSOCIATION FOR (1899), 33 Henriques Street, E.1.—*Gen. Sec.*, Michael Goldstein.

JEWS, LONDON SOCIETY FOR PROMOTING CHRISTIANITY AMONGST THE (1809), 16 Lincoln's Inn Fields, W.C.2.—*Secs.*, Rev. W. A. Curtis, B.SC.; Rev. E. F. Yorke, M.A.; Rev. G. H. Stevens, M.Th.

JEWS AND CHRISTIANS, LONDON SOCIETY OF (1927), 28 St. John's Wood Road, N.W.8.—*President*, The Dean of St. Paul's; *Joint Chairmen*, Rabbi Leslie I. Edgar, M.A., D.D.; The Ven. E. F. Carpenter, Ph.D., M.A., D.D.

JOHN INNES INSTITUTE (1910), Bayfordbury, Hertford.—*Director*, K. S. Dodds, Ph.D., D.Sc.

JOHNSON SOCIETY OF LONDON (1928).—*Hon. Sec.*, A. G. Dowdeswell, 92 St. Paul's Road, N.1.

JOINT AIR TRANSPORT COMMITTEE (of the Association of British Chambers of Commerce, Federation of British Industries and London Chamber of Commerce), 69 Cannon Street, E.C.4.—*Chairman*, J. S. Wills.

JOURNALISTS, THE INSTITUTE OF, 2–4 Tudor Street, E.C.4.—*Pres.*, H. H. Hayman; *Gen. Sec.*, R. F. Farmer.

JUSTICES' CLERKS' SOCIETY (1839).—*Hon. Sec.*, E. L. Bradley, 1 Park Road, Parkstone, Poole, Dorset.

KING EDWARD'S HOSPITAL FUND FOR LONDON (1897), 34 King Street, E.C.2.—Founded by King Edward VII. (then Prince of Wales) for the support, benefit or extension of the hospitals of London and incorporated by Act of Parliament in 1907. The Fund's capital amounts to some £9,000,000, the income of which is used for a wide variety of purposes. Since 1948 the Fund has developed its work in many directions, such as the establishment of the Hospital Centre and of training colleges for hospital administrators, matrons, ward sisters and caterers. Grants are made to hospitals for special purposes not covered by the National Health Service. *Chairman of Management Cttee.*, The Lord McCorquodale of Newton, P.C.; *Treas.*, The Lord Ashburton, K.C.V.O.; *Sec.*, R. E. Peers.

KING GEORGE'S FIELDS FOUNDATION (1936), 71 Eccleston Square, S.W.1.—*Chairman*, The Lord Luke, T.D.; *Hon. Sec. and Treas.*, W. W. Shaw-Zambra, C.V.O., C.B.E., T.D.

KING GEORGE'S FUND FOR SAILORS (1917), 1 Chesham Street, S.W.1. (the central fund for the Marine Benevolent Institutions in the United Kingdom). Over £200,000 is given annually to Marine Benevolent Institutions, working for the Royal Navy and Merchant Navy.—*Gen. Sec.*, Capt. S. H. Paton, C.B.E., R.N. (*ret.*).

KING GEORGE'S JUBILEE TRUST, 166 Piccadilly, W.1.—Inaugurated in 1935 in commemoration of the Silver Jubilee of King George V. Its objects are the advancement of the physical, mental and spiritual welfare of the younger generation.—*Sec.*, D. S. Miller, C.B.E.

KING'S FUND, THE (1940), State House, High Holborn, W.C.1.—To give temporary assistance in directions which are beyond the province of State liability to war-disabled members of the Navy, Army, Air Force, Auxiliary Services, Home Guard, Merchant Navy and Civil Defence organizations and to widows, children and other dependants of those who lost their lives through war service.

LABOUR PARTY, Transport House, Smith Square, S.W.1.—*Chairman*, D. H. Davies; *Gen. Sec.*, A. L. Williams.

LADIES IN REDUCED CIRCUMSTANCES, SOCIETY FOR THE ASSISTANCE OF (1886), Lancaster House, Malvern, Worcs.—*Sec.*. A. J. Weller.

LANCASTRIANS IN LONDON, ASSOCIATION OF (1892), 129 Kingsway, W.C.2.—*Hon. Sec.*, W. H. Butler.

LAND AGENTS' SOCIETY, CHARTERED (1902), 21 Lincoln's Inn Fields, W.C.2.—*Pres.* (1962–63), J. F. Croome; *Sec.*, W. H. Clifford.

LAND AND PROPERTY OWNERS, ASSOCIATION OF—*Sec.*, W. R. Gillespie, Abbey House, Victoria Street, S.W.1.

LAND-VALUE TAXATION LEAGUE, 177 Vauxhall Bridge Road, S.W.1.—*Pres.*, V. G. Saldji.

LANDS VALUATION ASSESSORS OF SCOTLAND, ASSOCIATION OF.—*Sec.*, H. B. Sturgeon, Telephone Exchange Building, Kirk Road, Bathgate, W. Lothian.

LAW REPORTING FOR ENGLAND AND WALES, INCORPORATED COUNCIL OF (1865), 3 Stone Buildings, Lincoln's Inn, W.C.2.

LEAGUE OF THE BRITISH COMMONWEALTH AND EMPIRE (Interchange of Teachers) (1901), 124 Belgrave Road, S.W.1.—*Chairman*, Sir Kenneth Bradley, C.M.G.; *Director and Sec.*, V. R. Shaw.

LEAGUE OF THE HELPING HAND, Southwood, Eaton Park, Cobham, Surrey.—*Sec.*, Mrs. J. W. Knight.

LEAGUE OF REMEMBRANCE (1914–45), 32 Great Ormond Street, W.C.1.—*Hon. Administrator*, Mrs. E. H. Gibson, C.B.E.

LEAGUE OF WELLDOERS (incorporated) (1893), 119 & 121 Limekiln Lane, Liverpool, 5.—*Warden and Sec.*, W. J. Horn.

LEATHER AND HIDE TRADES' PROVIDENT AND BENEVOLENT INSTITUTION (1860), 9 St. Thomas Street, S.E.1.—*Sec.*, R. H. Perrin.

LEPER GUILD (St. Francis) (1895), 20 The Boltons, S.W. 10.

LEPERS, THE MISSION TO (1874), 7 Bloomsbury Square, W.C.1.—*Chairman*, Sir Harry Greenfield, C.S.I., C.I.E.; *Gen. Sec.*, Rev. W. H. Russell, B.A.

LEVERHULME RESEARCH AWARDS COMMITTEE (1933), St. Bridget's House, Bridewell Place, E.C.4. Exists to promote research work by senior persons of established position and for the award of post-graduate scholarships for specified purposes abroad.—*Sec.*, Miss M. Branney.

LIBERAL CENTRAL ASSOCIATION, 58 Victoria Street, S.W.1.—*Sec.*, T. D. Nudds.

LIBERAL PARTY ORGANIZATION, 58 Victoria Street, S.W.1.—*Chairman of Executive Committee*, B. Wigoder; *Sec.*, P. W. Kemmis.

LIBERAL PUBLICATION DEPARTMENT (1887), 54 Victoria Street, S.W.1.—*Sec.*, Mrs. E. Hill.

LIBRARY ASSOCIATION (1877), Chaucer House, Malet Place, W.C.1.—*Sec.*, H. D. Barry.

LIFEBOATS. *See* "ROYAL NATIONAL."

LIFE OFFICES' ASSOCIATION, THE (1889), Aldermary House, Queen Street, E.C.4.—*Sec.*, R. W. Boss.

LINGUISTS, INSTITUTE OF (1910), 3 Craven Hill, W.2.—*Sec.*, B. Brook-Partridge.

LINNEAN SOCIETY OF LONDON, Burlington House, W.1.—*Pres.*, Prof. T. M. Harris, F.R.S.; *Treas.*, The Earl of Cranbrook, C.B.E.; *Secs.*, Prof. C. T. Ingold (*Botany*); Dr. H. G. Vevers, M.B.E. (*Zoology*); Dr. J. Smart (*Editorial*); *Gen. Sec.*, T. O'Grady.

LLOYD'S, Lime Street, E.C.3.—*Chairman* (1963), J. N. S. Ridgers; *Deputy Chairman*, R. W. Sturge; *Principal Clerk*, E. F. Phillips. International Insurance Market, Office of *Lloyd's List and Shipping Gazette, Shipping Index, Loading List, etc.*

LLOYD'S PATRIOTIC FUND (1803), Lloyd's Building, 5 Lime Street, E.C.3.—*Sec.*, Miss L. R. Wiggett. (In 1962 the Trustees distributed grants of £18,589 to 820 cases).

LLOYD'S REGISTER OF SHIPPING (1760), 71 Fenchurch Street, E.C.3.—*Chairman*, A. C. Grover; *Deputy Chairman and Chairman of the Sub-Committees of Classification*, R. M. Turnbull; *Deputy Chairman and Treas.*, G. Milling; *Chief Engineer Surveyor*, H. N. Pemberton; *Chief Ship Surveyor*, J. M. Murray, M.B.E., B.SC.; *Chief Executive* (*Administration*), W. J. Ferguson, M.Eng.; *Secretary*, R. B. Nancarrow. Office of *Lloyd's Register Book, Lloyd's Register of Yachts, etc.*

LOCAL AUTHORITIES, INTERNATIONAL UNION OF (1913), British Section, County Hall, S.E.1.—*Sec.*, F. E. Buckle.

LOCAL GOVERNMENT BARRISTERS, SOCIETY OF.—*Hon. Sec.*, J. A. Green, Council Offices, High Street, Bedworth, nr. Nuneaton, Warwicks.

LOCAL GOVERNMENT LEGAL SOCIETY.—*Hon. Sec.*, J. B. Chirnside, County Hall, Oxford.

LOCOMOTIVE ENGINEERS, INSTITUTION OF (1911), Locomotive House, Buckingham Gate, S.W.1.—*Sec. and Editor*, G. T. Hart, B.Sc.

LOMBARD ASSOCIATION (1930), 67 Lombard Street, E.C.3.—*Hon. Sec.*, D. J. Kent.

LONDON AND GREATER LONDON PLAYING FIELDS ASSOCIATION (1925), 38 Denison House, Vauxhall Bridge Road, S.W.1.—*Sec.*, Capt. T. L. Bratt, D.S.C., R.N. (*ret.*).

LONDON APPRECIATION SOCIETY (1932), 8 Scarsdale Villas, Kensington, W.8. Visits to places of historic and modern interest in and around London. Evening lectures.—*Hon. Sec.*, H. L. Bryant Peers.

LONDON BOARD OF CONGREGATIONAL MINISTERS, Memorial Hall, Farringdon Street, E.C.4.—*Chairman*, Rev. D. A. Douglass; *Sec.*, Rev. J. R. Plowman, M.A.

LONDON CITY MISSION (1835), The Mission House, 6 Eccleston Street, S.W.1.—*Sec.*, Rev. Canon C. E. Arnold, M.A.

LONDON CORNISH ASSOCIATION (1898), 48 Burnham Way, Ealing, W.13.—*Hon. Sec.*, J. M. St. Aubyn.

LONDON COURT OF ARBITRATION (1892), 69 Cannon Street, E.C.4.—*Chairman*, C. G. Hayes, C.C.; *Registrar*, J. G. Allanby.

LONDON DIOCESAN COUNCIL FOR MORAL WELFARE, St. Andrew's, St. Andrew Street, E.C.4.—*Org. Sec.*, Miss J. M. L. Watson.

LONDON DIOCESAN FUND AND LONDON DIOCESAN HOME MISSION, 33 Bedford Square, W.C.1.—*Sec.*, Ven. M. M. Hodgins.

LONDON GROUP, THE (Modern Painters and Sculptors).—*President*, Claude Rogers; *Hon. Treas.*, F. T. Nash; *Hon. Sec.*, E. A. Farrell, Stamford House, Blackfriars, S.E.1.

LONDON LABOUR PARTY, Herbert Morrison House, 195–7 Walworth Road, S.E.17.—*Sec.*, P. L. A. Robshaw.

LONDON LIBERAL PARTY, 58 Victoria Street, S.W.1.—*Hon. Sec.*, George B. Patterson.

LONDON LIBRARY, THE (1841), 14 St. James's Square, S.W.1.—*Secretary and Librarian*, S. G. Gillam.

LONDON MISSIONARY SOCIETY (1795), Livingstone House, Carteret Street, S.W.1.—*Gen. Sec.*, Rev. M. O. Janes, B.A., B.D. *Overseas Secs.*, Rev. A. F. Griffiths; Rev. C. Stuart Craig, B.A.; *Home Sec.*, Rev. R. O. Latham, M.A., B.D.; *Sec. for Candidates and Personnel*, Miss M. Cumber; *Financial Sec.*, Austen Spearing.

LONDON MUNICIPAL SOCIETY (1894), Palace Chambers, Bridge Street, S.W.1.—*Sec.*, Miss Phyllis Gelli, M.B.E.

LONDON NATURAL HISTORY SOCIETY (1858).—*Gen. Sec.*, Mrs. L. M. P. Small, 13 Woodfield Crescent, Ealing, W.5.

"LONDON OVER THE BORDER" CHURCH FUND (1878), Guy Harlings, New Street, Chelmsford.—*Sec.*, H. J. Matthews.

LONDON PLAYING FIELDS SOCIETY (1891), 21 Denison House, Vauxhall Bridge Road, S.W.1.

LONDON SOCIETY, THE (1912), 3 Dean's Yard, S.W.1.—*Hon. Sec.*, Miss E. B. Ashford.

LONDON SOLICITORS AND FAMILIES ASSOCIATION (formerly LAW ASSOCIATION) (1817), Maesgwyn, Glaziers Lane, Normandy, Guildford, Surrey.—*Sec.*, Miss K. M. Hugh-Jones.

LONDON SURVEY COMMITTEE (1894), c/o National Buildings Record, Fielden House, 10 Great College Street, S.W.1.

LONDON TOPOGRAPHICAL SOCIETY, 9 Rivercourt Road, W.6.—*Hon. Sec.*, P. D. Whitting, G.M.

LONDON WELSH ASSOCIATION, 157–163 Gray's Inn Road, W.C.1.—*Hon. Sec.*, P. A. Lloyd.

LORD KITCHENER NATIONAL MEMORIAL FUND. *See* p. 535.

LORD MAYOR TRELOAR COLLEGE, Froyle, nr. Alton, Hants.—*Warden*, F. M. Heywood, M.A.; *Sec. and Bursar*, Brig. H. W. Forsyth, C.B.E.

LORD'S DAY OBSERVANCE SOCIETY (1831), 55 Fleet Street, E.C.4.—*Gen. Sec.*, H. J. W. Legerton.

LUSO-BRAZILIAN COUNCIL (1943), Canning House, 2 Belgrave Square, S.W.1.—*Dir.-Gen.*, Sir John Walker, K.C.M.G., O.B.E.

MAGIC CIRCLE (1905), Hearts of Oak Building, Euston Road, N.W.1.—*Sec.*, P. Newcombe.

MAGISTRATES' ASSOCIATION (1920), Tavistock House South, Tavistock Square, W.C.1.—*Pres.*, The Lord Chancellor; *Sec.*, J. F. Madden.

MALAYAN COMMERCIAL ASSOCIATION OF GREAT BRITAIN INC. (1955), 54 Old Broad Street, E.C.2.—*Sec.*, W. C. S. Corry, C.B.E.

MALONE SOCIETY (for the study of Early English Drama).—*Hon. Sec.*, Miss K. M. Lea, Lady Margaret Hall. Oxford.

MANAGEMENT, BRITISH INSTITUTE OF, 80 Fetter Lane, E.C.4.—*Dir.*, John Marsh.

MARINE ARTISTS, SOCIETY OF, 6½ Suffolk Street, S.W.1.—*Pres.*, C. Muncaster, R.W.S., R.O.I., R.B.A.; *Sec.*, M. B. Bradshaw.

MARINE BIOLOGICAL ASSOCIATION OF THE U.K. (1884), The Laboratory, Citadel Hill, Plymouth.—*Sec. to Council and Director of Plymouth Laboratory*, F. S. Russell, C.B.E., D.S.C., D.F.C., D.Sc., LL.D., F.R.S.

MARINE ENGINEERS, INSTITUTE OF (1889), Memorial Building, 76 Mark Lane, E.C.3.—*Sec.*, J. Stuart Robinson, M.A.

MARINE SOCIETY (1756), Hanway House, Clark's Place, E.C.2. Ensures as far as possible that no boy is prevented by lack of means from going to sea in the capacity for which he is suited. Advice on training and entry of boys for the sea services.

MARKET AUTHORITIES, NATIONAL ASSOCIATION OF BRITISH, Markets Dept., Blackburn, Lancs.

MARKETING AND SALES MANAGEMENT, INSTITUTE OF (1911), Marketing House, Richbell Place, Lamb's Conduit Street, W.C.1.—*Sec.*, D. A. Chatt.

MARKET RESEARCH SOCIETY (1947), 39 Hertford Street, W.1.—*Hon. Sec.-Treas.*, L. H. Owens.

MARK MASTER MASONS, GRAND LODGE OF (1856), Mark Masons' Hall, 40 Upper Brook Street, W.1.—*Grand Master*, The Lord Harris, M.C.; *Deputy Grand Master*, Maj. R. L. Loyd, O.B.E., M.C.; *Grand Sec.*, Lt.-Col. J. W. Chitty, M.B.E.

MASONIC BENEVOLENT INSTITUTION, ROYAL (1842), 20 Great Queen Street, W.C.2.—*Sec.*, Sqn. Ldr. D. A. Lloyd, D.F.C., D.F.M.

MASONIC BENEVOLENT INSTITUTIONS IN IRELAND; *Masonic Girls' School* (1792); *Masonic Boys' School* (1867); *Victoria Jubilee Masonic Annuity Fund* (1887).—*Sec.*, D. S. Hope, 19 Molesworth Street, Dublin, 2.

MASONIC DEGREES—ORDER OF THE TEMPLE, Mark Masons' Hall, 40 Upper Brook Street, W.1.—*Grand Master*, The Lord Harris, M.C.; *Great Vice-Chancellor*, Lt.-Col. J. W. Chitty, M.B.E.

MASONIC INSTITUTION FOR BOYS, ROYAL (Incorporated) (1798).—*Sec.*, Col. H. J. Jones, T.D., 26 Great Queen Street, W.C.2.

MASONIC INSTITUTION FOR GIRLS, ROYAL (1788). *Schools*, Rickmansworth and Weybridge; *Offices*, 31 Great Queen Street, W.C.2.—*Sec.*, Dennis Haines, F.C.A.

MASTER BUILDERS, FEDERATION OF (1941), 33 John Street, W.C.1.—*Sec.*, L. B. Venning.

MASTERS OF FOXHOUNDS ASSOCIATION (1856), 51 Victoria Street, S.W.1.—*Hon. Sec.*, Lt.-Col. J. E. S. Chamberlayne.

MATERNAL AND CHILD WELFARE, NATIONAL ASSOCIATION FOR (1911), Tavistock House, North, Tavistock Square, W.C.1.—*Sec.*, Miss D. Hall.

MATHEMATICAL ASSOCIATION (1871).—*Pres.*, Prof. J. B. Morgan; *Hon. Sec.*, F. W. Kellaway, B.Sc., 87 Pixmore Way, Letchworth, Herts.

MATHEMATICAL SOCIETY, LONDON (1865), Burlington House, W.1.—*Hon. Secs.*, S. J. Taylor, Ph.D.; J. A. Todd, Ph.D., F.R.S.

MECHANICAL ENGINEERS, INSTITUTION OF, 1 Birdcage Walk, S.W.1.—*Pres.*, R. C. Bond; *Sec.*, K. H. Platt, M.B.E.

MEDICAL AUXILIARIES, THE BOARD OF REGISTRATION OF (1936), Tavistock House (North), Tavistock Square, W.C.1.—*Sec. and Registrar*, A. E. Vince.

MEDICAL OFFICERS OF HEALTH, SOCIETY OF (1856), Tavistock House South, W.C.1.—*Pres.*, H. M. Cohen; *Medical Sec.*, J. C. Hamilton.

MEDICAL OFFICERS OF HEALTH, GROUP AND ASSOCIATION OF COUNTY (England and Wales).—*Hon. Sec.*, G. Ramage, M.D., County Health Dept., Martin Street, Stafford.

MEDICAL SOCIETY OF LONDON (1773), 11 Chandos Street, Cavendish Square, W.1.—*Pres.*, A. L. Wingfield, M.D., F.R.C.S.; *Hon Sec.*, H. H. G. Eastcott, F.R.C.S.; *Registrar*, E. J. Tucker.

MEDICAL WOMEN'S FEDERATION (1917), Tavistock House (North), Tavistock Square, W.C.1.—*Pres.*, Dorothy McNair, M.D.; *Sec.*, Miss I. McCartan.

MEDICO-LEGAL SOCIETY (1901),—*Sec.*, J. P. Beaven, 40 Carey Street, Lincoln's Inn, W.C.2.

MEDICO-PSYCHOLOGICAL ASSOCIATION, ROYAL (1841), 11 Chandos Street, W.1.—*Hon. Gen. Sec.*, A. B. Monro, M.D., Ph.D.

MEN OF THE TREES SOCIETY (1922), Stansted Park Estate Office, Rowlands Castle, Hants.—*Sec.*, W. C. Browning.

MENTAL AFTER CARE ASSOCIATION, for the care and rehabilitation of those recovering from mental illness, 110 Jermyn Street, S.W.1.—*Sec.*, Mrs. E. Clifton.

MENTAL HEALTH, NATIONAL ASSOCIATION FOR, 39 Queen Anne Street, W.1.—*Gen. Sec.*, Miss M. Applebey, O.B.E.

MERCANTILE MARINE MASTERS AND OFFICERS BENEVOLENT FUND, Shipping Federation House, 146 Minories, E.C.3.—*Sec.*, Miss A. B. Talbot.

MERCANTILE MARINE SERVICE ASSOCIATION (1857) (Shipmasters in command), with which is amalgamated THE IMPERIAL MERCHANT SERVICE GUILD. Affiliated to the Officers (Merchant Navy) Federation. 6 Rumford Place, Liverpool.—*Gen. Sec.*, W. L. S. Harrison; *London Office*, 133 Whitechapel High Street, E.1.

MERCHANT NAVY RESIDENTIAL CLUBS AND CANTEENS (BRITISH SAILORS SOCIETY). Mariners' Hotel, 680 Commercial Road, E.14; Empire Residential Club, 747 Commercial Road, E.14. —*Gen. Sec.*, Stanley Heesom, O.B.E.

MERCHANT NAVY WELFARE BOARD (1948), 19 Lancaster Gate, W.2.—*Sec.*, R. E. Haerle.

MERSEY MISSION TO SEAMEN (1857). *Headquarters and Registered Office*, Kingston House, James Street, Liverpool 2. *Other Clubs*, Merchant Navy House, Liverpool; Pakistani and Indian Seamen's Clubs at Bootle and Birkenhead. *Gen. Sec.*, L. M. Robertson.

METALLURGISTS, THE INSTITUTION OF, 4 Grosvenor Gardens, S.W.1.—*Registrar-Secretary*, R. G. S. Ludlam.

METALS, INSTITUTE OF (1908), 17 Belgrave Square, S.W.1.—*Pres.*, Prof. H. Ford; *Sec.*, R. E. Moore.

METEOROLOGICAL SOCIETY, ROYAL (1850), 49 Cromwell Road, S.W.7.—*Pres.*, J. S. Sawyer, F.R.S.; *Hon. Secs.*, R. C. Frith, O.B.E., Ph.D.; F. H. Ludlam, D.Sc.

METHODIST MISSIONARY SOCIETY (1786), 25 Marylebone Road, N.W.1.—*Secs.*, Rev. D. W. Thompson; Rev. D. B. Childe; Rev. R. W. Pile, B.D.; Rev. P. A. Potter, M.Th.; *Med. Sec.*, Dr. T. F. Davey, C.B.E.; *Secs. for Women's Work*, Miss M. Stennett, B.A.; Mrs. L. R. M. Bingle, M.A.; Miss M. R. Anstey. Income, 1962, £1,750,363.

METROPOLITAN AND CITY POLICE ORPHANS FUND (1871), 30 Hazlewell Road, Putney, S.W.15—*Sec.*, E. R. Hall.

METROPOLITAN BOROUGHS' STANDING JOINT COMMITTEE (1912).—*Hon. Clerk*, A. G. Dawtry, M.B.E., T.D., LL.B. (Town Clerk of Westminster).

METROPOLITAN DRINKING FOUNTAIN AND CATTLE TROUGH ASSOCIATION (1859), 426 Lewisham High Street, S.E.13.—*Sec.*, Capt. J. M. Rymer-Jones, C.B.E., M.C.

METROPOLITAN HOSPITAL-SUNDAY FUND (1872), Mansion House, E.C., and 18 Queen Victoria Street, E.C.4. In 1962, £23,700 was distributed as maintenance grants and grants for specific purposes to Hospitals and Homes not controlled by the State; £15,600 for almoners at State hospitals to meet needs of patients not covered by the State services; £2,750 to Mental Hospitals for similar purposes; £1,000 to District Nursing Associations in London and £2,700 to other charities for the sick.—*Sec.*, Miss V. A. Miles.

METROPOLITAN PUBLIC GARDENS ASSOCIATION (1882), 58 Denison House, 296 Vauxhall Bridge Road, S.W.1.

MIDWIVES, ROYAL COLLEGE OF (1881), 15 Mansfield Street, W.1.—*Gen. Sec.*, Miss A. Wood.

MILITARY HISTORICAL SOCIETY.—*Hon. Sec.*, W. J. Steeple, Duke of York's Headquarters, Chelsea, S.W.3.

MINERALOGICAL SOCIETY (1876).—*Pres.*, Prof. L. R. Wager, M.A., SC.D., F.R.S.; *Hon. Gen. Sec.*, J. R. Butler, M.A., Ph.D., 41 Queen's Gate, S.W.7.

MINIATURE PAINTERS, SCULPTORS AND GRAVERS, ROYAL SOCIETY OF (1895), 6½ Suffolk Street, S.W.1.—*Pres.*, S. Shepherd, O.B.E.; *Sec.*, M. Bradshaw.

MINIATURISTS, SOCIETY OF (1895), 195 Piccadilly, W.1.—*Pres.*, Ernest Lloyd; *Sec.*, Reginald Blackmore.

MINING AND METALLURGY, INSTITUTION OF (1892), 44 Portland Place, W.1.—*Pres.*, Prof. K. C. Dunham, F.R.S.; *Sec.*, B. W. Kerrigan.

MINING ENGINEERS, THE INSTITUTION OF (1889), 3 Grosvenor Crescent, S.W.1.—*Pres.* (1963–64), F. G. Glossop, O.B.E.; *Sec.*, J. McDermid.

MINING INSTITUTE OF SCOTLAND, Royal College of Science and Technology, Glasgow.—*Sec.*, M. W. Bryce.

MISSIONARY SOCIETIES (*see* individual titles).

MISSIONS TO SEAMEN, THE, AND ST. ANDREW'S WATERSIDE CHURCH MISSION FOR SAILORS, 4 Buckingham Palace Gardens, S.W.1.—*Gen. Sec.*, Rev. Preb. C. J. Brown, O.B.E., M.A., Q.H.C.

MODERN CHURCHMEN'S UNION (1898), for the Advancement of Liberal Religious Thought—*Pres.*, The Bishop of Birmingham; *Hon. Sec.*, Rev. F. E. Compton, Caynham Vicarage, Ludlow, Salop.

MODERN LANGUAGE ASSOCIATION, 2 Manchester Square, W.1.—*Hon. Sec.*, W. L. Presswood.

MORAVIAN MISSIONS, LONDON ASSOCIATION IN AID OF (1817), 32 Great Ormond Street, W.C.1. —*Hon. Sec.*, Mrs. D. E. Hughes.

MORDEN COLLEGE (1695), Blackheath, S.E.3. *Clerk to the Trustees*, M. S. Graham.

(WILLIAM) MORRIS SOCIETY (1955).—*Hon. Sec.*, R. C. H. Briggs, 260 Sandycombe Road, Kew, Surrey.

MOTOR INDUSTRY, THE INSTITUTE OF THE (1920), Fanshaws, Brickendon, Herts.—*Sec.*, E. V. Tipper.

MULTIPLE SCLEROSIS SOCIETY, 10 Stratford Road, W.8.—*Sec.*, Capt. L. E. Porter, R.N.

MUNICIPAL CORPORATIONS, ASSOCIATION OF (1873), Victoria Station House, Victoria Street, S.W.1.—*Sec.*, J. C. Swaffield.

MUNICIPAL ENGINEERS, INSTITUTION OF (1873), 25 Eccleston Square, S.W.1.—*Sec.*, A. Banister, O.B.E., B.Sc.

MUNICIPAL TREASURERS AND ACCOUNTANTS, INSTITUTE OF (1885).—*Sec.*, L. F. Cheyney, O.B.E., 1 Buckingham Place, S.W.1.

MUSEUMS ASSOCIATION (1889), 87 Charlotte Street, W.1.—*Sec.*, P. James, C.B.E.

MUSICIANS' BENEVOLENT FUND, St. Cecilia's House, 7 Carlos Place, W.1. *Convalescent Home*, Westgate-on-Sea.—*Gen. Sec.*, D. Gowing.

MUSICIANS, INCORPORATED SOCIETY OF (1882), 48 Gloucester Place, W.1.—*Gen. Sec.*, D. H. R. Brearley.

MUSICIANS OF GREAT BRITAIN, ROYAL SOCIETY OF (1738), 10 Stratford Place, W.1.—*Hon. Treas.*, E. Cruft, M.V.O., O.B.E.

MUSIC SCHOOLS ASSOCIATION, RURAL, Little Benslow Hills, Hitchin, Herts.—*Director*, Miss H. Wright.

MUSIC SOCIETIES, NATIONAL FEDERATION OF (1935), 4 St. James's Square, S.W.1.—*Sec.*, Capt. T. A. K. Maunsell, R.N. (*ret.*).

MUTUAL HOUSEHOLDS ASSOCIATION LTD., 23 Haymarket, S.W.1.—*Sec.*, Miss J. Moore.

MYCOLOGICAL SOCIETY, BRITISH.—*Sec.*, R. C. F. Macer, Ph.D., Plant Breeding Institute, Cambridge.

NATIONAL ADULT SCHOOL UNION (1899), 35 Queen Anne Street, W.1.—*Gen. Sec.*, W. Arnold Hall, B.A., B.D.

NATIONAL ALLIANCE OF PRIVATE TRADERS (1943), 388 Corn Exchange, Hanging Ditch, Manchester 4.

NATIONAL AND LOCAL GOVERNMENT OFFICERS ASSOCIATION (NALGO) (1905), Nalgo House, 8 Harewood Row, N.W.1.—*Gen. Sec.*, W. C. Anderson.

NATIONAL AND UNIVERSITY LIBRARIES, STANDING CONFERENCE OF (1950).—*Hon. Sec.*, K. W. Humphreys, c/o The Library, The University, Edgbaston, Birmingham, 15.

NATIONAL ASSOCIATION OF FIRE OFFICERS, 5–6 Palace Chambers, Bridge Street, S.W.1.—*Gen. Sec.*, J. Camp.

NATIONAL ASSOCIATION OF PARISH COUNCILS (1947), 99 Great Russell Street, W.C.1.—*Sec.*, C. Arnold-Baker.

NATIONAL ASSOCIATION OF TRAINING CORPS FOR GIRLS (1942), Portland Chambers, 93 Great Titchfield Street, W.1.—Girls' Training Corps; Women's Junior Air Corps; Girls' Nautical Training Corps.

NATIONAL BENEVOLENT INSTITUTION (1812), 61 Bayswater Road, W.2.

NATIONAL BIRTHDAY TRUST FUND (1928), 57 Lower Belgrave Street, S.W.1. For Extension of Maternity Services.—*Sec.*, Miss D. V. Riddick, M.B.E.

NATIONAL BOOK LEAGUE (1944), 7 Albemarle Street, W.1.—*Dir. and Sec.*, J. E. Morpurgo.

NATIONAL BUILDINGS RECORD (1941), Fielden House, 10 Great College Street, S.W.1. —*Sec.*, Cecil Farthing, B.A., F.S.A.

NATIONAL CATTLE BREEDERS' ASSOCIATION, 32 Friar Street, Reading.—*Sec.*, W. G. Turpitt, M.B.E.

NATIONAL CHILDREN'S HOME (1869). *Chief Office*, Highbury Park, N.5.—*Principal*, Rev. John W. Waterhouse, O.B.E.; *Sec.*, T. O. Buck, B.com.

NATIONAL CORPORATION FOR THE CARE OF OLD PEOPLE, Nuffield Lodge, Regent's Park, N.W.1. —*Sec.*, M. R. F. Simson.

NATIONAL COUNCIL OF LABOUR COLLEGES, Tillicoultry, Clackmannanshire, Scotland.—*Gen. Sec.*, J. P. M. Millar.

NATIONAL COUNCIL OF WOMEN OF GREAT BRITAIN, 36 Lower Sloane Street, S.W.1.—*Sec.*, Mrs. Celia Gimpel, B.A.

NATIONAL FEDERATION OF OLD AGE PENSIONS ASSOCIATIONS, 15 Blakey Moor, Blackburn, Lancs.—*Sec.*, E. Melling.

NATIONAL FEDERATION OF YOUNG FARMERS' CLUBS (1,436 Clubs with 61,053 members), 55 Gower Street, W.C.1.—*Sec.*, K. R. Savage.

NATIONAL LIBERAL COUNCIL, 183–184 Palace Chambers, Bridge Street, S.W.1.—*Pres.*, Rt. Hon. J. S. Maclay, C.H., C.M.G., M.P.; *Chairman*, Gershom Stewart, C.B.E.; *Sec.*, J. Cherry.

NATIONAL MARITIME BOARD (1919), Portsoken House, Minories, E.C.3.—*Clerk in Charge*, Miss J. Neville.

NATIONAL MARKET TRADERS' FEDERATION (1899).—*Pres.*, A. Pether; *Gen. Sec.*, J. Coates, 87 Spital Hill, Sheffield, 4.

NATIONAL MARRIAGE GUIDANCE COUNCIL, 58 Queen Anne Street, W.1.—*Gen. Sec.*, A. J. Brayshaw.

NATIONAL PEACE COUNCIL (1908), 29 Great James Street, W.C.1.—*Gen. Sec.*, G. Delf.

NATIONAL SECULAR SOCIETY (1866), 103 Borough High Street, S.E.1.—*Sec.*, Colin McCall.

NATIONAL SOCIETY FOR CLEAN AIR (1899), Field House, Breams Buildings, E.C.4.—*Director*, Arnold Marsh, O.B.E.

NATIONAL SOCIETY FOR PROMOTING RELIGIOUS EDUCATION IN ACCORDANCE WITH THE PRINCIPLES OF THE CHURCH OF ENGLAND (1811), 69 Great Peter Street, S.W.1.—*Gen. Sec.*, Rev. Canon E. Wild, M.A.

NATIONAL SOCIETY FOR THE PREVENTION OF CRUELTY TO CHILDREN (1884) (Incorporated), *Central Office*, Victory House, Leicester Square, W.C.2.—*Chairman*, The Dowager Viscountess Hambleden, D.C.V.O.; *Treas.*, G. Edmiston; *Director*, Rev. Arthur Morton, O.B.E.

NATIONAL SUNDAY SCHOOL UNION.—*Headquarters*, Central Hall Buildings, Durnsford Road, S.W.19. (*Publication Dept.*, 104–105 Newgate Street, E.C.1.)

NATIONAL TRUST for places of Historic Interest or Natural Beauty (1895), 42 Queen Anne's Gate, S.W.1.—*Sec.*, J. F. W. Rathbone.

NATIONAL TRUST FOR SCOTLAND for places of historic interest or natural beauty (1931). 5 Charlotte Square, Edinburgh 2.—*Sec. and Treas.*, J. C. Stormonth Darling, M.C., W.S.

NATIONAL UNION OF STUDENTS, 3 Endsleigh Street, W.C.1.—*Chief Administration Officer*, H. P. Wetherell, M.B.E.

NATIONAL WOMEN CITIZENS' ASSOCIATION (1917), Incorporating the National Council for Equal Citizenship and Women for Westminster, 33 Denison House, 296 Vauxhall Bridge Road, S.W.1.—*Pres.*, Mrs. J. V. S. Petrie.

NATION'S FUND FOR NURSES, 21 Cavendish Square, W.1.—*Sec.*, Mrs. M. Wynne Williams.

NATURALISTS' ASSOCIATION, YOUNG.—*Gen. Sec.*, D. H. Smith, 22 Welton Road, Brough, Yorks.

NATURE CONSERVATION, BRITISH COMMITTEE FOR INTERNATIONAL (1949) c/o The Council for Nature, 41 Queen's Gate, S.W.7.—*Hon. Sec.*, D. J. B. Copp.

NATURE, COUNCIL FOR (1958), 41 Queen's Gate, S.W.7.—*Gen. Sec.*, D. J. B. Copp.

NATURE RESERVES, SOCIETY FOR PROMOTION OF (1912).—*Hon. Sec.*, N. D. Riley, C.B.E., c/o British Museum (Nat. Hist.), S.W.7.

NAUTICAL RESEARCH, SOCIETY FOR (1911), National Maritime Museum, Greenwich, S.E.10.—*Hon. Sec.*, G. P. B. Naish.

NAVAL, MILITARY AND AIR FORCE BIBLE SOCIETY (1780), Radstock House, Eccleston Street, S.W.1. Copies and portions of the Scriptures circulated to the Forces (1962), 185,363.—*Joint Secs.*, J. Mighell Smith; T. Wales.

NAVAL ARCHITECTS, ROYAL INSTITUTION OF (1860), 10 Upper Belgrave Street, S.W.1.—*Sec.*, L. A. Tiltman.

NAVIGATION, INSTITUTE OF, c/o Royal Geographical Society, 1 Kensington Gore, S.W.7.—*Sec.*, M. W. Richey.

NAVY LEAGUE (INC.) (1895), Grand Buildings, Trafalgar Square, W.C.2.—*Pres.*, The Earl Granville, M.C.; *Gen. Sec.*, H. T. Bishop, O.B.E.

NAVY RECORDS SOCIETY, Royal Naval College, Greenwich, S.E.10.—*Hon. Sec.*, Hon. D. Erskine.

NEWCOMEN SOCIETY (1920), for the Study of the History of Engineering and Technology, Science Museum, S.W.7.—*Hon. Sec.*, K. R. Gilbert.

NEW EDUCATION FELLOWSHIP (1915), *International Headquarters*, 55 Upper Stone Street, Tunbridge Wells, Kent.

NEW ENGLISH ART CLUB (1886), 6½ Suffolk Street, S.W.1.—*Hon. Sec.*, V. Lines; *Hon. Treas.*, G. Charlton; *Sec.*, M. B. Bradshaw.

NEWMAN ASSOCIATION (1942), *National Office and Newman International Centre*, 31 Portman Square, W.1.

NEWSPAPER EDITORS, GUILD OF BRITISH (1946), Whitefriars House, Carmelite Street, E.C.4.—*Pres.*, K. Loveland (*S. Wales Argus, Newport*); *Sec.-Treas.*, W. G. Ridd, M.V.O.

NEWSPAPER PRESS FUND (1864), Bouverie House, Fleet Street, E.C.4.—*Pres.*, Colonel the Lord Astor of Hever; *Sec.*, S. C. Reynolds.

NEWSPAPER PROPRIETORS ASSOCIATION (1906), 8 Bouverie Street, E.C.4.—*Joint Secs.*, Bernard Alton, M.V.O.; J. L. Wade.

NEWSPAPER SOCIETY (1836), Whitefriars House, Carmelite Street, E.C.4.—*Pres.*, K. M. Whitworth (*Provincial Newspapers Ltd.*); *Gen. Sec.*, W. G. Ridd, M.V.O.

NEWSVENDORS' BENEVOLENT INSTITUTION (1839), Memorial Hall Buildings, Farringdon Street, E.C.4.—*Sec.*, J. E. Llewellyn-Jones.

NEW WALES UNION, THE (Undeb Cymru Fydd) (1941), 24 Ffordd y Môr, Aberystwyth.—*Hon. Sec.*, T. I. Ellis, M.A.

NOISE ABATEMENT SOCIETY, 6 Old Bond Street, W.1.—*Hon. Sec.*, John Connell.

NORE R.N. AND R.M. CHILDREN'S TRUST (formerly R.N. and R.M. Children's Home, The Nore, Gillingham), H.M.S. *Pembroke*, Chatham.—*Sec.*, Lieut. E. W. Waters, R.N. (*ret.*).

NORTHERN IRELAND TOURIST BOARD, 6 and 10 Royal Avenue, Belfast 1.—*Gen. Manager*, R. J. Frizzell, O.B.E., B.A.

NORTHUMBERLAND AND DURHAM ASSOCIATION IN LONDON (1920).—*Hon. Sec.*, J. V. Witherspoon, 20 Argyle Road, West Ealing, W.13.

NORWOOD HOME FOR JEWISH CHILDREN (Jewish Orphanage) (1795), Knights Hill, West Norwood, S.E.27.—*Sec.* M. Finlay.

NUFFIELD CENTRE FOR FORCES OF THE CROWN (1943), 8 Adelaide Street, W.C.2.—*Sec.*, Miss Mary Cook.

NUFFIELD FOUNDATION (1943), Nuffield Lodge, Regent's Park, N.W.1.—*Dir.*, L. Farrer-Brown, C.B.E.

NUFFIELD PROVINCIAL HOSPITALS TRUST (1939), 3 Prince Albert Road, N.W.1.—*Sec. to Governing Trustees*, G. McLachlan.

NUMISMATIC SOCIETY, BRITISH.—*Hon. Sec.*, W. Slater, 63 West Way, Edgware, Middx.

NUMISMATIC SOCIETY, ROYAL, c/o Dept. of Coins and Medals, The British Museum, W.C.1.—*Pres.* P. Grierson, F.B.A., F.S.A.; *Hon. Sec.*, John Walker, C.B.E., D.Litt., F.B.A., F.S.A.

NURSERY SCHOOL ASSOCIATION OF GT. BRITAIN AND N. IRELAND, 89 Stamford Street, S.E.1.—*Sec.*, Miss D. E. Warren.

NURSES', ELDERLY, NATIONAL HOME FUND, The Home, Riverside Avenue, Holdenhurst, Bournemouth.—*Hon. Sec.*, J. A. Haley.

NURSES, ROYAL NATIONAL PENSION FUND FOR, 15 Buckingham Street, W.C.2.—*Manager and Actuary*, C. M. O'Brien, M.A.

NUTRITION SOCIETY (1941).—*Hon. Sec.*, Miss D. F. Hollingworth, c/o Ministry of Agriculture, Fisheries and Food, Great Westminster House, Horseferry Road, S.W.1.

OBSTETRICIANS AND GYNAECOLOGISTS, ROYAL COLLEGE OF (1929), 27 Sussex Place, Regent's Park, N.W.1.—*Pres.*, H. R. MacLennan.

OCEANOGRAPHY, NATIONAL INSTITUTE OF (1949), Wormley, Godalming, Surrey.—*Dir.*, G. E. R. Deacon, C.B.E., D.SC., F.R.S., F.R.S.E.

OFFICE MANAGEMENT, INSTITUTE OF (1915), 167 Victoria Street, S.W.1.—*Sec.*, J. L. Cousins.

OFFICERS' ASSOCIATION, THE (OFFICERS' BENEVOLENT DEPARTMENT OF THE BRITISH LEGION) (1920), 28 Belgrave Square, S.W.1. Affords relief and assistance to ex-officers, their widows and dependants.—*Gen. Sec.*, Maj.-Gen. Sir Peter St. Clair-Ford, K.B.E., C.B., D.S.O.

OFFICERS' FAMILIES FUND (1899), 27 Queen Anne's Gate, S.W.1.—*Sec.*, Miss Mary Gold.

OFFICERS (MERCHANT NAVY) FEDERATION (1928), Oceanair House, 133–137 Whitechapel High Street, E.1.—*Joint Gen. Managers*, D. S. Tennant, C.B.E.; W. L. S. Harrison; *Sec.*, D. Carmichael, M.B.E.

OFFICERS' PENSIONS SOCIETY, LTD., 171 Victoria Street, S.W.1.—*Gen. Sec.*, Capt. P. C. Bullock, O.B.E.

OIL PAINTERS, ROYAL INSTITUTE OF (1883), 195 Piccadilly, W.1.—*Pres.*, Iain Macnab, R.E.; *Treas.*, Clifford Hall; *Sec.*, Reginald Blackmore.

OLYMPIC ASSOCIATION, BRITISH (1906), 95 Mount Street, W.1.—*Sec.*, K. S. Duncan, M.B.E.

OPEN-AIR MISSION (1853), 19 John Street, Bedford Row, W.C.1.—*Sec.*, Ernest W. Jealous.

ORDERS AND MEDALS RESEARCH SOCIETY (1942)—*Hon. Sec.*, G. E. Lundberg, 49 Brooke Avenue, S. Harrow, Middx.

ORIENTAL CERAMIC SOCIETY (1921), 31B Torrington Square, W.C.1.—*Sec.*, Lt.-Col. J. D. Gage-Brown.

ORNITHOLOGISTS' CLUB, THE SCOTTISH, 21 Regent Terrace, Edinburgh.—*Sec.*, Mrs. George Waterston.

ORNITHOLOGISTS' UNION, BRITISH, c/o Bird Room, British Museum (Nat. History), Cromwell Road, S.W.7.—*Hon. Sec.*, Sir Hugh Elliott, Bt., O.B.E.

ORNITHOLOGY, BRITISH TRUST FOR (1932), Beech Grove, Tring, Herts.—*Sec.*, D. Wilson.

ORNITHOLOGY, FIELD, THE EDWARD GREY INSTITUTE OF (1938), Botanic Garden, Oxford.—*Director*, David Lack, F.R.S.

ORTHOPÆDIC ASSOCIATION, BRITISH (1918), c/o Royal College of Surgeons, Lincoln's Inn Fields, W.C.2.—*Hon. Sec.*, T. J. Fairbank, F.R.C.S.

OSTEOPATHS, GENERAL COUNCIL AND REGISTER OF (1937), 16 Buckingham Gate, S.W.1.—*Registrar*, R. F. Miller.

OUTWARD BOUND TRUST, 123 Victoria Street, S.W.1. Administers six schools for character-training through sea and mountain adventure at Aberdovey, Wales, Eskdale and Ullswater, Cumberland, Burghead, Morayshire and Ashburton, Devon (boys) and Towyn (girls).—*Dir.*, E. W. Dawson.

OVER-SEAS LEAGUE, ROYAL (1910), Over-Seas House, Park Place, St. James's Street, S.W.1.—*Dir.-General*, P. Crawshaw, C.B.E.

OWNERS OF CITY PROPERTIES, ASSOCIATED.—*Sec.*, W. R. Gillespie, 238 Abbey House, Victoria Street, S.W.1.

OXFORD AND CAMBRIDGE SCHOOLS EXAMINATION BOARD (1873). *Offices*, 10 Trumpington Street, Cambridge and Elsfield Way, Oxford.—*Secs.*, G. J. R. Potter, M.A., Oxford; A. E. E. McKenzie, M.A., Cambridge.

OXFORD PRESERVATION TRUST (1927).—*Sec.*, I. L. Phillips, C.B.E., Painted Room, 3 Cornmarket Street, Oxford; *Treas.*, Barclays Bank, High Street, Oxford.

OXFORD SOCIETY (1932), 18 Museum Road, Oxford.—*Sec.*, Mrs. D. M. Lennie.

OYSTER MERCHANTS' AND PLANTERS' ASSOCIATION, Fishmongers' Hall, E.C.4.—*Hon. Sec.*, J. S. Barclay, T.D.

PAINTER-ETCHERS AND ENGRAVERS, ROYAL SOCIETY OF (1880), 26 Conduit Street, W.1.—*Pres.*, R. S. Austin, R.A.; *Sec.*, M. Fry.

PAINTERS IN WATER COLOURS, ROYAL INSTITUTE OF (1831), 195 Piccadilly, W.1.—*Pres.*, Norman Wilkinson, C.B.E.; *Treas.*, A. Sykes; *Sec.*, Reginald Blackmore.

PAINTERS IN WATER COLOURS, ROYAL SOCIETY OF (1804), 26 Conduit Street, W.1.—*Pres.*, R. Austin, R.A.; *Sec. and Curator*, Malcolm Fry, F.R.S.A.

PAINTERS, SCULPTORS AND ENGRAVERS, NATIONAL SOCIETY OF (1930), 195 Piccadilly, W.1.—*Pres.*, Stanley Grimm, R.O.I., R.P.; *Sec.*, Reginald Blackmore.

PALÆONTOGRAPHICAL SOCIETY (1847), Burlington House, W.1.—*Sec.*, J. D. D. Smith, B.SC.

PALESTINE EXPLORATION FUND (1865), 2 Hinde Mews, Marylebone Lane, W.1.—*Chairman*, Rev. Canon C. B. Mortlock, F.S.A.

PARENTS' NATIONAL EDUCATIONAL UNION, P.N.E.U. (1888), Murray House, Vandon Street, S.W.1.—*Gen. Sec.*, Miss W. J. Denham, O.B.E.

PARLIAMENTARY AND SCIENTIFIC COMMITTEE.—*Sec.*, Lt.-Cdr. C. Powell, 7 Buckingham Gate, S.W.1.

PARLIAMENTARY LABOUR PARTY.—*Chairman and Leader*, Rt. Hon. J. H. Wilson, O.B.E., M.P.; *Vice-Chairman and Deputy Leader*, Rt. Hon. G. A. Brown, M.P.; *Chief Whip*, H. W. Bowden, C.B.E., M.P.; *Leader of Labour Peers*, The Earl Alexander of Hillsborough, P.C., C.H.; *Sec.*, F. H. Barlow.

PASTEL SOCIETY (1899), 195 Piccadilly, W.1.—*Pres.*, James Grant; *Sec.*, Reginald Blackmore.

PASTORAL PSYCHOLOGY, GUILD OF (1936), 25 Porchester Terrace, W.2.—*Hon. Sec.*, Mrs. W. Young.

PATENT AGENTS, CHARTERED INSTITUTE OF (1882), Staple Inn Buildings, W.C.1.—*Sec.*, P. E. Lincroft, M.B.E.

PATENTEES AND INVENTORS, INSTITUTE OF (1919), 207–208 Abbey House, Victoria Street, S.W.1.—*Gen. Sec.* (vacant).

PEACE SOCIETY, INTERNATIONAL (1816), Fellowship House, Browning Street, S.E.17. (*Continental Offices*, 5 rue Charles Bonnet, Geneva).—*Director and Sec.*, Rev. H. Rathbone Dunnico, LL.D.

PEDESTRIANS' ASSOCIATION FOR ROAD SAFETY, 4 College Hill, E.C.4.—*Sec.*, D. A. Wright.

P.E.N., INTERNATIONAL (1921), 62–3 Glebe Place, S.W.3. World association of writers.—*Gen. Sec.*, D. Carver.

PENSION FUNDS, NATIONAL ASSOCIATION OF (1923).—*Sec.*, F. B. Davis, Bank Chambers, 329 High Holborn, W.C.1.

PEOPLE'S DISPENSARY FOR SICK ANIMALS (1917), P.D.S.A. House, Clifford Street, W.1.

PERFORMING RIGHT SOCIETY LTD. (1914), 29–33 Berners Street, W.1.—*Gen. Manager*, H. L. Walter; *Sec.*, V. G. Tucker.

PERIODICAL PROPRIETORS ASSOCIATION LTD., Imperial House, Kingsway, W.C.2.—*Sec.*, H. MacDougall.

PERSONNEL MANAGEMENT, INSTITUTE OF (1913), 80 Fetter Lane, E.C.4.—*Dir.*, A. L. N. Stephens.

PETROLEUM, INSTITUTE OF (1913), 61 New Cavendish Street, W.1.—*Gen. Sec.*, D. A. Hough.

PHARMACEUTICAL SOCIETY OF GREAT BRITAIN, 17 Bloomsbury Square, W.C.1.—*Pres.*, C. W. Mablethorpe; *Secs.*, Sir Hugh N. Linstead, O.B.E., M.P.; F. W. Adams, B.SC.

PHARMACOLOGICAL SOCIETY, BRITISH.—*Sec.*, J. D. P. Graham, M.D., Dept. of Pharmacology, Welsh National School of Medicine, Cardiff.

PHILOLOGICAL SOCIETY (1842), University College, Gower Street, W.C.1.—*Hon. Secs.*, Prof. D. M. Jones; R. H. Robins.

PHILOSOPHICAL SOCIETY OF GLASGOW. *See* ROYAL.

PHILOSOPHICAL SOCIETY OF GREAT BRITAIN. *See* VICTORIA INSTITUTE.

PHILOSOPHY, ROYAL INSTITUTE OF, 14 Gordon Square, W.C.1.—*Director*, Prof. H. B. Acton, M.A., D.Phil.

PHONETIC ALPHABET ASSOCIATION (1955), 86 Dalmain Road, S.E.23.—*Hon. Sec.*, Miss B. Smoker.

PHOTOGRAPHERS, INSTITUTE OF BRITISH (1901), 38 Bedford Square, W.C.1.—*Gen. Sec.*, J. L. A. Hunt.

PHYSICAL RECREATION, CENTRAL COUNCIL OF (1935), 6 Bedford Square, W.C.1.—*Gen. Sec.*, W. Winterbottom, O.B.E.

PHYSICAL SOCIETY, *see* INSTITUTE OF PHYSICS AND PHYSICAL SOCIETY.

PHYSICIANS, ROYAL COLLEGE OF (1518), Pall Mall East, S.W.1.—*Pres.*, Sir Charles Dodds, M.V.O., M.D., F.R.S.; *Treas.*, R. R. Bomford, D.M.; *Registrar*, K. Robson, C.B.E., M.D.

PHYSICIANS AND SURGEONS, ROYAL COLLEGE OF (GLASGOW) (1599), 242 St. Vincent Street, Glasgow.—*Pres.*, Prof. Sir Charles Illingworth, C.B.E.; *Hon. Sec.*, G. B. Shaw.

PHYSICIANS OF EDINBURGH, ROYAL COLLEGE OF (1681), *Hall and Library*, 9 Queen Street, Edinburgh 2.—*Sec.*, R. F. Robertson.

PHYSICS AND PHYSICAL SOCIETY, INSTITUTE OF (1960), 47 Belgrave Square, S.W.1.—*Pres.*, Sir Alan Wilson, M.A., D.SC., F.R.S.; *Hon. Sec.*, C. G. Wynne, Ph.D.; *Sec.*, H. R. Lang, Ph.D.

PHYSIOLOGICAL SOCIETY (1876), Department of Physiology, Middlesex Hospital Medical School, W.1.—*Hon. Sec.*, C. G. Phillips, D.M., F.R.C.P. F.R.S.

PIG BREEDERS ASSOCIATION, NATIONAL (1884), 51a Clarendon Road, Watford, Herts.—*Sec.*, E. G. Wake.

PILGRIM TRUST, THE (1930), Millbank House, 2 Great Peter Street, S.W.1.—*Sec.*, The Lord Kilmaine, C.B.E.

PILGRIMS OF GREAT BRITAIN, THE (1902), Savoy Hotel, W.C.2.—*Chairman*, Sir Christopher Chancellor, C.M.G.; *Hon. Sec.*, Anthony Gishford.

PILGRIMS OF THE U.S., THE (1903).—*Pres.*, Hugh Bullock K.B.E.; *Hon. Sec.*, Edward K. Warren, C.B.E., 74 Trinity Place, New York, 6, N.Y., U.S.A.

PIT PONIES PROTECTION SOCIETY (1927).—*Sec.*, D. Jeffrey Williams, 50B Loudoun Road, N.W.8.

PLANT ENGINEERS, INSTITUTION OF, 2 Grosvenor Gardens, S.W.1.—*Sec.*, G. J. Lyons.

PLASTICS INSTITUTE, THE (1931), 6 Mandeville Place, W.1.—*Sec.*, J. N. Ratcliffe.

PLAYING FIELDS ASSOCIATION, NATIONAL (1925), 71 Eccleston Square, Belgrave Road, S.W.1.—*Chairman*, The Lord Luke, T.D.; *Gen Sec.*, Air Vice-Marshal R. A. R. Rae, C.B., O.B.E.

POETRY SOCIETY (INCORPORATED) (1909), 21 Earls Court Square, S.W.5.—*Pres.*, Sir Compton Mackenzie, O.B.E.; *Sec.*, Mrs. S. Moule.

POLAR RESEARCH INSTITUTE, SCOTT (1920), Cambridge.—*Director*, G. de Q. Robin, M.A.

POLIOMYELITIS AND OTHER CRIPPLING DISEASES, NATIONAL FUND FOR RESEARCH INTO (1952), Vincent House, Vincent Square, S.W.1.—*Dir.*, D. Guthrie.

POLITICAL AND ECONOMIC PLANNING (PEP) (1931), 16 Queen Anne's Gate, S.W.1.—*Dir.*, R. Bailey.

POOR CLERGY RELIEF CORPORATION (1856), 27 Medway Street, S.W.1.—*Sec.*, C. L. Talbot.

POULTRY AND EGG PRODUCERS ASSOCIATION OF GREAT BRITAIN (SPBA), LTD. (1915), 19 Compton Terrace, N.1.—*Gen. Sec.*, T. J. Aley.

POULTRY CLUB, THE (1877), (incorporating the British Bantam Association), Merriewood, Copthorne, Sussex.—*Gen. Sec.*, Mrs. E. Duckworth.

PRECEPTORS, COLLEGE OF, 23 Bloomsbury Square, W.C.1. All persons engaged in education who have obtained a Diploma of the College or have passed an examination satisfactory to the Council are admissible as members.—*Secretary*, J. V. Chapman.

PREHISTORIC SOCIETY (1908).—*Hon. Sec.*, N. de L' E. W. Thomas, M.A., F.S.A., City Museum, Birmingham 3.

PREPARATORY SCHOOLS, INCORPORATED ASSOCIATION OF.—*Sec.*, L. P. Dealtry, 31 Melbury Court, Kensington, W.8.

PRESBYTERIAN HISTORICAL SOCIETY OF ENGLAND (1913), Presbyterian Church House, 86 Tavistock Place, W.C.1.—*Hon. Sec.*, J. T. Darling, I.S.O.

PRESBYTERIAN HOUSING LIMITED (1929), 86 Tavistock Place, W.C.1.—*Sec.*, C. M. Manning.

PRESS ASSOCIATION (1868), 85 Fleet Street, E.C.4.—*Chairman* (1963), E. M. Clayson, *Birmingham Post*, Birmingham; *Gen. Manager*, G. C. Bloom; *Sec.*, E. J. Harvey.

PRIMROSE LEAGUE (1883), 54 Victoria Street, S.W.1. —*Grand Master*, The Rt. Hon. Sir Winston S. Churchill, K.G., O.M., C.H., M.P.; *Chancellor*, Sir Hamilton Kerr, Bt., M.P.; *Sec.*, Miss E. M. Killby, O.B.E.

PRINCESS LOUISE SCOTTISH HOSPITAL FOR LIMBLESS SAILORS AND SOLDIERS (1916), Erskine, Bishopton, Renfrewshire.—*Sec. and Tres.*, Maj. G. A. Rankin, 201 W. George Street, Glasgow, C.2.

PRINTERS' PENSION CORPORATION (1827), 61 Doughty Street, W.C.1. Homes of Rest at Basildon.—*Sec.*, A. Reynolds.

PRINTING, INSTITUTE OF (1961), 44 Bedford Row, W.C.1.—*Sec.*, M. A. Smith.

PRISON VISITORS, NATIONAL ASSOCIATION OF (1922), 71 Chaucer Road, Bedford.—*Hon. Sec.*, J. H. M. Sykes.

PROCURATORS, ROYAL FACULTY OF (1600).—*Treas., Clerk and Fiscal*, A. F. Ferguson, T.D., 34 West George Street, Glasgow, C.2.

PRODUCTION ENGINEERS, INSTITUTION OF, 10 Chesterfield Street, W.1.—*Sec.*, W. F. S. Woodford.

PROFESSIONAL CIVIL SERVANTS, INSTITUTION OF (1919), 3–7 Northumberland Street, W.C.2.—*Gen. Sec.*, W. McCall.

PROFESSIONAL CLASSES AID COUNCIL, 10 St. Christopher's Place, W.1.—*Sec.*, Miss P. Roden.

PROFESSIONAL WORKERS, NATIONAL FEDERATION OF (1920), Drayton House, Gordon Street, W.C.1.—*Gen. Sec.*, J. Fryd.

PROPAGATION OF THE GOSPEL IN FOREIGN PARTS, SOCIETY FOR THE (S.P.G.) (1701), 15 Tufton Street, S.W.1.—*Sec.*, Rt. Rev. E. J. Trapp; *Deputy Secs.*, J. Dudley Dixon, D.S.C.; Rev. A. E. A. Sulston; *Assist. Secs.*, F. Chappell; Rev. J. Redmayne; Rev. K. G. Symcox; Dr. Veronica Thres; Rev. M. S. Wheatley; Rev. J. D. Wilkinson; Miss R. M. Young. Income, 1962, £888,595.

PROTECTION OF LIFE FROM FIRE, SOCIETY FOR THE (1836), Chichester House, 278–82 High Holborn, W.C. 1.—*Sec.*, R. W. Hale.

PROTESTANT ALLIANCE, THE (1845), 119 Earlsfield Road, S.W.18.—*Hon. Sec.*, O. T. Taylor.

PROTESTANT REFORMATION SOCIETY (1827), 372 Caledonian Road, N.1.—*Sec.*, N. G. Wallace.

PROVIDENT CLERKS' BENEVOLENT FUND (1840), 25 Moorgate, E.C.2.—*Hon. Sec.*, E. C. Evans.

PROVINCIAL NOTARIES PUBLIC, INCORPORATED SOCIETY OF (1907), 7 Hampshire Terrace, Portsmouth, Hants.—*Sec.*, G. E. Delafield.

PSYCHICAL RESEARCH SOCIETY FOR (1882), 1 Adam and Eve Mews, W.8.—*Pres.*, D. J. West, M.D.

PSYCHOLOGICAL SOCIETY, THE BRITISH (1901), Tavistock House South, Tavistock Square, W.C.1.—*Pres.*, Prof. A. Summerfield; *Hon. Gen. Sec.*, H. G. Jones.

PUBLIC ADMINISTRATION, ROYAL INSTITUTE OF (1922), 24 Park Crescent, W.1.—*Dir.*, R. Nottage.

PUBLIC HEALTH AND HYGIENE, THE ROYAL INSTITUTE OF (1937), Postgraduate Medical School, 28 Portland Place, W.1.; Harben Laboratories, 23 Queen Square, W.C.1.—*Sec.*, A. R. Horsham.

PUBLIC HEALTH ENGINEERS, INSTITUTION OF (1895), 179–181 Vauxhall Bridge Road, S.W.1.—*Sec.*, E. V. Balsom, M.B.E.

PUBLIC HEALTH INSPECTORS, ASSOCIATION OF (1883), 19 Grosvenor Place, S.W.1.—*Sec.*, R. Johnson.

PUBLIC RELATIONS, INSTITUTE OF (1948), Templar House, 81–87 High Holborn, W.C.1.—*Director*, M. H. Archer.

PUBLIC SCHOOLS ASSOCIATION OF GOVERNING BODIES OF (BOYS) (1941).—*Hon. Sec.*, A. H. S. Vivian, 6 Wolsey Road, Moor Park, Northwood, Middlesex; *Sec.*, Brig. A. J. Knott, O.B.E., West Rood, West Hill, Harrow, Middx.

PUBLIC SCHOOLS, ASSOCIATION OF GOVERNING BODIES OF GIRLS' (1942), c/o Women's Employment Federation, 251 Brompton Road, S.W.3.—*Sec.*, Miss I. F. Hilton.

PUBLIC SCHOOLS APPOINTMENTS BUREAU, 17 Queen Street, W.1.—*Director*, A. N. Gilkes, M.A.

PUBLIC SCHOOLS BURSARS' ASSOCIATION (1932).—*Sec.*, D. M. Sherwood, Badminton School, Westbury-on-Trym, Bristol.

PUBLIC SUPPLIES, INSTITUTE OF (1949), 24 Park Crescent, W.1.—*Sec.*, A. M. Dawson.

PUBLIC TEACHERS OF LAW, SOCIETY OF (1908).—*Pres.*, Prof. A. H. Campbell; *Hon. Sec.*, Prof. E. R. Hardy Ivamy, Ph.D., Faculty of Laws, University College London, Gower Street, W.C.1.

PUBLIC TRANSPORT ASSOCIATION, INCORPORATED, Brettenham House, Lancaster Place, Strand, W.C.2.—*Sec.*, R. L. Howlett.

PUBLISHERS ASSOCIATION (1896), 18 Bedford Square, W.C.1.—*Pres.*, J. Brown; *Sec.*, R. E. Barker.

PURCHASING OFFICERS ASSOCIATION (1931), York House, Westminster Bridge Road, S.E.1. *Dir.*, P. F. H. Emery, M.P.

QUANTITY SURVEYORS, INSTITUTE OF, 98 Gloucester Place, W 1.

QUARRIER'S HOMES (1871), Bridge of Weir, Renfrewshire, Scotland.—*Sec.*, David Easton.

QUARRYING, INSTITUTE OF (1917), 62–64 Baker Street, W.1.—*Sec.*, Mary Roberts.

QUEEN ELIZABETH'S TRAINING COLLEGE FOR THE DISABLED (1934) (Bernhard Baron Memorial), Leatherhead Court, Surrey.—*Dir.*, R. N. Smith, M.C., T.D.

QUEEN VICTORIA CLERGY FUND (1897), *Central Fund*, Church House, Dean's Yard, S.W.1.—*Sec.*, H. Symons.

QUEEN'S INSTITUTE OF DISTRICT NURSING (1887), 57 Lower Belgrave Street, S.W.1.—*Gen. Supt.*, Miss L. J. Gray; *Gen. Sec.*, Mrs. I. Mumford.

RACE RELATIONS, INSTITUTE OF (1958), 36 Jermyn Street, S.W.1.—*Dir.*, P. Mason, C.I.E., O.B.E.

RADIO ENGINEERS, BRITISH INSTITUTION OF (1925), 9 Bedford Square, W.C.1.—*Sec.*, Graham D. Clifford.

RADIO SOCIETY OF GREAT BRITAIN (Incorporated), 28–30 Little Russell Street, W.C.1.—*Gen. Sec.*, John Clarricoats, O.B.E.

RADIOLOGISTS, FACULTY OF (1934), c/o Royal College of Surgeons, Lincoln's Inn Fields, W.C.2.—*Hon. Sec.*, C. J. Hodson, M.B., F.R.C.P.

RAILWAY BENEVOLENT INSTITUTION (1858), 29 John Street, W.C.1; Railway Orphanage at Derby.—*Gen. Sec.*, W. C. Wayland-Carr.

RAILWAY AND CANAL HISTORICAL SOCIETY.—*Hon. Sec.*, J. Bryant, 26 Clarence Street, Ulverston, Lancs.

RAILWAY OFFICERS' AND SERVANTS' ASSOCIATION, UNITED KINGDOM (1861), 85–86 London Wall, E.C.2.—*Sec.*, Albert T. Reynolds.

RAINER FOUNDATION (*formerly* London Police Court Mission), 2 Hobart Place, Eaton Square, S.W.1.—*Sec.*, G. J. M. Jacob, O.B.E.

RAMBLERS' ASSOCIATION (1935), 124 Finchley Road, N.W.3.—*Sec.*, T. Stephenson.

RANYARD MISSION (1857) and RANYARD NURSES (1868), St. Mark's Church, Kennington Park Road, S.E.11.—*Gen. Supt. and Sec.*, Miss Janet Filby.

RATEPAYERS' ASSOCIATIONS, NATIONAL UNION OF, 47 Victoria Street, S.W.1.

RATING AND VALUATION ASSOCIATION (1882), 29 Belgrave Square,,S.W.1.—*Sec.*, Frank L. Othick.

RED CROSS SOCIETY BRITISH. *See* BRITISH.

RED ENSIGN CLUB, SAILORS' HOME AND (1830), Dock Street, E.1.—*Gen. Manager*, Capt. E. W. Bush.

RED POLL CATTLE SOCIETY (1888), 10 Neale Street, Ipswich.—*Sec.*, D. J. A. Reynolds.

REEDHAM SCHOOL (Incorporated) (1844), Purley, Surrey.—*Sec.*, H. W. Richardson.

REED'S SCHOOL (1813). *Offices*, 32 Queen Victoria Street, E.C.4.—*Sec.*, Philip Horton.

REFRIGERATION, INSTITUTE OF (1900), New Bridge Street House, New Bridge Street, E.C.4.—*Sec.*, D. T. Lee.

REINDEER COUNCIL OF THE UNITED KINGDOM (1949), Newton Hill, Harston, Cambridge.—*Hon. Sec.*, Dr. E. J. Lindgren, M.A.

RELIGIOUS TRACT SOCIETY. *See* "UNITED SOCIETY."

RESEARCH DEFENCE SOCIETY, 11 Chandos Street, Cavendish Square, W.1.—*Hon. Sec.*, A. D. Macdonald, M.D.; *Sec.*, Mrs Katherine Williams.

RETIRED NAVAL OFFICERS, ASSOCIATION OF (Trafalgar Day, 1925), 117A Fulham Road, S.W.3.—*Gen. Sec.*, Cdr. J. N. K. Knight, D.S.C., R.N.

RIVERS PROTECTION, CENTRAL COUNCIL FOR, Fishmongers' Hall, E.C.4.—*Joint Hon. Secs.*, J. S. Barclay, T.D.; Leonard Millis, O.B.E.

ROAD TRANSPORT ENGINEERS (INCORPORATED), INSTITUTE OF (1945), 1 Cromwell Place, S.W.7.—*Sec.*, J. K. Bennett.

ROADS BEAUTIFYING ASSOCIATION (1928), 41 Kipling House, 43 Villiers Street, W.C.2.

ROADS IMPROVEMENT ASSOCIATION, Ruebilder House, Havelock Road, Southall, Middlesex.—*Gen. Sec.*, L. Bailey.

ROMAN AND MEDIAEVAL LONDON EXCAVATION COUNCIL.—*Hon. Sec.*, R. A. Woods, c/o Bank of England, E.C.2.

ROMAN STUDIES, SOCIETY FOR PROMOTION OF, 31–34 Gordon Square, W.C.1.—*Pres.*, Prof. F. W. Walbank, F.B.A.; *Sec.*, Mrs. P. Gilbert.

ROTARY INTERNATIONAL IN GREAT BRITAIN AND IRELAND (1914), Tavistock House South, Tavistock Square, W.C.1.—*Sec.*, R. W. Wordley, M.B.E.

ROYAL AFRICAN SOCIETY (1901), 18 Northumberland Avenue, W.C.2.—*Sec.*, H. Heather.

ROYAL AIR FORCE BENEVOLENT FUND (1919), 67 Portland Place, W.1.—*Controller*, Air Marshal Sir John Whitley, K.B.E., C.B., D.S.O., A.F.C.

ROYAL AIR FORCES ASSOCIATION, 43 Grove Park Road, W.4.—*Gen. Sec.*, G. R. Boak.

ROYAL ALEXANDRA AND ALBERT SCHOOL (1758). *Offices*, Gatton Park, Reigate, Surrey.—*Sec.*, Eric A. Corner.

ROYAL ALFRED MERCHANT SEAMEN'S SOCIETY (1865), 122–6 Balham High Road, S.W.12. Home for aged seamen, Belvedere. Outpensions to retired seamen of limited means. Samaritan and War Fund for general relief. Allowances for widows in distress.—*Gen. Sec.*, D. J. Lafferty.

ROYAL ARTILLERY ASSOCIATION, 58 Woolwich Common, S.E.18.—*Gen. Sec.*, Maj. F. C. Emery.

ROYAL ARTILLERY ASSOCIATION EMPLOYMENT BUREAU FOR FINDING WORK FOR EX-ARTILLERYMEN, 73 Elizabeth Street, S.W.1.

ROYAL ASIATIC SOCIETY, 56 Queen Anne Street, W.1.—*Sec.*, Mrs. M. Bunford, M.B.E.

ROYAL ASSOCIATION OF BRITISH DAIRY FARMERS (1876), 17 Devonshire Street, W.1.—*Sec.*, F. R. Francis.

ROYAL BRITISH NURSES ASSOCIATION, 194 Queen's Gate, S.W.7.—*Sec.*, Miss L. Macdonald, M.B.E.

ROYAL CALEDONIAN SCHOOLS (1815), Bushey, Herts.—*Sec.*, George Deans.

ROYAL CAMBRIDGE HOME FOR SOLDIERS' WIDOWS, 82–84 Hurst Road, East Molesey, Surrey.—*Sec.*, Miss E. M. Bennett.

ROYAL CENTRAL ASIAN SOCIETY (1901), 12 Orange Street, W.C.2.—*Pres.*, Marshal of the Royal Air Force Sir William Dickson, G.C.B., K.B.E., D.S.O., A.F.C.; *Sec.*, Miss M. K. Marsh.

ROYAL CHORAL SOCIETY (1871), Royal Albert Hall, S.W.7.—*Sec.*, Phyllis G. Dabbs.

ROYAL COLLEGE OF VETERINARY SURGEONS, 32 Belgrave Square, S.W.1.—*Pres.*, Prof. W. L. Weipers; *Registrar*, W. G. R. Oates.

ROYAL COMMONWEALTH SOCIETY (1868) (formerly Royal Colonial Institute and later Royal Empire Society), Northumberland Avenue, W.C.2.—*Chairman of Council*, Rt. Hon. Lord John Hope, M.P., (30,500 Fellows, Associates and Companions).—*Secretary-General*, D. K. Daniels, C.B.E.

ROYAL DESIGNERS FOR INDUSTRY, FACULTY OF (1936), (Royal Society of Arts), John Adam Street, W.C.2.—*Master*, L. Irving, O.B.E. *Sec.*, G. E. Mercer.

ROYAL DRAWING SOCIETY (1902), 6 Queen Square, W.C.1.—*Sec.*, R. J. Murton.

ROYAL ECONOMIC SOCIETY (1890), 21 Bentinck Street, W.1.—*Sec.*, E. A. G. Robinson, C.M.G., O.B.E.

ROYAL ENGINEERS, THE INSTITUTION OF (1875), Chatham.—*Sec.*, Brig. J. H. S. Lacey, C.B.E.

ROYAL FEMALE ORPHANAGE (1758), 743 London Road, High Wycombe, Bucks.—*Sec.*, Miss G. E. Miles.

ROYAL HIGHLAND AND AGRICULTURAL SOCIETY OF SCOTLAND (1784), 8 Eglinton Crescent, Edinburgh 12.—*Sec.*, R. M. Lemmon, O.B.E., B.L.

ROYAL HORTICULTURAL SOCIETY (1804).—*Offices*, Vincent Square, S.W.1. *Gardens*, Wisley, Ripley, Woking, Surrey.—*Sec.*, J. Hamer, M.B.E.

ROYAL HOSPITAL AND HOME FOR INCURABLES, PUTNEY (1854), West Hill, S.W.15.—*Sec.*, Brig. R. M. Villiers, D.S.O.

ROYAL HUMANE SOCIETY (1774).—In 1962, 832 persons were rewarded by the R.H.S. for saving 607 lives, and attempting to save the lives of 85 others.—*Offices*, Watergate House, York Buildings, Adelphi, W.C.2.

ROYAL INDIA, PAKISTAN AND CEYLON SOCIETY (1910) (Art and Letters), 2 Temple Chambers, Temple Avenue, E.C.4.—*Hon. Sec.*, Frederick Richter, C.B.E., M.A.

ROYAL INSTITUTE OF INTERNATIONAL AFFAIRS (1920), Chatham House, St. James's Square, S.W.1.—*Director*, Right Hon. K. G. Younger.

ROYAL INSTITUTION OF GREAT BRITAIN (1799), 21 Albemarle Street, W.1.—*Pres.*, The Lord

Fleck, K.B.E., D.SC., F.R.S.; *Sec.*, Brig. H. E. Hopthrow, C.B.E.

ROYAL INSTITUTION OF SOUTH WALES, Swansea (1835).—*Hon. Sec.*, Mrs. D. Griffiths.

ROYAL LIFE SAVING SOCIETY, THE (1891), Desborough House, 14 Devonshire Street, W.1.—*Chief Sec.*, Capt. E. Hale, C.B.E., R.N. (*ret.*).

ROYAL LITERARY FUND (1790), 11 Ludgate Hill, E.C.4. Grants to necessitous authors of some published work of approved literary merit or to their immediate dependants.—*Pres.*, Frank Swinnerton; *Sec.*, J. G. Broadbent.

ROYAL MEDICAL BENEVOLENT FUND (1836), 37 St. George's Road, Wimbledon, S.W.19.—*Sec.*, Cmdr. J. G. Hunt, R.N. (*ret.*).

ROYAL MEDICAL SOCIETY (1737), 7 Melbourne Place, Edinburgh, 1.—*Secs.*, D. I. Newble; A. M. Davison.

ROYAL MICROSCOPICAL SOCIETY, Tavistock House, South, Tavistock Square, W.C.1.—*Gen. Sec.*, G. G. Prince.

ROYAL MUSICAL ASSOCIATION (1874) 44 Philip Victor Road, Handsworth, Birmingham 21.—*Sec.*, Dr. N. Fortune.

ROYAL NATIONAL LIFE-BOAT INSTITUTION, THE (1824).—*Income* (1962), £1,355,792, expenditure £1,159,144; total number of lives rescued, over 84,000; rescued in 1962, 422. 150 life-boats are maintained on the coasts of Great Britain and Ireland. *Offices*, 42 Grosvenor Gardens, S.W.1. —*Sec.*, S. M. Whorlow.

ROYAL NATIONAL MISSION TO DEEP SEA FISHERMEN (1881), 43 Nottingham Place, W.1.—*Sec.*, Charles Laurie.

ROYAL NAVAL AND ROYAL MARINE CHILDREN'S HOME (1834), Portsmouth. *Sec.*, Miss B. H. W. Nimmo, Royal Naval Barracks, Portsmouth.

ROYAL NAVAL BENEVOLENT SOCIETY (1739), 1 Fleet Street, E.C.4.—*Sec.*, Capt. R. C. Steele, R.N. (*ret.*).

ROYAL NAVAL BENEVOLENT TRUST (1922) (Grand Fleet and Kindred Funds), High Street, Brompton, Gillingham, Kent (Local Committees at Chatham, Devonport and Portsmouth).—*Gen. Sec.*, Lt.-Comdr. H. B. Binks, O.B.E., D.S.C., R.N. (*ret.*).

ROYAL NAVAL FUND (1891). Administered by the Royal Naval Benevolent Trust. *See above.*

ROYAL PATRIOTIC FUND CORPORATION (1904), Wellington House, Buckingham Gate, S.W.1. Administers funds for the benefit of widows, children and other dependants of deceased officers and servicemen of the Armed Forces; also the Royal Victoria Patriotic School, Bedwell Park, Hatfield, Herts., for daughters of Sailors, Soldiers, Marines and Airmen.—*Sec.*, Maj.-Gen. R. F. H. Nalder, C.B., O.B.E.

ROYAL PHILANTHROPIC SOCIETY'S SCHOOL, Redhill, Surrey.—*Princ.*, R. Percival.

ROYAL PHILATELIC SOCIETY, LONDON (1869), 41 Devonshire Place, W.1.—*Hon. Sec.*, G. South, M.B.E.

ROYAL PHILHARMONIC SOCIETY (1813), 4 St. James's Square, S.W.1.—*Hon. Sec.*, L. Regan.

ROYAL PHOTOGRAPHIC SOCIETY (1853), 16 Princes Gate, S.W.7.—*Sec.*, L. E. Hallett.

"ROYAL SAILORS' RESTS" (Miss Agnes Weston's) (1876). *Head Office*, 31 Western Parade, Portsmouth. Rests for naval personnel, at Portsmouth, Devonport, Londonderry, Weymouth, Lossiemouth and Singapore. *Gen. Sec.*, Lt.-Cdr. F. M. Savage, R.N.

ROYAL SCHOOL OF NEEDLEWORK (1872), 25, Princes Gate, S.W.7.—*Sec.*, Miss V. Beames.

ROYAL SCOTTISH COUNTRY DANCE SOCIETY (1923), 12 Coates Crescent, Edinburgh 3.—*Sec.*, Miss M. F. Hadden.

ROYAL SCOTTISH SOCIETY FOR PREVENTION OF CRUELTY TO CHILDREN (1884), 16 Melville Street, Edinburgh, 3.—*Sec.*, C. A. Cumming Forsyth, O.B.E., B.L.

ROYAL SCOTTISH SOCIETY OF ARTS (1821) (Science and Technology).—*Secretary*, C. N. Kemp, 29 Alva Street, Edinburgh 2.

ROYAL SEAMEN'S PENSION FUND (Incorporated) (1919), 58 High Street, Sutton, Surrey—*Sec.*, W. G. Bowen.

ROYAL SOCIETY, THE (1660), Burlington House, Piccadilly W.1.—*Pres.*, Sir Howard Florey; *Treas. and Vice-Pres.*, The Lord Fleck, K.B.E., D.SC., F.R.S.; *Secretary and Vice-President*, Sir Lindor Brown, C.B.E.; *Secretary and Vice-President*, Sir William Hodge; *Foreign Secretary and Vice-President*, Sir Patrick Linstead, C.B.E.; *Executive Sec.*, Dr. D. C. Martin, C.B.E.

ROYAL SOCIETY FOR THE PREVENTION OF ACCIDENTS, Terminal House, 52 Grosvenor Gardens, S.W.1. —*Director-General*, Brig. R. F. E. Stoney, C.B.E., *Sec.*, R. F. B. Fenn.

ROYAL SOCIETY FOR THE PREVENTION OF CRUELTY TO ANIMALS (1824), 105 Jermyn Street, S.W.1. —*Chief Sec.*, John Hall.

ROYAL SOCIETY OF ARTS (1754), 6–8 John Adam Street, Adelphi, W.C.2.—*Chairman*, Sir Hilary Blood, G.B.E., K.C.M.G., *Sec.*, G. E. Mercer.

ROYAL SOCIETY OF BRITISH ARTISTS (1823), Suffolk Street, S.W.1.—*Pres.*, E. I. Halliday; *Hon. Sec.*, J. Brine; *Keeper*, M. B. Bradshaw.

ROYAL SOCIETY OF BRITISH SCULPTORS (1904) 6 Queen Square, W.C.1.—*Pres.*, E. Bainbridge Copnall, M.B.E.; *Sec.*, Grace Carter.

ROYAL SOCIETY OF EDINBURGH (1783), 22 George Street, Edinburgh 2.—*Pres.*, Prof. E. L. Hirst, C.B.E., LL.D., F.R.S.; *Gen. Sec.*, Norman Feather, Ph.D., F.R.S.; *Treas.*, Dr. J. R. Peddie, C.B.E.; *Curator*, Robert Schlapp, M.A., Ph.D.

ROYAL SOCIETY OF HEALTH (1876), to promote the health of the people, 90 Buckingham Palace Road, S.W.1.— *Sec.*, P. Arthur Wells, M.A., M.SC.

ROYAL SOCIETY OF LITERATURE (1823), 1 Hyde Park Gardens, W.2.—*Sec.*, Mrs. J. M. Patterson.

ROYAL SOCIETY OF MEDICINE (1805), 1 Wimpole Street, W.1.—*Pres.* T. Cawthorne; *Sec.* R. T. Hewitt, O.B.E.

ROYAL SOCIETY OF PORTRAIT PAINTERS (1891), 6½ Suffolk Street, S.W.1.—*Pres.*, Sir James Gunn, R.A.; *Hon. Sec.*, E. Halliday, P.R.B.A.; *Sec.*, M. B. Bradshaw.

ROYAL SOCIETY OF ST. GEORGE (1894), 4 Upper Belgrave Street, S.W.1.—*Gen. Sec.*, Major M. P. C. Hordern.

ROYAL STATISTICAL SOCIETY (1834), 21 Bentinck Street, W.1.—*Pres.*, Dr. J. O. Irwin; *Sec.*, Miss U. M. Croker.

ROYAL UNITED KINGDOM BENEFICENT ASSOCIATION (1863), Aldine House, 13 Bedford Street, W.C.2. —*Gen. Sec.*, Rear Adm. H. P. Currey, C.B., O.B.E.

ROYAL UNITED SERVICE INSTITUTION, Whitehall, S.W.1.—*Director and Chief Librarian*, Brig. J. Stephenson, O.B.E.; *Editor*, Lt.-Comdr. P. K. Kemp, O.B.E., R.N. (*ret.*).

RURAL ENGLAND, COUNCIL FOR THE PRESERVATION OF (1926), 4 Hobart Place, S.W.1.—*Gen. Sec.*, Sir Herbert Griffin, C.B.E.

RURAL INDUSTRIES BUREAU, 35 Camp Road, Wimbledon Common, S.W.19.—*Dir.*, J. Cosmo Clark, C.B.E., M.C., R.A.

RURAL SCOTLAND, ASSOCIATION FOR PRESERVATION OF (1927), 15 Rutland Square, Edinburgh, 1—*Sec.*, K. Macrae W.S.

RURAL WALES, COUNCIL FOR THE PROTECTION OF (1928), Y Plâs, Machynlleth, Montgomeryshire.—*Sec.*, Maj.-Gen. L. O. Pugh, C.B., C.B.E., D.S.O.

SAILORS' CHILDREN'S SOCIETY, THE (1821), Newland, Hull. Cares for British seamen's children who have lost a parent. (Provides welfare facilities for seamen in Humber area, including Home for aged seafarers.)—*Sec.*, L. Hartley.

ST. DEINIOL'S RESIDENTIAL LIBRARY (Gladstone Memorial), Hawarden, near Chester. *Warden*, Rev. J. S. Lawton, B.D., D.Phil.

ST. DUNSTAN'S, for men and women blinded on War Service, 191 Marylebone Road, N.W.1. In March, 1961, the number of blinded men and women in the care of the organization was 1,150 from World War I and 1,350 from World War II.—*Pres.*, Sir Neville Pearson, Bt.; *Chairman*, The Lord Fraser of Lonsdale, C.H., C.B.E.; *Hon. Treas.*, I. G. Orme; *Sec.*, A. D. Lloyds.

ST. GILES CHRISTIAN MISSION (1860), 60 Bride Street, Barnsbury, N.7.

ST. JOHN AMBULANCE ASSOCIATION, *Headquarters*, 10 Grosvenor Crescent, S.W.1.—*Dir.-Gen.*, Sir Philip Southwell, C.B.E., M.C.

ST. JOHN AMBULANCE BRIGADE, 8 Grosvenor Crescent, S.W.1.—*Sec.*, G. W. Woodhill. (Strength 1962, 121,000 men, 38,000 women, 43,000 boy cadets, 55,000 girl cadets.)

ST. VINCENT DE PAUL, SOCIETY OF (1844), 2 Iddesleigh House, Caxton Street, S.W.1.—*Sec.*, A. W. Barr.

SALMON AND TROUT ASSOCIATION (1903), Fishmongers' Hall, E.C.4.—*Hon. Sec.*, J. S. Barclay, T.D.

SALTIRE SOCIETY (1936), Gladstone's Land, 483 Lawnmarket, Edinburgh 1.—*Hon. Sec.*, Dr. R. M. Gorrie.

SALVAGE CORPS (FIRE)—
London (1866), 140 Aldersgate Street, E.C.1. *Chief Officer*, A. S. Pratten, O.B.E., G.M.
Liverpool (1842), 46 Derby Road, Liverpool, 20. *Chief Officer*, E. J. H. Catt.
Glasgow (1873) 201–203 Albion Street, Glasgow, C.1.—*Chief Officer*, T. Mundell.

SANITARY ENGINEERS, INSTITUTION OF. *See* PUBLIC HEALTH ENGINEERS.

SAVE THE CHILDREN FUND (1919), 29 Queen Anne's Gate, S.W.1.—*Dir. Gen.*, Brig. T. W. Boyce, O.B.E., M.C., M.M.

SAVINGS BANKS INSTITUTE, 22 Manchester Square, W.1.—*Sec.*, W. F. Rishton.

SCAPA SOCIETY, *see* ADVERTISING.

SCHOOL LIBRARY ASSOCIATION, Premier House, 150 Southampton Row, W.C.1.—*Hon. Sec.*, C. A. Stott, M.B.E.

SCHOOL NATURAL SCIENCE SOCIETY, 2 Bramley Mansions, Berrylands Road, Surbiton, Surrey.—*Hon. Gen. Sec.*, M. Jenny Sellers.

SCHOOLMASTERS' ASSOCIATION, SCOTTISH, 10 Atholl Crescent, Edinburgh, 3.—*Gen. Sec.*, P. J. Cannon.

SCHOOLMASTERS, NATIONAL ASSOCIATION OF, Swan Court, Hemel Hempstead, Herts.—*Sec.*, T. A. Casey.

SCHOOLMASTERS, SOCIETY OF (1798) (for the relief of Necessitous Schoolmasters and of their Widows and Orphans), 308 Galpins Road, Thornton Heath Surrey —*Sec.*, Mrs. H. E. Closs.

SCHOOLS' MUSIC ASSOCIATION, THE (1938), 4 Newman Road, Bromley, Kent.—*Hon. Sec.*, S. S. Moore.

SCIENCE AND LEARNING, SOCIETY FOR THE PROTECTION OF, c/o Society for Visiting Scientists, 19 Albemarle Street, W.1.—*President*, Prof. A. V. Hill, C.H., O.B.E., F.R.S.; *Sec.*, Miss E. Simpson, O.B.E.

SCIENCE EDUCATION, ASSOCIATION FOR (1963), 52 Bateman Street, Cambridge.

SCIENTIFIC FILM ASSOCIATION, 55a Welbeck Street, W.1.—*Sec.*, E. J. Cooper.

SCOTTISH CORPORATION, ROYAL (1611) (for the relief of Scottish poor), Fleur-de-Lis Court, Fetter Lane, E.C.4.

SCOTTISH COUNTRY INDUSTRIES DEVELOPMENT TRUST, 27 Walker Street, Edinburgh 3.—*Sec.*, Maj. H. C. Paterson, T.D.

SCOTTISH HISTORY SOCIETY (1886).—*Joint Secs.*, G. Donaldson, D.Litt.; G. G. Simpson, c/o Scottish Record Office, H.M. General Register House, Edinburgh 2.

SCOTTISH LANDOWNERS' FEDERATION (1906)—*Sec.*, M. Lorimer, 26, Rutland Square, Edinburgh.

SCOTTISH LIBERAL PARTY (1946), 2 Atholl Place, Edinburgh 3.—*Sec.*, A. A. Purdom.

SCOTTISH NATIONAL BLOOD TRANSFUSION ASSOCIATION 1940), 5 St. Colme Street, Edinburgh, 3.—*Sec.*, Neil A. Milne, W.S.

SCOTTISH NATIONAL PARTY, 59 Elmbank Street, Glasgow, C.2.—*Sec.*, M. B. Shaw.

SCOTTISH RECORD SOCIETY, Scottish Record Office, Edinburgh 2.—*Hon. Sec.*, A. L. Murray.

SCOTTISH SECONDARY TEACHERS' ASSOCIATION, 15 Dundas Street, Edinburgh, 3.—*Gen. Sec.*, A. G. Campbell, M.A., LL.B., B.Ed.

SCOTTISH SOCIETY FOR THE PREVENTION OF CRUELTY TO ANIMALS (1839), 19 Melville Street, Edinburgh, 3 —*Sec. and Treas.*, L. G. Langwill.

SCOTTISH SOCIETY FOR THE PROTECTION OF WILD BIRDS (1927), 125 Douglas Street, Glasgow. C.2.—*Sec.*, James M. MacKellar.

SCOTTISH THEATRICAL PROPRIETORS AND MANAGERS' ASSOCIATION, 132 West Regent Street, Glasgow, C.2.—*Sec.*, W. G. Bruce.

SCOTTISH TOURIST BOARD (1945), Rutland Place, Edinburgh 1.—*Dir.*, W. A. Nicholson.

SCOTTISH UNION OF STUDENTS, 30 Lothian Street, Edinburgh 8.—*Admin. Sec.*, Miss M. A. Hislop.

SCOTTISH UNIONIST ASSOCIATION.—*Sec.*, (*Eastern Council*), Ian M. Mowat, 9 Atholl Crescent, Edinburgh; (*Western Council*), Andrew Strong, M.B.E., 95 Bothwell, Street Glasgow.

SCRIBES AND ILLUMINATORS, THE SOCIETY OF.—*Hon. Sec.*, J. M. Cackett, 11 Dorchester Drive, Bedfont, Feltham, Middlesex.

SCRIPTURE GIFT MISSION (1888), Radstock House, Eccleston Street, S.W.1. Copies and selections of the Scriptures circulated (1962), 15,053,490.—*Joint Secs.*, J. Mighell Smith; T. Wales.

SCRIPTURE UNION AND CHILDREN'S SPECIAL SERVICE MISSION (1867), 5 Wigmore Street, W.1.—*Gen. Sec.*, J. M. Laird, M.B., Ch.B.

SEAFARERS' EDUCATION SERVICE (1919), Mansbridge House, 207 Balham High Road, S.W.17.—*Director*, Ronald Hope, O.B.E., M.A., D.Phil.

SEA FISHERMEN, ROYAL PROVIDENT FUND FOR (Incorporated).—*Sec.*, F. Page, 53 Eastcheap, E.C.3.

SEAMEN'S CHRISTIAN FRIEND SOCIETY (1846), 46 Denison House, Vauxhall Bridge Road, S.W.1.

SECRETARIES, CHARTERED INSTITUTE OF (1891), 14 New Bridge Street, E.C.4.—*Sec.*, J. F. Phillips, O.B.E., LL.M.

SECRETARIES, THE CORPORATION OF (1922), Devonshire House, 13 Devonshire Street, W.1.—*Sec.*, F. H. J. Wileman, LL.B.

SECRETARIES, FACULTY OF, 51 Tormead Road, Guildford.—*Executive Officer*, V. Rummery.

SELBORNE SOCIETY (1885). Founded in memory of Gilbert White of Selborne.—*Hon. Sec.*, Maj. G. A. Cattley, 57 Corfton Road, Ealing, W.5.

SELDEN SOCIETY (1887), 25 Russell Square, W.C.1.—*Pres.*, Rt. Hon. Lord Justice Upjohn, C.B.E.; *Sec.*, K. Howard Drake, M.A.

SHAFTESBURY HOMES AND "ARETHUSA" TRAINING SHIP (1843), 164 Shaftesbury Avenue, W.C.2.—*Gen. Sec.*, F A. Thorp.

SHAFTESBURY SOCIETY (1844), Shaftesbury House, 112 Regency Street, S.W.1.—Engaged in Christian social service among the poor and physically handicapped. Maintains inter-denominational missions, holiday homes and camps, residential centre for young men and 6 Residential Schools.—*Sec.*, G. Franklin.

SHAW SOCIETY (1941), 86 Dalmain Road, S.E.23.—*Hon. Gen. Sec.*, Miss B. Smoker.

SHIPBROKERS, INSTITUTE OF CHARTERED (1911), 25 Bury Street, E.C.3.—*Sec.*, J. L. Logan.

SHIPPING AND FORWARDING AGENTS, INSTITUTE OF (1944), 75 Cannon Street, E.C.4.—*Sec.*, D. J. Shearer.

SHIPPING OF THE UNITED KINGDOM, CHAMBER OF, Bury Court, St. Mary Axe, E.C.3.—*Pres.*, (1963–64), R. G. Grout; *Dir.*, H. E. Gorick, C.B.E.; *Sec.*, A. Watson, M.B.E.

SHIPPING, GENERAL COUNCIL OF BRITISH, Bury Court, St. Mary Axe, E.C.3.—*Chairman* (1963–64), D. F. Martin-Jenkins; *Joint Secs.*, Martin Hill, C.B.E.; H. E. Gorick, C.B.E.

SHIPWRECKED FISHERMEN AND MARINERS' ROYAL BENEVOLENT SOCIETY (1839), 16 Wilfred Street, S.W.1.—*Sec.*, Lt.-Cdr. H. E. Pinchin, R.N.

SHIRE HORSE SOCIETY (1878), Agricultural Office, 12 Priestgate, Peterborough.—*Sec.*, R. W. Bird.

SIR OSWALD STOLL FOUNDATION, 446 Fulham Road, S.W.6.—*Sec.*, Lt.-Cdr. P. Stent, R.N.

SMALL SHOPKEEPERS, NATIONAL UNION OF (1943), 13 Park Row, Nottingham.—*Gen. Sec.*, F. A. Neale.

SOCIAL CREDIT CO-ORDINATING CENTRE.—*Hon. Sec.*, V. R. Hadkins, Montagu Chambers, Mexborough, Yorkshire.

SOCIAL CREDIT SECRETARIAT, Penrhyn Lodge, Gloucester Gate, N.W.1.—*Sec.*, B. Hyatt.

SOCIAL SERVICE, NATIONAL COUNCIL OF (Incorporated), 26 Bedford Square, W.C.1.—*Dir.*, Sir George Haynes, C.B.E.

SOCIALIST PARTY OF GREAT BRITAIN (1904), 52 Clapham High Street, S.W.4.—*Gen. Sec.*, R. Weaver.

SOIL ASSOCIATION, New Bells Farm, Haughley, Stowmarket, Suffolk.—*Field Director*, Lady Eve Balfour.

SOLDIERS' AND AIRMEN'S SCRIPTURE READERS ASSOCIATION (1838), Havelock House, 35 Catherine Place, S W.1.—*Gen. Sec.*, Lt.-Col. G. G. S. Clarke, D.S.O.

SOLDIERS' DAUGHTERS' SCHOOL, ROYAL (1855) 65 Rosslyn Hill, Hampstead, N.W.3.—*Sec.*, Miss Rosina Sangston.

SOLDIERS', SAILORS' AND AIRMEN'S FAMILIES ASSOCIATION (1885), 23 Queen Anne's Gate, S.W.1.—*Chairman*, Lieut.-Gen. Sir Reginald Denning, K.B.E., C.B.; *Controller*, M. H. Nisbet, M.B.E.; *Sec.*, Lt.-Cdr. R. G. Brown, V.R.D., R.N.R.

SOLDIERS, SAILORS AND AIRMEN'S HELP SOCIETY (Incorporated) (1899), *see* FORCES HELP SOCIETY.

SOLICITORS' BENEVOLENT ASSOCIATION (1858), Clifford's Inn, Fleet Street, E.C.4.—*Sec.*, Miss A. H. Smith, M.B.E.

SOMERSET FOLK, SOCIETY OF—*Hon. Sec.*, Mrs. M. Porter, 208 Boston Road, Hanwell, W.7.

SONS OF THE CLERGY, CORPORATION OF THE (1655), 6 Woburn Square, W.C.1.—*Regr.*, Brig. G. O. N. Thompson, D.S.O., O.B.E.

SOROPTIMIST INTERNATIONAL ASSOCIATION, Federation of Soroptimist Clubs of Great Britain and Ireland, 63 Bayswater Road, W.2.—*Sec.*, Miss J. Grey.

S.O.S. SOCIETY, THE (1929), 24 Ashburn Place, S.W.7. Accommodation for those in need.—*Gen. Sec.*, E. A. Burrus.

SOUTH AFRICAN WAR VETERANS' ASSOCIATION—*Hon. Gen. Sec.*, P. Law, 95 Dalmeny Avenue, Norbury, S.W.16.

SOUTH AMERICAN MISSIONARY SOCIETY (1844), 20 John Street, W.C.1.

SOUTH WALES INSTITUTE OF ENGINEERS (1857), Institute Buildings, Park Place, Cardiff.—*Sec.*, Mrs. E. M. Davies (*acting*).

S.P.G.—*See* "PROPAGATION."

SPASTICS SOCIETY, THE (1952), 12 Park Crescent, W.1.—*Dir.*, Dr. C. P. Stevens.

SPURGEON'S HOMES (1867), Park Road, Birchington, Kent.—*Sec.*, P H. R. Hide.

STAFFORDSHIRE SOCIETY, THE.—*Hon. Sec.*, Mrs. A. C. Thwaites, 9 Burnham Way, Ealing, W.13.

STAIR SOCIETY (to encourage the study and advance the knowledge of the history of Scots Law).—*Sec.*, G. R. Thomson, T.D., Ph.D., 2 St. Giles' Street, Edinburgh 1.

STAR AND GARTER HOME FOR DISABLED SAILORS, SOLDIERS, AND AIRMEN (1916), Richmond, Surrey.—*Commandant*, Col. G. Anderton, O.B.E., M.B., B.S.

STATISTICIANS, INSTITUTE OF (1949), 55 Park Lane, W.1.—*Hon. Sec.*, R. Brech.

STEWART SOCIETY (1899), 50 Melville Street, Edinburgh.—*Hon. Sec.*, Col. C. Stewart Henderson, M.B.E., W.S., F.S.A.(Scot.).

STOCK EXCHANGE, THE, Throgmorton Street, E.C.2.—*Chairman*, The Lord Ritchie of Dundee; *Deputy Chairmen*, H. M. O. Knox; R. F. M. Wilkinson; *Sec.*, C. D. Morley.

STRUCTURAL ENGINEERS, INSTITUTION OF (1908), 11 Upper Belgrave Street, S.W.1.—*Sec.*, C. D. Morgan.

STUDENT CHRISTIAN MOVEMENT OF GREAT BRITAIN AND IRELAND (1889), Annandale, North End Road, N.W.11.—*Gen. Sec.*, Rt. Rev. R. A. Reeves.

SUNDAY, IMPERIAL ALLIANCE FOR DEFENCE OF, and CENTRAL SUNDAY CLOSING ASSOCIATION (1908), Alliance House, 12 Caxton Street, S.W.1.—*Sec.*, Ernest E. Attwell.

SUPERVISING ELECTRICAL ENGINEERS. ASSOCIATION OF (1914) 26 Bloomsbury Square, W.C.1.—*Gen. Sec.*, E. A. Bromfield.

SURGEONS OF ENGLAND, ROYAL COLLEGE OF (1800), Lincoln's Inn Fields, W.C.2.—*Pres.*, Sir Russell Brock; *Sec.*, R. S. Johnson-Gilbert.

SURGEONS OF EDINBURGH, ROYAL COLLEGE OF (1505), 18 Nicolson Street, Edinburgh.—*Sec.*, J. A. Ross, M.B.E.

SURGICAL AID SOCIETY, ROYAL (1862), 47 Victoria Street, S.W.1.—*Sec.*, Capt. K. S. Colquhoun, R.N.

SURGICAL TECHNICIANS, INSTITUTE OF BRITISH, 6 Holborn Viaduct, E.C.1.—*Hon. Sec.*, R. Nunn.

SURVEYORS, ROYAL INSTITUTION OF CHARTERED (1868), 12 Great George Street, S.W.1.—*Pres.*, (1963–64), C. D. Pilcher; *Sec.*, Rear-Admiral P. W. Burnett, C.B.E., D.S.O., D.S.C.

SUSSEX CATTLE SOCIETY (1870), 12 Lonsdale Gardens, Tunbridge Wells, Kent.—*Sec.*, R. E. Noakes.

SUTTON DWELLINGS TRUST (1901), Victoria House, Southampton Row, W.C.1.—*Sec.*, C. V. Baker.

SWEDENBORG SOCIETY (1810), 20–21 Bloomsbury Way, W.C.1.—*Hon. Sec.*, Freda G. Griffith, Ph.D., B.Sc.

TAIL WAGGERS CLUB (GREAT BRITAIN), LTD., 356–360 Gray's Inn Road, W.C.1.—*Sec.*, A. S. C. Michell.

TAXATION, INSTITUTE OF (1930), Cliffords Inn, E.C.4.—*Sec.*, A. A. Arnold.

TEACHERS, NATIONAL UNION OF, Hamilton House, Mabledon Place, W.C.1.—*Sec.*, Sir Ronald Gould, M.A.

TEACHERS' UNION, ULSTER (1919), 72 High Street, Belfast.—*Sec.*, J. King Carson, M.B.E., M.A.

TEACHERS IN COLLEGES AND DEPARTMENTS OF EDUCATION, ASSOCIATION OF, 151 Gower Street, W.C.1.—*Hon. Sec.*, Miss H. M. Simpson, O.B.E., B.A.

TEACHERS IN COMMERCE LTD., FACULTY OF, 20 Oakfield, Sale, Cheshire.—*Gen. Sec.*, J. Snowdon.

TEACHERS IN TECHNICAL INSTITUTIONS, ASSOCIATION OF (1904), Hamilton House, Mabledon Place, W.C.1.—*Sec.*, E. L. Britton, M.A.

TEACHERS OF DOMESTIC SCIENCE, ASSOCIATION OF, Hamilton House, Bidborough Street, W.C.1.—*Sec.*, Miss A. M. Crawley.

TEACHERS OF SPEECH AND DRAMA, SOCIETY OF, St. Bride's Institute, Fleet Street, E.C.4.—*Hon. Sec.*, Mona Swann.

TEACHING HOSPITALS ASSOCIATION, 12 Old Lambeth Palace Road, S.E.1.—*Sec.*, P. H. Constable, O.B.E.

TELEVISION AND SCREEN WRITERS' GUILD, 7 Harley Street, W.1.—*Gen. Sec.*, J. G. Johnson.

TELEVISION SOCIETY, 166 Shaftesbury Avenue, W.C.2.—*Hon. Sec.*, C. A. Marshall.

TEMPERANCE SOCIETIES:—

British Railways Temperance Union (1882), Culross Hall, King's Cross, N.W.1.—*Hon. Sec.*, G. W. Holland.

British National Temperance League (1834), Livesey-Clegg House, 44 Union Street, Sheffield, 1.—*Sec.*, W. H. Jaffray.

British Women's Temperance Association, S.C.U. (1876), 5 St. Andrew Square, Edinburgh, 2.—*Sec.* (vacant).

Church of England Temperance Society, Incorporated, Church Benefit House, 4 Palace Gate, W.8.—*Gen. Sec.*, Rev. J. B. Harrison.

Church of Scotland Committee on Temperance and Morals, 121 George Street, Edinburgh, 2.—*Convenor*, Rev. R. L. Small O.B.E., D.D.

Church of Scotland Women's Committee on Social Service, Temperance and Moral Welfare, 121 George Street, Edinburgh 2.—*Sec.*, Miss M.S. Ferguson.

Committee on Temperance and Gambling of the Presbyterian Church in Ireland, Church House, Belfast. —*Convener*, Rev. S. J. White, B.A.

Congregational Union of England and Wales, Temperance Committee, 112 Memorial Hall, Farringdon Street, E.C.4.

Department of Christian Citizenship of the Methodist Church, 1 Central Buildings, S.W.1.—*Gen. Sec.*, Rev. Edward Rogers, M.A., B.D.

Friends Temperance and Moral Welfare Union (1850), Friends' House, Euston Road, N.W.1.—*Sec.*, R. A. Smith.

Independent Order of Rechabites, Salford Unity Friendly Society (1835), North Parade, Deansgate, Manchester, 3.—*High Sec.*, D. Carr.

Independent Order of Rechabites, Salford Unity Friendly Society, London District (1870), No. 30, 18 Doughty Street, W.C.1.

National Association of Temperance Officials (1897), 16 Deansgate, Manchester, 3.—*Hon. Sec.*, J. Harrison.

National Commercial Temperance League of Business and Professional Men (1891), *Head Office*, 12 Caxton Street, S.W.1.—*Pres.*, H. C. Heath.

National Temperance Federation (1884), 12 Caxton Street, S.W.1.—*Hon. Sec.*, T. G. Waite.

National Unitarian and Free Christian Temperance Association (1893), 35 Oakington Manor Drive, Wembley.—*Hon. Sec.*, Rev. W. M. Long.

Order of the Sons of Temperance, 21 Victoria Avenue, Harrogate.—*Sec.*, K. Unsworth.

Royal Naval Temperance Society (auxiliary of Royal Sailors' Rests), 31 Western Parade, Portsmouth.—*Sec.*, Lt.-Cdr. F. M. Savage, R.N.

Scottish Temperance Alliance, 244 Bath Street, Glasgow, C.2.—*Sec.*, Colin Palmer.

Social Service Board of the Episcopal Church in Scotland (1919).—*Sec.*, F. C. B. Black, 13 Drumsheugh Gardens, Edinburgh, 3.

South Wales Temperance Union, 35 Windsor Place, Cardiff.—*Sec.*, A. C. Davey, M.SC.

Temperance Council of the Christian Churches (1915) (incorporating the Overseas Temperance Council), 27 Marylebone Road, N.W.1.—*Gen. Sec.*, Rev. A. C. Davies, B.A.,B.D.

Temperance Council of the Christian Churches of Wales, 35 Windsor Place, Cardiff.—*Joint Secs.*, Rev. A. Thomas, B.A.; A. C. Davey, M.SC.

Temperance Education Board (Ireland) (1919), 20 Lombard Street, Belfast.—*Sec.*, H. C. Jones.

United Kingdom Band of Hope Union, Hope House, 45 Great Peter Street, S.W.1.—*Gen. Sec.*, Robert Tayler.

TERRITORIAL AND AUXILIARY FORCES ASSOCIATIONS, COUNCIL OF (1908), Duke of York's Headquarters, Chelsea, S.W.3.—*Sec.*, Brig. W. N. Roper-Caldbeck, D.S.O.

TERRITORIAL ARMY RIFLE ASSOCIATION, 109 Kingsway, W.C.2.—*Sec.* Major D. J. Black, T.D.

TEXTILE INSTITUTE (1910), 10 Blackfriars Street, Manchester, 3.—*Gen. Sec.*. D. B. Moore, B.A.

THEATRE PRESS REPRESENTATIVES, ASSOCIATION OF LONDON (1950), 31 Queen's House, Leicester Square, W.C.2.—*Hon. Sec.*, F. Rainbow.

THEATRE RESEARCH, SOCIETY FOR (1949).—*Hon. Secs.*, Miss S. Rosenfeld; J. Reading, 103 Ralph Court, W.2.

THEATRICAL FUND, ROYAL GENERAL (1839), 11 Garrick Street, W.C.2.—*Sec.*, Mrs. H. Long.

THEATRICAL LADIES' GUILD (1892), 50 Great Russell Street, W.C.1.—*Sec.*, Miss F. A. Holdship.

THEATRICAL MANAGERS ASSOCIATION, Faraday House, 8/10 Charing Cross Road, W.C.2.—*Sec.*, T. Chapman-Mortimer.

THEOSOPHICAL SOCIETY IN ENGLAND (1875), 50 Gloucester Place, W.1.—*Gen. Sec.*, V. W. Slater.

THISTLE FOUNDATION, THE (1945), 22 Charlotte Square, Edinburgh 2.—*Secs.*, Graham, Smart and Annan, Chartered Accountants.

THORACIC SOCIETY, THE.—*Hon. Sec.*, H. M. Foreman, M.B.E., M.B., F.R.C.P., Sully Hospital, Penarth, Glamorgan.

TIN RESEARCH INSTITUTE (1932), Fraser Road, Perivale, Greenford, Middlesex.—*Dir.*, E. S. Hedges, Ph.D., D.SC.

TOC H (TALBOT HOUSE) (1915), *British Headquarters*, 15 Trinity Square, E.C.3.—*Gen. Sec.*, C. A. Cattell.

TOWN AND COUNTRY PLANNING ASSOCIATION, 28 King Street, Covent Garden, W.C.2.—*Dir.*, W. Thomas.

TOWN CLERKS, SOCIETY OF (1928).—*Hon. Sec.*, C. W. G. T. Kirk, LL.B. (Town Clerk of Hemel Hemspead).

TOWN PLANNING INSTITUTE (1914), 18 Ashley Place, S.W.1.—*Pres.*, (1963–64), D. W. Riley; *Sec.*, P. R. Rathbone, B.A.

TOWNSWOMEN'S GUILDS, NATIONAL UNION OF (1929), 2 Cromwell Place, S.W.7.—*Nat. Gen. Sec.*, Mrs. L. F. Norman, M.A.

TRADE, NATIONAL CHAMBER OF (1897), Enterprise House, 3 Hyde Park Place, W.2.—*Gen. Sec.*, J. W. Stevenson.

TRADE UNIONS, GENERAL FEDERATION OF (1899), Central House. Upper Woburn Place, W.C.1.—*Chairman*, R. Driver; *Sec.*, L Hodgson.

TRADES UNION CONGRESS, (T.U.C.)—*See* p. 1094.

TRAFFIC ADMINISTRATION, INSTITUTE OF (1944), 36 Victoria Street, S.W.1.—*Sec.*, A. C. Gibson.

TRANSPORT, INSTITUTE OF (1919), 80 Portland Place, W.1.—*Sec.*. F. W. Crews.

TRAVEL AGENTS, ASSOCIATION OF BRITISH (1950), 10 Mayfair Place, W.1.—*Sec.*, A. R. Colmer.

TROPICAL MEDICINE AND HYGIENE, ROYAL SOCIETY OF (1907), Manson House, 26 Portland Place, W.1.—*Pres.*, C. Wilcocks, C.M.G., M.D., F.R.C.P.; *Sec.*, Miss N. Hopper.

TRUSTEE SAVINGS BANKS ASSOCIATION (1887). 22 Manchester Square, W.1.—*Sec.*, R. T. H. Scott, M.B.E., C.A.

TUTORS IN ADULT EDUCATION, ASSOCIATION OF, 19 Lawn Avenue, West Drayton, Middlesex.—*Hon. Sec.*, L. Speak. M.A.

UFAW (Universities Federation for Animal Welfare) (1926), 7A Lamb's Conduit Passage, W.C.1; *Chairman*, Kenneth Bird, C.B.E.; *Sec. Gen.*, C. W. Hume, O.B.E., M.C., B.SC.

ULSTER ASSOCIATION, THE LONDON, 13 Lower Regent Street, S.W.1.—*Pres.*, Field-Marshal the Viscount Alanbrooke, K.G., G.C.B., G.C.V.O., O.M., D.S.O.; *Hon. Sec.*, Capt. J. Lindsay.

ULSTER TOURIST DEVELOPMENT ASSOCIATION (1924), 6 Royal Avenue, Belfast.—*Sec.*, W. B. Cowan.

ULSTER UNIONIST COUNCIL. *Headquarters*, 3 Glengall Street, Belfast, 12.—*Sec.*, W. Douglas, O.B.E.

UNIT TRUST MANAGERS, ASSOCIATION OF (1959), 306–8 Salisbury House, Finsbury Circus, E.C.2.—*Sec.*, W. G. N. Miller.

UNITED COMMERCIAL TRAVELLERS' ASSOCIATION OF GREAT BRITAIN AND IRELAND (U.K.C.T.A.), (1883) (Incorporated), 180 Tottenham Court Road, W.1.—*Gen. Sec.*, J. Maguire.

UNITED KINGDOM ALLIANCE FOR TOTAL SUPPRESSION OF LIQUOR TRAFFIC (1853), Alliance House, 12 Caxton Street, S.W.1.—*Pres.*, H. Cecil Heath, B.A.

UNITED NATIONS ASSOCIATION OF GREAT BRITAIN AND NORTHERN IRELAND (1945), 25 Charles Street, W.1.—*Dir.-Gen.*, Charles Judd, C.B.E.; *Sec.*, Lt.-Col. T. A. M. Twaddle.

UNITED SERVICES CORPS (1908), for employment of ex-regular Soldiers, Sailors and Airmen of exemplary character. *Headquarters*, 19 Hand Court, W.C.1.

UNITED SOCIETY FOR CHRISTIAN LITERATURE, THE comprising The Religious Tract Society (1799), The Christian Literature Society for India and Africa (1858), and The Christian Literature Society (Scotland) for China (1884). Headquarters, *Great Britain*, 4 Bouverie Street, E.C.4; *Africa*, Lusaka, Northern Rhodesia.—*Hon. Secs.*, Rev. Canon W. H. Murray Walton; Rev. G. E. Hickman Johnson; *Gen. Sec.*, Rev. Canon E. H. Wade; *Gen. Manager*, G. M. Lewis.

UNITED SYNAGOGUE (1870).—*Pres.*, Sir Isaac Wolfson, Bt.; *Sec.*, Alfred H. Silverman, Woburn House, Upper Woburn Place, W.C.1.

UNIVERSITIES' MISSION TO CENTRAL AFRICA (1857), Central Africa House, 35 Great Peter Street, S.W.1.—*Sec.*, Rev. Canon J. S. Kingsnorth.

UNIVERSITY TEACHERS, ASSOCIATION OF (1919), Laurie House, 21 Dawson Place, W.2.—*Hon. Gen. Sec.*, The Lord Chorley, M.A.

UNIVERSITY WOMEN, BRITISH FEDERATION OF (LTD.) (1907), Crosby Hall, Cheyne Walk, S.W.3.—*Sec.*, Miss K. Johnston, M.A.

UNIVERSITY WOMEN, INTERNATIONAL FEDERATION OF (1920), 17A, King's Road, Sloane Square, S.W.3.—*Sec.*, Miss S. F. Stallman, M.A.

UNMARRIED MOTHER AND HER CHILD, NATIONAL COUNCIL FOR THE (INCORPORATED), 255 Kentish Town Road, N.W.5.—*Gen. Sec.*, Mrs. M. E. Bramall, M.A.

VALUERS INSTITUTION, LTD., 3 Cadogan Gate, S.W.1.—*Sec.*, Lt.-Col. C. V. Watson-Gandy, O.B.E., M.A.

VEGETARIAN SOCIETY, LONDON (1888), 53 Marloes Road, W.8.—*Sec.*, R. Lightowler.

VEGETARIAN SOCIETY, THE (NATIONAL) (1847), *Headquarters*, Bank Square, Wilmslow, Cheshire.—*Sec.*, G. L. Rudd.

VENEREAL DISEASES, MEDICAL SOCIETY FOR THE STUDY OF, 11 Chandos Street, W.1.—*Hon. Sec.*, Dr. C. S. Nicol, Lydia Dept., St. Thomas' Hospital, S.E.1.

VICE-CHANCELLORS AND PRINCIPALS OF THE UNIVERSITIES OF THE UNITED KINGDOM, COMMITTEE OF, 36 Gordon Square, W.C.1.—*Chairman*, Prof. Sir William Mansfield Cooper, LL.M.; *Sec.*, J. F. Foster, M.A., LL.D.

VICTORIA LEAGUE (1901), 38 Chesham Place, Belgrave Square, S.W.1.—*Gen. Sec.*, J. V. Shaw.

VICTORY (EX-SERVICES) ASSOCIATION LTD. AND CLUB, THE, 63–79 Seymour Street, W.2.—*Sec.*, Lt.-Cdr. J. B. Williams, R.N.

VIKING SOCIETY FOR NORTHERN RESEARCH, University College, Gower Street, W.C.1.—*Hon. Secs.*, Prof. G. Turville-Petre, M.A., B.Litt.; P. G. Foote, M.A.

VITREOUS ENAMELLERS, INSTITUTE OF, Ripley, nr. Derby.—*Sec.*, J. D. Gardom.

VISUAL EDUCATION, COUNCIL FOR, 55 Park Lane, W.1.—*Sec.*, Mrs. M. Mathieson.

VOLUNTARY SERVICE OVERSEAS (1958), c/o Royal Commonwealth Society, 18 Northumberland Avenue, W.C.2.—*Sec.*, G. L. Stephenson.

WAIFS AND STRAYS, CHURCH OF ENGLAND INCORPORATED SOCIETY FOR PROVIDING HOMES FOR, *see* CHURCH OF ENGLAND CHILDREN'S SOCIETY.

WATER ENGINEERS, INSTITUTION OF, Parliament Mansions, Abbey Orchard Street, S.W.1.—*Pres.*, (1963–64), L. H. Brown; *Sec.*, W. O. Skeat.

WEIGHTS & MEASURES ADMINISTRATION, INSTITUTE OF.—*Hon. Sec.*, J. R. Roberts, Weights and Measures Office, 57A Newton Street, Piccadilly, Manchester, 1.

WELDING, INSTITUTE OF (1923) 54 Princes Gate, Exhibition Road, S.W.7.—*Sec.*, G. Parsloe.

WELLCOME TRUST (1936), 52 Queen Anne Street, W.1.—*Scientific Sec.*, P. O. Williams (*acting*).

WELSH ECONOMIC DEVELOPMENT COUNCIL, 177 Cathedral Road, Cardiff.—*Sec.*, Miss H. M. James.

WELSH JOINT EDUCATION COMMITTEE (1949), 30 Cathedral Road, Cardiff.—*Sec.*, H. Wyn Jones, C.B.E.

WELSH LEAGUE OF YOUTH (Cwmni Urdd Gobaith Cymru) (1922), Aberystwyth.—*Dir.*, R. E. Griffith, O.B.E.

WELSH NATIONALIST PARTY (Plaid Cymru), 8 Queen Street, Cardiff.—*Org. Sec.*, E. Roberts.

WELSH TOURIST AND HOLIDAYS BOARD, 7 Park Place, Cardiff and Llandrindod Wells.—*Sec.*, Lyn Howell, O.B.E.

WESLEY HISTORICAL SOCIETY (1893).—*Gen. Sec.*, Rev. T. Shaw, 94 Albany Road, Redruth, Cornwall.

WEST END THEATRE MANAGERS, SOCIETY OF, 8-10 Charing Cross Road, W.C.2.—*Sec.*, T. Chapman-Mortimer.

WEST INDIA COMMITTEE (1750), 40 Norfolk Street, W.C.2.—*Sec.*, Lt.-Col. M. R. Robinson, D.S.O.

WEST LONDON MISSION (1887), Kingsway Hall, W.C.2.—*Supt.*, Rev. D. O. Soper, M.A. Ph.D.

WHITE ENSIGN ASSOCIATION LTD. (1958), Suffolk House, 4 Laurence Pountney Hill, E.C.4.—*Sec.*, Cdr. C. B. Lamb, D.S.O., D.S.C., R.N.

WIDOWS, SOCIETY FOR THE RELIEF OF DISTRESSED (1823) (residing within five miles of Charing Cross and applying within two months of widowhood), 39 Buckingham Gate, S.W.1.—Sec., P. A. Marno.

WINE AND SPIRIT ASSOCIATION OF GREAT BRITAIN (1824), Vintners' Place, Upper Thames Street, E.C.4.—*Sec.*, J. W. Mahoney.

WINTER DISTRESS LEAGUE. *See* EMPLOYMENT FELLOWSHIP.

WOMEN, SOCIETY FOR PROMOTING THE TRAINING OF (1859), Court Farm, Hedgerley, Bucks.—*Sec.*, Mrs. W. M. Golding.

WOMEN'S ADVISORY COUNCIL ON SOLID FUEL (1943), 18 South Molton Street, W.1.

WOMEN'S EMPLOYMENT FEDERATION (1933), 251 Brompton Road, S.W.3.—*Organizing Sec.*, Miss I. F. Hilton.

WOMEN'S ENGINEERING SOCIETY (1919), 25 Foubert's Place, W.1.—*Sec.*, Mrs. N. Webb.

WOMEN'S HOLIDAY FUND (1895), 76 Denison House, Vauxhall Bridge Road, S.W.1.—*Sec.*, Mrs. A. Brown.

WOMEN'S INSTITUTES, NATIONAL FEDERATION OF (1917), 39 Eccleston Street, S.W.1.—*Gen. Sec.*, Miss Alison King.

WOMEN'S INTERNATIONAL LEAGUE FOR PEACE AND FREEDOM (1915), British Section, 29 Great James Street, W.C.1.—*Sec.*, Miss Alison Huntley.

WOMEN'S LIBERAL FEDERATION, 54 Victoria Street, S.W.1.—*Pres.*, Mrs. W. Grubb; *Sec.*, Miss G. Maxwell.

WOMEN'S MIGRATION AND OVERSEA APPOINTMENTS SOCIETY (1920), 43 Parliament Street, S.W.1.—*Dir.*, Miss E. Cumber O.B.E., M.A.

WOMEN'S PROTESTANT UNION (W.P.U.) and THE SENTINEL'S MISSIONARY UNION.—*Hon. Gen. Sec.*, L. de Wirtz, Clive Court, Ashdown Avenue, Saltdean, Sussex.

WOMEN'S ROYAL NAVAL SERVICE BENEVOLENT TRUST (1942), 2 Grosvenor Crescent, S.W.1.—*Gen. Sec.*, Miss E. G. W. Young.

WOMEN'S TRANSPORT SERVICE (FANY) (1907), 55-56 Sloane Street, S.W.1.

WOMEN'S VOLUNTARY SERVICE FOR CIVIL DEFENCE (WVS) (1938), 41 Tothill Street, S.W.1.

WOOD PRESERVING ASSOCIATION, BRITISH, 6 Southampton Place, W.C.1.—*Secretary*, W. E. Bruce.

WORCESTERSHIRE ASSOCIATION (1926). — *Hon. Treas.*, Leonard W. Whiteman, B.Sc., 709 Grenville House, Dolphin Square, S.W.1.

WORK STUDY, INSTITUTE OF (1941), 3 Cork Street, W.1.—*Hon. Gen. Sec.*, W. G. Neill.

WORKERS' EDUCATIONAL ASSOCIATION, Temple House, 27 Portman Square, W.1.—*Gen. Sec.*, H. Nutt.

WORKERS' EDUCATIONAL ASSOCIATIONS, INTERNATIONAL FEDERATION OF, 27 Portman Square, W.1.—*Sec.*, H. Nutt.

WORKING MEN'S CLUB AND INSTITUTE UNION, Club Union House, 251-256 Upper Street, N.1. —*Gen. Sec.*, F. R. Castle, M.B.E.

WORKS AND HIGHWAYS SUPERINTENDENTS, INSTITUTE OF (1938), Flat 5, Bloomsbury Mansion, 26 Bloomsbury Way, W.C.1.—*Hon. Sec.*, W. H. Bush.

WORKS MANAGERS, INSTITUTION OF, 34 Bloomsbury Way, W.C.1.—*Gen. Sec.*, G. J. West.

WORLD CONGRESS OF FAITHS (1934), Younghusband House, 23 Norfolk Square, W.2.—*Chairman*, Rev. R. W. Sorensen, M.P.

WORLD POWER CONFERENCE (1924). *Central Office*, 201-2 Grand Buildings, Trafalgar Square, W.C.2.—*Sec.*, *International Executive Council*, C. H. Gray, O.B.E.

WORLD PROHIBITION FEDERATION (1909), 32 Buckingham Palace Road, S.W.1.—*Sec.*, Mark H. C. Hayler.

WORLD UNIVERSITY SERVICE, 59 Gloucester Place, W.1.—*Gen. Sec.*, Mrs. E. R. Merriell.

WORLD ZIONIST ORGANISATION (1897).—*London Office*, 77 Great Russell Street, W.C.1.

YORKSHIRE AGRICULTURAL SOCIETY (1837), Cliftonfield, Shipton Road, York.—*Sec.*, F. M. Baldwin, M.B.E., B.SC.

YORKSHIREMEN IN LONDON, SOCIETY OF (1899), AND THE YORKSHIRE SOCIETY (1812), Porteous House, Porteous Road, W.2.

YOUNG MEN'S CHRISTIAN ASSOCIATION, *National Council*: 112 Great Russell Street, W.C.1.—*Gen. Sec.*, Sir Norman Tucker, O.B.E.

YOUNG WOMEN'S CHRISTIAN ASSOCIATION (1855), *National Headquarters*, Bedford House, 108 Baker Street, W.1.—*Nat. Gen. Sec.*, Miss Ruth Walder, O.B.E.

YOUTH CLUBS, NATIONAL ASSOCIATION OF, 30 Devonshire Street, W.1.—*Gen. Sec.*, Miss E. L. Sewell.

YOUTH CLUBS, NORTHERN IRELAND ASSOCIATION OF, 7 Wellington Place, Belfast 1.—*Sec.*, Miss C. M. P. Copeland.

YOUTH HOSTELS ASSOCIATION (ENGLAND AND WALES) (1930), *National Office*, Trevelyan House, St. Albans, Herts.—*Sec.*, H. L. Knapp.

YOUTH HOSTELS ASSOCIATION (SCOTTISH) (1931), *National Office*, 7 Bruntsfield Crescent, Edinburgh, 10.—*Gen. Sec.*, A. C. Cromar LL.B.

YOUTH HOSTEL ASSOCIATION OF NORTHERN IRELAND LTD. (1931), 28 Bedford Street, Belfast.—*Organizing Sec.*, R. G. Carinduff.

ZOOLOGICAL SOCIETY OF LONDON, Regent's Park, N.W.1.—*Sec.*, Prof. Sir Solly Zuckerman, C.B., D.SC., F.R.S.; *Controller*, Maj.-Gen. C. J. G. Dalton, C.B., C.B.E.; *Scientific Dir.*, L. Harrison Matthews, M.A. SC.D., F.R.S. Attendances (1962), Regent's Park, 1,640,541, and Whipsnade Park, 642,077.

ZOOLOGICAL SOCIETY OF SCOTLAND, ROYAL, Corstorphine Road, Edinburgh, 12.—*Dir. and Sec.*, G. D. Fisher.

LOCAL ARCHAEOLOGICAL SOCIETIES

England and Wales

Anglesey.—ANGLESEY ANTIQUARIAN SOCIETY. *Hon. Sec.*, D. O. Jones, County Library, Llangefni, Anglesey.

Bedfordshire. — BEDFORDSHIRE ARCHAEOLOGICAL COUNCIL. *Hon. Sec.*, L. A. Speed, Luton Museum, Luton.

SOUTH BEDFORDSHIRE ARCHÆOLOGICAL SOCIETY. *Hon. Sec.*, J. F. Dyer, 45 Ashcroft Road, Luton

Berkshire.—BERKSHIRE ARCHÆOLOGICAL SOCIETY. *Hon. Sec.*, F. M. Underhill, F.S.A., 32 Eton Road, Datchet, Bucks.

NEWBURY DISTRICT FIELD CLUB, Donnington Dene, Newbury. *Hon. Sec.*, E. G. Kaines-Thomas.

Buckinghamshire.—BUCKS ARCHÆOLOGICAL SOCIETY. *Hon. Sec.*, E. Viney, The Printing Works, Aylesbury, Bucks.

Cambridgeshire. — CAMBRIDGE ANTIQUARIAN SOCIETY. *Hon. Sec.*, Miss J. Liversidge, 20 Manor Court, Grange Road, Cambridge.

Cardiganshire. — CARDIGANSHIRE ANTIQUARIAN SOCIETY. *Hon. Sec.*, D. M. Jones, 26 Alban Square, Aberaeron.

Cheshire.—CHESTER AND NORTH WALES ARCHÆOLOGICAL SOCIETY, Grosvenor Museum, Chester. *Hon. Sec.*, D. M. Evans.

Cornwall.—ROYAL INSTITUTION OF CORNWALL, County Museum and Art Gallery, Truro. *Hon. Sec.*, A. J. Lyne.

Cumberland and Westmorland.—CUMBERLAND AND WESTMORLAND ANTIQUARIAN AND ARCHÆOLOGICAL SOCIETY. *Hon. Sec.*, H. Clegg, Affetside, Kilmidyke, Grange-over-Sands, Lancs.

Derbyshire.—DERBYSHIRE ARCHÆOLOGICAL SOCIETY, St. Mary's Bridge Chapel House, Derby. *Joint Hon. Secs.*, A. L. Thorpe; R. G. Hughes.

Devonshire.—DEVON ARCHÆOLOGICAL EXPLORATION SOCIETY. *Hon. Sec.*, E. G. Sandford, c/o The Museum, Queen Street, Exeter.

Dorset.—DORSET NATURAL HISTORY AND ARCHÆOLOGICAL SOCIETY, County Museum, Dorchester. *Curator and Sec.*, R. N. R. Peers.

Durham. — DURHAM AND NORTHUMBERLAND ARCHITECTURAL AND ARCHÆOLOGICAL SOCIETY. *Hon. Sec.*, C. W. Gibby, PH.D., F.S.A., Prebends' Gate, Durham.

SUNDERLAND ANTIQUARIAN SOCIETY. *Hon. Secs.*, A. Stewart, 9 Keswick Avenue, Sunderland; L. P. Crangle, 71 Hurstwood Road, Sunderland.

Essex.—ESSEX ARCHÆOLOGICAL SOCIETY, Holly Trees, Colchester. *Hon. Sec.*, J. S. Appleby.

Gloucestershire.—BRISTOL AND GLOUCESTERSHIRE ARCHÆOLOGICAL SOCIETY, Council House, Bristol, 1. *Hon. Sec.*, Miss E. Ralph.

UNIVERSITY OF BRISTOL SPELÆOLOGICAL SOCIETY, The University, Bristol 8. *Hon. Sec.*, J. J. P. Clokie.

Hampshire.—HAMPSHIRE FIELD CLUB AND ARCHÆOLOGICAL SOCIETY. *Hon. Sec.*, R. L. P. Jowitt, Gore Grange New Milton, Hants.

Herefordshire.—WOOLHOPE NATURALISTS' FIELD CLUB. *Hon. Sec.*, c/o The City Library, Broad Street, Hereford.

Hertfordshire.—EAST HERTFORDSHIRE ARCHÆOLOGICAL SOCIETY. *Hon. Sec.*, G. Moodey, 27 West Street, Hertford.

Kent.—KENT ARCHÆOLOGICAL SOCIETY, *Hon. Sec.*, c/o The Museum, Maidstone.

Leicestershire.—LEICESTERSHIRE ARCHÆOLOGICAL AND HISTORICAL SOCIETY, The Guildhall, Guildhall Lane, Leicester. *Hon. Sec.*, F. S. Cheney.

Lincolnshire.—LINCOLNSHIRE ARCHITECTURAL AND ARCHÆOLOGICAL SOCIETY, Jews' Court, Steep Hill, Lincoln. *Hon. Secs.*, G. S. Dixon; F. T. Baker.

Middlesex.—LONDON AND MIDDLESEX ARCHÆOLOGICAL SOCIETY, Bishopsgate Institute, E.C.2. *Hon. Sec.*, E. E. F. Smith.

Norfolk.—NORFOLK AND NORWICH ARCHÆOLOGICAL SOCIETY. *Hon. Gen. Sec.*, I. Cresswell, 32 The Close, Norwich.

Northamptonshire.—NORTHAMPTONSHIRE ANTIQUARIAN SOCIETY. *Hon. Sec.*, V. A. Hatley, 10 Watkin Terrace, Northampton.

Northumberland (*See also Durham*).—NEWCASTLE SOCIETY OF ANTIQUARIES, The Black Gate, Newcastle-upon-Tyne. *Hon. Sec.*, M. G. Cook.

Nottinghamshire.—THOROTON SOCIETY OF NOTTINGHAMSHIRE, Bromley House, Angel Row, Nottingham. *Hon. Sec.*, K. S. S. Train.

Radnorshire.—RADNORSHIRE SOCIETY. *Hon. Secs.*, E. V. Howells, Grammar School, Llandrindod Wells; C. W. Newman, County Library, Llandrindod Wells.

Salop.—SHROPSHIRE ARCHÆOLOGICAL AND PARISH REGISTER SOCIETY. *Hon. Sec.*, H. Beaumont, Silverdale, Severn Bank, Shrewsbury.

Somerset.—SOMERSET ARCHÆOLOGICAL AND NATURAL HISTORY SOCIETY, Taunton Castle, Taunton. *Secretary*, C. A. Cookson, O.B.E.

Staffordshire.—NORTH STAFFORDSHIRE FIELD CLUB, *Hon. Sec.*, Dr. J. T. Thomas, 34 Beresford Crescent, Newcastle, Staffs.

CITY OF STOKE-ON-TRENT MUSEUM ARCHÆOLOGICAL SOCIETY, City Museum, Stoke-on-Trent. *Hon. Sec.*, A. R. Mountford.

Suffolk.—SUFFOLK INSTITUTE OF ARCHÆOLOGY.—*Hon. Sec.*, M. J. Statham, County Record Office, Bury St. Edmunds.

Surrey.—SURREY ARCHÆOLOGICAL SOCIETY, Castle Arch, Guildford. *Hon. Sec.*, E. S. Wood, F.S.A.

Sussex.—SUSSEX ARCHÆOLOGICAL SOCIETY, Barbican House, High Street, Lewes. *Hon. Secs.*, T. T. Harris; A. E. Wilson, F.S.A.

Warwickshire.—BIRMINGHAM ARCHÆOLOGICAL SOCIETY, Birmingham and Midland Institute, Paradise Street, Birmingham. *Hon. Sec.*, Mrs. M. G. Sanders, F.S.A.

COVENTRY ARCHÆOLOGICAL SOCIETY. *Sec.*, H. J. Turner, c/o Herbert Art Gallery and Museum, Coventry.

Wight.—ISLE OF WIGHT NATURAL HISTORY AND ARCHÆOLOGICAL SOCIETY. *Sec.*, J. E. Cooper, Cliff Close, 99 Victoria Avenue, Shanklin, I.o.W.

Wiltshire.—WILTSHIRE ARCHÆOLOGICAL AND NATURAL HISTORY SOCIETY, The Museum, Devizes. *Hon. Sec.*, Rev. E. H. Steele.

Worcester. — WORCESTERSHIRE ARCHÆOLOGICAL SOCIETY. *Hon. Sec.*, R. F. Panton, Mayfield, 76 Graham Road, Malvern.

Yorkshire.—HUNTER ARCHÆOLOGICAL SOCIETY. *Hon. Sec.*, Miss D. Greene, F.S.A., 30 Clifton Mount, Rotherham.

YORKSHIRE ARCHÆOLOGICAL SOCIETY. *Hon. Sec.*, Miss E. M. Walker, F.S.A., 6 Aislabie Close, Ripon.

HALIFAX ANTIQUARIAN SOCIETY. *Hon. Sec.*, R. Bretton, 16 Mayfield Drive Halifax.

THORESBY SOCIETY, 16 Queen Square, Leeds 2. *Hon. Sec.*, K. J. Bonser.

Isle of Man, Channel Islands

ISLE OF MAN NATURAL HISTORY AND ANTIQUARIAN SOCIETY, c/o The Manx Museum, Douglas.

SOCIÉTÉ JERSIAISE, The Museum, Pier Road, St. Helier, Jersey. *Sec.*, G. C. H. Le Cocq.

Scotland

AYRSHIRE ARCHÆOLOGICAL AND NATURAL HISTORY SOCIETY, Carnegie Library, Ayr. *Hon. Sec.*, A. F. Sutherland, 11 Allanvale Road, Prestwick.

DUMFRIES AND GALLOWAY NATURAL HISTORY AND ANTIQUARIAN SOCIETY. *Hon. Sec.*, Mrs. S. M. Weeks, Querdon, Moss Road, Lochanhead Road, Dumfries.

GLASGOW ARCHÆOLOGICAL SOCIETY. *Hon. Secs.* H. B. Millar, F.S.A.Scot., 4 Clifton Street, Glasgow C.3.; J. Paterson, 49 Cumbernauld Road, Glasgow, E.3.

HAWICK ARCHÆOLOGICAL SOCIETY. *Hon. Sec.*, T. I. Storie, 3 Rinkvale Cottages, Hawick.

EMPLOYERS' ASSOCIATIONS

BAKERS, CONFECTIONERS AND CATERERS, NATIONAL ASSOCIATION OF MASTER, 13 Ashley Place, S.W.1.—*Dir.*, L. F. Cadwallader, O.B.E.

BAKERS, FEDERATION OF WHOLESALE AND MULTIPLE, 4 Lloyds Avenue, E.C.3.—*Sec.*, D. McKelvie.

BISCUIT MANUFACTURERS, NATIONAL ASSOCIATION OF, Scottish Union House, 25 Bucklersbury, E.C.4.—*Sec.*, C. T. Digby-Jones.

BOOT TRADES ASSOCIATION, LTD., ST. CRISPINS, St. Crispin's House, Desborough, nr. Kettering, Northants.

BRASSFOUNDRY ASSOCIATION, NATIONAL, 5 Greenfield Crescent, Edgbaston, Birmingham, 15.—*Sec.*, E. N. Hiley, M.B.E.

BRUSH MANUFACTURERS' ASSOCIATION, BRITISH, 80 Coleman Street, E.C.2.—*Sec.*, R. F. Knox.

BUILDING TRADES EMPLOYERS, NATIONAL FEDERATION OF (1878). 82 New Cavendish Street, W.1. —*Sec.*, C. G. Rowlands, O.B.E.

CABLE MAKERS' ASSOCIATION, High Holborn House, 52–54 High Holborn, W.C.1.—*Joint Managers*, E. H. Adams; G. E. Heard.

CALICO PRINTERS, FEDERATION OF, 20 Princess Street, Manchester 1.—*Sec.* A. E. Hall.

CARPET MANUFACTURERS, FEDERATION OF BRITISH (1960), 55–61 Moorgate, E.C.2.—*Sec.*, Hon. W. G. M. Spens, M.B.E.

CAST CONCRETE FEDERATION, BRITISH, 60 Buckingham Gate, S.W.1.—*Sec.*, R. W. Parks.

CATERERS' ASSOCIATION OF GREAT BRITAIN (1917), Victoria House, Vernon Place, Southampton Row, W.C.1.—*Sec.*, J. D. G. Hooper.

CEMENT MAKERS' FEDERATION, Terminal House, 52 Grosvenor Gardens, S.W.1.—*Sec.*, R. E. McGuire, C.M.G., O.B.E.

CHEMICAL MANUFACTURERS, ASSOCIATION OF BRITISH (1916), 86 Strand, W.C.2.—*Dir.*, G. Brearley.

CHINA AND GLASS RETAILERS' ASSOCIATION, 69 Cannon Street, E.C.4.—*Sec.*, J. R. Aldam.

CHINA CLAY PRODUCERS' FEDERATION, LTD., BRITISH, 5 High Cross Street, St. Austell, Cornwall.—*Sec.*, J. W. M. Graham.

CINEMATOGRAPH EXHIBITORS' ASSOCIATION OF GREAT BRITAIN AND IRELAND, 164 Shaftesbury Avenue, W.C.2.—*Gen. Sec.*, E. F. Pinkney.

CIVIL ENGINEERING CONTRACTORS, FEDERATION OF, Romney House, Tufton Street, S.W.1.—*Gen. Secs.*, P. R. O'Day; D. V. Gaulter.

CLAY INDUSTRIES, NATIONAL FEDERATION OF, Drayton House, 30 Gordon Street, W.C.1.—*Sec.*, G. K. Timperley.

CLOTHING MANUFACTURERS' FEDERATION OF GREAT BRITAIN, 70 Pall Mall, S.W.1.—*Sec.*, M. K. Reid, O.B.E.

COAL MERCHANTS' FEDERATION OF GREAT BRITAIN, Victoria House, Southampton Row, W.C.1.—*Dir. and Sec.*, J. W. Stewart, O.B.E.

COCOA, CHOCOLATE AND CONFECTIONERY ALLIANCE, 11 Green Street, W.1.—*Sec.*, J. E. Chapman.

COLD STORAGE AND ICE TRADES, NATIONAL FEDERATION OF, New Bridge Street House, E.C.4.—*Sec.*, D. T. Lee.

CONFECTIONERS, NATIONAL UNION OF RETAIL, 53 Christchurch Avenue, North Finchley, N.12.—*Sec.*, T. Hutchinson.

COOPERAGE FEDERATION, NATIONAL, 69 Cannon Street, E.C.4.—*Sec.*, J. R. Aldam.

CORN AND AGRICULTURAL MERCHANTS, NATIONAL ASSOCIATION OF, Cereal House, Mark Lane, E.C.3.—*Sec.*, C. G. Metson, O.B.E.

CUTLERY AND SILVERWARE MANUFACTURERS ASSOCIATION, UNITED KINGDOM, Light Trades House, Melbourne Avenue, Sheffield, 10.—*Sec.*, E. A. Tuxford.

CYCLE TRADERS, NATIONAL ASSOCIATION OF, 66 Grafton Way, W.1.—*Gen. Sec.*, A. E. Barnfather.

DRAPERS' CHAMBER OF TRADE, 4 Harley Street, W.1.—*Dir.*, J. Ramage, O.B.E.

ELECTRICAL AND ALLIED MANUFACTURERS ASSOCIATION, BRITISH (1905), 36 and 38 Kingsway, W.C.2.—*Dir.*, S. F. Steward, C.B.E.

ELECTRICAL APPLIANCE ASSOCIATION (R.T.R.A.) LTD., 19–21 Conway Street, Fitzroy Square, W.1. —*Dir.*, D. M. Keegan.

ELECTRICAL ASSOCIATION, NATIONAL FEDERATED, 14 Bedford Row, W.C.1.—*Sec.*, G. T. King.

ENGINEERING EMPLOYERS' FEDERATION, Broadway House, Tothill Street, S.W.1.—*Sec.*, E. C. Happold.

FARMERS' UNION, NATIONAL (1908), Agriculture House, Knightsbridge, S.W.1.—*Gen. Sec.*, J. K. Knowles, C.B.E.

FARMERS' UNION OF SCOTLAND, NATIONAL (1913), 17 Grosvenor Crescent, Edinburgh 12.—*Gen. Sec.*, H. G. Munro, T.D., W.S.

FILM PRODUCERS' ASSOCIATION, BRITISH, 49 Mount Street, W.1.—*Gen. Sec.*, J. P. H. Walton.

FISHMONGERS, NATIONAL FEDERATION OF, 20 Buckingham Street, W.C.2.—*Sec.*, P. Anderson.

FOOTWEAR MANUFACTURERS FEDERATION, BRITISH, 22 Gilbert Street, W.1.—*Dir.*, P. Glennie-Smith.

FREESTONE QUARRY OWNERS, NATIONAL FEDERATION OF, 138 Lord Street, Southport, Lancs.—*Sec.*, H. Hodson.

FUR TRADE ALLIANCE, BRITISH, 11 Great St. Thomas Apostle, E.C.4. *Sec.*, Miss P. Parratt, M.B.E.

FURNISHERS, NATIONAL ASSOCIATION OF RETAIL, 17 Berners Street, W.1.—*Sec.*, D. W. Edwards.

FURNITURE TRADE CONFEDERATION, BRITISH, 17 Berners Street, W.1.—*Joint Secs.*, D. D. Mitchell (*Manufacturers*); D. W. Edwards (*Retailers*).

GLASS MANUFACTURERS' FEDERATION, 19 Portland Place, W.1.—*Dir.*, D. Rider.

GROCERS' FEDERATION, NATIONAL, Federation House, 4 Endsleigh Street, W.C.1.—*Sec.* (vacant).

GROCERS AND PROVISION MERCHANTS, NATIONAL FEDERATION OF WHOLESALE, Panton House, 1 Howard Street, W.C.2.—*Sec.*, D. Ellam.

HAIRDRESSERS' FEDERATION, NATIONAL, 20 Cranbourne Gardens, Golders Green, N.W.11.—*Sec.*, T. Briggs.

HERRING TRADE ASSOCIATION, LTD., BRITISH, 22 Belmont Street, Aberdeen.—*Sec.*, W. B. Glennie.

IRON AND STEEL FEDERATION, BRITISH, Steel House, Tothill Street, S.W.1.—*Sec.* K. Donohue.

IRON ORE PRODUCERS, NATIONAL COUNCIL OF ASSOCIATED, 48 Meadow Road, Kettering, Northants.—*Sec.* P. T. M. Wilson.

JEWELLERS' ASSOCIATION, BRITISH, St. Dunstan's House, Carey Lane, E.C.2.—*Dir.*, H. B. Southam, M.B.E.

JUTE SPINNERS AND MANUFACTURERS ASSOCIATION, Chamber of Commerce Buildings, Panmure Street, Dundee.—*Sec.* G. A. S. Crombie.

LAUNDERERS, INSTITUTE OF BRITISH, LTD., 16–17 Lancaster Gate, W.2.—*Dir.*, E. W. Swetman.

LEATHER PRODUCERS' ASSOCIATION FOR ENGLAND, SCOTLAND AND WALES, Leather Trade House, 9 St. Thomas Street, S.E.1.—*Manager*, E. Bainbridge.

LINOLEUM AND FELT BASE EMPLOYERS' FEDERATION, 69 North End, Croydon, Surrey.—*Sec.*, C. M. Secrett.

MACHINE TOOL TRADES ASSOCIATION, 25–28 Buckingham Gate, S.W.1.—*Gen. Manager*, H. O. Barrett.

MALTSTERS' ASSOCIATION OF GREAT BRITAIN, 19 Southwark Street, S.E.1.—*Sec.*, Group Capt. V. Fairfield, O.B.E.

MEAT TRADERS' ASSOCIATIONS INCORPORATED, NATIONAL FEDERATION OF, 29 Linkfield Lane, Redhill, Surrey.—*Sec.*, J. B. Whalley, M.B.E.

MEAT TRADERS OF GREAT BRITAIN AND IRELAND, FEDERATION OF WHOLESALE FRESH, Lloyds Bank Buildings, 11–13 Victoria Street, Liverpool 2.—*Sec.*, J. F. Moore.

MILLERS, NATIONAL ASSOCIATION OF BRITISH AND IRISH, LTD. (1878), 21 Arlington Street, S.W.1.—*Sec.*, L. Carrington.

MOTOR AGENTS' ASSOCIATION, LTD., 201 Great Portland Street, W.1.—*Dir. Gen.* F. E. Higham.

MOTOR MANUFACTURERS AND TRADERS, SOCIETY OF (1902), Forbes House, Halkin Street, S.W.1.—*Sec.*, W. T. Williams.

NON-FERROUS METALS FEDERATION, BRITISH (1945), 6 Vicarage Road, Birmingham 15.—*Dir.*, K. Romer-Lee.

OUTFITTERS, NATIONAL ASSOCIATION OF, 21 Cavendish Place, W.1.—*Sec.*, K. E. Smith.

PAINTING AND DECORATING TRADE EMPLOYERS, CONFEDERATION OF, St. Stephen's House, Westminster, S.W.1.—*Sec.*, A. E. Wade.

PAPERMAKERS AND BOARDMAKERS, EMPLOYERS' FEDERATION OF, 1 Clements Inn, W.C.2.—*Gen. Sec.*, M. Lambert.

PAPER MERCHANTS, NATIONAL ASSOCIATION OF, 27 Chancery Lane, W.C.2.—*Gen. Sec.*, S. R. W. Bailey.

PLATE GLASS ASSOCIATION, THE, 6 Mount Row, W.1.—*Sec.*, L. F. Brett.

PLUMBERS AND DOMESTIC ENGINEERS, NATIONAL FEDERATION OF, 81 Gower Street, W.C.1.—*Sec.*, H. Leighton.

PLYWOOD AND VENEER MANUFACTURERS, ASSOCIATION OF BRITISH, Pinners Hall, Austin Friars, E.C.2.—*Sec.*, A. C. T. Dawe.

PORT EMPLOYERS, NATIONAL ASSOCIATION OF, Three Quays, Tower Hill, E.C.3.—*Gen. Manager*, J. M. Gifford.

POTTERY MANUFACTURERS' FEDERATION, BRITISH, Federation House, Station Road, Stoke-on-Trent.—*Sec.*, D. Turner.

PRINTERS, BRITISH FEDERATION OF MASTER, 11 Bedford Row, W.C.1.—*Dir.*, L. E. Kenyon, C.B.E.

QUARRY OWNERS OF GREAT BRITAIN, FEDERATED, Manfield House, 376–9 Strand, W.C.2.—*Sec.*, J. D. Mortimer.

RADIO AND TELEVISION RETAILERS' ASSOCIATION, 19–21 Conway Street, Fitzroy Square, W.1.—*Dir.*, D. M. Keegan.

ROAD HAULAGE ASSOCIATION, 22 Upper Woburn Place, W.C.1.—*Sec.-Gen.*, G. K. Newman.

ROOFING CONTRACTORS, NATIONAL FEDERATION OF, West Bar Chambers, 38 Boar Lane, Leeds 1.—*Sec.*, A. K. Davidson, M.B.E.

RUBBER INDUSTRY, INSTITUTION OF THE (1921), 4 Kensington Palace Gardens, W.8.—*Sec.*, G. E. Holmes-Siedle.

RUBBER MANUFACTURING EMPLOYERS' ASSOCIATION, 236 and 237 Royal Exchange, Manchester 2.—*Sec.*, A. Babbage.

SAND AND GRAVEL ASSOCIATION OF GREAT BRITAIN, 48 Park Street, W.1.—*Gen. Sec.*, C. B. Mills.

SAWMILLING ASSOCIATION, NATIONAL, 68–70 Queen Street, E.C.4.—*Sec.*, J. Bick.

SCIENTIFIC INSTRUMENT MANUFACTURERS' ASSOCIATION OF GREAT BRITAIN (1916), 20 Peel Street, W.8.—*Dir.*, Capt. R. A. Villiers, C.B.E., R.N. (*ret.*).

SEED CRUSHERS' ASSOCIATION, NATIONAL, Unilever House, Blackfriars, E.C.4.—*Sec.*, B. J. B. Thompson.

SHIPBUILDING EMPLOYERS' FEDERATION, 1 Chester Street, S.W.1.—*Sec.*, W. Watson, C.B.E.

SHIPPING FEDERATION (1890), 146–150 Minories, E.C.3.—*Dir.*, H. W. Greaney, C.B.E.

SPINNERS' AND DOUBLERS' ASSOCIATION, BRITISH, 5th Floor, Royal Exchange, Manchester 2.—*Sec.*, W. R. Hanks.

TAILORS OF GREAT BRITAIN, FEDERATION OF MERCHANT, 32 Savile Row, W.1.—*Sec.*, P. G. Clancy.

TEXTILE MANUFACTURERS' ASSOCIATION, UNITED KINGDOM, Midland Bank House, 26 Cross Street, Manchester 2.—*Sec.*, J. Gill.

TIMBER TRADE FEDERATION OF THE U.K., 69 Cannon Street, E.C.4.—*Sec.*, H. J. Bocking.

TOBACCONISTS, NATIONAL UNION OF RETAIL, 85 Gower Street, W.C.1.—*Sec.*, G. H. Scott.

TRAWLERS FEDERATION LTD., BRITISH, Albert Gardens, Cleethorpes Road, Grimsby, Lincs.—*Sec.*, J. H. Ray, O.B.E.

WATER COMPANIES ASSOCIATION, THE, 15 Great College Street, S.W.1.—*Sec.*, M. A. Liddell.

WATERWORKS ASSOCIATION, BRITISH, 34 Park Street, W.1.—*Sec.*, L. W. F. Millis, O.B.E.

WOOL FEDERATION, BRITISH, Commerce House, Bradford.—*Sec.*, E. Barlow.

BRITISH EMPLOYERS' CONFEDERATION

36 Smith Square, S.W.1.

The British Employers' Confederation was established in 1919. Its membership consists of 52 national employers' organizations which deal with labour questions in most of the principal industries, other than the nationalized industries.

President, E. J. Hunter, C.B.E.
Director, Sir George Pollock, Q.C.
Gen. Sec., F. J. C. Honey, C.B.E.

FEDERATION OF BRITISH INDUSTRIES

21, Tothill Street, S.W.1.

The Federation of British Industries was founded in 1916, and in 1923 was granted a Royal Charter. In the Charter, the F.B.I. is defined as an association of manufacturers founded for the "encouragement, promotion and protection of British Industries of all kinds."

The membership consists of individual firms engaged in productive industry (excluding the nationalized industries) and trade associations. More than 8,000 firms and 300 trade associations (representing about 40,000 firms) are members. The Federation has 12 regional and district offices and has representatives in 140 centres overseas.

President, P. F. Runge.
Director-General, Sir Norman Kipping, K.B.E.
Secretary, J. Gough.

NATIONAL ASSOCIATION OF BRITISH MANUFACTURERS

6, Holborn Viaduct, E.C.1

The National Association of British Manufacturers (formerly the National Union of Manufacturers) is a national organization representing manufacturing industry. Formed in 1915, its membership (restricted to manufacturers) now totals over 5,000 individual firms with 60 affiliated trade associations. It is regarded both by Government and by industry as the national representative of medium-sized and smaller firms in particular. It has no party-political affiliations. There are branches in London, Birmingham, Manchester, Liverpool, Nottingham, Leeds, Newcastle, Glasgow, Cardiff and N. Ireland.

President, Col. E. R. Mayer, T.D.
Director, H. J. Gray, C.M.G.

TRADES UNION CONGRESS (T.U.C.)

Congress House, 23–28 Great Russell Street, W.C.1
[Museum: 4030]

The Trades Union Congress, founded in 1868, is a voluntary association of Trade Unions, the primary purpose of which is to enable the representatives of unions to meet annually to consider matters of common concern to their members. The Congress has met annually since 1871 (with the exception of 1914) and in recent years has met normally on the first Monday in September, its sessions extending through the succeeding four days. Congress is constituted by delegates of the affiliated unions on the basis of one delegate for every 5,000 members, or fraction thereof, on whose behalf affiliation fees are paid. Affiliated unions (in 1962–63) totalled 176 with an aggregate membership of 8,315,332.

The main business of the annual Congress is to consider the report of its General Council dealing with the activities of the Congress year, along with resolutions from affiliated societies on questions of policy and organization. Although 176 trade union organizations are affiliated to Congress, some of these, especially in cotton, are themselves federal bodies including in total 150 more unions. Only two British unions with large membership are not affiliated to the T.U.C.

One of the important responsibilities of the annual Congress is to elect a General Council to keep watch on all industrial movements, legislation affecting labour and all matters touching the interest of the trade union movement, with authority to promote common action on general questions, and to assist trade unions in the work of organization. The General Council is elected by Congress and is composed of 34 members (32 representing 18 trade groups and two representing women workers). Following is a list of these trade groups with the aggregate membership of unions in each group (the woman membership included in the total being shown separately), and with the number of representatives each group is entitled to have on the General Council:—

Trade Group (with representation)	Membership	
	Total	Women
Mining and Quarrying (3)	563,990	12
Railways (3)	446,059	27,830
Transport (other) (3)	1,450,244	166,722
Shipbuilding	131,646	96
Engineering, Founding and Vehicle Building (3)	1,662,989	116,171
Iron and Steel and Minor Metal Trades (2)	208,287	7,717
Building, Woodworking and Furnishing (2)	530,194	13,808
Printing and Paper (1)	351,228	78,733
Cotton (2)	99,340	67,865
Textiles (other) (1)	89,285	37,107
Clothing (1)	163,921	128,006
Leather and Boot and Shoe (1)	99,495	43,777
Glass, Pottery, Food, Chemicals, etc. (2)	475,293	214,389
Agriculture (1)	135,000	7,500
Public Employees (1)	310,667	137,440
Civil Service (2)	499,286	161,939
Non-Manual (1)	310,681	94,522
General Workers (3)	787,727	177,369
TOTAL	8,315,332	1,481,003

Among the powers vested in it by consent of the Unions in Congress is the responsibility of adjusting disputes and differences between affiliated organizations; such cases being dealt with by a Disputes Committee of the General Council which investigates matters referred to it and issues its findings thereon, which are invariably accepted by the parties to the dispute. The General Council has power also, if there appears to be justification, to institute an investigation into the conduct of any affiliated organization on the ground that its activities are detrimental to the interests of the Trade Union Movement or contrary to the declared principles and policy of the Congress; but membership of the Congress is voluntary and Unions retain full control of their own affairs, and a penalty of suspension from membership of the Congress or exclusion from membership is the only measure that can be taken to enforce Congress decisions. Through the General Council the Trade Union Movement maintains organic relations with the Government and Government Departments, and with a large number of outside bodies. A major instrument for Government relations is the National Joint Advisory Council which functions on the Cabinet level; in this body the British Employers' Confederation and the Boards of nationalized industries are represented along with the T.U.C. for purposes of consultation and advice on matters of governmental policy and administration, affecting industry. The same bodies, together with the chairmen of the eleven Regional Boards for Industry and representatives of the Federation of British Industries, National Association of British Manufacturers and Association of British Chambers of Commerce, serve on the National Production Advisory Council on Industry which meets under the chairmanship of the Chancellor of the Exchequer, who is accompanied by Ministers of Departments concerned with aspects of production, to advise the government on production questions. The General Council is represented on the National Economic Development Council, established to examine problems associated with faster economic growth. Under the chairmanship of the Chancellor of the Exchequer, the Council includes the Minister of Labour, President of the Board of Trade, representatives of public and private industry and independent members. The General Council nominates members to serve on numerous other bodies, *e.g.* the National Savings Committee, National Insurance Advisory Committee, British Productivity Council, Consumers' Councils for the nationalized industries and numerous educational and miscellaneous bodies.

Chairman (1963–64), G. H. Lowthian, C.B.E.
General Secretary, G. Woodcock, C.B.E.
Assistant General Secretary, V. Feather, C.B.E.

SCOTTISH TRADES UNION CONGRESS

12, Woodlands Terrace, Glasgow, C.3.
Chairman (1963–64), F. H. Stephen.
General Secretary, J. Jack.

The Scottish Trades Union Congress was established in 1897 and it is pointed out that it is in no way a competitor of the British Congress, nor does it "justify its existence on strictly nationalist lines." Its objects are parallel to those of the T.U.C., with which it works in the closest co-operation.

In 1963 the Congress had 87 affiliated Unions and 41 Trades Councils with a membership of 786,533. The Annual Congress is held in April and a General Council of twelve members is elected.

TRADE UNIONS

A list of the Trade Unions affiliated to the Trades Union Congress in 1962-63 The number of members of each Union is shown in parenthesis.

ACTORS' EQUITY ASSOCIATION, BRITISH (11,052).—*Sec.*, G. Croasdell, O.B.E., 8 Harley Street, W.1.

AGRICULTURAL WORKERS, NATIONAL UNION OF (135,000).—*Sec.*, H. Collison, C.B.E., 308 Gray's Inn Road, W.C.1.

ASPHALT WORKERS, THE AMALGAMATED UNION OF (2,500).—*Sec.*, F. V. Jenkin, 84 Walworth Road, S.E.17.

ASSURANCE WORKERS, NATIONAL AMALGAMATED UNION OF LIFE (2,238).—*Sec.*, W. Hindson, 11 Mauldeth Road, Withington, Manchester, 20.

BAKERS, CONFECTIONERS AND ALLIED WORKERS, AMALGAMATED UNION OF OPERATIVE (30,192).—*Gen. Sec.*, A. E. Halliday, O.B.E., 8 Guilford Street, W.C.1.

BAKERS AND ALLIED WORKERS, SCOTTISH UNION OF (13,909).—*Sec.*, W. Mowbray, O.B.E., Baxterlee, 127 Fergus Drive, Glasgow, N.W.

BAKERS' UNION, LONDON JEWISH (48), 13 Sylvester Path, E.8.—*Sec.* (vacant)

BANK EMPLOYEES, NATIONAL UNION OF (59,134).—*Gen. Sec.*, A. G. Brooks, 28 Old Queen Street, S.W.1.

BASKET, CANE, WICKER AND FIBRE FURNITURE MAKERS OF GREAT BRITAIN AND IRELAND, NATIONAL UNION OF (112).—*Sec.*, T. Burrows, 9 District Road, Wembley, Middlesex.

BEAMERS, TWISTERS AND DRAWERS (HAND AND MACHINE), AMALGAMATED ASSOCIATION OF (2,692).—*Gen, Sec.*, A. Green, 21 Clayton Street, Blackburn.

BLASTFURNACEMEN, ORE MINERS, COKE WORKERS AND KINDRED TRADES, THE NATIONAL UNION OF (22,583).—*Sec.*, J. O'Hagan, O.B.E., 93 Borough Road West, Middlesborough.

BLIND OF GREAT BRITAIN AND IRELAND, NATIONAL LEAGUE OF THE (5,025).—*Sec.*, T. H. Smith, M.B.E., 262 Langham Road, N.15.

BOILERMAKERS, BLACKSMITHS, SHIPBUILDERS AND STRUCTURAL WORKERS, UNITED SOCIETY OF (99,668).—*Gen. Sec.*, E. J. Hill, Lifton House, Eslington Road, Newcastle upon Tyne, 2.

BOOT AND SHOE OPERATIVES, NATIONAL UNION OF (76,345).—*Gen. Sec.*, R. Gregson, The Grange, Earls Barton, Northampton.

BOOT, SHOE AND SLIPPER OPERATIVES, ROSSENDALE UNION OF (6,407).—*Sec.*, R. Driver, 7 Tenterfield Street, Waterfoot, Rossendale, Lancs.

BRASSTURNERS, FITTERS, FINISHERS AND INSTRUMENT MAKERS' ASSOCIATION, SCOTTISH (1,265), 221 West George Street, Glasgow, C.3.

BRITISH AIR LINES PILOTS ASSOCIATION (2,702).—*Gen. Sec.*, R. E. G. Waite, D.F.C., 81 New Road, Harlington, Hayes, Middlesex.

BROADCASTING STAFF, ASSOCIATION OF (8,971).—*Sec.*, T. L. Littlewood, 54-58 Uxbridge Road, W.5.

BRUSHMAKERS, NATIONAL SOCIETY OF (2,600).—*Sec.*, T. B. Thomas, 77 Kingsland Road, E.2.

BUILDING TECHNICIANS, ASSOCIATION OF (2,000).—*Sec.*, F. E. Shrosbree, 156 Waterloo Road, S.E.1.

BUILDING TRADE WORKERS OF GREAT BRITAIN AND IRELAND, AMALGAMATED UNION OF (80,363).—*Sec.*, G. H. Lowthian, C.B.E., " The Builders." Crescent Lane, Clapham Common, S.W.4.

CARD, BLOWING AND RING ROOM OPERATIVES, THE NATIONAL ASSOCIATION OF (34,404).—*Sec.*, J. King, 81 Fountain Street, Manchester, 2.

CARD SETTING MACHINE TENTERS' SOCIETY (262).—*Sec.*, R. Ashton, 326 Gibbet Street, Halifax, Yorks.

CARPET TRADE UNION, NORTHERN (950).—*Sec.*, Miss H. D. Pickles, 9 St. James Street, Halifax, Yorks.

CHAIN MAKERS AND STRIKERS ASSOCIATION (474).—*Sec.*, A. E. Head, M.B.E., Unity Villa, Sidney Road, Cradley Heath, Staffs.

CHEMICAL WORKERS' UNION (16,056).—*Sec.*, R. J. Edwards, M.P., 155 Kennington Park Road, S.E.11.

CIGARETTE MACHINE OPERATORS' SOCIETY (390).—R. E. Williams, 3 Mascot Road, Bedminister, Bristol 3.

CINEMATOGRAPH, TELEVISION AND ALLIED TECHNICIANS, ASSOCIATION OF (11,460).—*Sec.*, G. H. Elvin, 2 Soho Square, W.1.

CIVIL SERVICE CLERICAL ASSOCIATION (144,986).—*Sec.*, L. A. Wines, 215 Balham High Road, S.W.17.

CIVIL SERVICE UNION (25,717).—*Sec.*, J. O. N. Vickers, 17-21 Hatton Wall, E.C.1.

CLERICAL AND ADMINISTRATIVE WORKERS' UNION (68,479).—*Gen. Sec.*, H. Chapman, 70 St. George's Square, S.W.1.

CLOTH PRESSERS' SOCIETY (130).—*Sec.*, G. Kaye, 34 Southgate, Honley, Yorks.

COAL TRIMMERS' UNION, CARDIFF, PENARTH AND BARRY (92).—*Sec.*, A. W. Loxton, 13 Bute Crescent, Cardiff.

COLLIERY OVERMEN, DEPUTIES AND SHOTFIRERS, NATIONAL ASSOCIATION OF (34,571).—*Sec.*, J. Crawford, Argyle House, 29-31 Euston Road, N.W.1.

COMMERCIAL TRAVELLERS, NATIONAL UNION OF (315).—*Sec.*, J. F. Denning, 8-13 New Inn Street, E.C.2.

CONSTRUCTIONAL ENGINEERING UNION, THE (22,715).—*Sec.*, E. Patterson, 140 Lower Marsh, S.E.1.

CO-OPERATIVE OFFICIALS, NATIONAL UNION OF (8,678).—*Sec.*, A. W. Potts, 56 Market Street, Manchester, 1.

COOPERS' FEDERATION OF GREAT BRITAIN AND IRELAND (2,797).—*Sec.* E. H. Pettengell, 269 Burdett Road, Limehouse, E.14.

CORRECTORS OF THE PRESS, ASSOCIATION OF (1,448).—*Sec.*, O. F. McCarthy, 1 Gough Square, E.C.4.

DRAUGHTSMEN'S AND ALLIED TECHNICIANS' ASSOCIATION (68,903).—*Sec.*, G. H. Doughty, Onslow Hall, Little Green. Richmond, Surrey.

DYERS, BLEACHERS AND TEXTILE WORKERS, NATIONAL UNION OF (57,320).—*Gen. Sec.*, L. Sharp, M.B.E., Unity Chambers, 26 Manningham Lane, Bradford, 1.

ELECTRICAL POWER ENGINEERS' ASSOCIATION (20,018).—*Gen. Sec.*, H. Norton, O.B.E., 102 St. George's Square, S.W.1.

ELECTRICAL TRADES UNION (257,487).—*Sec.*, J. T. Byrne, O.B.E., Hayes Court, West Common Road, Hayes, Bromley, Kent.

ELECTROTYPERS AND STEREOTYPERS, NATIONAL SOCIETY OF (5,192).—*Sec.*, A. J. Buckle, 80 Blackfriars Road, S.E.1.

ENGINEERING UNION, AMALGAMATED (986,479).—*Sec.*, C. W. Hallett, 110 Peckham Road, S.E.15.

ENGINEERS' AND FIREMEN'S UNION, GRIMSBY STEAM AND DIESEL FISHING VESSELS (261).—*Sec.*, A. B. Stuart, 10 Orwell Street, Grimsby.

ENGINEER SURVEYORS' ASSOCIATION (2,080).—*Sec.*, A. Prestwich, Bermuda House, 4 Hall Street, Manchester, 2.

ENGINEMEN, FIREMEN, MECHANICS AND ELECTRICAL WORKERS, THE NATIONAL UNION OF (30,000).—

Sec., W. J. Tudor, Transport House, Smith Square, S.W.1.

ENGRAVERS, UNITED SOCIETY OF (966).—*Sec.*, D. Hill, 34 Anson Road, Manchester, 14.

FELT HATTERS AND ALLIED WORKERS, AMALGAMATED SOCIETY OF JOURNEYMEN (1,201).—*Sec.*, F. Worthington, O.B.E., 14 Walker Street, Denton, nr. Manchester.

FELT HAT TRIMMERS, WOOL FORMERS' AND ALLIED WORKERS, AMALGAMATED (1,228).—*Sec.*, F. Worthington, O.B.E., 14 Walker Street, Denton, nr. Manchester.

FILE TRADES, SHEFFIELD AMALGAMATED UNION OF (937).—*Sec.*, J. Thorpe, Queen Street Congregational School, North Church Street, Sheffield, 1,

FILM ARTISTS' ASSOCIATION, THE (2,328).—*Sec.*, S. Brannigan, 61 Marloes Road, W.8.

FIRE BRIGADES UNION, THE (27,000).—*Sec.*, J. Horner, 865 Fulham Road, S.W.6.

FOUNDRY WORKERS, AMALGAMATED UNION OF (70,514).—*Sec.*, D. Lambert, 164 Chorlton Road, Brooks's Bar, Manchester, 16.

FRENCH POLISHERS' SOCIETY, UNITED (1,402).—*Sec.*, W. C. Clifton, 95 Farringdon Road, E.C.1.

FUNERAL AND CEMETERY WORKERS, NATIONAL UNION OF (1,041).—*Sec.*, A. N. Pratt, 212 East Lane, N. Wembley, Middlesex.

FURNITURE TRADE OPERATIVES, NATIONAL UNION OF (64,688).—*Sec.*, A. G. Tomkins, C.B.E., Fairfields, Roe Green, Kingsbury, N.W.9.

GENERAL AND MUNICIPAL WORKERS, NATIONAL UNION OF (781,071), 4–8 Endsleigh Gardens, W.C.1.—*Gen. Sec.*, J. Cooper.

GLASS BEVELLERS AND KINDRED TRADES SOCIETY, MIDLAND (394).—*Sec.*, H. L. Bignell, 28 Hazel Croft, Northfield, Birmingham 31.

GLOVERS AND LEATHER WORKERS, NATIONAL UNION OF (1,928).—*Sec.*, E. C. G. Fear, 89a Middle Street, Yeovil, Somerset.

GOLD, SILVER AND ALLIED TRADES, NATIONAL UNION OF (2,493).—*Gen. Sec.*, J. W. Hodgkinson, Kean Chambers, 11 Mappin Street, Sheffield 1.

GOLDSMITHS, JEWELLERS AND KINDRED TRADES, THE SOCIETY OF (921).—*Sec.*, J. C. West, 331 Gray's Inn Road, W.C.1.

GRAPHICAL ASSOCIATION (80,232) (formerly the Typographical Association (1849) and London Typographical Society (1848), amalgamated 1963).—*Secs.*, J. M. Bonfield, Beechwood, Oak Drive, Fallowfield, Manchester 4; R. Willis, 3–7 New Street Square, E.C.4.

HEALDERS AND TWISTERS TRADE AND FRIENDLY SOCIETY, HUDDERSFIELD (252).—*Sec.* D. Ranfield, 26 Scotgate Road, Honley, Huddersfield.

HEALTH SERVICE EMPLOYEES, CONFEDERATION OF (64,713).—*Gen. Sec.*, W. J. Jepson, Glen House, High Street, Banstead, Surrey.

HEALTH VISITORS' ASSOCIATION (formerly WOMEN PUBLIC HEALTH OFFICERS ASSOCIATION) (3,954).—*Sec.*, Miss N. K. Ross, O.B.E., 36 Eccleston Square, S.W.1.

HEATING AND DOMESTIC ENGINEERS' UNION (21,809).—*Sec.*, L. Green, 917 Warwick Road, Solihull, Warwickshire.

HORSE AND MOTORMEN'S ASSOCIATION, SCOTTISH (20,000).—*Gen. Sec.*, A. H. Kitson, 308 Albert Drive, Glasgow, S.1.

HOSIERY FINISHERS' ASSOCIATION, NOTTINGHAM AND DISTRICT (2,817).—*Sec.* J. Charlesworth, 45a Lincoln Street, Basford, Nottingham.

HOSIERY TRIMMERS ASSOCIATION, LEICESTER AND LEICESTERSHIRE (1,547), Boot and Shoe Trade Hall, Earl Street, Leicester.—*Sec.*, W. Bee.

HOSIERY WORKERS, NATIONAL UNION OF (39,835).—*Sec.*, H. L. G. Gibson, 55 New Walk, Leicester.

INLAND REVENUE STAFF FEDERATION (42,541).—*Sec.*, C. T. H. Plant, 7–9 St. George's Square, S.W.1.

INSURANCE OFFICIALS, GUILD OF (21,060).—*Sec.*, M. W. Reynolds, 24 Railway Approach, S.E.1.

INSURANCE WORKERS, NATIONAL FEDERATION OF (36,834).—*Sec.*, T. Scrafton, 14–17 Holborn Hall, Gray's Inn Road, W.C.1.

IRON AND STEEL TRADES CONFEDERATION (104,962).—*Sec.*, H. Douglass, Swinton House, 324 Gray's Inn Road, W.C.1.

IRON FITTERS' ASSOCIATION, GENERAL (2,165).—*Sec.*, T. H. Young, 11 Callendar Riggs, Falkirk.

IRON, STEEL AND WOOD BARGE BUILDERS' AND HELPERS' ASSOCIATION (703).—*Sec.*, W. H. Harris, 32 Woolwich Road, S.E.10.

JOURNALISTS, NATIONAL UNION OF (16,881).—*Sec.*, H. J. Bradley, 22 Great Windmill Street, W.1.

JUTE, FLAX AND KINDRED TEXTILE OPERATIVES, UNION OF (5,003).—*Sec.*, R. Doyle, 93 Nethergate, Dundee.

LACE MAKERS AND AUXILIARY WORKERS, AMALGAMATED SOCIETY OF OPERATIVE (1,286).—*Sec.*, J. E. Flewitt, 1 North Road, The Park, Nottingham.

LAMINATED AND COIL SPRING WORKERS' UNION (272).—*Sec.*, F. M. Hynes, 144 Rural Lane, Wadsley, Sheffield, 6.

LEATHER WORKERS, AMALGAMATED SOCIETY OF (10,002).—*Sec.*, A. L. Barrett, M.B.E., 4 Mexborough Avenue, Leeds, 7.

LEATHER WORKERS AND ALLIED TRADES, NATIONAL UNION OF (4,813). 169 Old Street, E.C.1.—*Gen. Sec.*, C. J. Huggins.

LITHOGRAPHIC ARTISTS, DESIGNERS, ENGRAVERS AND PROCESS WORKERS, SOCIETY OF (14,837).—*Sec.*, H. G. Bellingham, 53–54 Doughty Street, W.C.1.

LITHOGRAPHIC PRINTERS, THE AMALGAMATED SOCIETY OF (10,814).—*Sec.*, R. Emerick, 137 Dickenson Road, Rusholme, Manchester, 14.

LOCK AND METAL WORKERS, NATIONAL UNION OF (3,633).—*Sec.*, J. Martin, Bellamy House, Wilkes Street, Willenhall, Staffs.

LOCOMOTIVE ENGINEERS AND FIREMEN, ASSOCIATED SOCIETY OF (49,559).—*Gen. Sec.*, A. E. Griffiths, 9 Arkwright Road, N.W.3.

LONDON COUNTY COUNCIL STAFF ASSOCIATION (10,581).—*Sec.*, F. T. Hollocks, Room B 73, County Hall, S.E.1.

LOOM OVERLOOKERS, THE GENERAL UNION OF ASSOCIATIONS OF (5,024).—*Gen. Sec.*, A. Howcroft, Derby Chambers, 6 The Rock, Bury.

MACHINE CALICO PRINTERS, TRADE SOCIETY OF (623).—*Sec.*, D. J. Barr, Room 43, 62 George Street, Manchester 1.

MANAGERS AND OVERLOOKERS' SOCIETY (1,858).—*Sec.*, D. Kirkbright, Textile Hall, Westgate, Bradford 1.

MEDICAL PRACTITIONERS' UNION (5,552).—*Sec.*, Dr. P. M. Elliot, Thorne House, 4–8 Endsleigh Gardens, W.C.1.

MERCHANT NAVY AND AIRLINE OFFICERS' ASSOCIATION (16,000).—*Sec.*, D. S. Tennant, C.B.E., Oceanair House, 133–137 Whitechapel High Street, E.1.

METAL DRESSERS AND KINDRED TRADES SOCIETY (5,260).—*Sec.*, E. Tullock, Lord's Chambers, 26 Corporation Street, Manchester 4.

METAL MECHANICS, NATIONAL SOCIETY OF (46,490).—*Sec.*, F. Briggs, 70 Lionel Street, Birmingham, 3.

METAL WORKERS AND ALLIED TRADES, ASSOCIATED (408), 347 Garratt Lane, Earlsfield, S.W.18.—*Sec.* (vacant).

MILITARY AND ORCHESTRAL MUSICAL INSTRUMENT MAKERS' TRADE SOCIETY (150).—*Sec.*, D. J. Lofthouse, 58 High Oaks, St. Albans, Herts.

MINEWORKERS, NATIONAL UNION OF (529,019).—*Sec.*, W. Paynter, 222 Euston Road, N.W.1.

MINISTRY OF LABOUR STAFF ASSOCIATION (11,393).—*Sec.*, J. L. Tindall, 22 St. George's Drive, S.W.1.

MOULDERS AND FOUNDRY WORKERS', ASSOCIATED SOCIETY OF (228).—*Sec.*, D. Davies, 47 Coronation Road, Llanelly, Carmarthenshire.

MOULDERS AND KINDRED INDUSTRIES TRADE UNION, AMALGAMATED (2,500).—*Sec.*, J. Banks, 2 Hamer Avenue, Blackburn.

MUSICIANS' UNION (30,189).—*Gen. Sec.*, H. Ratcliffe, 29 Catherine Place, Buckingham Gate, S.W.1.

NATIONAL COAL BOARD LABOUR STAFF ASSOCIATION (400).—*Sec.*, R. Gordon, 20 Pettycur Road, Kinghorn, Fife.

PACKING CASE MAKERS (WOOD AND TIN), BOX MAKERS, SAWYERS, AND MILLWORKERS, THE NATIONAL UNION OF (3,861).—*Sec.*, S. G. Reading, 95 Farringdon Road, E.C.1.

PAINTERS AND DECORATORS, AMALGAMATED SOCIETY OF (76,474).—*Sec.*, A. G. Austin, 4 Camp Street, Lower Broughton, Salford 7, Lancs.

PATTERNMAKERS' ASSOCIATION, UNITED (15,249).—*Sec.*, W. B. Beard, O.B.E., 15 Cleve Road, W. Hampstead, N.W.6.

PLASTERERS, THE NATIONAL ASSOCIATION OF OPERATIVE (12,472).—*Sec.*, A. Dunne, O.B.E., 1016 Harrow Road, Wembley, Middx.

PLUMBING TRADES UNION (55,730).—*Sec.*, H. Kelly, O.B.E., 15 Abbeville Road, Clapham, S.W.4.

POST OFFICE CONTROLLING OFFICERS, ASSOCIATION OF (13,915).—*Sec.*, S. A. R. Seaton, 52 Broadway, Bracknell, Berks.

POST OFFICE ENGINEERING UNION (78,029).—*Sec.* C. G. P. Smith, Greystoke House, Hanger Lane, Ealing, W.5.

POST OFFICE WORKERS, UNION OF (172,699).—*Sec.*, R. Smith, U.P.W. House, Crescent Lane, Clapham Common, S.W.4.

POTTERY WORKERS, NATIONAL SOCIETY OF (22,229).—*Sec.*, H. Hewitt, O.B.E., 5 Hillcrest Street, Hanley, Stoke-on-Trent.

POWER LOOM CARPET WEAVERS AND TEXTILE WORKERS' ASSOCIATION (4,535).—*Sec.*, C. S. Yarsley, Callow Lane, Kidderminster.

POWER LOOM OVERLOOKERS, YORKSHIRE ASSOCIATION OF (1,794).—*Sec.*, E. D. Sleeman, Textile Hall, Westgate, Bradford.

POWER LOOM TENTERS, SCOTTISH UNION OF (500).—*Sec.*, J. McCann, 33 Glenclova Terrace, Dundee.

PRESS TELEGRAPHISTS, NATIONAL UNION OF (1,513). *Sec.*, M. A. Clayton, 145 Fleet Street, E.C.4.

PRINT BLOCK ROLLER AND STAMP CUTTERS' SOCIETY (414).—*Sec.*, S. E. Ramsden, 18 Printon Avenue, Blackley, Manchester, 9.

PRINTERS AND ASSISTANTS, THE NATIONAL SOCIETY OF OPERATIVE (45,473).—*Gen. Sec.*, R. W. Briginshaw, 13–16 Borough Road, S.E.1.

PRINTING, BOOKBINDING AND PAPER WORKERS, THE NATIONAL UNION OF (164,756).—*Gen. Sec.*, T. J. Smith, 74 Nightingale Lane, S.W.12.

PROFESSIONAL FOOTBALLERS' AND TRAINERS' ASSOCIATION (2,158).—*Sec.*, C. Lloyd, 105–7 Corn Exchange Buildings, Cathedral Street, Manchester 4.

PUBLIC EMPLOYEES, NATIONAL UNION OF (215,000).—*Sec.*, S. Hill, 8 Aberdeen Terrace, Blackheath, S.E.3.

RADIO OFFICERS' UNION (3,521).—*Sec.* H. O'Neill, O.B.E., 4–6 Branfill Road, Upminster, Essex.

RAILWAYMEN, NATIONAL UNION OF (310,572).—*Sec.*, S. F. Greene, Unity House, Euston Road, N.W.1.

RETAIL BOOK, STATIONERY AND ALLIED TRADES EMPLOYEES' ASSOCIATION, THE (3,093).—*Sec.*, A. T. Johnson, 152–3 Temple Chambers, Temple Avenue, E.C.4.

ROLL TURNERS' TRADE SOCIETY, BRITISH (1,093).—*Sec.*, N. W. Goodchild, 12 Coverdale Road, Sheffield 7.

RUBBER WORKERS OF GREAT BRITAIN, THE UNITED (3,100).—*Sec.*, L. Walsh, 57 Ardwick Green North, Manchester, 12.

SALT AND CHEMICAL INDUSTRIES ALLIED WORKERS, UNION, MID-CHESHIRE (1,820).—*Sec.*, R. M. Moss, Central Palace Drive, Witton Street, Northwich.

SALT WORKERS, ALKALI WORKERS, MECHANICS AND GENERAL LABOURERS, FEDERATION OF TRADE UNIONS OF (1,736).—*Sec.*, G. Miles, Devonlow, Sandyhill Road, Swanlow, Winsford, Cheshire.

SAWMAKERS' PROTECTION SOCIETY, SHEFFIELD (352).—*Sec.*, H. Lambert, 46 Archer Lane, Sheffield, 7.

SCALEMAKERS, NATIONAL UNION OF (2,668).—*Gen. Sec.*, S. W. Parfitt, 33–34 Temple Chambers, Temple Avenue, E.C.4.

SCIENTIFIC WORKERS, THE ASSOCIATION OF (16,343).—*Sec.*, J. K. Dutton, 15 Half Moon Street, W.1.

SCREW, NUT, BOLT AND RIVET TRADE SOCIETY (2,300).—*Sec.*, H. Cater, 368 Dudley Road, Birmingham 18.

SEAMEN, NATIONAL UNION OF (62,500).—*Gen.* Sec., W. Hogarth, Maritime House, Old Town, Clapham, S.W.4.

SHEET METAL WORKERS AND COPPERSMITHS, NATIONAL UNION OF (50,288).—*Gen. Sec.*, L. W. Buck, 75–77 West Heath Road, N.W.3.

SHEET METAL WORKERS' SOCIETY, BIRMINGHAM AND MIDLAND (8,580).—*Sec.*, A. E. Cooper, 134 Bromsgrove Street, Birmingham, 5.

SHIPCONSTRUCTORS AND SHIPWRIGHTS' ASSOCIATION (21,624).—*Sec.* A. Williams, 8 Eldon Square, Newcastle-upon-Tyne, 1.

SHOP, DISTRIBUTIVE AND ALLIED WORKERS, UNION OF (356,038).—*Sec.*, A. W. Allen, 188 Wilmslow Road, Fallowfield, Manchester 14.

SHUTTLEMAKERS, SOCIETY OF (250).—*Sec.*, S. Brown, 6 Moyse Avenue, Walshaw, Bury.

SIGN AND DISPLAY TRADES UNION (3,001), 28 Downs Road, Clapton, E.5.—*Gen. Sec.*, A. C. Torode.

SILK WORKERS AND TEXTILE TRADES ASSOCIATION, NATIONAL (2,000).—*Gen. Sec.*, T. Molloy, 59 Park Green, Macclesfield, Cheshire.

SLATERS, TILERS AND ROOFING OPERATIVES SOCIETY, AMALGAMATED (2,012).—*Gen. Sec.*, L. Poupard, 430 Holderness Road, Hull.

SPINNERS AND TWINERS, THE AMALGAMATED ASSOCIATION OF OPERATIVE COTTON (5,074).—*Sec.*, J. W. Whitworth, 115 Newton Street, Manchester.

SPRING TRAPMAKERS' SOCIETY (90).—*Sec.*, J. Martin, Bellamy House, Wilks Street, Willenhall, Staffs.

STOVE GRATE AND GENERAL METAL WORKERS, THE NATIONAL UNION OF (5,825).—*Sec.*, J. Higham, M.B.E., Stove Grate Offices, Imperial Bldgs., High Street, Rotherham.

STREET MASONS, PAVIORS AND ROAD MAKERS, NATIONAL SOCIETY OF (1,400).—*Sec.*, W. Armitage, Kingston House, 1 Kingston Grove, Woodhouse Lane, Leeds, 2.

SUPERVISORY STAFFS, EXECUTIVES AND TECHNICIANS, ASSOCIATION OF (30,242).—*Gen. Sec.*, C. Jenkins, 2–4 Homerton High Street, Hackney, E.9.

TAILORS AND GARMENT WORKERS, NATIONAL UNION OF (115,102).—*Sec.*, J. E. Newton, 14 Kensington Square, W.8.

TECHNICAL CIVIL SERVANTS, SOCIETY OF (10,006).—*Sec.*, C. Cooper, 372 Wandsworth Road, S.W.8.

TEXTILE CRAFTSMEN, YORKSHIRE SOCIETY OF (1,200).—*Sec.*, C. Hall, Textile Hall, Westgate, Bradford, 1.

TEXTILE DAYMEN'S AND CLOTH PATTERN MAKERS ASSOCIATION (126).—*Sec.*, J. Halby, 18 Airedale Crescent, Bradford 3.

TEXTILE WAREHOUSEMEN, AMALGAMATED (5,500).—*Sec.*, T. Ashe, 6 The Rock, Bury.

TEXTILE WORKERS AND KINDRED TRADES, AMALGAMATED SOCIETY OF (5,800).—*Sec.*, H. Lisle, Foxlowe, Market Place, Leek, Staffs.

THEATRICAL AND KINE EMPLOYEES, THE NATIONAL ASSOCIATION OF (21,155).—*Sec.*, Sir Tom O'Brien, 17 Waterloo Place, S.W.1.

TOBACCO WORKERS' UNION, THE (16,326).—*Sec.*, P. Belcher, 218 Upper Street, Islington, N.1.

TRANSPORT AND GENERAL WORKERS' UNION (1,330,962).—*Sec.*, F. Cousins, Transport House, Smith Square, S.W.1.

TRANSPORT SALARIED STAFFS' ASSOCIATION (85,928).—*Gen. Sec.*, J. G. Bothwell, O.B.E., Walkden House, 10 Melton Street, N.W.1.

TRANSPORT WORKERS ASSOCIATION OF ENGLAND, THE UNITED ROAD (10,000).—*Sec.*, J. Moore, 28 Hathersage Road, Chorlton-on-Medlock, Manchester 13.

TYPOGRAPHICAL ASSOCIATION. *See* GRAPHICAL ASSOCIATION.

TYPOGRAPHICAL ASSOCIATION, SCOTTISH (7,082).—*Sec.*, P. Whigham, 136 West Regent Street, Glasgow, C.2.

TYPOGRAPHICAL SOCIETY, LONDON. *See* GRAPHICAL ASSOCIATION.

VARIETY ARTISTES' FEDERATION (3,147).—*Sec.*, R. W. Swinson, M.B.E., 18 Charing Cross Road, W.C.2.

VEHICLE BUILDERS, NATIONAL UNION OF (67,984).—*Gen. Sec.*, A. Roberts, 44 Hathersage Road, Oxford Road, Manchester 13.

WALL PAPER WORKERS' UNION (3,000).—*Sec.*, C. Heap, O.B.E., 223 Bury New Road, Whitefield, Manchester.

WARPDRESSERS, TWISTERS AND KINDRED TRADES ASSOCIATIONS, LEEDS AND DISTRICT (156).—*Sec.*, B. Jowett, 34 Green Hill Drive, Bramley, Leeds 13.

WATERMEN, LIGHTERMEN, TUGMEN AND BARGEMEN'S UNION (4,206).—*Sec.*, W. A. Lindley, 33 East India Dock Road, E.14.

WATERPROOF GARMENT WORKERS' TRADE UNION, THE (2,191).—*Sec.*, F. C. Henry, M.B.E., 88a Miller Street, Manchester, 4.

WEAVERS' AND WOOLEN TEXTILE WORKERS' ASSOCIATION, SADDLEWORTH AND DISTRICT (1,725).—*Sec.*, F. G. Battye, 4 Grains Road, Delph, nr. Oldham.

WEAVERS' ASSOCIATION, AMALGAMATED (46,646).—*Gen. Sec.*, L. T. Wright, Chronicle Buildings, 74 Corporation Street, Manchester, 4.

WIRE DRAWERS AND KINDRED WORKERS, THE AMALGAMATED SOCIETY OF (11,553).—*Sec.*, R. Birtwhistle, 21 Stirling Chambers, Campo Lane, Sheffield, 1.

WOOD-CUTTING MACHINISTS, AMALGAMATED SOCIETY OF (26,633).—*Sec.*, C. Stewart, 8 Fairfield Street, Manchester 1.

WOODWORKERS, AMALGAMATED SOCIETY OF (193,708).—*Sec.*, G. F. Smith, 9–11 Macaulay Road, S.W.4.

WOOL SHEAR WORKERS' TRADE UNION, SHEFFIELD (56).—*Sec.*, J. Billard, 19 Rivelin Park Drive, Sheffield 6.

WOOL SORTERS' SOCIETY, NATIONAL (2,085).—*Sec.*, N. Newton, 40 Little Horton Lane, Bradford 5.

WOOL YARN AND WAREHOUSE WORKERS' UNION (300).—*Sec.*, B. W. Berry, Textile Hall, Westgate, Bradford.

INDUSTRIAL RESEARCH ASSOCIATIONS

A notable development in modern industry is the growth in numbers and importance of Industrial Research Associations and their increasing influence on the scientific and economic life of the country. The total expenditure of these Associations in 1962 was £8,585,247 per annum, of which £1,964,000 was provided by the Department of Scientific and Industrial Research and the remainder by subscriptions of individual members.

The Government Scheme for Co-operative Industrial Research was launched by the Department of Scientific and Industrial Research in 1918. Its aim was to stimulate the industries of the United Kingdom to undertake co-operative research as a means of increasing their efficiency.

Research Associations formed under this scheme are registered companies, limited by guarantee of a nominal sum and working without the division of profits in the form of dividends. To assist the formation of such Associations the Board of Trade and the Department of Scientific and Industrial Research have drawn up a model Memorandum and Articles of Association, to which Research Associations under the scheme conform in all essential points.

The income of the Research Associations is derived from subscriptions from their individual members, supplemented in most cases by substantial grants from the Government, through the Department of Scientific and Industrial Research.

The Research Associations are autonomous bodies free to determine their own policy for the development of their research programmes and the use to be made of the results of their research. Membership is open to any British firm in the particular industry, subject to the approval of the Councils of the Research Associations.

There are now 47 Research Associations and 6 other organizations in receipt of grants from the Department. They cover most of the principal industries of the country, as follows:—

Baking.

BRITISH BAKING INDUSTRIES RESEARCH ASSOCIATION, Baking Industries Research Station, Chorleywood, Herts.—*Dir.*, G. A. H. Elton, D.SC., PH.D.

Boots and Shoes.

BRITISH BOOT, SHOE AND ALLIED TRADES RESEARCH ASSOCIATION, Satra House, Rockingham Road, Kettering, Northants.—*Dir.*, H. Bradley, C.B.E.

Brushes.

BRITISH BRUSH MANUFACTURERS' RESEARCH ASSOCIATION, 80 Coleman Street, E.C.2.—*Dir.*, D. I. Fothergill.

Cast Iron.

BRITISH CAST IRON RESEARCH ASSOCIATION, Bordesley Hall, Alvechurch, Birmingham.—*Dir.*, H Morrogh.

Ceramics.

BRITISH CERAMIC RESEARCH ASSOCIATION Queen's Road, Penkhull, Stoke-on-Trent.—*Dir.*, N. F. Astbury, SC.D.

Civil Engineering.

CIVIL ENGINEERING RESEARCH COUNCIL, Institution of Civil Engineers, Great George Street, S.W.1.—*Dir.*, M. F. Kaplan, Ph.D.

Coal Utilization.

BRITISH COAL UTILISATION RESEARCH ASSOCIATION, Randalls Road, Leatherhead, Surrey.—*Dir.-Gen.*, D. Hicks.

Coke.

BRITISH COKE RESEARCH ASSOCIATION, Coke Research Centre, Chesterfield, Derbyshire.—*Dir.*, G. W. Lee.

Cotton, Silk, etc.

COTTON SILK AND MAN-MADE FIBRES RESEARCH ASSOCIATION, Shirley Institute, Didsbury, Manchester, 20.—*Dir.*, D. W. Hill, D.Sc., Ph.D.

Cutlery.

CUTLERY AND ALLIED TRADES RESEARCH ASSOCIATION, Hoyle Street, Sheffield, 3.—*Dir.*, E. A. Oldfield.

Drop Forging.

DROP FORGING RESEARCH ASSOCIATION, Hoyle Street, Sheffield, 3.—*Director*, P. H. R. Lane, Ph.D.

Electrical.

BRITISH ELECTRICAL AND ALLIED INDUSTRIES RESEARCH ASSOCIATION, Cleeve Road, Leatherhead, Surrey.—*Dir.*, H. G. Taylor, D.Sc.

Felt.

BRITISH HAT AND ALLIED FELTMAKERS RESEARCH ASSOCIATION, Stanley House, Manchester Road, Fairfield, Droylsden, Manchester.—*Dir.*, T. Barr, Ph.D.

Files.

FILE RESEARCH COUNCIL, Hoyle Street, Sheffield, 3.—*Superintendent of Research*, R. H. Hancock.

Flour Milling.

RESEARCH ASSOCIATION OF BRITISH FLOUR-MILLERS, Cereals Research Station, Old London Road, St. Albans, Herts.—*Dir.*, T. Moran, C.B.E., D.Sc., Ph.D.

Food Manufacture.

BRITISH FOOD MANUFACTURING INDUSTRIES RESEARCH ASSOCIATION, Randalls Road, Leatherhead, Surrey.—*Dir.*, C. L. Cutting, Ph.D.

Fruit and Vegetable Canning.

FRUIT AND VEGETABLE CANNING AND QUICK FREEZING RESEARCH ASSOCIATION, Chipping Campden, Glos.—*Dir.*, W. B. Adam.

Furniture.

FURNITURE INDUSTRY RESEARCH ASSOCIATION, 11 Adelphi Terrace, Robert Street, W.C.2.—*Dir.*, G. A. McMillan.

Gelatine and Glue.

BRITISH GELATINE AND GLUE RESEARCH ASSOCIATION, 2a Dalmeny Avenue, Holloway, N.7.—*Dir.*, D. A. Sutton, Ph.D.

Glass.

BRITISH GLASS INDUSTRY RESEARCH ASSOCIATION, Northumberland Road, Sheffield 10.—*Dir.*, R. G. Newton, Ph.D.

Heating and Ventilating.

HEATING AND VENTILATING RESEARCH ASSOCIATION, Old Bracknell Lane, Bracknell, Berks.—*Dir.*, N. S. Billington.

Hosiery.

HOSIERY AND ALLIED TRADES RESEARCH ASSOCIATION, Thorneywood, Gregory Boulevard, Nottingham.—*Dir.*, W. A. Dutton.

Hydromechanics.

BRITISH HYDROMECHANICS RESEARCH ASSOCIATION South Road, Temple Fields, Harlow, Essex.—*Dir.*, L. E. Prosser.

Industrial Biology

BRITISH INDUSTRIAL BIOLOGICAL RESEARCH ASSOCIATION, Radnor House, 93–97 Regent Street, S.W.1.—*Dir.*, L. Golberg, D.Sc.

Industrial Psychology.

NATIONAL INSTITUTE OF INDUSTRIAL PSYCHOLOGY, 14 Welbeck Street, W.1.—*Dir.*, C. B. Frisby, Ph.D.

I.C. Engines.

BRITISH INTERNAL COMBUSTION ENGINE RESEARCH ASSOCIATION, 111–112 Buckingham Avenue, Trading Estate, Slough.—*Dir.*, W. P. Mansfield, Ph.D.

Iron and Steel.

BRITISH IRON AND STEEL RESEARCH ASSOCIATION, 11 Park Lane, W.1.—*Dir.*, Sir Charles Goodeve, O.B.E., D.Sc., F.R.S.

Jute.

BRITISH JUTE TRADE RESEARCH ASSOCIATION, Kinnoull Road, Kingsway West, Dundee, Scotland.—*Dir.*, H. P. Stout, Ph.D.

Lace.

LACE RESEARCH ASSOCIATION, Glaisdale Drive West, Bilborough, Nottingham.—*Dir.*, J. C. MacCallum, O.B.E.

Laundering.

BRITISH LAUNDERERS' RESEARCH ASSOCIATION, The Laboratories, Hill View Gardens, Hendon, N.W.4.—*Dir.*, J. Leicester.

Leather.

BRITISH LEATHER MANUFACTURERS' RESEARCH ASSOCIATION, Milton Park, Egham, Surrey.—*Dir.*, K. W. Pepper, D.Sc.

Lime.

CHALK LIME AND ALLIED INDUSTRIES RESEARCH ASSOCIATION, Laboratories, Church Street, Welwyn, Herts.—*Dir.*, G. E. Bessey.

Linen.

LINEN INDUSTRY RESEARCH ASSOCIATION, Research Institute, Lambeg, Lisburn, Co. Antrim.—*Dir.*, D. A. Derrett-Smith.

Machine Tools.

MACHINE TOOL INDUSTRY RESEARCH ASSOCIATION, 163 Kingsway, Manchester, 19.—*Dir.*, A. E. De Barr.

Motor Vehicles.

MOTOR INDUSTRY RESEARCH ASSOCIATION, Lindley, nr. Nuneaton, Warwickshire.—*Dir.*, A. Fogg, D.Sc.

Non-Ferrous Metals.

BRITISH NON-FERROUS METALS RESEARCH ASSOCIATION, Euston Street, N.W.1.—*Dir.*, G. L. Bailey, C.B.E.

Paint.

RESEARCH ASSOCIATION OF BRITISH PAINT, COLOUR AND VARNISH MANUFACTURERS, Paint Research Station. Waldegrave Road, Teddington, Middlesex.—*Dir.*, L. Valentine, Ph.D.

Paper.

BRITISH PAPER AND BOARD INDUSTRY RESEARCH ASSOCIATION, St. Winfred's Laboratories, Welcomes Road, Kenley, Surrey.—*Dir.*, N. R. Hood, O.B.E., Ph.D.

Printing and Packaging.

PRINTING, PACKAGING AND ALLIED TRADES RESEARCH ASSOCIATION, Patra House, Randalls Road, Leatherhead, Surrey.—*Dir.*, V. G. W. Harrison, Ph.D.

Production Engineering.

PRODUCTION ENGINEERING RESEARCH ASSOCIATION OF GREAT BRITAIN, Melton Mowbray, Leics.—*Dir.*, D. F. Galloway, Ph.D.

Rubber and Plastics.

RUBBER AND PLASTICS RESEARCH ASSOCIATION OF GREAT BRITAIN, Shawbury, Shrewsbury, Shropshire.—*Dir.*, W. F. Watson, D.Sc., Ph.D.

Scientific Instruments.

BRITISH SCIENTIFIC INSTRUMENT RESEARCH ASSOCIATION, South Hill, Chislehurst, Kent.—*Dir.* (vacant).

Ships.

BRITISH SHIP RESEARCH ASSOCIATION, Prince Consort House, 27–29 Albert Embankment, S.E.1.—*Dir.*, R. Hurst, G.M., Ph.D.

Springs.

SPRING MANUFACTURERS RESEARCH ASSOCIATION, Doncaster Street, Sheffield, 3.—*Dir.*, R. Haynes.

Steel Castings.

BRITISH STEEL CASTINGS RESEARCH ASSOCIATION, East Bank Road, Sheffield, 2.—*Dir.*, A. H. Sully, Ph.D.

Tar.

COAL TAR RESEARCH ASSOCIATION, Oxford Road, Gomersal, nr. Leeds.—*Dir.*, D. McNeil, Ph.D.

Timber.

TIMBER RESEARCH AND DEVELOPMENT ASSOCIATION, St. John's Road, Tylers Green, Penn, Bucks.—*Dir.*, J. S. McBride.

Water.

WATER RESEARCH ASSOCIATION, Ferry Lane, Medmenham, Marlow, Bucks.—*Dir.*, R. G. Allen, Ph.D.

Welding.

BRITISH WELDING RESEARCH ASSOCIATION, 19 Fitzroy Square, W.1.—*Dir.*, R. Weck, Ph.D.

Whiting.

WHITING AND INDUSTRIAL POWDERS RESEARCH COUNCIL, The Hall, 30 Church Street, Welwyn, Herts.—*Dir.*, D. C. Soul.

Wool.

WOOL INDUSTRIES RESEARCH ASSOCIATION, Torridon, Headingley Lane, Leeds, 6.—*Dir.*, A. B. D. Cassie, C.B.E., D.Sc., Ph.D.

AGRICULTURAL RESEARCH INSTITUTES AND UNITS

The following research institutes are under the direct control of the Agricultural Research Council (*see* pp. 360–361):—

Institute for Research on Animal Diseases, Compton, near Newbury, Berks.—*Director*, W. S. Gordon, C.B.E., Ph.D., M.R.C.V.S., F.R.S.E.

Unit of Insect Physiology, Department of Zoology, Cambridge.—*Director*, Prof. V. B. Wigglesworth, C.B.E., M.D., F.R.S.

Institute of Animal Physiology, Babraham Hall, Babraham, Cambs.—*Director*, J. H. Gaddum, M.A., Sc.D., M.R.C.S., L.R.C.P., F.R.S., F.R.S.E.

Animal Breeding Research Organisation, 6 South Oswald Road, Edinburgh, 9.—*Director*, H. P. Donald, D.Sc., Ph.D., F.R.S.E.

Poultry Research Centre, King's Buildings, West Mains Road, Edinburgh, 9.—*Director*, T. C. Carter, O.B.E., D.Sc., F.R.S.E.

Unit of Experimental Agronomy, Department of Agriculture, University of Oxford.—*Hon. Director*, Prof. G. E. Blackman, F.R.S.

Unit of Biometrical Genetics, Department of Genetics, University of Birmingham.—*Hon. Director*, Prof. K. Mather, C.B.E., D.Sc., Ph.D., F.R.S.

Unit of Microbiology, Department of Microbiology, The University, Sheffield, 10.—*Hon. Director*, Prof. S. R. Elsden, Ph.D.

Unit of Soil Physics, School of Agriculture, Huntingdon Road, Cambridge.—*Director*, E. C. Childs, Sc.D., Ph.D.

Unit of Embryology, Univ. College of N. Wales, Bangor.—*Hon. Director*, Prof. F. W. Rogers Brambell, D.Sc., Ph.D., F.R.S.

Unit of Statistics, University of Aberdeen.—*Director*, D. J. Finney, Sc.D., F.R.S., F.R.S.E.

Statistics Group, School of Agriculture, Cambridge.—*Officer-in-Charge*, R. C. Campbell, M.A., Ph.D.

Unit of Reproductive Physiology and Biochemistry, Molteno Institute, Cambridge.—*Director*, T. R. R. Mann, C.B.E., M.D., Sc.D., Ph.D., F.R.S.

Unit of Animal Genetics, University of Edinburgh, King's Buildings, West Mains Road, Edinburgh, 9.—*Hon. Director*, Prof. C. H. Waddington, C.B.E., Sc.D., F.R.S.

Radiobiological Laboratory, Letcombe Regis, Wantage, Berks.—*Director*, R. Scott Russell, M.Sc., Ph.D.

Systemic Fungicide Unit, Wye College, Ashford, Kent.—*Hon. Director*, Prof. R. L. Wain, D.Sc., Ph.D., F.R.S.

Virus Research Unit, Huntingdon Road, Cambridge.—*Director*, R. Markham, M.A., Ph.D., F.R.S.

Ditton Laboratory, Larkfield, Maidstone.—*Director*, R. G. Tomkins, M.A., Ph.D.

Covent Garden Laboratory, Inveresk House, 346 Strand, W.C.1.—*Officer-in-Charge*, J. C. Fidler, Ph.D.

Low Temperature Research Station, Downing Street, Cambridge.—*Director*, E. Bate-Smith, C.B.E., M.Sc., Ph.D.

Pest Infestation Laboratory, London Road, Slough, Bucks.—*Director*, G. V. B. Herford, C.B.E., M.Sc.

Unit of Flower Crop Physiology, Horticultural Research Laboratories Shinfield Grange, Shinfield, Reading, Berks. *Hon. Dir.*, Prof. O. V. S. Heath, D.Sc., F.R.S.

Unit of Plant Physiology, Imperial College of Science and Technology, Prince Consort Road, S.W.7.—*Director*, Prof. Helen K. Porter, D.Sc., F.R.S.

Unit of Plant Morphogenesis and Nutrition, Wye College, Ashford, Kent.—*Director*, F. J. Richards, D.Sc., F.R.S.

Weed Research Organization, Begbroke Hill, Kidlington, nr. Oxford.—*Director*, E. K. Woodford, O.B.E., M.Sc., Ph.D.

Farm Buildings Unit, Wrest Park Lodge, Silsoe, Beds.—*Hon. Director*, W. H. Cashmore, C.B.E., B.A.

GRANT-AIDED RESEARCH INSTITUTES

In addition to the above there are other institutes which, while retaining their own individuality, are financed wholly or in the main by grants made from Government funds. Most of these Institutes have governing bodies of their own to which they are directly responsible. The maintenance grants for Institutes in England and Wales are met from funds voted by Parliament and administered by the Agricultural Research Council; the Scottish Institutes are borne on the vote of the Department of Agriculture for Scotland. These Departments seek the advice of the Agricultural Research Council in the consideration of research programmes and estimates.

(a) Research affecting Plants and Soils

Soil Science and Plant Pathology

Rothamsted Experimental Station, Harpenden, Herts.—*Director*, F. C. Bawden, M.A., F.R.S.

Macaulay Institute for Soil Research, Craigiebuckler, Aberdeen.—*Director*, Prof. A. B. Stewart, C.B.E., M.A., B.Sc., Ph.D., F.R.I.C.

Plant Breeding

Hop Research Centre, Wye College, Ashford, Kent.

Plant Breeding Institute, Maris Lane, Trumpington, Cambridge.—*Director*, G. D. H. Bell, B.Sc., Ph.D.

Welsh Plant Breeding Station, Plas Gogerddan, nr.

Aberystwyth.—*Director*, Prof. P. T. Thomas, B.SC., Ph.D.

Scottish Plant Breeding Station, Pentlandfield, Roslin, Midlothian.—*Director*, J. W. Gregor, C.B.E., D.SC., Ph.D., F.L.S.

Horticulture

John Innes Institute, Bayfordbury, Hertford.—*Director*, K. S. Dodds, D.SC., Ph.D.

East Malling Research Station, Nr. Maidstone, Kent.—*Director*, F. R. Tubbs, C.B.E., M.SC., Ph.D.

Agricultural and Horticultural Research Station, Long Ashton, Bristol.—*Director*, Prof. H. G. H. Kearns, O.B.E., B.SC., Ph.D.

Scottish Horticultural Research Institute, Mylnefield, Invergowrie, Dundee.—*Director*, T. Swarbrick, M.SC., Ph.D.

Vegetables

National Vegetable Research Station, Wellesbourne, Warwickshire.—*Director*, J. Philp, Ph.D., F.L.S.

Grassland

Grassland Research Institute, Hurley, nr. Maidenhead, Berks.—*Director*, William Davies, D.SC.

Glasshouse Crops

Glasshouse Crops Research Institute, Worthing Road, Rustington, Littlehampton, Sussex.—*Director*, F. W. Toovey, O.B.E., B.SC.

(b) Research affecting Animals

Animal Diseases

Animal Diseases Research Association, Moredun Institute, Gilmerton, Edinburgh, 9.—*Director*, J. T. Stamp, D.SC., M.R.C.V.S., F.R.S.E.

Research Institute (Foot-and-Mouth Disease), Pirbright, Surrey.—*Director*, I. A. Galloway, D.SC., M.R.C.V.S.

Hill Farming

Hill Farming Research Organisation, 48 Palmerston Place, Edinburgh, 12.—*Director*, A. R. Wannop, O.B.E., F.R.S.E.

Dairying

National Institute for Research in Dairying, Shinfield, nr. Reading.—*Director*, Prof. R. G. Baskett, O.B.E., M.SC.

Hannah Dairy Research Institute, Kirkhill, Ayr.—*Director*, J. A. B. Smith, C.B.E., D.SC., Ph.D., F.R.S.E.

Nutrition

Rowett Research Institute, Bucksburn, Aberdeen.—*Director*, D. P. Cuthbertson, C.B.E., M.D., D.SC., F.R.S.E.

Poultry

Houghton Poultry Research Station,* Houghton Grange, Huntingdon.—*Director*, R. F. Gordon, D.SC., M.R.C.V.S.

(c) Research on Agricultural Engineering

National Institute of Agricultural Engineering, Wrest Park, Silsoe, Beds.—*Director*, W. H. Cashmore, C.B.E., B.A.

National Institute of Agricultural Engineering, Scottish Station, Bush and Dryden Estates, Milton Bridge, Penicuik, Midlothian.—*Director*, W. J. West, B.A.

* Financed jointly by the Agricultural Research Council and the Animal Health Trust.

PROGRESS OF THE NEW TOWNS (To March 31, 1963)

Town	New Industries		New shops	New houses and flats	Actual expenditure for all purposes
	Number of firms	Numbers employed			
Basildon	80	11,850	292	11,587	£38,710,000
Bracknell	27	6,669	75	4,963	18,117,000
Crawley	79	14,166	275	12,787	32,402,033
Harlow	89	13,852	247	15,489	44,873,000
Hatfield	16	762	99	3,445	8,787,000
Hemel Hempstead	59	8,854	295	11,562	36,956,552
Stevenage	54	12,887	233	11,797	37,898,000
Welwyn Garden City	47	5,078	109	5,191	16,167,000
Corby	20	2,084	171	4,900	13,293,000
Cwmbran	2	111	78	5,008	12,367,000
Newton Aycliffe	—	—	74	4,176	9,233,000
Peterlee	4	1,245	64	4,150	10,227,000
Cumbernauld	10	2,108	14	1,729	8,195,000
East Kilbride	58	7,728	127	9,286	25,985,000
Glenrothes	7	957	34	3,576	8,973,000
Livingston	—	—	—	—	29,000
Total Expenditure					£322,275,841

BRITISH STANDARDS INSTITUTION

British Standards House, 2 Park Street, W.1

The British Standards Institution is recognized as the organization responsible for preparing and publishing voluntary national standards for industrial and consumer products.

The Institution dates from 1901 when the Institutions of Civil, Mechanical and Electrical Engineers together with the Iron and Steel Institute and the Institution of Naval Architects formed a Joint Engineering Standards Committee, which eventually became the British Engineering Standards Association. Between 1923 and 1929 the building, chemical and textile industries joined in the work. In 1929 the organization was incorporated by Royal Charter under the title of "British Standards Institution."

British Standards are arrived at by common consent among authorized representatives of the industries which make and use the materials and goods concerned (mainly the engineering, chemical, building and textile industries). The 300 new and revised British Standards published each year specify agreed manufacturing processes, dimensions, methods of test and analysis, standards of safety and performance, and glossaries of terms.

The Institution has more than 11,000 subscribing members, consisting of public authorities, trade and technical institutions, distributors, manufacturers, engineers and other users.

President, G. Cunliffe.
Director, H. A. R. Binney, C.B.

Principal London Clubs

Club and Address	Secretary	Subscription Entr.	Subscription Ann.	Remarks
		G.	G.	
Aldwych (1911), 18 Exeter St., W.C.2.	P. Bell	*Nil*	5 & 2	Social: Non-political.
Alpine (1857), 74 S. Audley St., W.1.	A. K. Rawlinson (*Hon.*)	4	5–3	Mountaineering.
American (1919), 95 Piccadilly, W.1.	A. Saynes	£30	£30	Americans in London.
American Women's (1899), 1 Cadogan Gardens, S.W.3.	Mrs. K. E. Hayward	*Nil*	10–3	American Women in London.
Anglo-Belgian (1954), 6 Belgrave Square, S.W.1.	N. Charles	*Nil*	£8	Political, Social, Economic.
Army and Navy (1837), 36–39 and 46–47 Pall Mall, S.W.1.	J. Gordon	*Nil*	19, 10, & 9	Commissioned Officers of H.M. Forces.
Arts (1863), 40 Dover Street, W.1.	G. W. Stainer	10 (+ £10 share)	25 25	Art, Literature, Science.
The Athenæum (1824), 107 Pall Mall, S.W.1.	A. C. C. Peebles, C.V.O.	50	25	Literature and Science, Public Services, The Arts.
Authors' (1891), 2 Whitehall Court, S.W.1.	R. Goodfellow	7 & 1	20, 16, 12, & 7	Literary and Social.
The Bath (1896), 43 Brook St., W.1.	C. P. Frend	30	26	Naval, Military, Social.
Beefsteak (1876), 9 Irving St., W.C.2.	T. Russell	5	20	Dining and Social.
Boodle's (1762), 28 St. James's St., S.W.1.	Cdr. P. C. Eliot, R.N. (*ret.*)	40	40	Social: Non-political.
Brooks's (1764), St. James's St., S.W.1.	Maj. H. N. Lucas, M.B.E.	40	38	Social.
Buck's (1919), 18 Clifford Street, W.1.	(vacant)	*Nil*	30	Social: Non-political.
Caledonian (1897), 9 Halkin St., S.W.1.	Capt. G. G. Wilson, C.B.E., R.N. (*ret.*)	20 & 10	25–3½	Strictly Scottish.
Canning (1910), 1 Hamilton Place, W.1.	S. W. Chapman	*Nil*	15	Social: S. American.
Carlton (1832), 69 St. James's St., S.W.1.	M. R. D. Lord	30 & 15	35 & 22	Conservative.
Cavalry (1891), 127 Piccadilly, W.1.	Sqn.-Ldr. A. F. O'Connor (*Hon.*)	30	20	Officers of Mounted Services.
Challoner (1949), 59–61 Pont St., S.W.1.	Sqn.-Ldr. C. R. Brooke.	2	5 & 2	Social: Roman Catholic.
Chemical (1918), 2 Whitehall Court, S.W.1.	R. Goodfellow	7	16, 12 & 7	Social.
City Livery (1914), Sion College, E.C.4.	A. Stanley Bell, C.C. (*Hon.*)	15	7	Liverymen of City only.
City of London (1832), 19 Old Broad Street, E.C.2.	Cdr. A. C. Mathews, O.B.E., R.N.	100	30	Merchants, Bankers, &c.
City University (1885), 50 Cornhill, E.C.3.	H. W. Bundock	10	19	Oxford and Cambridge Graduates.
Civil Service (1953), 13–15 Great Scotland Yard, S.W.1.	C. F. Stewart	*Nil*	30*s.*–15*s.*	Serving or pensioned Civil Servants.
Constitutional (1883), c/o United Service Club, 116 Pall Mall, S.W.1.	Major P. G. A. Ennor	*Nil*	21 & 13	Social and Political.
Cowdray (1922), 20 Cavendish Sq., W.1.	(vacant)	£5 & £2 10*s.*	£8 10*s.*–£1 10*s.*	Nurses and Prof. Women and others.
Devonshire (1875), 50 St. James's St., S.W.1.	C. G. Dunning	30	30	Social.
East India and Sports' (1849), 16 St. James's Square, S.W.1.	J. Gledhill	30	25, 10 & 5	Service, Social, Sport.
Eccentric (1890), 9 Ryder Street, S.W.1.	Lt.-Cdr. W. E. V. Woods, R.N.	10	18	Social.
Farmers' (1842), 3 Whitehall Ct., S.W.1.	Lt.-Col. R. L. Henson, M.B.E.	3	7 & 4	Agricultural Interests.
Flyfishers' (1884), 3 Whitehall Ct., S.W.1.	D. J. Berry	5	12, 7 & 2	Flyfishing and Social.
Forum (1919), 42 Belgrave Sq., S.W.1.	Mrs. O. Ambler	*Nil*	18, 15, 12 & 5	Women: Social, etc.
Garrick (1831), 15 Garrick Street, W.C.2.	Cdr. E. S. Satterthwaite, R.N.	35	30	Dramatic and Literary.
Goat (1916), 179 New Bond St., W.1.	S. Pinhey	£2	6 & 4	R.N. and R.M. Officers.

Club and Address	Secretary	Subscription Entr.	Subscription Ann.	Remarks
		G.	G.	
Golfers' (1893), 2a Whitehall Ct., S.W.1.	Lt.-Col E. H. Thomas, M.B.E.	*Nil*	7–4	Members of Golf Clubs.
Green Room (1877), 8–9 Adam Street, W.C.2.	L. Syrett (*Hon.*).......	..	15	Dramatic Profession.
Gresham (1843), 15 Abchurch Lane, E.C.4.	Brig. A. A. J. Allen ...	50	20	Bankers, Merchants, Social.
Guards (1810), 16 Charles St., W.1.	C. E. Buss	15	£30, 23 & 16	Guards Officers only.
Hurlingham (1869), Ranelagh Gardens, S.W.6.	Capt. R. H. Rump, R.N. (*ret.*)	25	23	Tennis, Cricket, Swimming, Croquet, Squash, Bowls, Social.
International Sportsmen's (1929), 30 Upper Grosvenor Street, W.1	J. M. Hornsby	20	20	Ladies and Gentlemen.
Irish (1947), 82 Eaton Sq., S.W.1.	W. A. O'Hanlon (*Hon.*)	1	5	Social: Non-political.
Junior Army and Navy (1911), Horse Guards Avenue, S.W.1.	Lt.-Col. E. H. Thomas, M.B.E.	5	12, 10 & 5	Officers past and present.
Junior Carlton (1864), 30 Pall Mall, S.W.1.	Col. J. Masterton-Smith, C.B.E.	20	25, 14 & 3	Conservative.
Kempton Park (1878), Sunbury-on-Thames.	L. W. Hargreaves	*Nil*	£20	Racing.
Kennel (1873), 1–4 Clarges St., W.1.	E. Holland Buckley ...	*Nil*	5	For improving breed of dogs.
Ladies' Alpine (1907), c/o National Book League, 7 Albemarle Street, W.1.	Miss M. P. Darvall (*Hon.*)	1	3 & 2½	Mountaineering.
Lansdowne (1935), 9 Fitzmaurice Place, Berkeley Sq., W.1.	A. C. Heyman........	*Nil*	25, 16 & 10	Social, Sports and Residential.
London Fencing (1848), 83 Perham Road, W.14.	E. J. Morten (*Hon.*) ...	*Nil*	8	Fencing.
London Rowing (1856), Embankment, Putney, S.W.15.	A. J. Tressidder	£2	Various	Amateur Rowing.
M.C.C. (Marylebone Cricket Club) (1787), Lord's Cricket Ground, N.W.8.	S. C. Griffith, D.F.C.	£5	£6 & £4	Headquarters of Cricket.
Mining (1910), 3 London Wall Bldgs., E.C.2.	G. Sumner............	*Nil*	10, 4 & 3	Mining and Metallurgical Interests.
National (1845), 30–35 Pall Mall, S.W.1.	Brig. J. V. McCormack, O.B.E., M.C. (*Hon.*)	*Nil*	14	Clerical and Social.
National Liberal (1882), Whitehall Place, S.W.1.	C. Billson	*Nil*	20 & 10	Liberal and Social.
Naval and Military (1862), 94 Piccadilly, W.1.	Cdr. E. J. Webb, R.N. (*ret.*)	*Nil*	25–3	Officers of R.N., Army, Marines, R.A.F.
Oriental (1824), Stratford House, Stratford Place, W.1.	R. N. Rapson, M.V.O.	25	25–3	Social.
Oxford and Cambridge University (1830), 71–7 Pall Mall, S.W.1.	J. Harper.............	*Nil*	30	Oxford and Cambridge Univ.
Portland (1816), 18b Charles St., W.1.	H. E. Pretyman	50	30	Social: Non-political.
Pratt's (1841), 14 Park Place, S.W.1	Maj. H. N. Lucas, M.B.E.	*Nil*	£7 10s.	Social.
Press (1882), St. Bride's House, Salisbury Sq., E.C.4.	C. Lazenby...........	3 & 1	9, 2½ & 1	Strictly Journalistic.
Public Schools (1909), 100 Piccadilly, W.1.	T. J. R. Dashwood, O.B.E.	*Nil*	20, 9, & 3	Social: Public Schools.
Queen's (1886), W. Kensington, W.14.	R. J. Ritchie..........	15	22 & 18	Lawn Tennis, Tennis, Rackets and Squash Racquets.
Railway (1899), 320 High Holborn, W.C.1.	B. D. J. Walsh (*Hon.*)..	½	2 & 1	Railway interests.
Reform (1832), 104–5 Pall Mall, S.W.1.	C. J. L. Reynolds	10	36 & 5	Social.
Roehampton (1901), Roehampton Lane, S.W.15.	J. Maples.............	10 & 5	25 & 11	Golf, Lawn Tennis, Squash Racquets, Croquet, Swimming
Royal Aero (1901), 9 Fitzmaurice Place, Berkeley Square, W.1.	Col. R. L. Preston, C.B.E.	..	25	Aeronautics.
Royal Air Force (1917), 128 Piccadilly, W.1.	Group Capt. A. V. Rogers, A.F.C.	*Nil*	20 & 12	Officers of R.A.F., R.A.F.V.R., R.F.C. and R.N.A.S.
R.A.F. Reserves (1948), 14 South Street, W.1.	H. C. Room, M.B.E....	*Nil*	5–1	Officers of R.A.F., R.A.F.V.R., R.A.F. Reserve and ex-officers.

Club and Address	Secretary	Subscription Entr.	Subscription Ann.	Remarks
		G.	G.	
Royal Automobile (1897), 89–91 Pall Mall, S.W.1.	Cdr. D. P. Little, R.N.	20 & 10	21–8	And at Woodcote Park, Epsom.
Royal Cruising (1880), 42 Half Moon Street, Piccadilly, W.1.	D. C. L. Cree (*Hon.*)	4	4	Cruising and Social.
R.N.V.R. Officers (1943), 38 Hill Street, W.1.	Lt.-Cdr. C. H. Tross Youle, O.B.E.	10	5, 2, ½	Officers of R.N., R.M., R.N.R., R.N.V.R., and members of yacht clubs.
Royal Ocean Racing (1925), 20 St. James's Place, S.W.1.	A. H. Paul	6 & 3	6, 3 & 2	Long distance Yacht Racing.
Royal Societies (1894), 100 Piccadilly, W.1.	D. W. Milne (*Hon.*)	*Nil*	15, 6 & 4	Learned Societies, Professional, Social.
Royal Thames Yacht (1775), 60 Knightsbridge, S.W.1.	Col. N. Blair	25–10	25–2	Yachting and Social.
Royal Toxophilite Society (1781), 1 Albion Mews, W.2.	C. B. Edwards (*Hon.*)	5	5, 3, 1	Archery.
Royal Water Colour Society Art (1884), 26 Conduit Street, W.1.	M. Fry	2	2½	Exhibiting Art Society only.
St. James' (1859), 106 Piccadilly, W.1.	P. K. Hiller	25	40	Diplomatic and Social.
St. Stephen's (1870), 34 Queen Anne's Gate, S.W.1.	R. Lush	25–5	25–5	Conservative.
Sandown Park (1875), Esher, Surrey.	E. F. Legg	*Nil*	Various	Racing.
Savage (1857), c/o National Liberal Club, Whitehall Place, S.W.1.	A. H. Nash (*Hon.*)	20	20 & 12	Drama, Literature, Art, Music, Science, Law.
Savile (1868), 69 Brook Street, W.1	H. G. Vevers (*Hon*)	20	28	Social: Non-political.
Service Women's (1922), 52 Lower Sloane St., S.W.1.	Miss A. McNeil, C.B.E.	£2	4 & 3	Service Women, Past and Present
Sesame Imperial and Pioneer (1895), 49 Grosvenor Street, W.1.	Miss G. E. Martin	*Nil*	12–3	Social and Literary: Men and Women.
Ski Club of G.B. (1903), 118 Eaton Square, S.W.1.	M. N. H. Milne, O.B.E., E.D.	*Nil*	5–2	Ski-ing.
Spanish (Centro Español de Londres) (1920), 5 Cavendish Sq., W.1.	M. Blanch	*Nil*	15–£1 10*s.*	Social and Residential.
Thames Rowing (1860), Embankment, Putney.	J. P. M. Thomson; D. King (*Joint Hon.*).	£2	10	Amateur Rowing and Sculling.
Travellers' (1819), 106 Pall Mall, S.W.1.	R. P. McDouall	30	33	Social: Non-political.
Turf (1868), 85 Piccadilly, W.1.	(vacant)	15	30	Racing and Social.
Union (1800), 86 St. James's Street, S.W.1.	Lt.-Col. L. N. Barker-Simson, M.B.E.	21	33	Social: Non-political.
United Hunts (1928), 17 Upper Grosvenor Street, W.1.	Lt.-Cdr. C. H. Tyers.	10	10, 5 & 3	Social.
United Nursing Services (1921), 40 South Street, W.1.	Miss N. K. Allen	3	8–1	Ladies; Nursing Services and Social.
United Service (1815), 116 Pall Mall, S.W.1.	Cdr. J. C. Allan	£20	£25	Regular Officers.
United Sports (1903), 4 Whitehall Ct., S.W.1.	Lt.-Col. E. H. Thomas, M.B.E.	5	£10, £8 & £2	Social and Sporting.
United University (1821), 1 Suffolk Street, S.W.1.	G. Moore	*Nil*	33	Oxford and Cambbridge Univ.
United Wards (1877), Tallowchandlers' Hall, Dowgate Hill, E.C.4.	E. E. Taylor	1	2½	Freemen, Liverymen, Ward Club members in City: Civic.
University Women's (1886), 2 Audley Square, W.1.	Miss D. Cooper	3 & 2	11–9	University and Medical.
V.A.D. Ladies (1920), 44 Gt. Cumberland Place, W.1.	Miss M. A. Sample, M.B.E.	2	6 & 5	Red Cross and St. John.
Victoria (1860), 18 Wellington St., W.C.2.	G. Bailie	25	35	Sporting and Social.
Victory Ex-Services (1907), 63–79 Seymour Street, W.2.	Lt.-Cdr. J. B. Williams, R.N. (*ret.*)	*Nil*	£1	Social: For Ex-Service Men and Women.
West Indian (1898), 4 Whitehall Ct., S.W.1.	E. A. Davson (*Hon.*)	3	10, 6 & 2	Social: West Indian.
White's (1693), 37–8 St. James's St., S.W.1.	H. L. Webb	£50	30	Social: Non-political.
Women's Press (1943), 52 Carey St., W.C.2.	R. Sprooles	1	8–2	Women Journalists and Authors.

PRINCIPAL CLUBS OUTSIDE LONDON

Club (with date of foundation)	Address	Subscription		Secretary or *Hon. Sec.
		Entr.	Ann.	
		G.	G.	
Aldershot (Officers) (1854).......	Farnborough Road	*Nil*	Various	J. W. E. Huckstepp.
Bath (Bath and County) (1858) ..	21–22 Queen Square...	*Nil*	Various	*G. E. Fane.
(Bath and County Ladies) (1895)	25 Queen Square.....	1	5	Mrs. S. Carter.
Birmingham—				
(Chamber of Commerce) (1921)	75 Harborne Road....	*Nil*	10	*R. C. Booth, T.D.
(Conservative) (1871)..........	53 Temple Row......	20	20	*J. Seth-Smith.
(Midland) (1872)..............	5 Ethel Street.........	*Nil*	15	*F. B. Murray.
(Midland Conservative) (1882)..	Waterloo Street.......	10	18	*J. B. Boyd.
(St. Paul's) (1859)	34 St. Paul's Square ...	10	25	*W. J. Eley.
(Union) (1867)	87 Colmore Row.....	Various	Various	*F. W. Kenchington.
Bishop Auckland (The Club) (1866)	Victoria Street.......	5	5	*J. McM. Moore.
Blackburn (Union) (1849).......	45 Preston New Road	*Nil*	7	*R. B. Hargreaves.
Bolton (Constitutional) (1870)....	25 Mawdsley Street ...	*Nil*	9 & 4	*P. Nuttall.
Bournemouth (The Club) (1871)..	Pier Approach........	*Nil*	10, 6 & 3	*Group Capt. J. H. Herring, D.S.O., M.C.
Bradford (The Club) (1870).......	41 Bank Street........	5	18	W. E. B. Holroyd; G. R. Turner.
(Union) (1857)	Piece Hall Yard.......	10	22	*C. P. Wightman.
Bridport and West Dorset (1922)	12 South Street	5 & 2	3 & 1½	*R. de F. Ford.
Bristol (Clifton) (1882)	22 The Mall..........	*Nil*	13–3	Lt.-Col. C. T. Ingle.
(Constitutional) (1885)..........	Marsh Street..........	*Nil*	11	Rear Adm. B. Taylor, C.B., D.S.C.
(The Bristol Club) (1888)	38a Corn Street.	10 & 5	14 & 7	*V. R. Tamblyn.
(University and Literary) (1890)	20 Berkeley Square....	*Nil*	7	*E. F. Scudamore.
Buxton (Union) (1887)	St. John's Road.......	3 & 1	9–1	W. H. Finney.
Cambridge (Amateur Dramatic) (1855)	Park Street...........	2	1	*M. J. de C. Studdert.
(Hawks) (1871)	2 All Saints' Passage ...	2	6	*N. N. Browne.
(Union) (1815)	Bridge Street.........	1	5	S. A. Elwood (*Chief Clerk*).
Canterbury (Kent and Canterbury) (1868)	17 Old Dover Road...	3	5 & 4	D. F. Andrews.
Cardiff (Cardiff and County) (1866)	2 Westgate Street......	20	16	Lt.-Cdr. E. R. Tipple, M.B.E.
(Exchange Club) (1880).........	10 Mt. Stuart Square...	5	9	R. E. Collins.
(Glamorgan Wanderers) (1927)	Wyndham Arcade	4½	4½	*W. Eastman.
Carlisle (Border) (1862)..........	9 Portland Square.....	5	5	W. Shield.
(Cumberland County) (1870) ..	24 Lowther Street.....	*Nil*	10 & 2	*G. N. Worthington.
Cheltenham (The New Club) (1874)	Promenade...........	*Nil*	15–1½	*C. J. W. Lillie.
Chester (Grosvenor) (1866).......	3 Vicars Lane.........	*Nil*	13	*P. W. Wood.
(City) (1807)	St. Peter's Church Yd.	3	10–2	H. Dodd.
Chichester (W. Sussex County) (1874)	38 East Street........	*Nil*	5 & 3	*W. J. Higgins.
Colchester (The Club) (1874)	67–69 Culver Street....	..	8 & 5	F. J. Eves.
Devizes (Devizes & District) (1930)	27 St. John Street......	*Nil*	3 & 1	*C. S. Paige.
Douglas, Isle of Man (Ellan Vannin Club) (1893)	20 Finch Road........	1	5	*G. W. Howie, M.B.E.
Dudley (Conservative) (1884).....	Castle Hill	4	6	*S. W. Ordish.
Durham (County) (1890)	52 Old Elvet	*Nil*	6, 3 & 2	*G. W. Thompson, M.B.E.
Eastbourne (Devonshire) (1872) ..	Hartington Place......	*Nil*	10	*S. E. Worley.
Evesham (Evesham) (1900)	Dresden House	4	4 & 2	*N. H. F. Burrell.
Exeter (Exeter and County) (1870)	Southernhay House....	£4	9	*L. G. Coles.
Falmouth (The Club) (1829)......	Western Terrace	1	4	*R. J. Hold.
Folkestone (Radnor Club) (1874)..	136 Sandgate Road....	3	8–4½	*R. C. R. Land.
Guildford (County) (1882)	158 High Street.......	3 & 5	5–10	K. F. M. Loughnan.
Halifax (The Club) (1868)........	Fountain Street	*Nil*	18	*A. G. Hirst.
Harrogate (The Club) (1857).....	36 Victoria Avenue	5	12 & 5	T. D. Bertram.
Haverfordwest (Pembrokeshire County) (1877)	48 High Street........	3	3½	*T. G. Jones.
Henley-on-Thames (Leander) (1815)	Remenham Village, Henley.	6	4	*D. H. Mays-Smith, T.D.
(Phyllis Court) (1906)	Marlow Road........	*Nil*	12	Miss J. Crone.
Hove (The Club) (1882)	28 Fourth Avenue.....	*Nil*	10 & 5	*Maj. F. R. Clifton.
Huddersfield (Huddersfield and County Conservative) (1891)	Church Street	*Nil*	7, 4 & 3½	*H. M. Dyson.
Jersey (United) (1848)	Royal Sq., St. Helier.	£6	£7 10s.	*E. H. Stent.
(Victoria) (1853)	Beresford Street, St. Helier.	6 & 3	10 & 5	*Col. W. A. Cheeseman.

Club (with date of foundation)	Address	Subscription Entr.	Subscription Ann.	Secretary or *Hon. Sec.
		G.	G.	
Leamington (Tennis Court) (1846)	50 Bedford Street	*Nil*	10	*N. C. Adams.
Leeds (The Leeds Club) (1849)	3 Albion Place	10	16 & 8	*J. P. W. Wood.
Leicester (Constitutional) (1880)	1 Pocklington's Walk	3	9	A. O. Hallam.
(Leicestershire Club) (1873)	9 Welford Place	20	15	F. A. Lancashire.
Littlehampton (County) (1911)	16 Granville Road	*Nil*	5	*R. P. S. Walker, E.D.
Liverpool (Artists) (1898)	Eberle Street	5	10	*R. A. Gilroy.
(Athenæum) (1797)	Church Alley	*Nil*	20–5	*J. D. Newton.
(Constitutional) (1879)	11 Tithebarn Street	*Nil*	18	R. Whittingham.
(Exchange) (1832)	11 Fenwick Street	*Nil*	21	*H. H. Timson.
(Lyceum) (1801)	1 Bold Street	*Nil*	15 & 7½	F. A. Willett.
(Old Hall) (1909)	Cotton Exchge. Bldgs.	10	15	*C. C. Taylor.
(Palatine) (1836)	5 Union Court	20	20	*D. S. Syers-Gibson.
(Racquet) (1874)	102 Upper Parliament Street.	*Nil*	20	*A. R. Beddoe.
(University) (1895)	2 Mount Pleasant	*Nil*	13	*W. D. Herring; S. R. Whipple, D.F.C. (*joint*).
Manchester (Engineers) (1912)	17 Albert Square	*Nil*	21–7	*E. Wilkinson.
(The Old Rectory) (1911)	90 Deansgate	5	12	*J. E. Shortland.
(Reform) (1867)	81 King Street	10	20	A. W. Rothwell.
(St. James) (1961)	102 Mosley Street	10	21	M. F. L. Falkner; M. Pattison (*joint*)
Newbury (South Berks) (1888)	West Mills	*Nil*	6	*J. M. Laycock.
Newcastle on Tyne (Union) (1862)	Westgate Road	*Nil*	18–5	H. W. Dovey.
Northampton (Northampton and County) (1873)	George Row	5–2½	11, 7 & 6	W. Parry.
Norwich (Norfolk) (1864)	17 Upper King Street	7	£18–£5	Maj. W. F. Chapman, T.D.
Nottingham (Borough) (1893)	26 Market Street	*Nil*	20–5	W. W. B. Ball.
(Nottinghamshire) (1840)	Bridlesmith Gate	..	15	*Lt.-Col. G. A. Wharton, M.B.E., T.D.
Oxford (Clarendon) (1863)	54 Cornmarket Street	2½	7 & 3½	*A. Loose.
(Frewen) (1869)	98 St. Aldate's	5	5–3	W. H. Miller.
(O.U.D.S.) (1884)	O.U.D.S., Oxford	*Nil*	6*s*.	*G. D. Harley.
(Union Society) (1823)	Frewin Court	£1	£4 10*s*.	L. W. Crawte (*Steward*).
(Vincent's) (1863)	1a King Edward Street	£4	10	*R. A. Fletcher (*Treasurer*).
Paignton (The Paignton Club) (1882)	The Esplanade	3	5	*H. G. Hearn.
(Torbay) (1905)	Hyde Road	3	4	B. Moylan-Jones.
Peterborough (City and Counties) (1865)	21 Priestgate	£2	£8 & £6	*C. N. Morlin; J. W Bower (*Joint*).
Portsmouth (Royal Naval) (1867)	17 Pembroke Road	..	4	*Capt. H. S. P. Watch, O.B.E., R.N. (*ret*.).
Preston (Conservative) (1878)	Guildhall Street	*Nil*	5	*W. D. Fairclough.
Reading (Athenæum) (1842)	28 Friar Street	*Nil*	8–6	R. E. Beasley.
Richmond, Surrey (Richmond) (1880)	Northumberland Ho., Petersham Road.	*Nil*	7½	L. D. Greer.
Ripon (City Club) (1930)	3 Water Skellgate	*Nil*	£1 15*s*.	*G. C. Smith.
Rochester (Castle) (1865)	The Esplanade	5	9	*S. P. Harrison.
Rugby (The Rugby) (1866)	35 North Street	1	4	*F. P. Cronin.
Rye (Dormy House) (1895)	Rye	2	6 & 4	*J. L. S. Vidler.
St. Leonards on Sea (East Sussex) (1890)	Warrior Square	1	10 & 5	*Lt.-Col. V. Newton-Moss, M.C.
Scarborough (South Cliff) (1898)	5 West Street	*Nil*	5–2	*R. Bleach.
(St. James's) (1941)	St. James's Row	3	12	Mrs. M. Turner.
Shrewsbury (Shropshire) (1870)	The Square	..	8	A. N. Fielden, O.B.E.
Southwold (The Blyth Club) (1929)	81 High Street	1	4 & 2	*Maj. A. C. Brewitt, M.C.
Tavistock (West Devon) (1899)	Abbey Bridge	3	£5	*C. S. Pendrigh.
Teddington (Royal Canoe) (1866)	Trowlock Island	2	4	F. P. Penny.
Tunbridge Wells (Tunbridge Wells and Counties) (1872)	40 London Road	*Nil*	6 & 4	*Mrs. I. H. Barnes.
Winchester (Hampshire Club) (1857)	Southgate Street	*Nil*	9 & 5	*R. D. Utting.
Worcester (Worcestershire) (1861)	40 Foregate Street	..	8	*J. D. Schooling.
(Union) (1878)	2 The Cross	6	7	*H. F. Price.
Yeovil (Ivel Club) (1884)	Frederick Place	3 & 1	6 & 2	H. Cleave.
York (Yorkshire) (1839)	17 Museum Street	*Nil*	16 & 8	Miss M. O'Kelly.
(City) (1876)	4 Museum Street	2	7	*J. E. Walker.

Club (with date of foundation)	Address	Subscription Entr.	Subscription Ann.	Secretary or *Hon. Sec.
		G.	G.	
Scotland				
Aberdeen (Royal Northern) (1854)	9 Albyn Place	..	13 & 8	*W. S. Crosby.
Ayr (County) (1872)	Savoy Park Hotel	*Nil*	£4 10s.	*Lt.-Col. W. W. McHarg.
Dundee (Eastern) (1865)	1 Albert Square	10	18	Stuart and Stuart, C.A.
Edinburgh (Caledonian United Service and Northern) (1825)	3 Queensferry Street	10	17	*R. O. M. Williams, M.B.E., M.C., W.S.
(Ladies' Caledonian) (1908)	13–14 Charlotte Square.	7	10 & 9	Miss P. D. Bremner.
(New) (1787)	85 Princes Street	25	22, 16 & 13	C. Ballantyne.
(Queen's) (1897)	7 Frederick Street	10	12 & 11	Miss G. B. Kerr.
(Scottish Conservative) (1877)	112 Princes Street	10–2	18–3	Mrs. M. W. Hutton.
(University Union) (1889)	Park Place	£1	£5	A. A. Brown.
Glasgow (Art) (1867)	185 Bath Street	15 & 5	11 & 7	G. Middlemass.
(Conservative) (1880)	33 Bothwell Street	18 & 8	25–3	C. N. G. Orton.
(Kelvin) (1897)	19 Royal Exchange Sq.	8	13	Miss W. Hamilton.
(Royal Scottish Automobile) (1899)	11 Blythswood Square	25 & 7	10 & 4	(vacant)
(The Western Club) (1825)	147 Buchanan Street	£25	24	R. F. Maclauchlan.
Inverness (Highland) (1870)	39 High Street	12	12	Capt. J. MacLaren-Marshall, M.C.
Northern Ireland				
Belfast (Ulster) (1857)	Castle Place	10	18	*W. R. Knox.
(Ulster Reform) (1885)	4 Royal Avenue	10	18	*T. S. Duncan.
Enniskillen (Fermanagh County) (1883)	Church Street	4 & 3	4 & 3	*Lt.-Col. G. E. Liddle, C.B.E.
Omagh (Tyrone County) (1849)	High Street	*Nil*	5 & 2	*B.G.L. Glasgow, O.B.E.

YACHT CLUBS

Club (with date of foundation)	Address	Subscription Entr.	Subscription Ann.	Secretary or *Hon. Sec.
		G.	G.	
Beaumaris (Royal Anglesey) (1802)	6–7 Green Edge	3 & 2	4, 3 & 1	*R. R. M. Jones.
Bembridge, I. of W. (Sailing) (1886)	Isle of Wight	6	8 & 5	Cdr. W. A. R. Cartwright, R.N. (*ret.*).
Birkenhead (Royal Mersey) (1844)	8–10 Bedford Road, Rock Ferry.	3	6	*A. W. Tennant.
Bridlington (Royal Yorks) (1847)	1 Windsor Crescent	6	5	*B. V. Rhodes.
Burnham-on-Crouch (Royal Burnham) (1895)	The Quay	6	12	*Brig. H. J. R. Jackson.
(Royal Corinthian) (1872)	Burnham-on-Crouch, and The Parade, Cowes.	5	12	L. R. Billinghurst.
Caernarvon (Royal Welsh) (1847)	Porth-yr-Aur	3	4 & 2	*Capt. J. M. Jones.
Cowes (Royal Yacht Squadron) (1815)	The Castle, Cowes	£150	£35	Capt. M. H. Evelegh, R.N. (*ret.*).
(Royal London) (1838)	The Parade	5	10–3½	Lt.-Cdr. J. de G. Lamotte, R.N. (*ret.*).
Dover (Royal Cinque Ports) (1872)	Waterloo Crescent	3	7 & 4	*H. W. Andrews.
Fowey (Royal Fowey) (1894)	Fowey	2	5, 2 & 1	*S. W. Whiffen, O.B.E.
Harwich (Royal Harwich) (1843)	Woolverstone, nr. Ipswich.	6	6	Lt.-Col. A. L. Semmence.
Jersey (R.C.I.) (1862)	St. Aubin; St. Peter Port, Guernsey.	2	3 & 2½	Capt. D. R. Lane; R. Savage (*Guernsey*).
Kingswear (Royal Dart) (1866)	Kingswear, S. Devon	4 & 1	5–1	*Miss A. M. Hine-Haycock, M.B.E.
Leigh-on-Sea (Essex) (1890)	Leigh-on-Sea.	3	6	Capt. H. J. Patterson.
London (Cruising Association) (1908)	Chiltern Court, Baker Street, N.W.1.	2	3	Mrs. P. Wall.
(Royal Cruising) (1880)	42 Half Moon Street, W.1.	4	4	*D. C. L. Cree.

Club (with date of foundation)	Address	Subscription Entr.	Subscription Ann.	Secretary or *Hon. Sec.
		G.	G.	
Lowestoft (Royal Norfolk and Suffolk) (1859)	Royal Plain	5	10 & 6	L. F. Nicholson.
Penarth (Penarth) (1880)	The Esplanade	2	6	P. Skone-Rees.
Plymouth (Royal Western) (1827)	5 The Esplanade	2	6	*Capt. T. W. B. Shaw, D.S.C., R.N. (*ret.*).
(Royal Plymouth Corinthian) (1877)	Madeira Road	2	4	*C. N. P. Nicholson.
Poole (East Dorset Sailing) (1876)	Witley Pier, Parkstone	3	5	Miss A. Bailey.
(Parkstone) (1895)	Pearce Avenue, Parkstone.	2	6	W. T. Banner.
(Poole Harbour) (1949)	Salterns Way, Parkstone.	*Nil*	6 & 3	Mrs. E. M. Perry.
(Royal Motor Yacht) (1905)	Sandbanks, Panorama Rd., Poole	15	15	Lt.-Cdr. A.H.C. Booth, D.S.C.
(Yacht) (1865)	New Quay Road, Hamworthy.	4	4	Maj. R. J. Birbeck.
Ramsgate (Royal Temple) (1857)	Keel Haul.	2	4	D. Rhodes.
Ryde (Royal Victoria) (1844)	St. Thomas Street	3	3	*Cdr. H. W. Mole, D.S.C, R.N. (*ret.*).
Southampton:				
(Royal Air Force) (1932)	Riverside Ho., Hamble	..	5-½	Sqn.-Ldr. R. T. Edwards (*ret.*).
(Royal Southern) (1837)	Hamble, Hants.	5	12	*W. R. Thornback.
(Royal Southampton) (1875)	Northlands Road	10	13-3	Lt.-Cdr. A. G. C. Franklin, R.N. (*ret.*).
(Royal Thames) (1775)	Shore House, Warsash, Hants.	20 & 10	25-2	Col. N. Blair.
Southend (Alexandra) (1873)	The Cliffs	1	4	*B. J. Stuart.
Southsea (Royal Albert) (1864)	62 Clarence Parade	2	5	Capt. F. R. G. Holmes, V.R.D., R.N.V.R.
Swansea (Bristol Channel) (1875)	Southend, Mumbles	4	6 & 4	*P. G. Cawker.
Torquay (Royal Torbay) (1863)	Beacon Hill	2	4	*D. Roe.
Westcliff-on-Sea (Thames Estuary) (1947)	3 The Leas	1	4-1	*A. H. Woolverton.
Weymouth (Royal Dorset) (1875)	6 Charlotte Row	*Nil*	6	*Brig. T. H. Angus, D.S.O.
Windermere (Royal Windermere) (1860)	Bowness-on-Windermere.	8	7-5	*W. B. Smith.
Yarmouth (Royal Solent) (1878)	Yarmouth, I.O.W.	3	5 & 3	Gp.-Capt. F. R. Drew, C.B.E.
	Scotland			
Edinburgh (Royal Forth) (1868)	1 Boswall Road, Edinburgh, 5.	5	7	*K. L. Gumley.
Glasgow (Royal Clyde) (1856)	Royal Marine Hotel, Hunter's Quay, Argyll.	4	4-1½	R. M. Whyte, 147 Blythswood St., Glasgow, C.2.
(Clyde Corinthian) (1876)	(None)	1	1	*I. J. Scott, 118 Queen Street, Glasgow C.1.
(Mudhook) (1873)	(None)	5	1	*J. C. Robertson, 45 West Nile Street.
(Royal Gourock) (1894)	Ashton, Gourock	Various	Various	*H. Lyons.
(Royal Western) (1875)	(None)	1	1	*G. D. Jackson, Royal Exchange Bldgs.
Oban (Royal Highland) (1881)	Gt. Western Hotel	*Nil*	2	P. MacLeod, c/o Royal Bank of Scotland, Oban.
Rhu (Royal Northern) (1824)	Rhu, Dunbartonshire	3	Various	J. Ingoldby, 62 Templeton St., Glasgow.
	Northern Ireland			
Bangor (Royal Ulster) (1866)	Clifton Road, Bangor, Co. Down.	7	10	*J. B. Stark, D.F.C.

THE LONDON CLEARING BANKS

COMMITTEE OF LONDON CLEARING BANKERS (1821), 10 Lombard Street, E.C.3.

The Committee consists of the Chairmen of the eleven Clearing Banks listed in the Almanack (see pp. 1101–6) and meets regularly to discuss matters of common interest. It is the body through which the Bank of England communicates official policy to the banks and through which the banks may present their views to the Bank of England and the Treasury. The Committee controls the London Bankers' Clearing House.

Secretary, R. H. Barkshire.

Asst. Secretaries, L. M. Mears; M. C. Swift, M.C.; G. B. Scrine.

BANKERS' CLEARING HOUSE

10 Lombard Street, E.C.3.

This is the organization through which the Clearing Banks and the Bank of England exchange cheques drawn on each other and settle their indebtedness to one another. The clearing system came into being in London during the second half of the eighteenth century, and has served as a pattern for the Clearing Houses that have been established since throughout the world.

To obtain payment for any cheque received from a customer for his credit, a banker must present it for payment to the bank on which it is drawn, and the Bankers' Clearing House affords a quick and efficient means of doing this. On an average day almost 1,500,000 cheques, etc., are exchanged and paid for by the eleven Clearing Banks and the Bank of England on behalf of their branches, throughout England and Wales, which number over 10,000. Although, on an average day, the value of items exchanged may approach £1,000-millions in total, the member banks settle their net indebtedness only, each either paying or receiving through the Clearing House the net balance arising from the day's work.

At present two clearings operate, generally, each business day. Cheques drawn on, and paid into, any of the ninety-odd specified Town Clearing branches may be passed through the Town Clearing either at the morning session or, if the amount is £2,000 or over (£5,000 or over on Saturdays), at the afternoon session. All other cheques must be passed through the General Clearing each morning. Since April, 1960, a Credit Clearing has been operated, through which the member banks exchange, and pay for, credit items in respect of monetary transfers between their customers.

At the end of each business day each member bank works out the net balance resulting from its transactions in that day's Town Clearing, the previous day's General (cheque) Clearing and Credit Clearing, and such differences as need to be adjusted. This net balance is either credited to or deducted from the bank's own account at the Bank of England.

Chief Inspector, C. C. Hobday.

Deputy Inspector, E. A. Young.

PRINCIPAL BANKS OPERATING IN THE BRITISH COMMONWEALTH

* *Clearing Bankers.* ‡ *Army Agents.*

London Banking Hours are 10 a.m. to 3 p.m. (Saturdays 9 a.m. to 11.30 a.m.).

ALEXANDERS DISCOUNT CO., LTD. (1810), 24 Lombard St., E.C.3.—Capital, authorized, £3,000,000. Issued, £200,000 in £2 (fully-paid 6 p.c.) Cumulative Preference Shares, £2,700,000 £1 Ordinary Shares, fully paid; Reserves £2,700,000; Deposits, £149,158,733; Dividend, 1961, 6 p.c. on Cumulative Preference Shares; 12½ p.c. on Ordinary Shares.

ALLAHABAD BANK, LTD. (1865), *Calcutta*, India, Affiliated to The Chartered Bank.—Capital, authorized, Rs. 3,00,00,000. Issued and subscribed—67,500 Ordinary Shares of Rs. 100 each, fully paid; 15,000 6 p.c. Preference Shares of Rs. 100 each, fully paid; Reserve Fund, Rs. 1,28,25,000. Deposits, 31/12/62, Rs. 62,64,71,214. Dividend for 52 years to December 31, 1961, 12 p.c. and bonus 6 p.c. for 1962 on Ordinary Shares (89 Branches).

THE AMERICAN EXPRESS CO. Inc. The Subsidiary of American Express Co., New York (1868), 65 Broadway, *New York*, U.S.A.; 6 Haymarket, S.W.1.—Capital, $6,000,000 (Shares fully paid).

ANGLO-ISRAEL BANK LTD. (affiliated to the Bank Leumi Le-Israel B.M.), Bow Bells House, 11 Bread Street, E.C.4.—Capital: Authorized, £1,000,000; Issued and fully paid, 1,000,000 Ordinary Shares £1 each; Reserves, £315,000.

ANGLO-PORTUGUESE BANK, LTD. (1929), 7–9 Bishopsgate, E.C.2.—Capital, £2,500,000. Issued and fully paid, £2,000,000; Reserve £1,000,000; Deposits, 31/1/63, £17,166,176.

AUSTRALIA AND NEW ZEALAND BANK, LIMITED, *Head Office*, 71 Cornhill, E.C.3 (6 Albemarle Street, W.1., 15 Great Cumberland Place, W.1. and 263 Strand, W.C.2). Capital Authorized (£22,500,000) £A.28,237,500; Capital Issued and Paid up, (£11,000,000) £A.13,805,000; Reserve Fund at 30/9/62, (£7,500,000) £A.9,412,500; Total assets at 30/9/62, £A.525,616,280. (975 Branches, Sub-Branches and Agencies in Australia, New Zealand, Fiji, Papua, New Guinea and London.)

AUSTRALIA AND NEW ZEALAND SAVINGS BANK LIMITED, *Head Office*, 71 Cornhill, London, E.C.3. Capital Authorized (£5,000,000) £A.6,275,000; Capital Issued and Paid up (£1,600,000) £A.2,008,000. Deposits, etc., at 30/9/62, £A.107,497,440. Reserve Fund at 30/9/62, (£650,000) £A.815,750. Total Assets at 30/9/62, £A.110,565,327.

BANCO DE BILBAO (1857), *Bilbao* (Bilbao House, New Broad St., E.C.2. and 40 King Street, W.C.2).—Capital, Authorized and paid-up, *Pesetas* 482,866,000; Reserve Fund, *Pesetas* 1,617,950,000; Deposits, *Pesetas* 33 620,188,360; Dividends, 1962, 25·675 p.c. (208 Branches and Agencies in Spain, Canary Islds., Paris and London).

BANKERS TRUST COMPANY, 16 Wall St., *New York* (9 Queen Victoria Street, E.C.4 and 32–34 Grosvenor Square, W.1).—Capital (par value $10 per share), $80,779,000; Surplus Fund and Undivided Profits, $229,456,718; Deposits, 31/12/61, $3,390,921,255.

BANK OF ADELAIDE (1865), *Adelaide*, South Australia (11 Leadenhall St., E.C.3). Capital, Authorized £A.5,000,000; issued £A.1,750,000 (Stock in units of £A.1, with Reserve Liability of £A.1 each (£1 Stock Units, fully paid); Reserve Fund, £A.2,000,000. (171 Offices.)

BANK OF AMERICA NATIONAL TRUST AND SAVINGS ASSOCIATION, *San Francisco, California, U.S.A.* (27–29 Walbrook, E.C.4 and 29 Davies St., W.1).—Capital Funds, $803,708 547; Loan Reserves, $143,081,336; Deposits 31/12/62, $12,095,965,067.

BANK OF BARODA, LTD. (1908), *Baroda*, India (31–32 King Street, E.C.2.)—Capital Authorized Rs. 3,50,00,000; Issued and subscribed Rs.

3,00,00,000; Called up Rs. 1,50,00,000. Reserve Funds, Rs.1,81,24,560; Deposits Rs.94,45,57,989; Dividend, 1961, 17 p.c. (150 Branches in India, 1 in Pakistan, 8 in East Africa and 1 in Fiji).

BANK OF BERMUDA, LTD. (1889), *Hamilton*, Bermuda (*London Agents*, Midland Bank, Ltd.).—Capital paid up, £500,000 (100,000 Shares, £5 each); Total Reserves, £624,265; Resources, 31/12/62, £31,253,864; Dividends, 1962, £1 per share.

BANK OF N. T. BUTTERFIELD & SON, LTD., *Hamilton*, Bermuda. Established 1858, incorporated 1904. (*London Agents*, Westminster Bank, Ltd.).—Capital, fully paid, £500,000. Reserves and Undivided Profits, £627,000. Total Resources, £18,364,000.

BANK OF ENGLAND. *See* p. 445.

BANK OF INDIA, LTD. (1906), *Bombay* (17 Moorgate, E.C.2).—Capital paid up, Rs. 4,05,00,000 (7,10,000 shares Rs. 100., Rs. 50 paid; 1,00,000 shares Rs. 50); Reserve Fund, Rs. 4,11,50,000; Deposits, 31/12/62, Rs. 1,57,16,34,870; Dividend, 1962, 20 p.c. less Income Tax (120 Branches).

BANK OF IRELAND (1783), College Green, *Dublin* (*London Agents*, Bank of England; Coutts & Co.).—Capital (Authorized), £3,269,231; (Issued and Fully Paid), £3,263,566. Reserves, £5,390,369; Deposits, £98,912,252; Dividend, 1962, 21 p.c. (149 Branches and Sub-Branches).

BANK OF LONDON AND MONTREAL LTD. (1958), P.O. Box 1262, Nassau, Bahama Islands. Owned jointly by the Bank of London & South America and the Bank of Montreal. Capital (Authorized), £7,000,000; (Paid up), £5,000,000; Deposits, etc., £35,364,028. (29 Branches and Agencies.)

BANK OF LONDON & SOUTH AMERICA, LTD. (1862), 40-66 Queen Victoria Street, E.C.4.—Authorized Capital, £20,000,000; Paid-up Capital, £13,650,000. Reserve, £8,000,000. Deposits, etc., 31/12/62, £328,747,660. Dividend, 1962, 9½ p.c. (57 Branches and Agencies.)

BANK OF MONTREAL (1817), *Montreal*, Canada (47 Threadneedle St., E.C.2, and 9 Waterloo Place, S.W.1.)–Capital, authorized, $100,000,000; fully paid $60,750,000. Rest, $150,000,000; Deposits, 31/10/62, $3,712,565,329; Dividend, 1962, 21 p.c. (900 Branches and Agencies).

BANK OF NEW SOUTH WALES AND BANK OF NEW SOUTH WALES SAVINGS BANK LTD. (1817), Head Office, *Sydney*, N.S.W. (29 Threadneedle St., E.C.2, 47 Berkeley Square, W.1. and 14 Kingsway, W.C.2.)—Capital, authorized and paid up, £21,950,000; Reserve Fund £16,500,000; Reserve Liability of Proprietors, £21,950,000; Aggregate Assets on 30/9/62, £875,134,133; Dividend, 1962 9 p.c. plus bonus dividend of 2½ p.c. payable in Australian Currency. (1,144 Branches and Agencies in Australia, N.Z., New Guinea, Fiji and London.)

BANK OF NEW ZEALAND, Incorporated with Limited Liability in New Zealand (1861), *Wellington*, N.Z. (1 Queen Victoria St., E.C.4).—Capital, Subscribed and paid up, £6,328,125—Preference A £500,000 fully paid £1 shares; C Long term Mortgage shares of £1 each, fully paid £234,375. D Long term Mortgage Shares of £1 each, fully paid £468,750. Preference B £1,375,000 fully paid £1 shares; and £3,750,000 Ordinary Shares of £1 fully paid; Deposits, 31/3/63, £149,564,220; Dividend, Ordinary Shares, 1962–63, 8 p.c. in New Zealand Currency. (388 Branches and Agencies in New Zealand; also Branches in Melbourne, Sydney, in Fiji and at Apia (Bank of Western Samoa).

BANK OF NOVA SCOTIA (1832), *Halifax*, N.S.; General Manager's Office, *Toronto* Ontario, Canada (24–26, Walbrook, E.C.4)—Capital Authorized, $50,000,000; Paid-up $27,000,000 ($10 Shares); Reserve Fund, $92,000,000; Total Assets, $2,448,049,613; Deposits, etc., 31/12/62, $2,284,732,932; Dividend, 1962, $2.45 per Share. (650 Branches and Sub-Branches in Canada, West Indies, etc.)

BANK OF SCOTLAND (1695), The Mound, *Edinburgh*; 30 Bishopsgate, E.C.2; 16/18 Piccadilly, W.1; 1 Regent St., S.W.1; 332 Oxford St., W.1 and 140 Kensington High St.)—Capital £6,300,000. Reserve Fund and Balance carried forward, £7,040,299. Deposits and Credit Balances, 28/2/63, £191,146,951. (431 Branches and Sub-Branches.)

BANK OF TRINIDAD (GORDON GRANT) LTD. (1959) 10 St. Vincent Street, Port of Spain, Trinidad, West Indies.—(A Member of the United Dominions Trust Group) Established to take over former banking business of Gordon Grant & Co., Ltd. (1872), as from October 1, 1959. Capital, authorized, $5,000,000; paid up, $240,000.

BANK OF WEST AFRICA, LTD. (1894), 37 Gracechurch St., E.C.3.—Capital, authorized £6,000,000; Issued and paid up, £4,000,000. Reserve Fund, £2,700,000. Deposits, 31/3/63, £70,242,815; Dividend, 1962–63, 9 p.c. (118 Branches and Agencies.)

BANQUE BELGE LTD. (1934), 4 Bishopsgate, E.C.2.—Capital: Subscribed, £2,000,000; Paid-up, £1,000,000.

BANQUE CANADIENNE NATIONALE, *Montreal*, Canada (Bank of Hochelaga and Banque Nationale amalgamated).—Capital (issued), $12,000,000; Reserve, $36,000,000; Assets, more than $845,000,000. (600 Offices in Canada.)

*BARCLAYS BANK LIMITED (1896), *Head Office*, 54 Lombard St., E.C.3; *Chief Foreign Branch*, 168 Fenchurch St., E.C.3; *City Office*, 170 Fenchurch St., E.C.3; *Trustee Dept.*, P.O. Box 54, 37 King William St., E.C.4.—*Capital* Authorized £90,000,000. 30/6/63: Capital issued (converted into stock), £63,947,102; Reserve Fund, £28,987,983; Deposits (including reserves for contingencies and balance of Profit and Loss), £1,888,465,589; Dividend, 1962: Ord. Stock, 13 p.c.; Staff Stock, 20 p.c. Over 2,300 Branches in England and Wales. *Affiliated Companies* BARCLAYS BANK D.C.O.; BARCLAYS OVERSEAS DEVELOPMENT CORPORATION LTD.; BARCLAYS BANK (FRANCE) LTD.; BARCLAYS BANK EXECUTOR AND TRUSTEE COMPANY (CHANNEL ISLANDS) LTD.; THE BRITISH LINEN BANK. Barclays Bank Ltd. is closely associated with the UNITED DOMINIONS TRUST LTD.; in Belgium with the BANQUE DE BRUXELLES and BANQUE DE COMMERCE and in Spain with BANCO DEL DESARROLLO ECONOMICO ESPAÑOL (BANDESCO).

BARCLAYS BANK D.C.O., 54 Lombard St., E.C.3.—Authorized Capital, £25,000,000; Issued Capital, £17,000,000; Reserve Fund, £15,000,000; Deposits, 31/3/63, £765,400,527; Dividend, 1960–61, 10 p.c. actual on Ordinary Stock. (1,346 Branches, Sub-Branches and Agencies.)

BARING BROTHERS & CO., LTD. (1890), 8 Bishopsgate, E.C.2, and Liverpool. — Capital, Authorized, £4,100,000; Issued and fully paid, £3,075,000; Reserve, £2,000,000; Deposits, 31/12/62, £47,774,171.

BELFAST BANKING CO., LTD. (1827), Waring St., *Belfast*, 1 (*Affiliated to the* Midland Bank, Ltd.).—Subscribed Capital, £2,500,000; Paid-up Capital, £800,000 (200,000 Shares of £12 10s., £4 paid); Reserve Fund, £1,200,000; Deposits, 31/12/62, £44,518,036; Dividend, 1962, 13 p.c., less tax. (96 Offices.)

B. W. BLYDENSTEIN & CO. (1858), 54, 55 & 56 Threadneedle St., E.C.2.—Capital, £250,000. Provided half by The Twentsche Bank (London), Ltd. (Authorized and Subscribed Capital, £1,000,100) and half by the Netherlands Trading Society (London), Ltd. (Authorized and paid-up Capital, £220,100). Assets, 31/3/63, £9,286,662.

WM. BRANDT'S SONS & CO. LTD. (1805), 36 Fenchurch Street, E.C.3.—Capital Authorized, £2,000,000; Issued and Fully Paid, £1,250,000.

BRITISH AND FRENCH BANK LTD., Imrie House, 33-6 King William St., E.C.4. Capital authorized and fully paid, £2,000,000. Affiliate of the Banque Nationale pour le Commerce et l'Industrie–Paris.

BRITISH BANK FOR FOREIGN TRADE, LTD. (1911), 6 Broad St. Place, E.C.2—Subscribed Capital. £700,000; 7,000,000 Shares of 2*s*. each fully paid.

BRITISH BANK OF THE MIDDLE EAST (1889), 7 King William St., E.C.4.—Capital, authorized, issued and fully-paid, £2,500,000 (£1 shares): 31/12/62: Revenue Reserves, £2,937,134; Deposits, £116,543,010; Dividend, 1962–63, 16 p.c., less tax.

BRITISH LINEN BANK (1746), 38 St. Andrew Square, *Edinburgh* 2 (38 Threadneedle St., E.C.2, and 198 Piccadilly, W.1). *Affiliated to* Barclays Bank Ltd.—Capital, £1,250,000 fully paid; Reserve Funds, £3,000,000; Deposits, 30/9/62, £95,015,160; Dividend, 1962, 20 p.c. (210 Branches and Sub-Branches.)

BRITISH OVERSEAS BANK, LTD. 16 Bishopsgate, E.C.2.—In voluntary liquidation. (Current Banking business transferred to Glyn, Mills & Co.).

BROWN, SHIPLEY & CO. LTD. (1810), Founders Court, Lothbury, E.C.2.

BUNGE & CO., LIMITED (1905), Bunge House, St. Mary Axe, E.C.3. Capital subscribed and paid up £1,000,000; General Reserve, 31/12/62, £1,500,000; Carry Forward, £723,168.

CANADIAN IMPERIAL BANK OF COMMERCE (1961), *Toronto*, Ontario, Canada (2 Lombard St., E.C.3). —Capital Authorized $125,000,000 (12,500,000 shares of $10); Paid up $69,680,000. Reserve Fund $192,657,206; Total Assets, 31/10/62, $4,762,352,348; Dividend 1962, 21 p.c. (1,260 Branches in Canada and elsewhere.)

CATER RYDER & CO. LTD. (1960), 38 Lombard Street, E.C.3.—Capital authorized, £5,000,000; issued and fully paid, £4,677,000. Reserve and carry forward, £1,952,507. Deposits, etc., £162,240,662. Dividend 1962–63, 13 p.c.

CENTRAL BANK OF CEYLON (1950), 85 York Street, *Colombo*. (*London Correspondents*, The Bank of England). Capital, Rs. 15,000,000; Deposits, 31/3/63, Rs. 321,927,260.

CENTRAL BANK OF INDIA, LTD. (1911), *Bombay*. Authorized capital, Rs.6,30,72,700 (Shares of Rs.50). Paid-up capital, Rs.3,15,36,350 (Shares of Rs.25 each fully paid). Reserve Fund and Other Reserves, Rs. 4,77,57.322; Deposits, 31/12/62, Rs.2,36,51,71,215; Dividend paid 14 p.c. subject to Income Tax. (359 Branches, etc.)

CHARTERED BANK (1853), 38 Bishopsgate, E.C.2.—Capital, Authorized, £10,000,000 (divided into 10,000,000 shares of £1 each); Issued and converted into stock, £6,600,000; Reserve Fund, £7,525,000; Deposits, 31/12/62, £364,520.954; Dividend, 1962, 15 p.c. (104 Branches).

THE CHASE MANHATTAN BANK, *New York, U.S.A.* (6 Lombard St., E.C.3, and 46 Berkeley Square, W.1.).—Capital, $174,594,425; 31/12/62: Surplus and Undivided Profits, $574,276,769; Deposits, $9,631,947,815. Divided to shareholders, 1962, $2.60 per share.

CLIVE DISCOUNT COMPANY, LTD. (1946), 1 Royal Exchange Avenue, E.C.3.—Capital, Authorized, £2,000,000; Issued and fully paid, £1,820,000; Reserve Fund, £250,000.

CLYDESDALE BANK, LTD (1838), St. Vincent Place, *Glasgow*, C.1 (*Aberdeen*, Chief Office, 5 Castle St.) Chief London Office, 30 Lombard St., E.C.3. *Affiliated to* Midland Bank, Ltd.—Authorized Capital, £8,610,000; Paid-up Capital, £2,441,000; Reserve Fund, £3,900,000; Deposits, 31/12/62, £196,467,951. (Over 340 Branches in Scotland, 3 in Cumberland and 4 in London.)

COMMERCIAL BANK OF AUSTRALIA, LTD. (1866), Collins St., *Melbourne* (12 Old Jewry, E.C.2).—Paid-up Capital, £6,223,218 (£10 Preference, fully paid; 10*s*. Ordinary, fully paid); Reserve Funds, £3,610,000; Deposits, 30/6/62, £251,308,859; Dividend, 1961–62 4 p.c. on Pref. stock units in Australian currency, 10 p.c. on Ordinary stock units in Australian currency. (806 Branches and Agencies.)

COMMERCIAL BANK OF NEAR EAST, LTD. (1922), Bankside House, 107–112 Leadenhall Street, E.C.3.—*London Agents*, Lloyds Bank, Ltd., and Midland Bank, Ltd. Capital Authorized, Subscribed and fully paid up, £200,000; Reserve Fund, £140,000. Deposits, 31/12/62, £2,214,241.

COMMERCIAL BANK OF SCOTLAND, LTD., *see* NATIONAL COMMERCIAL BANK OF SCOTLAND, LIMITED.

COMMERCIAL BANKING CO., OF SYDNEY, LTD. (1834), 343 George St., *Sydney*, N.S.W. (27-32 Old Jewry, E.C.2.—Authorized Capital, £15,000,000 (Shares of £1 each); Issued and fully paid £8,500,000 (£1 Stock Units); Reserve Fund, £7,000,000; Deposits, 30/6/62, £208,539,410; Dividend, 1961–62, 9 p.c. (506 Branches in Australia.)

COMMONWEALTH SAVINGS BANK OF AUSTRALIA, *Sydney*, N.S.W. (8 Old Jewry, E.C.2 and Bush House, Aldwych, W.C.2.) Owned and guaranteed by the Government of the Commonwealth. Deposits, etc., 30/6/62, £A.872,852,767; Reserve Fund, £A.11,778,352. (Over 8,160 Branches and Agencies in Australia.)

COMMONWEALTH TRADING BANK OF AUSTRALIA (1953), *Sydney*, N.S.W. (8 Old Jewry, E.C.2; Australia House, Strand, W.C.2).—Owned and guaranteed by the Government of the Commonwealth. 30/6/62: Deposits, etc., £A.386,555,574; Reserve Fund, £A.4,238,068. (Over 856 Branches and Agencies in Australia.)

COMPTOIR NATIONAL D'ESCOMPTE DE PARIS (1889), 14 Rue Bergère, *Paris* (8–13 King William St., E.C.4) (Bank nationalized in 1946)—Capital, 30/5/63, *Francs* 60,000,000 (shares *Francs* 100 nominal); Reserve Fund, *Francs* 10,676,823; Deposits, *Francs* 6,662,649,331.

CO-OPERATIVE WHOLESALE SOCIETY, LTD. (1872), 1 Balloon St., *Manchester* (and 99 Leman St., E.1).—Capital paid up, £31,489,353; Deposits, 22/1/63, £149,181,179; Reserves and Insurance Fund, £34,256,260. Share Interest at 5 p.c. (23 Branches.)

COPLEYS BANK, LTD. (1916), Ludgate House, 107–11 Fleet Street, E.C.4.—Capital authorized, £1,000,000; paid up, £380,000.

*COUTTS & CO. (1692), 440 Strand, W.C.2; 15 Lombard St., E.C.3; 1 Old Park Lane, W.1; 16 Cavendish Square, W.1.; 1 Cadogan Place, Sloane Street, S.W.1.; and 108 Park Lane, W.1.—Capital issued and paid up, £1,000,000; Reserve Fund, £1,000,000; Deposits, 31/12/62,

£57,738,500. (*A subsidiary of* National Provincial Bank, Ltd.)

CREDIT FONCIER D'ALGERIE ET DE TUNISIE, *Paris* (62 Bishopsgate, E.C.2). Capital, *Frs.* 11,475,000. *Name changed to* SOCIÉTÉ DE BANQUE (C.F.A.T.) *on June* 1, 1963).

CREDIT INDUSTRIEL ET COMMERCIAL (1859), 66 Rue de la Victoire, *Paris* (96 Old Broad St., E.C.2).—Capital, *Frs.* 75,000,000 in 1,500,000 Shares of *Frs.* 50 fully paid. Reserve Fund, *Frs.* 61,026,607; Deposits and other creditors, 31/12/62, *Frs.* 2,137,094,319.

CREDIT LYONNAIS (1863), 19 Boulevard des Italiens, *Paris* (40 Lombard St., E.C.3; 25–27 Charles II St., Haymarket, S.W.1).—Capital, *Frs.* 120,000,000; Reserve Fund, *Frs.* 26,500,000 (Over 1,700 branches throughout the world).

DISCOUNT BANK (OVERSEAS) LTD., Ralli House, 30 St. Paul's Churchyard, E.C.4.

*DISTRICT BANK, LTD. (1829), 17 Spring Gardens, *Manchester* (75 Cornhill, E.C.3).—Authorized Capital £10,560,428; Paid-up Capital £9,000,000 in shares of £1 each fully paid; Reserves, £5,500,000; Deposits 31/12/62, £279,845,226; Dividend, 1962, 14½ p.c. (575 Branches.)

DOMINION BANK, *see* TORONTO-DOMINION BANK.

EASTERN BANK, LTD. (1909), Crosby Square, E.C.3—Capital, £2,000,000 (£10 Shares, £5 paid); Reserve Fund, £1,675,000; Current Accounts, Deposits, etc., 31/12/62, £66,641,715; Dividend, 1962, 8*s.* a share. (23 Branches).

ENGLISH, SCOTTISH AND AUSTRALIAN BANK, LTD. (1852), 55 Gracechurch St., E.C.3.—Capital, Paid up, £5,000,000 (£1 shares fully paid); Gen. Reserve, £3,000,000; Deposits, etc., 30/6/62, £131,957,094; Dividend, 1961–62, 9 p.c.

FIRST NATIONAL CITY BANK OF NEW YORK (1812), 399 Park Avenue, *New York*, 22 and 55 Wall St., *New York* 15, U.S.A. (117 Old Broad St., E.C.2 and 17 Bruton St., Berkeley Sq., W.1). 30/6/63: Capital, $260,803,720; Deposits, $9,236,297,630; Surplus and Undivided Profits, $577,709,171 (104 Branches in New York, 91 branches in 32 countries). Affiliate of First National City Bank for separate administration of trust functions—First National City Trust Company, 399 Park Avenue, *New York*, 22. Capital Funds, $24,866,188.

FLEMING (ROBERT) & CO., LTD. (1932), 8 Crosby Square, E.C.3.

ANTONY GIBBS & SONS, LTD. (1808), 22 Bishopsgate, E.C.2.

GILLETT BROTHERS DISCOUNT CO., LTD. (1867), 52 Cornhill, E.C.3. Issued Capital, £1,750,000; Reserve, £850,000; Deposits, 31/1/63, £102,020,582. Dividend, 1962–63, 15 p.c.

*‡GLYN, MILLS & CO. (1753), incorporating CHILD & CO. and HOLT & CO., 67 Lombard St., E.C.3; *Child's Branch*, 1 Fleet St., E.C.4; *Holt's Branch*, Kirkland House, Whitehall, S.W.1.; *Millbank Branch*, 25 Millbank, S.W.1.—Capital, £1,500,000 (Stock, fully paid); Reserve Fund, £1,500,000; Deposits, 31/12/62, £69,492,567.

GUARANTY TRUST COMPANY OF NEW YORK (1839). *See* MORGAN GUARANTY TRUST COMPANY.

GUINNESS, MAHON & CO. LTD. (1836), 53 Cornhill, E.C.3.

GUINNESS AND MAHON (1942), 17 College Green, *Dublin* (affiliated to Guinness, Mahon & Co. Ltd., London).

HAMBROS BANK, LTD. (1839). *Head Office*, 41 Bishopsgate, E.C.2; *West End Office*, 67 Pall Mall, S.W.1; *Holborn Office*, 1 Charterhouse St., E.C.1.—Authorized Capital, £8,000,000; Paid-up Capital, £4,500,000; Reserve, £8,005,000; Deposits, 31/3/63, £115,063,292; Dividend, 1962–63, 22½ p.c. on £10 and 5*s.* fully paid shares; 6 p.c. on "A" shares.

HANOVER BANK.—Merged on Sept. 8, 1961, with Manufacturers Trust Company. *See* MANUFACTURERS HANOVER TRUST COMPANY.

HARRODS, LTD. (1889), 87 Brompton Rd., S.W.1.

HELBERT, WAGG & CO., LTD. *See* J. HENRY SCHRODER WAGG & CO. LIMITED.

HIBERNIAN BANK, LTD. (1825), College Green, *Dublin* (*London Agents*, Lloyds Bank, Ltd.).—Capital, £2,000,000 (£4 Shares, £1 paid); Reserve Fund, £930,000; Deposits, 31/12/62, £34,320,370: Dividend, 1962–63, 18 p.c. (Over 100 Branches and Sub-Branches.)

(PHILIP) HILL, HIGGINSON, ERLANGERS LIMITED (1907), 34 Moorgate, E.C.2.

C. HOARE & CO. (1673), 37 Fleet St., E.C.4, and Aldford House, Park Lane, W.1.—Capital and Reserve Fund, £1,000,000.

HONGKONG AND SHANGHAI BANKING CORPORATION (1865), *Hong Kong* (9 Gracechurch St., E.C.3.)—Capital, authorized $HK100,000,000; Issued and fully paid $HK79,046,125 ($HK25 Shares); Reserve Funds, £15,000,000; Deposits, etc., 31/12/62, $HK3,683,996,744.

IMPERIAL BANK OF CANADA (1875). Amalgamated June 1, 1961, with Canadian Bank of Commerce. *See* CANADIAN IMPERIAL BANK OF COMMERCE.

INTERNATIONAL BANKING CORPORATION (1901), *New York Office*, 399 Park Avenue., *New York*, 22, U.S.A. (117 Old Broad St., E.C.2) (owned by First National City Bank of New York).—Capital, $3,500,000; Surplus and Undivided Profits, $6,955,085.

IONIAN BANK, LTD. (1839), 64 Coleman Street, E.C.2.—Capital, Authorized, £2,500,000; Issued and fully paid, £1,600,000; Reserve Fund, £725,000; Deposits, £15,569,937; Dividend, 1963, 10 p.c.

ISLE OF MAN BANK, LTD. (1865). (A subsidiary of National Provincial Bank Ltd.), *Douglas*, I.O.M. (*London Agents*, National Provincial Bank Ltd.).—Capital, £300,000 in 30,000 Shares of £10 each—£3 6*s.* 8*d.* paid up, £100,000; and £100,000 Stock. Reserve Fund, £370,000: Deposits, 31/12/62, £10,071,836. Dividend, 1962, 20 p.c. on paid up capital (15 Branches.)

S. JAPHET & CO., LTD. (1880), 30 St. Swithin's Lane, E.C.4.—Capital, authorized, £1,500,000; paid up, £1,300,000.

JESSEL, TOYNBEE & CO., LTD. (1922), 1 Grocers' Hall Garden, Princes Street, E.C.2.—Capital authorized, £2,000,000; paid up, £1,500,000.

A. KEYSER & CO., LTD. (Estd. 1868, Incorporated 1946), 31 Throgmorton St., E.C.2.

KING AND SHAXSON, LTD. (1866), 24 Birchin Lane, E.C.3. Capital authorized £2,000,000; issued and fully paid £1,400,000; Reserve Fund, £700,000.

KLEINWORT, BENSON LIMITED (1830 and 1961), St. Albans House, Goldsmith Street, E.C.2, Aldermanbury House, E.C.2, and at *Liverpool*.

LAZARD BROTHERS & CO., LTD. (1877), 11 Old Broad St., E.C.2. Capital authorized and paid up, £3,375,000.

*‡LLOYDS BANK, LIMITED (1865), *Head Office*, 71 Lombard St., E.C.3; *Branches Stock Office*, 111 Old Broad Street, E.C.2; *Overseas Department*, 6 Eastcheap, E.C.3; *Executor and Trustee Department*, 34 Threadneedle St., E.C.2; *Principal London Offices*:—City Office, 72 Lombard St., E.C.3; 39 Threadneedle St., E.C.2; 6 Pall Mall, S.W.1 (Cox's & King's Branch); 16 St. James's St., S.W.1; Law Courts, 222 Strand, W.C.2.—Capital authorized, £74,000,000; issued £53,606,638; Reserve Fund, £34,705,000; Current, Deposit and Other Accounts, 30/6/63, £1,466,872,882; Dividend 1962, interim 4½ p.c.,

final 5½ p.c. Over 2,000 Offices. Owns (*inter alia*) all capital of LLOYDS BANK EXECUTOR AND TRUSTEE CO. (CHANNEL ISLANDS) LTD., LLOYDS BANK (FOREIGN) LTD. and LLOYDS BANK PROPERTY CO. LTD., and is associated with the NATIONAL COMMERCIAL BANK OF SCOTLAND LTD., the BANK OF LONDON & SOUTH AMERICA LTD. (which in turn owns 50 p.c. of the capital of the BANK OF LONDON & MONTREAL LTD.), NATIONAL AND GRINDLAYS BANK LTD., THE NATIONAL BANK OF NEW ZEALAND LTD., and BANK OF WEST AFRICA LTD. Also owns 50 p.c. of the capital of LLOYDS & SCOTTISH LTD., and is associated with BOWMAKER LTD.

LLOYDS BANK (FOREIGN) LIMITED (1911), 10 Moorgate, E.C.2; 71 Haymarket, S.W.1; 43 Boulevard des Capucines, *Paris*.—Capital, £1,200,000 (£50 Shares, fully paid). (12 Branches.) (Wholly owned subsidiary of Lloyds Bank Ltd.)

MANUFACTURERS HANOVER TRUST COMPANY (1961), *New York*, U.S.A. (7 Princes Street, E.C.2 and 10 Mount Street, W.1.)—Capital, $175,780,005; Surplus, $200,000,000; Undivided Profits, 31/12/62, $86,767,553; Deposits 31/12/62, $5,674,454,983.

*MARTINS BANK, LTD. (1831), 4 Water St., Liverpool 2 (68 Lombard St., E.C.3.).—Capital paid up, £13,191,064 (52,764,256 shares of 5*s*. each, fully paid); Reserve Fund, £11,000,000; Deposits, 30/6/63, £369,658,824; Dividend, 1962, 15 p.c. (Over 600 Branches.)

MERCANTILE BANK, LTD. (1892), 15 Gracechurch St., E.C.3.—Issued Capital, £2,940,000 (2,940,000 Ordinary Shares, £1 each fully paid); Reserve Fund, £2,200,000; Deposits, £77,822,262. Share capital acquired in 1959 by Hong Kong and Shanghai Banking Corporation. (40 Branches and Agencies).

*MIDLAND BANK, LTD. (1836), *Head Office*, Poultry, E.C.2; *Principal City Branches*, Poultry and Princes St., E.C.2; 5 Threadneedle St., E.C.2; *Overseas Branch*, 60 Gracechurch Street, E.C.3 —Authorized Capital, £45,200,000; Issued Capital, £40,278,283 (Shares of £1 each, fully paid); Reserve Fund £30,000,000; Deposits, 30/6/63, £1,751,525,313; Dividend, 1962, 15 p.c. (2,400 offices in England and Wales). *Affiliations:* BELFAST BANKING CO. LTD., CLYDESDALE & NORTH OF SCOTLAND BANK, LTD., MIDLAND BANK EXECUTOR AND TRUSTEE CO., LTD., MIDLAND BANK EXECUTOR AND TRUSTEE CO. (CHANNEL ISLANDS), LTD.; BELFAST BANK EXECUTOR AND TRUSTEE CO., LTD.; FORWARD TRUST LTD.

MIDLAND BANK EXECUTOR AND TRUSTEE CO., LTD. (1909), *Head Office*, 6 Threadneedle Street, E.C.2. *Affiliated to the* Midland Bank. Ltd. Subscribed Capital, £1,000,000; Paid-up Capital, £250,000 (200,000 Shares of £5, £1 5*s*. paid); Reserve Fund, £250,000. (36 offices.)

SAMUEL MONTAGU & CO. LTD. (1853), 114 Old Broad St., E.C.2. Capital, authorized £2,750,000; paid up, £2,450,000.

MONTREAL CITY AND DISTRICT SAVINGS BANK (1846), *Montreal*, Canada (*London Agents*, Bank of Montreal). — Capital, $2,000,000 ($10 Shares, fully paid); Reserve Fund, $9,000,000; (60 Branches in Montreal and District.)

MORGAN GRENFELL & CO. LIMITED (1838), 23 Great Winchester St., E.C.2; Private limited Coy. (1934).—Authorized Capital, £2,500,000; Issued and fully paid £2,250,000.

MORGAN GUARANTY TRUST COMPANY OF NEW YORK (1839), 140 Broadway and 23 Wall Street, *New York*, U.S.A. (33 Lombard Street, E.C.3 and 31 Berkeley Sq., W.1).—Capital, $207,350,000 (8,294,000 shares—$25 par); Surplus Fund, $236,500,000; Undivided Profits Account, 30/6/63, $154,220,162; Deposits, 30/6/63, $4,070,423,895; Dividend, 16 p.c.

MOSCOW NARODNY BANK, LIMITED, 4 Moorgate, E.C.2.—Capital authorized and issued fully paid, £4,000,000; Deposits, 31/12/62, £83,448,434.

MUNSTER AND LEINSTER BANK, LTD. (1885), South Mall, *Cork*, Eire (*London Agents*, National Provincial Bank, Ltd.)—Capital authorized, £7,500,000 (3,000,000 Shares of £2 10*s*. each); paid up, £1,550,000 (1,550,000 Shares, £1 paid); Reserve Fund £1,550,000; Deposits 31/12/62, £105,513,988; Dividend 1962, 20 p.c. less Income Tax. (Offices throughout Ireland.)

*NATIONAL BANK, LTD. (1835), 13–17 Old Broad St., E.C.2, and 34–35 College Green, Dublin.—Capital, Authorized, £7,500,000 (£1 Shares); Issued, £2,000,000; Capital Reserves, £2,542,000; Deposits, 31/12/62, £129,440,843; Dividend, 1962, 18 p.c. (250 Branches and Sub-Branches in England, Wales and Ireland.)

NATIONAL BANK OF AUSTRALASIA, LTD., THE (1858), Collins St., *Melbourne* (6–8 Tokenhouse Yard, E.C.2).—Capital paid up £10,089,037; Reserve Fund, £7,500,000; Deposits, 30/9/62, £338,513,262. (The figures are stated in *Australian Currency*.) Dividend, 1961, 9 p.c. (931 Branches and Agencies in Australia.) The NATIONAL BANK SAVINGS BANK LIMITED, (Collins, Street, Melbourne) a wholly owned subsidiary of The National Bank of Australasia Limited was incorporated on May 16, 1962, with Capital, Authorized, £10,000,000; paid-up, £1,000,000.

NATIONAL BANK OF GREECE (1953), *Athens*, Greece (6 Old Jewry, E.C.2.). A merger of the National Bank of Greece (established 1841) and the Bank of Athens (established 1893). Capital, *Dr*. 581,407,680 in 404,880 shares of *Dr*. 1,436 each. Reserves, *Dr*. 105,000,000; Deposits, *Dr*. 11,159,907,453.

NATIONAL BANK OF MALTA (*Incorporating* ANGLO-MALTESE BANK and BANK OF MALTA), 45 Kingsway, Valletta, Malta. With which is affiliated Sciclunas Bank, Malta. Authorized Capital, £2,000,000; Paid-up Capital £1,000,000. (Branches in important centres of Malta and Gozo).

NATIONAL BANK OF NEW ZEALAND, LTD. (1872), 8 Moorgate, E.C.2.—Capital (Authorized, £6,000,000), Issued and fully-paid, £3,500,000; Reserve Fund, £2,650,000; Deposits, £69,949,274; Dividend, 1962–63, 10 p.c. (173 Branches and Agencies.)

NATIONAL COMMERCIAL BANK OF SCOTLAND LIMITED (1959), formed as a result of merger between The Commercial Bank of Scotland Limited (1810) and The National Bank of Scotland Limited (1825), 42 St. Andrew Square, Edinburgh, 2.—Capital Authorized, £9,275,000 (fully paid); Reserve Funds, £11,287,500; Deposits, £232,266,765.

NATIONAL DISCOUNT CO., LTD. (1856), 35 Cornhill, E.C.3.—Authorized Capital, £5,000,000—Paid-up Capital, £4,470,731; Reserves, £3,559,880; Deposits, 31/12/62, £202,833,965; Dividend, 1962, "A" Stock, 10 p.c.; "B" Stock, 12½ p.c.

NATIONAL AND GRINDLAYS BANK LIMITED 26 Bishopsgate, E.C.2.—Capital authorized £9,000,000 (12,000,000 Shares of 15*s*. each); issued and paid up, £5,703,000 (7,604,000 Shares of 15*s*. each); Reserve Funds, £5,250,000; Deposits 31/12/62, £264,696,336, Dividend 1962, 16 p.c. (165 Branches).

*NATIONAL PROVINCIAL BANK, LTD. (1833), *Head Office*, 15 Bishopsgate, E.C.2.—Authorized Capital, £60,000,000; Issued Capital, £38,406,500; Reserve Funds, £29,708,930 (incl. Share Premium A/c.); Deposits, 31/12/62, £994,623,165; Dividend, 1962, 14 p.c. (Over 1,550 Branches and Agencies in England and Wales) (*Affiliated Banks*, District Bank Ltd., Coutts & Co. *and* Isle of Man Bank Ltd.)

NETHERLANDS BANK OF SOUTH AFRICA LTD. (1951) *Johannesburg* (37 Lombard Street, E.C.3).—Capital Authorized, *R*7,000,000; Capital issued and paid up; *R*6,000,000; Reserves, *R*3,900,000; Deposits, 30/9/62, *R*110,265,481. Dividend, 1961–62, 10 p.c. Acquired from Nederlandse Bank voor Zuid-Africa N.V., Amsterdam (1888) their business in South Africa and the United Kingdom. (105 Branches and Agencies.)

NORTHERN BANK, LTD. (1824), *Belfast* (*London Agents*, Lloyds Bank, Ltd., 72 Lombard St., E.C.3).—Capital, £3,500,000 (£1 Shares); Capital, paid up, £1,100,000; Reserve Fund, £1,000,000; Share Premium Account, £400,000; Deposits, 31/12/62, £59,654,866; Dividend, 1962, 18 p.c. (184 Branches and Sub-Branches).

OTTOMAN BANK (1863), Bankalar Caddesi, Galata. *Istanbul*, Turkey (18/22 Abchurch Lane E.C.4), —Capital, £10,000,000 (£20 Shares, £10 paid), Statutory Reserve, £1,250,000. (Branches in Turkey, Cyprus, Sudan, Jordan, Arabian Gulf, Kenya, Uganda, Tanganyika, S. Rhodesia, France and Switzerland.).

PROVINCIAL BANK OF CANADA (1900) (BANQUE PROVINCIALE DU CANADA), 221 St. James St. West, *Montreal* (*London Agents*, Lloyds Bank Ltd.).—Capital $8,995,306 ($10 Shares, fully paid); Reserve Fund, $15,992,020; Deposits 31/10/62, $48,448,205; Regular dividend, 1962, 12 p.c.; Special, 2·5 p.c. (187 Branches and 172 Agencies.)

PROVINCIAL BANK OF IRELAND LTD. (1825), 5 College St., Dublin (*London Agents*, Barclays Bank, Ltd.)—Capital. £4,080,000; Issued, 1,130,000 Ordinary Shares of £1; Reserve Fund, £850,000; Deposits, 31/12/62, £56,641,221; Dividend, 1962, 9 p.c. on Old Capital; 7½ p.c. on New Capital (126 Branches and Sub-Branches.)

GERALD QUIN, COPE & CO. (1892), 7 Birchin Lane, E.C.3.

RALLI BROTHERS, LIMITED, 25 Finsbury Circus, E.C.2.—Capital authorized, £4,720,000; Issued and paid up, £3,720,000; Capital Reserves, £3,898 640; Revenue Reserves, £3,013,789.

RALLI BROTHERS (BANKERS) LTD., *Head Office*, Ralli House, 30 St. Paul's Churchyard, E.C.4; and 63-66 Hatton Garden, E.C.1. Capital, Authorized, £4,000,000; Issued and paid up, £3,500,000.

RELIANCE BANK, LTD. (1900), 111 Queen Victoria St., E.C.4.—Capital, £60,000; Reserve Fund, £90,000; Deposits, 31/3/63, £2,946,123.

RESERVE BANK OF NEW ZEALAND (1934), *Wellington, N.Z. Agencies at Christchurch and Auckland, N.Z.* (*London Agents, Bank of England*). *Owned by the New Zealand Government.*—Reserve Fund, £NZ1,500,000; Total Assets 31/3/63, £NZ185 039 602.

N. M. ROTHSCHILD & SONS (1804), New Court, St. Swithin's Lane, E.C.4. (During re-building—City Gate House, Finsbury Square, E.C.2).

ROYAL BANK OF CANADA (1869), *Montreal* (6 Lothbury, E.C.2, and 2 Cockspur St., S.W.1). —Capital, $100,000,000 ($10 Shares); Paid-up, $66,528 000; Rest Account, $243,071,200; Undivided Profits, $1,645,275; Assets, over $5,000,000,000; Deposits, 30/11/62, $4,673,708,399; Dividend, 1962, $2·25 per share plus extra distribution of 25 cents per share (1,080 Branches).

ROYAL BANK OF SCOTLAND (1727), St. Andrew Square, *Edinburgh* (3 Bishopsgate, E.C.2).—Capital, Authorized, £11,400,000; Issued, £9,500,000 (£1 units fully paid); Reserve Fund, £7,700,000; Deposits, 31/12/62, £143,899,692; Dividend, 1962, 15½ p.c. (241 Branches and Sub-Branches in Scotland and 7 offices in London). *Associate Banks*, Williams Deacon's Bank, Ltd., and Glyn, Mills & Co.

SALE & CO., (1908), Northgate House, Moorgate, E.C.2.

M. SAMUEL & CO., LTD. (1831), Shell House, 55 Bishopsgate, E.C.2.—Capital authorized, £4,000,000 (£3,600,000 in Ordinary Shares of £1 each and £400,000 in Unclassified Shares of £1 each) and Capital subscribed and paid up £3,600,000 (£3,600,000 in Ordinary Shares of £1 each).

DAVID SASSOON AND CO., LIMITED (1860), 11/12 St. Swithin's Lane, E.C.4.—Capital authorized, issued and paid up, £500,000.

E. D. SASSOON BANKING CO., LIMITED (1950) Nassau, N.P., Bahamas (37 Upper Brook Street, Park Lane, W.1).—Capital authorized and issued, £1,000,000; paid up, £500,000.

J. HENRY SCHRODER WAGG & CO. LIMITED. (1804), 145 Leadenhall St., E.C.3.—Capital: Authorized, £3,880,000; issued and paid up, £3,876,000.

SCOTTISH CO-OPERATIVE WHOLESALE SOCIETY LTD. (1868), 31 Morrison Street, *Glasgow*, C.5.

SELIGMAN BROTHERS (1864). Incorporated with WARBURG & COMPANY, LTD., on May 20, 1957.

SINGER AND FRIEDLANDER LTD. (1907), 20 Cannon Street, E.C.4.—Capital, Authorized, £2,000,000, Issued, £175,000 Cum. Red. Preference Shares of £1 each and £6,240,000 Ordinary Shares of 5*s*. each.

SMITH ST. AUBYN & CO. LTD. (1891), White Lion Court, Cornhill, E.C.3.—Capital authorized, £2,000,000; issued £1,620,000. Reserves, £1,000,000. Deposits and Contingency Reserve, 31/3/63, £8,004,976. Dividend, 1962–63, 22½ p.c.

SOCIÉTÉ GÉNÉRALE (1864), 29 Boulevard Haussmann, *Paris* (105–108 Old Broad St., E.C.2).—Subscribed Capital authorized, issued and paid up, *Francs* 150,000,000. Reserve Funds, *Francs* 75,000,000. (Over 1,500 Branches).

SOUTH AFRICAN RESERVE BANK (1920), *Pretoria*, Transvaal (*London Agents*, Bank of England).—Capital, fully paid, R.2,000,000 (£1,000,000); Reserve Fund *R*.9,413,101 (£4,706,550); Dividend, 1962–63, 10 p.c. (9 Branches.)

STANDARD BANK, LTD., THE (1862), 10 Clements Lane, and 77 King William St., E.C.4, 63 London Wall, E.C.2, 9 Northumberland Avenue, W.C.2 and Suffolk House, Park Lane.—Authorized Capital, £17,000,000; Subscribed and Paid-up Capital, £11,000,000; Reserve Fund, £11,100,000; Deposits, 31/3/63, £413,371,609; Dividend, 1962–63, 15 p.c. and Centenary Bonus 2½ p.c. (Over 900 Branches and Agencies in Africa.)

STATE BANK OF INDIA (1955), *Bombay, Calcutta, Madras, New Delhi* (25, Old Broad St., E.C.2). —Capital, Authorized, Rs. 20,00,00,000; Paid up, Rs. 5,62,50,000; Reserve, Rs. 8.75,00,000. (Over 1,000 Branches and Sub-Offices throughout India, Pakistan, Burma and Ceylon).

GEORGE STEUART & CO. LTD., *Colombo*, Ceylon (*London Correspondents*, Coutts & Co.).

JOHN STUART & CO., LTD. (1832), *Manchester* (*London Agents*, National Provincial Bank, Ltd.).—Capital, £35,200; Issued, £32,700 Preference; £2,500 Ordinary (£5 Shares, fully paid),

SWISS BANK CORPORATION (1872), *Basle* (99 Gresham Street, E.C.2; 18 Regent Street, S. W.1.)—Capital and Reserves. *Swiss Francs* 450,000,000; Dividend, 1962, 10 p.c. and capital increased 1 for 8 at price of *Sw. Frs.* 1,000. (64 Branches, etc.)

B. TAGLIAFERRO & SONS (1812), *Malta* (*London Agents*, Westminster Bank, Ltd.).

TORONTO-DOMINION BANK, *Toronto*, Ontario, Canada (an amalgamation (1955) of The Bank of Toronto (1856) and The Dominion Bank (1871)) (3 King William Street, E.C.4 and 103 Mount Street, W.1).—Capital (paid-up), $30,000,000; Rest Account, $84,000,000; Undivided Profits, $1,279,577; Deposits, 31/10/62, $2,104,630,153; Dividend, 50 cents quarterly. (614 Branches in Canada.)

ULLMANN & CO., LIMITED (1932), 85 Gracechurch St., E.C.3.

ULSTER BANK, LTD. (1836), *Head Office*, Waring St., *Belfast*. (*Affiliated to* Westminster Bank Ltd.).—Capital, £3,000,000 (£1 Shares); Issued and fully paid, £2,250,000; Reserve Fund, £2,050,000; Share Premium Account, £250,000; Deposits, 31/12/62, £68,664,732; Dividend, 1962, on Issued Capital, £2,250,000, (116 Offices and 96 Sub-Offices.)

UNION BANK OF INDIA LTD. (1919), 66–80 Apollo Street, Fort, *Bombay* 1. Capital: Authorized, *Rs.* 2,00,00,000; Issued and paid-up *Rs.* 1,00,00,000 (20,00,000 shares of *Rs.* 5 each fully paid-up); Reserve Fund, *Rs.*70,00,000; Deposits, *Rs.*42,62,00,000; Dividend, 1962, 11⅗ p.c. (65 branches in India).

UNION DISCOUNT COMPANY OF LONDON, LTD, (1885), 39 Cornhill, E.C.3.—Capital Issued. £6,652,800; in units of £1 each fully paid; Reserves and carry forward, £4,313,200; Deposits, other liabilities and reserve for contingencies, £289,269,743; Dividend, 1962, 12½ p.c.

UNITED COMMERCIAL BANK, LTD., 2 India Exchange Place, *Calcutta*.—Capital, Rs.2,23,33,937 (Shares of Rs.100. Rs.50 paid). Reserves Rs.3,03,00,000; Deposits, etc. 31/12/62 Rs.1,08,22,75,015. (Over 160 Branches.)

WARBURG (S. G.) & COMPANY, LIMITED (Incorporating Seligman Brothers), 30 Gresham Street, E.C.2.

*WESTMINSTER BANK, LTD. (1836). *Head Office*. 41 Lothbury, E.C.2; *Trustee Department Chief Office*, 41 Lothbury, E.C.2; *Lombard Street Office*. 21 Lombard Street, E.C.3; *Threadneedle Street Office*, 52 Threadneedle Street, E.C.2; *Overseas Branch*, 53 Threadneedle Street, E.C.2. Capital, Authorized: £33,000,000; (3,000,000 "A" Shares of £1 each; 30,000,000 "B" Shares of £1 each); Issued, 2,249,167 "A" Shares of £1 each F.P., converted into "A" Stock; 24,748,465 "B" Shares of £1 each F.P.) Reserve Fund, £26 654,864; Deposits, 31/12/62, £1,073,323,559; Dividend, 1962, 2*s*. 8*d*. per share for the year on "B" Shares; 12½ p.c. "A" Stock. (1,260 Branches, Sub-Branches and Agencies). *Affiliated Banks*, WESTMINSTER FOREIGN BANK, LTD.; ULSTER BANK, LTD. (*q.v.*).

WESTMINSTER FOREIGN BANK, LTD. (1913), 53 Threadneedle Street, E.C.2.

*WILLIAMS DEACON'S BANK, LTD. (1771), *Head Office*, Mosley St., *Manchester* (20 Birchin Lane, E.C.3).—Authorized Capital, £10,000,000; Paid-up Capital, £5,000,000 in shares of £1 each fully paid; Reserve Fund, £3,250,000. (248 Branches.)

YORKSHIRE BANK LIMITED (1911), 56–58 Cheapside, E.C.2 (2 Infirmary Street, *Leeds*). Capital, £2,750,000 (Capital paid up 2,250,000, £1 Shares fully paid); Reserve Fund, £2,250,000; Deposits, 30/6/63, £113,155,144. (156 Branches.)

INDUSTRIAL AND COMMERCIAL FINANCE CORPORATION LIMITED

Piercy House, Copthall Avenue, E.C.2.

[National: 4040]

Founded in 1945 by the English and Scottish joint-stock Banks, and the Bank of England, as a contribution to post-war reconstruction, with initial resources of £45,000,000, since enlarged by a series of debenture issues to more than £50,000,000. I.C.F.C. is independently managed and is not Government subsidized. It was formed for the specific purpose of providing long-term loan capital and share capital to small and medium sized businesses in Great Britain with no ready access to the capital market. In 18 years it has provided £90,000,000 to more than 1,200 businessses engaged in 52 industries and trades. Since 1951, branches have been established in Birmingham, Bristol, Cardiff, Edinburgh, Glasgow, Leeds, Leicester and Manchester.

Facilities, which range from £5,000 to £200,000 or more, are provided in the form of long-term loans and share capital. For its own requirements, and to assist its customers, I.C.F.C has an Industrial Department comprising engineers skilled in present-day production methods, and a staff of accountants versed in modern accounting and costing techniques. Rates, which vary with the security available and the inherent soundness and prospects of the business, are in line with the market rates current for long-term capital. The rate quoted in a particular case is generally fixed for the entire period of the loan, and is charged on the outstanding amount only. A small inclusive negotiation fee is charged on acceptance of an offer, out of which the Corporation pays its own investigation and legal costs. Facilities offered are of particular interest to private companies who wish to preserve their private status, or are not well situated to float, and to growing companies with good prospects.

Chairman, The Lord Piercy, C.B.E.

General Managers, L. V. D. Tindale; A. R. English.

Secretary, S. V. Warren.

SAVINGS BANKS

Post Office Savings Bank.—On Dec. 31, 1962, there were approximately 21,629,000 active deposit accounts in the *Post Office Savings Bank*, with the sum of £1,760,082,000 due to depositors. On December 31, 1962, Government Stock and Bonds to the amount of £1,079,780,000 stood to the credit of holders in the Post Office Savings Bank Section of the Post Office Register. Interest on Post Office Savings Bank deposits is allowed at 2½ per cent. per annum. A depositor may have more than one account but may not deposit more than a total of £5,000 in all accounts in his name, with certain exceptions for trust and trustee accounts.

In 1961 the *Average Amount due to each Depositor* in Active Accounts was £78 13*s*. 2*d*.

Trustee Savings Banks were started in the early years of the 19th century by public-spirited men who recognized the importance of individual thrift to the well-being of the community.

On Nov. 20, 1962, there were 9,905,753 active accounts in the Trustee Savings Banks. The total assets of the Banks amounted to £1,742,429,099 which comprised £1,517,129,672 due to depositors in the Ordinary and Special Investment Departments, £200,277,171 Stocks and Bonds held for depositors and £25,022,256 representing the accumulated surplus of the individual Trustee Savings Banks throughout the country. Information about these Banks and their offices, numbering 1,351 (principal and subordinate) in November, 1962, can be obtained from the *Trustee Savings Bank Association*, 22 Manchester Square, W.1.—*Chairman*, Sir Kenneth Stewart, Bt., G.B.E.; *Secretary*, R. T. H. Scott, M.B.E.

PREMIUM SAVINGS BONDS

One of the most popular forms of saving in the United Kingdom is through Premium Savings Bonds. These bonds are a United Kingdom Government security and were first introduced on November 1, 1956. Instead of earning interest, however, each bond offers to its holder the chance of winning a money prize in a monthly draw. Bonds are issued in values ranging from £1 to £500 and each £1 buys one bond, which has one chance in the monthly draw. Bonds are sold only to individuals, not to groups or corporate bodies. No more than 800 bonds can be held by any one person. The bonds are sold at Post Offices, Banks and Trustee Savings Banks. Holders may redeem bonds at any time by completing a form which is available at Post Offices and Banks.

Prizes are paid from a fund formed by the interest, at present 4½ per cent., carried into the draw by each eligible bond. A bond becomes eligible for the draw three clear calendar months following the month of purchase and goes into every subsequent draw whether or not it has won a prize. Prizes range in value from £5,000 to £25, the winning numbers being selected by the electronic random number indicator equipment—usually called "ERNIE." Winning numbers are printed monthly in the *London Gazette*. Bonds are eligible for inclusion in 12 monthly draws following the death of the holder. These terms also apply to bonds purchased before August 1, 1960 (Series "A").

It is estimated that by the end of May, 1963, bonds to the value of £526,800,000 had been sold. Of these £126,700,000 had been cashed, leaving £400,100,000 still invested. After the 73rd draw in June, 1963, more than 1,707,058 prizes had been distributed since the draws started. These prizes had a total value of £63,388,825.

NATIONAL SAVINGS CERTIFICATES

The amount, including accrued interest, remaining to the credit of investors in National Savings Certificates on March 31, 1963, was approximately £2,685,100,000. In 1962–63, £179,100,000 was subscribed and £167,900,000 (excluding interest) was repaid.

Note.—Certificates may be bought in denominations of 1, 2, 3, 4, 5, 10, 20, 50, 100 and 200 £1 units.

TERMS AND INTEREST

Issue and Maximum Holding	Unit Cost *s. d.*	Value after Years	Value after *s. d.*	Interest per unit
1st (1916–22) (500)	15 6	10	26 0	After 10 years, 1*d.* per completed month.* (1st–3rd issues)
2nd (1922–23) (500)	16 0	10	26 0	
3rd (1923–32) Conversion (1932) (500)	16 0	22	33 0	
4th (1932–33) (500)	16 0	20	29 0	After 20 years, 2½*d.* per completed 3 months.*
5th (1933–35) (500)	16 0	21	29 0	After 21 years, 2½*d.* per 3 months.*
6th (1935–39) (500)	15 0	22	27 0	After 22 years, 3*d.* per 3 months.*
7th (1939–47) (500)	15 0	10 22 29	20 6 27 6 35 0	After 10 years, bonus of 6*d.* and 3½*d.* per 6 months†; After 22 years, 3*d.* per 3 months and a bonus of 6*d.* at the end of 29th year.§
£1 (1943–47) (250)	20 0	10 22	23 0 27 0	After 10 years, bonus of 6*d.* and 1*d.* per completed 3 months.†
8th (1947–51) (1,000)	10 0	10 20	13 0 18 0	After 10 years, 1½*d.* added per 3 months.‡
9th (1951–56) (1,400)	15 0	10 17	20 3 26 0	After 1 yr., 3*d.* added; during 2nd year, ½*d.* per 2 months, 3rd–7th year, 1*d.* per 2 months; thereafter 1½*d.* per 2 months. After 10 yrs. 3*d.* per 4 months; 6*d.* bonus at end of 17th year. §
10th (1956–63) (1,200)	15 0	7 10	20 0 22 3	After 1 yr., 4*d.* added; during 2nd year, 1*d.* per 3 months; during 3rd year, 1½*d.* per 3 months; 4th and 5th years, 2*d.* per 3 months; 6th and 7th years, 3*d.* per 3 months; after 7th year, extra 6*d.* added. Then 3*d.* per 4 months.
11th (1963–) (300)	20 0	6	25 0	After 1 yr., 5*d.* added; during 2nd yr., 2*d.* per 4 months; during 3rd yr., 3*d.* per 4 months; 4th to 6th yrs., 4*d.* per 4 months; bonus of 4*d.* at end of 6th yr.

May be held from date of issue;* until further notice; † 22 years; ‡ 20 years, § 17 years, § 29 years.

THE NATIONAL BUILDINGS RECORD

Fielden House, 10 Great College Street, S.W.1.

The National Buildings Record is an organization established in 1941 under the direction of an Advisory Council. It is supported by an annual grant from the Treasury, and its functions are:

To maintain a library of photographs and measured drawings of English and Welsh architecture which is open to the public for consultation and study. There are over 550,000 photographs.

To supply copies of photographs where negatives are available. There are approximately 300,000 negatives.

To prepare and acquire additional records which are constantly being added to the library.

To maintain an index of architectural records (photographs, measured drawings, sketches, and engravings) in public and private possession.

Chairman of Advisory Council, The Lord Conesford, Q.C.

Secretary, Cecil Farthing, F.S.A.

PRINCIPAL SHIPPING LINES
LONDON OFFICES OR AGENCIES

ANCHOR LINE, LTD., 52 Leadenhall Street, E.C.3 and 9 Haymarket, S.W.1. *Head Office*: 12–16 St. Vincent Place, Glasgow, C.1.

ASIATIC STEAM NAVIGATION CO., LTD., 122 Leadenhall Street, E.C.3.

BELFAST STEAMSHIP CO., LTD. (Agents: Coast Lines, Ltd., *see below*).

BEN LINE STEAMERS, LTD., THE (Wm. Thomson & Co., Managers), 10 North St. David Street, Edinburgh 2. *Loading Brokers and Passenger Agents*, Killick Martin & Co., Ltd., 20 Mark Lane, E.C.3.

BERGEN LINE (Bergen Steamship Co. Ltd.), 21–24 Cockspur Street, S.W.1.

BIBBY LINE, LTD. (Agents: Alexr. Howden & Co., Ltd., 107–112 Leadenhall Street, E.C.3.)

BLUE FUNNEL LINE, 16 St. Helen's Place, E.C.3 (*Head Office*, India Buildings, Liverpool, 2).

BLUE STAR LINE LTD., Albion House, 34–5 Leadenhall Street, E.C.3.

BOWRING STEAMSHIP CO., LTD., 52 Leadenhall Street, E.C.3.

BRITISH & IRISH S. P. CO., LTD. (Agents: Coast Lines Ltd., *see below*).

BRITISH INDIA STEAM NAVIGATION CO., LTD., One Aldgate, E.C.3.

B P TANKER CO. LTD., Britannic House, Finsbury Circus, E.C.2.

BROCKLEBANK LINE (T. & J. Brocklebank Ltd.). London Agents: Alexr. Howden & Co. Ltd., 107–112 Leadenhall Street, E.C.3.

BROCKLEBANK'S WELL LINE, Gosman & Smith Ltd., 1–7 Crosswall, E.C.3.

BURNS AND LAIRD LINES LTD. (Agents: Coast Lines Ltd., *see below*).

CANADIAN PACIFIC RAILWAY COMPANY, Trafalgar Square, W.C.2.

CLAN LINE STEAMERS, LTD., THE; CAYZER, IRVINE & CO., LTD., 2 and 4 St Mary Axe, E.C.3.

COAST LINES LTD., London House, 3 New London Street, E.C.3, Seaway House, 338 The Highway, E.1 and 227 Regent Street, W.1.

CUNARD STEAM-SHIP CO. LTD., Cunard Building, Liverpool, 3; 15 Lower Regent Street, S.W.1 and 88 Leadenhall Street, E.C.3.

DONALDSON LINE, LTD., 31–35 Fenchurch Street, E.C.3.

ELDER DEMPSTER LINES, LTD., Dunster House, Mark Lane, E.C.3.

ELDERS & FYFFES, LTD., 15 Stratton Street, W.1.

ELLERMAN LINES LTD., 12-20 Camomile Street, E.C.3.

ELLERMAN AND BUCKNALL STEAMSHIP CO. LTD., 12–20 Camomile Street, E.C.3.

ELLERMAN'S WILSON LINE, LTD.: Agents: 108 Fenchurch Street, E.C.3.

EUROPE-CANADA LINE, 120 Pall Mall, S.W.1.

(WM.) FRANCE, FENWICK & CO., LTD., 23 Rood Lane, E.C.3.

FRENCH LINE, Compagnie Générale Transatlantique, Ltd., 20 Cockspur Street, S.W.1.

FURNESS, WITHY & CO., LTD., Furness House, Leadenhall Street, E.C.3.

GLEN LINE LTD., 16 St. Helen's Place. E.C.3.

HARRISON LINE: THOS. & JAS. HARRISON, LTD., Fountain House, Fenchurch Street, E.C.3.

HENDERSON LINE (P. HENDERSON & CO., LTD.), *Head Office*, 95 Bothwell Street, Glasgow, C.2.

P. HENDERSON & CO. (AGENCIES), LTD., Wellington Buildings, The Strand, Liverpool, 2.

HOLLAND-AMERICA LINE (LONDON), LTD., 120 Pall Mall, S.W.1.

HOULDER BROTHERS & CO., LTD., 53 Leadenhal Street, E.C.3.

HOUSTON LINE LIMITED, 4 St. Mary Axe, E.C.3.

LAMPORT & HOLT LINE, LTD., Asia House, 31–33 Lime Street, E.C.3.

MACANDREWS & CO., LTD., Plantation House, Mincing Lane, E.C.3.

MCILWRAITH, MCEACHARN, LTD., 154–156 Fenchurch Street, E.C.3.

MOSS HUTCHISON LINE, LTD., Three Quays, Tower Hill, E.C.3.

NEDERLAND LINE ROYAL DUTCH MAIL: Escombe, McGrath & Co., Ltd., General Passenger Agents, 120 Pall Mall, S.W.1.

NEW ZEALAND SHIPPING CO., LTD., 138 Leadenhall Street, E.C.3.

NIPPON YUSEN KAISHA, 104–6 Leadenhall Street, E.C.3.

ORIENT STEAM NAVIGATION CO., LTD., Amalgamated as P. & O.–Orient Lines (*see below*).

PACIFIC STEAM NAVIGATION CO., THE, Royal Mail House, Leadenhall Street, E.C.3.

P. & O. ORIENT LINES, Beaufort House, 29 Gravel Lane, E.1; 14 Cockspur Street, S.W.1.

PRINCE LINE, LTD., 56 Leadenhall Street, E.C.3.

ROYAL MAIL LINES, LTD., Royal Mail House, Leadenhall Street, E.C.3. and America House, Cockspur Street, S.W.1.

ROYAL ROTTERDAM LLOYD: Escombe, McGrath & Co., Ltd., General Passenger Agents, 120 Pall Mall, S.W.1.

SCOTTISH SHIRE LINE, LTD., THE, Cayzer House, 4 St. Mary Axe, E.C.3.

SHAW SAVILL LINE, 88 Leadenhall Street, E.C.3 and 11a Lower Regent Street, S.W.1.

SHELL TANKERS LTD., Shell Centre, S.E.1.

SMITH, SIR W. R., & SONS, LTD., 58–59 Fenchurch Street, E.C.3.

UNION-CASTLE MAIL STEAMSHIP CO., LTD., *Head Office*, 4 St. Mary Axe, E.C.3.

UNITED STATES LINES, 58 St. James's Street; *Passenger*, 50 Pall Mall, S.W.1; *Freight*, 38 Leadenhall Street, E.C.3.

WATTS WATTS & CO., LTD., 37 Threadneedle Street, E.C.2.

WEIR (ANDREW) & CO., LTD., 21 Bury Street, E.C.3.

LIGHTHOUSES

In 1961–62 the income of the General Lighthouse Fund was £4,687,923, made up of £4,520,605 United Kingdom Light Dues, £41 Bahamas Light Dues and £167,318 Miscellaneous Receipts. Expenditure during the year totalled £3,903,735 made up of £3,775,305 in respect of maintenance and operation of lighthouses, etc., under the control of the three General Lighthouse Authorities (*Trinity House, Commissioners of Northern Lighthouses*, and *Commissioners of Irish Lights*), £94,142 in respect of Lighthouses Abroad and £34,288 miscellaneous expenditure, including the cost of collecting dues. The surplus of £784,188 was carried to the Net Revenue Account. In September 1940, United Kingdom Light Dues were increased from 150 per cent. of the statutory rates laid down in the Merchant Shipping Act, 1894, to 200 per cent., and in March, 1942, to 300 per cent. The dues were reduced to 200 per cent. in January, 1946, but general increases in costs and expenditure on renewals and replacements necessitated increases up to 460 per cent. in April, 1956. As a consequence of the United Kingdom's adherence to the Convention on the Territorial Seas and Contiguous Zones, the Orders in Council under which Colonial Light Dues were collected were revoked with effect from March 25, 1960.

MERCHANT SHIPPING

Principal British Seaports

	Value of Trade, 1961				Volume of Trade†, 1962	
	Imports	Re-exports	Exports	Total	Arrived	Departed
	£	£	£	£	Tons	Tons
London	1,420,333,615	68,321,301	1,239,649,312	2,728,304,228	46,430,252	46,105,412
Liverpool	808,871,711	26,699,126	922,701,772	1,758,272,609	22,387,102	22,463,856
Hull	248,679,337	2,382,535	191,188,159	442,250,031	6,126,281	5,977,366
Manchester	235,780,340	1,102,217	113,642,013	350,524,570	6,804,164	6,599,239
Southampton	172,554,366	3,994,273	118,442,020	294,990,659	26,152,018	26,047,606
Glasgow	128,270,905	1,253,472	152,071,887	281,596,264	8,006,632	7,796,474
Bristol	165,449,519	823,589	21,603,833	187,876,941	6,123,810	5,831,664
Harwich	95,684,422	3,679,259	71,578,755	170,942,436	3,807,478*	3,815,099*
Dover	54,866,997	8,097,605	74,951,271	137,915,873	6,931,051*	6,914,260*
Swansea	50,864,155	2,647,203	61,663,105	115,174,463	4,364,427	4,374,387
Newcastle (including Nth. and Sth. Shields)	60,220,841	320,684	57,337,481	117,879,006	7,740,138	7,732,043

Value of imports and exports through United Kingdom *Airports* in 1961 was: Imports, £208,250,637; Re-exports, £30,174,264; Exports, £254,564,489; Total, £492,989,390.

* Excluding coastwise tonnages.

† Net registered tonnage of vessels that arrived and departed with cargoes and in ballast foreign and coastwise during 1962.

Passenger Movements at U.K. Ports, 1962

Port	Inward	Outward
United Kingdom and the Republic of Ireland		
Glasgow	27,000	26,000
Liverpool	136,000	132,000
Holyhead	404,000	394,000
Fishguard	126,000	126,000
Other ports	6,000	6,000
TOTAL	699,000	684,000
United Kingdom and Continent of Europe		
Southampton	71,000	75,000
Newhaven	142,000	145,000
Folkestone	460,000	436,000
Dover	1,535,000	1,513,000
London	44,000	40,000
Harwich	307,000	332,000
Hull	13,000	12,000
Tyne ports	69,000	70,000
Other ports	7,000	7,000
TOTAL	2,648,000	2,630,000
United Kingdom and Non-European Countries		
Glasgow	..	1,000
Liverpool	39,000	47,000
Bristol	1,000	1,000
Plymouth	5,000	2,000
Southampton	174,000	175,000
London	57,000	65,000
Other ports	10,000	9,000
TOTAL	286,000	300,000

Merchant Ships on U.K. Register

In July, 1962, there were in Lloyd's Register Book 2,031 steamships of 10,644,126 tons gross and 2,978 motorships of 11,014,016 tons; a total of 5,009 ships of 21,658,142 tons gross. Ships of less than 100 tons are not included.

Shipping Movements at U.K. Ports

Year	Entered (*a*) Vessels (Number)	Entered (*a*) Net tons ('000)	Cleared (*a*) Vessels (Number)	Cleared (*a*) Net tons ('000)
1957	14,308	19,033	21,549	46,952
1958	12,991	20,859	23,339	49,662
1959	13,853	22,301	23,824	54,269
1960	13,773	22,600	26,008	60,478
1961	14,623	22,180	27,119	61,266
1962	16,347	25,079	24,870	64,438

(*a*) With cargo and in ballast

Foreign Trade Movement, 1962

(Net Tonnage)

Flag	Entered‡	Cleared‡
Commonwealth	46,789,000	32,590,000
Belgian	1,843,000	1,695,000
Danish	2,257,000	1,599,000
Finnish	534,000	351,000
French	3,756,000	2,477,000
German	3,157,000	2,097,000
Greek	1,830,000	462,000
Italian	2,121,000	106,000
Liberian	5,815,000	193,000
Netherlands	7,168,000	5,422,000
Norwegian	9,445,000	3,388,000
Panamanian	1,206,000	148,000
Polish	174,000	188,000
Spanish	506,000	441,000
Swedish	3,612,000	1,375,000
U.S.A.	2,870,000	2,332,000
U.S.S.R.	616,000	257,000
Yugoslav	209,000	99,000
Other	1,527,000	1,098,000

Total movements of vessels with cargo in 1958–62 were:—

	Entered‡	Cleared‡
1958	79,865,000	51,392,000
1959	84,779,000	53,953,000
1960	91,626,000	54,806,000
1961	91,706,000	53,677,000
1962	95,434,000	56,318,000

‡ Net tonnage with cargo: vessels with mail only are excluded.

THE LARGEST SHIPS AFLOAT

As recorded in Lloyd's Register at July 1963

Name	Pro-pulsion	Flag	Tons Gross	Screws	Dimensions in Feet: Length Overall	Breadth Extreme	Draught Summer	Year Built	Owners
Passenger Liners									
Queen Elizabeth	Tb	Brit	83,673	4	1031·0	118·6	39·5	1940	Cunard S.S. Co. Ltd.
Queen Mary	Tb	Brit	81,237	4	1019·5	118·6	39·4	1936	Cunard S.S. Co. Ltd.
France	Tb	Fr	66,348	4	1035·2	110·9	34·4	1961	Cie. Générale Transatlantique
United States	Tb	U.S.A.	51,988	4	990·0	101·6	NR	1952	United States Lines Co.
Canberra	Tb	Brit	45,270	2	818·5	102·5	32·7	1961	P. & O. Steam Nav. Co.
Michelangelo	Tb	Italy	43,000	2	900·0	101·8	31·9	1963	" Italia " Soc. per Azioni di Nav.
Raffaello	Tb	Brit	43,000	2	900·0	101·8	31·9	1963	" Italia " Soc. per Azioni di Nav.
Oriana	Tb	Brit	41,915	2	804·0	97·2	32·0	1960	Orient Steam Nav. Co. Ltd.
Rotterdam	Tb	Neth	38,645	2	748·6	94·2	29·7	1959	N.V. Mailship " Rotterdam ".
Windsor Castle	Tb	Brit	37,640	2	783·1	92·5	32·1	1960	Union Castle Mail S.S. Co. Ltd.
Nieuw Amsterdam	Tb	Neth	36,982	2	758·5	88·4	31·5	1938	N.V. Nederl.-Amerik. Stoomv. Maats. (Holland-Amerika Lijn)
Mauretania	Tb	Brit	35,655	2	771·9	89·4	30·9	1939	Cunard S.S. Co. Ltd.
Caronia	Tb	Brit	34,172	2	715·0	91·4	31·6	1948	Cunard S.S. Co. Ltd.
Oceanic	Tb	Pan	34,000	2	774·3	96·5	NR	1963	Home Lines Inc.
America	Tb	U.S.A.	33,961	2	723·0	93·5	32·7	1940	United States Lines Co.
Leonardo Da Vinci	Tb	Ital	33,340	2	761·1	92·1	31·3	1960	" Italia " Soc. per Azioni di Nav.
Transvaal Castle	Tb	Brit	32,697	2	760·1	90·1	32·0	1961	Union Castle Mail S.S. Co. Ltd.
Bremen	Tb	W. Ger	32,336	4	696·9	90·3	30·6	1938	Bremer Nord-Atlantikdienst G.M.B.H.
Hanseatic	Tb	W. Ger	30,030	2	666·5	83·9	31·7	1930	Hamburg-Atlantik Line G.M.B.H. & Co.
Arcadia	Tb	Brit	29,664	2	721·3	90·7	31·0	1954	P. & O. Steam Nav. Co.
Oil Tankers etc.*									
Nissho Maru	Tb	Japan	74,868	1	954·7	141·4	54·4	1962	Idemitsu Kosan K.K
Universe Daphne	Tb	Lib	72,266	1	949·8	135·4	48·2	1960	Universe Tankships Inc.
Universe Apollo	Tb	Lib	72,132	1	949·8	135·4	48·0	1959	Universe Tankships Inc.
Manhattan	Tb	U.S.A.	65,740	2	940·4	132·5	49·4	1962	Manhattan Tankers Co. Inc.
Mobil Brilliant	Tb	Brit	56,000	1	900·0	127·4	NR	1963	Mobil Tankships Ltd.
Mobil Comet	Tb	Brit	56,000	1	900·0	127·4	NR	1963	Mobil Tankships Ltd.
Naess Champion	Tb	Brit	54,749	1	874·8	122·5	47·4	1962	Sovereign Shipping Co. Ltd.
Naess Sovereign	Tb	Brit	54,736	1	874·8	122·5	47·4	1961	Sovereign Shipping Co. Ltd.
Esso Den Haag	Tb	Neth	53,500	1	855·8	125·3	47·5	1963	Esso Nederland N.V.
Esso Deutschland	Tb	W.Ger	53,500	1	855·8	125·3	47·5	1963	Esso Tankscliff Reederei G.M.B.H.
Esso Libya	Tb	Brit	53,464	1	855·8	125·3	47·5	1962	Standard Tankers (Bahamas) Co. Ltd.
Esso Spain	Tb	Brit	53,423	1	855·8	125·3	46·8	1962	Standard Tankers (Bahamas) Co. Ltd.
Philip S. Niarchos	Tb	Lib	53,000	1	834·8	122·4	NR	1963	Andromeda Tanker Corp.
Universe Leader	Tb	Lib	51,400	1	854·8	125·4	46·0	1956	Universe Tankships Inc.
Universe Commander	Tb	Lib	51,398	1	854·8	125·6	46·2	1957	Universe Tankships Inc.
Frisia	Tb	Lib	51,321	1	854·8	125·4	46·2	1957	Universe Tankships Inc.
George Champion	Tb	Lib	51,320	1	854·8	125·3	46·2	1958	Universe Tankships Inc.
Harold H. Helm	Tb	Lib	51,320	1	854·8	125·4	46·2	1958	Universe Tankships Inc.
Universe Admiral	Tb	Lib	51,320	1	854·8	125·4	46·2	1958	Universe Tankships Inc.
Universe Defiance	Tb	Lib	51,320	1	855·8	125·4	46·2	1957	Universe Tankships Inc.

* All oil tankers unless otherwise stated Oe = Oil Engines Tb = Turbine Engines NR = Not recorded

MERCHANT SHIPPING

MERCHANT FLEETS OF THE WORLD

From Lloyd's Register Books, 1939 and 1962

FLAG	1939 Total		1962 Steamships		1962 Motorships		1962 Total	
	No.	Tons Gross	No.	Tons Gross	No.	Tons Gross	No.	Tons Gross
United Kingdom	6,722	17,891,134*	2,031	10,644,126	2,978	11,014,016	5,009	21,658,142
Canada	792	1,223,961	344	1,184,755	719	518,794	1,063	1,703,549
Other Commonwealth Countries	1,463	1,886,830	626	1,834,945	903	1,715,647	1,529	3,550,592
Total: British Commonwealth	8,977	21,001,925	3,001	13,663,826	4,600	13,248,457	7,601	26,912,283
Argentina	295	290,602	156	694,061	176	567,969	332	1,262,030
Brazil	293	484,870	225	687,801	205	516,250	430	1,204,051
Denmark	705	1,174,944	42	174,654	831	2,224,591	873	2,399,245
France	1,231	2,933,933	264	1,958,269	1,198	3,203,852	1,462	5,162,121
Germany (West)	2,459	4,482,662	298	1,124,957	2,194	3,798,889	2,492	4,923,846
Greece	607	1,780,666	584	4,551,402	584	1,986,017	1,168	6,537,419
Italy	1,227	3,424,804	456	2,686,776	922	2,724,876	1,378	5,411,652
Japan	2,337	5,629,845	382	1,853,994	3,990	7,016,161	4,372	8,870,155
Liberia	..	..	632	8,929,514	221	1,643,644	853	10,573,158
Netherlands	1,523	2,969,578	170	1,921,844	1,737	3,244,328	1,907	5,166,172
Norway	1,987	4,833,813	323	1,737,572	2,402	10,773,510	2,725	12,511,082
Panama	159	717,525	374	3,052,280	218	798,879	592	3,851,159
Russia (U.S.S.R.)	699	1,305,959	632	2,042,092	681	2,641,985	1,313	4,684,077
Spain	777	902,251	635	808,547	940	1,186,541	1,575	1,995,088
Sweden	1,231	1,577,120	143	413,883	1,090	3,752,845	1,233	4,166,728
United States of America	2,853	11,361,533	2,746	22,328,697	1,003	944,159	3 749	23,272,856†
Other Countries	2,403	3,637,462	1,661	5,007,686	2,945	6,069,005	4,606	11,076,691
World Total	29,763	68,509,432	12,724	73,637,855	25,937	66,341,958	38,661	139,979,813

* Including Eire (134 ships of 188,077 tons gross). † Including ships of the United States Reserve Fleet.

TONNAGE CLASSED WITH LLOYD'S REGISTER

At July 1962 92% of the tonnage in the British Commonwealth was classed by Lloyd's Register. Of the total tonnage owned in the World, 56,557,000 tons were classed with that Society.

MERCHANT SHIPPING

STEAMSHIPS AND MOTORSHIPS LAUNCHED IN THE WORLD* DURING 1962

As recorded in Lloyd's Register

Showing (*a*) the countries *in which* new ships were built (*b*) the countries *for which* they were built.

(*a*) Country of Build	Steamships		Motorships		Total		(*b*) Country of Registration	Total Steamships and Motorships	
	No.	Tons Gross	No.	Tons Gross	No.	Tons Gross		No.	Tons Gross
United Kingdom	14	376,791	173	695,722	187	1,072,513	United Kingdom	190	1,476,831
Australia	1	22,334	7	21,693	8	44,027	Australia	7	22,312
Canada	6	97,392	39	31,770	45	129,162	Canada	50	147,566
India	1	420	4	21,796	5	22,216	India	19	71,882
Other Commonwealth Countries	..	..	14	5,947	14	5,947	Other Commonwealth Countries	39	138,155
Total: British Commonwealth	22	496,937	237	776,928	259	1,273,865	Total: British Commonwealth	305	1,856,746
Argentina	..	..	4	11,805	4	11,805	Argentina	9	39,177
Belgium	1	29,699	8	46,982	9	76,681	Belgium	8	51,346
Brazil	1	7,500	9	22,731	10	30,231	Brazil	13	38,525
Denmark	1	29,000	34	201,470	35	230,470	China (Nationalist)	6	12,750
Egypt (U.A.R.)	..	..	5	4,352	5	4,352	Denmark	54	146,052
Faroe Is.	..	..	1	273	1	273	Finland	14	34,997
Finland	..	..	43	140,135	43	140,135	France	61	173,996
France	4	94,881	80	385,697	84	480,578	Germany (West)	138	327,317
Germany (West)	11	350,233	223	659,465	234	1,009,698	Greece	24	243,776
Greece	..	..	6	1,515	6	1,515	Indonesia	24	13,503
Hungary	..	..	1	120	1	120	Irish Republic	4	20,378
Indonesia	..	..	11	2,388	11	2,388	Israel	6	59,603
Irish Republic	..	..	2	16,501	2	16,501	Italy	47	322,171
Italy	3	90,300	48	257,896	51	348,196	Japan	483	1,306,353
Japan	24	776,583	534	1,406,564	558	2,183,147	Liberia	27	555,414
Madagascar	..	..	2	508	2	508	Netherlands	104	283,188
Netherlands	5	117,784	146	300,710	151	418,494	Norway	153	1,325,216
Norway	..	..	95	376,444	95	376,444	Panama	4	27,461
Poland	..	..	44	189,412	44	189,412	Poland	†	†
Portugal	..	..	7	11,934	7	11,934	Portugal	10	14,679
South Africa	..	..	1	360	1	360	Spain	71	66,152
Spain	5	27,501	87	97,753	92	125,254	Sweden	58	366,600
Sweden	5	180,925	69	660,097	74	841,022	Turkey	9	39,237
Turkey	2	2,396	5	2,240	7	4,636	United States of America	89	448,620
United States of America	34	407,225	56	41,825	90	449,050	Yugoslavia	7	35,970
Yugoslavia	..	..	25	147,685	25	147,685	Other Countries	173	565,527
World Total	118	2,610,964	1,783	5,763,790	1,901	8,374,754	World Total	1,901	8,374,754

* Returns from The People's Republic of China, East Germany and U.S.S.R. are not available. † Details not available

TONNAGE LAUNCHED TO LLOYD'S REGISTER CLASS

Of the World tonnage launched during 1962, 39 per cent (3,248,957 tons) was to Lloyd's Register Class. This figure includes 996,132 tons (93 per cent) of the tonnage built in British yards.

BRITISH RAILWAYS IN 1962

The *British Transport Commission* set up by the terms of the *Transport Act*, 1947, organized the Railways of Britain in six Regions under the control of the Railway Executive.

(1) The *London Midland Region*, corresponding to the system of the London, Midland and Scottish Company in England and Wales.

(2) The *Western Region*, corresponding to the system of the Great Western Railway.

(3) The *Southern* Region, corresponding to the system of the Southern Railway.

(4) The *Eastern Region*, corresponding to the Southern Area of the London and North Eastern Railway.

(5) The *North Eastern Region*, corresponding to the North Eastern Area of the London and North Eastern Railway.

(6) The *Scottish Region*, corresponding to the Scottish systems of the London, Midland and Scottish and London and North Eastern Railway.

Certain revisions in the Regional boundaries have subsequently taken place, notably in the cases of the London Midland, Southern and Western Regions.

By the terms of the *Transport Act*, 1953, the Railway Executive ceased to exist on September 30, 1953, when its functions, together with those of the other Executives excepting the London Transport Executive, were assumed by the British Transport Commission.

The *Transport Act*, 1962, provided for the dissolution of the Commission and for the creation in its place of four new statutory boards—the British Railways Board, the London Transport Board, the British Transport Docks Board and the British Waterways Board—and a Transport Holding Company. These bodies assumed the liabilities, responsibilities and assets of the Commission on January 1, 1963. The Act gave the Railways Board greater commercial freedom and a new financial structure.

BRITISH TRANSPORT COMMISSION RESULTS

OPERATING RATIOS.—Working expenses of the British Transport Commission in the operation of railways in 1962 amounted to 122 per cent. of gross receipts, compared with 118 per cent. in 1961 and 114 per cent. in 1960; in the operation of ships, working expenses were 80 per cent. of gross receipts in 1962 compared with 81 per cent. in 1961 and 80 per cent. in 1960.

£million

	1959	1960	1961	1962
Gross Revenue				
Railways				
Passenger Receipts	140·0	151·3	157·5	161·2
Freight (including parcels and mail)	307·4	316·9	306·7	293·1
Miscellaneous Receipts	9·9	10·4	10·5	10·8
Ships				
Passenger Receipts	7·5	7·4	7·9	8·2
Freight (including parcels and mail)	9·3	10·2	11·0	11·8
Miscellaneous	1·5	1·6	1·7	1·7
TOTAL REVENUE	475·6	497·8	495·3	486 8
Gross Expenditure				
Railways				
Operating Expenses	189·2	201·9	200·3	199·1
Maintenance of Rolling Stock	106·6	116·3	127·0	126·0
Other Traffic Exports	83·5	93·1	94·4	97·3
Signalling Expenses	34·0	37·8	39·1	40·8
Maintenance of Way and Structures	75·6	83·7	85·5	88·1
General	10·4	13·4	15·3	17·7
Ships	14·4	15·3	16·7	17·4
TOTAL EXPENDITURE	513·7	561·5	578·3	586·4
DEFICIT	38·1	63·7	83·0	99·6

BRITISH RAILWAY FARES, 1938–1962

The following table shows rail fares for 12 specimen journeys in 1938, in 1946 and in each year thereafter, and the fares current in September, 1963 when a change was made. The fares are 3rd or 2nd class ordinary returns, January each year. In 1957 the 3rd class was renamed 2nd.

LONDON TO:—	JANUARY																						SEPT.	
	1938		1946		1947		1948		1953		1956		1958		1960		1961		1962		1963	
	s.	*d.*	*s.*	*d.*	*s.*	*d.*	*s.*	*d.*	*s.*	*d.*	*s.*	*d.*	*s.*	*d.*	*s.*	*d.*	*s.*	*d.*	*s.*	*d.*	*s.*	*d*
Birmingham (New St.)	19	8	22	11	26	3	30	6	32	6	34	10	37	6	42	0	47	0	51	0	55	6
Bournemouth (Central)	18	11	22	1	25	3	30	6	31	6	34	0	36	0	41	0	45	0	50	0	54	0
Brighton	9	2	10	8	12	3	14	3	15	0	16	0	17	0	19	6	21	6	23	6	25	6
Bristol	21	0	24	6	28	0	32	7	34	6	37	0	39	4	45	0	50	0	55	0	59	0
Edinburgh (Waverley)	69	4	80	11	92	5	107	6	114	8	123	4	131	0	142	0	142	0	142	0	162	0
Glasgow (*viâ* Carlisle)	70	4	82	1	93	9	109	0	117	4	126	2	134	0	144	0	144	0	144	0	168	0
Liverpool	34	8	40	5	46	3	53	9	56	8	60	10	64	8	73	0	81	0	89	0	97	0
Manchester	32	3	37	8	43	0	50	0	53	8	57	10	61	4	69	0	77	0	85	0	92	0
Norwich	20	6	23	11	27	4	31	9	33	8	36	2	38	4	44	0	46	0	53	0	57	6
Oxford	11	3	13	2	15	0	17	5	18	8	20	2	21	4	24	0	27	0	29	6	32	0
Sheffield	28	1	32	9	37	5	43	6	46	6	50	6	53	0	60	0	67	0	73	0	79	6
York	33	1	38	7	44	1	51	3	55	2	59	4	63	0	71	0	79	0	87	0	94	6

LONDON SUBURBAN RAIL AND COACH FARES, 1938–1963

London Underground Railways Return Fares

Specimen Journey	JANUARY 1938	1951	1953	1954	1956	1957	1958	1959	1960	1963	SEPT. 1963
	s. d.	*s. d.*	*s. d.*	*s. d.*	*s. d.*	*s. d.*	*s. d.*	*s. d.*	*s. d.*	*s. d.*	*s. d.*
Tottenham Court Rd.-Morden	1 2	1 8	2 0	2 2	2 4	2 10	3 0	3 4	3 6	4 0	4 8
Liverpool Street-Ealing Broadway	1 2	1 11	2 4	2 6	2 8	3 0	3 4	3 8	3 10	4 4	5 0
Tower Hill-Putney Br.	1 2	1 6	1 10	2 0	2 2	2 8	2 8	2 8	2 10	3 4	3 10
Piccadilly Circus-Cockfosters	1 6	2 2	2 6	2 8	2 10	3 4	3 8	3 10	4 0	4 8	5 4

The fare for each of the above journeys rose by 2*d.* between January and June, 1962.

Southern Region of British Railways 2nd Class Return Fares

Specimen Journey	JANUARY 1938	1946	1947	1948	1953	1956	1958	1960	1961	1962	1963
	s. d.	*s. d.*	*s. d.*	*s. d.*	*s. d.*	*s. d.*	*s. d.*	*s. d.*	*s. d.*	*s. d.*	*s. d.*
Charing X-Orpington	3 5	3 5	3 11	4 6	4 2	4 6	4 8	5 4	5 10	6 6	7 0
Waterloo-Esher*	2 8	2 8	3 0	3 6	4 2	4 6	5 0	5 8	6 4	7 0	7 6
Victoria-Sanderstead	2 9	2 9	3 1	3 7	3 10	4 2	4 4	5 0	5 6	6 0	6 6
Charing X-Bexleyheath	2 9	2 9	3 1	3 7	3 10	4 2	4 4	5 0	5 6	6 0	6 6

* This return fare also rose by 4*d.* in 1957.

Green Line Coach Return Fares

Specimen Journey	JANUARY 1938	1947	1948	1951	1953	1954	1956	1958	1960	1963	SEPT. 1963
	s. d.	*s. d.*	*s. d.*	*s. d.*	*s. d.*	*s. d.*	*s. d.*	*s. d.*	*s. d.*	*s. d.*	*s. d.*
Hyde Park Corner-Bromley South Stn.	1 6	3 4	4 0	3 2	3 6	3 8	4 0	4 4	4 8	5 4	6 0
Marble Arch-Purley	1 9	3 4	4 0	3 0	3 10	4 0	4 4	4 8	5 0	5 8	6 4
Marble Arch-Enfield Town Station	1 6	2 8	3 0	2 10	3 0	3 2	3 6	3 10	4 0	4 8	5 8
Aldgate-Romford Market Place	1 6	2 8	3 0	2 10	3 4	3 6	3 10	4 2	4 4	5 0	5 8

The fare for each of the above journeys rose by 2*d.* between January and June, 1962.

OPERATING STATISTICS

At the end of 1962, British Railways had 47,417 miles of standard gauge lines and sidings in use, including 17,471 miles of first track of which 1,560 miles were electrified. The total length of electrified track in 1962 was 4,138 miles. Standard rail on main lines has a weight of 109 lbs. per yard. British railways had 12,628 locomotives (steam, 8,767; diesel and diesel electric, 3,683 and electric, 178); 2,445 multiple-unit diesel power cars and 2,982 multiple-unit electric power cars in 1962. Engine miles run in passenger service totalled 258,620,000. 33,607 passenger-carrying vehicles had a total of 1,952,896 seats or berths. 997,718,000 passenger journeys were made during the year, including 327,271,000 made by holders of season tickets. The average distance of each passenger journey on ordinary fare was 21·85 miles; and on season ticket, 15·65 miles. Passenger stations in use in 1962 numbered 4,347 and freight stations 2,382.

Freight.—There were 862,640 freight vehicles and 12,482 other vehicles in the non-passenger-carrying stock. 35,943,000 tons of merchandise and livestock were carried in 1962, 145,041,000 tons of coal and coke and 47,115,000 tons of other minerals. Engine miles run in freight service totalled 130,707,000. 34,561 railway road vehicles were in use in 1962 and 46,535 containers.

Staff and Wages

On Dec. 31, 1962, British Railways employed a total staff of 475,222 persons. Average weekly earnings at April 14, 1962 (with numbers of staff), were:—Men (435,684) £15 4*s*.; Women (29,611) £9 15*s*.; Youths and Boys (23,397) £7 11*s*.; and Girls (2,879) £5 0*s*.

Train Accidents on British Railways

	Average 1958–62	1962
Fatal Accidents	28	33
Passengers killed	11	20
Passengers seriously injured	40	35
Railwaymen killed	6	2
Railwaymen seriously injured	28	24
Other persons killed	14	11
Other persons seriously injured	12	12
Passengers carried per passenger killed	96,700,000	49,900,000
Passenger miles run per passenger killed	1,977,800,000	988,600,000

RAILWAY ACCIDENTS IN WHICH 20 PERSONS AND OVER WERE KILLED IN THE UNITED KINGDOM SINCE 1879

Year	Date	Name of Accident	Railway	Number Killed	Cause
1879	Dec. 28	Tay Bridge	N.B.	78	Bridge failed.
1884	July 16	Bullhouse	M.S. & L.	24	Derailment.
1887	Sept. 16	Hexthorpe	M.S. & L.	25	Collision.
1889	June 12	Armagh	G.N. (Ireland)	80	Collision.
1905	July 27	Hall Road	L. & Y.	21	Collision.
1906	July 1	Salisbury	L. & S.W.	28	Derailment.
1906	Dec. 28	Elliot Jct	N.B. & Cal.	22	Collision.
1915	May 22	Quintinshill	Caledonian	227	Collision.
1928	June 27	Darlington	L. & N.E.	25	Collision.
1937	Dec. 10	Castle Cary	L. & N.E.	35	Collision.
1940	Nov. 4	Norton Fitzwarren	G.W.	27	Derailment.
1941	Dec. 30	Eccles	L.M. & S.	23	Collision.
1945	Sept. 30	Bourne End	L.M. & S.	43	Points at excessive speed.
1946	Jan. 1	Lichfield (T.V.)	L.M. & S.	20	Point mechanism jammed.
1947	Oct. 24	South Croydon	S.R.	32	Collision in fog.
1947	Oct. 26	Goswick	L. & N.E.	28	Derailment.
1948	Apl. 17	Winsford	L.M. Region	24	Collision.
1952	Oct. 8	Harrow	L.M. Region	112	Collision.
1957	Dec. 4	Lewisham	S. Region	90	Collision in fog.

MODERNIZATION

The British Transport Commission announced early in 1955, the Modernization and Re-equipment Plan for British Railways at a then estimated cost of £1,240,000,000. It has since made significant progress. The complete plan, covering a period of 15 years, envisages the provision of some 2,500 main-line diesel locomotives; about 8,200 vehicles for multiple-unit trains, of which some 3,600 are for electric and the remainder for diesel powered trains; a large number of diesel-shunting engines; electrification of certain main-line and suburban services; major improvements to goods marshalling yards and goods stations, and certain passenger stations; the provision of new rolling stock and carriage cleaning facilities.

Details of some of the major works and of new equipment provided under the Programme, include the following:—

Track and Signalling.—Long welded rails, giving lower maintenance costs, reduced train vibration and noise and diminished wear and tear of rolling stock, are now being produced in all six Regions of British Railways at the rate of 350 miles a year and by 1963 well over 1,000 track miles had been laid. Modern signalling, including electric colour-light signals, more track circuits and power-operated signal boxes, and the extension of the automatic warning system, is now being installed on a large scale. The 1959–63 programme provides for 2,000 miles of colour-light signalling and the reduction of the number of existing signal boxes from about 9,000 to 8,400.

Electrification.—Following approval by the Minister of Transport in January, 1961, for the whole of the London Midland main line electrification scheme, the second stage between Crewe and Liverpool was completed and full electric passenger and freight services began operating in June, 1962. Engineering work continues on the remaining sections between Crewe and London (Euston) and it is intended that full electric services will be operating by 1967. In Scotland work on the second phase of the Glasgow electrification scheme involving electrification of suburban lines south of the Clyde has now been completed. Electric services also commenced running in the Eastern Region on the London, Tilbury and Shoeburyness line, and between Liverpool Street and Clacton/Walton-on-Sea. In the Southern Region electric trains were introduced on all routes comprising the second phase of the Kent Coast electrification scheme.

Diesel Traction.—Of the 2,700 main line diesel locomotives ordered, 1,900 had been delivered by July, 1963; by the end of 1963 about 2,000 were expected to be in service. Nearly 2,000 diesel shunting engines are in use, and over 4,000 diesel multiple-unit train vehicles. The 22 3,300 h.p. Deltic locomotives ordered for the East Coast main line services between London (King's Cross) and Edinburgh, now replace 55 steam locomotives. These diesel-electrics are the most powerful in service and their use has led to spectacular reductions in timings.

Passenger Stations.—Improvements are in progress or have been carried out at many stations, including major schemes of reconstruction at Plymouth, Coventry, Stafford, Tamworth and Ashford (Kent). Work continued in 1963 on demolition work at Euston Station, the first stage of a major scheme of rebuilding.

Freight Yards.—New freight marshalling yards at Perth, Newport (Tees-side), Millerhill (Edinburgh), Lamesley (Tyneside) and Kingmoor (Carlisle) were completed and brought into operational use and work is in progress on new yards at Bescot, Healey Mills (near Wakefield), Scunthorpe and Tinsley (Sheffield). A modern coal concentration depot designed to handle 50,000 tons of solid fuel a year, previously dealt with at thirteen stations was brought into use at Enfield Chase. Work continued on other freight depots including those at Gateshead and Grimesthorpe (Sheffield).

INLAND WATERWAYS

There are about 2,400 miles of inland waterways in use in Great Britain. Of these about 2,000 miles are administered by the British Waterways Board. In the year 1962, 9,263,000 tons of goods—coal and other fuel, liquids in bulk and general merchandise—were carried on the Board's waterways, compared with 10,800,000 tons in 1951. Total staff employed in December, 1962, was 4,051.

The Thames Conservancy had 136 miles of waterways in use in 1962 and carried 104,327 tons of goods; Manchester Ship Canal (36 miles) carried 14,737,434 tons and its Bridgewater Department 28½ (miles) carried 129,586 tons of goods.

LONDON RAILWAY STATIONS AND SYSTEMS

London Midland Region

EUSTON, off Euston Road.—for trains to Rugby, Coventry, Stafford, Crewe, North Wales, Manchester, Liverpool, Warrington, Carlisle, and Scotland *viâ* old London and North-Western route; boat trains to Holyhead (for Dún Laoghaire); Liverpool (for Dublin and Belfast); Heysham (for Belfast); Stranraer (for Larne). Also short-distance trains to Watford, etc.

ST. PANCRAS, Euston Road.—For trains to Bedford, Leicester, Derby, Nottingham, Manchester, Sheffield, etc. and to Scotland *viâ* old Midland route. Also short-distance trains to St. Albans, Luton, etc.

BROAD STREET.—City terminus of the former North London line to Richmond *viâ* Willesden Junction and for trains to Watford.

MARYLEBONE.—For trains to Rugby, Leicester and Nottingham and for some shorter-distance trains, *e.g.* to Harrow, High Wycombe and Aylesbury (*see also* Metropolitan Line).

Eastern Region

KING'S CROSS.—For trains to Peterborough, Grantham, Doncaster, York, Darlington, Durham, Newcastle and Edinburgh *viâ* old London and North-Eastern route; Lincolnshire and East Riding. Also short distance trains to parts of Hertfordshire.

LIVERPOOL STREET, City.—For trains to East Anglia—Chelmsford, Colchester, Ipswich, Norwich, Cromer, Yarmouth, etc.; boat-trains to Harwich. Also short-distance trains to outer N.E. London suburbs and to most parts of Essex.

FENCHURCH STREET, City.—Is terminus for the Tilbury and Southend Line.

Western Region

PADDINGTON, Praed Street, W.2.—For trains to Reading, Swindon, Bristol, Taunton, Exeter, Plymouth, Penzance, Newport, Cardiff, Swansea and other parts of South Wales, Cheltenham, Gloucester, Oxford, Worcester and Hereford, Birmingham (Snow Hill), Wolverhampton, Chester and Birkenhead. Also short-distance trains to parts of Middlesex and Thames Valley.

Southern Region

VICTORIA, end of Victoria Street, S.W.1.—Boat trains for Dover, Folkestone and Newhaven. Trains to Kent and Sussex coast. Short-distance trains to many parts of Kent and Surrey.

WATERLOO, Waterloo Road, S.E.1.—Trains to Southampton, Portsmouth (for Isle of Wight), Lymington (for Isle of Wight), Bournemouth, Basingstoke, Winchester, Salisbury, Exeter, Ilfracombe and Bude. Short-distance trains to many parts of Surrey, Middlesex and Thames Valley.

LONDON BRIDGE, south of London Bridge, S.E.1.—Trains to South Coast and many short-distance trains on Southern Electric system.

CHARING CROSS.—Trains to all parts of Kent and East Sussex and many short-distance trains.

CANNON STREET, City.—City terminus for trains covering largely same routes as Charing Cross.

HOLBORN VIADUCT, City.—Used mostly for short-distance trains to South London and parts of Kent. BLACKFRIARS is on the Holborn Viaduct Line, but is a terminus for some trains.

LONDON TRANSPORT UNDERGROUND SYSTEM

Bakerloo Line

Elephant and Castle,* Lambeth North, Waterloo,* Charing Cross,* Trafalgar Square, Piccadilly Circus,* Oxford Circus,* Regent's Park, Baker Street*—then *Stanmore Branch* (St. John's Wood, Swiss Cottage, Finchley Road,* West Hampstead, Kilburn, Willesden Green, Dollis Hill, Neasden, Wembley Park,* Kingsbury, Queensbury, Canons Park, Stanmore) or *Watford Branch* (Marylebone, Edgware Road,* Paddington,* Warwick Avenue, Maida Vale, Kilburn Park, Queen's Park, Kensal Green, Willesden Junction, Harlesden, Stonebridge Park, Wembley Central, North Wembley, South Kenton, Kenton, Harrow and Wealdstone, Headstone Lane, Hatch End, Carpenders Park, Bushey and Oxhey, Watford High Street, Watford Junction).

Central Line

From Ruislip.—West Ruislip, Ruislip Gardens, South Ruislip, Northolt, Greenford, Perivale, Hanger Lane.

From Ealing.—Ealing Broadway, West Acton.

Then (both branches) North Acton, East Acton, White City, Shepherd's Bush, Holland Park, Notting Hill Gate,* Queensway, Lancaster Gate, Marble Arch, Bond Street, Oxford Circus,* Tottenham Court Road,* Holborn,* Chancery Lane, St. Paul's, Bank,* Liverpool Street,* Bethnal Green, Mile End,* Stratford, Leyton, Leytonstone.

Then **Hainault Branch** *viâ* Wanstead (Wanstead, Redbridge, Gants Hill, Newbury Park, Barkingside, Fairlop, Hainault).

Or **EppingBranch** (Snaresbrook, South Woodford, Woodford, Buckhurst Hill, Loughton, Debden, Theydon Bois, Epping, North Weald, Blake Hall, Ongar). Change at Woodford for Roding Valley, Chigwell, Grange Hill and Hainault.

Circle Line

Charing Cross,* Westminster, St. James's Park, Victoria, Sloane Square, South Kensington,* Gloucester Road,* High Street Kensington, Notting Hill Gate,* Bayswater, Paddington,* Edgware Road,* Baker Street,* Great Portland Street, Euston Square, King's Cross and St. Pancras,* Farringdon, Aldersgate, Moorgate,* Liverpool Street,* Aldgate, Tower Hill, Monument,* Cannon Street, Mansion House, Blackfriars, Temple, Charing Cross.*

District Line

Upminster, Upminster Bridge, Hornchurch, Elm Park, Dagenham East, Dagenham Heathway, Becontree, Upney, Barking, East Ham, Upton Park, Plaistow, West Ham, Bromley, Bow Road, Mile End,* Stepney Green, Whitechapel,* Aldgate East, Tower Hill (for Tower Hill–Gloucester Road and Edgware Road, *see* Circle Line), Earl's Court.*

Change at Earl's Court for Kensington (Olympia).

Then **Wimbledon Branch.**—West Brompton, Fulham Broadway, Parsons Green, Putney Bridge, East Putney, Southfields, Wimbledon Park, Wimbledon.

Or **Richmond, Hounslow or Ealing Branches,** Common as far as Turnham Green *viâ* West Kensington, Barons Court, Hammersmith,* Ravenscourt Park, Stamford Brook.

Richmond Branch.—Gunnersbury, Kew Gardens, Richmond.

Hounslow Branch.—Chiswick Park, Acton Town,* then as Piccadilly Line.

Ealing Branch.—Chiswick Park, Acton Town,* Ealing Common,* Ealing Broadway.*

Metropolitan Line

From Barking as District to Aldgate East, then as Circle Line, Liverpool Street – Baker Street *viâ* King's Cross. Change at Whitechapel for Shoreditch and for Shadwell, Wapping, Rotherhithe, Surrey Docks and New Cross or New Cross Gate.

From Baker Street—**Hammersmith Branch.**—

* Interchange Stations.

Edgware Road,* Paddington,* Royal Oak, Westbourne Park, Ladbroke Grove, Latimer Road, Shepherd's Bush, Goldhawk Road, Hammersmith.*

Or **Uxbridge, Watford and Amersham Branches.** Common as far as Harrow-on-the-Hill (Finchley Road.* Wembley Park,* Preston Road, Northwick Park.)

Uxbridge Branch—West Harrow, Rayners Lane,* then as Piccadilly Line.

Watford and Amersham Branches.—Common as far as Moor Park via North Harrow, Pinner, Northwood Hills, Northwood.
Then Croxley and Watford.

Or Rickmansworth, Chorley Wood, Chalfont and Latimer, Amersham. Change at Chalfont and Latimer for Chesham.

Northern Line

Morden, South Wimbledon, Collier's Wood, Tooting Broadway, Tooting Bec, Balham, Clapham South, Clapham Common, Clapham North, Stockwell, Oval, Kennington.

Then **City Branch**—Elephant and Castle,* Borough, London Bridge, Bank,* Moorgate,* Old Street.* Angel, King's Cross and St. Pancras,* Euston,* Camden Town,* *see below*. (Change at Moorgate for *Northern City Line*—Old Street,* Essex Road, Highbury and Islington, Drayton Park and Finsbury Park.*)

Or **West End Branch**—Waterloo,* Charing Cross,* Strand, Leicester Square,* Tottenham Court Road,* Goodge Street, Warren Street, Euston*, Mornington Crescent, Camden Town*.
Then **Edgware Branch**—Chalk Farm, Belsize Park, Hampstead, Golders Green, Brent, Hendon Central. Colindale, Burnt Oak, Edgware.

Or **Barnet and Mill Hill East Branches.**—Kentish Town, Tufnell Park, Archway, Highgate, East Finchley, Finchley Central, West Finchley, Woodside Park, Totteridge, High Barnet. (Mill Hill East trains diverge after Finchley Central.)

Piccadilly Line

Cockfosters, Oakwood, Southgate, Arnos Grove, Bounds Green, Wood Green, Turnpike Lane, Manor House, Finsbury Park,* Arsenal, Holloway Road, Caledonian Road, King's Cross and St. Pancras,* Russell Square, Holborn,* Covent Garden, Leicester Square,* Piccadilly Circus,* Green Park, Hyde Park Corner, Knightsbridge, South Kensington,* Gloucester Road,* Earls Court,* Barons Court, Hammersmith,* Acton Town.*

Then **Hounslow Branch.**—South Ealing, Northfields, Boston Manor, Osterley, Hounslow East, Hounslow Central. Hounslow West.

Or **Uxbridge Branch.**—Ealing Common,* North Ealing, Park Royal, Alperton, Sudbury Town, Sudbury Hill, South Harrow, Rayners Lane,* Eastcote, Ruislip Manor, Ruislip, Ickenham, Hillingdon, Uxbridge.

Waterloo and City Line
(*British Railways*)
Direct trains between Waterloo* and Bank.*

* Interchange Stations.

GREEN LINE COACH ROUTES

701. Gravesend – Dartford – Victoria – Staines – Ascot.
702. Gravesend – Dartford – Victoria – Staines – Sunningdale.
703. Wrotham – Swanley – Victoria – Wembley – Amersham.
704. Tunbridge Wells – Sevenoaks – Victoria – Slough – Windsor.
705. Sevenoaks – Westerham – Victoria – Slough – Windsor.
706. Westerham – Croydon – Victoria – Watford – Aylesbury.
707. Oxted – Croydon – Victoria – Watford – Aylesbury.
708. East Grinstead – Caterham – Victoria – Watford – Hemel Hempstead.
709. Godstone – Caterham – Oxford Circus – Uxbridge – Chesham.
710. Crawley – Redhill – Oxford Circus – Uxbridge – Amersham.
711. Reigate – Sutton – Oxford Circus – Uxbridge – High Wycombe.
712. Dorking – Epsom – Victoria – St. Albans – Luton.
712A. Dorking – Epsom – Victoria – St. Albans – Whipsnade Zoo (Summer Sats. and Sundays).
713. Dorking – Epsom – Victoria – St. Albans – Dunstable.
714. Dorking – Kingston – King's Cross – St. Albans – Luton.
715. Guildford – Esher – Oxford Circus – Enfield – Hertford.
715A. Marble Arch – Oxford Circus – Edmonton – Hertford.
716. Chertsey – Kingston – Baker Street – Barnet – Hitchin.
716A. Woking – Kingston – Baker Street – Barnet – Stevenage.
717. Victoria – Baker Street – Barnet – Welham Green – Welwyn Garden City.
718. Windsor – Kingston – Victoria – Chingford – Epping – Harlow New Town.
719. Hemel Hempstead – Leverstock Green – Garston – Watford – Victoria.
720. Bishop's Stortford – Harlow – Epping – Woodford – Aldgate.
720A. Harlow New Town – Epping – Woodford – Aldgate.
721. Brentwood – Gidea Park – Romford – Ilford – Aldgate.
722. Upminster – Hornchurch – Becontree Heath – Aldgate.
723. Tilbury Ferry – Chadwell St. Mary – Grays – Purfleet – Aldgate.
723A. Grays – Belhus – Aldgate.
723B. Tilbury Ferry – Dock Road – Grays – Purfleet – Aldgate.
725. Gravesend – Bromley – Croydon – Kingston – Windsor.
726. Harold Hill – Romford – Baker Street – Barnet – St. Albans – Whipsnade Zoo (summer only).

AERODROMES AND AIRPORTS

A list of 167 aerodromes in the United Kingdom, Isle of Man, the Channel Islands, etc., available to civil aircraft, showing the class of aerodrome and the length in feet of the longest runway, grass or beach landing strip. Civil Aircraft are not permitted to land at aerodromes in U.K. other than those listed below, except in cases of genuine emergency in flight or where special permission has been obtained from the appropriate authority.

S=Airfield owned or controlled by the Ministry of Aviation; airports available for International air services are also shown in bold type (22).
J=Aerodrome licensed for joint use of Royal Air Force, Royal Navy and civil aircraft (56).
M=Municipal aerodrome, owned or controlled by the local authority (22).
Pu.=Aerodrome licensed for public use (30).
U=Unlicensed aerodrome; *available with prior permission to civil aircraft (18).
Priv.=Aerodrome licensed for private use (37).
C=Aerodrome or airport with Customs and Immigration facilities, continuously or on call.
H=Helicopter Station only.

England and Wales (140)

Abingdon. J. (6,600).
Acklington. J. (5,850).
Andover, Hants. J. (4,200).
Aylesbury (Thame). Priv. U. (3,550).
Barrow (Walney Island). Priv. (3,925)
Bassingbourn. J. (6,000).
Bath Racecourse (Lansdowne). Priv. U. (1,450).
Bedford (Castle Mill). Priv. U. (1,400).
Bembridge, I.O.W. Pu. (2,700).
Benson, Oxon. J. (6,006).
Biggin Hill. Priv. J. (2,960).
Biggleswade (Old Warden). Priv. U. (2,100).
Birmingham. MC. (5,006).
Bitteswell, Warwickshire. Priv. (5,999).
Blackpool. M.Pu.C. (6,001).
Bognor Regis. Priv. U. (2,500).
Boston, Lincs. Priv. U. (2,000).
Bournemouth (Hurn). SC. (6,031).
Bovingdon, Herts. J. (4,902).
Bristol (Filton). Priv. U. (8,175).
Bristol (Lulsgate). Pu.C. (4,600).
Brough, Hull. Priv. (3,900).
Cambridge. Pu. (5,307).
Cardiff (Rhoose). SC. (4,534).
Carlisle (Crosby). Pu. (6,035).
Chivenor. J. (6,048).
Christchurch, Hants. Priv. (2,500).
Church Fenton. J. (6,000).
Colerne. J. (5,860).
Coltishall. J. (7,500).
Cosford J. (3,720).
Coventry. Pu.M. (5,300).
Cranfield, Bedford. Pu. (6,000).
Cranwell North. J. (3,000).
Cranwell South. J. (6,830).
Culdrose J. (6,000).
Denham, Bucks. Priv. (2,700).
Derby (Burnaston). Pu.M.C (3,590).
Dishforth. J. (5,970).
Elstree, Herts. Priv. (2,100).
Exeter. Pu.C. (6,120).
Fairoaks, Woking. Priv. (2,880).
Gloucester, Cheltenham (Staverton). Pu.M. (3,240).
Goodwood. Priv. (4,320).
Halfpenny Green. Priv. (3,865).
Halton. J. (3,400).
Hamble, Hants. Priv. (3,930).
Hatfield. Priv. U. (6,000).
Haverfordwest (Withybush). U.M. (4,200).
Hawarden, Flintshire. Priv. (4,713). (Licensed for scheduled passenger services).
Hucknall. Priv. U. (7,000).
Hucknall South. Priv. (2,650). (Available only by day during periods when flying has ceased on the paved runway—within boundary of Hucknall Aerodrome).
Huddersfield (Crosland Moor). U.Priv. (2,136).
Hullavington. J. (4,054).
Ipswich. Pu.M. (4,280).
Kemble. J. (6,110).
Land's End (St. Just). S. (2,450).
Leavesden, Watford. Priv. (3,030).
Leconfield. J. (7,500).
Leeds and Bradford. Pu.C.M. (3,970).
Leeming. J. (7,500).
Leicester (East). Priv.U. (5,925).
— (Rearsby). Pu. (3,100).
Lindholme. J. (5,919).
Linton-on-Ouse. J. (6,000).
Little Rissington. J. (4,800).
Liverpool. Pu.C.M. (5,627).
London (Heathrow) Airport SC. (11,000; 9,312; 7,734; 7,560; 6,225).
—**(Gatwick)**. SC. (7,000).
— (Westland Heliport, London). H.
Luton. Pu.M.C. (5,532).
Lydd, Kent. Priv.C. (4,050).
Lympne, Kent. Pu.C. (3,500).
Lyneham. J. (7,800).
Manby, Lincs. J. (4,257).
Manchester. Pu.CM. (7,000).
— (Barton). Priv. (2,100).
Manston. J. (9,018).
Middleton St. George. J. (7,500).
Nether Thorpe, Worksop. U. (1,555).
Newcastle-upon-Tyne (Woolsington). Pu.CM. (5,300).
Newmarket Heath. Priv. (3,500).
Newton. J. (4,200).
Northampton (Sywell). Priv. (4,500).
Northolt, Middx. J. (5,520).
North Weald. J. (6,300).
Nottingham (Tollerton). Priv. (3,470).
Oakington. J. (6,110).
Ouston, Newcastle. J. (6,000).
Oxford (Kidlington). Pu.M. (3,600).
Panshanger, Herts. Priv. (3,830).
Peterborough (Westwood). Priv.U. (2,800).
Plymouth, Roborough. Pu.M. (3,140).
Portsmouth. Pu.M. (3,170).
Preston/Blackburn (Samlesbury). Priv.U. (5,100).
Radlett, Herts. Priv. (6,910).
Ramsgate. Pu. (2,550).
Redhill, Surrey. Priv.U. (3,702).
Rochester. Priv.M. (3 665).
Rufforth. J. (6,042).
St. Mawgan. J. (9,040).
Salisbury (Old Sarum). J. (3,300).
Sandown, I.O.W. (Lea). Pu. (3,990).
Seighford. Priv. (6,030).
Shawbury, Shrewsbury. J. (6,000).
Shoreham, Sussex. Pu.M. (2,810).
Skegness (Ingoldmells). Priv. (2,060).
Southampton. Pu.M.C. (5,050).
— (Southampton Water). Priv.U. (9,000).
South Cerney. J. (3,300).
Southend. Pu.CM. (5,265).
South Marston. Priv. (6,000).
Southport (Birkdale Sands). Priv.M. (2,500).
— (Hesketh Park). Priv.M. (1,500).

Southport (Woodvale). J. (5,412).
Stansted, Essex. SC. (10,000).
Stapleford Tawney, Essex. Priv. (2,200).
Stradishall. J. (6,000).
Swansea. Priv.M. (4,280).
Swinderby. J. (6,056).
Syerston. J. (5,940).
Tangmere. J. (6,042).
Ternhill. J. (3,192).
Thorney Island. J. (6,000).
Thruxton, nr. Andover, Hants. Priv. (4,680).
Topcliffe. J. (6.009).
Upavon, Wilts. J. (3,600).
Valley. JC. (6,000).
Warton. Priv. U. (7,995).
Waterbeach. J. (6,000).
Wattisham. J. (7,500).
Weston-super-Mare. Pu. (4,197).
White Waltham. U. (3,600).
Wolverhampton. Pu.M. (3,575).
Woodford, nr. Macclesfield. Priv. (7,470).
Wroughton, Wilts. J. (4,890).
Yeovil, Som. Priv. (5,200).

Scotland (19)

Aberdeen (Dyce). S. (6,002).
Arbroath. J. (3,960).
Barra, Hebrides. Priv. (3,000).
Benbecula, Hebrides. S. (6,016).
Edinburgh (Turnhouse). SC. (6,000).
Inverness (Dalcross). S. (5,476).
Islay (Port Ellen). S. (4,040).
Kinloss. J. (6,080).
Kirkwall. S. (3,880).
Leuchars. J. (8,454).
Lossiemouth. J. (9,140).
Machrihanish, Argyll. S. (10,000).
Perth (Scone). Pu. (3,810).
Prestwick, Ayrshire. SC. (9,800).
Glasgow (Renfrew). SC. (5,789).
Stornoway, Hebrides. S. (6,035).
Sumburgh Head, Zetland. S. (4,065).
Tiree, Argyll. S. (5,500).
Wick, Caithness. S. (6,000).

Northern Ireland (4)

Aldergrove, Antrim. J. (6,025).
Ballykelly, Londonderry. J. (6,020).
Belfast (Nutts Corner). SC. (6,014).
— (Sydenham). Priv. (6,000).
Newtownards. Priv. (3,970).

Isle of Man (2)

Jurby, Ramsey, I.O.M. J.C. (3,570).
Ronaldsway, Ballasalla, nr. Douglas Pu.C. (5,200).

Channel Islands, etc. (4)

Alderney (States of Guernsey). C. (2,887).
Guernsey (States of Guernsey). C. (4,800).
Jersey (St. Peter). Pu.C. (5,100).
Scilly Isles (St. Mary's). S. (1,872).

Cost of the State Airports

Under the Civil Aviation Act, 1946, 21 civil airports are operated by the Ministry of Aviation. They include the three major international airports, London (Heathrow), London (Gatwick) and Prestwick; and ten other airports which either cater in part for international traffic or are locally important—Aberdeen, Belfast, Bournemouth, Cardiff, Edinburgh, Inverness, Isles of Scilly, Land's End, Glasgow (Renfrew) and Stansted. The remainder are used by air services operated to meet the need for air communication in the Scottish highlands and islands—Benbecula, Islay, Kirkwall, Machrihanish, Stornoway, Sumburgh, Tiree and Wick. Following are brief details of revenue and expenditure of the state airports in 1961–62. Assets (land, runways and aprons, buildings, plant, services and equipment) were valued at £49,821,799 on March 31, 1962. The following figures of Revenue and Expenditure exclude cost of services to overflying aircraft.

Airport	*Revenue*	*Expenditure*	*Net Cost, 1961–62*
London (Heathrow)	£8,692,937	£7,252,538	—£1,440,399
London (Gatwick)	836,615	1,755,335	918,720
Prestwick	1,259,596	1,397,295	137,699
Scottish airports operated to meet social needs	95,957	721,944	625,987
Other United Kingdom airports*	1,436,411	3,044,505	1,608,094
ALL STATE AIRPORTS	£12,321,516	£14,171,617	£1,850,101

* Aberdeen, Belfast, Bournemouth, Blackpool, Cardiff, Edinburgh, Glasgow (Renfrew), Isles of Scilly and Land's End.

AIRLINES

STATE AIRLINES

In 1962 the United Kingdom Airways Corporations, British European Airways and British Overseas Airways, together with private companies operating scheduled services, flew respectively 36,176,000, 62,849,000 and 19,111,000 aircraft miles, and carried 4,797,000, 910,000 and 2,000,000 passengers. Passenger miles flown were 1,679,386,000, 2,778,725,000 and 418,654,000 respectively. Total freight and mail ton-miles flown were 25,386,000, 96,692,000 and 23,471,000 respectively.

Air Traffic between U.K. and Abroad

Detail	1961	1962
Number of flights	190,500	192,250
By Aircraft registered in U.K.	100,500	96,131
Do. abroad	90,000	96,119
Passengers carried	6 513,000	7.317,778
In Aircraft registered in U.K.	3,412,400	3,784,992
Do. abroad	3,100,600	3,532,786

Aircraft Types

B.O.A.C.

The operational fleet of the British Overseas Airways Corporation: Bristol *Britannia* 312, 17; Douglas DC7F, 2; de Havilland *Comet* 4, 19; Boeing 707, 20. The following aircraft are on order: Vickers VC10, (1964–1965), 12; Super VC10, 30.

B.E.A.

The British European Airways Corporation had the following aircraft in service in 1963: Vickers *Vanguard* 951, 6; *Vanguard* 953, 14; Vickers *Viscount* 802, 20; *Viscount* 806, 19; D. H. *Comet IVB*, 13; Handley Page *Herald*, 3; Whitworth Gloster *Argosy*, freighter, 3; D. H. *Rapide*, 3; D. H. *Heron*, 2; *Helicopters:* Westland *Sikorsky*, S.55, 2; Bristol 171, 1; Augusta-Bell 47B3, 1; 47J, 1. New aircraft on order for B.E.A.: D.H. 121 *Trident* (80–100 seater, with speed of 600 miles per hour) 24 (1963–66); *Trident* IF (128-seater), 10; *Sikorsky* 5-6N (25-seater) twin-engined helicopter, 2.

Operating Statistics
(All U.K. Scheduled Operators)

Detail	1961	1962*
Number of stage flights	310,000	317,000
Average length (miles)	375	373
Aircraft miles flown	116,395,000	118,136,000
Passengers carried	6,851,000	7,707,000
Do. miles flown	4,531,024,000	4,876,764,000
Cargo carried (short-tons)	267,650	311 521
Freight	252 760	294 440
Mail	14,889	17 082
Load short-ton miles	559,246,000	609,304,000
Passenger	432,703,000	463,756,000
Freight	91,619,000	113,301,000
Mail	34,925,000	32,247,000

* Provisional figures

Accidents on Regular Passenger Carrying Services of U.K. Operators

	1958–1962	1962
Fatal Accidents	5	2
Passengers Killed	55	9
Passengers seriously injured	39	6
Crew killed	18	4
Crew seriously injured	4	—
Passengers carried per passenger killed	529,400	856,500
Passengers miles flown per passenger killed	348,822,400	541,893,400

INDEPENDENT AIRLINES

The following are among air transport companies operating independently in and from the United Kingdom in 1962.

BRITISH EAGLE AIRWAYS LTD., 15 Lower Regent Street, S.W.1.—Scheduled passenger and freight services; London–Bermuda, Nassau, Jamaica, Miami; London–Dinard, Luxemburg, Innsbruck, La Baule, Pisa, Rimini and Perpignan; Manchester–Bergen; Birmingham–Palma. (Boeing 707, 2; Bristol *Britannia*, 2; Vickers *Viscount*, 4; Douglas DC6C, 5).

BRITISH UNITED AIRWAYS, Portland House, Victoria Street, S.W.1. Scheduled passenger services to East, West and Central Africa, Canary Islands, Gibraltar, Spain, Netherlands, Switzerland, France and Italy; within U.K. and contract services worldwide. Helicopter operations; engineering and specialized services; aeronautical training. (Bristol *Britannia*; Vickers *Viscount*; Douglas DC6 and DC4, Handley Page *Dart Herald*, Carvair and Bristol 170, etc.).

BRITISH UNITED AIR FERRIES, Portland House, Victoria Street, S.W.1.—Scheduled services, passengers, vehicles and freight; Southend to Calais, Ostend, Rotterdam, Basle, Geneva and Strasbourg; Lydd to Ostend, Calais and Le Touquet; Hurn to Channel Islds. and Cherbourg. Passenger and Freight Charter; Livestock Carriage. (ATL 98 *Carvair*, 3; Bristol *Freighter*, 25).

DERBY AVIATION LTD., 78 Buckingham Gate, S.W.1.—Scheduled services: Derby to Belfast, Cork, Dublin, Channel Islds., I.O.M., Basle, Rotterdam and Ostend; Birmingham, Cambridge, Gloucester, Luton, Northampton–Channel Islds.; Bristol and Cardiff–Amsterdam, Barcelona, Luxemburg, Ostend and Palma; Carlisle–London (Gatwick); Birmingham–Isle of Wight and Newcastle. (21 aircraft).

FAIREY AIR SURVEYS LTD., White Waltham Aerodrome, nr. Maidenhead, Berks. Photography. (*Dakota*, D.H. *Dove*, D.H. *Rapide*, 5).

HUNTING SURVEYS LTD., 6 Elstree Way, Boreham Wood, Herts.—Air and ground survey; Photogrammetric mapping; Geophysics; Geology, etc. (*Prince*, *Dakota*, D.H. *Rapide*, *Autocar*, 8).

MANX AIRLINES LTD., Ronaldsway Airport, Ballasalla, I.O.M.—Scheduled services in U.K.; Freight; Charter; Ambulance. (*Dakota* 7).

MERCURY AIRLINES LTD., 22 Broad Street, St. Helier, Jersey.—Passenger and freight charter and scheduled services from Manchester. (D.H. *Heron* 1B, 2).

MERIDIAN AIRMAPS LTD., Commerce Way, Lancing, Sussex.—Vertical and oblique aerial photography; Photogrammetric, geophysical and geological surveys; Architectural and terrain models.

SKYWAYS COACH AIR SERVICES, LTD., 7 Berkeley Street, W.1.—Scheduled pass. services to Paris, Lyons, Tours; Vichy/Montpellier; Passenger and freight charter. (Avro 748, 3; DC3, 4).

UNITED KINGDOM AIRBORNE TRADE

The following table illustrates the steady rise during the past five years in the proportion of United Kingdom trade carried by air.

Year	Imports			Exports			Re-Exports		
	Total	Airborne		Total	Airborne		Total	Airborne	
	£'000,000	£'000,000	% of Total	£'000,000	£'000,000	% of Total	£'000,000	£'000,000	% of Total
1958	3,747·5	99·0	2·6	3,176·2	103·7	3·3	141·2	27·6	19·5
1959	3,983·4	137·4	3·4	3,330·1	142·9	4·3	130·9	24·5	18·7
1960	4,540·7	176·1	3·9	3,554·8	177·7	5·0	141·2	29·0	20·5
1961	4,397·9	202·9	4·6	3,682·4	219·7	6·0	158·5	30·1	19·0
1962	4,512·3	231·8	5·1	3,793·3	252·1	6·6	157·3	41·1	26·1

WORLD SPEED RECORDS

Air.—Lt.-Col. Robert R. Robinson (U.S. Marine Corps) achieved a maximum speed of 1,606 m.p.h. (2,585 kilometres per hour) on Nov. 22, 1961. *Women.*—Mme. Jacqueline Auriol achieved an average speed of 1148·89 m.p.h. on a closed circuit on June 22, 1962.

Land.—The late John R. Cobb, in a *Railton Mobil* achieved a speed of 394·196 m.p.h., taking 9·1325 secs. for 2 runs over a measured mile from a flying start at Bonneville Flats, Utah, on Sept. 16, 1947.

Water.—Donald Campbell averaged 260·35 m.p.h. in 2 consecutive runs over a measured kilometre (·621 miles) on Lake Coniston on May 14, 1959. Previous record, 248·62 m.p.h., Nov. 10, 1958.

ROADS

The total mileage of public roads in Great Britain is 196,135 miles, of which 167,815 are in *England and Wales* and 28,320 in *Scotland*. The roads of Great Britain are classified, and out of the total mileage of 196,135 there are 8,484 miles of Trunk Roads, 19,758 of Class I, 17,615 of Class II and 48,955 of Class III roads. The remainder are unclassified.

Highway Authorities.—The Minister of Transport became the highway authority for some 8,190 miles of road in Great Britain under the Trunk Roads Acts of 1936 and 1946 (now consolidated in the Highways Act, 1959). These roads which comprise the national system of routes for through traffic, are known as trunk roads and the Minister (in Scotland from April 1, 1956, the Secretary of State) is responsible for their maintenance and improvement. Under the Local Government Act, 1929, county councils in England and Wales became (from April 1, 1930) the highway authorities for all roads in rural districts except trunk roads, and all country roads (which include Class I, Class II and Class III Roads) outside county boroughs and metropolitan boroughs. County boroughs are responsible for all roads within their boundaries with the exception of trunk roads. Borough and urban district councils are the highway authorities for roads other than trunk roads and county roads which lie within their areas. In Scotland similar provisions have been made. In England and Wales under the Act of 1929, provision is made for borough councils and urban district councils in certain circumstances to act as highway authorities for country roads.

Grants made to Highway Authorities for the years 1962–63 amounted to £68,442,000 (provisional figure), an increase of £1,089,000 over the previous year. Payments for work carried out on trunk roads (including motorways) in England and Wales were estimated at £75,906,000, compared with £61,076,000 in the previous year. £6,424,000 was spent on trunk roads in Scotland in 1961–2.

Motorways.—The network is based on five main motorways: the Birmingham–Lancashire Motorway, the Birmingham–South Wales Motorway, the London–South Wales Motorway, the London–Yorkshire Motorway, and the Medway Towns Motorway. Shorter motorways known as the Midland Links will connect the three main motorways converging on Birmingham from London, from South Wales, and from the North-West. Other lengths of motorway are planned to radiate from London to Basingstoke, Crawley and Bishop's Stortford. On the Great North Road (A.1) motorways will bypass Stevenage, Baldock, Doncaster, Darlington and Durham; a motorway is also planned to run across the Pennines between Lancashire and Yorkshire.

In August 1963, 260 miles of motorway were open to traffic and a further 125 miles were under construction. 126 miles of motorway between London and Lancashire were in use and the remaining 34 miles of the section from the north of Birmingham to Preston were scheduled for completion before the end of the year. A continuous 48 mile motorway was also in use from the southern outskirts of Birmingham to Ross in Monmouthshire. The By-passes of Slough and Maidenhead on the London–South Wales Motorway were open and work was under way on the Chiswick to Langley and Newport By-pass sections, as well as on the huge suspension bridge over the River Severn. The Medway Towns Motorway (26 miles) was complete affording a much easier journey to the Channel Ports. 39 miles of the motorway from Crick (near Rugby) to Doncaster were also under construction, as was the 13 mile motorway By-Pass of Darlington on the Great North Road. In addition to these schemes a further 600 miles of motorway were in various stages of survey or preparation.

Trunk Roads—During 1963 a number of investigations were authorized to determine the future needs of trunk road traffic. Important traffic surveys were undertaken in the North East of England, in the Hull area and on Tees-side.

In London, the £5,000,000 Hyde Park Corner Scheme was opened to traffic in October, 1962. In the same month work was started on the Strand Underpass which, including part of the old Kingsway tram tunnel, will provide a route for light traffic in one direction between Lancaster Place and Kingsway. The underpass was expected to be completed early in 1964 at a cost of about £1,300,000. In December, 1962, a start was made on a £1,600,000 scheme to improve the southern approach to Waterloo Bridge. It will take about 2 years to complete and will include a sunken pedestrian concourse accessible by an extensive subway system to segregate pedestrians from vehicles at this very busy junction. At the northern approach to Blackfriars Bridge the construction of an east-west underpass was started in November, 1962. The work involves extending the river wall under Blackfriars Bridge and reclaiming land from the Thames. The whole scheme is estimated to cost about £3,500,000 and is due to be completed by the end of 1965. It will form part of a larger scheme for a southern by-pass of the City.

Inner Ring Road, Croydon.—Extensive redevelopment of Croydon's town centre is proceeding. A major and indispensable project is the construction of an Inner Ring Road estimated at £10,000,000. It will be built in stages and work started in January, 1962, on the first stage which includes the provision of dual carriageways in Wellesley Road and Park Lane (B.274) and the construction of a vehicular underpass at their junction with George Street in the town centre. George Street (A.232) is also being widened to give dual carriageways and the railway bridge at East Croydon Station is being considerably widened. It is estimated that this first stage will cost about £1,370,000, three quarters of which will be borne by Ministry grants, and will be comleted by December, 1964.

Outside London, work was completed on, for instance, the Hessle Road Bridge, Hull. The Birmingham, Wolverhampton, Leicester and Southampton Inner Ring Roads have been partially opened to traffic. And in Plymouth, the Laira and Tamar bridges are now completed.

Newcastle's Urban Motorway.—Commencement of work on the Pilgrim Street roundabout and the associated underpass leading to the Inner Ring Road was made in January, 1963. Further stages of the Inner Ring Road when completed will free the city centre for extensive redevelopment. The cost of the ring road will be about £6,250,000, of which the Government will be paying about £4,250,000.

Scotswood Bridge.—Work has started this year on the £2 million Scotswood Bridge scheme. The existing Scotswood Bridge, on the western outskirts of Newcastle, is narrow and can take only one line of traffic at a time: it is also weight-restricted. It is to be replaced by a new bridge carrying 24 ft. dual carriageways, and there will also be provision for future widening. The immediate approach roads will also be extensively improved.

Tyne Tunnel.—Work started in 1961 on the driving of the new road tunnel under the River Tyne between Jarrow and Howden. At present there is no vehicular crossing of the Tyne between Newcastle and the sea, except by ferries. The tunnel with its approach roads, will connect the Gateshead–Sunderland Road (A.184) to the Newcastle–Tynemouth Road (A.1058), and proposed extensions of the approach roads will provide a by-pass round the east side of the main Tyneside urban area for traffic from the Great North Road. The tunnel itself will be nearly one mile long and has a single 24 ft. carriageway within its internal diameter of 31 ft. 3 in. Separate tunnels for cyclists and pedestrians were opened in 1951 but the main scheme was deferred because of restrictions on capital expenditure on roadworks. Part of the cost will be recovered by tolls. The project will take about 5 years to complete and will cost approximately £12,500,000 towards which the Ministry of Transport is making grants and loans amounting to £9,500,000.

New Thames Road Tunnel.—The driving of a new road tunnel under the Thames, from Dartford, Kent, to Purfleet, Essex, started on March 21, 1957. The project was authorized by Acts of Parliament in 1930 and 1937 and a pilot tunnel was completed in 1938, but progress was interrupted by the war. The scheme has taken 6½ years to complete and cost about £11,000,000, of which three-quarters is to be repaid by toll revenue from 3,000,000 vehicles expected to use the tunnel each year. The tunnel and its approach roads will connect the London–Southend Road (A.13) and the London–Rochester Road (A.2), passing over or under intervening roads.

Situated in the Long Reach of the Thames, where the river is half a mile wide, the project provides for a single tunnel 4,700 feet long, carrying a roadway for two lanes of traffic. The roadway will fall from the tunnel entrances towards the river on gradients of 1 in 28 with a short section practically level underneath the river. At the lowest point in the tunnel the roadway is 100 ft. below the high water level. The tunnel is iron lined to an internal diameter of 28 ft., using some 34,000 tons of cast iron and 260,000 bolts. The existing pilot tunnel of 12 ft. diameter was dismantled as construction of the full tunnel proceeded and its lining recovered for use elsewhere. The carriageway in the tunnel, carried on a re-inforced concrete structure, will be 21 ft. wide between the kerbs, with minimum vertical head-room of 16 ft. at the kerb. Pedestrians are not admitted to the tunnel.

Duplication of Blackwall Tunnel.—In June, 1960, work started on the duplication of the road traffic tunnel under the Thames at Blackwall. The new tunnel will be about 250 yards downstream from the old one. It will have a 20 ft. carriageway and on completion in 1965 will take southbound traffic only, while the old tunnel will carry north-bound traffic. The northern approaches have been redesigned accordingly. The tunnel will cost about £6,700,000, towards which the Ministry of Transport will make a grant of about £5,000,000.

New Clyde Road Tunnel.—Work has been proceeding since June, 1957, on driving twin road tunnels under the River Clyde in Glasgow. This scheme, authorized by Act of Parliament in 1947, links A.814 at Whiteinch with A.8 at Linthouse at a total cost now estimated at more than £11,000,000. Each tunnel is designed to provide a 24 ft. carriageway with a nominal headroom of 16 ft. 6 ins. and will cater for cyclists and pedestrians below the main carriageway. The first tunnel and the immediate approaches for both tunnels have been completed and were opened to traffic on July 3, 1963, by Her Majesty the Queen. The second tunnel is expected to be ready for use by mid-1964.

New Road Bridge across the Firth of Forth.—Under powers conferred on the Forth Road Bridge Joint Board by Acts of Parliament between 1947 and 1960, a suspension bridge is being built to carry A.90 across the Firth of Forth at South Queensferry. Construction began in September, 1958, and is expected to cost about £18,500,000, of which £13,350,000 will be found by Government loan to be repaid from tolls charged for the use of the bridge. The new bridge is about half a mile upstream from the famous railway bridge and its clear centre span of 3,300 ft. will be the longest in Europe. Dual carriageways each of 24 ft. and, outside the main cables, cycle tracks and footpaths of 9 ft. and 6 ft. respectively will be provided. The main towers, rising to 500 feet above sea level, and the suspension cable anchorages were completed in 1961 and the spinning of the suspension cables by a process new on this side of the Atlantic in 1962. The bridge deck, which will carry the roadway, was being laid in 1963 and work on the construction of approach viaducts and roads on each side of the Firth was also in progress.

New Road Bridge across the River Tay.—A road bridge is being built across the River Tay between Dundee and Newport by the Tay Road Bridge Joint Board under powers conferred by Act of Parliament in 1962. The bridge, which will be 1½ miles long, will link the road system of central Dundee with A.92 near Newport. It is estimated to cost £4,500,000, of which £1,500,000 will be met by Government loan and the rest by loans from the constituent authorities of the Joint Board. Constructional work on the scheme began in March, 1963, and is expected to continue for about four years. The bridge will have dual 24 ft. carriageways, with a central footpath 10 ft. wide. It will be carried on piers supporting a series of spans, four of which have been designed to allow shipping to pass under them.

Motoring Offences.—A total of £3,365,996 in fines was paid by motorists in 1962. The number of persons charged in respect of 989,812 offences was 755,753. In addition written warnings were sent to 262,750 persons in respect of 290,379 alleged offences. Of the 755,753 persons prosecuted, 17,795 were arrested.

Convictions numbered 953,600 (against 861,548 in 1961) and a sentence of imprisonment without the option of a fine was passed on 3,392 persons for 6,984 offences. The number of motorists fined was 722,582 for 927,645 offences. Endorsement of licences numbered 298,581, of which 49,050 involved disqualification.

British Road Accident Statistics

Road accident figures were first recorded in Great Britain in 1909. In that year about 100,000 motor vehicles were licensed; and there were 1,070 fatal road accidents and 26,091 accidents resulting in non-fatal injuries, excluding those accidents attributed to pedal cycles. As the number of motor vehicles on the road increased, so did the annual casualty figures. Statistics of road accident deaths and injuries were first recorded in 1926. In that year there were 4,803 fatal and 119,484 non-fatal accidents, resulting in 4,886 deaths and 133,888 serious and slight injuries; and by then there were about 1,720,000 vehicles in use. Road casualty figures have been compiled, in increasing detail, since that time by the Ministry of Transport.

1926–1962

Year	Killed	Injured	Year	Killed	Injured
1926	4,886	133,888	1945	5,256	133,042
1927	5,329	148,575	1946	5,062	157,484
1928	6,138	164,838	1947	4,881	161,318
1929	6,696	170,917	1948	4,513	148,884
1930	7,305	177,895	1949	4,773	172,006
1931	6,691	202,119	1950	5,012	196,313
1932	6,667	206,450	1951	5,250	211,243
1933	7,202	216,328	1952	4,706	203,306
1934	7,343	231,603	1953	5,090	221,680
1935	6,502	221,726	1954†	5,010	233,271
1936	6,561	227,813	1955	5,526	262,396
1937	6,633	226,402	1056	5,367	262,593
1938	6,648	226,711	1957	5,550	268,308
1939	8,272	*	1952	5,970	293,797
1940	8,609	*	1959	6,520	326,933
1941	9,169	*	1960	6,970	340,581
1942	6,926	140,618	1961	6,908	342,859
1943	5,796	116,740	1962	6,709	334,987
1944	6,416	124,458			

* Not available.
† 30-day limit for fatalities introduced.

The accompanying table lists the total of road deaths and injuries in this country since 1926. The reporting of non-fatal injuries was suspended during the early part of the last war; and in fact during the rest of the war the reporting of slight injury cases was probably incomplete. Fatalities now exclude those occurring after 30 days. Over the years the volume of road traffic has increased steadily, particularly since the war: deaths and injuries, particularly the latter, have also tended to rise, but not to the same extent.

In 1962 there were 341,696 road casualties, including 6,709 deaths, showing reductions compared with 1961. There are 10,505,000 motor vehicles on British roads today; *i.e.* 54 vehicles per mile of road (the roads cover over 196,000 miles, one vehicle for every 33 yards, and, on average, there is a death every 78 minutes and an injury every 94 seconds. Each day 18 road users are killed and 918 injured (a quarter of them seriously). Thus, despite the alarming rise in road accidents and casualties this century, reflecting the growth of traffic in this age of the motor vehicle, the tendency has been for accident *rates* to decline steadily. Thus for example, in 1935 personal-injury accidents per 100 vehicles licensed numbered 7·6, a rate which dropped to 6·3 just before the war. Soon after the war the rate was 4·4, and by 1962 it had fallen to 2·5. To consider the death rate is even more favourable. Just after the war the number of deaths per 10,000 vehicles was over 16, whereas today the rate, having fallen rapidly in the intervening years, is down to 6·4.

Casualties in 1962

	Fatal	Serious	Slight	Total
Pedestrians	2,681	20,062	49,498	72,241
Pedal Cyclists	583	8,461	31,624	40,668
Riders of motor cycles, scooters and mopeds	1,122	20,294	49,202	70,618
Riders' passengers	201	3,962	11,832	15,995
Drivers	1,011	13,966	44,134	59,111
Drivers' passengers	1,111	17,170	64,782	83,063

Taxation of Road Vehicles

Description	Number* 1962	Gross Tax Receipts 1961–62
Mechanically propelled:—		£
Cars	6,556,000	102,720,788
Motor-cycles	1,865,700	4,055,517
Goods vehicles:—		
(*a*) Agricultural Vans and Lorries	57,500	1,017,587
(*b*) Showmen's and General Haulage	1,412,500	50,463,853
Motor Hackneys†	92,700	2,391,729
Tramcars	300	229
Tractors—		
(*a*) Agricultural, etc. (£2 10*s.* class)	452,700	1,118,286
(*b*) Showmen's and General Haulage	5,800	291,936
Exempt Vehicles	61,000	*Nil*
Trade Licences	61,100	876,653
Miscellaneous receipts (fees for driving licences, etc.)	..	4,845,584
Total	..	167,782,162

* Licences current at any time during Quarter ended Sept. 30, 1962. Since 1961 the census of road motor vehicles has been conducted on a sample basis, which accounts for the rounding of the figures. † Includes 1,500 trolley vehicles (electrically propelled).

METROPOLITAN WATER BOARD STORAGE RESERVOIRS

THAMES VALLEY

Reservoir (with date of inauguration)	Available Storage Capacity	Water Area
	Million Gallons	Acres
Queen Mary, Littleton (1925)	6,679	707
King George the Sixth, Staines (1947)	4,450	350
Queen Elizabeth II, Walton (1962)	4,300	317
Staines, North (1902)	1,584	178
Staines, South (1902)	1,749	246
Knight, Walton (1907)	454	52
Bessborough, Walton (1907)	677	74
Island Barn, East Molesey (1911)	823	121
Total	20,716,000,000 gallons	

LEA VALLEY

Reservoir (with date of inauguration)	Available Storage Capacity	Water Area
	Million Gallons	Acres
King George's, Chingford (1913)	2,729	420
William Girling, Chingford (1951)	3,493	334
Banbury, Walthamstow (1903)	625	91
Lockwood, Walthamstow (1903)	478	74
Total	7,325,000,000 gallons	

There are also 16 smaller reservoirs in the Thames Valley and 10 in the Lea Valley, the total available storage capacity of these two groups amounting to 2,063 million gallons.

OWNERSHIP AND USE OF MOTOR CARS

A series of motoring surveys was instituted by the Ministry of Transport in 1961 to provide data on the use of motor cars, which now account for more than half of total traffic on the roads. It is hoped that these surveys will provide a continuing measure of the use of motor cars and facilitate the study of vehicle mileage and passenger mileage by both car and other forms of transport. The following data are drawn from the first Motoring Survey taken in October, 1961.

It was estimated that of 6,000,000 cars licensed for private use at the time of the survey about 92 per cent. were owned by or were at the sole disposal of private households. These 5,500,000 cars, described below as *household cars*, were covered by the Motoring Survey. The remaining 8 per cent, include cars owned by car hire firms or motoring schools, or fleet cars held by firms and not placed at the sole disposal of private households, and licensed cars held by dealers. The survey showed that nearly one-third of all households in Great Britain had the use of a car in 1961; of these households, 7 per cent. had two or more cars at their disposal. Some 7 per cent. of household cars were found to be owned by the employer of a member of the household but placed solely at the employee's disposal for private as well as business use; 12 per cent. of household cars were owned by self-employed members of households and would be used for both business and private use. Cars receiving no subsidy recorded very little business use and two-thirds of the journeys recorded were not connected with work.

AGE AND SIZE OF CARS, 1962

The following table analyses by sizes and year of first registration the total of 6,556,000 cars for which licences were current during the September quarter 1962. Vehicles first registered and licensed as goods vehicles but subsequently operated and licensed as private cars are included.

thousands

Year of original registration	Cylinder capacity: Not over 1,000 c.c.	1,000 c.c. to 1,400 c.c.	1,400 c.c. to 1,800 c.c.	Over 1,800 c.c.	All capacities	Percentage in Great Britain
1962*	258	93	202	65	618	19·8 (1962–1961)
1961	302	104	192	80	679	
1960	346	89	236	97	768	21·4 (1960–1959)
1959	203	115	225	94	637	
1958	161	140	182	82	564	21·7 (1958–1956)
1957	134	125	117	64	440	
1956	110	153	83	74	420	
1955	152	169	96	92	509	20·7 (1955–1952)
1954	102	139	66	75	381	
1953	68	97	52	68	285	
1952	30	63	31	55	180	
1951	17	41	20	44	123	8·6 (1951–1947)
1950	16	35	22	44	117	
1949	22	52	21	37	131	
1948	17	29	17	26	89	
1947	31	41	19	13	104	
1946 or earlier†	204	208	67	32	510	7·8
Total	2,173	1,693	1,648	1,042	6,556	100·0

* Up to September 30. † These cars were classified by horsepower and the c.c. equivalents are approximations.

MILEAGES

17 per cent. of all household cars in Great Britain were located in Greater London. A week's mileage recorded during the survey in 1961 showed an average of 117 and drivers estimated their annual mileage at 8,400, compared with a national average of 135 recorded miles per week and a national estimate of 8,800 miles annually.

Mileage by age of car

	Percentage of all household cars	Recorded week's mileage October 1961	Driver's estimate of annual mileage
1961 (up to October)	9	211	15,500
1960	12	183	11,300
1959	11	166	10,000
1958	9	142	8,900
1957	7	121	7,600
1956–52	32	113	7,400
1951–47	11	106	6,200
1946 and earlier	9	84	5,600
All years	100	135	8,800

Mileage by size of car

	Percentage of all household cars	Recorded week's mileage October 1961	Driver's estimate of annual mileage
Up to 1,000 c.c.	36	136	8,900
Over 1,000 c.c. to 1,250 c.c.	22	119	7,400
Over 1,250 c.c. to 1,500 c.c.	18	152	9,200
Over 1,500 c.c. to 2,000 c.c.	11	136	10,000
Over 2,000 c.c. to 2,500 c.c.	8	125	8,300
Over 2,500 c.c.	5	163	10,300
All sizes	100	135	8,800

Purpose and Length of Journey—A sample consisting of 15,284 car journeys showed that 38 per cent. had been made to or from work, the national average length of journey being 5·5 miles; in the London area the percentage was 29 for this purpose. 16 per cent. of journeys were made in the course of employment (average mileage, 12·8), in the London area 20 per cent. 46 per cent. of all car journeys had no connection with work (average mileage, 9·8); in the London area 51 per cent. of journeys were not connected with work. The average length of all car journeys recorded in the survey was 8·6 miles.

Occupancy of Cars—It was found that on 52 per cent. of all journeys (45 per cent. of all mileage) by household cars there was one person in the car for half or more of the journey; on 31 per cent. of all journeys there were 2 persons in the car; and on 17 per cent. of all journeys, 3 or more persons. On 64 per cent. of journeys made to or from work, 77 per cent. of journeys in the course of employment and 33 per cent. of journeys not connected with work there was one person in the car. The average rate of occupancy of cars was 1·93 persons—on journeys to or from work, 1·54; in the course of employment, 1·35; and on other journeys, 2·39 persons per car.

OWNERSHIP AND SUBSIDY BY EMPLOYERS

81 per cent. of all household cars were owned by private persons other than self-employed and 28 per cent. of their weekly mileage was run on journeys mainly to or from work and 12 per cent. in the course of employment. 52 per cent. of their week's mileage was not connected with work. 12 per cent. of all household cars were owned by self-employed persons and ran 53 per cent. of their week's mileage in the course of employment. 7 per cent. of household cars were owned by firms and did 55 per cent. of their week's mileage in the course of employment.

Where employers subsidized the running costs of household cars wholly or in part, 47 per cent. of the week's mileage was run in the course of employment, 30 per cent. on journeys not connected with work and 23 per cent. on journeys to or from work. 6 per cent. of household cars had their running costs covered by employers to the extent of three-quarters or more, 2 per cent. had half to three-quarters covered and 7 per cent. had less than half their running costs covered by employers.

Ownership and Subsidy—By size and age. percentages

	Household cars owned by		Degree of subsidy		
	Firms	Private persons	All or part of running costs paid by an employer	Owner self-employed	Cars not subsidized by employer
Cylinder capacity					
Up to 1,000	39	35	45	17	37
1,001 to 1,500	33	41	36	42	40
1,501 to 2,000	15	11	9	13	12
2,001 and over	13	13	10	28	11
	100	100	100	100	100
Year of original registration					
1961* to 1957	93	45	73	64	40
1956 to 1952	5	33	21	29	34
1951 to 1947	2	12	4	6	14
1946 or earlier	—	10	2	1	12
	100	100	100	100	100

* Up to October 1961.

LIFE ASSURANCE AND FIRE AND GENERAL INSURANCE

LIFE ASSURANCE

THE list on the following two pages contains the names of all the more important British Life offices, and of Commonwealth companies (marked C), all of which transact business in this country.

CLASS OF BUSINESS.—The second column shows whether the company is conducted on the Mutual system whereby the whole of the divisible profit is allotted to participating policy-holders (M), or whether the company has proprietors by whom part (usually a very small proportion) of such profit is received (P). Life offices transacting other insurance business are marked (O) in this column. In such cases the Life funds are kept separately, and are not liable for the claims of other departments. The Share Capital is usually liable for the claims of all branches. Those having an Industrial branch are indicated by letter (I).

FIGURES.—These are taken from the latest annual accounts available at date of going to press, and in the majority of cases refer to annual reports for the financial year ended December 31, 1962.

LIFE FUNDS.—The amounts of these funds, though interesting, are not in themselves a sufficient indication of the financial stability of a company, which cannot be judged unless liabilities are actuarially compared with assets.

PREMIUM INCOME.—The annual premium income is in all cases stated after deduction of the amount paid to other companies for reassuring parts of the risks.

CONSIDERATION FOR ANNUITIES.—These are the amounts received to provide various types of Annuities.

EXPENSES.—The expenses of a Life office include in all cases where paid, commission to agents. The amount of expenses is less important in itself than in relation to premium income, consequently the percentage of the premium income absorbed in expenses is shown. The average percentage of British offices is about 16½%, of which about 5½% is expended on commission and 11% on other expenses. This ratio taken by itself is frequently misleading, because, if the proportion of new business is large, the percentage of the total premiums absorbed in expenses may legitimately be higher than where the new business is small. Moreover, where rates of premium are below the average any comparisons of percentage should be considered, with due regard to this feature, a gain to the policy holder through reduced premium being equivalent to an immediate cash bonus.

INTEREST.—The rate of interest earned is important for comparison with the rate assumed in valuing liabilities, since the greater the margin between these rates the greater is the surplus available from this source for bonus. The rate of interest given is before deduction of Income Tax except where marked (N)—net.

VALUATIONS.—The valuation returns which are required to be made by the companies to the Board of Trade indicate liability under existing policies, after making allowance for the amounts to be paid and received. It is assumed that deaths will occur in accordance with a mortality table (various tables are used), and that interest will be earned at a certain rate. If a company assumes that it will earn a high rate of interest in the future the net liability will appear less than if it assumes a low rate, while the liability on account of mortality appears greater by some tables than by others. The position of an office is most satisfactory when a stringent basis of valuation is adopted, because the margin between the calculated and experienced liability is larger and the surplus available for bonuses is greater. The lower the rate of interest assumed the more stringent is the valuation. The foregoing remarks, however, do not apply in the case of an office which has adopted a Bonus Reserve Valuation.

FIRE INSURANCE RATES

MOST large fire offices belong to the tariff association, charging identical rates of premium. There are, however, a number of non-tariff offices which claim to assess individual risks independently on merits. Tariff rates of premium per £100 insured against fire for the more common classes of risk are as follows:—

Private Dwelling Houses, built of brick or stone and tiled or slated and in no hazardous proximity 1*s*. 6*d*.

Household goods therein, usually 2*s*.

A number of companies issue "comprehensive" policies embracing in one contract all risks incidental to private houses and contents.

Shops and Warehouses, similarly built and circumstanced, in which no hazardous goods are deposited nor hazardous trades carried on, from 3*s*. 6*d*.

Stock and Utensils in trade fixtures, and household furniture in such shops and warehouses, from 3*s*. 6*d*.

Most fire insurance companies transact accident (including Motor) and miscellaneous business, and if a strong company be selected it will probably be found to the advantage of an insurer that he should effect with it all such policies as he may require, in place of dividing them amongst several companies. The "comprehensive" policies, previously referred to, combine in one contract protection against damage by fire to the contents of a house, or from burglary, housebreaking, larceny, theft, etc., and insurance against domestic servants' employers' liability, damage from storm or tempest, third party risks, and other hazards. This can usually be arranged for an annual premium of 5*s*. per £100 of the full value of the contents of the house. Fire insurance of the house itself is not included, however, in this estimate, but can be included under the same policy, if desired. The advantage of a policy of this description is that it obviates the inconvenience of payments of small amounts in insurance premiums at different dates, and that in one comprehensive form it supplies protection at a moderate cost for all a householder's ordinary insurance requirements.

NOTE.—As Insurance is highly technical, particularly where business risks are involved, the advice and assistance of a qualified Insurance Broker can be utilized with considerable advantage.

PRINCIPAL LIFE ASSURANCE COMPANIES

Established	Class	Name of Office	Annual Accounts: Life & Annuity Funds	Annual Accounts: Life Premium Income	Annual Accounts: Consideration for Annuities	Annual Accounts: % of Expenses to Prems:	Annual Accounts: Rate of Interest Earned	Interest % assumed at Valuation
			£	£	£		£ s. d.	£
1824	PO	Alliance	50,499,738	3,810,165	1,151,905	—	6 2 9	2¼
1808	PO	Atlas	53,065,962	5,419,352	537,852	12·0	6 15 6	2¼ & 2½
1849	M	Australian Mutual (C)	466,323,407	50,543,763	1,059,033	15·15	5 19 5	2½
1925	PO	Avon	1,056,355	166,704	76,998	12·45	6 12 4	2½
1883	PO	Beacon	13,688,272	1,750,514	134,315	25·84	5 15 10	2¼
1839	PIO	Blackburn (Ord.)	2,552,997	374,275	—	15·9	5 14 1	2½
1866	PIO	Britannic (Ord.)	51,499,494	5,571,471	102,622	14·53	6 11 1	2½
1920	PO	British National	1,559,458	178,521	171,777	42·5	7 1 2	2½
1805	PO	Caledonian	28,616,375	2,296,503	2,801,928	13·4	5 14 3	2¼ & 2½
1847	M	Canada Life (C)	277,342,966	25,159,164	9,059,883	—	5 13 1	1¾ to 4
1862	MI	City of Glasgow	1,364,737	197,100	—	11·2	4 10 9	2½
1824	P	Clerical, Medical & Gen.	46,597,647	4,175,456	2,191,375	—	7 0 2	2½
1873	MO	Colonial Mutual (C)..£A.	216,418,438	29,578,269	7,723,480	17·08	5 13 5(N)	2½ to 4½
1861	PO	Commercial Union	95,037,632	7,667,202	4,290,151	11·6	6 7 3	3 & 4
1871	P	Confederation (C)	161,014,346	17,066,069	2,915,005	—	5 8 10(N)	2¼ to 3½
1867	MIO	Co-operative (Ord.)	109,617,349	13,075,298	87,681	14·8	6 0 6	2½
1900	P	Crown Life†	121,781,204	17,719,823	3,361,080	—	5 10 10	2½ to 3½
1899	PO	Crusader	12,959,747	2,380,022	258,006	26·13	6 1 1	2½ & 3
1904	PO	Eagle Star*	183,647,519	20,114,383	2,361,772	9·86	5 9 3	2½
1887	PO	Ecclesiastical*	1,548,189	123,654	40,412	7·62	4 17 7	2 & 2½
1901	PO	Economic	1,386,443	153,436	55,137	11·43	5 10 7	2½
1762	M	Equitable	46,149,604	3,807,560	733,504	7·6	6 5 6	3¾ Bonus Reserve
1844	P	Equity & Law	99,477,511	10,058,639	4,580,664	17·2	7 13 4	2½ & 2¾
1925	M	Federation Mutual	562,737	86,413	5,439	6·73	5 17 7	2 & 2¾
1832	M	Friends Prov. & Cent.	112,794,057	9,372,008	8,005,783	16·81	6 7 0	2½*
1837	P	General	31,147,022	4,533,459	199,168	16·07	6 0 0	2½
1848	P	Gresham	35,156,724	4,755,732	113,254	24·35	5 3 6(N)	2½ & 2¾
1821	PO	Guardian	95,846,159	9.086,265	13,254,564	—	6 15 5	2¼ & 2½
1932	PO	Ideal†	1,197,875	147,221	2,039	14·2	4 5 5	3
1897	P	Imperial Life of Can. (C)	109,636,245	10,520,585	1,883,366	26·0	5 8 10(N)	2½ & 3
1939	PI	Irish Life	21,176,580	2,584,520	379,562	13·44	5 5 3	2½, 3 & 4
1806	PO	Law Union & Rock	28,020,160	2,133,312	980,415	16·31	4 19 2(N)	2¾
1836	PO	Legal & General	503,079,100	60,030,049	2,450,553	14·30	5 13 3(N)	2½ to 4
1890	PO	Licenses & General	6,247,080	697,052	624,919	—	6 8 0	2½
1838	P	Life Assoc. of Scotland	16,765,733	1,893,482	725,257	15·7	6 3 7	2½
1836	PO	L'pool, Lond. & Globe	39,696,680	2,341,243	1,592,118	11·44	4 16 1	2¼
1843	MI	Liverpool Victoria	36,552,033	4,046,858	—	14·09	5 7 0	3 Bonus Reserve
1869	PIO	London & Manch. (Ord.)	39,968,028	4,313,567	29,838	18·04	7 6 2	2½
1720	PO	London Assurance	38,449,745	3,385,590	1,110,110	17·55	6 7 0	2¼
1806	M	London Life	58,232,894	4,550,562	1,936,476	8·02	6 7 9	3+ 3¼ Bonus Reserve
1887	P	Manufacturers Life (C)	391,243,271	32,426,072	18,435,486	—	5 13 0(N)	2½ to 4
1852	M	Marine & General	12,611,790	1,456,197	6,935	25·1	6 10 11	2½
1884	M	Medl, Sickness Ann. & Life	7,347,884	700,254	45,160	14·47	4 18 4(N)	2½
1898	PO	Midland Employers	9,084,399	1,135,957	28,791	13·0	6 2 10	2½ & 2¾
1886	PI	Mutual Life & Citizens	176,782,258	22,181,032	31,329	15·61	5 18 6	3
1890	M	Natl. & Local Govt. Offrs.	2,266,184	208,904	—	6·0	5 9 7	2½
1935	P	Natl. Employers Life	2,479,534	945,686	127,027	27·9	4 16 5	3¼
1910	MO	Natl. Farmers Union	22,356,893	2,233,800	726,611	11·68	6 2 7	2½ & 3
1830	M	Natl. Mutual	23,085,100	2,175,435	1,834,086	16·7	6 1 8	4 Bonus Reserve
1869	M	Natl.Mut.of Austr.(C)*.£A	227,495,855	28,703,283	79,440	10·9	5 10 9(N)	2½ & 3
1835	M	National Provident	50,041,547	4,751,185	1,730,341	18·42	6 17 11	2½
1925	PI	New Ireland (Ord.)	10,965,765	1,421,485	3,058	14·80	6 0 3	3 & 3½
1823	PO	North. Brit. & Merc.	91,486,074	4,483,043	3,914,095	9·0	5 18 3	2½
1836	PO	Northern	63,560,902	6,183,344	3,388,292	—	6 16 7	2¼ & 2¾
1808	M	Norwich Union Life	253,790,789	31,927,229	4,625,704	18·4	6 2 2	2½
1864	PIO	Pearl	139,655,536	17,609,138	377,970	21·07	7 6 8	2½
1782	PO	Phoenix	65,490,427	6,413,420	292,507	21·15	6 6 1	2¼
1891	PI	Pioneer* (Ord.)	2,284,244	400,323	28,985	34·54	6 6 2(N)	2 & 2¾
1877	P	Prov. Life Assoc. of Ldn.	29,382,537	3,042,329	1,341,056	25·9	5 3 9	2½
1840	M	Provident Mutual	33,617,840	4,606,000	589,634	18·84	6 14 11	3¼ Bonus Reserve
1848	PIO	Prudential (Ord.)	636,812,295	84,080,488	3,141,869	16·4	6 12 6	2½

PRINCIPAL LIFE ASSURANCE COMPANIES—*continued*

Estab-lished	Class	Name of Office	Annual Accounts: Life & Annuity Funds	Life Premium Income	Considera-tion for Annuities	% of Ex-penses to Prems:	Rate of Interest Earned	Interest % assumed at Valuation
			£	£	£		£ s. d.	£
1864	PIO	Refuge (Ord.)	87,721,970	10,382,697	158,396	14·10	6 4 8	2½
1911	MI	Reliance Mutual (Ord.)	1,299,321	314,176	3,958	35·6	4 15 6(N)	2½ & 2¾
1845	PO	Royal*	150,436,153	10,565,158	6,625,203	14·27	4 19 0	2¼
1720	PO	Royal Exchange	48,154,972	4,774,839	2,602,854	16·33	6 19 11	2½
1850	M	Royal Liver	18,429,210	2,223 455	—	13·80	5 4 2	2½
1861	MIO	Royal London	48,589,280	5,237,777	7,450	18·01	6 15 6	2¼
1867	PI	Salvation Army	7,284,417	773,414	5,000	19·96	4 5 11	2½
1826	M	Scottish Amicable	107,763,712	13,916,533	355,845	13·04	6 3 2	2½
1831	M	Scottish Equitable	33,835,502	3,498,108	550,073	20·71	6 13 6	2¼
1852	MI	Scottish Legal	1,896,567	260,176	—	37·63	5 16 5	2½ & 3
1881	P	Scottish Life	36,705,976	4,631,568	697,999	18·41	6 14 3	2½
1883	MO	Scottish Mutual	25,459,112	2,915,673	589,646	17·34	6 18 4	2½
1837	M	Scottish Provident	68,414,632	6,100,759	2,781,635	12·57	6 18 4	2½
1824	PO	Scottish Union & Natl.	39,434,081	3,901,306	257,400	16·86	6 14 6	2½
1815	M	Scottish Widows	180,797,152	16,456,058	4,176,900	11·6	6 18 11	2¼
1904	P	Sentinel*	2,204,661	684,261	24,025	25·51	—	3¾
1825	M	Standard*	362,216,561	41,795,817	6,010,285	9·37	6 4 4	2
1810	P	Sun Life	190,663,708	24,386,628	7,930,928	12·93	6 2 8	2¼, 2½, 2¾
1865	M	Sun Life of Canada (C)	766,512,726	58,418,259	12,019,640	—	4 18 10(N)	2½, 3 & 3½
1936	M	Teachers*	3,337,466	444,241	—	14·5	6 0 5	2 & 2½
1839	M	Tunstall & District	1,961,478	123,318	—	11·38	5 2 0	2½
1908	P	United Friendly	3,973,224	836,302	—	24·68	6 5 5	3
1804	M	United Kingdom Prov.	67,677,894	6,043,478	1,113,929	14·5	6 16 6	2¼ & 2½
1825	P	University	5,887,619	763,949	474,979	7·1	6 3 2	3¾ Bonus Reserve
1841	MIO	Wesleyan & General	18,952,319	2,218,788	70,747	15·69	6 0 2	2¾
1824	PO	Yorkshire	71,026,506	7,326,954	2,458,447	18·48	6 3 5	2¾

INDUSTRIAL COMPANIES

Estab-lished	Class	Name of Office	Life Funds	Life Premium Income	%of Ex-penses to Prems.	Rate of Interest Earned	Interest assumed at Valuation
1839	PO	Blackburn	9,556,938	1,266,869	36·9	6 2 10	2½
1866	PO	Britannic	81,264,452	11,340,658	30·56	6 13 10	2½
1862	M	City of Glasgow	5,397,259	701,558	32·2	4 10 9	2½
1867	MO	Co-operative	177,382,510	30,685,624	28·1	6 0 6	3
1939	P	Irish Life	16,076,995	2,991,995	34·2	5 4 1	3
1843	M	Liverpool Victoria	161,568,293	20,472,754	31·31	5 8 4	2½
1869	PO	London & Manchester	38,938,142	47,47,616	31·70	7 6 5	2½
1925	P	New Ireland	5,355,705	1,738,300	40·4	7 0 10	3½
1864	PO	Pearl	175,773,040	25,273,166	30·67	7 7 7	2½
1891	P	Pioneer	1,594,013	239,570	43·75	6 0 3	2¾
1848	PO	Prudential	532,507,632	66,360,824	29·99	6 18 2	2½
1864	PO	Refuge	86,645,344	12,597,142	30·10	6 8 10	3
1911	M	Reliance Mutual	2,545,014	520,247	39·17	4 15 6	2¾
1850	M	Royal Liver	78,308,348	10,387,141	35·14	5 3 5	2½ & 3
1861	MO	Royal London	114,513,537	12,360,746	36·42	6 17 4	2¼
1867	P	Salvation Army	15,435,775	2,123,007	35·40	5 4 6	2½
1852	M	Scottish Legal	23,234,648	2,485,926	67·95	4 12 7	2½ to 3¼
1841	MO	Wesleyan & General	21,112,563	3,057,663	36·15	6 2 9	3

C—Commonwealth Office. † 1961 figures.
* Eagle Star—Including funds of acquired businesses.
* Ecclesiastical—Year ending Feb 28, 1963.
* Friends Prov. & Cent.—Discounting 2¾% net prems.
* Nat. Mut. of Austrl. Year ending Sept. 30, 1962.
* Pioneer—Year ending March 31, 1963.
* Royal—Including figures of associated companies.
* Sentinel—Year ending March 31, 1962.
* Standard—Year ending Nov. 15, 1962.
* Teachers—year ending Sept. 30, 1962.

LIFE ASSURANCES IN FORCE

British Life Assurance Statistics show that 11,300,000 ordinary assurance policies to the amount of £11,600,000,000 were in force at the end of 1962, with total yearly premiums of £340,000,000. The 1961 figures include the Ordinary Branch business of Friendly Societies.

IMMEDIATE ANNUITIES (payable half-yearly, in arrear) FOR EVERY £100 PAID.

	Males				Females			
	Age 50	Age 60	Age 65	Age 70	Age 50	Age 60	Age 65	Age 70
	£ s. d.	£ s. d.	£ s. d.	£ s. d.	£ s. d.	£ s. d.	£ s. d.	£ s. d.
Alliance	7 17 8	9 12 10	11 1 8	13 2 6	7 7 3	8 13 4	9 14 7	11 5 0
Atlas*	7 15 3	9 9 10	10 18 4	12 19 0	7 5 1	8 10 5	9 11 5	11 1 6
Avon*	7 15 10	9 12 10	11 3 4	13 6 10	7 5 0	8 12 2	9 14 7	11 6 9
Beacon	7 16 4	9 15 4	11 4 5	13 6 0	7 6 2	8 15 7	9 16 10	11 7 7
Britannic*	7 19 10	9 14 11	11 3 11	13 5 5	7 9 8	8 15 2	9 16 5	11 7 2
British National*	7 17 5	9 15 7	11 6 4	13 9 0	7 6 0	8 14 5	9 17 4	11 8 4
Caledonian*	7 10 6	9 6 3	10 15 7	12 17 5	6 19 11	8 6 4	9 7 11	10 18 11
Canada Life	6 17 5	8 14 2	10 2 10	12 3 7	6 6 0	7 13 11	8 15 10	10 6 2
City of Glasgow	7 7 10	9 5 10	10 15 2	12 16 5	6 11 6	8 4 3	9 7 3	11 1 1
Clerical, Medical & General*	7 19 4	9 15 4	11 5 2	13 7 6	7 8 10	8 15 2	9 17 0	11 8 6
Commercial Union	7 18 2	9 14 1	11 3 8	13 5 11	7 7 8	8 14 0	9 15 9	11 7 0
Co-operative Ins.	7 17 2	9 13 0	11 2 8	13 5 0	7 6 8	8 12 10	9 14 8	11 6 0
Crown Life	7 4 0	8 17 5	10 3 8	12 10 8	6 11 1	7 16 5	8 17 5	10 6 7
Crusader	7 6 11	9 9 11	10 19 5	13 1 5	6 17 0	8 9 11	9 11 7	11 2 8
Eagle Star*	8 1 3	9 16 10	11 6 1	13 8 1	7 9 10	8 15 9	9 17 4	11 8 4
Ecclesiastical	7 17 2	9 13 6	11 3 8	13 6 8	7 6 6	8 13 2	9 15 2	11 7 0
Equitable*	7 19 7	9 15 8	11 5 6	13 8 1	7 9 2	8 15 5	9 17 2	11 8 10
Equity & Law*	7 12 4	9 7 4	10 15 10	12 16 6	7 4 0	8 11 6	9 14 0	11 6 7
Friends Prov. & Cent.*	7 17 4	9 12 8	11 2 0	13 4 0	7 7 0	8 12 8	9 14 4	11 5 4
General Life*	7 13 10	9 11 8	11 3 0	13 2 4	7 0 10	8 7 0	9 8 4	10 19 0
Gresham*	7 19 4	9 15 0	11 4 8	13 6 8	7 8 0	8 14 4	9 15 8	11 6 8
Guardian*	7 10 6	9 6 3	10 15 7	12 17 5	6 19 11	8 6 4	9 7 11	10 18 11
Irish Life*	7 16 9	9 14 7	11 4 7	13 7 5	7 3 3	8 1 1	9 9 4	11 1 0
Law Union & Rock	7 19 10	9 15 6	11 4 8	13 6 4	7 9 2	8 15 8	9 17 4	11 8 2
Legal & General*	7 19 4	9 15 0	11 4 8	13 6 8	7 8 0	8 14 4	9 15 8	11 6 8
Licenses & General*	7 10 6	9 6 3	10 15 7	12 17 5	6 19 11	8 6 4	9 7 11	10 18 11
Life Assoc. of Scotland*	7 12 8	9 8 10	10 18 2	13 0 2	7 2 4	8 8 10	9 10 6	11 1 8
Liverpool & London & Globe	7 19 10	9 15 6	11 4 8	13 6 4	7 9 2	8 15 8	9 17 4	11 8 2
London & Manchester	7 6 2	9 4 2	10 13 7	12 15 7	6 15 10	8 4 3	9 5 10	10 16 10
London Assurance	7 16 4	9 15 4	11 4 5	13 6 0	7 6 2	8 15 7	9 16 10	11 7 7
London Life*	7 13 3	9 9 7	10 19 7	13 2 10	7 2 5	8 9 3	9 11 7	11 3 3
Manufacturers	7 4 6	8 17 4	10 4 4	12 2 8	6 12 5	7 17 9	8 19 8	10 11 5
Marine & General*	7 18 0	9 12 6	11 1 0	13 2 0	7 8 0	8 13 0	9 14 0	11 4 6
Medl. Sickness An. & Life	7 17 0	9 12 5	11 1 9	13 3 7	7 6 8	8 12 7	9 14 0	11 5 0
Midland Employers' Mutual	7 11 10	9 8 0	10 17 10	13 0 2	7 1 4	8 7 10	9 9 8	11 1 2
Natl. Employers Life	7 11 8	9 10 4	11 2 8	13 9 8	6 18 4	8 4 8	9 6 8	10 18 4
National Farmers Union*	7 15 10	9 12 10	11 3 4	13 6 10	7 5 0	8 12 2	9 14 7	11 6 9
National Mutual	7 12 3	9 7 11	10 17 3	12 18 11	7 1 9	8 8 0	9 9 7	11 0 6
Natl. Mut. of Austr.	7 2 2	9 5 0	10 14 4	12 16 2	6 11 6	8 0 6	9 6 6	10 17 6
National Provident*	7 14 0	9 9 0	10 18 0	12 19 0	7 3 0	8 9 0	9 11 0	11 1 0
North British & Mercantile	7 18 2	9 14 1	11 3 8	13 5 11	7 7 8	8 14 0	9 15 9	11 7 0
Northern*	8 1 1	9 16 6	11 5 9	13 7 6	7 10 10	8 16 7	9 18 1	11 9 0
Norwich Union Life*	7 19 11	9 17 1	11 5 9	13 6 9	7 8 10	8 16 7	9 17 7	11 7 11
Pearl*	7 13 6	9 9 2	10 18 6	13 0 8	7 3 2	8 9 2	9 10 8	11 1 10
Phoenix	7 17 8	9 13 0	11 2 2	13 3 8	7 7 2	8 13 4	9 14 8	11 5 8
Pioneer	8 2 0	9 19 0	11 9 0	13 13 0	7 12 0	8 18 0	10 0 0	11 12 0
Prov. Life Assoc. of London	7 16 4	9 11 10	11 1 0	13 2 6	7 5 10	8 12 0	9 13 6	11 4 4
Provident Mutual	7 15 7	9 9 8	10 17 10	12 8 1	7 5 7	8 10 6	9 11 2	11 0 11
Prudential*	7 18 0	9 14 0	11 4 0	13 6 0	7 8 0	8 14 0	9 16 0	11 8 0
Refuge	7 6 0	9 2 4	10 12 0	12 14 8	6 15 8	8 2 0	9 4 0	10 15 8
Reliance	7 14 10	9 5 2	11 0 0	13 2 0	7 4 5	8 10 5	9 12 0	11 3 3
Royal	7 19 10	9 15 6	11 4 8	13 6 4	7 9 2	8 15 8	9 17 4	11 8 2
Royal Exchange*	7 15 3	9 9 10	10 18 4	12 19 0	7 5 1	8 10 5	9 11 5	11 1 6
Royal London*	7 19 0	9 14 0	11 3 0	13 4 0	7 9 0	8 14 0	9 15 0	11 6 0
Scottish Amicable*	7 3 0	8 19 0	10 8 7	12 10 7	6 12 5	7 19 0	9 0 10	10 12 0
Scottish Equitable*	7 17 4	9 12 2	11 0 10	13 1 6	7 7 2	8 12 10	9 13 10	11 4 0
Scottish Life	7 18 0	9 13 6	11 2 10	13 5 0	7 7 8	8 13 6	9 15 2	11 6 2
Scottish Mutual*	7 16 2	9 13 8	11 4 2	13 7 4	7 3 8	8 11 8	9 14 4	11 6 6
Scottish Provident	7 18 2	9 13 9	11 3 2	13 5 5	7 7 9	8 13 9	9 15 5	11 6 6
Scottish Union & Natl.*	7 19 11	9 17 1	11 5 9	13 6 9	7 8 10	8 16 7	9 17 7	11 7 11
Scottish Widows*	7 15 3	9 10 7	10 19 11	13 1 11	7 5 0	8 10 9	9 12 2	11 3 2
Sentinel	7 18 0	9 17 0	11 7 0	13 11 0	7 9 0	8 16 0	9 18 0	11 10 0
Standard*	7 18 0	9 13 0	11 3 0	13 5 0	7 8 0	8 13 0	9 15 0	11 5 0
Sun Life*	7 12 0	9 8 0	10 18 0	13 0 4	7 1 4	8 8 0	9 9 8	11 1 4
United Kingdom*	7 15 10	9 11 0	11 0 0	13 1 6	7 5 8	8 11 3	9 12 7	11 3 3
University*	7 17 2	9 14 10	11 5 7	13 9 2	7 6 5	8 14 0	9 16 0	11 8 10
Wesleyan & General	7 17 4	9 12 4	11 0 10	13 1 10	7 7 0	8 12 10	9 14 0	11 4 4
Yorkshire	7 19 0	9 14 0	11 3 0	13 3 0	7 9 0	8 14 0	9 16 0	11 6 0

Note P.P.—Purchase Price. *Increase in rate of Annuity as shown. Atlas—2*s.*% for amount of P.P. which exceeds £2,000. Avon—2*s* 6*d.*% if P.P. £2,500 or over. Britannic—2*s.*% if P.P. £5,000 or over. British National—3*s.*% if P.P. exceeds £2,000. If less than £1,000 deduct £1 from Annuity. Caledonian—2*s*.% if P.P. £1,000–£2,499. 3*s*.% £2,500–£4,999 4*s*.% £5,000 or over. Clerical Med. & Gen.—Minimum P.P. £500. Deduct £2 10*s*. 0*d*. per contract. Eagle Star—Deduct £2 10*s*. 0*d*. per contract. Equitable—4*s*.% if P.P. not less than £10,000. Equity & Law—2*s*. 6*d*.% if P.P. £2,500 or over. Friends Prov. & Cent.—2*s*.% if P.P. £5,000–£9,999. 4*s*.% £10,000 or over. General Life—Increased if P.P. £3,000 or over. Gresham—2*s*.% for amount of P.P. which exceeds £1,500. Guardian—4*s*.% if P.P. £1,000–£2,499. 6*s*.% £2,500–£4,999. 8*s*.% £5,000 or over. Irish Life—Rates for P.P. of at least £2,000. Legal & General—Rates improved if P.P. exceeds £1,500. Licenses & General—Increased according to amount of P.P. Life Assoc. of Scotland—2*s*. 6*d*. % if P.P. £10,000 or over. London Life—2*s*.% if P.P. £5,000 or over. Marine & Genl.—1*s*.% if P.P. not less than £2,500. 2*s*. 6*d*.% £5,000 or over. Natl. Farmers Union—2*s*. 6*d*.% if P.P. £2,500 or over. Natl. Provident—1% if P.P. £5,000 or over. Northern—Rates for P.P. of £10,000 or over. If less than £10,000 deduct £1 from Annuity. Norwich Union—Deduct £4 from Annuity if P.P. in excess of £2,000. Rate reduced by 4*s*. if less than £2,000. Pearl—3*s*.% if P.P. £2,500–£4,999. 6*s*.% £5,000 or over. Prudential—Deduct £1 10*s*. 6*d*. per contract if P.P. £500 or over. 6*s*.% if less than £500. Royal Exchange—2*s*.% for amount of P.P. which exceeds £2,000. Royal London—Add £1 per contract for any amount of P.P. Scottish Amicable—Rates are for £1,000 P.P. Scottish Equitable—Increased for larger P.P. Scottish Mutual—Deduct 10*s*. from Annual Annuity. Scottish Union & Natl.—Deduct £4 from Annuity if P.P. £2,000 or more. Rate reduced by 4*s*. if less than £2,000. Scottish Widows—Deduct £1 5*s*. 0*d*. per contract if P.P. £500 or over. 5*s*.% if less than £500. Standard—Deduct £1 5*s*. 0*d*. per contract. Sun Life—4*s*.% if P.P. £5,000 or over. United Kingdom—2*s*.% if P.P. £5,000 or over. University—Deduct £2 per contract.

BONUSES

The following table gives examples of Bonus last declared on Whole Life and Endowment Assurances for £100. In each case the rate given is in respect of a policy effected at age 30 next birthday, and the Endowment Bonus is based on a Policy maturing at age 60.

Office	Last* Valuation	Bonus declared on Whole Life Assurances	Bonus declared on Endowment Assurances	Interim Bonus
Alliance	1958	£2/6/0 compound	£2/6/0 compound	£2/10/0 compound
Atlas	1961*	£2/15/0 compound*	£2/15/0 compound*	£2/15/0 compound
Australian Mutual	1962A	£2/9/0 compound	£2/5/0 compound	At rate last declared
Avon	1958	£2/0/0	£2/0/0	£2/15/0
Beacon	1962*	£3/5/0	£3/5/0	£2/15/0
Blackburn	1962A	£2/10/0	£2/10/0	£2/10/0
Britannic	1962A	£2/14/0	£2/14/0	£2/14/0
British National Life	1962	£2/5/0	£2/5/0	£2/5/0
Caledonian	1962*	£3/10/0*	£3/6/0*	At rate last declared
Canada Life	1962A	Vary with age,	plan and duration	Allowed on death after first year
City of Glasgow Friendly	1959	£1/8/0	£1/8/0	£1/8/0
Clerical, Medical & Gen.	1960	£3/5/0	£3/5/0	£3/5/0
Colonial Mutual	1962	£2/14/0 compound	£2/10/0 compound	At rate last declared
Commercial Union	1960*	£2/15/0 compound	£2/15/0 compound	£2/18/0 compound
Confederation	1962	Vary	with age, plan and	duration
Co-operative	1962A	£2/12/0	£2/12/0	£2/12/0
Crusader*	1962A	£3/5/0	£2/15/0	At rate last declared
Eagle Star	1960*	£2/15/0	£2/15/0	£2/15/0
Ecclesiastical	1959*	£2/15/0 compound	£2/15/0 compound	£2/15/0 compound
Economic	1960	£2/10/0 compound	£2/10/0 compound	£2/10/0 compound
Equitable	1961	£4/10/0 to £22/10/0 (according to duration)	£4/0/0 plus £2/10/0 on existing Bonus	Wh. Life—£3/10/0 to £11/15/0 Endmt.—£3/10/0 plus £1/15/0
Equity & Law	1961*	£3/2/0*	£3/2/0*	£2/18/0*
Federation Mutual	1961	£2/5/0	£2/5/0	£2/5/0
Friends Prov. & Century	1959	£2/12/6 compound	£2/12/6 compound	£2/15/0 compound
General	1960	£3/0/0	£2/15/0	At rate last declared
Gresham	1960	£2/2/0 to £5/10/0*	£2/2/0 to £3/11/0*	At rate last declared
Guardian	1962	£3/15/0	£3/10/0	At rate last declared
Ideal Life	1959*	£1/8/0	£1/8/0	£1/8/0
Imperial Life of Canada	1962	Vary with age, plan	and duration	Allowed at death
Law Union & Rock	1959	£2/2/0 compound (Home)	£2/2/0 compound (Home)	£2/2/0 compound
Legal & General	1962*	£2/17/6	£2/17/6	£2/15/0
Licenses & General	1962	£3/0/0	£3/0/0	£3/0/0
Life Assoc. of Scotland	1960*	£3/0/0	£3/0/0	£3/0/0
Liverpool, London & Globe	1958	£2/15/0	£2/15/0	£2/15/0
Liverpool Victoria	1959*	£2/8/0	£2/8/0	£2/8/0
London & Manchester	1962A	£2/14/0	£2/14/0	£2/14/0
London Assurance	1960	£3/15/0 compound	£3/15/0 compound	£2/15/0 compound
London Life	1961A	£2/12/6 compound for year	beginning July 1, 1963	Nil
Marine & General	1960	£3/5/0*	£3/0/0*	At rate last declared
Med. Sickness, An. & Life	1961	£3/0/0	£3/0/0	£3/0/0
Midland Employers	1961	£2/15/0	£2/15/0	£2/15/0
Mutual Life	1962	£2/8/0 compound	£2/6/0 compound	At rate last declared
N.A.L.G.O.	1960	£2/15/0*	£2/15/0*	£2/15/0

Office	Last* Valuation	Bonus declared on Whole Life Assurances	Bonus declared on Endowment Assurances	Interim Bonus
National Employers Life	1962	Special	Profit-Sharing System	
Nat. Farmers' Union	1962	£3/0/0	£3/0/0	£3/0/0
National Mutual	1962*	£2/15/0 compound*	£2/10/0 compound*	At rate last declared
Natl. Mut. of Austr.	1962*	£2/13/6 compound	£2/6/0 compound	At rate last declared
National Provident	1960*	£4/12/6	£4/0/0	£3/2/6 & £2/10/0
New Ireland	1962A	£2/6/0	£2/6/0	£2/6/0
North British & Mercantile	1959	£2/12/0 compound	£2/12/0 compound	£2/15/0 compound
Northern	1960	£2/18/0	£2/18/0	£3/2/0
Norwich Union	1962*	£3/10/0	£3/0/0	At rate last declared
Pearl	1962A	£2/18/0	£2/18/0	£2/18/0
Phoenix	1960	£2/15/0	£2/15/0	£2/15/0
Pioneer	1963*	£2/14/0	£2/14/0	£2/14/0
Provident Life Association of London	1962A	£3/0/0	£3/0/0	£3/0/0
Provident Mutual	1960	£3/0/0—Age 65 or over £2/15/0—Under age 65	£2/10/0	Whole Life—£2/17/6 & £2/12/6 Endowment—£2/7/6
Prudential	1962A	£3/2/0*	£3/2/0*	At rate last declared
Refuge	1962A	£2/12/0	£2/12/0	£2/12/0
Reliance Mutual	1960	£2/0/0	£2/0/0	£2/0/0
Royal Exchange	1960*	£3/0/0	£3/0/0	£3/0/0
Royal	1958	£2/15/0	£2/15/0	£2/15/0
Royal Liver Friendly	1962A	£2/17/0	£2/17/0	£2/17/0
Royal London	1960	£2/10/0*	£2/10/0*	£3/0/0
Salvation Army	1962A	£2/4/0	£2/4/0	—
Scottish Amicable	1960	£2/12/6 compound	£2/12/6 compound	£2/12/6 compound
Scottish Equitable	1962	£3/0/0 compound	£3/0/0 compound	£2/15/0 compound
Scottish Legal Life	1962	£2/10/0	£2/10/0	£2/10/0
Scottish Life	1960	£2/18/0	£2/18/0	£2/18/0
Scottish Mutual	1961*	£2/12/6 compound	£2/12/6 compound	£2/12/6
Scottish Provident	1958	£1/15/0 and £2/0/0*	£2/10/0 compound*	£2/16/0
Scottish Union	1962	£3/10/0	£3/0/0	At rate last declared
Scottish Widows	1958	£2/10/0 compound*	£2/10/0 compound*	£2/10/0*
Sentinel	1962*	£3/0/0	£3/0/0	£3/0/0
Standard	1961*	£2/2/0*	£2/2/0*	At rate last declared
Sun Life	1960*	£2/16/0	£2/16/0	£2/16/0
Sun Life of Canada	1962A	Vary with age, plan	and duration	—
Teachers	1960	£2/7/0	£2/7/0	£2/7/0
Tunstall & District	1960	£2/14/0	£2/14/0	£2/14/0
United Friendly	1962	£2/15/0	£2/15/0	—
United Kingdom	1962*	£2/16/0 Temperance* £2/15/0 General	Temperance* £2/15/0	£2/14/0 & £2/13/0 Temperance*
University Life	1962	£4/8/0	£4/0/0	£3/6/0 & £3/0/0
Wesleyan & General	1962A	£2/10/0	£2/10/0	£2/10/0
Yorkshire	1962*	£3/5/0	£3/5/0	£3/5/0

* NOTE.—The Valuation period is for the 5 years ending in December of the year stated, unless otherwise marked.

A —Annual Valuation.

Atlas—Three years ending December 31, 1961. Plus special Bonus 15% of Bonuses already attaching.

Beacon—Three years ending December 31, 1962—United Kingdom only.

Caledonian.—Three years ending December 31, 1962. Plus special Bonus—7½% of Bonuses attaching.

Commercial Union—Three years ending Dec. 31, 1960.

Crusader—Rates for United Kingdom only.

Eagle Star.—Three years ending December 31, 1960.

Ecclesiastical.—Five years ending February 28, 1959.

Equity & Law.—Three years ending Dec. 31, 1961. Plus £2 on existing Bonus. Interim Rate—plus £1/16/0. Further revisionary bonus on existing bonus additions.

Gresham—According to duration in force irrespective of age or term.

Ideal Life —Three vears ending December 31, 1959.

Legal & Genl.—Three years ending Dec. 31, 1962. United Kingdom only.

Licenses & Genl.—Three years ending Dec. 31, 1962.

Life Assoc. of Scot. – Three years ending Dec. 31, 1960.

Liverpool Victoria.—Three years ending Dec. 31, 1959.

Marine & Genl.—Plus £1/10/0% on Policies in force prior to 1st Jan. 1958.

N.A.L.G.O.—Plus single Bonus £2/10/0% for Policies in force throughout quinquennium.

National Mutual—One year ending December 31, 1962. Plus £1% on existing Bonus for 1961 and 1962.

National Mut. of Austr.—One year ending Sept. 30, 1962.

National Provident.—Three years ending Dec. 31, 1960.

Norwich Union—Rates for United Kingdom only. Plus 10% of Bonus attaching.

Pioneer —One vear ending March 31, 1963.

Prudential.—Plus special additions.

Royal Exchange.–Three years ending December 31. 1960.

Royal London—Additional Bonus 10s.% for 1956 to 1960.

Scottish Mutual.—Three years ending Dec. 31, 1961.

Scottish Provident—Under special distinctive System.

Sentinel—One year ending March 31, 1962.

Scottish Widows.—Plus special additions.

Standard.—One year ending November 15, 1962. Plus special additions.

Sun Life.—Three years ending December 31, 1960.

United Kingdom.—Three years ending December 31, 1962. Policies effected on or after Jan. 1, 1960.

Yorkshire.—Two years ending December 31. 1962.

ANNUAL PREMIUMS FOR WHOLE LIFE ASSURANCE

Life assurance may be effected either with or without participation in profits. If with participation then a higher premium is charged and the Policy is entitled to a Bonus, which is a share in the profits made by the Office, as and when declared. Valuations are made by Offices at periods varying from one to five years and the rate of Bonus then declared is usually in respect of each year since the previous valuation. These Bonuses are normally payable with the Sum Assured for their full amount, but, if desired, they can be applied to reduce the premium or surrendered for a cash payment. If a Policy is effected without participation the Sum Assured only is payable.

The ages applicable to the life and endowment assurance (but not the annuity) rates as hereafter given are "next birthday" unless otherwise stated.

AVERAGE ANNUAL PREMIUMS FOR WHOLE LIFE ASSURANCE OF £100

Age at Entry	With Profits	Without Profits	Age at Entry	With Profits	Without Profits	Age at Entry	With Profits	Without Profits
	£ s. d.	£ s. d.		£ s. d.	£ s. d.		£ s. d.	£ s. d.
21	1 18 9	1 6 0	31	2 9 9	1 14 1	41	3 5 7	2 8 5
22	1 19 9	1 6 9	32	2 11 1	1 15 2	42	3 7 9	2 10 5
23	2 0 9	1 7 6	33	2 12 6	1 16 4	43	3 10 1	2 12 6
24	2 1 9	1 8 3	34	2 13 11	1 17 6	44	3 12 5	2 14 8
25	2 2 10	1 9 0	35	2 15 5	1 18 10	45	3 14 10	2 16 10
26	2 3 11	1 9 9	36	2 16 11	2 0 2	46	3 17 4	2 19 2
27	2 5 1	1 10 6	37	2 18 7	2 1 8	48	4 2 8	3 4 3
28	2 6 3	1 11 4	38	3 0 3	2 3 2	50	4 9 3	3 9 10
29	2 7 5	1 12 2	39	3 1 11	2 4 9	55	5 9 1	4 7 10
30	2 8 7	1 13 1	40	3 3 10	2 6 6	60	6 13 11	5 10 5

The next table shows the annual premiums payable throughout life [with some Offices premiums cease at age 85] for a policy of £100 payable at death, with and without profits. It is not sufficient to judge a life office by premium rates only. An office charging a high premium may give higher bonuses than one charging a low premium, and therefore bonus results and prospects as well as premiums have to be considered. Most offices grant interim bonuses between valuation periods, and it is important to ascertain if this is the case before an assurance is effected, and how such interim bonuses compare with valuation bonuses, especially in cases of endowment assurance. A without profit Insurance provides the maximum amount of cover at the lowest cost and if an Office, as in some cases, is prepared to allow the option of converting the Insurance at any time to "with" profits either for whole of Life or on the Endowment plan, this gives an attractive contract. The change would, of course, entail a higher premium being paid but under this arrangement the highest cover can be obtained in the early years and the alteration made when the increased cost can be met.

ANNUAL PREMIUMS FOR ASSURANCE OF £100 PAYABLE AT DEATH.
MALE LIVES (lower premiums are quoted by many offices for female lives)

NAME OF OFFICE	WITH PROFITS					WITHOUT PROFITS			
	Age 30	Age 35	Age 40	Age 50	Age 60	Age 30	Age 40	Age 50	Age 60
	£ s. d.	£ s. d.	£ s. d.	£ s. d.	£ s. d.	£ s. d.	£ s. d.	£ s. d.	£ s. d.
★Alliance	2 10 8	2 16 11	3 4 11	4 8 2	6 8 1	1 10 8	2 3 7	3 5 7	5 4 5
★Atlas	2 12 8	2 19 4	3 7 11	4 12 11	6 17 7	1 12 4	2 5 10	3 8 11	5 10 1
★Australian Mutual	2 3 5	2 10 2	2 18 8	4 3 7	6 9 2	1 10 8	2 3 10	3 7 3	5 10 0
★Avon	2 6 7	2 13 1	3 1 3	4 5 6	6 8 7	1 7 9	2 0 6	3 2 5	5 0 3
★Beacon	2 3 6	2 10 4	2 19 1	4 4 2	6 5 11	1 8 10	2 2 0	3 4 8	5 4 0
★Blackburn	2 11 6	2 18 8	3 7 5	4 13 5	6 19 0	1 18 7	2 12 10	3 17 1	6 0 11
★Britannic	2 7 0	2 13 9	3 2 3	4 6 10	6 7 10	1 11 5	2 4 6	3 6 9	5 5 2
British National Life	2 7 1	2 13 8	3 2 0	4 6 2	6 9 7	1 8 6	2 1 5	3 3 11	5 3 8
★Caledonian	2 12 1	2 18 10	3 7 0	4 11 7	6 15 7	1 8 8	2 1 11	3 4 3	5 2 11
★Canada Life	1 19 6	2 6 0	2 14 4	3 19 8	6 6 8	1 11 11	2 4 9	3 7 3	5 7 7
★Clerical, Medical & General	2 6 2	2 12 10	3 1 2	4 5 9	6 10 10	1 11 5	2 3 9	3 5 2	5 2 5
★Colonial Mutual	2 7 3	2 14 6	3 3 7	4 8 2	6 15 2	1 8 3	2 0 4	3 2 0	5 1 5
★Commercial Union	2 12 3	2 18 9	3 6 11	4 10 10	6 10 9	1 9 10	2 3 0	3 5 7	5 5 9
★Confederation	2 2 4	2 8 5	2 16 5	4 0 8	6 4 9	1 5 10	1 18 8	3 0 5	4 17 9
★Co-operative	2 11 8	2 18 7	3 7 5	4 16 4	6 19 8		Not	issued	
★Crown Life	1 14 10	2 0 7	2 8 6	3 12 7	5 16 1	1 8 9	2 2 2	3 5 4	5 7 1
★Crusader	2 15 2	3 2 5	3 11 4	4 17 3	7 2 7	1 11 11	2 5 0	3 7 4	5 5 11
★Eagle Star	2 6 3	2 13 4	3 2 2	4 8 0	6 13 0	1 9 8	2 2 8	3 4 10	5 5 7
Ecclesiastical	2 5 7	2 12 2	3 0 5	4 4 11	6 8 4	1 7 4	2 0 0	3 1 8	4 19 0
★Economic	2 12 0	2 18 8	3 7 0	4 11 8	6 15 7	1 10 2	2 2 6	3 5 2	5 6 10
★Equitable	2 13 0	2 18 0	3 5 0	4 6 0	6 4 0	1 7 2	1 18 10	2 18 5	4 14 0
★Equity & Law	2 6 11	2 14 7	3 4 6	4 13 5	7 4 4	1 8 0	2 0 9	3 2 7	5 0 5
★Federation Mutual	2 12 7	2 19 7	3 8 3	4 13 8	6 18 5	1 10 4	2 3 2	3 5 4	5 3 7
★Friends' Prov. & Cen.	2 10 5	2 17 8	3 6 8	4 12 10	6 18 5	1 10 4	2 3 5	3 5 7	5 4 1
★General Life	2 5 0	2 12 0	3 1 0	4 6 3	6 8 0	1 6 6	2 0 0	3 3 0	5 3 6
★Gresham	2 7 11	2 14 3	3 2 2	4 6 6	6 10 6	1 10 8	2 3 1	3 4 8	5 4 2
★Guardian	2 9 3	2 16 4	3 5 2	4 10 8	6 13 3	1 8 8	2 1 11	3 4 3	5 2 11
★Ideal Life	2 7 0	2 13 5	3 1 8	4 5 11	6 8 10	1 16 0	2 9 7	3 12 8	5 14 6

NAME OF OFFICE	WITH PROFITS Age 30	WITH PROFITS Age 35	WITH PROFITS Age 40	WITH PROFITS Age 50	WITH PROFITS Age 60	WITHOUT PROFITS Age 30	WITHOUT PROFITS Age 40	WITHOUT PROFITS Age 50	WITHOUT PROFITS Age 60
	£ s. d.	£ s. d.	£ s. d.	£ s. d.	£ s. d.	£ s. d.	£ s. d.	£ s. d.	£ s. d.
*Impl. Life of Canada....	1 17 1	2 3 6	2 11 7	3 17 10	6 8 2	1 7 6	1 19 8	3 1 5	4 19 7
*Irish Life..............		Not	published			1 14 1	2 7 9	3 11 7	5 13 7
*Law Union & Rock.....	2 9 8	2 16 1	3 4 4	4 8 5	6 10 2	1 19 4	2 3 4	3 5 8	5 5 6
*Legal & General........	2 11 4	2 17 8	3 5 8	4 12 2	6 17 11	1 10 8	2 3 1	3 4 8	5 4 2
*Licenses & General.....		Not	Issued			1 8 8	2 1 11	3 4 3	5 2 11
*Life Assoc. of Scotland..	2 7 4	2 14 5	3 3 2	4 8 4	6 9 8	1 12 2	2 5 2	3 7 2	5 5 1
*L'pool & Lond. & Gl....	2 6 10	2 14 4	3 3 8	4 10 4	6 13 2	1 10 4	2 3 4	3 5 8	5 5 6
L'pool Victoria F'dly....	2 7 11	2 15 7	3 5 3	4 13 10	7 4 6	1 18 3	2 13 6	3 19 7	6 7 5
*London & Manchester..	2 9 3	2 16 3	3 5 0	4 10 6	6 14 9	1 11 10	2 5 6	3 8 10	5 11 0
*London Assurance	2 10 6	2 17 3	3 5 9	4 10 6	6 14 0	1 8 10	2 2 10	3 4 8	5 4 0
*London Life...........	2 6 10	2 13 8	3 1 8	4 5 8	6 9 3	1 8 0	1 19 10	2 19 10	4 16 0
*Manufacturers..........	1 14 6	2 0 11	2 9 5	3 14 7	5 18 6	1 3 10	1 16 8	2 18 7	4 15 10
*Marine & General	2 8 11	2 15 8	3 4 2	4 9 2	6 13 5	1 11 5	2 4 3	3 6 6	5 5 0
*Med. Sickness An. & Life	2 3 3	2 10 0	2 18 6	4 3 2	6 4 0	1 10 0	2 2 11	3 5 0	5 3 4
*Midland Employers.....	2 8 5	2 15 1	3 3 7	4 8 3	6 9 6	1 12 7	2 5 9	3 8 5	5 7 8
Mutual Life	2 1 1	2 7 4	2 15 4	3 18 9	6 0 8	1 9 2	2 2 8	3 5 9	5 6 9
*Natl. & Local Gov. Officers	2 4 10	2 11 8	3 0 5	4 4 10	—	1 10 3	2 3 11	3 6 4	—
*Natl. Employers Life ..	1 12 8	1 18 4	2 5 8	3 8 0	5 8 0	All Policies Participate			
*National Farmers' Union	2 4 7	2 11 1	2 19 3	4 3 6	6 6 7	1 6 10	1 18 11	3 0 5	4 18 3
*National Mutual........	2 17 0	3 4 0	3 13 0	4 17 0	6 17 0	1 14 0	2 6 0	3 8 0	5 8 0
*Nat. Mut'l of Australasia.	2 6 9	2 13 4	3 1 6	4 7 3	6 9 8	1 9 10	2 2 6	3 4 6	5 2 11
*National Provident....	2 6 7	2 14 0	3 3 5	4 10 7	6 15 9	1 12 1	2 4 7	3 4 11	5 5 4
New Ireland..........	2 4 9	2 11 10	3 0 7	4 6 10	6 13 2	1 13 2	2 6 3	3 8 6	5 7 1
*North. Brit. & Mercan...	2 10 0	2 16 6	3 4 10	4 9 3	6 14 1	1 9 10	2 3 0	3 5 7	5 5 9
*Northern..............	2 3 5	2 10 4	2 19 0	4 3 8	6 6 6	1 4 5	1 16 8	2 17 10	4 14 3
*Norwich Union.........	2 8 10	2 16 0	3 5 4	4 11 1	6 14 4	1 9 0	2 1 3	3 2 8	5 2 2
*Pearl..................	2 5 6	2 12 8	3 1 9	4 7 8	6 10 3	1 11 11	2 5 1	3 7 6	5 6 5
*Phoenix...............	2 7 4	2 14 3	3 3 1	4 8 4	6 10 7	1 9 4	2 2 4	3 4 7	5 3 3
Pioneer	2 9 0	2 19 0	3 11 0	4 13 0	6 15 0	1 18 0	2 10 0	3 13 0	5 17 0
*Prov. Life Assoc. of Lond.	2 7 6	2 14 5	3 2 10	4 7 10	6 14 6	1 10 7	2 3 6	3 5 8	5 5 2
*Provident Mutual.......	2 7 2	2 14 2	3 3 0	4 8 10	6 15 0	1 8 11	2 1 9	3 4 2	5 3 7
*Prudential.............	2 2 0	2 9 6	2 19 0	4 6 0	6 10 6	1 7 0	2 0 0	3 3 0	5 4 0
*Refuge.................	2 12 4	2 19 4	3 7 8	4 13 4	7 0 0	—	2 10 4	3 14 8	5 19 8
*Reliance..............	2 6 6	2 13 3	3 1 6	4 5 8	6 5 10	1 12 1	2 5 3	3 7 1	5 5 0
*Royal..................	2 6 10	2 14 4	3 3 8	4 10 4	6 13 2	1 10 4	2 3 4	3 5 8	5 5 6
*Royal Exchange........	2 9 6	2 16 6	3 5 3	4 10 7	6 13 11	1 12 4	2 5 10	3 8 11	5 10 1
Royal Liver Friendly...	2 5 11	2 13 0	3 2 5	4 9 9	6 19 2	1 16 2	2 11 1	3 16 9	6 2 10
*Royal London.........	2 4 0	2 11 3	3 0 4	4 6 8	6 11 3	—	2 1 4	3 5 3	5 7 9
*Salvation Army........	2 7 7	2 15 0	3 4 4	4 11 9	7 1 1	1 13 4	2 7 7	3 12 8	5 16 10
*Scottish Amicable	2 11 7	2 18 5	3 6 11	4 12 1	6 13 2	1 11 0	2 4 5	3 7 0	5 6 2
*Scottish Equitable	2 13 2	2 19 8	3 8 2	4 12 6	6 13 0	1 12 0	2 4 10	3 7 0	5 5 6
Scottish Legal Life......	2 4 6	2 12 7	3 2 10	4 12 9	7 7 4		Not	published	
*Scottish Life...........	2 9 10	2 16 8	3 5 1	4 9 5	6 9 6	1 11 4	2 3 8	3 5 0	5 2 10
*Scottish Mutual........	2 7 8	2 14 2	3 2 8	4 7 10	6 11 2	1 6 6	1 19 4	3 2 0	5 1 8
*Scottish Provident	2 10 5	2 17 1	3 5 8	4 10 0	6 11 3	1 10 0	2 2 11	3 5 0	5 3 3
*Scott. Union & Nat.....	2 9 4	2 16 8	3 5 11	4 12 8	6 17 10	1 9 0	2 1 3	3 2 8	5 2 2
*Scottish Widows.......	2 14 3	3 1 7	3 10 10	4 14 6	6 13 3	1 8 2	2 0 9	3 2 6	5 1 2
*Sentinel...............	2 4 8	2 11 9	3 0 8	4 6 3	6 8 5	1 7 6	2 0 4	3 2 8	5 1 5
*Standard..............	2 13 0	2 18 0	3 6 0	4 8 0	6 9 0	1 9 0	2 1 0	3 1 0	4 17 0
*Sun Life..............	2 8 5	2 15 3	3 3 8	4 8 5	6 9 5	1 10 5	2 3 5	3 5 8	5 4 8
*Sun Life of Canada.....	2 10 5	2 16 6	3 4 6	4 8 8	6 13 3	1 13 4	2 6 8	3 9 5	5 12 10
Teachers	2 2 2	2 8 11	2 16 7	4 1 6	6 4 7	1 8 4	2 1 0	3 3 5	5 1 5
*United Friendly	2 12 9	3 0 10	3 10 9	4 19 9	7 10 8	1 13 11	2 8 11	3 14 6	6 1 0
*United Kingdom Prov...	2 10 1	2 16 7	3 4 10	4 8 9	6 8 10	1 8 3	2 1 3	3 3 9	5 3 11
*University Life.........	1 19 0	2 6 0	2 16 0	4 0 0	6 0 0	1 2 0	1 13 7	2 13 7	4 10 7
Wesleyan & General....	2 6 10	2 13 10	3 2 7	4 8 4	6 13 5	1 8 2	2 0 5	3 2 2	5 0 10
*Yorkshire.............	2 7 0	2 13 0	3 2 0	4 7 0	6 10 0	1 10 0	2 3 0	3 5 0	5 5 0

* † For notes see p. 1144.

ENDOWMENT ASSURANCES.

Endowment Assurances are very popular, and are extremely attractive to persons who desire to combine a provision for their dependants, in event of premature death, with the investment of savings for the realization of a fund for their own personal enjoyment in later life. For the investment of small annual sums there is no medium promising more satisfactory results than an Endowment assurance participating in profits in a good bonus-paying life office. The selection of such an office is all-important, as so much depends upon profit-earning capacity—*see* first page of Life Assurance.

Under endowment assurances the sum assured is paid after a given number of years, or on the attainment of a fixed age. Should the life assured, however, die during the endowment period, the sum assured is paid at death together with any Bonuses attaching under a " with profit " Policy.

The following table shows the annual premiums, for various ages at entry, charged by the offices named, to secure £100 at the end of 15, 20 and 25 years, or at death, if previous, with profits.

MALE LIVES (lower premiums are quoted by many offices for female lives)

NAME OF OFFICE	SUM ASSURED PAYABLE AT DEATH, OR AT THE END OF 15 YEARS			20 YEARS			25 YEARS			
	Age 35	Age 40	Age 45	Age 30	Age 35	Age 40	Age 25	Age 30	Age 35	Age 40
	£ s. d.	£ s. d.	£ s. d.	£ s. d.	£ s. d.	£ s. d.	£ s. d.	£ s. d.	£ s. d.	£ s. d.
★Alliance	7 4 7	7 6 0	7 8 7	5 7 5	5 8 4	5 10 4	4 6 6	4 7 2	4 8 7	4 11 2
★Atlas	7 7 9	7 9 2	7 11 10	5 9 10	5 10 10	5 12 10	4 8 6	4 9 2	4 10 8	4 13 5
★Australian Mutual	6 12 0	6 13 5	6 16 3	4 16 6	4 17 6	4 19 6	3 15 2	3 15 11	3 17 4	4 0 0
★Avon	7 0 9	7 2 3	7 4 8	5 2 9	5 3 11	5 5 11	4 1 5	4 2 4	4 3 11	4 6 7
★Beacon	6 19 4	7 0 10	7 3 7	5 3 3	5 4 3	5 6 3	4 1 3	4 2 0	4 3 6	4 6 3
★Blackburn	7 5 5	7 6 11	7 9 6	5 8 4	5 9 6	5 11 7	4 5 8	4 6 7	4 8 4	4 11 1
★Britannic	7 1 8	7 3 1	7 5 10	5 5 5	5 6 5	5 8 5	4 3 5	4 4 1	4 5 7	4 8 4
British National Life	7 2 6	7 4 2	7 6 9	5 6 3	5 7 5	5 9 8	4 4 2	4 5 2	4 6 10	4 9 9
★Caledonian	7 4 8	7 6 1	7 8 6	5 9 2	5 10 4	5 12 4	4 7 9	4 8 7	4 10 2	4 12 11
★Canada Life	6 13 0	6 14 8	6 17 6	4 15 10	4 17 2	4 19 5	3 13 10	3 14 9	3 16 6	3 19 6
City of Glasgow Friendly	6 9 6	6 11 8	6 15 2	4 13 2	4 14 10	4 17 6	3 11 10	3 12 10	3 15 0	3 18 8
★Clerical, Med. & Gen.	7 3 5	7 4 9	7 6 9	5 7 7	5 8 7	5 10 4	4 6 0	4 6 9	4 8 1	4 10 5
★Colonial Mutual	7 1 1	7 2 9	7 5 3	5 4 4	5 5 6	5 7 10	4 2 1	4 3 2	4 4 11	4 8 2
★Commercial Union	7 3 6	7 5 0	7 7 8	5 8 10	5 9 9	5 11 9	4 7 10	4 8 5	4 10 0	4 12 7
★Confederation	6 12 11	6 14 4	6 16 11	4 16 9	4 17 11	4 19 10	3 15 0	3 16 2	3 17 11	4 1 0
★Co-operative	7 5 4	7 6 10	7 9 6	5 7 8	5 8 10	5 11 0	4 6 0	4 6 11	4 8 5	4 11 2
★Crown Life	6 6 0	6 7 10	6 10 11	4 8 7	4 10 0	4 12 6	3 7 1	3 7 11	3 9 9	3 12 10
★Crusader	7 8 5	7 9 10	7 12 5	5 12 0	5 13 3	5 15 4	4 10 0	4 10 11	4 12 6	4 15 3
★Eagle Star	7 2 7	7 4 1	7 6 8	5 5 3	5 6 7	5 8 8	4 3 1	4 4 1	4 5 9	4 8 9
Ecclesiastical	6 17 2	6 18 9	7 1 2	5 2 2	5 3 4	5 5 5	4 1 1	4 1 11	4 3 7	4 6 5
★Economic	7 4 8	7 6 2	7 8 11	5 9 7	5 10 6	5 12 6	4 8 4	4 9 0	4 10 5	4 13 0
★Equitable	7 2 0	7 3 2	7 5 2	5 6 10	5 7 2	5 8 10	4 4 10	4 5 2	4 6 5	4 8 5
★Equity & Law	7 13 7	7 15 8	7 19 0	5 7 11	5 9 11	5 13 5	4 2 2	4 3 10	4 6 6	4 10 8
★Federation Mutual	7 4 3	7 5 8	7 8 2	5 8 6	5 9 8	5 11 9	4 6 10	4 7 9	4 9 5	4 12 1
★Friends' Prov. & Cent.	7 3 3	7 4 11	7 8 3	5 6 2	5 7 5	5 9 7	4 4 8	4 5 7	4 7 4	4 10 4
★General Life	6 18 9	7 0 3	7 3 0	5 3 0	5 4 0	5 5 9	4 1 0	4 1 6	4 3 0	4 5 9
★Gresham	6 19 9	7 1 3	7 3 10	5 3 9	5 5 0	5 7 0	4 2 4	4 3 3	4 4 11	4 7 8
★Guardian	7 2 11	7 4 6	7 6 11	5 6 11	5 8 2	5 10 3	4 5 2	4 6 1	4 7 9	4 10 7
★Ideal Life	6 17 5	6 18 10	7 1 4	5 2 5	5 3 7	5 5 7	4 1 4	4 2 2	4 3 9	4 6 6
Imperial Life of Canada	6 14 7	6 16 6	6 19 8	4 16 5	4 17 10	5 0 4	3 15 1	3 16 2	3 18 0	4 1 5
★Irish Life	7 3 7	7 4 7	7 6 9	5 7 0	5 7 7	5 8 10	4 4 7	4 4 10	4 5 6	4 7 1
★Law Union & Rock	7 1 9	7 3 1	7 5 4	5 6 4	5 7 5	5 9 3	4 5 1	4 5 11	4 7 4	4 9 10
★Legal & General	7 5 10	7 6 11	7 8 11	5 7 5	5 8 4	5 9 11	4 6 7	4 7 3	4 8 6	4 10 8
★Life Assoc. of Scotland	7 4 9	7 6 2	7 8 10	5 8 7	5 9 7	5 11 6	4 6 8	4 7 4	4 8 9	4 11 4
★L'pool & Lond. & Gl.	7 5 2	7 6 9	7 9 5	5 8 10	5 10 0	5 12 2	4 6 5	4 7 2	4 8 9	4 11 10
L'pool Vict. Friendly	7 3 10	7 5 7	7 8 2	5 5 9	5 7 1	5 9 4	4 2 6	4 3 7	4 5 4	4 8 5
★London & Manchester	7 3 2	7 4 8	7 7 1	5 7 7	5 8 9	5 10 9	4 6 1	4 6 11	4 8 6	4 11 2
★London Assurance	7 3 2	7 4 8	7 7 4	5 7 4	5 8 4	5 10 5	4 5 9	4 6 5	4 7 11	4 10 8
★London Life	7 0 0	7 1 3	7 3 8	5 3 3	5 4 0	5 5 8	4 2 0	4 2 5	4 4 0	4 6 5
★Manufacturers'	6 6 4	6 8 7	6 12 3	4 9 6	4 11 2	4 14 1	3 7 8	3 8 11	3 11 1	3 14 8
★Marine & General	7 3 7	7 5 0	7 7 7	5 6 3	5 7 6	5 9 6	4 4 7	4 5 5	4 7 1	4 9 11
★Med. Sickness An. & Life	6 18 10	7 0 3	7 2 11	5 3 0	5 4 0	5 5 11	4 1 3	4 1 11	4 3 3	4 5 11
★Midland Employers	7 2 4	7 3 9	7 6 5	5 6 6	5 7 7	5 9 7	4 5 0	4 5 8	4 7 2	4 9 11
Mutual Life	6 13 1	6 15 4	6 18 3	4 16 7	4 18 9	5 1 6	3 14 6	3 16 8	3 19 3	4 2 0
★Nat. & Local Gov. Officers	7 1 5	7 3 4	7 6 3	5 5 4	5 6 3	5 9 2	4 2 11	4 3 10	4 5 10	4 8 9
★Natl. Employers Life	5 18 8	6 0 4	6 3 0	4 4 8	4 5 8	4 7 8	3 4 8	3 5 4	3 6 8	3 9 4
★Nat. Farmers' Union	6 18 9	7 0 3	7 2 8	5 0 9	5 1 11	5 3 11	3 19 5	4 0 4	4 1 11	4 4 7
★National Mutual	7 5 0	7 6 0	7 9 0	5 10 0	5 11 0	5 13 0	4 9 0	4 10 0	4 12 0	4 14 0
★Natl. Mut. of Austr.	6 9 10	6 11 4	6 14 0	4 14 10	4 15 10	4 17 11	3 13 10	3 14 6	3 15 11	3 18 10
★National Provident	6 16 11	6 19 10	7 4 0	5 0 6	5 2 10	5 6 2	3 18 0	3 19 10	4 2 7	4 7 10
New Ireland	7 1 3	7 2 11	7 5 7	5 3 9	5 5 1	5 7 3	4 1 2	4 2 2	4 3 10	4 6 11
★North Brit. & Mercan.	7 1 9	7 3 2	7 5 10	5 6 6	5 7 5	5 9 5	4 5 7	4 6 2	4 7 7	4 10 2
★Northern	7 1 3	7 2 10	7 5 4	5 4 6	5 5 9	5 7 11	4 2 3	4 3 2	4 4 10	4 7 9
★Norwich Union	7 6 4	7 7 7	7 10 0	5 7 11	5 8 9	5 10 6	4 5 2	4 5 8	4 6 10	4 9 3
★Pearl	7 3 1	7 4 7	7 7 4	5 6 6	5 7 6	5 9 7	4 4 0	4 4 8	4 6 3	4 9 2
★Phoenix	7 5 11	7 7 4	7 10 1	5 8 7	5 9 7	5 11 7	4 6 2	4 6 10	4 8 4	4 11 1
Pioneer	7 10 1	7 12 0	7 14 0	5 13 0	5 14 0	5 16 0	4 10 0	4 11 0	4 13 0	4 16 0
★Prov. Life Assoc. of Lond.	7 0 7	7 2 2	7 4 9	5 4 8	5 5 11	5 8 0	4 3 0	4 3 10	4 5 5	4 8 3
★Provident Mutual	6 18 10	7 0 4	7 2 10	5 3 3	5 4 6	5 6 6	4 1 9	4 2 7	4 4 3	4 7 0
★Prudential	7 0 6	7 2 6	7 4 6	5 4 0	5 5 0	5 7 6	4 1 6	4 2 6	4 4 0	4 7 0
★Refuge	7 7 0	7 8 4	7 10 8	5 10 0	5 11 0	5 12 8	4 8 0	4 9 0	4 10 4	4 12 8
★Reliance	6 19 3	7 0 8	7 3 3	5 3 10	5 5 0	5 7 0	4 2 6	4 3 5	4 5 0	4 7 11
★Royal	7 5 2	7 6 9	7 9 5	5 8 10	5 10 0	5 12 2	4 6 5	4 7 2	4 8 9	4 11 10
★Royal Exchange	7 3 0	7 4 5	7 7 1	5 6 11	5 7 10	5 9 11	4 4 11	4 5 8	4 7 1	4 9 10
Royal Liver Friendly	6 19 5	7 1 7	7 4 8	5 2 11	5 4 3	5 6 11	4 0 4	4 1 4	4 3 2	4 6 7
★Royal London	7 3 3	7 4 9	7 7 3	5 6 0	5 7 3	5 9 4	4 3 7	4 4 6	4 6 1	4 8 10
★Salvation Army	7 4 11	7 6 7	7 9 2	5 8 0	5 9 3	5 11 5	4 5 10	4 6 9	4 8 6	4 11 6
★Scottish Amicable	7 3 0	7 4 7	7 7 0	5 8 4	5 9 7	5 11 7	4 7 1	4 8 0	4 9 7	4 12 4
★Scottish Equitable	7 6 8	7 8 0	7 10 8	5 10 8	5 11 8	5 13 8	4 9 4	4 10 0	4 11 6	4 14 2

NAME OF OFFICE	Sum Assured Payable at Death or at the End of									
	15 Years			20 Years			25 Years			
	Age 35	Age 40	Age 45	Age 30	Age 35	Age 40	Age 25	Age 30	Age 35	Age 40
	£ s. d.	£ s. d.	£ s. d.	£ s. d.	£ s. d.	£ s. d.	£ s. d.	£ s. d.	£ s. d.	£ s. d.
Scottish Legal Life	7 6 4	7 8 2	7 11 3	5 6 3	5 7 8	5 10 1	4 2 5	4 3 5	4 5 4	4 8 6
*Scottish Life	7 5 2	7 6 6	7 9 0	5 8 10	5 9 9	5 11 9	4 6 10	4 7 8	4 9 3	4 12 0
*Scottish Mutual	6 18 10	7 0 2	7 2 10	5 3 8	5 4 8	5 6 8	4 2 6	4 3 2	4 4 6	4 7 4
*Scottish Provident	7 3 5	7 4 9	7 7 5	5 7 1	5 8 0	5 10 0	4 5 8	4 6 3	4 7 8	4 10 3
*Scottish Un. & Nat.	7 5 8	7 7 2	7 9 11	5 7 0	5 8 0	5 10 1	4 5 6	4 6 3	4 7 8	4 10 7
*Scottish Widows'	7 9 2	7 10 10	7 13 7	5 11 3	5 12 7	5 14 10	4 9 6	4 10 7	4 12 4	4 15 3
*Sentinel	7 1 0	7 2 6	7 5 3	5 5 0	5 6 0	5 8 1	4 2 9	4 3 6	4 4 11	4 7 9
*Standard	7 0 0	7 1 0	7 4 0	5 5 0	5 6 0	5 8 0	4 5 0	4 6 0	4 8 0	4 10 0
*Sun Life	7 2 10	7 4 3	7 7 0	5 7 3	5 8 3	5 10 5	4 5 8	4 6 5	4 7 10	4 10 8
*Sun Life of Canada	7 4 3	7 5 9	7 8 9	5 7 6	5 8 8	5 10 9	4 5 10	4 6 6	4 8 0	4 10 10
Teachers	6 13 3	6 15 2	6 18 0	4 17 9	4 18 9	5 0 8	3 16 8	3 17 8	3 19 7	4 2 5
Tunstall & District	7 0 1	7 2 9	7 7 2	5 2 1	5 4 11	5 8 4	3 19 8	4 1 10	4 4 8	4 9 5
*United Friendly	7 3 10	7 5 7	7 8 3	5 5 6	5 6 10	5 9 2	4 4 11	4 6 0	4 7 10	4 11 0
United Kingdom Prov	7 3 0	7 4 5	7 7 1	5 7 9	5 8 8	5 10 8	4 6 7	4 7 2	4 8 7	4 11 3
*University Life	6 17 0	6 18 0	7 0 0	4 18 0	5 0 0	5 2 0	3 16 0	3 17 0	3 19 0	4 2 0
Wesleyan & Gen.	7 1 11	7 3 2	7 5 2	5 5 5	5 6 4	5 8 0	4 3 7	4 4 3	4 5 7	4 7 9
*Yorkshire	7 3 0	7 4 0	7 7 0	5 7 0	5 8 0	5 10 0	4 5 0	4 5 0	4 7 0	4 9 0

* Reductions allowed are as shown, and some offices allow further reductions for sums assured of £5,000 and over.

Alliance—1/-% £2,000–£4,999.

Atlas—Rates for £500–£999. 1/-% £1,000–£1,499. 2/-% £1,500–£2,499. 3/-% £2,500–£4,999.

Australian Mut.—1/-% £2,000–£4,999.

Avon—1/-% £2,500–£4,999.

Beacon—Rates for £1000 to £2,499.

Blackburn—1/-% £500–£999. 2/-% £1,000 and over.

Britannic—Rates for £1,000–£2,499. 1/-% £2,500 and over.

Caledonian—1/6% £1,000–£2,499. 2/6% £2,500–£4.999.

Canada Life—Ages nearest birthday. 2/-% £1,000–£2,499. 4/-% £2,500–£9,999. 5/-% £10,000 or more.

Clerical Medl. & Gen.—5/-% for excess over £1,000.

Colonial Mutual—1/-% £2,500–£4,999.

Commercial Union—2/-% £2,000–£4,999

Confederation—2/-% £2,500–£4,999.

Co-operative—2/-% £500 or over.

Crown Life—Add £3 per Policy. Min. £500.

Crusader—Reductions £1,000 and over with profits. £500 and over, without.

Eagle Star—Rates for £500–£1,999. 1/-% £2,000–£4,999.

Economic—1/-% £2,500–£4,999.

Equitable—2/-% £1,000–£2,499. 3/-% £2,500 and over.

Equity & Law—1/-% £2,500–£4,999.

Fedn. Mutl.—1/-% £1,000–£1,999. 2/-% £2,000–4,999.

Friends Prov. & Cent.—1/-% £2,500–£4,999.

Genl. Life—Prems: subject to addition of £2 per policy.

Gresham—Over £500 deduct 5/-% on excess above £500.

Guardian—1/6% £1,000–£2,499. 2/6% £2,500–£4,999.

Ideal—2/6% £1,000 or over.

Irish Life—Rates for £1.000–£4,999. Increased for less.

Law Union & Rock.—£500 and over deduct 4/-% and add £2 per policy. Under £500 add 4/-%.

Legal & General—1/-% £500–£999. 2/6% £1000 or over. Further 2/-% on excess of £1,000. with profits.

Life Assn. of Scot.—1/6% £1,000–£2,499; 3/-% £2,500–£4,999.

L'pool & L'don & Globe—Rates for £1,000. Under £500 add 4/-%. Deduct 4/-% and add £2 per policy other amounts.

Lon. & Man.—1/-% £2,500–£4,999. Endowment.

Lond. Assur.—Rates for £1,000–£2,499.

London Life—Rates for £500–£2,000. 4/-% on excess of £2,000

Manufacturers'—Rates subject to addition of £3 per Policy.

Marine & Gen.—1/-% £1,000–£2,499. 2/6% £2,500–£4,999.

Medical Sickness—Special reductions £1,000 and over.

Midl. Emp.—1/6% £1,000–£2,499. 2/6% £2,500–£4,999.

N.A.L.G.O.—1/-% £1,000 or over.

Natl. Emp. Life—1/-% £1,000–£1,999. 2/-% £2,000–£4,999. Policies share in profits without extra charge.

National Farmers' Union—1/-% £2,500–£4,999.

National Mutual—1/-% £1,000–£2,499. 2/-% £2,500–£3,999. 3/-% £4,000–£4,999.

Natl. Mut. of Aust.—Ages nearest birthday. 1/-% £2,000–£4,999.

National Provident—Rates for £1,000–£1,999. 1/-% £2,000–£4,999. Increased if less than £1,000.

North Brit. & Merc.—2/-% £2,000–£4,999.

Northern—Add 6/-% under £500. Over £500 add £1/10/0 per policy.

Norwich Union—Rates for £1,000–£1,999. 1/6% £2,000–£4,999. Less than £1,000 add £1 to calculated premium.

Pearl—Rates for £1,000–£2,499. 1/-% £2,500–£4,999. Less than £1,000 add 5/- per Policy.

Phoenix—Rates for £1,000–£2,499. 1/-% £2,500–£4,999. Increased if less than £1,000.

Prov. Life Assoc. of London—Rates for £500–£1,999. Reduced £2,000 or over.

Prov. Mut.—Rates for £1,000–£1,999. 1/-% £2,000–£4,999 Add 5/- per Policy under £1,000.

Prudential—Sums assured £500 and over add £1/10/0 per Policy. Less than £500 add 6/-%.

Refuge—1/-% £250–£499; 2/-% £500–£999; 3/-% £1,000–£2,499; 4/-% £2,500 or over.

Reliance—Rates for £1,000. 3/-% on excess of £1,000. Increased for less than £1,000.

Royal—Rates for £1,000. Under £500 add 4/-%. Deduct 4/-% and add £2 per Policy other amounts.

Royal Exchange—Rates for £500–£999 1/-% £1,000–£2,499. 2/-% £2,500–£4,999.

Royal London—Add £1 per policy, any amount.

Salvation Army—1/-% £500–£999; 1/6% £1,000 or over.

Scottish Amicable—Rates for £1,000. Reduced for larger and increased for smaller amounts.

Scottish Equitable—Rates reduced for larger policies.

Scottish Life—2/-% £1,000–£2,499. 3/6% £2,500–£4,999.

Scottish Mutual—Rates for £1,000 and over, plus £2 on calculated premium. Increased for less.

Scottish Prov.—1/-% £2,500–£4,999.

Scot U. & Natl.—Rates for £1,000–£1,999. 1/6% £2,000–£4,999. Less than £1,000 add £1 to calculated premium.

Scottish Widows'—Rates for £1,000–£2,499. 1/-% £2,500–£4,999. Add 1/6% for less than £1,000.

Sentinel—Rates for £1,000–£2,500.

Standard—£500 and over add £1/5/0 per Policy with profits and £1/15/0 without profits.

Sun Life—1/-% £2,500–£4,999.

Sun Life of Canada—Rates for £750–£1,249 with profits. £1,000–£1,249 without profits. Increased for less. Reduced 2/-% £1,250–£2,499. 3/-% £2,500 and over.

United Friendly—1/-% £500–£999. 2/-% £1,000–£1,499. 3/-% £1.500–£1,999. 4/-% £2,000–£4,999.

University Life.—Plus £2 per policy.

Yorkshire—1/-% £1,000–£1,999. 2/-% £2,000–£4,999.

LIFE INSURANCE NEW BUSINESS, 1962

The following tables shows the net business (after allowing for amount reassured) and net annual and single premiums received during the year ending December 31, 1962 unless otherwise stated.

Name of Office	No. of Policies issued	Net sums assured	Net annual premiums	Net single premiums
		£	£	£
Alliance	12,691	26,635,452	421,400	66,645
Atlas	6,380	21,083,378	504,277	85,089
Asutralian Mutual Prov.	164,656	293,089,462	—	—
Avon	940	1,580,331	28,125	1,347
Beacon	8,381	13,893,810	220,254	40,786
Blackburn (Ord.)	2,010	1,807,880	67,412	1,872
Britannic (Ord.)	18,115	15,560,445	596,347	90,055
British National Life	900	1,780,114	47,635	47
Caledonian	6,037	22,679,490	446,779	49,277
Canada Life	35,619	182,495,780	2,717,159	35,497
City of Glasgow Friendly	1,054	392,586	23,118	36,830
Clerical, Medl. & Genl.	12,692	25,579,825	795,592	31,687
Colonial Mutual	120,562	212,288,955	4,841,236	686,262
Commerical Union	18,821	61,013,711	1,052,060	118,956
Confederation Life	6,104	12,299,605	310,831	12,239
Co-operative (Ord.)	73,414	62,705,918	1,915,794	57,846
Crown Life†	28,476	218,779,102	2,376,709	187,672
Crusader	13,447	22,365,713	493,411	12,173
Eagle Star	10,093	100,416,013	2,804,935	260,170
Ecclesiastical	604	722,890	19,830	3,289
Economic	375	858,022	22,005	270
Equitable Life	12,030	10,796,726	513,920	588,214
Equity & Law	12,481	29,266,375	1,132,448	41,972
Federation Mutual	365	252,233	10,973	3,491
Friends Prov.	16,298	75,947,529	1,770,912	76,624
General Life	9,243	25,106,832	652,580	38,767
Gresham Life	10,735	18,979,782	612,967	21,917
Guardian	16,500	67,930,000	2,275,225	309,441
Ideal	576	463,209	12,831	747
Imperial	16,133	49,807,635	1,065,771	15,158
Irish Life	9,668	9,948,121	444,843	381,519
Law Union & Rock	7,419	12,931,156	196,538	113,509
Legal & General	76,666	198,399,800	13,740,918	2,791,656
Licenses & General	2,165	5,637,529	109,228	15,098
Life Assoc. of Scotland	5,289	9,942,920	301,603	49,588
Liverpool & London and Globe	9,216	26,999,942	475,084	392,609
Liverpool Victoria	23,518	6,273,801	338,798	22,998
London & Manchester (Ord.)	13,481	13,109,395	607,770	42,801
London Assurance	19,952	19,210,639	391,767	58,953
London Life	5,507	13,428,610	431,237	79,498
Manufacturers' Life*	5,987	21,916,273	425,659	34,413
Marine & General	4,032	6,502,784	208,498	10,859
Medical Sickness	1,347	3,812,260	73,085	9,510
Midland Employers	2,666	9,130,902	99,239	21,691
Mutual Life	70,181	97,401,467	—	—
Natl. Employers Life	5,390	20,184,892	481,793	11,020
National & Local Govt.	1,170	1,383,239	21,770	336
Nat. Farmers Union	6,300	13,852,873	271,308	13,227
Nat. Mutl. of Aust.*	76,878	188,729,153	3,745,955	735,215
Nat. Mutual Life	2,343	7,341,289	413,624	10,763
Natl. Prov.	9,208	16,742,807	594,059	28,275
New Ireland (Ord.)	5,777	5,120,182	198,955	3,058
North Brit. & Merc.	8,420	31,017,927	473,971	56,376
Northern*	14,096	70,129,665	951,232	254,496
Norwich Union	112,967	233,257,000	4,667,828	5,250,750
Pearl (Ord.)	66,487	70,360,235	2,229,294	1,095,630
Phoenix	15,228	40,394,388	591,408	61,691
Pioneer*	12,111	2,496,582	131,489	2,021
Prov. Life Assoc. of London	12,922	21,914,838	456,993	4,068
Prov. Mutual	33,787	23,289,215	618,374	13,606
Prudential (Ord.)	177,390	404,865,104	7,364,430	291,291
Refuge (Ord.)	38,285	27,447,133	1,092,913	734,024
Reliance Mutual	2,518	4,104,599	60,847	1,413
Royal Exchange	10,742	29,495,998	952,860	48,335
Royal*	40,397	107,511,462	2,082,367	2,503,277
Royal Liver (Ord.)	—	4,108,975	237,951	19,342
Royal London (Ord.)	17,323	18,677,921	545,639	40,309
Salvation Army (Ord.)	4,042	1,584,550	74,535	4,667
Scottish Amicable	10,814	30,003,144	795,280	23,956

Name of Office	No. of policies issued	Net sums assured	Net annual premiums	Net single premiums
	£	£	£	£
Scottish Equitable	6,875	18,728,640	470,384	31,529
Scottish Legal (Ord.)	1,925	476,020	28,059	3,882
Scottish Life	8,896	23,013,074	711,190	30,192
Scottish Mutual	7,648	14,115,068	384,393	12,775
Scottish Prov.	5,360	23,327,753	904,403	125,702
Scottish Union & Natl.	3,859	14,369,182	284,830	18,858
Scottish Widows	15,299	64,567,344	1,052,557	41,368
Sentinel*	1,400	2,483,083	90,885	87,051
Standard*	29,145	149,469,344	2,067,183	104,308
Sun Life of Canada	93,746	346,462,479	5,575,251	401,250
Sun Life	26,977	111,036,327	2,865,291	116,930
Teachers	2,351	2,241,369	67,709	Nil
Tunstall & District	270	72,800	4,265	Nil
United Friendly	5,223	4,204,810	173,526	1,482
United Kingdom	12,901	24,293,338	809,725	26,626
University Life	1,051	1,962,288	54,079	18,197
Wesleyan & Gen. (Ord.)	6,095	7,543,401	216,114	16,475
Yorkshire	17,157	67,914,239	1,122,360	83,704

Industrial Companies

Office	Policies Issued	Net sums Assured	Office	Policies Issued	Net sums Assured
Blackburn	40,520	2,611,934	Pioneer	10,218	657,779
Britannic	320,342	22,042,767	Prudental	1,488,349	138,605,098
City of Glasgow Friendly	27,361	1,837,000	Refuge	307,404	23,508,229
Co-operative	839,069	59,203,766	Reliance Mutual	33,444	2,516,870
Irish Life	111,958	7,794,750	Royal Liver	—	20,058,748
Liverpool Victoria	620,243	44,613,915	Royal London	323,254	31,338,167
London and Manchester	111,208	9,009,998	Salvation Army	66,545	3,398,407
New Ireland	51,854	2,323,234	Scottish Legal	77,627	3,893,300
Pearl	680,164	56,656,729	Wesleyan and General	76,139	6,157,210

Manufacturers Life—United Kingdom only. Natl. Mutual of Australasia, year ending September 30, 1962. Northern, including figures of associated companies. Pioneer, year ending March 31, 1963. Royal, including figures of associated companies. Sentinel, year ending March 31, 1962. Standard, year ending November 15, 1962. † 1961 figures.

DIRECTORY OF INSURANCE COMPANIES

The class of Insurance undertaken is shown in the second column as follows :— A—Accident (which includes Motor, Employers' Liability, etc.); F—Fire (including Burglary) ; L—Life: and M—Marine.

Est'd.	Nature of Business	Name of Company	Address of Head and London Offices
1961	L	Abbey Life	St. Paul's Corner, 1–3, St. Paul's Churchyard, E.C.4.
1904	Annuities	African Life	*Johannesburg:* City Wall House, Finsbury Pavement, E.C.2.
1951	AFM	Albion	Albion House, 34–35 Leadenhall St., E.C.3.
1824	AFLM	Alliance	Bartholomew-lane, E.C.2.
1921	L	American Life	*Delaware,* U.S.A. 50, Pall Mall, S.W.1.
1904	AFM	Army, Navy, & General	Woodruffe Ho., Coopers Row, Trinity Square, E.C.3.
1808	AFLM	Atlas	92, Cheapside, E.C.2.
1849	L	Australian Mutual Provident	*Sydney:* 73-76, King William St., E.C 4.
1925	AFL	Avon	*Stratford-on-Avon:* 88–89, Gracechurch Street, E.C.3.
1905	AFM	Baptist	4, Southampton-row, W.C.1.
1883	AFLM	Beacon	*Birmingham:* 3, Berkeley Square, W.1.
1894	AFM	Bedford General	Fairfax Ho., Fulwood Pl., High Holborn, W.C.1.
1961	L	Bedford Life	Fairfax Ho., Fulwood Pl., High Holborn, W C.1
1839	L	Blackburn Assurance	151, Dale-street, Kingsway, *Liverpool,* 2.
1925	AFM	Black Sea and Baltic	106, Fenchurch Street, E.C.3.
1866	AFL	Britannic	*Birmingham:* 44–46, Kingsway, W.C.2.
1863	M	British & Foreign Marine	*Liverpool:* Lime-street, E.C.3.
1878	Machinery	British Engine, &c.	*Manchester:* 80, Lombard St., E.C.3.
1854	AFL	British Equitable	Royal Exchange, Cornhill, E.C.3.
1904	AFM	British General	36–44, Moorgate, E.C.2.
1888	AFM	British Law	31 & 32, King-street, Cheapside, E.C.2
1896	L	British Life	*Tunbridge Wells:* 123–127, Cannon Street, E.C.4.

Est'd.	Nature of Business	Name of Company	Address of Head and London Offices
1920	AFL	British Nat. Life	4, South-place, Moorgate, E.C.2.
1920	AF	British Merchants...........	92–94, Gracechurch St., E.C.3.
1908	AFM	British Oak.................	81-82, Cornhill, E.C.3.
1881	A	Builders' Accident	31 & 32, Bedford-street, Strand, W.C.2.
1805	AFLM	Caledonian	*Edinburgh:* 5. Lothbury, E.C.2.
1934	AFM	Cambrian...................	15, Lime St., E.C.3.
1847	L	Canada Life................	*Toronto:* 6, Charles II Street, S.W.1,
1932	Dog Ins.	Canine Ins. Assoc............	90, Gracechurch-street, E.C.3.
1903	AFM	Car & General	83, Pall Mall, S.W.1.
1899	AFM	Central....................	1, Cornhill, E.C.3. [E.C.3.
1885	AFM	Century....................	18, Charlotte-sq., *Edin.*; 7, Leadenhall-street,
1922	AFMex-motor	Chemists' Mutual............	4 & 5, Queen-sq., W.C.1.
1862	L	City of Glasgow Friendly	*Glasgow:* 160 Bishopsgate, E.C.2.
1824	L	Clerical, Medical, & Gen.	15, St. James's-square, S.W.1.
1873	L & Pers. Acc.	Colonial Mutual.............	*Melbourne:* 24, Ludgate Hill, E.C.4.
1919	AFM	Comrcl. Ins. Co. of Ireland...	10, Donegall Square, S., *Belfast.*
1861	AFLM	Commercial Union..........	24, Cornhill, E.C.3. Life Dept., 66, Cheapside.
1871	L	Confederation..............	*Toronto:* 120, Regent Street, W.1. [E.C. 2,
1891	AF	Congregational.............	21–22, Apsley Crescent, *Bradford* 8.
1867	AFLM	Co-operative...............	*Manchester:* 42, Kingsway, W.C.2.
1905	AFM	Cornhill...................	32, Cornhill, E.C.3.
1807	AFM	County Fire	50, Regent-street, W.1.
1900	L	Crown Life.................	*Toronto:* 21-24, Cockspur Street, S.W.1.
1899	AFLM	Crusader	Woodhatch, Reigate, Surrey; 52, Lime St., E.C.3.
1908	AFM	Dominion..................	*Edinburgh:* 12–13, Hatton Garden, E.C.1.
1904	AFLM	Eagle Star.................	1, Threadneedle-street. E.C.2. Life Dept. 22, [Arlington-street, S.W.1.
1887	AFL	Ecclesiastical..............	Aldwych House, W.C.2.
1901	AFLM	Economic..................	105, Fenchurch-street, E.C.3.
1823	AFM	Edinburgh.................	24, Cornhill, E.C.3.
1880	AFLM	Employers' Liability	Hamilton House, Victoria Embankment, E.C.4.
1762	L	Equitable Life	19, Coleman-street, E.C.2.
1844	L	Equity & Law...............	20, Lincoln's Inn Fields, W.C.2.
1802	AF	Essex & Suffolk	*Colchester:* 7 & 8, King-street, E.C2.
1894	AFM	Excess....................	13, Fenchurch-avenue, E.C.3.
1900	AF	Farmers' Finance and Ins......	10, Davygate, York.
1904	AF	Federated Employers'.........	*Manchester:* 34–35, Leadenhall St., E.C.3.
1925	AFL	Federation Mutual	*Redhill:* 64, West Smithfield, E.C.1.
1890	AF	Fine Art & General..........	64, Cornhill, E.C.3.
1832	L	Friends' Prov. & Century....	7, Leadenhall-street, E.C.3. Life Dept., Dorking Surrey.
1885	AFLM	General Accident............	General-buildings, Aldwych, W.C.2.
1837	L	General Life................	4–5, Grosvenor Place Hyde Park Corner, S.W.1.
1848	L	Gresham Life...............	Barrington Ho., 59, Gresham St., E.C.2.
1910	AFM	Gresham Fire & Accident.....	188–190, Fleet-st., E.C.4.
1840	AFM	Guarantee Society...........	36, Old Jewry, E.C.2.
1821	AFLM	Guardian..................	68, King William-street, E.C.4. Life Dept., 66–73, Shoe Lane, E.C.4.
1919	AFM	Guildhall..................	83, Queen St., E.C.4.
1908	AFM	Hibernian..................	48 & 49, Dame-street. *Dublin.* [W.7.
1932	FL	Ideal	*Birmingham*, 13. 5, The Broadway, Hanwell,
1897	L	Imperial Life of Canada......	*Toronto:* 28-29, St. James's-square, S.W.1.
1824	M	Indemnity Marine...........	4, Fenchurch-avenue, E.C.3.
1935	AFM	Insurance Corpn. of Ireland...	34–36, Dame-street, *Dublin*, C.1. [C.3.
1939	L	Irish Life..................	Hammam Bldgs., Upper O'Connell St., *Dublin*,
1880	A	Iron Trades Employers'......	Iron Trades Ho., 21-24, Grosvenor Pl., S.W.1.
1892	AFM	Law Accident..............	5, Chancery-lane, W.C.2.
1845	AF	Law Fire..................	114, Chancery-lane, W.C.2.
1806	AFLM	Law Union & Rock	7, Chancery-lane, W.C.2.
1907	AFM	Legal.....................	24-28, Lombard Street, E.C.3.
1836	AFLM	Legal and General..........	Temple Court, 11, Queen Victoria St., E.C.4.
1890	AFLM	Licenses & General..........	24-28, Moorgate, E.C.2.
1838	L	Life Assoc. of Scotland.......	82, Princes-st., *Edin.:* 61–62 Coleman St., E.C.2.
1836	AFLM	L'pool & London & Globe....	1, Dale-street, *Liverpool:* 1, Cornhill, E.C.3.
1866	Plate Glass	L'pool & London Plate Glass.	14, Dale-st., *Liverpool:* 30, Walbrook, E.C.4.
1918	AFM	Liverpool Marine & General ..	7, Leadenhall-street, E.C.3.
1843	L	Liverpool Victoria Friendly...	Victoria House, Southampton-row, W.C.1.
1890	AFM	Local Government Guarantee.	Byron House, 7-9, St. James's-street, S.W.1.
1836	AFM	Lombard Insurance	3 & 4, Lime St., E.C.3.
1720	AFLM	London Assurance...........	1, King William-street, E.C.4.
1869	AFM	London Guar. & Accident....	4-5, King William-street, E.C.4.
1861	AFM	London & Lancashire........	7, Chancery-lane. W.C.2 (Chief Administration).
1806	L	London Life................	81, King William-street, E.C.4.
1919	AFLM	London & Edinburgh	1, Seething-lane, E.C.3.

Est'd.	Nature of Business	Name of Company	Address of Head and London Offices
1869	AFL	London & Manchester	50, Finsbury-square, E.C.2.
1885	Plate Glass	London & Manch. Plate Glass	30–37, Walbrook, E.C.4.
1860	AFM	London & Provincial Marine..	4, Fenchurch-avenue, E.C.3.
1862	AFM	London & Scottish..........	Northern House, Gresham-street, E.C.2.
1887	L	Manufacturers.............	*Toronto:* 197, Knightsbridge, S.W.7.
1836	M	Marine...................	159, Leadenhall-street, E.C.3.
1852	L	Marine & General..........	1, St. Swithin's Lane, E.C.4.
1864	M	Maritime.................	*Liverpool:* Lloyd's-buildings, E.C.3.
1884	L Sickness A	Med., Sickness, Ann. and Life.	7–10, Chandos Street, Cavendish Sq. W.1.
1907	Reinsurance	Mercantile & General........	Moorfields House, Tenter St., E.C.2.
1871	M	Merchants' Marine..........	36–38, Cornhill, E.C.3.
1872	AF	Methodist................	51, Spring-gardens, *Manchester.*
1898	AFLM	Midland Employers' Mutual..	*Birmingham:* 52–54, Leadenhall St., E.C.3.
1934	L	Migdal...................	*Jerusalem:* 5, Fenchurch St., E C.3.
1940	AFM	Minster..................	Minster House, Arthur-street, E.C.4.
1909	AFM	Monument................	98-106, Cannon-street, E.C.4.
1906	AFM	Motor Union..............	10, St. James's-street, S.W.1.
1903	AF	Municipal Mutual..........	22, Old Queen-street, Westminster, S.W.1.
1886	L	Mutual Life & Citizens'......	*Sydney:* 1, Lancaster-place, Strand, W.C.2.
1925	AFL	Nation Life & Gen..........	Nation Ho., Teddington, Mdx.
1890	AFL	National & Loc. Gov. Officers	Nalgo Ho., 8, Harewood Row, N.W.1.
1864	Boilers, etc.	National Boiler............	*Manchester:* Empire House, St. Martin's-le-Grand, E.C.1.
1935	L	National Employers' Life.....	Moor House, London Wall, E.C.2
1914	AFM	National Employers' Mutual..	National Employers House, Bury-street, E.C.3.
1910	AFL	National Farmers' Union.....	*Stratford-on-Avon:* 88–89, Gracechurch Street, E.C.3.
1863	Fidelity Guar. etc.	National Guaran. & Suretyship	*Edinburgh:* Granville Ho., Arundel-st., W.C.2.
1830	L	National Mutual Life........	5, Bow Churchyard (off Cheapside), E.C.4.
1869	L	National Mutual of Austral....	*Melbourne:* Austral., Ho., Basinghall Avenue, E.C.2.
1835	L	National Provident..........	48, Gracechurch-street, E.C.3.
1854	Plate Glass	National Provincial.........	St. Swithin's House, Walbrook, E.C.4.
1921	Naval Officers risks, etc.	Navigators & General........	Woodruffe Ho., Coopers Row, Trinity Square, E.C.3.
1924	L	New Ireland..............	12, Dawson-street. *Dublin,* C.2.
1809	AFLM	North British & Mercantile...	*Edinburgh:* 24, Cornhill, E.C.3. Life Dept., 66, Cheapside, E.C.2.
1862	FM	North Pacific..............	*Hong Kong:* 78-80, Cornhill, E.C.3.
1836	AFLM	Northern.................	1, Moorgate, E.C.2 and 1, Union Terrace, Aberdeen.
1797	AFM	Norwich Union Fire.........	*Norwich:* 51–54, Fenchurch-street, E.C.3.
1808	L	Norwich Union Life	*Norwich:* 51–54, Fenchurch-street, E.C.3.
1871	AFM	Ocean Accident............	36-44, Moorgate, E.C.2.
1859	M	Ocean Marine	37-9, Lime-street. E.C.3.
1931	AFM	Orion....................	70–72, King William St., E.C.4.
1886	AF	Palatine..................	24, Cornhill, E.C.3.
1824	AF	Patriotic.................	9, College Green, Dublin.
1864	AFLM	Pearl....................	High Holborn, W.C.1.
1958	Sickness & Acc.	Permanent Sickness..........	7–10, Chandos Street, Cavendish Sq. W.1.
1782	AFLM	Phœnix..................	Phœnix House, King William-street, E.C.4.
1891	L	Pioneer..................	31, Dale-street, *Liverpool,* 2.
1920	AFM	Planet Assurance...........	63, Threadneedle-street, E.C.2.
1919	Motor	Premier Motor Policies......	Melbourne Ho., Aldwych, W.C.2.
1877	L	Prov. Life Assocn. of London.	Provident House, Bishopsgate, E.C.2.
1840	L	Provident Mutual Life.......	25-31, Moorgate, E.C.2.
1903	AFM	Provincial................	*Kendal:* Provincial Ho., 100, Cannon-st., E.C.4.
1848	AFLM	Prudential................	Holborn-bars, E.C.1.
1886	AFM	Queensland...............	*Sydney:* 22, Birchin-lane, E.C.3.
1849	AF	Railway Passengers.........	64, Cornhill, E.C.3.
1864	AFL	Refuge...................	Oxford-st., *Manchester:* 34, Leadenhall St., E.C.3.
1911	L	Reliance Mutual	*Tunbridge Wells:* 123–7, Cannon Street, E.C.4.
1906	AF	Reliance Fire & Accident	*Tunbridge Wells:* 123–7, Cannon-street, E.C.4.
1881	AFM	Reliance Marine	*Liverpool:* 51, Lime-street, E.C.3.
1823	Reversions	Reversionary Interest Society..	19, Coleman-street, E.C.2.
1918	AF	Road Transport & General ...	Grosvenor Buildings, Hyde Park, S.W.1.
1845	AFLM	Royal....................	*Liverpool:* 24-28, Lombard-street. E.C.3.
1720	AFL	Royal Exchange............	Royal Exchange, E.C.3. Life Dept.: 36, Cheapside, E.C.2.
1850	L	Royal Liver Friendly........	*Liverpool:* 8-9, Giltspur-street, E.C.1.
1861	AFL	Royal London	Royal London House, Finsbury-square, E.C.2.
1887	L	Royal Nat. Pensions (Nurses).	(Temp.) Eastbury Ho., Albert Embankment, S.E.1.

Est'd.	Nature of Business	Name of Company	Address of Head and London Offices
1867	L	Salvation Army	220–226, Tottenham Court-road, W.1.
1909	AFM	Salvation Army Fire	4, Holywell Hill, St. Albans, Herts.
1826	L	Scottish Amicable	*Glasgow:* 17, Tokenhouse Yard, E.C.2.
1881	FM	Scottish Boiler	*Glasgow:* 36, Old Jewry, E.C.2.
1831	L	Scottish Equitable	28, St. Andrew-sq., *Edinb.:* 13, Cornhill, E.C.3.
1919	AFM	Scottish General	*Glasgow:* 99, Aldwych, W.C.2.
1877	AFLM	Scottish Insurance	115, George-st., *Edinb.:* 38, Eastcheap, E.C.3.
1852	L	Scottish Legal	95 Bothwell-st., *Glasgow*, C.2.
1881	L	Scottish Life	*Edinburgh:* 6, Old Jewry, E.C.2.
1876	AF	Scottish Metropolitan	Northern House, Gresham-street, E.C.2.
1883	AL	Scottish Mutual	*Glasgow*, C.2; 6, Bell Yard, Law Courts, W.C.2.
1837	L	Scottish Provident	*Edinburgh:* 3, Lombard-st., E.C.3.
1824	AFLM	Scottish Union & National	*Edinburgh:* 25, Bucklersbury, E.C.3.
1815	L	Scottish Widows'	*Edinburgh:* 28, Cornhill, E.C.3.
1875	AFM	Sea	*Liverpool:* 7, Lothbury, E.C.2.
1904	AFL	Sentinel	11–13, Holborn Viaduct, E.C.1.
1872	AFM	South British	*New Zealand:* 4, Fenchurch Avenue, E.C.3.
1899	L	Stamford Mutual	21 & 23, Stamford Street, S.E.1.
1825	L	Standard Life	*Edinburgh:* 3, Abchurch Yard, Cannon St., E.C.4.
1871	M	Standard Marine	*Liverpool.*
1891	AFM	State	*Liverpool:* 30, Walbrook, E.C.4.
1710	AFM	Sun	63, Threadneedle-street, E.C.2.
1810	L	Sun Life	107, Cheapside, E.C.2.
1865	L	Sun Life of Canada	*Montreal:* 2, 3 & 4, Cockspur-st., S.W.1.
1936	FL	Teachers' Assurance	Hamilton Ho., Mabledon Pl., W.C.1.
1860	M	Thames & Mersey	*Liverpool:* 3-6, Lime-street, E.C.3.
1894	FM	Thistle	3, Lombard-street, E.C.3.
1850	FM	Triton	*Calcutta:* 3–4, Lime-st., E.C.3.
1839	L	Tunstall & District Assurance Collecting Society	Station Chambers, Tunstall, *Stoke on Trent.*
1867	M	Ulster Marine	1, Linen Hall-street, *Belfast.*
1714	AFM	Union Assurance	1 & 2, Royal Exchange-buildings, E.C.3.
1835	AFM	Union Ins. Soc. of Canton	*Hongkong:* 81, Cornhill, E.C.3.
1863	M	Union Marine	*Liverpool:* Lloyd's Building, E.C.3.
1915	AFM	United British	Byron House, 7-9, St. James's-street, S.W.1.
1908	AFL	United Friendly	42, Southwark Bridge Road, S.E.1.
1840	L	United Kingdom Prov.	33–36, Gracechurch-street, E.C.3.
1912	AFM	United Scottish	20, Billiter-street, E.C.3.
1825	L	University	19a Coleman St., E.C.2.
1919	Reinsurance	Victory Insurance	73-76 King William-street, E.C.4.
1859	Machinery	Vulcan Boiler and General	*Manchester 2:* 25, Birchin Lane, E.C.3.
1875	AFM	Warden	24–28, Lombard-st., E.C.3.
1949	AFLM	Welfare	110, Cannon Street, E.C.4.
1911	AF	Welsh Insurance Corpn.	*Cardiff:* Northern Ho., Gresham-st., E.C.2.
1841	AFL	Wesleyan & General	*Birmingham* 4: Candlewick House, Cannon-st., E.C.4.
1886	AF	West of Scotland	*Glasgow:* 24, Cornhill, E.C.3.
1851	AFM	Western	*Toronto:* Kent Ho., Telegraph-st., E.C.2.
1912	AFLM	Western Australian	*Perth:* 107/111 Fleet St., E.C.4.
1717 / 1906	AF	Westminster Fire	27, King-street, Covent-garden, W.C.2.
1865	AF	White Cross	Northern House, 29, Gresham-street, E.C.2.
1919	AFM	World Auxily. Ins. Corpn.	4 & 7, Fenchurch-avenue, E.C.3.
1894	AFM	World Marine & General	4 & 7, Fenchurch-avenue, E.C.3.
1824	AFLM	Yorkshire	St. Helen's-square, *York:* Becket House, 36-37, Old Jewry, E.C.2.
1872	AF	Zurich	*Zurich:* Fairfax Ho., Fulwood-place, W.C.1.

Co-operative Societies—Great Britain

During the 10 years ended 1962 Co-operative Retail Trading Societies (almost all General Supply Stores) expanded their membership and assets by 18 per cent. and 25 per cent respectively as shown by the following particulars covering the 903 societies on the register at the end of 1962 and 1,107 societies in 1952:

Year	Number of Members	Share Capital	Sales	Year's Surplus	Interest on Shares	Dividends on Sales	Total Assets
		£000's	£000's	£000's	£000's	£000's	£000's
1962	12,893,000	254,912	1,019,419	55,720	7,515	43,648	497,142
1952	10,932,000	224,411	704,245	45,965	5,956	35,625	394,692

In addition, 146 Co-operative Wholesale and Productive Trading Societies (with a total membership of 52,000) were on the register at the end of 1962. The total figures for these societies are dominated by those of the two main Wholesale Trading Societies (with their "Joint" undertaking) whose combined sales for 1962 amounted to £571,739,000, their assets at the end of the year totalling £185,556,000.

Friendly Societies—Great Britain

Acts 1896–1958

In spite of the expansion of *Compulsory* "Health" insurance since the introduction of the *State* scheme in 1912 and its extension in 1948, the *Voluntary* business of Friendly Societies registered under the Friendly Societies Act, 1896, still continues on a large scale, as shown by the following comparative totals—those in ordinary type relate to registered Friendly Societies proper (embracing both "Centralized" societies and "Orders with Branches"); those in *italics* "Collecting" societies which, although registered under the Friendly Societies Acts, are subject also to the special provisions of the Industrial Assurance Acts:—

End of Year	No. of Societies on Register		Membership	Assurances or Policies	Total Funds	
			Thousands		£000's	
1961	10,467	*91*	5,968	*31,980*	257,319	*332,449*
1938	19,600	*149*	8,491	*25,738*	151,613	*84,837*
1913	25,475	*71*	6,783	*7,481*	51,489	*11,165*

Although recent years have seen the growth of societies registered for such specific purposes as the provision of institutional treatment or assuring annuities and pensions, most friendly societies continue to provide the customary benefits in sickness and at death. During 1961 Friendly Societies proper paid out £5,635,000 in sickness benefit and £2,162,000 in death benefit while payments on death claims by collecting societies amounted to £10,574,000.

Many societies still operate mainly on the old system of accumulating funds on a mutual basis. Others, usually termed deposit societies, allocate all or the greater part of their funds annually to the individual credit of the members to be withdrawn by them as the rules provide. Apart from the National Deposit Society's method of a uniform contribution throughout membership there are several systems operated on individual account lines, one of which (known as the "Holloway" principle) is worked by a contribution increasing with each year of attained age after the member reaches age 30 up to age 65.

The membership and funds figures—as at the end of 1961—set out below indicate the strength of several leading old established societies, including the three largest Orders which operate through registered districts and branches subject to a central body:—

FRIENDLY Socs.—Name with (in brackets) Year Established	Membership	Total Funds
		£
National Deposit Friendly Society (1868)	560,000	24,575,000
Hearts of Oak Benefit Society (1842)	553,000	18,093,000
Independent Order of Odd Fellows, Manchester Unity (1810)	410,000	28,339,000
Ancient Order of Foresters (1834)	339,000	20,266,000
Independent Order of Rechabites, Salford Unity (1835)	179,000	7,245,000

COLLECTING Socs.—Name and Year Established	No. of Assurances: Premium Paying	No. of Assurances: Free Paid-up	Total Funds
			£
Liverpool Victoria Friendly Society (1843)	12,202,000	4,072,000	186,658,000
Royal Liver Friendly Society (1850)	7,408,000	2,086,000	93,632,000
Scottish Legal Life Assurance Society (1852)	2,526,000	935,000	24,905,000

The present National Insurance scheme with its provision of "cradle to the grave" benefits has had serious repercussions on the Voluntary Friendly Societies. The total membership at the end of 1961 of 5,968,000 represents a decrease of nearly 30 per cent. on the membership at the end of 1938. The decrease in membership continues year by year although only at a rate of about 1 per cent. It is perhaps surprising that the membership has remained so nearly steady over the past ten years for even when the modest scheme of 1912 was introduced some people doubted the Voluntary Friendly Societies' ability to survive for long. Nevertheless, until 1948 they continued to grow in the face of keen competition. Their remarkable expansion naturally brought many societies up to a point where they found it increasingly difficult to maintain a sufficient inflow of new, young entrants to replace membership losses due to death and other causes.

In considering how far the general body of members comprising the Friendly Societies movement can afford to continue their voluntary insurances along with State scheme contributions which are likely to continue to increase in the future, it must not be overlooked that present-day wage levels are substantially higher for all classes of workers than before the war and successive Governments have said that continued Voluntary insurance to supplement State benefits, wherever one's means permit, should be encouraged.

Moreover, in addition to the widespread *branch* units of the better known "Orders," there are numerous small independent societies whose membership is maintained more easily than in the large societies, by age-long custom of family and social ties within their own locality, and there still exist a few such societies whose formation dates back far beyond any "Friendly Society" legislation. In fact, long before the term "Friendly Society" came into use, the seeds of voluntary mutual insurance had been sown in the ancient religious and trade "Guilds." As is evident from the many extant parchment returns detailing their rules and possessions under a decree of Richard II, Guilds had become widespread in Britain by the 14th century. By then, the purely charitable character of the original Guilds had largely changed with the emergence of numerous small institutions adopting primitive mutual insurance methods of a regular flat rate contribution in order to obtain relief when sick or in old age and a payment to the widow in the event of death.

The present register of Friendly Societies includes several societies which have been in existence for upwards of 200 years, the oldest operating in Scotland, being the "Incorporation of Carters in Leith" established as long ago as 1555. The two oldest in England were both formed in London—the "Society of Lintot", (estd. 1708) and the "Society for the Mutual Help of Swiss in London" (est. 1703), the first of these having been formed by Huguenot refugees from the Protestant persecution under Louis XIV.

The first Act for the encouragement and protection of "Friendly Societies" in this country was not passed until 1793, but various amending Acts were put on the Statute Book during the next century as the result of the recommendations of successive Select Committees (including a Royal Commission in 1871). For example, it was not until the 1829 Act that all registered Friendly Societies were required to keep proper records of individual sickness and mortality amongst their members, which data enabled the construction of standard actuarial tables showing the expected (average) duration of sickness at successive ages, and also (with data from the Census) the corresponding mortality rates.

The rules and other documents of societies deposited with local justices passed into the custody of the Registrar following the Act of 1846 and are of considerable interest to social historians. Those relating to some societies no longer on the register have been transferred to the Public Record Office for permanent preservation.

The present consolidating Act of 1896 allows various specific classes other than "Friendly Societies" to be registered thereunder, but exemption from income tax (irrespective of the extent of interest income) is enjoyed only by registered "Friendly Societies."

The Friendly Societies Act, 1955, extended the purposes for which societies may be registered under the Acts, and authorized societies to invest their surplus funds in other registered societies.

Building Societies—Great Britain

Act 1962.

Building Societies are, with few exceptions, associations incorporated with limited liability under the Building Societies Act. All Building Societies are required to register their rules and file their accounts with the Registry of Friendly Societies. The following particulars showing the growth of Building Societies (as also that of Co-operative and Friendly Societies tabulated on pp. 1149 and 1150) are based on the Chief Registrar's Annual Reports. The Editor is also indebted to the publishers of the "Building Societies Year Book" for details of individual societies from which the second table hereunder has been compiled.

The building societies movement has played a considerable part in the expansion of home ownership since the war. Since 1946 building societies have advanced nearly £6,500,000,000 on mortgage, the bulk of it to assist owner-occupiers to buy their homes. Advances during 1962 amounted to £613,000,000, the highest total ever recorded in a single year and an increase of £67,000,000 on the previous year.

The number of societies on the register dropped from 706 at the beginning of 1962 to 681 at the end of the year. Twenty-eight societies were removed from the register during the year, twenty-four of them as a result of unions or transfers of engagements. Three societies were added to the register during the year; of these only one was a new society, the other two having been formed by the union of existing societies. The average number of new societies registered during the years 1958 to 1960 was eight per year. The Chief Registrar comments in his Report for 1962 that the effect the more stringent requirements of the 1960 legislation has had on the number of new societies is readily apparent.

Shareholders and depositors added £776,000,000 to their accounts during 1962 while £537,000,000 was withdrawn from these accounts. The total assets increased by £379,000,000 to £3,815,000,000. Of this total, mortgage balances accounted for £3,138,000,000, the remainder consisting chiefly of investments in securities of the Government and local authorities and cash. The investments in which societies may invest their surplus funds are restricted to those authorised by the Building Societies (Authorised Investments) Order, 1962.

For the year 1962 interest received by societies from borrowers amounted to £199,000,000. Interest payments to shareholders and depositors totalled £122,000,000. Management costs, at £22,000,000 for 1962, averaged only about 1¾*d.* per £1 of the mean mortgage assets. Of this total advertising accounted for 7 per cent. and commission and agency fees 11 per cent.

The rate of interest usually charged on mortgage advances to owner-occupiers is now 6 per cent. Interest rates paid on share and deposit accounts are usually 3½ and 3¼ per cent. respectively (income tax on both share and deposit interest being paid by the societies).

Section 1 of the House Purchase and Housing Act, 1959, empowered the Chief Registrar to designate building societies for the purposes of the section. Societies that had been designated up to the time of going to press are marked "D" in the list which follows. Deposits in a designated building society rank as "narrower-range investments requiring advice" and shares in such a society as "wider-range investments" under the First Schedule to the Trustee Investments Act, 1961.

The Building Societies Act, 1962, which consolidated into one statute the greater part of the previously existing enactments relating to building societies, consists of eight parts with 135 sections and ten schedules. It deals first with the constitution of societies, including establishment and incorporation, membership, unions and transfers of engagements. It then proceeds to Advances on Mortgage bringing together provisions from the 1939 Act and those of the 1960 Act which placed restrictions on " special advances " (that is advances to bodies corporate or exceeding £5,000). Part III deals with Borrowing Powers and Depositors.

Part IV sets out the various powers of control exercisable by the Chief Registrar. Section 11 of the Prevention of Fraud (Investments) Act, 1958, under which the Registrar had prohibited certain societies from inviting investments was repealed by the 1960 Act (but without prejudice to any order currently in force) and the Chief Registrar was empowered to direct that a building society shall not advertise at all or to give directions to a particular society as to the matter included in its advertisements. In addition he may make an order prohibiting a building society from accepting further investments. The Chief Registrar's Report to Parliament for 1962 disclosed that at the end of that year 17 orders under the 1958 Act were still in force while 5 orders under the 1960 Act prohibiting the acceptance of further investments were in force at the end of 1962 (of which one was revoked in April 1963).

Matters of internal administration of societies regulated by Parts V and VI of the 1962 Act include the keeping of books of account and register of members, the preparation of annual accounts in a form prescribed by the Chief Registrar, the qualifications, appointment and removal of auditors, the form and content of directors' and auditors' reports, the right of members to receive copies of the accounts and reports, the calling and conduct of general meetings and the duties of directors. Part VII deals with winding up and dissolution while Part VIII contains a variety of miscellaneous and supplementary provisions.

The standard rules for meetings of building societies formerly contained in the Fifth Schedule to the 1960 Act are now to be found in the Ninth Schedule of the 1962 Act.

BUILDING SOCIETIES, GREAT BRITAIN, 1962—with 1961 totals in italics.

Class	Number	Share Investors	Advances during Year	Share Capital	Due to Depositors and other Creditors	General Reserve and Balance C/fd.	Mortgage Assets	Invests. and other Assets
Assets over			£000's	£000's	£000's	£000's	£000's	£000's
£10m.	53	3,711,910	515,807	2,726,576	206,100	136,639	2,619,042	572,393
Other Socs.	628	778,526	97,176	538,326	36,093	31,918	519,040	104,857
1962 TOTALS	681	4,490,436	612,983	3,264,902	242,193†	168,557	3,138,082*	677,250
1961 "	*706*	*4,122,084*	*545,761*	*2,920,890*	*225,503*	*150,933*	*2,870,553*	*566,198*

† Total Depositors, 578,603. * Total Borrowers, 2,509,759.

SOCIETIES WITH TOTAL ASSETS EXCEEDING £500,000—AT END OF FINANCIAL YEAR, 1962

Year Estabd.	* Name of Society (abbreviated) Head Office	Share Investors	Total Assets
	ENGLAND.		£
1869D	Accrington Savings and Bldg. Soc. 15 Dutton St., Accrington	1,440	1,126,000
1853D	Barnsley P., Permanent Bldg., Regent St., Barnsley...............	10,009	7,815,000
1851D	Barnstaple, Bridge Buildings, Barnstaple	2,812	1,811,000
1868D	" — Queen Anne, Queen Anne Chambers, The Strand Barnstaple	1,002	613,000
1953D	Bath Investment and Bldg. Soc., 20, Charles St., Bath	3,865	1,170,000
1870D	" Liberal, 1 South Parade, Bath.	1,682	1,394,000
1881D	Bedford Crown P., 107, Midland Rd., Bedford..................	1,213	663,000
1879D	" P., 41 Midland Road, Bedford	3,074	1,730,000
1924D	" — Bedfordshire, 77–83 Harpur St., Bedford	16,966	13,852,000
1866	Beverley, 16, Lairgate, Beverley.............................	1,955	656,000
1914D	Bexhill-on-Sea, 2, Devonshire Square, Bexhill-on-Sea	1,161	1,134,000
1853D	Bideford and North Devon, 5 The Quay, Bideford, Devon.........	941	702,000
1862D	" —Western Counties, 1 Grenville St., Bideford	3,433	3,459,000
1851D	Bingley, Main Street, Bingley	38,491	41,417,000
1889D	Birmingham Citizens P., 20 Bennetts Hill, Birmingham	6,423	8,195,000
1847D	" Incorporated, 42-44 Waterloo St., Birmingham	11,848	15,163,000
1903D	Birmingham—Blackheath, 12, Long Lane, Blackheath, Birmingham	1,976	1,284,000
1857	Bishop Auckland P., 56, N. Bondgate, Bishop Auckland, Co. Durham	544	500,000
1888D	Bishop's Stortford—Herts and Essex P., 4 Market Square, Bishop's Stortford..	1,079	1,095,000
1868D	Blyth—Northumbria P.B., 11 Beaconsfield St., Blyth, Nbld........	817	698,000
1934D	Bournemouth and Christchurch, 162 Old Christchurch Road, Bournemouth..............................	1,677	2,152,000
1949D	" —Wessex P., 115 Old Christchurch Rd., Bournemouth	2,472	3,026,000

*P.=Permanent: B.=Benefit. Head Office Town is shown first followed by a dash where it is not the first word in a Society's name.

Year Estabd.	Name of Society (abbreviated) Head Office	Share Investors	Total Assets
			£
1851D	Bradford Equit. 45 & 47 Bank St., Bradford	45,572	51,981,000
1885D	„ P., 57–63 Sunbridge Rd., Bradford	27,658	32,277,000
1849D	„ —Provincial, Market St., Bradford 1 and Albion St., Leeds, 1	97,807	108,510,000
1880	Brentwood—Orient P., 77 High St., Brentwood, Essex	797	870,000
1921D	Bridgwater, 1 King Sq., Bridgwater	15,469	13,114,000
1865D	Brighton & Shoreham, 115 Western Rd., Brighton	566	652,000
1865D	„ & Southern Counties P., 13 Ship St., Brighton	1,392	1,075,000
1863D	„ —Alliance, Princes Ho., North St., Brighton	77,669	96,158,000
1995D	„ —Citizens P., Marlborough Pl., Brighton	3,473	3,582,000
1930D	„ —Regency, 3 Marlborough Place, Brighton	677	767,000
1850D	Bristol & W., St. Stephen's Ho., Bristol	34,741	37,226,000
1853D	„ P. Econ., 40, Broad St., Bristol	1,801	1 602,000
1883D	Bromley, 180 High St., Bromley, Kent	682	653,000
1880D	Burgess Hill—Mid-Sussex, P., Church Rd., Burgess Hill	1,238	872,000
1850D	Burnley, Grimshaw St., Burnley	60,224	77,515,000
1874D	„ —Borough, Parker Lane, Burnley	33 082	22,078,000
1866D	Bury St. Edmund's P.B., 59 Abbeygate St., Bury St. Edmund's	1,074	865,000
1850D	Cambridge, 6 Post Office Terrace, Cambridge	4,038	4,002,000
1850D	Carlisle—Cumberland, 38 Fisher St., Carlisle	14,410	9,256,000
1907D	Chalfont St. Giles—Buckinghamshire, High St., Chalfont St. Giles, Bucks.	3,285	1,621,000
1898D	Chatham Reliance, Manor Rd., Chatham	5,280	3,758,000
1850D	Cheltenham & Gloucester, Clarence St., Cheltenham	42,272	44,695,000
1845D	Chesham, 12 Market Sq., Chesham	1,131	881,000
1888	„ and Dt. M and P., Norfolk Hse., Station Rd., Chesham	647	521,000
1861D	Cheshunt, 100 Crossbrook St., Cheshunt, Waltham Cross	5,272	4,486,000
1937	Chislehurst—Lion, Chislehurst, Kent	7,078	5,206,000
1859	Chorley and District, 51 St. Thomas's Road, Chorley	3,105	896,000
1912D	Coalville P., 19 London Rd., Coalville	987	753,000
1869D	Colchester Equitable, 3 Pelham's Lane, High St., Colchester	1,171	1,412,000
1856D	„ P. B., 11 Sir Isaac's Walk, Colchester	1,186	1,272,000
1866	Colne, Albert Rd., Colne	2,835	2,601,000
1884D	Coventry Economic, 19 & 20 High St., Coventry	40,856	29,422,000
1892D	„ Mut., 11 Priory Row, Coventry	3,598	3,203,000
1872D	„ Provident 25Warwick Rd., Coventry	7,135	6,292,000
1906	Cradley Heath & Dt. B., 194 High St., Cradley Heath	1,903	1,252,000
1864D	Croydon—Vigilant, 7, Norfolk Hse., Wellesley Rd., Croydon	1,618	1,469,000
1946D	Darlington, Church Row, Market Place, Darlington	11,231	9,342,000
1869D	Darwen,—Over Darwen, 24, Railway Rd., Darwen	824	543,000
1859D	Derbyshire, 7 Iron Gate, Derby	28,546	24,143,000
1866D	Dewsbury & W. Riding, Church St., Dewsbury	12,313	11,409,000
1858	Dudley & Dist. B., 224 Market Place, Dudley	4,779	3,414,000
1852D	Dunstable, 9, West St., Dunstable	849	831,000
1857D	Earl Shilton, 22 The Hollow, Earl Shilton	2,982	1,535,000
1877D	Eastbourne Mut., 147 Terminus Rd., Eastbourne	8,455	9,547,000
1880D	Enfield, 47 London Rd., Enfield	3,453	2,945,000
1860	Frome Selwood P., Bath St., Frome	1,594	1,157,000
1865D	Furness & S. Cumb., 36 Cornwallis St., Barrow-in-Furness	8,681	5,836,000
1911	Gainsborough, 26, Lord St., Gainsborougth, Lincs	587	590,000
1863D	Gateshead-Newcastle and Gateshead, 46, West Street, Gateshead	1,426	1,382,000
1866D	Gravesend—North Kent P. B., 27 Windmill St., Gravesend, Kent	1,221	924,000
1880D	Grays 22 New Rd., Grays	4,685	3,477,000
1847D	„ —Essex Equit. 13 Orsett Rd., Grays,	964	900,000
1899D	„ —Essex and Kent P., 1, Orsett Rd., Grays	683	773,000
1848D	Grimsby & North Lincs. Osborne Chambers, Osborne St., Grimsby	639	866,000
1849	Halesowen B., Old Public Offices, Great Cornbow, Halesowen, Worcs.	730	503,000
1851D	„ Hasbury, Cradley and Dt.B., 5 Summer Hill, Halesowen	1,338	904,000
1853D	Halifax, Permanent Bldgs., Halifax	623,517	623,400,000
1854D	Hanley Econ., 42 Cheapside, Hanley, Stoke-on-Trent	7,083	5,294,000
1882D	Harrow, Cunningham Ho., Bessboro' Rd., Harrow	2,665	2,402,000
1851D	Hastings and East Sussex, Wellington Pl., Hastings	15,081	10,991,000
1890D	Haywards Heath & Dist. 33 The Broadway, Haywards Heath	4,669	3,266,000
1884D	Hemel Hempstead, 43 Marlowes Hemel Hempstead	1,894	1,978,000
1888	Herne Bay, 1, Midland Bank Chambers, Herne Bay, Kent	736	691,000
1870D	Hexham P. B., 2 Cattle Market, Hexham	854	776,000
1853D	Hinckley & Country, 9 Castle St., Hinckley	4,235	4,117,000
1865D	„ P., 31 Castle St., Hinckley	5,504	3,470,000
1870D	„ —Leicestershire, 19–21 The Borough, Hinckley	22,972	18,660,000
1856D	Horsham, 30, Carfax Horsham, Sussex	630	616,000
1872	Hove—Sussex Mutual, Sussex House, 126–127 Western Road, Hove.	5,009	5,127,000
1864D	Huddersfield, Britannia Bldgs., Huddersfield	41,885	44 460,000
1853D	Ilkeston P., Queen St., Ilkeston	1,007	698,000
1876D	Ipswich & District, 8 Northgate St., Ipswich	2,294	1,231,000

Year Estabd.	Name of Society (abbreviated) Head Office	Share Investors	Total Assets
			£
1849	Ipswich & Suffolk P. B., 44 Upper Brook St., Ipswich	9,610	3,866,000
1855D	„ —Eastern Counties, 13 and 15 Queen St., Ipswich	10,164	9,633,000
1877D	Jarrow—Tyne Commercial P., 10 Grange Road West, Jarrow	1,312	1,288,000
1851D	Keighley & Craven, Town Hall Square, Keighley	10,631	14,313,000
1851	Kidderminster P.B., 29 Church St., Kidderminster	734	611,000
1868	Kingston—Globe, Neville House, 55 Eden St., Kingston-on-Thames.	2,372	2,306,000
1865D	„ 6 Eden St., Kingston-on-Thames	3,304	2,939,000
1853D	Leamington Spa, 10 Euston Place, Leamington Spa	1,493	1,462,000
1875D	Leeds and Holbeck, 105 Albion St., Leeds	23,734	22,992,000
1848D	„ P., Permanent House, The Headrow, Leeds	153,662	160,889,000
1856D	Leek & Moorlands, New Stockwell Ho., Leek	40 633	75 740,000
1863D	„ United & Midlands, 50 St. Edward St., Leek	17,730	11,415,000
1853D	Leicester P., Welford Ho., Welford Place, Leicester	71,407	87,112,000
1875D	„ Temp., Halford House, Charles St., Leicester	26,162	29,014,000
1870D	Lewes, 11 High St., Lewes	4,154	3,052,000
1877D	Liverpool Investment, Investment Bldgs. Lord St., Liverpool	11,917	12,918,000
1854	„ & Provincial, 13 Tempest Hey, Liverpool	690	779,000
1917	„ —King Edward, 19 Castle St., Liverpool	1,102	541,000
	London :—		
1849D	Abbey National, Abbey House, Baker St., N.W.1.	778,542	485,225,000
1870D	Argyle, 105 Seven Sisters Rd., Holloway, N.7.	2,983	1,461,000
1864	Bolton, 213, Baker St., N.W.1.	602	541,000
1878D	Chelsea, 110/112 King's Road, S.W.3	8,535	9,061,000
1882D	Church of England, 6/7 New Bridge St., E.C.4.	13,791	14,121,000
1946D	City & Metropolitan, 145, Moorgate, E.C.2.	2,839	2,539,000
1862D	City of London, 34 London Wall, E.C.2.	7,884	9,408,000
1908	City Prudential, 131–2 Park Lane, W.1.	9,035	9,506,000
1931D	Civil Service, 20 Victoria St., S.W.1	3,117	2,822,000
1884D	Co-operative P., New Oxford Ho., W.C.1.	471,347	280,042,000
1956	Eagle, Chancery House, Chancery Lane W.C.2.	1,322	902,000
1927D	Ealing and Acton, 55 The Mall, Ealing, W.5.	1,048	1,162,000
1879D	Equity 164A Strand, W.C.2	2,196	1,409,000
1902D	Finchley, 767 High Rd., N. Finchley, N.12	3,865	4,316,000
1896D	Fourth P.O. Brettenham Ho., Lancaster Pl., W.C.2	14,464	14,590,000
1946	General, 51 Grosvenor St., W.1	377	761,000
1876D	Goldhawk Mut. B., 15–17 High Rd., Chiswick, W.4	4,571	4,348,000
1852D	Greenwich, 281 Greenwich High Rd., S.E.10	2,756	2,961,000
1871D	Guardian, Guardian House, 120, High Holborn, W.C.1.	13,221	15,575,000
1849D	Hastings and Thanet, 12–14, Wigmore St., W. 1.	56,334	49,853,000
1875D	Hearts of Oak P., 47–49 Oxford St., W.1	6,178	7,254,000
1926D	Hendon, 81 Church Rd., Hendon, N.W.4	1,994	1,172,000
1957D	Holloway and City Terminus, 246, Upper St., N.1	1,852	1,470,000
1852D	Lambeth, 118/120 Westminster Bridge Rd., S.E.1	9,568	10,732,000
1883D	London and Essex, 2 Romford Rd., Stratford, E.15	1,974	2,072,000
1863D	London Commercial, Guilford Hse., Gray's I. Rd., W.C.1	1,208	871,000
1962D	Magnet and North West, North West Hse., Marylebone Rd., N.W.1.	11,998	11,826,000
1886	Metrogas, 709, Old Kent Rd., S.E.15.	1,273	567,000
1866D	Mornington P., 240 Kentish Town Road, N.W.5	4,622	2,636,000
1866D	New Cross Equitable, 470 New Cross Rd., S.E.14	1,373	1,512,000
1886	North London, 407 Holloway Rd., N.7.	485	681,000
1879	Paddington, 17–19 Gt. Western Rd., W.9.	731	705,000
1879D	Peckham Mutual, Hanover Park House, Peckham, S.E.15	1,610	1,365,000
1855D	Peckham P., 6-8 Queen's Road, Peckham, S.E.15	925	692,000
1847D	People's, 99 Lewisham High St., S.E.13	1,647	1,321,000
1848D	Planet, Planet Ho., Finsbury Sq., E.C.2	13,526	14,714,000
1881D	Portman, Portman Sq., W.1.	18,449	20,598,000
1961	Productive, 231–232, Strand, W.C.,	475	515,000
1941D	Property Owners' 4, Cavendish Place, W.1.	2,863	4,583,000
1886	Queen Victoria St., 123–125, Queen Victoria St., E.C.4.	699	709,000
1937	St. Pancras, 200 Finchley Road, N.W.3	2,674	2,541,000
1922D	Shern Hall (Methodist), 306 Hoe St., Walthamstow, E.17	6,149	5,361,000
1875D	South London, 45, Streatham Hill, S.W.2	10 500	9 353,000
1876D	South Western, 6 Station Parade, Balham High Rd., S.W.12	4,330	2,051,000
1854D	Temperance P., 223-227 Regent St., W.1.	42,783	52,591,000
1877D	Walthamstow, 223 Hoe St., Walthamstow, E.17	5,153	5,842,000
1885D	Westbourne Pk., W'bourne House, W'bourne Grove, W.2	31,667	39,945,000
1879D	West London Inv., West London House, Shepherd's Bush, W.12.	3,456	3,594,000
1850D	West London P., 246, Upper Richmond Rd. West, S.W. 14	763	727,000
1875	Wimbledon, 22a Wimbledon Bridge, S.W.19	597	650,000
1847D	Woolwich Equitable, Equitable House, Woolwich, S.E.18.	284,660	222,549,000
1867D	Loughborough P., 16 Baxter Gate, Loughborough	2,248	2,359,000
1866D	Luton, 24 King St., Luton	2,621	3,251,000
1870D	Macclesfield—Cheshire, Castle St., Macclesfield	10,915	6,929,000

Year Estabd.	Name of Society (abbreviated) Head Office	Share Investors	Total Assets
			£
1859D	Maidenhead, 58 King St.. Maidenhead	8 405	9,367,000
1922	Manchester, 49, Princess St., Manchester	618	662,000
1956	,, —Mancunian, 14, St. Peter's Sq., Manchester, 2	1,687	1,175,000
1870D	Mansfield, Regent St., Mansfield	3,986	4,383,000
1870D	Market Harborough, Welland House, The Square, Market Harboro'	7,986	4,259,000
1875D	Melton Mowbray, 14 Nottingham St., Melton Mowbray	3,492	3,713,000
1872D	Middleton, 99 Long St., Middleton, Manchester	10,402	4,871,000
1860D	Nelson—Marsden, 2 Russell St., Nelson	15,274	10,520,000
1856D	Newbury, 17–20 Bartholomew St., Newbury	4,574	4,712,000
1861D	Newcastle upon Tyne P., 37/41 Grainger St., Newcastle upon Tyne.	9,595	9,875,000
1876D	,, ,, Globe P., 21 Eldon Sq., ,, ,, ,,	1,562	1,965,000
1957D	,, ,, —Grainger and Percy, Hood St., ,, ,, ,,	8,804	10,160,000
1850D	,, ,, —Northern Counties P., 2 Market St., ,, ,,	25 518	23,364,000
1865D	,, ,, —Rock, Market St., ,, ,,	26,128	22,066,000
1870D	,, ,, —Royal Arcade, 25 Grey St., ,, ,,	736	656,000
1867	,, ,, —St. Andrew's P., 3 Ellison Place, ,, ,,	892	933,000
1863D	,, ,, —Universal, 36 Grey St., ,, ,,	7,436	7,012,000
1869D	Newport—Mon'shire. & S. Wales, Friars Chrs., Newport	2,999	3,798,000
1888D	Northampton & Midlands, 60, Gold St., Northampton	8,640	6 304,000
1848D	,, Town & County, 85 Abington St., Northampton	73,897	55,896,000
1895D	North Shields—Mercantile, 25 Northumberland Square, N. Shields	1,984	1,895,000
1875D	,, P., 75 Howard St., N. Shields	2,596	2,043,000
1875D	,, —Standard, 64 Church Way, North Shields	1,671	1,076,000
1855D	,, —Tynemouth, 53–55 Howard St., North Shields	1,673	1,520,000
1887D	,, —Tynemouth Vict. Jub. P., 23,W. Percy St., N. Shields	1,717	1,735,000
1848D	Northwich, 1 High St., Bull Ring, Northwich	5,480	3,997,000
1852D	Norwich, St. Andrew's House, Norwich	10,365	13,490,000
1850D	Nottingham, Friar Lane. Nottingham	10,562	12,452,000
1935	,, Oddfellows, Imperial Building, Victoria St., Nottingham	1,168	584,000
1888D	Old Hill—Rowley Regis & Dist. B., 269 Halesowen Rd., Old Hill.	3,848	2,444,000
1867D	Oldham—Lancashire, 127 Union St., Oldham, Lancs.	1,357	1,215,000
1848D	Otley, 34 Boroughgate, Otley	3,031	2,912,000
1877D	Padiham, Burnley Rd., Padiham	3,276	3,299,000
1877D	Penrith, St. Andrew's Churchyard, Penrith	941	682,000
1860D	Peterborough, 5, Market Place, Peterborough	5,440	5,486,000
1896D	Portsmouth, 166 London Rd., Portsmouth	2,104	2,649,000
1866D	,, —Hampshire, 44 Commercial Rd., Portsmouth	2,217	2,090,000
1846D	Ramsbury, The Square, Ramsbury	3,874	3,848,000
1859D	Redditch B., Church Green West, Redditch	8,019	6,066,000
1903D	Redhill—East Surrey, 12 London Rd., Redhill	2,636	1,613,000
1855D	Reigate—Holmesdale B., 43 Church St., Reigate	2,613	2,403,000
1866D	Rugby, Temple Bldgs., Rugby	11,105	6,458,000
1861D	,, Provident, 34 North St., Rugby	2,014	1,254,000
1849D	Saffron Walden B., King St., Saffron Walden	1,196	1,305,000
1858D	St. Helens and Rainford, 82 Church St., St. Helens	634	694,000
1875	Sandy 6, Bedford Road, Sandy, Beds,	868	842,000
1846D	Scarborough, York Ho., York Pl., Scarborough	4,545	3,711,000
1935D	Sheffield, 99, Queen Street., Sheffield	504	744,000
1879D	Shepshed, P. B., Bull Ring, Shepshed	2,162	1,194,000
1901D	Shotton,—Summers', Hawarden Bridge Steel Works, Shotton	3,616	904,000
1853D	Skipton, 59 High St., Skipton	35,102	22,212,000
1855D	Smethwick, 364 High Street, Smethwick	1,396	958,000
1876D	Somercotes, Leabrooks Rd., Somercotes	2,962	1,194,000
1891D	Southend-on-Sea—South East Essex P., 28 Clarence St., Southend-on-Sea	2,094	2,335,000
1875D	South Shields Commercial P., Barrington St., South Shields	1,317	1,643,000
1866D	,, ,, —Corporation, 99, Fowler St., South Shields	2,489	1,608,000
1874D	,, ,, —Eligible and United, 91, Fowler St., South Shields	1,521	1,301,000
1928	,, ,, —Hadrian, 3, Winchester St. South Shields.	753	599,000
1877D	,, ,, Nelson P., Queen St., South Shields	1,271	1,058,000
1919D	,, ,, —Victory, Victory Hse, Burrow St., South Shields	539	543,000
1867D	Stafford and County P.. 1 Martin St.. Stafford	1,717	2,120,000
1877D	,, Railway, 4 Market Sq., Stafford	2,208	2,146,000
1873D	Steyning & Sussex County, 62 High St., Steyning	2,993	2,948,000
1898	Stockport Mersey P., 79a, Wellington Rd., S., Stockport, Ches	593	530,000
1924D	,, Vernon, 26, St. Petersgate, Stockport	1,545	1,717,000
1852D	Stoke-on-Trent P.. Victoria Chambers, Liverpool Rd., Stoke-on-Trent.	790	1,059,000
1852D	,, —Tunstall, Victoria Chambers, 48 The Boulevard, Tunstall, Stoke-on-Trent	2,032	1,140,000
1889D	Stourbridge, Lye and Dist. P., Victoria Chambers, 94 High St., Stourbridge	1,680	1,280,000
1849D	,, —Brierley Hill & Stourbridge Incorpd., 82 High St., Stourbridge	2,783	1,929,000

Year Estabd.	Name of Society (abbreviated) Head Office	Share Investors	Total Assets
			£
1850D	Stroud, 4 Rowcroft, Stroud	2,860	2,674,000
1853D	Sunderland, 51, Fawcett St., Sunderland	8,331	6,065,000
1854D	,, —Indus. and Provt. P., 23 John St., Sunderland	2,534	2,324,000
1877D	,, —North of England, 57 Fawcett St., Sunderland	6,051	6,324,000
1868D	Swindon P., 1 Commercial Road, Swindon	1,742	1,804,000
1883D	,, —New Swindon, 36 Regent Circus, Swindon	792	1,035,000
1899D	,, —North Wilts. Equit., 18 to 20, Commercial Rd., Swindon	1,236	1,159,000
1854D	Tamworth P. B., 6. Victoria Rd., Tamworth	1,399	962,000
1883D	Tewkesbury & Dist. P. B., 142–3 High St., Tewkesbury	1,080	949,000
1901D	Tipton & Coseley P., 60 High St., Tipton	3.508	1 685,000
1866D	Tyldesley, Dist. Bank Chambers, Chapel St., Tyldesley	1,588	1,282,000
1869D	Uxbridge P.B., 54 High St., Uxbridge, Middlesex	594	583,000
1846D	Wakefield, 57 Westgate, Wakefield	11,794	6,696,000
1881	Wallingford and Dt. P., 7 St. Martin's St., Wallingford	771	773,000
1863D	Walsall Mutual, 41–45 Bridge St., Walsall	4,796	4,434,000
1847D	Waltham Abbey, 5 Church St., Waltham Abbey, Essex	2,413	2,568,000
1854D	Warwick & W'shire. P., 24–26 Jury Street, Warwick	5.641	3,646,000
1851D	Wednesbury, 52 Lower High St., Wednesbury	6,642	4,127,000
1934	Wembley-Atlas, 293 Harrow Rd., Wembley	1,588	1,243,000
1849D	West Bromwich, 321 High St., W. Bromwich	22,105	18,071,000
1873	Wigan, Midland Bank Chambers, 1 Library St., Wigan	652	637,000
1877D	Wolverhampton & Dist. P., 41 Lichfield St., Wolverhampton	8 829	9,258,000
1849D	,, F'holders'. P., 37 Queen Sq., Wolverhampton	12,003	10,076,000
1902D	,, —S. Staffs., 5 Princess St., Wolverhampton	12 219	8,529,000
1859D	Worcester, 5 Foregate St., Worcester	6.605	4,172,000
1870	Workington P.B., 6 Nook St., Workington	991	777,000
1882	,, and W. Cumberland P.B., 29, Finkle St., Workington	772	601,000
	WALES		
1922	Barry Mutual, Lombard Buildings, Barry, Glam.	621	562,000
1865D	Cardiff, 75 St. Mary St., Cardiff	768	1,110,000
1874	,, —Hibernian P., 55, Churchill Way, Cardiff	745	584,000
1860D	,, —Principality, Principality Bldgs., Queen St., Cardiff	10,673	11,587,000
1866	Pontypridd and Provincial, Town Hall Chambers, Pontypridd	450	581,000
	SCOTLAND		
1869	Dunfermline, 56 East Port, Dunfermline	14 595	12,534,000
1870D	Edinburgh, 39 Melville St., Edinburgh	987	986,000
1899	,, —Century, 21–23 Albany Street, Edinburgh	1,003	1,184,000
1952D	,, —Dunedin, 32 Castle St., Edinburgh	1.413	1,276,000
1933D	,, —Prudential Investment, 1 Leopold Place, Edinburgh	541	643,000
1848D	,, —Scottish, 4, York Place, Edinburgh	1,285	1,271,000
1891	Inverness, 21–23 Union St., Inverness	2,124	1,384,000
1853D	Paisley, 8 Gilmour St., Paisley	2.348	1,977,000

MORTGAGE REPAYMENT TABLE

Calendar monthly subscriptions required to pay off principal and interest of mortgages at 6 per cent. interest* over various periods of years. Intermediate amounts can be determined by addition of subscription rates, *e.g.*, Calendar monthly subscription for a mortgage of £3,200 over 20 years—£21 17*s.* 6*d.* + £1 9*s.* 2*d.* = £23 6*s.* 8*d.*

Period of Years	£100	£200	£300	£500	£1,000	£2,000	£3,000
	£ *s.* *d.*	£ *s.* *d.*	£ *s.* *d.*	£ *s.* *d.*	£ *s.* *d.*	£ *s.* *d.*	£ *s.* *d.*
5	1 19 7	3 19 2	5 18 9	9 17 11	19 15 10	39 11 8	59 7 6
10	1 2 8	2 5 4	3 8 0	5 13 4	11 6 8	22 13 4	34 0 0
11	1 1 2	2 2 4	3 3 6	5 5 10	10 11 8	21 3 4	31 15 0
12	19 11	1 19 10	2 19 9	4 19 7	9 19 2	19 18 4	29 17 6
13	18 10	1 17 8	2 16 6	4 14 2	9 8 4	18 16 8	28 5 0
14	18 0	1 16 0	2 14 0	4 10 0	9 0 0	18 0 0	27 0 0
15	17 2	1 14 4	2 11 6	4 5 10	8 11 8	17 3 4	25 15 0
16	16 6	1 13 0	2 9 6	4 2 6	8 5 0	16 10 0	24 15 0
17	15 11	1 11 10	2 7 9	3 19 7	7 19 2	15 18 4	23 17 6
18	15 5	1 10 10	2 6 3	3 17 1	7 14 2	15 8 4	23 2 6
19	15 0	1 10 0	2 5 0	3 15 0	7 10 0	15 0 0	22 10 0
20	14 7	1 9 2	2 3 9	3 12 11	7 5 10	14 11 8	21 17 6
21	14 3	1 8 6	2 2 9	3 11 3	7 2 6	14 5 0	21 7 6
22	13 11	1 7 10	2 1 9	3 9 7	6 19 2	13 18 4	20 17 6
23	13 7	1 7 2	2 0 9	3 7 11	6 15 10	13 11 8	20 7 6
24	13 4	1 6 8	2 0 0	3 6 8	6 13 4	13 6 8	20 0 0
25	13 1	1 6 2	1 19 3	3 5 5	6 10 10	13 1 8	19 12 6

* Most of the Building Societies were charging 6 per cent. on mortgages to owner-occupiers in 1963.

Legal Notes

ADOPTION OF CHILDREN

In England and Wales the adoption of children is regulated mainly by the Adoption of Children Acts, 1926 to 1949, and the Adoption Act, 1958. An order of court is necessary to legalize the adoption. Adoption puts the child adopted practically on the same footing as a child born to the adopter in lawful wedlock, in all matters of custody, education and maintenance; further, it is provided by the Act of 1958 that an adopted child shall be treated as the child of the adopter (and not the child of its natural parents) for the purpose of the devolution of property on an intestacy occurring, or under any disposition made, after the date of the adoption order. Applications are made to the High Court (Chancery), County Court, or Magistrates Court. Orders will not usually be made for a man to be *sole* adopter of a girl, and the applicant must be either:—

(*a*) Twenty-five years of age or over; or
(*b*) Twenty-one years of age or over and a relative (as defined in the Act of 1958) of the infant; or
(*c*) the mother or father of the infant.

Two spouses may jointly adopt an infant, but unless one of them is the mother or father of the infant, condition (*a*) or (*b*) above must be satisfied in respect of one of the applicants *and* the other spouse must have attained the age of twenty-one.

The consent of the child's parents or guardian is required before an adoption order will be made, but in certain circumstances (e.g., where the parent or guardian has ill-treated or neglected the child) the Court may dispense with this consent. Since the 1949 Act, marriage between the adopter and the adoptee is prohibited, but marriages of that kind, solemnized before the passing of the Act, are not thereby invalidated.

The 1958 Act places restrictions on societies which make arrangements for the adoption of children.

Scotland.—The Adoption of Children (Scotland) Acts, 1930 to 1949, and the Adoption Act, 1958, cover the law relating to the adoption of children in Scotland, where an Adopted Children Register is maintained. Applications are made to the Court of Session, or the Sheriff Court within whose jurisdiction either the applicant or the child resides at the date of application. The Adoption Act, 1958, which is a consolidating Act, also applies, with modifications, to Scotland, and reference is also made to the Adoption Act, 1960 which amends the law with respect to revocation of adoption orders. Owing to divergence of the laws of England and Scotland there is not, however, complete uniformity in this branch of the law in both countries. Thus, in regard to property rights, an adopted child in Scotland remains a member of the family of his actual parents, and an adoption order does not deprive him of any legal rights competent to him in the estate of his parents, nor are any rights conferred on him as the child of the adopter.

All adoptions in Great Britain are registered in the Registers of Adopted Children kept by the Registrars General in London and Edinburgh respectively. Certificates from these registers, including short certificates which contain no reference to adoptions, can be obtained on conditions similar to those relating to birth certificates. (See below.)

BIRTHS (REGISTRATION)

When a birth takes place, personal information of it must be given to the Registrar of Births and Deaths for the sub-district in which the birth occurred, and the register signed in his presence, by one of the following persons:—

1. The father or mother of the child. If they fail; 2. the occupier of the house in which the birth happened; 3. a person present at the birth; or, 4. the person having charge of the child. The duty of attending to the registration therefore rests firstly on the parents. The mother is responsible for the registration of the birth of an illegitimate child. The registration is required to be made within 42 days (*Scotland* 21 days) of the birth. Failure to do this, without reasonable cause, involves liability to a penalty of forty shillings (in Scotland the penalty is £1). The registration of a birth will be free when it takes place within 42 days (in *Scotland* 21 days). In England or Wales, the informant, instead of attending before the registrar of the sub-district where the birth occurred, may make a declaration of the particulars required to be registered in the presence of any registrar. The fee payable for this is 3*s.* 0*d.* There are special provisions relating to late registration. Under the Public Health Act, 1936, and the Public Health (London) Act, 1936, notice of every birth must be given by the father, or person in attendance on the mother, to the district medical officer of health by post within 36 hours of the birth. *This is in addition to the registration already mentioned.*

A "Stillbirth" must be registered and a certificate signed by the doctor or midwife who was present at the birth or has examined the body of the child must be produced to the registrar. The certificate must, where possible, state the cause of death and the estimated duration of the pregnancy.

The re-registration of the birth of a person legitimated by the subsequent marriage of the parents is provided for in the Births and Deaths Registration Act, 1953. In *Scotland* re-registration of a child legitimated *per subsequens matrimonium* or whose birth entry is affected by a Decree of Court respecting status or paternity is provided for by the Registration of Births, etc. (Scotland), Amendment Act, 1934.

Birth at Sea: The master of a British ship must record any birth on board and send particulars to the Registrar General of Shipping.

Birth Abroad: Consular Officers are authorized to register births of British subjects occurring abroad. Certificates are procurable in due course at Registrar General's office, London.

The registration of births occurring out of the United Kingdom among members of the armed forces, or occurring on board H.M. ships and aircraft, is provided for by the Registration of Births, Deaths and Marriages (Special Provisions) Act 1957, applicable also to Scotland.

CERTIFICATES

OF BIRTHS, MARRIAGES, OR DEATHS

England and Wales.—Certificates of Births, Deaths, or Marriages can be obtained at the General Register Office, Somerset House, on payment of fees amounting to 5*s.* 3*d.*, viz., 1*s.* 6*d.* for search, and 3*s.* 9*d.* for the certificate. (When application is made by post the charges are 10*s.*) They can also be obtained from the Superintendent Registrar having the legal custody of the register containing the entry of which a certificate is required. Certificates of marriages can also be obtained from the incumbent of the church in which the marriage took place (the customary fee being 3*s*. 9*d*.); or from the Nonconformist minister (or other "authorized person") where the marriage takes place in a registered building (See *post* under Marriage).

Certificates at reduced rates can be obtained for the purposes of certain Acts of Parliament, and under Births and Deaths Registration Act, 1953, a modified form of birth certificate, showing the names, sex and date of birth and certain other particulars, but not the parentage, may be obtained from the Registrar General, or the appropriate Superintendent Registrar or Registrar, on payment of a fee of 9*d*. (inclusive of search) and on furnishing certain particulars.

English Registers.—Records of births, deaths and marriages registered in England and Wales since 1837 are kept at the General Register Office, Somerset House. *The Society of Genealogists*, 37 Harrington Gardens, S.W.7, possesses many records of Baptisms, Marriages and Deaths prior to 1837, including copies, in whole or in part, of about 4,000 Parish Registers.

Scottish Registers of Births, Deaths and Marriages.—Certificates of births, deaths or marriages registered from 1855 when compulsory registration commenced in Scotland can be obtained personally at the General Registry Office, New Register House, Edinburgh, or from the appropriate local Registrar, on payment of the fee of 5*s*. 3*d*., viz.:—1*s*. 6*d*. for search and 3*s*. 9*d*. for the certificate; postal application since 1 March, 1962—inclusive fee, Registrar General's office, 10*s*., local Registrar, 7*s*. 6*d*. Certificates are issued at reduced rates for specified purposes as in England & Wales and similar provision exists for abbreviated birth certificates (fee 9*d*).

There are also available at the General Registry Office old parish registers of date prior to 1855, which were formerly kept under the administration of the Established Church of Scotland. An extract of an entry in these registers may be obtained at the fee of 5*s*. 3*d*. A fee of 20*s*. is payable for a general search of all the Scottish registers.

BRITISH NATIONALITY AND CITIZENSHIP OF THE UNITED KINGDOM AND COLONIES

General.—The law as to British Nationality is now to be found mainly in the British Nationality Act, 1948, which came into force on Jan. 1, 1949. The Act introduces a new term, "citizenship." Every person who under the Act is a citizen of the United Kingdom and Colonies, or any citizen (by virtue of legislation in that country) of Canada, Australia, New Zealand, India, Pakistan, Ghana, the Federation of Malaya, Nigeria, Sierra Leone, Tanganyika, Jamaica, Trinidad and Tobago, and Uganda (hereafter referred to as "the Dominions") has by virtue of that citizenship the status of a British subject, and may be known either as a British Subject or as a Commonwealth citizen. Under s. 2 of the Newfoundland (Consequential Provisions) Act, 1950, potential citizens of Newfoundland under the British Nationality Act, 1948, are deemed to have been potential citizens of Canada.

Nationality *before* Jan. 1, 1949, was determined mainly by the British Nationality and Status of Alien Acts, 1914–1943, though these Acts did not affect the status of any person born *before* Jan. 1, 1915.

Retention of nationality by persons born in or who are citizens of Eire (now by virtue of the Ireland Act, 1949, styled the Republic of Ireland).

By the Ireland Act, 1949, a person who was born before Dec. 6, 1922, in what is now the Republic of Ireland (Eire) and was a British subject immediately before Jan. 1, 1949, is not deemed to have ceased to be a British subject unless either (i) he was domiciled in the Irish Free State on Dec. 6, 1922, or (ii) was on or after April 10, 1935, and before Jan. 1, 1949, permanently resident there, or (iii) had before Jan. 1, 1949, been registered as a citizen of Eire under the laws of that country.

In addition by the British Nationality Act, 1948, any citizen of Eire who immediately before Jan. 1, 1949, was also a British subject can retain that status by submitting at any time a claim to the Home Secretary on any of the following grounds: (*a*) he has been in the service of the United Kingdom government; (*b*) he holds a British passport issued in the United Kingdom or in any colony, protectorate, United Kingdom mandated or trust territory; (*c*) he has associations by way of descent, residence or otherwise with any such place; or on complying with similar legislation in any of the "Dominions."

Citizenship of the United Kingdom and Colonies.

In the majority of cases, a person who is a British subject becomes also a "citizen," either of one of the "Dominions" by virtue of legislation in that country, or of the United Kingdom and Colonies under the 1948 Act. In the latter case, citizenship is acquired by:—

1. *Birth* on or after Jan. 1, 1949, in the United Kingdom and Colonies (which term does not include the "Dominions"), except
   - (*a*) children born to non-citizen fathers enjoying diplomatic immunity from suit or legal process;
   - (*b*) children born to fathers who are enemy aliens in enemy occupied territory.

2. *Descent*, if the father was a citizen by *birth*. If the father was a citizen by *descent* only, the child acquires citizenship by descent if either:—
   - (*a*) the child is or his father was born in a protectorate, protected state, mandated territory or trust territory, or in a foreign country where Her Majesty then had jurisdiction over British subjects; or
   - (*b*) the birth (occurring elsewhere than (*a*)) is registered at a United Kingdom consulate within one year; or
   - (*c*) the father is at the time of birth in the service of the Crown under Her Majesty's United Kingdom government; or
   - (*d*) the child is born in one of the "Dominions" in which a citizenship law has then taken effect and does not become a citizen thereof by birth.

3. *Registration* by the Home Secretary upon application by:—
   - (*a*) a citizen of one of the "Dominions" or of the Republic of Ireland who can show that he has been (a) ordinarily resident in the United Kingdom; or (b) in Crown service under Her Majesty's Government in the United Kingdom; or (c) partly the one and partly the other throughout the period of five years ending with the date of his application, or such shorter period so ending as the Home Secretary may in the special circumstances of any particular case accept; or, in certain circumstances, if he is serving under an international organization of which the United Kingdom Government is a member, or is in the employment of a body established in the United Kingdom;
   - (*b*) a woman married to a United Kingdom, etc. citizen. If she is a British protected person or an alien she must take an oath of allegiance. (A woman who marries on or after Jan. 1, 1949, does not by virtue of that marriage acquire citizenship.)

A minor child of a citizen can be registered upon application being made by his parent or guardian.

A person in respect of whom a recommendation for deportation or a deportation order is in force under the Commonwealth Immigrants Act, 1962, is not entitled to be registered, although the Home Secretary may register such a person.

4 *Naturalization.*—In order to be eligible for a certificate of naturalization an alien must:—

(*a*) during the eight years preceding his application have resided for not less than five years (of which not less than one year immediately preceding the application *must* have been spent in the United Kingdom) in the United Kingdom or in any colony, protectorate, United Kingdom mandated or trust territory, or have been for five years in the service of the Crown; and

(*b*) be of good character and have a sufficient knowledge of the English language; and

(*c*) intend to reside in the United Kingdom or any colony, etc., or to enter or continue in the service of the Crown or in the service of certain organizations.

A British protected person who satisfies (*b*) and (*c*) above can apply for naturalization if he can show that he has been (a) ordinarily resident in the United Kingdom; or (b) in Crown service under Her Majesty's Government in the United Kingdom; or (c) partly the one and partly the other throughout the period of five years ending with the date of his application, or such shorter period as the Home Secretary may in a particular case accept.

Instructions for the guidance of persons desiring to apply for a Certificate of Naturalization are supplied with the form of application which may be obtained from H.M. Stationery Office.

5. *Incorporation of Territory* when citizenship is granted to such persons as are specified by Order in Council.

6. *Transitional Provisions,* which confer citizenship on a person who was a British subject immediately before Jan. 1, 1949, if either:—

(i) (*a*) he would, if born after that date, have qualified for citizenship by birth; or

(*b*) he is a person naturalized in the United Kingdom and Colonies; or

(*c*) he became a British subject by reason of annexation of territory which on Jan. 1, 1949, was included in the United Kingdom and Colonies; or

(ii) at the time of his birth his father was a British subject and possessed any of the above qualifications; or

(iii) he was born within territory comprised on Jan. 1, 1949, in a protectorate, protected state or United Kingdom trust territory; or

(iv) he was not on that date a citizen or potential citizen of one of the "Dominions"; or

(v) being a woman, had before Jan. 1, 1949, been married to a man who becomes, or would but for his death have become, a citizen.

A British subject who is merely a potential citizen of one of the "Dominions" continues as a British subject without citizenship until he becomes a citizen of such "Dominion" or of the Republic of Ireland, or an alien. If none of these has happened at the date when a citizenship law is passed in the country of which he is potentially a citizen, he becomes a citizen by descent of the United Kingdom and Colonies.

A woman who lost British nationality by reason of marriage to an alien regained it on Jan. 1, 1949.

By the Adoption Act, 1958, an adopted child becomes a citizen of the United Kingdom and Colonies as from the date of the adoption order if the adopter or, in the case of a joint adoption, the male adopter, is a citizen of the United Kingdom and Colonies.

Citizenship of the United Kingdom and Colonies can be lost:—

(i) by declaration in the prescribed manner by a person who is also a citizen of a "Dominion" or of the Republic of Ireland or a national of a foreign country. The Home Secretary can withhold registration of the declaration in time of war;

(ii) where the Home Secretary is satisfied that citizenship by registration or naturalization was obtained by fraud, false representation, etc.;

(iii) by the Home Secretary depriving a *naturalized* person of citizenship if such person has:—

(*a*) shown himself by act or speech to be disloyal or disaffected towards Her Majesty; or

(*b*) in time of war, traded with the enemy; or

(*c*) within five years after becoming naturalized, been sentenced in any country to a term of twelve months' imprisonment; or

(*d*) continuously resided in foreign countries for seven years, and during that period has neither at any time been in the service of the Crown or of certain international organizations, nor registered annually at a United Kingdom consulate his intention to retain citizenship;

and the Home Secretary is satisfied that it is not conducive to the public good that such person should retain his citizenship;

(iv) where a naturalized person is deprived of citizenship of a "Dominion" or of the Republic of Ireland, the Home Secretary can also deprive him of citizenship of the United Kingdom and Colonies.

(v) Under sect. 2 of the British Nationality Act, 1958, which contains special provisions with regard to citizens of Ghana.

(vi) Under sect. 4 of the Cyprus Act, 1960, which contains special provisions with regard to Cyprus.

(vii) Under sect. 2 of the Nigeria Independence Act, 1960, which contains special provisions with regard to Nigeria.

(viii) Under sect. 2 of the Sierra Leone Independence Act, 1961, which contains special provisions with regard to Sierra Leone.

(ix) Under sect. 2 of the Tanganyika Independence Act, 1961, which contains special provisions with regard to Tanganyika.

(x) Under sect. 2 of the Jamaica Independence Act, 1962, which contains special provisions with regard to Jamaica.

(xi) Under sect. 2 of the Trinidad and Tobago Independence Act, 1962, which contains special provisions with regard to Trinidad and Tobago.

(xii) Under sect. 2 of the Uganda Independence Act, 1962, which contains special provisions with regard to Uganda.

(xiii) Under sect. 1 of the South Africa Act, 1962, under which persons who were British subjects by virtue only of citizenship of South Africa ceased to be British subjects. Provision is made, however, for registration of South Africans as citizens of the

United Kingdom and Colonies on application made before 1966.

STATUS OF ALIENS.—Property may be held by an alien in the same manner as by a natural-born British subject, but he may not hold public office, exercise the franchise or own a British ship or air-craft. The Republic of Ireland Act, 1949, declares that the Republic, though not part of H.M. Dominions, is not a foreign country, and any reference in an Act of Parliament to foreigners, aliens, foreign countries, etc., shall be construed accordingly.

CROWN—PROCEEDINGS AGAINST

Before 1947 proceedings against the Crown were generally possible only by a procedure known as a petition of right, which placed the litigant at a considerable disadvantage and which was not normally available at all in cases of tort (i.e., civil wrongs other than breach of contract). Thus, no proceedings would normally lie against the Government if a subject were injured by the negligent driving of a Government vehicle (although the driver could be sued) or if a Government employee were injured by the defective condition of the Crown premises on which he worked. Now, however, by the Crown Proceedings Act, 1947, which came into operation on Jan. 1, 1948, the Crown, in its public capacity, is largely placed in the same position as a subject, although some procedural disadvantages remain. Among exceptions to the Act are the following: (*a*) No action lies in tort against the Crown *or the individual Crown servant* for anything done or omitted to be done in relation to any postal packet or telephone communication, except for loss of a registered inland postal packet (in which case the action must be brought within one year of posting), not being a telegram. (*b*) The Crown *and any member of the armed forces* are immune from liability in tort in respect of death of, or personal injury to, another member of the armed forces on duty, provided that the death or injury is attributable to service for purposes of pension.

Scotland.—The Act extends to Scotland and has the effect of bringing the practice of the two countries as closely together as the different legal systems will permit. While formerly actions against the Crown, when permissible, were confined to the Court of Session, proceedings may now be brought in the Sheriff Court. The Lord Advocate is the proper defender in proceedings against the Crown.

The Act lays down that arrestment of money in the hands of the Crown or of a Government Department is competent in any case where arrestment in the hands of a subject would have been competent, but an exception is made in respect of Post Office Savings Bank deposits. On the other hand, the former rule that the wages and salaries of the servants of the Crown are not arrestable remains unaltered.

DEATHS, BURIAL AND CREMATION

DEATHS

(For Certificates, *see* under BIRTHS)

In England and Wales.—When a death takes place, personal information of it must be given to the local Registrar of Births and Deaths, and the register signed in his presence, by one of the following persons:—1. A relative of the deceased present at the death, or in attendance during the last illness. If they fail, 2. Some other of relative the deceased. In default of any relatives, 3. A person present at the death; or, the occupier of the house in which the death happened. If all the above-named fail, 4. An inmate of the house, or, the person causing the disposal of the body. Relatives present or in attendance are first required to attend to the registration. The registration must be made within five days of the death, or within the same time written notice of the death sent to the Registrar. If the deceased was attended during his last illness by a registered medical practitioner, a certificate of cause of death must be sent by the doctor to the registrar. The doctor must give to the informant of the death a written notice of the signing of the certificate, which must be delivered to the registrar. It is essential that a certificate for disposal should be obtained from the registrar before the funeral and delivered to the clergyman or other person in charge of the churchyard or cemetery. No fee is chargeable for this certificate. If the death is not registered within five days (or fourteen days if written notice of the occurrence of the death is sent to him) the Registrar may require any one of the above-mentioned persons to attend to register at a stated time and place. Failure to comply involves a penalty of forty shillings. The registration of a death is free of charge when it takes place within the above-mentioned periods. After twelve months no death can be registered without the Registrar General's consent and on payment of fees amounting to fifteen shillings.

A body must not be disposed of until (1) either the Registrar has given a certificate to the effect that he has registered or received notice of the death, or (2) until the Coroner has made a disposal order (*Births and Deaths Registration Act*, 1926, s. 1).

A person disposing of a body must within ninety-six hours deliver to the Registrar a notification as to the date, place, and means of the disposal of the body (*ib.* s. 3).

"Still-born" child. (*See* under Births (Registration), p. 1157.)

Death at Sea.—The master of a British ship must record any death on board and send particulars to the Registrar General of Shipping.

Death Abroad.—Consular Officers are authorized to register deaths of British subjects occurring abroad. Certificates are procurable at the Registrar General's Office, London. If the deceased was of *Scottish* domicile, particulars are sent to the Registrar General for Scotland.

With regard to the registration of deaths of members of the armed forces, and deaths occurring on H.M. ships and aircraft, see the Registration of Births, etc. Act, 1957.

In *Scotland*, the rules of registration are similar, but (1) the death must be registered within 8 days, failure to do so involving a penalty of from £1 to £2; (2) the medical man concerned must give a certificate of death to the Registrar in terms of the Registration of Births, &c. (Scotland) Act, 1854, within 7 days; (3) the informant of a death receives from the Registrar a certificate that the death has been registered. This is given to the undertaker, who delivers it to the keeper of the cemetery. Failure to comply is under penalty in all cases. The Registration of Births, etc., Act, 1957, applies without modification to Scotland.

BURIAL

The duty of burial is incumbent on the deceased person's Executors (if any appointed); it is also a recognized obligation of the husband of a woman, and the parent of a child, also of a householder where the body lies. Funeral expenses of a reasonable amount will be repayable out of deceased's estate in priority to any other claims. Directions as to place and mode of burial are frequently contained in the deceased's will or in some memorandum placed with private papers, or may have been communicated verbally to a relative. Consequently steps should immediately be taken to ascertain the deceased's wishes from the above sources. If the wishes are considered objectionable, they are not necessarily enforceable: legal advice should be taken. A person may legally leave directions for the anatomical examination of his body. As to the place of burial—unless closed by Order in Council—the parish churchyard is the normal burying place for parishioners, or any person dying in the Parish, but nowadays this will apply only in villages and the smaller towns. In populous districts cemeteries and crematoria have been established either by the local council, or a private company, and burials will take place there in accordance with the regulations. For an exclusive right to a burial space in the churchyard a faculty is required from the Ecclesiastical Court. Poor persons may be buried at the public expense by the local authority. As to the necessity for obtaining a registrar's certificate or authority from the Coroner for disposal, *see* above.

CREMATION

Under the Cremation Acts, 1902 and 1952, regulations are made by the Home Secretary dealing fully with the cremation of a body, disposal of ashes, etc., and containing numerous essential safeguards.

If Cremation is desired it is advisable for instructions to be left in writing to that effect. Cremation may not take place if deceased has prohibited that form of disposal.

To arrange for Cremation the Executor or near relative should instruct the undertaker to that effect and obtain from him the Statutory Forms required as given in the Cremation Regulations issued in 1930 (Statutory Rules and Orders, 1930, No. 1016).

DIVORCE, ETC.

Preliminary.—Matrimonial Suits may be conveniently divided into three classes, viz. (1) those in which a declaration that there has never been a marriage is sought; (2) those in which the duties arising from marriage are sought to be upheld; and (3) those in which, the marriage being admitted, it is sought to end the marriage or the duties arising from it.

(1) *Nullity of Marriage.*—Marriage is void *ab initio* if the parties were in the prohibited degrees of affinity, if it was bigamous, if there was no sufficient consent on the part of one or both of the parties, if one of the parties was insane, or if one of the parties was under the age of consent, *i.e.*, 16—Marriage Act, 1949. Where the *formalities* of the marriage were defective, the marriage is generally void if *both* parties knew of the defect (*e.g.*, where marriage took place otherwise than in an authorized building). But absence of the consent of parents or guardians (or of the Court or other authority, in lieu thereof) in the case of minors does not invalidate the marriage. Inability to consummate a marriage may also be a ground for a nullity decree; but in this case, the marriage is only voidable and remains valid until the decree is made.

Under the Matrimonial Causes Act, 1950, which does not apply to Scotland, a marriage is also voidable (*i.e.*, a decree of nullity may be obtained) on the following grounds—(*a*) respondent's wilful refusal to consummate the marriage; (*b*) that either party at the time of marriage was a mentally disordered person or subject to recurrent attacks of insanity or epilepsy; (*c*) that at the time of marriage the respondent was suffering from communicable venereal disease; (*d*) that at the time of the marriage the respondent was pregnant by another man. In cases, (*b*), (*c*) and (*d*), the petitioner must have been ignorant of the grounds at the date of the marriage and must not have agreed to intercourse taking place since discovering the grounds, and proceedings must be instituted within a year of the marriage.

By the Matrimonial Causes Act, 1950, and, as to Scotland, by the Law Reform (Miscellaneous Provisions) Act, 1949, it is provided that a decree of nullity in respect of a voidable marriage shall not operate so as to bastardize any child, who would have been the legitimate child of the parties to the marriage if the marriage had been dissolved instead of annulled. Further, even if a marriage is void, a child of such a union can sometimes be treated as legitimate if at the time of conception or of the marriage (if later) either or both of the parties reasonably believed that the marriage was valid (Legitimacy Act, 1959).

A spouse's insistence upon the use of contraceptives will not constitute wilful refusal to consummate within (*a*) above, even though there has been no normal intercourse, but it may in certain circumstances enable a petition for *Divorce* to be brought on the grounds of cruelty (as to which see below). Further it has been allowed as a *defence* to a charge of desertion against the aggrieved party.

In one High Court case the judge held that a husband's insistence on the practice of *coitus interruptus* amounted to wilful refusal to consummate the marriage, where there had been no other intercourse. In other High Court cases the judges have disagreed with this view, but held that, in the circumstances of the particular cases, a divorce could be granted on the ground of legal cruelty.

(2) *Restitution of Conjugal Rights.*—This is a form of relief generally sought by a spouse who has been deserted. Disobedience to a decree of restitution of conjugal rights is a ground for obtaining judicial separation.

(3) *Judicial Separation and Divorce.*—The third class of suit includes a suit for judicial separation (which does not dissolve a marriage) and a suit for divorce (which, if successful, dissolves the marriage altogether and leaves the parties at liberty to marry again). Either spouse may petition for judicial separation on the same grounds as those for divorce and also on the ground specified in (2) above.

Divorce.—Complete divorce is now obtainable by either husband or wife upon any one of the following grounds: adultery of respondent since marriage; desertion by respondent for 3 years immediately before petition; cruelty to petitioner; incurable insanity (under certain conditions); and by the wife, also on commission by the husband of certain criminal sexual offences. Matrimonial Causes Act, 1950, s. 1.

The foregoing is subject to a clause prohibiting any petition for divorce (but not for judicial separation) before the lapse of three years from the date of marriage, except in the case of exceptional hardship (upon petitioner) or of exceptional depravity of respondent.

Cruelty, in a legal sense, is conduct of such a character as to have caused injury or a reasonable apprehension of injury to life, limb, or health (bodily or mental). A course of conduct which the sufferer should not be expected to endure, continued until health breaks down or is likely to break down constitutes legal cruelty, without proof of any intention to injure, so that the respondent's insanity is no defence to a charge of cruelty.

Desertion may be defined as a voluntary withdrawal from cohabitation by one spouse without just cause and against the wishes of the other. Where one spouse is guilty of conduct of a serious nature which forces the other to leave, the party at fault is said to be guilty of constructive desertion.

If, upon disputes arising, the parties *agree* to live apart, then in general neither can be said to have deserted the other.

When the decree will be refused—A decree *must* be refused, even if the suit is undefended, if the allegations in the petition for divorce are not proved. (There is no such thing in the Divorce Court as judgment against the respondent by default.) Other *absolute* bars to relief are (i) connivance at the *adultery* of the respondent; (ii) collusion, as where the initiation of the suit is procured by agreement or bargain (but this does not prevent a fresh suit being brought free from collusion); (iii) condonation of the respondent's *adultery or cruelty, i.e.*, complete forgiveness which restores the *status quo* (although the offence may be revived by later misconduct). There are also certain *discretionary* bars, as *e.g.*, where the petitioner has been guilty of adultery; of unreasonable delay; of cruelty; or of wilful neglect or misconduct conducing to the adultery, insanity, or desertion alleged. (1950 Act, s. 4.)

Intervention by Queen's Proctor.—At any time during the progress of a suit, and before the decree *nisi* is made absolute, the Queen's Proctor may intervene.

Decree Absolute.—Every decree of dissolution or nullity is in the first instance a decree *nisi*. The marriage subsists until the decree is made absolute, usually three months after decree *nisi*. After that date either spouse may marry again; but as to marriage within "Prohibited Degrees" see Marriage—Miscellaneous Notes, p. 1171. By the Matrimonial Proceedings (Children) Act, 1958 a decree *nisi* cannot be made absolute until the Court is satisfied that arrangements have been made for the care and upbringing of every child of the family who has not attained the age of sixteen which are satisfactory or the best which can be devised in the circumstances or that it is impracticable for the parties before the Court to make any such arrangements.

Maintenance, etc.—The Court has wide powers to make orders as to maintenance or alimony (usually payable to an innocent wife), and as to costs. The husband can be ordered to pay his wife's costs, even if she is unsuccessful in her suit or defence. A guilty co-respondent may be ordered to pay costs and damages.

By the Matrimonial Causes Act, 1950, the High Court in England may, where the husband has wilfully neglected to provide reasonable maintenance for the wife or children, order the husband to make provision for them, *even though* no matrimonial suit is pending between the parties to the marriage, and while such an order is in force the Court may also deal with custody of and access to the children.

CUSTODY OF CHILDREN

In suits for nullity, divorce or judicial separation, whether the suit succeeds or is dismissed, the Court can make orders as to the custody of and access to the children and as to their upkeep and education, and these orders can be made not only in respect of children of the marriage but also in respect of a child of one party who has been accepted as one of the family by the other party. A guilty spouse will normally be entitled to reasonable access to the children and may even be awarded the custody if the Court thinks fit. The paramount consideration is always the welfare of the child.

A spouse who has been deprived of the custody of a child will not thereby be deprived of his other rights as the child's *guardian* unless the Court expressly so orders.

SEPARATION BY AGREEMENT

Husband and wife may agree, with or without consideration, to separate and live apart, but the agreement, to be valid, must be followed by an immediate separation. It is most desirable to consult a solicitor in every such case.

MAGISTRATE'S SEPARATION AND MAINTENANCE ORDERS

When a husband has been guilty of adultery or has been convicted of certain assaults or has deserted his wife, or has been guilty of persistent cruelty to her or to an infant child of the family, or of wilful neglect to maintain her or such a child, or where he is an habitual drunkard or drug addict, or insists on having intercourse while suffering from a venereal disease, or compels her to submit herself to prostitution, the wife may obtain relief from the local magistrates' court. A husband may apply on similar grounds, so far as they are applicable to him. In particular a wife can sometimes be guilty of the offence of wilful neglect to provide reasonable maintenance for her husband or children and an order can be made against her (there is no such remedy in the High Court). The Court may declare that the complainant is no longer bound to cohabit with the defendant. It may order the husband to pay a weekly sum not exceeding £7 10*s*. to the wife and may order her to make a similar payment to him if his earning capacity is impaired by age or illness. Provision may be made for legal custody of and access to any child of the family who is under the age of 16 years and for payment by either or both of the spouses of up to 50*s*. weekly to the person entrusted with legal custody in respect of each child of the family up to the age of 16. If the court thinks the child would still be a dependant although over that age, similar payments may be ordered for support of the child up to the age of 21. The court cannot make an order that the parties need no longer cohabit or that either spouse shall support the other where the complainant has committed adultery during the marriage, unless the defendant has condoned or connived at, or by wilful neglect or misconduct conduced to, that act of adultery. The court has wide powers of revocation, revival and variation of orders already made. The order must be revoked if the parties have resumed cohabitation, and must be revoked, except so far as the order relates to the children, if the complainant is subsequently proved to have committed adultery since the marriage and the defendant has not condoned or connived at or by wilful neglect or misconduct conduced to that act of adultery. Complaints based on desertion or failure to maintain can be made whilst the offence continues. Complaints based on adultery must usually be made within 6 months of the complainant discovering it, all other complaints within 6 months of the offence itself. The Magistrates' Courts Act, 1952, separates the hearing of matrimonial disputes from ordinary Court business; specifies the persons allowed to be present; limits newspaper reports, etc. etc.

SCOTLAND

DIVORCE

Proceedings are brought in the Court of Session and it is necessary that the husband be domiciled in Scotland, or, he not being domiciled in the United Kingdom or in the Channel Islands or the Isle of Man, that the wife is resident in Scotland and has been ordinarily resident there for a period of three years immediately preceding commencement of proceedings.

The following are the grounds for divorce:—

1. *Adultery.*—A mere confession by the defender is of itself insufficient; there must be proof of the facts. Direct evidence is not required, if facts can be established which give rise to an inevitable inference of adultery. There must be no collusion between the parties, and the pursuer is required to swear to this. It is not collusion, however, for a guilty spouse to give information of an act of adultery already committed. It is a defence to an action of divorce for adultery to plead that the

innocent spouse has condoned the misconduct on which the action is founded.

2. *Desertion.*— The defender must have wilfully and without reasonable cause deserted the pursuer and persisted in such desertion for a period of not less than three years. It must be shown that the desertion was without reasonable cause, and that the pursuer has throughout the period been willing to adhere. Refusal by one spouse to have marital relations with the other for any period of three years without any overt act of desertion does not constitute desertion. Here also, collusion is fatal to the success of the action.

3. *Incurable Insanity.*—The defender must, for five years preceding the raising of the action, have been under care and treatment as an insane person.

4. *Cruelty.*—The degree of cruelty to be established depends on the circumstances of each individual case, but the test, generally speaking, is that the conduct complained of must be such as to endanger the health of the pursuer. Cruelty may take the form of habitual drunkenness on the part of one of the spouses. The fraudulent activity of one spouse involving the other may amount to cruelty.

5. *Unnatural Sexual Offences.*—An extract of the criminal conviction is sufficient proof.

Effect of Divorce on Property.—A husband or wife obtaining decree of divorce against the other, except on the ground of incurable insanity. is entitled to claim his or her legal rights, *jus relicti*, however, being excluded, as if the offender was dead. Where there has been a successful cross-action the effect is the same as though both spouses had died at the date of decree.

Nullity of Marriage.—A declaration of nullity of marriage may be obtained on the ground of any impediment, viz., consanguinity and affinity, subsistence of a previous marriage, non-age of one of the parties, incapacity or insanity of one of the parties, or by the absence of genuine consent.

SEPARATION

A decree of judicial separation may be obtained by one spouse against the other on the grounds of (*a*) adultery, (*b*) cruelty. This entitles the parties to live apart, but does not dissolve the marriage. The husband, if the guilty party, is liable for aliment.

CUSTODY OF CHILDREN

In actions for divorce and separation, the Court has a discretion in awarding the custody of the children of the parties. The welfare of the children is the paramount consideration, and the mere fact that a spouse is the guilty party in the action does not of itself deprive him or her of the right to claim custody, though where the considerations of welfare are equally balanced the Court will have regard to the element of guilt.

HIRE-PURCHASE

ENGLAND AND WALES

Protection of the hirer against unscrupulous dealings and against delivery of shoddy goods is given by the Hire-Purchase Act, 1938 (as amended by the Hire-Purchase Act, 1954), which applies to a hire-purchase agreement under which the hire-purchase price *i.e.*, the total sum payable by the hirer to complete the purchase of the goods, does not exceed £1000 for livestock, or £300 in any other case.

Before any agreement is made, the owner of the goods must state in writing to the hirer the cash price at which the goods can be purchased, and there must be a memorandum of the agreement signed by the hirer himself and by or on behalf of the owner and any guarantor. The memorandum must contain (i) the cash price, (ii) the hire-purchase price, (iii) the amount of each instalment, (iv) when each instalment falls due, (v) a list of the goods, and (vi) a notice informing the hirer of his right to terminate the agreement (*below*), and of the restrictions on the owner's right to recover the goods (*below*), and a copy of the memorandum must be sent to the hirer within seven days of the agreement being made. In breach of any of these conditions the owner can neither recover the goods from the hirer nor enforce the agreement or any security given, although the Court can dispense with any of the conditions save that as to the signed memorandum. The same result ensues (while default continues) if the owner fails without reasonable cause within four days after written request (with a tender of 1*s*. for expenses) to supply to the hirer a copy of the agreement and a statement of amounts paid, in arrear, and not yet payable. Before the last instalment becomes due, the hirer may by writing determine the agreement, and, although he will not thereby escape liability for any instalments which have already become due he will be under no further obligation *under the agreement*. Under the Act, however, he must allow the owner to retake the goods and, if one-half of the hire-purchase price exceeds the total of the sums paid and due, he must pay the difference to the owner. These rights of the hirer cannot be taken away from him, but he can enforce more favourable rights (if any) under the agreement.

Any provision in the agreement giving the owner a right to enter any premises for the purpose of seizing the goods is invalidated by the Act. Further, even though the agreement may have been terminated because the hirer has broken it, or because the owner has exercised a right to terminate it, if one-third of the hire-purchase price has been paid or tendered, the owner cannot recover the goods otherwise than by action in a County Court, in which the Court can ensure that the hirer is fairly treated. If the owner disregards this provision, the hirer cannot recover the goods, but can recover all sums paid under the agreement.

SCOTLAND

The Hire Purchase and Small Debt (Scotland) Act, 1932, provides that no contract of hire purchase to which the Act applies is binding on the hirer unless (1) it is signed by him and (2) either a copy is acknowledged by him to have been delivered at the time of his signature or sent to him by registered post within fourteen days thereafter. Any contract which limits any right conferred by the Act on the hirer is void to that extent. The hirer may terminate the contract at any time by (1) re-delivery of the article in a good state of repair, fair wear and tear excepted, and (2) paying any instalment then due together with the amount, if any, by which one-third of the total payments stipulated for in the contract by way of instalment exceeds the *cumulo* amount of the instalments due. Even after the owner has obtained decree of delivery of an article, the hirer is entitled to retain it in his possession or to recover it if, within fourteen days of the decree, he pays the whole instalment which is due, with expenses.

The above Act was extended by the Hire Purchase Act, 1954, to apply to articles exceeding £300 in value. The Credit Sale Agreements (Scotland) Act, 1961 provides for the application in Scotland of the English Act of 1938 in so far as it relates to credit sale agreements.

ILLEGITIMACY AND LEGITIMATION

ENGLAND AND WALES

A man may be summoned to petty sessions on the application of the mother of a bastard child, or by the Public Assistance Authority where the child becomes chargeable to the local authority, and the Justices, on his being proved to be the father of the child, may make an order requiring him to pay for its maintenance and education a sum not exceeding 50*s*. a week. The evidence of the woman must be *corroborated* in a material particular. The mother has the custody of her bastard children. *Prima facie* every child born of a married woman during a marriage is legitimate; and this presumption can only be rebutted by strong, distinct, satisfactory and conclusive evidence. If however the husband and wife are separated under an Order of the Court, a child conceived by the wife during such separation is presumed not to be the husband's child.

LEGITIMATION.—By the *Legitimacy Act*, 1926, which came into force on Jan. 1, 1927, where the parents of an illegitimate person marry, or have married, whether before or after that date, the marriage, if the father is at the date thereof domiciled in England or Wales, renders that person, if living, legitimate as from Jan. 1, 1927, or from the date of the marriage, whichever last happens. Under the Act of 1959, marriage legitimates a person even though the father or mother was married to a third person at the time when the illegitimate person was born. It is the duty of the parents to supply to the Registrar General information for re-registration of the birth of a legitimated child.

Declarations of Legitimacy.—A person claiming that he, his parent, or any remoter ancestor has become legitimated, may petition the High Court or the County Court for the necessary declaration.

Rights and Duties of Legitimated Persons.—A legitimated person, his spouse or issue may take property under an intestacy occurring after the date of legitimation, or under any disposition (*e.g.*, a will) coming into operation after such date, as if he had been legitimate.

He must maintain all persons whom he would be bound to maintain had he been born legitimate, and he is entitled to the benefit of any Act of Parliament which confers rights on legitimate persons to recover damages or compensation. The Act specially provides that nothing therein contained is to render any person capable of succeeding to or transmitting a right to any dignity or title.

SCOTLAND

Illegitimate Children (Scotland) Act, 1930.—The mother of an illegitimate child may raise an action of affiliation and aliment against the father, either in the Court of Session or, more usually, in the Sheriff Court. Where in any such action the Court finds that the defender is the father of the child, the Court shall, in awarding inlying expenses, or aliment, have regard to the means of the parties, and the whole circumstances of the case. The Court may, upon application by the mother or by the father of any illegitimate child, or in any action for aliment for an illegitimate child, make such order as it may think fit regarding the custody of such child and the right of access thereto of either parent, having regard to the welfare of the child and to the conduct of the parents and to the wishes as well of the mother as of the father and may on the application of either parent recall or vary such order. The obligation of the mother and of the father of an illegitimate child to provide aliment for such child shall (without prejudice to any obligation attaching at common law) endure until the child attains the age of sixteen years.

By Scots Law an illegitimate child is legitimated by the subsequent marriage of its parents provided there was no impediment to the marriage of the parents at the time of the conception of the child. Such legitimation is recognized by International Law so far as the laws of particular countries allow it and is valid to that extent in England. By the Legitimacy Act, 1926, an illegitimate child may, in certain circumstances, succeed on intestacy. By the Registration of Births, Deaths and Marriages (Scotland) Amendment Act, 1934, a child so legitimated, who has already been registered as illegitimate, may, in certain circumstances be re-registered as legitimate. The consent of the father of an illegitimate child to its adoption is not required.

INTESTACY

ENGLAND AND WALES

As regards deaths on or after January 1, 1953, the position is governed by the Administration of Estates Act, 1925, as amended by the Intestates' Estates Act, 1952. The latter Act considerably increased the benefits of a surviving spouse of an intestate, and also extended the provisions of the Inheritance (Family Provision) Act, 1938 (*see under* "Wills"), to intestacies. These notes deal with the position under the 1952 Act, so that if the death occurred before 1953 reference must be made elsewhere. If the intestate leaves a spouse and issue, the spouse takes (i) the "personal chattels"; (ii) £5,000 with interest at 4 per cent. from death until payment; and (iii) a life interest in half of the rest of the estate. This life interest can be capitalized at the option of the spouse. "Personal chattels" are articles of household use or ornament (including motor-cars), not used for business purposes. The rest of the estate goes to the issue. If the intestate leaves a spouse and no issue, but leaves a parent or brother or sister of the whole blood or issue of such brothers and sisters the spouse takes (i) the "personal chattels"; (ii) £20,000 with interest at 4 per cent. from death until payment, and (iii) half of the rest of the estate absolutely. The other half of the rest of the estate goes to the parents, equally if more than one, or, if none, to the brothers and sisters of the whole blood. If the intestate leaves a spouse, but no issue, no parents, and no brothers or sisters of the whole blood or their issue, the spouse takes the whole estate absolutely. If resident therein at the intestate's death, the surviving spouse may generally require the personal representatives to appropriate the interest of the intestate in the matrimonial home in or towards satisfaction of any absolute interest of the spouse, including the capitalized value of a life interest. In certain cases, leave of Court is required. On a partial intestacy any benefit (other than personal chattels specifically bequeathed) received by the surviving spouse under the will must be brought into account against the statutory legacy of £5,000 or £20,000 as the case may be. If there is no surviving spouse, the estate is distributed among those who survive the intestate in the following order (those entitled under earlier numbers taking to the exclusion of those entitled under later numbers):—(1) issue; (2) father or mother (equally, if both alive); (3) brothers and sisters of the whole blood; (4) brothers and sisters of the half blood; (5) grandparents (equally, if more than one alive); (6) uncles and aunts of the whole blood; (7) uncles and aunts of the half blood; (8) the Crown.

In cases (1), (3), (4), (6) and (7) the persons entitled lose their interests unless they or their issue not only survive the intestate, but also attain twenty-one or marry under that age, their shares going to the other persons (if any) within the same group who do attain twenty-one or marry. Moreover, in the same cases, succession is not *per capita*, but *per stirpes*, *i.e.*, by stocks or families. Thus, if the intestate leaves one child and two grandchildren, being the children of a child of the intestate who pre-deceased the intestate, the two grandchildren represent their deceased parent and take between them one-half of the issue's share, the remaining half going to the surviving child. Similarly, nephews and nieces represent a deceased brother, and so on.

When the deceased died partially intestate (*i.e.*, leaving a will which disposed of only part of his property), the above rules apply to the intestate part.

Children must bring into account (hotchpot) any substantial advances received from the intestate during his lifetime before claiming any further share under the intestacy. Special hotchpot provisions apply to partial intestacy.

For further details, *see* Administration of Estates Act, 1925, as amended by the Intestates' Estates Act, 1952.

The Legitimacy Act, 1926, contains special provisions concerning the intestacy of an illegitimate child or the mother of an illegitimate child.

SCOTLAND

Heritage.—The lines of succession are: (1) descendants; (2) collaterals; (3) ascendants and their collaterals and so on in the ascending scale. Males have preference over females and the rule of primogeniture obtains. Regard is had, however, to the right of representation; thus, if the eldest son of the deceased, being his heir, has predeceased him leaving issue, the issue (whether male or female) are preferred to the younger sons of the deceased. Daughters only succeed if there are neither sons nor the issue of predeceasing sons, and where there are more than one, they share equally. There being no descendants, brothers, etc., will succeed, those of the full blood excluding those of the half blood. Among collaterals it is noted that the deceased's immediate younger brother is preferred to an elder brother. Failing a younger brother and his issue the estate ascends to the next elder brother and so on. If there are no brothers and sisters, nor the issue of brothers and sisters, the estate goes to the father and failing him to his collaterals; failing these the estate ascends to the paternal grandfather and his collaterals. The succession never ascends to the mother and her relations; even the mother's own estate, after vesting in her son or daughter, never ascends to the maternal line again.

By the Intestate Husband's Estate (Scotland) Acts, 1911, 1919 and 1959, the widow of a man dying intestate and without lawful issue is entitled to the whole estate both heritable and moveable if under £5,000 in value; if over that amount, she takes £5,000 with interest at 4 per cent. from the date of death, out of the heritable and moveable estate rateably before any division is made, and without prejudice to her rights of terce and *jus relictæ* (see *post*, p. 1174–5). Section 5 of the Law Reform (Miscellaneous Provisions) (Scotland) Act, 1940, gives like rights to a surviving husband. The same section covers the case of partial intestacy.

Moveable.—One-third of the moveable estate goes to the surviving spouse as *jus relicti* (*relictæ*); one-third to surviving children as *legitim* (see *post*, p. 1175); and one-third to surviving children and issue of predeceasing children *per stirpes*, *i.e.*, the share which would have fallen to a predeceased parent, if alive, is divided equally among the children. Where no children or issue of children survive, half of the estate goes to the surviving spouse and half to the heirs *in mobilibus*, *i.e.*, nearest heirs including representatives of predecessors, subject to the spouse's right to £5,000 (*supra*). The lines of succession are the same as in heritable succession, but the right of representation (*supra*) only applies where there are next of kin or the issue of predeceasing next of kin, Intestate Moveable Succession (Scotland) Act, 1855 (amended 1919). Beyond that relationship heirs take *per capita*. Where an intestate leaves no issue and is predeceased by his father, his mother is entitled to the same rights as the father would have had on survivance (1919 Act).

JURY SERVICE

Liability to Jury Service depends upon inclusion in the local Jury Book. This is compiled from the Electors Lists for each year (see *post* under "Voters' Qualifications"). The names of all persons who are on 10th October qualified and liable to serve as jurors are marked with the letter "J" on the Electors Lists. The marked Electors Lists are published, and anyone whose name is improperly marked may before the following 17th December claim that, although *qualified* to serve [see below] he is *exempt* from service [see below]; the marks will be removed from the names of exempted persons. The remaining marked names are thereafter included in the Jury Book. No one whose name actually appears in the Jury Book may claim exemption on any ground whatever except illness or, if a woman, for medical reasons.

QUALIFICATIONS

England and Wales—Every man and woman between the ages of 21 and 60 years [persons over 60 are exempt but not disqualified] residing in England or Wales being the owner, legally or under a trust, of freehold land worth £10 a year or more, or of leasehold land worth £20 a year or more (if the lease is for at least 21 years) in the county in which they live; or being a householder rated in respect of premises of a net annual value of at least £20 (or in London or Middlesex £30); is qualified and liable to serve on juries in the superior courts (civil and criminal), and at Assizes in their own county, and on petty juries in the local County Court or Quarter Sessions. Also all burgesses of boroughs having separate quarter sessions or a borough civil court are qualified and liable to serve on juries therein. Special regulations govern the qualifications and method of listing common jurors in the City of London; and jurors for a coroner's inquest. By the Juries Act, 1949, a person attending for jury service is entitled to be paid travelling and subsistence allowances together with compensation for loss of earnings and other loss or expenses.

Disqualifications.—Any person who has been attainted of treason or felony, or convicted of any infamous crime (unless he has obtained a free pardon) is disqualified from service on all juries.

Exemptions.—The persons who are exempt from serving on juries (including coroner's juries) include: peers; M.P.'s; judges; ministers of religion (Christian and Jewish); practising lawyers; officers of the Courts; coroners; prison, etc., officers; keepers of public mental hospitals; practising M.R.C.S.'s, M.R.C.P.'s and L.R.C.P.'s; practising apothecaries, doctors and chemists, registered practising dentists, veterinary practitioners; midwives; members of the armed forces; members of the Territorial Army (in certain cases) or the Royal Auxiliary Air Force; members of the Mersey Docks and Harbour Board, and of the Port of London Authority; certain members of Trinity House, Deptford Strond; masters of buoy and light vessels under the Trinity Houses, and all licensed water pilots; household servants of the Crown; officers of the Post Office, customs and excise; sheriff's officers; police officers; special constables; metropolitan magistrates and their court clerks and servants; officers of the Houses of Parliament.

As to their own counties: members of the L.C.C., and commissioners of income tax.

As to their local counties: borough councillors and J.P.'s., town clerks and borough treasurers; burgesses of boroughs having separate Quarter Sessions are exempt from serving on the County Sessions.

As to their own area of jurisdiction: J.P.'s.

Moreover a juror can never be called upon to serve oftener than once in each year; this period of exemption is longer in certain counties.

JURY SERVICE IN SCOTLAND

It is the duty of the Sheriff in each county to make up a list of persons qualified and liable to serve as jurors. The list is compiled from information which every householder is required to provide. From this list the General Jury Book is made up. Part II of the Juries Act, 1949 (amended by the Juries Act, 1954 with Regulations following thereon), applies only to Scotland and provides, *inter alia*, for the payment of travelling expenses and subsistence allowances to jurors, and for compensation for loss of earnings, recently increased.

QUALIFICATIONS

Every man or woman between the ages of 21 and 60 is qualified, who is possessed of heritable property of the yearly value of at least £5, or of moveable property of the value of at least £200 sterling.

Exemptions.—The persons who are exempt from serving on juries include: peers, judges of the supreme courts, sheriffs, magistrates of Royal Burghs, ministers of religion, parochial schoolmasters, practising lawyers, clerks and officers of court, prison officers, university professors, physicians, surgeons and dentists, officers in the Navy or Army on full pay, customs officers, messengers-at-arms and other officers of the law, lighthouse keepers and their assistants, soldiers, members of the Territorial Army and the Auxiliary Air Force (in certain circumstances), Inland Revenue officials and officers of the Post Office.

Jurors failing to attend without good cause are liable to a penalty.

LANDLORD AND TENANT
ENGLAND AND WALES

Although basically the relationship between the parties to the lease is governed by the lease itself, the law on this subject is complicated by the mass of legislation thereon, and no attempt is made here to deal in any detail with that legislation. Some of the statutes which govern specific aspects of the topic are set out at the end of this note with brief particulars. The few points dealt with may show the desirability of seeking professional assistance in these matters. Important statutes include:—

(1) As to agricultural holdings—the Agricultural Holdings Act, 1948. Among other things, this Act regulates the length of notice necessary to determine an agricultural tenancy, the tenant's right to remove fixtures on the land, his right to compensation for damage done by game, for improvements and for disturbance, and his right to require the consent of the Agricultural Land Tribunal to the operation of a notice to quit.

(2) As to business premises—the Landlord and Tenant Acts, 1927 and 1954, which do not extend to Scotland. Part II of the 1954 Act gives security of tenure to the tenant of most business premises, and in effect he can only be ousted on one or more of the seven grounds set out in the Act. In some cases, where the landlord can resume possession, the tenant is entitled to compensation.

(3) As to unfurnished dwelling houses—the complicated mass of legislation generally known as the Rent Acts. If a house is within these Acts, the tenant may have a personal right to reside in the house and can only be ousted on certain grounds. Further, each house within the Acts has a rent limit, and the rent recoverable by the landlord is limited to this rent. The Landlord and Tenant (Furniture and Fittings) Act, 1959, makes it an offence in connection with a grant, renewal or assignment of a tenancy of a house within the Rent Acts on terms which require the purchase of furniture to offer the furniture (which includes fittings and other articles) at a price which the vendor knows or ought to know is unreasonably high. It is also an offence under the Act to fail to furnish to a person seeking to obtain or retain such accommodation and who is provided with particulars of the tenancy a written inventory of the furniture, specifying the price sought for each item.

Houses let at a rent which includes board or substantial attendance or furniture are governed by the Furnished Houses (Rent Control) Act, 1946, as amended by the Landlord and Tenant (Rent Control) Act, 1949, if within the limits of rent control imposed by the Rent Act, 1957 (*see below*).

Since the Rent Act, 1957, the Rent Acts do not apply to a lease of a dwelling house granted for a term certain exceeding twenty-one years, but Part I of the Landlord and Tenant Act, 1954, gives protection in such cases, provided the rateable value does not exceed £100 in London and elsewhere in England and Wales, £75. Under this Act, the contractual tenancy is automatically extended until brought to an end in the manner prescribed by the Act, and in effect the landlord can only get possession on one of the grounds specified in the Act.

The Rent Act, 1957, has made considerable inroads into the importance of rent control by removing many houses from control altogether and fixing new maximum rent limits for all houses which remain subject to control. The principal changes effected by this Act are as follows:

1. Any house whose rateable value on November 7, 1956, exceeded £40 in London and elsewhere £30, is automatically decontrolled (and the operation of the Furnished Houses (Rent Control) Act is restricted to houses within the same limits of rateable value).

2. No tenancies beginning on or after July 6, 1957, are subject to control unless the person to whom the tenancy is granted is already a protected tenant of that house.

3. For all houses remaining subject to control the maximum rent is determined by reference to the gross value shown in the rating valuation list on November 7, 1956. The maximum rent is then computed as follows:—(*a*) where the tenant is not responsible for repairs other than internal decorative—twice the 1956 gross value; (*b*) where the landlord is responsible for all repairs including internal decorative—7/3 of the gross value; (*c*) where the tenant is responsible for all repairs—4/3 of the gross value. (There are varying proportions in certain other cases.) In all cases there may be added, (*a*) rates borne by the landlord; (*b*) a reasonable charge for services provided by the landlord.

4. A notice to quit *any* dwelling house must be given at least four weeks before it is to take effect.

(5) Under the Housing Act, 1961 (which does not extend to Scotland), in a lease of a dwelling-house granted after 24 October, 1961, for a term of less than 7 years, there is implied a covenant by the landlord (a) to keep in repair the structure and exterior of the house and (b) to keep in repair and proper working order the installations in the house (i) for the supply of water, gas and electricity, and for sanitation, and (ii) for space heating or heating water.

SCOTLAND

A Lease is a Contract, the relationship of the parties being governed by the terms thereof. As is also the case in England (see the foregoing Section) legislation has played an important part in regulating that relationship. Thus, what at Common Law was an Agreement binding only the parties to the deed, becomes in virtue of Statute 1449 c. 17, a contract binding the landlord's successors, as purchasers or creditors, provided the following four conditions are observed; (1) the lease, if for more than one year, must be in writing, (2) there must be a rent, (3) there must be a term of expiry, and (4) the tenant must have entered into possession.

It would be impracticable in a brief section of these Notes to enter upon a general discussion of this branch of the law and, accordingly, the plan adopted in the preceding Section of quoting a few important Statutes is followed here.

The Agricultural Holdings (Scotland) Act, 1949 (amended by the Agriculture Act, 1958), which is a consolidating act applicable to Scotland, contains provisions similar to those in the English Act, alluded to in the preceding Section. It cannot here be analysed in detail.

It is of interest to note that the Small Landholders Act, 1911, provided for the setting up of the Land Court which has jurisdiction over a large proportion of agricultural and pastoral land in Scotland.

In Scotland business premises are not controlled by Statute to so great an extent as in England, but the Tenancy of Shops (Scotland) Act, 1949, gives a measure of security to tenants of shops. This Act enables the tenant of a shop who is threatened with eviction to apply to the Sheriff for a renewal of the tenancy. If the landlord has offered to sell the subjects to the tenant at an agreed price the application for a renewal of the tenancy may be dismissed. Reference should be made to Section 1 (3) of the Act for particulars of other circumstances under which the Sheriff has a discretion to dismiss an application. The Act applies to premises held by the Crown or Government Departments, either as landlord or tenant.

The series of complicated statutes known as The Rent and Mortgage Interest (Restrictions) Acts, 1920 to 1939, largely govern the relations between landlord and tenant in regard to certain unfurnished houses—including parts thereof if let as separate dwellings—and it is important to note that notwithstanding conditions in the lease of a controlled house providing for the removal of the tenant, it is not possible to contract out of the Acts. The Landlord and Tenant (Furniture and Fittings) Act, 1959 (*ante*, under England and Wales), applies to Scotland. Employees occupying premises by virtue of their employment are not tenants and so cannot claim protection. The Housing (Repairs and Rents) (Scotland) Act, 1954, provides for increase in rent of a controlled dwelling house on which repairs of a certain value have been carried out. The Rent of Furnished Houses Control (Scotland) Act, 1943 contains provisions applicable to houses or parts of houses let with furniture and with or without services, as also to unfurnished premises let with services. These Acts have however been substantially altered or modified by the Rent Act, 1957. The changes in the law are *inter alia* as follows:—(1) Dwelling houses, the rateable value of which was on November 7, 1956, over £40, are released from control. (2) All tenancies coming into operation on or after July 6, 1957, are free from control, except where a new tenancy is granted to a statutory tenant already in occupation. (3) Provision is made for the increase of rent by a maximum of one quarter of all controlled houses. (4) The repairs increase of two-fifths provided for in the 1954 Act is increased to one-half.

The Rent Act, 1957, further provides that a notice to quit a dwelling house (furnished or unfurnished) must be sent at least four weeks before the date on which it is to take effect.

The Landlord and Tenant Act, 1954, referred to in the preceding section, does not apply to Scotland.

LEGAL AID

LEGAL AID IN CIVIL PROCEEDINGS

The Legal Aid and Advice Act, 1949, is designed to make legal aid and advice more readily available for persons of small and moderate means. The main structure of the new service is contained in the Act itself and the Regulations made thereunder but the administrative details are embodied in a scheme made by the Law Society.

Legal aid is available for proceedings (including matrimonial causes) in the House of Lords, Court of Appeal, High Court, County Courts, certain local courts, and civil proceedings in Magistrates Courts. In any event, an application for legal aid will not be approved if it appears that the applicant would gain only a trivial advantage from the proceedings. Further, proceedings wholly or partly in respect of defamation, breach of promise of marriage, seduction, inducement of one spouse to leave or remain apart from the other are excepted from the scheme, as are also relator actions, election petitions and proceedings by way of judgment summons.

Eligibility for legal aid in civil proceedings depends upon an applicant's "disposable income" and "disposable capital." Legal aid cannot be granted if the former exceeds £700 per annum, and a person may be refused assistance if he has a disposable capital of more than £500 and it appears that he can afford to proceed without legal aid. Even so, the applicant *may* be required to contribute up to one third the excess of his disposable income above £250, together with the whole excess of his disposable capital above £125. Disposable income is calculated by making deductions from gross income in respect of certain matters such as dependants, interest on loans, income tax, rates, rent and other matters for which the applicant must or reasonably may provide. Disposable capital is calculated by excluding from gross capital the value of the house in which the applicant resides, of furniture and household possessions; a deduction of up to £75 may be made in respect of dependants. Except in matrimonial proceedings or cases where the spouses are living apart, any resources of a person's wife or husband are to be treated as that person's resources. These figures will be assessed by the National Assistance Board, and will be certified to a Local Committee, who will determine whether reasonable grounds exist for the grant of a civil aid certificate. Appeal from refusal of a certificate lies to an Area Committee. A person resident in England or Wales desiring legal aid may apply for a certificate to any Local Committee; if resident elsewhere, application should be made to the Local Committee for London. However, if the application is made in respect of proceedings in an *appellate* court and the applicant is resident in England or Wales, application should generally be made to any *Area* Committee—if resident elsewhere, to the *Area* Committee for London. If a certificate is granted, the applicant may select his solicitor, and, if necessary, counsel, from a panel. The costs of the assisted person's solicitor and counsel will be paid out of the legal aid fund. There is no power at present to order payments to be made out of this fund to unassisted parties, but legislation to alter this is likely to come soon.

LEGAL ADVICE

Legal advice from a solicitor on the Legal Aid Panel is now available to anyone over the age of sixteen. Persons on National Assistance can get it free of charge, whilst those whose means are within the limits set out below can get it for 2*s*. 6*d*. An application form should be obtained from a Citizens' Advice Bureau, Court Office or from one of the Law Society's Legal Aid Offices, or from a solicitor whose name is on the panel, and, after completing the form, it should be taken to a solicitor on the panel and an interview requested. A person is entitled to advice on any one legal question only from one solicitor; and for not more than one hour and thirty minutes, but application for further advice may be made to the Area Committee. Lists of solicitors concerned may be consulted at the places mentioned above.

Legal advice is available for 2*s*. 6*d*. to a person whose capital is £125 or less and whose income has not been more than £7 10*s*. during the seven days up to and including the day of application for legal advice. Capital and income of husband and wife must be added together for this purpose, unless they are living apart or the applicant seeks advice on a matter in which the spouse has a contrary interest. In working out capital, the value of the applicant's house, its contents and the value of clothing and tools can be ignored. In working out income, a deduction of £2 5*s*. may be made for a spouse living with or maintained by the applicant, of £1 7*s*. for each child maintained by the applicant, and of £2 5*s*. for any other adult person maintained by the applicant. There may also be deducted any income tax and any National Insurance, Industrial Injuries or National Health contributions paid by the applicant during the week immediately before the date of obtaining legal advice.

Quite apart from the above statutory scheme for legal advice, there exists a voluntary scheme under which any person may apply to a solicitor who is on the panel for advice for a fee of £1 for up to thirty minutes. If the matter cannot be disposed of in thirty minutes, the solicitor should give an estimate of the approximate cost of any further advice or steps which may be necessary.

It should be mentioned that under both schemes a solicitor, even though he is on the panel, is entitled to decline to give advice to the applicant without giving any reason to the applicant.

OTHER LEGAL AID

Neither of the advice schemes covers further action such as writing letters. If however a person wants something more than advice but something less than proceedings, he may obtain a certificate to take steps to assert or dispute a claim where the question of proceedings has not yet arisen, but if it did arise legal aid could be granted for those proceedings. This type of legal aid could cover writing letters, obtaining evidence, and negotiating settlements. The certificate limits the amount to be spent under it, and does not cover any step in proceedings, nor can counsel be instructed. It is available to a person whose disposable capital does not exceed £125 and who was either receiving National Assistance at the date of his application or has a disposable income not exceeding £325 per annum. In assessing disposable capital deductions are made in respect of dependants, and further deductions for them are made in assessing disposable income. Where the applicant's disposable income exceeds £253 he must pay a contribution of up to £1 for each £3 above £250.

LEGAL AID IN CRIMINAL CASES

The Poor Prisoners' Defence Act, 1930, provides for free legal aid in criminal proceedings in specified cases, and official lists are kept of solicitors and barristers willing to undertake the defence of poor prisoners. On trial for an *indictable offence* (*i.e.* before the higher courts, such as Assizes or Quarter Sessions) the person charged may have free legal aid, if Justices, on committal for trial, or Judge of trial court grant a *Defence Certificate.* If the person's means are insufficient, such Certificate *may* be granted in cases where desirable, and *must* be given for a murder charge. In Magistrates' Courts, a Defence Certificate may be granted to a person of insufficient means if it is considered desirable to do so owing to gravity of charge or exceptional circumstances. The Legal Aid and Advice Act, 1949, provides that application for free legal aid under the Poor Prisoners' Defence Act, 1930, may be made by letter by any person arrested or summoned for an offence, as well as by a person charged with an offence. The letter should be addressed to the clerk to the Justices and must give particulars of the offence charged and set out the grounds of the application. Refusal of a legal aid certificate by a Justice after such application does not prevent the applicant being granted a legal aid certificate at the hearing. Legal aid is also available under the 1930 Act in proceedings on the question of the sentence to be passed, and after as well as before the defendant has pleaded or been found guilty.

Provision is also made for applications for legal aid in the event of an appeal under the Criminal Appeal Act, 1907, and the Summary Jurisdiction (Appeals) Act, 1933.

In any application for aid under the Poor Prisoners' Defence Act, 1930, the Summary Jurisdiction (Appeals) Act, 1933, or the Criminal Appeal Act, 1907, if any doubt exists as to whether the applicant can afford to provide his own legal aid, or whether it is desirable in the interests of justice that he should have free legal aid, such doubt is to be resolved in favour of the applicant. Further, the Justices have an almost absolute discretion in deciding applications.

SCOTLAND

Civil Proceedings

The Legal Aid and Solicitors (Scotland) Acts, 1949 and 1960 provide a scheme which is limited to civil actions in the Court of Session and in the Sheriff Courts except actions in respect of defamation or verbal injury, breach of promise of marriage, the inducement of one spouse to leave or remain apart from the other, election petitions (under the Parliamentary Elections Act, 1868, or the Elections (Scotland) (Corrupt and Illegal Practices) Act, 1890), and small debt proceedings (*i.e.*, under £20) and proceedings for summary removing, in both of which liability for the debt and the amount thereof are admitted.

As to those to whom legal aid is available, the same considerations as to income and capital apply in Scotland as in England. (See the preceding paragraph.) A person believing himself to be eligible may instruct any solicitor of his own choice who is on the official lists, or he may apply for a solicitor to one of the various Legal Aid Committees which are set up to administer the scheme. Application for a certificate granting legal aid is thereafter made to the appropriate Committee by the applicant's solicitor, who is required to prepare, for the signature of the applicant, a memorandum setting forth the grounds of the proposed action. Investigation into the applicant's financial means is carried out by the National Assistance Board after the Committee has considered the memorandum and, on a suitable contribution, if any, by the applicant being approved, a Certificate is granted enabling the applicant to proceed with his action.

LEGAL ADVICE

Since March, 1959, legal advice, as distinct from legal aid in proceedings, is available to anyone in Scotland on terms similar to those stated in a preceding paragraph dealing with legal advice in England. Application forms are available in the offices of all Legal Aid Committees and Citizens' Advice Bureaux.

Criminal Proceedings

In every sheriffdom there are Solicitors for the poor, and in the Court of Session there are Counsel and Solicitors for the poor, all of whom act gratuitously. No Court dues are payable in the first instance. The means that preclude a person from the benefit of the Poors' Roll are not fixed, and each application depends on its own circumstances.

MARRIAGE

A.—MARRIAGE ACCORDING TO RITES OF THE CHURCH OF ENGLAND

1. Marriage by Banns.—The Marriage Act, 1949, prescribes audible publication according to the rubric, on three Sundays preceding the ceremony during morning service or, if there is no morning service on a Sunday on which the banns are to be published, during evening service. Where the parties reside in different parishes, the banns must be published in both. Under the Act, banns may be published and the marriage solemnized in the parish church, *which is the usual place of worship* of the persons to be married or either of them, although neither of such persons dwells in such parish; but this publication of banns is *in addition* to any other publication required by law and does not apply if the church or the residence of either party is in Wales. The Act provides specially for the case where one of the parties resides in Scotland and the other in England, the publication being then in the parish in England in which one party resides, and, according to the law and custom in Scotland, in the place where the other party resides. After the lapse of three months from the last time of publication, the banns become useless, and the parties must either obtain a licence (*see below*), or submit to the republication of banns.

2. Marriage by Licence.—Marriage licences are of two kinds:—

(i) *A Common Licence*, dispensing with the necessity for banns, granted by the Archbishops and Bishops through their Surrogates, for marriages in any church or chapel duly licensed for marriages. A Common Licence can be obtained in London by application at the Faculty Office (1 The Sanctuary, Westminster, S.W.1) and (for marriages in London) at the Bishop of London's Diocesan Registry (1 The Sanctuary, S.W.1), by one of the parties about to be married. In the country they may be obtained at the offices of the Bishops' Registrars, but licences obtained at the Bishop's Diocesan Registry only enable the parties to be married in the diocese in which they are issued; those procured at the Faculty Office are available for *all* England and Wales. No instructions, either verbal or in writing, can be received, except from one of the parties. Affidavits are prepared from the personal instructions of one of the parties about to be married, and the licence is delivered to the party upon payment of fees amounting to thirty shillings. [The cost of licences through a clerical Surrogate in the country (*see below*) is £2 15s.] *No previous notice is required and the licence is available as soon as it is issued.* Before a licence can be granted one of the parties must make an affidavit that there is no legal impediment to the intended marriage; and also that one of such parties has had his or her usual place of abode for the space of fifteen days immediately preceding the issuing of the licence within the parish or ecclesiastical district of the church in which the marriage is to be solemnized, *or* the church in which the marriage is to be solemnized is the usual place of worship of the parties or one of them. In the country there may generally be found a parochial clergyman (Surrogate) before whom the affidavit may be taken, and whose office it is to deliver the licence personally to the applicant. (In some dioceses it is necessary for the Surrogate to procure the licence from the Bishop's Registry.) The licence continues in force for three months from its date.

(ii) *A Special Licence* granted by the Archbishop of Canterbury, under special circumstances, for marriage at any place with or without previous residence in the district, or at any time, etc.; but the reasons assigned must meet with his Grace's approval. Application must be made to the Faculty Office. Fees for licence, etc., £25.

3. Marriage under Superintendent Registrar's Certificate.—A marriage may be performed in church on the Superintendent Registrar's Certificate (as to which see below) without banns, provided that the incumbent's consent is obtained. One of the parties must be resident within the ecclesiastical parish of the church in which the marriage is to take place unless the church is the usual place of worship of the parties or one of them.

Marriage Fees.—The Church Commissioners settle tables of fees for all parishes. The usual fees are paid although a stranger-clergyman be invited to perform the service.

B.—MARRIAGE UNDER SUPERINTENDENT REGISTRAR'S CERTIFICATE

The following marriages may be solemnized on the authority of a Superintendent Registrar's Certificate (either with or without a licence):—

(*a*) A marriage in a registered building (*e.g.*, a nonconformist church registered for the solemnization of marriages therein).

(*b*) A marriage in a register office.

(*c*) A marriage according to the usages of the Society of Friends (commonly called Quakers).

(*d*) A marriage between two persons professing the Jewish religion according to the usages of the Jews.

(*e*) A marriage according to the rites of the Church of England (see above—in this case the marriage can only be *without* licence).

Notice.—Notice of the intended marriage must be given as follows:—

(i) Marriage by certificate (*without* licence)—If both parties reside in the same registration district, they must both have resided there for seven days before the notice can be given. It may then be given by either party. If the parties reside in different registration districts, notice must be given by each to the Superintendent Registrar of the district in which he or she resides, and the preliminary residential qualification of seven days must be fulfilled by each before either notice can be given.

(ii) Marriage by certificate (*with* licence)—One notice only is necessary, whether the parties live in the same or in different registration districts. Either party may give the notice, which must be given to the Superintendent Registrar of any registration district in which one of the parties has resided for the period of fifteen days immediately preceding the giving of notice, but both parties must be resident in England or Wales on the day notice is given.

The notice (in either case) must be in the prescribed form and must contain particulars as to names, marital status, occupation, residence, length of residence, and the building in which the marriage is to take place. The notice must also contain or have added at the foot thereof a solemn declaration that there is no legal impediment to the marriage, and, in the case of minors, that the consent of the person whose consent to the marriage is required by law (*see below*) has been duly given, and that the residential qualifications (mentioned above) have been complied with. A person making a false declaration renders himself or herself liable to prosecution for perjury. The notice is entered in the marriage notice book.

ISSUE OF CERTIFICATE:

(i) *Without* licence.—The notice (or an exact copy thereof) is affixed in some conspicuous place in the Superintendent Registrar's office for 21 days next after the notice was entered in the marriage notice book. After the lapse of this period the Superintendent Registrar may, provided no impediment is shown, issue his certificate for the marriage, which can then take place at any time within three months from the date of the entry of the notice.

(ii) *With* licence.—The notice in this case is not affixed in the office of the Superintendent Registrar. After the lapse of one whole day (other than a Sunday, Christmas Day or Good Friday) from the date of entry of the notice, the Superintendent Registrar may, provided no impediment is shown, issue his certificate and licence for the marriage, which can then take place on any day within three months from the date of entry of the notice.

SOLEMNIZATION OF THE MARRIAGE:

(i) *In a Registered Building.*—The marriage must generally take place at a building within the district of residence of one of the parties, but if the usual place of worship of either is outside the district of his or her residence, it may take place in such usual place of worship. Further, if there is not within the district of residence of one of the parties a registered building within which marriages are solemnized according to the rites and ceremonies which the parties desire to adopt in solemnizing their marriage, it may take place in an appropriate registered building in the nearest district.

The presence of a Registrar of Marriages is not necessary at marriages at registered buildings which have adopted the provisions of section 43 of the Marriage Act, 1949. This section provides for the appointment of an "authorized person" (a person, usually the minister or an official of the building, certified by the trustees or governing body as having been duly authorized for the purpose) who must be present and must register the marriage.

The marriage must be solemnized between the hours of 8 a.m. and 6 p.m. with open doors in the presence of two or more witnesses. The parties must at some time during the ceremony make the following declaration—"I do solemnly declare that I know not of any lawful impediment why I, A. B., may not be joined in matrimony to C. D." Also each of the parties must say to the other: "I call upon these persons here present to witness that I, A. B., do take thee, C. D., to be my lawful wedded wife [or husband]," *or*, if the marriage is solemnized in the presence of an authorized person without the presence of a Registrar, each party may say in lieu thereof: "I, A. B., do take thee, C. D., to be my wedded wife [or husband]."

(ii) *In a Register Office.*—The marriage may be solemnized in the office of the Superintendent Registrar to whom notice of the marriage has been given. The marriage must be solemnized between the hours of 8 a.m. and 6 p.m., with open doors in the presence of the Superintendent Registrar and a Registrar of the registration district of that Superintendent Registrar, and in the presence of two witnesses. The parties must make the following declaration: "I do solemnly declare that I know not of any lawful impediment why I, A. B., may not be joined in matrimony to C. D.," and each party must say to the other: "I call upon these persons here present to witness that I, A. B., do take thee, C. D., to be my lawful wedded wife [or husband]." No religious ceremony may take place in the Registry Office, though the parties may, on production of their marriage certificate, go through a subsequent religious ceremony in any church or persuasion of which they are members.

(iii) *Other Cases.*—If both parties are members of the Society of Friends (Quakers), or if, not being in membership, they have been authorized by the Society of Friends to solemnize their marriage in accordance with its usages, they may be married in a Friends' meeting-house. The marriage must be registered by the registering officer of the Society appointed to act for the district in which the meeting house is situated. The presence of a Registrar of Marriages is not necessary.

If both parties are Jews they may marry according to their usages in a synagogue, which has a certified marriage secretary, or private dwelling-house at any hour; the building may be situated within or without the district of residence. The marriage must be registered by the secretary of the synagogue of which the man is a member. The presence of a Registrar of Marriages is not necessary.

FEES OF SUPERINTENDENT REGISTRARS.

	s.	d.
For entering notice of a marriage by certificate (with or without licence) in the marriage notice book............	1	6
For a certificate for marriage (with or without licence)..................	1	6
For a licence for marriage..............	46	6
For a marriage by certificate (without licence) in the presence of a Registrar...	7	6
For a marriage by certificate (with licence) in the presence of a Registrar..........	15	0

MISCELLANEOUS NOTES

Consanguinity and Affinity.—A marriage between persons within the prohibited degrees of consanguinity or affinity is void. Relaxations have, however, been made by various statutes which have now been replaced by the Marriage Act, 1949 (see the 1st Schedule to the Act) and the Marriage (Enabling) Act, 1960. It is now permitted to contract a marriage with:—

Sister, aunt or niece of a former wife (whether living or not). Former wife of brother, uncle or nephew (whether living or not).

No clergyman can be compelled to solemnize any of the foregoing marriages, but he may allow his church to be used for the purpose by another minister.

Minors.—Persons under 21 years of age are generally required to obtain the consent of certain persons (see Marriage Act, 1949, section 3 and 2nd Schedule). Where both parents are living, both must consent; where one is dead, the survivor, or, if there is a guardian appointed by the deceased parent, the guardian and the survivor. No consent is required in the case of an infant's second marriage. In certain exceptional cases consent may be dispensed with, *e.g.*, the insanity of a parent. If consent is refused the Court may, on application being made, consent to the marriage; application can be made for this purpose to the High Court, the County Court, or a Court of Summary Jurisdiction. The Act *prohibits* any marriage where either party is under 16 years of age.

C.—MARRIAGE IN ENGLAND OR WALES WHEN ONE PARTY LIVES IN SCOTLAND OR NORTHERN IRELAND

Notice for a marriage by a Superintendent Registrar's certificate in a register office or registered building may be given in the usual way by the party resident in England. As regards Scotland, the party there, after a residence of fifteen days, should either apply to the session clerk to publish banns or give notice of marriage to the registrar; as regards Northern Ireland, the party there, after a residence of seven days, must give notice to the District Registrar of Marriages. Notice cannot be given for such marriages to take place by Certificate *with* licence of the Superintendent Registrar.

Marriage of such parties may take place in a church of the Church of England after the publication of banns, or by Ecclesiastical licence.

MARRIAGES IN SCOTLAND

According to the law of Scotland, marriage is a contract which is completed by the mutual consent of parties.

Impediments to marriage: These render the marriage null and void. (*a*) Age: If either party is under the age of 16. (*b*) Forbidden Degrees: If the parties are within certain degrees of relationship. (*c*) Subsisting previous marriage. (*d*) Impotency of either party. (*e*) Non-residence, *i.e.*, if the legal requirement of prior residence of one or other of the parties in Scotland have not been complied with. (*f*) Insanity of either party.

No consent of parents or guardians is necessary. Marriages may be regular or "irregular."

Regular Marriages.

A regular marriage is one which is celebrated by a Minister of religion or authorized Registrar after due notice by the proclamation of banns or publication by the Registrar. Any Minister of any denomination (including a person officiating at a Quaker wedding) who performs the ceremony is reckoned to be a minister of religion. It must be performed before two witnesses and one of the parties must either have his or her usual residence in the Registration District, or have resided there for at least 15 days before the ceremony or have a parent so residing there. No form, place or hours are prescribed by law. There are no canonical hours as in England. Public proclamation is made by (*a*) banns or (*b*) notice by the Registrar. Banns must be proclaimed in the parish church of both parties. It is ordered that the proclamation of banns should be made three times, but by immemorial practice proclamation on one Sunday is sufficient. The Clerk of the Kirk Session of the Parish takes in notices of banns and issues certificates of proclamation. The fee for proclamation may not exceed 3*s*. A certificate of proclamation of banns is only valid for three months.

Under the Marriage Notices (Scotland) Act, 1878, amended by the Marriage (Scotland) Act, 1956, a notice posted up in a conspicuous or accessible place on the board or outer wall of the Registrar's office is equivalent to the proclamation of banns, but a minister of the Church of Scotland is not bound, although he is entitled, to celebrate a marriage not preceded by banns. The statute is limited to persons with qualifying residence in Scotland or having parents so residing. Exhibition is made for 7 consecutive days, during which time any person may appear personally and lodge an objection in writing subscribed by him. If no objections are lodged the Registrar issues a certificate: fees, 3*s*. Such certificate of publication is only valid for three months. The Naval Marriages Act, 1908, regulates the publication of banns or of notice on board H.M. ships and the granting of certificates by the Officer-Commanding.

Marriage before Registrar: After obtaining a certificate of due publication as above, it is competent for the parties to contract the marriage in the office of the authorized Registrar in his presence and in the presence of two witnesses. Such a marriage is regular and valid in all respects.

Marriage by Licence: In unforeseen and exceptional circumstances—see Section 2 of the Marriage (Scotland) Act, 1939—where normal methods of publication cannot be carried through, the Sheriff, on application by the parties may grant a licence which is deemed in all respects to be equivalent to a certificate of publication.

Irregular Marriages.

Since the passing of the Marriage (Scotland) Act, 1939, only one form of irregular marriage is recognized, viz. marriage by co-habitation and habit and repute. If parties live together constantly as husband and wife, and if they are held to be such by the general repute of the neighbourhood, then there may arise a presumption from which marriage can be inferred. Before such marriage can be registered, however, a decree of declarator of marriage must be obtained from the Court of Session.

MASTER AND SERVANT

WAGES AND HOLIDAYS

Under the Truck Acts, it is in general forbidden for an employer to pay wages other than in current coin of the realm, and it is illegal for an employer to deduct from the employee's wages sums alleged to be due to the employer. However, the application of these Acts is confined to workmen, and domestic servants are specifically excluded from their operation. Even in the case of payments to workmen, certain deductions, including rent and the price of food to be consumed on the employers' premises, are not forbidden where the employee's written consent is obtained. Further, under the Payment of Wages Act, 1960, it is permissible for wages to be paid otherwise than in cash at the request of the employee, *e.g.*, by cheque, money order, postal order or into a banking account. The Truck Acts did not relate to the amount of wage to be paid to the employee, but to-day minimum wage rates for particular trades are prescribed by numerous statutes. The Wages Councils Act, 1945, established Wages Councils, which are given power to fix minimum wages in respect of a number of trades and industries. The Councils may also direct as to the length of holidays for workers in such trades and industries, and for payment of wages during holidays, under the Holidays with Pay Act, 1938. Subject to this Act, a servant's right to a holiday is a matter of contract. The terms of the contract may be express or implied; but if there is a right to a holiday once in a year and if the servant is rightfully dismissed before the end of that year, he cannot successfully claim pay in respect of the loss of the holiday.

RECEIPTS

Receipts should be kept for six years from the date of payment, after which period no action can be brought concerning the goods, etc., received.

In *Scotland*, as in England, inability to produce receipts does not necessarily bar defence to an action for payment.

TOWN AND COUNTRY PLANNING

The Town and Country Planning Act, 1962, contains very far-reaching provisions affecting the liberty of an owner of land to develop and use it as he will. A person has generally to get planning permission before carrying out any development on his land from the Local Planning Authority. Development charge is not payable in respect of operations begun or uses of land instituted on or after the 18th November, 1952.

What is Development:—

(*a*) Carrying out of building, engineering, mining or other operations.

(*b*) Making a material change in use.

It is expressly provided that if one dwelling-house is converted into two or more dwelling-houses, this involves a material change in use.

Examples of what is not Deemed Development:—

(*a*) Maintaining, improving or altering the interior of a building (except works for making good war damage), provided there is no material change to the exterior.

(*b*) Change of use of property within the curtilage of a dwelling-house for a purpose incidental to the use of the dwelling-house as such. (It will, however, be development if building operations are carried out.)

Application can be made to the Local Planning Authority to determine whether or not an operation or change of use constitutes development.

Planning Permission.—Application for such permission is not always necessary, as the Minister may make Development Orders giving general permission for a specified type of development. Thus a General Development Order of 1950 specified a number of types of development for which no permission is required *e.g.*, enlargement of a dwelling-house (including erection of a garage), so long as the cubic content of the original dwelling (external measurement) is not exceeded by more than 1,750 cubic feet or one-tenth whichever is greater, subject to a maximum of 4,000 cubic feet.

Appeal against refusal of permission lies to the Minister, and from the Minister, in limited circumstances, to the High Court. If the result of the appeal is unsatisfactory, an applicant may in certain circumstances require the Council to purchase the land.

Enforcement Notice.—If development is carried out without permission, or in defiance of conditions attached to such permission, the Local Planning Authority may serve an enforcement notice on the owner of the land calling upon him to demolish or alter any building, or to discontinue the use of land, or to comply with the said conditions. If the notice is not complied with, the Local Planning Authority may take appropriate steps to enforce it, recovering their expenses from the owner for the time being of the land. Appeal against an enforcement order lies to the Minister.

Scotland.

In Scotland special provisions, on similar lines, have been made by the Town and Country Planning (Scotland) Act, 1947, which incorporates certain provisions of the Town and Country Planning (Scotland) Act, 1945, all other earlier planning Acts being repealed. The financial provisions of the 1947 Act, have, however, been amended by the Town and Country Planning Act, 1953, which abolished development charges, and by the Town and Country Planning (Scotland) Act, 1954, which set up a new Scheme of compensation. *See also* the Town and Country Planning (Scotland) Act, 1959.

VOTERS' QUALIFICATIONS

The franchise is governed by the Representation of the People Acts, the latest of which, the Acts of 1948 and 1949, amended in some respects, have made important changes in the law. Those entitled to vote as electors at a parliamentary election in any constituency are those resident there on the qualifying date who, at that date and on the date of the poll, are British subjects of at least twenty-one years of age and not subject to any legal incapacity to vote; but registration as an elector in the register to be used at the election in question in that constituency is a prerequisite, and at a general election no person may vote in more than one constituency. Since the Electoral Registrars Act of 1949, the registers are prepared once in each year only. Under the Electoral Registers Act, 1953, the Register (of parliamentary and local government electors or, in Northern Ireland, of parliamentary electors) is published not later than February 15 in each year and is for use in the period of 12 months commencing on February 16. The qualifying date referred to is, in England, Wales and Scotland the preceding October 10, and in Northern Ireland the preceding September 15. It is, however, provided that any person who is not of full age on the relevant qualifying date, but is of full age on June 15, and is otherwise duly qualified, is entitled to vote at elections held in Great Britain between October 2 of that year and February 15 of the following year. Detailed provisions are laid down as to the meaning of "residence" in doubtful cases.

The Act of 1948 abolished the university constituencies and the business premises vote.

The Register is prepared by the Registration Officer in each constituency in Great Britain. It is the registration officer's duty to have a house to house or other official inquiry made as to the persons entitled to be registered and to publish preliminary electors lists showing the persons appearing to him to be entitled to be registered. Any person whose name is omitted may claim registration, and any person on the list may object to the inclusion therein of other persons' names: the registration officer determines the claims and objections. The procedure is slightly different for Northern Ireland.

Special provision is made for "Service voters," who include wives of Service voters resident with their husbands outside the United Kingdom. Such persons may make a Service declaration in a prescribed form and are then treated as resident at the address specified in the declaration. Service voters may vote by post or by proxy, on making the necessary application to the registration officer.

Certain other persons (*e.g.*, those unable to go in person to the polling station owing to the general nature of their occupation, blindness or other physical incapacity, etc.) may vote by post or, in some cases, by proxy as "absent voters."

The local government franchise now depends upon either residence in the area or the possession of a non-resident qualification, *i.e.*, occupation as owner or tenant of rateable lands or premises of the yearly value of not less than £10, excluding occupation of furnished dwelling-houses let for less than nine weeks and excluding occupation as a lodger. There are provisions, similar to those relating to the parliamentary franchise, for the preparation of registers, etc., and in fact the same register is used, as far as possible, with a mark indicating those persons entitled to vote for local government purposes only.

The Acts apply generally to Scotland where certain matters relating to local government and parliamentary elections are further regulated by Representation of the People (Scotland) Regulations, 1949.

WILLS

IMPORTANT NOTE.—*The following notes must be read subject to the provisions of the Inheritance (Family Provision) Act*, 1938, *which is liable to affect or modify the will of any person (domiciled in England) dying after July* 13, 1939. This Act empowers the High Court to order maintenance out of the testator's estate for the benefit of certain "dependants," *i.e.*, a surviving wife or husband; an unmarried (or invalid) daughter; an infant (or invalid) son. Such order can be made if the will does not itself make "reasonable provision" for the maintenance of the dependant who seeks the order. An application must normally be made within six months of probate. A legally adopted child comes within the definition of a "son" or "daughter" under the Act. For further details as to the limits of an order, the Act itself should be consulted.

Since the object of the Act is to provide *maintenance* for dependants, an application is not likely to be successful where the estate is very small, *e.g.*, two or three hundred pounds.

There are similar provisions under the Matrimonial Causes (Property and Maintenance Act), 1958, whereby the court may order provision out of a deceased's estate for the support of a *former* husband or wife where the marriage has been dissolved or annulled.

REASONS FOR MAKING A WILL.—Every person should make a will. However small the estate, it is safer in every case to protect the interests of the survivors by a will, and by the appointment of one or more trustworthy persons as executors to carry the testator's wishes into effect. The help of a lawyer in making a will is not in every case essential, but it is always advisable, particularly where there is a desire on a testator's part to provide for his property being "settled" as it is called—*e.g.*, the income being paid to his widow and the capital being ultimately divided among his children, for this requires the skill of a practised lawyer. When property is thus "settled," there may be a saving in death duties. Assuming a lawyer is not employed, a person having resolved to make a will must remember that it is only after a person is dead, and cannot explain his meaning, that his will can be open to dispute. It is the more necessary, therefore, to express what is meant in language of the utmost clearness, avoiding the use of any word or expression that admits of another meaning than the one intended. Avoid the use of "legal terms," such as "heirs" and "issue," when the same thing may be expressed in plain language. If in writing the will a mistake be made, it is better to rewrite the whole. Before a will is executed (see below) an alteration *may* be made by striking through the words with a pen, but opposite to such alteration the testator and witnesses should write their names or place their initials. Never scratch out a word with a knife or other instrument, and no alteration *of any kind whatever* must be made after the will is executed. If the testator afterwards wishes to change the disposition of his estate, it is best to make a new will, revoking the old one. The use of *codicils* should be left to the lawyer. *A will should be written in ink and very legibly, on a single sheet of paper.* Although, of course, forms of wills must vary to suit different cases, the following forms may be found useful to those who, in cases of emergency, are called upon to draw up wills, either for themselves or others.

Nothing more complicated should be attempted. The forms should be studied in conjunction with the notes following.

This is the last will and testament of me [*Thomas Smith*] of [*Vine Cottage, Silver Street, Reading, Berks*] which I make this [*thirteenth*] day of [*February*, 1964] and whereby I revoke all previous wills and testamentary dispositions.

1. I hereby appoint [*John Green of* —— *and Richard Brown of* ——] to be the executor(s) of this my will.

2. I give all my property real and personal to [*my wife Mary* or *my sons Raymond and David equally* or as the case may be].

Signed by the testator in the presence of us both present at the same time who, at his request, in his presence and in the presence of each other have hereunto set our names as witnesses.

Thomas Smith
Signature of Testator:

William Jones (*signed*) of Green Gables, South Street, Reading, tailor.

Henry Morgan (*signed*) of 16, North Street, Reading, butcher.

Should it be desired to give legacies and or gifts of specific property, instead of giving the whole estate to one or more persons, the form above should be used with the substitution for clause 2 of the following clauses:—

2. I give to —— of —— the sum of £—— and to —— of —— the sum of £—— and to —— of —— all my books (*or as the case may require*).

3. All the residue of my property real and personal I give to —— of ——.

TERMS.—Real property includes freehold land and houses; while personal property includes debts due, arrears of rents, money, leasehold property, house furniture, goods, assurance policies, stocks and shares in companies, and the like. The words "my money," apart from the context, will normally only include actual ready money. The expression "goods and chattels" should not be used. In giving *particular* property, ordinary language is sufficient, *e.g.*, "my house, Vine Cottage, Silver Street, Reading, Berks." Such specific gifts fail if not owned by the testator at his death.

RESIDUARY LEGATEES.—It is well in all cases where legacies or specific gifts are made, to leave to some person or persons "the residue of my property," although it may be thought that the whole of the property has been disposed of in legacies, etc., already mentioned in the will. *It should be remembered that a will operates on property acquired after it has been made.*

EXECUTION OF A WILL, AND WITNESSES.—The testator should sign his name at the foot or end of the will, in presence of two witnesses, who will immediately afterwards sign their names in his and in each other's presence. A person who has been left any gift or share of residue in the will, or whose wife or husband has been left such a gift, should not be an attesting witness. Their attestation would be good, but they would forfeit the gift. It is better that a person named as executor should not be a witness. Husband and wife may both be witnesses, provided neither is a legatee. If a solicitor be appointed executor, it is lawful to direct that his ordinary fees and charges shall be paid; but in this case he (as an interested party) must not be a witness to the will.

It is desirable that the witnesses should be fully described, as they may possibly be wanted at some future time. If the testator should be too ill to sign, even by a mark, another person may sign the testator's name to the will for him, in his presence and by his direction, and in this case it should be shown that the testator knew the contents of the document. The attestation clause should therefore be worded: "Signed by Thomas Brown, by the direction and in the presence of the testator, Thomas Smith, in the joint presence of us, who thereupon signed our names in his presence and in the presence of each other, the will having been first read over to the testator, who appeared fully to understand the same."

A *blind person* may make a will in Braille. If the testator be blind the will should be read aloud to him in the presence of the witnesses, and the fact mentioned in the attestation clause. A blind person cannot witness a will.

If by inadvertence the testator should have signed his will without the witnesses being present, then the attestation should be:—"The testator acknowledged his signature already made as his signature to his last will and testament, in the joint presence," etc. Any omission in the observance of these details may invalidate the will. *The stringency of the law as to signature and witnessing of a will is only relaxed in favour of soldiers, sailors and airmen in certain circumstances.*

EXECUTORS.—It is usual to appoint two executors, although one is sufficient; any number up to and including four may be appointed. The name and address of each executor should be given in full. An executor may be a legatee. Thus a child of full age or wife to whom the whole or a portion of the estate is left may be appointed sole executor, or one of two executors. The addresses of the executors are not essential; but it is desirable here as elsewhere, to avoid ambiguity or vagueness.

LAPSED LEGACIES.—If a legatee die in the lifetime of the testator, the legacy generally lapses and falls into the residue. Where a residuary legatee pre-deceases the testator, his share of the residuary estate will not generally pass to the other residuary legatees, but will pass to the persons entitled on the deceased's intestacy. In all such cases it is desirable to make a new will.

TESTAMENTARY CAPACITY.—A minor cannot make a will except, in certain circumstances, if he be a soldier, sailor or airman. A married woman (married on or since January 1, 1883) may dispose by will of any real or personal property as if she were a man.

REVOCATION.—A will is revoked by a subsequent will (but, if it does not expressly revoke former wills, only so far as such subsequent will operates as an implied revocation as by making other provisions inconsistent with the previous will, for this reason a will should always have a clause revoking previous testamentary dispositions), or by burning, tearing or otherwise *destroying* the same with the intention of revoking it. Such destruction must either be by the testator or by some other person in his presence and at his direction. *It is not sufficient to obliterate the will with a pen.* Marriage in every case acts as the revocation of a will, unless, in the case of a will made on or after Jan. 1, 1926, it is expressed to have been made in contemplation of a particular marriage (Law of Property Act, 1925, s. 177); so that after marriage a new will should be made, except in this last case.

PERSONAL APPLICATION FOR PROBATE OR LETTERS OF ADMINISTRATION

Application for probate or for letters of administration may be made *in person* at the Principal Probate Registry, or at a district registry, by the executors or persons entitled to a grant of administration. Applicants should bring (1) the will, if any; (2) a certificate of death; (3) particulars of property liable to estate duty; and (4) generally, a list of debts and funeral expenses. In an application for administration, the applicant will be required to enter into a bond for due administration, generally with two sureties who must attend at the Registry, although they need not do so at the same time as the applicant.

WHERE TO FIND A PROVED WILL

A will proved since 1858 must have been proved either at the Principal Registry at Somerset House, or a District Registry. In the former case the original will itself is carefully preserved at Somerset House, the copy of which probate has been granted is in the hands of the executors who proved the will, and another copy for Parliament is bound up in a folio volume of wills made by testators of that initial and date; the indices to these volumes fill a room of considerable size at Somerset House, where the indices may be examined and a copy of any will read on payment of a search fee of one shilling. In the latter case, the original will proved in the District Registry, is there kept, and may be seen or a *copy* obtained, but a copy is sent to and filed at Somerset House, where also it may be seen. A general index of grants, both probates and administrations, is prepared and printed annually in lexicographical form, and may be seen at either the Principal or a District Registry. This index is usually ready by about October of the following year.

SCOTS LAW OF WILLS

A domiciled Scotsman, unlike a domiciled Englishman, cannot in certain circumstances dispose of the entirety of his estate. If he leave a widow and children, the widow is entitled to a one-third share in the whole of the moveable estate (her *jus relictae*), and the children are entitled to another one-third share equally between them (their *legitim*). If he leave a widow but no children—or children but no widow—the *jus relictae* or *legitim* is increased to a one-half share in the estate. The remaining portion is known as the *dead's part*. The widow is also entitled to terce, *i.e.*, a life rent in one-third of her husband's heritable property. A surviving husband and children have comparable rights in the wife's estate. The *dead's part* is the only portion of which the testator can freely dispose. All burdens falling upon the representatives in moveables are payable out of the whole of the moveables before any division. Burdens in the nature of legacies are payable out of the *dead's part*. Pupils cannot make wills. Minors may dispose of moveables without the consent of any other person; but minors (unless they be serving in H.M. forces) cannot dispose of heritage. A will must be in writing (except that a person may leave a legacy verbally if the amount of that legacy does not exceed 100 pounds Scots (£8 6*s*. 8*d*. sterling) and may be typewritten or even in pencil. A will may be either (1) *holograph*, *i.e.*, written by the testator himself, in which case no witnesses are necessary; a printed form filled up by the testator is not necessarily *holograph* but may be made effectual when it has clearly been adopted as *holograph*. Words written on erasure or marginal additions or interlineations in *holograph* writings, it proved to be in the handwriting of the maker of the deed, are valid; (2) *tested*, i.e., signed in presence of two witnesses. It is not necessary that these witnesses should sign in presence of one another, or even that they should see the testator signing so long as the testator acknowledges his signature to the witnesses. If the testator cannot write, or is blind, his will may be authenticated by a notary and two witnesses. It is better that the will be not witnessed by a beneficiary thereunder, although this circumstance will not invalidate the attestation of the will or (as it would in England) the gift. A parish minister may act as a notary for the purpose of subscribing a will in his own parish. Wills are registered in the Books of the County in which the deceased died domiciled, and in the Books of Council and Session, H.M. General Register House, Edinburgh. The original deed may be inspected on payment of a small fee and a certified official copy may be obtained. A Scottish will is not revoked by the subsequent marriage of the testator. The subsequent birth of a child, no testamentary provision having been made for him, may revoke a will in whole or in part. A will is revoked by a subsequent will, either expressly or by implication; but in so far as the two can be read together both wills have effect.

"Confirmation," the Scottish equivalent of Probate, is obtained in the Sheriff Court of the County in which the deceased was domiciled at the date of his death or, where he had no fixed domicile or died abroad, in the commissariat of Edinburgh. Executors are either "nominate" or "dative." An Executor nominate is one nominated by the deceased in his will. An Executor dative is one appointed by the Court (1) in the case of intestacy or (2) where the deceased had failed to name an executor in his will. In the former case the deceased's next-of-kin are all entitled to be declared executors dative. An inventory of the deceased's estate and a schedule of debts, together with an affidavit, must first be given up. In estates under £500 confirmation is obtained under a simplified procedure at reduced fees.

THE OFFICES, SHOPS AND RAILWAY PREMISES ACT, 1963.

This Act, which comes into operation on a day or days to be appointed, applies to office premises, shop premises and railway premises being, in, each case, premises where persons are employed to work. Shop premises include a building which is not a shop but of which the main use is the carrying on there of a retail trade or business; a building occupied by a wholesaler where goods are kept for sale wholesale (except a warehouse belonging to the owner of a dock, wharf or quay); and a building to which the public can resort for the purpose of having goods repaired. However, the Act does not apply to premises if the only employees are the spouse, parent, grandparent, child, grandchild or brother or sister of the employer, and it does not apply to premises if the period of time worked there during each week does not normally exceed 21 hours.

The following is a very brief summary of the main provisions affecting premises to which the Act applies—

1. The premises and all furniture etc., must be kept clean, and no dirt or refuse must be allowed to accumulate.

2. No overcrowding so as to cause risk of injury to health is permitted.

3. Provisions must be made for maintaining a reasonable temperature in rooms, and a thermometer must be provided on each floor of a building.

4. Provision must be made for securing adequate ventilation.

5. Provision must be made for securing sufficient and suitable lighting.

6. Suitable and sufficient sanitary conveniences and washing facilities (including a supply of clean, running hot and cold or warm water and, in addition, soap and clean towels or other suitable means of cleaning or drying) must be provided at accessible places; and also an adequate supply of wholesome drinking water.

7. Accommodation must be provided for clothing which is not in use.

8. For each sedentary worker there must be provided a seat of a design, construction and dimensions suitable for that worker.

9. Where persons employed to work in shop premises eat meals there, suitable and sufficient facilities for eating them must be provided.

10. All floors, stairs and passages must be of sound construction and properly maintained.

11. Every dangerous part of any machinery must be securely fenced, unless it is in such a position or of such construction as to be as safe as if it were fenced. No person under 18 can clean machinery if he is thereby exposed to risk of injury from a moving part.

12. No person can be required to lift or carry a load so heavy as to be likely to injure him.

13. A first-aid box or cupboard must be provided.

14. Means of escape in case of fire must be provided, as must appropriate fire-fighting equipment.

15. Where an accident occurs which causes death to an employee or disables him from working for more than 3 days, the occupier of the premises must at once send notice of the accident to the appropriate authority.

PROFESSIONAL FEES

SOLICITORS' FEES

Solicitors and their clients may (subject to certain rules designed to prevent undercutting) make special agreements as to remuneration in non-contentious business (including conveyancing) under Section 57 of the Solicitors Act, 1957. In the absence of any such agreement the solicitor's remuneration is governed by Orders made under Section 56 of that Act. There are two methods of charging under the Orders. One is by a scale based upon the amount of money involved; the other is by a charge (usually known as a Schedule II charge) determined by reference to all the circumstances of the case, the amount of money involved being only one factor amongst many. Usually a scale charge is payable in conveyancing matters, provided the transaction has not been abortive, but a solicitor has an option to elect, before undertaking any business, to be paid a Schedule II charge instead. For negotiating sales or purchases the charges are always under Schedule II. *In addition to solicitors' charges, disbursements such as Government stamp duty, search fees and Land Registry fees may be payable.*

The Solicitors' Remuneration Order (1959) and The Solicitors' Remuneration (Registered Land) Order, 1959, increased the scales of permitted charges in the case of certain conveyancing transactions where the consideration does not exceed £1,000.

In sales by auction further charges may be payable, which will be computed under Schedule II below, *e.g.* for preparing or perusing Particulars of Sale and poster and attending the sale.

The following sections illustrate the scales of charges on sales, purchases and mortgages based upon the amount of money involved:—

I. For Unregistered Land

(Land, including houses, having a title which is not registered at the Land Registry).

For the following, charges are the same:—

Vendor's solicitor for deducing title to freehold or leasehold property, and perusing and completing conveyance (including preparation of contract or conditions of sale, if any);

Purchaser's solicitor for investigating title to freehold or leasehold property, and preparing and completing conveyance (including perusal and completion of contract, if any);

Mortgagor's solicitor for deducing title to freehold or leasehold property, perusing mortgage and completing;

Mortgagee's solicitor for investigating title to freehold or leasehold property, and preparing and completing mortgage.;

Value of Land or Amount of Charge	Scale of Remuneration
Under £100	£9 9s.
£100 or over, but not exceeding £150	£10 10s.
Over £150 but not exceeding £200	£11 11s.
Over £200 but not exceeding £300	£12 12s.
Over £300 but not exceeding £350	£12 15s
For each additional £50 thereafter up to £1,000	15s. per £50
For the second and third £1,000	£1 10s. per £100
For the fourth and each subsequent £1,000 up to £10,000	15s. per £100
For the remainder without limit	10s. per £100

Vendor's solicitor for conducting a sale of property by public auction, including the conditions of sale:—

When the property is sold:—For the first £1,000, 30s. per £100; for the second and third £1,000, 15s. per £100; for the fourth and each subsequent £1,000 up to £10,000, 7s. 6d. per £100; for the remainder without limit, 3s. 9d. per £100. When the property is not sold, half the scale rates are charged on the reserved price.

NOTE:—A minimum charge of £7 10s. is to be made whether a sale is effected or not.

Mortgagor's solicitor for negotiating loan:—For the first, second and third £1,000, 16s. 10½d. per £100; for the fourth and each subsequent £1,000 up to £10,000, 5s. 7½d. per £100; for the remainder without limit 3s. 9d. per £100. These charges apply equally to land having a registered title.

Mortgagee's solicitor for negotiating loan:— For the first, second and third £1,000, 33s. 9d. per £100; for the fourth and each subsequent £1,000 up to £10,000, 11s. 3d. per £100; for the remainder without limit, 7s. 6d. per £100. These charges apply equally to land having a registered title.

Title registered after completion.—Where the title is registered under the Land Registration Act, 1925, after completion, charges under Schedule II are payable in addition in respect of the first registration.

II. For Registered Land

(Land including houses having a title registered at the Land Registry.)

Scale of solicitor's charges for Transfers on Sale, Charges, Sub-Charges, Mortgages, Sub-Mortgages and Transfers thereof.

Value of Land or Amount of Charge	Scale of Remuneration
(1) Under £100	£5 15s. 6d.
£100 to £150	£6 6s.
Over £150 to £200	£7 7s.
Over £200 to £300	£8 8s.
Over £300 to £350	£8 10s.
For each additional £50 thereafter up to £1,000	10s. per £50
For the second and third £1,000	£1 per £100.
For the fourth £1,000	10s. per £100.
For each subsequent £1,000 up to £13,000	7s. 6d. per £100.
For each subsequent £1,000 up to £17,000	5s. per £100.
For the remainder without limit	4s. per £100.

(2) Above £1,000, fractions of £100 under £50 are to be reckoned as £50, fractions of £100 above £50 are to be reckoned as £100.

ACCOUNTANTS

The Councils of the three Institutes of Chartered Accountants and of the Association of Certified and Corporate Accountants have not laid down any scale of fees for their members. There are no statutory scales of fees except for certain special appointments such as Approved Auditors under the Industrial and Provident Societies Act.

Accountancy and auditing.—The Council of the Institute of Chartered Accountants in England and Wales has stated that chartered accountants' charges should generally be calculated by reference to the skill and knowledge required for the type of work involved, the seniority of the persons necessarily engaged on the work, the time occupied by each person engaged and the nature of the responsibility. The normal practice is therefore to calculate charges at an appropriate rate per day for the principal and for each of the clerks engaged on the work.

Special Work.—Substantially higher charges are appropriate where the work requires special skill or has other special features, for example work calling for priority of attention. Prospectus reports, investigations, back duty and acting as financial adviser are in this category.

Receivers, Liquidators and Trustees in Bankruptcy.—By long-standing custom and sometimes by statutory requirement the remuneration is often calculated by a percentage on the amount realised and a percentage on the amount distributed in dividend.

Taxation.—The rates charged for taxation matters are generally higher than those for audits. The Councils of the recognized accountancy bodies have intimated that a member undertaking taxation work on the basis that he should be remunerated by a percentage on the amount recovered, or receive no remuneration if no recovery results would be liable to be regarded as acting discreditably.

Expenses.—Out-of-pocket expenses, in particular travelling expenses, attributable to the work done for the client are normally charged in addition to the professional fees.

ARCHITECTS

Conditions of Engagement

A. Members of the Royal Institute of British Architects are governed by the Charters, Bye-laws and Code of Professional Conduct of the Royal Institute.

B. The Architect shall give such periodical supervision and inspection as may be necessary to ensure that the works are being executed in general accordance with the contract; constant supervision does not form part of the duties undertaken by him.

C. In cases where constant superintendence is required a Clerk of Works shall be employed for this purpose. He shall be nominated or approved by the Architect, and appointed and paid by the Client. He shall be under the Architect's direction and control.

D. The Architect shall not make any material deviation, alteration, addition to or omission from the approved design without the knowledge and consent of the Client and shall inform the Client if the total authorized expenditure is likely to be exceeded and if the contract period is likely to be varied.

E. The Architect has authority to give orders on behalf of the Client if such are necessitated by constructional requirements provided that the Client shall be immediately notified thereof.

F. The Architect shall, if requested to do so, at the completion of the work, prepare small-scale drawings thereof showing the main lines of drainage and other essential services as executed.

G. The following Architects' charges do not include for Surveyors' work for which see Clauses 11–17 which are those of the Royal Institution of Chartered Surveyors adopted by the R.I.B.A.

H. The employment of Consultants shall be at the Architect's discretion in agreement with the Client and Consultants shall be nominated or approved by the Architect, and appointed and paid by the Client. Where it is agreed to retain the services of Consultants the Architect's fee may by prior written agreement be reduced, but in no case shall the reduction exceed one-third on the cost of the work upon which the services of the Consultants are retained, provided always that the Architect's fee on the cost of the whole scheme shall not be reduced by more than one-sixth.

I. An engagement entered into between the Architect and the Client may be terminated at any time by either party upon reasonable notice being given.

J. Copyright in all drawings and in the work executed from them will remain the property of the Architect.

K. Under these Conditions of Engagement, the fees and charges payable to the Architect shall be in accordance with the following Scale of Charges, unless a higher charge is agreed between Architect and Client when the former is commissioned.

Scale of Charges

1. *New Works*

For taking the Client's instructions, preparing sketch designs, making approximate estimate of cost, submitting applications for licences, town planning, bye-law and/or Building Act approvals, preparing working drawings, specification or such particulars as may be necessary for the preparation of bills of quantities by an independent Quantity Surveyor, or for the purpose of obtaining tenders, advising on tenders and preparation of contract, nominating and instructing Consultants (if any), preparing for the use of the Contractor, two copies of all drawings, specification, or other particulars and of such further details as are necessary for the proper carrying out of the works, giving general supervision as defined in the Conditions of Engagement, issuing certificates for payment, certifying accounts and preparing such drawings as may be required under Condition F exclusive of the services enumerated in Clauses 5 and 11, the charge is to be a percentage on the total cost of all executed works as follows:

	Total Cost of Executed Works	*Percentage Fee*	*Minimum*
(i)	Up to £700	10	
	£700–£1,600	9½	£70
	£1,600–£2,500	9	£152
	£2,500–£3,400	8½	£225
	£3,400–£4,300	8	£289
	£4,300–£5,200	7½	£344
	£5,200–£6,100	7	£390
	£6,100–£7,000	6½	£427
	Over £7,000	6	£455

(ii) The fees set out in the Scale of Charges are in all cases exclusive of the cost of all prints and other reproductions of drawings and documents, travelling and hotel expenses and other reasonable disbursements.

(iii) When work is executed wholly or in part with old materials, or where material, labour or carriage is provided by the Client, the percentage shall be calculated as if the works had been executed wholly by the Contractor supplying all labour and materials.

(iv) In addition to a percentage on the total cost of executed works, the Architect is entitled to charge in respect of all works included in the tenders, but subsequently omitted, two-thirds of the charge which would have been payable had they been executed.

2. *Variations of Charges*

The above Scale of Charges is subject to variation by prior written agreement as to the percentage fee between Client and Architect in respect of the following:

(i) Repetitive Works: In the case of extensive works of a simple repetitive character, the charge may be reduced by one-sixth. This sub-clause shall not apply in the case of schemes of housing of a repetitive character, fees for which are governed by the provisions of the Application of the R.I.B.A. Scale of Professional Charges to Repetitive Housing Work: nor shall it apply to repetitive schemes for private house-builders, fees for which schemes are governed by the R.I.B.A. Scale of Fees for Private House Building (based on selling price).

(ii) Works to Existing Buildings: In the case of works to existing buildings a higher percentage is chargeable, not exceeding twice the amount payable under the Scale for new works of the same cost, and depending upon the intricacy of the work involved.

(iii) Special Works: In works involving special services in respect of fittings, furniture, decorations, exhibitions, garden or landscape design, special fees appropriate to the circumstances are chargeable.

3. *Partial Services*

In cases where the Architect performs partial services for any reason, including the abandonment, deferment, substitution or omission of any project and/or works, or part thereof, or if the services of the Architect are terminated, the charges in respect of the services performed are as follows:

(i) For taking Client's instructions and preparing preliminary sketch designs to illustrate possibilities of a site or cost of a scheme the charge is on *quantum meruit*.

(ii) For taking Client's instructions, preparing sketch designs sufficient to indicate the Architect's interpretation of the Client's instructions (but not in detail adequate to enable bills of quantities to be prepared), making approximate estimate of cost and making application for outline Town Planning approval, the charge is on *quantum meruit* and shall not exceed one-sixth of the percentage due under Clause 1 or 2 (as the case may be) on the Architect's estimated cost of such works.

(iii) For taking Client's instructions, preparing sketch designs sufficient to indicate the Architect's interpretation of the Client's instructions, and preparing drawings and particulars sufficient to enable applications to be made for Town Planning, Bye-law and/or Building Act approvals, the charge is one-third of the percentage due under Clause 1 or 2 (as the case may be) on the estimated cost of such works.

(iv) For taking Client's instructions, preparing sketch designs, making approximate estimate of cost and preparing working drawings, specification or such particulars as may be necessary for the preparation of bills of quantities by an independent Quantity Surveyor, or for the purpose of obtaining tenders, the charge is two-thirds of the percentage due under Clause 1 or 2 (as the case may be) on the Architect's estimated cost of such works.

(v) If the project or any part thereof is abandoned or deferred or any part omitted or submitted on the Client's instructions during the preparation of the working drawings, the charge is two-thirds of the appropriate percentage on the Architect's estimated cost of such works less a *quantum meruit* charge for bringing the working drawings and other particulars up to the stage defined in Clause 3 (iv).

(vi) In all cases where fees are assessed on the basis of *quantum meruit* regard must be had to all relevant factors.

4. *The Layout of Housing Estates*

(i) Where the Architect is employed to prepare a layout but not to design any dwellings and the layout shows the siting only of dwellings and other works, the fee shall be ½ per cent. on the estimated cost of such dwellings and other works.

(ii) Where the Architect is employed to prepare a layout only of the roads and public paths to a scale of 1/500th, the fee shall be 1 per cent. on the cost or estimated cost, as the case may be, of such roads and public paths.

(iii) Where the Architect is employed for the services specified in Clause 1 in connection with the construction of roads and sewers, the fee shall be based on the cost of the executed works in accordance with Clause 1.

5. *Services not Included in the Scale*

Charges assessed on the basis of *quantum meruit* in accordance with Clause 3 (vi) shall be payable in respect of any additional services involved:

(i) In advising as to the selection and suitability of sites. Negotiating as to sites or buildings. Surveying sites or buildings and taking levels, and making surveys, measurements, and plans of existing buildings.

(ii) In preparing for the use of the Client special drawings in addition to working drawings, and preparing drawings for negotiations with ground landlords, adjoining owners, public authorities, licensing authorities or others.

(iii) In amending working drawings or preparing new working drawings to give effect to alterations of the Client's instructions or changes in design due to causes outside the control of the Architect.

(iv) In negotiations arising from applications for licences, town planning, bye-law and/or Building Act approvals, and negotiations in connection with Party Walls, Rights of Light and other easements, reservations or restrictions.

(v) Arising out of delay in building operations due to causes outside the control of the Architect.

6. *Mode and Time of Payment*

The Architect is entitled to payment in stages as follows:

(i) On the completion of sketch designs one-sixth of the total fees payable.

(ii) On the completion of the drawings and particulars sufficient to enable applications to be made for Town Planning, Bye-law and/or Building Act approvals, one-third of the total fees payable less the amounts of any payments already received by the Architect pursuant to sub-clause 6 (i).

(iii) During the preparation of working drawings and other particulars instalments consistent with the amount of work completed by the Architect.

(iv) On completion of the said working drawings and other particulars, two-thirds of the total fees payable less the amount of any payments already received by the Architect pursuant to sub-Clauses 6 (i), 6 (ii) and 6 (iii).

(v) The remaining one-third of the total fees to be paid by instalments as the building work proceeds consistent with the value of the said building work as certified from time to time.

7. *Inspections and Reports*

For making inspections, preparing reports or giving advice on the condition of premises, the charge is on *quantum meruit* in accordance with Clause 3 (vi).

8. *Litigation and Arbitration*

For qualifying to give evidence, settling proofs, conferences with Solicitors and Counsel, attendance in Court or before Arbitrations or other tribunals, charge is based upon the time occupied at the minimum rate of £3 3*s*. per hour to which shall be added charges for Assistant's time, out-of-pocket expenses and other disbursements.

Architects acting as Arbitrators are recommended to base their charges upon the total time occupied in dealing with a case at a minimum rate of £3 3s. an hour exclusive of out-of-pocket expenses and other disbursements (minimum fee £21).

9. *Travelling Time*

An additional charge may be made by prior written agreement if the work should be at such a distance as to lead to an exceptional expenditure of time in travelling.

10. *Time Charges*

In cases in which charges are based upon time occupied the minimum fee for Principal's time is 2 guineas per hour to which shall be added charges for Assistants' time and office overheads thereon.

STRUCTURAL ENGINEERS

The following charges are those usually in operation among Consulting Structural Engineers who are not connected with any firm of contractors and who receive remuneration for their services directly from their clients. Full details of the scales which it authorizes can be obtained from the Institution of Structural Engineers, 11 Upper Belgrave Street, S.W.1.

Reports and Other Advisory Work.

For reports, advisory work, or valuations of plant and undertakings, a fee dependent on the professional standing of the Engineer, on the matter under consideration and on any special circumstances. In such cases, the fee will normally be computed on a time basis in accordance with the following paragraph or an agreed lump sum, or a combination thereof, or alternatively computed as an agreed percentage of the estimated capital value.

Fees Based on Time.

Where fees are based on the time occupied, an Engineer is entitled to charge for work done by himself and by his technical assistants, but not (unless otherwise agreed) by his clerical staff. Alternatively, an Engineer may charge for his technical assistants on a time basis, together with a fixed fee for his personal services. An Engineer is entitled to charge for time spent by himself and his technical assistants in travelling.

The time rates currently in force are:—

(i) Partners: Dependent on the standing of the Engineer, on the nature of the work, and on any special circumstances, but not less than 3½ guineas per hour.

(ii) Technical Staff: 3s. od. per hour per £100 or part thereof of annual salary (including bonus, if any).

Inspection Work.

Charges for inspection work, where not already covered by the basic fee, will usually be calculated as a percentage of the cost of the materials to be inspected, or on a time basis, or as a lump sum fee, or as a combination thereof. In addition out-of-pocket expenses are reimbursable.

Arbitration, Evidence, etc.

(i) When an Engineer acts as Arbitrator or Umpire, the fee shall be a lump sum plus a charge of not less than 5 guineas per hour, depending on the nature of the reference and on the professional standing of the Engineer.

(ii) When an Engineer attends at Parliamentary Committees, Courts of Law, Arbitrations or Official Enquiries, the fee shall usually be a lump sum, plus an appropriate hourly charge—not less than 3 hours being chargeable for attendance, however short, either before or after a mid-day adjournment. The Engineer is also entitled to a refresher for each day on which he is requested to hold himself in readiness to attend, but is subsequently not required, in the sum of three hours' remuneration.

(iii) Fees are also chargeable on a time basis for work done by an Engineer's technical assistants.

(iv) When computing fees chargeable under this paragraph on a time basis, an Engineer is entitled to include time spent by him or his assistants in travelling, attendance at consultations, considering documents, making inspections or otherwise qualifying for and preparing evidence. All travelling hotel and other out-of-pocket expenses, properly incurred are reimbursable—either at actual cost or as may be otherwise agreed.

Constructional Work.

A lump sum of £200* per Contract or concurrent group of Contracts for work on one site, plus a percentage of the Cost of the Works in accordance with the following table:—

Cost of the Works	*Fee per cent.*	*Additional fee for Reinforced and Prestressed Concrete per cent.*
On the first £50,000	7	3
„ „ next £50,000	6	3
„ „ „ £100,000	5½	3
„ „ remainder	5	3

*If the total cost of the Works is below £5,000 the lump sum of £200 shall be reduced *pro rata* to the cost of the Works, with a minimum of £25. 0. 0.

NOTE: The above fees do not apply in cases where the demands on the Engineer's time are out of proportion to the estimated or actual Cost of the Works—*e.g.* alteration or additions to existing works. In such cases, the renumeration payable shall be on a higher percentage rate, or on a time basis, or as may be otherwise agreed.

CONSULTING ENGINEERS

The fees payable to Consulting Engineers for design and supervision are based on a percentage scale and for project reports, inspections, etc., on a lump sum or time scale. Full details can be obtained from the Association of Consulting Engineers Abbey House, 2 Victoria Street, S.W.1.

A booklet "Conditions of Engagement and Scales of Fees" which gives full details of fees in addition to containing Model Forms of Agreement between a Client and a Consulting Engineer is issued at 5s. per copy.

STOCKBROKERS

The Rules and Regulations drawn up by the London Stock Exchange Council are voluminous and technical. On British Government stocks the scale of brokerage is ⅜ per cent. on Stock up to £10,000 Stock and ⅛ per cent. on Stock on any balance in excess of £10,000 Stock. On shares the commission is 1¼ per cent. on consideration. There are minimum charges of 5s. on less than £20; 10s. on less than £100; and £1 on £100 and over. In certain circumstances the above charges may be modified. Copies of the Rules and Scales of Commission may be obtained from the Secretary.

AUCTIONEERS AND ESTATE AGENTS

(Summary based on the Scales of Charges of the Professional Societies. In all cases expenses are excluded)

Sales by Private Treaty or by Auction

Freehold Property and Leasehold Property, where the rent is less than 2/3rds. of the rateable value, including in the case of auctions the preparation of particulars and advising as to reserves:—On the first £500, 5 per cent.; on the next £4,500, 2½ per cent.; on the residue, 1½ per cent. Minimum Fee, £7 10s.

In addition to the above charges:—On payments for goodwill, 5 per cent. on the first £1,000 and 2½ per cent. on the residue; and on amounts paid by the purchaser for *Chattels, Fixtures, Fittings, Furniture, Plant and Machinery, Trade Stocks, Book Debts,* and other *Movable Effects, Timber,* and *Tenant-right,* 5 per cent. to include inventory and valuation if required.

Where the division of an estate into a number of lots involves substantial additional work, an extra fee may be charged.

Sales before Auction

After acceptance of instructions, whether sale arranged by auctioneer or not, the same scale as for sale by auction.

Non-Sale

In the event of non-sale at the auction, a fee, the amount of which is a matter of arrangement, is payable.

Sales within 3 Months after Auction

Whether arranged by auctioneer or not, same commission as for sale by auction merging any fee for non-sale previously paid.

Disposal of Leasehold Property

On disposing of all leases (other than those to which the foregoing sale scale applies and building leases) either by private treaty or by auction (whether effected by assignment, surrender or otherwise):—On the rent, the same commission as for a letting (*see below*); *and*, on the premium and any consideration equivalent thereto, 5 per cent. on the first £1,000 and 2½ per cent. on the residue; *and*, where the necessary instructions are held, on payments for goodwill, 5 per cent. on the first £1,000 and 2½ per cent. on the residue; and on payments for *Chattels, Fixtures, etc.*:—As for Freehold Property (*see above*).

NOTE.—Where two Agents are co-operating at the request of the owner, the commission shall be at the rate of a scale and a half.

Other Sales

On sales of *Furniture, Trade Stocks, Book Debts* and *Chattels* on the vendor's premises, 7½ per cent. on the amount realized.

On sales of *Plant* and *Machinery*, 5 per cent. on the amount realized.

On sales of *Live and Dead Farming Stock*, except Horses, Pedigree Live Stock,* Recorded Cattle,* Bulls, Rams and Boars, and Poultry, 2½ per cent. on live stock and 5 per cent. dead stock, on the amount realized.

On sale of *Horses, Pedigree Live Stock,* Recorded Cattle,* Bulls, Rams* and *Boars*, and *Poultry*, 5 per cent. on amount realized.

On marking, valuing and selling, timber and timber-like trees and selling underwood, 7½ Guineas on the first £1,000; and 5 Guineas per cent. on the residue of the amount realized; the fee to cover a felling licence if required. Minimum Fee, 7½ Guineas. Alternatively by prior arrangement, a fee on a time basis.

Purchases

Freehold and Leasehold Property.—For seeking and negotiating the purchase of a property to suit a client's requirements:—2½ per cent. on the first £5,000; 1½ per cent on the next £10,000; and 1 per cent. on the residue. In the case of leaseholds, in addition to the foregoing a fee on the rent equal to that payable under the appropriate letting scale (*see below*). For abortive work a fee to be fixed by arrangement. For negotiating the purchase of a particular property named by the client:—1½ per cent. on the first £15,000; and 1 per cent. on the residue. In the case of leaseholds, in addition to the foregoing, a fee on the rent equal to three-quarters of that payable under the appropriate letting scale (*see below*). If no purchase is effected, the usual scale for valuation should be charged: one guinea per cent. on first £1,000; half a guinea on next £9,000; and a quarter of a guinea per cent. beyond on the residue. Minimum fee, £7 17*s*. 6*d*.

Lettings

NOTES.—(*a*) Should the rent be a progressive one, the commission is based on the average rent for the period up to the first possible break of the tenancy. (*b*) When a property, which an Agent has been instructed to let or sell, is let with an option to purchase, and the tenant afterwards exercises his option, or becomes the purchaser within the period of the option, the commission for selling, less the commission already paid on the letting, will then become payable. (*c*) " Letting " includes a letting to a sitting tenant (including negotiating and agreeing a new rent) or to a nominee of the landlord. (*d*) For the purposes of these scales " rent " means (except where otherwise stated) the rent reserved by the letting plus any payment such as a service charge, made to the landlord for which the tenant is responsible, irrespective of the purpose to which the payment is subsequently applied; (*e*) In cases where two agents are co-operating at the request of the owner, the commission shall be at the rate of Scale and a half.

(1) *Unfurnished Premises*.—(*a*) Where there is a premium or any equivalent consideration and the rent (exclusive of any payment in respect of rates, heat, light, water, service or other incidental charges) is less than two-thirds of the rateable value, the same commission as is payable for the sale of such property (*see above*); (*b*) in all other cases, where the letting is for a term certain of twelve months or more, 10 per cent. on one year's rent; where there is a periodic tenancy which subsists for twelve months or more, a fee to be fixed by arrangement subject to a maximum of 10 per cent. on one year's rent; where there is a periodic tenancy which subsists for less than twelve months, 10 per cent. on the amount of the rent payable under the letting; and *in addition* a commission on the premium or goodwill as for the disposal of leasehold property (*see above*).

(2) *Furnished Premises*, including collection of rent. if required, but excluding the making and checking of inventories: (*a*) for lettings of 12 months or less, 10 per cent. on the amount of rent payable under the letting; (*b*) for lettings of more than 12 months, 10 per cent. on one year's rent, and, *in addition*, 7½ per cent. on the amount of rent payable during any period for which the premises are let in excess of twelve months.

(3) *Sporting Rights*, including collection of rent if required—10 per cent. on one year's rent or, where letting is for less than one year, 10 per cent. on the amount of rent payable under the letting.

(4) *Farms and Agricultural Land*.—10 per cent. on the first £250 and 7½ per cent. on the residue, of 1 year's rent.

(5) *Land on Building Lease, or at a Fee Farm Rent*.—100 per cent. on the first £100; 50 per cent. on the next £900; and 25 per cent. on the residue, of one year's ground rent; *and in addition* where a premium is paid, a Commission of 5 per cent. on the first £1,000 and 2½ per cent. on the residue.

---

* Where a full catalogue with details of pedigree or milk records respectively is provided, the 5 per cent. scale applies.

TAXES, STAMP DUTIES AND LICENCES

INCOME TAX 1963–64

Income Tax is a tax on annual income, represented by money, or money's worth. In general, the charge to tax is on the full amount of income arising for the year of assessment, the fiscal year which runs from 6th April in one year to 5th April in the next, subject to the deductions authorised by the Income Tax Acts. Under Schedule D, however, the assessment is made on the profits or gains of a continuing trade or profession for the year preceding the year of assessment, which is called the "basis year." The profits are arrived at on ordinary accountancy principles and then adjusted for tax purposes. The profits for the accounting year of the trade or profession which ends in the year preceding the year of assessment, are the profits of the "basis year."

Broadly, the charge to tax is on income arising in the United Kingdom, or on income received from home or abroad, by residents in the United Kingdom. An individual is resident and ordinarily resident in the United Kingdom if he is living here in the ordinary course of his life, or for an extended period; also, though normally he lives here, if he is abroad for occasional residence only; or if he visits the United Kingdom year by year, even though his main home is abroad.

The income of a married woman living with her husband is aggregated with his income. Separate assessment may be claimed, but the tax due remains the same.

Income Tax is imposed at the rates specified by the annual Finance Acts. There are graduated rates of tax, the principal rate being called the "Standard Rate," which for 1963/64 is 7/9*d.* in the £. There is an additional income tax on higher incomes called "Sur-tax." The enactments relating to income tax were consolidated in the Income Tax Act, 1952, as amended by subsequent Finance Acts.

The Tables which follow show the income tax payable for 1963/64 and surtax (if any) for 1962/63, payable in 1963/64 by an individual on the amount of income specified, after deduction of the personal allowance, an allowance for National Insurance contributions, children's allowance (where appropriate) and, in the case of earned income, the earned income relief. The taxpayer, however, may be entitled to further reliefs which would reduce the tax payable below the amounts shown in the Tables.

Under Schedule A.—Landlords under short leases (not exceeding 50 years) are taxed on the annual value of houses and lands. This is based on an estimate of the rent obtainable on a letting from year to year when landlord bears the cost of repairs, insurance and maintenance and tenant pays rates. The tax is collected from the occupier who has the right to deduct it from the next succeeding payment of rent. Leaseholders paying ground rents, rent charges or feu duties under long leases (exceeding 50 years) from which they are entitled to deduct tax at source, are also assessable under this schedule but the assessment is limited to the amount of the ground rent, etc.

Owner-occupiers who were previously charged under this schedule are exempt from 1963/64 onwards. The whole schedule has been abolished with effect from 1964/65 when all rents other than mineral rents will be assessed on the recipient under a new Case VIII of Schedule D (see below). The distinction between short and long leases will then disappear and ground rents, rent charges and feu duties will be payable without deduction of tax.

(1) Single Persons

Income	All Earned Income					All Investment Income				
	Income Tax (and Surtax if any)			Effective Rate		Income Tax (and Surtax if any)			Effective Rate	
£	£	*s.*	*d.*	*s.*	*d.*	£	*s.*	*d.*	*s.*	*d.*
225	—			—		—			—	
250	—			—		—			—	
300	2	5	4	–	2	1	9	4	–	1
350	10	0	10	–	7	9	4	10	–	6½
400	17	16	5	–	10½	17	0	5	–	10
500	40	1	4	1	7	52	4	0	2	1
600	63	8	0	2	1½	102	4	0	3	5
700	88	13	11	2	6½	147	8	6	4	2½
800	118	16	8	2	11½	186	3	6	4	8
900	148	19	6	3	3½	224	18	6	5	0
1,000	179	2	3	3	7	263	13	6	5	3½
1,250	254	9	2	4	1	360	11	0	5	9
1,500	329	16	2	4	5	457	8	6	6	1
1,750	405	3	1	4	7½	554	6	0	6	4
2,000	480	10	0	4	9½	651	3	6	6	6
2,500	631	3	11	5	0½	892	14	6	7	1½
3,000	781	17	10	5	2½	1,148	8	6	7	8
4,000	1,083	5	7	5	5	1,709	16	6	8	6½
5,000	1,427	10	2	5	8½	2,321	4	6	9	3½
6,000	1,868	4	11	6	2½	2,982	12	6	9	11½
7,000	2,361	15	3	6	9	3,694	0	6	10	6½
8,000	2,894	3	4	7	3	4,406	10	6	11	0
9,000	3,465	9	3	7	8½	5,167	18,	6	11	6
10,000	4,080	0	0	8	2	5,930	8	6	11	10½
12,000	5,526	12	0	9	2½	7,554	6	6	12	7
15,000	7,885	14	0	10	6	10,140	14	6	13	6½
20,000	12,205	12	0	12	2½	14,577	13	6	14	7
25,000	16,643	2	0	13	4	19,015	3	6	15	2½
30,000	21,080	12	0	14	0½	23,452	13	6	15	7½
40,000	29,955	12	0	14	11½	32,327	13	6	16	2
50,000	38,830	12	0	15	6½	41,202	13	6	16	6
100,000	83,205	12	0	16	7½	85,577	13	6	17	1½

Maintenance Relief.—The relief previously available to occupiers has been abolished consequent upon the abolition of Schedule A tax. In 1963/64 landlords are entitled to claim relief for the cost of repairs, insurance and maintenance based on the average expenditure in the previous five years, except where property is newly acquired during the year when the claim is based on the actual expenditure in the year. From 1964/65 onwards the relief ceases altogether and expenditure of this nature will be allowed as a deduction from the rents assessable under Case VIII of Schedule D.

Under Schedule B.—From 1963/64 onwards the charge under this Schedule is restricted to woodlands in the United Kingdom managed on a commercial basis and with a view to the realization of profits. Amenity lands such as parks and gardens are no longer assessable to tax. The assessment on woodlands will be based on one-third of the annual value of the land arrived at on the normal rating basis on the assumption that the lands were let and occupied in their natural and unimproved state. The taxpayer has the option to be assessed under Schedule D Case I on the results shown by accounts instead.

Under Schedule C.—Dividends, interest, annuities from public revenue on actual year basis. Income Tax is deducted at source.

Under Schedule D.—This schedule is divided into eight cases as follows:—Cases I and II—Profits of trades, businesses, commercial activities on land including farming, professions or vocations.

Case III—Interest on Government stocks not taxed at source (*e.g.* War Loan, Defence Bonds), bank deposit interest, discounts, etc. Interest on Post Office Savings Bank and Trustee Savings Bank accounts up to £15 is exempt from income tax but assessable to Sur-tax grossed at standard rate.

Cases IV and V—Income from Foreign or Commonwealth securities, rents and possessions including businesses and pensions: for persons domiciled and ordinarily resident in Great Britain this income is assessable whether remitted or not. Persons not domiciled or British subjects not ordinarily resident in Great Britain are assessable only on remittances to the United Kingdom of this income in any year in which they become resident. Income from Trades or Professions carried on abroad is assessable only to extent that it is remitted, and then only when person entitled thereto is resident in United Kingdom.

Case VI—Sundry profits not included above, such as profits from letting of Furnished Houses, etc., and Excess Rents arising when rent of unfurnished house, less an allowance for repairs, exceeds Schedule A assessment.

(2) Married Couples without Children
(see introductory notes)

Income	All Earned Income					All Investment Income				
	Income Tax (and Surtax) if any)			Effective Rate		Income Tax (and Surtax if any)			Effective Rate	
£	£	*s.*	*d.*	*s.*	*d.*	£	*s.*	*d.*	*s.*	*d.*
350	—			—		—			—	
400	—			—		—			—	
500	9	7	6	–	4½	25	0	0	1	0
600	27	8	0	–	11	66	4	0	2	2½
700	50	14	8	1	5½	100	18	6	2	10½
800	74	1	4	1	10	139	13	6	3	6
900	102	9	6	2	3½	178	8	6	3	11½
1,000	132	12	3	2	8	217	3	6	4	4
1,250	207	19	2	3	4	314	1	0	5	0½
1,500	283	6	2	3	9½	410	18	6	5	5½
1,750	358	13	1	4	1	507	16	0	5	9½
2,000	434	0	0	4	4	604	13	6	6	0½
2,500	584	13	11	4	8	836	4	6	6	8½
3,000	735	7	10	4	11	1,089	8	6	7	3
4,000	1,036	15	7	5	2	1,645	16	6	8	2½
5,000	1,381	0	2	5	6½	2,252	4	6	9	0
6,000	1,809	4	11	6	0½	2,908	12	6	9	8½
7,000	2,297	15	3	6	7	3,615	0	6	10	4
8,000	2,825	3	4	7	1	4,327	10	6	10	10
9,000	3,391	9	3	7	6½	5,083	18	6	11	3½
10,000	4,001	0	0	8	0	5,846	8	6	11	8½
12,000	5,442	12	0	9	1	7,465	6	6	12	5½
15,000	7,796	14	0	10	4½	10,046	14	6	13	4½
20,000	12,109	2	0	12	1½	14,481	3	6	14	6
25,000	16,546	12	0	13	3	18,918	13	6	15	1½
30,000	20,984	2	0	14	0	23,356	3	6	15	7
40,000	29,859	2	0	14	11	32,231	3	6	16	1½
50,000	38,734	2	0	15	6	41,106	3	6	16	5½
100,000	83,109	2	0	16	7½	85,481	3	6	17	1

Premiums on leases.—From 1963/64 onwards premiums and certain sums treated as such, payable in connection with leases not exceeding fifty years, will be taxable subject to a deduction of 2% for each year after the first year. In 1963/64 this charge will be made under Case VI. "Lease" includes any tenancy but leases granted in pursuance of a contract entered into before April 4th, 1963 are excluded. From 1964/65 onwards Excess Rents and most premiums will be assessed as rents under Case VIII (see below).

Case VII—*Short-term gains.*—Gains made as a result of the acquisition and disposal, both being after April 10th, 1962, of (a) land, where the disposal takes place not more than three years after the acquisition, and (b) in the case of other property; *e.g.*, stocks and shares, where the disposal takes place not more than six months after acquisition. The principal exceptions are for owner-occupied dwelling houses, business premises and tangible moveable property. Losses are allowable against gains for the year, or subsequent years, until exhausted. Liability is confined to persons resident and ordinarily resident in the U.K. Case VIII—Profits arising in respect of rents and certain other receipts from land of an income nature, other than mineral rents or royalties, and premiums in connection with leases will from 1964/65 be assessable under this Case. Expenditure on maintenance, insurance and repairs and certain other expenses will be allowable as deductions.

Under Schedule E.—Income from all Offices, Employments and Pensions, including Salaries, Wages, Emoluments, Directors Fees, etc. taxed by deduction on payment under P.A.Y.E. (pay-as-you-earn) on actual year basis. Necessary expenses are allowable, including fees and subscriptions to certain professional bodies and learned societies.

Tax is charged on the emoluments of an office or employment if the holder is resident, and ordinarily resident within the United Kingdom, provided the duties are not performed wholly abroad. A person not resident (or if resident, then not ordinarily resident) in the United Kingdom is charged only on emoluments for duties performed in the United Kingdom.

Income from employments exercised abroad is assessable only to the extent that it is received in the United Kingdom, and then only when employee is resident in United Kingdom.

Expense allowances and payments in kind (less expenses incurred in performance of duties) to Directors and employees enjoying emoluments of £2,000 p.a. or more are assessable. Certain payments made on retirement or removal from a person's office or employment (in excess of £5,000) are assessable to tax on him. Where any person has premises available for his use by reason of his employment and either pays no rent or pays less than the annual value he will be charged to tax on the annual value less any rent paid.

Exemptions.—Unemployment, sickness and maternity benefit and grant, and death grant payable under the National Insurance Acts are not assessable to income tax, but retirement (old age) pensions and family allowances are included in the charge under this schedule.

TAXABLE INCOME is Statutory Income less Allowances and Deductions as under:

Personal Allowance.—To single person... £200
To married man living with or normally maintaining his wife.................. £320

When either husband or wife is absent from United Kingdom throughout a complete fiscal year they are treated as separate entities for tax

(3) Married Couples with one Child

Income	All Earned Income					
	One Child not over 11		One Child over 11, but not over 16		One Child over 16	
	Income Tax (and Surtax, if any)	Effective Rate	Income Tax (and Surtax, if any)	Effective Rate	Income Tax (and Surtax, if any)	Effective Rate
£	£ s. d.	s. d.	£ s. d.	s. d.	£ s. d.	s. d.
500	—	—	—	—	—	—
600	1 18 8	– 1	—	—	—	—
700	17 9 9	– 6	12 9 9	– 4½	7 9 9	– 2½
800	39 11 4	1 0	32 1 4	– 9½	24 11 4	– 7½
900	62 18 0	1 5	55 8 0	1 3	47 18 0	1 1
1,000	88 1 0	1 9	78 14 8	1 7	71 4 8	1 5
1,250	163 7 11	2 7½	153 14 2	2 5½	144 0 5	2 3½
1,500	238 14 11	3 2	229 1 2	3 0½	219 7 5	2 11
1,750	314 1 10	3 7	304 8 1	3 5½	294 14 4	3 4½
2,000	389 8 9	3 10½	379 15 0	3 9½	370 1 3	3 8½
2,500	540 2 8	4 4	530 8 11	4 3	520 15 2	4 2
3,000	690 16 7	4 7½	681 2 10	4 6½	671 9 1	4 5½
4,000	992 4 4	4 11½	982 10 7	4 11	972 16 10	4 10½
5,000	1,336 8 11	5 4	1,326 15 2	5 3½	1,317 1 5	5 3
6,000	1,752 3 8	5 10	1,739 7 5	5 9½	1,726 11 2	5 9
7,000	2,235 14 0	6 4½	2,221 12 9	6 4	2,207 11 6	6 3½
8,000	2,758 2 1	6 10½	2,742 15 10	6 10½	2,727 9 7	6 10
9,000	3,319 8 0	7 4½	3,302 16 9	7 4	3,286 5 6	7 3½
10,000	3,923 18 9	7 10	3,906 2 6	7 9½	3,888 6 3	7 9½
12,000	5,360 10 9	8 11	5,341 9 6	8 11	5,322 8 3	8 10½
15,000	7,709 12 9	10 3½	7,689 6 6	10 3	7,669 0 3	10 2½
20,000	12,014 10 9	12 0	11,992 7 0	12 0	11,970 3 3	11 11½
25,000	16,452 0 9	13 2	16,429 17 0	13 1½	16,407 13 3	13 1½
30,000	20,889 10 9	13 11	20,867 7 0	13 11	20,845 3 3	13 11
40,000	29,764 10 9	14 10½	29,742 7 0	14 10½	29,720 3 3	14 10½
50,000	38,639 10 9	15 5½	38,617 7 0	15 5½	38,595 3 3	15 5½
100,000	83,014 10 9	16 7	82,992 7 0	16 7	82,970 3 3	16 7

purposes, each entitled to Single Personal Allowance. A married woman permanently separated from her husband is treated as a single woman.

Children.—For each child under 16 (or over that age at the beginning of the fiscal year and receiving full time instruction at a recognized educational establishment, or who is articled or apprenticed) and who does not have income in that year exceeding £115 in his own right, the allowances are:—

(*a*) Child over 16 at commencement of fiscal year........................ £165
(*b*) Child over 11 at commencement of fiscal year........................ £140
(*c*) Other children (each).............. £115

Scholarship or bursary does not count for this purpose. From 1964/65 onwards marginal relief will be given where a child's income exceeds £115. The child relief will then be reduced by £1 for each £1 by which the child's income will exceed £115. "Child" includes step-child and adopted child. Child allowance is due to the person who has the custody and who maintains the child. If more than one person could claim the allowance; *e.g.* if a husband and wife are divorced or separated, the allowance will be apportioned between them, as necessary.

The " Family Allowance " for children ranks as the father's income subject to Earned Income Allowance.

Dependent Relatives.—A maximum deduction for each dependent relative of £75. This allowance is reduced by £1 for every £1 by which the relative's own income (excluding voluntary allowance) exceeds £180. Claimant must maintain relative who must be incapacitated by old age or infirmity from maintaining himself or herself, except in the case of his or his wife's widowed mother (which includes any woman living apart from her husband, or whose marriage has been dissolved or annulled). If more than one person gives support to the dependent relative then allowance is divided *pro rata*. The dependent person must not be in receipt of an income exceeding £255.

Daughter.—A person who by reason of his or her own age or infirmity, has to retain the services of a daughter resident with him or her is entitled to an allowance of £40.

Housekeeper or person looking after children.—An allowance of £75 is granted to:—

(*a*) any male taxpayer entitled to single personal allowances, any female tax-payer who was either working full time in some employment or business or was totally incapacitated throughout the year, and a married man entitled to married personal allowance whose wife is totally incapacitated throughout the whole of the year, who has a female person resident with and maintained or employed by him or her for the purpose of having care of any child or children for whom the taxpayer is entitled to claim child relief.

(*b*) a widow or widower who has a female relative (or, if no relative is available, a female person) resident with her or him in the capacity of Housekeeper.

A widow or widower (and certain single persons) entitled to the allowance for children but with no resident-housekeeper, is entitled to an allowance of £40.

(4) Married Couples with Two Children not over 11
(See introductory notes)

Income	Income All Earned Income					
	Two Children not over 11		Two Children over 11, but not over 16		Two Children over 16	
	Income Tax (and Surtax if any)	Effective Rate	Income Tax (and Surtax if any)	Effective Rate	Income Tax (and Surtax if any)	Effective Rate
£	£ s. d.	s. d.	£ s. d.	s. d.	£ s. d.	s. d.
600	—	—	—	—	—	—
700	—	—	—	—	—	—
800	10 0 10	– 3	– – 10	—	—	—
900	28 8 0	– 7½	15 12 0	– 4	5 12 0	– 1½
1,000	51 14 8	1 0½	36 14 8	– 9	21 14 8	– 5
1,250	118 16 8	1 11	99 9 2	1 7	80 1 8	1 3½
1,500	194 3 8	2 7	174 16 2	2 4	155 8 8	2 1
1,750	269 10 7	3 1	250 3 1	2 10½	230 15 7	2 7½
2,000	344 17 6	3 5½	325 10 0	3 3	306 2 6	3 0½
2,500	495 11 5	3 11½	476 3 11	3 9½	456 16 5	3 8
3,000	646 5 4	4 3½	626 17 10	4 2	607 10 4	4 0½
4,000	947 13 1	4 9	928 5 7	4 7½	908 18 1	4 6½
5,000	1,291 17 8	5 2	1,272 10 2	5 1	1,253 2 8	5 0
6,000	1,695 2 5	5 8	1,669 9 11	5 7	1,644 12 3	5 6
7,000	2,173 12 9	6 2½	2,145 10 3	6 1½	2,117 7 9	6 0½
8,000	2,691 0 10	6 8½	2,660 8 4	6 8	2,629 15 10	6 7
9,000	3,247 6 9	7 2½	3,214 4 3	7 1½	3,181 1 9	7 1
10,000	3,846 17 6	7 8½	3,811 5 0	7 7½	3,775 12 6	7 6½
12,000	5,278 9 6	8 9½	5,240 7 0	8 9	5,202 4 6	8 8
15,000	7,622 11 6	10 2	7,581 19 0	10 1½	7,541 6 6	10 0½
20,000	11,919 19 6	11 11	11,875 12 0	11 10½	11,831 4 6	11 10
25,000	16,357 9 6	13 1	16,313 2 0	13 0½	16,268 14 6	13 0
30,000	20,794 19 6	13 10½	20,750 12 0	13 10	20,706 4 6	13 9½
40,000	29,669 19 6	14 10	29,625 12 0	14 10	29,581 4 6	14 9½
50,000	38,544 19 6	15 5	38,500 12 0	15 5	38,456 4 6	15 4½
100,000	82,919 19 6	16 7	82,875 12 0	16 7	82,831 4 6	16 7

Blind persons.—An allowance of £100 less 7/9ths of any tax free disability receipts may be claimed by a registered blind person, of a greater amount than £100, provided that the Daughter's allowance of £40 is not also claimed. Where both spouses are blind the maximum allowance is £200 less 7/9ths of any tax free disability receipts.

Earned Income.—Allowance of the following fractions of earned income (after deducting allowances for necessary expenses, superannuation, etc.):—

Up to £4,005—Two-ninths.
The next £5,940—One-ninth.
Maximum amount on which relief can be obtained is thus £9,945.

Married woman earning income in her own right has deduction of two-ninths of such earnings and, in addition, an allowance equal to seven-ninths of her earnings subject to a maximum of £200 plus Reduced Rate Reliefs as shown below.

Small Income Relief.—All incomes up to £450 are treated as earned income; *i.e.* relief of two-ninths of income is allowed. Marginal relief is given where income slightly exceeds £450 up to a maximum of £680.

Age Relief.—Allowance of two-ninths of unearned income where taxpayer (or his wife) attains 65 years subject to total income not exceeding £900. Where the total income exceeds £900, marginal relief is given so that the full tax on the investment income scale is not payable until the marginal relief runs out.

Age exemption.—Persons over 65 years of age are exempt from tax if their total incomes do not exceed:—

Single person.............................. £325
Married couple (either being over 65)........ £520

Marginal relief is given where income slightly exceeds these amounts, up to a maximum of £75.

Pension Contributions.—Contributions by both employed and self-employed persons to officially approved superannuated funds, or premiums paid (within certain limits) to provide for *retirement annuities* are allowed as deductions.

National Insurance Contributions.—Certain deductions are allowable in respect of contributions payable under the national insurance scheme by employed, self-employed and non-employed persons respectively. The general allowance for employed adults is £22. Taxpayer paying "employer's" contribution in respect of personal or domestic servants may deduct whole of such contribution from his income.

Life Assurance Premiums.—Relief is given for premiums paid under assurance policies on life of taxpayer or his wife. A capital sum must be payable at death. Where the total premiums available for relief to taxpayer and his wife do not exceed £25 an amount of £10 or total premiums, whichever is less, may be deducted from assessable income. Where total premiums exceed £25 the deduction is two-fifths of the premiums. Where annual premium exceeds 7 per cent. of capital sum assured, relief is limited to sum equal to 7 per cent. The amount on which relief is given must not exceed one-sixth of net total income. Relief is also given on sums paid under Act of Parliament or under terms of employment for securing deferred annuity to widow or provision for children after death of the taxpayer.

Purchased Life Annuities.—The capital element of annuities for a term referable to a life, which are purchased for money or money's worth from a person whose business is to grant annuities (with certain exceptions) is not taxable as income.

Reduced Rate Relief.—Rates of tax on taxable income are:—

	in the £
On first £100	4s. od.
On next £200	6s. od.
On balance	7s. 9d.

Repayment Claims.—Where relief or allowance due has not been given in the assessment of the taxpayer, or where tax has been deducted from income received in excess of the amount of tax due in respect of total income, repayment may be claimed in general, within six years after the end of the year of assessment.

Error or Mistake.—Relief may be claimed if an assessment is excessive because of some error or mistake in the return or statement made by the taxpayer. Application for relief must be made to the Inspector within six years after the end of the fiscal year in which the assessment was made.

Building Society Interest.—Majority of societies operate under special arrangement with Inland Revenue and interest is paid to depositors and shareholders "free of income tax." But such interest must be included in taxpayer's total income for assessment to surtax, grossed at the standard rate.

Surtax is an additional duty of income tax, chargeable on total income of individuals in excess of £2,000. Total income is the amount of income chargeable to income tax by assessment or deduction, less yearly interest or other annual sums payable under deduction of tax. Loss relief, and interest payable to banks and building societies are deductible. Personal allowances, child allowances, housekeeper, dependent relative and similar reliefs (to the extent they exceed £200) are also deductible.

There is deductible from total income, earned income relief, and also an earnings allowance of £2,000, or less so as to reduce the earned income (after deducting earned income relief) to £2,000. Broadly earned income is not charged to surtax if less than £5,000, or more if personal reliefs are due.

Surtax is payable on 1st January following year of assessment, so that surtax for 1963–64 is payable on 1st January 1965. Surtax is chargeable on a sliding scale as follows:—

On each £ of first	£500	2s.	in the £
„ next	£500	2s. 6d.	„
„	£1,000	3s. 6d.	„
„	£1,000	4s. 6d.	„
„	£1,000	5s. 6d.	„
„	£2,000	6s. 6d.	„
„	£2,000	7s. 6d.	„
„	£2,000	8s. 6d.	„
„	£3,000	9s. 6d.	„
of remainder		10s. in the £	

Seven-year Covenants.—Where covenant to pay annual sums of money is made for other than valuable and sufficient consideration, the period of the covenant must be for a term which can exceed six years if the Covenantor wishes to divest himself of such income for income tax purposes. Any such covenant entered into after 10th April, 1946, must be in favour of an individual, not employed in any way by Covenantor (and not, for example, a charitable body) in order to divest the Covenantor of the income for Surtax purposes.

Settlements in favour of taxpayer's own infant children.—The Income of any such Settlement made since 22nd April, 1936, is treated as that of the Settlor for all income tax purposes if:—

(*a*) the Settlement can be revoked within a period of six years (unless the child becomes bankrupt).

(*b*) the income can be paid to or for the benefit of the child during the lifetime of the settlor. This ceases to apply at the end of the fiscal year in which the child attains 21 years or marries.

Double Taxation Relief.—Agreements for the avoidance of Double Taxation have been made between the United Kingdom and Aden Colony, Antigua, Argentina, Australia, Austria, Barbados, Basutoland, Bechuanaland, Belgium, British Guiana, British Honduras, British Solomon Islands Protectorate, Brunei, Burma, Canada, Ceylon, Cyprus, Denmark, Dominica, Falkland Islands, Faroe Islands, Federation of Rhodesia and Nyasaland, Fiji, Finland, France, Gambia, Germany (Federal Rep.), Ghana, Gilbert and Ellice Islands, Greece, Grenada, Guernsey, Iceland, Iran, Ireland (Rep.), Isle of Man, Israel, Italy, Jamaica, Japan, Jersey, Kenya, Malaya, Malta, Mauritius, Montserrat, Netherlands, Netherlands Antilles, New Zealand, Nigeria, North Borneo, Norway, Pakistan, St. Christopher and Nevis, St. Lucia, St. Vincent, Sarawak, Seychelles, Sierra Leone, Singapore, South Africa, South West Africa, Swaziland, Sweden, Switzerland, Tanganyika, Trinidad, Uganda, United States of America, Virgin Islands and Zanzibar.

Relief may further be obtained by residents of the United Kingdom in respect of any income tax payable in any other Country, Colony or Dominion, than the above-mentioned, when that income is also liable to British income tax.

Persons Resident Abroad.—Persons normally resident outside the United Kingdom are liable, in general, in respect of income from United Kingdom sources but not on the interest from:—

3½% War Stock 1952 or after; 4% Victory Bonds; 4% Funding Loan 1960–90; 3% Savings Bonds (all issues); 5½% Funding Loan 1982–84; 3% Defence Bonds (1st, 2nd, 3rd and 4th issues) and 2½% Defence Bonds.

Such persons become resident in the United Kingdom if they visit for a period or periods exceeding six months in any fiscal year. Also if they visit for any period in a year in which they have retained a place of abode in the United Kingdom, except such persons as are engaged in full-time employment abroad. They would then be liable to United Kingdom Tax on all remittances of income arising abroad. If they visit the United Kingdom in four consecutive years for periods averaging three months or more per annum they would be regarded as ordinarily resident here.

A person who is not resident in the United Kingdom who has income which is liable to United Kingdom tax cannot claim any of the normal income tax allowances unless he is:

(*a*) a British subject;

(*b*) a present or former servant of the Crown; or widow of a former Crown servant;

(*c*) employed by any missionary society controlled from the United Kingdom or a servant of a native State under British protection;

(*d*) a resident of the Isle of Man or the Channel Islands or

(*e*) was previously resident in the United Kingdom but resides abroad for the sake of his health or the health of a member of his family.

Post War Credits.—Those Credits arising out of the temporary reduction of certain income tax allowances during the years 1941–42 to 1945–46 inclusive are repayable to women over 55 and men over 60 years of age, and to widows entitled to Credits in their own right. Where a man or woman has died, repayment is made to personal representatives or beneficiaries, irrespective of age.

Holders of Credits are also entitled to repayment if certified as blind persons or in-patients of hospitals or nursing homes, or if in receipt of any of the following: National Assistance, Constant Attendance Allowance or Unemployability Supplement, Sickness or Injury Benefit, Disablement Pensions, Workmen's Compensation 1956 Supplement; or if registered as unemployed. There is a qualifying period of 26 weeks in certain categories (12 weeks for National Assistance). Interest from 1st October 1959 will be added to the sum repayable. Forms for claiming repayment may be obtained at any Post Office.

INCOME TAX ADMINISTRATION

Income Tax under Schedules A, B, D and E, is assessed by H.M. Inspector of Taxes. Schedules A and B assessments are made by H.M. Inspector for the district in which the land or property is situated. Assessments under Schedules D and E are made by H.M. Inspector of Taxes for the district in which Trade, Profession or Employment is carried on, or from which the Pension is paid, otherwise assessments are made in the district in which the taxpayer resides. Notices of Assessment are sent to taxpayer who should make a formal appeal against any assessment which he disputes direct to H.M. Inspector by whom the notice was issued within the time limit for such appeals, as stated on the notice. The grounds of appeal should be given. If the assessment cannot be agreed with H.M. Inspector, the appeal will be heard by the General Commissioners. Alternatively, certain appeals are made to the Special Commissioners. An appeal may be made by way of Case Stated from the Appeal Commissioners' decision to the High Court on points of law.

Income Tax is payable to the Collector of Taxes.

Surtax is assessable by the Special Commissioners of Income Tax to whom returns of total income are made, except where a full return of income is made to H.M. Inspector of Taxes. Appeals are made to the Special Commissioners and thence to the Courts by way of Case Stated.

Surtax is payable to the Special Commissioners.

Penalties may be incurred for failure to make proper returns of income.

Every person chargeable to income tax must give notice of chargeability within one year (unless an income tax return has been already made).

P.A.Y.E

Income Tax payable under Schedule E is deducted by employer, who accounts for it to the Collector of Taxes. The amount of tax deduction from each payment of salary, wage, pension, etc., is determined by reference to Tax Tables issued by H.M. Inspector of Taxes to employer, in conjunction with the taxpayer's Code Number. This Code Number is an interpretation of the taxpayer's Allowances and Reliefs. Notices of Coding are issued by H.M. Inspector of Taxes and they may take into account income assessable under other Schedules. Notice of Coding should be checked on receipt and H.M. Inspector of Taxes informed of any necessary amendment in order that no considerable over or under-deduction of income tax may take place. The tax deductions are on a cumulative basis and can be carried on by successive employers should changes in employment take place during fiscal year. When leaving one employment a statement (Form P45) showing code number, remuneration, and tax deductions to date should be obtained from old employer and handed, in due course, to new employer. At the end of fiscal year employer should give employee a statement (Form P60) showing total remuneration and tax deductions for the year.

DEDUCTION OF TAX

Tax is deductible at the standard rate from annual interest, annuities and annual payments such as ground rents and mortgage interest. The tax deducted may be retained by the payer unless he has not borne tax himself at the standard rate on an equivalent amount of income, in which case he must account to the Revenue for the tax deducted in respect of the excess. The tax paid under Schedule A by an occupier is normally deductible from the next rent paid by him to the landlord.

STANDARD RATES OF INCOME TAX SINCE 1925

	s.	*d.*		*s.*	*d.*
1925–30.......	4	0	1940–41.......	8	6
1930–31.......	4	6	1941–46.......	10	0
1931–34.......	5	0	1946–51.......	9	0
1934–36.......	4	6	1951–53.......	9	6
1936–37.......	4	9	1953–55.......	9	0
1937–38.......	5	0	1955–59.......	8	6
1938–39.......	5	6	1959–60......	7	9
1939–40.......	7	0	1960–64......	7	9

PROFITS TAX

Corporate bodies are subject to income tax at the standard rate but are not entitled to personal allowances and reliefs. In addition they are liable to Profits Tax. This tax was first introduced two years before the last war when it was called the National Defence Contribution. It is a further tax on income based on the actual profits of chargeable accounting periods which are usually the periods for which the body concerned makes up its accounts. The bodies chargeable include limited companies, building societies, industrial and provident societies, foreign companies carrying on business in the United Kingdom, and trustees of unit trusts.

The tax is charged on the profits of any trade or business carried on in the United Kingdom, or carried on anywhere in the world by bodies ordinarily resident in the United Kingdom. The holding of investments or property is by statute deemd to be a business for this purpose. Subject to certain modifications, profits are ascertained as for income tax under the rules applicable to Case I of *Schedule D*. (*See* p. 1182). To this is added income from property and investments other than "franked investment income", which is defined as income received directly or indirectly by way of dividend or distribution of profits from another body corporate carrying on a trade or business which is itself subject to profits tax. A double charge to profits tax in respect of the same income is thus avoided but the exemption does not apply to dividends received from foreign companies which are not themselves subject to profits tax in this country. Rents, premiums under leases not exceeding fifty years, income from Government securities and other income chargeable to income tax by deduction at source are all included in the amount brought into charge to profits tax, as are short term gains assessable under Case VII of *Schedule D*.

The rate at which profits tax is chargeable has varied from time to time and is at present 15 per cent. If the profits of a 12 months chargeable accounting period are less than £2,000 they are exempt and there is a reduction in the charge if the profits do not exceed £12,000. The reduction is known as "abatement" and is computed by deducting the profits for the period from £12,000, taking one-fifth of the balance remaining and deducting this from the chargeable profits. Tax on the remaining sum is then charged at 15 per cent. If the chargeable accounting period is less than twelve months the figures of £2,000 and £12,000 are proportionately reduced. Franked investment income has to be included in the computation of the abatement and the abatement itself has to be apportioned between the chargeable profits and the franked investment income.

Between January 1, 1947 and March 31, 1958, the tax was charged at two different rates according to whether the profits were distributed or not. Profits retained by the company were given non-distribution relief and were charged at a lower rate while the higher rate was payable on any distributions. There were elaborate provisions to avoid evasion of the higher charge and profits originally retained but distributed at a later date were subject to a distribution charge.

Allowable deductions.—As explained above, profits are generally ascertained by applying income tax rules but for profits tax the gross amount of annual payments such as interest, annuities, royalties or ground rents paid less income tax at standard rate are deductible from the profits as adjusted for income tax. All capital allowances given for income tax are allowable for profits tax. Investment allowances are given in the chargeable accounting period in which the expenditure is incurred. Other capital allowances computed for income tax purposes for fiscal years have to be apportioned to chargeable accounting periods unless these periods coincide with years of assessment in which case the allowances for the fiscal year may be deducted for profits tax purposes.

Losses incurred in any chargeable accounting period can be carried forward and are allowed against profits of subsequent periods. Any such losses must, however, be deducted from the profit of the first available subsequent period and before applying the rules relating to exemption and abatement.

Directors' remuneration.—Special limits apply to the amounts allowed to be charged against profits in respect of the remuneration of " controlling directors ". If these limits are exceeded, the excess will be disallowed in the profits tax computation and profits tax will be payable thereon. This does not affect the income tax position. For income tax the full remuneration is allowed as a charge in the company's accounts but assessed to tax in the hands of the directors concerned.

" Director " for this purpose includes a manager who is remunerated out of the funds of the trade or business and is the beneficial owner of not less than 20 per cent. of the ordinary share capital of the company and any person in accordance with whose instructions the directors are accustomed to act. The limitation does not apply to a " whole-time service director " who is defined as a director who is required to devote substantially the whole of his time to the service of the company in a managerial or technical capacity and who does not own or control more than 5 per cent of the ordinary share capital of the company. A company is director-controlled and the directors rank as " controlling directors " for the purpose of these provisions if the directors together have power to control the decision of the company in general meeting.

Where a company is director-controlled the allowable remuneration of the directors (other than whole-time service directors) is limited to a maximum of £15,000 or the greatest of the following three amounts:—(*i*) 15 per cent. of the profits (computed before deducting any remuneration of directors other than whole-time service directors), or (*ii*) a figure calculated at the rate of £3,000 per annum over the period, or (*iii*) if for more than half the chargeable accounting period there are two directors who are required to devote substantially the whole of their time to the service of the company in a managerial or technical capacity but are not whole-time service directors, £5,000; if there are three such directors £7000; if there are four or more such directors £9,000. These limitations apply to annual sums and are reduced proportionately for shorter periods. In no circumstances is a total sum exceeding the remuneration actually payable to the directors allowable as a deduction. Rents and annual payments, such as interest, made to controlling directors are also disallowed.

Groups of companies.—Each limited company is separately assessed to profits tax but interest and other annual payments between companies forming part of a group (*i.e.* where one company is a subsidiary of the other or both are subsidiaries of a third) are disallowed in the computation of the paying company and not included as a receipt in the computation of the profits of the receiving company. Where one company (the principal company) is the beneficial owner of not less than three-quarters of the ordinary share capital of another company (the subsidiary) and both are resident in and engaged in trade in the United Kingdom, the principal company may elect to be jointly assessed for profits tax purposes in which case all profits and losses of the subsidiary are treated as profits and losses of the principal company in the corresponding chargeable accounting period, franked investment income of the subsidiary company is included in the franked investment income of the principal company and franked investment income paid between the two companies is disregarded. A grouping notice, once given, applies to all future chargeable accounting periods and cannot be revoked.

Anti-avoidance provisions.—If, in the opinion of the Commissioners of Inland Revenue, any transaction or transactions had as its main purpose or one of its main purposes the avoidance or reduction of liability to profits tax, the Commissioners have power to direct such adjustment as respects liability to profits tax as they consider appropriate to counteract such avoidance or reduction. There is no corresponding power in the Income Tax Acts and the Revenue is thus provided with a powerful weapon against attempted avoidance of the tax. The taxpayer has the right of appeal to the Special Commissioners.

Administration.—Profits tax is assessed and collected by the Commissioners of Inland Revenue who may require returns from any person carrying on a business, the profits of which are chargeable to the tax. Assessments must be made within six years of the end of the chargeable accounting period to which they apply except in case of fraud or wilful default. The tax is payable within one month of the date of the assessment. If the assessment exceeds £1,000 and the tax is unpaid for more than three months, interest is payable at the rate of 3 per cent per annum. Appeals against assessments may be made either to the General Commissioners or to the Special Commissioners, within thirty days of the service of the notice of assessment. From the decision of either body a further appeal by way of a case stated lies to the High Court. Penalty provisions similar to those in force for income tax are applicable.

THE CONSUMER COUNCIL

3 Cornwall Terrace, N.W.1

[Hunter 1658]

The Consumer Council was set up in March 1963 by the President of the Board of Trade. Its functions are to inform itself about the consumer's problems and about matters affecting his interests, and to consider what action should be taken to deal with these, either by itself, by the Government, or by other interested organizations. The Council will not undertake comparative test reports on consumer goods or take up complaints on behalf of individual consumers: the latter function will be the concern of the Citizen's Advice Bureaux. An annual report will be published, and other material on particular aspects of consumer protection.

There are twelve members of the Council, including the Chairman and the Director, appointed by the President of the Board of Trade. They are appointed for a period of three years. The Chairman receives £1,000 a year and the members £500 a year each.

The Council receives an annual grant from the Board of Trade. For 1963/64, the first year of operation, the amount was £60,000.

Chairman, The Baroness Elliot of Harwood, D.B.E.

Members, Miss E. Ackroyd; Mrs. C. Calvert; L. Cohen; T. Cynog Jones, O.B.E.; A. L. Diamond; Mrs. W. Jenkins; W. G. McClelland; Mrs. F. Palmer; The Lord Peddie; Mrs. P. Perks.

Director, Miss E. Ackroyd.

PERSONAL EXPENDITURE

A table showing personal expenditure on consumer goods and services with totals of consumers' expenditure in U.K. and abroad: (*a*) in 1952 and 1962 at current market prices: and (*b*) in 1962 at 1958 prices.

Heads of Expenditure	£ million		
	(*a*) 1952	(*a*) 1962	(*b*) 1962
Food	3,198	5,152	4,865
Household Expenditure	2,837	4,580	4,323
Bread and Cereals	486	611	556
Meat and Bacon	652	1,220	1,183
Fish	96	154	142
Oils and Fats	129	225	202
Sugar, Preserves and Confectionery	264	449	410
Dairy Products	496	684	670
Fruit	159	289	275
Potatoes and Vegetables	338	526	480
Beverages	127	282	275
Other manufactured food	90	140	130
Other personal expenditure	361	572	542
Alcoholic Drink	779	1,123	1,088
Beer	521	665	655
Wines, Spirits, Cider, etc.	258	458	433
Tobacco	821	1,242	1,055
Cigarettes	706	1,086	927
Pipe Tobacco, Cigars and Snuff	115	156	128
Housing	879	1,773	1,477
Rent, Rates and Water	702	1,481	1,215
Maintenance, Repairs, etc.	177	292	262
Fuel and Light	424	894	829
Coal	178	301	256
Electricity	101	328	333
Gas	100	159	145
Other	45	106	95
Durable Household Goods	462	876	860
Furniture and Floor Coverings	250	436	394
Radio and Electrical Goods	212	440	466
Other Household Goods	362	576	538
Textiles, Soft Furnishings and Hardware	221	373	357
Matches, Soap and other Cleaning Materials	141	203	181

Heads of Expenditure	£ million		
	(*a*) 1952	(*a*) 1962	(*b*) 1962
Clothing	1,097	1,723	1,629
Footwear	196	304	272
Other Clothing:			
Men's and Boys' Wear	312	488	458
Women's, Girls' and Infants' Wear	589	931	899
Recreational Goods	326	605	555
Books	37	61	54
Newspapers	92	162	135
Magazines	35	52	40
Other	162	330	326
Chemists' Goods	151	272	255
Other Goods	152	251	244
Private Motoring:—			
Vehicles, New and Used	111	514	556
Running Costs	149	579	536
Travel	424	624	521
Railway	107	156	112
Other	317	468	409
Communication Services	74	155	145
Postal	42	73	67
Telephone and Telegraph	32	82	78
Entertainments	225	280	277
Cinema	112	60	51
Other	113	220	226
Domestic Service	95	84	71
Insurance	95	197	} 1,407
Other Services	758	1,391	}
Expenditure not included above	68	45	42
Deduct Expenditure by Foreign Tourists, etc. in U.K.	−104	−214	−190
Personal Expenditure:— in the United Kingdom	10,546	18,142	16,760
abroad	161	310	291
TOTAL	10,707	18,452	17,051

BETTING AND GAMING PERMITS AND LICENCES (Great Britain)

In the year ending May 31, 1962, under the Betting and Gaming Act, 1960, 1,521 applications were made in Great Britain for Bookmakers' Permits, 17 being refused and 1,427 granted. Applications for Betting Agency Permits numbered 312 of which 270 were granted. 5,852 Betting Office Licences were granted and 985 refused.

On June 1, 1962, 10,712 Bookmakers' Permits were in force—2·09 per 10,000 of population.

Permits and Licences Current, June, 1962

	Bookmakers' Permits	Betting Agency Permits	Betting Office Licences
England	9,090	160	10,318
Wales and Monmouth	402	8	1,240
Scotland	1,220	184	1,782
GREAT BRITAIN	10,712	352	13,340

OTHER TAXES AND STAMP DUTIES

NOTE.—(1) The instruments for which the use of adhesive postage stamps is "permitted" include:—
Agreements liable to the duty of 6d.—s. 22. Bills of exchange (including cheques), for payment of money on demand—s. 34 (1). Policies of Insurance (not life)—s. 99. Receipts—s. 101 (2).

(2) The Commissioners as a general rule allow deeds, etc., to be stamped after execution:—

WITHOUT PENALTY, ON PAYMENT OF DUTY ONLY:

Deeds and instruments not otherwise excepted, within 30 days of *first* execution.

NOTE.—Where wholly executed *abroad*, the period begins to run from the date of arrival here.

PENALTIES ENFORCEABLE ON STAMPING, IN ADDITION TO DUTY:—

	£	s.	d.
Agreements under hand only. Attested copies or contracts: after 30 days from their first execution....	10	0	0
Receipts, within 14 days after they have been given................	5	0	0
Receipts, after 14 days, but within one month......................	10	0	0
Other Instruments presented after the proper time (subject to special provisions in some cases).........	10	0	0

	£	s.	d.
AGREEMENT for Lease, *see* LEASES.			
AGREEMENT FOR SALE OF PROPERTY—charged with *ad val.* duty as if an actual conveyance on sale (see *post*, pp. 1190–1) with certain exceptions, *e.g.* agreements for the sale of land, stocks and shares, goods, wares or merchandise, or a ship (*see* s. 59 (1), Stamp Act, 1891). If *ad val.* duty is paid on an agreement in accordance with this provision, the subsequent conveyance or transfer is not chargeable with any *ad val.* duty and the Commissioners will upon application either place a denoting stamp on such conveyance or transfer or will transfer the *ad val.* duty thereto. Further, if such an agreement is rescinded, not performed, etc., the Commissioners will return the *ad val.* duty paid.			
AGREEMENT, not otherwise charged with duty, under hand only........	0	0	6
N.B.—The following agreements are exempt:—			
(*a*) Where the value of the subject-matter is less than £5.			
(*b*) For the hire of any labourer, artificer, manufacturer, or menial servant.			
(*c*) For the sale of any goods, wares, or merchandise (but hire purchase agreements, *post*, p. 1180, are not exempt).			
Not otherwise charged with duty, under seal or with clause of registration............................	0	10	0
APPOINTMENT of a new trustee or in exercise of a power over property, not being by a will; also on retirement of trustee, although no new trustee be appointed..............	0	10	0
ASSIGNMENT:			
By way of security—*see* Mortgage.			
By way of sale—*see* Conveyance.			
By way of gift—*see* Voluntary Disposition.			
ASSURANCE—*see* Insurance Policies.			
BANK NOTE for money payable on demand:			
Not exceeding £1..................	0	0	5
" " 2..................	0	0	10
" " 5..................	0	1	3
" " 10..................	0	1	9
" " 20..................	0	2	0
" " 30..................	0	3	0
" " 50..................	0	5	0
" " 100..................	0	8	6
BANKER'S CHEQUES..................	0	0	2

BEARER INSTRUMENT:

Inland bearer instrument i.e., share warrant, stock certificate to bearer or any other instrument to bearer by which stock can be transferred, issued by a company or body formed or established in U.K. Duty of an amount equal to three times the transfer duty (usually £3% of the market value).

Overseas bearer instrument i.e., such an instrument issued in G.B. by a company formed out of the U.K. Duty equal to twice the transfer duty (usually £2% of the market value). Even if issued out of G.B. the instrument must be stamped before transfer in G.B.

	£	s.	d.
BILL OF SALE, Absolute, *see* CONVEYANCE ON SALE; by way of Security, *see* MORTGAGE, &c.			
BILLS OF EXCHANGE and promissory notes..........................	0	0	2
BOND for payment of money, *see* MORTGAGE BOND, etc.			
For securing an annuity (not being a Superannuation Annuity, as to which, *see post*, under Contract or Grant for payment of a Superannuation Annuity):—			
1. Where the total amount ultimately payable is ascertainable. Same as MORTGAGE BOND, etc.			
2. Collateral. Where the total amount is ascertainable. Same as MORTGAGE BOND, Collateral, etc.			
3. Where the payments are for the term of life, or other indefinite period:—			
For every £5, and every fractional part of £5 payable—			
If as primary security..........	0	2	6
If as collateral security.........	0	0	6
Of any kind whatever, not specifically charged (including Fidelity Bonds), same as MORTGAGE BOND, etc., but not to exceed..................	0	10	0
CAPITAL DUTY (Share).—Companies and Corporations with limited liability, on every £100 or fraction of £100 of the nominal capital.....	0	10	0
Statement of amount of any increase of registered capital shall be delivered duly stamped within fifteen days after the resolution of the company authorizing the increase (Companies Act, 1948).			

	£ s. d.
CAPITAL DUTY (Loan).—Per £100 or part of £100	0 2 6
(Subject to deduction of 2*s.* for each £100 which is applied in conversion or consolidation of existing Loan Capital.)	
CHEQUES, or drafts, payable on demand or at sight or on presentation or within three days after date or sight	0 0 2

COLLATERAL SECURITY, *see* MORTGAGE, BOND, etc., *post.*

CONTRACT, *see* AGREEMENT.

CONTRACT NOTE for the sale or purchase of any stock or marketable security: where the value of the stock or marketable security—

			£ s. d.
Is £5 and does not exceed		£100	0 1 0
Exceeds £100 and does not exceed		£500	0 2 0
,, 500	,, ,,	1,000	0 4 0
,, 1,000	,, ,,	1,500	0 6 0
,, 1,500	,, ,,	2,500	0 8 0
,, 2,500	,, ,,	5,000	0 12 0
,, 5,000	,, ,,	7,500	0 16 0
,, 7,500	,, ,,	10,000	1 0 0
,, 10,000	,, ,,	12,500	1 4 0
,, 12,500	,, ,,	15,000	1 8 0
,, 15,000	,, ,,	17,500	1 12 0
,, 17,500	,, ,,	20,000	1 16 0
,, 20,000			2 0 0

(Special adhesive stamps.)

Option Contract Notes are chargeable with half the above rates only, unless the option is a double one.

Contract Note following a duly stamped option contract note chargeable with half the above rates only.

	£ s. d.
CONTRACT OR GRANT FOR PAYMENT OF A SUPERANNUATION ANNUITY: for every £5 or fractional part of £5	0 0 6

CONVEYANCE OR TRANSFER on sale or by way of gift *inter vivos* of Stock or Marketable Securities: where the purchase money (or in the case of a gift the middle market value on the date of the transaction) does not exceed £1 5*s.*; 3*d.*

Exceeding £1 5*s.*	not exceeding		£2 10*s.*	6*d.*
,, 2 10*s.*	,,	,,	3 15*s.*	9*d.*
,, 3 15*s.*	,,	,,	5	1*s.*
,, 5	,,	,,	10	2*s.*
,, 10	,,	,,	15	3*s.*
,, 15	,,	,,	20	4*s.*
,, 20	,,	,,	35	5*s.*
,, 35	,,	,,	60	10*s.*
,, 60	,,	,,	80	15*s.*
,, 80	,,	,,	100	20*s.*
,, 100	,,	,,	300	5*s.* per £25
,, 300 per every £50 or part				10*s.*

NOTE. The rate chargeable in respect of a transfer of commonwealth government stock is a quarter those set out above. Where the consideration does not exceed £5 the duty is 3*d.*

"Marketable Security" includes the Registered Bonds and Debentures generally of Companies, Corporations, and Public Bodies.

	£ s. d.
CONVEYANCE OR TRANSFER ON SALE (in the case of a Voluntary Disposition, *see* below, p. 1193) of any property (*except* stock or marketable securities for which, *see* above), where the consideration for the sale does not exceed £4,500	nil
Exceeds £4,500 but does not exceed £6,000 for every £50 and any fraction of £50	0 5 0
Exceeds £6,000, for every £50 and any fraction of £50	0 10 0

If the consideration does not exceed £4,500 (or £6,000, as the case may be) the Conveyance or Transfer on Sale must contain a certificate of value certifying that the transaction does not form part of a larger transaction or series of transactions in respect of which the amount or value or the aggregate amount or value of the consideration exceeds £4,500 (or £6,000, as the case may be).

If the Conveyance or Transfer on Sale does not contain the appropriate statement duty at the full rate of 10*s.* for every £50 or fraction of £50 will be payable whatever the amount of the consideration.

However, if the consideration does not exceed £300, and the instrument does not contain a certificate of value, then if the consideration for the sale does not exceed £1 5*s.* the duty is 3*d.*

Where the consideration:

Exceeds £1 5*s.*	but does not exceed		£2 10*s.*	6*d.*
,, 2 10*s.*	,,	,,	3 15*s.*	9*d.*
,, 3 15*s.*	,,	,,	5	1*s.*
,, 5	,,	,,	10	2*s.*
,, 10	,,	,,	15	3*s.*
,, 15	,,	,,	20	4*s.*
,, 20	,,	,,	35	5*s.*
,, 35	,,	,,	60	10*s.*
,, 60	,,		80	15*s.*
,, 80	,,	,,	100	20*s.*
,, 100		,,	300	5*s.* per £25

If in such a case the instrument is certified at £6000 it is stamped at ½ the above rates.

	£ s. d.
CONVEYANCE OR TRANSFER of any other kind ... fixed duty	0 10 0

Included under this head are Transfers for nominal consideration within any of the following categories:—

(*a*) Transfers vesting the property in trustees on the appointment of a new trustee of a pre-existing trust, or on the retirement of a trustee.

(*b*) Transfers, where no beneficial interest in the property passes, (i) to a mere nominee of the transferor, (ii) from a mere nominee of the transferee, (iii) from one nominee to another nominee of the same beneficial owner.

(*c*) Transfers by way of security for a loan or re-transfer to the original transferor on repayment of a loan.

(*d*) Transfer to a residuary legatee of stock, etc., forming part of the residue divisible under a will.

£ s. d.

(*e*) Transfers to a beneficiary under a will of a specific legacy of stock, etc. (*Note.*—Transfers by executors in discharge, or partial discharge, of a pecuniary legacy (unless made under an express power of appropriation) are chargeable with *ad valorem* duty on the amount of the legacy so discharged.)

(*f*) Transfers of stock, etc., forming part of an intestate's estate to the person entitled to it.

(*g*) Transfers to a beneficiary under settlement on a distribution of the trust funds of stock, etc., forming the share or part of the share of those funds to which the beneficiary is entitled in accordance with the terms of the settlement.

(*h*) Transfers on the occasion of a marriage to trustees of stocks, etc., to be held on the terms of a settlement made in consideration of marriage.

(*i*) Transfers by the liquidator of a company of stocks, etc., forming part of the assets of the company to the persons who were shareholders, in satisfaction of their rights on a winding-up.

The evidence necessary to establish that a transfer is liable to the fixed duty of 10*s.* should take the form of a certificate setting forth the facts of the transaction. In cases falling within (*b*) or (*c*) such a certificate should be signed by (1) both transferor and transferee or (2) a member of a Stock Exchange or a solicitor acting for one or other of the parties or (3) an accredited representative of a bank; in the last case when the bank or its official nominee is a party to the transfer, the certificate, instead of setting out the facts, may be to the effect that "the transfer is excepted from Section 74 of the Finance (1909-10) Act, 1910." A certificate in other cases should be signed by a solicitor or other person (*e.g.*, a bank acting as trustee or executor) having a full knowledge of the facts.

Registering Officers will in any case in which a Marking Officer's certificate has not been given require such evidence in order to satisfy themselves that a transfer stamped with the 10*s.* fixed duty is duly stamped.

COVENANT—For repayment of money, *see* MORTGAGE.
For original creation and sale of any annuity, *see* CONVEYANCE.
For an annuity (except on original creation and sale) or other periodical payments, *see* BOND.
Separate Deed of, made on occasion of sale or mortgage, but not being an instrument chargeable with *ad valorem* duty as a Conveyance or Mortgage: same duty as a Conveyance on sale, or a Mortgage, but not to exceed.................. 0 10 0

DEATH DUTIES, *see* ESTATE DUTY. £ s. d.

DECLARATION OF TRUST, not being a Will or Settlement................ 0 10 0

DEED of any kind not charged under some special head................. 0 10 0

DEMISE, *see* LEASE.

DUPLICATE OR COUNTERPART.
Same duty as original, but not to exceed........................... 0 5 0

EQUITABLE MORTGAGES under hand only
For every £100 or part thereof..... 0 1 0

ESTATE DUTY:
In the case of every person dying on or after April 4, 1963, where the principal value of all property, real or personal, settled or not settled, passing on the death of such person,

Exceeds	Does not exceed	Rate *per cent.*
	£5,000	Nil
£5,000	6,000	1
6,000	7,000	2
7,000	8,000	3
8,000	10,000	4
10,000	12,500	6
12,500	15,000	8
15,000	17,500	10
17,500	20,000	12
20,000	25,000	15
25,000	30,000	18
30,000	35,000	21
35,000	40,000	24
40,000	45,000	28
45,000	50,000	31
50,000	60,000	35
60,000	75,000	40
75,000	100,000	45
100,000	150,000	50
150,000	200,000	55
200,000	300,000	60
300,000	500,000	65
500,000	750,000	70
750,000	1,000,000	75
1,000,000		80

Lower rates of duty are payable in certain circumstances on property passing on two deaths occurring within 5 years of one another. (Finance Act, 1958.)

A reduction of 45 per cent. of the above rates is applied to the "agricultural value" of agricultural property; and (as respects deaths on and after 30th July, 1954) to certain business assets, viz.: "industrial hereditaments" and "machinery or plant" (Finance Act, 1954, s. 28).

Gifts made by deceased during his life for public or charitable purposes are liable for duty, unless made more than twelve months before death; other gifts are liable for duty, unless made more than five years before death, (although if the donor dies at any time within the third year after making the gift, the value of the property the subject of the gift is for estate duty purposes reduced by 15 per cent.; if he dies within the fourth year it is reduced by 30 per cent.; and if he dies within the fifth year it is reduced by 60 per cent.) gifts made in consideration of marriage, or as part of deceased's reasonable normal expenditure, excepted. Gifts not exceeding £100 in value or amount (or in certain circumstances £500) also excepted. — £ s. d.

Payment of Estate Duty may, by agreement with the Commissioners, be made, wholly or in part, in the form of real or leasehold property comprised in the estate.

Interest at 2 per cent. per annum is also payable on the Estate Duty on personalty from the date of the death up to that of delivery of the affidavit or account.

The Estate Duty on real property may be paid, if desired, by eight yearly or sixteen half-yearly instalments, and 2 per cent. interest is charged on all unpaid instalments from twelve months after death.

Marginal relief may be claimed where the value of the estate is slightly above a figure at which the estate becomes liable to a higher rate of duty. In such a case the amount of duty will be the top value at the lower rate plus the excess value of estate over that top value. Thus, if an estate is valued at £8,050, duty at 4% would be £322; but the duty will actually be 3% on £8000 = £240 + £50 = £290.

FEES are taken in all Public Departments by means of Stamps: such payments are accounted for to the Exchequer under the heading of Miscellaneous Revenue.

	£ s. d.
FIRE INSURANCE POLICY..............	0 0 6
GIFT (*see* VOLUNTARY DISPOSITION, p. 1193).	
GUARANTEE:	
If under hand only................	0 0 6
If under seal......................	0 10 0

N.B.—(i) If the instrument contains a charge on property duty will be payable as an Equitable Mortgage, col. 1, if under hand only, or on a Mortgage, Bond, etc., (col. 2), if under seal. (ii) A guarantee by a third party for the payment of the purchase price of goods, wares and merchandise is exempt from duty if under hand only as an agreement within exemption (*c*), p. 1189.

	£ s. d.
HIRE-PURCHASE AGREEMENTS:	
Under hand......................	0 0 6
Under seal.......................	0 10 0

(Finance Act, 1907, s. 7.)

N.B.—If the agreement amounts to a "credit-sale" the position is the same.

	£ s. d.
INSURANCE POLICIES:	
Other than life insurance............	0 0 6
Life:—	
For any sum not exceeding £10....	0 0 1
Exc. £10, and not exc. £25........	0 0 3
Exc. £25, and not exc. £500, for every £50 or fractional part of £50	0 0 6
Exc. £500, and not exc. £1,000, for every £100 or fractional part of £100..........................	0 1 0
Exc. £1,000, for every £1,000 or any fractional part of £1,000.........	0 10 0

LEASES:—Lease or tack for any definite term less than a year of any furnished dwelling-house or apartments where the rent for such term exceeds £100, 10*s.*; of any lands, tenements, etc., in consideration of any rent, according to the following table:—

Annual rent not exceeding	* Term not exceeding 7 years	35 years	100 years	Term exceeding 100 years
£	£ s. d.	£ s. d.	£ s. d.	£ s. d.
5	Nil	1 0	6 0	12 0
10	Nil	2 0	12 0	1 4 0
15	Nil	3 0	18 0	1 16 0
20	Nil	4 0	1 4 0	2 8 0
25	Nil	5 0	1 10 0	3 0 0
50	Nil	10 0	3 0 0	6 0 0
75	Nil	15 0	4 10 0	9 0 0
100	Nil	1 0 0	6 0 0	12 0 0
Exceeding £100, for every £50 or fraction of £50	5 0	10 0	3 0 0	6 0 0

* If the term is indefinite the same duty is payable as if the term did not exceed 7 years.

Agreement for lease not exceeding 35 years, same as actual lease.

Where a consideration other than rent is payable and duty is charged on that consideration at conveyance rates, the same graduation applies where the consideration does not exceed £6,000 as under Conveyance or Transfer on Sale (except stock or marketable securities), provided that any rent payable does not exceed £50 a year.

	£ s. d.
MINERAL RIGHTS DUTY.—This is payable in respect of minerals which are the subject of a mining lease, or which are being worked by the proprietor of the minerals. Duty is payable annually on the rental value of all rights to work minerals and of all mineral wayleaves. Rate, per 20*s.* of the rental value..................	0 1 0
MORTGAGE under hand only, *see* EQUITABLE MORTGAGE.	
MORTGAGE, BOND, ETC., not exceeding £10......................	0 0 3
Not exceeding £25................	0 0 8
" " 50................	0 1 3
" " 100................	0 2 6
" " 150................	0 3 9
" " 200................	0 5 0
" " 250................	0 6 3
" " 300................	0 7 6
Exceeding £300, for every £100 and fractional part of £100..........	0 2 6
Transfer of Mortgage (except marketable securities), for every £100...	0 0 6
Reconveyance, Release, etc., per £100..........................	0 0 6

£ s. d.

No stamp duty is payable on discharge of a Building Society mortgage, or on the discharge of a local authority mortgage.

Collateral, or auxiliary, or additional, or substituted security (other than an equitable mortgage), when the principal security is duly stamped; for every £100, or fraction of £100, 6*d*., up to a maximum of .. 0 10 0

POWER OF ATTORNEY, etc., for receiving certain prize-money or wages 0 1 0

For the receipt of any money, or bill, or note, not exceeding £20, or of any periodical payments not exceeding £10 annually............ 0 5 0

For the receipt of dividends or interest of any stock, if for one payment only.................. 0 1 0

Ditto in any other case............ 0 5 0

Power of attorney of any other kind 0 10 0

An order, request, or direction under hand only from the proprietor of any stocks or shares to any Company or to any officer of any Company or to any banker to pay the dividends or interest arising therefrom to any person therein named is not chargeable with duty.

PROCURATION, Deed, etc., of......... 0 10 0

PROMISSORY NOTE, *see* BILLS or EXCHANGE.

PROPERTY AND INCOME TAX, *see* INCOME TAX, pp. 1181–86.

RECEIPTS, £2 or upwards............ 0 0 2

RECEIPTS FOR SALARIES, Wages, and Superannuation, and other like allowances are exempted by Sect. 36 Finance Act, 1924.

£ s. d.

REVOCATION of any Trust of Property not being a Will................ 0 10 0

SURTAX, *see* p. 1185.

TRANSFER OF STOCK, *see* CONVEYANCE.

UNIT TRUST INSTRUMENT—Any trust instrument of a unit trust scheme—For every £100, and also for any fractional part of £100, of the amount or value of the property subject to the trusts created or recorded by the instrument.................. 0 5 0

VOLUNTARY DISPOSITION *inter vivos*:—

On any instrument being a voluntary disposition (*inter vivos*) of any property (except stock or marketable securities, *see ante*, under Conveyance or Transfer) where the value of the property conveyed or transferred does not exceed £4,500 .... nil

Exceeds £4,500, but does not exceed £6,000, for every £50 and fraction of £50........................ 0 5 0

Exceeds £6,000, for every £50 and fraction of £50.................... 0 10 0

The instrument must contain similar certificates of value as a Conveyance or Transfer on Sale (*see* p. 1190), with the substitution of the words "property conveyed or transferred" for the word "consideration."

If the value of the property does not exceed £300, the same graduated rates apply as under Conveyance or Transfer on Sale (except Stock or marketable securities).

N.B.—The instrument is not deemed to be duly stamped unless it has been adjudicated, *i.e.* the instrument has been lodged with the Commissioner who will adjudge the value of the property and the duty payable.

LOCAL TAXATION LICENCES

DOG, GAME AND GUN LICENCES

In England and Wales, Dog, Game and Gun Licences are administered by the respective County Councils and County Borough Councils and the proceeds retained by them; and in Scotland by the Commissioners of Customs and Excise. Licences are issued for the Councils by the Post Office.

£ s. d.

DOGS, of any kind (annually, from first day of month of issue), Great Britain........................ 0 7 6

Dogs under 6 months of age, and those kept solely for the purpose of tending sheep or cattle on a farm, or by shepherds, or by blind persons for their guidance, exempt from Duty.

GAME AND GUN LICENCES.—A licence is required by every person who hunts, shoots, or takes game, except persons (in Great Britain) taking woodcock and snipe with nets or springs; proprietors, or tenants, on enclosed land, killing rabbits; persons hunting deer, or hares, with hounds; owners or occupiers, or their servants, killing deer on their own enclosed land; beaters and others, not holding guns, attending holders of game licences. Occupiers of enclosed land, or owners, having the right to kill game, may themselves kill hares, or authorize others to do so, without a licence, but such authority must be limited to one person at a time in any one parish, and must be registered with the clerk of the Justices of the Petty Sessional Division in which the land is situate. Even when the quarry is not what is legally known as "game," a "gun" licence is necessary. A game licence, however, covers a gun licence. Sailors, soldiers, airmen, territorial soldiers, or constables, *on duty or at practice*, need not take out a gun licence, nor need occupiers of land scaring birds or killing vermin on such land, or persons so acting under the orders of occupiers holding a licence. Unless, however, the occupier is himself licensed, he cannot authorize any unlicensed person to carry a gun. "Scaring" birds is not to be regarded as including killing of any birds, and "vermin" does not include rabbits. The rates of duty are as follows:—

£ s. d.

GAME LICENCES, if taken out after 31st July and before 1st Nov., to expire on 31st July following........... 3 0 0

After 31st July, to expire 31st Oct... 2 0 0

After 31st Oct., to expire 31st July.. 2 0 0

For a continuous period of 14 days.. 1 0 0

Gamekeeper's (Great Britain), to expire 31st July........................ 2 0 0

Game-Dealer's Licence, to expire 1st July, annually.................. 2 0 0

GUN LICENCES (gun, air gun or pistol). 0 10 0

A *Firearm Certificate* (5/- for the first, 2/6 subsequently—renewable every 3 years) is also necessary (with certain exceptions) for any person in possession of a firearm, other than a smooth bore gun with a barrel not less than 20 inches in length, or an air weapon.

A person under 17 may not purchase or hire and (with certain exceptions) a person under 14 may not have in his possession a firearm.

Firearm regulations are strictly enforced.

OTHER LOCAL LICENCES

Power to levy the duties on the following licences was transferred to county and county borough councils by the Finance Act, 1949.

	£	s.	d.
HAWKERS, annual licence	2	0	0
MONEYLENDERS, annual licence (to July 31)	15	0	0
February to July	10	0	0
PAWNBROKERS, annual licence	7	10	0
REFRESHMENT HOUSES, annual licence	1	1	0

An abatement of 17*s.* 10*d.* may be obtained by a person also taking out a wine retailer's on-licence in respect of a refreshment house not open after 10 p.m.

MECHANICALLY PROPELLED VEHICLES

Road licences and driving licences for mechanically-propelled vehicles are issued in England and Wales by county councils and by county borough councils (Scotland, 4 cities and Greenock, Motherwell, and Paisley), on behalf of the Ministry of Transport. Renewal licences are issued in certain circumstances by the Post Office. Details of the excise duties chargeable on motor vehicles are set out in the Vehicles (Excise) Act, 1962, which provides *inter alia* that any vehicle kept on a public road but not used on roads is chargeable to excise duty as if it were in use.

	£	s.	d.
Bicycles (other than electrically propelled):			
(*a*) If the cylinder capacity of the engine does not exceed 150 cubic centimetres	†1	0	0
(*b*) Exceeds 150 c.c. but does not exceed 250 c.c.	†2	5	0
(*c*) Exceeds 250 c.c.	*4	10	0
Bicycles which are electrically propelled	†1	0	0
†Additional if used for drawing trailer or side-car	0	12	0
* Additional if used for drawing trailer or side-car	1	10	0

Reduced duty on certain bicycles.—Where the cylinder capacity of the engine of a bicycle exceeds 250 c.c. and the bicycle (*a*) is one in respect of which a licence was taken out before Jan. 1, 1933, and (*b*) does not exceed 224 lb. unladen weight, the bicycle shall be treated for the purpose of the above table as if the cylinder capacity of the engine exceeded 150 c.c. but not 250 c.c.

	£	s.	d.
Tricycles (neither constructed nor adapted for use nor used for the carriage of a driver or passenger)	2	10	0
Other tricycles	6	0	0

	£	s.	d.
Vehicles other than mowing machines, being vehicles with more than three wheels neither constructed nor adapted for use nor used for the carriage of a driver or passenger	3	15	0

Hackney Carriages.

	£	s.	d.
Tramcars	0	15	0
Other hackney carriages	12	0	0
Additional for each person above 20 (excluding the driver) for which the vehicle has seating capacity	0	10	0

Licensing of Public Vehicles.

Public vehicles and also the persons concerned with driving and conducting them must be licensed. Vehicles are licensed by the Traffic Commissioners; licensing of personnel is effected by the authority in the area in which they live—not the area where the vehicle is to operate. Addresses of the Licensing Authorities can be obtained from local Police Stations. See also *Driving Licence Rates*, p. 1195.

Tractors, Cranes, Excavators, Agricultural Vehicles, etc.

	£	s.	d.
Locomotive ploughing engines, tractors, agricultural tractors and other agricultural engines, not used for hauling on roads any objects except their own necessary gear, etc.	2	10	0
Vehicles designed, constructed and used for the purpose of trench digging or any kind of excavating or shovelling work which (1) are used on public roads only for that purpose or for the purpose of proceeding to and from the place where they are to be used for that purpose, and (2) when so proceeding neither carry nor haul any load other than such as is necessary for their propulsion or equipment	2	10	0
Vehicles designed and constructed as mobile cranes which (1) are used on public roads only either as cranes in connection with work being carried on at a site in the immediate vicinity or for the purpose of proceeding to and from a place where they are to be used as cranes; and (2) when so proceeding neither carry nor haul any load other than such as is necessary for their propulsion or equipment	2	10	0
Mowing machines	2	10	0

Vehicles (other than vehicles in respect of which duty is chargeable under the foregoing provisions) which are constructed and used on public roads for haulage solely and not for the purpose of carrying or having superimposed upon them any load except such as is necessary for their propulsion or equipment:—

	£	s.	d.
(i) Showmen's vehicles:—			
Not excdg. 7¼ tons unladen	30	0	0
Excdg. 7¼ but not excdg. 8 tons	36	0	0
Excdg. 8 but not excdg. 10 tons	42	0	0
Excdg. 10 tons unladen—			
For the first 10 tons	42	0	0
For each additional ton or part	6	0	0
(ii) Other such vehicles—			
Not excdg. 2 tons unladen	30	0	0
Excdg. 2 but not excdg. 4 tons	48	0	0
Excdg. 4 but not excdg. 6 tons	66	0	0
Excdg. 6 but not excdg. 7¼ tons	84	0	0
Excdg. 7¼ but not excdg. 8 tons	102	0	0
Excdg. 8 tons in weight unladen—			
For the first 8 tons	102	0	0
For each additional ton or part	18	0	0

Goods Vehicles.

Electrically propelled goods vehicles, including tower wagons whether electrically propelled or not but not including farmers' or showmen's goods vehicles or local authorities' watering vehicles.

Exceeding	Not excdg.	Initial £ s. d.	*Additional £ s. d.
—	12 cwt.	12 0 0	—
12 cwt.	16 cwt.	15 0 0	—
16 cwt.	1 ton	18 0 0	—
1 ton	2 tons	18 0 0	1 10 0
2 tons	3 tons	24 0 0	3 0 0
3 tons	6 tons	36 0 0	1 10 0
6 tons	—	54 0 0	3 0 0

Goods vehicles which are propelled by steam or are constructed or adapted to use gas as fuel, other than farmers' or showmen's goods vehicles or local authorities' watering vehicles:—

Exceeding	Not excdg.	Initial £ s. d.	*Additional £ s. d.
—	12 cwt.	12 0 0	—
12 cwt.	16 cwt.	15 0 0	—
16 cwt.	1 ton	18 0 0	—
1 ton	3 tons	18 0 0	3 0 0
3 tons	4 tons	42 0 0	4 10 0
4 tons	6 tons	60 0 0	6 0 0
6 tons	—	108 0 0	4 10 0

Farmers' goods vehicles:—

Exceeding	Not excdg.	Initial £ s. d.	*Additional £ s. d.
—	12 cwt.	12 0 0	—
12 cwt.	1¼ tons	12 0 0	0 15 0
1¼ tons	2 tons	14 5 0	0 10 0
2 tons	2½ tons	15 15 0	15 0
2½ tons	3¼ tons	17 5 0	1 0 0
3¼ tons	—	20 5 0	0 10 0

Showmen's goods vehicles:—

Exceeding	Not excdg.	Initial £ s. d.	*Additional £ s. d.
—	12 cwt.	12 0 0	—
12 cwt.	16 cwt.	13 5 0	—
16 cwt.	1 ton	14 10 0	—
1 ton	1¼ tons	15 10 0	—
1¼ tons	—	15 10 0	1 5 0

Local authorities' watering vehicles, electrically propelled:—

Exceeding	Not excdg.	Initial £ s. d.	*Additional £ s. d.
—	1¼ tons	7 0 0	—
1¼ tons	2 tons	7 0 0	3 0 0
2 tons	3 tons	16 0 0	0 15 0
3 tons	5 tons	19 0 0	1 0 0
5 tons	—	29 0 0	—

Local authorities' watering vehicles, not electrically propelled:—

Exceeding	Not excdg.	Initial £ s. d.	*Additional £ s. d.
—	12 cwt.	12 0 0	—
12 cwt.	16 cwt.	15 0 0	—
16 cwt.	1 ton	18 0 0	—
1 ton	2 tons	18 0 0	3 0 0
2 tons	4 tons	30 0 0	2 0 0
4 tons	5 tons	46 0 0	1 10 0
5 tons	—	58 0 0	—

Goods vehicles not included in any of the foregoing provisions:—

Exceeding	Not excdg.	Initial £ s. d.	*Additional £ s. d.
—	12 cwt.	12 0 0	—
12 cwt.	16 cwt.	15 0 0	—
16 cwt.	1 ton	18 0 0	—
1 ton	3 tons	18 0 0	3 0 0
3 tons	4 tons	42 0 0	4 10 0
4 tons	—	60 0 0	6 0 0

* For each ¼ ton or part of a ¼ ton over the weight in column 2.

Goods Vehicles.

Used for drawing trailers

	£ s. d.
Showmen's goods vehicles used for drawing showmen's trailers	12 0 0
Local Authorities' watering vehicles	7 0 0
Other goods vehicles:—	
Not exceeding 2½ tons unladen	12 0 0
Exceeding 2½ tons but not 4 tons	18 0 0
" 4 tons	24 0 0

Other Vehicles.

	£ s. d.
Electrically propelled vehicles	9 0 0
Other vehicles—	
(*a*) If registered under the Roads Act, 1920, for the first time before January 1, 1947—	
Not exceeding 6 horsepower	10 15 0
Exceeding 6 horsepower but not exceeding 7 horsepower	12 10 0
(*b*) Other vehicles not included under (*a*) above	15 0 0

Motor-cars and cycles must be registered with, and licences to drive obtained from, the respective Clerks of the County Councils or County Borough Councils.

Driving Licences

Under the Road Traffic Act, 1956, driving licences valid for a period of three years were introduced over the years 1957–60.

Licence Rates	£ s. d.
Three-year Driving Licence	0 15 0
Replacement of lost or defaced licence	0 2 6
Amendment of licence (*e.g.* for additional Group of vehicles), for the unexpired period	0 5 0
Provisional Driving Licence: 6 months	0 10 0
Public Service Vehicle Driving Licence: 3 years†	0 3 0

† Additional to ordinary driving licence. *See* under Hackney Carriages.

COMPANIES

(Registered by the Board of Trade *Registrar of Companies*, Companies House, 55–71 City Road, E.C.1. The *Registry of Business Names* is also located at Companies House.)

In 1935 there were 14,826 public and 124,143 private Companies on the Register with paid-up capital of £3,963,000,000 and £1,730,000,000 respectively.

During 1962, 34,473 new Companies having a share capital were registered in Great Britain (England and Wales, 33,351; Scotland, 1,122), with nominal capital of £224,773,000. On December 31, 1962, there were 444,039 Companies on the register. Companies having a share capital were 10,668 Public Companies with total paid-up Capital, £5,024,000,000, and 412,515 Private Companies, with total paid-up capital, £2,833,000,000.

WEIGHTS AND MEASURES

The Weights and Measures Act of 1963, enacts the legal measures for Great Britain, basing them upon "United Kingdom primary standards" in the custody of the Standards Department of the Board of Trade. The primary standards are the yard, pound, metre and kilogramme. The GALLON, the capacity standard, wet or dry, is based upon the Pound. The Act of 1963 defines the GALLON as the space occupied by 10 pounds weight of distilled water of density 0·998 859 gramme per millilitre weighed in air of density 0·001 217 gramme per millilitre against weights of density 8·136 grammes per millilitre. The METRE and the LITRE have the meanings assigned by order of the Board of Trade to reproduce in English the international definition of these measures in force at the time of making of the orders.

New definitions for an *international yard* and *pound* were adopted on Jan. 1, 1959, by the standards laboratories of the United Kingdom, Canada, Australia, New Zealand, South Africa and the United States:

international yard = 0·914 4 metre. *international pound* = 0·453 592 37 kilogramme.

The following list shows the definitions of measures set out in the Weights and Measures Act, 1963 and some useful conversions. *See also* Conversion Tables, p. 1199.

Measurement of Length

Imperial Units

Mile = 1,760 yards.
Furlong = 220 yards.
Chain = 22 yards.
YARD = 0·914 4 metre.
Foot = ⅓ yard.
Inch = 1/36 yard.

1 mil = 1/1000 inch.
12 inches (*in.*) = 1 foot (*ft.*).
3 feet = 1 yard (*yd.*).
6 feet = 1 fathom.
22 yards = 1 chain = 100 links.
10 chains = 1 furlong.
8 furlongs = 1 mile = 1,760 yards.

Metric Units

Kilometre = 1,000 metres.
METRE (*see* above) = 1·094 yards.
Decimetre = 1/10 metre.
Centimetre = 1/100 metre.
Millimetre = 1/1000 metre.

10 millimetres (*mm.*) = 1 centimetre (*cm.*) = 0·393 701 inch.
10 centimetres = 1 decimetre (*dm.*) = 3·937 011 inches.
10 decimetres = 1 METRE (*m.*) = 1·093 614 yards.
10 metres = 1 dekametre (*dam.*) = 10·936 143 yards.
10 dekametres = 1 hectometre (*hm.*) = 109·361 43 yards.
10 hectometres = 1 kilometre (*km.*) = 0·621 371 mile.

A kilometre is approximately *five-eighths* of a mile, so that 8 kilometres may be regarded as 5 miles.

Measurement of Area

Imperial Units

Square mile = 640 acres
Acre = 4,840 square yards.
Rood = 1,210 square yards.
SQUARE YARD = a superficial area equal to that of a square each side of which measures one yard
Square foot = 1/9 square yard
Square inch = 1/144 square foot.

144 sq. inches = 1 sq. foot.
9 sq. feet = 1 sq. yard.
4 roods = 1 acre.
10 square chains = 1 acre = 4,840 sq. yards.
640 acres = 1 square mile.

Metric Units

Hectare = 100 ares.
Dekare = 10 ares.
Are = 100 square metres.
SQUARE METRE = a superficial area equal to that of a square each side of which measures one metre.
Square decimetre = 1/100 square metre.
Square centimetre = 1/100 square decimetre.
Square millimetre = 1/100 square centimetre.

1 sq. centimetre = 0·155 sq. inch.
1 sq. METRE = 10·763 9 sq. feet = 1·195 99 sq. yds.
1 are (*a.*) = 0·098 8 rood.
1 hectare (10,000 sq. metres) (*ha.*) = 2·471 05 acres.
1 sq. kilometre = 0·386 102 sq. mile.

Measurement of Volume

Imperial Units

CUBIC YARD = a volume equal to that of a cube each edge of which measures one yard.
Cubic foot = 1/27 cubic yard.
Cubic inch = 1/1728 cubic foot.

1,728 cubic inches = 1 cubic foot.
27 cubic feet = 1 cubic yard.

Metric Units

CUBIC METRE = a volume equal to that of a cube each edge of which measures one metre.
Cubic decimetre = 1/1000 cubic metre.
Cubic centimetre = 1/1000 cubic decimeter.

1 cubic metre (*cbm.* or m^3.) = 35·314 7 cu. ft. = 1·307 95 cu. yds.
(1 stere (= 1 cu. metre) is used as a unit of measurement of timber.)
1 cubic cm. (water) = 1 gram; 1,000 cubic cm. (water) or 1 litre = 1 kilogram; 1 cubic metre (1,000 litres, 1,000 kilograms) = 1 metric ton.

Measurement of Capacity

Imperial Units

GALLON (*see* above)
Quart = ¼ gallon.
Pint = ½ quart.
Gill = ¼ pint.
Fluid ounce = 1/20 pint.

4 gills = a pint.
2 pints = 1 quart.
4 quarts = 1 GALLON.
1 gallon = 160 fluid ounces.
= 277·274 cubic inches.

Bushel = 8 gallons.
Peck = 2 gallons

2 gallons = 1 peck.
4 pecks = 1 bushel.
8 bushels = 1 quarter.
A chaldron is 36 bushels = 4½ quarters.

1 hectolitre = 2·749 69 bushels.
1 hectolitre per hectare = 1·11 bushels per acre.
1 quintal = 3·6743 bushels.
1 quintal per hectare = 1·49 bushels per acre.

Measurement of Capacity—*continued*

Fluid drachm = ⅛ fluid ounce. | *See* Apothecaries Weight (*below*)
Minim = 1/60 fluid drachm.

Metric Units

Hectolitre = 100 litres.

LITRE = The volume occupied by the mass of 1 kilogramme of pure water at its temperature of maximum density and under a pressure of one standard atmosphere (14·696 lb. per sq. inch).

Decilitre = 1/10 litre.

Centilitre = 1/100 litre.

Millilitre = 1/1000 litre.

1 centilitre (*cl.*) = 0·070 4 gill.

1 decilitre (*dl.*) = 0·175 98 pint.

1 LITRE* (1/1,000 cubic metre) (*lit.*) = 1·759 8 pints = 0·88 Imp. quart = 0·22 Imp. gallon = 61·025 5 cu. inch = 0·035 315 7 cu. ft.

1 hectolitre (*hl.*) = 21·997 5 Imp. gallons = 26·417 1 U.S. gallons = 2·749 Imp. bushels = 2·837 7 U.S. bushels.

Measurement of Mass or Weight

Imperial Units

Ton = 2,240 pounds.
Hundredweight = 112 pounds.
Cental = 100 pounds.
Quarter = 28 pounds.
Stone = 14 pounds.
POUND = 0·453 592 37 kilogramme.
Ounce = 1/16 pound.
Dram = 1/16 ounce.
Grain = 1/7000 pound.

7000 grains (*gr.*) = 1 pound (*lb.*).
16 drams (*dr.*) = 1 ounce.
16 ounces = 1 POUND.
14 pounds = 1 stone.
28 pounds = 1 quarter (of a *cwt.*).
4 quarters (112 *lb.*) = 1 hundredweight (*cwt.*).
20 hundredweight (2,240 *lb.*) = 1 ton.

Ounce Troy = 480 grains
Pennyweight = 24 grains

20 pennyweights (*dwt.*) = 1 Troy ounce.
For gold and silver the ounce, divided decimally, and *not* into grains, is the sole unit of weight. The Troy ounce is the same as the Apothecaries' ounce = 480 Avoirdupois grains (31·1035 *Grammes*) in weight. A Troy POUND (= 5,760 grains) is legalized in the United States.

Ounce apothecaries' = 480 grains. | *See* Apothecaries Weight (*below*)
Drachm = ⅛ ounce apothecaries.
Scruple = ⅓ drachm.

Metric Units

Metric ton = 1,000 kilogrammes.
Quintal = 100 kilogrammes.

1 centigram (*cg.*) = 0·154 32 grains.
1 decigram (*dg.*) = 1·543 2 grains.
1 gramme (*grm.*) = 15·432 4 grains.
1 dekagram (*dag.*) = 5·643 8 drams.
1 hectogram (*hg.*) = 3·527 4 oz.
1 KILOGRAM (*kg.*) = 32·150 7 oz. Troy = 35·273 4 oz. Avoirdupois = 2·204 62 lb. Avoirdupois.
1 myriagram = 22·046 2 lb. Avoirdupois.
1 quintal (*q.*) = 100 kg. = 220·5 lb. Avoirdupois = 1·968 4 cwt.
1 tonne (*t.*) = 0·984 207 U.K. or long ton = 1·102 31 U.S. or short ton.

Measurement of Electricity

Units of measurement of electricity, the AMPERE (unit of electical current), the OHM (unit of electrical resistance), the VOLT (unit of difference of electrical potential) and the WATT (unit of electrical power) have the meanings assigned to them respectively by order of the Board of Trade, to reproduce in English the international definition in force at the date of the making of the order.

Kilowatt = 1000 watts. Megawatt = 1,000,000 watts.

Apothecaries' Weight

Measures of Weight.

20 grains = 1 scruple (℈1).
3 scruples = 1 drachm (ʒ1).
8 drachms = 1 ounce.

Measures of Capacity.

60 minims (*min.*) = 1 fluid drachm.
8 fluid drachms = 1 fluid ounce.
5 fluid ounces = 1 gill.
4 gills = 1 pint.
8 pints = 1 GALLON.

The Apothecaries' grain is the Avoirdupois grain, and the Apothecaries' ounce is the Troy ounce, of 480 grains. The Apothecaries' *drachm* is not the same as the Avoirdupois *dram*, and is spelled differently. A fluid ounce of distilled water at a temperature of 62° Fahrenheit is equal in weight to the Avoirdupois ounce (437·5 grains). A fluid *drachm* (54·6875 grains) is equal in weight to TWO Avoirdupois *drams*.

Angular or Circular Measure

60 seconds (″) = 1 minute (′).
60 minutes = 1 degree (°).
90 degrees = 1 right angle or quadrant.
Diameter of circle × 3·1416 = circumference.
Diameter squared × ·7854 = area of circle.
Diameter squared × 3·1416 = surface of sphere.
Diameter cubed × ·5236 = solidity of sphere.
One degree of circumference × 57·3 = radius.*

Diameter of cylinder × 3·1416; product by length or height, gives the surface.

Diameter squared × ·7854; product by length or height, gives solid content.

* Or, one radian (the angle subtended at the centre of a circle by an arc of the circumference equal in length to the radius) = 57·3 degrees, nearly.

Note.—A circle of 7 yards diameter has, in practice, a circumference of 22 yards = 1 chain.

Water Measures.

Cubic inch.............. = 252·458 grains.
Gallon (277·274 cu. in.) ... = 10 lb. (distilled).
Cubic foot.............. = 62·321 lb.
35·943 cubic ft. (224 gals.). = 1 ton.

Water for Ships: Tun, 210 gals., Butt 110, Puncheon 72, Barrel 36, Kilderkin 18 gals.

An *Inch of Rain* on the surface of an acre (43,560 sq. feet) = 3,630 cubic feet = 100·992 tons.

Cisterns: A cistern 4 feet by 2½ and 3 deep will hold brimful 186·963 gallons, weighing 16 cwt. 2 qrs. 21·6 lbs. in addition to its own weight.

Million, Billion, etc.

Value in the United Kingdom

Million.................thousand × thousand (10^6)
Billion.................million × million (10^{12})
Trillion................million × billion (10^{18})
Quadrillion............million × trillion (10^{24})

Value in U.S.A

Million..............thousand × thousand (10^6)
Billion...............thousand × million (10^9)
Trillion..............million × million (10^{12})
Quadrillion ....million × billion U.S. (10^{15})

United Kingdom (and other European) usage above follows the decision of the 9th Gen. Conference on Weights and Measures, 1948.

NAUTICAL MEASURES

Distance is measured in nautical (or sea) miles. The nautical mile is traditionally defined as the length of a minute of arc of a great circle of the earth; but as this length varies in different latitudes (owing to the fact that the earth is not a perfect sphere), 6,080 feet, a "rounded off value" of the mean length, has been adopted in British practice as the standard length of the nautical mile. On this basis 33 nautical miles exactly equal 38 statute miles; the statute (land) mile contains 5,280 feet. A *cable*, as a measure used by seamen, is 600 feet (100 fathoms) approximately one-tenth of a nautical mile. *Soundings at sea* are recorded in fathoms (6 feet).

6 feet = 1 fathom.
100 fathoms = 1 cable length.
10 cables = 1 nautical mile.

Note.—Some other countries, including the United States in 1954, have adopted the nautical mile of 1,852 metres as recommended by the International Hydrographic Bureau in 1929.

Speed is measured in *nautical miles per hour*, called *knots*. A knot is a measure of speed and is not used to express distance. A ship moving at the rate of 30 nautical miles per hour is said to be "doing 30 knots" and as the nautical mile is longer than the land or statute mile this represents a land speed of over 34½ miles per hour. In 1945 the *Royal Air Force* adopted the knot and the nautical mile as the standard measurements for speed and distance.

Knots	m.p.h.	Knots	m.p.h.	Knots	m.p.h.
1	1·1515	15	17·2727	29	33·3939
2	2·3030	16	18·4242	30	34·5454
3	3·4545	17	19·5757	31	35·6969
4	4·6060	18	20·7272	32	36·8484
5	5·7575	19	21·8787	33	38·0000
6	6·9090	20	23·0303	34	39·1515
7	8·0606	21	24·1818	35	40·3030
8	9·2121	22	25·3333	36	41·4545
9	10·3636	23	26·4848	37	42·6060
10	11·5151	24	27·6363	38	43·7575
11	12·6666	25	28·7878	39	44·9090
12	13·8180	26	29·9393	40	46·0606
13	14·9696	27	31·0908	41	47·2121
14	16·1212	28	32·2424	42	48·3636

Gross tonnage.—The total volume of all the enclosed spaces of a vessel, the unit of measurement being a ton of 100 cubic feet.

Net tonnage.—The gross tonnage less certain deductions for crew space, engine room, water ballast and other spaces not used for passengers or cargo.

F C+R+32

$R = \dfrac{4(F-32)}{9}$ $F = \dfrac{9R}{4} + 32$

CONVERSION.
Let F = Fahr.
" C = Cent.
" R = Réaum.

$°F = \dfrac{9C}{5} + 32$

$C = \dfrac{5(F-32)}{9}$

NOTE.—The *normal* temperature of the *human body* is 98·4° F., or 37° (36·9°) C., or 29·5° R. *Freezing* point = 32° F. = 0° C. = 0° R.; *Boiling* point = 212° F. = 100° C. = 80° R.

"*Absolute*" *Temperature* is Temperature reckoned from "*Absolute Zero*," which is at 273° C. below 0° C., 459·4° below 0° F., and 218·4° below 0° R. and is denoted by the letter "K."

• Below 32° F. *subtract* 32.

THERMOMETER COMPARISONS

Comparison between Scales of Fahrenheit Réaumur, and Centigrade.

CENT.	FAH'T.	RMR.	CENT.	FAH'T	RMR.
°	°	°	°	°	°
100B.	212B.	80B.	25	77	20·0
99	210·2	79·2	24	75·2	19·2
98	208·4	78·4	23	73·4	18·4
97	206·6	77·6	22	71·6	17·6
96	204·8	76·8	21	69·8	16·8
95	203	76	20	68	16
94	201·2	7 ·2	19	66·2	15·2
93	199·4	74·4	18	64·4	14·4
92	197·6	73·6	17	62·6	13·6
91	195·8	72·8	16	60·8	12·8
90	194	72	15	59	12
89	192·2	71·2	14	57·2	11·2
88	190·4	70·4	13	55·4	10·4
87	188·6	69·6	12	53·6	9·6
86	186·8	68·8	11	51·8	8·8
85	185	68	10	50	8·0
84	183·2	67·2	9	48·2	7·2
83	181·4	66·4	8	46·4	6·4
82	179·6	65·6	7	44·6	5·6
81	177·8	64·8	6	42·8	4·8
80	176	64	5	41	4
79	174·2	63	4	39·2	3·2
78	172·4	62·4	3	37·4	2·4
77	170·6	61·6	2	35·6	1·6
76	168·8	60·8	1	33·8	0·8
75	167	60	*zero*	32	*zero*
74	165·2	59·2	1	30·2	0·8
73	163·4	58·4	2	28·4	1·6
72	161·6	57·6	3	26·6	2·4
71	159·8	56·8	4	24·8	3·2
70	158	56	5	23	4
69	156·2	55·2	6	21·2	4·8
68	154·4	54·4	7	19·4	5·6
67	152·6	53·6	8	17·6	6·4
66	150·8	52·8	9	15·8	7·2
65	149	52	10	14	8
64	147·2	51·2	11	12·2	8·8
63	145·4	50·4	12	10·4	9·6
62	143·6	49·6	13	8·6	10·4
61	141·8	48·8	14	6·8	11·2
60	140	48	15	5	12
59	138·2	47·2	16	3·2	12·8
58	136·4	46·4	17	1·4	13·6
57	134·6	45·6	18	*0·4*	14·4
56	132·8	44·8	19	2·2	15·2
55	131	44	20	4	16
54	129·2	43·2	21	5·8	16·8
53	127·4	42·4	22	7·6	17·6
52	125·6	41·6	23	9·3	18·4
51	123·8	40·8	24	11·2	19·2
50	122	40	25	13	20
49	120·2	39·2	26	14·8	20·8
48	118·4	38·4	27	16·6	21·6
47	116·6	37·6	28	18·4	22·4
46	114·8	36·8	29	20·2	23·2
45	113	36	30	22	24
44	111·2	35·2	31	23·8	24·8
43	109·4	34·4	32	25·6	25·6
42	107·6	33·6	33	27·4	26·4
41	105·8	32·8	34	29·2	27·2
40	104	32	35	31	28
39	102·2	31·2	36	32·8	28·8
38	100·4	30·4	37	34·6	29·6
37	98·6	29·6	38	36·4	30·4
36	96·8	28·8	39	38·2	31·2
35	95	28	40	40	32
34	93·2	27·2	41	41·8	32·8
33	91·4	26·4	42	43·6	33·6
32	89·6	25·6	43	45·4	34·4
31	87·8	24·8	44	47·2	35·2
30	86	24	45	49	36
29	84·2	23·2	46	50·8	36·8
28	82·4	22·4	47	52·6	37·6
27	80·6	21·6	48	54·4	38·4
26	78·8	20·8	49	56·2	39·2

CONVERSION TABLES FOR WEIGHTS AND MEASURES

NOTE.—The central figures in heavy type represent either of the two columns beside them, as the case may be. *Examples:*—1 centimetre=0·394 inch and 1 inch=2·540 centimetres. 1 metre=1·094 yards and 1 yard=0·914 metre. 1 kilometre=0·621 mile and 1 mile=1·609 kilometres.

Length			Area			Volume			Weight (Mass.)					
Centi-metres.		Inches.	Square Centi-metres.		Square Inches.	Cubic Centi-metres.		Cubic Inches.	Long Tons.		Short Tons.	Metric Tonnes.		Short Tons.
2·540	**1**	0·394	6·452	**1**	0·155	16.387	**1**	0·061	0·893	**1**	1·120	0·907	**1**	1·102
5·080	**2**	0·787	12·903	**2**	0·310	32·774	**2**	0·122	1·786	**2**	2·240	1·814	**2**	2·205
7·620	**3**	1·181	19·355	**3**	0·465	49·161	**3**	0·183	2·679	**3**	3·360	2·722	**3**	3·307
10·160	**4**	1·575	25·806	**4**	0·620	65·548	**4**	0·244	3·571	**4**	4·480	3·629	**4**	4·409
12·700	**5**	1·969	32·258	**5**	0·775	81·936	**5**	0·305	4·464	**5**	5·600	4·536	**5**	5·512
15·240	**6**	2·362	38·710	**6**	0·930	98·323	**6**	0·366	5·357	**6**	6·720	5·443	**6**	6·614
17·780	**7**	2·756	45·161	**7**	1·085	114·710	**7**	0·427	6·250	**7**	7·840	6·350	**7**	7·716
20·320	**8**	3·150	51·613	**8**	1·240	131·097	**8**	0·488	7·143	**8**	8·960	7·257	**8**	8·818
22·860	**9**	3·543	58·064	**9**	1·395	147·484	**9**	0·549	8·036	**9**	10·080	8·165	**9**	9·921
25·400	**10**	3·937	64·516	**10**	1·550	163·871	**10**	0·610	8·929	**10**	11·200	9·072	**10**	11·023
50·800	**20**	7·874	129·032	**20**	3·100	327·742	**20**	1·220	17·857	**20**	22·400	18·144	**20**	22·046
76·200	**30**	11·811	193·548	**30**	4·650	491·613	**30**	1·831	26·786	**30**	33·600	27·216	**30**	33·069
101·600	**40**	15·748	258·064	**40**	6·200	655·484	**40**	2·441	35·714	**40**	44·800	36·287	**40**	44·092
127·000	**50**	19·685	322·580	**50**	7·750	819·355	**50**	3·051	44·643	**50**	56·000	45·359	**50**	55·116
152·400	**60**	23·622	387·096	**60**	9·300	983·226	**60**	3·661	53·571	**60**	67·200	54·431	**60**	66·139
177·800	**70**	27·559	451·612	**70**	10·850	1147·097	**70**	4·272	62·500	**70**	78·400	63·503	**70**	77·162
203·200	**80**	31·496	516·128	**80**	12·400	1310·968	**80**	4·882	71·429	**80**	89·600	72·575	**80**	88·185
228·600	**90**	35·433	580·644	**90**	13·950	1474·839	**90**	5·492	80·357	**90**	100·800	81·647	**90**	99·208
254·000	**100**	39·370	645·160	**100**	15·500	1638·710	**100**	6·102	89·286	**100**	112·000	00·710	**100**	110·231

Metres		Yards.	Square Metres.		Square Yards.	Cubic Metres		Cubic Yards.	Metric Tonnes.		Long Tons.	Kilo-grams.		Av. Pounds.
0·914	**1**	1·094	0·836	**1**	1·196	0·765	**1**	1·308	1·016	**1**	0·984	0·454	**1**	2·205
1·829	**2**	2·187	1·672	**2**	2·392	1·529	**2**	2·616	2·032	**2**	1·968	0·907	**2**	4·409
2·743	**3**	3·281	2·508	**3**	3·588	2·294	**3**	3·924	3·048	**3**	2·953	1·361	**3**	6·614
3·658	**4**	4·374	3·345	**4**	4·784	3·058	**4**	5·232	4·064	**4**	3·937	1·814	**4**	8·819
4·572	**5**	5·468	4·181	**5**	5·980	3·823	**5**	6·540	5·080	**5**	4·921	2·268	**5**	11·023
5·486	**6**	6·562	5·017	**6**	7·176	4·587	**6**	7·848	6·096	**6**	5·905	2·722	**6**	13·228
6·401	**7**	7·655	5·853	**7**	8·372	5·352	**7**	9·156	7·112	**7**	6·889	3·175	**7**	15·432
7·315	**8**	8·749	6·689	**8**	9·568	6·116	**8**	10·464	8·128	**8**	7·874	3·629	**8**	17·637
8·230	**9**	9·843	7·525	**9**	10·764	6·881	**9**	11·772	9·144	**9**	8·858	4·082	**9**	19·842
9·144	**10**	10·936	8·361	**10**	11·960	7·646	**10**	13·080	10·161	**10**	9·842	4·536	**10**	22·046
18·288	**20**	21·872	16·723	**20**	23·920	15·291	**20**	26·159	20·321	**20**	19·684	9·072	**20**	44·092
27·432	**30**	32·808	25·084	**30**	35·880	22·937	**30**	39·239	30·481	**30**	29·526	13·608	**30**	66·139
36·576	**40**	43·745	33·445	**40**	47·840	30·582	**40**	52·318	40·642	**40**	39·368	18·144	**40**	88·185
45·720	**50**	54·681	41·806	**50**	59·799	38·228	**50**	65·398	50·802	**50**	49·210	22·680	**50**	110·231
54·864	**60**	65·617	50·168	**60**	71·759	45·873	**60**	78·477	60·963	**60**	59·052	27·216	**60**	132·277
64·008	**70**	76·553	58·529	**70**	83·719	53·519	**70**	91·557	71·123	**70**	68·894	31·752	**70**	154·324
73·152	**80**	87·489	66·890	**80**	95·679	61·164	**80**	104·636	81·284	**80**	78·737	36·287	**80**	176·370
82·296	**90**	98·425	75·251	**90**	107·639	68·810	**90**	117·716	91·444	**90**	88·579	40·823	**90**	198·416
91·440	**100**	109·361	83·613	**100**	119·599	76·455	**100**	130·795	101·605	**100**	98·421	45·359	**100**	220·462

Kilo-metres.		Miles.	Square Kilo-metres.		Square Miles.	Litres.		Gallons	Bushels U.S.		Bushels U.K.	Hectares.		Acres.
1·609	**1**	0·621	2·590	**1**	0·386	4·546	**1**	0·220	1·032	**1**	0·969	0·405	**1**	2·471
3·219	**2**	1·243	5·180	**2**	0·772	9·092	**2**	0·440	2·064	**2**	1·938	0·809	**2**	4·942
4·828	**3**	1·864	7·770	**3**	1·158	13·638	**3**	0·660	3·096	**3**	2·907	1·214	**3**	7·413
6·437	**4**	2·485	10·360	**4**	1·544	18·184	**4**	0·880	4·128	**4**	3·876	1·619	**4**	9·884
8·047	**5**	3·107	12·950	**5**	1·931	22·730	**5**	1·100	5·160	**5**	4·845	2·023	**5**	12·355
9·656	**6**	3·728	15·540	**6**	2·317	27·276	**6**	1·320	6·192	**6**	5·814	2·428	**6**	14·826
11·265	**7**	4·350	18·130	**7**	2·703	31·822	**7**	1·540	7·224	**7**	6·783	2·833	**7**	17·297
12·875	**8**	4·971	20·720	**8**	3·089	36·368	**8**	1·760	8·256	**8**	7·752	3·237	**8**	19·769
14·484	**9**	5·592	23·310	**9**	3·475	40·914	**9**	1·980	9·288	**9**	8·721	3·642	**9**	22·240
16·093	**10**	6·214	25·900	**10**	3·861	45·460	**10**	2·200	10·321	**10**	9·689	4·047	**10**	24·711
32·187	**20**	12·427	51·800	**20**	7·722	90·919	**20**	4·400	20·641	**20**	19·379	8·094	**20**	49·421
48·280	**30**	18·641	77·700	**30**	11·583	136·379	**30**	6·599	30·962	**30**	29·068	12·140	**30**	74·132
64·374	**40**	24·855	103·600	**40**	15·444	181·839	**40**	8·799	41·282	**40**	38·758	16·187	**40**	98·842
80·467	**50**	31·069	129·499	**50**	19·305	227·298	**50**	10·999	51·603	**50**	48·447	20·234	**50**	123·553
96·561	**60**	37·282	155·399	**60**	23·166	272·758	**60**	13·199	61·923	**60**	58·137	24·281	**60**	148·263
112·654	**70**	43·496	181·299	**70**	27·027	318·217	**70**	15·398	72·244	**70**	67·826	28·328	**70**	172·974
128·748	**80**	49·710	207·199	**80**	30·888	363·677	**80**	17·598	82·564	**80**	77·516	32·375	**80**	197·684
144·841	**90**	55·923	233·099	**90**	34·749	409·137	**90**	19·798	92·885	**90**	87·205	36·422	**90**	222·395
160·934	**100**	62·137	258·999	**100**	38·610	454·596	**100**	21·998	103·205	**100**	96·895	40·469	**100**	247·105

PAPER AND BOOK MEASURES

Writing Paper		*Printing Paper*	
480 sheets	= 1 ream	516 sheets	= 1 ream
24 sheets	= 1 quire	2 reams	= 1 bundle
20 quires	= 1 ream	5 bundles	= 1 bale

Sizes of Writing and Drawing Papers

Emperor	=	72 × 48	inches
Antiquarian	=	53 × 31	,,
Double Elephant	=	40 × 26¾	,,
Grand Eagle	=	42 × 28¾	,,
Atlas	=	34 × 26	,,
Colombier	=	34½ × 23½	,,
Imperial	=	30 × 22	,,
Elephant	=	28 × 23	,,
Cartridge	=	26 × 21	,,
Super Royal	=	27 × 19	,,
Royal	=	24 × 19	,,
Medium	=	22 × 17½	,,
Large Post	=	21 × 16½	,,
Copy or Draft	=	20 × 16	,,
Demy	=	20 × 15½	,,
Post	=	19 × 15¼	,,
Pinched Post	=	18½ × 14¾	,,
Foolscap	=	17 × 13½	,,
Sheet and ⅓ Foolscap	=	22 × 13½	,,
Sheet and ½ Foolscap	=	24½ × 13½	,,
Double Foolscap	=	26½ × 16½	,,
Double Post	=	30½ × 19	,,
Double Large Post	=	33 × 21	,,
Double Demy	=	31 × 20	,,
Brief	=	16½ × 13¼	,,
Pott	=	15 × 12½	,,

Sizes of Brown Papers

Casing	=	46 × 36	inches
Double Imperial	=	45 × 29	,,
Elephant	=	34 × 24	,,
Double Four Pound	=	31 × 21	,,
Imperial Cap	=	29 × 22	,,
Haven Cap	=	26 × 21	,,
Bag Cap	=	24 × 19½	,,
Kent Cap	=	21 × 18	,,

Sizes of Printing Papers

Foolscap	=	17 × 13½	inches
Double Foolscap	=	27 × 17	,,
Crown	=	20 × 15	,,
Double Crown	=	30 × 20	,,
Quad Crown	=	40 × 30	,,
Double Quad Crown	=	60 × 40	,,
Post	=	19¼ × 15½	,,
Double Post	=	31½ × 19½	,,
Double Large Post	=	33 × 21	,,
Sheet and ½ Post	=	23½ × 19½	,,
Demy	=	22½ × 17½	,,
Double Demy	=	35 × 22½	,,
Quad Demy	=	45 × 35	,,
Music Demy	=	20 × 15½	,,
Medium	=	23 × 18	,,
Royal	=	25 × 20	,,
Super Royal	=	27½ × 20½	,,
Elephant	=	28 × 23	,,
Imperial	=	30 × 22	,,

Sizes of Bound Books

Demy 16mo	=	5⅝ × 4⅜	inches
Demy 18mo	=	5¾ × 3¾	,,
Foolscap Octavo (8vo)	=	6¾ × 4¼	,,
Crown 8vo	=	7½ × 5	,,
Large Crown 8vo	=	8 × 5¼	,,
Demy 8vo	=	8⅜ × 5⅝	,,
Medium 8vo	=	9½ × 6	,,
Royal 8vo	=	10 × 6¼	,,
Super Royal 8vo	=	10¼ × 6⅞	,,
Imperial 8vo	=	11 × 7½	,,
Foolscap Quarto (4to)	=	8½ × 6¾	,,
Crown 4to	=	10 × 7½	,,
Demy 4to	=	11¼ × 8¾	,,
Royal 4to	=	12½ × 10	inches
Imperial 4to	=	15 × 11	,,
Crown Folio	=	15 × 10	,,
Demy Folio	=	17½ × 11¼	,,
Royal Folio	=	20 × 12½	,,
Music	=	14 × 10¼	,,

NOTE.—*Folio* means a sheet folded in half, *quarto* folded into four, and so on; thus, a crown 8vo page is one-eighth the size of a crown sheet. Books are usually bound up in sheets of 16 or 32 pages. Octavo books are generally printed 64 pages at a time (32 pages on each side of a sheet of quad); a crown octavo book of 320 pages will therefore require 5 sheets of quad crown, or 10 reams per 1,000 copies, the odd 16 sheets in each ream being allowed as waste. Newspapers (and some books in editions of 50,000 or over) are printed on rotary presses, for which the paper is supplied in continuous reels.

Sizes of Types

The type size chiefly used in "Whitaker" is 5½ point, or *Ruby*, set on a 6 point "body." The column contains 78 lines, and is 12 Pica ems wide; on an average every column contains about 3,100 letters, or 710 words.

Today type up to 14 point size is usually set by a keyboard machine, and mechanically cast in single letters or in complete lines of type (e.g. Monotype and Linotype). All type is cast to one uniform height ("type high"), which is ¹¹⁄₁₂ inch. Individual letters vary in *breadth*, but the "body" of each character is of uniform *depth* throughout the alphabet in each size. The unit of *breadth* is the Pica M (*Em*) 6 of which, side by side, occupy one inch of space. The unit of *depth* is the Point (72 Points=1 inch), so that 6 lines of 12 Point occupy 1 inch in depth. The names of the various sizes are:—

Brilliant (3½ point). A column the size of this in "Whitaker," if set in Brilliant would contain 132 lines, and about 1,450 words.

Printing is the art of producing impressions, from characters or figures

Diamond (4½ point) is the next size; the column would contain 102 lines, and about 1,020 words.

Printing is the art of producing impressions, from characters or figures

5 point (*Pearl*), 92 lines, 830 words—

Printing is the art of producing impressions, from character

Ruby (5½ point), 84 lines, 710 words—

Printing is the art of producing impressions, from ch

6 point (*Nonpareil*), 77 lines, 600 words—

Printing is the art of producing impressions, fro

7 point (*Minion*), 66 lines, 500 words—

Printing is the art of producing impressions

8 point (*Brevier*), 58 lines, 410 words—

Printing is the art of producing impressi

9 point (*Bourgeois*), 51 lines, 340 words—

Printing is the art of producing impr

10 point (*Long Primer*), 46 lines, 300 words—

Printing is the art of producing im

11 point (*Small Pica*), 44 lines, 270 words—

Printing is the art of producing

12 point (*Pica*), 38 lines, 230 words—

Printing is the art of produ

14 point (*English*), 33 lines, 180 words—

Printing is the art of pro

18 point (*Great Primer*), 25 lines, 110 words—

Printing is the art o

Further point sizes used are 24, 30, 36, 42, 48, 60 and 72

SYMBOLS FOR CORRECTING PROOFS

Supplied by WILLIAM CLOWES & SONS LTD, Beccles, Suffolk, Printers of "WHITAKER"

Letter(s) or word(s) requiring alteration should be struck through IN INK in the text and the substitution should be written in the nearest margin followed by / (the symbol used to denote that the marginal mark is concluded). Insertions should be indicated by ⅄ or ^ at the conclusion of the marginal mark *and* at the desired place in the text.

Alteration required	*Mark in margin*	*Mark in text*
Delete (take out)	*or*	/ *or* —— Vertical stroke to delete one or two letters; horizontal line to delete more
Delete and close up	*or*	Strike out letter(s) not required and add "close up" mark above and below
Close up: delete space between letters		linking letters or words
Use ligature (fi, fl, ffl, etc.) or diphthong (æ, œ)	*enclosing ligature or diphthong required*	enclosing letters to be altered
Insert space between letters or words	#⅄	⅄
Leave as printed (i.e. a cancellation of previous marking)	stet	.... under letter(s) or word(s) crossed out but to be retained
Invert type (of letter(s) upside down)		Encircle letter(s) to be altered
"Battered" letter(s) to be replaced by similar but undamaged characters	X	Encircle letter(s) or word(s) to be replaced and write the correct letter(s) in the margin
Push down space or "high" letter(s) or word(s)		Encircle space, letter(s), or word(s) affected
Transpose	tr. *or* trs.	between letters or words, numbered when necessary
Take letter(s) or word(s) from end of one line to beginning of next line	take over *or* over	

Alteration required	*Mark in margin*	*Mark in text*
Take letter(s) or word(s) from beginning of one line to end of preceding line	back *or* take back	
Begin a new paragraph	n.p.	[before first word of new paragraph
No new para. here or run on previous matter with later matter	run on	between paras. or other matter
Spell out in full the abbreviation, contraction, or figure	spell out	Encircle words, etc., or figures concerned
Insert omitted portion of copy	out-see copy	⅄ Attach the relevant copy to the proof, indicating omitted portion
Inserted or substituted letter(s), figure(s), or sign(s) under which this is placed to be superscript (i.e. high alignment) [1]	(*see footnote*)	⅄ for insertions For substitutions encircle letter(s), figure(s), or sign(s) to be altered
Inserted or substituted letter(s), figure(s), or sign(s) over which this is placed to be subscript (low alignment) [2]	(*see footnote*)	⅄ for insertions For substitutions encircle letter(s), figure(s), etc., to be altered
Change to lower case	l.c.	Encircle letter(s) to be altered
Replace "wrong fount" by letter(s) of correct fount	w.f.	Encircle letter(s) or word(s) to be altered
Change to capital letters	caps.	≡ under letter(s) or word(s) to be altered
Change to small capitals	s.c.	= under letter(s) or word(s) to be altered

1 indicates a superior (superscript) figure one   2 indicates an inferior (subscript) figure two

Alteration required	*Mark in margin*	*Mark in text*
Use capital letters for initial letter(s) (as desired) and small capitals for rest of word(s)	caps & s.c.	≡ under initial letter(s) and = under the remainder of the word(s)
Change to bold type	(bold)	Draw wavy line under letter(s) or word(s) to be altered
Change to roman type	(rom.)	Encircle letter(s) or word(s) to be altered
Change to italic type	(italic)	Draw this straight line under letter(s) or word(s) to be altered
Letter(s) or word(s) to be underlined	(underline)	under letter(s), word(s), etc., to be underlined
Equalize space between words	eq. #	between words
Reduce space	less #	between words
Space to be inserted between lines or paragraphs	#>	*Amount of space should be indicated*
To be placed in centre of line, etc.	(centre)	Position to be indicated by ⌐ ¬
Indent one en (approx. space occupied by n of type in use)	en □ ⅄	indicating approximate position
Indent one em (approx. space occupied by M of type in use)	em □ ⅄	Ditto
Indent two ems (approx. space occupied by MM of type in use)	□□ ⅄	Ditto
Move to the left		Ditto
Move to the right		Ditto
Move lines to the right		at left side of group of lines to be moved (indicating approx. position)
Move lines to the left		at right side of group of lines to be moved (indicating approx. position)
Move portion of matter so that it is positioned as indicated	[ ]	[ ] at limits of required position
Raise lines	(raise)	↑ over lines to be raised
Lower lines	(lower)	↓ under lines to be lowered
Correct the vertical alignment	‖	‖
Straighten lines	=	= through lines to be straightened
Insert parentheses (round-shaped brackets)	(/) or (/)/	⅄ ⅄⅄
Insert [square] brackets	[/] or [/]/	⅄ ⅄⅄
Insert hyphen	-/	⅄
Insert en (=half-em) rule (*see above*)	en/	⅄
Insert one-em rule (*see above*)	em/	⅄
Insert two-em rule (*see above*)	2 em/	⅄
Insert apostrophe	ʼ	⅄
Insert single quotation marks	‘ ’	⅄ ⅄
Insert double quotation marks	“ ”	⅄ ⅄
Insert ellipsis	.../	⅄
Insert leader (*visual guide to alignment in contents pages, etc.*)	(...) (..) (.)	⅄ (*three, two, or one dot*)
Insert shilling stroke (oblique)	(/)	⅄

Punctuation ,⅄ ,/ ;⅄ ;/ ⊙ (:) ?⅄ ?/ !⅄ !/

HALL-MARKS ON GOLD AND SILVER WARES

Hall-marks are the symbols stamped on gold or silver articles to indicate that they have been chemically tested and that they conform to one of the legal standards. With certain exceptions, all gold or silver articles are required by law to be hall-marked before they are offered for sale. Hall-marking was instituted in 1300 under a statute of Edward I.

Normally a complete modern hall-mark consists of four symbols—the maker's mark, assay office mark, standard mark and date letter. Additional marks have been authorized from time to time.

Maker's Mark.—Instituted in 1363, the maker's mark was originally a device such as a bird or *fleur-de-lys* and now consists invariably of the initials of the Christian and surnames of the maker or of the firm.

Assay Office Mark.—The existing assay offices and their distinguishing marks are:—

LONDON (Goldsmiths' Hall).
A leopard's head (uncrowned from 1300 to 1478–9, when it became crowned until 1821, since when it has been uncrowned). From 1697–1720 this mark was used in London for gold only and not for silver.

BIRMINGHAM......................An anchor.
SHEFFIELD.........................A crown.
EDINBURGH.........................A castle.
GLASGOW......Tree, salmon, bell, and bird and ring.

Offices formerly existed in other towns, *e.g.* Chester, Newcastle, Exeter, York and Norwich, each having its own distinguishing mark.

Standard Mark.—Instituted in 1544. The current legal standards and their marks are as follows:—

SILVER.—Sterling silver (92·5 per cent. silver) is marked by English assay offices with a *lion passant*; by the Edinburgh Assay Office with a *thistle*; and by the Glasgow Assay Office with a *thistle* followed by a *lion rampant*. A full-length figure

of *Britannia* was impressed on fine silver plate (95·84 per cent. silver) between 1697 and 1720 and this mark is still used occasionally by all British assay offices.

GOLD.—22 carat articles (91·6 per cent. gold) are marked by English offices with a crown followed by the figure 22; by the Edinburgh and Glasgow offices with the figure 22 following their respective standard marks as for sterling silver (*see* above).

18 carat articles (75 per cent. gold) are marked by English assay offices with a crown followed by the figure 18 and by Scottish offices as for 22 carat articles.

All British assay offices mark 14 carat gold (58·5 per cent. gold) with the figures 14·585 and 9 carat gold (37·5 per cent. gold) with the figures 9.375.

Date Letter.—Instituted in 15th Century. The date letter denotes the year in which an article was assayed or hall-marked. Each alphabetical cycle has a distinctive style of lettering or shape of shield. The date letters are different at the various assay offices and the particular office must be established from the assay office mark before reference is made to tables of date letters. The date letter is changed at the London Office in May each year and at Birmingham and Sheffield in July. Specimen shields and letters used by the London Office in each period from 1438 to date are shown below.

OTHER MARKS

Duty Mark.—In 1784 an additional mark of the reigning sovereign's head was introduced to signify that the excise duty had been paid. The mark became obsolete on the abolition of the duty in 1890.

Silver Jubilee and Coronation Marks.—Voluntary marks were authorized to be used at manufacturers' request to commemorate the silver jubilee of King George V and Queen Mary and the Coronation of Her Majesty Queen Elizabeth II. The Jubilee Mark was used on silver made in 1933, 1934 and 1935 and the Coronation Mark on gold and silver with date letter 1952/3 or 1953/4.

Foreign Wares.—Since 1842 foreign wares imported into Great Britain have been required to be hall-marked before sale. The marks consist of the importer's mark, a special assay office mark (*see below*), the decimal figures denoting fineness (together with the carat figure in the case of gold) and the annual date letter. The current assay office marks for foreign wares are as follows:—

LONDON.—The sign of the Constellation Leo.
BIRMINGHAM.—Equilateral triangle.
SHEFFIELD.—The sign of the Constellation Libra.
EDINBURGH.—St. Andrew's Cross.
GLASGOW.—Double block letter F inverted.

London (Goldsmiths' Hall) Date Marks
From 1438 *to* 1976.

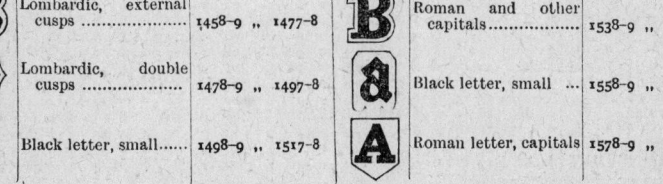

	Lombardic, simple......	1438–9 to 1457–8	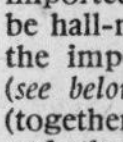	Lombardic	1518–9 „ 1537–8
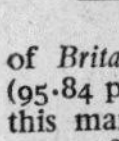	Lombardic, external cusps	1458–9 „ 1477–8	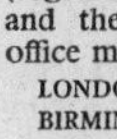	Roman and other capitals..................	1538–9 „ 1557–8
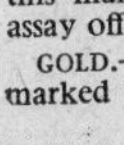	Lombardic, double cusps	1478–9 „ 1497–8	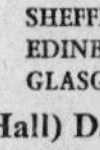	Black letter, small ...	1558–9 „ 1577–8
	Black letter, small......	1498–9 „ 1517–8		Roman letter, capitals	1578–9 „ 1597–8

	Lombardic, external cusps	1598–9 „ 1617–8
	Italic letter, small ...	1618–9 „ 1637–8
	Court hand	1638–9 „ 1657–8
	Black letter, capitals	1658–9 „ 1677–8
	Black letter, small ...	1678–9 „ 1696–7
	Court hand	1697 „ 1715–6 (From March 1697 only.)
	Roman letter, capitals	1716–7 to 1735–6
	Roman letter, small	1736–7 „ 1755–6
	Old English, capitals	1756–7 to 1775–6
	Roman letter, small...	1776–7 „ 1795–6
	Roman letter, capitals	1796–7 „ 1815–6
	Roman letter, small...	1816–7 „ 1835–6
	Old English, capitals	1836–7 „ 1855–6
	Old English, small ...	1856–7 „ 1875–6
	Roman letter, capitals [A to M *square* shield N to Z as shown.]	1876–7 „ 1895–6
	Roman letter, small...	1896–7 „ 1915–6
	Black letter, small ...	1916–7 „ 1935–6
	Roman letter, capital	1936–7 „ 1955–6
	Italic letter, small ...	1956–7 „ 1975–6

TABLE OF INCOME OR WAGES

Per Year	Per Month	Per Week	Per Day
£ s.	s. d.	s. d.	s. d.
0 10	0 10	0 2¼	0 0¼
1 0	1 8	0 4½	0 0¾
1 10	2 6	0 7	0 1
2 0	3 4	0 9	0 1¼
2 2	3 6	0 9½	0 1½
2 10	4 2	0 11½	0 1¾
3 0	5 0	1 1¾	0 2
3 3	5 3	1 2½	0 2
3 10	5 10	1 4¼	0 2¼
4 0	6 8	1 6½	0 2¾
4 4	7 0	1 7½	0 2¾
4 10	7 6	1 8¾	0 3
5 0	8 4	1 11	0 3¼
5 5	8 9	2 0¼	0 3½
5 10	9 2	2 1½	0 3¾
6 0	10 0	2 3¾	0 4
6 6	10 6	2 5	0 4¼
6 10	10 10	2 6	0 4¼
7 0	11 8	2 8¼	0 4½
7 7	12 3	2 10	0 4¾
7 10	12 6	2 10½	0 5

Per Year	Per Month	Per Week	Per Day
£ s.	£ s. d.	s. d.	s. d.
8 0	0 13 4	3 1	0 5¼
8 8	0 14 0	3 2¾	0 5½
8 10	0 14 2	3 3¼	0 5½
9 0	0 15 0	3 5½	0 6
9 9	0 15 9	3 7½	0 6¼
10 0	0 16 8	3 10¼	0 6½
10 10	0 17 6	4 0½	0 7
11 0	0 18 4	4 2¾	0 7¼
11 11	0 19 3	4 5¼	0 7½
12 0	1 0 0	4 7½	0 8
12 12	1 1 0	4 10¼	0 8¼
13 0	1 1 8	5 0	0 8½
13 13	1 2 9	5 3	0 9
14 0	1 3 4	5 4½	0 9¼
14 14	1 4 6	5 7¾	0 9¾
15 0	1 5 0	5 9¼	0 9¾
15 15	1 6 3	6 0¾	0 10¼
16 0	1 6 8	6 1¾	0 10½
16 16	1 8 0	6 5½	0 11
17 0	1 8 4	6 6½	0 11¼
17 17	1 9 9	6 10½	0 11¼

Per Year	Per Month	Per Week	Per Day
£ s.	£ s. d.	£ s. d.	£ s. d.
18 0	1 10 0	0 6 11	0 0 11¾
18 18	1 11 6	0 7 3¼	0 1 0½
19 0	1 11 8	0 7 3¾	0 1 0½
20 0	1 13 4	0 7 8¼	0 1 1¼
30 0	2 10 0	0 11 6½	0 1 7¾
40 0	3 6 8	0 15 4¼	0 2 2¼
50 0	4 3 4	0 19 2¾	0 2 9
60 0	5 0 0	1 3 1	0 3 3½
70 0	5 16 8	1 6 11	0 3 10
80 0	6 13 4	1 10 9¼	0 4 4½
90 0	7 10 0	1 14 7½	0 4 11¼
100 0	8 6 8	1 18 5½	0 5 5¾
200 0	16 13 4	3 16 11	0 10 11½
300 0	25 0 0	5 15 4½	0 16 5¼
400 0	33 6 8	7 13 10¼	1 1 11
500 0	41 13 4	9 12 3¾	1 7 4¾
600 0	50 0 0	11 10 9¼	1 12 10½
700 0	58 6 8	13 9 2¾	1 18 4¼
800 0	66 13 4	15 7 8¼	2 3 10
900 0	75 0 0	17 6 1¾	2 9 3¾
1000 0	83 6 8	19 4 7¼	2 14 9½

EQUIVALENT INVESTMENTS

Examples:—To ascertain the yield of Consols at a price of £83 6*s*. 8*d*. look in the column headed 2½ per cent. for 83⅓, and it will be seen that the yield (column headed Return Per Cent.) is £3 0*s*. 0*d*. Similarly, shares paying a fixed dividend of 6 per cent., if purchased at £189, will yield £3 3*s*. 6*d*. per cent.; while 5 per cent. shares at £152 10*s*. 0*d*. yield £3 5*s*. 7*d*. per cent.

Return Per Cent.	1 p.c.	1½ p.c.	2 p.c.	2½ p.c.	2¾ p.c.	3 p.c.	3¼ p.c.	3½ p.c.	4 p.c.	4½ p.c.	5 p.c.	5½ p.c.	6 p.c.	7 p.c.	7½ p.c.
£2 10 0	40	60	80	100	110	120	130	140	160	180	200	220	240	280	300
2 12 6	38	57 1/7	76⅕	95¼	104¾	114 2/7	123 6/7	133⅓	152⅓	171⅓	190⅓	209½	228½	266⅔	285¾
2 13 9	37⅕	55⅘	74⅖	93	102⅓	111⅔	12 1	130⅓	149	167½	186	204⅔	223⅓	260⅔	279⅓
2 15 0	36⅓	54⅓	72 5/7	90⅚	100	109	118	127⅙	145⅓	163½	181⅔	200	218	254½	272⅔
2 17 6	34¾	52⅙	69 4/7	87	95⅝	104⅓	113	121⅔	139	156½	174	191¼	208⅔	243⅓	260⅔
3 0 0	33⅓	50	66⅔	83⅓	91⅔	100	108¼	116⅔	133⅓	150	166⅔	183⅓	200	233⅓	250
3 0 7	33	49½	66	82½	90¾	99	107¼	115½	132	148½	165	181½	198	231	247½
3 1 6	32½	48⅘	65	81¼	89⅜	97½	105¾	113¾	130	146¼	162½	178¾	195	227½	243¾
3 2 6	32	48	64	80	88	96	104	112	128	144	160	176	192	224	240
3 3 6	31½	47¼	63	78¾	86⅝	94½	102¼	110¼	126	141¾	157½	173¼	189	220½	236¼
3 4 6	31	46½	62	77½	85¼	93	100¾	108½	124	139½	155	170½	186	217	232½
3 5 7	30½	45¾	61	76¼	83⅞	91½	99¼	106¾	122	137¼	152½	167¾	183	213½	228¾
3 6 8	30	45	60	75	82½	90	97½	105	120	135	150	165	180	210	225
3 7 10	29½	44¼	59	73¾	81⅛	88½	95¾	103¼	118	132¾	147½	162¼	177	206½	221¼
3 9 0	29	43½	58	72½	79¾	87	94¼	101½	116	130½	145	159½	174	203	217½
3 10 2	28½	42¾	57	71¼	78⅜	85½	92¾	99¾	114	128¼	142½	156¾	171	199½	213¾
3 11 5	28	42	56	70	77	84	91	98	112	126	140	154	168	196	210
3 12 9	27½	41¼	55	68¾	75⅝	82½	89⅓	96¼	110	123¾	137½	151¼	165	192½	206¼
3 14 1	27	40½	54	67½	74¼	81	87¾	94½	108	121½	135	148½	162	189	202½
3 15 6	26½	39¾	53	66¼	72⅞	79½	86¼	92¾	106	119⅓	132½	145⅔	159	185½	198¾
3 16 11	26	39	52	65	71½	78	84½	91	104	117	130	143	156	182	195
3 18 5	25½	38¼	51	63¾	70⅛	76½	82¾	89¼	102	114¾	127½	140¼	153	178½	191¼
4 0 0	25	37½	50	62½	68¾	75	81¼	87½	100	112½	125	137½	150	175	187½
4 1 7	24½	36¾	49	61¼	67⅜	73½	79⅔	85¾	98	110¼	122½	134¾	147	171½	183¾
4 3 4	24	36	48	60	66	72	78	84	96	108	120	132	144	168	180
4 5 1	23½	35¼	47	58¾	64⅝	70½	76½	82¼	94	105¾	117½	129¼	141	164½	176¼
4 6 11	23	34½	46	57½	63¼	69	74¾	80½	92	103½	115	126½	138	161	172½
4 8 11	22½	33¾	45	56¼	61⅞	67½	73¼	78¾	90	101¼	112½	123¾	135	157½	168¾
4 10 11	22	33	44	55	60½	66	71½	77	88	99	110	121	132	154	165
4 13 0	21½	32¼	43	53¾	59⅛	64½	69¾	75¼	86	96¾	107½	118⅛	129	150½	161¼
4 15 3	21	31½	42	52½	57¾	63	68¼	73½	84	94½	105	115½	126	147	157½
4 17 7	20½	30¾	41	51¼	56⅜	61½	66¾	71¾	82	92¼	102½	112¾	123	143½	153¾
5 0 0	20	30	40	50	55	60	65	70	80	90	100	110	120	140	150
5 2 7	19½	29¼	39	48¾	53⅝	58½	63⅓	68¼	78	87¾	97½	107¼	117	136½	146¼
5 5 3	19	28½	38	47½	52¼	57	61¾	66½	76	85½	95	104½	114	133	142½
5 8 1	18½	27¾	37	46¼	50⅞	55½	60¼	64¾	74	83¼	92½	101¾	111	129½	138¾
5 11 1	18	27	36	45	49½	54	58½	63	72	81	90	99	108	126	135
5 14 3	17½	26¼	35	43¾	48⅛	52½	56¾	61¼	70	78¾	87½	96¼	105	122½	131¼
5 17 8	17	25½	34	42½	46¾	51	55¼	59½	68	76½	85	93½	102	119	127½
6 0 0	16⅔	25	33⅓	41⅔	45⅞	50	54¼	58⅓	66⅔	75	83⅓	91⅔	100	116⅔	125
6 2 5	16⅓	24½	32⅔	40⅚	44⅞	49	53	57⅙	65⅓	73½	81⅔	89⅔	98	114⅓	122½
6 5 0	16	24	32	40	44	48	52	56	64	72	80	88	96	112	120
6 7 8	15⅔	23½	31⅓	39⅙	43⅛	47	50¾	54⅚	62⅔	70½	78⅓	86⅙	94	109⅔	117½
6 10 5	15⅓	23	30⅔	38⅓	42⅛	46	49¾	53⅔	61⅓	69	76⅔	84⅓	92	107⅓	115
6 13 4	15	22½	30	37½	41¼	45	48¾	52½	60	67½	75	82½	90	105	112½
6 16 4	14⅔	22	29⅓	36⅔	40⅓	44	47¾	51⅓	58⅔	66	73⅓	80⅔	88	102⅔	110
6 19 6	14⅓	21½	28⅔	35⅚	39⅜	43	46½	50⅙	57⅓	64½	71⅔	78⅚	86	100⅓	107½
7 2 10	14	21	28	35	38½	42	45½	49	56	63	70	77	84	98	105
7 6 4	13⅔	20½	27⅓	34⅙	37½	41	44½	47⅚	54⅚	61½	68⅓	75⅙	82	95⅔	102½
7 10 0	13⅓	20	26⅔	33⅓	36⅔	40	43⅓	46⅔	53⅓	60	66⅔	73⅓	80	93⅓	100
7 13 10	13	19½	26	32½	35¾	39	42¼	45½	52	58½	65	71½	78	91	97½
7 17 11	12⅔	19	25⅓	31⅔	34⅞	38	41	44⅓	50⅔	57	63⅓	69⅔	76	88⅔	95
8 2 2	12⅓	18½	24⅔	30⅚	33⅞	37	40	43⅙	49⅓	55½	61⅔	67⅚	74	86⅓	92½
8 6 8	12	18	24	30	33	36	39	42	48	54	60	66	72	84	90
8 11 5	11⅔	17½	23⅓	29⅙	32⅛	35	37¾	40⅚	46⅔	52½	58⅓	64⅙	70	81⅔	87⅗
8 16 6	11⅓	17	22⅔	28⅓	31⅙	34	36¾	39⅔	45⅓	51	56⅔	62⅓	68	79⅓	85
9 1 10	11	16½	22	27½	30¼	33	35¾	38½	44	49½	55	60½	66	77	82½
9 7 6	10⅔	16	21⅓	26⅔	29⅓	32	34¾	37⅓	42⅔	48	53⅓	58⅔	64	74⅔	80
9 13 7	10⅓	15½	20⅔	25⅚	28⅖	31	33½	36⅙	41⅓	46½	51⅔	50⅚	62	72⅓	77½
10 0 0	10	15	20	25	27½	30	32½	35	40	45	50	55	60	70	75

"WHITAKER" ADVERTISEMENTS, 1964

BANKING, INSURANCE AND INVESTMENT

CHARITABLE APPEALS

MISCELLANEOUS

SPECIAL TRAINING COLLEGES

PRINCIPAL CHARITABLE BEQUESTS OF THE YEAR

The following list shows the principal charitable bequests noted since our last issue. Apart from individual legacies to societies, the amounts receivable by beneficiaries under the terms residue or remainder are the balances payable after the deduction of liabilities at death, probate charges, estate duty and bequests. Final benefits, in some cases, are also subject to life interests as shown in the list. Bequests are not necessarily payable during the current year and are subject to direction by testators to the executors as to the mode of payment, which may take the form of giving the executors powers to pay bequests as and when they determine and in some cases "in their sole and absolute discretion".

The latest Treasury figures show the yearly yield of Estate Duty up by £25 million to £261 million, but the only relief afforded in this year's Finance Bill is the raising of the exemption figure to £5,000, with reduction of rates of duty up to £8,000. This will hardly allay the anxiety of charitable bodies regarding their expectations in the larger estates, where death duties make the heaviest inroads. Mr. Nicholas Greenham, of Worthing, left the residue of his £418,082 estate to the Institute of Cancer Research and after estate duty of £264,643, a total of £140,000 is left for the purposes of the Institute. In this publication, 50 years ago, under the feature "Exchequer Windfalls in 1914", rates of duty then payable on a £400,000 estate were shown at 12 per cent, thus in half a century a bequest of this nature drops from £360,213 to £140,000. Captain Oliver Bird, whose fortune came from the custard powder concern, and who, in his lifetime, among other charitable gifts, gave £450,000 to the Nuffield Trust to help victims of osteo-arthritis, made the suggestion that "as hospitals have been taken over by the State the very heavy death duties payable on my estate must be taken to be applied for the maintenance of the Hospitals for which I would otherwise have made provision in my Will".

A feature of this year's list is other large bequests for research into the causes and defeat of cancer and a total of over £500,000 is shown as left to the various societies engaged in this work, including £20,000 by Mrs. Ethel Foster, of Wolverhampton, who for 30 years kept a front room small shop in the district, and over £200,000 by Mrs. Marjorie Hosack, "on condition that it is utilized for the benefit of those suffering from cancer in their own homes and who have not been admitted to any institution or hospital, preference being given to residents in the county of Caithness or elsewhere in Scotland".

Mrs. Violet Barlow left over £60,000 to the R.A.F. Benevolent Fund in memory of her son who was killed in an accident while serving with the Royal Air Force in 1938, and Mrs. Laura M. K. Capel left over £70,000 to her trustees for distribution in their discretion, expressing the wish that particular attention be paid to institutions established for the benefit of ex-servicemen disabled in body and mind. A single bequest of £10,000, under the Will of Miss Annette W. Clegg, falls to the Royal U.K. Beneficent Association, and £20,000, from Settled Funds, is left by Mrs. Mariska C. Joicey, to the Distressed Gentlefolks Aid Society, who also receive the residence of Mrs. Mary L. Powell as a home for elderly middle aged persons together with the residue of her £267,605 estate for the upkeep of same. The balance of the estate of Miss Mildred A. Carr, of Bath, amounting to some £90,000, is left to St. Dunstans and the R.N.L.I., and she also bequeathed "my spring chair" to the Royal National Hospital for Rheumatic Diseases, Bath. The Society for the Propagation of the Gospel in Foreign Parts benefit by some £40,000 under the Will of Mr. Richard Altham and other charities who receive bequests of £10,000 or over include the National Council for the Unmarried Mother and her Child, The Guide Dogs for the Blind Association, St. Dunstans, Dr. Barnardo's Homes, the N.P.S.C.C., the Salvation Army, the Church Army, the Forces Help Society, Lord Roberts' Workshops, the British Red Cross Society, the Sunshine Home for Blind Babies and the R.S.P.C.A. Over £180,000, under the Will of Mr. Fred Davidson, is left to various Jewish charities and bodies. By contrast to these bequests the Financial Statement of the Y.M.C.A. for the current year contains the item "legacies received during the year £21,118".

This year saw the establishment of the British Heart Foundation under the presidency of Field Marshal the Earl Alexander of Tunis, for research into heart diseases. More than £1 million was promised at the inception of the campaign towards the target of £3,500,000 to defeat what has been described as "Killer No. 1 and a problem three times as great as that of Cancer".

Among directions in Wills in recent years the bequest of eyes for therapeutic purposes to aid the blind has greatly increased, and this year saw the world's first eye bank for preserving corneas at nearly 100 deg. F. below zero being established at the Queen Victoria Hospital, East Grinstead. This meets a great need as the several other eye banks in Britain are only able to preserve corneas for a few days, whereas the new technique ensures preservation for up to two months.

Under the Ministry of Education a register of over 30,000 charitable trusts has been set up in London and actual inspection of trust deeds is now possible by the public although the whole of the work has not been finally completed. Among the deeds available are a photostat copy of the Churchill Endowment Fund, with a reproduction of Sir Winston's signature at the end of the document.

Name	Gross Value	
Mrs. Alice May Allott, of Great Crosby, Lancs.	£132,271	The residue equally between the Liverpool Personal Service Society, the Liverpool Union of Girls & Mixed Clubs, the Liverpool Boys Association, the Girls Friendly Society (Liverpool Diocese), the Friends of the Liverpool Radium Institute, St. Dunstans and the R.N.L.I.

(*continued on page viii*)

Name	Gross Value	
Mr. Richard Altham, of Holcombe Brook, Lancs.	£73,280	The residue to the Society for the Propagation of the Gospel in Foreign Parts.
Miss Clara Margaret Elsie Austin, of Amblecote, Staffs.	£40,423	The residue equally between the Royal Wolverhampton School and the National Children's Home.
Mrs. Violet Ethel Barlow of Bell Moor, N.W.3.	£198,476	The residue to the R.A.F. Benevolent Fund
Mrs. Frances Ethel Beddington, of Welbeck Street, W.1.	£97,020	The residue equally between the Salvation Army and the R.N.L.I.
Mr. John Bruce, of Dolphin Square, S.W.1.	£44,076	The residue to the National Council for the Unmarried Mother and her Child.
Mrs. Sarah Jane Bunting, of Matlock, Derbyshire.	£48,014	The residue equally between the Guide Dogs for the Blind Association and the Imperial Cancer Research Fund.
Mrs. Laura Mary Katherine Capel, of St. James Court, S.W.1.	£245,172	The residue for charitable institutions or objects in the United Kingdom at the discretion of her executors.
Miss Mildred Alice Carr, of Bath.	£298,437	The residue equally between St. Dunstans and the R.N.L.I.
Miss Annette Wild Clegg, of Whitehall Court, S.W.1.	£524,126	£10,000 to the Royal United Kingdom Beneficent Association.

(*continued on page x*)

Name	Gross Value	
Mr. Henry James Cutler, of Malvern, Worcs.	£35,741	One third of his property each to Dr. Barnardo's Homes and the Church of England Children's Society, and one sixth each to the N.S.P.C.C. and the Homeless Children's Aid and Adoption Society and F. B. Meyer Children's Home.
Mr. Fred Davidson, of Grosvenor Square, W.1.	£429,024	All of his property to eighteen Jewish institutions and charities.
Mrs. Fanny Davis, of Grange-over-Sands, Lancs.	£70,033	All of her property equally between St. Dunstans and Dr. Barnado's Homes.
Mrs. Levina Mary Devenish, of Angmering-on-Sea.	£353,663	The residue equally between the National Trust, the N.S.P.C.C., and the R.S.P.C.A.
Mr. Hugh William Alexander Dunn, of Whitehall Place, S.W.1.	£706,028	One fifth of the residue each to Orphan Homes of Scotland, Bridge of Weir, Dr. Barnardo's Homes, the Salvation Army and the R.N.L.I., and one fifth for charitable purposes as his Trustees think fit.
Mrs. Evangeline Du Pré Moore, of 19 Pelham Court, S.W.3.	£75,872	The residue to Dr. Barnardo's Homes.

(*continued on page xii*)

Name	Gross Value	
Miss Edith Owen Finer, of Windsor Road, E.7.	£73,362	The residue equally between The Church Army, The Salvation Army, and the British Union for the Abolition of Vivisection.
Miss Mary Dorothy Firth, of Bexhill-on-Sea.	£16,120	All of her property, including funds passing under a Will, to the Imperial Cancer Research Fund.
Mrs. Ethel Foster, of Wolverhampton.	£25,901	The residue to the Imperial Cancer Research Fund.
Mr. Nicholas John Henry Greenham, of Worthing.	£418,082	The residue to the Institute of Cancer Research.
Miss Emily Gracie Cecil Grove, of Bath.	£27,963	Subject to a life interest the remainder to the R.S.P.C.A.
Mrs Hilda Mary Hardy, of Park Hall Road, S.E.21.	£26,025	The residue to The Forces' Help Society and Lord Roberts' Workshops.

(*continued on page xiv*)

Name	Gross Value	
Mr. Robert Roy Herron, of Guildford, Surrey.	£73,228	The residue equally between the Imperial Cancer Research Fund, the British Red Cross Society, the Guide Dogs for the Blind Association and the R.S.P.C.A.
Dr. Cecil Walpole Richard Preston-Hillary, M.R.C.S. L.R.C.P., of Hastings.	£56,274	Subject to a life interest the remainder to the R.N.L.I.
Mr. Jacob Hodgins, of Millbrook, Southampton.	£22,309	The residue to the Institute of Cancer Research.
Mrs. Marjorie Hosack, of Watten, Caithness.	£534,204	The residue to the Marie Curie Memorial Foundation.
Mr. Thomas Vernon James, of North Bersted, Sussex.	£174,835	The residue equally between the British Empire Cancer Campaign and a body to be nominated by the British Medical Association for research into bronchial asthma.
Mrs. Mariska Christabel Joicey, of Richmond, Surrey.	£31,908	£20,000, from settled funds, to the Distressed Gentlefolks' Aid Association, and the remainder of such funds to the R.N.L.I.
Mrs. Katie Maude Nelson Leighton, of Farnham, Surrey.	£48,691	The residue equally between St. Dunstans and the Distressed Gentlefolks Aid Association.

(*continued on page xvi*)

Name	Gross Value	
Mr. Stanley Lord, of Littleborough, Lancs.	£47,313	The residue to the Imperial Cancer Research Fund.
Colonel Walter Francis Lucey, of Fulwith Brow, Yorks.	£88,148	Subject to a life interest two thirds of the remainder to the N.S.P.C.C., and one third to the R.S.P.C.A.
Dr. Nina Gertrude MacCarthy, of Drayton Gardens, S.W.10.	£210,209	The residue to the R.S.P.C.A.
Mr. Raoul Henry Nicole, of 39 Egerton Gardens, S.W.3.	£250,947	£5,000 to the Distressed Gentlefolks Aid Association.
Mrs. Ethel Parrett, of Market Harborough, Leics.	£74,026	The residue to Charitable Institutions and Societies in England as a relative may select.
Mrs. Mary Louise Powell, of Ruthin, N. Wales.	£267,605	The residue to the Distressed Gentlefolks Aid Association.
Mrs. Grace Lillian Russell Roberts, of Blackpool.	£23,262	All of her property equally between the Royal Humane Society and the League Against Cruel Sports.
Lady Annie Maude Rowbotham, of Bournemouth	£62,589	The residue to the Distressed Gentlefolks Aid Association.
Mrs. Helen Adele Saffery, of Melbury Road, W.14.	£69,005	Subject to a life interest the remainder to the Church Army.
Mr. Thomas Edgar Sanderson, of Nottingham.	£112,080	The residue to Dr. Barnardo's Homes.

(*continued on page xviii*)

Name	Gross Value	
Miss Elsie Grace Scott, of Walton-on-Thames.	£42,882	The residue to the Distressed Gentlefolks Aid Association.
Mr. George Francis Sharpe, of Poole, Dorset.	£71,837	The residue equally between St. Dunstans and the Disabled Sailors & Soldiers Workshops, Bournemouth
Mrs. Alice Maud Smith, of Huntley Street, W.C.1.	£94,471	All her freehold or leasehold property to Dr. Barnardo's Homes, and the residue to the Sunshine Home for Blind Babies.
Mrs. Mabel Thorne, of Deal, Kent.	£23,698	The residue equally between St. Dunstans and the British Red Cross Society.
Mrs. Nellie Tullie, of Pudsey, Yorks.	£25,903	Subject to a life interest the remainder to the Imperial Cancer Research Fund.
Mr. James Wheeldon, J.P., of Broken Cross, Ches.	£400,474	The residue equally between the National Children's Home, Dr. Barnado's Homes, N.S.P.C.C., and the Imperial Cancer Research Fund.
Mr. Pierce Williams, of Liverpool.	£411,779	Subject to a life interest the remainder to St. Dunstans.
Mrs. Jean Wilson, of Hove, Sussex.	£24,593	One half of the residue to the Salvation Army.
Miss Clara Henrietta Wootton, of Maidenhead, Berks.	£308,466	The residue for charitable or other purposes at the discretion of her Trustees.

(*continued on page xx*)

Name	Gross Value	
Mr. Hugh Francis Yeoman, of Roehampton, S.W.15.	£290,771	1/7th of the residue each to the Royal National Institute for the Blind, the National Institute for the Deaf, National Society for Cancer Relief, Imperial Cancer Research Fund, the Church of England Children's Society, the Fairbridge Society and the Church Army.

Multiple Sclerosis Society

The Society encourages medical research by establishing Fellowships in Multiple (Disseminated) Sclerosis (cause and cure of which are both unknown) and Allied Nervous Diseases. Through its welfare work it brings help to those who have M.S. In the past seven years the Society has authorised £108,000 in Research Grants and has spent £77,000 on Welfare. *Please support the Society by*

LEGACIES, DONATIONS AND SUBSCRIPTIONS

(Registered as a Charity in accordance with the National Assistance Act, 1948)

DEPT. WA. 10 STRATFORD ROAD, LONDON, W.8

METROPOLITAN SOCIETY FOR THE BLIND AND INDIGENT BLIND VISITING SOCIETY

51 Denison House, 296 Vauxhall Bridge Road, London, S.W.1

(Registered in accordance with the National Assistance Act 1948)

Agents for the Worshipful Company of Clothworkers

To visit the Blind in Hospitals, Institutions, and in their own homes. White sticks given to all who need them. Grants are given to individual blind persons in respect of a wide variety of needs, no reasonable request being refused if the funds are available. Talking Book machines provided in co-operation with the Nuffield Talking Book Library. Maintenance and installation of wireless sets. The Society organises eleven weekly afternoon social Clubs. Christmas parties and a summer Outing arranged for Club members. Hackney House, in Amhurst Road, E.8, provides 12 self-contained flats, which are let unfurnished to blind men and women. A Home for 50 blind men and women at Maldon, Essex. Residential, recuperative and Holiday Home for 75 blind men and women, The Armitage, Marine Parade, Worthing.

Organising Secretary: Mrs. M. Davie

THE MISSION TO LEPERS

International **Interdenominational**

Since its foundation in 1874 The Mission to Lepers has been in the forefront of service to sufferers from leprosy. It co-operates with 58 Christian Societies in their crusade against leprosy, and itself administers a number of Leprosy Homes and Hospitals in 30 different countries. Legacies, Annual Subscriptions and Donations will be gratefully received.

Full information may be obtained from Headquarters:

7, Bloomsbury Square, London, W.C.1

YET ANOTHER STEP FORWARD

The new Guest House at Weston-super-Mare, Somerset, will be ready by May 1964.

The Lauriston is in an ideal position, one minute from the sea, with rooms for 47 guests. This new venture will ensure that in future a greater number of blind and partially sighted persons will be able to enjoy themselves with their families by the sea.

The London Association also provides Workshops, Flats and Residential Homes, including those for the aged, and its Benevolent and Pensions Fund helps hundreds of those in need.

Founded in 1857, this national charity remains an independent body relying on legacies and voluntary contributions for the furtherance of its work and is grateful for every gift, large or small.

The Lauriston, Knightstone Road, Weston-super-Mare

Patron: H.R.H. PRINCESS ALEXANDRA, THE HON. MRS. ANGUS OGILVY, G.C.V.O

LONDON ASSOCIATION FOR THE BLIND

Head Office: **PELICAN HOUSE, 88/92, PECKHAM ROAD, LONDON, S.E.15**

(*Registered in accordance with the National Assistance Act,* 1948, *and as a National Charity under the Charities Act,* 1960)

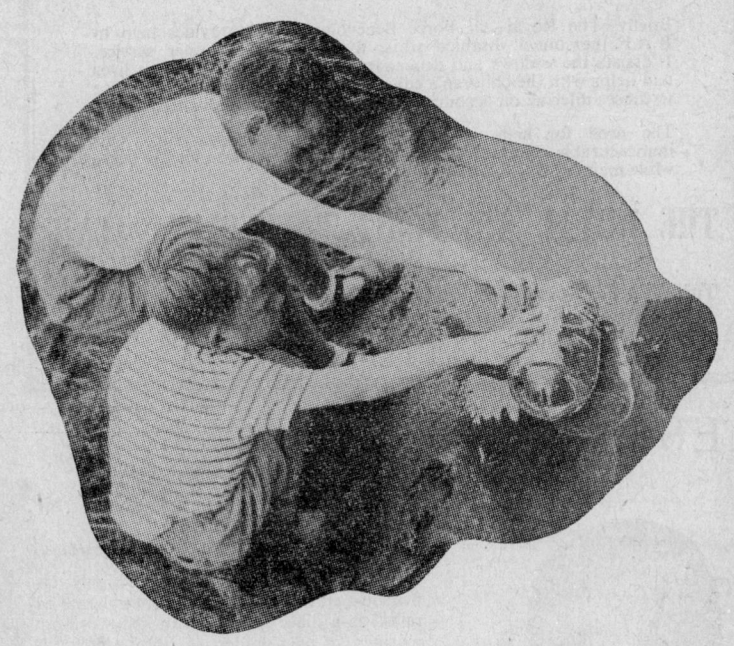

By Will or Codicil or Covenant...

May we suggest to Legal or Financial Advisers that when questions of their clients' benefactions arise the worthiness of the Royal Air Force Benevolent Fund may be whole-heartedly and deservedly commended.

Briefly, The Royal Air Force Benevolent Fund provides help to R.A.F. personnel disabled while flying or during other service. It assists the widows and dependants of those who lose their lives and helps with the children's education. It gives practical assistance to those suffering on account of sickness and general distress.

The need for help in nowise lessens in peace or war. Our immeasurable gratitude to that "Immortal Few" can hardly cease while memory itself endures.

THE ROYAL AIR FORCE BENEVOLENT FUND

More detailed information will be gladly sent by the Hon. Treasurer

The R.A.F. Benevolent Fund, 67 Portland Place, London, W.1

Telephone: Langham 8343

(Registered under the War Charities Act, 1940)

RESOLUTION which founded the *Royal Alfred*

MANSION HOUSE, JULY 17TH, 1857

Chairman: The Rt. Hon. Lord Mayor Sir Thomas Quested Finnis

Sir Thomas Quested Finnis
THE RT. HON. LORD MAYOR 1856-7

"This meeting . . . considers it highly expedient that a hospital or hospitals should be raised as a place of refuge for the worn-out mariner of all grades of the Mercantile Marine when aged and disabled and having none to care for him, and that a scheme of out-pensions should be grafted on it. . . ."

130 infirm or aged seamen are now cared for in the ROYAL ALFRED home. 1,000 aged seamen are receiving out-pensions. Seamen's widows and dependants in distress are also assisted.

Patron: H.M. The Queen

Please help by a gift or bequest

Hon. Treasurer:
Sir Ernest H. Murrant, K.C.M.G., M.B.E.

ROYAL ALFRED Merchant Seamen's Society
126H Balham High Road, London, S.W.12

THE BEST WAY TO SAY

"THANK YOU, NURSE"

Give to

THE ROYAL COLLEGE OF NURSING AND NATIONAL COUNCIL OF NURSES OF THE UNITED KINGDOM

Patrons: Her Majesty the Queen, Her Majesty Queen Elizabeth the Queen Mother

The College works unceasingly to promote the science and art of nursing. Funds are urgently needed for

expansion, research, maintenance.

Remember the nurses who help you in times of sickness. Help them to maintain their College which serves the public through the nursing profession.

Please send a subscription or donation NOW or make a bequest.

All gifts gratefully received by The Appeals Secretary, 1A Henrietta Place, Cavendish Square, London, W.1

THE ROYAL ASSOCIATION IN AID OF THE DEAF AND DUMB

7-11 ARMSTRONG ROAD, ACTON, W.3.

Founded 1840.

(Registered in accordance with the National Assistance Act, 1948)

Dioceses of London, Chelmsford, Guildford, Rochester, Southwark, and Croydon (Canterbury)

Patron: H.M. THE QUEEN

President: THE ARCHBISHOP OF CANTERBURY

AREA OF WORK: LONDON, MIDDLESEX, SURREY, ESSEX AND WEST KENT

There are more than 6,000 Deaf and Dumb in this area

OBJECTS.

To promote the spiritual, social and general welfare of the Deaf and Dumb.

Association has established 12 Centres of its own and hires rooms for services, lectures, clubs, etc.

Gifts and Legacies gratefully acknowledged by:

Secretary, R.A.D.D. 7-11 Armstrong Road, Acton, W.3.

ROYAL BLIND PENSION SOCIETY

Patron—HER MAJESTY THE QUEEN

Treasurer: Mr. P. LAURENCE POCOCK

Bankers: BANK OF ENGLAND

This Society grants Pensions to the Blind Poor at their own homes in sums of various amounts.

There are about 580 pensioners, residing in various parts of the Kingdom, among whom over £5,700 are annually distributed.

To be eligible, applicants must be totally blind, and of good moral character. Amount of Income at the discretion of the Committee. No distinction is made in regard to sex or creed.

Application must be made on the printed forms provided by the Society.

Contributions will be gratefully received by the Treasurer or by the BANK OF ENGLAND.

145-147 NORTH END, CROYDON, SURREY L. E. WATTS, *Secretary.* [3

SOLDIERS' SAILORS' AND AIRMEN'S FAMILIES ASSOCIATION

Patrons:
Her Majesty The Queen. Her Majesty Queen Elizabeth the Queen Mother

---

FOR OVER SEVENTY-SEVEN YEARS SSAFA has been giving help and advice to thousands of service and ex-service families in distress. Broken homes sudden bereavement, separated families and resettlement in civilian life are a few of the problems with which SSAFA deals. SSAFA has an active Overseas organisation which is available to all service families abroad who may be in need of help or advice. SSAFA assists the widows and dependants of ex-servicemen in time of need.

SSAFA is maintained almost entirely by voluntary subscriptions.

Donations and legacies gratefully received by

The Director of Appeals

SOLDIERS' SAILORS' AND AIRMEN'S FAMILIES ASSOCIATION

23, Queen Anne's Gate, London, S.W.I.

THE TOLL OF THE SEA

Last year this Society Cared for 333 survivors from 43 vessels.

Gave IMMEDIATE RELIEF to **162 dependants of men lost at sea during the year.**

Over 3,500 aged seamen, fishermen and their families were assisted.

Relief Expenditure for the year—£51,000.

Legacies are solicited Please help this National Work

SHIPWRECKED Fishermen and MARINERS' Royal Benevolent SOCIETY

PATRON: HER MAJESTY THE QUEEN

(B2) 16 WILFRED STREET, WESTMINSTER, LONDON, S.W.1